Mailing Lists & Marketing Services
For The Education Market

Patterson's Educational Mailing Lists are available from **Educational Directories Inc.**, the publisher of *PATTERSON'S AMERICAN EDUCATION, PATTERSON'S ELEMENTARY EDUCATION* and *PATTERSON'S SCHOOLS CLASSIFIED*. For over 100 years, educators have relied on Patterson's publications as **THE** guide to school's in the United States. Now you can use this same data to market your products and services.

Public, Private and Catholic High, Junior High, Middle, Elementary Schools and School Districts. Addresses can be selected by state, county, city, cities by size, MSA's, radius, sectional center, zip code, enrollment, grade, wealth, urban suburban, ethnic breakdown and random sample.

Other services available are merging, personal names of principals and superintendents, attention lines, phone numbers, fax numbers and presort barcoding.

Post-Secondary Schools. Selections can be made using any combination of colleges and universities, community colleges, career schools, home study, handicapped and hospital schools. Additional selections can be made by academic discipline.

Database Selectivity. EDI can optimize your productivity by scoring prospects using the "demographics" of your current customers. The system determines market segments; arrays your prospects from best to worse; and will produce addressed lists based on the depth you wish to promote.

Others Lists Available. Public libraries, churches, hospitals, Canadian schools, nursery schools, correctional institutions, YMCA, YWCA, summer camps, park and recreation directors, police departments and many others.

Increase Your Response Rate

By Getting Lists For Schools Who Meet Your Criteria. The accuracy of our list selections is a direct result of the work that goes into our directories. Our directories have been tested for accuracy and completeness every year for the past 100 years by people working in the education field. They verify the information in the books with each use. No other label supplier is subjected to this degree of scrutiny.

By Getting Lists That Are Deliverable. We guarantee our lists 100% deliverable. Our use of phone and fax verification, custom reports from state and local school authorities plus our own annual mailings to addresses contained in our publications, on an "address service requested" basis, assures you the most current and accurate addresses possible.

**Let Educational Directories Inc. *"The Education Specialists"*
Help Your Business Grow**
EDI provides top quality information and personalized
service at very competitive prices.

For a copy of our Mailing List Catalog . . . call, email or visit our website.

Educational Directories Inc.
PO Box 68097 Schaumburg IL 60168-0097
Telephone (800) 357-6183   Fax (847) 891-0945
www.ediusa.com - info@ediusa.com

D1250577

PATTERSON'S

AMERICAN EDUCATION

2007 Edition
VOLUME CIII

Editorial Staff
Editor   Wayne Moody
Assistant Editor   Rita Ostdick
Assistant Editor   James Thiessen
Assistant Editor   Gloria Busch

EDUCATIONAL DIRECTORIES INC.

Educational Directories Inc.
PO Box 68097
Schaumburg IL 60168-0097
(847) 891-1250 or (800) 357-6183
www.ediusa.com

First edition published 1904. One Hundred Third edition 2007

ISBN 0-9771602-3-8
ISSN 0079-0230
Library of Congress Catalog Card Number: 04-012953
Printed in the United States of America

CONTENTS

HOW TO USE THIS DIRECTORY

Patterson's AMERICAN EDUCATION (published annually since 1904) is THE standard directory to secondary schools and is the first in a series of school directories published by Educational Directories Inc. Patterson's ELEMENTARY EDUCATION (published annually since 1989) is identical in format to Patterson's AMERICAN EDUCATION but is a directory to elementary schools; and Patterson's SCHOOLS CLASSIFIED (published annually since 1951) is the most comprehensive directory to post-secondary schools available. The three volumes combined fulfill the need for a single, systematized, comprehensive directory to our nation's schools from kindergarten through post-graduate studies.

Patterson's AMERICAN EDUCATION contains 10,920 public school districts, 30,425 public secondary schools, 6,387 private and Catholic secondary schools and more than 7,000 post-secondary schools in an easy-to-use and consistent format. It is an invaluable resource for anyone involved in education or educational research. School registrars, guidance counselors, principals, superintendents, directors of admissions, financial aid officers, schools of education, public libraries, government agencies, armed forces, and business people find it a welcome replacement for the multitude of other directories required for national coverage of our nation's school systems with their variation in size, content, format and publishing date.

One of the primary objectives of this directory is to make available the latest, most comprehensive information about secondary and post-secondary schools in a condensed and easily accessible format. Its general organization is geographical. Entries are arranged alphabetically, by state, then by community (post office) and then by District and School name. Each state begins with a listing of the officials in its Department of Education followed by the head of the State Board of Education. If a state has intermediate superintendents (a level of superintendent between the state superintendent of schools and the superintendents who actually supervise the schools) they appear in a table preceding the community listings. Community listings follow and include the community name, county name, community population, district name, total district student enrollment, the superintendent's name, address, telephone, fax number and website where available followed by a listing of the district schools, showing their enrollment, grade range and the principal's name, address, telephone number and fax number. A district may be responsible for schools in more than one community. To achieve consistency, the district office is listed in the community in which it is located. A cross-reference is provided to and from the schools of the district located in other communities.

A short line may appear at the end of the listing of public secondary schools. This line separates the public secondary schools from the private and Catholic secondary schools and the post-secondary schools located in the community. Private and Catholic school listings include their enrollment, grade range and the principal's name, address, telephone number and fax number. Post-secondary school listings include their name, address and telephone number. Please refer to page vi, "Guide to Editorial Style," for an example of how these elements work together to provide an easy-to-use format.

Schools Listed

Patterson's AMERICAN EDUCATION lists the following types of schools

- **Middle Schools** usually teach any combination of grades five through eight.

- **Junior High Schools** usually teach grades seven through nine.

- **Junior-Senior High Schools** usually teach any combination of grades five through eight and include nine through twelve.

- **High Schools** usually teach grades nine through twelve or ten through twelve.

- **K-12 Schools**

- **Vocational-Technical Schools**

The following are included:

- All graded state approved public secondary schools.

- All graded secondary schools belonging to the National Catholic Education Association.

- All graded, regionally accredited, private secondary schools.

- Private secondary schools belonging to the member associations of the Council of American Private Education.

Non graded, special education schools and other non-traditional secondary schools are not listed.

Patterson's ELEMENTARY EDUCATION lists Kindergarten Schools, Primary Schools, Elementary Schools, Middle Schools and K-12 Schools.

ABBREVIATIONS

AVC. . .	Area Vocational Center	JUNHSD	Joint Union High School District
AVTS . .	Area Vocational Technical School	JUSD . .	Joint Unified School District
CCSD. .	Community Consolidated School District	JVSD . .	Joint Vocational School District
CDC . .	Child Development Center	K	Kindergarten
CESD . .	Consolidated Elementary School District	MS . . .	Middle School
CISD . .	City Independent School District	MSHS. .	Middle School High School
CSD. . .	City School District	PS . . .	Primary School
CUSD. .	Community Unit School District	RHSD. .	Rural High School District
ECC. . .	Early Childhood Center	RISD . .	Rural Independent School District
ECCSD .	Elementary Community Consolidated School District	ROC . .	Regional Occupational Center
EHSD. .	Elementary-High School District	ROP . .	Regional Occupational Program
ES . . .	Elementary School	RSD. . .	Reorganized School District
ESD. . .	Elementary School District	S	School
EVD. . .	Exempted Village District	SAD. . .	School Administrative District
HS . . .	High School	SC . . .	School Corporation
HSD. . .	High School District	SD . . .	School District
IS. . . .	Intermediate School	SHS. . .	Senior High School
ISD . . .	Independent School District	SSD. . .	Separate School District
JESD . .	Joint Elementary School District	UESD. .	Unified Elementary School District
JHS . . .	Junior High School	UFD. . .	Union Free District
JSD . . .	Joint School District	UHSD. .	Unified High School District
JSHS . .	Junior-Senior High School	UNESD .	Union Elementary School District
JUESD .	Joint Unified Elementary School District	UNHSD .	Union High School District
JUHSD .	Joint Unified High School District	UNSD. .	Union School District
JUNESD	Joint Union Elementary School District	USD. . .	Unified School District
		Vo/Tech.	Vocational/Technical

GUIDE TO EDITORIAL STYLE

1. State.

2. City, county and city population.

3. Community school districts - school district name (refer to page v for abbreviations), address, superintendent's name and website.

4. Enrollment, grade range, phone number and fax number.

5. Community schools - school name, address and principal's name.

6. If the school district office is not located in this city, a cross-reference will show office location.

7. Private and Catholic secondary schools appear below a short line in the cities where they are located.

8. Post-secondary schools also appear below the line in the cities where they are located.

SECONDARY SCHOOL COUNTS BY STATE

State	Districts	Public 5-9	Public 7-12	Public 9-12	Public 10-12	Public K-12	Private	Catholic	Total
Alabama	131	222	93	191	9	80	109	10	845
Alaska	54	34	18	33	0	179	15	3	336
Arizona	111	206	8	173	7	4	39	13	561
Arkansas	253	163	151	93	49	2	37	7	755
California	415	1,240	45	897	8	6	616	122	3,349
Colorado	177	261	68	213	5	5	81	11	821
Connecticut	123	169	9	146	1	1	52	28	529
Delaware	16	31	1	23	0	0	36	7	114
District Of Columbia	1	20	0	14	0	0	13	8	56
Florida	67	513	40	346	3	13	484	37	1,503
Georgia	175	431	19	323	5	4	195	12	1,164
Hawaii	1	36	6	33	0	6	35	7	124
Idaho	108	94	36	70	15	11	25	1	360
Illinois	489	705	48	600	11	0	112	83	2,048
Indiana	292	319	100	243	4	3	88	24	1,073
Iowa	341	262	110	238	8	0	27	31	1,017
Kansas	295	225	97	232	9	0	33	18	909
Kentucky	171	224	26	206	1	4	47	28	707
Louisiana	69	206	62	172	2	66	86	55	718
Maine	118	96	15	95	1	9	37	4	375
Maryland	24	232	7	181	2	4	116	38	604
Massachusetts	227	288	44	217	2	2	97	54	931
Michigan	521	576	98	456	18	28	186	55	1,938
Minnesota	330	217	186	160	21	9	56	30	1,009
Mississippi	148	151	62	130	6	42	80	10	629
Missouri	447	332	203	280	13	2	65	49	1,391
Montana	161	215	0	167	1	0	12	7	563
Nebraska	256	102	173	96	7	0	14	30	678
Nevada	16	89	12	66	2	5	22	2	214
New Hampshire	76	85	2	75	1	1	41	6	287
New Jersey	266	386	37	280	8	0	112	75	1,164
New Mexico	89	136	20	88	7	0	44	3	387
New York	646	778	199	647	18	68	368	138	2,862
North Carolina	115	442	13	344	4	5	208	4	1,135
North Dakota	159	37	119	39	4	3	7	5	373
Ohio	610	623	128	575	14	1	118	85	2,154
Oklahoma	428	272	34	369	50	2	36	4	1,195
Oregon	179	199	33	171	3	25	69	11	690
Pennsylvania	498	498	165	382	36	1	240	92	1,912
Rhode Island	32	51	1	42	0	1	19	10	156
South Carolina	85	230	18	166	7	2	101	4	613
South Dakota	158	164	0	161	0	1	11	7	502
Tennessee	119	290	42	232	4	19	92	11	809
Texas	972	1,336	151	944	60	114	278	56	3,911
Utah	40	122	22	32	53	2	44	4	319
Vermont	52	28	21	27	1	10	24	2	165
Virginia	132	325	35	274	16	2	123	15	922
Washington	247	339	46	236	29	24	110	14	1,045
West Virginia	55	125	17	94	5	2	35	8	341
Wisconsin	379	344	61	341	7	15	94	53	1,294
Wyoming	46	54	11	45	5	7	5	2	175
Total	10,920	14,523	2,912	11,658	542	790	4,994	1,393	47,732

Part I SECONDARY SCHOOLS

ALABAMA

ALABAMA DEPARTMENT OF EDUCATION
50 N Ripley St, Montgomery 36130-1001
Telephone 334-242-9700
Fax 334-242-9708
Website http://www.alsde.edu

State Superintendent of Education   Joseph Morton

ALABAMA BOARD OF EDUCATION
50 N Ripley St, Montgomery 36130-1001

President   Governor Bob Riley

PUBLIC, PRIVATE AND CATHOLIC SECONDARY SCHOOLS

Abbeville, Henry, Pop. 2,954
Henry County SD — 2,700/K-12
PO Box 635 36310 — 334-585-2206
Dennis Coe, supt. — Fax 585-2551
www.henrycountyboe.org/
Abbeville HS — 300/9-12
PO Box 519 36310 — 334-585-2065
Dale Barnes, prin. — Fax 585-6562
Abbeville MS — 300/6-8
200 Gilliam St 36310 — 334-585-2185
Larry Calloway, prin. — Fax 585-6378
Other Schools – See Headland

Abbeville Christian Academy — 200/K-12
PO Box 9 36310 — 334-585-5100
Barbara Lindsey, prin. — Fax 585-5100

Adamsville, Jefferson, Pop. 4,921
Jefferson County SD
Supt. — See Birmingham
Bottonfield MS — 1,000/6-8
400 Hillcrest Rd 35005 — 205-379-2550
Dr. Jennifer Maye, prin. — Fax 379-2553
Minor HS — 900/10-12
2285 Minor Pkwy 35005 — 205-379-4750
David Pike, prin. — Fax 379-4795

Addison, Winston, Pop. 715
Winston County SD
Supt. — See Double Springs
Addison HS — 300/7-12
PO Box 240 35540 — 256-747-2286
Olen Bolzle, prin. — Fax 747-6410

Akron, Hale, Pop. 513
Hale County SD
Supt. — See Greensboro
Akron Community HS East — 200/7-12
PO Box 38 35441 — 205-372-3787
Fredrica Jimerson, prin. — Fax 372-3782

Alabaster, Shelby, Pop. 25,462
Shelby County SD
Supt. — See Columbiana
Thompson HS — 1,300/9-12
100 Warrior Dr 35007 — 205-682-5700
Robin Thomas, prin. — Fax 682-5705
Thompson MS — 1,200/6-8
1509 Kent Dairy Rd 35007 — 205-682-5710
Nicke Gaspers, prin. — Fax 682-5715

Kingwood Christian S — 300/PK-12
1351 Royalty Dr 35007 — 205-663-3973

Albertville, Marshall, Pop. 17,891
Albertville CSD — 3,600/K-12
107 W Main St 35950 — 256-891-1183
Robert Sparkman, supt. — Fax 891-6303
www.albertk12.org
Alabama Avenue MS — 500/7-8
600 E Alabama Ave 35950 — 256-878-2341
Darryl Cooper, prin. — Fax 891-6334
Albertville HS — 900/9-12
402 E Mccord Ave 35950 — 256-878-6580
Paul McAbee, prin. — Fax 891-6305

Marshall County SD
Supt. — See Guntersville
Asbury S — 900/K-12
1990 Asbury Rd 35951 — 256-878-4068
Bill Aaron, prin. — Fax 878-5233

Alexander City, Tallapoosa, Pop. 14,966
Alexander City SD — 3,500/K-12
375 Lee St 35010 — 256-234-5074
Dr. Thomas R. Bice, supt. — Fax 234-8649
www.alex.k12.al.us
Alexander City MS — 600/7-8
359 State St 35010 — 256-234-8660
Tracy McGhee, prin. — Fax 234-8659
Russell HS — 1,000/9-12
225 Heard Blvd 35010 — 256-234-8611
Jim Davidson, prin. — Fax 234-8680

Central Alabama Community College — Post-Sec.
PO Box 699 35011 — 256-234-6346

Alexandria, Calhoun
Calhoun County SD
Supt. — See Anniston

Alexandria HS — 1,100/5-12
PO Box 180 36250 — 256-741-4400
Ronald Chambless, prin. — Fax 820-7161

Aliceville, Pickens, Pop. 2,505
Pickens County SD
Supt. — See Carrollton
Aliceville JSHS — 500/7-12
417 3rd St SE 35442 — 205-373-6378
Minnie Washington, prin. — Fax 373-6730

Alpine, Talladega
Talladega County SD
Supt. — See Talladega
Winterboro HS — 400/5-12
22601 AL Highway 21 35014 — 256-315-5370
Vicky Ozment, prin. — Fax 315-5380

Andalusia, Covington, Pop. 8,610
Andalusia CSD — 1,700/K-12
122 6th Ave 36420 — 334-222-3186
Dr. Beverly McAnulty, supt. — Fax 222-8631
andalusia.k12.al.us/
Andalusia HS — 500/9-12
701 3rd St 36420 — 334-222-7569
Dr. Daniel Shakespeare, prin. — Fax 222-5834
Andalusia MS — 400/6-8
1201 C C Baker Ave, — 334-222-6542
Ted Watson, prin. — Fax 222-3875

Covington County SD — 3,200/K-12
PO Box 460 36420 — 334-222-7571
Ronnie Driver, supt. — Fax 222-7573
www.cov.k12.al.us/
Pleasant Home S — 500/K-12
12548 Falco Rd 36420 — 334-222-1315
James Garner, prin. — Fax 222-4415
Straughn HS — 600/7-12
29324 Straughn School Rd, — 334-222-2511
John Thomasson, prin. — Fax 222-4010
Other Schools – See Florala, Red Level

Lurleen B. Wallace Community College — Post-Sec.
PO Box 1418 36420 — 334-222-6591

Anniston, Calhoun, Pop. 23,750
Anniston CSD — 2,600/K-12
PO Box 1500 36202 — 256-231-5000
Dr. Sammy Felton, supt. — Fax 231-5073
www.annistonschools.com/
Anniston HS — 600/9-12
1301 Woodstock Ave 36207 — 256-231-5010
George Jordan, prin. — Fax 231-5069
Anniston MS — 600/6-8
4800 Mcclellan Blvd 36206 — 256-231-5020
Lywood Hawkins, prin. — Fax 231-5024

Calhoun County SD — 8,900/K-12
PO Box 2084 36202 — 256-741-7400
H. Jacky Sparks, supt. — Fax 237-5332
www.calhoun.k12.al.us
Saks HS — 600/8-12
4401 Saks Rd 36206 — 256-741-7000
Larry Skinner, prin. — Fax 236-5121
Wellborn HS — 700/7-12
135 Pinson Rd 36201 — 256-741-7600
Charles E. Whatley, prin. — Fax 237-7071
White Plains HS — 400/7-12
250 White Plains Rd 36207 — 256-741-7800
Davine Miller, prin. — Fax 237-3301
Other Schools – See Alexandria, Jacksonville, Ohatchee, Weaver

Cornerstone Christian Academy — 50/K-12
2885 Choccolocco Rd 36207 — 256-236-1603
Sharon Cox, prin. — Fax 236-1120
Donoho S — 400/PK-12
2501 Henry Rd 36207 — 256-237-5477
Janice Hurd, hdmstr. — Fax 237-6474
Faith Christian S — 300/K-12
4100 Ronnaki Rd 36207 — 256-236-4499
Dr. Ben Character, hdmstr. — Fax 236-4673
Gadsden Business College — Post-Sec.
1809 Hillyer Robinson Pky 36207 — 256-831-3838
Gadsden State Community College — Post-Sec.
1801 Coleman Rd 36207 — 256-835-5400
Sacred Heart S — 200/PK-12
16 Morton Rd 36205 — 256-237-4231
Charlie Maniscalco, prin. — Fax 237-2353

Arab, Marshall, Pop. 7,305
Arab CSD — 2,700/K-12
750 Arabian Dr NE 35016 — 256-586-6011
John Mullins, supt. — Fax 586-6013
www.arabcityschools.org
Arab HS — 1,000/9-12
511 Arabian Dr NE 35016 — 256-586-6026
Patrick Crowder, prin. — Fax 586-1948
Arab JHS — 600/6-8
911 Old Cullman Rd SW 35016 — 256-586-6074
John Ingram, prin. — Fax 586-1348

Ardmore, Limestone, Pop. 1,080
Limestone County SD
Supt. — See Athens
Ardmore HS — 800/6-12
30285 Ardmore Ave 35739 — 256-423-2685
Mike Owens, prin. — Fax 423-4991

Ariton, Dale, Pop. 758
Dale County SD
Supt. — See Ozark
Ariton S — 600/K-12
PO Box 750 36311 — 334-762-2371
James Blanchard, prin. — Fax 762-2126

Arley, Winston, Pop. 289
Winston County SD
Supt. — See Double Springs
Meek HS — 300/7-12
PO Box 168 35541 — 205-384-5825
Danny Stallings, prin. — Fax 384-6825

Ashford, Houston, Pop. 1,879
Houston County SD
Supt. — See Dothan
Ashford JSHS — 700/7-12
607 Church St 36312 — 334-899-5411
James Odom, prin. — Fax 899-7450
Houston County AVC — Vo/Tech
PO Box 3005 36312 — 334-899-3308
Glenn Maloy, prin. — Fax 899-8854

Ashford Academy — 200/K-12
1100 N Broadway St 36312 — 334-899-3286
David Griggs, prin. — Fax 899-7503

Ashland, Clay, Pop. 1,926
Clay County SD — 2,000/K-12
PO Box 278 36251 — 256-354-5414
Ben H. Griffin, supt. — Fax 354-5415
Clay County S — 500/7-12
220 3rd St SW 36251 — 256-354-7510
Anthony Wilkinson, prin. — Fax 354-7511
Other Schools – See Lineville

Ashville, Saint Clair, Pop. 2,356
Saint Clair County SD — 7,300/PK-12
33205 US Highway 231 35953 — 205-594-7131
Tom Sanders, supt. — Fax 594-4441
www.stclaircountyschools.net
Ashville HS — 400/9-12
33215 US Highway 231 35953 — 205-594-7943
Jody Whaley, prin. — Fax 594-4349
Ashville MS — 400/5-8
PO Box 340 35953 — 205-594-7044
Phillip Johnson, prin. — Fax 594-2241
Eden Career-Technical Center — Vo/Tech
45 County Road 33 35953 — 205-594-7055
James King, dir. — Fax 594-4124
Other Schools – See Moody, Odenville, Ragland, Springville

Athens, Limestone, Pop. 19,869
Athens CSD — 2,700/K-12
313 E Washington St 35611 — 256-233-6600
Dr. Orman Bridges, supt. — Fax 233-6640
www.acs-k12.org
Athens HS — 800/9-12
PO Box 109 35612 — 256-233-6615
Chris Bolen, prin. — Fax 233-6617
Athens MS — 500/7-8
601 S Clinton St 35611 — 256-233-6620
Joe Jackson, prin. — Fax 233-6623

Limestone County SD — 8,000/K-12
300 S Jefferson St 35611 — 256-232-5353
Barry L. Carroll Ed.D., supt. — Fax 233-6461
www.lcsk12.org
Clements S — 1,100/K-12
7730 US Highway 72 35611 — 256-729-6564
Donald Wilson, prin. — Fax 729-1029

East Limestone S   900/6-12
15641 E Limestone Rd 35613   256-233-6660
Dennis Black, prin.   Fax 230-9366
Limestone Co. Career Technical Center   Vo/Tech
505 E Sanderfer Rd 35611   256-233-6463
Charlotte Craig, prin.   Fax 233-6667
Other Schools – See Ardmore, Elkmont, Lester, Tanner

Athens Bible S   300/K-12
507 Hoffman St 35611   256-232-3525
Joseph Olson, prin.   Fax 232-5417
Athens State University   Post-Sec.
300 N Beaty St 35611   256-233-8100
Faith Christian Academy   200/PK-12
705 W Sanderfer Rd 35611   256-233-3778
Wayne Forsythe, admin.

Atmore, Escambia, Pop. 7,497
Escambia County SD
Supt. — See Brewton
Escambia County HS   600/9-12
1215 S Presley St 36502   251-368-9181
Kyle Ferguson, prin.   Fax 368-0674
Escambia County MS   700/5-8
PO Box 1236 36504   251-368-9105
Zickeyous Byrd, prin.   Fax 368-0969

Escambia Academy   200/K-12
268 Cowpen Creek Rd 36502   251-368-2080
Judy Branum, prin.   Fax 368-1950
Jefferson Davis Community College   Post-Sec.
PO Box 1119 36504   251-368-8118

Attalla, Etowah, Pop. 6,394
Attalla CSD   1,800/PK-12
101 Case Ave SE 35954   256-538-8051
Danny Golden, supt.   Fax 538-8388
www.attalla.k12.al.us
Etowah HS   700/9-12
201 Case Ave SE 35954   256-538-8381
John Serafini, prin.   Fax 538-2136
Etowah MS   500/6-8
429 4th St SW 35954   256-538-3236
Jerald Cardin, prin.   Fax 538-3232

Etowah County SD
Supt. — See Gadsden
Career Technical Center   Vo/Tech
105 Burke Ave SE 35954   256-538-3312
Herman McMurtrey, dir.   Fax 538-1090

Auburn, Lee, Pop. 46,923
Auburn CSD   4,700/K-12
PO Box 3270 36831   334-887-2100
Dr. J. Terry Jenkins, supt.   Fax 887-2107
auburnschools.org
Auburn HS   1,000/10-12
405 S Dean Rd 36830   334-887-4970
Dr. Cathy Long, prin.   Fax 887-4177
Auburn JHS   800/8-9
332 E Samford Ave 36830   334-887-1960
Jason Wright, prin.   Fax 887-4160

Auburn University 36849   Post-Sec.
334-844-4000
Lee-Scott Academy   700/PK-12
1601 Academy Dr 36830   334-821-2430
Don Roberts, hdmstr.   Fax 821-0876

Autaugaville, Autauga, Pop. 848
Autauga County SD
Supt. — See Prattville
Autaugaville S   400/K-12
PO Box 9 36003   334-365-8329
John Clay, prin.   Fax 365-8043

Bay Minette, Baldwin, Pop. 7,845
Baldwin County SD   26,000/K-12
2600 Hand Ave 36507   251-937-0306
Faron Hollinger Ed.D., supt.   Fax 937-0318
www.bcbe.org
Baldwin County HS   1,200/9-12
1 Tiger Dr 36507   251-937-2341
Eddie Mitchell, prin.   Fax 937-2933
Bay Minette MS   900/6-8
600 Blackburn Ave 36507   251-937-9243
Tammie Fleming, prin.   Fax 937-3721
North Baldwin Center for Tech   Vo/Tech
505 W Hurricane Rd 36507   251-937-6751
John Cabaniss, prin.   Fax 937-4688
Other Schools – See Daphne, Elberta, Fairhope, Foley,
Gulf Shores, Robertsdale, Spanish Fort

James H. Faulkner State Comm. College   Post-Sec.
1900 S US Highway 31 36507   251-580-2100

Bayou La Batre, Mobile, Pop. 2,754
Mobile County SD
Supt. — See Mobile
Alba MS   600/6-8
14180 S Wintzell Ave 36509   251-824-4134
James Gill, prin.   Fax 824-1324

Bear Creek, Marion, Pop. 1,015
Marion County SD
Supt. — See Hamilton
Phillips HS   200/7-12
142 School Ave 35543   205-486-3737
Lynda Hall, prin.   Fax 486-1716

Beatrice, Monroe, Pop. 404
Monroe County SD
Supt. — See Monroeville
Shields HS   200/7-12
17688 State Highway 21 N 36425   251-789-2168
Marion McIntosh, prin.   Fax 789-2715

Berry, Fayette, Pop. 1,225
Fayette County SD
Supt. — See Fayette
Berry JSHS   300/7-12
18242 Highway 18 E 35546   205-689-4467
Vic Herren, prin.   Fax 689-8819

Rhema Christian Academy   50/K-12
21506 Highway 18 E 35546   205-689-1274
Sheila Clark, prin.   Fax 932-4427

Bessemer, Jefferson, Pop. 29,108
Bessemer CSD   4,200/K-12
PO Box 1230 35021   205-432-3000
Deborah Horn Ed.D., supt.   Fax 432-3085
www.bessk12.org
Bessemer Center for Technology   Vo/Tech
50 High School Dr 35022   205-432-3798
Dr. Keith Mahaffey, prin.   Fax 432-3811
Davis MS   900/6-8
1224 Clarendon Ave 35020   205-432-3600
Albert Soles, prin.   Fax 432-3607
Lanier HS   1,100/9-12
100 High School Dr 35022   205-432-3700
Jerome Cook, prin.   Fax 432-3791

Jefferson County SD
Supt. — See Birmingham
Oak Grove HS   800/6-12
9494 Oak Grove Pkwy 35023   205-379-5000
Alan Pruden, prin.   Fax 379-5045

Bessemer State Technical College   Post-Sec.
PO Box 308 35021   205-426-7389
ITT Technical Institute   Post-Sec.
6270 Park South Dr 35022   205-497-5700
Rock Creek Academy   50/1-12
901 Glaze Dr 35023   205-436-3757
Nick Hope, hdmstr.

Billingsley, Autauga, Pop. 116
Autauga County SD
Supt. — See Prattville
Billingsley S   800/K-12
PO Box 118 36006   205-755-1629
Van Smith, prin.   Fax 755-1633

Birmingham, Jefferson, Pop. 236,620
Birmingham CSD   33,200/K-12
PO Box 10007 35202   205-231-4600
Dr. Wayman Shiver, supt.   Fax 231-4761
www.bhm.k12.al.us
Alabama Fine Arts JSHS   1,000/7-12
1800 8th Ave N 35203   205-252-9241
John Northrop, prin.   Fax 251-9541
Arrington MS   500/6-8
2101 Jefferson Ave SW 35211   205-231-1130
Sherene Carpenter, prin.   Fax 231-1133
Banks MS   500/6-8
721 86th St S 35206   205-231-5190
Jessie Dabert, prin.   Fax 231-5218
Bush Magnet MS   700/6-8
1112 25th Street Ensley 35218   205-231-6000
Aurlinda Hagler, prin.   Fax 231-6007
Carver HS   1,300/9-12
3900 24th St N 35207   205-231-3900
Darrell Hudson, prin.   Fax 231-3973
Center Street MS   600/6-8
1832 Center Way S 35205   205-231-7187
Cassandra Fincher Fells, prin.   Fax 231-7231
Ensley Magnet HS   700/9-12
2301 Avenue J 35218   205-231-6250
Ethel Ransom Knight, prin.   Fax 231-6925
Gaskins MS   600/6-8
200 Dalton Dr 35215   205-231-9200
Millard Hicks, prin.   Fax 231-9253
Glenn MS   400/6-8
901 16th St W 35208   205-231-6370
Dr. Cleo Larry, prin.   Fax 231-6954
Green Acres MS   500/6-8
1220 67th St W 35228   205-231-1370
Evelyn Baugh, prin.   Fax 231-1414
Hayes HS   700/9-11
505 43rd St N 35222   205-231-8440
Vanessa Byrd, prin.   Fax 231-8939
Huffman Magnet HS   1,300/9-12
950 Springville Rd 35215   205-231-5000
Willie Goldsmith, prin.   Fax 231-5056
Huffman Magnet MS   300/6-8
517 Huffman Rd 35215   205-231-5370
Marilyn Gibson, prin.   Fax 231-5426
Jackson-Olin HS   600/9-12
510 12th Street Ensley 35218   205-231-6431
Linda Parson, prin.   Fax 231-6527
Kirby MS   300/6-8
1328 28th St N 35234   205-231-3370
Ponzella Fuller, prin.   Fax 231-3414
Olin Vocational HS   Vo/Tech
1054 Avenue F 35218   205-783-6126
Linda Parson, prin.
Parker HS   1,100/9-12
900 4th St N 35204   205-231-2370
Joseph Martin, prin.   Fax 231-2916
Payne MS   400/6-8
1500 Daniel Payne Dr 35214   205-231-3190
Pinnie Yarbrough, prin.   Fax 231-3236
Putnam Magnet MS   400/6-8
1757 Montclair Rd 35210   205-231-8680
Michael Scott, prin.   Fax 231-8685
Smith MS   500/6-8
1124 Five Mile Rd 35215   205-231-5675
Charles Willis, prin.   Fax 231-5899
Wenonah HS   1,000/9-12
2916 Wilson Rd SW 35221   205-231-1675
Regina Carr Hunter, prin.   Fax 231-1921
West End HS   800/9-12
1840 Pearson Ave SW 35211   205-231-1740
Allen Lewis, prin.   Fax 231-1976
Wilkerson MS   500/6-8
116 11th Ct N 35204   205-231-2740
Constance Burns, prin.   Fax 231-2790
Woodlawn Magnet HS   900/9-12
5620 1st Ave N 35212   205-231-8000
Shirley Graham, prin.   Fax 231-8084

Hoover CSD
Supt. — See Hoover
Berry HS   1,100/6-8
4500 Jaguar Dr 35242   205-439-2000
Dr. Kathleen Wheaton, prin.   Fax 439-2001
Spain Park HS   1,300/9-12
4700 Jaguar Dr 35242   205-439-1400
Billy Broadway, prin.   Fax 439-1401

Jefferson County SD   35,000/K-12
2100 18th St S 35209   205-379-2000
Dr. Phil Hammonds, supt.   Fax 379-2311
www.jefcoed.com/
Erwin JSHS   1,100/7-12
532 23rd Ave NW 35215   205-379-3400
Van Phillips, prin.   Fax 856-6663
Fultondale JSHS   500/7-12
1450 Carson Rd N 35217   205-379-3500
Donna Williamon, prin.   Fax 379-3545
Gresham MS   500/6-8
2650 Gresham Dr 35243   205-379-3800
Margaret McCullough, prin.   Fax 379-3845
Shades Valley Technical Academy   Vo/Tech
5191 Pine Whispers Dr 35210   205-379-3300
Zsolt Batizy, prin.   Fax 951-1347
Other Schools – See Adamsville, Bessemer,
Gardendale, Hueytown, Irondale, Kimberly, Mc Calla,
Morris, Pinson, Pleasant Grove, Trussville, Warrior

Shelby County SD
Supt. — See Columbiana
Oak Mountain HS   1,700/9-12
5476 Caldwell Mill Rd 35242   205-682-5200
Randy Fuller, prin.   Fax 682-5205
Oak Mountain MS   1,300/6-8
5650 Cahaba Valley Rd 35242   205-682-5210
Larry Haynes, prin.   Fax 682-5215
Riverchase MS   1,100/6-8
853 Willow Oak Dr 35244   205-682-5510
Charles Smith, prin.   Fax 682-5515

Tarrant CSD
Supt. — See Tarrant
Tarrant City MS   500/5-8
1 Wildcat Dr 35217   205-849-0168
Judy Mattews, prin.   Fax 849-3728

Alabama State College of Barber Styling   Post-Sec.
9480 Parkway E 35215   205-836-2404
Altamont S   400/5-12
PO Box 131429 35213   205-879-2006
Thomas M.S. Wheelock, prin.   Fax 871-5666
American Academy for Young Professionals   50/7-12
1627 Dennison Ave SW 35211   205-925-4673
Juliet Arrington, admin.   Fax 925-4673
American Sentinel University   Post-Sec.
2101 Magnolia Ave S Ste 200 35205   205-323-6191
Andrew Jackson University   Post-Sec.
10 Old Montgomery Hwy 35209   205-871-9288
Baptist Health System   Post-Sec.
PO Box 830605 35283   205-715-5319
Birmingham-Southern College   Post-Sec.
900 Arkadelphia Rd 35254   800-523-5793
Briarwood Christian S   1,800/PK-12
2204 Briarwood Way 35243   205-776-5800
Byrle Kynerd, admin.   Fax 776-5815
Carraway Methodist Medical Center   Post-Sec.
1600 Carraway Blvd 35234   205-226-6000
Carroll HS   900/9-12
300 Lakeshore Pkwy 35209   205-940-2400
David Chauvette, prin.   Fax 945-7429
Central Park Christian S   200/K-12
1900 43rd St W 35208   205-786-4811
Fax 786-0140
Ephesus Junior Academy   200/K-12
829 McMillon Ave SW 35211   205-786-2194
Willie Walker, prin.   Fax 786-0857
Holy Family HS   200/9-12
2001 19th Street Ensley 35218   205-787-9937
John Ippolito, prin.   Fax 787-8530
Jefferson State Community College   Post-Sec.
2601 Carson Rd 35215   205-853-1200
Lawson State Community College   Post-Sec.
3060 Wilson Rd SW 35221   205-925-2515
Miles College   Post-Sec.
PO Box 3800 35208   205-929-1000
New Generation Christian S   50/PK-12
924 41st St N 35212   205-591-5552
John Davis, hdmstr.
Parkway Christian Academy   500/PK-12
959 Huffman Rd 35215   205-833-2410
Rachel Howze, prin.   Fax 833-4692
Samford University   Post-Sec.
800 Lakeshore Dr 35229   205-726-3673
Southeastern Bible College   Post-Sec.
2545 Valleydale Rd 35244   205-970-9200
University of Alabama at Birmingham   Post-Sec.
Univ Sta 35205   205-934-4011
University of Alabama Hospital   Post-Sec.
619 19th St S 35249   205-934-5490
Virginia College   Post-Sec.
65 Bagby Dr 35209   205-802-1200
Winewood Christian S   50/PK-12
2974 Winewood Rd 35215   205-853-9906
John Davis, hdmstr.   Fax 854-9629

Blountsville, Blount, Pop. 1,844
Blount County SD
Supt. — See Oneonta
Moore HS   500/7-12
4040 Susan Moore Rd 35031   205-466-7663
Clay Daughtry, prin.   Fax 466-7858
Pennington HS   500/7-12
81 College St 35031   205-429-4101
Craig Sosebee, prin.   Fax 429-4104

Boaz, Marshall, Pop. 7,628
Boaz CSD   2,200/K-12
PO Box 721 35957   256-593-8180
Leland Dishman, supt.   Fax 593-8181
www.boazk12.org/
Boaz HS   700/9-12
907 Brown St 35957   256-593-2401
Lowell Smith, prin.   Fax 593-2403
Boaz MS   600/6-8
140 Newt Parker Dr 35957   256-593-0799
Ray Landers, prin.   Fax 593-0729

Snead State Community College   Post-Sec.
Walnut St 35957   256-593-5120

Brantley, Crenshaw, Pop. 901
Crenshaw County SD
Supt. — See Luverne

Brantley S   600/PK-12
PO Box 86 36009   334-527-8879
Waylon Bush, prin.   Fax 527-3405

Bremen, Cullman
Cullman County SD
Supt. — See Cullman
Cold Springs HS   400/7-12
PO Box 130 35033   256-287-1787
William Calvert, prin.   Fax 287-2841

Brewton, Escambia, Pop. 5,348
Brewton CSD   1,400/K-12
811 Belleville Ave 36426   251-867-8400
Lynn Smith, supt.   Fax 867-8403
www.brewtoncityschools.org/
Brewton MS   500/5-8
301 Liles Blvd 36426   251-867-8420
Douglas Prater, prin.   Fax 867-8422
Miller HS   400/9-12
1835 Douglas Ave 36426   251-867-8430
Donald Rotch, prin.   Fax 867-8432

Escambia County SD   4,600/K-12
PO Box 307 36427   251-867-6251
Melvin Powell, supt.   Fax 867-6252
escambiak12.net
Escambia-Brewton Area Career/Tech Center   Vo/Tech
2824 Pea Ridge Rd 36426   251-867-7829
Jane Henderson, prin.   Fax 867-7064
Other Schools – See Atmore, East Brewton, Flomaton

Jefferson Davis Community College   Post-Sec.
PO Box 958 36427   251-867-4832

Bridgeport, Jackson, Pop. 2,673
Jackson County SD
Supt. — See Scottsboro
Bridgeport MS   200/5-8
620 Jacobs Ave 35740   256-495-2967
Darrell Kirk, prin.   Fax 495-2850

Brilliant, Marion, Pop. 730
Marion County SD
Supt. — See Hamilton
Brilliant HS   200/7-12
PO Box 90 35548   205-465-2322
Jack Hayes, prin.   Fax 465-2382

Brookwood, Tuscaloosa, Pop. 1,482
Tuscaloosa County SD
Supt. — See Tuscaloosa
Brookwood HS   800/9-12
15981 Highway 216 35444   205-342-5005
Laura McBride, prin.   Fax 556-8972

Brundidge, Pike, Pop. 2,328
Pike County SD
Supt. — See Troy
Pike County JSHS   500/7-12
552 S Main St 36010   334-735-2389
Mike Hall, prin.   Fax 735-3176

Bryant, Jackson

Mountain View Christian Academy   100/PK-12
3665 AL Highway 73 35958   256-597-3467
Trudy Shadrick, prin.   Fax 597-3467

Butler, Choctaw, Pop. 1,839
Choctaw County SD   1,500/K-12
107 Tom Orr Dr 36904   205-459-3031
William Boggs, supt.   Fax 459-3037
choctawboe.k12.al.us/
Choctaw County HS   500/7-12
277 Tom Orr Dr 36904   205-459-2139
Dyana Thomas, prin.   Fax 459-2277
Orr Career Technical Center   Vo/Tech
105 Tom Orr Dr 36904   205-459-3031
B. Smith, prin.   Fax 459-3037
Other Schools – See Gilbertown

Patrician Academy   400/K-12
901 S Mulberry Ave 36904   205-459-3605
Marcus Walters Ph.D., prin.   Fax 459-4802

Calera, Shelby, Pop. 5,130
Shelby County SD
Supt. — See Columbiana
Calera MSHS   600/6-12
8454 Highway 31 35040   205-682-6100
Ken Mobley, prin.   Fax 682-6105

Camden, Wilcox, Pop. 2,224
Wilcox County SD   2,500/PK-12
PO Box 160 36726   334-682-4716
Malcolm Cain, supt.   Fax 682-4179
Camden S of Arts & Technology   400/7-8
PO Box 698 36726   334-682-4514
Andre Saulsberry, prin.   Fax 682-5934
Wilcox Central HS   700/9-12
PO Box 1089 36726   334-682-9239
James Thomas, prin.   Fax 682-5411

Wilcox Academy, PO Box 1149 36726   300/K-12
Buddy Sumner, prin.   334-682-9619

Camp Hill, Tallapoosa, Pop. 1,212
Tallapoosa County SD
Supt. — See Dadeville
Bell S   300/K-12
PO Box 490 36850   256-896-2865
Glenda Mennifee, prin.   Fax 896-2527

Lyman Ward Military Academy   200/6-12
PO Box 550 36850   800-798-9151
Dr. Chester C. Carroll, pres.   Fax 896-4661

Carbon Hill, Walker, Pop. 2,048
Walker County SD
Supt. — See Jasper
Carbon Hill HS   300/9-12
PO Box 579 35549   205-924-8821
Dr. Diane Jones, prin.   Fax 924-8877

Carrollton, Pickens, Pop. 961
Pickens County SD   3,300/K-12
PO Box 32 35447   205-367-2080
Dr. Leonard Duff, supt.   Fax 367-8404
www.pcboe.org
Carrollton Unit S   400/K-12
PO Box 320 35447   205-367-8152
Anissa Ball, prin.   Fax 367-8908
LaDow Technology Center   Vo/Tech
377 Ladow Center Cir 35447   205-367-8194
Mike Maughan, prin.   Fax 367-2123
Other Schools – See Aliceville, Gordo, Reform

Pickens Academy   400/PK-12
225 Ray Bass Rd 35447   205-367-8144
Louis Mc Bride, prin.   Fax 367-2164

Cedar Bluff, Cherokee, Pop. 1,496
Cherokee County SD
Supt. — See Centre
Cedar Bluff S   600/K-12
3655 Old Highway 9 35959   256-779-6211
Bobby Mintz, prin.   Fax 779-8328

Centre, Cherokee, Pop. 3,273
Cherokee County SD   4,200/PK-12
130 E Main St 35960   256-927-3362
Brian Johnson, supt.   Fax 927-3399
www.cherokeek12.org/
Centre MS   400/6-8
350 E Main St 35960   256-927-5656
Renee Miller, prin.   Fax 927-4656
Cherokee Co. Career & Technology Center   Vo/Tech
600 Bay Springs Rd 35960   256-927-5351
Mitchell Guice, prin.   Fax 927-3501
Cherokee County HS   500/9-12
910 Warrior Dr 35960   256-927-3625
Paul Hyche, prin.   Fax 927-6445
Other Schools – See Cedar Bluff, Gaylesville, Leesburg, Spring Garden

Cahawba Christian Academy   100/PK-12
2415 Montevallo Rd 35042   205-926-4676
Diane Thompson, prin.

Chatom, Washington, Pop. 1,177
Washington County SD   3,600/K-12
PO Box 1359 36518   251-847-2401
Tim Savage, supt.   Fax 847-3611
washingtoncounty.al.schoolwebpages.com
Washington County AVC   Vo/Tech
PO Box 1298 36518   251-847-2040
Harold Crouch, prin.   Fax 847-3489
Washington County JSHS   600/5-12
PO Box 1329 36518   251-847-2851
Sidney Hinton, prin.   Fax 847-2825
Other Schools – See Fruitdale, Leroy, Mc Intosh, Millry

Chelsea, Shelby, Pop. 3,493
Shelby County SD
Supt. — See Columbiana
Chelsea HS   600/9-12
PO Box 639 35043   205-682-7200
Pat Grey, prin.   Fax 682-7205
Chelsea MS   500/6-8
PO Box 600 35043   205-682-7210
Mike Burns, prin.   Fax 682-7215

Cherokee, Colbert, Pop. 1,195
Colbert County SD
Supt. — See Tuscumbia
Cherokee HS   200/9-12
850 High School Dr 35616   256-359-4434
Ricky Willingham, prin.   Fax 359-4060
Cherokee MS   300/5-8
4595 Old Lee Hwy 35616   256-359-6432
Larry Grissom, prin.   Fax 359-6543

Chickasaw, Mobile, Pop. 6,099
Mobile County SD
Supt. — See Mobile
Clark S of Math & Science   800/4-8
50 12th Ave 36611   251-221-2106
Dianne McWain, prin.   Fax 221-2108

Childersburg, Talladega, Pop. 4,996
Talladega County SD
Supt. — See Talladega
Childersburg HS   500/9-12
122 Faye S Perry Dr 35044   256-315-5475
Kevin Maddox, prin.   Fax 315-5495
Childersburg MS   600/5-8
800 4th St SE 35044   256-315-5505
Jena Jones, prin.   Fax 315-5520

Citronelle, Mobile, Pop. 3,675
Mobile County SD
Supt. — See Mobile
Citronelle HS   600/9-12
19325 Rowe St 36522   251-221-3444
Alex Crane, prin.   Fax 221-3448
Lott MS   600/6-8
17740 Celeste Rd 36522   251-221-2240
Thomas Campbell, prin.   Fax 221-2247

Clanton, Chilton, Pop. 8,096
Chilton County SD   7,100/PK-12
1705 Lay Dam Rd 35045   205-280-3000
Mildred Ellison, supt.   Fax 755-6549
www.chilton.k12.al.us
Chilton County HS   600/9-12
1214 7th St 35045   205-280-2710
Larry Mahaffey, prin.   Fax 755-0618
Clanton MS   600/6-8
835 Temple Rd 35045   205-280-2750
Don Finlayson, prin.   Fax 755-2446

LeCroy Career Tech Center   Vo/Tech
2829 4th Ave N 35045   205-280-2920
David Conway, prin.   Fax 755-2035
Other Schools – See Jemison, Maplesville, Thorsby, Verbena

Clayton, Barbour, Pop. 1,420
Barbour County SD   700/PK-12
PO Box 429 36016   334-775-3453
Vic Adkison, supt.   Fax 775-7301
Barbour County HS   400/9-12
PO Box 339 36016   334-775-3545
David Hobdy, prin.   Fax 775-8861
Other Schools – See Louisville

Cleveland, Blount, Pop. 1,306
Blount County SD
Supt. — See Oneonta
Blount County Center of Technology   Vo/Tech
PO Box 125 35049   205-625-3424
Philip Cleveland, dir.   Fax 625-3427
Cleveland HS   400/7-12
71 High School Av 35049   205-274-9915
Denise Martin, prin.   Fax 274-0201

Coffeeville, Clarke, Pop. 355
Clarke County SD
Supt. — See Grove Hill
Coffeeville JSHS   100/7-12
PO Box 130 36524   251-276-3227
Janice Richardson, prin.   Fax 276-0349

Collinsville, DeKalb, Pop. 1,649
De Kalb County SD
Supt. — See Rainsville
Collinsville S   600/K-12
PO Box 269 35961   256-524-2111
Paulette Davis, prin.   Fax 524-7526

Columbia, Houston, Pop. 805
Houston County SD
Supt. — See Dothan
Houston County JSHS   400/7-12
PO Box 519 36319   334-696-2221
Scott Stephens, prin.   Fax 696-4677

Columbiana, Shelby, Pop. 3,526
Shelby County SD   23,700/K-12
PO Box 1910 35051   205-682-7000
Evan Major, supt.   Fax 682-7005
www.shelbyk.k12.al.us
Columbiana MS   600/6-8
222 Joiner Town Rd 35051   205-682-6610
David Dixon, prin.   Fax 682-6615
School of Technology   Vo/Tech
701 Highway 70 35051   205-682-6650
Tim Eliff, prin.   Fax 682-6655
Shelby County HS   600/9-12
101 Washington St 35051   205-682-6600
Gene Rogers, prin.   Fax 682-6605
Other Schools – See Alabaster, Birmingham, Calera, Chelsea, Montevallo, Pelham, Vincent

Cornerstone Christian S   200/PK-12
24975 Highway 25 35051   205-669-7777
Laurie Porter, hdmstr.   Fax 669-5283

Cordova, Walker, Pop. 2,340
Walker County SD
Supt. — See Jasper
Bankhead MS   300/5-8
110 School St 35550   205-483-7245
Dr. Gypsy Stovall, prin.   Fax 483-7244
Cordova HS   300/9-12
1 Blue Devil Way 35550   205-483-7404
Dr. Jason Adkins, prin.   Fax 483-1934

Cottondale, Tuscaloosa
Tuscaloosa CSD
Supt. — See Tuscaloosa
Bryant HS   800/9-12
6315 Mary Harmon Bryant Dr 35453   205-759-3538
Amanda Cassity, prin.   Fax 759-8315
Eastwood MS   900/6-8
6314 Mary Harmon Bryant Dr 35453   205-759-3612
   Fax 759-3798

Tuscaloosa County SD
Supt. — See Tuscaloosa
Davis - Emerson MS   500/6-8
1550 Prude Mill Rd 35453   205-342-2750
Dwight Monroe, prin.   Fax 633-1155

Tuscaloosa Christian S   300/PK-12
PO Box 250 35453   205-553-4303
Dan Lancaster, prin.

Cottonwood, Houston, Pop. 1,167
Houston County SD
Supt. — See Dothan
Cottonwood S   800/K-12
663 Houston St 36320   334-691-2587
Judy Fowler, prin.   Fax 691-4200

Courtland, Lawrence, Pop. 759
Lawrence County SD
Supt. — See Moulton
Hubbard S   500/K-12
12905 Jessie Jackson Pkwy 35618   256-637-3010
Dr. Denise Stovall, prin.   Fax 637-3006

Crossville, DeKalb, Pop. 1,438
De Kalb County SD
Supt. — See Rainsville
Crossville HS   700/6-12
PO Box 38 35962   256-528-7858
David Uptain, prin.   Fax 528-7840

Cullman, Cullman, Pop. 14,395
Cullman CSD   2,700/K-12
301 1st St NE 35055   256-734-2233
Jan Harris Ed.D., supt.   Fax 737-9621
www.cullmancats.net
Cullman City Career Tech S   Vo/Tech
800 2nd Ave NE 35055   256-734-7959
Bridgette Chandler, prin.   Fax 734-7711
Cullman HS   900/9-12
510 13th St NE 35055   256-734-3923
Patrick Lane Hill, prin.   Fax 734-9570

Cullman MS
800 2nd Ave NE 35055 — 400/7-8 — 256-734-7959
Jayne Barnett, prin. — Fax 734-7711

Cullman County SD — 9,900/PK-12
PO Box 1590 35056 — 256-734-2933
Dr. Nancy Horton, supt. — Fax 736-2402
www.ccboe.org/
Cullman Area Career Center — Vo/Tech
17640 US Highway 31 35058 — 256-734-7740
Rebecca Eason, prin. — Fax 734-7464
Fairview HS — 500/9-12
841 Welcome Rd 35058 — 256-796-5106
Stanley Burden, prin. — Fax 796-9025
Fairview MS — 400/6-8
841 Welcome Rd 35058 — 256-796-0883
Mickey Tankersley, prin. — Fax 796-0885
Good Hope HS — 400/9-12
210 Good Hope School Rd 35057 — 256-734-3807
Dr. Anita Kilpatrick, prin. — Fax 734-3427
Good Hope MS — 300/6-8
216 Good Hope School Rd 35057 — 256-734-9600
Wayne Weissend, prin. — Fax 734-9704
West Point HS — 600/9-12
4314 County Road 1141 35057 — 256-734-5375
Darrell Brock, prin. — Fax 775-6047
Other Schools – See Bremen, Hanceville, Holly Pond, Vinemont

St. Bernard Prep HS — 100/9-12
101 Saint Bernard Ave SE 35055 — 256-739-6682
Rev. Joel Martin, prin. — Fax 734-2925

Dadeville, Tallapoosa, Pop. 3,153
Tallapoosa County SD — 3,200/K-12
125 N Broadnax St Rm 113 36853 — 256-825-1020
Ginger East, supt. — Fax 825-1003
tallapoosa.k12.al.us/~bpage/Schools/schools.html
Dadeville HS — 600/8-12
227 Weldon St 36853 — 256-825-7848
Jason Yohn, prin. — Fax 825-0697
Other Schools – See Camp Hill, New Site, Notasulga

Daleville, Dale, Pop. 4,611
Daleville CSD — 1,600/K-12
626 N Daleville Ave 36322 — 334-598-2456
Andrew Kelley, supt. — Fax 598-9006
www.daleville.k12.al.us
Daleville HS — 600/9-12
626 N Daleville Ave 36322 — 334-598-4461
Mike McDuffie, prin. — Fax 598-3850
Daleville MS — 500/5-8
626 N Daleville Ave 36322 — 334-598-4463
Kenneth Seay, prin. — Fax 598-9006

Danville, Morgan
Lawrence County SD
Supt. — See Moulton
Speake S — 500/K-12
6559 County Road 81 35619 — 256-974-9201
Dr. Tommy Whitlow, prin. — Fax 905-2483

Morgan County SD
Supt. — See Decatur
Danville HS — 300/9-12
9235 Danville Rd 35619 — 256-773-9909
Gilmer Ellis, prin. — Fax 773-5622
Danville MS — 400/5-8
5933 Highway 36 W 35619 — 256-773-7723
Gary Walker, prin. — Fax 773-7708

Daphne, Baldwin, Pop. 17,697
Baldwin County SD
Supt. — See Bay Minette
Daphne HS — 1,600/9-12
9300 Lawson Rd 36526 — 251-626-8787
Barry Pennington, prin. — Fax 626-3024
Daphne MS — 700/7-8
1 Jodie Davis Cir 36526 — 251-626-2845
Anthony Sampson, prin. — Fax 626-0025

Bayside Academy — 700/PK-12
303 Dryer Ave 36526 — 251-626-2840
Thomas Johnson, prin. — Fax 626-2899
United States Sports Academy — Post-Sec.
1 Academy Dr 36526 — 251-626-3303

Deatsville, Elmore, Pop. 358
Elmore County SD
Supt. — See Wetumpka
Holtville HS — 400/9-12
10425 Holtville Rd 36022 — 334-569-3034
Jimmy Hull, prin. — Fax 569-1013
Holtville MS — 500/5-8
655 Bulldog Ln 36022 — 334-569-3574
Verna Webb, prin. — Fax 569-3258

J. F. Ingram State Technical College — Post-Sec.
PO Box 220350 36022 — 334-285-7870

Decatur, Morgan, Pop. 54,239
Decatur CSD — 9,100/PK-12
302 4th Ave NE 35601 — 256-552-3000
Dr. Samuel L. Houston, supt. — Fax 552-3981
www.dcs.edu
Austin HS — 1,400/9-12
1625 Danville Rd SW 35601 — 256-552-3060
Dr. Donald Snow, prin. — Fax 350-7802
Brookhaven MS — 700/6-8
1302 5th Ave SW 35601 — 256-552-3045
Dr. Larry Collier, prin. — Fax 552-3047
Cedar Ridge MS — 800/6-8
2715 Danville Rd SW 35603 — 256-552-4622
Dr. Elizabeth Lacy, prin. — Fax 552-4623
Decatur HS — 1,000/9-12
1011 Prospect Dr SE 35601 — 256-552-3011
Mike Ward, prin. — Fax 308-2535
Oak Park MS — 700/6-8
1218 16th Ave SE 35601 — 256-552-3035
Dwight Satterfield, prin. — Fax 552-3082

Morgan County SD — 7,700/K-12
1325 Point Mallard Pkwy 35601 — 256-309-2105
Don Murphy, supt. — Fax 309-2187
www.morgank12.org
Priceville HS — 800/6-12
317 Highway 67 S 35603 — 256-353-1950
Guy Bowling, prin. — Fax 353-2802

Other Schools – See Danville, Falkville, Somerville, Trinity

Calhoun Community College — Post-Sec.
PO Box 2216 35609 — 256-306-2500
Decatur Heritage Christian Academy — 400/PK-12
PO Box 5659 35601 — 256-351-4275
Scott Mayo, hdmstr. — Fax 355-4738

Demopolis, Marengo, Pop. 7,372
Demopolis CSD — 2,300/PK-12
PO Box 759 36732 — 334-289-1670
W. Wesley Hill, supt. — Fax 289-1689
www.demopolishighschool.org
Demopolis HS — 600/9-12
701 US Highway 80 W 36732 — 334-289-0294
Dr. Isaac Espy, prin. — Fax 289-8777
Demopolis MS — 600/6-8
300 E Pettus St 36732 — 334-289-4242
Clarence Jackson, prin. — Fax 289-2670

Marengo County SD
Supt. — See Linden
Essex S — 300/K-12
70 Hornet Dr 36732 — 334-289-3504
Loretta McCoy, prin. — Fax 289-3591

West Alabama Preparatory S — 200/PK-12
1908 Mauvilla Dr 36732 — 334-289-0452
John Holley, prin. — Fax 289-0464

Dixons Mills, Marengo
Marengo County SD
Supt. — See Linden
Marengo S — 500/K-12
212 Panther Dr 36736 — 334-992-2395
George Green, prin. — Fax 992-2197

Dora, Walker, Pop. 2,359
Walker County SD
Supt. — See Jasper
Dora HS — 500/9-12
330 Glenn C Gant Cir 35062 — 205-648-6863
Ricky Pate, prin. — Fax 648-4709

Dothan, Houston, Pop. 60,036
Dothan CSD — 8,800/K-12
500 Dusy St 36301 — 334-793-1397
Dr. Sam Nichols, supt. — Fax 794-1499
www.dothan.k12.al.us
Beverlye MS — 600/6-8
1025 S Beverlye Rd 36301 — 334-794-1432
James Larry Norris, prin. — Fax 792-0886
Carver S for Math Science & Technology — 500/6-8
1001 Webb Rd 36303 — 334-794-1440
Dr. James Kelley, prin. — Fax 794-1587
Dothan HS — 1,400/9-12
1236 S Oates St 36301 — 334-794-1400
Dr. Jimmy McCarty, prin. — Fax 677-0099
Dothan Technology Center — Vo/Tech
3165 Reeves St 36303 — 334-794-1436
Greg Allen, prin. — Fax 794-1439
Girard MS — 500/6-8
600 Girard Ave 36303 — 334-794-1426
Greg Yance, prin. — Fax 794-6373
Honeysuckle MS — 600/6-8
1665 Honeysuckle Rd 36305 — 334-794-1420
Patsy Slaughter, prin. — Fax 678-6546
Northview HS — 1,100/9-12
3209 Reeves St 36303 — 334-794-1410
Ron Snell, prin. — Fax 702-4802

Houston County SD — 5,700/K-12
PO Box 1688 36302 — 334-792-8331
Tim Pitchford, supt. — Fax 792-1016
hcboe.us/
Rehobeth HS — 600/9-12
373 Malvern Rd 36301 — 334-677-7002
Matt Swann, prin. — Fax 677-2699
Rehobeth MS — 500/6-8
5631 County 203 Rd 36301 — 334-677-5153
John Dixon, prin. — Fax 677-5947
Other Schools – See Ashford, Columbia, Cottonwood, Newton

Emmanuel Christian S — 400/K-12
178 Earline Rd 36305 — 334-792-0935
Mark Redmond, prin. — Fax 702-7410
Flowers Hospital — Post-Sec.
PO Box 6907 36302 — 334-793-5000
George C. Wallace State Comm College — Post-Sec.
1141 Wallace Dr 36303 — 334-983-3521
Houston Academy — 600/PK-12
901 Buena Vista Dr 36303 — 334-794-4106
John O'Connell, prin. — Fax 793-4053
Providence Christian S — 600/1-12
4847 Murphy Mill Rd 36303 — 334-702-8933
Gary Waddell, admin. — Fax 702-0700
Southeast Alabama Medical Center — Post-Sec.
PO Box 6987 36302 — 334-793-8100
Troy University — Post-Sec.
PO Box 8368 36304 — 334-983-6556

Double Springs, Winston, Pop. 979
Winston County SD — 2,800/K-12
PO Box 9 35553 — 205-489-5018
Sue Reed, supt. — Fax 489-3203
www.winstonk12.org
Double Springs MS — 300/5-8
PO Box 669 35553 — 205-489-3813
Ben Aderholt, prin. — Fax 489-8832
Winston County HS — 300/9-12
PO Box 549 35553 — 205-489-5593
Jeff Cole, prin. — Fax 489-8204
Winston Co. Technical Center — Vo/Tech
PO Box 1000 35553 — 205-489-2121
Shandy Porter, prin. — Fax 489-2121
Other Schools – See Addison, Arley, Lynn

Douglas, Marshall, Pop. 549
Marshall County SD
Supt. — See Guntersville
Douglas HS — 500/9-12
PO Box 300 35964 — 256-593-2810
Sarah Mitchell, prin. — Fax 840-5489
Douglas MS — 500/6-8
PO Box 269 35964 — 256-593-1240
Larry Wilson, prin. — Fax 593-1259

East Brewton, Escambia, Pop. 2,445
Escambia County SD
Supt. — See Brewton
Neal HS — 400/9-12
801 Andrew Jackson St 36426 — 251-867-4645
Phillip Ellis, prin. — Fax 867-4642
Neal MS — 400/5-8
PO Box 2385, — 251-867-5035
Gayle Fountain, prin. — Fax 867-5051

Eclectic, Elmore, Pop. 1,083
Elmore County SD
Supt. — See Wetumpka
Eclectic MS — 600/5-8
170 S Ann St 36024 — 334-541-2131
Matt Coker, prin. — Fax 541-3556
Elmore County JSHS — 900/7-12
155 N College Ave 36024 — 334-541-3662
James Adams, prin. — Fax 541-4441

Eight Mile, See Prichard

Alpha & Omega Christian S — 100/K-12
2420 S Shelton Beach Rd 36613 — 251-452-0545
Deborah Stokes, prin. — Fax 457-3421

Elba, Coffee, Pop. 4,192
Coffee County SD — 1,900/K-12
400 Reddoch Hill Rd 36323 — 334-897-5016
Dr. Linda Ingram, supt. — Fax 897-6207
www.coffeecountyschools.org
Other Schools – See Jack, Kinston, New Brockton

Elba CSD — 1,000/K-12
131 Tiger Dr 36323 — 334-897-2801
Danny Weeks, supt. — Fax 897-5601
www.elbaed.com
Elba Area Vocational HS — Vo/Tech
371 Tiger Dr 36323 — 334-897-2266
Larry Goodson, prin. — Fax 897-5106
Elba HS — 500/7-12
371 Tiger Dr 36323 — 334-897-2266
Johnny Dunn, prin. — Fax 897-5106

Elberta, Baldwin, Pop. 571
Baldwin County SD
Supt. — See Bay Minette
Elberta MS — 600/4-8
13355 Main St 36530 — 251-986-8127
Jane Peacock, prin. — Fax 986-7472

Elkmont, Limestone, Pop. 475
Limestone County SD
Supt. — See Athens
Elkmont S — 1,000/K-12
25630 Evans Ave 35620 — 256-732-4291
Mickey Glass, prin. — Fax 732-3418

Enterprise, Coffee, Pop. 21,861
Enterprise CSD — 5,400/K-12
PO Box 311790 36331 — 334-347-9531
Dr. Jim Reese, supt. — Fax 347-5102
www.enterpriseschools.net/
Dauphin JHS — 400/8-9
425 Dauphin St 36330 — 334-347-1141
Perry Vickers, prin. — Fax 347-0845
Enterprise JHS — 400/8-9
401 W College St 36330 — 334-347-1733
Greg Faught, prin. — Fax 347-1009
Enterprise SHS — 1,200/10-12
500 E Watts St 36330 — 334-347-2640
Rick Rainer, prin. — Fax 347-3144

Enterprise-Ozark Community College — Post-Sec.
PO Box 1300 36331 — 334-347-2623

Eufaula, Barbour, Pop. 13,651
Eufaula CSD — 2,900/PK-12
420 Sanford Ave 36027 — 334-687-1100
Barry R. Sadler, supt. — Fax 687-1150
www.ecs.k12.al.us
Eufaula HS — 800/9-12
530 Lake Dr 36027 — 334-687-1110
Gary Atkins, prin. — Fax 687-1121
Moorer MS — 800/6-8
101 Saint Francis Rd 36027 — 334-687-1130
Tharel Shirah, prin. — Fax 687-1138

Lakeside S — 300/PK-12
1020 Lake Dr 36027 — 334-687-5748
Traci Murph, hdmstr. — Fax 687-6306
Wallace Community College Sparks Campus — Post-Sec.
PO Box 580 36072 — 334-687-3543

Eutaw, Greene, Pop. 1,844
Greene County SD — 1,600/K-12
220 Main St 35462 — 205-372-3114
Dr. Douglas L. Ragland, supt. — Fax 372-3247
www.greene.k12.al.us
Carver MS — 500/4-8
PO Box 659 35462 — 205-372-4816
Isaac Atkins, prin. — Fax 372-4828
Greene County HS — 400/9-12
PO Box 658 35462 — 205-372-3789
Carolyn Young, prin. — Fax 372-3404
Kirksey AVC — Vo/Tech
836 County Road 131 35462 — 205-372-4636
Rhinnie Scott, prin. — Fax 372-2358

Warrior Academy — 100/K-12
PO Box 920 35462 — 205-372-3546
John Santoro, prin. — Fax 372-9744

Evergreen, Conecuh, Pop. 3,530
Conecuh County SD — 1,600/PK-12
100 Jackson St 36401 — 251-578-1752
Ronnie Brogden, supt. — Fax 578-7061
Hillcrest HS — 500/8-12
1989 Jaguar Dr 36401 — 251-578-1126
Preston Fluker, prin. — Fax 578-7071

Reid State Technical College — Post-Sec.
PO Box 588 36401 — 251-578-1313
Sparta Academy, 200 Pierce St 36401 — 300/PK-12
Wayne Hammonds, prin. — 251-578-2852

Excel, Monroe, Pop. 579
Monroe County SD
Supt. — See Monroeville
Excel S 1,000/K-12
PO Box 429 36439 251-765-2351
Kevin York, prin. Fax 765-9153

Fairfield, Jefferson, Pop. 11,918
Fairfield CSD 2,500/K-12
6405 Avenue D 35064 205-783-6850
Dr. Anthony Greene, supt. Fax 783-6805
www.fairfield.k12.al.us
Fairfield Area Vocational HS Vo/Tech
610 Valley Rd 35064 205-785-5176
Dr. Gordon Fears, prin. Fax 783-6748
Fairfield Preparatory HS 700/9-12
610 Valley Rd 35064 205-785-5176
Dr. Gordon Fears, prin. Fax 783-6748
Forest Hills MS 600/6-8
7000 Grasselli Rd 35064 205-783-6841
Ardrene Bishop, prin. Fax 783-6753

Restoration Academy 200/PK-12
4600 Carnegie Ave 35064 205-785-8805
Carl Lynn, admin. Fax 785-8809

Fairhope, Baldwin, Pop. 14,138
Baldwin County SD
Supt. — See Bay Minette
Fairhope HS 1,200/9-12
1 Pirate Dr 36532 251-928-8309
Dr. Beverly Thomas, prin. Fax 990-2053
Fairhope MS 700/6-8
408 N Section St 36532 251-928-2573
Dr. Deadra Powe, prin. Fax 990-0403

Falkville, Morgan, Pop. 1,168
Morgan County SD
Supt. — See Decatur
Falkville JSHS 400/7-12
43 Clark Dr 35622 256-784-5248
Sue Wood, prin. Fax 784-9438

Fayette, Fayette, Pop. 4,769
Fayette County SD 2,700/K-12
PO Box 686 35555 205-932-4611
Reba Anderson, supt. Fax 932-7246
www.fayette.k12.al.us
Fayette County HS 500/9-12
202 14th Ct NE 35555 205-932-6313
Radford Hester, prin. Fax 932-8361
Fayette MS 500/5-8
418 3rd Ave NE 35555 205-932-7660
Debbie Deavours, prin. Fax 932-7661
Hubbertville S 400/K-12
7360 County Road 49 35555 205-487-2845
Tim Dunavant, prin. Fax 487-3375
Other Schools – See Berry

Bevill State Community College Post-Sec.
2631 Temple Ave N 35555 800-526-5755

Flomaton, Escambia, Pop. 1,562
Escambia County SD
Supt. — See Brewton
Flomaton HS 300/9-12
21200 Highway 31 36441 251-296-2627
Scott Hammond, prin. Fax 296-2625

Florala, Covington, Pop. 1,885
Covington County SD
Supt. — See Andalusia
Florala City MS 100/7-8
22975 7th Ave 36442 334-858-3642
Rodney Drish, prin. Fax 858-7181
Florala HS 200/9-12
PO Box 218 36442 334-858-3765
Terry Holley, prin. Fax 858-6925

Florence, Lauderdale, Pop. 35,852
Florence CSD 2,900/K-12
541 Riverview Dr 35630 256-768-3015
Dr. Kendy Behrends, supt. Fax 768-3006
www.fcs.k12.al.us/
Florence Career Technical Education Vo/Tech
541 Riverview Dr 35630 256-768-3021
Jeanette Custer, prin. Fax 768-3010
Florence Freshman Center 100/9-9
648 N Cherry St 35630 256-768-2400
Gerald Johnson, prin. Fax 768-2405
Florence HS 600/10-12
1201 Bradshaw Dr 35630 256-768-2200
Mike Lewey, prin. Fax 768-2205
Florence MS 7-8
648 N Cherry St 35630 256-768-3100
William Griffin, prin. Fax 768-3105

Lauderdale County SD 9,100/K-12
PO Box 278 35631 256-760-1300
Jerry Fulmer, supt. Fax 766-5815
www.lcschools.org
Central S 1,300/K-12
3000 County Road 200 35633 256-764-2903
David Corl, prin. Fax 764-5409
Rogers S 1,300/K-12
300 Rogers Ln 35634 256-757-3106
Timothy Tubbs, prin. Fax 757-9625
Wilson S 1,400/K-12
7601 Highway 17 35634 256-764-8470
Larry Hill, prin. Fax 764-1304
Other Schools – See Killen, Lexington, Rogersville, Waterloo

Heritage Christian University Post-Sec.
PO Box HCU 35630 800-367-3565
Mars Hill Bible S 600/K-12
698 Cox Creek Pkwy 35630 256-767-1203
Dr. Kenny Barfield, hdmstr. Fax 767-6304
Shoals Christian S 300/K-12
301 Heathrow Dr 35633 256-767-7070
Thomas Hughes, hdmstr. Fax 766-5677
University of North Alabama Post-Sec.
Univ Sta 35632 256-765-4100

Foley, Baldwin, Pop. 9,689
Baldwin County SD
Supt. — See Bay Minette
Foley HS 1,100/9-12
1 Pride Pl 36535 251-943-2221
Kenneth Dinges, prin. Fax 943-3538
Foley MS 700/6-8
201 N Pine St 36535 251-943-1255
James Shoots, prin. Fax 943-8221

Fort Deposit, Lowndes, Pop. 1,257
Lowndes County SD
Supt. — See Hayneville
Lowndes County MS 300/6-8
PO Box 393 36032 334-227-4206
Sonja Taylor, prin. Fax 227-4125

Fort Payne, DeKalb, Pop. 13,279
Fort Payne CSD 2,600/K-12
PO Box 681029 35968 256-845-0915
James B. Cunningham, supt. Fax 845-4962
Fort Payne HS 800/9-12
201 45th St NE 35967 256-845-0535
Ronnie Crabtree, prin. Fax 845-7868
Fort Payne MS 600/6-8
4910 Martin Ave NE 35967 256-845-7501
Deborah Baker, prin. Fax 845-8292

Frisco City, Monroe, Pop. 1,408
Monroe County SD
Supt. — See Monroeville
Frisco City S 200/K-12
PO Box 70 36445 251-267-3261
Fax 267-3728

Fruitdale, Washington
Washington County SD
Supt. — See Chatom
Fruitdale S 500/K-12
PO Box 448 36539 251-827-6655
Dr. Alfred Taylor, prin. Fax 827-6573

Fyffe, DeKalb, Pop. 1,001
De Kalb County SD
Supt. — See Rainsville
Fyffe S 900/K-12
PO Box 7 35971 256-623-2116
Ricky Bryant, prin. Fax 623-4388

Gadsden, Etowah, Pop. 37,619
Etowah County SD 8,600/K-12
3200 W Meighan Blvd 35904 256-549-7578
Dr. Tommy Mosley, supt. Fax 549-7582
www.ecboe.org/
Gaston S 600/K-12
4550 US Highway 411 35901 256-547-8828
Ronald Moland, prin. Fax 543-7124
Hokes Bluff MS 400/5-8
5425 Main St 35903 256-492-1963
Dr. Marguerite W. Early, prin. Fax 492-1950
Southside HS 700/9-12
2150 Highway 77 35907 256-442-2172
Charles Gardner, prin. Fax 442-2183
Other Schools – See Attalla, Glencoe, Hokes Bluff, Rainbow City, Sardis City, Walnut Grove

Gadsden CSD 5,200/K-12
PO Box 184 35902 256-543-3512
Bob Russell, supt. Fax 549-2950
www.gcs.k12.al.us
Cory MS 300/6-8
715 Raley St 35903 256-492-6793
Kimberly Smith, prin. Fax 494-9958
Disque MS 500/6-8
612 Tracy St 35901 256-547-6341
Joel Gulledge, prin. Fax 547-6323
Forrest MS 400/6-8
2000 W Meighan Blvd 35904 256-546-4992
Ronald Mayes, prin. Fax 543-3796
Gadsden HS 600/9-12
607 S 12th St 35901 256-547-5446
Peter Rowe, prin. Fax 547-5448
Litchfield HS 400/9-12
1109 Hoke St 35903 256-492-3061
Johnnie Parker, prin. Fax 492-4010
Sansom HS 500/9-12
2210 W Meighan Blvd 35904 256-546-3316
Terry Harris, prin. Fax 543-1060
Weaver Technical Center Vo/Tech
1515 Campbell Ave 35903 256-492-6441
Tony Reddick, prin. Fax 492-4954

Coosa Christian S 200/K-12
771 Whites Chapel Rd 35901 256-547-1841
C. Michael Davis, prin.
Gadsden Business College Post-Sec.
PO Box 8365 35902 256-546-2863
Gadsden State Community College Post-Sec.
PO Box 227 35902 256-549-8200

Gardendale, Jefferson, Pop. 12,106
Jefferson County SD
Supt. — See Birmingham
Bragg MS 800/6-8
840 Ash Ave 35071 205-379-2600
Carol Yarborough, prin. Fax 379-2645
Gardendale HS 900/9-12
800 Main St 35071 205-379-3600
Dr. Anna Vacca, prin. Fax 379-3645

Gaylesville, Cherokee, Pop. 140
Cherokee County SD
Supt. — See Centre
Gaylesville S 400/PK-12
760 Trojan Way 35973 256-422-3401
Paul McWhorter, prin. Fax 422-3165

Geneva, Geneva, Pop. 4,330
Geneva CSD 1,300/K-12
505 Panther Dr 36340 334-684-7757
James Bixby, supt. Fax 684-3128
Geneva HS 400/9-12
505 Panther Dr 36340 334-684-9379
Ricky Bennett, prin. Fax 684-3128
Geneva MS 300/6-8
501 Panther Dr 36340 334-684-6431
Elizabeth Mitchell, prin. Fax 684-0476

Geneva County SD 2,700/K-12
PO Box 250 36340 334-684-5690
David Snell, supt. Fax 684-5601
Other Schools – See Hartford, Samson, Slocomb

Georgiana, Butler, Pop. 1,636
Butler County SD
Supt. — See Greenville
Georgiana HS 300/7-12
PO Box 680 36033 334-376-9130
Keith York, prin. Fax 376-2956

Geraldine, DeKalb, Pop. 801
De Kalb County SD
Supt. — See Rainsville
Geraldine S 1,100/K-12
PO Box 157 35974 256-659-2142
Larry Lingerfelt, prin. Fax 659-4296

Gilbertown, Choctaw, Pop. 178
Choctaw County SD
Supt. — See Butler
Southern Choctaw HS 300/7-12
10941 Highway 17 36908 251-843-5645
Betty McBride, prin. Fax 843-5649

Glencoe, Etowah, Pop. 5,187
Etowah County SD
Supt. — See Gadsden
Glencoe HS 300/9-12
803 Lonesome Bend Rd 35905 256-492-2250
Marion Smith, prin. Fax 492-2265
Glencoe MS 300/5-8
809 Lonesome Bend Rd 35905 256-492-5627
Ginger Smith, prin. Fax 492-7076

Gordo, Pickens, Pop. 1,619
Pickens County SD
Supt. — See Carrollton
Gordo JSHS 400/7-12
630 4th St NW 35466 205-364-7353
Steve Street, prin. Fax 364-6160

Goshen, Pike, Pop. 296
Pike County SD
Supt. — See Troy
Goshen JSHS 400/7-12
101 Eagle Cir 36035 334-484-3245
Gene Nelson, prin. Fax 484-3247

Grand Bay, Mobile, Pop. 3,383
Mobile County SD
Supt. — See Mobile
Grand Bay MS 700/6-8
12800 Cunningham Rd 36541 251-865-6511
Suzanne Crist, prin. Fax 865-6182

Grant, Marshall, Pop. 668
Marshall County SD
Supt. — See Guntersville
Smith DAR HS 400/9-12
6077 Main St 35747 256-728-4238
Stacy Anderton, prin. Fax 728-8900
Smith DAR MS 400/5-8
6077 Main St 35747 256-728-5950
Susan Keller, prin. Fax 728-8447

Greensboro, Hale, Pop. 2,644
Hale County SD 3,300/PK-12
PO Box 360 36744 334-624-8836
Joseph F. Stegall, supt. Fax 624-3415
www.halek12.org
Greensboro East HS 400/7-12
PO Box 460 36744 334-624-9156
Anne Jones, prin. Fax 624-9157
Greensboro West HS 300/7-12
PO Box 40 36744 334-624-7932
Jack Clayton, prin. Fax 624-0470
Hale County Technology Center Vo/Tech
PO Box 517 36744 334-624-3691
James Essex, prin. Fax 624-1090
Other Schools – See Akron, Moundville, Newbern

Southern Academy 300/K-12
407 College St 36744 334-624-8111
James Davis, prin. Fax 624-3778

Greenville, Butler, Pop. 7,048
Butler County SD 3,600/K-12
215 Administrative Dr 36037 334-382-2665
Mike Looney, supt. Fax 382-8607
www.butlerco.k12.al.us
Butler County Area Vocational HS Vo/Tech
100 Tiger Dr 36037 334-382-0266
Joseph West, prin. Fax 382-8607
Greenville HS 800/9-12
100 Tiger Dr 36037 334-382-2608
Dr. Kathy Murphy, prin. Fax 382-7202
Greenville MS 800/5-8
300 Overlook Rd 36037 334-382-3450
Jai Hill, prin. Fax 382-0686
Other Schools – See Georgiana, Mc Kenzie

Fort Dale Academy 500/K-12
1100 Gamble St 36037 334-382-2606
David Brantley, prin. Fax 382-0912

Grove Hill, Clarke, Pop. 1,400
Clarke County SD 3,400/PK-12
PO Box 936 36451 251-275-3255
Gerald Stephens, supt. Fax 275-8061
www.southalabama.edu/ccbe
Clarke County HS 400/9-12
PO Box 937 36451 251-275-3368
Debra Dennis, prin. Fax 275-4132
Wilson Hall MS 400/5-8
PO Box 906 36451 251-275-8993
Larry Bagley, prin. Fax 275-4688
Other Schools – See Coffeeville, Jackson

Clarke Preparatory S 400/PK-12
20100 Highway 43 36451 251-275-8576
Billy Pritchett, prin.

Guin, Marion, Pop. 2,258
Marion County SD
Supt. — See Hamilton
Marion County HS 200/7-12
PO Box 549 35563 205-468-3377
Van Nelson, prin. Fax 468-8047

Gulf Shores, Baldwin, Pop. 5,682
Baldwin County SD
Supt. — See Bay Minette

Gulf Shores HS 600/9-12
PO Box 3729 36547 251-968-4747
Eddie Tyler, prin. Fax 968-4770
Gulf Shores MS 500/6-8
450 E 15th Ave 36542 251-968-8719
Sherry Frazier, prin. Fax 967-1577

Guntersville, Marshall, Pop. 7,533
Guntersville CSD 1,800/K-12
PO Box 129 35976 256-582-3159
Andrew Lee, supt. Fax 582-6158
www.guntersvilleboe.com
Carlisle Park MS 400/6-8
801 Sunset Dr 35976 256-582-5182
Shirl Dollar, prin. Fax 582-4477
Guntersville HS 500/9-12
14227 US Highway 431 35976 256-582-2046
Bill Wharton, prin. Fax 582-4742

Marshall County SD 5,300/PK-12
12380 US Highway 431 35976 256-582-3171
Dr. Barry Kirkland, supt. Fax 582-3178
www.marshallk12.org
Brindlee Mountain HS 9-12
994 Scant City Rd 35976 256-753-2800
Keith Buchanan, prin. Fax 753-2802
Brindlee Mountain MS 400/6-8
994 Scant City Rd 35976 256-753-2820
Tim Nabors, prin. Fax 753-2802
Marshall Technical HS Vo/Tech
12312 US Highway 431 35976 256-582-5629
Cindy Wigley, prin. Fax 582-2580
Other Schools – See Albertville, Douglas, Grant

Gurley, Madison, Pop. 885
Madison County SD
Supt. — See Huntsville
Madison County HS 500/9-12
174 Brock Rd 35748 256-776-6247
Freddie Hargett, prin. Fax 776-4302

Hackleburg, Marion, Pop. 1,472
Marion County SD
Supt. — See Hamilton
Hackleburg S 600/K-12
PO Box 310 35564 205-935-3223
Jerry Kuykendall, prin. Fax 935-8092

Haleyville, Winston, Pop. 4,128
Haleyville CSD 1,700/PK-12
2011 20th St 35565 205-486-9231
Dr. Clint A. Baggett, supt. Fax 486-8833
www.havc.k12.al.us
Haleyville Center of Technology Vo/Tech
2007 20th St 35565 205-486-9481
Gary Warren, prin. Fax 486-8735
Haleyville JSHS 800/7-12
2001 20th St 35565 205-486-3122
Roger Satcher, prin. Fax 486-1660

Hamilton, Marion, Pop. 6,524
Marion County SD 3,700/K-12
188 Winchester Dr 35570 205-921-9319
Bravell Jackson, supt. Fax 921-7336
www.mcbe.net
Hamilton HS 400/9-12
211 Aggie Ave 35570 205-921-3281
Ronnie Miller, prin. Fax 921-2333
Hamilton MS 500/5-8
400 Military St S 35570 205-921-7030
Steven Deavours, prin. Fax 921-3821
Other Schools – See Bear Creek, Brilliant, Guin,
Hackleburg

Bevill State Community College Post-Sec.
PO Box 9 35570 205-921-3177

Hampton, Tallapoosa
Huntsville CSD
Supt. — See Huntsville
Hampton Cove MS 400/6-8
261 Old Highway 431, 256-428-8380
Dr. Debi Edwards, prin. Fax 428-8383

Hanceville, Cullman, Pop. 2,984
Cullman County SD
Supt. — See Cullman
Hanceville HS 300/9-12
801 Commercial St SE 35077 256-352-6111
Robert Burgess, prin. Fax 352-6491
Hanceville MS 300/6-8
805 Commercial St SE 35077 256-352-6175
Gary McHan, prin. Fax 352-9741

Wallace State Community College Post-Sec.
PO Box 2000 35077 256-352-8000

Hartford, Geneva, Pop. 2,335
Geneva County SD
Supt. — See Geneva
Geneva County HS 200/9-12
301 Lily St 36344 334-588-2943
Mike Whitaker, prin. Fax 588-3650
Geneva County MS 200/6-8
301 Lily St 36344 334-588-2943
Mike Whitaker, prin. Fax 588-3650

Hartselle, Morgan, Pop. 12,557
Hartselle CSD 3,200/K-12
305 College St NE 35640 256-773-5419
Dr. Mike Reed, supt. Fax 773-5433
www.hartselletigers.org
Hartselle AVC Vo/Tech
904 Sparkman St SW 35640 256-773-5426
Jerry Reeves, prin. Fax 773-5572
Hartselle HS 900/9-12
904 Sparkman St SW 35640 256-773-5426
Jerry Reeves, prin. Fax 773-5572
Hartselle JHS 800/6-8
130 Petain St SW 35640 256-773-6094
Don Pouncey, prin. Fax 773-3499

Harvest, Madison, Pop. 1,922
Madison County SD
Supt. — See Huntsville
Sparkman HS 1,900/9-12
2616 Jeff Rd 35749 256-837-0331
Manuel Wallace, prin. Fax 837-7673

Hayden, Blount, Pop. 500
Blount County SD
Supt. — See Oneonta
Hayden HS 900/7-12
125 Atwood Rd 35079 205-647-0397
Allen Hargett, prin. Fax 647-8633

Hayneville, Lowndes, Pop. 1,178
Lowndes County SD 2,400/K-12
PO Box 755 36040 334-548-2131
Dr. J. Wm. Covington, supt. Fax 548-2161
www.lowndesboe.org
Central HS 400/9-12
145 Main St 36040 334-563-7311
Kenneth Hart, prin. Fax 563-7299
Hayneville MS 300/6-8
PO Box 307 36040 334-548-2184
Harvey Means, prin. Fax 548-5237
Lowndes Co. Career Technical Ctr Vo/Tech
147 Main St 36040 334-563-7389
Donald Dotson, prin. Fax 563-9233
Other Schools – See Fort Deposit, Letohatchee

Hazel Green, Madison, Pop. 2,208
Madison County SD
Supt. — See Huntsville
Hazel Green HS 1,100/9-12
14380 Highway 231 431 N 35750 256-828-0764
John Fanning, prin. Fax 828-6203
Meridianville MS 800/6-8
12975 Highway 231 431 N 35750 256-829-1165
Tom Highfield, prin. Fax 829-1104

Headland, Henry, Pop. 3,575
Henry County SD
Supt. — See Abbeville
Headland HS 400/9-12
8 Sporman St 36345 334-693-2442
Steve Williams, prin. Fax 693-5255
Headland MS 300/6-8
1 Martin Luther King Dr 36345 334-693-3764
Rickey Allen, prin. Fax 693-9058

Heflin, Cleburne, Pop. 3,120
Cleburne County SD 2,600/K-12
93 Education St 36264 256-463-5624
Scott Coefield, supt. Fax 463-5709
www.cleburneschools.net
Cleburne Co. Career Technical S Vo/Tech
11200 Highway 46 36264 256-748-2961
Bill Ayers, prin. Fax 748-3904
Cleburne County HS 800/7-12
520 Evans Bridge Rd 36264 256-463-2012
Dennis Magouirk, prin. Fax 463-5504
Other Schools – See Ranburne

Higdon, Jackson
Jackson County SD
Supt. — See Scottsboro
North Sand Mountain S 700/K-12
PO Box 129 35979 256-597-2111
Mark Guffey, prin. Fax 597-2505

Highland Home, Crenshaw
Crenshaw County SD
Supt. — See Luverne
Highland Home S 800/PK-12
18434 Montgomery Hwy 36041 334-537-4369
Joseph Eiland, prin. Fax 537-9805

Hokes Bluff, Etowah, Pop. 4,241
Etowah County SD
Supt. — See Gadsden
Hokes Bluff HS 400/9-12
1865 Appalachian Hwy 35903 256-492-1360
Jeff Lasseter, prin. Fax 492-7502

Holly Pond, Cullman, Pop. 691
Cullman County SD
Supt. — See Cullman
Holly Pond HS 500/7-12
160 New Hope Rd 35083 256-796-5169
Kim Butler, prin. Fax 796-5199

Hollywood, Jackson, Pop. 938
Jackson County SD
Supt. — See Scottsboro
Pruett Center of Technology Vo/Tech
29490 US Highway 72 35752 256-574-6079
Dana Moore, prin. Fax 259-1644

Holt, Tuscaloosa, Pop. 4,125
Tuscaloosa County SD
Supt. — See Tuscaloosa
Holt HS 500/9-12
3801 Alabama Ave NE 35404 205-342-2768
Cliff Booth, prin. Fax 553-8225

Homewood, Jefferson, Pop. 24,399
Homewood CSD 3,300/K-12
PO Box 59366 35259 205-870-4203
Dr. Jodi Newton, supt. Fax 877-4544
www.homewood.k12.al.us
Homewood HS 1,000/9-12
1901 Lakeshore Dr S 35209 205-871-9663
Dyer Carlisle, prin. Fax 879-0879
Homewood MS 800/6-8
395 Mecca Ave 35209 205-870-0878
Dr. Bill Cleveland, prin. Fax 877-4573

Herzing College Post-Sec.
280 W Valley Ave 35209 205-916-2800

Hoover, Jefferson, Pop. 65,070
Hoover CSD 11,700/K-12
2810 Metropolitan Way 35243 205-439-1015
Dr. Connie Williams, supt. Fax 439-1001
www.hoover.k12.al.us
Bumpus MS 800/6-8
1730 Lake Cyrus Club Dr 35244 205-439-2200
Dr. Joy Brown, prin. Fax 439-2201
Hoover HS 2,000/9-12
1000 Buccaneer Dr 35244 205-439-1200
Dr. Sandra Spivey, prin. Fax 439-1201
Simmons JHS 800/6-8
1575 Patton Chapel Rd 35226 205-439-2100
Carol Barber, prin. Fax 439-2101
Other Schools – See Birmingham

Hoover Christian S 100/K-10
2113 Old Rocky Ridge Rd 35216 205-987-3376
Mark Grice, prin. Fax 987-4428
Shades Mountain Christian S 500/PK-12
2290 Old Tyler Rd 35226 205-978-6001
Brian Benscoter, hdmstr. Fax 978-9120

Hope Hull, Montgomery

Hooper Academy 400/K-12
380 Fischer Rd 36043 334-288-5980
John Niblett, prin. Fax 288-9171

Hueytown, Jefferson, Pop. 15,377
Jefferson County SD
Supt. — See Birmingham
Hueytown HS 1,000/9-12
131 Dabbs Ave 35023 205-379-4150
Dr. Judson Jones, prin. Fax 379-4195
Hueytown MS 800/6-8
701 Sunrise Blvd 35023 205-379-5150
Randy McCarty, prin. Fax 379-5195

Garywood Christian S 200/PK-12
2750 Allson Bonnett Mmrl Dr 35023 205-744-4390
Amanda Kleiser, prin. Fax 332-0225

Huntsville, Madison, Pop. 164,237
Huntsville CSD 22,400/K-12
PO Box 1256 35807 256-428-6800
Dr. Ann Roy Moore, supt. Fax 428-6817
www.hsv.k12.al.us
Butler HS 1,100/9-12
3401 Holmes Ave NW 35816 256-428-7950
Van Barnes, prin. Fax 428-7951
Challenger MS 600/6-8
13555 Chaney Thompson Rd SE 35803
256-428-7620
Edith Pickens, prin. Fax 428-7621
Chapman MS 400/6-8
2001 Reuben Dr NE 35811 256-428-7640
Walker McGinniss, prin. Fax 428-7641
Columbia HS 9-12
300 Explorer Blvd NW 35806 256-428-7576
Dr. Jennifer Garrett, prin. Fax 428-7879
Davis Hills MS 500/6-8
3221 Mastin Lake Rd NW 35810 256-428-7660
Bryon McGlathery, prin. Fax 428-7661
Grissom HS 1,900/9-12
7901 Bailey Cove Rd SE 35802 256-428-8000
B.T. Drake, prin. Fax 428-8001
Huntsville Center for Technology Vo/Tech
2800 Drake Ave SW 35805 256-428-7810
Eddie Turner, prin. Fax 428-7811
Huntsville HS 1,100/9-12
2304 Billie Watkins St SW 35801 256-428-8050
Leslie Esneault, prin. Fax 428-8051
Huntsville MS 600/6-8
817 Adams St SE 35801 256-428-7700
Jim Caneer, prin. Fax 428-7701
Johnson HS 800/9-12
6201 Pueblo Dr NW 35810 256-428-8100
Dr. Fredonia Williams, prin. Fax 428-8118
Johnson HS International Education 9-12
6201 Pueblo Dr NW 35810 256-428-8100
Dr. Fredonia Williams, prin. Fax 428-8118
Lee Creative & Performing Arts HS 9-12
606 Forrest Cir NE 35811 256-428-8150
Brenda Chunn, prin. Fax 428-8151
Lee HS 900/9-12
606 Forrest Cir NE 35811 256-428-8150
Brenda Chunn, prin. Fax 428-8151
Lee Pre-Engineering HS 9-12
606 Forrest Cir NE 35811 256-428-8150
Brenda Chunn, prin. Fax 428-8151
Mountain Gap MS 500/6-8
821 Mountain Gap Rd SE 35803 256-428-7720
John Timlin, prin. Fax 428-7721
New Century Technology S Vo/Tech
300 Explorer Blvd NW 35806 256-428-7800
Paul Glover, prin. Fax 428-7801
Stone MS 500/6-8
2620 Clinton Ave W 35805 256-428-7740
Guinever Givens, prin. Fax 428-7741
Westlawn MS 400/6-8
4217 9th Ave SW 35805 256-428-7760
Fraizier Barnes, prin. Fax 428-7761
White MS 700/6-8
4800 Sparkman Dr NW 35810 256-428-7680
Annie Savage, prin. Fax 428-7681
Whitesburg MS 600/6-8
107 Sanders Rd SW 35802 256-428-7780
Mike Bible, prin. Fax 428-7781
Other Schools – See Hampton

Madison County SD 16,800/K-12
PO Box 226 35804 256-852-2557
Elam Swaim, supt. Fax 852-2538
www.madison.k12.al.us
Madison County Career Academy Vo/Tech
1275 Jordan Rd 35811 256-852-2170
William Starnes, prin. Fax 851-9790
Monrovia MS 1,000/6-8
1216 Jeff Rd NW 35806 256-430-4499
Derrell Brown, prin. Fax 726-0230
Riverton MS 600/6-8
399 Homer Nance Rd 35811 256-859-3667
Richard Medlen, prin. Fax 851-2610
Other Schools – See Gurley, Harvest, Hazel Green, New Hope, New Market, Toney

Catholic HS 100/9-12
4810 Bradford Dr NW 35805 256-430-1760
Vince Aquila, prin. Fax 430-1766
Huntsville Bible College Post-Sec.
PO Box 3493 35810 256-539-0834
Huntsville Hospital Post-Sec.
101 Sivley Rd SW 35801 256-533-8123
J. F. Drake State Technical College Post-Sec.
3421 Meridian St N 35811 256-539-8161
Oakwood Adventist Academy 300/K-12
7000 Adventist Blvd 35896 256-726-7010
Gilbert B. Cooper, prin. Fax 726-7016
Oakwood College Post-Sec.
Oakwood Rd NW 35896 256-726-7000

Pivot Point the Masters — Post-Sec.
8215 Stephanie Dr SW 35802 — 256-881-8587
Providence Classical S — 100/K-10
PO Box 302 35804 — 256-852-8884
Pattie Steward, admin.
Randolph S — 700/K-12
1005 Drake Ave SE 35802 — 256-881-1701
M. Edward Krenson, hdmstr. — Fax 881-1784
University of Alabama in Huntsville — Post-Sec.
PO Box 1247 35899 — 256-890-6120
Valley Fellowship Christian Academy — 200/PK-12
3616 Holmes Ave NW 35816 — 256-533-5248
Patti Simon, prin. — Fax 533-5253
Virginia College — Post-Sec.
2800 Bob Wallace Ave SW #A 35805 — 256-533-7387
Westminster Christian Academy — 800/PK-12
1400 Evangel Dr NW 35816 — 256-705-8000
Robert Illman, hdmstr. — Fax 705-8001

Ider, DeKalb, Pop. 678
De Kalb County SD
Supt. — See Rainsville
Ider S — 800/K-12
PO Box 127 35981 — 256-632-2302
Steven Street, prin. — Fax 632-3481

Indian Springs, Shelby, Pop. 1,520
Indian Springs S — 300/8-12
190 Woodward Dr 35124 — 205-988-3350
Melville Mackay, dir. — Fax 988-3797

Irondale, Jefferson, Pop. 9,710
Jefferson County SD
Supt. — See Birmingham
Shades Valley HS — 1,200/9-12
6100 Old Leeds Rd 35210 — 205-379-5350
Jane Baker, prin. — Fax 379-5395

Irvington, Mobile
Mobile County SD
Supt. — See Mobile
Bryant Career Technical S — Vo/Tech
8950 Padgett Switch Rd 36544 — 251-957-2845
Thomas Reed, prin. — Fax 957-3170
Bryant HS — 1,500/9-12
14001 Hurricane Blvd 36544 — 251-824-3213
Larry Mouton, prin. — Fax 824-3221

Jack, Coffee
Coffee County SD
Supt. — See Elba
Zion Chapel S — 700/K-12
29256 Highway 87 36346 — 334-897-6275
Jerry Barnes, prin. — Fax 897-5136

Jackson, Clarke, Pop. 5,271
Clarke County SD
Supt. — See Grove Hill
Jackson HS — 500/9-12
321 Stanley Dr 36545 — 251-246-2571
Robert Hagood, prin. — Fax 246-3190
Jackson MS — 300/7-8
235 College Ave 36545 — 251-246-3597
Jessie Taylor, prin. — Fax 246-6017

Jackson Academy — 200/K-12
PO Box 838 36545 — 251-246-5552

Jacksonville, Calhoun, Pop. 8,565
Calhoun County SD
Supt. — See Anniston
Calhoun Co. Career Technical Center — Vo/Tech
1200 Church Ave SE 36265 — 256-741-4600
David Talley, prin. — Fax 435-4221
Pleasant Valley HS — 500/7-12
4141 Pleasant Valley Rd 36265 — 256-741-6700
Charlton Giles, prin. — Fax 435-0171

Jacksonville CSD — 1,700/K-12
123 College St SW 36265 — 256-782-5682
Dr. Eric George MacKey, supt. — Fax 782-5685
www.jacksonville.k12.al.us
Jacksonville HS — 700/K-12
1000 George Douthit Dr SW 36265 — 256-435-4177
Mike Newell, prin. — Fax 435-3015

Jacksonville Christian Academy — 200/K-12
831 Alexandria Rd SW 36265 — 256-435-3333
Tommy Miller, prin. — Fax 435-2059
Jacksonville State University — Post-Sec.
700 Pelham Rd N 36265 — 256-782-5000

Jasper, Walker, Pop. 13,910
Jasper CSD — 2,600/K-12
PO Box 500 35502 — 205-384-6880
Philip Woods, supt. — Fax 387-5213
www.jasper.k12.al.us/
Maddox MS — 600/6-8
1 Panther Trl 35501 — 205-384-3235
Patsy Stricklin, prin. — Fax 387-5208
Walker HS — 800/9-12
1601 Highland Ave 35501 — 205-221-9277
Daniel Gambrell, prin. — Fax 387-5228

Walker County SD — 8,300/PK-12
PO Box 311 35502 — 205-387-0555
Dr. Harvey Sanford, supt. — Fax 384-0810
www.walkercountyschools.com/
Curry HS — 700/9-12
155 Yellow Jacket Dr 35503 — 205-384-3887
Bobby Gann, prin. — Fax 221-7381
Curry MS — 400/5-8
115 Yellow Jacket Dr 35503 — 205-384-3441
David Hendon, prin. — Fax 384-1110
Walker County Center for Tech — Vo/Tech
1100 Viking Dr 35501 — 205-387-0561
Debra Ellis, prin. — Fax 384-5170
Other Schools – See Carbon Hill, Cordova, Dora, Oakman, Parrish

Bevill State Community College — Post-Sec.
1411 Indiana Ave 35501 — 800-777-0372

Jemison, Chilton, Pop. 2,321
Chilton County SD
Supt. — See Clanton

Jemison HS — 500/9-12
25195 US Highway 31 35085 — 205-280-4860
Margo Gibson, prin. — Fax 688-4761
Jemison MS — 600/5-8
25125 US Highway 31 35085 — 205-280-4840
Mark Knight, prin. — Fax 688-2302

Killen, Lauderdale, Pop. 1,090
Lauderdale County SD
Supt. — See Florence
Brooks JSHS — 800/7-12
4300 Highway 72 35645 — 256-757-2115
Dale Mathis, prin. — Fax 757-1136
Thornton Career Technical Center — Vo/Tech
7252 Highway 72 35645 — 256-757-2101
Kenneth Angel, prin. — Fax 757-8692

Kimberly, Jefferson, Pop. 2,192
Jefferson County SD
Supt. — See Birmingham
North Jefferson MS — 600/6-8
8350 Warrior Kimberly Rd 35091 — 205-379-4000
Pam Horton, prin. — Fax 379-4045

Kinston, Coffee, Pop. 609
Coffee County SD
Supt. — See Elba
Kinston S — 500/K-12
201 College St 36453 — 334-565-3016
Mark Coale, prin. — Fax 565-3494

Lafayette, Chambers, Pop. 3,108
Chambers County SD — 4,400/K-12
202 1st Ave SE 36862 — 334-864-9343
Leonard Riley, supt. — Fax 864-0119
www.chambersk12.org
Chambers County Career Tech Center — Vo/Tech
PO Box 318 36862 — 334-864-8863
Mike Riley, prin. — Fax 864-9394
Lafayette HS — 300/9-12
214 1st Ave SE 36862 — 334-864-9881
Florence Moore, prin. — Fax 864-0650
Powell MS — 300/6-8
621 1st St SE 36862 — 334-864-8876
Terry Reed, prin. — Fax 864-8169
Other Schools – See Valley

Chambers Academy — 200/K-12
15048 US Highway 431 36862 — 334-864-9852
Jim Childers, prin. — Fax 864-9691

Lanett, Chambers, Pop. 7,610
Lanett CSD — 1,000/K-12
105 N Lanier Ave 36863 — 334-644-5900
Charles Looser, supt. — Fax 644-5996
www.lanettcityschools.org
Lanett HS — 300/9-12
1301 S 8th Ave 36863 — 334-644-5965
Joan Gilbert, prin. — Fax 644-5979
Lanett JHS — 300/6-8
1302 Cherry Dr 36863 — 334-644-5950
Sanford Isom, prin. — Fax 644-5964

Springwood S — 400/PK-12
PO Box 1030 36863 — 334-644-2191
Theresa Williams, hdmstr. — Fax 644-2194

Leeds, Jefferson, Pop. 10,912
Leeds CSD — 1,300/K-12
PO Box 1083 35094 — 205-699-5437
Dr. Billy J. Paul, supt. — Fax 699-6629
www.leedscityschools.org
Leeds HS — 400/9-12
8404 Greenwave Dr 35094 — 205-699-4510
Mark Ford, prin. — Fax 699-4515
Leeds MS — 300/6-8
1721 Moton St NW 35094 — 205-699-4505
Elliot Harris, prin. — Fax 699-4509

Leesburg, Cherokee, Pop. 815
Cherokee County SD
Supt. — See Centre
Sand Rock S — 1,000/K-12
1950 Sand Rock Ave 35983 — 256-523-3564
Ben East, prin. — Fax 523-3507

Leighton, Colbert, Pop. 837
Colbert County SD
Supt. — See Tuscumbia
Colbert County HS — 600/7-12
2200 High School St 35646 — 256-446-8214
Jackie Hubbard-Witt, prin. — Fax 446-8951

Leroy, Washington
Washington County SD
Supt. — See Chatom
Leroy S — 800/K-12
PO Box 40 36548 — 251-246-2000
Larry Massey, prin. — Fax 246-2199

Lester, Limestone, Pop. 109
Limestone County SD
Supt. — See Athens
West Limestone S — 900/K-12
10945 W School House Rd 35647 — 256-233-6687
Stan Davis, prin. — Fax 233-8034

Letohatchee, Lowndes
Lowndes County SD
Supt. — See Hayneville
Calhoun HS — 400/9-12
8213 County Road 33 36047 — 334-227-4515
Robert O. Gardner, prin. — Fax 548-5322

Lexington, Lauderdale, Pop. 825
Lauderdale County SD
Supt. — See Florence
Lexington S — 900/K-12
101 School St 35648 — 256-229-6622
Larry Smith, prin. — Fax 229-6636

Lincoln, Talladega, Pop. 4,787
Talladega County SD
Supt. — See Talladega
Drew MS — 300/7-8
450 Drew Ave 35096 — 256-315-5280
Dr. Rhonda Lee, prin. — Fax 315-5290
Lincoln HS — 400/9-12
78989 AL Highway 77 35096 — 256-315-5295
Terry Roller, prin. — Fax 315-5315

Linden, Marengo, Pop. 2,374
Linden CSD — 600/K-12
PO Box 480609 36748 — 334-295-8802
Dr. Walter E. Davis, supt. — Fax 295-8801
www.lindencity.org/
Austin JHS — 100/6-8
PO Box 480699 36748 — 334-295-5378
Terry Gosa, prin. — Fax 295-5376
Linden HS — 200/9-12
PO Box 480729 36748 — 334-295-4287
Timothy Thurman, prin. — Fax 295-0988
Marengo Co. Technology Center — Vo/Tech
2450 E Coats Ave 36748 — 334-295-4237
George Baldwin, prin. — Fax 295-1177

Marengo County SD — 1,700/K-12
PO Box 480339 36748 — 334-295-4123
Luke Hallmark, supt. — Fax 295-2259
Other Schools – See Demopolis, Dixons Mills, Sweet Water, Thomaston

Marengo Academy — 400/K-12
PO Box 480639 36748 — 334-295-4151
H.D. Russell, prin.

Lineville, Clay, Pop. 2,360
Clay County SD
Supt. — See Ashland
Lineville JSHS — 400/7-12
18 W Main St 36266 — 256-396-2466
Demita Parson, prin. — Fax 396-6935

Livingston, Sumter, Pop. 3,103
Sumter County SD — 2,600/K-12
PO Box 10 35470 — 205-652-9605
Dr. Fred Primm, supt. — Fax 652-9641
www.sumter.k12.al.us
Bell-Brown Career Technical Center — Vo/Tech
PO Box 1380 35470 — 205-652-9469
Travis Bailey, prin. — Fax 652-9487
Livingston HS — 400/9-12
PO Box 40 35470 — 205-652-2464
Eric Hines, prin. — Fax 652-2475
Other Schools – See York

University of West Alabama — Post-Sec.
Hwy 11 35470 — 205-652-3400

Loachapoka, Lee, Pop. 164
Lee County SD
Supt. — See Opelika
Loachapoka HS — 300/7-12
PO Box 187 36865 — 334-887-8038
Jimmy Wilkerson, prin. — Fax 887-5228

Locust Fork, Blount, Pop. 1,104
Blount County SD
Supt. — See Oneonta
Locust Fork HS — 600/7-12
77 School Rd 35097 — 205-681-7846
Daniel Smith, prin. — Fax 681-6175

Louisville, Barbour, Pop. 587
Barbour County SD
Supt. — See Clayton
Barbour County MS — 6-8
PO Box 459 36048 — 334-266-6151
Jimmie Fryer, prin. — Fax 226-5991

Dixie Academy, PO Box 67 36048 — 100/K-12
Glenda Green, prin. — 334-266-5311

Lowndesboro, Lowndes, Pop. 134
Lowndes Academy, PO Box 99 36752 — 300/K-12
Randy Skipper, prin. — 334-278-3366

Luverne, Crenshaw, Pop. 2,570
Crenshaw County SD — 2,400/PK-12
183 Votec Dr 36049 — 334-335-6519
Kathi H. Wallace, supt. — Fax 335-6510
Crenshaw County AVTS — Vo/Tech
183 Votec Dr 36049 — 334-335-3319
Yvonne Noble, prin. — Fax 335-4119
Luverne S — 1,000/PK-12
194 First Ave 36049 — 334-335-3331
Earl Franks, prin. — Fax 335-2241
Other Schools – See Brantley, Highland Home

Crenshaw Christian Academy — 200/K-12
608 Country Club Dr 36049 — 334-335-5749
Angela Carpenter, prin. — Fax 335-6422

Lynn, Winston, Pop. 597
Winston County SD
Supt. — See Double Springs
Lynn HS — 200/8-12
531 E Main St 35575 — 205-893-5471
Greg Pendley, prin. — Fax 893-2484

Mc Calla, Jefferson
Jefferson County SD
Supt. — See Birmingham
McAdory HS — 1,400/6-12
4800 McAdory School Rd 35111 — 205-379-4700
Samuel Staggs, prin. — Fax 481-8037

Mc Intosh, Washington, Pop. 252
Washington County SD
Supt. — See Chatom
Mc Intosh HS — 300/6-12
PO Box 359 36553 — 251-944-2441
David Davis, prin. — Fax 944-8779

Mc Kenzie, Butler, Pop. 441
Butler County SD
Supt. — See Greenville
Mc Kenzie S — 300/K-12
PO Box 158 36456 — 334-374-2711
J. Randy Williams, prin. — Fax 374-8108

Madison, Madison, Pop. 34,080
Madison CSD — 7,500/K-12
211 Celtic Dr 35758 — 256-464-8370
Dr. Steve Nowlin, supt. — Fax 774-0404
www.madisoncity.k12.al.us

Discovery MS 800/7-9
1304 Hughes Rd 35758 256-837-3735
Sharon Willis, prin. Fax 837-1573
Jones HS 1,500/10-12
650 Hughes Rd 35758 256-772-2547
Robert Parker, prin. Fax 772-6698
Liberty MS 900/7-9
281 Dock Murphy Dr 35758 256-430-0001
Sally Bruer, prin. Fax 430-0282

Madison Academy 800/K-12
325 Slaughter Rd 35758 256-971-1620
Robert Burton, prin. Fax 971-1436

Maplesville, Chilton, Pop. 683
Chilton County SD
Supt. — See Clanton
Isabella S 800/K-12
11338 County Road 15 36750 205-280-2770
Ricky Porter, prin. Fax 755-8549
Maplesville S 500/K-12
PO Box 146 36750 334-366-2991
Maggie Hicks, prin. Fax 366-2531

Marbury, Autauga
Autauga County SD
Supt. — See Prattville
Marbury HS 500/7-12
PO Box A 36051 205-755-2118
Don Hulin, prin. Fax 755-3168

Marion, Perry, Pop. 3,514
Perry County SD 2,200/K-12
PO Box 900 36756 334-683-6528
John Heard, supt. Fax 683-8427
Marion JSHS 500/7-12
PO Box 150 36756 334-683-6741
Bob Coley, prin. Fax 683-8838
Other Schools – See Uniontown

Judson College Post-Sec.
302 Bibb St 36756 800-447-9472
Marion Military Institute Post-Sec.
1101 Washington St 36756 800-664-1842
Marion Military Institute 100/9-12
1101 Washington St 36756 334-683-2303
Col. James Benson, pres. Fax 683-2383

Midfield, Jefferson, Pop. 5,440
Midfield CSD 1,200/K-12
417 Parkwood St 35228 205-923-2262
Donnie Breaseale, supt. Fax 929-0585
www.midfield.k12.al.us/
Midfield Area Vo HS Vo/Tech
1600 High School Dr, Birmingham AL 35221
205-923-2833
Larry Thornton, prin. Fax 929-0593
Midfield HS 400/9-12
1600 High School Dr, Birmingham AL 35221
205-923-2833
Charles Anthony, prin. Fax 929-0593
Rutledge MS 400/5-8
1221 8th St 35228 205-780-8647
Nikita Williams, prin. Fax 780-3664

Southeastern School of Cosmetology Post-Sec.
26B Phillips Dr 35228 205-925-0011

Midland City, Dale, Pop. 1,754
Dale County SD
Supt. — See Ozark
Dale County HS 400/9-12
PO Box 1140 36350 334-983-3541
Levy Boutwell, prin. Fax 983-1549

Millbrook, Elmore, Pop. 12,455
Elmore County SD
Supt. — See Wetumpka
Millbrook MS 1,500/4-8
4228 Chapman Rd 36054 334-285-2100
Dr. Oliver Boone, prin. Fax 285-2102
Stanhope-Elmore HS 1,100/9-12
4300 Main St 36054 334-285-4263
Bruce Fulmer, prin. Fax 285-4575

Millport, Lamar, Pop. 1,080
Lamar County SD
Supt. — See Vernon
South Lamar S 600/K-12
300 Sls Rd 35576 205-662-4411
Garth Moss, prin. Fax 662-4544

Millry, Washington, Pop. 606
Washington County SD
Supt. — See Chatom
Millry S 600/K-12
PO Box 65 36558 251-846-2987
Larry Odom, prin. Fax 846-2986

Mobile, Mobile, Pop. 193,464
Mobile County SD 64,100/PK-12
PO Box 1327 36633 251-221-4000
Dr. Harold Dodge, supt. Fax 221-4399
www.mcpss.com
Baker HS 1,500/9-12
8901 Airport Blvd 36608 251-221-3000
Clem Richardson, prin. Fax 221-3004
Burns MS 1,100/6-8
6175 Girby Rd 36693 251-221-2025
John Adams, prin. Fax 221-2021
Calloway-Smith MS 500/6-8
350 N Lawrence St 36603 251-221-2042
Dorothy Robinson, prin. Fax 221-2041
Causey MS 1,200/6-8
2205 McFarland Rd 36695 251-221-2060
Mary Wood, prin. Fax 221-2062
Chastang MS 800/6-8
2800 Berkley Ave 36617 251-221-2081
Zad Douglas, prin. Fax 221-2080
Davidson HS 1,400/9-12
3900 Pleasant Valley Rd 36609 251-221-3084
Lewis Copeland, prin. Fax 221-3083
Denton MS 600/6-8
3800 Pleasant Valley Rd 36609 251-221-2148
Lori Taylor, prin. Fax 221-2152
Dunbar Magnet S 700/4-8
500 Saint Anthony St 36603 251-221-2160
Rhonda Boone, prin. Fax 221-2162

Eanes MS 900/6-8
1901 Hurtel St 36605 251-221-2189
Douglas July, prin. Fax 221-2191
Hillsdale MS 300/6-8
6301 Biloxi Ave 36608 251-221-2223
Elden Byrd, prin. Fax 221-2221
Le Flore HS 1,500/9-12
700 Donald St 36617 251-221-3125
Alvin Dailey, prin. Fax 221-3134
Murphy Area Technical Center Vo/Tech
100 S Carlen St 36606 251-221-3200
Djuna Jackson, prin. Fax 221-3199
Murphy HS 2,400/9-12
100 S Carlen St 36606 251-221-3186
Doug Estle, prin. Fax 221-3196
Phillips Preparatory S 800/6-8
3255 Old Shell Rd 36607 251-221-2287
Brenda Hartzog, prin. Fax 221-2285
Pillans MS 900/6-8
2051 Gatotkoco Dr 36605 251-221-2300
Gloria Burks, prin. Fax 221-2312
Rain HS 700/9-12
3125 Dauphin Island Pkwy 36605 251-221-3233
Robert Blakely, prin. Fax 470-3229
Scarborough MS 700/6-8
1800 Phillips Ln 36618 251-221-2323
Arnold Tillman, prin. Fax 221-2321
Shaw HS 700/9-12
5960 Arlberg St 36608 251-221-3305
Sylvia Ward, prin. Fax 221-3304
Washington MS 500/6-8
1961 Andrews St 36617 251-221-2361
Rosalyn Dean, prin. Fax 221-2367
Williamson HS 900/9-12
1567 E Dublin St 36605 251-221-3411
Terrence Mixon, prin. Fax 221-3414
Continuous Learning Center Adult
1870 Pleasant Ave 36617 251-221-2122
Grady Gordon, prin. Fax 221-2124
Other Schools – See Bayou La Batre, Chickasaw,
Citronelle, Grand Bay, Irvington, Prichard, Saraland,
Satsuma, Semmes, Theodore

Bishop State Community College Post-Sec.
925 Dauphin Island Pkwy 36605 251-479-0003
Bishop State Community College-Carver Post-Sec.
414 Stanton Rd 36617 251-473-8692
Bishop State Community College-Central Post-Sec.
1365 Martin Luther King Ave 36603 251-405-4400
Bishop State Community College-Main Post-Sec.
351 N Broad St 36603 251-690-6419
Blue Cliff School of Therapeutic Massage Post-Sec.
2970 Cottage Hill Rd # 175 36606 251-665-9900
CAPPS College Post-Sec.
3590 Pleasant Valley Rd 36609 251-473-1393
Cottage Hill Christian Academy 200/9-12
7355 Creekwood Dr 36695 251-634-2513
Dr. Charles Lang, supt. Fax 634-2566
Faith Academy 1,700/PK-12
8650 Tanner Williams Rd 36608 251-633-7267
Tim Skelton, hdmstr. Fax 633-9133
McGill-Toolen HS 1,200/9-12
1501 Old Shell Rd 36604 251-432-0784
Michelle Haas, prin. Fax 433-8356
Mobile Christian S 700/K-12
5900 Cottage Hill Rd 36609 251-661-1613
James M. Powell, pres. Fax 661-1396
Murray S at Wilmer Hall Childrens Home 60/6-12
3811 Old Shell Rd 36608 251-342-4931
Margie Sumlin, prin. Fax 342-4466
Remington College Post-Sec.
828 Downtowner Loop W 36609 251-343-8200
St. Paul's Episcopal S 1,600/PK-12
161 Dogwood Ln 36608 251-342-6700
Robert Rutledge, hdmstr. Fax 342-1844
Spring Hill College Post-Sec.
4000 Dauphin St 36608 251-380-4000
UMS Wright Prep S 1,300/K-12
65 Mobile St 36607 251-479-6551
Tony Havard, prin. Fax 470-9050
University of Mobile Post-Sec.
PO Box 13220 36663 251-675-5990
University of South Alabama Post-Sec.
307 University Blvd N 36688 251-460-6101

Monroeville, Monroe, Pop. 6,748
Monroe County SD 4,400/PK-12
PO Box 967 36461 251-575-2168
Dennis Mixon, supt. Fax 575-5818
www.monroe.k12.al.us/
Monroe County Career Technical Center Vo/Tech
230 Tiger Dr 36460 251-575-4381
C. Al Brown, prin. Fax 575-2017
Monroe County HS 600/9-12
212 Tiger Dr 36460 251-575-3258
Larry Turner, prin. Fax 575-2019
Monroeville JHS 500/6-8
201 York St 36460 251-575-4121
Lana Wilson, prin. Fax 575-2934
Other Schools – See Beatrice, Excel, Frisco City, Uriah

Alabama Southern Community College Post-Sec.
PO Box 2000 36461 251-575-3156
Monroe Academy, PO Box 927 36461 600/PK-12
Clark McKinley, hdmstr. 251-743-3932

Montevallo, Shelby, Pop. 5,033
Shelby County SD
Supt. — See Columbiana
Montevallo HS 400/9-12
980 Oak St 35115 205-682-6400
Judy Simmons, prin. Fax 682-6405
Montevallo MS 300/6-8
235 Samford St 35115 205-682-6410
Vanessa Nason, prin. Fax 682-6415

Shelby Academy 200/PK-12
9178 Highway 22 35115 205-668-2299
DeWayne Kervin, prin. Fax 668-1912
University of Montevallo Post-Sec.
Station 6030 35115 205-665-6000

Montgomery, Montgomery, Pop. 200,123
Montgomery County SD 32,200/PK-12
PO Box 1991 36102 334-223-6700
Dr. Carlinda Purcell, supt. Fax 269-3076
www.mps.k12.al.us

Baldwin Art & Academics Magnet S 600/6-8
410 S McDonough St 36104 334-269-3870
Jannette Wright, prin. Fax 269-3918
Bellingrath JHS 800/7-9
3488 S Court St 36105 334-269-3623
Angela Mangum, prin. Fax 269-0237
Brewbaker JHS 1,200/7-9
4425 Brewbaker Dr 36116 334-284-8008
Cheryl Fountain, prin. Fax 284-8052
Brewbaker Technology Magnet HS 500/9-12
4405 Brewbaker Dr 36116 334-284-7100
Mitzi McLaurine, prin. Fax 284-7110
Capitol Heights JHS 700/7-9
116 Federal Dr 36107 334-260-1000
Lorenza Pharrams, prin. Fax 260-1049
Carver HS 1,400/9-12
2001 W Fairview Ave 36108 334-269-3636
Cynthia Tucker, prin. Fax 269-3912
Davis SHS 1,300/10-12
3420 Carter Hill Rd 36111 334-269-3712
Marie Kostick, prin. Fax 269-3695
Floyd MS 500/6-8
3444 Le Bron Rd 36111 334-284-7130
Robert Hunter, prin. Fax 284-7125
Goodwyn JHS 800/7-9
209 Perry Hill Rd 36109 334-260-1021
Vince Johnson, prin. Fax 260-1079
Houston Hill JHS 300/7-9
215 Hall St 36104 334-269-3694
Thomas Cochran, prin. Fax 269-3695
Lanier SHS 900/10-12
1756 S Court St 36104 334-269-3726
Lewis Washington, prin. Fax 269-3961
Lee SHS 1,600/10-12
225 Ann St 36107 334-269-3742
David Sikes, prin. Fax 269-3888
Loveless Academic Magnet HS 400/9-12
921 W Jeff Davis Ave 36108 334-269-3839
Veverly Arrington, prin.
McIntyre MS, 1220 Hugh St 36108 500/6-8
Gary Hall, prin. 334-269-3755
McKee JHS 800/7-9
4017 McInnis Dr 36116 334-284-7528
Bobby Abrams, prin. Fax 284-7615
Southlawn MS 700/6-8
5333 Mobile Hwy 36108 334-284-8086
Tina Minott, prin.
Washington Magnet HS 500/9-12
632 S Union St 36104 334-269-3618
Quesha Starks, prin. Fax 269-6140
Other Schools – See Pike Road

Alabama Christian Academy 1,000/K-12
4700 Wares Ferry Rd 36109 334-277-1985
Ronnie Sewell, prin. Fax 279-0604
Alabama State University Post-Sec.
PO Box 271 36101 334-229-4200
Auburn University at Montgomery Post-Sec.
PO Box 244023 36124 334-244-3000
Baptist Medical Center Post-Sec.
301 Brown Springs Rd 36117 334-273-4400
Community College of the Air Force Post-Sec.
130 W Maxwell Blvd 36112 334-953-5033
Cool Preparatory Academy 50/8-12
3019 N Colonial Dr 36111 334-268-4144
Dr. C. Andrew Phillips, admin.
Eastwood Christian S 300/K-12
1701 E Trinity Blvd 36106 334-272-8195
John Geiger, hdmstr. Fax 386-2399
Evangel Christian Academy 300/K-12
3975 Vaughn Rd 36106 334-272-3882
Rev. Victor Tubbs, prin. Fax 272-5662
Faulkner University Post-Sec.
5345 Atlanta Hwy 36109 334-272-5820
Freedom Life Christian Academy 100/PK-12
221 W Fleming Rd 36105 334-284-1461
Annetta Tate, admin. Fax 281-1912
Huntingdon College Post-Sec.
1500 E Fairview Ave 36106 334-833-4222
Montgomery Academy 600/K-12
3240 Vaughn Rd 36106 334-272-8210
Archibald Douglas, hdmstr. Fax 277-3240
Montgomery Catholic HS 200/9-12
5350 Vaughn Rd 36116 334-272-7220
Susan Vaughn, prin. Fax 272-2440
Montgomery Catholic MS 7-8
5350 Vaughn Rd 36116 334-272-2465
Anne Ceasar, prin. Fax 272-2330
Montgomery Job Corps Center Post-Sec.
1145 Air Base Blvd 36108 334-262-8883
Prince Institute of Professional Studies Post-Sec.
7735 Atlanta Hwy 36117 334-271-1670
St. James S 1,200/PK-12
6010 Vaughn Rd 36116 334-277-8033
Fax 277-2542
St. Jude Educational Institute 200/9-12
2048 W Fairview Ave 36108 334-264-5376
John Mitchell, prin. Fax 264-6669
Southern Christian University Post-Sec.
1200 Taylor Rd 36117 800-351-4040
South University Post-Sec.
5355 Vaughn Rd 36116 334-395-8800
The Robert B. Adams/LabCorp CLS Program Post-Sec.
543 S Hull St 36104 334-263-5745
Trenholm State Technical College Post-Sec.
1225 Air Base Blvd 36108 334-832-9000
Trenholm State Technical College Post-Sec.
3920 Troy Hwy 36116 334-420-4200
Trinity Presbyterian S 1,000/K-12
1700 E Trinity Blvd 36106 334-277-0370
Brian Willett, hdmstr. Fax 272-9262
Troy University Montgomery Post-Sec.
PO Box 4419 36103 334-834-1400

Moody, Saint Clair, Pop. 9,324
Saint Clair County SD
Supt. — See Ashville
Moody HS 600/9-12
714 High School Dr 35004 205-640-5127
Ken Storie, prin. Fax 640-2300
Moody JHS 400/7-8
600 High School Dr 35004 205-640-2040
Ronald McFarling, prin. Fax 640-3036

Morris, Jefferson, Pop. 1,843
Jefferson County SD
Supt. — See Birmingham

Jordan JSHS 900/7-12
8601 Old Highway 31 35116 205-379-4850
Dr. Byron Campbell, prin. Fax 379-4895

Moulton, Lawrence, Pop. 3,257
Lawrence County SD 6,100/K-12
14131 Market St 35650 256-905-2400
Dexter Rutherford, supt. Fax 905-2406
www.lawrenceal.org
Lawrence Co. Center of Technology Vo/Tech
PO Box 606 35650 256-974-3751
Wade Fleming, prin. Fax 905-2482
Lawrence County JSHS 600/8-12
102 College St 35650 256-905-2440
Joe Lang, prin. Fax 905-2444
Other Schools – See Courtland, Danville, Mount Hope, Town Creek, Trinity

Moundville, Hale, Pop. 1,997
Hale County SD
Supt. — See Greensboro
Hale County HS 400/7-12
PO Box 188 35474 205-371-8920
Brian Clayton, prin. Fax 371-6800

Mountain Brook, Jefferson, Pop. 19,938
Mountain Brook CSD 4,100/K-12
3 Church St, Birmingham AL 35213 205-871-4608
Charles Mason, supt. Fax 877-8303
www.mtnbrook.k12.al.us
Mountain Brook JHS 1,000/7-9
205 Overbrook Rd, Birmingham AL 35213
205-871-3516
Garry Rickard, prin. Fax 969-8113
Mountain Brook SHS 900/10-12
3650 Bethune Dr 35223 205-414-3800
Richard Barlow, prin. Fax 969-8113

Mount Hope, Lawrence
Lawrence County SD
Supt. — See Moulton
Mount Hope S 300/K-12
8455 County Road 23 35651 256-905-2470
Tony Rutherford, prin. Fax 905-2471

Munford, Talladega
Talladega County SD
Supt. — See Talladega
Munford HS 600/7-12
300 Cedars Rd 36268 256-315-5220
Judson Warlick, prin. Fax 315-5240

Muscle Shoals, Colbert, Pop. 12,249
Muscle Shoals CSD 2,500/PK-12
PO Box 2610 35662 256-389-2600
Jeff Wooten, supt. Fax 389-2605
www.mscs.k12.al.us
Muscle Shoals Center for Technology Vo/Tech
PO Box 2186 35662 256-389-2660
Sylvia Coleman, prin. Fax 389-2662
Muscle Shoals HS 700/9-12
1900 Avalon Ave 35661 256-389-2682
H.L. Noah, prin. Fax 389-2689
Muscle Shoals MS 600/6-8
100 Trojan Dr 35661 256-389-2640
Mary Ann Stegall, prin. Fax 389-2647

Northwest-Shoals Community College Post-Sec.
PO Box 2545 35662 256-331-5200

Newbern, Perry, Pop. 229
Hale County SD
Supt. — See Greensboro
Sunshine S 400/K-12
3125 County Road 10 36765 334-624-8747
Herbert Pickens, prin. Fax 624-8781

New Brockton, Coffee, Pop. 1,242
Coffee County SD
Supt. — See Elba
New Brockton HS 400/7-12
210 S Tyler St 36351 334-894-2350
Dale Kelley, prin. Fax 894-5204

New Hope, Madison, Pop. 2,774
Madison County SD
Supt. — See Huntsville
New Hope HS 400/9-12
5216 Main Dr 35760 256-723-4226
Brenda Goodwin, prin. Fax 723-4063

New Market, Madison, Pop. 1,094
Madison County SD
Supt. — See Huntsville
Buckhorn HS 1,000/9-12
4123 Winchester Rd 35761 256-379-2123
Tom Ledbetter, prin. Fax 379-5311

New Site, Tallapoosa, Pop. 833
Tallapoosa County SD
Supt. — See Dadeville
Horseshoe Bend S 800/K-12
10684 Highway 22 E 36256 256-329-9110
Glenn Fuller, prin. Fax 329-9119

Newton, Dale, Pop. 1,709
Houston County SD
Supt. — See Dothan
Wicksburg S 800/K-12
1172 S State Highway 123 36352 334-692-5549
James Murrey, prin. Fax 692-3184

Normal, Madison

Alabama A & M University Post-Sec.
PO Box 908 35762 256-372-5000

Northport, Tuscaloosa, Pop. 20,106
Tuscaloosa County SD
Supt. — See Tuscaloosa
Collins-Riverside MS 400/6-8
1400 3rd St 35476 205-342-2680
Bryant Williams, prin. Fax 752-8024
Echols MS 500/6-8
2701 Echols Ave 35476 205-342-2884
Nancy Terry, prin. Fax 339-1064
Northside HS 400/9-12
19230 Northside Pkwy 35475 205-342-2755
David W. Patrick, prin. Fax 339-3437

Northside MS 300/6-8
19130 Northside Rd 35475 205-342-2740
June Traweek, prin. Fax 339-4680
Tuscaloosa County HS 1,600/9-12
12500 Wildcat Dr 35475 205-342-2670
Dr. Steve Benson, prin. Fax 339-5086
Wood MS 600/6-8
2300 26th Ave 35476 205-342-2690
Greg Hurst, prin. Fax 339-6642

Notasulga, Macon, Pop. 880
Macon County SD
Supt. — See Tuskegee
Notasulga S 500/K-12
PO Box 10 36866 334-257-3510
Tommy Thompson, prin. Fax 257-4228

Tallapoosa County SD
Supt. — See Dadeville
Reeltown S 800/K-12
4085 AL Highway 120 36866 334-257-3784
Joseph C. Windle, prin. Fax 257-3978

Oakman, Walker, Pop. 951
Walker County SD
Supt. — See Jasper
Oakman JSHS 400/7-12
PO Box 286 35579 205-622-3381
Joel Hagood, prin. Fax 622-3542

Odenville, Saint Clair, Pop. 1,174
Saint Clair County SD
Supt. — See Ashville
Odenville MS 500/5-8
PO Box 610 35120 205-629-2280
Debra Carroll, prin. Fax 620-2282
St. Clair Co. HS 500/9-12
PO Box 550 35120 205-629-6222
Brian Terry, prin. Fax 629-2228

Ohatchee, Calhoun, Pop. 1,213
Calhoun County SD
Supt. — See Anniston
Ohatchee HS 400/7-12
100 Cherokee Trl 36271 256-741-4900
Robin Kines, prin. Fax 892-9181

Oneonta, Blount, Pop. 6,034
Blount County SD 7,800/K-12
PO Box 578 35121 205-625-4102
James E. Carr, supt. Fax 625-4100
www.blountcountyschools.net
Appalachian S 700/K-12
350 County Highway 12 35121 205-274-9712
Steven Love, prin. Fax 274-9706
Other Schools – See Blountsville, Cleveland, Hayden, Locust Fork

Oneonta CSD 1,300/K-12
27605 State Highway 75 35121 205-625-4106
Henry Housch, supt. Fax 274-2910
www.oneonta.k12.al.us/
Oneonta City HS 600/7-12
27605 State Highway 75 35121 205-625-3801
Keith Bender, prin. Fax 625-5015

Opelika, Lee, Pop. 23,608
Lee County SD 9,300/K-12
PO Box 120 36803 334-745-9770
John Painter, supt. Fax 745-9774
www.lee.k12.al.us
Beauregard HS 500/9-12
7343 AL Highway 51 36804 334-745-5916
Richard Brown, prin. Fax 749-6421
Sanford MS 700/5-8
1500 Lee Road 11 36804 334-745-5023
Michelle Rutherford, prin. Fax 745-5685
Other Schools – See Loachapoka, Salem, Smiths Station, Valley

Opelika CSD 4,300/K-12
PO Box 2469 36803 334-745-9700
Fax 745-9706
www.opelikaschools.org
Opelika HS 1,200/9-12
1700 Lafayette Pkwy 36801 334-745-9715
Stan Cox, prin. Fax 745-9721
Opelika MS 1,100/6-8
1206 Denson Dr 36801 334-745-9726
Kenneth Burton, prin. Fax 745-9730

Southern Union State Community College Post-Sec.
1701 Lafayette Pkwy 36801 334-745-6437
Trinity Christian S 200/K-12
1010 India Rd 36801 334-745-2464
Sharon Miller, prin. Fax 745-4856

Opp, Covington, Pop. 6,426
Opp CSD 1,400/K-12
PO Box 840 36467 334-493-3173
Dr. Earl Weeks, supt. Fax 493-3060
oppcityschools.com/
Opp HS 400/9-12
502 N Maloy St 36467 334-493-4561
Ruth Walker, prin. Fax 493-2146
Opp MS 400/5-8
303 E Stewart Ave 36467 334-493-6332
Michael Smithart, prin. Fax 493-1120

LBW Community College Post-Sec.
PO Box 910 36467 334-493-3573

Orange Beach, Baldwin, Pop. 4,281

Columbia Southern University Post-Sec.
25326 Canal Rd 36561 251-981-3771

Orrville, Dallas, Pop. 216
Dallas County SD
Supt. — See Selma
Keith MSHS 300/7-12
1166 County Road 115 36767 334-875-4155
Grady Broadnax, prin. Fax 996-8464

Oxford, Calhoun, Pop. 15,470
Oxford CSD 4,000/PK-12
310 E 2nd St 36203 256-831-0243
Dr. Jeff Goodwin, supt. Fax 831-8620
www.oxford.k12.al.us/
Oxford Area Vo HS Vo/Tech
915 Stewart St 36203 256-831-7505
William Holladay, prin. Fax 831-8142
Oxford HS 1,000/9-12
915 Stewart St 36203 256-831-7505
William Holladay, prin. Fax 831-8142
Oxford MS 900/6-8
1750 US Highway 78 W 36203 256-835-8955
Wayne Caldwell, prin. Fax 835-8813

Ozark, Dale, Pop. 14,987
Dale County SD 2,700/K-12
PO Box 948 36361 334-774-2355
Phillip Parker, supt. Fax 774-3503
www.dalecountyboe.org/
Other Schools – See Ariton, Midland City, Pinckard, Skipperville

Ozark CSD 5,200/K-12
1044 Andrews Ave 36360 334-774-5197
Dr. Daniel C. Payant, supt. Fax 774-2685
ocbecobalt.ocbe.k12.al.us
Carroll HS 900/9-12
455 Forest Ave 36360 334-774-4915
Terry Casey, prin. Fax 774-1865
Ozark Carroll HS Career Center Vo/Tech
227 Faust Ave 36360 334-774-4949
Fax 774-8314
Smith MS 700/6-8
994 Andrews Ave 36360 334-774-4913
Sylvia Malone, prin. Fax 774-2685

Parrish, Walker, Pop. 1,256
Walker County SD
Supt. — See Jasper
Parrish JSHS 200/7-12
35 Tornado Aly 35580 205-686-7701
David Beason, prin. Fax 686-9350

Pelham, Shelby, Pop. 17,396
Shelby County SD
Supt. — See Columbiana
Pelham HS 1,100/9-12
2500 Panther Cir 35124 205-682-5500
Bob Lavett, prin. Fax 682-5505

Pell City, Saint Clair, Pop. 10,315
Pell City CSD 4,000/K-12
25 Williamson Dr 35125 205-884-4440
Dr. Bobby Hathcock, supt. Fax 338-7999
www.pellcityschools.net
Duran JHS 700/7-8
309 Williamson Dr 35125 205-338-2825
Cynthia Williamson, prin. Fax 884-6502
Pell City HS 1,100/9-12
1300 Cogswell Ave 35125 205-338-2250
Bob McCool, prin. Fax 338-2838

Victory Christian S 600/PK-12
PO Box 710 35125 205-338-2901
David Weir, prin. Fax 338-3916

Phenix City, Russell, Pop. 28,444
Phenix City SD 7,300/K-12
PO Box 460 36868 334-298-0534
Larry DiChiara, supt. Fax 298-6038
www.pcboe.net
Central HS 1,400/9-12
2400 Dobbs Dr 36870 334-298-3626
Jan Funderburk, prin. Fax 298-7690
South Girard S 400/8-8
521 Fontaine Rd 36869 334-298-2527
Reginald Sparks, prin. Fax 297-8274

Russell County SD 3,600/K-12
PO Box 400 36868 334-298-8791
Dr. Rebecca Lee, supt. Fax 448-8825
www.russellcountyschools.org
Other Schools – See Seale

Chattahoochee Valley Community College Post-Sec.
2602 College Dr 36869 334-291-4900
Troy University - Phenix City Post-Sec.
1 University Pl 36869 334-297-1007

Phil Campbell, Franklin, Pop. 1,054
Franklin County SD
Supt. — See Russellville
Phil Campbell HS 400/7-12
PO Box 849 35581 205-993-5311
William Smith, prin. Fax 993-5312

Piedmont, Calhoun, Pop. 4,986
Piedmont CSD 1,000/K-12
502 W Hood St 36272 256-447-8831
Matthew Akin, supt. Fax 447-6486
Piedmont HS 300/9-12
750 Highway 200 36272 256-447-2829
Hugh McWhorter, prin. Fax 447-8722
Piedmont MS 300/6-8
401 N Main St 36272 256-447-6165
Brenda Formby, prin. Fax 447-8070

Pike Road, Montgomery, Pop. 304
Montgomery County SD
Supt. — See Montgomery
Washington JHS 800/7-9
696 Georgia Washington Rd 36064 334-215-8290
Janet Reese, prin. Fax 215-0112

Pinckard, Dale, Pop. 656
Dale County SD
Supt. — See Ozark
South Dale MS 300/5-8
PO Box D 36371 334-983-3077
David Lee, prin. Fax 983-5882

Pinson, Jefferson, Pop. 10,987
Jefferson County SD
Supt. — See Birmingham
Clay-Chalkville HS 1,400/9-12
6623 Roe Chandler Rd 35126 205-379-3050
Randle Cassady, prin. Fax 680-8128

Pinson Valley HS 1,000/9-12
6895 Highway 75 35126 205-379-5100
June Houge, prin. Fax 379-5145
Rudd MS 800/6-8
4526 Rudd School Rd 35126 205-379-5300
Steven Laney, prin. Fax 379-5345

Pisgah, Jackson, Pop. 701
Jackson County SD
Supt. — See Scottsboro
Pisgah S 600/K-12
PO Box 249 35765 256-451-3241
John Kirby, prin. Fax 451-3457

Plantersville, Dallas
Dallas County SD
Supt. — See Selma
Dallas County HS 600/9-12
PO Box 145 36758 334-366-2232
Don Ingram, prin. Fax 366-4015

Pleasant Grove, Jefferson, Pop. 10,293
Jefferson County SD
Supt. — See Birmingham
Pleasant Grove JSHS 1,000/7-12
805 7th Ave 35127 205-379-5250
Wayne Byram, prin. Fax 379-5295

Prattville, Autauga, Pop. 26,657
Autauga County SD 9,100/K-12
153 W 4th St 36067 334-365-5706
Larry Butler, supt. Fax 361-3828
www.autaugacountyschool.org
Autauga County Tech Center Vo/Tech
1301 Upper Kingston Rd 36067 334-361-0258
Charles Y. Riddle, prin. Fax 361-3839
Prattville HS 2,000/9-12
1315 Upper Kingston Rd 36067 334-365-8804
Lee Hicks, prin. Fax 358-0011
Prattville JHS 1,100/7-8
1089 Martin Luther King Dr 36067 334-365-6697
Jason Wingate, prin. Fax 361-3870
Other Schools – See Autaugaville, Billingsley, Marbury

Autauga Academy 200/K-12
497 Golson Rd 36067 334-365-4343
Gerald Carter, prin. Fax 365-7713
Prattville Christian Academy 200/PK-12
Old Farm Ln N 36066 334-285-0077
Ron Mitchell, prin.

Prichard, Mobile, Pop. 27,983
Mobile County SD
Supt. — See Mobile
Blount HS 600/9-12
838 W Main St 36610 251-221-3070
Don Mitchell, prin. Fax 221-3075
Faulkner Career Technical S Vo/Tech
33 W Elm St 36610 251-221-5431
Ronald Coleman, prin. Fax 221-5433
Mobile County Training MS 400/6-8
800 Whitley St 36610 251-221-2267
Aaron Guyton, prin. Fax 221-2269
Vigor HS 1,100/9-12
913 N Wilson Ave 36610 251-221-3045
Leland Whidden, prin. Fax 221-3050

Princeton, Jackson
Jackson County SD
Supt. — See Scottsboro
Paint Rock Valley S 100/K-12
PO Box 150 35766 256-776-2628
Paul Kennamer, prin. Fax 776-0042

Ragland, Saint Clair, Pop. 1,972
Saint Clair County SD
Supt. — See Ashville
Ragland S 600/K-12
1060 Main St 35131 205-472-2123
Hanley Hardy, prin. Fax 472-0086

Rainbow City, Etowah, Pop. 8,760
Etowah County SD
Supt. — See Gadsden
Rainbow MS 600/6-8
454 Lumbley Rd 35906 256-442-1095
Alan Cosby, prin. Fax 442-1028

Westbrook Christian S 600/PK-12
100 Westminster Dr 35906 256-442-7457
Cynthia Greer, prin. Fax 442-7635

Rainsville, DeKalb, Pop. 4,699
De Kalb County SD 7,500/K-12
PO Box 1668 35986 256-638-6921
Charles D. Warren, supt. Fax 638-9720
www.dekalbk12.org
De Kalb Technology Center Vo/Tech
PO Box 469 35986 256-638-4421
Conner Runyan, prin. Fax 638-4420
Plainview S 1,200/K-12
PO Box 469 35986 256-638-3510
Ronald Bell, prin. Fax 638-6274
Other Schools – See Collinsville, Crossville, Fyffe,
Geraldine, Ider, Sylvania, Valley Head

Northeast Alabama Community College Post-Sec.
PO Box 159 35986 256-638-4418

Ranburne, Cleburne, Pop. 476
Cleburne County SD
Supt. — See Heflin
Ranburne HS 400/7-12
21045 Main St 36273 256-568-3402
Fred Lovvorn, prin. Fax 568-2605

Red Bay, Franklin, Pop. 3,293
Franklin County SD
Supt. — See Russellville
Red Bay S 800/K-12
PO Box 1518 35582 256-356-4408
Wesley Thigpen, prin. Fax 356-4418

Red Level, Covington, Pop. 544
Covington County SD
Supt. — See Andalusia
Red Level S 700/K-12
PO Box D 36474 334-469-5315
Johny Odom, prin. Fax 469-6192

Reform, Pickens, Pop. 1,905
Pickens County SD
Supt. — See Carrollton
Pickens County JSHS 400/7-12
PO Box 1239 35481 205-375-2344
Delynn Bouldin, prin. Fax 375-8151

Roanoke, Randolph, Pop. 6,489
Roanoke CSD 1,400/K-12
PO Box 1367 36274 334-863-2628
Chuck Marcum, supt. Fax 863-2849
www.roanokecityschools.org/home.asp
Handley HS 400/9-12
PO Box 1393 36274 334-863-6815
Jim Holley, prin. Fax 863-6284
Handley MS 500/4-8
PO Box 725 36274 334-863-4174
Greg Foster, prin. Fax 863-6129

Robertsdale, Baldwin, Pop. 4,366
Baldwin County SD
Supt. — See Bay Minette
Central Baldwin MS 800/6-8
PO Box 930 36567 251-947-2327
Keith McClammy, prin. Fax 947-1949
Robertsdale HS 1,300/9-12
PO Box 69 36567 251-947-4154
Theresa Bryant, prin. Fax 947-2666
South Baldwin Center for Tech Vo/Tech
PO Box 549 36567 251-947-5041
Kendall Mowdy, prin. Fax 947-4837

Central Christian S 300/PK-12
17395 State Highway 104 36567 251-947-5043
Tim Shelton, admin. Fax 947-2572
Faith Presbyterian Christian S 100/PK-12
PO Box 950 36567 251-947-5012
Marcy Barnhart, prin. Fax 947-5012

Rockford, Coosa, Pop. 410
Coosa County SD 1,600/K-12
PO Box 37 35136 256-377-4913
Todd Wingard, supt. Fax 377-2385
coosaschools.k12.al.us/
Central HS of Coosa County 400/9-12
RR 2 Box 62 35136 256-377-4384
Keith Bullard, prin. Fax 377-4658
Central MS of Coosa County 600/5-8
RR 2 Box 65 35136 256-377-1490
Dr. James Martin, prin. Fax 377-1493
Coosa County Science & Technology Center Vo/Tech
RR 2 Box 52 35136 256-377-4678
Calvin McKinney, prin. Fax 377-4589

Rogersville, Lauderdale, Pop. 1,180
Lauderdale County SD
Supt. — See Florence
Lauderdale County S 1,000/K-12
PO Box 220 35652 256-247-3414
James Stejskal, prin. Fax 247-3444

Russellville, Franklin, Pop. 8,783
Franklin County SD 2,600/K-12
PO Box 610 35653 256-332-1360
Bill Moss, supt. Fax 331-0069
www.franklin.k12.al.us/
Belgreen S 500/K-12
14220 Highway 187 35653 256-332-1376
Ed Britton, prin. Fax 332-7209
Franklin Co. Career Tech Ctr Vo/Tech
85 Jail Springs Rd 35653 256-332-2127
Orval Seay, prin. Fax 332-2219
Tharptown S 400/K-10
145 Highway 80 35654 256-332-3404
David Riddle, prin. Fax 332-3402
Other Schools – See Phil Campbell, Red Bay, Vina

Russellville CSD 2,300/K-12
PO Box 880 35653 256-331-2000
Dr. Wayne Ray, supt. Fax 332-7323
www.rcs.k12.al.us
Russellville HS 700/9-12
PO Box 730 35653 256-332-8460
Rex Mayfield, prin. Fax 332-8447
Russellville MS 600/6-8
PO Box 1213 35653 256-332-8450
Frankie Hammock, prin. Fax 332-8453

Salem, Lee
Lee County SD
Supt. — See Opelika
Wacoochee JHS 900/7-8
125 Lee Road 254 36874 334-745-3062
Joey Biddle, prin. Fax 745-3565

Samson, Geneva, Pop. 2,017
Geneva County SD
Supt. — See Geneva
Samson HS 200/9-12
209 N Broad St 36477 334-898-2371
Mavis Rials, prin. Fax 898-7576
Samson MS, 209 N Broad St 36477 200/7-8
Mavis Rials, prin. 334-898-1317

Saraland, Mobile, Pop. 12,507
Mobile County SD
Supt. — See Mobile
Adams MS 900/6-8
401 Baldwin Rd 36571 251-221-2000
John Powell, prin. Fax 221-2004

Sardis City, DeKalb, Pop. 1,737
Etowah County SD
Supt. — See Gadsden
Sardis JSHS 600/7-12
1420 Church St 35956 256-593-5221
Gerald Beard, prin. Fax 593-5223

Satsuma, Mobile, Pop. 5,872
Mobile County SD
Supt. — See Mobile
Satsuma HS 1,300/9-12
1 Gator Cir 36572 251-221-3269
Deborah Altman, prin. Fax 221-3274

Scottsboro, Jackson, Pop. 14,776
Jackson County SD 6,000/K-12
PO Box 490 35768 256-259-9500
Jerry W. Jeffery, supt. Fax 259-0076
www.jackson.k12.al.us/

Skyline S 600/K-12
897 County Road 25 35768 256-587-6561
Douglas Graden, prin. Fax 587-6562
Other Schools – See Bridgeport, Higdon, Hollywood,
Pisgah, Princeton, Section, Stevenson, Woodville

Scottsboro CSD 2,800/K-12
906 S Scott St 35768 256-218-2100
Dr. Judith Berry, supt. Fax 218-2190
www.scottsboroschools.net
Scottsboro HS 700/9-12
25053 John T Reid Pkwy 35768 256-218-2000
Anthony Ball, prin. Fax 218-2090
Scottsboro JHS 500/7-8
1601 Jefferson St 35768 256-218-2300
Hal Luse, prin. Fax 218-2390

Gaither Beauty College Post-Sec.
414 E Willow St 35768 256-259-1001
Scottsboro Christian Academy 100/K-12
9545 AL Highway 79 35768 256-259-5398
Debbie Johnson, admin. Fax 574-3639

Seale, Russell
Russell County SD
Supt. — See Phenix City
Russell County HS 1,100/9-12
4699 Highway 431 36875 334-855-4378
Dr. Janet Womack, prin. Fax 855-4334
Russell County MS 1,000/6-8
4716 Highway 431 36875 334-855-4453
Larry Screws, prin. Fax 855-4437

Section, Jackson, Pop. 763
Jackson County SD
Supt. — See Scottsboro
Section S 600/K-12
PO Box 10 35771 256-228-6718
Dr. Camille Wright, prin. Fax 228-6252

Selma, Dallas, Pop. 19,630
Dallas County SD 4,600/K-12
PO Box 1056 36702 334-875-3440
Dr. Fannie Major-McKenzie, supt. Fax 876-4493
www.dallask12.org
Dallas County Career Technical Center Vo/Tech
1306 Roosevelt St 36701 334-872-8031
Don Willingham, prin. Fax 872-5697
Martin MS 400/7-8
2863 Dallas County Road 81 36703 334-872-6417
Finis Sanders, prin. Fax 875-4013
Southside HS 500/9-12
7975 US Highway 80 E 36701 334-872-0518
Bailey Dawson, prin. Fax 872-0295
Tipton MS 400/7-8
2500 Tipton St 36701 334-872-8080
Hattie Shelton, prin. Fax 872-8008
Other Schools – See Orrville, Plantersville

Selma CSD 4,200/PK-12
PO Box 350 36702 334-874-1600
Dr. James Carter, supt. Fax 876-4430
www.selmacityschools.org
Selma Area Vo HS Vo/Tech
2180 Broad St 36701 334-874-1680
Roosevelt Wilson, prin. Fax 874-9450
Selma HS 1,000/9-12
2180 Broad St 36701 334-874-1680
Roosevelt Wilson, prin. Fax 874-9450
Selma MS CHAT Academy 600/7-8
1701 Summerfield Rd 36701 334-874-1675
Bertram Pickney, prin. Fax 874-1679

Central Christian Academy 200/1-12
1 Bell St 36701 334-877-1581
Jimmy Barlow, prin.
Concordia College Post-Sec.
PO Box 1329 36702 334-874-5700
George C. Wallace State Comm College Post-Sec.
PO Box 2530 36702 334-876-9227
Meadowview Christian S 400/PK-12
1512 Old Orrville Rd 36701 334-872-8448
Dr. Michael Gaylor, prin. Fax 872-8447
Morgan Academy 600/K-12
PO Box 1587 36702 334-875-4464
Dr. Christopher De Buzna, prin.
Selma University Post-Sec.
1501 Lapsley St 36701 334-872-2533

Semmes, Mobile
Mobile County SD
Supt. — See Mobile
Montgomery MS 1,700/9-12
4275 Snow Rd N 36575 251-221-3153
George Romano, prin. Fax 221-3150
Semmes MS 1,500/6-8
4566 Ed George Rd 36575 251-221-2344
Brenda Shenesey, prin. Fax 221-2347

Sheffield, Colbert, Pop. 9,286
Sheffield CSD 1,300/K-12
300 W 6th St 35660 256-383-0400
Richard L. Gardner, supt. Fax 386-5704
www.scs.k12.al.us/
Sheffield HS 400/9-12
2800 E 19th Ave 35660 256-383-6052
Ronnie Wicks, prin. Fax 386-5707
Sheffield JHS 200/7-8
1803 E 30th St 35660 256-386-5735
Brezofski Anderson, prin. Fax 386-5706

Skipperville, Dale
Dale County SD
Supt. — See Ozark
Long HS 400/7-12
2565 County Road 60 36374 334-774-2380
Jason Steed, prin. Fax 774-3937

Slocomb, Geneva, Pop. 2,002
Geneva County SD
Supt. — See Geneva
Slocomb HS 300/9-12
PO Box 380 36375 334-886-2008
Max Whittaker, prin. Fax 886-9889
Slocomb MS 300/6-8
PO Box 380 36375 334-886-2008
Max Whittaker, prin. Fax 886-9889

Smiths, Lee, Pop. 3,456

Glenwood S — 600/K-12
5801 Summerville Rd 36877 — 334-297-3614
Phillip R. Elder, prin. — Fax 214-9027

Smiths Station, Lee, Pop. 4,488
Lee County SD
Supt. — See Opelika
Smiths Station HS — 1,500/9-12
1100 Lee Road 298 36877 — 334-298-0969
Mike Walton, prin. — Fax 298-1304

Somerville, Morgan, Pop. 349
Morgan County SD
Supt. — See Decatur
Brewer HS — 900/9-12
59 Eva Rd 35670 — 256-778-8634
Frances Couey, prin. — Fax 778-8012
Brewer Vocational HS — Vo/Tech
59 Eva Rd 35670 — 256-778-8634
Greg Hudson, prin. — Fax 778-9119

Spanish Fort, Baldwin, Pop. 5,584
Baldwin County SD
Supt. — See Bay Minette
Spanish Fort JSHS — 1,400/7-12
PO Box 7504 36577 — 251-625-3259
Michael Lucci, prin. — Fax 615-5648

Chi Alpha Academy — 200/PK-12
PO Box 7174 36577 — 251-626-6801
Mike McPherson, admin. — Fax 626-6858

Spring Garden, Cherokee
Cherokee County SD
Supt. — See Centre
Spring Garden S — 600/K-12
PO Box 31 36275 — 256-447-7045
Michael Welsh, prin. — Fax 447-6947

Springville, Saint Clair, Pop. 2,800
Saint Clair County SD
Supt. — See Ashville
Springville HS — 500/9-12
8295 US Highway 11 35146 — 205-467-7833
Robert Harris, prin. — Fax 467-2734
Springville MS — 700/4-8
6691 US Highway 11 35146 — 205-467-2740
Virgil Winslett, prin. — Fax 467-2742

Stevenson, Jackson, Pop. 1,751
Jackson County SD
Supt. — See Scottsboro
North Jackson HS — 500/9-12
PO Box 848 35772 — 256-437-2136
Frank Stevens, prin. — Fax 437-2400
Stevenson MS — 300/5-8
701 Kentucky Ave 35772 — 256-437-2945
Dr. Dianne Brooks, prin. — Fax 437-2747

Sulligent, Lamar, Pop. 2,048
Lamar County SD
Supt. — See Vernon
Sulligent S — 900/K-12
PO Box 367 35586 — 205-698-9254
Craig Weeks, prin. — Fax 698-8497

Sumiton, Walker, Pop. 2,602

Bevill State Community College — Post-Sec.
PO Box 800 35148 — 205-648-3271

Sweet Water, Marengo, Pop. 233
Marengo County SD
Supt. — See Linden
Sweet Water S — 600/K-12
PO Box 127 36782 — 334-994-4263
Stan Stokley, prin. — Fax 994-4686

Sylacauga, Talladega, Pop. 12,607
Sylacauga CSD — 2,300/K-12
605 W 4th St 35150 — 256-245-5256
Jane Cobia, supt. — Fax 245-6665
www.sylacauga.k12.al.us
Nichols-Lawson MS — 500/6-8
1550 Talladega Hwy 35150 — 256-245-4376
Gerald Douglass, prin. — Fax 245-4071
Sylacauga HS — 700/9-12
701 N Broadway Ave 35150 — 256-249-8692
Tommy Porch, prin. — Fax 245-1026

Talladega County SD
Supt. — See Talladega
Comer Memorial HS — 500/7-12
801 Seminole Ave 35150 — 256-315-5400
Linda McAdam, prin. — Fax 315-5420
Fayetteville S — 500/K-12
170 WW Averitte Dr 35151 — 256-315-5550
Joan Doyle, prin. — Fax 315-5575

Sylvania, DeKalb, Pop. 1,226
De Kalb County SD
Supt. — See Rainsville
Sylvania S — 900/K-12
PO Box 390 35988 — 256-638-2030
Gary Carlyle, prin. — Fax 638-7839

Talladega, Talladega, Pop. 17,066
Talladega CSD — 2,900/K-12
501 South St E 35160 — 256-315-5600
Leonard Messer, supt. — Fax 315-5606
www.talladega-cs.net/default.aspx
Ellis JHS — 500/7-8
414 Elm St 35160 — 256-315-5700
Scott Bailey, prin. — Fax 315-5704
Talladega Career Tech HS — Vo/Tech
110 Piccadilly Dr 35160 — 256-315-5688
Dr. Trellys Riley, prin. — Fax 315-5690
Talladega HS — 800/9-12
1177 McMillan St E 35160 — 256-315-5666
Darren Douthitt, prin. — Fax 315-5670

Talladega County SD — 7,800/K-12
PO Box 887 35161 — 256-315-5100
Dr. Cynthia Elsberry, supt. — Fax 315-5126
www.tcboe.org
Talladega County Central HS — 300/7-12
5104 Howell Cove Rd 35160 — 256-315-5340
John Galloway, prin. — Fax 315-5350
Other Schools – See Alpine, Childersburg, Lincoln, Munford, Sylacauga

---

Alabama Institute for the Deaf and Blind — Post-Sec.
PO Box 698 35161
St. Peter's Episcopal MS — 50/6-8
208 North St E 35160 — 256-315-0026
Fax 362-1048
Talladega College — Post-Sec.
627 Battle St W 35160 — 256-362-0206

Tallassee, Elmore, Pop. 4,951
Tallassee CSD — 1,900/K-12
308 King St 36078 — 334-283-6864
Dr. James Jeffers, supt. — Fax 283-4338
tallassee.al.schoolwebpages.com
Southside MS — 600/5-8
901 EB Payne Sr Dr 36078 — 334-283-2151
Ron McDaniel, prin. — Fax 283-3577
Tallassee HS — 600/9-12
502 Barnett Blvd 36078 — 334-283-2187
Carl Stewart, prin. — Fax 283-6210

Tanner, Limestone
Limestone County SD
Supt. — See Athens
Tanner S — 800/K-12
12060 Sommers Rd 35671 — 256-233-6682
Billy Owens, prin. — Fax 233-6449

Tarrant, Jefferson, Pop. 7,554
Tarrant CSD — 1,400/K-12
1318 Alabama St 35217 — 205-849-3700
Dr. Marti Rizzato, supt. — Fax 849-3728
www.tarrant.k12.al.us/
Tarrant City HS — 400/9-12
830 Jefferson Blvd 35217 — 205-849-0172
Cas McWaters, prin. — Fax 849-3728
Other Schools – See Birmingham

Theodore, Mobile, Pop. 6,509
Mobile County SD
Supt. — See Mobile
Hankins MS — 1,300/6-8
5771 Katherine Hankins Dr 36582 — 251-221-2200
Cheryl Wittner, prin. — Fax 221-2204
Theodore HS — 1,700/9-12
6201 Swedetown Rd N 36582 — 251-221-3351
Ronald Rowell, prin. — Fax 221-3355

Magnolia Springs Baptist Academy — 200/PK-12
6058 Theodore Dawes Rd 36582 — 251-653-0251
Bob Ramirez, prin. — Fax 653-2668

Thomaston, Marengo, Pop. 380
Marengo County SD
Supt. — See Linden
Johnson S — 400/K-12
PO Box 67 36783 — 334-627-3364
Lepolean Peterson, prin. — Fax 627-3396

Thomasville, Clarke, Pop. 4,593
Thomasville CSD — 1,600/K-12
PO Box 458 36784 — 334-636-9955
Roger Speed, supt. — Fax 636-4096
www.thomasvilleschools.org/
Thomasville HS — 500/9-12
777 Gates Dr 36784 — 334-636-4451
Leon Clark, prin. — Fax 636-0022
Thomasville MS — 500/5-8
781 Gates Dr 36784 — 334-636-4928
Terry Norton, prin. — Fax 636-4924

Alabama Southern Community College — Post-Sec.
PO Box 2000 36784 — 334-636-4429

Thorsby, Chilton, Pop. 1,920
Chilton County SD
Supt. — See Clanton
Thorsby S — 900/K-12
54 Opportunity Dr 35171 — 205-280-4880
Russ Bryan, prin. — Fax 646-2197

Toney, Madison
Madison County SD
Supt. — See Huntsville
Sparkman MS — 700/6-8
2697 Carters Gin Rd 35773 — 256-852-0112
Ronnie Blair, prin. — Fax 852-4368

Harmony Christian S — 50/K-12
PO Box 428 35773 — 256-852-5607
Sharon DeMontgomery, prin. — Fax 852-5607

Town Creek, Lawrence, Pop. 1,201
Lawrence County SD
Supt. — See Moulton
Hatton JSHS — 400/7-12
6909 AL Highway 101 35672 — 256-685-4010
Larry Hancock, prin. — Fax 685-4007
Hazlewood JSHS — 300/7-12
PO Box 819 35672 — 256-685-4030
Clyde Goode, prin. — Fax 685-4009

Toxey, Choctaw, Pop. 145

South Choctaw Academy — 300/K-12
PO Box 160 36921 — 251-843-2426

Trinity, Morgan, Pop. 1,708
Lawrence County SD
Supt. — See Moulton
East Lawrence HS — 500/8-12
55 County Road 370 35673 — 256-905-2430
Karen Hitt, prin. — Fax 905-2424
East Lawrence MS — 700/4-8
99 County Road 370 35673 — 256-905-2420
Cindy Praytor, prin. — Fax 905-2477

Morgan County SD
Supt. — See Decatur
West Morgan HS — 700/5-12
261 S Greenway Dr 35673 — 256-353-5214
Billy Hopkins, prin. — Fax 351-0161

Troy, Pike, Pop. 13,587
Pike County SD — 2,100/K-12
101 W Love St 36081 — 334-566-1850
Mark Bazzell, supt. — Fax 566-2580
www.pikecountyschools.com
Troy-Pike Regional Center for Technology — Vo/Tech
285 Gibbs St 36081 — 334-566-5395
Al Griffin, prin. — Fax 566-1690
Other Schools – See Brundidge, Goshen

Troy CSD — 2,400/K-12
PO Box 529 36081 — 334-566-3741
Dr. Linda Felton-Smith, supt. — Fax 566-1425
www.troyschools.net
Henderson HS — 600/9-12
PO Box 1006 36081 — 334-566-3510
Frank Brown, prin. — Fax 566-4940
Henderson MS — 600/6-8
PO Box 925 36081 — 334-566-5770
David Helms, prin. — Fax 566-3071

New Life Christian Academy — 100/PK-12
PO Box 1085 36081 — 334-566-0424
Annie Blackmon, dir. — Fax 566-8938
Pike Liberal Arts S — 300/K-12
PO Box 329 36081 — 334-566-2023
Larry Pickett, hdmstr. — Fax 566-7091
Troy University 36082 — Post-Sec.
334-670-3100

Trussville, Jefferson, Pop. 14,604
Jefferson County SD
Supt. — See Birmingham
Clay-Chalkville MS — 1,200/6-8
6700 Trussville Clay Rd 35173 — 205-379-3100
Mo Williams, prin. — Fax 379-3145

Trussville City SD — 3,900/K-12
113 N Chalkville Rd 35173 — 205-228-3000
Dr. Suzanne Freeman, supt. — Fax 228-3001
trussvillecityschools.com/
Hewitt-Trussville HS — 1,200/9-12
5275 Trussville Clay Rd 35173 — 205-228-3500
Phyllis Montalto, prin. — Fax 228-3501
Hewitt-Trussville MS — 900/6-8
301 Parkway Dr 35173 — 205-228-3700
Dr. Sunderland Williams, prin. — Fax 228-3701

Tuscaloosa, Tuscaloosa, Pop. 79,294
Tuscaloosa CSD — 9,300/PK-12
PO Box 038991 35403 — 205-759-3530
Dr. Joyce Levy, supt. — Fax 759-3711
www.tusc.k12.al.us
Central HS — 500/9-12
1715 ML King Jr Blvd 35401 — 205-759-3720
Herbert Ragsdale, prin. — Fax 759-3756
Northridge HS — 900/9-12
2901 Northridge Rd 35406 — 205-759-3590
Margaret O'Neal, prin. — Fax 759-3605
Tuscaloosa Center for Technology — Vo/Tech
1300 37th St E 35405 — 205-759-3649
James Adkins, coord. — Fax 759-3767
Tuscaloosa MS — 1,000/6-8
315 McFarland Blvd E 35404 — 205-759-3653
Ann Hewitt, prin. — Fax 759-3784
Westlawn MS — 500/6-8
2800 ML King Jr Blvd 35401 — 205-759-3673
Dr. Barbara Allen, prin. — Fax 759-3770
Night HS — Adult
1715 ML King Jr Blvd 35401 — 205-759-3519
Walter Bishop, dir. — Fax 759-3793
Other Schools – See Cottondale

Tuscaloosa County SD — 16,200/K-12
PO Box 2568 35403 — 205-758-0411
Dr. Frank Costanzo, supt. — Fax 758-2990
www.tcss.net/
Hillcrest HS — 1,200/9-12
300 Patriot Pkwy 35405 — 205-342-2800
Jeffery Hyche, prin. — Fax 758-3018
Hillcrest MS — 1,000/6-8
401 Hillcrest School Rd 35405 — 205-342-2820
Wayne Vickers, prin. — Fax 752-2467
Other Schools – See Brookwood, Cottondale, Holt, Northport, Vance

---

American Christian Academy — 900/PK-12
2300 Veterans Memorial Pkwy 35404 — 205-553-5963
Dan Carden, hdmstr. — Fax 553-5942
DCH Regional Medical Center — Post-Sec.
809 University Blvd E 35401 — 205-759-7177
Holy Spirit HS — 200/7-12
601 37th St E 35405 — 205-553-5606
Judy Halli, prin. — Fax 566-7103
Open Door Christian S — 300/PK-12
1785 McFarland Blvd N 35406 — 205-349-4881
Rebekah Ensor, admin. — Fax 349-3246
Shelton State Community College — Post-Sec.
9500 Old Greensboro Rd 35405 — 205-759-1541
Stillman College — Post-Sec.
PO Box 1430 35403 — 205-349-4240
Tuscaloosa Academy — 400/PK-12
420 Rice Valley Rd N 35406 — 205-758-4462
Dr. George B. Elder, hdmstr. — Fax 758-4418
University of Alabama — Post-Sec.
PO Box 870132 35487 — 205-348-6010

Tuscumbia, Colbert, Pop. 7,967
Colbert County SD — 3,300/K-12
1101 Highway 72 E 35674 — 256-386-8565
Billy Hudson, supt. — Fax 381-9375
colbert.k12.al.us/
Colbert Heights HS — 500/7-12
6825 Woodmont Dr 35674 — 256-383-7875
Leroy Willis, prin. — Fax 383-5526
Other Schools – See Cherokee, Leighton

Tuscumbia CSD | 1,400/K-12
300 E 7th St 35674 | 256-389-2900
Royce Massey, supt. | Fax 389-2903
www.tuscumbia.k12.al.us
Deshler Area Vocational HS | Vo/Tech
200 N Commons E 35674 | 256-389-2910
Larry Danley, prin. | Fax 389-2915
Deshler HS | 500/9-12
200 N Commons St E 35674 | 256-389-2910
Larry Danley, prin. | Fax 389-2915
Northside MS | 300/6-8
598 N High St 35674 | 256-389-2920
Robert Mullen, prin. | Fax 389-2921

Covenant Christian S | 300/PK-12
1900 Covenant Dr 35674 | 256-383-4436
Becky Odell, admin. | Fax 381-4437

Tuskegee, Macon, Pop. 11,662
Macon County SD | 3,600/PK-12
PO Box 830090 36083 | 334-727-1600
Willie C. Thomas, supt. | Fax 724-9990
www.maconk12.org
Washington HS | 1,000/9-12
3803 W Mrtn Luther King Hwy 36083 | 334-727-0073
Dr. Kenneth Oliver, prin. | Fax 724-0222
Other Schools – See Notasulga, Tuskegee Institute

Southern Community College | Post-Sec.
PO Box 830688 36083 | 334-727-5220

Tuskegee Institute, See Tuskegee
Macon County SD
Supt. — See Tuskegee
Tuskegee Institute MS | 700/6-8
1809 Franklin Rd 36088 | 334-727-2580
Dr. Dorothy Hooks, prin. | Fax 727-5089

Tuskegee University 36088 | Post-Sec.
334-727-8011

Union Springs, Bullock, Pop. 3,566
Bullock County SD | 1,800/K-12
PO Box 231 36089 | 334-738-2860
Keith Allen Stewart, supt. | Fax 738-2802
bullock.k12.al.us/
Bullock County AVC | Vo/Tech
304 Blackmon Ave E 36089 | 334-738-4370
Charles Cook, prin. | Fax 738-4369
Bullock County HS | 800/7-12
PO Box 5108 36089 | 334-738-2198
Robert McDaniel, prin. | Fax 738-2606

Uniontown, Perry, Pop. 1,555
Perry County SD
Supt. — See Marion
Hatch JSHS | 400/7-12
PO Box 709 36786 | 334-628-4061
Leslie Turner, prin. | Fax 683-4935

Uriah, Monroe
Monroe County SD
Supt. — See Monroeville
Blacksher S | 500/PK-12
PO Box 68 36480 | 251-862-2130
Keith Cardwell, prin. | Fax 862-2808

Valley, Chambers, Pop. 8,888
Chambers County SD
Supt. — See Lafayette
Burns MS | 700/6-8
292 Johnson St 36854 | 334-756-3567
Priscilla Holley, prin. | Fax 756-7511
Valley HS | 800/9-12
501 US Highway 29 36854 | 334-756-4105
Vickie Lynn, prin. | Fax 756-9602

Lee County SD
Supt. — See Opelika
Beulah HS | 500/7-12
4848 Lee Road 270 36854 | 334-745-5010
Jerry Southwell, prin. | Fax 749-1914

Valley Head, DeKalb, Pop. 628
De Kalb County SD
Supt. — See Rainsville
Valley Head S | 500/K-12
PO Box 145 35989 | 256-635-6228
William Monroe, prin. | Fax 635-6229

Vance, Tuscaloosa, Pop. 489
Tuscaloosa County SD
Supt. — See Tuscaloosa
Brookwood MS | 800/6-8
17021 Brookwood Pkwy 35490 | 205-342-2748
Irene Byrd, prin. | Fax 553-9910

Verbena, Chilton
Chilton County SD
Supt. — See Clanton
Verbena S | 500/K-12
PO Box 128 36091 | 205-280-2820
Larry Raines, prin. | Fax 755-0393

Vernon, Lamar, Pop. 2,006
Lamar County SD | 2,500/K-12
PO Box 1379 35592 | 205-695-7615
Terry Robinson, supt. | Fax 695-7678
Lamar County S | 700/4-12
8990 Highway 18 35592 | 205-695-7717
Don Harding, prin. | Fax 695-8218
Lamar County School of Technology | Vo/Tech
43880 Highway 17 35592 | 205-695-7129
Jeff Newman, prin. | Fax 695-6153
Other Schools – See Millport, Sulligent

Vestavia Hills, Jefferson, Pop. 30,909
Vestavia Hills CSD | 5,200/K-12
1204 Montgomery Hwy 35216 | 205-402-5100
Jamie Blair, supt. | Fax 402-5134
www.vestavia.k12.al.us
Pizitz MS | 1,200/6-8
2020 Pizitz Dr 35216 | 205-402-5350
David Miles, prin. | Fax 402-5354
Vestavia Hills HS | 1,500/9-12
2235 Lime Rock Rd 35216 | 205-402-5250
Ann C. Jones, prin. | Fax 402-5262

Vina, Franklin, Pop. 398
Franklin County SD
Supt. — See Russellville
Vina S | 300/K-12
PO Box 36 35593 | 256-356-4733
James Pharr, prin. | Fax 356-4731

Vincent, Shelby, Pop. 1,914
Shelby County SD
Supt. — See Columbiana
Vincent MSHS | 500/6-12
42505 Highway 25 35178 | 205-682-7300
Gary Minnick, prin. | Fax 682-7305

Vinemont, Cullman
Cullman County SD
Supt. — See Cullman
Vinemont HS | 300/9-12
PO Box 189 35179 | 256-734-0571
Ronald Barnes, prin. | Fax 739-8605
Vinemont MS | 300/6-8
170 High School Rd 35179 | 256-739-1943
Michael Grantham, prin. | Fax 737-1664
West Point MS | 500/6-8
4545 County Road 1141 35179 | 256-734-5904
Hank Allen, prin. | Fax 736-2354

Wadley, Randolph, Pop. 636
Randolph County SD
Supt. — See Wedowee
Wadley S | 400/K-12
PO Box 49 36276 | 256-395-2286
Joe Wilkerson, prin. | Fax 395-4488

Southern Union State Community College | Post-Sec.
PO Box 1000 36276 | 256-395-2211

Walnut Grove, Etowah, Pop. 704
Etowah County SD
Supt. — See Gadsden
West End HS | 400/7-12
4515 Elm St 35990 | 205-589-6421
Mark Stancil, prin. | Fax 589-4782

Warrior, Jefferson, Pop. 3,056
Jefferson County SD
Supt. — See Birmingham
Corner S | 1,000/K-12
10005 Corner School Rd 35180 | 205-379-3200
Ronald Cooper, prin. | Fax 379-3245

Waterloo, Lauderdale, Pop. 207
Lauderdale County SD
Supt. — See Florence

Waterloo S | 400/K-12
PO Box 68 35677 | 256-766-3100
Ronnie Lee, prin. | Fax 766-3194

Weaver, Calhoun, Pop. 2,561
Calhoun County SD
Supt. — See Anniston
Weaver HS | 500/7-12
917 Clairmont Dr 36277 | 256-741-7200
Frances Shipp, prin. | Fax 820-0811

Wedowee, Randolph, Pop. 808
Randolph County SD | 2,400/K-12
PO Box 288 36278 | 256-357-4611
Wayne Wortham, supt. | Fax 357-4844
www.randolph.k12.al.us/
Randolph County S | 800/K-12
PO Box 490 36278 | 256-357-4751
Byron Nix, prin. | Fax 357-2310
Randolph-Roanoke Career Tech | Vo/Tech
960 Main St S 36278 | 256-357-2839
Stanley Clark, prin. | Fax 357-4580
Other Schools – See Wadley, Woodland

New Hope Independent S | 50/PK-12
3500 County Road 56 36278 | 256-357-4968
Mary Ward, admin. | Fax 357-4968

West Blocton, Bibb, Pop. 1,381
Bibb County SD
Supt. — See Centreville
Bibb County Career/Technical Center | Vo/Tech
17191 Highway 5 35184 | 205-938-7434
Dennis Duncan, prin. | Fax 938-2037
West Blocton HS | 300/9-12
4734 Truman Aldrich Pkwy 35184 | 205-938-9002
Suzanne Jones, prin. | Fax 938-9546
West Blocton MS | 400/5-8
4721 Truman Aldrich Pkwy 35184 | 205-938-2451
Judson Locke, prin. | Fax 938-3261

Wetumpka, Elmore, Pop. 6,510
Elmore County SD | 10,700/K-12
PO Box 817 36092 | 334-567-1200
Jeffery Langham, supt. | Fax 567-1405
www.elmoreco.com
Elmore Co. Technical Center | Vo/Tech
800 Kelly Fitzpatrick Dr 36092 | 334-567-1219
Carl Thomas, dir. | Fax 567-1417
Wetumpka HS | 1,000/9-12
1251 Coosa River Pkwy 36092 | 334-567-5158
Richard Dennis, prin. | Fax 567-1178
Wetumpka JHS | 600/7-8
409 Alabama St 36092 | 334-567-1248
Steve McKenzie, prin. | Fax 567-1407
Other Schools – See Deatsville, Eclectic, Millbrook

Winfield, Marion, Pop. 4,622
Winfield CSD | 1,300/K-12
PO Box 70 35594 | 205-487-4255
Terrel W. Kirkpatrick, supt. | Fax 487-4603
www.winfieldal.org/
Winfield HS | 400/9-12
232 Pirate Cv 35594 | 205-487-6900
Benny Parrish, prin. | Fax 487-4257
Winfield MS | 400/5-8
481 Apple Ave 35594 | 205-487-6901
Christopher Cook, prin. | Fax 487-4603

Woodland, Randolph, Pop. 203
Randolph County SD
Supt. — See Wedowee
Woodland S | 800/K-12
PO Box 157 36280 | 256-449-2315
Rick Murphy, prin. | Fax 449-2316

Woodville, Jackson, Pop. 752
Jackson County SD
Supt. — See Scottsboro
Woodville S | 500/K-12
290 County Road 63 35776 | 256-776-2874
Shane Small, prin. | Fax 776-4718

York, Sumter, Pop. 2,697
Sumter County SD
Supt. — See Livingston
Sumter County HS | 400/9-12
902 4th Ave 36925 | 205-392-4771
Ellis Levy, prin. | Fax 392-4788

Sumter Academy | 300/K-12
181 Sumter Academy Rd 36925 | 205-392-5238
Paul Kirchharr, hdmstr.

ALASKA

ALASKA DEPARTMENT OF EDUCATION
801 W 10th St Ste 200, Juneau 99801-1878
Telephone 907-465-2800
Fax 907-465-4165
Website http://www.educ.state.ak.us/

Commissioner of Education   Roger Sampson

ALASKA BOARD OF EDUCATION
801 W 10th St, Juneau 99801-1823

Chairperson   Richard I. Mauer

PUBLIC, PRIVATE AND CATHOLIC SECONDARY SCHOOLS

Akhiok, Kodiak Island, Pop. 75
Kodiak Island Borough SD
  Supt. — See Kodiak
Akhiok S   100/K-12
  PO Box 5049 99615   907-836-2223
  Bill Watkins, prin.   Fax 836-2206

Akiachak, Bethel, Pop. 481
Yupiit SD   400/K-12
  PO Box 51190 99551   907-825-3600
  Joseph Slats, supt.   Fax 825-3655
  www.yupiit.org/
Akiachak S   200/K-12
  PO Box 51100 99551   907-825-3616
  Eugene Avey, prin.   Fax 825-3690
Other Schools – See Akiak, Tuluksak

Akiak, Bethel, Pop. 317
Yupiit SD
  Supt. — See Akiachak
Akiak S   100/K-12
  PO Box 52049 99552   907-765-4600
  Dan Reum, prin.   Fax 765-4642

Akutan, Aleutians East, Pop. 745
Aleutian East Borough SD
  Supt. — See Sand Point
Akutan S   50/PK-12
  PO Box 25 99553   907-698-2205
  Alan Swanborough, prin.   Fax 698-2216

Alakanuk, Wade Hampton, Pop. 678
Lower Yukon SD
  Supt. — See Mountain Village
Alakanuk S   200/PK-12
  PO Box 9 99554   907-238-3312
  Nancy Mazurek, prin.   Fax 238-3417

Allakaket, Yukon-Koyukuk, Pop. 94
Yukon-Koyukuk SD
  Supt. — See Fairbanks
Allakaket S   50/PK-12
  PO Box 69 99720   907-968-2205
  Heidi Imhof, prin.   Fax 968-2250

Ambler, Northwest Arctic, Pop. 316
Northwest Arctic Borough SD
  Supt. — See Kotzebue
Ambler S   100/PK-12
  PO Box 109 99786   907-445-2154
  Doni Newell, prin.   Fax 445-2159

Anaktuvuk Pass, North Slope, Pop. 274
North Slope Borough SD
  Supt. — See Barrow
Nunamiut S   100/PK-12
  PO Box 21029 99721   907-661-3226
  David Sharstrom, prin.   Fax 661-3402

Anchorage, Anchorage, Pop. 270,951
Alaska Vocational Technical SD
  Supt. — See Seward
AVTEC Allied Health Dept
  1251 Muldoon Rd Ste 11 99504   Vo/Tech
  Fred Esposito, prin.   907-334-2230
                                              Fax 334-2287

Aleutian Region SD   100/K-12
  PO Box 92230 99509   907-277-2648
  Joe Beckford, supt.   Fax 277-2649
Adak S   50/K-12
  100 Mechanics Rd 99515   907-592-3820
  Joe Beckford, prin.   Fax 592-2249
Other Schools – See Atka, Nikolski

Anchorage SD   48,600/PK-12
  PO Box 196614 99519   907-742-4312
  Carol Comeau, supt.   Fax 742-4318
  www.asdk12.org
Bartlett HS   2,000/9-12
  1101 Muldoon Rd 99506   907-742-1800
  Mary McKean, prin.   Fax 742-1825
Central MS of Science   800/7-8
  1405 E St 99501   907-742-5100
  Johanna Naylor, prin.   Fax 742-5125
Clark MS   900/7-8
  150 Bragaw St 99508   907-742-4700
  Cessilye Williams, prin.   Fax 742-4756

Dimond HS   2,300/9-12
  2909 W 88th Ave 99502   907-742-7000
  Cheryl Guyett, prin.   Fax 742-7007
East HS   2,200/9-12
  4025 E Northern Lights Blvd 99508 907-742-2100
  Michael Graham, prin.   Fax 742-2134
Goldenview MS   900/7-8
  15800 Golden View Dr 99516   907-348-8626
  Julie Maker, prin.   Fax 742-8273
Hanshew MS   1,000/7-8
  10121 Lake Otis Pkwy 99507   907-349-1561
  Sherry Ellers, prin.   Fax 349-2835
King Career Center   Vo/Tech
  2650 E Northern Lights Blvd 99508 907-742-8900
  Guy Okada, prin.   Fax 742-8907
Mears MS   1,100/7-8
  2700 W 100th Ave 99515   907-349-3332
  Michael Perkins, prin.   Fax 349-3389
Romig MS   800/7-8
  2500 Minnesota Dr 99503   907-742-5200
  Trudy Genne, prin.   Fax 742-5252
Service HS   2,500/9-12
  5577 Abbott Rd 99507   907-742-8100
  Lou Pondolfino, prin.   Fax 742-6615
South Anchorage HS   800/9-12
  13400 Elmore Rd 99516   907-742-6200
  Chuck Fannin, prin.   Fax 742-6207
Wendler MS   800/7-8
  2905 Lake Otis Pkwy 99508   907-742-7300
  Joel Roylance, prin.   Fax 742-7307
West HS   1,800/9-12
  1700 Hillcrest Dr 99517   907-742-2500
  Jim Bailey, prin.   Fax 742-2525
Whaley S   400/PK-12
  2220 Nichols St 99508   907-742-2350
  Colleen Castaneda, prin.   Fax 742-2360
Other Schools – See Chugiak, Eagle River

Chugach SD   300/PK-12
  9312 Vanguard Dr #100 99507   907-522-7400
  Bob Crumley, supt.   Fax 522-3399
  www.chugachschools.com
Other Schools – See Chenega Bay, Tatitlek, Whittier

──────────────────

Alaska Pacific University   Post-Sec.
  4101 University Dr 99508   800-252-7528
Anchorage Christian S   800/PK-12
  6401 E Northern Lights Blvd 99504 907-337-9575
  Tom Cobaugh, admin.   Fax 338-3903
Career Academy   Post-Sec.
  1415 E Tudor Rd 99507   907-563-7575
Charter College   Post-Sec.
  2221 E Northern Lights Blvd 99508 907-277-1000
Grace Christian S   700/K-12
  12407 Pintail St 99516   907-345-4814
  Nate Davis, admin.   Fax 644-2260
Heritage Christian S   400/K-12
  9251 Lake Otis Pkwy 99507   907-349-8032
  Richard Satterfield, prin.   Fax 349-8275
Holy Rosary Academy   100/K-12
  1010 W Fireweed Ln 99503   907-276-5822
  Barbara Doermer, prin.   Fax 258-1055
Lumen Christi JSHS   100/8-12
  8110 Jewel Lake Rd Bldg D 99502 907-245-9231
  James Yeargan, prin.   Fax 245-9232
University of Alaska Anchorage   Post-Sec.
  PO Box 141629 99514   907-786-1800

Anchor Point, Kenai Peninsula, Pop. 866
Kenai Peninsula Borough SD
  Supt. — See Soldotna
Nikolaevsk S   100/K-12
  PO Box 5129 99556   907-235-8972
  Sharon Conley, prin.   Fax 235-3617

Anderson, Denali, Pop. 336
Denali Borough SD
  Supt. — See Healy
Anderson S   100/K-12
  PO Box 3120 99744   907-582-2700
  Fred Deussing, prin.   Fax 582-2000

Angoon, Skagway-Yakutat-Angoon, Pop. 493
Chatham SD   200/K-12
  PO Box 109 99820   907-788-3302
  Vance Cortez-Rucker, supt.   Fax 788-3252
  www.chathamsd.org/
Angoon S   100/K-12
  PO Box 209 99820   907-788-3811
  Ryan Dorsey, prin.   Fax 788-3812
Other Schools – See Gustavus, Haines, Tenakee Springs

Aniak, Bethel, Pop. 585
Kuspuk SD   500/PK-12
  PO Box 49 99557   907-675-4250
  Dr. Martin Laster, supt.   Fax 675-4305
  www.kuspuk.org
Aniak JSHS   100/7-12
  PO Box 29 99557   907-675-4300
  Christian Justice, prin.   Fax 675-4256
Other Schools – See Chuathbaluk, Crooked Creek,
  Kalskag, Red Devil, Sleetmute, Stony River

Anvik, Yukon-Koyukuk, Pop. 101
Iditarod Area SD
  Supt. — See Mc Grath
Blackwell S   50/K-12
  PO Box 90 99558   907-663-6348
  Julia Walker, prin.   Fax 663-6349

Arctic Village, Yukon-Koyukuk, Pop. 96
Yukon Flats SD
  Supt. — See Fort Yukon
Arctic Village S   50/PK-12
  PO Box 22049 99722   907-587-5211
  Caroline Tritt-Frank, prin.   Fax 587-5210

Atka, Aleutians West, Pop. 141
Aleutian Region SD
  Supt. — See Anchorage
Netsvetov S   50/K-12
  PO Box 47050 99547   907-839-2210
  Ethan Petticrew, prin.   Fax 839-2212

Atmautluak, Bethel, Pop. 258
Lower Kuskokwim SD
  Supt. — See Bethel
Alexie Memorial S   100/PK-12
  PO Box ATT 99559   907-553-5112
  Larry Strunk, prin.   Fax 553-5129

Atqasuk, North Slope, Pop. 221
North Slope Borough SD
  Supt. — See Barrow
Meade River S   100/PK-12
  General Delivery 99791   907-633-6315
  Mike Wetherbee, prin.   Fax 633-6215

Barrow, North Slope, Pop. 4,421
North Slope Borough SD   2,100/PK-12
  PO Box 169 99723   907-852-5311
  Trent Blankenship, supt.   Fax 852-9503
  www.nsbsd.org/
Barrow HS   300/9-12
  PO Box 960 99723   907-852-8950
  Mac Whyte, prin.   Fax 852-8969
Hopson Memorial MS   300/6-8
  PO Box 509 99723   907-852-3880
  Bob Thompson, prin.   Fax 852-7794
Other Schools – See Anaktuvuk Pass, Atqasuk, Kaktovik,
  Nuiqsut, Point Hope, Point Lay, Wainwright

──────────────────

Ilisagvik College   Post-Sec.
  PO Box 749 99723   907-852-3333

Beaver, Yukon-Koyukuk, Pop. 103
Yukon Flats SD
  Supt. — See Fort Yukon
Cruikshank S   50/PK-12
  PO Box 24050 99724   907-628-6313
  Ann Fisher, prin.   Fax 628-6615

Bethel, Bethel, Pop. 5,983
Lower Kuskokwim SD   3,900/PK-12
  PO Box 305 99559   907-543-4800
  Bill Ferguson, supt.   Fax 543-4904
  www.lksd.org

Bethel Regional HS 500/6-12
PO Box 700 99559 907-543-3957
James Lehman, prin. Fax 543-2327
Other Schools – See Atmautluak, Chefornak, Eek, Goodnews Bay, Kasigluk, Kipnuk, Kongiganak, Kwethluk, Kwigillingok, Mekoryuk, Napakiak, Napaskiak, Newtok, Nightmute, Nunapitchuk, Quinhagak, Toksook Bay, Tuntutuliak, Tununak

University of Alaska Kuskokwim Campus Post-Sec.
PO Box 368 99559 907-543-4500

Big Lake, Matanuska-Susitna, Pop. 1,477
Matanuska-Susitna Borough SD
Supt. — See Palmer
Houston HS 400/9-12
PO Box 521060 99652 907-892-9400
Mike Vrvilo, prin. Fax 892-9460
Houston MS 400/6-8
PO Box 521060 99652 907-892-9250
Andy Murr, prin. Fax 892-6193

Brevig Mission, Nome, Pop. 274
Bering Strait SD
Supt. — See Unalakleet
Brevig Mission S 100/PK-12
General Delivery 99785 907-642-4021
Robin Gray, prin. Fax 642-4031

Buckland, Northwest Arctic, Pop. 416
Northwest Arctic Borough SD
Supt. — See Kotzebue
Buckland S 200/K-12
PO Box 91 99727 907-494-2127
Richard Dennis, prin. Fax 494-2106

Cantwell, Denali, Pop. 147
Denali Borough SD
Supt. — See Healy
Cantwell S 100/K-12
PO Box 29 99729 907-768-2372
Pete Hauschka, prin. Fax 768-2500

Central, Yukon-Koyukuk, Pop. 52
Yukon Flats SD
Supt. — See Fort Yukon
Far North S 50/K-12
PO Box 30049 99730 907-520-5114
Jack Von Thaer, prin. Fax 520-5151

Chalkyitsik, Yukon-Koyukuk, Pop. 90
Yukon Flats SD
Supt. — See Fort Yukon
Tsuk Taih S 50/PK-12
General Delivery 99788 907-848-8113
Margaret Waldrup, prin. Fax 848-8312

Chefornak, Bethel, Pop. 404
Lower Kuskokwim SD
Supt. — See Bethel
Chaptnquak S 100/PK-12
PO Box 50 99561 907-867-8700
Bruce Sheehan, prin. Fax 867-8727

Chenega Bay, Valdez-Cordova, Pop. 94
Chugach SD
Supt. — See Anchorage
Chenega Bay Community S 50/PK-12
PO Box 8030 99574 907-573-5123
Steve Grajewski, prin. Fax 573-5137

Chevak, Wade Hampton, Pop. 796
Kashunamiut SD 400/K-12
985 KSD Way 99563 907-858-7713
Gary Stevens, supt. Fax 858-7328
Chevak S 400/K-12
985 KSD Way 99563 907-858-7712
Delbert Lantz, prin. Fax 858-7264

Chignik, Lake and Peninsula, Pop. 66
Lake & Peninsula SD
Supt. — See King Salmon
Chignik Bay S 50/PK-12
PO Box 9 99564 907-749-2213
Adam Mokelke, lead tchr. Fax 749-2261

Chignik Lagoon, Lake and Peninsula, Pop. 53
Lake & Peninsula SD
Supt. — See King Salmon
Chignik Lagoon S 50/K-12
PO Box 50 99565 907-840-2210
Adam Mokelke, lead tchr. Fax 840-2265

Chignik Lake, Lake and Peninsula, Pop. 133
Lake & Peninsula SD
Supt. — See King Salmon
Chignik Lake S 50/PK-12
General Delivery 99548 907-845-2210
Mike Flanagan, prin. Fax 845-2254

Chiniak, Kodiak Island, Pop. 69
Kodiak Island Borough SD
Supt. — See Kodiak
Chiniak S 100/K-10
PO Box 5529 99615 907-486-8323
Bill Watkins, prin. Fax 486-3185

Chuathbaluk, Bethel, Pop. 122
Kuspuk SD
Supt. — See Aniak
Crow Village Sam S 50/PK-12
PO Box Chu 99557 907-467-4229
Conrad Detering, prin. Fax 467-4122

Chugiak, See Anchorage
Anchorage SD
Supt. — See Anchorage
Chugiak HS 2,000/9-12
16525 Birchwood Loop Rd 99567 907-742-3050
Rick Volk, prin. Fax 742-3148

Mirror Lake MS 700/6-8
22901 Lake Hill Dr 99567 907-742-3500
Jeanne Fisher, prin. Fax 742-3545

Circle, Yukon-Koyukuk, Pop. 73
Yukon Flats SD
Supt. — See Fort Yukon
Circle S 50/PK-12
PO Box 49 99733 907-773-1250
Paula Noel, prin. Fax 773-1259

Coffman Cove, Prince of Wales-Outer Ketchikan, Pop. 189
Southeast Island SD
Supt. — See Thorne Bay
Valentine S 50/K-12
PO Box 18002 99918 907-329-2244
Jenny Vermaas, prin. Fax 329-2210

Cold Bay, Aleutians East, Pop. 85
Aleutian East Borough SD
Supt. — See Sand Point
Cold Bay S 50/PK-12
PO Box 128 99571 907-532-2409
Kurt Schmidt, prin. Fax 532-2421

Copper Center, Valdez-Cordova, Pop. 449
Copper River SD
Supt. — See Glennallen
Kenny Lake S 100/1-12
HC 60 Box 224 99573 907-822-3870
Reed Carlson, prin. Fax 822-3794

Cordova, Valdez-Cordova, Pop. 2,332
Cordova CSD 500/PK-12
PO Box 140 99574 907-424-3265
Don Clark, supt. Fax 424-3271
cordova.schoolaccess.net
Cordova JSHS 200/7-12
PO Box 140 99574 907-424-3266
Don Clark, prin. Fax 424-5215

Craig, Prince of Wales-Outer Ketchikan, Pop. 1,280
Craig CSD 800/PK-12
PO Box 800 99921 907-826-3274
Ronald Erickson, supt. Fax 826-3322
www.craigschools.com
Craig HS 100/9-12
PO Box 800 99921 907-826-2274
Doug Rhodes, prin. Fax 826-3016
Craig MS 100/6-8
PO Box 800 99921 907-826-3274
Camille Booth, prin. Fax 826-3309

Crooked Creek, Bethel, Pop. 106
Kuspuk SD
Supt. — See Aniak
John S 50/PK-12
General Delivery 99575 907-432-2205
Conrad Detering, prin. Fax 432-2206

Deering, Northwest Arctic, Pop. 138
Northwest Arctic Borough SD
Supt. — See Kotzebue
Deering S 100/PK-12
PO Box 36009 99736 907-363-2121
Rod Pruitt, prin. Fax 363-2128

Delta Junction, Southeast Fairbanks, Pop. 801
Delta-Greely SD 900/PK-12
PO Box 527 99737 907-895-4658
Dan Beck, supt. Fax 895-4246
www.dgsd.k12.ak.us/
Delta Junction HS 200/9-12
PO Box 647 99737 907-895-4460
Rod Schug, prin. Fax 895-4049
Ft. Greely S 200/6-8
PO Box 546 99737 907-869-1305
Brian Schaffer, prin. Fax 869-3382
Gerstle River S 100/PK-12
PO Box 527 99737 907-895-4655
Brian Schaffer, prin. Fax 895-4246

Dillingham, Dillingham, Pop. 2,480
Dillingham CSD 500/PK-12
PO Box 170 99576 907-842-5223
Arnold Watland, supt. Fax 842-5634
www.dcsd.k12.ak.us
Dillingham JSHS 300/6-12
PO Box 170 99576 907-842-5221
Brian Midles, prin. Fax 842-4395

Southwest Region SD 700/K-12
PO Box 90 99576 907-842-5287
Jack Foster, supt. Fax 842-5428
dlg.swrsd.org/do/doHomePage.shtml
Other Schools – See Koliganek, Manokotak, New Stuyahok, Togiak

University of Alaska Bristol Bay Campus Post-Sec.
PO Box 1070 99576 907-842-5109

Diomede, Nome, Pop. 145
Bering Strait SD
Supt. — See Unalakleet
Diomede S 100/PK-12
PO Box 7099 99762 907-686-3021
Elsie Davis, prin. Fax 686-3022

Dot Lake, Southeast Fairbanks, Pop. 70
Alaska Gateway SD
Supt. — See Tok
Dot Lake S 50/K-12
PO Box 2280 99737 907-882-2663
William Sprott, prin. Fax 882-2112

Eagle, Southeast Fairbanks, Pop. 122
Alaska Gateway SD
Supt. — See Tok
Eagle Community S 50/K-12
PO Box 168 99738 907-547-2210
Ross Bolding, prin. Fax 547-2302

Eagle River, See Anchorage
Anchorage SD
Supt. — See Anchorage
Eagle River HS 9-12
8701 Yosemite Dr 99577 907-742-2700
Natalie Burnett, prin. Fax 742-2710
Gruening MS 600/7-8
9601 Lee St 99577 907-742-3600
Sven Gustafson, prin. Fax 742-3666

Eagle River Christian S 200/PK-12
10336 E Eagle River Loop Rd 99577 907-694-4602
Denny Archer, admin. Fax 694-4141

Eek, Bethel, Pop. 288
Lower Kuskokwim SD
Supt. — See Bethel
Eek S 100/PK-12
PO Box 50 99578 907-536-5228
Dan Walker, prin. Fax 536-5628

Egegik, Lake and Peninsula, Pop. 98
Lake & Peninsula SD
Supt. — See King Salmon
Egegik S 50/PK-12
PO Box 10 99579 907-233-2210
Lee Webster, lead tchr. Fax 233-2254

Eielson AFB, Fairbanks North Star, Pop. 5,251
Fairbanks-North Star Borough SD
Supt. — See Fairbanks
Eielson JSHS 600/7-12
675 Ravens Way 99702 907-372-3110
Larry Martin, prin. Fax 372-3202

Elim, Nome, Pop. 312
Bering Strait SD
Supt. — See Unalakleet
Aniguiin S 100/PK-12
PO Box 29 99739 907-890-3021
Steve Sammons, prin. Fax 890-3031

Emmonak, Wade Hampton, Pop. 799
Lower Yukon SD
Supt. — See Mountain Village
Emmonak S 200/PK-12
General Delivery 99581 907-949-1248
Gregory Lelvis, prin. Fax 949-1148

Fairbanks, Fairbanks North Star, Pop. 30,970
Fairbanks-North Star Borough SD 14,700/PK-12
520 5th Ave 99701 907-452-2000
Dr. Ann E. Shortt, supt. Fax 451-0541
www.northstar.k12.ak.us
Guided Independent Study 300/K-12
520 5th Ave 99701 907-452-2000
Wayne Gerke, lead tchr. Fax 451-1009
Hutchison HS Vo/Tech
3750 Geist Rd 99709 907-479-2261
Bill McLeod, prin. Fax 479-8286
Lathrop HS 1,400/9-12
901 Airport Way 99701 907-456-7794
Mario Gatto, prin. Fax 452-6735
Ryan MS 500/7-8
951 Airport Way 99701 907-452-4751
Carol Digou, prin. Fax 451-8834
Smith MS 500/7-8
1401 Bainbridge Blvd 99701 907-458-7600
Jim Currie, prin. Fax 458-7676
Tanana MS 600/7-8
600 Trainor Gate Rd 99701 907-452-8145
Edwina Strange, prin. Fax 456-2780
West Valley HS 1,400/9-12
3800 Geist Rd 99709 907-479-4221
Marianne Carlson, prin. Fax 474-8901
Other Schools – See Eielson AFB, North Pole

Yukon-Koyukuk SD 1,000/PK-12
4762 Old Airport Way 99709 907-374-9400
Christopher Simon, supt. Fax 374-9440
www.yksd.com
Other Schools – See Allakaket, Hughes, Huslia, Juneau, Kaltag, Manley Hot Springs, Minto, Nulato, Ruby

Fairhill Christian S 200/PK-12
101 City Lights Blvd 99712 907-457-2167
Marilyn Buchanan, prin. Fax 457-4382
Far North Christian S 100/K-12
1110 20th Ave 99701 907-452-7979
Kevin Taylor, admin. Fax 452-5327
Lighthouse Community Christian S 100/PK-12
1524 Westwood Way 99709 907-457-5227
Fax 457-5227
Monroe Catholic HS 200/7-12
615 Monroe St 99701 907-452-2044
Vince Fantazzi, prin. Fax 452-5978
University of Alaska Fairbanks Post-Sec.
PO Box 757480 99775 907-474-7581
University of Alaska Interior Campus Post-Sec.
PO Box 756720 99775 907-474-7211
University of Alaska Tanana Valley Cmps Post-Sec.
PO Box 758000 99775 907-474-7400

False Pass, Aleutians East, Pop. 61
Aleutian East Borough SD
Supt. — See Sand Point
False Pass S 100/PK-12
PO Box 30 99583 907-548-2224
Ernest McKay, prin. Fax 548-2304

Fort Yukon, Yukon-Koyukuk, Pop. 578
Yukon Flats SD 400/PK-12
PO Box 350 99740 907-662-2515
Linda Evans, supt. Fax 662-3094
www.yukonflats.net
Fort Yukon S 100/PK-12
PO Box 129 99740 907-662-2352
Susan Johnson, prin. Fax 662-2958
Other Schools – See Arctic Village, Beaver, Central, Chalkyitsik, Circle, Stevens Village, Venetie

Fritz Creek, Kenai Peninsula, Pop. 1,426
Kenai Peninsula Borough SD
Supt. — See Soldotna
Kachemak Selo S   100/K-12
  PO Box 15007 99603   907-235-5552
  Randy Creamer, prin.   Fax 235-5644
Voznesenka S   100/K-12
  PO Box 15336 99603   907-235-8549
  Ray Hillman, prin.   Fax 235-6086

Galena, Yukon-Koyukuk, Pop. 658
Galena CSD   200/PK-12
  PO Box 299 99741   907-656-1205
  Jim Smith, supt.   Fax 656-2238
  www.galenaalaska.org
Galena JSHS   100/7-12
  PO Box 299 99741   907-656-1205
  Chris Reitan, prin.   Fax 656-1368

Gambell, Nome, Pop. 646
Bering Strait SD
Supt. — See Unalakleet
Gambell S   200/PK-12
  PO Box 169 99742   907-985-5515
  Steve Petz, prin.   Fax 985-5435

Glennallen, Valdez-Cordova, Pop. 451
Copper River SD   600/K-12
  PO Box 108 99588   907-822-3234
  Kathy Gearhart, supt.   Fax 822-3949
  www.crsd.k12.ak.us
Glennallen JSHS   200/7-12
  PO Box 108 99588   907-822-5286
  Ron Dempsay, prin.   Fax 822-8501
Other Schools – See Copper Center, Slana

Alaska Bible College   Post-Sec.
  PO Box 289 99588   907-822-3201

Golovin, Nome, Pop. 143
Bering Strait SD
Supt. — See Unalakleet
Olson S   100/PK-12
  PO Box 62040 99762   907-779-3021
  Gay Jacobson, prin.   Fax 779-3031

Goodnews Bay, Bethel, Pop. 236
Lower Kuskokwim SD
Supt. — See Bethel
Rocky Mountain S   100/PK-12
  PO Box 153 99589   907-967-8213
  Christopher Carmichael, prin.   Fax 967-8228

Grayling, Yukon-Koyukuk, Pop. 189
Iditarod Area SD
Supt. — See Mc Grath
David-Louis Memorial S   100/K-12
  PO Box 90 99590   907-453-5135
  Jeff Ralston, prin.   Fax 453-5165

Gustavus, Skagway-Yakutat-Angoon, Pop. 258
Chatham SD
Supt. — See Angoon
Gustavus S   100/K-12
  PO Box 120 99826   907-697-2248
  Abigail Calkin, prin.   Fax 697-2378

Haines, Haines, Pop. 1,265
Chatham SD
Supt. — See Angoon
Klukwan S   50/K-12
  PO Box 1409 99827   907-767-5551
  Cheryl Stickler, prin.   Fax 767-5573

Haines Borough SD   300/K-12
  PO Box 1289 99827   907-766-2644
  Woody Wilson, supt.   Fax 766-2508
  glacierbears.hbsd.net/
Haines HS   100/9-12
  PO Box 1289 99827   907-766-2411
  Charlie Jones, prin.   Fax 766-2416

Healy, Denali, Pop. 487
Denali Borough SD   400/K-12
  PO Box 280 99743   907-683-2278
  Robert Lang, supt.   Fax 683-2514
  denali.ak.schoolwebpages.com/
Tri-Valley S   200/K-12
  PO Box 400 99743   907-683-2267
  Anne Olson, prin.   Fax 683-2632
Other Schools – See Anderson, Cantwell

Holy Cross, Yukon-Koyukuk, Pop. 222
Iditarod Area SD
Supt. — See Mc Grath
Holy Cross S   100/K-12
  PO Box 210 99602   907-476-7131
  Kay Holbrook, prin.   Fax 476-7161

Homer, Kenai Peninsula, Pop. 5,149
Kenai Peninsula Borough SD
Supt. — See Soldotna
Homer HS   500/9-12
  600 E Fairview Ave 99603   907-235-8186
  Ron Keffer, prin.   Fax 235-8933
Homer MS   200/7-8
  500 Sterling Hwy 99603   907-235-5291
  Jim Cammon, prin.   Fax 235-5747
Razdolna S   100/K-12
  PO Box 15098 99603   907-235-6870
  Ray Hillman, prin.   Fax 235-6485

Hoonah, Skagway-Yakutat-Angoon, Pop. 766
Hoonah CSD   200/K-12
  PO Box 157 99829   907-945-3611
  Howard Diamond, supt.   Fax 945-3492
  www3.hcs.k12.ak.us/
Hoonah JSHS   100/7-12
  PO Box 157 99829   907-945-3613
  Michael Byer, prin.   Fax 945-3607

Hooper Bay, Wade Hampton, Pop. 1,055
Lower Yukon SD
Supt. — See Mountain Village
Hooper Bay S   400/PK-12
  General Delivery 99604   907-758-4826
  Terry Bentley, prin.   Fax 758-4012

Hope, Kenai Peninsula, Pop. 161
Kenai Peninsula Borough SD
Supt. — See Soldotna
Hope S   200/K-12
  PO Box 47 99605   907-782-3202
  Mark Norgren, admin.   Fax 782-3140

Hughes, Yukon-Koyukuk, Pop. 76
Yukon-Koyukuk SD
Supt. — See Fairbanks
Oldman S   100/K-12
  PO Box 30 99745   907-889-2204
  Joan Jones, prin.   Fax 889-2220

Huslia, Yukon-Koyukuk, Pop. 284
Yukon-Koyukuk SD
Supt. — See Fairbanks
Huntington S   100/PK-12
  PO Box 110 99746   907-829-2205
  John Christian, prin.   Fax 829-2270

Hydaburg, Prince of Wales-Outer Ketchikan, Pop. 359
Hydaburg CSD   100/K-12
  PO Box 109 99922   907-285-3591
  William Raduenz, supt.   Fax 285-3391
Hydaburg JSHS   50/7-12
  PO Box 109 99922   907-285-3591
  Kenneth Hagel, prin.   Fax 285-3391

Hyder, Prince of Wales-Outer Ketchikan, Pop. 99
Southeast Island SD
Supt. — See Thorne Bay
Hyder S   50/K-12
  PO Box 110 99923   250-636-2100
  Kathy Shirley, prin.   Fax 636-2112

Igiugig, Bristol Bay, Pop. 33
Lake & Peninsula SD
Supt. — See King Salmon
Igiugig S   50/PK-12
  PO Box 4010 99613   907-533-3220
  Todd Washburn, lead tchr.   Fax 533-3221

Iliamna, Lake and Peninsula, Pop. 94
Lake & Peninsula SD
Supt. — See King Salmon
Newhalen S   100/K-12
  PO Box 89 99606   907-571-1211
  Reta Doland, prin.   Fax 571-1466

Juneau, Juneau, Pop. 30,751
Juneau Borough SD   5,500/PK-12
  10014 Crazy Horse Dr 99801   907-463-1700
  Peggy Cowan, supt.   Fax 463-1768
  www.jsd.k12.ak.us
Dryden MS   700/6-8
  10014 Crazy Horse Dr 99801   907-463-1850
  Tom Milliron, prin.   Fax 463-1828
Heeni MS   700/6-8
  10014 Crazy Horse Dr 99801   907-463-1899
  Barb Mecum, prin.   Fax 463-1877
Juneau-Douglas HS   1,700/9-12
  10014 Crazy Horse Dr 99801   907-463-1900
  Bernie Sorenson, prin.   Fax 463-1919

Yukon-Koyukuk SD
Supt. — See Fairbanks
Alyeska Central S   400/K-12
  3141 Channel Dr Ste 100 99801   907-586-1566
  Roxie Quick, prin.   Fax 586-8106

University of Alaska Southeast   Post-Sec.
  11120 Glacier Hwy 99801   907-465-6457

Kake, Wrangell-Petersburg, Pop. 674
Kake CSD   200/K-12
  PO Box 450 99830   907-785-3741
  Eric Gebhart, supt.   Fax 785-6439
Kake HS   100/7-12
  PO Box 450 99830   907-785-3741
  Eric Gebhart, prin.   Fax 785-6439

Kaktovik, North Slope, Pop. 284
North Slope Borough SD
Supt. — See Barrow
Kaveolook S   100/PK-12
  PO Box 20 99747   907-640-6626
  Brad Allen, prin.   Fax 640-6718

Kalskag, Bethel, Pop. 186
Kuspuk SD
Supt. — See Aniak
Morgan HS   100/7-12
  General Delivery 99607   907-471-2288
  Bill Gilliland, prin.   Fax 471-2242

Kaltag, Yukon-Koyukuk, Pop. 225
Yukon-Koyukuk SD
Supt. — See Fairbanks
Kaltag S   50/PK-12
  PO Box 30 99748   907-534-2204
  Irene Bowie, prin.   Fax 534-2227

Kasigluk, Bethel, Pop. 425
Lower Kuskokwim SD
Supt. — See Bethel
Akiuk Memorial S   100/PK-12
  General Delivery 99609   907-477-6829
  Carl Williams, prin.   Fax 477-6314
Akula Elitnaurvik S   100/K-12
  PO Box 79 99609   907-477-6615
  Felicia Kleven, prin.   Fax 477-6715

Kenai, Kenai Peninsula, Pop. 7,347
Kenai Peninsula Borough SD
Supt. — See Soldotna
Kenai Central HS   500/9-12
  9583 Kenai Spur Hwy 99611   907-283-7524
  Alan Fields, prin.   Fax 283-3230
Kenai MS   400/6-8
  201 N Tinker Ln 99611   907-283-4896
  Paul Sorenson, prin.   Fax 283-3180

Ketchikan, Ketchikan Gateway, Pop. 7,453
Ketchikan Gateway Borough SD   2,100/PK-12
  333 Schoenbar Rd 99901   907-247-2142
  Harry Martin, supt.   Fax 247-3822
  www.kgbsd.org
Ketchikan HS   600/9-12
  2610 4th Ave 99901   907-225-9815
  Larry Eklund, prin.   Fax 247-5761
Revilla JSHS   200/7-12
  3131 Baranof Ave 99901   907-225-6681
  Doug Gregg, prin.   Fax 247-6681
Schoenbar MS   300/7-8
  217 Schoenbar Rd 99901   907-225-5138
  Bob Hewitt, prin.   Fax 225-5761

Southeast Island SD
Supt. — See Thorne Bay
Hollis S   50/1-12
  PO Box HYL 99950   907-530-7108
  Julie Vasquez, prin.   Fax 530-7111
Naukati S   50/K-12
  PO Box NKI 99950   907-629-4121
  Mary Lou Smart, prin.   Fax 629-4121
Port Protection S   50/K-12
  PO Box PPV 99950   907-489-2228
  Frank Pickett, prin.   Fax 489-2260

Ketchikan Christian Academy   50/1-12
  PO Box 7400 99901   907-225-2891
  Rev. Bill White, admin.   Fax 225-2890
University of Alaska Southeast-Ketchikan   Post-Sec.
  2600 7th Ave 99901   907-225-6177

Kiana, Northwest Arctic, Pop. 395
Northwest Arctic Borough SD
Supt. — See Kotzebue
Kiana S   100/PK-12
  PO Box 190 99749   907-475-2115
  Ken Carr, prin.   Fax 475-2120

King Cove, Aleutians East, Pop. 725
Aleutian East Borough SD
Supt. — See Sand Point
King Cove S   100/PK-12
  PO Box 69 99612   907-497-2354
  Herman Gerving, prin.   Fax 497-2408

King Salmon, Bristol Bay, Pop. 696
Lake & Peninsula SD   500/PK-12
  PO Box 498 99613   907-246-4280
  Steve Atwater, supt.   Fax 246-4473
  www.lpsd.com
Other Schools – See Chignik, Chignik Lagoon, Chignik
  Lake, Egegik, Igiugig, Iliamna, Kokhanok, Levelock,
  Nondalton, Pedro Bay, Perryville, Pilot Point, Port
  Alsworth, Port Heiden

Kipnuk, Bethel, Pop. 470
Lower Kuskokwim SD
Supt. — See Bethel
Chief Paul Memorial S   200/PK-12
  PO Box 19 99614   907-896-5011
  Gloria Ingle, prin.   Fax 896-5428

Kivalina, Northwest Arctic, Pop. 386
Northwest Arctic Borough SD
Supt. — See Kotzebue
McQueen S 99750   100/PK-12
  Gerald Pickner, prin.   907-645-2125
     Fax 645-2124

Klawock, Prince of Wales-Outer Ketchikan, Pop. 801
Klawock CSD   200/K-12
  PO Box 9 99925   907-755-2228
  Rich Carlson, supt.   Fax 755-2320
  www.klawockschool.com/
Klawock S   200/K-12
  PO Box 9 99925   907-755-2220
  Donald Spink, prin.   Fax 755-2913

Kodiak, Kodiak Island, Pop. 6,302
Kodiak Island Borough SD   2,800/K-12
  722 Mill Bay Rd 99615   907-486-9210
  Betty Walters, supt.   Fax 486-9277
  www.kodiak.k12.ak.us
Kodiak HS   800/9-12
  722 Mill Bay Rd 99615   907-481-2502
  Bob Meade, prin.   Fax 481-2505
Kodiak MS   400/7-8
  722 Mill Bay Rd 99615   907-486-9213
  Porfiria Lopez-Trout, prin.   Fax 486-9061
Other Schools – See Akhiok, Chiniak, Larsen Bay, Old
  Harbor, Ouzinkie, Port Lions

Kodiak College   Post-Sec.
  117 Benny Benson Dr 99615   907-486-1235

Kokhanok, Lake and Peninsula, Pop. 152
Lake & Peninsula SD
Supt. — See King Salmon
Kokhanok S   50/K-12
  General Delivery 99606   907-282-2210
  Todd Washburn, prin.   Fax 282-2247

Koliganek, Dillingham, Pop. 181
Southwest Region SD
Supt. — See Dillingham
Koliganek S   100/K-12
  PO Box 5052 99576   907-596-3444
  Nancy McManus, prin.   Fax 596-3484

Kongiganak, Bethel, Pop. 294
Lower Kuskokwim SD
Supt. — See Bethel
Kiunva Memorial S 100/PK-12
PO Box 5109 99545 907-557-5126
Doyle Horton, prin. Fax 557-5639

Kotlik, Wade Hampton, Pop. 616
Lower Yukon SD
Supt. — See Mountain Village
Kotlik S 200/PK-12
PO Box 20129 99620 907-899-4415
Vic Lewin, prin. Fax 899-4515

Kotzebue, Northwest Arctic, Pop. 3,156
Northwest Arctic Borough SD 2,400/PK-12
PO Box 51 99752 907-442-3472
Robert Boyle, supt. Fax 442-2246
www.nwarctic.org/
Alaska Technical Center Vo/Tech
PO Box 51 99752 907-442-3733
Cheryl Edenshaw, dir. Fax 442-2764
Kotzebue MSHS 400/6-12
PO Box 264 99752 907-442-3341
Norm Eck, prin. Fax 442-2141
Other Schools – See Ambler, Buckland, Deering, Kiana,
Kivalina, Noatak, Noorvik, Selawik, Shungnak

University of Alaska Chuchi Campus Post-Sec.
PO Box 297 99752 907-442-3400

Koyuk, Nome, Pop. 296
Bering Strait SD
Supt. — See Unalakleet
Koyuk-Malemute S 100/PK-12
PO Box 53009 99753 907-963-3021
Dave Foshee, prin. Fax 963-2428

Kwethluk, Bethel, Pop. 732
Lower Kuskokwim SD
Supt. — See Bethel
Ket'acik Aap'alluk Memorial S 200/PK-12
PO Box 150 99621 907-757-6014
Gary White, prin. Fax 757-6013

Kwigillingok, Bethel, Pop. 278
Lower Kuskokwim SD
Supt. — See Bethel
Kwigillingok S 100/PK-12
PO Box 109 99622 907-588-8629
Walt Betz, prin. Fax 588-8613

Larsen Bay, Kodiak Island, Pop. 107
Kodiak Island Borough SD
Supt. — See Kodiak
Larsen Bay S 100/K-12
PO Box 70 99624 907-847-2252
Bill Watkins, prin. Fax 847-2260

Levelock, Lake and Peninsula, Pop. 105
Lake & Peninsula SD
Supt. — See King Salmon
Levelock S 50/PK-12
PO Box 89 99625 907-287-3060
Ty Mase, lead tchr. Fax 287-3021

Mc Grath, Yukon-Koyukuk, Pop. 491
Iditarod Area SD 500/PK-12
PO Box 90 99627 907-524-3033
Joe Banghort, supt. Fax 524-3217
www.iditarodsd.org/
Lime Village S 50/PK-12
PO Box LVD 99627 907-526-5112
Art Woodard, prin. Fax 526-5225
Mc Grath S 100/K-12
PO Box 290 99627 907-524-3388
RIchard Edison, prin. Fax 524-3751
Other Schools – See Anvik, Grayling, Holy Cross,
Nikolai, Shageluk, Takotna

Manley Hot Springs, Yukon-Koyukuk, Pop. 96
Yukon-Koyukuk SD
Supt. — See Fairbanks
Manley Hart Springs Gladys Dart S 50/PK-12
PO Box 29 99756 907-672-3202
Heidi Wright, prin. Fax 672-3201

Manokotak, Dillingham, Pop. 400
Southwest Region SD
Supt. — See Dillingham
Manokotak S 100/K-12
PO Box 30 99628 907-289-1013
Priscilla McIntyre, prin. Fax 289-2050

Marshall, Wade Hampton, Pop. 362
Lower Yukon SD
Supt. — See Mountain Village
Marshall S 100/PK-12
PO Box 89 99585 907-679-6112
Jason Moen, prin. Fax 679-6637

Mekoryuk, Bethel, Pop. 215
Lower Kuskokwim SD
Supt. — See Bethel
Nuniwaarmiut S 50/PK-12
PO Box 49 99630 907-827-8415
Kevin McCalla, prin. Fax 827-8613

Mentasta Lake, Valdez-Cordova, Pop. 96
Alaska Gateway SD
Supt. — See Tok
Mentasta Lake S 50/K-12
PO Box 6039 99780 907-291-2327
Barbara Dalke, prin. Fax 291-2325

Metlakatla, Prince of Wales-Outer Ketchikan, Pop. 1,407
Annette Islands SD 300/K-12
PO Box 7 99926 907-886-6332
Brett Agenbroad, supt. Fax 886-5130
aisd.k12.ak.us

Leask MS 100/7-8
PO Box 7 99926 907-886-6003
Richard Montgomery, prin. Fax 886-6019
Metlakatla HS 100/9-12
PO Box 7 99926 907-886-6000
Richard Montgomery, prin. Fax 886-5120

Minto, Yukon-Koyukuk, Pop. 218
Yukon-Koyukuk SD
Supt. — See Fairbanks
Minto S 100/PK-12
PO Box 81 99758 907-798-7212
Kim Ray, prin. Fax 798-7282

Mountain Village, Wade Hampton, Pop. 785
Lower Yukon SD 2,000/PK-12
PO Box 32089 99632 907-591-2411
Robert J. Robertson, supt. Fax 591-2449
Beans S 300/PK-12
PO Box 32105 99632 907-591-2829
Doc Kieckbusch, prin. Fax 591-2214
Other Schools – See Alakanuk, Emmonak, Hooper Bay,
Kotlik, Marshall, Pilot Station, Russian Mission, Saint
Marys, Scammon Bay, Sheldon Point

Naknek, Bristol Bay, Pop. 575
Bristol Bay Borough SD 200/K-12
PO Box 169 99633 907-246-4225
Richard Hebhardt, supt. Fax 246-6857
alaska.ihigh.com/bristolbay/
Bristol Bay MSHS 100/7-12
PO Box 169 99633 907-246-4265
Kelly Castleberry, prin. Fax 246-4447

Nanwalek, Kenai Peninsula
Kenai Peninsula Borough SD
Supt. — See Soldotna
Nanwalek S 100/K-12
PO Box 8007 99603 907-281-2210
Mike Sellers, prin. Fax 281-2211

Napakiak, Bethel, Pop. 361
Lower Kuskokwim SD
Supt. — See Bethel
Miller Memorial S 100/PK-12
PO Box 50 99634 907-589-2420
Bruce Kleven, prin. Fax 589-2515

Napaskiak, Bethel, Pop. 399
Lower Kuskokwim SD
Supt. — See Bethel
Qugcuun Memorial S 100/PK-12
PO Box 6199 99559 907-737-7214
Christopher Woodward, prin. Fax 737-7211
Williams S 100/K-12
PO Box 6089 99559 907-737-7212
Sandra King, prin. Fax 737-7967

Nelson Lagoon, Aleutians East, Pop. 83
Aleutian East Borough SD
Supt. — See Sand Point
Nelson Lagoon S 50/PK-12
PO Box 19 99571 907-989-2225
Joan Eddy, prin. Fax 989-2228

Nenana, Yukon-Koyukuk, Pop. 391
Nenana CSD 1,400/PK-12
PO Box 10 99760 907-832-5400
Dr. Kenneth Eggleston, supt. Fax 832-2008
Nenana City S 200/PK-12
PO Box 10 99760 907-832-5464
Ellie Cole, prin. Fax 832-5625

New Stuyahok, Dillingham, Pop. 472
Southwest Region SD
Supt. — See Dillingham
Chief Blunka S 99636 200/K-12
Mitzi Garrison, prin. 907-693-3144
Fax 693-3163

Newtok, Bethel, Pop. 207
Lower Kuskokwim SD
Supt. — See Bethel
Ayaprun S 100/K-12
PO Box WWT 99559 907-237-2505
Grant Kashatok, prin. Fax 237-2506

Nightmute, Bethel, Pop. 213
Lower Kuskokwim SD
Supt. — See Bethel
Nightmute S 100/PK-12
General Delivery 99690 907-647-6313
Mitchell Pioch, prin. Fax 647-6227

Nikiski, Kenai Peninsula, Pop. 2,743
Kenai Peninsula Borough SD
Supt. — See Soldotna
Nikiski MSHS 500/7-12
PO Box 7112 99635 907-776-3456
John O'Brien, prin. Fax 776-3486

Nikolai, Yukon-Koyukuk, Pop. 97
Iditarod Area SD
Supt. — See Mc Grath
Top of the Kuskokwim S 50/K-12
PO Box 9190 99691 907-293-2427
Mary Groat, prin. Fax 293-2214

Nikolski, Aleutians West, Pop. 35
Aleutian Region SD
Supt. — See Anchorage
Nikolski S 50/K-12
General Delivery 99638 907-576-2200
Sally Swetzof, prin. Fax 576-2230

Ninilchik, Kenai Peninsula, Pop. 456
Kenai Peninsula Borough SD
Supt. — See Soldotna
Ninilchik S 200/K-12
PO Box 39010 99639 907-567-3301
Terry Martin, prin. Fax 567-3504

Noatak, Northwest Arctic, Pop. 333
Northwest Arctic Borough SD
Supt. — See Kotzebue
Napaaqtugmiut S 200/PK-12
PO Box 49 99761 907-485-2153
Harlen Heinrich, prin. Fax 485-2150

Nome, Nome, Pop. 3,502
Nome CSD 700/PK-12
PO Box 131 99762 907-443-2231
Stan Lujan, supt. Fax 443-5144
www.nomeschools.com
Nome-Beltz JSHS 300/7-12
PO Box 131 99762 907-443-5201
Owen Carter, prin. Fax 443-3626

University of Alaska Northwest Campus Post-Sec.
PO Box 400 99762 907-443-2201

Nondalton, Lake and Peninsula, Pop. 188
Lake & Peninsula SD
Supt. — See King Salmon
Nondalton S 100/K-12
100 School Rd 99640 907-294-2210
Ed Cox, prin. Fax 294-2265

Noorvik, Northwest Arctic, Pop. 647
Northwest Arctic Borough SD
Supt. — See Kotzebue
Aqqaluk / Noorvik S 200/K-12
PO Box 165 99763 907-636-2178
Darrell Johnston, prin. Fax 636-2160

North Pole, Fairbanks North Star, Pop. 1,645
Fairbanks-North Star Borough SD
Supt. — See Fairbanks
North Pole HS 900/9-12
601 NPHS Blvd 99705 907-488-3761
A.C. Woolnough, prin. Fax 488-1488
North Pole MS 600/6-8
300 E 8th Ave 99705 907-488-2271
Ernie Manzie, prin. Fax 488-9213

North Pole Christian S 100/PK-12
PO Box 55306 99705 907-488-0133
Ethan Gelineau, prin. Fax 488-8248

Northway, Southeast Fairbanks, Pop. 123
Alaska Gateway SD
Supt. — See Tok
Northway S 100/K-12
PO Box 519 99764 907-778-2287
Dale Lackner, prin. Fax 778-2221

Nuiqsut, North Slope, Pop. 411
North Slope Borough SD
Supt. — See Barrow
Nuiqsut Trapper S 100/PK-12
3310 3rd Ave 99789 907-480-6712
John Luhrs, prin. Fax 480-6621

Nulato, Yukon-Koyukuk, Pop. 328
Yukon-Koyukuk SD
Supt. — See Fairbanks
Demoski S 100/PK-12
PO Box 65029 99765 907-898-2204
Teresa Cox, prin. Fax 898-2340

Nunapitchuk, Bethel, Pop. 479
Lower Kuskokwim SD
Supt. — See Bethel
Tobeluk Memorial S 200/PK-12
PO Box 150 99641 907-527-5325
John Wachmann, prin. Fax 527-5610

Old Harbor, Kodiak Island, Pop. 222
Kodiak Island Borough SD
Supt. — See Kodiak
Old Harbor S 100/K-12
PO Box 49 99643 907-286-2213
Bill Watkins, prin. Fax 286-2222

Ouzinkie, Kodiak Island, Pop. 213
Kodiak Island Borough SD
Supt. — See Kodiak
Ouzinkie S 100/K-12
PO Box 49 99644 907-680-2204
Bill Watkins, prin. Fax 680-2288

Palmer, Matanuska-Susitna, Pop. 5,742
Matanuska-Susitna Borough SD 14,700/PK-12
501 N Gulkana St 99645 907-746-9255
Robert Doyle, supt. Fax 761-4076
www.matsuk12.us
Beryozava S, 501 N Gulkana St 99645 400/K-12
Laurine Domke, prin. 907-746-9239
Colony HS 1,000/9-12
9550 E Colony Schools Dr 99645 907-746-9500
Cydney Duffin, prin. Fax 746-9572
Colony MS 600/6-8
9250 E Colony Schools Dr 99645 907-761-1500
John Miller, prin. Fax 761-1592
Glacier View S 100/K-12
HC 3 Box 8454 99645 907-745-5122
Wendy Taylor, prin. Fax 746-5560
Palmer HS 900/9-12
1170 W Arctic Ave 99645 907-745-3241
Wolfgang Winter, prin. Fax 746-0569
Palmer MS 700/6-8
1159 S Chugach St 99645 907-745-3812
Lesley Parkin, prin. Fax 745-4833
Other Schools – See Big Lake, Talkeetna, Wasilla

Matanuska Christian S 100/PK-12
248 E Elmwood Ave 99645 907-746-6789
Scott Richardson, admin. Fax 746-6788
University of Alaska Matanuska-Susitna Post-Sec.
PO Box 2889 99645 907-745-9774

Pedro Bay, Lake and Peninsula, Pop. 42
Lake & Peninsula SD
  Supt. — See King Salmon
Dena'ina S   50/K-12
  General Delivery 99647   907-850-2207
  Reta Doland, lead tchr.   Fax 850-2254

Pelican, Skagway-Yakutat-Angoon, Pop. 142
Pelican CSD   50/PK-12
  PO Box 90 99832   907-735-2236
  Connie Newman Ph.D., supt.   Fax 735-2263
Pelican S   50/PK-12
  PO Box 90 99832   907-735-2236
  Connie Newman, prin.   Fax 735-2263

Perryville, Lake and Peninsula, Pop. 108
Lake & Peninsula SD
  Supt. — See King Salmon
Perryville S   50/K-12
  PO Box 103 99648   907-853-2210
  Adam Mokelke, lead tchr.   Fax 853-2267

Petersburg, Wrangell-Petersburg, Pop. 3,019
Petersburg CSD   700/K-12
  PO Box 289 99833   907-772-4271
  Dr. Gary Jacobasen, supt.   Fax 772-4719
  www.psgsd.k12.ak.us
Mitkof MS   200/6-8
  PO Box 289 99833   907-772-3860
  David Morris, prin.   Fax 772-3617
Petersburg HS   200/9-12
  PO Box 289 99833   907-772-3861
  David Morris, prin.   Fax 772-4168

Pilot Point, Lake and Peninsula, Pop. 84
Lake & Peninsula SD
  Supt. — See King Salmon
Pilot Point S   50/PK-12
  PO Box 467 99649   907-797-2210
  Mike Flanagan, prin.   Fax 797-2267

Pilot Station, Wade Hampton, Pop. 572
Lower Yukon SD
  Supt. — See Mountain Village
Pilot Station S   200/PK-12
  PO Box 5090 99650   907-549-3212
  Max Lunt, prin.   Fax 549-3335

Point Hope, North Slope, Pop. 734
North Slope Borough SD
  Supt. — See Barrow
Tikigaq S   300/PK-12
  PO Box 148 99766   907-852-4711
  Steve Pile, prin.   Fax 852-4713

Point Lay, North Slope, Pop. 139
North Slope Borough SD
  Supt. — See Barrow
Kali S   100/PK-12
  PO Box 59077 99759   907-833-2311
  Kitza Durkop, prin.   Fax 833-2315

Port Alexander, Wrangell-Petersburg, Pop. 77
Southeast Island SD
  Supt. — See Thorne Bay
Port Alexander S   50/K-12
  PO Box 8170 99836   907-568-2205
  Nick Higson, prin.   Fax 568-2261

Port Alsworth, Lake and Peninsula, Pop. 55
Lake & Peninsula SD
  Supt. — See King Salmon
Tanalian S   50/PK-12
  General Delivery 99653   907-781-2210
  Ed Cox, lead tchr.   Fax 781-2254

Port Graham, Kenai Peninsula, Pop. 166
Kenai Peninsula Borough SD
  Supt. — See Soldotna
Port Graham S   100/K-12
  PO Box 5550 99603   907-284-2210
  Mike Sellers, prin.   Fax 284-2213

Port Heiden, Lake and Peninsula, Pop. 101
Lake & Peninsula SD
  Supt. — See King Salmon
Meshik S   50/K-12
  General Delivery 99549   907-837-2210
  Mike Flanagan, lead tchr.   Fax 837-2265

Port Lions, Kodiak Island, Pop. 241
Kodiak Island Borough SD
  Supt. — See Kodiak
Port Lions S   50/K-12
  PO Box 109 99550   907-454-2237
  Bill Watkins, prin.   Fax 454-2377

Quinhagak, Bethel, Pop. 569
Lower Kuskokwim SD
  Supt. — See Bethel
Kuinerrarmiut Elitnaurviat S   200/PK-12
  General Delivery 99655   907-556-8628
  David Bauer, prin.   Fax 556-8228

Red Devil, Bethel, Pop. 53
Kuspuk SD
  Supt. — See Aniak
Willis S   100/K-12
  General Delivery 99656   907-447-3213
  Conrad Detering, prin.   Fax 447-3214

Ruby, Yukon-Koyukuk, Pop. 181
Yukon-Koyukuk SD
  Supt. — See Fairbanks
Kangas S   50/PK-12
  PO Box 68110 99768   907-468-4465
  Bruce Buffmire, prin.   Fax 468-4444

Russian Mission, Wade Hampton, Pop. 308
Lower Yukon SD
  Supt. — See Mountain Village

Russian Mission S   100/PK-12
  PO Box 90 99657   907-584-5615
  Mike Hull, prin.   Fax 584-5412

Saint George Island, Aleutians West, Pop. 59
Pribilof SD
  Supt. — See Saint Paul Island
St. George S   100/K-12
  PO Box 959 99591   907-859-2228
  Brooke Statan, prin.   Fax 859-2229

Saint Marys, Wade Hampton, Pop. 577
Lower Yukon SD
  Supt. — See Mountain Village
Pitkas Point S   50/PK-12
  PO Box 161 99658   907-438-2571
  Claudia Pinto, prin.   Fax 438-2948

Saint Mary's SD   200/K-12
  PO Box 9 99658   907-438-2411
  Dr. Kathryn Godinet, supt.   Fax 438-2831
St. Mary's S   200/K-12
  PO Box 9 99658   907-438-2736
  Dr. Kathryn Godinet, prin.   Fax 438-2831

Saint Michael, Nome, Pop. 366
Bering Strait SD
  Supt. — See Unalakleet
Andrews S   100/PK-12
  100 Baker St 99659   907-923-3041
  Jeannie Odenbach, prin.   Fax 923-3031

Saint Paul Island, Aleutians West, Pop. 400
Pribilof SD   200/K-12
  PO Box 905 99660   907-546-2221
  Malcolm Fleming, supt.   Fax 546-2327
  www.pribilofs.k12.ak.us/
St. Paul S   100/K-12
  PO Box 905 99660   907-546-2221
  Jamie Stacks, prin.   Fax 546-2356
  Other Schools – See Saint George Island

Sand Point, Aleutians East, Pop. 951
Aleutian East Borough SD   400/PK-12
  PO Box 429 99661   907-383-5222
  Dennis Maasjo, supt.   Fax 383-3496
  www.aebsd.org
Sand Point S   100/PK-12
  PO Box 269 99661   907-383-2393
  Don Johnson', prin.   Fax 383-3833
  Other Schools – See Akutan, Cold Bay, False Pass, King
  Cove, Nelson Lagoon

Savoonga, Nome, Pop. 642
Bering Strait SD
  Supt. — See Unalakleet
Kingeekuk Memorial S   200/K-12
  PO Box 200 99769   907-984-6811
  Margaret Koegler, prin.   Fax 984-6413

Scammon Bay, Wade Hampton, Pop. 484
Lower Yukon SD
  Supt. — See Mountain Village
Scammon Bay S   200/PK-12
  General Delivery 99662   907-558-5312
  Harley Sundown, prin.   Fax 558-5320

Selawik, Northwest Arctic, Pop. 789
Northwest Arctic Borough SD
  Supt. — See Kotzebue
Davis-Ramoth S   300/K-12
  PO Box 29 99770   907-484-2142
  Douglas Walker, prin.   Fax 484-2127

Seldovia, Kenai Peninsula, Pop. 295
Kenai Peninsula Borough SD
  Supt. — See Soldotna
English S   100/K-12
  PO Box 171 99663   907-234-7616
  Curtis Liberty, prin.   Fax 234-7617

Seward, Kenai Peninsula, Pop. 2,880
Alaska Vocational Technical SD
  PO Box 889 99664   907-224-4140
  Fred Esposito, supt.   Fax 224-4143
  www.avtec.alaska.edu
Alaska Vocational Technical Center   Vo/Tech
  PO Box 889 99664   907-224-4140
  Fred Esposito, prin.   Fax 224-4143
  Other Schools – See Anchorage

Kenai Peninsula Borough SD
  Supt. — See Soldotna
Seward HS   300/9-12
  PO Box 1049 99664   907-224-3351
  Steve Pautz, prin.   Fax 224-3306
Seward MS   100/7-8
  PO Box 1049 99664   907-224-3351
  John Cote, admin.   Fax 224-3306

Alaska Vocational Technical School   Post-Sec.
  PO Box 889 99664   907-224-4159

Shageluk, Yukon-Koyukuk, Pop. 126
Iditarod Area SD
  Supt. — See Mc Grath
Innoko River S   50/PK-12
  PO Box 53 99665   907-473-8233
  Timothy Stathis, prin.   Fax 473-8268

Shaktoolik, Nome, Pop. 227
Bering Strait SD
  Supt. — See Unalakleet
Shaktoolik S   100/PK-12
  PO Box 40 99771   907-955-3021
  Edna Apatiki, prin.   Fax 955-3031

Sheldon Point, Wade Hampton, Pop. 121
Lower Yukon SD
  Supt. — See Mountain Village

Sheldon Point S   100/PK-12
  PO Box 32, Nunam Iqua AK 99666   907-498-4112
  Alex Russin, prin.   Fax 498-4235

Shishmaref, Nome, Pop. 560
Bering Strait SD
  Supt. — See Unalakleet
Shishmaref S   200/PK-12
  1 Seaview Ln 99772   907-649-3021
  Joe Braach, prin.   Fax 649-3031

Shungnak, Northwest Arctic, Pop. 261
Northwest Arctic Borough SD
  Supt. — See Kotzebue
Shungnak S   100/PK-12
  PO Box 79 99773   907-437-2151
  Megan Reinseth, prin.   Fax 437-2177

Sitka, Sitka, Pop. 8,510
Mt. Edgecumbe HSD   300/9-12
  1330 Seward Ave 99835   907-966-3200
  Bill K. Denkinger, supt.   Fax 966-2442
  www.mehs.us
Mt. Edgecumbe HS   300/9-12
  1330 Seward Ave 99835   907-966-3202
  Bernie Gurule, prin.   Fax 966-2442
Sitka SD   1,600/PK-12
  300 Kostrometinoff St 99835   907-747-8622
  Steve Bradshaw, supt.   Fax 966-1260
  www.ssd.k12.ak.us
Blatchley MS   300/6-8
  601 Halibut Point Rd 99835   907-747-8672
  Charlie Robison, prin.   Fax 966-1460
Sitka HS   400/9-12
  1000 Lake St 99835   907-747-3263
  Howard Wayne, prin.   Fax 747-3229

Sheldon Jackson College   Post-Sec.
  801 Lincoln St 99835   907-747-5220
University of Alaska Sitka Campus   Post-Sec.
  1332 Seward Ave 99835   907-747-6653

Skagway, Skagway-Yakutat-Angoon, Pop. 818
Skagway CSD   100/K-12
  PO Box 497 99840   907-983-2960
  Dr. Michael G. Dickens, supt.   Fax 983-2964
Skagway S   100/K-12
  PO Box 497 99840   907-983-2960
  Dr. Michael Dickens, prin.   Fax 983-2964

Slana, Valdez-Cordova, Pop. 63
Copper River SD
  Supt. — See Glennallen
Slana S   100/1-12
  PO Box 870 99586   907-822-5868
  Bob Snedigar, prin.   Fax 822-3850

Sleetmute, Bethel, Pop. 106
Kuspuk SD
  Supt. — See Aniak
Egnaty S   50/K-12
  General Delivery 99668   907-449-4216
  Conrad Detering, prin.   Fax 449-4217

Soldotna, Kenai Peninsula, Pop. 4,000
Kenai Peninsula Borough SD   9,700/PK-12
  148 N Binkley St 99669   907-714-8888
  Dr. Donna Peterson, supt.   Fax 262-9645
  www.kpbsd.k12.ak.us
Skyview HS   600/9-12
  46188 Sterling Hwy 99669   907-262-7675
  Randy Neill, prin.   Fax 262-6555
Soldotna HS   500/9-12
  425 W Marydale Ave 99669   907-262-7411
  Todd Syverson, prin.   Fax 262-4288
Soldotna MS   500/7-8
  426 W Redoubt Ave 99669   907-262-4344
  Sharon Moock, prin.   Fax 262-7036
  Other Schools – See Anchor Point, Fritz Creek, Homer,
  Hope, Kenai, Nanwalek, Nikiski, Ninilchik, Port
  Graham, Seldovia, Seward, Tyonek

Cook Inlet Academy   200/PK-12
  45872 Kalifornsky Beach Rd 99669   907-262-5101
  Kevin Spence, prin.   Fax 262-1541
Kenai Peninsula College   Post-Sec.
  34820 College Dr 99669   907-262-0300

Stebbins, Nome, Pop. 547
Bering Strait SD
  Supt. — See Unalakleet
Tukurngailnguq S   200/PK-12
  General Delivery 99671   907-934-3041
  Terry Peppers, prin.   Fax 934-3031

Sterling, Kenai Peninsula, Pop. 3,802

Academy of Higher Learning   50/K-12
  PO Box 682 99672   907-260-7741
  Catherine Gibson, prin.   Fax 260-7741

Stevens Village, Yukon-Koyukuk, Pop. 102
Yukon Flats SD
  Supt. — See Fort Yukon
Old Stevens S   50/PK-12
  General Delivery 99774   907-478-7116
  Doris McDaniel, prin.   Fax 478-7893

Stony River, Bethel, Pop. 51
Kuspuk SD
  Supt. — See Aniak
Michael S   50/K-12
  General Delivery 99557   907-537-3226
  Conrad Detering, prin.   Fax 537-3237

Takotna, Yukon-Koyukuk, Pop. 38
Iditarod Area SD
  Supt. — See Mc Grath

Takotna S   50/K-12
  PO Box 90   99675   907-298-2115
  Robert Absher, prin.   Fax 298-2316

Talkeetna, Matanuska-Susitna, Pop. 250
  Matanuska-Susitna Borough SD
  Supt. — See Palmer
  Susitna Valley JSHS   200/7-12
    PO Box 807   99676   907-733-2241
    Matthew Clark, prin.   Fax 733-1363

Tanana, Yukon-Koyukuk, Pop. 300
  Tanana CSD   100/K-12
    PO Box 89   99777   907-366-7207
    Dorothy Jordan, coord.   Fax 366-7201
  Sommer S   100/K-12
    PO Box 89   99777   907-366-7207
    Dorothy Jordan, prin.   Fax 366-7201

Tatitlek, Valdez-Cordova, Pop. 119
  Chugach SD
  Supt. — See Anchorage
  Tatitlek Community S   50/K-12
    PO Box 167   99677   907-325-2252
    Jea Palmer, prin.   Fax 325-2299

Teller, Nome, Pop. 265
  Bering Strait SD
  Supt. — See Unalakleet
  Isabell S   100/PK-12
    100 Airport Ave   99778   907-642-3041
    Jay Thomas, prin.   Fax 642-3031

Tenakee Springs, Skagway-Yakutat-Angoon, Pop. 94
  Chatham SD
  Supt. — See Angoon
  Tenakee Springs S   50/K-12
    PO Box 2204   99841   907-736-2204
    Diane Zemanek, prin.   Fax 736-2204

Thorne Bay, Prince of Wales-Outer Ketchikan, Pop. 518
  Southeast Island SD   300/K-12
    PO Box 19569   99919   907-828-8254
    Jim Nygaard, supt.   Fax 828-8257
    www.sisd.org
  Thorne Bay S   100/K-12
    PO Box 5   99919   907-828-3921
    Amy McDonald, prin.   Fax 828-3901
  Other Schools – See Coffman Cove, Hyder, Ketchikan,
    Port Alexander

Togiak, Dillingham, Pop. 809
  Southwest Region SD
  Supt. — See Dillingham
  Togiak S   200/K-12
    PO Box 500   99678   907-493-5829
    David Wick, prin.   Fax 493-5933

Tok, Southeast Fairbanks, Pop. 935
  Alaska Gateway SD   500/PK-12
    PO Box 226   99780   907-883-5151
    Ross Bolding, supt.   Fax 883-4356
    tok.schoolaccess.net/
  Tetlin S   50/PK-12
    General Delivery   99780   907-324-2104
    Margie Grant, prin.   Fax 324-2120
  Tok S   300/K-12
    PO Box 249   99780   907-883-5161
    Gordon Kron, prin.   Fax 883-5165
  Other Schools – See Dot Lake, Eagle, Mentasta Lake,
    Northway

Toksook Bay, Bethel, Pop. 546
  Lower Kuskokwim SD
  Supt. — See Bethel
  Nelson Island S   200/PK-12
    General Delivery   99637   907-427-7815
    Talbert Bentley, prin.   Fax 427-7612

Tuluksak, Bethel, Pop. 383
  Yupiit SD
  Supt. — See Akiachak
  Tuluksak S   200/K-12
    PO Box 115   99679   907-695-5625
    Vaughn Dosko, prin.   Fax 695-5645

Tuntutuliak, Bethel, Pop. 300
  Lower Kuskokwim SD
  Supt. — See Bethel
  Angapak Memorial S   100/PK-12
    General Delivery   99680   907-256-2415
    Frank Cook, prin.   Fax 256-2527

Tununak, Bethel, Pop. 338
  Lower Kuskokwim SD
  Supt. — See Bethel
  Albert Memorial S   100/K-12
    PO Box 49   99681   907-652-6827
    Gayle Miller, prin.   Fax 652-6028

Tyonek, Kenai Peninsula, Pop. 154
  Kenai Peninsula Borough SD
  Supt. — See Soldotna
  Tebughna S   100/K-12
    PO Box 82010   99682   907-583-2291
    Sandra Miller, prin.   Fax 583-2692

Unalakleet, Nome, Pop. 744
  Bering Strait SD   1,800/PK-12
    PO Box 225   99684   907-624-3611
    John Davis, supt.   Fax 624-3099
    www.bssd.org
  Unalakleet S   200/PK-12
    PO Box 130   99684   907-624-3444
    Ben Howard, prin.   Fax 624-3388
  Other Schools – See Brevig Mission, Diomede, Elim,
    Gambell, Golovin, Koyuk, Saint Michael, Savoonga,
    Shaktoolik, Shishmaref, Stebbins, Teller, Wales, White
    Mountain

Unalaska, Aleutians West, Pop. 4,071
  Unalaska CSD   400/PK-12
    PO Box 570   99685   907-581-3151
                                                 Fax 581-3152
    www.ucsd.net
  Unalaska JSHS   200/5-12
    PO Box 570   99685   907-581-1222
    John Conwell, prin.   Fax 581-2428

Valdez, Valdez-Cordova, Pop. 4,060
  Valdez CSD   900/K-12
    PO Box 398   99686   907-835-4357
    Dr. Lance Bowie, supt.   Fax 835-4964
    www.valdezcityschools.org/
  Gilson JHS   100/7-8
    PO Box 827   99686   907-835-2244
    Rodney Morrison, prin.   Fax 835-2540
  Valdez HS   300/9-12
    PO Box 1629   99686   907-835-4767
    Geary Cantrell, prin.   Fax 835-2596

  Prince William Sound Community College   Post-Sec.
    PO Box 97   99686   907-834-1600

Venetie, Yukon-Koyukuk, Pop. 182
  Yukon Flats SD
  Supt. — See Fort Yukon
  Fredson S   100/PK-12
    PO Box 39   99781   907-849-8415
    George Renfrow, prin.   Fax 849-8630

Wainwright, North Slope, Pop. 529
  North Slope Borough SD
  Supt. — See Barrow
  Alak S   200/PK-12
    PO Box 10   99782   907-763-2541
    Ken Meacham, prin.   Fax 763-2550

Wales, Nome, Pop. 149
  Bering Strait SD
  Supt. — See Unalakleet
  Wales S   100/PK-12
    PO Box 490   99783   907-664-3021
    Craig Probst, prin.   Fax 664-3031

Wasilla, Matanuska-Susitna, Pop. 7,084
  Matanuska-Susitna Borough SD
  Supt. — See Palmer
  Teeland MS   700/6-8
    2788 N Seward Meridian Rd   99654   907-352-7500
    Larry Jacobson, prin.   Fax 352-7585
  Wasilla HS   1,100/9-12
    701 Bogard Rd   99654   907-376-5341
    Dwight Probasco, prin.   Fax 376-5348
  Wasilla MS   700/6-8
    650 Bogard Rd   99654   907-376-5308
    Amy Spargo, prin.   Fax 376-9625

  Cornerstone Christian S   100/K-12
    4001 E Darrington Village   99654   907-357-9798
    Karen Armstrong, prin.   Fax 357-9799
  Wasilla Lake Christian S   200/K-12
    2001 Palmer Wasilla Hwy   99654   907-373-6439
    Colleen Hamblen, admin.   Fax 373-5439

White Mountain, Nome, Pop. 201
  Bering Strait SD
  Supt. — See Unalakleet
  White Mountain S   100/PK-12
    PO Box 55   99784   907-638-3021
    Andy Haviland, prin.   Fax 638-3031

Whittier, Valdez-Cordova, Pop. 174
  Chugach SD
  Supt. — See Anchorage
  Whittier Community S   100/PK-12
    PO Box 638   99693   907-472-2575
    Doug Penn, prin.   Fax 472-2409

Wrangell, Wrangell-Petersburg, Pop. 2,163
  Wrangell SD   400/K-12
    PO Box 2319   99929   907-874-2347
    Susan Sciabbarrasi, supt.   Fax 874-3137
    www.wrangellschools.org
  Stikine MS   100/6-8
    PO Box 1935   99929   907-874-3393
    Monty Buness, prin.   Fax 874-3149
  Wrangell HS   100/9-12
    PO Box 651   99929   907-874-3395
    Monty Buness, prin.   Fax 874-3143

Yakutat, Skagway-Yakutat-Angoon, Pop. 534
  Yakutat SD   100/PK-12
    PO Box 429   99689   907-784-3317
    Timothy Macdonald Ph.D., supt.   Fax 784-3446
    yakutatschools.org
  Yakutat S   100/PK-12
    PO Box 429   99689   907-784-3317
    Timothy Macdonald Ph.D., prin.   Fax 784-3446

ARIZONA

ARIZONA DEPARTMENT OF EDUCATION
1535 W Jefferson St, Phoenix 85007-3280
Telephone 602-542-5393
Fax 602-542-5440
Website http://www.ade.az.gov/
Superintendent of Public Instruction   Tom Horne

ARIZONA BOARD OF EDUCATION
1535 W Jefferson St #418, Phoenix 85007-3209
President   Matthew Diethelm

COUNTY SUPERINTENDENTS OF SCHOOLS

Apache County Office of Education
  Dr. Pauline Begay, supt. — 928-337-7539
  PO Box 548, Saint Johns 85936 — Fax 337-2033
  www.co.apache.az.us/live/default.asp
Cochise County Office of Education
  Trudy Berry, supt. — 520-432-8950
  PO Box 208, Bisbee 85603 — Fax 432-7136
  www.co.cochise.az.us/ccwebsite/Default.asp
Coconino County Office of Education
  Cecilia Owen, supt. — 928-779-6591
  110 E Cherry Ave, Flagstaff 86001 — Fax 779-6571
  www.coconino.az.gov
Gila County Office of Education
  Dr. Linda O'Dell, supt. — 928-425-3231
  1400 E Ash St, Globe 85501 — Fax 402-0038
  www.governet.net/AZ/CO/GIL/home.cfm
Graham County Office of Education
  Donna McGaughey, supt. — 928-428-2880
  921 W Thatcher Blvd — Fax 428-3982
  Safford 85546
  206.169.149.67/county_offices.asp

Greenlee County Office of Education
  Tom Powers, supt. — 928-865-2822
  PO Box 1595, Clifton 85533 — Fax 865-4417
  www.governet.net/AZ/CO/GRE/schools.cfm
Lapaz County Office of Education
  Janice Shelton, supt. — 928-669-6183
  1112 S Joshua Ave, Parker 85344 — Fax 669-4406
  www.co.la-paz.az.us/
Maricopa County Office of Education
  Dr. Sandra Dowling, supt. — 602-506-3866
  301 W Jefferson St Ste 660 — Fax 506-3753
  Phoenix 85003
  www.maricopa.gov/schools/default.asp
Mohave County Office of Education
  Michael File, supt. — 928-753-0747
  PO Box 7000, Kingman 86402 — Fax 753-5822
  www.mcss.k12.az.us/
Navajo County Office of Education
  Linda L. Morrow, supt. — 928-524-4204
  PO Box 668, Holbrook 86025 — Fax 524-4209
  www.co.navajo.az.us/

Pima County Office of Education
  Dr. Linda Arzoumanian, supt. — 520-740-8451
  130 W Congress St Fl 4 — Fax 623-9308
  Tucson 85701
  www.schools.pima.gov/
Pinal County Office of Education
  Jack Harmon, supt. — 520-866-6565
  PO Box 769, Florence 85232 — Fax 866-4671
  www.pinalcounty.org
Santa Cruz County Office of Education
  Dr. Lynn Gillman, supt. — 520-375-7940
  2150 N Congress Dr #107 — Fax 375-7958
  Nogales 85621
  www.sccedu.org
Yavapai County Office of Education
  Tim Carter, supt. — 928-771-3326
  1015 Fair St Rm 324 — Fax 771-3329
  Prescott 86305
  www.co.yavapai.az.us/
Yuma County Office of Education
  Thomas Tyree, supt. — 928-373-1006
  210 S 1st Ave, Yuma 85364 — Fax 329-2008
  www.co.yuma.az.us/

PUBLIC, PRIVATE AND CATHOLIC SECONDARY SCHOOLS

Ajo, Pima, Pop. 2,919
Ajo USD 15 — 600/K-12
  PO Box 68 85321 — 520-387-5618
  Robert Dooley Ed.D., supt. — Fax 387-6545
Ajo S — 600/K-12
  PO Box 68 85321 — 520-387-7601
  Don German Ed.D., prin. — Fax 387-7603

Apache Junction, Pinal, Pop. 34,027
Apache Junction USD 43 — 5,700/PK-12
  1575 W Southern Ave Ste 3 85220 — 480-982-1110
  Gregg Wyman, supt. — Fax 982-6474
  www.ajusd.org
Apache Junction HS — 1,500/9-12
  2525 S Ironwood Dr 85220 — 480-982-1110
  Chad Wilson, prin. — Fax 982-3787
Desert Shadows MS — 600/6-8
  801 W Southern Ave 85220 — 480-982-1110
  Robert Pappalardo, prin. — Fax 983-4913
Thunder Mountain MS — 800/6-8
  3700 E 16th Ave 85219 — 480-982-1110
  Russell Sgro, prin. — Fax 671-1427

Central Arizona College — Post-Sec.
  273 E US Highway 60 85219 — 480-982-7261

Ash Fork, Yavapai
Ash Fork JUSD 31 — 200/K-12
  PO Box 247 86320 — 928-637-2561
  Gary Spiker, supt. — Fax 637-2623
Ash Fork HS — 50/9-12
  PO Box 247 86320 — 928-637-2561
  Colleen McDougall, prin. — Fax 637-2623
Ash Fork MS — 100/6-8
  PO Box 247 86320 — 928-637-2561
  Colleen McDougall, prin. — Fax 637-2623

Avondale, Maricopa, Pop. 54,710
Agua Fria UNHSD 216 — 4,400/9-12
  750 E Riley Dr 85323 — 623-932-7000
  Doug Wilson, supt. — Fax 932-2796
  www.aguafria.org
Agua Fria Union HS — 1,700/9-12
  530 E Riley Dr 85323 — 623-932-7300
  Bryce Anderson, prin. — Fax 932-0650
Other Schools – See Goodyear

Tolleson UNHSD 214
  Supt. — See Tolleson
La Joya Community HS — 1,100/9-12
  11650 W Whyman Ave 85323 — 623-478-4400
  Cheryl Ingram, prin. — Fax 478-7225
Westview HS — 2,400/9-12
  10850 W Garden Lakes Pkwy 85323 — 623-877-2438
  Brandi Haskins, prin. — Fax 877-4989

Estrella Mountain Community College — Post-Sec.
  3000 N Dysart Rd 85323 — 623-935-8015
Maricopa Beauty College — Post-Sec.
  515 W Western Ave 85323 — 623-932-4414
Universal Technical Institute — Post-Sec.
  10695 W Pierce St 85323 — 623-245-4600

Bagdad, Yavapai, Pop. 1,858
Bagdad USD 20 — 300/PK-12
  PO Box 427 86321 — 928-633-4101
  Marvin Smith, supt. — Fax 633-4345
Bagdad HS — 100/9-12
  PO Box 427 86321 — 928-633-2201
  Rodney Wilhelm, prin. — Fax 633-2541

Benson, Cochise, Pop. 4,879
Benson USD 9 — 1,000/PK-12
  360 S Patagonia St 85602 — 520-586-2213
  Bob McKenzie, supt. — Fax 586-2506
  www.bensonsd.k12.az.us/
Benson HS — 400/9-12
  360 S Patagonia St 85602 — 520-586-2213
  Bryan Bullington, prin. — Fax 586-2310
Benson MS — 300/5-8
  360 S Patagonia St 85602 — 520-586-2213
  Jomel Jansson, prin. — Fax 586-2253

Bisbee, Cochise, Pop. 5,957
Bisbee USD 2 — 1,000/PK-12
  100 Old Douglas Rd 85603 — 520-432-5381
  Paul McDonald, supt. — Fax 432-7622
  www.busd.k12.az.us
Bisbee HS — 400/9-12
  100 Old Douglas Rd 85603 — 520-432-5714
  Vince Creviston, prin. — Fax 432-6105
Lowell JHS — 200/7-8
  100 Old Douglas Rd 85603 — 520-432-6125
  Terri Romo, prin. — Fax 432-6106

Bowie, Cochise
Bowie USD 14 — 100/K-12
  PO Box 157 85605 — 520-847-2545
  Bruce Brown, supt. — Fax 847-2546
  www.bowieusd.k12.az.us
Bowie HS — 50/9-12
  PO Box 157 85605 — 520-847-2545
  Bruce Brown, prin. — Fax 847-2546

Buckeye, Maricopa, Pop. 8,921
Buckeye UNHSD 201 — 1,400/9-12
  902 E Eason Ave 85326 — 623-386-9701
  Beverly Hurley, supt. — Fax 386-9705
  www.buhsd.org
Buckeye Union HS — 1,100/9-12
  902 E Eason Ave 85326 — 623-386-9716
  Mary Ann Sphar, prin. — Fax 386-9711

Other Schools – See Goodyear
Litchfield ESD 79
  Supt. — See Litchfield Park
Verrado MS — 6-8
  20880 W Main St, — 623-527-1300
  Heather Cruz, prin. — Fax 853-2358

Bullhead City, Mohave, Pop. 36,255
Bullhead City ESD 15 — 3,900/K-8
  1004 Hancock Rd 86442 — 928-758-3961
  Dr. Ted Fadler, supt. — Fax 758-4996
  www.bullheadschools.com
Bullhead City JHS — 700/6-8
  1062 Hancock Rd 86442 — 928-758-3921
  Pat Young, prin. — Fax 758-7428
Fox Creek JHS — 600/6-8
  3101 Desert Sky Dr 86442 — 928-704-2500
  Melinda Sobraske, prin. — Fax 704-2504

Colorado River UNHSD 2
  Supt. — See Fort Mohave
Mohave HS — 1,400/9-12
  2251 Highway 95 86442 — 928-758-3916
  Jim Daly, prin. — Fax 758-7145

Camp Verde, Yavapai, Pop. 9,945
Camp Verde USD 28 — 1,500/PK-12
  410 Camp Lincoln Rd 86322 — 928-567-8000
  Ron Maughan, supt. — Fax 567-8004
  www.cvaz.org/cvs
Camp Verde HS — 400/9-12
  PO Box 728 86322 — 928-567-8033
  Steve Marshall, prin. — Fax 567-8045
Camp Verde MS — 400/6-8
  370 Camp Lincoln Rd 86322 — 928-567-8014
  Dan Brown, prin. — Fax 567-8022

Casa Grande, Pinal, Pop. 29,700
Casa Grande ESD 4 — 5,700/PK-8
  1460 N Pinal Ave 85222 — 520-836-2125
  Frank Davidson, supt. — Fax 426-3712
  www.cgelem.k12.az.us
Cactus MS — 900/6-8
  1220 E Kortsen Rd 85222 — 520-421-3330
  Jeffrey Lavender, prin. — Fax 421-7425
Casa Grande MS — 1,000/6-8
  300 W McMurray Blvd 85222 — 520-836-7310
  William Eddings, prin. — Fax 836-2399

Casa Grande UNHSD 82 — 2,300/9-12
  1362 N Casa Grande Ave 85222 — 520-316-3303
  Nancy Pifer, supt. — Fax 316-3352
  cguhs.org
Casa Grande Union HS — 2,300/9-12
  2730 N Trekell Rd 85222 — 520-836-8500
  Keith Greer, prin. — Fax 316-3353

Cashion, See Avondale
Littleton ESD 65 — 2,300/PK-8
PO Box 280 85329 — 623-478-5600
Patricia Williams Ed.D., supt. — Fax 478-5625
www.littletonaz.org
Underdown JHS — 300/7-8
PO Box 280 85329 — 623-478-5800
Lenora Owoyemi, prin. — Fax 478-5600

Chandler, Maricopa, Pop. 211,299
Chandler USD 80 — 27,400/PK-12
1525 W Frye Rd 85224 — 480-812-7000
Dr. Camille Casteel, supt. — Fax 812-7015
ww2.chandler.k12.az.us/
Andersen JHS — 1,200/7-8
1255 N Dobson Rd 85224 — 480-883-5300
Jim Anderson, prin. — Fax 883-5320
Basha HS — 1,900/9-12
5990 S Val Vista Dr 85249 — 480-224-2100
Kristine Marchiando, prin. — Fax 224-2120
Bogle JHS — 1,000/7-8
1600 W Queen Creek Rd 85248 — 480-883-5500
Susie Avey, prin. — Fax 883-5520
Chandler HS — 2,600/9-12
350 N Arizona Ave 85225 — 480-812-7700
Terry Williams, prin. — Fax 812-7720
Hamilton HS — 3,200/9-12
3700 S Arizona Ave 85248 — 480-883-5000
Dr. Fred DePrez, prin. — Fax 883-5020
Santan JHS — 7-8
1550 E Chandler Heights Rd 85249 — 480-883-4600
Frank Narducci, prin. — Fax 883-4620
Willis JHS — 1,100/7-8
401 S McQueen Rd 85225 — 480-883-5700
Paul Bollard, prin. — Fax 883-5720
Other Schools – See Gilbert

Kyrene ESD 28
Supt. — See Tempe
Kyrene Aprende MS — 1,200/6-8
777 N Desert Breeze Blvd E 85226 — 480-783-2200
Gerri Shaw, prin. — Fax 940-0657
Kyrene Del Pueblo MS — 1,100/6-8
360 S Twelve Oaks Blvd 85226 — 480-783-2400
Tom Seiger, prin. — Fax 961-4152

Mesa USD 4
Supt. — See Mesa
Hendrix JHS — 1,000/7-9
1550 W Summit Pl 85224 — 480-472-3300
David Jeffrey, prin. — Fax 472-3320

Artistic Beauty College — Post-Sec.
2978 N Alma School Rd Ste 3 85224 — 480-855-7901
Chandler-Gilbert Community College — Post-Sec.
2626 E Pecos Rd 85225 — 480-732-7000
Golf Academy of Arizona — Post-Sec.
670 N Arizona Ave Ste 13 85225 — 800-342-7342
International Academy of Hair Design — Post-Sec.
3350 N Arizona Ave Ste 4 85225 — 480-820-9422
Quantum Helicopters — Post-Sec.
2370 S Airport Blvd 85249 — 480-814-8118
Seton Catholic HS — 500/9-12
1150 N Dobson Rd 85224 — 480-963-1900
Patricia Collins, prin. — Fax 963-1974
Valley Christian HS — 400/9-12
6900 W Galveston St 85226 — 480-705-8888
Clark Stephens, admin. — Fax 705-8889

Chinle, Apache, Pop. 5,059
Chinle USD 24 — 4,100/PK-12
PO Box 587 86503 — 928-674-9600
Dr. Leon Ben, supt. — Fax 674-9608
www.chinleusd.k12.az.us/
Chinle HS — 1,100/9-12
PO Box 587 86503 — 928-674-9507
Douglas Clauschee, prin. — Fax 674-9432
Chinle JHS — 500/7-8
PO Box 587 86503 — 928-674-9505
Jaquline Price, prin. — Fax 674-9424

Chino Valley, Yavapai, Pop. 8,816
Chino Valley USD 51 — 2,600/PK-12
PO Box 225 86323 — 928-636-2458
Linda Nelson, supt. — Fax 636-1434
www.cvsd.k12.az.us
Chino Valley HS — 800/9-12
PO Box 225 86323 — 928-636-2298
Jeff St. Clair, prin. — Fax 636-6219
Heritage MS — 700/6-8
PO Box 225 86323 — 928-636-4464
Harold Tenney, prin. — Fax 636-6214

Trinity Christian S — 100/PK-12
PO Box 3825 86323 — 928-636-6306
Kyle Maestri, admin. — Fax 636-5131

Clifton, Greenlee, Pop. 2,257
Clifton USD 3 — 200/PK-12
PO Box 1567 85533 — 928-865-2752
Sharron Redden, supt. — Fax 865-2792
Clifton HS — 100/9-12
PO Box 1567 85533 — 928-865-3262
Sharron Redden, prin. — Fax 865-2792

Colorado City, Mohave, Pop. 3,901
Colorado City USD 14 — 400/PK-12
PO Box 309 86021 — 928-875-9000
Fax 875-8099
www.ccusd.net
Colorado City S — 400/PK-12
PO Box 309 86021 — 928-875-9001
Carol Timpson, prin. — Fax 875-9098

Coolidge, Pinal, Pop. 8,362
Coolidge USD 21 — 2,900/K-12
221 W Central Ave 85228 — 520-723-2042
Dr. Bill Christen, supt. — Fax 723-2442
www.cusd.k12.az.us/
Coolidge HS — 600/9-12
800 W Northern Ave 85228 — 520-723-2305
Tim Hamilton, prin. — Fax 723-2306
Hohokam MS — 700/6-8
800 N 9th St 85228 — 520-723-2202
Macon Thompson, prin. — Fax 723-2203

Central Arizona College — Post-Sec.
8470 N Overfield Rd 85228 — 520-426-4444

Cottonwood, Yavapai, Pop. 10,192
Cottonwood-Oak Creek ESD 6 — 1,800/PK-8
1 N Willard St 86326 — 928-634-2288
Julia S. Larson, supt. — Fax 634-2309
www.cocsd.k12.az.us
Cottonwood MS — 700/6-8
1 N Willard St 86326 — 928-634-2231
Michelle Stadelman, prin. — Fax 634-2874

Mingus UNHSD 4 — 1,200/9-12
1801 E Fir St 86326 — 928-634-8901
Sharyl Allen, supt. — Fax 649-4399
muhs.com
Mingus Union HS — 1,200/9-12
1801 E Fir St 86326 — 928-634-7531
Christopher Schultz, prin. — Fax 634-0546

Cornerstone Christian Academy — 50/7-12
2080 S Highway 260 86326 — 928-646-9299
Jill Rhoton, prin. — Fax 646-8213

Dewey, Yavapai, Pop. 3,640
Humboldt USD 22
Supt. — See Prescott Valley
Bradshaw Mountain MS — 400/6-8
12255 E Turquoise Cir 86327 — 928-759-4900
Brian Buchholtz, prin. — Fax 759-4920

Dolan Springs, Mohave, Pop. 1,090
Kingman USD 20
Supt. — See Kingman
Mt. Tipton S — 300/K-12
PO Box 248 86441 — 928-767-3350
Bill Harness, prin. — Fax 767-4330

Douglas, Cochise, Pop. 16,556
Douglas USD 27 — 4,200/PK-12
PO Box 1237 85608 — 520-364-2447
Gail Zamar, supt. — Fax 364-7470
www.dusd.k12.az.us
Borane MS — 400/6-8
PO Box 1237 85608 — 520-364-2461
Diane Drury, prin. — Fax 364-5537
Douglas HS — 1,100/9-12
PO Box 1237 85608 — 520-364-3462
Gloria Lopez, prin. — Fax 805-4171
Huber JHS — 600/6-8
PO Box 1237 85608 — 520-364-2840
George Watkins, prin. — Fax 364-2421

Duncan, Greenlee, Pop. 714
Duncan USD 2 — 500/K-12
PO Box 710 85534 — 928-359-2472
John Payne, supt. — Fax 359-2807
duncan.k12.az.us
Duncan HS — 200/9-12
PO Box 710 85534 — 928-359-2474
John Payne, prin. — Fax 359-1141
Duncan MS — 200/4-8
PO Box 710 85534 — 928-359-2471
Don Smith, prin. — Fax 359-1105

Elfrida, Cochise
Valley UNHSD 22 — 200/9-12
PO Box 158 85610 — 520-642-3492
Karl Uterhardt, supt. — Fax 642-3523
Valley Union HS — 200/9-12
PO Box 158 85610 — 520-642-3492
Karl Uterhardt, prin. — Fax 642-3523

El Mirage, Maricopa, Pop. 18,261
Dysart USD 89
Supt. — See Surprise
Dysart HS — 1,300/9-12
11425 N Dysart Rd 85335 — 623-876-7500
Teddy Irvine, prin. — Fax 876-7521

Eloy, Pinal, Pop. 10,805
Eloy ESD 11 — 1,200/PK-8
1011 N Sunshine Blvd 85231 — 520-466-2100
Ruby James, supt. — Fax 466-2101
Eloy JHS — 300/7-8
1011 N Sunshine Blvd 85231 — 520-466-2140
Danny Rogers, prin. — Fax 466-2150

Santa Cruz Valley UNHSD 840 — 500/9-12
900 N Main St 85231 — 520-466-2237
Lionel Goar, supt. — Fax 466-2222
www.santacruzdustdevils.us
Santa Cruz Valley HS — 500/9-12
900 N Main St 85231 — 520-466-2200
Mary Griffith, prin. — Fax 466-2222

Toltec ESD 22 — 1,000/PK-8
3315 N Toltec Rd 85231 — 520-466-2360
Dick Lesher, supt. — Fax 466-2398
www.toltec.k12.az.us
Toltec MS — 600/4-8
3315 N Toltec Rd 85231 — 520-466-2350
Korrin Ledbetter, prin. — Fax 466-2399

Flagstaff, Coconino, Pop. 55,893
Flagstaff USD 1 — 11,500/PK-12
3285 E Sparrow Ave 86004 — 928-527-6000
Dr. Kevin Brown, supt. — Fax 527-6015
www.flagstaff.k12.az.us
Coconino HS — 1,400/9-12
2801 N Izabel St 86004 — 928-773-8200
David Roth, prin. — Fax 773-8247
Flagstaff HS — 1,400/9-12
400 W Elm Ave 86001 — 928-773-8100
Tony Cullen, prin. — Fax 773-8146
Flagstaff MS — 700/7-8
755 N Bonito St 86001 — 928-773-8150
Robert Kuhn, prin. — Fax 773-8169
Mount Elden/Renaissance Magnet MS — 900/7-8
3323 N 4th St 86004 — 928-773-8250
Rodney Johnson, prin. — Fax 773-8269
Sinagua HS — 1,000/9-12
3950 E Butler Ave 86004 — 928-527-5500
Ute Salisbury, prin. — Fax 527-5561

Artistic Beauty College — Post-Sec.
1790 E Route 66 86004 — 928-774-7146
Coconino Community College — Post-Sec.
2800 S Lone Tree Rd 86001 — 928-527-1222
CollegeAmerica — Post-Sec.
1800 S Milton Rd 86001 — 928-526-0763
Montessori S of Flagstaff — 50/6-8
2212 E Cedar Ave 86004 — 928-774-1600
Marlane Spencer, prin. — Fax 774-0424
Northern Arizona University — Post-Sec.
PO Box 4084 86011 — 928-523-9011

Florence, Pinal, Pop. 15,375
Florence USD 1 — 2,100/PK-12
PO Box 2850 85232 — 520-866-3500
Dr. Richard Sagar, supt. — Fax 868-2302
florence.k12.az.us
Florence HS — 400/9-12
PO Box 2850 85232 — 520-866-3560
Nick McVicker, prin. — Fax 868-2329

Fort Defiance, Apache, Pop. 4,489
Window Rock USD 8 — 3,100/K-12
PO Box 559 86504 — 928-729-6705
Thomas Jackson, supt. — Fax 729-5780
www.wrschool.net
Tse Ho Tsoh MS — 500/7-8
PO Box 559 86504 — 928-729-6802
Chuck Foster, prin. — Fax 729-7572
Window Rock HS — 900/9-12
PO Box 559 86504 — 928-729-7004
Glenn Haven, prin. — Fax 729-7661

Fort Huachuca, See Sierra Vista
Fort Huachuca Accommodation SD 00 — 1,300/PK-8
PO Box 12954 85670 — 520-458-5082
Dr. Ronda Frueauff, supt. — Fax 515-5972
www.fthuachuca.k12.az.us
Smith MS — 400/6-8
PO Box 12954 85670 — 520-459-8892
Robert Henderson, prin. — Fax 459-8939

Fort Mohave, Mohave
Colorado River UNHSD 2 — 2,100/9-12
5221 S Highway 95 Ste 5 86426 — 928-768-1665
Mark Schnizlein, supt. — Fax 768-1702
www.cruhsd.org
Other Schools – See Bullhead City, Mohave Valley

Fort Thomas, Graham
Fort Thomas USD 7 — 600/K-12
PO Box 28 85536 — 928-485-9423
Jerry Hancock, supt. — Fax 485-2058
www.ftthomas.k12.az.us
Fort Thomas JSHS — 300/7-12
PO Box 28 85536 — 928-485-2427
Carter McEuen, prin. — Fax 485-2834

Fountain Hills, Maricopa, Pop. 22,159
Fountain Hills USD 98 — 3,300/PK-12
16000 E Palisades Blvd 85268 — 480-664-5011
Dr. Marian Hermie, supt. — Fax 664-5099
fhusd.org
Fountain Hills HS — 900/9-12
16100 E Palisades Blvd 85268 — 480-664-5500
Patrick Sweeney, prin. — Fax 837-5699
Fountain Hills MS — 700/6-8
15414 N McDowell Mountain R 85268 — 480-664-5400
Tom Lawrence, prin. — Fax 664-5499
Four Peaks IS — 1,000/4-8
17300 E Calaveras Ave 85268 — 480-664-5100
Rebecca Romans, prin. — Fax 664-5199

Fredonia, Coconino, Pop. 1,057
Fredonia-Moccasin USD 6 — 400/K-12
PO Box 247 86022 — 928-643-7333
Steve Nielsen, supt. — Fax 643-7044
www.fredonia.org/
Fredonia-Moccasin HS — 100/9-12
PO Box 247 86022 — 928-643-7333
Steve Nielsen, prin. — Fax 643-7044

Ganado, Apache, Pop. 1,257
Ganado USD 20 — 2,100/K-12
PO Box 1757 86505 — 928-755-1099
Dr. Phillip Bluehouse, supt. — Fax 755-1005
www.ganado.k12.az.us/
Ganado HS — 800/9-12
PO Box 1757 86505 — 928-755-1402
Ann Wilyard, prin. — Fax 755-1401
Ganado MS — 300/7-8
PO Box 1757 86505 — 928-755-1220
Lucinda Swedberg, prin. — Fax 755-1298

Gila Bend, Maricopa, Pop. 2,058
Gila Bend USD 24 — 500/PK-12
PO Box V 85337 — 928-683-2225
James Mosley, supt. — Fax 683-2671
gila.az.schoolwebpages.com
Gila Bend HS — 100/9-12
PO Box V 85337 — 928-683-2286
James Mosley, prin. — Fax 683-6415

Gilbert, Maricopa, Pop. 145,250
Chandler USD 80
Supt. — See Chandler

Payne JHS | 7-8
7655 S Higley Rd 85297 | 480-224-2400
Craig Gilbert, prin. | Fax 224-2420

Gilbert USD 41 | 35,000/PK-12
140 S Gilbert Rd 85296 | 480-497-3300
Brad Barrett Ph.D., supt. | Fax 497-3398
www.gilbert.k12.az.us/
Gilbert HS | 3,000/9-12
1101 E Elliot Rd 85234 | 480-497-0177
Dr. Charles Santa Cruz, prin. | Fax 497-5673
Gilbert JHS | 1,000/7-8
1016 N Burk St 85234 | 480-892-6908
Kevin Rainey, prin. | Fax 813-8240
Greenfield JHS | 1,500/7-8
101 S Greenfield Rd 85296 | 480-813-1770
Jill Bowers, prin. | Fax 813-7279
Highland HS | 2,300/9-12
4301 E Guadalupe Rd 85234 | 480-813-0051
Ken James, prin. | Fax 813-0258
Mesquite HS | 3,000/9-12
500 S McQueen Rd 85233 | 480-632-4750
Dominic Marchiando, prin. | Fax 632-4777
Mesquite JHS | 1,000/7-8
130 W Mesquite St 85233 | 480-926-1433
Ron Izzett, prin. | Fax 813-9002
South Valley JHS | 7-8
2034 S Lindsay Rd 85296 | 480-855-0015
Marti Farmer, prin. | Fax 855-3542
Other Schools – See Mesa

Higley USD 60
Supt. — See Higley
Higley HS | 1,100/9-12
4068 E Pecos Rd 85297 | 480-279-7300
Robert Mileham, prin. | Fax 279-7305

Conservatory of Recording Arts/Sciences | Post-Sec.
1205 N Fiesta Blvd 85233 | 480-858-9400
Surrey Garden Christian S | 400/K-12
1424 S Promenade Ln 85296 | 480-279-1366
Tim Ihms, admin. | Fax 279-5433

Glendale, Maricopa, Pop. 232,838
Alhambra ESD 68
Supt. — See Phoenix
Barcelona MS | 900/4-8
6130 N 44th Ave 85301 | 623-842-8616
Tyson Kelly, prin. | Fax 842-1384

Deer Valley USD 97
Supt. — See Phoenix
Deer Valley HS | 2,200/9-12
18424 N 51st Ave 85308 | 602-467-6700
Barbara Dobbs, prin. | Fax 467-6780
Desert Sky MS | 1,000/7-8
5130 W Grovers Ave 85308 | 602-467-6500
Don Morrison, prin. | Fax 467-6580
Hillcrest MS | 1,000/7-8
22833 N 71st Ave 85310 | 623-376-3300
Dannene Truett, prin. | Fax 376-3380
Mountain Ridge HS | 2,700/9-12
22800 N 67th Ave 85310 | 623-376-3000
Debra Poulson, prin. | Fax 376-3080
O'Connor HS | 2,300/9-12
25250 N 35th Ave 85310 | 623-445-7100
Jack Dillard, prin. | Fax 445-7180

Glendale ESD 40 | 12,400/PK-8
7301 N 58th Ave 85301 | 623-842-8100
Dr. Perry Hill, supt. | Fax 842-8198
www.gesd40.org/
Challenger MS | 900/7-8
6905 W Maryland Ave 85303 | 623-842-8314
Bob Wallace, prin. | Fax 842-8324
Glendale Landmark MS | 1,000/6-8
5730 W Myrtle Ave 85301 | 623-842-8304
John Dalmolin, prin. | Fax 842-8330

Glendale UNHSD 205 | 14,200/9-12
7650 N 43rd Ave 85301 | 623-435-6000
Vernon E. Jacobs, supt. | Fax 435-6078
guhsdaz.org
Apollo HS | 1,700/9-12
8045 N 47th Ave 85302 | 623-435-6300
Brian Capistran, prin. | Fax 435-6369
Glendale HS | 1,500/9-12
6216 W Glendale Ave 85301 | 623-435-6200
Deborah Jordan, prin. | Fax 435-6270
Independence HS | 1,700/9-12
6602 N 75th Ave 85303 | 623-435-6100
Mark Farison, prin. | Fax 435-6157
Other Schools – See Phoenix

Peoria USD 11 | 36,500/PK-12
6330 W Thunderbird Rd 85306 | 623-486-6000
Jack Erb, supt. | Fax 486-6009
portal.peoriaud.k12.az.us/default.aspx
Cactus HS | 1,800/9-12
6330 W Greenway Rd 85306 | 623-412-5000
Debbie McKintosh, prin. | Fax 412-5020
Ironwood HS | 2,100/9-12
6051 W Sweetwater Ave 85304 | 623-486-6400
Pat Redl, prin. | Fax 486-6424
Kellis HS | 9-12
8990 W Orangewood Ave 85305 | 623-412-5425
Shona Miranda, prin. | Fax 412-5447
Other Schools – See Peoria

Tolleson UNHSD 214
Supt. — See Tolleson
Copper Canyon HS | 9-12
9126 W Camelback Rd 85305 | 623-478-4800
Sharon Wagner, prin. | Fax 478-4802

Arizona Automotive Institute | Post-Sec.
6829 N 46th Ave 85301 | 623-934-7273
Arizona College of Allied Health | Post-Sec.
4425 W Olive Ave Ste 300 85302 | 602-222-9300

Artistic Beauty College | Post-Sec.
10820 N 43rd Ave 85304 | 623-937-2749
Glendale Community College | Post-Sec.
6000 W Olive Ave 85302 | 623-845-3000
Midwestern University | Post-Sec.
19555 N 59th Ave 85308 | 623-572-3275
Thunderbird The Garvin School | Post-Sec.
15249 N 59th Ave 85306 | 602-978-7011

Globe, Gila, Pop. 7,254
Globe USD 1 | 2,100/PK-12
501 E Ash St 85501 | 928-425-3211
Dr. Timothy Trent, supt. | Fax 425-8912
www.globeusd.org
Globe HS | 700/9-12
501 E Ash St 85501 | 928-425-3211
Susanne Morgan, prin. | Fax 425-8909
High Desert MS | 700/5-8
4000 High Desert Rd 85501 | 928-402-5700
Steve Doerksen, prin. | Fax 402-5788

Goodyear, Maricopa, Pop. 31,968
Agua Fria UNHSD 216
Supt. — See Avondale
Desert Edge HS | 1,100/9-12
15778 W Yuma Rd 85338 | 623-932-7500
Dr. Bob Rossi, prin. | Fax 932-7502
Millennium HS | 1,600/9-12
14802 W Wigwam Blvd 85338 | 623-932-7500
Dr. Dennis Runyan, prin. | Fax 932-7204

Buckeye UNHSD 201
Supt. — See Buckeye
Estrella Foothills HS | 300/9-12
13033 S Estrella Pkwy 85338 | 623-327-2400
Eric Godfrey, admin. | Fax 327-2420
Litchfield ESD 79
Supt. — See Litchfield Park
Western Sky MS | 1,000/6-8
4905 N 144th Ave 85338 | 623-535-6300
Alan Harper, prin. | Fax 935-9536

Grand Canyon, Coconino
Grand Canyon USD 4 | 300/K-12
PO Box 519 86023 | 928-638-2461
Sheila Breen, supt. | Fax 638-2461
www.grandcanyonschool.org
Grand Canyon S | 300/K-12
PO Box 519 86023 | 928-638-2461
Robert Kelso, prin. | Fax 638-2428

Heber, Navajo, Pop. 1,581
Heber-Overgaard USD 6 | 600/PK-12
PO Box 547 85928 | 928-535-4622
Ken VanWinkle, supt. | Fax 535-5146
Capps MS / Mogollon JHS | 200/4-8
PO Box 820 85928 | 928-535-4667
Ron Tenney, prin. | Fax 535-9044
Mogollon HS | 200/9-12
PO Box 279 85928 | 928-535-4238
Rick Honsinger, prin. | Fax 535-3933

Higley, Maricopa
Higley USD 60 | 4,700/PK-12
3333 E Vest Ave 85236 | 480-279-7000
Joyce Lutrey, supt. | Fax 279-7005
www.husd.org
Other Schools – See Gilbert

Holbrook, Navajo, Pop. 5,095
Holbrook USD 3 | 2,000/K-12
PO Box 640 86025 | 928-524-6144
Mary Koury, supt. | Fax 524-3073
www.holbrook.k12.az.us
Holbrook HS | 800/9-12
PO Box 640 86025 | 928-524-2815
Travis Udall, prin. | Fax 524-3537
Holbrook JHS | 400/6-8
PO Box 640 86025 | 928-524-3959
Linda Crumrine, prin. | Fax 524-3766

Holbrook SDA Indian S | 100/K-12
PO Box 910 86025 | 928-524-6845
| Fax 524-3190
Northland Pioneer College | Post-Sec.
PO Box 610 86025 | 928-524-7606

Joseph City, Navajo
Joseph City USD 2 | 500/PK-12
PO Box 8 86032 | 928-288-3307
Hollis Merrell, supt. | Fax 288-3309
www.myweb.cableone.net/joecity
Joseph City JSHS | 200/7-12
PO Box 8 86032 | 928-288-3361
Bryan Fields, prin. | Fax 288-3825

Kayenta, Navajo, Pop. 4,372
Kayenta USD 27 | 2,600/PK-12
PO Box 337 86033 | 928-697-2012
William L. Allsbrooks, supt. | Fax 697-2160
www.kayenta.k12.az.us
Kayenta MS | 600/6-8
PO Box 337 86033 | 928-697-2298
Jack Gilmore, prin. | Fax 697-2308
Monument Valley HS | 1,000/9-12
PO Box 337 86033 | 928-697-2228
Blane Baker, prin. | Fax 697-2195

Keams Canyon, Navajo, Pop. 393
Cedar USD 25 | 400/K-12
PO Box 367 86034 | 928-738-2366
Damon Clarke, supt. | Fax 738-5404
www.cedarusd.org
White Cone HS, PO Box 367 86034 | 9-12
Darrel Brinkerhoff, prin. | 928-654-3451

Kearny, Pinal, Pop. 2,479
Ray USD 3 | 600/PK-12
PO Box 427 85237 | 520-363-5515
Joseph W. Bullmore, supt. | Fax 363-5642

Ray HS | 200/9-12
PO Box 427 85237 | 520-363-5513
David Orzell, prin. | Fax 363-5642
Ray MS | 200/5-8
PO Box 427 85237 | 520-363-5511
Curt Cook, prin. | Fax 363-5005

Kingman, Mohave, Pop. 22,875
Kingman USD 20 | 7,300/PK-12
3033 McDonald Ave 86401 | 928-753-5678
Dr. Maurice Flores, supt. | Fax 753-6910
www.kusd.org
Kingman HS South | 700/9-9
400 Grandview Ave 86401 | 928-753-6216
Gary Blanton, prin. | Fax 753-4042
Kingman JHS | 1,000/7-8
1969 Detroit Ave 86401 | 928-753-3588
Jerry Arave, prin. | Fax 753-1336
Kingman SHS North | 1,600/10-12
4182 N Bank St, | 928-692-6480
Pat Mickelson, prin. | Fax 692-6418
Other Schools – See Dolan Springs

Mohave Community College | Post-Sec.
1971 E Jagerson Ave, 86409 | 928-757-0879

Lake Havasu City, Mohave, Pop. 49,124
Lake Havasu USD 1 | 6,000/PK-12
2200 Havasupai Blvd 86403 | 928-855-7861
Gail Malay, supt. | Fax 855-5908
www.havasu.k12.az.us/
Daytona MS | 500/6-8
98 Swanson Plz 86403 | 928-855-4200
Hector Fimbres, prin. | Fax 855-6323
Lake Havasu HS | 1,800/9-12
2675 Palo Verde Blvd S 86403 | 928-855-4011
Kathy Cox, prin. | Fax 855-5795
Thunderbolt MS | 1,100/6-8
695 Thunderbolt Ave 86406 | 928-855-4066
Paul Olson, prin. | Fax 855-0041

Bethany Christian S | 50/1-12
1200 Park Terrace Ave 86404 | 928-855-2661
Rev. Jerry Adams, prin.
Charles of Italy Beauty College | Post-Sec.
1987 McCulloch Blvd #205 86403 | 928-453-6666

Lakeside, Navajo, Pop. 3,492
Blue Ridge USD 32 | 2,600/PK-12
1200 W White Mountain Blvd 85929 | 928-368-6126
W. Michael Aylstock, supt. | Fax 368-5570
www.brusd.k12.az.us/
Blue Ridge HS | 800/9-12
1200 W White Mountain Blvd 85929 | 928-368-6328
Gerard Ball, prin. | Fax 368-8308
Blue Ridge JHS | 500/7-8
1200 W White Mountain Blvd 85929 | 928-368-6377
Greg Schalow, prin. | Fax 368-6378

Laveen, Maricopa
Laveen ESD 59 | 2,600/PK-8
PO Box 29 85339 | 602-237-9100
Ron Dickson, supt. | Fax 237-3376
www.laveeneld.org/
Vista del Sur MS | 400/7-8
PO Box 630 85339 | 602-237-3046
Steve Preis, admin. | Fax 237-9139

Phoenix UNHSD 210
Supt. — See Phoenix
Chavez HS | 2,400/9-12
3921 W Baseline Rd 85339 | 602-764-4000
James McElroy, prin. | Fax 764-4054

Litchfield Park, Maricopa, Pop. 3,933
Litchfield ESD 79 | 6,300/PK-8
553 E Plaza Cir 85340 | 623-935-6000
L. Thomas Heck, supt. | Fax 935-1448
www.lesd.k12.az.us/
Wigwam Creek MS | 1,100/6-8
553 E Plaza Cir 85340 | 623-547-1100
David Mayer, prin. | Fax 535-8083
Other Schools – See Buckeye, Goodyear

Littlefield, Mohave
Littlefield USD 9 | 400/K-12
PO Box 730 86432 | 928-347-5796
| Fax 347-5795
Beaver Dam HS, PO Box 730 86432 | 9-12
R. Lawrence, prin. | 928-347-5252

Marana, Pima, Pop. 20,333
Marana USD 6 | 12,700/K-12
11279 W Grier Rd 85653 | 520-682-3243
Dennis Dearden, supt. | Fax 682-2421
www.maranausd.org
Marana Career and Technical HS | Vo/Tech
11279 W Grier Rd Ste 128 85653 | 520-682-4773
Lynne Prouty, prin. | Fax 682-4106
Marana MS | 1,000/7-8
11279 W Grier Rd Ste 105 85653 | 520-682-4730
David Liss, prin. | Fax 682-4790
Other Schools – See Tucson

Maricopa, Pinal
Maricopa USD 20 | 1,400/PK-12
45012 W Honeycutt Ave 85239 | 520-568-5100
Alma Farrell, supt. | Fax 568-5151
www.musd20.org/
Maricopa JSHS | 600/6-12
45012 W Honeycutt Ave 85239 | 520-568-8102
Burnie Hubbard, prin. | Fax 568-7104
Maricopa MS | 7-8
45012 W Honeycutt Ave 85239 | 520-568-7102
Stephanie Sharp, prin. | Fax 568-7104

Mayer, Yavapai
Mayer USD 43 | 600/PK-12
PO Box 1059 86333 | 928-642-1005
Patrick Dallabetta, supt. | Fax 632-4005

Mayer JSHS — 300/7-12
PO Box 1059 86333 — 928-642-1201
Jim Dean, prin. — Fax 632-5714

Orme S — 200/7-12
HC 63 Box 3040 86333 — 928-632-7601
— Fax 632-7605

Mesa, Maricopa, Pop. 432,376
East Valley Institute of Tech. SD 401
1601 W Main St 85201 — 480-461-4150
Sally Downey Ed.D., supt. — Fax 461-4169
evit.com
East Valley Institute of Technology — Vo/Tech
1601 W Main St 85201 — 480-898-6100
Dr. Janet Cox, dir. — Fax 461-4169

Gilbert USD 41
Supt. — See Gilbert
Desert Ridge HS — 1,500/9-12
10045 E Madero Ave, — 480-984-8947
Daniel Coombs, prin. — Fax 354-5090
Desert Ridge JHS — 800/7-8
10211 E Madero Ave, — 480-635-2025
Jean Woods, prin. — Fax 635-2044
Highland JHS — 1,300/7-8
6915 E Guadalupe Rd 85212 — 480-632-4739
George Bowers, prin. — Fax 632-4729

Mesa USD 4 — 74,100/PK-12
63 E Main St Ste 101 85201 — 480-472-0000
Dr. Debra Duvall, supt. — Fax 472-0204
www.mpsaz.org
Brimhall JHS — 1,400/7-9
4949 E Southern Ave 85206 — 480-472-2600
Dr. Barbara Remondini, prin. — Fax 472-2698
Carson JHS — 1,300/7-9
525 N Westwood 85201 — 480-472-2900
Robert Crispin, prin. — Fax 472-2899
Dobson SHS — 2,500/10-12
1501 W Guadalupe Rd 85202 — 480-472-3000
Steve Green, prin. — Fax 472-3075
Fremont JHS — 1,500/7-9
1001 N Power Rd 85205 — 480-472-8300
Patricia Christie, prin. — Fax 472-8333
Kino JHS — 1,200/7-9
848 N Horne 85203 — 480-472-2400
Domonic Salce, prin. — Fax 472-2549
Mesa JHS — 1,100/7-9
828 E Broadway Rd 85204 — 480-472-1300
Catherine McDaniel, prin. — Fax 472-1319
Mesa SHS — 2,700/10-12
1630 E Southern Ave 85204 — 480-472-5900
Pete Lesar, prin. — Fax 472-5995
Mountain View SHS — 2,700/10-12
2700 E Brown Rd 85213 — 480-472-6900
Craig Luketich, prin. — Fax 472-6983
Poston JHS — 1,400/7-9
2433 E Adobe St 85213 — 480-472-2100
Catherine Pletchette, prin. — Fax 472-2105
Powell MS — 1,300/7-9
855 W 8th Ave 85210 — 480-472-1000
Nancy Roberts, prin. — Fax 472-1110
Red Mountain SHS — 2,400/10-12
7301 E Brown Rd 85207 — 480-472-8000
Gerald Slemmer, prin. — Fax 472-8008
Rhodes JHS — 1,200/7-9
1860 S Longmore 85202 — 480-472-2300
Matt Devlin, prin. — Fax 472-2299
Shepherd JHS — 1,500/7-9
1407 N Alta Mesa Dr 85205 — 480-472-1800
Eileen Cahoon, prin. — Fax 472-1888
Skyline HS — 1,900/9-12
845 S Crismon Rd 85208 — 480-472-9400
Denise Griffin, prin. — Fax 472-9406
Smith JHS — 1,500/7-9
10100 E Adobe Rd 85207 — 480-472-9900
Bruce Cox, prin. — Fax 472-9999
Stapley JHS — 1,400/7-9
3250 E Hermosa Vista Dr 85213 — 480-472-2700
Ken Erickson, prin. — Fax 472-2828
Taylor JHS — 1,200/7-9
705 S 32nd St 85204 — 480-472-1500
Dale Cox, prin. — Fax 472-1616
Westwood SHS — 2,300/10-12
945 W 8th St 85201 — 480-472-4400
Helen Riddle, prin. — Fax 472-4509
Other Schools – See Chandler

Apollo College — Post-Sec.
630 W Southern Ave 85210 — 480-831-6585
Arizona Sch of Dentistry & Oral Health — Post-Sec.
5850 E Still Cir 85206 — 480-219-6000
Arizona School of Health Sciences — Post-Sec.
5850 E Still Cir 85206 — 480-219-6000
Arizona State University Polytechnic — Post-Sec.
7001 E Williams Field Rd 85212 — 480-727-3278
Earl's Academy of Beauty — Post-Sec.
2111 S Alma School Rd #21 85210 — 480-897-1688
Faith Christian S — 100/K-12
PO Box 31300 85275 — 480-833-1983
Dick Buckingham, admin. — Fax 833-1649
International Academy of Beauty — Post-Sec.
42 N Stapley Dr 85203 — 480-964-8675
International Institute of the Americas — Post-Sec.
925 S Gilbert Rd Ste 201 85204 — 480-545-8755
Keller Graduate School of Management — Post-Sec.
1201 S Alma School Rd #5450 85210 — 480-827-1511
Mesa Community College — Post-Sec.
1833 W Southern Ave 85202 — 480-461-7000
Pima Medical Institute — Post-Sec.
957 S Dobson Rd 85202 — 480-644-0267
Providence Classical S — 100/K-12
3426 E University Dr 85213 — 480-830-7211
Chris Traffanstedt, hdmstr. — Fax 813-3637
Redeemer Christian S — 100/K-12
719 N Stapley Dr 85203 — 480-962-5003
Denise Monroe Ed.D., hdmstr. — Fax 833-7502

Miami, Gila, Pop. 1,863
Miami USD 40 — 1,100/PK-12
PO Box H 85539 — 928-425-3271
Don E. Nelson, supt. — Fax 425-7419
miami.az.schoolwebpages.com/education/district/distri
Kornegay JHS — 200/7-8
PO Box H 85539 — 928-425-3271
Susan Hocking, prin. — Fax 425-5470
Miami HS — 300/9-12
PO Box H 85539 — 928-425-3271
Sherrill Stephens, prin. — Fax 425-7027

Mohave Valley, Mohave, Pop. 6,962
Colorado River UNHSD 2
Supt. — See Fort Mohave
River Valley HS — 700/9-12
2250 Laguna Rd 86440 — 928-768-2300
Bud Scully, prin. — Fax 768-6156

Mohave Valley ESD 16 — 1,700/PK-8
PO Box 5070 86446 — 928-768-2507
Phil Sauceman, supt. — Fax 768-2510
www.mvesd16.org
Mohave Valley JHS — 500/7-8
6565 Girard Ave 86440 — 928-768-9196
Whitney Crow, prin. — Fax 768-1129

Morenci, Greenlee, Pop. 1,799
Morenci USD 18 — 1,000/PK-12
PO Box 1060 85540 — 928-865-2081
David Woodall, supt. — Fax 865-3130
www.morenci.k12.az.us/
Morenci JSHS — 400/7-12
PO Box 1060 85540 — 928-865-3631
Duane Howard, prin. — Fax 865-3614

Nogales, Santa Cruz, Pop. 20,980
Nogales USD 1 — 5,700/K-12
310 W Plum St 85621 — 520-287-0800
Dr. Guillermo Zamudio, supt. — Fax 287-3586
www.nusd.k12.az.us
Carpenter Middle Academy — 700/6-8
595 W Kino St 85621 — 520-287-0820
Liza Montiel, prin. — Fax 287-0817
Desert Shadows MS — 800/6-8
340 Boulevard Del Rey David 85621 — 520-377-2646
Joan Molera, prin. — Fax 377-2674
Nogales HS — 1,700/9-12
1905 N Apache Blvd 85621 — 520-377-2021
Mark Valenzuela, prin. — Fax 281-4448
Pierson Vocational HS — Vo/Tech
451 N Arroyo Blvd 85621 — 520-287-0915
Joel Kramer, lead tchr. — Fax 287-0918

Lourdes HS — 100/9-12
555 E Patagonia Hwy 85621 — 520-287-5659
Sr. Barbara Monsegur, prin. — Fax 287-2910

Oro Valley, Pima, Pop. 34,355
Amphitheater USD 10
Supt. — See Tucson
Ironwood Ridge HS — 1,700/9-12
2475 W Naranja Dr, — 520-696-3900
Sam McClung, prin. — Fax 696-3999

Page, Coconino, Pop. 6,923
Page USD 8 — 3,000/PK-12
PO Box 1927 86040 — 928-608-4100
Jim Walker, supt. — Fax 608-4109
www.pageud.k12.az.us
Page HS — 1,100/9-12
PO Box 1927 86040 — 928-608-4138
Perry Berry, prin. — Fax 645-9285
Page MS — 800/6-8
PO Box 1927 86040 — 928-608-4306
Eric Bonniksen, prin. — Fax 645-9285

Paradise Valley, Maricopa, Pop. 14,169

Phoenix Country Day S — 700/PK-12
3901 E Stanford Dr 85253 — 602-955-8200
Geoffrey Campbell, hdmstr. — Fax 955-1286

Parker, LaPaz, Pop. 3,064
Parker USD 27 — 1,900/PK-12
PO Box 1090 85344 — 928-669-9244
Kevin Uden, supt. — Fax 669-2515
www.parkerusd.k12.az.us
Parker HS — 600/9-12
PO Box 1090 85344 — 928-669-2202
Le Roy Shontz, prin. — Fax 669-2315
Wallace JHS — 200/7-8
PO Box 1090 85344 — 928-669-2141
Jay Sandusky, prin. — Fax 669-2515

Patagonia, Santa Cruz, Pop. 854
Patagonia ESD 6 — 100/PK-8
PO Box 295 85624 — 520-394-3050
Susan Stropko, supt. — Fax 394-3051
patagonia.echalk.com
Patagonia MS — 50/6-8
PO Box 254 85624 — 520-394-3000
Peter Fagergren, prin. — Fax 394-3001

Patagonia UNHSD — 100/9-12
PO Box 254 85624 — 520-394-3050
Susan Stropko, supt. — Fax 394-3051
Patagonia Union HS — 100/9-12
PO Box 254 85624 — 520-394-3000
Susan Stropko, prin. — Fax 394-3001

Payson, Gila, Pop. 14,301
Payson USD 10 — 2,700/PK-12
PO Box 919 85547 — 928-474-2070
Sue Myers, supt. — Fax 472-2013
www.pusd.k12.az.us/
Payson HS — 900/9-12
PO Box 919 85547 — 928-474-2233
Roy Sandoval, prin. — Fax 472-2010

Rim Country MS — 600/6-8
PO Box 919 85547 — 928-474-4511
Monica Nitzsche, prin. — Fax 472-2013

Payson Community Christian S — 100/PK-12
213 S Colcord Rd 85541 — 928-474-8050
Teresa Purtee, admin. — Fax 468-1176

Peach Springs, Mohave, Pop. 787
Peach Springs USD 8 — 300/K-12
PO Box 360 86434 — 928-769-2202
Eugene Thomas Ph.D., supt. — Fax 769-2676
www.psusd.k12.az.us/
Music Mountain JSHS — 100/7-12
PO Box 360 86434 — 928-769-2202
Dr. Eugene Thomas, prin. — Fax 769-2412

Peoria, Maricopa, Pop. 127,580
Peoria USD 11
Supt. — See Glendale
Centennial HS — 2,000/9-12
14388 N 79th Ave 85381 — 623-412-4400
Jim Davis, prin. — Fax 412-4420
Liberty HS — 9-12
9621 W Speckled Gecko Dr 85383 — 623-773-6525
Ali Bridgewater, prin. — Fax 773-6540
Peoria HS — 2,700/9-12
11200 N 83rd Ave 85345 — 623-486-6300
Dr. Kayla Carter, prin. — Fax 486-6330
Sunrise Mountain HS — 2,300/9-12
21200 N 83rd Ave 85382 — 623-487-5125
Jerry Nunez, prin. — Fax 487-5140

Southwest Indian S — 50/1-12
14202 N 73rd Ave 85381 — 623-979-6008
Debbie McKelvey, prin. — Fax 486-5243

Phoenix, Maricopa, Pop. 1,388,416
Alhambra ESD 68 — 14,700/PK-8
4510 N 37th Ave 85019 — 602-336-2920
Dr. Jim Rice, supt. — Fax 336-2270
www.alhambra.k12.az.us
Andalucia MS — 1,200/4-8
4730 W Campbell Ave 85031 — 623-848-8646
Kathy Moore, prin. — Fax 846-6044
Cordova MS — 800/4-8
5631 N 35th Ave 85017 — 602-841-0704
Barbara Marshall, prin. — Fax 973-8416
Granada East MS — 1,300/4-8
3022 W Campbell Ave 85017 — 602-589-0110
Sandra Kennedy, prin. — Fax 589-0140
Simpson MS — 1,100/4-8
5330 N 23rd Ave 85015 — 602-246-0699
Cynthia Nicholas, prin. — Fax 246-4305
Other Schools – See Glendale

Cartwright ESD 83 — 17,900/PK-8
3401 N 67th Ave 85033 — 623-691-4000
Michael Martinez, supt. — Fax 691-5920
www.cartwright.k12.az.us
Atkinson MS — 1,000/7-8
4315 N Maryvale Pkwy 85031 — 623-691-1700
Raul Pina, prin. — Fax 691-1720
Borman MS — 1,000/7-8
3637 N 55th Ave 85031 — 623-691-5000
Susan Jurkunas, prin. — Fax 691-5020
Desert Sands MS — 900/7-8
6308 W Campbell Ave 85033 — 623-691-4900
Jim Paczosa, prin. — Fax 691-4920
Estrella MS — 1,100/7-8
3733 N 75th Ave 85033 — 623-691-5400
Patricia Heichel, prin. — Fax 691-5420

Deer Valley USD 97 — 32,800/PK-12
20402 N 15th Ave 85027 — 623-445-5000
Dr. Virginia McElyea, supt. — Fax 445-5086
www.dvusd.org
Boulder Creek HS — 9-12
40404 N Gavilan Peak Pkwy 85086 — 623-445-8600
C. Kevin Imes, prin. — Fax 445-8680
Deer Valley MS — 1,000/7-8
21100 N 27th Ave 85027 — 623-445-3300
Dr. Dan Courson, prin. — Fax 445-3380
Goldwater HS — 2,200/9-12
2820 W Rose Garden Ln 85027 — 623-445-3000
Dr. Mike Anderson, prin. — Fax 445-3080
Other Schools – See Glendale

Fowler ESD 45 — 3,100/PK-8
1617 S 67th Ave 85043 — 623-707-4500
Dr. Randall Blecha, supt. — Fax 707-4561
www.fesd.org
Santa Maria MS — 500/6-8
7250 W Lower Buckeye Rd 85043 — 623-707-1100
Frank Larby, prin. — Fax 707-1110
Western Valley MS — 400/6-8
6250 W Durango St 85043 — 623-707-2200
Louis Daniels, prin. — Fax 707-2204

Glendale UNHSD 205
Supt. — See Glendale
Cortez HS — 1,200/9-12
8828 N 31st Ave 85051 — 623-915-8200
Tom Hernandez, prin. — Fax 915-8244
Greenway HS — 1,700/9-12
3930 W Greenway Rd 85053 — 623-915-8500
Elizabeth Tataseo, prin. — Fax 915-8560
Moon Valley HS — 1,700/9-12
3625 W Cactus Rd 85029 — 623-915-8000
Linda Rosness, prin. — Fax 915-8070
Sunnyslope HS — 1,600/9-12
35 W Dunlap Ave 85021 — 623-915-8760
John Croteau, prin. — Fax 915-8762
Thunderbird HS — 1,700/9-12
1750 W Thunderbird Rd 85023 — 623-915-8900
Norman Smalley, prin. — Fax 915-8971
Washington HS — 1,500/9-12
2217 W Glendale Ave 85021 — 623-915-8400
Virginia Gibney, prin. — Fax 915-8437

Isaac ESD 5 9,200/PK-8
3348 W McDowell Rd 85009 602-455-6700
Dr. Kent Paredes Scribner, supt. Fax 455-6701
www.isaacschools.org
Isaac MS 1,000/6-8
3402 W McDowell Rd 85009 602-455-6800
John Fernandez, prin. Fax 455-6899
Pueblo Del Sol MS 1,000/6-8
3449 N 39th Ave 85019 602-455-6900
Gloria Garino Spencer, prin. Fax 484-4118
Smith MS 6-8
4301 W Fillmore St 85043 602-442-2850
Rosalind Fisher, prin. Fax 442-2897

Kyrene ESD 28
Supt. — See Tempe
Kyrene Akimel A-al MS 1,100/6-8
2720 E Liberty Ln 85048 480-783-1600
Ernie Broderson, prin. Fax 759-7688
Kyrene Altadena MS 1,200/6-8
14620 S Desert Fthills Pkwy 85048 480-783-1300
Nancy Corner, prin. Fax 460-2094
Kyrene Centennial MS 1,200/6-8
13808 S 36th St 85044 480-783-2500
Kathy Cranson, prin. Fax 496-6110

Madison ESD 38 5,200/PK-8
5601 N 16th St 85016 602-664-7900
Linda Schmitt, supt. Fax 664-7999
www.msd38.org
Madison I MS 900/5-8
5525 N 16th St 85016 602-664-7100
Ann Roberts, prin. Fax 664-7199
Madison Meadows MS 700/5-8
225 W Ocotillo Rd 85013 602-664-7600
Ralph Schneider, prin. Fax 664-7699
Madison Park MS 800/4-8
1431 E Campbell Ave 85014 602-664-7500
Richard Ramos, prin. Fax 664-7599

Osborn ESD 8 3,700/K-8
1226 W Osborn Rd 85013 602-707-2000
Wilma Basnett, supt. Fax 707-2040
www.osbornnet.org
Osborn MS 700/7-8
1102 W Highland Ave 85013 602-707-2400
Marty Makar, prin. Fax 707-2440

Paradise Valley USD 69 34,800/PK-12
15002 N 32nd St 85032 602-867-5100
John A. Kriekard Ed.D., supt. Fax 867-5251
www.pvusd.k12.az.us
Explorer MS 600/7-8
22401 N 40th St 85050 480-419-5600
Marianne Bursi, prin. Fax 419-5608
Greenway MS 800/7-8
3002 E Nisbet Rd 85032 602-493-6300
Jesse Acosta, prin. Fax 971-6385
Mountain Trail MS 900/7-8
2323 E Mountain Gate Pass 85024 480-538-7100
Tanya Beckwith, prin. Fax 538-7100
North Canyon HS 2,400/9-12
1700 E Union Hills Dr 85024 623-780-4200
Carol Pollack, prin. Fax 780-4304
Paradise Valley HS 2,000/9-12
3950 E Bell Rd 85032 602-867-5505
Cara Herkamp, prin. Fax 867-5592
Pinnacle HS 1,900/9-12
3535 E Mayo Blvd 85050 480-419-4400
Richard Zielinski, prin. Fax 419-4412
Shadow Mountain HS 1,900/9-12
2902 E Shea Blvd 85028 602-867-5326
Heather Glaeser, prin. Fax 867-5317
Shea MS 900/7-8
2728 E Shea Blvd 85028 602-493-6440
Dan Knak, prin. Fax 787-0915
Star Tech Professional Center Vo/Tech
3950 E Bell Rd 85032 602-867-5571
Jacque Boyer, dir. Fax 867-5596
Vista Verde MS 900/7-8
2826 E Grovers Ave 85032 602-493-6013
Elaine Jacobs, prin. Fax 493-7656
Other Schools – See Scottsdale

Pendergast ESD 92 9,400/PK-8
3802 N 91st Ave 85037 623-772-2200
Ron Richards, supt. Fax 877-8188
www.pesd92.org/
Westwind IS 400/5-8
9040 W Campbell Ave 85037 623-772-2460
Claudio Coria, prin. Fax 872-0327

Phoenix ESD 1 8,100/PK-8
1817 N 7th St 85006 602-257-3755
Dr. Georgina Takemoto, supt. Fax 257-3783
www.phxelem.k12.az.us
Phoenix Preparatory Academy 1,100/5-8
735 E Fillmore St 85006 602-257-4840
John Ewing, prin. Fax 257-4852

Phoenix UNHSD 210 21,500/9-12
4502 N Central Ave 85012 602-271-3100
Raj Chopra Ph.D., supt. Fax 271-3131
www.phxhs.k12.az.us
Alhambra HS 2,600/9-12
3839 W Camelback Rd 85019 602-764-6022
Marty Hoeffel, prin. Fax 271-3497
Browne HS 2,600/9-12
7402 W Catalina Dr 85033 602-764-8516
Virginia Corder, prin. Fax 440-6803
Camelback HS 2,300/9-12
4612 N 28th St 85016 602-764-7001
Pete Garcia, prin. Fax 271-2295
Central HS 2,200/9-12
4525 N Central Ave 85012 602-764-7500
Nancy Kloss, prin. Fax 271-2385
Hayden HS 2,200/9-12
3333 W Roosevelt St 85009 602-764-3000
Steve Ybarra, prin. Fax 229-8387

Maryvale HS 2,400/9-12
3415 N 59th Ave 85033 602-764-2009
Phillip Verdugo, prin. Fax 271-2597
Metro Tech HS Vo/Tech
1900 W Thomas Rd 85015 602-764-8008
Frank Rasmussen, prin. Fax 764-8215
North HS 2,400/9-12
1101 E Thomas Rd 85014 602-764-6500
Zachary Munoz, prin. Fax 271-2765
South Mountain HS 2,100/9-12
5401 S 7th St 85040 602-764-5000
Alvin Watson, prin. Fax 271-2880
Other Schools – See Laveen

Riverside ESD 2 300/K-8
1414 S 51st Ave 85043 602-477-8900
Jack Bliss, supt. Fax 272-8378
www.riverside.k12.az.us/
Kings Ridge MS 5-8
3650 S 64th Ln 85043 602-477-8960
Dr. Jaime Rivera, prin. Fax 936-5531

Roosevelt ESD 66 11,500/K-8
6000 S 7th St 85042 602-243-4800
Grace Wright Ed.D., supt. Fax 243-2637
www.rsd.k12.az.us
Greenfield MS 700/4-8
7009 S 10th St 85042 602-232-4240
Juan Gallardo, prin. Fax 243-4973
Julian MS 300/5-8
2149 E Carver Dr 85040 602-232-4950
Louise Henderson, prin. Fax 243-4906

Scottsdale USD 48 25,900/PK-12
3811 N 44th St 85018 480-484-6100
Dr. John Baracy, supt. Fax 484-6293
www.susd.org/
Arcadia HS 1,200/9-12
4703 E Indian School Rd 85018 480-484-6300
Anne-Marie Woolsey, prin. Fax 484-6301
Ingleside MS 800/6-8
5402 E Osborn Rd 85018 480-484-4900
Cindy Hans, prin. Fax 484-4901
Other Schools – See Scottsdale

Tempe UNHSD 213
Supt. — See Tempe
Desert Vista HS 2,800/9-12
16440 S 32nd St 85048 480-706-7900
Anna Battle, prin. Fax 706-7976
Mountain Pointe HS 2,300/9-12
4201 E Knox Rd 85044 480-759-8449
Brenda Mayberry, prin. Fax 759-8458

Washington ESD 6 24,300/PK-8
8610 N 19th Ave 85021 602-347-2600
Dr. Susie Cook, supt. Fax 347-2720
www.wesd.k12.az.us
Cholla MS 900/7-8
3120 W Cholla St 85029 602-896-5400
Brenda Case, prin. Fax 896-5420
Desert Foothills JHS 900/7-8
3333 W Banff Ln 85053 602-896-5500
Kenneth Wamsley, prin. Fax 896-5520
Mountain Sky JHS 900/7-8
16225 N 7th Ave 85023 602-896-6100
Linda Marlar, prin. Fax 896-6120
Palo Verde MS 1,300/7-8
7502 N 39th Ave 85051 602-347-2500
Luanne Herman, prin. Fax 347-2520
Royal Palm MS 1,200/7-8
8520 N 19th Ave 85021 602-347-3200
Sheryl Schaver, prin. Fax 347-3220

Wilson ESD 7 1,400/PK-8
3025 E Fillmore St 85008 602-683-2200
Antonio Sanchez, supt. Fax 275-7517
www.wsd.k12.az.us
Wilson MS 700/4-8
2929 E Fillmore St 85008 602-683-2400
Cindy Campton, prin. Fax 275-8677

American Indian Coll of Assemblies/God Post-Sec.
10020 N 15th Ave 85021 602-944-3335
American Institute of Technology Post-Sec.
440 S 54th Ave 85043 602-233-2222
Apollo College Post-Sec.
2701 W Bethany Home Rd 85017 602-433-1333
Apollo College Post-Sec.
8503 N 27th Ave 85051 602-864-1571
Argosy University/Phoenix Post-Sec.
2233 W Dunlap Ave 85021 866-216-2777
Arizona Lutheran Academy 200/9-12
6036 S 27th Ave 85041 602-268-8686
Daniel Johnson, prin. Fax 243-1353
Arizona State University West Post-Sec.
PO Box 37110 85069 602-543-5500
Art Institute of Phoenix Post-Sec.
2233 W Dunlap Ave 85021 602-331-7500
Artistic Beauty College Post-Sec.
2727 W Glendale Ave Ste 200 85051 623-939-8364
Bourgade Catholic HS 300/9-12
4602 N 31st Ave 85017 602-973-4000
Sr. Mary McGreevy, prin. Fax 973-5854
Brophy College Prep HS 1,200/9-12
4701 N Central Ave 85012 602-264-5291
Edwin Hearn, prin. Fax 234-1669
Bryman School Post-Sec.
2250 W Peoria Ave Ste A100 85029 602-274-4300
CollegeAmerica Post-Sec.
6533 N Black Canyon Hwy 85015 602-246-3041
DeVry University Post-Sec.
2149 W Dunlap Ave 85021 602-870-9220
Everest College Post-Sec.
10400 N 25th Ave Ste 190 85021 602-942-4141
Gateway Community College Post-Sec.
108 N 40th St 85034 602-392-5000
Grand Canyon University Post-Sec.
3300 W Camelback Rd 85017 602-249-3300

High-Tech Institute Post-Sec.
1515 E Indian School Rd 85014 602-279-9700
International Import-Export Institute Post-Sec.
11225 N 28th Dr Ste B201 85029 602-648-5750
International Institute of the Americas Post-Sec.
6049 N 43rd Ave 85019 602-242-6265
International Institute of the Americas Post-Sec.
4136 N 75th Ave Ste 211 85033 623-849-8208
Long Technical College Post-Sec.
13450 N Black Canyon # 104 85029 602-548-1955
Long Technical College Post-Sec.
4646 E Van Buren St Ste 350 85008 602-252-2171
Motorcycle Mechanics Institute Post-Sec.
2844 W Deer Valley Rd 85027 623-869-9644
Mundus Institute Post-Sec.
2001 W Camelback Rd Ste 400 85015 602-246-7111
91st Psalm Christian S 100/K-12
2020 E Baseline Rd 85042 602-243-1900
Scott Ranney, prin. Fax 243-5919
Northwest Christian S 1,500/PK-12
16401 N 43rd Ave 85053 602-978-5134
Dave Young, supt. Fax 978-5804
Paradise Valley Community College Post-Sec.
18401 N 32nd St 85032 602-787-7411
Phoenix Christian JSHS 500/7-12
1751 W Indian School Rd 85015 602-265-4707
Robert L. Byrd, supt. Fax 277-7170
Phoenix College Post-Sec.
1202 W Thomas Rd 85013 602-264-2492
Phoenix First Pastors College Post-Sec.
1220 E Rosemonte Dr 85024 602-867-4587
Phoenix Institute of Herbal Medicine Post-Sec.
301 E Bethany Home Rd #A100 85012
602-274-1885
Phoenix Seminary Post-Sec.
4222 E Thomas Rd Ste 400 85018 602-850-8000
Refrigeration School Post-Sec.
4210 E Washington St 85034 602-275-7133
Roberto-Venn Guitar Making School Post-Sec.
4011 S 16th St 85040 602-243-1179
St. Marys Catholic HS 800/9-12
2525 N 3rd St 85004 602-254-6371
Mark Mauro, prin. Fax 253-0337
St. Paul's Preparatory Academy 100/9-12
2645 E Osborn Rd 85016 602-956-9090
Fax 956-3018
Scottsdale Christian Academy 1,100/PK-12
14400 N Tatum Blvd 85032 602-992-5100
Dr. Gary Damore, supt. Fax 992-0575
South Mountain Community College Post-Sec.
7050 S 24th St 85042 602-243-8000
Southwestern College Post-Sec.
2625 E Cactus Rd 85032 800-247-2697
The Paralegal Institute Post-Sec.
PO Box 11408 85061 602-212-0501
University of Phoenix Post-Sec.
4615 E Elwood St 85040 480-966-9577
Valley Lutheran HS 100/9-12
5199 N 7th Ave 85013 602-230-1600
Fax 230-1602
Western International University Post-Sec.
9215 N Black Canyon Hwy 85021 602-943-2311
Xavier College Prep HS 1,100/9-12
4710 N 5th St 85012 602-277-3772
Sr. Joan Fitzgerald, prin. Fax 279-1346

Pima, Graham, Pop. 1,979
Pima USD 6 600/K-12
PO Box 429 85543 928-485-0529
Stan Smith, supt. Fax 485-2343
www.pima.k12.az.us/
Pima HS 200/9-12
PO Box 429 85543 928-485-2421
Tony Goodman, prin. Fax 485-0790
Pima JHS, PO Box 429 85543 100/7-8
Joseph Farnsworth, prin. 928-485-2273

Pinon, Navajo, Pop. 468
Pinon USD 4 1,500/PK-12
PO Box 839 86510 928-725-2100
Larry Wallen, supt. Fax 725-2123
www.pusdatsa.org
Pinon Accelerated MS 400/6-8
PO Box 839 86510 928-725-2300
Dorothy R. Yazzie, prin. Fax 725-2370
Pinon HS 400/9-12
PO Box 839 86510 928-725-3484
James Lesher, prin. Fax 725-2470

Prescott, Yavapai, Pop. 37,576
Prescott USD 1 5,200/K-12
146 S Granite St 86303 928-445-5400
Kevin J. Kapp, supt. Fax 713-3207
www.prescottschools.com
Granite Mountain MS 600/6-8
1800 N Williamson Valley Rd 86305 928-717-3253
Michael Harlan, prin. Fax 717-3284
Prescott HS 1,800/9-12
1050 Ruth St 86301 928-445-2322
Totsy McCraley, prin. Fax 778-6106
Prescott Mile High MS 600/6-8
300 S Granite St 86303 928-717-3241
Joe Howard, prin. Fax 717-3298

Artistic Beauty College Post-Sec.
410 W Goodwin St 86303 928-778-5064
Embry-Riddle Aeronautical University Post-Sec.
3700 Willow Creek Rd 86301 800-888-3728
Northcentral University Post-Sec.
505 Whipple St 86301 928-541-7777
Prescott College Post-Sec.
220 Grove Ave 86301 928-778-2090
Yavapai College Post-Sec.
1100 E Sheldon St 86301 928-445-7300

Prescott Valley, Yavapai, Pop. 28,223
Humboldt USD 22 — 5,200/PK-12
  8766 E State Route 69 86314 — 928-759-4000
  Dr. Henry E. Schmitt, supt. — Fax 759-4020
  www.humboldt.k12.az.us
Bradshaw Mountain HS — 1,400/9-12
  6000 E Long Look Dr 86314 — 928-759-4100
  Jerry Nunez, prin. — Fax 759-4120
Bradshaw Mountain HS East — 9-12
  6411 N Robert Rd 86314 — 928-759-5100
  Connie Kudrna, prin. — Fax 759-5120
Glassford Hill MS — 700/6-8
  6901 Panther Path 86314 — 928-759-4600
  Kristen Rex, prin. — Fax 759-4620
Other Schools – See Dewey

Queen Creek, Maricopa, Pop. 7,515
J.O. Combs ESD 44 — 600/K-8
  301 E Combs Rd 85242 — 480-987-5300
  Jan Langer, supt. — Fax 987-3487
  www.jocombs.org/
Combs MS — 100/7-8
  37327 N Gantzel Rd 85242 — 480-987-5320
  Eric Samuels, prin. — Fax 987-5009

Queen Creek USD 95 — 2,500/PK-12
  20740 S Ellsworth Rd 85242 — 480-987-5935
  Dr. James D. Murlless, supt. — Fax 987-9714
  www.qcusd.org/
Queen Creek HS — 800/9-12
  22149 E Ocotillo Rd 85242 — 480-987-5973
  Angela Chomokos, prin. — Fax 987-5979
Queen Creek MS — 600/6-8
  20435 S Ellsworth Rd 85242 — 480-987-5940
  Tom Lindsey, prin. — Fax 987-5947

Rio Rico, Santa Cruz, Pop. 100
Santa Cruz Valley USD 35 — 2,600/PK-12
  1374 W Frontage Rd 85648 — 520-375-8261
  Daniel Fontes, supt. — Fax 281-7093
  www.santacruz.k12.az.us
Calabasas MS — 800/6-8
  1374 W Frontage Rd 85648 — 520-375-8600
  Rod Rich, prin. — Fax 375-8690
Rio Rico HS — 800/9-12
  1374 W Frontage Rd 85648 — 520-375-8200
  Kate Mueller, prin. — Fax 375-8700

Sacaton, Pinal, Pop. 1,452
Sacaton ESD 18 — 500/PK-8
  PO Box 98 85247 — 520-562-8600
  Dr. James E. Christensen, supt. — Fax 763-4410
Sacaton MS — 100/6-8
  PO Box 98 85247 — 520-562-8600
  Tom Cox, prin. — Fax 763-4410

Safford, Graham, Pop. 8,956
Safford USD 1 — 2,900/PK-12
  734 W 11th St 85546 — 928-348-7000
  Mark Tregaskes, supt. — Fax 348-7001
  www.saffordusd.k12.az.us
Safford HS — 800/9-12
  734 W 11th St 85546 — 928-348-7050
  Rich DeRidder, prin. — Fax 348-7051
Safford MS — 400/7-8
  734 W 11th St 85546 — 928-348-7040
  Robert Beeman, prin. — Fax 348-7041

Safford College of Beauty Culture — Post-Sec.
  1550 W Thatcher Blvd 85546 — 928-428-0331

Sahuarita, Pima, Pop. 3,806
Sahuarita USD 30 — 2,600/PK-12
  350 W Sahuarita Rd 85629 — 520-625-3502
  Jay St. John, supt. — Fax 625-4609
  sahuarita.k12.az.us
Sahuarita HS — 800/9-12
  350 W Sahuarita Rd 85629 — 520-625-3502
  Larry McKee, prin. — Fax 399-1223
Sahuarita MS — 600/6-8
  350 W Sahuarita Rd 85629 — 520-625-3502
  Katherin Shiba, prin. — Fax 399-1870

Saint David, Cochise, Pop. 1,468
Saint David USD 21 — 500/PK-12
  PO Box 70 85630 — 520-720-4781
  Troy Thygerson, supt. — Fax 720-4783
  www.stdavidschool.net/
Saint David HS — 200/9-12
  PO Box 70 85630 — 520-720-4781
  Mark Goodman, dean — Fax 720-4783

Saint Johns, Apache, Pop. 3,513
Saint Johns USD 1 — 1,100/PK-12
  PO Box 3030 85936 — 928-337-2255
  Larry Heap, supt. — Fax 337-2263
  www.sjusd.net
Saint Johns HS — 400/9-12
  PO Box 429 85936 — 928-337-2221
  Roger Heap, prin. — Fax 337-2867
Saint Johns MS — 400/4-8
  PO Box 3060 85936 — 928-337-2132
  Ed Burgoyne, prin. — Fax 337-3147

Saint Michaels, Apache, Pop. 1,119

St. Michael HS — 200/9-12
  PO Box 650 86511 — 928-871-4443
  — Fax 871-3191

Salome, LaPaz
Bicentennial UNHSD 76 — 100/9-12
  PO Box 519 85348 — 928-859-3453
  Dave Perey, supt. — Fax 859-4663
  www.salomehs.org
Salome HS — 100/9-12
  PO Box 519 85348 — 928-859-3453
  Dave Perey, prin. — Fax 859-3875

San Carlos, Gila, Pop. 2,918
San Carlos USD 20 — 1,300/PK-12
  PO Box 207 85550 — 928-475-2315
  John Bush, supt. — Fax 475-2301
San Carlos HS — 300/9-12
  PO Box 207 85550 — 928-475-2378
  William Stiner, prin. — Fax 475-2697
San Carlos JHS — 300/6-8
  PO Box 207 85550 — 928-475-2262
  Elberta Monroe, prin. — Fax 475-2431

Sanders, Apache
Sanders USD 18 — 1,100/K-12
  PO Box 250 86512 — 928-688-4755
  Alex Martinez, supt. — Fax 688-4766
  www.susd.k12.az.us
Sanders MS — 300/6-8
  PO Box 250 86512 — 928-688-4772
  James Bingham, prin. — Fax 688-4773
Valley HS — 300/9-12
  PO Box 250 86512 — 928-688-4200
  Scott Shakespeare, prin. — Fax 688-4202

San Luis, Yuma, Pop. 19,001
Gadsden ESD 32 — 4,600/PK-8
  PO Box 6870 85349 — 928-627-6540
  Raymond Aguilera, supt. — Fax 627-3635
  www.gesd32.org
San Luis MS — 1,200/7-8
  PO Box 6870 85349 — 928-627-6920
  Carlos Robles, prin. — Fax 627-9339
Southwest JHS — 7-8
  PO Box 6870 85349 — 928-627-6580
  Richard West, prin. — Fax 627-9266

Yuma UNHSD 70
  Supt. — See Yuma
San Luis HS — 1,800/9-12
  1250 N 8th Ave 85349 — 928-502-6100
  Mary Lynn Coleman, prin. — Fax 502-6222

San Manuel, Pinal, Pop. 4,009
Mammoth/San Manuel USD 8 — 1,300/PK-12
  PO Box 406 85631 — 520-385-2337
  Dr. Ron Rickel, supt. — Fax 385-2621
  www.msmusd.k12.az.us
San Manuel JSHS — 600/7-12
  PO Box 406 85631 — 520-385-2336
  John Ryan, prin. — Fax 385-3035

San Simon, Cochise
San Simon USD 18 — 100/K-12
  PO Box 38 85632 — 520-845-2275
  Michael Reed, supt. — Fax 845-2480
  www.sansimon.k12.az.us
San Simon HS — 50/9-12
  PO Box 38 85632 — 520-845-2275
  Michael Reed, prin. — Fax 845-2480

Scottsdale, Maricopa, Pop. 217,989
Cave Creek USD 93 — 5,400/PK-12
  33606 N 60th St 85262 — 480-575-2016
  Dr. Tacy Ashby, supt. — Fax 488-7055
  cavecreek.schoolnet.com/
Cactus Shadows HS — 1,400/9-12
  5802 E Dove Valley Rd 85262 — 480-575-2400
  Dr. Gaye Leo, prin. — Fax 488-6701
Desert Arroyo MS — 700/6-8
  33401 N 56th St 85262 — 480-575-2300
  Ann Orlando, prin. — Fax 488-7059
Sonoran Trails MS — 600/6-8
  33606 North 6th Street 85262 — 480-575-2200
  Dr. Skot Beazley, prin. — Fax 488-2386

Paradise Valley USD 69
  Supt. — See Phoenix
Desert Shadows MS — 800/7-8
  5858 E Sweetwater Ave 85254 — 602-493-6000
  Carol Kendrick, prin. — Fax 494-9266
Horizon HS — 2,400/9-12
  5601 E Greenway Rd 85254 — 602-953-4104
  Anthony Capuano, prin. — Fax 953-4144
Sunrise MS — 800/7-8
  4960 E Acoma Dr 85254 — 602-493-6030
  Gregory Martin, prin. — Fax 493-6037

Scottsdale USD 48
  Supt. — See Phoenix
Chaparral HS — 1,800/9-12
  6935 E Gold Dust Ave 85253 — 480-484-6500
  Mary Lou Muccino, prin. — Fax 484-6501
Cocopah MS — 1,100/6-8
  6615 E Cholla St 85254 — 480-484-4400
  Dr. Tere Peterson, prin. — Fax 484-4401
Copper Ridge MS — 500/6-8
  10101 E Thompson Peak Pkwy 85255 — 480-484-1500
  Marla Zimmerman, prin. — Fax 484-1501
Coronado HS — 1,200/9-12
  2501 N 74th St 85257 — 480-484-6800
  John Biera, prin. — Fax 484-6801
Desert Canyon MS — 800/6-8
  10203 E McDowell Mntn Ranch 85255 — 480-484-4600
  Tracy Olson, prin. — Fax 484-4601
Desert Mountain HS — 2,400/9-12
  12575 E Via Linda 85259 — 480-484-7000
  Greg Millbrandt, prin. — Fax 484-7001
Mohave MS — 700/7-8
  5520 N 86th St 85250 — 480-484-5200
  Chris Sawyer, prin. — Fax 484-5201
Mountainside MS — 1,000/6-8
  11256 N 128th St 85259 — 480-484-5500
  Mark Blomgren, prin. — Fax 484-5501
Saguaro HS — 1,700/9-12
  6250 N 82nd St 85250 — 480-484-7100
  Tyrus Timbrooks, prin. — Fax 484-7201
Supai MS — 700/7-8
  6720 E Continental Dr 85257 — 480-484-5800
  Daniel Cooper, prin. — Fax 484-5801

Artistic Beauty College — Post-Sec.
  7730 E McDowell Rd 85257 — 480-949-7557
Devereux-Arizona Treatment Network — Post-Sec.
  6436 E Sweetwater Ave 85254 — 480-998-2920
Frank Lloyd Wright Sch of Architecture — Post-Sec.
  Taliesin West 85261 — 480-860-2700
Keller Graduate School of Management — Post-Sec.
  9201 E Mountn View Rd #115 85258 — 480-657-3223
Notre Dame Preparatory HS — 1,000/9-12
  9701 E Bell Rd 85260 — 480-634-8200
  David Gonsalves, prin. — Fax 634-8299
RainStar University — Post-Sec.
  8370 E Via De Ventura K-100 85258 — 480-423-0375
Scott Cole Academy — Post-Sec.
  7201 E Camelback Rd Ste 100 85251 — 480-994-4222
Scottsdale Community College — Post-Sec.
  9000 E Chaparral Rd 85256 — 480-423-6000
Scottsdale Culinary Institute — Post-Sec.
  8100 E Camelback Rd 85251 — 480-990-3773
Sonoran Desert Institute — Post-Sec.
  10245 E Via Linda Ste 102 85258 — 480-314-2102
Thunderbird Adventist Academy — 100/9-12
  7410 E Sutton Dr 85260 — 480-948-3300
  — Fax 443-4944

Sedona, Coconino, Pop. 10,905
Sedona-Oak Creek JUSD 9 — 1,300/PK-12
  221 Brewer Rd Ste 100 86336 — 928-204-6800
  Kim Randall, supt. — Fax 282-0232
  www.sedona.k12.az.us/
Sedona Red Rock HS — 400/9-12
  995 Upper Red Rock Loop Rd 86336 — 928-204-6700
  Russ Snider, prin. — Fax 282-5992

Oak Creek Ranch S — 100/6-12
  PO Box 4329 86340 — 928-634-5571
Verde Valley S — 100/9-12
  3511 Verde Valley School Rd 86351 — 928-284-2272
  — Fax 284-0432

Seligman, Yavapai
Seligman USD 40 — 200/K-12
  PO Box 650 86337 — 928-422-3233
  Todd Kissick, supt. — Fax 422-3642
Seligman HS — 100/9-12
  PO Box 650 86337 — 928-422-3233
  Patrick Kissick, prin. — Fax 422-3642

Sells, Pima, Pop. 2,750
Indian Oasis-Baboquivari USD 40 — 1,200/K-12
  PO Box 85634 — 520-623-1031
  Joe Frazier, supt. — Fax 383-5441
  www.iobusd40.org
Baboquivari HS — 300/9-12
  PO Box 248 85634 — 520-383-6800
  Paula Hart, prin. — Fax 383-4852
Baboquivari MS — 200/7-8
  PO Box 248 85634 — 520-383-6800
  Paula Hart, prin. — Fax 383-4852

Tohono O'odham Community College — Post-Sec.
  PO Box 3129 85634 — 520-383-8401

Show Low, Navajo, Pop. 8,765
Show Low USD 10 — 2,500/PK-12
  500 W Old Linden Rd 85901 — 928-537-6000
  Kevin Brackney, supt. — Fax 537-6009
  www.show-low.k12.az.us
Show Low HS — 800/9-12
  500 W Old Linden Rd 85901 — 928-537-6200
  Farrell Adams, prin. — Fax 537-6299
Show Low JHS — 400/7-8
  500 W Old Linden Rd 85901 — 928-537-6100
  Connie Lewis, prin. — Fax 537-6149

Sierra Vista, Cochise, Pop. 39,841
Sierra Vista USD 68 — 6,600/PK-12
  3555 E Fry Blvd 85635 — 520-515-2714
  Renae Humburg, supt. — Fax 515-2721
  www.sierravistapublicschools.com
Apache MS — 700/6-8
  3555 E Fry Blvd 85635 — 520-515-2920
  Jeff Spencer, prin. — Fax 515-2900
Buena HS — 2,600/9-12
  3555 E Fry Blvd 85635 — 520-515-2800
  Tad Bloss, prin. — Fax 515-2877
Sierra Vista MS — 900/6-8
  3555 E Fry Blvd 85635 — 520-515-2930
  Jim Sprigg, prin. — Fax 515-2941

Cochise College — Post-Sec.
  901 Colombo Ave 85635 — 520-515-5412
DeVoe College of Beauty — Post-Sec.
  750 Bartow Dr 85635 — 520-458-8660
Shiloh Christian S — 100/K-12
  200 North Ave 85635 — 520-459-2869
  Angela Tumpkin, prin. — Fax 459-7436
Veritas Christian Community S — 100/K-12
  215 Taylor Dr 85635 — 520-417-1113
  Karen Bolton, hdmstr. — Fax 417-0180

Snowflake, Navajo, Pop. 4,788
Snowflake USD 5 — 2,500/K-12
  682 W School Bus Ln 85937 — 928-536-4156
  Monte Silk, supt. — Fax 536-2634
  www.snowflake.k12.az.us
Snowflake HS — 800/9-12
  682 W School Bus Ln 85937 — 928-536-4156
  Larry Titus, prin. — Fax 536-2756
Snowflake JHS — 400/7-8
  682 W School Bus Ln 85937 — 928-536-4156
  Edna Jean LaMarca, prin. — Fax 536-2634

Somerton, Yuma, Pop. 8,534
Somerton ESD 11 — 2,500/PK-8
  PO Box 3200 85350 — 928-341-6005
  Judith Bobbitt, supt. — Fax 341-6090
  www.somerton.k12.az.us

Somerton MS | 900/6-8
PO Box 3200 85350 | 928-341-6100
George Brick, prin. | Fax 627-6190

Springerville, Apache, Pop. 1,937
Round Valley USD 10 | 1,400/PK-12
PO Box 610 85938 | 928-333-6580
Dennis Bigelow, supt. | Fax 333-2823
www.elks.net
Round Valley HS | 500/9-12
PO Box 610 85938 | 928-333-6800
Renita Kirkham, prin. | Fax 333-6820
Round Valley MS | 300/6-8
PO Box 610 85938 | 928-333-6700
Alan Bingham, prin. | Fax 333-5252

Sun City, Maricopa, Pop. 38,400

Walter Boswell Memorial Hospital | Post-Sec.
10401 W Thunderbird Blvd 85351 | 623-977-7211

Superior, Pinal, Pop. 3,307
Superior USD 15 | 600/PK-12
199 N Lobb Ave 85273 | 520-689-5291
Pete Guzman, supt.
Superior HS | 200/9-12
100 W Mary Dr 85273 | 520-689-3101
David Pastor, prin. | Fax 689-3197
Superior JHS | 100/7-8
199 N Lobb Ave 85273 | 520-689-3100
David Pastor, prin. | Fax 689-3197

Surprise, Maricopa, Pop. 50,585
Dysart USD 89 | 10,900/K-12
15802 N Parkview Pl 85374 | 623-876-7000
Dr. Mark S. Maksimowicz, supt. | Fax 876-7042
www.dysart.org
Valley Vista HS | 9-10
15550 N Parkview Pl 85374 | 623-523-8800
Dr. Tammy Hall, prin. | Fax 523-8811
Willow Canyon HS | 900/9-12
17901 W Lundberg St, | 623-876-8000
Kathy Vogt, prin. | Fax 523-8011
Other Schools – See El Mirage

Teec Nos Pos, Apache, Pop. 317
Red Mesa USD 27 | 900/PK-12
HC 61 Box 40 86514 | 928-656-4100
William Bean, supt. | Fax 656-4106
www.rmusd.net
Red Mesa HS | 300/9-12
HC 61 Box 40 86514 | 928-656-4177
Tim Benally, prin. | Fax 656-4178

Immanuel Mission S | 100/K-8
PO Box 2000 86514 | 928-674-3616
John Bloom, prin. | Fax 826-8120

Tempe, Maricopa, Pop. 158,880
Kyrene ESD 28 | 18,400/PK-8
8700 S Kyrene Rd 85284 | 480-783-4000
David Schauer Ed.D., supt. | Fax 783-4141
www.kyrene.org
Kyrene MS | 1,100/6-8
1050 E Carver Rd 85284 | 480-783-1000
Susan Poole, prin. | Fax 831-0169
Other Schools – See Chandler, Phoenix

Tempe ESD 3 | 14,000/K-8
PO Box 27708 85285 | 480-730-7100
Dr. Arthur Tate, supt. | Fax 730-7177
www.tempeschools.org
Connolly MS | 1,000/6-8
2002 E Concorda Dr 85282 | 480-967-8933
Kathryn Mullery, prin. | Fax 929-9695
Fees MS | 1,100/6-8
1600 E Watson Dr 85283 | 480-897-6063
Reynaldo Cruz, prin. | Fax 838-0853
Gililland MS | 1,000/6-8
1025 S Beck Ave 85281 | 480-966-7114
Rick Horvath, prin. | Fax 829-6178
McKemy MS | 1,000/6-8
2250 S College Ave 85282 | 480-921-9003
Ardie Sturdivant, prin. | Fax 829-6179

Tempe UNHSD 213 | 13,200/9-12
500 W Guadalupe Rd 85283 | 480-839-0292
Dr. Shirley Miles, supt. | Fax 413-0685
www.tempehighschools.org
Corona Del Sol HS | 2,700/9-12
1001 E Knox Rd 85284 | 480-752-8888
James Denton, prin. | Fax 820-3632
Marcos De Niza HS | 2,000/9-12
6000 S Lakeshore Dr 85283 | 480-838-3200
Frank Mirizio, prin. | Fax 730-7665
McClintock HS | 1,800/9-12
1830 E Del Rio Dr 85282 | 480-839-4222
Kim Hilgers, prin. | Fax 752-8622
Tempe HS | 1,400/9-12
1730 S Mill Ave 85281 | 480-967-1661
Mark Yslas, prin. | Fax 736-4096
Other Schools – See Phoenix

Arizona State University | Post-Sec.
PO Box 870112 85287 | 480-965-9011
Carsten Institute of Hair and Beauty | Post-Sec.
3345 S Rural Rd 85282 | 480-491-0449
College of the Humanities and Sciences | Post-Sec.
1105 E Broadway Rd 85282 | 480-317-5955
Collins College School of Design & Tech. | Post-Sec.
1140 S Priest Dr 85281 | 480-966-3000
Conservatory of Recording Arts/Sciences | Post-Sec.
2300 E Broadway Rd 85282 | 480-858-9400
International Baptist College | Post-Sec.
2150 E Southern Ave 85282 | 480-838-7070
ITT Technical Institute | Post-Sec.
5005 S Wendler Dr 85282 | 602-437-7500
Lamson College | Post-Sec.
1126 N Scottsdale Rd Ste 17 85281 | 480-898-7000

Remington College | Post-Sec.
875 W Elliot Rd 85284 | 480-834-1000
Rio Salado Community College | Post-Sec.
2323 W 14th St 85281 | 480-517-8000
Southwest Coll of Naturopathic Medicine | Post-Sec.
2140 E Broadway Rd 85282 | 480-858-9100
Southwest Institute of Healing Arts | Post-Sec.
1100 E Apache Blvd 85281 | 480-994-9244
University of Advancing Technology | Post-Sec.
2625 W Baseline Rd 85283 | 800-658-5744

Thatcher, Graham, Pop. 4,043
Thatcher USD 4 | 1,200/K-12
PO Box 65552 | 928-348-7200
Janice Given, supt. | Fax 348-7220
www.thatcherud.k12.az.us
Thatcher HS | 400/9-12
601 N 3rd Ave 85552 | 928-348-7272
Paul Nelson, prin. | Fax 348-7273
Thatcher MS | 200/7-8
1300 N 4th Ave 85552 | 928-348-7262
Matt Petersen, prin. | Fax 348-7263

Eastern Arizona College | Post-Sec.
3714 W Church St 85552 | 928-428-8233

Tolleson, Maricopa, Pop. 5,848
Tolleson UNHSD 214 | 5,500/9-12
9419 W Van Buren St 85353 | 623-478-4000
Kino Flores, supt. | Fax 936-5048
www.tuhsd.org
Tolleson Union HS | 2,000/9-12
9419 W Van Buren St 85353 | 623-478-4200
Harold Crenshaw, prin. | Fax 936-9366
Other Schools – See Avondale, Glendale

Union ESD 62 | 200/K-8
3834 S 91st Ave 85353 | 623-936-8711
Justin Greene, supt. | Fax 936-4944
www.uesd.org
Union S | 200/5-8
3834 S 91st Ave 85353 | 623-478-5000
Justin Greene, prin. | Fax 478-5026

Tombstone, Cochise, Pop. 1,547
Tombstone USD 1 | 1,000/PK-12
PO Box 1000 85638 | 520-457-2217
Ron Hennings, supt. | Fax 457-3270
www.tombstone.k12.az.us/
Tombstone HS | 400/9-12
PO Box 1000 85638 | 520-457-2215
Thomas Yarborough, prin. | Fax 457-4003

Tonalea, Coconino
San Juan SD
Supt. — See Blanding, UT
Navajo Mountain HS | 50/9-12
PO Box 10040 86044 | 435-678-1287
Lewis Singer, prin. | Fax 678-1289

Tonopah, Maricopa
Saddle Mountain USD 90 | 700/PK-12
38201 W Indian School Rd 85354 | 623-386-5688
Roxanne Morris, supt. | Fax 386-3364
Tonopah Valley HS | 9-12
38201 W Indian School Rd 85354 | 623-386-5688
John Sigala, prin. | Fax 386-3364

Tsaile, Apache, Pop. 1,043

Din College 86556 | Post-Sec.
| 928-724-3311

Tuba City, Coconino, Pop. 7,323
Tuba City USD 15 | 2,600/PK-12
PO Box 67 86045 | 928-283-1006
Hector Tahu, supt. | Fax 283-5105
www.tcusd.org
Tuba City HS | 1,000/9-12
PO Box 67 86045 | 928-283-1045
Ralph Navarre, prin. | Fax 283-1129
Tuba City JHS | 600/6-8
PO Box 67 86045 | 928-283-1055
Lee Tsinigine, prin. | Fax 283-1094

Tucson, Pima, Pop. 507,658
Altar Valley ESD 51 | 800/PK-8
HC 1 Box 130 85736 | 520-822-1484
Douglas Roe, supt. | Fax 822-1798
Altar Valley MS | 400/5-8
HC 1 Box 130 85736 | 520-822-9343
John Holt, prin. | Fax 822-5801

Amphitheater USD 10 | 16,800/PK-12
701 W Wetmore Rd 85705 | 520-696-5000
Vicki Balentine Ph.D., supt. | Fax 696-5015
www.amphi.com
Amphitheater HS | 1,700/9-12
125 W Yavapai Rd 85705 | 520-696-5340
Patsy Harris, prin. | Fax 696-5410
Amphitheater MS | 900/6-8
315 E Prince Rd 85705 | 520-696-6230
Chuck Bermudez, prin. | Fax 696-6236
Canyon Del Oro HS | 1,900/9-12
25 W Calle Concordia 85704 | 520-696-5560
Mike Gemma, prin. | Fax 696-5590
Cross MS | 1,000/6-8
1000 W Chapala Dr 85704 | 520-696-5920
Robert Vinyard, prin. | Fax 696-5996
La Cima MS | 700/6-8
5600 N La Canada Dr 85704 | 520-696-6730
Gail Gault, prin. | Fax 696-6792
Other Schools – See Oro Valley

Catalina Foothills USD 16 | 5,000/PK-12
2101 E River Rd 85718 | 520-299-6446
Mary Kamerzell, supt. | Fax 577-5307
www.cfsd.k12.az.us
Catalina Foothills HS | 1,900/9-12
4300 E Sunrise Dr 85718 | 520-577-5090
Wagner Van Vlack, prin. | Fax 577-5094

Espercro Canyon MS | 600/6-8
5801 N Sabino Canyon Rd 85750 | 520-577-5330
Brian Lorimer, prin. | Fax 577-5334
Orange Grove MS | 700/6-8
1911 E Orange Grove Rd 85718 | 520-577-5315
Phil Woodall, prin. | Fax 577-5319

Flowing Wells USD 8 | 6,000/PK-12
1556 W Prince Rd 85705 | 520-696-8800
Dr. Nicholas Clement, supt. | Fax 690-2400
www.flowingwells.k12.az.us
Flowing Wells HS | 1,900/9-12
3725 N Flowing Wells Rd 85705 | 520-696-8000
Jim Brunenkant, prin. | Fax 690-2379
Flowing Wells JHS | 1,000/7-8
4545 N La Cholla Blvd 85705 | 520-696-8550
Deborah Schreiner, prin. | Fax 690-2420

Marana USD 6
Supt. — See Marana
Marana HS | 1,600/9-12
12000 W Emigh Rd 85743 | 520-616-6400
Jim Doty, prin. | Fax 616-6426
Mountain View HS | 2,100/9-12
3901 W Linda Vista Blvd 85742 | 520-579-4400
Jill Atlas, prin. | Fax 579-4505
Tortolita MS | 1,100/7-8
4101 W Hardy Rd 85742 | 520-579-4600
Jane D'Amore, prin. | Fax 579-4646

Sunnyside USD 12 | 16,700/K-12
2238 E Ginter Rd 85706 | 520-545-2000
Raul Bejarano Ph.D., supt. | Fax 545-2120
www.susd12.org
Apollo MS | 1,000/6-8
265 W Nebraska St 85706 | 520-545-4500
Wendy Conger, prin. | Fax 545-4516
Challenger MS | 1,000/6-8
100 E Elvira Rd 85706 | 520-545-4600
Jud Jones, prin. | Fax 545-4616
Chaparral MS | 900/6-8
3700 E Alvord Rd 85706 | 520-545-4700
Norma Garcia, prin. | Fax 545-4716
Desert View HS | 1,500/9-12
4101 E Valencia Rd 85706 | 520-545-5100
Jonathon Hanson, prin. | Fax 545-5116
S.T.A.R. Academic Center | 1,700/6-12
5093 S Liberty Ave 85706 | 520-545-2300
Pamela Cornell, prin. | Fax 545-2316
Sierra MS | 1,100/6-8
5801 S Del Moral Blvd 85706 | 520-545-4800
Art Menchaca, prin. | Fax 545-4816
Sunnyside HS | 2,000/9-12
1725 E Bilby Rd 85706 | 520-545-5300
Raul Nido, prin. | Fax 545-5316

Tanque Verde USD 13 | 1,400/PK-12
11150 E Tanque Verde Rd 85749 | 520-749-5751
Michael Schwanenberger, supt. | Fax 749-5400
www.tanq.org
Gray JHS | 400/7-9
4201 N Melpomene Way 85749 | 520-749-3838
Robert Lombardi, prin. | Fax 749-9668
Tanque Verde HS | 10-12
4201 N Melpomene Way 85749 | 520-749-3838
Robert Lombardi, prin. | Fax 749-9668

Tucson USD 1 | 62,200/PK-12
1010 E 10th St 85719 | 520-225-6000
Roger F. Pfeuffer, supt. | Fax 225-6174
www.tusd.k12.az.us
Carson MS | 800/6-8
7777 E Stella Rd 85730 | 520-584-4700
Mary Quinnan, prin. | Fax 584-4701
Catalina Magnet HS | 1,500/9-12
3645 E Pima St 85716 | 520-232-8400
W. Daniel Bailey, prin. | Fax 232-8401
Cholla Magnet HS | 1,600/9-12
2001 W Starr Pass Blvd 85713 | 520-225-4000
Marcia Volpe Ph.D., prin. | Fax 225-4001
Dodge Magnet MS | 400/6-8
5831 E Pima St 85712 | 520-731-4100
Catherine Comstock, prin. | Fax 731-4101
Doolen MS | 900/6-8
2400 N Country Club Rd 85716 | 520-232-6900
Charlotte Patterson, prin. | Fax 232-6901
Gridley MS | 800/6-8
350 S Harrison Rd 85748 | 520-731-4600
Kathleen Scheppe, prin. | Fax 731-4601
Hohokam MS | 700/6-8
7400 S Settler Ave 85746 | 520-908-3700
John Michel, prin. | Fax 908-3701
Magee MS | 1,000/6-8
8300 E Speedway Blvd 85710 | 520-731-5000
Jerry Holmes, prin. | Fax 731-5001
Mansfeld MS | 900/6-8
1300 E 6th St 85719 | 520-225-1800
David Berry, prin. | Fax 225-1801
Maxwell MS | 600/6-8
2802 W Anklam Rd 85745 | 520-225-2000
Javier Fuentes, prin. | Fax 225-2001
Naylor MS | 800/6-8
1701 S Columbus Blvd 85711 | 520-584-6800
Alice McBride, prin. | Fax 584-6801
Palo Verde Magnet HS | 1,600/9-12
1302 S Avenida Vega 85710 | 520-584-7400
Richard Gastellum, prin. | Fax 584-7441
Pistor MS | 1,100/6-8
5455 S Cardinal Ave 85746 | 520-908-5400
Kathryn Manley-Crockett, prin. | Fax 908-5401
Pueblo Magnet HS | 1,900/9-12
3500 S 12th Ave 85713 | 520-225-4300
Patricia Dienz, prin. | Fax 225-4301
Rincon HS | 1,200/9-12
421 N Arcadia Ave 85711 | 520-232-5600
Angela Julien, prin. | Fax 232-5601
Sabino HS | 1,700/9-12
5000 N Bowes Rd 85749 | 520-584-7700
Valerie Payne, prin. | Fax 584-7701

Sahuaro HS 2,000/9-12
545 N Camino Seco 85710 520-731-7100
Sam Giangardella, prin. Fax 731-7101
Santa Rita HS 1,300/9-12
3951 S Pantano Rd 85730 520-731-7500
Mark Kershner, prin. Fax 731-7501
Secrist MS 600/6-8
3400 S Houghton Rd 85730 520-731-5300
Jim Christ, prin. Fax 731-5301
Townsend MS 600/6-8
2120 N Beverly Ave 85712 520-232-7900
Barbara Kohl, prin. Fax 232-7901
Tucson Magnet HS 2,800/9-12
400 N 2nd Ave 85705 520-225-5000
Dr. Abel Morado, prin. Fax 225-5221
University HS 600/9-12
421 N Arcadia Ave 85711 520-232-5900
Stuart Baker, prin. Fax 235-5901
Utterback Magnet MS 1,100/6-8
3233 S Pinal Vis 85713 520-225-3500
Debbie Summers, prin. Fax 225-3501
Vail MS 800/6-8
5350 E 16th St 85711 520-584-5400
David Ross, prin. Fax 584-5401
Valencia MS 800/6-8
4400 W Irvington Rd 85746 520-908-4500
Violet Bingham, prin. Fax 908-4501
Wakefield MS 600/6-8
101 W 44th St 85713 520-225-3800
Carmen Kemery, prin. Fax 225-3801

Vail USD 20
Supt. — See Vail
Desert Sky MS 700/6-8
9850 E Rankin Loop 85747 520-762-2700
Kevin Carney, prin. Fax 762-2701
Empire HS 9-12
10701 E Mary Ann Cleveland 85747 520-762-3000
Cindy Lee, prin. Fax 762-3001

Apollo College Post-Sec.
3550 N Oracle Rd 85705 520-888-5885
Arizona Academy of Beauty Post-Sec.
5631 E Speedway Blvd 85712 520-885-4120
Arizona Academy of Beauty - North Post-Sec.
4066 N Oracle Rd 85705 520-888-0170
AZ School of Acupuncture & Oriental Med Post-Sec.
4646 E Ft Lowell Rd Ste 105 85712 520-795-0787
AZ State School for the Deaf & Blind Post-Sec.
PO Box 85000 85754 520-770-3719
Artistic Beauty College Post-Sec.
3210 E Speedway Blvd 85716 520-327-6544
Asian Institute of Medical Studies Post-Sec.
3131 N Country Club Rd #100 85716 520-322-6330
Carondelet Saint Marys Hospital Post-Sec.
1601 W Saint Marys Rd 85745 520-622-5833
Chaparral College Post-Sec.
4585 E Speedway Blvd #204 85712 520-327-6866
Desert Christian HS 200/9-12
PO Box 31240 85751 520-298-5817
Allen Neilsen, admin. Fax 298-9312
Desert Christian MS 200/6-8
7525 E Speedway Blvd 85710 520-795-7161
Dennis O'Reilly, prin. Fax 795-3386
Desert Institute of the Healing Arts Post-Sec.
639 N 6th Ave 85705 520-882-0899
Fenster S of Southern Arizona 100/9-12
8500 E Ocotillo Dr 85750 520-749-3340
Fax 749-3349
Green Fields Country Day S 200/K-12
6000 N Camino De La Tierra 85741 520-297-2288
Dr. Gerald Barkan, hdmstr. Fax 297-2072
HDS Truck Driving Institute Post-Sec.
PO Box 17600 85731 520-721-5825
Immaculate Heart HS 100/9-12
625 E Magee Rd 85704 520-297-2851
Dan Ethridge, prin. Fax 797-7374
International Institute of the Americas Post-Sec.
5441 E 22nd St 85711 520-748-9799
ITT Technical Institute Post-Sec.
1455 W River Rd 85704 520-408-7488
Pima Community College Post-Sec.
4905 E Broadway Blvd 85709 520-206-4500
Pima Medical Institute Post-Sec.
3350 E Grant Rd 85716 520-326-1600
Pusch Ridge Christian Academy 500/6-12
9500 N Oracle Rd 85704 520-797-0107
Dr. Eric Abrams, prin. Fax 797-0598
River of Life Christian S 100/PK-12
6902 E Golf Links Rd 85730 520-790-7082
Denise Garcia, prin. Fax 790-3891
St. Augustine Catholic HS 100/9-12
8800 E 22nd St 85710 520-751-8300
Velma Castaneda-Titone, prin. Fax 751-8304
St. Gregory College Preparatory S 400/6-12
3231 N Craycroft Rd 85712 520-327-6395
Fax 327-8276
Salpointe Catholic HS 1,300/9-12
1545 E Copper St 85719 520-327-6581
Jeffrey Mounts, prin. Fax 327-8477
San Miguel HS 100/9-11
PO Box 22199 85734 520-294-6403
Br. Nick Gonzalez, prin. Fax 294-6417
The Art Center Design College Post-Sec.
2525 N Country Club Rd 85716 520-325-0123
Tucson College Post-Sec.
7310 E 22nd St 85710 520-296-3261
University of Arizona 85721 Post-Sec.
520-621-3237
University of Arizona Medical Center Post-Sec.
1501 N Campbell Ave 85724 520-694-4660
Vision Quest Lodgemakers Learning Center 100/7-12
PO Box 12948 85732 520-299-8993

Vail, Pima
Vail USD 20 5,500/K-12
PO Box 800 85641 520-762-2000
Calvin Baker, supt. Fax 762-2001
vail.k12.az.us
Cienega HS 1,300/9-12
12775 Mary Ann Cleveland 85641 520-762-2800
Tricia Pena, prin. Fax 762-2801
Corona Foothills MS 6-8
16705 S Houghton Rd 85641 520-762-3500
Margaret Steuer, prin. Fax 762-3501
Old Vail MS 600/6-8
13299 E Colossal Cave Rd 85641 520-762-2400
Laurie Emery, prin. Fax 762-5840
Pantano HS 200/9-12
12775 E Old Vail Rd 85641 520-762-2000
Heather Pletnick, prin. Fax 762-2930
Other Schools – See Tucson

Wellton, Yuma, Pop. 1,863
Antelope UNHSD 50 300/9-12
9168 S Avenue 36 E 85356 928-785-4041
Robert Klee, supt. Fax 785-4588
Antelope Union HS 300/9-12
9168 S Avenue 36 E 85356 928-785-3344
Randall O'Donnell, prin. Fax 785-9566

Whiteriver, Navajo, Pop. 3,775
Whiteriver USD 20 2,400/PK-12
PO Box 190 85941 928-338-4842
Earl Pettit, supt. Fax 338-5124
www.wusd.k12.az.us/
Alchesay HS 700/9-12
PO Box 190 85941 928-338-4848
Jeff Fuller, prin. Fax 338-4840
Canyon Day JHS 400/7-8
PO Box 190 85941 928-338-1040
Brian Gum, prin. Fax 338-4850

East Fork Lutheran S 50/K-12
PO Box 489 85941 928-338-4455
Richard Carver, prin. Fax 338-1575

Wickenburg, Maricopa, Pop. 5,345
Wickenburg USD 9 1,300/K-12
40 W Yavapai St 85390 928-668-5350
Archy D. Hamm, supt. Fax 668-5390
www.wickenburg.k12.az.us
Vulture Peak MS 300/6-8
920 S Vulture Mine Rd 85390 928-684-6700
Brett Richards, prin. Fax 684-6746
Wickenburg HS 600/9-12
1090 S Vulture Mine Rd 85390 928-684-6600
Thomas Newton, prin. Fax 684-6628

Gospel Outreach Christian S 50/K-12
515 W Wickenburg Way 85390 928-684-5227
Donald Fisher, admin. Fax 684-2878

Willcox, Cochise, Pop. 3,753
Willcox USD 13 1,400/PK-12
480 N Bisbee Ave 85643 520-384-4211
Dr. Donald L. Roberts, supt. Fax 384-2025
www.willcox.k12.az.us
Willcox HS 500/9-12
240 N Bisbee Ave 85643 520-384-4214
Joel Todd, prin. Fax 384-5401
Willcox MS 500/4-8
360 N Bisbee Ave 85643 520-384-4218
Doris Jones, prin. Fax 384-6322

Williams, Coconino, Pop. 2,959
Williams USD 2 800/PK-12
PO Box 427 86046 928-635-4473
Thomas L. McCraley Ed.D., supt. Fax 635-4767
www.wusd2.org
Williams HS 200/9-12
PO Box 427 86046 928-635-4474
Steve Hudgens, prin. Fax 635-2796

Winkelman, Gila, Pop. 445
Hayden/Winkelman USD 41 500/K-12
PO Box 409 85292 520-356-7876
Jeff Gregorich, supt. Fax 356-7303
www.hwusd.k12.az.us/
Hambly MS 200/6-8
PO Box 409 85292 520-356-7876
Jacob Kame, prin. Fax 356-7303
Hayden HS 100/9-12
PO Box 409 85292 520-356-7876
Jacob Kame, prin. Fax 356-7303

Winslow, Navajo, Pop. 9,824
Winslow USD 1 2,600/PK-12
PO Box 580 86047 928-288-8101
Robert Mansell, supt. Fax 288-8292
www.winslowsd.k12.az.us/
Winslow HS 900/9-12
PO Box 580 86047 928-288-8100
Doug Watson, prin. Fax 288-8290
Winslow JHS 400/7-8
PO Box 580 86047 928-288-8300
Jim MacLean, prin. Fax 288-8393

Young, Gila
Young ESD 5 100/PK-12
PO Box 390 85554 928-462-3244
Rick Ullery, supt. Fax 462-3283
Young Teaching HS 50/9-12
PO Box 390 85554 928-462-3244
Rick Ullery, prin. Fax 462-3283

Yuma, Yuma, Pop. 81,605
Crane ESD 13 5,200/PK-8
4250 W 16th St 85364 928-373-3403
Cindy Didway, supt. Fax 782-6831
craneschools.org/
Centennial MS 600/7-8
2650 W 20th St 85364 928-373-3300
Rich Skuletich, prin. Fax 376-7742
Crane MS 700/7-8
4450 W 32nd St 85364 928-373-3200
Linda Huff, prin. Fax 344-6821

Yuma ESD 1 10,300/K-8
450 W 6th St 85364 928-502-4300
Thomas Rushin, supt. Fax 502-4442
www.yuma.org
Castle Dome MS 1,000/6-8
2353 S Otondo Dr 85365 928-341-1600
Harriet Williams, prin. Fax 341-1700
Fourth Avenue JHS 600/7-8
450 S 4th Ave 85364 928-782-2193
Rob Monson, prin. Fax 783-2195
Gila Vista JHS 700/6-8
2245 S Arizona Ave 85364 928-782-5174
Rusty Tyndall, prin. Fax 782-1483
Woodard JHS 800/6-8
2250 S 8th Ave 85364 928-782-6546
Alan Sullivan, prin. Fax 782-4596

Yuma UNHSD 70 9,200/9-12
3150 S Avenue A 85364 928-502-4600
Tim Foist, supt. Fax 502-4740
www.yumaunion.com
Cibola HS 2,800/9-12
4100 W 20th St 85364 928-502-5700
Tony Steen, prin. Fax 502-6046
Kofa HS 2,100/9-12
3100 S Avenue A 85364 928-502-5400
Jamie Sheldahl, prin. Fax 502-5693
Yuma HS 2,600/9-12
400 S 6th Ave 85364 928-502-5000
Jeff Magin, prin. Fax 502-5338
Other Schools – See San Luis

Arizona Western College Post-Sec.
PO Box 929 85366 928-317-6000
Yuma Catholic HS 400/9-12
2100 W 28th St 85364 928-317-7900
Sr. Adrianna Schouten, prin. Fax 317-8558

ARKANSAS

ARKANSAS DEPARTMENT OF EDUCATION
4 State Capitol Rm 304A, Little Rock 72201
Telephone 501-682-4475
Fax 501-682-1079
Website arkedu.state.ar.us
Commissioner of Education   T. Kenneth James

ARKANSAS BOARD OF EDUCATION
4 State Capitol, Little Rock 72201
Chairperson   Diane Tatum

EDUCATION SERVICE COOPERATIVES (ESC)

Arch Ford ESC
Phillip Young, dir.   501-354-2269
101 Bulldog Dr, Plumerville 72127   Fax 354-0167
www.afsc.k12.ar.us/
Arkansas River ESC
Carolyn McCoy, dir.   870-534-6129
912 W 6th Ave, Pine Bluff 71601   Fax 534-2847
Crowley's Ridge ESC
Jim Parrish, dir.   870-578-5426
PO Box 377, Harrisburg 72432   Fax 578-5896
crowleys.crsc.k12.ar.us/
Dawson ESC
R. Saunders, dir.   870-246-3077
711 Clinton St, Arkadelphia 71923   Fax 246-5892
www.dawson.dsc.k12.ar.us
De Queen/Mena ESC
J. Scott, dir.   870-386-2251
PO Box 110, Gillham 71841   Fax 386-7731
nexus.dmsc.k12.ar.us/

Great Rivers ESC
Suzann McCommon, dir.   870-338-6461
PO Box 2837, West Helena 72390   Fax 338-7905
griver.grsc.k12.ar.us/
Northcentral Arkansas ESC
Dennis Martin, dir.   870-368-7955
PO Box 739, Melbourne 72556   Fax 368-4920
naesc.k12.ar.us/
Northeast Arkansas ESC
Harrell Austin, dir., 211 W Hickory St 870-886-7717
Walnut Ridge 72476   Fax 886-7719
thor.nesc.k12.ar.us/
Northwest Arkansas ESC
Burton Elliott, dir.   479-267-7450
409 N Thompson St   Fax 267-7456
Springdale 72764
starfish.k12.ar.us/

Ozarks Unlimited ESC
Steve Brewer, dir.   870-743-9100
525 Old Bellefonte Rd   Fax 743-9099
Harrison 72601
www.oursc.k12.ar.us/
South Central ESC
Marsha Daniels, dir.   870-836-2213
400 Maul Rd, Camden 71701   Fax 836-5347
www.scsc.k12.ar.us/
Southeast Arkansas ESC
Bruce Terry, dir.   870-367-6848
1022 Scogin Dr, Monticello 71655   Fax 367-9877
se.sesc.k12.ar.us/
Southwest Arkansas ESC
Anthony Gadberry, dir.   870-777-3076
500 S Spruce St, Hope 71801   Fax 777-5793
Western Arkansas ESC
Guy Fenter, dir.   479-965-2191
RR 1 Box 104, Branch 72928   Fax 965-2723
Wilbur D. Mills ESC
Rodger Harlan, dir.   501-882-5467
PO Box 1016, Beebe 72012   Fax 882-2155
wdmweb.wmsc.k12.ar.us/

PUBLIC, PRIVATE AND CATHOLIC SECONDARY SCHOOLS

Alma, Crawford, Pop. 4,345
Alma SD   3,000/K-12
PO Box 2359 72921   479-632-4791
Charles Dyer, supt.   Fax 632-4793
almasd.net
Alma HS   900/9-12
PO Box 2139 72921   479-632-2162
Jerry Valentine, prin.   Fax 632-5070
Alma MS   700/6-8
PO Box 2229 72921   479-632-2168
Pat Whorton, prin.   Fax 632-2160

Alpena, Boone, Pop. 378
Alpena SD   500/K-12
PO Box 270 72611   870-437-2220
Robert Smalley, supt.   Fax 437-2133
Alpena JSHS   200/7-12
PO Box 270 72611   870-437-2228
David Bennett, prin.   Fax 437-5638

Altheimer, Jefferson, Pop. 1,176
Altheimer USD   400/PK-12
PO Box 640 72004   870-766-0001
Dr. William Thomas, supt.   Fax 766-0016
Altheimer MS   6-8
PO Box 640 72004   870-766-0012
Brenda Barnes, prin.   Fax 766-0014
Altheimer-Sherrill HS   200/9-12
PO Box 640 72004   870-766-0005
Michael Anthony, prin.   Fax 766-0007

Amity, Clark, Pop. 747
Centerpoint SD   700/K-12
755 Highway 8 E 71921   870-356-2912
Lewis Diggs, supt.   Fax 356-4637
www.centerpoint.dsc.k12.ar.us/
Centerpoint JHS   7-9
755 Highway 8 E 71921   870-356-3612
Dewayne Curry, prin.   Fax 356-4519
Centerpoint SHS   200/10-12
755 Highway 8 E 71921   870-356-3612
Deric Owens, prin.   Fax 356-4519

Arkadelphia, Clark, Pop. 11,036
Arkadelphia SD   2,200/K-12
235 N 11th St 71923   870-246-5564
Tony Prothro, supt.   Fax 246-1144
apsd.k12.ar.us/
Arkadelphia HS   700/9-12
401 High School Rd 71923   870-246-7373
Odas Parsons, prin.   Fax 246-1154
Goza JHS   500/6-8
1305 Caddo St 71923   870-246-4291
Angela Garner, prin.   Fax 246-1153

Arkadelphia Beauty College   Post-Sec.
2708 Pine St 71923   870-246-6726
Henderson State University   Post-Sec.
1100 Henderson St 71999   870-230-5000

Ouachita Baptist University   Post-Sec.
410 Ouachita St 71998   870-245-5000

Armorel, Mississippi
Armorel SD   400/K-12
PO Box 99 72310   870-763-6639
Chuck Hanson, supt.   Fax 763-0028
armorel.crsc.k12.ar.us
Armorel JSHS   200/7-12
PO Box 99 72310   870-763-7121
Steven Noble, prin.   Fax 763-7020

Ashdown, Little River, Pop. 4,662
Ashdown SD   1,800/K-12
511 N 2nd St 71822   870-898-3208
Mike Walker, supt.   Fax 898-3709
www.ashdownschools.org
Ashdown JHS   400/7-9
600 S Ellen Dr 71822   870-898-5138
Lin Johnson, prin.   Fax 898-4472
Ashdown SHS   300/10-12
751 Rankin St 71822   870-898-3562
John Crowder, prin.   Fax 898-4452

Atkins, Pope, Pop. 2,831
Atkins SD   1,100/K-12
302 Avenue 2 NW 72823   479-641-7871
Alton Davidson, supt.   Fax 641-7569
ahs.afsc.k12.ar.us/
Atkins HS   400/9-12
302 Avenue 2 NW 72823   479-641-7872
Robert Travis, prin.   Fax 641-1306
Atkins MS   400/5-8
302 Avenue 2 NW 72823   479-641-1008
Allen D. Wilbanks, prin.   Fax 641-5504

Augusta, Woodruff, Pop. 2,500
Augusta SD   600/K-12
320 Sycamore St 72006   870-347-2241
Richard Blevins, supt.   Fax 347-5423
www.geocities.com/ahs_east/Augusta_Public_Schools
.htm
Augusta HS   200/9-12
320 Sycamore St 72006   870-347-2515
Robert Moore, prin.   Fax 347-8113

Bald Knob, White, Pop. 3,303
Bald Knob SD   1,300/K-12
103 W Park Ave 72010   501-724-3273
R. Wayne Fawcett, supt.   Fax 724-6621
bkps.wmsc.k12.ar.us
ASU Area Career Center   Vo/Tech
103 W Park Ave 72010   501-724-3614
Preston Haynie, dir.   Fax 724-6865
Bald Knob HS   400/9-12
901 N Hickory St 72010   501-724-3843
Steve Landers, prin.   Fax 724-6621
Bald Knob MS   400/5-8
103 W Park Ave 72010   501-724-5652
David Clark, prin.   Fax 724-6621

Batesville, Independence, Pop. 9,479
Batesville SD   2,800/K-12
330 E College St 72501   870-793-6831
Ted Hall, supt.   Fax 793-6760
www.batesvilleschools.com
Batesville HS   500/10-12
1 Pioneer Dr 72501   870-793-6846
David Campbell, prin.   Fax 793-0607
Batesville JSHS   500/7-9
2 Pioneer Dr 72501   870-793-7533
Harry Crossett, prin.   Fax 793-0626

Southside SD   1,400/K-12
70 Scott Dr 72501   870-251-2341
Danny L. Foley, supt.   Fax 251-3316
southside.k12.ar.us/
Southside HS   400/9-12
70 Scott Dr 72501   870-251-2662
Roger Reid, prin.   Fax 251-3316
Southside MS   400/5-8
70 Scott Dr 72501   870-251-2332
Joel W. Franks, prin.   Fax 251-3316

Bee-Jay's Hairstyling Academy   Post-Sec.
130 W Main St 72501   870-793-3898
Lyon College   Post-Sec.
PO Box 2317 72503   870-793-9813
University of Arkansas Community College Post-Sec.
PO Box 3350 72503   870-793-7581

Bauxite, Saline, Pop. 425
Bauxite SD   1,100/K-12
800 School St 72011   501-557-5453
Mickey Billingsley, supt.   Fax 557-2235
miners.k12.ar.us/default2.htm
Bauxite JSHS   500/7-12
800 School St 72011   501-557-5303
Keith Baker, prin.   Fax 557-2274

Bay, Craighead, Pop. 1,926
Bay SD   600/K-12
PO Box 39 72411   870-781-3711
Chip Layne, supt.   Fax 781-3712
yellowjackets.k12.ar.us/
Bay JSHS   300/7-12
PO Box 39 72411   870-781-3297
Jodi Cobb, prin.   Fax 781-3687

Bearden, Ouachita, Pop. 1,072
Bearden SD   700/K-12
PO Box 195 71720   870-687-2236
Denny Rozenberg, supt.   Fax 687-3683
www.scsc.k12.ar.us/bearden/
Bearden HS   200/9-12
PO Box 195 71720   870-687-3670
James Bonsall, prin.   Fax 687-2514
Bearden MS   200/5-8
PO Box 195 71720   870-687-3503
Iva Lou Stoker, prin.   Fax 687-3683

28

Beebe, White, Pop. 5,407
Beebe SD   2,100/PK-12
1201 W Center St 72012   501-882-5463
Belinda Shook, supt.   Fax 882-5465
thor.k12.ar.us
Beebe HS   700/9-12
1201 W Center St 72012   501-882-3311
Sheena Williamson, prin.   Fax 882-8405
Beebe JHS   400/7-8
1201 W Center St 72012   501-882-8414
Donald Sandlin, prin.   Fax 882-8416

Arkansas State University - Beebe   Post-Sec.
PO Box 1000 72012   501-882-6452
Servants of Christ S   50/PK-12
1809 Edgewood Cv 72012   501-454-3678
Charlotte Sutton, admin.

Bee Branch, Van Buren
South Side SD   500/K-12
334 Southside Rd 72013   501-654-2633
Billy Jackson, supt.   Fax 654-2336
ssbb.k12.ar.us
Southside JSHS   200/7-12
334 Southside Rd 72013   501-654-2242
Travis Love, prin.   Fax 654-8113

Benton, Saline, Pop. 23,749
Benton SD   4,300/K-12
PO Box 939 72018   501-778-4861
Dr. Fred Dawson, supt.   Fax 776-5777
bentonschooldistrict.dsc.k12.ar.us/
Benton JHS   700/8-9
411 N Border St 72015   501-778-7698
Roger Burton, prin.   Fax 776-5744
Benton SHS   900/10-12
211 N Border St 72015   501-778-3288
John Dedman, prin.   Fax 776-5783

Harmony Grove SD   800/K-12
2621 N Highway 229 72015   501-778-6271
Daniel Henley, supt.   Fax 778-6271
cardinals.dsc.k12.ar.us/default.htm
Harmony Grove HS   200/9-12
2621 N Highway 229 72015   501-776-2337
William Gibbs, prin.   Fax 778-6271
Harmony Grove MS   200/5-8
2621 N Highway 229 72015   501-860-6796
Sarah Gober, prin.   Fax 778-6271

Bentonville, Benton, Pop. 26,397
Bentonville SD   8,000/K-12
400 NW 2nd St 72712   479-254-5000
Dr. Gary Compton, supt.   Fax 271-1159
www.bentonville.k12.ar.us
Bentonville HS   1,900/9-12
1901 SE J St 72712   479-254-5100
Steve Jacoby, prin.   Fax 271-1180
Lincoln JHS   700/7-8
1206 Leopard Ln 72712   479-254-5250
Rose Peterson, prin.   Fax 464-1128
Washington JHS   600/7-8
1501 NE Wildcat Way 72712   479-254-5345
Kim Garrett, prin.   Fax 271-1191

Ambassadors For Christ Academy   200/K-12
PO Box 924 72712   479-273-5635
David Welshenbaugh, admin.   Fax 273-0684
Northwest Arkansas Community College   Post-Sec.
1 College Dr 72712   479-636-9222

Bergman, Boone, Pop. 425
Bergman SD   900/K-12
PO Box 1 72615   870-741-5213
Joe Couch, supt.   Fax 741-6701
bergman.oursc.k12.ar.us/
Bergman HS   400/7-12
PO Box 1 72615   870-741-1414
Clyde Atchley, prin.   Fax 741-6701

Berryville, Carroll, Pop. 4,687
Berryville SD   1,700/K-12
PO Box 408 72616   870-423-7065
Michael H. Cox, supt.   Fax 423-6824
bobcat.oursc.k12.ar.us
Berryville HS   500/9-12
PO Box 408 72616   870-423-3312
Ron Harvell, prin.   Fax 423-6028
Berryville MS   400/6-8
PO Box 408 72616   870-423-4512
Matt Summers, prin.   Fax 423-3195

Bigelow, Perry, Pop. 336
East End SD   700/K-12
PO Box 360 72016   501-759-2808
Mark A. Tyler, supt.   Fax 759-2667
bigelow.afsc.k12.ar.us
Bigelow JSHS   300/7-12
PO Box 360 72016   501-759-2602
Paul Gottsponer, prin.   Fax 759-3081

Biggers, Randolph, Pop. 352
Corning SD
Supt. — See Corning
Biggers-Reyno JSHS   100/7-12
PO Box 82 72413   870-769-2480
Ralph Morrow, prin.   Fax 769-2811

Bismarck, Hot Spring
Bismarck SD   1,100/K-12
11636 Highway 84 71929   501-865-4888
Dr. Ernest Huff, supt.   Fax 865-3626
www.bsd-lions.net/
Bismarck HS   300/9-12
11636 Highway 84 71929   501-865-4888
Jarrod Bray, prin.   Fax 865-4512
Bismarck MS   300/5-8
11636 Highway 84 71929   501-865-4888
Jerry Gill, prin.   Fax 865-4505

Black Rock, Lawrence, Pop. 713
Black Rock SD   400/K-12
PO Box 240 72415   870-878-6273
David Foley, supt.   Fax 878-6051
www.blackrock.k12.ar.us
Black Rock JSHS   200/7-12
PO Box 240 72415   870-878-6461
Steve Morris, prin.   Fax 878-6051

Blevins, Hempstead, Pop. 367
Blevins SD   700/K-12
PO Box 98 71825   870-874-2801
Donnie Davis, supt.   Fax 874-2889
hornet.swsc.k12.ar.us/
Blevins JSHS   200/7-12
PO Box 98 71825   870-874-2281
Billy Lee, prin.   Fax 874-2450
Other Schools – See Emmet

Blytheville, Mississippi, Pop. 17,092
Blytheville SD   3,200/K-12
PO Box 1169 72316   870-762-2053
Bruce Daniels, supt.   Fax 762-0141
blytheville.k12.ar.us
Blytheville HS   900/9-12
600 N 10th St 72315   870-762-2772
Suzanne Kenner, prin.   Fax 762-0175
Blytheville MS   500/7-8
700 Chickasawba St 72315   870-762-2983
Richard Atwill, prin.   Fax 762-0174

Arkansas Northeastern College   Post-Sec.
2501 S Division St 72315   870-762-1020
Blytheville Academy of Cosmetology   Post-Sec.
100 E Main St 72315   870-763-6326
Pathway Christian Academy   100/K-12
PO Box 466 72316   870-763-4561
Kim Brown, prin.   Fax 763-7277

Booneville, Logan, Pop. 4,138
Booneville SD   1,500/K-12
381 W 7th St 72927   479-675-3504
Bobby Ashley, supt.   Fax 675-3186
www.booneville.k12.ar.us/
Booneville HS   400/9-12
945 N Plum St 72927   479-675-3277
Steve Halter, prin.   Fax 675-3214
Booneville MS   500/5-8
835 E 8th St 72927   479-675-5247
Scotty Pierce, prin.   Fax 675-0793

Bradford, White, Pop. 819
Bradford SD   600/K-12
PO Box 60 72020   501-344-2707
Donald Swiney, supt.   Fax 344-2707
bradford.wmsc.k12.ar.us/
Bradford JSHS   300/7-12
PO Box 60 72020   501-344-2607
Nicholas Benson, prin.   Fax 344-2607

Bradley, Lafayette, Pop. 578
Bradley SD 20   400/K-12
521 School Dr 71826   870-894-3313
Lynn Roe King, supt.   Fax 894-3344
bradleyweb.swsc.k12.ar.us/
Bradley HS   200/7-12
521 School Dr 71826   870-894-3316
Jeff Fairris, prin.   Fax 894-3344

Branch, Franklin, Pop. 359
County Line SD   600/K-12
12092 W State Highway 22 72928   479-635-2222
Ashley Whitman, supt.   Fax 635-2087
indians.wsc.k12.ar.us/
County Line JSHS   300/7-12
12092 W State Highway 22 72928   479-635-2441
Steven Breedlove, prin.   Fax 635-2452

Briggsville, Yell
Two Rivers SD
Supt. — See Plainview
Fourche Valley JSHS   100/7-12
18148 W Highway 28 72828   479-299-6220
David Murdock, prin.   Fax 299-6212

Brinkley, Monroe, Pop. 3,658
Brinkley SD   1,000/K-12
200 Tigers Dr 72021   870-734-5000
Dr. Randy Byrd, supt.   Fax 734-5187
www.brinkleyschools.com
Brinkley HS   500/7-12
100 Tigers Dr 72021   870-734-5005
Randy Cannon, prin.   Fax 734-1354

Brockwell, Izard
Izard County Consolidated SD   500/K-12
PO Box 115 72517   870-258-7700
Fred Walker, supt.   Fax 258-3140
icc.k12.ar.us/
Izard County Consolidated JSHS   200/7-12
PO Box 115 72517   870-258-7788
David Harmon, prin.   Fax 258-3140

Brookland, Craighead, Pop. 1,396
Brookland SD   600/K-12
100 W School St 72417   870-932-2080
Gene Goza, supt.   Fax 932-2088
brookland.crsc.k12.ar.us/
Brookland JHS   7-9
100 W School St 72417   870-932-2080
Keith McDaniel, prin.   Fax 932-2088
Brookland SHS   200/10-12
100 W School St 72417   870-932-2080
Steven Hovis, prin.   Fax 932-2088

Bryant, Saline, Pop. 12,177
Bryant SD   6,400/K-12
200 NW 4th St 72022   501-847-5600
Dr. Richard Abernathy, supt.   Fax 847-5603
www.bryantschools.org
Bryant HS North   900/9-10
200 NW 4th St 72022   501-847-5620
Delton Kitchell, prin.   Fax 847-5627

Bryant HS South   800/11-12
200 NW 4th St 72022   501-847-5605
Danny Spadoni, prin.   Fax 847-5612
Bryant MS   1,500/6-8
200 NW 4th St 72022   501-847-5651
Sue Reeves, prin.   Fax 847-5654
Other Schools – See Paron

Burdette, Mississippi, Pop. 121

Cotton Boll Technical Institute   Post-Sec.
PO Box 36 72321   870-763-1486

Cabot, Lonoke, Pop. 18,148
Cabot SD   8,300/K-12
602 N Lincoln St 72023   501-843-3363
Dr. Frank A. Holman, supt.   Fax 843-0576
cabot.k12.ar.us
Cabot HS   1,600/10-12
401 N Lincoln St 72023   501-843-3562
Dr. Tony Thurman, prin.   Fax 843-4231
Cabot JHS North   1,000/7-9
38 Spirit Dr 72023   501-605-8470
Georgia Chastain, prin.   Fax 605-8472
Cabot JHS South   900/7-9
38 Panther Trl 72023   501-843-2788
Henry Hawkins, prin.   Fax 941-7746

Calico Rock, Izard, Pop. 1,004
Calico Rock SD   500/K-12
PO Box 220 72519   870-297-8339
Jerry Skidmore, supt.   Fax 297-4233
pirates.k12.ar.us/
Calico Rock JSHS   300/7-12
PO Box 220 72519   870-297-3745
Dewayne Treat, prin.   Fax 297-3168

Camden, Ouachita, Pop. 12,520
Camden Fairview SD   2,900/K-12
625 Clifton St 71701   870-836-4193
Dr. Jerry Guess, supt.   Fax 836-6039
www.scsc.k12.ar.us/camdenfairview/
Camden Fairview HS   1,000/9-12
1750 Cash Rd SW 71701   870-837-1300
Peggy Burton, prin.   Fax 837-2330
Camden Fairview MS   700/6-8
647 Jefferson Dr NW 71701   870-836-9361
Rodney Williams, prin.   Fax 836-3717

Harmony Grove SD   1,000/K-12
401 Ouachita Rd 88 71701   870-574-0971
Harold Davidson, supt.   Fax 574-2765
www.scsc.k12.ar.us/harmonygrove/
Harmony Grove JSHS   400/7-12
401 Ouachita Rd 88 71701   870-574-0867
Robert A. McAdoo, prin.   Fax 574-2765
Other Schools – See Sparkman

Camden Christian Academy   100/K-12
1245 California Ave SW 71701   870-836-3716
Bob Taynor, admin.   Fax 836-4511
Professional Cosmetology Education Ctr   Post-Sec.
PO Box 429 71711   870-836-5481
Southern Arkansas University Tech   Post-Sec.
100 Carr Rd 71701   870-574-4500

Caraway, Craighead, Pop. 1,355
Riverside SD
Supt. — See Lake City
Riverside JHS   200/7-9
PO Box 699 72419   870-482-3327
Polly Owens, prin.   Fax 482-3328

Carlisle, Lonoke, Pop. 2,379
Carlisle SD   700/PK-12
520 Center St 72024   870-552-3931
Sherry Holliman, supt.   Fax 552-7967
bison.wmsc.k12.ar.us
Carlisle JSHS   300/7-12
716 E 5th St 72024   870-552-3196
Floyd Marshall, prin.   Fax 552-3032

Cave City, Sharp, Pop. 1,992
Cave City SD   1,300/K-12
PO Box 600 72521   870-283-5391
Steven Green, supt.   Fax 283-6887
www.cavecity.k12.ar.us
Cave City JSHS   400/7-12
PO Box 600 72521   870-283-5392
Marc Walling, prin.   Fax 283-6887
Other Schools – See Evening Shade

Cedarville, Crawford, Pop. 1,179
Cedarville SD   900/K-12
PO Box 97 72932   479-474-7220
David Smith, supt.   Fax 410-1804
chs.wsc.k12.ar.us/
Cedarville HS   300/9-12
PO Box 97 72932   479-474-7021
Glennis Cook, prin.   Fax 410-1804
Cedarville MS   300/5-8
PO Box 97 72932   479-474-5847
Curt Ledbetter, prin.   Fax 471-7036

Center Ridge, Conway
Nemo Vista SD   400/K-12
5690 Highway 9 72027   501-893-2925
Cody Beene, supt.   Fax 893-2367
nemo.k12.ar.us/
Nemo Vista JSHS   200/7-12
5690 Highway 9 72027   501-893-2811
Jeff Andrews, prin.   Fax 893-2367

Charleston, Franklin, Pop. 2,985
Charleston SD   700/K-12
PO Box 188 72933   479-965-7160
Jeff Stubblefield, supt.   Fax 965-9989
tigers.wsc.k12.ar.us/
Charleston HS   300/9-12
PO Box 188 72933   479-965-7150
Shane Storey, prin.   Fax 965-7140
Charleston MS   7-8
PO Box 188 72933   479-965-7170
Melissa Moore, prin.   Fax 965-9989

Cherry Valley, Cross, Pop. 704
Cross County SD 7   600/K-12
   PO Box 180 72324   870-588-3338
   Don Smith, supt.   Fax 588-3565
   crosscountyschooldistrict.com/
Cross County HS   400/7-12
   PO Box 180 72324   870-588-3337
   Ed Ross, prin.   Fax 588-4606

Clarendon, Monroe, Pop. 1,879
Clarendon SD   600/K-12
   PO Box 248 72029   870-747-3351
   George LaFargue, supt.   Fax 747-5963
Clarendon HS   300/7-12
   PO Box 248 72029   870-747-3326
   Robert Age, prin.   Fax 747-5444

Clarksville, Johnson, Pop. 8,084
Clarksville SD   2,200/K-12
   1701 W Clark Rd 72830   479-705-3200
   Don Johnston, supt.   Fax 754-3748
   panthernet.wsc.k12.ar.us/
Clarksville JHS   500/7-9
   1801 W Clark Rd 72830   479-705-3224
   Paul Dean, prin.   Fax 754-7431
Clarksville SHS   400/10-12
   1703 W Clark Rd 72830   479-705-3212
   Steven Wyatt, prin.   Fax 754-2492

University of the Ozarks   Post-Sec.
   415 N College Ave 72830   479-979-1000

Clinton, Van Buren, Pop. 2,431
Clinton SD   1,400/K-12
   851 Yellowjacket Ln 72031   501-745-6000
   Curtis Turner, supt.   Fax 745-2475
   clinton.k12.ar.us/
Alread JSHS   50/7-12
   20308 Highway 16 W 72031   501-745-5337
   Frank McMurry, prin.   Fax 745-8525
Clinton HS   300/10-12
   849 Edd St 72031   501-745-6035
   Danny Thomas, prin.   Fax 745-2450
Clinton JHS   300/7-9
   848 Walker St 72031   501-745-6079
   Mark Gammill, prin.   Fax 745-6065
Other Schools – See Scotland

Coal Hill, Johnson, Pop. 1,026
Westside SD
   Supt. — See Hartman
Westside JSHS   300/7-12
   PO Box 189 72832   479-497-1171
   John H. Burke, prin.   Fax 497-1537

Concord, Cleburne, Pop. 261
Concord SD   600/K-12
   PO Box 10 72523   870-668-3844
   David Burnley, supt.   Fax 668-3380
   concord.k12.ar.us
Concord JSHS   200/7-12
   PO Box 358 72523   870-668-3522
   Mike Hopper, prin.   Fax 668-3522
Other Schools – See Wilburn

Conway, Faulkner, Pop. 47,840
Conway SD   8,200/K-12
   2220 Prince St 72034   501-450-4800
   James Simmons, supt.   Fax 450-4898
   www.conwayschools.afsc.k12.ar.us
Conway Area Career Center   Vo/Tech
   2300 Prince St 72034   501-450-4888
   Nicholas Stroman, prin.   Fax 450-6658
Conway HS East   1,300/9-10
   1815 Prince St 72034   501-450-4860
   Mickey Siler, prin.   Fax 450-6651
Conway HS West   1,100/11-12
   2300 Prince St 72034   501-450-4880
   John Tyler, prin.   Fax 450-4884
Courtway MS   1,000/6-8
   1200 Bob Courtway Dr 72032   501-450-4832
   Jerry Whitmore, prin.   Fax 450-4839
Stuart MS   1,000/6-8
   2745 Carl Stuart St 72034   501-329-2782
   Bob Hill, prin.   Fax 450-4848

Arkansas Beauty School - Conway   Post-Sec.
   1061 Markham St 72032   501-329-8303
Central Baptist College   Post-Sec.
   1501 College Ave 72034   501-329-6872
Conway Christian S   400/PK-12
   701 Polk St 72032   501-336-9067
   Gloria Gwatney, prin.   Fax 336-0706
Hendrix College   Post-Sec.
   1600 Washington Ave 72032   501-329-6811
St. Joseph HS   600/7-12
   502 Front St 72032   501-329-5741
   Joe Mallett, prin.   Fax 513-6804
University of Central Arkansas   Post-Sec.
   201 Donaghey Ave 72035   501-450-5000

Corning, Clay, Pop. 3,537
Corning SD   1,300/K-12
   PO Box 479 72422   870-857-6818
   John M. Eddington, supt.   Fax 857-5086
   www.corningschools.k12.ar.us/
Corning JSHS   500/7-12
   PO Box 479 72422   870-857-3041
   Stan Johnson, prin.   Fax 857-5086
Other Schools – See Biggers

Cotter, Baxter, Pop. 964
Cotter SD   600/K-12
   PO Box 70 72626   870-435-6171
   Don Sharp, supt.   Fax 435-1300
   cotter.oursc.k12.ar.us/
Cotter JSHS   300/7-12
   PO Box 70 72626   870-435-6323
   Dennis Copeland, prin.   Fax 435-1300

Cove, Polk, Pop. 383
Van Cove SD   400/K-12
   110 S 5th St 71937   870-387-6832
   Lyn Graves, supt.   Fax 387-2350
   vancove.dmsc.k12.ar.us/
Van-Cove JSHS   200/7-12
   110 S 5th St 71937   870-387-2744
   Terry Thompson, prin.   Fax 387-7961

Crossett, Ashley, Pop. 5,919
Crossett SD   2,400/K-12
   219 Main St 71635   870-364-3112
   Janice Warren, supt.   Fax 364-5499
   csd.k12.ar.us/crossett/Main.htm
Crossett SHS   500/10-12
   219 Main St 71635   870-364-2625
   Roosevelt Early, prin.   Fax 364-4792
Norman JHS   600/7-9
   219 Main St 71635   870-364-4712
   Steve Garrison, prin.   Fax 364-3771

Abiding Faith Christian S   100/PK-12
   1552 Highway 52 W 71635   870-364-3844
   Br. Blaine Beck, dir.   Fax 364-6651
Forest Echoes Technical Institute   Post-Sec.
   1326 Highway 82W 71635   870-364-6414
University of Arkansas - Monticello   Post-Sec.
   1326 Highway 52 W 71635   870-364-6414

Cushman, Independence, Pop. 463
Cushman SD   400/K-12
   PO Box 370 72526   870-793-6321
   Gary Anderson, supt.   Fax 793-7266
   bulldog.k12.ar.us/
Cushman JSHS   200/7-12
   PO Box 370 72526   870-793-6321
   Roger Fisher, prin.   Fax 793-5312

Danville, Yell, Pop. 2,463
Danville SD   800/K-12
   PO Box 939 72833   479-495-4800
   Mickey Billingsley, supt.   Fax 495-4803
   www.dps-littlejohns.net/
Danville JSHS   400/7-12
   PO Box 939 72833   479-495-4810
   Jimmy Cunningham, prin.   Fax 495-4832

Dardanelle, Yell, Pop. 4,319
Dardanelle SD   1,800/K-12
   209 Cedar St 72834   479-229-4111
   John Thompson, supt.   Fax 229-1387
   lizardlink.afsc.k12.ar.us/
Dardanelle HS   500/9-12
   1079 N State Highway 28 72834   479-229-4655
   Marcia Lawrence, prin.   Fax 229-4687
Dardanelle MS   300/7-8
   2032 State Highway 7 N 72834   479-229-4550
   Avis Cotton, prin.   Fax 229-1697

Decatur, Benton, Pop. 1,334
Decatur SD   400/PK-12
   PO Box 97 72722   479-752-3986
   Mike Parrish, supt.   Fax 752-2490
   decatur.k12.ar.us/
Decatur HS   200/8-12
   PO Box 97 72722   479-752-3983
   Tom Pannell, prin.   Fax 752-2491

Deer, Newton
Deer / Mt. Judea SD   500/K-12
   PO Box 56 72628   870-428-5433
   Richard Denniston, supt.   Fax 428-5901
   antler.oursc.k12.ar.us/
Deer JSHS   100/7-12
   PO Box 56 72628   870-428-5288
   Junior C. Edgmon, prin.   Fax 428-5901
Other Schools – See Mount Judea

Delaplaine, Greene, Pop. 127
Greene County Technical SD
   Supt. — See Paragould
Delaplaine JSHS   200/7-12
   PO Box 68 72425   870-249-3216
   Marilyn Jerome, prin.   Fax 249-3898

Delight, Pike, Pop. 303
Delight SD   400/K-12
   PO Box 8 71940   870-379-2214
   Curtis Turner, supt.   Fax 379-2448
Delight JSHS   200/7-12
   PO Box 8 71940   870-379-2214
   Tanya Wilcher, prin.   Fax 379-2448

De Queen, Sevier, Pop. 5,746
De Queen SD   2,000/K-12
   PO Box 950 71832   870-584-4312
   Bill Blackwood, supt.   Fax 642-8881
   leopards.k12.ar.us/
De Queen HS   400/10-12
   1803 W Coulter Ave 71832   870-642-2426
   Judi Jenkins, prin.   Fax 642-4931
De Queen MS   600/6-9
   1803 W Coulter Ave 71832   870-642-2428
   Bob Sikes, prin.   Fax 642-5857

Cossatot Community College Univ. of AR   Post-Sec.
   PO Box 960 71832   870-584-4471

Dermott, Chicot, Pop. 3,562
Dermott SD   600/K-12
   PO Box 380 71638   870-538-1000
   Alton Newton, supt.   Fax 538-1005
   dermott.k12.ar.us
Dermott HS   200/9-12
   PO Box 380 71638   870-538-1030
   Orin Shaw, prin.   Fax 538-1005
Dermott MS   200/6-8
   PO Box 380 71638   870-538-1020
   Terry Murry, prin.   Fax 538-1005

Des Arc, Prairie, Pop. 1,888
Des Arc SD   700/K-12
   600 Main St 72040   870-256-4164
   Rick Green, supt.   Fax 256-3701
   www.geocities.com/desarceagles/
Des Arc JSHS   300/7-12
   600 Main St 72040   870-256-4166
   Ricky Burns, prin.   Fax 256-3701

De Valls Bluff, Prairie, Pop. 762
De Valls Bluff SD   400/K-12
   710 E Sycamore St 72041   870-998-2412
   Charles Eads, supt.   Fax 998-7150
   dvbsd.k12.ar.us/
De Valls Bluff JSHS   200/7-12
   710 E Sycamore St 72041   870-998-2361
   Vernard Metcalf, prin.   Fax 998-7150

De Witt, Arkansas, Pop. 3,442
De Witt SD   1,000/K-12
   422 W 1st St 72042   870-946-3576
   Tom Wilson, supt.   Fax 946-1491
De Witt HS   400/9-12
   1614 S Grandview Dr 72042   870-946-4661
   Glenn Johnston, prin.   Fax 946-2746
De Witt MS   300/6-8
   301 N Jackson St 72042   870-946-3708
   Rick Garner, prin.   Fax 946-1301
Other Schools – See Gillett

Dierks, Howard, Pop. 1,243
Dierks SD   600/K-12
   PO Box 124 71833   870-286-2191
   Terry Ray, supt.   Fax 286-2450
Dierks JSHS   300/7-12
   PO Box 124 71833   870-286-3234
   Gary Bobo, prin.   Fax 286-2450

Donaldson, Hot Spring, Pop. 334
Ouachita SD   400/K-12
   166 Schoolhouse Rd 71941   501-384-2318
   David Hopkins, supt.   Fax 384-5615
Ouachita JSHS   200/7-12
   258 Schoolhouse Rd 71941   501-384-2323
   Ronnie Kissire, prin.   Fax 384-5614

Dover, Pope, Pop. 1,340
Dover SD   1,400/K-12
   PO Box 325 72837   479-331-2916
   Danny Lovelady, supt.   Fax 331-2205
   pirates.afsc.k12.ar.us
Dover HS   400/9-12
   PO Box 325 72837   479-331-2120
   Jamie Churchill, prin.   Fax 331-3286
Dover MS   400/6-8
   PO Box 325 72837   479-331-4814
   Michael Lee, prin.   Fax 331-4965

Dumas, Desha, Pop. 4,966
Dumas SD   1,600/K-12
   213 Adams St 71639   870-382-4571
   Dr. Tom Cox, supt.   Fax 382-4874
   dumas.sesc.k12.ar.us/
Dumas JHS   400/7-9
   315 S College St 71639   870-382-4476
   Paul Morara, prin.   Fax 382-2162
Dumas SHS   300/10-12
   Dan Gill Dr 71639   870-382-4151
   Kelvin Gragg, prin.   Fax 382-8904

Earle, Crittenden, Pop. 2,938
Earle SD   500/K-12
   PO Box 637 72331   870-792-8486
   Jack Crumbly, supt.   Fax 792-8897
Dunbar MS   5-8
   PO Box 637 72331   870-792-8401
   Tagwunda Smith, prin.   Fax 792-8403
Earle HS   200/9-12
   PO Box 637 72331   870-792-8716
   Rickey Nicks, prin.   Fax 792-1004

Elaine, Phillips, Pop. 799
Elaine SD   300/K-12
   PO Box 179 72333   870-827-6395
   Don Hamilton, supt.   Fax 827-6601
   elaine.grsc.k12.ar.us
Elaine JSHS   200/7-12
   PO Box 419 72333   870-827-6345
   Jimmy Lowery, prin.   Fax 827-3908

El Dorado, Union, Pop. 20,849
El Dorado SD   4,600/K-12
   200 W Oak St 71730   870-864-5001
   Bob Watson, supt.   Fax 864-5004
   www.eldoradopublicschools.com
Barton JHS   700/7-8
   400 W Faulkner St 71730   870-864-5051
   Larry Walters, prin.   Fax 864-5064
El Dorado HS   1,300/9-12
   501 Timberlane Dr 71730   870-864-5100
   Bonnie Haynie, prin.   Fax 863-3309
Union S   300/K-12
   6049 Moro Bay Hwy 71730   870-862-4800
   Beverly Overturf, supt.   Fax 862-4807

Parkers Chapel SD   700/K-12
   401 Parkers Chapel Rd 71730   870-862-4641
   John Gross, supt.   Fax 881-5092
Parkers Chapel JSHS   400/7-12
   401 Parkers Chapel Rd 71730   870-862-2360
   Mike LaRue, prin.   Fax 881-5095

South Arkansas Community College   Post-Sec.
   PO Box 7010 71731   870-862-8131

Elkins, Washington, Pop. 1,550
Elkins SD   800/K-12
   PO Box 322 72727   479-643-2172
   Dr. Robert Allen, supt.   Fax 643-3605
   elks.k12.ar.us/
Elkins HS   300/9-12
   PO Box 322 72727   479-643-3381
   Rebecca Martin, prin.   Fax 643-2726

Elkins MS 200/7-8
PO Box 322 72727 479-643-2552
Steve Denzer, prin. Fax 643-4272

Emerson, Columbia, Pop. 355
Emerson - Taylor SD 600/K-12
PO Box 129 71740 870-547-2218
James G. Hines, supt. Fax 547-2077
www.scsc.k12.ar.us/emerson/default2.htm
Emerson HS 200/7-12
400 Church St 71740 870-547-2862
Jim L. Deloach, prin. Fax 547-2077
Other Schools – See Taylor

Emmet, Nevada, Pop. 486
Blevins SD
Supt. — See Blevins
Emmet JSHS 100/7-12
PO Box 330 71835 870-887-2319
Frank Henson, prin. Fax 887-2941

England, Lonoke, Pop. 2,982
England SD 900/K-12
PO Box 410 72046 501-842-2996
Paula Henderson, supt. Fax 842-3698
England HS 300/9-12
501 Pine Bluff Hwy 72046 501-842-2031
Brian Cossey, prin. Fax 842-3263
England MS 200/6-8
1500 NE 1st St 72046 501-842-9606
Sally Loretz, prin. Fax 842-9951

Eudora, Chicot, Pop. 2,664
Eudora SD 600/K-12
111 N Archer St 71640 870-355-6000
Willie Easter, supt. Fax 355-6005
Eudora HS 300/7-12
111 N Archer St 71640 870-355-6040
Alberta Dunbar, prin. Fax 355-6045

Eureka Springs, Carroll, Pop. 2,308
Eureka Springs SD 700/K-12
42 Greenwood Hollow Rd 72632 479-253-5999
Reck Wallis, supt. Fax 253-5955
www.eurekaspringshighschool.com
Eureka Springs HS 200/9-12
44 Kingshighway 72632 479-253-8875
David Childers, prin. Fax 253-8390
Eureka Springs MS 200/5-8
142 Greenwood Hollow Rd 72632 479-253-7716
Dr. Linda Trice, prin. Fax 253-7809

Clear Spring S 100/PK-12
PO Box 511 72632 479-253-7888
Fax 253-0768

Evening Shade, Sharp, Pop. 481
Cave City SD
Supt. — See Cave City
Evening Shade HS 100/7-12
200 School Dr 72532 870-266-3391
Jerry Elkins, prin. Fax 266-3657

Everton, Marion, Pop. 172
Ozark Mountain SD
Supt. — See Saint Joe
Bruno-Pyatt JSHS 200/7-12
4754 Highway 125 S 72633 870-427-5227
Rusty Blevins, prin. Fax 427-5255

Farmington, Washington, Pop. 4,053
Farmington SD 1,400/K-12
42 S Double Springs Rd 72730 479-266-1800
Ron Wright, supt. Fax 267-6030
farmington.k12.ar.us
Farmington HS 500/9-12
278 W Main St 72730 479-266-1860
Blaine Hipes, prin. Fax 267-6065
Lynch MS 600/5-8
359 Rheas Mill Rd 72730 479-266-1840
Carolyn Odom, prin. Fax 267-6051

Fayetteville, Washington, Pop. 62,078
Fayetteville SD 7,600/PK-12
PO Box 849 72702 479-444-3000
Dr. Bobby New, supt. Fax 444-3004
www.fayar.net
Fayetteville SHS East Campus 1,700/10-12
1001 W Stone St 72701 479-444-3050
Dr. Randy Willison, prin. Fax 444-3056
NWACC Regional Technology Center Vo/Tech
2350 W Old Farmington Rd 72701 479-444-3060
Dr. Lee Haight, prin. Fax 444-3017
Ramay JHS 700/8-9
401 S Sang Ave 72701 479-444-3064
Nick Tschepikow, prin. Fax 444-3013
Woodland JHS 600/8-9
15 E Poplar St 72703 479-444-3067
Anita Lawson, prin. Fax 444-3039

Arkansas Aviation Technologies Center Post-Sec.
4248 S School Ave 72701 479-443-2283
Fayetteville Beauty College Post-Sec.
2167 W 6th St 72701 479-442-5181
Fayetteville Christian S 300/PK-12
2006 E Mission Blvd 72703 479-442-2565
Brad Jones, supt. Fax 444-6156
University of Arkansas at Fayetteville Post-Sec.
1 University Of Arkansas 72701 479-575-2000

Flippin, Marion, Pop. 1,364
Flippin SD 900/K-12
210 Alford St 72634 870-453-2270
Dale Query, supt. Fax 453-5059
flippin.ar.schoolwebpages.com
Flippin HS 300/9-12
103 Alford St 72634 870-453-2233
Dr. John Carey, prin. Fax 453-7380
Flippin MS 200/6-8
308 N 1st St 72634 870-453-6464
Robert Gray, prin. Fax 453-6465

Fordyce, Dallas, Pop. 4,513
Fordyce SD 1,200/PK-12
PO Box 706 71742 870-352-3005
Pam Blake, supt. Fax 352-7187
redbugs.dsc.k12.ar.us
Fordyce HS 400/9-12
100 Redbug Blvd 71742 870-352-2126
Bobby Brown, prin. Fax 352-7187
Fordyce MS 400/5-8
75 Redbug Blvd 71742 870-352-7121
Crystal Williams, prin. Fax 352-7187

Foreman, Little River, Pop. 1,086
Foreman SD 500/K-12
PO Box 480 71836 870-542-7211
Larry Lairmore, supt. Fax 542-7225
www.theforemangators.com
Foreman JSHS 300/7-12
PO Box 480 71836 870-542-7212
James Luther, prin. Fax 542-7227

Forrest City, Saint Francis, Pop. 14,351
Forrest City SD 3,500/K-12
845 N Rosser St 72335 870-633-1485
Lee Vent, supt. Fax 633-1415
mustang.grsc.k12.ar.us/
Forrest City JHS 600/8-9
1133 N Division St 72335 870-633-3230
William Ferguson, prin. Fax 633-6066
Forrest City SHS 700/10-12
467 Victoria St 72335 870-633-1464
Abbie Robinson, prin. Fax 261-1844

Palestine Wheatley SD 600/PK-12
7920 Highway 70 W 72335 870-581-2646
John Manning, supt. Fax 581-4420
Other Schools – See Palestine, Wheatley

Calvary Christian S 200/K-12
1611 N Washington St 72335 870-633-5333
Suzanne Hess, prin. Fax 633-6238
Crowley's Ridge Technical Institute Post-Sec.
1620 Newcastle Rd 72335 870-633-5411
East Arkansas Community College Post-Sec.
1700 New Castle Rd 72335 870-633-4480

Fort Smith, Sebastian, Pop. 81,562
Fort Smith SD 12,700/K-12
PO Box 1948 72902 479-785-2501
Ben Gooden Ed.D., supt. Fax 785-1722
www.fssc.k12.ar.us/
Chaffin JHS 700/7-9
3025 Massard Rd 72903 479-452-2226
Dr. Ralph Spencer, prin. Fax 478-3103
Darby JHS 600/7-9
616 N 14th St 72901 479-783-4159
Michael Farrell, prin. Fax 784-8165
Kimmons JHS 700/7-9
2201 N 50th St 72904 479-785-2451
Martin Mahan, prin. Fax 784-8177
Northside SHS 1,300/10-12
2301 N B St 72901 479-783-1171
Ray Martin, prin. Fax 784-8114
Ramsey JHS 900/7-9
3201 Jenny Lind Rd 72901 479-783-5115
Dennis Siebenmorgen, prin. Fax 784-8119
Southside SHS 1,500/10-12
4100 Gary St 72903 479-646-7371
Wayne Haver, prin. Fax 648-8204
Adult Education Adult
501 S 20th St 72901 479-785-1232
Sharon Ellis, dir. Fax 784-8184

Mellie's Beauty College Post-Sec.
311 S 16th St 72901 479-782-5059
Trinity JHS 200/7-9
1205 S Albert Pike Ave 72903 479-782-2451
Ann Finch, prin. Fax 782-7263
Union Christian Academy 700/PK-12
4201 Windsor Dr 72904 479-782-0282
Tom Waller, prin. Fax 782-6622
University of Arkansas at Fort Smith Post-Sec.
PO Box 3649 72913 479-788-7000

Fouke, Miller, Pop. 844
Fouke SD 1,000/K-12
PO Box 20 71837 870-653-4311
Paulette Smith, supt. Fax 653-2856
Fouke HS 300/9-12
PO Box 20 71837 870-653-4551
Rhonda Souter, prin. Fax 653-7823
Fouke MS 200/6-8
PO Box 20 71837 870-653-2304
Faye Kay Brown, prin. Fax 653-7840

Fox, Stone
Mountain View SD
Supt. — See Mountain View
Rural Special HS 100/7-12
13237 Highway 263 72051 870-363-4202
Brent Howard, prin. Fax 363-4222

Gassville, Baxter, Pop. 1,866

North Central Christian S 100/PK-12
190 Whitaker Ln 72635 870-424-6622
Judi Meador, prin. Fax 424-6622

Gentry, Benton, Pop. 2,468
Gentry SD 1,400/K-12
201 S Giles Ave 72734 479-736-2253
Dr. Randy Barrett, supt. Fax 736-2245
gentrypioneers.com/
Gentry HS 400/9-12
995 Pioneer Ln 72734 479-736-2666
Robert King, prin. Fax 736-5202
Gentry MS 300/6-8
1055 Pioneer Ln 72734 479-736-2251
Larry Cozens, prin. Fax 736-5198

Ozark Adventist Academy 200/9-12
20997 Dawn Hill East Rd 72734 479-736-2221
Dr. Lyle Hansen, prin. Fax 736-2224

Gillett, Arkansas, Pop. 795
De Witt SD
Supt. — See De Witt
Gillett JSHS 100/7-12
PO Box 179 72055 870-548-2316
Jon Howell, prin. Fax 548-2281

Gosnell, Mississippi, Pop. 3,765
Gosnell SD 1,300/K-12
600 N State Highway 181 72315 870-532-4000
Stan Williams, supt. Fax 532-4002
pirates.crsc.k12.ar.us
Gosnell JSHS 600/7-12
600 N State Highway 181 72315 870-532-4010
Bonard Mace, prin. Fax 532-4031

Gravette, Benton, Pop. 2,142
Gravette SD 1,600/PK-12
609 Birmingham St SE 72736 479-787-4100
Curtis Spann, supt. Fax 787-4108
lions.k12.ar.us/
Gravette HS 500/9-12
607 Dallas St SE 72736 479-787-4180
Jo Ellen Hastings, prin. Fax 787-4188
Gravette JHS 300/7-8
605 Dallas St SE 72736 479-787-4160
Mitchell Wilber, prin. Fax 787-4178

Greenbrier, Faulkner, Pop. 3,357
Greenbrier SD 2,400/K-12
4 School Dr 72058 501-679-4808
Mike Mertens, supt. Fax 679-1024
gps.k12.ar.us/
Greenbrier JHS 400/8-9
10 School Dr 72058 501-679-3433
Amy Burchfield, prin. Fax 679-1055
Greenbrier SHS 500/10-12
72 Green Valley Dr 72058 501-679-4236
Steve Lucas, prin. Fax 679-5765

Green Forest, Carroll, Pop. 2,822
Green Forest SD 1,200/K-12
PO Box 1950 72638 870-438-5201
Dr. Larry Bennett, supt. Fax 438-6214
www.gf.k12.ar.us
Green Forest JSHS 500/8-12
PO Box 1950 72638 870-438-5203
Dave Borg, prin. Fax 438-4588

Greenland, Washington, Pop. 974
Greenland SD 1,000/K-12
PO Box 57 72737 479-521-2366
Ronald Browner, supt. Fax 521-1480
Greenland HS 200/9-12
PO Box 57 72737 479-521-2366
Jay Gardenhire, prin. Fax 521-1350
Greenland MS 300/5-8
PO Box 57 72737 479-521-2366
David Hudgens, prin. Fax 251-1203

Greenwood, Sebastian, Pop. 7,493
Greenwood SD 3,200/K-12
420 N Main St 72936 479-996-4142
Dr. Kay Johnson, supt. Fax 996-4143
www.greenwoodarkansasschools.com
Greenwood SHS 700/10-12
440 E Gary St 72936 479-996-4141
Jerry Efurd, prin. Fax 996-6548
Wells JHS 500/8-9
1211 Raymond E Wells Dr 72936 479-996-7440
Kevin Hesslen, prin. Fax 996-7469

Greers Ferry, Cleburne, Pop. 946
West Side SD 500/K-12
7295 Greers Ferry Rd 72067 501-825-6258
Russell A. Hester, supt. Fax 825-6258
westside.afsc.k12.ar.us/
West Side JSHS 300/7-12
7295 Greers Ferry Rd 72067 501-825-7241
Rick Waters, prin. Fax 825-6258

Gurdon, Clark, Pop. 2,276
Gurdon SD 900/K-12
314 School St 71743 870-353-4454
Bobby Smithson, supt. Fax 353-4455
Cabe MS 300/5-8
7780 Highway 67 S 71743 870-353-4311
Libby White, prin. Fax 353-5149
Gurdon HS 300/9-12
7777 Highway 67 S 71743 870-353-5123
Leonard Gills, prin. Fax 353-5131

Guy, Faulkner, Pop. 205
Guy-Perkins SD 400/K-12
492 Highway 25 N 72061 501-679-7224
Kerry Saylors, supt. Fax 679-3508
thunderbird.k12.ar.us/
Guy-Perkins HS 200/7-12
492 Highway 25 N 72061 501-679-3507
David Westenhover, prin. Fax 679-3508

Hackett, Sebastian, Pop. 724
Hackett SD 600/K-12
102 N Oak St 72937 479-638-8822
William C. Pittman, supt. Fax 638-7106
Hackett JSHS 300/7-12
102 N Oak St 72937 479-638-7003
Neal Perrin, prin. Fax 638-8210

Hamburg, Ashley, Pop. 2,895
Hamburg SD 1,700/PK-12
521 E Lincoln St 71646 870-853-9851
Carlton Lawrence, supt. Fax 853-2842
se.sesc.k12.ar.us/hamburg/
Hamburg JHS 400/7-9
521 E Lincoln St 71646 870-853-2811
Bob Davis, prin. Fax 853-2835
Hamburg SHS 300/10-12
1109 S Main St 71646 870-853-9856
John L. Wesson, prin. Fax 853-2850

Hampton, Calhoun, Pop. 1,529
Hampton SD 700/K-12
PO Box 1176 71744 870-798-2229
Max N. Dyson, supt. Fax 798-2239
www.scsc.k12.ar.us/Hampton/

Hampton JSHS | 300/7-12
PO Box 1176 71744 | 870-798-2742
William Anders, prin. | Fax 798-2239

Hardy, Sharp, Pop. 753
Highland SD | 1,600/K-12
PO Box 419 72542 | 870-856-3275
Ronnie Brogdon, supt. | Fax 856-2765
highlandrebels.k12.ar.us/
Highland JSHS | 600/8-12
PO Box 419 72542 | 870-856-3273
Don Carithers, prin. | Fax 856-2765

Harrisburg, Poinsett, Pop. 2,180
Harrisburg SD | 1,100/K-12
207 W Estes St 72432 | 870-578-2416
Danny Sample, supt. | Fax 578-9366
sting.k12.ar.us
Harrisburg HS | 300/9-12
207 W Estes St 72432 | 870-578-2417
Steve Rorex, prin. | Fax 578-2338
Harrisburg MS | 400/5-8
207 W Estes St 72432 | 870-578-2410
Karli Saracini, prin. | Fax 578-2338

Harrison, Boone, Pop. 12,375
Harrison SD | 2,800/K-12
400 S Sycamore St 72601 | 870-741-7600
Dr. Jerry Moody, supt. | Fax 741-4520
harrison.k12.ar.us/
Harrison JHS | 700/7-9
515 S Pine St 72601 | 870-741-3496
Mike Stokes, prin. | Fax 741-0101
Harrison SHS | 600/10-12
925 Goblin Dr 72601 | 870-741-8223
Ronny Brown, prin. | Fax 741-2606

Grace Christian S | 100/PK-12
PO Box 7 72602 | 870-741-8505
Yvonne Adamson, prin. | Fax 741-6605
North Arkansas College | Post-Sec.
1515 Pioneer Ridge Dr 72601 | 870-743-3000

Hartford, Sebastian, Pop. 777
Hartford SD | 400/K-12
PO Box 489 72938 | 479-639-5002
John Hunt, supt. | Fax 639-2158
Hartford JSHS | 200/7-12
PO Box 489 72938 | 479-639-2239
Gary Walker, prin. | Fax 639-2158

Hartman, Johnson, Pop. 612
Westside SD | 600/K-12
122 Thompson St 72840 | 479-497-1991
Roy L. Hester, supt. | Fax 497-9037
westsiderebels.k12.ar.us
Other Schools – See Coal Hill

Hattieville, Conway
Wonderview SD | 500/K-12
2436 Highway 95 72063 | 501-354-0211
Steve Thomas, supt. | Fax 354-6071
wonder.k12.ar.us
Wonderview JSHS | 200/7-12
2436 Highway 95 72063 | 501-354-8668
Danny Heard, prin. | Fax 354-8602

Havana, Yell, Pop. 392
Western Yell County SD | 400/K-12
PO Box 214 72842 | 479-476-4116
Brad Spikes, supt. | Fax 476-4115
wolverines.k12.ar.us
Western Yell County JSHS | 200/7-12
PO Box 214 72842 | 479-476-4100
Barry Fisher, prin. | Fax 476-4111

Hazen, Prairie, Pop. 1,585
Hazen SD | 400/K-12
477 N Hazen Ave 72064 | 870-255-4549
Danny Hazelwood, supt. | Fax 255-4508
Hazen JSHS | 200/7-12
477 N Hazen Ave 72064 | 870-255-4546
Roxanne Bradow, prin. | Fax 255-4508

Heber Springs, Cleburne, Pop. 6,740
Heber Springs SD | 1,700/K-12
800 W Moore St 72543 | 501-362-6712
Rick Rana, supt. | Fax 362-0613
hssdweb.afsc.k12.ar.us/
Heber Springs HS | 500/9-12
800 W Moore St 72543 | 501-362-3141
Harold Wilson, prin. | Fax 362-9931
Heber Springs MS | 400/6-8
800 W Moore St 72543 | 501-362-2488
Stanley Wildman, prin. | Fax 362-2193

Hector, Pope, Pop. 501
Hector SD | 700/K-12
11520 SR 27 72843 | 479-284-2021
Eric Armour, supt. | Fax 284-2350
wildcats.afsc.k12.ar.us/
Hector JSHS | 300/7-12
11601 SR 27 72843 | 479-284-3536
David Waddell, prin. | Fax 284-5023

Helena, Phillips, Pop. 5,817
Helena-West Helena SD | 3,200/K-12
305 Valley Dr 72342 | 870-338-4425
Rudolph Howard, supt. | Fax 338-4434
hwh.grsc.k12.ar.us/
Other Schools – See West Helena

Phillips Comm. Coll. of the Univ. of AR | Post-Sec.
PO Box 785 72342 | 870-338-6474

Hermitage, Bradley, Pop. 774
Hermitage SD | 600/K-12
PO Box 38 71647 | 870-463-2246
John Jordan, supt. | Fax 463-8520
se.sesc.k12.ar.us/hermitage
Hermitage JSHS | 300/7-12
PO Box 190 71647 | 870-463-2235
Neish Robinson, prin. | Fax 463-2122

Hope, Hempstead, Pop. 10,453
Hope SD | 2,700/K-12
117 E 2nd St 71801 | 870-722-2700
Kenneth Muldrew, supt. | Fax 777-4087
hope.k12.ar.us
Hope HS | 700/9-12
1701 S Main St 71801 | 870-777-3451
Tommy Morrison, prin. | Fax 722-2736
Yerger MS | 400/7-8
400 E 9th St 71801 | 870-722-2770
Larry Muldrew, prin. | Fax 722-2707

Spring Hill SD | 500/K-12
633 Highway 355 W 71801 | 870-777-8236
Don Collins, supt. | Fax 777-9200
Spring Hill JSHS | 300/7-12
633 Highway 355 W 71801 | 870-722-7430
Dani Elledge, prin. | Fax 722-7425

University of Arkansas Community College | Post-Sec.
PO Box 140 71802 | 870-777-5722

Horatio, Sevier, Pop. 988
Horatio SD | 800/PK-12
PO Box 435 71842 | 870-832-2340
Joseph Cornelison, supt. | Fax 832-2174
Horatio JSHS | 400/7-12
PO Box 435 71842 | 870-832-2341
James Dobbins, prin. | Fax 832-2174

Hot Springs National Park, Garland, Pop. 36,356
Cutter-Morning Star SD | 600/K-12
2801 Spring St 71901 | 501-262-2414
Carl Hughes, supt. | Fax 262-0670
eaglesnest.dsc.k12.ar.us/
Cutter-Morning Star JSHS | 300/7-12
2801 Spring St 71901 | 501-262-1220
Charles Ferriter, prin. | Fax 262-3771

Fountain Lake SD | 1,100/K-12
4207 Park Ave 71901 | 501-623-5655
Dr. Lowell Hightower, supt. | Fax 623-6447
flcobra.k12.ar.us/
Fountain Lake JSHS | 500/7-12
4207 Park Ave 71901 | 501-623-5101
Steve Campbell, prin. | Fax 624-4053

Hot Springs SD | 3,400/K-12
400 Linwood Ave 71913 | 501-624-3372
Roy Rowe, supt. | Fax 620-7829
hsprings.dsc.k12.ar.us
Hot Springs HS | 800/9-12
701 Emory St 71913 | 501-624-5286
Jim Gentry, prin. | Fax 620-7820
Hot Springs MS | 800/6-8
700 Main St 71913 | 501-624-5228
Danny Stanford, prin. | Fax 620-7833

Lakeside SD | 2,500/K-12
2837 Malvern Ave 71901 | 501-262-1880
Shawn Cook, supt. | Fax 262-2732
lakeside.rams.dsc.k12.ar.us
Lakeside JHS | 500/8-9
2865 Malvern Ave 71901 | 501-262-1316
James Fotioo, prin. | Fax 262-6232
Lakeside SHS | 600/10-12
2871 Malvern Ave 71901 | 501-262-1530
Darn Beckwith, prin. | Fax 262-6205

Arkansas Career Training Institute | Post-Sec.
105 Reserve St 71901 | 501-624-4411
Christian Ministries Academy | 100/K-12
PO Box 8500 71910 | 501-624-1952
Paul Kern, prin. | Fax 318-2624
Crossgate Christian Academy | 200/K-12
3102 E Grand Ave 71901 | 501-262-4222
Charles Utt, prin. | Fax 262-9825
Hot Springs Beauty College | Post-Sec.
100 Cones Rd 71901 | 501-624-0203
Lighthouse Christian S | 50/PK-12
2535 E Grand Ave 71901 | 501-262-4560
National Park Community College | Post-Sec.
101 College Dr 71913 | 501-760-4222

Hoxie, Lawrence, Pop. 2,771
Hoxie SD | 900/K-12
PO Box 240 72433 | 870-886-2401
Dennis Truxler, supt. | Fax 886-4252
green.nesc.k12.ar.us/
Hoxie JSHS | 400/7-12
PO Box 240 72433 | 870-886-4254
Tim Gardner, prin. | Fax 886-4253

Hughes, Saint Francis, Pop. 1,770
Hughes SD | 700/K-12
PO Box 9 72348 | 870-339-2570
Randy Crowder, supt. | Fax 339-3317
hughes.grsc.k12.ar.us/
Hughes JSHS | 400/7-12
PO Box 9 72348 | 870-339-2580
Judy Manning, prin. | Fax 339-3317

Huntsville, Madison, Pop. 1,992
Huntsville SD | 2,500/K-12
PO Box F 72740 | 479-738-2011
Dr. Alvin L. Lievsay, supt. | Fax 738-2563
eagle.nwsc.k12.ar.us/
Huntsville HS | 700/9-12
PO Box 1377 72740 | 479-738-2500
Michael Gray, prin. | Fax 738-2849
Huntsville MS | 300/7-8
PO Box G 72740 | 479-738-6520
Mike Cain, prin. | Fax 738-6259
Other Schools – See Saint Paul

Huttig, Union, Pop. 718
Strong-Huttig SD
Supt. — See Strong
Huttig JHS | 50/7-8
PO Box 408 71747 | 870-943-2202
James Jones, prin. | Fax 943-2883

Imboden, Lawrence, Pop. 660
Sloan-Hendrix SD | 600/K-12
PO Box 1080 72434 | 870-869-2384
Michael Holland, supt. | Fax 869-2384
shsd.k12.ar.us
Sloan-Hendrix JSHS | 300/7-12
PO Box 1080 72434 | 870-869-2361
Mitch Walton, prin. | Fax 869-2361

Jacksonville, Pulaski, Pop. 30,393
Pulaski County Special SD
Supt. — See Little Rock
Jacksonville JHS - Boys | 700/8-9
1320 School Dr 72076 | 501-982-1587
Mike Nellums, prin. | Fax 241-2139
Jacksonville MS - Girls | 900/6-8
201 Sharp Dr 72076 | 501-982-9407
Angela Romney, prin. | Fax 241-2108
Jacksonville SHS | 800/10-12
2400 Linda Ln 72076 | 501-982-2128
Ken Clark, prin. | Fax 982-1692
North Pulaski HS | 900/9-12
718 Harris Rd 72076 | 501-982-9436
Brenda Allen, prin. | Fax 241-2256

Arthur's Beauty College | Post-Sec.
2600 John Harden Dr 72076 | 501-982-8987

Jasper, Newton, Pop. 498
Jasper SD | 700/K-12
PO Box 446 72641 | 870-446-2223
Chuck Archer, supt. | Fax 446-2305
jhspirates.k12.ar.us/
Jasper JSHS | 200/7-12
PO Box 446 72641 | 870-446-2223
Charles Emmett, prin. | Fax 446-2305
Other Schools – See Kingston, Oark

Jessieville, Garland
Jessieville SD | 800/K-12
PO Box 4 71949 | 501-984-5381
George Foshee, supt. | Fax 984-4200
Jessieville JSHS | 400/7-12
PO Box 4 71949 | 501-984-5011
Steve Wright, prin. | Fax 984-4200

Jonesboro, Craighead, Pop. 57,435
Jonesboro SD | 4,900/PK-12
2506 Southwest Sq 72401 | 870-933-5800
Steve Singleton, supt. | Fax 933-5838
www.jps.k12.ar.us/
Area Technical Center | Vo/Tech
1727 S Main St 72401 | 870-933-5891
Carmack Sanders, prin. | Fax 933-5890
Camp JHS | 600/7-9
1814 W Nettleton Ave 72401 | 870-933-5820
| Fax 933-5837
Jonesboro SHS | 1,000/10-12
301 Hurricane Dr 72401 | 870-933-5881
Terry Trotter, prin. | Fax 933-5812
MacArthur JHS | 600/7-9
1615 Wilkins Ave 72401 | 870-933-5840
Dr. Brad Faught, prin. | Fax 933-5848

Nettleton SD | 2,600/K-12
2616 Progress St 72401 | 870-910-7800
James Dunivan, supt. | Fax 910-7854
nettletonschools.net
Nettleton JHS | 600/7-9
4208 Chieftan Ln 72401 | 870-910-7819
Grace Petersen, prin. | Fax 910-6984
Nettleton SHS | 500/10-12
4201 Chieftan Ln 72401 | 870-910-7805
Tommy Fowler, prin. | Fax 910-7804

Valley View SD | 1,200/K-12
2131 Valley View Dr 72404 | 870-935-6200
Dr. Radius Baker, supt. | Fax 972-0373
blazers.k12.ar.us/
Valley View JHS | 400/7-9
2118 Valley View Dr Ste A 72404 | 870-935-4602
Barry Jones, prin. | Fax 935-6202
Valley View SHS | 300/10-12
2118 Valley View Dr Ste B 72404 | 870-932-3737
Robert Lindley, prin. | Fax 935-6202
Adult Education Center | Adult
2311 E Nettleton Ave 72401 | 870-933-5896
Steve Clayton, prin. | Fax 933-5889

Westside Consolidated SD | 1,400/K-12
1630 Highway 91 W 72404 | 870-935-7503
Dr. James Best, supt. | Fax 935-2123
warriors.crsc.k12.ar.us/
Westside JHS | 8-9
1630 Highway 91 W 72404 | 870-935-7502
Eddie Mitchell, prin. | Fax 268-9111
Westside SHS | 300/10-12
1630 Highway 91 W 72404 | 870-935-7501
Pat Lundahl, prin. | Fax 268-9119

Ridgefield Christian S | 300/PK-12
3824 Casey Springs Rd 72404 | 870-932-7540
Randy Johnson, admin. | Fax 931-9711

Judsonia, White, Pop. 2,077
Riverview SD
Supt. — See Searcy
Riverview-Judsonia MS | 200/5-8
916 Judson Ave 72081 | 501-729-3371
Tony Stark, prin. | Fax 729-5306

White County Central SD | 700/K-12
3259 Highway 157 72081 | 501-729-3992
Monty Betts, supt. | Fax 729-3992
wccsdweb.wmsc.k12.ar.us/
White County Central JSHS | 300/7-12
3259 Highway 157 72081 | 501-729-3947
Jerry Lacy, prin. | Fax 729-3947

Junction City, Union, Pop. 709
Junction City SD | 600/K-12
PO Box 790 71749 | 870-924-4575
Gary Wayman, supt. | Fax 924-4565
www.scsc.k12.ar.us/junctioncity/

Junction City JSHS 300/7-12
PO Box 790 71749 870-924-4576
Dale Hux, prin. Fax 924-4565

Kensett, White, Pop. 1,715
Riverview SD
Supt. — See Searcy
Riverview-Kensett MS 200/5-8
701 W Dandridge St 72082 501-742-3346
Pat Falcinelli, prin. Fax 742-5539

Kingston, Madison
Jasper SD
Supt. — See Jasper
Kingston JSHS 7-12
PO Box 149 72742 479-665-2995
Earl Rowe, prin. Fax 665-2577

Kirby, Pike
Kirby SD 400/K-12
PO Box 9 71950 870-398-4212
Jeff Alexander, supt. Fax 398-4442
kirby.dsc.k12.ar.us
Kirby JSHS 200/7-12
PO Box 9 71950 870-398-4211
Carla Golden, prin. Fax 398-5413

Lake City, Craighead, Pop. 1,982
Riverside SD 800/K-12
PO Box 178 72437 870-237-4329
Larry Nowlin, supt. Fax 237-4867
Riverside SHS 200/10-12
PO Box 178 72437 870-237-4328
Tommy Knight, prin. Fax 237-4867
Other Schools – See Caraway

Lake Village, Chicot, Pop. 2,702
Lakeside SD 1,000/PK-12
1110 S Lakeshore Dr 71653 870-265-2284
Joyce L. Vaught, supt. Fax 265-5466
lakeside.k12.ar.us/
Lakeside HS 300/9-12
1110 S Lakeshore Dr 71653 870-265-2232
Linda Armour, prin. Fax 265-7302
Lakeside MS 300/6-8
1110 S Lakeshore Dr 71653 870-265-2970
Arthur Gray, prin. Fax 265-7309

Lamar, Johnson, Pop. 1,508
Lamar SD 800/K-12
301 Elberta St 72846 479-885-3907
Dennis Meins, supt. Fax 885-2380
www.serve.com/warriors/
Lamar HS 400/9-12
301 Elberta St 72846 479-885-3344
Mary Jean Nordin, prin. Fax 885-3842
Lamar MS 5-8
301 Elberta St 72846 479-885-6511
Johanna Kenner, prin. Fax 885-2384

Lavaca, Sebastian, Pop. 1,918
Lavaca SD 800/K-12
PO Box 8 72941 479-674-5611
John Ciesla, supt. Fax 674-2271
lavacapublicschools.k12.ar.us/
Lavaca HS 300/9-12
PO Box 8 72941 479-674-5612
Jason Lockhart, prin. Fax 674-2271
Lavaca MS 300/5-8
PO Box 8 72941 479-674-5618
Marcia Ford, prin. Fax 674-5518

Leachville, Mississippi, Pop. 1,874
Buffalo Island Central SD
Supt. — See Monette
Buffalo Island Central JHS 200/7-9
PO Box 110 72438 870-539-6883
Randy Rose, prin. Fax 539-6696

Lead Hill, Boone, Pop. 289
Lead Hill SD 400/K-12
PO Box 20 72644 870-436-5249
Dr. Shari Marshall, supt. Fax 436-5946
Lead Hill JSHS 200/7-12
PO Box 20 72644 870-436-5677
Alan King, prin. Fax 436-6827

Lepanto, Poinsett, Pop. 2,091
East Poinsett County SD 800/K-12
502 McClellan St 72354 870-475-2472
Michael Pierce, supt. Fax 475-3531
epc.k12.ar.us/
East Poinsett County JSHS 400/7-12
502 McClellan St 72354 870-475-2331
Gary Williams, prin. Fax 475-2206

Leslie, Searcy, Pop. 460
Searcy County SD
Supt. — See Marshall
Leslie MSHS 6-12
RR 1 Box 100 72645 870-447-2431
Connie Richardson, prin. Fax 447-2831
North Central Career Center Vo/Tech
PO Box 187 72645 870-447-6111
Fax 447-2872

Lewisville, Lafayette, Pop. 1,243
Lafayette County SD 1,000/K-12
PO Box 950 71845 870-921-5500
Dr. Winston Simpson, supt. Fax 921-4277
lafayette.k12.ar.us/
Lafayette County MS 300/5-8
PO Box 950 71845 870-921-4275
Sammy Bray, prin. Fax 921-3812
Other Schools – See Stamps

Lexa, Phillips, Pop. 310
Barton-Lexa SD 700/K-12
9546 Highway 85 72355 870-572-7294
Roy Kirkland, supt. Fax 572-4713
blsd.grsc.k12.ar.us
Barton JSHS 300/7-12
9546 Highway 85 72355 870-572-6867
David Bagley, prin. Fax 572-4713

Lincoln, Washington, Pop. 1,860
Lincoln Consolidated SD 1,100/K-12
PO Box 1127 72744 479-824-3010
Jim Lewis, supt. Fax 824-3045
wolfpride.k12.ar.us
Lincoln HS 300/9-12
201 E School St 72744 479-824-3010
Rebecca Guthrie, prin. Fax 824-3042
Lincoln MS 300/6-8
201 E School St 72744 479-824-3010
Elaine King, prin. Fax 824-3042

Little Rock, Pulaski, Pop. 184,053
Little Rock SD 24,800/PK-12
810 W Markham St 72201 501-447-1000
Dr. Roy G. Brooks, supt. Fax 447-1001
www.lrsd.org/
Central HS 2,100/9-12
1500 S Park St 72202 501-447-1400
Nancy Rousseau, prin. Fax 447-1401
Cloverdale Magnet MS 800/6-8
6300 Hinkson Rd 72209 501-447-2500
Frederick Fields, prin. Fax 447-2501
Dunbar Magnet MS 800/6-8
1100 Wright Ave 72206 501-447-2600
Eunice Thrasher, prin. Fax 447-2601
Fair Magnet HS 1,000/9-12
13420 David O Dodd Rd 72210 501-447-1700
Randy Rutherford, prin. Fax 447-1701
Forest Heights MS 800/6-8
5901 Evergreen Dr 72205 501-447-2700
Dr. Deborah Price, prin. Fax 447-2701
Hall HS 1,300/9-12
6700 H St 72205 501-447-1900
John Bacon, prin. Fax 447-1901
Henderson Magnet MS 700/6-8
401 John Barrow Rd 72205 501-447-2800
Marvin Burton, prin. Fax 447-2801
Mann Magnet MS 900/6-8
1000 E Roosevelt Rd 72206 501-447-3100
James Fullerton, prin. Fax 447-3101
McClellan Magnet HS 1,000/9-12
9417 Geyer Springs Rd 72209 501-447-2100
Lawrence Buck, prin. Fax 447-2101
Metropolitan Career-Tech Center Vo/Tech
7701 Scott Hamilton Dr 72209 501-447-1200
Mike Peterson, prin. Fax 447-1201
Parkview Magnet HS 1,100/9-12
2501 John Barrow Rd 72204 501-447-2300
Dr. Linda Brown, prin. Fax 447-2301
Pulaski Heights MS 700/6-8
401 N Pine St 72205 501-447-3200
Dr. Daniel W. Whitehorn, prin. Fax 447-3201
Southwest MS 500/6-8
3301 S Bryant St 72204 501-447-3400
David Smith, prin. Fax 447-3401
Adult Education Center Adult
4800 W 26th St 72204 501-447-1850
Paulette Martin, prin. Fax 447-1851
Other Schools – See Mabelvale

Pulaski County Special SD 18,700/PK-12
PO Box 8601 72216 501-490-2000
Dr. Robert Clowers, supt. Fax 490-0483
www.pcssd.org
Fuller MS 700/6-8
808 E Dixon Rd 72206 501-490-5730
Don Booth, prin. Fax 490-5736
Mills HS 1,000/9-12
1205 E Dixon Rd 72206 501-490-5700
Bill Barnes, prin. Fax 490-5709
Robinson HS 700/9-12
21501 Highway 10 72223 501-868-2400
Joy Plants, prin. Fax 868-2405
Robinson MS 500/6-8
21001 Highway 10 72223 501-868-2410
John Pearce, prin. Fax 868-2441
Other Schools – See Jacksonville, North Little Rock,
Sherwood

Arkansas Baptist College Post-Sec.
1600 Bishop St 72202 501-372-6883
Arkansas Baptist JSHS 300/7-12
8400 Ranch Blvd 72223 501-868-5121
Randy Goldsmith, prin. Fax 868-5403
Arkansas Beauty School Post-Sec.
5108 Baseline Rd 72209 501-562-5673
Arkansas School for the Blind Post-Sec.
PO Box 668 72203 501-296-1810
Arkansas School for the Deaf Post-Sec.
PO Box 3811 72203 501-324-9514
Baptist Schools of Allied Health Post-Sec.
11900 Colonel Glenn Rd 72210 501-202-7415
Bee-Jay's Hairstyling Academy Post-Sec.
1907 Hinson Loop Rd 72212 501-224-2442
Catholic HS for Boys 700/9-12
6300 Father Tribou St 72205 501-664-3939
Steve Straessle, prin. Fax 664-6549
Central Arkansas Radiation Therapy Inst. Post-Sec.
PO Box 55050 72215 501-664-8573
Eastern College of Health Vocations Post-Sec.
6423 Forbing Rd 72209 501-568-0211
Eaton Beauty Stylist College Post-Sec.
814 W 7th St 72201 501-375-0211
Episcopal Collegiate S 400/6-12
1701 Cantrell Rd 72201 501-372-1194
Mercer Neale, hdmstr. Fax 372-2160
ITT Technical Institute Post-Sec.
4520 S University Ave 72204 501-565-5550
Little Rock Christian Academy 1,200/K-12
PO Box 17450 72222 501-868-9822
Boyd Chitwood, pres. Fax 868-8766
Lutheran HS 200/9-12
6711 W Markham St 72205 501-663-5117
Mary Kathryn Stein, prin. Fax 663-1017
Mt. St. Mary Academy 600/9-12
3224 Kavanaugh Blvd 72205 501-664-8006
Becky Henle, prin. Fax 664-4382
Philander Smith College Post-Sec.
812 W 13th St 72202 501-375-9845

Pulaski Academy 1,300/PK-12
12701 Hinson Rd 72212 501-604-1923
Ellis Arnold, prin. Fax 225-1974
Remington College Post-Sec.
19 Remington Rd 72204 501-312-0007
St. Vincent Infirmary Medical Center Post-Sec.
2 Saint Vincent Cir 72205 501-660-3910
Southwest Christian Academy 500/PK-12
11301 Geyer Springs Rd 72209 501-565-3276
Sharon Stewart, prin. Fax 565-3567
University of Arkansas at Little Rock Post-Sec.
2801 S University Ave 72204 501-569-3000
University of Arkansas/Medical Sciences Post-Sec.
4301 W Markham St 72205 501-686-5000
Velvatex College of Beauty Culture Post-Sec.
1520 Dr Martin Luther King 72202 501-372-9678
Word of Outreach Christian Academy 200/PK-12
3300 Asher Ave 72204 501-663-0300
Cheryl Washington, admin. Fax 558-0203

Lockesburg, Sevier, Pop. 712
Lockesburg SD 400/K-12
PO Box 88 71846 870-289-5161
Velma Owens, supt. Fax 289-5189
Lockesburg JSHS 200/7-12
PO Box 88 71846 870-289-2431
Brenda Leeper, prin. Fax 289-3264

Lonoke, Lonoke, Pop. 4,444
Lonoke SD 1,800/K-12
401 W Holly St 72086 501-676-2042
Sharron Havens Ed.D., supt. Fax 676-7074
lonokeschools.org/
Lonoke HS 600/9-12
501 W Academy St 72086 501-676-2476
Phynaus Wilson, prin. Fax 676-3716
Lonoke MS 400/6-8
200 E Locust St 72086 501-676-6670
Jeannie Holt, prin. Fax 676-7013

Lynn, Lawrence, Pop. 312
Hillcrest SD
Supt. — See Strawberry
Hillcrest JHS 100/7-9
PO Box 70 72440 870-528-3462
Gregg Cooper, prin. Fax 528-3766

Mabelvale, Pulaski
Little Rock SD
Supt. — See Little Rock
Mabelvale Magnet MS 700/6-8
10811 Mabelvale West Rd 72103 501-447-3000
Ann Blaylock, prin. Fax 447-3001

Mc Crory, Woodruff, Pop. 1,862
McCrory SD 600/K-12
PO Box 930 72101 870-731-2535
Barry Scott, supt. Fax 731-2536
mccrorynt.wrnsc.k12.ar.us/
Mc Crory JSHS 300/7-12
PO Box 930 72101 870-731-2851
Lincoln Daniels, prin. Fax 731-2574

Mc Gehee, Desha, Pop. 4,527
McGehee SD 1,200/K-12
PO Box 767 71654 870-222-3670
Diane Barrett, supt. Fax 222-6957
owls.k12.ar.us/
Mc Gehee JSHS 500/7-12
PO Box 767 71654 870-222-5026
Remmel Grayson, prin. Fax 222-5838

Baptist School of Nursing-SE Post-Sec.
Highway 1 NE 71654

Magazine, Logan, Pop. 912
Magazine SD 500/K-12
292 E Priddy St 72943 479-969-2566
Jarad Cleveland, supt. Fax 969-8740
magazinerattlers.k12.ar.us
Leftwich JS 200/7-12
292 E Priddy St 72943 479-969-2640
Sandra Beck, prin. Fax 969-8740

Magnolia, Columbia, Pop. 10,547
Magnolia SD 3,000/PK-12
PO Box 649 71754 870-234-4933
Dr. John H. Moore, supt. Fax 901-2508
panther.scsc.k12.ar.us/
Magnolia JHS 700/7-9
540 E North St 71753 870-234-2206
Chris Hurley, prin. Fax 234-1293
Magnolia SHS 600/10-12
1400 High School Dr 71753 870-234-2610
Roger Loper, prin. Fax 901-2509

Columbia Christian S 200/K-12
250 Columbia Road 61 71753 870-234-2831
John Steelman, prin. Fax 234-1497
Southern Arkansas University Post-Sec.
100 E University 71753 870-235-4000

Malvern, Hot Spring, Pop. 9,011
Glen Rose SD 700/K-12
14334 Highway 67 72104 501-332-6764
Nathan Gills, supt. Fax 332-3031
gr1.dsc.k12.ar.us
Glen Rose HS 300/9-12
14334 Highway 67 72104 501-332-3520
Vic Gandolph, prin. Fax 332-3902
Glen Rose MS 5-8
14334 Highway 67 72104 501-332-3694
Tim Holicer, prin. Fax 332-3031

Magnet Cove SD 800/K-12
472 Magnet School Rd 72104 501-332-5468
Gail McClure, supt. Fax 337-4119
magnetcove.k12.ar.us
Magnet Cove HS 400/7-12
472 Magnet School Rd 72104 501-332-5466
Gail McClure, prin. Fax 337-8711

Malvern Special SD 2,200/K-12
1517 S Main St 72104 501-332-7500
Ron Holt, supt. Fax 332-7501
malvern.dsc.k12.ar.us/
Malvern JHS 400/7-8
1910 Roosevelt St 72104 501-332-7530
Danny Lindsey, prin. Fax 332-7532
Malvern SHS 600/9-12
525 E Highland Ave 72104 501-332-6905
Steve Williams, prin. Fax 332-7523

Ouachita Technical College Post-Sec.
1 College Cir 72104 501-332-3658

Mammoth Spring, Fulton, Pop. 1,135
Mammoth Spring SD 400/K-12
410 Goldsmith Ave 72554 870-625-3612
Ronald Taylor, supt. Fax 625-3609
Mammoth Spring JSHS 200/7-12
410 Goldsmith Ave 72554 870-625-7212
Brian Davis, prin. Fax 625-3609

Manila, Mississippi, Pop. 2,883
Manila SD 1,000/K-12
PO Box 670 72442 870-561-4419
Pamela Castor, supt. Fax 561-4410
mps.crsc.k12.ar.us
Manila JSHS 500/7-12
PO Box 670 72442 870-561-4417
Pamela D. Chipman, prin. Fax 561-4243

Mansfield, Scott, Pop. 1,099
Mansfield SD 700/K-12
402 Grove St 72944 479-928-4006
Jim Hattabaugh, supt. Fax 928-4482
www.mansfieldtigers.com
Mansfield HS 300/9-12
2500 S Highway 71 E 72944 479-928-1105
Tina Smith, prin.
Mansfield MS 5-8
400 Grove St 72944 479-928-4451
Kenny Burnett, prin. Fax 928-4323

Marianna, Lee, Pop. 4,889
Lee County SD 1,900/K-12
188 W Chestnut St 72360 870-295-7100
Wayne Thompson, supt. Fax 295-7125
lcsd1.grsc.k12.ar.us/
Lee HS 500/9-12
523 Forest Ave 72360 870-295-7130
Irish Williams, prin. Fax 295-7313
Strong MS 400/6-8
214 S Alabama St 72360 870-295-7140
Robert Rose, prin. Fax 295-7314

Marion, Crittenden, Pop. 9,108
Marion SD 3,400/K-12
200 Manor St 72364 870-739-5100
Dan Shepherd, supt. Fax 739-5156
marion.crsc.k12.ar.us/
Marion JHS 600/8-9
2 Patriot Dr 72364 870-739-5140
John Heath, prin. Fax 739-5142
Marion SHS 700/10-12
1 Patriot Dr 72364 870-739-5130
John Lowry, prin. Fax 739-5135

Marked Tree, Poinsett, Pop. 2,751
Marked Tree SD 700/K-12
406 Saint Francis St 72365 870-358-2913
Gary Masters, supt. Fax 358-3953
mtree.crsc.k12.ar.us/
Marked Tree JSHS 300/7-12
406 Saint Francis St 72365 870-358-2891
Annesa Thompson, prin. Fax 358-3953

Delta Technical Institute Post-Sec.
PO Box 280 72365 870-358-2117

Marmaduke, Greene, Pop. 1,162
Marmaduke SD 800/K-12
1010 Greyhound Dr 72443 870-597-4693
Debbie Smith, supt. Fax 597-4336
marmaduke.nesc.k12.ar.us/
Marmaduke JSHS 400/7-12
1010 Greyhound Dr 72443 870-597-4693
Keith Richey, prin. Fax 597-4336

Marshall, Searcy, Pop. 1,264
Searcy County SD 800/K-12
PO Box 310 72650 870-448-3011
Andrew Vining, supt. Fax 448-3012
searcycounty.ar.schoolwebpages.com/
Marshall JSHS 400/7-12
PO Box 310 72650 870-448-3331
Jimmy Yarbrough, prin. Fax 448-5306
Other Schools – See Leslie

Marvell, Phillips, Pop. 1,281
Marvell SD 600/PK-12
PO Box 1870 72366 870-829-2101
Ulicious Reed, supt. Fax 829-2044
marvell.grsc.k12.ar.us/
Marvell JSHS 300/7-12
PO Box 1870 72366 870-829-2594
Fax 829-9700

Mayflower, Faulkner, Pop. 1,717
Mayflower SD 800/K-12
PO Box 127 72106 501-470-0506
Rhonda Bradford, supt. Fax 470-1343
Mayflower HS 300/9-12
PO Box 127 72106 501-470-0388
Joel Linn, prin. Fax 470-2106
Mayflower MS 200/6-8
PO Box 127 72106 501-470-2111
Dr. Robert Toney, prin. Fax 470-2116

Maynard, Randolph, Pop. 369
Maynard SD 500/K-12
PO Box 499 72444 870-647-2051
Phillip Mielke, supt. Fax 647-2301
maynard.nesc.k12.ar.us/
Maynard JSHS 300/7-12
PO Box 499 72444 870-647-2210
Larry Sullinger, prin. Fax 647-8207

Melbourne, Izard, Pop. 1,667
Melbourne SD 900/K-12
PO Box 250 72556 870-368-7070
Gerald Cooper, supt. Fax 368-7071
bearkatz.k12.ar.us/
Melbourne JSHS 200/7-12
PO Box 250 72556 870-368-4345
Kelly Powell, prin. Fax 368-7071
Other Schools – See Mount Pleasant

Ozarka College Post-Sec.
PO Box 10 72556 870-368-7371

Mena, Polk, Pop. 5,603
Mena SD 2,000/K-12
501 Hickory Ave 71953 479-394-1710
John Ponder, supt. Fax 394-1713
170.211.34.2/Mena%20Public%202000/index.htm
Mena HS 600/9-12
700 Morrow St S 71953 479-394-1144
Connie Davis, prin. Fax 394-1145
Mena MS 500/6-8
320r Mena St 71953 479-394-2572
Ken Marshall, prin. Fax 394-0258

Ouachita River SD 700/K-12
143 Polk Road 96 71953 479-394-2348
Marcus O. Willborg, supt. Fax 394-6687
Acorn JSHS 200/7-12
143 Polk Road 96 71953 479-394-5544
Steve Crumpler, prin. Fax 394-6687
Other Schools – See Oden

Rich Mountain Community College Post-Sec.
1100 College Dr 71953 479-394-7622

Mineral Springs, Howard, Pop. 1,277
Mineral Springs SD 600/PK-12
PO Box 189 71851 870-287-4748
Max Adcock, supt. Fax 287-5301
mssd.dmsc.k12.ar.us/
Mineral Springs JSHS 200/7-12
PO Box 189 71851 870-287-4747
Doug Booker, prin. Fax 287-5300
Other Schools – See Saratoga

Monette, Craighead, Pop. 1,183
Buffalo Island Central SD 800/K-12
PO Box 730 72447 870-486-5411
George Holland, supt. Fax 486-2657
bic.crsc.k12.ar.us
Buffalo Island Central SHS 200/10-12
PO Box 730 72447 870-486-5512
Homer Craig, prin. Fax 486-2657
Other Schools – See Leachville

Monticello, Drew, Pop. 9,079
Drew Central SD 1,000/K-12
440 Highway 83 S 71655 870-367-5369
Michael S. Reeves, supt. Fax 367-1932
www.drewcentral.org/
Drew Central JSHS 500/7-12
440 Highway 83 S 71655 870-367-6076
Frank Ferguson, prin. Fax 367-1932

Monticello SD 2,100/K-12
935 Scogin Dr 71655 870-367-4000
Norman Hill, supt. Fax 367-1531
www.billies.org
Monticello HS 700/9-12
390 Clyde Ross Dr 71655 870-367-4050
Kenny Pennington, prin. Fax 367-3699
Monticello MS 500/6-8
180 Clyde Ross Dr 71655 870-367-4040
J.J. Humphries, prin. Fax 367-5437
Occupational Education Center Vo/Tech
741 Scogin Dr 71655 870-367-4060
Cornelious Branch, prin. Fax 367-1385

University of Arkansas at Monticello Post-Sec.
PO Box 3600 71656 870-367-6811

Morrilton, Conway, Pop. 6,532
South Conway County SD 1,800/K-12
704 E Church St 72110 501-354-9400
Douglas S. Adams, supt. Fax 354-9464
www.sccsd.org
Morrilton HS 700/9-12
701 E Harding St 72110 501-354-9430
Brian Bunch, prin. Fax 354-9468
Morrilton JHS 7-8
1400 Poor Farm Rd 72110 501-354-9437
Shawn Halbrook, prin. Fax 354-9429
River Valley Vocational Center Vo/Tech
1905 Poor Farm Rd 72110 501-354-9475
Bruce Bryant, dir. Fax 354-9441

Sacred Heart S 200/K-12
106 N Saint Joseph St 72110 501-354-8113
Brian Bailey, prin. Fax 354-2001
University of Arkansas Community College Post-Sec.
1 Bruce St 72110 501-354-2465

Mountainburg, Crawford, Pop. 701
Mountainburg SD 800/K-12
129 Highway 71 SW 72946 479-369-2121
Dr. James A. Bridges, supt. Fax 369-2138
dragonsweb.wsc.k12.ar.us/
Mountainburg HS 300/9-12
129 Highway 71 SW 72946 479-369-2146
Barton Hunter, prin. Fax 369-2845
Mountainburg MS 200/5-8
129 Highway 71 SW 72946 479-369-4506
Alan Love, prin. Fax 369-4355

Mountain Home, Baxter, Pop. 11,405
Mountain Home SD 3,800/K-12
2465 Rodeo Dr 72653 870-425-1201
Dr. Charles Scriber, supt. Fax 425-1316
bombers.k12.ar.us/
Mountain Home HS 1,200/9-12
500 Bomber Blvd 72653 870-425-1215
Dana Brown, prin. Fax 508-6097
Mountain Home JHS 300/8-8
2301 Rodeo Dr 72653 870-425-1231
Wesley Henderson, prin. Fax 424-4797

Arkansas State University Mountain Home Post-Sec.
1600 S College St 72653 870-508-6100
Marsha Kay Beauty College Post-Sec.
408 Highway 201 N 72653 870-425-7575

Mountain Pine, Garland, Pop. 815
Mountain Pine SD 700/K-12
PO Box 1 71956 501-767-1540
Ron Looper, supt. Fax 767-1589
Mountain Pine JSHS 300/7-12
PO Box 1 71956 501-767-6917
Darwin Foshee, prin. Fax 767-0170

Mountain View, Stone, Pop. 2,958
Mountain View SD 1,700/K-12
210 High School Rd 72560 870-269-3443
Mark A. Rector, supt. Fax 269-3446
mvschools.k12.ar.us
Mountain View JSHS 600/7-12
210 High School Rd 72560 870-269-3943
Mark Mallett, prin. Fax 269-3446
Other Schools – See Fox, Timbo

Mount Ida, Montgomery, Pop. 962
Mount Ida SD 600/K-12
PO Box 1230 71957 870-867-2323
Benny Weston, supt. Fax 867-3734
Mount Ida JSHS 300/7-12
PO Box 1230 71957 870-867-4517
Heath Bennett, prin. Fax 867-3734

Mount Judea, Newton
Deer / Mt. Judea SD
Supt. — See Deer
Mount Judea JSHS 100/7-12
PO Box 40 72655 870-434-5362
Sammie Bye, prin. Fax 434-5359

Mount Pleasant, Izard, Pop. 401
Melbourne SD
Supt. — See Melbourne
Mount Pleasant JSHS 200/7-12
PO Box 144 72561 870-346-5481
Conny Johnson, prin. Fax 346-5337

Mount Vernon, Faulkner, Pop. 144
Mount Vernon-Enola SD 500/K-12
PO Box 43 72111 501-849-2220
Ronnie Greer, supt. Fax 849-3076
mve.k12.ar.us/
Mount Vernon-Enola JSHS 200/7-12
PO Box 43 72111 501-849-2221
Rudy Beavers, prin. Fax 849-2221

Mulberry, Crawford, Pop. 1,661
Mulberry SD 600/K-12
PO Box D 72947 479-997-1715
Kerry Schneider, supt. Fax 997-1897
www.mulberryyellowjackets.homestead.com
Mulberry JSHS 200/7-12
PO Box D 72947 479-997-1363
Chris Rink, prin. Fax 997-1897
Other Schools – See Ozark

Murfreesboro, Pike, Pop. 1,725
Murfreesboro SD 600/K-12
PO Box 339 71958 870-285-2201
Dr. Bernie Hellums, supt. Fax 285-2276
Murfreesboro JSHS 200/7-12
PO Box 339 71958 870-285-3678
Mike Jackson, prin. Fax 285-2276

Nashville, Howard, Pop. 4,915
Nashville SD 1,800/K-12
600 N 4th St 71852 870-845-3425
Danny Howard, supt. Fax 845-7344
scrappers.k12.ar.us/
Nashville JHS 500/7-9
1000 N 8th St 71852 870-845-3418
Joe Kell, prin. Fax 845-7334
Nashville SHS 400/10-12
1301 Mount Pleasant Dr 71852 870-845-3261
Jan Booker, prin. Fax 845-7345

Newark, Independence, Pop. 1,217
Cedar Ridge SD 600/K-12
1502 N Hill St 72562 870-799-8691
Guy Santucci, supt. Fax 799-8647
www.klln.com
Cedar Ridge JSHS 200/7-12
1500 N Hill St 72562 870-799-8691
Rhonda Dickey, prin. Fax 799-3225

Newport, Jackson, Pop. 7,386
Newport SD 1,600/PK-12
406 Wilkerson Dr 72112 870-523-1311
Dr. Ron Wilson, supt. Fax 523-1388
newport.crsc.k12.ar.us/
Newport HS 500/9-12
406 Wilkerson Dr 72112 870-523-1321
Danny Ebbs, prin. Fax 523-1383
Newport JHS 200/7-8
406 Wilkerson Dr 72112 870-523-1346
Suzanne Bailey, prin. Fax 523-1388

Arkansas State University - Newport Post-Sec.
7648 Victory Blvd 72112 870-512-7800

Norfork, Baxter, Pop. 486
Norfork SD 400/K-12
44 Fireball Ln 72658 870-499-5228
Mike Seay, supt. Fax 499-5109
panthers.k12.ar.us
Norfork JSHS 200/7-12
136 Mildred Simpson Dr 72658 870-499-7191
Bob Hulse, prin. Fax 499-5659

Norman, Montgomery, Pop. 414
Caddo Hills SD 600/K-12
2268 Highway 8 E 71960 870-356-4495
Donald Henley, supt. Fax 356-3426
caddohills.dsc.k12.ar.us/
Caddo Hills JSHS 300/7-12
2268 Highway 8 E 71960 870-356-3857
Stacy Vines, prin. Fax 356-3426

Norphlet, Union, Pop. 810
Norphlet SD 500/K-12
PO Box 50 71759 870-546-2781
Eddie G. Miller, supt. Fax 546-2345
www.scsc.k12.ar.us/norphlet/
Norphlet JSHS 200/7-12
PO Box 50 71759 870-546-2781
Keith Coleman, prin. Fax 546-2345

North Little Rock, Pulaski, Pop. 59,687
North Little Rock SD 9,700/PK-12
2700 N Poplar St 72114 501-771-8000
Kenneth Kirspel, supt. Fax 771-8067
www.nlrsd.k12.ar.us
Lakewood MS 600/7-8
2300 Lakeview Rd 72116 501-771-8250
Dr. Ginger Wallace, prin. Fax 771-8268
North Little Rock HS - East Campus 1,500/9-10
2400 Lakeview Rd 72116 501-771-8200
Lee Tackett, prin. Fax 771-8213
North Little Rock HS - West Campus 2,100/6-12
101 W 22nd St 72114 501-771-8100
Anita Cameron, prin. Fax 771-8123
Rose City MS 200/7-8
5500 Lynch Dr 72117 501-955-3600
Penny Elliott, prin. Fax 955-3603

Pulaski County Special SD
Supt. — See Little Rock
Northwood MS 700/6-8
10200 Bamboo Ln 72120 501-833-1170
Thelma Jones-Ramsey, prin. Fax 833-1178
Oak Grove JSHS 1,000/6-12
10025 Oakland Dr 72118 501-851-5350
Richard Heien, prin. Fax 851-5356

AR College of Barbering & Hair Design Post-Sec.
200 Washington Ave 72114 501-376-9696
Central Arkansas Christian S 1,100/K-12
1 Windsong Dr 72113 501-758-3160
Carter Lambert, pres. Fax 791-7975
Lee's School of Cosmetology Post-Sec.
2700 W Pershing Blvd 72114 501-758-2800
New Tyler Barber College Post-Sec.
1221 E 7th St 72114 501-375-0377
Pulaski Technical College Post-Sec.
3000 W Scenic Dr 72118 501-771-1000

Oark, Johnson
Jasper SD
Supt. — See Jasper
Oark JSHS 100/7-12
General Delivery 72852 479-292-3353
Anita Cooper, prin. Fax 292-3435

Oden, Montgomery, Pop. 213
Ouachita River SD
Supt. — See Mena
Oden JSHS 100/7-12
PO Box 150 71961 870-326-4311
Doug Carmack, prin. Fax 326-5552

Ola, Yell, Pop. 1,212
Two Rivers SD
Supt. — See Plainview
Ola JSHS 300/7-12
PO Box 279 72853 479-489-4154
Kenneth McCoy, prin. Fax 489-4167

Omaha, Boone, Pop. 169
Omaha SD 400/K-12
522 College Rd 72662 870-426-3366
Dr. David Land, supt. Fax 426-3360
omaha.k12.ar.us/
Omaha HS 200/7-12
522 College Rd 72662 870-426-3373
Martha Hicks, prin. Fax 426-2926

Osceola, Mississippi, Pop. 8,335
Osceola SD 1,500/K-12
PO Box 528 72370 870-563-2561
Milton Washington, supt. Fax 563-2181
osceola.ar.schoolwebpages.com
Osceola HS 500/9-12
PO Box 528 72370 870-563-2192
Doug Caldwell, prin. Fax 622-1003
Osceola JHS 200/6-8
PO Box 528 72370 870-563-2918
Sharon McGee, prin. Fax 622-1030

Ozark, Franklin, Pop. 3,558
Mulberry SD
Supt. — See Mulberry
Pleasant View JSHS 100/7-12
5750 Hornet Ln 72949 479-997-8469
Shane Vincent, prin. Fax 997-1667

Ozark SD 1,600/K-12
PO Box 135 72949 479-667-4118
Donald S. Stone, supt. Fax 667-4092
ozark.k12.ar.us/
Ozark JHS 300/8-9
1301 Walden Dr 72949 479-667-4747
Jerrod Burns, prin. Fax 667-0898
Ozark SHS 300/10-12
3500 Jeffers Dr 72949 479-667-4116
Jody Jenkins, prin. Fax 667-5921

Arkansas Valley Technical Institute Post-Sec.
PO Box 506 72949 479-667-2117
Cass Civilian Conservation Job Corps Ctr Post-Sec.
21424 N Highway 23 72949 479-667-3686

Palestine, Saint Francis, Pop. 754
Palestine Wheatley SD
Supt. — See Forrest City
Palestine Wheatley HS 200/9-12
PO Box 790 72372 870-581-2425
Greg Jackson, prin. Fax 581-4421

Pangburn, White, Pop. 653
Pangburn SD 700/K-12
1100 Short St 72121 501-728-4511
Larry Moore, supt. Fax 728-4514
Pangburn JSHS 400/7-12
1100 Short St 72121 501-728-3513
Pat Rose, prin. Fax 728-4514

Paragould, Greene, Pop. 22,888
Greene County Technical SD 2,500/PK-12
5413 W Kingshighway 72450 870-236-2762
Sheila Ford, supt. Fax 236-7333
www.gctsd.k12.ar.us/
Greene County Technical HS 600/10-12
5201 W Kingshighway 72450 870-236-6113
Gene Weeks, prin. Fax 239-6976
Greene County Technical JHS 400/8-9
5207 W Kingshighway 72450 870-239-2147
Michael Todd, prin. Fax 239-2148
Other Schools - See Delaplaine

Paragould SD 2,600/PK-12
631 W Court St 72450 870-239-2105
Dr. Aaron Hosman, supt. Fax 239-4697
paragould.k12.ar.us/
Paragould HS 800/9-12
1701 W Court St 72450 870-236-7744
Brett Gibson, prin. Fax 239-2934
Paragould JHS 500/7-8
1701 W Court St 72450 870-236-7744
James Brittingham, prin. Fax 239-0185

Crowleys Ridge Academy 300/PK-12
606 Academy Dr 72450 870-236-6909
Dale Horn, pres. Fax 236-6988
Crowley's Ridge College Post-Sec.
100 College Dr 72450 870-236-6901

Paris, Logan, Pop. 3,699
Paris SD 1,100/K-12
602 N 10th St 72855 479-963-3243
Jim Loyd, supt. Fax 963-3620
paris.wsc.k12.ar.us/
Paris HS 300/9-12
2000 E Wood St 72855 479-963-2247
Gary Montgomery, prin. Fax 963-8018
Paris MS 300/6-8
602 N 10th St 72855 479-963-6995
Martha Dodson, prin. Fax 963-8052

Parkin, Cross, Pop. 1,563
Parkin SD 300/K-12
116 Lake St 72373 870-755-2742
Sylvia R. Moore, supt. Fax 755-2929
Parkin JSHS 200/7-12
116 Lake St 72373 870-755-2791
Lonzo Gatlin, prin. Fax 755-2929

Paron, Saline
Bryant SD
Supt. — See Bryant
Paron JSHS 100/7-12
22265 Highway 9 72122 501-594-5622
Larry Freeman, prin. Fax 594-5712

Pearcy, Garland
Lake Hamilton SD 3,800/K-12
205 Wolf St 71964 501-767-2306
Dr. Barbara Wood, supt. Fax 767-1219
wolves.dsc.k12.ar.us
Lake Hamilton JHS 600/8-9
281 Wolf St 71964 501-767-2731
Shawn Higginbotham, prin. Fax 767-1711
Lake Hamilton SHS 900/10-12
280 Wolf St 71964 501-767-9311
Vernon Brooks, prin. Fax 767-9318

Pea Ridge, Benton, Pop. 2,658
Pea Ridge SD 1,200/K-12
781 W Pickens Rd 72751 479-451-8181
Michael Van Dyke, supt. Fax 451-8235
www.prs.k12.ar.us/
Pea Ridge HS 400/9-12
781 W Pickens Rd 72751 479-451-8182
Rick Neal, prin. Fax 451-0323
Pea Ridge MS 400/5-8
1460 N Davis St 72751 479-451-1555
Holly Dayberry, prin. Fax 451-9635

Perryville, Pulaski, Pop. 1,474
Perryville SD 900/K-12
823 N Ash St 72126 501-889-2327
Bobby Miller, supt. Fax 889-5191
Perryville JSHS 400/7-12
823 N Ash St 72126 501-889-2326
John Parrish, prin. Fax 889-5006

Piggott, Clay, Pop. 3,731
Piggott SD 1,000/K-12
PO Box 387 72454 870-598-2572
Bruce Evans, supt. Fax 598-5283
piggotths.k12.ar.us
Piggott HS 500/7-12
PO Box 387 72454 870-598-3815
Barry DeHart, prin. Fax 598-1560

Pine Bluff, Jefferson, Pop. 53,905
Dollarway SD 1,500/K-12
4900 Dollarway Rd 71602 870-534-7003
Thomas Gathen, supt. Fax 534-1455
www.dollarway.org/
Dollarway HS 400/9-12
4900 Dollarway Rd 71602 870-534-3878
Terry Julian, prin. Fax 534-1455
Dollarway MS 400/6-8
2602 W Fluker Ave 71601 870-534-5243
Dorothea Hobbs, prin. Fax 535-1215

Pine Bluff SD 6,000/K-12
PO Box 7678 71611 870-543-4200
Frank Anthony, supt. Fax 543-4208
pbweb.arsc.k12.ar.us/
Pine Bluff SHS 1,200/10-12
711 W 11th Ave 71601 870-543-4300
Rodney Matheney, prin. Fax 543-4302
Robey JHS 1,000/8-9
4101 S Olive St 71603 870-543-4280
Robbie Williams, prin. Fax 850-2027

Watson Chapel SD 3,100/K-12
4100 Camden Rd 71603 870-879-0220
Charles Knight, supt. Fax 879-0588
watson2.arsc.k12.ar.us
Watson Chapel JHS 900/7-9
3900 Camden Rd 71603 870-879-4420
Henry Webb, prin. Fax 879-4426
Watson Chapel SHS 700/10-12
4000 Camden Rd 71603 870-879-3230
Leydel Willis, prin. Fax 879-1842

Jefferson Regional Medical Center Post-Sec.
1515 W 42nd Ave 71603 870-541-7269
St. Joseph SHS 200/7-12
1501 W 73rd Ave 71603 870-540-0413
Peter Rivera, prin. Fax 540-0345
Southeast Arkansas College Post-Sec.
1900 S Hazel St 71603 870-543-5900
University of Arkansas at Pine Bluff Post-Sec.
1200 University Dr 71601 870-543-8000

Plainview, Yell, Pop. 756
Two Rivers SD 1,000/K-12
PO Box 187 72857 479-272-3113
Earl Jamison, supt. Fax 272-3125
tworivers.k12.ar.us
Plainview-Rover JSHS 100/7-12
PO Box 190 72857 479-272-3111
Kerry Cunningham, prin. Fax 272-3125
Other Schools - See Briggsville, Ola

Pleasant Plains, Independence, Pop. 270
Midland SD 600/K-12
PO Box 630 72568 501-345-8844
Tommy Thompson, supt. Fax 345-2086
Midland JSHS 300/7-12
PO Box 630 72568 501-345-2852
Vickie Crawford, prin. Fax 345-2086

Pocahontas, Randolph, Pop. 6,583
Pocahontas SD 1,800/K-12
2300 N Park St 72455 870-892-4573
Daryl Blaxton, supt. Fax 892-8857
www.nesc.k12.ar.us/
Pocahontas HS 400/10-12
2312 Stadium Dr 72455 870-892-4573
David Almany, prin. Fax 892-8857
Pocahontas JHS 500/7-9
2405 N Park St 72455 870-892-4573
Byron Busby, prin. Fax 892-8857

Black River Technical College Post-Sec.
PO Box 468 72455 870-892-4565

Pottsville, Pope, Pop. 1,320
Pottsville SD 1,200/K-12
63 W Cedar St 72858 479-968-8101
Randall Williams, supt. Fax 968-6339
apache.afsc.k12.ar.us
Pottsville HS 300/9-12
500 Apache Dr 72858 479-968-6334
Larry Dugger, prin. Fax 968-3442
Pottsville MS 400/5-8
6926 State Rd 247 72858 479-890-6631
Houston Townsend, prin. Fax 968-6446

Poyen, Grant, Pop. 276
Poyen SD 500/K-12
PO Box 209 72128 501-332-2939
Jerry Newton, supt. Fax 332-7800
www.poyenschool.com/
Poyen JSHS 200/7-12
PO Box 209 72128 501-337-5424
Bobby Daniel, prin. Fax 332-7800

Prairie Grove, Washington, Pop. 2,825
Prairie Grove SD 1,400/K-12
110 School St 72753 479-846-4213
Chris Webb, supt. Fax 846-2015
tiger.nwsc.k12.ar.us
Prairie Grove HS 400/9-12
500 Cole Dr 72753 479-846-4212
Ron Bond, prin. Fax 846-4207
Prairie Grove MS 400/5-8
807 Catlett St 72753 479-846-4221
Janet Collins, prin. Fax 846-4275

Prescott, Nevada, Pop. 3,799
Prescott SD 1,100/K-12
762 Martin St 71857 870-887-3016
Hyacinth Deon, supt. Fax 887-5021
McRae MS 400/5-8
1030 E 5th St N 71857 870-887-2521
Jamye Barnes, prin. Fax 887-3717
Prescott HS 400/9-12
736 Martin St 71857 870-887-3123
James C. Purtle, prin. Fax 887-3682

Quitman, Cleburne, Pop. 725
Quitman SD 600/K-12
PO Box 178 72131 501-589-3156
Robert Stewart, supt. Fax 589-3156
quitnet.afsc.k12.ar.us/
Quitman JSHS 300/7-12
PO Box 178 72131 501-589-2554
James Williams, prin. Fax 589-2554

Ravenden Springs, Randolph, Pop. 136
Twin Rivers SD
Supt. — See Williford
Oak Ridge Central JSHS 100/7-12
5749 Oak Ridge Rd 72460 870-869-2479
Susie Adams, prin. Fax 869-3067

Rector, Clay, Pop. 1,904
Rector SD — 700/K-12
  PO Box 367 72461 — 870-595-3151
  Robert Louder, supt. — Fax 595-9067
Rector HS — 300/7-12
  PO Box 367 72461 — 870-595-3553
  Wade Williams, prin. — Fax 595-9067

Redfield, Jefferson, Pop. 1,164
White Hall SD
  Supt. — See White Hall
Redfield JHS — 100/7-9
  PO Box 350 72132 — 501-397-2253
  James Kight, prin. — Fax 397-6534

Rison, Cleveland, Pop. 1,297
Cleveland County SD — 800/K-12
  PO Box 600 71665 — 870-325-6344
  Scott Holderfield, supt. — Fax 325-7094
  www.risonschools.org
Rison JSHS — 300/7-12
  PO Box 600 71665 — 870-325-6241
  Brian Brown, prin. — Fax 325-6799

Woodlawn SD — 600/K-12
  6760 Highway 63 71665 — 870-357-8108
  Billy Williams, supt. — Fax 357-8718
  bears.k12.ar.us
Woodlawn JSHS — 300/7-12
  6760 Highway 63 71665 — 870-357-8171
  Jeff Wylie, prin. — Fax 357-8718

Rogers, Benton, Pop. 42,795
Rogers SD — 11,900/K-12
  212 S 3rd St 72756 — 479-636-3910
  Dr. Janie Darr, supt. — Fax 631-3504
  www.rogers.k12.ar.us
Elmwood JHS — 900/8-9
  1610 S 13th St 72758 — 479-631-3600
  Bob White, prin. — Fax 631-3603
Oakdale JHS — 1,000/8-9
  511 N Dixieland Rd 72756 — 479-631-3615
  James Goodwin, prin. — Fax 631-3617
Rogers HS Sophomore Campus — 1,000/10-10
  1114 S Mountie Blvd 72756 — 479-631-3579
  Dr. Larry Ben, prin. — Fax 631-3580
Rogers SHS — 1,500/11-12
  2300 S Dixieland Rd 72758 — 479-636-2202
  Bill Stringer, prin. — Fax 631-3554

New Covenant Christian Academy — 50/PK-12
  2298 S 13th St 72758 — 479-636-9186
  Jody Bricker, prin. — Fax 631-1553

Rose Bud, White, Pop. 444
Rose Bud SD — 800/K-12
  124 School Rd 72137 — 501-556-5815
  Jeff Williams, supt. — Fax 556-4201
  rbsd.wmsc.k12.ar.us
Rose Bud JSHS — 400/7-12
  124 School Rd 72137 — 501-556-5404
  Fred Ramsey, prin. — Fax 556-5781

Rosston, Nevada, Pop. 250
Nevada SD — 400/K-12
  PO Box 50 71858 — 870-871-2418
  Rick McAfee, supt. — Fax 871-2419
Nevada JSHS — 200/7-12
  PO Box 50 71858 — 870-871-2478
  Frank Bradley, prin. — Fax 871-2419

Russellville, Pope, Pop. 24,719
Russellville SD — 5,100/K-12
  PO Box 928 72811 — 479-968-1306
  Danny Taylor, supt. — Fax 968-6381
  rsdweb.k12.ar.us/
Russellville Area Vo-Technical Center — Vo/Tech
  2201 S Knoxville Ave 72802 — 479-968-5422
  Jim Franks, prin. — Fax 968-7918
Russellville JHS — 800/8-9
  2000 W Parkway Dr 72802 — 479-890-1599
  Alene Bynum, prin. — Fax 890-6419
Russellville SHS — 1,200/10-12
  2203 S Knoxville Ave 72802 — 479-968-3151
  Wesley White, prin. — Fax 968-4264

Arkansas Tech University — Post-Sec.
  215 W O St 72801 — 479-968-0389

Saint Joe, Searcy, Pop. 83
Ozark Mountain SD — 800/K-12
  PO Box 69 72675 — 870-439-2213
  James Trammell, supt. — Fax 439-2604
Saint Joe JSHS — 100/7-12
  PO Box 69 72675 — 870-439-2213
  Ronnie Ruff, prin. — Fax 439-2604
Other Schools – See Everton, Western Grove

Saint Paul, Madison, Pop. 162
Huntsville SD
  Supt. — See Huntsville
Saint Paul JSHS — 200/7-12
  PO Box 125 72760 — 479-677-2411
  Rick Land, prin. — Fax 677-2210

Salem, Fulton, Pop. 1,587
Salem SD — 700/K-12
  313 Highway 62 E Ste 1 72576 — 870-895-2516
  Ken Rich, supt. — Fax 895-4062
  salem.k12.ar.us/
Salem JSHS — 400/7-12
  313 Highway 62 E Ste 2 72576 — 870-895-3293
  Wayne Guiltner, prin. — Fax 895-4062

Saratoga, Howard, Pop. 200
Mineral Springs SD
  Supt. — See Mineral Springs
Saratoga HS — 100/7-12
  PO Box 90 71859 — 870-388-9262
  Lavon Flaherty, prin. — Fax 388-9205

Scotland, Van Buren
Clinton SD
  Supt. — See Clinton

Scotland JSHS — 100/7-12
  PO Box 4 72141 — 501-592-3313
  Dale Stokes, prin. — Fax 592-3732

Scranton, Logan, Pop. 242
Scranton SD — 400/K-12
  103 N 10th St 72863 — 479-938-7121
  Larry Garland, supt. — Fax 938-7564
  www.rocketnet.k12.ar.us
Scranton JSHS — 200/7-12
  103 N 10th St 72863 — 479-938-7121
  Mark Siebenmorgen, prin. — Fax 938-7564

Searcy, White, Pop. 19,714
Riverview SD — 1,300/K-12
  800 Raider Dr 72143 — 501-279-0540
  Hugh Burge, supt. — Fax 279-0737
Riverview HS — 400/9-12
  810 Raider Dr 72143 — 501-279-7700
  Kennedy Simmons, prin. — Fax 279-2848
Other Schools – See Judsonia, Kensett

Searcy SD — 3,600/K-12
  801 N Elm St 72143 — 501-268-3517
  James T. Wood, supt. — Fax 278-2220
  ssweb.wmsc.k12.ar.us/
Ahlf JHS — 600/7-8
  308 W Vine Ave 72143 — 501-268-3158
  Bill Dunaway, prin. — Fax 268-2212
Searcy HS — 1,000/9-12
  301 N Ella St 72143 — 501-268-8315
  Bill Derryberry, prin. — Fax 268-2249

Arkansas State University Searcy Campus — Post-Sec.
  PO Box 909 72145 — 501-268-6191
Harding Academy — 500/K-12
  PO Box 10775 72149 — 501-279-7200
  Mark Benton M.Ed., hdmstr. — Fax 279-7213
Harding University — Post-Sec.
  900 E Center Ave 72149 — 501-279-4000
Searcy Beauty College — Post-Sec.
  1004 S Main St 72143 — 501-268-6300

Sheridan, Grant, Pop. 4,125
Sheridan SD — 3,700/K-12
  400 N Rock St 72150 — 870-942-3135
  Scott Spainhour, supt. — Fax 942-2931
  www.sheridanschools.org/
Sheridan Freshman Academy — 9-9
  510 W Church St 72150 — 870-942-3232
  Dr. Phil Clark, prin. — Fax 942-3296
Sheridan MS — 900/6-8
  500 N Rock St 72150 — 870-942-3813
  Charles Tadlock, prin. — Fax 942-3034
Sheridan SHS — 900/10-12
  700 W Vine St 72150 — 870-942-3137
  Donna Yancey, prin. — Fax 942-7546

Sherwood, Pulaski, Pop. 22,111
Pulaski County Special SD
  Supt. — See Little Rock
Sylvan Hills HS — 1,200/9-12
  484 Bear Paw Rd 72120 — 501-833-1100
  Kim Forrest, prin. — Fax 833-1104
Sylvan Hills MS — 900/6-8
  401 Dee Jay Hudson Dr 72120 — 501-833-1120
  Leon Hays, prin. — Fax 833-1137

Abundant Life S — 400/PK-12
  9200 Highway 107 72120 — 501-835-3120
  Russell Eudy, supt. — Fax 835-4428

Shirley, Van Buren, Pop. 338
Shirley SD — 500/K-12
  154 School Dr 72153 — 501-723-8191
  Jack Robinson, supt. — Fax 723-4020
Shirley JSHS — 200/7-12
  154 School Dr 72153 — 501-723-4902
  Randy Moore, prin. — Fax 723-8114

Siloam Springs, Benton, Pop. 12,704
Siloam Springs SD — 3,100/K-12
  PO Box 798 72761 — 479-524-3191
  Kendall D. Ramey, supt. — Fax 524-8002
  sssd.k12.ar.us/
Siloam Springs HS — 900/9-12
  1500 W Jefferson St 72761 — 479-524-5134
  Charles D. Abernathy, prin. — Fax 524-8211
Siloam Springs MS — 800/6-8
  1500 N Mount Olive St 72761 — 479-524-6184
  Teresa Morgan, prin. — Fax 524-3228

John Brown University — Post-Sec.
  2000 W University St 72761 — 479-524-9500

Smackover, Union, Pop. 1,957
Smackover SD — 800/K-12
  PO Box 109 71762 — 870-725-3132
  Darrell Porter, supt. — Fax 725-2385
  www.scsc.k12.ar.us/smackover
Smackover HS — 300/7-12
  1 Buckaroo Ln 71762 — 870-725-3101
  Donald Smeltzer, prin. — Fax 725-2540

Sparkman, Dallas, Pop. 551
Harmony Grove SD
  Supt. — See Camden
Sparkman S — 200/K-12
  PO Box 37 71763 — 870-678-2242
  Walton Pigott, prin. — Fax 678-2911

Springdale, Washington, Pop. 52,471
Springdale SD — 13,700/PK-12
  PO Box 8 72765 — 479-750-8800
  Dr. Jim Rollins, supt. — Fax 750-8812
  www.springdaleschools.org
Central JHS — 1,000/8-9
  2811 W Huntsville Ave 72762 — 479-750-8854
  Darrell Watts, prin. — Fax 750-8700
George JHS — 8-9
  3200 Powell St 72764 — 479-750-8750
  David Nelson, prin. — Fax 750-8756

Har-Ber HS — 10-12
  300 Jones Rd 72762 — 479-750-8777
  Danny Brackett, prin. — Fax 750-8704
Southwest JHS — 1,100/8-9
  1807 Princeton Ave 72762 — 479-750-8849
  Brice Wagner, prin. — Fax 750-8704
Springdale HS — 2,700/10-12
  1103 W Emma Ave 72764 — 479-750-8832
  Dr. Allen Williams, prin. — Fax 750-8811

Baptist School of Nursing-NW — Post-Sec.
  610 E Emma Ave 72764 — 479-750-6200
Ecclesia College — Post-Sec.
  9653 Nations Dr 72762 — 800-735-9926
Leon's Hair Training Academy — Post-Sec.
  200 Holcomb St 72764 — 479-756-6060
Northwest Technical Institute — Post-Sec.
  PO Box 2000 72765 — 479-751-8824
Shiloh Christian S — 700/PK-12
  1707 Johnson S 72762 — 479-756-1140
  Bruce Perkins, pres. — Fax 756-7107

Stamps, Columbia, Pop. 2,050
Lafayette County SD
  Supt. — See Lewisville
Lafayette County HS — 100/9-12
  1209 Alexander Ln 71860 — 870-533-4464
  Opal Anderson, prin. — Fax 533-2367

Star City, Lincoln, Pop. 2,362
Star City SD — 1,600/K-12
  206 Cleveland St 71667 — 870-628-4237
  Rhonda Mullikin, supt. — Fax 628-4228
  www.starcityschools.com
Star City HS — 400/9-12
  206 Cleveland St 71667 — 870-628-4111
  Mike Walker, prin. — Fax 628-4228
Star City MS — 400/6-8
  206 Cleveland St 71667 — 870-628-5125
  Susan White, prin. — Fax 628-4228

State University, Craighead

Arkansas State University — Post-Sec.
  PO Box 1630 72467 — 870-972-2100

Stephens, Ouachita, Pop. 1,088
Stephens SD — 300/K-12
  315 W Chert St 71764 — 870-786-5443
  Mark Keith, supt. — Fax 786-5095
  www.scsc.k12.ar.us/stephens/
Stephens JSHS — 200/7-12
  315 W Chert St 71764 — 870-786-5442
  Jeff Alphin, prin. — Fax 786-5095

Strawberry, Lawrence, Pop. 281
Hillcrest SD — 400/K-12
  PO Box 50 72469 — 870-528-3856
  Greg Crabtree, supt. — Fax 528-3383
Hillcrest HS — 100/10-12
  PO Box 50 72469 — 870-528-3856
  George Green, prin. — Fax 528-3383
Other Schools – See Lynn

Strong, Union, Pop. 645
Strong-Huttig SD — 500/K-12
  PO Box 735 71765 — 870-797-7322
  Saul Lusk, supt. — Fax 797-2257
Strong HS — 100/9-12
  PO Box 735 71765 — 870-797-2312
  William Neikirk, prin. — Fax 797-2257
Other Schools – See Huttig

Stuttgart, Arkansas, Pop. 9,398
Stuttgart SD — 1,100/K-12
  2501 S Main St 72160 — 870-673-3561
  Dr. Laura Bednar, supt. — Fax 673-7337
  sps.k12.ar.us
Meekins MS — 50/7-8
  2501 S Main St 72160 — 870-673-3561
  Randy Deaton, prin. — Fax 673-7337
Stuttgart HS — 600/9-12
  2501 S Main St 72160 — 870-673-3561
  Donnie Boothe, prin. — Fax 673-7337

Grand Prairie Ev. Methodist Christian S — 50/K-12
  PO Box 728 72160 — 870-673-2087
  Thomas Bormann, prin. — Fax 673-4718

Subiaco, Logan, Pop. 444

Subiaco Academy — 200/9-12
  405 N Subiaco Ave 72865 — 479-934-1005
  Mike Berry, hdmstr. — Fax 936-1033

Swifton, Jackson, Pop. 819
Jackson County SD
  Supt. — See Tuckerman
Swifton JSHS — 100/7-12
  PO Box 556 72471 — 870-485-2381
  Larry Lee, prin. — Fax 485-2711

Taylor, Columbia, Pop. 555
Emerson - Taylor SD
  Supt. — See Emerson
Taylor JSHS — 100/7-12
  506 E Pine St 71861 — 870-694-2251
  Mike Lyons, prin. — Fax 694-2901

Texarkana, Miller, Pop. 28,900
Genoa Central SD — 1,000/PK-12
  12472 Highway 196 71854 — 870-653-4343
  Albert Murphy, supt. — Fax 653-2624
  dragons1.k12.ar.us/dragons/
Cobb MS — 300/5-8
  11986 Highway 196 71854 — 870-653-2132
  Deloris Coe, prin. — Fax 653-6944
Genoa Central HS — 300/9-12
  12472 Highway 196 71854 — 870-653-2272
  Bobby Hart, prin. — Fax 653-6967

Texarkana Arkansas SD 4,400/K-12
3512 Grand Ave 71854 870-772-3371
Dr. Paul Dee Human, supt. Fax 773-2602
www.tasd7.net
Arkansas HS 1,200/9-12
3512 Grand Ave 71854 870-774-7641
Dr. Richard Young, prin. Fax 773-8408
North Heights JHS 700/7-8
3512 Grand Ave 71854 870-773-1091
Gerald Hatley, prin. Fax 772-2722

Trinity Christian S 400/PK-12
3107 Trinity Blvd 71854 870-779-1009
Greg Jones, supt. Fax 772-1258

Tillar, Desha, Pop. 227

Cornerstone Christian Academy 100/K-12
PO Box 129 71670 870-392-2482
Monica Daniels, admin. Fax 392-2328

Timbo, Stone
Mountain View SD
Supt. — See Mountain View
Timbo JSHS 100/7-12
PO Box 6 72680 870-746-4303
Shade Gilbert, prin. Fax 746-4844

Trumann, Poinsett, Pop. 6,873
Trumann SD 1,700/K-12
221 N Pine Ave 72472 870-483-6444
Ronald J. Waleszonia, supt. Fax 483-2602
wildcat.crsc.k12.ar.us/
Trumann JSHS 800/7-12
221 N Pine Ave 72472 870-483-5301
Jimmy Montgomery, prin. Fax 483-2602

Tuckerman, Jackson, Pop. 1,743
Jackson County SD 900/K-12
PO Box 1070 72473 870-349-2232
Chester Shannon, supt. Fax 349-2355
Tuckerman JSHS 300/7-12
PO Box 1070 72473 870-349-2657
Cathy Tanner, prin. Fax 349-2355
Other Schools – See Swifton

Turrell, Crittenden, Pop. 925
Turrell SD 400/K-12
PO Box 369 72384 870-343-2533
Alfred Hogan, supt. Fax 343-2823
Turrell JSHS 200/7-12
PO Box 369 72384 870-343-2655
Charles Webster, prin. Fax 343-2876

Umpire, Howard
Wickes SD
Supt. — See Wickes
Umpire JSHS 50/7-12
PO Box 60 71971 870-583-2141
Allen Blackwell, prin. Fax 583-6364

Valley Springs, Boone, Pop. 168
Valley Springs SD 1,000/K-12
PO Box 640 72682 870-429-8371
Mark Sanders, supt. Fax 429-5551
valley.k12.ar.us
Valley Springs HS 300/9-12
PO Box 640 72682 870-429-8120
Charles Trammell, prin. Fax 429-5551
Valley Springs MS 300/5-8
PO Box 640 72682 870-429-8101
Rick Still, prin. Fax 429-8121

Van Buren, Crawford, Pop. 20,154
Van Buren SD 5,600/K-12
2221 E Pointer Trl 72956 479-474-7942
Dr. Merle Dickerson, supt. Fax 471-3146
vbschools.k12.ar.us/
Butterfield JHS 700/7-9
319 N 12th St 72956 479-474-6838
Todd Marshell, prin. Fax 471-3101
Coleman JHS 700/7-9
821 E Pointer Trl 72956 479-471-3160
Dan Roberts, prin. Fax 471-0249
Van Buren HS 1,200/10-12
2001 E Pointer Trl 72956 479-474-6821
Tom Watkins, prin. Fax 471-3171

Vilonia, Faulkner, Pop. 2,498
Vilonia SD 2,600/K-12
PO Box 160 72173 501-796-3500
Dr. Frank Mitchell, supt. Fax 796-3134
vilonia.k12.ar.us/
Vilonia JHS 400/8-9
PO Box 160 72173 501-796-2037
Jim Binan, prin. Fax 796-4326
Vilonia SHS 600/10-12
PO Box 160 72173 501-796-2111
Ed Sellers, prin. Fax 796-8895

Viola, Fulton, Pop. 385
Viola SD 400/K-12
PO Box 380 72583 870-458-2323
Marvin Newton, supt. Fax 458-2214
Viola JSHS 200/7-12
PO Box 380 72583 870-458-2213
John May, prin. Fax 458-2214

Waldo, Columbia, Pop. 1,532
Waldo SD 300/K-12
PO Box 367 71770 870-693-5731
Dr. Richard Britt, supt. Fax 693-2057
www.scsc.k12.ar.us/waldo/
Waldo JSHS 200/7-12
PO Box 367 71770 870-693-5825
Edgar Montgomery, prin. Fax 693-2057

Waldron, Scott, Pop. 3,491
Waldron SD 1,700/K-12
1560 W 6th St 72958 479-637-3179
Boyce Watkins, supt. Fax 637-3177
waldron.k12.ar.us
Waldron HS 500/9-12
36 W Highway 80 72958 479-637-3405
Bruce Sikes, prin. Fax 637-5624
Waldron MS 600/5-8
2075 Rice St 72958 479-637-4549
Dan Breshears, prin. Fax 637-3165

Walnut Ridge, Lawrence, Pop. 4,849
Walnut Ridge SD 800/K-12
508 E Free St 72476 870-886-6634
Terry E. Belcher, supt. Fax 886-6635
wrhsbobcats.nesc.k12.ar.us/
Walnut Ridge HS 200/9-12
508 E Free St 72476 870-886-6623
Charles Lee, prin. Fax 886-6624

Williams Baptist College Post-Sec.
PO Box 3665 72476 870-886-6741

Warren, Bradley, Pop. 6,368
Warren SD 1,600/K-12
PO Box 1210 71671 870-226-8500
Andrew Tolbert, supt. Fax 226-8531
se.sesc.k12.ar.us/warren/
Warren HS 500/9-12
803 N Walnut St 71671 870-226-6736
Jimmy Don Dupuy, prin. Fax 226-8527
Warren MS 400/6-8
PO Box 1210 71671 870-226-2484
Glenetta Burks, prin. Fax 226-8511

Weiner, Poinsett, Pop. 763
Weiner SD 400/K-12
313 N Garfield St 72479 870-684-2253
Betty McGruder, supt. Fax 684-7574
cardinal.k12.ar.us/
Weiner JSHS 200/7-12
313 Garfield St 72479 870-684-2250
Fax 684-7574

Western Grove, Newton, Pop. 409
Ozark Mountain SD
Supt. — See Saint Joe
Western Grove JSHS 100/7-12
300 School St 72685 870-429-5215
Cynthia Hearn, prin. Fax 429-5276

West Fork, Washington, Pop. 2,174
West Fork SD 1,100/K-12
359 School Ave 72774 479-839-2231
Dr. Joey Walters, supt. Fax 839-8412
www.westforktigers.k12.ar.us
West Fork HS 300/9-12
359 School Ave 72774 479-839-3131
John Karnes, prin. Fax 839-8412
West Fork MS 400/5-8
359 School Ave 72774 479-839-3342
David Skelton, prin. Fax 839-8412

West Helena, Phillips, Pop. 8,062
Helena-West Helena SD
Supt. — See Helena
Central HS 900/9-12
103 School Rd 72390 870-572-4503
Dr. Chris Gelenter, prin. Fax 572-4502
Miller JHS 600/7-8
106 Miller Loop 72390 870-572-3705
Ernest Simpson, prin. Fax 572-4525

De Soto S 300/K-12
PO Box 2807 72390 870-572-6717
E.G. Morris, hdmstr. Fax 572-9531

West Memphis, Crittenden, Pop. 28,014
West Memphis SD 6,000/K-12
PO Box 826 72303 870-735-1915
Bill Kessinger, supt. Fax 732-8643
west.grsc.k12.ar.us
East JHS 400/7-9
1151 Goodwin Ave 72301 870-735-2081
Arther Quarrels, prin. Fax 732-8583
West JHS 500/7-9
331 W Barton Ave 72301 870-735-3161
Jon Collins, prin. Fax 732-8566
West Memphis SHS 1,100/10-12
501 W Broadway St 72301 870-735-3660
Woodrow Burton, prin. Fax 732-8510
Wonder JHS 600/7-9
1401 Madison Ave 72301 870-735-8522
Dan Henderson, prin. Fax 732-8584

American Professional Institute Post-Sec.
103 S Avalon St 72301
Calvary Baptist Academy 50/PK-12
1600 N Avalon St 72301 870-735-5219
Barbara Stokes, admin. Fax 735-6396
Mid-South Community College Post-Sec.
2000 W Broadway St 72301 870-733-6722
Southern Institute of Cosmetology Post-Sec.
103 S Avalon St 72301 870-735-2800
West Memphis Christian S 300/K-12
PO Box 5669 72303 870-735-0341
Mark Lay, prin. Fax 400-4001

Wheatley, Saint Francis, Pop. 356
Palestine Wheatley SD
Supt. — See Forrest City
Palestine Wheatley MS 200/5-8
PO Box 109 72392 870-457-2121
Bobbie Fingers, prin. Fax 457-4840

White Hall, Jefferson, Pop. 4,979
White Hall SD 3,000/K-12
1020 W Holland Ave 71602 870-247-2196
Gary Kees, supt. Fax 247-3707
whsd.arsc.k12.ar.us/
White Hall JHS 600/7-9
8106 Dollarway Rd 71602 870-247-2711
Vicki Scott, prin. Fax 247-4879
White Hall SHS 700/10-12
700 Bulldog Dr 71602 870-247-3255
Bill Mitchell, prin. Fax 247-2756
Other Schools – See Redfield

Wickes, Polk, Pop. 686
Wickes SD 600/K-12
130 School Dr 71973 870-385-7101
Lendall Martin, supt. Fax 385-2238
Wickes HS 200/9-12
130 School Dr 71973 870-385-2366
Andy Curry, prin. Fax 385-7333
Wickes MS 200/5-8
130 School Dr 71973 870-385-2363
Rick Ward, prin. Fax 385-7212
Other Schools – See Umpire

Wilburn, Cleburne
Concord SD
Supt. — See Concord
Wilburn JSHS 100/7-12
PO Box 1000 72179 501-362-3302
Oneta Williams, prin. Fax 362-0836

Williford, Sharp, Pop. 65
Twin Rivers SD 500/K-12
423 College Ave 72482 870-966-4331
David Gilliard, supt. Fax 966-4490
willifordschool.tripod.com/williford.html
Williford JSHS 100/7-12
423 College Ave 72482 870-966-4331
Roy Causbie, prin. Fax 966-4490
Other Schools – See Ravenden Springs

Wilson, Mississippi, Pop. 877
South Mississippi County SD 900/K-12
22 N Jefferson St 72395 870-655-8633
Rogers Ford, supt. Fax 655-8841
Rivercrest HS 400/9-12
1700 W State Highway 14 72395 870-655-8111
Mitzi S. Smith, prin. Fax 655-8507
Rivercrest JHS 5-8
50 Cortez Kennedy Ave 72395 870-655-8421
Ronnie Parnell, prin. Fax 655-9980

Wynne, Cross, Pop. 8,466
Wynne SD 2,800/K-12
PO Box 69 72396 870-238-5000
Darrell Smith, supt. Fax 238-5011
wynne.k12.ar.us/
Wynne HS 800/9-12
PO Box 69 72396 870-238-5001
Carl Easley, prin. Fax 238-5009
Wynne JHS 700/6-8
PO Box 69 72396 870-238-5040
Darrell Mills, prin. Fax 238-5043

Yellville, Marion, Pop. 1,296
Yellville-Summit SD 1,000/K-12
1124 N Panther Ave 72687 870-449-4061
Dr. Jack Leatherman, supt. Fax 449-5003
yspanthers.k12.ar.us/
Yellville-Summit HS 300/9-12
1124 N Panther Ave 72687 870-449-4066
Ralph Bishop, prin. Fax 449-4773
Yellville-Summit MS 300/5-8
1124 N Panther Ave 72687 870-449-6533
Carl Jones, prin. Fax 449-4330

CALIFORNIA

CALIFORNIA DEPARTMENT OF EDUCATION
1430 N St, Sacramento 95814-5901
Telephone 916-319-0800
Fax 916-319-0100
Website http://www.cde.ca.gov

Superintendent of Public Instruction   Jack O'Connell

CALIFORNIA BOARD OF EDUCATION
1430 N St, Sacramento 95814-5901

President   Glee Johnson

COUNTY SUPERINTENDENTS OF SCHOOLS

Alameda County Office of Education
Sheila Jordan, supt.   510-887-0152
313 W Winton Ave, Hayward 94544   Fax 670-4146
www.alameda-coe.k12.ca.us/
Alpine County Office of Education
James Parsons, supt.   530-694-2230
43 Hawkside Dr   Fax 694-2379
Markleeville 96120
www.alpinecoe.k12.ca.us
Amador County Office of Education
Michael Carey, supt.   209-257-5353
217 Rex Ave, Jackson 95642   Fax 257-5360
www.co.amador.ca.us/
Butte County Office of Education
Don McNelis, supt.   530-532-5650
1859 Bird St, Oroville 95965   Fax 532-5762
www.bcoe.org/
Calaveras County Office of Education
John Brophy, supt.   209-736-4662
PO Box 760, Angels Camp 95222   Fax 736-2138
www.ccoe.k12.ca.us
Colusa County Office of Education
Kay Spurgeon, supt.   530-458-0350
146 7th St, Colusa 95932   Fax 458-8054
www.ccoe.net/
Contra Costa County Office of Education
Joseph Ovick, supt.   925-942-3388
77 Santa Barbara Rd   Fax 472-0875
Pleasant Hill 94523
www.cocoschools.org/
Del Norte County Office of Education
Jan Moorehouse, supt.   707-464-6141
301 W Washington Blvd   Fax 464-0238
Crescent City 95531
www.delnorte.k12.ca.us
El Dorado County Office of Education
Vicki Barber, supt.   530-622-7130
6767 Green Valley Rd   Fax 621-2543
Placerville 95667
www.edcoe.k12.ca.us
Fresno County Office of Education
Peter Mehas, supt.   559-265-3000
1111 Van Ness Ave, Fresno 93721   Fax 559-3053
www.fcoe.k12.ca.us
Glenn County Office of Education
Dr. Joni Samples, supt.   530-934-6575
311 S Villa Ave, Willows 95988   Fax 934-6576
www.glenncoe.org
Humboldt County Office of Education
Gary T. Eagles, supt.   707-445-7000
901 Myrtle Ave, Eureka 95501   Fax 445-7143
www.humboldt.k12.ca.us
Imperial County Office of Education
John Anderson, supt.   760-312-6464
1398 Sperber Rd, El Centro 92243   Fax 312-6565
www.icoe.k12.ca.us
Inyo County Office of Education
George Lozito, supt.   760-878-2426
PO Box G, Independence 93526   Fax 878-2279
www.inyo.k12.ca.us/
Kern County Office of Education
Larry Reider, supt.   661-636-4000
1300 17th St, Bakersfield 93301   Fax 636-4130
www.kern.org/
Kings County Office of Education
John Stankovich, supt.   559-584-1441
1144 W Lacey Blvd, Hanford 93230   Fax 589-7000
www.kings.k12.ca.us
Lake County Office of Education
William Cornelison, supt.   707-262-4100
1152 S Main St, Lakeport 95453   Fax 263-0197
www.lake-coe.k12.ca.us

Lassen County Office of Education
Robert Owens, supt.   530-257-2196
472-013 Johnstonville Rd   Fax 257-2518
Susanville 96130
www.lassencoe.org
Los Angeles County Office of Education
Darline P. Robles, supt.   562-922-6111
9300 Imperial Hwy, Downey 90242   Fax 922-6768
www.lacoe.edu
Madera County Office of Education
Sally Frazier Ed.D., supt.   559-673-6051
28123 Avenue 14, Madera 93638   Fax 673-5569
www.maderacoe.k12.ca.us
Marin County Office of Education
Mary Jane Burke, supt.   415-472-4110
PO Box 4925, San Rafael 94913   Fax 491-6625
www.marin.k12.ca.us
Mariposa County Office of Education
Patrick Holland, supt.   209-742-0250
PO Box 8, Mariposa 95338   Fax 966-4549
www.mariposa.k12.ca.us/
Mendocino County Office of Education
Paul Tichinin, supt.   707-467-5000
2240 Old River Rd, Ukiah 95482   Fax 462-0379
www.mcoe.k12.ca.us
Merced County Office of Education
Lee Andersen, supt.   209-381-6600
632 W 13th St, Merced 95340   Fax 381-6767
www.mcoe.org
Modoc County Office of Education
Vanston Shaw, supt.   530-233-7100
139 Henderson St, Alturas 96101   Fax 233-5531
www.modoccoe.k12.ca.us/
Mono County Office of Education
Richard McAteer, supt.   760-932-7311
PO Box 477, Bridgeport 93517   Fax 932-7278
www.monocoe.k12.ca.us
Monterey County Office of Education
William Barr, supt.   831-755-0300
PO Box 80851, Salinas 93912   Fax 755-6473
www.monterey.k12.ca.us
Napa County Office of Education
Barbara Nemko, supt.   707-253-6800
2121 Imola Ave, Napa 94559   Fax 253-6841
www.ncoe.k12.ca.us
Nevada County Office of Education
Terence McAteer, supt.   530-478-6400
112 Nevada City Hwy   Fax 478-6410
Nevada City 95959
www.nevco.k12.ca.us/
Orange County Office of Education
William Habermehl, supt.   714-966-4000
PO Box 9050, Costa Mesa 92628   Fax 662-3570
www.ocde.k12.ca.us
Placer County Office of Education
Alfred Nobili, supt.   530-889-8020
360 Nevada St, Auburn 95603   Fax 888-1367
www.placercoe.k12.ca.us
Plumas County Office of Education
Michael Chelotti, supt.   530-283-6500
50 Church St, Quincy 95971   Fax 283-6509
www.pcoe.k12.ca.us
Riverside County Office of Education
David Long, supt.   951-826-6530
PO Box 868, Riverside 92502   Fax 826-6199
www.rcoe.k12.ca.us
Sacramento County Office of Education
David Gordon, supt.   916-228-2500
PO Box 269003   Fax 228-2403
Sacramento 95826
www.scoe.net
San Benito County Office of Education
Tim Foley, supt.   831-637-5393
460 5th St, Hollister 95023   Fax 637-0140
sbcoe.k12.ca.us

San Bernardino Co. Office of Education
Herbert Fischer, supt.   909-386-2400
601 N E St, San Bernardino 92410   Fax 386-2941
www.sbcss.k12.ca.us
San Diego County Office of Education
Rudy Castruita, supt.   858-292-3500
6401 Linda Vista Rd   Fax 569-7851
San Diego 92111
www.sdcoe.k12.ca.us
San Francisco County Office of Education
Arlene Ackerman, supt.   415-241-6121
555 Franklin St   Fax 241-6012
San Francisco 94102
www.sfusd.edu
San Joaquin County Office of Education
Frederick Wentworth, supt.   209-468-4800
PO Box 213030, Stockton 95213   Fax 468-4975
www.sjcoe.org
San Luis Obispo Co. Office of Education
Julian Crocker, supt., PO Box 8105   805-543-7732
San Luis Obispo 93403   Fax 541-2605
www.slocs.k12.ca.us
San Mateo County Office of Education
Jean Holbrook, supt.   650-802-5300
101 Twin Dolphin Dr   Fax 802-5564
Redwood City 94065
www.smcoe.k12.ca.us
Santa Barbara County Office of Education
William Cirone, supt.   805-964-4711
PO Box 6307, Santa Barbara 93160   Fax 964-4712
www.sbceo.org
Santa Clara County Office of Education
Colleen Wilcox Ph.D., supt.   408-453-6500
1290 Ridder Park Dr   Fax 453-6811
San Jose 95131
www.sccoe.org
Santa Cruz County Office of Education
Dr. Diane Siri, supt.   831-476-7140
809 Bay Ave Ste H, Capitola 95010   Fax 476-5294
www.santacruz.k12.ca.us
Shasta County Office of Education
Carol M. Whitmer, supt.   530-225-0200
1644 Magnolia Ave   Fax 225-0329
Redding 96001
www.shastacoe.org/
Sierra County Office of Education
Mary Genasci, supt.   530-994-1044
PO Box 157, Sierraville 96126   Fax 994-1045
Siskiyou County Office of Education
Barbara Dillman, dir.   530-842-8400
609 S Gold St, Yreka 96097   Fax 842-8436
www.sisnet.ssku.k12.ca.us
Solano County Office of Education
Dee Alarcon, supt.   707-399-4400
5100 Business Center Dr   Fax 863-4175
Fairfield
www.solanocoe.k12.ca.us
Sonoma County Office of Education
Carl Wong, supt., 5340 Skylane Blvd   707-524-2600
Santa Rosa 95403   Fax 578-0220
www.sonoma.k12.ca.us
Stanislaus County Office of Education
Martin Petersen, supt.   209-525-4900
1100 H St, Modesto 95354   Fax 525-5147
www.stan-co.k12.ca.us
Sutter County Office of Education
Jeff Holland, supt.   530-822-2900
970 Klamath Ln, Yuba City 95993   Fax 671-3422
www.sutter.k12.ca.us
Tehama County Office of Education
Robert Douglas, supt.   530-527-5811
PO Box 689, Red Bluff 96080   Fax 529-4120
www.tehama.k12.ca.us

Trinity County Office of Education
James French, supt. 530-623-2861
PO Box 1256, Weaverville 96093 Fax 623-4489
www.tcoek12.org/
Tulare County Office of Education
Jim Vidak, supt. 559-733-6300
PO Box 5091, Visalia 93278 Fax 737-4378
www.tcoe.k12.ca.us

Tuolumne County Office of Education
Joe Silva, supt. 209-536-2000
175 Fairview Ln, Sonora 95370 Fax 536-2003
www.tuolcoe.k12.ca.us

Ventura County Office of Education
Charles Weis, supt. 805-383-1900
5189 Verdugo Way Fax 383-1908
Camarillo 93012
www.vcss.k12.ca.us
Yolo County Office of Education
Jorge Ayala, supt. 530-668-6700
1280 Santa Anita Ct Ste 100 Fax 668-3848
Woodland 95776
www.ycoe.org
Yuba County Office of Education
Richard Teagarden, supt. 530-741-6231
935 14th St, Marysville 95901 Fax 741-6500
www.yubacoe.k12.ca.us/

PUBLIC, PRIVATE AND CATHOLIC SECONDARY SCHOOLS

Acampo, San Joaquin

Mokelumne River S 300/K-12
18950 N Highway 99 95220 209-368-7271
Shannon Woodard, prin. Fax 368-7569

Acton, Los Angeles, Pop. 1,471
Acton-Agua Dulce USD 1,800/K-12
32248 Crown Valley Rd 93510 661-269-0750
Linda Wagner, supt. Fax 269-0849
aadusd.k12.ca.us/
High Desert MS 500/6-8
3620 Antelope Woods Rd 93510 661-269-0310
Gerald Watkins, prin. Fax 269-9336
Vasquez HS 600/9-12
33630 Red Rover Mine Rd 93510 661-269-0410
Martin Young, prin. Fax 269-5325

Adelanto, San Bernardino, Pop. 20,002
Adelanto ESD 6,500/K-8
PO Box 70 92301 760-246-8691
Chris Van Zee, supt. Fax 246-4259
www.aesd.net
Columbia MS 7-8
14409 Aster St 92301 760-530-1950
Dr. David Grohosky, prin. Fax 530-1953
Other Schools – See Victorville

Agoura Hills, Los Angeles, Pop. 21,784
Las Virgenes USD
Supt. — See Calabasas
Agoura HS 2,200/9-12
28545 Driver Ave 91301 818-889-1262
Larry Misel, prin. Fax 597-0816
Lindero Canyon MS 1,200/6-8
5844 Larboard Ln 91301 818-889-2134
Ronald Kaiser, prin. Fax 889-9432

Alameda, Alameda, Pop. 71,805
Alameda City USD 11,100/PK-12
2200 Central Ave 94501 510-337-7000
Ardella Dailey, supt. Fax 522-6926
www.alameda.k12.ca.us
Alameda HS 1,800/9-12
2201 Encinal Ave 94501 510-337-7022
Mike Janvier, prin. Fax 521-4740
Alameda Science & Technical Institute Vo/Tech
2200 Central Ave 94501 510-337-7059
Sean McPhetridge, prin. Fax 337-7163
Chipman MS 700/6-8
401 Pacific Ave 94501 510-748-4017
Laurie McLachlan-Fry, prin. Fax 523-5304
Encinal HS 1,200/9-12
210 Central Ave 94501 510-748-4023
Bill Sonneman, prin. Fax 521-4956
Lincoln MS 900/6-8
1250 Fernside Blvd 94501 510-748-4018
Fax 523-6217
Wood MS 800/6-8
420 Grand St 94501 510-748-4015
Valerie Williams, prin. Fax 523-8829
Alameda Adult S Adult
2250 Central Ave 94501 510-522-3858
Peggy McCarthy, prin. Fax 522-0846

Regional Occupational Center & Program
Supt. — None
Oakland-Alameda ROP Vo/Tech
2200 Central Ave 94501 510-337-7094
Sean McPhetridge, dir. Fax 337-7163

Alameda Beauty College Post-Sec.
2318 Central Ave 94501 510-523-1050
Armstrong University Post-Sec.
1301 Marina Village Pkwy 94501 510-865-1336
College of Alameda Post-Sec.
555 Atlantic Ave 94501 510-522-7221
St. Joseph Notre Dame HS 500/9-12
1011 Chestnut St 94501 510-523-1526
Anthony Aiello, prin. Fax 523-2181

Alamo, Contra Costa, Pop. 12,277
San Ramon Valley USD
Supt. — See Danville
Stone Valley MS 700/6-8
3001 Miranda Ave 94507 925-552-5640
Shawn McElroy, prin. Fax 838-5680

Albany, Alameda, Pop. 16,400
Albany USD 3,300/K-12
904 Talbot Ave 94706 510-558-3750
Dr. William Wong, supt. Fax 559-6560
www.albany.k12.ca.us
Albany HS 1,100/9-12
603 Key Route Blvd 94706 510-559-6550
Ron Rosenbaum, prin. Fax 559-6584
Albany MS 900/6-8
1259 Brighton Ave 94706 510-558-3600
Robin Davis, prin. Fax 559-6547
Albany Adult S Adult
601 San Gabriel Ave 94706 510-559-6580
Barry Shapiro, prin. Fax 559-6583

Alhambra, Los Angeles, Pop. 87,754
Alhambra City SD 19,300/K-12
15 W Alhambra Rd 91801 626-308-2200
Dr. Julie Hadden, supt. Fax 281-4020
www.alhambra.k12.ca.us
Alhambra HS 3,200/9-12
101 S 2nd St 91801 626-308-2342
Maria Sanchez, prin. Fax 308-2344
Keppel HS 2,200/9-12
501 E Hellman Ave 91801 626-572-2242
Russell Yamanaka, prin. Fax 572-2258
Alhambra Community Adult S Adult
101 S 2nd St 91801 626-308-2309
Jenny Schulz Mitchell, prin. Fax 308-2747
Garfield Community Adult S Adult
217 N Garfield Ave 91801 626-308-2247
Ana Escobedo, dir. Fax 308-2749
Keppel Community Adult S Adult
501 E Hellman Ave 91801 626-572-2209
Other Schools – See Rosemead, San Gabriel

Alhambra Beauty College Post-Sec.
PO Box 7494 91802 626-282-6433
Alliant International University Post-Sec.
1000 S Fremont Ave 91803 626-284-2777
Bryman College Post-Sec.
2215 W Mission Rd 91803 626-979-4940
Platt College Post-Sec.
1000 S Fremont Ave # A9W 91803 626-300-5444
Ramona Convent Secondary S 600/7-12
1701 W Ramona Rd 91803 626-282-4151
Kathleen Pillon, prin. Fax 281-0797

Aliso Viejo, Orange, Pop. 40,450
Capistrano USD
Supt. — See San Juan Capistrano
Aliso Niguel HS 2,900/9-12
28000 Wolverine Way 92656 949-831-5590
Dr. Charles Salter, prin. Fax 448-9854
Aliso Viejo MS 1,200/6-8
111 Park Ave 92656 949-831-2622
Peggy Swanson, prin. Fax 643-2784
Avila MS 1,300/6-8
26278 Wood Canyon Dr 92656 949-362-0348
Chris Carter, prin. Fax 362-9076

Saddleback Christian Academy 300/K-12
150 Columbia 92656 949-587-9650
Tracey Hodge, hdmstr.
Soka University of America Post-Sec.
1 University Dr 92656 949-480-4000

Alpaugh, Tulare
Alpaugh USD 300/K-12
PO Box 9 93201 559-949-8413
Robert Hudson, supt. Fax 949-8173
Alpaugh JSHS 100/7-12
PO Box 9 93201 559-949-8413
Leonard Cruz, admin. Fax 949-8173

Alpine, San Diego, Pop. 9,695
Alpine UNSD 2,400/PK-8
1323 Administration Way 91901 619-445-3236
Greg Ryan, supt. Fax 445-7045
alpineschooldistrict.net/
MacQueen MS 800/6-8
2001 Tavern Rd 91901 619-445-3245
Katy Woodward, prin. Fax 445-6503

Altadena, Los Angeles, Pop. 44,300
Pasadena USD
Supt. — See Pasadena
Eliot MS 1,100/6-8
2184 Lake Ave 91001 626-794-7121
Jerry Cradduck, prin. Fax 794-7238

Sahag-Mesrob Christian S 300/PK-12
2501 Maiden Ln 91001 626-798-5020
Levon Filian, admin. Fax 798-0036

Alta Loma, San Bernardino
Alta Loma ESD 7,500/K-8
9390 Baseline Rd 91701 909-484-5151
Janet Morey, supt. Fax 484-5155
www.alsd.k12.ca.us
Alta Loma JHS 1,000/7-8
9000 Lemon Ave 91701 909-484-5100
Judith Neiuber, prin. Fax 484-5105
Vineyard JHS 1,100/7-8
6440 Mayberry Ave 91737 909-484-5120
Catherine Perry, prin. Fax 484-5125

Chaffey JUNHSD
Supt. — See Ontario
Alta Loma HS 2,900/9-12
8880 Baseline Rd 91701 909-989-5511
William Bertrand, prin. Fax 987-8321

Chaffey College Post-Sec.
5885 Haven Ave 91737 909-987-1737

Altaville, Calaveras
Bret Harte UNHSD
Supt. — See Angels Camp
Bret Harte Union HS 800/9-12
PO Box 208 95221 209-736-2507
Aaron Rosander, prin. Fax 736-8383

Alturas, Modoc, Pop. 2,877
Modoc JUSD 1,200/K-12
906 W 4th St 96101 530-233-7201
Douglas Squellati, supt. Fax 233-4362
www.modoc.k12.ca.us
Modoc HS 300/9-12
900 N Main St 96101 530-233-7501
Don Demsher, prin. Fax 233-7306
Modoc MS 200/6-8
906 W 4th St 96101 530-233-7201
Lane Bates, prin. Fax 233-7503
Modoc Community Adult S Adult
802 N East St 96101 530-233-7201
Ron Handel, prin. Fax 233-5158

Regional Occupational Center & Program
Supt. — None
Modoc ROP Vo/Tech
139 Henderson St 96101 530-233-7102
Randy Wise, admin. Fax 233-5531

American Canyon, Napa, Pop. 13,135
Napa Valley USD
Supt. — See Napa
American Canyon MS 800/6-8
300 Benton Way 94503 707-259-8592
Roseann Gasser, prin. Fax 259-8800

Anaheim, Orange, Pop. 332,361
Anaheim UNHSD 32,800/7-12
501 N Crescent Way 92801 714-999-3511
Joseph Farley Ed.D., supt. Fax 808-9090
www.auhsd.k12.ca.us/
Anaheim HS 2,700/9-12
811 W Lincoln Ave 92805 714-999-3717
Ben Sanchez, prin. Fax 772-6537
Ball JHS 1,500/7-8
1500 W Ball Rd 92802 714-999-3663
Diane Bethencourt, prin. Fax 563-9214
Brookhurst JHS 1,400/7-8
601 N Brookhurst St 92801 714-999-3613
Russel Earnest, prin. Fax 999-1764
Dale JHS 1,400/7-8
900 S Dale Ave 92804 714-220-4210
Kirsten Schaefer, prin. Fax 220-4076
Katella HS 2,300/9-12
2200 E Wagner Ave 92806 714-999-3621
Jack Jensen, prin. Fax 535-3991
Loara HS 2,200/9-12
1765 W Cerritos Ave 92804 714-999-3677
Pam Krey, prin. Fax 999-3703
Magnolia HS 1,700/9-12
2450 W Ball Rd 92804 714-220-4221
Ken Fox, prin. Fax 220-4233
Orangeview JHS 1,400/7-8
3715 W Orange Ave 92804 714-220-4205
Denise Selbe, prin. Fax 220-3023
Savanna HS 3,500/7-12
301 N Gilbert St 92801 714-220-4262
Marsha Wagner, prin. Fax 995-2544
South JHS 1,700/7-8
2320 E South St 92806 714-999-3667
Mike Brennan, prin. Fax 999-3721
Sycamore JHS 2,000/7-8
1801 E Sycamore St 92805 714-999-3616
Manuel Colon, prin. Fax 776-3879
Western HS 1,800/9-12
501 S Western Ave 92804 714-220-4040
John Dahlem, prin. Fax 220-4027
Adult Education Adult
1800 W Ball Rd 92804 714-999-5616
Fax 999-5650
Other Schools – See Cypress, La Palma

Orange USD
Supt. — See Orange
Canyon HS 2,000/9-12
220 S Imperial Hwy 92807 714-532-8000
Gloria Duncan, prin. Fax 921-0278

Placentia Yorba Linda USD
Supt. — See Placentia
Esperanza HS 3,000/9-12
1830 N Kellogg Dr 92807 714-779-7870
Dave Flynn, prin. Fax 693-7527

Regional Occupational Center & Program
Supt. — None
North Orange County ROP Vo/Tech
385 N Muller St 92801 714-502-5800
Patricia Frank, supt. Fax 535-0891

American Career College Post-Sec.
1200 N Magnolia Ave 92801 714-952-9066
Anaheim Discovery Christian HS 100/6-12
622 N Gilbert St 92801 714-535-2535
Carol Caltharp, admin. Fax 991-5418
Bethesda Christian University Post-Sec.
730 N Euclid St 92801 714-517-1945
Brownson Technical School Post-Sec.
1110 S Technology Cir Ste D 92805 714-774-9443

Bryman College   Post-Sec.
  511 N Brookhurst St Ste 300 92801   714-953-6500
California Career School   Post-Sec.
  1100 S Technology Cir 92805   714-635-6585
Calvary Chapel Anaheim S   200/PK-12
  270 E Palais Rd 92805   714-563-9620
  Michael Moddelmog, prin.   Fax 563-9520
Career Academy of Beauty   Post-Sec.
  663 N Euclid St 92801   714-776-8400
Connelly HS   200/9-12
  2323 W Broadway 92804   714-776-1717
  Sr. Francine Gunther, prin.   Fax 776-2534
Fairmont Private HS   600/7-12
  2200 W Sequoia Ave 92801   714-999-5055
  Uwe Gemba, hdmstr.   Fax 999-0150
Integrity Christian S   100/K-12
  4905 E La Palma Ave 92807   714-693-2022
  Shelly Kitada, admin.
ITT Technical Institute   Post-Sec.
  525 N Muller St 92801   714-535-3700
Maric College   Post-Sec.
  1360 S Anaheim Blvd 92805   714-758-1500
Orange County Christian S   200/PK-12
  641 S Western Ave 92804   714-821-6227
  Elaine Findley, admin.   Fax 952-8823
Saints of Glory S   50/K-12
  1210 W Park Ave 92801   714-875-9387
  Ichiro Tsuruoka, admin.   Fax 817-0612
Servite HS   800/9-12
  1952 W La Palma Ave 92801   714-774-7575
  Raymond Dunne, prin.   Fax 774-1404
South Baylo University   Post-Sec.
  1126 N Brookhurst St 92801   714-533-1495
Southern California Institute of Tech   Post-Sec.
  1900 W Crescent Ave 92801   714-520-5552
Vineyard Christian S   300/PK-12
  5340 E La Palma Ave 92807   714-777-5462
  Jim Wilkinson, prin.   Fax 777-5422
Westwood College   Post-Sec.
  1551 S Douglass Rd 92806   714-704-2727

Anderson, Shasta, Pop. 9,894
Anderson UNHSD   2,200/9-12
  1469 Ferry St 96007   530-378-0568
  Randy Palomino, supt.   Fax 378-0834
  www.anderson.k12.ca.us/
Anderson HS   900/9-12
  1471 Ferry St 96007   530-365-2741
  Mike Koontz, prin.   Fax 365-5446
Other Schools – See Cottonwood

Cascade UNESD   1,500/K-8
  1645 Mill St 96007   530-378-7000
  John Almond, supt.   Fax 378-7001
  www.shastalink.k12.ca.us/cascade/
Anderson MS   500/6-8
  1646 Ferry St 96007   530-378-7060
  Wesley Smith, prin.   Fax 378-7061

Happy Valley UNESD   600/K-8
  16300 Cloverdale Rd 96007   530-357-2134
  Robert Ferrera, supt.   Fax 357-4143
  www.shastalink.k12.ca.us/happyvalley/
Happy Valley MS   300/5-8
  17480 Palm Ave 96007   530-357-2111
  Steve Westaby, prin.   Fax 357-4193

American Christian Academy   1,200/1-12
  PO Box 805 96007   530-365-2950
  Jim Rose, supt.   Fax 365-2950

Angels Camp, Calaveras, Pop. 2,997
Bret Harte UNHSD   800/9-12
  PO Box 7000 95221   209-736-8340
  Joseph W. Wilimek, supt.   Fax 736-8367
  www.bhuhsd.k12.ca.us
Other Schools – See Altaville

Calaveras County Office of Education
  PO Box 760 95222   209-736-4662
  John Brophy, supt.   Fax 736-2138
  www.ccoe.k12.ca.us
Calaveras County Adult Education   Adult
  PO Box 760 95221   209-736-6033
  W. Patrick Miller, dir.   Fax 736-2138

Regional Occupational Center & Program
  Supt. – None
Calaveras County ROP   Vo/Tech
  PO Box 760 95221   209-736-6033
  W. Patrick Miller, dir.   Fax 736-2138

Angwin, Napa, Pop. 3,503

Pacific Union College   Post-Sec.
  1 Angwin Ave 94508   707-965-6311
Pacific Union/College Prep S   100/9-12
  1 Angwin Ave 94508   707-965-7272
      Fax 965-6689

Antelope, Sacramento, Pop. 70
Center USD   4,300/K-12
  8408 Watt Ave 95843   916-338-6330
  Dr. Kevin Jolly, supt.   Fax 338-6411
  www.centerusd.k12.ca.us
Center HS   1,700/9-12
  3111 Center Court Ln 95843   916-338-6420
  Bill Newton, prin.   Fax 338-6370
Other Schools – See Roseville

Dry Creek ESD
  Supt. — See Roseville
Antelope Crossing MS   1,100/6-8
  9200 Palmerson Dr 95843   916-745-2100
  Gordon Medd, prin.   Fax 745-2135

Antioch, Contra Costa, Pop. 101,124
Antioch USD   20,200/K-12
  PO Box 768 94509   925-706-4100
  Dennis Goettsch, supt.   Fax 757-2937
  www.antioch.k12.ca.us
Antioch HS   2,800/9-12
  700 W 18th St 94509   925-706-5300
  Jeff Reich, prin.   Fax 706-1875

Antioch MS   1,100/6-8
  1500 D St 94509   925-706-5316
  Stephanie Anello, prin.   Fax 706-5430
Black Diamond MS   1,300/6-8
  4730 Sterling Hill Dr 94531   925-776-5500
  Clarence Isadore, prin.   Fax 779-2600
Dallas Ranch MS   1,300/6-8
  1401 Mount Hamilton Dr 94531   925-706-4491
  Bob Sanchez, prin.   Fax 706-1933
Deer Valley HS   3,300/9-12
  4700 Lone Tree Way 94531   925-776-5555
  Jo Ella Allen, prin.   Fax 754-8094
Park MS   1,300/6-8
  1 Spartan Way 94509   925-706-5314
  Scott Bergerhouse, prin.   Fax 706-2376
Antioch Adult & Community Education Ctr.   Adult
  820 W 2nd St 94509   925-706-5365
  Jim Hollingsworth, prin.   Fax 778-5843

Antioch Hilltop Christian SDA S   100/K-10
  2200 Country Hills Dr 94509   925-778-0214
  Monica Greene, prin.   Fax 778-7418
Cornerstone Christian S   500/PK-12
  1745 E 18th St 94509   925-754-1241
      Fax 754-0769
Heritage Baptist Academy   200/K-12
  5200 Heidorn Ranch Rd 94531   925-778-2234
  Dr. John Mincy, admin.
Western Career College   Post-Sec.
  2157 Country Hills Dr 94509   925-522-7777

Anza, Riverside
Hemet USD
  Supt. — See Hemet
Hamilton HS   7-12
  57430 Mitchell Rd 92539   951-763-1865
  Jim Allured, prin.   Fax 763-5420

Apple Valley, San Bernardino, Pop. 60,076
Apple Valley USD   13,900/K-12
  22974 Bear Valley Rd 92308   760-247-8001
  Steven Webb, supt.   Fax 247-4103
  www.avusd.org
Apple Valley HS   2,000/9-12
  11837 Navajo Rd 92308   760-247-7206
  Lois Osborn, prin.   Fax 247-2092
Apple Valley MS   1,600/6-8
  12555 Navajo Rd 92308   760-247-7267
  Stella Kemp, prin.   Fax 247-1226
Granite Hills HS   2,100/9-12
  22900 Esaws Ave 92307   760-961-2290
  Matt Schulenberg, prin.   Fax 961-8755
Vista Campana MS   1,700/6-8
  20700 Thunderbird Rd 92307   760-242-7011
  Sonia Waterman, prin.   Fax 242-7005

Apple Valley Christian S   300/PK-12
  22434 Nisqually Rd 92308   760-247-8412
  Ann Hainley, prin.   Fax 247-6988
Valley Christian S   50/K-12
  19923 Bear Valley Rd 92308   760-247-2933
  Mary Ann Beaumont, prin.   Fax 247-4903

Aptos, Santa Cruz, Pop. 9,061
Pajaro Valley USD
  Supt. — See Watsonville
Aptos HS   2,000/9-12
  100 Mariner Way 95003   831-688-6565
  Diane Burbank, prin.   Fax 688-6430
Aptos JHS   700/7-8
  1001 Huntington Dr 95003   831-688-3234
  Ray Blute, prin.   Fax 728-8139

Cabrillo College   Post-Sec.
  6500 Soquel Dr 95003   831-479-6100

Arbuckle, Colusa, Pop. 1,912
Pierce JUSD   1,200/K-12
  PO Box 239 95912   530-476-2892
  Patricia Hamilton, supt.   Fax 476-2289
  www.pierce.k12.ca.us
Johnson JHS   300/6-8
  938 Wildwood Rd 95912   530-476-3261
  John Ithurburn, prin.   Fax 476-2017
Pierce HS   400/9-12
  960 Wildwood Rd 95912   530-476-2277
  Doug Kaelin, prin.   Fax 476-3285

Arcadia, Los Angeles, Pop. 55,443
Arcadia USD   9,900/K-12
  234 Campus Dr 91007   626-821-8300
  Mimi Hennessy, supt.   Fax 821-8647
  www.ausd.k12.ca.us
Arcadia HS   3,600/9-12
  234 Campus Dr 91007   626-821-8370
  David Vannasdall, prin.   Fax 821-1712
Dana MS   800/6-8
  234 Campus Dr 91007   626-821-8361
  Joseph Fox, prin.   Fax 447-1965
First Avenue MS   800/6-8
  234 Campus Dr 91007   626-821-8362
  Beverly Klatt, prin.   Fax 446-1660
Foothills MS   900/6-8
  234 Campus Dr 91007   626-821-8363
  Patricia Hartline, prin.   Fax 303-7983

Rio Hondo Preparatory S   200/6-12
  PO Box 662080 91066   626-444-9531
  Arlis Dowd, prin.   Fax 442-1113

Arcata, Humboldt, Pop. 16,891
Arcata ESD   800/K-8
  1435 Buttermilk Ln 95521   707-822-0351
  Douglas White, supt.   Fax 822-6589
  www.humboldt.k12.ca.us/arcata_sd/index.htm
Sunny Brae MS   300/6-8
  1430 Buttermilk Ln 95521   707-822-5988
  Carlena Moss, prin.   Fax 822-7002

Northern Humboldt UNHSD
  Supt. — See Mc Kinleyville
Arcata HS   1,000/9-12
  1720 M St 95521   707-825-2400
  Bob Wallace, prin.   Fax 825-2407

Pacific Coast HS   200/9-12
  1720 M St 95521   707-825-2443
  David Navarre, prin.   Fax 825-2407

Humboldt State University   Post-Sec.
  1 Harpst St 95521   707-826-3011

Armona, Kings, Pop. 3,122
Armona UNESD   1,000/K-8
  PO Box 368 93202   559-583-5000
  Steve Bogan, supt.   Fax 583-5004
  www.kings.k12.ca.us/armona/
Parkview MS   500/5-8
  11075 C St 93202   559-583-5020
  Phil Holloway, prin.   Fax 583-5030

Armona Union Academy   100/K-12
  PO Box 397 93202   559-582-4468
      Fax 582-6609

Arroyo Grande, San Luis Obispo, Pop. 16,373
Lucia Mar USD   11,100/K-12
  602 Orchard Ave 93420   805-474-3000
  Deborah Flores Ph.D., supt.   Fax 481-1398
  www.luciamar.k12.ca.us/
Arroyo Grande HS   2,300/9-12
  495 Valley Rd 93420   805-474-3200
  Ryan Pinkerton, prin.   Fax 473-4222
Mesa MS   800/6-8
  2555 S Halcyon Rd 93420   805-474-3400
  Barb LoCoco, prin.   Fax 473-4396
Paulding MS   600/7-8
  600 Crown Hill St 93420   805-474-3500
  Gary Moore, prin.   Fax 473-5525
Other Schools – See Nipomo, Pismo Beach

Regional Occupational Center & Program
  Supt. — None
Santa Lucia ROP   Vo/Tech
  602 Orchard Ave 93420   805-474-3000
  James Souza, dir.   Fax 473-5593

Coastal Christian S   200/K-12
  1220 Farroll Ave 93420   805-489-1213
  Lance Tullis, admin.   Fax 489-5394
Valley View Adventist Academy   100/K-10
  230 Vernon St 93420   805-489-2687
  Donald Ramey, prin.   Fax 489-2704

Artesia, Los Angeles, Pop. 16,812
ABC USD
  Supt. — See Cerritos
Ross MS   600/7-8
  17707 Elaine Ave 90701   562-924-8331
  Cheryl Bodger, prin.   Fax 402-6145

Arvin, Kern, Pop. 14,009
Arvin UNESD   4,300/K-8
  737 Bear Mountain Blvd 93203   661-854-6500
  Ken Bergevin, supt.   Fax 854-2362
  arvin.k12.ca.us
Haven Drive MS   900/6-8
  737 Bear Mountain Blvd 93203   661-854-6540
  David Bowling, prin.   Fax 854-1440

Kern HSD
  Supt. — See Bakersfield
Arvin HS   2,400/9-12
  PO Box 518 93203   661-854-5561
  Blanca Cavazos, prin.   Fax 854-5943

Atascadero, San Luis Obispo, Pop. 27,015
Atascadero USD   5,600/K-12
  5601 West Mall 93422   805-462-4200
  John Rogers, supt.   Fax 466-2941
  www.atas.k12.ca.us
Atascadero Fine Arts Academy   200/4-8
  6100 Olmeda Ave 93422   805-460-2500
  Cheryl Hockett, prin.   Fax 460-2522
Atascadero HS   1,700/9-12
  1 High School Hill Rd 93422   805-462-4300
  Kimberley Spinks, prin.   Fax 462-4387
Atascadero JHS   800/7-8
  6501 Lewis Ave 93422   805-462-4360
  Kirk Smith, prin.   Fax 462-4373

North County Christian S   200/K-12
  PO Box 6017 93423   805-466-4457
  Rich Jessup, admin.   Fax 466-7948

Atherton, San Mateo, Pop. 7,067
Menlo Park City ESD   2,000/K-8
  181 Encinal Ave 94027   650-321-7140
  Kenneth Ranella, supt.   Fax 321-7184
  www.mpcsd.org
Other Schools – See Menlo Park

Sequoia UNHSD
  Supt. — See Redwood City
Menlo-Atherton HS   2,100/9-12
  555 Middlefield Rd 94027   650-322-5311
  Denise Plante, prin.   Fax 323-1411

Menlo College   Post-Sec.
  1000 El Camino Real 94027   650-688-3753
Menlo S   800/6-12
  50 Valparaiso Ave 94027   650-330-2000
      Fax 330-2002
Sacred Heart Prep S   900/PK-12
  150 Valparaiso Ave 94027   650-322-1866
  Richard Dioli, prin.   Fax 322-7151

Atwater, Merced, Pop. 26,515
Atwater ESD   5,000/K-8
  1401 Broadway Ave 95301   209-357-6100
  Melinda Hennes, supt.   Fax 357-6163
  www.aesd.edu
Mitchell Sr ES   1,000/7-8
  1753 5th St 95301   209-357-6124
  Bob Ellis, prin.   Fax 357-6506

Merced UNHSD — 9,300/9-12
3430 A St 95301 — 209-385-6400
Robert Fore Ph.D., supt. — Fax 385-6442
muhsd.k12.ca.us
Atwater HS — 1,800/9-12
PO Box 835 95301 — 209-357-6000
Linda Lucas, prin. — Fax 357-6067
Buhach Colony HS — 1,500/9-12
PO Box 753 95301 — 209-357-6600
Ernest Sopp, prin. — Fax 357-6602
Other Schools – See Livingston, Merced

Auburn, Placer, Pop. 12,522
Auburn UNESD — 2,900/K-8
255 Epperle Ln 95603 — 530-885-7242
Michele Schuetz, supt. — Fax 885-5170
www.auburn.k12.ca.us/
Cain MS — 900/6-8
150 Palm Ave 95603 — 530-823-6106
Laurie Hockerson, prin. — Fax 823-0943

Placer UNHSD — 12,200/9-12
PO Box 5048 95604 — 530-886-4400
Bart O'Brien, supt. — Fax 886-4439
www.puhsd.k12.ca.us/
Placer HS — 1,700/9-12
275 Orange St 95603 — 530-885-4581
Dave Horsey, prin. — Fax 823-5770
Placer S for Adults — Adult
390 Finley St 95603 — 530-885-8585
Gregg Ramseth, prin. — Fax 823-1406
Other Schools – See Colfax, Foresthill, Loomis

Regional Occupational Center & Program
Supt. — None
Forty-Niner ROP — Vo/Tech
360 Nevada St 95603 — 530-889-5940
Randy Scott, admin. — Fax 887-1704
_____

Forest Lake Christian S — 700/K-12
12515 Combie Rd 95602 — 530-269-1535
Jean Schoellerman, dir. — Fax 269-1541
Pine Hills Adventist Academy — 100/K-12
13500 Richards Ln 95603 — 530-885-9447
— Fax 885-5237

Avalon, Los Angeles, Pop. 3,312
Long Beach USD
Supt. – See Long Beach
Avalon S — 800/K-12
PO Box 557 90704 — 310-510-0790
Sally Gregory, prin. — Fax 510-2986

Avenal, Kings, Pop. 15,813
Reef-Sunset USD — 2,500/K-12
205 N Park Ave 93204 — 559-386-9083
Dr. Nancy Mellor, supt. — Fax 386-5303
www.kings.k12.ca.us/rsusd/
Avenal HS — 600/9-12
601 E Mariposa St 93204 — 559-386-5253
Felipe Meraz, prin. — Fax 386-9413
Reef-Sunset MS — 500/6-8
608 N 1st Ave 93204 — 559-386-4128
Dorothy Crass, prin. — Fax 386-4918

Avery, Calaveras, Pop. 900
Vallecito UNSD — 900/K-8
PO Box 329 95224 — 209-795-8000
Michael Chimente, supt. — Fax 795-8005
www.vsd.k12.ca.us
Avery MS — 400/K-8
PO Box 329 95224 — 209-795-8045
Thomas Kevin Hart, prin. — Fax 795-8048

Azusa, Los Angeles, Pop. 46,962
Azusa USD — 13,700/K-12
PO Box 500 91702 — 626-967-6211
C. Cervantes McGuire, supt. — Fax 858-6123
www.azusausd.k12.ca.us
Azusa HS — 1,400/9-12
PO Box 500 91702 — 626-815-5212
Rick Stoecklein, prin. — Fax 815-5206
Center MS — 900/6-8
PO Box 500 91702 — 626-815-5189
Bob Ware, prin. — Fax 815-5534
Foothill MS — 1,000/6-8
PO Box 500 91702 — 626-815-5132
Jackie Littrell, prin. — Fax 815-1027
Slauson MS — 1,000/6-8
PO Box 500 91702 — 626-815-5144
Armando Marentes, prin. — Fax 815-5147
Other Schools – See Covina, Glendora
_____

Azusa Pacific University — Post-Sec.
901 E Alosta Ave 91702 — 626-969-3434

Baker, San Bernardino
Baker Valley USD — 300/K-12
PO Box 460 92309 — 760-733-4567
Mark Kemp, supt. — Fax 733-4605
www.baker.k12.ca.us/
Baker HS, PO Box 460 92309 — 100/9-12
Robert McGrew, prin. — 760-733-4567
Baker JHS, PO Box 460 92309 — 50/7-8
Robert McGrew, prin. — 760-733-4567
Baker Valley Adult S — Adult
PO Box 460 92309 — 760-733-4567

Bakersfield, Kern, Pop. 271,035
Bakersfield CSD — 29,400/K-8
1300 Baker St 93305 — 661-631-4600
Michael Lingo, supt. — Fax 326-1485
www.bcsd.com
Chipman JHS — 800/7-8
2905 Eissler St 93306 — 661-631-5210
Russell Taylor, prin. — Fax 631-3229
Compton JHS — 700/7-8
3211 Pico Ave 93306 — 661-631-5230
Linda Carbajal, prin. — Fax 631-3168
Curran MS — 1,000/6-8
1116 Lymric Way 93309 — 661-631-5240
Kim Edwards, prin. — Fax 631-4538
Emerson MS — 1,000/6-8
801 4th St 93304 — 661-631-5260
Kempton Coman, prin. — Fax 631-3157

Sequoia MS — 1,000/6-8
900 Belle Ter 93304 — 661-631-5940
Hugh McGowan, prin. — Fax 631-3236
Sierra MS — 800/6-8
3017 Center St 93306 — 661-631-5470
Tomas Prieto, prin. — Fax 631-4541
Stiern MS — 1,500/6-8
2551 Morning Dr 93306 — 661-631-5480
Warren Ramay, prin. — Fax 631-3241
Washington MS — 700/6-8
1101 Noble Ave 93305 — 661-631-5810
Armando Carrillo, prin. — Fax 631-3172

Beardsley ESD — 1,900/K-8
1001 Roberts Ln 93308 — 661-393-8550
Ken Chapman, supt. — Fax 393-5965
www.beardsleyschool.org/
Beardsley JHS — 400/7-8
1001 Roberts Ln 93308 — 661-392-9254
Rocky Johnson, prin. — Fax 399-3925

Edison ESD — 900/K-8
9600 Eucalyptus Dr 93306 — 661-363-5394
Barbara Clark, supt. — Fax 363-4631
www.edisonschooldistrict.org
Edison MS — 400/5-8
721 S Edison Rd 93307 — 661-366-8216
Loreda Clevenger, prin. — Fax 366-0922

Fairfax ESD — 1,000/K-8
1500 S Fairfax Rd 93307 — 661-366-7221
Desiree Von Flue, supt. — Fax 366-1901
www.fairfax.k12.ca.us/
Fairfax MS — 600/6-8
1500 S Fairfax Rd 93307 — 661-366-4461
Terry Wolfe, prin. — Fax 366-5831

Fruitvale ESD — 3,100/K-8
7311 Rosedale Hwy 93308 — 661-589-3830
Dr. Carl Olsen, supt. — Fax 589-3674
www.fruitvale.k12.ca.us/
Fruitvale JHS — 800/7-8
2114 Calloway Dr 93312 — 661-589-3933
John Hefner, prin. — Fax 588-3259

Greenfield UNESD — 7,800/K-8
1624 Fairview Rd 93307 — 661-837-6000
Gary Rice, supt. — Fax 832-2873
www.gfusd.k12.ca.us/
Greenfield MS — 1,000/6-8
1109 Pacheco Rd 93307 — 661-837-6110
Scott McArthur, prin. — Fax 832-7431
McKee MS, 205 McKee Rd 93307 — 800/6-8
Carol Schaefer, prin. — 661-837-6060
Ollivier MS — 1,000/6-8
7310 Monitor St 93307 — 661-837-6120
Sheila Johnson, prin. — Fax 396-0963

Kern HSD — 35,900/9-12
5801 Sundale Ave 93309 — 661-827-3154
Donald E. Carter, supt. — Fax 827-3302
www.kernhigh.org/
Bakersfield HS — 2,900/9-12
1241 G St 93301 — 661-324-9841
David Reese, prin. — Fax 324-3401
Centennial HS — 2,300/9-12
8601 Hageman Rd 93312 — 661-588-8601
David Olds, prin. — Fax 588-8608
East Bakersfield HS — 2,100/9-12
2200 Quincy Dr 93306 — 661-871-7221
John Gibson, prin. — Fax 872-6980
Foothill HS — 2,200/9-12
501 Park Dr 93306 — 661-366-4491
Mark Richardson, prin. — Fax 363-6223
Frontier HS — 9-12
6401 Allen Rd, — 661-829-1107
Dr. Bill Bruce, prin. — Fax 829-1185
Golden Valley HS — 1,100/9-12
801 Hosking Ave 93307 — 661-827-0800
William Sandoval, prin. — Fax 827-0480
Highland HS — 2,000/9-12
2900 Royal Scots Way 93306 — 661-872-2777
Robert Schneider, prin. — Fax 871-6052
Liberty HS — 2,500/9-12
925 Jewetta Ave 93312 — 661-587-0925
Pat Preston, prin. — Fax 587-1299
North HS — 2,200/9-12
300 Galaxy Ave 93308 — 661-399-3351
Bryon Schaefer, prin. — Fax 393-5918
Ridgeview HS — 2,200/9-12
8501 Stine Rd 93313 — 661-398-3100
Bill Jones, prin. — Fax 398-9758
Ruggenberg Career Center — Vo/Tech
610 Ansol Ln 93306 — 661-366-4401
Lu Ellen Fleming, admin. — Fax 363-0828
Schuetz Career Center — Vo/Tech
8600 Shannon Dr 93307 — 661-827-4800
Jim Bennett, prin. — Fax 827-4804
South HS — 2,300/9-12
1101 Planz Rd 93304 — 661-831-3680
Librado Vasquez, prin. — Fax 837-2756
Stockdale HS — 2,500/9-12
2800 Buena Vista Rd 93311 — 661-665-2800
Ramon Hendrix, prin. — Fax 665-0914
West HS — 2,400/9-12
1200 New Stine Rd 93309 — 661-832-2822
Dean McGee, prin. — Fax 831-5606
Bakersfield Adult HS — Adult
501 S Mount Vernon Ave 93307 — 661-835-1855
Susan Handy, prin. — Fax 835-9612
Other Schools – See Arvin, Lake Isabella, Shafter

Norris SD — 2,100/K-8
6940 Calloway Dr 93312 — 661-387-7000
Wallace McCormick Ph.D., supt. — Fax 399-9750
www.norris.k12.ca.us/
Norris MS — 700/6-8
6940 Calloway Dr 93312 — 661-387-7060
Dianne Doremus, prin. — Fax 399-9356

Panama-Buena Vista UNSD — 14,000/K-8
4200 Ashe Rd 93313 — 661-831-8331
Douglas Miller, supt. — Fax 398-2141
www.pbvusd.k12.ca.us
Actis JHS — 700/7-8
2400 Westholme Blvd 93309 — 661-833-1250
Bill Galloway, prin. — Fax 833-9656
Tevis JHS — 900/7-8
3901 Pin Oak Park Blvd 93311 — 661-664-7211
Robert Machado, prin. — Fax 664-9659
Thompson JHS, Fred L. — 800/7-8
4200 Planz Rd 93309 — 661-832-8011
Jon Dean, prin. — Fax 832-5165
Warren JHS — 1,000/7-8
4615 Mountain Vista Dr 93311 — 661-665-9210
George Thornburgh, prin. — Fax 665-9507

Regional Occupational Center & Program
Supt. — None
Kern County ROP — Vo/Tech
1300 17th St 93301 — 661-824-9313
Armando Vazquez, admin. — Fax 824-9316
Kern HSD ROP — Vo/Tech
501 S Mount Vernon Ave 93307 — 661-831-3327
Sandra Banducci, admin. — Fax 398-8239

Rio Bravo-Greeley ESD — 800/K-8
6521 Enos Ln, — 661-589-2696
Gerald Higbee, supt. — Fax 589-2218
www.rbgusd.k12.ca.us
Rio Bravo-Greeley MS — 500/4-8
6601 Enos Ln, — 661-589-2505
Art Folsom, prin. — Fax 588-7204

Rosedale UNESD — 4,200/K-8
2553 Old Farm Rd 93312 — 661-588-6000
Jamie Henderson, supt. — Fax 588-6009
www.rosedale.k12.ca.us
Freedom MS — 600/7-8
11445 Noriega Rd 93312 — 661-588-6044
Sue Lemon, prin. — Fax 588-6048
Rosedale MS — 600/7-8
12463 Rosedale Hwy 93312 — 661-588-6030
Maria Toretta, prin. — Fax 588-6039

Standard ESD — 2,700/K-8
1200 N Chester Ave 93308 — 661-392-2110
Erich Kwek Ed.D., supt. — Fax 392-0681
www.standard.k12.ca.us
Standard MS — 900/6-8
1222 N Chester Ave 93308 — 661-392-2130
Tonny Gisbertz, prin. — Fax 392-2134

Vineland ESD — 900/K-8
14713 Weedpatch Hwy 93307 — 661-845-3713
Adolph Wirth, supt. — Fax 845-8449
www.vinelandschooldistrict.com
Sunset MS — 400/5-8
8301 Sunset Blvd 93307 — 661-845-1320
Mike Gonzalez, prin. — Fax 845-3952
_____

Bakersfield Adventist Academy — 200/K-12
3333 Bernard St 93306 — 661-871-1591
Alex Federowski, prin. — Fax 871-1594
Bakersfield Christian HS — 400/9-12
12775 Stockdale Hwy, — 661-410-7000
David Meek, prin. — Fax 410-7007
Bakersfield College — Post-Sec.
1801 Panorama Dr 93305 — 661-395-4011
Bethel Apostolic Academy — 100/K-12
1418 W Columbus St 93301 — 661-323-2851
Kevin Bradford, prin.
California State University-Bakersfield — Post-Sec.
9001 Stockdale Hwy 93311 — 661-664-2011
Eternity Preparatory HS — 100/9-12
48 Manor St 93308 — 661-327-5921
Dr. James Turner, admin. — Fax 327-5953
Garces Memorial HS — 700/9-12
2800 Loma Linda Dr 93305 — 661-327-2578
Robert Garcia, prin. — Fax 327-5427
Lighthouse Christian S — 100/3-12
1417 H St 93301 — 661-324-2751
Lisa Kane, admin. — Fax 861-9217
Lyle's Bakersfield College of Beauty — Post-Sec.
2935 F St 93301 — 661-327-9784
Maric College — Post-Sec.
1914 Wible Rd 93304 — 866-574-5550
Real Park S — 100/K-12
3612 Ora Vista Ave 93309 — 661-398-3052
Doris Parrott, prin.
San Joaquin Valley College — Post-Sec.
201 New Stine Rd 93309 — 661-834-1026
Santa Barbara Business College — Post-Sec.
211 S Real Rd 93309 — 661-835-1100

Baldwin Park, Los Angeles, Pop. 78,747
Baldwin Park USD — 17,700/PK-12
3699 Holly Ave 91706 — 626-962-3311
Mark Skvarna, supt. — Fax 856-4901
www.bpusd.net
Baldwin Park HS — 2,400/9-12
3900 Puente Ave 91706 — 626-960-5431
Julie Infante, prin. — Fax 856-4059
Holland MS — 700/6-8
4733 Landis Ave 91706 — 626-962-8412
Luis Cruz, prin. — Fax 813-6148
Jones JHS — 800/7-8
14250 Merced Ave 91706 — 626-962-8312
Cindy Cuevas, prin. — Fax 856-4291
Olive MS — 600/6-8
13701 Olive St 91706 — 626-962-8416
Richard Novlett, prin. — Fax 856-4568
Santa Fe S — 400/3-8
4650 Baldwin Park Blvd 91706 — 626-856-1525
Burke Hamilton, prin. — Fax 813-0614
Sierra Vista HS — 2,000/9-12
3600 Frazier St 91706 — 626-962-1300
Jackie White, prin. — Fax 856-4577
Sierra Vista JHS — 800/7-8
13400 Foster Ave 91706 — 626-962-1300
Angela Salazar, prin. — Fax 856-4577
Baldwin Park Adult & Community Education — Adult
4640 Maine Ave 91706 — 626-939-4456
John Kerr, prin. — Fax 856-4384

Baldwin Park Adult S | Adult
13307 Francisquito Ave 91706 | 626-338-5115
John Kerr, prin. | Fax 856-4384

Ballico, Merced
Ballico-Cressey ESD | 300/K-8
PO Box 49 95303 | 209-632-5371
Robert Wear, supt. | Fax 632-8929
Ballico S | 200/4-8
PO Box 49 95303 | 209-632-5371
Robert Wear, prin. | Fax 632-8929

Banning, Riverside, Pop. 27,284
Banning USD | 4,000/K-12
161 W Williams St 92220 | 951-922-0201
Kathleen McNamara Ed.D., supt. | Fax 922-0227
www.banning.k12.ca.us
Banning HS | 1,200/9-12
100 W Westward Ave 92220 | 951-922-0285
Dr. Jim Broncatello, prin. | Fax 922-2137
Nicolet MS | 400/7-8
101 E Nicolet St 92220 | 951-922-0280
Jim Alvarado, prin. | Fax 922-2748

Calvary Christian S | 200/K-12
PO Box 457 92220 | 951-849-1877
Richard Szydlowski, admin.

Barstow, San Bernardino, Pop. 23,073
Barstow USD | 5,500/K-12
551 S Avenue H 92311 | 760-255-6006
Jerry Bergmans, supt. | Fax 255-6007
www.barstow.k12.ca.us/
Barstow HS | 1,700/9-12
551 S Avenue H 92311 | 760-255-6105
Claire Ellis, prin. | Fax 256-4076
Barstow JHS | 500/7-8
551 S Avenue H 92311 | 760-255-6200
Carolyn Norman, prin. | Fax 255-6205

Barstow Community College | Post-Sec.
2700 Barstow Rd 92311 | 760-252-2411

Beaumont, Riverside, Pop. 15,083
Beaumont USD | 4,700/K-12
PO Box 187 92223 | 951-845-1631
Dr. Frank Passarella, supt. | Fax 845-2319
www.beaumontusd.k12.ca.us/
Beaumont HS | 1,200/9-12
PO Box 187 92223 | 951-845-3171
Dr. Kathryn Norwood, prin. | Fax 769-9289
Mountain View MS | 1,200/6-8
PO Box 187 92223 | 951-845-1627
Victor Kezer, prin. | Fax 845-8679
San Gorgonio MS, PO Box 187 92223 | 6-8
Brian Wood, prin. | 951-769-4391

Bell, Los Angeles, Pop. 37,694
Los Angeles USD
Supt. — See Los Angeles
Bell HS | 4,600/9-12
4328 Bell Ave 90201 | 323-560-1800
Onofre DiStefano, prin. | Fax 560-7874

Cynthia's Beauty Academy | Post-Sec.
4130 Gage Ave 90201 | 323-560-2207

Bellflower, Los Angeles, Pop. 74,863
Bellflower USD | 15,100/K-12
16703 Clark Ave 90706 | 562-866-9011
Rick Kemppainen, supt. | Fax 866-7713
www.busd.k12.ca.us
Bellflower MSHS | 3,300/7-12
15301 Mcnab Ave 90706 | 562-920-1801
Tracy Rutkoski, prin. | Fax 804-2387
Bellflower Adult S | Adult
9242 Laurel St 90706 | 562-461-2218
Pat Dixon, prin. | Fax 461-2221
Other Schools – See Lakewood

American Beauty College | Post-Sec.
16512 Bellflower Blvd 90706 | 562-866-0728
St. John Bosco HS | 1,100/9-12
13640 Bellflower Blvd 90706 | 562-920-1734
Pat Lee, prin. | Fax 867-5322

Bell Gardens, Los Angeles, Pop. 45,491
Montebello USD
Supt. — See Montebello
Bell Gardens HS | 3,100/9-12
6119 Agra St 90201 | 323-826-5151
Victor Chavez, prin. | Fax 887-7959
Bell Gardens S | 2,300/5-8
5841 Live Oak St 90201 | 562-927-1319
 | Fax 806-5131
Suva IS | 1,600/5-8
6660 Suva St 90201 | 562-927-2679
Glenda Golobay, prin. | Fax 806-5132
Bell Gardens Adult Education | Adult
6119 Agra St 90201 | 323-887-7955
Kathy Brendzal, prin. | Fax 887-7958
Ford Park Adult | Adult
7800 Scout Ave 90201 | 562-927-7750
Rosemary Grebel, prin. | Fax 806-5133

Faith Christian Academy | 200/K-12
6100 Florence Ave 90201 | 562-806-7540
Ray Marin, prin. | Fax 806-7574

Belmont, San Mateo, Pop. 24,499
Belmont-Redwood Shores ESD | 2,500/K-8
2960 Hallmark Dr 94002 | 650-637-4800
John McIntosh, supt. | Fax 637-4811
www.belmont.k12.ca.us
Ralston IS, 2675 Ralston Ave 94002 | 800/6-8
Maggie O'Reilly, prin. | 650-637-4880

Sequoia UNHSD
Supt. — See Redwood City
Carlmont HS | 1,900/9-12
1400 Alameda De Las Pulgas 94002 | 650-595-0210
Andrea Jenoff, prin. | Fax 591-6067

Notre Dame de Namur University | Post-Sec.
1500 Ralston Ave 94002 | 650-593-1601
Notre Dame HS | 700/9-12
1540 Ralston Ave 94002 | 650-595-1913
Rita Gleason, prin. | Fax 593-9330

Benicia, Solano, Pop. 26,941
Benicia USD | 5,000/PK-12
350 E K St 94510 | 707-747-8300
Shalee Cunningham Ph.D., supt. | Fax 748-0146
www.benicia.k12.ca.us
Benicia HS | 1,800/9-12
1101 Military W 94510 | 707-747-8325
JoAnn Severson, prin. | Fax 745-6769
Benicia MS | 1,300/6-8
1100 Southampton Rd 94510 | 707-747-8340
Susan Hutchinson, prin. | Fax 747-8349

Ben Lomond, Santa Cruz, Pop. 7,884
San Lorenzo Valley USD | 3,000/K-12
325 Marion Ave 95005 | 831-336-5194
Julie Haff, supt. | Fax 336-9531
www.slv.k12.ca.us
Other Schools – See Felton

Berkeley, Alameda, Pop. 102,049
Berkeley USD | 18,900/K-12
2134 Mrtn Lther King Jr Way 94704 | 510-644-6206
Michele Lawrence, supt. | Fax 540-5358
www.berkeley.k12.ca.us
Berkeley HS | 3,000/9-12
2246 Milvia St 94704 | 510-644-6120
Jim Slemp, prin. | Fax 548-4221
King MS | 900/6-8
1781 Rose St 94703 | 510-644-6280
Kit Pappenheimer, prin. | Fax 644-8783
Longfellow Arts & Technology MS | 500/6-8
1500 Derby St 94703 | 510-644-6360
Rebecca Cheung, prin. | Fax 644-8707
Willard MS | 600/6-8
2425 Stuart St 94705 | 510-644-6330
Robert Ithurburn, prin. | Fax 548-4219
Berkeley Adult S | Adult
1701 San Pablo Ave 94702 | 510-644-6130
Margaret Kirkpatrick, prin. | Fax 644-6784

Acupuncture & Integrative Medicine Coll. | Post-Sec.
2550 Shattuck Ave 94704 | 510-666-8248
American Baptist Seminary of the West | Post-Sec.
2606 Dwight Way 94704 | 510-841-1905
Arrowsmith Academy | 100/9-12
2300 Bancroft Way 94704 | 510-540-0440
Saul Drevitch, hdmstr.
Berkeley City College | Post-Sec.
2020 Milvia St 94704 | 510-981-2800
Church Divinity School of the Pacific | Post-Sec.
2451 Ridge Rd 94709 | 510-204-0700
Dominican School of Philosophy/Theology | Post-Sec.
2301 Vine St 94708 | 510-849-2030
Franciscan School of Theology | Post-Sec.
1712 Euclid Ave 94709 | 510-848-5232
Graduate Theological Union | Post-Sec.
2400 Ridge Rd 94709 | 510-649-2400
Jesuit School of Theology at Berkeley | Post-Sec.
1735 Le Roy Ave 94709 | 510-549-5000
Pacific Lutheran Theological Seminary | Post-Sec.
2770 Marin Ave 94708 | 510-524-5264
Pacific School of Religion | Post-Sec.
1798 Scenic Ave 94709 | 510-848-0528
St. Marys College HS | 600/9-12
1294 Albina Ave 94706 | 510-526-9242
Peter Imperial, prin. | Fax 559-6277
Starr King School for the Ministry | Post-Sec.
2441 Le Conte Ave 94709 | 510-845-6232
University of California | Post-Sec.
110 Sproul Hall 94720 | 510-642-6000
Wright Institute | Post-Sec.
2728 Durant Ave 94704 | 510-841-9230

Bermuda Dunes, Riverside, Pop. 4,571

Christian School of the Desert | 500/PK-12
40700 Yucca Ln, | 760-345-2848
David Fulton, prin. | Fax 345-8173

Beverly Hills, Los Angeles, Pop. 34,941
Beverly Hills USD | 11,400/K-12
255 S Lasky Dr 90212 | 310-551-5100
Jeffrey Hubbard, supt. | Fax 286-2138
www.beverlyhills.k12.ca.us
Beverly Hills HS | 2,100/9-12
241 S Moreno Dr 90212 | 310-229-3685
Dan Stepenosky, prin. | Fax 286-7446
Beverly Hills Adult S | Adult
255 S Lasky Dr 90212 | 310-551-5150
John Borsum, prin. | Fax 277-6932

West Coast Ultrasound Institute | Post-Sec.
291 S La Cienega Blvd # 500 90211 | 310-289-5123

Bieber, Lassen
Big Valley JUSD | 300/K-12
PO Box 157 96009 | 530-294-5266
Mark Evans, supt. | Fax 294-5396
www.bigvalleyschool.org/
Big Valley HS | 100/9-12
PO Box 157 96009 | 530-294-5231
Mark Evans, prin. | Fax 294-5100
Big Valley IS | 100/4-8
PO Box 157 96009 | 530-294-5214
Ron Shaull, prin. | Fax 294-5109
Big Valley Adult S | Adult
PO Box 157 96009 | 530-294-5231

Big Bear Lake, San Bernardino, Pop. 5,889
Bear Valley USD | 3,100/K-12
PO Box 1529 92315 | 909-866-4631
Allan Pelletier, supt. | Fax 866-2040
www.bigbear.k12.ca.us
Big Bear HS | 900/9-12
PO Box 1708 92315 | 909-585-6892
Dr. Rick Jameson, prin. | Fax 585-6809

Big Bear MS | 600/7-8
PO Box 1607 92315 | 909-866-4634
Julie Chamberlin, prin. | Fax 866-5679

Biggs, Butte, Pop. 1,813
Biggs USD | 800/K-12
300 B St 95917 | 530-868-1281
Lee Funk, supt. | Fax 868-1615
www.biggs.org/
Biggs HS, 300 B St 95917 | 200/9-12
Ralph Vandro, prin. | 530-868-5825
Biggs MS, 300 B St 95917 | 200/7-8
Ralph Vandro, prin. | 530-868-5825

Big Pine, Inyo, Pop. 1,158
Big Pine USD | 200/K-12
PO Box 908 93513 | 760-938-2005
Margaret Dame, supt. | Fax 938-2310
Big Pine HS | 100/9-12
PO Box 908 93513 | 760-938-2222
Margaret Dame, prin. | Fax 938-2310

Regional Occupational Center & Program
Supt. — None
Inyo County ROP | Vo/Tech
PO Box 970 93513 | 760-938-2936
Jim Meadowcroft, dir. | Fax 837-3127

Big Sur, Monterey
Pacific USD | 50/K-12
69325 Highway 1 93920 | 805-927-4507
Dr. Ivan Kolozsvari, supt. | Fax 927-8123
www.pacificvalleyschool.com
Pacific Valley S | 50/K-12
69325 Highway 1 93920 | 805-927-4507
Dr. Ivan Kolozsvari, prin. | Fax 927-8123

Bishop, Inyo, Pop. 3,646
Bishop JUNHSD | 800/9-12
301 N Fowler St 93514 | 760-872-3680
Mark Geyer, supt. | Fax 872-6016
www.buhs.k12.ca.us
Bishop Union HS | 700/9-12
301 N Fowler St 93514 | 760-873-4275
Maggie Kingsbury, prin. | Fax 873-3065

Bishop UNESD | 1,400/K-8
800 W Elm St 93514 | 760-872-4352
Mark Geyer, supt. | Fax 872-1063
www.buesd.k12.ca.us
Home Street MS, 201 Home St 93514 | 500/6-8
Bill Kennedy, prin. | 760-872-1381

Bloomington, San Bernardino, Pop. 15,116
Colton JUSD
Supt. — See Colton
Bloomington HS | 2,800/9-12
10750 Laurel Ave 92316 | 909-580-5004
Ignacio Cabrera, prin. | Fax 876-6326
Bloomington MS | 900/7-8
18829 Orange St 92316 | 909-876-4101
Dan Rocha, prin. | Fax 876-4195
Harris MS | 900/7-8
11150 Alder Ave 92316 | 909-876-6300
David Grohosky Ed.D., prin. | Fax 820-2238

Bloomington Christian S | 1,000/PK-12
PO Box 355 92316 | 909-877-2810
Yvonna Williams, admin. | Fax 877-2960

Blythe, Riverside, Pop. 21,679
Palo Verde USD | 3,500/K-12
295 N 1st St 92225 | 760-922-4164
Dr. Alan Jensen, supt. | Fax 922-5942
www.pvusd-bly.k12.ca.us
Blythe MS | 800/6-8
825 N Lovekin Blvd 92225 | 760-922-1300
Jim Stier, prin. | Fax 922-3748
Palo Verde Valley HS | 900/9-12
667 N Lovekin Blvd 92225 | 760-922-7148
Michael Gilmore, prin. | Fax 922-8916
Twin Palms Continuation & Adult S | Adult
190 N 5th St 92225 | 760-922-4884
Robert Jeppson, prin. | Fax 922-1177

Palo Verde College | Post-Sec.
1 College Dr 92225 | 760-921-5500

Bonsall, San Diego, Pop. 1,881
Bonsall UNESD | 1,500/K-8
31505 Old River Rd 92003 | 760-631-5200
Jeffrey Schleiger, supt. | Fax 941-4409
www.sdcoe.k12.ca.us/districts/bonsall/
Sullivan MS | 600/6-8
7350 W Lilac Rd 92003 | 760-631-5210
John Heckman, prin. | Fax 631-5230

Boonville, Mendocino
Anderson Valley USD | 600/PK-12
PO Box 457 95415 | 707-895-3774
James Collins, supt. | Fax 895-2665
www.avusd.k12.ca.us
Anderson Valley JSHS | 300/7-12
PO Box 130 95415 | 707-895-3496
James Collins, prin. | Fax 895-3153
Anderson Valley Adult S | Adult
PO Box 457 95415 | 707-895-2953
Donna Pierson-Pugh, prin. | Fax 895-2665

Boron, Kern, Pop. 2,101
Muroc JUSD
Supt. — See North Edwards
Boron JSHS | 300/7-12
26831 Prospect St 93516 | 760-762-5121
Paul Kostopoulos, prin. | Fax 762-5040

Borrego Springs, San Diego, Pop. 2,244
Borrego Springs USD | 500/K-12
1315 Palm Canyon Dr 92004 | 760-767-5357
Consuela Smith, supt. | Fax 767-0494
www.sdcoe.k12.ca.us/districts/borrego/
Borrego Springs HS | 100/9-12
1315 Palm Canyon Dr 92004 | 760-767-5335
Gary Gernandt, prin. | Fax 767-5999

Borrego Springs MS 100/6-8
1315 Palm Canyon Dr 92004 760-767-5335
Gary Gernandt, prin. Fax 767-5999

Brawley, Imperial, Pop. 22,010
Brawley ESD 3,500/K-8
261 D St 92227 760-344-2330
Terri L. Decker, supt. Fax 344-8928
www.icoe.k12.ca.us/ICOE/Schools/BESD/
Worth JHS 900/7-8
385 D St 92227 760-344-2153
Gerardo Roman, prin. Fax 351-5043

Brawley UNHSD 1,700/9-12
480 N Imperial Ave 92227 760-312-5819
Roberto Moreno, supt. Fax 344-9520
www.brawleyhigh.org
Brawley HS 1,700/9-12
480 N Imperial Ave 92227 760-312-5819
Tony Munguia, prin. Fax 344-9520

Brawley Christian Academy 100/PK-12
430 N 2nd St 92227 760-344-3911
Robert Feist, prin. Fax 344-5864

Brea, Orange, Pop. 37,889
Brea-Olinda USD 6,100/K-12
PO Box 300 92822 714-990-7800
Tim Harvey, supt. Fax 529-2137
bousd.k12.ca.us
Brea JHS 1,100/7-8
400 N Brea Blvd 92821 714-990-7500
Pam Gallarda, prin. Fax 990-7585
Brea-Olinda HS 2,000/9-12
789 Wildcat Way 92821 714-990-7850
Jerry Halpin, prin. Fax 990-7547

Brea School of Exceptional Children Post-Sec.
875 N Brea Blvd 92821

Brentwood, Contra Costa, Pop. 36,234
Brentwood UNSD 5,900/K-8
255 Guthrie Ln 94513 925-513-6300
J. Douglas Adams, supt. Fax 634-8583
www.brentwood.k12.ca.us
Adams MS, 401 American Ave 94513 6-8
Adam Clark, prin. 925-513-6480
Bristow MS 900/6-8
855 Minnesota Ave 94513 925-513-6460
Molleen Barnes, prin. Fax 516-8725
Hill MS 1,000/6-8
140 Birch St 94513 925-513-6440
Eric Prater, prin. Fax 513-0696

Liberty UNHSD 4,800/9-12
20 Oak St 94513 925-634-2166
Daniel Smith, supt. Fax 634-1687
www.libertyuhsd.k12.ca.us
Liberty HS 2,300/9-12
850 2nd St 94513 925-634-3521
Tim Halloran, prin. Fax 513-2739
Liberty Adult Education S Adult
929 2nd St 94513 925-634-2565
Gene Clare, dir. Fax 634-5317
Other Schools – See Oakley

Gateway Christian S 200/K-12
657 McClarren Rd 94513 925-634-0493
David Stutzman, admin. Fax 634-0402

Bridgeport, Mono
Eastern Sierra USD 500/K-12
PO Box 575 93517 760-932-7443
Larry Plew, supt. Fax 932-7140
www.esusd.org
Other Schools – See Coleville, Lee Vining

Mono County Office of Education
PO Box 477 93517 760-932-7311
Richard McAteer, supt. Fax 932-7278
www.monocoe.k12.ca.us
Other Schools – See Mammoth Lakes

Bridgeville, Humboldt
Southern Trinity JUSD 200/K-12
HC 33 Box 156 95526 707-574-6237
David Albee, supt. Fax 574-6538
www.tcoe.trinity.k12.ca.us
Southern Trinity HS 50/9-12
HC 33 Box 155 95526 707-574-6239
David Albee, prin. Fax 574-1067

Brisbane, San Mateo, Pop. 3,487
Brisbane ESD 700/K-8
1 Solano St 94005 415-467-0550
Steve Waterman, supt. Fax 467-2914
brisbane.ca.campusgrid.net/home
Lipman MS 200/6-8
1 Solano St 94005 415-467-9541
Pennie Pine, prin. Fax 467-5073

Broderick, See West Sacramento
Washington USD
Supt. — See West Sacramento
Golden State MS 1,000/7-8
1100 Carrie St 95605 916-375-7700
Paul Orlando, prin. Fax 375-7709

Buellton, Santa Barbara, Pop. 3,804
Buellton UNESD 600/K-8
595 2nd St 93427 805-686-2767
Tom Cooper, supt. Fax 686-2719
Jonata S 400/K-K, 4-8
301 2nd St 93427 805-688-4222
Patricia Garrett, prin. Fax 688-6611

Buena Park, Orange, Pop. 78,934
Buena Park ESD 6,400/K-8
6885 Orangethorpe Ave 90620 714-522-8412
Lew Becker, supt. Fax 994-1506
www.ocde.k12.ca.us/bpsd
Buena Park JHS 1,300/7-8
6931 Orangethorpe Ave 90620 714-522-8491
Debra Diaz, prin. Fax 523-1602

Fullerton JUNHSD
Supt. — See Fullerton
Buena Park HS 2,000/9-12
8833 Academy Dr 90621 714-992-8600
Maggie Buchan, prin. Fax 992-8619

Bethel Baptist Academy 100/K-12
8433 Philodendron Way 90620 714-521-5586
Sharon Wallace, admin.
Rossier Park S, 7100 Knott Ave 90620 200/K-12
Maria Wagner-Chappelear, dir. 714-562-0441
Speech and Language Development Ctr 300/K-12
8699 Holder St 90620 714-821-3620
Dawn O'Connor, prin.

Burbank, Los Angeles, Pop. 103,359
Burbank USD 19,500/K-12
1900 W Olive Ave 91506 818-729-4400
Dr. Gregory A. Bowman, supt. Fax 729-4483
www.burbank.k12.ca.us
Burbank HS 2,500/9-12
902 N 3rd St 91502 818-558-4700
Bruce Osgood, prin. Fax 845-6122
Burbank MS 1,100/6-8
3700 W Jeffries Ave 91505 818-558-4646
Anita Schackmann, prin. Fax 842-3727
Burroughs HS 2,400/9-12
1920 W Clark Ave 91506 818-558-4777
Emilio Urioste, prin. Fax 846-9268
Jordan MS 1,200/6-8
420 S Mariposa St 91506 818-558-4622
Mary Margaret Kljunak, prin. Fax 843-3509
Muir MS 1,600/6-8
1111 N Kenneth Rd 91504 818-558-5320
Dr. Daniel Hacking, prin. Fax 841-4637
Burbank Adult S Adult
3811 W Allan Ave 91505 818-558-4611
Dr. Cherise Moore, dir. Fax 558-4620

Bellarmine Jefferson HS 400/9-12
465 E Olive Ave 91501 818-972-1400
Sr. Cheryl Milner, prin. Fax 559-6387
Elegante Beauty College Post-Sec.
200 N San Fernando Blvd 91502 818-954-8894
Holmes Institute Post-Sec.
2600 W Magnolia Blvd 91505 818-556-7757
Intercoast Colleges Post-Sec.
401 S Glenoaks Blvd Ste 211 91502 818-500-8400
Make-up Designory Post-Sec.
129 S San Fernando Blvd 91502 818-729-9420
Providence HS 600/9-12
511 S Buena Vista St 91505 818-846-8141
Michele Schulte, prin. Fax 843-8421
Woodbury University Post-Sec.
7500 N Glenoaks Blvd 91504 818-767-0888

Burlingame, San Mateo, Pop. 27,387
Burlingame ESD 2,400/K-8
1825 Trousdale Dr 94010 650-259-3800
Sonny DaMarto Ed.D., supt. Fax 259-3820
www.burlingameschools.com/
Burlingame IS 900/6-8
1715 Quesada Way 94010 650-259-3830
Ted Barone, prin. Fax 259-3843

San Mateo UNHSD
Supt. — See San Mateo
Burlingame HS 1,300/9-12
400 Carolan Ave 94010 650-558-2899
Matt Biggar, prin. Fax 762-0122

Mercy HS 400/9-12
2750 Adeline Dr 94010 650-343-3631
Laura Held, prin. Fax 343-3358
Mills Peninsula Health Services Post-Sec.
1783 El Camino Real 94010 650-696-5678

Burney, Shasta, Pop. 3,423
Fall River JUSD 1,500/K-12
20375 Tamarack Ave 96013 530-335-4538
Larry Snelling, supt. Fax 335-3115
www.shastalink.k12.ca.us/frjusd/
Burney JSHS 300/7-12
37571 Mountain View Rd 96013 530-335-4576
Larry Hutchinson, prin. Fax 335-3554
Other Schools – See Mc Arthur

Byron, Contra Costa
Byron UNESD 1,300/K-8
14301 Byron Hwy 94514 925-634-6644
Thomas Meyer, supt. Fax 634-9421
www.byron.k12.ca.us
Excelsior MS 400/6-8
14301 Byron Hwy 94514 925-240-7360
Nancie Castro, prin. Fax 634-5120

Calabasas, Los Angeles, Pop. 20,889
Las Virgenes USD 12,200/K-12
4111 Las Virgenes Rd 91302 818-880-4000
Dr. Sandra Smyser, supt. Fax 880-4200
www.lvusd.org
Calabasas HS 1,900/9-12
22855 Mulholland Hwy 91302 818-222-7177
Dave Jackson, prin. Fax 223-8477
Stelle MS 900/6-8
22450 Mulholland Hwy 91302 818-224-4107
Mary Sistrunk, prin. Fax 224-4989
Wright MS 1,000/6-8
4029 Las Virgenes Rd 91302 818-880-4614
Steve Rosentsweig, prin. Fax 878-0453
Other Schools – See Agoura Hills

Arbor Academy 100/1-12
26245 Hatmor Dr 91302 818-880-6029
Lisa Jackson, dir.
Mesivta of Greater Los Angeles S 50/9-12
25115 Mureau Rd 91302 818-876-0550
Rabbi Shlomo Gottesman, dir. Fax 876-0537
Viewpoint S 1,200/K-12
23620 Mulholland Hwy 91302 818-340-2901
Dr. Robert Dworkoski, hdmstr. Fax 591-0834

Calexico, Imperial, Pop. 32,517
Calexico USD 9,200/K-12
PO Box 792 92232 760-768-3888
David Alvarez, supt. Fax 357-0842
www.calexico.k12.ca.us/
Calexico SHS 1,800/10-12
PO Box 792 92232 760-768-3980
Gilbert Barraza, prin. Fax 357-9640
De Anza JHS 800/7-8
PO Box 792 92232 760-768-3950
Rebecca Ayala-Rodriguez, prin. Fax 357-8251
Moreno JHS 1,100/7-9
PO Box 792 92232 760-768-3960
Kevin Dorward, prin. Fax 768-1905
Morales Adult Education Center Adult
PO Box 792 92232 760-357-7471
Clara Rendon, prin. Fax 357-7246

Calexico Mission S 400/K-12
601 E 1st St 92231 760-357-3711
Susan Smith, prin. Fax 357-3713
Vincent Memorial HS 200/9-12
525 Sheridan St 92231 760-357-3461
Sr. Lilia Barba, prin. Fax 357-0902

California City, Kern, Pop. 11,221
Mojave USD
Supt. — See Mojave
California City MS 400/6-8
9736 Redwood Blvd 93505 760-373-3241
Cheri Newlander, prin. Fax 373-1355

Calimesa, Riverside, Pop. 7,633

Mesa Grande Academy 400/K-12
975 Fremont St #A 92320 909-795-1112
Alfred Riddle, prin. Fax 795-1653

Calipatria, Imperial, Pop. 7,601
Calipatria USD 1,200/K-12
501 W Main St 92233 760-348-2892
James Hanks, supt. Fax 344-8926
mail.calipatria.k12.ca.us/
Calipatria HS 300/9-12
601 W Main St 92233 760-348-2254
Virginia Calsada Medina, prin. Fax 348-2431
Young MS 300/5-8
220 S International Blvd 92233 760-348-2842
Joe Derma, prin. Fax 348-2848

Calistoga, Napa, Pop. 5,254
Calistoga JUSD 900/K-12
1520 Lake St 94515 707-942-4703
Jeff Johnson, supt. Fax 942-6589
www.calistoga.k12.ca.us
Calistoga JSHS 400/7-12
1608 Lake St 94515 707-942-6278
Kevin Eisenberg, prin. Fax 942-6592

Camarillo, Ventura, Pop. 60,445
Oxnard UNHSD
Supt. — See Oxnard
Camarillo HS 2,500/9-12
4660 Mission Oaks Blvd 93012 805-389-6406
Glenn Lipman, prin. Fax 484-8087

Pleasant Valley ESD 7,300/PK-8
600 Temple Ave 93010 805-482-2763
Thomas R. Dase, supt. Fax 987-5511
www.pvsd.k12.ca.us
Las Colinas MS 900/6-8
5750 Fieldcrest Dr 93012 805-484-0461
Pat Fitzgerald, prin. Fax 482-2443
Los Altos MS 700/6-8
700 Temple Ave 93010 805-482-4656
Sue Eastman, prin. Fax 388-9059
Monte Vista MS 800/6-8
888 Lantana St 93010 805-482-8891
Sara Davis, prin. Fax 987-8951

Regional Occupational Center & Program
Supt. — None
Ventura County ROP Vo/Tech
465 Horizon Way 93010 805-388-4421
Peggy Velarde, prin. Fax 388-4428

California State University Channel Isle Post-Sec.
1 University Dr 93012 805-437-8400
Cornerstone Christian S 600/PK-12
1777 Arneill Rd 93010 805-987-8621
Lory Selby, supt. Fax 987-8208

Cambria, San Luis Obispo, Pop. 5,382
Coast USD 900/K-12
2950 Santa Rosa Creek Rd 93428 805-927-3880
Pamela Martens, supt. Fax 927-0312
www.cambria.k12.ca.us
Coast Union HS 400/9-12
2950 Santa Rosa Creek Rd 93428 805-927-3889
Karl Dearie, prin. Fax 924-2933
Santa Lucia MS 200/6-8
2850 Schoolhouse Ln 93428 805-927-3693
Denis deClercq, prin. Fax 927-4615

Cameron Park, El Dorado, Pop. 11,897
Buckeye UNSD
Supt. — See Shingle Springs
Camerado Springs MS 800/6-8
2480 Merrychase Dr 95682 530-677-1658
Meg Enns, prin. Fax 677-9537

Campbell, Santa Clara, Pop. 37,149
Campbell UNHSD
Supt. — See San Jose
Westmont HS 1,700/9-12
4805 Westmont Ave 95008 408-378-1500
Owen Hege, prin. Fax 379-1720

Campbell UNSD 6,600/K-8
155 N 3rd St 95008 408-364-4200
Johanna VanderMolen, supt. Fax 341-7280
www.campbellusd.k12.ca.us
Campbell MS 900/5-8
295 Cherry Ln 95008 408-364-4222
Susan Zimmer, prin. Fax 341-7150
Other Schools – See Los Gatos, San Jose

California College of Communication — Post-Sec.
700 W Hamilton Ave Ste 210 95008 — 408-374-5066
Pioneer Family Academy — 200/K-12
1799 Winchester Blvd 95008 — 408-313-5113
Kathy Kistler, hdmstr.
Veritas Christian Academy — 50/6-12
400 Llewellyn Ave Unit 2 95008 — 408-984-1255
David Wallace, prin. — Fax 871-7929

Canoga Park, See Los Angeles
Los Angeles USD
Supt. — See Los Angeles
Canoga Park HS — 2,300/9-12
6850 Topanga Canyon Blvd 91303 — 818-340-3221
Dennis Thompson, prin. — Fax 702-8942
Columbus MS — 1,400/6-8
22250 Elkwood St 91304 — 818-348-5601
Saundra Collins, prin. — Fax 348-2894
Sutter MS — 1,500/6-8
7330 Winnetka Ave 91306 — 818-341-6661
Michael Smith, prin. — Fax 341-3039

AGBU Manoogian-Demirdjian S — 800/K-12
6844 Oakdale Ave 91306 — 818-883-2428
Hagop Hagopian, prin. — Fax 883-8353
Coutin S — 100/1-12
7119 Owensmouth Ave 91303 — 818-992-0301
Faith Baptist S — 1,300/PK-12
7644 Farralone Ave 91304 — 818-340-6131
Dr. Roland Rasmussen, dir. — Fax 592-0279

Canyon Country, See Santa Clarita
William S. Hart UNHSD
Supt. — See Santa Clarita
Canyon HS — 2,900/9-12
19300 Nadal St 91351 — 661-252-6110
Bob Messina, prin. — Fax 251-8512
Sierra Vista JHS — 1,500/7-8
19425 Stillmore St 91351 — 661-252-3113
Randy Parker, prin. — Fax 252-2790

Clarita Career College — Post-Sec.
27125 Sierra Hwy Ste 329 91351 — 661-251-1864
Cornerstone Christian S — 200/1-12
27945 Oakgale Ave 91351 — 661-251-9732
Dean Hadfield, prin.
Santa Clarita Christian S — 600/K-12
27249 Luther Dr 91351 — 661-252-7371
Lee Duncan, admin. — Fax 252-4354

Canyon Lake, Riverside, Pop. 10,941

Hope Learning Academy — 50/9-12
24370 Canyon Lake Dr N # 10 92587
Rev. Chris Suitt, admin. — 951-244-2177

Capitola, Santa Cruz, Pop. 9,802
Regional Occupational Center & Program
Supt. — None
Santa Cruz County ROP — Vo/Tech
809 Bay Ave Ste H 95010 — 831-479-5335
Robert Rieber, dir. — Fax 462-6457

Soquel UNESD — 1,800/K-8
620 Monterey Ave 95010 — 831-464-5630
Kathleen Howard, supt. — Fax 475-5196
www.soqueldo.santacruz.k12.ca.us/
New Brighton MS — 800/6-8
250 Washburn Ave 95010 — 831-464-5660
Sydney Renwick, prin.

Carlsbad, San Diego, Pop. 87,372
Carlsbad USD — 9,300/K-12
6225 El Camino Real 92009 — 760-331-5000
John A. Roach Ed.D., supt. — Fax 331-5094
www.carlsbadusd.k12.ca.us
Aviara Oaks MS — 800/6-8
6880 Ambrosia Ln, — 760-331-6100
Steve VanZant, prin. — Fax 438-7894
Calavera Hills MS — 6-8
4104 Tamarack Ave 92008 — 760-331-6400
Devin Vodicka, prin. — Fax 729-3040
Carlsbad HS — 2,800/9-12
3557 Monroe St 92008 — 760-331-5100
Scott Wright, prin. — Fax 729-6830
Valley MS — 1,200/6-8
1645 Magnolia Ave 92008 — 760-331-5300
Carolyn Millikin, prin. — Fax 720-2326

San Dieguito UNHSD
Supt. — See Encinitas
La Costa Canyon HS — 2,700/9-12
3451 Camino de los Coches 92009 — 760-436-6136
Amy Carlin, prin. — Fax 943-3539

Applied Professional Training — Post-Sec.
PO Box 131717 92013 — 800-483-8488
Army and Navy Academy — 400/7-12
PO Box 3000 92018 — 760-729-2385
Stephen Bliss, pres. — Fax 720-7121
Gemological Institute of America — Post-Sec.
5345 Armada Dr 92008 — 760-603-4000

Carmel, Monterey, Pop. 4,084
Carmel USD — 3,500/K-12
PO Box 222700 93922 — 831-624-1546
Marvin Biasotti, supt. — Fax 626-4052
www.carmelunified.org
Carmel HS — 800/9-12
PO Box 222780 93922 — 831-624-1821
Karl Pallastrini, prin. — Fax 626-4313
Carmel MS — 600/6-8
PO Box 222740 93922 — 831-624-2785
Edmund Gross, prin. — Fax 624-0839
Carmel Adult Education — Adult
PO Box 222700 93922 — 831-624-1714
Patricia Beebe, prin. — Fax 624-3855

Carmichael, Sacramento, Pop. 49,900
San Juan USD — 43,700/K-12
PO Box 477 95609 — 916-971-7700
Steven Enoch, supt. — Fax 971-7070
www.sanjuan.edu

Barrett MS — 900/6-8
4243 Barrett Rd 95608 — 916-971-7842
Mark Roberts, prin. — Fax 971-7839
Churchill MS — 900/6-8
4900 Whitney Ave 95608 — 916-971-7324
Gloria Baker, prin. — Fax 971-7856
Starr King MS — 500/6-8
4848 Cottage Way 95608 — 916-971-7320
Ethan Hoff, prin. — Fax 971-7920
Other Schools – See Citrus Heights, Fair Oaks,
Orangevale, Sacramento

College of Career Training — Post-Sec.
7220 Fair Oaks Blvd Ste A 95608 — 916-481-9001
Heritage Christian Academy — 100/K-12
PO Box 2423 95609 — 916-487-1250
Lorraine Velasco, admin.
Jesuit HS — 1,000/9-12
1200 Jacob Ln 95608 — 916-482-6060
Rev. Edward Fassett, prin. — Fax 480-2119
Sacramento Adventist Academy — 400/K-12
5601 Winding Way 95608 — 916-481-2300
Bettesue Constanzo, prin. — Fax 481-7426
Victory Christian HS - Garfield Campus — 300/7-12
3045 Garfield Ave 95608 — 916-488-5601
John Huffman, prin. — Fax 488-2589

Carpinteria, Santa Barbara, Pop. 14,037
Carpinteria USD — 2,300/K-12
1400 Linden Ave 93013 — 805-684-4511
Paul Cordeiro, supt. — Fax 684-0218
www.cusd.net
Carpinteria HS — 900/9-12
4810 Foothill Rd 93013 — 805-684-4107
Gerardo Cornejo, prin. — Fax 566-5952
Carpinteria MS — 500/7-8
5351 Carpinteria Ave 93013 — 805-684-4544
Felicia Sexsmith, prin. — Fax 566-3839

Cate S — 300/9-12
PO Box 5005 93014 — 805-684-4127
Benjamin Williams, hdmstr. — Fax 684-8940
Pacifica Graduate Institute — Post-Sec.
249 Lambert Rd 93013 — 805-969-3626
Truck Marketing Institute — Post-Sec.
1090 Eugenia Pl Ste 101 93013 — 805-684-4558

Carson, Los Angeles, Pop. 93,747
Long Beach USD
Supt. — See Long Beach
California Academy of Math & Science — 600/9-12
1000 E Victoria St 90747 — 310-243-2025
Kathleen Clark, prin. — Fax 516-4041

Los Angeles USD
Supt. — See Los Angeles
Carnegie MS — 1,900/6-8
21820 Bonita St 90745 — 310-830-1330
Susan Price, prin. — Fax 830-9015
Carson HS — 3,400/9-12
22328 Main St 90745 — 310-835-0181
Kenneth Keener, prin. — Fax 518-5817
Curtiss MS — 1,500/6-8
1254 E Helmick St 90746 — 310-537-3551
William Elkins, prin. — Fax 537-2115
White MS — 1,900/6-8
22102 Figueroa St 90745 — 310-328-7540
James Noble, prin. — Fax 782-8954

California State Univ.-Dominguez Hills — Post-Sec.
1000 E Victoria St 90747 — 310-243-3300
Carson Christian S — 100/K-12
21828 Avalon Blvd 90745 — 310-538-5370
Marian Alexander, prin.
CEI — Post-Sec.
20700 Avalon Blvd # 210 90746 — 310-532-6328

Caruthers, Fresno, Pop. 1,603
Caruthers USD — 1,500/K-12
PO Box 127 93609 — 559-864-3274
Dwight Miller, supt. — Fax 864-8857
www.caruthers.k12.ca.us
Caruthers HS — 600/9-12
PO Box 545 93609 — 559-864-3224
Jim Sargent, prin. — Fax 864-8303

Castaic, Los Angeles
Castaic UNSD
Supt. — See Valencia
Castaic MS — 1,600/4-8
28900 Hillcrest Pkwy 91384 — 661-257-4550
Marcia Dains, prin. — Fax 294-9714

Castro Valley, Alameda, Pop. 59,300
Castro Valley USD — 8,200/K-12
PO Box 2146 94546 — 510-537-3000
James Fitzpatrick, supt. — Fax 886-8962
www.cv.k12.ca.us
Canyon MS — 1,400/6-8
PO Box 2146 94546 — 510-538-8833
Mark Croghan, prin. — Fax 247-9439
Castro Valley HS — 2,600/9-12
PO Box 2146 94546 — 510-537-5910
Debbie Coco, prin. — Fax 582-3924
Creekside MS — 800/6-8
PO Box 2146 94546 — 510-581-6617
Mary Ann DeGrazia, prin. — Fax 886-0375
Castro Valley Adult S — Adult
PO Box 2146 94546 — 510-886-1000
Jerry Green, dir. — Fax 537-8537

Hayward USD
Supt. — See Hayward
Adult Education - Laurel Site — Adult
2652 Vergil Ct 94546 — 510-293-8599
Mahnoush Harirsa, prin.

Castroville, Monterey, Pop. 5,272
North Monterey County USD
Supt. — See Moss Landing
North Monterey County HS — 1,600/9-12
13990 Castroville Blvd 95012 — 831-633-5221
Steve Hirt, prin. — Fax 633-2520

North Montgomery County MS — 300/7-8
10301 Seymour St 95012 — 831-633-3391
Murry Schekman, prin. — Fax 633-3680
North Monterey County Adult S — Adult
13990 Castroville Blvd 95012 — 831-633-7050
Ken Jordan, prin. — Fax 633-7095

Cathedral City, Riverside, Pop. 48,528
Palm Springs USD
Supt. — See Palm Springs
Cathedral City HS — 2,600/9-12
69250 Dinah Shore Dr 92234 — 760-770-0100
Guillermo Chavez, prin. — Fax 770-0149
Coffman MS — 1,200/6-8
34603 Plumley Rd 92234 — 760-770-8617
Terri Simon, prin. — Fax 770-8623
Workman MS — 1,500/6-8
69300 30th Ave 92234 — 760-770-8540
Joseph Aguanno, prin. — Fax 770-8545

Calvary Christian S — 100/PK-12
68550 Dinah Shore Dr 92234 — 760-324-2355
Pam Chesterman, prin. — Fax 321-5901
Coachella Valley Technical Skills Center — Post-Sec.
35325 Date Palm Dr Ste 101 92234 — 760-328-5554

Cedarville, Modoc
Surprise Valley JUSD — 300/K-12
PO Box 100 96104 — 530-279-6141
Dr. Michael Sherrod, supt. — Fax 279-2210
surprisevalleyhs.org/
Surprise Valley HS — 100/9-12
PO Box 100 96104 — 530-279-6146
Dr. Michael Sherrod, prin. — Fax 279-2210

Central Valley, Shasta, Pop. 4,340
Gateway USD
Supt. — See Redding
Central Valley HS — 1,000/9-12
4066 La Mesa Ave 96019 — 530-275-7075
Charlie Hoffman, prin. — Fax 275-7065

Ceres, Stanislaus, Pop. 37,828
Ceres USD — 9,300/K-12
PO Box 307 95307 — 209-556-1500
Walt Hanline Ed.D., supt. — Fax 537-7301
www.ceres.k12.ca.us
Blaker-Kinser JHS — 700/7-8
PO Box 307 95307 — 209-541-0542
Geoffrey Barney, prin. — Fax 541-0174
Central Valley HS — 9-12
PO Box 307 95307 — 209-556-1900
Fred Van Vleck, prin. — Fax 531-2748
Ceres HS — 2,300/9-12
PO Box 307 95307 — 209-538-0130
Bob Palous, prin. — Fax 538-8978
Hensley JHS — 900/7-8
PO Box 307 95307 — 209-556-1820
Lynda Maben, prin. — Fax 538-9428

Central Valley Christian Academy — 300/PK-12
2020 Academy Pl 95307 — 209-537-4521
Donald Krpalek, prin. — Fax 538-0706

Cerritos, Los Angeles, Pop. 52,800
ABC USD — 21,900/K-12
16700 Norwalk Blvd 90703 — 562-926-5566
Dr. Gary Smuts, supt. — Fax 404-1092
www.abcusd.k12.ca.us
Carmenita MS — 700/7-8
13435 166th St 90703 — 562-926-4405
Valencia Mayfield, prin. — Fax 404-7807
Cerritos HS — 2,200/9-12
12500 183rd St 90703 — 562-865-5310
Jeff Green, prin. — Fax 924-3187
Gahr HS — 1,900/9-12
11111 Artesia Blvd 90703 — 562-402-4523
George Kambeitz, prin. — Fax 924-8136
Haskell MS — 600/7-8
11525 Del Amo Blvd 90703 — 562-860-6529
Susan Hixson Ed.D., prin. — Fax 809-7250
Tetzlaff MS — 700/7-8
12351 Del Amo Blvd 90703 — 562-865-9539
Rebecca Caudillo Ed.D., prin. — Fax 402-6412
Whitney JSHS — 1,000/7-12
16800 Shoemaker Ave 90703 — 562-229-7745
Patricia Hager, prin. — Fax 926-2751
ABC Adult HS — Adult
12254 Cuesta Dr 90703 — 562-926-5566
Augustin Jaramillo, prin. — Fax 921-9958
Other Schools – See Artesia, Hawaiian Gardens,
Lakewood

Regional Occupational Center & Program
Supt. — None
Southeast LA County ROP — Vo/Tech
20122 Cabrillo Ln 90703 — 562-860-1927
Harold Horchover, supt. — Fax 860-1829

Professional Career Institute — Post-Sec.
17215 Studebaker Rd Ste 310 90703 — 562-916-5055
Valley Christian HS — 700/9-12
10818 Artesia Blvd 90703 — 562-865-0281
Scott Edwards, prin. — Fax 865-0082
Valley Christian MS — 300/7-8
18100 Dumont Ave 90703 — 562-865-6519
Jason Schrock, prin. — Fax 403-3159
Western College of Southern California — Post-Sec.
10900 183rd St Ste 290 90703 — 562-809-5100

Chatsworth, See Los Angeles
Los Angeles USD
Supt. — See Los Angeles
Chatsworth HS — 3,100/9-12
10027 Lurline Ave 91311 — 818-341-6211
Jeffrey Davis, prin. — Fax 709-6952
Lawrence MS — 2,100/6-8
10100 Variel Ave 91311 — 818-882-1214
Christopher Rosas, prin. — Fax 349-4539

Chaminade MS — 700/6-8
19800 Devonshire St 91311 — 818-363-8127
Christine Hunter, prin. — Fax 363-1219
Learning Tree University — Post-Sec.
20916 Knapp St 91311 — 818-882-5685

Cherry Valley, Riverside, Pop. 5,945

Cherry Valley Brethren S | 100/K-12
39205 Vineland St 92223 | 951-845-2653
Judy Polman, prin. | Fax 845-2026

Chester, Plumas, Pop. 2,082
Plumas USD
Supt. — See Quincy
Chester JSHS | 300/7-12
PO Box 797 96020 | 530-258-2126
Michael Jordan, prin. | Fax 258-2306

Chico, Butte, Pop. 67,509
Chico USD | 12,900/K-12
1163 E 7th St 95928 | 530-891-3000
Dr. Chet Francisco, supt. | Fax 891-3220
www.chicousd.org
Bidwell JHS, 2376 North Ave 95926 | 800/7-8
Rob Williams, prin. | 530-891-3080
Chico HS | 2,100/9-12
901 Esplanade 95926 | 530-891-3026
Jim Hanlon, prin. | Fax 891-3284
Chico JHS | 700/7-8
280 Memorial Way 95926 | 530-891-3066
John Mealley, prin. | Fax 891-3264
Marsh JHS, 2253 Humboldt Rd 95928 | 600/7-8
Steve Piluso, prin. | 530-895-4110
Pleasant Valley HS | 2,000/9-12
1475 East Ave 95926 | 530-879-5100
Michael Rupp, prin. | Fax 879-5263

Regional Occupational Center & Program
Supt. — None
Butte County ROP | Vo/Tech
2491 Carmichael Dr Ste 100 95928 | 530-879-7457
Paul Watters, dir. | Fax 879-7458

American Christian Academy | 100/1-12
13 San Ramon Dr 95973 | 530-896-1150
Julie Clark, admin.
California State University-Chico | Post-Sec.
95929 | 530-898-6116
Champion Christian JSHS | 100/7-12
1184 East Ave 95926 | 530-345-8008
Rick Stout, prin. | Fax 345-5405
Pleasant Valley Baptist S | 100/K-12
13539 Garner Ln 95973 | 530-343-2949
Tim Ruhl, prin.

Chino, San Bernardino, Pop. 71,928
Chino Valley USD | 33,100/K-12
5130 Riverside Dr 91710 | 909-628-1201
Edmond Heatley Ed.D., supt. | Fax 590-4911
www.chino.k12.ca.us
Chino HS | 2,800/9-12
5472 Park Pl 91710 | 909-627-7351
Rigoberto Vasquez, prin. | Fax 548-6004
Lugo HS | 2,300/9-12
13400 Pipeline Ave 91710 | 909-591-3902
Preston Carr, prin. | Fax 548-6020
Magnolia JHS | 1,000/7-8
13150 Mountain Ave 91710 | 909-627-9263
Bonnie Cardinale, prin. | Fax 627-2165
Ramona JHS | 1,000/7-8
4575 Walnut Ave 91710 | 909-627-9144
Mike Finkbiner, prin. | Fax 517-9258
Chino Community Adult | Adult
5130 Riverside Dr 91710 | 909-628-1201
Richard Meyer, prin. | Fax 548-6016
Other Schools – See Chino Hills, Ontario

Chino Valley Christian Academy | 100/K-12
12205 Pipeline Ave 91710 | 909-464-8255
Dennis Leonard, dir.

Chino Hills, San Bernardino, Pop. 73,886
Chino Valley USD
Supt. — See Chino
Ayala HS | 2,700/9-12
14255 Peyton Dr 91709 | 909-627-3584
 | Fax 464-9239
Canyon Hills JHS | 1,200/7-8
2500 Madrugada Dr 91709 | 909-464-9938
Mike Hunkins, prin. | Fax 590-3959
Chino Hills HS | 2,200/9-12
16150 Pomona Rincon Rd 91709 | 909-606-7540
Carl Hampton, prin. | Fax 548-6041
Townsend JHS | 1,200/7-8
15359 Ilex Dr 91709 | 909-591-2161
Melody Kohn, prin. | Fax 597-4153

Chowchilla, Madera, Pop. 14,518
Alview-Dairyland UNESD | 400/K-8
12861 Avenue 18 1/2 93610 | 559-665-2394
Dr. Darrel White, supt. | Fax 665-7347
www.adusd.k12.ca.us
Dairyland S | 200/4-8
12861 Avenue 18 1/2 93610 | 559-665-2394
Dr. Darrel White, prin. | Fax 665-7347

Chowchilla ESD | 1,700/K-8
PO Box 910 93610 | 559-665-8000
Duncan B. Hobbs, supt. | Fax 665-3036
www.chowchillaelem.k12.ca.us
Wilson MS | 600/6-8
PO Box 910 93610 | 559-665-8070
Tara Bright, prin. | Fax 665-8004

Chowchilla UNHSD | 800/9-12
805 Humboldt Ave 93610 | 559-665-1331
Dr. Donna White, supt. | Fax 665-4659
www.chowchillahigh.k12.ca.us
Chowchilla HS | 800/9-12
805 Humboldt Ave 93610 | 559-665-1331
Ron Seals, prin. | Fax 665-1074

Chula Vista, San Diego, Pop. 199,060
Sweetwater UNHSD | 73,900/7-12
1130 5th Ave 91911 | 619-691-5500
Bruce Husson, supt. | Fax 498-1997
www.suhsd.k12.ca.us
Bonita Vista HS | 2,800/9-12
751 Otay Lakes Rd 91913 | 619-216-5000
Thomas Gray, prin. | Fax 656-1203

Bonita Vista MS | 1,200/7-8
650 Otay Lakes Rd 91910 | 619-397-2200
Bettina Batista, prin. | Fax 482-9356
Castle Park HS | 2,400/9-12
1395 Hilltop Dr 91911 | 619-691-5600
Maria Castilleja, prin. | Fax 427-5967
Castle Park MS | 1,500/7-8
160 Quintard St 91911 | 619-691-5490
George Ohnesorgen, prin. | Fax 427-8045
Chula Vista MS | 1,800/7-9
415 5th Ave 91910 | 619-691-5655
Doug Jenkins, prin. | Fax 427-5723
Chula Vista SHS | 2,000/10-12
820 4th Ave 91911 | 619-691-5765
Gary Chapman, prin. | Fax 427-5824
Eastlake HS | 2,700/9-12
1120 Eastlake Pkwy 91915 | 619-216-5055
Robert Barrett, prin. | Fax 656-9736
Eastlake MS | 900/7-8
900 Duncan Ranch Rd 91914 | 619-591-4000
Victoria Kreiser, prin. | Fax 482-0553
Hilltop HS | 2,300/9-12
555 Claire Ave 91910 | 619-691-5640
Jerry Rindone, prin. | Fax 425-3284
Hilltop MS | 1,200/7-8
44 E J St 91910 | 619-498-2700
Linda Stanley, prin. | Fax 585-3576
Otay Ranch HS | 1,900/9-12
1250 Olympic Pkwy 91913 | 619-591-5000
Jose Brosz, prin. | Fax 591-5010
Rancho del Rey MS | 1,600/7-8
1174 E J St 91910 | 619-216-5077
Sebastian Perez, prin. | Fax 656-3810
Chula Vista Adult S | Adult
1034 4th Ave 91911 | 619-691-5760
Tony Alfaro Ed.D., prin. | Fax 425-5447
Other Schools – See Imperial Beach, National City, San Diego, San Ysidro

Calvary Christian Academy | 400/PK-12
1771 E Palomar St 91913 | 619-591-2260
Dr. Chapin Marsh, hdmstr. | Fax 591-2261
Covenant Christian S | 100/K-12
505 E Naples St 91911 | 619-421-8822
Thomas M. McManus, prin. | Fax 216-9846
Pima Medical Institute - Chula Vista | Post-Sec.
780 Bay Blvd Ste 101 91910 | 619-425-3200
Southwestern College | Post-Sec.
900 Otay Lakes Rd 91910 | 619-421-6700

Citrus Heights, Sacramento, Pop. 88,515
San Juan USD
Supt. — See Carmichael
Mesa Verde HS | 1,300/9-12
7501 Carriage Dr 95621 | 916-971-5288
Paul Oropallo, prin. | Fax 971-5215
San Juan HS | 1,100/9-12
7551 Greenback Ln 95610 | 916-971-5150
Dave Terwilliger, prin. | Fax 971-5150
Sunrise Tech Center | Vo/Tech
7322 Sunrise Blvd 95610 | 916-971-5049
Margaret Holiday, prin. | Fax 971-7695
Sylvan MS | 900/7-8
7137 Auburn Blvd 95610 | 916-971-7873
Jim Shoemake, prin. | Fax 971-7896

American Christian Academy | 200/K-12
7412 Hollyhock Ct 95621 | 916-725-8316
Karen Davis, admin.
National Career Education | Post-Sec.
6060 Snrs Vista Dr #3000 95610 | 916-969-4900
Western Career College | Post-Sec.
7301 Greenback Ln Ste A 95621 | 916-722-8200

City of Industry, Los Angeles, Pop. 616
Bassett USD
Supt. — See La Puente
Torch Magnet MS | 900/6-8
751 Vineland Ave 91746 | 626-931-2700
Joe Medina, prin. | Fax 931-2702

Hacienda La Puente USD | 49,100/K-12
PO Box 60002 91716 | 626-933-1000
Dr. Edward Lee Vargas, supt. | Fax 855-3505
www.hlpusd.k12.ca.us/
Workman HS | 1,300/9-12
16303 Temple Ave 91744 | 626-933-8800
Sergio Garcia, prin. | Fax 855-3148
Other Schools – See Hacienda Heights, La Puente

Regional Occupational Center & Program
Supt. — None
La Puente Valley ROP | Vo/Tech
18501 Gale Ave Ste 100 91748 | 626-810-3300
Cynthia Parulan-Colfer, supt. | Fax 581-9108

Bryman College | Post-Sec.
12801 Crossroads Pkwy S 91746 | 562-908-2500
Elegante Beauty College | Post-Sec.
1600 S Azusa Ave Unit 244 91748 | 626-965-2532

Claremont, Los Angeles, Pop. 34,964
Claremont USD | 6,900/K-12
2080 N Mountain Ave 91711 | 909-398-0609
Sheralyn Smith Ed.D., supt. | Fax 621-0180
www.cusd.claremont.edu
Claremont HS | 2,200/9-12
1601 N Indian Hill Blvd 91711 | 909-624-9053
Carrie Allen, prin. | Fax 624-2128
El Roble IS | 1,100/7-8
665 N Mountain Ave 91711 | 909-398-0343
Kevin Grier, prin. | Fax 398-0399
San Antonio HS | 100/9-12
125 W San Jose Ave 91711 | 909-398-0316
Steven Boyd, prin. | Fax 398-0384
Claremont Adult S | Adult
170 W San Jose # 100 91711 | 909-398-0609
Bill Teague, prin. | Fax 626-5109

Claremont Graduate University | Post-Sec.
170 E 10th St 91711 | 909-621-8000
Claremont McKenna College | Post-Sec.
500 E 9th St 91711 | 909-621-8000

Claremont School of Theology | Post-Sec.
1325 N College Ave 91711 | 909-626-3521
Harvey Mudd College | Post-Sec.
301 E 12th St 91711 | 909-621-8000
Keck Graduate Institute | Post-Sec.
535 Watson Dr 91711 | 909-607-7855
Pitzer College | Post-Sec.
1050 N Mills Ave 91711 | 909-621-8219
Pomona College | Post-Sec.
333 N College Way 91711 | 909-621-8000
Scripps College | Post-Sec.
1030 Columbia Ave 91711 | 909-621-8000
Webb S | 400/9-12
1175 W Baseline Rd 91711 | 909-626-3587
Susan Nelson, hdmstr. | Fax 621-4582

Clarksburg, Yolo
River Delta USD
Supt. — See Rio Vista
Clarksburg MS | 100/7-9
PO Box 99 95612 | 916-744-1717
Ceil Wiegand, prin. | Fax 744-5704
Delta HS | 300/9-12
PO Box 100 95612 | 916-744-1714
Paul Gengler, prin. | Fax 744-1673

Clayton, Contra Costa, Pop. 11,042
Mt. Diablo USD
Supt. — See Concord
Diablo View MS | 600/6-8
300 Diablo View Ln 94517 | 925-672-0898
Michele Cooper, prin. | Fax 672-4327

Clearlake, Lake, Pop. 14,225
Konocti USD
Supt. — See Lower Lake
Oak Hill MS | 500/7-8
PO Box 7087 95422 | 707-994-6447
Marie Friedrich, prin. | Fax 994-5047

Cloverdale, Sonoma, Pop. 7,480
Cloverdale USD | 1,600/K-12
97 School St 95425 | 707-894-1920
Claudia Rosatti, supt. | Fax 894-1922
www.cusd.org/
Cloverdale HS | 400/9-12
509 N Cloverdale Blvd 95425 | 707-894-1900
Gene Lile, prin. | Fax 894-4804
Washington MS | 600/4-8
129 S Washington St 95425 | 707-894-1940
Connie Sumner, prin. | Fax 894-1946

Clovis, Fresno, Pop. 78,558
Clovis USD | 37,900/K-12
1450 Herndon Ave 93611 | 559-327-9000
Terry Bradley Ed.D., supt. | Fax 327-9109
www.clovisusd.k12.ca.us
Alta Sierra IS | 1,600/7-8
380 W Teague Ave, | 559-327-3500
Devin Blizzard, prin. | Fax 327-3590
Buchanan HS | 2,700/9-12
1560 Minnewawa Ave 93612 | 559-327-3000
Don Ulrich, prin. | Fax 327-3090
Clark IS | 1,300/7-8
902 5th St 93612 | 559-327-1500
Scott Steele, prin. | Fax 327-1556
Clovis East HS | 700/9-9
4343 N Leonard Ave, | 559-327-4000
Jeff Eben, prin. | Fax 327-4190
Clovis HS | 2,400/9-12
1055 Fowler Ave 93611 | 559-327-1000
Norm Anderson, prin. | Fax 327-1010
Reyburn IS | 1,400/7-8
4300 N DeWolf Ave, | 559-327-4500
Stacy Dunnicliff, prin. | Fax 327-4791
Clovis Adult S | Adult
1452 David E Cook Way 93611 | 559-327-2800
John Ballinger, prin. | Fax 327-2889
Other Schools – See Fresno

Clovis Christian S | 200/PK-12
3105 Locan Ave, | 559-291-6302
Phil Laughlin, admin. | Fax 291-6278
Institute of Technology - Clovis Campus | Post-Sec.
564 W Herndon Ave 93612 | 559-297-4500
San Joaquin College of Law | Post-Sec.
901 5th St 93612 | 559-323-2100
Tower Christian S | 300/K-12
8753 Chickadee Ln, | 559-298-2772
Ann Raber, admin.

Coachella, Riverside, Pop. 28,021
Coachella Valley USD
Supt. — See Thermal
Cahuilla Desert Academy | 1,300/7-8
82489 Avenue 52 92236 | 760-398-0097
Estella Palacio, prin. | Fax 398-0088
Coachella Valley Adult Education | Adult
1099 Orchard St 92236 | 760-398-6302
Guillermo Mendoza, prin. | Fax 398-0436

Coalinga, Fresno, Pop. 16,101
Coalinga/Huron USD | 4,300/K-12
657 Sunset St 93210 | 559-935-7500
Dr. William McDermott, supt. | Fax 935-5329
www.chusd.k12.ca.us
Coalinga HS | 1,100/9-12
750 Van Ness St 93210 | 559-935-7520
Roger Campbell, prin. | Fax 935-3571
Coalinga MS | 700/6-8
265 Cambridge Ave 93210 | 559-935-7550
Dawn Contreras-Douglas, prin. | Fax 934-1311
Other Schools – See Huron

Faith Christian Academy | 100/K-12
450 W Elm Ave 93210 | 559-935-9209
Tara Davis, prin. | Fax 935-0745
West Hills Community College | Post-Sec.
300 W Cherry Ln 93210 | 559-935-0801

Coarsegold, Madera
Chawanakee USD
Supt. — See North Fork
Chawanakee Adult Education | Adult
28420 Yosemite Springs Pkwy 93614 | 559-683-0808
Doug Waltner, prin. | Fax 683-8604

Coleville, Mono
Eastern Sierra USD
Supt. — See Bridgeport
Coleville HS 100/9-12
111591 US Highway 395 96107 530-495-2231
Jason Reid, prin. Fax 495-2730

Colfax, Placer, Pop. 1,667
Placer UNHSD
Supt. — See Auburn
Colfax HS 1,000/9-12
24995 Ben Taylor Rd 95713 530-346-2284
Rick Spears, prin. Fax 346-6476

Aviation & Electronic School of America Post-Sec.
PO Box 1810 95713 800-345-2742

Colma, San Mateo, Pop. 1,216
Jefferson ESD
Supt. — See Daly City
Franklin IS 600/7-8
700 Stewart Ave, Daly City CA 94015 650-991-1202
James Parrish, prin. Fax 756-5475

Colton, San Bernardino, Pop. 50,602
Colton JUSD 24,800/PK-12
1212 Valencia Dr 92324 909-580-5000
Dennis Byas, supt. Fax 876-6395
www.colton.k12.ca.us
Colton HS 3,300/9-12
777 W Valley Blvd 92324 909-580-5005
John Steven Coke, prin. Fax 876-4093
Colton MS 1,100/7-8
670 W Laurel St 92324 909-580-5009
Chris Marin, prin. Fax 876-4095
Other Schools – See Bloomington, Grand Terrace

Rialto USD
Supt. — See Rialto
Jehue MS 1,600/6-8
1500 N Eucalyptus Ave 92324 909-421-7377
Leonard Buckner, prin. Fax 421-7376

Arrowhead Regional Medical Center Post-Sec.
400 N Pepper Ave 92324 909-580-1000
Four-D College Post-Sec.
1020 E Washington St 92324 909-783-9331

Colusa, Colusa, Pop. 5,662
Colusa USD 1,400/K-12
745 10th St 95932 530-458-7791
Larry Yeghoian, supt. Fax 458-4030
www.colusa.k12.ca.us
Colusa HS 400/9-12
901 Colus Ave 95932 530-458-2156
Robert Hulbert, prin. Fax 458-5783
Egling MS 500/4-8
813 Webster St 95932 530-458-7631
Ed Conrado, prin. Fax 458-8107

Compton, Los Angeles, Pop. 95,835
Compton USD 32,000/PK-12
500 S Santa Fe Ave 90221 310-639-4321
Dr. Jesse L. Gonzales, supt. Fax 632-3014
www.compton.k12.ca.us
Bunche MS 1,100/6-8
12338 S Mona Blvd 90222 310-898-6010
Frank Sifuentes, prin. Fax 638-4935
Centennial HS 1,300/9-12
2600 N Central Ave 90222 310-635-2715
Dr. Richard Chavez, prin. Fax 631-9164
Compton HS 2,600/9-12
601 S Acacia Ave 90220 310-635-3881
Jesse Jones, prin. Fax 635-3051
Davis MS 1,400/6-8
621 W Poplar St 90220 310-898-6020
Marrio Walker, prin. Fax 631-5725
Dominguez HS 2,300/9-12
15301 S San Jose Ave 90221 562-630-0142
Cuauhtemoc Avila, prin. Fax 408-2367
Enterprise MS 800/6-8
2600 W Compton Blvd 90220 310-898-6030
Dr. Teodor Brancov, prin. Fax 632-4183
Roosevelt MS 1,400/6-8
1200 E Alondra Blvd 90221 310-898-6040
JaMaiia Bond, prin. Fax 631-3298
Walton MS 700/6-8
900 W Greenleaf Blvd 90220 310-898-6060
Gipson Lyles, prin. Fax 631-3409
Whaley MS 1,300/6-8
14401 S Gibson Ave 90221 310-898-6070
Dr. Mark Jones, prin. Fax 638-7079
Willowbrook MS 700/6-8
2601 N Wilmington Ave 90222 310-898-6080
Valerie Quarles, prin. Fax 537-2932
Compton Adult S Adult
1104 E 148th St 90220 310-898-6470
Saundra Bishop, prin. Fax 898-6477
Other Schools – See Los Angeles

Regional Occupational Center & Program
Supt. — None
Compton Unified ROP Vo/Tech
700 N Bullis Rd # 12 90221 310-898-6000
Reena Singh, dir. Fax 763-3871

Compton Community College Post-Sec.
1111 E Artesia Blvd 90221 310-900-1600
James Academic Development S 100/K-12
1901 W Reeve St 90220 310-631-6235
Bertha James, prin. Fax 631-9471
Universal College of Beauty Post-Sec.
718 W Compton Blvd 90220 310-635-6969

Concord, Contra Costa, Pop. 124,977
Mt. Diablo USD 34,900/K-12
1936 Carlotta Dr 94519 925-682-8000
Gary McHenry, supt. Fax 680-2505
www.mdusd.k12.ca.us
Clayton Valley HS 1,900/9-12
1101 Alberta Way 94521 925-682-7474
Gary Swanson, prin. Fax 825-7859
Concord HS 1,400/9-12
4200 Concord Blvd 94521 925-687-2030
Ronald Miller, prin. Fax 682-4613
El Dorado MS 1,000/6-8
1750 West St 94521 925-682-5700
Barbara Weil, prin. Fax 685-1460
Glenbrook MS 700/6-8
2351 Olivera Rd 94520 925-685-6835
Gary McAdam, prin. Fax 671-9532
Mt. Diablo HS 1,500/9-12
2450 Grant St 94520 925-682-4030
Bev Hansen, prin. Fax 687-9658
Oak Grove MS 900/6-8
2050 Minert Rd 94518 925-682-1843
Teresa McCormick, prin. Fax 682-2083
Pine Hollow MS 800/6-8
5522 Pine Hollow Rd 94521 925-672-5444
Marcie Brown, prin. Fax 672-9751
Ygnacio Valley HS 1,500/9-12
755 Oak Grove Rd 94518 925-685-8414
Carolyn Plath, prin. Fax 685-1435
Loma Vista Adult Center Adult
1266 San Carlos Ave 94518 925-685-7340
Fax 687-8217
Other Schools – See Clayton, Pittsburg, Pleasant Hill, Walnut Creek

---

Carondelet HS 900/9-12
1133 Winton Dr 94518 925-686-5353
Sr. Marien Dyer, prin. Fax 671-9429
Concord Academy 100/K-12
PO Box 21383 94521 925-798-2097
Ronald Myers, admin.
Concord Christian S 100/K-12
2120 Olivera Ct 94520 925-825-1370
Lisa Coniglio, admin. Fax 682-5981
De La Salle HS 1,000/9-12
1130 Winton Dr 94518 925-686-3310
Br. Christopher Brady, prin. Fax 686-3474
Heald College Concord Post-Sec.
5130 Commercial Cir 94520 925-827-1300
Paris Beauty College Post-Sec.
1950 Market St 94520 925-685-7600

Corcoran, Tulare, Pop. 21,586
Corcoran JUSD 3,100/K-12
1520 Patterson Ave 93212 559-992-3104
Rich Merlo, supt. Fax 992-3957
www.corcoran.k12.ca.us
Corcoran HS 900/9-12
1520 Patterson Ave 93212 559-992-5061
Gloria Gravalle, prin. Fax 992-5066
Muir MS 700/6-8
1520 Patterson Ave 93212 559-992-4167
Mike Graville, prin. Fax 992-4423

Corning, Tehama, Pop. 6,924
Corning UNESD 2,300/K-8
1590 South St 96021 530-824-7700
Stephen Kelish, supt. Fax 824-2493
www.cuesd.tehama.k12.ca.us
Maywood MS 700/6-8
1666 Marguerite Ave 96021 530-824-7730
Bobbi Abold, prin. Fax 824-7742

Corning UNHSD 1,000/9-12
643 Blackburn Ave 96021 530-824-8000
Melinda Self, supt. Fax 824-8005
Corning HS 1,000/9-12
643 Blackburn Ave 96021 530-824-8000
Bruce Cole, prin. Fax 824-8005

Corona, Riverside, Pop. 142,454
Corona-Norco USD
Supt. — See Norco
Auburndale IS 1,200/7-8
1255 River Rd 92880 951-736-3231
Linda Lanyi, prin. Fax 736-3360
Centennial HS 2,900/9-12
1820 Rimpau Ave 92881 951-739-5670
Sam Buenrostro, prin. Fax 739-5693
Citrus Hills IS 1,600/7-8
3211 S Main St 92882 951-736-4600
Michael Ridgway, prin. Fax 736-4623
Corona Fundamental IS 1,000/7-8
1230 S Main St 92882 951-736-3321
Bonnie Paskey, prin. Fax 736-3417
Corona HS 2,800/9-12
1150 W 10th St 92882 951-736-3211
Robert Taylor, prin. Fax 736-3408
El Cerrito MS 700/6-8
7610 El Cerrito Rd 92881 951-736-3216
Lisa Simon, prin. Fax 736-3286
Raney IS 1,600/6-8
1010 W Citron St 92882 951-736-3221
Don Ward, prin. Fax 736-3439
River Heights IS 7-8
7227 Cleveland Ave 92880 951-736-8285
Karen Fisher, prin.
Roosevelt HS 9-12
7447 Cleveland Ave 92880 951-736-8284
Julie Vitale, prin.
Santiago HS 3,600/9-12
1395 Foothill Pkwy 92881 951-739-5600
Rupertino Cisneros, prin. Fax 739-5639
Corona-Norco Adult Education Adult
300 S Buena Vista Ave 92882 951-736-3325
Judy Guerard, prin. Fax 736-7159

Amor Christian Academy 50/1-12
PO Box 2650 92878 951-735-6609
Jesse Reyes, admin. Fax 735-5185
Central CA School of Continuing Educ. Post-Sec.
271 Ott St Ste 23 92882 951-549-0693
Christian Heritage S 400/K-12
PO Box 1780 92878 951-736-3033
Arleen Morris, admin.
Corona Christian S 100/PK-12
1901 W Ontario Ave 92882 951-734-5683
Dr. David Howard, admin. Fax 734-3809

Coronado, San Diego, Pop. 23,784
Coronado USD 2,900/K-12
201 6th St 92118 619-522-8900
Susan Coyle, supt. Fax 437-6570
www.coronado.k12.ca.us
Coronado HS 1,000/9-12
650 D Ave 92118 619-522-8907
Karl Mueller, prin. Fax 437-0236
Coronado MS 700/6-8
550 F Ave 92118 619-522-8921
Nancy Girvin Ed.D., prin. Fax 522-6948

Costa Mesa, Orange, Pop. 109,563
Newport-Mesa USD 21,800/PK-12
2985 Bear St 92626 714-424-5000
Dr. Robert Barbot, supt. Fax 424-5018
www.nmusd.us
Costa Mesa JSHS 1,900/7-12
2650 Fairview Rd 92626 714-424-8700
John Garcia, prin. Fax 424-8770
Estancia HS 1,200/9-12
2323 Placentia Ave 92627 949-515-6500
Tom Antal, prin. Fax 515-6571
TeWinkle MS 1,100/6-8
3224 California St 92626 714-424-7965
Dan Diehl, prin. Fax 424-5680
Other Schools – See Newport Beach

Regional Occupational Center & Program
Supt. — None
Coastline ROP Vo/Tech
1001 Presidio Sq 92626 714-979-1955
Paul Snyder, supt. Fax 557-6812

James Albert School of Cosmetology Post-Sec.
281 E 17th St 92627 949-642-0606
Orange Coast College Post-Sec.
PO Box 5005 92628 714-432-0202
Pacific College Post-Sec.
3160 Red Hill Ave 92626 714-662-4402
Paul Mitchell The School Post-Sec.
1534 Adams Ave 92626 714-546-8786
Vanguard University of Southern CA Post-Sec.
55 Fair Dr 92626 714-556-3610
Whittier College School of Law Post-Sec.
3333 Harbor Blvd 92626 714-444-4141

Cottonwood, Shasta, Pop. 1,747
Anderson UNHSD
Supt. — See Anderson
West Valley HS 1,100/9-12
3805 Happy Valley Rd 96022 530-347-7171
Karl Stemmler, prin. Fax 347-0481

Cottonwood UNESD 1,200/K-8
20512 1st St 96022 530-347-3165
Dale H. Hansen, supt. Fax 347-0247
www.shastalink.k12.ca.us/cotton
West Cottonwood JHS 700/4-8
20512 1st St 96022 530-347-3123
Barry Espil, prin. Fax 347-0247

Evergreen USD 900/K-8
19500 Learning Way 96022 530-347-7955
Harley North, supt. Fax 347-7954
www.eusd.tehama.k12.ca.us
Evergreen MS 400/5-8
19500 Learning Way 96022 530-347-7950
Brad Mendenhall, prin. Fax 347-7953

Coulterville, Mariposa
Mariposa County USD
Supt. — See Mariposa
Coulterville HS 100/9-12
PO Box 480 95311 209-878-3955
Dr. Stella Pizelo, prin. Fax 878-3816

Covelo, Mendocino, Pop. 1,057
Round Valley USD 400/K-12
PO Box 276 95428 707-983-6171
Joy Muhleck, supt. Fax 983-6655
Round Valley HS 100/9-12
PO Box 276 95428 707-983-6171
John Nickel, prin. Fax 983-6179

Covina, Los Angeles, Pop. 48,160
Azusa USD
Supt. — See Azusa
Gladstone HS 1,500/9-12
1340 N Enid Ave 91722 626-815-5157
Scott Magnuson, prin. Fax 815-5155

Charter Oak USD 6,700/K-12
PO Box 9 91723 626-966-8331
Norm Kirschenbaum Ed.D., supt. Fax 967-9580
www.cousd.k12.ca.us
Charter Oak HS 2,100/9-12
PO Box 9 91723 626-915-5841
Richard Evers, prin. Fax 915-3398
Royal Oak IS 1,700/6-8
PO Box 9 91723 626-967-6354
Scott Wollam, prin. Fax 331-2074

Covina-Valley USD 14,400/K-12
PO Box 269 91723 626-974-7000
Louis Pappas, supt. Fax 974-7032
www.cvusd.k12.ca.us
Covina HS 1,400/9-12
PO Box 269 91723 626-974-6020
Fax 974-6045
Las Palmas MS 1,100/6-8
PO Box 269 91723 626-974-7200
Josie Paredes, prin. Fax 974-7215
Northview HS 1,400/9-12
PO Box 269 91723 626-974-6120
Lynn Carmen-Day, prin. Fax 974-6145
Sierra Vista MS 1,200/6-8
PO Box 269 91723 626-974-7300
Robert Shivers, prin. Fax 974-7315
Business Center, PO Box 269 91723 Adult
Vincent VanDetta, prin. 626-974-6800
Tri Community Adult Ed.-Griswold Center Adult
PO Box 269 91723 626-974-6800
Vincent VanDetta, dir. Fax 974-6815
Other Schools – See West Covina

American Graduate University Post-Sec.
733 N Dodsworth Ave 91724 626-966-4576

Sonrise Christian S 400/4-8
1220 E Ruddock St 91724 626-331-0559
Dr. John Free, prin. Fax 339-8029
Western Christian HS 500/9-12
1115 E Puente St 91724 626-967-0733
Russ Grelling, prin. Fax 915-8824
Western Christian ISP 500/K-12
124 N Armel Dr 91722 626-332-9981
Marilyn Stephens, dir.

Crescent City, Del Norte, Pop. 7,319
Del Norte County Office of Education
301 W Washington Blvd 95531 707-464-6141
Jan Moorehouse, supt. Fax 464-0238
www.delnorte.k12.ca.us
Del Norte County Alternative Education K-12
400 W Harding Ave 95531 707-464-0750
Gerry Riley, dir. Fax 465-5116

Del Norte County USD 4,200/K-12
301 W Washington Blvd 95531 707-464-6141
Jan Moorehouse, supt. Fax 464-0238
www.delnorte.k12.ca.us
Crescent Elk MS 700/6-8
994 G St 95531 707-464-0320
Billy Hartwick, prin. Fax 464-0326
Del Norte County HS 1,100/9-12
1301 El Dorado St 95531 707-464-0260
Patrick Finley, prin. Fax 465-6923

Regional Occupational Center & Program
Supt. — None
Del Norte County ROP Vo/Tech
1301 El Dorado St 95531 707-464-0274
Patrick Finley, dir. Fax 465-6923

Crockett, Contra Costa, Pop. 3,228
John Swett USD 1,800/K-12
341 B St 94525 510-787-1141
Michael Roth, supt. Fax 787-2079
www.jsusd.k12.ca.us
Carquinez MS 500/6-8
1099 Pomona St 94525 510-787-1081
Linda Steensrud, prin. Fax 787-2359
Swett HS 600/9-12
1098 Pomona St 94525 510-787-1088
Steven Peters, prin. Fax 787-1930

Cudahy, Los Angeles, Pop. 25,236
Los Angeles USD
Supt. — See Los Angeles
Elizabeth S 2,800/K-12
4811 Elizabeth St 90201 323-562-0175
Barbara Gee, prin. Fax 560-8412

Culver City, Los Angeles, Pop. 39,788
Culver City USD 10,700/K-12
4034 Irving Pl 90232 310-842-4220
Laura McGaughey, supt. Fax 842-4205
www.ccusd.k12.ca.us
Culver City HS 2,100/9-12
4401 Elenda St 90230 310-842-4200
Pamela Magee, prin. Fax 842-4303
Culver City MS 1,700/6-8
4601 Elenda St 90230 310-842-4200
Patricia Jaffe, prin. Fax 842-4304
Culver City Adult S Adult
4501 Elenda St 90230 310-842-4300
Dr. Marvin Brown, prin. Fax 842-4343

Antioch University Southern California Post-Sec.
400 Corporate Pointe 90230 310-578-1080
Gemological Institute of America Post-Sec.
600 Corporate Point Ste 100 90230 310-670-2100
Kayne ERAS Center 200/K-12
5350 Machado Ln 90230 310-737-9393
Dwight Counsel, prin.
West Los Angeles College Post-Sec.
4800 Freshman Dr 90230 310-287-4200

Cupertino, Santa Clara, Pop. 50,479
Cupertino UNESD 15,200/K-8
10301 Vista Dr 95014 408-252-3000
Phil Quon Ph.D., supt. Fax 255-4450
cupertino.ca.campusgrid.net
Hyde MS 1,000/6-8
19325 Bollinger Rd 95014 408-252-6290
Todd Shimada, prin. Fax 255-3288
Kennedy MS 1,400/6-8
821 Bubb Rd 95014 408-253-1525
Russ Ottey, prin. Fax 257-5777
Lawson MS 6-8
10401 Vista Dr 95014 408-255-7500
Cici O'donnell, prin. Fax 446-4987
Other Schools – See San Jose, Sunnyvale

Fremont UNHSD
Supt. — See Sunnyvale
Cupertino HS 1,500/9-12
10100 Finch Ave 95014 408-366-7380
Cary Matsuoka, prin. Fax 996-3060
Homestead HS 1,800/9-12
21370 Homestead Rd 95014 408-522-2500
Graham Clark, prin. Fax 738-8631
Monta Vista HS 2,300/9-12
21840 McClellan Rd 95014 408-366-7600
April Scott, prin. Fax 252-1519

DeAnza College Post-Sec.
21250 Stevens Creek Blvd 95014 408-864-5678
Our Savior Lutheran S 100/K-12
5825 Bollinger Rd 95014 408-252-0250
Fax 252-0558

Cypress, Orange, Pop. 47,215
Anaheim UNHSD
Supt. — See Anaheim
Cypress HS 2,200/9-12
9801 Valley View St 90630 714-220-4144
Ben Carpenter, prin. Fax 220-4174
Lexington JHS 1,200/7-8
4351 Orange Ave 90630 714-220-4201
Jodie Wales, prin. Fax 761-4989
Oxford Academy 1,100/7-12
5172 Orange Ave 90630 714-220-3055
Carolyn Houston, prin. Fax 527-7128

Cypress College Post-Sec.
9200 Valley View St 90630 714-484-7000
Touro University International Post-Sec.
5665 Plaza Dr Fl 3 90630 714-816-0366

Daly City, San Mateo, Pop. 100,819
Bayshore ESD 400/K-8
1 Martin St 94014 415-467-5443
Stephen J. Waterman, supt. Fax 467-1542
www.bayshore.k12.ca.us
Robertson IS 200/4-8
1 Martin St 94014 415-467-5443
Norman D. Fobert, prin. Fax 467-1542

Jefferson ESD 6,100/K-8
101 Lincoln Ave 94015 650-991-1000
Barbara B. Wilson Ph.D., supt. Fax 992-2265
www.jsd.k12.ca.us/
Pollicita MS 600/6-8
550 E Market St 94014 650-991-1216
Joseph J. Spaulding, prin. Fax 755-2170
Rivera IS 500/7-8
1255 Southgate Ave 94015 650-991-1225
Jan Hopkins, prin. Fax 755-6273
Other Schools – See Colma

Jefferson UNHSD 12,200/9-12
699 Serramonte Blvd #100 94015 650-550-7900
Michael Crilly, supt. Fax 550-7888
www.juhsd.net
Jefferson HS 1,300/9-12
6996 Mission St 94014 650-550-7700
Alice Campbell, prin. Fax 550-7790
Westmoor HS 1,800/9-12
131 Westmoor Ave 94015 650-550-7400
Richard Morosi, prin. Fax 550-7490
Adult Education Divison Adult
699 Serramonte Blvd #111 94015 650-550-7890
Dana Rumney, prin. Fax 550-7889
Other Schools – See Pacifica

Hilltop Beauty School Post-Sec.
6317 Mission St 94014 650-756-2720

Dana Point, Orange, Pop. 35,745
Capistrano USD
Supt. — See San Juan Capistrano
Dana Hills HS 2,800/9-12
33333 Golden Lantern St 92629 949-496-6666
Carolyn Williams, prin. Fax 489-8317

Danville, Contra Costa, Pop. 42,547
San Ramon Valley USD 21,500/K-12
699 Old Orchard Dr 94526 925-552-5500
Robert Kessler, supt. Fax 838-3147
www.srvusd.net/
Diablo Vista MS 700/6-8
4100 Camino Tassajara 94506 925-648-8560
Becky Ingram, prin. Fax 648-7167
Los Cerros MS 700/6-8
968 Blemer Rd 94526 925-552-5620
Lisa Ward, prin. Fax 837-3512
Monte Vista HS 2,200/9-12
3131 Stone Valley Rd 94526 925-552-5530
Rebecca Smith, prin. Fax 743-1744
San Ramon Valley HS 2,000/9-12
140 Love Ln 94526 925-552-5580
David Lorden, prin. Fax 838-7802
Wood MS 1,000/6-8
600 El Capitan Dr 94526 925-552-5600
Sandy Budde, prin. Fax 820-1857
Other Schools – See Alamo, San Ramon

Athenian S 400/6-12
2100 Mount Diablo Scenic Bl 94506 925-837-5375
Eleanor Dase, hdmstr. Fax 831-1120

Davis, Yolo, Pop. 64,348
Davis JUSD 8,800/K-12
526 B St 95616 530-757-5300
David Murphy, supt. Fax 757-5423
www.djusd.k12.ca.us
Davis SHS 1,900/10-12
315 W 14th St 95616 530-757-5400
Michael Cawley, prin. Fax 757-5492
Emerson JHS 1,000/7-9
2121 Calaveras Ave 95616 530-757-5430
Diane Studley, prin. Fax 757-5434
Harper JHS 7-9
4000 E Covell Blvd 95616 530-759-2182
David Inns, prin. Fax 759-2321
Holmes JHS 1,100/7-9
1220 Drexel Dr 95616 530-757-5455
Bev Maul, prin. Fax 757-5435
Davis Adult S Adult
315 W 14th St 95616 530-757-5380
Laurel Clumpner, prin. Fax 757-5381

D-Q University Post-Sec.
PO Box 409 95617 530-758-0470
University of California Post-Sec.
1 Shields Ave 95616 530-752-1011

Delano, Kern, Pop. 42,801
Delano JUNHSD 4,900/9-12
1747 Princeton St 93215 661-725-4000
Sherrill Hufnagel, supt. Fax 721-9390
www.djuhsd.org/
Chavez HS 1,600/9-12
1747 Princeton St 93215 661-720-4502
Saul D. Gonzalez, prin. Fax 725-8875
Delano HS 2,600/9-12
1747 Princeton St 93215 661-720-4121
Richard Smithey, prin. Fax 720-4119
Delano Adult Adult
1747 Princeton St 93215 661-720-4171
Alfred Sanchez, prin. Fax 725-5852

Delano UNSD 7,100/K-8
1405 12th Ave 93215 661-721-5000
Ronald A.Garcia, supt. Fax 725-2446
www.duesd.org
Almond Tree MS 1,100/6-8
1405 12th Ave 93215 661-721-3641
Michael Dobrenen, prin. Fax 721-3649
Cecil Avenue MS 1,200/6-8
1405 12th Ave 93215 661-721-5030
Jason Kashwer, prin. Fax 721-5097

Bakersfield College Post-Sec.
1942 Randolph St 93215 661-725-8020
Sequoia Christian Academy 50/K-12
PO Box 1876 93216 661-721-2721
Roberta Hunter, prin. Fax 721-2721

Delhi, Merced, Pop. 3,280
Delhi USD 2,800/K-12
9716 Hinton Ave 95315 209-656-2000
Bill Baltazar, supt. Fax 668-6133
www.delhi.k12.ca.us
Delhi HS 500/9-12
9716 Hinton Ave 95315 209-669-3178
George Grijalva, prin. Fax 669-3168
Delhi MS 400/7-8
9716 Hinton Ave 95315 209-669-3178
Dave Woods, prin. Fax 669-3168
Delhi Adult S Adult
9716 Hinton Ave 95315 209-669-6154
Francisca Briones, prin. Fax 669-6165

Denair, Stanislaus, Pop. 3,693
Denair USD 1,200/K-12
3460 Lester Rd 95316 209-632-7514
Edward Parraz, supt. Fax 632-9194
dusd.k12.ca.us
Denair HS 400/9-12
3431 Lester Rd 95316 209-632-9911
Jerry Savelson, prin. Fax 632-8153
Denair MS 300/5-8
3460 Lester Rd 95316 209-632-2510
Darrin Allen, prin. Fax 632-0269

Providence Christian Academy 200/K-12
PO Box 616 95316 209-656-0744
Paulette Applegate, prin.

Desert Hot Springs, Riverside, Pop. 17,902
Palm Springs USD
Supt. — See Palm Springs
Desert Hot Springs HS 1,400/9-12
65850 Pierson Blvd 92240 760-288-7000
Brian Murray, prin. Fax 288-7010
Desert Springs MS 1,500/6-8
66755 Two Bunch Palms Trl 92240 760-251-7200
Mike Swize, prin. Fax 251-7206

Image School of Cosmetology Post-Sec.
13070 Palm Dr 92240 760-251-5373
Palm Springs Christian S 50/7-12
66675 Pierson Blvd 92240 760-329-5466
Dr. Alon Barak, hdmstr. Fax 329-9324

Diamond Bar, Los Angeles, Pop. 58,160
Pomona USD
Supt. — See Pomona
Lorbeer MS 1,000/7-8
501 S Diamond Bar Blvd 91765 909-397-4527
Kathrine Morillo-Shope, prin. Fax 396-9022

Walnut Valley USD
Supt. — See Walnut
Chaparral MS 1,300/6-8
1405 Spruce Tree Dr 91765 909-861-6227
Dr. Michael Chavez, prin. Fax 396-0749
Diamond Bar HS 3,100/9-12
21400 Pathfinder Rd 91765 909-594-1405
Denis Paul, prin. Fax 595-8301

Diamond Springs, El Dorado, Pop. 2,872
El Dorado UNHSD
Supt. — See Placerville
El Dorado Adult HS Adult
2227 Pleasant Valley Rd 95619 530-622-7090
Don Buchheit, prin. Fax 642-2291

Regional Occupational Center & Program
Supt. — None
Central Sierra ROP Vo/Tech
PO Box 1450 95619 530-295-2296
Dave Soper, dir. Fax 295-1273

Dinuba, Tulare, Pop. 17,871
Dinuba USD 5,300/K-12
1327 E El Monte Way 93618 559-595-7200
Jerry L. Sessions, supt. Fax 591-3334
www.dinubausd.com
Dinuba HS 1,500/9-12
1327 E El Monte Way 93618 559-595-7220
Yolanda Valdez, prin. Fax 591-3655
Washington IS 800/7-8
1327 E El Monte Way 93618 559-595-7252
Mark Dutra, prin. Fax 595-8158
Dinuba Adult S Adult
1327 E El Monte Way 93618 559-595-7242
Bill Weller, prin. Fax 595-7248

Dinuba Jr. Academy 50/K-10
218 S Crawford Ave 93618 559-591-0194
Emily Villeda, prin. Fax 591-4835

Dixon, Solano, Pop. 16,210
Dixon USD 3,800/K-12
180 S 1st St Ste 6 95620 707-678-5582
Wally Holbrook, supt. Fax 678-0726
www.dixonusd.org
Dixon HS 1,100/9-12
455 E A St 95620 707-678-2391
Brian Dolan, prin. Fax 678-9318
Jacobs IS 600/7-8
200 N Lincoln St 95620 707-678-9222
Yolanda Falkenberg, prin. Fax 678-1245

Dorris, Siskiyou, Pop. 879
Butte Valley USD 300/K-12
PO Box 709 96023 530-397-3840
Ed Traverso, supt. Fax 397-3842
www.bvalusd.org/
Butte Valley HS 100/9-12
PO Box 709 96023 530-397-4161
Ed Traverso, prin. Fax 397-2311
Butte Valley Adult S Adult
PO Box 709 96023 530-397-3363
Ed Traverso, prin. Fax 397-3360
Other Schools – See Macdoel

Dos Palos, Merced, Pop. 4,863
Dos Palos Oro Loma JUSD 2,500/K-12
2041 Almond St 93620 209-392-6101
Brian Walker, supt. Fax 392-3347
www.dpol.net
Bryant MS 600/6-8
16695 Bryant Ave 93620 209-392-6186
Katy Miller, prin. Fax 392-2636
Dos Palos HS 700/9-12
1701 E Blossom St 93620 209-392-2131
Mike Ashmore, prin. Fax 392-2705

Downey, Los Angeles, Pop. 110,360
Downey USD 23,400/K-12
PO Box 7017 90241 562-469-6500
Dr. Wendy Doty, supt. Fax 469-6515
www.dusd.net/
Downey HS 3,600/9-12
11040 Brookshire Ave 90241 562-869-7301
Tom Houts, prin. Fax 469-7340
East MS 1,300/6-8
10301 Woodruff Ave 90241 562-904-3586
Brent Shubin, prin. Fax 469-7240
Griffiths MS 1,400/6-8
9633 Tweedy Ln 90240 562-904-3580
Gregg Stapp, prin. Fax 469-7260
Sussman MS 1,500/6-8
12500 Birchdale Ave 90242 562-904-3572
Gloria Widmann, prin. Fax 469-7280
Warren HS 3,300/9-12
8141 De Palma St 90241 562-869-7306
Eileen Wannett, prin. Fax 469-7360
West MS 1,400/6-8
11985 Old River School Rd 90242 562-904-3565
Craig Bertsch, prin. Fax 469-7300
Downey Adult S Adult
12340 Woodruff Ave 90241 562-940-6200
R. Brossmer, prin. Fax 940-6221

Regional Occupational Center & Program
Supt. — None
Los Angeles County ROP Vo/Tech
9300 Imperial Hwy 90242 562-922-6850
Dr. Nancy Wagner, dir. Fax 940-1877

Calvary Chapel Christian S 1,200/K-12
12808 Woodruff Ave 90242 562-803-6556
Jeff Johnson, admin. Fax 803-9916
Keystone Academy 300/K-12
8615 Florence Ave Ste 207 90240 562-862-7134
Philip Trout, hdmstr.
Los Amigos Research & Education Inst. Post-Sec.
PO Box 3500 90242 562-401-8111
St. Matthias HS 500/9-12
7851 Gardendale St 90242 562-861-2271
Margaret Meland, prin. Fax 869-8652

Downieville, Sierra
Sierra-Plumas JUSD
Supt. — See Sierraville
Downieville JSHS 50/7-12
PO Box B 95936 530-289-3473
James Berardi, prin. Fax 289-3693

Duarte, Los Angeles, Pop. 22,196
Duarte USD 4,600/K-12
1620 Huntington Dr 91010 626-599-5000
Dr. Dean Conklin, supt. Fax 599-5072
www.duarte.k12.ca.us
Duarte HS 1,200/9-12
1620 Huntington Dr 91010 626-599-5700
Bill Martinez, prin. Fax 599-5784
Northview IS 800/7-8
1620 Huntington Dr 91010 626-599-5600
Miriam Fox, prin. Fax 599-5684

City of Hope Medical Center Post-Sec.
1500 Duarte Rd 91010 626-359-8111

Dublin, Alameda, Pop. 35,581
Dublin USD 4,500/K-12
7471 Larkdale Ave 94568 925-828-2551
Dr. John Sugiyama, supt. Fax 829-6532
www.dublin.k12.ca.us
Dublin HS 1,300/9-12
8151 Village Pkwy 94568 925-833-3300
Carol Shimizu, prin. Fax 833-3322
Fallon MS 6-8
Gleason Rd 94568 925-828-2551
Tess Thomas, prin. Fax 829-7261
Wells MS 1,100/6-8
6800 Penn Dr 94568 925-828-6227
Kathy Rosselle, prin. Fax 829-8851

Valley Christian JSHS 500/7-12
7506 Inspiration Dr 94568 925-560-6200
Jane Kitchen, prin. Fax 828-5658

Dunsmuir, Siskiyou, Pop. 1,896
Dunsmuir JUNHSD 200/9-12
5805 High School Way 96025 530-235-4835
Leonard Foreman, supt. Fax 235-2224
tiger.sisnet.ssku.k12.ca.us/
Dunsmuir HS 100/9-12
5805 High School Way 96025 530-235-4835
Leonard Foreman, prin. Fax 235-2224

Durham, Butte, Pop. 4,784
Durham USD 1,300/K-12
PO Box 300 95938 530-895-4675
Dr. Penny Chennell, supt. Fax 895-4692
www.durhamunified.org/
Durham HS 400/9-12
PO Box 600 95938 530-895-4680
Paul Arnold, prin. Fax 895-4688
Durham IS 300/6-8
PO Box 310 95938 530-895-4690
Rick Desimone, prin. Fax 895-4305
Durham Adult, PO Box 300 95938 Adult
Don McNelis, prin.

Earlimart, Tulare, Pop. 5,881
Earlimart ESD 1,800/K-8
PO Box 11970 93219 661-849-3386
Dr. Marcella Smith, supt. Fax 849-2352
www.earlimart.org
Earlimart MS 600/6-8
PO Box 11970 93219 661-849-2611
Judith Cunningham, prin. Fax 849-4214

East Palo Alto, San Mateo, Pop. 31,915
Ravenswood City SD 3,300/PK-8
2160 Euclid Ave 94303 650-329-2800
Maria De La Vega, supt. Fax 329-6778
www.ravenswood.k12.ca.us
Chavez ES 500/4-8
2450 Ralmar Ave 94303 650-329-6700
Cammie Harris, prin. Fax 326-8902
San Francisco 49er Academy 100/6-8
2086 Clarke Ave 94303 650-614-4300
Vera Clark, dir. Fax 614-4310

Edwards, Kern
Muroc JUSD
Supt. — See North Edwards
Desert HS 400/9-12
1575 Payne Ave 93523 661-258-4411
Joan Fincher, prin. Fax 258-5029
Edwards MS 300/7-8
1575 Payne Ave 93523 661-258-4411
Joan Fincher, prin. Fax 258-5029

El Cajon, San Diego, Pop. 95,159
Cajon Valley UNESD 17,600/K-8
PO Box 1007 92022 619-588-3000
Janice L. Cook Ed.D., supt. Fax 588-7653
www.cajonvalley.net/
Cajon Valley MS 1,100/6-8
395 Ballantyne St 92020 619-588-3092
Rod Girvin, prin. Fax 579-4817
Emerald MS 1,100/6-8
1221 Emerald Ave 92020 619-588-3097
James Raymond, prin. Fax 588-3225
Greenfield MS 1,000/7-8
1495 Greenfield Dr 92021 619-588-3103
Froylan Villanueva, prin. Fax 588-3648
Hillsdale MS 1,500/6-8
1301 Brabham St 92019 619-441-6156
Don Hohimer, prin. Fax 441-6185
Montgomery MS 1,100/6-8
1570 Melody Ln 92019 619-588-3107
Kelly Madden, prin. Fax 441-6122

Grossmont UNHSD 21,200/9-12
1100 Murray Dr 92020 619-644-8000
Terry Ryan, supt. Fax 465-1349
www.guhsd.net
El Cajon Valley HS 2,200/9-12
1035 E Madison Ave 92021 619-401-4300
Paul Dautremont, prin. Fax 447-3943
Granite Hills HS 2,700/9-12
1719 E Madison Ave 92019 619-593-5500
Georgette Torres, prin. Fax 588-9389
Grossmont HS 2,400/9-12
1100 Murray Dr 92020 619-668-6000
Theresa Kemper, prin. Fax 463-7108
Valhalla HS 1,800/9-12
1725 Hillsdale Rd 92019 619-593-5300
Larry Martinsen, prin. Fax 588-9713
Adult Education-Foothill Adult
1550 Melody Ln 92019 619-401-4200
Colette Fleming, prin. Fax 579-9291
Other Schools – See Lakeside, Santee, Spring Valley

Advanced Training Associates Post-Sec.
1810 Gillespie Way Ste 104 92020 619-596-2766
Christian HS 600/7-12
2100 Greenfield Dr 92019 619-440-1531
Mark Wever, supt. Fax 590-1717
Cuyamaca College Post-Sec.
900 Rancho San Diego Pkwy 92019 619-660-4000
Grossmont College Post-Sec.
8800 Grossmont College Dr 92020 619-644-7000
Je Boutique College of Beauty Post-Sec.
1073 E Main St 92021 619-442-3407
San Diego Christian College Post-Sec.
2100 Greenfield Dr 92019 619-441-2200
Southern California Seminary Post-Sec.
2075 E Madison Ave 92019 619-442-9841
Venture Christian HS 200/9-12
367 N Magnolia Ave # 101 92020 619-447-8124
Loren Naffziger, prin. Fax 447-4176

El Centro, Imperial, Pop. 37,985
Central UNHSD 4,200/9-12
351 W Ross Ave 92243 760-336-4500
C. Thomas Budde Ph.D., supt. Fax 353-3606
www.cuhsd.net
Central Union HS 1,700/9-12
1001 W Brighton Ave 92243 760-336-4300
Emma Jones, prin. Fax 353-3570
Southwest HS 2,100/9-12
2001 Ocotillo Dr 92243 760-336-4100
Joe Evangelist, prin. Fax 353-0467
Central Adult Education Adult
1302 S 3rd St 92243 760-336-4544
Sherry Spencer, dir. Fax 336-4547

El Centro ESD 5,900/K-8
1256 Broadway St 92243 760-352-5712
Michael Klentschy, supt. Fax 312-9522
www.ecsd.k12.ca.us/
Kennedy MS 800/6-8
900 N 6th St 92243 760-352-0444
Renato Montano, prin. Fax 353-0325
Wilson JHS 900/7-8
600 S Wilson St 92243 760-352-5341
Matt Phillips, prin. Fax 337-3800

Regional Occupational Center & Program
Supt. — None
Imperial Valley ROP Vo/Tech
687 W State St 92243 760-482-2600
Mary Camacho, supt. Fax 482-2751

Christ Community S 200/K-12
585 W Orange Ave 92243 760-337-9408
Susan Arroyave, prin. Fax 337-1558

El Cerrito, Contra Costa, Pop. 23,339
West Contra Costa USD
Supt. — See Richmond
El Cerrito HS 1,500/9-12
540 Ashbury Ave 94530 510-525-0234
Vince Rhea, prin. Fax 525-1810
Portola MS 700/6-8
1021 Navellier St 94530 510-524-0405
Kal Phan, prin. Fax 599-8784

El Dorado, El Dorado
El Dorado UNHSD
Supt. — See Placerville
Union Mine HS 800/9-10
6530 Koki Ln 95623 530-621-4003
Carl Fickle, prin. Fax 622-6034

El Dorado Hills, El Dorado, Pop. 6,395
Buckeye UNSD
Supt. — See Shingle Springs
Rolling Hills MS 800/6-8
7141 Silva Valley Pkwy 95762 916-933-9290
Gloria Silva, prin. Fax 939-7454

El Dorado UNHSD
Supt. — See Placerville
Oak Ridge HS 1,800/9-12
1120 Harvard Way 95762 916-933-6980
Stephen Wehr, prin. Fax 933-6987

Rescue UNESD
Supt. — See Rescue
Marina Village MS 700/6-8
1901 Francisco Dr 95762 916-933-3993
Colleen Johnson, prin. Fax 933-3995

Elk Creek, Glenn
Stony Creek JUSD 300/K-12
PO Box 68 95939 530-968-5361
Greg Beale, supt. Fax 968-5102
www.glenn-co.k12.ca.us/ech/
Elk Creek JSHS 100/7-12
PO Box 68 95939 530-968-5361
Charles Beath, prin. Fax 968-5102

Elk Grove, Sacramento, Pop. 82,499
Elk Grove USD 54,500/PK-12
9510 Elk Grove Florin Rd 95624 916-686-5085
Steven Ladd Ed.D., supt. Fax 686-7787
www.egusd.k12.ca.us
Albiani MS 7-8
9140 Bradshaw Rd 95624 916-686-5210
Ramona Nelson, prin. Fax 686-5538
Eddy MS 1,100/7-8
9329 Soaring Oaks Dr 95758 916-683-1302
Peter Lambert, prin. Fax 684-6142
Elk Grove HS 2,700/9-12
9800 Elk Grove Florin Rd 95624 916-686-7741
Catherine Guy, prin. Fax 685-5515
Franklin HS 2,300/9-12
6400 Poppy Ridge Rd, 916-714-8150
Charlotte Phinizy, prin. Fax 714-8155
Harris MS 7-8
8691 Power Inn Rd 95624 916-688-0075
Felicia Bessent, prin. Fax 688-0084
Johnson MS 1,500/7-8
10099 Franklin High Rd, 916-714-8181
Patrick McDougall, prin. Fax 714-8177
Kerr MS 1,600/7-8
8865 Elk Grove Blvd 95624 916-686-7728
Patricia Dwairi, prin. Fax 685-2952
Laguna Creek HS 2,400/9-12
9050 Vicino Dr 95758 916-683-1339
Douglas Craig, prin. Fax 683-3128
Monterey Trail HS 9-12
8661 Power Inn Rd 95624 916-688-0050
Terry Chapman, prin. Fax 688-0058
Pleasant Grove HS 9-12
9531 Bond Rd 95624 916-686-0230
Frank Lucia, prin. Fax 686-0239
Other Schools – See Sacramento

DeVry University Post-Sec.
2218 Kausen Dr 95758 916-478-2847
Sacramento Lutheran HS 100/9-12
9270 Bruceville Rd 95758 916-691-2277
David C. Kretzmann, dir. Fax 714-3834

El Monte, Los Angeles, Pop. 121,740
El Monte City ESD 11,400/K-8
3540 Lexington Ave 91731 626-453-3700
Jeffrey Seymour, supt. Fax 442-1063
www.emcsd.org/
Durfee IS 700/4-8
12233 Star St 91732 626-443-3900
Suzanne Seymour, prin. Fax 579-0451

El Monte UNHSD 9,700/9-12
3537 Johnson Ave 91731 626-444-9005
Kathy M. Furnald, supt. Fax 350-1095
www.emuhsd.k12.ca.us
Arroyo HS 2,300/9-12
4921 Cedar Ave 91732 626-444-9201
Keith Richardson, prin. Fax 443-1175
El Monte HS 2,000/9-12
3048 Tyler Ave 91731 626-444-7701
Joel Kyne, prin. Fax 442-6594
Mountain View HS 1,900/9-12
2900 Parkway Dr 91732 626-443-6181
Sandra Stevens, prin. Fax 442-7284
El Monte/Rosemead Adult Education Adult
10807 Ramona Blvd 91731 626-443-9491
Victor Chavez, prin. Fax 258-5809
Other Schools – See Rosemead, South El Monte

Mountain View ESD 10,200/K-8
3320 Gilman Rd 91732 626-652-4000
Gary Rapkin, supt. Fax 652-4052
www.mtview.k12.ca.us
Kranz IS 1,300/7-8
12460 Fineview St 91732 626-652-4200
Toni Bias, prin. Fax 652-4215
Madrid MS 1,300/6-8
3300 Gilman Rd 91732 626-652-4300
Sylvia Rivera, prin. Fax 652-4315

International Theological Seminary Post-Sec.
3225 N Tyler Ave 91731 626-448-0023
Logos Evangelical Seminary Post-Sec.
9358 Telstar Ave 91731 626-571-5110
Palladium Technical Academy Post-Sec.
10507 Valley Blvd Ste 806 91731 626-444-0880
Professional Institute of Beauty Post-Sec.
10801 Valley Mall 91731 626-443-9401

Paso Robles, San Luis Obispo, Pop. 20,187
Paso Robles JUSD 6,500/K-12
PO Box 7010 93447 805-238-2222
Patrick Sayne Ed.D., supt. Fax 237-3339
www.pasoschools.org/
Flamson MS 900/6-8
PO Box 7010 93447 805-237-3350
Frank Galicia, prin. Fax 237-3427
Lewis MS 700/6-8
PO Box 7010 93447 805-237-3450
Rick Oyler, prin. Fax 237-3458
Paso Robles HS 2,000/9-12
PO Box 7010 93447 805-237-3333
Ed Railsback, prin. Fax 237-3424

Advanced Christian Training S 100/K-12
PO Box 97 93447 805-239-0707
William Thompson, admin. Fax 238-1133
Design School of Cosemetology Post-Sec.
715 24th St Ste E 93446 805-237-8575
Solid Rock Christian Academy 50/K-12
4918 Sparrowhawk Ln 93446 805-610-5318
Yasmin Nason, dir.

El Portal, Mariposa
Mariposa County USD
Supt. — See Mariposa
Yosemite Park HS 100/9-12
PO Box 49 95318 209-379-2414
Phyllis Weber, admin. Fax 379-2414

El Segundo, Los Angeles, Pop. 16,483
El Segundo USD 3,200/K-12
641 Sheldon St 90245 310-615-2650
Bruce Auld Ed.D., supt. Fax 640-8272
www.elsegundousd.com
El Segundo HS 1,100/9-12
641 Sheldon St 90245 310-615-2662
Jim Garza, prin. Fax 640-8079
El Segundo MS 800/6-8
641 Sheldon St 90245 310-615-2690
Marian Chiarra, prin. Fax 640-9634

El Sobrante, Contra Costa, Pop. 9,852
West Contra Costa USD
Supt. — See Richmond
Crespi JHS 900/7-8
1121 Allview Ave 94803 510-223-8611
Sherry Bell, prin. Fax 243-2090

Calvary Christian Academy 100/PK-8
4892 San Pablo Dam Rd 94803 510-222-3828
Susan Blankenchip, admin. Fax 222-3702
East Bay Waldorf S 300/K-12
3800 Clark Rd 94803 510-223-3570
Morgan Cleveland, admin. Fax 222-3141
El Sobrante Christian S 500/K-12
5100 Argyle Rd 94803 510-223-2242
C Scott Wells, prin. Fax 223-8453

Elverta, Sacramento
Elverta JESD 300/K-8
8920 Elwyn Ave 95626 916-991-4726
Dianna Mangerich Ed.D., supt. Fax 991-5888
www.elverta.k12.ca.us/
Alpha Technology MS 100/6-8
8920 Elwyn Ave 95626 916-991-4726
Dianna Mangerich, supt. Fax 991-5888

Emeryville, Alameda, Pop. 7,325
Emery USD 800/K-12
4727 San Pablo Ave 94608 510-601-4000
Anthony Smith Ph.D., supt. Fax 601-4913
www.emeryusd.k12.ca.us
Emery HS 400/7-12
1100 47th St 94608 510-601-4961
Mark Miller, prin. Fax 601-4988

Expression College for Digital Arts Post-Sec.
6601 Shellmound St 94608 510-654-2934
Western Career College Post-Sec.
6001 Shellmound St 2nd Flr 94608 510-601-0133

Empire, Stanislaus
Empire UNESD
Supt. — See Modesto
Teel MS 800/6-8
PO Box 1300 95319 209-526-0684
Nancy Fox, prin. Fax 544-8401

Encinitas, San Diego, Pop. 60,340
San Dieguito UNHSD 11,600/7-12
710 Encinitas Blvd 92024 760-753-6491
Peggy Lynch Ed.D., supt. Fax 943-1542
www.sduhsd.net
Diegueno MS 1,100/7-8
710 Encinitas Blvd 92024 760-944-1892
Marilyn Pugh, prin. Fax 944-3717
Oak Crest MS 900/7-8
710 Encinitas Blvd 92024 760-753-6241
Terry Calen, prin. Fax 942-0520
San Dieguito HS Academy 1,500/9-12
710 Encinitas Blvd 92024 760-753-1121
Barbara Gauthier, prin. Fax 753-8142

San Dieguito Adult HS Adult
710 Encinitas Blvd 92024 760-753-7073
Denise Stanley, prin. Fax 436-8376
Other Schools – See Carlsbad, San Diego, Solana
Beach

Encino, See Los Angeles

Crespi Carmelite HS 500/9-12
5031 Alonzo Ave 91316 818-345-1672
Fr. Paul Henson, prin. Fax 705-0209
Holy Martyrs S 300/6-12
5300 White Oak Ave 91316 818-784-6228
John Kossakian, prin.
Phillips Graduate Institute Post-Sec.
5445 Balboa Blvd 91316 818-386-5600
Westmark S 200/2-12
5461 Louise Ave 91316 818-986-5045
Dr. Leslie Barnebey, hdmstr. Fax 986-2605

Escalon, San Joaquin, Pop. 6,855
Escalon USD 3,100/K-12
1520 Yosemite Ave 95320 209-838-3591
Bob Wallace, supt. Fax 838-6703
www.escalonusd.org/
El Portal MS 700/6-8
805 1st St 95320 209-838-7095
Pam Collingsworth, prin. Fax 838-3017
Escalon HS 1,000/9-12
1528 Yosemite Ave 95320 209-838-7073
Joel Johannsen, prin. Fax 838-6127

Escondido, San Diego, Pop. 136,093
Escondido UNESD 18,300/PK-8
1330 E Grand Ave 92027 760-432-2400
Mike Caston Ed.D., supt. Fax 745-8896
www.eusd4kids.org/
Bear Valley MS 6-8
3003 Bear Valley Pkwy S 92025 760-432-4060
Julie Rich, prin. Fax 504-0158
Del Dios MS 1,100/6-8
1400 W 9th Ave 92029 760-432-2439
George Robinson, prin. Fax 432-0728
Grant MS 1,500/6-8
939 E Mission Ave 92025 760-432-2452
Randy Garcia, prin. Fax 737-9085
Hidden Valley MS 1,500/6-8
2700 Reed Rd 92027 760-432-2457
Kyle Ruggles, prin. Fax 480-0845
Rincon MS 1,700/6-8
925 Lehner Ave 92026 760-432-2491
Brenda Jones, prin. Fax 743-6713

Escondido UNHSD 16,500/9-12
302 N Midway Dr 92027 760-291-3200
Ed Nelson, supt. Fax 480-3163
euhsd.k12.ca.us
Escondido HS 2,400/9-12
1535 N Broadway 92026 760-291-4000
Sue Emerson, prin. Fax 739-7313
Orange Glen HS 2,200/9-12
2200 Glenridge Rd 92027 760-291-5000
Dianna Carberry, prin. Fax 739-7314
San Pasqual HS 2,300/9-12
3300 Bear Valley Pkwy S 92025 760-291-6000
Martin Griffin, prin. Fax 739-7315
Valley HS 400/9-12
410 N Hidden Trails Rd 92027 760-291-3275
Saundra Uribe-Silverman, prin. Fax 741-7605
Escondido Adult S Adult
3750 Mary Ln 92025 760-739-7300
Dom Gagliardi, prin. Fax 739-7310

Calvin Christian JSHS 400/6-12
2000 N Broadway 92026 760-489-6430
Frank Steidl, prin. Fax 489-7055
Christian LIFE Academy 200/K-12
PO Box 300038 92030 760-741-7651
Escondido Adventist Academy 300/K-12
1233 W 9th Ave 92029 760-746-1800
Kristine Fuentes, prin. Fax 743-3499
Westminster Theological Seminary Post-Sec.
1725 Bear Valley Pkwy 92027 760-480-8474

Esparto, Yolo, Pop. 1,487
Esparto USD 900/K-12
26675 Plainfield St 95627 530-787-3446
Tom Michaelson, supt. Fax 787-3033
Esparto HS 300/9-12
26675 Plainfield St 95627 530-787-3405
Cheryl Bremer, prin. Fax 787-4850
Esparto MS 200/6-8
26675 Plainfield St 95627 530-787-4151
Rick Martinez, prin. Fax 787-3890

Etiwanda, See Rancho Cucamonga
Chaffey JUNHSD
Supt. — See Ontario
Etiwanda HS 3,400/9-12
13500 Victoria St 91739 909-899-2531
Lynne Ditfurth, prin. Fax 899-3661

Etiwanda SD 11,300/K-8
6061 East Ave 91739 909-899-2451
Shawn Judson, supt. Fax 899-1656
www.etiwanda.k12.ca.us
Day Creek IS 6-8
12345 Coyote Dr 91739 909-803-3300
Terry Embleton, prin. Fax 803-3309
Etiwanda IS 1,300/6-8
6925 Etiwanda Ave 91739 909-899-1701
Janella Cantu-Myricks, prin. Fax 899-5676
Summit IS 1,500/6-8
5959 East Ave 91739 909-899-1704
Lori Arita, prin. Fax 899-7596
Other Schools – See Fontana

Etna, Siskiyou, Pop. 774
Etna UNHSD
Supt. — See Fort Jones
Etna HS 300/9-12
PO Box 721 96027 530-467-3244
Jim Isbell, prin. Fax 467-5763

Scott River Adult S Adult
PO Box 59 96027 530-467-5279
Ken Fowle, admin. Fax 467-3459

Eureka, Humboldt, Pop. 25,808
Eureka City SD 4,800/K-12
3200 Walford Ave 95503 707-441-2400
James Scott Ed.D., supt. Fax 441-3326
www.eurekacityschools.org
Eureka HS 1,700/9-12
1915 J St 95501 707-441-2508
Bob Steffen, prin. Fax 445-1956
Winship MS 600/6-8
2500 Cypress St 95503 707-441-2487
Kim Cobine, prin. Fax 441-2490
Zane MS 700/6-8
2155 S St 95501 707-441-2470
Teddie Lyons, prin. Fax 441-0286
Eureka Adult Education Adult
674 Allard Ave 95503 707-441-2448
Kim Kellenberg, prin. Fax 442-1403

Regional Occupational Center & Program
Supt. — None
Humboldt County ROP Vo/Tech
901 Myrtle Ave 95501 707-445-7180
Art Cardoza, prin. Fax 445-7143

Frederick and Charles Beauty College Post-Sec.
831 F St 95501 707-443-2733
Gospel Outreach S 50/K-12
PO Box 1022 95502 707-445-1167
David Sczepanski, prin. Fax 445-1562
Redwoods Community College Post-Sec.
7351 Tompkins Hill Rd 95501 707-476-4100
St. Bernard HS 200/7-12
222 Dollison St 95501 707-443-2735
Patrick Daly, prin. Fax 443-4723

Exeter, Tulare, Pop. 9,699
Exeter UNSD 3,000/K-12
134 S E St 93221 559-592-9421
Renee Whitson, supt. Fax 592-9445
www.exeterpublicschools.org/
Exeter Union HS 1,000/9-12
505 Rocky Hill Dr 93221 559-592-2127
Don Brinkman, prin. Fax 592-3539
Wilson MS 700/6-8
265 Albert Ave 93221 559-592-2144
Rebecca Mestaz, prin. Fax 592-5536

Sierra View Junior Academy 100/K-10
19933 Avenue 256 93221 559-592-3689
Gail Cook, prin. Fax 592-5615

Fairfax, Marin, Pop. 7,186
Ross Valley SD
Supt. — See San Anselmo
White Hill MS 600/6-8
101 Glen Dr 94930 415-454-8390
Michele Patterson, prin. Fax 454-3980

Fairfield, Solano, Pop. 102,762
Fairfield-Suisun USD 24,100/K-12
1975 Pennsylvania Ave 94533 707-399-5000
Woodrow Carter Ph.D., supt. Fax 399-1250
www.fsusd.k12.ca.us
Armijo HS 2,300/9-12
824 Washington St 94533 707-438-3378
Richard Vaccaro, prin. Fax 438-3390
Dover MS 900/6-8
301 E Alaska Ave 94533 707-421-4145
Tom McKay, prin. Fax 421-4252
Fairfield HS 2,400/9-12
205 E Atlantic Ave 94533 707-438-3000
Vic Ramos, prin. Fax 421-3977
Grange MS 700/7-8
1975 Blossom Ave 94533 707-421-4175
Eric Tretten, prin. Fax 422-4004
Green Valley MS 800/7-8
1350 Gold Hill Rd, 707-646-7000
Greg Hubbs, prin. Fax 863-7916
Rodriguez HS 1,900/9-12
5000 Red Top Rd, 707-863-7950
Kevin French, prin. Fax 863-7974
Sullivan MS 800/7-8
2195 Union Ave 94533 707-421-4115
Reginald Marsh, prin. Fax 421-3964
Fairfield-Suisun Adult Education Adult
1100 Civic Center Dr 94533 707-421-4155
Vickie Good, prin. Fax 421-4158
Other Schools – See Suisun City

Regional Occupational Center & Program
Supt. — None
Solano County ROP Vo/Tech
2460 Clay Bank Rd 94533 707-399-4800
Janet Harden, dir. Fax 429-1360

Travis USD 5,300/K-12
2751 De Ronde Dr 94533 707-437-4604
Kate Wren Gavlak, supt. Fax 437-3378
travisusd.k12.ca.us
Golden West MS 900/7-8
2651 De Ronde Dr 94533 707-437-8240
Jim Bryan, prin. Fax 437-3416
Vanden HS 1,300/9-12
2951 Markeley Ln 94533 707-437-8270
Sheila McCabe, prin. Fax 437-8295

Solano Community College Post-Sec.
4000 Suisun Valley Rd, 707-864-7000

Fair Oaks, Sacramento, Pop. 28,300
San Juan USD
Supt. — See Carmichael
Bella Vista HS 1,900/9-12
8301 Madison Ave 95628 916-971-5052
Marilyn Pino-Jones, prin. Fax 971-5011
Del Campo HS 1,800/9-12
4925 Dewey Dr 95628 916-971-5664
Gail Pierce, prin. Fax 971-5640
Rogers MS 900/7-8
4924 Dewey Dr 95628 916-971-7889
Monty Muller, prin. Fax 971-7903

Freedom Christian S | 100/PK-12
7736 Sunset Ave 95628 | 916-962-3247
Annette Coller, supt. | Fax 962-0783
Sacramento Waldorf S | 400/PK-12
3750 Bannister Rd 95628 | 916-961-3900
Elizabeth Beaven, admin. | Fax 961-3970

Fallbrook, San Diego, Pop. 22,095
Fallbrook UNESD | 6,100/K-8
321 Iowa St 92028 | 760-723-7020
Janice Schultz Ed.D., supt. | Fax 723-3895
www.fuesd.k12.ca.us
Potter IS | 1,100/7-8
1743 Reche Rd 92028 | 760-731-4150
Lisa Denham, prin. | Fax 723-5740

Fallbrook UNHSD | 3,100/9-12
2234 S Stagecoach Ln 92028 | 760-723-6332
Thomas Anthony, supt. | Fax 723-1795
www.fuhsd.net
Fallbrook HS | 2,900/9-12
2400 S Stagecoach Ln 92028 | 760-723-6300
Ruth Hellams, prin. | Fax 731-6192

Farmersville, Tulare, Pop. 9,285
Farmersville Unified SD | 2,400/K-12
571 E Citrus 93223 | 559-592-2010
Janet Jones, supt. | Fax 592-2203
www.farmersville.k12.ca.us
Farmersville HS | 600/9-12
631 E Walnut Ave 93223 | 559-594-4567
Ernie Flores, prin. | Fax 594-5287
Farmersville JHS | 500/6-8
650 N Virginia Ave 93223 | 559-747-0764
Jenifer Ahlstrand, prin. | Fax 747-2704

Felton, Santa Cruz, Pop. 5,350
San Lorenzo Valley USD
Supt. — See Ben Lomond
San Lorenzo Valley HS | 1,100/9-12
7105 Highway 9 95018 | 831-335-4425
Craig Lewis, prin. | Fax 335-1531
San Lorenzo Valley JHS | 500/7-8
7179 Hacienda Way 95018 | 831-335-4452
Chris Mercer, prin. | Fax 335-3812

St. Lawrence Academy | 100/K-12
6184 Highway 9 95018 | 831-335-0328
Wendell Woodthorp, prin. | Fax 335-0353

Ferndale, Humboldt, Pop. 1,388
Ferndale USD | 500/K-12
1231 Main St 95536 | 707-786-5900
Alan Brainerd, supt. | Fax 786-4865
www.ferndalek12.org/
Ferndale HS | 200/9-12
1231 Main St 95536 | 707-786-5900
Alan Brainerd, prin. | Fax 786-4865

Fillmore, Ventura, Pop. 14,949
Fillmore USD | 3,900/K-12
PO Box 697 93016 | 805-524-6000
Jane Kampbell, supt. | Fax 524-6060
www.fillmore.k12.ca.us
Fillmore HS | 1,100/9-12
PO Box 697 93016 | 805-524-6100
Rebecca Larkin, prin. | Fax 524-6121
Fillmore MS | 1,000/6-8
PO Box 697 93016 | 805-524-6055
Patricia Gradias, prin. | Fax 524-6063

Firebaugh, Madera, Pop. 6,688
Firebaugh-Las Deltas USD | 2,700/K-12
1976 Morris Kyle Dr 93622 | 559-659-1476
Wayne Walters Ed.D., supt. | Fax 659-2355
www.fldusd.k12.ca.us/
Firebaugh HS | 700/9-12
1976 Morris Kyle Dr 93622 | 559-659-1415
Patrick Flattley, prin. | Fax 659-2636
Firebaugh MS | 600/6-8
1976 Morris Kyle Dr 93622 | 559-659-1481
 | Fax 659-7106
Firebaugh-Las Deltas Adult S | Adult
1976 Morris Kyle Dr 93622 | 559-659-3899
Ana Apodaca, prin. | Fax 659-1511

Folsom, Sacramento, Pop. 62,628
Folsom-Cordova USD | 19,200/K-12
125 E Bidwell St 95630 | 916-355-1100
Patrick Godwin, supt. | Fax 985-0722
www.fcusd.k12.ca.us
Folsom HS | 2,500/9-12
1655 Iron Point Rd 95630 | 916-355-1115
Paul Richards, prin. | Fax 355-1110
Folsom MS | 1,100/6-8
500 Blue Ravine Rd 95630 | 916-983-4466
Karen Knight, prin. | Fax 983-3462
Sutter MS | 1,000/6-8
715 Riley St 95630 | 916-985-3644
Charles Linebarger, prin. | Fax 985-7044
Other Schools – See Rancho Cordova

Folsom Lake College | Post-Sec.
100 Scholar Way 95630 | 916-608-6500

Fontana, San Bernardino, Pop. 151,903
Etiwanda SD
Supt. — See Etiwanda
Heritage IS | 1,400/6-8
13766 S Heritage Cir 92336 | 909-357-1345
Laura Rowland, prin. | Fax 357-8945

Fontana USD | 40,500/PK-12
9680 Citrus Ave 92335 | 909-357-5000
Charles D. Milligan Ph.D., supt. | Fax 357-5128
fontana.k12.ca.us
Alder MS | 1,700/6-8
7555 Alder Ave 92336 | 909-357-5330
Richard Roth, prin. | Fax 357-5348
Almeria MS | 1,600/6-8
7723 Almeria Ave 92336 | 909-357-5350
Dr. Marlin Brown, prin. | Fax 357-5360
Fontana HS | 4,000/9-12
9453 Citrus Ave 92335 | 909-357-5500
Thomas Reasin, prin. | Fax 357-5629

Fontana MS | 1,400/6-8
8425 Mango Ave 92335 | 909-357-5370
Giovanni Annous, prin. | Fax 357-5391
Kaiser HS | 2,600/9-12
11155 Almond Ave 92337 | 909-357-5900
Bryan Malloy, prin. | Fax 357-5997
Miller HS | 3,700/9-12
PO Box 5085 92334 | 909-357-5800
Dr. Kenneth Hendershot, prin. | Fax 823-5283
Ruble MS | 6-8
6762 Juniper Ave 92336 | 909-357-5530
Crystal Whitley, prin. | Fax 357-5539
Sequoia MS | 1,400/7-8
9452 Hemlock Ave 92335 | 909-357-5400
Anne Roth, prin. | Fax 357-5419
Southridge MS | 1,400/6-8
14500 Live Oak Ave 92337 | 909-357-5420
Gary Soto, prin. | Fax 822-4609
Summit HS | 9-12
15551 Summit Ave 92336 | 909-357-5000
Michael Andrus, prin. | Fax 357-5129
Truman MS | 1,200/6-8
6224 Mallory Dr 92335 | 909-357-5190
Doug Reid, prin. | Fax 357-5199
Fontana Adult S | Adult
9453 Citrus Ave 92335 | 909-357-5555
Pat Meagher, prin. | Fax 357-5556

Agape Christian S | 200/K-12
17777 Merrill Ave 92335 | 909-350-1101
Joyce Alex, prin.

Foresthill, Placer, Pop. 1,409
Foresthill UNESD | 600/K-8
24750 Main St 95631 | 530-367-2966
Jim Roberts, supt. | Fax 367-2470
www.fusd.org
Foresthill Divide MS | 300/5-8
22888 Foresthill Rd 95631 | 530-367-3782
Shannon Jacinto, prin. | Fax 367-4526

Placer UNHSD
Supt. — See Auburn
Foresthill HS | 9-12
23319 Foresthill Rd 95631 | 530-367-5244
Sue Lunsford, prin. | Fax 367-4623

Forestville, Sonoma, Pop. 2,443
West Sonoma CUHSD
Supt. — See Sebastopol
El Molino HS | 1,100/9-12
7050 Covey Rd 95436 | 707-824-6550
Frank Anderson, prin. | Fax 887-0448

Fort Bragg, Mendocino, Pop. 6,867
Fort Bragg USD | 2,200/K-12
312 S Lincoln St 95437 | 707-961-2850
Steve Lund, supt. | Fax 964-5002
www.fbusd.org
Fort Bragg HS | 600/9-12
300 Dana St 95437 | 707-961-2880
Allen Urbani, prin. | Fax 961-2884
Fort Bragg MS | 500/6-8
500 N Harold St 95437 | 707-961-2870
Marli Bock, prin. | Fax 964-9416
Coastal Adult S | Adult
250 S Sanderson Way 95437 | 707-961-2889
Mike Presley, prin. | Fax 964-1017

Fort Irwin, San Bernardino
Silver Valley USD
Supt. — See Yermo
Fort Irwin MS | 700/4-8
1700 Pork Chop Hill St 92310 | 760-386-1133
Joni James, prin. | Fax 386-2448

Fort Jones, Siskiyou, Pop. 651
Etna UNHSD | 500/7-12
PO Box 705 96032 | 530-468-4158
Winifred Walker, supt. | Fax 468-4170
www.sisnet.ssku.k12.ca.us/~ehsdftp/
Scott Valley JHS | 100/7-9
PO Box 607 96032 | 530-468-5565
Winifred Walker, prin. | Fax 468-5658
Other Schools – See Etna

Fortuna, Humboldt, Pop. 10,868
Fortuna UNESD | 800/K-8
843 L St 95540 | 707-725-2293
David Hochman, supt. | Fax 725-2228
www.humboldt.k12.ca.us/fortuna_un/
Fortuna MS | 400/5-8
843 L St 95540 | 707-725-3415
Jim Stewart, prin. | Fax 725-2228

Fortuna UNHSD | 1,500/9-12
379 12th St 95540 | 707-725-4461
Dave Moss, supt. | Fax 725-5511
www.humboldt.k12.ca.us/fortuna_hi/
East HS | 400/9-12
392 16th St 95540 | 707-725-4461
Gordon Dexter, prin. | Fax 725-9746
Fortuna Union HS | 1,100/9-12
379 12th St 95540 | 707-725-4461
Kathy Harrison, prin. | Fax 725-5511
Fortuna Adult Education | Adult
379 12th St 95540 | 707-725-4482
Stephanie Bennett, coord. | Fax 725-4482

Rohnerville ESD | 600/K-8
3850 Rohnerville Rd 95540 | 707-725-7823
Dena McCullough, supt. | Fax 725-4941
www.humboldt.k12.ca.us/rohnerville_sd/index.html
Thomas MS | 300/4-8
2800 Thomas St 95540 | 707-725-5197
Linda Meitner, prin. | Fax 725-8637

New Life Christian S | 100/PK-12
1736 Newburg Rd 95540 | 707-725-9136
Anita Horner, admin. | Fax 725-1638

Foster City, San Mateo, Pop. 28,866
San Mateo-Foster City SD
Supt. — See San Mateo

Bowditch MS | 1,000/6-8
1450 Tarpon St 94404 | 650-312-7680
David Holcombe, prin. | Fax 312-7639

Fountain Valley, Orange, Pop. 55,747
Fountain Valley ESD | 6,300/K-8
10055 Slater Ave 92708 | 714-843-3200
Marc Ecker, supt. | Fax 841-0356
www.fvsd.k12.ca.us
Fulton MS | 700/6-8
8778 El Lago Cir 92708 | 714-375-2816
Chris Christensen, prin. | Fax 375-2825
Masuda MS | 800/6-8
17415 Los Jardines W 92708 | 714-378-4250
Cara Robinson, prin. | Fax 378-4259
Other Schools – See Huntington Beach

Garden Grove USD
Supt. — See Garden Grove
Los Amigos HS | 2,100/9-12
16566 Newhope St 92708 | 714-663-6288
Connie Van Luit, prin. | Fax 663-6518

Huntington Beach UNHSD
Supt. — See Huntington Beach
Fountain Valley HS | 3,000/9-12
17816 Bushard St 92708 | 714-962-3301
Chris Herzfeld, prin. | Fax 964-0491

Ocean View SD
Supt. — See Huntington Beach
Vista View MS | 900/6-8
16250 Hickory St 92708 | 714-842-0626
Anne Silavs, prin. | Fax 843-9156

Coastline Community College | Post-Sec.
11460 Warner Ave 92708 | 714-546-7600
Ivory Dental Technology College | Post-Sec.
16600 Harbor Blvd Ste I 92708 | 714-899-8382
Modern Technology School | Post-Sec.
16560 Harbor Blvd Ste K 92708 | 714-418-9100
Sycamore Tree | 100/K-12
17150 Newhope St Ste 701 92708 | 714-668-1343
Sandra Gogel, dir.

Fowler, Fresno, Pop. 4,398
Fowler USD | 2,300/K-12
658 E Adams Ave 93625 | 559-834-2591
John Cruz, supt. | Fax 834-3390
www.fowler.k12.ca.us
Fowler HS | 700/9-12
701 E Main St 93625 | 559-834-2564
Russell Freitas, prin. | Fax 834-3284
Sutter MS | 500/6-8
701 E Walter Ave 93625 | 559-834-6300
Mark Archon, prin. | Fax 834-4739

Fremont, Alameda, Pop. 204,525
Fremont USD | 31,800/K-12
PO Box 5008 94537 | 510-657-2350
Dr. John Rieckewald, supt. | Fax 659-2597
www.fremont.k12.ca.us
American HS | 1,900/9-12
36300 Fremont Blvd 94536 | 510-796-1776
Connie White, prin. | Fax 791-5331
Centerville JHS | 1,100/7-8
37720 Fremont Blvd 94536 | 510-797-2072
Garo Mirigian, prin. | Fax 794-7588
Hopkins JHS | 1,000/7-8
600 Driscoll Rd 94539 | 510-656-3500
Leesa Jack, prin. | Fax 656-3731
Horner JHS | 1,000/7-8
41365 Chapel Way 94538 | 510-656-4000
Art Johnson, prin. | Fax 656-2793
Irvington HS | 2,000/9-12
41800 Blacow Rd 94538 | 510-656-5711
Pete Murchison, prin. | Fax 623-9805
Kennedy HS | 1,300/9-12
39999 Blacow Rd 94538 | 510-657-4070
Vivienne Paratore, prin. | Fax 438-9287
Mission San Jose HS | 2,000/9-12
41717 Palm Ave 94539 | 510-657-3600
Stuart Kew, prin. | Fax 657-2302
Thornton JHS | 1,100/7-8
4357 Thornton Ave 94536 | 510-793-9090
Ron Echandia, prin. | Fax 793-9756
Walters JHS | 800/7-8
39600 Logan Dr 94538 | 510-656-7211
Khristel Johnson, prin. | Fax 656-4056
Washington HS | 2,000/9-12
38442 Fremont Blvd 94536 | 510-505-7300
Milt Werner, prin. | Fax 794-8437
Fremont Adult S | Adult
4700 Calaveras Ave 94538 | 510-793-6465
Ron Cass, prin. | Fax 793-2271

Regional Occupational Center & Program
Supt. — None
Mission Valley ROC/P | Vo/Tech
40230 Laiolo Rd 94538 | 510-657-1865
Charles Brown, supt. | Fax 438-0378

California School for the Blind | Post-Sec.
500 Walnut Ave 94536
California School for the Deaf | Post-Sec.
39350 Gallaudet Dr 94538 | 510-794-3684
DeVry University | Post-Sec.
6600 Dumbarton Cir 94555 | 510-574-1100
Fremont Christian S | 1,400/PK-12
4760 Thornton Ave 94536 | 510-744-2200
Rev. C.K. Rankin, supt. | Fax 744-2255
Northwestern Polytechnic University | Post-Sec.
47671 Westinghouse Dr 94539 | 510-657-5911
Ohlone College | Post-Sec.
PO Box 3909 94539 | 510-659-6000
Queen of the Holy Rosary College | Post-Sec.
43326 Mission Blvd 94539 | 510-657-2468
Sequoia Institute | Post-Sec.
200 Whitney Pl 94539 | 510-490-6900

Fresno, Fresno, Pop. 451,455
Central USD | 10,600/K-12
4605 N Polk Ave 93722 | 559-276-5206
Marilou Ryder Ed.D., supt. | Fax 271-8200
www.centralusd.k12.ca.us

Central HS East Campus 2,100/10-12
3535 N Cornelia Ave 93722 559-276-0280
Chuck Howell, prin. Fax 276-5653
Central HS West Campus 9-12
2045 N Dickenson Ave, 559-276-5276
Kevin Wagner, prin. Fax 276-6380
El Capitan MS 800/7-8
4443 W Weldon Ave 93722 559-276-5270
John Barber, prin. Fax 276-3121
Rio Vista MS 1,200/7-8
6240 N Palo Alto Ave 93722 559-276-3185
Tim Swain, prin. Fax 276-3199
Central Unified Adult Education Adult
2698 N Brawley Ave 93722 559-276-5230
Fran Bergmann, prin. Fax 276-8204

Clovis USD
Supt. — See Clovis
Clovis West HS 2,800/9-12
1070 E Teague Ave 93720 559-327-2000
Jeanne Hatfield, prin. Fax 327-2490
Kastner IS 1,400/7-8
7676 N 1st St 93720 559-327-2500
Rick Gold, prin. Fax 327-2790

Fresno USD 78,100/PK-12
2309 Tulare St 93721 559-457-3000
Michael Hanson, supt. Fax 457-3786
www.fresno.k12.ca.us/
Ahwahnee MS 800/7-8
1127 E Escalon Ave 93710 559-451-4300
Elizabeth DeLeon, prin. Fax 439-1808
Baird MS 600/5-8
5500 N Maroa Ave 93704 559-451-4310
Keith A. Herzog, prin. Fax 432-4075
Bullard HS 2,600/9-12
5445 N Palm Ave 93704 559-451-4320
Tim Belcher, prin. Fax 451-4339
Carver Academy 400/5-8
2463 Martin L King Jr Blvd 93706 559-457-2620
Carolyn Major, prin. Fax 237-0460
Computech MS 700/7-8
555 E Belgravia Ave 93706 559-457-2640
Tanis DeRuosi, prin. Fax 457-2643
Cooper MS 800/7-8
2277 W Bellaire Way 93705 559-248-7050
Martha Michals, prin. Fax 224-7255
Duncan Polytechnical HS Vo/Tech
4330 E Garland Ave 93726 559-248-7080
Carol Gaab Hansen, prin. Fax 222-6186
Edison HS 2,400/9-12
540 E California Ave 93706 559-457-2650
Jim Bowen, prin. Fax 457-2742
Ft. Miller MS 1,000/7-8
1302 E Dakota Ave 93704 559-248-7100
Debbie Buckman, prin. Fax 221-7548
Fresno HS 3,100/9-12
1839 N Echo Ave 93704 559-457-2780
Bob Reyes, prin. Fax 457-2801
Hoover HS 2,400/9-12
5550 N 1st St 93710 559-451-4000
Doug Jones, prin. Fax 451-4072
Kings Canyon MS 1,000/7-8
5117 E Tulare Ave 93727 559-253-6470
Clark Mello, prin. Fax 253-6474
McLane HS 2,500/9-12
2727 N Cedar Ave 93703 559-248-5100
Frank Silvestro, prin. Fax 226-5232
Roosevelt HS 2,900/9-12
4250 E Tulare St 93702 559-253-5200
Maria Romero, prin. Fax 253-5319
Scandinavian MS 900/7-8
3232 N Sierra Vista Ave 93726 559-253-6510
John Jimenez, prin. Fax 252-7608
Sequoia MS 1,000/7-8
4050 E Hamilton Ave 93702 559-457-3210
Maureen Moore, prin. Fax 497-1745
Sunnyside HS 2,900/9-12
1019 S Peach Ave 93727 559-253-6700
Sheryl Weaver, prin. Fax 253-6799
Tehipite MS 800/7-8
630 N Augusta St 93701 559-457-3420
Richard Pascual, prin. Fax 457-3423
Tenaya MS 1,000/7-8
1239 W Mesa Ave 93711 559-451-4570
Maria Mazzoni, prin. Fax 431-0771
Terronez MS 1,000/7-8
2300 S Willow Ave 93725 559-253-6571
David Gonzalez, prin. Fax 253-6572
Tioga MS 900/7-8
3232 E Fairmont Ave 93726 559-248-7280
Wendy Tukloff, prin. Fax 226-1296
Wawona MS 800/7-8
4524 N Thorne Ave 93704 559-248-7310
Mike Darling, prin. Fax 227-5206
Yosemite MS 900/7-8
1292 N 9th St 93703 559-457-3450
Kathy Chambas, prin. Fax 264-0933
Fresno Adult Education Center Adult
2500 Stanislaus St 93721 559-457-6000
Mark Wilson, prin. Fax 457-6033

Regional Occupational Center & Program
Supt. — None
Fresno ROP Vo/Tech
1111 Van Ness Ave #5 93721 559-497-3850
Nancy Masich, admin. Fax 497-3806

Washington UNHSD 1,100/9-12
6041 S Elm Ave 93706 559-485-8805
John Pestorich, supt. Fax 485-4435
www.washingtonunion.net
Washington HS 1,100/9-12
6041 S Elm Ave 93706 559-485-8805
Joey Campbell, prin. Fax 485-4435

West Fresno ESD 900/PK-8
2888 S Ivy Ave 93706 559-485-2272
D. Kent Ashworth, admin. Fax 264-0805
West Fresno MS 300/6-8
2888 S Ivy Ave 93706 559-485-5607
Vinita Armstrong, prin. Fax 485-3006

Alliant International University Post-Sec.
5130 E Clinton Way 93727 559-456-2777

California Christian College Post-Sec.
4881 E University Ave 93703 559-251-4215
California State University-Fresno Post-Sec.
93740 559-278-4240
Central Valley Christian Academy 100/K-12
4147 E Dakota Ave 93726 559-226-4644
Timothe Addelsee, prin. Fax 248-2775
Fresno Adventist Academy 200/K-12
5397 E Olive Ave 93727 559-251-5548
Daniel Kittle, prin. Fax 456-1735
Fresno Christian S - Peoples Campus 600/3-12
7280 N Cedar Ave 93720 559-299-1695
Gary Schultz, prin. Fax 299-1051
Fresno City College Post-Sec.
1101 E University Ave 93741 559-442-4600
Fresno Pacific University Post-Sec.
1717 S Chestnut Ave 93702 559-453-2000
Galen College Medical & Dental Assts. Post-Sec.
1325 N Wishon Ave 93728 559-264-9700
Heald College Post-Sec.
255 W Bullard Ave 93704 559-438-4222
Lyle's College of Beauty Post-Sec.
6735 N 1st St Ste 112 93710 559-431-6060
Lyle's Fresno College of Beauty Post-Sec.
3125 W Shaw Ave 93711 559-222-6060
Manchester Beauty College Post-Sec.
3756 N Blackstone Ave 93726 559-224-4242
MCed Career College Post-Sec.
2002 N Gateway Blvd 93727 559-456-0623
Mennonite Brethren Biblical Seminary Post-Sec.
4824 E Butler Ave 93727 559-251-8628
San Joaquin Memorial HS 600/9-12
1406 N Fresno St 93703 559-268-9251
Rev. Vincent Lopez, prin. Fax 268-1351
San Joaquin Valley College Post-Sec.
295 E Sierra Ave 93710 559-448-8282
San Joaquin Valley College Post-Sec.
4985 E Andersen Ave 93727 559-453-0380
Sierra Valley Business College Post-Sec.
4747 N 1st St # D 93726 559-222-0947
Truth Tabernacle Christian S 100/K-12
PO Box 5393 93755 559-225-1027
Diane Estes, prin. Fax 225-0465

Fullerton, Orange, Pop. 131,249
Fullerton ESD 13,800/K-8
1401 W Valencia Dr 92833 714-447-7400
Cameron M. McCune, supt. Fax 447-7414
www.fsd.k12.ca.us
Ladera Vista JHS 1,000/7-8
1700 E Wilshire Ave 92831 714-447-7765
Margy Price, prin. Fax 447-7554
Nicolas JHS 1,300/7-8
1100 W Olive Ave 92833 714-447-7775
Allan Waterman, prin. Fax 447-7586
Parks JHS 900/7-8
1710 Rosecrans Ave 92833 714-447-7785
Larry Beaver, prin. Fax 447-7753

Fullerton JUNHSD 14,900/9-12
1051 W Bastanchury Rd 92833 714-870-2801
George Giokaris Ed.D., supt. Fax 870-2807
www.fjuhsd.k12.ca.us
Fullerton HS 2,200/9-12
201 E Chapman Ave 92832 714-626-3800
Cathy Gach, prin. Fax 626-3839
Sunny Hills HS 2,300/9-12
1801 Warburton Way 92833 714-626-4200
Ed Atkinson, prin. Fax 738-3728
Troy HS 2,200/9-12
2200 Dorothy Ln 92831 714-626-4400
Chuck Maruca, prin. Fax 626-4492
Other Schools – See Buena Park, La Habra

California State University-Fullerton Post-Sec.
PO Box 34080 92834 714-278-2011
College of Information Technology Post-Sec.
2701 E Chapman Ave Ste 101 92831 714-879-5100
Eastside Christian S 500/PK-12
2505 Yorba Linda Blvd 92831 714-879-2187
David Schoen, supt. Fax 526-5074
Fullerton College Post-Sec.
321 E Chapman Ave 92832 714-992-7000
Fullerton SDA S 50/K-12
2353 W Valencia Dr 92833 714-526-5039
Barbara Irish, prin. Fax 526-7761
Hope International University Post-Sec.
2500 Nutwood Ave 92831 714-879-3901
Rosary HS 700/9-12
1340 N Acacia Ave 92831 714-879-6302
Terry Gonzalez, prin. Fax 879-0853
Southern California College of Optometry Post-Sec.
2575 Yorba Linda Blvd 92831 714-449-7450
Western State University College of Law
1111 N State College Blvd 92831 714-738-1000

Galt, Sacramento, Pop. 22,578
Galt JUNESD 4,300/K-8
1018 C St #210 95632 209-744-4545
Jeffery Jennings, supt. Fax 744-4553
www.galt.k12.ca.us/
Greer MS 800/6-8
248 W A St 95632 209-745-2641
Robert Nacario, prin. Fax 745-9202
McCaffrey MS 700/6-8
997 Park Terrace Dr 95632 209-745-5462
Ron Rammer, prin. Fax 745-5465

Galt JUNHSD 2,000/9-12
417 C St #B 95632 209-745-3061
Thomas Gemma, supt. Fax 745-0881
www.ghsd.k12.ca.us/
Galt HS 2,000/9-12
145 N Lincoln Way 95632 209-745-3081
Bernie Olmos, prin. Fax 745-4786
Adult Education Adult
150 Camellia Way 95632 209-745-5852
Karen Liu, dir. Fax 745-7026

Valley Christian S 50/K-10
501 B St 95632 209-745-2049
Larry Brand, admin. Fax 745-9009

Garberville, Humboldt
Southern Humbolt JUSD 900/K-12
PO Box 129 95542 707-923-2789
Clifton Anderson, supt. Fax 923-2055
www.humboldt.k12.ca.us/sohumb_usd/school/
Other Schools – See Miranda

Gardena, Los Angeles, Pop. 59,941
Los Angeles USD
Supt. — See Los Angeles
Gardena HS 3,100/9-12
1301 W 182nd St 90248 310-327-5900
Russell Thompson, prin. Fax 366-6943
Peary MS 2,300/6-8
1415 W Gardena Blvd 90247 310-324-6606
L. Gail Garrett, prin. Fax 329-3957
Gardena-Carson Community Adult S Adult
18120 S Normandie Ave 90248 310-323-2686
Donna Brashear, prin. Fax 323-8981

American College of Medical Technology Post-Sec.
555 W Redondo Bch Blvd #100 90248 310-324-1000
Bryman College Post-Sec.
1045 W Rdnd Bch Blvd #275 90247 310-527-7105
Junipero Serra HS 500/9-12
14830 Van Ness Ave 90249 310-324-6675
Rev. Sal Pilato, prin. Fax 352-4953

Garden Grove, Orange, Pop. 167,029
Garden Grove USD 49,600/K-12
10331 Stanford Ave 92840 714-663-6000
Laura Schwalm Ed.D., supt. Fax 663-6100
www.ggusd.k12.ca.us
Alamitos IS 1,000/7-8
12381 Dale St 92841 714-663-6101
Bill Gates, prin. Fax 663-6277
Bell IS 800/7-8
12345 Springdale St 92845 714-663-6466
David Binasz, prin. Fax 663-6995
Bolsa Grande HS 1,500/9-12
9401 Westminster Ave 92844 714-663-6424
Denise Jay, prin. Fax 663-6029
Doig IS, 12752 Trask Ave 92843 900/7-8
Margaret Feliciani, prin. 714-663-6241
Garden Grove HS 2,000/9-12
11271 Stanford Ave 92840 714-663-6115
Dr. Colleen Cross, prin. Fax 663-6030
Irvine IS 900/7-8
10552 Hazard Ave 92843 714-663-6551
John Casato, prin. Fax 663-6013
Jordan IS 700/7-8
9821 Woodbury Ave 92844 714-663-6124
Steve Osborne, prin. Fax 663-6123
Pacifica HS 1,900/9-12
6851 Lampson Ave 92845 714-663-6515
Mary Jane Hibbard, prin.
Ralston IS 600/7-8
10851 Lampson Ave 92840 714-663-6366
Jan Cody, prin. Fax 663-7155
Rancho Alamitos HS 1,800/9-12
11351 Dale St 92841 714-663-6415
Gene Campbell, prin.
Santiago HS, 12342 Trask Ave 92843 2,100/9-12
Benjamin Wolf, prin. 714-663-6215
Walton IS 800/7-8
12181 Buaro St 92840 714-663-6040
Terry Haxton, prin. Fax 534-4814
Garden Grove Adult S Adult
11262 Garden Grove Blvd 92843 714-663-6305
James Delong, dir.
Other Schools – See Fountain Valley, Santa Ana,
Westminster

Career Academy of Beauty Post-Sec.
12471 Valley View St 92845 714-897-3010
Concorde Career Institute Post-Sec.
12951 Euclid St Ste 101 92840 714-703-1900
Crystal Cathedral Academy 400/PK-12
13280 Chapman Ave 92840 714-971-4159
Sheila Coleman, prin. Fax 971-4028
Kim Anh Academy of Beauty Post-Sec.
12141 Brookhurst St Ste 101 92840 714-896-9847
Lola Beauty College Post-Sec.
11883 Valley View St 92845 714-894-3366
Orangewood Adventist Academy 300/PK-12
13732 Clinton St 92843 714-534-4694
Ruben Escalante, prin. Fax 534-5931
Thanh Le College School of Cosmetology Post-Sec.
12875 Chapman Ave 92840 714-971-5644
Village Bible Academy 200/1-12
12671 Buaro St 92840 714-537-5344
Chris Zuniga, admin.

Garden Valley, El Dorado
Black Oak Mine USD
Supt. — See Georgetown
Golden Sierra HS 600/9-12
PO Box 175 95633 530-333-8330
Audrey Keebler, prin. Fax 333-8333

Georgetown, El Dorado
Black Oak Mine USD 2,000/K-12
PO Box 4510 95634 530-333-8300
Rob Schamberg, supt. Fax 333-8303
www.bomusd.k12.ca.us
Other Schools – See Garden Valley

Geyserville, Sonoma
Geyserville USD 300/K-12
1300 Moody Ln 95441 707-857-3592
Joseph F. Carnation, supt. Fax 431-8148
www.gusd.com
Geyserville HS, 1300 Moody Ln 95441 100/9-12
Katherine Hadden, prin. 707-857-3592
Geyserville MS, 1300 Moody Ln 95441 100/6-8
Katherine Hadden, prin. 707-857-3592

Gilroy, Santa Clara, Pop. 43,817
Gilroy USD 9,200/K-12
7810 Arroyo Cir 95020 408-847-2700
Edwin Diaz, supt. Fax 847-4717
www.gusd.k12.ca.us

Brownell MS 1,000/6-8
 7800 Carmel St 95020 408-847-3377
 Joseph DiSalvo, prin. Fax 846-7521
Gilroy HS 2,400/9-12
 750 W 10th St 95020 408-847-2424
 James Maxwell, prin. Fax 842-3311
Solorsano MS 6-8
 7121 Grenache Way 95020 408-848-4121
 Sal Tomasello, prin.
South Valley MS 1,000/6-8
 385 Ioof Ave 95020 408-847-2828
 John Perales, prin. Fax 847-5708

Regional Occupational Center & Program
 Supt. — None
Santa Clara County ROP South Vo/Tech
 700 W 6th St Ste L 95020 408-842-0361
 Dr. David Matuszak, dir. Fax 842-0653

Anchorpoint Christian HS 100/7-12
 2220 Pacheco Pass Hwy 95020 408-846-6642
 Sondra Cole, prin. Fax 848-4426
Gavilan Community College Post-Sec.
 5055 Santa Teresa Blvd 95020 408-847-1400

Glendale, Los Angeles, Pop. 200,499
Glendale USD 28,200/K-12
 223 N Jackson St 91206 818-241-3111
 Michael Escalante Ed.D., supt. Fax 548-9041
 www.gusd.net/
Glendale HS 3,300/9-12
 1440 E Broadway 91205 818-242-3161
 Kathy Fundukian, prin. Fax 244-6309
Hoover HS 2,700/9-12
 651 Glenwood Rd 91202 818-242-6801
 Kevin Welsh, prin. Fax 247-8825
Roosevelt MS 1,000/7-8
 1017 S Glendale Ave 91205 818-242-6845
 Maria Gandera, prin. Fax 552-5188
Toll MS 1,300/7-8
 700 Glenwood Rd 91202 818-244-8414
 Jan Canfield, prin. Fax 500-1487
Wilson MS 1,200/7-8
 1221 Monterey Rd 91206 818-244-8145
 Richard Lucas, prin. Fax 244-2050
Other Schools – See La Crescenta

Glendale Adventist Academy 700/K-12
 700 Kimlin Dr 91206 818-244-8671
 Dr. Glen Baker, prin. Fax 546-1180
Glendale Career College Post-Sec.
 1015 Grandview Ave 91201 818-243-1131
Glendale Community College Post-Sec.
 1500 N Verdugo Rd 91208 818-240-1000
Holy Family HS 300/9-12
 400 E Lomita Ave 91205 818-241-3178
 Dr. Michelle Purghart, prin. Fax 241-7753
Moro Beauty College Post-Sec.
 124 N Brand Blvd 91203 818-246-7376
North American Computer Consultants Post-Sec.
 570 W Stocker St Unit 311 91202 818-500-7227
Northwest College Medical Dental Assts. Post-Sec.
 221 N Brand Blvd 91203 818-242-0205
Tobinworld S, 920 E Broadway 91205 300/K-12
 Judith Weber, dir. 818-247-7474
Uni Health America/Glendale Mem Hospital Post-Sec.
 1420 S Central Ave 91204 818-502-2334

Glendora, Los Angeles, Pop. 50,853
Azusa USD
 Supt. — See Azusa
Azusa Adult Educ Center Adult
 1134 S Barranca Ave 91740 626-852-8400
 Mary Ketza, prin. Fax 852-8407

Glendora USD 7,800/K-12
 500 N Loraine Ave 91741 626-963-1611
 Catherine Nichols, supt. Fax 335-2196
 www.glendora.k12.ca.us
Glendora HS 2,700/9-12
 1600 E Foothill Blvd 91741 626-963-5731
 Rick Bartman, prin. Fax 963-2880
Goddard HS 1,000/6-8
 859 E Sierra Madre Ave 91741 626-852-4500
 Dominic DiGrazia, prin. Fax 852-4520
Sandburg MS 1,000/6-8
 819 W Bennett Ave 91741 626-852-4530
 Michelle Hunter, prin. Fax 852-4521

Citrus College Post-Sec.
 1000 W Foothill Blvd 91741 626-963-0323
St. Lucy Priory HS 900/9-12
 655 W Sierra Madre Ave 91741 626-335-3322
 Fax 335-4373

Gold River, Sacramento

Northwestern College Post-Sec.
 2317 Gold Meadow Way 95670 866-649-2400

Goleta, Santa Barbara, Pop. 28,522
Santa Barbara SD
 Supt. — See Santa Barbara
Dos Pueblos HS 2,300/9-12
 7266 Alameda Ave 93117 805-968-2541
 Quentin Panek, prin. Fax 968-2891
Goleta Valley JHS 900/7-8
 6100 Stow Canyon Rd 93117 805-967-3486
 Veronica Rogers, prin. Fax 967-8176

Gonzales, Monterey, Pop. 8,510
Gonzales USD 3,000/K-12
 PO Box G 93926 831-675-0100
 Ernest S. Zermeno, supt. Fax 675-2763
 www.gusd-district.org
Fairview MS 700/5-8
 PO Box G 93926 831-675-3704
 Joni Madolora, prin. Fax 675-3274
Gonzales HS 700/9-12
 PO Box G 93926 831-675-2495
 Liz Modena, prin. Fax 675-8054

Granada Hills, See Los Angeles
Los Angeles USD
 Supt. — See Los Angeles

Frost MS 1,700/6-8
 12314 Bradford Pl 91344 818-360-2146
 Joyce Edelson, prin. Fax 360-9584
Henry MS 1,500/6-8
 17340 San Jose St 91344 818-363-7401
 Michael Bennett, prin. Fax 368-7333
Kennedy HS 3,000/9-12
 11254 Gothic Ave 91344 818-363-6794
 Christine Clark, prin. Fax 368-2087
Porter MS 1,700/6-8
 15960 Kingsbury St 91344 818-891-1807
 Laura Hale, prin. Fax 891-7826
Kennedy-San Fernando Adult Education Adult
 11254 Gothic Ave 91344 818-368-3702
 Carlynn Huddleston, prin. Fax 368-5518

Hillcrest Christian S 800/K-12
 17531 Rinaldi St 91344 818-368-7071
 David Kendrick, supt. Fax 363-4455
Newberry School of Beauty Post-Sec.
 16860 Devonshire St 91344 818-366-3211

Grand Terrace, San Bernardino, Pop. 12,205
Colton JUSD
 Supt. — See Colton
Terrace Hills MS 1,100/7-8
 22579 De Berry St 92313 909-876-4256
 Julia Nichols, prin. Fax 783-3836

Keystone S 700/K-12
 11980 Mount Vernon Ave 92313 909-783-8400
 Stacy Thompson, dir.

Granite Bay, Placer
Eureka UNSD 4,300/K-8
 5455 Eureka Rd 95746 916-791-4939
 Bob Schultz, supt. Fax 791-5527
 www.eureka-usd.k12.ca.us
Cavitt JHS 600/7-8
 7200 Fuller Dr 95746 916-791-4152
 John Montero, prin. Fax 791-7414
Other Schools – See Roseville

Roseville JUNHSD
 Supt. — See Roseville
Granite Bay HS 1,100/9-10
 1 Grizzly Way 95746 916-786-8676
 Ron Severson, prin. Fax 786-7232

Grass Valley, Nevada, Pop. 11,629
Grass Valley ESD 1,500/K-8
 10840 Gilmore Way 95945 530-273-4483
 Jon Byerrum, supt. Fax 273-0248
 www.gvsd.k12.ca.us
Gilmore MS 600/6-8
 10837 Rough and Ready Hwy 95945 530-273-8479
 Stephanie Perez, prin. Fax 273-1675

Nevada JUNHSD 4,300/9-12
 11645 Ridge Rd 95945 530-273-3351
 Maggie Deetz, supt. Fax 273-3372
 www.nuhsd.org
Bear River HS 1,100/9-12
 11130 Magnolia Rd 95949 530-268-3700
 David Wilk, prin. Fax 268-8372
Nevada Union HS 2,700/9-12
 11761 Ridge Rd 95945 530-273-4431
 Marty Mathiesen, prin. Fax 477-9317
Nevada Union Technical HS Vo/Tech
 11761 Ridge Rd 95945 530-273-4431
 Linda Campbell, admin. Fax 477-9317
Nevada Adult Education Adult
 350 Buena Vista St 95945 530-272-2643
 Trisha Dellis, prin. Fax 272-3422

Pleasant Ridge UNESD 2,100/K-8
 22580 Kingston Ln 95949 530-268-2800
 Linda Kramer, supt. Fax 268-2804
 www.pleasantridge.k12.ca.us
Magnolia IS 800/6-8
 22431 Kingston Ln 95949 530-268-2815
 Mark Rodriguez, prin. Fax 268-2819

Christian Encounter HS 50/9-12
 PO Box 1022 95945 530-268-0877
 Tom Kern, prin. Fax 268-9077

Greenfield, Monterey, Pop. 12,953
Greenfield UNSD 2,800/K-8
 493 El Camino Real 93927 831-674-2840
 Tom Guajardo, supt. Fax 674-3712
 www.greenfield.k12.ca.us/
Vista Verde MS 800/6-8
 1199 Elm Ave 93927 831-674-1420
 Ron Garcia, prin. Fax 674-1425

King City JUNHSD
 Supt. — See King City
Greenfield HS 900/9-12
 2025 El Camino Real 93927 831-674-2751
 Rudy Garcia, prin. Fax 674-2646
King City Adult Education Adult
 2015 El Camino Real 93927 831-674-3275
 Dan Andrus, prin. Fax 674-1187

Greenville, Plumas, Pop. 1,396
Plumas USD
 Supt. — See Quincy
Greenville JSHS 200/7-12
 117 Grand St 95947 530-284-7197
 Kevin Wickersham, prin. Fax 284-6710

Gridley, Butte, Pop. 5,670
Gridley USD 2,100/K-12
 429 Magnolia St 95948 530-846-4721
 Clark S. Redfield, supt. Fax 846-4595
 www.gridley.k12.ca.us/
Gridley HS 700/9-12
 300 E Spruce St 95948 530-846-4791
 Joan Zappettini, prin. Fax 846-3412
Sycamore MS 500/6-8
 1125 Sycamore St 95948 530-846-3636
 James Walters, prin. Fax 846-6796

Groveland, Tuolumne, Pop. 2,753
Big Oak Flat-Groveland USD 600/K-12
 PO Box 1397 95321 209-962-5765
 John Triolo Ed.D., supt. Fax 962-6108
 www.bofg.k12.ca.us/
Tioga HS 100/9-12
 19304 Ferretti Rd 95321 209-962-4763
 Sandra Bradley, prin. Fax 962-4507
Big Oak Flat-Groveland Adult S Adult
 PO Box 1397 95321 209-962-5765
  Fax 962-6108

Other Schools – See La Grange

Guadalupe, Santa Barbara, Pop. 5,869
Guadalupe UNESD 1,200/K-8
 PO Box 788 93434 805-343-2114
 Hugo Lara, supt. Fax 343-6155
 www.sbceo.org/districts/guadalupeusd/
McKenzie JHS 400/6-8
 PO Box 788 93434 805-343-1951
 Celia Ramos, prin. Fax 343-6931

Gustine, Merced, Pop. 5,346
Gustine USD 1,900/K-12
 1500 Meredith Ave 95322 209-854-3784
  Fax 854-9164
 www.gustine.k12.ca.us
Gustine HS 500/9-12
 501 North Ave 95322 209-854-6414
 Dennis Shaw, prin. Fax 854-1955
Gustine MS 500/6-8
 685 Wallis Ave 95322 209-854-6404
 Sharon Brown, prin. Fax 854-9575

Hacienda Heights, Los Angeles, Pop. 53,300
Hacienda La Puente USD
 Supt. — See City of Industry
Cedarlane MS 500/6-8
 16333 Cedarlane Dr 91745 626-933-8000
 Yvette Meneses, prin. Fax 855-3819
Los Altos HS 1,800/9-12
 15325 Los Robles Ave 91745 626-934-5400
 William Roberts, prin. Fax 855-3145
Newton MS 600/6-8
 15616 Newton St 91745 626-933-2400
 Stephen Lee, prin. Fax 855-3832
Orange Grove MS 700/6-8
 14505 Orange Grove Ave 91745 626-933-7000
  Fax 855-3837
Wilson HS 1,800/9-12
 16455 Wedgeworth Dr 91745 626-934-4440
 Albert Clegg, prin. Fax 855-3792

Morning Star Christian S 100/K-12
 15716 Tetley St 91745 626-333-7784
 Marlene Guerrero, admin. Fax 330-8636

Half Moon Bay, San Mateo, Pop. 12,143
Cabrillo USD 3,800/K-12
 498 Kelly Ave 94019 650-712-7100
 John Bayless, supt. Fax 726-0279
 www.cabrillo.k12.ca.us/
Cunha IS 800/6-8
 498 Kelly Ave 94019 650-712-7190
 Michael Andrews, prin. Fax 712-7195
Half Moon Bay HS 1,200/9-12
 498 Kelly Ave 94019 650-712-7200
 Susan Milliion, prin. Fax 712-7232
Cabrillo Adult S Adult
 498 Kelly Ave 94019 650-712-7224
 Elizabeth Schuck, prin. Fax 712-7225

Hamilton City, Glenn, Pop. 1,811
Hamilton UNHSD 400/9-12
 PO Box 488 95951 530-826-3261
 Ray Odom, supt. Fax 826-0440
 www.glenn-co.k12.ca.us/ham-hs
Hamilton Union HS 300/9-12
 PO Box 488 95951 530-826-3261
 Ray Odom, prin. Fax 826-0440
Hamilton Adult S Adult
 PO Box 488 95951 530-826-3531
 Jeannie Robinson, dir. Fax 826-3929

Hanford, Kings, Pop. 45,368
Hanford ESD 5,400/K-8
 PO Box 1067 93232 559-585-3601
 Rebecca Presley, supt. Fax 584-7833
 www.hesd.k12.ca.us/
Kennedy JHS 600/7-8
 PO Box 1067 93232 559-585-3850
 Karen McConnell, prin. Fax 585-2374
Wilson JHS 600/7-8
 PO Box 1067 93232 559-585-3870
 Dave Perkins, prin. Fax 585-2336

Hanford JUNHSD 3,500/9-12
 823 W Lacey Blvd 93230 559-583-5901
 William Fishbough, supt. Fax 589-9769
 www.kings.k12.ca.us/huhsd
Hanford HS 1,700/9-12
 120 E Grangeville Blvd 93230 559-583-5902
 Steve France, prin. Fax 582-5229
Hanford West HS 1,700/9-12
 1150 W Lacey Blvd 93230 559-583-5903
 John Davis, prin. Fax 583-6708
Hanford Adult S Adult
 905 Campus Dr 93230 559-583-5905
 Mark Dutra, prin. Fax 589-9564

Lakeside UNESD 400/K-8
 9100 Jersey Ave 93230 559-582-2868
 John Partin, supt. Fax 582-7638
 www.kings.k12.ca.us/lakeside/
Lakeside ES 200/4-8
 9100 Jersey Ave 93230 559-582-2868
 Darin Denney, prin. Fax 582-7638

Regional Occupational Center & Program
 Supt. — None
Kings County ROP Vo/Tech
 1144 W Lacey Blvd 93230 559-589-7026
 Tim Bowers, admin. Fax 589-7007

Happy Camp, Siskiyou
Siskiyou UNHSD
Supt. — See Mount Shasta
Happy Camp HS 100/9-12
PO Box 437 96039 530-493-2697
Ernie Micheli, prin. Fax 493-2605

Harbor City, See Los Angeles
Los Angeles USD
Supt. — See Los Angeles
Narbonne HS 3,300/9-12
24300 Western Ave 90710 310-326-0920
Pat Donahoe, prin. Fax 326-1805

Hawaiian Gardens, Los Angeles, Pop. 15,357
ABC USD
Supt. — See Cerritos
Fedde MS 800/7-8
21409 Elaine Ave 90716 562-924-2309
Paul Gonzales, prin. Fax 809-6895
Adult Education Center Adult
11949 215th St 90716 562-229-7970
Jean Rose, prin.

Way Out Ministries Christian Academy 50/7-12
22427 Norwalk Blvd 90716 562-429-2397
Terryl Bruce, prin. Fax 497-0348

Hawthorne, Los Angeles, Pop. 86,173
Centinela Valley UNHSD
Supt. — See Lawndale
Hawthorne HS 2,900/9-12
4859 W El Segundo Blvd 90250 310-263-4400
Fax 675-7017

Hawthorne SD 10,100/K-8
14120 Hawthorne Blvd 90250 310-676-2276
Donald Carrington, supt. Fax 675-9464
www.hawthorne.k12.ca.us
Carson MS, 13838 Yukon Ave 90250 900/6-8
Patricia Jordan, prin. 310-676-1908
Hawthorne MS 900/6-8
4366 W 129th St 90250 310-676-0167
Wendy Ostenson, prin.
Prairie Vista MS 900/6-8
13600 Prairie Ave 90250 310-679-1003
Christine Fagnano, prin.

Wiseburn ESD 2,000/K-8
13530 Aviation Blvd 90250 310-643-3025
Dr. Don Brann, supt. Fax 643-7659
www.wiseburn.k12.ca.us/
Dana MS 700/6-8
13500 Aviation Blvd 90250 310-643-6165
Matthew Wunder, prin. Fax 643-0208

Hawthorne Academy 100/K-12
12500 Ramona Ave 90250 310-644-8841
Dennis Richard, dir.
International School of Cosmetology Post-Sec.
13613 Hawthorne Blvd 90250 310-973-7774
New Journey Christian S 100/PK-12
14204 Prairie Ave 90250 310-676-9042
Colette Arce, prin. Fax 676-9043

Hayfork, Trinity, Pop. 2,605
Mountain Valley USD 600/K-12
PO Box 339 96041 530-628-5265
David Schumaker, supt. Fax 628-5267
www.mvusd.us
Hayfork HS 200/9-12
PO Box 10 96041 530-628-5261
Tom Barnett, prin. Fax 628-3091

Hayfork SDA S 50/1-12
PO Box 580 96041 530-628-1601
Fax 628-4064

Hayward, Alameda, Pop. 141,336
Hayward USD 43,300/PK-12
PO Box 5000 94540 510-784-2600
Janis A. Duran, supt. Fax 784-2641
www.husd.k12.ca.us
Chavez MS 800/7-8
PO Box 5000 94540 510-293-8581
Olga Pineda, prin. Fax 538-8478
Harte MS 600/7-8
PO Box 5000 94540 510-293-8578
Shelly Jones, prin. Fax 886-5926
Hayward HS 2,100/9-12
PO Box 5000 94540 510-293-8586
Mary Ann Heather, prin. Fax 581-3145
King MS 800/7-8
PO Box 5000 94540 510-293-8528
Ricardy Anderson, prin. Fax 786-4139
Mt. Eden HS 2,400/9-12
PO Box 5000 94540 510-293-8539
Fax 786-2269
Ochoa MS 600/7-8
PO Box 5000 94540 510-293-8532
Delores Connors, prin. Fax 786-0559
Tennyson HS 2,000/9-12
PO Box 5000 94540 510-293-8591
Theresa McEwen, prin. Fax 582-0964
Winton MS 800/7-8
PO Box 5000 94540 510-293-8583
Fax 733-9043
Hayward Adult Education Center Adult
PO Box 5000 94540 510-293-8595
Mahnoush Harirsa, prin. Fax 727-1139
Other Schools – See Castro Valley

New Haven USD
Supt. — See Union City
Conley-Caraballo HS 9-12
541 Blanche St 94544 510-471-5126
Judy Silver, prin. Fax 475-3949

Regional Occupational Center & Program
Supt. — None
Eden Area ROP Vo/Tech
26316 Hesperian Blvd 94545 510-293-2900
Cyril Bonnano, dir. Fax 783-2955

Bryman College Post-Sec.
22336 Main St 94541 510-582-9500
California State University-East Bay Post-Sec.
25800 Carlos Bee Blvd 94542 510-885-3000
Chabot College Post-Sec.
25555 Hesperian Blvd 94545 510-723-6600
Heald College Post-Sec.
25500 Industrial Blvd 94545 510-783-2100
Life Chiropractic College West Post-Sec.
25001 Industrial Blvd 94545 800-788-4476
Moreau HS 1,200/9-12
27170 Mission Blvd 94544 510-881-4300
Terry Lee, prin. Fax 581-5669

Healdsburg, Sonoma, Pop. 11,187
Healdsburg SD 1,800/K-12
1028 Prince Ave 95448 707-431-3117
Robert Carter, supt. Fax 433-8403
www.husd.com
Healdsburg HS 1,000/9-12
1024 Prince Ave 95448 707-431-3420
Karen Ricketts, prin. Fax 431-3467
Healdsburg JHS 600/6-8
315 Grant St 95448 707-431-3410
John Curry, prin. Fax 431-3593

Rio Lindo Adventist Academy 200/9-12
3200 Rio Lindo Ave 95448 707-431-5100
Doug Schmidt, prin. Fax 431-5115

Helendale, San Bernardino
Helendale ESD 600/K-8
PO Box 249 92342 760-952-1180
Mark Sumpter, supt. Fax 952-1178
www.sbcss.k12.ca.us/helendale
Riverview MS 200/6-8
PO Box 249 92342 760-952-1266
Brian Dietz, prin. Fax 952-1180

Hemet, Riverside, Pop. 65,044
Hemet USD 19,200/K-12
2350 W Latham Ave 92545 951-765-5100
Dr. Philip Pendley, supt. Fax 765-5115
www.hemetusd.k12.ca.us
Acacia MS 1,500/6-8
1200 E Acacia Ave 92543 951-765-1620
John Huber, prin. Fax 765-5149
Dartmouth MS 1,200/6-8
41535 Mayberry Ave 92544 951-765-2550
Sandra Watkins, prin. Fax 765-2559
Diamond Valley MS 6-8
291 W Chambers Ave 92543 951-925-2899
Christine Goennier, prin. Fax 925-6297
Hemet HS 2,400/9-12
41701 Stetson Ave 92544 951-765-5150
Bill Black, prin. Fax 765-5177
Santa Fe MS 1,500/6-8
831 E Devonshire Ave 92543 951-765-6440
Jacqueline Luzak, prin. Fax 765-6444
West Valley HS 2,700/9-12
3401 Mustang Way 92545 951-765-1600
Mark Lenoir, prin. Fax 765-1607
Hemet Adult Education Adult
26866 San Jacinto St 92543 951-765-5190
Walter Brubaker, prin. Fax 765-5195
Other Schools – See Anza

Baptist Christian S 500/PK-12
26089 Girard St 92544 951-658-3203
Leslie Wilhelm, prin. Fax 658-0723
Image School of Cosmetology Post-Sec.
2627 W Florida Ave 92545 951-766-5759

Hercules, Contra Costa, Pop. 21,602
West Contra Costa USD
Supt. — See Richmond
Hercules MSHS 1,700/6-12
1900 Refugio Valley Rd 94547 510-245-5000
Guy Zakrevsky, prin. Fax 245-1089

Herlong, Lassen
Fort Sage USD 200/K-12
PO Box 35 96113 530-827-2129
Guy Zakrevsky, supt. Fax 827-2019
Fort Sage MS 50/6-8
PO Box 35 96113 530-827-2126
Guy Zakrevsky, prin. Fax 827-3239
Herlong HS 100/9-12
PO Box 97 96113 530-827-2101
Guy Zakrevsky, prin. Fax 827-3362

Hermosa Beach, Los Angeles, Pop. 19,429
Hermosa Beach CSD 1,000/K-8
1645 Valley Dr 90254 310-937-5877
Sharon L. McClain Ed.D., supt. Fax 376-4974
www.hbcsd.org
Hermosa Valley MS 700/3-8
1645 Valley Dr 90254 310-937-5888
Linda Cohen, prin. Fax 798-4365

Hope Chapel Academy 200/K-12
2420 Pacific Coast Hwy 90254 310-374-4673
Rev. Zachary Nazarian, prin.

Hesperia, San Bernardino, Pop. 69,179
Hesperia USD 15,900/K-12
15576 Main St 92345 760-244-4411
Richard Bray, supt. Fax 244-2806
www.hesperia.org
Hesperia HS 2,200/9-12
9898 Maple Ave 92345 760-244-9898
Larry Porras, prin. Fax 244-0939
Hesperia JHS 1,400/7-8
10275 Cypress Ave 92345 760-244-9386
Larry Silverman, prin. Fax 244-0595
Ranchero MS 1,400/7-8
17607 Ranchero Rd 92345 760-948-0175
Cindy Costa, prin. Fax 948-0381
Sultana HS 2,400/9-12
17311 Sultana St 92345 760-947-6777
Robert McCollum, prin. Fax 947-6788

Hesperia Christian S 500/PK-12
16775 Olive St 92345 760-244-6164
Sharon Romero, admin. Fax 244-9756

Highland, San Bernardino, Pop. 48,516
Redlands USD
Supt. — See Redlands
Beattie MS, 7800 Boulder Ave 92346 6-8
Carol Purvine, prin. 909-307-2400

San Bernardino City USD
Supt. — See San Bernardino
Serrano MS 1,200/7-8
3131 Piedmont Dr 92346 909-388-6530
Julie Swan, prin. Fax 864-6232

Citrus Valley Christian Academy 100/K-12
7171 Tiara Ave 92346 909-556-7201
Douglas Van Gelder, admin.
Universal Training Center Post-Sec.
3875 Atlantic Ave 92346 909-864-1918

Hillsborough, San Mateo, Pop. 10,578
Hillsborough CSD 1,400/K-8
300 El Cerrito Ave 94010 650-342-5193
Marilyn Loushin-Miller, supt. Fax 342-6964
www.hcsd.k12.ca.us/
Crocker MS 500/6-8
2600 Ralston Ave 94010 650-342-6331
Janet Chun, prin. Fax 579-5943

Crystal Springs Uplands S 400/6-12
400 Uplands Dr 94010 650-342-4175
Amy Richards, hdmstr. Fax 342-7623

Hilmar, Merced, Pop. 3,392
Hilmar USD 2,300/K-12
7807 Lander Ave 95324 209-667-5701
David Miller Ph.D., supt. Fax 667-1721
www.hilmar.k12.ca.us
Hilmar HS 700/9-12
7807 Lander Ave 95324 209-667-5903
Steve Gomes, prin. Fax 667-7628
Hilmar MS 600/6-8
7807 Lander Ave 95324 209-632-8847
Andres Zamora, prin. Fax 667-7018

Hollister, San Benito, Pop. 36,555
Hollister SD 6,200/K-8
2690 Cienega Rd 95023 831-630-6300
Ronald Crates Ed.D., supt. Fax 634-2080
www.hsd.k12.ca.us
Maze MS 1,000/6-8
900 Meridian St 95023 831-636-4480
Bernice Smith, prin. Fax 636-4488
Rancho San Justo MS 1,000/6-8
1201 Rancho Dr 95023 831-636-4450
Don Knapp, prin. Fax 634-4952

San Benito HSD 2,800/9-12
1220 Monterey St 95023 831-637-5831
Jean Burns Slater Ed.D., supt. Fax 637-6524
www.sbhsd.k12.ca.us
San Benito HS 2,800/9-12
1220 Monterey St 95023 831-637-5831
Debbie Padilla, prin. Fax 637-6524

Calvary Christian S 100/K-12
1900 Highland Dr 95023 831-637-2909
Walt Lindquist, prin.
Grace Bible Christian S 50/1-12
634 Monterey St 95023 831-638-1394
Robin Sando, admin. Fax 638-0460

Hollywood, See Los Angeles
Los Angeles USD
Supt. — See Los Angeles
Le Conte MS 2,200/6-8
1316 N Bronson Ave 90028 323-461-4741
Christine Zardeneta, prin. Fax 856-3053

Academy Pacific Travel College Post-Sec.
1777 Vine St # 30 90028 323-462-3211
American Academy of Dramatic Arts Post-Sec.
1336 N La Brea Ave 90028 800-222-2867
Elegance International Post-Sec.
1622 N Highland Ave 90028 323-871-8318
Musicians Institute Post-Sec.
1655 N McCadden Pl 90028 323-462-1384

Holtville, Imperial, Pop. 5,536
Holtville USD 1,900/K-12
621 E 6th St 92250 760-356-2974
Patricia Salcido, supt. Fax 356-4936
www.holtville.k12.ca.us/
Holtville HS 600/9-12
755 Olive Ave 92250 760-356-2926
Jackie Hester, prin. Fax 356-1206
Holtville JHS 400/6-8
800 Beale Ave 92250 760-356-2811
Tish Lyon, prin. Fax 356-5741

Honeydew, Humboldt
Mattole USD 200/K-12
29289 Chambers Rd 95545 707-629-3311
Richard Graey, supt. Fax 629-3575
www.humboldt.k12.ca.us/mattole_usd/
Other Schools – See Petrolia

Hoopa, Humboldt
Klamath-Trinity JUSD 1,200/K-12
PO Box 1308 95546 530-625-4255
Douglas Oliveira, supt. Fax 625-4133
www.humboldt.k12.ca.us/kt_usd/K-T/home.html
Hoopa Valley HS 300/9-12
PO Box 1308 95546 530-625-4218
John Greene, prin. Fax 625-4200

Hughson, Stanislaus, Pop. 5,498
Hughson USD 2,000/K-12
PO Box 189 95326 209-883-4428
Jim Rallis, supt. Fax 883-4639
www.hughson.k12.ca.us/

Hughson HS 800/9-12
PO Box 99 95326 209-883-0460
Debra Davis, prin. Fax 883-0870
Ross MS 400/6-8
PO Box 189 95326 209-883-4425
Matthew Shipley, prin. Fax 883-2017

Keyes UNESD
Supt. — See Keyes
Spratling MS 6-8
5277 Washington Rd 95326 209-664-3833
Mike Richter, prin. Fax 656-2384

Huntington Beach, Orange, Pop. 194,248
Fountain Valley ESD
Supt. — See Fountain Valley
Talbert MS 600/6-8
9101 Brabham Dr 92646 714-378-4220
Cathie Abdel, prin. Fax 378-4229

Huntington Beach City SD 6,300/K-8
20451 Craimer Ln 92646 714-964-8888
Roberta DeLuca, supt. Fax 963-9565
www.hbcsd.k12.ca.us
Dwyer MS 1,200/6-8
1502 Palm Ave 92648 714-536-7507
Donald Ruisinger, prin. Fax 960-0955
Sowers MS 1,200/6-8
9300 Indianapolis Ave 92646 714-962-7738
Paul Morrow Ed.D., prin. Fax 968-5580

Huntington Beach UNHSD 19,100/9-12
5832 Bolsa Ave 92646 714-903-7000
Van W. Riley, supt. Fax 892-5750
www.hbuhsd.org
Edison HS 2,100/9-12
21400 Magnolia St 92646 714-962-1356
D'Liese Melendrez, prin. Fax 963-4280
Huntington Beach HS 2,400/9-12
1905 Main St 92648 714-536-2514
David Linzey, prin. Fax 960-7042
Marina HS 2,600/9-12
15871 Springdale St 92649 714-893-6571
Stephen Roderick, prin. Fax 892-7855
Ocean View HS 1,600/9-12
17071 Gothard St 92647 714-848-0656
Karen Gilden, prin. Fax 843-0541
Huntington Beach Adult Education Adult
16666 Tunstall Ln 92647 714-847-2873
Doris Longmead, prin. Fax 841-2283
Other Schools – See Fountain Valley, Westminster

Ocean View SD 10,200/PK-8
17200 Pinehurst Ln 92647 714-847-2551
Karen Colby, supt. Fax 847-1430
www.ovsd.org
Marine View MS 900/6-8
5682 Tilburg Dr 92649 714-846-0624
Elizabeth Williams, prin. Fax 846-2074
Mesa View MS 800/6-8
17601 Avilla Ln 92647 714-842-6608
Leona Olson, prin. Fax 842-8798
Spring View MS 900/6-8
16662 Trudy Ln 92647 714-846-2891
Cameron Malotte, prin. Fax 377-9821
Other Schools – See Fountain Valley

Brethren Christian HS 500/7-12
21141 Strathmoor Ln 92646 714-962-6617
Rick Niswonger, admin. Fax 962-3171
Golden West College Post-Sec.
15744 Goldenwest St 92647 714-892-7711
Hebrew Academy 400/PK-12
14401 Willow Ln 92647 714-898-0051
Rabbi Yitzchok Newman, dir. Fax 898-0633
Liberty Christian S 400/K-12
7661 Warner Ave 92647 714-842-5992
Thom Doney, prin. Fax 848-7484
Platt College Post-Sec.
7755 Center Ave Ste 400 92647 714-373-3240

Huntington Park, Los Angeles, Pop. 63,139
Los Angeles USD
Supt. — See Los Angeles
Gage MS 3,700/6-8
2880 E Gage Ave 90255 323-587-5271
Veronica Aragon, prin. Fax 589-6925
Huntington Park HS 4,400/9-12
6020 Miles Ave 90255 323-583-3333
Robert Hinojosa, prin. Fax 583-0463
Nimitz MS 3,700/6-8
6021 Carmelita Ave 90255 323-585-0957
Francisco Vasquez, prin. Fax 773-5201
Huntington Park-Bell Community Adult S Adult
6020 Miles Ave 90255 323-581-0168
Juan Jimenez, prin. Fax 581-5515

California Learning Center Post-Sec.
6812 Pacific Blvd 90255 323-581-0600
ICDC College Post-Sec.
6330 Pacific Blvd Ste 200 90255 323-655-9100

Huron, Fresno, Pop. 6,991
Coalinga/Huron USD
Supt. — See Coalinga
Huron MS 400/6-8
PO Box 99 93234 559-945-2926
Irene Fernandez, prin. Fax 945-8482

Idyllwild, Riverside, Pop. 2,853

Idyllwild Arts Academy 300/8-12
PO Box 38 92549 951-659-2171
William Lowman, prin. Fax 659-5463

Imperial, Imperial, Pop. 8,885
Imperial USD 2,800/K-12
219 N E St 92251 760-355-3200
Barbara Layaye, supt. Fax 355-4511
iusd.imperial.k12.ca.us/
Imperial HS 700/9-12
517 W Barioni Blvd 92251 760-355-3220
Lisa Tabarez, prin. Fax 355-0869
Wright IS 500/7-8
515 W 10th St 92251 760-355-3240
Chuck Bush, prin. Fax 355-3256

Imperial Valley College Post-Sec.
PO Box 158 92251 760-352-8320

Imperial Beach, San Diego, Pop. 27,151
Sweetwater UNHSD
Supt. — See Chula Vista
Mar Vista HS 2,300/9-12
505 Elm Ave 91932 619-628-3074
Dr. Louise Phipps, prin. Fax 424-6232

Independence, Inyo
Owens Valley USD 100/K-12
PO Box E 93526 760-878-2405
Joel Hampton, supt. Fax 878-2626
Owens Valley HS 50/9-12
PO Box E 93526 760-878-2405
Joel Hampton, prin. Fax 878-2626

Indio, Riverside, Pop. 58,241
Desert Sands USD
Supt. — See La Quinta
Glenn MS of International Studies 1,400/6-8
79655 Miles Ave 92201 760-200-3700
Jean Carroll, prin. Fax 200-3709
Indio HS 2,400/9-12
81750 Avenue 46 92201 760-775-3550
Rudy Ramirez, prin. Fax 775-3565
Indio MS 1,100/6-8
81195 Miles Ave 92201 760-775-3800
Dan Miller, prin. Fax 775-3807
Jefferson MS 700/6-8
83089 US Highway 111 92201 760-863-3660
Esther Lopez, prin. Fax 775-3597
Wilson MS 600/6-8
83501 Dillon Ave 92201 760-775-3880
Harry Munoz, prin. Fax 775-3885

Inglewood, Los Angeles, Pop. 115,208
Inglewood USD 31,300/K-12
401 S Inglewood Ave 90301 310-419-2700
Dr. Pamela Short-Powell, supt. Fax 680-5144
inglewood.k12.ca.us
City Honors HS 400/9-12
115 W Kelso St 90301 310-680-4880
Thelma Brown, prin. Fax 680-5144
Crozier MS 800/7-8
151 N Grevillea Ave 90301 310-680-5280
Beverly Pye, prin. Fax 680-5299
Inglewood HS 2,100/9-12
231 S Grevillea Ave 90301 310-680-5200
Debra Tate, prin. Fax 680-5201
Monroe MS 1,400/6-8
10711 S 10th Ave 90303 310-680-5310
Reginald Sirls, prin. Fax 680-5317
Morningside HS 1,600/9-12
10500 Yukon Ave 90303 310-680-5230
Evlyn Mainor, prin. Fax 680-5257
Inglewood Adult Education Adult
106 E Manchester Blvd 90301 310-330-5222
Lacy Alexander, prin. Fax 330-5218

Daniel Freeman Mem. Hospital Post-Sec.
333 N Prairie Ave 90301 310-674-7050
Marinello School of Beauty Post-Sec.
240 S Market St 90301 310-674-8100
St. Marys Academy 300/9-12
701 Grace Ave 90301 310-674-8470
Sr. Fay Hagen, prin. Fax 674-6255
South Bay Lutheran HS 100/6-12
3600 W Imperial Hwy 90303 310-672-1101
Joe Bennett, prin. Fax 672-1115
University of West Los Angeles Post-Sec.
9920 S La Cienega Blvd 90301 310-342-5200
Westwood College of Aviation Technology Post-Sec.
8911 Aviation Blvd 90301 310-337-4444

Ione, Amador, Pop. 7,514
Amador County USD
Supt. — See Jackson
Ione JHS 400/7-8
450 S Mill St 95640 209-274-2491
Bill Murray, prin. Fax 274-0671

Irvine, Orange, Pop. 170,561
Irvine USD 25,600/PK-12
5050 Barranca Pkwy 92604 949-936-5000
Dean Waldfogel, supt. Fax 936-5259
www.iusd.org
Irvine HS 1,800/9-12
4321 Walnut Ave 92604 949-936-7000
Gail Richards, prin. Fax 936-7009
Lakeside MS 700/7-8
3 Lemongrass 92604 949-936-6100
Craig Ritter, prin. Fax 936-6109
Northwood HS 1,900/9-12
4515 Portola Pkwy 92620 949-936-7200
Cassie Parham, prin. Fax 936-7209
Rancho San Joaquin MS 900/7-8
4861 Michelson Dr 92612 949-936-6500
Richard Behn, prin. Fax 936-6509
Sierra Vista MS 900/7-8
2 Liberty 92620 949-936-6600
Beverly Khalil-White, prin. Fax 936-6609
South Lake MS 600/7-8
655 W Yale Loop 92614 949-936-6700
Bruce Baron, prin. Fax 936-6709
University HS 2,200/9-12
4771 Campus Dr 92612 949-936-7600
John Pehrson, prin. Fax 936-7609
Venado MS 800/7-8
4 Deerfield Ave 92604 949-936-6800
Fran Antenore, prin. Fax 936-6809
Woodbridge HS 2,100/9-12
2 Meadowbrook 92604 949-936-7800
Tom Nelson, prin. Fax 936-7809
Irvine Adult S Adult
311 W Yale Loop 92604 949-936-7450
Karen Bautista, dir. Fax 936-7459
Tustin USD
Supt. — See Tustin
Beckman HS 9-12
3588 Bryan 92602 714-734-2900
Adele Heuer, prin. Fax 505-9676

Alliant International University Post-Sec.
2500 Michelson Dr Bldg 250 92612 949-833-2651
Concordia University Post-Sec.
1530 Concordia 92612 949-854-8002
DeVry University Post-Sec.
3333 Michelson Dr Ste 420 92612 949-752-5631
Executive 2000 Post-Sec.
2041 Business Center Dr 92612 949-794-9090
FIDM/The Fashion Institute Post-Sec.
17590 Gillette Ave 92614 949-851-6200
Irvine Valley College Post-Sec.
5500 Irvine Center Dr 92618 949-451-5100
St. Michael the Archangel Academy 300/K-12
4790 Irvine Blvd Ste 105 92620 714-730-9114
Marcia Neill, dir. Fax 730-9114
Tarbut V'Torah Day S 600/K-12
5200 Bonita Canyon Dr 92603 949-509-9500
Bernice Tabak, prin. Fax 856-2400
University of California 92697 Post-Sec.
949-824-5011

Irwindale, Los Angeles, Pop. 1,480

CEI Post-Sec.
4900 Rivergrade Rd Ste E210 91706 626-338-8886
Premiere Career College Post-Sec.
12901 Ramona Blvd Ste D 91706 626-814-2080
Public Health Foundation Enterprises Post-Sec.
12781 Schabarum Ave 91706 626-856-6376

Jackson, Amador, Pop. 4,102
Amador County USD 4,500/K-12
217 Rex Ave 95642 209-223-1750
Mike Carey, supt. Fax 223-1733
www.teachnet.k12.ca.us/main.html
Argonaut HS 600/9-12
217 Rex Ave 95642 209-257-7700
Peggy Gardner, prin. Fax 223-3149
Jackson JHS 400/6-8
217 Rex Ave 95642 209-257-5310
Dave Vicari, prin. Fax 257-5311
Other Schools – See Ione, Sutter Creek

Regional Occupational Center & Program
Supt. — None
Amador County ROP Vo/Tech
217 Rex Ave 95642 209-267-5274
Elizabeth Chapin-Pinotti, dir. Fax 267-5497

Jamul, San Diego, Pop. 2,258
Jamul-Dulzura UNESD 1,200/K-8
14581 Lyons Valley Rd 91935 619-669-7700
Dr. Roberta Zapf, supt. Fax 669-0254
www.jdusd.k12.ca.us/
Oak Grove MS 500/6-8
14344 Olive Vista Dr 91935 619-669-2700
Jeannie Lopez, prin. Fax 669-7632

Joshua Tree, San Bernardino, Pop. 3,898

Boston S, PO Box 708 92252 200/K-12
David Zimmerman, dir. 760-366-8658
Copper Mountain College Post-Sec.
PO Box 1398 92252 760-366-3791

Julian, San Diego, Pop. 1,284
Julian UNESD 400/K-8
PO Box 337 92036 760-765-0661
Kevin Ogden, supt. Fax 765-0220
www.sdcoe.k12.ca.us/districts/julianel/
Julian JHS 100/7-8
PO Box 337 92036 760-765-0575
Brian Duffy, prin. Fax 765-3340

Julian UNHSD 200/9-12
PO Box 417 92036 760-765-3208
Brian E. Bristol, supt. Fax 765-2926
julianhs.sdcoe.net/
Julian HS 200/9-12
PO Box 417 92036 760-765-0606
Brian E. Bristol, prin. Fax 765-2782

Kelseyville, Lake, Pop. 2,861
Kelseyville USD 1,800/K-12
4410 Konocti Rd 95451 707-279-1511
Boyce McClain, supt. Fax 279-9221
www.kusd.lake.k12.ca.us
Kelseyville HS 600/9-12
5480 Main St 95451 707-279-4923
Matt Cockerton, prin. Fax 279-9173
Mountain Vista MS 400/6-8
5081 Konocti Rd 95451 707-279-4060
John Berry, prin. Fax 279-8835

Kentfield, Marin, Pop. 6,030
Kentfield ESD 1,000/K-8
699 Sir Francis Drake Blvd 94904 415-925-2230
Robert Caine, supt. Fax 925-2238
www.kentfieldschools.org/district/
Kent MS 500/5-8
250 Stadium Way 94904 415-458-5970
Skip Kniesche, prin. Fax 458-5973

College of Marin Post-Sec.
835 College Ave 94904 415-457-8811
Marin Catholic HS 800/9-12
675 Sir Francis Drake Blvd 94904 415-464-3800
Don Ritchie, prin. Fax 461-7161

Kerman, Fresno, Pop. 9,765
Kerman USD 3,800/K-12
151 S 1st St 93630 559-846-5383
Roger Halbert, supt. Fax 846-5941
www.kermanusd.k12.ca.us
Kerman HS 1,100/9-12
205 S 1st St 93630 559-842-2500
Jim Volkoff, prin. Fax 846-4229

Kerman MS
601 S 1st St 93630
Homar Garza, prin.
600/7-8
559-842-3000
Fax 846-5217
Kerman Adult S
15405 W Sunset Ave 93630
Nellie Neri, prin.
Adult
559-842-3500
Fax 846-5371

Keyes, Stanislaus, Pop. 2,878
Keyes UNESD
PO Box 310 95328
Tom Changon, supt.
Other Schools – See Hughson
600/K-8
209-669-2921
Fax 669-2923

King City, Monterey, Pop. 11,323
King City JUNHSD
800 Broadway St 93930
Wayne Brown, supt.
www.kingcity.k12.ca.us/
King City HS
720 Broadway St 93930
Todd Dearden, prin.
Other Schools – See Greenfield
2,400/9-12
831-385-0606
Fax 385-0695
1,200/9-12
831-385-5461
Fax 385-0901

King City UNESD
800 Broadway St 93930
Wayne Brown, supt.
www.kingcity.k12.ca.us/
San Lorenzo MS
415 Pearl St 93930
Kelly Green, prin.
2,800/K-8
831-385-1144
Fax 385-0695
900/6-8
831-385-5446
Fax 386-0372

Kingsburg, Fresno, Pop. 10,504
Kingsburg JUNHSD
1900 18th Ave 93631
Linda E. Clark, supt.
www.kjuhsd.k12.ca.us/
Kingsburg HS, 1900 18th Ave 93631
Linda E. Clark, prin.
1,000/9-12
559-897-5156
Fax 897-7759
1,000/9-12
559-897-5156

La Canada Flintridge, Los Angeles, Pop. 20,980
La Canada USD
5039 Palm Dr 91011
Jim Stratton, supt.
www.lcusd.net
La Canada JSHS
4463 Oak Grove Dr 91011
Dr. Damon Dragos, prin.
4,300/K-12
818-952-8300
Fax 952-8309
2,300/7-12
818-952-4200
Fax 952-4214

Flintridge Prep S
4543 Crown Ave 91011
Peter Bachmann, prin.
Flintridge Sacred Heart Academy
440 Saint Katherine Dr 91011
Sr. Celeste Botello, prin.
Renaissance Academy
4490 Cornishon Ave 91011
Ann Hazen, prin.
St. Francis HS
200 Foothill Blvd 91011
Thomas Moran, prin.
500/7-12
818-790-1178
Fax 952-6247
400/9-12
626-685-8300
Fax 685-8305
100/K-12
818-952-3055
Fax 952-3069
600/9-12
818-790-0325
Fax 790-5542

La Crescenta, Los Angeles, Pop. 16,968
Glendale USD
Supt. — See Glendale
Clark Magnet HS
4747 New York Ave 91214
Douglas Dall, prin.
Crescenta Valley HS
2900 Community Ave 91214
Mike Livingston, prin.
Rosemont MS
4725 Rosemont Ave 91214
Sally T. Buckley, prin.
600/9-10
818-248-8324
Fax 957-2954
2,800/9-12
818-249-5871
Fax 541-9531
1,400/7-8
818-248-4224
Fax 248-3790

Ladera Ranch, Orange
Capistrano USD
Supt. — See San Juan Capistrano
Ladera Ranch MS
29551 Sienna Pkwy 92694
Eamonn O'Donovan, prin.
800/6-8
949-234-5922

Ladera Ranch JHS
26122 ONeill Dr 92694
Sherry Worel, supt.
100/7-8
949-429-3812
Fax 429-3820

Lafayette, Contra Costa, Pop. 24,574
Acalanes UNHSD
1212 Pleasant Hill Rd 94549
Jim Negri, supt.
www.acalanes.k12.ca.us
Acalanes HS
1200 Pleasant Hill Rd 94549
John Nickerson, prin.
Other Schools – See Moraga, Orinda, Walnut Creek
5,900/9-12
925-942-9602
Fax 938-2846
1,300/9-12
925-935-2600
Fax 210-0320

Lafayette ESD
PO Box 1029 94549
Linda Weesner, supt.
www.lafsd.k12.ca.us
Stanley MS
3455 School St 94549
Sandy Bruketta, prin.
3,400/K-8
925-299-3502
Fax 284-1525
1,300/6-8
925-283-6282
Fax 283-1797

Bentley S - Lafayette Campus
1000 Upper Happy Valley Rd 94549
Laurie Kahn, prin.
300/9-12
510-843-2512
Fax 299-0469

La Grange, Stanislaus
Big Oak Flat-Groveland USD
Supt. — See Groveland
Pedro HS
3090 Merced Falls Rd 95329
Dr. Lana Rosing, prin.
100/9-12
209-852-2864
Fax 852-2125

Laguna Beach, Orange, Pop. 24,126
Laguna Beach USD
550 Blumont St 92651
Theresa Daem, supt.
www.lagunabeachschools.org
Laguna Beach HS
625 Park Ave 92651
Nancy Blade, prin.
Thurston MS
2100 Park Ave 92651
Joanne Culverhouse, prin.
2,700/K-12
949-497-7700
Fax 497-6021
800/9-12
949-497-7750
Fax 497-7766
700/6-8
949-497-7785
Fax 497-7798

Laguna College of Art and Design
2222 Laguna Canyon Rd 92651
Post-Sec.
949-376-6000

Laguna Hills, Orange, Pop. 32,181
Saddleback Valley USD
Supt. — See Mission Viejo
Laguna Hills HS
25401 Paseo De Valencia 92653
Ed Adams, prin.
1,900/9-12
949-770-5447
Fax 830-0295

Allied Business School
22952 Alcalde Dr 92653
Post-Sec.
949-598-0875

Laguna Niguel, Orange, Pop. 64,326
Capistrano USD
Supt. — See San Juan Capistrano
Niguel Hills MS
29070 Paseo De La Escuela 92677
Jim Hansen, prin.
1,600/6-8
949-234-5360
Fax 249-2069

Laguna Niguel Adventist S
29702 Kensington Dr 92677
Jennie Mende, prin.
50/K-10
949-495-0311
Fax 363-7006

La Habra, Orange, Pop. 59,703
Fullerton JUNHSD
Supt. — See Fullerton
La Habra HS
801 Highlander Ave 90631
Jennifer Leeman, prin.
Sonora HS
401 S Palm St 90631
Rich Peterson, prin.
2,300/9-12
562-266-5000
Fax 691-8280
2,000/9-12
562-266-2001
Fax 266-2040

La Habra City ESD
PO Box 307 90633
Richard Hermann, supt.
www.lhcsd.k12.ca.us
Imperial MS
PO Box 307 90633
Cathy Seighman, prin.
Washington MS
PO Box 307 90633
Gary Mantey, prin.
6,500/K-8
562-690-2300
Fax 690-4154
1,100/6-8
562-690-2344
Fax 526-3678
1,100/6-8
562-690-2374
Fax 690-7834

Whittier Christian HS
501 N Beach Blvd 90631
Robert Brown, prin.
600/9-12
562-694-3803
Fax 697-1673

La Jolla, See San Diego
San Diego City USD
Supt. — See San Diego
La Jolla HS
750 Nautilus St 92037
Dana Shelburne, prin.
Muirlands MS
1056 Nautilus St 92037
Christine Hargrave, prin.
1,700/9-12
858-454-3081
Fax 459-2188
1,100/6-8
858-459-4211
Fax 459-8075

Bishops S
7607 La Jolla Blvd 92037
Michael Teitelman, hdmstr.
La Jolla Country Day S
9490 Genesee Ave 92037
Dr. Judith Glickman, prin.
National University
11255 N Torrey Pines Rd 92037
Scripps Memorial Hospital
9888 Genesee Ave 92037
Scripps Research Institute
10550 N Torrey Pines Rd 92037
University of California
9500 Gilman Dr 92093
800/7-12
858-459-4021
Fax 459-3914
1,000/PK-12
858-453-3440
Fax 453-8210
Post-Sec.
858-642-8000
Post-Sec.
858-457-6100
Post-Sec.
858-784-8469
Post-Sec.
858-534-2230

Lake Arrowhead, San Bernardino, Pop. 6,539
Rim of the World USD
PO Box 430 92352
Clint Harwick Ed.D., supt.
www.rimsd.k12.ca.us
Henck IS
PO Box 430 92352
Dr. Tom Battle, prin.
Rim of the World HS
PO Box 430 92352
Guy Bonanno, prin.
5,500/K-12
909-336-2031
Fax 337-4527
1,000/7-8
909-336-0360
Fax 336-3449
1,800/9-12
909-336-2038
Fax 336-0254

Faith Academy
PO Box 910 92352
Bill Norton, prin.
200/K-12
909-337-9341
Fax 337-6169

Lake Elsinore, Riverside, Pop. 34,914
Lake Elsinore USD
545 Chaney St 92530
Frank Passarella, supt.
www.leusd.k12.ca.us
Canyon Lake MS
33005 Canyon Hills Rd 92532
Mike Sepulveda, prin.
Elsinore MS
1203 W Graham Ave 92530
Nori Holland, prin.
Lakeside HS
32593 Riverside Dr 92530
Lorie Reitz, prin.
Temescal Canyon HS
28755 El Toro Rd 92532
Patrick Kelleher, prin.
Terra Cotta MS
29291 Lake St 92530
Kip Meyer, prin.
Valley Adult S
520 Chaney St 92530
Cindy Dickinson, prin.
Other Schools – See Wildomar
19,500/K-12
951-253-7000
Fax 253-7084
1,200/6-8
951-244-2123
Fax 244-2103
900/6-8
951-674-2118
Fax 674-6302
9-12
951-253-7300
Fax 253-7335
2,700/9-12
951-245-4484
Fax 245-2974
1,500/6-8
951-674-0641
Fax 674-5191
Adult
951-245-2093
Fax 245-1988

Lake Forest, Orange, Pop. 76,738
Saddleback Valley USD
Supt. — See Mission Viejo
El Toro HS
25255 Toledo Way 92630
Dave Ellick, prin.
2,600/9-12
949-586-6333
Fax 380-9874

Serrano IS
24642 Jeronimo Rd 92630
Linda Garza, prin.
1,500/7-8
949-586-3221
Fax 586-3773

CEI
25361 Commercentre Dr #100 92630
Elegante Beauty College
23635 El Toro Rd Ste K 92630
Lake Forest Beauty College
23600 Rockfield Blvd Ste 3C 92630
Post-Sec.
949-472-4192
Post-Sec.
949-586-4900
Post-Sec.
949-951-8883

Lake Isabella, Kern, Pop. 3,323
Kern HSD
Supt. — See Bakersfield
Kern Valley HS
3340 Erskine Creek Rd 93240
Jeanie Brachear, prin.
700/9-12
760-379-2611
Fax 379-8314

Kernville UNESD
PO Box 3077 93240
Mary C. Barlow, supt.
www.kernville.usd.org
Wallace JHS
PO Box 3077 93240
Todd Farr, prin.
900/K-8
760-379-3651
Fax 379-3812
300/6-8
760-379-4646
Fax 379-1322

Lakeport, Lake, Pop. 5,186
Lakeport USD
2508 Howard Ave 95453
Erin Smith-Hagberg, supt.
www.lakeport.k12.ca.us
Clear Lake HS
2508 Howard Ave 95453
Steve Gentry, prin.
Terrace MS
2508 Howard Ave 95453
Jill Falconer, prin.
1,700/K-12
707-262-3000
Fax 263-7332
500/9-12
707-262-3010
Fax 262-3026
700/4-8
707-262-3007
Fax 262-5532

Regional Occupational Center & Program
Supt. — None
Lake County ROP
1152 S Main St 95453
Dave Geck, dir.
Vo/Tech
707-262-3498
Fax 262-5625

Lakeside, San Diego, Pop. 56,225
Grossmont UNHSD
Supt. — See El Cajon
El Capitan HS
10410 Ashwood St 92040
Pat Price, prin.
2,000/9-12
619-443-1081
Fax 390-8503

Lakeside UNESD
12335 Woodside Ave 92040
Stephen Halfaker, supt.
www.lsschools.k12.ca.us/lakeside/default.htm
Lakeside MS
11833 Woodside Ave 92040
Steve Mull, prin.
Tierra Del Sol MS
9611 Petite Ln 92040
David Nichols, prin.
4,500/K-8
619-390-2600
Fax 561-7929
800/6-8
619-390-2636
Fax 390-2643
800/6-8
619-390-2670
Fax 390-2518

Lakewood, Los Angeles, Pop. 81,300
ABC USD
Supt. — See Cerritos
Artesia HS
12108 Del Amo Blvd 90715
Sergio Garcia, prin.
1,800/9-12
562-402-2015
Fax 809-5604

Bellflower USD
Supt. — See Bellflower
Mayfair MSHS
6000 Woodruff Ave 90713
Joseph Perry, prin.
3,500/7-12
562-925-9981
Fax 804-1656

Long Beach USD
Supt. — See Long Beach
Hoover MS
3501 Country Club Dr 90712
Michael Troyer, prin.
Lakewood HS
4400 Briercrest Ave 90713
Allan Taylor, prin.
1,200/6-8
562-421-1213
Fax 421-8063
4,300/9-12
562-425-1281
Fax 421-9616

St. Joseph HS
5825 Woodruff Ave 90713
Dr. Mary Mendoza, prin.
800/9-12
562-925-5073
Fax 925-3315

La Mesa, San Diego, Pop. 54,571
La Mesa-Spring Valley ESD
4750 Date Ave 91941
Brian Marshall, supt.
www.lmsvsd.k12.ca.us
La Mesa MS
4200 Parks Ave 91941
Dennis Munden, prin.
Parkway MS
9009 Park Plaza Dr 91942
Cyndi Sutton, prin.
Other Schools – See Spring Valley
14,300/K-8
619-668-5700
Fax 668-5809
1,300/6-8
619-668-5730
Fax 668-8303
1,200/6-8
619-668-5810
Fax 668-5779

California Hair Design Academy
8011 University Ave # A-2 91941
La Mesa Christian S
9407 Jericho Rd 91942
Post-Sec.
619-461-8600
100/PK-12
619-463-5591

La Mirada, Los Angeles, Pop. 48,887
Norwalk-La Mirada USD
Supt. — See Norwalk
Benton MS
15709 Olive Branch Dr 90638
Craig Hauke, prin.
Hutchinson MS
13900 Estero Rd 90638
Bob Euston, prin.
La Mirada HS
13520 Adelfa Dr 90638
Don Jones, prin.
Los Coyotes MS
14640 Mercado Ave 90638
Dr. Sylvia Begtrup, prin.
Norwalk Adult S
15920 Barbata Rd 90638
Sharon Renfro, dir.
800/6-8
562-943-1553
Fax 947-3861
600/6-8
562-944-3268
Fax 944-3269
2,400/9-12
562-868-0431
Fax 943-7872
600/6-8
714-523-2051
Fax 739-2368
Adult
562-670-9279
Fax 670-1654

Biola University | Post-Sec.
13800 Biola Ave 90639 | 562-903-6000
Foundation Christian S | 200/K-12
16450 Phoebe Ave 90638 | 714-865-9211
Jenette Sovilla, admin. |
Heights Christian JHS | 300/7-8
12900 Bluefield Ave 90638 | 562-947-3309
Rolland Esslinger, prin. | Fax 947-1001

Lamont, Kern, Pop. 11,517
Lamont ESD | 3,000/K-8
7915 Burgundy Ave 93241 | 661-845-0751
James R. Bates, supt. | Fax 845-0689
www.lamontschooldistrict.org/
Mountain View MS | 600/7-8
7915 Burgundy Ave 93241 | 661-845-2291
Fred Molina, prin. | Fax 845-1839

Lancaster, Los Angeles, Pop. 125,896
Antelope Valley UNHSD | 22,400/9-12
44811 Sierra Hwy 93534 | 661-948-7655
David J. Vierra, supt. | Fax 942-8744
www.avdistrict.org
Antelope Valley Union HS | 2,900/9-12
44900 Division St 93535 | 661-948-8552
Trish Lockhart, prin. | Fax 945-4867
Eastside HS | 9-12
3200 E Avenue J8 93535 | 661-948-7655
Tom Grady, prin. | Fax 946-3850
Lancaster HS | 3,100/9-12
44701 Eagle Way 93536 | 661-726-7649
Cheri Kreitz, prin. | Fax 726-7694
Antelope Valley Adult HS | Adult
45110 3rd St E 93535 | 661-942-3042
Terry O'Connor, prin. | Fax 948-0846
Other Schools – See Littlerock, Palmdale, Quartz Hill

Eastside UNSD | 2,700/K-8
45006 30th St E 93535 | 661-952-1200
Gregory Riccio Ph.D., supt. | Fax 952-1220
www.eastside.k12.ca.us
Cole MS | 1,000/6-8
3126 E Avenue I 93535 | 661-946-1041
Steve Smith, prin. | Fax 946-0166

Lancaster ESD | 15,600/K-8
44711 Cedar Ave 93534 | 661-948-4661
Dr. Stephen Gocke, supt. | Fax 948-9398
www.lancaster.k12.ca.us
Amargosa Creek MS | 1,600/6-8
44333 27th St W 93536 | 661-729-6064
Lexy Conte, prin. | Fax 729-6858
Endeavour MS | 6-8
831 E Avenue K2 93535 | 661-723-0351
Robert Porter, prin. | Fax 723-1362
New Vista MS | 1,300/6-8
753 E Avenue K2 93535 | 661-726-4271
Deborah Lewis, prin. | Fax 726-4278
Park View MS | 1,300/6-8
808 W Avenue J 93534 | 661-942-0496
Eric George, prin. | Fax 940-5732
Piute MS | 1,300/6-8
425 E Avenue H11 93535 | 661-942-9508
Kathy Lee, prin. | Fax 940-6676

Westside UNESD | 9,500/K-8
41914 50th St W 93536 | 661-722-0716
Regina Rossalli, supt. | Fax 772-5223
www.westside.k12.ca.us
Other Schools – See Palmdale, Quartz Hill

Wilsona SD
Supt. — See Palmdale
Challenger MS | 700/6-8
41725 170th St E 93535 | 661-264-1790
Mary Gerard, prin. | Fax 264-1793

Antelope Valley Christian S | 400/PK-12
3700 W Avenue L 93536 | 661-943-0044
Karen Hester, prin. | Fax 943-6774
Antelope Valley College | Post-Sec.
3041 W Avenue K 93536 | 661-722-6300
Bethel Christian S | 500/PK-12
3100 W Avenue K 93536 | 661-943-2224
Mathias Konnerth, prin. | Fax 943-6574
Calvary Chapel Christian S | 200/1-12
1935 W Avenue L 93534 | 661-942-0404
Tina McMillen, prin. |
Country Christian S | 200/1-12
2343 W Avenue K 93536 | 661-729-0142
Rebekah Wilson, prin. |
Desert Christian HS | 500/9-12
2340 W Avenue J8 93536 | 661-723-7441
Don Phillips, prin. | Fax 723-7437
Desert Christian MS | 400/6-8
44662 15th St W 93534 | 661-723-0665
Brian Roseborough, prin. | Fax 723-6774
Lancaster Baptist S | 500/K-12
4020 E Lancaster Blvd 93535 | 661-946-4668
Ray Cazis, prin. | Fax 946-7374
Lancaster Beauty School | Post-Sec.
44646 10th St W 93534 | 661-948-1672
Paraclete HS | 700/9-12
42145 30th St W 93536 | 661-943-3255
John Anson, prin. | Fax 722-9455
Seton S, 44751 Date Ave 93534 | 700/K-12
Richard Ellis, dir. | 661-948-8881

La Palma, Orange, Pop. 15,903
Anaheim UNHSD
Supt. — See Anaheim
Kennedy HS | 2,300/9-12
8281 Walker St 90623 | 714-220-4101
Kelly Wilson, prin. | Fax 995-1833
Walker JHS | 1,300/7-8
8132 Walker St 90623 | 714-220-4051
Chelsea Smith, prin. | Fax 220-2237

La Puente, Los Angeles, Pop. 42,143
Bassett USD | 7,500/K-12
904 Willow Ave 91746 | 626-931-3000
Robert Watanabe, supt. | Fax 918-3105
www.bassett.k12.ca.us

Bassett HS | 1,400/9-12
755 Ardilla Ave 91746 | 626-931-2800
Carolyn Pruitt, prin. | Fax 931-2850
Bassett Adult S Florence Flanner Campus | Adult
1314 N Le Borgne Ave 91746 | 626-931-7950
Matthew Smith, dir. | Fax 931-7915
Other Schools – See City of Industry

Hacienda La Puente USD
Supt. — See City of Industry
La Puente HS | 1,700/9-12
15615 Nelson Ave 91744 | 626-934-6700
Ava Smalley, prin. | Fax 855-3798
Sierra Vista MS | 800/6-8
15801 Sierra Vista Ct 91744 | 626-933-4000
Steve Behar, prin. | Fax 855-3817
Sparks MS | 1,000/6-8
15100 Giordano St 91744 | 626-933-5000
Barbara Wolfinbarger, prin. | Fax 855-3848
Hacienda La Puente Valley Adult Ed | Adult
14101 Nelson Ave 91746 | 626-934-2800

Rowland USD
Supt. — See Rowland Heights
Nogales HS | 2,500/9-12
401 Nogales St 91744 | 626-965-3437
Karen Coggins, prin. | Fax 965-4587

Bishop Amat HS | 1,400/9-12
14301 Fairgrove Ave 91746 | 626-962-2495
Dr. Merritt Hemenway, prin. | Fax 960-0994
Hacienda LaPuente Valley Adult Education | Post-Sec.
14101 Nelson Ave 91746 | 626-934-2800

La Quinta, Riverside, Pop. 32,139
Desert Sands USD | 24,800/K-12
47950 Dune Palms Rd 92253 | 760-777-4200
Dr. Doris Wilson, supt. | Fax 771-8505
www.dsusd.us
La Quinta HS | 2,500/9-12
79255 Westward Ho Dr 92253 | 760-772-4150
Donna Salazar, prin. | Fax 772-4166
La Quinta MS | 900/6-8
78900 Avenue 50 92253 | 760-777-4220
Janet Seto, prin. | Fax 777-4216
Desert Sands Adult S | Adult
47950 Dune Palms Rd 92253 | 760-863-3693
Pam Rutledge, prin. | Fax 863-3696
Other Schools – See Indio, Palm Desert

Larkspur, Marin, Pop. 11,827
Larkspur ESD | 1,000/K-8
230 Doherty Dr 94939 | 415-927-6960
Valerie Pitts, supt. | Fax 927-6964
www.larkspurschools.org
Hall MS | 300/6-8
200 Doherty Dr 94939 | 415-927-6978
Daniel A. Norbutas, prin. | Fax 927-6985

Tamalpais UNHSD | 3,600/9-12
PO Box 605 94977 | 415-945-3720
Bob Ferguson, supt. | Fax 945-3719
www.tamdistrict.org
Redwood HS | 1,400/9-12
395 Doherty Dr 94939 | 415-924-6200
Nancy Neu, prin. | Fax 945-3675
Other Schools – See Mill Valley, San Anselmo

La Selva Beach, Santa Cruz

Monterey Bay Academy | 200/9-12
783 San Andreas Rd 95076 | 831-728-1481
Tim Kubrock, prin. | Fax 728-1485

Las Flores, Orange
Capistrano USD
Supt. — See San Juan Capistrano
Las Flores MS | 1,800/6-8
25862 Antonio Pkwy, Rcho Sta Marg CA 92688
| 949-589-6543
Holly Feldt, prin. | Fax 589-9286

Lathrop, San Joaquin, Pop. 12,181

ITT Technical Institute | Post-Sec.
16916 S Harlan Rd 95330 | 209-858-0077

Laton, Fresno, Pop. 1,415
Laton JUSD | 900/PK-12
PO Box 248 93242 | 559-922-4015
James Brooks, supt. | Fax 923-4791
www.laton.k12.ca.us
Laton HS | 200/9-12
PO Box 278 93242 | 559-922-4080
Larry Rowe, prin. | Fax 923-4072

La Verne, Los Angeles, Pop. 33,005
Bonita USD
Supt. — See San Dimas
Bonita HS | 1,800/9-12
3102 D St 91750 | 909-971-8220
Robert Ketterling, prin. | Fax 971-8229
Ramona MS | 1,400/6-8
3490 Ramona Ave 91750 | 909-971-8260
Mark Rodgers, prin. | Fax 971-8269

Calvary Baptist S | 200/PK-12
2990 Damien Ave 91750 | 909-593-4672
Taylora Dial, prin. | Fax 392-9533
Damien HS | 1,100/9-12
2280 Damien Ave 91750 | 909-596-1946
Fr. Patrick Travers, prin. | Fax 596-6112
Lutheran HS | 100/9-12
3960 Fruit St 91750 | 909-593-4494
Jeremy Lowe, prin. | Fax 596-3744
University of La Verne | Post-Sec.
1950 3rd St 91750 | 909-593-3511

Lawndale, Los Angeles, Pop. 32,490
Centinela Valley UNHSD | 7,500/9-12
14901 Inglewood Ave 90260 | 310-263-3200
Dr. Cheryl White, supt. | Fax 263-6571
www.centinela.k12.ca.us/

Lawndale HS | 1,200/9-12
14901 Inglewood Ave 90260 | 310-263-3102
Fred Gomeztrejo, prin. | Fax 263-3120
Leuzinger HS | 3,100/9-12
4118 Rosecrans Ave 90260 | 310-263-2200
Sonia Miller, prin. | Fax 675-7023
Centinela Valley Adult S | Adult
4953 Marine Ave 90260 | 310-263-3165
Dr. Fe Woods, prin. | Fax 644-6142
Other Schools – See Hawthorne

Lawndale ESD | 6,100/K-8
4161 W 147th St 90260 | 310-973-1300
Joseph Condon Ed.D., supt. | Fax 675-6462
www.lawndale.k12.ca.us
Rogers MS | 1,300/7-8
4161 W 147th St 90260 | 310-676-1197
Martha Funes, prin. | Fax 675-0489

Laytonville, Mendocino, Pop. 1,133
Laytonville USD | 500/K-12
PO Box 868 95454 | 707-984-6414
John Markatos, supt. | Fax 984-8223
Laytonville HS | 200/9-12
PO Box 868 95454 | 707-984-6108
Joan Potter, prin. | Fax 984-8066

Lebec, Kern
El Tejon USD | 1,400/K-12
PO Box 876 93243 | 661-248-6247
John Wight, supt. | Fax 248-6714
www.el-tejon.k12.ca.us
El Tejon MS | 600/4-8
PO Box 876 93243 | 661-248-6680
Shelly Mason, prin. | Fax 248-5203
Frazier Mountain HS | 500/9-12
PO Box 876 93243 | 661-248-0310
Dan Penner, prin. | Fax 248-0403

Lee Vining, Mono
Eastern Sierra USD
Supt. — See Bridgeport
Lee Vining JSHS | 50/7-12
PO Box 268 93541 | 760-647-6366
Frank Romero, prin. | Fax 647-6695

Leggett, Mendocino
Leggett Valley USD | 200/K-12
PO Box 186 95585 | 707-925-6285
Bill Raebe, supt. | Fax 925-6396
leggett.k12.ca.us
Leggett Valley HS | 50/9-12
PO Box 186 95585 | 707-925-6230
Katie Sommer, prin. | Fax 925-6396
Other Schools – See Whitethorn

Le Grand, Merced, Pop. 1,205
Le Grand UNHSD | 600/9-12
12961 Le Grand Rd 95333 | 209-389-9403
George Hinds, supt. | Fax 389-9414
www.lghs.k12.ca.us/
Le Grand Union HS | 500/9-12
12961 Le Grand Rd 95333 | 209-389-9400
Donna Alley, prin. | Fax 389-4065

Lemon Grove, San Diego, Pop. 24,935
Lemon Grove SD | 4,400/K-8
8025 Lincoln St 91945 | 619-825-5600
Ernie Anastos, supt. | Fax 462-7959
www.lgsd.k12.ca.us
Lemon Grove MS | 900/6-8
7866 Lincoln St 91945 | 619-825-5628
David Torres, prin. | Fax 825-5781
Palm MS | 700/6-8
8425 Palm St 91945 | 619-825-5641
Russell Little, prin. | Fax 628-5786

Lemoore, Kings, Pop. 21,584
Lemoore UNESD | 3,200/K-8
100 Vine St 93245 | 559-924-6800
Ronald Meade, supt. | Fax 924-6809
www.kings.k12.ca.us/luesd/
Liberty MS | 700/7-8
100 Vine St 93245 | 559-924-6860
Eric Smyers, prin. | Fax 924-6869

Lemoore UNHSD | 2,000/9-12
5 Powell Ave 93245 | 559-924-6610
Dr. Paul Terry, supt. | 924-9212
www.luhsd.k12.ca.us/
Lemoore HS | 2,000/9-12
101 E Bush St 93245 | 559-924-6600
James Bennett, prin. | Fax 924-5086
Lemoore Adult S | Adult
351 E Bush St 93245 | 559-924-6620
Sandi Lowe, prin. | Fax 924-6637

Kings Christian S | 300/PK-12
900 E D St 93245 | 559-924-8301
Duane Daniel, admin. | Fax 924-0607

Lennox, Los Angeles, Pop. 22,757
Lennox SD | 7,000/K-8
10319 Firmona Ave 90304 | 310-330-4950
Dr. Bruce McDaniel, supt. | Fax 674-7804
www.lennox.k12.ca.us
Lennox MS | 2,300/6-8
10319 Firmona Ave 90304 | 310-419-1800
Brian Johnson, prin. | Fax 677-4635

Lincoln, Placer, Pop. 23,080
Western Placer USD | 1,700/K-12
810 J St 95648 | 916-645-6350
Roger Yohe, supt. | Fax 645-6356
www.wpusd.k12.ca.us
Edwards MS | 900/6-8
204 L St 95648 | 916-645-6370
Mary Boyle, prin. | Fax 645-6379
Lincoln HS | 9-12
790 J St 95648 | 916-645-6360
David Butler, prin. | Fax 645-6349

Linden, San Joaquin, Pop. 1,339
Linden USD | 2,700/K-12
18527 Main St 95236 | 209-887-3894
Ronald Estes, supt. | Fax 887-2250
www.sjcoe.net

Linden HS
18527 E Front St 95236
Stephanie Markle, prin.
Other Schools – See Stockton
700/9-12
209-887-3073
Fax 887-3815

Lindsay, Tulare, Pop. 10,611
Lindsay USD
519 E Honolulu St 93247
Janet Kliegl, supt.
www.lindsay.k12.ca.us
3,700/K-12
559-562-5111
Fax 562-6145
Garvey JHS
340 N Harvard Ave 93247
Rebecca Mestaz, prin.
600/7-8
559-562-1311
Fax 562-1411
Lindsay HS
1701 E Tulare Rd 93247
Lana Weatherly, prin.
900/9-12
559-562-5911
Fax 562-4291

Littlerock, Los Angeles, Pop. 1,320
Antelope Valley UNHSD
Supt. — See Lancaster
Littlerock HS
10833 E Avenue R 93543
Lisa Oates, prin.
2,800/9-12
661-944-5209
Fax 944-5191

Keppel UNESD
Supt. — See Pearblossom
Almondale MS
9330 E Avenue U 93543
Dawn Evenson, prin.
600/7-8
661-944-2152
Fax 944-0694

Live Oak, Sutter, Pop. 6,487
Live Oak USD
2201 Pennington Rd 95953
Tom Pritchard, supt.
www.lodo.santacruz.k12.ca.us/
2,000/K-12
530-695-5400
Fax 695-5460
Live Oak HS
2351 Pennington Rd 95953
Bill Cornelius, prin.
500/9-12
530-695-5415
Fax 695-5422
Live Oak MS
2082 Pennington Rd 95953
Joanne Bass, prin.
600/5-8
530-695-5435
Fax 695-5443

Livermore, Alameda, Pop. 77,744
Livermore Valley JUSD
685 E Jack London Blvd 94551
Brenda Miller, supt.
www.livermoreschools.com
13,300/K-12
925-606-3200
Fax 606-3328
Christenson MS
5757 Haggin Oaks Ave 94551
Janet Loughran-Smith, prin.
700/6-8
925-606-4702
Fax 606-4705
East Avenue MS
3951 East Ave 94550
Vicki Scudder, prin.
900/6-8
925-606-4711
Fax 606-4763
Granada HS
400 Wall St 94550
Chris Van Schaack, prin.
2,000/9-12
925-606-4800
Fax 606-4808
Junction Avenue MS
298 Junction Ave 94550
Vicki Scudder, prin.
900/6-8
925-606-4720
Fax 606-3318
Livermore HS
600 Maple St 94550
Dr. Jim Green, prin.
2,000/9-12
925-606-4812
Fax 606-4851
Mendenhall MS
1701 El Padro Dr 94550
Helen Foster, prin.
900/6-8
925-606-4731
Fax 606-4737
Livermore Adult Community Education
543 Sonoma Ave 94550
Nancy Steele, prin.
Adult
925-606-4722
Fax 606-3389

Regional Occupational Center & Program
Supt. — None
Tri-Valley ROP
2600 Kitty Hawk Rd Ste 117 94551
Robert Kreitz, dir.
Vo/Tech
925-455-4800
Fax 449-9126

Las Positas College
3033 Collier Canyon Rd 94551
Post-Sec.
925-373-5800

Livingston, Merced, Pop. 11,484
Livingston UNSD
922 B St 95334
Henry Escobar, supt.
www.lusd.k12.ca.us
2,400/K-8
209-394-5400
Fax 394-5401
Livingston MS
101 F St 95334
Filomena Sousa, prin.
900/6-8
209-394-5450
Fax 394-5451

Merced UNHSD
Supt. — See Atwater
Livingston HS
1617 Main St 95334
Nancy Edmiston, prin.
1,100/9-12
209-394-7961
Fax 358-1093

Lodi, San Joaquin, Pop. 61,027
Lodi USD
1305 E Vine St 95240
William Huyett, supt.
www.lodiusd.k12.ca.us
30,400/K-12
209-331-7000
Fax 331-7256
Career Education
421 S Pleasant Ave 95240
Tami Somera, dir.
Vo/Tech
209-331-7642
Fax 331-7526
Lodi HS
3 S Pacific Ave 95242
Bill Atterbery, prin.
2,500/9-12
209-331-7815
Fax 331-7779
Lodi MS
945 S Ham Ln 95242
Dawn Vetica, prin.
1,200/7-8
209-331-7544
Fax 331-7550
Millswood MS
233 N Mills Ave 95242
Sheree Flemmer, prin.
7-8
209-331-8332
Fax 331-8347
Tokay HS
1111 W Century Blvd 95240
Erik Sandstrom, prin.
2,900/9-12
209-331-7850
Fax 331-7168
Lodi Adult S
542 E Pine St 95240
Steve Colwell, prin.
Other Schools – See Stockton
Adult
209-331-7607
Fax 331-7167

Elliot Christian HS
2695 W Vine St 95242
David Couchman, admin.
200/9-12
209-368-2800
Fax 333-5208
Lodi Academy
1230 S Central Ave 95240
100/9-12
209-368-2781
Fax 368-6142

Zion MS
105 S Ham Ln 95242
Jason Tacderan, prin.
50/5-8
209-369-1910
Fax 369-0811

Loma Linda, San Bernardino, Pop. 20,089

Loma Linda Academy
10656 Anderson St 92354
Dr. L. Roo McKenzie, prin.
1,500/K-12
909-796-0161
Fax 478-6829
Loma Linda University 92350
Post-Sec.
909-558-1000

Lomita, Los Angeles, Pop. 20,548
Los Angeles USD
Supt. — See Los Angeles
Fleming MS
25425 Walnut St 90717
Janice Hackett, prin.
2,000/6-8
310-326-4242
Fax 326-9071

Coastal Academy
25501 Oak St 90717
M. Grace Di Pasquale, dir.
200/K-12
310-644-0433

Lompoc, Santa Barbara, Pop. 41,167
Lompoc USD
PO Box 8000 93438
Dr. Frank Lynch, supt.
www.lusd.org
13,400/K-12
805-742-3300
Fax 735-8452
Cabrillo HS
PO Box 8000 93438
Betty McCallum, prin.
1,600/9-12
805-742-2900
Fax 733-4156
El Camino MS
PO Box 8000 93438
Kathleen Woods, prin.
500/6-8
805-742-2550
Fax 735-1474
Lompoc HS
PO Box 8000 93438
Art Diaz, prin.
1,600/9-12
805-742-3000
Fax 735-1411
Lompoc Valley MS
PO Box 8000 93438
Jeff Wagonseller, prin.
1,200/6-8
805-742-2600
Fax 737-9480
Vandenberg MS
PO Box 8000 93438
Tom Klepper, prin.
1,100/6-8
805-742-2700
Fax 734-1790
Lompoc Adult Education
PO Box 8000 93438
Susan Williams, prin.
Adult
805-742-3100
Fax 736-3089

Lone Pine, Inyo, Pop. 1,818
Lone Pine USD
PO Box 159 93545
Diane Ogden, supt.
500/K-12
760-876-5579
Fax 876-5438
Lone Pine HS
PO Box 159 93545
Beverle Jeans, prin.
100/9-12
760-876-5577
Fax 876-1037
Lone Pine Adult S, PO Box 159 93545
Diane Ogden, prin.
Adult
760-876-5577

Long Beach, Los Angeles, Pop. 475,460
Long Beach USD
1515 Hughes Way 90810
Christopher Steinhauser, supt.
www.lbusd.k12.ca.us
93,300/PK-12
562-997-8000
Fax 997-8280
Bancroft MS
5301 E Centralia St 90808
Penelope O'Toole, prin.
1,500/6-8
562-425-7461
Fax 425-9741
Cabrillo HS
2001 Santa Fe Ave 90810
Mel Collins, prin.
3,100/9-12
562-951-7700
Fax 951-7797
DeMille MS
7025 E Parkcrest 90808
Timothy Spivey, prin.
1,300/6-8
562-421-8424
Fax 429-1054
Franklin MS
540 Cerritos Ave 90802
David Taylor, prin.
1,500/6-8
562-435-4952
Fax 432-6308
Hamilton MS
1060 E 70th St 90805
Connie Jensen, prin.
1,700/6-8
562-602-0302
Fax 602-1354
Hill MS
1100 Iroquois Ave 90815
Peter Davis, prin.
1,100/6-8
562-598-7611
Fax 598-6329
Hughes MS
3846 California Ave 90807
Monica Daley, prin.
1,500/6-8
562-595-0831
Fax 595-9221
Jefferson MS
750 Euclid Ave 90804
Helen Compton-Harris, prin.
1,200/6-8
562-438-9904
Fax 439-3718
Jordan 9th Grade Academy
171 W Bort St 90805
Rosalind Morgan, prin.
9-9
562-984-3710
Fax 423-0781
Jordan HS
6500 Atlantic Ave 90805
Kelly Hurley, prin.
4,300/9-12
562-423-1471
Fax 422-9091
Lindbergh MS
1022 E Market St 90805
Dr. Avery Hall, prin.
1,400/6-8
562-422-2845
Fax 423-8176
Long Beach Polytechnic HS
1600 Atlantic Ave 90813
Shawn Ashley, prin.
Vo/Tech
562-591-0581
Fax 591-0631
Marshall MS
5870 E Wardlow Rd 90808
Sherryl Johnson, prin.
1,400/6-8
562-429-7013
Fax 496-1489
Millikan HS
2800 Snowden Ave 90815
Jefferey Cornejo, prin.
3,900/9-12
562-425-7441
Fax 425-1151
Renaissance HS for the Arts
235 E 8th St 90813
Mark Zahn, prin.
500/9-12
562-901-0168
Fax 435-7147
Rogers MS
365 Monrovia Ave 90803
Thomas Huff, prin.
900/6-8
562-434-7411
Fax 434-0581
Stanford MS
5871 E Los Arcos St 90815
1,400/6-8
562-594-9793
Fax 594-8591
Stephens MS
1830 W Columbia St 90810
Diane Brown, prin.
1,600/6-8
562-595-0841
Fax 426-5631
Washington MS
1450 Cedar Ave 90813
Deborah Stark, prin.
1,300/4-8
562-591-2434
Fax 591-6888
Wilson HS
4400 E 10th St 90804
Alejandro Flores, prin.
4,400/9-12
562-433-0481
Fax 433-2731
Evening S
1515 Hughes Way 90810
Matthew Saldana, prin.
Adult
562-989-7872
Fax 997-8650

Long Beach School for Adults
3701 E Willow St 90815
Fitzgerald Jones, prin.
Other Schools – See Avalon, Carson, Lakewood
Adult
562-595-8893
Fax 988-1924

Regional Occupational Center & Program
Supt. — None
Long Beach USD ROC/P
3701B E Willow St 90815
Matt Saldana, dir.
Vo/Tech
562-595-8893
Fax 424-8976

American Institute of Health Science
3501 Atlantic Ave 90807
Post-Sec.
562-988-2278
Brooks College
4825 E Pacific Coast Hwy 90804
Post-Sec.
562-597-6611
California State University-Long Beach
1250 N Bellflower Blvd 90840
Post-Sec.
562-985-4111
DeVry University
3880 Kilroy Airport Way 90806
Post-Sec.
562-427-0861
First Baptist Church S
1000 Pine Ave 90813
James Allen, prin.
200/K-12
562-432-8447
Fax 499-6847
Gethsemane Baptist Christian S
6095 Orange Ave 90805
Dr. David Smith, prin.
100/K-12
562-422-4206
John Wesley Intl. Barber/Beauty Coll
717 Pine Ave 90813
Post-Sec.
562-435-7060
Long Beach City College
4901 E Carson St 90808
Post-Sec.
562-938-4111
National Institute of Technology
2161 Technology Pl 90810
Post-Sec.
562-437-0501
New Life Christian Academy
PO Box 5217 90805
100/PK-12
562-423-9000
Fax 423-4019
Pacific Baptist S
3332 Magnolia Ave 90806
Dr. Joseph Esposito, prin.
200/K-12
562-426-5214
St. Anthony HS
620 Olive Ave 90802
Gina Rushing, pres.
200/9-12
562-435-4496
Fax 437-3055
Southwestern Longview Private S
4747 Daisy Ave 90805
Clarence Horton, dir.
200/K-12
562-422-1582

Loomis, Placer, Pop. 6,312
Placer UNHSD
Supt. — See Auburn
Del Oro HS
3301 Taylor Rd 95650
Bob Christiansen, prin.
1,600/9-12
916-652-7243
Fax 652-3706

Los Alamitos, Orange, Pop. 11,697
Los Alamitos USD
10293 Bloomfield St 90720
Carol Hart, supt.
www.losalusd.k12.ca.us
9,100/PK-12
562-799-4700
Fax 799-4711
Los Alamitos HS
3591 Cerritos Ave 90720
Kelley Godfrey, prin.
3,000/9-12
562-799-4780
Fax 799-4798
McAuliffe MS
4112 Cerritos Ave 90720
Dennis Sackett, prin.
1,200/6-8
714-816-3320
Fax 816-3362
Oak MS
10821 Oak St 90720
David Downing, prin.
1,100/6-8
562-799-4740
Fax 799-4773

Los Altos, Santa Clara, Pop. 27,173
Los Altos ESD
201 Covington Rd 94024
Tim Justus, supt.
www.losaltos.k12.ca.us
4,100/K-8
650-947-1150
Fax 947-0118
Blach IS
1120 Covington Rd 94024
Arthur Harris, prin.
400/7-8
650-934-3800
Fax 968-3918
Egan IS
100 W Portola Ave 94022
Brenda Dyckman, prin.
500/7-8
650-917-2200
Fax 949-3748

Mountain View-Los Altos UNHSD
Supt. — See Mountain View
Los Altos HS
201 Almond Ave 94022
Wynne Satterwhite, prin.
1,600/9-12
650-968-6571
Fax 948-8672

Los Altos Hills, Santa Clara, Pop. 8,097

Foothill College
12345 S El Monte Rd 94022
Post-Sec.
650-949-7777
Pinewood S - Upper Campus
26800 W Fremont Rd 94022
Scott Riches, pres.
300/7-12
650-941-1532
Fax 941-4727

Los Angeles, Los Angeles, Pop. 3,819,951
Compton USD
Supt. — See Compton
Vanguard Learning Center
13305 S San Pedro St 90061
Sonja Bankston-Cullen, prin.
1,100/4-8
310-898-6050
Fax 327-7180

Los Angeles USD
333 S Beaudry Ave 90017
Roy Romer, supt.
www.lausd.k12.ca.us
750,200/PK-12
213-241-7000
Fax 241-8442
Adams MS
151 W 30th St 90007
Joseph Santana, prin.
2,200/6-8
213-744-1502
Fax 749-8542
Audubon MS
4120 11th Ave 90008
Laverne Brunt, prin.
2,000/6-8
323-299-2882
Fax 296-2433
Bancroft MS
929 N Las Palmas Ave 90038
Annie Lykes Webb, prin.
1,400/6-8
323-461-3174
Fax 461-8246
Belmont HS
1575 W 2nd St 90026
Gary Yoshinobu, prin.
5,000/9-12
213-250-0244
Fax 250-9706
Belvedere MS
312 N Record Ave 90063
2,500/6-8
323-266-3730
Fax 269-6769
Berendo MS
1157 S Berendo St 90006
Jeanette Stevens, prin.
3,200/6-8
213-382-1343
Fax 382-8599
Bethune MS
155 W 69th St 90003
Daryl Narimatsu, prin.
2,600/6-8
323-971-3646
Fax 759-1271

Bravo Medical Magnet HS 1,700/9-12
1200 Cornwell St 90033 323-342-0428
Maria Flores, prin. Fax 342-9139
Burbank MS 2,100/6-8
6460 N Figueroa St 90042 323-255-0108
Omar Del Cueto, prin. Fax 257-7420
Burroughs MS 2,300/6-8
600 S Mccadden Pl 90005 323-938-9146
Mirta McKay, prin. Fax 934-9051
Carver MS 2,700/6-8
4410 McKinley Ave 90011 323-233-3261
Evelyn Wesley, prin. Fax 232-5344
Clay MS 1,900/6-8
12226 S Western Ave 90047 323-757-4181
Pamela Gartrell Jackson, prin. Fax 777-6056
Crenshaw HS 2,800/9-12
5010 11th Ave 90043 323-296-5370
Charles Didinger, prin. Fax 292-6712
Dorsey HS 2,000/9-12
3537 Farmdale Ave 90016 323-296-7120
George Bartleson, prin. Fax 298-8501
Downtown Business HS 1,100/9-12
1081 W Temple St 90012 213-481-0371
Jessica White, prin. Fax 482-0792
Drew MS 2,600/6-8
8511 Compton Ave 90001 323-583-6961
Joyce Brown, prin. Fax 583-6030
Eagle Rock JSHS 2,800/7-12
1750 Yosemite Dr 90041 323-254-6891
Salvador Antoni Velasco, prin. Fax 255-3398
Edison MS 2,400/6-8
6500 Hooper Ave 90001 323-587-5108
Faye Banton, prin. Fax 581-8389
El Sereno MS 2,400/6-8
2839 N Eastern Ave 90032 323-223-2441
Arthur Duardo, prin. Fax 223-9024
Emerson MS 1,400/6-8
1650 Selby Ave 90024 310-475-8417
Charlotte Lerchenmuller, prin. Fax 474-6517
Fairfax HS 2,800/9-12
7850 Melrose Ave 90046 323-651-5200
Heather Daims, prin. Fax 651-5803
Fashion Careers Magnet S Vo/Tech
1081 W Temple St 90012 213-481-0371
Fax 482-0792
Franklin HS 3,200/9-12
820 N Avenue 54 90042 323-254-7104
Luis Manuel Lopez, prin. Fax 258-5940
Fremont HS 4,800/9-12
7676 S San Pedro St 90003 323-758-4141
Rosa Denny, prin. Fax 971-5890
Garfield HS 4,600/9-12
5101 E 6th St 90022 323-268-9361
Guadalupe Paramo, prin. Fax 268-4957
Gompers MS 1,800/6-8
234 E 112th St 90061 323-757-9211
Diana Garcia, prin. Fax 418-0778
Griffith MS 2,200/6-8
4765 E 4th St 90022 323-266-6106
Joseph Caldera, prin. Fax 268-6375
Hamilton HS 2,800/9-12
2955 S Robertson Blvd 90034 310-836-1602
Joseph Guidetti, prin. Fax 842-8663
Harte Prep MS 1,700/6-8
9301 S Hoover St 90044 323-757-9143
Linda Kay, prin. Fax 757-0408
Hollenbeck MS 2,700/6-8
2510 E 6th St 90023 323-268-0176
Victoria Castro, prin. Fax 265-0865
Hollywood HS 3,000/9-12
1521 N Highland Ave 90028 323-461-3891
Fonna Bishop, prin. Fax 957-0238
Irving MS 1,700/6-8
3010 Estara Ave 90065 323-256-2123
Edward Zubiate, prin. Fax 254-6447
Jefferson HS 3,600/9-12
1319 E 41st St 90011 323-232-2261
Juan Flecha, prin. Fax 231-4755
Jordan HS 2,500/9-12
2265 E 103rd St 90002 323-567-0531
Stephen Strachan, prin. Fax 249-4709
King-Drew Medical Magnet HS 1,700/9-12
1601 E 120th St 90059 323-566-0420
Juanita Woods, prin. Fax 567-1429
King MS 3,000/6-8
4201 Fountain Ave 90029 323-664-1176
Charlene Hirotsu, prin. Fax 913-3594
LA Center for Enriched Studies 1,600/6-12
5931 W 18th St 90035 323-938-1620
Margaret Kim, prin. Fax 938-8737
Lincoln HS 2,700/9-12
3501 N Broadway 90031 323-223-4021
James Molina, prin. Fax 223-1291
Locke HS 2,800/9-12
325 E 111th St 90061 323-757-9381
Frank Wells, prin. Fax 779-1322
Los Angeles Academy 2,900/6-8
644 E 56th St 90011 323-232-7820
Maria Borges, prin. Fax 231-0136
Los Angeles HS 4,600/9-12
4650 W Olympic Blvd 90019 323-937-3210
Frank Nishimura, prin. Fax 936-8455
Los Angeles Technology Center Vo/Tech
3721 W Washington Blvd 90018 323-732-0153
Maxine Hammond, prin. Fax 731-1568
Mann MS 1,400/6-8
7001 S St Andrews Pl 90047 323-778-9450
Cynthia Arceneaux, prin. Fax 758-8203
Manual Arts HS 3,900/9-12
4131 S Vermont Ave 90037 323-232-1121
Hugo Pedroza, prin. Fax 232-0837
Marina Del Rey MS 1,300/6-8
12500 Braddock Dr 90066 310-822-6788
Erick Mata, prin. Fax 821-3248
Markham MS 1,900/6-8
1650 E 104th St 90002 323-564-6951
Miyahara Allwelt, prin. Fax 569-6066
Marshall HS 4,400/9-12
3939 Tracy St 90027 323-660-1440
Thomas Abraham, prin. Fax 665-8682
Mt. Vernon MS 1,700/6-8
4066 W 17th St 90019 323-733-2157
Scott Schmerelson, prin. Fax 733-9106

Muir MS 2,200/6-8
5929 S Vermont Ave 90044 323-971-4361
Bernard Kleiner, prin. Fax 778-9824
Nightingale MS 1,900/6-8
3311 N Figueroa St 90065 323-221-2128
Manuel Diaz, prin. Fax 222-4506
Palms MS 1,900/6-8
10860 Woodbine St 90034 310-837-5236
Bonnie Murrow, prin. Fax 559-0397
Roosevelt HS 4,700/9-12
456 S Mathews St 90033 323-268-7241
Cecilia Quemada, prin. Fax 269-5473
South Los Angeles Area HS 9-12
1921 Maple Ave 90011 213-763-1000
Vince Carbino, prin. Fax 742-9883
Stevenson MS 2,400/6-8
725 S Indiana St 90023 323-262-4101
Teresa Hurtado, prin. Fax 265-3952
Thirty Second Street USC Magnet S 1,000/K-12
822 W 32nd St 90007 213-748-0126
Gail Greer, prin. Fax 744-1608
Twain MS 1,300/6-8
2224 Walgrove Ave 90066 310-397-2125
Jeffrey Felz, prin. Fax 398-1627
University HS 2,300/9-12
11800 Texas Ave 90025 310-478-9833
Elois McGehee, prin. Fax 478-6535
Venice HS 2,900/9-12
13000 Venice Blvd 90066 310-306-7981
Janice Davis, prin. Fax 306-3249
Virgil MS 2,600/6-8
152 N Vermont Ave 90004 213-388-0347
Barbara Sandusky, prin. Fax 389-8973
Washington Prep HS 2,800/9-12
10860 S Denker Ave 90047 323-757-9281
Herbert Jones, prin. Fax 754-3517
Webster MS 1,300/6-8
11330 Graham Pl 90064 310-478-2041
Kendra Nichols Wallace, prin. Fax 477-0146
Westchester HS 2,500/9-12
7400 W Manchester Ave 90045 310-670-4003
Anita Barner, prin. Fax 410-1067
Wilson HS 2,800/9-12
4500 Multnomah St 90032 323-223-1131
Robert Martinez, prin. Fax 223-7936
Wright MS 1,400/6-8
6550 W 80th St 90045 310-670-5666
Stephen Rochelle, prin. Fax 568-8942
Belmont Community Adult Education Adult
1575 W 2nd St 90026 213-250-9133
Roger Miller, prin. Fax 250-9272
Central Adult HS Adult
211 W 17th St 90015 213-745-6079
Fax 749-7628
Crenshaw/Washington Adult Education Adult
5010 11th Ave 90043 323-292-9184
Fax 294-8783
East Los Angeles Skills Center Adult
3921 Selig Pl 90031 323-227-0018
Pete Fernandez, prin. Fax 222-2351
Evans Community Adult Education Adult
717 N Figueroa St 90012 213-626-7151
Jean Batey, prin. Fax 626-4487
Franklin Adult Education Adult
820 N Avenue 54 90042 323-256-2144
Dianne Baird, prin. Fax 256-2790
Fremont Community Adult S Adult
7676 S San Pedro St 90003 323-778-1651
Michael Wada, prin. Fax 778-8531
Friedman Occupational Center Adult
1646 S Olive St 90015 213-745-2013
Howard Saxe, prin. Fax 748-7406
Garfield Adult Education Adult
5101 E 6th St 90022 323-262-5163
Wanda Chang, prin. Fax 266-3294
Hollywood Community Adult Education Adult
1521 N Highland Ave 90028 323-467-6191
Eva Green, prin. Fax 467-3382
Jefferson Adult S Adult
1319 E 41st St 90011 323-231-1166
France Wong, prin. Fax 233-9658
Jordan-Locke Adult Education Adult
325 E 111th St 90061 323-757-8296
Fax 757-9416
Los Angeles Adult Education Adult
4650 W Olympic Blvd 90019 323-931-1026
Claudine Ajeti, prin. Fax 936-5496
Manual Arts-Crenshaw Community Adult S Adult
4131 S Vermont Ave 90037 323-234-9177
Maureen Jensen, prin. Fax 234-1310
Metropolitan Skills Center Adult
2801 W 6th St 90057 213-386-7269
Cynthia Moore, prin. Fax 386-4554
Roosevelt Community Adult S Adult
456 S Mathews St 90033 323-263-9388
Clifton De Cordoba, prin. Fax 263-5040
Venice Community Adult S Adult
13000 Venice Blvd 90066 310-306-8111
Fred Webb Hermosillo, prin. Fax 306-7336
Waters Employment Preparation Center Adult
10925 S Central Ave 90059 323-564-4451
Janet Clark, prin. Fax 566-0147
Westchester-Emerson Community Adult S Adult
7400 W Manchester Ave 90045 310-641-4867
Patricia Colby, prin. Fax 645-8043
Westside Community Adult S Adult
7850 Melrose Ave 90046 323-653-4085
Paul Hamel, prin. Fax 653-3004
Wilson-Lincoln Adult Education Adult
4500 Multnomah St 90032 323-223-3311
Gertrude Hawkins, prin. Fax 221-0543
Other Schools – See Bell, Canoga Park, Carson, Chatsworth, Cudahy, Gardena, Granada Hills, Harbor City, Hollywood, Huntington Park, Lomita, Maywood, Mission Hills, North Hollywood, Northridge, Pacoima, Rancho Palos Verdes, Reseda, San Fernando, San Pedro, Sepulveda, Sherman Oaks, South Gate, Sunland, Sun Valley, Sylmar, Tarzana, Tujunga, Van Nuys, Wilmington, Woodland Hills

Regional Occupational Center & Program
Supt. — None
Los Angeles USD ROC/P Vo/Tech
333 S Beaudry Ave 90017 213-241-3801
Dominick Cistone, admin. Fax 241-6836

American Career College Post-Sec.
4021 Rosewood Ave 90004 323-383-2862
American Film Institute Post-Sec.
2021 N Western Ave 90027 323-856-7600
American InterContinental University Post-Sec.
12655 W Jefferson Blvd 90066 310-302-2000
Archer S for Girls 500/6-12
11725 W Sunset Blvd 90049 310-873-7000
Arlene Hogan, hdmstr. Fax 873-7070
Arshag Dickranian Armenian S 300/PK-12
1200 N Cahuenga Blvd 90038 323-461-4377
Vartkes Kourouyan, prin. Fax 461-4247
Associated Technical College Post-Sec.
1670 Wilshire Blvd 90017 213-353-1845
Bais Chana Chabad HS 100/9-12
9017 W Pico Blvd 90035 310-278-8995
Batya Lisker, prin. Fax 278-9256
Bais Yaakov S 200/9-12
7353 Beverly Blvd 90036 323-938-3231
Rabbi Yoel Bursztyn, prin. Fax 930-0477
Bishop Conaty-Our Lady Loretta HS 400/9-12
2900 W Pico Blvd 90006 323-737-0012
Sharon Morano, prin. Fax 737-1749
Bishop Mora Salesian HS 400/9-12
960 S Soto St 90023 323-261-7124
Manuel Villarreal, prin. Fax 261-7600
Brentwood S 600/7-12
100 S Barrington Pl 90049 310-476-9633
Dr. Michael Pratt, hdmstr. Fax 476-4087
Bryan College Post-Sec.
2333 Beverly Blvd 90057 213-484-8850
Bryman College Post-Sec.
3460 Wilshire Blvd Ste 500 90010 213-388-9950
Bryman College Post-Sec.
3000 S Robertson Blvd 90034 310-840-5777
California Design College Post-Sec.
3440 Wilshire Blvd Ste 700 90010 213-251-3636
California Healing Arts College Post-Sec.
12217 Santa Monica Blvd 90025 310-826-7622
California State University-Los Angeles Post-Sec.
5151 State University Dr 90032 323-343-3000
Cathedral HS 600/9-12
1253 Bishop Rd 90012 323-225-2438
Br. John Montgomery, prin. Fax 222-7223
CEI Post-Sec.
3699 Wilshire Blvd Fl 4 90010 213-351-2000
Charles R. Drew Univ. of Med. & Science Post-Sec.
1621 E 120th St 90059 323-563-4800
Chase College Post-Sec.
3580 Wilshire Blvd Fl 4 90010 213-365-1999
Children's Hospital of Los Angeles Post-Sec.
4650 W Sunset Blvd 90027 323-669-2301
Cleveland Chiropractic College of LA Post-Sec.
590 N Vermont Ave 90004 323-660-6166
Colburn School Post-Sec.
200 S Grand Ave 90012 213-621-2200
Concord Law School Post-Sec.
10866 Wilshire Blvd # 1200 90024 800-439-4794
Dongguk Royal University Post-Sec.
440 Shatto Pl 90020 213-487-0110
East Los Angeles Occupational Center Post-Sec.
2100 Marengo St 90033 323-223-1283
Escuelas Leicester Post-Sec.
1940 S Figueroa St 90007 213-746-7666
FIDM/The Fashion Institute Post-Sec.
919 S Grand Ave 90015 213-624-1200
Golden Day S 400/K-12
4508 Crenshaw Blvd 90043 323-296-6280
Clark Parker, prin. Fax 290-0190
Harvard-Westlake S 700/7-9
700 N Faring Rd 90077 310-274-7281
Thomas Hudnut, hdmstr. Fax 288-3331
Hebrew Union College Post-Sec.
3077 University Ave 90007 213-749-3424
ICDC College Post-Sec.
5422 W Sunset Blvd 90027 323-468-0404
Immaculate Heart HS 500/9-12
5515 Franklin Ave 90028 323-461-3651
Sr. Virginia Hurst, prin. Fax 462-0610
Immaculate Heart MS 200/6-8
5515 Franklin Ave 90028 323-461-3651
Ann Phelps, prin. Fax 462-0610
Institute of Computer Technology Post-Sec.
3200 Wilshire Blvd Fl 4 90010 213-381-3333
International Christian Education Coll. Post-Sec.
3807 Wilshire Blvd Ste 730 90010 213-368-0316
John Scholastic Academy 100/7-12
100 E 49th St 90011 323-234-2400
Nancy Baker Orduna, admin. Fax 234-2492
John Tracy Clinic Post-Sec.
806 W Adams Blvd 90007 213-748-5481
Le Lycee Francais de Los Angeles 1,000/PK-12
3261 Overland Ave 90034 310-836-3464
Alain Anselme, dir. Fax 558-8069
Liberty Training Institute Post-Sec.
2706 Wilshire Blvd 90057 213-383-9545
Little Citizens Westside Academy 100/1-12
4256 S Western Ave 90062 323-293-9775
Angela Moore, admin.
Los Angeles Adventist Academy 300/PK-12
846 E El Segundo Blvd 90059 323-321-2585
Dr. Lilly Nelson, prin. Fax 324-3207
Los Angeles City College Post-Sec.
855 N Vermont Ave 90029 323-953-4000
Los Angeles Co. Coll. Nursing/Alld Hlth Post-Sec.
1200 N State St 90033 323-226-4911
Los Angeles Southwest College Post-Sec.
1600 W Imperial Hwy 90047 323-241-5225
Los Angeles Trade-Technical College Post-Sec.
400 W Washington Blvd 90015 213-744-9058
Loyola HS 1,200/9-12
1901 Venice Blvd 90006 213-381-5121
Bill Thomason, prin. Fax 368-3819
Loyola Marymount University Post-Sec.
PO Box 15019 90015 213-736-1180
Loyola Marymount University Post-Sec.
7900 Loyola Blvd 90045 310-338-2700
Lycee International De Los Angeles 500/PK-12
4155 Russell Ave 90027 323-665-4526
Elizabeth Chaponot, dir. Fax 665-2607
Marinello School of Beauty Post-Sec.
716 S Broadway Fl 2 90014 213-627-5561
Marinello School of Beauty Post-Sec.
6111 Wilshire Blvd 90048 323-938-2005

Marinello School of Beauty — Post-Sec.
2700 Colorado Blvd Ste 266 90041 — 323-254-6226
Marlborough HS — 500/7-12
250 S Rossmore Ave 90004 — 323-935-1147
Barbara Wagner, hdmstr. — Fax 933-0542
Marymount HS — 400/9-12
10643 W Sunset Blvd 90077 — 310-472-1205
Mary Gozdecki, prin. — Fax 476-0910
Medical Institute — Post-Sec.
5170 Santa Monica Blvd #300 90029 — 323-663-2700
Mt. St. Mary's College — Post-Sec.
12001 Chalon Rd 90049 — 310-954-4000
Mt. St. Mary's College - Doheny Campus — Post-Sec.
10 Chester Pl 90007 — 213-746-0450
Murphy Catholic HS — 400/9-12
241 S Detroit St 90036 — 323-935-1161
Denis Munoz, prin. — Fax 935-1621
Netan Eli HS — 50/9-12
1445 S Robertson Blvd 90035 — 310-553-7150
Rabbi Sholom Weil, prin. — Fax 553-2199
New Covenant Academy — 100/6-12
1111 W Sunset Blvd 90012 — 213-250-1600
Jason Song, admin. — Fax 250-1601
New West Technical Academy — 100/5-12
10531 S Vermont Ave 90044 — 310-241-1850
Dr. Andrew Manley, pres.
Notre Dame Academy for Girls — 500/9-12
2851 Overland Ave 90064 — 310-839-5289
— Fax 839-7957
Occidental College — Post-Sec.
1600 Campus Rd 90041 — 323-259-2500
Ohr Haemet Institute — 50/9-12
1030 S Robertson Blvd 90035 — 310-854-3006
David Akhamzadeh, dir. — Fax 854-6689
Optimist HS — 200/7-12
PO Box 411076 90041 — 310-443-3100
Alan Eskot, dir. — Fax 443-3264
Otis College of Art and Design — Post-Sec.
9045 Lincoln Blvd 90045 — 310-665-6800
Pacific Hills S — 300/6-12
8628 Holloway Dr 90069 — 310-276-3068
Richard Makoff, hdmstr. — Fax 657-3831
Pacific States University — Post-Sec.
1516 S Western Ave 90006 — 323-731-2383
Pacific Union College — Post-Sec.
1720 E Cesar E Chavez Ave 90033 — 323-268-5000
Pepperdine University — Post-Sec.
6100 Center Dr 90045 — 310-568-5500
Pilgrim S — 400/PK-12
540 S Commonwealth Ave 90020 — 213-385-7351
Mark Brooks, prin. — Fax 386-7264
Pilibos Armenian S — 700/K-12
1615 N Alexandria Ave 90027 — 323-668-2661
Viken Yacoubian, prin. — Fax 662-0332
Price S — 300/PK-12
7901 S Vermont Ave 90044 — 323-565-4199
Veon Bradford, prin. — Fax 753-6770
Ribet Academy — 500/K-12
2911 N San Fernando Rd 90065 — 323-344-4330
Teresa Ruiz, prin. — Fax 344-4339
Sacred Heart of Jesus HS — 400/9-12
2111 Griffin Ave 90031 — 323-225-2209
Sr. Mary Diane Scott, prin. — Fax 225-5046
Samra University of Oriental Medicine — Post-Sec.
3000 S Robertson Blvd Fl 4 90034 — 310-202-6444
Shalhevet HS — 300/5-12
910 S Fairfax Ave 90036 — 323-930-9333
Ken Milman, prin.
Southern California Inst. Architecture — Post-Sec.
960 E 3rd St 90013 — 213-613-2200
Southwestern University School of Law — Post-Sec.
675 S Westmoreland Ave 90005 — 213-738-6700
Summit View S - Westside — 200/1-12
12101 W Washington Blvd 90066 — 310-751-1100
Nancy Rosenfelt, dir.
SUTECH School of Voc/Tech Training — Post-Sec.
PO Box 23098 90023 — 323-262-3210
UCLA Center for the Health Sciences — Post-Sec.
10833 Le Conte Ave 90095 — 310-825-5654
Universal College of Beauty — Post-Sec.
8619 S Vermont Ave 90044 — 323-750-5750
Universal College of Beauty — Post-Sec.
3419 W 43rd Pl 90008 — 323-298-0045
University of California 90095 — Post-Sec.
— 310-825-4321
University of Judaism — Post-Sec.
15600 Mulholland Dr 90077 — 310-476-9777
University of Southern California — Post-Sec.
Health Science Campus 90033 — 323-226-6501
University of Southern California — Post-Sec.
Univ Park 90089 — 213-740-2311
Verbum Dei HS — 200/9-12
11100 S Central Ave 90059 — 323-564-6651
Susan B. Abelein, prin. — Fax 564-9009
Village Glen S - Westside — 200/K-12
4160 Grand View Blvd 90066 — 310-751-1101
Pamela Clark, dir.
Virginia School Center — Post-Sec.
1033 S Broadway 90015 — 213-747-8292
Vista S — 300/K-12
3200 Motor Ave 90034 — 310-836-1223
Donna Baker, dir. — Fax 836-3506
West Los Angeles Baptist S — 100/1-12
1609 S Barrington Ave 90025 — 310-826-2050
James Lennon, prin. — Fax 826-0970
West Los Angeles VA Medical Center — Post-Sec.
Wilshire & Sawtelle Blvds 90073 — 310-824-3132
Westview S, 2000 Stoner Ave 90025 — 100/6-12
Judith Gordon, prin. — 310-478-5544
Westwood College — Post-Sec.
3250 Wilshire Blvd 4th Flr 90010 — 213-739-9999
Wildwood Secondary S — 400/7-12
11811 W Olympic Blvd 90064 — 310-478-7189
Hope Boyd, hdmstr. — Fax 478-6875
Windward S — 500/7-12
11350 Palms Blvd 90066 — 310-391-7127
Thomas Gilder, hdmstr. — Fax 397-5655
Wise Temple S — 1,500/K-12
15500 Stephen S Wise Dr 90077 — 310-889-2282
Metuka Benjamin, dir. — Fax 476-2353
World Mission University — Post-Sec.
500 Shatto Pl Ste 600 90020 — 213-385-2322
Yeshiva Gedola of Los Angeles HS — 100/9-12
5444 W Olympic Blvd 90036 — 323-938-2071
Rabbi Yaakov Gross, dir. — Fax 938-4650

Yeshiva Ohr Elchonon Chabad — Post-Sec.
7215 Waring Ave 90046 — 323-937-3763
Yeshiva Ohr Elchonon Chabad West Coast — 100/9-12
7215 Waring Ave 90046 — 323-937-3763
Rabbi Ezra Schochet, dean — Fax 937-9456
Yeshiva University Boys HS — 300/9-12
9760 W Pico Blvd 90035 — 310-229-0936
Dovid Landesman, prin. — Fax 203-3199
Yeshiva University Girls HS — 200/9-12
1619 S Robertson Blvd 90035 — 310-203-0755
Deborah Shrier, prin. — Fax 551-0312
Yo San Univ. of Traditional Chinese Med. — Post-Sec.
13315 W Washington Blvd 90066 — 310-577-3000

Los Banos, Merced, Pop. 30,538
Los Banos USD — 8,400/K-12
1717 S 11th St 93635 — 209-826-3801
Paul Alderete, supt. — Fax 826-6810
www.losbanosusd.k12.ca.us
Los Banos HS — 2,100/9-12
1966 S 11th St 93635 — 209-826-6033
Dan Martin, prin. — Fax 827-4156
Los Banos JHS — 1,300/7-8
1750 San Luis St 93635 — 209-826-0867
Paul Enos, prin. — Fax 826-8532

Merced College-Los Banos Campus — Post-Sec.
16570 S Mercey Springs Rd 93635 — 209-826-3431

Los Gatos, Santa Clara, Pop. 27,976
Campbell UNSD
Supt. — See Campbell
Rolling Hills MS — 1,000/5-8
1585 More Ave 95032 — 408-364-4235
Kathleen Gibbs, prin. — Fax 341-7010

Loma Prieta JUNESD — 800/K-8
23800 Summit Rd 95033 — 408-353-1101
Henry Castaniada, supt. — Fax 353-8051
www.loma.k12.ca.us
English MS — 300/6-8
23800 Summit Rd 95033 — 408-353-1123
Diana Hallock, prin. — Fax 353-5024

Los Gatos UNESD — 2,600/K-8
17010 Roberts Rd 95032 — 408-335-2000
Suzanne Boxer-Gassman Ed.D., supt. — Fax 395-6481
www.lgusd.k12.ca.us
Fisher MS — 1,000/6-8
19195 Fisher Ave 95032 — 408-335-2000
Lisa Fraser, prin. — Fax 335-2328

Los Gatos-Saratoga JUNHSD — 2,900/9-12
17421 Farley Rd W 95030 — 408-354-2520
Cynthia Ranii, supt. — Fax 354-3375
www.lgsuhsd.org
Los Gatos HS — 1,600/9-12
20 High School Ct 95030 — 408-354-2730
Trudy McCulloch, prin. — Fax 354-3742
Other Schools — See Saratoga

Los Molinos, Tehama, Pop. 1,709
Los Molinos USD — 600/K-12
7851 Highway 99 E 96055 — 530-384-7826
Dave Pilger, supt. — Fax 384-7832
www.lmusd.tehama.k12.ca.us
Los Molinos HS — 200/9-12
PO Box 609 96055 — 530-384-7900
Dave Pilger, prin. — Fax 384-1534

Los Nietos, Los Angeles, Pop. 24,164
Los Nietos ESD — 2,400/K-8
PO Box 2405 90610 — 562-692-0271
Lillian Maldonado-French, supt. — Fax 699-3395
www.losnietos.k12.ca.us
Los Nietos MS — 800/6-8
11425 Rivera Rd 90606 — 562-695-0637
Les Mazon, prin. — Fax 695-3805

Los Olivos, Santa Barbara

Dunn S — 200/6-12
PO Box 98 93441 — 805-688-6471
Carlos Ortiz, admin. — Fax 686-2078
Midland S — 100/9-12
PO Box 8 93441 — 805-688-5114
David S. Lourie, hdmstr. — Fax 686-2470

Los Osos, San Luis Obispo, Pop. 14,377
San Luis Coastal USD
Supt. — See San Luis Obispo
Los Osos MS — 600/6-8
1555 El Morro Ave 93402 — 805-534-2835
Diane Frost, prin. — Fax 528-5133

Lost Hills, Kern, Pop. 1,212
Lost Hills Union SD — 600/K-8
PO Box 158 93249 — 661-797-2626
Jerry Scott, supt. — Fax 797-2580
Thomas MS — 200/5-8
PO Box 158 93249 — 661-797-3019
Donna Jackson, prin. — Fax 797-3015

Lower Lake, Lake, Pop. 1,217
Konocti USD — 3,400/K-12
PO Box 5000 95457 — 707-994-6475
Louise Nan, supt. — Fax 994-0210
www.konoctiusd.lake.k12.ca.us/
Lower Lake HS — 900/9-12
PO Box 799 95457 — 707-994-6471
Dan Herrera, prin. — Fax 994-4050
Konocti Adult S — Adult
PO Box 309 95457 — 707-994-7142
Bill MacDougall, prin. — Fax 994-4421
Other Schools — See Clearlake

Loyalton, Sierra, Pop. 847
Sierra-Plumas JUSD
Supt. — See Sierraville
Loyalton HS — 200/9-12
PO Box 37 96118 — 530-993-4454
Lisa Evans, prin. — Fax 993-4667
Loyalton MS — 100/6-8
PO Box 5 96118 — 530-993-4186
Penny Berry, prin. — Fax 993-0828

Lucerne Valley, San Bernardino
Lucerne Valley UNSD — 1,000/K-12
10790 Barstow Rd 92356 — 760-248-6108
Dr. Jim Buckley, supt. — Fax 248-6677
www.lvsd.k12.ca.us/
Lucerne Valley HS — 300/9-12
10790 Barstow Rd 92356 — 760-248-2124
Tom Hunter, prin. — Fax 248-2162
Lucerne Valley MS — 200/7-8
10790 Barstow Rd 92356 — 760-248-2124
Tom Hunter, prin. — Fax 248-2162

Lynwood, Los Angeles, Pop. 71,619
Lynwood USD — 24,700/K-12
11321 Bullis Rd 90262 — 310-886-1600
Dr. Dhyan Lal, supt. — Fax 608-7483
www.lynwood.k12.ca.us
Chavez MS, 3898 Abbott Rd 90262 — 7-8
Dr. Nick Velasquez, prin. — 310-886-1600
Firebaugh HS — 9-9
5246 Martin Luther King Blv 90262 — 310-886-1600
Jonas Silverio, prin.
Hosler MS — 3,300/6-8
11300 Spruce St 90262 — 310-603-1447
— Fax 764-4124
Lynwood HS — 3,400/10-12
4050 E Imperial Hwy 90262 — 310-603-1582
Jose Urias, prin. — Fax 638-9253
Lynwood MS — 3,100/7-8
12124 Bullis Rd 90262 — 310-603-1466
Dr. Anim Mener, prin. — Fax 638-2156
Lynwood Adult S — Adult
4050 E Imperial Hwy 90262 — 310-604-3096
Jean Jones, prin. — Fax 635-9107

St. Francis Career College — Post-Sec.
3630 E Imperial Hwy 90262 — 310-603-1830

Mc Arthur, Shasta
Fall River JUSD
Supt. — See Burney
Fall River JSHS — 300/7-12
44215 Walnut St, — 530-336-5515
Elizabeth Kyle, prin. — Fax 336-6256

Mc Cloud, Siskiyou, Pop. 1,555
Siskiyou UNHSD
Supt. — See Mount Shasta
McCloud HS — 50/9-12
PO Box 1530, — 530-964-2181
James Burger, admin. — Fax 964-2011

Macdoel, Siskiyou
Butte Valley USD
Supt. — See Dorris
Butte Valley JHS — 100/7-9
13001 Old State Hwy 96058 — 530-398-4415
Ed Traverso, prin. — Fax 398-4401

Mc Farland, Kern, Pop. 7,133
McFarland USD — 2,900/K-12
601 2nd St 93250 — 661-792-3081
Jim Schiffman, supt. — Fax 792-2447
www.mcfarlandusd.com
Mc Farland HS — 700/9-12
259 W Sherwood Ave 93250 — 661-792-3126
Gabriel McCurtis, prin. — Fax 792-2315
Mc Farland MS — 700/6-8
405 Mast Ave 93250 — 661-792-3340
David Diaz, prin. — Fax 792-5681

Mc Kinleyville, Humboldt, Pop. 10,749
Mc Kinleyville UNESD — 1,300/K-8
2275 Central Ave, — 707-839-1549
Alan Jorgensen, supt. — Fax 839-1540
www.nohum.k12.ca.us/msd/
Mc Kinleyville MS — 500/6-8
2285 Central Ave, — 707-839-1508
Doug Oliveira, prin. — Fax 839-2548

Northern Humboldt UNHSD — 2,100/9-12
2755 McKinleyville Ave 95519 — 707-839-6470
Kenny Richards, supt. — Fax 839-6477
www.nohum.k12.ca.us
Mc Kinleyville HS — 800/9-12
1300 Murray Rd, — 707-839-6400
David Lonn, prin. — Fax 839-6407
Northern Humboldt Adult S — Adult
2755 McKinleyville Ave, — 707-839-6460
Brian Stephens, prin. — Fax 839-6457
Other Schools – See Arcata

Madera, Madera, Pop. 47,952
Golden Valley USD — 1,600/K-12
37479 Avenue 12, — 559-645-7500
Marilyn K. Shepherd, supt. — Fax 645-7144
www.gvusd.k12.ca.us
Liberty HS — 300/9-12
12220 Road 36, — 559-645-3500
Andy Alvarado, prin. — Fax 645-0174
Ranchos MS, 12220 Road 36, — 200/7-8
Ruben Diaz, prin. — 559-645-3550

Madera County Office of Education — 559-673-6051
28123 Avenue 14 93638 — Fax 673-5569
Sally Frazier Ed.D., supt.
www.maderacoe.k12.ca.us
Pioneer Technical Center — Vo/Tech
1025 S Madera Ave 93637 — 559-664-1600
Steve Carney, dir. — Fax 664-9501

Madera USD — 18,100/K-12
1902 Howard Rd 93637 — 559-675-4500
Julia O'Kane, supt. — Fax 671-7764
www.madera.k12.ca.us
Desmond MS — 7-8
26490 Martin St 93638 — 559-664-1775
Michael Lennemann, prin. — Fax 664-1308
Jefferson MS — 1,000/7-8
1407 Sunset Ave 93637 — 559-673-9286
Jesse Carrasco, prin. — Fax 673-6930
King MS — 1,000/7-8
601 Lilly St 93638 — 559-674-4681
Robert Chavez, prin. — Fax 674-4261

Madera HS North Campus | 4,000/9-12
200 S L St 93637 | 559-675-4444
Ron Pisk, prin. | Fax 675-4531
Madera HS South Campus | 9-12
26433 Avenue 13 93637 | 559-675-4450
Mike Rivard, prin. | Fax 675-9985
Madera Adult S | Adult
26355 Avenue 13 93637 | 559-675-4425
Dan Lindstrom, prin. | Fax 675-4562

Madera Beauty College | Post-Sec.
325 N Gateway Dr 93637 | 559-673-9201

Magalia, Butte, Pop. 8,987
Paradise USD
Supt. — See Paradise
Mountain Ridge MS | 300/6-8
13835 W Park Dr 95954 | 530-873-3864
Steve Harrington, prin. | Fax 873-4011

Malibu, Los Angeles, Pop. 13,223
Santa Monica-Malibu USD
Supt. — See Santa Monica
Malibu JSHS | 1,300/6-12
30215 Morning View Dr 90265 | 310-457-6801
Dr. Mark Kelly, prin. | Fax 457-4984

Pepperdine University | Post-Sec.
24255 Pacific Coast Hwy 90263 | 310-506-4000

Mammoth Lakes, Mono, Pop. 7,304
Mammoth USD | 1,200/K-12
PO Box 3509 93546 | 760-934-6802
Stan Halperin, supt. | Fax 934-6803
Mammoth HS | 300/9-12
PO Box 3149 93546 | 760-934-8541
Mike DeRisi, prin. | Fax 934-3008
Mammoth MS | 300/6-8
PO Box 2429 93546 | 760-934-7072
Gloria Vasquez, prin. | Fax 934-6803

Mono County Office of Education
Supt. — See Bridgeport
Mono County Adult S | Adult
PO Box 130 93546 | 760-934-0031
Janice Work, prin. | Fax 934-1443

Manhattan Beach, Los Angeles, Pop. 36,007
Manhattan Beach USD | 6,800/K-12
325 S Peck Ave 90266 | 310-318-7345
Gwen E. Gross, supt. | Fax 303-3822
www.manhattan.k12.ca.us
Manhattan Beach MS | 1,300/6-8
325 S Peck Ave 90266 | 310-545-4878
John Jackson, prin. | Fax 303-3829
Mira Costa HS | 2,400/9-12
325 S Peck Ave 90266 | 310-318-7337
Julie Ruisinger, prin. | Fax 303-3814

Manteca, San Joaquin, Pop. 59,500
Manteca USD | 29,700/K-12
PO Box 32 95336 | 209-825-3200
Cathy Nichols-Washer Ed.D., supt. | Fax 825-3295
www.mantecausd.net/
East Union HS | 1,800/9-12
1700 N Union Rd 95336 | 209-825-3125
John Alba, prin. | Fax 825-3148
Manteca HS | 1,600/9-12
450 E Yosemite Ave 95336 | 209-825-3150
Steve Winter, prin. | Fax 825-3158
Sierra HS | 1,900/9-12
1700 Thomas St 95337 | 209-825-3175
Rick Arucan, prin. | Fax 825-3198
Lindbergh Adult S | Adult
311 E North St 95336 | 209-825-3100
Howard Holtsman, prin. | Fax 825-3110
Other Schools – See Stockton

Maricopa, Kern, Pop. 1,154
Maricopa USD | 400/K-12
955 Stanislaus St 93252 | 661-769-8231
Barry Lindaman, supt. | Fax 769-8168
www.maricopaschools.org/
Maricopa HS | 100/9-12
955 Stanislaus St 93252 | 661-769-8234
Debra Marker, prin. | Fax 769-8168

Marina, Monterey, Pop. 18,919
Monterey Peninsula USD
Supt. — See Monterey
Los Árboles MS | 700/6-8
294 Hillcrest Ave 93933 | 831-384-3550
Shannon Lueken, prin. | Fax 384-6353

Mariposa, Mariposa, Pop. 1,152
Mariposa County USD | 2,600/K-12
PO Box 8 95338 | 209-742-0250
Patrick J. Holland Ed.D., supt. | Fax 966-4549
mariposa.k12.ca.us
Mariposa County HS | 700/9-12
PO Box 127 95338 | 209-742-0260
Rock Carlson, prin. | Fax 742-0264
Mariposa MS | 300/7-8
5171 Silva Rd 95338 | 209-742-0320
Bill Atwood, prin. | Fax 742-0382
Other Schools – See Coulterville, El Portal

Markleeville, Alpine
Alpine County Office of Education
43 Hawkside Dr 96120 | 530-694-2230
James Parsons, supt. | Fax 694-2379
www.alpinecoe.k12.ca.us
Alpine County Adult Education | Adult
43 Hawkside Dr 96120 | 530-694-2230
James W. Parsons, prin.

Martinez, Contra Costa, Pop. 36,595
Martinez USD | 5,400/K-12
921 Susana St 94553 | 925-313-0480
Dan White, supt. | Fax 313-0476
www.martinez.k12.ca.us/
Alhambra HS | 1,300/9-12
150 E St 94553 | 925-313-0440
Toni Taylor, prin. | Fax 229-2097

Martinez JHS | 1,100/6-8
1600 Court St 94553 | 925-313-0414
Louanne Petty, prin. | Fax 370-0143
Martinez Adult Center | Adult
600 F St 94553 | 925-228-3276
Marshall Burgamy, dir. | Fax 228-6989

Martinez Adult Education | Post-Sec.
600 F St 94553 | 925-228-3276
New Vistas Christian S | 50/6-12
68 Morello Ave 94553 | 925-370-7767
Maria Zablah, admin. | Fax 370-6395

Marysville, Yuba, Pop. 12,498
Marysville JUSD | 9,400/PK-12
1919 B St 95901 | 530-741-6000
Gay Todd Ph.D., supt. | Fax 742-0573
www.mjusd.k12.ca.us
Alicia IS | 600/6-8
1208 Pasado Rd 95901 | 530-741-6103
Jack Stokes, prin. | Fax 741-6129
Foothill IS | 300/6-8
5351 Fruitland Rd 95901 | 530-741-6130
Ken Doglio, prin. | Fax 741-6017
Marysville HS | 1,100/9-12
12 E 18th St 95901 | 530-741-6180
Gary Cena, prin. | Fax 741-7828
McKenney IS | 600/6-8
1904 Huston St 95901 | 530-741-6187
Charles Ward, prin. | Fax 741-6004
Marysville Adult S, 1919 B St 95901 | Adult
Carolyn Tindel, prin. | 530-741-6005
Other Schools – See Olivehurst

New Life Christian S | 200/PK-12
5736 Arboga Rd 95901 | 530-742-3033
Alison Harrell, admin. | Fax 741-8221
Yuba College | Post-Sec.
2088 N Beale Rd 95901 | 530-741-6700

Mather, Sacramento, Pop. 4,885

Institute of Technology - Sacramento | Post-Sec.
3695 Bleckely St 95655 | 916-363-4300
Institute of Technology - Sacramento | Post-Sec.
3695 Bleckely St 95655 | 916-363-4300

Maxwell, Colusa
Maxwell USD | 400/K-12
PO Box 788 95955 | 530-438-2052
Ron Turner, supt. | Fax 438-2693
www.maxwell.k12.ca.us
Maxwell HS | 100/9-12
PO Box 788 95955 | 530-438-2291
Ron Turner, prin. | Fax 438-2693

Maywood, Los Angeles, Pop. 28,751
Los Angeles USD
Supt. — See Los Angeles
Southeast Area Learning Center | 9-12
6125 Pine Ave 90270 | 323-832-4600
Sandra English, prin. | Fax 562-1020

Meadow Vista, Placer, Pop. 3,067
Placer Hills UNESD | 1,400/K-8
PO Box 68 95722 | 530-878-2606
David J. Dominguez, supt. | Fax 878-2663
www.phusd.k12.ca.us/
Other Schools – See Weimar

Mendocino, Mendocino
Mendocino USD | 800/K-12
PO Box 1154 95460 | 707-937-5868
| Fax 937-0714
musd.mcn.org/
Mendocino HS | 300/9-12
PO Box 226 95460 | 707-937-5871
Gail Dickenson, prin. | Fax 937-1552
Mendocino MS | 200/6-8
PO Box 226 95460 | 707-937-0564
Bronwyn Rhoades, prin. | Fax 937-4753

Mendota, Fresno, Pop. 8,473
Mendota USD | 2,500/K-12
115 McCabe Ave 93640 | 559-655-4942
Gilbert Rossette, supt. | Fax 655-4944
www.mendotausd.k12.ca.us/
McCabe JHS | 300/7-8
115 McCabe Ave 93640 | 559-655-4991
Perry Jensen, prin. | Fax 655-1229
Mendota HS | 600/9-12
115 McCabe Ave 93640 | 559-655-1993
Victor Villar, prin. | Fax 655-0223

Menifee, Riverside, Pop. 100
Menifee UNESD | 5,900/K-8
30205 Menifee Rd 92584 | 951-672-1851
Linda Callaway Ed.D., supt. | Fax 672-6447
www.menifeeusd.org
Bell Mountain MS | 1,000/6-8
28525 La Piedra Rd 92584 | 951-301-8496
Paul Drob, prin. | Fax 301-5286
Menifee Valley MS | 1,100/6-8
26255 Garbani Rd 92584 | 951-672-6400
Cynthia Deavers, prin. | Fax 672-6415

Perris UNHSD
Supt. — See Perris
Paloma Valley HS | 2,400/9-12
31375 Bradley Rd 92584 | 951-672-6030
Jim Smolenski, prin. | Fax 672-6037

Revival Christian Academy | 100/K-12
29220 Scott Rd 92584 | 951-672-3157
Diana Miller, dir. | Fax 672-9187

Menlo Park, San Mateo, Pop. 29,811
Las Lomitas ESD | 1,000/K-8
1011 Altschul Ave 94025 | 650-854-2880
Mary Ann Somerville, supt. | Fax 854-0882
www.llesd.k12.ca.us
La Entrada MS | 500/4-8
2200 Sharon Rd 94025 | 650-854-3962
Deanna Brummett, prin. | Fax 854-5947

Menlo Park City ESD
Supt. — See Atherton
Hillview MS | 700/6-8
1100 Elder Ave 94025 | 650-326-4341
Michael Moore, prin. | Fax 325-3861

Sequoia UNHSD
Supt. — See Redwood City
Sequoia District Adult S | Adult
3247 Middlefield Rd 94025 | 650-306-8866
Patricia Cocconi, prin. | Fax 365-2420

Mid-Peninsula HS | 200/9-12
1340 Willow Rd 94025 | 650-321-1991
Dr. Douglas Thompson, hdmstr. | Fax 321-9921
St. Patrick's Seminary & University | Post-Sec.
320 Middlefield Rd 94025 | 650-325-5621

Merced, Merced, Pop. 69,512
Merced City ESD | 10,400/K-8
444 W 23rd St 95340 | 209-385-6600
Terry Brace, supt. | Fax 385-6316
mcsd.k12.ca.us
Cruickshank MS | 1,100/6-8
601 Cormorant Dr 95340 | 209-385-6330
Trisha Wylie, prin. | Fax 385-6338
Hoover MS | 900/6-8
800 E 26th St 95340 | 209-385-6631
Tammy McDaniel, prin. | Fax 385-6799
Rivera MS | 1,000/6-8
945 Buena Vista Dr 95348 | 209-385-6680
Joe Havel, prin. | Fax 385-6702
Tenaya MS | 1,000/6-8
760 W 8th St 95340 | 209-385-6687
Leon Cope, prin. | Fax 385-6365

Merced UNHSD
Supt. — See Atwater
Golden Valley HS | 2,300/9-12
PO Box 2188 95344 | 209-385-8000
Ralf Swenson, prin. | Fax 385-8002
Merced HS | 2,500/9-12
PO Box 2167 95344 | 209-385-6465
Thomas Scheidt, prin. | Fax 385-6696
Merced Adult S | Adult
50 E 20th St 95340 | 209-385-6524
Carole Roberds, prin. | Fax 385-6430

Regional Occupational Center & Program
Supt. — None
Merced County ROP | Vo/Tech
632 W 13th St 95340 | 209-381-6677
Lee Anderson, supt. | Fax 381-6766

Weaver UNESD | 1,700/K-8
3076 E Childs Ave 95340 | 209-723-7606
Steve Becker, supt. | Fax 725-7128
www.weaverusd.k12.ca.us
Weaver ES | 900/4-8
3076 E Childs Ave 95340 | 209-723-2174
Brenda Jones, prin. | Fax 725-7116

Merced College | Post-Sec.
3600 M St 95348 | 209-384-6000
Sierra College of Beauty | Post-Sec.
1340 W 18th St 95340 | 209-723-2989
Stone Ridge Christian HS | 100/9-12
500 Buena Vista Dr 95348 | 209-386-0322
Dr. Mike Myers, admin. | Fax 386-0334

Middletown, Lake
Middletown USD | 1,900/K-12
20932 Big Canyon Rd 95461 | 707-987-4100
Donald Martin Ed.D., supt. | Fax 987-4105
www.musd.lake.k12.ca.us/
Middletown HS | 500/9-12
20932 Big Canyon Rd 95461 | 707-987-4140
Chris Heller, prin. | Fax 987-4146
Middletown MS | 300/7-8
20932 Big Canyon Rd 95461 | 707-987-4160
Tony Limoges, prin. | Fax 987-4162
Middletown Adult S | Adult
20932 Big Canyon Rd 95461 | 707-987-4175
| Fax 987-4171

Midway City, Orange, Pop. 4,400

Huntington College of Dental Technology | Post-Sec.
14848 Monroe St 92655 | - -

Millbrae, San Mateo, Pop. 20,040
Millbrae ESD | 2,100/K-8
555 Richmond Dr 94030 | 650-697-5693
Karen Philip, supt. | Fax 697-6865
www.smcoe.k12.ca.us/msd/do/do.htm
Taylor MS | 900/6-8
850 Taylor Blvd 94030 | 650-697-4096
John Corry, prin. | Fax 697-8435

San Mateo UNHSD
Supt. — See San Mateo
Mills HS | 1,500/9-12
400 Murchison Dr 94030 | 650-558-2599
Christopher Moore, prin. | Fax 652-1029

Mill Valley, Marin, Pop. 13,418
Mill Valley ESD | 2,200/K-8
411 Sycamore Ave 94941 | 415-389-7700
Ken Benny, supt. | Fax 389-7773
www.mvschools.org
Mill Valley MS | 800/6-8
425 Sycamore Ave 94941 | 415-389-7711
Matt Huxley, prin. | Fax 389-7780

Tamalpais UNHSD
Supt. — See Larkspur
Tamalpais HS | 1,100/9-12
700 Miller Ave 94941 | 415-388-3292
Chris Holleran, prin. | Fax 380-3526

Golden Gate Baptist Theological Seminary | Post-Sec.
201 Seminary Dr 94941 | 415-380-1300

Milpitas, Santa Clara, Pop. 63,081
Milpitas USD   14,300/K-12
  1331 E Calaveras Blvd 95035 408-945-2310
  Karl Black Ed.D., supt. Fax 945-2421
  www.musd.org
Milpitas HS   2,700/9-12
  1285 Escuela Pkwy 95035 408-945-5500
  Charles Gary, prin. Fax 945-5506
Rancho Milpitas MS   700/7-8
  1915 Yellowstone Ave 95035 408-945-5561
  Leticia Villa-Gascon, prin. Fax 945-2492
Russell MS   800/7-8
  1500 Escuela Pkwy 95035 408-945-2333
  Laura Foegal, prin. Fax 945-2491
Milpitas Adult S   Adult
  1331 E Calaveras Blvd 95035 408-945-2392
  Daniel Kreuzer, dir. Fax 945-2378

Heald College   Post-Sec.
  341 Great Mall Pkwy # A 95035 408-934-4900
Plantation Christian S   100/1-12
  PO Box 36073 95036 408-956-1557
  Stephen Burns, dir.

Mira Loma, Riverside, Pop. 15,786
Jurupa USD
  Supt. — See Riverside
Jurupa Valley HS   2,900/9-12
  10551 Bellegrave Ave 91752 951-360-2600
  Ron Shecklin, prin. Fax 360-2612

Miranda, Humboldt
Southern Humbolt JUSD
  Supt. — See Garberville
South Fork HS   400/8-12
  PO Box 188 95553 707-943-3144
  Paula Kelso, prin. Fax 943-3129

Mission Hills, Los Angeles, Pop. 3,112
Los Angeles USD
  Supt. — See Los Angeles
North Valley Occupational Center Vo/Tech
  11450 Sharp Ave 91345 818-365-9645
  Juan Urdiales, prin. Fax 365-2695

Bishop Alemany HS   1,500/9-12
  11111 Alemany Dr 91345 818-365-3925
  Dr. Jack Monnig, prin. Fax 365-2064

Mission Viejo, Orange, Pop. 95,831
Capistrano USD
  Supt. — See San Juan Capistrano
Capistrano Valley HS   2,200/9-12
  26301 Via Escolar 92692 949-364-6100
  Tom Ressler, prin. Fax 347-0514
Newhart MS   1,600/6-8
  25001 Veterans Way 92692 949-855-0162
  Tim Reece, prin. Fax 770-1262

Saddleback Valley USD   34,200/K-12
  25631 Peter A Hartman Way 92691 949-586-1234
  Steven Fish Ed.D., supt. Fax 951-0994
  www.svusd.k12.ca.us
La Paz IS   1,300/7-8
  25151 Pradera Dr 92691 949-830-1720
  Allan Mucerino, prin. Fax 830-3320
Los Alisos IS   1,300/7-8
  25171 Moor Ave 92691 949-830-9700
  Dr. Jerry Ray, prin. Fax 472-3968
Mission Viejo HS   2,700/9-12
  25025 Chrisanta Dr 92691 949-837-7722
  Marilyn McDowell, prin. Fax 830-0782
Trabuco Hills HS   2,800/9-12
  27501 Mustang Run 92691 949-768-1934
  Dan Sullivan, prin. Fax 588-0763
Adult Education Center   Adult
  25598 Peter A Hartman Way 92691 949-837-8830
  Dr. Linda Cistone-Albers, dean Fax 837-1921
Other Schools – See Laguna Hills, Lake Forest, Rancho
  Santa Margarita

Agape Academy   100/K-12
  23632 Via Calzada 92691 949-770-5690
  Denise Justiniano, admin.
Grace Academy   100/K-12
  24242 Castilla Ln 92691 949-583-1783
  Christine Anderson, admin.
Master's Academy   50/K-12
  23052 Alicia Pkwy #H107 92692 949-457-1586
  Daniel R. Gammie, admin. Fax 457-1586
Saddleback College   Post-Sec.
  28000 Marguerite Pkwy 92692 949-582-4500

Modesto, Stanislaus, Pop. 206,872
Empire UNESD   4,100/K-8
  116 N McClure Rd 95357 209-521-2800
  Dr. Robert Price, supt. Fax 526-6421
  www.empire.k12.ca.us
Glick MS   600/6-8
  400 Frazine Rd 95357 209-577-3945
  Melva Rush, prin. Fax 577-3975
Other Schools – See Empire

Modesto CSD   36,200/K-12
  426 Locust St 95351 209-576-4011
  James Enochs, supt. Fax 576-4184
  www.monet.k12.ca.us
Beyer HS   3,000/9-12
  1717 Sylvan Ave 95355 209-576-4311
  Randy Fillpot, prin. Fax 576-4352
Davis HS   3,000/9-12
  1200 W Rumble Rd 95350 209-576-4500
  Jeff Albritton, prin. Fax 576-4028
Downey HS   2,600/9-12
  1000 Coffee Rd 95355 209-576-4211
  Phil Alfano, prin. Fax 576-4258
Enochs HS   9-12
  3201 Sylvan Ave 95355 209-575-8545
  Michael Coats, prin. Fax 575-8597
Hanshaw MS   1,100/7-8
  1725 Las Vegas St 95358 209-576-4847
  Ed Miller, prin. Fax 576-4723
Johansen HS   2,900/9-12
  641 Norseman Dr 95357 209-576-4702
  Thor Harrison, prin. Fax 576-4752

La Loma JHS   1,000/7-8
  1800 Encina Ave 95354 209-576-4627
  Mike Henderson, prin. Fax 576-4631
Modesto HS   3,000/9-12
  18 H St 95351 209-576-4401
  Melda Gaskins, prin. Fax 576-4434
Roosevelt JHS   900/7-8
  1330 College Ave 95350 209-576-4871
  Dave Kline, prin. Fax 569-2713
Twain JHS   1,000/7-8
  707 S Emerald Ave 95351 209-576-4814
    Fax 576-4843
Elliott Adult Education Center   Adult
  1440 Sunrise Ave 95350 209-576-4621
  Hugo Ramos, dir. Fax 576-4863

Regional Occupational Center & Program
  Supt. — None
Yosemite ROP   Vo/Tech
  1100 H St 95354 209-525-5093
  Judie Piscitello, dir. Fax 525-5108

Stanislaus UNESD   3,300/K-8
  3601 Carver Rd 95356 209-529-9546
  Keith Daniel Ed.D., supt. Fax 529-0243
  www.stanunion.k12.ca.us
Prescott Sr ES   700/7-8
  2243 W Rumble Rd 95350 209-529-9892
  Tom Freeman Ed.D., prin. Fax 529-4406

Sylvan Union SD   7,700/K-8
  605 Sylvan Ave 95350 209-574-5000
  Dr. John Halverson, supt. Fax 524-2672
  www.sylvan.k12.ca.us
Savage MS   6-8
  1900 Maid Mariane Ln 95355 209-552-3300
  Dave Garcia, prin.
Somerset MS   1,200/6-8
  1037 Floyd Ave 95350 209-574-5300
  Janice Latham, prin. Fax 529-1110
Ustach MS   1,600/6-8
  2701 Kodiak Dr 95355 209-552-3000
  Mitch Wood, prin. Fax 552-3010

Big Valley Christian S   1,100/PK-12
  4040 Tully Rd # D 95356 209-527-3481
  Dr. Richard Odegaard, supt. Fax 569-0138
Brethren Heritage S   100/K-12
  3549 Dakota Ave 95358 209-543-7860
  Betsy Johns, prin. Fax 543-7862
California Beauty College   Post-Sec.
  1115 15th St 95354 209-524-5184
Calvary Temple Christian S   300/PK-12
  1601 Coffee Rd 95355 209-529-7154
  Jerry Grimshaw, supt. Fax 529-1129
Central Catholic HS   400/9-12
  200 S Carpenter Rd 95351 209-524-9611
  Melissa Bengtson, prin. Fax 524-4913
Community Business College   Post-Sec.
  3800 McHenry Ave 95356 209-529-3648
Computer Tutor Business & Technical Inst Post-Sec.
  4306 Sisk Rd 95356 209-545-5200
Galen College Medical & Dental Assts. Post-Sec.
  1604 Ford Ave Ste 10 95350 209-527-5084
Heritage Christian S   50/K-12
  812 Thieman Rd 95356 209-545-9009
  Kimberly Meyer, prin. Fax 545-9009
Institute of Technology - Modesto Campus Post-Sec.
  5737 Stoddard Rd 95356 209-545-3100
Modesto Christian S   300/9-12
  5755 Sisk Rd 95356 209-529-5510
  Cynthia A. Jewell, prin. Fax 545-0584
Modesto Christian MS   200/5-8
  5901 Sisk Rd 95356 209-529-5510
  Rod Lemburg, prin. Fax 545-1369
Modesto Junior College   Post-Sec.
  435 College Ave 95350 209-575-6498
North Adrian's Beauty College   Post-Sec.
  124 Floyd Ave 95350 209-526-2040
San Joaquin Valley College   Post-Sec.
  1700 McHenry Village Way #6 95350 209-527-7582
Western Pacific Truck School   Post-Sec.
  2316 Nickerson Dr 95358 209-531-9226
Wood Colony Brethren S   100/K-12
  2524 Finney Rd 95358 209-544-9227
  Renee Dutter, admin. Fax 544-9229

Mojave, Kern, Pop. 3,763
Mojave USD   2,700/K-12
  3500 Douglas Ave 93501 661-824-4001
  Larry Beers, supt. Fax 824-2686
  www.mojave.k12.ca.us/
Joshua MS   400/4-8
  3200 Pat Ave 93501 661-824-2411
  Starletta Darbeau, prin. Fax 824-5251
Mojave HS   600/9-12
  15732 O St 93501 661-824-4088
  Jim Walsh, prin. Fax 824-3406
Other Schools – See California City

Monrovia, Los Angeles, Pop. 37,996
Monrovia USD   10,700/PK-12
  325 E Huntington Dr 91016 626-471-2000
  Louise Taylor, supt. Fax 471-2077
  www.monroviaschools.net
Clifton MS   800/6-8
  226 S Ivy Ave 91016 626-471-2600
  Deb Rinder, prin. Fax 471-2610
Monrovia HS   1,700/9-12
  845 W Colorado Blvd 91016 626-471-2800
  Frank Zepeda, prin. Fax 471-2810
Santa Fe MS   800/6-8
  148 W Duarte Rd 91016 626-471-2700
  Ron Letourneau, prin. Fax 471-2710
Monrovia Community Adult Education   Adult
  920 S Mountain Ave 91016 626-471-3035
  Esther McDonald, prin. Fax 471-3036

Excellence in Education Academy   600/K-12
  2640 S Myrtle Ave 91016 626-821-0025
  Carolyn Forte, prin. Fax 821-0216
Mt. Sierra College   Post-Sec.
  101 E Huntington Dr 91016 626-873-2100

Montclair, San Bernardino, Pop. 34,776
Chaffey JUNHSD
  Supt. — See Ontario
Montclair HS   3,200/9-12
  4725 Benito St 91763 909-621-6781
  Michael Hook, prin. Fax 621-1882

Ontario-Montclair SD
  Supt. — See Ontario
Serrano MS   900/7-8
  4725 San Jose St 91763 909-624-0029
  Ellen Lugo, prin. Fax 445-1687
Vernon MS   900/7-8
  9775 Vernon Ave 91763 909-624-5036
  Brian Bettger, prin. Fax 445-1720

Montebello, Los Angeles, Pop. 63,747
Montebello USD   35,300/K-12
  123 S Montebello Blvd 90640 323-887-7900
  Edward Velasquez, supt. Fax 887-5890
  www.montebello.k12.ca.us
Eastmont IS   1,800/5-8
  400 Bradshawe St 90640 323-721-5133
  Robert Cornejo, prin. Fax 887-3058
La Merced IS   2,000/5-8
  215 E Avenida De La Merced 90640 323-722-7262
  Suzette Montano, prin. Fax 887-5816
Montebello HS   3,200/9-12
  2100 W Cleveland Ave 90640 323-728-0121
  Jeffrey Schwartz, prin. Fax 887-7848
Montebello IS   2,100/5-8
  1600 W Whittier Blvd 90640 323-721-5111
  Susan Donnelly, prin. Fax 887-3192
Schurr HS   3,100/9-12
  820 N Wilcox Ave 90640 323-887-3090
  Art Sanchez, prin. Fax 887-3097
Montebello Adult Education   Adult
  149 N 21st St 90640 323-887-7844
  Robert Martinez, prin. Fax 724-4175
Schurr Adult Education   Adult
  820 N Wilcox Ave 90640 323-887-3088
  Sharon Brannon, prin. Fax 887-3098
Other Schools – See Bell Gardens, Monterey Park

Cantwell Sacred Heart of Mary HS   500/9-12
  329 N Garfield Ave 90640 323-887-2066
  David Chambers, prin. Fax 724-4332
Montebello Beauty College   Post-Sec.
  2201 W Whittier Blvd 90640 323-727-7851
National Polytechnic College   Post-Sec.
  2465 W Whittier Blvd # 201 90640 323-728-9636

Monterey, Monterey, Pop. 29,960
Monterey Peninsula USD   11,700/PK-12
  PO Box 1031 93942 831-645-1200
  John Lamb, supt. Fax 649-4175
  www.mpusd.k12.ca.us
Monterey HS   1,400/9-12
  101 Herrmann Dr 93940 831-658-1532
  Dan Albert, prin. Fax 649-5149
Del Monte Adult S   Adult
  222 Casa Verde Way 93940 831-373-4600
  Ann Kilty, dir. Fax 373-1819
Other Schools – See Marina, Seaside

Monterey Institute of Intl. Studies   Post-Sec.
  460 Pierce St 93940 831-647-4100
Monterey Peninsula College   Post-Sec.
  980 Fremont St 93940 831-646-4010
Santa Catalina S   600/PK-12
  1500 Mark Thomas Dr 93940 831-655-9300
  Sr. Claire Barone, hdmstr. Fax 649-3056
York S   200/8-12
  9501 York Rd 93940 831-372-7338
  Chuck Harmon, hdmstr. Fax 372-8055

Monterey Park, Los Angeles, Pop. 62,213
Montebello USD
  Supt. — See Montebello
Macy IS   1,300/5-8
  2101 Lupine Ave 91755 323-722-0260
  Deborah De La Torre, prin. Fax 887-3068

East Los Angeles College   Post-Sec.
  1301 Avenida Cesar Chavez 91754 323-265-8650
Newbridge College - Monterey Park   Post-Sec.
  583 Monterey Pass Rd 91754 626-576-2444

Montgomery Creek, Shasta
Mountain UNESD   100/K-8
  PO Box 368 96065 530-337-6214
  Michael J. Grady, supt. Fax 337-6215
  www.shastalink.k12.ca.us/muesd/
Montgomery Creek MS   100/4-8
  PO Box 368 96065 530-337-6214
  Michael J. Grady, prin. Fax 337-6215

Moorpark, Ventura, Pop. 35,168
Moorpark USD   8,500/K-12
  5297 Maureen Ln 93021 805-378-6300
  Ellen Smith, supt. Fax 529-8592
  www.mrpk.k12.ca.us
Chaparral MS   900/6-8
  280 Poindexter Ave 93021 805-378-6302
  Creig Nicks, prin. Fax 378-6324
Mesa Verde MS   900/6-8
  14000 Peach Hill Rd 93021 805-378-6309
  Kelli Hays, prin. Fax 531-6622
Moorpark HS   2,400/9-12
  4500 Tierra Rejada Rd 93021 805-378-6305
  Kirk Miyashiro, prin. Fax 531-6498

Moorpark College   Post-Sec.
  7075 Campus Rd 93021 805-378-1400

Moraga, Contra Costa, Pop. 16,701
Acalanes UNHSD
  Supt. — See Lafayette
Campolindo HS   1,300/9-12
  300 Moraga Rd 94556 925-376-5986
  Carol Kitchens, prin. Fax 376-6189

Moraga ESD — 1,900/K-8
PO Box 158 94556 — 925-376-5943
Richard Schafer, supt. — Fax 376-8132
www.moraga.k12.ca.us
Moraga IS — 700/6-8
1010 Camino Pablo 94556 — 925-376-7206
Paul Simonin, prin. — Fax 376-6836

St. Mary's College — Post-Sec.
1928 Saint Marys Rd 94556 — 925-631-4000

Moreno Valley, Riverside, Pop. 157,063
Moreno Valley USD — 35,300/K-12
25634 Alessandro Blvd 92553 — 951-571-7500
Rowena Lagrosa, supt. — Fax 571-7550
www.mvusd.k12.ca.us
Badger Springs MS — 1,400/6-8
24750 Delphinium Ave 92553 — 951-571-4200
Willie Williams, prin. — Fax 571-4205
Canyon Springs HS — 2,800/9-12
23100 Cougar Canyon Dr 92557 — 951-571-4760
Tammy Guzzetta, prin. — Fax 571-4765
Landmark MS — 1,400/6-8
15261 Legendary Dr 92555 — 951-571-4220
Jackie Tafoya, prin. — Fax 571-4225
Moreno Valley HS — 2,300/9-12
23300 Cottonwood Ave 92553 — 951-571-4820
Maribel Mattox, prin. — Fax 571-4825
Mountain View MS — 1,500/6-8
13130 Morrison St 92555 — 951-571-4240
Deborah Fay, prin. — Fax 571-4245
Palm MS — 1,500/6-8
11900 Slawson Ave 92557 — 951-571-4260
Nancy Ross, prin. — Fax 571-4265
Sunnymead MS — 1,100/6-8
23996 Eucalyptus Ave 92553 — 951-571-4280
Gitta Williams, prin. — Fax 571-4285
Valley View HS — 2,500/9-12
13135 Nason St 92555 — 951-571-4850
Kim Kruger, prin. — Fax 571-4855
Vista Del Lago HS — 2,000/9-12
15150 Lasselle St 92551 — 951-571-4880
Mary Jones, prin. — Fax 571-4885
Vista Heights MS — 1,500/6-8
23049 Old Lake Dr 92557 — 951-571-4300
Mike Newcomb, prin. — Fax 571-4305
Moreno Valley Adult HS — Adult
24551 Dracaea Ave 92553 — 951-571-4790
Janine Brauer, admin. — Fax 571-4795

Val Verde USD
Supt. — See Perris
Rancho Verde HS — 2,900/9-12
17750 Lasselle St 92551 — 951-485-6200
Michael McCormick, prin. — Fax 485-6218
Vista Verde MS — 1,400/6-8
25777 Krameria St 92551 — 951-485-6270
Gary Roughton, prin. — Fax 485-6278

Calvary Chapel Christian S — 600/K-12
11960 Pettit St 92555 — 951-485-6088
John Milhouse, admin. — Fax 485-6718
Elegante Beauty College — Post-Sec.
24741 Alessandro Blvd 92553 — 951-247-2047
Kings Chapel Christian Academy — 100/PK-12
13027 Perris Blvd Ste 110 92553 — 951-242-2210
Kisha Montgomery, admin. — Fax 601-1565
Riverside Community College — Post-Sec.
16130 Lasselle St 92551 — 951-571-6100
Sage College — Post-Sec.
12125 Day St Ste L 92557 — 951-781-2727

Morgan Hill, Santa Clara, Pop. 34,128
Morgan Hill USD — 11,700/K-12
15600 Concord Cir 95037 — 408-201-6023
Dr. Alan Nishino, supt. — Fax 779-2124
www.mhu.k12.ca.us
Britton MS — 800/7-8
80 W Central Ave 95037 — 408-779-5200
Russom Mesfun, prin. — Fax 778-2550
Live Oak HS — 2,000/9-12
1505 E Main Ave 95037 — 408-201-6100
Nick Boden, prin. — Fax 776-9097
Sobrato HS — 9-12
401 Burnett Ave 95037 — 408-201-6200
Rich Knapp, prin. — Fax 465-2467
Community Adult Education — Adult
17940 Monterey St 95037 — 408-779-5261
Dennis Browne, prin. — Fax 779-8367
Other Schools – See San Jose

Shadow Mountain Baptist S — 100/K-12
280 Llagas Rd 95037 — 408-782-7806
David Warthan, prin.

Morro Bay, San Luis Obispo, Pop. 10,372
San Luis Coastal USD
Supt. — See San Luis Obispo
Morro Bay HS — 1,000/9-12
235 Atascadero Rd 93442 — 805-771-1845
Peter Zotovich, prin. — Fax 772-5944

Moss Landing, Monterey
North Monterey County USD — 4,700/PK-12
8142 Moss Landing Rd 95039 — 831-633-3343
Carolyn Post, supt. — Fax 633-4188
www.nmcusd.org
Other Schools – See Castroville

Mountain Center, Riverside, Pop. 300

Morning Sky Residential School — Post-Sec.
PO Box 379 92561 — 951-659-4044

Mountain View, Santa Clara, Pop. 69,366
Mountain View-Los Altos UNHSD — 15,300/9-12
1299 Bryant Ave 94040 — 650-940-4668
Richard Fischer, supt. — Fax 961-7008
www.mvla.net/
Mountain View HS — 1,700/9-12
3535 Truman Ave 94040 — 650-940-4600
Keith Moody, prin. — Fax 961-6349

Mountain View/Los Altos Adult Education — Adult
333 Moffett Blvd 94043 — 650-940-1333
Laura Stefanski, dir. — Fax 967-4699
Other Schools – See Los Altos

Mountain View-Whisman SD — 4,000/K-8
750A San Pierre Way 94043 — 650-526-3500
Maurice Ghysels, supt. — Fax 964-8907
www.mvwsd.org/
Crittenden MS — 600/6-8
1701 Rock St 94043 — 650-903-6945
Karen Robinson, prin. — Fax 903-6952
Graham MS — 700/6-8
1175 Castro St 94040 — 650-526-3570
Alicia Henderson, prin. — Fax 965-9278

Girls' MS, 180 N Rengstorff Ave 94043 — 100/6-8
Deborah Hof, hdmstr. — 650-968-8338
Mountain View Academy — 200/9-12
360 S Shoreline Blvd 94041 — 650-967-2324
— Fax 967-6886
St. Francis HS — 1,300/9-12
1885 Miramonte Ave 94040 — 650-968-1213
Patricia Tennant, prin. — Fax 968-1706

Mount Shasta, Siskiyou, Pop. 3,614
Mount Shasta UNSD — 700/K-8
595 E Alma St 96067 — 530-926-6007
Steve Mitrovich, supt. — Fax 926-6103
sisnet.ssku.k12.ca.us/~msusdftp/index.html
Sisson S — 500/4-8
601 E Alma St 96067 — 530-926-3846
Karen Snell, prin. — Fax 926-2152

Siskiyou UNHSD — 800/9-12
624 Everitt Memorial Hwy 96067 — 530-926-3006
Richard Holmes, supt. — Fax 926-3113
siskuhsd2.sisnet.ssku.k12.ca.us/
Mount Shasta HS — 400/9-12
710 Everitt Memorial Hwy 96067 — 530-926-2614
Jim Cox, prin. — Fax 926-5162
Other Schools – See Happy Camp, Mc Cloud, Weed

Murrieta, Riverside, Pop. 66,729
Murrieta Valley USD — 18,100/K-12
41870 Mcalby Ct 92562 — 951-696-1600
Dr. Stan Scheer, supt. — Fax 696-1641
www.murrieta.k12.ca.us
Murrieta Valley HS — 3,600/9-12
42200 Nighthawk Way 92562 — 951-696-1408
Renate Jefferson, prin. — Fax 304-1803
Shivela MS — 1,600/6-8
24515 Lincoln Ave 92562 — 951-696-1406
Gary Farmer, prin. — Fax 304-1643
Thompson MS — 1,600/6-8
24040 Hayes Ave 92562 — 951-696-1410
Dale Velk, prin. — Fax 304-1691
Vista Murrietta HS — 2,100/9-12
28251 Clinton Keith Rd 92563 — 951-894-5750
Darren Daniel, prin. — Fax 304-1832
Warm Springs MS — 1,200/6-8
39245 Calle de Fortuna 92563 — 951-696-3503
Timothy Custer, prin. — Fax 304-1611

Temecula Valley USD
Supt. — See Temecula
Bella Vista MS — 6-8
31650 Browning St 92563 — 951-294-6600
Pam Keller, prin. — Fax 294-6624

Calvary Chapel Christian S — 1,600/K-12
24225 Monroe Ave 92562 — 951-677-5667
Desmond Starr, supt. — Fax 698-4896
Oak Grove Institute - Jack Weaver — 100/K-12
24275 Jefferson Ave 92562 — 909-677-5599
Dr. Michael Brown, dir.
Sierra Springs Christian S — 100/1-12
40960 California Oaks Rd 92562 — 951-304-3304
Pamela Healey, admin.

Napa, Napa, Pop. 75,560
Napa Valley USD — 18,600/K-12
2425 Jefferson St 94558 — 707-253-3511
John P. Glaser, supt. — Fax 253-3855
www.nvusd.k12.ca.us
Harvest MS — 900/6-8
2449 Old Sonoma Rd 94558 — 707-259-8866
Linda Beckstrom, prin. — Fax 253-4013
Napa HS — 2,500/9-12
2475 Jefferson St 94558 — 707-253-3711
Barb Franco, prin. — Fax 253-3906
New Technology HS — Vo/Tech
920 Yount St 94559 — 707-259-8557
Monica Tipton, prin. — Fax 253-8558
Redwood MS — 1,200/6-8
3600 Oxford St 94558 — 707-253-3415
Michael Pearson, prin. — Fax 259-0718
Silverado MS — 1,000/6-8
1133 Coombsville Rd 94558 — 707-253-3688
Mike Mansuy, prin. — Fax 253-3830
Vintage HS — 2,300/9-12
1375 Trower Ave 94558 — 707-253-3601
Eric Schneider, prin. — Fax 253-3604
Napa Adult Education — Adult
1600 Lincoln Ave 94558 — 707-253-3594
Rhonda Slota, prin. — Fax 253-3828
Other Schools – See American Canyon

Regional Occupational Center & Program
Supt. — None
Napa County ROP — Vo/Tech
2121 Imola Ave 94559 — 707-253-6830
M.L. Oxford, dir. — Fax 253-6917

Justin-Siena HS — 600/9-12
4026 Maher St 94558 — 707-255-0950
Gregory Schmitz, prin. — Fax 255-0334
Napa Christian S — 300/K-12
2201 Pine St 94559 — 707-255-5233
Dr. Larry Kromann, prin. — Fax 255-8530
Napa State Hospital — Post-Sec.
2100 Napa Vallejo Hwy 94558 — 707-253-5428
Napa Valley College — Post-Sec.
2277 Napa Vallejo Hwy 94558 — 707-253-3000

New Life Academy — 50/K-12
PO Box 5478 94581 — 707-255-1062
Susan Leport, prin. — Fax 226-5433

National City, San Diego, Pop. 58,292
Sweetwater UNHSD
Supt. — See Chula Vista
Granger JHS — 1,200/7-9
2101 Granger Ave 91950 — 619-472-6000
Susan Mitchell, prin. — Fax 267-4107
National City MS — 900/7-8
1701 D Ave 91950 — 619-336-2600
Margaret Harding, prin. — Fax 474-1756
Sweetwater HS — 2,700/9-12
2900 Highland Ave 91950 — 619-336-7009
Wes Braddock, prin. — Fax 474-7635
National City Adult S — Adult
517 Mile Of Cars Way 91950 — 619-336-7037
Ralph Mora, prin. — Fax 336-0641

Bay Vista College of Beauty — Post-Sec.
1520 E Plaza Blvd 91950 — 619-474-6607
Faithful Ambassadors Bible Baptist Acdmy — 100/K-12
2432 E 18th St 91950 — 619-434-2265
Ireneo Austria, admin.
San Diego Academy — 300/K-12
2800 E 4th St 91950 — 619-267-9550
Wayne Longhofer, prin. — Fax 267-8662
Southport Christian Academy — 100/K-12
142 E 16th St 91950 — 619-474-2834
Carolyn Nichols, prin. — Fax 474-0201

Needles, San Bernardino, Pop. 5,276
Needles USD — 1,200/K-12
1900 Erin Dr 92363 — 760-326-3891
Dave Renquest, supt. — Fax 326-4218
www.needles.k12.ca.us/
Needles HS — 300/9-12
1900 Erin Dr 92363 — 760-326-2191
Mike Kincaid, prin. — Fax 326-1212
Needles MS — 200/6-8
1900 Erin Dr 92363 — 760-326-3894
Jim Rolls, prin. — Fax 326-4052

Nevada City, Nevada, Pop. 3,009
Nevada City SD — 1,400/K-8
800 Hoover Ln 95959 — 530-265-1826
Roger Steel, supt. — Fax 265-1822
www.ncsd.k12.ca.us
Seven Hills IS — 500/6-8
700 Hoover Ln 95959 — 530-265-1840
Joe Limov, prin. — Fax 265-1846

Woolman Semester — 50/11-12
13075 Woolman Ln 95959 — 530-273-3183
Shana Maziarz, hdmstr. — Fax 273-9028

Newark, Alameda, Pop. 43,042
Newark USD — 7,600/PK-12
5715 Musick Ave 94560 — 510-818-4112
John C. Bernard, supt. — Fax 794-2199
www.nusd.k12.ca.us
Newark JHS — 1,200/7-8
6201 Lafayette Ave 94560 — 510-818-3000
Don Gill, prin. — Fax 794-2079
Newark Memorial HS — 2,100/9-12
39375 Cedar Blvd 94560 — 510-818-4300
Bill Morones, prin. — Fax 794-2120
Newark Adult S — Adult
35777 Cedar Blvd 94560 — 510-818-3701
Carolyn Scott, prin. — Fax 794-2654

Newbury Park, See Thousand Oaks
Conejo Valley USD
Supt. — See Thousand Oaks
Newbury Park HS — 1,800/9-12
456 N Reino Rd 91320 — 805-498-3676
Max Beaman, prin. — Fax 499-3549
Sequoia MS — 1,200/6-8
2855 Borchard Rd 91320 — 805-498-3617
Vivian Vina-Hunt, prin. — Fax 375-5605

Newbury Park Adventist Academy — 100/9-12
180 Academy Dr 91320 — 805-498-2191
Dr. Harold Crook, prin. — Fax 499-1165
Trinity Pacific Christian S — 400/K-12
3538 Gerald Dr 91320 — 805-492-0863
Lorraine Dilworth, prin.

New Cuyama, Santa Barbara
Cuyama JUSD — 300/K-12
PO Box 271 93254 — 661-766-2482
Jan Hensley, supt. — Fax 766-2255
Cuyama Valley HS — 100/9-12
PO Box 271 93254 — 661-766-2293
Don Wilson, prin. — Fax 766-2593

Newhall, See Santa Clarita
William S. Hart UNHSD
Supt. — See Santa Clarita
Hart HS — 3,000/9-12
24825 Newhall Ave 91321 — 661-259-7575
Gary Fuller, prin. — Fax 254-6436
Placerita JHS — 1,600/7-8
25015 Newhall Ave 91321 — 661-259-1551
Rob Gapper, prin. — Fax 287-9748

Master's College and Seminary — Post-Sec.
21726 Placerita Canyon Rd 91321 — 661-259-3540

Newman, Stanislaus, Pop. 7,874
Newman-Crows Landing USD — 2,400/K-12
890 Main St 95360 — 209-862-2933
Rick Fauss, supt. — Fax 862-0113
www.nclusd.k12.ca.us/
Orestimba HS — 700/9-12
707 Hardin Rd 95360 — 209-862-2916
Joe Terra, prin. — Fax 862-0259
Yolo MS — 500/6-8
901 Hoyer Rd 95360 — 209-862-2984
Kathy McWilliams, prin. — Fax 862-3734

Newport Beach, Orange, Pop. 78,043
Newport-Mesa USD
Supt. — See Costa Mesa

Corona Del Mar JSHS   2,100/7-12
2101 Eastbluff Dr 92660   949-515-6000
Fal Asrani, prin.   Fax 515-6070
Ensign IS   1,200/7-8
2000 Cliff Dr 92663   949-515-6910
Ed Wong, prin.   Fax 515-3370
Newport Harbor HS   2,400/9-12
600 Irvine Ave 92663   949-515-6300
Michael Vossen, prin.   Fax 515-6370

Interior Designers Institute   Post-Sec.
1061 Camelback St 92660   949-675-4451

Newport Coast, Orange

Sage Hill   500/9-12
20402 Newport Coast Dr 92657   949-219-0100
Clint Wilkins, hdmstr.

Nicolaus, Sutter

East Nicolaus JUNHSD   300/9-12
2454 Nicolaus Ave 95659   530-656-2255
Dr. Wayne B. Tierney, supt.   Fax 656-1065
www.eastnicolaus.k12.ca.us
East Nicolaus HS   300/9-12
2454 Nicolaus Ave 95659   530-656-2255
Dr. Wayne Tierney, prin.   Fax 656-1065

Nipomo, San Luis Obispo, Pop. 7,109
Lucia Mar USD
Supt. — See Arroyo Grande
Nipomo HS   1,300/9-12
525 N Thompson Ave 93444   805-474-3300
Robert Mistele, prin.   Fax 929-2551

Highland Preparatory S   100/K-12
PO Box 238 93444   805-929-4059
Kristin Holder, admin.   Fax 929-1837

Norco, Riverside, Pop. 26,265
Corona-Norco USD   46,700/K-12
2820 Clark Ave 92860   951-736-5000
Lee V. Pollard, supt.   Fax 736-5016
www.cnusd.k12.ca.us
Kennedy HS, 1951 3rd St 92860   10-12
Don Ward, prin.   951-736-8283
Norco HS   2,600/9-12
2065 Temescal Ave 92860   951-736-3241
John Johnson, prin.   Fax 736-3282
Norco IS   1,200/7-8
2711 Temescal Ave 92860   951-736-3206
Allen Pietrok, prin.   Fax 736-3208
Other Schools – See Corona

North Edwards, Kern, Pop. 1,259
Muroc JUSD   2,300/K-12
17100 Foothill Ave 93523   760-769-4821
Michael Summerbell, supt.   Fax 769-4241
www.muroc.k12.ca.us
McGowan HS   50/9-12
17100 Lorraine Ave, Edwards CA 93523
   760-769-4333
Paul Kostopoulos, prin.   Fax 769-1131
Other Schools – See Boron, Edwards

North Fork, Madera
Chawanakee USD   600/K-12
PO Box 400 93643   559-877-6209
Dr. Stephen Foster, supt.   Fax 877-4802
www.chawanakee.k12.ca.us
Other Schools – See Coarsegold, O Neals

North Highlands, Sacramento, Pop. 44,600
Grant JUNHSD
Supt. — See Sacramento
Highlands HS   1,400/9-12
6601 Guthrie St 95660   916-286-1701
Gary Bly, prin.   Fax 263-6487
Julio JHS   800/7-8
6444 Walerga Rd 95660   916-286-1800
John Stephens, prin.   Fax 286-1871
Pacific Careers & Technology HS   Vo/Tech
3800 Bolivar Ave 95660   916-286-1970
Michael Crosetti, prin.   Fax 263-6404
Campos Verdes Adult Education Center   Adult
3701 Stephen Dr 95660   916-263-6505
Hal Steward, dir.   Fax 263-6512

North Hills, Los Angeles

Centers of Learning   100/PK-12
PO Box 2037 91393   818-894-3213
Debra Grill, prin.   Fax 893-8074
Los Angeles Baptist JSHS   1,000/7-12
9825 Woodley Ave 91343   818-894-5742
Tim Piatt, prin.   Fax 892-5018

North Hollywood, See Los Angeles
Los Angeles USD
Supt. — See Los Angeles
Madison MS   2,400/6-8
13000 Hart St 91605   818-765-7796
Joanna Kunes, prin.   Fax 765-4692
North Hollywood HS   4,400/9-12
5231 Colfax Ave 91601   818-769-8510
Randall Delling, prin.   Fax 508-7124
Reed MS   2,100/6-8
4525 Irvine Ave 91602   818-762-0691
Sally Burford, prin.   Fax 766-9069
North Hollywood Adult Education   Adult
5231 Colfax Ave 91601   818-252-5627
Kathleen Javaheri, prin.   Fax 766-8247

Campbell Hall S   1,000/K-12
PO Box 4036 91617   818-980-7280
Julian Bull, hdmstr.   Fax 505-5362
Concorde Career College   Post-Sec.
12412 Victory Blvd 91606   818-766-8151
Harvard-Westlake S   800/10-12
3700 Coldwater Canyon Ave 91604   818-980-6692
Thomas Hudnut, hdmstr.   Fax 487-6631
Maric College   Post-Sec.
6180 Laurel Canyon Ste 101 91606   818-763-2563
Marinello School of Beauty   Post-Sec.
6219 Laurel Canyon Blvd 91606   818-980-1300

Oakwood S   500/7-12
11600 Magnolia Blvd 91601   818-752-4400
James Astman, hdmstr.   Fax 752-4408
Summit View   200/2-12
6455 Coldwater Canyon Ave 91606   818-623-6300
Nancy Rosenfelt, dir.
Valley Torah Girls' HS   100/9-12
12003 Riverside Dr 91607   818-755-1697
Rochel Grossman, prin.   Fax 755-1694

Northridge, See Los Angeles
Los Angeles USD
Supt. — See Los Angeles
Holmes MS   1,500/6-8
9351 Paso Robles Ave 91325   818-886-3404
Valerie Turner, prin.   Fax 886-3358
Nobel MS   2,300/6-8
9950 Tampa Ave 91324   818-349-4200
Bob Coburn, prin.   Fax 701-9480
Northridge Academy HS   9-12
9601 Zelzah Ave 91330   818-700-2222
Constance Semf, prin.   Fax 718-2239
Northridge MS   1,200/6-8
17960 Chase St 91325   818-885-8253
Deborah Wiltz, prin.   Fax 885-1461

CA National University Advanced Studies   Post-Sec.
8550 Balboa Blvd Ste 210 91325   800-782-2422
California State University-Northridge   Post-Sec.
18111 Nordhoff St 91330   818-677-1200
Highland Hall Waldorf S   400/PK-12
17100 Superior St 91325   818-349-1394
Ed Eadon, dir.   Fax 349-2390
San Fernando Valley Academy   200/PK-12
17601 Lassen St 91325   818-349-1373
Arsenio Hernandez, prin.   Fax 773-6353

North San Juan, Nevada
Sierra-Plumas JUSD
Supt. — See Sierraville
Pliocene Ridge JSHS   50/7-12
1999 Ridge Rd 95960   530-288-3247
James Berardi, prin.   Fax 288-3221

Norwalk, Los Angeles, Pop. 107,155
Little Lake City ESD
Supt. — See Santa Fe Springs
Lakeside MS   900/6-8
11000 Kenney St 90650   562-868-9422
Sandra Sanders Ed.D., prin.   Fax 863-9252

Norwalk-La Mirada USD   23,500/PK-12
12820 Pioneer Blvd 90650   562-868-0431
Ginger Shattuck, supt.   Fax 864-9857
www.nlmusd.k12.ca.us
Corvallis MS   1,000/6-8
11032 Leffingwell Rd 90650   562-868-2678
Matthew Fraijo, prin.   Fax 863-4755
Glenn HS   1,900/9-12
13520 Shoemaker Ave 90650   562-868-0431
Linda Granillo, prin.   Fax 802-1596
Hargitt MS   900/6-8
12940 Foster Rd 90650   562-864-2593
Dr. Karen Cresswell, prin.   Fax 863-8195
Los Alisos MS   1,100/6-8
14800 Jersey Ave 90650   562-868-0865
Ligia Hallstrom, prin.   Fax 864-2967
Norwalk HS   2,300/9-12
11356 Leffingwell Rd 90650   562-868-0431
Dina Leslie, prin.   Fax 864-0796
Waite MS   1,000/6-8
14320 Norwalk Blvd 90650   562-921-7981
Dr. Linda Haley, prin.   Fax 921-8114
Norwalk Adult S   Adult
15711 Pioneer Blvd 90650   562-868-9858
Frances Kusumoto, dir.   Fax 863-2159
Other Schools — See La Mirada

Adcon Technical Institute   Post-Sec.
12440 Firestone Blvd # 2001 90650   562-864-0506
Cerritos College   Post-Sec.
11110 Alondra Blvd 90650   562-860-2451
Grace Christian S   50/PK-12
12722 Woods Ave 90650   562-868-2398
Rev. Robert Rockhill, prin.
New Harvest Christian S   200/PK-12
PO Box 529 90651   562-929-0774
Richard Salazar, dir.   Fax 484-3260
NTMA Training Center of Southern CA   Post-Sec.
14926 Bloomfield Ave 90650   562-921-3722
Pioneer Baptist S   200/K-12
11717 Pioneer Blvd 90650   562-863-5817
Gerald Mitchell, prin.   Fax 868-2943

Novato, Marin, Pop. 48,383
Novato USD   7,400/K-12
1015 7th St 94945   415-897-4201
Jan La Torre-Derby, supt.   Fax 898-5790
www.nusd.org
Hill MS   600/6-8
720 Diablo Ave 94947   415-893-1557
Louise Koenig, prin.   Fax 898-3910
Novato HS   1,100/9-12
625 Arthur St 94947   415-898-2125
Rey Mayoral, prin.   Fax 897-4242
San Jose MS   500/6-8
1000 Sunset Pkwy 94949   415-883-7831
Dale Ravazzini, prin.   Fax 883-0624
San Marin HS   1,100/9-12
15 San Marin Dr 94945   415-898-2121
Loeta Andersen, prin.   Fax 892-8284
Sinaloa MS   800/6-8
2045 Vineyard Rd 94947   415-897-2111
Kit Gabbard, prin.   Fax 892-1201

College of Marin   Post-Sec.
1800 Ignacio Blvd 94949   415-883-2211
North Bay Christian Academy   100/K-12
6965 Redwood Blvd 94945   415-892-8921
Pam Carraher, prin.   Fax 893-1750

Nuevo, Riverside, Pop. 3,010
Nuview UNSD   1,400/K-8
29780 Lakeview Ave 92567   951-928-0066
Jay Hoffman, supt.   Fax 928-0324
www.nuview.k12.ca.us
Mountain Shadows MS   500/6-8
30401 Reservoir Ave 92567   951-928-3836
Manuel Peredia, prin.   Fax 928-3015

Oakdale, Stanislaus, Pop. 17,440
Oakdale JUSD   4,900/K-12
168 S 3rd Ave 95361   209-848-4884
Wendell Chun, supt.   Fax 847-0155
www.oakdale.k12.ca.us
Oakdale HS   1,500/9-12
739 W G St 95361   209-847-3007
Richard Jones, prin.   Fax 848-0314
Oakdale JHS   800/7-8
400 S Maag Ave 95361   209-847-2294
Marc Malone, prin.   Fax 847-8521
Oakdale Adult Education   Adult
200 Hinkley Ave 95361   209-847-9609
Mike Riley, prin.   Fax 848-4359

Oakhurst, Madera, Pop. 2,602
Bass Lake JUNESD   1,200/K-8
40096 Indian Springs Rd 93644   559-642-1555
Michael MacChesney Ed.D., supt.   Fax 642-1556
www.basslakejuesd.com
Oak Creek IS   300/6-8
40094 Indian Springs Rd 93644   559-642-1570
Dr. Bob Guizar, prin.   Fax 683-7279

Yosemite UNHSD   1,400/9-12
50200 Road 427 93644   559-683-8801
Bill McCabe, supt.   Fax 683-4160
www.yosemiteuhsd.com
Yosemite HS   1,200/9-12
50200 Road 427 93644   559-683-4667
Steve Raupp, prin.   Fax 683-8392
Yosemite Community Education Center   Adult
50200 Road 427 93644   559-683-4667
Roberta Tackett, prin.   Fax 683-4160

Oakland, Alameda, Pop. 398,844
Oakland USD   44,200/PK-12
1025 2nd Ave 94606   510-879-8200
Randolph E. Ward Ed.D., supt.   Fax 879-8800
www.ousd.k12.ca.us/
Best HS   700/9-12
2607 Myrtle St 94607   510-879-3030
Lynne Dodd, prin.   Fax 879-3039
Brewer JHS   700/6-8
3748 13th Ave 94610   510-879-2100
Jamie Marantz, prin.   Fax 879-2109
Business & Information Technology   9-12
8601 MacArthur Blvd 94605   510-879-3010
Richard Gaston, prin.   Fax 879-3019
Carter MS   400/6-8
4521 Webster St 94609   510-879-2140
Carolyn Howard-McBride, prin.   Fax 879-2149
Claremont MS   500/6-8
5750 College Ave 94618   510-879-2010
David Chambliss, prin.   Fax 879-2019
Cole MS   200/6-8
1011 Union St 94607   510-879-1090
Toby Hopstone, prin.   Fax 879-1099
College Prep & Architecture Academy   9-12
4610 Foothill Blvd 94601   510-879-1131
Daniel Hurst, prin.   Fax 879-8874
East Oakland Community   9-12
8251 Fontaine St 94605   510-879-1040
Eric DeMeulenaere, prin.   Fax 879-1049
East Oakland School of the Arts   9-12
8601 MacArthur Blvd 94605   510-879-3010
Matin Abdel-Qawi, prin.   Fax 879-2535
Elmhurst MS   1,000/6-8
1800 98th Ave 94603   510-879-2020
Matthew Duffy, prin.   Fax 879-2029
Excell HS, 2607 Myrtle St 94607   9-12
Yetunde Reeves, prin.   510-879-3030
Frick JHS   700/6-8
2845 64th Ave 94605   510-879-2030
Calvin Criddle, prin.   Fax 879-2039
Harte JHS   1,000/6-8
3700 Coolidge Ave 94602   510-879-2060
Mary Hamadeh, prin.   Fax 879-2069
Havenscourt JHS   700/6-8
1390 66th Ave 94621   510-879-2070
Jackie Phillips, prin.   Fax 879-2079
KIPP Bridge College Prep S   300/6-8
991 14th St 94607   510-879-2421
David Ling, prin.   Fax 879-3182
Kizmet MS, 2607 Myrtle St 94607   6-8
Lynn Dodd, prin.   510-879-3030
Leadership Preparatory HS   1,700/9-12
8601 Macarthur Blvd 94605   510-879-3010
Denise Jeffrey, prin.   Fax 879-1997
Life Academy   200/9-12
2111 International Blvd 94606   510-879-4110
Allison McDonald, prin.   Fax 879-4129
Lowell MS   500/6-8
991 14th St 94607   510-879-2090
Carolyn Howard, prin.   Fax 879-2099
Madison MS   400/6-8
400 Capistrano Dr 94603   510-879-2150
Michael Lyons, prin.   Fax 879-2159
Mandela HS   500/9-12
4610 Foothill Blvd 94601   510-879-1141
Robin Glover-Bailer, prin.   Fax 879-8876
Media College Prep   400/9-12
4610 Foothill Blvd 94601   510-879-1597
Benjamin Schmoolder, prin.   Fax 879-1236
Metwest HS   300/9-12
314 E 10th St 94606   510-879-0235
Matt Spengler, prin.   Fax 879-0235
Montera JHS   900/6-8
5555 Ascot Dr 94611   510-879-2110
Cheryl Rodby, prin.   Fax 879-2119
Oakland HS   2,100/9-12
1023 Macarthur Blvd 94610   510-879-3040
Clement Mok, prin.   Fax 879-3049
Oakland Technical HS   Vo/Tech
4351 Broadway 94611   510-879-3050
Sheliagh Andujar, prin.   Fax 879-3059

Robeson S of Visual & Performing Arts   400/9-12
   4610 Foothill Blvd 94601   510-879-1237
   Anisa Rasheed, prin.   Fax 879-3127
Roosevelt MS   900/6-8
   1926 E 19th St 94606   510-879-2120
   Darcel Stockey, prin.   Fax 879-2129
Simmons MS   900/6-8
   2101 35th Ave 94601   510-879-2050
   Gregory McNamara, prin.   Fax 879-2059
Skyline HS   2,100/9-12
   12250 Skyline Blvd 94619   510-879-3060
   Amy Hansen, prin.   Fax 879-3069
Westlake MS   700/6-8
   2629 Harrison St 94612   510-879-2130
   Misha Karigaca, prin.   Fax 879-2139
Youth Empowerment S   500/9-12
   8251 Fontaine St 94605   510-879-8877
   Maureen Benson, prin.   Fax 879-8879
Oakland Evening Adult   Adult
   750 International Blvd 94606   510-879-4020
   Brigitte Marshall, prin.   Fax 879-4029
Pleasant Valley Adult   Adult
   920 53rd St 94608   510-879-4090
   Chris Nelson, prin.   Fax 879-1806
Shands Adult S   Adult
   2455 Church St 94605   510-879-4040
   Chris Nelson, admin.   Fax 879-4044

Regional Occupational Center & Program
   Supt. — None
Oakland-Alameda ROP   Vo/Tech
   1025 2nd Ave 94606   510-879-8474
   Allie Whitehurst, dir.   Fax 879-1845

Academy of Chinese Culture & Health Sci.   Post-Sec.
   1601 Clay St 94612   510-763-7787
Bentley S   700/K-12
   1 Hiller Dr 94618   510-843-2512
   Rick Fitzgerald, hdmstr.   Fax 843-5162
Bishop O'Dowd HS   1,000/9-12
   9500 Stearns Ave 94605   510-577-9100
   Joseph Salamack, prin.   Fax 638-3259
California College of the Arts   Post-Sec.
   5212 Broadway 94618   510-594-3600
California School of Podiatric Medicine   Post-Sec.
   370 Hawthorne Ave 94609   510-869-8727
College Preparatory S   300/9-12
   6100 Broadway 94618   510-652-0111
   Murray Cohen, prin.   Fax 652-7467
Golden Gate Academy   100/K-12
   3800 Mountain Blvd 94619   510-531-0110
          Fax 531-9434
Head-Royce S   800/K-12
   4315 Lincoln Ave 94602   510-531-1300
   Paul D. Chapman, hdmstr.   Fax 531-2649
Holy Names HS   300/9-12
   4660 Harbord Dr 94618   510-450-1110
   Sr. Sally Slyngstad, prin.   Fax 547-3111
Holy Names University   Post-Sec.
   3500 Mountain Blvd 94619   510-436-1000
Laney College   Post-Sec.
   900 Fallon St 94607   510-834-5740
Lincoln University   Post-Sec.
   401 15th St 94612   510-628-8010
Merritt College   Post-Sec.
   12500 Campus Dr 94619   510-531-4911
Mills College   Post-Sec.
   5000 Macarthur Blvd 94613   510-430-2255
Mohammed S   100/K-12
   1652 47th Ave 94601   510-436-7755
   Carla Ali, prin.   Fax 437-1715
Moler Barber College   Post-Sec.
   3815 Telegraph Ave 94609   510-652-4177
Morgan S for Girls   200/6-8
   PO Box 9966 94613   510-632-6000
   Ann Clarke, hdmstr.
Muhammad University of Islam   100/K-12
   5277 Foothill Blvd 94601   510-436-0206
   Sr. Salamah Muhammad, admin.
Patten Academy of Christian Education   200/K-12
   2433 Coolidge Ave 94601   510-533-3121
   Sharon Anderson, prin.   Fax 535-9381
Patten University   Post-Sec.
   2433 Coolidge Ave 94601   510-261-8500
St. Andrew Mission Baptist S   200/K-12
   PO Box 70378 94612   510-465-8023
   Dr. Robeth Lacy, admin.   Fax 465-0725
St. Elizabeth HS   300/9-12
   1530 34th Ave 94601   510-532-8947
   Sr. Liam Brock, prin.   Fax 532-9754
St. Martin de Porres S   100/6-8
   1630 10th St 94607   510-832-1757
   Sr. Barbara Dawson, prin.   Fax 832-6481
Samuel Merritt College   Post-Sec.
   370 Hawthorne Ave 94609   510-869-6511
Sierra Academy of Aeronautics   Post-Sec.
   Oakland Intl Airport 94614   510-568-6100

Oakley, Contra Costa, Pop. 26,349
Liberty UNHSD
   Supt. — See Brentwood
Freedom HS   1,900/9-12
   1050 Neroly Rd 94561   925-625-5900
   Eric Volta, prin.   Fax 625-0396

Oakley UNESD   4,500/K-8
   91 Mercedes Ln 94561   925-625-0700
   Richard K. Rogers Ed.D., supt.   Fax 625-1863
   www.ouesd.k12.ca.us
Delta Vista MS   800/6-8
   4901 Frank Hengel Way 94561   925-625-6840
   Greg Hetrick, prin.   Fax 625-6850
O'Hara Park MS   800/6-8
   1100 OHara Ave 94561   925-625-5060
   Jeanne Donovan, prin.   Fax 625-5096

Faith Christian Learning Center   50/K-12
   5400 Main St 94561   925-625-2161
   Karen Lyles, admin.   Fax 625-2161

Oak Park, Ventura, Pop. 2,412
Oak Park USD   3,900/PK-12
   5801 Conifer St 91377   818-735-3200
   Anthony Knight, supt.   Fax 879-0372
   www.opusd.k12.ca.us

Medea Creek MS   1,000/6-8
   1002 Doubletree Rd 91377   818-707-7922
   Laurel Ford, prin.   Fax 865-8641
Oak Park HS   1,100/9-12
   899 Kanan Rd 91377   818-735-3300
   Lynn McCormack, prin.   Fax 707-7970

Occidental, Sonoma, Pop. 1,300
Harmony UNSD   300/K-8
   1935 Bohemian Hwy 95465   707-874-3280
   Fred Adam, supt.   Fax 874-1226
   www.harmony.k12.ca.us
Salmon Creek MS   200/5-8
   1935 Bohemian Hwy 95465   707-874-1205
   Brian Burke, prin.   Fax 874-1226

Oceanside, San Diego, Pop. 167,082
Oceanside USD   21,500/K-12
   2111 Mission Ave 92054   760-757-2560
   Kenneth Noonan, supt.   Fax 721-9714
   www.oside.k12.ca.us
El Camino HS   2,900/9-12
   400 Rancho Del Oro Dr 92057   760-757-8550
   Dan Daris, prin.   Fax 757-5321
Jefferson MS   1,400/6-8
   823 Acacia Ave 92054   760-757-6060
   Duane Coleman, prin.   Fax 757-5791
King MS   1,900/6-8
   1290 Ivey Ranch Rd 92057   760-967-1122
   Martha Munden, prin.   Fax 967-4154
Lincoln MS   1,500/6-8
   2000 California St 92054   760-757-0153
   Bob Mueller, prin.   Fax 433-2035
Oceanside HS   2,300/9-12
   1 Pirates Cove Way 92054   760-722-8201
   Kimo Marquardt, prin.   Fax 757-2419

Vista USD
   Supt. — See Vista
Madison MS   1,300/6-8
   4930 Lake Blvd 92056   760-940-0176
   Dr. Robert Pack, prin.   Fax 940-2081
Roosevelt MS   1,400/6-8
   850 Sagewood Dr 92057   760-726-8003
   Raif Henry, prin.   Fax 726-8596

Futures International High School   Post-Sec.
   2204 S El Camino Real #312 92054   760-721-0121
Mira Costa College   Post-Sec.
   1 Barnard Dr 92056   760-757-2121
Oceanside College of Beauty   Post-Sec.
   1575 S Coast Hwy 92054   760-757-6161
Victory Christian S   50/2-12
   PO Box 1760 92051   760-439-6431
   Teresa Brugger, prin.   Fax 439-6431

Ojai, Ventura, Pop. 8,006
Ojai USD   3,700/K-12
   PO Box 878 93024   805-640-4300
   Dr. Timothy Baird, supt.   Fax 640-4321
   www.ojai.k12.ca.us
Matilija JHS   700/7-8
   703 El Paseo Rd 93023   805-640-4355
   Doug Becker, prin.   Fax 640-4398
Nordhoff HS   1,300/9-12
   1401 Maricopa Hwy 93023   805-640-4343
   Dan Musick, prin.   Fax 640-4335

Happy Valley S   100/9-12
   PO Box 850 93024   805-646-4343
   Adrian Sweet, admin.   Fax 646-4371
Laurel Springs S   1,900/K-12
   PO Box 1440 93024   805-646-2473
   Marilyn Mosley-Gordanier, dir.   Fax 646-0186
Mother of Divine Grace S   500/K-12
   PO Box 1810 93024   805-646-5818
   Laura Berquist, dir.
Oak Grove S   200/PK-12
   220 W Lomita Ave 93023   805-646-8236
   Ellen Hall, dir.   Fax 646-6509
Oak Meadow S, PO Box 1626 93024   100/K-12
   Rebecca Lowe, admin.   805-646-4510
Ojai Valley S   400/PK-12
   723 El Paseo Rd 93023   805-646-1423
   Michael Hermes, pres.   Fax 646-0362
Thacher S   200/9-12
   5025 Thacher Rd 93023   805-646-4377
   Michael Mulligan, hdmstr.   Fax 640-1322
Villanova Preparatory S   200/9-12
   12096 N Ventura Ave 93023   805-646-1464
   Anthony Sabatino, hdmstr.   Fax 646-4430

Olivehurst, Yuba, Pop. 9,738
Marysville JUSD
   Supt. — See Marysville
Lindhurst HS   1,300/9-12
   4446 Olive Ave 95961   530-741-6150
   Dean Miller, prin.   Fax 741-6171
Yuba Gardens IS   700/6-8
   1964 11th Ave 95961   530-741-6194
   Cindy Thomas, prin.   Fax 741-7847

Olympic Valley, Placer

Squaw Valley Academy   100/6-12
   PO Box 2667 96146   530-583-1558
   Donald Rees, hdmstr.   Fax 581-1111

O Neals, Madera
Chawanakee USD
   Supt. — See North Fork
Mountain Oaks HS   9-12
   PO Box 210 93645   559-868-4444
   Marihelen Westrick, prin.   Fax 868-3407

Ontario, San Bernardino, Pop. 167,402
Chaffey JUNHSD   18,400/9-12
   211 W 5th St 91762   909-988-8511
   Barry Cadwallader, supt.   Fax 984-1164
   www.cjuhsd.k12.ca.us
Chaffey HS   3,500/9-12
   1245 N Euclid Ave 91762   909-988-5560
   Tim Ward, prin.   Fax 988-0146

Ontario HS   2,500/9-12
   901 W Francis St 91762   909-988-7411
   Rod Hust, prin.   Fax 986-2181
Chaffey Adult S   Adult
   211 W 5th St 91762   909-988-8511
   Gabe Petrocelli, prin.   Fax 983-9916
Other Schools – See Alta Loma, Etiwanda, Montclair,
   Rancho Cucamonga

Chino Valley USD
   Supt. — See Chino
Woodcrest JHS   500/7-8
   2725 S Campus Ave 91761   909-923-3455
   Diana Yarboi, prin.   Fax 923-0851

Mountain View ESD   3,500/K-8
   2585 S Archibald Ave 91761   909-947-2205
   Dr. Rick Carr, supt.   Fax 947-2291
   www.mtnview.k12.ca.us
Yokley JHS, 2947 S Turner Ave 91761   1,200/6-8
   Bruce Perry, prin.   909-947-6774

Ontario-Montclair SD   26,900/PK-8
   950 W D St 91762   909-459-2500
   Dr. Sharon McGehee, supt.   Fax 459-2542
   www.omsd.k12.ca.us
Danks MS   1,200/6-8
   1020 N Vine Ave 91762   909-983-2691
   Jeanette Troesh, prin.   Fax 459-2959
De Anza MS   1,000/6-8
   1450 S Sultana Ave 91761   909-986-8577
   Kathy Kinley, prin.   Fax 459-2673
Oaks MS   1,100/7-8
   1221 S Oaks Ave 91762   909-988-2050
   Jack Young, prin.   Fax 988-2081
Wiltsey MS   1,000/7-8
   1450 E G St 91764   909-986-5838
   Lisa Somerville, prin.   Fax 459-2834
Other Schools – See Montclair

Bryman College   Post-Sec.
   1460 S Milliken Ave 91761   909-984-5027
Franklin Career College   Post-Sec.
   1274 Slater Cir 91761   909-937-9007
Marinello School of Beauty   Post-Sec.
   940 N Mountain Ave 91762   909-984-5884
Montecito Baptist S   100/K-12
   2560 S Archibald Ave 91761   909-923-8455
   Luis Lobos, prin.
NTMA Training Center of Southern CA   Post-Sec.
   1717 S Grove Ave 91761   909-947-9363
Ontario Christian HS   400/9-12
   931 W Philadelphia St 91762   909-984-1756
   Tim Hoekstra, prin.   Fax 460-0176
Platt College   Post-Sec.
   3700 Inland Empire # 400 91764   909-941-9410
Richard's Beauty College   Post-Sec.
   200 N Euclid Ave 91762   909-988-7584
San Antonio Christian S   100/K-10
   1722 E 8th St 91764   909-982-2301
   Richard L. Butterfield, prin.   Fax 982-0921
Westech College   Post-Sec.
   3491 Concours 91764   909-980-4474

Orange, Orange, Pop. 132,197
Orange USD   28,600/PK-12
   PO Box 11022 92856   714-628-4040
   Thomas A. Godley Ed.D., supt.   Fax 628-4041
   www.orangeusd.k12.ca.us
Career Education Center   Vo/Tech
   250 S Yorba St 92869   714-997-6066
   Teryl Snyder, coord.   Fax 997-6035
El Modena HS   2,100/9-12
   3920 E Spring St 92869   714-997-6331
   Brent Bailey, prin.   Fax 997-0705
Orange HS   2,300/9-12
   525 N Shaffer St 92867   714-997-6211
   S.K. Johnson, prin.   Fax 633-6460
Portola MS   900/6-8
   270 N Palm Dr 92868   714-997-6361
   Debra Thompson, prin.   Fax 978-0274
Yorba MS   700/7-8
   935 N Cambridge St 92867   714-997-6161
   Frank Huerta, prin.   Fax 532-4759
Other Schools – See Anaheim, Villa Park

Chapman University   Post-Sec.
   1 University Dr 92866   714-997-6815
Colleen O'Hara's Beauty Academy   Post-Sec.
   102 N Glassell St 92866   714-633-5950
Eldorado S for the Gifted Child   200/PK-12
   4100 E Walnut Ave 92869   714-633-4774
   Dr. Glory Ludwick, dir.   Fax 744-3304
Lutheran HS of Orange County   1,200/9-12
   2222 N Santiago Blvd 92867   714-998-5151
   Dr. Kenneth Ellwein, dir.   Fax 998-1371
St. Joseph Hospital   Post-Sec.
   1100 W Stewart Dr 92868   714-771-8111
Santiago Canyon College   Post-Sec.
   8045 E Chapman Ave 92869   714-564-4000
South Coast College   Post-Sec.
   2011 W Chapman Ave 92868   714-635-6464
University of California-Irvine Med. Ctr   Post-Sec.
   101 The City Dr S 92868   714-456-5678

Orange Cove, Fresno, Pop. 8,993
Kings Canyon JUSD
   Supt. — See Reedley
Citrus MS   600/6-8
   1400 Anchor Ave 93646   559-626-4194
   Rodney Cisneros, prin.   Fax 626-7255
Orange Cove HS   9-12
   1700 Anchor Ave 93646   559-626-5900
   Roger Trujillo, prin.   Fax 626-7217

Orangevale, Sacramento, Pop. 26,800
San Juan USD
   Supt. — See Carmichael
Carnegie MS   900/7-8
   5820 Illinois Ave 95662   916-971-7853
   Kent Kern, prin.   Fax 971-7849
Casa Roble Fundamental HS   1,800/9-12
   9151 Oak Ave 95662   916-971-5452
   Vera Vaccaro, prin.   Fax 971-5495

Pasteur MS 1,000/7-8
8935 Elm Ave 95662 916-971-7891
Kamaljit Pannu, prin. Fax 971-7893

Orcutt, Santa Barbara
Orcutt UNESD 5,000/K-8
PO Box 2310 93457 805-938-8900
Dr. Sharon McHolland, supt. Fax 938-8919
www.orcutt-schools.net
Orcutt JHS 600/7-8
608 Pinal Ave 93455 805-938-8700
Alan Majewski, prin. Fax 938-8749
Other Schools – See Santa Maria

Orinda, Contra Costa, Pop. 18,091
Acalanes UNHSD
Supt. — See Lafayette
Miramonte HS 1,400/9-12
750 Moraga Way 94563 925-280-3930
Luanne Wright, prin. Fax 280-3930
Orinda UNSD 2,400/K-8
8 Altarinda Rd 94563 925-254-4901
Frank Brunetti Ph.D., supt. Fax 254-5261
www.orinda.k12.ca.us
Orinda HS 900/6-8
80 Ivy Dr 94563 925-376-4402
Michael Randall, prin. Fax 631-7985

Orinda Academy 100/7-12
19 Altarinda Rd 94563 925-254-7553
Ronald Graydon, dir. Fax 254-4768

Orland, Glenn, Pop. 6,412
Orland USD 2,400/K-12
1320 6th St 95963 530-865-1200
Chris von Kleist, supt. Fax 865-1202
www.orlandusd.net
Orland HS 700/9-12
1320 6th St 95963 530-865-1210
Dan Raner Ed.D., prin. Fax 865-1215
Price IS 500/6-8
1320 6th St 95963 530-865-1225
Jeffrey Patch, prin. Fax 865-1227

Orosi, Tulare, Pop. 5,486
Cutler-Orosi JUSD 4,200/K-12
12623 Avenue 416 93647 559-528-4763
Frank N. Murphy, supt. Fax 528-3132
www.cojusd.org
El Monte JHS 600/7-8
42111 Road 128 93647 559-528-3017
Roel Alvarado, prin. Fax 528-2822
Orosi HS 800/9-12
41815 Road 128 93647 559-528-4731
Gene Etheridge, prin. Fax 528-4930
Cutler-Orosi Adult S Adult
12623 Avenue 416 93647 559-528-6949
Melissa Calvero, prin. Fax 528-3562

Oroville, Butte, Pop. 13,137
Golden Feather UNESD 200/K-8
11679 Nelson Bar Rd 95965 530-533-3833
Al Keller, supt. Fax 533-3887
www.bcoe.org/home/districts/golden.htm
Concow MS 100/4-8
11679 Nelson Bar Rd 95965 530-533-6033
Al Keller, supt. Fax 533-3887
Oroville City ESD 3,200/K-8
2795 Yard St 95966 530-532-3000
Donald Remley, supt. Fax 532-3050
www.ocesd.org/
Central MS 800/7-8
2565 Mesa Ave 95966 530-532-3002
Richard Hilliard, prin. Fax 532-3042
Ishi Hills MS 6-8
2255 Foothill Blvd 95966 530-532-3078
Patricia Garrison, prin. Fax 532-3040
Oroville UNHSD 2,700/9-12
2211 Washington Ave 95966 530-538-2300
Oran Roberts, supt. Fax 538-2308
www.ouhsd.org
Las Plumas HS 1,500/9-12
2380 Las Plumas Ave 95966 530-538-2310
Sandy Dovell, prin. Fax 534-5974
Oroville HS 1,200/9-12
1535 Bridge St 95966 530-538-2320
Paul Broughton, prin. Fax 534-6203
Oroville Adult Education Adult
78 Table Mountain Blvd 95965 530-538-5350
Dwayne Robinson, prin. Fax 538-5396

Thermalito UNSD 2,300/K-8
400 Grand Ave 95965 530-538-2900
Gregory Kampf, supt. Fax 538-2909
www.thermalito.org/
Nelson Avenue MS 600/6-8
2255 6th St 95965 530-538-2940
Ken Atterbury, prin. Fax 538-2949

Butte College Post-Sec.
3536 Butte Campus Dr 95965 530-895-2511
Feather River Adventist S 100/K-10
27 Cox Ln 95965 530-533-8848
Fax 533-6496

Oxnard, Ventura, Pop. 180,872
Hueneme ESD
Supt. — See Port Hueneme
Blackstock JHS 1,300/6-8
701 E Bard Rd 93033 805-488-3644
Adrian Palazuelos, prin. Fax 488-1250
Green JHS 1,200/6-8
3739 S C St 93033 805-986-8750
Joel Lovstedt, prin. Fax 986-8756

Ocean View ESD 2,500/K-8
4200 Olds Rd 93033 805-488-4441
Nancy Carroll, supt. Fax 986-6797
www.ovsd.k12.ca.us
Ocean View JHS 800/6-8
4300 Olds Rd 93033 805-488-6421
Sharon Anderson, prin. Fax 488-4132

Oxnard ESD 16,900/K-8
1051 S A St 93030 805-487-3918
Rick Miller, supt. Fax 483-7426
www.oxnardsd.org
Frank IS 1,300/7-8
1051 S A St 93030 805-981-1733
Doug Livingston, prin. Fax 981-1754
Fremont IS 1,300/7-8
1051 S A St 93030 805-485-5900
Laura Rynott, prin. Fax 485-2486
Haydock IS 1,000/7-8
1051 S A St 93030 805-487-6797
Frank Barba, prin. Fax 487-7159
Oxnard UNHSD 26,600/9-12
309 S K St 93030 805-385-2500
Judy Dunlap Ed.D., supt. Fax 483-3069
www.ouhsd.k12.ca.us
Channel Islands HS 2,700/9-12
1400 Raiders Way 93033 805-385-2756
Sylvia Jackson, prin. Fax 385-2748
Hueneme HS 2,300/9-12
500 W Bard Rd 93033 805-385-2651
John Saunders, prin. Fax 385-2817
Oxnard HS 2,800/9-12
3400 W Gonzales Rd, 805-278-2906
James Edwards, prin. Fax 278-2912
Pacifica HS 2,300/9-11
600 E Gonzales Rd, 805-278-5000
William E. Dabbs, prin. Fax 278-7187
Rio Mesa HS 2,100/9-12
545 Central Ave, 805-278-5500
Rene Rickard, prin. Fax 278-5525
Oxnard Adult S Adult
1101 W 2nd St 93030 805-385-2584
Wayne Edmonds, prin. Fax 385-2581
Other Schools – See Camarillo

Rio ESD 4,100/K-8
3300 Cortez St, 805-485-3111
Sherianne Cotterell, supt. Fax 983-0221
www.rio.k12.ca.us
Rio Del Valle MS 900/7-8
3300 Cortez St, 805-485-3119
Maria Hernandez, prin. Fax 981-7737

Academy Education Services Post-Sec.
3151 W 5th St Ste E101 93030 805-984-2511
ITT Technical Institute Post-Sec.
2051 Solar Dr Ste 150, 805-988-0143
Modern Beauty Academy Post-Sec.
699 S C St 93030 805-483-4994
Morgan Creek Christian Academy 100/K-12
723 S D St 93030 805-486-4656
Ginger Paschal, admin. Fax 486-5256
Oxnard College Post-Sec.
4000 S Rose Ave 93033 805-986-5800
St. John's Regional Medical Center Post-Sec.
1600 N Rose Ave 93030 805-988-2500
Santa Clara S 200/9-12
2121 Saviers Rd 93033 805-483-9502
Siobhan O'Reilly-Hill, prin. Fax 483-1588

Pacifica, San Mateo, Pop. 37,291
Jefferson UNHSD
Supt. — See Daly City
Oceana HS 600/9-12
401 Paloma Ave 94044 650-550-7300
Samuel Butscher, prin. Fax 550-7310
Terra Nova HS 1,500/9-12
1450 Terra Nova Blvd 94044 650-550-7600
Sherry Segalas, prin. Fax 550-7690

Pacifica SD 2,700/K-8
375 Reina Del Mar Ave 94044 650-738-6600
Michele Garside Ph.D., supt. Fax 557-9672
www.pacificasd.org/
Lacy MS 700/6-8
1427 Palmetto Ave 94044 650-738-6665
Kitty Mindel, prin. Fax 738-6669

Alma Heights Christian Academy 300/K-12
1295 Seville Dr 94044 650-359-0555
Joseph Gross, admin. Fax 359-5020

Pacific Grove, Monterey, Pop. 15,444
Pacific Grove USD 6,700/K-12
555 Sinex Ave 93950 831-646-6520
Patrick Perry, supt. Fax 646-6500
pgusd.org
Pacific Grove HS 700/9-12
615 Sunset Dr 93950 831-646-6590
Stan Dodd, prin. Fax 646-6660
Pacific Grove MS 500/6-8
835 Forest Ave 93950 831-646-6568
Matt Bell, prin. Fax 646-6662
Pacific Grove Adult Education Adult
1025 Lighthouse Ave 93950 831-646-6580
Maria Nunez, prin. Fax 646-6578

Calvary Chapel HS 100/9-12
1002 David Ave 93950 831-656-9434
Skip Joannes, prin. Fax 656-9670
Stanford University Post-Sec.
Hopkins Marine Station 93950 831-373-0464

Pacoima, See Los Angeles
Los Angeles USD
Supt. — See Los Angeles
MacLay MS 1,500/6-8
12540 Pierce St 91331 818-899-7492
Karen O'Riley, prin. Fax 834-1012
Pacoima MS 2,200/6-8
9919 Laurel Canyon Blvd 91331 818-899-5291
Paul Rosario, prin. Fax 834-2021

Palermo, Butte, Pop. 5,260
Palermo UNSD 1,400/K-8
7390 Bulldog Way 95968 530-533-4842
Sam Chimento, supt. Fax 532-1047
www.palermoschools.org
Palermo MS 600/5-8
7350 Bulldog Way 95968 530-533-4708
Kathleen Coleman, prin. Fax 532-7801

Palmdale, Los Angeles, Pop. 127,759
Antelope Valley UNHSD
Supt. — See Lancaster
Highland HS 3,600/9-12
39055 25th St W 93551 661-538-0304
Stacy Bryant, prin. Fax 538-0405
Knight HS 2,300/9-12
37423 70th St E 93552 661-533-9000
Brett Neal, prin. Fax 533-0111
Palmdale HS 3,500/9-12
2137 E Avenue R 93550 661-273-3181
Eric Riegert, prin. Fax 273-1093
Palmdale ESD 22,100/K-8
39139 10th St E 93550 661-947-7191
Roger Gallizzi, supt. Fax 273-5137
www.psd.k12.ca.us
Cactus MS 1,000/6-8
38060 20th St E 93550 661-273-0847
Kate Laferriere, prin. Fax 273-5514
Desert Willow IS 6-8
36555 Sunny Ln 93550 661-285-5866
Thomas Pitts, prin. Fax 456-1145
Juniper IS 1,100/7-8
39066 Palm Tree Way 93551 661-947-0181
David Ellms, prin. Fax 456-1576
Mesa IS 1,000/6-8
3243 E Avenue R8 93550 661-947-0188
Ruth James, prin. Fax 456-1338
Shadow Hills IS 900/7-8
37315 60th St E 93552 661-533-7400
Suresh Bajnath, prin. Fax 533-7445

Regional Occupational Center & Program
Supt. — None
Antelope Valley ROP Vo/Tech
1156 E Avenue S 93550 661-575-1025
June Battey, dir. Fax 575-1037

Westside UNESD
Supt. — See Lancaster
Hillview MS 900/7-8
40525 Peonza Ln 93551 661-722-9993
Joe Andrews, prin. Fax 722-9483
Wilsona SD 2,100/K-8
18050 E Avenue O 93591 661-264-1111
Ned McNabb, prin. Fax 261-3259
Other Schools – See Lancaster

Palm Desert, Riverside, Pop. 45,624
Desert Sands USD
Supt. — See La Quinta
Palm Desert HS 1,900/9-12
43570 Phyllis Jackson Ln 92260 760-862-4300
Patrick Walsh, prin. Fax 862-4390
Palm Desert MS 1,300/6-8
74200 Rutledge Way 92260 760-862-4320
Sallie Fraser, prin. Fax 862-4327

College of the Desert Post-Sec.
43500 Monterey Ave 92260 760-346-8041

Palm Springs, Riverside, Pop. 45,228
Palm Springs USD 25,200/PK-12
980 E Tahquitz Canyon Way 92262 760-416-6000
Michael Sellwood Ed.D., supt. Fax 416-6015
www.psusd.k12.ca.us
Cree MS 1,100/6-8
1011 E Vista Chino 92262 760-416-8283
Clarence Nolan, prin. Fax 416-8287
Palm Springs HS 1,800/9-12
2401 E Baristo Rd 92262 760-778-0400
Ricky Wright, prin. Fax 778-0481
Palm Springs Adult Education Adult
333 S Farrell Dr 92262 760-416-8450
Virginia Eberhard, prin. Fax 416-8454
Other Schools – See Cathedral City, Desert Hot Springs

Desert Career College Post-Sec.
490 S Farrell Dr Ste C200 92262 760-864-1356
Desert Chapel Christian S 400/K-12
630 S Sunrise Way 92264 760-327-2772
Frank Marshall, admin. Fax 325-7048

Palo Alto, Santa Clara, Pop. 57,233
Palo Alto USD 10,200/K-12
25 Churchill Ave 94306 650-329-3737
Mary Frances Callan, supt. Fax 321-3810
www.pausd.org
Gunn HS 1,700/9-12
780 Arastradero Rd 94306 650-354-8200
Noreen Likins, prin. Fax 493-7801
Jordan MS 900/6-8
750 N California Ave 94303 650-494-8120
Suzanne Barbarasch, prin. Fax 858-1310
Palo Alto HS 1,700/9-12
50 Embarcadero Rd 94301 650-329-3701
Scott Laurence, prin. Fax 329-3753
Stanford MS 800/6-8
480 E Meadow Dr 94306 650-856-5188
Don Cox, prin. Fax 856-3248
Terman MS 600/6-8
655 Arastradero Rd 94306 650-856-9810
Carmen Giedt, prin. Fax 856-9878

Castilleja S 400/6-12
1310 Bryant St 94301 650-328-3160
Joan Lonergan, prin. Fax 326-8036
Eastside College Preparatory S 200/6-12
1041 Myrtle St 94303 650-688-0850
Chris Bischof, prin.
Institute of Transpersonal Psychology Post-Sec.
1069 E Meadow Cir 94303 650-493-4430
Pacific Graduate School of Psychology Post-Sec.
935 E Meadow Dr 94303 650-843-3500

Palo Cedro, Shasta
Junction ESD 500/K-8
9087 Deschutes Rd 96073 530-547-5494
Gregg Haulk, supt. Fax 547-4829
www.shastalink.k12.ca.us/junction/
Junction IS 200/6-8
9019 Deschutes Rd 96073 530-547-5494
Gregg Haulk, prin. Fax 547-4829

Shasta UNHSD
Supt. — See Redding
Foothill HS 1,700/9-12
9733 Deschutes Rd 96073 530-547-1700
Jim Cloney, prin. Fax 245-2700

Bishop Quinn HS 100/9-12
21893 Old 44 Dr 96073 530-547-2900
Karl Hanf, prin. Fax 547-5349
St. Francis MS 200/6-8
21945 Old 44 Dr 96073 530-547-2900
Karl Hanf, prin. Fax 547-5349

Palos Verdes Estates, Los Angeles, Pop. 13,827
Palos Verdes Peninsula USD 10,400/K-12
3801 Via La Selva 90274 310-378-9966
Ira J. Toibin Ph.D., supt. Fax 378-0732
www.pvpusd.k12.ca.us
Palos Verdes HS 800/9-10
600 Cloyden Rd 90274 310-378-8471
Christopher Bowles, prin. Fax 378-0311
Palos Verdes IS 1,000/6-8
2161 Via Olivera 90274 310-544-4816
Diawn Stanley, prin. Fax 265-5944
Other Schools – See Rancho Palos Verdes, Rolling Hills

Rolling Hills Prep S 300/6-12
300 Paseo Del Mar 90274 310-791-1101
Peter McCormack, prin. Fax 373-4931

Palos Verdes Peninsula, See Rolling Hills Estates

Chadwick S 800/K-12
26800 Academy Dr 90274 310-377-1543
Frederick Hill, hdmstr. Fax 377-0380

Panorama City, See Los Angeles

Maric College Post-Sec.
14355 Roscoe Blvd 91402 818-672-8907
St. Genevieve HS 400/9-12
13967 Roscoe Blvd 91402 818-894-6417
Daniel Horn, prin. Fax 892-9853
San Fernando Beauty Academy Post-Sec.
8700 Van Nuys Blvd 91402 818-894-9550

Paradise, Butte, Pop. 26,796
Paradise USD 4,900/K-12
6696 Clark Rd 95969 530-872-6400
Stephen Jennings, supt. Fax 872-6409
www.paradise.k12.ca.us
Paradise HS 1,700/9-12
5911 Maxwell Dr 95969 530-872-6425
Mike Lerch, prin. Fax 872-6427
Paradise IS 600/6-8
5657 Recreation Dr 95969 530-872-6465
Michael Ervin, prin. Fax 876-1852
Other Schools – See Magalia

Lighthouse Christian S 50/K-12
PO Box 399 95967 530-872-9029
Wendy Lightbody, prin. Fax 877-2246
Paradise Adventist Academy 200/K-12
PO Box 2169 95967 530-877-6540
Ken Preston, prin. Fax 877-0870

Paramount, Los Angeles, Pop. 56,660
Paramount USD 20,500/K-12
15110 California Ave 90723 562-602-6000
David Verdugo Ed.D., supt. Fax 602-8111
www.paramount.k12.ca.us
Jackson MS 4-8
7220 Jackson St 90723 562-602-8020
Lupe Hernandez, prin. Fax 602-8021
Paramount HS 2,800/10-12
14429 Downey Ave 90723 562-602-6064
Jim Monico, prin. Fax 602-6099
Paramount HS - West Campus 9-9
14708 Paramount Blvd 90723 562-602-8073
Morrie Kosareff, prin. Fax 602-8075
Paramount Adult Education Adult
14507 Paramount Blvd 90723 562-602-8080
Frank Peck, prin. Fax 602-8081

Paramount School of Beauty Post-Sec.
8527 Alondra Blvd Ste 129 90723 714-998-7461

Parlier, Fresno, Pop. 12,358
Parlier USD 3,300/K-12
900 S Newmark Ave 93648 559-646-2731
Maria Trejo Ed.D., supt. Fax 888-0210
www.parlierunified.org/
Parlier HS 800/9-12
601 3rd St 93648 559-646-3573
Elida Padron, prin. Fax 646-2610
Parlier JHS 500/7-8
1200 E Parlier Ave 93648 559-646-1660
Martin Mares, prin. Fax 646-1633

Pasadena, Los Angeles, Pop. 141,114
Pasadena USD 22,600/K-12
351 S Hudson Ave 91101 626-795-6981
Dr. Percy Clark, supt. Fax 795-5309
www.pusd.us/
Blair HS 1,200/7-12
1201 S Marengo Ave 91106 626-441-2201
Rich Boccia, prin. Fax 441-6148
Marshall Fundamental JSHS 1,800/6-12
990 N Allen Ave 91104 626-798-0713
Steven R. Miller, prin. Fax 798-0643
Muir HS 1,400/9-12
1905 Lincoln Ave 91103 626-798-7881
Dan Webb, prin. Fax 791-3499
Pasadena HS 2,500/9-12
2925 E Sierra Madre Blvd 91107 626-798-8901
Dr. Derick F. Evans, prin. Fax 798-1875
Roosevelt S 1,800/K-12
315 N Pasadena Ave 91103 626-795-9501
Fax 795-5180
Washington MS 700/6-8
1505 N Marengo Ave 91103 626-798-6708
Michael Rochin, prin. Fax 798-2844
Wilson MS 1,400/6-8
300 Madre St 91107 626-449-7390
Margaret Abrahamson, prin. Fax 584-9895
Other Schools – See Altadena

Art Center College of Design Post-Sec.
1700 Lida St 91103 626-396-2000
California Institute of Technology Post-Sec.
1201 E California Blvd 91125 626-395-6811
California School of Culinary Arts Post-Sec.
521 E Green St 91101 626-403-8490
Emmanuel Bible College Post-Sec.
1605 E Elizabeth St 91104 626-791-2575
Frostig Center 100/1-12
971 N Altadena Dr 91107 626-791-1255
Tobey Shaw, prin.
Fuller Theological Seminary Post-Sec.
135 N Oakland Ave 91182 626-584-5200
Huntington Memorial Hospital Post-Sec.
100 W California Blvd 91105 626-397-5000
Integrated Digital Technologies Post-Sec.
2555 E Colorado Blvd # 200 91107 626-585-6300
La Salle HS 800/9-12
3880 E Sierra Madre Blvd 91107 626-351-8951
Patrick Bonacci, prin. Fax 351-0275
Maranatha HS 600/9-12
169 S Saint John Ave 91105 626-817-4000
Charles E. Crane, prin. Fax 817-4040
Mayfield HS 300/9-12
500 Bellefontaine St 91105 626-799-9121
Rita McBride, prin. Fax 799-8576
Northwest College Medical Dental Assts. Post-Sec.
530 E Union St 91101 626-796-5815
Pacific Oaks College Post-Sec.
5 Westmoreland Pl 91103 626-397-1300
Pasadena City College Post-Sec.
1570 E Colorado Blvd 91106 626-585-7123
Polytechnic S 900/K-12
1030 E California Blvd 91106 626-792-2147
Deborah E. Reed, hdmstr. Fax 796-2249
St. Monica Academy 100/1-12
301 N Orange Grove Blvd 91103 626-229-0351
Jae Yup Kim, hdmstr.
Westridge S 500/4-12
324 Madeline Dr 91105 626-799-1153
Fran Norris Scoble, hdmstr. Fax 799-9236

Patterson, Stanislaus, Pop. 14,239
Patterson JUSD 4,700/K-12
PO Box 547 95363 209-892-3700
Patrick Sweeney, supt. Fax 892-5803
www.stan-co.k12.ca.us/Patterson/welcome.htm
Creekside MS 1,100/6-8
535 Peregrine Dr 95363 209-892-3600
Debra Herzog, prin. Fax 892-7101
Patterson HS 1,200/9-12
201 N 9th St 95363 209-892-7453
Miguel Guerrero, prin. Fax 892-5935

Patton, San Bernardino, Pop. 1,000

Patton State Hospital Post-Sec.
3102 E Highland Ave 92369 909-425-7297

Pearblossom, Los Angeles
Keppel UNESD 3,000/K-8
PO Box 186 93553 661-944-2155
Dr. Linda Wagner, supt. Fax 944-2933
www.keppel.k12.ca.us
Other Schools – See Littlerock

Pebble Beach, Monterey, Pop. 3,600

Stevenson S 800/K-12
3152 Forest Lake Rd 93953 831-626-5300
Joseph Wandke, pres. Fax 625-5208

Penn Valley, Nevada, Pop. 1,242
Pleasant Valley ESD 700/K-8
14806 Pleasant Valley Rd 95946 530-432-7311
James Voss, supt. Fax 432-7314
www.pvsdnc.k12.ca.us/
Pleasant Valley S 400/4-8
14685 Pleasant Valley Rd 95946 530-432-7333
Clint Johnson, prin. Fax 432-7338

Perris, Riverside, Pop. 41,208
Perris UNHSD 6,200/7-12
155 E 4th St 92570 951-943-6369
Dennis Murray, supt. Fax 940-5378
www.puhsd.org/
Perris HS 2,400/9-12
175 E Nuevo Rd 92571 951-657-2171
Grant Bennett, prin. Fax 940-5717
Pinacate MS 1,300/7-8
1990 S A St 92570 951-943-6441
Dennis Bixler, prin. Fax 940-5344
Perris Community Adult Education Adult
418 W Ellis Ave 92570 951-657-7357
Dorothy Brown, prin. Fax 940-5305
Other Schools – See Menifee

Val Verde USD 12,900/PK-12
975 Morgan St 92571 951-940-6100
C. Fred Workman Ed.D., supt. Fax 940-6121
www.valverde.edu
Citrus Hill HS 9-12
18150 Wood Rd 92570 951-490-0400
John Simonson, prin. Fax 490-0405
Lakeside MS 900/6-8
27720 Walnut St 92571 951-443-2440
Robert Block, prin. Fax 443-2445
Rivera MS 1,000/6-8
21675 Martin St 92570 951-940-8570
Ernesto Lizarraga, prin. Fax 940-6133
Other Schools – See Moreno Valley

Pescadero, San Mateo
La Honda-Pescadero USD 400/K-12
PO Box 189 94060 650-879-0286
Timothy Beard, supt. Fax 879-0816
Pescadero HS 100/9-12
PO Box 730 94060 650-879-0274
Amy Wooliever, prin. Fax 879-0589

Petaluma, Sonoma, Pop. 55,175
Petaluma SD 9,000/K-12
200 Douglas St 94952 707-778-4604
Greta Viguie, supt. Fax 778-4736
www.petalumacityschools.org
Casa Grande HS 1,800/9-12
333 Casa Grande Rd 94954 707-778-4677
Ron Everett, prin. Fax 778-4687
Kenilworth JHS 1,000/7-8
800 Riesling Rd 94954 707-778-4710
Toni Beal, prin. Fax 766-8231
Petaluma HS 1,600/9-12
201 Fair St 94952 707-778-4651
Michael Simpson, prin. Fax 778-4767
Petaluma JHS 900/7-8
700 Bantam Way 94952 707-778-4724
John Lehmann, prin. Fax 778-4600
Petaluma Adult S Adult
200 Douglas St 94952 707-778-4634
Carol Waxman, prin. Fax 778-4785

St. Vincent de Paul HS 400/9-12
PO Box 517 94953 707-763-1032
John Walker, prin. Fax 763-9448
Santa Rosa Junior College Post-Sec.
680 Sonoma Mountain Pkwy 94954 707-778-2415
Sonoma College Post-Sec.
1304 Southpoint Blvd # 280 94954 707-283-0800

Petrolia, Humboldt
Mattole USD
Supt. — See Honeydew
Mattole Triple Junction HS 50/9-12
PO Box 211 95558 707-629-3250
Richard Graey, prin. Fax 629-3551

Phelan, San Bernardino
Snowline JUSD 6,800/K-12
PO Box 296000 92329 760-868-5817
Arthur Golden, supt. Fax 868-5309
snowline.k12.ca.us
Pinon Mesa MS 1,000/6-8
PO Box 296000 92329 760-868-3126
Bob Tait, prin. Fax 868-3033
Quail Valley MS 900/6-8
PO Box 296000 92329 760-949-4888
Dennis Zimmerman, prin. Fax 949-3663
Serrano HS 2,300/9-12
PO Box 296000 92329 760-868-3222
Sharon Schlegel, prin. Fax 868-3803

Pico Rivera, Los Angeles, Pop. 65,317
El Rancho USD 15,400/PK-12
9333 Loch Lomond Dr 90660 562-942-1500
Norbert D. Genis, supt. Fax 942-1598
www.erusd.k12.ca.us
Burke MS 800/6-8
8101 Orange Ave 90660 562-801-5059
Sam Genis, prin. Fax 801-5067
El Rancho HS 3,200/9-12
6501 Passons Blvd 90660 562-801-5355
Julie Ellis, prin. Fax 801-5293
North Park MS 1,100/6-8
4450 Durfee Ave 90660 562-801-5137
Yolanda Aguerrebere, prin. Fax 801-5143
Rivera MS 1,100/6-8
7200 Citronell Ave 90660 562-801-5088
Andrew Alvidrez, prin. Fax 801-9158
El Rancho Adult Education Adult
9515 Haney St 90660 562-801-5009
Dwight Jones, prin. Fax 948-2041

Armenian Mesrobian S 300/PK-12
8420 Beverly Rd 90660 562-699-2054
Hilda Saliba, prin. Fax 699-0757

Piedmont, Alameda, Pop. 10,846
Piedmont City USD 2,600/K-12
760 Magnolia Ave 94611 510-594-2600
Constance Hubbard, supt. Fax 654-7374
www.piedmont.k12.ca.us
Piedmont HS 900/9-12
800 Magnolia Ave 94611 510-594-2626
Pam Bradford, prin.
Piedmont MS 600/6-8
740 Magnolia Ave 94611 510-594-2660
Carol King, prin.
Piedmont Adult S Adult
800 Magnolia Ave 94611 510-594-2655
Tra Holloway-Boxer, dir. Fax 595-8173

Pine Valley, San Diego, Pop. 1,297
Mountain Empire USD 1,500/K-12
3291 Buckman Springs Rd 91962 619-473-9022
Patrick Judd, supt. Fax 473-9728
www.meusd.net
Mountain Empire JSHS 600/7-12
3305 Buckman Springs Rd 91962 619-473-8601
Jan Hagan, prin. Fax 473-8038

Pinole, Contra Costa, Pop. 19,433
West Contra Costa USD
Supt. — See Richmond
Pinole JHS 800/7-8
1575 Mann Dr 94564 510-724-4042
Mary Allen, prin. Fax 724-9583
Pinole Valley HS 1,700/9-12
2900 Pinole Valley Rd 94564 510-758-4664
Haidee Foust, prin. Fax 758-6054

Pismo Beach, San Luis Obispo, Pop. 8,560
Lucia Mar USD
Supt. — See Arroyo Grande
Judkins MS 600/7-8
680 Wadsworth Ave 93449 805-474-3600
Bryant Smith, prin. Fax 473-4376

Pittsburg, Contra Costa, Pop. 61,004
Mt. Diablo USD
Supt. — See Concord
Riverview MS 900/6-8
205 Pacifica Ave 94565 925-458-3216
Denise Rugani, prin. Fax 458-0875

Pittsburg USD 13,300/PK-12
2000 Railroad Ave 94565 925-473-4000
Reed McLaughlin, supt. Fax 473-4274
www.pittsburg.k12.ca.us
Central JHS 1,200/6-8
1201 Stoneman Ave 94565 925-473-4450
Robert Bass, prin. Fax 473-4454
Hillview JHS 1,000/6-8
333 Yosemite Dr 94565 925-473-4400
Todd Whitmire, prin. Fax 473-4406
Pittsburg HS 2,200/9-12
250 School St 94565 925-473-4100
Tim Galli, prin. Fax 473-4183
Pittsburg Adult Education Center Adult
1151 Stoneman Ave 94565 925-473-4460
Bob Beck, prin. Fax 473-4470

Christian Center S 300/PK-12
1210 Stoneman Ave 94565 925-439-2552
Linda Miller, prin. Fax 439-2333
Los Medanos College Post-Sec.
2700 E Leland Rd 94565 925-439-2181

Placentia, Orange, Pop. 48,210
Placentia Yorba Linda USD 26,000/K-12
1301 E Orangethorpe Ave 92870 714-996-2550
Dennis Smith Ed.D., supt. Fax 524-3034
www.pylusd.org/
El Dorado Park 2,100/9-12
1651 Valencia Ave 92870 714-993-5350
Karen Wilkins, prin. Fax 524-2458
Kraemer MS 1,700/6-8
645 N Angelina Dr 92870 714-996-1551
Minerva Gandara, prin. Fax 996-8407
Tuffree MS 600/7-8
2151 N Kraemer Blvd 92870 714-996-1881
Sharon Cordes, prin. Fax 993-6359
Valencia HS 2,300/9-12
500 N Bradford Ave 92870 714-996-4970
Bill Cline, prin. Fax 996-3159
Other Schools – See Anaheim, Yorba Linda

Placerville, El Dorado, Pop. 10,123
El Dorado UNHSD 5,800/9-12
4675 Missouri Flat Rd 95667 530-622-5081
Sherry J. Smith, supt. Fax 622-5087
www.eduhsd.k12.ca.us
El Dorado HS 1,300/9-12
561 Canal St 95667 530-622-3634
Jerry Smith, prin. Fax 622-1802
Other Schools – See Diamond Springs, El Dorado, El
Dorado Hills, Shingle Springs

Gold Oak UNESD 700/K-8
3171 Pleasant Valley Rd 95667 530-626-3150
Richard Williams, supt. Fax 626-3145
www.gousd.k12.ca.us
Pleasant Valley MS 300/6-8
4120 Pleasant Valley Rd 95667 530-644-9620
Mary Zaun, prin. Fax 644-9622

Gold Trail UNSD 600/K-8
1575 Old Ranch Rd 95667 530-626-3194
Joe Murchison, supt. Fax 626-3199
www.gtusd.k12.ca.us/
Gold Trail S 400/4-8
889 Cold Springs Rd 95667 530-626-2595
Stephany Rewick, prin. Fax 626-3289

Mother Lode UNESD 1,600/K-8
3783 Forni Rd 95667 530-622-6464
Shanda G. Hahn, supt. Fax 622-6163
Green MS 600/6-8
3781 Forni Rd 95667 530-622-4668
Tim Smith, prin. Fax 622-4680

Placerville UNESD 1,300/K-8
1032 Thompson Way 95667 530-622-7216
David Freeman, supt. Fax 622-0336
www.pusd.k12.ca.us/
Markham MS 400/6-8
2800 Moulton Dr 95667 530-622-0403
Marc Nigel, prin. Fax 622-5584

Consumnes River College-Eldorado Center Post-Sec.
6699 Campus Dr 95667 530-642-5621
El Dorado Adventist S 200/K-12
1900 Broadway 95667 530-622-3560
Larry Ballew, prin. Fax 622-2604

Planada, Merced, Pop. 3,531
Planada ESD 900/K-8
PO Box 236 95365 209-382-0756
Jose L. Banda, supt. Fax 382-1750
www.planada.k12.ca.us/
Chavez MS 300/6-8
PO Box 236 95365 209-382-0768
Jose L. Banda, prin. Fax 382-0775

Playa Del Rey, See Los Angeles

St. Bernard HS 600/9-12
9100 Falmouth Ave 90293 310-823-4651
James McClune, prin. Fax 827-3365

Pleasant Hill, Contra Costa, Pop. 33,859
Mt. Diablo USD
Supt. — See Concord
College Park HS 2,000/9-12
201 Viking Dr 94523 925-682-7670
Barbara Oaks, prin. Fax 676-7892
Pleasant Hill MS 800/6-8
1 Santa Barbara Rd 94523 925-256-0791
Jonathan Roslin, prin. Fax 937-6271
Sequoia MS 900/6-8
265 Boyd Rd 94523 925-934-8174
Vivian Boyd, prin. Fax 946-9063
Valley View MS 800/6-8
181 Viking Dr 94523 925-686-6136
Nadine Rosenzweig, prin. Fax 825-8908
Pleasant Hill Adult Center Adult
3100 Oak Park Blvd 94523 925-937-1530
Fax 937-6271

Regional Occupational Center & Program
Supt. — None
Contra Costa County ROP Vo/Tech
77 Santa Barbara Rd 94523 925-942-3368
Marie McClaskey, dir. Fax 934-1057

Diablo Valley College Post-Sec.
321 Golf Club Rd 94523 925-685-1230
John F. Kennedy University Post-Sec.
100 Ellinwood Way 94523 925-969-3300
Pleasant Hill Adventist Academy 300/K-12
796 Grayson Rd 94523 925-934-9261
Alexis Emmerson, prin. Fax 934-5871
Western Career College Post-Sec.
380 Civic Dr Ste 300 94523 925-609-6650

Pleasanton, Alameda, Pop. 65,982
Pleasanton USD 14,000/K-12
4665 Bernal Ave 94566 925-462-5500
John M. Casey, supt. Fax 426-8216
www.pleasanton.k12.ca.us
Amador Valley HS 2,200/9-12
1155 Santa Rita Rd 94566 925-461-6100
Bill Coupe, prin. Fax 461-6133
Foothill HS 2,200/9-12
4375 Foothill Rd 94588 925-461-6650
Kevin Johnson, prin. Fax 461-6633
Hart MS 1,100/6-8
4433 Willow Rd 94588 925-426-3102
Steve Maher, prin. Fax 460-0799
Harvest Park MS 1,100/6-8
4900 Valley Ave 94566 925-426-4444
Jim Hansen, prin. Fax 426-9613
Pleasanton MS 1,300/6-8
5001 Case Ave 94566 925-426-4390
John Whitney, prin. Fax 426-1382
Amador Valley Adult Ed. & Comm. Services Adult
215 Abbie St 94566 925-461-6150
Glen Sparks, prin. Fax 846-5317

Point Arena, Mendocino, Pop. 478
Point Arena JUNHSD 200/9-12
PO Box 87 95468 707-882-2803
Mark Iacuaniello, supt. Fax 882-2848
Point Arena HS 200/9-12
PO Box 7 95468 707-882-2134
Warren Galletti, prin. Fax 882-3453

Pollock Pines, El Dorado, Pop. 4,291
Pollock Pines ESD 800/K-8
6181A Pine St 95726 530-644-5416
Molly Helms, supt. Fax 644-5483
www.ppsd.k12.ca.us
Sierra Ridge MS 400/5-8
2700 Amber Trl 95726 530-644-2031
Jeanne Harper, prin. Fax 644-0198

Pomona, Los Angeles, Pop. 154,147
Pomona USD 33,500/K-12
800 S Garey Ave 91766 909-397-4800
Patrick Leier, supt. Fax 397-4881
www.pusd.org
Diamond Ranch HS 1,800/9-12
100 Diamond Ranch Rd 91766 909-397-4715
M. Tourville-Principe, prin. Fax 591-9374
Emerson MS 1,100/6-8
635 Lincoln Ave 91767 909-397-4516
Patti Formica, prin. Fax 397-5280
Fremont MS 900/7-8
725 W Franklin Ave 91766 909-397-4521
Susan M. Williams, prin. Fax 620-6229
Ganesha HS 1,700/9-12
1151 Fairplex Dr 91768 909-397-4400
Michael Hernandez, prin. Fax 629-4069
Garey HS 2,200/9-12
321 W Lexington Ave 91766 909-397-4451
Curtis Donaldson, prin. Fax 620-1575
Garey Village S 9-9
2350 S Garey Ave 91766 909-397-5060
Curtis Donaldson, prin.
Marshall MS 1,100/6-8
1921 Arroyo Ave 91768 909-397-4532
Lilia Villa, prin. Fax 629-8275
Palomares MS 900/6-8
2211 N Orange Grove Ave 91767 909-397-4539
Mary Storm, prin. Fax 625-0337
Pomona HS 1,700/9-12
475 Bangor St 91767 909-397-4498
Marilyn Ghirelli, prin. Fax 629-1410
Simons MS 1,400/6-8
900 E Franklin Ave 91766 909-397-4544
Darren Knowles, prin. Fax 623-4691
Village Academy Vo/Tech
1444 E Holt Ave 91767 909-397-4900
Carol A. Aseltine, prin. Fax 865-9250
Adult & Career Education Adult
1515 W Mission Blvd #5 91766 909-469-2333
Barbara Thompson, prin. Fax 623-3841
Other Schools – See Diamond Bar

Regional Occupational Center & Program
Supt. — None
San Antonio ROP Vo/Tech
1425 E Holt Ave Ste 101 91767 909-469-2304
Jose Castro, dir. Fax 620-5770

California State Polytechnic University Post-Sec.
3801 W Temple Ave 91768 909-869-2000
CEI Post-Sec.
980 Corporate Center Dr 91768 909-865-9008
City of Knowledge S 200/K-12
3285 N Garey Ave 91767 909-382-0251
Dr. Haleema Shaikley, prin.
DeVry University Post-Sec.
901 Corporate Center Dr 91768 909-622-8866
Northwest College Medical Dental Assts. Post-Sec.
134 W Holt Ave 91768 909-623-1552
Pomona Catholic HS 300/9-12
533 W Holt Ave 91768 909-623-5297
Fax 620-6057
Western University of Health Sciences Post-Sec.
309 E 2nd St 91766 909-623-6116

Porterville, Tulare, Pop. 42,484
Burton ESD 2,900/K-8
264 N Westwood St 93257 559-781-8020
Donald Brown, supt. Fax 781-1403
burton.k12.ca.us
Burton MS 700/7-8
1155 N Elderwood St 93257 559-781-2671
David Huchingson, prin. Fax 788-6424
Porterville USD 14,000/K-12
600 W Grand Ave 93257 559-793-2455
John Snavely Ed.D., supt. Fax 793-1088
www.portervilleschools.org
Bartlett MS 700/7-8
355 N G St 93257 559-782-7100
Lisa Whitworth, prin. Fax 784-3432
Granite Hills HS 9-12
1701 E Putnam Ave 93257 559-782-7075
Veryl Ann Duncan, prin. Fax 789-9357
Monache HS 1,900/9-12
960 N Newcomb St 93257 559-782-7150
Shirley Houser, prin. Fax 781-3377
Pioneer MS 900/7-8
255 E College Ave 93257 559-782-7200
Isaac Nunez, prin. Fax 784-3507
Porterville HS 1,900/9-12
465 W Olive Ave 93257 559-782-7210
Steve Graybehl, prin. Fax 782-7215
Sequoia MS 7-8
1450 W Castle Ave 93257 559-793-7627
Joe Santos, prin.
Porterville Adult S Adult
900 Pioneer Ave 93257 559-782-7030
Bob Perez, dir. Fax 781-4943
Other Schools – See Strathmore

Landmark Christian Academy 50/K-12
2380 W Olive Ave 93257 559-781-9500
Bertha Hearne, prin. Fax 784-2861
Porterville College Post-Sec.
100 E College Ave 93257 559-791-2200
Porterville Development Center Post-Sec.
PO Box 2000 93258 559-782-2753

Port Hueneme, Ventura, Pop. 21,837
Hueneme ESD 8,400/K-8
205 N Ventura Rd 93041 805-488-3588
Dr. Jerry Dannenberg, supt. Fax 986-8755
www.huensd.k12.ca.us
Other Schools – See Oxnard

Portola, Plumas, Pop. 2,219
Plumas USD
Supt. — See Quincy
Portola JSHS 400/7-12
155 6th Ave 96122 530-832-4284
Rex Coffman, prin. Fax 832-5682

Portola Valley, San Mateo, Pop. 4,418
Portola Valley ESD 700/K-8
4575 Alpine Rd 94028 650-851-1777
Anne Campbell, supt. Fax 851-3700
www.pvsd.net
Corte Madera MS 400/4-8
4575 Alpine Rd 94028 650-851-1777
Joel Willen, prin. Fax 529-8553

Woodside Priory S 200/6-8
302 Portola Rd 94028 650-851-8221
Dora Arrendondo-Marron, prin. Fax 851-2839
Woodside Priory S 300/9-12
302 Portola Rd 94028 650-851-8221
Tim Molak, prin. Fax 851-2839

Potter Valley, Mendocino
Potter Valley Community USD 300/K-12
PO Box 219 95469 707-743-2101
Michael Distefano, supt. Fax 743-1930
ntap.k12.ca.us/pvhs/pvcusd.htm
Potter Valley HS 100/7-12
PO Box 219 95469 707-743-1142
Scott Paulin, prin. Fax 743-2879

Poway, San Diego, Pop. 49,201
Poway USD 34,600/K-12
13626 Twin Peaks Rd 92064 858-748-0010
Dr. Donald Phillips, supt. Fax 679-2642
www.powayusd.com
Meadowbrook MS 1,600/6-8
12320 Meadowbrook Ln 92064 858-748-0802
Cathy Brose, prin. Fax 679-0149
Poway HS 3,100/9-12
15500 Espola Rd 92064 858-748-0245
Scott Fisher, prin. Fax 679-6879
Twin Peaks MS 1,700/6-8
14640 Tierra Bonita Rd 92064 858-748-5131
Lyn Antrim, prin. Fax 679-6823
Poway Adult S Adult
13230 Evening Creek Dr S 92064 858-668-4000
Kathleen Porter, dir. Fax 748-7423
Other Schools – See San Diego

Poway Academy of Hair Design Post-Sec.
13266 Poway Rd 92064 858-748-1490

Prather, Fresno, Pop. 30
Sierra USD 2,400/K-12
29143 Auberry Rd 93651 559-855-3662
Dr. Don A. Witzansky, supt. Fax 855-3585
www.sierra.k12.ca.us
Foothill MS 400/6-8
29147 Auberry Rd 93651 559-855-3551
Brent Patten, prin. Fax 855-5350
Other Schools – See Tollhouse

Princeton, Colusa
Princeton JUSD 300/K-12
PO Box 8 95970 530-439-2261
Jess Modesto, supt. Fax 439-2113
www.pjusd.org/
Princeton JSHS 100/7-12
PO Box 8 95970 530-439-2261
Jess Modesto, prin. Fax 439-2113

Prunedale, Monterey, Pop. 7,393

Prunedale Christian Academy 100/PK-12
8145 Prunedale North Rd 93907 831-663-2183
Dr. E.L. Moon, admin. Fax 663-1663

Quartz Hill, Los Angeles, Pop. 9,626
Antelope Valley UNHSD
Supt. — See Lancaster
Quartz Hill HS 3,200/9-12
6040 W Avenue L 93536 661-718-3100
Mark Bryant, prin. Fax 943-8203

Westside UNESD
Supt. — See Lancaster
Walker MS 900/7-8
5632 W Avenue L8 93536 661-943-3258
Robert Garza, prin. Fax 943-2969

Covenant Christian S 100/1-12
2763 W Avenue L 93536 661-274-8285
Susan Mitchell, admin.

Quincy, Plumas, Pop. 4,271
Plumas USD 3,000/K-12
50 Church St 95971 530-283-6500
Mike Chelotti, supt. Fax 283-6509
www.pcoe.k12.ca.us
Quincy JSHS 500/7-12
6 Quincy Junction Rd 95971 530-283-6510
Tim Gallagher, prin. Fax 283-6519
Other Schools – See Chester, Greenville, Portola

Regional Occupational Center & Program
Supt. — None
Plumas County ROP Vo/Tech
50 Church St #B 95971 530-283-6500
Terry Oestreich, dir. Fax 283-6509

Feather River Community College Post-Sec.
570 Golden Eagle Ave 95971 530-283-0202
Plumas Christian S 100/K-12
49 S Lindan Ave 95971 530-283-0415
John Sturley, admin. Fax 283-2933

Ramona, San Diego, Pop. 13,040
Ramona USD 6,600/K-12
720 9th St 92065 760-787-2000
Pete Schiff, supt. Fax 789-9168
www.ramonausd.net/
Peirce MS 1,100/7-8
1521 Hanson Ln 92065 760-787-2400
Linda Solis, prin. Fax 788-5014
Ramona HS 2,000/9-12
1401 Hanson Ln 92065 760-787-4000
Steve Petsche, prin. Fax 789-4596

New Life Christian Academy 100/K-12
PO Box 788 92065 760-789-7543
Hayden Williams, prin. Fax 789-9977

Rancho Cordova, Sacramento, Pop. 56,500
Folsom-Cordova USD
Supt. — See Folsom
Cordova HS 2,100/9-12
2239 Chase Dr 95670 916-362-1104
Jacquelyn Levy, prin. Fax 362-1447
Mills MS 1,100/6-8
10439 Coloma Rd 95670 916-363-6544
Dennis Willeford, prin. Fax 361-3744
Mitchell MS 700/6-8
2100 Zinfandel Dr 95670 916-635-8460
DeAnn Kamilos, prin. Fax 635-8979
Folsom-Cordova Adult Education Adult
10850 Gadsten Way 95670 916-635-6810
Dax Bryson, prin. Fax 635-0905

Heald College Rancho Cordova Post-Sec.
2910 Prospect Park Dr 95670 916-638-1616
IHS Christian S, PO Box 2191 95741 100/K-12
Leanne Kramp, admin. 916-638-7755
ITT Technical Institute Post-Sec.
10863 Gold Center Dr 95670 916-851-3900
San Joaquin Valley College Post-Sec.
11050 Olson Dr 95670

Rancho Cucamonga, San Bernardino, Pop. 151,640
Central SD 5,300/K-8
10601 Church St Ste 112 91730 909-989-8541
Sharon Nagel, supt. Fax 941-1732
www.csd.k12.ca.us/
Cucamonga MS 1,000/6-8
7611 Hellman Ave 91730 909-987-1788
Jeffrey Koenig, prin. Fax 483-3201
Musser MS 1,100/5-8
10789 Terra Vista Pkwy 91730 909-980-1230
David Soden, prin. Fax 980-3042

Chaffey JUNHSD
Supt. — See Ontario
Rancho Cucamonga HS 2,800/9-12
11801 Lark Dr 91701 909-989-1600
Todd Haag, prin. Fax 945-5355
Cucamonga ESD 2,900/K-8
8776 Archibald Ave 91730 909-987-8942
Claudia Maidenberg, supt. Fax 980-3628
www.cuca.k12.ca.us
Rancho Cucamonga MS 900/6-8
10022 Feron Blvd 91730 909-980-0969
Bruce LaVallee, prin. Fax 481-5381

Regional Occupational Center & Program
Supt. — None
Baldy View ROP Vo/Tech
8265 Aspen St Ste 100 91730 909-980-6490
Dr. Larry Weigel, supt. Fax 980-8364

San Joaquin Valley College Post-Sec.
10641 Church St 91730 909-948-7582
Universal Technical Institute Post-Sec.
9494 Haven Ave 91730 909-484-1929

Rancho Mirage, Riverside, Pop. 15,297

Eisenhower Memorial Hospital Post-Sec.
39000 Bob Hope Dr 92270 760-340-3911
Marywood Palm Valley S 300/6-12
35525 Da Vall Dr 92270 760-328-0861
Graham Hookey, admin. Fax 770-4541

Rancho Palos Verdes, Los Angeles, Pop. 42,265
Los Angeles USD
Supt. — See Los Angeles
Dodson MS 1,900/6-8
28014 S Montereina Dr 90275 310-832-5342
Elmore Collier, prin. Fax 832-4709

Palos Verdes Peninsula USD
Supt. — See Palos Verdes Estates
Miraleste IS 1,000/6-8
29323 Palos Verdes Dr E 90275 310-732-0900
John Letcher, prin. Fax 521-8915

Marymount College Post-Sec.
30800 Palos Verdes Dr E 90275 310-377-5501

Rancho Santa Fe, San Diego, Pop. 7,000
Rancho Sante Fe ESD 800/K-8
PO Box 809 92067 858-756-1141
Lindy Delaney, supt. Fax 756-0712
www.rsf.k12.ca.us
Rancho Santa Fe MS 200/7-8
PO Box 809 92067 858-756-1141
Blake Isaac, prin. Fax 759-0712

Rancho Santa Margarita, Orange, Pop. 49,142
Capistrano USD
Supt. — See San Juan Capistrano
Tesoro HS 2,600/9-12
1 Tesoro Creek Rd 92688 949-234-5310
Dr. Daniel Burch, prin. Fax 766-3370

Saddleback Valley USD
Supt. — See Mission Viejo
Rancho Santa Margarita IS 1,700/7-8
21931 Alma Aldea 92688 949-459-8253
Dan Graham, prin. Fax 459-8258

Santa Margarita HS 1,800/9-12
22062 Antonio Pkwy 92688 949-766-6000
Br. Lawrence Monroe, prin. Fax 766-6005

Red Bluff, Tehama, Pop. 13,690
Antelope ESD 700/K-8
22630 Antelope Blvd 96080 530-527-1272
Emily Houck, supt. Fax 527-2931
www.asd.tehama.k12.ca.us/
Berrendos MS 200/6-8
401 Chestnut Ave 96080 530-527-6700
Emily Houck, prin. Fax 527-2506

Red Bluff JUNHSD 1,800/9-12
PO Box 1507 96080 530-529-8700
Kathleen Wheeler, supt. Fax 529-8709
www.rbuhsd.k12.ca.us/
Red Bluff HS 1,700/9-12
PO Box 1507 96080 530-529-8710
Patrick Gleason, prin. Fax 529-8739

Red Bluff UNESD 2,200/K-8
1755 Airport Blvd 96080 530-527-7200
Charles Allen, supt. Fax 527-9308
www.rbuesd.tehama.k12.ca.us
Vista MS 500/7-8
1770 S Jackson St 96080 530-527-7840
Mark Klinesteker, prin. Fax 527-9374

Regional Occupational Center & Program
Supt. — None
Tehama County ROP Vo/Tech
PO Box 689 96080 530-528-7341
Larry Champion, admin. Fax 529-4120

Mercy HS 200/9-12
233 Riverside Way 96080 530-527-8313
Cheryl Ramirez, prin. Fax 527-3058

Redding, Shasta, Pop. 87,579
Columbia ESD 1,000/K-8
10140 Old Oregon Trl 96003 530-223-1915
Frank Adelman, supt. Fax 223-4168
www.shastalink.k12.ca.us/columbia
Mountain View MS 400/6-8
675 Shasta View Dr 96003 530-221-6224
Andrea McClure, prin. Fax 221-5620

Enterprise ESD 3,500/K-8
1155 Mistletoe Ln 96002 530-224-4100
Tom Armelino, supt. Fax 224-4101
www.enterprise.k12.ca.us
Parsons MS 800/6-8
750 Hartnell Ave 96002 530-224-4190
Cheryl Kirschman, prin. Fax 224-4191

Gateway USD 3,000/K-12
4411 Mountain Lakes Blvd 96003 530-245-7900
John Strohmayer, supt. Fax 245-7920
www.gwusd.org
Buckeye MS 300/6-8
3500 Tamarack Dr 96003 530-225-0456
Laura Kelly, prin. Fax 225-0499
Other Schools – See Central Valley

Pacheco UNESD 700/K-8
7433 Pacheco Rd 96002 530-224-4589
Richard Rhodes, supt. Fax 224-4595
www.pacheco.k12.ca.us
Pacheco S 500/4-8
7430 Pacheco School Rd 96002 530-224-4585
Michael Kurth, prin. Fax 224-4588

Redding SD 3,700/K-8
PO Box 992418 96099 530-225-0011
Diane Kempley, supt. Fax 225-0015
www.shastalink.k12.ca.us/rsd
Sequoia MS 1,000/6-8
PO Box 992418 96099 530-225-0020
Wendy Pace, prin. Fax 225-0029

Regional Occupational Center & Program
Supt. — None
Shasta-Trinity ROP Vo/Tech
4659 Eastside Rd 96001 530-246-3302
Eleanor Townsend, supt. Fax 246-3306

Shasta UNHSD 5,300/9-12
2200 Eureka Way #B 96001 530-241-3261
Michael Stuart, supt. Fax 225-8499
www.suhsd.net
Enterprise HS 1,400/9-12
3411 Churn Creek Rd 96002 530-222-6601
Chris Adams, prin. Fax 222-5138
Shasta HS 1,700/9-12
2500 Eureka Way 96001 530-241-4161
Milan Woollard, prin. Fax 241-9571
Other Schools – See Palo Cedro

Grace Baptist S 300/K-12
3782 Churn Creek Rd 96002 530-222-2232
Stephen Roberts, supt. Fax 222-1784
Hope S International 200/K-12
2250 Churn Creek Rd 96002 530-222-2095
Dee Haselhuhn, prin. Fax 222-5819
Lake College Post-Sec.
2655 Bechelli Ln 96002 530-224-7227
Redding Adventist Academy 200/K-12
1356 E Cypress Ave 96002 530-222-1018
Timothy Erich, prin. Fax 222-4260
Redding Christian S 500/K-12
777 Loma Vista Dr 96002 530-223-1226
Leilani Guido, admin. Fax 223-4755
Shasta Bible College & Graduate School Post-Sec.
2951 Goodwater Ave 96002 530-221-4275
Shasta College Post-Sec.
PO Box 496006 96049 530-225-4600
Simpson University Post-Sec.
2211 College View Dr 96003 530-224-5600

Redlands, San Bernardino, Pop. 67,859
Redlands USD 25,300/K-12
PO Box 3008 92373 909-307-5300
Robert Hodges, supt. Fax 307-5321
www.redlands.k12.ca.us
Clement MS 1,700/6-8
501 E Pennsylvania Ave 92374 909-307-5400
John Massie, prin. Fax 307-5414
Cope MS 1,600/6-8
1000 W Cypress Ave 92373 909-307-5420
Brad Mason, prin. Fax 307-5436
Moore MS 1,500/6-8
1550 E Highland Ave 92374 909-307-5440
Dale Whitehurst, prin. Fax 307-5453
Redlands East Valley HS 3,300/9-12
31000 Colton Ave 92374 909-389-2500
John Maloney, prin. Fax 389-2517
Redlands HS 3,200/9-12
840 E Citrus Ave 92374 909-307-5500
Christina Rivera, prin. Fax 307-5527
Redlands Adult HS Adult
7 W Delaware Ave 92374 909-748-6930
Cheryl Bordelon, prin. Fax 307-5324
Other Schools – See Highland

Regional Occupational Center & Program
Supt. — None
Colton-Redlands-Yucaipa ROP Vo/Tech
1214 Indiana Ct 92374 909-793-3115
Dalene Morris, supt. Fax 793-6901

American College of Health Professions Post-Sec.
700 E Redlands Blvd # U227 92373 909-307-6022
Arrowhead Christian Academy 600/6-12
105 Tennessee St 92373 909-793-0601
Steve Hicok, admin. Fax 792-5691
Calvary Chapel Christian S 300/K-12
9700 Alabama St 92374 909-793-4984
William Johnson, prin. Fax 307-1852
Community Christian College Post-Sec.
251 Tennessee St 92373 909-335-8863
Redlands Adventist Academy 500/K-12
130 Tennessee St 92373 909-793-1000
Dustin Saxton, prin. Fax 793-9862
University of Redlands Post-Sec.
PO Box 3080 92373 909-793-2121

Redondo Beach, Los Angeles, Pop. 66,337
Redondo Beach Unified SD 7,800/PK-12
1401 Inglewood Ave 90278 310-379-5449
Steven Keller Ed.D., supt. Fax 372-5269
www.rbusd.org/
Adams MS 800/6-8
1401 Inglewood Ave 90278 310-798-8636
Karen Westberg, prin. Fax 318-3064
Parras MS 800/6-8
1401 Inglewood Ave 90278 310-798-8616
Sallie Tahajian, prin. Fax 798-8660
Redondo Union HS 2,200/9-12
1401 Inglewood Ave 90278 310-798-8665
Mary Little, prin. Fax 798-4685
South Bay Adult HS Adult
1401 Inglewood Ave 90278 310-937-3340
Gerald Striff, prin. Fax 937-3345

Gates College Post-Sec.
4450 182nd St 90278 310-542-4411
South Bay Faith Academy 400/K-12
PO Box 7000 90277 310-379-8242
Roslyn Ballard, prin.

Redwood City, San Mateo, Pop. 73,472
Redwood City ESD 7,500/PK-8
750 Bradford St 94063 650-423-2200
Jan Christensen, supt. Fax 423-2204
www.rcsd.k12.ca.us

Kennedy MS 1,000/6-8
2521 Goodwin Ave 94061 650-365-4611
Warren Sedar, prin. Fax 367-4362
McKinley Institute of Technology 400/6-8
400 Duane St 94062 650-366-3827
Cheryl Bracco, prin. Fax 367-4363
North Star Academy 500/3-8
400 Duane St 94062 650-482-5973
Ray Dawley, prin. Fax 482-5980

Regional Occupational Center & Program
Supt. — None
San Mateo County ROP Vo/Tech
101 Twin Dolphin Dr 94065 650-802-5411
Diane Centoni, dir. Fax 802-5414

Sequoia UNHSD 17,400/9-12
480 James Ave 94062 650-369-1411
Patrick Gemma, supt. Fax 306-8870
www.seq.org
Sequoia HS 1,500/9-12
1201 Brewster Ave 94062 650-367-9780
Morgan Marchbanks, prin. Fax 368-5180
Other Schools – See Atherton, Belmont, Menlo Park, Woodside

Canada College Post-Sec.
4200 Farm Hill Blvd 94061 650-306-3100

Redwood Valley, Mendocino
Ukiah USD
Supt. — See Ukiah
Eagle Peak MS 500/6-8
8601 West Rd 95470 707-485-8154
Carolyn Johnson, prin. Fax 485-9542

Deep Valley Christian S 200/PK-12
PO Box 9 95470 707-485-8778
Jim Burnham, admin. Fax 485-8804

Reedley, Fresno, Pop. 21,549
Kings Canyon JUSD 8,600/K-12
675 W Manning Ave 93654 559-637-1210
Juan Garza, supt. Fax 637-1292
www.kc-usd.k12.ca.us
Grant MS 700/6-8
360 N East Ave 93654 559-637-1266
Bill Wachtel, prin. Fax 638-6772
Navelencia MS 500/6-8
22620 Wahtoke Ave 93654 559-637-1251
Jeremy Brown, prin. Fax 637-1316
Reedley HS 2,200/9-12
740 W North Ave 93654 559-637-1250
Jeff Wiggams, prin. Fax 637-0458
Kings Canyon Adult S Adult
675 W Manning Ave 93654 559-637-1246
Cecil Trinidad, dir. Fax 637-9563
Other Schools – See Orange Cove

Immanuel HS 400/7-12
1128 S Reed Ave 93654 559-638-2529
Jerry Meadows, supt. Fax 638-7030
Immanuel JSHS 300/7-12
1128 S Reed Ave 93654 559-638-2529
Jerry Meadows, supt.
Reedley College Post-Sec.
995 N Reed Ave 93654 559-638-3641

Rescue, El Dorado
Rescue UNESD 3,600/K-8
2390 Bass Lake Rd 95672 530-677-5446
Carol Bly Ed.D., supt. Fax 677-0719
www.rescue.k12.ca.us/
Pleasant Grove MS 700/6-8
2540 Green Valley Rd 95672 530-672-4400
Reid Briggs, prin. Fax 677-5829
Other Schools – See El Dorado Hills

Reseda, See Los Angeles
Los Angeles USD
Supt. — See Los Angeles
Cleveland HS 3,600/9-12
8140 Vanalden Ave 91335 818-349-8410
Robert Marks, prin. Fax 727-0964
Reseda HS 2,800/9-12
18230 Kittridge St 91335 818-342-6186
Alfredo Tarin, prin. Fax 776-0452
Reseda Adult Education Adult
18230 Kittridge St 91335 818-343-1977
Anna Madrid, prin. Fax 343-2107

Bryman College Post-Sec.
18040 Sherman Way # 400 91335 818-774-0550
Marinello School of Beauty Post-Sec.
18442 Sherman Way 91335 818-881-2521
Trinity Lutheran JSHS 100/7-12
18425 Kittridge St 91335 818-342-7855
Jerry Romsa, prin. Fax 342-4491

Rialto, San Bernardino, Pop. 98,091
Rialto USD 30,400/K-12
182 E Walnut Ave 92376 909-820-7700
Edna D. Herring, supt. Fax 873-0448
www.rialto.k12.ca.us
Eisenhower HS 3,600/9-12
1321 N Lilac Ave 92376 909-820-7777
Reginald Thompkins, prin. Fax 421-7640
Frisbie MS 1,500/6-8
1442 N Eucalyptus Ave 92376 909-820-7887
Robin Santiago, prin. Fax 820-7885
Kolb MS 1,400/6-8
2351 N Spruce Ave 92377 909-820-7849
Felix Avila, prin. Fax 875-0374
Kucera MS 1,600/6-8
2140 W Buena Vista Dr 92377 909-421-7662
Monique Conway, prin. Fax 421-7681
Rialto HS 4,200/9-12
595 S Eucalyptus Ave 92376 909-421-7500
Mehran Akhtarkhavari, prin. Fax 421-7584
Rialto MS 1,400/6-8
324 N Palm Ave 92376 909-820-7838
Mark Bline, prin. Fax 820-7940
Rialto Adult S Adult
595 S Eucalyptus Ave 92376 909-820-7785
Peggy Wheeler, prin.
Other Schools – See Colton

Lighthouse Christian Academy 100/PK-12
PO Box 520 92377 909-820-2191
Sharon Pierce, prin. Fax 820-2323

Richgrove, Tulare, Pop. 1,899
Richgrove ESD 500/K-8
PO Box 540 93261 661-725-2427
Frank Chavez, supt. Fax 725-5772
www.richgrove.org
Richgrove JHS 6-8
20908 Grove Dr 93261 661-725-0315
Frank Chavez, prin.

Richmond, Contra Costa, Pop. 102,327
West Contra Costa USD 33,100/K-12
1108 Bissell Ave 94801 510-234-3825
Fax 236-6784
www.wccusd.k12.ca.us
Adams MS 700/6-8
5000 Patterson Cir 94805 510-235-5464
Bonnie Glover, prin. Fax 233-9450
De Anza HS 1,400/9-12
5000 Valley View Rd 94803 510-223-3811
Vera Rowsey, prin. Fax 223-7984
DeJean MS 1,000/6-8
3400 Macdonald Ave 94805 510-412-8300
Antoinette Henry-Evans, prin. Fax 236-6680
Kennedy HS 1,000/9-12
4300 Cutting Blvd 94804 510-235-2291
Julio Franco, prin. Fax 235-1915
Richmond HS 1,800/9-12
1250 23rd St 94804 510-237-8770
Terry Ishmael, prin. Fax 235-0316
Adult Education Adult
5625 Sutter Ave 94804 510-559-2660
Jim Trombley, prin. Fax 559-2664
West CC Adult Ed Center Adult
6028 Ralston Ave 94805 510-215-4666
Tim Shaw, prin. Fax 215-0430
Other Schools – See El Cerrito, El Sobrante, Hercules, Pinole, San Pablo

---

Argosy University/San Francisco Campus Post-Sec.
999 Canal Blvd Ste A 94804 510-215-0277
Kaiser Permanente Medical Center Post-Sec.
901 Nevin Ave 94801 510-307-2412
La Cheim S 50/1-12
2853 Groom Dr 94806 510-243-2360
Karen Jackson, dir. Fax 243-2370
Salesian HS 400/9-12
2851 Salesian Ave 94804 510-234-4434
Tim Chambers, prin. Fax 236-4636

Ridgecrest, Kern, Pop. 25,635
Sierra Sands USD 6,100/K-12
113 W Felspar Ave 93555 760-375-3363
Joanna Rummer, supt. Fax 375-3338
www.ssusd.org
Burroughs HS 1,600/9-12
500 E French Ave 93555 760-375-4476
Ernie Bell, prin. Fax 375-1735
Monroe MS 600/6-8
340 W Church Ave 93555 760-375-1301
Dave Ostash, prin. Fax 375-8781
Murray MS 800/6-8
921 E Inyokern Rd 93555 760-446-5525
Kirsti Smith, prin. Fax 446-3838
Sierra Sands Adult S Adult
140 Drummond Ave 93555 760-446-5872
Ingrid Larsen, prin. Fax 499-7053

Calvary Christian S 50/K-12
PO Box 2138 93556 760-375-3133
Glenn Hill, prin. Fax 375-2694
Cerro Coso Community College Post-Sec.
3000 College Heights Blvd 93555 760-384-6100
Immanuel Christian S 200/PK-12
201 W Graaf Ave 93555 760-446-6114
Dr. Wes Johnston, prin. Fax 446-7035

Rio Dell, Humboldt, Pop. 3,148
Rio Dell ESD 300/K-8
95 Center St 95562 707-764-5694
Mary Varner, supt. Fax 764-2656
internet.humboldt.k12.ca.us/riodell_sd/
Monument MS 100/7-8
95 Center St 95562 707-764-3783
Jeff Northern, prin. Fax 764-2656

Rio Linda, Sacramento, Pop. 9,481
Grant JUNHSD
Supt. — See Sacramento
Rio Linda HS 1,800/9-12
6309 Dry Creek Rd 95673 916-286-4500
Stephen Liles, prin. Fax 263-6462
Rio Linda JHS 600/7-8
1101 G St 95673 916-286-1601
Harjinder Mattu, prin. Fax 263-4674

Rio Vista, Solano, Pop. 6,142
River Delta USD 2,400/K-12
445 Montezuma St 94571 707-374-6381
Dr. Alan Newell, supt. Fax 374-2995
www.riverdelta.k12.ca.us/
Rio Vista HS 400/9-12
410 S 4th St 94571 707-374-6336
Dennis Wallin, prin. Fax 374-6810
Riverview MS 300/5-8
525 S 2nd St 94571 707-374-2345
James Lake, prin. Fax 374-5623
Wind River Adult S Adult
410 S 4th St 94571 707-374-5610
Robert Hubbell, prin. Fax 374-2944
Other Schools – See Clarksburg

Ripon, San Joaquin, Pop. 12,150
Ripon USD 3,000/K-12
304 N Acacia Ave 95366 209-599-2131
Leo Zuber, supt. Fax 599-6271
www.riponusd.net/
Ripon HS, 301 N Acacia Ave 95366 800/9-12
Jeff Frase, prin. 209-599-4287
Ripon Adult S Adult
304 N Acacia Ave 95366 209-599-2131
Lisa Boje, prin.

Ripon Christian HS 300/9-12
435 Maple Ave 95366 209-599-2155
William Finley, prin. Fax 599-2170

Riverbank, Stanislaus, Pop. 17,847
Riverbank USD 3,000/K-12
6715 7th St 95367 209-869-2538
Joseph Galindo, supt. Fax 869-1487
www.riverbank.k12.ca.us/home
Cardozo MS 800/6-8
3525 Santa Fe St 95367 209-869-2591
Richard Shahbazian, prin. Fax 869-2714
Riverbank HS 800/9-12
6200 Claus Rd 95367 209-869-1891
Ken Geisick, prin. Fax 869-2116

Riverdale, Fresno, Pop. 1,980
Riverdale USD 1,500/K-12
PO Box 1058 93656 559-867-8200
Elaine Cash, supt. Fax 867-6722
www.riverdale.k12.ca.us
Riverdale ES 600/4-8
PO Box 338 93656 559-867-3589
Mark Allein, prin. Fax 867-3393
Riverdale HS 500/9-12
PO Box 726 93656 559-867-3562
Peter Faragia, prin. Fax 867-4750

Riverside, Riverside, Pop. 281,514
Alvord USD 19,300/K-12
10365 Keller Ave 92505 951-509-5070
Paul Jessup, supt. Fax 509-6070
www.alvord.k12.ca.us
Arizona MS 1,200/6-8
10365 Keller Ave 92505 951-351-9343
Chuck Fischer, prin. Fax 351-2187
La Sierra HS 2,800/9-12
10365 Keller Ave 92505 951-351-9238
Robert Cunard, prin. Fax 351-9307
Loma Vista MS 1,100/6-8
10365 Keller Ave 92505 951-351-9216
Kevin Hawkins, prin. Fax 351-2153
Norte Vista HS 2,300/9-12
10365 Keller Ave 92505 951-351-9201
Santos Campos, prin. Fax 351-9249
Villegas MS 1,400/6-8
10365 Keller Ave 92505 951-351-6622
Julie Koehler-Mount, prin. Fax 351-7515
Wells MS 1,000/6-8
10365 Keller Ave 92505 951-351-9241
Patricia Nilsen, prin. Fax 351-6606

Jurupa USD 20,600/K-12
4850 Pedley Rd 92509 951-360-4100
Elliott Duchon, supt. Fax 360-4194
www.jusd.k12.ca.us
Jurupa MS 1,100/7-8
8700 Galena St 92509 951-360-2846
Walter Lancaster, prin. Fax 360-8928
Mira Loma MS 1,200/7-8
5051 Steve St 92509 951-360-2883
Cindy Freeman, prin. Fax 685-7405
Mission MS 1,100/7-8
5961 Mustang Ln 92509 951-222-7842
Luz Mendez, prin. Fax 369-1407
Rubidoux HS 2,600/9-12
4250 Opal St 92509 951-222-7821
Jay Trujillo, prin. Fax 779-1035
Adult Education Adult
4041 Pacific Ave 92509 951-222-7739
George Monge, prin. Fax 788-8689
Other Schools – See Mira Loma

Regional Occupational Center & Program
Supt. — None
Riverside County ROP Vo/Tech
PO Box 868 92502 951-826-6797
Kevin Rubow, dir. Fax 826-6440

Riverside USD 43,600/K-12
PO Box 2800 92516 951-788-7134
Dr. Susan Rainey, supt. Fax 788-7110
www.rusd.k12.ca.us
Arlington HS 2,200/9-12
2951 Jackson St 92503 951-788-7240
David Hansen, prin. Fax 788-7542
Central MS 800/7-8
4795 Magnolia Ave 92506 951-788-7282
Antonio Garcia, prin. Fax 276-2028
Chemawa MS 1,300/7-8
8830 Magnolia Ave 92503 951-352-8244
Susan Baltagi, prin. Fax 687-6949
Earhart MS 1,500/7-8
20202 Aptos St 92508 951-697-5700
Barbara Carpenter, prin. Fax 697-5733
Gage MS 1,200/7-8
6400 Lincoln Ave 92506 951-788-7350
Charles Hiroto, prin. Fax 787-8067
King HS 2,600/9-12
9301 Wood Rd 92508 951-789-5690
Karen Stevenson, prin. Fax 789-5692
North HS 2,400/9-12
1550 3rd St 92507 951-788-7311
Dale Kinnear, prin. Fax 276-2075
Polytechnic HS Vo/Tech
5450 Victoria Ave 92506 951-788-7203
Frank Paredes, prin. Fax 784-2306
Ramona HS 2,000/9-12
7675 Magnolia Ave 92504 951-352-8429
Mike Neece, prin. Fax 352-8446
Sierra MS 1,000/7-8
4950 Central Ave 92504 951-788-7501
Wade Coe, prin. Fax 788-7561
University Heights MS 1,000/7-8
1155 Massachusetts Ave 92507 951-788-7388
Patricia Grice, prin. Fax 276-7649
Riverside Adult S Adult
6735 Magnolia Ave 92506 951-788-7185
Cliff Weaver, prin. Fax 369-4966

Bethel Christian S 300/PK-12
2425 Van Buren Blvd 92503 951-359-1123
Dr. Carl Vaughn, admin. Fax 359-1719
California Baptist University Post-Sec.
8432 Magnolia Ave 92504 951-689-5771
CEI Post-Sec.
1635 Spruce St 92507 951-276-1704
Huntington College of Health Sciences Post-Sec.
7339 Lakeside Dr 92509 800-290-4226
La Sierra Academy 700/K-12
4900 Golden Ave 92505 951-351-1445
Dr. Cyril Connelly, prin. Fax 689-3708
La Sierra University Post-Sec.
4700 Pierce St 92505 951-785-2022
Notre Dame HS 600/9-12
7085 Brockton Ave 92506 951-275-5896
Dr. JoDean Salley, prin. Fax 781-9020
Olive Tree Christian S 400/K-12
4864 Rockingham Pl 92509 951-685-6325
Rebecca Kocsis, admin.
Riverside Christian HS 500/7-12
3532 Monroe St 92504 951-687-0077
Morris Lewis, supt. Fax 687-3340
Riverside Community College Post-Sec.
4800 Magnolia Ave 92506 951-222-8000
Somerset Educational Services 200/7-12
PO Box 20529 92516 951-789-4405
Joseph McCoy, dir.
University of California Post-Sec.
900 University Ave 92521 951-827-1012
Woodcrest Christian S 700/7-12
18401 Van Buren Blvd 92508 951-780-2010
Randy Thompson, supt. Fax 780-2079

Rocklin, Placer, Pop. 46,937
Rocklin USD 8,900/K-12
2615 Sierra Meadows Dr 95677 916-624-2428
Kevin Brown, supt. Fax 630-2229
www.rocklin.k12.ca.us
Granite Oaks MS 800/7-8
2600 Wyckford Blvd 95765 916-315-9009
Mike Melton, prin. Fax 315-9885
Rocklin HS 2,500/9-12
5301 Victory Ln 95765 916-632-1600
Mike Garrison, prin. Fax 632-0305
Spring View MS 800/7-8
5040 5th St 95677 916-624-3381
Marjorie Crawford, prin. Fax 624-5737
Whitney HS 9-12
701 Wildcat Blvd 95765 916-632-6500
Debra Hawkins, prin. Fax 435-2542

Sierra Christian Academy 500/PK-12
6900 Destiny Dr 95677 916-772-1440
Cynthia White, admin. Fax 773-0304
Sierra College Post-Sec.
5000 Rocklin Rd 95677 916-624-3333

Rohnert Park, Sonoma, Pop. 41,871
Cotati-Rohnert Park USD 7,300/K-12
5860 Labath Ave 94928 707-792-4722
Michael Watenpaugh, supt. Fax 792-4537
www.crpusd.org/
Creekside MS 900/6-8
5154 Snyder Ln 94928 707-588-5600
Bob Dahlstet, prin. Fax 588-5607
Mountain Shadows MS 1,000/6-8
7165 Burton Ave 94928 707-792-4800
Laura Mason, prin. Fax 792-4516
Rancho Cotate HS 2,000/9-12
5450 Snyder Ln 94928 707-792-4750
Joseph Williams, prin. Fax 792-4758
Technology HS Vo/Tech
1801 E Cotati Ave 94928 707-792-4825
Kay Dorner, prin. Fax 792-4727

Sonoma State University Post-Sec.
1801 E Cotati Ave 94928 707-664-2880

Rolling Hills, Los Angeles, Pop. 1,931
Palos Verdes Peninsula USD
Supt. — See Palos Verdes Estates
Palos Verdes Peninsula HS 2,800/9-12
27118 Silver Spur Rd 90274 310-377-4888
Kelly Johnson, prin. Fax 544-1839
PVPUSD Adult Education Adult
38 Crest Rd W 90274 310-541-7626
Rosemary Humphrey, prin. Fax 265-5967

Rosamond, Kern, Pop. 7,430
Southern Kern USD 3,100/K-12
PO Box CC 93560 661-256-5000
Rodney Van Norman, supt. Fax 256-1247
www.skusd.k12.ca.us
Rosamond HS 700/9-12
PO Box CC 93560 661-256-5020
Jeffrey Fisher, prin. Fax 256-6880
Tropico MS 800/6-8
PO Box CC 93560 661-256-5040
Rebecca Evers, prin. Fax 256-0630
Southern Kern Adult S Adult
PO Box CC 93560 661-256-5090
Mike Luckenbill, prin. Fax 256-6868

Rosemead, Los Angeles, Pop. 55,262
Alhambra City SD
Supt. — See Alhambra
Southeast Community Adult S Adult
7422 Garvey Ave 91770 626-572-2280
John Kao, prin. Fax 573-4308

El Monte UNHSD
Supt. — See El Monte
Rosemead HS 2,000/9-12
9063 Mission Dr 91770 626-286-3141
Diane Bladen, prin. Fax 286-6396

Garvey ESD 6,600/K-8
2730 Del Mar Ave 91770 626-307-3400
Virginia Peterson Ed.D., supt. Fax 307-1964
www.garvey.k12.ca.us
Garvey IS 800/7-8
2720 Jackson Ave 91770 626-307-3385
Lindsey Ma, prin. Fax 307-3443
Temple IS 500/7-8
8470 Fern Ave 91770 626-307-3360
C.P. Cheung, prin. Fax 307-8162

Rosemead SD 3,300/K-8
3907 Rosemead Blvd 91770 626-312-2900
Amy Enomoto-Perez Ed.D., supt. Fax 312-2906
www.rosemead.k12.ca.us
Muscatel MS 700/7-8
4201 Ivar Ave 91770 626-287-1139
Dean Wharton, prin. Fax 292-1741

Don Bosco Technical Institute Post-Sec.
1151 San Gabriel Blvd 91770 626-307-6500
Don Bosco Technical Institute 1,000/9-12
1151 San Gabriel Blvd 91770 626-940-2000
Fr. Michael Gergen, prin. Fax 940-2001
Edgewood College of California Post-Sec.
4930 Earle Ave 91770 626-291-5000
Rosemead Beauty School Post-Sec.
8531 Valley Blvd 91770 626-286-2147
University of the West Post-Sec.
1409 Walnut Grove Ave 91770 626-571-8811

Roseville, Placer, Pop. 98,359
Center USD
Supt. — See Antelope
Riles MS 6-8
4747 PFE Rd 95747 916-787-8100
Joyce Duplissea, prin. Fax 773-4131

Dry Creek ESD 7,000/K-8
9707 Cook Riolo Rd 95747 916-771-0646
Kelvin Lee, supt. Fax 771-0650
www.drycreek.k12.ca.us
Silverado MS 1,300/6-8
2525 Country Club Dr 95747 916-780-2620
Kevin Kurtz, prin. Fax 780-2635
Other Schools – See Antelope

Eureka UNSD
Supt. — See Granite Bay
Olympus JHS 500/7-8
2625 La Croix Dr 95661 916-782-1667
Kelly Graham, prin. Fax 782-1339

Roseville City ESD 7,500/K-8
1000 Darling Way 95678 916-771-1600
Richard Pierrucci, supt. Fax 786-5098
www.rcsdk8.org
Buljan MS 900/6-8
100 Hallissey Dr 95678 916-773-2059
Greg Gunn, prin. Fax 773-2696
Cooley MS 800/6-8
9300 Prairie Woods Way 95747 916-786-3030
Karen Calkins, prin. Fax 786-3003
Eich IS 500/7-8
1509 Sierra Gardens Dr 95661 916-783-5245
Christine Hudson, prin. Fax 783-7292

Roseville JUNHSD 6,500/9-12
1750 Cirby Way 95661 916-786-2051
Tony Monetti, supt. Fax 786-2681
www.rjuhsd.k12.ca.us
Oakmont HS 1,600/9-12
1710 Cirby Way 95661 916-782-3781
Kathleen Sirovy, prin. Fax 782-4943
Roseville HS 1,700/9-12
1 Tiger Way 95678 916-782-3753
John Montgomery, prin. Fax 786-5281
Woodcreek HS 2,100/9-12
2551 Woodcreek Oaks Blvd 95747 916-771-6565
Jess Borjon, prin. Fax 771-6596
Roseville Adult S Adult
200 Branstetter St 95678 916-782-3952
Joyce Lude, dir. Fax 782-4361
Other Schools – See Granite Bay

Christian Life Academy 50/K-12
628 Royer St 95678 916-956-4662
Peggy Gubitz, prin. Fax 786-7916
Cornerstone Christian S 200/K-12
143 Clinton Ave 95678 916-783-7779
Dr. D. Craig Garbe, hdmstr. Fax 783-1856
Heald College Post-Sec.
7 Sierra Gate Plz 95678 916-789-8600
Valley Christian Academy 300/PK-12
301 W Whyte Ave 95678 916-728-5500
Dr. Brad Gunter, admin. Fax 721-3305

Ross, Marin, Pop. 2,298

Branson HS 300/9-12
PO Box 887 94957 415-454-3612
Peter Esty, hdmstr. Fax 454-2327

Rowland Heights, Los Angeles, Pop. 49,900
Rowland USD 18,900/K-12
1830 Nogales St 91748 626-965-2541
Dr. Maria Ott, supt. Fax 854-8302
www.rowland-unified.org
Alvarado IS 1,200/7-8
1901 Desire Ave 91748 626-964-2358
Nancy Padilla, prin. Fax 810-5579
Rowland HS 2,500/9-12
2000 Otterbein Ave 91748 626-965-3448
Bill Weirich, prin. Fax 810-4859
Rowland Adult & Continuing Education Adult
2100 Lerona Ave 91748 626-965-5975
Rocky Bettar, prin. Fax 854-1191
Other Schools – See La Puente, West Covina

Sacramento, Sacramento, Pop. 445,335
Elk Grove USD
Supt. — See Elk Grove
Florin HS 2,400/9-12
7956 Cottonwood Ln 95828 916-689-8600
Philip Moore, prin. Fax 689-7430
Jackman MS 1,400/7-8
7925 Kentwall Dr 95823 916-393-2352
William Del Bonta, prin. Fax 393-4053
Rutter MS 1,400/7-8
7350 Palmer House Dr 95828 916-422-7590
Sara Noguchi, prin. Fax 422-8354
Sheldon HS 3,300/9-12
8333 Kingsbridge Dr 95829 916-681-7500
Paula Duncan, prin. Fax 681-7505
Smedberg MS 1,800/7-8
8239 Kingsbridge Dr 95829 916-681-7525
Fax 681-7530
Valley HS 2,300/9-12
6300 Ehrhardt Ave 95823 916-689-6500
Roger Stock, prin. Fax 682-1528
Adult/Community Education Adult
8401 Gerber Rd 95828 916-686-7717
Dr. Tim Taylor, prin. Fax 689-5752
Always Learning Adult
8401 Gerber Rd # A 95828 916-686-7783
Maureen Sawyer, admin. Fax 689-4372

Grant JUNHSD 12,300/7-12
1333 Grand Ave 95838 916-286-4800
Larry Buchanan Ed.D., supt. Fax 263-6247
www.grant.k12.ca.us
Foothill Farms JHS 1,000/7-8
5001 Diablo Dr 95842 916-286-1400
Leslie Mankoski, prin. Fax 263-3756
Foothill HS 1,500/9-12
5000 McCloud Dr 95842 916-286-1300
Larry Tosta, prin. Fax 263-4685
Grant HS - Main Campus 2,200/9-12
1400 Grand Ave 95838 916-286-1000
Craig Murray, prin. Fax 263-6326
Grant West HS 9-12
1221 South Ave 95838 916-286-1200
Larry Brown, prin. Fax 263-6686
King JHS 1,100/7-8
3051 Fairfield St 95815 916-286-4700
Samuel Harris, prin. Fax 263-6701
Norwood JHS 600/7-8
4601 Norwood Ave 95838 916-649-6600
Roxanne Mitchell, prin. Fax 649-6696
Rio Tierra JHS 700/7-8
3201 Northstead Dr 95833 916-286-1500
Leo Burns, prin. Fax 263-6971
Vista Nueva Career & Tech HS Vo/Tech
2035 North Ave 95838 916-286-1100
Michael Crossetti, prin. Fax 263-6498
Grant Dist Skills/Adult Center Adult
577 Las Palmas Ave 95815 916-286-7527
Hal Steward, dir.
Other Schools – See North Highlands, Rio Linda

Natomas USD 7,600/K-12
1901 Arena Blvd 95834 916-567-5400
Dr. Steve Farrar, supt. Fax 567-5405
www.natomas.k12.ca.us
Greene MS 800/6-8
2950 W River Dr 95833 916-567-5560
Bob Evans, prin. Fax 567-5569
Inderkum HS 9-12
2500 New Market Dr 95835 916-567-5640
Ben Flores, prin. Fax 567-5649
Natomas HS 2,100/9-12
3301 Fong Ranch Rd 95834 916-641-4960
Troy Johnston, prin. Fax 641-5455
Natomas MS 900/6-8
3700 Del Paso Rd 95834 916-567-5540
Carla Najera-Kunsemiller, prin. Fax 567-5549
Sacramento Valley Technical HS Vo/Tech
2500 New Market Dr 95835 916-567-5880
Tanya Parker, dir. Fax 567-5889

Regional Occupational Center & Program
Supt. — None
Sacramento County ROP Vo/Tech
PO Box 269003 95826 916-228-2459
Linda Mitchell, prin. Fax 228-2459

Sacramento City USD 55,600/K-12
5735 47th Ave 95824 916-643-7400
Dr. Maggie Mejia, supt. Fax 643-9480
www.scusd.edu
Bacon Basic MS 1,000/6-8
4140 Cuny Ave 95823 916-433-5000
Gloria Nogales-Talley, prin. Fax 433-5166
Brannan MS 1,100/7-8
5301 Elmer Way 95822 916-264-4350
Nancy Purcell, prin. Fax 264-4481
Burbank HS 2,400/9-12
3500 Florin Rd 95823 916-433-5100
Ted Appel, prin. Fax 433-5199
California MS 900/7-8
1600 Vallejo Way 95818 916-264-4550
Elizabeth Vigil, prin. Fax 264-4477
Carson MS 700/6-8
5301 N St 95819 916-277-6750
Catherine Beckworth, prin. Fax 277-6550
Einstein MS 1,000/7-8
9325 Mirandy Dr 95826 916-228-5800
Fax 228-5813
Goethe MS 800/7-8
2250 68th Ave 95822 916-433-5400
Harriet Young, prin. Fax 433-5518
Johnson HS 2,400/9-12
6879 14th Ave 95820 916-277-6300
Lynne Tafoya, prin. Fax 277-6740
Johnson HS West Campus 800/9-12
5022 58th St 95820 916-277-6400
John Becker, prin. Fax 277-6593
Kennedy HS 2,500/9-12
6715 Gloria Dr 95831 916-433-5200
Mary Shelton, prin. Fax 433-5511
McClatchy HS 2,500/9-12
3066 Freeport Blvd 95818 916-264-4400
Dr. Daisy Lee, prin. Fax 264-4499
Rosemont HS 1,200/9-12
9594 Kiefer Blvd 95827 916-228-5844
Rob Jones, prin. Fax 228-5733
Sutter MS 1,200/7-8
3150 I St 95816 916-264-4150
Greg Purcell, prin. Fax 264-3436
Wood MS 1,000/7-8
6201 Lemon Hill Ave 95824 916-382-5900
James Wong, prin. Fax 382-5914
Florin Technology Education Center Adult
2401 Florin Rd 95822 916-433-2844
Mary Prather, prin.

Fremont S for Adults | Adult
2420 N St 95816 | 916-277-6620
John Miller, prin. | Fax 277-6617
Jones Skills Center | Adult
5451 Lemon Hill Ave 95824 | 916-433-2600
Kirk Williams, prin. | Fax 433-2640
McClaskey Adult Education Center | Adult
5241 J St 95819 | 916-277-6625
Susan Gilmore, prin. | Fax 277-6810
Old Marshall Adult Education Center | Adult
2718 G St 95816 | 916-264-4113
Mary Prather, prin. | Fax 264-4098

San Juan USD
Supt. — See Carmichael
Arcade Fundamental MS | 600/6-8
3500 Edison Ave 95821 | 916-971-7300
Tony Oddo, prin. | Fax 971-7821
Arden MS | 700/6-8
1640 Watt Ave 95864 | 916-971-7306
Peggy Picardo, prin. | Fax 971-7830
El Camino Fundamental HS | 1,700/9-12
4300 El Camino Ave 95821 | 916-971-7430
Ernie Boone, prin. | Fax 971-7429
Encina HS | 800/9-12
1400 Bell St 95825 | 916-971-7538
Myrtle Berry, prin. | Fax 971-7555
Mira Loma HS | 1,800/9-12
4000 Edison Ave 95821 | 916-971-7485
Christopher Hoffman, prin. | Fax 971-7483
Rio Americano HS | 1,800/9-12
4540 American River Dr 95864 | 916-971-7494
Rob Hollingsworth, prin. | Fax 971-7513
Salk MS | 500/6-8
2950 Hurley Way 95864 | 916-971-7312
Jody Graf, prin. | Fax 971-7694
Orange Grove Adult Education | Adult
4640 Orange Grove Ave 95841 | 916-971-7399
Jan Brewer, prin. | Fax 482-3540
Winterstein Adult Center | Adult
900 Morse Ave 95864 | 916-971-7419
Bill Bettencourt, prin. | Fax 482-8857

Alliant International University | Post-Sec.
425 University Ave Ste 211 95825 | 916-565-2955
American River College | Post-Sec.
4700 College Oak Dr 95841 | 916-484-8011
Bradshaw Christian S | 900/PK-12
8324 Bradshaw Rd 95829 | 916-688-0521
Brett Mowery, prin. | Fax 688-0502
California State University-Sacramento | Post-Sec.
6000 J St 95819 | 916-278-6011
Calvary Christian S | 300/K-12
5051 47th Ave 95824 | 916-393-3633
Jeffrey Stone, prin. | Fax 393-5000
Capital Christian HS | 600/6-12
9470 Micron Ave 95827 | 916-856-5611
Todd Jacobs, prin. | Fax 856-5950
Christian Brothers HS | 900/9-12
4315 Mrtn Lthr King Jr Blvd 95820 | 916-733-3600
Raymond Burnell, prin. | Fax 733-3657
Cosumnes River College | Post-Sec.
8401 Center Pkwy 95823 | 916-691-7344
Elite Progressive School of Cosmetology | Post-Sec.
5522 Garfield Ave 95841 | 916-338-1885
Federico College of Hairstyling | Post-Sec.
1515 Sports Dr 95834 | 916-929-4242
Florin Christian S | 200/K-12
8144 Florin Rd 95828 | 916-386-9792
Gloria Flores, prin.
High-Tech Institute | Post-Sec.
9738 Lincoln Village Dr 95827 | 866-502-2627
Loretto HS | 400/9-12
2360 El Camino Ave 95821 | 916-482-7793
Sr. Barbara Nelson, prin. | Fax 482-3621
Maric College - Sacramento Campus | Post-Sec.
4330 Watt Ave Ste 400 95821 | 916-649-8168
MTI College | Post-Sec.
5221 Madison Ave 95841 | 916-339-1500
My-Le's Beauty College | Post-Sec.
5972 Stockton Blvd 95824 | 916-422-0223
Precision Technical Institute | Post-Sec.
9342 Tech Center Dr # 600 95826 | 916-366-3431
Sacramento City College | Post-Sec.
3835 Freeport Blvd 95822 | 916-558-2111
Sacramento Country Day S | 600/PK-12
2636 Latham Dr 95864 | 916-481-8811
Stephen T. Repsher, prin. | Fax 481-6016
Sacramento Medical Foundation Blood Bank | Post-Sec.
1625 Stockton Blvd 95816 | 916-456-1500
St. Francis HS | 800/9-12
5900 Elvas Ave 95819 | 916-452-3461
Andreas Agos, prin. | Fax 452-1591
Success HS, 2245 Florin Rd 95822 | 200/9-12
James Scott, dir. | 916-392-5277
Trinity Life Bible College | Post-Sec.
5225 Hillsdale Blvd 95842 | 916-348-4689
Truck Driving Academy | Post-Sec.
5711 Florin Perkins Rd 95828 | 916-381-2285
Universal Technical Institute | Post-Sec.
4400 E Commerce Dr 95834
University of California-Davis | Post-Sec.
2315 Stockton Blvd 95817 | 916-453-3096
University of the Pacific-McGeorge Sch. | Post-Sec.
3200 5th Ave 95817 | 916-739-7105
Western Career College | Post-Sec.
8909 Folsom Blvd 95826 | 916-361-1660
Western Pacific Truck School | Post-Sec.
8720 Fruitridge Rd 95826 | 800-333-1233

Saint Helena, Napa, Pop. 6,028
St. Helena USD | 1,500/K-12
465 Main St 94574 | 707-967-2708
Allan Gordon, supt. | Fax 963-1335
www.sthelena.k12.ca.us
St. Helena HS | 500/9-12
1401 Grayson Ave 94574 | 707-967-2740
James Zoll, prin. | Fax 967-2735
Stevenson MS | 300/6-8
1316 Hillview Pl 94574 | 707-967-2725
Lance Hanson, prin. | Fax 967-2734

Culinary Institute of America Greystone | Post-Sec.
2555 Main St 94574 | 800-888-7850

Salida, Stanislaus, Pop. 4,499
Salida UNESD | 3,400/K-8
4801 Sisk Rd 95368 | 209-545-0339
Antonio L. Borba Ed.D., supt. | Fax 545-2682
www.salida.k12.ca.us/
Salida MS - Vella Campus | 1,000/6-8
5041 Toomes Rd 95368 | 209-545-1633
Mike Kinsey, prin. | Fax 545-0831

Maric College | Post-Sec.
5172 Kiernan Ct 95368 | 209-543-7000

Salinas, Monterey, Pop. 147,840
Regional Occupational Center & Program
Supt. — None
Mission Trails ROP | Vo/Tech
867 E Laurel Dr 93905 | 831-753-4209
Eric Deleissegues, dir. | Fax 422-5115
Salinas UNHSD | 31,700/7-12
431 W Alisal St 93901 | 831-796-7000
Roger Anton, supt. | Fax 796-7005
www.salinas.k12.ca.us
Alisal HS | 2,200/9-12
777 Williams Rd 93905 | 831-796-7610
Dan Burns, prin. | Fax 796-7605
El Sausal MS | 900/7-8
1155 E Alisal St 93905 | 831-796-7200
Sylvia Echeverri, prin. | Fax 796-7205
Everret Alvarez HS | 2,200/9-12
1900 Independence Blvd 93906 | 831-796-7810
Darren Sylvia, prin. | Fax 796-7805
Harden MS | 1,200/7-8
1561 McKinnon St 93906 | 831-796-7310
Abel Valdez, prin. | Fax 796-7305
La Paz MS | 1,100/7-8
1300 N Sanborn Rd 93905 | 831-796-7900
Steve Oliver, prin. | Fax 796-7905
North Salinas HS | 2,000/9-12
55 Kip Dr 93906 | 831-796-7500
Augie Caresani, prin. | Fax 796-7505
Salinas HS | 2,600/9-12
726 S Main St 93901 | 831-796-7400
John Macias, prin. | Fax 796-7405
Washington MS | 1,300/7-8
560 Iverson St 93901 | 831-796-7100
Candy McCarthy, prin. | Fax 796-7105
Salinas Adult S | Adult
20 Sherwood Pl 93906 | 831-796-6900
Corinne Price, prin. | Fax 796-6905

Santa Rita UNESD | 3,100/K-8
57 Russell Rd 93906 | 831-443-7200
James Fontana, supt. | Fax 442-1729
www.santaritaschools.org
Gavilan View MS | 1,100/6-8
18250 Van Buren Ave 93906 | 831-443-7212
Tom Dietrich, prin. | Fax 443-0908

Spreckels UNESD
Supt. — See Spreckels
Buena Vista MS | 300/6-8
18250 Tara Dr 93908 | 831-455-8936
Eric Tarallo, prin. | Fax 455-8832

Washington UNESD | 1,000/K-8
43 San Benancio Rd 93908 | 831-484-2166
Catherine Gallegos, supt. | Fax 484-2828
schools.monterey.k12.ca.us/~sbenanci/
San Benancio MS | 400/6-8
43 San Benancio Rd 93908 | 831-484-1172
Walt Robison, prin.

Hartnell College | Post-Sec.
156 Homestead Ave 93901 | 831-755-6700
Heald College | Post-Sec.
1450 N Main St 93906 | 831-443-1700
Notre Dame HS | 400/9-12
455 Palma Dr 93901 | 831-751-1850
Sally Donnelly, prin. | Fax 757-5749
Palma HS | 700/7-12
919 Iverson St 93901 | 831-422-6391
Br. Patrick Dunne, prin. | Fax 422-5065

San Andreas, Calaveras, Pop. 2,115
Calaveras USD | 4,000/K-12
PO Box 788 95249 | 209-754-3504
Jim Frost, supt. | Fax 754-5361
www.calaveras.k12.ca.us
Calaveras HS | 1,100/9-12
PO Box 607 95249 | 209-754-1811
Mike Merrill, prin. | Fax 754-0276
Other Schools – See Valley Springs

San Anselmo, Marin, Pop. 12,132
Ross Valley SD | 1,500/K-8
110 Shaw Dr 94960 | 415-454-2162
Cheryl Crawley, supt. | Fax 454-6840
rvsd.marin.k12.ca.us
Other Schools – See Fairfax

Tamalpais UNHSD
Supt. — See Larkspur
Sir Francis Drake HS | 1,000/9-12
1327 Sir Francis Drake Blvd 94960 | 415-453-8770
Don Drake, prin. | Fax 458-3429

San Domenico HS | 100/9-12
1500 Butterfield Rd 94960 | 415-258-1939
Tekakwitha Wise, prin. | Fax 258-1901
San Domenico MS | 100/6-8
1500 Butterfield Rd 94960 | 415-258-1908
Jay Buckley, prin. | Fax 258-1901
San Francisco Theological Seminary | Post-Sec.
105 Seminary Rd 94960 | 415-451-2800

San Bernardino, San Bernardino, Pop. 195,357
Regional Occupational Center & Program
Supt. — None
San Bernadino County ROP | Vo/Tech
601 N E St 92410 | 909-386-2449
Mark Lyons, dir. | Fax 386-2479

San Bernardino City USD | 66,200/K-12
777 N F St 92410 | 909-381-1100
Dr. Arturo Delgado, supt. | Fax 388-1451
www.sbcusd.k12.ca.us
Arrowview MS | 1,600/7-8
2299 N G St 92405 | 909-881-8109
Arwyn Wild, prin. | Fax 881-8119
Arroyo Valley HS | 3,100/9-12
1881 W Base Line St 92411 | 909-381-4605
Karen Craig, prin. | Fax 386-2577
Cajon HS | 2,600/9-12
1200 W Hill Dr 92407 | 909-881-8120
Brett Killeen, prin. | Fax 881-8141
Chavez MS | 6-8
6650 N Magnolia Ave 92407 | 909-381-1186
Stephanie Cereceres, prin.
Curtis MS | 1,300/6-8
1472 E 6th St 92410 | 909-388-6332
Jim Dilday, prin. | Fax 388-6339
Del Vallejo MS | 1,500/6-8
1885 E Lynwood Dr 92404 | 909-881-8280
Charles McWilliams, prin. | Fax 881-8285
Golden Valley MS | 1,400/6-8
3800 N Waterman Ave 92404 | 909-881-8168
Steve Perlut, prin. | Fax 881-5196
King MS | 1,400/6-8
1250 Medical Center Dr 92411 | 909-388-6350
James Espinoza, prin. | Fax 388-6361
Pacific HS | 2,600/9-12
1020 Pacific St 92404 | 909-388-6419
Kenneth Martinez, prin. | Fax 388-6427
Richardson Prep JHS | 600/6-8
455 S K St 92410 | 909-388-6438
James Kissinger, prin. | Fax 383-0368
San Bernardino HS | 2,500/9-12
1850 N E St 92405 | 909-881-8217
Darryl Adams, prin. | Fax 881-8245
San Gorgonio HS | 3,000/9-12
2299 Pacific St 92404 | 909-388-6524
Sandra Robbins, prin. | Fax 889-3439
Shandin Hills MS | 1,800/6-8
4301 Little Mountain Dr 92407 | 909-880-6666
Toni Miller, prin. | Fax 880-6672
San Bernardino Adult S | Adult
1200 N E St 92405 | 909-388-6000
| Fax 381-2887

Other Schools – See Highland

Aquinas HS | 300/9-12
2772 Sterling Ave 92404 | 909-886-4659
Daryl Sequeira, prin. | Fax 886-7717
Art Institute of CA Inland Empire | Post-Sec.
630 E Brier 92408 | 909-915-2100
Bryman College | Post-Sec.
217 E Club Center Dr Ste A 92408 | 909-777-3300
California State Univ.-San Bernardino | Post-Sec.
5500 University Pkwy 92407 | 909-880-5000
Concorde Career College | Post-Sec.
201 E Airport Dr # A 92408 | 909-884-8891
Dikaios Christian Academy | 200/K-12
PO Box 9067 92427 | 909-473-0118
Von Sommerville, admin.
Hair Masters University of Beauty | Post-Sec.
208 W Highland Ave 92405 | 909-882-2987
Inland Technical Skills Center | Post-Sec.
320 N E St Ste 513 92401 | - -
ITT Technical Institute | Post-Sec.
670 Carnegie Dr 92408 | 909-889-3800
Marinello School of Beauty | Post-Sec.
721 W 2nd St # E 92410 | 909-884-8747
San Bernardino Valley College | Post-Sec.
701 S Mount Vernon Ave 92410 | 909-888-6511
Temple Learning Center | 100/PK-12
1777 W Base Line St 92411 | 909-885-4695
Rev. Raymond Turner, admin. | Fax 885-5650

San Bruno, San Mateo, Pop. 39,602
San Bruno Park ESD | 2,700/K-8
500 Acacia Ave 94066 | 650-624-3100
David Hutt, supt. | Fax 266-9626
sbpsd.k12.ca.us
Parkside IS | 600/7-8
1801 Niles Ave 94066 | 650-624-3180
Angela Addiego, prin. | Fax 877-8195

San Mateo UNHSD
Supt. — See San Mateo
Capuchino HS | 1,100/9-12
1501 Magnolia Ave 94066 | 650-558-2799
Edward Marquez, prin. | Fax 558-2759

Highlands Christian S | 900/PK-12
1900 Monterey Dr 94066 | 650-873-4090
Vernita Sheley, supt. | Fax 742-6228
Skyline College | Post-Sec.
3300 College Dr 94066 | 650-738-4100

San Carlos, San Mateo, Pop. 27,004
San Carlos ESD | 500/5-8
826 Chestnut St 94070 | 650-508-7333
Patty Wool, supt. | Fax 508-7340
www.sancarlos.k12.ca.us
Central MS | 500/5-8
828 Chestnut St 94070 | 650-508-7321
Jerrie Welch, prin. | Fax 508-7342

San Clemente, Orange, Pop. 57,768
Capistrano USD
Supt. — See San Juan Capistrano
Ayer MS | 800/6-8
1271 Calle Sarmentoso 92673 | 949-366-9607
Dr. Cheryl Baughn, prin. | Fax 366-1519
San Clemente HS | 2,900/9-12
700 Avenida Pico 92673 | 949-492-4165
Dr. Charles Hinman, prin. | Fax 361-5175
Shorecliffs MS | 1,200/6-8
240 Via Socorro 92672 | 949-498-1660
Kenny Moe, prin. | Fax 498-0826
Vista del Mar MS | 400/6-8
1130 Avenida Talega 92673 | 949-234-5955
James Sieger, prin.

St. Michael's Academy 200/K-12
107 W Marquita 92672 949-366-9468
Daniel Sharp, prin. Fax 492-7238

San Diego, San Diego, Pop. 1,266,753
Poway USD
Supt. — See Poway
Bernardo Heights MS 1,900/6-8
12990 Paseo Lucido 92128 858-485-4850
Elaine Johnson, prin. Fax 485-4865
Black Mountain MS 1,300/6-8
9353 Oviedo St 92129 858-484-1300
David Hall, prin. Fax 538-9440
Mesa Verde MS 1,600/6-8
8375 Entreken Way 92129 858-538-5478
Greg Mizel, prin. Fax 538-8636
Mt. Carmel HS 2,500/9-12
9550 Carmel Mountain Rd 92129 858-484-1180
Dr. Tom McCoy, prin. Fax 538-9426
Oak Valley MS 6-8
16055 Wine Creek Rd 92127 858-487-2939
Sonya Wrisley, prin. Fax 457-0991
Rancho Bernardo HS 3,200/9-12
13010 Paseo Lucido 92128 858-485-4800
Paul Robinson, prin. Fax 485-4822
Westview HS 2,200/9-12
13500 Camino del Sur 92129 858-780-2000
Dawn Kastner, prin. Fax 780-2054

Regional Occupational Center & Program
Supt. — None
San Diego County ROP Vo/Tech
6401 Linda Vista Rd # 408 92111 858-292-3529
Richard Smith, dir. Fax 268-9726

San Diego City USD 122,800/PK-12
4100 Normal St 92103 619-725-8000
Dr. Carl Cohn, supt. Fax 291-7182
www.sandi.net/
Bell JHS 1,800/7-9
620 Briarwood Rd 92139 619-479-7111
Janice Roudebush, prin. Fax 470-6054
Business HS 9-12
1405 Park Blvd 92101 619-525-7455
Joseph Austin, prin. Fax 525-7337
Challenger MS 1,100/6-8
10810 Parkdale Ave 92126 858-586-7001
Lamont Jackson, prin. Fax 271-5203
Clairemont HS 1,400/9-12
4150 Ute Dr 92117 858-273-0201
Nellie Meyer, prin. Fax 272-4219
Clark MS 1,700/6-8
4388 Thorn St 92105 619-563-6801
Fax 563-9653
Communications Investigations HS 9-12
1405 Park Blvd 92101 619-525-7455
Cesar Alcantar, prin. Fax 525-7259
Community Health and Medical Practices 9-12
4191 Colts Way 92115 619-583-2500
Kenneth Hurst, prin. Fax 229-9088
Correia JHS 1,000/7-8
4302 Valeta St 92107 619-222-0476
Linda Taggert, prin. Fax 221-0147
Creative Performing & Media Arts S 700/6-8
5095 Arvinels Ave 92117 858-278-5917
Ginger Blackmon, prin. Fax 293-7235
De Portola MS 1,000/6-8
11010 Clairemont Mesa Blvd 92124 858-496-8080
Listy Gillingham, prin. Fax 576-4419
Digital and Media Design 9-12
7651 Wellington Way 92111 858-496-8370
Cheryl Hibbeln, prin. Fax 278-6349
Farb MS 1,000/6-8
4880 La Cuenta Dr 92124 858-496-8090
Susan Levy, prin. Fax 576-0931
Foster Construction Tech Academy 9-12
7651 Wellington Way 92111 858-496-8370
Glenn Hillegas, dir. Fax 496-4907
Gompers Magnet JSHS 1,800/7-12
1005 47th St 92102 619-263-2171
Vince Riveroll, prin. Fax 262-5341
Henry HS 2,400/9-12
6702 Wandermere Dr 92120 619-286-7700
Patricia Crowder, prin. Fax 229-0370
Hoover HS 2,100/9-12
4474 El Cajon Blvd 92115 619-283-6281
Douglas Williams, prin. Fax 280-5837
International Business 9-12
7651 Wellington Way 92111 858-496-8370
Ana Diaz-Booz, prin. Fax 496-8379
International Studies HS 2,800/9-12
1405 Park Blvd 92101 619-525-7455
Karen Wroblewski, prin. Fax 744-7651
Invention & Design Educational Academy 1,700/9-12
4191 Colts Way 92115 619-583-2500
John Spiegel, dir. Fax 582-4173
Keiller MS 600/6-8
7270 Lisbon St 92114 619-263-9266
Patricia Ladd, prin. Fax 262-2217
Kroc MS 900/7-8
5050 Conrad Ave 92117 858-496-8150
Susan Manning, prin. Fax 292-5296
Law and Business 9-12
4191 Colts Way 92115 619-583-2500
Monique Robertson, prin. Fax 229-2005
Lead Explore Achieve Discover & Serve HS 9-12
1405 Park Blvd 92101 619-525-7455
Scott Giusti, prin. Fax 744-7676
Lewis MS 1,200/6-8
5170 Greenbrier Ave 92120 619-583-3233
Dr. Barbara Forcier, prin. Fax 229-1338
Madison HS 1,500/9-12
4833 Doliva Dr 92117 858-496-8410
Virginia Eves, prin. Fax 496-8421
Mann MS 1,400/6-8
4345 54th St 92115 619-582-8990
Valerie Voss, prin. Fax 583-2637
Marshall MS 1,000/6-8
11778 Cypress Canyon Rd 92131 858-549-8840
Rick Novack, prin. Fax 549-4910
Marston MS 1,200/6-8
3799 Clairemont Dr 92117 858-273-2030
Dr. Elizabeth Cook, prin. Fax 272-3460

Media Visual & Performing Arts HS 9-12
1405 Park Blvd 92101 619-525-7455
Shirley Rehkopf, prin. Fax 744-7680
Mira Mesa HS 2,500/9-12
10510 Reagan Rd 92126 858-566-2262
Jeff Olivero, prin. Fax 549-9541
Mission Bay HS 1,700/9-12
2475 Grand Ave 92109 858-273-1313
Thomas Yount, prin. Fax 270-8294
Montgomery MS 700/6-8
2470 Ulric St 92111 858-496-8330
Fax 292-0125
Morse HS 3,000/9-12
6905 Skyline Dr 92114 619-262-0763
Rocio Weiss, prin. Fax 262-6835
Multimedia and Visual Arts 9-12
4191 Colts Way 92115 619-583-2500
Diego Gutierrez, dir. Fax 229-9225
Pacific Beach MS 800/6-8
4676 Ingraham St 92109 858-273-9070
Michelle Bishop-Irwin, prin. Fax 270-8063
Pershing MS 900/6-8
8204 San Carlos Dr 92119 619-465-3234
Sarah Sullivan, prin. Fax 461-5447
Point Loma HS 1,900/9-12
2335 Chatsworth Blvd 92106 619-223-3121
Barbara Samilson, prin. Fax 225-1298
Roosevelt MS 1,100/6-8
3366 Park Blvd 92103 619-293-4450
Dr. Julie Martel, prin. Fax 497-0918
San Diego Met HS Vo/Tech
7250 Mesa College Dr 92111 619-388-2299
Mildred Phillips, prin.
School of Creative & Performing Arts 1,500/6-12
2425 Dusk Dr 92139 619-470-0555
Liz Laughlin, prin. Fax 470-9430
Science Connections & Technology HS 9-12
7651 Wellington Way 92111 858-496-8370
Rochelle Dawes, dir. Fax 715-9504
SCITECH HS 9-12
1405 Park Blvd 92101 619-525-7455
Dianne Cordero, prin. Fax 744-7677
Scripps Ranch HS 2,300/9-12
10410 Treena St 92131 858-621-9020
Donna Campbell, prin. Fax 621-0646
Serra HS 2,000/9-12
5156 Santo Rd 92124 858-496-8342
Donna Somerville, prin. Fax 571-3457
Standley MS 1,300/6-8
6298 Radcliffe Dr 92122 858-455-0550
Godwin Higa, prin. Fax 546-7627
Taft MS 700/6-8
9191 Gramercy Dr 92123 858-496-8245
Barbara Balser, prin. Fax 496-8138
University City HS 1,900/9-12
6949 Genesee Ave 92122 858-457-3040
Ernest Smith, prin. Fax 458-9432
Wangenheim MS 1,400/6-8
9230 Gold Coast Dr 92126 858-578-1400
Robert Grano, prin. Fax 578-9481
Wilson MS 1,200/6-8
3838 Orange Ave 92105 619-280-1661
Bernadette Nguyen, prin. Fax 280-6437
Other Schools – See La Jolla

San Dieguito UNHSD
Supt. — See Encinitas
Canyon Crest Academy 9-10
5951 Village Center Loop Rd 92130 858-350-0253
David Jaffe, prin. Fax 350-0280
Carmel Valley MS 1,200/7-8
3800 Mykonos Ln 92130 858-481-8221
Michael Grove, prin. Fax 481-8256
Torrey Pines HS 3,400/9-12
3710 Del Mar Heights Rd 92130 858-755-0125
Rich Schmitt, prin. Fax 481-0098

Sweetwater UNHSD
Supt. — See Chula Vista
Mar Vista MS 1,300/7-8
1267 Thermal Ave 92154 619-628-5100
Samuel Montes, prin. Fax 423-8431
Montgomery HS 2,500/9-12
3250 Palm Ave 92154 619-628-3007
Robin Fiege, prin. Fax 424-6473
Montgomery MS 1,200/7-8
1051 Picador Blvd 92154 619-662-4000
Ernie Zamudo, prin. Fax 428-6517
San Ysidro HS 1,200/9-12
5353 Airway Rd 92154 619-710-2300
Hector Espinoza, prin. Fax 710-2318
Southwest HS 2,500/9-12
1685 Hollister St 92154 619-628-3023
Sid Salazar, prin. Fax 423-8253
Southwest MS 1,300/7-9
2710 Iris Ave 92154 619-628-4000
Thomas Rodrigo, prin. Fax 423-1151
Montgomery Adult S Adult
3240 Palm Ave 92154 619-628-3017
Dr. Thomas Teagle, prin. Fax 423-7876

Academy of Our Lady of Peace 800/9-12
4860 Oregon St 92116 619-297-2266
Sr. Dolores Anchondo, prin. Fax 297-2473
Alliant International University Post-Sec.
10455 Pomerado Rd 92131 858-635-4772
Art Institute of California Post-Sec.
7650 Mission Valley Rd 92108 858-598-1200
Associated Technical College Post-Sec.
1445 6th Ave 92101 619-234-2181
Avance Beauty College Post-Sec.
750 Beyer Way Ste B 92154 619-575-1511
Balboa City S, 525 Hawthorn St 92101 100/1-12
Dr. Stephen Parker, dir. 619-298-2990
California College San Diego Post-Sec.
2820 Camino Del Rio S # 300 92108 619-295-5785
California Western School of Law Post-Sec.
225 Cedar St 92101 619-239-0391
Cathedral Catholic HS 1,600/9-12
5555 Del Mar Heights Rd 92130 858-523-4000
Timothy Derenthal, prin. Fax 523-4097
Childrens Creative/Performing Arts Acad. 300/K-12
6365 Lake Atlin Ave 92119 619-697-7724
Janet Cherif, prin. Fax 697-7746

City Learning Center 400/9-12
5945 Mission Gorge Rd Ste 8 92120 619-282-7900
Greg Haberman, admin.
Coleman College Post-Sec.
8888 Balboa Ave 92123 858-499-0202
Concorde Career Institute Post-Sec.
4393 Imperial Ave Ste 100 92113 619-688-0800
Cook Education Center 100/6-12
2255 Camino Del Rio S 92108 619-243-1325
Dr. Suzanne Fitch, prin.
Court Reporting Institute Post-Sec.
8665 Gibbs Dr Ste 204 92123 619-294-5700
Design Institute of San Diego Post-Sec.
8555 Commerce Ave 92121 858-566-1200
Fashion Careers College Post-Sec.
1923 Morena Blvd 92110 619-275-4700
FIDM/The Fashion Institute Post-Sec.
1010 2nd Ave Ste 200 92101 800-243-3436
Futures HS 50/7-12
5333 Mission Center Rd 92108 619-297-5311
Carolyn Lindstrom, dir. Fax 297-5313
Grace Christian S 50/K-12
3656 Ruffin Rd 92123 858-541-0373
Steve Coffman, admin. Fax 576-9070
Heritage Christian S of San Diego 1,200/K-12
PO Box 262099 92196 858-689-2254
Jeff Wells, prin.
Horizon JSHS 600/7-12
5331 Mount Alifan Dr 92111 858-244-0333
Jason Cook, prin. Fax 654-3054
International Prof School of Body Work Post-Sec.
1366 Hornblend St 92109 858-272-4142
ITT Technical Institute Post-Sec.
9680 Granite Ridge Dr 92123 858-571-8500
Keller Graduate School of Management Post-Sec.
2655 Cmno Del Rio N #201 92108 619-683-2446
Lutheran HS of San Diego 100/9-12
2755 55th St 92105 619-262-4444
Hanne E. Krause, prin. Fax 262-6297
Marian Catholic HS 500/9-12
1002 18th St 92154 619-423-2121
George Milke, prin. Fax 423-6910
Maric College Post-Sec.
9055 Balboa Ave 92123 858-279-4500
Maric College East County Post-Sec.
6160 Mission Gorge Rd #108 92120 619-282-9000
Marinello School of Beauty Post-Sec.
1226 University Ave 92103 619-298-7187
Midway Baptist S 400/K-12
2460 Palm Ave 92154 619-424-7875
Stephen Johnson, prin. Fax 424-9204
Mueller College of Holistic Massage Post-Sec.
4607 Park Blvd 92116 619-291-9811
National University School of Law Post-Sec.
3580 Aero Ct 92123 619-563-7300
Newschool of Architecture & Design Post-Sec.
1249 F St 92101 619-235-4100
Occupational Training Services Post-Sec.
8799 Balboa Ave Ste 100 92123 858-560-0411
Pacific College of Oriental Medicine Post-Sec.
7445 Mssn Valley Rd #105 92108 619-574-6909
Parker S 700/6-12
6501 Linda Vista Rd 92111 858-569-7900
Timothy McIntire, hdmstr. Fax 569-0621
Platt College Post-Sec.
6250 El Cajon Blvd 92115 619-265-0107
Point Loma Nazarene University Post-Sec.
3900 Lomaland Dr 92106 619-849-2200
Remington College Post-Sec.
123 Cmino De La Reina #100N 92108 619-686-8600
St. Augustine HS 700/9-12
3266 Nutmeg St 92104 619-282-2184
Jim Horne, prin. Fax 282-1203
San Diego City College Post-Sec.
1313 Park Blvd 92101 619-230-2400
San Diego Jewish Academy 700/K-12
11860 Carmel Creek Rd 92130 858-704-3700
Larry Acheatel, dir.
San Diego Mesa College Post-Sec.
7250 Mesa College Dr 92111 858-627-2600
San Diego Miramar College Post-Sec.
10440 Black Mountain Rd 92126 619-388-7800
San Diego State University Post-Sec.
5500 Campanile Dr 92182 619-594-5200
Stein Education Center 100/K-12
6145 Decena Dr 92120 619-281-5511
Dr. Elizabeth McInnis, dir.
Thomas Jefferson School of Law Post-Sec.
2121 San Diego Ave 92110 619-297-9700
Torah HS of San Diego 100/9-12
9001 Towne Centre Dr 92122 858-558-6880
Rabbi Michoel Peikes, prin. Fax 558-6835
Travel University International Post-Sec.
3870 Murphy Canyon Rd #310 92123 858-292-9755
United Truck & Car Driving School Post-Sec.
2425 Camino Del Rio S 92108 619-296-2020
University of California Medical Center Post-Sec.
200 W Arbor Dr # H-910C 92103 619-543-6654
University of San Diego Post-Sec.
5998 Alcala Park 92110 619-260-4600
Veterans Affairs Medical Center Post-Sec.
3350 La Jolla Village Dr 92161 858-552-8585

San Dimas, Los Angeles, Pop. 36,000
Bonita USD 10,000/K-12
115 W Allen Ave 91773 909-971-8200
Dr. Robert C. Otto, supt. Fax 971-8329
www.bonita.k12.ca.us
Lone Hill MS 1,100/6-8
115 W Allen Ave 91773 909-971-8270
Ray Arredondo, prin. Fax 971-8279
San Dimas HS 1,400/9-12
115 W Allen Ave 91773 909-971-8230
Kristine Kulow, prin. Fax 971-8239
Other Schools – See La Verne

Life Pacific College Post-Sec.
1100 W Covina Blvd 91773 800-356-0001

San Fernando, Los Angeles, Pop. 24,253
Los Angeles USD
Supt. — See Los Angeles
San Fernando HS 4,400/9-12
11133 Omelveny Ave 91340 818-365-1121
Jose Rodriguez, prin. Fax 365-7255

San Fernando MS 2,100/6-8
130 N Brand Blvd 91340 818-361-0181
Eloisa Marquez, prin. Fax 365-8911

Calvary Baptist Christian S 100/PK-12
12928 Vaughn St 91340 818-899-8206
Aaron Jackson, prin. Fax 890-0277

San Francisco, San Francisco, Pop. 751,682
Regional Occupational Center & Program
Supt. — None
San Francisco County ROP Vo/Tech
1098 Harrison St 94103 415-355-7711
Marigrace Cohen, coord. Fax 355-7744

San Francisco USD 53,200/PK-12
555 Franklin St 94102 415-241-6000
Gwen Chan, supt. Fax 555-5555
www.sfusd.edu
Aptos MS 900/6-8
105 Aptos Ave 94127 415-469-4520
Ericka Lovrin, prin. Fax 333-9038
Balboa HS 900/9-12
1000 Cayuga Ave 94112 415-469-4090
Patricia Gray, prin. Fax 469-0859
Burbank MS 400/6-8
325 La Grande Ave 94112 415-469-4547
Karen Morgan, prin. Fax 586-5217
Burton HS 1,900/9-12
400 Mansell St 94134 415-469-4550
Eric Marshall, prin. Fax 239-6806
Davis College Prep Academy 1,200/6-12
1195 Hudson Ave 94124 415-695-5390
Matt Livingston, prin. Fax 920-5067
Denman MS 700/6-8
241 Oneida Ave 94112 415-469-4535
Gary Pacini, prin. Fax 585-8402
Downtown HS 300/9-12
110 Bartlett St 94110 415-695-5860
Richard Maggi, prin. Fax 695-5863
Everett MS 600/6-8
450 Church St 94114 415-241-6344
Francisco Duran, prin. Fax 241-6361
Francisco MS 500/6-8
2190 Powell St 94133 415-291-7900
Margarett Anne Centrella, prin. Fax 291-7910
Galileo Academy of Science & Technology 2,000/9-12
1150 Francisco St 94109 415-749-3430
Margaret Chiu, prin. Fax 771-2322
Giannini MS 1,300/6-8
3151 Ortega St 94122 415-759-2770
Leslie Trook, prin. Fax 664-8541
Hoover MS 1,200/6-8
2290 14th Ave 94116 415-759-2783
Judy Dong, prin. Fax 759-2881
King Academic MS 500/6-8
350 Girard St 94134 415-330-1500
Gil Cho, prin. Fax 468-7295
Lick MS 600/6-8
1220 Noe St 94114 415-695-5675
Carmelo Sgarlato, prin. Fax 695-5360
Lincoln HS 2,500/9-12
2162 24th Ave 94116 415-759-2700
Ron Pang, prin. Fax 566-2224
Lowell HS 2,600/9-12
1101 Eucalyptus Dr 94132 415-759-2730
Paul Cheng, prin. Fax 759-2742
Mann MS 600/6-8
3351 23rd St 94110 415-695-5881
Gene Barrcsi, prin. Fax 282-7868
Marina MS 1,100/6-8
3500 Fillmore St 94123 415-749-3495
Dennis Chew, prin. Fax 921-7539
Marshall HS 1,000/9-12
45 Conkling St 94124 415-695-5612
Michael Eddings, prin. Fax 285-5283
Maxwell MS 200/6-8
655 De Haro St 94107 415-695-5905
Marcus Blacksher, prin. Fax 695-5914
Mission HS 900/9-12
3750 18th St 94114 415-241-6240
Kevin Truitt, prin. Fax 626-1641
Newcomer HS 400/9-12
2340 Jackson St 94115 415-241-6584
Balrai Thiara, prin. Fax 474-9618
O'Connell HS 900/9-12
2355 Folsom St 94110 415-695-5370
Janet Schulze, prin. Fax 695-5379
Presidio MS 1,200/6-8
450 30th Ave 94121 415-750-8435
Alvin Dea, prin. Fax 750-8445
Roosevelt MS 800/6-8
460 Arguello Blvd 94118 415-750-8446
Diane Panagotacos, prin. Fax 750-8455
Visitacion Valley MS 500/6-8
450 Raymond Ave 94134 415-469-4590
James Dierke, prin. Fax 469-4703
Wallenberg HS 700/9-12
40 Vega St 94115 415-749-3469
Aileen Murphy, prin. Fax 346-7303
Washington HS 2,300/9-12
600 32nd Ave 94121 415-750-8400
Andrew Ishibashi, prin. Fax 750-8417

Academy of Art University Post-Sec.
79 New Montgomery St 94105 415-274-2200
American College of California Post-Sec.
760 Market St Ste 1009 94102 415-677-9717
American Coll of Traditional Chinese Med Post-Sec.
455 Arkansas St 94107 415-282-7600
American Conservatory Theater Post-Sec.
30 Grant Ave 94108 415-439-2350
Archbishop Riordan HS 700/9-12
175 Phelan Ave 94112 415-586-8200
Gabriel Crotti, prin. Fax 587-1310
Art Institute of California - San Fran Post-Sec.
1170 Market St 94102 888-493-3261
Bay S of San Francisco 100/9-12
35 Keyes Ave 94129 415-561-5800
Rev. Malcolm Manson, hdmstr.
Bridgemont JSHS 100/6-12
777 Brotherhood Way 94132 415-333-7600
Peter Tropper, admin. Fax 333-7603
Bryman College Post-Sec.
814 Mission St Ste 500 94103 415-777-2500
California College of the Arts Post-Sec.
450 Irwin St 94107 415-703-9500
California Culinary Academy Post-Sec.
625 Polk St 94102 415-771-3536
California Institute of Integral Studies Post-Sec.
1453 Mission St 94103 415-575-6100
City College of San Francisco Post-Sec.
50 Phelan Ave 94112 415-239-3000
Convent of the Sacred Heart HS 200/9-12
2222 Broadway St 94115 415-563-2900
Douglas Grant, prin. Fax 929-0553
Cornerstone Academy 500/6-12
501 Cambridge St 94134 415-585-5183
Derrick Wong, prin. Fax 469-9600
De Marillac MS 100/6-8
175 Golden Gate Ave 94102 415-552-5220
John Omernil, prin. Fax 621-5632
Discovery Center 300/K-12
65 Ocean Ave 94112 415-333-6609
Drew S 300/9-12
2901 California St 94115 415-409-3739
Samuel Cuddeback, prin. Fax 346-0720
FIDM/The Fashion Institute Post-Sec.
55 Stockton St 94108 415-433-6691
French-American International S 900/PK-12
150 Oak St 94102 415-558-2000
Jane Camblin, hdmstr. Fax 558-2024
Golden Gate University Post-Sec.
536 Mission St 94105 415-442-7000
Heald College Post-Sec.
350 Mission St 94105 415-808-3000
Hebrew Academy of San Francisco 200/PK-12
645 14th Ave 94118 415-752-7333
Rabbi Pinchas Lipner, dean Fax 752-5851
Hospitality Management Training Inst. Post-Sec.
760 Market St Ste 1009 94102 415-677-9717
Immaculate Conception Academy 300/9-12
3625 24th St 94110 415-824-2052
Sr. Janice Wellington, prin. Fax 821-4677
Jewish Community HS of the Bay 200/9-12
1835 Ellis St 94115 415-345-9777
Rabbi Sheldon Dorph, hdmstr. Fax 345-1888
Keller Graduate School of Management Post-Sec.
455 Market St Ste 1650 94105 415-243-8585
Lick-Wilmerding HS 400/9-12
755 Ocean Ave 94112 415-333-4021
Albert Adams, hdmstr. Fax 586-0737
Lycee Francais-Laperouse S 700/K-12
755 Ashbury St 94117 415-661-5232
Alain Cuzin, hdmstr. Fax 661-0246
Mercy HS 600/9-12
3250 19th Ave 94132 415-334-0525
Dorothy McCrea, prin. Fax 334-9726
Miss Marty's Sch. Beauty & Hairstyling Post-Sec.
1087 Mission St 94103 415-227-4240
New College School of Law Post-Sec.
50 Fell St 94102 415-241-1300
Oxman College Post-Sec.
375 3rd Ave 94118 415-751-6461
Sacred Heart Cathedral Prep S 1,200/9-12
1055 Ellis St 94109 415-775-6626
Dr. Ken Hogarty, prin. Fax 931-6941
St. Ignatius College Prep S 1,400/9-12
2001 37th Ave 94116 415-731-7500
Charles Dullea, prin. Fax 731-2227
San Francisco Art Institute Post-Sec.
800 Chestnut St 94133 415-771-7020
San Francisco Christian S 300/K-12
25 Whittier St 94112 415-586-1117
Mark Asire, admin.
San Francisco Conservatory of Music Post-Sec.
50 Oak St 94102 800-899-7326
San Francisco State University Post-Sec.
1600 Holloway Ave 94132 415-338-1111
San Francisco University HS 400/9-12
3065 Jackson St 94115 415-447-3100
Dr. Michael Diamonti, hdmstr. Fax 447-5801
San Francisco Waldorf HS 100/9-12
245 Valencia St 94103 415-431-2736
Joan Caldarera, prin. Fax 431-1712
Saybrook Graduate School Post-Sec.
747 Front St Fl 3 94111 800-825-4480
Sonoma College - San Francisco Post-Sec.
301 Howard St Ste 510 94105 888-649-7801
Stuart Hall HS 200/9-12
1715 Octavia St 94109 415-345-5811
Gordon Sharafinski, hdmstr. Fax 931-9161
University of California Post-Sec.
Parnassus And 3rd Ave 94143 415-476-9000
University of CA Hastings College of Law Post-Sec.
200 McAllister St 94102 415-565-4600
University of San Francisco Post-Sec.
2130 Fulton St 94117 415-422-5555
University of the Pacific Post-Sec.
2155 Webster St 94115 415-929-6400
Urban S of San Francisco 300/9-12
1563 Page St 94117 415-626-2919
Mark Salkind, dir. Fax 626-1125
Voice of Pentecost Academy 200/K-12
1970 Ocean Ave 94127 415-334-0105
Sherwood Jansen, prin.
Woodside International S 100/6-12
1555 Irving St 94122 415-564-1063
John Edwards, hdmstr. Fax 564-2511

San Gabriel, Los Angeles, Pop. 40,987
Alhambra City SD
Supt. — See Alhambra
San Gabriel HS 2,500/9-12
801 S Ramona St 91776 626-308-2352
Marsha Gilbert, prin. Fax 308-2332
San Gabriel Community Adult Center Adult
801 S Ramona St 91776 626-308-2319
Fax 308-2748

San Gabriel USD 5,600/K-12
408 Junipero Serra Dr 91776 626-451-5400
Berjouhi Koukeyan, supt. Fax 451-5494
www.sgusd.k12.ca.us
Gabrielino HS 1,700/9-12
1327 S San Gabriel Blvd 91776 626-573-2453
Eugene Murphy Ed.D., prin. Fax 573-5089
Jefferson MS 1,200/6-8
1340 E Live Oak St 91776 626-287-5260
John Fox, prin. Fax 285-5387

San Gabriel Mission HS 300/9-12
254 S Santa Anita Ave 91776 626-282-3181
Carolyn Nelson, prin. Fax 282-4209
San Gabriel SDA Academy 700/K-12
8827 E Broadway 91776 626-292-1156
Robert Peeke, prin. Fax 285-4949

Sanger, Fresno, Pop. 20,113
Regional Occupational Center & Program
Supt. — None
Valley ROP Vo/Tech
1305 Q St 93657 559-876-2122
Debbe Marvin-Deeter, dir. Fax 876-2102

Sanger USD 7,100/K-12
1905 7th St 93657 559-875-6521
Marcus Johnson, supt. Fax 875-0311
www.sanger.k12.ca.us
Sanger HS 2,100/9-12
1045 Bethel Ave 93657 559-875-7121
Dan Chacon, prin. Fax 875-5721
Washington Academic MS 900/7-8
1705 10th St 93657 559-875-5561
Cathy Padilla, prin. Fax 875-6365

San Jacinto, Riverside, Pop. 26,929
San Jacinto USD 7,100/K-12
2045 S San Jacinto Ave 92583 951-929-7700
Shari Fox Ed.D., supt. Fax 658-3574
www.sanjacinto.k12.ca.us/
Monte Vista MS 900/6-8
181 N Ramona Blvd 92583 951-654-9361
Sharon Raffiee, prin. Fax 654-0173
North Mountain MS 1,200/6-8
1202 E 7th St 92583 951-487-7797
Garry Packham, prin. Fax 487-7799
San Jacinto HS 1,600/9-12
500 Idyllwild Dr 92583 951-654-7374
Gwen Smith, prin. Fax 654-7702

Alpha Omega Christian S 50/K-12
950 N Ramona Blvd Ste 5 92582 951-487-2079
Susan Hall, prin. Fax 487-0828
Mt. San Jacinto College Post-Sec.
1499 N State St 92583 951-487-6752

San Joaquin, Fresno, Pop. 3,530
Golden Plains USD 2,100/K-12
PO Box 937 93660 559-693-1115
Joann Evans, supt. Fax 693-4366
www.gpusd.k12.ca.us
Golden Plains Adult Educ-San Joaquin Adult
PO Box 937 93660 559-693-2401
Aurora Ramirez, prin. Fax 693-2519
Other Schools – See Tranquillity

San Jose, Santa Clara, Pop. 898,349
Alum Rock UNESD 14,300/PK-8
2930 Gay Ave 95127 408-928-6800
Anthony P. Russo Ed.D., supt. Fax 928-6416
www.arusd.org/
Fischer MS 800/6-8
1720 Hopkins Dr 95122 408-928-7500
Hilaria Bauer, prin. Fax 928-7501
George MS 600/6-8
277 Mahoney Dr 95127 408-928-7600
Amparo Barrera, prin. Fax 928-7601
Mathson MS 600/6-8
2050 Kammerer Ave 95116 408-928-7950
Glenn VanderZee, prin. Fax 928-7951
Ocala MS 800/6-8
2800 Ocala Ave 95148 408-928-8350
Oscar Leon, prin. Fax 928-8351
Pala MS 600/6-8
149 N White Rd 95127 408-928-8500
Sid Haro, prin. Fax 928-8501
Sheppard MS 700/6-8
480 Rough and Ready Rd 95133 408-928-8800
Donita Grace, prin. Fax 928-8801

Berryessa UNSD 8,500/K-8
1376 Piedmont Rd 95132 408-923-1800
Marc Liebman Ph.D., supt. Fax 923-0623
www.berryessa.k12.ca.us
Morrill MS 900/6-8
1970 Morrill Ave 95132 408-923-1930
Ron Fairchild, prin. Fax 946-0776
Piedmont MS 1,000/6-8
955 Piedmont Rd 95132 408-923-1945
Bobbie Infelise, prin. Fax 251-2392
Sierramont MS 1,000/6-8
3155 Kimlee Dr 95132 408-923-1955
Joseph Amelio, prin. Fax 729-5840

Campbell UNHSD 7,300/9-12
3235 Union Ave 95124 408-371-0960
Rhonda Farber, supt. Fax 558-3006
www.cuhsd.org/
Branham HS 1,400/9-12
1570 Branham Ln 95118 408-267-1020
Tom Utic, prin. Fax 267-2676
Del Mar HS 1,200/9-12
1224 Del Mar Ave 95128 408-298-0260
Jim Russell, prin. Fax 295-9476
Leigh HS 1,700/9-12
5210 Leigh Ave 95124 408-377-4470
Donna Hope, prin. Fax 265-7525
Other Schools – See Campbell, Saratoga

Campbell UNSD
Supt. — See Campbell
Monroe MS 900/5-8
1055 S Monroe St 95128 408-556-0360
Shelly Viramontez, prin. Fax 341-7020

Cupertino UNESD
Supt. — See Cupertino
Miller MS 1,200/6-8
6151 Rainbow Dr 95129 408-252-3755
Richard Taylor, prin. Fax 255-5269

East Side UNHSD | 22,100/9-12
830 N Capitol Ave 95133 | 408-347-5000
Bob Nunez, supt. | Fax 347-5045
www.esuhsd.org/
Hill HS | 2,000/9-12
3200 Senter Rd 95111 | 408-347-4100
Dave Riley, prin. | Fax 347-4115
Independence HS | 4,100/9-12
1776 Educational Park Dr 95133 | 408-928-9500
Carol Blackerby, prin. | Fax 928-9515
Lick HS | 1,100/9-12
57 N White Rd 95127 | 408-347-4400
Bill Rice, prin. | Fax 347-4415
Mt. Pleasant HS | 2,000/9-12
1750 S White Rd 95127 | 408-937-2800
Grettel Castro-Stanley, prin. | Fax 937-2815
Oak Grove HS | 2,600/9-12
285 Blossom Hill Rd 95123 | 408-347-6500
Dr. Geraldine Forte, dir. | Fax 347-6515
Overfelt HS | 1,500/9-12
1835 Cunningham Ave 95122 | 408-347-5900
Diego Certa, prin. | Fax 347-5915
Piedmont Hills HS | 2,000/9-12
1377 Piedmont Rd 95132 | 408-347-3800
Dan Moser, prin. | Fax 347-3805
Santa Teresa HS | 2,100/9-12
6150 Snell Ave 95123 | 408-347-6200
Kathy Prasch, prin. | Fax 347-6215
Silver Creek HS | 2,400/9-12
3434 Silver Creek Rd 95121 | 408-347-5600
Thelma Boac, prin. | Fax 347-5615
Yerba Buena HS | 1,600/9-12
1855 Lucretia Ave 95122 | 408-347-4700
Juan Cruz, prin. | Fax 347-4715
East Side Adult Center | Adult
625 Educational Park Dr 95133 | 408-928-9300
Cari Vaeth, dir. | Fax 928-9309

Evergreen ESD | 12,500/K-8
3188 Quimby Rd 95148 | 408-270-6800
Clif Black, supt. | Fax 274-3894
www.eesd.org/
Chaboya MS | 1,000/7-8
3276 Cortona Dr 95135 | 408-270-6900
Bette Samdahl, prin. | Fax 270-6916
LeyVa MS | 1,000/6-8
1865 Monrovia Dr 95122 | 408-270-4992
Chris Corpus, prin. | Fax 270-5462
Quimby Oak MS | 1,000/7-8
3190 Quimby Rd 95148 | 408-270-6735
Phil Bond, prin. | Fax 223-4533

Franklin-McKinley SD | 9,900/K-8
645 Wool Creek Dr 95112 | 408-283-6000
Dr. John Porter, supt. | Fax 283-6022
www.fmsd.k12.ca.us
Fair MS | 800/7-8
1702 Mclaughlin Ave 95122 | 408-283-6400
Beverly Hill, prin. | Fax 283-6419
Sylvandale JHS | 1,000/7-8
653 Sylvandale Ave 95111 | 408-363-5700
Rafael Cruz, prin. | Fax 363-5649

Fremont UNHSD
Supt. — See Sunnyvale
Lynbrook HS | 1,700/9-12
1280 Johnson Ave 95129 | 408-366-7700
Mike White, prin. | Fax 257-0551

Moreland SD | 4,000/K-8
4711 Campbell Ave 95130 | 408-874-2900
Dr. Leslie M. Adelson, supt. | Fax 374-8863
www.moreland.k12.ca.us
Castro MS | 700/6-8
4600 Student Ln 95130 | 408-874-3300
Tom Kennedy, prin. | Fax 379-3622
Rogers MS | 700/6-8
4835 Doyle Rd 95129 | 408-874-3500
Norma Jean Ready, prin. | Fax 253-7321

Morgan Hill USD
Supt. — See Morgan Hill
Murphy MS | 600/7-8
141 Avenida Espana 95139 | 408-281-1500
Rhoda Wolfskehl, prin. | Fax 281-0312

Mt. Pleasant ESD | 2,800/K-8
3434 Marten Ave 95148 | 408-223-3700
George L. Perez, supt. | Fax 223-3715
www.mountpleasant.k12.ca.us
Boeger MS | 700/7-8
1944 Flint Ave 95148 | 408-223-3770
Norm Robbins, prin. | Fax 223-6959

Oak Grove SD | 11,500/K-8
6578 Santa Teresa Blvd 95119 | 408-227-8300
Manny Barbara, supt. | Fax 257-2719
www.ogsd.k12.ca.us
Bernal IS | 900/7-8
6610 San Ignacio Ave 95119 | 408-578-5731
Ginny Maiwald, prin. | Fax 578-7367
Davis IS | 900/7-8
5035 Edenview Dr 95111 | 408-227-0616
Jeanette Crawford, prin. | Fax 224-8957
Herman IS | 800/7-8
5955 Blossom Ave 95123 | 408-226-1886
Barry Whittall, prin. | Fax 226-1897

Regional Occupational Center & Program
Supt. — None
Central Santa Clara Occupational Center | Vo/Tech
760 Hillsdale Ave 95136 | 408-723-6464
Tim Hallett, supt. | Fax 723-7266

San Jose USD | 30,000/K-12
855 Lenzen Ave 95126 | 408-535-6000
Don Iglesias, supt. | Fax 535-2362
Burnett MS | 700/6-8
850 N 2nd St 95112 | 408-535-6267
Dr. Robert Perez, prin. | Fax 298-1675
Castillero MS | 1,200/6-8
6384 Leyland Park Dr 95120 | 408-535-6385
Susan Walker, prin. | Fax 268-4489

Community Career Academy | Vo/Tech
2105 Forest Ave 95128 | 408-947-2852
Linda Ferdig-Riley, prin.
Gunderson HS | 1,100/9-12
622 Gaundabert Ln 95136 | 408-535-6340
Carrie Catching, prin. | Fax 224-2209
Harte MS | 1,300/6-8
7050 Bret Harte Dr 95120 | 408-535-6270
Don McCloskey, prin. | Fax 927-0698
Hoover MS | 1,100/6-8
1635 Park Ave 95126 | 408-535-6274
Marc Sosa, prin. | Fax 286-4864
Leland HS | 1,800/9-12
6677 Camden Ave 95120 | 408-535-6290
Bob Setterlund, prin. | Fax 927-6448
Lincoln HS | 1,800/9-12
555 Dana Ave 95126 | 408-535-6300
Chris Funk, prin. | Fax 535-2352
Muir MS | 900/6-8
1260 Branham Ln 95118 | 408-535-6281
Shannon McGee, prin. | Fax 535-2319
Pioneer HS | 1,400/9-12
1290 Blossom Hill Rd 95118 | 408-535-6310
Sandy Engel, prin. | Fax 535-2357
San Jose HS Academy | 1,100/9-12
275 N 24th St 95116 | 408-535-6320
Betsy Doss, prin. | Fax 535-2355
Willow Glen HS | 1,300/9-12
2001 Cottle Ave 95125 | 408-535-6330
Elaine Farace, prin. | Fax 535-2353
Willow Glen MS | 1,100/6-8
2105 Cottle Ave 95125 | 408-535-6277
John Tavella, prin. | Fax 535-2353

Union ESD | 3,900/K-8
5175 Union Ave 95124 | 408-377-8010
Phil Quon, supt. | Fax 377-7182
www.unionsd.org
Dartmouth MS | 800/6-8
5575 Dartmouth Dr 95118 | 408-264-1122
Carole Carlson, prin. | Fax 264-9332
Union MS | 800/6-8
2130 Los Gatos Almaden Rd 95124 | 408-371-0366
Laurie Marcellin, prin. | Fax 371-1217

———

Archbishop Mitty HS | 1,400/9-12
5000 Mitty Way 95129 | 408-252-6610
Timothy Brosnan, prin. | Fax 252-6967
Bellarmine College Prep S | 1,300/9-12
960 W Hedding St 95126 | 408-294-9224
Mark Pierotti, prin. | Fax 297-5585
Bryman College | Post-Sec.
1245 S Wnchstr Blvd #102 95128 | 408-246-0859
Center of Employment Training | Post-Sec.
701 Vine St 95110 | 408-287-7924
Evergreen Valley College | Post-Sec.
3095 Yerba Buena Rd 95135 | 408-274-7900
Five Branches Institute | Post-Sec.
3031 Tisch Way Ste 605 95128 | 408-260-0208
Golden State Private S | 500/9-12
5440 Thornwood Dr Ste F 95123 | 408-226-4494
Anthony Zimmer, dir.
Harker S | 1,500/K-8
PO Box 9067 95157 | 408-249-2510
Christopher Nikolo, hdmstr. | Fax 984-2325
Liberty Baptist S | 300/PK-12
2790 S King Rd 95122 | 408-274-5613
Russel Barnes, prin. | Fax 274-1363
National Hispanic University | Post-Sec.
14271 Story Rd 95127 | 408-273-2680
Notre Dame HS | 400/9-12
596 S 2nd St 95112 | 408-294-1113
Diane Saign, prin. | Fax 293-9779
Palmer College of Chiropractic West | Post-Sec.
90 E Tasman Dr 95134 | 408-944-6000
Presentation HS | 600/9-12
2281 Plummer Ave 95125 | 408-264-1664
Mary Miller, prin. | Fax 266-3028
Sacred Heart Nativity S | 200/6-8
310 Edwards Ave 95110 | 408-993-1293
Kevin Eagleson, prin. | Fax 292-0675
St. Thomas More S | 200/K-12
1565 S White Rd 95127 | 408-258-6888
Tim Selway, prin.
San Jose City College | Post-Sec.
2100 Moorpark Ave 95128 | 408-298-2181
San Jose State University | Post-Sec.
1 Washington Sq 95192 | 408-924-1000
Valley Christian HS | 1,200/9-12
100 Skyway Dr 95111 | 408-513-2400
Dr. Joel Torode, prin. | Fax 513-2424
Valley Christian JHS | 500/6-8
100 Skyway Dr #140 95111 | 408-513-2460
Robert Bridges, prin. | Fax 513-2466
Valley Christian Schools Discovery Ctr | 50/K-12
1450 Leigh Ave 95125 | 408-362-2645
Betty Ruth Bridgen, dir. | Fax 362-2647
Western Career College | Post-Sec.
6201 San Ignacio Ave 95119 | 408-360-0840
White Road Baptist Academy | 50/K-12
480 S White Rd 95127 | 408-272-7713
Chris Dona, admin. | Fax 272-7666
William Jessup University | Post-Sec.
1190 Saratoga Ave Ste 210 95129 | 408-278-4343
Willow Vale Christian Children's Center | 100/PK-12
1730 Curtner Ave 95125 | 408-448-0656
Carollyn Ellis, admin. | Fax 264-2817

———

San Juan Bautista, San Benito, Pop. 1,675
Aromas/San Juan USD | 1,400/K-12
2300 San Juan Hwy 95045 | 831-623-4500
Jacquelyn B. Munoz, supt. | Fax 623-4907
www.asjusd.k12.ca.us
Anzar HS | 300/9-12
2000 San Juan Hwy 95045 | 831-623-7660
Charlene McKowen, prin. | Fax 623-7676
Adult Education | Adult
100 Nyland Dr 95045 | 831-623-9622
Jose Luis Palacios, lead tchr. | Fax 623-0614

San Juan Capistrano, Orange, Pop. 34,796
Capistrano USD | 54,300/K-12
32972 Calle Perfecto 92675 | 949-489-7000
Dr. James Fleming, supt. | Fax 240-6241
www.capousd.org/

Forster MS | 1,600/6-8
25601 Camino Del Avion 92675 | 949-493-1133
Carrie Bertini, prin.
Capistrano Unified Adult Education | Adult
31431 El Camino Real 92675 | 949-493-0658
Beverly de Nicola, prin. | Fax 489-1421
Other Schools – See Aliso Viejo, Dana Point, Ladera
Ranch, Laguna Niguel, Las Flores, Mission Viejo,
Rancho Santa Margarita, San Clemente

Regional Occupational Center & Program
Supt. — None
Capistrano-Laguna Beach ROP | Vo/Tech
31522 El Camino Real 92675 | 949-496-3118
Richard Bogart, dir. | Fax 496-1850

———

Capistrano Valley Christian S | 600/PK-12
32032 Del Obispo St 92675 | 949-493-5683
Dr. Dave Baker, supt. | Fax 493-6057
Junipero Serra HS | 300/9-12
26351 Junipero Serra Rd 92675 | 949-493-9307
Thomas Waszak, prin. | Fax 493-9308
Saddleback Valley Christian S | 600/PK-12
26333 Oso Rd 92675 | 949-443-4050
Edward Carney, admin. | Fax 443-3941
St. Margaret Episcopal S | 1,200/PK-12
31641 La Novia Ave 92675 | 949-661-0108
Marcus D. Hurlbut, hdmstr. | Fax 489-8042

San Leandro, Alameda, Pop. 80,139
San Leandro USD | 8,400/K-12
14735 Juniper St 94579 | 510-667-3500
Laura Aguayo-Guevara, supt. | Fax 667-3569
www.sanleandro.k12.ca.us
Bancroft MS | 1,000/6-8
1150 Bancroft Ave 94577 | 510-667-3560
Mary Ann Valles, prin. | Fax 895-4113
Muir MS | 1,200/6-8
1444 Williams St 94577 | 510-667-3571
Belen Magers, prin. | Fax 667-3545
San Leandro HS | 2,400/9-12
2200 Bancroft Ave 94577 | 510-667-3540
Amy Furtado, prin. | Fax 614-0986
San Leandro Adult S | Adult
2255 Bancroft Ave 94577 | 510-667-6087
Susanne Wong, prin. | Fax 352-2183

San Lorenzo USD
Supt. — See San Lorenzo
Washington Manor MS | 900/6-8
1170 Fargo Ave 94579 | 510-317-5500
Jocelyn Lee, prin. | Fax 317-5597

———

Chinese Christian S | 900/K-12
750 Fargo Ave 94579 | 510-351-4957
Robin Hom, supt. | Fax 351-1789
Community Christian S | 300/K-12
562 Lewelling Blvd 94579 | 510-351-3684
Susan McCarrie, admin. | Fax 351-4906
Seneca Center | 100/K-12
2275 Arlington Dr 94578 | 510-481-1222
Scott Osborn, dir.
Western Career College | Post-Sec.
15555 E 14th St Ste 500 94578 | 510-276-3888

San Lorenzo, Alameda, Pop. 19,987
San Lorenzo USD | 11,400/K-12
15510 Usher St 94580 | 510-317-4600
Arnie Glassberg, supt. | Fax 278-3048
www.slzusd.org
Arroyo HS | 1,800/9-12
15701 Lorenzo Ave 94580 | 510-317-4000
Richard Lloyd, prin. | Fax 278-9067
Bohannon MS | 1,000/6-8
800 Bockman Rd 94580 | 510-317-3800
| Fax 317-3890
Edendale MS | 900/6-8
16160 Ashland Ave 94580 | 510-317-5100
Janet Clayton, prin. | Fax 317-5190
San Lorenzo HS | 1,600/9-12
50 E Lewelling Blvd 94580 | 510-317-3000
Sheryl Cambra, prin. | Fax 278-0547
San Lorenzo Adult S | Adult
820 Bockman Rd 94580 | 510-317-4200
Darryl Stucker, prin. | Fax 317-4291
Other Schools – See San Leandro

———

Redwood Christian HS | 500/7-12
1000 Paseo Grande 94580 | 510-317-8990
John Bakker, prin. | Fax 278-5064

San Luis Obispo, San Luis Obispo, Pop. 44,202
San Luis Coastal USD | 8,500/K-12
1500 Lizzie St 93401 | 805-549-1200
Edward Valentine, supt. | Fax 549-9074
www.slcusd.org
Laguna MS | 800/7-8
11050 Los Osos Valley Rd 93405 | 805-596-4055
Steve Anderson, prin. | Fax 544-2449
San Luis Obispo HS | 1,500/9-12
1499 San Luis Dr 93401 | 805-596-4040
Will Jones, prin. | Fax 542-9075
Adult S | Adult
1500 Lizzie St Bldg G 93401 | 805-549-1222
Greg Halfman, prin. | Fax 544-0638
Other Schools – See Los Osos, Morro Bay

———

California Polytechnic State University | Post-Sec.
93407 | 805-756-1111
Central CA School of Continuing Educ. | Post-Sec.
3195 McMillan Ave Ste F 93401 | 805-543-9123
Cuesta College | Post-Sec.
PO Box 8106 93403 | 805-546-3100
Mission College Preparatory Catholic HS | 300/9-12
682 Palm St 93401 | 805-543-2131
Rev. Charles Tilley, prin. | Fax 543-4359

San Marcos, San Diego, Pop. 64,242
San Marcos USD | 14,000/K-12
1 Civic Center Dr Ste 300 92069 | 760-752-1299
Edward Brand, supt. | Fax 471-4928
www.smusd.org/

Mission Hills HS 9-12
1 E Mission Hills Ct 92069 760-290-2700
Brad Lichtman, prin.
San Elijo MS 6-8
1600 Schoolhouse Way 92078 760-290-2800
Doug Hall, prin. Fax 290-2828
San Marcos HS 3,100/9-12
1615 W San Marcos Blvd 92078 760-290-2200
Nancy Peterson, prin. Fax 736-8275
San Marcos MS 1,800/6-8
650 W Mission Rd 92069 760-290-2500
Brian Randall, prin. Fax 736-2223
Woodland Park MS 1,500/6-8
1270 Rock Springs Rd 92069 760-290-2455
Melissa Hunt, prin. Fax 741-6178

California State University-San Marcos Post-Sec.
92096 760-750-4000
CEI Post-Sec.
1050 Los Vallecitos Blvd 92069 760-471-9300
Coleman College Post-Sec.
1284 W San Marcos Blvd #110 92069 760-747-3990
Palomar College 760-744-1150
1140 W Mission Rd 92069
Palomar College of Cosmetology Post-Sec.
355 Via Vera Cruz Ste 3 92078 760-744-7900

San Marino, Los Angeles, Pop. 13,230
San Marino USD 3,300/K-12
1665 West Dr 91108 626-299-7000
Jack R. Rose, supt. Fax 299-7010
www.san-marino.k12.ca.us
Huntington MS 800/6-8
1700 Huntington Dr 91108 626-299-7060
Gary McGuigan, prin. Fax 299-7064
San Marino HS 1,200/9-12
2701 Huntington Dr 91108 626-299-7020
Loren Kleinrock, prin. Fax 299-7037

Southwestern Academy 200/6-12
2800 Monterey Rd 91108 626-799-5010
Kenneth Veronda, prin. Fax 799-0407

San Mateo, San Mateo, Pop. 91,157
San Mateo UNHSD 8,100/9-12
650 N Delaware St 94401 650-558-2299
Samuel Johnson, supt. Fax 762-0249
www.smuhsd.k12.ca.us
Aragon HS 1,500/9-12
900 Alameda De Las Pulgas 94402 650-558-2999
Kirk Black, prin. Fax 558-2952
Hillsdale HS 1,300/9-12
3115 Del Monte St 94403 650-558-2699
Yvonne Shiv, prin. Fax 574-4173
San Mateo HS 1,400/9-12
506 N Delaware St 94401 650-558-2399
Jacqueline McEvoy, prin. Fax 762-0265
San Mateo Adult S Adult
789 E Poplar Ave 94401 650-558-2100
Lawrence Teshara, prin. Fax 762-0232
Other Schools – See Burlingame, Millbrae, San Bruno

San Mateo-Foster City SD 10,100/K-8
PO Box K 94402 650-312-7700
Pendery A. Clark Ed.D., supt. Fax 312-7779
www.smfc.k12.ca.us
Abbott MS 800/6-8
600 36th Ave 94403 650-312-7600
Cathy Ennon, prin. Fax 312-7605
Bayside MS 800/6-8
2025 Kehoe Ave 94403 650-312-7660
Jeanne Elliot, prin. Fax 312-7634
Borel MS 900/6-8
425 Barneson Ave 94402 650-312-7670
Clathel Zach, prin. Fax 312-7644
Other Schools – See Foster City

Alpha Beacon Christian S 200/PK-12
525 42nd Ave 94403 650-212-4222
Lillian Mark, supt. Fax 212-1026
College of San Mateo Post-Sec.
1700 W Hillsdale Blvd 94402 650-574-6161
Junipero Serra HS 900/9-12
451 W 20th Ave 94403 650-345-8207
Lars Lund, prin. Fax 573-6638

San Pablo, Contra Costa, Pop. 31,041
West Contra Costa USD
Supt. — See Richmond
Helms MS 1,300/6-8
2500 Rd 20 94806 510-233-3988
Harriet MacLean, prin. Fax 234-5977

Contra Costa College Post-Sec.
2600 Mission Bell Dr 94806 510-235-7800

San Pedro, See Los Angeles
Los Angeles USD
Supt. — See Los Angeles
Dana MS 1,900/6-8
1501 S Cabrillo Ave 90731 310-833-5235
Terry Ball, prin. Fax 514-9925
San Pedro HS 3,300/9-12
1001 W 15th St 90731 310-547-2491
Diana Gelb, prin. Fax 547-3183
Harbor Community Adult S Adult
950 W Santa Cruz St 90731 310-547-4425
Lanny Nelms, prin. Fax 832-3489
Harbor Occupational Center Adult
740 N Pacific Ave 90731 310-547-5551
Gertrude Hawkins, prin. Fax 547-4979

Mary Star of the Sea HS 400/9-12
810 W 8th St 90731 310-547-1138
Rita Dever, prin. Fax 547-1827

San Rafael, Marin, Pop. 55,805
Dixie ESD 1,800/K-8
380 Nova Albion Way 94903 415-492-3700
Thomas Lohwasser, supt. Fax 492-3707
dixiesd.marin.k12.ca.us/
Miller Creek MS 700/6-8
2255 Las Gallinas Ave 94903 415-492-3760
Greg Johnson, prin. Fax 492-3765

Regional Occupational Center & Program
Supt. — None
Marin County ROP Vo/Tech
1111 Las Gallinas Ave 94903 415-499-5892
Gene Abbott, coord. Fax 491-6622

San Rafael CSD 5,600/K-12
310 Nova Albion Way 94903 415-492-3233
Dr. Laura D. Alvarenga, supt. Fax 492-3245
www.srcs.org
Davidson MS 900/6-8
280 Woodland Ave 94901 415-485-2400
Ed Colucci, prin. Fax 485-2476
San Rafael HS 1,000/9-12
185 Mission Ave 94901 415-485-2330
Judy Colton, prin. Fax 485-2345
Terra Linda HS 1,000/9-12
320 Nova Albion Way 94903 415-492-3100
Carole Ramsey, prin. Fax 492-3105
San Rafael Adult Education Adult
150 Lovell Ave 94901 415-492-3226
Sue Gatlin, prin. Fax 492-3246

Dominican University of California Post-Sec.
50 Acacia Ave 94901 415-457-4440
Marin Academy 400/9-12
1600 Mission Ave 94901 415-453-4550
Bodie Brizendine, prin. Fax 453-8538

San Ramon, Contra Costa, Pop. 45,907
San Ramon Valley USD
Supt. — See Danville
California HS 2,300/9-12
9870 Broadmoor Dr 94583 925-803-7400
Mark Corti, prin. Fax 803-9341
Iron Horse MS 1,000/6-8
12601 Alcosta Blvd 94583 925-824-2820
Kirby Hoy, prin. Fax 824-2830
Pine Valley MS 1,000/6-8
3000 Pine Valley Rd 94583 925-803-7420
Marilyn Nachtman, prin. Fax 828-1972
Windemere Ranch MS 6-8
11611 E Branch Pkwy, 925-479-7400
David Bolin, prin. Fax 479-7469

Santa Ana, Orange, Pop. 342,510
Garden Grove USD
Supt. — See Garden Grove
Fitz IS, 4600 W McFadden Ave 92704 1,000/7-8
Vicki Braddock, prin. 714-663-6351

Regional Occupational Center & Program
Supt. — None
Central County ROP Vo/Tech
2323 N Broadway Ste 301 92706 714-541-5537
Diana Schneider, dir. Fax 541-5214

Santa Ana USD 59,200/PK-12
1601 E Chestnut Ave 92701 714-558-5501
Al Mijares Ph.D., supt. Fax 558-5610
www.sausd.k12.ca.us
Carr IS 1,700/6-8
2120 W Edinger Ave 92704 714-431-7600
P. Yrarrazaval-Correa, prin. Fax 431-7699
Century HS 2,500/9-12
1401 S Grand Ave 92705 714-568-7000
Greg Rankin, prin. Fax 568-7038
Lathrop IS 1,800/6-8
1111 S Broadway 92707 714-567-3300
Lucinda Clear, prin. Fax 567-3399
MacArthur Fundamental IS 1,300/6-8
600 W Alton Ave 92707 714-513-9800
Marvin Smulowitz, prin. Fax 513-9899
McFadden IS 1,600/6-8
2701 S Raitt St 92704 714-435-3700
Esther Severy, prin. Fax 435-3799
Mendez Fundamental IS 1,400/6-8
2000 N Bristol St 92706 714-972-7800
Cynthia Landsiedel, prin. Fax 972-7899
Saddleback HS 3,100/9-12
2802 S Flower St 92707 714-513-2900
Esther Jones, prin. Fax 513-2911
Santa Ana HS 3,900/9-12
520 W Walnut St 92701 714-567-4900
Dan Salcedo, prin. Fax 567-4952
Segerstrom HS 9-12
2301 W MacArthur Blvd 92704 714-241-5000
Lyn Maher, prin. Fax 241-5999
Sierra IS 1,200/5-8
1901 N McClay St 92705 714-567-3500
Brenda McGaffigan, prin. Fax 567-3591
Spurgeon IS 1,700/6-8
2701 W 5th St 92703 714-480-2200
Robert Laxton, prin. Fax 480-2215
Valley HS 3,100/9-12
1801 S Greenville St 92704 714-241-6410
Antonio Espinosa, prin. Fax 241-6547
Villa Fundamental IS 1,400/6-8
1441 E Chestnut Ave 92701 714-558-5100
Dawn Miller, prin. Fax 558-5103
Willard IS 1,800/5-8
1342 N Ross St 92706 714-480-4800
Jeff Bishop, prin. Fax 480-4899

Tustin USD
Supt. — See Tustin
Foothill HS 2,400/9-12
19251 Dodge Ave 92705 714-730-7464
Al Marzilli, prin. Fax 573-9376
Hewes MS 1,000/6-8
13232 Hewes Ave 92705 714-730-7348
Tracey VanderHayden, prin. Fax 730-7315

Argosy University/Orange County Post-Sec.
3501 W Sunflower Ave 92704 714-338-6200
Art Institute of California Post-Sec.
3601 W Sunflower Ave 92704 714-830-0200
Bethel Baptist S 300/K-12
901 S Euclid St 92704 714-839-3600
Dr. Terry Cantrell, admin. Fax 839-4953
California Coast University Post-Sec.
700 N Main St 92701 714-547-9625
Calvary Chapel S 1,800/K-12
3800 S Fairview St 92704 714-556-0965
Jay Henry, supt. Fax 751-3718

Colleen O'Hara's Beauty Academy Post-Sec.
109 W 4th St Flr 2 92701 714-568-5399
College of Automotive Management Post-Sec.
3000 W MacArthur Blvd Fl 3 92704 714-755-6894
Health Staff Training Institute Post-Sec.
1505 E 17th St Ste 122 92705 714-543-9828
Kensington College Post-Sec.
2428 N Grand Ave Ste D 92705 714-542-8086
Mater Dei HS 2,100/9-12
1202 W Edinger Ave 92707 714-754-7711
Frances Clare, prin. Fax 754-1880
Newbridge College Post-Sec.
1840 E 17th St # 140 92705 714-550-8000
Santa Ana College 714-564-6000
1530 W 17th St 92706
William Howard Taft University Post-Sec.
3700 S Susan St 92704 714-850-4800

Santa Barbara, Santa Barbara, Pop. 88,251
Regional Occupational Center & Program
Supt. — None
Santa Barbara County ROP South Vo/Tech
PO Box 6307 93160 805-964-4711
John Ingram, dir. Fax 569-2507

Santa Barbara SD 15,100/K-12
720 Santa Barbara St 93101 805-963-4331
J. Brian Sarvis, supt. Fax 962-3146
www.sbceo.k12.ca.us/~sbsdweb/
La Colina JHS 1,000/7-8
4025 Foothill Rd 93110 805-967-4506
David Ortiz, prin. Fax 967-3056
La Cumbre MS 600/6-8
2255 Modoc Rd 93101 805-687-0761
JoAnn Caines, prin. Fax 563-4636
San Marcos HS 2,100/9-12
4750 Hollister Ave 93110 805-967-4581
Craig Morgan, prin. Fax 967-8358
Santa Barbara HS 2,400/9-12
700 E Anapamu St 93103 805-966-9101
Paul Turnbull, prin. Fax 965-6872
Santa Barbara JHS 1,000/7-8
721 E Cota St 93103 805-963-7751
Susan Salcido, prin. Fax 962-7196
Other Schools – See Goleta

Anacapa S 100/7-12
814 Santa Barbara St 93101 805-965-0228
Fax 899-2758
Antioch University Post-Sec.
801 Garden St Ste 101 93101 805-962-8179
Avalon Beauty College Post-Sec.
504 N Milpas St 93103 805-966-1931
Bishop Garcia Diego HS 400/9-12
4000 La Colina Rd 93110 805-967-1266
Fr. Tom Elewaut, prin. Fax 964-3178
Brooks Institute of Photography Post-Sec.
801 Alston Rd 93108 805-966-3888
Devereux California Post-Sec.
PO Box 6784 93160 805-968-2525
Fielding Graduate University Post-Sec.
2112 Santa Barbara St 93105 805-687-1099
Laguna Blanca S 400/K-12
4125 Paloma Dr 93110 805-687-2461
Douglas W. Jessup, hdmstr. Fax 682-2553
Santa Barbara Business College Post-Sec.
5266 Hollister Ave 93111 805-967-9677
Santa Barbara City College Post-Sec.
721 Cliff Dr 93109 805-965-0581
Santa Barbara Coll. of Oriental Medicine Post-Sec.
1919 State St 93101 800-549-6299
Santa Barbara Cottage & Gen. Hosp. Post-Sec.
PO Box 689 93102 805-569-7290
Santa Barbara Middle S 200/6-9
2300 Garden St 93105 805-682-2989
Stephen Lane, hdmstr.
University of California 93106 Post-Sec.
805-893-8000
Westmont College Post-Sec.
955 La Paz Rd 93108 805-565-6000

Santa Clara, Santa Clara, Pop. 102,095
Santa Clara USD 13,600/K-12
PO Box 397 95052 408-423-2000
Rod Adams, supt. Fax 423-2285
www.scu.k12.ca.us
Buchser MS 900/6-8
1111 Bellomy St 95050 408-423-3000
Kyle Eaton, prin. Fax 423-3080
Cabrillo MS 900/6-8
2550 Cabrillo Ave 95051 408-423-3700
Stan Garber, prin. Fax 423-3780
Santa Clara HS 1,600/9-12
3000 Benton St 95051 408-423-2600
Brad Syth, prin. Fax 985-2681
Wilcox HS 2,000/9-12
3250 Monroe St 95051 408-423-2400
Tab Taber, prin. Fax 423-2480
Santa Clara Adult Comm Education Center Adult
1840 Benton St 95050 408-984-6220
Daniene Marciano, dir. Fax 423-3580
Other Schools – See Sunnyvale

California Cosmetology College Post-Sec.
955 Monroe St 95050 408-247-2200
Institute for Business and Technology Post-Sec.
2400 Walsh Ave 95051 408-727-1060
Mission College Post-Sec.
3000 Mission College Blvd 95054 408-988-2200
North Valley Baptist S 300/K-12
941 Clyde Ave 95054 408-988-8883
Daniel Azzarello, prin.
St. Lawrence Academy 300/9-12
2000 Lawrence Ct 95051 408-296-3013
Christie Filios, prin. Fax 296-3794
Santa Clara University Post-Sec.
500 El Camino Real 95053 408-554-4000
Sierra S, 220 Blake Ave 95051 100/K-12
Linda Wesley, prin. 408-247-4740

Santa Clarita, Los Angeles, Pop. 162,742
Regional Occupational Center & Program
Supt. — None

Hart ROP — Vo/Tech
21515 Centre Pointe Pkwy 91350 — 661-259-0033
Jan Burns, dir. — Fax 254-8653

William S. Hart UNHSD — 22,500/7-12
21515 Centre Pointe Pkwy 91350 — 661-259-0033
Jaime Castellanos, supt. — Fax 254-8653
www.hartdistrict.org
Golden Valley HS — 9-12
22501 Robert E Lee Pkwy 91321 — 661-298-8140
Jacque Snyder, prin. — Fax 250-8362
La Mesa JHS — 1,300/7-8
26623 May Way 91351 — 661-250-0022
Pete Fries, prin. — Fax 252-3326
Golden Oak Adult S — Adult
23201 Dalbey Dr 91355 — 661-253-0583
Lynda Rick, prin. — Fax 260-1371
Other Schools – See Canyon Country, Newhall, Saugus, Stevenson Ranch, Valencia

Advantage Preparatory S — 200/K-12
PO Box 802274 91380 — 661-296-5466
Cynthia Grant, prin.
College of the Canyons — Post-Sec.
26455 Rockwell Canyon Rd 91355 — 661-259-7800

Santa Cruz, Santa Cruz, Pop. 54,262
Live Oak SD — 1,900/K-8
984 Bostwick Ln Ste 1 95062 — 831-475-6333
Dr. David Paine, supt. — Fax 475-2638
www.lodo.santacruz.k12.ca.us
Shoreline MS — 600/6-8
855 17th Ave 95062 — 831-475-6565
Barbara Keesaw, prin. — Fax 462-1653

Santa Cruz CSD
Supt. — See Soquel
Branciforte MS — 500/6-8
315 Poplar Ave 95062 — 831-429-3883
Kris Munro, prin. — Fax 429-3962
Harbor HS — 1,200/9-12
300 La Fonda Ave 95062 — 831-429-3810
Nancy Tocchini, prin. — Fax 429-3982
Mission Hill MS — 700/6-8
425 King St 95060 — 831-429-3860
Dona Abrahams-Johnson, prin. — Fax 427-4846
Santa Cruz HS — 1,200/9-12
415 Walnut Ave 95060 — 831-429-3960
Karen Edmunds, prin. — Fax 429-3944
Santa Cruz Adult Education — Adult
2931 Mission St 95060 — 831-429-3966
Mary Powers, prin. — Fax 429-3061

Five Branches Institute — Post-Sec.
200 7th Ave 95062 — 831-476-9424
Kirby Preparatory S — 200/6-12
117 Union St 95060 — 831-423-0658
Joshua Karter Ph.D., hdmstr.
Santa Cruz Waldorf HS — 100/9-12
111 Errett Cir 95060 — 831-420-0565
Jennipher Lommen, admin. — Fax 425-1326
University of California-Santa Cruz — Post-Sec.
95064 — 831-459-0111

Santa Fe Springs, Los Angeles, Pop. 17,032
Little Lake City ESD — 5,200/K-8
10515 Pioneer Blvd 90670 — 562-868-8241
Phillip Perez Ph.D., supt. — Fax 868-1192
www.littlelake.k12.ca.us
Lake Center MS — 1,000/6-8
10503 Pioneer Blvd 90670 — 562-868-4977
Linda Erdman, prin. — Fax 929-4527
Other Schools – See Norwalk

Whittier UNHSD
Supt. — See Whittier
Santa Fe HS — 2,600/9-12
10400 Orr and Day Rd 90670 — 562-698-8121
Monica Oviedo, prin. — Fax 868-8277

NTMA Training Center of Southern CA — Post-Sec.
13230 E Firestone Blvd # A 90670 — 562-404-4295
St. Paul HS — 900/9-12
9635 Greenleaf Ave 90670 — 562-698-6246
Frank Laurenzello, prin. — Fax 696-8396

Santa Maria, Santa Barbara, Pop. 81,944
Orcutt UNESD
Supt. — See Orcutt
Lakeview JHS — 700/7-8
3700 Orcutt Rd 93455 — 805-938-8600
Robert Bush, prin. — Fax 938-8649

Regional Occupational Center & Program
Supt. — None
Santa Barbara County ROP North — Vo/Tech
4893 Bethany Ln 93455 — 805-937-8427
Ken Main, dir. — Fax 937-7489

Santa Maria JUNHSD — 6,400/9-12
2560 Skyway Dr 93455 — 805-922-4573
Jeffrey Hearn Ph.D., supt. — Fax 928-9916
www.smjuhsd.k12.ca.us
Pioneer Valley HS — 9-12
675 Fremont St 93454 — 805-922-1305
Dee Ringstead, prin. — Fax 928-9916
Righetti HS — 2,600/9-12
941 E Foster Rd 93455 — 805-937-2051
Catherine Ulrich, prin. — Fax 934-0819
Santa Maria HS — 3,800/9-12
901 S Broadway 93454 — 805-925-2567
Esther Prieto-Chavez, prin. — Fax 922-0215
Santa Maria Adult S — Adult
251 E Clark Ave 93455 — 805-937-6356
Craig Huseth, prin. — Fax 934-4743

Santa Maria-Bonita SD — 12,200/K-8
708 S Miller St 93454 — 805-928-1783
David Francis, supt. — Fax 928-7874
www.smbsd.org/
Arellanes JHS — 400/7-8
1890 Sandalwood Dr 93455 — 805-361-6820
Patty Grady, prin. — Fax 346-8535

El Camino JHS — 1,000/7-8
219 W El Camino St 93458 — 805-361-7800
Mark Muller, prin. — Fax 346-1851
Fesler JHS — 900/7-8
1100 E Fesler St 93454 — 805-361-7880
Barbara Walker, prin. — Fax 346-1849
Kunst JHS — 7-8
930 Hidden Pines Way 93458 — 805-361-5800
Ed Cora, prin. — Fax 925-8239

Allan Hancock College — Post-Sec.
800 S College Dr 93454 — 805-922-6966
Crossroads Christian JHS — 100/7-8
1550 S College Dr 93454 — 805-922-0237
Susan Pruett, admin. — Fax 925-9690
St. Joseph HS — 700/9-12
4120 S Bradley Rd 93455 — 805-937-2038
Joseph Myers, prin. — Fax 937-4248
Santa Barbara Business College — Post-Sec.
303 Plaza Dr 93454 — 805-922-8256
Valley Christian Academy — 300/K-12
2970 Santa Maria Way 93455 — 805-937-6317
Charles Mason, prin. — Fax 934-2563

Santa Monica, Los Angeles, Pop. 87,162
Santa Monica-Malibu USD — 12,100/PK-12
1651 16th St 90404 — 310-450-8338
John Deasy, supt. — Fax 450-1667
www.smmusd.org
Adams MS — 1,200/6-8
2425 16th St 90405 — 310-452-2326
Irene Ramos, prin. — Fax 452-5352
Lincoln MS — 1,300/6-8
1501 California Ave 90403 — 310-393-9227
Kathy Scott, prin. — Fax 393-4297
Santa Monica HS — 3,400/9-12
601 Pico Blvd 90405 — 310-395-3204
Dr. Ilene Straus, prin. — Fax 395-5842
Santa Monica-Malibu Adult Education — Adult
2510 Lincoln Blvd 90405 — 310-664-6222
Stephen Martinez, prin. — Fax 664-6220
Other Schools – See Malibu

Art Institute of California — Post-Sec.
2900 31st St 90405 — 310-752-4700
Concord HS — 100/9-12
1831 Wilshire Blvd Ste B 90403 — 310-828-9443
Susan Packer Davis, prin.
Crossroads S for Arts & Sciences — 1,100/K-12
1714 21st St 90404 — 310-829-7391
Roger Weaver, prin. — Fax 828-5636
Emperor's Coll. of Trad. Oriental Med. — Post-Sec.
1807 Wilshire Blvd Ste B 90403 — 310-453-8300
Lighthouse Christian Academy — 100/9-12
1424 Yale St 90404 — 310-829-2522
George Neos, prin.
Lighthouse S — 200/PK-12
1220 20th St 90404 — 310-829-1741
Rob Scribner, prin. — Fax 829-2743
New Roads HS — 200/9-12
3131 Olympic Blvd 90404 — 310-828-5582
David Bryan, hdmstr. — Fax 828-2582
New Roads MS — 100/6-8
1238 Lincoln Blvd 90401 — 310-587-2255
David Bryan, hdmstr. — Fax 587-2258
Pacifica Christian HS — 50/9-12
1730 Wilshire Blvd 90403 — 310-828-7015
Jim Knight, hdmstr. — Fax 829-2063
Pardee RAND Grad Sch of Policy Studies — Post-Sec.
PO Box 2138 90407 — 310-393-0411
St. Monica HS — 600/9-12
1030 Lincoln Blvd 90403 — 310-394-3701
Thom Gasper, prin. — Fax 458-1353
Santa Monica College — Post-Sec.
1900 Pico Blvd 90405 — 310-434-4000

Santa Paula, Ventura, Pop. 28,879
Briggs ESD — 500/K-8
12465 Foothill Rd 93060 — 805-525-7540
Mike McLaughlin, supt. — Fax 933-1111
www.briggs.k12.ca.us
Briggs MS — 200/5-8
14438 W Telegraph Rd 93060 — 805-525-7151
Deborah Cuevas, prin. — Fax 933-3565

Santa Paula ESD — 4,000/K-8
201 S Steckel Dr 93060 — 805-933-8800
Luis C. Villegas Ed.D., supt. — Fax 525-0546
www.spesd.org/
Isbell MS — 1,300/6-8
221 S 4th St 93060 — 805-933-8880
Fernando Rivera, prin. — Fax 933-5582

Santa Paula UNHSD — 1,700/9-12
500 E Santa Barbara St 93060 — 805-525-0988
David Gomez, supt. — Fax 525-6128
www.spuhsd.k12.ca.us
Santa Paula HS — 1,600/9-12
404 N 6th St 93060 — 805-525-4406
J. Antonio Gaitan, prin. — Fax 525-1690
Santa Paula Adult Education — Adult
333 N Palm Ave 93060 — 805-525-9502
Lorenzo Moraza, prin. — Fax 525-2294

Thomas Aquinas College — Post-Sec.
10000 Ojai Rd 93060 — 800-634-9797

Santa Rosa, Sonoma, Pop. 153,386
Oak Grove UNSD — 600/K-8
5285 Hall Rd 95401 — 707-545-0171
Noel Buehler, supt. — Fax 545-0176
www.ogusd.org/
Willowside MS — 300/6-8
5285 Hall Rd 95401 — 707-542-3322
Lisa Saxon, prin. — Fax 525-4439

Piner-Olivet UNESD — 1,600/K-6
3450 Coffey Ln 95403 — 707-522-3000
Rod Buchignani, supt. — Fax 522-3007
www.pousd.k12.ca.us
Career Academy at Piner-Olivet — Vo/Tech
3450 Coffey Ln 95403 — 707-292-9222
Helen Ramstad, dir. — Fax 522-3007

Regional Occupational Center & Program
Supt. — None
Sonoma County ROP — Vo/Tech
5340 Skylane Blvd 95403 — 707-524-2720
Stephen Jackson, dir. — Fax 524-2789

Santa Rosa CSD — 17,500/K-12
211 Ridgeway Ave 95401 — 707-528-5352
Sharon Liddell, supt. — Fax 528-5487
www.srcs.k12.ca.us
Allen HS — 1,600/9-12
599 Bellevue Ave 95407 — 707-528-5020
Mary Gail Stablein, prin. — Fax 528-5023
Carillo HS — 1,500/9-12
6975 Montecito Blvd 95409 — 707-528-5790
Mark Klick, prin. — Fax 528-5789
Comstock MS — 700/7-8
2750 W Steele Ln 95403 — 707-528-5266
Raul Guerrero, prin. — Fax 528-5480
Cook MS — 800/7-8
2480 Sebastopol Rd 95407 — 707-528-5156
Harriet Gray, prin. — Fax 528-5163
Montgomery HS — 1,900/9-12
1250 Hahman Dr 95405 — 707-528-5191
William Stirnus, prin. — Fax 528-5056
Piner HS — 1,500/9-12
1700 Fulton Rd 95403 — 707-528-5245
Janet Olson, prin. — Fax 528-5246
Rincon Valley MS — 900/7-8
4650 Badger Rd 95409 — 707-528-5255
Arlen Agapinan, prin. — Fax 528-5644
Santa Rosa HS — 2,000/9-12
1235 Mendocino Ave 95401 — 707-528-5291
Toni Negri, prin. — Fax 528-5724
Santa Rosa MS — 800/7-8
500 E St 95404 — 707-528-5281
Kathy Coker, prin. — Fax 528-5283
Slater MS — 1,000/7-8
3500 Sonoma Ave 95405 — 707-528-5241
Jason Lea, prin. — Fax 528-5733
Lewis Adult Education Center — Adult
2230 Lomitas Ave 95404 — 707-522-3280
Stephen Nielsen, prin. — Fax 522-3289

Cardinal Newman HS — 500/9-12
50 Ursuline Rd 95403 — 707-546-6470
Grahm Rutherford, prin. — Fax 544-8502
Covenant Christian Academy — 50/PK-12
1315 Pacific Ave 95404 — 707-579-0661
Dawna Wiemeyer, admin. — Fax 579-0661
Empire College School of Business — Post-Sec.
3035 Cleveland Ave 95403 — 707-546-4000
Lytle's Redwood Empire Beauty College — Post-Sec.
186 Wikiup Dr 95403 — 707-545-8490
Redwood Adventist Academy — 200/PK-12
385 Mark West Springs Rd 95404 — 707-545-1697
Rob Fenderson, prin. — Fax 545-8020
Rincon Valley Christian S — 400/PK-12
4585 Badger Rd 95409 — 707-539-1486
Tor Benestad, prin. — Fax 539-1493
Santa Rosa Christian S — 300/K-12
950 S Wright Rd 95407 — 707-542-6414
Dr. Lois Sowers, hdmstr. — Fax 542-0421
Santa Rosa Junior College — Post-Sec.
1501 Mendocino Ave 95401 — 707-527-4011
Sonoma Academy — 200/9-12
50 Mark West Springs Rd 95403 — 707-545-1770
Janet Durgin, hdmstr. — Fax 636-2474
Summerfield Waldorf S — 400/PK-12
655 Willowside Rd 95401 — 707-575-7194
Bill Ritch, admin. — Fax 575-3217
Ursuline HS — 400/9-12
90 Ursuline Rd 95403 — 707-524-1130
Barbara Johannes, prin. — Fax 524-0131

Santa Ynez, Santa Barbara, Pop. 4,200
Santa Ynez Valley UNHSD — 1,100/9-12
PO Box 398 93460 — 805-688-6487
Fred Van Leuven, supt. — Fax 686-4454
www.syvuhsd.org
Santa Ynez Valley Union HS — 1,100/9-12
PO Box 398 93460 — 805-688-6487
Norman Clevenger, prin. — Fax 688-1913

Santee, San Diego, Pop. 52,942
Grossmont UNHSD
Supt. — See El Cajon
Santana HS — 1,800/9-12
9915 N Magnolia Ave 92071 — 619-448-5500
Gary Schwartzwald, prin. — Fax 449-3119
West Hills HS — 2,300/9-12
8756 Mast Blvd 92071 — 619-596-3600
Brian Wilbur, prin. — Fax 562-9342

Institute for Creation Research Grad Sch — Post-Sec.
10946 Woodside Ave N 92071 — 619-448-0900

San Ysidro, See San Diego
San Ysidro ESD — 4,900/PK-8
4350 Otay Mesa Rd 92173 — 619-428-4476
Tim Allen, supt. — Fax 428-1505
www.sysd.k12.ca.us
San Ysidro MS — 1,000/7-8
4345 Otay Mesa Rd 92173 — 619-428-5551
Carolina Flores, prin. — Fax 690-2837

Sweetwater UNHSD
Supt. — See Chula Vista
San Ysidro Adult S — Adult
4220 Otay Mesa Rd 92173 — 619-662-4026
Lenora Neely, prin. — Fax 428-0295

New Life Christian Academy — 100/K-12
3747 Sunset Ln 92173 — 619-428-0967
Jose Perez, admin.

Saratoga, Santa Clara, Pop. 29,309
Campbell UNHSD
Supt. — See San Jose
Prospect HS — 1,200/9-12
18900 Prospect Rd 95070 — 408-253-1662
Rita Matthews, prin. — Fax 973-1759

Los Gatos-Saratoga JUNHSD
Supt. — See Los Gatos
Saratoga HS — 1,300/9-12
20300 Herriman Ave 95070 — 408-867-3411
Fax 867-3577

Saratoga Union Elem SD — 2,400/K-8
20460 Forrest Hills Dr 95070 — 408-867-3424
Lane Weiss, supt. — Fax 867-2312
www.saratogausd.org
Redwood MS — 900/6-8
13925 Fruitvale Ave 95070 — 408-867-3042
Beth Polito, prin. — Fax 867-3195

West Valley College — Post-Sec.
14000 Fruitvale Ave 95070 — 408-867-2200

Saugus, See Santa Clarita
William S. Hart UNHSD
Supt. — See Santa Clarita
Saugus HS — 2,700/9-12
21900 Centurion Way 91350 — 661-297-3900
William Bolde, prin. — Fax 297-7491

Sausalito, Marin, Pop. 7,223
Sausalito Marin City SD — 200/K-8
630 Nevada St 94965 — 415-332-3190
Rose Marie Roberson Ed.D., supt. — Fax 332-9643
www.sausalitomarincityschooldistrict.org/
King Jr Academy — 100/7-8
630 Nevada St 94965 — 415-332-3573
Ruby Wilson, prin. — Fax 332-2492

Scotts Valley, Santa Cruz, Pop. 11,284
Scotts Valley USD — 2,700/K-12
4444 Scotts Valley Dr Ste 5 95066 — 831-438-1820
Dr. Susan Silver, supt. — Fax 438-2314
www.svusd.santacruz.k12.ca.us
Scotts Valley HS — 800/9-12
555 Glenwood Dr 95066 — 831-439-9555
Gregg Gunkel, prin. — Fax 439-9501
Scotts Valley MS — 700/6-8
8 Bean Creek Rd 95066 — 831-438-0610
Mary Lonhart, prin. — Fax 439-8935

Bethany University — Post-Sec.
800 Bethany Dr 95066 — 831-438-3800

Seaside, Monterey, Pop. 33,897
Monterey Peninsula USD
Supt. — See Monterey
Fitch MS — 600/6-8
999 Coe Ave 93955 — 831-899-7080
Ken Harbord, prin. — Fax 899-0663
Seaside HS — 1,400/9-12
2200 Noche Buena St 93955 — 831-899-7033
Sheila Keifetz, prin. — Fax 899-5781
Cabrillo Adult Education — Adult
1295 La Salle Ave 93955 — 831-899-1615
Ann Kilty, dir.

California State University-Monterey Bay — Post-Sec.
100 Campus Ctr 93955 — 831-582-3000

Sebastopol, Sonoma, Pop. 7,732
Gravenstein UNESD — 500/PK-8
3840 Twig Ave 95472 — 707-823-7008
Linda LaMarre, supt. — Fax 823-2108
www.grav.k12.ca.us/
Hillcrest S — 200/6-8
725 Bloomfield Rd 95472 — 707-823-7653
Linda LaMarre, prin. — Fax 823-4630
Sebastopol UNESD — 1,100/K-8
7611 Huntley St 95472 — 707-829-4570
Robert A. Haley, supt. — Fax 829-7427
www.sebusd.org/
Brook Haven MS — 500/6-8
7905 Valentine Ave 95472 — 707-829-4590
David Wheeler, prin. — Fax 829-6285

Twin Hills UNSD — 700/K-8
700 Watertrough Rd 95472 — 707-823-0871
Donald F. Armstrong, supt. — Fax 823-5832
thusd.k12.ca.us
Twin Hills MS — 300/6-8
1685 Watertrough Rd 95472 — 707-823-7446
Catherine Bosch, prin. — Fax 823-6470

West Sonoma CUHSD — 2,900/9-12
462 Johnson St 95472 — 707-824-6403
Keller McDonald, supt. — Fax 824-6490
wscuhsd.k12.ca.us
Analy HS — 1,400/9-12
6950 Analy Ave 95472 — 707-824-2300
Martin Webb, prin. — Fax 824-2306
New Vista Adult Education — Adult
462 Johnson St 95472 — 707-824-6485
Ross Bickford, prin. — Fax 824-7910
Other Schools – See Forestville

Selma, Fresno, Pop. 21,176
Selma USD — 6,000/K-12
3036 Thompson Ave 93662 — 559-898-6500
Anthony A. Monreal Ed.D., supt. — Fax 896-7147
www.selma.k12.ca.us
Lincoln MS — 1,000/7-8
1239 Nelson Blvd 93662 — 559-898-6600
Norma Barajas-Ruiz, prin. — Fax 896-0733
Selma HS — 1,500/9-12
3125 Wright St 93662 — 559-898-6550
Mark Babiarz, prin. — Fax 891-1110
Selma Adult S — Adult
3125 Wright St 93662 — 559-898-6590
Teresa Wood, coord. — Fax 896-4333

Sepulveda, See Los Angeles
Los Angeles USD
Supt. — See Los Angeles
Monroe HS — 4,600/9-12
9229 Haskell Ave 91343 — 818-892-4311
Lynda Schwarz, prin. — Fax 892-5622
Sepulveda MS — 2,600/6-8
15330 Plummer St 91343 — 818-892-3151
Barbara Charness, prin. — Fax 891-5754

Shafter, Kern, Pop. 13,720
Kern HSD
Supt. — See Bakersfield
Shafter HS — 1,300/9-12
526 Mannel Ave 93263 — 661-746-4961
Jaime Quinonez, prin. — Fax 746-6743

Richland SD — 3,000/K-8
331 N Shafter Ave 93263 — 661-746-8600
Lyle Mack, supt. — Fax 746-8614
www.richland.k12.ca.us
Richland JHS — 1,000/6-8
331 N Shafter Ave 93263 — 661-746-8630
Kathy Mayes, prin. — Fax 746-8614

Shandon, San Luis Obispo
Shandon JUSD — 300/K-12
PO Box 79 93461 — 805-238-0286
Chris Crawford, supt. — Fax 238-0777
shandon.echalk.com
Shandon HS — 100/7-12
PO Box 79 93461 — 805-238-0286
Chris Crawford, prin. — Fax 238-0777

Sherman Oaks, See Los Angeles
Los Angeles USD
Supt. — See Los Angeles
Millikan MS — 2,100/6-8
5041 Sunnyslope Ave 91423 — 818-788-5020
Derek Horowitz, prin. — Fax 990-7651

Bridgeport S — 100/K-12
13130 Burbank Blvd 91401 — 818-781-0360
Pamela Clark, prin.
Buckley S — 800/K-12
3900 Stansbury Ave 91423 — 818-783-1610
Elizabeth McGregor, hdmstr. — Fax 461-6714
DeVry University — Post-Sec.
15301 Ventura Blvd Ste 100 91403 — 888-610-0800
Notre Dame HS — 1,100/9-12
13645 Riverside Dr 91423 — 818-933-3600
Stephanie Connelly, prin.
Village Glen S — 200/1-12
13130 Burbank Blvd 91401 — 818-781-0360
Pamela Clark, prin.

Shingle Springs, El Dorado, Pop. 2,049
Buckeye USD — 4,200/K-8
PO Box 547 95682 — 530-677-2261
Teresa Wenig, supt. — Fax 677-1015
www.buckeye.k12.ca.us
Other Schools – See Cameron Park, El Dorado Hills

El Dorado UNHSD
Supt. — See Placerville
Ponderosa HS — 1,900/9-12
3661 Ponderosa Rd 95682 — 530-677-2281
Joyce Boesch, prin. — Fax 676-1401

Latrobe SD — 200/K-8
7900 S Shingle Rd 95682 — 916-677-0260
Jean Pinotti, supt. — Fax 672-0463
www.latrobeschool.com/
Millers Hill S — 100/4-8
7900 S Shingle Rd 95682 — 530-677-0260
Jean Pinotti, prin. — Fax 672-0463

Shingletown, Shasta
Black Butte UNESD — 300/K-8
7752 Ponderosa Way 96088 — 530-474-3125
Don Aust, supt. — Fax 474-3118
www.shastalink.k12.ca.us/bbutte/
Black Butte JHS — 100/7-8
7946 Ponderosa Way 96088 — 530-474-3441
Don Aust, prin. — Fax 474-1361

Shoshone, Inyo
Death Valley USD — 100/K-12
PO Box 217 92384 — 760-852-4303
James Copeland, supt. — Fax 852-4395
Death Valley Academy — 50/7-12
PO Box 217 92384 — 760-852-4303
James Copeland, prin. — Fax 852-4395

Sierra Madre, Los Angeles, Pop. 10,936

Alverno HS — 300/9-12
200 N Michillinda Ave 91024 — 626-355-3463
Fax 355-3153

Sierraville, Sierra
Regional Occupational Center & Program
Supt. — None
Rouse ROP — Vo/Tech
PO Box 157 96126 — 530-994-1044
Mary Genasci, supt. — Fax 994-1045

Sierra-Plumas JUSD — 700/K-12
PO Box 157 96126 — 530-994-1044
Fax 994-1045
www.spjusd.org
Other Schools – See Downieville, Loyalton, North San
Juan

Signal Hill, Los Angeles, Pop. 10,159

Institute of Network Technology — Post-Sec.
2525 Cherry Ave Ste 110, — 562-424-9200

Silverado, Orange

St. Michaels Preparatory S — 100/9-12
19292 El Toro Rd 92676 — 949-858-0222
Rev. Gabriel Stack, prin. — Fax 858-7365

Simi Valley, Ventura, Pop. 117,115
Simi Valley USD — 33,400/K-12
875 Cochran St 93065 — 805-520-6500
Kathryn Scroggin Ed.D., supt. — Fax 520-6504
www.simi.k12.ca.us
Hillside MS — 1,200/6-8
2222 Fitzgerald Rd 93065 — 805-520-6810
Susanne Wolf, prin. — Fax 520-6156
Royal HS — 2,800/9-12
1402 Royal Ave 93065 — 805-306-4875
Daniel Houghton, prin. — Fax 520-6644

Santa Susana HS — 1,100/9-12
3570 Cochran St 93063 — 805-520-6800
Pamela Carter, prin. — Fax 579-6385
Simi Valley HS — 2,500/9-12
5400 Cochran St 93063 — 805-577-1400
Stephen Pietrolungo, prin. — Fax 520-6633
Sinaloa JHS — 1,200/6-8
601 Royal Ave 93065 — 805-520-6830
Leslie Frank, prin. — Fax 520-6835
Valley View JHS — 1,500/6-8
3347 Tapo St 93063 — 805-520-6820
Terry Webb, prin. — Fax 520-6157
Simi Valley Adult Education — Adult
3192 E Los Angeles Ave 93065 — 805-579-6200
Marirose Kozak, dir. — Fax 522-8902

Grace Brethren JSHS — 400/7-12
1350 Cherry Ave 93065 — 805-522-4667
John Hynes, supt. — Fax 522-5617
Heritage Christian Academy — 100/K-12
1559 Rosita Dr 93065 — 805-520-0273
Cheryl Neher, admin.
Simi Valley Adult Education — Post-Sec.
3192 E Los Angeles Ave 93065 — 805-579-6200
Stoneridge Prep S — 50/6-12
1625 Tierra Rejada Rd 93065 — 805-581-9110
MaLuisa Arnold, dir. — Fax 581-2864

Snelling, Merced
Merced River UNESD — 200/K-8
2241 Turlock Rd 95369 — 209-722-4581
Dr. Helio Brasil, supt. — Fax 563-1045
www.mercedriver.k12.ca.us
Other Schools – See Winton

Solana Beach, San Diego, Pop. 12,993
San Dieguito UNHSD
Supt. — See Encinitas
Warren MS — 600/7-8
155 Stevens Ave 92075 — 858-755-1558
Anna Pedroza, prin. — Fax 755-0891

Santa Fe Christian S — 1,000/K-12
838 Academy Dr 92075 — 858-755-8900
Jim Hopson, hdmstr. — Fax 755-2480

Soledad, Monterey, Pop. 25,248
Soledad USD — 3,800/K-12
PO Box 186 93960 — 831-678-3987
Jorge Guzman, supt. — Fax 678-2866
mainst.monterey.k12.ca.us
Ledesma ES — 7-8
973 Vista de Soledad 93960 — 831-678-6320
Larry Newman, prin. — Fax 678-8029
Main Street MS — 900/6-8
441 Main St 93960 — 831-678-6460
Lori Villanueva, prin. — Fax 678-0797
Soledad HS — 900/9-12
425 Gabilan Dr 93960 — 831-678-6400
Roberto Nunez, prin. — Fax 678-0449

Somerset, El Dorado
Pioneer UNSD — 500/K-8
PO Box 8 95684 — 530-620-3556
Richard Williams, supt. — Fax 620-4932
Mountain Creek MS — 200/6-8
PO Box 690 95684 — 530-620-4393
Jeannine Wheeler, prin. — Fax 620-6509

Sonoma, Sonoma, Pop. 9,521
Sonoma Valley USD — 4,800/K-12
17850 Railroad Ave 95476 — 707-935-6000
D. Kim Jamieson Ed.D., supt. — Fax 939-2235
www.sonomavly.k12.ca.us
Altimira MS — 600/6-8
17805 Arnold Dr 95476 — 707-935-6020
Micaela Philpot, prin. — Fax 935-6027
Harrison MS — 500/6-8
1150 Broadway 95476 — 707-935-6080
Dan Scudero, prin. — Fax 935-6083
Sonoma Valley HS — 1,600/9-12
20000 Broadway 95476 — 707-935-4010
Robert Castro, prin. — Fax 935-4205
Sonoma Valley Adult S — Adult
20000 Broadway 95476 — 707-933-4033
Pam Garramone, prin. — Fax 933-4205

New Song S — 200/K-12
121 Lichtenberg Ave 95476 — 707-481-3709
Alison Lasley, admin.

Sonora, Tuolumne, Pop. 4,632
Sonora UNHSD — 1,700/9-12
251 Barretta St 95370 — 209-533-8510
Robert Gaskill, supt. — Fax 533-0991
www.sonorahs.k12.ca.us/district
Sonora Union HS — 1,600/9-12
430 N Washington St 95370 — 209-532-5511
Terry Clark, prin. — Fax 533-1158

Columbia College — Post-Sec.
11600 Columbia College Dr 95370 — 209-588-5100
Mother Lode Adventist Junior Academy — 100/K-10
80 N Forest Rd 95370 — 209-532-2855
Robert Chinnock, prin. — Fax 532-7757

Soquel, Santa Cruz, Pop. 9,188
Santa Cruz CSD — 12,100/K-12
405 Old San Jose Rd 95073 — 831-429-3410
Alan Pagano, supt. — Fax 429-3439
www.sccs.santacruz.k12.ca.us
Soquel HS — 1,400/9-12
401 Old San Jose Rd 95073 — 831-429-3909
Jennifer Kollmann, prin. — Fax 429-3311
Other Schools – See Santa Cruz

South El Monte, Los Angeles, Pop. 21,776
El Monte UNHSD
Supt. — See El Monte
South El Monte HS — 1,400/9-12
1001 Durfee Ave 91733 — 626-442-0218
Silvia Montero, prin. — Fax 442-4794

Valle Lindo ESD 1,400/K-8
  1431 Central Ave 91733 626-580-0610
  Mary Labrucherie, supt. Fax 575-1534
  www.vallelindo.k12.ca.us/
Shively MS 800/4-8
  1431 Central Ave 91733 626-580-0610
  John Gannon, prin. Fax 575-1534

United Beauty College Post-Sec.
  9324 Garvey Ave Ste D 91733 626-433-1371

South Gate, Los Angeles, Pop. 98,966
Los Angeles USD
  Supt. — See Los Angeles
International Studies Learning Center 6-11
  2560 Tweedy Blvd 90280 323-568-3155
  Sherrie Quach, prin. Fax 568-3153
Southeast Area MS 6-8
  2560 Tweedy Blvd 90280 323-568-3100
  Walter R. Flores, prin. Fax 564-9398
Southeast HS 9-12
  2720 Tweedy Blvd 90280 323-568-3400
  Jesus Angulo, prin. Fax 566-7918
South Gate HS 4,800/9-12
  3351 Firestone Blvd 90280 323-567-2333
  Patrick Moretta, prin. Fax 249-0237
South Gate MS 4,100/6-8
  4100 Firestone Blvd 90280 323-567-1431
  Michael Perez, prin. Fax 564-7434
South Gate Adult Education Adult
  3351 Firestone Blvd 90280 323-569-7104
  James Chacon, prin. Fax 569-7107

Advanced College Post-Sec.
  13180 Paramount Blvd 90280 562-408-6969
Career College of America Post-Sec.
  5612 Imperial Hwy 90280 562-861-8702

South Lake Tahoe, El Dorado, Pop. 23,912
Lake Tahoe USD 4,200/K-12
  1021 Al Tahoe Blvd 96150 530-541-2850
  Dr. James Tarwater, supt. Fax 541-5930
  www.ltusd.k12.ca.us/
South Tahoe HS 1,500/9-12
  1735 Lake Tahoe Blvd 96150 530-541-4111
  Marcia Kaster, prin. Fax 541-4157
South Tahoe MS 1,300/6-8
  2940 Lake Tahoe Blvd 96150 530-541-6404
  Jackie Nelson, prin. Fax 541-4624

Lake Tahoe Community College Post-Sec.
  1 College Dr 96150 530-541-4660

South Pasadena, Los Angeles, Pop. 24,847
South Pasadena USD 4,200/K-12
  1020 El Centro St 91030 626-441-5800
  Kenneth Moffett Ed.D., supt. Fax 441-5815
  www.spusd.net
South Pasadena HS 1,500/9-12
  1401 Fremont Ave 91030 626-441-5820
  Janet Anderson, prin. Fax 441-5825
South Pasadena MS 1,100/6-8
  1600 Oak St 91030 626-441-5830
  Mercedes Metz, prin. Fax 441-5835

Almansor Center 100/K-12
  1137 Huntington Dr 91030 323-257-3006
  Dr. Albert Hernandez, prin.

South San Francisco, San Mateo, Pop. 59,415
South San Francisco USD 9,000/PK-12
  398 B St 94080 650-877-8700
  Barbara Olds, supt. Fax 583-4717
  www.ssfusd.k12.ca.us
Alta Loma MS 800/6-8
  116 Romney Ave 94080 650-877-8797
  Lou Delorio, prin. Fax 877-8824
El Camino HS 1,400/9-12
  1320 Mission Rd 94080 650-877-8806
  Adele Berg, prin. Fax 589-2343
Parkway Heights MS 800/6-8
  825 Park Way 94080 650-877-8788
  Jay Rowley, prin. Fax 225-9427
South San Francisco HS 1,500/9-12
  400 B St 94080 650-877-8754
  Michael Coyne, prin. Fax 871-7943
Westborough MS 700/6-8
  2570 Westborough Blvd 94080 650-877-8848
  Beth Orofino, prin. Fax 871-5356
South San Francisco Adult Adult
  825 Southwood Dr 94080 650-877-8844
  Jim Murphy, prin. Fax 877-8786

Spreckels, Monterey
Spreckels UNESD 900/K-8
  PO Box 7362 93962 831-455-2550
  Harold Kahn Ed.D., supt. Fax 455-1871
Other Schools – See Salinas

Spring Valley, San Diego, Pop. 27,100
Grossmont UNHSD
  Supt. — See El Cajon
Monte Vista HS 1,900/9-12
  3230 Sweetwater Springs Blv 91977 619-660-9902
  Paul Wargo, prin. Fax 670-9749
Mt. Miguel HS 2,100/9-12
  8585 Blossom Ln 91977 619-644-8400
  Steve Coover, prin. Fax 589-1143
Steele Canyon HS 1,900/9-12
  12440 Campo Rd 91978 619-660-7100
  Brian Smith, prin. Fax 660-7199

La Mesa-Spring Valley ESD
  Supt. — See La Mesa
La Presa MS 1,200/6-8
  1001 Leland St 91977 619-668-5720
  Mike Allman, prin. Fax 668-8305
Spring Valley MS 1,300/6-8
  3900 Conrad Dr 91977 619-668-5750
  Claudia Bender, prin. Fax 668-8302

Stanford, Santa Clara, Pop. 18,097

Stanford University Post-Sec.
  520 Lasuen Mall Un 232 94305 650-723-2300

Stanton, Orange, Pop. 37,853

Newbridge College - Stanton Post-Sec.
  12362 Beach Blvd Ste 100 90680 714-901-9447

Stevenson Ranch, Los Angeles
William S. Hart UNHSD
  Supt. — See Santa Clarita
Rancho Pico JHS 7-8
  26250 Valencia Blvd 91381 661-284-3260
  Dave LeBarron, prin. Fax 255-7523
West Ranch HS 9-12
  26255 Valencia Blvd 91381 661-222-1220
  Bob Vincent, prin. Fax 255-7261

Stockton, San Joaquin, Pop. 271,466
Lincoln USD 8,200/PK-12
  2010 W Swain Rd 95207 209-953-8700
  Steve Lowder, supt. Fax 474-7817
  www.lusd.net
Lincoln HS 2,700/9-12
  6844 Alexandria Pl 95207 209-953-8920
  Debbi Holmerud, prin. Fax 952-4646
Sierra MS 500/7-8
  6776 Alexandria Pl 95207 209-953-8749
  Terry Asplund, prin. Fax 953-8747

Linden USD
  Supt. — See Linden
Waterloo MS 500/5-8
  7007 Pezzi Rd 95215 209-931-0818
  Mike McCandless, prin. Fax 931-2915

Lodi USD
  Supt. — See Lodi
Bear Creek HS 2,500/9-12
  10555 Thornton Rd 95209 209-953-8234
  Daryl Camp, prin. Fax 953-8247
Delta Sierra MS 1,000/7-8
  2255 Wagner Heights Rd 95209 209-953-8510
  Irene Outlaw, prin. Fax 953-8139
Elkhorn MS 300/3-8
  10505 Davis Rd 95209 209-331-7330
  Neil Young, prin. Fax 953-8319
McAuliffe MS 7-8
  3838 Iron Canyon Cir 95209 209-953-9431
  Darla Briggs, prin. Fax 953-9432
McNair HS 9-12
  9550 Ronald E McNair Way 95210 209-953-9244
  Jim Davis, prin. Fax 953-9261
Morada Eastview MS 1,000/7-8
  5001 Eastview Dr 95212 209-953-8490
  Steve Takemoto, prin. Fax 953-8128

Manteca USD
  Supt. — See Manteca
Weston Ranch HS 1,200/9-12
  4606 McCuen Ave 95206 209-982-5387
  Clara Schmiedt, prin. Fax 982-5765

Regional Occupational Center & Program
  Supt. — None
San Joaquin County ROC/P Vo/Tech
  PO Box 213030 95213 209-468-9210
  Doug Martin, dir. Fax 468-4984

Stockton USD 38,600/K-12
  701 N Madison St 95202 209-933-7070
  George Ridler, supt. Fax 933-7071
  www.stockton.k12.ca.us
Chavez HS 9-12
  2929 Windflower Ln 95212 209-933-7480
  Fax 469-3681
Edison HS 2,700/9-12
  1425 S Center St 95206 209-933-7425
  Mark Hagemann, prin. Fax 942-2106
Franklin HS 3,100/9-12
  300 N Gertrude Ave 95215 209-933-7435
  Scott Luhn, prin. Fax 464-4708
Fremont MS 1,400/7-8
  2021 E Flora St 95205 209-933-7385
  Marlesse Cavazos, prin. Fax 466-7342
Hamilton MS 1,500/7-8
  2245 E 11th St 95206 209-933-7395
  Dr. Gurmel Singh, prin. Fax 464-4851
Marshall MS 1,400/7-8
  1141 Lever Blvd 95206 209-933-7405
  Dr. Ron Small, prin. Fax 466-4962
Stagg HS 3,000/9-12
  1621 Brookside Rd 95207 209-933-7445
  Edward Burns, prin. Fax 954-9037
Weber Institute Vo/Tech
  302 W Weber Ave 95203 209-933-7330
  Knute Momberg, dir. Fax 466-7548
Webster MS 1,400/7-8
  2725 Michigan Ave 95204 209-933-7415
  Margaret Salazar Huerta, prin. Fax 948-2960
School for Adults Adult
  1525 Pacific Ave 95204 209-933-7455
  Carol Hirota, prin. Fax 464-4917

Brookside Christian HS 100/9-12
  915 Rosemarie Ln 95207 209-954-7651
  Dennis Gildea, admin. Fax 954-7657
Children's Home of Stockton 100/K-12
  PO Box 201068 95201 209-466-0853
  Michael Dutra, prin.
Emergency Medical Sciences Training Inst Post-Sec.
  343 E Main St Ste 906 95202 209-461-5550
Heald College Post-Sec.
  1605 E March Ln 95210 209-477-1114
Humphreys College Post-Sec.
  6650 Inglewood Ave 95207 209-478-0800
Maric College Post-Sec.
  722 W March Ln 95207 209-462-8777
MTI Business College of Stockton Post-Sec.
  6006 N El Dorado St 95207 209-957-3030
St. Mary HS 1,000/9-12
  PO Box 7247 95267 209-957-3340
  Peter Morelli, prin. Fax 957-0861

San Joaquin Delta College Post-Sec.
  5151 Pacific Ave 95207 209-954-5151
San Joaquin General Hospital Post-Sec.
  PO Box 1020 95201 209-468-6600
Stockton Christian S 400/K-12
  9021 West Ln 95210 209-957-3043
  Percel Graves, prin. Fax 957-4120
University of the Pacific Post-Sec.
  3601 Pacific Ave 95211 209-946-2011
Western Career College Post-Sec.
  1313 W Robinhood Dr Ste B 95207 209-956-1240
Western Pacific Truck School Post-Sec.
  1002 N Broadway Ave 95205 209-465-1191

Strathmore, Tulare, Pop. 2,353
Porterville USD
  Supt. — See Porterville
Strathmore HS 9-12
  22568 Avenue 196 93267 559-568-1731
  Mike Henson, prin. Fax 568-0091

Strathmore UNESD 800/K-8
  PO Box 247 93267 559-568-1283
  David DePaoli, supt. Fax 568-1262
  www.suesd.k12.ca.us
Strathmore MS 200/6-8
  PO Box 247 93267 559-568-9293
  Evelyn Erquhart, prin. Fax 568-2944

Studio City, See Los Angeles

Bridges Academy 100/6-12
  3921 Laurel Canyon Blvd 91604 818-506-1091
  Carl Sabatino, hdmstr. Fax 506-8094

Suisun City, Solano, Pop. 26,968
Fairfield-Suisun USD
  Supt. — See Fairfield
Crystal MS 700/6-8
  400 Whispering Bay Ln 94585 707-435-5800
  Roxanne Rice, prin. Fax 435-5806

Sunland, See Los Angeles
Los Angeles USD
  Supt. — See Los Angeles
Mt. Gleason MS 1,600/6-8
  10965 Mount Gleason Ave 91040 818-352-1466
  John McLaughlin, prin. Fax 352-6209

Fairhaven Christian Academy 100/K-12
  10438 Oro Vista Ave 91040 818-434-7533
  Rev. Marc Goodwin, prin.
Sunland Christian S 300/K-12
  PO Box 4070 91041 818-951-9652
  Terrence Neven, prin.

Sunnyvale, Santa Clara, Pop. 128,549
Cupertino UNESD
  Supt. — See Cupertino
Cupertino MS 1,100/6-8
  1650 S Bernardo Ave 94087 408-245-0303
  Kara Butler, prin. Fax 732-4152

Fremont UNHSD 27,300/9-12
  589 W Fremont Ave 94087 408-522-2200
  Stephen R. Rowley Ph.D., supt. Fax 245-5325
  www.fuhsd.org
Fremont HS 1,900/9-12
  1279 Sunnyvale Saratoga Rd 94087 408-522-2400
  Peggy Raun-Linde, prin. Fax 522-2403
Adult & Community Education Adult
  591 W Fremont Ave 94087 408-522-2700
  Dennis Frese, dir. Fax 737-9926
Other Schools – See Cupertino, San Jose

Regional Occupational Center & Program
  Supt. — None
Santa Clara County ROP North Vo/Tech
  575 W Fremont Ave 94087 408-733-0881
  Alyssa Lynch, dir. Fax 733-0894

Santa Clara USD
  Supt. — See Santa Clara
Peterson MS 1,300/6-8
  1380 Rosalia Ave 94087 408-423-2800
  David Kennedy, prin. Fax 423-2880

Sunnyvale SD 6,000/K-8
  PO Box 3217 94088 408-522-8200
  Joseph Rudnicki, supt. Fax 522-8338
  www.sesd.org
Columbia MS 900/6-8
  739 Morse Ave 94085 408-522-8247
  Jocelyn Lee, prin. Fax 522-8254
Sunnyvale MS 1,000/6-8
  1080 Mango Ave 94087 408-522-8288
  Frances Dampier, prin. Fax 522-8296

Brooks College Post-Sec.
  1120 Kifer Rd 94086 408-328-5700
Cogswell College Post-Sec.
  1175 Bordeaux Dr 94089 408-541-0100
King's Academy 800/6-12
  562 N Britton Ave 94085 408-481-9900
  Bob Kellogg, prin. Fax 481-9932
University of East West Medicine Post-Sec.
  970 W El Camino Real 94087 408-733-1878

Sun Valley, See Los Angeles
Los Angeles USD
  Supt. — See Los Angeles
Byrd MS 1,900/6-8
  9171 Telfair Ave 91352 818-767-9550
  Gerald Horowitz, prin. Fax 767-8125
Francis Polytechnic HS 3,900/9-12
  12431 Roscoe Blvd 91352 818-767-4860
  Janis Martinez, prin. Fax 771-0452
Sun Valley MS 2,900/6-8
  7330 Bakman Ave 91352 818-765-3010
  Antonio Delgado, prin. Fax 503-9846

Sol del Valle Christian S 50/K-12
  10725 Penrose St 91352 818-252-7305
  Jessenal Arroyo, prin. Fax 767-5176

Village Christian HS 600/9-12
8930 Village Ave 91352 818-767-8382
Barret Luketic, prin. Fax 768-2006
Village Christian MS 500/6-8
8930 Village Ave 91352 818-767-8382
Thomas Nare, prin. Fax 768-2006

Susanville, Lassen, Pop. 17,584
Lassen UNHSD 1,100/9-12
55 S Weatherlow St 96130 530-257-5134
Dan Lewis, supt. Fax 257-0796
www.lassenhigh.org
Lassen Union HS 1,100/9-12
1110 Main St 96130 530-257-2141
Fax 251-1173
Lassen Adult S Adult
814 Cottage St 96130 530-257-5566

Regional Occupational Center & Program
Supt. — None
Lassen County ROP Vo/Tech
472-013 Johnstonville Rd 96130 530-257-2196
Jud Jensen, dir. Fax 257-2518

Susanville SD 1,300/K-8
109 S Gilman St 96130 530-257-8200
Mark Evans, supt. Fax 257-8246
www.susanvillesd.org
Diamond View MS 300/7-8
850 Richmond Rd 96130 530-257-5144
Patricia Gunderson, prin. Fax 257-7232

Lassen Community College Post-Sec.
PO Box 3000 96130 530-257-6181
New Horizons Christian S 100/PK-12
995 Paiute Ln 96130 530-257-6420
Rebecca Guess, admin. Fax 257-6423

Sutter, Sutter, Pop. 2,606
Sutter UNHSD 800/9-12
PO Box 498 95982 530-822-5161
Ryan Robison, supt. Fax 822-5168
www.sutterhigh.k12.ca.us/
Sutter HS 800/9-12
PO Box 498 95982 530-822-5161
Ryan Robison, prin. Fax 822-5168

Sutter Creek, Amador, Pop. 2,402
Amador County USD
Supt. — See Jackson
Amador HS 800/9-12
330 Spanish St 95685 209-267-5244
Eli Johnson, prin. Fax 267-5942

Sylmar, See Los Angeles
Los Angeles USD
Supt. — See Los Angeles
Olive Vista MS 2,000/6-8
14600 Tyler St 91342 818-367-1071
Jean Whitaker, prin. Fax 367-8273
Sylmar HS 3,400/9-12
13050 Borden Ave 91342 818-367-1971
Jan Lyons, prin. Fax 364-1037

Delphi Academy of Los Angeles 200/K-12
11341 Brainard Ave 91342 818-583-1070
Maggie Reinhart, prin.
First Lutheran JSHS 100/7-12
13361 Glenoaks Blvd 91342 818-362-9223
Rick Klein, prin. Fax 362-9713
ITT Technical Institute Post-Sec.
12669 Encinitas Ave 91342 818-364-5151
Los Angeles Lutheran HS 300/6-12
13750 Eldridge Ave 91342 818-362-5861
Dale Wolfgram, prin. Fax 367-0043
Los Angeles Mission College Post-Sec.
13356 Eldridge Ave 91342 818-364-7600
Olive View/UCLA Medical Centers Post-Sec.
14445 Olive View Dr 91342 818-364-4224

Taft, Kern, Pop. 9,047
Regional Occupational Center & Program
Supt. — None
West Side ROP Vo/Tech
PO Box 1337 93268 661-765-7185
Dale Countryman, dir. Fax 765-7187

Taft CSD 2,200/K-8
820 6th St 93268 661-763-1521
Michael Harris, supt. Fax 763-1495
www.taftcity.k12.ca.us
Lincoln JHS 700/6-8
810 6th St 93268 661-765-2127
Dr. Kathy Orrin, prin. Fax 763-3970

Taft UNHSD 1,000/9-12
701 7th St 93268 661-763-2300
Curtis T. Dubost Ed.D., supt. Fax 763-1445
taft.ca.schoolwebpages.com
Taft Union HS 900/9-12
701 7th St 93268 661-763-2300
Marilyn Brown, prin. Fax 763-4736

Taft College Post-Sec.
29 Emmons Park Dr 93268 661-763-7700

Tahoe City, Placer, Pop. 1,643
Tahoe-Truckee USD
Supt. — See Truckee
North Tahoe HS 500/9-12
PO Box 5099 96145 530-581-7000
Bill Frey, prin. Fax 581-3252
North Tahoe MS 400/6-8
PO Box 5099 96145 530-581-7050
Dave Curry, prin. Fax 581-1237

Tarzana, See Los Angeles
Los Angeles USD
Supt. — See Los Angeles
Portola MS 2,300/6-8
18720 Linnet St 91356 818-342-6173
Adrienne Marvee, prin. Fax 996-0292

Columbia College Hollywood Post-Sec.
18618 Oxnard St 91356 800-785-0585

Hypnosis Motivation Institute Post-Sec.
18607 Ventura Blvd Ste 310 91356 800-479-9464

Tecate, San Diego

Tecate Christian S 100/1-12
PO Box 1000 91980 619-468-3355
Ronald Hoffman, prin. Fax 478-5910

Tehachapi, Kern, Pop. 11,434
Tehachapi USD 4,600/K-12
400 S Snyder Ave 93561 661-822-2100
Dr. Marian B. Stephens, supt. Fax 822-2159
www.teh.k12.ca.us
Jacobsen MS 1,200/6-8
711 Anita Dr 93561 661-822-2150
Eric Triguerio, prin. Fax 822-2156
Tehachapi HS 1,400/9-12
801 S Dennison Rd 93561 661-822-2130
Michael Arredondo, prin. Fax 822-1854
Tehachapi Adult S Adult
20569 Eumatilla 93561 661-822-2124
Ria Maaskant, prin. Fax 822-2188

Heritage Oak S 100/K-12
20915 Schout Rd 93561 661-823-0885
Vanessa Cross, admin. Fax 823-0863

Temecula, Riverside, Pop. 76,836
Temecula Valley USD 22,700/K-12
31350 Rancho Vista Rd 92592 951-676-2661
David Allmen, supt. Fax 695-7121
www.tvusd.k12.ca.us
Chaparral HS 3,000/9-12
27215 Nicolas Rd 92591 951-695-4200
Fax 695-4219
Day MS 1,300/6-8
40770 Camino Campos Verde 92591 951-699-8138
Greg Cooke, prin. Fax 699-4198
Gardner MS 700/6-8
45125 Via Del Coronado 92592 951-699-0080
Jim Flesuras, prin. Fax 699-0081
Great Oak HS 9-12
32555 Deer Hollow Way 92592 951-294-6450
Tim Ritter, prin. Fax 294-6477
Margarita MS 1,200/6-8
30600 Margarita Rd 92591 951-695-7370
Karen Hayes, prin. Fax 695-7378
Temecula MS 1,400/6-8
42075 Meadows Pkwy 92592 951-302-5151
Rob Sousa, prin. Fax 302-5160
Temecula Valley HS 3,600/9-12
31595 Rancho Vista Rd 92592 951-695-7300
Scott Schaufele, prin. Fax 695-7311
Vail Ranch MS 900/6-8
33340 Camino Piedra Rojo 92592 951-302-5188
Kevin Groepper, prin. Fax 302-5195
Temecula Valley Adult S Adult
31340 Rancho Vista Rd 92592 951-506-7996
Juanita Hernandez, prin. Fax 695-7336
Other Schools – See Murrieta

Linfield Christian S 900/K-12
31950 Pauba Rd 92592 951-676-8111
Karen Raftery, supt. Fax 695-1291
Professional Golfers Career College Post-Sec.
26109 Ynez Rd 92591 800-877-4380
Royale College of Beauty Post-Sec.
27485 Commerce Center Dr 92590 951-676-0833

Temple City, Los Angeles, Pop. 36,325
Temple City USD 5,600/K-12
9700 Las Tunas Dr 91780 626-548-5000
Joan Hillard, supt. Fax 548-5022
www.templecity.k12.ca.us
Oak Avenue IS 1,000/7-8
6623 Oak Ave 91780 626-548-5060
David Mintz, prin. Fax 548-5170
Temple City HS 1,900/9-12
9501 Lemon Ave 91780 626-548-5040
Ray Plutko, prin. Fax 548-5045
Temple City Adult Education Adult
9229 Pentland St 91780 626-548-5050
Doug Sears, prin. Fax 548-5118
Temple City Community Learning Center Adult
9229 Pentland St 91780 626-548-5101
Doug Sears, prin. Fax 548-5118

U. S. Arts Education Center 400/K-12
9451 1/2 Las Tunas Dr 91780 626-287-7204
Curie Hu, dir.

Templeton, San Luis Obispo, Pop. 2,887
Templeton USD 2,300/K-12
960 Old County Rd 93465 805-434-5800
Deborah Bowers Ed.D., supt. Fax 434-5879
www.tusdnet.k12.ca.us
Eagle Canyon HS 9-12
964 Old County Rd 93465 805-434-5833
Gary Duke Ed.D., prin. Fax 434-3879
Templeton HS 800/9-12
1200 S Main St 93465 805-434-5888
Jim Fotinakes, prin. Fax 434-0743
Templeton MS 600/6-8
925 Old County Rd 93465 805-434-5813
Jon Lorimer, prin. Fax 434-5812

Terra Bella, Tulare, Pop. 2,740
Terra Bella UNESD 900/K-8
9121 Road 240 93270 559-535-4451
Frank Betry, supt. Fax 535-0314
Smith MS 200/6-8
23825 Avenue 92 93270 559-535-4451
Guadalupe Roman, prin. Fax 535-0829

Thermal, Riverside
Coachella Valley USD 15,100/K-12
PO Box 847 92274 760-399-5137
Foch Pensis, supt. Fax 399-1052
www.coachella.k12.ca.us
Coachella Valley HS 2,900/9-12
83800 Airport Blvd 92274 760-399-5183
Manuel Arredondo, prin. Fax 399-0089

Toro Canyon MS 900/7-8
86150 Avenue 66 92274 760-397-2244
Carolyn Weston, prin. Fax 397-8760
West Shores HS 900/7-12
2381 Shore Hawk Ave 92274 760-394-4331
David Shepard, prin. Fax 394-0971
Other Schools – See Coachella

Thousand Oaks, Ventura, Pop. 124,192
Conejo Valley USD 22,500/K-12
1400 E Janss Rd 91362 805-497-9511
Dr. Robert Fraisse, supt. Fax 371-9170
www.conejo.k12.ca.us
Colina MS 1,200/6-8
1500 E Hillcrest Dr 91362 805-495-7429
Michael Waters, prin. Fax 374-1163
Los Cerritos MS 1,100/6-8
2100 E Ave De Las Flores 91362 805-492-3538
Eleanor Love, prin. Fax 493-8854
Redwood MS 1,300/6-8
233 W Gainsborough Rd 91360 805-497-7264
Lou Lichtl, prin. Fax 497-3734
Thousand Oaks HS 2,600/9-12
2323 N Moorpark Rd 91360 805-495-7491
Timothy Carpenter, prin. Fax 374-1165
Conejo Valley Adult Education Adult
1025 Old Farm Rd 91360 805-497-2761
Mike Berger, prin. Fax 374-1167
Other Schools – See Newbury Park, Westlake Village

California Lutheran University Post-Sec.
60 W Olsen Rd 91360 805-492-2411
Hillcrest Christian S 400/PK-12
384 Erbes Rd 91362 805-497-7501
Steve Allen, hdmstr. Fax 494-9355
La Reina HS 600/7-12
106 W Janss Rd 91360 805-495-6494
Cecilia Coe, prin. Fax 494-4966

Tiburon, Marin, Pop. 8,688
Reed UNESD 1,100/K-8
277 Karen Way 94920 415-381-1112
Christine Carter, supt. Fax 384-0890
rusd.marin.k12.ca.us/
Del Mar IS 400/6-8
105 Avenida Miraflores 94920 415-435-1468
Sandy Kuzma, prin. Fax 435-6190

Tollhouse, Fresno
Sierra USD
Supt. — See Prather
Sierra HS 900/9-12
33326 Lodge Rd 93667 559-855-8311
Melissa Ireland, prin. Fax 855-2162

Tomales, Marin
Shoreline USD 700/K-12
10 John St 94971 707-878-2266
Dr. Stephen Rosenthal, supt. Fax 878-2554
shoreline.marin.k12.ca.us/
Tomales HS 200/9-12
PO Box 198 94971 707-878-2286
Trina Legacy, prin. Fax 878-2787

Torrance, Los Angeles, Pop. 142,621
Regional Occupational Center & Program
Supt. — None
Southern California ROC Vo/Tech
2300 Crenshaw Blvd 90501 310-224-4200
Christine Hoffman, supt. Fax 320-1029

Torrance USD 25,100/K-12
2335 Plaza Del Amo 90501 310-972-6500
George Mannon Ed.D., supt. Fax 972-6012
www.tusd.k12.ca.us
Calle Mayor MS 900/6-8
4800 Calle Mayor 90505 310-533-4548
Tabitha Swiger, prin. Fax 972-6389
Casimir MS 700/6-8
17220 Casimir Ave 90504 310-533-4498
Susan Holmes, prin. Fax 972-6391
Hull MS 800/6-8
2080 W 231st St 90501 310-533-4516
Andrew Heughins, prin. Fax 972-6397
Jefferson MS 700/6-8
21717 Talisman St 90503 310-533-4794
James Jones, prin. Fax 972-6398
Lynn MS 700/6-8
5038 Halison St 90503 310-533-4495
Leroy Jackson, prin. Fax 972-6401
Madrona MS 800/6-8
21364 Madrona Ave 90503 310-533-4562
Ron Alatorre, prin. Fax 972-6402
Magruder MS 800/6-8
4100 W 185th St 90504 310-533-4527
Chris Vanderleest, prin. Fax 972-6403
North HS 2,200/9-12
3620 W 182nd St 90504 310-533-4412
Annette Alpern, prin. Fax 972-6404
Richardson MS 700/6-8
23751 Nancylee Ln 90505 310-533-4790
Mario Liberati, prin. Fax 972-6405
South HS 2,000/9-12
4801 Pacific Coast Hwy 90505 310-533-4352
Scott McDowell, prin. Fax 972-6454
Torrance HS 2,200/9-12
2200 W Carson St 90501 310-533-4396
John O'Brien, prin. Fax 972-6455
West HS 2,000/9-12
20401 Victor St 90503 310-533-4299
Tim Stowe, prin. Fax 972-6483
Griffith Adult Education Center Adult
2291 Washington Ave 90501 310-533-4454
Rick Long, prin. Fax 972-6394
Hamilton Adult Education Center Adult
2606 W 182nd St 90504 310-533-4459
Richard Rose, prin. Fax 972-6395

Bishop Montgomery HS 1,100/9-12
5430 Torrance Blvd 90503 310-540-2021
Rosemary Libbon, prin. Fax 543-5102
El Camino College Post-Sec.
16007 Crenshaw Blvd 90506 310-660-3670
International Bilingual S 100/K-12
23800 Hawthorne Blvd 90505 310-373-0430

ITT Technical Institute — Post-Sec.
20050 S Vermont Ave 90502 — 310-380-1555
Los Angeles Co. Harbor UCLA Medical Ctr. — Post-Sec.
1000 W Carson St 90502 — 310-533-2101
South Bay Junior Academy — 200/K-10
4400 Del Amo Blvd 90503 — 310-370-6215
Susan Vlach, prin. — Fax 793-8665
South Bay Lutheran HS — 100/9-12
2150 Sepulveda Blvd 90501 — 310-530-1231
Southern CA Regional Occupational Center — Post-Sec.
2300 Crenshaw Blvd 90501 — 310-224-4220
Westwood College - South Bay Campus — Post-Sec.
19700 S Vermont Ave Ste 100 90502 — 310-965-0888

Tracy, San Joaquin, Pop. 72,456
Jefferson ESD — 2,000/K-8
7500 W Linne Rd 95304 — 209-836-3388
Ed Quinn, supt. — Fax 836-2930
www.jeffersonschooldistrict.com/
Jefferson S — 600/5-8
7500 W Linne Rd 95304 — 209-835-3053
Jim Bridges, prin. — Fax 835-4419

Tracy JUSD — 15,000/K-12
1875 W Lowell Ave 95376 — 209-830-3200
James Franco, supt. — Fax 830-3259
www.tracy.k12.ca.us
Monte Vista MS — 1,000/6-8
751 W Lowell Ave 95376 — 209-831-5260
Steve Donahue, prin. — Fax 831-5580
Tracy HS — 2,200/9-12
315 E 11th St 95376 — 209-831-5100
Pat Anastasio, prin. — Fax 831-5117
West HS — 2,800/9-12
1775 W Lowell Ave 95376 — 209-831-5430
Herman Calad, prin. — Fax 831-5433
Williams MS — 1,300/6-8
1600 Tennis Ln 95376 — 209-831-5289
Barbara Montgomery, prin. — Fax 831-5294
Tracy Adult S — Adult
1902 N Corral Hollow Rd 95376 — 209-830-3384
Walter Gouveia, prin. — Fax 830-3385

Tranquillity, Fresno
Golden Plains USD
Supt. — See San Joaquin
Tranquillity HS — 500/9-12
PO Box 457 93668 — 559-698-7205
Brian Wall, prin. — Fax 698-7632

Trona, San Bernardino
Trona JUSD — 300/K-12
83600 Trona Rd 93562 — 760-372-2861
Charles Raff, supt. — Fax 372-4534
www.trona.k12.ca.us/
Trona JSHS — 200/7-12
83600 Trona Rd 93562 — 760-372-2865
Charles Raff, prin. — Fax 372-4504

Truckee, Nevada, Pop. 14,930
Tahoe-Truckee USD — 3,800/K-12
11839 Donner Pass Rd 96161 — 530-582-2500
Dennis K. Williams, supt. — Fax 582-7606
www.ttusd.org
Alder Creek MS — 6-8
10931 Alder Dr 96161 — 530-582-2750
Susan Phebus, prin. — Fax 582-7640
Tahoe-Truckee HS — 900/9-12
11725 Donner Pass Rd 96161 — 530-582-2600
Mike Finney, prin. — Fax 582-7636
Other Schools – See Tahoe City

Tujunga, See Los Angeles
Los Angeles USD
Supt. — See Los Angeles
Verdugo Hills HS — 2,300/9-12
10625 Plainview Ave 91042 — 818-353-1171
Cheryl Dellepiane, prin. — Fax 352-3577

Skyward Christian S — 200/K-12
7747 Apperson St 91042 — 818-353-5159
Richard Lowe, hdmstr.
Smart Christian S — 50/K-12
7754 McGroarty St 91042 — 818-951-7182
Brendan Moore, prin. — Fax 951-7183

Tulare, Tulare, Pop. 47,421
Regional Occupational Center & Program
Supt. — None
Tulare Co. Organization/Vocational Ed. — Vo/Tech
4136 N Mooney Blvd 93274 — 559-688-0571
Ron Johnson, dir. — Fax 688-5913

Tulare City ESD — 7,800/K-8
600 N Cherry St 93274 — 559-685-7200
John Beck, supt. — Fax 685-7287
www.tcsd.k12.ca.us
Cherry Avenue MS — 700/6-8
540 N Cherry St 93274 — 559-685-7320
Joe Terri, prin. — Fax 685-7323
Live Oak MS — 700/6-8
980 N Laspina St 93274 — 559-685-7310
Paula Adair, prin. — Fax 685-7313
Los Tules MS — 6-8
801 W Gail Ave 93274 — 559-687-3156
Gary Yentes, prin. — Fax 685-7374
Mulcahy MS — 600/6-8
1001 W Sonora Ave 93274 — 559-685-7250
John Pendleton, prin. — Fax 685-7252

Tulare JUNHSD — 5,600/9-12
426 N Blackstone St 93274 — 559-688-2021
Gerald Benton, supt. — Fax 687-7317
tulare.k12.ca.us
Countryside HS — 300/9-12
1070 S Pratt St 93274 — 559-687-7384
Michelle Nunley, prin. — Fax 687-7388
Tulare Tech Prep S — Vo/Tech
737 W Bardsley Ave 93274 — 559-687-7400
Janis Lehmann, prin. — Fax 687-7414
Tulare Union HS — 1,900/9-12
755 E Tulare Ave 93274 — 559-686-4761
Howard Berger, prin. — Fax 687-7367
Tulare Western HS — 2,000/9-12
824 W Maple Ave 93274 — 559-686-8751
Vern Barlogio, prin. — Fax 687-7341

Tulare Adult S — Adult
575 W Maple Ave 93274 — 559-686-0225
Susan Pasquini, prin. — Fax 687-7447

Tulare Beauty College — Post-Sec.
1400 W Inyo Ave 93274 — 559-688-2901

Tulelake, Siskiyou, Pop. 1,019
Tulelake Basin JUSD — 600/K-12
PO Box 640 96134 — 530-667-2295
William Figgess, supt. — Fax 667-4298
www.tulelake.k12.ca.us
Tulelake HS — 300/7-12
PO Box 640 96134 — 530-667-2292
William Figgess, prin. — Fax 667-2290

Tuolumne, Tuolumne
Summerville UNHSD — 700/9-12
17555 Tuolumne Rd 95379 — 209-928-4228
John H. Keiter, supt. — Fax 928-1422
www.summbears.k12.ca.us/
Summerville HS — 600/9-12
17555 Tuolumne Rd 95379 — 209-928-4228
David Urquhart, prin. — Fax 928-1422

Mother Lode Christian S — 200/PK-12
18393 Gardner Ave 95379 — 209-928-4126
Anna Noonan, admin. — Fax 928-4613

Turlock, Stanislaus, Pop. 63,467
Chatom UNESD — 700/K-8
7201 Clayton Rd 95380 — 209-664-8505
Barbara Patman, supt. — Fax 664-8508
www.chatom.k12.ca.us
Mountain View MS — 200/6-8
10001 Crows Landing Rd 95380 — 209-664-8515
Cherise Olvera, prin. — Fax 669-1733

Turlock USD — 14,200/PK-12
PO Box 819013 95381 — 209-667-0632
William H. Gibson Ed.D., supt. — Fax 667-6520
www.turlock.k12.ca.us
Pitman HS — 1,900/9-12
2525 W Christoffersen Pkwy 95382 — 209-656-1592
Rod Hollars, prin. — Fax 656-1639
Turlock HS — 2,600/9-12
1600 E Canal Dr 95380 — 209-667-2055
Dana Trevethan, prin. — Fax 634-2698
Turlock JHS — 1,500/7-8
3951 N Walnut Rd 95382 — 209-667-0881
Heidi Lawler, prin. — Fax 668-3985
Turlock Adult Education — Adult
1574 E Canal Dr 95380 — 209-667-0643
Don Wilkins, prin. — Fax 667-0695

Adrian's Beauty College of Turlock — Post-Sec.
2253 Geer Rd 95382 — 209-632-2233
California State University-Stanislaus — Post-Sec.
801 W Monte Vista Ave 95382 — 209-667-3122
Turlock Christian HS — 300/7-12
PO Box 1540 95381 — 209-632-2337
Eric Davis, prin. — Fax 632-5859

Tustin, Orange, Pop. 68,478
Tustin USD — 18,700/K-12
300 S C St 92780 — 714-730-7305
Brock Wagner, supt. — Fax 730-7436
www.tustin.k12.ca.us
Columbus Tustin MS — 900/6-8
17952 Beneta Way 92780 — 714-730-7352
James Christensen, prin. — Fax 730-7512
Currie MS — 900/6-8
1402 Sycamore Ave 92780 — 714-730-7360
Karla Wells, prin. — Fax 730-7593
Pioneer MS — 1,000/6-8
2700 Pioneer Rd 92782 — 714-730-7534
Mike Mattos, prin. — Fax 730-5405
Tustin HS — 2,200/9-12
1171 El Camino Real 92780 — 714-730-7414
Margie Sepulveda, prin. — Fax 730-7568
Utt MS — 800/6-8
13601 Browning Ave 92780 — 714-730-7573
Christine Matos, prin. — Fax 750-7576
Sycamore HS / Tustin Adult S — Adult
13780 Orange St 92780 — 714-730-7395
Betty Sarell, prin. — Fax 730-4895
Other Schools – See Irvine, Santa Ana

Adcon Technical Institute — Post-Sec.
17821 E 17th St Ste 120 92780 — 714-730-7080
Spirit Academy — 200/K-12
1372 Irvine Blvd 92780 — 714-731-2630
Sandi Metsch, admin. — Fax 731-2639

Twain Harte, Tuolumne, Pop. 2,170
Twain Harte-Long Barn UESD — 700/K-8
18995 Twain Harte Dr 95383 — 209-586-0999
Mike Brusa, supt. — Fax 586-0662
Twain Harte MS — 200/6-8
18815 Manzanita Ct 95383 — 209-586-3266
Mike Woicicki, prin. — Fax 586-3975

Twentynine Palms, San Bernardino, Pop. 25,971
Morongo USD — 9,700/K-12
PO Box 1209 92277 — 760-367-9191
James Majchrzak, supt. — Fax 367-7189
www.morongo.k12.ca.us
Twentynine Palms HS — 1,000/9-12
72750 Wild Cat Way 92277 — 760-367-9591
Amy Woods, prin. — Fax 367-2106
Twentynine Palms JHS — 600/7-8
5798 Utah Trl 92277 — 760-367-9507
Jolie Kelley, prin. — Fax 367-0742
Other Schools – See Yucca Valley

Twin Peaks, San Bernardino

Lake Arrowhead Christian S — 100/PK-12
PO Box 870 92391 — 909-337-3739
Randall Leonard, prin. — Fax 337-4550

Ukiah, Mendocino, Pop. 15,661
Regional Occupational Center & Program
Supt. — None
Mendocino County ROP — Vo/Tech
2240 Old River Rd 95482 — 707-467-5123
Nona Olsen, dir. — Fax 468-8212

Ukiah USD — 8,000/K-12
925 N State St 95482 — 707-463-5200
Raymond Chadwick, supt. — Fax 463-2120
www.uusd.net/
Pomolita MS — 700/6-8
740 N Spring St 95482 — 707-463-5224
Meredith Rosenberg, prin. — Fax 463-5203
Ukiah HS — 1,900/9-12
1000 Low Gap Rd 95482 — 707-463-5253
Ken Montoya, prin. — Fax 463-4859
Ukiah Adult Education — Adult
1056 N Bush St 95482 — 707-463-5217
Gordon Bourke, prin. — Fax 463-0718
Other Schools – See Redwood Valley

Mendocino College — Post-Sec.
PO Box 3000 95482 — 707-468-3000
Ukiah Junior Academy — 100/K-10
180 Stipp Ln 95482 — 707-462-6350
David Schwartz, prin. — Fax 462-4026

Union City, Alameda, Pop. 69,309
New Haven USD — 12,300/K-12
34200 Alvarado Niles Rd 94587 — 510-471-1100
Pat Jaurequi, supt. — Fax 471-7108
www.nhusd.k12.ca.us
Alvarado MS — 1,100/6-8
31604 Alvarado Blvd 94587 — 510-489-0700
Yvonne Hull, prin. — Fax 475-3936
Barnard-White MS — 800/6-8
725 Whipple Rd 94587 — 510-471-5363
Gustavo Samaniego, prin. — Fax 471-8372
Chavez MS — 1,100/6-8
2801 Hop Ranch Rd 94587 — 510-487-1700
Mireya Casarez, prin. — Fax 475-3938
Logan HS — 4,000/9-12
1800 H St 94587 — 510-471-2520
Don Montoya, prin. — Fax 471-0514
New Haven Adult S — Adult
600 G St 94587 — 510-489-2185
Nancy George, prin. — Fax 471-0554
Other Schools – See Hayward

Upland, San Bernardino, Pop. 72,040
Upland USD — 12,100/K-12
390 N Euclid Ave 91786 — 909-985-1864
Gary Rutherford Ed.D., supt. — Fax 949-7862
www.upland.k12.ca.us
Pioneer JHS — 1,000/7-8
245 W 18th St 91784 — 909-949-7770
Brett O'Connor, prin. — Fax 949-7778
Upland HS — 3,600/9-12
565 W 11th St 91786 — 909-949-7880
Guy Roubian, prin. — Fax 949-7895
Upland JHS — 1,100/7-8
444 E 11th St 91786 — 909-949-7810
Cedric de Visser, prin. — Fax 949-7817

Upland Christian S — 700/K-12
100 W 9th St 91786 — 909-920-5858
Susan Chiappone, prin. — Fax 920-5866
Westwood College - Inland Empire — Post-Sec.
20 W 7th St 91786 — 909-931-7500

Upper Lake, Lake
Upper Lake UNESD — 600/K-8
PO Box 36 95485 — 707-275-2357
Kurt Herndon, supt. — Fax 275-2205
Upper Lake Union MS — 200/6-8
PO Box 36 95485 — 707-275-0223
Rick Winer, prin. — Fax 275-2911

Upper Lake UNHSD — 400/9-12
675 Clover Valley Rd 95485 — 707-275-2655
Jerry Boudreaux, supt. — Fax 275-0239
www.ulhs.k12.ca.us
Upper Lake Union HS — 400/9-12
675 Clover Valley Rd 95485 — 707-275-2338
Dave Hansen, prin. — Fax 275-0239

Vacaville, Solano, Pop. 94,129
Vacaville USD — 13,200/K-12
751 School St 95688 — 707-453-6100
John T. Aycock, supt. — Fax 453-6999
www.vacavilleusd.org
Jepson MS — 1,000/7-8
580 Elder St 95688 — 707-453-6280
Fax 447-7128
Vaca Pena MS — 1,200/7-8
200 Keith Way 95687 — 707-453-6270
Kristine Golomb, prin. — Fax 451-9501
Vacaville HS — 2,100/9-12
100 W Monte Vista Ave 95688 — 707-453-6065
Kari Gibson, prin. — Fax 447-5604
Wood HS — 2,100/9-12
998 Marshall Rd 95687 — 707-453-6900
Chris Strong, prin. — Fax 451-3656

Vacaville Christian S — 1,600/PK-12
1117 Davis St 95687 — 707-446-1776
Karen Winter, supt. — Fax 446-1538

Valencia, See Santa Clarita
Castaic UNSD — 3,600/K-8
28131 Livingston Ave 91355 — 661-257-4500
Beverly W. Silsbee, supt. — Fax 257-3596
www.castaic.k12.ca.us/
Other Schools – See Castaic

William S. Hart UNHSD
Supt. — See Santa Clarita
Arroyo Seco JHS — 1,400/7-8
27171 Vista Delgado Dr 91354 — 661-296-0991
Rhondi Durand, prin. — Fax 296-3436
Rio Norte JHS — 800/7-8
28771 Rio Norte Dr 91354 — 661-295-3700
John Krinkle, prin. — Fax 257-1413
Valencia HS — 3,500/9-12
27801 Dickason Dr 91355 — 661-294-1188
Paul Priesz, prin. — Fax 294-3828

California Institute of the Arts | Post-Sec.
24700 McBean Pkwy 91355 | 661-255-1050

Vallejo, Solano, Pop. 119,708
Vallejo City USD | 20,200/K-12
211 Valle Vista Ave 94590 | 707-556-8921
Dr. Richard J. Damelio, admin. | Fax 649-3907
www.vallejo.k12.ca.us
Bethel HS | 1,600/9-12
1800 Ascot Pkwy 94591 | 707-556-5700
Lilli Rollins, prin. | Fax 556-5703
Franklin MS | 1,100/6-8
501 Starr Ave 94590 | 707-556-8470
Lender Golden, prin. | Fax 556-8475
Hogan HS | 1,900/9-12
850 Rosewood Ave 94591 | 707-556-8510
Mike Santos, prin. | Fax 556-8529
Solano MS | 900/6-8
1025 Corcoran Ave 94589 | 707-556-8600
Rusty Clark, prin. | Fax 556-8615
Springstowne MS | 1,200/6-8
2833 Tennessee St 94591 | 707-556-8620
Sharon Babot, prin. | Fax 556-8624
Vallejo HS | 2,100/9-12
840 Nebraska St 94590 | 707-556-1700
Phillip Saroyan, prin. | Fax 556-8729
Vallejo MS | 1,000/6-8
1347 Amador St 94590 | 707-556-8650
Gigi Patrick, prin. | Fax 556-8666
Vallejo Adult Education | Adult
1140 Capitol St 94590 | 707-556-8680
Kay Hartley, prin. | Fax 556-8686

California Maritime Academy | Post-Sec.
PO Box 1392 94590 | 707-654-1000
North Hills Christian S | 600/PK-12
200 Admiral Callaghan Ln 94591 | 707-644-5284
Richard Porter, admin. | Fax 644-5295
St. Patrick-St. Vincent HS | 600/9-12
1500 Benicia Rd 94591 | 707-644-4425
Mary Ellen Ryan, prin. | Fax 644-3107
Touro Univ. Coll. / Osteopathic Medicine | Post-Sec.
1310 Johnson Ln 94592 | 707-638-5270

Valley Center, San Diego, Pop. 1,711
Valley Center-Pauma USD | 4,000/K-12
28751 Cole Grade Rd 92082 | 760-749-0464
Karen Jobe, supt. | Fax 749-1208
www.vcpusd.k12.ca.us
Valley Center HS | 1,500/9-12
28751 Cole Grade Rd 92082 | 760-751-5500
Lucy Haines, prin. | Fax 751-5509
Valley Center MS | 800/6-8
28751 Cole Grade Rd 92082 | 760-751-4295
Chris Sommer, prin. | Fax 751-4259

Valley Springs, Calaveras
Calaveras USD
Supt. — See San Andreas
Toyon MS | 600/7-8
3412 Double Springs Rd 95252 | 209-754-2137
John Peckler, prin. | Fax 754-5327

Valley Village, See Los Angeles

Valley Torah Boys HS | 200/9-12
12517 Chandler Blvd 91607 | 818-505-7999
Rabbi Avroham Stulberger, prin. | Fax 505-7997

Van Nuys, See Los Angeles
Los Angeles USD
Supt. — See Los Angeles
Birmingham HS | 3,500/9-12
17000 Haynes St 91406 | 818-881-1581
Marsha Coates, prin. | Fax 342-5877
East Valley Area MS | 6-8
15040 Roscoe Blvd 91402 | 818-901-2727
Suzanne Blake, prin. | Fax 901-2740
Fulton College Prep S | 2,800/6-9
7477 Kester Ave 91405 | 818-785-8624
Robert Garcia, prin. | Fax 994-2284
Grant HS | 3,000/9-12
13000 Oxnard St 91401 | 818-781-1400
Linda Ibach, prin. | Fax 908-0774
Mulholland MS | 1,700/6-8
17120 Vanowen St 91406 | 818-345-5446
John White, prin. | Fax 345-1933
Van Nuys HS | 3,800/9-12
6535 Cedros Ave 91411 | 818-781-2371
Judith Vanderbok, prin. | Fax 781-5181
Van Nuys MS | 1,600/6-8
5435 Vesper Ave 91411 | 818-785-5475
Sandra Cruz, prin. | Fax 909-7274
Van Nuys Adult Education | Adult
6535 Cedros Ave 91411 | 818-785-5427
Philip MacMillan, prin. | Fax 782-8354

California Institute of Locksmithing | Post-Sec.
14719 1/2 Oxnard St 91411 | 818-994-7425
ICDC College | Post-Sec.
14434 Sherman Way 91405 | 818-787-0007
Los Angeles Valley College | Post-Sec.
5800 Fulton Ave 91401 | 818-947-2600
Montclair College Preparatory S | 500/6-12
8071 Sepulveda Blvd 91402 | 818-787-5290
Dr. Vernon Simpson, prin. | Fax 786-3382
Nick Harris Detective Academy | Post-Sec.
14721 Oxnard St 91411 | 818-343-6611
The Kings College and Seminary | Post-Sec.
14800 Sherman Way 91405 | 818-779-8040

Ventura, Ventura, Pop. 102,000
Ventura USD | 24,700/K-12
255 W Stanley Ave 93001 | 805-641-5000
Dr. Trudy Tuttle Arriaga, supt. | Fax 653-7855
www.ventura.k12.ca.us/
Anacapa MS | 1,100/6-8
100 S Mills Rd 93003 | 805-289-7900
Ken Magdaleno, prin. | Fax 289-7909
Balboa MS | 1,400/6-8
247 S Hill Rd 93003 | 805-289-1800
Tom Temprano, prin. | Fax 289-1806

Buena HS | 2,100/9-12
5670 Telegraph Rd 93003 | 805-289-1826
Kyunghae Schwartz, prin. | Fax 289-1854
Cabrillo MS | 1,000/6-8
1426 E Santa Clara St 93001 | 805-641-5155
Glory Page, prin. | Fax 641-5377
De Anza MS | 800/6-8
2060 Cameron St 93001 | 805-641-5165
Val Murphy, prin. | Fax 641-5282
Foothill Technology HS | Vo/Tech
100 Day Rd 93003 | 805-289-0023
Joe Bova, prin. | Fax 289-0029
Ventura HS | 2,100/9-12
2 N Catalina St 93001 | 805-641-5116
Larry Emrich, prin. | Fax 641-5310
Ventura Adult and Continuing Education | Adult
5200 Valentine Rd 93003 | 805-289-7925
Denise McMillan, prin. | Fax 289-7931

St. Bonaventure HS | 800/9-12
3167 Telegraph Rd 93003 | 805-648-6836
Br. Paulinus Horkan, prin. | Fax 648-4903
Ventura College | Post-Sec.
4667 Telegraph Rd 93003 | 805-654-6400
Ventura County Christian S | 200/K-12
96 MacMillan Ave 93001 | 805-641-0187
Lisa Darby, admin. | Fax 641-0252

Victorville, San Bernardino, Pop. 74,987
Adelanto ESD
Supt. — See Adelanto
Mesa Linda MS | 900/7-8
13001 Mesa Linda Ave 92392 | 760-956-7355
Jeff Youskievicz, prin. | Fax 956-7456

Victor Valley UNHSD | 8,900/7-12
16350 Mojave Dr, | 760-955-3200
Greg Lundeen, supt. | Fax 245-3128
www.vvuhsd.k12.ca.us/
Cobalt MS | 700/7-8
13801 Cobalt Rd 92392 | 760-955-2530
Greg Johnson, prin. | Fax 955-2437
High Desert Academy | 7-12
15411 Village Dr 92394 | 760-843-7445
Anthony Chambers, dir. | Fax 245-9541
Hook JHS | 1,000/7-8
15000 Hook Blvd 92394 | 760-955-3360
James Nason, prin. | Fax 245-5839
Silverado HS | 3,300/9-12
14048 Cobalt Rd 92392 | 760-955-3353
Susan Levine, prin. | Fax 955-3439
Victor Valley HS | 2,300/9-12
16500 Mojave Dr, | 760-955-3300
Elvin Momon, prin. | Fax 955-3319
Victor Valley JHS | 800/7-8
16925 Forrest Ave, | 760-955-3400
Richard Rojas, prin. | Fax 955-1992
Victor Valley Adult Education | Adult
15733 1st St, | 760-955-3440
Gloria McGee, prin.

Victor Valley Beauty College | Post-Sec.
16515 Mojave Dr, | 760-245-2522
Victor Valley Christian S | 600/PK-12
15260 Nisqually Rd, | 760-241-8827
Dr. Linda Byrd, admin. | Fax 243-0654
Victor Valley Community College | Post-Sec.
18422 Bear Valley Rd, | 760-245-4271

Villa Park, Orange, Pop. 6,039
Orange USD
Supt. — See Orange
Cerro Villa MS | 1,100/7-8
17852 Serrano Ave 92861 | 714-997-6251
Aileen Sterling, prin. | Fax 921-9331
Villa Park HS | 2,200/9-12
18042 Taft Ave 92861 | 714-532-8020
Benjamin Rich, prin. | Fax 628-4302

Visalia, Tulare, Pop. 100,612
Visalia USD | 41,900/K-12
5000 W Cypress Ave 93277 | 559-730-7300
Stan A. Carrizosa, supt. | Fax 730-7559
www.visalia.k12.ca.us
Divisadero MS | 900/7-8
1200 S Divisadero St 93277 | 559-730-7661
Steve Moody, prin. | Fax 730-7908
El Diamante HS | 1,600/9-12
5100 W Whitendale Ave 93277 | 559-735-3501
Drew Sorensen, prin. | Fax 735-3579
Golden West HS | 2,200/9-12
1717 N McAuliff St 93292 | 559-730-7801
Bob Cesena, prin. | Fax 730-7408
Green Acres MS | 1,000/7-8
1147 N Mooney Blvd 93291 | 559-730-7671
Dave Tonini, prin. | Fax 730-7918
La Joya MS | 1,000/7-8
4711 W La Vida Ave 93277 | 559-730-7921
Mary Whitfield, prin. | Fax 730-7505
Mt. Whitney HS | 1,800/9-12
900 S Conyer St 93277 | 559-730-7602
Henry Pasquini, prin. | Fax 730-7679
Redwood HS | 2,000/9-12
1001 W Main St 93291 | 559-730-7367
James Bushman, prin. | Fax 730-7741
Valley Oak MS | 1,200/7-8
2000 N Lovers Ln 93292 | 559-730-7681
Cindy Alonzo, prin. | Fax 730-7822
Visalia Adult Education | Adult
3110 E Houston Ave 93292 | 559-730-7655
Jill Rojas, prin. | Fax 635-0372

Central Valley Christian S | 1,000/PK-12
5600 W Tulare Ave 93277 | 559-734-9481
John DeLeeuw, prin. | Fax 734-7963
College of the Sequoias | Post-Sec.
915 S Mooney Blvd 93277 | 559-730-3700
Estes Inst. Cosmetology Arts & Sciences | Post-Sec.
324 E Main St 93291 | 559-733-3617
Golden State College | Post-Sec.
3356 S Fairway St 93277 | 559-733-4040
San Joaquin Valley College | Post-Sec.
8400 W Mineral King Ave 93291 | 559-651-2500

Visalia Christian Academy | 200/6-12
3737 W Walnut Ave 93277 | 559-737-9710
Tamara Olson, prin. | Fax 737-9714

Vista, San Diego, Pop. 91,813
Vista USD | 24,000/K-12
1234 Arcadia Ave 92084 | 760-726-2170
Dr. Dave Cowles, supt. | Fax 630-0196
www.vusd.k12.ca.us
Lincoln MS | 1,300/6-8
1234 Arcadia Ave 92084 | 760-726-5766
Larrie Hall, prin. | Fax 945-4273
Rancho Buena Vista HS | 3,200/9-12
1234 Arcadia Ave 92084 | 760-727-7284
Rich Alderson, prin. | Fax 598-7062
Vista HS | 3,400/9-12
1234 Arcadia Ave 92084 | 760-726-5611
Larry White, prin. | Fax 630-9738
Washington MS | 1,300/6-8
1234 Arcadia Ave 92084 | 760-724-7115
Janet Whiddon, prin. | Fax 941-6912
Vista Adult S | Adult
1234 Arcadia Ave 92084 | 760-758-7122
Dick Crane, prin. | Fax 726-3277
Other Schools – See Oceanside

Calvary Christian S | 300/K-12
885 E Vista Way 92084 | 760-724-4590
Ronald Barger, admin. | Fax 560-0607
Golf Academy of San Diego | Post-Sec.
1910 Shadowridge Dr Ste 111, | 800-342-7342
Maric College | Post-Sec.
2022 University Dr 92083 | 760-630-1555
Tri City Christian S | 1,200/PK-12
302 N Emerald Dr 92083 | 760-724-3016
Don Hulin, supt. | Fax 724-6643

Walnut, Los Angeles, Pop. 31,089
Walnut Valley USD | 15,300/K-12
880 S Lemon Ave 91789 | 909-595-1261
Dr. Kent L. Bechler, supt. | Fax 444-3435
www.walnutvalley.k12.ca.us
South Pointe MS | 1,300/6-8
20671 Larkstone Dr 91789 | 909-595-8171
Anne Neal, prin. | Fax 468-5201
Suzanne MS | 1,500/6-8
525 Suzanne Rd 91789 | 909-594-1657
Jan Keating, prin. | Fax 598-6741
Walnut HS | 2,600/9-12
400 Pierre Rd 91789 | 909-594-1333
Russell Lee-Sung, prin. | Fax 598-7282
Walnut Valley Adult S | Adult
476 S Lemon Ave 91789 | 909-595-1261
Lisa Raigosa, prin. | Fax 594-1272
Other Schools – See Diamond Bar

Mt. San Antonio College | Post-Sec.
1100 N Grand Ave 91789 | 909-594-5611
Southlands Christian S | 600/PK-12
1920 Brea Canyon Cut Off Rd 91789 | 909-598-9733
Glenn Duncan, admin. | Fax 468-9943

Walnut Creek, Contra Costa, Pop. 65,151
Acalanes UNHSD
Supt. — See Lafayette
Las Lomas HS | 1,700/9-12
1460 S Main St 94596 | 925-935-4110
Patrick Lickiss, prin. | Fax 935-5353
Acalanes Adult S & Center | Adult
1963 Tice Valley Blvd 94595 | 925-935-0170
Laura Canciamilla, dir. | Fax 935-0170

Mt. Diablo USD
Supt. — See Concord
Foothill MS | 1,100/6-8
2775 Cedro Ln 94598 | 925-939-8600
Robert Johnson, prin. | Fax 256-4281
Northgate HS | 1,500/9-12
425 Castle Rock Rd 94598 | 925-938-0900
Martha Riley, prin. | Fax 945-6429

Walnut Creek ESD | 3,300/K-8
960 Ygnacio Valley Rd 94596 | 925-944-6850
Michael De Sa, supt. | Fax 944-1768
www.wcsd.k12.ca.us
Walnut Creek IS | 1,300/6-8
2425 Walnut Blvd 94597 | 925-944-6840
Kevin Collins, prin. | Fax 933-1922

Berean Christian HS | 400/9-12
245 El Divisadero Ave 94598 | 925-945-6464
Nelson Noriega, prin. | Fax 945-7473
Contra Costa Christian S | 400/PK-12
2721 Larkey Ln 94597 | 925-934-4964
B. J. Huizenga, supt. | Fax 934-4966
Legacy Academy | 100/1-12
1283 Boulevard Way 94595 | 925-262-4102
Brad Smith, dir.

Warner Springs, San Diego
Warner USD | 300/PK-12
PO Box 8 92086 | 760-782-3517
Dr. Richard Swanson, supt. | Fax 782-9117
www.sdcoe.k12.ca.us/districts/warner/
Warner HS | 200/6-12
PO Box 8 92086 | 760-782-3517
Ron Koenig Ph.D., prin. | Fax 782-0605

Wasco, Kern, Pop. 22,476
Regional Occupational Center & Program
Supt. — None
North Kern Vocational Training Center | Vo/Tech
2150 7th St 93280 | 661-758-3045
Glenda Santillan, dir. | Fax 758-5956

Wasco UNESD | 3,000/K-8
639 Broadway St 93280 | 661-758-7100
Gary Bray, supt. | Fax 758-7110
www.wuesd.org
Jefferson MS | 700/7-8
305 Griffith Ave 93280 | 661-758-7140
William Elliott, prin. | Fax 758-9366

Wasco UNHSD 1,300/9-12
2100 7th St 93280 661-758-8447
Elizabeth McCray, supt. Fax 758-4946
www.wasco.k12.ca.us/
Wasco HS 1,300/9-12
1900 7th St 93280 661-758-7400
Joseph Elwood, prin. Fax 758-9201

Waterford, Stanislaus, Pop. 8,038
Waterford USD 1,900/K-12
12420 Bentley St 95386 209-874-1809
Frank Cranley, supt. Fax 874-3109
www.waterford.k12.ca.us
Waterford HS 600/9-12
121 S Reinway Ave 95386 209-874-9060
Don Davis, prin. Fax 874-9065
Waterford MS 600/5-8
12916 Bentley St 95386 209-874-2382
Jose Aldaco, prin. Fax 874-3652

Watsonville, Santa Cruz, Pop. 46,159
Pajaro Valley USD 17,800/K-12
294 Green Valley Rd 95076 831-786-2100
Terry McHenry, supt. Fax 728-4288
www.pvusd.net
Hall MS 900/6-8
201 Brewington Ave 95076 831-728-6270
Artemisa Cortez, prin. Fax 761-6150
Lakeview MS 1,000/6-8
2350 E Lake Ave 95076 831-728-6454
Casey O'Brien, prin. Fax 728-6480
Pajaro MS 600/6-8
250 Salinas Rd 95076 831-728-6238
Stella Moreno, prin. Fax 728-6219
Rolling Hills MS 900/6-8
130 Herman Ave 95076 831-728-6341
Rick Ito, prin. Fax 724-7323
Watsonville HS 3,100/9-12
250 E Beach St 95076 831-728-6390
Fax 761-6013
Adult Education Downtown Center Adult
280 Main St 95076 831-728-6330
Bob Harper, coord. Fax 728-6245
Adult Education Green Valley Center Adult
294 Green Valley Rd 95076 831-786-2160
Bob Harper, dir. Fax 786-2193
Other Schools – See Aptos

Monte Vista Christian S 900/6-12
2 School Way 95076 831-722-8178
Stephen Sharp, supt. Fax 722-6003
Mt. Madonna S 200/PK-12
491 Summit Rd 95076 408-847-2717
Dr. Sarada Diffenbaugh, prin. Fax 847-5633
St. Francis Central Coast Catholic HS 50/9-12
2400 E Lake Ave 95076 831-724-5933
Keith Mathews, prin. Fax 724-5995

Weaverville, Trinity, Pop. 3,370
Trinity UNHSD 600/9-12
PO Box 1227 96093 530-623-6104
Robert Lowden, supt. Fax 623-3418
www.trinitywolves.org
Trinity HS 400/9-12
PO Box 1060 96093 530-623-6127
Michael McAllister, prin. Fax 623-6661
Trinity Adult S Adult
PO Box 2789 96093 530-623-2541
Lynn Kelly, prin. Fax 623-6026

Weed, Siskiyou, Pop. 2,977
Siskiyou UNHSD
Supt. — See Mount Shasta
Weed HS 200/9-12
909 Hillside Dr 96094 530-938-4774
Michael Matheson, prin. Fax 938-1319

College of the Siskiyous Post-Sec.
800 College Ave 96094 530-938-4461

Weimar, Placer, Pop. 1,300
Placer Hills UNESD
Supt. — See Meadow Vista
Weimar Hills MS 500/6-8
PO Box 255 95736 530-637-4121
Steve Schaumleffel, prin. Fax 637-4054

Weldon, Kern
South Fork UNESD 400/K-8
5225 S Kelso Valley Rd 93283 760-378-4000
Robin Shive, supt. Fax 378-3046
www.southforkschool.org
South Fork MS 200/6-8
5225 S Kelso Valley Rd 93283 760-378-1300
Robin Shive, prin. Fax 378-9113

West Covina, Los Angeles, Pop. 108,251
Covina-Valley USD
Supt. — See Covina
South Hills HS 1,800/9-12
645 S Barranca St 91791 626-974-6220
Judith North, prin. Fax 974-6245
Traweek MS 1,200/6-8
1941 E Rowland Ave 91791 626-974-7400
Jeff Wilson, prin. Fax 974-7415
Tri Community Adult Ed.-Pioneer Center Adult
1651 E Rowland Ave 91791 626-974-6821
Bruce Krall, prin. Fax 974-6830

Regional Occupational Center & Program
Supt. — None
East San Gabriel Valley ROP Vo/Tech
1501 Del Norte St 91790 626-962-5080
Laurel Adler, supt. Fax 472-5145

Rowland USD
Supt. — See Rowland Heights
Giano IS 1,000/7-8
3223 S Giano Ave 91792 626-965-2461
Stephen Hansen, prin. Fax 854-2212
Rincon IS 700/7-8
2800 E Hollingworth St 91792 626-965-1696
Debi Klotz, prin. Fax 810-4916

West Covina USD 9,000/K-12
1717 W Merced Ave 91790 626-939-4600
Liliam Leis-Castillo, supt. Fax 939-4701
www.wcusd.k12.ca.us
Edgewood MS 1,500/6-8
1625 W Durness St 91790 626-939-4900
James Mandala, prin. Fax 939-4999
Hollencrest MS 700/6-8
2101 E Merced Ave 91791 626-931-1760
Kathy Granger, prin. Fax 931-1762
West Covina HS 2,700/9-12
1609 E Cameron Ave 91791 626-859-2900
Jim Coombs, prin. Fax 859-3950

ITT Technical Institute Post-Sec.
1530 W Cameron Ave 91790 626-960-8681
Marinello School of Beauty Post-Sec.
118 Plaza Dr 91790 626-962-1021
Northwest College Medical Dental Assts. Post-Sec.
2121 W Garvey Ave N 91790 626-960-5046

West Hills, Ventura

Chaminade College Prep S 1,100/9-12
7500 Chaminade Ave 91304 818-347-8300
Br. Tom Fahy, prin. Fax 348-8374
New Community Jewish HS 300/9-12
7353 Valley Circle Blvd 91304 818-348-0048
Dr. Bruce Powell, hdmstr.
West Valley Christian S 400/K-12
22450 Sherman Way 91307 818-884-4710
Dr. Robert Lozano, admin. Fax 884-4749

Westlake Village, Los Angeles, Pop. 8,575
Conejo Valley USD
Supt. — See Thousand Oaks
Westlake HS 2,200/9-12
100 N Lakeview Canyon Rd 91362 805-497-6711
Ronald Lipari, prin. Fax 497-2606

Malibu Cove Private S 100/K-12
32412 Lake Pleasant Dr 91361 805-267-4818
J. Alfonso, pres.
Oaks Christian S 900/6-12
31749 La Tienda Rd 91362 818-575-9900
Jeffrey Woodcock, hdmstr. Fax 575-9951

Westminster, Orange, Pop. 89,493
Garden Grove USD
Supt. — See Garden Grove
La Quinta HS 1,700/9-12
10372 McFadden Ave 92683 714-663-6315
Louise Milner, prin.
McGarvin IS, 9802 Bishop Pl 92683 600/7-8
Jane Jones, prin. 714-663-6218

Huntington Beach UNHSD
Supt. — See Huntington Beach
Westminster HS 2,600/9-12
14325 Goldenwest St 92683 714-893-1381
Shirley Vaughn, prin. Fax 898-4721

Westminster SD 10,200/K-8
14121 Cedarwood St 92683 714-894-7311
Sheri Loewenstein, supt. Fax 899-2781
www.wsd.k12.ca.us
Johnson MS 900/6-8
13603 Edwards St 92683 714-894-7244
Marc Patterson, prin. Fax 379-0784
Warner MS 900/6-8
14171 Newland St 92683 714-894-7281
Christine Fullerton, prin. Fax 895-2378

Asian American Intl Beauty College Post-Sec.
7871 Westminster Blvd 92683 714-891-0508
Covenant Christian Academy 50/K-12
10101 Cunningham Ave 92683 714-531-9950
Nancy Gorrell, prin. Fax 531-9926
H.O.P.E. Christian Academy 200/K-12
6458 Westminster Blvd 92683 714-373-4673
Dan Haller, dir. Fax 373-4473

West Sacramento, Yolo, Pop. 37,897
Washington USD 6,700/K-12
930 Westacre Rd 95691 916-375-7600
Steven Lawrence Ph.D., supt. Fax 375-7619
www.wusd.k12.ca.us
River City HS 1,600/9-12
1100 Clarendon St 95691 916-375-7800
Stuart MacKay, prin. Fax 375-7809
Washington Adult S Adult
920 Westacre Rd 95691 916-375-7740
Morton Geivett, prin. Fax 375-7744
Other Schools – See Broderick

Wyotech Post-Sec.
980 Riverside Pkwy 95605 916-376-8888
Wyotech Post-Sec.
980 Riverside Dr 93003 916-376-8888

Westwood, Lassen, Pop. 2,017
Westwood USD 700/K-12
PO Box 1225 96137 530-256-2311
Henry Bietz, supt. Fax 256-3539
Westwood JSHS 200/7-12
PO Box 1510 96137 530-256-3235
Henry Bietz, prin. Fax 256-3693

Lake Almanor Christian S 50/1-12
2610 Highway A13 96137 530-596-3683
Gwen Meinhardt, prin. Fax 596-4682

Wheatland, Yuba, Pop. 2,840
Wheatland ESD 1,300/K-8
PO Box 818 95692 530-633-3130
Debra Pearson, supt. Fax 633-4807
www.wheatland.k12.ca.us/
Bear River MS 500/4-8
100 Wheatland Park Dr 95692 530-633-3135
Julie Tyler, prin. Fax 633-3142

Wheatland UNHSD 700/9-12
1010 Wheatland Rd 95692 530-633-3100
Glenn Sewell, supt. Fax 633-3109
www.wheatlandhigh.org
Wheatland Union HS 700/9-12
1010 Wheatland Rd 95692 530-633-3100
Glenn Sewell, prin. Fax 633-3109

Whitethorn, Humboldt
Leggett Valley USD
Supt. — See Leggett
Whale Gulch HS 50/9-12
76811 Usal Rd 95589 707-986-7131
Bill Raebe, prin. Fax 986-1355

Whittier, Los Angeles, Pop. 85,368
East Whittier City ESD 9,100/K-8
14535 Whittier Blvd 90605 562-698-0351
Dorothy Fagan, supt. Fax 696-9256
www.ewcsd.k12.ca.us
East Whittier MS 1,100/6-8
14421 Whittier Blvd 90605 562-693-3766
Dorka Duron, prin. Fax 945-3542
Granada MS 1,100/6-8
15337 Lemon Dr 90604 562-943-0283
Charles Royce, prin. Fax 943-5413
Hillview MS 1,100/6-8
10931 Stamy Rd 90604 562-946-7446
Toni Eannareno, prin. Fax 946-3066

Lowell JESD 3,300/K-8
11019 Valley Home Ave 90603 562-943-0211
Dr. Patricia Howell, supt. Fax 947-7874
www.ljsd.org
Rancho-Starbuck IS 800/7-8
16430 Woodbrier Dr 90604 562-902-4261
Kim Likert, prin. Fax 947-9911

Regional Occupational Center & Program
Supt. — None
Tri-Cities ROP Vo/Tech
12519 Washington Blvd 90602 562-698-9571
Esperanza Fernandez, supt. Fax 696-5352

South Whittier ESD 4,300/K-8
PO Box 3037 90605 562-944-6231
Richard Graves, supt. Fax 944-9659
www.swhittier.k12.ca.us/
Graves MS 1,000/7-8
13243 Los Nietos Rd 90605 562-944-0135
Kathy Cardiff, prin. Fax 944-9433

Whittier City ESD 7,200/PK-8
7211 Whittier Ave 90602 562-789-3075
Dr. Carmella Franco, supt. Fax 698-6534
www.whittiercity.k12.ca.us
Dexter MS 1,300/6-8
11532 Floral Dr 90601 562-789-3090
Diane Kinnart, prin. Fax 789-3095
Edwards MS 1,100/6-8
6812 Norwalk Blvd 90606 562-789-3115
Monica Sena, prin. Fax 789-3133

Whittier UNHSD 17,900/9-12
9401 Painter Ave 90605 562-698-8121
Sandra Thorstenson, supt. Fax 693-0221
www.wuhsd.k12.ca.us
California HS 2,500/9-12
9800 Mills Ave 90604 562-698-8121
Richard Boline, prin. Fax 946-6094
La Serna HS 2,100/9-12
15301 Youngwood Dr 90605 562-698-8121
Martin Plourde, prin. Fax 698-6918
Pioneer HS 1,600/9-12
10800 Ben Avon St 90606 562-698-8121
Alex Flores, prin. Fax 692-9194
Whittier HS 2,100/9-12
12417 Philadelphia St 90601 562-698-8121
Loring Davies, prin. Fax 698-8925
Adult Education Center Adult
9401 Painter Ave 90605 562-698-8121
Leonard Rivera, prin. Fax 693-5354
Other Schools – See Santa Fe Springs

Marinello School of Beauty Post-Sec.
6538 Greenleaf Ave 90601 562-698-0068
Morningstar Christian Academy 200/1-12
16241 Leffingwell Rd 90603 562-943-0297
Eva Flanders, admin.
Primanti Montessori S - Whittier 100/K-11
10947 Valley Home Ave 90603 562-943-0246
Christine Komaki, dir.
Remnant Christian S 50/K-12
7346 Painter Ave 90602 562-464-2554
James Vaughn, admin. Fax 464-2556
Rio Hondo College Post-Sec.
3600 Workman Mill Rd 90601 562-692-0921
Southern CA University of Health Science Post-Sec.
16200 Amber Valley Dr 90604 562-947-8755
Whittier Christian JHS 200/7-8
6548 Newlin Ave 90601 562-698-0527
Robert Sowell, admin. Fax 698-2859
Whittier College Post-Sec.
PO Box 634 90608 562-907-4200

Wildomar, Riverside, Pop. 10,411
Lake Elsinore USD
Supt. — See Lake Elsinore
Brown MS 1,300/6-8
21861 Grand Ave 92595 951-678-8400
Billie Davolt, prin. Fax 678-8408
Elsinore HS 2,500/9-12
21800 Canyon Dr 92595 951-253-7200
John Hurst, prin. Fax 253-7209

California Lutheran HS 100/9-12
PO Box 1570 92595 951-678-7000
Rev. Gregory Bork, prin. Fax 678-0172
Cornerstone Christian S 300/K-12
34570 Monte Vista Dr 92595 951-674-9381
Jim Phillips, dir. Fax 674-8462
Faith Baptist Academy 200/K-12
PO Box 1030 92595 951-245-8748
Greg Beil, admin.

Williams, Colusa, Pop. 3,925
Williams USD
  PO Box 7 95987   1,100/K-12
  Dr. Merrill Grant, supt.   530-473-2550
  www.williams.k12.ca.us/   Fax 473-5894
Williams HS
  PO Box 7 95987   300/9-12
  Dan Flanigan, prin.   530-473-5369
Williams MS   Fax 473-5026
  PO Box 7 95987   400/4-8
  Arthur Estrada, prin.   530-473-5304
    Fax 473-5928

Willits, Mendocino, Pop. 5,139
Willits USD
  120 Pearl St 95490   2,200/K-12
  Steven Jorgensen, supt.   707-459-5314
  www.ctap1.org/wusd/   Fax 459-7862
Baechtel Grove MS   500/6-8
  1150 Magnolia St 95490   707-459-2417
  Rick Jordan, prin.   Fax 459-7881
Willits HS   600/9-12
  299 N Main St 95490   707-459-7700
  Gordon Oslund, prin.   Fax 459-7741
Willits Adult S   Adult
  120 N Main St 95490   707-459-4801
  Catherine Scott, prin.   Fax 459-7862

Willow Creek, Humboldt, Pop. 1,576

Willow Creek Christian S   100/K-12
  PO Box 1568 95573   530-629-3332
  Marie Smith, prin.   Fax 629-3332

Willows, Glenn, Pop. 6,320
Glenn County Office of Education
  311 S Villa Ave 95988   530-934-6575
  Dr. Joni Samples, supt.   Fax 934-6576
  www.glenncoe.org
Glenn Adult Program   Adult
  511 S Villa Ave 95988   530-934-6320
  Coleen Parker, dir.   Fax 934-6325

Regional Occupational Center & Program
  Supt. — None
Glenn County ROP   Vo/Tech
  525 W Sycamore St 95988   530-934-6575
  Coleen Parker, supt.   Fax 934-6576

Willows USD   1,800/K-12
  334 W Sycamore St 95988   530-934-6600
  Ronald Mongini, supt.   Fax 934-6609
  www.willowsunified.org/home.htm
Willows HS   500/9-12
  203 N Murdock Ave 95988   530-934-6611
  Preston Persky, prin.   Fax 934-6619
Willows IS   500/5-8
  1145 W Cedar St 95988   530-934-6633
  Steve Sailsbery, prin.   Fax 934-6697
Willows Community HS   Adult
  823 W Laurel St 95988   530-934-6605
  Mike Rutherglen, prin.   Fax 934-6384

Wilmington, See Los Angeles
Los Angeles USD
  Supt. — See Los Angeles
Banning HS   3,200/9-12
  1527 Lakme Ave 90744   310-549-7500
  Michael Summe, prin.   Fax 830-5515
Wilmington MS   2,300/6-8
  1700 Gulf Ave 90744   310-518-1120
  Shannon Lee, prin.   Fax 549-5307

Los Angeles Harbor College   Post-Sec.
  1111 Figueroa Pl 90744   310-522-8200
National Polytechnic College   Post-Sec.
  272 S Fries Ave 90744   310-834-2501
Pacific Harbor Christian S   400/PK-12
  1530 N Wilmington Blvd 90744   310-835-5665
  Angie Colclasure, supt.   Fax 835-6361

Windsor, Sonoma, Pop. 24,412
Windsor USD   3,700/K-12
  9291 Old Redwood Hwy 95492   707-837-7700
  Steven Herrington Ph.D., supt.   Fax 838-4031
  www.wusd.org
Windsor HS   1,300/9-12
  8695 Windsor Rd 95492   707-837-7767
  Patricia Law, prin.   Fax 837-7773
Windsor MS   1,000/6-8
  9500 Brooks Rd S 95492   707-837-7737
  Loren Barker, prin.   Fax 837-7743

Windsor Christian Academy   300/PK-12
  PO Box 1880 95492   707-838-3757
  Tad Theiss, prin.   Fax 838-3542

Winterhaven, Imperial
San Pasqual Valley USD   800/PK-12
  676 Base Line Rd 92283   760-572-0222
  Suzanne Smith, supt.   Fax 572-0711
  www.sanpasqual.k12.ca.us
San Pasqual Valley HS   200/9-12
  676 Base Line Rd 92283   760-572-0222
  Lynda Schoonover, prin.   Fax 572-0881
San Pasqual Valley MS   200/6-8
  676 Base Line Rd 92283   760-572-0222
  Lynda Schoonover, prin.   Fax 572-0881

Winters, Yolo, Pop. 6,658
Winters JUSD   2,300/K-12
  909 W Grant Ave 95694   530-795-6100
  Dale J. Mitchell, supt.   Fax 795-6114
  www.winters.k12.ca.us

Winters HS   700/9-12
  101 Grant Ave 95694   530-795-6140
  George Griffin, prin.   Fax 795-6147
Winters MS   500/6-8
  425 Anderson Ave 95694   530-795-6130
  Suzanne Martin, prin.   Fax 795-6137

Winton, Merced, Pop. 7,559
Merced River UNESD
  Supt. — See Snelling
Washington MS   100/4-8
  4402 Oakdale Rd 95388   209-358-5679
  Dr. Helio Brasil, prin.   Fax 358-2855

Winton SD   1,800/K-8
  PO Box 8 95388   209-357-6175
  Michael Crass, supt.   Fax 357-1994
  www.winton.k12.ca.us
Winton MS   600/6-8
  PO Box 1299 95388   209-357-6189
  Randall Heller, prin.   Fax 358-5889

Woodlake, Tulare, Pop. 6,938
Woodlake UNSD   2,500/K-12
  300 W Whitney Ave 93286   559-564-8081
  Steve Tietjen, supt.   Fax 564-3831
Woodlake Union HS   800/9-12
  400 W Whitney Ave 93286   559-564-3307
  Tim Hire, prin.   Fax 564-3320
Woodlake Valley MS   600/6-8
  497 N Palm St 93286   559-564-8061
  David East, prin.   Fax 564-0702

Woodland, Yolo, Pop. 50,988
Regional Occupational Center & Program
  Supt. — None
Yolo County ROP   Vo/Tech
  1240 Harter Ave 95776   530-668-3770
  Ronda Adams, dir.   Fax 668-3850

Woodland JUSD   10,700/K-12
  630 Cottonwood St 95695   530-662-0201
  Jacki L. Cottingim Ph.D., supt.   Fax 662-6956
  www.wjusd.net
Douglass MS   900/7-8
  525 Granada Dr 95695   530-666-2191
  Jonathan Brunson, prin.   Fax 668-9217
Lee MS   700/7-8
  520 West St 95695   530-662-0251
  Garth Lewis, prin.   Fax 662-9423
Pioneer HS   900/9-12
  1400 Pioneer Ave 95776   530-406-1140
  Nick McNicholas, prin.   Fax 662-3661
Woodland HS   2,200/9-12
  21 N West St 95695   530-662-4678
  Evelia Genera Ed.D., prin.   Fax 662-7464
Woodland Adult Education   Adult
  575 Hays St 95695   530-662-0798
  Susan Moylan, dir.   Fax 662-8039

Woodland Christian S   600/PK-12
  1616 West St 95695   530-666-6615
  Jim Lokkesmoe, admin.   Fax 666-3470

Woodland Hills, See Los Angeles
Los Angeles USD
  Supt. — See Los Angeles
El Camino Real HS   3,700/9-12
  5440 Valley Circle Blvd 91367   818-888-8920
  Kenneth Lee, prin.   Fax 710-9023
Hale MS   2,300/6-8
  23830 Califa St 91367   818-346-1851
  Neal Siegel, prin.   Fax 346-7517
Parkman MS   1,300/6-8
  20800 Burbank Blvd 91367   818-348-8770
  Ann Allocca, prin.   Fax 716-0649
Taft HS   3,500/9-12
  5461 Winnetka Ave 91364   818-348-7171
  Sharon Thomas, prin.   Fax 592-0877
El Camino Real Adult Education   Adult
  5440 Valley Circle Blvd 91367   818-888-1491
  Joanna McConaghy, prin.   Fax 888-6714
West Valley Occupational Center   Adult
  6200 Winnetka Ave 91367   818-346-3540
  Maureen Jensen, prin.   Fax 346-3858

Los Angeles Pierce College   Post-Sec.
  6201 Winnetka Ave 91371   818-347-0551
Louisville HS   500/9-12
  22300 Mulholland Dr 91364   818-346-8812
    Fax 346-9483
University of West Los Angeles   Post-Sec.
  6400 Canoga Ave Ste 271 91367   818-883-0529

Woodside, San Mateo, Pop. 5,256
Sequoia UNHSD
  Supt. — See Redwood City
Woodside HS   1,900/9-12
  199 Churchill Ave 94062   650-367-9750
  Linda Common, prin.   Fax 367-7263

Yermo, San Bernardino
Silver Valley USD   2,600/PK-12
  PO Box 847 92398   760-254-2916
  David Kincaid, supt.   Fax 254-2091
  www.silvervalley.k12.ca.us
Silver Valley HS   500/9-12
  PO Box 847 92398   760-254-2963
  Dr. Michael Davitt, prin.   Fax 254-3043
Silver Valley Adult S   Adult
  PO Box 847 92398   760-254-2715
  Jim Swor, prin.   Fax 254-2194
Other Schools – See Fort Irwin

Yorba Linda, Orange, Pop. 62,358
Placentia Yorba Linda USD
  Supt. — See Placentia
Yorba Linda MS   700/6-8
  4777 Casa Loma Ave 92886   714-528-7090
  Virginia Trapani, prin.   Fax 996-2752
Yorba MS   1,000/7-8
  5350 Fairmont Blvd 92886   714-970-0650
  Harry Dolen, prin.   Fax 970-1647
Adult Education S   Adult
  4175 Fairmont Blvd 92886   714-779-6042
  Jackie Howland, admin.   Fax 779-6825

Friends Christian MS   500/5-8
  4231 Rose Dr 92886   714-524-5240
  Ron Ralston, prin.   Fax 524-5784

Yreka, Siskiyou, Pop. 7,204
Regional Occupational Center & Program
  Supt. — None
Siskiyou County ROP   Vo/Tech
  431 Knapp St 96097   530-842-5161
  Kim Greene, dir.   Fax 842-1759

Yreka UNESD   1,100/K-8
  309 Jackson St 96097   530-842-1168
  Jerome Jereb, supt.   Fax 842-4576
  sisnet.ssku.k12.ca.us/~yesftp
Jackson Street MS   500/5-8
  405 Jackson St 96097   530-842-3561
  Valerie Herman, prin.   Fax 842-1716
Yreka UNHSD   900/9-12
  431 Knapp St 96097   530-842-2521
  Mark Greenfield, supt.   Fax 842-1759
  sisnet.ssku.k12.ca.us/~yuhsdftp/
Discovery HS   100/9-12
  431 Knapp St 96097   530-842-1659
  Marie Caldwell, prin.   Fax 841-1057
Yreka HS   800/9-12
  431 Knapp St 96097   530-842-6151
  Jennifer McKinnon, prin.   Fax 841-0740
Yreka Union HS Adult Education   Adult
  431 Knapp St 96097   530-842-7829
  Maria Rosenlund, dir.   Fax 842-1759

Yreka SDA Christian S   100/K-10
  346 Payne Ln 96097   530-842-7071
    Fax 842-7463

Yuba City, Sutter, Pop. 48,998
Regional Occupational Center & Program
  Supt. — None
Tri-County ROP   Vo/Tech
  970 Klamath Ln 95993   530-822-2952
  Randy Page, dir.   Fax 822-3003

Yuba City USD   11,400/K-12
  750 N Palora Ave 95991   530-822-5200
  Nancy Aaberg, supt.   Fax 671-2454
  www.ycusd.k12.ca.us
Gray Avenue MS   800/6-8
  808 Gray Ave 95991   530-822-5240
  Dave Morrow, prin.   Fax 822-5057
Karperos MS   1,300/5-8
  1666 Camino De Flores 95993   530-822-5262
  Bob Chiechi, prin.   Fax 671-5356
River Valley HS   9-12
  801 El Margarita Rd 95993   530-822-2500
  Don Beno, prin.   Fax 822-2589
Yuba City HS   2,900/9-12
  850 B St 95991   530-674-4900
  Mario Johnson Ph.D., prin.   Fax 671-7814

Faith Christian HS   200/7-12
  PO Box 1690 95992   530-674-5474
  Steve Finlay, prin.   Fax 674-0194

Yucaipa, San Bernardino, Pop. 46,171
Yucaipa-Calimesa JUSD   11,100/K-12
  12797 3rd St 92399   909-797-0174
  Mitchell Hovey, supt.   Fax 790-6103
  www.yucaipaschools.com
Canyon MS   400/7-8
  35948 Susan St 92399   909-790-8580
  Melissa Moore, prin.   Fax 790-8584
Park View MS   1,100/7-8
  34875 Tahoe Dr 92399   909-790-3285
  Jeff Litel, prin.   Fax 790-3295
Yucaipa HS   2,100/10-12
  33000 Yucaipa Blvd 92399   909-797-0106
  Bernie Cavanagh, prin.   Fax 790-3200
Yucaipa HS Ninth Grade Campus   700/9-9
  12358 6th St 92399   909-797-5181
  Sherry Smith, prin.   Fax 790-6192
Yucaipa Adult S   Adult
  12787 3rd St 92399   909-797-0121
  Nancy Greening, prin.   Fax 790-6115

Crafton Hills College   Post-Sec.
  11711 Sand Canyon Rd 92399   909-794-2161

Yucca Valley, San Bernardino, Pop. 18,301
Morongo USD
  Supt. — See Twentynine Palms
La Contenta JHS   900/7-8
  7050 La Contenta Rd 92284   760-228-1802
  Jean Johnson, prin.   Fax 369-6324
Yucca Valley HS   1,500/9-12
  7600 Sage Ave 92284   760-365-3391
  Carl Phillips, prin.   Fax 365-1845

Joshua Springs Christian S   500/PK-12
  57373 Joshua Ln 92284   760-365-3599
  Fem Ontiveros, admin.   Fax 369-0315

COLORADO

COLORADO DEPARTMENT OF EDUCATION
201 E Colfax Ave, Denver 80203-1704
Telephone 303-866-6600
Fax 303-830-0793
Website http://www.cde.state.co.us

Commissioner of Education   William Moloney

COLORADO BOARD OF EDUCATION
201 E Colfax Ave, Denver 80203-1704

Chairperson   Pamela Jo Suckla

BOARDS OF COOPERATIVE EDUCATIONAL SERVICES (BOCES)

Adams County BOCES
Dave Carroll, dir.
602 E 64th Ave, Denver 80229   303-286-7294
Fax 853-1156
Centennial BOCES
Dale McCall, dir.
830 S Lincoln St, Longmont 80501   303-772-4420
Fax 776-0504
www.cboces.org
Centennial BOCES
Dale McCall, dir., 821 W Platte Ave
Fort Morgan 80701   970-867-8297
Fax 867-6129
www.cboces.org
East Central BOCES
David Van Sant, dir.
PO Box 910, Limon 80828   719-775-2342
Fax 775-9714
www.ecboces.org
Expeditionary BOCES
Jim McDermott, dir.
1700 S Holly St, Denver 80222   303-759-2076
Fax 757-7442
www.rmsel.org/
Front Range BOCES
Susan Sparks, dir.
PO Box 173364, Denver 80217   303-556-6028
Fax 556-6060
frontrangeboces.org/
Grand Valley BOCES
Kerry Youngblood, dir.
2508 Blichman Ave   970-255-2600
Grand Junction 81505   Fax 255-2626

Larimer BOCES
Jack Hale, dir.
2880 Monroe Ave, Loveland 80538   970-613-5173
Fax 613-5184
Mountain BOCES
Edward Vandertook, dir.
1713 Mount Lincoln Dr W   719-486-2603
Leadville 80461   Fax 486-2109
www.mtnboces.k12.co.us/
Mount Evans BOCES
Joyce Conrey, dir.
PO Box 3399, Idaho Springs 80452   303-567-4467
Fax 567-2208
Northeast Colorado BOCES
Tim Sanger, dir.
PO Box 98, Haxtun 80731   970-774-6152
Fax 774-6157
www.neboces.com
Northwest Colorado BOCES
Jane Toothaker, dir., PO Box 773390   970-879-0391
Steamboat Springs 80477   Fax 879-0442
www.nwboces.k12.co.us
Pikes Peak BOCES
Dr. Corinne Harmon, dir.
4825 Lorna Pl   719-570-7474
Colorado Springs 80915   Fax 380-9685
www.ppboces.org

Rio Blanco BOCES
Donna Day, dir.
402 W Main St Ste 135   970-675-2064
Rangely 81648   Fax 675-5738
San Juan BOCES
Tom Lawson, dir.
201 E 12th St, Durango 81301   970-247-3261
Fax 247-8333
www.sjbocs.org/index.htm
San Luis Valley BOCES
John Tillman, dir.
PO Box 1198, Alamosa 81101   719-589-5851
Fax 589-5007
www.slvbocs.org
Santa Fe Trail BOCES
Sandy Malouff, dir.
PO Box 980, La Junta 81050   719-383-2623
Fax 383-2627
South Central BOCES
Cynthia Seidel, dir.
323 S Purcell Blvd, Pueblo 81007   719-647-0023
Fax 647-0136
www.scboces.k12.co.us
Southeastern BOCES
Jo Autrey, dir.
PO Box 1137, Lamar 81052   719-336-9046
Fax 336-9679
www.seboces.k12.co.us/
Southwest BOCES
Victor Bruce, dir.
PO Box 1420, Cortez 81321   970-565-8411
Fax 565-1203
Uncompahgre BOCES
Sharon Davarn, dir.
PO Box 728, Ridgway 81432   970-626-2977
Fax 626-2978
www.unbocs.org/

PUBLIC, PRIVATE AND CATHOLIC SECONDARY SCHOOLS

Agate, Elbert, Pop. 100
Agate SD 300   100/PK-12
PO Box 118 80101   719-764-2741
Wendy Dunaway, supt.   Fax 764-2751
Agate JSHS   100/6-12
PO Box 118 80101   719-764-2741
Wendy Dunaway, prin.   Fax 764-2751

Aguilar, Las Animas, Pop. 582
Aguilar RSD 6   200/PK-12
PO Box 567 81020   719-941-4614
Nancy Gjovik, supt.   Fax 941-4439
Aguilar JSHS   100/7-12
PO Box 567 81020   719-941-4640
Dennis Hoyt, prin.   Fax 941-4439

Akron, Washington, Pop. 1,649
Akron SD R-1   400/K-12
PO Box 429 80720   970-345-2268
Jim Pagel, supt.   Fax 345-6508
www.akronrams.net/homepage2.htm
Akron HS   100/9-12
600 Elm Ave 80720   970-345-2268
Bryce Monasmith, prin.   Fax 345-6508

Alamosa, Alamosa, Pop. 8,570
Alamosa SD RE-11J   2,400/PK-12
209 Victoria Ave 81101   719-587-1600
Henry Herrera, supt.   Fax 587-1712
www.alamosa.k12.co.us/
Alamosa HS, 805 Craft Dr 81101   600/9-12
Shelly Swayne, prin.   719-587-6000
Ortega MS, 401 Victoria Ave 81101   600/6-8
Neil Seneff, prin.   719-587-1650

Adams State College   Post-Sec.
208 Edgemont Blvd 81101   800-824-6494

Anton, Washington, Pop. 40
Arickaree SD R-2   100/PK-12
12155 County Road NN 80801   970-383-2202
Richard Walter, supt.   Fax 383-2205
Arickaree JSHS   50/7-12
12155 County Road Nn 80801   970-383-2202
Richard Walter, prin.   Fax 383-2205

Antonito, Conejos, Pop. 839
South Conejos SD RE-10   300/PK-12
PO Box 398 81120   719-376-5512
Carlos A. Garcia, supt.   Fax 376-5425
scsd.echalk.com/home.asp
Antonito HS   100/9-12
PO Box 398 81120   719-376-5468
Virginia Goddard, prin.   Fax 376-5425

Antonito JHS   50/7-8
PO Box 398 81120   719-376-5468
Virginia Goddard, prin.   Fax 376-5425

Arvada, Jefferson, Pop. 101,972
Jefferson County SD R-1
Supt. — See Golden
Arvada HS   1,700/9-12
7951 W 65th Ave 80004   303-982-0162
Al Aguayo, prin.   Fax 982-0163
Arvada MS   400/7-8
5751 Balsam St 80002   303-982-1240
Beverly Eidmann, prin.   Fax 982-1241
Arvada West HS   1,700/9-12
11325 Allendale Dr 80004   303-982-1303
Priscilla Straughn, prin.   Fax 982-1304
Drake MS   900/7-9
12550 W 52nd Ave 80002   303-982-1510
Linda Rice, prin.   Fax 982-1511
Moore MS   800/7-8
8455 W 88th Ave 80005   303-982-0400
John White, prin.   Fax 982-0462
North Arvada MS   500/7-8
7285 Pierce St 80003   303-982-0528
Mike Little, prin.   Fax 982-0529
Oberon MS   800/7-8
7300 Quail St 80005   303-982-2020
Dana Ellis, prin.   Fax 982-2021
Pomona HS   1,700/9-12
8101 W Pomona Dr 80005   303-982-0710
Dan Cohan, prin.   Fax 982-0709
Ralston Valley HS   1,300/9-12
13355 W 80th Ave 80005   303-982-5600
Jim Elkins, prin.   Fax 982-5601

Faith Christian HS   400/9-12
4890 Carr St 80002   303-424-7310
Andrew Hasz, prin.   Fax 403-2730
Faith Christian MS   300/6-8
6250 Wright St 80004   303-424-7310
Randy Ziemer, prin.   Fax 403-2720
Maranatha Christian Center   900/PK-12
7180 Oak St 80004 – Pat Loser, dir.   303-431-5653

Aspen, Pitkin, Pop. 5,850
Aspen SD 1   1,400/PK-12
235 High School Rd 81611   970-925-3760
Dr. Diana Sirko, supt.   Fax 925-5721
www.aspenk12.net/
Aspen HS   500/9-12
235 High School Rd 81611   970-925-3760
Kendall Evans, prin.   Fax 925-1205
Aspen MS   400/5-8
235 High School Rd 81611   970-925-3760
Griff Smith, prin.   Fax 925-8374

Ault, Weld, Pop. 1,411
Ault-Highland SD RE-9   900/K-12
PO Box 68 80610   970-834-1345
Dennis Scheer Ed.D., supt.   Fax 834-1347
www.weldre9.k12.co.us
Highland HS   300/9-12
PO Box 68 80610   970-834-2816
Randy Ward, prin.   Fax 834-2858
Highland MS   200/6-8
PO Box 68 80610   970-834-2829
Todd Bissell, prin.   Fax 834-2858

Aurora, Arapahoe, Pop. 290,418
Aurora SD   31,300/PK-12
1085 Peoria St 80011   303-344-8060
John Barry, supt.   Fax 326-1280
www.aps.k12.co.us
Aurora Central HS   2,200/9-12
11700 E 11th Ave 80010   303-340-1600
Dean Stecklein, prin.   Fax 326-1270
Aurora Hills MS   1,100/6-8
1009 S Uvalda St 80012   303-341-7450
Jinger Haberer, prin.   Fax 326-1250
Columbia MS   1,000/6-8
17600 E Columbia Ave 80013   303-690-6570
James O'Tremba, prin.   Fax 326-1251
East MS   1,000/6-8
1275 Fraser St 80011   303-340-0660
Fred Quinonez, prin.   Fax 326-1252
Gateway HS   1,700/9-12
1300 S Sable Blvd 80012   303-755-7160
James Bailey, prin.   Fax 326-1272
Hinkley HS   1,700/9-12
1250 Chambers Rd 80011   303-340-1500
Gerald Califano, prin.   Fax 326-1274
Mrachek MS   1,300/6-8
1955 S Telluride St 80013   303-750-2836
Linda Witulski, prin.   Fax 326-1254
North MS   800/6-8
12095 Montview Blvd 80010   303-364-7411
Paula Arroyo, prin.   Fax 326-1256
Pickens Technical Center   Vo/Tech
500 Airport Blvd 80011   303-344-4910
Art Bogardus, prin.   Fax 326-1277
Rangeview HS   2,100/9-12
17599 E Iliff Ave 80013   303-695-6848
Rob Bishop, prin.   Fax 326-1276
South MS   1,000/6-8
12310 E Parkview Dr 80011   303-364-7623
Kevin Gates, prin.   Fax 326-1258
West MS   1,000/6-8
10100 E 13th Ave 80010   303-366-2671
Dale Krueger, prin.   Fax 326-1260

Cherry Creek SD 5
 Supt. — See Greenwood Village
Cherokee Trail HS | 1,800/9-12
 25901 E Arapahoe Pkwy N 80016 | 720-886-1900
 Mary Jarvis, prin. | Fax 886-1989
Eaglecrest HS | 2,700/9-12
 5100 S Picadilly St 80015 | 720-886-1000
 Jeanne Piper, prin. | Fax 886-1097
Falcon Creek MS | 1,100/6-8
 6100 S Genoa St 80016 | 720-886-7700
 John Kennedy, prin. | Fax 886-7788
Grandview HS | 2,500/9-12
 20500 E Arapahoe Rd 80016 | 720-886-6500
 Dr. Harry Bull, prin. | Fax 886-6698
Horizon Community MS | 1,400/6-8
 3981 S Reservoir Rd 80013 | 720-886-6100
 Tony Davis, prin. | Fax 886-6253
Laredo MS | 1,400/6-8
 5000 S Laredo St 80015 | 720-886-5200
 Mark Wahlstrom, prin. | Fax 886-5298
Liberty HS | 1,000/6-8
 21500 E Dry Creek Rd 80016 | 720-886-2400
 Scott Siegfried, prin. | Fax 886-2688
Overland HS | 2,000/9-12
 12400 E Jewell Ave 80012 | 720-747-3700
 Jane Frieler, prin. | Fax 747-3895
Prairie MS | 1,600/6-8
 12600 E Jewell Ave 80012 | 720-747-3000
 Kandy Cassaday, prin. | Fax 747-3113
Sky Vista MS | 6-8
 4500 S Himalaya Cir 80015 | 720-886-4700
 Tony Poole, prin. | Fax 886-4788
Smoky Hill HS | 2,700/9-12
 16100 E Smoky Hill Rd 80015 | 720-886-5300
 Jeannine Brown, prin. | Fax 886-5408
Thunder Ridge MS | 1,500/6-8
 5250 S Picadilly St 80015 | 720-886-1500
 Mark Sneden, prin. | Fax 886-1582

American Health Science University | Post-Sec.
 1010 S Joliet St Ste 107 80012 | 303-340-2054
Aurora Christian Academy | 100/K-12
 11001 E Alameda Ave # A 80012 | 303-344-2530
 Adam Luna, admin. | Fax 344-9255
Cambridge College | Post-Sec.
 350 Blackhawk St 80011 | 866-502-2627
CedarWood Christian Academy | 100/K-12
 PO Box 111389 80042 | 303-361-6456
 Gene Oborny, admin. | Fax 340-0971
Community College of Aurora | Post-Sec.
 16000 E Centretech Pkwy 80011 | 303-360-4700
Concorde Career College | Post-Sec.
 111 Havana St 80010 | 303-861-1151
Excelsior HS | 200/7-12
 15001 E Oxford Ave 80014 | 303-693-1550
 Jann Clevenger, prin. | Fax 693-2415
Parks College | Post-Sec.
 14280 E Jewell Ave 80012 | 303-367-2757
Pickens Technical Center | Post-Sec.
 500 Airport Blvd 80011 | 303-344-4910
Platt College | Post-Sec.
 3100 S Parker Rd 80014 | 303-369-5151
Regis Jesuit HS for Boys | 800/9-12
 6400 S Lewiston Way 80016 | 303-269-8000
 Charlie Saulino, prin. | Fax 766-2240
Regis Jesuit HS for Girls | 100/9-12
 6300 S Lewiston Way 80016 | 303-269-8100
 Gretchen Kessler, prin. | Fax 221-4772
Xenon Intl School of Hair Design III | Post-Sec.
 2231 S Peoria St 80014 | 303-752-1560

Bailey, Park, Pop. 150
Platte Canyon SD 1 | 1,400/PK-12
 57393 US Highway 285 80421 | 303-838-7666
 Jim Walpole Ed.D., supt. | Fax 679-7504
Fitzsimmons MS | 500/6-8
 57093 US Highway 285 80421 | 303-838-7666
 Susan Hickel, prin. | Fax 679-7506
Platte Canyon HS | 500/9-12
 57243 US Highway 285 80421 | 303-838-7666
 Bryan Krause, prin. | Fax 679-7497

Basalt, Pitkin, Pop. 2,969
Roaring Fork SD RE-1
 Supt. — See Glenwood Springs
Basalt HS | 400/9-12
 600 Southside Dr 81621 | 970-384-5959
 Jim Waddick, prin. | Fax 384-5955
Basalt MS | 500/5-8
 51 School St 81621 | 970-384-5650
 Christian Kingsbury, prin. | Fax 384-5905

Alpine Christian Academy | 100/PK-12
 20449 Highway 82 81621 | 970-927-9106
 Mick Bennett, hdmstr. | Fax 927-3705

Bayfield, LaPlata, Pop. 1,625
Bayfield SD 10 JT-R | 1,100/PK-12
 24 S Clover Ln 81122 | 970-884-2496
 Donald Magill, supt. | Fax 884-4284
 www.bayfield.k12.co.us
Bayfield HS | 400/9-12
 24 S Clover Ln 81122 | 970-884-9521
 Michael Gearheart, prin. | Fax 884-4226
Bayfield MS | 300/6-8
 24 S Clover Ln 81122 | 970-884-9592
 Michael Lister, prin. | Fax 884-4110

Bennett, Adams, Pop. 2,271
Bennett SD 29J | 1,100/PK-12
 615 7th St 80102 | 303-644-3234
 Dr. George Sauter, supt. | Fax 644-4121
 www.bennett29j.k12.co.us
Bennett HS | 300/9-12
 610 7th St 80102 | 303-644-3234
 Richard Coleman, prin. | Fax 644-3894
Bennett MS | 300/6-8
 455 8th St 80102 | 303-644-3234
 Amy Burns, prin. | Fax 644-4398

Berthoud, Larimer, Pop. 5,098
Thompson SD R-2J
 Supt. — See Loveland
Berthoud HS | 700/9-12
 850 Spartan Ave 80513 | 970-613-7700
 Leonard Sherman, prin. | Fax 613-7728

Turner MS | 500/6-8
 950 Massachusetts Ave 80513 | 970-613-7400
 Sheila Pottorff, prin. | Fax 532-4377

Bethune, Kit Carson, Pop. 225
Bethune SD R-5 | 100/PK-12
 PO Box 127 80805 | 719-346-7513
 Don Anderson, supt. | Fax 346-5048
Bethune JSHS, PO Box 127 80805 | 100/7-12
 Don Anderson, prin. | 719-343-7513

Black Hawk, Gilpin, Pop. 110
Gilpin County SD RE-1 | 400/PK-12
 10595 Highway 119 80403 | 303-582-3444
 Ken Ladouceur, supt. | 303 582-3346
 gilpin.k12.co.us
Gilpin County JSHS | 200/7-12
 10595 Highway 119 80403 | 303-582-3444
 Alexis Donaldson, prin. | Fax 582-3346

Blanca, Costilla, Pop. 386
Sierra Grande SD R-30 | 300/PK-12
 17523 E Highway 160 81123 | 719-379-3259
 Robert Rael, supt. | Fax 379-2572
 www.sierragrande.k12.co.us
Sierra Grande HS | 100/9-12
 17523 E Highway 160 81123 | 719-379-3257
 Dennis Lopez, prin. | Fax 379-2572
Sierra Grande JHS | 50/7-8
 17523 E Highway 160 81123 | 719-379-3257
 Dennis Lopez, prin. | Fax 379-2572

Boulder, Boulder, Pop. 93,051
Boulder Valley SD RE-2 | 25,500/PK-12
 PO Box 9011 80301 | 303-447-1010
 Dr. George Garcia, supt. | Fax 447-5024
 www.bvsd.k12.co.us
Arapahoe Ridge HS | 9-12
 6600 Arapahoe Rd 80303 | 303-447-5284
 Dave Krassowski, prin. | Fax 447-5258
Boulder HS | 1,900/9-12
 1604 Arapahoe Ave 80302 | 303-442-2430
 Bud Jenkins, prin. | Fax 447-5317
Boulder Technical Education Center | Vo/Tech
 6600 Arapahoe Rd 80303 | 303-447-5220
 Michael Rask, prin. | Fax 447-5228
Casey MS | 300/6-8
 2410 13th St 80304 | 303-442-5235
 Alison Boggs, prin. | Fax 939-9626
Centennial MS | 600/6-8
 2205 Norwood Ave 80304 | 303-443-3760
 Cheryl Scott, prin. | Fax 443-3761
Fairview HS | 1,900/9-12
 1515 Greenbriar Blvd 80305 | 303-499-7600
 Don Stensrud, prin. | Fax 447-5353
Manhattan S of Arts and Academics | 600/6-8
 290 Manhattan Dr 80303 | 303-494-0335
 Candy Hyatt, prin. | Fax 494-0336
New Vista HS | 300/9-12
 700 20th St 80302 | 303-494-8037
 Rona Wilensky, prin. | Fax 447-5094
Platt MS | 500/6-8
 6096 Baseline Rd 80303 | 303-499-6800
 Alice Lindemann, prin. | Fax 499-0628
Southern Hills MS | 500/6-8
 1500 Knox Dr 80305 | 303-444-2866
 Terry Gillach, prin. | Fax 494-2867
Other Schools – See Broomfield, Lafayette, Louisville, Nederland

Boulder College of Massage Therapy | Post-Sec.
 6255 Longbow Dr 80301 | 303-530-2100
Naropa University | Post-Sec.
 2130 Arapahoe Ave 80302 | 303-444-0202
Rolf Institute of Structural Integration | Post-Sec.
 5055 Chaparral Ct Ste 103 80301 | 303-449-5903
September S | 100/9-12
 1902 Walnut St 80302 | 303-443-9933
Shining Mountain Waldorf S | 300/K-12
 999 Violet Ave 80304 | 303-444-7697
 Robert Schiappacasse, admin. | Fax 444-7701
Tara Performing Arts HS | 50/9-12
 4180 19th St 80304 | 303-440-4510
 Greg Fisher, admin. | Fax 448-0090
University of Colorado 80309 | Post-Sec.
 | 303-492-1411

Branson, Las Animas, Pop. 79
Branson RSD 82 | 50/K-12
 PO Box 128 81027 | 719-946-5531
 Troy Mayfield, supt. | Fax 946-5619
 www.bransonschoolonline.com
Branson JSHS | 50/7-12
 PO Box 128 81027 | 719-946-5531
 | Fax 946-5620

Briggsdale, Weld, Pop. 225
Briggsdale SD RE-10 | 100/K-12
 PO Box 125 80611 | 970-656-3417
 Rick Mondt, supt. | Fax 656-3479
 www.briggsdaleschool.org/
Briggsdale JSHS | 100/7-12
 PO Box 125 80611 | 970-656-3417
 Rick Mondt, prin. | Fax 656-3479

Brighton, Adams, Pop. 25,459
Brighton SD 27J | 6,600/PK-12
 630 S 8th Ave 80601 | 303-655-2900
 Tonda Potts, supt. | Fax 655-2870
 www.brightnps27j.k12.co.us
Brighton HS | 1,700/9-12
 270 S 8th Ave 80601 | 303-655-4200
 Tom Delgado, prin. | Fax 655-2883
Overland Trail MS | 600/6-8
 455 N 19th Ave 80601 | 303-655-4000
 Mary Truax, prin. | Fax 655-2880
Vikan MS | 500/6-8
 879 Jessup St 80601 | 303-655-4050
 Mary Jones, prin. | Fax 655-2881

Brighton Adventist Academy | 100/PK-11
 820 S 5th Ave 80601 | 303-659-1223
 Arthur Leavitt, prin. | Fax 558-8837

Broomfield, Boulder, Pop. 42,169
Boulder Valley SD RE-2
 Supt. — See Boulder

Broomfield Heights MS | 600/6-8
 1555 Daphne St 80020 | 303-466-2387
 Gayle Burke, prin. | Fax 466-2386
Broomfield HS | 1,300/9-12
 1 Eagle Way 80020 | 303-466-7344
 Ginger Ramsey, prin. | Fax 447-5390
Northglenn-Thornton 12 SD
 Supt. — See Thornton
Legacy HS | 1,900/9-12
 2701 W 136th Ave 80020 | 720-972-6700
 Cathy Nolan, prin. | Fax 972-6899
Westlake MS | 1,100/6-8
 2800 W 135th Ave 80020 | 720-972-5200
 Paul Gordon, prin. | Fax 972-5239

Cortiva Institute - Colorado | Post-Sec.
 390 Interlocken Cres # 450 80021 | 303-996-5050
Holy Family HS | 500/9-12
 5195 W 144th Ave 80020 | 303-410-1411
 Sr. Mary Lieb, prin. | Fax 466-1935
Westwood College of Aviation Technology | Post-Sec.
 10851 W 120th Ave 80021 | 800-888-3995

Brush, Morgan, Pop. 5,173
Brush SD RE-2(J) | 1,600/PK-12
 PO Box 585 80723 | 970-842-5176
 Bret Miles, supt. | Fax 842-4481
 www.brushschools.org
Brush HS | 500/9-12
 PO Box 585 80723 | 970-842-5171
 Tom George, prin. | Fax 842-2804
Brush MS | 400/6-8
 PO Box 585 80723 | 970-842-5035
 Ken Miller, prin. | Fax 842-3009

Riverview Christian S | 100/PK-12
 PO Box 665 80723 | 970-842-4604
 Larry French, admin. | Fax 842-4604

Buena Vista, Chaffee, Pop. 2,189
Buena Vista SD R-31 | 900/PK-12
 PO Box 2027 81211 | 719-395-7000
 Dr. Doug Price, supt. | Fax 395-7007
Buena Vista HS | 300/9-12
 PO Box 2027 81211 | 719-395-7100
 Michael Kruger, prin. | Fax 395-7106
McGinnis MS | 200/6-8
 PO Box 2027 81211 | 719-395-7060
 Scott Cope, prin. | Fax 395-7090

Mountain BOCES
 Supt. — See Leadville
Arrowhead Learning Center | 5-9
 PO Box 1199 81211 | 719-395-4675
 | Fax 395-4676

Patterson Christian Academy | 100/PK-12
 PO Box 1243 81211 | 719-395-6046
 Erik Ritschard, admin. | Fax 395-2055

Burlington, Kit Carson, Pop. 3,640
Burlington SD RE-6J | 800/PK-12
 PO Box 369 80807 | 719-346-8737
 Don Davis, supt. | Fax 346-8541
 www.burlingtonk12.org/
Burlington HS | 200/9-12
 380 Mike Lounge Dr 80807 | 719-346-8455
 Duane Arntt, prin. | Fax 346-5599
Burlington MS | 200/5-8
 2600 Rose Ave 80807 | 719-346-5440
 Greg Swiatkowski, prin. | Fax 346-7900

Byers, Arapahoe, Pop. 1,065
Byers SD 32J | 600/PK-12
 444 E Front St 80103 | 303-822-5292
 Tom Turrell, supt. | Fax 822-9592
 www.byers32j.k12.co.us
Byers HS | 200/7-12
 444 E Front St 80103 | 303-822-5292
 Terrell Price, prin. | Fax 822-8616

Calhan, El Paso, Pop. 910
Calhan SD RJ-1 | 600/PK-12
 PO Box 800 80808 | 719-347-2541
 Robert Selle, supt. | Fax 347-2144
Calhan HS | 200/9-12
 PO Box 800 80808 | 719-347-2766
 David MacKenzie, prin. | Fax 347-2108
Calhan MS | 100/6-8
 PO Box 800 80808 | 719-347-2766
 Linda Miller, prin. | Fax 347-2108

Campo, Baca, Pop. 139
Campo SD RE-6 | 100/PK-12
 PO Box 70 81029 | 719-787-2226
 Nikki Johnson, supt. | Fax 787-0140
Campo JSHS | 50/7-12
 PO Box 70 81029 | 719-787-2226
 Sharon Kay Maes, prin. | Fax 787-0140

Canon City, Fremont, Pop. 15,780
Canon City SD Fremont RE-1 | 3,700/K-12
 101 N 14th St 81212 | 719-276-5700
 Dr. Robin Gooldy, supt. | Fax 276-5739
 www.canoncityschools.org/
Canon City HS | 1,300/9-12
 1313 College Ave 81212 | 719-276-5870
 Dr. Cindy Compton, prin. | Fax 276-5950
Canon City MS | 600/7-8
 1215 Main St 81212 | 719-276-5740
 Ken Trujillo, prin. | Fax 276-5795

Colorado Institute of Taxidermy | Post-Sec.
 708 Royal Gorge Blvd 81212 | 719-276-2883

Carbondale, Garfield, Pop. 5,625
Roaring Fork SD RE-1
 Supt. — See Glenwood Springs
Carbondale MS | 300/6-8
 455 S 3rd St 81623 | 970-384-5700
 Cliff Colia, prin. | Fax 384-5705
Roaring Fork HS | 300/9-12
 180 Snowmass Dr 81623 | 970-384-5757
 Dale Parker, prin. | Fax 384-5755

Colorado Rocky Mountain S 200/9-12
1493 County Road 106 81623 970-963-2562
Andrew Menke, prin. Fax 963-9865

Castle Rock, Douglas, Pop. 29,869
Douglas County SD RE-1 40,000/PK-12
620 Wilcox St 80104 303-387-0100
Jim Christensen, supt. Fax 387-0107
www.dcsd.k12.co.us
HS #8 9-12
5254 N Meadows Dr, 303-387-5492
Lisle Gates, prin. Fax 387-5426
Castle Rock MS 1,100/7-8
2575 Meadows Pkwy, 303-387-1300
Terry Olson, prin. Fax 387-1301
Douglas County HS 2,400/9-12
2842 Front St 80104 303-387-1000
Edna Doherty, prin. Fax 387-1001
Other Schools – See Highlands Ranch, Littleton, Parker

Cedaredge, Delta, Pop. 2,042
Delta County SD 50(J)
Supt. — See Delta
Cedaredge HS 300/9-12
575 SE Deer Creek Dr 81413 970-856-6882
Kathy Perkins, prin. Fax 856-6616
Cedaredge MS 200/6-8
845 SE Deer Creek Dr 81413 970-856-3118
Todd Markley, prin. Fax 856-3235

Centennial, Arapahoe, Pop. 98,586
Littleton SD 6
Supt. — See Littleton
Arapahoe HS 2,200/9-12
2201 E Dry Creek Rd 80122 303-347-6000
Ron Booth, prin. Fax 347-6004
Newton MS 800/6-8
4001 E Arapahoe Rd 80122 303-347-7900
Tara Strohm, prin. Fax 347-7930

Jones International University Post-Sec.
9697 E Mineral Ave 80112 303-784-8045

Center, Rio Grande, Pop. 2,491
Center Consolidated SD 26JT 700/PK-12
500 S Broadway 81125 719-754-3442
George Welsh, supt. Fax 754-3952
www.center.k12.co.us
Center HS, 500 S Broadway 81125 200/9-12
Charleen Schaeffer, prin. 719-754-2232
Skoglund MS, 500 S Broadway 81125 200/6-8
Charleen Schaeffer, prin. 719-754-2232

Redeemer Ranch S 50/7-12
7528 County Road 50 81125 719-754-0559
Del Groen, dir.

Cheraw, Otero, Pop. 210
Cheraw SD 31 200/PK-12
PO Box 160 81030 719-853-6655
Rick Lovato, supt. Fax 853-6322
cheraw.k12.co.us
Cheraw HS, PO Box 160 81030 100/9-12
Kenny Bridges, prin. 719-853-6655
Cheraw MS, PO Box 160 81030 100/6-8
Kenny Bridges, prin. 719-853-6655

Cheyenne Wells, Cheyenne, Pop. 926
Cheyenne County SD RE-5 200/PK-8
PO Box 577 80810 719-767-5866
David Marx, supt. Fax 767-8773
www.cheyennesd.net/
Cheyenne Wells MS 100/6-8
PO Box 577 80810 719-767-5656
Laurie Kjosness, prin.

Clifton, Mesa, Pop. 12,671
Mesa County Valley SD 51
Supt. — See Grand Junction
Mt. Garfield MS 600/6-8
3475 Front St 81520 970-464-0533
David Spellman, prin. Fax 464-0536

Collbran, Mesa, Pop. 402
Plateau Valley SD 50 300/PK-12
56600 Highway 330 81624 970-487-3547
Gregory Randall, supt. Fax 487-3876
www.plateauvalley.k12.co.us/
Plateau Valley HS 100/9-12
56600 Highway 330 81624 970-487-3547
Ted Okey, prin. Fax 487-3876
Plateau Valley MS 100/6-8
56600 Highway 330 81624 970-487-3547
Ted Okey, prin. Fax 487-3876

Colorado City, Pueblo, Pop. 1,149
Pueblo County Rural SD 70
Supt. — See Pueblo
Craver MS 200/6-8
PO Box 19369 81019 719-676-3030
Chuck Scott, prin. Fax 676-3511

Colorado Springs, El Paso, Pop. 370,448
Academy SD 20 17,000/PK-12
1110 Chapel Hills Dr 80920 719-234-1200
Dr. Ken Vedra, supt. Fax 234-1299
www.d20.co.edu
Aspen Valley HS 100/9-12
1450 Chapel Hills Dr 80920 719-234-6000
George Stone, prin. Fax 234-6099
Challenger MS 800/6-8
10215 Lexington Dr 80920 719-234-3000
Tony Scott, prin. Fax 234-3199
Eagleview MS 1,100/6-8
1325 Vindicator Dr 80919 719-234-3400
Karon Cofield, prin. Fax 234-3599
Liberty HS 1,400/9-12
8720 Scarborough Dr 80920 719-234-2200
Tom Weston, prin. Fax 234-2399
Mountain Ridge MS 1,200/6-8
9150 Lexington Dr 80920 719-234-3200
Joy Porter, prin. Fax 234-3399
Pine Creek HS 1,300/9-12
10750 Thunder Mountain Ave 80908 719-234-2600
Todd Morse, prin. Fax 234-2799
Rampart HS 1,500/9-12
8250 Lexington Dr 80920 719-234-2000
Gil Bierman, prin. Fax 234-2199
Timberview MS 1,000/6-8
8680 Scarborough Dr 80920 719-234-3600
David Peak, prin. Fax 234-3799
Other Schools – See USAF Academy

Cheyenne Mountain SD 12 4,000/PK-12
1118 W Cheyenne Rd 80906 719-475-6100
Harlan Else, supt. Fax 475-6106
www.cmsd.k12.co.us
Cheyenne Mountain HS 1,400/9-12
1200 Cresta Rd 80906 719-475-6110
Paul Martin, prin. Fax 475-6116
Cheyenne Mountain JHS 700/7-8
1200 W Cheyenne Rd 80906 719-475-6120
Donald Wallace, prin. Fax 475-6123

Colorado Springs SD 11 29,700/PK-12
1115 N El Paso St 80903 719-520-2000
Sharon Thomas Ph.D., supt. Fax 577-4546
www.d11.org/
Coronado HS 1,700/9-12
1590 W Fillmore St 80904 719-328-3600
Susan Humphrey, prin. Fax 328-3601
Doherty HS 2,100/9-12
4515 Barnes Rd 80917 719-328-6400
Jill Martin, prin. Fax 328-6401
East MS 500/6-8
1600 N Union Blvd 80909 719-328-2200
Clay Gomez, prin. Fax 448-0498
Holmes MS 800/6-8
2455 Mesa Rd 80904 719-328-3800
Brenda Lebrasse, prin. Fax 448-0358
Irving MS 900/6-8
1702 N Murray Blvd 80915 719-328-6900
Karen Gidley, prin. Fax 573-5094
Jenkins MS 900/6-8
6410 Austin Bluffs Pkwy 80923 719-328-5300
Ken Potman, prin. Fax 266-5276
Mann MS 700/6-8
1001 E Van Buren St 80907 719-328-2300
Rusty Moomey, prin. Fax 488-0354
Mitchell HS 1,700/9-12
1205 Potter Dr 80909 719-328-6600
Jerry Anderson, prin. Fax 328-6601
North MS 700/6-8
612 E Yampa St 80903 719-328-2400
Martha Crisp, prin. Fax 448-0268
Palmer HS 2,000/9-12
301 N Nevada Ave 80903 719-328-5000
Thomas Kelly, prin. Fax 328-5001
Russell MS 800/6-8
3825 Montebello Dr W 80918 719-328-5200
Jeannice Swift, prin. Fax 531-5520
Sabin MS 700/6-8
3605 N Carefree Cir 80917 719-328-7000
Berry Swenson, prin. Fax 573-4960
Wasson HS 1,600/9-12
2115 Afton Way 80909 719-328-2000
Robert Slauson, prin. Fax 520-2966
West Intergenerational Center MS 500/6-8
1920 W Pikes Peak Ave 80904 719-328-3900
Joe Torrez, prin. Fax 448-0141
Adult Education Center Adult
917 E Moreno Ave 80903 719-328-2975
M. Burkhardt-Shields, prin. Fax 578-8757
Doherty Night S Adult
4515 Barnes Rd 80917 719-328-6441
Carol Salaba, prin. Fax 328-6444
Palmer Night S Adult
301 N Nevada Ave 80903 719-328-5040
Lara Disney, prin. Fax 328-5109

Falcon SD 49
Supt. — See Falcon
Horizon MS 700/6-8
1750 Piros Dr 80915 719-574-7700
Michelle McAteer, prin. Fax 495-5209
Sand Creek HS 1,400/9-12
7005 N Carefree Cir 80922 719-572-0924
Lois Bay, prin. Fax 495-1196
Skyview MS 700/6-8
6350 Windom Peak Blvd 80923 719-638-2736
Sandy Rivera, prin. Fax 495-5591

Hanover SD 28 300/K-12
17050 S Peyton Hwy 80928 719-683-2247
Dr. Henry Roman, supt. Fax 683-4602
Hanover JSHS 100/7-12
17050 S Peyton Hwy 80928 719-683-2247
Mike Moore, prin. Fax 683-3805

Harrison SD 2 9,400/PK-12
1060 Harrison Rd 80906 719-579-2000
Vic Meyers, supt. Fax 579-2019
www.harrison.k12.co.us
Carmel MS 600/6-8
1740 Pepperwood Dr 80910 719-579-3210
Derryck Gowie, prin. Fax 579-2695
Fox Meadow MS 6-8
1450 Cheyenne Meadows Rd 80906 719-527-7100
Chuck Stovall, prin. Fax 527-7174
Harrison HS 1,100/9-12
2755 Janitell Rd 80906 719-579-2080
Cheri Martinez, prin. Fax 579-2454
Panorama MS 800/6-8
2145 S Chelton Rd 80916 719-579-3220
Teresa Newbold, prin. Fax 579-2756
Sierra HS 1,200/9-12
2250 Jet Wing Dr 80916 719-579-2090
Bryan Wright, prin. Fax 579-2536

Widefield SD 3 8,200/PK-12
1820 Main St 80911 719-391-3000
Dr. Mark Hatchell, supt. Fax 390-4372
wsd3.k12.co.us
Mesa Ridge HS 1,200/9-12
6070 Mesa Ridge Pkwy 80911 719-391-3600
Joe Garrett, prin. Fax 390-9697
Sproul JHS 400/7-8
235 Sumac Dr 80911 719-391-3218
Larry Borchik, prin. Fax 392-3459
Watson JHS 400/7-8
136 Fontaine Blvd 80911 719-391-3255
Kirsten Toy, prin. Fax 392-3419
Widefield HS 1,300/9-12
615 Widefield Dr 80911 719-391-3200
Jim Felice, prin. Fax 391-8072
Other Schools – See Fountain

Americana Beauty College II Post-Sec.
3650 Austin Bluff Pky #174 80918 719-598-4188
Blair College Post-Sec.
1815 Jet Wing Dr 80916 719-638-6580
CollegeAmerica - Colorado Springs Post-Sec.
3645 Citadel Dr S 80909 719-637-0600
Colorado College Post-Sec.
14 E Cache La Poudre St 80903 719-389-6000
Colorado Sch. of Professional Psychology Post-Sec.
555 E Pikes Peak Ave # 108 80903 877-442-0505
Colorado School for the Deaf and Blind Post-Sec.
33 N Institute St 80903
Colorado Springs Christian HS 500/9-12
4825 Mallow Rd 80907 719-535-2727
Dr. Roland DeRenzo, supt. Fax 268-2121
Colorado Springs Christian MS 300/6-8
4845 Mallow Rd 80907 719-535-8968
Dr. Roland DeRenzo, supt. Fax 268-2122
Colorado Springs S 600/PK-12
21 Broadmoor Ave 80906 719-475-9747
Charles Landry, prin. Fax 475-9864
Colorado Technical University Post-Sec.
4435 N Chestnut St 80907 719-598-0200
DeVry University Post-Sec.
1175 Kelly Johnson Blvd 80920 719-632-3000
Evangelical Christian Academy 200/7-12
4050 Nonchalant Cir S 80917 719-597-3675
Paul Finch, prin. Fax 597-6983
Fountain Valley S 200/9-12
6155 Fountain Valley School 80911 719-390-7035
John Creeden, hdmstr. Fax 392-6138
Hilltop Baptist S 200/K-12
6915 Palmer Park Blvd 80915 719-597-1880
Carl Adams, prin. Fax 597-8168
IntelliTec College Post-Sec.
2315 E Pikes Peak Ave 80909 719-632-7626
IntelliTec Medical Institute Post-Sec.
2345 N Academy Blvd 80909 719-596-7400
International Beauty Academy Post-Sec.
1360 N Academy Blvd 80909 719-598-4188
Memorial Hospital Post-Sec.
1400 E Boulder St 80909 719-365-5000
National American University Post-Sec.
5125 N Academy Blvd 80918 719-277-0588
Nazarene Bible College Post-Sec.
1111 Academy Park Loop 80910 719-596-5110
Penrose-St. Francis Health System Post-Sec.
2215 N Cascade Ave 80907 719-776-5111
Pikes Peak Christian S 600/PK-12
5905 Flintridge Dr 80918 719-598-8610
Ken Preslar, dir. Fax 598-1491
Pikes Peak Community College Post-Sec.
5675 S Academy Blvd 80906 719-576-7711
Remington College Post-Sec.
6050 Erin Park Dr # 250 80918 719-532-1234
St. Mary HS 400/9-12
2501 E Yampa St 80909 719-635-7540
Patty Beckert, prin. Fax 471-7623
Shepherd of the Springs Lutheran HS 50/7-12
8595 Explorer Dr 80920 719-598-7446
TONI@GUY Hairdressing Academy Post-Sec.
332 Main St 80911 719-390-9898
University of Colorado Post-Sec.
1420 Austin Bluffs Pkwy 80918 719-262-3000

Commerce City, Adams, Pop. 26,228
Adams County SD 14 7,700/PK-12
4720 E 69th Ave 80022 303-853-3333
John Lange, supt. Fax 286-9753
www.acsd14.k12.co.us
Adams City HS 1,500/9-12
4625 E 68th Ave 80022 303-289-3111
Wesley Paxton, prin. Fax 288-6113
Adams City MS 700/6-8
4451 E 72nd Ave 80022 303-289-5881
Philip Sorensen, prin. Fax 288-8574
Arnold JSHS 800/7-12
6500 E 72nd Ave 80022 303-289-2983
Allan Hollenbeck, prin. Fax 289-7167
Kearney MS 800/6-8
6160 Kearney St 80022 303-287-0261
Sophia Masewicz, prin. Fax 287-0432

Conifer, Jefferson, Pop. 600
Jefferson County SD R-1
Supt. — See Golden
Conifer HS 1,000/9-12
10441 Highway 73 80433 303-982-5255
Cynthia Whitlock, prin. Fax 982-5256
West Jefferson MS 700/6-8
9449 Barnes Ave 80433 303-982-3056
Jean Kelley, prin. Fax 982-3057

Cortez, Montezuma, Pop. 8,181
Montezuma-Cortez SD RE-1 3,100/K-12
PO Box R 81321 970-565-7282
Stacy Houser, supt. Fax 565-2161
www.cortez.k12.co.us
Cortez MS 700/6-8
450 W 2nd St 81321 970-565-7824
Jamie Haukeness, prin. Fax 565-5120
Montezuma-Cortez HS 900/9-12
206 W 7th St 81321 970-565-3722
Ember Conley, prin. Fax 565-5118

Southwest BOCES
PO Box 1420 81321 970-565-8411
Victor Bruce, dir. Fax 565-1203
Adult Education Program Adult
PO Box 1420 81321 970-565-8411

San Juan Basin Technical College Post-Sec.
PO Box 970 81321 970-565-8457

Cotopaxi, Fremont, Pop. 130
Cotopaxi SD RE-3 300/PK-12
345 County Road 12 81223 719-942-4131
Geoffrey Gerk, supt. Fax 942-4134
cotopaxire3.org/
Cotopaxi JSHS 200/7-12
345 County Road 12 81223 719-942-4131
Peggy Murphy-Gerk, prin. Fax 942-4134

Craig, Moffat, Pop. 9,282
Moffat County SD RE-1 2,400/K-12
775 Yampa Ave 81625 970-824-3268
Pete Bergmann, supt. Fax 824-6655
moffatsd.org/

Craig MS 400/7-8
915 Yampa Ave 81625 970-824-3289
Bill Toovey, prin. Fax 824-3858
Moffat County HS 700/9-12
900 Finley Ln 81625 970-824-7036
Jane Krogman, prin. Fax 824-3130

Creede, Mineral, Pop. 397
Creede Consolidated SD 1 200/PK-12
PO Box 429 81130 719-658-2220
Buck Stroh, supt. Fax 658-2942
www.creedek12.net
Creede JSHS 100/7-12
PO Box 429 81130 719-658-2220
John Goss, prin. Fax 658-2942

Crested Butte, Gunnison, Pop. 1,505
Gunnison Watershed SD RE 1J
Supt. — See Gunnison
Crested Butte S 400/K-12
PO Box 339 81224 970-641-7720
Stephanie Niemi, prin. Fax 641-7729

Crested Butte Academy 50/9-12
PO Box 1180 81224 970-349-1805
Mark White, dean Fax 349-0997

Cripple Creek, Teller, Pop. 1,084
Cripple Creek-Victor SD RE-1 600/PK-12
PO Box 897 80813 719-689-2685
Guy F. Arseneau, supt. Fax 689-2256
www.ccvschools.com
Cripple Creek-Victor JSHS 300/7-12
PO Box 897 80813 719-689-2661
Joan Rook, prin. Fax 389-2256

De Beque, Mesa, Pop. 469
De Beque SD 49JT 200/PK-12
PO Box 70 81630 970-283-5418
Mike Henwood, supt. Fax 283-5213
www.debeque.k12.co.us
De Beque JSHS 100/7-12
PO Box 70 81630 970-283-5596
Sue Taylor, prin. Fax 283-5598

Deer Trail, Arapahoe, Pop. 589
Deer Trail SD 26J 200/PK-12
PO Box 129 80105 303-769-4421
Dr. Jerre Doss, supt. Fax 769-4600
deertrail26j.k12.co.us
Deer Trail JSHS 100/6-12
PO Box 129 80105 303-769-4421
Mary J. Lynch, prin. Fax 769-4600

Del Norte, Rio Grande, Pop. 1,625
Del Norte SD C-7 700/K-12
PO Box 159 81132 719-657-4040
Michael Salvato, supt. Fax 657-2546
www.del-norte.k12.co.us/
Del Norte HS 200/9-12
PO Box 159 81132 719-657-4030
Ernie Rivale, prin. Fax 657-4024
Del Norte MS 200/6-8
PO Box 159 81132 719-657-4050
Nathan Smith, prin. Fax 657-0329

Delta, Delta, Pop. 7,788
Delta County SD 50(J) 5,000/K-12
7655 2075 Rd 81416 970-874-4438
Mike McMillan, supt. Fax 874-5744
www.deltaschools.com
Delta HS 600/9-12
1400 Pioneer Rd 81416 970-874-8031
Delaine Hudson, prin. Fax 874-8034
Delta MS 500/6-8
910 Grand Ave 81416 970-874-8046
Kurt Clay, prin. Fax 874-8049
Other Schools – See Cedaredge, Hotchkiss, Paonia

Denver, Denver, Pop. 557,478
Adams County SD 50
Supt. — See Westminster
Carpenter MS 600/6-8
7001 Lipan St 80221 303-428-8583
Patrick Sanchez, prin. Fax 657-3962
Clear Lake MS 600/6-8
1940 Elmwood Ln 80221 303-428-7526
B.J. Buchmann, prin. Fax 430-6465
Hodgkins MS 600/6-8
3475 W 67th Ave 80221 303-428-7503
Carol Peters, prin. Fax 657-3943
Ranum HS 1,500/9-12
2401 W 80th Ave 80221 303-428-9577
Kircher Leday, prin. Fax 657-3952

Denver County SD 1 67,500/PK-12
900 Grant St 80203 720-423-3200
Michael Bennet, supt. Fax 423-3413
www.dpsk12.org/
CEC Middle College of Denver Vo/Tech
2650 Eliot St 80211 720-423-6600
Scott Springer, prin. Fax 423-6604
Denver S of the Arts 800/6-12
7111 Montview Blvd 80220 720-424-1700
Patricia Bippus, prin. Fax 424-1845
East HS 1,900/9-12
1545 Detroit St 80206 720-423-8300
Kathy Callum, prin. Fax 423-8306
Grant MS 400/6-8
1751 S Washington St 80210 720-423-9360
Ricardo Concha, prin. Fax 423-9385
Griffith Opportunity S Vo/Tech
1250 Welton St 80204 720-423-4700
Les Lindauer, dir. Fax 423-4840
Hamilton MS 1,000/6-8
8600 E Dartmouth Ave 80231 720-423-9500
Reina Gutierrez, prin. Fax 423-9445
Henry MS 800/6-8
3005 S Golden Way 80227 720-423-9560
Wendy Lanier, prin. Fax 424-9585
Hill MS 700/6-8
451 Clermont St 80220 720-423-9680
Don Roy, prin. Fax 423-9705
Jefferson HS 1,100/9-12
3950 S Holly St 80237 303-691-7000
Sandra Just, prin. Fax 423-7058
Kennedy HS 1,600/9-12
2855 S Lamar St 80227 720-423-4300
Jeannie Peppel, prin. Fax 423-4309
Kepner MS 1,100/6-8
911 S Hazel Ct 80219 720-424-0000
Deborah Lanman, prin. Fax 424-0023
King MS 1,200/6-8
19535 E 46th Ave 80249 720-424-0042
Michael Gaither, prin. Fax 424-0557
Kunsmiller MS 900/6-8
2250 S Quitman Way 80219 720-424-0200
Miguel Salazar, prin. Fax 424-0145
Lake MS 800/6-8
1820 Lowell Blvd 80204 720-424-0260
Dave Debus, prin. Fax 424-0294
Lincoln HS 1,400/9-12
2285 S Federal Blvd 80219 720-423-5000
Scott Mendelsberg, prin. Fax 423-5098
Mann MS 600/6-8
4130 Navajo St 80211 720-423-9800
Linda Torres, prin. Fax 423-9850
Manual Arts & Cultural HS 400/9-12
1700 E 28th Ave 80205 720-423-6330
Phillip Gallegos, prin. Fax 423-6302
Manual Leadership HS 300/9-12
1700 E 28th Ave 80205 720-423-6350
Marsha Pointer, prin. Fax 423-6463
Manual Millenium Quest HS 300/9-12
1700 E 28th Ave 80205 720-423-6348
Ethan Dalton, prin. Fax 423-6433
Merrill MS 700/6-8
1551 S Monroe St 80210 720-424-0600
Ann Greenfield, prin. Fax 424-0625
Montbello HS 1,400/9-12
5000 Crown Blvd 80239 720-423-5700
Antwan Wilson, prin. Fax 423-5801
Morey MS 600/6-8
840 E 14th Ave 80218 720-424-0700
Doris Claunch, prin. Fax 424-0727
Noel MS 900/6-8
5290 Kittredge St 80239 720-424-0800
Patricia Slaughter, prin. Fax 424-0945
North HS 1,500/9-12
2960 N Speer Blvd 80211 720-423-2700
Darlene LeDoux, prin. Fax 423-2708
Place MS 600/6-8
7125 Cherry Creek North Dr 80224 720-424-0960
Keith Mills, prin. Fax 424-0985
Randolph MS 700/6-8
3955 Steele St 80205 720-424-1080
Bruce Randolph, prin. Fax 424-1241
Rishel MS 900/6-8
451 S Tejon St 80223 720-424-1260
Sylvia Bookhardt, prin. Fax 424-1350
Skinner MS 700/6-8
3435 W 40th Ave 80211 720-424-1420
Pat Sandos, prin. Fax 424-1446
Smiley MS 500/6-8
2540 Holly St 80207 720-424-1540
Nathaniel Howard, prin. Fax 424-1565
South HS 1,400/9-12
1700 E Louisiana Ave 80210 720-423-6000
William Kohut, prin. Fax 423-6280
Washington HS 1,600/9-12
655 S Monaco Pkwy 80224 720-423-8600
Mario Williams, prin. Fax 423-8614
West HS 1,700/9-12
951 Elati St 80204 720-423-5300
Angie Bodenhamer, prin. Fax 423-5410

Jefferson County SD R-1
Supt. — See Golden
D'Evelyn JSHS 1,400/7-12
10359 W Nassau Ave 80235 303-982-2600
Mark Hartshorne, prin. Fax 982-2601

Mapleton SD 1 12,100/PK-12
591 E 80th Ave 80229 303-853-1000
Charlotte Ciancio, supt. Fax 853-1087
www.mapleton.us
Global Leadership Academy 2,100/6-12
7480 Conifer Rd 80221 303-853-1930
Elaine Curcurio, prin.
Mapleton Early College HS 9-12
601 E 64th Ave 80229 303-853-1960
Jeff Park, dir.
Mapleton Preparatory HS 1,500/9-12
601 E 64th Ave 80229 303-853-1960
Mari Ruddy, dir.
Welby New Technology HS 1,500/9-12
1200 E 78th Ave 80229 303-853-1660
Matt Flores, dir. Fax 853-1670
York International S 2,600/K-12
9200 York St 80229 303-853-1600
Paul Frank, dir. Fax 853-1656
Other Schools – See Thornton

Northglenn-Thornton 12 SD
Supt. — See Thornton
Niver Creek MS 900/6-8
9450 Pecos St 80260 720-972-5120
Jacque Kerr, prin. Fax 972-5159

Accelerated Schools Foundation 200/K-12
2160 S Cook St 80210 303-758-2003
Fax 757-4336
American University of Paris Post-Sec.
950 S Cherry St Ste 210 80246 303-757-6333
Arrupe Jesuit HS 100/9-12
4343 Utica St 80212 303-455-7449
Michael O'Hagan, prin. Fax 455-7453
Art Institute of Colorado Post-Sec.
1200 Lincoln St 80203 800-275-2420
Aspen University Post-Sec.
501 S Cherry St Ste 350 80246 800-441-4746
Bel-Rea Institute of Animal Technology Post-Sec.
1681 S Dayton St, 303-751-8700
Beth Jacob HS of Denver 100/9-12
5100 W 14th Ave 80204 303-893-1333
Esther Melamid, prin. Fax 573-4932
Bishop Machebeuf Catholic HS 500/9-12
458 Uinta Way 80230 303-344-0082
Lisa Switzer, prin. Fax 344-1582
Centura-St. Anthony Hospital Post-Sec.
4231 W 16th Ave 80204 303-629-4350
CHANGE Christian Academy 100/PK-12
12505 Elmendorf Pl 80239 303-373-5200
Evelyn Bryant, dir. Fax 373-1908
CollegeAmerica - Colorado Post-Sec.
1385 S Colorado Blvd Fl 5 80222 303-691-9756
Colorado Academy 900/PK-12
3800 S Pierce St 80235 303-986-1501
Christopher Babbs, hdmstr. Fax 914-2583
Colorado Christian S 200/PK-12
200 S University Blvd 80209 303-777-7723
Christine Sadozai, dir. Fax 765-2642
Colorado Ctr for Medical Laboratory Sci. Post-Sec.
1719 E 19th Ave 80218 303-839-6485
CO Sch of Traditional Chinese Medicine Post-Sec.
1441 York St Ste 202 80206 303-329-6355
Community College of Denver Post-Sec.
PO Box 173363 80217 303-556-2600
Denver Automotive & Diesel College Post-Sec.
PO Box 9366 80209 303-722-5724
Denver Campus for Jewish Education 400/K-12
2450 S Wabash St 80231 303-755-1846
Fax 755-3614
Denver Christian HS 400/9-12
2135 S Pearl St 80210 303-733-2421
Mark Swalley, prin. Fax 733-7734
Denver Health Medical Center Post-Sec.
660 Bannock St 80204 303-436-6611
Denver Lutheran HS 200/9-12
3201 W Arizona Ave 80219 303-934-2345
Loren Otte, prin. Fax 934-0455
Denver Waldorf S 300/PK-12
940 Fillmore St 80206 303-777-0531
Judy Lucas, prin. Fax 744-1216
Emily Griffith Opportunity School Post-Sec.
1250 Welton St 80204 720-423-4700
Heritage College Post-Sec.
12 Lakeside Ln 80212 303-477-7240
Iliff School of Theology Post-Sec.
2201 S University Blvd 80210 303-744-1287
Johnson & Wales University Post-Sec.
7150 Montview Blvd 80220 303-256-9300
Metropolitan State College Post-Sec.
PO Box 173362 80217 303-556-3018
Mile High Adventist Academy 200/PK-12
711 E Yale Ave 80210 303-744-0812
Dennis Dickerson, prin. Fax 744-1060
Mullen HS 1,000/9-12
3601 S Lowell Blvd 80236 303-761-1764
Linda Brady, prin. Fax 761-0502
National American University Post-Sec.
1325 S Colorado Blvd #100 80222 303-758-6700
National Theatre Conservatory Post-Sec.
1050 13th St 80204 303-446-4855
Parks College Post-Sec.
9065 Grant St 80229 303-457-2757
Phlebotomy Learning Center Post-Sec.
1780 S Bellaire St Ste 780 80222 303-584-0575
Pima Medical Institute Post-Sec.
1701 W 72nd Ave Ste 130 80221 303-426-1800
Regis University Post-Sec.
3333 Regis Blvd 80221 303-458-4100
Teikyo Loretto Heights University Post-Sec.
3001 S Federal Blvd 80236 303-936-8441
University of Colorado at Denver Post-Sec.
PO Box 173364 80217 303-556-2400
University of Colorado Health Sciences Post-Sec.
4200 E 9th Ave Box C245 80262 303-372-0000
University of Denver Post-Sec.
2199 S University Blvd 80208 303-871-2000
University of Denver University College Post-Sec.
2211 S Josephine St 80208 303-871-3354
Westwood College - Denver North Post-Sec.
7350 Broadway 80221 303-426-7000
Westwood College - Denver South Post-Sec.
3150 S Sheridan Blvd 80227 303-934-2790
Yeshiva Toras Chaim 100/9-12
PO Box 40067 80204 303-629-8200
Dr. Daniel Peckman, prin. Fax 623-5949
Yeshiva Toras Chaim Talmudic Seminary Post-Sec.
1555 Stuart St 80204 303-629-8200

Dolores, Montezuma, Pop. 848
Dolores SD RE-4A 800/PK-12
17631 Highway 145 81323 970-882-7255
Larry Archibeque, supt. Fax 882-7685
www.dolores.k12.co.us
Dolores HS 200/9-12
17631 Highway 145 81323 970-882-7288
Laura Harper, prin. Fax 882-7289
Dolores MS 200/6-8
17631 Highway 145 81323 970-882-7288
Laura Harper, prin. Fax 882-7289

Dove Creek, Dolores, Pop. 693
Dolores County SD RE 2J 300/PK-12
PO Box 459 81324 970-677-2522
Steve Strong, supt. Fax 677-2712
www.dolorescounty.k12.co.us
Dove Creek HS 100/7-12
PO Box 459 81324 970-677-2237
Stephen Baroch, prin. Fax 677-2927

Durango, LaPlata, Pop. 14,741
Durango SD 9-R 4,500/PK-12
201 E 12th St 81301 970-247-5411
Dr. Mary Barter, supt. Fax 247-9581
www.durango.k12.co.us
Durango HS 1,500/9-12
2390 Main Ave 81301 970-259-1630
Greg Spradling, prin. Fax 385-1493
Escalante MS 500/6-8
141 Baker Ln 81303 970-247-9490
Amy Kendziorski, prin. Fax 385-1194
Miller MS 500/6-8
2608 Junction St 81301 970-247-1418
Bruce Hanson, prin. Fax 385-1191

Colorado Timberline Academy 50/9-12
35554 Highway 550 81301 970-247-5898
Durango Air Service Post-Sec.
1340 Airport Rd 81303 970-247-5535
Fort Lewis College Post-Sec.
1000 Rim Dr 81301 970-247-7010
Grace Preparatory Academy of Durango 50/K-12
PO Box 3777 81302 970-759-9677
Catherine Spriggs, admin.

Eads, Kiowa, Pop. 664
Kiowa County SD RE-1 200/PK-12
210 W 10th St 81036 719-438-2218
Glenn Smith, supt. Fax 438-2272
www.eadseagles.com

Eads HS   100/9-12
210 W 10th St 81036   719-438-2214
Glenn Smith, prin.   Fax 438-2272
Eads JHS   50/6-8
900 Maine St 81036   719-438-2216
Glenn Smith, prin.   Fax 438-2090

Eagle, Eagle, Pop. 3,508
Eagle County SD RE-50J   4,800/PK-12
PO Box 740 81631   970-328-6321
John Brendza, supt.   Fax 328-1024
www.eagleschools.net
Battle Mountains HS   700/9-12
750 Eagle Rd 81631   970-328-2930
Brian Hester, prin.   Fax 949-1550
Eagle Valley MS   300/6-8
PO Box 1019 81631   970-328-6224
Jerry Santoro, prin.   Fax 328-6430
Red Canyon HS   100/9-12
PO Box 4807 81631   970-926-8107
Wade Hill, prin.   Fax 926-8133
Other Schools – See Edwards, Gypsum, Minturn

Eaton, Weld, Pop. 3,652
Eaton SD RE-2   1,600/K-12
200 Park Ave 80615   970-454-3402
John Nuspl, supt.   Fax 454-5193
www.eaton.k12.co.us
Eaton HS   400/9-12
114 Park Ave 80615   970-454-3374
Mark Naill, prin.   Fax 454-5190
Eaton MS   400/6-8
225 Juniper Ave 80615   970-454-3358
Camille Agone, prin.   Fax 454-1337

Edgewater, Jefferson, Pop. 5,356
Jefferson County SD R-1
Supt. — See Golden
Jefferson HS   700/9-12
2305 Pierce St 80214   303-982-6056
Jose Martinez, prin.   Fax 982-6057

Edwards, Eagle, Pop. 500
Eagle County SD RE-50J
Supt. — See Eagle
Berry Creek MS   300/6-8
PO Box 1416 81632   970-328-2960
Robert Cuevas, prin.   Fax 926-4137

Vail Christian HS   100/9-12
PO Box 2023 81632   970-926-3015
Gene Hagerman, hdmstr.   Fax 926-5682

Elbert, Elbert, Pop. 150
Elbert SD 200   300/PK-12
PO Box 38 80106   303-648-3030
Kelli Loflin, supt.   Fax 648-3652
elbertschool.org
Elbert JSHS   100/7-12
PO Box 38 80106   303-648-3030
Bob Beebe, prin.   Fax 648-3652

Elizabeth, Elbert, Pop. 1,520
Elizabeth SD C-1   2,500/PK-12
PO Box 610 80107   303-646-4441
Rod Blunck, supt.   Fax 646-3362
elizabeth.k12.co.us/
Elizabeth HS   800/9-12
PO Box 660 80107   303-646-4616
Jim Trevino, prin.   Fax 646-6030
Elizabeth MS   600/6-8
PO Box 369 80107   303-646-4520
Robert McMullen, prin.   Fax 646-0980
Frontier HS   100/9-12
PO Box 610 80107   303-646-1798
Robin Gaffney, prin.   Fax 646-1329

Ellicott, El Paso
Ellicott SD 22   900/K-12
395 S Ellicott Hwy 80808   719-683-2700
Terry Ebert, supt.   Fax 683-4442
www.ellicottschools.org
Ellicott HS   300/9-12
375 S Ellicott Hwy 80808   719-683-2700
Steve Oberg, prin.   Fax 683-2705
Ellicott MS   300/5-8
350 S Ellicott Hwy 80808   719-683-2700
Chris Smith, prin.   Fax 683-5430

Englewood, Arapahoe, Pop. 32,762
Cherry Creek SD 5
Supt. — See Greenwood Village
Campus MS   1,400/6-8
4785 S Dayton St 80111   720-554-2700
Donna McCarl, prin.   Fax 554-2782
Career & Technical Education   Vo/Tech
9150 E Union Ave 80111   720-554-4553
   Fax 554-4531
Cherry Creek HS   3,500/9-12
9300 E Union Ave 80111   720-554-2000
Dr. Kathleen Smith, prin.   Fax 554-2239

Englewood SD 1   3,400/PK-12
4101 S Bannock St 80110   303-761-7050
Larry Nisbet, supt.   Fax 806-2064
www.englewood.k12.co.us
Englewood HS   1,000/9-12
3800 S Logan St,   303-806-2266
Robert Barrows, prin.   Fax 806-2298
Flood MS   400/6-8
3695 S Lincoln St,   303-761-1226
Mandy Braun, prin.   Fax 806-2199
Sinclair MS   300/6-8
300 W Chenango Ave 80110   303-781-7817
Randy Johnson, prin.   Fax 806-2399

Columbia HealthOne   Post-Sec.
501 E Hampden Ave,   303-788-6484
Kent Denver S   700/6-12
4000 E Quincy Ave,   303-770-7660
Todd Horn, prin.   Fax 770-7137
Misers Inspection and Training   Post-Sec.
2401 S Raritan St 80110   303-761-8860
Misers Inspection and Training   Post-Sec.
1825 W Baker Ave 80110   303-922-8821
St. Mary's Academy   200/6-12
4545 S University Blvd,   303-762-8300
   Fax 783-6201

St. Mary's Academy   300/9-12
4545 S University Blvd,   303-762-8300
Kathryn McNamee, prin.   Fax 783-6201
Tri-County Health Nutrition Services   Post-Sec.
7000 E Blleview Ave #301 80111   303-220-9200

Erie, Weld, Pop. 8,904
St. Vrain Valley SD RE-1J
Supt. — See Longmont
Erie HS   300/9-12
3180 County Road 5 80516   303-828-4213
Steven Payne, prin.   Fax 494-3873
Erie MS   6-8
650 Main St 80516   303-828-3391
Ella Padilla, prin.   Fax 828-3817

Vista Ridge Academy   100/K-10
3100 Ridgeview Dr 80516   303-828-4944
Carol Schneider, prin.   Fax 828-1525

Estes Park, Larimer, Pop. 5,655
Park SD R-3   1,400/PK-12
1701 Brodie Ave 80517   970-586-2361
Linda Chapman, supt.   Fax 586-1108
www.estesschools.org/
Estes Park HS   400/9-12
1600 Manford Ave 80517   970-586-5321
Diane Rastatter, prin.   Fax 586-1102
Estes Park MS   300/6-8
1500 Manford Ave 80517   970-586-4439
Micheal Jobman, prin.   Fax 586-1100

Eagle Rock S   100/9-12
PO Box 1770 80517   970-586-0600
Robert Burkhardt, hdmstr.   Fax 586-4805

Evergreen, Jefferson, Pop. 7,582
Clear Creek SD RE-1
Supt. — See Idaho Springs
Clear Creek HS   300/9-12
185 Beaver Brook Canyon Rd 80439   303-679-4600
Frank Reeves, prin.   Fax 679-4603

Jefferson County SD R-1
Supt. — See Golden
Evergreen HS   900/9-12
29300 Buffalo Park Rd 80439   303-982-5140
Jane Sutera, prin.   Fax 982-5141
Evergreen MS   700/6-8
2059 Hiwan Dr 80439   303-982-5020
Roslin Marshall, prin.   Fax 982-5021

Fairplay, Park, Pop. 674
Park County SD RE-2   500/PK-12
PO Box 189 80440   719-836-3114
Charles Soper, supt.   Fax 836-2275
www.parkcountyschools.org
Silverheels MS   100/6-8
PO Box 189 80440   719-836-4406
Jane Newman, prin.   Fax 836-2275
South Park HS   100/9-12
PO Box 189 80440   719-836-2007
Jane Newman, prin.   Fax 836-2275

Falcon, El Paso, Pop. 200
Falcon SD 49   8,800/K-12
10850 E Woodmen Rd 80831   719-495-3601
Steven Hull Ph.D., supt.   Fax 495-0832
www.d49.org
Falcon HS   800/9-12
9755 Towner Ave 80831   719-495-2261
Beverly Ray, prin.   Fax 495-2264
Falcon MS   500/7-8
11990 Swingline Rd 80831   719-495-3661
Bill Noxon, prin.   Fax 495-5237
Other Schools – See Colorado Springs

Federal Heights, Adams, Pop. 11,850

Cornerstone Christian Academy   100/K-12
2300 W 90th Ave 80260   303-451-1421
Larry Zimbelman, admin.   Fax 280-0361

Flagler, Kit Carson, Pop. 612
Arriba-Flagler SD C-20   300/PK-12
PO Box 218 80815   719-765-4684
Mark Ricken, supt.   Fax 765-4418
www.arriba-flaglercsd20.net
Flagler MSHS, PO Box 218 80815   100/5-12
Tom Arensdorf, prin.   719-765-4684

Fleming, Logan, Pop. 451
Frenchman SD RE-3   200/PK-12
506 N Fremont Ave 80728   970-265-2111
John Condie, supt.   Fax 265-2815
www.flemingschools.org
Fleming HS   100/9-12
506 N Fremont Ave 80728   970-265-2022
Joseph Skerjanec, prin.   Fax 265-2029

Florence, Fremont, Pop. 3,705
Florence RE-2 SD   1,800/K-12
403 W 5th St 81226   719-784-6312
John Merriam, supt.   Fax 784-4140
www.re-2.org/
Florence HS   600/9-12
215 Maple St 81226   719-784-6414
Jim Lucas, prin.   Fax 784-3821
Fremont MS   400/5-8
500 W 5th St 81226   719-784-4856
Gary Strubel, prin.   Fax 784-4060
Other Schools – See Penrose

Florence Christian S   50/PK-12
303 E 3rd St 81226   719-784-6352
Dr. Howard Glen, admin.

Fort Carson, El Paso, Pop. 11,309
Fountain SD 8
Supt. — See Fountain
Carson MS   500/6-8
6200 Prussman Blvd 80913   719-382-1610
Steve Jerman, prin.   Fax 382-8526

Fort Collins, Larimer, Pop. 125,740
Poudre SD R-1   23,000/PK-12
2407 La Porte Ave 80521   970-490-3604
Dr. Jerry Wilson, supt.   Fax 490-3514
www.psd.k12.co.us
Blevins JHS   600/7-9
2101 S Taft Hill Rd 80526   970-488-4000
David Linehan, prin.   Fax 488-4011
Boltz JHS   900/7-9
720 Boltz Dr 80525   970-472-3700
Dana Calkins, prin.   Fax 472-3730
Fort Collins SHS   1,600/10-12
3400 Lambkin Way 80525   970-488-8021
Mark Eversole, prin.   Fax 488-8008
Fossil Ridge HS   10-12
5400 Ziegler Rd 80528   970-488-6260
Dierdre Cook, prin.   Fax 488-6263
Kinard Core Knowledge JHS   7-9
5400 Ziegler Rd 80528   970-472-3933
Joe Cuddemi, prin.   Fax 472-3930
Lesher JHS   600/7-9
1400 Stover St 80524   970-472-3800
Edwin Ginty, prin.   Fax 472-3880
Lincoln JHS   700/7-9
1600 Lancer Dr 80521   970-484-3073
Lou Marchesano, prin.   Fax 484-9462
Poudre SHS   1,700/10-12
201 S Impala Dr 80521   970-488-6011
Sandra Lundt, prin.   Fax 488-6060
Preston JHS   1,000/7-9
4901 Corbett Dr 80528   970-419-7300
Richard Ramirez, prin.   Fax 419-7307
Rocky Mountain SHS   1,800/10-12
1300 W Swallow Rd 80526   970-488-7023
Tom Lopez, prin.   Fax 488-7001
Webber JHS   900/7-9
4201 Seneca St 80526   970-488-7800
Sandra Bickel, prin.   Fax 488-7811
Other Schools – See Laporte, Wellington

Cheeks Intl Academy of Beauty Culture   Post-Sec.
4025 S Mason St # 5 80525   970-226-1416
CollegeAmerica - Fort Collins   Post-Sec.
4601 S Mason St 80525   970-223-6060
Colorado State University   Post-Sec.
102 Administration 80523   970-491-1101
Front Range Baptist Academy   100/PK-12
625 E Harmony Rd 80525   970-223-2173
Jamison Coppola, prin.   Fax 223-5826
Front Range Community College   Post-Sec.
4616 S Shields St 80526   970-226-2500
Hair Dynamics Education Center   Post-Sec.
6464 S College Ave 80525   970-223-9943
Heritage Christian S   300/PK-12
4800 Wheaton Dr 80525   970-482-0868
George Cuff, admin.   Fax 482-1501
Institute of Business & Medical Careers   Post-Sec.
1609 Oakridge Dr Ste 102 80525   970-223-2669
Weston Distance Learning   Post-Sec.
2001 Lowe St 80525   800-347-7899

Fort Lupton, Weld, Pop. 7,071
Weld County SD RE-8   2,600/PK-12
301 Reynolds St 80621   303-857-3200
Mark Payler, supt.   Fax 857-3219
www.ftlupton.k12.co.us
Fort Lupton HS   700/9-12
530 Reynolds St 80621   303-857-7100
Michael Campbell, prin.   Fax 857-7179
Fort Lupton MS   600/6-8
201 S McKinley Ave 80621   303-857-7200
Carey Sanchez, prin.   Fax 857-7287

Fort Morgan, Morgan, Pop. 10,995
Ft. Morgan SD RE-3   3,300/PK-12
715 W Platte Ave 80701   970-867-5633
Dr. Daniel Patterson, supt.   Fax 867-0262
www.morgan.k12.co.us
Fort Morgan HS   800/9-12
709 E Riverview Ave 80701   970-867-5648
Ed Raines, prin.   Fax 867-3347
Fort Morgan MS   500/7-8
300 Deuel St 80701   970-867-8253
Patrick Haley, prin.   Fax 867-4876
Lincoln HS   50/9-12
900 State St 80701   970-867-2924
Stan Bills, prin.   Fax 867-4958

Morgan Community College   Post-Sec.
17800 County Road 20 80701   970-542-3100

Fountain, El Paso, Pop. 15,709
Fountain SD 8   5,800/PK-12
425 W Alabama Ave 80817   719-382-1300
Dwight Jones, supt.   Fax 382-7338
www.ffc8.org
Fountain-Fort Carson HS   1,200/9-12
900 Jimmy Camp Rd 80817   719-382-1640
James Calhoun, prin.   Fax 382-3228
Fountain MS   800/6-8
515 N Santa Fe Ave 80817   719-382-1580
Debra Keiley, prin.   Fax 382-9065
Other Schools – See Fort Carson

Widefield SD 3
Supt. — See Colorado Springs
Janitell JHS   500/7-8
7635 Fountain Mesa Rd 80817   719-391-3295
Aaron Hoffman, prin.   Fax 390-7869

Fowler, Otero, Pop. 1,156
Fowler SD R-4J   400/K-12
PO Box 218 81039   719-263-4224
Larry Vibber, supt.   Fax 263-4625
www.fowler.k12.co.us/
Fowler HS   100/9-12
PO Box 218 81039   719-263-4279
Willis Lowther, prin.   Fax 263-4625
Fowler JHS   50/7-8
PO Box 218 81039   719-263-4224
Willis Lowther, prin.   Fax 263-4625

Franktown, Douglas, Pop. 350

Brookstone Christian Academy   100/K-12
389 Castlewood Canyon Rd 80116   303-841-1370
Debbie Winegar, prin.   Fax 841-1145

Frederick, Weld, Pop. 5,273
St. Vrain Valley SD RE-1J
  Supt. — See Longmont
Frederick HS   600/9-12
  600 5th St 80530 303-833-3533
  Jim Sundberg, prin. Fax 833-4664

Frisco, Summit, Pop. 2,490
Summit SD RE-1 2,800/PK-12
  PO Box 7 80443 970-668-3011
  Dr. Millie Hamner, supt. Fax 668-0361
  summit.k12.co.us
Summit HS 800/9-12
  PO Box 7 80443 970-547-9311
  Jim Hesse, prin. Fax 547-1061
Summit MS 700/6-8
  PO Box 7 80443 970-668-5037
  Iva Katz-Hesse, prin. Fax 668-5038

Summit County Christian S 100/PK-12
  PO Box 1130 80443 970-668-2173
  Connie Moody, admin. Fax 668-1198

Fruita, Mesa, Pop. 6,751
Mesa County Valley SD 51
  Supt. — See Grand Junction
Fruita MS 700/6-8
  239 N Maple St 81521 970-254-6570
  Ken Haptonstall, prin. Fax 858-0486
Fruita Monument HS 1,700/9-12
  1815 Wildcat Ave 81521 970-254-6600
  John Vail, prin. Fax 254-6668

Gilcrest, Weld, Pop. 1,159
Weld County SD RE-1 2,000/PK-12
  PO Box 157 80623 970-737-2403
  Jo Barbie, supt. Fax 737-2516
  www.weld-re1.k12.co.us
Valley HS 600/9-12
  PO Box 156 80623 970-737-2494
  Ben Rainbolt, prin. Fax 737-2203
Other Schools – See La Salle, Platteville

Glenwood Springs, Garfield, Pop. 8,333
Roaring Fork SD RE-1 4,700/PK-12
  1405 Grand Ave 81601 970-384-6000
  Judy Haptonstall, supt. Fax 384-6005
  www.rfsd.k12.co.us
Glenwood Springs HS 700/9-12
  1340 Pitkin Ave 81601 970-384-5555
  Paul Freeman, prin. Fax 384-5556
Glenwood Springs MS 400/6-8
  120 Soccer Field Rd 81601 970-384-5500
  Robert Farris, prin. Fax 384-5505
Roaring Fork Career Center Vo/Tech
  504A 27th St 81601 970-384-5980
  Judy Haptonstall, prin. Fax 384-5985
Other Schools – See Basalt, Carbondale

Colorado Mountain College Post-Sec.
  PO Box 10001 81602 800-621-8559
Glenwood Beauty Academy Post-Sec.
  51241 Highway 6 Ste 1 81601 970-945-0485

Golden, Jefferson, Pop. 17,550
Jefferson County SD R-1 82,900/PK-12
  PO Box 4001 80401 303-982-6500
  Dr. Cindy Stevenson, supt. Fax 982-6667
  jeffcoweb.jeffco.k12.co.us/
Bell MS 700/7-8
  1001 Ulysses St 80401 303-982-4280
  Griff Wirth, prin. Fax 982-4281
Golden HS 1,300/9-12
  701 24th St 80401 303-982-4200
  Mike Murphy, prin. Fax 982-4201
Other Schools – See Arvada, Conifer, Denver,
  Edgewater, Evergreen, Lakewood, Littleton,
  Westminster, Wheat Ridge

Colorado School of Mines Post-Sec.
  1500 Illinois St 80401 303-273-3000

Granada, Prowers, Pop. 626
Granada SD RE-1 300/K-12
  PO Box 259 81041 719-734-5492
  Leo Laprarie, supt. Fax 734-5495
Granada JSHS 100/7-12
  PO Box 259 81041 719-734-5492
  Ty Kemp, prin. Fax 734-5495

Granby, Grand, Pop. 1,546
East Grand SD 2 1,300/PK-12
  PO Box 125 80446 970-887-2581
  Robb Rankin, supt. Fax 887-2635
  www.egsd.org
East Grand MS 300/6-8
  PO Box 2210 80446 970-887-3382
  Nancy Karas, prin. Fax 887-9234
Middle Park HS 400/9-12
  PO Box 130 80446 970-887-2104
  Dale Fleming, prin. Fax 887-9454

Grand Junction, Mesa, Pop. 44,382
Mesa County Valley SD 51 20,200/PK-12
  2115 Grand Ave 81501 970-254-5100
  Dr. J. Tim Mills, supt. Fax 254-5282
  www.mesa.k12.co.us
Bookcliff MS 500/6-8
  2935 Orchard Ave 81504 970-243-6350
  Marty Bassett, prin. Fax 242-8066
Career Occupational Ed Ctr Vo/Tech
  2935 North Ave 81504 970-243-3142
  Dean Blair, prin. Fax 243-9829
Central HS 1,600/9-12
  550 Warrior Way 81504 970-254-6200
  Jody Frost, prin. Fax 254-6169
Deep River S 200/K-12
  2813 Patterson Rd 81506
East MS 400/6-8
  830 Gunnison Ave 81501 970-242-0133
  Leigh Grasso, prin. Fax 242-0513
Grand Junction HS 1,600/9-12
  1400 N 5th St 81501 970-254-6900
  Kevin Schott, prin. Fax 243-2573
Grand Mesa MS 700/6-8
  583 31 1/2 Rd 81504 970-254-6270
  Debra Bailey, prin. Fax 254-6307

Orchard Mesa MS 600/6-8
  2736 C Road 81503 970-242-5563
  Brett Livingston, prin. Fax 245-7343
Redlands MS 600/6-8
  2200 Broadway 81503 970-245-6084
  Kimberly Heutzenroeder, prin. Fax 245-1985
West MS 400/6-8
  123 W Orchard Ave 81505 970-254-5090
  Jody Mimmack, prin. Fax 243-0574
Other Schools – See Clifton, Fruita, Palisade

Academy of Beauty Culture Post-Sec.
  2992 North Ave 81504 970-245-5570
Cornerstone Christian S 100/K-12
  3099 F Rd 81504 970-434-4619
  Karen Sherman, admin. Fax 434-4620
IntelliTec College Post-Sec.
  772 Horizon Dr 81506 970-245-8101
Intermountain Adventist Academy 50/PK-10
  1704 N 8th St 81501 970-242-5116
  David Priest, prin. Fax 242-5659
Mesa State College Post-Sec.
  1100 North Ave 81501 970-248-1020
MJM Institute of Cosmetology Post-Sec.
  1048 Independent Ave #A113 81505 970-241-9060

Greeley, Weld, Pop. 83,414
Weld County SD 6 16,000/PK-12
  1025 9th Ave 80631 970-348-6000
  Renae Dreier, supt. Fax 348-6231
  www.greeleyschools.org
Brentwood MS 600/6-8
  2600 24th Avenue Ct 80634 970-348-3000
  John Diebold, prin. Fax 348-3030
Evans MS 800/6-8
  2900 15th Ave 80631 970-348-3600
  Guy Newland, prin. Fax 348-3630
Franklin MS 700/6-8
  818 35th Ave 80634 970-348-3200
  Terri Gesick-Pappas, prin. Fax 348-3230
Greeley Central HS 1,300/9-12
  1515 14th Ave 80631 970-348-5000
  Mary Lauer, prin. Fax 348-5030
Greeley West HS 1,500/9-12
  2401 35th Ave 80634 970-348-5400
  Bob Harr, prin. Fax 348-5430
Heath MS 900/6-8
  2223 16th St 80631 970-348-3400
  Mark Rangel, prin. Fax 348-3430
Maplewood MS 500/6-8
  1201 21st Ave 80631 970-348-3800
  Robert Billings, prin. Fax 348-3830
Northridge HS 1,200/9-12
  100 N 71st Ave 80634 970-348-5200
  John Borman, prin. Fax 348-5230
Weld Opportunity HS Vo/Tech
  2505 1st Ave 80631 970-351-7472
  Chris Ingram, prin. Fax 351-7568
Night S, 1401 22nd Ave 80631 Adult
  Joan Rhodes, prin. 970-348-3550

Aims Community College Post-Sec.
  PO Box 69 80632 970-330-8008
Cheeks Intl Academy of Beauty Culture Post-Sec.
  2547 11th Ave Ste B 80631 970-352-4500
Dayspring Christian S 400/PK-12
  3734 W 20th St 80634 970-330-1151
  Harley Lowe, prin. Fax 330-0565
University of Northern Colorado Post-Sec.
  501 20th St 80639 970-351-1890

Greenwood Village, Arapahoe, Pop. 12,731
Cherry Creek SD 5 47,300/PK-12
  4700 S Yosemite St 80111 303-773-1184
  Dr. Monte Moses, supt. Fax 773-9884
  www.cherrycreekschools.org
Other Schools – See Aurora, Englewood, Littleton

College for Financial Planning Post-Sec.
  8000 E Maplewood Ave 80111 303-220-1200
DeVry Institute of Technology Post-Sec.
  5775 DTC Blvd 80111 303-694-6600

Grover, Weld, Pop. 154
Pawnee SD RE-12 100/K-12
  PO Box 220 80729 970-895-2222
  Douglas J. Pfau, supt. Fax 895-2221
  www.pawneeschool.com
Pawnee JSHS 100/7-12
  PO Box 220 80729 970-895-2222
  Douglas J. Pfau, supt. Fax 895-2221

Gunnison, Gunnison, Pop. 5,313
Gunnison Watershed SD RE 1J 1,600/K-12
  800 N Boulevard St 81230 970-641-7760
  Bill Chambliss, supt. Fax 641-7777
  www.gunnisonschools.net/
Gunnison HS 300/9-12
  800 W Ohio Ave 81230 970-641-7700
  Mike Adams, prin. Fax 641-7709
Gunnison MS 300/6-8
  1099 N 11th St 81230 970-641-7710
  Doug Tredway, prin. Fax 641-7739
Gunnison Valley HS 50/9-12
  600 N 8th St 81230 970-641-7755
  Bill Chambliss, prin. Fax 641-7777
Other Schools – See Crested Butte

Western State College of Colorado Post-Sec.
  600 N Adams St 81231 970-943-0120

Gypsum, Eagle, Pop. 4,553
Eagle County SD RE-50J
  Supt. — See Eagle
Eagle Valley HS 600/9-12
  PO Box 188 81637 970-328-8960
  Mark Strakbein, prin. Fax 524-5607
Gypsum Creek MS 300/6-8
  PO Box 5129 81637 970-328-8980
  Steve Smith, prin. Fax 524-7393

Haxtun, Phillips, Pop. 984
Haxtun SD RE-2J 300/PK-12
  201 W Powell St 80731 970-774-6111
  James Poole, supt. Fax 774-7568
  www.haxtun.k12.co.us

Haxtun HS 100/9-12
  201 W Powell St 80731 970-774-6111
  Darcy Garretson, prin. Fax 774-7568

Hayden, Routt, Pop. 1,585
Hayden SD RE-1 500/PK-12
  PO Box 70 81639 970-276-3864
  Michael Luppes, supt. Fax 276-4217
  www.haydensd.org
Hayden HS 100/9-12
  PO Box 70 81639 970-276-3761
  Troy Zabel, prin. Fax 276-4376
Hayden MS, PO Box 70 81639 100/6-8
  Troy Zabel, prin. 970-276-3762

Highlands Ranch, Douglas, Pop. 10,181
Douglas County SD RE-1
  Supt. — See Castle Rock
Cresthill MS 1,000/7-8
  9195 Cresthill Ln 80130 303-387-2800
  Sally Stanley, prin. Fax 387-2801
Highlands Ranch HS 1,800/9-12
  9375 Cresthill Ln 80130 303-387-2500
  Jerry Goings, prin. Fax 387-2501
Mountain Ridge MS 900/7-8
  10590 Mountain Vista Rdg 80126 303-387-1800
  Kara Shepherd, prin. Fax 387-1801
Mountain Vista HS 800/9-10
  10585 Mountain Vista Rdg 80126 303-387-1500
  Steve Johnson, prin. Fax 387-1501
Ranch View MS 800/7-8
  1731 W Wildcat Reserve Pkwy 80129 303-387-2300
  Bryan Breuer, prin. Fax 387-2301
Rock Canyon HS 1,000/9-12
  5810 McArthur Ranch Rd 80124 303-387-3000
  Dan McMinimee, prin. Fax 387-3001
Thunderridge HS 1,500/9-12
  1991 W Wildcat Reserve Pkwy 80129 303-387-2000
  Carole Jennings, prin. Fax 387-2001

Cherry Hills Christian MS 200/6-8
  3900 Grace Blvd 80126 303-791-5500
  Evan Dalrymple, prin. Fax 683-5252
Elliot Christian S 100/7-12
  2680 E County Line Rd 80126 303-922-0011
  Frank Daugherity, admin. Fax 922-0159

Hoehne, Las Animas, Pop. 150
Hoehne RSD 3 400/PK-12
  PO Box 91 81046 719-846-4457
  Hal Roueche, supt. Fax 846-4450
  www.hoehne.k12.co.us
Hoehne HS, PO Box 91 81046 100/9-12
  Paul Molano, prin. 719-846-4457
Hoehne JHS, PO Box 91 81046 100/7-8
  Paul Molano, prin. 719-846-4457

Holly, Prowers, Pop. 1,024
Holly SD RE-3 400/PK-12
  PO Box 608 81047 719-537-6616
  Carlyn Yokum, supt. Fax 537-0315
  www.holly.k12.co.us
Holly JSHS 200/7-12
  PO Box 608 81047 719-537-6512
  Ruth Ann Cullen, prin. Fax 537-6519

Holyoke, Phillips, Pop. 2,266
Holyoke SD RE-1J 700/K-12
  435 S Morlan Ave 80734 970-854-3634
  Stephen Bohrer, supt. Fax 854-4049
  www.hcosd.org
Holyoke JSHS 300/7-12
  545 E Hale St 80734 970-854-2284
  Dave Rice, prin. Fax 854-2441

Hotchkiss, Delta, Pop. 1,024
Delta County SD 50(J)
  Supt. — See Delta
Hotchkiss HS 300/9-12
  438 Bulldog St 81419 970-872-3882
  Mike Beard, prin. Fax 872-2390

Hugo, Lincoln, Pop. 837
Genoa-Hugo SD C113 200/PK-12
  PO Box 247 80821 719-743-2428
  Robert Ring, supt. Fax 743-2194
Genoa-Hugo MSHS 100/6-12
  PO Box 247 80821 719-743-2428
  Charla Hannigan, prin. Fax 743-2194

Idaho Springs, Clear Creek, Pop. 1,884
Clear Creek SD RE-1 1,300/PK-12
  PO Box 3399 80452 303-567-3850
  Mike Greek, supt. Fax 567-3861
  www.ccsdre1.org
Clear Creek Career & Technical S Vo/Tech
  PO Box 3399 80452 303-567-3848
  Frank Reeves, prin.
Clear Creek MS 200/7-8
  PO Box 3369 80452 303-567-4461
  Jake Dingman, prin. Fax 567-3856
Other Schools – See Evergreen

Idalia, Yuma, Pop. 100
Idalia SD RJ-3 100/PK-12
  PO Box 40 80735 970-354-7298
  Tim Gribben, supt. Fax 354-7416
Idalia JSHS 100/7-12
  PO Box 40 80735 970-354-7298
  Tim Gribben, prin. Fax 354-7416

Ignacio, LaPlata, Pop. 671
Ignacio SD 11 JT 900/K-12
  PO Box 460 81137 970-563-0500
  Juvie Jones, supt. Fax 563-4524
  www.ignacio.k12.co.us
Ignacio HS 200/9-12
  PO Box 460 81137 970-563-0515
  Mark Huffmyer, prin. Fax 563-9465
Ignacio JHS 100/7-8
  PO Box 460 81137 970-563-0600
  Roy Lyons, prin. Fax 563-1030

Iliff, Logan, Pop. 220
Valley SD RE-1
  Supt. — See Sterling
Caliche JSHS 100/7-12
  26308 Buffalo Rd 80736 970-522-8200
  Helen Duncan, prin. Fax 522-9400

Joes, Yuma, Pop. 75
Liberty SD J-4 — 100/K-12
PO Box 112 80822 — 970-358-4288
Milton C. Roeder, supt. — Fax 358-4282
www.libertyschoolj4.com
Liberty JSHS, PO Box 112 80822 — 50/7-12
Milton C. Roeder, prin. — 970-358-4288

Johnstown, Weld, Pop. 5,595
Weld County SD RE-5J
Supt. — See Milliken
Roosevelt HS — 500/9-12
616 N 2nd St 80534 — 970-587-6000
John Bruce, prin. — Fax 587-2608

Julesburg, Sedgwick, Pop. 1,426
Julesburg SD RE-1 — 400/PK-12
102 W 6th St 80737 — 970-474-3365
Shawn Ehnes, supt. — Fax 474-3742
Julesburg JSHS — 200/7-12
102 W 6th St 80737 — 970-474-3364
Shawn Ehnes, prin. — Fax 474-3592

Karval, Lincoln, Pop. 50
Karval SD RE-23 — 100/PK-12
PO Box 5 80823 — 719-446-5311
Martin Adams, supt. — Fax 446-5332
Karval JSHS — 50/7-12
PO Box 5 80823 — 719-446-5311
Martin Adams, prin. — Fax 446-5332

Keenesburg, Weld, Pop. 1,117
Weld County SD RE-3J — 1,800/PK-12
PO Box 269 80643 — 303-536-2000
Dr. Marvin Wade, supt. — Fax 536-2010
www.rebel-net.tec.co.us/
Weld Central HS — 500/9-12
4977 County Road 59 80643 — 303-536-2100
Steve Jones, prin. — Fax 536-2110
Weld Central JHS — 300/7-8
4977 Weld County Road 59 80643 — 303-536-2100
Steve Jones, prin. — Fax 536-2110

Kersey, Weld, Pop. 1,371
Weld County SD RE-7 — 1,100/PK-12
PO Box 485 80644 — 970-336-8500
E. Glenn McClain, supt. — Fax 336-8511
Platte Valley HS — 300/9-12
PO Box 487 80644 — 970-336-8700
Brad Joens, prin. — Fax 336-8794
Platte Valley MS — 300/6-8
PO Box 515 80644 — 970-336-8610
Bruce Parker, prin. — Fax 336-8635

Kim, Las Animas, Pop. 66
Kim RSD 88 — 100/PK-12
PO Box 100 81049 — 719-643-5295
Ramona McMillian, supt. — Fax 643-5299
www.kim.k12.co.us/
Kim JSHS — 50/7-12
PO Box 100 81049 — 719-643-5295
Ramona McMillan, prin. — Fax 643-5295

Kiowa, Elbert, Pop. 612
Kiowa SD C-2 — 400/PK-12
PO Box 128 80117 — 303-621-2220
Bret L. Robinson, supt. — Fax 621-2876
www.kiowaschool.org
Kiowa HS — 100/9-12
PO Box 128 80117 — 303-621-2115
Jason Westfall, prin. — Fax 621-2566
Kiowa MS — 100/6-8
PO Box 128 80117 — 303-621-2785
Jason Westfall, prin. — Fax 621-2566

Kit Carson, Cheyenne, Pop. 235
Kit Carson SD R-1 — 100/K-12
PO Box 185 80825 — 719-962-3219
Gerald Keefe, supt. — Fax 962-3317
www.kcsdr1.org
Carson JSHS — 100/K-12
PO Box 185 80825 — 719-962-3219
Gerald Keefe, prin. — Fax 962-3317

Kremmling, Grand, Pop. 1,610
West Grand SD 1-JT — 600/K-12
PO Box 515 80459 — 970-724-3217
Dr. Jeff Perry, supt. — Fax 724-9373
www.westgrand.k12.co.us/
West Grand HS — 200/9-12
PO Box 515 80459 — 970-724-3425
Philip Bonds, prin. — Fax 724-3450
West Grand MS — 100/6-8
PO Box 515 80459 — 970-724-3489
Eddy Liddle, prin. — Fax 724-9052

Lafayette, Boulder, Pop. 23,654
Boulder Valley SD RE-2
Supt. — See Boulder
Angevine MS — 700/6-8
1150 W South Boulder Rd 80026 — 303-665-5540
Isobel Stevenson, prin. — Fax 661-0354
Centaurus HS — 1,000/9-12
10300 E South Boulder Rd 80026 — 303-665-9211
Deirdre Pilch, prin. — Fax 447-5368

Dawson S — 400/K-12
10455 Dawson Dr 80026 — 303-665-6679
Anthony Kandel Ph.D., hdmstr. — Fax 665-0757

La Jara, Conejos, Pop. 838
North Conejos SD RE 1J — 1,200/PK-12
PO Box 72 81140 — 719-274-5174
John D. Jordan, supt. — Fax 274-5621
Centauri HS — 400/9-12
PO Box 72 81140 — 719-274-5178
Curt Wilson, prin. — Fax 274-5637
Centauri MS — 300/6-8
PO Box 72 81140 — 719-274-4301
Tom Salazar, prin. — Fax 274-4301

La Junta, Otero, Pop. 7,379
East Otero SD R-1 — 1,600/K-12
1802 Colorado Ave Ste 200 81050 — 719-384-6900
Jim Sullivan, supt. — Fax 384-6910
www.lajunta.k12.co.us
La Junta HS — 500/9-12
1817 Smithland Ave 81050 — 719-384-4467
Bud Ozzello, prin.

La Junta MS — 400/6-8
901 Smithland Ave 81050 — 719-384-4371
Paul Jebe, prin.

Otero Junior College — Post-Sec.
1802 Colorado Ave 81050 — 719-384-6831

Lake City, Hinsdale, Pop. 360
Hinsdale County SD RE 1 — 100/PK-12
PO Box 39 81235 — 970-944-2314
Karen Thormalen, supt. — Fax 944-2662
Lake City Community S — 100/PK-12
PO Box 39 81235 — 970-944-2314
Karen Thormalen, prin. — Fax 944-2662

Lakewood, Jefferson, Pop. 142,474
Jefferson County SD R-1
Supt. — See Golden
Alameda HS — 1,100/9-12
1255 S Wadsworth Blvd 80232 — 303-982-8160
Richard Zarkowski, prin. — Fax 982-8161
Bear Creek HS — 1,900/9-12
3490 S Kipling St 80227 — 303-982-8855
Phyllis Emrich, prin. — Fax 982-8856
Carmody MS — 800/7-8
2050 S Kipling St 80227 — 303-982-8930
John Schalk, prin. — Fax 982-8931
Creighton MS — 700/7-8
75 Independence St 80226 — 303-982-6282
Terry Robertson, prin. — Fax 982-6283
Dunstan MS — 800/7-8
1855 S Wright St 80228 — 303-982-9270
Linda Burton, prin. — Fax 982-9269
Green Mountain HS — 1,600/9-12
13175 W Green Mountain Dr 80228 — 303-982-9500
Barbara Goings, prin. — Fax 982-9501
Jefferson County Open S — 1,000/PK-12
7655 W 10th Ave 80214 — 303-982-7045
Danielle Romero, prin. — Fax 982-7046
Lakewood HS — 1,600/9-12
9700 W 8th Ave 80215 — 303-982-7096
Ron Castagna, prin. — Fax 982-7098
O'Connell MS — 600/7-8
1275 S Teller St 80232 — 303-982-8370
Pati Montgomery, prin. — Fax 982-8371
Warren Occupational Tech Ctr — Vo/Tech
13300 W 2nd Pl 80228 — 303-982-8600
Joe Shaw, prin. — Fax 982-8622

Artistic Beauty College — Post-Sec.
1225 Wadsworth Blvd 80214 — 303-238-7501
Christian Fellowship MSHS — 200/6-12
7700 W Woodard Dr 80227 — 720-974-0252
Truman Abbott, prin. — Fax 974-0262
Colorado Christian University — Post-Sec.
180 S Garrison St 80226 — 303-202-0100
Colorado School of Healing Arts — Post-Sec.
7655 W Mississippi #100 80226 — 303-986-2320
Colorado School of Trades — Post-Sec.
1575 Hoyt St 80215 — 303-233-4697
Mile High Baptist S — 100/K-12
8100 W Hampden Ave 80227 — 303-986-2183
— Fax 980-8105
Ohio Center for Broadcasting - Colorado — Post-Sec.
1310 Wadsworth Blvd Ste 100 80214 — 303-937-7070
Red Rocks Community College — Post-Sec.
13300 W 6th Ave 80228 — 303-988-6160
Remington College - Denver Campus — Post-Sec.
11011 W 6th Ave 80215 — 303-445-0500
Remington College Online — Post-Sec.
11011 W 6th Ave 80215 — 800-829-5488
Rocky Mountain College of Art & Design — Post-Sec.
1600 Pierce St 80214 — 800-888-2787
Silver State Baptist S — 200/PK-12
460 S Kipling St 80226 — 303-922-8850
Daniel Brock, prin. — Fax 922-4573

Lamar, Prowers, Pop. 8,630
Lamar SD RE-2 — 1,700/PK-12
210 W Pearl St 81052 — 719-336-3251
Wayne Graybeal, supt. — Fax 336-2817
www.lamar.k12.co.us
Lamar HS — 500/9-12
1900 S 11th St 81052 — 719-336-3488
Allan Medina, prin. — Fax 336-3026
Lamar MS — 400/6-8
104 W Park St 81052 — 719-336-7436
Verna Milnes, prin. — Fax 336-5457

Lamar Community College — Post-Sec.
2401 S Main St 81052 — 719-336-2248

Laporte, Larimer, Pop. 1,500
Poudre SD R-1
Supt. — See Fort Collins
Cache La Poudre JHS — 400/7-9
3511 W County Road 54G 80535 — 970-488-7400
Brian Williams, prin. — Fax 488-7433

Larkspur, Douglas, Pop. 286

Griffith Center — 100/6-12
PO Box 95 80118 — 303-681-2400

La Salle, Weld, Pop. 1,786
Weld County SD RE-1
Supt. — See Gilcrest
North Valley MS — 300/6-8
PO Box 248 80645 — 970-284-5508
Mel Sussman, prin. — Fax 284-6595

Las Animas, Bent, Pop. 2,575
Las Animas SD RE-1 — 600/PK-12
1021 2nd St 81054 — 719-456-0161
Scott Cuckow, supt. — Fax 456-1117
www.lasanimas.k12.co.us
Las Animas HS — 100/9-12
300 Grove Ave 81054 — 719-456-0211
Dennis Veal, prin. — Fax 456-0932
Las Animas MS — 100/6-8
1021 2nd St 81054 — 719-456-0228
Dennis Veal, prin. — Fax 456-0241

La Veta, Huerfano, Pop. 905
La Veta SD RE-2 — 300/PK-12
PO Box 85 81055 — 719-742-3562
Wayne Graybeal, supt. — Fax 742-3959
www.laveta.k12.co.us

La Veta JSHS — 100/7-12
PO Box 85 81055 — 719-742-3662
Wayne Graybeal, prin. — Fax 742-5799

Leadville, Lake, Pop. 2,712
Lake County SD R-1 — 1,200/PK-12
107 Spruce St 80461 — 719-486-6800
Dr. Bette Bullock, supt. — Fax 486-2048
www.lakecountyschools.net/
Lake County HS — 300/9-12
1000 W 4th St 80461 — 719-486-6950
Rhett Parham, prin. — Fax 486-3767
Lake County MS — 400/5-8
1000 W 6th St 80461 — 719-486-6830
Deb Forkner, prin. — Fax 486-6880

Mountain BOCES
1713 Mount Lincoln Dr W 80461 — 719-486-2603
Edward Vandertook, dir. — Fax 486-2109
www.mtnboces.k12.co.us/
Other Schools – See Buena Vista

Colorado Mountain College — Post-Sec.
901 US Highway 24 80461 — 800-621-8559

Limon, Lincoln, Pop. 2,014
Limon SD RE-4J — 600/K-12
PO Box 249 80828 — 719-775-2350
Harvey Goodman, supt. — Fax 775-9052
www.plains.net/~lps/
Limon HS — 300/6-12
PO Box 249 80828 — 719-775-2350
— Fax 775-9052

Littleton, Arapahoe, Pop. 40,599
Cherry Creek SD 5
Supt. — See Greenwood Village
West MS — 1,400/6-8
5151 S Holly St 80121 — 720-554-5100
Sheila Graham, prin. — Fax 554-5181

Douglas County SD RE-1
Supt. — See Castle Rock
Rocky Heights MS — 400/7-8
11033 Monarch Blvd 80124 — 303-387-3300
Pat Dierberger, prin. — Fax 387-3301

Jefferson County SD R-1
Supt. — See Golden
Chatfield HS — 2,100/9-12
7227 S Simms St 80127 — 303-982-3670
Keith Mead, prin. — Fax 982-3671
Columbine HS — 1,700/9-12
6201 S Pierce St 80123 — 303-982-4400
Frank DeAngelis, prin. — Fax 982-4401
Dakota Ridge HS — 1,600/9-12
13399 W Coal Mine Ave 80127 — 303-982-1970
Jim Jelinek, prin. — Fax 982-1971
Deer Creek MS — 700/7-8
9201 W Columbine Dr 80128 — 303-982-3820
Heather Beck, prin. — Fax 982-3821
Falcon Bluffs MS — 500/7-8
8449 S Garrison St 80128 — 303-982-9900
Wendy Rubin, prin. — Fax 982-9901
Ken Caryl MS — 700/7-8
6509 W Ken Caryl Ave 80128 — 303-982-4710
Mary Ellen Hansen, prin. — Fax 982-4711
Summit Ridge MS — 900/7-8
11809 W Coal Mine Dr 80127 — 303-982-9013
Lisa Myles, prin. — Fax 982-8998

Littleton SD 6 — 15,500/PK-12
5776 S Crocker St 80120 — 303-347-3300
Scott Murphy, supt. — Fax 347-3439
www.littletonpublicschools.net
Euclid MS — 900/6-8
777 W Euclid Ave 80120 — 303-347-7800
Gary Hein, prin. — Fax 347-7830
Goddard MS — 900/6-8
3800 W Berry Ave 80123 — 303-347-7850
Amy Oaks, prin. — Fax 347-7880
Heritage HS — 1,900/9-12
1401 W Geddes Ave 80120 — 303-347-7600
Kenneth Moritz, prin. — Fax 347-7603
Littleton HS — 1,700/9-12
199 E Littleton Blvd 80121 — 303-347-7700
Kathy Dinmore, prin. — Fax 347-7775
Powell MS — 1,000/6-8
8000 S Corona Way 80122 — 303-347-7800
Becky Friend, prin. — Fax 347-3975
Other Schools – See Centennial

Arapahoe Community College — Post-Sec.
5900 S Santa Fe Dr 80120 — 303-797-4222
Denver Seminary — Post-Sec.
6399 S Santa Fe Dr 80120 — 303-762-6982
Front Range Christian HS — 300/7-12
6637 W Ottawa Ave 80128 — 303-979-4582
Rogene Lowe, prin. — Fax 979-3591
Rock Solid HS — 100/9-12
6570 S Broadway # B 80121 — 303-797-1005
Gail Arthur, prin. — Fax 797-1005
St. Marys MS — 300/4-8
6833 S Prince St 80120 — 303-798-2875
Mary Cohen, prin. — Fax 283-4756

Lonetree, See Littleton

University of Phoenix — Post-Sec.
10004 Park Meadows Dr 80124 — 303-755-9090

Longmont, Boulder, Pop. 79,556
St. Vrain Valley SD RE-1J — 19,500/PK-12
395 S Pratt Pkwy 80501 — 303-776-6200
Randy Zila, supt. — Fax 682-7343
www.stvrain.k12.co.us
Altoona MS — 6-8
4600 Clover Basin Dr 80503 — 720-494-3730
Joe Mehsling, prin.
Heritage MS — 800/6-8
233 E Mountain View Ave 80501 — 303-772-7900
Mark Spencer, prin. — Fax 776-4376
Longmont HS — 1,400/9-12
1040 Sunset St 80501 — 303-776-6014
Rick Olsen, prin. — Fax 678-7583
Longs Peak MS, 1500 14th Ave 80501 — 700/6-8
Nancy Wesorick, prin. — 303-776-5611

Niwot HS | 1,200/9-12
8989 Niwot Rd 80503 | 303-652-2550
Dennis Daly, prin. | Fax 440-9399
Silver Creek HS | 800/9-12
4901 Nelson Rd 80503 | 720-494-3721
Sherri Schumann, prin. | Fax 494-1848
Skyline HS | 1,400/9-12
600 E Mountain View Ave 80501 | 720-494-3741
Tom Stumpf, prin.
Sunset MS, 1300 S Sunset St 80501 | 700/6-8
Dawn Macy, prin. | 303-776-3963
Trail Ridge MS | 6-8
1000 Button Rock Dr 80501 | 720-494-3820
Valerie Millert, prin.
Westview MS | 700/6-8
1651 Airport Rd 80503 | 303-772-3134
Cathy O'Donnell, prin. | Fax 772-0596
Adult Education Lincoln Center | Adult
619 Bowen St 80501 | 303-678-5662
Mary Willoughby, prin.
Other Schools – See Erie, Frederick, Lyons, Mead

Faith Baptist S | 300/K-12
833 15th Ave 80501 | 303-776-5677
Randy Peterson, prin. | Fax 776-5723
Longmont Christian S | 400/PK-12
550 Coffman St 80501 | 303-776-3254
Donnie Bennett, prin. | Fax 485-6937

Louisville, Boulder, Pop. 18,387
Boulder Valley SD RE-2
Supt. — See Boulder
Louisville MS | 500/6-8
1341 Main St 80027 | 303-666-6503
Adam Fels, prin. | Fax 665-3703
Monarch HS | 1,600/9-12
329 Campus Dr 80027 | 303-665-5888
Bill Johnson, prin. | Fax 245-5650

Loveland, Larimer, Pop. 56,436
Thompson SD R-2J | 14,600/K-12
2890 N Monroe 80538 | 970-613-5000
Dr. Dan Johnson, supt. | Fax 613-5095
www.thompson.k12.co.us
Ball MS | 800/6-8
2660 Monroe Ave 80538 | 970-613-7300
Diane Lauer, prin. | Fax 613-7371
Clark MS | 800/6-8
2605 Carlisle Dr 80537 | 970-613-5400
Kelly Boren, prin. | Fax 613-5420
Erwin MS | 800/6-8
4700 Lucerne Ave 80538 | 970-613-7600
David Steward, prin. | Fax 613-7619
Loveland HS | 1,500/9-12
920 W 29th St 80538 | 970-613-5200
Dr. Doug Deason, prin. | Fax 613-7191
Mountain View HS | 1,200/9-12
3500 Mountain Lion Dr 80537 | 970-613-7800
Kevin Aten, prin. | Fax 613-7820
Reed MS | 700/6-8
370 W 4th St 80537 | 970-613-7200
Todd Ball, prin. | Fax 613-7287
Thompson Valley HS | 1,400/9-12
1669 Eagle Dr 80537 | 970-613-7900
Mark Johnson, prin. | Fax 613-7909
Other Schools – See Berthoud

Campion Academy | 200/9-12
300 42nd St SW 80537 | 970-667-5592
John Winslow, prin. | Fax 667-5104
Loveland Christian HS | 50/9-12
3901 14th St SW 80537 | 970-667-6300
Cherylann Dozier, admin. | Fax 593-1961
Resurrection Christian S | 500/K-12
6502 E Crossroads Blvd 80538 | 970-667-1610
Doug Roth, prin. | Fax 667-1643

Lyons, Boulder, Pop. 1,606
St. Vrain Valley SD RE-1J
Supt. — See Longmont
Lyons MSHS | 400/6-12
PO Box 619 80540 | 303-823-6631
Mark Mills, prin. | Fax 823-5492

Mc Clave, Bent, Pop. 150
McClave SD RE-2 | 300/PK-12
PO Box 1 81057 | 719-829-4517
Ron Nordin, supt. | Fax 829-4430
Mc Clave JSHS | 100/7-12
PO Box 1 81057 | 719-829-4517
Terry Weber, prin. | Fax 829-4430

Mancos, Montezuma, Pop. 1,140
Mancos SD RE-6 | 400/PK-12
395 Grand Ave 81328 | 970-533-7748
Michael Canzona, supt. | Fax 533-7954
www.mancosre6.edu
Mancos HS | 100/9-12
355 Grand Ave 81328 | 970-533-7746
J. Gary Hill, prin. | Fax 533-7537
Mancos MS | 100/6-8
100 S Beech 81328 | 970-533-9143
J. Gary Hill, prin. | Fax 533-1463

Manitou Springs, El Paso, Pop. 5,036
Manitou Springs SD 14 | 1,300/PK-12
405 El Monte Pl 80829 | 719-685-2024
Roy C. Crawford, supt. | Fax 685-4536
mssd14.org
Manitou Springs HS | 500/9-12
401 El Monte Pl 80829 | 719-685-2074
Rob Cody, prin. | Fax 685-4755
Manitou Springs MS | 300/6-8
415 El Monte Pl 80829 | 719-685-2127
Keith Elsberry, prin. | Fax 685-4552

Manzanola, Otero, Pop. 506
Manzanola SD 3J | 200/K-12
PO Box 148 81058 | 719-462-5527
Ernie Vigil, supt. | Fax 462-5708
www.manzanola.k12.co.us/
Manzanola JSHS | 100/7-12
PO Box 148 81058 | 719-462-5528
Todd Werner, prin. | Fax 462-5115

Mead, Weld, Pop. 2,140
St. Vrain Valley SD RE-1J
Supt. — See Longmont

Mead MS | 500/6-8
620 Welker Ave 80542 | 970-535-4446
Victoria Teague, prin. | Fax 535-4434

Meeker, Rio Blanco, Pop. 2,210
Meeker SD RE-1 | 600/PK-12
PO Box 1089 81641 | 970-878-9040
Dan Evig, supt. | Fax 878-3682
www.meeker.k12.co.us
Barone MS | 100/6-8
PO Box 690 81641 | 970-878-9060
Pam Stranathan, prin. | Fax 878-4291
Meeker HS | 200/9-12
PO Box 159 81641 | 970-878-9070
Dwayne Newman, prin. | Fax 878-3633

Merino, Logan, Pop. 277
Buffalo SD RE-4J | 300/K-12
PO Box 198 80741 | 970-522-7424
Dave Kautz, supt. | Fax 522-1541
www.merino.k12.co.us
Merino JSHS | 100/7-12
PO Box 198 80741 | 970-522-7424
Dave Kautz, prin. | Fax 522-1541

Milliken, Weld, Pop. 4,635
Weld County SD RE-5J | 2,400/K-12
110 Centennial Dr Ste A 80543 | 970-587-6050
Dr. Marti Foster, supt. | Fax 587-2607
www.weldre5j.k12.co.us
Milliken MS | 500/6-8
PO Box 339 80543 | 970-587-6300
Trevor Long, prin. | Fax 587-5749
Other Schools – See Johnstown

Minturn, Eagle, Pop. 1,131
Eagle County SD RE-50J
Supt. — See Eagle
Minturn MS | 200/6-8
PO Box 280 81645 | 970-328-2920
Toni Boush, prin. | Fax 827-5805

Moffat, Saguache, Pop. 119
Moffat SD 2 | 100/PK-12
PO Box 428 81143 | 719-256-4710
Eli Dokson, supt. | Fax 256-4730
www.moffat.k12.co.us
Moffat HS, PO Box 428 81143 | 50/9-12
Michelle Hashbarger, prin. | 719-256-4710
Moffat MS, PO Box 428 81143 | 50/6-8
Michelle Hashbarger, prin. | 719-256-4710

Monte Vista, Rio Grande, Pop. 4,370
Monte Vista SD C-8 | 1,100/PK-12
345 E Prospect Ave 81144 | 719-852-5996
Don Wilkinson, supt. | Fax 852-6184
www.monte.k12.co.us
Monte Vista HS | 300/9-12
349 E Prospect Ave 81144 | 719-852-3586
James Szoka, prin. | Fax 852-6121
Monte Vista MS | 300/6-8
3720 Sherman Ave 81144 | 719-852-5984
John Wilson, prin. | Fax 852-6199

Sargent SD RE-33J | 400/K-12
7090 N County Road 2 E 81144 | 719-852-4023
Lyle Oliver, supt. | Fax 852-9890
www.sargent.k12.co.us
Sargent JSHS | 200/7-12
7090 N County Road 2 E 81144 | 719-852-4025
Stan Dodds, prin. | Fax 852-9672

Montrose, Montrose, Pop. 14,195
Montrose County SD RE-1J | 5,300/K-12
PO Box 10000 81402 | 970-249-7726
Dr. George Voorhis, supt. | Fax 249-7173
www.mcsd.org
Centennial MS | 500/6-8
PO Box 10000 81402 | 970-249-2576
Kirk Henwood, prin. | Fax 240-6461
Columbine MS | 600/6-8
PO Box 10000 81402 | 970-249-2581
Ben Stephenson, prin. | Fax 240-6404
Montrose HS | 1,200/9-12
PO Box 10000 81402 | 970-249-6636
Jill Myers, prin. | Fax 240-6414
Other Schools – See Olathe

Colorado West Christian S | 200/K-10
2705 Sunnyside Rd 81401 | 970-249-1094
Raymond Fell, admin. | Fax 249-7988

Monument, El Paso, Pop. 2,500
Lewis-Palmer SD 38 | 4,800/PK-12
PO Box 40 80132 | 719-488-4700
Dave Dilley, supt. | Fax 488-5951
www.lewispalmer.org
Creekside MS | 600/6-8
1330 Creekside Dr 80132 | 719-481-1099
Susan Hansen, prin. | Fax 481-0681
Lewis-Palmer HS | 1,700/9-12
1300 Higby Rd 80132 | 719-488-4720
Mark Brewer, prin. | Fax 488-4723
Lewis-Palmer MS | 600/6-8
1776 Woodmoor Dr 80132 | 719-488-4776
Terry Miller, prin. | Fax 488-4780

Mosca, Alamosa, Pop. 180
Sangre De Cristo SD RE-22J | 300/PK-12
PO Box 145 81146 | 719-378-2321
Lynn Howard, supt. | Fax 378-2327
Sangre De Cristo JSHS | 200/7-12
PO Box 145 81146 | 719-378-2321
Nathan Smith, prin. | Fax 378-2327

Naturita, Montrose, Pop. 673
West End SD Re-2 | 200/PK-12
PO Box 190 81422 | 970-865-2290
Duane Denny, supt. | Fax 865-2573
www.westendschools.org
Other Schools – See Nucla

Nederland, Boulder, Pop. 1,355
Boulder Valley SD RE-2
Supt. — See Boulder
Nederland MSHS | 400/6-12
597 Eldora Rd 80466 | 303-258-3212
Rich Salaz, prin. | Fax 258-8699

New Castle, Garfield, Pop. 2,675
Garfield SD RE-2
Supt. — See Rifle
Coal Ridge HS | 9-12
35947 Highway 6 81647 | 970-625-6710
Jeanie Humble, prin. | Fax 625-6701
Riverside S | 500/5-8
804 Main Dr 81647 | 970-625-7800
Bill Nickell, prin. | Fax 625-7846

New Raymer, Weld, Pop. 109
Prairie SD RE-11 | 100/PK-12
PO Box 68 80742 | 970-437-5351
R. Joe Kimmel, supt. | Fax 437-5732
prairieschool.org
Prairie JSHS | 100/7-12
PO Box 68 80742 | 970-437-5351
Leann R. Smith, prin. | Fax 437-5732

Northglenn, Adams, Pop. 32,943
Northglenn-Thornton 12 SD
Supt. — See Thornton
Huron MS | 800/6-8
10900 Huron St 80234 | 720-972-5000
Tracy Webber, prin. | Fax 972-5039
Northglenn HS | 2,400/9-12
601 W 100th Pl 80260 | 720-972-4600
Julie Enger, prin. | Fax 972-4739
Northglenn MS | 800/6-8
1123 Muriel Dr 80233 | 720-972-5080
Paula Redig, prin. | Fax 972-5119

Community Christian S | 300/K-12
11980 Irma Dr 80233 | 303-452-7514
Scott E. Bruns, admin. | Fax 452-4904
North Lutheran HS | 50/9-12
11700 Irma Dr 80233 | 720-887-9031
Kevin Wilaby, prin. | Fax 439-0698
Rocky Mountain Lutheran HS | 100/9-12
11700 Irma Dr 80233 | 303-346-1947
John Barenz, prin. | Fax 451-0817

Norwood, San Miguel, Pop. 471
Norwood SD R-2J | 300/PK-12
PO Box 448 81423 | 970-327-4336
Bob Conder, supt. | Fax 327-4116
Norwood HS | 100/9-12
PO Box 448 81423 | 970-327-4336
James Hoffman, prin. | Fax 327-4116

Nucla, Montrose, Pop. 743
West End SD Re-2
Supt. — See Naturita
Nucla JSHS | 100/7-12
PO Box 570 81424 | 970-864-7641
John Smith, prin. | Fax 864-7269

Oak Creek, Routt, Pop. 819
South Routt SD RE-3 | 400/PK-12
PO Box 158 80467 | 970-736-2313
Steve Jones, supt. | Fax 736-2458
www.southroutt.k12.co.us
Soroco HS, PO Box 158 80467 | 100/9-12
James Chamberlin, prin. | 970-736-2531
Soroco MS, PO Box 158 80467 | 100/6-8
James Chamberlain, prin. | 970-736-8531

Olathe, Montrose, Pop. 1,648
Montrose County SD RE-1J
Supt. — See Montrose
Olathe HS | 300/9-12
410 Highway 50 81425 | 970-252-7950
Andy Hanks, prin. | Fax 323-5947
Olathe MS | 300/6-8
410 Highway 50 81425 | 970-252-7950
Andy Hanks, prin. | Fax 323-5947

Ordway, Crowley, Pop. 1,194
Crowley County SD Re-1-J | 600/K-12
117 W 3rd St 81063 | 719-267-3117
John McCleary, supt. | Fax 267-3130
Crowley County HS | 200/9-12
PO Box 338 81063 | 719-267-3582
Rick Walter, prin. | Fax 267-3585
Crowley County MS | 200/6-8
1001 Main St 81063 | 719-267-9880
John McCleary, prin. | Fax 267-9881

Otis, Washington, Pop. 524
Lone Star SD 101 | 100/K-12
44940 County Road 54 80743 | 970-848-2778
Gena Ramey, supt. | Fax 848-0340
www.lonestar.k12.co.us/
Lone Star JSHS | 50/7-12
44940 County Road 54 80743 | 970-848-2778
Gena Ramey, prin. | Fax 848-0340

Otis SD R-3 | 200/K-12
518 Dungan St 80743 | 970-246-3413
Jeff Durbin, supt. | Fax 246-0518
www.osdco.com
Otis JSHS | 100/7-12
301 West St 80743 | 970-246-3486
Jim Anderson, prin. | Fax 246-3487

Ouray, Ouray, Pop. 832
Ouray SD R-1 | 300/PK-12
PO Box N 81427 | 970-325-4505
Heidi McDuffie, supt. | Fax 325-7343
www.ouray.k12.co.us/
Ouray HS | 100/9-12
PO Box N 81427 | 970-325-4218
Heidi McDuffie, prin. | Fax 325-7343

Ovid, Sedgwick, Pop. 327
Platte Valley SD RE-3 | 100/PK-12
PO Box 369 80744 | 970-463-5414
William Pile, supt. | Fax 463-5493
www.plattevsd.k12.co.us/
Revere JSHS | 100/7-12
PO Box 369 80744 | 970-463-5477
Henry Armknecht, prin. | Fax 463-5669

Pagosa Springs, Archuleta, Pop. 1,528
Archuleta SD 50 JT | 1,600/K-12
PO Box 1498 81147 | 970-264-2228
Duane Noggle, supt. | Fax 264-4631
www.pagosa.k12.co.us

Pagosa Springs HS | 500/9-12
PO Box 1498 81147 | 970-264-2231
William Esterbrook, prin. | Fax 264-2239
Pagosa Springs JHS | 300/7-8
PO Box 1498 81147 | 970-264-2794
Chris Hinger, prin. | Fax 264-6112

Palisade, Mesa, Pop. 2,650
Mesa County Valley SD 51
Supt. — See Grand Junction
Palisade HS | 900/9-12
3679 G Rd 81526 | 970-464-5937
Matthew Diers, prin. | Fax 464-5102

Paonia, Delta, Pop. 1,586
Delta County SD 50(J)
Supt. — See Delta
Paonia JSHS | 300/6-12
846 Grand Ave 81428 | 970-527-4882
Brent Curtice, prin. | Fax 527-4080

Parachute, Garfield, Pop. 1,055
Garfield County SD 16 | 1,000/PK-12
PO Box 68 81635 | 970-285-5701
Dr. Steven McKee, supt. | Fax 285-5711
www.garcoschools.org
Grand Valley HS | 200/9-12
PO Box 68 81635 | 970-285-5705
Larry Brady, prin. | Fax 285-5715
L.W. St. John MS | 200/7-8
PO Box 68 81635 | 970-285-5704
Scott Pankow, prin. | Fax 285-5714

Parker, Douglas, Pop. 34,527
Douglas County SD RE-1
Supt. — See Castle Rock
Chaparral HS | 1,800/9-12
15655 Brookstone Dr 80134 | 303-387-3500
Ron Peterson, prin. | Fax 387-3501
Ponderosa HS | 1,800/9-12
7007 E Bayou Gulch Rd 80134 | 303-387-4000
Cathy Brondos, prin. | Fax 387-4001
Sagewood MS | 900/7-8
4725 Fox Sparrow Rd 80134 | 303-387-4300
Ralph Montgomery, prin. | Fax 387-4301
Sierra MS | 1,000/7-8
6651 E Pine Ln 80138 | 303-387-3800
Karen Tarbell, prin. | Fax 387-3801

Lutheran HS of the Rockies | 100/9-12
11249 Newlin Gulch Blvd 80134 | 303-841-5551
Juls Clausen, prin. | Fax 842-1015

Peetz, Logan, Pop. 232
Plateau SD RE-5 | 200/PK-12
PO Box 39 80747 | 970-334-2435
Dean Koester, supt. | Fax 334-2360
Peetz HS | 100/9-12
PO Box 39 80747 | 970-334-2361
Dean Koester, prin. | Fax 334-2360

Penrose, Fremont, Pop. 2,235
Florence RE-2 SD
Supt. — See Florence
Penrose MS | 200/6-8
100 Illinois Ave 81240 | 719-372-6777
Dominic Carochi, prin. | Fax 372-0719

Peyton, El Paso, Pop. 200
Peyton SD 23 JT | 700/PK-12
13990 Bradshaw Rd 80831 | 719-749-2330
Rich Campbell, supt. | Fax 749-2368
www.peyton.k12.co.us/
Peyton HS | 200/9-12
13885 Bradshaw Rd 80831 | 719-749-2244
Tim Kistler, prin. | Fax 749-2567
Peyton MS, 18220 Main St 80831 | 200/6-8
Tim Kistler, prin. | 719-749-2244

Platteville, Weld, Pop. 2,547
Weld County SD RE-1
Supt. — See Gilcrest
South Valley MS | 200/6-8
1004 Main St 80651 | 970-785-2205
Jeff Angus, prin. | Fax 785-2180

Pritchett, Baca, Pop. 127
Pritchett SD RE-3 | 100/PK-12
PO Box 7 81064 | 719-523-4045
Stephanie Hund, supt. | Fax 523-6991
Pritchett JSHS | 50/6-12
PO Box 7 81064 | 719-523-4045
Stephanie Hund, prin. | Fax 523-6991

Pueblo, Pueblo, Pop. 103,648
Pueblo CSD 60 | 16,200/PK-12
315 W 11th St 81003 | 719-549-7100
Dr. Joyce F. Bales, supt. | Fax 549-7112
www.pueblo60.k12.co.us
Centennial HS | 1,200/9-12
2525 Mountview Dr 81008 | 719-549-7335
Miguel Elias, prin. | Fax 549-7634
Central HS | 1,100/9-12
216 E Orman Ave 81004 | 719-549-7300
Robert Gonzales, prin. | Fax 549-7306
Corwin MS | 300/6-8
1500 Lakeview Ave 81004 | 719-549-7400
Dr. Kathy DeNiro, prin. | Fax 564-2773
East HS | 1,000/9-12
9 Macneil Rd 81001 | 719-549-7222
Alan Nelms, prin. | Fax 545-0389
Freed MS | 500/6-8
715 W 20th St 81003 | 719-549-7410
Cheryl Madrill-Stringham, prin. | Fax 562-0816
Heaton MS | 700/6-8
6 Adair Rd 81001 | 719-549-7420
Denise Garcia-Cooper, prin. | Fax 549-7838
Pitts MS | 700/6-8
29 Lehigh Ave 81005 | 719-549-7430
John Huff, prin. | Fax 549-7878
Risley MS | 400/6-8
625 N Monument Ave 81001 | 719-549-7440
Rena Jimenez, prin. | Fax 549-7926
Roncalli MS | 700/6-8
4202 W State Highway 78 81005 | 719-549-7450
Bradley Farbo, prin. | Fax 549-7469
South HS | 1,400/9-12
1801 Hollywood Dr 81005 | 719-549-7255
James Wessely, prin. | Fax 549-7759

Keating Education Center | Adult
215 E Orman Ave 81004 | 719-549-7371
Greg Millard, prin. | Fax 549-7704

Pueblo County Rural SD 70 | 7,500/PK-12
24951 E US Highway 50 81006 | 719-542-0220
Daniel Lere, supt. | Fax 542-0225
www.district70.org/
Pleasant View MS | 400/6-8
23600 Everett Rd 81006 | 719-542-7813
Margery Dudley, prin. | Fax 542-6291
Pueblo County HS | 800/9-12
1050 35th Ln 81006 | 719-948-3352
Jose Perea, prin. | Fax 948-0196
Pueblo Technical Academy | Vo/Tech
900 W Orman Ave 81004 | 719-549-3317
Kent Muckel, prin.
Vineland MS | 300/6-8
1132 36th Ln 81006 | 719-948-3336
Laurie Stratman, prin. | Fax 948-2323
Other Schools — See Colorado City, Pueblo West, Rye

Colorado State University - Pueblo | Post-Sec.
2200 Bonforte Blvd 81001 | 719-549-2100
IntelliTec College | Post-Sec.
3673 Parker Blvd Ste 250 81008 | 719-542-3181
Park Hill Christian Academy | 100/PK-12
PO Box 8147 81008 | 719-544-6174
| Fax 544-6175
Parkview Medical Center | Post-Sec.
400 W 16th St 81003 | 719-584-4573
Pueblo Community College | Post-Sec.
900 W Orman Ave 81004 | 719-549-3200

Pueblo West, Pueblo, Pop. 4,386
Pueblo County Rural SD 70
Supt. — See Pueblo
Pueblo West HS | 1,000/9-12
661 W Capistrano Ave 81007 | 719-547-8050
Martha Nogare, prin. | Fax 547-8053
Pueblo West MS | 400/6-8
484 S Maher Dr 81007 | 719-547-3752
Phillip Compton, prin. | Fax 547-3753
Sky View MS | 500/6-8
1047 S Camino De Bravo 81007 | 719-547-1175
Anna Lou White, prin.

Summit Classical Christian Academy | 50/K-12
694 E Spaulding Ave 81007 | 719-565-3343
Charlene Dengler, admin.

Rangely, Rio Blanco, Pop. 2,065
Rangely SD RE-4 | 600/PK-12
550 River Rd 81648 | 970-675-2207
Jim Day, supt. | Fax 675-5143
www.rangelyk12.org/
Rangely HS | 200/9-12
234 S Jones Ave 81648 | 970-675-2253
Patrick Moore, prin. | Fax 675-5403
Rangely MS | 100/6-8
550 River Rd 81648 | 970-675-5021
Jim Day, prin. | Fax 675-5143

Colorado Northwestern Community College | Post-Sec.
500 Kennedy Dr 81648 | 800-562-1105

Ridgway, Ouray, Pop. 737
Ridgway SD R-2 | 200/PK-12
PO Box 230 81432 | 970-626-4320
Douglas Bissonette, supt. | Fax 626-4337
ridgway.co.schoolwebpages.com/
Ridgway MS, PO Box 230 81432 | 6-8
Christopher Martin, prin. | 970-626-5468
Ridgway Secondary S | 100/9-12
PO Box 230 81432 | 970-626-5468
Michael Roggero, prin. | Fax 626-5597

Rifle, Garfield, Pop. 7,483
Garfield SD RE-2 | 3,800/PK-12
839 Whiteriver Ave 81650 | 970-625-7600
Dr. Gary Pack, supt. | Fax 625-7623
www.garfieldre2.k12.co.us
Rifle HS | 900/9-12
1350 Prefontaine Ave 81650 | 970-625-7725
Todd Ellis, prin. | Fax 625-7785
Rifle MS | 700/5-8
753 Railroad Ave 81650 | 970-625-7900
Susan Birdsey, prin. | Fax 625-7930
Other Schools — See New Castle

Rocky Ford, Otero, Pop. 4,137
Rocky Ford SD R-2 | 800/K-12
601 S 8th St 81067 | 719-254-7423
Nancy Aschermann, supt. | Fax 254-7425
www.rockyford.k12.co.us/
Jefferson MS | 200/6-8
901 S 11th St 81067 | 719-254-7669
Monica Johnson, prin. | Fax 254-4307
Rocky Ford HS | 200/9-12
100 W Washington Ave 81067 | 719-254-7431
Russell Bates, prin. | Fax 254-7436

Rush, El Paso, Pop. 100
Miami-Yoder SD 60 JT | 400/K-12
420 S Rush Rd 80833 | 719-478-2186
Paul Dellacroce, supt. | Fax 478-5380
Miami-Yoder JSHS | 200/7-12
420 S Rush Rd 80833 | 719-478-2186
Chris Whetzel, prin. | Fax 478-5380

Rye, Pueblo, Pop. 204
Pueblo County Rural SD 70
Supt. — See Pueblo
Rye HS, PO Box 10 81069 | 200/9-12
Richard Sanchez, prin. | 719-489-2271

Saguache, Saguache, Pop. 600
Mountain Valley SD RE-1 | 200/K-12
PO Box 127 81149 | 719-655-0267
Brady Stagner, supt. | Fax 655-0269
www.valley.k12.co.us
Mountain Valley HS | 100/9-12
PO Box 127 81149 | 719-655-2578
Brady Stagner, prin. | Fax 655-2875
Mountain Valley MS | 50/6-8
PO Box 127 81149 | 719-655-2578
Brady Stagner, prin. | Fax 655-2875

Salida, Chaffee, Pop. 5,494
Salida SD R-32 | 1,200/K-12
310 E 9th St 81201 | 719-530-5252
James Wilson, supt. | Fax 539-6220
www.salida.k12.co.us/
Salida HS | 400/9-12
905 D St 81201 | 719-530-5400
Robert Carrick, prin. | Fax 539-2407
Salida MS | 400/5-8
520 Milford St 81201 | 719-530-5300
Rebecca Minnis, prin. | Fax 530-5364

Sanford, Conejos, Pop. 795
Sanford SD 6J | 400/PK-12
PO Box 39 81151 | 719-274-5167
Kevin Edgar, supt. | Fax 274-5830
Sanford JSHS | 200/7-12
PO Box 39 81151 | 719-274-5167
David Judd, prin. | Fax 274-5830

San Luis, Costilla, Pop. 720
Centennial SD R-1 | 200/PK-12
PO Box 350 81152 | 719-672-3322
Diana Cortez, supt. | Fax 672-3345
centennialschoolsr-1.com
Centennial HS, PO Box 350 81152 | 100/9-12
David Judd, prin. | 719-672-3322
Centennial JHS, PO Box 350 81152 | 50/7-8
David Judd, prin. | 719-672-3322

Seibert, Kit Carson, Pop. 182
Hi-Plains SD R-23
Supt. — See Vona
Hi-Plains JSHS | 100/7-12
PO Box 238 80834 | 970-664-2616
Steven McCracken, prin. | Fax 664-2622

Sheridan, Arapahoe, Pop. 5,577
Sheridan SD 2 | 1,600/PK-12
4000 S Lowell Blvd 80110 | 720-833-6991
Michael Poore, supt. | Fax 833-6649
www.sheridank12.org
Sheridan HS | 600/9-12
3201 W Oxford Ave 80110 | 720-833-6987
Greg Gotchey, prin. | Fax 833-6833
Sheridan MS | 400/6-8
4107 S Federal Blvd 80110 | 720-833-6988
William Wooddell, prin. | Fax 833-6903

Sheridan Lake, Kiowa, Pop. 61
Plainview SD RE-2 | 100/K-12
13997 County Road 71 81071 | 719-729-3331
Garry Coulter, supt. | Fax 727-4471
Plainview JHSH | 50/6-12
13997 County Road 71 81071 | 719-729-3331
Garry Coulter, prin.

Silverton, San Juan, Pop. 545
Silverton SD 1 | 100/K-12
PO Box 128 81433 | 970-387-5543
Kim White, supt. | Fax 387-5791
www.silvertonschool.org
Silverton JSHS | 50/6-12
PO Box 128 81433 | 970-387-5543
Kim White, prin. | Fax 387-5791

Simla, Elbert, Pop. 715
Big Sandy SD 100J | 300/K-12
PO Box 68 80835 | 719-541-2292
Steve Wilson, supt. | Fax 541-2186
Simla JSHS | 200/6-12
PO Box 68 80835 | 719-541-2291
Rik Dahl, prin. | Fax 541-2443

Springfield, Baca, Pop. 1,439
Springfield SD RE-4 | 300/PK-12
389 Tipton St 81073 | 719-523-6654
Michael Salvato, supt. | Fax 523-4192
www.springfield.k12.co.us/
Springfield HS | 100/9-12
389 Tipton St 81073 | 719-523-6522
Richard Hargrove, prin. | Fax 523-4361
Springfield JHS | 50/7-8
389 Tipton St 81073 | 719-523-6522
Richard Hargrove, prin. | Fax 523-4361

Steamboat Springs, Routt, Pop. 9,390
Steamboat Springs SD RE-2 | 1,900/K-12
PO Box 774368 80477 | 970-879-1530
Donna Howell, supt. | Fax 879-3943
www.sssd.k12.co.us
Steamboat Springs HS | 600/9-12
PO Box 774368 80477 | 970-879-1562
Mike Knezevich, prin. | Fax 879-8039
Steamboat Springs MS | 500/6-8
PO Box 774368 80477 | 970-879-1058
Tim Bishop, prin. | Fax 870-0368

Christian Heritage S | 100/K-12
27285 Brandon Cir 80487 | 970-879-1760
Tim Calkins, hdmstr. | Fax 879-5511
Colorado Mountain College | Post-Sec.
PO Box 775288 80477 | 800-621-8559
Whiteman S | 100/9-12
42605 County Road 36 80487 | 970-879-1350
Walt Daub, prin. | Fax 879-0506

Sterling, Logan, Pop. 12,785
Valley SD RE-1 | 2,000/PK-12
415 Beattie St 80751 | 970-522-0792
Dr. Betty Summers, supt. | Fax 522-0525
www.re1valleyschools.org/
Sterling HS | 700/9-12
407 W Broadway St 80751 | 970-522-2944
Doug Stutzman, prin. | Fax 522-2900
Sterling MS | 600/6-8
1177 Pawnee Ave 80751 | 970-522-1041
Robert Hall, prin. | Fax 522-0306
Other Schools — See Iliff

Northeastern Junior College | Post-Sec.
100 College Ave 80751 | 970-522-6600

Strasburg, Adams, Pop. 1,200
Strasburg SD 31J | 900/PK-12
PO Box 207 80136 | 303-622-9211
Dr. David VanSant, supt. | Fax 622-9224
www.strasburg31j.com

Strasburg HS | 300/9-12
PO Box 207 80136 | 303-622-9211
Jeffrey Rasp, prin. | Fax 622-9224
Strasburg JHS, PO Box 207 80136 | 100/7-8
Jeffrey Rasp, prin. | 303-622-9211

Stratton, Kit Carson, Pop. 657
Stratton SD R-4 | 300/PK-12
219 Illinois Ave 80836 | 719-348-5369
Eric Moser, supt. | Fax 348-5555
www.strattonschools.org
Stratton HS | 100/9-12
219 Illinois Ave 80836 | 719-348-5369
Vici Jennings, prin. | Fax 348-5555
Stratton MS, PO Box 266 80836 | 50/7-8
Vici Jennings, prin. | 719-348-5369

Swink, Otero, Pop. 691
Swink SD 33 | 400/K-12
PO Box 487 81077 | 719-384-8103
Pat Lesar, supt. | Fax 384-5471
www.swink.k12.co.us/
Swink JSHS | 200/7-12
PO Box 487 81077 | 719-384-8103
Dianna Milenski, prin. | Fax 384-5471

Telluride, San Miguel, Pop. 2,321
Telluride SD R-1 | 600/K-12
725 W Colorado Ave 81435 | 970-728-6617
Mary Rubadeau, supt. | Fax 728-9490
www.tellurideschool.org
Telluride MSHS | 300/6-12
725 W Colorado Ave 81435 | 970-728-4377
Peter Mueller, prin. | Fax 728-0257

Thornton, Adams, Pop. 96,584
Mapleton SD 1
Supt. — See Denver
Mapleton Expeditionary S of the Arts | 6-12
8990 York St 80229 | 303-853-1270
Mike Johnston, dir.
Skyview Academy HS | 9-12
8990 York St 80229 | 303-853-1900
Eldon Wire, dir.
Skyview SHS | 300/12-12
8990 York St 80229 | 303-853-1200
Jim Hamilton, dir. | Fax 853-1256

Northglenn-Thornton 12 SD | 30,900/PK-12
1500 E 128th Ave 80241 | 720-972-4000
Mike Paskewicz, supt. | Fax 972-4169
www.adams12.org
Bollman Technical Education Center | Vo/Tech
9451 Washington St 80229 | 720-972-5820
Kim Howell, prin. | Fax 972-5869
Century MS | 1,300/6-8
13000 Lafayette St 80241 | 720-972-5240
Phil Friedrich, prin. | Fax 972-5279
Horizon HS | 2,100/9-12
5321 E 136th Ave 80602 | 720-972-4400
Randy Swanson, prin. | Fax 972-4599
Rocky Top MS, 14150 York St 80602 | 6-8
Jami C. Miller, prin. | 720-972-2200
Shadow Ridge MS | 1,300/6-8
12551 Holly St 80241 | 720-972-5040
Dennis J. Kennedy, prin. | Fax 972-5079
Thornton HS | 2,300/9-12
9351 Washington St 80229 | 720-972-4800
Kerry Moynihan, prin. | Fax 972-4999
Thornton MS | 900/6-8
9451 Hoffman Way 80229 | 720-972-5160
Barb Galicia, prin. | Fax 972-5199
High Plains Adult Evening HS | Adult
455 Eppinger Blvd 80229 | 720-972-5818
Nancy MacDonnell, prin. | Fax 972-5819
Other Schools – See Broomfield, Denver, Northglenn, Westminster

Artistic Beauty College | Post-Sec.
3811 E 120th Ave 80233 | 303-451-5808
Denver Career College | Post-Sec.
500 E 84th Ave Ste W200 80229 | 800-848-0550
HealthONE North Suburban Medical Center | Post-Sec.
9191 Grant St 80229 | 303-451-7800
ITT Technical Institute | Post-Sec.
500 E 84th Ave 80229 | 303-288-4488

Trinidad, Las Animas, Pop. 9,152
Trinidad SD 1 | 1,400/K-12
215 S Maple St 81082 | 719-846-3324
Dr. Frank Lucero, supt. | Fax 846-2957
www.trinidad.k12.co.us/
Trinidad HS | 500/9-12
816 West St 81082 | 719-846-2971
Jenifer Mason, prin. | Fax 846-7488
Trinidad MS | 300/6-8
614 Park St 81082 | 719-846-4411
Deana Dunford, prin. | Fax 846-4740

Trinidad State Junior College | Post-Sec.
600 Prospect St 81082 | 719-846-5621

USAF Academy, El Paso, Pop. 9,062
Academy SD 20
Supt. — See Colorado Springs
Air Academy HS | 1,500/9-12
6910 Carlton Dr, | 719-234-2400
Dr. Erik Fredell, prin. | Fax 234-2599

United States Air Force Academy | Post-Sec.
| 719-333-1110

Vail, Eagle, Pop. 4,603

Vail Mountain S | 300/K-12
3000 Booth Falls Rd 81657 | 970-476-3850
Peter Abuisi, prin. | Fax 476-3860

Vilas, Baca, Pop. 103
Vilas SD RE-5 | 100/PK-12
PO Box 727 81087 | 719-523-6738
Joseph Shields, supt. | Fax 523-4818
www.vilas.k12.co.us
Vilas Undivided HS | 100/7-12
PO Box 727 81087 | 719-523-6738
Joe Shields, prin. | Fax 523-4818

Vona, Kit Carson, Pop. 93
Hi-Plains SD R-23 | 100/PK-12
PO Box 9 80861 | 970-664-2636
Ronald Conrad, supt. | Fax 664-2283
Other Schools – See Seibert

Walden, Jackson, Pop. 690
North Park SD R-1 | 300/PK-12
PO Box 798 80480 | 970-723-3300
Sandra Hall, supt. | Fax 723-8486
www.northpark.k12.co.us
North Park JSHS | 100/7-12
PO Box 798 80480 | 970-723-3300
Mark Pretz, prin. | Fax 723-4702

Walsenburg, Huerfano, Pop. 4,017
Huerfano SD RE-1 | 500/PK-12
611 W 7th St 81089 | 719-738-1520
Glenn Davis, supt. | Fax 738-3148
huerfano.k12.co.us
Mall HS | 300/7-12
335 W Pine St 81089 | 719-738-1610
Paul Heesaker, prin. | Fax 738-2541

Walsh, Baca, Pop. 697
Walsh SD RE-1 | 200/PK-12
PO Box 68 81090 | 719-324-5632
Kyle Hebberd, supt. | Fax 324-5426
www.walsheagles.com
Walsh JSHS | 100/7-12
PO Box 68 81090 | 719-324-5221
Tom A. Meardon, prin. | Fax 324-5734

Weldona, Morgan, Pop. 325
Weldon Valley SD RE-20(J) | 200/PK-12
911 North Ave 80653 | 970-645-2411
Robert Petterson, supt. | Fax 645-2377
Weldon Valley HS | 100/9-12
911 North Ave 80653 | 970-645-2411
Francine Covelli, prin.
Weldon Valley JHS | 50/7-8
911 North Ave 80653 | 970-645-2411
Francine Covelli, prin.

Wellington, Larimer, Pop. 2,632
Poudre SD R-1
Supt. — See Fort Collins
Wellington JHS | 300/7-9
4001 Wilson Ave 80549 | 970-568-3944
Alicia Durand, prin. | Fax 568-3901

Westcliffe, Custer, Pop. 460
Custer County SD C-1 | 500/PK-12
PO Box 730 81252 | 719-783-2357
Steve Marantino, supt. | Fax 783-2334
bobcats.ccs.k12.co.us/district/district.html
Custer County HS | 200/9-12
PO Box 730 81252 | 719-783-2291
Lance Villers, prin. | Fax 783-4944
Custer County JHS | 100/6-8
PO Box 730 81252 | 719-783-2291
Lance Villers, prin.

Westminster, Adams, Pop. 103,391
Adams County SD 50 | 10,400/PK-12
4476 W 68th Ave 80030 | 303-428-3511
Dr. Roberta Selleck, supt. | Fax 428-2810
www.adams50.org
Hidden Lake HS | Vo/Tech
7300 Lowell Blvd 80030 | 303-428-2600
Cheryl Gregg, prin. | Fax 428-2142
Shaw Heights MS | 600/6-8
8780 Circle Dr 80031 | 303-428-9533
Myla Shepherd, prin. | Fax 650-6859
Westminster HS | 1,400/9-12
4276 W 68th Ave 80030 | 303-428-9541
Byron Wiehe, prin. | Fax 657-3988
Other Schools – See Denver

Jefferson County SD R-1
Supt. — See Golden
Carle MS, 10200 W 100th Ave 80021 | 7-8
Greg Bushey, prin. | 303-982-6540
Mandalay MS | 900/7-8
9651 Pierce St 80021 | 303-982-9802
Karen Quanbeck, prin. | Fax 982-9813
Standley Lake HS | 1,700/9-12
9300 W 104th Ave 80021 | 303-982-3311
Todd Engels, prin. | Fax 982-3312

Northglenn-Thornton 12 SD
Supt. — See Thornton
Mountain Range HS | 9-12
12500 Huron St 80234 | 720-972-6300
Julie Enger, prin. | Fax 972-6498

Artistic Beauty College | Post-Sec.
3049 W 74th Ave Ste A 80030 | 303-428-5100
Belleview Christian S | 400/PK-12
3455 W 83rd Ave 80031 | 303-427-5459
Gary Dickinson, prin. | Fax 426-6768
Colorado Institute of Reading & Writing | 50/K-12
Dixon Dr 80031 | 303-466-3520
Denver Academy of Court Reporting | Post-Sec.
9051 Harlan St Ste 20 80031 | 303-427-5292
Devereux/Wallace Center | 100/K-12
8405 Church Ranch Blvd 80021 | 303-466-7391
DeVry University | Post-Sec.
1870 W 122nd Ave 80234 | 303-280-7600
Front Range Community College | Post-Sec.
3645 W 112th Ave 80031 | 303-466-8811

Hyland Christian S | 100/K-12
5255 W 98th Ave 80020 | 303-466-1673
LIFE Christian Academy | 300/PK-12
11500 Sheridan Blvd 80020 | 303-438-1260
Kenneth Walsh, supt. | Fax 438-1866

Weston, Las Animas, Pop. 200
Primero RSD 2 | 200/PK-12
20200 State Highway 12 81091 | 719-868-2715
Mike Sparaco, supt. | Fax 868-2241
Primero JSHS | 100/6-12
20200 State Highway 12 81091 | 719-868-2715
Mike Sparaco, supt. | Fax 868-2241

Wheat Ridge, Jefferson, Pop. 31,782
Jefferson County SD R-1
Supt. — See Golden
Everitt MS | 600/7-8
3900 Kipling St 80033 | 303-982-1580
Kathleen Norton, prin. | Fax 982-1581
Wheat Ridge HS | 1,500/9-12
9505 W 32nd Ave 80033 | 303-982-7695
Pat Harrison, prin. | Fax 982-7696
Wheat Ridge MS | 400/7-8
7101 W 38th Ave 80033 | 303-982-2833
B.J. Pell, prin. | Fax 982-2834

Beth Eden Baptist S | 200/K-12
2600 Wadsworth Blvd 80033 | 303-232-2313
Steve Curtis M.A., prin. | Fax 232-3027
Colorado Catholic Academy | 100/1-12
11180 W 44th Ave 80033 | 303-422-9549
Stephen Doyle, prin. | Fax 422-9549
Foothills Academy | 200/PK-12
4725 Miller St 80033 | 303-431-0920
Mary Faddick, prin. | Fax 431-9505

Wiggins, Morgan, Pop. 922
Wiggins SD RE-50(J) | 600/PK-12
320 Chapman St 80654 | 970-483-7762
Dr. Sharol Little, supt. | Fax 483-6205
www.wiggins50.k12.co.us/
Wiggins HS | 300/7-12
320 Chapman St 80654 | 970-483-7763
Richard Jones, prin. | Fax 483-7796

Wiley, Prowers, Pop. 475
Wiley SD RE-13 JT | 300/PK-12
PO Box 247 81092 | 719-829-4806
Mike Doyle, supt. | Fax 829-4805
www.wiley.k12.co.us
Wiley JSHS | 200/7-12
PO Box 247 81092 | 719-829-4806
Ruth Ann Cullen, prin. | Fax 829-4805

Windsor, Weld, Pop. 13,086
Weld County SD RE-4 | 2,800/PK-12
PO Box 609 80550 | 970-686-8000
Karen Trusler, supt. | Fax 686-5280
www.windsor.k12.co.us
Windsor HS | 800/9-12
1100 Main St 80550 | 970-686-8100
Kirk Salmela, prin. | Fax 686-0935
Windsor MS | 700/6-8
900 Main St 80550 | 970-686-8200
Douglas Englert, prin. | Fax 686-7122

Woodland Park, Teller, Pop. 6,751
Woodland Park SD RE-2 | 3,100/PK-12
PO Box 99 80866 | 719-687-6048
John Pacheco, supt. | Fax 687-8408
www.wpsdk12.org/
Woodland Park HS | 1,100/9-12
PO Box 6820 80866 | 719-686-2067
Jo Spry, prin. | Fax 687-3880
Woodland Park MS | 800/6-8
PO Box 6790 80866 | 719-686-2200
John Jamison, prin. | Fax 687-8458

Woodrow, Washington, Pop. 20
Woodlin SD R-104 | 100/PK-12
PO Box 185 80757 | 970-386-2223
Rose Cronk, supt. | Fax 386-2241
www.woodlinschool.com
Woodlin Undivided HS | 50/7-12
PO Box 185 80757 | 970-386-2223
Rose Cronk, prin.

Wray, Yuma, Pop. 2,165
Wray SD RD-2 | 700/PK-12
PO Box 157 80758 | 970-332-5764
Ron Howard, supt. | Fax 332-5773
www.wrayschools.org
Buchanan MS | 200/5-8
PO Box 157 80758 | 970-332-4723
Myra Westfall, prin. | Fax 332-3356
Wray HS | 200/9-12
PO Box 157 80758 | 970-332-5758
George Purnell, prin. | Fax 332-4476

Yoder, El Paso, Pop. 40
Edison SD 54 JT | 100/PK-12
14550 Edison Rd 80864 | 719-478-2125
David Grosche, supt. | Fax 478-3000
www.edison54jt.org
Edison JSHS, 14550 Edison Rd 80864 | 50/6-12
Rachel Paul, prin. | 719-478-2125

Yuma, Yuma, Pop. 3,269
Yuma SD 1 | 900/PK-12
PO Box 327 80759 | 970-848-5831
Dick Heger, supt. | Fax 848-2256
www.yumaschools.org
Yuma HS | 300/9-12
1000 S Albany St 80759 | 970-848-5488
David Wells, prin. | Fax 848-0314
Yuma MS | 300/5-8
500 S Elm St 80759 | 970-848-2000
Donna Fields, prin. | Fax 848-4261

CONNECTICUT

CONNECTICUT DEPARTMENT OF EDUCATION
165 Capitol Ave, Hartford 06106-1659
Telephone 860-566-8792
Fax 860-566-8964
Website http://www.state.ct.us/sde

Commissioner of Education   Betty Sternberg

CONNECTICUT BOARD OF EDUCATION
165 Capitol Ave, Hartford 06106-1659

Chairperson   Allan Taylor

REGIONAL EDUCATIONAL SERVICE CENTERS

Area Coop. Educational Services RESC
Cheryl Saloom Ed.D., dir.   203-498-6800
350 State St, North Haven 06473   Fax 498-6890
www.aces.k12.ct.us
Capitol Region Education Council RESC
Dr. Bruce Douglas, dir.   860-524-4063
111 Charter Oak Ave   Fax 548-9924
Hartford 06106
www.crec.org

Cooperative Educational Services RESC
Nancy Cetorelli, dir.   203-365-8803
40 Lindeman Dr, Trumbull 06611   Fax 365-8804
www.ces.k12.ct.us
Eastconn RESC
Paula Colen, dir.   860-455-0707
376 Hartford Tpke, Hampton 06247 Fax 455-8026
www.eastconn.org

Education Connection RESC
Danuta Thibodeau, dir.   860-567-0863
PO Box 909, Litchfield 06759   Fax 567-3381
www.educationconnection.org
Learn RESC
Virginia Seccombe, dir.   860-434-4800
44 Hatchetts Hill Rd   Fax 434-4820
Old Lyme 06371
www.learn.k12.ct.us

PUBLIC, PRIVATE AND CATHOLIC SECONDARY SCHOOLS

Ansonia, New Haven, Pop. 18,818
Ansonia SD   2,700/PK-12
42 Grove St 06401   203-736-5095
Dr. Edward Favolise, supt.   Fax 736-5098
www.ansonia.org
Ansonia HS   700/9-12
20 Pulaski Hwy 06401   203-736-5060
Wilhemenia Christon, prin.   Fax 736-5068
Ansonia MS   700/6-8
115 Howard Ave 06401   203-736-5070
Lynn Bennett-Wallick, prin.   Fax 736-1044

Connecticut Technical HS System
Supt. — See Middletown
O'Brien Technical HS   Vo/Tech
141 Prindle Ave 06401   203-732-1800
Lisa Hylwa-Colandro, dir.   Fax 735-6236

Avon, Hartford
Avon SD   3,200/PK-12
34 Simsbury Rd 06001   860-404-4700
Richard Kisiel, supt.   Fax 404-4702
www.avon.k12.ct.us
Avon HS   900/9-12
510 W Avon Rd 06001   860-404-4740
Lawrence Sparks, prin.   Fax 404-4743
Avon MS   500/7-8
375 W Avon Rd 06001   860-404-4770
Jody Goeler, prin.   Fax 404-4773

Avon Old Farms S   400/9-12
500 Old Farms Rd 06001   860-404-4100
Kenneth LaRocque, hdmstr.   Fax 404-4135

Baltic, New London

Academy of the Holy Family   100/9-12
PO Box 691 06330   860-822-9272
Sr. Mary Patrick Mulready, prin.   Fax 822-1318

Beacon Falls, New Haven
Regional SD 16
Supt. — See Prospect
Woodland Regional HS   700/9-12
135 Back Rimmon Rd 06403   203-881-5551
Dr. Arnold Frank, prin.   Fax 881-2015

Berlin, Hartford
Berlin SD   3,300/PK-12
238 Kensington Rd 06037   860-828-6581
Dr. Michael Cicchetti, supt.   Fax 829-0832
www.berlinschools.org
Berlin HS   1,100/9-12
139 Patterson Way 06037   860-828-6577
George Synnott, prin.   Fax 829-2169
McGee MS   800/6-8
899 Norton Rd 06037   860-828-0323
Brian Benigni, prin.   Fax 828-0676

Bethany, New Haven
Regional SD 5
Supt. — See Woodbridge
Amity Regional MS   400/7-8
190 Luke Hill Rd 06524   203-393-3102
Richard Dellinger, prin.   Fax 393-0583

Bethel, Fairfield, Pop. 8,835
Bethel SD   3,200/K-12
PO Box 253 06801   203-794-8601
Gary Chesley, supt.   Fax 794-8723
www.bethel.k12.ct.us

Bethel HS   1,000/9-12
300 Whittlesey Dr 06801   203-794-8620
Patricia Cosentino, prin.   Fax 794-8618
Bethel MS   800/6-8
600 Whittlesey Dr 06801   203-794-8663
Kevin Smith, prin.   Fax 794-8718

Bethlehem, Litchfield

Woodhall S   50/9-12
PO Box 550 06751   203-266-7788
                                   Fax 266-5896

Bloomfield, Hartford, Pop. 7,200
Bloomfield SD   2,000/PK-12
1133 Blue Hills Ave 06002   860-769-4200
David G. Title, supt.   Fax 769-4215
www.bloomfieldschools.org/
Arace MS   400/7-8
390 Park Ave 06002   860-286-2622
Barbara Maybin, prin.   Fax 242-0347
Big Picture HS   9-12
44 Griffin Rd S 06002   860-769-6600
Patricia Hymes, prin.   Fax 769-6605
Bloomfield HS   700/9-12
5 Huckleberry Ln 06002   860-286-2630
Irene Zytka, prin.   Fax 242-9491

Bolton, Tolland
Bolton SD   1,000/K-12
108 Notch Rd 06043   860-643-1569
Thomas Cronin, supt.   Fax 647-8452
Bolton HS, 72 Brandy St 06043   300/9-12
Paul Smith, prin.   860-643-2768

King's S   100/5-12
PO Box 9175 06043   860-645-6466
James Kirch, prin.   Fax 645-1889

Branford, New Haven, Pop. 27,603
Branford SD   3,700/PK-12
1111 Main St 06405   203-315-7800
Dr. Kathleen Halligan, supt.   Fax 315-3505
www.branford.k12.ct.us
Branford HS   1,200/9-12
185 E Main St 06405   203-488-7291
Edmund Higgins, prin.   Fax 315-6740
Walsh IS   1,200/5-8
185 Damascus Rd 06405   203-488-8317
Robin Goeler, prin.   Fax 481-2785

Branford Hall Career Institute   Post-Sec.
1 Summit Pl 06405   203-488-2525
Connecticut School of Electronics Post-Sec.
221 W Main St 06405   203-315-1060

Bridgeport, Fairfield, Pop. 139,664
Bridgeport SD   22,400/PK-12
45 Lyon Ter Rm 203 06604   203-576-7302
John Ramos Ed.D., supt.   Fax 337-0150
www.bridgeportedu.com
Bassick HS   1,200/9-12
1181 Fairfield Ave 06605   203-576-7350
Ronald Remey, prin.   Fax 576-7736
Central HS   2,200/9-12
1 Lincoln Blvd 06606   203-576-7377
Alejandro Ortiz, prin.   Fax 576-7855
Harding HS   1,600/9-12
1734 Central Ave 06610   203-576-7330
Hector Sanchez, prin.   Fax 576-7762

Connecticut Technical HS System
Supt. — See Middletown
Bullard-Havens Technical HS   Vo/Tech
500 Palisade Ave 06610   203-579-6333
Joseph LaVorgna, dir.   Fax 579-6904

Bridgeport Hospital   Post-Sec.
267 Grant St 06610   203-384-3464
Bridgeport Hospital School of Nursing Post-Sec.
200 Mill Hill Ave 06610   203-384-3022
Butler Business School   Post-Sec.
2710 North Ave 06604   203-333-3601
Housatonic Community College   Post-Sec.
900 Lafayette Blvd 06604   203-332-5000
Kolbe Cathedral HS   300/9-12
33 Calhoun Pl 06604   203-335-2554
Jo Anne Jakab, prin.   Fax 335-2556
Leon Institute of Hair Design   Post-Sec.
111 Wall St 06604   203-333-1465
St. Vincent's College   Post-Sec.
2800 Main St 06606   203-576-5235
University of Bridgeport   Post-Sec.
126 Park Ave 06604   203-576-4000

Bristol, Hartford, Pop. 60,722
Bristol SD   9,000/PK-12
PO Box 450 06011   860-584-7002
Dr. Michael J. Wasta, supt.   Fax 584-7611
www.bristol.k12.ct.us
Bristol Central HS   1,400/9-12
480 Wolcott St 06010   860-584-7732
Dennis Siegmann, prin.   Fax 584-7713
Bristol Eastern HS   1,400/9-12
632 King St 06010   860-584-7852
V. Everett Lyons, prin.   Fax 584-4886
Chippins Hill MS   1,000/6-8
551 Peacedale St 06010   860-584-3881
Michael Cerruto, prin.   Fax 584-4833
Memorial Boulevard MS   500/6-8
70 Memorial Blvd 06010   860-584-7882
Walter Ives, prin.   Fax 584-3889
Northeast MS   600/6-8
530 Stevens St 06010   860-584-7839
Rochelle Schwartz, prin.   Fax 584-7837

St. Paul HS   400/6-12
1001 Stafford Ave 06010   860-584-0911
Craig Hill, prin.   Fax 585-8815

Broad Brook, Hartford, Pop. 3,585
East Windsor SD
Supt. — See East Windsor
East Windsor MS   500/5-8
38 Main St 06016   860-623-4488
James Slattery, prin.   Fax 654-1915

Brookfield, Fairfield
Brookfield SD   3,100/PK-12
PO Box 5194 06804   203-775-7620
John A. Goetz, supt.   Fax 740-9008
www.brookfield.k12.ct.us/
Brookfield HS   900/9-12
45 Long Meadow Hill Rd 06804   203-775-7725
Richard Nabel, prin.   Fax 775-7773
Whisconier MS   1,000/5-8
17 W Whisconier Rd 06804   203-775-7710
Eugenia Slone, prin.   Fax 775-7615

94

Brooklyn, Windham
Brooklyn SD 1,000/PK-8
119 Gorman Rd 06234 860-774-9153
Louise Berry, supt. Fax 774-6938
www.brooklyn.ctschool.net
Brooklyn MS 400/5-8
119 Gorman Rd 06234 860-774-9153
Matthew Carroll, prin. Fax 774-6938

Burlington, Hartford
Regional SD 10 2,700/PK-12
24 Lyon Rd 06013 860-673-2538
Paula Schwartz, supt. Fax 675-4976
www.region10ct.org
Har-Bur MS 700/6-8
26 Lyon Rd 06013 860-673-6163
Kenneth Platz, prin. Fax 673-3481
Mills HS 700/9-12
26 Lyon Rd 06013 860-673-0423
Karissa Niehoff, prin. Fax 673-9128

Canterbury, Windham
Canterbury SD 600/PK-8
45 Westminster Rd 06331 860-546-6950
Sandra Suplicki, supt. Fax 546-6423
Baldwin MS 300/5-8
45 Westminster Rd 06331 860-546-9421
Kathleen Boyhan-Maus, prin. Fax 546-6289

Central Village, Windham
Plainfield SD
Supt. — See Plainfield
Plainfield HS 700/9-12
PO Box 218 06332 860-564-6417
Susan Rourke, prin. Fax 564-2116

Chaplin, Windham
Regional SD 11 300/7-12
PO Box 277 06235 860-455-9306
Dr. Edward Malvey, supt. Fax 455-1263
www.parishhill.org/
Parish Hill JSHS 300/7-12
PO Box 275 06235 860-455-9584
Fax 455-9081

Cheshire, New Haven, Pop. 25,684
Cheshire SD 5,200/PK-12
29 Main St 06410 203-250-2420
Greg Florio, supt. Fax 250-2453
www.cheshire.k12.ct.us/
Cheshire HS 1,600/9-12
525 S Main St 06410 203-250-2511
Judy Gallagher, prin. Fax 250-2563
Dodd MS 800/7-8
100 Park Pl 06410 203-272-3249
Donald Wailonis, prin. Fax 250-7614

Cheshire Academy 400/6-12
10 Main St 06410 203-272-5396
Ralph Van Inwagen, hdmstr. Fax 250-7209

Clinton, Middlesex, Pop. 3,439
Clinton SD 2,100/PK-12
137 Glenwood Rd # B 06413 860-664-6500
Albert Coviello, supt. Fax 664-6580
www.clintonpublic.org
Eliot MS 500/6-8
69 Fairy Dell Rd 06413 860-664-6503
Linda Tucker, prin. Fax 664-6583
Morgan S 600/9-12
27 Killingworth Tpke 06413 860-664-6504
William Barney, prin. Fax 664-6584

Colchester, New London, Pop. 3,212
Colchester SD 3,100/K-12
127 Norwich Ave #202 06415 860-537-7260
Karen Loiselle, supt. Fax 537-1252
www.colchesterct.org/
Bacon Academy HS 900/9-12
611 Norwich Ave 06415 860-537-2378
Jeffry Mathieu, prin. Fax 537-5410
Johnston MS 800/6-8
360 Norwich Ave 06415 860-537-2313
Candace Sullivan, prin. Fax 537-6258

Collinsville, Hartford, Pop. 2,591
Canton SD 1,400/PK-12
4 Market St Ste 100 06019 860-693-7704
Dr. Anthony Serio, supt. Fax 693-7706
www.cantonschools.org
Canton HS 500/9-12
76 Simonds Ave 06019 860-693-7707
Gary Gula, prin. Fax 693-7812
Canton MS 7-8
76 Simonds Ave 06019 860-693-7712
Joseph Scheideler, prin. Fax 693-7812

Coventry, Tolland, Pop. 10,063
Coventry SD 2,100/PK-12
1700 Main St 06238 860-742-7317
Donna Bernard, supt. Fax 742-4567
www.coventrypublicschools.org/
Coventry HS 600/9-12
78 Ripley Hill Rd 06238 860-742-7346
Charles Britton, prin. Fax 742-4591
Hale MS 500/6-8
1776 Main St 06238 860-742-7334
Marie Castle-Good, prin. Fax 742-4565

Cromwell, Middlesex
Cromwell SD 1,900/PK-12
9 Mann Memorial Dr 06416 860-632-4830
Dr. Mark Cohan, supt. Fax 632-4865
www.cromwellschools.org/
Cromwell HS 500/9-12
34 Evergreen Rd 06416 860-632-4841
Barbara Miles, prin. Fax 613-3363
Cromwell MS 600/5-8
6 Mann Memorial Dr 06416 860-632-4853
Harry Dumeer, prin. Fax 632-4863

Holy Apostles College and Seminary Post-Sec.
33 Prospect Hill Rd 06416 860-632-3000

Danbury, Fairfield, Pop. 77,353
Connecticut Technical HS System
Supt. — See Middletown
Abbott Technical HS Vo/Tech
21 Hayestown Ave 06811 203-797-4460
Robert Sandagata, dir. Fax 797-4382

Danbury SD 9,700/PK-12
63 Beaver Brook Rd 06810 203-797-4701
Eddie L. Davis Ph.D., supt. Fax 830-6560
www.danbury.k12.ct.us
Broadview MS 1,100/6-8
72 Hospital Ave 06810 203-797-4861
Edward Robbs, prin. Fax 790-2856
Danbury HS 2,800/9-12
43 Clapboard Ridge Rd 06811 203-797-4803
Catherine Richard, prin. Fax 797-4730
Rogers Park MS 1,100/6-8
21 Memorial Dr 06810 203-797-4881
Jose Olavarria, prin. Fax 790-2829

Regional SD 4 900/7-12
49A High Ridge Rd 06811 860-526-2417
Thomas S. Forcella, supt. Fax 526-5469
www.reg4.k12.ct.us
Other Schools – See Deep River

American Academy of Cosmetology Post-Sec.
109 South St 06810 203-744-0900
Danbury Hospital Post-Sec.
24 Hospital Ave 06810 203-797-7210
Hudson Country Montessori S 200/PK-12
44A Shelter Rock Rd 06810 203-744-8088
Mark Meyer, prin. Fax 748-3403
Immaculate HS 400/9-12
73 Southern Blvd 06810 203-744-1510
Richard Stoops Ed.D., prin. Fax 744-1275
Western Connecticut State University Post-Sec.
181 White St 06810 203-837-8200
Wooster S 500/K-12
91 Miry Brook Rd 06810 203-830-3900
George N. King, hdmstr. Fax 790-7147

Danielson, Windham, Pop. 4,273
Connecticut Technical HS System
Supt. — See Middletown
Ellis Technical HS Vo/Tech
613 Upper Maple St 06239 860-774-8511
Brian Mignault, dir. Fax 779-1563

Killingly SD 2,900/PK-12
PO Box 210 06239 860-779-6600
William Silver, supt. Fax 779-3798
www.killingly.k12.ct.us
Killingly HS 1,000/9-12
79 Westfield Ave 06239 860-779-6620
Mary Christian, prin. Fax 774-0846
Other Schools – See Dayville

Quinebaug Valley Community College Post-Sec.
742 Upper Maple St 06239 860-774-1160

Darien, Fairfield, Pop. 18,130
Darien SD 4,300/PK-12
PO Box 1167 06820 203-656-7412
Donald Fiftal, supt. Fax 656-3052
www.darien.k12.ct.us
Darien HS 1,000/9-12
80 High School Ln 06820 203-655-3981
Jerome Auclair, prin. Fax 655-0462
Middlesex MS 1,000/6-8
204 Hollow Tree Ridge Rd 06820 203-655-2518
Debi Boccanfuso, prin. Fax 655-1627

Dayville, Windham
Killingly SD
Supt. — See Danielson
Killingly IS 800/5-8
1599 Upper Maple St 06241 860-779-6700
Sheryl Kempain, prin. Fax 779-9639

Deep River, Middlesex, Pop. 2,520
Regional SD 4
Supt. — See Danbury
Valley Regional HS 500/9-12
256 Kelsey Hill Rd 06417 860-526-5328
Alan K. Frishman, prin. Fax 526-8123
Winthrop JHS 300/7-8
PO Box 187 06417 860-526-9546
David Russell, prin. Fax 526-3721

Derby, New Haven, Pop. 12,593
Derby SD 1,500/PK-12
PO Box 373 06418 203-736-5027
Janet Robinson, supt. Fax 736-5031
www.derbyps.org/
Derby JSHS 700/7-12
8 Nutmeg Ave 06418 203-736-5032
Craig Drezek, prin. Fax 736-5031

Durham, Middlesex, Pop. 2,650
Regional SD 13 2,100/PK-12
135A Pickett Ln 06422 860-349-7200
Susan Viccaro, supt. Fax 349-7203
www.rsd13ct.org/
Coginchaug Regional HS 600/9-12
PO Box 280 06422 860-349-7215
Steven Wysowski, prin. Fax 349-7136
Strong MS 400/7-8
PO Box 435 06422 860-349-7222
Scott Nicol, prin. Fax 349-7225

Lake Grove School at Durham Post-Sec.
459R Wallingford Rd 06422 860-349-3467

East Granby, Hartford
East Granby SD 900/K-12
PO Box 674 06026 860-653-6486
Robert Kozaczka, supt. Fax 413-9075
www.eastgranby.k12.ct.us/
East Granby HS 200/9-12
95 S Main St 06026 860-653-2541
Dr. Christine Mahoney, prin. Fax 413-9092
East Granby MS 200/6-8
95 S Main St 06026 860-653-2541
Linda Carlson, prin. Fax 413-9092

East Hampton, Middlesex, Pop. 2,167
East Hampton SD 2,100/PK-12
94 Main St 06424 860-365-4000
William Troy, supt. Fax 365-4004
East Hampton HS 500/9-12
50 N Maple St 06424 860-365-4030
Linda Berry, prin. Fax 365-4034
East Hampton MS 500/6-8
19 Childs Rd 06424 860-365-4060
Carol Wheeler, prin. Fax 365-4064

East Hartford, Hartford, Pop. 49,400
Capitol Region Education Council RESC
Supt. — See Hartford
Two Rivers Magnet MS 6-8
337 E River Dr 06108 860-290-3114
Tom Scarice, prin. Fax 290-5330

East Hartford SD 7,900/PK-12
1110 Main St 06108 860-622-5107
Marion Martinez, supt. Fax 622-5119
www.easthartford.org
CT International Baccalaureate Academy 100/9-12
857 Forbes St 06118 860-622-5560
Paul Clapp, dir. Fax 622-5555
East Hartford HS 2,300/9-12
869 Forbes St 06118 860-622-5200
Craig Jordan, prin. Fax 622-5223
East Hartford MS 1,100/7-8
777 Burnside Ave 06108 860-622-5600
Catherine Carbone, prin. Fax 622-5619

Connecticut Institute of Hair Design Post-Sec.
1000 Main St 06108 860-528-5032
Goodwin College Post-Sec.
745 Burnside Ave 06108 860-528-4111
New Testament Baptist Church S 100/PK-12
111 Ash St 06108 860-290-6696
Mark Davis, prin. Fax 290-6698

East Haven, New Haven, Pop. 28,600
East Haven SD 3,900/PK-12
35 Wheelbarrow Ln 06513 203-468-3261
Martin DeFelice, supt. Fax 468-3918
www.east-haven.k12.ct.us/ehsd/
East Haven Academy 200/3-8
200 Tyler St 06512 203-468-3219
Dolores Butcher, prin. Fax 468-3961
East Haven HS 1,100/9-12
35 Wheelbarrow Ln 06513 203-468-3267
John J. Smith, prin. Fax 468-3818
Melillo MS 600/7-8
67 Hudson St 06512 203-468-3227
John Petonito, prin. Fax 468-3866

East Lyme, New London
East Lyme SD 3,200/PK-12
PO Box 176 06333 860-739-3966
Paul Smotas, supt. Fax 739-1215
www.eastlymeschools.org
East Lyme HS 1,200/9-12
PO Box 210 06333 860-739-6946
Lawrence Roberts, prin. Fax 739-1241
Other Schools – See Niantic

Easton, Fairfield
Easton SD
Supt. — See Monroe
Keller MS 500/5-8
360 Sport Hill Rd 06612 203-268-8651
Joan Parker, prin. Fax 268-6105

East Windsor, Hartford
East Windsor SD 1,600/PK-12
70 S Main St 06088 860-623-3346
Dr. Joseph Gallucci, supt. Fax 292-6817
www.ewindsor.k12.ct.us/home
East Windsor HS 500/9-12
76 S Main St 06088 860-623-3361
Joseph Kopf, prin. Fax 623-7197
Other Schools – See Broad Brook

Ellington, Tolland
Ellington SD 2,400/PK-12
PO Box 179 06029 860-896-2300
Dr. Richard Packman, supt. Fax 896-2312
www.ellingtonschools.org
Ellington HS 700/9-12
PO Box 149 06029 860-896-2352
Neil Rinaldi, prin. Fax 896-2366
Ellington MS 400/7-8
46 Middle Butcher Rd 06029 860-896-2339
David Pearson, prin. Fax 896-2351

Enfield, Hartford, Pop. 45,500
Enfield SD 6,600/PK-12
27 Shaker Rd 06082 860-253-6531
John Gallacher, supt. Fax 253-6515
www.enfieldschools.org
Enfield HS 1,000/9-12
1264 Enfield St 06082 860-253-5540
Thomas Duffy, prin. Fax 253-5555
Fermi HS 1,200/9-12
124 N Maple St 06082 860-763-8800
Paul Newton, prin. Fax 763-8810
Kennedy MS 1,100/7-8
155 Raffia Rd 06082 860-763-8855
Timothy Neville, prin. Fax 763-8888

Asnuntuck Community College | Post-Sec.
170 Elm St 06082 | 860-253-3000
Porter and Chester Institute | Post-Sec.
138 Weymouth Rd 06082 | 860-741-2561

Fairfield, Fairfield, Pop. 54,400
Fairfield SD | 8,800/PK-12
PO Box 320189, | 203-255-8371
Ann Clark, supt. | Fax 255-8245
www.fairfield.k12.ct.us
Fairfield Ludlowe HS | 9-12
785 Unquowa Rd, | 203-255-7201
Nancy Larsen, prin. | Fax 255-7213
Fairfield Warde HS | 2,300/9-12
755 Melville Ave, | 203-255-8449
James Coyne, hdmstr. | Fax 255-8284
Fairfield Woods MS | 700/6-8
1115 Fairfield Woods Rd, | 203-255-8334
Lynda Cox, prin. | Fax 255-8210
Ludlowe MS | 800/6-8
689 Unquowa Rd, | 203-255-8345
Glenn Mackno, prin. | Fax 255-8214
Tomlinson MS | 600/6-8
200 Unquowa Rd, | 203-255-8336
Connee Dawson, prin. | Fax 255-8211

Fairfield College Prep S | 800/9-12
1073 N Benson Rd, | 203-254-4000
Dr. Robert A. Perrotta, prin. | Fax 254-4108
Fairfield University | Post-Sec.
1073 N Benson Rd, | 203-254-4000
Notre Dame HS | 600/9-12
220 Jefferson St, | 203-372-6521
Rev. William Sangiovanni, prin. | Fax 374-0387
Sacred Heart University | Post-Sec.
5151 Park Ave, | 203-371-7999

Falls Village, Litchfield
Regional SD 1 | 600/9-12
246 Warren Tpke 06031 | 860-824-0855
Patricia Chamberlain, supt. | Fax 824-1271
Housatonic Valley Regional HS | 600/9-12
246 Warren Tpke 06031 | 860-824-5123
Dr. Gretchen Foster-Mosca, prin. | Fax 824-5419

Farmington, Hartford, Pop. 2,500
Farmington SD | 4,300/PK-12
1 Monteith Dr 06032 | 860-673-8268
Robert Villanova, supt. | Fax 673-8224
www.fpsct.org
Farmington HS | 1,300/9-12
10 Monteith Dr 06032 | 860-673-2514
Kevin Ryan, prin. | Fax 673-7284
Robbins MS | 700/7-8
20 Wolf Pit Rd 06032 | 860-677-2683
Kelly Lyman, prin. | Fax 676-0697

Miss Porter's S | 300/9-12
60 Main St 06032 | 860-409-3500
M. Burch Tracy Ford, hdmstr. | Fax 409-3525
Tunxis Community College | Post-Sec.
271 Scott Swamp Rd 06032 | 860-677-7701
University of Connecticut Health Center | Post-Sec.
263 Farmington Ave 06032 | 860-679-2000

Gales Ferry, New London
Ledyard SD
Supt. — See Ledyard
Ledyard MS | 500/7-8
1860 Route 12 06335 | 860-464-0200
Louis Gabordi, prin. | Fax 464-2155

Glastonbury, Hartford, Pop. 27,901
Glastonbury SD | 6,600/PK-12
PO Box 191 06033 | 860-652-7961
Alan Bookman, supt. | Fax 652-7979
www.glastonburyus.org
Glastonbury HS | 1,900/9-12
330 Hubbard St 06033 | 860-652-7200
Matthew Dunbar, prin. | Fax 652-7267
Smith MS | 1,100/7-8
216 Addison Rd 06033 | 860-652-7040
Donna Schilke, prin. | Fax 652-4450

Granby, Hartford
Granby SD | 2,200/K-12
15B N Granby Rd 06035 | 860-844-5250
Gwen Van Dorp, supt. | Fax 844-6081
www.granby.k12.ct.us
Granby Memorial HS | 600/9-12
315 Salmon Brook St 06035 | 860-844-3014
Alan Addley, prin. | Fax 844-3026
Granby Memorial MS | 400/7-8
321 Salmon Brook St 06035 | 860-844-3029
Shellie Pierce, prin. | Fax 844-3039

Greens Farms, Fairfield

Greens Farms Academy | 600/K-12
PO Box 998, | 203-256-0717
Janet Hartwell, hdmstr. | Fax 256-7501

Greenwich, Fairfield, Pop. 57,100
Greenwich SD | 8,600/K-12
290 Greenwich Ave 06830 | 203-625-7400
Larry Leverett Ed.D., supt. | Fax 618-9379
www.greenwichschools.org
Central MS | 700/6-8
9 Indian Rock Ln 06830 | 203-661-8500
Carol Walsh, prin. | Fax 661-2576
Greenwich HS | 2,600/9-12
10 Hillside Rd 06830 | 203-625-8000
Alan Capasso, prin. | Fax 863-8888
Western MS | 600/6-8
1 Western Junior Hwy 06830 | 203-531-5700
Stacey Gross, prin. | Fax 531-5220
Other Schools – See Riverside

Brunswick S | 800/PK-12
100 Maher Ave 06830 | 203-625-5800
Thomas W. Philip, hdmstr. | Fax 625-5889
Convent of Sacred Heart S | 600/PK-12
1177 King St 06831 | 203-531-6500
Sr. Joan Magnetti, prin. | Fax 531-5206
Greenwich Academy | 800/PK-12
200 N Maple Ave 06830 | 203-625-8900
Molly King, hdmstr. | Fax 869-6580

Griswold, See Jewett City
Griswold SD | 2,300/PK-12
267 Slater Ave 06351 | 860-376-7600
Elizabeth Osga, supt. | Fax 376-7604
griswold.k12.ct.us
Griswold HS | 800/9-12
267 Slater Ave 06351 | 860-376-7640
Mark Frizzell, prin. | Fax 376-7684
Griswold MS | 500/6-8
211 Slater Ave 06351 | 860-376-7630
Preston Shaw, prin. | Fax 376-7631

Groton, New London, Pop. 10,237
Connecticut Technical HS System
Supt. — See Middletown
Grasso Southeastern Technical HS | Vo/Tech
189 Fort Hill Rd 06340 | 860-448-0220
Richard Steel, dir. | Fax 446-9895

Groton SD
Supt. — See Mystic
Fitch HS | 1,400/9-12
101 Groton Long Point Rd 06340 | 860-449-7200
John Luciano, prin. | Fax 449-7255
Fitch MS | 500/6-8
61 Fort Hill Rd 06340 | 860-449-5620
Robert Pendolphi, prin. | Fax 449-5623
West Side MS | 300/6-8
250 Brandegee Ave 06340 | 860-449-5630
K. Michael Talbot, prin. | Fax 449-5628

Connecticut Center for Massage Therapy | Post-Sec.
1154 Poquonnock Rd 06340 | 877-295-2268
University of Connecticut | Post-Sec.
1084 Shennecossett Rd 06340 | 860-486-4444

Guilford, New Haven, Pop. 19,848
Guilford SD | 3,900/PK-12
PO Box 367 06437 | 203-453-8200
Dr. Thomas Forcella, supt. | Fax 453-8211
www.guilford.k12.ct.us/
Adams MS | 700/7-8
233 Church St 06437 | 203-453-2755
Catherine Walker, prin. | Fax 453-8446
Guilford HS | 1,100/9-12
605 New England Rd 06437 | 203-453-2741
Bruce Hall, prin. | Fax 453-6768

Hamden, New Haven, Pop. 52,600
Connecticut Technical HS System
Supt. — See Middletown
Whitney Technical HS | Vo/Tech
71 Jones Rd 06514 | 203-397-4031
E. Paulett Moore, dir. | Fax 397-4129

Hamden SD | 6,100/K-12
60 Putnam Ave 06517 | 203-407-2000
Alida Begina Ed.D., supt. | Fax 407-2001
www.hamden.org
Hamden HS | 2,200/9-12
2040 Dixwell Ave 06514 | 203-407-2040
Vincent Iezzi, prin. | Fax 407-2041
Hamden MS | 1,000/7-8
550 Newhall St 06517 | 203-407-3140
Frank Pepe, prin. | Fax 407-3141

New Haven SD
Supt. — See New Haven
Fair Haven MS | 900/5-8
164 Grand Ave 06517 | 203-691-2600
Kevin Miller, prin. | Fax 691-2697

Eli Whitney Regional Voc. Tech. School | Post-Sec.
71 Jones Rd 06514 | 203-397-4037
Goodwin Institute | Post-Sec.
1315 Dixwell Ave 06514 | 800-889-3282
Hamden Hall Country Day S | 600/PK-12
1108 Whitney Ave 06517 | 203-865-6158
Robert Izzo, prin. | Fax 752-2651
New England Technical Institute | Post-Sec.
109 Sanford St 06514 | 203-287-7300
Paier College of Art | Post-Sec.
20 Gorham Ave 06514 | 203-287-3032
Quinnipiac University | Post-Sec.
275 Mount Carmel Ave 06518 | 203-582-8200
Sacred Heart Academy | 500/9-12
265 Benham St 06514 | 203-288-2309
Sr. Ritamary Schulz, prin. | Fax 230-9680
St. Martin dePorres Academy | 100/5-8
43 Jones Rd 06514 | 203-389-1777
Mary Surowiecki, prin. | Fax 387-0777
Sawyer School | Post-Sec.
1125 Dixwell Ave 06514 | 203-865-2900
Stone Academy | Post-Sec.
1315 Dixwell Ave 06514 | 203-288-7474
West Woods Christian Academy | 200/K-12
2105 State St 06517 | 203-562-9922
William Kane, admin. | Fax 786-4730

Hartford, Hartford, Pop. 124,387
Capitol Region Education Council RESC | 400/
111 Charter Oak Ave 06106 | 860-524-4063
Dr. Bruce Douglas, dir. | Fax 548-9924
www.crec.org
Greater Hartford Academy of the Arts | 9-12
15 Vernon St 06106 | 860-757-6385
Herbert Sheppard, prin. | Fax 757-6382

Greater Hartford Academy of Math/Science | 9-12
15 Vernon St 06106 | 860-757-6316
Howard Thiery, prin. | Fax 757-6382
Metropolitan Learning Center Magnet | 6-12
1551 Blue Hills Ave, | 860-242-7834
Anne McKernan, prin. | Fax 242-7836
Other Schools – See East Hartford, Manchester

Connecticut Technical HS System
Supt. — See Middletown
Prince Technical HS | Vo/Tech
500 Brookfield St 06106 | 860-951-7112
William Chaffin, dir. | Fax 951-1529

Hartford SD | 23,000/PK-12
960 Main St 06103 | 860-695-8401
Robert Henry, supt. | Fax 722-8502
www.hartfordschools.org
Belizzi MS | 700/6-8
215 South St 06114 | 860-695-2400
Ana Ortiz, prin. | Fax 956-9993
Bulkeley HS | 1,700/9-12
300 Wethersfield Ave 06114 | 860-695-1000
Miriam Taylor, prin. | Fax 247-3491
Capital Preparatory Magnet S | 6-12
950 Main St 06103 | 860-695-9800
Steven Perry, prin. | Fax 722-8520
Fox MS | 800/7-8
305 Greenfield St 06112 | 860-695-6560
Shirley Harrison, prin. | Fax 722-8813
Greater Hartford Magnet S | 500/6-8
85 Woodland St 06105 | 860-695-9100
Timothy Sullivan, prin. | Fax 722-6449
Hartford HS | 1,200/9-12
55 Forest St 06105 | 860-695-1300
Zandralyn Gordon, prin. | Fax 722-8779
Hartford Magnet MS | 600/6-8
53 Vernon St 06106 | 860-757-6200
Cecilia Green, prin. | Fax 947-9935
Quirk MS | 1,000/7-8
85 Edwards St 06120 | 860-695-2140
Amador Mojica, prin. | Fax 527-0346
Sports & Medical Science Academy | 400/9-12
275 Asylum St 06103 | 860-695-6900
Eduardo Genao, prin. | Fax 722-8017
University HS | 9-12
30 Elizabeth St 06105 | 860-695-9020
Elizabeth Colli, prin. | Fax 722-6408
Weaver HS | 1,300/9-12
415 Granby St 06112 | 860-695-1640
Paul Stringer, prin. | Fax 242-6241
Other Schools – See Windsor

Capital Community College | Post-Sec.
950 Main St 06103 | 860-906-5000
Connecticut Childrens Medical Center | Post-Sec.
282 Washington St 06106 | 860-545-8514
Connecticut Culinary Institute | Post-Sec.
85 Sigourney St 06105 | 860-677-7869
Connecticut Institute for the Blind | Post-Sec.
120 Holcomb St 06112 |
Hartford College for Women | Post-Sec.
1265 Asylum Ave 06105 | 860-236-1215
Hartford Conservatory | Post-Sec.
834 Asylum St 06105 | 860-246-2588
Hartford Hospital | Post-Sec.
PO Box 5037 06102 | 860-545-2100
Hartford Seminary | Post-Sec.
77 Sherman St 06105 | 860-509-9500
Institute of Living Schools | Post-Sec.
400 Washington St 06106 |
Prince Regional Vocational Tech School | Post-Sec.
500 Brookfield St 06106 | 860-246-8594
Rensselaer at Hartford | Post-Sec.
275 Windsor St 06120 | 860-548-2400
Sawyer School | Post-Sec.
141 Washington St 06106 | 860-568-1554
Trinity College | Post-Sec.
300 Summit St 06106 | 860-297-2000
Watkinson S | 300/6-12
180 Bloomfield Ave 06105 | 860-236-5618
John Bracker, hdmstr. | Fax 233-8295

Hebron, Tolland
Regional SD 8 | 1,600/7-12
33 Pendleton Dr 06248 | 860-228-9417
Robert Siminski Ed.D., supt. | Fax 228-2912
www.reg8.k12.ct.us/
RHAM HS | 1,000/9-12
85 Wall St 06248 | 860-228-9474
Scott Leslie, prin. | Fax 228-9209
RHAM MS | 500/7-8
25 RHAM Rd 06248 | 860-228-9423
Linda Crossman, prin. | Fax 228-2471

Allen Inst. Ctr. for Innovative Learning | Post-Sec.
PO Box 100 06248 | 866-666-6910

Higganum, Middlesex, Pop. 1,692
Regional SD 17 | 2,400/PK-12
PO Box 568 06441 | 860-345-4534
Gary Mala, supt. | Fax 345-2817
rsd17.org
Haddam-Killingworth HS | 600/9-12
PO Box 569 06441 | 860-345-8541
Charles Macunas, prin. | Fax 345-8252
Haddam-Killingworth MS | 400/7-8
PO Box 540 06441 | 860-345-8567
Miriam Wagner, prin. | Fax 345-7610

Kensington, Hartford, Pop. 8,306

Mooreland Hill S | 100/5-9
166 Lincoln St 06037 | 860-223-6428
| Fax 223-3318

Kent, Litchfield

Kent S   500/9-12
  PO Box 2006 06757   860-927-6000
                Fax 927-6014
Marvelwood S   100/9-12
  PO Box 3001 06757   860-927-0047
                Fax 927-5325

Lakeville, Litchfield

Hotchkiss S   600/9-12
  PO Box 800 06039   860-435-2591
  Robert Mattoon, hdmstr.   Fax 435-8056

Lebanon, New London
Lebanon SD   1,500/PK-12
  891 Exeter Rd 06249   860-642-3560
  Robert McGray, supt.   Fax 642-4589
  www.lebanonct.org/default.htm
Lebanon MS   400/5-8
  891 Exeter Rd 06249   860-642-4702
  James Worth, prin.   Fax 642-3534
Lyman Memorial HS   600/9-12
  917 Exeter Rd 06249   860-642-7567
  Stephen Salisbury, prin.   Fax 642-3521

Ledyard, New London
Ledyard SD   3,000/PK-12
  4 Blonder Park Rd 06339   860-464-9255
  Michael H. Graner, supt.   Fax 464-8589
  www.ledyardschools.org
Ledyard HS   1,000/9-12
  24 Gallup Hill Rd 06339   860-464-9600
  Marcia Griffin, prin.   Fax 464-1990
Other Schools – See Gales Ferry

Litchfield, Litchfield, Pop. 1,331
Litchfield SD   1,400/PK-12
  PO Box 110 06759   860-567-7500
  Dr. Dominick Vita, supt.   Fax 567-7508
  www.litchfieldschools.org
Litchfield JSHS   700/7-12
  PO Box 110 06759   860-567-7530
  Dr. Timothy Breslin, prin.   Fax 567-7538

Regional SD 6   1,100/K-12
  98 Wamogo Rd 06759   860-567-7400
  Anthony J. Bivona, supt.   Fax 567-6652
  rsd6.org
Wamogo Regional JSHS   500/7-12
  98 Wamogo Rd 06759   860-567-7410
  Janet Garagliano, prin.   Fax 567-6651

Connecticut Junior Republic   Post-Sec.
  PO Box 161 06759
Forman S   200/9-12
  12 Norfolk Rd 06759   860-567-8712
                Fax 567-8317

Madison, New Haven, Pop. 15,485
Madison SD   3,500/K-12
  PO Box 71 06443   203-245-6300
  Dr. H. Kaye Griffin, supt.   Fax 245-6336
  www.madison.k12.ct.us
Hand HS   1,000/9-12
  286 Green Hill Rd 06443   203-245-6350
  Barbara Britton, prin.   Fax 245-6356
Polson MS   600/7-8
  302 Green Hill Rd 06443   203-245-6480
  Frank Henderson, prin.   Fax 245-6494

Manchester, Hartford, Pop. 52,500
Capitol Region Education Council RESC
  Supt. — See Hartford
Great Path Academy   11-12
  PO Box 1046 06045   860-512-3560
  Thomas Danehy, prin.

Connecticut Technical HS System
  Supt. — See Middletown
Cheney Technical HS   Vo/Tech
  791 Middle Tpke W 06040   860-649-5396
  Bruce Sievers, dir.   Fax 649-5263

Manchester SD   7,500/PK-12
  45 N School St 06040   860-647-3441
  Kathleen M. Ouellette, supt.   Fax 647-5042
  www.ci.manchester.ct.us
Bennet MS   800/6-8
  1151 Main St 06040   860-647-3571
  Dr. Ann Richardson, prin.   Fax 647-3577
Illing MS   900/6-8
  227 Middle Tpke E 06040   860-647-3400
  Bo Cuprak, prin.   Fax 647-5008
Manchester HS   2,200/9-12
  134 Middle Tpke E 06040   860-647-3530
  Donald Sierakowski, prin.   Fax 646-3727

Cornerstone Christian S   200/K-12
  236 Main St 06040   860-643-0792
  Edward Campolongo, hdmstr.   Fax 647-9291
East Catholic HS   700/9-12
  115 New State Rd,   860-649-5336
                Fax 649-7191
Manchester Community College   Post-Sec.
  PO Box 1046 06045   860-647-6000

Meriden, New Haven, Pop. 58,962
Area Coop. Educational Services RESC
  Supt. — See North Haven
Edison Magnet MS   6-8
  1355 N Broad St 06450   203-639-8403
  Patricia Joaquim, prin.   Fax 639-8323

Connecticut Technical HS System
  Supt. — See Middletown
Wilcox Technical HS   Vo/Tech
  298 Oregon Rd 06451   203-238-6260
  Richard Cavallaro, dir.   Fax 238-6602

Meriden SD   8,800/PK-12
  22 Liberty St 06450   203-630-4171
  Mary N. Cortright, supt.   Fax 630-0110
  www.meriden.k12.ct.us
Lincoln MS   700/6-8
  164 Centennial Ave 06451   203-238-2381
  John Lineen, prin.   Fax 238-7258
Maloney HS   1,300/9-12
  121 Gravel St 06450   203-238-2334
  Robert Angeli, prin.   Fax 630-7011
Platt HS   1,100/9-12
  220 Coe Ave 06451   203-235-7963
  Timothy Gaffney, prin.   Fax 630-4011
Washington MS   1,000/6-8
  1225 N Broad St 06450   203-235-6606
  Jean Privitera, prin.   Fax 235-6040

Brio Academy of Cosmetology   Post-Sec.
  1231 E Main St 06450   203-237-6683

Middlebury, New Haven, Pop. 4,100
Regional SD 15   4,500/PK-12
  PO Box 395 06762   203-758-8258
  Dr. Frank Sippy, supt.   Fax 758-1908
  www.region15.org
Memorial MS   500/6-8
  PO Box 903 06762   203-758-2496
  John Sieller, prin.   Fax 758-9594
Other Schools – See Southbury

Westover S   200/9-12
  PO Box 847 06762   203-758-2423
  Ann Pollina, hdmstr.   Fax 577-4585

Middletown, Middlesex, Pop. 46,918
Connecticut Technical HS System
  25 Industrial Park Rd 06457   860-807-2200
  Abigail Hughes, supt.   Fax 807-2156
  www.cttech.org
Vinal Technical HS   Vo/Tech
  60 Daniels St 06457   860-344-7100
  Sheila Fredson, dir.   Fax 344-2622
  Other Schools – See Ansonia, Bridgeport, Danbury, Danielson, Groton, Hamden, Hartford, Manchester, Meriden, Milford, New Britain, Norwich, Stamford, Torrington, Waterbury, Willimantic

Middletown SD   5,200/PK-12
  311 Hunting Hill Ave 06457   860-638-1401
  Michael J. Frechette Ph.D., supt.   Fax 638-1495
  www.middletownschools.org
Middletown HS   1,300/9-12
  370 Hunting Hill Ave 06457   860-704-4500
  Robert Fontaine, prin.   Fax 347-2044
Wilson MS   800/7-8
  1 Wilderman Way 06457   860-347-8594
  Eugene Nocera, prin.   Fax 347-2158

Mercy HS   600/9-12
  1740 Randolph Rd 06457   860-346-6659
  Sr. Mary McCarthy, prin.   Fax 344-9887
Middlesex Community College   Post-Sec.
  100 Training Hill Rd 06457   860-343-5800
Wesleyan University 06459   Post-Sec.
                860-685-2000
Xavier HS   800/9-12
  181 Randolph Rd 06457   860-346-7735
  William Garrity, prin.   Fax 346-6859

Milford, New Haven, Pop. 51,734
Connecticut Technical HS System
  Supt. — See Middletown
Platt Technical HS   Vo/Tech
  600 Orange Ave,   203-783-5300
  Gene LaPorta, dir.   Fax 783-3970

Milford SD   7,500/PK-12
  70 W River St 06460   203-783-3402
  Gregory A. Firn, supt.   Fax 783-3475
  www.milforded.org
East Shore MS   600/6-8
  240 Chapel St 06460   203-783-3559
  Catherine Williams, prin.   Fax 301-5060
Foran HS   1,000/9-12
  80 Foran Rd 06460   203-783-3502
  Michael Cummings, prin.   Fax 783-3635
Harborside MS   700/6-8
  175 High St 06460   203-783-3523
  Raymond Vitali, prin.   Fax 783-3687
Law HS   1,000/9-12
  20 Lansdale Ave 06460   203-783-3574
  Janet Garagliano, prin.   Fax 783-3586
West Shore MS   600/6-8
  50 Kay Ave 06460   203-783-3553
  John Barile, prin.   Fax 783-4827

Academy of Our Lady of Mercy   500/9-12
  200 High St 06460   203-877-2786
  Ann Pratson, prin.   Fax 876-9760
Berean Christian Academy   100/K-12
  989 New Haven Ave 06460   203-876-2126
  James Loomer, hdmstr.   Fax 874-0492

Monroe, Fairfield
Easton SD   1,100/PK-8
  605 Main St 06468   203-261-2513
  Dr. Allen Fossbender, supt.   Fax 261-4549
  www.er9.org
Other Schools – See Easton

Monroe SD   4,300/PK-12
  375 Monroe Tpke 06468   203-452-6501
  Alan Beitman, supt.   Fax 452-5818
  www.monroeps.org
Jockey Hollow S   700/7-8
  365 Fan Hill Rd 06468   203-452-2281
  Anita Healy, prin.   Fax 452-2263

Masuk HS   1,300/9-12
  1014 Monroe Tpke 06468   203-452-5823
  John Battista, prin.   Fax 452-5835
Redding SD   1,200/K-8
  605 Main St 06468   203-261-2513
  Dr. Allen Fossbender, supt.   Fax 261-4549
  www.er9.org
Other Schools – See West Redding
Regional SD 9   900/9-12
  605 Main St 06468   203-261-2513
  Alan Fossbender, supt.   Fax 261-4549
  www.er9.org
Other Schools – See Redding

Moodus, Middlesex, Pop. 1,170
East Haddam SD   1,400/PK-12
  PO Box 401 06469   860-873-5090
  Steven Durham, supt.   Fax 873-5092
  www.easthaddam.k12.ct.us
Hale-Ray HS   300/9-12
  PO Box 404 06469   860-873-5065
  Linda Dadona, prin.   Fax 873-5074
Hale-Ray MS   500/5-8
  PO Box 363 06469   860-873-5081
  Judy Deleeuw, prin.   Fax 873-5086

Mystic, New London, Pop. 2,618
Groton SD   5,700/PK-12
  1300 Flanders Rd 06355   860-572-2100
  James E. Mitchell Ph.D., supt.   Fax 572-2107
  www.groton.k12.ct.us
Cutler MS   500/6-8
  160 Fishtown Rd 06355   860-572-5830
  Monson Lane, prin.   Fax 572-5834
Other Schools – See Groton

Stonington SD
  Supt. — See Old Mystic
Mystic MS   500/5-8
  204 Mistuxet Ave 06355   860-536-9613
  Susan Dumas, prin.   Fax 536-4508

Westlawn Institute of Marine Technology   Post-Sec.
  PO Box 6000 06355   860-572-7900

Naugatuck, New Haven, Pop. 31,700
Naugatuck SD   5,300/PK-12
  380 Church St 06770   203-720-5265
  Robert D. Cronin Ph.D., supt.   Fax 720-5272
  www.naugy.net
City Hill MS   600/7-8
  441 City Hill St 06770   203-720-5246
  Francis Serratore, prin.   Fax 720-5256
Hillside MS   300/7-8
  51 Hillside Ave 06770   203-720-5260
  Brian Sullivan, prin.   Fax 720-5209
Naugatuck HS   1,600/9-12
  543 Rubber Ave 06770   203-720-5400
  Lori Ferreira, prin.   Fax 720-5444

New Britain, Hartford, Pop. 71,572
Connecticut Technical HS System
  Supt. — See Middletown
Goodwin Regional Technical HS   Vo/Tech
  735 Slater Rd 06053   860-827-7736
  Stephen Anderson, dir.   Fax 827-7862

New Britain SD   10,800/PK-12
  PO Box 1960 06050   860-827-2204
  Dr. Doris J. Kurtz, supt.   Fax 612-1533
  www.new-britain.k12.ct.us
New Britain MS   3,000/9-12
  110 Mill St 06051   860-225-6351
  Thomas Reale, prin.   Fax 826-5079
Pulaski MS   1,000/6-8
  757 Farmington Ave 06053   860-225-7665
  Ann Carabillo, prin.   Fax 233-3840
Roosevelt MS   700/6-8
  40 Goodwin St 06051   860-612-3334
  Vaughn Ramseur, prin.   Fax 826-1162
Slade MS   900/6-8
  183 Steele St 06052   860-225-6395
  Mark Fernandes, prin.   Fax 826-7894

Central Connecticut State University   Post-Sec.
  1615 Stanley St 06053   860-832-3200
Charter Oak State College   Post-Sec.
  55 Paul Manafort Dr 06053   860-832-3800
New England Technical Institute   Post-Sec.
  200 John Downey Dr 06051   860-225-8641
St. Francis of Assisi MS   100/6-8
  30 Pendleton Rd 06053   860-225-8729
  Sr. Marie Murphy, prin.   Fax 224-1532

New Canaan, Fairfield, Pop. 17,864
New Canaan SD   4,000/PK-12
  39 Locust Ave 06840   203-594-4000
  Dr. David E. Abbey, supt.   Fax 594-4035
  www.newcanaan.k12.ct.us
New Canaan HS   1,100/9-12
  11 Farm Rd 06840   203-594-4600
  Tony Pavia, prin.   Fax 594-4619
Saxe MS   1,300/6-8
  468 South Ave 06840   203-594-4500
  Gregory Macedo, prin.   Fax 594-4565

St. Luke's S   500/5-12
  PO Box 1148 06840   203-966-5612
  Mark Davis, hdmstr.   Fax 972-3450

New Fairfield, Fairfield, Pop. 12,911
New Fairfield SD   3,100/PK-12
  3 Brush Hill Rd 06812   203-312-5770
  Joseph Castagnola, supt.   Fax 312-5609
  www.newfairfieldschools.org
New Fairfield HS   900/9-12
  54 Gillotti Rd 06812   203-312-5805
  Alicia Roy, prin.   Fax 312-5803

New Fairfield MS | 700/6-8
56 Gillotti Rd 06812 | 203-312-5886
Diane Hartman-Chesley, prin. | Fax 312-5887

New Haven, New Haven, Pop. 124,512
Area Coop. Educational Services RESC
Supt. — See North Haven
Educational Center for the Arts | 9-12
55 Audubon St 06510 | 203-777-5451
Leo Lavallee, prin. | Fax 782-3596

New Haven SD | 18,800/PK-12
54 Meadow St 06519 | 203-946-8888
Dr. Reginald Mayo, supt. | Fax 946-7300
www.nhps.net
Cross HS | 1,700/9-12
181 Mitchell Dr 06511 | 203-946-8728
Robert Canelli, prin. | Fax 946-6932
Cross HS Annex | 9-12
45 Nash St 06511 | 203-946-8635
| Fax 946-6487
Hillhouse HS | 1,300/9-12
480 Sherman Pkwy 06511 | 203-946-8484
Lonnie Garris, prin. | Fax 946-8487
Hill Regional Career HS | Vo/Tech
140 Legion Ave 06519 | 203-946-5845
Rose Coggins, prin. | Fax 946-5949
Hooker MS | 5-8
804 State St 06511 | 203-946-6610
| Fax 946-6376
Jepson Magnet MS | 5-8
460 Lexington Ave 06513 | 203-946-2992
Peggy Pelley, prin. | Fax 946-8606
Ross Arts MS | 500/5-8
150 Kimberly Ave 06519 | 203-946-8974
Peggy Moore, prin. | Fax 946-5824
Sheridan Academy for Excellence | 500/5-8
191 Fountain St 06515 | 203-946-8828
Eleanor Turner, prin. | Fax 946-5661
Troup Magnet Academy of Science | 600/5-8
259 Edgewood St 06511 | 203-946-8854
Richard Kaliszewski, prin. | Fax 946-7276
Adult & Continuing Education Center | Adult
580 Ella T Grasso Blvd 06519 | 203-946-5884
Alicia Caraballo, prin. | Fax 946-6384
Other Schools – See Hamden

Albertus Magnus College | Post-Sec.
700 Prospect St 06511 | 203-773-8550
Berkeley Divinity School | Post-Sec.
363 Saint Ronan St 06511 | 203-764-9300
Gateway Community College | Post-Sec.
60 Sargent Dr 06511 | 203-285-2000
Hopkins S | 700/7-12
986 Forest Rd 06515 | 203-397-1001
Barbara Masters Riley, hdmstr. | Fax 389-2249
Southern Connecticut State University | Post-Sec.
501 Crescent St 06515 | 203-392-5200
Yale-New Haven Hospital | Post-Sec.
20 York St 06504 | 203-785-5074
Yale University | Post-Sec.
38 Hillhouse Ave 06511 | 203-432-4771
Yeshiva of New Haven | 50/9-12
765 Elm St 06511 | 203-777-7199
Rabbi Daniel Greer, prin. | Fax 777-7198

Newington, Hartford, Pop. 29,300
Newington SD | 4,600/PK-12
131 Cedar St 06111 | 860-665-8610
Ernest Perlini, supt. | Fax 665-8616
www.newington-schools.org
Kellogg MS | 700/5-8
155 Harding Ave 06111 | 860-666-5418
Jeffrey Schumann, prin. | Fax 667-5925
Newington HS | 1,400/9-12
605 Willard Ave 06111 | 860-666-5611
William Collins, prin. | Fax 666-8224
Wallace MS | 700/5-8
71 Halleran Dr 06111 | 860-667-5888
David Milardo, prin. | Fax 667-5893

Connecticut Center for Massage Therapy | Post-Sec.
75 Kitts Ln 06111 | 860-667-1886
Hanger Orthopedic Group | Post-Sec.
181 Patricia M Genova Dr 06111 | 860-667-5304

New London, New London, Pop. 26,201
Learn RESC
Supt. — See Old Lyme
Regional Multicultural Magnet S | K-12
1 Bulkeley Pl 06320 | 860-437-7775
Richard Virgin, prin. | Fax 437-1585

New London SD | 3,000/PK-12
134 Williams St 06320 | 860-447-6000
Christopher Clouet, supt. | Fax 447-6016
www.newlondon.org
Jackson MS | 700/6-8
36 Waller St 06320 | 860-437-6480
Jaye Wilson, prin. | Fax 437-6494
New London HS | 700/9-12
490 Jefferson Ave 06320 | 860-437-6400
Daniel Sullivan, prin. | Fax 271-4036
Science & Technology Magnet HS | 9-12
490 Jefferson Ave 06320 | 860-447-6000
Louis Allen, dir.
New London Adult Education | Adult
3 Shaws Cv 06320 | 860-437-2385
Daniel Gaynor, dir. | Fax 437-6460

Connecticut College | Post-Sec.
270 Mohegan Ave 06320 | 860-447-1911
Mitchell College | Post-Sec.
437 Pequot Ave 06320 | 860-701-5000
Ridley-Lowell Business & Technical Inst. | Post-Sec.
PO Box 652 06320 | 860-443-7441
United States Coast Guard Academy | Post-Sec.
15 Mohegan Ave 06320 | 800-883-8724

Williams S | 300/7-12
182 Mohegan Ave 06320 | 860-443-5333
Charlotte Rea, prin. | Fax 439-2796

New Milford, Litchfield, Pop. 5,775
New Milford SD | 5,200/PK-12
50 East St 06776 | 860-355-8406
JeanAnn Paddyfote, supt. | Fax 210-4132
www.new-milford.k12.ct.us/
New Milford HS | 1,500/9-12
388 Danbury Rd 06776 | 860-350-6647
Greg Shugrue, prin. | Fax 210-2256
Schaghticoke MS | 900/7-8
23 Hipp Rd 06776 | 860-354-2204
Dana Ford, prin. | Fax 210-2217

Canterbury S | 400/9-12
PO Box 5000 06776 | 860-210-3800
Thomas Sheehy, hdmstr. | Fax 350-4455
Faith Academy | 200/PK-12
600 Danbury Rd Ste 2 06776 | 203-798-1787
Josephine DuBois, prin.

Newtown, Fairfield, Pop. 1,847
Newtown SD | 5,400/PK-12
31 Pecks Ln 06470 | 203-426-7621
Evan Pitkoff Ed.D., supt. | Fax 270-6199
www.newtown.k12.ct.us
Newtown MS | 800/7-8
11 Queen St 06470 | 203-426-7642
Diane Sherlock, prin. | Fax 270-6102
Other Schools – See Sandy Hook

Niantic, New London, Pop. 3,048
East Lyme SD
Supt. — See East Lyme
East Lyme MS | 1,000/5-8
31 Society Rd 06357 | 860-739-4491
Paul Freeman, prin. | Fax 739-1219

North Branford, New Haven, Pop. 12,996
North Branford SD
Supt. — See Northford
North Branford HS | 700/9-12
49 Caputo Rd 06471 | 203-484-1465
David Perry, prin. | Fax 484-1233
North Branford IS | 600/6-8
654 Foxon Rd 06471 | 203-484-1500
Alan Davis, prin. | Fax 484-1505

Northford, New Haven, Pop. 3,200
North Branford SD | 2,500/PK-12
PO Box 129 06472 | 203-484-1440
Dr. Robert Wolfe, supt. | Fax 484-1445
www.northbranfordschools.org
Other Schools – See North Branford

North Grosvenordale, Windham, Pop. 1,705
Thompson SD | 1,400/PK-12
785 Riverside Dr 06255 | 860-923-9581
Michael Jolin Ed.D., supt. | Fax 923-9638
www.thompson.ctschool.net
Thompson MS | 500/5-8
785 Riverside Dr 06255 | 860-923-9380
Anthony Salutari, prin. | Fax 923-9638
Tourtellotte Memorial HS | 400/9-12
785 Riverside Dr 06255 | 860-923-9303
| Fax 923-3752

North Haven, New Haven, Pop. 22,249
Area Coop. Educational Services RESC
350 State St 06473 | 203-498-6800
Cheryl Saloom Ed.D., dir. | Fax 498-6890
www.aces.k12.ct.us
Other Schools – See Meriden, New Haven

North Haven SD | 3,800/PK-12
5 Linsley St 06473 | 203-239-2581
Sara-Jane R. Querfeld, supt. | Fax 234-9811
www.north-haven.k12.ct.us/
North Haven HS | 1,100/9-12
222 Maple Ave 06473 | 203-239-1641
Patricia Brozek, prin. | Fax 234-2602
North Haven MS | 900/6-8
55 Bailey Rd 06473 | 203-239-1683
| Fax 234-2846

Gal Mar Academy of Hairdressing | Post-Sec.
97 Washington Ave Ste 8 06473 | 203-281-4477

North Stonington, New London
North Stonington SD | 800/K-12
297 Norwich Westerly Rd 06359 | 860-535-2800
Natalie Pukas, supt. | Fax 535-1470
www.northstonington.k12.ct.us
Wheeler HS | 300/9-12
298 Norwich Westerly Rd 06359 | 860-535-0377
Stephen Bickford, prin. | Fax 535-2536
Wheeler MS | 200/6-8
298 Norwich Westerly Rd 06359 | 860-535-0377
Stephen Bickford, prin. | Fax 535-2536

North Stonington Christian Academy | 200/PK-12
12 Stillman Rd 06359 | 860-599-5071
Pamela Wilkinson, dir. | Fax 599-2815

Norwalk, Fairfield, Pop. 84,170
Norwalk SD | 11,100/PK-12
PO Box 6001 06852 | 203-854-4000
Dr. Salvatore J. Corda, supt. | Fax 838-3299
www.norwalk.k12.ct.us
Briggs HS | Vo/Tech
350 Main Ave 06851 | 203-899-2820
| Fax 899-2824
Center for Global Studies | 9-12
300 Highland Ave 06854 | 203-852-9488
Joan Glass, prin. | Fax 899-2813
Hale MS | 600/6-8
176 Strawberry Hill Ave 06851 | 203-899-2910
Robert McCain, prin. | Fax 899-2914

McMahon HS | 1,400/9-12
300 Highland Ave 06854 | 203-852-9488
Joseph Rodriguez, prin. | Fax 899-2814
Norwalk HS | 1,700/9-12
23 Calvin Murphy Dr 06851 | 203-838-4481
Roz McCarthy, prin. | Fax 899-2815
Ponus Ridge MS | 700/6-8
21 Hunters Ln 06850 | 203-847-3557
Linda Sumpter, prin. | Fax 889-2924
Roton MS | 500/6-8
201 Highland Ave 06853 | 203-899-2930
Joseph Vellucci, prin. | Fax 899-2934
West Rocks MS | 800/6-8
81 W Rocks Rd 06851 | 203-899-2970
Lynne Moore, prin. | Fax 899-2974

Gibbs College | Post-Sec.
10 Norden Pl 06855 | 800-845-5333
Norwalk Community College | Post-Sec.
188 Richards Ave 06854 | 203-857-7000
Norwalk Hospital | Post-Sec.
24 Stevens St 06850 | 203-852-2211

Norwich, New London, Pop. 36,227
Connecticut Technical HS System
Supt. — See Middletown
Norwich Technical HS | Vo/Tech
590 New London Tpke 06360 | 860-889-8453
Nikitoula Menounos, dir. | Fax 886-4632

Endowed & Incorporated Academies | 2,300/9-12
305 Broadway 06360 | 860-887-2505
Mary Lou Bargnesi, supt. | Fax 887-2004
www.norwichfreeacademy.com
Norwich Free Academy | 2,300/9-12
305 Broadway 06360 | 860-887-2505
Mary Lou Bargnesi, prin. | Fax 887-2004
Endowed & Incorporated Academies | 100/9-12
191 Hickory St 06360 | 860-823-4256
| Fax 892-4377
Thames Academy | 9-12
191 Hickory St 06360 | 860-823-4256
Edward Derr, prin. | Fax 892-4377

Norwich SD | 4,000/PK-12
90 Town St 06360 | 860-823-4245
Donald Steinman Ph.D., supt. | Fax 823-1880
www.norwichpublicschools.org
Kelly MS | 700/6-8
25 Mahan Dr 06360 | 860-823-4211
Scott Fain, prin. | Fax 892-4302
Teachers Memorial MS | 500/6-8
15 Teachers Dr 06360 | 860-823-4212
William Peckham, prin. | Fax 823-4277

Three Rivers Community Technical College | Post-Sec.
Mahan Dr 06360 | 860-886-0177
Three Rivers Community Technical College | Post-Sec.
574 New London Tpke 06360 | 860-823-2845

Oakdale, New London
Montville SD | 2,900/PK-12
Old Colchester Rd 06370 | 860-848-1228
David Erwin, supt. | Fax 848-0589
www.montvilleschools.org
Montville HS | 800/9-12
800 Old Colchester Rd 06370 | 860-848-9208
Thomas Amanti, prin. | Fax 848-3872
Tyl MS | 700/6-8
166 Chesterfield Rd 06370 | 860-848-2822
Peter DeLisa, prin. | Fax 848-8854

St. Thomas More S | 200/8-12
45 Cottage Rd 06370 | 860-859-1900
James Hanrahan, hdmstr. | Fax 823-3863

Oakville, Litchfield, Pop. 8,741
Watertown SD
Supt. — See Watertown
Swift MS | 600/7-8
250 Colonial St 06779 | 860-945-4830
Marylu Lerz, prin. | Fax 945-6449

Old Lyme, New London
Learn RESC
44 Hatchetts Hill Rd 06371 | 860-434-4800
Virginia Seccombe, dir. | Fax 434-4820
www.learn.k12.ct.us
Other Schools – See New London

Regional SD 18 | 1,600/PK-12
4 Davis Rd W 06371 | 860-434-7238
David Klein, supt. | Fax 434-9959
www.region18.org
Lyme-Old Lyme HS | 500/9-12
69 Lyme St 06371 | 860-434-1651
Jan Guarino-Rhone, prin. | Fax 434-8234
Lyme-Old Lyme MS | 400/6-8
53 Lyme St 06371 | 860-434-2568
Jeffrey Ostroff, prin. | Fax 434-0717

Lyme Academy College of Fine Arts | Post-Sec.
84 Lyme St 06371 | 860-434-5232

Old Mystic, New London
Stonington SD | 2,600/PK-12
PO Box 479 06372 | 860-572-0506
Michael McKee, supt. | Fax 572-1470
www.stoningtonschools.org
Other Schools – See Mystic, Pawcatuck

Old Saybrook, Middlesex, Pop. 9,552
Old Saybrook SD | 1,600/PK-12
50 Sheffield St 06475 | 860-395-3157
Salvatore Pascarella, supt. | Fax 395-3162
www.oldsaybrook.k12.ct.us

Old Saybrook HS 400/9-12
1111 Boston Post Rd 06475 860-395-3175
Scott Schoonmaker, prin. Fax 395-3179
Old Saybrook MS 600/4-8
60 Sheffield St 06475 860-395-3168
Michael Rafferty, prin. Fax 395-3350

Orange, New Haven, Pop. 12,830
Regional SD 5
Supt. — See Woodbridge
Amity Regional MS 400/7-8
100 Ohman Ave 06477 203-392-3200
Robert Slie, prin. Fax 387-7603

Beth Chana Acad/New Haven Hebrew Day S 200/K-12
261 Derby Ave 06477 203-795-5261
Rabbi Hecht, prin. Fax 891-9719

Oxford, New Haven
Oxford SD 1,400/PK-8
1 Great Hill Rd 06478 203-888-7754
Judith A. Palmer, supt. Fax 888-2468
www.oxfordpublicschools.org
Great Oak MS 400/6-8
50 Great Oak Rd 06478 203-888-5418
Frank Samuelson, prin. Fax 888-7798

Pawcatuck, New London, Pop. 5,289
Stonington SD
Supt. — See Old Mystic
Pawcatuck MS 300/5-8
40 Field St 06379 860-599-5696
Jane Giulini, prin. Fax 599-8948
Stonington HS 700/9-12
176 S Broad St 06379 860-599-5781
Stephen Murphy, prin. Fax 599-5784

Plainfield, Windham, Pop. 14,363
Plainfield SD 2,600/PK-12
651 Norwich Rd 06374 860-564-6403
Mary Conway, supt. Fax 564-6412
www.plainfieldschools.org/
Plainfield Central MS 600/6-8
75 Canterbury Rd 06374 860-564-6437
Jerry Davis, prin. Fax 564-1147
Other Schools – See Central Village

Plainville, Hartford, Pop. 17,932
Plainville SD 2,600/PK-12
47 Robert Holcomb Way 06062 860-793-3200
Kathleen Binkowski, supt. Fax 747-6790
www.plainvilleschools.org
Plainville HS 800/9-12
47 Robert Holcomb Way 06062 860-793-3220
Gregory Ziogas, prin. Fax 793-3224
MS of Plainville 700/6-8
150 Northwest Dr 06062 860-793-3250
Carole Alvaro, prin. Fax 793-3265

Plantsville, Hartford, Pop. 7,000
Southington SD
Supt. — See Southington
Kennedy MS 800/6-8
1071 S Main St 06479 860-628-3275
Angelo Campagnano, prin. Fax 628-3404

Pomfret, Windham

Pomfret S 300/9-12
PO Box 128 06258 860-963-6100
Bradford Hastings, hdmstr. Fax 963-2086
Rectory S 200/5-9
PO Box 68 06258 860-928-7759
Thomas Army, hdmstr. Fax 963-2355

Portland, Middlesex, Pop. 5,645
Portland SD 1,200/PK-12
PO Box 231 06480 860-342-6790
Dr. Sally Doyen, supt. Fax 342-6791
www.portlandct.org
Portland HS 300/9-12
PO Box 73 06480 860-342-1720
Donald Gates, prin. Fax 342-2906
Portland MS 200/7-8
PO Box 686 06480 860-342-1880
William Grimm, prin. Fax 342-3934

Preston, New London
Preston SD 400/PK-8
325 Shetucket Tpke 06365 860-889-6098
Dr. John Welch, supt. Fax 889-8685
www.prestonschools.org/
Preston Plains MS 200/6-8
1 Route 164 06365 860-889-3831
Raymond Bernier, prin. Fax 204-0126

Prospect, New Haven, Pop. 7,775
Regional SD 16 2,600/PK-12
207 New Haven Rd 06712 203-758-6401
Dr. Maggie V. Shook, supt. Fax 758-5797
www.region16ct.org
Long River MS 600/6-8
Columbia Ave 06712 203-758-4421
Kenneth Ross, prin. Fax 758-6948
Other Schools – See Beacon Falls

Putnam, Windham, Pop. 9,031
Putnam SD 1,400/PK-12
126 Church St 06260 860-963-6900
Margo Marvin, supt. Fax 963-6903
www.putnam.k12.ct.us/
Putnam HS 400/9-12
152 Woodstock Ave 06260 860-963-6905
Linda Joyal, prin. Fax 963-6911
Putnam MS 300/6-8
35 Wicker St 06260 860-963-6920
Joseph Morris, prin. Fax 963-6921

Redding, Fairfield
Regional SD 9
Supt. — See Monroe

Barlow HS 900/9-12
100 Black Rock Tpke 06896 203-938-2508
Ross Calabro, prin. Fax 938-9602

Ridgefield, Fairfield, Pop. 6,363
Ridgefield SD 5,500/PK-12
70 Prospect St 06877 203-431-2800
Dr. Kenneth R. Freeston, supt. Fax 431-2810
www.ridgefield.org
East Ridge MS 800/6-8
10 E Ridge Rd 06877 203-438-3744
Martin Fiedler, prin. Fax 431-2843
Ridgefield HS 1,500/9-12
700 N Salem Rd 06877 203-438-3785
Dr. Dianna Lindsay, prin. Fax 438-4002
Scotts Ridge MS 600/6-8
750 N Salem Rd 06877 203-894-3400
Marie Doyon, prin. Fax 894-3411

Riverside, Fairfield
Greenwich SD
Supt. — See Greenwich
Eastern MS 700/6-8
51 Hendrie Ave 06878 203-637-1744
Ralph Mayo, prin. Fax 637-3567

Rocky Hill, Hartford, Pop. 16,554
Rocky Hill SD 2,500/PK-12
PO Box 627 06067 860-258-7701
J. A. Camille Vautour Ph.D., supt. Fax 258-7710
www.rockyhillps.us
Griswold MS 600/6-8
144 Bailey Rd 06067 860-258-7741
Richard Watson, prin. Fax 258-7746
Rocky Hill HS 700/9-12
50 Chapin Ave 06067 860-258-7721
Robert Pitocco, prin. Fax 258-7735

Salisbury, Litchfield

Salisbury S 300/9-12
251 Canaan Rd 06068 860-435-5700
Chisholm Chandler, hdmstr. Fax 435-5750

Sandy Hook, Fairfield
Newtown SD
Supt. — See Newtown
Newtown HS 1,600/9-12
12 Berkshire Rd 06482 203-426-7646
Arlene Gottesman, prin. Fax 426-6573

Seymour, New Haven, Pop. 14,288
Seymour SD 2,700/PK-12
98 Bank St 06483 203-888-4565
Thomas Petruny, supt. Fax 888-1704
www.seymourschools.org
Seymour HS 900/9-12
2 Botsford Rd 06483 203-888-2561
Michael Valovcin, prin. Fax 888-7476
Seymour MS 700/6-8
211 Mountain Rd 06483 203-888-4513
Christine Syriac, prin. Fax 881-7535

Shelton, Fairfield, Pop. 39,121
Shelton SD 5,600/PK-12
382 Long Hill Ave 06484 203-924-1023
Robin Willink, supt. Fax 924-5894
www.sheltonpublicschools.org
Shelton HS 1,700/9-12
120 Meadow St 06484 203-924-9578
Donald Ramia, prin. Fax 924-8236
Shelton IS 900/7-8
675 Constitution Blvd N 06484 203-926-2000
Howard Gura, prin. Fax 926-2017

New England Technical Institute Post-Sec.
8 Progress Dr 06484 203-929-0592

Simsbury, Hartford, Pop. 22,023
Simsbury SD 5,000/PK-12
933 Hopmeadow St 06070 860-651-3361
Diane Ullman, supt. Fax 651-4343
www.simsbury.k12.ct.us
James Memorial MS 800/7-8
155 Firetown Rd 06070 860-651-3341
Erin Murray, prin. Fax 658-3629
Simsbury HS 1,500/9-12
34 Farms Village Rd 06070 860-658-0451
Neil Sullivan, prin. Fax 658-2439

Walker S 200/6-12
230 Bushy Hill Rd 06070 860-658-4467
Susanna Jones, hdmstr. Fax 658-6763
Westminster S 400/9-12
PO Box 337 06070 860-408-3000
W. Graham Cole, hdmstr. Fax 408-3001

Somers, Tolland
Somers SD 1,700/PK-12
55 9th District Rd 06071 860-749-2279
Angelo Vespe Ph.D., supt. Fax 763-0748
www.somers.k12.ct.us
Avery MS 400/6-8
55 9th District Rd 06071 860-763-0723
Nancy Barry, prin. Fax 763-2073
Somers HS 600/9-12
55 9th District Rd 06071 860-749-0719
Daniel Lynch, prin. Fax 749-9264

New England Tractor Trailer Training Post-Sec.
PO Box 326 06071 860-749-0711

Southbury, New Haven, Pop. 15,818
Regional SD 15
Supt. — See Middlebury
Pomperaug Regional HS 1,300/9-12
234 Judd Rd 06488 203-262-3200
James Agostine, prin. Fax 262-6806

Rochambeau MS 600/6-8
100 Peter Rd 06488 203-264-2711
Lauren Robinson, prin. Fax 264-6638

Southington, Hartford, Pop. 39,200
Southington SD 6,500/PK-12
49 Beecher St 06489 860-628-3202
Harvey Polansky, supt. Fax 628-3205
www.southingtonschools.org
DePaolo MS 800/6-8
385 Pleasant St 06489 860-628-3260
David Telesca, prin. Fax 628-3403
Southington HS 2,100/9-12
720 Pleasant St 06489 860-628-3229
Kathleen McGrath, prin. Fax 628-3397
Other Schools – See Plantsville

Branford Hall Career Institute Post-Sec.
35 N Main St 06489 860-276-0600
Briarwood College Post-Sec.
2279 Mount Vernon Rd 06489 860-628-4751

South Kent, Litchfield

South Kent S 100/9-12
40 Bulls Bridge Rd 06785 860-927-3539
Fax 927-1161

South Windsor, Hartford, Pop. 22,090
South Windsor SD 5,000/K-12
1737 Main St 06074 860-291-1205
Joseph Wood, supt. Fax 291-1291
www.swindsor.k12.ct.us
Edwards MS 1,200/6-8
100 Arnold Way 06074 860-648-5030
Janice Tirinzonie, prin. Fax 648-5029
South Windsor HS 1,500/9-12
161 Nevers Rd 06074 860-648-5000
John Dilorio, prin. Fax 648-5013

Stafford Springs, Tolland, Pop. 4,100
Stafford SD 2,000/PK-12
PO Box 147 06076 860-684-4211
Therese Fishman, supt. Fax 684-5172
www.stafford.ctschool.net/
Stafford HS 600/9-12
PO Box 87 06076 860-684-4233
Francis Kennedy, prin. Fax 684-0424
Stafford MS 400/6-8
PO Box 106 06076 860-684-2785
Kenneth Valentine, prin. Fax 684-4671

Stamford, Fairfield, Pop. 120,107
Connecticut Technical HS System
Supt. — See Middletown
Wright Technical HS Vo/Tech
PO Box 1416 06904 203-324-7363
Sidney Abramowitz, dir. Fax 324-1196

Stamford SD 14,700/PK-12
PO Box 9310 06904 203-977-4543
Dr. Joshua Starr, supt. Fax 977-5964
www.stamfordpublicschools.org/
Academy of Information Technology Vo/Tech
381 High Ridge Rd 06905 203-977-4336
Paul Gross, dir. Fax 977-6638
Cloonan MS 700/6-8
11 W North St 06902 203-977-4544
David Rudolph, prin. Fax 977-4867
Dolan MS 700/6-8
51 Toms Rd 06906 203-977-4441
Charmaine Tourse, prin. Fax 977-4880
Scofield Magnet MS 600/6-8
641 Scofieldtown Rd 06903 203-977-2750
Carol Walsh, prin. Fax 977-2766
Stamford HS 2,000/9-12
55 Strawberry Hill Ave 06902 203-977-4227
Suzanne Brown-Koroshclz, prin. Fax 356-1720
Turn of River MS 600/6-8
117 Vine Rd 06905 203-977-4284
Rodney Bass, prin. Fax 977-5037
Westhill HS 2,000/9-12
125 Roxbury Rd 06902 203-977-4838
Camille Figluizzi, prin. Fax 977-4996

Beth Benjamin Academy of Connecticut Post-Sec.
132 Prospect St 06901 203-325-4351
King & Low-Heywood Thomas S 700/PK-12
1450 Newfield Ave 06905 203-322-3496
Thomas B. Main, hdmstr. Fax 329-0291
Sacred Heart Academy 100/9-12
200 Strawberry Hill Ave 06902 203-323-3173
Sr. Jeanne Paulella, prin. Fax 975-7804
Stamford Hospital Post-Sec.
PO Box 9317 06904 203-276-7877
Trinity Catholic HS 400/9-12
926 Newfield Ave 06905 203-322-3401
Robert F. D'Aquila, prin. Fax 322-5330
Trinity Catholic MS 300/6-8
948 Newfield Ave 06905 203-322-7383
Rev. Cyprian LaPastina, prin. Fax 322-4435
Yeshiva Bais Binyomin 100/9-12
132 Prospect St 06901 203-325-4351
Fax 323-6073

Storrs, Tolland, Pop. 12,198
Mansfield SD 1,400/PK-8
4 S Eagleville Rd 06268 860-429-3350
Gordon Schimmel, supt. Fax 429-3379
www.mansfieldct.org
Mansfield MS 700/5-8
205 Spring Hill Rd 06268 860-429-9341
Jeffrey Cryan, prin. Fax 429-1020

Regional SD 19 — 1,300/9-12
  1235 Storrs Rd 06268 — 860-487-1862
  Bruce Silva, supt. — Fax 429-0085
  www.eosmith.org
Smith HS — 1,300/9-12
  1235 Storrs Rd 06268 — 860-487-0877
  Louis DeLoreto, prin. — Fax 429-7892

University of Connecticut 06269 — Post-Sec.
— 860-486-2000

Stratford, Fairfield, Pop. 50,100
Stratford SD — 7,400/PK-12
  1000 E Broadway 06615 — 203-385-4210
  Irene Cornish, supt. — Fax 381-2012
  www.stratford.k12.ct.us
Bunnell HS — 1,400/9-12
  1 Bulldog Blvd 06614 — 203-385-4250
  Robert Tremaglio, prin. — Fax 381-2014
Flood MS — 700/7-8
  490 Chapel St 06614 — 203-385-4280
  Carol Aloi, prin. — Fax 381-2033
Stratford HS — 1,000/9-12
  45 N Parade St 06615 — 203-385-4230
  Margaret Lasek, prin. — Fax 381-2021
Wooster MS — 600/7-8
  150 Lincoln St 06614 — 203-385-4275
  Linda Paslov, prin. — Fax 381-6918

Porter and Chester Institute — Post-Sec.
  670 Lordship Blvd 06615 — 203-375-4463

Suffield, Hartford
Suffield SD — 1,800/PK-12
  350 Mountain Rd 06078 — 860-668-3800
  William Troy, supt. — Fax 668-3805
  www.suffield.org
Suffield HS — 600/6-8
  350 Mountain Rd 06078 — 860-668-3820
  John Warrington, prin. — Fax 668-3088
Other Schools – See West Suffield

Connecticut Culinary Institute — Post-Sec.
  1760 Mapleton Ave 06078 — 860-668-3518
International Coll. of Hospitality Mgmt. — Post-Sec.
  1760 Mapleton Ave 06078 — 860-668-3515
Suffield Academy — 400/9-12
  PO Box 999 06078 — 860-668-7315
  Charles Cahn, hdmstr. — Fax 668-2966

Terryville, Litchfield, Pop. 5,426
Plymouth SD — 1,800/PK-12
  77 Main St 06786 — 860-314-8005
  Anthony Distasio Ph.D., supt. — Fax 314-2766
  www.plymouth.k12.ct.us/
Fisher MS — 500/6-8
  79 N Main St 06786 — 860-314-2790
  Michael Buzzi, prin. — Fax 314-2786
Terryville HS — 500/9-12
  21 N Main St 06786 — 860-314-2777
  Andrea Lavery, prin. — Fax 314-2785

Thomaston, Litchfield, Pop. 6,947
Thomaston SD — 1,300/PK-12
  PO Box 166 06787 — 860-283-4796
  Lynda Mitchell, supt. — Fax 283-6708
  www.thomastonschools.net/
Thomaston HS — 600/7-12
  185 Branch Rd 06787 — 860-283-3030
  James Wenker, prin. — Fax 283-3040

Thompson, Windham

Marianapolis Prep S — 200/9-12
  PO Box 304 06277 — 860-923-9565
  Marilyn Ebbitt, hdmstr. — Fax 923-3730

Tolland, Tolland
Tolland SD — 3,000/PK-12
  51 Tolland Grn 06084 — 860-870-6850
  William D. Guzman, supt. — Fax 870-7737
  www.tolland.k12.ct.us
Tolland HS — 900/9-12
  1 Eagle Hill Dr 06084 — 860-870-6860
  Joseph Bacewicz, prin. — Fax 870-8168
Tolland MS — 900/5-8
  96 Old Post Rd 06084 — 860-875-2564
  Michael Seroussi, prin. — Fax 872-7126

Torrington, Litchfield, Pop. 35,756
Connecticut Technical HS System
  Supt. — See Middletown
Wolcott Technical HS — Vo/Tech
  75 Oliver St 06790 — 860-496-5300
  Daniel Kushman, dir. — Fax 496-9022

Torrington SD — 4,800/K-12
  355 Migeon Ave 06790 — 860-489-2327
  Susan W. O'Brien Ed.D., supt. — Fax 489-0726
  www.torrington.org
Torrington HS — 1,300/9-12
  50 Major Besse Dr 06790 — 860-489-2294
  Veronica LeDuc, prin. — Fax 489-2853
Torrington MS — 1,300/6-8
  200 Middle School Dr 06790 — 860-496-4050
  John Hudson, prin. — Fax 496-1089

St. Francis of Assisi S — 200/3-8
  360 Prospect St 06790 — 860-489-4177
  Jo Anne Gauger, prin. — Fax 489-1590

Trumbull, Fairfield, Pop. 34,600
Trumbull SD — 6,500/PK-12
  6254 Main St 06611 — 203-452-4301
  Ralph Iassogna, supt. — Fax 452-4305
  www.trumbullps.org
Hillcrest MS — 800/6-8
  530 Daniels Farm Rd 06611 — 203-452-4466
  Rosemary Seaman, prin. — Fax 452-4479

Madison MS — 800/6-8
  4630 Madison Ave 06611 — 203-452-4499
  Valerie Forshaw, prin. — Fax 452-4490
Trumbull HS — 1,900/9-12
  72 Strobel Rd 06611 — 203-452-4555
  Robert Tremaglio, prin. — Fax 452-4593

Christian Heritage S — 500/K-12
  575 White Plains Rd 06611 — 203-261-6230
  Barry Giller, hdmstr. — Fax 452-1531
St. Joseph HS — 800/9-12
  2320 Huntington Tpke 06611 — 203-378-9378
  Dr. Matthew Kenney, prin. — Fax 378-7306

Uncasville, New London, Pop. 2,975

St. Bernard Academy — 100/6-8
  1593 Norwich New London Tpk 06382
— 860-848-3007
  Mary Dillman, prin. — Fax 848-0261
St. Bernard HS — 400/9-12
  1593 Norwich New London Tpk 06382
— 860-848-1271
  Br. Robert Daszkiewicz, prin. — Fax 848-1274

Vernon Rockville, Tolland, Pop. 28,900
Vernon SD — 4,000/PK-12
  PO Box 10066 06066 — 860-870-6000
  Stephen Cullinan, supt. — Fax 870-6008
  www.vernonschools.com
Rockville HS — 1,300/9-12
  70 Loveland Hill Rd 06066 — 860-870-6050
  Brian Levesque, prin. — Fax 870-6314
Vernon Center MS — 1,000/6-8
  777 Hartford Tpke 06066 — 860-870-6070
  Beth Katz, prin. — Fax 870-6318

Wallingford, New Haven, Pop. 41,700
Wallingford SD — 7,100/PK-12
  142 Hope Hill Rd 06492 — 203-949-6500
  Kenneth V. Henrici, supt. — Fax 949-6550
  www.wallingford.k12.ct.us
Hall HS — 1,200/9-12
  70 Pond Hill Rd 06492 — 203-294-5350
  David Bryant, prin. — Fax 294-5353
Hammarskjold MS — 800/6-8
  106 Pond Hill Rd 06492 — 203-294-5340
  Enrico Buccilli, prin. — Fax 294-5322
Moran MS — 900/6-8
  141 Hope Hill Rd 06492 — 203-741-2900
  Robert Cyr, prin. — Fax 741-2939
Sheehan HS — 1,000/9-12
  142 Hope Hill Rd 06492 — 203-294-5900
  Rosemary Duthie, prin. — Fax 294-5980

Choate Rosemary Hall S — 900/9-12
  333 Christian St 06492 — 203-697-2000
  Edward Shanahan, prin. — Fax 697-2720

Washington, Litchfield
Regional SD 12
  Supt. — See Washington Depot
Shepaug Valley HS — 400/9-12
  159 South St 06793 — 860-868-7326
  Eugene Horrigan, prin. — Fax 868-0622
Shepaug Valley MS — 300/6-8
  159 South St 06793 — 860-868-7326
  Lorrie Rodrigue, prin. — Fax 868-0622

Devereux Center in Connecticut — Post-Sec.
  81 Sabbaday Ln 06793 — 860-868-7377
Glenholme S — 100/4-12
  81 Sabbaday Ln 06793 — 860-868-7377
  Gary L. Fitzherbert, hdmstr. — Fax 868-7413
Gunnery — 300/9-12
  99 Green Hill Rd 06793 — 860-868-7334
  Susan Graham, hdmstr. — Fax 868-7205

Washington Depot, Litchfield
Regional SD 12 — 1,100/K-12
  PO Box 386 06794 — 860-868-6100
  Richard E. Carmelich Ph.D., supt. — Fax 868-6103
  www.region-12.org
Other Schools – See Washington

Waterbury, New Haven, Pop. 108,130
Connecticut Technical HS System
  Supt. — See Middletown
Kaynor Technical HS — Vo/Tech
  43 Tompkins St 06708 — 203-596-4302
  Robert Axon, dir. — Fax 596-4308

Waterbury SD — 17,500/PK-12
  236 Grand St 06702 — 203-574-8004
  Dr. David Snead, supt. — Fax 574-8010
  www.waterbury.k12.ct.us/
Crosby HS — 1,300/9-12
  300 Pierpont Rd 06705 — 203-574-8061
  Barbara Carrington, prin. — Fax 574-8072
Kennedy HS — 1,400/9-12
  422 Highland Ave 06708 — 203-574-8150
  Anthony Azzara, prin. — Fax 574-8154
North End MS — 1,200/6-8
  534 Bucks Hill Rd 06704 — 203-574-8097
  Michael LoRusso, prin. — Fax 574-8203
Wallace MS — 1,400/6-8
  3465 E Main St 06705 — 203-574-8140
  Louis Padua, prin. — Fax 574-8141
Waterbury Arts Magnet S — 6-12
  16 S Elm St 06706 — 203-573-6300
  Alan Kramer, prin. — Fax 573-6325
West Side MS — 1,500/6-8
  483 Chase Pkwy 06708 — 203-574-8120
  Charles Nappi, prin. — Fax 574-8130
Wilby HS — 1,100/9-12
  568 Bucks Hill Rd 06704 — 203-574-8100
  Robyn Apicella, prin. — Fax 574-6896

Chase Collegiate S — 500/PK-12
  565 Chase Pkwy 06708 — 203-236-9560
  John Fixx, hdmstr. — Fax 236-9494
Goodwin Institute Business School — Post-Sec.
  101 Pierpont Rd 06705 — 203-756-5500
Holy Cross HS — 900/9-12
  587 Oronoke Rd 06708 — 203-757-9248
  Timothy McDonald, prin. — Fax 757-3423
Industrial Management and Training — Post-Sec.
  233 Mill St 06706 — 203-753-7910
Naugatuck Valley Community College — Post-Sec.
  750 Chase Pkwy 06708 — 203-575-8044
Post University — Post-Sec.
  800 Country Club Rd 06708 — 203-596-4500
Sacred Heart HS — 500/9-12
  142 S Elm St 06706 — 203-753-1605
  Jacqueline C. Jennings, prin. — Fax 597-1686
St. Mary's Hospital — Post-Sec.
  56 Franklin St 06706 — 203-574-6300
University of Connecticut — Post-Sec.
  32 Hillside Ave 06710 — 203-757-1231

Waterford, New London, Pop. 17,930
Waterford SD — 3,000/K-12
  PO Box 284 06385 — 860-444-5801
  Randall Collins, supt. — Fax 444-5870
  www.waterfordschools.org
Clark Lane MS — 800/6-8
  105 Clark Ln 06385 — 860-443-2837
  Michael Lovetere, prin. — Fax 437-6985
Waterford HS — 1,000/9-12
  20 Rope Ferry Rd 06385 — 860-437-6956
  Donald Macrino, prin. — Fax 447-7928

Watertown, Litchfield, Pop. 6,000
Watertown SD — 3,500/PK-12
  10 Deforest St 06795 — 860-945-4801
  Dr. Joseph Erardi, supt. — Fax 945-2775
  www.watertownctschools.org
Watertown HS — 900/9-12
  324 French St 06795 — 860-945-4810
  Thad Hasbrouck, prin. — Fax 945-3348
Other Schools – See Oakville

Porter and Chester Institute — Post-Sec.
  320 Sylvan Lake Rd 06779 — 860-274-9294
Taft S — 600/9-12
  110 Woodbury Rd 06795 — 860-945-7777
  William MacMullen, hdmstr. — Fax 945-7858

Westbrook, Middlesex, Pop. 2,060
Westbrook SD — 1,000/PK-12
  158 McVeagh Rd 06498 — 860-399-6432
  Dr. John Sullivan, supt. — Fax 399-8817
  www.westbrookctschools.org/
Westbrook HS — 300/9-12
  156 Mcveagh Rd 06498 — 860-399-6214
  Robert Hale, prin. — Fax 399-2007
Westbrook MS — 300/6-8
  152 Mcveagh Rd 06498 — 860-399-2010
  Philip House, prin. — Fax 399-2007

Oxford Academy — 50/9-12
  1393 Boston Post Rd 06498 — 860-399-6247
— Fax 399-6805

West Hartford, Hartford, Pop. 64,300
West Hartford SD — 9,800/PK-12
  28 S Main St, — 860-523-3500
  David Sklarz, supt. — Fax 523-3523
  www.whps.org
Bristow MS, 34 Highland St, — 6-8
  Jeanne Camperchioli, prin. — 860-523-3500
Conard HS — 1,400/9-12
  110 Berkshire Rd, — 860-231-5000
  Alphonse Landroche, prin. — Fax 521-6699
Hall HS — 1,600/9-12
  975 N Main St, — 860-232-4561
  Donald Slater, prin. — Fax 236-0366
King Philip MS — 1,100/6-8
  100 King Philip Dr, — 860-233-8236
  Mary Hourdequin, prin. — Fax 233-0812
Sedgwick MS — 1,000/6-8
  128 Sedgwick Rd, — 860-521-0610
  Ben Skaught, prin. — Fax 521-7502

American School for the Deaf — Post-Sec.
  139 N Main St, — 860-570-2309
Fox Institute of Business — Post-Sec.
  99 South St, — 860-947-2299
Hartt Community Division — Post-Sec.
  200 Bloomfield Ave, — 860-768-7768
Kingswood-Oxford S — 600/6-12
  170 Kingswood Rd, — 860-233-9631
  Lee Levison, hdmstr. — Fax 232-3843
Northwest Catholic HS — 600/9-12
  29 Wampanoag Dr, — 860-236-4221
  Margaret Williamson, prin. — Fax 586-0911
St. Joseph College — Post-Sec.
  1678 Asylum Ave, — 860-232-4571
St. Timothy MS — 100/6-8
  225 King Philip Dr, — 860-236-0614
  Christian Cashman, prin. — Fax 920-0293
University of Connecticut — Post-Sec.
  1800 Asylum Ave, — 860-241-4700
University of Hartford — Post-Sec.
  200 Bloomfield Ave, — 860-768-4100

West Haven, New Haven, Pop. 53,004
West Haven SD — 8,900/PK-12
  25 Ogden St 06516 — 203-937-4310
  Paul Tortora, supt. — Fax 937-4315
  www.whschools.org
Bailey MS — 900/6-8
  106 Morgan Ln 06516 — 203-937-4380
  Anthony Cordone, prin. — Fax 937-4385

Carrigan MS 1,000/6-8
2 Tetlow St 06516 203-937-4390
Patricia Libero, prin. Fax 937-4393
Stiles Alternative Learning Ctr 1,800/9-12
575 Main St 06516 203-931-6860
Lester Hawley, prin. Fax 931-6863
West Haven HS 1,800/9-12
1 McDonough Plz 06516 203-937-4360
Ronald Stancil, prin. Fax 934-4370

Living Word Christian Academy 200/PK-12
225 Meloy Rd 06516 203-931-7750
Lawrence Batza, prin. Fax 931-7540
Notre Dame HS 700/9-12
24 Ricardo St 06516 203-933-1673
Ralph Proto, prin. Fax 933-2474
University of New Haven Post-Sec.
300 Boston Post Rd 06516 203-932-7000

Weston, Fairfield
Weston SD 1,900/PK-12
24 School Rd 06883 203-291-1401
Lynne B. Pierson Ed.D., supt. Fax 291-1415
www.westonk12-ct.org
Weston HS 700/9-12
115 School Rd 06883 203-291-1600
Rose Marie Cipriano, prin. Fax 291-1603
Weston MS 600/6-8
135 School Rd 06883 203-291-1500
Lisa Wolak, prin. Fax 291-1516

Westport, Fairfield, Pop. 24,407
Westport SD 5,100/PK-12
110 Myrtle Ave 06880 203-341-1025
Elliott Landon, supt. Fax 341-1029
www.westport.k12.ct.us/
Bedford MS 800/5-8
88 North Ave 06880 203-341-1510
Angela Wormser, prin. Fax 341-1508
Coleytown MS 500/6-8
255 North Ave 06880 203-341-1610
Kris Biendowski, prin. Fax 341-1603
Staples HS 1,400/9-12
70 North Ave 06880 203-341-1200
John Dodig, prin. Fax 341-1202

Connecticut Center for Massage Therapy Post-Sec.
25 Sylvan Rd S 06880 203-221-7325

West Redding, Fairfield
Redding SD
Supt. — See Monroe
Read MS 600/5-8
Route 53 06896 203-938-2533
Dianne Martin, prin. Fax 938-8667

West Simsbury, Hartford, Pop. 2,149

Master's S 300/PK-12
36 Westledge Rd 06092 860-651-9361
Rick Burslem, hdmstr. Fax 651-9363

West Suffield, Hartford
Suffield SD
Supt. — See Suffield
Suffield HS 800/9-12
1060 Sheldon St 06093 860-668-3810
Thomas Jones, prin. Fax 668-3037

Wethersfield, Hartford, Pop. 26,400
Wethersfield SD 4,000/K-12
127 Hartford Ave 06109 860-571-8110
Patrick Proctor Ed.D., supt. Fax 571-8130
www.wethersfield.k12.ct.us/
Deane MS 600/7-8
551 Silas Deane Hwy 06109 860-571-8300
James Collin, prin. Fax 563-0563
Wethersfield HS 1,100/9-12
411 Wolcott Hill Rd 06109 860-571-8200
Thomas Moore, prin. Fax 571-8240

Connecticut Childrens Medical Center Post-Sec.
170 Ridge Rd 06109 860-545-8551
Porter and Chester Institute Post-Sec.
125 Silas Deane Hwy 06109 860-529-2519

Willimantic, Windham, Pop. 14,746
Connecticut Technical HS System
Supt. — See Middletown
Windham Technical HS Vo/Tech
210 Birch St 06226 860-456-3879
Kirk Murad, dir. Fax 450-0630

Windham SD 3,600/PK-12
322 Prospect St 06226 860-465-2310
Paul K. Perzanoski, supt. Fax 456-2311
www.windham.k12.ct.us
Windham HS 1,000/9-12
355 High St 06226 860-465-2480
Gene Blain, prin. Fax 465-2463
Windham MS 1,100/5-8
123 Quarry St 06226 860-465-2351
Robert Musial, prin. Fax 465-2353

Eastern Connecticut State University Post-Sec.
83 Windham St 06226 860-456-5000
Windham Community Memorial Hospital Post-Sec.
112 Mansfield Ave 06226 860-456-6800
Windham Regional Vocational Tech School Post-Sec.
210 Birch St 06226 860-456-3789

Willington, Tolland
Willington SD 600/PK-8
40 Old Farms Rd # A 06279 860-487-3130
Corinne Berglund, supt. Fax 487-3132
www.willingtonct.org
Hall Memorial MS 400/4-8
111 River Rd 06279 860-429-9391
David Harding, prin. Fax 429-5682

Wilton, Fairfield, Pop. 7,200
Wilton SD 4,200/PK-12
PO Box 277 06897 203-762-3381
Gary G. Richards, supt. Fax 762-2177
www.wilton.k12.ct.us/
Middlebrook MS 1,000/6-8
131 School Rd 06897 203-762-8388
Julia Harris, prin. Fax 762-1716
Wilton HS 1,200/9-12
395 Danbury Rd 06897 203-762-0381
Timothy Canty, prin. Fax 834-0164

Windsor, Hartford, Pop. 27,817
Hartford SD
Supt. — See Hartford
Pathways to Technology Vo/Tech
184 Windsor Ave 06095 860-695-9450
Gail Rowe, dir. Fax 722-6442

Windsor SD 4,400/PK-12
601 Matianuck Ave 06095 860-687-2000
Elizabeth E. Feser Ed.D., supt. Fax 687-2009
www.windsorct.org
Sage Park MS 1,100/6-8
25 Sage Park Rd 06095 860-687-2030
Paul Cavaliere, prin. Fax 687-2039
Windsor HS 1,500/9-12
50 Sage Park Rd 06095 860-687-2020
Joseph Arcarese, prin. Fax 687-2029

Branford Hall Career Institute Post-Sec.
995 Day Hill Rd 06095 860-683-4900
Loomis Chaffee S 700/9-12
4 Batchelder Rd 06095 860-687-6000
Russell Weigel, hdmstr. Fax 687-1100
Praise Power & Prayer Christian S 100/K-12
PO Box 474 06095 860-285-8898
Rev. Raymond McMahon, prin.

Windsor Locks, Hartford, Pop. 12,358
Windsor Locks SD 1,900/PK-12
58 S Elm St 06096 860-292-5000
Dr. Greg W. Little, supt. Fax 292-5003
www.wlps.org
Windsor Locks HS 600/9-12
58 S Elm St 06096 860-292-5032
Matt Bisceglia, prin. Fax 292-5039
Windsor Locks MS 500/6-8
7 Center St 06096 860-292-5012
Gregory Blanchfield, prin. Fax 292-5017

Baran Institute of Technology Post-Sec.
PO Box 06088 06096 800-688-3353

Baran Institute of Technology Post-Sec.
225 Ella Grasso Tpke 06096 860-688-3353

Winsted, Litchfield, Pop. 8,254
Endowed & Incorporated Academies 500/9-12
200 Williams Ave 06098 860-379-8521
Dr. David Cressy, supt. Fax 379-6163
gilbertschool.org
Gilbert S 500/9-12
200 Williams Ave 06098 860-379-8521
Daniel Hatch, prin. Fax 379-6163
Regional SD 7 1,100/7-12
PO Box 656 06098 860-379-1084
Dr. Roberta Ohotnicky, supt. Fax 379-0618
www.nwr7.com
Northwestern Regional HS 700/9-12
100 Battistoni Rd 06098 860-379-8525
Wayne Conner, prin. Fax 738-6059
Northwestern Regional MS 400/7-8
100 Battistoni Rd 06098 860-379-7243
Paul Osypuk, prin. Fax 738-6205
Winchester SD 1,100/PK-8
30 Elm St 06098 860-379-0706
Clay Krevolin, supt. Fax 379-6521
www.winchesterschools.org/
Pearson MS 400/6-8
2 Wetmore Ave 06098 860-379-7588
Clay Krevolin, prin. Fax 379-0406

Northwestern CT Comm. Technical College Post-Sec.
2 Park Pl 06098 860-738-6300

Wolcott, New Haven, Pop. 13,700
Wolcott SD 2,900/PK-12
154 Center St 06716 203-879-8183
Dr. Thomas M. Smyth Jr., supt. Fax 879-8182
www.wolcottps.org
Tyrrell MS 800/6-8
500 Todd Rd 06716 203-879-8151
Karen Habegger, prin. Fax 879-8419
Wolcott HS 800/9-12
457 Bound Line Rd 06716 203-879-8164
Gary Cotzin, prin. Fax 879-8167

Connecticut Institute of Hair Design Post-Sec.
1681 Meriden Rd 06716 203-879-4247

Woodbridge, New Haven, Pop. 7,924
Regional SD 5 2,300/7-12
25 Newton Rd 06525 203-392-2106
Dr. John Brady, supt. Fax 397-4864
www.amityregion5.org
Amity Regional HS 1,400/9-12
25 Newton Rd 06525 203-397-4830
Edward Goldstone, prin. Fax 397-4866
Other Schools – See Bethany, Orange

Woodbury, Litchfield, Pop. 8,131
Regional SD 14 2,300/K-12
PO Box 469 06798 203-263-4330
David Pendleton, supt. Fax 263-0372
www.ctreg14.org
Nonnewaug HS 800/9-12
PO Box 469 06798 203-263-2186
John Vecchitto, prin. Fax 263-3570
Woodbury MS 500/6-8
67 Washington Ave 06798 203-263-4306
Ellen Solek, prin. Fax 263-0825

Woodstock, Windham
Endowed & Incorporated Academies 1,100/9-12
57 Academy Rd 06281 860-928-6575
Richard Foye, hdmstr. Fax 963-7222
www.woodstockacademy.org
Woodstock Academy 1,100/9-12
57 Academy Rd 06281 860-928-6575
Richard Foye, hdmstr. Fax 963-7222

Woodstock SD 1,000/PK-8
147 Route 169 06281 860-928-7453
Dr. Francis A. Baron, supt. Fax 928-0206
www.woodstockschools.net
Woodstock MS 400/5-8
147 Route 169 06281 860-963-6575
Paul Gamache, prin. Fax 963-6577

Hyde S 200/9-12
PO Box 237 06281 860-963-9096
Duncan McCrann, hdmstr. Fax 928-0612

DELAWARE

DELAWARE DEPARTMENT OF EDUCATION
401 Federal St Ste 2, Dover 19901-3639
Telephone 302-739-4601
Fax 302-739-4654
Website http://www.doe.k12.de.us

Secretary of Education   Valerie Woodruff

DELAWARE BOARD OF EDUCATION
PO Box 1402, Dover 19903-1402

President   Joseph Pika

PUBLIC, PRIVATE AND CATHOLIC SECONDARY SCHOOLS

Bear, New Castle

Caravel Academy | 1,100/PK-12
2801 Del Laws Rd 19701 | 302-834-8938
Donald C. Keister, hdmstr. | Fax 834-3658
Fairwinds Christian S | 200/PK-12
801 Seymour Rd 19701 | 302-328-7404
Neil Webster, prin. | Fax 328-0190
Red Lion Christian Academy | 900/PK-12
1390 Red Lion Rd 19701 | 302-834-2526
Donald Cook, hdmstr. | Fax 836-6346

Bridgeville, Sussex, Pop. 1,518
Woodbridge SD
Supt. — See Greenwood
Wheatley MS | 700/5-8
48 Church St 19933 | 302-337-3469
Delores Tunstall, prin. | Fax 337-6016
Woodbridge HS | 500/9-12
307 S Laws St 19933 | 302-337-8289
Gary Rosenthal, prin. | Fax 337-0631

Camden Wyoming, Kent, Pop. 1,045
Caesar Rodney SD | 6,500/PK-12
PO Box 188 19934 | 302-697-2173
Harold Roberts Ed.D., supt. | Fax 697-3406
www.k12.de.us/caesarrodney/
Fifer MS | 800/6-8
109 E Camden Wyoming Ave 19934 | 302-698-8400
David Sechler, prin. | Fax 698-8409
Postlethwait MS | 800/6-8
2841 S State St 19934 | 302-698-8410
Michael Noel, prin. | Fax 698-8419
Rodney HS | 1,700/9-12
239 Old North Rd 19934 | 302-697-2161
Kevin Fitzgerald Ed.D., prin. | Fax 697-6888
Other Schools – See Dover

Claymont, New Castle, Pop. 9,800
Brandywine SD | 10,400/K-12
1000 Pennsylvania Ave 19703 | 302-793-5000
Bruce Harter Ph.D., supt. | Fax 792-3823
www.bsd.k12.de.us
Other Schools – See Wilmington

Archmere Academy | 500/9-12
3600 Philadelphia Pike 19703 | 302-798-6632
Rev. John Zagarella, hdmstr. | Fax 798-7290

Dagsboro, Sussex, Pop. 537
Indian River SD
Supt. — See Selbyville
Indian River HS | 700/9-12
29772 Armory Rd 19939 | 302-732-1500
Mark Steele, prin. | Fax 732-1514

National Massage Therapy Institute | Post-Sec.
Route 113 Box 144D 19939 | 800-264-9835

Delmar, Sussex, Pop. 1,453
Delmar SD | 1,100/6-12
200 N 8th St 19940 | 302-846-9544
David Ring Ed.D., supt. | Fax 846-2793
www.k12.de.us/delmar
Delmar HS | 600/9-12
200 N 8th St 19940 | 302-846-9544
Giffin Bowen, prin. | Fax 846-2793
Delmar MS | 500/6-8
200 N 8th St 19940 | 302-846-9544
Giffin Bowen, prin. | Fax 846-2793

Dover, Kent, Pop. 32,808
Caesar Rodney SD
Supt. — See Camden Wyoming
Dover AFB MS | 200/6-8
3100 Hawthorne Dr 19901 | 302-674-3284
Ernestine Adams, prin. | Fax 730-4283

Capital SD | 5,900/PK-12
945 Forest St 19904 | 302-672-1500
Michael D. Thomas Ed.D., supt. | Fax 672-1714
www.k12.de.us/capital/
Central MS | 1,000/7-8
211 Delaware Ave 19901 | 302-672-1772
Darren Guido, prin. | Fax 672-1733
Dover HS | 1,600/9-12
1 Pat Lynn Dr 19904 | 302-672-1526
Gene Montano, prin. | Fax 672-1565

Bayhealth Medical Center | Post-Sec.
640 S State St 19901 | 302-674-7001
Calvary Christian Academy | 300/PK-12
1143 E Lebanon Rd 19901 | 302-697-7860
Rosalia Martinez, admin. | Fax 697-0284
Capitol Baptist S | 100/K-12
401 Kesselring Ave 19904 | 302-678-9190
Thomas Horne, prin. | Fax 674-5957
Delaware State University | Post-Sec.
1200 N Dupont Hwy 19901 | 302-857-6060
Delaware Technical & Community College | Post-Sec.
100 Campus Dr 19904 | 302-857-1000
Kent Christian Academy | 100/K-12
3282 N Dupont Hwy 19901 | 302-678-3837
Jeanette Berry, prin. | Fax 678-5135
Star Technical Institute | Post-Sec.
655 S Bay Rd Ste 562 19901 | 302-736-6111
Wesley College | Post-Sec.
120 N State St 19901 | 302-736-2300

Felton, Kent, Pop. 798
Lake Forest SD | 3,400/PK-12
5423 Killens Pond Rd 19943 | 302-284-3020
Dr. Daniel Curry, supt. | Fax 284-4491
www.k12.de.us/lakeforest
Lake Forest HS | 800/9-12
5407 Killens Pond Rd 19943 | 302-284-9291
Dean Ivory, prin. | Fax 284-5833
Other Schools – See Harrington

Georgetown, Sussex, Pop. 4,811
Indian River SD
Supt. — See Selbyville
Sussex Central HS | 1,100/9-12
26026 Patriots Way 19947 | 302-934-3166
Donna Hall Ed.D., prin. | Fax 934-3234

Sussex Technical SD |
PO Box 351 19947 | 302-856-2542
Patrick Savini Ed.D., supt. | Fax 856-7078
www.sussexvt.k12.de.us
Sussex Technical HS | Vo/Tech
PO Box 351 19947 | 302-856-0961
Curt Bunting, prin. | Fax 856-1760

Delaware Technical & Community College | Post-Sec.
PO Box 610 19947 | 302-856-5400
Delmarva Christian HS | 50/9-12
150 Airport Rd 19947 | 302-856-4040
William Kemerling, prin. | Fax 856-6878

Greenville, New Castle
Red Clay Consolidated SD
Supt. — See Wilmington
DuPont HS | 1,200/9-12
50 Hillside Rd 19807 | 302-651-2626
Jeffrey Lawson, prin. | Fax 651-2757
DuPont MS | 500/6-8
3130 Kennett Pike 19807 | 302-651-2690
Theodore Boyer, prin. | Fax 425-4585

Greenwood, Sussex, Pop. 860
Woodbridge SD | 1,800/PK-12
PO Box 869 19950 | 302-349-1421
Kevin Carson Ed.D., supt. | Fax 349-1427
www.wsd.k12.de.us
Other Schools – See Bridgeville

Greenwood Mennonite S | 300/K-12
12802 Mennonite School Rd 19950 | 302-349-4131
Larry Crossgrove, admin. | Fax 349-5076

Harrington, Kent, Pop. 3,161
Lake Forest SD
Supt. — See Felton
Chipman MS | 500/7-8
101 N Center St 19952 | 302-398-8197
Linda Noel-Batiste Ph.D., prin. | Fax 398-8375

Hockessin, New Castle
Red Clay Consolidated SD
Supt. — See Wilmington
DuPont MS | 1,000/6-8
735 Meeting House Rd 19707 | 302-239-3420
John Kennedy, prin. | Fax 239-3450

Sanford S | 700/PK-12
PO Box 888 19707 | 302-239-5263
Douglas MacKelcan, hdmstr. | Fax 239-5389
Tall Oaks Classical S | 100/K-12
1514 Brackenville Rd 19707 | 302-239-3600
Donald H. Post, admin. | Fax 657-8373
Towle Institute | 200/K-12
PO Box 580 19707 | 302-234-4442
Kathleen Todd, prin. | Fax 832-3449
Wilmington Christian S | 600/PK-12
825 Loveville Rd 19707 | 302-239-2121
 | Fax 239-2778

Laurel, Sussex, Pop. 3,752
Laurel SD | 2,000/PK-12
1160 S Central Ave 19956 | 302-875-6100
Keith Duda, supt. | Fax 875-6106
www.laurelschooldistrict.org
Laurel Central MS | 300/7-8
801 S Central Ave 19956 | 302-875-6110
Julie Bradley, prin. | Fax 875-6148
Laurel HS | 500/9-12
1133 S Central Ave 19956 | 302-875-6120
Dr. Diane Stetina, prin. | Fax 875-6123

Lewes, Sussex, Pop. 3,006
Cape Henlopen SD | 3,700/K-12
1270 Kings Hwy 19958 | 302-645-6686
George Stone Ed.D., supt. | Fax 645-6684
www.k12.de.us/capehenlopen
Beacon MS | 600/6-8
19483 John J Williams Hwy 19958 | 302-645-6288
T.S. Buckmaster, prin. | Fax 644-6118
Cape Henlopen HS | 1,200/9-12
1250 Kings Hwy 19958 | 302-645-7711
Edward Waples, prin. | Fax 645-1356
Other Schools – See Milton

Beebe Medical Center School of Nursing | Post-Sec.
424 Savannah Rd 19958 | 302-645-3251

Lincoln, Sussex

Christian Tabernacle Academy | 200/PK-12
PO Box 148 19960 | 302-422-6471
Ronald Hill, admin. | Fax 422-9207

Magnolia, Kent, Pop. 227

St. Thomas More Academy | 100/9-12
133 Thomas More Dr 19962 | 302-697-8100
Dr. Jonathan Grant, prin. | Fax 697-8122

Middletown, New Castle, Pop. 6,496
Appoquinimink SD
Supt. — See Odessa
Meredith MS | 900/6-8
504 S Broad St 19709 | 302-378-5001
Dr. Claude McAllister, prin. | Fax 378-5008
Middletown HS | 1,700/9-12
120 Silver Lake Rd 19709 | 302-376-4141
Donna Mitchell, prin. | Fax 378-5268
Redding MS | 700/6-8
201 New St 19709 | 302-378-5030
James Comegys, prin. | Fax 378-5080

St. Andrew's S 300/9-12
350 Noxontown Rd 19709 302-378-9511
Daniel Roach, hdmstr. Fax 378-7120

Milford, Sussex, Pop. 6,991
Milford SD 3,700/PK-12
906 Lakeview Ave 19963 302-422-1600
Robert D. Smith Ed.D., supt. Fax 422-1608
www.milfordschooldistrict.com
Milford HS 1,000/9-12
1019 N Walnut St 19963 302-422-1610
Phyllis Kohel, prin. Fax 424-5463
Milford MS 900/6-8
612 Lakeview Ave 19963 302-422-1620
Kevin Dickerson, prin. Fax 424-5466

Millsboro, Sussex, Pop. 2,467
Indian River SD
Supt. — See Selbyville
Sussex Central MS 1,000/6-8
PO Box 668 19966 302-934-3200
Vincent Catania, prin. Fax 934-3215

Milton, Sussex, Pop. 1,750
Cape Henlopen SD
Supt. — See Lewes
Mariner MS 500/6-8
16391 Harbeson Rd 19968 302-684-8516
Brian Curtis, prin. Fax 684-5606

Newark, New Castle, Pop. 29,821
Christina SD
Supt. — See Wilmington
Christiana HS 1,300/9-12
190 Salem Church Rd 19713 302-454-2123
Scott Flowers, prin. Fax 454-3490
Gauger/Cobbs MS 1,100/7-8
50 Gender Rd 19713 302-454-2358
Amy Levitz, prin. Fax 454-3482
Glasgow HS 1,400/9-12
1901 S College Ave 19702 302-454-2381
Todd Harvey, prin. Fax 454-5453
Kirk MS 1,000/7-8
140 Brennen Dr 19713 302-454-2164
Donald Patton, prin. Fax 454-3491
Newark HS 1,900/9-12
750 E Delaware Ave 19711 302-454-2151
Emmanuel Caulk, prin. Fax 454-2155
Shue-Medill MS 1,000/7-8
1550 Capitol Trl 19711 302-454-2171
Eleanor Ludwigsen, prin. Fax 454-3492

New Castle County Voc-Tech SD
Supt. — See Wilmington
Hodgson Vocational-Technical HS Vo/Tech
2575 Glasgow Ave 19702 302-834-0990
Gerald Allen, prin. Fax 834-0598

Delaware Technical & Community College Post-Sec.
400 Stanton Christiana Rd 19713 302-454-3900
Schilling-Douglas School of Hair Design Post-Sec.
70 Amstel Ave 19711 302-737-5100
University of Delaware 19711 Post-Sec.
302-831-2000

New Castle, New Castle, Pop. 4,787
Colonial SD 9,900/K-12
318 E Basin Rd 19720 302-323-2700
George Meney Ed.D., supt. Fax 323-2748
www.colonial.k12.de.us
Bedford MS 1,200/6-8
801 Coxneck Rd 19720 302-832-6280
Dusty Blakey, prin. Fax 834-6729
New Castle MS 600/6-8
903 Delaware St 19720 302-323-2880
Steve Haber, prin. Fax 323-2897
Penn HS 2,200/9-12
713 E Basin Rd 19720 302-323-2800
Jeff Menzer, prin. Fax 323-2955
Read MS 1,100/6-8
314 E Basin Rd 19720 302-323-2760
Paul Walmsley, prin. Fax 323-2763

New Castle Christian Academy 300/PK-12
901 E Basin Rd 19720 302-328-7026
Kevin Gephart, admin. Fax 328-7886

Wilmington College Post-Sec.
320 N Dupont Hwy 19720 302-328-9401

Odessa, New Castle, Pop. 282
Appoquinimink SD 6,400/PK-12
PO Box 4010 19730 302-376-4128
Dr. Tony Marchio, supt. Fax 378-5016
apposchooldistrict.com
Other Schools – See Middletown

Seaford, Sussex, Pop. 6,948
Seaford SD 3,500/K-12
390 N Market Street Ext 19973 302-629-4587
Dr. Russell Knorr, supt. Fax 629-2619
www.seaford.k12.de.us
Seaford HS 900/9-12
399 N Market St 19973 302-629-4587
Clarence Davis, prin. Fax 628-4417
Seaford MS 800/6-8
500 E Stein Hwy 19973 302-629-4587
Stephanie Smith, prin. Fax 628-4485

Seaford Christian Academy 300/PK-12
110 Holly St 19973 302-629-7161
David McGown, admin. Fax 629-7726

Selbyville, Sussex, Pop. 1,711
Indian River SD 7,900/PK-12
31 Hoosier St 19975 302-436-1000
Lois Hobbs, supt. Fax 436-1034
www.irsd.net/
Selbyville MS 600/6-8
80 Bethany Rd 19975 302-436-1020
Michael Kline, prin. Fax 436-1035
Other Schools – See Dagsboro, Georgetown, Millsboro

Smyrna, Kent, Pop. 6,207
Smyrna SD 3,800/K-12
22 S Main St 19977 302-653-8585
Deborah Wicks, supt. Fax 653-3149
www.smyrna.k12.de.us
Smyrna HS 900/9-12
500 Duck Creek Pkwy 19977 302-653-8581
Anthony Soligo, prin. Fax 653-3139
Smyrna MS 600/7-8
700 Duck Creek Pkwy 19977 302-653-8584
Patrik Williams, prin. Fax 653-3424

Wilmington, New Castle, Pop. 72,051
Brandywine SD
Supt. — See Claymont
Brandywine HS 1,300/9-12
1400 Foulk Rd 19803 302-479-1600
Richard Gregg, prin. Fax 479-1604
Concord HS 1,100/9-12
2501 Ebright Rd 19810 302-475-3951
Fax 529-3094
Hanby MS 700/7-8
2523 Berwyn Rd 19810 302-479-1631
Ronald Mendenhall, prin. Fax 479-1643
Mt. Pleasant HS 900/9-12
5201 Washington Blvd 19809 302-762-7125
Gregg Robinson, prin. Fax 762-7042
Springer MS 600/7-8
2220 Shipley Rd 19803 302-479-1621
Michael Gliniak, prin. Fax 479-1628
Talley MS 500/7-8
1110 Cypress Rd 19810 302-475-3976
Barbara Starkey, prin. Fax 475-3998

Christina SD 18,400/PK-12
600 N Lombard St 19801 302-552-2600
Dr. Joseph J. Wise, supt. Fax 429-4109
www.christina.k12.de.us/
Other Schools – See Newark

New Castle County Voc-Tech SD
1417 Newport Rd 19804 302-995-8000
Steven Godowsky Ed.D., supt. Fax 995-8038
www.nccvotech.com/
Delcastle Technical HS Vo/Tech
1417 Newport Rd 19804 302-995-8100
Laurence Monaghan, prin. Fax 995-8197
Howard HS of Technology Vo/Tech
401 E 12th St 19801 302-571-5400
Evelyn Edney, prin. Fax 571-5843

Delaware Skills Center Adult
13th & Clifford Brown Walk 19801 302-654-5392
Robert Marshall, prin. Fax 654-9418
Other Schools – See Newark

Red Clay Consolidated SD 14,900/K-12
2916 Duncan Rd 19808 302-683-6600
Dr. Robert J. Andrzejewski, supt. Fax 636-8775
www.redclay.k12.de.us
Calloway School of Arts 800/6-12
100 N Dupont Rd 19807 302-651-2700
Julie Rumschlag, prin. Fax 425-4594
Conrad MS 600/6-8
201 Jackson Ave 19804 302-992-5545
Burton Watson, prin. Fax 992-5585
Dickinson HS 1,000/9-12
1801 Milltown Rd 19808 302-992-5500
Chad Carmack, prin. Fax 992-5506
McKean HS 1,100/9-12
301 Mckennans Church Rd 19808 302-992-5520
Tim Nolan, prin. Fax 992-5525
Skyline MS 700/6-8
2900 Skyline Dr 19808 302-454-3410
Dr. Nick Manolakos, prin. Fax 454-3541
Stanton MS 700/6-8
1800 Limestone Rd 19804 302-992-5540
Carolyn Zogby, prin. Fax 992-5586
Groves Adult Education Adult
100 N Dupont Rd 19807 302-651-2709
Les Henry, prin. Fax 658-7137
Other Schools – See Greenville, Hockessin

Christiana Care Health Services Post-Sec.
PO Box 1668 19899 302-428-2571
Concord Christian Academy 200/K-12
2510 Marsh Rd 19810 302-475-3247
Jeffrey Bergey, prin. Fax 475-6462
Dawn Training Centre Post-Sec.
3700 Lancaster Pike 19805 302-633-9075
Deep Muscle Therapy School Post-Sec.
5341 Limestone Rd 19808 302-234-8525
Delaware Technical & Community College Post-Sec.
333 N Shipley St 19801 302-571-5474
Goldey-Beacom College Post-Sec.
4701 Limestone Rd 19808 302-998-8814
Harrison Career Institute Post-Sec.
631 W Newport Pike 19804 302-999-7827
Padua Academy 600/9-12
905 N Broom St 19806 302-421-3739
Fax 421-3748
St. Edmond's Academy 300/4-8
2120 Veale Rd 19810 302-475-5370
Br. Michael Smith, hdmstr. Fax 475-2256
St. Elizabeth HS 400/9-12
1500 Cedar St 19805 302-656-3369
Fax 656-7513
St. Marks HS 1,600/9-12
2501 Pike Creek Rd 19808 302-738-3300
Mark Freund, prin. Fax 738-5132
Salesianum S 1,000/9-12
1801 N Broom St 19802 302-654-2495
Fax 654-7767
Tatnall S 700/PK-12
1501 Barley Mill Rd 19807 302-998-2292
Eric Ruoss, hdmstr. Fax 892-4389
Tower Hill S 700/PK-12
2813 W 17th St 19806 302-575-0550
Christopher Wheeler, hdmstr. Fax 657-8373
Ursuline Academy 700/PK-12
1106 Pennsylvania Ave 19806 302-658-7158
Veronica Harrington, prin. Fax 658-4297
Widener University School of Law Post-Sec.
PO Box 7474 19803 302-477-2100
Wilmington Friends S 800/PK-12
101 School Rd 19803 302-576-2900
Leo Dressel, hdmstr. Fax 576-2939

Woodside, Kent, Pop. 188
Polytech SD
PO Box 22 19980 302-697-2170
Dianne Sole Ed.D., supt. Fax 697-6749
www.polytech.k12.de.us
Polytech HS Vo/Tech
PO Box 97 19980 302-697-3255
Bruce Curry Ed.D., prin. Fax 697-4536

DISTRICT OF COLUMBIA

DISTRICT OF COLUMBIA PUBLIC SCHOOLS
825 N Capitol St NE, Washington 20002-4210
Telephone 202-442-5635
Website http://www.k12.dc.us

Superintendent   Clifford B. Janey

DISTRICT OF COLUMBIA BOARD OF EDUCATION
825 N Capitol St NE, Washington 20002-4210

President   Peggy Cafritz

PUBLIC, PRIVATE AND CATHOLIC SECONDARY SCHOOLS

Washington, District of Columbia, Pop. 563,384

District of Columbia SD — 59,300/PK-12
825 N Capitol St NE 20002 — 202-724-4222
Clifford B. Janey Ed.D., supt. — Fax 442-5026
www.k12.dc.us/
Anacostia HS — 600/9-12
1601 16th St SE 20020 — 202-698-2155
James Wilson, prin. — Fax 645-3019
Backus MS — 500/6-8
5171 S Dakota Ave NE 20017 — 202-576-6110
Alfonso Powell, prin. — Fax 576-6112
Ballou HS — 1,100/9-12
3401 4th St SE 20032 — 202-645-3400
Karen Smith, prin. — Fax 767-7297
Banneker HS — 400/9-12
800 Euclid St NW 20001 — 202-673-7322
Anita Berger, prin. — Fax 673-2231
Bell Multi-Cultural HS — 700/9-12
3145 Hiatt Pl NW 20010 — 202-673-7314
Maria Tukeva, prin. — Fax 673-7581
Browne JHS, 850 26th St NE 20002 — 500/7-9
Keith Stephenson, prin. — 202-724-4547
Brown MS, 4800 Meade St NE 20019 — 400/6-8
Rita O. Johnson, prin. — 202-724-4632
Cardozo HS — 800/9-12
1200 Clifton St NW 20009 — 202-673-7385
Reginald Ballard, prin. — Fax 673-2232
Coolidge HS — 800/9-12
6315 5th St NW 20011 — 202-576-6143
Cecil Robinson, prin. — Fax 576-6263
Deal JHS — 900/7-9
3815 Fort Dr NW 20016 — 202-282-0100
Melissa Kim, prin. — Fax 282-1116
Dunbar HS — 900/9-12
1301 New Jersey Ave NW 20001 — 202-673-7233
Harriett Kargbo, prin. — Fax 673-2233
Eastern HS — 900/9-12
1700 E Capitol St NE 20003 — 202-698-4500
Jacqueline Williams, prin. — Fax 724-8744
Eliot JHS — 300/7-9
1830 Constitution Ave NE 20002 — 202-673-8666
Andre Roach, prin. — Fax 543-4500
Ellington HS of the Arts — 500/9-12
3500 R St NW 20007 — 202-282-0123
Mitzi Yates Lizarraga, prin. — Fax 282-1106
Francis JHS — 400/7-9
2425 N St NW 20037 — 202-724-4841
Stephanie Crutchfield, prin. — Fax 724-3957
Garnet-Patterson MS — 400/5-8
2001 10th St NW 20001 — 202-673-7329
Veda Usilton, prin. — Fax 673-6543
Hardy MS — 500/5-8
1819 35th St NW 20007 — 202-282-0057
Patrick Pope, prin. — Fax 282-2303
Hart MS — 600/6-8
601 Mississippi Ave SE 20032 — 202-645-3420
Willie Bennett, prin. — Fax 645-3426
Hine JHS — 700/7-9
335 8th St SE 20003 — 202-698-3330
Duane Ross, prin. — Fax 724-4775
Jefferson JHS — 800/7-9
801 7th St SW 20024 — 202-724-4881
MenSa Ankh Maa, prin. — Fax 724-2459
Johnson JHS — 700/7-9
1400 Bruce Pl SE 20020 — 202-698-1017
Sylvia S. Dark, prin. — Fax 645-3693
Kramer MS — 400/6-8
1700 Q St SE 20020 — 202-698-1188
Kenneth Parker, prin. — Fax 645-3553
Lincoln MS, 1800 Perry St NE 20018 — 300/6-8
Lydia Blazquez, prin. — 202-576-5392
MacFarland MS — 600/6-8
4400 Iowa Ave NW 20011 — 202-576-6207
Antonia Peters, prin.
McKinley Technology HS — Vo/Tech
151 T St NE 20002 – Dan Gohl, prin. — 202-281-3950
Miller MS, 301 49th St NE 20019 — 6-8
Robert Gill, prin. — 202-388-6870

Moore Academy — 200/9-12
5600 E Capitol St NE 20019 — 202-388-8950
Reginald Elliott, prin.
Roosevelt HS — 800/9-12
4301 13th St NW 20011 — 202-576-6130
Benjamin Hosch, prin. — Fax 576-6259
Shaw JHS — 500/7-9
925 Rhode Island Ave NW 20001 — 202-673-7203
Gregory Thomas, prin. — Fax 673-2364
Sousa MS — 400/6-8
3650 Ely Pl SE 20019 — 202-645-3170
William Lipscomb, prin. — Fax 582-2953
Spingarn HS — 600/9-12
2500 Benning Rd NE 20002 — 202-724-4525
Reginald Burke, prin. — Fax 724-8746
Stuart-Hobson MS — 400/5-8
410 E St NE 20002 — 202-698-4700
Brandon Eatman, prin. — Fax 724-4985
Terrell JHS — 300/7-9
100 Pierce St NW 20001 — 202-535-2000
Francis Nicol, prin. — Fax 724-4901
Washington Career Development S — Vo/Tech
27 O St NW 20001 — 202-673-7224
L. Nelson Burton, prin. — Fax 673-7229
Wilson HS — 1,400/9-12
3950 Chesapeake St NW 20016 — 202-282-0120
Stephen Tarason, prin. — Fax 282-0077
Woodson HS — 700/9-12
5500 Eads St NE 20019 — 202-724-4500
Aona Jefferson, prin. — Fax 727-9360
Ballou STAY S — Adult
3401 4th St SE 20032 — 202-645-3390
Wilbert Miller, prin. — Fax 645-3397
Roosevelt STAY — Adult
4301 13th St NW 20011 — 202-576-8399
Linda Gray, prin.
Spingarn STAY S — Adult
2500 Benning Rd NE 20002 — 202-724-4538
Erline Whitaker, prin.

Academia de la Recto Porta Christian S — 50/PK-12
7614 Georgia Ave NW 20012 — 202-726-8737
Annette Miles, admin. — Fax 726-8759
American University — Post-Sec.
4400 Massachusetts Ave NW 20016 — 202-885-1000
Archbishop Carroll HS — 600/9-12
4300 Harewood Rd NE 20017 — 202-529-0900
John Butler, prin. — Fax 526-8879
Bennett Beauty Institute — Post-Sec.
700 Monroe St NE 20017 — 202-526-1400
Burke S — 300/6-12
2955 Upton St NW 20008 — 202-362-8882
David Shapiro, prin. — Fax 362-1914
Catholic University of America — Post-Sec.
620 Michigan Ave NE 20064 — 202-319-5000
Corcoran College of Art & Design — Post-Sec.
500 17th St NW 20006 — 202-639-1814
Dominican House of Studies — Post-Sec.
487 Michigan Ave NE 20017 — 202-529-5300
Dudley Beauty College — Post-Sec.
2031 Rhode Island Ave NE 20018 — 202-269-3666
Dupont Park Adventist S — 300/PK-10
3942 Alabama Ave SE 20020 — 202-583-8500
Lafese Quinnonez, prin. — Fax 583-0650
Field S — 300/7-12
2301 Foxhall Rd NW 20007 — 202-295-5800
Dale Johnson, prin. — Fax 295-5858
Gallaudet University — Post-Sec.
800 Florida Ave NE 20002 — 202-651-5000
Georgetown Day S — 500/9-12
4200 Davenport St NW 20016 — 202-274-3200
Peter Branch, hdmstr. — Fax 364-9603
Georgetown University — Post-Sec.
37th And O St NW 20057 — 202-687-0100
Georgetown Visitation Prep HS — 500/9-12
1524 35th St NW 20007 — 202-337-3350
Daniel Kerns, hdmstr. — Fax 342-5733
George Washington University — Post-Sec.
2035 H St NW 20052 — 202-994-1000

Gonzaga College HS — 900/9-12
19 I St NW 20001 — 202-336-7100
Michael Pakenham, hdmstr. — Fax 454-1188
Howard University — Post-Sec.
2400 6th St NW 20059 — 202-806-6100
Howard University School of Divinity — Post-Sec.
1400 Shepherd St NE 20017 — 202-806-0500
Johns Hopkins University
1740 Massachusetts Ave NW 20036 — 202-663-5600
Lab S of Washington — 300/K-12
4759 Reservoir Rd NW 20007 — 202-965-6600
Dr. Sally L. Smith, dir. — Fax 454-2270
Levine School of Music — Post-Sec.
2801 Upton St NW 20008 — 202-686-8000
Maret S — 600/K-12
3000 Cathedral Ave NW 20008 — 202-939-8800
Marjo Talbott, hdmstr. — Fax 939-8884
Model Secondary School for the Deaf — Post-Sec.
800 Florida Ave NE 20002 — 202-651-5466
National Cathedral S — 600/4-12
3612 Woodley Rd NW 20016 — 202-537-6300
Kathleen O. Jamieson, hdmstr. — Fax 537-5743
National Conservatory of Dramatic Arts — Post-Sec.
1556 Wisconsin Ave NW 20007 — 202-333-2202
Our Lady of Perpetual Help S — 100/5-8
1604 Morris Rd SE 20020 — 202-678-0211
Charlene Hursey, prin. — Fax 610-1519
Parkmont S — 100/6-12
4842 16th St NW 20011 — 202-726-0740
— Fax 726-0748
Potomac College — Post-Sec.
4000 Chesapeake St NW 20016 — 202-686-0876
Rock Creek International S — 200/PK-10
1550 Foxhall Rd NW 20007 — 202-965-8700
Daniel Hollinger, prin. — Fax 965-8973
St. Alban's S — 600/4-12
Mount Saint Alban 20016 — 202-537-6435
Vance Wilson, hdmstr. — Fax 537-5613
St. Anselms Abbey S — 200/6-12
4501 S Dakota Ave NE 20017 — 202-269-2350
Rev. Peter Weigand, prin. — Fax 269-2373
St. Johns College HS — 1,000/9-12
2607 Military Rd NW 20015 — 202-363-2316
Jeffrey Mancabelli, prin. — Fax 686-5162
San Miguel MS — 100/6-8
1525 Newton St NW 20010 — 202-232-1193
Br. Francis Eells, prin. — Fax 232-3987
Sidwell Friends S — 1,100/PK-12
3825 Wisconsin Ave NW 20016 — 202-537-8100
Bruce Stewart, hdmstr. — Fax 537-8138
Southeastern University — Post-Sec.
501 I St SW 20024 — 202-488-8162
Strayer University — Post-Sec.
1133 15th St NW 20005 — 202-419-2400
The Institute of World Politics — Post-Sec.
1521 16th St NW 20036 — 202-462-2101
Trinity University — Post-Sec.
125 Michigan Ave NE 20017 — 202-884-9000
University of the D.C. School of Law — Post-Sec.
4200 Connecticut Ave NW 20008 — 202-274-5000
University of the District of Columbia — Post-Sec.
4200 Connecticut Ave NW 20008 — 202-274-5100
Walter Reed Medical Center — Post-Sec.
6825 16th St NW 20307 — 202-782-6104
Washington Conservatory of Music — Post-Sec.
PO Box 5758 20016 — 202-320-2770
Washington Hospital Center — Post-Sec.
110 Irving St NW 20010 — 202-877-6101
Washington International S — 800/6-12
3100 Macomb St NW 20008 — 202-243-1800
Richard Hall, hdmstr. — Fax 243-1802
Washington Jesuit Academy — 100/6-8
800 3rd St NE 20002 — 202-543-5250
John Hoffman, hdmstr. — Fax 543-5901
Washington Theological Union — Post-Sec.
6896 Laurel St NW 20012 — 202-726-8800
Wesley Theological Seminary — Post-Sec.
4500 Massachusetts Ave NW 20016 — 202-885-8600

FLORIDA

FLORIDA DEPARTMENT OF EDUCATION
325 W Gaines St, Tallahassee 32399-0400
Telephone 850-245-0505
Fax 850-245-9667
Website http://www.fldoe.org/
Commissioner of Education   John Winn

FLORIDA BOARD OF EDUCATION
325 W Gaines St, Tallahassee 32399-0400
Chairperson   F. Philip Handy

PUBLIC, PRIVATE AND CATHOLIC SECONDARY SCHOOLS

Alachua, Alachua, Pop. 6,759
Alachua County SD
 Supt. — See Gainesville
Mebane MS   500/6-8
 16401 NW 140th St 32615   386-462-1648
 Dr. Chester Sanders, prin.   Fax 462-9094
Santa Fe HS   1,200/9-12
 16213 NW US Highway 441 32615 386-462-1125
 Bill Herschleb, prin.   Fax 462-1711

Altamonte Springs, Seminole, Pop. 40,942
Seminole County SD
 Supt. — See Sanford
Lake Brantley HS   3,300/9-12
 991 Sand Lake Rd 32714   407-320-3450
 Darvin Boothe, prin.   Fax 320-3600
Teague MS   1,600/6-8
 1350 Mcneil Rd 32714   407-320-1550
 Adrienne DeRienzo, prin.   Fax 320-1545

Altamonte Christian S   300/PK-12
 601 Palm Springs Dr 32701   407-831-0950
 Rev. Scott Carlson, dir.   Fax 831-6840
Champion Preparatory Academy   300/PK-12
 721 W Lake Brantley Rd 32714   407-788-0018
 Vicki Falco, dir.   Fax 788-7625
Golf Academy of the South   Post-Sec.
 1200 E Altamonte Dr #1010 32701 800-342-7342

Altha, Calhoun, Pop. 500
Calhoun County SD
 Supt. — See Blountstown
Altha S   700/PK-12
 PO Box 67 32421   850-762-3121
 Ronnie Hand, prin.   Fax 762-9502

Alva, Lee, Pop. 1,036
Lee County SD
 Supt. — See Fort Myers
Alva MS   700/6-8
 PO Box 128 33920   239-728-2525
 Stephen Hutnik, prin.   Fax 728-2835

Apalachicola, Franklin, Pop. 2,310
Franklin County SD   1,100/PK-12
 155 Avenue E 32320   850-653-8831
 Jo Ann Gander, supt.   Fax 653-3705
 www.franklincountyschools.org/
Apalachicola JSHS   300/6-12
 1 Shark Blvd 32320   850-653-8811
 Nick O'Grady, prin.   Fax 653-2782
Franklin County Adult S   Adult
 155 Avenue E 32320   850-653-8831
 Nan Collins, dir.   Fax 653-8984
Other Schools – See Carrabelle

Apopka, Orange, Pop. 30,703
Orange County SD
 Supt. — See Orlando
Apopka 9th Grade Center   9-9
 800 Wells St 32712   407-905-5500
 Scott Sherman, prin.
Apopka HS, 555 Martin St 32712   3,900/9-12
 William Floyd, prin.   407-905-5500
Apopka MS   1,500/6-8
 425 N Park Ave 32712   407-884-2208
 Douglas Guthrie, prin.   Fax 884-2217
Apopka Piedmont Lakes Relief MS   6-8
 1725 W Ponkan Rd 32712   407-317-3200
 Dr. Cathy Thornton, prin.
Piedmont Lakes MS   1,600/6-8
 2601 Lakeville Rd 32703   407-884-2265
 David Magee, prin.   Fax 884-2287

Forest Lake Academy   600/9-12
 3909 E Semoran Blvd 32703   407-862-8411
 John Wheaton, prin.   Fax 862-7050

Arcadia, DeSoto, Pop. 6,902
De Soto County SD   4,800/PK-12
 PO Box 2000 34265   863-494-4222
 Adrian Cline, supt.   Fax 494-9675
 www.desotoschools.com
DeSoto HS   1,200/9-12
 1710 E Gibson St 34266   863-494-3434
 Daniel Dubbert, prin.   Fax 494-7867
DeSoto MS   1,100/6-8
 420 E Gibson St 34266   863-494-4133
 Dave Bremer, prin.   Fax 494-6263
DeSoto County Adult Education Center   Adult
 310 W Whidden St 34266   863-993-1333
 Martha Jo Markey, prin.   Fax 993-9181

Atlantic Beach, Duval, Pop. 13,565
Duval County SD
 Supt. — See Jacksonville
Mayport MS   900/6-8
 2600 Mayport Rd 32233   904-247-5977
 Karen Davis, prin.   Fax 247-5987

Auburndale, Polk, Pop. 11,956
Polk County SD
 Supt. — See Bartow
Auburndale HS   1,800/9-12
 1 Bloodhound Trl 33823   863-965-6200
 Ernest Joe, prin.   Fax 965-6245
Stambaugh MS   1,000/6-8
 226 N Main St 33823   863-965-5494
 Allison Kalbfleisch, prin.   Fax 965-5496
East Area Adult & Community S   Adult
 300 E Bridgers Ave 33823   863-965-5475
 Keith Windham, prin.   Fax 965-5477

Florida Technical College   Post-Sec.
 298 Havendale Blvd 33823   863-967-8822

Avon Park, Highlands, Pop. 8,684
Highlands County SD
 Supt. — See Sebring
Avon Park HS   1,000/9-12
 700 E Main St 33825   863-452-4311
 Stuart Guthrie, prin.   Fax 452-4324
Avon Park MS   700/6-8
 401 S Lake Ave 33825   863-452-4333
 Dan Johnson, prin.   Fax 452-4341

South Florida Community College   Post-Sec.
 600 W College Dr 33825   863-453-6661
Walker Memorial Academy   200/K-12
 1525 W Avon Blvd 33825   863-453-3131
 William Farmer, dir.   Fax 453-4925

Babson Park, Polk, Pop. 1,125

Webber International University   Post-Sec.
 PO Box 96 33827   863-638-1431

Baker, Okaloosa
Okaloosa County SD
 Supt. — See Fort Walton Beach
Baker S   1,400/PK-12
 1369 14th St 32531   850-689-7279
 Tom Shipp, prin.   Fax 689-7416

Baldwin, Duval, Pop. 1,616
Duval County SD
 Supt. — See Jacksonville
Baldwin MSHS   900/6-12
 291 Mill St W 32234   904-266-1200
 Donna Richardson, prin.   Fax 266-1220

Bartow, Polk, Pop. 15,574
Polk County SD   76,200/PK-12
 PO Box 391 33831   863-534-0521
 Dr. Gail F. McKinzie, supt.   Fax 519-8231
 www.pcsb.k12.fl.us/
Bartow HS   1,200/9-12
 1270 S Broadway Ave 33830   863-534-7400
 Ron Pritchard, prin.   Fax 534-0077
Bartow MS   900/6-8
 550 E Clower St 33830   863-534-7415
 Harry Williams, prin.   Fax 534-7418
Union Academy MS   400/6-8
 1795 E Wabash St 33830   863-534-7435
 Steve Petrie, prin.   Fax 534-7487
Other Schools – See Auburndale, Davenport, Dundee,
 Eagle Lake, Fort Meade, Frostproof, Haines City, Lake
 Alfred, Lakeland, Lake Wales, Mulberry, Winter Haven

Bell, Gilchrist, Pop. 377
Gilchrist County SD
 Supt. — See Trenton
Bell HS   700/6-12
 930 S Main St 32619   352-463-3232
 H.H. Schofield, prin.   Fax 463-3294

Belle Glade, Palm Beach, Pop. 15,206
Palm Beach County SD
 Supt. — See West Palm Beach
Glades Central Community HS   1,200/9-12
 1001 SW Avenue M 33430   561-993-4400
 Edward Harris, prin.   Fax 993-4414
Lake Shore MS   1,200/6-8
 425 W Canal St N 33430   561-829-1100
 Floyd Henry, prin.   Fax 829-1190

Glades Central Community HS   Adult
 39600 SW Avenue M 33430   561-993-4404
 Dick Brinker, prin.   Fax 993-4414

Glades Day S   600/PK-12
 400 Gator Blvd 33430   561-996-6769
 Mandy Perez, dir.   Fax 992-9274

Belleview, Marion, Pop. 3,654
Marion County SD
 Supt. — See Ocala
Belleview HS   1,800/9-12
 10400 SE 36th Ave 34420   352-671-6210
 Jim Wohrley, prin.   Fax 671-6212
Belleview MS   1,200/6-8
 10500 SE 36th Ave 34420   352-671-6235
 Lisa Krysalka, prin.   Fax 671-6239

Blountstown, Calhoun, Pop. 2,387
Calhoun County SD   2,200/PK-12
 20859 Central Ave E Ste G20 32424 850-674-5927
 Mary Sue Neves, supt.   Fax 674-5814
 www.paec.org/calhoun/district/
Blountstown HS   400/9-12
 17586 Main St N 32424   850-674-5724
 Keith Summers, prin.   Fax 674-8865
Blountstown MS   300/6-8
 21089 SE Mayhaw Dr 32424   850-674-8234
 Mike Johnson, prin.   Fax 674-6480
Calhoun County Adult Education Center   Adult
 17283 NW Charlie Johns St 32424 850-674-8661
 Willy Pitts, prin.   Fax 237-2355
Other Schools – See Altha

Boca Raton, Palm Beach, Pop. 78,449
Palm Beach County SD
 Supt. — See West Palm Beach
Boca Raton Community HS   1,800/9-12
 1501 NW 15th Ct 33486   561-338-1400
 Geoffrey McKee, prin.   Fax 338-1440
Boca Raton Community MS   1,200/6-8
 1251 NW 8th St 33486   561-416-8700
 Jack Thompson, prin.   Fax 416-8777
Eagles Landing MS   1,600/6-8
 19500 Coral Ridge Dr 33498   561-470-7000
 Ira Margulies, prin.   Fax 470-7030
Estridge High Tech MS   6-8
 1798 NW Spanish River Blvd 33431 561-989-7800
 Debra Johnson, prin.   Fax 989-7810
Loggers Run Community MS   1,500/6-8
 11584 W Palmetto Park Rd 33428 561-883-8000
 Carol Blacharski, prin.   Fax 883-8027
Olympic Heights Community HS   2,600/9-12
 20101 Lyons Rd 33434   561-852-6900
 Peter Licata, prin.   Fax 852-6974
Omni MS   1,400/6-8
 5775 Jog Rd 33496   561-989-2900
 Mark Stenner, prin.   Fax 989-2851
Spanish River Community HS   3,300/9-12
 5100 Jog Rd 33496   561-241-2200
 Constance Tuman-Rugg, prin.   Fax 241-2236
West Boca Raton Community HS   9-12
 12811 Glades Rd 33498   561-672-2001
 Francis Giblin, prin.   Fax 672-2014
Boca Raton Community HS   Adult
 1501 NW 15th Ct 33486   561-338-1420
 Cheryl Lombard, prin.   Fax 338-1440
Loggers Run Community MS   Adult
 11584 W Palmetto Park Rd 33428 561-883-8000
 Susan Stanley, prin.   Fax 883-8027
Spanish River Community HS   Adult
 5100 Jog Rd 33496   561-241-2205
 Elizabeth Albury, prin.   Fax 241-2236

Boca Raton Christian S   600/PK-12
 315 NW 4th St 33432   561-391-2727
 Robert Tennies Ed.D., hdmstr.   Fax 367-6808
Boca Raton Preparatory S   100/PK-12
 10333 Diego Dr S 33428   561-852-1410
 Karleene Gill, prin.   Fax 470-6124
Claremont Montessori S   100/PK-12
 2450 NW 5th Ave 33431   561-394-7674
 Harvey Hallenberg, prin.   Fax 394-9792
Everglades University   Post-Sec.
 5002 T Rex Ave Ste 100 33431   561-912-1211
Florida Atlantic University   Post-Sec.
 PO Box 3091 33431   561-297-3000
Grandview Preparatory S   300/PK-12
 336 NW Spanish River Blvd 33431 561-416-9737
 Jacqueline Westerfield, prin.   Fax 416-9739
Klein Jewish Academy   700/K-12
 9701 Donna Klein Blvd 33428   561-852-3300
 Karen Feller, hdmstr.   Fax 852-3327

Lynn University Post-Sec.
3601 N Military Trl 33431 561-237-7000
Lynn University Conservatory of Music Post-Sec.
3601 N Military Trl 33431 561-237-9001
PC Professor Post-Sec.
7056 Beracasa Way 33433 561-750-7879
Pope John Paul II HS 800/9-12
4001 N Military Trl 33431 561-314-2100
Sr. Eileen Sullivan, prin. Fax 989-8582
St. Andrew's S 1,100/PK-12
3900 Jog Rd 33434 561-210-2010
Rev. George E. Andrews, hdmstr. Fax 210-2017
Weinbaum Yeshiva HS 200/9-12
7902 Montoya Cir N 33433 561-417-7422
Shimmie Kaminetsky, dir. Fax 417-7028
West Boca Medical Center Post-Sec.
21644 State Road 7 33428 561-488-8000

Bonifay, Holmes, Pop. 2,669
Holmes County SD 3,400/PK-12
701 E Pennsylvania Ave 32425 850-547-9341
Steve Griffin, supt. Fax 547-0381
www.hdsb.org
Bethlehem S 600/PK-12
2676 Highway 160 32425 850-547-3621
T.C. Clemmons, prin. Fax 547-4856
Bonifay MS 500/5-8
401 Mclaughlin Ave 32425 850-547-2754
Bill Gilley, prin. Fax 547-3685
Holmes County HS 500/9-12
825 W Highway 90 32425 850-547-9000
Janis Johnson, prin. Fax 547-6694
Other Schools – See Graceville, Ponce de Leon

Bonita Springs, Lee, Pop. 36,230
Lee County SD
Supt. — See Fort Myers
Bonita Springs MS 900/6-8
10141 W Terry St 34135 239-992-4422
Joe Williams, prin. Fax 992-9157

Grace Community S 100/PK-12
8971 Brighton Ln 34135 239-948-7878
Rev. Jeremy Walker, prin. Fax 949-1597
Lee County Independent Private S 100/K-12
26801 Pine Ave 34135 239-992-6381
Kathleen Sprafka, prin. Fax 992-6473

Boynton Beach, Palm Beach, Pop. 64,384
Palm Beach County SD
Supt. — See West Palm Beach
Boynton Beach Community HS 2,400/9-12
4975 Park Ridge Blvd 33426 561-752-1200
Kathleen Perry, prin. Fax 752-1205
Congress MS 1,300/6-8
101 S Congress Ave 33426 561-374-5600
Kathy Harris, prin. Fax 374-5642
McAuliffe MS 1,500/6-8
6500 Le Chalet Blvd 33437 561-374-6600
Terry Costa, prin. Fax 374-6636
Odyssey MS 1,300/6-8
6161 W Woolbright Rd 33437 561-752-1300
Bonnie Fox, prin. Fax 752-1305
South Technical Education Center Vo/Tech
1300 SW 30th Ave 33426 561-369-7000
James Kidd, prin. Fax 369-7024

Bethesda Memorial Hospital Post-Sec.
2815 S Seacrest Blvd 33435 561-737-7733
Lake Worth Christian S 400/PK-12
7592 High Ridge Rd 33426 561-586-8216
Robert Hook, admin. Fax 586-4382
St. Vincent DePaul Regional Seminary Post-Sec.
10701 S Military Trl 33436 561-732-4424

Bradenton, Manatee, Pop. 52,498
Manatee County SD 36,800/PK-12
PO Box 9069 34206 941-708-8770
Dr. Roger Dearing, supt. Fax 708-8680
www.manatee.k12.fl.us
Bayshore HS 1,800/9-12
5401 34th St W 34210 941-751-7004
David Underhill, prin. Fax 753-0953
Braden River HS 9-12
6545 State Road 70 E 34203 941-751-8230
Jim Pauley, prin. Fax 751-8250
Braden River MS 1,300/6-8
6215 River Club Blvd 34202 941-751-7080
Randy Petrilla, prin. Fax 751-7085
Haile MS 1,200/6-8
9501 E State Road 64 34212 941-714-7240
Janet Kerley, prin. Fax 714-7245
Harllee MS 700/6-8
6423 9th St E 34203 941-751-7027
Carol Felton, prin. Fax 751-7030
Johnson MS 900/6-8
2121 26th Ave E 34208 941-741-3344
Ann McDonald, prin. Fax 741-3345
King MS 1,000/6-8
6545 State Road 70 E 34203 941-751-8230
Joe Stokes, prin. Fax 751-8250
Lakewood Ranch HS 2,400/9-12
5500 Lakewood Ranch Blvd 34211 941-727-6100
Mike Wilder, prin. Fax 727-6099
Lee MS 1,000/6-8
4000 53rd Ave W 34210 941-727-6500
Scot Boice, prin. Fax 727-6513
Manatee HS 2,100/9-12
1 Hurricane Ln 34205 941-714-7300
Jeff Asher, prin. Fax 741-3443
Manatee Technical Institute Vo/Tech
5603 34th St W 34210 941-751-7900
Mary Cantrell, prin. Fax 751-7927
Manatee Technical Institute East Vo/Tech
5520 Lakewood Ranch Blvd 34211 941-752-8100
Dr. Patricia Haflich, prin. Fax 727-6254
Nolan MS 6-8
6615 Greenbrook Blvd 34202 941-751-8200
Ron Hirst, prin. Fax 751-8210
Southeast HS 1,900/9-12
1200 37th Ave E 34208 941-741-3366
Mike Horne, prin. Fax 741-3372
Sugg MS 900/6-8
3801 59th St W 34209 941-741-3157
Angela Essig, prin. Fax 741-3514
Community HS Adult
5603 34th St W 34210 941-751-7900
Omar Edwards, dir. Fax 751-7927
Other Schools – See Palmetto

Beauty and Barber Academy Post-Sec.
5505 Manatee Ave W 34209 941-761-4400
Bradenton Academy 300/PK-12
7900 40th Ave W 34209 941-792-7838
Dr. Murray Gerber, prin. Fax 798-9920
Bradenton Christian S 600/PK-12
3304 43rd St W 34209 941-792-5454
Dan van der Kooy, admin. Fax 795-7190
Community Christian S 300/PK-12
5500 18th St E 34203 941-756-8748
Charles Sartor, prin. Fax 753-7057
Edison Academic Center 200/PK-12
7431 Manatee Ave W 34209 941-794-3630
Barbara Iannarelli, prin. Fax 794-3955
Florida College of Natural Health Post-Sec.
616 67th Street Cir E 34208 941-954-8999
Gulfcoast Christian Academy 50/K-12
1700 51st Ave E 34203 941-755-1690
Brenda Timms, admin. Fax 755-0332
Lake Erie College\Osteopathic Medicine Post-Sec.
5000 Lakewood Ranch Blvd 34211 941-756-0690
Manatee Community College Post-Sec.
5840 26th St W 34207 941-752-5000
Manatee Technical Institute Post-Sec.
5603 34th St W 34210 941-751-7900
Manatee Technical Institute East Campus Post-Sec.
5520 Lakewood Ranch Blvd 34211 941-752-8100
Pendleton S 400/PK-12
5500 34th St W 34210 941-739-3964
Dick Townsend, prin. Fax 739-6483
Providence Community S 100/PK-12
5512 26th St W 34207 941-727-6860
Barry Batson, admin.
St. Stephen's Episcopal S 800/PK-12
315 41st St W 34209 941-746-2121
Jan Pullen, hdmstr. Fax 746-5699

Brandon, Hillsborough, Pop. 83,200
Hillsborough County SD
Supt. — See Tampa
Brandon HS 2,000/9-12
1101 Victoria St 33510 813-744-8120
Leslie Granich, prin. Fax 744-8129
Burns MS 1,100/7-8
615 Brooker Rd 33511 813-744-8383
Brenda Nolte, prin. Fax 740-3623
Mann MS 900/6-8
409 E Jersey Ave 33510 813-744-8400
Nancy Trathowen, prin. Fax 744-6707
McLane MS 1,600/6-8
306 N Knights Ave 33510 813-744-8100
James Elliott, prin. Fax 744-8135
Brandon Adult & Community Center Adult
1101 Victoria St 33510 813-744-8131
James Rich, admin. Fax 664-8393

Faith Baptist Christian S 100/PK-12
1118 N Parsons Ave 33510 813-654-4936
Dr. Gene Reynolds, prin. Fax 654-7239

Branford, Suwannee, Pop. 721
Suwannee County SD
Supt. — See Live Oak
Branford HS 700/6-12
405 Reynolds St NE 32008 386-935-1231
Ted Roush, prin. Fax 935-3867

Bristol, Liberty, Pop. 874
Liberty County SD 1,100/PK-12
PO Box 429 32321 850-643-2275
David H. Summers, supt. Fax 643-2533
www.firn.edu/schools/liberty/liberty
Liberty County HS 300/9-12
PO Box 519 32321 850-643-2241
Gary Lewis, prin. Fax 643-4153
Liberty County Adult S Adult
PO Box 429 32321 850-643-2275
Melissa Muza, prin. Fax 643-2533

Bronson, Levy, Pop. 1,006
Levy County SD 6,300/PK-12
PO Box 129 32621 352-486-5231
Cliff Norris, supt. Fax 486-5237
www.levy.k12.fl.us
Bronson MSHS 600/6-12
PO Box 189 32621 352-486-5261
Valerie Boughanem, prin. Fax 486-5263
Other Schools – See Cedar Key, Chiefland, Williston

Brooksville, Hernando, Pop. 7,436
Hernando County SD 18,400/PK-12
919 N Broad St 34601 352-797-7000
Wendy Tellone Ed.D., supt. Fax 797-7101
www.hcsb.k12.fl.us
Central HS 1,800/9-12
14075 Ken Austin Pkwy 34613 352-797-7020
Dennis McGeehan, prin. Fax 797-7121
Hernando HS 1,200/9-12
700 Bell Ave 34601 352-797-7015
Betty Harper, prin. Fax 797-7115
Nature Coast Technical HS Vo/Tech
4057 California St 34604 352-797-7088
Margaret Schoelles, prin. Fax 797-7188
Parrott MS 1,000/6-8
19220 Youth Dr 34601 352-797-7075
Marvin Gordon, prin. Fax 797-7175
Powell MS 1,200/6-8
4100 Barclay Ave 34609 352-797-7095
Earl Deen, prin. Fax 797-7195
West Hernando MS 1,300/6-8
14325 Ken Austin Pkwy 34613 352-797-7035
Joe Clifford, prin. Fax 797-7135
Other Schools – See Spring Hill

Hernando Christian Academy 500/PK-12
7200 Emerson Rd 34601 352-796-0616
David Holtzhouse, supt. Fax 799-3400
Pasco-Hernando Community College Post-Sec.
11415 Ponce De Leon Blvd 34601 352-796-6726

Bunnell, Flagler, Pop. 2,258
Flagler County SD 7,300/PK-12
PO Box 755 32110 386-437-7526
Bill Delbrugge, supt. Fax 437-7577
www.flaglerschools.com
Flagler Palm Coast HS 2,400/9-12
PO Box 488 32110 386-437-7540
Jeff Miller, prin. Fax 437-7546
Taylor MS 1,200/6-8
PO Box 815 32110 386-446-6700
Winnie Oden, prin. Fax 446-6711
Other Schools – See Palm Coast

Bushnell, Sumter, Pop. 2,056
Sumter County SD 5,300/PK-12
2680 W C 476 33513 352-793-2315
Richard Shirley, supt. Fax 793-4180
www.sumter.k12.fl.us
South Sumter HS 1,000/9-12
706 N Main St 33513 352-793-3131
Dr. Preston Morgan, prin. Fax 793-2992
Other Schools – See Sumterville, Webster, Wildwood

Callahan, Nassau, Pop. 963
Nassau County SD
Supt. — See Fernandina Beach
Callahan MS 800/6-8
450121 Old Dixie Hwy 32011 904-491-7935
Ellen Ryan, prin. Fax 879-2860
West Nassau County HS 1,000/9-12
1 Warrior Dr 32011 904-491-7942
Ronald Booker, prin. Fax 879-5843

Cantonment, Escambia, Pop. 4,500
Escambia County SD
Supt. — See Pensacola
Ransom MS 1,400/6-8
1000 W Kingsfield Rd 32533 850-937-2220
Jeff Pomeroy, prin. Fax 937-2232
Tate HS 2,000/9-12
PO Box 68 32533 850-937-2300
Rick Shackle, prin. Fax 937-2328

Cape Coral, Lee, Pop. 118,737
Lee County SD
Supt. — See Fort Myers
Baker HS 9-12
3500 Agualinda Blvd 33914 239-458-6690
Joe Vetter, prin. Fax 458-6691
Caloosa MS 1,300/6-8
610 Del Prado Blvd S 33990 239-574-3232
John Wortham, prin. Fax 574-2660
Cape Coral HS 2,200/9-12
2300 Santa Barbara Blvd 33991 239-574-6766
Nancy Graham, prin. Fax 574-7799
Diplomat MS 1,300/6-8
1039 NE 16th Ter 33909 239-574-5257
Elizabeth Maxwell, prin. Fax 574-4008
Gulf MS 1,300/6-8
1809 SW 36th Ter 33914 239-549-0606
William Lane, prin. Fax 549-2806
Lee County HS Tech Center North Vo/Tech
360 Santa Barbara Blvd 33991 239-574-4440
Michael Schiffer, prin. Fax 458-3721
Mariner HS 2,200/9-12
701 Chiquita Blvd N 33993 239-772-3324
Erik Cioffi, prin. Fax 772-4880
Mariner MS 500/6-8
425 Chiquita Blvd N 33993 239-772-1848
Richard Hagy, prin.
Trafalgar MS 1,400/6-8
2120 SW Trafalgar Pkwy 33991 239-283-2001
Dr. Angela Pruitt, prin. Fax 283-5620

Cape Coral Beauty School Post-Sec.
1214 SE 47th St 33904 239-549-1819
Cape Coral Christian S 200/PK-12
811 Santa Barbara Blvd 33991 239-574-3707
Christopher Roy, prin. Fax 574-0947
Lee County High Tech Center North Post-Sec.
360 Santa Barbara Blvd N 33993 239-574-4440
Radiation Therapy Services Post-Sec.
1419 SE 8th Ter 33990 239-772-3202

Carrabelle, Franklin, Pop. 1,292
Franklin County SD
Supt. — See Apalachicola
Carrabelle S 500/PK-12
1001 Gray Ave 32322 850-697-3815
Richard Key, prin. Fax 697-4136

Casselberry, Seminole, Pop. 23,707
Seminole County SD
Supt. — See Sanford
South Seminole MS 1,200/6-8
101 S Winter Park Dr 32707 407-320-1350
Robin Dehlinger, prin. Fax 320-1420

City College Post-Sec.
853 Semoran Blvd Ste 200 32707 407-831-9816
Regent Academy 100/K-12
910 S Winter Park Dr 32707 407-740-0561
Benny Phillips, prin. Fax 740-5654

Cedar Key, Levy, Pop. 896
Levy County SD
Supt. — See Bronson
Cedar Key S 300/PK-12
951 Whiddon Ave 32625 352-543-5223
Dan Faircloth, prin. Fax 543-5988

Century, Escambia, Pop. 1,783
Escambia County SD
Supt. — See Pensacola
Northview HS 500/9-12
4100 W Highway 4 32535 850-327-6681
Gayle Weaver, prin. Fax 327-4015

Chiefland, Levy, Pop. 2,038
Levy County SD
Supt. — See Bronson
Chiefland HS 500/9-12
808 N Main St 32626 352-493-6000
Bob Hastings, prin. Fax 493-6018
Chiefland MS 400/6-8
811 NW 4th Dr 32626 352-493-6025
Bobbie Turnipseed, prin. Fax 493-6048
Adult HS Adult
114 Rodgers Blvd 32626 352-493-9533
Rayanne Giddis, prin. Fax 493-9994

Chipley, Washington, Pop. 3,600
Washington County SD 2,600/PK-12
652 3rd St 32428 850-638-6222
Calvin Stevenson, supt. Fax 638-6226
www.firn.edu/schools/washington/wash/
Chipley HS 9-12
1545 Brickyard Rd 32428 850-638-6100
George French, prin. Fax 638-6017
Roulhac MS 600/5-8
1535 Brickyard Rd 32428 850-638-6170
Mike Park, prin. Fax 638-6319
Washington-Holmes Tech Center Vo/Tech
757 Hoyt St 32428 850-638-1180
Olin Gilbert, dir. Fax 638-6177
Other Schools – See Vernon

Washington Holmes Technical Center Post-Sec.
757 Hoyt St 32428 850-638-1180

Citra, Marion
Marion County SD
Supt. — See Ocala
North Marion HS 1,600/9-12
151 W Highway 329 32113 352-671-6010
Kathy Quelland, prin. Fax 671-6011
North Marion MS 900/6-8
2085 W Highway 329 32113 352-671-6035
Jerome Brown, prin. Fax 671-6044

Citrus Springs, Citrus, Pop. 2,213
Citrus County SD
Supt. — See Inverness
Citrus Springs MS 900/6-8
150 W Citrus Springs Blvd 34434 352-344-2244
David Stephens, prin. Fax 344-5615

Clearwater, Pinellas, Pop. 108,272
Pinellas County SD
Supt. — See Largo
Clearwater HS 2,100/9-12
540 S Hercules Ave 33764 727-298-1620
Nicklas Grasso, prin. Fax 469-5981
Coachman Fundamental MS 500/6-8
2235 NE Coachman Rd 33765 727-669-1190
Dawn Coffin, prin. Fax 669-1194
Countryside HS 2,400/9-12
3000 State Road 580 33761 727-725-7956
Gerald Schlereth, prin. Fax 725-7990
Kennedy MS 1,100/6-8
1660 Palmetto St 33755 727-298-1609
Susan W. Keller, prin. Fax 298-1614
Oak Grove MS 1,100/6-8
1370 S Belcher Rd 33764 727-524-4430
Patricia Bell, prin. Fax 524-4416
PTEC Clearwater Vo/Tech
6100 154th Ave N 33760 727-538-7167
Warren Laux, dir. Fax 538-7203
Clearwater Adult Education Center Adult
540 S Hercules Ave 33764 727-469-4190
Christy E. Richards, admin. Fax 469-4193

Allendale Academy Private S 700/K-12
7208 Amhurst Way 33764 727-531-2481
Patricia Carter, prin. Fax 531-6491
Calvary Christian HS 200/9-12
110A N McMullen Booth Rd 33759 727-449-2247
Thomas J. Cathey, prin. Fax 461-5421
Clearwater Academy International 200/PK-12
801 Drew St 33755 727-446-1722
Jim Zwers, prin. Fax 443-5252
Clearwater Central Catholic HS 700/9-12
2750 Haines Bayshore Rd 33760 727-531-1449
Dulce Roman, prin. Fax 535-7034
Clearwater Christian College Post-Sec.
3400 Gulf To Bay Blvd 33759 727-726-1153
EduTech Centers Post-Sec.
410 Park Place Blvd 33759 727-724-1037
FL Metropolitan Univ. - Pinellas Post-Sec.
2471 N McMullen Booth Rd 33759 727-725-2688
Lakeside Christian S 200/PK-12
1897 Sunset Point Rd 33765 727-461-3311
Jim Jensen, prin. Fax 445-1835
National Aviation Academy Post-Sec.
6225 Ulmerton Rd 33760 727-531-2080
Pinellas Technical Education Center Post-Sec.
6100 154th Ave N 33760 727-538-7167
Sunstate Academy of Hair Design Post-Sec.
18453 US Highway 19 N 33764 727-538-3827

Clermont, Lake, Pop. 10,577
Lake County SD
Supt. — See Tavares
Clermont MS 900/6-8
301 East Ave 34711 352-243-2460
Dave Coggshall, prin. Fax 243-1407
East Ridge HS 2,300/9-12
13322 Excalibur Rd 34711 352-242-2080
Aurelia Cole, prin. Fax 242-2090
Windy Hill MS 1,200/6-8
3575 Hancock Rd 34711 352-394-2123
David Tucker, prin. Fax 394-7901

Clewiston, Hendry, Pop. 6,770
Hendry County SD
Supt. — See La Belle
Clewiston HS 1,000/9-12
1501 S Francisco St 33440 863-983-1520
Robert Egley, prin. Fax 983-2168
Clewiston MS 900/6-8
601 W Pasadena Ave 33440 863-983-1530
Garry Ensor, prin. Fax 983-1541
Clewiston Adult S Adult
1501 S Francisco St 33440 863-983-1578
James Way, prin. Fax 983-1595

Cocoa, Brevard, Pop. 16,429
Brevard County SD
Supt. — See Melbourne
Clearlake MS 600/7-8
1225 Clearlake Rd 32922 321-633-3660
Mark Mullins, prin. Fax 617-7731
Cocoa HS 1,400/9-12
2000 Tiger Trl 32926 321-632-5300
Lorena Backus, prin. Fax 636-1218
McNair Magnet MS 500/6-8
1 Challenger Dr 32922 321-633-3630
Rosette Brown, prin. Fax 633-3639
Space Coast JSHS 2,000/7-12
6150 Banyan St 32927 321-638-0750
Robert Spinner, prin. Fax 638-0766

Brevard Community College Post-Sec.
1519 Clearlake Rd 32922 321-632-1111
Brevard Independent Private S 100/PK-12
202 River Heights Dr 32922 321-636-2754
Elizabeth Graham, prin. Fax 636-5981

Cocoa Beach, Brevard, Pop. 12,432
Brevard County SD
Supt. — See Melbourne
Cocoa Beach JSHS 1,500/7-12
1500 Minutemen Cswy 32931 321-783-1776
Tim Cool, prin. Fax 868-6602

Coconut Creek, Broward, Pop. 48,198
Broward County SD
Supt. — See Fort Lauderdale

Atlantic Technical Center Vo/Tech
4700 Coconut Creek Pkwy 33063 754-321-5100
Robert Crawford, prin. Fax 321-5380
Coconut Creek HS 2,500/9-12
1400 NW 44th Ave 33066 754-322-0350
John Bowen, prin. Fax 322-0480
Lyons Creek MS 2,100/6-8
4333 Sol Press Blvd 33073 754-322-3700
Washington Collado, prin. Fax 322-3785
Monarch HS 1,400/9-12
5050 Wiles Rd 33073 754-322-1400
Kathy Collins, prin. Fax 322-1530

Broward Community College-North Campus Post-Sec.
1000 Coconut Creek Blvd 33066 954-972-9100
North Broward Preparatory Schools 1,900/PK-12
7600 Lyons Rd 33073 954-247-0011
Dr. Michael Rossi, hdmstr. Fax 247-0012
Randazzo S 300/PK-12
2251 NW 36th Ave 33066 954-968-1750
Dr. Ronald Simon, hdmstr. Fax 968-1857

Coconut Grove, See Miami
Miami-Dade County SD
Supt. — See Miami
Carver MS 1,000/6-8
4901 Lincoln Dr 33133 305-444-7388
Libia Gonzalez, prin. Fax 529-5148

Carrollton S of the Sacred Heart 700/PK-12
3747 Main Hwy 33133 305-446-5673
Sr. Suzanne Cooke, prin. Fax 446-4160
La Salle HS 600/9-12
3601 S Miami Ave 33133 305-854-2334
Sr. Patricia Roche, prin. Fax 858-5971

Cooper City, Broward, Pop. 28,853
Broward County SD
Supt. — See Fort Lauderdale
Cooper City HS 2,500/9-12
9401 Stirling Rd 33328 754-323-0200
Wendy Doll, prin. Fax 323-0330
Pioneer MS 1,800/6-8
5350 SW 90th Ave 33328 754-323-4100
Linda Arnold, prin. Fax 323-4185

Coral Gables, Dade, Pop. 42,539
Miami-Dade County SD
Supt. — See Miami
Coral Gables HS 3,900/8-12
450 Bird Rd 33146 305-443-4871
Dr. Alexis Martinez, prin. Fax 441-8094
Ponce De Leon MS 1,500/6-8
5801 Augusto St 33146 305-661-1611
Joanne D. Gans, prin. Fax 666-3140
Coral Gables SHS Adult Education Center Adult
450 Bird Rd 33146 305-443-4871
Alonzo Kilpatrick, prin. Fax 446-2507

New Professions Technical Institute Post-Sec.
4000 W Flagler St 33134 305-461-2223
University of Miami Post-Sec.
PO Box 248006 33124 305-284-2211

Coral Springs, Broward, Pop. 127,005
Broward County SD
Supt. — See Fort Lauderdale
Coral Glades HS 9-12
2700 Sportsplex Dr 33065 754-322-1250
David Jones, prin. Fax 322-1380
Coral Springs HS 2,900/9-12
7201 W Sample Rd 33065 754-322-0500
Anne Lynch, prin. Fax 322-0630
Coral Springs MS 1,100/6-8
10300 Wiles Rd 33076 754-322-3000
Victoria Kaufman, prin. Fax 322-3085
Forest Glen MS 1,300/6-8
6501 Turtle Run Blvd 33067 754-322-3400
James McDermott, prin. Fax 322-3485
Ramblewood MS 1,600/6-8
8505 W Atlantic Blvd 33071 754-322-4300
Desmond Blackburn, prin. Fax 322-4385
Sawgrass Springs MS 1,300/6-8
12500 W Sample Rd 33065 754-322-4500
Adeline Andreano, prin. Fax 322-4585
Taravella HS 3,400/9-12
10600 Riverside Dr 33071 754-322-2300
Shawn Cerra, prin. Fax 322-2430

Academy HS - Coral Springs Campus 200/8-12
648 Riverside Dr 33071 954-752-5038
Nina Kaufman, prin. Fax 752-1470
Coral Springs Christian Academy 1,100/PK-12
2251 Riverside Dr 33065 954-752-2870
Robert Clampett, hdmstr. Fax 840-1101

Cottondale, Jackson, Pop. 852
Jackson County SD
Supt. — See Marianna
Cottondale JSHS 500/6-12
2680 Levy St 32431 850-482-9821
Don Wilson, prin. Fax 482-9827

Crawfordville, Wakulla
Wakulla County SD 4,300/K-12
PO Box 100 32326 850-926-0065
David Miller, supt. Fax 926-0123
www.firn.edu/schools/wakulla/wakulla/
Riversprings MS 500/6-8
800 Spring Creek Hwy 32327 850-926-2300
Dod Walker, prin. Fax 926-2111
Wakulla County HS 1,300/9-12
3237 Coastal Hwy 32327 850-926-7125
Randy Newland, prin. Fax 926-8571
Wakulla MS 600/6-8
22 Jean Dr 32327 850-926-7143
JoAnn Daniels, prin. Fax 926-3752

Crescent City, Putnam, Pop. 1,780
Putnam County SD
Supt. — See Palatka
Crescent City JSHS 900/7-12
2201 S US Highway 17 32112 386-698-1629
Joe Warren, prin. Fax 698-3073

Crestview, Okaloosa, Pop. 15,826
Okaloosa County SD
Supt. — See Fort Walton Beach
Crestview HS 1,900/9-12
1250 N Ferdon Blvd 32536 850-689-7177
Andy Johnson, prin. Fax 689-7332

Davidson MS 900/6-8
6261 Old Bethel Rd 32536 850-683-7500
Beth Walthall, prin. Fax 683-7523
Richbourg MS 700/6-8
500 Alabama St 32536 850-689-7229
Bob Jones, prin. Fax 689-7245

Crossroads Christian S 300/K-12
PO Box 295 32536 850-423-1291
Dorothy Chatterton, prin. Fax 423-1291
Tall Pines Academy 200/PK-12
100 Duggan Ave 32536 850-682-2730
Mike Hinson, dir. Fax 682-0087

Cross City, Dixie, Pop. 1,801
Dixie County SD 2,200/PK-12
PO Box 890 32628 352-498-6131
Dennis Bennett, supt. Fax 498-1308
www.dixie.k12.fl.us/
Dixie County HS 600/9-12
PO Box 1180 32628 352-498-6410
Charlotte Lord, prin. Fax 498-1287
Rains MS 500/6-8
PO Box 2159 32628 352-498-1346
Beverly Baumer, prin. Fax 498-1283
Dixie County Adult Center Adult
PO Box 890 32628 352-498-6149
Anne Engers, prin. Fax 498-1308

Crystal River, Citrus, Pop. 3,565
Citrus County SD
Supt. — See Inverness
Crystal River HS 1,300/9-12
1205 NE 8th Ave 34428 352-795-4641
Patrick Simon, prin. Fax 795-4519
Crystal River MS 900/6-8
344 NE Crystal St 34428 352-795-2116
Mark McCoy, prin. Fax 795-2378

Westcoast Christian S 100/PK-12
718 NW 1st Ave 34428 352-795-2079
R. Marlene Pringle, dir. Fax 795-1104

Dade City, Pasco, Pop. 6,476
Pasco County SD
Supt. — See Land O Lakes
Centennial MS 700/6-8
38505 Centennial Rd 33525 352-524-9700
Thomas Rulison, prin. Fax 524-9791
Pasco Comprehensive HS 1,300/9-12
36850 State Road 52 33525 352-524-5500
Pat Reedy, prin. Fax 524-5591
Pasco MS 800/6-8
13925 14th St 33525 352-524-8400
Jim Lane, prin. Fax 524-8441
Moore-Mickens Education Center Adult
38301 Martin Luther King Bl 33525 352-524-9000
Steve Cox, prin. Fax 524-9091

East Pasco Adventist Academy 100/PK-10
38434 Centennial Rd 33525 352-567-3646
Jeffrey Foote, prin. Fax 567-1907
Pasco-Hernando Community College Post-Sec.
34727 Blanton Rd 33523 352-567-6701

Dania, Broward, Pop. 14,456
Broward County SD
Supt. — See Fort Lauderdale
Olsen MS 2,000/6-8
330 SE 11th Ter 33004 754-323-3800
Kim Flynn, prin. Fax 323-3885

Key College Post-Sec.
225 E Dania Beach Blvd #130 33004 954-923-4440

Davenport, Polk, Pop. 1,986
Polk County SD
Supt. — See Bartow
Ridge Community HS 9-12
500 Orchid Dr 33837 863-419-3315
Sherry Wells, prin. Fax 419-3321

Davie, Broward, Pop. 80,364
Broward County SD
Supt. — See Fort Lauderdale
McFatter Tech Center Vo/Tech
6500 Nova Dr 33317 754-321-5785
Mark Thomas, prin. Fax 321-5980
Nova HS 2,000/9-12
3600 College Ave 33314 754-323-1650
John LaCasse, prin. Fax 323-1780
Nova MS 1,500/6-8
3602 College Ave 33314 754-323-3700
Ricardia Garcia, prin. Fax 323-3785
Western HS 2,300/9-12
1200 SW 136th Ave 33325 754-323-2400
Scott Fiske, prin. Fax 323-2530

Academy HS - Davie Campus 200/8-12
4850 S Pine Island Rd 33328 954-434-2722
Nina Kaufman, prin. Fax 752-1470
Alternative Education Institute 600/PK-12
5071 SW 64th Ave 33314 954-649-2274
Krista Sallop, dir.
ASM Beauty World Academy Post-Sec.
6423 Stirling Rd 33314 954-321-8411
ITT Technical Institute Post-Sec.
3401 SW University Dr 33328 954-476-9300
Kentwood Preparatory S 100/1-12
4650 SW 61st Ave 33314 954-570-6400
Adrian Thomas, prin. Fax 649-6142
Nova Southeastern University Post-Sec.
3301 College Ave 33314 954-262-7300
Nova Southeastern Univ Health Profession Post-Sec.
3200 S University Dr 33328 954-262-1101
Westlake Preparatory S 100/6-12
4190 S University Dr 33328 954-236-2300
Shirley Gil, hdmstr. Fax 473-0770
William T. McFatter Technical Center Post-Sec.
6500 Nova Dr 33317 954-370-8324

Daytona Beach, Volusia, Pop. 64,581
Volusia County SD
Supt. — See De Land
Campbell MS, 625 S Keech St 32114 1,000/6-8
Vickie Presley, prin. 386-258-4661
Hinson MS 6-8
1860 N Clyde Morris Blvd 32117 386-258-4682
Ted Petrucciani, prin.

Mainland HS 2,100/9-12
125 S Clyde Morris Blvd 32114 386-258-4665
Patsy Graham, prin.
Seabreeze HS 1,800/9-12
2700 N Oleander Ave 32118 386-258-4674
Bob Wallace, prin. Fax 676-1451

Bethune-Cookman College Post-Sec.
640 Dr Mary Mclod Bthn Blvd 32114 800-448-0228
Daytona Beach Community College Post-Sec.
PO Box 2811 32120 386-255-8131
Embry-Riddle Aeronautical University Post-Sec.
PO Box 11767 32120 800-862-2416
Father Lopez HS 400/9-12
960 Madison Ave 32114 386-253-5213
Linda Dowdy, prin. Fax 252-6101
Halifax Medical Center Post-Sec.
PO Box 2830 32120 386-254-4065
Keiser College Post-Sec.
1800 Business Park Blvd 32114 386-274-5060
Phoenix East Aviation Post-Sec.
561 Pearl Harbor Dr 32114 386-258-0703

Deerfield Beach, Broward, Pop. 65,694
Broward County SD
Supt. — See Fort Lauderdale
Deerfield Beach HS 2,800/9-12
910 SW 15th St 33441 754-322-0650
Kathleen Martinez, prin. Fax 322-0780
Deerfield Beach MS 1,700/6-8
701 SE 6th Ave 33441 754-322-3300
Vincent Alessi, prin. Fax 322-3385

Zion Lutheran Christian S 700/K-12
959 SE 6th Ave 33441 954-421-3146
Ron Kooy, prin. Fax 421-4250

De Funiak Springs, Walton, Pop. 5,250
Walton County SD 6,000/PK-12
145 S Park St #2 32435 850-892-1100
Carlene Anderson, supt. Fax 892-1191
www.walton.k12.fl.us
Walton Career Development Center Vo/Tech
761 N 20th St 32433 850-892-1240
Gail Cole, dir. Fax 892-1249
Walton HS 700/9-12
555 Walton Rd 32433 850-892-1270
Mike Davis, prin. Fax 892-1279
Walton MS 700/6-8
625 Park Ave 32435 850-892-1280
Russell Hughes, prin. Fax 892-1289
Other Schools – See Freeport, Paxton, Santa Rosa Beach

De Land, Volusia, Pop. 21,902
Volusia County SD 61,400/PK-12
PO Box 2118 32721 386-734-7190
Margaret Smith, supt. Fax 943-3423
www.volusia.k12.fl.us
DeLand HS 2,900/9-12
800 N Hill Ave 32724 386-822-6909
Mitch Moyer, prin. Fax 822-6556
DeLand MS 1,500/6-8
1400 Aquarius Ave 32724 386-822-5678
Matt Krajewski, prin. Fax 822-6583
Southwestern MS 600/6-8
605 W New Hampshire Ave 32720 386-822-6815
Mamie Oatis, prin. Fax 822-6708
Other Schools – See Daytona Beach, Deltona, Holly Hill, New Smyrna Beach, Ormond Beach, Pierson, Port Orange

Childrens House Montessori S 100/PK-12
509 E Pennsylvania Ave 32724 386-736-3632
Dora Mallett, admin. Fax 736-3667
Florida Technical College Post-Sec.
1199 S Woodland Blvd 32720 386-734-3303
Lighthouse Christian Academy 500/PK-12
126 S Ridgewood Ave 32720 386-734-5380
Luke Pearson, prin. Fax 734-5627
Stetson University Post-Sec.
421 N Woodland Boulevard 32720 386-822-7000

Delray Beach, Palm Beach, Pop. 63,321
Palm Beach County SD
Supt. — See West Palm Beach
Atlantic Community HS 2,000/9-12
2455 W Atlantic St 33445 561-243-1500
Kathleen Weigel, prin. Fax 243-1532
Carver Community MS 1,400/6-8
101 Barwick Rd 33445 561-638-2100
Mary Stratos, prin. Fax 638-2181
Atlantic Community HS Adult
2501 Seacrest Blvd 33444 561-243-1520
Dick Brinker, prin. Fax 243-1532
Delray Full Service Center Adult
301 SW 14th Ave 33444 561-243-1566
Lena Roundtree, prin. Fax 243-1591

American Heritage S of Boca/Delray 1,000/K-12
6200 Linton Blvd 33484 561-495-7272
Robert Stone, dir. Fax 495-1606
TLC Christian Academy 100/PK-12
111-115 SW 10th Ave 33444 561-278-3115
Queen Owens, prin. Fax 278-4629

Deltona, Volusia, Pop. 76,597
Volusia County SD
Supt. — See De Land
Deltona HS 2,800/9-12
100 Wolf Pack Run 32725 386-575-4153
Gary Marks, prin. Fax 789-9843
Deltona MS 1,400/6-8
250 Enterprise Rd 32725 386-575-4150
Tom Russell, prin. Fax 860-3383
Galaxy MS 1,800/6-8
2400 Eustace Ave 32725 386-575-4144
Julian Jones, prin. Fax 789-7058
Heritage MS, 1001 Parnell Ct 32738 1,400/6-8
Dennis Neal, prin. 386-575-4113
Pine Ridge HS 2,400/9-12
925 Howland Blvd 32738 386-575-4195
Dr. Michael Mongelli, prin.

Deltona Christian S 200/PK-12
1200 Providence Blvd 32725 386-574-1971
Byron Herchenroder, admin. Fax 574-1771
Trinity Christian Academy 600/PK-12
875 Elkcam Blvd 32725 386-789-4515
Dennis Robinson, dir. Fax 789-0210

Volusia County Christian Academy 50/PK-12
PO Box 391091 32739 386-532-8005
Donald Morgan, prin. Fax 532-8005

Destin, Okaloosa, Pop. 11,769
Okaloosa County SD
Supt. — See Fort Walton Beach
Destin MS 700/6-8
400 Regatta Bay Blvd 32541 850-833-7655
Sherri Houp, prin. Fax 833-7677

Doral, Dade, Pop. 3,126
ITT Technical Institute Post-Sec.
7955 NW 12th St 33126 305-477-3080
Polytechnic University of the Americas Post-Sec.
8180 NW 36th St 33166 305-418-4220

Dundee, Polk, Pop. 2,986
Polk County SD
Supt. — See Bartow
Dundee Ridge MS 1,000/6-8
5555 Lake Trask Rd 33838 863-419-3088
Kathryn Blackburn, prin. Fax 419-3157

Dunedin, Pinellas, Pop. 36,715
Pinellas County SD
Supt. — See Largo
Dunedin Highland MS 1,100/6-8
70 Patricia Ave 34698 727-469-4112
Margaret Landers, prin. Fax 469-4115
Dunedin HS 1,900/9-12
1651 Pinehurst Rd 34698 727-469-4100
Paul Summa, prin. Fax 469-4143

Dunedin Academy 200/PK-12
1408 County Road 1 34698 727-733-9148
Dale Porter, dir. Fax 733-6696
Schiller International University Post-Sec.
453 Edgewater Dr 34698 727-736-5082

Dunnellon, Marion, Pop. 1,954
Marion County SD
Supt. — See Ocala
Dunnellon HS 1,300/9-12
10055 SW 180th Avenue Rd 34432 352-465-6745
Michelle Lewis, prin. Fax 465-6746
Dunnellon MS 900/6-8
21005 Chestnut St 34431 352-465-6720
Jane Ashman, prin. Fax 465-6721

Cambridge Academy 500/6-12
PO Box 3 34430 352-489-7999
Tanzee Nahas, prin. Fax 489-4994
Dunnellon Christian Academy 200/PK-12
20831 Powell Rd 34431 352-489-7716
Rev. Russell Randall, dir. Fax 489-0337

Eagle Lake, Polk, Pop. 2,493
Polk County SD
Supt. — See Bartow
Lake Region HS 2,000/9-12
1995 Thunder Rd 33839 863-297-3099
Joel McGuire, prin. Fax 297-3097

Eagle Lake Christian S 100/PK-12
670 N Eagle Dr 33839 863-294-7259
Pamela Henderson, prin. Fax 299-7509

Eatonville, Orange, Pop. 2,411
Orange County SD
Supt. — See Orlando
Hungerford Preparatory HS 400/9-12
100 E Kennedy Blvd 32751 407-622-8200
Dr. Gladys White, prin. Fax 645-0236

Englewood, Sarasota, Pop. 15,025
Charlotte County SD
Supt. — See Port Charlotte
Lemon Bay HS 1,400/9-12
2201 Placida Rd 34224 941-474-7702
Dan Jeffers, prin. Fax 475-5260

Heritage Christian Academy 100/PK-12
75 Pine St 34223 941-474-5884
Bill Ingham, prin. Fax 473-1797

Estero, Lee, Pop. 3,177
Lee County SD
Supt. — See Fort Myers
Estero HS 2,000/9-12
21900 River Ranch Rd 33928 239-947-9400
George Clover, prin. Fax 947-5017

Eustis, Lake, Pop. 16,316
Lake County SD
Supt. — See Tavares
Eustis HS - Curtright Campus 9-9
1801 Bates Ave 32726 352-589-1510
Michael Elchenko, prin. Fax 589-1605
Eustis MS 1,100/6-8
18725 Bates Ave 32736 352-357-3366
Albert Larry, prin. Fax 357-5963
Eustis SHS 800/10-12
1300 E Washington Ave 32726 352-357-4447
Michael Elchenko, prin. Fax 357-7449
Lake Technical Center Vo/Tech
2001 Kurt St 32726 352-589-2250
Terry Miller, prin. Fax 357-4776

Blue Lake Academy 300/PK-12
PO Box 1947 32727 352-357-8655
Roger Cox, hdmstr. Fax 357-6956
Gold Medal Honors Academy 100/K-12
38832 Ilex Trl 32736 386-785-0440
Lily Schwarz, prin. Fax 740-8064
Lake Technical Center Post-Sec.
2001 Kurt St 32726 352-589-2250

Everglades City, Collier
Collier County SD
Supt. — See Naples
Everglades City S 200/PK-12
PO Box 170 34139 239-377-9800
Bobby Jones, prin. Fax 377-9801

Fernandina Beach, Nassau, Pop. 11,059
Nassau County SD 10,100/PK-12
1201 Atlantic Ave 32034 904-491-9900
John Ruis, supt. Fax 277-9042
www.nassau.k12.fl.us

Fernandina Beach HS 1,700/9-12
435 Citrona Dr 32034 904-491-7937
Jane Arnold, prin. Fax 277-3754
Fernandina Beach MS 800/6-8
315 Citrona Dr 32034 904-491-7938
John Mazzella, prin. Fax 261-8919
Nassau County Adult S Adult
1201 Atlantic Ave 32034 904-491-9898
Tom Jenkins, prin. Fax 225-2183
Other Schools – See Callahan, Hilliard, Yulee

Faith Christian Academy 200/PK-12
134 Brady Point Rd 32034 904-321-2137
Wendy Lannon, admin. Fax 321-1707

Fern Park, Seminole, Pop. 8,294
Americare School of Nursing Post-Sec.
7275 Estapona Cir 32730 407-673-7406

Florahome, Putnam
Putnam County SD
Supt. — See Palatka
Roberts MS 300/6-8
901 State Road 100 32140 386-659-1737
Randy Hedstern, prin. Fax 659-1986

Fort Lauderdale, Broward, Pop. 162,917
Broward County SD 250,500/PK-12
600 SE 3rd Ave 33301 754-321-2600
Dr. Frank Till, supt. Fax 321-2701
www.browardschools.com
Ashe MS 1,100/6-8
1701 NW 23rd Ave 33311 754-322-2800
Luwando Wright-Hines, prin. Fax 322-2880
Dandy MS 1,400/6-8
2400 NW 26th St 33311 754-322-3200
Casandra Robinson, prin. Fax 322-3285
Dillard HS 2,200/9-12
2501 NW 11th St 33311 754-322-0800
Merceda Stanley, prin. Fax 322-0930
Fort Lauderdale HS 1,800/9-12
1600 NE 4th Ave 33305 754-322-1100
Gina Eyerman, prin. Fax 322-1230
New River MS 1,600/6-8
3100 Riverland Rd 33312 754-323-3600
Jan Beal, prin. Fax 323-3685
Parkway MS 1,900/6-8
3600 NW 5th Ct 33311 754-322-4000
David Hall, prin. Fax 322-4085
Stranahan HS 2,200/9-12
1800 SW 5th Pl 33312 754-323-2100
Deborah Owens, prin. Fax 323-2230
Sunrise MS 1,500/6-8
1750 NE 14th St 33304 754-322-4700
Rebecca Dahl, prin. Fax 322-4799
Whiddon-Rodgers Education Center Adult
700 SW 26th St 33315 754-321-7550
Linda Thomas, prin. Fax 321-7590
Whiddon-Rodgers Education Center Annex Adult
1300 SW 32nd Ct 33315 754-321-7600
Linda Thomas, prin. Fax 321-7649
Other Schools – See Coconut Creek, Cooper City, Coral Springs, Dania, Davie, Deerfield Beach, Hallandale, Hollywood, Lauderdale Lakes, Lauderhill, Margate, Miramar, North Lauderdale, Oakland Park, Parkland, Pembroke Pines, Plantation, Pompano Beach, Sunrise, Tamarac, Weston

Archbishop Edward McCarthy HS 1,000/9-12
5451 S Flamingo Rd 33330 954-434-8820
Dr. Richard Perhla, prin. Fax 680-4835
Art Institute of Fort Lauderdale Post-Sec.
1799 SE 17th St 33316 954-463-3000
ATI Career Training Center Post-Sec.
2890 W Cypress Creek Rd 33309 954-973-4760
Atlantic Institute of Oriental Medicine Post-Sec.
100 E Broward Blvd Ste 100 33301 954-763-9840
Broward Community College Post-Sec.
225 E Las Olas Blvd 33301 954-475-6500
Calvary Christian Academy 1,200/PK-12
2401 W Cypress Creek Rd 33309 954-556-4400
David Salvatelli, prin. Fax 556-4480
Cardinal Gibbons HS 1,100/9-12
2900 NE 47th St 33308 954-491-2900
Paul Ott, prin. Fax 772-1025
City College Post-Sec.
2000 W Commercial Blvd 33309 954-492-5353
Coral Ridge Nurse's Asst Training School Post-Sec.
2740 E Oakland Park Blvd 33306 954-561-2022
Fort Lauderdale Christian S 300/PK-12
6330 NW 31st Ave 33309 954-972-3444
Gerald A. Mitchell, hdmstr. Fax 977-2681
Fort Lauderdale Preparatory S 200/PK-12
3275 W Oakland Park Blvd 33311 954-485-7500
Anita Lonstein, prin. Fax 485-1732
Keiser College Post-Sec.
1500 NW 49th St 33309 954-776-4456
Knox Theological Seminary Post-Sec.
5554 N Federal Hwy 33308 954-771-0376
Nur Ul-Islam Academy 300/PK-12
10600 SW 59th St 33328 954-434-3288
Kem Hussain, dir. Fax 434-9333
Oxford Academy 100/10-12
1919 NE 45th St Ste 115 33308 954-772-4512
Laurie Pittman, prin. Fax 772-4514
Pine Crest S 2,500/PK-12
1501 NE 62nd St 33334 954-492-4100
Robert Goldberg, hdmstr. Fax 492-4167
St. Thomas Aquinas HS 1,900/9-12
2801 SW 12th St 33312 954-581-0700
Tina Jones, prin. Fax 581-8263
University S of Nova Southeastern Univ 1,600/6-12
3301 College Ave 33314 954-262-4400
Dr. Jerome Chermak, hdmstr. Fax 262-3971
Westminster Academy 1,000/PK-12
5601 N Federal Hwy 33308 954-771-4600
Greg Beaupied, hdmstr. Fax 491-3021

Fort Meade, Polk, Pop. 5,724
Polk County SD
Supt. — See Bartow
Fort Meade MSHS 800/6-12
700 Edgewood Dr N 33841 863-285-1180
Tom Ereditario, prin. Fax 285-1186

Fort Myers, Lee, Pop. 51,028
Lee County SD 61,400/PK-12
2055 Central Ave 33901 239-334-1102
Dr. James W. Browder, supt. Fax 337-8378
www.lee.k12.fl.us

Cypress Lake HS 2,000/9-12
6750 Panther Ln 33919 239-481-2233
Tracy Perkins, prin. Fax 481-6094
Cypress Lake MS 1,200/6-8
8901 Cypress Lake Dr 33919 239-481-1533
Jeananne Folaros, prin. Fax 481-3121
Dunbar HS 1,200/9-12
3800 Edison Ave 33916 239-461-5322
Carl Burnside, prin. Fax 461-5110
Dunbar MS 1,200/6-8
4750 Winkler Avenue Ext, 239-334-1357
Beth Ellen Bolger, prin. Fax 334-7633
Fort Myers HS 2,100/9-12
2635 Cortez Blvd 33901 239-334-2167
Richard Shafer, prin. Fax 334-3095
Fort Myers Middle Academy 800/6-8
3050 Central Ave 33901 239-936-1759
Louise Hollins, prin. Fax 936-4350
Lee County HS Tech Center Central Vo/Tech
3800 Michigan Ave 33916 239-334-4544
Robert Durham, prin. Fax 332-4839
Lee MS 700/6-8
1333 Marsh Ave 33905 239-337-1333
Vivian Smith, prin. Fax 334-4144
Lexington MS 6-8
16760 Bass Rd 33908 239-454-6130
Linda Caprarotta, prin. Fax 489-3419
Riverdale HS 1,900/6-12
2600 Buckingham Rd 33905 239-694-4141
Gerald Demming, prin. Fax 694-3527
South Fort Myers HS 9-12
14020 Plantation Rd 33912 239-561-0060
Tommy O'Connell, prin. Fax 561-3612
Three Oaks MS 1,100/6-8
18500 3 Oaks Pkwy, 239-267-5757
Mike Carson, prin. Fax 267-4007
Adult & Community Education Adult
2266 2nd St 33901 239-334-7172
Fax 334-4568
Dunbar Community S Adult
1857 High St 33916 239-334-2941
Dr. Betty Bowers, admin. Fax 334-3519
Other Schools – See Alva, Bonita Springs, Cape Coral, Estero, Lehigh Acres, North Fort Myers

Bishop Verot HS 700/9-12
5598 Sunrise Dr 33919 239-274-6700
Rev. Christian Beretta, prin. Fax 274-6798
Canterbury S 700/PK-12
8141 College Pkwy 33919 239-481-4323
R. Mason Goss, hdmstr. Fax 481-8339
Edison College Post-Sec.
PO Box 60210 33906 239-489-9300
Evangelical Christian S 1,200/PK-12
8237 Beacon Blvd 33907 239-936-3319
John Hunte, hdmstr. Fax 939-1445
Florida Christian Institute 200/K-12
2830 Winkler Ave Ste 201 33916 239-274-5935
Keith Leonardo, dir. Fax 274-5939
Florida Gulf Coast University Post-Sec.
10501 FGCU Blvd 33965 239-590-1000
Heritage Institute Post-Sec.
6811 Palisades Park Ct 33912 239-936-5822
International College Post-Sec.
4501 Colonial Blvd 33912 239-482-0019
Lee County High Tech Center Central Post-Sec.
3800 Michigan Ave 33916 239-334-4544
Sonshine Chistian Academy 200/PK-12
12925 Palm Beach Blvd 33905 239-694-8882
Ken Norvell, prin. Fax 694-8885
Southwest Florida Christian Academy 600/K-12
3750 Colonial Blvd, 239-936-8865
Dr. Phil Tingle, hdmstr. Fax 936-7095
Southwest Florida College Post-Sec.
1685 Medical Ln 33907 239-939-4766
Sunstate Academy of Hair Design Post-Sec.
2418 Colonial Blvd 33907 239-278-1311

Fort Pierce, Saint Lucie, Pop. 37,841
St. Lucie County SD 32,400/PK-12
4204 Okeechobee Rd 34947 772-429-3600
Michael J. Lannon, supt.
www.stlucie.k12.fl.us/index.html
Forest Grove MS 1,300/6-8
3201 S 25th St 34981 772-468-5885
Charles Cuomo, prin. Fax 595-1187
Fort Pierce Central HS 1,900/9-12
1101 Edwards Rd 34982 772-468-5888
John Williams, prin. Fax 468-5761
Fort Pierce Magnet S of the Arts 1,300/K-12
1100 Delaware Ave 34950 772-467-4278
Dr. David Washington, prin. Fax 460-3094
Fort Pierce Westwood HS 1,600/9-12
1801 Panther Ln 34947 772-468-5400
Linda Bushore, prin. Fax 468-5465
Lincoln Park Academy 1,800/6-12
1806 Avenue I 34950 772-468-5474
Margaret Anderson, prin. Fax 468-5485
McCarty MS 1,200/6-8
1201 Mississippi Ave 34950 772-468-5700
Catherine Smith, prin. Fax 595-1124
Other Schools – See Port Saint Lucie

Ari Ben Aviator Post-Sec.
3800 Saint Lucie Blvd 34946 772-466-4822
Bible Baptist S 200/PK-12
4401 S 25th St 34981 772-461-7215
Dave Piero, dir. Fax 461-7215
Faith Baptist S 300/PK-12
3607 Oleander Ave 34982 772-461-3607
Terry Booher, dir. Fax 461-4732
Fort Pierce Beauty Academy Post-Sec.
3028 S US 1 34982 772-464-4885
Golden Rule Academy 50/PK-12
3891 Edwards Rd 34981 772-466-0034
Rev. Rick George, prin. Fax 466-8102
Indian River Community College Post-Sec.
3209 Virginia Ave 34981 772-462-4700
John Carroll HS 500/9-12
3402 Delaware Ave 34947 772-464-5200
Ben Hopper, prin. Fax 464-5233
Orange Avenue Baptist S 100/PK-12
100 Cyclone Dr 34945 772-461-1225
Wanda Hurt, prin. Fax 461-0605
Palm Vista Christian S 100/PK-12
700 S 33rd St 34947 772-464-1591
Terrell Ray, dir. Fax 464-6861
Sampson Memorial SDA S 50/K-10
3201 Memory Ln 34981 772-465-8386

Fort Walton Beach, Okaloosa, Pop. 19,936
Okaloosa County SD 28,700/PK-12
120 Lowery Pl SE 32548 850-833-3100
Don Gaetz, supt. Fax 833-3436
www.okaloosaschools.com/
Bruner MS 1,100/6-8
322 Holmes Blvd NW 32548 850-833-3266
Dr. Diane Kelley, prin. Fax 833-3434
Choctawhatachee HS 1,800/9-12
110 Racetrack Rd NW 32547 850-833-3414
Cindy Massarelli, prin. Fax 833-3410
Fort Walton Beach HS 2,000/9-12
400 Hollywood Blvd SW 32548 850-833-3300
Alexis Tibbetts, prin. Fax 833-3311
Pryor MS 800/6-8
201 Racetrack Rd NW 32547 850-833-3613
Vivian Green, prin. Fax 833-4276
UWF/OCSD Common Campus Vo/Tech
1976 Lewis Turner Blvd 32547 850-833-3500
Fax 833-3466
Other Schools – See Baker, Crestview, Destin, Laurel Hill, Niceville, Shalimar, Valparaiso

Calvary Christian Academy 400/PK-12
535 Clifford St 32547 850-862-1414
Jon Gross, admin. Fax 862-9826
Okaloosa Applied Technical Center Post-Sec.
1976 Lewis Turner Blvd 32547 850-833-3500

Fort White, Columbia, Pop. 428
Columbia County SD
Supt. — See Lake City
Fort White HS 1,200/6-12
17828 SW State Road 47 32038 386-497-5952
Keith Hatcher, prin. Fax 497-5951

Freeport, Walton, Pop. 1,353
Walton County SD
Supt. — See De Funiak Springs
Freeport HS 300/9-12
12615 US Highway 331 S 32439 850-892-1200
Michael Murphy, prin. Fax 892-1209
Freeport MS 300/6-8
360 Kylea Laird Dr 32439 850-892-1220
Beth Tucker, prin. Fax 892-1229

Frostproof, Polk, Pop. 2,940
Polk County SD
Supt. — See Bartow
Frostproof MSHS 1,200/6-12
1000 N Palm Ave 33843 863-635-7809
Stephen White, prin. Fax 635-7812

Fruitland Park, Lake, Pop. 3,393

Holy Trinity Episcopal S 50/6-12
2201 Spring Lake Rd 34731 352-787-8855
Thomas J. Boyd, hdmstr. Fax 787-8063

Gainesville, Alachua, Pop. 109,146
Alachua County SD 27,100/PK-12
620 E University Ave 32601 352-955-7300
Dr. W. Daniel Boyd, supt. Fax 955-6700
www.sbac.edu/
Bishop MS 1,100/6-8
1901 NE 9th St 32609 352-955-6701
Jeff Charbonnet, prin. Fax 955-6966
Buchholz HS 2,600/9-12
5510 NW 27th Ave 32606 352-955-6702
Vince Perez, prin. Fax 955-7285
Eastside HS 1,800/9-12
1201 SE 43rd St 32641 352-955-6704
Michael Thorne, prin. Fax 955-7291
Ft. Clarke MS 900/6-8
9301 NW 23rd Ave 32606 352-333-2800
Donna Kidwell, prin. Fax 333-2806
Gainesville HS 1,900/9-12
1900 NW 13th St 32609 352-955-6707
Dr. Wiley Dixon, prin. Fax 955-7283
Kanapaha MS 900/6-8
5005 SW 75th St 32608 352-955-6960
Jennifer Wise, prin. Fax 955-6858
Lincoln MS 900/6-8
1001 SE 12th St 32641 352-955-6711
Don Lewis, prin. Fax 955-7133
Loften HS Vo/Tech
3000 E University Ave 32641 352-955-6839
Dr. Ellen West, prin. Fax 955-6999
Westwood MS 900/6-8
3215 NW 15th Ave 32605 352-955-6718
James Tenbieg, prin. Fax 955-6897
Other Schools – See Alachua, Hawthorne, Newberry

City College Post-Sec.
2400 SW 13th St 32608 352-335-4000
Cornerstone Academy 200/PK-12
3536 NW 8th Ave 32605 352-378-9337
Leigh Glover, prin. Fax 378-7708
Countryside Christian S 100/PK-12
10926 NW 39th Ave 32606 352-332-9731
David L. Keith, prin. Fax 332-4153
Dragon Rises College Oriental Medicine Post-Sec.
901 NW 8th Ave Ste B5 32601 352-371-2833
Florida School of Massage Post-Sec.
6421 SW 13th St 32608 352-378-7891
Oak Hall S 400/6-12
8009 SW 14th Ave 32607 352-332-3609
Richard Gehman, prin. Fax 332-4975
Rock S 200/PK-12
9818 SW 24th Ave 32607 352-331-7625
Bob Carter, prin. Fax 331-9760
St. Francis HS 9-12
11500 NW 39th Ave 32606 352-376-6545
Ernest Herrington, prin. Fax 376-7568
Santa Fe Community College Post-Sec.
3000 NW 83rd St 32606 352-395-5000
University of Florida Post-Sec.
PO Box 114000 32611 352-392-3261
Westwood Hills Christian S 300/PK-12
1520 NW 34th St 32605 352-378-5190
Jay Jethro, prin. Fax 371-6782
Windsor Christian Academy 50/1-12
918 SE County Road 234 32641 352-375-1144
Mike Redmond, admin. Fax 375-7316

Gibsonton, Hillsborough, Pop. 7,706
Hillsborough County SD
Supt. — See Tampa
East Bay HS 2,200/9-12
7710 Big Bend Rd 33534 813-671-5134
Clyde Trathowen, prin. Fax 671-5139

Eisenhower MS 1,800/6-8
7620 Big Bend Rd 33534 813-671-5121
Tim Ducker, prin. Fax 671-5039
East Bay Adult & Community Center Adult
7710 Big Bend Rd 33534 813-672-5113
Richard Garrett, prin. Fax 672-5122

Glen Saint Mary, Baker, Pop. 537
Baker County SD
Supt. — See Macclenny
Baker County HS 1,300/9-12
1 Wildcat Dr 32040 904-259-6286
John David Crawford, prin. Fax 259-5617

Gotha, Orange

Central Florida Preparatory S 200/PK-12
PO Box 817 34734 407-290-8073
Rowena Flanders, dir. Fax 298-6443

Goulds, Dade, Pop. 7,284
Miami-Dade County SD
Supt. — See Miami
Mays MS 1,100/6-8
11700 SW 216th St 33170 305-233-2300
Kenneth Cooper, prin. Fax 251-5462

Graceville, Jackson, Pop. 2,357
Holmes County SD
Supt. — See Bonifay
Poplar Springs S 300/PK-12
3726 Atomic Dr 32440 850-263-6260
Patty Segrest, prin. Fax 263-1252
Jackson County SD
Supt. — See Marianna
Graceville JSHS 400/6-12
5539 Brown St 32440 850-263-4451
Laurence Pender, prin. Fax 263-3605

The Baptist College of Florida Post-Sec.
5400 College Dr 32440 800-328-2660

Grand Ridge, Jackson, Pop. 779
Jackson County SD
Supt. — See Marianna
Grand Ridge S 600/PK-12
6925 Florida St 32442 850-482-9835
Beth Westmoreland, prin. Fax 482-9834

Greenacres, Palm Beach, Pop. 31,111
Palm Beach County SD
Supt. — See West Palm Beach
Leonard HS 2,500/9-12
4701 10th Ave N 33463 561-641-1000
Reginald Myers, prin. Fax 357-1100
Swain MS 6-8
5332 Lake Worth Rd 33463 561-649-6900
Camille Long-Coleman, prin. Fax 649-6910

Keiser Career College Post-Sec.
6812 Forest Hill Blvd # D1 33413 561-433-2330

Green Cove Springs, Clay, Pop. 5,671
Clay County SD 31,200/PK-12
900 Walnut St 32043 904-284-6500
David Owens, supt. Fax 284-6525
www.clay.k12.fl.us/
Clay HS 1,300/9-12
2025 State Road 16 W 32043 904-529-2110
Pete McCabe, prin. Fax 529-2112
Green Cove Springs JHS 900/7-8
1220 Bonaventure Ave 32043 904-529-2140
Kenneth Francis, prin. Fax 529-2144
Lake Asbury JHS 7-8
2851 Sandridge Rd 32043 904-291-5582
Ed Paulk, prin. Fax 291-5593
Other Schools – See Keystone Heights, Middleburg, Orange Park

Greensboro, Gadsden, Pop. 607
Gadsden County SD
Supt. — See Quincy
West Gadsden HS 300/7-12
PO Box 10 32330 850-442-9500
Rocky Pace, prin. Fax 442-6126

Greenville, Madison, Pop. 824

Greenville Hills Academy 200/6-12
742 SW Greenville Hills Rd 32331 850-948-1200
John Chancyn, prin. Fax 948-1330

Groveland, Lake, Pop. 3,951
Lake County SD
Supt. — See Tavares
Gray MS 800/6-8
205 E Magnolia St 34736 352-429-3322
Janice Boyd, prin. Fax 429-0133
South Lake HS 1,300/9-12
15600 Silver Eagle Rd 34736 352-394-2100
Dave Bordenkircher, prin. Fax 394-1972

Gulf Breeze, Santa Rosa, Pop. 6,199
Santa Rosa County SD
Supt. — See Milton
Gulf Breeze HS 1,500/9-12
675 Gulf Breeze Pkwy 32561 850-916-4100
Cherry Fitch, prin. Fax 916-4109
Gulf Breeze MS 900/6-8
649 Gulf Breeze Pkwy 32561 850-934-4080
Jennifer Granse, prin. Fax 934-4085
Woodlawn Beach MS 800/6-8
1500 Woodlawn Way 32563 850-934-4010
C.J. Lovallo, prin. Fax 934-4015

Gulfport, Pinellas, Pop. 12,586
Pinellas County SD
Supt. — See Largo
Boca Ciega HS 2,100/9-12
924 58th St S 33707 727-893-2780
John M. Leanes, prin. Fax 893-1382

Stetson University Post-Sec.
1401 61st St S 33707 727-345-1121

Haines City, Polk, Pop. 13,956
Polk County SD
Supt. — See Bartow
Boone MS 1,000/6-8
225 S 22nd St 33844 863-421-3302
Pamela Henderson, prin. Fax 421-3305

Haines City HS 2,100/9-12
2800 Hornet Dr 33844 863-421-3281
Duane Collins, prin. Fax 421-3283
Jenkins Academy of Technology Vo/Tech
701 Ledwith Ave 33844 863-421-3267
Eileen Killebrew, prin. Fax 421-3269

Landmark Christian S 300/PK-12
2020 E Hinson Ave 33844 863-422-2037
Wallace Hill, admin. Fax 419-1256

Hallandale, Broward, Pop. 31,163
Broward County SD
Supt. — See Fort Lauderdale
Gulfstream MS 6-8
120 SW 4th Ave 33009 754-323-4700
Debra Patterson, prin. Fax 323-5940
Hallandale HS 1,600/9-12
720 NW 9th Ave 33009 754-323-0900
Rosemary Chambers, prin. Fax 323-1030
Hallandale Adult & Comm Ctr Adult
1000 SW 3rd St 33009 754-321-7050
Linda Lopez, prin. Fax 321-7135

Academy for Five Element Acupuncture Post-Sec.
1170a E Hllndale Beach Blvd 33009 954-456-6336
Florida S of Excellence 100/10-12
640 W Hallandale Beach Blvd 33009 954-455-9990
Alexander Guignard, dir. Fax 559-9973

Havana, Gadsden, Pop. 1,685
Gadsden County SD
Supt. — See Quincy
East Gadsden HS 1,100/9-12
27001 Blue Star Hwy 32333 850-539-2882
William Harvey, prin.
Havana MS 300/6-8
1100 E 9th Ave 32333 850-539-6736
Verna Norris, prin. Fax 539-4191

Tallavana Christian S 200/PK-12
5840 Havana Hwy 32333 850-539-5300
Natalie Alday, prin. Fax 539-8785

Hawthorne, Alachua, Pop. 1,454
Alachua County SD
Supt. — See Gainesville
Hawthorne JSHS 600/6-12
21403 SE 69th Ave 32640 352-481-1900
Dr. Susan Arnold, prin. Fax 481-4859

Hialeah, Dade, Pop. 226,401
Miami-Dade County SD
Supt. — See Miami
American HS 2,900/9-12
18350 NW 67th Ave 33015 305-557-3770
Dr. Louis J. Algaze, prin. Fax 828-7380
Filer MS 1,500/6-8
531 W 29th St 33012 305-822-6601
Luis Diaz, prin. Fax 822-2063
Goleman HS 4,700/8-12
14100 NW 89th Ave 33018 305-362-0676
Carlos Artime, prin. Fax 827-0249
Hialeah HS 4,200/9-12
251 E 47th St 33013 305-822-1500
Lorenzo Ladaga, prin. Fax 828-5513
Hialeah-Miami Lakes HS 3,400/9-12
7977 W 12th Ave 33014 305-823-1330
Karen L. Robinson, prin. Fax 362-4188
Hialeah MS 1,300/6-8
6027 E 7th Ave 33013 305-681-3527
Martha H. Montiel, prin. Fax 681-6225
Marti MS 1,600/6-8
5701 W 24th Ave 33016 305-557-5931
Jose Bueno, prin. Fax 596-6917
Miami Lakes MS 1,600/6-8
6425 Miami Lakeway N 33014 305-557-3900
Joaquin Hernandez, prin. Fax 828-6753
Palm Springs MS 2,300/6-9
1025 W 56th St 33012 305-821-2460
Melissa Wolin, prin. Fax 828-3987
American SHS Adult Education Adult
18350 NW 67th Ave 33015 305-557-3770
Eddie Colletti, prin. Fax 827-7935
Hialeah-Miami Lakes HS Adult Ed Center Adult
7977 W 12th Ave 33014 305-823-1330
Nilda Diaz, prin. Fax 828-8929
Hialeah SHS Adult Education Center Adult
251 E 47th St 33013 305-822-1500
James Bishop, prin. Fax 821-6018

Advance Science Institute Post-Sec.
3750 W 12th Ave 33012 305-827-5452
Beauty Schools of America Post-Sec.
1060 W 49th St 33012 305-362-9003
Champagnat Catholic S 300/PK-12
369 E 10th St 33010 305-888-3760
Maria Alonso, prin. Fax 883-1174
Compu-Med Vocational Careers Post-Sec.
2900 W 12th Ave Ste 3 33012 305-888-9200
Edison Private S 400/PK-12
3720 E 4th Ave 33013 305-824-0303
Margarita Jiminez, prin. Fax 822-4205
First Baptist S 200/PK-12
140 E 7th St 33010 305-888-9776
Hilda Solares, dir. Fax 888-9783
Florida National College Post-Sec.
4425 W 20th Ave 33012 305-821-3333
Horeb Christian S 300/PK-12
795 W 68th St 33014 305-557-6811
Ana L. Morales-Gonzalez, prin. Fax 821-5048
Keiser Career College Post-Sec.
17395 NW 59th Ave 33015 305-820-5003
La Belle Beauty School Post-Sec.
775 W 49th St Ste 5 33012 305-558-0562
Lincoln-Marti S 400/PK-12
1750 E 4th Ave 33010 305-643-4888
Fax 649-2767
Lincoln-Marti S 500/PK-12
90 W 11th St 33010 305-643-4888
Fax 649-2767
Miami Dade Christian Academy 50/9-12
1840 W 49th St Ste 520 33012 305-823-8111
Rodolfo Alfonso, prin. Fax 823-8111
Miami Lakes Educational Center Post-Sec.
5780 NW 158th St 33014 305-557-1100
National School of Technology Post-Sec.
4410 W 16th Ave Ste 52 33012 305-558-9500
Nouvelle Institute Post-Sec.
500 W 49th St Fl 2 33012 305-557-3017

Paradise Christian S 200/PK-12
6184 W 21st Ct 33016 305-828-7477
Dr. Eileen Fluney, dir. Fax 828-1950
The Praxis Institute Post-Sec.
4162 W 12th Ave 33012 305-556-1424

Hialeah Gardens, Dade, Pop. 19,867

Youth Co-op Training Institute Post-Sec.
12051 W Okeechobee Rd 33018 305-819-8855

Hilliard, Nassau, Pop. 2,812
Nassau County SD
Supt. — See Fernandina Beach
Hilliard MSHS 800/6-12
1 Flashes Ave 32046 904-491-7940
Dale Braddock, prin. Fax 845-7662

Hobe Sound, Martin, Pop. 11,507

Florida Unschoolers 200/K-12
8680 SE Eagle Ave 33455 772-546-0257
Nance Confer, prin.
Hobe Sound Bible College Post-Sec.
PO Box 1065 33475 772-546-5534
Hobe Sound Christian Academy 200/K-12
PO Box 1065 33475 772-545-1455
William Marshall, dir. Fax 545-1454

Holiday, Pasco, Pop. 19,360

Webster College Post-Sec.
2127 Grand Blvd 34690 727-942-0069

Holly Hill, Volusia, Pop. 12,586
Volusia County SD
Supt. — See De Land
Holly Hill MS 1,000/6-8
1200 Center Ave 32117 386-258-4663
John Polsinelli, prin. Fax 239-6314

Hollywood, Broward, Pop. 143,408
Broward County SD
Supt. — See Fort Lauderdale
Apollo MS 1,500/6-8
6800 Arthur St 33024 754-323-2900
Aimee Zekofsky, prin. Fax 323-2985
Attucks MS 700/6-8
3500 N 22nd Ave 33020 754-323-3000
Carletha Shaw, prin. Fax 323-3085
Driftwood MS 1,900/6-8
2751 NW 70th Ter 33024 754-323-3100
Jody Perry, prin. Fax 323-3185
Hollywood Hills HS 2,400/9-12
5400 Stirling Rd 33021 754-323-1050
Joyce Ferguson, prin. Fax 323-1180
McArthur HS 2,600/9-12
6501 Hollywood Blvd 33024 754-323-1200
Carol Roland, prin. Fax 323-1330
McNicol MS 1,600/6-8
1602 S 27th Ave 33020 754-323-3400
Kelvin Lee, prin. Fax 323-3485
Sheridan Technical Center Vo/Tech
5400 Sheridan St 33021 754-321-5400
Daniel Boegli, prin. Fax 321-5680
South Broward HS 2,400/9-12
1901 N Federal Hwy 33020 754-323-1800
Alan Strauss, prin. Fax 323-1930

Aukela Christian Military Academy 100/PK-12
2835 Madison St 33020 954-929-7010
Audrey Rodriguez, prin. Fax 927-2523
Chaminade-Madonna College Prep HS 900/9-12
500 E Chaminade Dr 33021 954-989-5150
M. Gloria Ramos, prin. Fax 983-4663
Hollywood Christian S 600/PK-12
1708 N State Road 7 33021 954-322-4350
Tobin Wilkins, prin. Fax 966-0097
Ross Medical Education Center Post-Sec.
6847 Taft St 33024 954-963-0043
Sheridan Hills Christian S 500/PK-12
3751 Sheridan St 33021 954-966-7995
Chesley A. Steele, hdmstr. Fax 961-1395
Sheridan Technical Center Post-Sec.
5400 Sheridan St 33021 754-321-5400

Homestead, Dade, Pop. 34,182
Miami-Dade County SD
Supt. — See Miami
Campbell Drive MS 1,300/6-8
31110 SW 157th Ave 33033 305-248-7911
Luz Navarro, prin. Fax 248-3518
Homestead HS 3,300/9-12
2351 SE 12th Ave 33034 305-245-7000
Dr. Henry Crawford, prin. Fax 247-5757
Homestead MS 1,300/6-8
650 NW 2nd Ave 33030 305-247-4221
Vanessa Strickland, prin. Fax 247-1098
Redland MS 1,700/6-8
16001 SW 248th St 33031 305-247-6112
Craig DePriest, prin. Fax 248-0628
South Dade HS 2,700/9-12
28401 SW 167th Ave 33030 305-247-4244
L.M. Mijuskovic, prin. Fax 248-3867
South Dade Adult Education Center Adult
109 NE 8th St 33030 305-248-5723
Gilda Santalla, prin. Fax 248-9164

Barrington Academy 200/PK-12
1013 N Redland Rd 33034 305-248-3400
Gwendolyn Thomas, prin. Fax 248-3732
Colonial Christian S 200/PK-12
17105 SW 296th St 33030 305-246-8608
Stephen Hager, prin. Fax 246-1542
First Assembly Christian Academy 100/PK-12
824 W Palm Dr 33034 305-248-2273
Julie Alexander, prin. Fax 246-5030
Redland Christian Academy 200/PK-12
17700 SW 280th St 33031 305-247-7399
Sharon Waldbillig, dir. Fax 247-1147

Hudson, Pasco, Pop. 7,344
Pasco County SD
Supt. — See Land O Lakes
Hudson HS 1,600/9-12
14410 Cobra Way 34669 727-774-4200
Angie Stone, prin. Fax 774-4291
Hudson MS 1,200/6-8
14540 Cobra Way 34669 727-774-8200
Steve Van Gorden, prin. Fax 774-8291

Grace Christian S 200/PK-12
9403 Scot St 34669 727-863-1825
Glenwood Pratt, prin. Fax 862-4484

Immokalee, Collier, Pop. 14,120
Collier County SD
Supt. — See Naples
Immokalee HS 1,200/9-12
701 Immokalee Dr 34142 239-377-1800
Armando Touron, prin. Fax 377-1801
Immokalee MS 1,200/6-8
401 N 9th St 34142 239-377-4200
Lisa Rivera-Scallan, prin. Fax 377-4201

Lorenzo Walker Institute of Technology Post-Sec.
614 S 5th St 34142

Indialantic, Brevard, Pop. 2,958
Brevard County SD
Supt. — See Melbourne
Hoover MS 600/7-8
2000 Hawk Haven Dr 32903 321-727-1611
Barbara Rodrigues, prin. Fax 725-0076

Indiantown, Martin, Pop. 4,794
Martin County SD
Supt. — See Stuart
Indiantown MS 500/5-8
16303 SW Farm Rd 34956 772-597-2146
Debbie Henderson, prin. Fax 597-5854

Interlachen, Putnam, Pop. 1,485
Putnam County SD
Supt. — See Palatka
Interlachen HS 900/9-12
126 N County Road 315 32148 386-684-2116
Susan Mathe, prin. Fax 684-3915
Price MS 600/6-8
140 N County Road 315 32148 386-684-2113
Sandra Gilyard, prin. Fax 684-3908

Inverness, Citrus, Pop. 7,184
Citrus County SD 15,000/PK-12
1007 W Main St 34450 352-726-1931
Sandra Himmel, supt. Fax 726-1246
www.citrus.k12.fl.us
Citrus HS 1,600/9-12
600 W Highland Blvd 34452 352-726-2241
Leigh Ann Bradshaw, prin. Fax 726-1368
Inverness MS 1,200/6-8
1950 Highway 41 N 34450 352-726-1471
Bill Farrell, prin. Fax 726-4535
Withlachoochee Technical Institute Vo/Tech
1201 W Main St 34450 352-726-2430
Andrew Buchanan, dir. Fax 726-5842
Other Schools – See Citrus Springs, Crystal River, Lecanto

Withlacoochee Technical Institute Post-Sec.
1201 W Main St 34450 352-726-2430

Islamorada, Monroe, Pop. 1,220

Island Christian S 200/PK-12
83250 Overseas Hwy 33036 305-664-4933
Richard Oates, prin. Fax 664-8170

Jacksonville, Duval, Pop. 773,781
Duval County SD 123,000/PK-12
1701 Prudential Dr 32207 904-390-2000
Dr. Nancy Snyder, supt. Fax 390-2586
www.educationcentral.org
Anderson HS of the Arts 1,000/9-12
2445 San Diego Rd 32207 904-346-5620
Jackie Cornelius, prin. Fax 346-5636
Arlington MS 1,000/6-8
8141 Lone Star Rd 32211 904-720-1680
Debbie Smith, prin. Fax 720-1702
Butler MS 600/6-8
900 Acorn St 32209 904-630-6900
Nongongama Majova-Seana, prin. Fax 630-6913
Darnell-Cookman MS 1,300/6-8
1701 N Davis St 32209 904-630-6805
Cheryl Hough, prin. Fax 630-6811
Davis MS 1,500/6-8
7050 Melvin Rd 32210 904-573-1060
Royce Turner, prin. Fax 573-1066
DuPont MS 1,100/6-8
2710 Dupont Ave 32217 904-739-5200
Gary Finger, prin. Fax 739-5321
Englewood HS 1,900/9-12
4412 Barnes Rd 32207 904-739-5212
Michael Kemp, prin. Fax 739-5324
First Coast HS 2,000/9-12
590 Duval Station Rd 32218 904-757-0080
Crystal Sisler, prin. Fax 696-8721
Forrest HS 1,600/9-12
5530 Firestone Rd 32244 904-573-1170
Tim Ahearn, prin. Fax 573-1177
Ft. Caroline MS 1,100/6-8
3787 University Club Blvd 32277 904-745-4927
Kathy Kassees, prin. Fax 745-4937
Gilbert MS 700/6-8
1424 Franklin St 32206 904-630-6700
Tony Bellamy, prin. Fax 630-6713
Grand Park Career Center Vo/Tech
2335 W 18th St 32209 904-630-6894
John Lumpkin, prin. Fax 630-6897
Highlands MS 1,600/6-8
10913 Pine Estates Rd E 32218 904-696-8771
Bill Permenter, prin. Fax 696-8782
Jackson HS 1,500/9-12
3816 N Main St 32206 904-630-6950
Lance Barnett, prin. Fax 630-6955
Johnson MS 1,200/6-8
1840 W 9th St 32209 904-630-6640
Marilyn Myrick, prin. Fax 630-6653
Kernan MS 1,300/6-8
2271 Kernan Blvd S 32246 904-220-1350
David Gilmore, prin. Fax 220-1355
Kirby-Smith MS 1,000/6-8
2034 Hubbard St 32206 904-630-6600
Dana Krizner, prin. Fax 630-6605
Lake Shore MS 1,300/6-8
2519 Bayview Rd 32210 904-381-7440
Iranetta Wright, prin. Fax 381-7437
Landmark MS 1,600/6-8
101 Kernan Blvd N 32225 904-221-7125
Connie Hall, prin. Fax 221-8847

Landon MS 900/6-8
1819 Thacker Ave 32207 904-346-5650
Jacquelyn Christopher, prin. Fax 346-5657
LaVilla S of the Arts 1,100/6-8
501 N Davis St 32202 904-633-6069
Janelle Wagoner, prin. Fax 633-8089
Lee HS 1,900/9-12
1200 McDuff Ave S 32205 904-381-3930
Denise Hall, prin. Fax 381-3945
Mandarin HS 2,800/9-12
4831 Greenland Rd 32258 904-260-3911
Larry Roziers, prin. Fax 260-5439
Mandarin MS 1,700/6-8
5100 Hood Rd 32257 904-292-0555
Joy Recla, prin. Fax 260-5415
Northwestern MS 1,000/6-8
2100 W 45th St 32209 904-924-3100
Saryn Hatcher, prin. Fax 924-3284
Oceanway MS 700/6-8
143 Oceanway Ave 32218 904-714-4680
John Cochran, prin. Fax 714-4685
Parker HS 2,200/9-12
7301 Parker School Rd 32211 904-720-1650
Paige French, prin. Fax 720-1700
Paxon HS for Advanced Studies 1,600/9-12
3239 Norman E Thagard Blvd 32254 904-693-7583
Jim Williams, prin. Fax 693-7597
Paxon MS 900/6-8
3276 Norman E Thagard Blvd 32254 904-693-7600
Pam Pierce, prin. Fax 693-7661
Peterson Academy of Technology Vo/Tech
7450 Wilson Blvd 32210 904-573-1150
John Holechek, prin. Fax 573-3206
Raines HS 1,600/9-12
3663 Raines Ave 32209 904-924-3049
Carol Daniels, prin. Fax 924-3058
Randolph Academies of Technology Vo/Tech
1157 Golfair Blvd 32209 904-924-3011
Lorenda Tiscornia, prin. Fax 924-3125
Ribault HS 1,100/9-12
3701 Winton Dr 32208 904-924-3092
Stephen Schyck, prin. Fax 924-3154
Ribault MS 700/6-8
3610 Ribault Scenic Dr 32208 904-924-3062
George Maxey, prin. Fax 924-3167
Sandalwood HS 3,100/9-12
2750 John Prom Blvd 32246 904-646-5100
Victoria Schultz, prin. Fax 646-5126
Southside MS 1,100/6-8
2948 Knights Ln E 32216 904-739-5238
Mary Jeffrey, prin. Fax 739-5244
Stanton College Preparatory HS 1,500/9-12
1149 W 13th St 32209 904-630-6760
Jim Jaxon, prin. Fax 630-6758
Stilwell MS 1,300/6-8
7840 Burma Rd 32221 904-693-7523
Lawrence Dennis, prin. Fax 693-7539
Stuart MS 1,100/6-8
4815 Wesconnett Blvd 32210 904-573-1000
Jeanne Ballentine, prin. Fax 573-3213
Twin Lakes Academy 1,600/6-8
8050 Point Meadows Dr 32256 904-538-0825
Don Nelson, prin. Fax 538-0840
White HS 2,000/9-12
1700 Old Middleburg Rd N 32210 904-693-7620
James Clark, prin. Fax 693-7639
Wolfson HS 2,000/9-12
7000 Powers Ave 32217 904-739-5265
Hammond Gracey, prin. Fax 739-5272
Other Schools – See Atlantic Beach, Baldwin, Jacksonville Beach, Neptune Beach

St. John's County SD
Supt. — See Saint Augustine
Bartram Trail HS 2,100/9-12
2050 Roberts Rd 32259 904-287-6767
James Forson, prin. Fax 819-8345
Fruit Cove MS 900/6-8
3180 Race Track Rd 32259 904-287-2211
Clay Carmichael, prin. Fax 819-7885
Switzerland Point MS 1,000/6-8
777 Greenbriar Rd 32259 904-819-8650
Sue Sparkman, prin. Fax 819-8645

Arlington Country Day S 500/PK-12
5725 Fort Caroline Rd 32277 904-744-0466
Dr. Fred Lichtward, dir. Fax 744-0859
Baptist Medical Centers Post-Sec.
800 Prudential Dr 32207 904-393-2001
Baptist/St. Vincent's Health System Post-Sec.
1800 Barrs St 32204 904-387-7300
Bishop John J. Snyder HS 500/9-12
5001 Samaritan Way 32210 904-771-1029
David Yazdiya, prin. Fax 908-8988
Bishop Kenny HS 1,600/9-12
PO Box 5544 32247 904-398-7545
Todd Orlando, prin. Fax 398-5728
Bolles S 1,800/K-12
7400 San Jose Blvd 32217 904-733-9292
Dr. John E. Trainer, pres. Fax 739-9363
Bolles S - Bartrum Campus 400/6-8
2264 Bartram Rd 32207 904-724-8850
Richard Anderson, prin. Fax 724-8862
Broach S - Westside 200/1-12
440 Lenox Sq 32254 904-389-5106
Dr. Cheryl Wright, prin. Fax 388-1077
Cedar Creek Christian S 200/PK-12
1372 Lane Ave S 32205 904-781-9151
Jacquelyn Pitts, prin. Fax 781-9182
Concorde Career Institute Post-Sec.
7960 Arlington Expy 32211 904-725-0525
Coral Ridge Baptist S 50/1-12
2967 Huffman Blvd 32246 904-642-2726
Cornerstone Christian S 200/PK-12
4000 Spring Park Rd 32207 904-730-5500
Deborah Wagner, prin. Fax 730-5502
Eagle's View Academy 400/K-12
7788 Ramona Blvd W 32221 904-786-1411
Scott Kinlaw, admin. Fax 786-1445
Edward Waters College Post-Sec.
1658 Kings Rd 32209 904-355-3030
Episcopal HS 900/6-12
4455 Atlantic Blvd 32207 904-396-5751
Charles F. Zimmer, hdmstr. Fax 396-7209
Esprit De Corps Center for Learning 100/PK-12
9840 Wagner Rd 32219 904-924-2000
Betty White, prin. Fax 766-8870
Euro Hair Design Institute Post-Sec.
5995 University Blvd W #3 32216 904-731-4766
First Coast Academy 900/9-12
2725 College St 32205 904-381-1935
Barbara Cornelius, prin. Fax 381-0135
First Coast Christian S 600/PK-12
7587 Blanding Blvd 32244 904-777-3040
Morry Kemple, prin. Fax 777-3045
Florida Coastal School of Law Post-Sec.
7555 Beach Blvd 32216 904-680-7700
Florida Community College Post-Sec.
101 State St W 32202 904-633-8100
Florida Community College Post-Sec.
3939 Roosevelt Blvd 32205 904-381-3400
Florida Community College Post-Sec.
4501 Capper Rd 32218 904-766-6500
Florida Community College Post-Sec.
11901 Beach Blvd 32246 904-646-2111
Florida Technical College Post-Sec.
8711 Lone Star Rd 32211 904-724-2229
Global Impact Ministries Academy 100/PK-12
8550 Arlington Expy 32211 904-725-3750
Pamela Knopf, prin. Fax 398-0494
Greenwood S 200/1-12
9920 Regency Square Blvd 32225 904-726-5000
Beverly Connell, prin. Fax 726-5056
Hendricks Methodist Day S 300/PK-10
4000 Spring Park Rd 32207 904-720-0398
Sally Lott, dir. Fax 720-0435
Heritage Institute Post-Sec.
4130 Salisbury Rd Ste 1100 32216 904-332-0910
ITT Technical Institute Post-Sec.
6600 Youngerman Cir Ste 10 32244 904-573-9100
Jacksonville Adventist Academy 100/PK-12
4298 Livingston Rd 32257 904-268-2433
David Gardner, dir. Fax 268-7770
Jacksonville University Post-Sec.
2800 University Blvd N 32211 904-744-3950
Jones College Post-Sec.
5353 Arlington Expy 32211 904-743-1122
Little Country S 100/PK-12
862 Baisden Rd 32218 904-757-8200
Dr. Lola Jay, dir.
Mandarin Christian S 600/K-10
10850 Old St Augustine Rd 32257 904-268-8667
Pat Stuart, hdmstr. Fax 880-3251
Maxville Christian Academy 50/PK-12
9140 US Highway 301 S 32234 904-289-9727
Gail Bushbee, prin. Fax 289-9732
Normandy Beauty School of Jacksonville Post-Sec.
5373 Lenox Ave 32205 904-786-6250
Potters House Christian Academy 600/PK-12
5732 Normandy Blvd 32205 904-786-0028
Narlene McLaughlin, admin. Fax 695-2034
Providence Christian S 2,500/PK-12
2701 Hodges Blvd 32224 904-223-5270
Don Barfield, hdmstr. Fax 223-3028
Remington College Post-Sec.
7011 A C Sknnr Pky #140 32256 904-296-3435
Riverside Hairstyling Academy Post-Sec.
3530 Beach Blvd 32207 904-398-0502
St. Luke's Hospital/Mayo Clinic Post-Sec.
4201 Belfort Rd 32216 904-296-3733
Sanford-Brown Institute Post-Sec.
10255 Fortune Pkwy Ste 501 32256 904-363-6221
Seacoast Christian Academy 500/PK-12
9570 Regency Square Blvd 32225 904-725-5544
Marla Stremmel, admin. Fax 727-6748
Shands Jacksonville Medical Center Post-Sec.
655 W 8th St 32209 904-244-0411
Shekinah Christian Academy 200/K-12
10551 Beach Blvd 32246 904-421-1015
Saundra Armour, prin. Fax 421-1022
Southeastern School of Neuromuscular Post-Sec.
9424 Baymeadows Rd Ste 200 32256 904-448-9499
Stenotype Inst. Court Reporting School Post-Sec.
3986 Blvd Center Dr #200 32207 904-246-7466
Success Academy 200/PK-12
2103 Grand St 32208 904-766-6212
Marian Williams-Johnson, admin. Fax 768-5013
Trinity Baptist College Post-Sec.
800 Hammond Blvd 32221 904-596-2400
Trinity Christian Academy 1,700/PK-12
800 Hammond Blvd 32221 904-596-2400
Clayton Lindstam, admin. Fax 596-2531
Tulsa Welding School Post-Sec.
3500 Southside Blvd 32216 904-646-9353
University Christian S 900/PK-12
5520 University Blvd W 32216 904-737-6330
Richard L. Spain, dir. Fax 737-3359
University of North Florida Post-Sec.
4567 Saint Johns Bluff Rd S 32224 904-620-1000
Victory Christian Academy 300/PK-12
10613 Lem Turner Rd 32218 904-764-7781
Jan Van Delinder, dir. Fax 764-7297
West Meadows Baptist Academy 100/K-12
11711 Normandy Blvd 32221 904-786-9308
Dr. Bruce Armstrong, admin. Fax 786-2712

Jacksonville Beach, Duval, Pop. 21,339
Duval County SD
Supt. — See Jacksonville
Fletcher MS 1,400/6-8
2000 3rd St N 32250 904-247-5929
Jill Budd, prin. Fax 247-5940

Foundation Academy 200/K-12
107 3rd Ave S 32250 904-241-3515
Nadia Hionides, prin. Fax 241-9857

Jasper, Hamilton, Pop. 1,825
Hamilton County SD 2,000/PK-12
4280 SW County Road 152 32052 386-792-1228
Harry Pennington, supt. Fax 792-3681
www.firn.edu/schools/hamilton/hamilton/
Hamilton County HS 800/7-12
5683 US Highway 129 S 32052 386-792-6540
Gene Starr, prin. Fax 792-6594
Hamilton Vo-Tech Center Vo/Tech
4280 SW County Road 152 32052 386-792-6529
Rex Mitchell, prin. Fax 792-6623

Jay, Santa Rosa, Pop. 635
Santa Rosa County SD
Supt. — See Milton
Jay JSHS 500/7-12
13863 Alabama St 32565 850-675-4507
Dale Westmoreland, prin. Fax 675-8573

Jensen Beach, Martin, Pop. 9,884
Martin County SD
Supt. — See Stuart
Jensen Beach HS 9-12
2875 NW Goldenrod Rd 34957 772-232-3500
Ginger Featherstone, prin. Fax 232-3699

Trinity United Methodist S 100/PK-12
2221 NE Savannah Rd 34957 772-334-4828
Diana Weber, prin. Fax 334-7834

Juno Beach, Palm Beach, Pop. 3,347

Batt Private S 100/PK-12
13205 US Highway 1 Ste 211 33408 561-630-9980
Vicki Griswold, dir. Fax 624-4632

Jupiter, Palm Beach, Pop. 45,100
Palm Beach County SD
Supt. — See West Palm Beach
Independence MS 1,300/6-8
4001 Greenway Dr 33458 561-799-7500
Gwendolyn Johnson, prin. Fax 799-7505
Jupiter Community HS 2,300/9-12
500 Military Trl 33458 561-744-7900
Paula Nessmith, prin. Fax 744-7978
Jupiter MS 1,000/6-8
15245 Military Trl 33458 561-745-7200
Butch Mondy, prin. Fax 745-7246
Jupiter Community HS Adult
500 Military Trl 33458 561-744-7931
Paula Nessmith, prin. Fax 744-7978

Jupiter Christian S 600/PK-12
1300 Mohawk St 33458 561-746-7800
Leslie Downs, pres. Fax 748-9528

Key Biscayne, Dade, Pop. 10,319
Miami-Dade County SD
Supt. — See Miami
MAST Academy 600/9-12
3979 Rickenbacker Cswy 33149 305-365-6278
Dr. Consuelo Dominguez, prin. Fax 361-0996

Keystone Heights, Clay, Pop. 1,384
Clay County SD
Supt. — See Green Cove Springs
Keystone Heights JSHS 1,300/7-12
900 Orchid Ave 32656 352-473-2761
Dr. Susan Sailor, prin. Fax 473-5920

Key West, Monroe, Pop. 25,031
Monroe County SD 8,800/PK-12
PO Box 1788 33041 305-293-1400
Randy Acevedo, supt. Fax 293-1408
www.keysschools.com
Key West HS 1,400/9-12
2100 Flagler Ave 33040 305-293-1549
John Welsh, prin. Fax 293-1547
O'Bryant MS 800/6-8
1105 Leon St 33040 305-296-5628
Frank Spoto, prin. Fax 293-1644
Other Schools – See Marathon, Tavernier

Florida Keys Community College Post-Sec.
5901 College Rd 33040 305-296-9081

Kissimmee, Osceola, Pop. 54,598
Osceola County SD 39,000/PK-12
817 Bill Beck Blvd 34744 407-870-4600
Blaine A. Muse, supt. Fax 870-4010
www.osceola.k12.fl.us
Celebration HS 1,500/9-12
1809 Celebration Blvd 34747 321-939-6600
Dan White, prin. Fax 939-6652
Denn John MS 1,300/6-8
2001 Denn John Ln 34744 407-935-3560
Rob Paswaters, prin. Fax 935-3572
Discovery IS 1,400/6-8
5350 San Miguel Rd 34758 407-343-7300
Annette Campbell, prin. Fax 343-7310
Gateway HS 2,700/9-12
93 Panther Paws Trl 34744 407-935-3600
Terry Andrews, prin. Fax 935-3609
Horizon MS 1,200/6-8
2020 Ham Brown Rd 34746 407-943-7240
Michael Allen, prin. Fax 943-7250
Kissimmee MS 1,200/6-8
2410 Dyer Blvd 34741 407-870-0857
Paula Evans, prin. Fax 870-5669
Neptune MS 1,600/6-8
2727 Neptune Rd 34744 407-935-3500
Judy Zieg, prin. Fax 935-3519
Osceola County S for the Arts 500/6-12
3151 N Orange Blossom Trl 34744 407-931-4803
Michael Vondracek, prin. Fax 931-3019
Osceola HS 2,400/9-12
420 S Thacker Ave 34741 407-518-5400
Charles Paradiso, prin. Fax 943-7909
Parkway MS 1,200/6-8
857 Florida Pkwy 34743 407-344-7000
Jeannette Paul-Rivers, prin. Fax 348-2797
PATHS @ TECO Vo/Tech
501 Simpson Rd 34744 407-344-5080
Laura Rhinehart, dir. Fax 344-2467
Poinciana HS 2,100/9-12
2300 S Poinciana Blvd 34758 407-870-4860
George Sullivan, prin. Fax 870-0382
Technical Education Center Vo/Tech
501 Simpson Rd 34744 407-344-5080
Laura Rhinehart, dir. Fax 344-5089
Adult Learning Center Adult
705 Simpson Rd 34744 407-518-8140
Dave Welty, dir. Fax 518-8141
Other Schools – See Saint Cloud

Florida Christian College Post-Sec.
1011 Bill Beck Blvd 34744 407-847-8966
Heartland Christian Academy 300/PK-12
2874 E Irlo Bronson Mem Hwy 34744 407-847-5184
Kathy Harkema, prin. Fax 870-2679
Heritage Christian S 600/K-12
1500 E Vine St 34744 407-847-4087
Karla Beever, admin. Fax 932-2806
Life Assembly of God Life Academy 200/K-12
2269 Partin Settlement Rd 34744 407-847-8222
Margaret Olmo, prin. Fax 932-4431
North Kissimmee Christian S 200/PK-12
425 W Donegan Ave 34741 407-847-2877
Yvonne Johnson, prin. Fax 847-5372
Pleasant Hill Academy 100/PK-12
PO Box 453536 34745 407-518-0002
Carmen Caban-Ruiz, prin. Fax 518-0032
Technical Education Center - Osceola Post-Sec.
501 Simpson Rd 34744 407-344-5080

La Belle, Hendry, Pop. 3,302
Hendry County SD — 7,500/PK-12
PO Box 1980 33975 — 863-674-4550
Thomas Conner, supt. — Fax 674-4090
www.hendry-schools.org
La Belle HS — 1,000/9-12
4050 E Cowboy Way 33935 — 863-674-4120
Daniel Gilbertson, prin. — Fax 674-4571
La Belle MS — 900/6-8
8000 E Cowboy Way 33935 — 863-674-4646
Teresa Baker, prin. — Fax 674-4645
Labelle Community Adult S — Adult
PO Box 2738, — 863-674-4118
James Way, prin. — Fax 674-4117
Other Schools – See Clewiston

Lake Alfred, Polk, Pop. 3,924
Polk County SD
Supt. — See Bartow
Addair Career Academy — Vo/Tech
925 N Buena Vista Dr 33850 — 863-295-5988
Asonja Cross, prin. — Fax 295-5989

Lake Butler, Union, Pop. 1,986
Union County SD — 2,100/PK-12
55 SW 6th St 32054 — 386-496-2045
Carlton Faulk, supt. — Fax 496-2580
www.union.k12.fl.us/
Lake Butler MS — 700/5-8
150 SW 6th St 32054 — 386-496-3046
Mark Bracewell, prin. — Fax 496-4352
Union County HS — 600/9-12
1000 S Lake Ave 32054 — 386-496-3040
Gale Lappalainen, prin. — Fax 496-4187
Union County Adult HS — Adult
208 SE 6th St 32054 — 386-496-1300
Barry Sams, prin.

Lake City, Columbia, Pop. 10,471
Columbia County SD — 9,600/PK-12
372 W Duval St 32055 — 386-755-8000
Grady D. Markham, supt. — Fax 755-8029
www.columbia.k12.fl.us
Columbia HS — 1,800/9-12
469 SE Fighting Tiger Dr 32025 — 386-755-8080
Terry Huddleston, prin. — Fax 755-8082
Lake City MS — 1,100/6-8
843 SW Arlington Blvd 32025 — 386-758-4800
Tom Dorsett, prin. — Fax 758-4839
Richardson MS — 700/6-8
646 SE Pennsylvania St 32025 — 386-755-8130
Keith Couey, prin. — Fax 755-8154
Vocational Adult & Community Education — Vo/Tech
409 SW St Johns St 32025 — 386-755-8190
Melvin Goggins, prin.
Other Schools – See Fort White

Lake City Christian Academy — 200/K-12
3035 SW Pinemount Rd 32024 — 386-758-0055
Tana Espenship, prin. — Fax 758-3018
Lake City Community College — Post-Sec.
149 SE College Pl 32025 — 386-752-1822

Lakeland, Polk, Pop. 87,860
Polk County SD
Supt. — See Bartow
Chiles MS Academy — 600/6-8
400 N Florida Ave 33801 — 863-499-2742
Sharon Neuman, prin. — Fax 499-2774
Crystal Lake MS — 1,000/6-8
2410 N Crystal Lake Dr 33801 — 863-499-2970
Christopher Canning, prin. — Fax 603-6267
Jenkins HS — 2,100/9-12
6000 Lakeland Highlands Rd 33813 — 863-648-3566
Buddy Thomas, prin. — Fax 648-3573
Kathleen HS — 1,500/9-12
2600 Crutchfield Rd 33805 — 863-499-2655
Cecil McClellan, prin. — Fax 499-2726
Kathleen MS — 800/6-8
3627 Kathleen Pnes 33810 — 863-853-6040
Sam Wright, prin. — Fax 853-6037
Lake Gibson HS — 1,700/9-12
7007 N Socrum Loop Rd 33809 — 863-853-6100
Ralph Gilchrest, prin. — Fax 853-6108
Lake Gibson MS — 1,100/6-8
6901 N Socrum Loop Rd 33809 — 863-853-6181
John Barber, prin. — Fax 853-6171
Lakeland Highlands MS — 1,100/6-8
740 Lake Miriam Dr 33813 — 863-648-3500
Robert Hartley, prin. — Fax 648-3580
Lakeland HS — 2,000/9-12
726 Hollingsworth Rd 33801 — 863-499-2900
Mark Thomas, prin. — Fax 499-2917
Sleepy Hill MS — 1,000/6-8
2115 Sleepy Hill Rd 33810 — 863-815-6577
Lee Brackman, prin. — Fax 815-6586
Southwest MS — 1,000/6-8
2815 Eden Pkwy 33803 — 863-499-2840
John Wilson, prin. — Fax 499-2762
Traviss Technical Center — Vo/Tech
3225 Winter Lake Rd 33803 — 863-499-2700
Kenneth James, prin. — Fax 499-2706
West Area Adult & Community S — Adult
604 S Central Ave 33815 — 863-499-2835
Loretta Cameron, prin. — Fax 499-2727

Families of Faith Cristian Academy — 800/K-12
1248 George Jenkins Blvd 33815 — 863-686-7755
James Lawson, prin. — Fax 686-7086
FL Metropolitan Univ. - Lakeland — Post-Sec.
995 E Memorial Blvd Ste 110 33801 — 863-686-1444
Florida Southern College — Post-Sec.
111 Lake Hollingsworth Dr 33801 — 863-680-4111
Geneva Classical Academy — 100/PK-10
4410 E County Road 540A 33813 — 863-644-1408
Tim Bullock, prin. — Fax 619-5841
Highlands Christian Academy — 100/PK-12
4210 Lakeland Highlands Rd 33813 — 863-646-5031
Robert Wamsley, admin. — Fax 646-2267
Keiser College — Post-Sec.
3515 Aviation Dr 33811 — 863-701-7789
Lakeland Christian S — 1,000/K-12
1111 Forest Park St 33803 — 863-688-2771
Michael Sligh, hdmstr. — Fax 682-5637
Lakeland Regional Medical Center — Post-Sec.
1324 Lakeland Hills Blvd 33805 — 863-687-1100
New Jerusalem Christian Academy — 100/PK-10
1129 N Missouri Ave 33805 — 863-683-0414
Jimmie Downing, prin. — Fax 683-0495
Santa Fe Catholic HS — 200/9-12
3110 US Highway 92 E 33801 — 863-665-4188
Glenda Pierce, prin. — Fax 665-4151

Sonrise Christian S — 200/PK-12
3151 Hardin Combee Rd 33801 — 863-665-4187
Donna Ready, dir. — Fax 665-6065
Southeastern University — Post-Sec.
1000 Longfellow Blvd 33801 — 863-667-5000
Traviss Technical Center — Post-Sec.
3225 Winter Lake Rd 33803 — 863-499-2700

Lake Mary, Seminole, Pop. 13,260
Seminole County SD
Supt. — See Sanford
Greenwood Lakes MS — 1,600/6-8
601 Lake Park Dr 32746 — 407-320-7650
Kate Eglof, prin. — Fax 320-7699
Lake Mary HS — 2,800/9-12
655 Longwood Lake Mary Rd 32746 — 407-320-9550
Boyd Karns, prin. — Fax 320-9512

ITT Technical Institute — Post-Sec.
1400 S International Pkwy 32746 — 407-660-2900
Lake Mary Preparatory S — 600/PK-12
650 Rantoul Ln 32746 — 407-805-0095
Dr. Pounrh Alcott, prin. — Fax 322-3872

Lake Placid, Highlands, Pop. 1,714
Highlands County SD
Supt. — See Sebring
Lake Placid HS — 800/9-12
202 Green Dragon Dr 33852 — 863-699-5010
Ruth Heckman, prin. — Fax 699-5094
Lake Placid MS — 600/6-8
201 S Tangerine Dr 33852 — 863-699-5030
Derrel Bryan, prin. — Fax 699-5029

Lake Wales, Polk, Pop. 11,194
Polk County SD
Supt. — See Bartow
Lake Wales HS — 1,400/9-12
1 Highlander Way 33853 — 863-678-4222
Clark Berry, prin. — Fax 678-4064
McLaughlin MS — 900/6-8
800 S 4th St 33853 — 863-678-4233
Sharon Kurschner, prin. — Fax 678-4033
Roosevelt Academy — 300/6-12
115 E St 33853 — 863-678-4252
Ron Rizer, prin. — Fax 678-4250

Vanguard S — 100/5-12
22000 Hwy 27 33859 — 863-676-6091
James R. Moon Ph.D., dir. — Fax 676-8297
Warner Southern College — Post-Sec.
5301 US Highway 27 S 33859 — 863-638-1426

Lake Worth, Palm Beach, Pop. 35,612
Palm Beach County SD
Supt. — See West Palm Beach
Lake Worth Community HS — 3,200/9-12
1701 Lake Worth Rd 33460 — 561-533-6300
Anna Meehan, prin. — Fax 533-6334
Lake Worth MS — 1,500/6-8
1300 Barnett Dr 33461 — 561-540-5500
Robert Hatcher, prin. — Fax 540-5559
Park Vista Community HS — 9-12
7900 Jog Rd 33467 — 561-491-8400
Nora Rosensweig, prin. — Fax 493-6854
Tradewinds MS — 6-8
5090 Haverhill Rd 33463 — 561-493-6400
Kathleen Orloff, prin. — Fax 493-6410
Woodlands MS — 1,800/6-8
5200 Lyons Rd 33467 — 561-357-0300
May Gamble, prin. — Fax 357-0307
Lake Worth Community HS — Adult
1701 Lake Worth Rd 33460 — 561-533-6363
Rick Swearingen, prin. — Fax 533-6334

Academy of Healing Arts Massage — Post-Sec.
3141 S Military Trl 33463 — 561-965-4686
Cornerstone Academy — 100/PK-12
6863 S Congress Ave 33462 — 561-968-9633
Dr. Rex Allen, prin. — Fax 968-1110
Medical Career Institute South Florida — Post-Sec.
802 S Dixie Hwy 33460 — 561-493-5022
Palm Beach Community College — Post-Sec.
4200 S Congress Ave 33461 — 561-439-8000
Trinity Christian Academy — 700/PK-12
7259 S Military Trl 33463 — 561-967-1900
Cindy Ansell, prin. — Fax 965-4347

Land O Lakes, Pasco, Pop. 7,892
Pasco County SD — 53,700/PK-12
7227 Land O Lakes Blvd 34638 — 813-794-2000
Heather Fiorentino Ph.D., supt. — Fax 794-2716
www.pasco.k12.fl.us
Land O'Lakes HS — 2,000/9-12
20325 Gator Ln, — 813-794-9400
Ray Bonti, prin. — Fax 794-9491
Pine View MS — 1,600/6-8
5334 Parkway Blvd 34639 — 813-794-4800
David Estabrook, prin. — Fax 794-4891
Other Schools – See Dade City, Hudson, New Port Richey, Port Richey, Wesley Chapel, Zephyrhills

Academy at the Lakes — 300/PK-12
2220 Collier Pkwy 34639 — 813-948-2133
Richard J. Wendlek, hdmstr. — Fax 948-2943
Land O'Lakes Christian S — 200/PK-12
5105 School Rd, — 813-995-9040
Denise Smith, dir. — Fax 996-9742

Lantana, Palm Beach, Pop. 9,665
Palm Beach County SD
Supt. — See West Palm Beach
Lantana Community MS — 1,000/6-8
1225 W Drew St 33462 — 561-540-3400
Ann Clark, prin. — Fax 540-3435
Santaluces Community HS — 3,100/9-12
6880 Lawrence Rd 33462 — 561-642-6200
Glenn Heyward, prin. — Fax 642-6255
Lantana Community MS — Adult
1225 W Drew St 33462 — 561-533-6382
Richard Valentine, prin. — Fax 533-6414
Santaluces Community HS — Adult
6880 Lawrence Rd 33462 — 561-642-6212
Frank Fiedor, prin. — Fax 642-6255

Largo, Pinellas, Pop. 71,166
Pinellas County SD — 110,600/PK-12
PO Box 2942 33779 — 727-588-1818
Dr. Clayton Wilcox, supt. — Fax 588-6200
www.pinellas.k12.fl.us

Fitzgerald MS — 1,300/6-8
6410 118th Ave 33773 — 727-547-4526
Bill Corbett, prin. — Fax 547-4530
Largo HS — 2,200/9-12
410 Missouri Ave N 33770 — 727-588-3758
Jeffrey Haynes, prin. — Fax 588-4037
Largo MS — 1,400/6-8
155 8th Ave SE 33771 — 727-588-4600
Fred Ulrich, prin. — Fax 588-3720
Pinellas Park HS — 2,300/9-12
6305 118th Ave 33773 — 727-538-7410
Denise Hart, prin. — Fax 507-6174
Other Schools – See Clearwater, Dunedin, Gulfport, Madeira Beach, Palm Harbor, Pinellas Park, Safety Harbor, Saint Petersburg, Seminole, Tarpon Springs

Indian Rocks Christian S — 1,000/PK-12
12685 Ulmerton Rd 33774 — 727-596-4321
Don Mayes, supt. — Fax 593-5485
Lighthouse Christian Academy — 400/K-12
8200 Bryan Dairy Rd 33777 — 727-319-0700
Glen Aulgur, prin. — Fax 289-0405
Remington College — Post-Sec.
8550 Ulmerton Rd Ste 100 33771 — 727-532-1999
Westside Christian S — 100/K-12
13650 Walsingham Rd 33774 — 727-517-2153
Dr. Jerry Forrester, admin. — Fax 593-7700

Lauderdale Lakes, Broward, Pop. 31,571
Broward County SD
Supt. — See Fort Lauderdale
Anderson HS — 2,700/9-12
3050 NW 41st St 33309 — 754-322-0200
Dr. Timothy Gadson, prin. — Fax 322-0330
Lauderdale Lakes MS — 1,000/6-8
3911 NW 30th Ave 33309 — 754-322-3500
Martin Reid, prin. — Fax 322-3585

Concorde Career Institute — Post-Sec.
4000 N State Rd 7 33319 — 954-731-8880
Hope Career Institute — Post-Sec.
3714 W Oakland Park Blvd 33311 — 954-741-0088
Sanford Brown Institute — Post-Sec.
4780 N State Rd 7 #100 33319 — 954-733-8900
The School of Health Careers — Post-Sec.
3190 N State Road 7 33319 — 954-777-0083

Lauderhill, Broward, Pop. 59,096
Broward County SD
Supt. — See Fort Lauderdale
Lauderhill MS — 1,100/6-8
1901 NW 49th Ave 33313 — 754-322-3600
Phillip Patton, prin. — Fax 322-3685

Upperroom Christian Academy — 300/K-12
3944 NW 19th St 33311 — 954-730-9697
Pastor Jimmie Butler, prin. — Fax 730-8206

Laurel Hill, Okaloosa, Pop. 570
Okaloosa County SD
Supt. — See Fort Walton Beach
Laurel Hill S — 400/PK-12
8078 4th St 32567 — 850-652-4111
Rodney Nobles, prin. — Fax 652-4659

Lecanto, Citrus, Pop. 1,243
Citrus County SD
Supt. — See Inverness
Lecanto HS — 1,600/9-12
3810 W Educational Path 34461 — 352-746-2334
Kelly Tyler, prin. — Fax 746-1675
Lecanto MS — 800/6-8
3800 W Educational Path 34461 — 352-746-2050
James Kusmaul, prin. — Fax 746-3639

Seven Rivers Christian S — 400/PK-12
4221 W Gulf to Lake Hwy 34461 — 352-746-5696
Joel Satterly, hdmstr. — Fax 746-5520

Leesburg, Lake, Pop. 17,216
Lake County SD
Supt. — See Tavares
Carver MS — 800/6-8
1200 Beecher St 34748 — 352-787-7868
Linda Shepherd, prin. — Fax 787-1339
Leesburg HS — 1,800/9-12
1401 W Meadows Ave 34748 — 352-787-5224
Nancy Velez, prin.
Oak Park MS — 700/6-8
2101 South St 34748 — 352-787-3232
Sue Mullen, prin. — Fax 326-2177

Beacon College — Post-Sec.
105 E Main St 34748 — 352-787-7660
First Academy — 400/K-12
219 N 13th St 34748 — 352-787-7762
Gregory Frescoln, admin. — Fax 323-1773
Lake-Sumter Community College — Post-Sec.
9501 US Highway 441 34788 — 352-787-3747

Lehigh Acres, Lee, Pop. 13,611
Lee County SD
Supt. — See Fort Myers
East Lee County HS — 9-12
1200 Homestead Rd N 33936 — 239-369-2932
Merle Winder, prin. — Fax 369-3213
Lehigh Acres MS — 1,300/6-8
104 Arthur Ave 33936 — 239-369-6108
Ray Bowers, prin. — Fax 369-8808
Lehigh HS — 1,900/9-12
901 Gunnery Rd N 33971 — 239-693-5353
Peter Bohatch, prin. — Fax 693-6702
Varsity Lakes MS — 6-8
801 Gunnery Rd N 33971 — 239-694-3464
Ron Davis, prin. — Fax 694-7093

Dayspring Independent S — 50/K-12
101 Xelda Ave N 33971 — 239-369-5008
Robert Wiedeman, admin.

Leisure City, Dade, Pop. 19,379
Miami-Dade County SD
Supt. — See Miami
South Dade Skill Ctr — Vo/Tech
28300 SW 152nd Ave 33033 — 305-247-7839
Evelyn Davis, prin. — Fax 247-2375

Lithia, Hillsborough
Hillsborough County SD
Supt. — See Tampa

Newsome HS 1,100/9-12
16550 Fishhawk Blvd 33547 813-740-4600
Rebecca Anderson, prin. Fax 740-4604
Randall MS 1,100/6-8
16510 Fishhawk Blvd 33547 813-740-3900
Marcia Elliott, prin. Fax 740-3910

Live Oak, Suwannee, Pop. 6,670
Suwannee County SD 5,900/PK-12
702 2nd St NW 32064 386-364-2601
Walter Boatright, supt. Fax 364-2635
www.suwannee.k12.fl.us
Suwannee-Hamilton Technical Ctr Vo/Tech
415 Pinewood Dr SW 32064 386-364-2750
Dianne Westcott, prin. Fax 364-4698
Suwannee HS 1,200/9-12
1314 Pine Ave SW 32064 386-364-2639
Dawn Lamb, prin. Fax 364-2794
Suwannee MS 1,100/6-8
1730 Walker Ave SW 32064 386-364-2730
Norri Steele, prin. Fax 208-1474
Other Schools – See Branford

Melody Christian Academy 200/PK-12
PO Box 1448 32064 386-364-4800
Amanda Davis, dir. Fax 364-1889
Suwannee-Hamilton Technical Center Post-Sec.
415 Pinewood Dr SW 32064 386-364-2750

Longwood, Seminole, Pop. 13,674
Seminole County SD
Supt. — See Sanford
Lyman HS 2,400/9-12
865 S Ronald Reagan Blvd 32750 407-320-2050
Frank Casillo, prin. Fax 320-2024
Milwee MS 1,200/6-8
1341 S Ronald Reagan Blvd 32750 407-320-3850
Lois Chavis, prin. Fax 320-3899
Rock Lake MS 1,200/6-8
250 Slade Dr 32750 407-320-9350
Michelle Clopton, prin. Fax 320-9399

PACE - Brantley Hall S 100/1-11
3221 Sand Lake Rd 32779 407-869-8882
Kathleen Shatlock, prin. Fax 869-8717

Loxahatchee, Palm Beach
Palm Beach County SD
Supt. — See West Palm Beach
Osceola Creek MS 6-8
6775 180th Ave N 33470 561-422-2500
Susan Atherley, prin. Fax 422-2510
Seminole Ridge Community HS 9-12
4601 Seminole Pratt Whitney 33470 561-422-2600
Lynne McGee, prin. Fax 422-2623

Family Tree Private S 200/PK-12
17626 94th St N 33470 561-721-3683
Nancy Moral, prin. Fax 383-6956

Lutz, Hillsborough, Pop. 10,552
Hillsborough County SD
Supt. — See Tampa
Martinez MS 900/6-8
5601 W Lutz Lake Fern Rd 33558 813-558-1190
Kathleen A. Flanagan, prin. Fax 558-1226

Lynn Haven, Bay, Pop. 14,238
Bay County SD
Supt. — See Panama City
Mosley HS 2,200/9-12
501 Mosley Dr 32444 850-872-4400
Bill Husfelt, prin. Fax 872-7528
Mowat MS 900/6-8
1903 W Highway 390 32444 850-271-6140
Shirley Baker, prin. Fax 265-2179

Macclenny, Baker, Pop. 4,838
Baker County SD 4,100/PK-12
392 South Blvd E 32063 904-259-6251
Paula Barton, supt. Fax 259-2825
www.baker.k12.fl.us
Baker County MS 1,100/6-8
211 E Jonathan St 32063 904-259-2226
David Davis, prin. Fax 259-7955
Baker County Adult Center Adult
270 South Blvd E 32063 904-259-6251
Dr. Garlon Webb, prin. Fax 259-2825
Other Schools – See Glen Saint Mary

Madeira Beach, Pinellas, Pop. 4,459
Pinellas County SD
Supt. — See Largo
Madeira Beach MS 1,100/6-8
591 Madeira Beach Cswy 33708 727-547-7697
Brenda Poff, prin. Fax 547-7528

Madison, Madison, Pop. 3,140
Madison County SD 3,000/PK-12
210 NE Duval Ave 32340 850-973-5022
Lou Miller, supt. Fax 973-5027
www.madison.k12.fl.us
Madison County HS 800/9-12
2649 W Us 90 32340 850-973-5061
Ben Killingsworth, prin. Fax 973-5066

North Florida Community College Post-Sec.
1000 Turner Davis Dr 32340 850-973-2288

Maitland, Orange, Pop. 11,857
Orange County SD
Supt. — See Orlando
Maitland MS 1,200/6-8
1901 Choctaw Trl 32751 407-623-1462
Dr. Cathy Thornton, prin. Fax 623-1474

Florida College of Natural Health Post-Sec.
2600 Lake Lucien Dr Ste 140 32751 407-261-0319
Orangewood Christian S 600/PK-12
1221 Trinity Woods Ln 32751 407-339-0223
LuAnne Schendel, hdmstr. Fax 339-4148

Malone, Jackson, Pop. 1,666
Jackson County SD
Supt. — See Marianna
Malone S 600/PK-12
PO Box 68 32445 850-482-9950
Linda Hall, prin. Fax 482-9981

Marathon, Monroe, Pop. 10,143
Monroe County SD
Supt. — See Key West
Marathon HS 700/7-12
350 Sombrero Beach Rd 33050 305-289-2480
Dr. John Pertner, prin. Fax 289-2486

Margate, Broward, Pop. 54,954
Broward County SD
Supt. — See Fort Lauderdale
Margate MS 1,300/6-8
500 NW 65th Ave 33063 754-322-3800
Bettye Brown, prin. Fax 322-3885

Atlantic Technical Center Post-Sec.
4700 Coconut Creek Pkwy 33063 954-977-2000
Faith Christian S 300/PK-12
6950 Royal Palm Blvd 33063 954-974-2404
Dan Riley, dir. Fax 974-0139
Margate School of Beauty Post-Sec.
5281 Coconut Creek Pkwy 33063 954-972-9630

Marianna, Jackson, Pop. 6,112
Jackson County SD 6,900/PK-12
PO Box 5958 32447 850-482-1200
Daniel Sims, supt. Fax 482-1299
web.jcsb.org
Academy at Marianna HS Vo/Tech
3546 Caverns Rd 32446 850-482-9666
James Sims, prin. Fax 482-9800
Marianna HS 700/9-12
3546 Caverns Rd 32446 850-482-9605
Randy Ward, prin. Fax 482-1247
Marianna MS 700/6-8
4144 South St 32448 850-482-9609
Dr. Gayle Westbrook, prin. Fax 482-9795
Marianna Adult Center Adult
2971 Guyton St 32446 850-482-9617
Durrance Britt, admin. Fax 482-1201
Other Schools – See Cottondale, Graceville, Grand Ridge, Malone, Sneads

Chipola College Post-Sec.
3094 Indian Cir 32446 850-526-2761
Masters Academy of NW FL 50/PK-12
PO Box 6302 32447 850-482-3828
Anna Lopez-Wooden, admin. Fax 482-6984

Mayo, Lafayette, Pop. 1,013
LaFayette County SD 1,100/PK-12
363 NE Crawford St 32066 386-294-1351
Fredric Ward, supt. Fax 294-3072
hornet.lafayette.k12.fl.us
LaFayette JSHS 500/6-12
160 NE Hornet Ln 32066 386-294-1701
Derek Hembree, prin. Fax 294-4197
Adult Education Adult
363 NE Crawford St 32066 386-294-4120
Debra Land, prin. Fax 294-3072

Melbourne, Brevard, Pop. 74,545
Brevard County SD 71,200/PK-12
2700 Jdge Fran Jamieson Way 32940 321-633-1000
Dr. Richard DiPatri, supt. Fax 633-3432
www.brevard.k12.fl.us
Eau Gallie HS 2,300/9-12
1400 Commodore Blvd 32935 321-242-6400
Thomas Sawyer, prin. Fax 242-6427
Johnson MS 1,100/7-8
2155 Croton Rd 32935 321-242-6430
Robert Fish, prin. Fax 242-6436
Melbourne SHS 1,600/10-12
74 Bulldog Blvd 32901 321-952-5880
James Willcoxon, prin. Fax 952-5898
Palm Bay HS 2,400/9-12
101 Pirate Ln 32901 321-952-5900
John Thomas, prin. Fax 676-2891
Stone MS 800/7-8
1101 E University Blvd 32901 321-723-0741
Andrew Johnson, prin. Fax 951-1497
West Shore JSHS 900/7-12
250 W Brevard Dr 32935 321-242-4730
Cynthia Van Meter, prin. Fax 242-4740
South Area Adult/Community Educ. Ctr. Adult
1362 S Babcock St 32901 321-952-5977
Fax 952-5831
Other Schools – See Cocoa, Cocoa Beach, Indialantic, Merritt Island, Palm Bay, Rockledge, Satellite Beach, Titusville, West Melbourne

Community Christian S 100/PK-12
1616 Ferndale Ave 32935 321-259-1590
Laurel Earls, prin. Fax 259-5301
Florida Air Academy 500/6-12
1950 Academy Dr 32901 321-723-3211
Antiny White, prin. Fax 676-0422
Florida Institute of Technology Post-Sec.
150 W University Blvd 32901 321-674-8000
FL Metropolitan Univ. - Melbourne Campus Post-Sec.
2401 N Harbor City Blvd 32935 321-253-2929
Holy Trinity Episcopal Academy 900/PK-12
5625 Holy Trinity Dr 32940 321-723-8323
Catherine Ford, hdmstr. Fax 308-9077
Keiser College Post-Sec.
900 S Babcock St 32901 321-255-2255
Melbourne Beauty School Post-Sec.
686 N Wickham Rd 32935 321-259-0001
Melbourne Central Catholic HS 700/9-12
100 E Florida Ave 32901 321-727-0793
Sue Rauch, prin. Fax 727-0798
New Covenant Christian S 100/K-12
4028 S Babcock St 32901 321-724-9603
Sandra Hancock, prin. Fax 952-8218
Wade Christian Academy 100/K-12
4300 N Wickham Rd 32935 321-259-6788
Jack Snyder, prin. Fax 259-0399
West Melbourne Christian Academy 200/PK-12
3150 Milwaukee Ave 32904 321-725-3743
Pastor Kerry Siler, prin. Fax 725-4813

Merritt Island, Brevard, Pop. 36,800
Brevard County SD
Supt. — See Melbourne
Edgewood JSHS 1,300/7-12
180 E Merritt Ave 32953 321-454-1030
Kenneth Winn, prin. Fax 452-1176
Jefferson MS 600/7-8
1275 S Courtenay Pkwy 32952 321-453-5154
Eric Fleming, prin. Fax 459-2854
Merritt Island HS 1,800/9-12
100 Mustang Way 32953 321-454-1000
Gary Shiffrin, prin. Fax 454-1014

Advanced/Basic Hair Design Training Ctr Post-Sec.
85 Richland Ave 32953 321-452-8490
Merritt Island Christian S 700/PK-12
140 Magnolia Ave 32952 321-453-2710
Chris Harmon, hdmstr. Fax 452-6580

Miami, Dade, Pop. 376,815
Miami-Dade County SD 354,700/PK-12
1450 NE 2nd Ave 33132 305-995-1000
Dr. Rudolph F. Crew, supt. Fax 995-1488
www.dadeschools.net/
Allapattah MS 1,300/6-8
1331 NW 46th St 33142 305-634-9787
Brian Hamilton, prin. Fax 638-8254
Ammons MS 1,100/6-8
17990 SW 142nd Ave 33177 305-971-0158
Irwin Adler, prin. Fax 971-0179
Arvida MS 1,900/6-8
10900 SW 127th Ave 33186 305-385-7144
Herbert Koross, prin. Fax 383-9472
Baker Aviation S Vo/Tech
3275 NW 42nd Ave 33142 305-871-3143
Ruby B. Jones, prin. Fax 871-5840
Bell MS 1,600/6-8
11800 NW 2nd St 33182 305-220-2075
Ingrid Soto, prin. Fax 229-0798
Braddock HS 4,900/8-12
3601 SW 147th Ave 33185 305-225-9729
Manuel S. Garcia, prin. Fax 221-3312
Brownsville MS 1,300/7-9
4899 NW 24th Ave 33142 305-633-1481
Guillermo Munoz, prin. Fax 635-8702
Centennial MS 1,100/6-8
8601 SW 212th St 33189 305-235-1581
Elvoyd Fischer, prin. Fax 234-8071
Chiles MS 2,000/6-8
8190 NW 197th St 33015 305-816-9101
Alan J. Stevens, prin. Fax 816-9248
Citrus Grove MS 1,500/6-8
2153 NW 3rd St 33125 305-642-5055
Emirce Ladaga, prin. Fax 642-9349
Coral Reef HS 2,800/9-12
10101 SW 152nd St 33157 305-232-2044
Adrianne Leal, prin. Fax 252-3454
Curry MS 900/6-8
15750 SW 47th St 33185 305-222-2775
Caridad Montano, prin. Fax 229-1521
Cutler Ridge MS 1,400/6-8
19400 Gulfstream Rd 33157 305-235-4761
Thomas Ennis, prin. Fax 254-3746
Dario MS 1,100/6-8
350 NW 97th Ave 33172 305-226-0179
Barbara Mendizabal, prin. Fax 559-0919
Design & Architectural Magnet HS Vo/Tech
4001 NE 2nd Ave 33137 305-573-7135
Dr. Stacy Mancuso, prin. Fax 573-8253
Diego MS 1,300/6-8
3100 NW 5th Ave 33127 305-573-7229
Concepcion Martinez, prin. Fax 572-9705
Doolin MS 1,700/6-8
6401 SW 152nd Ave 33193 305-386-6656
Eduardo Tillet, prin. Fax 408-3068
Doral MS 1,200/6-8
5005 NW 112th Ct 33178 305-592-2822
Tatiana De Miranda, prin. Fax 597-3853
Drew MS 1,200/6-8
1801 NW 60th St 33142 305-633-6057
Dr. Gwendolyn Coverson, prin. Fax 638-1307
Ferguson HS 1,600/9-12
15900 SW 56th St 33185 305-408-2700
Dr. Donald A. Hoecherl, prin. Fax 408-6487
Glades MS 1,500/6-8
9451 SW 64th Ter 33173 305-271-3342
Elio Falcon, prin. Fax 271-0402
Hammocks MS 2,500/6-8
9889 Hammocks Blvd 33196 305-385-0896
Rafael Villalobos, prin. Fax 382-0861
Hopkins Tech Center Vo/Tech
750 NW 20th St 33127 305-324-6070
James Parker, prin. Fax 545-6397
Jefferson MS 900/7-9
525 NW 147th St 33168 305-681-7481
Ellen Wright, prin. Fax 688-5912
Kinloch Park MS 1,400/6-8
4340 NW 3rd St 33126 305-445-5467
V. M. Santiesteban-Pardo, prin. Fax 445-3110
Krop HS 3,900/8-12
1410 NE 215th St 33179 305-652-6808
Matthew Welker, prin. Fax 651-8043
Madison MS 1,200/6-8
3400 NW 87th St 33147 305-836-2610
Anne Marie Duboulay, prin. Fax 696-5249
Mann MS 1,200/6-8
8950 NW 2nd Ave 33150 305-757-9537
Carol Wright, prin. Fax 754-0724
McMillan MS 1,700/6-8
13100 SW 59th St 33183 305-385-6877
Dr. Winston Whyte, prin. Fax 387-9641
Miami Central HS 3,000/9-12
1781 NW 95th St 33147 305-696-4161
Dr. Rosa Simmons, prin. Fax 836-2872
Miami Coral Park HS 4,400/9-12
8865 SW 16th St 33165 305-226-6565
Dr. Nicholas P. Jacangelo, prin. Fax 553-4658
Miami Edison HS 1,800/9-12
6161 NW 5th Ct 33127 305-751-7337
Dr. Jean Teal, prin. Fax 759-4561
Miami Edison MS 1,000/6-8
6101 NW 2nd Ave 33127 305-754-4683
Dr. Onetha Gilliard, prin. Fax 757-2219
Miami HS 3,100/9-12
2450 SW 1st St 33135 305-649-9800
Victoriano Lopez, prin. Fax 649-9475
Miami Jackson HS 2,000/9-12
1751 NW 36th St 33142 305-634-2621
Deborah Love, prin. Fax 634-7477
Miami Killian HS 3,800/9-12
10655 SW 97th Ave 33176 305-271-3311
Ricardo Rodriguez, prin. Fax 270-9142
Miami MacArthur South HS 200/9-12
11035 SW 84th St 33173 305-279-5422
Steve J. Rummel, prin. Fax 279-8973
Miami Norland JSHS 3,500/6-12
1050 NW 195th St 33169 305-653-1416
Gale Cunningham, prin. Fax 651-6175
Miami Northwestern HS 2,800/9-12
1100 NW 71st St 33150 305-836-0991
Dr. Alvin Brennan, prin. Fax 691-4955
Miami Palmetto HS 3,400/9-12
7460 SW 118th St 33156 305-235-1360
Howard Weiner, prin. Fax 378-9724

Miami Southridge HS 3,900/9-12
19355 SW 114th Ave 33157 305-238-6110
Carzell Morris, prin. Fax 253-4456
Miami Sunset JSHS 3,700/8-12
13125 SW 72nd St 33183 305-385-4255
Dr. Lucia Cox, prin. Fax 385-6458
Norland MS 2,000/6-8
1235 NW 192nd Ter 33169 305-653-1210
Cheryl Nelson, prin. Fax 654-1237
Palmetto MS 1,800/7-9
7351 SW 128th St 33156 305-238-3911
Paul Merker, prin. Fax 233-4849
Reagan/Doral HS 9-12
8600 NW 107th Ave 33178 305-805-1900
Douglas Rodriguez, prin. Fax 805-1901
Richmond Heights MS 1,600/6-8
15015 SW 103rd Ave 33176 305-238-2316
Dr. Mona Jackson, prin. Fax 251-3712
Riviera MS 900/6-8
10301 SW 48th St 33165 305-226-4286
Valerie Carrier, prin. Fax 226-1025
Rockway MS 1,500/6-8
9393 SW 29th Ter 33165 305-221-8212
Maria Cedeno, prin. Fax 221-5940
School for Applied Technology Vo/Tech
225 NE 34th St 33137 305-573-5499
Michael Guthrie, prin. Fax 573-2184
Shenandoah MS 1,400/6-8
1950 SW 19th St 33145 305-856-8282
Lourdes Delgado, prin. Fax 285-4792
South Miami HS 2,900/9-12
6856 SW 53rd St 33155 305-666-5871
Craig V. Speziale, prin. Fax 666-6359
Southwest Miami HS 3,300/9-12
8855 SW 50th Ter 33165 305-274-0181
James Haj, prin. Fax 596-7370
Southwood MS 1,800/6-8
16301 SW 80th Ave 33157 305-251-5361
Michele Bush, prin. Fax 251-7464
Thomas MS 1,400/6-8
13001 SW 26th St 33175 305-995-3800
Dr. Verona McCarthy, prin. Fax 995-3537
Turner Technical Arts HS Vo/Tech
10151 NW 19th Ave 33147 305-691-8324
Valmarie Rhoden, prin. Fax 693-9463
Varela HS 4,700/9-12
15255 SW 96th St 33196 305-752-7900
Caryl Grant, prin. Fax 386-8987
Washington HS 1,500/9-12
1200 NW 6th Ave 33136 305-324-8900
Dr. Rosann Sidener, prin. Fax 324-4676
West Miami MS 1,600/6-8
7525 SW 24th St 33155 305-261-8383
Gilberto D. Bonce, prin. Fax 267-8204
Westview MS 1,200/6-8
1901 NW 127th St 33167 305-681-6647
Lavette Hunter, prin. Fax 685-3192
Dorsey Education Center Adult
7100 NW 17th Ave 33147 305-693-2490
Rose Martin, prin. Fax 691-7492
English Center Adult
3501 SW 28th St 33133 305-445-7731
Rosy Diaz-Duque, prin. Fax 441-2150
Miami Coral Park HS Adult Education Ctr. Adult
8865 SW 16th St 33165 305-226-6565
Robert D. Novak, prin. Fax 559-7415
Miami HS Adult Education Center Adult
2450 SW 1st St 33135 305-649-9800
Eunice Soto, prin. Fax 647-2395
Miami Jackson HS Adult Education Center Adult
1751 NW 36th St 33142 305-634-2621
Judy Hunter, prin. Fax 633-8191
Miami Northwestern HS Adult Ed Center Adult
1100 NW 71st St 33150 305-836-0991
Rose L. Martin, prin. Fax 691-9927
Miami Palmetto HS Adult Education Center Adult
7460 SW 118th St 33156 305-235-1360
Dr. Edward Gehret, prin. Fax 253-3898
Miami Southridge Adult Education Center Adult
19355 SW 114th Ave 33157 305-238-6110
Fax 253-4456
Miami Sunset HS Adult Education Center Adult
13125 SW 72nd St 33183 305-385-4255
Dulce de Villa, prin. Fax 386-9218
Southwest Miami HS Adult Education Ctr. Adult
8855 SW 50th Ter 33165 305-274-0181
Clifton Lewis, prin. Fax 274-3351
Turner Tech Arts Adult Ed Center Adult
10151 NW 19th Ave 33147 305-691-8324
Fax 693-9463
Other Schools – See Coconut Grove, Coral Gables, Goulds, Hialeah, Homestead, Key Biscayne, Leisure City, Miami Beach, Miami Gardens, Miami Lakes, Miami Springs, North Miami, North Miami Beach, Opa Locka, Perrine, South Miami

---

Acupuncture & Massage College Post-Sec.
10506 N Kendall Dr 33176 305-595-9500
Adams HS 200/12-12
8345 NW 66th St # 8179 33166 888-612-9705
Frederick Orlander, prin. Fax 366-4217
American Academy 400/10-12
12651 S Dixie Hwy Ste 314 33156 305-233-5723
Robert Kunzler, dir. Fax 233-6225
American Academy HS 50/12-12
19151 S Dixie Hwy Ste 209 33157 888-701-3192
Joel Suarez, prin. Fax 675-0844
American HS Academy 400/6-12
10300 SW 72nd St Ste 470-A 33173 305-270-1440
Reinaldo Valentino, prin. Fax 270-1440
Archbishop Coleman Carroll HS 600/9-12
10300 SW 167th Ave 33196 305-388-6700
Dr. Richard Fenchak, prin. Fax 388-4371
Archbishop Curley-Notre Dame HS 500/9-12
4949 NE 2nd Ave 33137 305-751-8367
Br. Patrick Sean Moffet, prin. Fax 751-3517
ATI Career Training Center Post-Sec.
7265 NW 25th St 33122 305-573-1600
ATI College of Health Post-Sec.
1395 NW 167th St Ste 200 33169 305-628-1000
Atlantis Academy 200/K-12
9600 SW 107th Ave 33176 305-271-9771
Carlos Aballi, prin. Fax 271-7078
Beauty Schools of America Post-Sec.
1176 SW 67th Ave 33144
Belen Jesuit Prep HS 1,000/6-12
500 SW 127th Ave 33184 305-223-8600
Rev. Marcelino Garcia, prin. Fax 227-2565
Brito Miami Private S 400/PK-12
2732 SW 32nd Ave 33133 305-448-1463
Antonio Brito, dir. Fax 448-0181
Calusa Preparatory S 300/K-12
12515 SW 72nd St 33183 305-596-3787
Dr. Linton T. Fowler, prin. Fax 596-7589
Carlos Albizu University Post-Sec.
2173 NW 99th Ave 33172 305-593-1223
Champagnat Catholic S 200/PK-12
2609 NW 7th St 33125 305-642-4132
Dr. Reinaldo Alfonso, dir. Fax 305-6488
Cherish Academy 100/K-12
61 NW 47th St 33127 305-691-4600
Eva Miller, prin. Fax 696-5560
City College Post-Sec.
9300 S Dadeland Blvd Ste PH 33156 305-666-9242
College of Business & Technology Post-Sec.
8991 SW 107th Ave # 200 33176 305-273-4499
Columbus HS 1,300/9-12
3000 SW 87th Ave 33165 305-223-5650
Br. Patrick McNamara, prin. Fax 559-4306
Compu-Med Vocational Careers Post-Sec.
9738 SW 24th St 33165 305-553-2898
Dade Christian S 1,300/PK-12
6601 NW 167th St 33015 305-822-7690
Dr. Mike Hiltibidal, admin. Fax 826-4072
DeVry University Post-Sec.
200 S Biscayne Blvd Ste 500 33131 786-425-1113
Educating Hands School of Massage Post-Sec.
120 SW 8th St 33130 305-285-6991
Florida Career College Post-Sec.
1321 SW 107th Ave Ste 201B 33174 305-553-6065
Florida Christian S 1,400/PK-12
4200 SW 89th Ave 33165 305-226-8152
Dr. Robert Andrews, dir. Fax 226-8166
Florida College of Natural Health Post-Sec.
7925 NW 12th St Ste 201 33126 305-597-9599
Florida International University Post-Sec.
Tamiami Trl 33199 305-348-2000
Florida National College Post-Sec.
11865 SW 26th St 33175 305-266-9999
Florida Regents Academy 100/6-12
600 Brickell Ave 33131 305-579-4779
David Cardona, prin. Fax 579-4791
George T. Baker Aviation School Post-Sec.
3275 NW 42nd Ave 33142 305-871-3143
Greater Miami Academy 200/9-12
500 NW 122nd Ave 33182 305-220-5955
Luis Cortes, prin. Fax 220-5970
Guadalupe Vocational Institute Post-Sec.
2500 SW 107th Ave Ste 29 33165 305-559-7728
Gulliver Prep S 700/9-12
6575 SW 88th St 33156 305-666-7937
Marian Krutulis, dir. Fax 668-3791
Hope Center Post-Sec.
PO Box 10789 33101 305-545-7572
International Training Careers Post-Sec.
7360 Coral Way 33155 305-263-9696
Jackson Memorial Medical Center Post-Sec.
1611 NW 12th Ave 33136 305-585-6754
Jones College Post-Sec.
11430 N Kendall Dr Ste 200 33176 305-275-9996
Keystone National HS 100/9-12
12840 NW 1st Ct 33168 866-257-6011
Clarence Watson, prin. Fax 257-6013
Killian Oaks Academy 100/PK-12
10545 SW 97th Ave 33176 305-274-2221
Mercedes Ricon, prin. Fax 279-5460
La Belle Beauty Academy Post-Sec.
2960 SW 8th St 33135 305-649-4899
Landow Yeshiva/Bais Chana HS 100/PK-12
17330 NW 7th Ave 33169 305-653-8770
Shevy Sossonko, prin. Fax 653-6790
La Progressiva Presbyterian S 300/PK-12
2480 NW 7th St 33125 305-642-8600
Lessly Lacayo, dir. Fax 642-2169
Lincoln-Marti S 700/PK-12
931 SW 1st St 33130 305-643-4888
Fax 649-2767
Lincoln-Marti S 500/PK-12
949 SW 1st St 33130 305-643-4888
Fax 649-2767
Lindsey Hopkins Technical Education Ctr Post-Sec.
750 NW 20th St 33127 305-324-6070
Miami Christian S 500/PK-12
200 NW 109th Ave 33172 305-221-7754
Dr. Lorena Morrison, admin. Fax 221-7783
Miami Country Day S 1,000/PK-12
PO Box 380608 33238 305-779-7230
John Davies Ed.D., hdmstr. Fax 758-5107
Miami-Dade College Post-Sec.
300 NE 2nd Ave 33132 305-237-3316
Miami-Dade Community College Post-Sec.
11380 NW 27th Ave 33167 305-237-1245
Miami-Dade Community College Post-Sec.
11011 SW 104th St 33176 305-237-2000
Miami-Dade Community College-Medical Ctr Post-Sec.
950 NW 20th St 33127 305-347-4101
Miami International Univ of Art & Design Post-Sec.
1501 Biscayne Blvd 33132 800-225-9023
National School of Technology Post-Sec.
9020 SW 137th Ave 33186 305-386-9900
National School of Technology Post-Sec.
111 NW 183rd St Ste 200 33169 305-949-9500
New Concept Massage & Beauty School Post-Sec.
2022 SW 1st St 33135 305-642-3020
New World Academy 100/K-12
6101 NW 7th Ave 33127 305-762-4191
Olivia Janis, prin. Fax 754-7623
New World School of the Arts Post-Sec.
300 NE 2nd Ave 33132 305-237-7007
Northwest Christian Academy 400/PK-12
951 NW 136th St 33168 305-685-8734
Susan Nay, admin. Fax 685-5341
Nouvelle Institute Post-Sec.
3271 NW 7th St Ste 106 33125 305-643-3360
Our Lady of Lourdes Academy 900/9-12
5525 SW 84th St 33143 305-667-1623
Sr. Sheila Foy, prin. Fax 663-3121
Palmer Trinity S 600/6-12
7900 SW 176th St 33157 305-251-2230
Sean Murphy, hdmstr. Fax 254-8812
Professional Training Center Post-Sec.
13926 SW 47th St 33175 305-220-4120
Ransom-Everglades MS 400/6-8
2045 S Bayshore Dr 33133 305-250-6850
Shelly Stamler, dir. Fax 250-4205
Ransom Everglades S 900/9-12
3575 Main Hwy 33133 305-460-8800
Ellen Y. Moceri, hdmstr. Fax 854-1846
Robert Morgan Educational Center Post-Sec.
18180 SW 122nd Ave 33177 305-253-9920
St. Brendan HS 1,200/9-12
2950 SW 87th Ave 33165 305-223-5181
Br. Felix Elardo, prin. Fax 220-7434
St. John Vianney College Seminary Post-Sec.
2900 SW 87th Ave 33165 305-223-4561
Sha'arei Bina Torah Academy for Girls 50/6-9
137 NE 19th St 33132 305-438-1802
Rabbi Elchonon Abramchik, prin. Fax 438-1803
South Florida Institute of Technology Post-Sec.
2141 SW 1st St Ste 104 33135 305-649-2050
Technical Career Institute Post-Sec.
7757 W Flagler St Ste 23 33144 305-863-1818
Temple Beth Am Day S 200/PK-10
5950 N Kendall Dr 33156 305-665-6228
Dr. Mindy Pincus, prin. Fax 668-6340
The English Center Post-Sec.
3501 SW 28th St 33133 305-445-7731
The Praxis Institute Post-Sec.
1850 SW 8th St 33135 305-642-4104
TLC Christian Academy #3 100/PK-12
6565 NW 32nd Ave 33147 561-278-3115
Queen Owens Dunmore, prin. Fax 278-3022
Trinity International University Post-Sec.
111 NW 183rd St Ste 500 33169 305-577-4600
Universidad FLET Post-Sec.
14540 SW 136th St Ste 202 33186 305-378-8700
University HS 200/10-12
14707 S Dixie Hwy 33176 786-242-6577
Donna Nelson, prin. Fax 242-5622
University of Miami Post-Sec.
4600 Rickenbacker Cswy 33149 305-361-4000
US International Christian Academy 50/9-12
7601 W Flagler St Ste 215 33144 305-265-5858
Ricardo Alfonso, dir. Fax 244-9355
Westminster Christian HS 400/9-12
6855 SW 152nd St 33157 305-233-2030
Robert Stephens, prin. Fax 253-9623
Westminster Christian MS 300/6-8
6855 SW 152nd St 33157 305-233-2030
John Manoogian, prin. Fax 253-9623
Westwood Christian S 400/6-12
5801 SW 120th Ave 33183 305-274-3380
Edwin Oksanen, hdmstr. Fax 595-7519
World Hope Academy 200/9-12
10661 N Kendall Dr Ste 227 33176 305-270-9830
Dr. Alan Perez, prin. Fax 270-9780

Miami Beach, Dade, Pop. 89,312
Miami-Dade County SD
Supt. — See Miami
Miami Beach HS 2,400/9-12
2231 Prairie Ave 33139 305-532-4515
Dr. Jeanne Friedman, prin. Fax 531-9209
Nautilus MS 1,400/7-8
4301 N Michigan Ave 33140 305-532-3481
Caridad Figueredo, prin. Fax 532-8906
Feinberg-Fisher Community Center Adult
1424 Drexel Ave 33139 305-531-0451
Martha Montaner, prin. Fax 531-2352
Miami Beach Adult Center Adult
2231 Prairie Ave 33139 305-531-0451
Wanda Y. Williams, prin. Fax 531-2352

Landow Yeshiva S 400/7-12
1140 Alton Rd 33139 305-532-9820
Rabbi Abraham Korf, dean Fax 653-5664
Mechina HS of South Florida 100/7-12
1965 Alton Rd 33139 305-538-5543
Rabbi Eliyohu Schmelczer, prin. Fax 532-3627
Miami Ad School Post-Sec.
955 Alton Rd 33139 305-538-3193
Mt. Sinai Medical Center Post-Sec.
4300 Alton Rd 33140 305-674-2222
RASG Hebrew Academy 600/PK-12
2400 Pine Tree Dr 33140 305-532-6421
Jody Steele, prin. Fax 672-6191
Talmudic College of Florida Post-Sec.
1910 Alton Rd 33139 305-534-7050
Yeshiva Gedolah Rabbinical College Post-Sec.
1140 Alton Rd 33139 305-673-5664
Yeshiva Tichon HS 100/9-12
PO Box 403222 33140 800-539-4743
Rabbi Mordechai Friedman, prin. Fax 539-4743

Miami Gardens, Broward
Miami-Dade County SD
Supt. — See Miami
Carol City MS 1,300/6-8
3737 NW 188th St, 305-624-2652
Dr. Mark Soffian, prin. Fax 623-2955
Lake Stevens MS 1,500/6-8
18484 NW 48th Pl, 305-620-1294
Derick McKoy, prin. Fax 620-1345
Miami Carol City HS 2,600/9-12
3422 NW 187th St, 305-621-5681
Kim Cox, prin. Fax 620-8862
Parkway MS 1,000/6-8
2349 NW 175th St, 305-624-9613
Eugene Butler, prin. Fax 623-9756
Miami Carol City Adult S Adult
3422 NW 187th St, 305-621-5681
Lourdes Garcia, prin. Fax 624-9317

Miami Job Corps Center Post-Sec.
3050 NW 183rd St, 305-626-7800

Miami Lakes, Dade, Pop. 22,666
Miami-Dade County SD
Supt. — See Miami
Miami Lakes Educational Center Vo/Tech
5780 NW 158th St 33014 305-557-1100
James Parker, prin. Fax 364-9279

Florida Christian Academy 50/9-12
6625 Miami Lakes Dr E # 348 33014 305-777-3823
Ricardo Alfonso, prin. Fax 244-9355
Goliath Academy 100/10-12
15025 NW 77th Ave Ste 216 33014 305-512-5994
Consuelo Goliath, prin. Fax 512-5996
Miami Lake Christian Academy 200/PK-12
6250 Miami Lakes Dr E 33014 305-823-3888
Will Ortiz, dir. Fax 823-7219

Miami Shores, Dade, Pop. 10,234

Barry University Post-Sec.
11300 NE 2nd Ave 33161 305-899-3000

Miami Springs, Dade, Pop. 13,585
Miami-Dade County SD
Supt. — See Miami
Miami Springs HS 3,500/9-12
751 Dove Ave 33166 305-885-3585
Edward Smith, prin. Fax 884-2632

Miami Springs MS 2,000/6-8
150 S Royal Poinciana Blvd 33166 305-888-6457
Dr. Gail Senita, prin. Fax 887-5281
Miami Springs HS Adult Education Center Adult
751 Dove Ave 33166 305-885-3585
Robert Hernandez, prin. Fax 884-2632

Middleburg, Clay, Pop. 6,223
Clay County SD
Supt. — See Green Cove Springs
Middleburg HS 1,600/9-12
3750 County Road 220 32068 904-213-2100
David Broskie, prin. Fax 291-5462
Wilkinson JHS 1,100/7-8
5025 County Road 218 32068 904-291-5500
Dr. David McDonald, prin. Fax 291-5510

Calvary Christian Academy 100/K-12
1532 Long Bay Rd 32068 904-282-0407
Dr. Ken Pledger, prin. Fax 282-6212
Madeira Christian Academy 100/K-12
1650 Blanding Blvd 32068 904-291-1875
Marsha Sealey, prin. Fax 291-1884

Milton, Santa Rosa, Pop. 7,740
Santa Rosa County SD 23,800/PK-12
5086 Canal St 32570 850-983-5000
John Rogers, supt. Fax 983-5011
www.santarosa.k12.fl.us/
Avalon MS 800/6-8
5445 King Arthurs Way 32583 850-983-5540
Erma Fillingim, prin. Fax 983-5545
Central JSHS 300/7-12
6180 Central School Rd 32570 850-983-5640
Kenny Owens, prin. Fax 983-5645
Hobbs MS 600/6-8
5317 Glover Ln 32570 850-983-5630
Buddy Powell, prin. Fax 983-5635
King MS 700/6-8
5928 Stewart St 32570 850-983-5660
Charlotte Hatcher, prin. Fax 983-5665
Locklin Technical Center Vo/Tech
5330 Berryhill Rd 32570 850-983-5700
Charles Etheredge, prin. Fax 983-5715
Milton HS 1,800/9-12
5445 Stewart St 32570 850-983-5600
Lewis Lynn, prin. Fax 983-5610
Santa Rosa County Adult HS Adult
5330 Berryhill Rd 32570 850-983-5710
Donna Christopher, prin. Fax 983-5715
Other Schools – See Gulf Breeze, Jay, Navarre, Pace

Radford M. Locklin Technical Center Post-Sec.
5330 Berryhill Rd 32570 850-983-5700
Santa Rosa Christian S 300/PK-12
PO Box 643 32572 850-623-4671
Doris Peppard, prin. Fax 623-9559
West Florida Baptist Academy 300/K-12
5621 Highway 90 32583 850-623-9306
Alan Stewart, dir.

Miramar, Broward, Pop. 96,646
Broward County SD
Supt. — See Fort Lauderdale
Everglades HS 2,600/9-12
17100 SW 48th Ct 33027 754-323-0500
Paul Fetscher, prin. Fax 323-0640
Miramar HS 2,700/9-12
3601 SW 89th Ave 33025 754-323-1350
David Gordon, prin. Fax 323-1480
New Renaissance MS 1,600/6-8
10701 Miramar Blvd 33025 754-323-3500
Dr. Shirley McCray, prin. Fax 323-3585
Perry MS 1,500/6-8
3400 Wildcat Way 33023 754-323-3900
Steven Frazier, prin. Fax 323-3985

Continental Academy 1,000/9-12
3241 Executive Way 33025 800-285-3514
Lee Taylor, prin. Fax 820-9230
DeVry University Post-Sec.
2300 SW 145th Ave 33027 954-499-9700
Florida Bible Christian S 700/PK-12
9300 Pembroke Rd 33025 954-431-6770
Robert McCann, prin. Fax 431-5475
Le Cordon Bleu College of Culinary Arts Post-Sec.
3221 Enterprise Way 33025 954-438-8882

Monticello, Jefferson, Pop. 2,546
Jefferson County SD 1,400/K-12
1490 W Washington St 32344 850-342-0100
Phil Barker, supt. Fax 342-0108
www.firn.edu/schools/jefferson/jefferson/home.html
Howard MS 400/5-8
1145 Second St 32344 850-342-0125
Juliette Jackson, prin. Fax 342-0127
Jefferson County HS 400/9-12
50 David Rd 32344 850-997-3555
Michael Bryan, prin. Fax 997-4773
Jefferson County Adult Center Adult
375 S Water St 32344 850-342-0140
Artis Johnson, prin. Fax 342-0402

Aucilla Christian Academy 400/PK-12
7803 Aucilla Rd 32344 850-997-3597
Richard Finlayson, dir. Fax 997-3598

Montverde, Lake, Pop. 911

Montverde Academy 400/PK-12
17235 7th St 34756 407-469-2561
Kasey Kesselring, hdmstr. Fax 469-3711

Moore Haven, Glades, Pop. 1,734
Glades County SD 1,000/K-12
PO Box 459 33471 863-946-2083
Wayne Aldrich, supt. Fax 946-1549
www.firn.edu/schools/glades/glades
Moore Haven JSHS 400/7-12
PO Box 99 33471 863-946-0811
Jean Prowant, prin. Fax 946-1532

Mount Dora, Lake, Pop. 10,284
Lake County SD
Supt. — See Tavares
Mount Dora HS 900/9-12
700 N Highland St 32757 352-383-2177
Claude Pennacchia, prin. Fax 383-6466
Mount Dora MS 600/6-8
1405 Lincoln Ave 32757 352-383-6101
Thomas Sanders, prin. Fax 383-4949

Christian Home & Bible S 800/PK-12
301 W 13th Ave 32757 352-383-2155
David Pahman, prin. Fax 383-3112
Solid Rock Christian S 100/PK-12
21951 US Highway 441 32757 352-735-5777
Diana Bunting, prin. Fax 735-1084

Mulberry, Polk, Pop. 3,233
Polk County SD
Supt. — See Bartow
Mulberry HS 900/9-12
1 Panther Pl 33860 863-701-1104
George Hatch, prin. Fax 701-1109
Mulberry MS 800/6-8
500 Dr Mlk Jr Ave 33860 863-701-1066
Patricia Barnes, prin. Fax 701-1068

Florida Career Institute Post-Sec.
5925 Imperial Pkwy Ste 200 33860 863-646-1400
Southern Lutheran Academy 50/9-12
4440 Academy Dr 33860 863-425-6635
Eric Brown, prin. Fax 425-6637

Naples, Collier, Pop. 21,284
Collier County SD 38,500/PK-12
5775 Osceola Trl 34109 239-377-0001
Ray Baker, supt. Fax 377-0206
www.collier.k12.fl.us
Collier HS 2,200/9-12
5600 Cougar Dr 34109 239-377-1200
Ronald Miller, prin. Fax 377-1201
Corkscrew MS 1,200/6-8
1165 County Road 858 34120 239-377-3400
Dennis Snider, prin. Fax 377-3401
East Naples MS 1,200/6-8
4100 Estey Ave 34104 239-377-3600
Ken Fairbanks, prin. Fax 377-3601
Golden Gate HS 9-12
2925 Magnolia Pond Dr 34116 239-377-1601
Robert Spano, prin. Fax 377-1601
Golden Gate MS 1,000/6-8
2701 48th Ter SW 34116 239-377-3800
Mary Murray, prin. Fax 377-3801
Gulf Coast HS 3,000/9-12
7878 Immokalee Rd 34119 239-377-1400
David Stump, prin. Fax 377-1401
Gulfview MS 700/6-8
255 6th St S 34102 239-377-4000
Kevin Saba, prin. Fax 377-4001
Lely HS 2,300/9-12
1 Lely High School Blvd 34113 239-377-2001
Michael Parrish, prin. Fax 377-2001
Manatee MS 600/6-8
1920 Manatee Rd 34114 239-377-4400
Scholastica Choi, prin. Fax 377-4401
Naples HS 2,200/9-12
1100 Golden Eagle Cir 34102 239-377-2200
Dr. Rosanne Winter, prin. Fax 377-2201
North Naples MS 6-8
16165 Livingston Rd 34110 239-377-4600
Frank Zencuch, prin. Fax 377-4601
Oakridge MS 1,500/6-8
14975 Collier Blvd 34119 239-377-4800
John Kasten, prin. Fax 377-4801
Palmetto Ridge HS 9-12
1655 Victory Ln 34120 239-377-2400
Roy Terry, prin. Fax 377-2401
Pine Ridge MS 1,300/6-8
1515 Pine Ridge Rd 34109 239-377-5000
George Brenco, prin. Fax 377-5001
Walker Institute of Technology Vo/Tech
3702 Estey Ave 34104 239-377-0900
Jeanette Johnson, dir. Fax 377-0901
Other Schools – See Everglades City, Immokalee

Ave Maria University Post-Sec.
1025 Commons Circle 34119 877-283-8648
Community S of Naples 800/PK-12
13275 Livingston Rd 34109 239-597-7575
John Zeller, prin. Fax 598-2973
International College Post-Sec.
2655 Northbrooke Dr 34119 239-513-1122
Lorenzo Walker Institute of Technology Post-Sec.
3702 Estey Ave 34104 239-430-6900
Nicaea Academy 200/PK-12
2200 Santa Barbara Blvd 34116 239-455-9090
Rev. Barton McIntyre, admin. Fax 348-0499
St. John Neumann HS 300/9-12
3000 53rd St SW 34116 239-455-3044
Laura Campbell, prin. Fax 455-2966
Seacrest Country Day S 500/PK-10
7100 Davis Blvd 34104 239-793-1986
Lynne Powell Ed.D., prin. Fax 793-1460

Navarre, Santa Rosa
Santa Rosa County SD
Supt. — See Milton
Holley-Navarre MS 800/6-8
1976 Williams Creek Dr 32566 850-936-6040
Donald Bowersox, prin. Fax 939-6049
Navarre HS 1,600/9-12
8600 High School Blvd 32566 850-936-6080
Bill Emerson, prin. Fax 936-6088

Neptune Beach, Duval, Pop. 7,179
Duval County SD
Supt. — See Jacksonville
Fletcher HS 2,300/9-12
700 Seagate Ave 32266 904-247-5905
Helene Kirkpatrick, prin. Fax 247-5911

Newberry, Alachua, Pop. 3,505
Alachua County SD
Supt. — See Gainesville
Newberry HS 600/9-12
400 SW 258th St 32669 352-472-1101
Hershel Lyons, prin. Fax 472-1116
Oak View MS 500/6-8
1203 SW 250th St 32669 352-472-1102
Karen Clarke, prin. Fax 472-1131

New Port Richey, Pasco, Pop. 16,711
Pasco County SD
Supt. — See Land O Lakes
Bayonet Point MS 1,000/6-8
11125 Little Rd 34654 727-774-7400
Beth Brown, prin. Fax 774-7491
Gulf HS 1,500/9-12
5355 School Rd 34652 727-774-3300
Tom Imerson, prin. Fax 774-3391
Gulf MS 1,100/6-8
6419 Louisiana Ave 34653 727-774-8000
Stan Trapp, prin. Fax 774-8091
Marchman Tech Education Center Vo/Tech
7825 Campus Dr 34653 727-774-1700
Rob Aguis, prin. Fax 774-1791
Mitchell HS 2,200/9-12
2323 Little Rd 34655 727-774-9200
Tina Tiede, prin. Fax 774-9291
Ridgewood HS 1,800/9-12
7650 Orchid Lake Rd 34653 727-774-3900
Randall Koenigsfeld, prin. Fax 774-3991
River Ridge HS 1,900/9-12
11646 Town Center Rd 34654 727-774-7200
Jim Michaels, prin. Fax 774-7291
River Ridge MS 6-8
11646 Town Center Rd 34654 727-774-7200
Jason Joens, prin. Fax 774-7291
Seven Springs MS 1,800/6-8
2441 Little Rd 34655 727-774-6700
Chris Christoff, prin. Fax 774-6791
Schwettman Adult Education Center Adult
5520 Grand Blvd 34652 727-774-0000
John Letvin, prin. Fax 774-0091

Benes International School of Beauty Post-Sec.
7127 US Highway 19 34652 727-848-8415
Elfers Christian S 200/PK-12
5630 Olympia St 34652 727-845-0235
Harold Lippert, admin. Fax 848-5135
Pasco-Hernando Community College Post-Sec.
10230 Ridge Rd 34654 727-847-2727
Renaissance Academy 100/K-12
8431 Corporate Way 34653 727-845-8150
Dr. Janine Walker Caffrey, prin. Fax 845-8069
Trinity College of Florida Post-Sec.
2430 Welbilt Blvd 34655 727-376-6911

New Smyrna Beach, Volusia, Pop. 20,742
Volusia County SD
Supt. — See De Land
New Smyrna Beach HS 2,000/9-12
100 Barracuda Blvd 32169 386-424-2555
Dr. Carole Kelley, prin. Fax 409-5625
New Smyrna Beach MS 1,600/6-8
1200 S Myrtle Ave 32168 386-424-2550
Jim Tager, prin. Fax 426-7476

Niceville, Okaloosa, Pop. 12,235
Okaloosa County SD
Supt. — See Fort Walton Beach
Niceville HS 2,300/9-12
800 John Sims Pkwy E 32578 850-833-4114
Janie Varner, prin. Fax 833-4267
Ruckel MS 900/6-8
201 Partin Dr N 32578 850-833-4142
Janet Hays, prin. Fax 833-3291

Okaloosa-Walton College Post-Sec.
100 College Blvd E 32578 850-678-5111
Rocky Bayou Christian S 800/PK-12
2101 Partin Dr N 32578 850-678-7358
Don Larson, supt. Fax 729-2513

North Fort Myers, Lee, Pop. 42,900
Lee County SD
Supt. — See Fort Myers
North Fort Myers HS 2,200/9-12
5000 Orange Grove Blvd 33903 239-995-2117
Kim Lunger, prin. Fax 995-1243

Grace Community S 200/PK-12
4735 Orange Grove Blvd 33903 239-997-3727
Rev. Daniel McIntyre, prin. Fax 997-7336
Temple Christian S 100/PK-12
18841 State Road 31 33917 239-543-3222
Maribeth Singleton, prin. Fax 543-6112

North Lauderdale, Broward, Pop. 33,534
Broward County SD
Supt. — See Fort Lauderdale
Silver Lakes MS 1,200/6-8
7600 Tam Oshanter Blvd 33068 754-322-4600
Jacquelyn Vernon, prin. Fax 322-4685

North Miami, Dade, Pop. 59,310
Miami-Dade County SD
Supt. — See Miami
North Miami HS 3,200/9-12
800 NE 137th St 33161 305-891-6590
Carnell A. White, prin. Fax 895-1788
North Miami MS 1,600/7-9
13105 NE 7th Ave 33161 305-891-5611
Arnold Montgomery, prin. Fax 891-4057
North Miami HS Adult Education Center Adult
800 NE 137th St 33161 305-891-6590
Leslie Prudent, prin. Fax 895-6248

Florida International University Post-Sec.
Biscayne Blvd and 151st St 33181 305-940-5625
Johnson & Wales University Post-Sec.
1701 NE 127th St 33181 305-892-7000
Miami Union Academy 300/PK-12
12600 NW 4th Ave 33168 305-953-9907
Regina Harris, prin. Fax 953-3602

North Miami Beach, Dade, Pop. 40,345
Miami-Dade County SD
Supt. — See Miami
Highland Oaks MS 2,500/6-8
2375 NE 203rd St, Miami FL 33180 305-932-3810
Sally J. Alayon, prin. Fax 932-0676
Kennedy MS 2,000/6-8
1075 NE 167th St 33162 305-947-1451
Kay Mikulas, prin. Fax 949-9046
North Miami Beach HS 3,000/9-12
1247 NE 167th St 33162 305-949-8381
Raymond Fontana, prin. Fax 949-0491

Allison Academy 100/6-12
1881 NE 164th St 33162 305-940-3922
Sarah Allison, prin. Fax 940-1820
Beth Jacob S 300/6-12
1110 NE 163rd St 33162 305-957-1670
Rabbi Ephraim Leizerson, prin. Fax 957-1677
Hillel Community Day S 1,100/PK-12
19000 NE 25th Ave, Miami FL 33180 305-931-2831
Dr. Richard Barbieri, hdmstr. Fax 932-7463
Rohr MS 100/6-8
1051 N Miami Beach Blvd 33162 305-947-7779
Rabbi Ephraim Palgon, prin. Fax 947-7221

Spirit of Christ Child Development Ctr 100/K-12
18801 W Dixie Hwy, Miami FL 33180 305-935-5001
Camelon Lamb-Pope, prin. Fax 935-5057
Yeshiva Toras Chaim 100/7-12
1025 NE Miami Gardens Dr 33179 305-944-5344
Rabbi Bentzion Chait, prin. Fax 947-5021

North Palm Beach, Palm Beach, Pop. 12,612

Benjamin S 1,300/PK-12
11000 Ellison Wilson Rd 33408 561-626-3747
Eugene Gross, hdmstr. Fax 626-8752

North Port, Sarasota, Pop. 30,945
Sarasota County SD
Supt. — See Sarasota
Heron Creek MS 1,500/6-8
6501 W Price Blvd 34286 941-480-3371
Scott Wilson, prin. Fax 480-3398
North Port HS 1,500/9-12
6400 W Price Blvd 34286 941-423-8558
Dr. George Kinney, prin. Fax 480-3199

Active Learning Academy 800/PK-12
14503 Tamiami Trl 34287 941-235-2077
Terry Ingram, prin. Fax 235-2073

Oakland Park, Broward, Pop. 31,462
Broward County SD
Supt. — See Fort Lauderdale
Northeast HS 2,200/9-12
700 NE 56th St 33334 754-322-1550
William Kemp, prin. Fax 322-1680
Rickards MS 1,100/6-8
6000 NE 9th Ave 33334 754-322-4400
Ronald Forsman, prin. Fax 322-4485

ATI Career Training Center Post-Sec.
3501 Powerline Rd 33309 954-563-5899

Ocala, Marion, Pop. 47,921
Marion County SD 38,500/PK-12
PO Box 670 34478 352-671-7700
James M. Yancey, supt. Fax 671-7581
www.marion.k12.fl.us/
Forest HS 1,700/9-12
5000 SE Maricamp Rd 34480 352-671-4700
Rick Lankford, prin. Fax 671-4702
Fort King MS 900/6-8
545 NE 17th Ave 34470 352-671-4725
Don Cox, prin. Fax 671-4726
Howard MS 1,300/6-8
1108 NW Martin Luther King 34475 352-671-7225
Kathy Collins, prin. Fax 671-7226
Lake Weir HS 1,700/9-12
10351 SE Maricamp Rd 34472 352-671-4820
Cynthia Saunders, prin. Fax 671-4829
Marion Technical Institute Vo/Tech
1614 E Ft King St 34471 352-671-4765
Mark Vianello, prin. Fax 671-4766
Osceola MS 1,000/6-8
526 SE Tuscawilla Ave 34471 352-671-7100
Julie Shealy, prin. Fax 671-7101
Vanguard HS 1,800/9-12
7 NW 28th St 34475 352-671-4900
David Ellers, prin. Fax 671-4903
West Port HS 1,500/9-12
3733 SW 80th Ave 34481 352-291-4000
Jane Ellspermann, prin. Fax 291-4001
West Port MS 1,200/6-8
3733 SW 80th Ave 34481 352-291-4050
Greg Dudley, prin. Fax 291-4051
Comm Adult Education Center Adult
1014 SW 7th Rd 34474 352-671-7200
Debbie Jenkins, dir. Fax 629-1117
Other Schools – See Belleview, Citra, Dunnellon, Summerfield

Academy Biblical Character Development 100/K-12
850 NE 36th Ter 34470 352-694-2223
Tom Ranew, dir. Fax 694-2223
Central Florida Community College Post-Sec.
PO Box 1388 34478 352-854-2322
Hale Academy 100/PK-12
3443 SW 20th St 34474 352-854-8835
Jeffrey Magnoli, prin. Fax 861-8822
Marion Co. School Radiologic Technology Post-Sec.
1014 SW 7th Rd 34474 352-671-7200
Ocala Christian Academy 300/PK-12
1714 SE 36th Ave 34471 352-694-4178
Randy Swartz, admin. Fax 694-7192
Ocala Word of Faith Academy 300/K-12
4741 SW 20th St #1 34474 352-861-0700
James Watts, dir. Fax 861-0533
Oceans S 200/9-12
121 NE 13th Ave 34470 352-236-4406
Ray Cates, prin. Fax 629-1573
St. John Lutheran S 600/PK-12
1915 SE Lake Weir Ave 34471 352-622-7275
Richard Rath, prin. Fax 622-5564
Shores Christian Academy 200/PK-12
10515 SE 115th Ave 34472 352-687-4454
Rev. Stephen Davison, admin. Fax 687-1462
Trinity Catholic HS 200/9-12
2600 SW 42nd St 34474 352-622-9025
Br. Andrew Prendergast, prin. Fax 861-8164
Webster College Post-Sec.
2221 SW 19th Avenue Rd 34474 352-629-1941

Ocoee, Orange, Pop. 27,133
Orange County SD
Supt. — See Orlando
Ocoee HS 9-12
1925 Crown Point Pkwy 34761 407-905-3000
Mike Armbruster, prin. Fax 905-3099
Ocoee MS 1,500/6-8
300 S Bluford Ave 34761 407-877-5035
Katherine Clark, prin. Fax 877-5045

Central Florida Christian Academy 600/PK-12
8800 W Colonial Dr 34761 407-293-8062
Dave Bess, prin. Fax 290-1579
Victory Christian Academy 200/PK-12
1601 A D Mims Rd 34761 407-656-1295
Bradley Phillips, dir. Fax 656-6895

Odessa, Hillsborough, Pop. 1,200
Hillsborough County SD
Supt. — See Tampa

Walker MS 1,000/6-8
8282 N Mobley Rd 33556 813-631-4726
Marc Hutek, prin. Fax 631-4738

Okeechobee, Okeechobee, Pop. 5,563
Okeechobee County SD 6,800/PK-12
700 SW 2nd Ave 34974 863-462-5000
Dr. Patricia G. Cooper, supt. Fax 462-5151
www.okee.k12.fl.us/web.nsf
Okeechobee Freshman Campus 500/9-9
610 SW 2nd Ave 34974 863-462-5288
Andy Brewer, prin. Fax 462-5258
Okeechobee HS 1,200/10-12
2800 US Highway 441 N 34972 863-462-5025
Toni Wiersma, prin. Fax 462-5037
Osceola MS 900/6-8
825 SW 28th St 34974 863-462-5070
Theda Bass, prin. Fax 462-5076
Yearling MS 700/6-8
925 NW 23rd Ln 34972 863-462-5056
Brian Greseth, prin. Fax 462-5062

Grace Christian S 100/PK-12
701 S Parrott Ave 34974 863-763-3072
David Ogden, prin. Fax 213-1339

Oldsmar, Pinellas, Pop. 13,609

Oldsmar Christian S 300/PK-12
650 Burbank Rd 34677 813-855-5746
Rev. Eddie Preston, prin. Fax 855-4476

Old Town, Dixie

Dixie County Learning Academy 50/K-12
PO Box 672 32680 352-542-3306
Dr. Sylvia Lamenta, prin. Fax 542-7291

Opa Locka, Dade, Pop. 15,081
Miami-Dade County SD
Supt. — See Miami
North Dade MS 1,000/6-8
1840 NW 157th St 33054 305-624-8415
Eunice Davis, prin. Fax 628-2954

Florida Memorial University Post-Sec.
15800 NW 42nd Ave 33054 305-626-3600
Monsignor Edward Pace HS 1,100/9-12
15600 NW 32nd Ave 33054 305-624-8534
Ana Garcia, prin. Fax 521-0185
North Dade Academy 100/PK-10
13850 NW 26th Ave 33054 305-725-4755
Santarvis Brown, prin. Fax 687-0098
St. Thomas University Post-Sec.
16401 NW 37th Ave 33054 305-625-6000

Orange Park, Clay, Pop. 9,210
Clay County SD
Supt. — See Green Cove Springs
Fleming Island HS 1,600/9-12
2233 Village Square Pkwy 32003 904-541-2100
Sam Ward, prin. Fax 541-2085
Lakeside JHS 1,400/7-8
2750 Moody Ave 32073 904-213-2980
Randy Oliver, prin. Fax 213-2987
Orange Park HS 2,400/9-12
2300 Kingsley Ave 32073 904-272-8110
Mike Wingate, prin. Fax 213-2944
Orange Park JHS 1,200/7-8
1500 Gano Ave 32073 904-278-2000
James Young, prin. Fax 278-2009
Ridgeview HS 1,800/9-12
466 Madison Ave 32065 904-272-3003
Toni McCabe, prin. Fax 213-3033
Clay Co. Center for Community Education Adult
2306 Kingsley Ave 32073 904-272-8170
Bill Smith, admin. Fax 272-8149

American Heritage Academy 200/K-12
4325 Highway 17 S 32003 904-269-2405
Melissa Kager, prin. Fax 264-9791
Berean Christian Academy 100/PK-12
4459 US Highway 17 32003 904-264-5333
David Wright, prin. Fax 264-9185
Citizen's High School Post-Sec.
PO Box 66089 32065 904-276-1700
Citizens HS 100/9-12
188 College Dr 32065 904-276-1700
Larry Lark, prin. Fax 272-6702
Lighthouse Christian S 200/1-12
1542 Kingsley Ave 32073 904-637-0637
Elaine Ludwig, prin. Fax 637-0638
National Heavy Equipment Operator School Post-Sec.
PO Box 65789 32065 904-272-4000
National Training Post-Sec.
PO Box 65789 32065 904-272-4000
North Florida Institute Post-Sec.
560 Wells Rd 32073 904-269-7086
Orange Park Christian Academy 200/K-12
1324 Kingsley Ave 32073 904-269-0096
Jerry Stigliano, prin. Fax 269-7445
St. Johns Country Day S 800/PK-12
3100 Doctors Lake Dr 32073 904-264-9572
Gregory Foster, prin. Fax 264-0375

Orlando, Orange, Pop. 199,336
Orange County SD 159,000/PK-12
445 W Amelia St 32801 407-317-3200
Ronald Blocker, supt. Fax 317-3401
www.ocps.k12.fl.us
Boone HS 3,200/9-12
2000 S Mills Ave 32806 407-893-7200
Christopher Bernier, prin. Fax 897-2466
Carver MS 1,000/6-8
4500 Columbia St 32811 407-296-5110
Marilyn Doyle, prin. Fax 296-6407
Chain of Lakes MS 1,300/6-8
8700 Conroy Windermere Rd 32835 407-909-5400
Carol Kindt, prin. Fax 909-5410
Colonial 9th Grade Center 9-9
7775 Valencia College Ln 32807 407-249-6369
Robert Allen, prin.
Colonial HS 3,700/9-12
6100 Oleander Dr 32807 407-482-6300
Dr. Paul Mitchell, prin. Fax 737-1450
Conway MS 1,400/6-8
4600 Anderson Rd 32812 407-249-6420
Claudia Vogt, prin. Fax 249-6429
Corner Lakes MS 1,500/6-8
1700 Chuluota Rd 32820 407-568-0510
Judith Frank, prin. Fax 568-0920

Cypress Creek HS 2,900/9-12
1101 Bear Crossing Dr 32824 407-852-3400
Susan Storch, prin. Fax 850-5160
Discovery MS 1,800/6-8
601 Woodbury Rd 32828 407-384-1555
Dr. Stefanie Shames, prin. Fax 384-1580
Edgewater HS 3,300/9-12
3100 Edgewater Dr 32804 407-835-4900
Arthur Anderson, prin. Fax 245-2758
Evans 9th Grade Center 9-9
2751 N Apopka Vineland Rd 32818 407-296-6468
Reginald Forbes, prin.
Evans HS 2,900/9-12
4949 Silver Star Rd 32808 407-522-3400
Karen Wilson, prin. Fax 522-6048
Freedom HS 2,500/9-12
2500 W Taft Vineland Rd 32837 407-816-5600
Mark Brown, prin. Fax 816-5616
Freedom MS 6-8
2850 Taft Vineland Rd 32837 407-858-6130
Timothy Smith, prin. Fax 858-6132
Glenridge MS 1,300/6-8
2900 Upper Park Rd 32814 407-623-1415
Michele Erickson, prin. Fax 623-1427
Howard MS 800/6-8
800 E Robinson St 32801 407-245-1780
Carl Cartwright, prin. Fax 245-1785
Hunters Creek MS 2,100/6-8
13400 Town Loop Blvd 32837 407-858-4620
Harold Border, prin. Fax 858-4621
Jackson MS 1,200/6-8
6000 Stonewall Jackson Rd 32807 407-249-6430
Joseph Miller, prin. Fax 249-6438
Jones HS 1,100/9-12
801 S Rio Grande Ave 32805 407-835-2300
Lorenzo Phillips, prin. Fax 245-2765
Lee MS 1,200/6-8
1201 Maury Rd 32804 407-245-1800
Tom Pylant, prin. Fax 245-1809
Legacy MS 6-8
11398 Lake Underhill Rd 32825 407-658-5330
Todd Trimble, prin. Fax 658-5334
Liberty MS 1,300/6-8
3405 S Chickasaw Trl 32829 407-249-6440
Elisha Bonnewitz, prin. Fax 249-6449
Lockhart MS 1,100/6-8
3411 Dr Love Rd 32810 407-296-5120
Margaret McMillen, prin. Fax 296-6549
Meadowbrook MS 1,000/6-8
6000 North Ln 32808 407-296-5130
Valeria Maxwell, prin. Fax 296-5139
Meadow Woods MS 1,800/6-8
1800 Rhode Island Woods Cir 32824 407-850-5180
Isom Rivers, prin. Fax 850-5190
Memorial MS 800/6-8
2220 29th St 32805 407-245-1810
Gail Burke, prin. Fax 245-1820
Mid Florida Tech Vo/Tech
2900 W Oak Ridge Rd 32809 407-251-6047
Robert Clark, prin. Fax 251-6197
Oak Ridge HS 2,500/9-12
6000 Winegard Rd 32809 407-852-3200
Maxine Risper, prin. Fax 850-5152
Odyssey MS 1,300/6-8
9290 Lee Vista Blvd 32829 407-207-3850
Patricia Bowen-Painter, prin. Fax 207-3873
Olympia HS 3,000/9-12
4301 S Apopka Vineland Rd 32835 407-905-6400
Robert Avossa, prin. Fax 905-6465
Orlando Tech Ctr Vo/Tech
301 W Amelia St 32801 407-246-7060
Joseph McCoy, prin. Fax 317-3372
Phillips 9th Grade Center 9-9
6500 Turkey Lake Rd 32819 407-355-3200
Steve McKinney, prin. Fax 370-7232
Phillips HS 3,500/9-12
6500 Turkey Lake Rd 32819 407-355-3200
Eugene Trochinski, prin. Fax 370-7232
Robinswood MS 1,300/6-8
6305 Balboa Dr 32818 407-296-5140
Bridget Williams, prin. Fax 296-5148
Southwest MS 1,300/6-8
6450 Dr Phillips Blvd 32819 407-370-7200
Dr. Anne Carcara, prin. Fax 370-7210
Timber Creek HS 2,900/9-12
1001 Avalon Blvd 32828 321-235-7800
John Wright, prin. Fax 253-7821
Union Park MS 1,400/6-8
1844 Westfall Dr 32817 407-249-6309
Kris Viles, prin. Fax 249-4404
University HS 3,400/9-12
11501 Eastwood Dr 32817 407-482-8700
David Christiansen, prin. Fax 737-1455
Walker MS 1,100/6-8
150 Amidon Ln 32809 407-858-3210
Stephen Frankenstein, prin. Fax 858-3218
Westridge MS 1,200/6-8
3800 W Oak Ridge Rd 32809 407-354-2640
Nelson Pinder, prin. Fax 354-2637
East Tech ACE Center Adult
6100 Oleander Dr 32807 407-482-6304
Tony Encinias, prin.
South Tech ACE Center Adult
2000 S Mills Ave 32806 407-893-7204
Mike Painter, prin.
Transition Education ACE Center Adult
3723 Vision Blvd 32839 407-836-3590
Tim Holmes, prin.
West Tech ACE Center Adult
6500 Turkey Lake Rd 32819 407-355-3204
Lynne Voltaggio, prin.
Other Schools – See Apopka, Eatonville, Maitland, Ocoee, Windermere, Winter Garden, Winter Park

---

Agape Christian Academy 500/PK-12
2425 N Hiawassee Rd 32818 407-298-1111
Carol Fairweather, prin. Fax 298-0400
Asbury Theological Seminary Post-Sec.
8401 Valencia College Ln 32825 407-482-7500
Audio Recording Technology Institute Post-Sec.
4525 Vineland Rd Ste 201B 32811 407-423-2784
Avalon S, 5002 Andrus Ave 32804 100/K-12
Katherine Shafer, prin. 407-297-4353
Bishop Moore HS 1,200/9-12
3901 Edgewater Dr 32804 407-293-7561
Maureen Kane, prin. Fax 296-8135
Career Training Institute Post-Sec.
3318 Edgewater Dr 32804 407-884-1816
Central Florida Blood Bank Post-Sec.
8669 Commodity Cir 32819 407-849-6100
Christian Victory Academy 100/K-12
PO Box 721436 32872 407-281-6244
Paula Williamson, prin. Fax 281-6244

Devereux-Florida Treatment Network — Post-Sec.
5850 T G Lee Blvd Ste 400 32822 — 407-812-4555
DeVry University — Post-Sec.
4000 Millenia Blvd 32839 — 407-345-2800
DeVry University — Post-Sec.
1800 Pembrook Dr Ste 160 32810 — 407-659-0900
Downey Christian S — 300/PK-12
10201 E Colonial Dr 32817 — 407-275-0340
Dr. Charles Dees, prin. — Fax 275-1481
Eastland Christian S — 300/PK-12
6000 E Colonial Dr 32807 — 407-277-5858
Dolores Green, admin. — Fax 658-1013
Everglades University — Post-Sec.
5600 Lake Underhill Rd #200 32807 — 866-289-1078
Faith Christian Academy — 900/K-12
2008 N Goldenrod Rd 32807 — 407-275-8031
Chuck Smith, admin. — Fax 281-3710
First Academy — 900/PK-12
2667 Bruton Blvd 32805 — 407-206-8600
Steve Whitaker, hdmstr. — Fax 206-8771
Florida College of Integrative Medicine — Post-Sec.
7100 Lake Ellenor Dr 32809 — 407-888-8689
Florida Hospital College of Health Sci — Post-Sec.
800 Lake Estelle Dr 32803 — 407-303-9798
FL Metropolitan Univ. - Orlando College — Post-Sec.
5421 Diplomat Cir 32810 — 407-628-5870
FL Metropolitan Univ. - South Orlando — Post-Sec.
9200 S Park Center Loop 32819 — 407-851-2525
Florida Technical College — Post-Sec.
12689 Challenger Pkwy # 130 32826 — 407-678-5600
Heritage Prep S — 300/PK-12
6000 W Colonial Dr 32808 — 407-293-6000
Lloyd Elliott, hdmstr. — Fax 292-7246
High-Tech Institute — Post-Sec.
3710 Maguire Blvd 32803 — 407-893-7400
International Academy of Design & Tech — Post-Sec.
5959 Lake Ellenor Dr 32809 — 407-857-2300
Keiser College — Post-Sec.
5600 Lake Underhill Rd 32807 — 407-273-5800
Lake Highland Prep S — 1,900/PK-12
901 N Highland Ave 32803 — 407-206-1900
Warren P. Hudson, pres. — Fax 206-1911
Lake Rose Christian Academy — 100/K-12
4340 N Hiawassee Rd 32818 — 407-292-0244
Kathy Jones, prin. — Fax 297-7887
Motorcycle Mechanics Institute — Post-Sec.
9751 Delegates Dr 32837 — 407-240-2422
Muslim Academy of Central Florida — 200/PK-12
1021 N Goldenrod Rd 32807 — 407-382-9900
Michael Baker, prin. — Fax 277-4190
Orange Technical Educ. Center-Mid FL — Post-Sec.
2900 W Oak Ridge Rd 32809 — 407-855-5880
Orange Technical Educ. Center-Orlando — Post-Sec.
301 W Amelia St 32801 — 407-246-7060
Orlando Christian Prep S — 500/PK-12
500 S Semoran Blvd 32807 — 407-823-9744
Dr. Mike Zobel, admin. — Fax 380-1186
Orlando Lutheran Academy — 100/6-12
550 N Econlockhatchee Trl 32825 — 407-275-7750
Dr. Wade Jensen, prin. — Fax 277-1288
Pine Castle Christian Academy — 600/PK-12
5933 Randolph Ave 32809 — 407-438-2737
Dr. Lorne Wenzel, hdmstr. — Fax 438-2764
Princeton House Academy — 200/1-12
4832 Fairview Ave 32804 — 407-539-1301
Carol Tucker, prin. — Fax 523-7187
South Orlando Christian Academy — 200/PK-12
5815 Makoma Dr 32839 — 407-859-9511
Elizabeth Campo, prin. — Fax 859-1510
Teachers Hands Academy — 200/PK-12
3057 Curry Ford Rd Ste 2 32806 — 407-897-7477
Barbara Serianni, prin. — Fax 897-6690
University of Central Florida — Post-Sec.
PO Box 25000 32816 — 407-823-3000
Valencia Community College — Post-Sec.
PO Box 3028 32802 — 407-299-5000
Valencia Community College East Campus — Post-Sec.
701 N Econlockhatchee Trl 32825 — 407-299-5000
West Oaks Academy — 100/PK-12
8624 A D Mims Rd 32818 — 407-292-8481
Thomas Parlier, prin. — Fax 292-8838

Ormond Beach, Volusia, Pop. 37,617
Volusia County SD
Supt. — See De Land
Ormond Beach MS — 1,700/6-8
151 Domicilio Ave 32174 — 386-258-4667
Carl Persis, prin. — Fax 676-1258

Calvary Christian Academy — 300/PK-12
1687 W Granada Blvd 32174 — 386-672-2081
Anthony Arnett, prin. — Fax 615-3736
Harry Wendelstedt Umpire School — Post-Sec.
88 S Saint Andrews Dr 32174 — 386-672-4879

Otter Creek, Levy, Pop. 124

Creekside Christian S — 100/PK-12
171 SW 3rd St 32683 — 352-486-2112
William Keith, prin. — Fax 486-2171

Oviedo, Seminole, Pop. 27,940
Seminole County SD
Supt. — See Sanford
Chiles MS — 1,200/6-8
1240 Sanctuary Dr 32766 — 407-871-7050
Jim Shupe, prin. — Fax 871-7099
Hagerty HS — 9-12
3225 Lockwood Blvd 32765 — 407-871-0750
Sam Momary, prin. — Fax 871-0749
Jackson Heights MS — 1,200/6-8
141 Academy Ave 32765 — 407-320-4550
Winston Bailey, prin. — Fax 320-4599
Oviedo HS — 3,200/9-12
601 King St 32765 — 407-320-4050
Robert Lundquist, prin. — Fax 320-4000
Tuskawilla MS — 1,200/6-8
1801 Tuskawilla Rd 32765 — 407-320-8550
Michael Mizwicki, prin. — Fax 320-8599

Master's Academy — 1,000/K-12
1500 Lukas Ln 32765 — 407-971-2221
Dr. William Harris, supt. — Fax 706-0254
Reformed Theological Seminary — Post-Sec.
1231 Reformation Dr 32765 — 407-366-9493

Pace, Santa Rosa, Pop. 6,277
Santa Rosa County SD
Supt. — See Milton
Pace HS — 1,900/9-12
4065 Norris Rd 32571 — 850-995-3600
Frank Lay, prin. — Fax 995-3620

Sims MS — 900/6-8
5500 Education Dr 32571 — 850-995-3676
Wanda Knowles, prin. — Fax 995-9696

Pahokee, Palm Beach, Pop. 6,263
Palm Beach County SD
Supt. — See West Palm Beach
Pahokee MSHS — 800/7-12
900 Larrimore Rd 33476 — 561-924-6400
Marvin Bain, prin. — Fax 924-6457

Palatka, Putnam, Pop. 10,462
Putnam County SD — 11,900/PK-12
200 S 7th St 32177 — 386-329-0510
David Buckles, supt. — Fax 329-0520
www.putnamschools.org
Beasley MS — 700/6-8
1100 S 18th St 32177 — 386-329-0569
James Roach, prin. — Fax 329-0670
Jenkins MS — 800/6-8
1100 N 19th St 32177 — 386-329-0588
Debbie Decubellis, prin. — Fax 329-0636
Palatka HS — 1,700/9-12
302 Mellon Rd 32177 — 386-329-0579
Karen Hughes, prin. — Fax 329-0624
Other Schools – See Crescent City, Florahome, Interlachen

Peniel Baptist Academy — 300/PK-12
110 Peniel Church Rd 32177 — 386-328-1707
Lester Jenkins, prin. — Fax 328-0950
St. John's River Community College — Post-Sec.
5001 Saint Johns Ave 32177 — 386-312-4200

Palm Bay, Brevard, Pop. 85,076
Brevard County SD
Supt. — See Melbourne
Bayside HS — 2,100/9-12
1901 Degroodt Rd SW 32908 — 321-956-5000
John Tuttle, prin. — Fax 956-5009
Southwest MS — 1,400/7-8
451 Eldron Blvd SE 32909 — 321-952-5800
Robin Novelli, prin. — Fax 952-5819

Covenant Christian S — 300/K-12
720 Emerson Dr NE 32907 — 321-727-2661
Paul Rumbley, hdmstr. — Fax 728-9574
Darlyne McGee's Academy of Cosmetology — Post-Sec.
4711 Babcock St NE Ste 26 32905 — 321-951-0595
North Atlantic Schools — 500/K-12
5240 Babcock St NE 32905 — 321-956-6959
Stephen Moitozo, prin. — Fax 956-6222
Palm Bay Baptist Academy — 100/PK-12
2601 Emerson Dr SE 32909 — 321-723-3773
Lisa Greene, prin. — Fax 723-8730

Palm Beach Gardens, Palm Beach, Pop. 41,834
Palm Beach County SD
Supt. — See West Palm Beach
Duncan MS — 1,200/6-8
5150 117th Ct N 33418 — 561-776-3500
Joseph Lee, prin. — Fax 776-3550
Dwyer HS — 2,000/9-12
13601 N Military Trl 33410 — 561-625-7800
David Culp, prin. — Fax 625-7870
Palm Beach Gardens HS — 2,700/9-12
4245 Holly Dr 33410 — 561-694-7300
Jonathan Prince, prin. — Fax 691-0515
Watkins MS — 1,000/6-8
9480 MacArthur Blvd 33403 — 561-776-3600
Daniel Smith, prin. — Fax 776-3603
Palm Beach Gardens HS Adult Ed Center — Adult
4245 Holly Dr 33410 — 561-694-7330
Steven Martin, prin. — Fax 694-7397

Palm City, Martin, Pop. 3,925
Martin County SD
Supt. — See Stuart
Hidden Oaks MS — 1,500/6-8
2801 SW Martin Hwy 34990 — 772-219-1655
Jenny Lambdin, prin. — Fax 219-1663

Palm Coast, Flagler, Pop. 37,266
Flagler County SD
Supt. — See Bunnell
Indian Trails MS — 800/6-8
5505 Belle Terre Pkwy 32137 — 386-446-6732
Michele Crosby, prin. — Fax 445-7662
Matanzas HS — 9-10
3535 Old Kings Rd N 32137
Chris Pryor, prin.
Flagler County Adult & Comm Education S — Adult
1 Corporate Plaza Dr 32137 — 386-446-7612
Mary Gilbert, prin. — Fax 446-7620

FAA Center for Management Development — Post-Sec.
4500 Palm Coast Pkwy SE 32137 — 386-446-7136
Palm Coast Christian S — 100/PK-12
94 Whiteview Pkwy 32164 — 386-445-6339
Cindy Pryor, dir. — Fax 446-1750

Palmetto, Manatee, Pop. 12,767
Manatee County SD
Supt. — See Bradenton
Lincoln MS — 1,100/6-8
305 17th St E 34221 — 941-721-6840
Reid Wallace, prin. — Fax 721-6853
Palmetto HS — 1,600/9-12
1200 17th St W 34221 — 941-723-4848
Debra Valcarcel, prin. — Fax 723-4952

Palm Harbor, Pinellas, Pop. 61,400
Pinellas County SD
Supt. — See Largo
Carwise MS — 1,400/6-8
3301 Bentley Dr 34684 — 727-724-1442
Garrison T. Linder, prin. — Fax 724-1446
Palm Harbor MS — 1,500/6-8
1800 Tampa Rd 34683 — 727-669-1146
Ward Kennedy, prin. — Fax 669-1244
Palm Harbor University HS — 2,300/9-12
1900 Omaha St 34683 — 727-669-1131
Harry Brown, prin. — Fax 725-7936
Palm Harbor Community S — Adult
1900 Omaha St 34683 — 727-669-1140
Suzanne B. Wester, admin. — Fax 725-7936

Central Florida Institute — Post-Sec.
30522 US Highway 19 N 34684 — 727-786-4707

Palm Springs, Palm Beach, Pop. 13,673

MedVance Institute — Post-Sec.
1630 S Congress Ave 33461 — 561-304-3466

Panama City, Bay, Pop. 37,085
Bay County SD — 24,400/PK-12
1311 Balboa Ave 32401 — 850-872-7700
James McCalister, supt. — Fax 872-4367
www.bay.k12.fl.us
Arnold HS — 1,300/9-12
550 N Alf Coleman Rd 32407 — 850-236-3070
John Haley, prin. — Fax 236-3068
Bay HS — 1,500/9-12
1200 Harrison Ave 32401 — 850-872-4600
Larry Bolinger, prin. — Fax 872-4651
Brown MS — 900/6-8
5044 Merritt Brown Way 32404 — 850-872-4740
Charlotte Marshall, prin. — Fax 872-7625
Everitt MS — 900/6-8
608 School Ave 32401 — 850-872-4790
Linda Landen, prin. — Fax 872-7721
Haney Technical Center — Vo/Tech
3016 Highway 77 32405 — 850-747-5500
Sandra Davis, prin. — Fax 747-5555
Haney Technical HS — 200/9-12
3016 Highway 77 32405 — 850-747-5500
Sandra Davis, prin. — Fax 747-5555
Harris HS — 300/9-12
819 E 11th St 32401 — 850-872-4590
Anita Dillard, prin. — Fax 747-5799
Jinks MS — 800/6-8
600 W 11th St 32401 — 850-872-4695
Anna McLain, prin. — Fax 872-7612
Rosenwald MS — 800/6-8
924 Bay Ave 32401 — 850-872-4580
Mike Riley, prin. — Fax 872-7615
Rutherford HS — 1,800/9-12
1000 School Ave 32401 — 850-872-4500
Mike Kennedy, prin. — Fax 872-4827
Surfside MS — 1,100/6-8
300 Nautilus St 32413 — 850-233-5180
Sue Harrell, prin. — Fax 233-5193
Shaw Adult Center — Adult
162 Detroit Ave 32401 — 850-872-4555
Mike Heptinstall, prin. — Fax 872-7587
Other Schools – See Lynn Haven

Bay Medical Center — Post-Sec.
615 N Bonita Ave 32401 — 800-422-2418
Covenant Christian S — 400/PK-12
2350 Frankford Ave 32405 — 850-769-7448
Tom Bingham, admin. — Fax 763-2104
Fellowship Christian Academy — 100/PK-12
2511 E 3rd St 32401 — 850-769-5442
Dr. Vernette Rosier, prin. — Fax 769-0313
Gulf Coast Community College — Post-Sec.
5230 W Highway 98 32401 — 850-769-1551
Panama City Christian S — 300/PK-12
1104 Balboa Ave 32401 — 850-769-6000
Dr. Doug Boucher, prin. — Fax 785-5212
Tom P. Haney Technical Center — Post-Sec.
3016 Highway 77 32405 — 850-747-5500

Parkland, Broward, Pop. 19,861
Broward County SD
Supt. — See Fort Lauderdale
Stoneman HS — 4,300/9-12
5901 Pine Island Rd 33076 — 754-322-2150
Daniel Traeger, prin. — Fax 322-2280
Westglades MS — 1,800/6-8
11000 Holmberg Rd 33076 — 754-322-4800
Christine Flynn, prin. — Fax 322-4885

Paxton, Walton, Pop. 733
Walton County SD
Supt. — See De Funiak Springs
Paxton S — 700/PK-12
PO Box 1168 32538 — 850-892-1230
Mike Anderson, prin. — Fax 892-1239

Pembroke Pines, Broward, Pop. 148,927
Broward County SD
Supt. — See Fort Lauderdale
Flanagan HS — 3,700/9-12
12800 Taft St 33028 — 754-323-0650
Sharon Shaulis, prin. — Fax 323-0780
Flanagan HS Annex — 9-9
201 SW 172nd Ave 33029 — 954-450-5030
Fax 450-5044
Glades MS — 6-8
201 SW 172nd Ave 33029 — 754-323-4600
Krista Herrera, prin. — Fax 323-4685
Pines MS — 1,500/6-8
200 N Douglas Rd 33024 — 754-323-4000
Carlton Campbell, prin. — Fax 323-4085
Young Resource Center MS — 1,800/6-8
901 NW 129th Ave 33028 — 754-323-4500
Diane Hall, prin. — Fax 323-4585

Broward Community College-South Campus — Post-Sec.
7200 Pines Blvd 33024 — 954-963-8835
Florida Career College — Post-Sec.
7891 Pines Blvd 33024 — 954-965-7272
PC Professor — Post-Sec.
600 N Hiatus Rd Ste 105 33026 — 954-704-4444
Pelican Flight Training Center — Post-Sec.
1601 SW 75th Ave 33023 — 954-966-9750

Pensacola, Escambia, Pop. 54,897
Escambia County SD — 42,000/PK-12
215 W Garden St 32502 — 850-469-6121
Jim Paul, supt. — Fax 469-6379
www.escambia.k12.fl.us
Bailey MS — 1,600/6-8
4110 Bauer Rd 32506 — 850-492-6136
Judy Pippin, prin. — Fax 492-9860
Bellview MS — 1,200/6-8
6201 Mobile Hwy 32526 — 850-941-6080
Vicki Gibowksi, prin. — Fax 941-6089
Brentwood MS — 700/6-8
201 Hancock Ln 32503 — 850-494-5640
Marsha Higgins, prin. — Fax 494-5699
Brown Barge MS — 500/6-8
151 E Fairfield Dr 32503 — 850-595-6900
Patricia Kerrigan, prin. — Fax 595-6920
Brownsville Arts & Science Academy — 700/6-8
3700 W Avery St 32505 — 850-595-6860
Sandra Riley-Rush, prin. — Fax 595-6866
Escambia HS — 1,700/9-12
1310 N 65th Ave 32506 — 850-453-3221
Ruth Mims, prin. — Fax 453-9381

Ferry Pass MS 1,000/6-8
8355 Yancey Ave 32514 850-494-5650
Ann Bookout, prin. Fax 494-5653
Pensacola HS 1,700/9-12
500 W Maxwell St 32501 850-595-1500
Sara Lewis, prin. Fax 595-1519
Pine Forest HS 1,600/9-12
2500 Longleaf Dr 32526 850-941-6150
Barbara Patterson, prin. Fax 941-6163
Stone Career Center Center Vo/Tech
2400 Longleaf Dr 32526 850-941-6200
Eric Smith, prin. Fax 941-6215
Washington HS 1,700/9-12
6000 College Pkwy 32504 850-475-5257
Steve Marcanio, prin. Fax 494-7297
Wedgewood MS 700/6-8
3420 W Pinestead Rd 32505 850-494-5660
Larry Reid, prin. Fax 494-5672
West Florida HS 1,100/9-12
2400 Longleaf Dr 32526 850-941-6200
Lesa Morgan, prin. Fax 941-6215
Woodham HS 1,300/9-12
150 E Burgess Rd 32503 850-494-7140
Michael Roberts, prin. Fax 494-7484
Workman MS 900/6-8
6299 Lanier Dr 32504 850-494-5665
Juanita Edwards, prin. Fax 494-5697
Other Schools – See Cantonment, Century, Walnut Hill, Warrington

---

Aletheia Christian Academy 200/PK-12
1700 Woodchuck Ave 32504 850-969-0088
Jeff Caulfield-James, admin. Fax 969-0906
East Hill Christian S 400/PK-12
1301 E Gadsden St 32501 850-435-7741
James Sidbury, admin. Fax 435-7280
Florida Institute of Ultrasound Post-Sec.
8800 University Pkwy Ste A4 32514 850-478-7300
George Stone Vocational Technical Ctr. Post-Sec.
2400 Longleaf Dr 32526 850-941-6200
Jubilee Christian Academy 200/PK-12
PO Box 30269 32503 850-494-2477
Angela Fox, hdmstr. Fax 494-2900
Medical Career Center Post-Sec.
19 W Garden St 32502 850-436-8444
Pensacola Catholic HS 600/9-12
3043 W Scott St 32505 850-436-6400
Sr. Kierstin Martin, prin. Fax 436-6405
Pensacola Christian Academy 2,600/PK-12
10 Brent Ln 32503 850-478-8483
Troy A. Shoemaker, dir. Fax 479-6572
Pensacola Christian College Post-Sec.
PO Box 18000 32523 850-478-8496
Pensacola Junior College Post-Sec.
1000 College Blvd 32504 850-484-1000
Trinitas Christian S 100/K-12
3301 E Johnson Ave 32514 850-484-3515
Kenneth Trotter, admin. Fax 484-3590
University of West Florida Post-Sec.
11000 University Pkwy 32514 850-474-2000

Perrine, Dade, Pop. 15,576
Miami-Dade County SD
Supt. — See Miami
Morgan Education Center 1,300/9-12
18180 SW 122nd Ave 33177 305-253-9920
Gregory Zawyer, prin. Fax 259-1495

Perry, Taylor, Pop. 6,749
Taylor County SD 3,100/K-12
318 N Clark St 32347 850-838-2500
Oscar Howard, supt. Fax 838-2501
www.taylor.k12.fl.us
Taylor County HS 800/9-12
900 N Johnson Stripling Rd 32347 850-838-2525
Michael Thompson, prin. Fax 838-2521
Taylor County MS 700/6-8
601 E Lafayette St 32347 850-838-2516
Paul Dyal, prin. Fax 838-2559
Taylor Technical Institute Vo/Tech
3233 S Byron Butler Pkwy 32348 850-838-2545
Ken Olsen, prin. Fax 838-2546

Taylor Technical Institute Post-Sec.
3233 Highway 19 S 32347 850-838-2545

Pierson, Volusia, Pop. 2,602
Volusia County SD
Supt. — See De Land
Taylor MSHS 1,000/6-12
100 E Washington Ave 32180 386-740-9800
R. Marty Schmidt, prin. Fax 749-6836

Pinellas Park, Pinellas, Pop. 46,449
Pinellas County SD
Supt. — See Largo
Pinellas Park MS 1,200/6-8
6940 70th Ave 33781 727-545-6400
Lori Potenza, prin. Fax 547-7894

Center Academy - Pinellas Park 100/4-12
6710 86th Ave 33782 727-541-5716
John Porter, prin. Fax 544-8186
First Baptist Christian S 200/K-12
5495 Park Blvd 33781 727-541-2785
Jerry Forrester, prin. Fax 541-3308
Humanities Center Inst. of Allied Health Post-Sec.
4045 Park Blvd 33781 727-541-5200

Plantation, Broward, Pop. 84,929
Broward County SD
Supt. — See Fort Lauderdale
Plantation HS 3,100/9-12
6901 NW 16th St 33313 754-322-1850
Susan Bruining, prin. Fax 322-1980
Plantation MS 1,300/6-8
6600 W Sunrise Blvd 33313 754-322-4100
David Olafson, prin. Fax 322-4185
Seminole MS 1,400/6-8
6200 SW 16th St 33317 754-323-4200
Sherry Rose Patire, prin. Fax 323-4285
South Plantation HS 2,600/9-12
1300 SW 54th Ave 33317 754-323-1950
Joel Herbst, prin. Fax 323-2080

American Academy 500/1-12
12200 W Broward Blvd 33325 954-470-0022
William Laurie, prin. Fax 472-3088
American Heritage S 1,900/PK-12
12200 W Broward Blvd 33325 954-472-0022
William Laurie, prin. Fax 472-3088
American InterContinental University Post-Sec.
8151 Peters Rd Ste 1000 33324 954-835-0939
Broward Christian S 100/PK-12
1490 N Flamingo Rd 33323 954-472-5750
Dr. Ray Nichols, prin. Fax 472-1295
Posnack Hebrew Day S 700/K-12
6511 W Sunrise Blvd 33313 954-583-6100
Geri Stief, prin. Fax 791-5463

Plant City, Hillsborough, Pop. 31,117
Hillsborough County SD
Supt. — See Tampa
Durant HS 2,500/9-12
4748 Cougar Path 33567 813-757-9075
Pamela Bowden, prin. Fax 707-7079
Marshall MS 900/6-8
18 S Maryland Ave, 813-757-9360
Josie Sanders, prin. Fax 707-7385
Plant City HS 2,500/9-12
1 Raider Pl, 813-757-9370
Dr. David Steele, prin. Fax 757-9135
Simmons Career Center Vo/Tech
1202 W Grant St, 813-707-7430
Leslie Morris, prin. Fax 707-7435
Tomlin MS 1,500/6-8
501 N Woodrow Wilson St, 813-757-9400
Dr. Beverly Carbaugh, prin. Fax 707-7024
Turkey Creek MS 1,100/6-8
5005 Turkey Creek Rd 33567 813-757-9442
Mark West, prin. Fax 757-9451
Plant City Adult & Community Center Adult
1 Raider Pl, 813-707-7147
Stephen A. Barta, prin. Fax 707-7149

Hillsborough Community College Post-Sec.
1206 N Park Rd, 813-757-2100
Hope Christian Academy 100/1-12
1109 W Grant St, 813-752-1000
Michelle Hagel, admin. Fax 752-1367

Pompano Beach, Broward, Pop. 88,064
Broward County SD
Supt. — See Fort Lauderdale
Crystal Lake MS 1,800/6-8
3551 NE 3rd Ave 33064 754-322-3100
James Neer, prin. Fax 322-3185
Ely HS 2,800/9-12
1201 NW 6th Ave 33060 754-322-0950
Edmond Wade, prin. Fax 322-1080
Pompano Beach HS 900/9-12
600 NE 13th Ave 33060 754-322-2000
William Bell, prin. Fax 322-2130
Pompano Beach MS 1,200/6-8
310 NE 6th St 33060 754-322-4200
Sonja Braziel, prin. Fax 322-4285
Thomas Education Center Adult
180 SW 2nd St 33060 754-321-6750
Linda Wilhoit, prin. Fax 321-6790

Florida Barber Academy Post-Sec.
3269 N Federal Hwy 33064 954-781-6066
Florida College of Natural Health Post-Sec.
2001 W Sample Rd Ste 100 33064 954-975-6400
FL Metropolitan Univ. Post-Sec.
225 N Federal Hwy 33062 954-568-1600
Highlands Christian Academy 900/PK-12
501 NE 48th St 33064 954-421-1747
Ken Lopez, prin. Fax 421-2429

Ponce de Leon, Holmes, Pop. 464
Holmes County SD
Supt. — See Bonifay
Ponce De Leon JSHS 400/6-12
1477 Ammons Rd 32455 850-836-4242
Buddy Brown, prin. Fax 836-5388

Ponte Vedra Beach, Saint Johns
St. John's County SD
Supt. — See Saint Augustine
Landrum MS 1,000/6-8
230 Landrum Ln 32082 904-285-9080
Beverly Gordon, prin. Fax 819-8415

Port Charlotte, Charlotte, Pop. 47,600
Charlotte County SD 17,500/PK-12
1445 Education Way 33948 941-255-0808
Dr. David Gayler, supt. Fax 255-0413
www.ccps.k12.fl.us
Charlotte Technical Center Vo/Tech
18300 Toledo Blade Blvd 33948 941-255-7500
Barbara Witte, dir. Fax 255-7509
Murdock MS 1,100/6-8
17325 Mariner Way 33948 941-255-7525
Dr. Christine Dollinger, prin. Fax 255-7533
Port Charlotte HS 2,000/9-12
18200 Toledo Blade Blvd 33948 941-255-7485
Steve Dionisio, prin. Fax 255-7493
Port Charlotte MS 1,100/6-8
23000 Midway Blvd 33952 941-255-7460
Demetrius Revelas, prin. Fax 255-7469
Adult & Community Education Adult
1441 Tamiami Trl Unit 365 33948 941-255-7555
Mike Riley, dir. Fax 255-7433
Other Schools – See Englewood, Punta Gorda, Rotonda West

Charlotte Technical Center Post-Sec.
18300 Toledo Blade Blvd 33948 941-255-7500
Community Christian S 300/PK-12
20035 Quesada Ave 33952 941-625-0008
Margaret Adkins, admin. Fax 625-1735
Port Charlotte Christian S 50/PK-12
3279 Sherwood Rd 33980 941-625-4450
Rev. Daniel Kolenda, prin. Fax 243-0586
Port Charlotte SDA S 100/K-11
2100 Loveland Blvd 33980 941-625-5237
Marcia Moore, prin. Fax 625-8460

Port Orange, Volusia, Pop. 50,930
Volusia County SD
Supt. — See De Land
Atlantic HS 1,500/9-12
1250 Reed Canal Rd 32129 386-322-6100
Ron Pagano, prin. Fax 322-5649
Creekside MS 1,300/6-8
6801 Airport Rd 32128 386-322-6155
Deborah Drawdy, prin. Fax 304-5508
Silver Sands MS 1,400/6-8
1300 Herbert St 32129 386-322-6175
Dr. Leslie Potter, prin. Fax 322-7574
Spruce Creek HS 2,600/9-12
801 Taylor Rd 32127 386-322-6272
Timothy Egnor, prin. Fax 756-7270

Palmer College of Chiropractic Florida Post-Sec.
4777 City Center Pkwy 32129 386-763-2709

Port Richey, Pasco, Pop. 3,221
Pasco County SD
Supt. — See Land O Lakes
Chasco MS 1,000/6-8
7702 Ridge Rd 34668 727-774-1300
Lawrence Albano, prin. Fax 774-1391

Port Saint Joe, Gulf, Pop. 4,150
Gulf County SD 2,300/PK-12
150 Middle School Rd 32456 850-229-8256
Tim Wilder, supt. Fax 229-6089
www.gulf.k12.fl.us
Port Saint Joe HS 400/9-12
100 Shark Dr 32456 850-229-8251
Duane McFarland, prin. Fax 227-1803
Port Saint Joe MS 300/6-8
191 Middle School Rd 32456 850-227-3211
Juanise Griffin, prin. Fax 229-9078
Gulf County Adult S Adult
2855 Long Ave 32456 850-227-1744
Don Rich, prin. Fax 229-2724
Other Schools – See Wewahitchka

Faith Christian S 100/PK-12
801 20th St 32456 850-229-6707
Lorelei Beightol, admin. Fax 227-1307

Port Saint Lucie, Saint Lucie, Pop. 98,538
St. Lucie County SD
Supt. — See Fort Pierce
Northport MS 1,200/6-8
250 NW Floresta Dr 34983 772-340-4700
Eric Seymour, prin. Fax 340-7116
Port Saint Lucie HS 2,100/9-12
1201 SE Jaguar Ln 34952 772-337-6770
Terry Davis, prin. Fax 337-6780
St. Lucie West Centennial HS 2,200/9-12
1485 SW Cashmere Blvd 34986 772-785-6660
Gayle Pike, prin. Fax 785-6679
St. Lucie West MS 1,100/6-8
1001 SW Juliet Ave 34953 772-785-6630
Pam Frederick, prin. Fax 785-6632
Southern Oaks MS 1,100/6-8
5500 NW Saint James Dr 34983 772-785-5640
John Lynch, prin. Fax 785-5660
Southport MS 1,100/6-8
2420 SE Morningside Blvd 34952 772-337-5900
Mary Mosley, prin. Fax 337-5903
Treasure Coast HS 9-12
1000 SW Darwin Blvd 34953 772-807-4300
Helen Roberts, prin.

Keiser Career College Post-Sec.
9468 S US 1 34652 727-398-9990
Morningside Academy 700/K-12
2180 SE Morningside Blvd 34952 561-335-2096
William Turner, prin. Fax 335-2095
Olivet Private S, PO Box 7865 34985 200/K-12
Cathie Mouring, dir. 772-879-3917
Port St. Lucie Beauty Academy Post-Sec.
7644 S US 1 34983 772-340-3540
Treasure Coast Christian Academy 200/PK-12
590 NW Peacock Blvd Ste 5 34986 772-343-8088
Cynthia Netwig, prin. Fax 879-6975
Victory Forge Military Academy 50/7-12
638 SW Biltmore St 34983 772-879-7181
Alan Weierman, prin. Fax 878-8160

Princeton, Dade, Pop. 7,073

Princeton Christian S 500/PK-12
PO Box 924916 33092 305-257-3644
Cynthia Stone, prin. Fax 257-5799

Punta Gorda, Charlotte, Pop. 16,720
Charlotte County SD
Supt. — See Port Charlotte
Charlotte HS 2,200/9-12
1250 Cooper St 33950 941-575-5450
Bernard Duffy, prin. Fax 575-5464
Punta Gorda MS 1,100/6-8
825 Carmalita St 33950 941-575-5485
Dr. Donna DiGrazia, prin. Fax 575-5491

IMPAC University Post-Sec.
900 W Marion Ave 33950 941-639-7512

Quincy, Gadsden, Pop. 6,915
Gadsden County SD 6,400/PK-12
35 Martin Luther King Jr Bl 32351 850-627-9651
Reginald C. James, supt. Fax 627-2760
www.gcps.k12.fl.us
Gadsden Technical Institute Vo/Tech
201 Martin Luther King Jr B 32351 850-875-8324
Debra Rackley, prin. Fax 875-7269
Shanks MS 800/6-8
1400 W King St 32351 850-875-8737
Rosalyn Smith, prin. Fax 875-8775
Gadsden Adult Education Center Adult
201 Martin Luther King Jr B 32351 850-875-8324
Debra Rackley, prin. Fax 875-7269
Other Schools – See Greensboro, Havana

Community Learning Institute 200/PK-12
523 S Pat Thomas Pkwy 32351 850-627-8150
Willie Green, prin. Fax 627-1807
Munroe Day S 300/PK-12
91 Old Mt Pleasant Rd 32352 850-856-5500
Michael Knight, prin. Fax 856-5856

Riverview, Hillsborough, Pop. 6,478
Hillsborough County SD
Supt. — See Tampa
Giunta MS 6-8
4202 Falkenburg Rd S 33569 813-740-4888
Scott Fritz, prin. Fax 740-4892
Riverview HS 2,600/9-12
11311 Boyette Rd 33569 813-671-5011
Robert Heilmann, prin. Fax 671-5012
Rodgers MS 1,600/6-8
11910 Tucker Rd 33569 813-671-5288
Clara Davis, prin. Fax 671-5245
Spoto HS, 8538 Eagle Palm Dr 33569 9-12
Clyde Trathowen, prin. 813-672-5405

East Bay Christian S 100/PK-12
10102 Old Big Bend Rd 33569 813-677-5236
Bruce DuBois, prin. Fax 672-0808
EduTech Centers Post-Sec.
2262 S Falkenburg Rd 33569 800-485-0717
Providence Christian S 400/PK-12
5416 Providence Rd 33569 813-661-0588
Stephen Weer, dir. Fax 681-3852
Tropical Acres Baptist S 50/K-12
12107 Rhodine Rd 33569 813-677-8036
Rev. Thomas Saxe, dir. Fax 677-8036

Riviera Beach, Palm Beach, Pop. 31,733
Palm Beach County SD
Supt. — See West Palm Beach
Inlet Grove Community HS Vo/Tech
7071 Garden Rd 33404 561-881-4600
Michael Murgio, prin. Fax 881-4668
Kennedy MS 1,100/6-8
1901 Avenue S 33404 561-845-4500
Donald Greene, prin. Fax 845-4537
Suncoast HS 1,400/9-12
600 W 28th St 33404 561-882-3400
Gloria Crutchfield, prin. Fax 882-3443

Hendley Christian Education Center 400/PK-12
2800 Avenue R 33404 561-881-8015
Charley Hendley, dir. Fax 840-0716
North Technical Education Center Post-Sec.
7071 Garden Rd 33404 561-881-4600

Rockledge, Brevard, Pop. 22,239
Brevard County SD
Supt. — See Melbourne
Kennedy MS 800/6-8
2100 Fiske Blvd 32955 321-633-3500
Richard Myers, prin. Fax 633-3509
Rockledge HS 1,600/9-12
220 Raider Rd 32955 321-636-3711
Anthony Hines, prin. Fax 632-6064

Rotonda West, Charlotte
Charlotte County SD
Supt. — See Port Charlotte
Ainger MS 1,100/6-8
245 Cougar Way 33947 941-697-5800
Marcia Louden, prin. Fax 697-5470

Royal Palm Beach, Palm Beach, Pop. 28,506
Palm Beach County SD
Supt. — See West Palm Beach
Crestwood MS 1,500/6-8
64 Sparrow Dr 33411 561-753-5000
Vera Garcia, prin. Fax 753-5035
Royal Palm Beach HS 3,100/9-12
10600 Okeechobee Blvd 33411 561-753-4000
Jose Garcia, prin. Fax 753-4015

Ruskin, Hillsborough, Pop. 6,046
Hillsborough County SD
Supt. — See Tampa
Lennard HS 9-12
2002 Shell Point Rd 33570 813-641-5611
Denny Oest, prin.
Shields MS 6-8
3908 19th Ave NE 33573 813-672-5338
Jerry Jackson, prin. Fax 672-5342
South County Career Center Vo/Tech
4646 S Highway 41 33570 813-233-3335
John Sherman, prin. Fax 233-3339

First Baptist/Ruskin Christian S 300/PK-12
820 College Ave W 33570 813-645-6441
Rev. Barry Rumsey, dir. Fax 641-2073

Safety Harbor, Pinellas, Pop. 17,424
Pinellas County SD
Supt. — See Largo
Safety Harbor MS 1,500/6-8
901 1st Ave N 34695 727-724-1400
Alison Kennedy, prin. Fax 724-1407

Saint Augustine, Saint Johns, Pop. 11,915
St. John's County SD 22,000/PK-12
40 Orange St 32084 904-819-7500
Joseph Joyner Ed.D., supt. Fax 819-7515
www.stjohns.k12.fl.us
Menendez HS 1,500/9-12
600 State Road 206 W 32086 904-819-8660
Robert Allten, prin. Fax 819-8675
Murray MS 700/6-8
150 N Holmes Blvd 32084 904-819-8470
Meredith Strickland, prin. Fax 819-8475
Nease HS 1,600/9-12
10550 Ray Rd 32081 904-819-8300
Dr. Linda Thomson, prin. Fax 819-8305
Rogers MS 1,000/6-8
6250 US Highway 1 S 32086 904-819-8700
Randy Johnson, prin. Fax 819-8705
Saint Augustine HS 1,500/9-12
3205 Varella Ave 32084 904-819-8530
Dr. Michael O'Loughlin, prin. Fax 819-8535
St. Johns Technical HS Vo/Tech
2980 Collins Ave 32084 904-819-8500
Jay Willets, prin. Fax 819-8505
Sebastian MS 800/6-8
2955 Lewis Speedway 32084 904-819-3840
Paul Abbatinozzi, prin. Fax 819-3845
Webster S 1,000/PK-12
420 N Orange St 32084 904-819-3860
Mary Davis, prin. Fax 819-3865
Other Schools – See Jacksonville, Ponte Vedra Beach

First Coast Technical Institute Post-Sec.
2980 Collins Ave 32084 904-829-1010
Flagler College Post-Sec.
PO Box 1027 32085 904-829-6481
Florida School for the Deaf and Blind Post-Sec.
207 San Marco Ave 32084
Mill Creek Baptist Christian Academy 200/PK-12
6019A State Road 16 32092 904-940-0344
Rev. David Beecher, dir. Fax 940-9833
St. John's Academy 100/PK-12
1533 Wildwood Dr 32086 904-824-9224
Wallis Brooks, prin. Fax 823-1145
St. Joseph Academy 400/9-12
155 State Rd 207 32084 904-824-0431
Michael Heubeck, prin. Fax 826-4477
Univ. of St. Augustine for Health Sci. Post-Sec.
1 University Blvd 32086 904-826-0084

Saint Cloud, Osceola, Pop. 21,480
Osceola County SD
Supt. — See Kissimmee
Harmony HS 9-12
3601 Arthur J Gallagher 34771 407-933-9900
Debra Pace, prin. Fax 933-9901
Saint Cloud HS 2,600/9-12
2000 Bulldog Ln 34769 407-891-3100
Scott Muri, prin. Fax 891-3114
Saint Cloud MS 800/6-8
1975 Michigan Ave 34769 407-891-3200
Robert Studly, prin. Fax 891-3206

Southland Christian S 400/PK-12
2901 17th St 34769 407-891-7723
Rob Ennis, prin. Fax 891-7734

St Georges Isle, Franklin

North Tennessee Bible Inst. & Seminary Post-Sec.
556 W Bayshore Dr 32328 850-927-4711

Saint Leo, Pasco, Pop. 782

St. Leo University Post-Sec.
PO Box 6665 33574 352-588-8200

Saint Petersburg, Pinellas, Pop. 247,610
Pinellas County SD
Supt. — See Largo
Azalea MS 1,300/6-8
7855 22nd Ave N 33710 727-893-2606
Teresa Anderson, prin. Fax 893-2624
Bay Point MS 1,200/6-8
2151 62nd Ave S 33712 727-893-1153
Starla Metz, prin. Fax 893-1181
Gibbs HS 2,100/9-12
850 34th St S 33711 727-893-5452
Herman Allen, prin. Fax 893-5461
Hollins HS 2,000/9-12
4940 62nd St N 33709 727-547-7876
Michael Bohnet, prin. Fax 547-7727
Hopkins MS 1,400/6-8
701 16th St S 33705 727-893-2400
Maureen Thornton, prin. Fax 893-1600
Lakewood HS 1,700/9-12
1400 54th Ave S 33705 727-893-2916
Dennis Duda, prin. Fax 893-1387
Marshall MS 600/6-8
3901 22nd Ave S 33711 727-552-1737
Joan Minnis, prin. Fax 552-1741
Meadowlawn MS 1,300/6-8
6050 16th St N 33703 727-570-3097
Gregory Cardone, prin. Fax 570-3396
Northeast HS 2,000/9-12
5500 16th St N 33703 727-570-3138
Patricia Wright, prin. Fax 217-7318
PTEC St. Petersburg Vo/Tech
901 34th St S 33711 727-893-2500
Dorothy Bailey, dir. Fax 893-2123
Riviera MS 1,200/6-8
501 62nd Ave NE 33702 727-570-5150
Albert Bennett, prin. Fax 570-3094
St. Petersburg HS 2,400/9-12
2501 5th Ave N 33713 727-893-1842
Dr. Julie Janssen, prin. Fax 893-1399
Southside Fundamental MS 600/6-8
1701 10th St S 33705 727-893-2742
Michael Miller, prin. Fax 893-2129
Tyrone MS 1,100/6-8
6421 22nd Ave N 33710 727-893-1819
Stephanie A. Adkinson, prin. Fax 893-1946
Hollins Evening Adult Education Ctr Adult
4940 62nd St N 33709 727-547-7872
Brenda Vlach, admin. Fax 547-7873
Lakewood Community S Adult
1400 54th Ave S 33705 727-893-2955
Dr. Jane Huber, admin. Fax 893-1375
Northeast Community S Adult
1717 54th Ave N 33714 727-570-3193
Dr. Kathy K. Gregg, admin. Fax 570-3193
Tomlinson Adult Learning Center Adult
296 Mirror Lake Dr N 33701 727-893-2723
Dr. Debby VanderWoude, dir. Fax 893-2782

Admiral Farragut Academy 400/K-12
PO Box 43010 33743 727-384-5500
Robert Fine, hdmstr. Fax 384-5507
Bayfront Medical Center Post-Sec.
701 6th St S 33701 727-893-6604
Broach S 100/1-12
4500 43rd St N 33714 727-526-5700
Susan Ray, prin. Fax 525-4322
Canterbury S of Florida 400/PK-12
901 58th Ave NE 33703 727-525-1419
Mac Hall, hdmstr. Fax 521-4739
Eckerd College Post-Sec.
4200 54th Ave S 33711 727-867-1166
Florida Blood Services Post-Sec.
10100 Dr Mrtn Lthr King St 33716 727-568-5433
Galen Health Institute Post-Sec.
9549 Koger Blvd N Ste 100 33702 727-577-1497
Keswick Christian S 600/PK-12
10101 54th Ave N 33708 727-393-9100
Steven Sinclair, hdmstr. Fax 397-5378
Loraine's Academy Post-Sec.
1012 58th St N 33710 727-347-4247
Northside Christian S 800/PK-12
7777 62nd Ave N 33709 727-541-7593
Mary Brandes, hdmstr. Fax 546-5836
Pinellas Technical Education Center Post-Sec.
901 34th St S 33711 727-893-2500
Poynter Institute for Media Studies Post-Sec.
801 3rd St S 33701 727-821-9494
St. Petersburg Catholic HS 600/9-12
6333 9th Ave N 33710 727-344-4065
Rev. John Serio, prin. Fax 343-9311
St. Petersburg College Post-Sec.
PO Box 13489 33733 727-341-3600
St. Petersburg Theological Seminary Post-Sec.
10830 Navajo Dr 33708 727-399-0276
Shorecrest Preparatory S 1,000/PK-12
5101 1st St NE 33703 727-522-2111
Michael Murphy, hdmstr. Fax 527-4191
University of South Florida Post-Sec.
140 7th Ave S 33701 727-893-9536

Sanford, Seminole, Pop. 43,556
Seminole County SD 64,600/PK-12
400 E Lake Mary Blvd 32773 407-320-0000
Dr. Bill Vogel, supt. Fax 320-0281
www.scps.k12.fl.us
Millennium MS 1,900/6-8
21 Lakeview Ave 32773 407-320-6550
Brennan Asplen, prin. Fax 320-6599
Sanford MS 1,300/6-8
1700 S French Ave 32771 407-320-6150
Mark Russi, prin. Fax 320-6265
Seminole HS 2,800/9-12
2701 Ridgewood Ave 32773 407-320-5050
Walt Griffin, prin. Fax 320-5024
Other Schools – See Altamonte Springs, Casselberry, Lake Mary, Longwood, Oviedo, Winter Park, Winter Springs

Delta Connection Academy Post-Sec.
2700 Flightline Ave 32773 407-430-4112
Liberty Christian S 200/K-12
2626 S Palmetto Ave 32773 407-323-1583
Rev. Ron Williams, dir. Fax 323-1588
Seminole Community College Post-Sec.
100 Weldon Blvd 32773 407-328-4722

Santa Rosa Beach, Walton
Walton County SD
Supt. — See De Funiak Springs
Emerald Coast MS 6-8
6694 W County Highway 30A 32459 850-622-5025
John Haro, prin. Fax 622-5027
South Walton HS 400/9-12
645 Greenway Trl 32459 850-622-5020
Mark Ewing, prin. Fax 622-5039

Sarasota, Sarasota, Pop. 53,259
Sarasota County SD 35,900/PK-12
1960 Landings Blvd 34231 941-927-9000
Dr. Gary Norris, supt. Fax 361-6049
www.sarasota.k12.fl.us
Booker HS 1,600/9-12
3201 N Orange Ave 34234 941-355-2967
Jill Dorsett, prin. Fax 359-5757
Booker MS 1,300/6-8
2250 Myrtle St 34234 941-359-5824
William Maher, prin. Fax 359-5898
Brookside MS 1,300/6-8
3636 S Shade Ave 34239 941-361-6472
Karen Rose, prin. Fax 361-6508
Gulf Coast Vocational Institute Vo/Tech
1684 11th St 34236 941-361-6502
Derrick Mays, dir. Fax 361-6646
McIntosh MS 1,100/6-8
701 McIntosh Rd 34232 941-361-6520
Robert Hagemann, prin. Fax 361-6340
Riverview HS 2,600/9-12
1 Ram Way 34231 941-923-1484
Linda Nook, prin. Fax 361-6175
Sarasota County Technical Institute Vo/Tech
4748 Beneva Rd 34233 941-924-1365
Bruce Andersen, dir. Fax 921-7902
Sarasota HS 2,600/9-12
1000 S School Ave 34237 941-955-0181
Jeff Hradek, prin. Fax 361-6380
Sarasota MS 1,300/6-8
4826 Ashton Rd 34233 941-361-6464
Dr. Page Dettmann, prin. Fax 361-6798
Adult & Community Education Center Adult
1086 S Shade Ave 34237 941-361-6590
Jeanne Goble, prin. Fax 361-6382
Other Schools – See North Port, Venice

Argosy University/Sarasota Post-Sec.
5250 17th St 34235 800-331-5995
Cardinal Mooney HS 600/9-12
4171 Fruitville Rd 34232 941-371-4917
Stephen Christie, prin. Fax 371-6924
East West College of Natural Medicine Post-Sec.
3808 N Tamiami Trl 34234 941-355-9080
Everglades University Post-Sec.
6001 Lake Osprey Dr 34240 866-907-2262
Fashion Focus Hair Academy Post-Sec.
2184 Gulf Gate Dr 34231 941-921-4877
Keiser College Post-Sec.
6151 Lake Osprey Dr 34240 941-907-3900
Morningstar Learning Center 100/K-12
PO Box 5502 34277 941-377-6484
Maximillian Mayerhofer, prin. Fax 377-6484
New College of Florida Post-Sec.
5700 N Tamiami Trl 34243 941-359-4310
New Gate S 300/PK-12
5237 Ashton Rd 34233 941-922-4949
Paul Wenninger, prin. Fax 922-7660
Out of Door Academy-Upper S 100/7-12
5950 Deer Dr 34240 941-907-1159
David Mahler, hdmstr. Fax 907-1251
Potter's Wheel Academy 100/K-12
PO Box 50203 34232 886-335-1098
Reed Palmer, prin.
Ringling School of Art & Design Post-Sec.
2700 N Tamiami Trl 34234 941-351-5100
Sarasota Christian S 600/K-12
5415 Bahia Vista St 34232 941-371-6481
Eugene Miller, admin. Fax 371-0898
Sarasota County Technical Institute Post-Sec.
4748 Beneva Rd 34233 941-924-1365
Sarasota Memorial Hospital Post-Sec.
1700 S Tamiami Trl 34239 941-917-1080
Sarasota School of Massage Therapy Post-Sec.
1932 Ringling Blvd 34236 941-957-0577
Sonhaven Preparatory Academy 50/K-12
PO Box 50517 34232 941-360-0033
Dr. Carolyn Hilt, prin. Fax 355-6127
Sunstate Academy of Hair Design Post-Sec.
4424 Bee Ridge Rd 34233 941-377-4880
West Florida Christian S 200/PK-12
4311 Wilkinson Rd 34233 941-921-6311
Mary McClintic, prin. Fax 921-4046

Satellite Beach, Brevard, Pop. 9,752
Brevard County SD
Supt. — See Melbourne
DeLaura MS 900/7-8
300 Jackson Ave 32937 321-773-7581
Jeremy Salmon, prin. Fax 773-0702
Satellite HS 2,100/9-12
300 Scorpion Ct 32937 321-779-2000
Mark Elliott, prin. Fax 773-0703

Sebastian, Indian River, Pop. 17,744
Indian River County SD
Supt. — See Vero Beach
Sebastian River HS 1,800/9-12
9001 90th Ave 32958 772-564-4170
Dr. Margaret Jones, prin. Fax 564-4182
Sebastian River MS 1,300/6-8
9400 County Road 512 32958 772-564-5111
Eileen Shirah, prin. Fax 564-5113

Sebring, Highlands, Pop. 9,878
Highlands County SD 11,500/PK-12
426 School St 33870 863-471-5555
Wally Cox, supt. Fax 471-5622
www.highlands.k12.fl.us
Hill-Gustat MS 700/6-8
4700 Schumacher Rd 33872 863-471-5437
David Robinson, prin. Fax 314-5245
Sebring HS 1,500/9-12
3514 Kenilworth Blvd 33870 863-471-5500
Toni Stivender, prin. Fax 471-5507
Sebring MS 800/6-8
500 E Center Ave 33870 863-471-5700
Sandi Whidden, prin. Fax 471-5710
Other Schools – See Avon Park, Lake Placid

Grace Academy 100/PK-12
3704 Valerie Blvd 33870 863-386-1020
Don Roberts, admin. Fax 386-1001
Heartland Christian S 200/PK-12
1160 Persimmon Ave 33870 863-385-5752
David Noel, hdmstr. Fax 385-6926
Liberty Christian Academy 50/PK-12
PO Box 372 33871 863-385-0400
Jerry Case, admin. Fax 385-0400

Seffner, Hillsborough, Pop. 5,371
Hillsborough County SD
Supt. — See Tampa
Armwood HS 1,800/9-12
12000 E US Highway 92 33584 813-744-8040
Maria Singfield, prin. Fax 744-8048
Burnett MS 900/6-8
1010 N Kingsway Rd 33584 813-744-6745
Herbert Peeples, prin. Fax 744-8973
Jennings MS 1,300/6-8
8799 Williams Rd 33584 813-740-4575
Sarah Governor, prin. Fax 740-4579
Eastern Region Adult S Adult
12000 E US Highway 92 33584 813-740-3944
Tammy Crawford-Morse, prin. Fax 744-8048

Seffner Christian Academy 700/PK-12
11605 E US Highway 92 33584 813-626-0001
Roger Duncan, dir. Fax 627-0330

Seminole, Pinellas, Pop. 16,628
Pinellas County SD
Supt. — See Largo
Osceola HS 1,700/9-12
9751 98th St 33777 727-547-7717
Carol Moore, prin. Fax 545-6412
Osceola MS 1,200/6-8
9301 98th St 33777 727-547-7689
Bob Vicari, prin. Fax 547-7667
Seminole HS 2,100/9-12
8401 131st St 33776 727-547-7536
Richard Misenti, prin. Fax 547-7503
Seminole MS 1,200/6-8
8701 131st St 33776 727-547-4520
Judy Leboeuf, prin. Fax 547-7741
Seminole Vocational Education Center Vo/Tech
12611 86th Ave 33776 727-545-6405
Matt Fischer, dir. Fax 545-6408

Shalimar, Okaloosa, Pop. 731
Okaloosa County SD
Supt. — See Fort Walton Beach
Meigs MS 700/6-8
150 Richbourg Ave 32579 850-833-4301
Dr. Lamar White, prin. Fax 833-9392

Sneads, Jackson, Pop. 1,899
Jackson County SD
Supt. — See Marianna
Sneads JSHS 500/6-12
8066 Old Spanish Trl 32460 850-482-9007
Patricia Dickson, prin. Fax 482-9058

Victory Christian Academy 100/PK-12
2271 River Rd 32460 850-593-6699
Rev. David Pipping, admin. Fax 593-3341

South Daytona, Volusia, Pop. 13,799

International Academy Post-Sec.
2550 S Ridgewood Ave 32119 386-767-4600
Warner Christian Academy 700/PK-12
1730 S Ridgewood Ave 32119 386-767-5451
Dr. Samuel Smith, hdmstr. Fax 760-6834

South Miami, Dade, Pop. 11,355
Miami-Dade County SD
Supt. — See Miami
South Miami MS 800/7-8
6750 SW 60th St 33143 305-661-3481
Meracita Minns, prin. Fax 665-6728

South Miami Christian S 200/PK-12
6767 Sunset Dr 33143 305-666-5171
Dr. Jack Zimmerman, prin. Fax 666-2317

Spring Hill, Hernando, Pop. 85,900
Hernando County SD
Supt. — See Brooksville
Fox Chapel MS 1,300/6-8
9412 Fox Chapel Ln 34606 352-797-7025
David Schoelles, prin. Fax 797-7125
Springstead HS 1,700/9-12
3300 Mariner Blvd 34609 352-797-7010
Susan Duval, prin. Fax 797-7110

Bishop McLaughlin HS 500/9-12
13651 Hays Rd 34610 727-857-2600
Jane Moerschbacher, prin. Fax 857-2610
Spring Hill Christian Academy 300/PK-12
3140 Mariner Blvd 34609 352-683-8485
Charles Gottshall, prin. Fax 683-5087
West Hernando Christian S 200/PK-12
2250 Osowaw Blvd 34607 352-688-9918
Marti Covert, admin. Fax 683-1184

Wider Horizons S 200/PK-12
4060 Castle Ave 34609 352-686-1934
Dr. Domenick Maglio, prin. Fax 688-4371

Starke, Bradford, Pop. 5,665
Bradford County SD 3,800/PK-12
501 W Washington St 32091 904-966-6800
Harry M. Hatcher, supt. Fax 966-6030
www.bradford.k12.fl.us
Bradford HS 1,100/9-12
582 N Temple Ave 32091 904-966-6091
Randy Whytsell, prin. Fax 966-6020
Bradford MS 800/6-8
527 N Orange St 32091 904-966-6704
Jeff Cable, prin. Fax 966-6714
Bradford Union Vocational Ctr Vo/Tech
609 N Orange St 32091 904-966-6766
Clarence DeSue, dir. Fax 966-6786

Bradford-Union Area Vo-Tech Center Post-Sec.
609 N Orange St 32091 904-966-6760
Hope Christian Academy 100/PK-12
3900 SE State Route 100 32091 352-473-4040
Joseph Murphy, admin. Fax 473-8176
Northside Christian Academy 100/PK-12
7415 NW County Road 225 32091 904-964-7124
Tobias Roehm, prin. Fax 964-7141
Sunrise Academy 50/5-8
222 Bradford Dr 32091 904-704-2292
Michael Duffy, dir. Fax 964-4916

Stuart, Martin, Pop. 14,891
Martin County SD 16,900/PK-12
500 SE Ocean Blvd 34994 772-219-1200
Dr. Sara Wilcox, supt. Fax 219-1231
www.sbmc.org
Anderson MS 6-8
7000 SE Atlantic Ridge Dr 34997 772-219-1200
Dr. Larthenia Howard, prin.
Martin County HS 2,800/9-12
2801 S Kanner Hwy 34994 772-219-1800
Joan Hunt, prin. Fax 219-1821
Murray MS 1,100/6-8
4400 SE Murray St 34997 772-219-1670
Kit Weir, prin. Fax 219-1677
South Fork HS 2,300/9-12
10205 SW Pratt Whitney Rd 34997 772-219-1840
Patricia Schmoyer, prin. Fax 219-1860
Stuart MS 1,300/6-8
575 SE Georgia Ave 34994 772-219-1685
Sigrid George, prin. Fax 219-1690
Adult Education Adult
800 SE Monterey Rd 34994 772-220-7260
William Connolly, prin. Fax 220-7264
Other Schools – See Indiantown, Jensen Beach, Palm City

Chapman School of Seamanship Post-Sec.
4343 SE Saint Lucie Blvd 34997 772-283-8130
Community Christian Academy 300/PK-12
777 SE Salerno Rd 34997 772-288-7227
Norma Hammond, admin. Fax 600-2727
Star Academy for Pet Stylists Post-Sec.
2201 SE Indian St Ste C6 34997 772-221-9330

Summerfield, Marion
Marion County SD
Supt. — See Ocala
Lake Weir MS 1,300/6-8
10220 SE Sunset Harbor Rd 34491 352-671-6120
Walt Miller, prin. Fax 671-6121

Sumterville, Sumter
Sumter County SD
Supt. — See Bushnell
Sumter County Adult Center Adult
1425 County Road 526A 33585 352-793-5719
Gloria Croft, prin. Fax 793-6508

Sunrise, Broward, Pop. 89,136
Broward County SD
Supt. — See Fort Lauderdale
Bair MS 1,700/6-8
9100 NW 21st Mnr 33322 754-322-2900
Ellen Etling, prin. Fax 322-2985
Cypress Bay 9th Annex 9-9
270 N New River Cir 33326 754-323-1500
Charles Neely, prin. Fax 323-1535
Piper HS 3,400/9-12
8000 NW 44th St 33351 754-322-1700
Anthony Taylor, prin. Fax 322-1830
Westpine MS 1,500/6-8
9393 NW 50th St 33351 754-322-4900
Paula Meadows, prin. Fax 322-4985

Tallahassee, Leon, Pop. 153,938
Leon County SD 30,600/PK-12
2757 W Pensacola St 32304 850-487-7100
William Montford, supt. Fax 487-7141
www.leon.k12.fl.us
Belle Vue MS 600/6-8
2214 Bellevue Way 32304 850-488-4467
Reginald Griffin, prin. Fax 922-8494
Chiles HS 1,800/9-12
7200 Lawton Chiles Ln 32312 850-488-1756
Allan Cox, prin. Fax 488-1218
Cobb MS 800/6-8
915 Hillcrest St 32308 850-488-3364
Shannon Meeks, prin. Fax 922-2452
Deerlake MS 1,300/6-8
9902 Deer Lk W 32312 850-922-6545
Jackie Pons, prin. Fax 488-3275
Fairview MS 900/6-8
3415 Zillah St 32305 850-488-6880
Roger Pinholster, prin. Fax 922-6326
Godby HS 1,400/9-12
1717 W Tharpe St 32303 850-488-1325
Randy Pridgeon, prin. Fax 922-4162
Griffin MS 800/6-8
800 Alabama St 32304 850-488-8436
Michelle Gayle, prin. Fax 922-4226
Leon HS 1,800/9-12
550 E Tennessee St 32308 850-488-1971
Rocky Hanna, prin. Fax 922-5311
Lincoln HS 1,800/9-12
3838 Trojan Trl 32311 850-487-2110
Martha Bunch, prin. Fax 922-4173
Lively-Technical Center Vo/Tech
500 Appleyard Dr 32304 850-487-7555
Jean Ferguson, prin. Fax 922-3880
Nims MS 600/6-8
723 W Orange Ave 32310 850-488-5960
Pam Hayman, prin. Fax 922-0203

Raa MS 800/6-8
401 W Tharpe St 32303 850-488-6287
Pat Keen, prin. Fax 922-5835
Rickards HS 1,300/9-12
3013 Jim Lee Rd 32301 850-488-1783
Pink Hightower, prin. Fax 922-7104
Swift Creek MS 1,000/6-8
2100 Pedrick Rd 32317 850-487-4868
Alice Caswell, prin. Fax 414-2650
Leon Countywide Adult Education Adult
283 Trojan Trl 32311 850-922-5343
Barbara Van Camp, prin. Fax 922-5352

Atlantis Academy of Tallahassee 100/1-12
1500 Miccosukee Rd 32308 850-893-4692
Duwayne Baum, prin. Fax 893-4464
Core Institute Post-Sec.
223 W Carolina St 32301 866-830-0108
Florida A&M University 32307 Post-Sec.
850-599-3000
Florida State University Post-Sec.
600 W College Ave 32306 850-644-2525
John Paul II HS 300/9-12
5100 Terrebonne Dr 32311 850-201-5744
Dr. Randall Felton, prin. Fax 205-3299
Keiser College Post-Sec.
1700 Halstead Blvd 32309 850-906-9494
Lively Area Vocational Technical Center Post-Sec.
3290 Capital Cir SW 32310 850-488-2460
Lively Area Vocational Technical School Post-Sec.
500 Appleyard Dr 32304 850-487-7555
Maclay S 1,000/PK-12
3737 N Meridian Rd 32312 850-893-2138
William Jablon, hdmstr. Fax 893-7434
Maranatha Christian S 200/PK-12
2532 W Tharpe St 32303 850-385-5920
Alan Risk, prin. Fax 386-7785
North Florida Christian S 1,200/PK-12
3000 N Meridian Rd 32312 850-386-6327
Charles Fielding, admin. Fax 385-7188
North Florida Cosmetology Institute Post-Sec.
2424 Allen Rd 32312 850-878-5269
Tallahassee Community College Post-Sec.
444 Appleyard Dr 32304 850-201-8595
Tallahassee Memorial Hospital Post-Sec.
1300 Miccosukee Rd 32308 850-681-5385

Tamarac, Broward, Pop. 57,967
Broward County SD
Supt. — See Fort Lauderdale
Millennium MS 1,500/6-8
5803 NW 94th Ave 33321 754-322-3900
Dr. Cheryl Cendan, prin. Fax 322-3985

Tampa, Hillsborough, Pop. 317,647
Hillsborough County SD 177,200/PK-12
PO Box 3408 33601 813-272-4000
Mary Ellen Elia, supt. Fax 272-4510
www.sdhc.k12.fl.us/
Adams MS 1,200/6-8
10201 N Boulevard 33612 813-975-7665
Odalys Pritchard, prin. Fax 632-6889
Alonso HS 2,400/9-12
8302 Montague St 33635 813-356-1525
Dr. Sandy Bunkin, prin. Fax 356-1529
Benito MS 1,300/6-8
10101 Cross Creek Blvd 33647 813-631-4694
Bobby Smith, prin. Fax 631-4706
Blake HS 1,600/9-12
1701 N Boulevard 33607 813-272-3422
Jackie Haynes, prin. Fax 272-3715
Bowers/Whitley Career Center Vo/Tech
13609 N 22nd St 33613 813-558-1750
Anthony Colucci, prin. Fax 558-1761
Brewster Tech Center Vo/Tech
2222 N Tampa St 33602 813-276-5448
Janice Carter-Collier, prin. Fax 276-5756
Buchanan MS 900/6-8
1001 W Bearss Ave 33613 813-975-7600
Dr. Dwight Raines, prin. Fax 975-7610
Chamberlain HS 2,100/9-12
9401 N Boulevard 33612 813-975-7677
Pam Campbell-Peralta, prin. Fax 975-7687
Coleman MS 900/6-8
1724 S Manhattan Ave 33629 813-872-5335
Maribeth Franklin, prin. Fax 872-5338
Davidsen MS 1,300/6-8
10501 Montague St 33626 813-558-5300
Rebecca Kaskeski, prin. Fax 558-5299
Dowdell MS 1,000/6-8
1208 Wishing Well Way 33619 813-744-8322
Robert Lawson, prin. Fax 740-3616
Erwin Tech Center Vo/Tech
2010 E Hillsborough Ave 33610 813-231-1800
Michael Donohue, prin. Fax 231-1820
Farnell MS 1,200/6-8
13912 Nine Eagles Dr 33626 813-356-1640
John Cobb, prin. Fax 356-1644
Ferrell Magnet MS 700/6-8
4302 N 24th St 33610 813-276-5608
Charles Dixon, prin. Fax 276-5615
Franklin MS 700/6-8
3915 E 21st Ave 33605 813-744-8108
John Copeland, prin. Fax 744-8579
Gaither HS 2,400/9-12
16200 N Dale Mabry Hwy 33618 813-975-7340
Brenda Grasso, prin. Fax 975-7349
Hill MS 1,200/6-8
5200 Ehrlich Rd 33624 813-975-7325
Angela Oliver, prin. Fax 975-4819
Hillsborough HS 2,000/9-12
5000 N Central Ave 33603 813-276-5620
Dr. William Orr, prin. Fax 276-5629
Jefferson HS 1,800/9-12
4401 W Cypress St 33607 813-872-5241
Lou Diaz, prin. Fax 872-5250
King HS 2,100/9-12
6815 N 56th St 33610 813-744-8333
Carla Bruning, prin. Fax 744-8343
Learey Technical S Vo/Tech
5410 N 20th St 33610 813-231-1907
Susan Miller, prin. Fax 231-1855
Leto HS 1,900/9-12
4409 W Sligh Ave 33614 813-872-5300
Daniel Bonilla, prin. Fax 872-5314
Liberty MS 1,400/6-8
17400 Commerce Park Blvd 33647 813-558-1180
Debbie Rodgers, prin. Fax 558-1184
Madison MS 900/6-8
4444 W Bay Vista Ave 33611 813-272-3050
Kathleen Hoffman, prin. Fax 233-2796

Memorial MS 1,300/6-8
4702 N Central Ave 33603 813-872-5230
John Haley, prin. Fax 872-5238
Middleton Magnet HS 1,900/9-12
4801 N 22nd St 33610 813-233-3360
James Gatlin, prin. Fax 233-3364
Monroe MS 700/6-8
4716 W Montgomery Ave 33616 813-272-3020
Joseph Brown, prin. Fax 272-3027
Orange Grove Magnet MS 600/6-8
3415 N 16th St 33605 813-276-5717
Debra Arias, prin. Fax 276-5857
Pierce MS 1,100/6-8
5511 N Hesperides St 33614 813-872-5344
Victor Fernandez, prin. Fax 871-7978
Plant HS 2,000/9-12
2415 S Himes Ave 33629 813-272-3033
Eric Bergholm, prin. Fax 272-0624
Progress Village MS 800/6-8
8113 Zinnia Dr 33619 813-671-5110
Walt Shaffner, prin. Fax 671-5240
Robinson HS 1,200/9-12
6311 S Lois Ave 33616 813-272-3006
Laura Zavatkay, prin. Fax 272-3014
Sickles HS 2,200/9-12
7950 Gunn Hwy 33626 813-631-4742
Jake Russell, prin. Fax 631-4754
Sligh MS 900/6-8
2011 E Sligh Ave 33610 813-276-5596
Juanita Underwood, prin. Fax 276-5606
Stewart MS 700/6-8
1125 W Spruce St 33607 813-276-5691
Barry Davis, prin. Fax 276-5698
Tampa Bay Technical HS Vo/Tech
6410 Orient Rd 33610 813-744-8360
William Person, prin. Fax 744-8368
Van Buren MS 900/6-8
8715 N 22nd St 33604 813-975-7652
Vince Aguero, prin. Fax 631-4312
Waters Career Center Vo/Tech
2704 N Highland Ave 33602 813-233-2655
Veronica Knight, admin. Fax 233-2659
Webb MS 900/6-8
6035 Hanley Rd 33634 813-872-5351
Carmen Aguero, prin. Fax 872-5359
Wharton HS 2,100/9-12
20150 Bruce B Downs Blvd 33647 813-631-4710
George Gaffney, prin. Fax 631-4722
Williams MS 800/6-8
5020 N 47th St 33610 813-744-8600
Patricia Harrell, prin. Fax 744-8665
Wilson MS 600/6-8
1005 W Swann Ave 33606 813-276-5682
Stephanie Woodford, prin. Fax 233-2540
Young Magnet MS 700/6-8
1807 E Dr Martn Lthr King 33610 813-276-5739
Faychone Durant, prin. Fax 276-5893
Adult Education Center Adult
2222 N Tampa St 33602 813-276-5654
Shirley Robbins, prin. Fax 276-5662
Aparicio/Levy Adult Technical S Adult
10119 E Ellicott St 33610 813-740-4884
Todd Bowden, prin. Fax 740-4885
Central Region S Adult
2222 N Tampa St 33602 813-247-8483
Edward Wickham, prin. Fax 247-8532
Chamberlain Adult & Community Center Adult
9401 N Boulevard 33612 813-631-4500
Linda Peterson, prin. Fax 631-4513
Gaither Adult & Community Center Adult
16200 N Dale Mabry Hwy 33618 813-632-6823
Georgene Diaz, prin. Fax 975-7349
Gary Adult S Adult
3610 E 10th Ave 33605 813-276-5439
Terry Zartman, prin. Fax 272-3658
Jefferson Adult & Community Center Adult
4401 W Cypress St 33607 813-356-1288
Janelle Buck, prin. Fax 356-1291
Leto Adult & Community Center Adult
4409 W Sligh Ave 33614 813-872-5300
Michelle Loango, prin. Fax 872-5314
Middleton Adult & Community S Adult
4801 N 22nd St 33610 813-233-3360
Bob Davis, prin. Fax 233-3364
Tampa Bay Technical Adult Evening S Adult
6410 Orient Rd 33610 813-744-8360
Candace Odierna, admin. Fax 744-8368
West Region Adult Education Adult
1701 N Boulevard 33607 813-233-2400
Eria Chester, prin. Fax 233-2402
Other Schools – See Brandon, Gibsonton, Lithia, Lutz, Odessa, Plant City, Riverview, Ruskin, Seffner, Temple Terrace, Valrico

---

Academy of the Holy Names HS 300/9-12
3319 Bayshore Blvd 33629 813-839-5371
Sarah Regan, prin. Fax 839-1486
American Youth Academy 300/PK-12
5905 E 130th Ave 33617 813-987-9282
Magda Saleh, prin. Fax 987-9262
Argosy University/Tampa Post-Sec.
4401 N Himes Ave Ste 150 33614 813-740-1108
Art Institute of Tampa Post-Sec.
4401 N Himes Ave Suite 150 33614 813-873-2112
Bayshore Christian S 400/PK-12
3909 S MacDill Ave 33611 813-839-4297
Donna Brooks, prin. Fax 835-1404
Berean Academy 200/K-12
10948 N Central Ave 33612 813-932-0552
Conrad Bray, admin. Fax 930-2134
Berkeley Preparatory S 1,200/PK-12
4811 Kelly Rd 33615 813-885-1673
Joseph Merluzzi, prin. Fax 886-6933
Cambridge S 700/PK-12
6101 N Habana Ave 33614 813-872-6744
Ron Whipple, hdmstr. Fax 872-6013
Citrus Park Christian S 500/PK-12
7705 Gunn Hwy 33625 813-920-3960
Herman Meister, dir. Fax 926-1240
Concorde Career Institute Post-Sec.
4202 W Spruce St 33607 813-874-0094
DeVry University Post-Sec.
3030 N Rocky Point Dr # 100 33607 813-288-8994
D.G. Erwin Technical Center Post-Sec.
2010 E Hillsborough Ave 33610 813-231-1800
Faith Outreach Academy 100/PK-12
7607 Sheldon Rd 33615 813-887-5546
Julie A. Sierra, prin. Fax 249-6896
FL Metropolitan Univ. - Brandon Post-Sec.
3924 Coconut Palm Dr 33619 813-621-0041
FL Metropolitan Univ. - Tampa Campus Post-Sec.
3319 W Hillsborough Ave 33614 813-879-6000
Gulf Coast College Post-Sec.
3910 N US Highway 301 33619 813-620-1446
Henry W. Brewster Technical Center Post-Sec.
2222 N Tampa St 33602 813-276-5464
Hillsborough Community College Post-Sec.
1404 Tech Blvd 33619 813-253-7000
Hillsborough Community College Post-Sec.
PO Box 30030 33630 813-253-7000
Hillsborough Community College Ybor Camp Post-Sec.
PO Box 5096 33675 813-253-7601
International Academy of Design & Tech Post-Sec.
5104 Eisenhower Blvd 33634 813-881-0007
ITT Technical Institute Post-Sec.
4809 Memorial Hwy 33634 813-885-2244
James Haley Veteran's Hospital Post-Sec.
13000 Bruce B Downs Blvd 33612 813-972-2000
Jesuit HS 700/9-12
4701 N Himes Ave 33614 813-877-5344
Joseph Sabin, prin. Fax 872-1853
Libertas Academy 100/K-12
14018 N Boulevard 33613 813-964-1779
Hannah Vickery, prin. Fax 514-1283
Manhattan Beauty School Post-Sec.
2317 E Fletcher Ave 33612 813-264-3535
Manhattan Hairstyling Academy Post-Sec.
1906 W Platt St 33606 813-837-2525
Mary Help of Christians S 100/6-8
6400 E Chelsea St 33610 813-626-6191
Stuart Miller, prin. Fax 621-5461
Remington College Tampa Campus Post-Sec.
2410 E Busch Blvd 33612 813-935-5700
Sanford Brown Institute Post-Sec.
5701 E Hllsbrgh Av #1417 33610 813-621-0072
Stepping Stones S 100/9-12
19046 Bruce B Downs Blvd 33647 813-973-0619
Linda Decubellis, prin.
Strayer University Post-Sec.
6302 E M L King Blvd # 450 33619 813-663-0100
Strayer University Post-Sec.
4902 Eisenhower Blvd # 100 33634 813-882-0100
Suncoast Center for Natural Health Post-Sec.
2005 Pan Am Cir Ste 100 33607 813-287-1099
Tampa Adventist Academy 100/PK-10
3205 N Boulevard 33603 813-228-7950
David Matthews, prin. Fax 228-0170
Tampa Baptist Academy 400/PK-12
300 E Sligh Ave 33604 813-238-3229
Dr. Barbara Bode, admin. Fax 237-3426
Tampa Catholic HS 700/9-12
4630 N Rome Ave 33603 813-870-0860
Patricia Landry, prin. Fax 877-9136
Tampa General Hospital Post-Sec.
PO Box 1289 33601 813-844-7985
Tampa Preparatory S 700/6-12
727 W Cass St 33606 813-251-8481
D. Gordon MacLeod, prin. Fax 254-2106
Temple Heights Christian S 200/PK-12
8406 N 46th St 33617 813-988-5143
Ronald Sainsbury, prin. Fax 985-7247
Universal Academy of Florida 300/PK-12
6801 Orient Rd 33610 813-664-0695
Moosa Yahya, dir. Fax 664-4506
University of South Florida Post-Sec.
3702 Spectrum Blvd Ste 180 33612 813-974-4031
University of South Florida Post-Sec.
4202 E Fowler Ave 33620 813-974-3350
University of Tampa Post-Sec.
401 W Kennedy Blvd 33606 813-253-3333
West Gate Christian S 400/PK-12
5121 Kelly Rd 33615 813-884-5147
Walt Boehm, dir. Fax 888-5368

Tarpon Springs, Pinellas, Pop. 22,240
Pinellas County SD
Supt. — See Largo
East Lake HS 2,200/9-12
1300 Silver Eagle Dr 34688 727-942-5419
Clayton Snare, prin. Fax 942-5441
Tarpon Springs HS 1,900/9-12
1411 Gulf Rd 34689 727-943-4900
Evert Vermeer, prin. Fax 943-4907
Tarpon Springs MS 1,600/6-8
501 N Florida Ave 34689 727-943-5511
Felita Lott, prin. Fax 943-5519

St. Petersburg College Post-Sec.
600 Klosterman Rd W 34689 727-791-2400

Tavares, Lake, Pop. 10,831
Lake County SD 29,200/PK-12
201 W Burleigh Blvd 32778 352-253-6500
Anna Cowin, supt. Fax 343-0198
www.lake.k12.fl.us/
Tavares HS 1,100/9-12
603 N New Hampshire Ave 32778 352-343-3007
Kathy Tatro, prin. Fax 343-0892
Tavares MS 1,000/6-8
13032 Lane Park Cutoff 32778 352-343-4545
Mike Herring, prin. Fax 343-7212
Other Schools – See Clermont, Eustis, Groveland, Leesburg, Mount Dora, Umatilla

---

Liberty Christian Academy 300/PK-12
2451 Dora Ave 32778 352-343-0061
Mark Curtis, prin. Fax 343-2424

Tavernier, Monroe, Pop. 2,433
Monroe County SD
Supt. — See Key West
Coral Shores HS 800/9-12
89901 Old Hwy 33070 305-853-3222
Ron Martin, prin. Fax 853-3228

Temple Terrace, Hillsborough, Pop. 21,860
Hillsborough County SD
Supt. — See Tampa
Greco MS 1,200/6-8
6925 E Fowler Ave 33617 813-987-6926
Dr. Judith Kennedy, prin. Fax 987-6863

Florida College Post-Sec.
119 N Glen Arven Ave 33617 813-988-5131

Titusville, Brevard, Pop. 41,752
Brevard County SD
Supt. — See Melbourne
Astronaut HS 1,700/9-12
800 War Eagle Blvd 32796 321-264-3000
Terry Humphrey, prin. Fax 264-3013
Jackson MS 700/7-8
1515 Knox Mcrae Dr 32780 321-269-1812
James Hickey, prin. Fax 269-7811
Madison MS 800/7-8
3375 Dairy Rd 32796 321-264-3120
Joan Sparks, prin. Fax 264-3124
Titusville HS 1,900/9-12
150 Terrier Trl S 32780 321-264-3100
Mark Rendell, prin. Fax 264-3103

Helicopter Adventures Post-Sec.
365 Golden Knights Blvd 32780 321-385-2919
Temple Christian S 200/PK-12
1400 N US Highway 1 32796 321-269-2837
Scott Hallock, prin. Fax 383-9101

Trenton, Gilchrist, Pop. 1,720
Gilchrist County SD 2,800/PK-12
310 NW 11th Ave 32693 352-463-3200
James Vickers, supt. Fax 463-3276
www.gilchristschools.org
Trenton HS 700/6-12
1013 N Main St 32693 352-463-3210
Lynette Langford, prin. Fax 463-3264
Other Schools – See Bell

Victory Christian S 100/7-12
6191 SW County Road 344 32693 352-463-1473
Rev. Carl Cornwell, dir. Fax 796-2687

Umatilla, Lake, Pop. 2,416
Lake County SD
Supt. — See Tavares
Umatilla HS 800/9-12
320 N Trowell Ave 32784 352-669-3131
June Dalton, prin. Fax 669-5481
Umatilla MS 800/6-8
305 E Lake St 32784 352-669-3171
Bill Miller, prin. Fax 669-5424

Living Word Academy 200/PK-12
19624 Quails Nest Run 32784 352-669-8966
Elaine Christensen, prin.

Valparaiso, Okaloosa, Pop. 6,358
Okaloosa County SD
Supt. — See Fort Walton Beach
Lewis MS 600/6-8
281 Mississippi Ave 32580 850-833-4130
Dr. Linda Smith, prin. Fax 833-4197

Valrico, See Brandon
Hillsborough County SD
Supt. — See Tampa
Bloomingdale HS 2,300/9-12
1700 Bloomingdale Ave 33594 813-744-8018
Mark West, prin. Fax 744-8026
Mulrennan MS 1,200/6-8
4215 Durant Rd 33594 813-651-2100
Quincenia Bell, prin. Fax 651-2104

Grace Christian S 300/K-12
1300 N Valrico Rd 33594 813-689-8815
Dr. Robert Gustafson, dir. Fax 681-7396
Manhattan Hairstyling Academy Post-Sec.
3244 Lithia Pinecrest #103 33594 813-655-4545

Venice, Sarasota, Pop. 19,351
Sarasota County SD
Supt. — See Sarasota
Venice Area MS 700/6-8
1900 Center Rd 34292 941-486-2100
Jack Turgeon, prin. Fax 486-2108
Venice HS 2,200/9-12
1 Indian Ave 34285 941-488-6726
Candace Millington, prin. Fax 486-2034

Vernon, Washington, Pop. 745
Washington County SD
Supt. — See Chipley
Vernon HS 400/9-12
PO Box 386 32462 850-535-2046
Bobbie Dawson, prin. Fax 535-6244
Vernon MS 200/7-8
3206 Moss Hill Rd 32462 850-535-2807
Julia Morales, prin. Fax 535-1683

Vero Beach, Indian River, Pop. 17,357
Indian River County SD 15,600/PK-12
1990 25th St 32960 772-564-3000
Duncan Pritchett Ed.D., supt. Fax 564-3128
www.indian-river.k12.fl.us/
Gifford MS 1,300/6-8
4530 28th Ct 32967 772-564-3550
Dave Kramek, prin. Fax 564-3561
Oslo MS 1,200/6-8
480 20th Ave SW 32962 772-564-3980
Deborah Long, prin. Fax 564-4029
Vero Beach Freshman Learning Center 9-9
1507 19th St 32960 772-564-4820
Jane Hudson, prin. Fax 564-4928
Vero Beach HS 2,700/9-12
1707 16th St 32960 772-564-4620
Jane Hudson, prin. Fax 564-4720
Indian River Adult Education Adult
1426 19th St 32960 772-564-4955
John Fontana, prin. Fax 564-4977
Other Schools – See Sebastian

FlightSafety International Post-Sec.
PO Box 2708 32961 772-564-7600
Master's Academy of Vero Beach 300/PK-10
1105 58th Ave 32966 772-794-4655
Dr. H. Grant Powell, hdmstr. Fax 563-9714
St. Edward's S 900/PK-12
1895 Saint Edwards Dr 32963 772-231-4136
Dr. Charles F. Clark, hdmstr. Fax 231-6158

Walnut Hill, Escambia
Escambia County SD
Supt. — See Pensacola
Ward MS 400/6-8
7650 Highway 97 32568 850-327-4283
Nancy Gindl, prin. Fax 327-4991

Warrington, Escambia, Pop. 16,040
Escambia County SD
Supt. — See Pensacola
Warrington MS 800/6-8
450 S Old Corry Field Rd, Pensacola FL 32507
850-453-7440
Christine Nixon, prin. Fax 453-7572

Wauchula, Hardee, Pop. 4,406
Hardee County SD 5,200/PK-12
PO Box 1678 33873 863-773-9058
Dennis Jones, supt. Fax 773-0069
www.hardee.k12.fl.us
Hardee HS 1,200/9-12
830 Altman Rd 33873 863-773-3181
Mike Wilkinson, prin. Fax 773-4390
Hardee JHS 1,200/6-8
200 S Florida Ave 33873 863-773-3147
Mae Robinson, prin. Fax 773-3167
Family Service Center Adult
901 W Main St 33873 863-773-3173
Gerald Kapusta, prin. Fax 773-3127

Webster, Sumter, Pop. 809
Sumter County SD
Supt. — See Bushnell
South Sumter MS 900/6-8
773 NW 10th Ave 33597 352-793-2232
Kathy Dustin, prin. Fax 793-3976

Wellington, Palm Beach, Pop. 46,604
Palm Beach County SD
Supt. — See West Palm Beach
Palm Beach Central HS 2,400/9-12
8499 Forest Hill Blvd, 561-304-1000
Dr. Ian B. Saltzman, prin. Fax 304-1017
Polo Park MS 1,600/6-8
11901 Lake Worth Rd 33414 561-333-5500
Connie B. Gregory, prin. Fax 333-5505
Wellington Community HS 3,100/9-12
2101 Greenview Shores Blvd 33414 561-795-4900
Cheryl Alligood, prin. Fax 795-4934
Wellington Landings MS 1,600/6-8
1100 Aero Club Dr 33414 561-792-8100
Mario Crocetti, prin. Fax 792-8106

Wellington Christian S 800/PK-12
1000 Wellington Trce 33414 561-793-1017
Joseph Austin, prin. Fax 798-9622

Wesley Chapel, Pasco, Pop. 1,200
Pasco County SD
Supt. — See Land O Lakes
Wesley Chapel HS 1,800/9-12
30651 Wells Rd 33544 813-794-8700
Andrew Frelick, prin. Fax 794-8791

Faith Baptist Academy 50/PK-12
6300 Oakley Blvd 33544 813-907-9462
Travis Hartsfield, admin. Fax 907-9986
Saddlebrook Preparatory S 100/K-12
5700 Saddlebrook Way 33543 813-907-4300
Larry Robison, hdmstr. Fax 991-4713

West Melbourne, Brevard, Pop. 12,334
Brevard County SD
Supt. — See Melbourne
Central MS 1,200/7-8
2600 Wingate Blvd 32904 321-722-4150
Pamela Mitchell, prin. Fax 722-4165

Brevard Christian S 200/PK-12
1100 Dorchester Ave 32904 321-727-2038
Michael Branch, prin. Fax 729-4212
Space Coast Health Institute Post-Sec.
1070 S Wickham Rd 32904 321-729-9000

West Miami, Dade, Pop. 6,009

Florida Education Institute Post-Sec.
5818 SW 8th St 33144 305-444-1515

Weston, Broward, Pop. 62,243
Broward County SD
Supt. — See Fort Lauderdale
Cypress Bay HS 4,300/9-12
18600 Vista Park Blvd 33332 754-323-0350
Charles Neely, prin. Fax 323-0363
Falcon Cove MS 2,700/6-8
4251 Bonaventure Blvd 33332 754-323-3200
Mark Kaplan, prin. Fax 323-3285
Tequesta Trace MS 1,700/6-8
1800 Indian Trce 33326 754-323-4400
Paul Micensky, prin. Fax 323-4485

Sagemont S - Upper Campus 400/6-12
2585 Glades Cir 33327 954-389-2454
Brent Goldman, hdmstr. Fax 389-8106

West Palm Beach, Palm Beach, Pop. 88,932
Palm Beach County SD 160,900/PK-12
3300 Forest Hill Blvd 33406 561-434-8000
Arthur C. Johnson Ph.D., supt. Fax 434-8571
www.palmbeach.k12.fl.us
Bak MS of the Arts 1,400/6-8
1725 Echo Lake Dr 33407 561-882-3870
Elizabeth Perlman, prin. Fax 882-3879
Bear Lakes MS 1,000/6-8
3505 Shenandoah Rd 33409 561-615-7700
Cheryl McKeever, prin. Fax 615-7756
Conniston Community MS 1,000/6-8
673 Conniston Rd 33405 561-802-5400
Sheila Henry, prin. Fax 802-5409
Dreyfoos S of the Arts 1,300/9-12
501 S Sapodilla Ave 33401 561-802-6000
Ellen VanArsdale, prin. Fax 802-6059
Forest Hill Community HS 1,500/9-12
6901 Parker Ave 33405 561-540-2400
Mayra Stafford, prin. Fax 540-2440
Jeaga MS 1,200/6-8
3777 N Jog Rd 33411 561-242-8000
John Stevens, prin. Fax 242-8005
Okeeheelee MS 1,600/6-8
2200 Pinehurst Dr 33413 561-434-3200
David Samore, prin. Fax 434-3244
Palm Beach Lakes Community HS 2,600/9-12
3505 Shiloh Dr 33407 561-640-5000
Nathan Collins, prin. Fax 688-5340
Palm Springs Community MS 1,800/6-8
1560 Kirk Rd 33406 561-434-3300
Sandra Jinks, prin. Fax 434-3303
Roosevelt Community MS 1,300/6-8
1900 Australian Ave 33404 561-822-0200
George Lockhart, prin. Fax 882-0222
Western Pines MS 1,600/6-8
5949 140th Ave N 33411 561-792-2500
Peggy Campbell, prin. Fax 792-2530
Adult Education Center of Palm Beach Adult
2161 N Military Trl 33409 561-640-5074
Cynthia Smith, prin. Fax 688-5209
Conniston Community MS Adult
673 Conniston Rd 33405 561-687-7166
Jim Utterback, prin. Fax 364-7922
Other Schools – See Belle Glade, Boca Raton, Boynton Beach, Delray Beach, Greenacres, Jupiter, Lake Worth, Lantana, Loxahatchee, Pahokee, Palm Beach Gardens, Riviera Beach, Royal Palm Beach, Wellington

---

Academy for Practical Nursing/Health Occ Post-Sec.
5154 Okechobee Blvd #201 33417 561-683-1400
Berean Christian S 700/PK-12
8350 Okeechobee Blvd 33411 561-798-9300
Embree Bolton, hdmstr. Fax 792-3073
Cardinal Newman HS 900/9-12
512 Spencer Dr 33409 561-683-6266
John Clarke, prin. Fax 683-7307
Ephesus Junior Academy 100/K-10
4011 N Shore Dr 33407 561-832-9789
Karen Jones, prin. Fax 832-3567
Hope Career Institute Post-Sec.
3101 Forest Hill Blvd 33406
King's Academy 1,400/PK-12
8401 Belvedere Rd 33411 561-686-4244
Jeffrey M. Loveland, pres. Fax 686-8017
New England Institute of Technology Post-Sec.
2410 Metrocentre Blvd 33407 561-842-8324
Northwood University Post-Sec.
2600 N Military Trl 33409 800-458-8325
Palm Beach Atlantic University Post-Sec.
PO Box 24708 33416 561-803-2000
PC Professor Post-Sec.
6080 Okeechobee Blvd 33417 561-684-3333
Progressive S 200/PK-12
1950 Prairie Rd 33406 561-642-3100
Dennis Kelley, prin. Fax 969-1950
Ross Medical Education Center Post-Sec.
2601 S Military Trl Ste 29 33415 561-433-1288
South University Post-Sec.
1760 N Congress Ave 33409 561-697-9200
Summit Christian S 1,500/PK-12
4900 Summit Blvd 33415 561-686-8081
Sam Skelton, hdmstr. Fax 640-7613

Wewahitchka, Gulf, Pop. 1,700
Gulf County SD
Supt. — See Port Saint Joe
Wewahitchka HS 300/9-12
1 Gator Cir 32465 850-639-2228
Larry White, prin. Fax 639-5394
Wewahitchka MS 300/6-8
190 Aligator Aly 32465 850-639-6840
Pam Lister, prin. Fax 639-6929

Wildwood, Sumter, Pop. 3,625
Sumter County SD
Supt. — See Bushnell
Wildwood HS 500/9-12
700 Huey St 34785 352-748-1314
Richard Hampton, prin. Fax 748-7668
Wildwood MS 300/6-8
200 Cleveland Ave 34785 352-748-1510
Chuck Sullivan, prin. Fax 748-7639

Williston, Levy, Pop. 2,395
Levy County SD
Supt. — See Bronson
Williston HS 700/9-12
427 W Noble Ave 32696 352-528-3542
Gary Clark, prin. Fax 528-2723
Williston MS 500/6-8
20550 NE 42nd Pl 32696 352-528-2941
Ernst Kordgien, prin. Fax 528-2941

Windermere, Orange, Pop. 1,924
Orange County SD
Supt. — See Orlando
Gotha MS 1,700/6-8
9155 Gotha Rd 34786 407-521-2360
Daniel Axtell, prin. Fax 521-2361

Crenshaw S 200/K-12
PO Box 1159 34786 407-876-9122
Brenda Crenshaw, prin. Fax 876-9424
Windemere Preparatory S 400/PK-12
6189 State Road 535 34786 407-905-7737
Leigh Byron, prin. Fax 905-7710

Winter Garden, Orange, Pop. 20,307
Orange County SD
Supt. — See Orlando
Lakeview MS 1,300/6-8
1200 W Bay St 34787 407-877-5010
Debra Lucas, prin. Fax 877-5019
West Orange 9th Grade Center 9-9
1625 Beulah Rd 34787 407-905-2400
Mark Brown, prin. Fax 656-4989
West Orange HS 3,800/9-12
1625 Beulah Rd 34787 407-905-2400
Daniel Buckman, prin. Fax 656-4970

Calvary Christian S 200/PK-12
631 S Dillard St 34787 407-656-3001
Jack Kelley, dir. Fax 656-1210
Foundation Academy 600/PK-12
125 E Plant St 34787 407-656-3677
Dr. Russell Richards, admin. Fax 656-0118
Orange Technical Educ. Center-Westside Post-Sec.
955 E Story Rd 34787 407-905-2001

Winter Haven, Polk, Pop. 27,137
Polk County SD
Supt. — See Bartow
Denison MS 1,000/6-8
400 Avenue A SE 33880 863-291-5353
Linda Williams, prin. Fax 291-5347
Jewett Academy 600/6-8
601 Avenue T NE 33881 863-291-5320
Gary McDaniel, prin. Fax 297-3049
Ridge Technical Center Vo/Tech
7700 State Highway 544 33881 863-419-3060
Carolyn Ramsey, prin. Fax 419-3062
Westwood MS 1,000/6-8
3520 Avenue J NW 33881 863-965-5484
Carolyn Williams, prin. Fax 965-5585
Winter Haven HS 1,800/9-12
600 6th St SE 33880 863-291-5330
Michael Tucker, prin. Fax 297-3024

All Saints' Academy 700/PK-12
5001 State Road 540 W 33880 863-293-5980
Michael Wyman, hdmstr. Fax 294-2819
Haven Christian Academy 200/PK-12
2105 King Rd 33880 863-293-0930
Stace Alcala, prin. Fax 293-0429
Polk Community College Post-Sec.
999 Avenue H NE 33881 863-297-1000
Ridge Vocational-Technical Center Post-Sec.
7700 State Rd 544 33881 863-419-3060

Winter Park, Orange, Pop. 26,755
Orange County SD
Supt. — See Orlando
Winter Park 9th Grade Center 9-9
528 Huntington Ave 32789 407-623-1476
David Stanley, prin. Fax 623-1485
Winter Park HS 3,500/9-12
2100 Summerfield Rd 32792 407-622-3200
Dr. William Gordon, prin. Fax 975-2434
Winter Park Tech Center Vo/Tech
901 W Webster Ave 32789 407-622-2900
Diane Culpepper, prin. Fax 975-2435
Central Tech ACE Center Adult
2100 Summerfield Rd 32792 407-622-3204
Neal Alford, prin.

Seminole County SD
Supt. — See Sanford
Lake Howell HS 2,000/9-12
4200 Dike Rd 32792 407-320-9050
Shanne Storch, prin. Fax 320-9025

Central Christian Academy 800/1-12
PO Box 6000 32793 407-332-6988
Leslie Rawle, dir. Fax 332-4413
Central Florida College Post-Sec.
1573 W Fairbanks Ave #100 32789 407-843-3984
Florida Institute of Animal Arts Post-Sec.
3776 Howell Branch Rd 32792 407-657-8088
Full Sail - Real World Education Post-Sec.
3300 University Blvd 32792 407-679-0100
Geneva S 500/PK-12
2025 State Road 436 32792 407-332-6363
Robert Ingram, hdmstr. Fax 332-1664
Herzing College Post-Sec.
1595 S Semoran Blvd #1501 32792 407-478-0500
International Community S 500/PK-12
1021 N New York Ave 32789 407-645-2343
Robyn Terwilleger, prin. Fax 645-2366
Morningstar Academy 900/K-12
1 Purlieu Pl 32792 866-582-2223
Howard Mandel, prin. Fax 509-7294
Orange Technical Educ. Ctr.-Winter Park Post-Sec.
901 W Webster Ave 32789 407-622-2900
Rollins College Post-Sec.
1000 Holt Ave 32789 407-646-2000
Trinity Prep S 800/6-12
5700 Trinity Prep Ln 32792 407-671-4140
Craig Maughan, hdmstr. Fax 671-6935

Winter Springs, Seminole, Pop. 31,808
Seminole County SD
Supt. — See Sanford
Indian Trails MS 1,500/6-8
415 Tuskawilla Rd 32708 407-320-4350
Eugene Petty, prin. Fax 320-4399
Winter Springs HS 2,700/9-12
130 Tuskawilla Rd 32708 407-320-8750
Michael Blasewitz, prin. Fax 320-8700

Yulee, Nassau, Pop. 6,915
Nassau County SD
Supt. — See Fernandina Beach
Yulee HS 9-12
PO Box 160 32041 904-491-7949
Diane Romon, prin. Fax 225-3656
Yulee MS 300/6-8
PO Box 2800 32041 904-491-7944
Deonia Simmons, prin. Fax 225-0104

Zephyrhills, Pasco, Pop. 11,554
Pasco County SD
Supt. — See Land O Lakes
Stewart MS 1,000/6-8
38505 10th Ave, 813-794-6500
Jackson Johnson, prin. Fax 794-6591
Weightman MS 1,600/6-8
30649 Wells Rd 33544 813-794-0200
Shae Davis, prin. Fax 794-0291
Zephyrhills HS 1,400/9-12
6335 12th St, 813-794-6100
Gerri Painter, prin. Fax 794-6191

Zephyrhills Christian Academy 100/PK-12
5353 5th St, 813-779-1648
Michael Smith, prin. Fax 799-9829

GEORGIA

GEORGIA DEPARTMENT OF EDUCATION
2054 Twin Towers East, Atlanta 30334
Telephone 404-656-2800
Fax 404-651-6867
Website http://www.doe.k12.ga.us

State Superintendent of Schools   Kathy Cox

GEORGIA BOARD OF EDUCATION
2053 Twin Towers East, Atlanta 30334

Chief Executive Officer   Kathy Cox

REGIONAL EDUCATIONAL SERVICE AGENCIES (RESA)

Central Savannah River Area RESA
  Dr. Terry Nelson, dir.   706-556-6225
  PO Box 609, Dearing 30808   Fax 556-8891
  www.csraresa.org/resa/
Chattahoochee-Flint RESA
  Norman Carter, dir.   229-937-5341
  PO Box 1150, Ellaville 31806   Fax 937-5754
  www.cfresa.org/
Coastal Plains RESA
  Harold Chambers, dir.   229-546-4094
  245 N Robinson St, Lenox 31637   Fax 546-4167
  www.cpresa.org
First District RESA
  Dr. Linda Lewis, dir.   912-842-5000
  PO Box 780, Brooklet 30415   Fax 842-5161
  www.fdresa.org/
Griffin RESA
  Dr. Stephanie Gordy, dir.   770-229-3247
  PO Box H, Griffin 30224   Fax 228-7316
  www.griffinresa.net/

Heart of Georgia RESA
  June Bradfield, dir.   478-374-2240
  1141 Cochran Hwy   Fax 374-1524
  Eastman 31023
  www.hgresa.org/
Metro RESA
  Dr. Fran Davis Perkins, dir.   770-432-2404
  1870 Teasley Dr SE, Smyrna 30080   Fax 432-6105
  www.ciclt.com/mresa/
Middle Georgia RESA
  Carolyn Williams, dir.   478-825-3132
  PO Box 1148, Fort Valley 31030   Fax 825-8248
  www.mgresa.org/
Northeast Georgia RESA
  Dr. Russell Cook, dir.   706-742-8292
  375 Winter St, Winterville 30683   Fax 742-8928
  www.ciclt.com/negaresa/
North Georgia RESA
  Larry Harmon, dir.   706-276-1111
  4731 Old Highway 5 S   Fax 276-1114
  Ellijay 30540
  www.ngresa.org/

Northwest Georgia RESA
  Mona Tucker, dir.   706-295-6189
  3167 Cedartown Hwy SE   Fax 295-6098
  Rome 30161
  www.nwgaresa.com/
Oconee RESA
  Dr. Mike Walker, dir.   478-552-5178
  PO Box 699, Sandersville 31082   Fax 552-6499
  www.ga-edtech.org/oconee/
Okefenokee RESA
  Dr. Teresa Pack, dir.   912-285-6151
  1450 N Augusta Ave   Fax 287-6650
  Waycross 31503
  www.okresa.org/
Pioneer RESA
  Dr. Sandy Addis, dir.   706-865-2141
  PO Box 1789, Cleveland 30528   Fax 865-6748
  www.pioneerresa.org/
Southwest Georgia RESA
  Milton Callaway, dir.   229-294-6750
  118 McLaughlin St SW   Fax 294-6777
  Pelham 31779
  www.sw-georgia.resa.k12.ga.us
West Georgia RESA
  Dr. Ronnie Williams, dir.   770-583-2528
  99 Brown School Dr   Fax 583-3223
  Grantville 30220
  www.garesa.org/

PUBLIC, PRIVATE AND CATHOLIC SECONDARY SCHOOLS

Abbeville, Wilcox, Pop. 2,407
Wilcox County SD   1,400/PK-12
  103 Broad St N 31001   229-467-2141
  Charles Bloodsworth, supt.   Fax 467-2302
  www.wilcox.k12.ga.us/
  Other Schools – See Rochelle

Acworth, Cobb, Pop. 17,434
Cobb County SD
  Supt. — See Marietta
Barber MS   6-8
  4222 Cantrell Rd NW 30101   770-975-6764
  Lisa Williams, prin.   Fax 529-0325
Durham MS   1,700/6-8
  2891 Mars Hill Rd NW 30101   770-975-6641
  Linda Clark, prin.   Fax 975-6643

North Metro Technical College   Post-Sec.
  5198 Ross Rd SE 30102   770-975-4000

Adairsville, Bartow, Pop. 2,979
Bartow County SD
  Supt. — See Cartersville
Adairsville HS   700/9-12
  519 Old Highway 41 NW 30103   770-606-5841
  Tammy Griffith, prin.   Fax 773-2722
Adairsville MS   600/6-8
  100 College St 30103   770-606-5842
  Gordon Scoggins, prin.   Fax 606-5842

Adel, Cook, Pop. 5,295
Cook County SD   2,500/PK-12
  1109 N Parrish Ave 31620   229-896-2294
  Dr. Fred Rayfield, supt.   Fax 896-3443
  www.cook.k12.ga.us/
Cook HS   900/9-12
  1200 N Hutchinson Ave 31620   229-896-2213
  Charles Bell, prin.   Fax 896-3423
  Other Schools – See Sparks

Alamo, Wheeler, Pop. 2,420
Wheeler County SD   1,100/PK-12
  PO Box 427 30411   912-568-7198
  William R. Clark, supt.   Fax 568-1985
  www.wheelercountyschools.org
Wheeler County MSHS   600/6-12
  RR 1 Box 145 30411   912-568-7166
  William Black, prin.   Fax 568-7141

Albany, Dougherty, Pop. 76,202
Dougherty County SD   15,700/PK-12
  PO Box 1470 31702   229-431-1285
  Dr. Sally Whatley, supt.   Fax 431-1276
  www.docoschools.org
Albany HS   800/9-12
  801 W Residence Ave 31701   229-431-3300
  Sheila Marshall, prin.   Fax 431-3481

Albany MS   600/6-8
  1700 Cordell Ave 31705   229-431-3325
  Gloria Jones-Baker, prin.   Fax 431-3474
Cross MS   600/6-8
  324 Lockett Station Rd,   229-431-3362
  Holly Thursby, prin.   Fax 431-3476
Dougherty HS   1,200/9-12
  1800 Pearce Ave 31705   229-431-3310
  Horace Reid, prin.   Fax 431-1302
Dougherty MS   700/6-8
  1800 Massey Dr 31705   229-431-3328
  Thelma Chunn, prin.   Fax 431-3475
Merry Acres MS   900/6-8
  1601 Florence Dr 31707   229-431-3326
  Larry Worthy, prin.   Fax 431-1204
Monroe HS   1,100/9-12
  900 Lippitt Dr 31701   229-431-3316
  Deloris Spears, prin.   Fax 431-3380
Radium Springs MS   600/6-8
  2600 Radium Springs Rd 31705   229-431-3345
  Geraldine Hudley, prin.   Fax 431-3552
Southside MS   600/6-8
  1615 Newton Rd 31701   229-431-3351
  Johnny Scott, prin.   Fax 431-1209
Westover HS   1,300/9-12
  2600 Partridge Dr 31707   229-431-3320
  Gene Melvin, prin.   Fax 431-3349

Albany State University   Post-Sec.
  504 College Dr 31705   229-430-4600
Albany Technical College   Post-Sec.
  1704 S Slappey Blvd 31701   229-430-3500
Byne Memorial Baptist Church S   300/PK-12
  2832 Ledo Rd 31707   229-436-0173
  Jon Davis, hdmstr.   Fax 434-0039
Darton College   Post-Sec.
  2400 Gillionville Rd 31707   229-430-6000
Deerfield-Windsor S   800/PK-12
  PO Box 71149 31708   229-435-1301
  W.T. Henry, hdmstr.   Fax 888-6085
Sherwood Christian Academy   600/PK-12
  1418 Old Pretoria Rd,   229-883-5677
  Glen Schultz, hdmstr.   Fax 883-5794
Turner Job Corps Center   Post-Sec.
  2000 Schilling Ave 31705   229-883-8500

Alma, Bacon, Pop. 3,187
Bacon County SD   1,900/PK-12
  601 N Pierce St 31510   912-632-7363
  Richard Wheeler, supt.   Fax 632-2454
  www.bcraiders.com/
Bacon County HS   500/9-12
  901 N Pierce St 31510   912-632-4414
  Eddie Mosley, prin.   Fax 632-6603
Bacon County MS   400/6-8
  901 N Pierce St 31510   912-632-4662
  Gavin Vickers, prin.   Fax 632-6603

Alpharetta, Fulton, Pop. 35,139
Fulton County SD
  Supt. — See Atlanta
Alpharetta HS   9-12
  3595 Webb Bridge Rd 30005   770-521-7640
  Bucke Green, prin.   Fax 521-7653
Autrey Mill MS   1,000/6-8
  4110 Old Alabama Rd 30022   770-521-7622
  Dr. Ann Ferrell, prin.   Fax 521-7630
Chattahoochee HS   2,100/9-12
  5230 Taylor Rd 30022   770-521-7600
  Tim Duncan, prin.   Fax 521-7659
Haynes Bridge MS   900/6-8
  10665 Haynes Bridge Rd 30022   770-740-7030
  Debbie Reeves, prin.   Fax 667-2842
Holcomb Bridge MS   800/6-8
  2700 Holcomb Bridge Rd 30022   770-594-5280
  Emmett Shaffer, prin.   Fax 643-3333
Hopewell MS   6-8
  13060 Cogburn Rd 30004   678-297-3240
  Frances Boyd, prin.   Fax 297-3250
Milton HS   2,600/9-12
  13025 Birmingham Hwy 30004   770-740-7000
  Ronald Tesch, prin.   Fax 667-2844
Northwestern MS   1,700/6-8
  12805 Birmingham Hwy 30004   770-667-2870
  Norm Barchi, prin.   Fax 667-2878
Taylor Road MS   900/6-8
  5150 Taylor Rd 30022   770-740-7090
  Ed Williamson, prin.   Fax 619-5609
Webb Bridge MS   1,200/6-8
  4455 Webb Bridge Rd 30005   770-667-2940
  Elizabeth Fogartie, prin.   Fax 667-2948

DeVry University   Post-Sec.
  2555 Northwinds Pkwy 30004   770-521-4900
Forsyth Christian S   100/K-12
  1250 Alpha Dr 30004   770-781-4385
  Christopher Walls, admin.
Mill Springs Academy   300/1-12
  13660 New Providence Rd 30004   770-360-1336
  Robert Moore, pres.   Fax 360-1341
Mt. Pisgah Christian S   1,000/PK-12
  9820 Nesbit Ferry Rd 30022   678-336-3000
  Chris Alexander, hdmstr.   Fax 336-3349

Americus, Sumter, Pop. 16,886
Sumter County SD   5,400/PK-12
  100 Learning Ln,   229-931-8500
  Dr. Dennis McMahon, supt.   Fax 931-8555
  www.sumter.k12.ga.us
Americus Sumter HS South Campus   500/10-12
  805 Harrold Ave 31709   229-924-3653
  Tony Overstreet, prin.   Fax 924-1556
Americus Sumter HS North Campus   200/9-9
  101 Industrial Blvd,   229-924-5914
  Victoria Harris, prin.   Fax 928-2827

Staley MS 700/6-8
915 N Lee St, 229-924-3168
Keith Lee, prin. Fax 928-2135
Sumter County MS 700/6-8
439 Bumphead Rd, 229-924-1010
Carolyn Hamilton, prin. Fax 928-5571

Georgia Southwestern State University Post-Sec.
800 Wheatley St 31709 229-928-1279
South Georgia Technical College Post-Sec.
900 S Georgia Tech Pkwy 31709 229-931-2394
Southland Academy 800/PK-12
PO Box 1127 31709 229-924-4406
Adam W. Smith, prin. Fax 924-2996

Appling, Columbia
Columbia County SD 20,100/PK-12
6430 Pollards Pond Rd 30802 706-541-0650
Thomas Price, supt. Fax 541-2344
www.ccboe.net
Other Schools – See Evans, Grovetown, Harlem

Armuchee, Floyd
Floyd County SD
Supt. — See Rome
Armuchee MS 500/6-8
471 Floyd Springs Rd NE 30105 706-378-7924
Bill Gilbert, prin. Fax 378-7983

Ashburn, Turner, Pop. 4,435
Turner County SD 1,800/K-12
PO Box 609 31714 229-567-3338
Ray Jordan, supt. Fax 567-3285
www.turner.k12.ga.us/
Turner County HS 500/9-12
316 Lamar St 31714 229-567-4377
Craig Matthews, prin. Fax 567-9243
Turner County MS 400/6-8
316 Lamar St 31714 229-567-4343
Tommy Day, prin. Fax 567-9243

Moultrie Technical College Post-Sec.
222 Rock House Rd 31714

Athens, Clarke, Pop. 102,663
Clarke County SD 11,400/PK-12
PO Box 1708 30603 706-546-7721
Dr. Lewis Holloway, supt. Fax 369-1804
www.clarke.k12.ga.us
Burney-Harris-Lyons MS 500/6-8
1600 Tallassee Rd 30606 706-548-7208
Robbie Hooker, prin. Fax 357-5263
Cedar Shoals HS 1,600/9-12
1300 Cedar Shoals Dr 30605 706-546-5375
Dr. Tommy Craft, prin. Fax 357-5291
Clarke Central HS 1,500/9-12
350 S Milledge Ave 30605 706-357-5200
Dr. Maxine Easom, prin. Fax 357-5269
Clarke MS 700/6-8
1235 Baxter St 30606 706-543-6547
Dr. Ken Sherman, prin. Fax 548-0257
Coile MS 700/6-8
110 Old Elberton Rd 30601 706-357-5318
Staughton Jennings, prin. Fax 357-5321
Hilsman MS 700/6-8
870 Gaines School Rd 30605 706-548-7281
Dr. Tony Price, prin. Fax 357-5295

Athens Academy 800/PK-12
PO Box 6548 30604 706-549-9225
Robert Chambers, hdmstr. Fax 354-3775
Athens Christian S 800/K-12
1270 Highway 29 N 30601 706-549-7586
Dr. Buhl Cummings, hdmstr. Fax 549-2899
Athens Technical College Post-Sec.
800 Highway 29 N 30601 706-355-5000
Georgia Institute of Cosmetology Post-Sec.
3531 Atlanta Hwy 30606 706-549-6003
Msgr. Walter J. Donovan HS 500/9-12
590 Lavender Rd 30606 706-433-0223
Geoffray Estes, prin. Fax 433-0229
Prince Avenue Christian S 400/K-12
PO Box 1112 30603 706-353-1993
William Pevey, prin. Fax 613-7553
University of Georgia 30602 Post-Sec.
706-542-3000

Atlanta, Fulton, Pop. 423,019
Atlanta CSD 47,800/PK-12
130 Trinity Ave SW 30303 404-802-2820
Dr. Beverly Hall, supt. Fax 802-1803
www.atlanta.k12.ga.us
Brown MS, 765 Peeples St SW 30310 700/6-8
Dr. Sharon R. Ordu, prin. 404-756-6414
Bunche MS 800/6-8
1925 Niskey Lake Rd SW 30331 404-346-2503
Aaron Fernander, prin. Fax 346-2537
Carson Prep MS 800/6-8
1890 Donald L Hollowell Pky 30318 404-792-5944
Nash Alexander, prin. Fax 792-5924
Coan MS 600/6-8
1550 Hosea L Williams Dr NE 30317 404-371-4854
Dr. Andre Williams, prin. Fax 371-7135
Crim HS 600/9-12
256 Clifton St SE 30317 404-371-4881
Dr. Angelisa Cummings, prin. Fax 371-4889
Douglass HS 1,900/9-12
225 Hamilton E Holmes Dr NW 30318 404-792-5925
Dr. Eldrick Horton, prin. Fax 792-5736
Early College HS 500/9-12
55 McDonough Blvd SE 30315 404-802-4405
Marcene Thornton, prin.
Grady HS 1,000/9-12
929 Charles Allen Dr NE 30309 404-802-3001
Dr. Vincent Murray, prin. Fax 853-4099
Harper-Archer MS 600/6-8
3399 Collier Dr NW 30331 404-699-4794
Ben Pennington, prin. Fax 699-4569
Inman MS 700/6-8
774 Virginia Ave NE 30306 404-802-3200
Dr. Betsy Bockman, prin. Fax 853-4085
Kennedy MS 600/6-8
225 James P Brawley Dr NW 30314 404-802-3600
Linda Cumberlander, prin.
King MS 500/6-8
545 Hill St SE 30312 404-330-4979
Tresa Riney, prin. Fax 330-4196
Long MS 700/6-8
3200 Latona Dr SW 30354 404-669-2257
Dr. Elizabeth Harris, prin. Fax 669-2266

Mays HS 1,700/9-12
3450 Benjamin E Mays Dr SW 30331 404-699-4537
Dr. Tyronne Smith, prin. Fax 699-6781
North Atlanta HS 1,400/9-12
2875 Northside Dr NW 30305 404-351-0895
Scott Bursmith, prin. Fax 351-8763
Parks MS 600/6-8
1090 Windsor St SW 30310 404-752-0742
Merita Brown, prin. Fax 752-0791
Price MS 900/6-8
1670 Benjamin W Bickers SE 30315 404-624-5128
Sheila Barker, prin. Fax 624-2118
School of Entrepreneurship 9-12
55 McDonough Blvd SE 30315 404-802-4400
Abigail Crawford, prin.
School of Health Sciences & Research 9-12
55 McDonough Blvd SE 30315 404-802-4420
Dr. Darien Jones, prin.
School of Technology 9-12
55 McDonough Blvd SE 30315 404-802-4410
Rodney Ray, prin.
School of the Arts 9-12
55 McDonough Blvd SE 30315 404-802-4415
Dr. Marvin Pryor, prin.
South Atlanta HS 1,300/9-12
800 Hutchens Rd SE 30354 404-362-5057
Esmie Gaynor, prin. Fax 608-8114
Southside HS 1,000/9-12
801 Glenwood Ave SE 30316 404-624-2064
Dr. Shirlene Carter, prin. Fax 624-2111
Sutton MS 700/6-8
4191 Northside Dr NW 30342 404-256-6920
Mark Mygrant, prin. Fax 705-0100
Sylvan Hills MS 600/6-8
1461 Sylvan Rd SW 30310 404-752-0711
Gwendolyn Atkinson, prin. Fax 756-2290
Therrell HS 1,000/9-12
3099 Panther Trl SW 30311 404-346-2523
Algie Davis, prin. Fax 346-3097
Turner MS 600/6-8
98 Anderson Ave NW 30314 404-792-5539
Dr. Joyce Clarke, prin.
Walden MS 300/6-8
320 Irwin St NE 30312 404-330-4173
Dr. Flora Goolsby, prin. Fax 521-1596
Washington HS 1,600/9-12
2250 Perry Blvd NW 30318 404-792-5900
Carter Coleman, prin.
Young MS 900/6-8
3116 Benjamin E Mays Dr SW 30311 404-699-4533
Dr. Thomas Kenner, prin. Fax 699-6794
Crim Evening Classes Adult
256 Clifton St SE 30317 404-371-7105
Dr. Angelisa Cummings, prin.
Washington Evening HS Adult
256 Clifton St SE 30317 404-371-7105
Carl Shivers, prin.

DeKalb County SD
Supt. — See Decatur
Chamblee MS 600/7-8
4680 Chamblee Dunwoody Rd 30338 678-874-8202
Cynthia Jackson, prin. Fax 874-8210
Cross Keys HS 900/9-12
1626 N Druid Hills Rd NE 30319 678-874-6102
Ron Hutcheson, prin. Fax 874-6110
DeKalb S of the Arts 8-12
2415 N Druid Hills Rd NE 30329 678-676-2502
Susan McCauley, prin. Fax 676-2510
Lakeside HS 1,400/9-12
3801 Briarcliff Rd NE 30345 678-874-6702
Wayne Chelf, prin. Fax 874-6710
McNair HS 1,200/9-12
1804 Bouldercrest Rd SE 30316 678-874-4902
Chris Beal, prin. Fax 874-4910
Open Campus SHS 1,000/11-12
2415 N Druid Hills Rd NE 30329 678-676-2602
Mattie Small, prin. Fax 676-2610

Fulton County SD 69,800/PK-12
786 Cleveland Ave SW 30315 404-768-3600
James Wilson, supt. Fax 763-6798
www.fultonschools.org
North Springs HS 1,700/9-12
7447 Roswell Rd NE 30328 770-551-2490
Vicky Ferguson, prin. Fax 551-2498
Ridgeview MS 600/6-8
5340 Trimble Rd NE 30342 404-843-7710
Karen Cox, prin. Fax 847-3292
Riverwood HS 1,200/9-12
5900 Heards Dr NW 30328 404-847-1980
Edward Echols, prin. Fax 255-8709
Sandtown MS 6-8
5400 Campbellton Rd SW 30331 404-346-6500
Sandra McGary-Ervin, prin. Fax 346-6510
Sandy Springs MS 800/6-8
8750 Colonel Dr 30350 770-552-4970
Cathi Barlow, prin. Fax 643-3334
Westlake HS 1,200/9-12
2370 Union Rd SW 30331 404-346-6400
Darron Franklin, prin. Fax 346-6410
Other Schools – See Alpharetta, College Park, Duluth, East Point, Fairburn, Roswell

---

American InterContinental University Post-Sec.
6600 Peachtree Dunwoody Rd 30328 404-965-6500
American InterContinental University Post-Sec.
3330 Peachtree Rd NE 30326 404-965-5700
American Red Cross Blood Services Post-Sec.
1925 Monroe Dr NE 30324 404-881-9800
Argosy University/Atlanta Post-Sec.
980 Hammond Dr NE Ste 100 30328 770-671-1200
Art Institute of Atlanta Post-Sec.
6600 Peachtree Dunwoody Rd 30328 800-275-4242
Atlanta Adventist Academy 100/9-12
3870 Cascade Rd SW 30331
Atlanta International S 900/PK-12
2890 N Fulton Dr NE 30305 404-841-3840
Robert Brindley, hdmstr. Fax 841-3873
Atlanta Job Corps Center Post-Sec.
239 W Lake Ave NW 30314 404-794-9512
Atlanta Medical Center Post-Sec.
303 Parkway Dr NE 30312 404-265-4203
Atlanta Metro College Post-Sec.
1630 Metropolitan Pkwy SW 30310 404-756-4000
Atlanta School of Massage Post-Sec.
2 Dunwoody Park 30338 770-454-7167
Atlanta Technical College Post-Sec.
1560 Metropolitan Pkwy SW 30310 404-756-3700

Bauder College Post-Sec.
384 Northyards Blvd NW #190 30313 404-237-7573
Beulah Heights Bible College Post-Sec.
PO Box 18145 30316 404-627-2681
Brandon Hall S 100/4-12
1701 Brandon Hall Dr 30350 770-394-8177
Paul Stockhammer, pres. Fax 804-8821
Brown Coll. of Court Reporting & Med. Post-Sec.
1740 Peachtree St NW 30309 404-876-1227
Brown Mackie College Post-Sec.
6600 Peachtree Dunwoody NE 30328 770-638-0121
Carver Bible College Post-Sec.
PO Box 4335 30302 800-262-4253
Clark Atlanta University Post-Sec.
223 James P Brawley Dr SW 30314 404-880-8000
Creative Circus Post-Sec.
812 Lambert Dr NE 30324 404-607-8880
DeVry University Post-Sec.
3575 Piedmont Rd NE # P-100 30305 404-296-7400
DeVry University Post-Sec.
2 Ravinia Dr Ste 350 30346 770-671-1744
DeVry University Post-Sec.
100 Galleria Pkwy SE #100 30339 678-424-5630
Emory University Post-Sec.
200B Jones Ctr 30322 404-727-6123
Emory University Hospital Post-Sec.
1364 Clifton Rd NE 30322 404-712-4881
Franklin Academy 100/9-12
1585 Clifton Rd NE 30329 404-633-7404
Galloway S 700/PK-12
215 W Wieuca Rd NW 30342 404-252-8389
Linda Martinson, hdmstr. Fax 252-7770
Georgia Institute of Technology Post-Sec.
225 North Ave NW 30332 404-894-2000
Georgia Medical Institute Post-Sec.
101 Marietta St NW Ste 600 30303 404-525-1111
Georgia Medical Institute Post-Sec.
1706 Northeast Expy NE 30329 404-327-8787
Georgia State University Post-Sec.
PO Box 4009 30302 404-651-2000
Grady Health System Post-Sec.
PO Box 26189 30303 404-616-4252
Greater Atlanta Adventist Academy 100/9-12
401 Hamilton E Holmes Dr NW 30318 404-799-0337
Fax 799-0977
Herzing College Post-Sec.
3355 Lenox Rd NE Ste 100 30326 404-816-4533
Holy Innocents' Episcopal S 1,300/PK-12
805 Mount Vernon Hwy NW 30327 404-255-4026
Kirk Duncan, hdmstr. Fax 250-0815
Holy Spirit Preparatory S 200/PK-12
4449 Northside Dr NW 30327 678-904-2811
Gareth Genner, prin. Fax 904-4983
Howard S 100/PK-12
1246 Ponce De Leon Ave NE 30306 404-377-7436
Marifred Cilella, hdmstr. Fax 377-0884
Interdenominational Theological Center Post-Sec.
700 Mrtn Lthr King Jr Dr SW 30314 404-527-7700
International School of Skin/Nailcare Post-Sec.
5600 Roswell Rd NE 30342 404-843-1005
Javelin Technical Training Center Post-Sec.
4501 Circle 75 Ste C-3180 30339 770-859-9779
Lovett S 1,500/K-12
4075 Paces Ferry Rd NW 30327 404-262-3032
Dr. William Peeble, hdmstr. Fax 261-1967
Marist HS 1,000/7-12
3790 Ashford Dunwoody Rd NE 30319
770-457-7201
Fr. Joel Konzen, prin. Fax 457-8402
Mercer University in Atlanta Post-Sec.
3001 Mercer University Dr 30341 678-547-6000
Mohammed Schools of Atlanta 200/PK-12
735 Fayetteville Rd SE 30316 404-378-4219
Safiyyah Shahid, prin. Fax 378-4600
Morehouse College Post-Sec.
830 Westview Dr SW 30314 404-681-2800
Morehouse School of Medicine Post-Sec.
720 Westview Dr SW 30310 404-752-1500
Mt. Vernon Presbyterian S 700/PK-12
471 Mount Vernon Hwy NE 30328 404-252-3448
Dr. Jeff Jackson, hdmstr. Fax 252-6777
Oglethorpe University Post-Sec.
4484 Peachtree Rd NE 30319 404-261-1441
Pace Academy 900/K-12
966 W Paces Ferry Rd NW 30327 404-262-1345
Fred Assaf, hdmstr. Fax 264-9376
Paideia S 900/PK-12
1509 Ponce De Leon Ave NE 30307 404-377-3491
Paul Bianchi, hdmstr. Fax 377-0032
Portfolio Center Post-Sec.
125 Bennett St NW 30309 404-351-5055
Rising Spirit Inst. of Natural Health Post-Sec.
4536 Chamblee Dunwoody Rd 30338 770-457-2021
St. Joseph's Hospital Post-Sec.
5665 Pchtree Dunwoody Rd NE 30342
404-851-7120
St. Pius X HS 1,100/9-12
2674 Johnson Rd NE 30345 404-636-3023
Steven Spellman, prin. Fax 633-8387
Savannah College of Art and Design Post-Sec.
PO Box 77300 30357 404-253-2700
Southwest Atlanta Christian Academy 300/PK-12
PO Box 310750 31131 404-346-2080
Geraldine Thompson, hdmstr. Fax 346-2085
Spelman College Post-Sec.
350 Spelman Ln SW 30314 800-982-2411
Strayer University Post-Sec.
3355 Northeast Expy NE #100 30341 770-454-9270
Strayer University Post-Sec.
3101 TowerCreek Pkwy SE 700 30339 770-612-2170
Temima HS 100/9-12
1985B Lavista Rd NE 30329 404-315-0507
Miriam Feldman, prin. Fax 634-2111
The Psychological Studies Institute Post-Sec.
2055 Mount Paran Rd NW 30327 404-233-3949
Ultrasound Diagnostic School Post-Sec.
1140 Hammond Dr NE # 8-1150 30328
404-248-9070
Westminster S 1,800/K-12
1424 W Paces Ferry Rd NW 30327 404-355-8673
William Clarkson, pres. Fax 355-6606
Westwood College Post-Sec.
1100 Spring St NW Ste 102 30309 404-745-9096
Westwood College Post-Sec.
2220 Parklake Dr NE 30345 404-962-2999
Yeshiva Atlanta HS 100/9-12
3130 Raymond Dr 30340 770-451-5299
Dewey Holbrook, prin. Fax 451-5571
Yeshiva Ohr Yisroel 50/9-12
1810 Briarcliff Rd NE 30329 404-320-1444
Rabbi Mayer Neuberger, dir. Fax 320-1609

Augusta, Richmond, Pop. 193,101
Richmond County SD — 33,100/PK-12
864 Broad St 30901 — 706-826-1000
Dr. Charles Larke, supt.
www.richmond.k12.ga.us — Fax 826-4613
Academy of Richmond County Comp. HS — 1,300/9-12
910 Russell St 30904 — 706-737-7152
David Robbins, prin. — Fax 737-7155
Butler Comprehensive HS — 1,200/9-12
2011 Lumpkin Rd 30906 — 706-796-4959
Walter Reeves, prin. — Fax 796-4780
Cross Creek HS — 1,300/9-12
3855 Old Waynesboro Rd 30906 — 706-772-8140
Lynn Warr, prin. — Fax 772-8153
Davidson Magnet JSHS — 700/6-12
615 12th St 30901 — 706-823-6924
Vicky Addison, prin. — Fax 823-4373
East Augusta MS — 500/6-8
320 Kentucky Ave 30901 — 706-823-6960
Dr. Velma Curtis, prin. — Fax 823-6963
Glenn Hills HS — 1,300/9-12
2840 Glenn Hills Dr 30906 — 706-796-4924
Jessie Chambers, prin. — Fax 796-4932
Glenn Hills MS — 1,200/6-8
2941 Glenn Hills Dr 30906 — 706-796-4705
Hartley Gibbons, prin. — Fax 796-4716
Johnson Health Professions HS — 400/9-12
1324 Laney Walker Blvd 30901 — 706-823-6933
Deborah Walker, prin. — Fax 823-6931
Josey Comprehensive HS — 1,000/9-12
1701 15th St 30901 — 706-737-7360
Quentin Motley, prin. — Fax 737-7363
Laney Comprehensive HS — 600/9-12
1339 Laney Walker Blvd 30901 — 706-823-6900
Dr. Hawthorne Welcher, prin. — Fax 823-6918
Langford MS — 700/6-8
3019 Walton Way Ext 30909 — 706-737-7301
Cheryl Fry, prin. — Fax 737-7302
Sego MS — 900/6-8
3420 Julia Ave 30906 — 706-796-4944
Ronald Wiggins, prin. — Fax 796-4670
Tubman MS — 600/6-8
1740 Walton Way 30904 — 706-737-7250
Rickey Lumpkin, prin. — Fax 737-7246
Tutt MS — 600/6-8
495 Boy Scout Rd 30909 — 706-737-7288
Charles Thompson, prin. — Fax 481-1620
Westside HS — 900/9-12
1002 Patriots Way 30907 — 706-868-4030
Tim Spivey, prin. — Fax 868-4005
Josey Evening S — Adult
804 Katherine St 30904 — 706-731-8805
Winnette Bradley, prin. — Fax 737-7271
Other Schools – See Hephzibah

Alleluia Community S — 200/K-12
2819 Peach Orchard Rd 30906 — 706-793-9663
Dan Funsch, prin. — Fax 560-2759
Aquinas HS — 300/9-12
1920 Highland Ave 30904 — 706-736-5516
Robert Larcher, prin. — Fax 736-2678
Augusta State University — Post-Sec.
2500 Walton Way 30904 — 706-737-1400
Augusta Technical College — Post-Sec.
3116 Deans Bridge Rd 30906 — 706-771-4000
Curtis Baptist S — 400/PK-12
1326 Broad St 30901 — 706-722-2201
Philip Musgrave, hdmstr. — Fax 722-1881
Georgia Institute of Cosmetology — Post-Sec.
2803 Wrightsboro Rd 30909
Medical College of Georgia — Post-Sec.
1120 15th St 30912 — 706-721-0211
Paine College — Post-Sec.
1235 15th St 30901 — 800-476-7703
Savannah River College — Post-Sec.
2528 Center West Pkwy # A 30909 — 706-738-5046
Shekinah Glory Christian Academy — 50/9-12
815 12th St 30901 — 706-722-1011
Dr. Marilyn McDonald, admin. — Fax 722-3701
Southgate Christian S — 100/K-12
2226 Peach Orchard Rd 30906 — 706-798-2473
University Hospital Health System — Post-Sec.
1350 Walton Way 30901 — 706-722-9011
Westminster S of Augusta — 500/PK-12
3067 Wheeler Rd 30909 — 706-731-7780
Jim Adare, hdmstr. — Fax 731-5274

Austell, Cobb, Pop. 6,430
Cobb County SD
Supt. — See Marietta
Cooper MS — 1,000/6-8
4605 Ewing Rd 30106 — 770-819-2438
Peggy Martin, prin. — Fax 819-2440
Garrett MS — 900/6-8
5235 Powder Springs Rd 30106 — 770-819-2466
Dr. Phillip Page, prin. — Fax 819-2468
South Cobb HS — 2,000/9-12
1920 Clay Rd 30106 — 770-819-2611
Dr. Grant Rivera, prin. — Fax 819-2613

Avondale Estates, DeKalb, Pop. 2,630
DeKalb County SD
Supt. — See Decatur
Avondale HS — 1,100/9-12
1192 Clarendon Ave 30002 — 678-874-0402
Mike Worthington, prin. — Fax 874-0410
Avondale MS — 1,000/6-8
3131 Old Rockbridge Rd 30002 — 678-875-0102
Bernetta Jordan, prin. — Fax 875-0110

Bainbridge, Decatur, Pop. 11,823
Decatur County SD — 5,700/PK-12
100 S West St, — 229-248-2200
Ralph D. Jones, supt. — Fax 248-2252
www.dcboe.com
Bainbridge HS — 1,500/9-12
1301 E College St, — 229-248-2230
Tommie Howell, prin. — Fax 248-2260
Hutto MS — 700/6-8
1201 Martin Luther King Jr, — 229-248-2224
Dr. Marvin Thomas, prin. — Fax 243-5303
West Bainbridge MS — 600/6-8
1417 Dothan Rd, — 229-248-2206
Robert McIntosh, prin. — Fax 248-2270

Bainbridge College — Post-Sec.
2500 E Shotwell St, — 229-248-2500
Grace Christian Academy — 200/PK-12
PO Box 1930, — 229-243-8851
Dennis Moore, prin. — Fax 243-0515

Barnesville, Lamar, Pop. 5,890
Lamar County SD — 2,000/PK-12
3 Trojan Way 30204 — 770-358-5891
Dr. Jerry Stinchcomb, supt. — Fax 358-5897
www.lamar.k12.ga.us
Lamar County Comprehensive HS — 700/9-12
1 Trojan Way 30204 — 770-358-8641
Charles Bonner, prin. — Fax 358-8649
Lamar County MS — 700/6-8
100 Burnette Rd 30204 — 770-358-8652
Diane Harvey, prin. — Fax 358-8657

Gordon College — Post-Sec.
419 College Dr 30204 — 770-358-5000

Baxley, Appling, Pop. 4,379
Appling County SD — 3,400/PK-12
249 Blackshear Hwy 31513 — 912-367-8600
Janice Sellers, supt. — Fax 367-1011
www.appling.k12.ga.us
Appling County HS — 900/9-12
482 Blackshear Hwy 31513 — 912-367-8610
Phil Murphy, prin. — Fax 366-9877
Appling County MS — 800/6-8
2997 Blackshear Hwy 31513 — 912-367-8630
Keith Johnson, prin. — Fax 367-8803

Bellville, Evans, Pop. 137

Pinewood Christian Academy — 600/K-12
PO Box 7 30414 — 912-739-1272
Dewey Hulsey, hdmstr. — Fax 739-2321

Blackshear, Pierce, Pop. 3,302
Pierce County SD — 3,300/PK-12
PO Box 349 31516 — 912-449-2044
Dr. Joy B. Williams, supt. — Fax 449-2046
www.pierce.k12.ga.us/
Pierce County HS — 900/9-12
4850 County Farm Rd 31516 — 912-449-2055
Anthony Smith, prin. — Fax 449-2061
Pierce County MS — 800/6-8
5216 County Farm Rd 31516 — 912-449-2077
Terri DeLoach, prin. — Fax 449-2075

Blairsville, Union, Pop. 696
Towns County SD
Supt. — See Hiawassee
Mountain Education Center — Adult
218 Church St 30512 — 706-745-9575
Wade Smith, prin. — Fax 745-3588

Union County SD — 2,600/K-12
10 Hughes St 30512 — 706-745-2322
Tommy Stephens, supt. — Fax 745-5025
www.union.k12.ga.us
Union County HS — 700/9-12
604 Panther Cir 30512 — 706-745-2216
Ed Rohrbaugh, prin. — Fax 745-4122
Union County MS — 600/6-8
448 Wellborn St 30512 — 706-745-2483
Karen Roxbury, prin. — Fax 745-3920
Other Schools – See Suches

North Georgia Technical College — Post-Sec.
434 Meeks Ave 30512 — 706-781-2300

Blakely, Early, Pop. 5,588
Early County SD — 2,700/PK-12
11927 Columbia St, — 229-723-4337
Betty Orange, supt. — Fax 723-8183
www.early.k12.ga.us
Early County HS — 800/9-12
12020 Columbia St, — 229-723-3006
Jim Morrell, prin. — Fax 723-8690
Early County MS — 600/6-8
12053 Columbia St, — 229-723-3746
James McCoy, prin. — Fax 723-3942

Albany Technical College — Post-Sec.
40 Harold Regan Blvd, — 229-724-2100

Blue Ridge, Fannin, Pop. 1,191
Fannin County SD — 3,200/K-12
2290 E First St 30513 — 706-632-3771
Sandra Mercier, supt. — Fax 632-7583
www.fannin.k12.ga.us
Fannin County Career & Technology Center — Vo/Tech
2346 E 1st St 30513 — 706-632-2013
Jeff Wilbanks, dir. — Fax 632-6552
Fannin County Comprehensive HS — 1,000/9-12
2346 E First St 30513 — 706-632-2081
Douglas Davenport, prin. — Fax 632-4442
Fannin County MS — 700/6-8
4560 Old Highway 76 30513 — 706-632-6100
Angela Berrong, prin. — Fax 632-0461

Bogart, Clarke, Pop. 1,101
Oconee County SD
Supt. — See Watkinsville
Malcom Bridge MS — 500/6-8
2500 Malcom Bridge Rd 30622 — 770-725-2319
Tom Odom, prin. — Fax 725-0961
North Oconee HS — 9-12
1081 Rocky Branch Rd 30622 — 706-769-7760
John Osborne, prin. — Fax 769-4766

Bonaire, Houston
Houston County SD
Supt. — See Perry
Bonaire MS — 1,000/6-8
125 GA Highway 96 31005 — 478-929-6236
Cindy Randall, prin. — Fax 929-6245

Bowdon, Carroll, Pop. 1,958
Carroll County SD
Supt. — See Carrollton
Bowdon HS — 400/9-12
504 W College St 30108 — 770-258-5408
Chuck Taylor, prin. — Fax 258-7278
Jonesville MS — 500/6-8
129 N Jonesville Rd 30108 — 770-258-1778
Barry Williams, prin. — Fax 258-4374
Open Campus HS — Adult
225 E College St 30108 — 770-258-4403
Dot Sayer, prin. — Fax 258-8205

Bremen, Haralson, Pop. 5,057
Bremen CSD — 1,600/PK-12
504 Laurel St 30110 — 770-537-5508
Dr. Stanley McCain, supt. — Fax 537-0610
www.bremencs.com
Bremen HS — 400/9-12
504 Georgia Ave S 30110 — 770-537-2592
Duane McManus, prin. — Fax 537-0714
Sewell MS — 400/6-8
515 Laurel St 30110 — 770-537-4874
David Clay, prin. — Fax 537-5043

Brooklet, Bulloch, Pop. 1,100
Bulloch County SD
Supt. — See Statesboro
Southeast Bulloch HS — 800/9-12
9184 Brooklet Denmark Rd 30415 — 912-842-2131
Joni Walker-Seier, prin. — Fax 842-9411
Southeast Bulloch MS — 700/6-8
9124 Brooklet Denmark Rd 30415 — 912-842-9555
Alan Putz, prin. — Fax 842-9559

Brunswick, Glynn, Pop. 15,984
Glynn County SD — 12,100/PK-12
PO Box 1677 31521 — 912-267-4100
Dr. Michael Bull, supt. — Fax 265-2011
www.glynn.k12.ga.us
Brunswick HS — 1,700/9-12
3920 Habersham St 31520 — 912-267-4200
Terry Graff, prin. — Fax 261-4433
Glynn Academy — 1,700/9-12
PO Box 1678 31521 — 912-267-4210
Baker Davis, prin. — Fax 267-4246
Glynn MS — 700/6-8
901 George St 31520 — 912-267-4150
Ricky Rentz, prin. — Fax 267-4158
Macon MS — 900/6-8
3885 Altama Ave 31520 — 912-265-3337
Scott Spence, prin. — Fax 267-4118
Needwood MS — 800/6-8
669 Harry Driggers Blvd 31525 — 912-261-4488
Dr. Joan Boorman, prin. — Fax 261-4491
Risley MS — 500/6-8
2900 Albany St 31520 — 912-267-4160
Robert Jaudon, prin. — Fax 267-4161

Brunswick Christian Academy — 100/K-12
4231 US Highway 17 N 31525 — 912-264-4546
Christian Renewal Academy — 200/K-12
4265 Norwich Street Ext 31520 — 912-264-5491
Rick Postell, admin. — Fax 264-0799
Coastal Georgia Community College — Post-Sec.
3700 Altama Ave 31520 — 912-264-7235
Emmanuel Christian S — 100/K-12
1010 Old Jesup Rd 31520 — 912-265-9647

Buchanan, Haralson, Pop. 977
Haralson County SD — 3,900/PK-12
10 Van Wert St 30113 — 770-646-3882
William Johnson, supt. — Fax 646-8628
www.haralson.k12.ga.us
Other Schools – See Tallapoosa

Buena Vista, Marion, Pop. 1,657
Marion County SD — 1,700/PK-12
PO Box 391 31803 — 229-649-2234
Richard McCorkle, supt. — Fax 649-7423
www.marion.k12.ga.us/
Marion MS — 600/5-8
PO Box 16 31803 — 229-649-2145
Janie Downer, prin. — Fax 649-5570
Tri-County HS — 500/9-12
PO Box 177 31803 — 229-649-7520
Glenn Tidwell, prin. — Fax 649-5945

Buford, Gwinnett, Pop. 10,820
Buford CSD — 2,300/K-12
70 Wiley Dr Ste 200 30518 — 770-945-5035
Sue H. Morris, supt. — Fax 945-4629
www.bufordcityschools.org
Buford HS — 700/9-12
2750 Sawnee Ave 30518 — 770-945-6768
Steve Miller, prin. — Fax 932-7570
Buford MS — 600/6-8
2700 Robert Bell Pkwy 30518 — 770-904-3690
Rachel Adams, prin. — Fax 904-3689

Gwinnett County SD
Supt. — See Suwanee
Jones MS — 6-8
3575 Ridge Rd 30519 — 770-904-5450
Dr. Richard Holland, prin. — Fax 904-5452
Lanier MS — 2,900/6-8
918 Buford Hwy 30518 — 770-945-8419
Jaime Espinosa, prin. — Fax 271-5108

Butler, Taylor, Pop. 1,928
Taylor County SD — 1,300/PK-12
PO Box 1930 31006 — 478-862-5224
Wayne Smith, supt. — Fax 862-5818
www.taylor.k12.ga.us
Taylor County HS — 400/9-12
PO Box 1927 31006 — 478-862-3314
Clarence Mathise, prin. — Fax 862-5818
Taylor County MS — 400/6-8
PO Box 580 31006 — 478-862-5285
Anzy Hardman, prin. — Fax 862-5368

Byron, Peach, Pop. 3,062
Peach County SD
Supt. — See Fort Valley
Byron MS — 500/6-8
201 Linda Dr 31008 — 478-956-4999
Ken Banter, prin. — Fax 956-3916

Cairo, Grady, Pop. 9,342
Grady County SD — 4,500/PK-12
122 N Broad St, — 229-377-3701
Steven A. Wooten, supt. — Fax 377-3437
www.grady.k12.ga.us
Cairo HS — 1,200/9-12
455 5th St SE, — 229-377-2222
Tim Helms, prin. — Fax 377-2812
Washington MS — 800/6-8
1277 Booker Hill Blvd SW, — 229-377-2106
Arthur Anderson, prin. — Fax 377-7779

Calhoun, Gordon, Pop. 12,342
Calhoun CSD — 3,000/PK-12
380 Barrett Rd 30701 — 706-629-2900
Mike Davis, supt. — Fax 629-3235
www.calhounschools.org
Calhoun HS — 700/9-12
315 S River St 30701 — 706-629-9213
Wanda Westmoreland, prin. — Fax 602-6652
Calhoun MS — 600/6-8
399 S River St 30701 — 706-629-3340
Bob Orfield, prin. — Fax 629-0236

Gordon County SD — 6,400/PK-12
PO Box 12001 30703 — 706-629-7366
Mike Stanton, supt. — Fax 625-5671
www.gcbe.org
Ashworth MS — 700/6-8
PO Box 12001 30703 — 706-625-9545
W.H. Robbie Robison, prin. — Fax 625-0114
Gordon Central HS — 1,700/9-12
PO Box 12001 30703 — 706-629-7391
Allen Fort, prin. — Fax 625-5376
Sonoraville East MS — 800/6-8
PO Box 12001 30703 — 706-629-0793
Clark Maggart, prin. — Fax 629-2983
Sonoraville HS — 9-12
PO Box 12001 30703 — 706-879-3209
 — Fax 602-0321

Coosa Valley Technical College — Post-Sec.
1151 Highway 53 Spur SW 30701
Georgia Cumberland Academy — 200/9-12
397 Academy Dr SW 30701 — 706-629-4591
Greg Gerard, prin. — Fax 629-1272

Camilla, Mitchell, Pop. 5,609
Mitchell County SD — 2,300/PK-12
108 S Harney St 31730 — 229-336-2100
Beauford Hicks, supt. — Fax 336-1615
www.mitchell.k12.ga.us
Mitchell-Baker HS — 800/9-12
1000 Newton Rd 31730 — 229-336-0970
Robert Adams, prin. — Fax 336-2171
Mitchell County MS — 500/6-8
55 Griffin Rd 31730 — 229-336-0980
Rodney Bullard, prin. — Fax 336-2139

Westwood S — 300/PK-12
255 Fuller St 31730 — 229-336-7992
Betty Shiver, prin. — Fax 336-0982

Canton, Cherokee, Pop. 13,195
Cherokee County SD — 28,500/PK-12
PO Box 769, — 770-479-1871
Dr. Frank Petruzielo, supt. — Fax 479-7758
www.cherokee.k12.ga.us
Cherokee HS — 2,000/9-12
930 Marietta Hwy 30114 — 770-479-4112
Pam Biser, prin. — Fax 479-8421
Creekland MS — 6-8
1555 Owens Store Rd 30115 — 770-479-3200
Dr. Deborah Wiseman, prin. — Fax 479-3210
Creekview HS — 9-12
1550 Owens Store Rd 30115 — 770-720-7600
Bob Eddy, prin.
Freedom MS — 7-8
10550 Bells Ferry Rd 30114 — 770-345-4100
Dr. Lou Manzella, prin. — Fax 345-4140
Rusk MS — 1,100/7-8
4695 Hickory Rd 30115 — 770-345-2832
Elaine Daniel, prin. — Fax 345-5073
Sequoyah HS — 2,000/9-12
4485 Hickory Rd 30115 — 770-345-1474
Elliott Berman, prin. — Fax 345-5498
Teasley MS — 1,200/7-8
8871 Knox Bridge Hwy 30114 — 770-479-7077
Lory Hill, prin. — Fax 479-3275
Other Schools – See Woodstock

Carnesville, Franklin, Pop. 586
Franklin County SD — 3,600/K-12
PO Box 99 30521 — 706-384-4554
Dr. Rio Ayer, supt. — Fax 384-7472
www.franklin.k12.ga.us
Franklin County HS — 1,000/9-12
PO Box 543 30521 — 706-384-4525
Diane Toney, prin. — Fax 384-2201
Franklin County MS — 900/6-8
PO Box 544 30521 — 706-384-4581
Lucy Floyd, prin. — Fax 384-2284

Carrollton, Carroll, Pop. 20,615
Carroll County SD — 14,400/PK-12
164 Independence Dr 30116 — 770-832-3568
John Zauner, supt. — Fax 834-6399
www.carrollcountyschools.com/
Central HS — 1,200/9-12
113 Central High Rd 30116 — 770-834-3386
Gail Stewart, prin. — Fax 832-0103
Central MS — 1,000/6-8
155 Whooping Creek Rd 30116 — 770-832-8114
Terry Jones, prin. — Fax 836-2782
Technical HS of Carroll Co. — Vo/Tech
1075 Newnan Rd 30116 — 770-832-8380
Cindy Clanton, prin. — Fax 830-5037
Other Schools – See Bowdon, Mount Zion, Temple, Villa Rica

Carrollton CSD — 3,000/K-12
106 Trojan Dr 30117 — 770-832-9633
Thomas Wilson, supt. — Fax 836-2830
www.carrolltoncityschools.net/
Carrollton HS — 1,100/9-12
202 Trojan Dr 30117 — 770-834-7726
Dr. Kent Edwards, prin. — Fax 834-8714
Carrollton JHS — 800/6-8
510 Ben Scott Blvd 30117 — 770-832-6535
David Hicks, prin. — Fax 832-7003

Oak Mountain Academy — 200/K-12
222 Cross Plains Rd 30116 — 770-834-6651
Ricky Parmer, hdmstr. — Fax 834-6785
University of West Georgia 30118 — Post-Sec.
 — 770-836-6500
West Central Technical College — Post-Sec.
997 Newnan Rd 30116 — 770-836-6800

Cartersville, Bartow, Pop. 17,221
Bartow County SD — 9,400/PK-12
PO Box 200007 30120 — 770-606-5800
Dr. Abbe Boring, supt. — Fax 606-5857
www.bartow.k12.ga.us
Cass HS — 1,300/9-12
738 Grassdale Rd NW 30121 — 770-606-5845
Mike Nelson, prin. — Fax 606-3825
Cass MS — 1,100/6-8
195 Fire Tower Rd NW 30120 — 770-606-5846
Kristy Arnold, prin. — Fax 606-3835
Woodland HS — 1,900/8-12
800 Old Alabama Rd SE 30120 — 770-606-5870
Brian Newhall, prin. — Fax 606-2080
Other Schools – See Adairsville, Emerson, Kingston

Cartersville CSD — 3,900/PK-12
PO Box 3310 30120 — 770-382-5880
Dr. J. Howard Hinesley, supt. — Fax 387-7476
www.cartersville.k12.ga.us
Cartersville HS — 1,000/9-12
320 E Church St 30120 — 770-382-3200
Jay Floyd, prin. — Fax 382-0701
Cartersville MS — 900/6-8
825 Douthit Ferry Rd 30120 — 770-382-3666
Jeff Hogan, prin. — Fax 387-7495

Excel Christian Academy — 400/K-12
325 Old Mill Rd 30120 — 770-382-9488
A. Tommy Harris, admin. — Fax 606-9884

Cave Spring, Floyd, Pop. 992

Georgia School for the Deaf — Post-Sec.
232 Perry Farm Rd SW 30124 — 706-777-2200

Cedartown, Polk, Pop. 9,583
Polk County SD — 7,100/PK-12
PO Box 128 30125 — 770-748-3821
Dr. Darrell Sorrells, supt. — Fax 748-5131
www.polk.k12.ga.us/
Cedartown HS — 1,100/9-12
167 Frank Lott Dr 30125 — 770-748-0490
Dr. Ken Prichard, prin. — Fax 749-1872
Cedartown MS — 1,000/6-8
1664 Syble Brannon Pkwy 30125 — 770-749-8850
Lucy Cromer, prin. — Fax 749-2795
Other Schools – See Rockmart

Vineyard Harvester Christian Academy — 100/K-12
40 Lake Creek Rd 30125 — 770-748-9320
Kenneth Meadors, hdmstr. — Fax 748-5374

Centerville, Houston, Pop. 5,268
Houston County SD
Supt. – See Perry
Thomson MS — 6-8
301 Thomson St 31028 — 478-953-0489
Tammy Dunn, prin. — Fax 953-0484

Chamblee, DeKalb, Pop. 9,228
DeKalb County SD
Supt. — See Decatur
Henderson MS — 1,400/6-8
2830 Henderson Mill Rd 30341 — 678-874-2902
Terese Allen, prin. — Fax 874-2910

Interactive College of Technology — Post-Sec.
5303 New Peachtree Rd 30341 — 770-216-2960

Chatsworth, Murray, Pop. 3,768
Murray County SD — 7,600/PK-12
PO Box 40 30705 — 706-695-4531
Dr. Charlotte Pipkin, supt. — Fax 695-8425
www.murray.k12.ga.us
Bagley MS — 700/6-8
4600 Highway 225 N 30705 — 706-695-1115
Danny Dunn, prin. — Fax 695-7269
Gladden MS — 1,000/6-8
700 Old Dalton Ellijay Rd 30705 — 706-695-7448
Maria Bradley, prin. — Fax 517-2479
Murray County HS — 1,800/9-12
1001 Green Rd 30705 — 706-695-1414
Gary Mealer, prin. — Fax 517-2625
Adult Education — Adult
273 Harris St 30705 — 706-695-4641
Joe Jackson, prin. — Fax 695-9103

Chickamauga, Walker, Pop. 2,392
Chickamauga CSD — 1,300/PK-12
402 Cove Rd 30707 — 706-382-3100
Melody Day, supt. — Fax 375-5364
www.chickamaugacityschools.org/
Lee HS — 500/9-12
105 Lee Cir 30707 — 706-382-3100
Randall Barker, prin. — Fax 375-4103
Lee MS — 300/6-8
300 Crescent Ave 30707 — 706-382-3100
Kristen Bradley, prin. — Fax 375-7988

Chula, Tift

Tiftarea Academy — 600/PK-12
PO Box 10 31733 — 229-382-0436
Ron Drummonds, prin. — Fax 382-7742

Clarkesville, Habersham, Pop. 1,347
Habersham County SD — 5,000/PK-12
PO Box 70 30523 — 706-754-2118
Dr. Judy C. Forbes, supt. — Fax 754-1549
www.habershamschools.com/
North Habersham MS — 500/7-8
1500 Wall Bridge Rd 30523 — 706-754-2915
Dr. Ben Desper, prin. — Fax 754-8218
Other Schools – See Cornelia, Demorest, Mount Airy

North Georgia Technical College — Post-Sec.
PO Box 65 30523 — 706-754-7700

Clarkston, DeKalb, Pop. 7,122
DeKalb County SD
Supt. — See Decatur
Clarkston HS — 1,100/7-12
618 N Indian Creek Dr 30021 — 678-676-5302
Joe Jenkins, prin. — Fax 676-5310
DeKalb Alternative Night S — Adult
955 N Indian Creek Dr 30021 — 678-676-2876
Tom Willis, prin. — Fax 676-2878

Atlanta Area School for the Deaf — Post-Sec.
890 N Indian Creek Dr 30021 — 404-296-7101
DeKalb Technical College — Post-Sec.
495 N Indian Creek Dr 30021 — 404-297-9522
Georgia Perimeter College — Post-Sec.
555 N Indian Creek Dr 30021 — 404-244-5090

Claxton, Evans, Pop. 2,394
Evans County SD — 1,800/PK-12
613 W Main St 30417 — 912-739-3544
Marion A. Shaw, supt. — Fax 739-2492
www.evans.k12.ga.us
Claxton HS — 500/9-12
102 N Clark St 30417 — 912-739-3993
Neal Hammack, prin. — Fax 739-2029
Claxton MS — 500/6-8
4 N College St 30417 — 912-739-3646
Diane Holland, prin. — Fax 739-7217

Clayton, Rabun, Pop. 2,065
Rabun County SD — 2,100/PK-12
41 Education St 30525 — 706-746-5376
Robert Arthur, supt. — Fax 746-3084
www.rabun.k12.ga.us
Other Schools – See Tiger

Cleveland, White, Pop. 2,225
White County SD — 3,500/PK-12
113 Brooks St 30528 — 706-865-2315
Dr. Paul Shaw, supt. — Fax 865-7784
www.white.k12.ga.us
White County HS — 700/10-12
2600 Highway 129 N 30528 — 706-865-2312
Bryan Dorsey, prin. — Fax 865-5981
White County MS — 900/6-8
283 Old Blairsville Rd 30528 — 706-865-4060
Sheila Fussell, prin. — Fax 865-1947
White County Ninth Grade Academy — 9-9
328 Old Blairsville Rd 30528 — 706-865-0727
Rodney Green, prin. — Fax 865-0737

Truett McConnell College — Post-Sec.
100 Alumni Dr 30528 — 706-865-2134
White Creek Christian Academy — 100/K-12
67 Academy Dr 30528 — 706-865-1917
Judy Kinsey, prin. — Fax 865-0862

Cochran, Bleckley, Pop. 4,501
Bleckley County SD — 2,400/PK-12
PO Box 516 31014 — 478-934-2821
Dr. L.C. Evans, supt. — Fax 934-9595
www.bleckley.k12.ga.us
Bleckley County HS — 600/9-12
1 Royal Dr 31014 — 478-934-6258
W. Richard Smith, prin. — Fax 934-9707
Bleckley County MS — 600/6-8
RR 6 Box 480 31014 — 478-934-7270
Flora Bryant, prin. — Fax 934-6502

Middle Georgia College — Post-Sec.
1100 2nd St SE 31014 — 478-934-6221

College Park, Fulton, Pop. 18,940
Clayton County SD
Supt. — See Jonesboro
North Clayton HS — 1,500/9-12
1525 Norman Dr, — 770-994-4035
Derrick Manning, prin. — Fax 994-4038
North Clayton MS — 1,000/6-8
5517 W Fayetteville Rd, — 770-994-4025
Clarence Jackson, prin. — Fax 994-4028

Fulton County SD
Supt. — See Atlanta
Banneker HS — 1,400/9-12
5935 Feldwood Rd, — 770-969-3410
Gregory Middleton, prin. — Fax 969-3418
Camp Creek MS — 1,000/6-8
4345 Welcome All Rd SW, — 404-669-8030
Minnie Miller, prin. — Fax 669-8228
McNair MS — 1,000/6-8
2800 Burdett Rd, — 770-991-4160
Ronald Taylor, prin. — Fax 991-4165

Woodward Academy — 2,900/PK-12
1662 Rugby Ave 30337 — 404-765-4000
Dr. Harry Payne, pres. — Fax 765-4009

Collins, Tattnall, Pop. 528
Tattnall County SD
Supt. — See Reidsville
Collins MS — 200/6-8
720 N Main St 30421 — 912-693-2455
Chris Freeman, prin. — Fax 693-9046

Colquitt, Miller, Pop. 1,909
Miller County SD — 1,200/PK-12
PO Box 188, — 229-758-5592
Robert Phillips, supt. — Fax 758-4138
www.miller.k12.ga.us/
Miller County HS — 300/9-12
96 Perry St, — 229-758-4130
Ginger Webster, prin. — Fax 758-4152
Miller County MS — 300/6-8
96 Perry St, — 229-758-4131
Frank Killingsworth, prin. — Fax 758-4152

Columbus, Muscogee, Pop. 185,702
Muscogee County SD — 32,400/PK-12
PO Box 2427 31902 — 706-748-2019
Dr. John A. Phillips, supt. — Fax 748-2001
www.mcsdga.net/
Arnold Magnet Academy — 700/6-8
2011 51st St 31904 — 706-748-2436
Jose Negron, prin. — Fax 748-2435
Baker MS — 600/6-8
1215 Benning Dr 31903 — 706-683-8721
Dr. JoAnn Brown, prin. — Fax 683-8731
Blackmon Road MS — 900/6-8
7251 Blackmon Rd 31909 — 706-565-2998
Gary Shouppe, prin. — Fax 565-3006
Carver Magnet HS — 1,500/9-12
3100 8th St 31906 — 706-748-2499
Chris Lindsey, prin. — Fax 748-2512
Columbus HS — 1,300/9-12
1700 Cherokee Ave 31906 — 706-748-2534
Susan Bryant, prin. — Fax 748-2546
Double Churches MS — 900/6-8
7611 Whitesville Rd 31904 — 706-748-2678
Dr. Mike Hudson, prin. — Fax 748-2682

East Columbus Magnet Academy 800/6-8
6100 Georgetown Dr 31907 706-565-3026
Dr. Carol Hutcheson, prin. Fax 565-3031
Eddy MS 700/6-8
2100 S Lumpkin Rd 31903 706-683-8782
Dr. Cleo Griswould, prin. Fax 683-8789
Fort MS 600/6-8
2900 Woodruff Farm Rd 31907 706-569-3740
Lillia Bernard, prin. Fax 569-3616
Hardaway HS 1,400/9-12
2901 College Dr 31906 706-748-2766
Matt Bell, prin. Fax 748-2776
Jordan Vocational HS Vo/Tech
3200 Howard Ave 31904 706-748-2819
Dwain Tovey, prin. Fax 748-2829
Kendrick HS 1,000/9-12
6015 Georgetown Dr 31907 706-565-2960
Dr. Ed Barnwell, prin. Fax 565-2971
Marshall MS 500/6-8
1830 Shepherd Dr 31906 706-748-2900
Dr. Carlos Stepnes, prin. Fax 748-2908
Northside HS 1,000/9-12
2002 American Way 31909 706-748-2920
Dr. Renee Mallory, prin. Fax 748-2931
Richards MS 700/6-8
2892 Edgewood Rd 31906 706-569-3697
Mike Johnson, prin. Fax 569-3704
Rothschild MS 700/6-8
1136 Hunt Ave 31907 706-569-3709
Chris Cox, prin. Fax 569-3717
Shaw HS 1,200/9-12
7601 Schomburg Rd 31909 706-569-3638
Dr. Jim Arnold, prin. Fax 569-3648
Spencer HS 1,100/9-12
4340 Victory Dr 31903 706-683-8701
Olivia Rutledge, prin. Fax 683-8716
Muscogee Evening S Adult
1042 Manchester Expy 31904 706-748-2600
Dr. Isaac Neal, prin. Fax 748-2602
Tillinghurst Adult Education Adult
514 Morris Rd 31906 706-683-8741
Karl Roberts, prin. Fax 683-8743
Other Schools – See Midland

Beacon University Post-Sec.
6003 Veterans Pkwy 31909 706-323-5364
Brookstone S 900/PK-12
440 Bradley Park Dr 31904 706-324-1392
Scott Wilson, hdmstr. Fax 571-0178
Calvary Christian S 600/PK-12
7556 Old Moon Rd 31909 706-323-0467
Len McWilliams, hdmstr. Fax 323-1941
Christian Heritage Academy 200/K-12
3564 Forest Rd 31907 706-568-1251
Michael Hall, prin. Fax 568-1431
Columbus State University Post-Sec.
4225 University Ave 31907 706-568-2001
Columbus Technical College Post-Sec.
928 Manchester Expy 31904 706-649-1800
Edgewood Christian S 100/K-12
1909 Morris Rd 31907 706-563-4414
Grace Christian S 200/PK-12
2915 14th Ave 31904 706-323-9161
Jeffrey Amsbaugh, prin. Fax 323-8554
Medical Center Post-Sec.
PO Box 951 31902 706-571-1200
Pacelli HS 200/9-12
3556 Trinity Dr 31907 706-561-8243
John Albert, prin. Fax 561-3243
Rivertown School of Beauty Post-Sec.
4747 Hamilton Rd Ste B 31904 706-653-9223
Southeastern Beauty School Post-Sec.
PO Box 12483 31917 706-687-1054
Southeastern Beauty School Post-Sec.
PO Box 12483 31917 706-687-1054
Turner S 100/9-12
2917 University Ave 31907 706-561-3518

Commerce, Jackson, Pop. 5,333
Commerce CSD 1,400/K-12
PO Box 29 30529 706-335-5500
Dr. James McCoy, supt. Fax 335-5214
www.commerce-city.k12.ga.us
Commerce HS 400/9-12
272 Lakeview Dr 30529 706-335-5942
Donald Drew, prin. Fax 336-6955
Commerce MS 300/6-8
7690 Jefferson Rd 30529 706-335-5594
Mary Evans, prin. Fax 335-6222

Jackson County SD
Supt. — See Jefferson
East Jackson MS 700/6-8
1880 Hoods Mill Rd 30529 706-335-2083
Frank Sarratt, prin. Fax 335-0935

Conyers, Rockdale, Pop. 12,034
Rockdale County SD 14,200/PK-12
PO Box 1199 30012 770-860-4211
Samuel King, supt. Fax 860-4285
www.rockdale.k12.ga.us
Conyers MS 1,100/6-8
400 Sigman Rd NW 30012 770-483-3371
Eugene Baker, prin. Fax 483-9448
Edwards MS 1,300/6-8
2633 Stanton Rd SE 30094 770-483-3255
Tonya Bloodworth, prin. Fax 483-3676
Heritage HS 1,500/9-12
2400 Granade Rd SW 30094 770-483-5428
Greg Fowler, prin. Fax 483-9435
Magnet S for Science/Technology 9-12
1174 Bulldog Cir NE 30012 770-483-8737
Mary Ann Suddeth, dir. Fax 483-7379
Memorial MS 1,300/6-8
3205 Underwood Rd SE 30013 770-922-0139
Emilio Garza, prin. Fax 922-6192
Rockdale Career Academy Vo/Tech
1064 Culpepper Dr SW 30094 770-483-4713
Timothy Melvin, prin.
Rockdale County HS 1,400/9-12
1174 Bulldog Cir NE 30012 770-483-8754
Cynthia Hudson, prin. Fax 483-8708
Salem HS 1,400/9-12
3551 Underwood Rd SE 30013 770-929-0176
Robert Cresswell, prin. Fax 922-1292
Evening Academy Adult
3551 Underwood Rd SE 30013 770-929-0176
Robert Cresswell, dir. Fax 483-6164
Other Schools – See Stockbridge

Georgia Career Institute Post-Sec.
1820 Highway 20 SE Ste 200 30013 770-922-7653
Georgia Driving Academy Post-Sec.
1449 V F W Dr SW 30012 770-918-8501
Peachtree Academy 500/PK-12
1801 Ellington Rd 30013 770-860-8900
JaNice VanNess, admin. Fax 761-0883
Philadelphia Christian S 200/PK-12
2360 Old Covington Hwy SW 30012 770-483-7789
Victory Christian S 400/PK-12
1151 Flat Shoals Rd SE 30013 770-929-3758
DeShuan Mills, prin. Fax 929-8848
Young Americans Christian S 400/PK-12
1701 Honey Creek Rd SE 30013 770-760-7902
Jan Taylor, dir. Fax 760-7981

Cordele, Crisp, Pop. 11,500
Crisp County SD 4,100/PK-12
PO Box 729 31010 229-276-3400
Judy Bean Ed.D., supt. Fax 276-3406
www.crisp.k12.ga.us
Crisp County HS 1,100/9-12
2402 Cougar Aly 31015 229-276-3430
Michael Overstreet, prin. Fax 276-3430
Crisp County MS 1,000/6-8
1116 E 24th Ave 31015 229-276-3460
Michael Lehr, prin. Fax 276-3466

Crisp Academy 300/PK-12
150 Crisp Academy Dr 31015 229-273-6330
Danny Greene, prin. Fax 273-4141
South Georgia Technical College Post-Sec.
402 N Midway Rd 31015 229-271-4040

Cornelia, Habersham, Pop. 3,730
Habersham County SD
Supt. — See Clarkesville
South Habersham MS 500/7-8
237 Old Athens Hwy 30531 706-778-7121
Angela Robinson, prin. Fax 778-2110

Covington, Newton, Pop. 13,152
Newton County SD 14,700/PK-12
PO Box 1469 30015 770-787-1330
E. Clamp, supt. Fax 784-2950
www.newtoncountyschools.org
Alcovy HS 9-12
14567 Highway 36 30014 770-784-4995
Dave Easterday, prin. Fax 784-4996
Clements MS 900/6-8
66 Jack Neely Rd 30016 770-784-2934
Dr. Sylvia Jordan, prin. Fax 784-2992
Cousins MS 700/6-8
8187 Carlton Trl NW 30014 770-786-7311
Scott Sauls, prin. Fax 784-2991
Eastside HS 1,400/9-12
10245 Eagle Dr 30014 770-784-2920
Dr. Robert Daria, prin. Fax 784-2918
Indian Creek MS 900/6-8
11051 S Covington By-Pass 30014 770-385-6453
Samantha Fuhrey, prin. Fax 385-6456
Newton HS 2,300/9-12
140 Ram Dr 30014 770-787-2250
Joe Gheesling, prin. Fax 784-2957
Veterans Memorial MS 1,000/6-8
13357 Brown Bridge Rd 30016 770-385-6893
Gary Mistovich, prin. Fax 385-6899

Cumming, Forsyth, Pop. 5,034
Forsyth County SD 21,500/PK-12
1120 Dahlonega Hwy 30040 770-887-2461
Paula H. Gault, supt. Fax 781-6632
www.forsyth.k12.ga.us
Forsyth Central HS 1,700/9-12
520 Tribble Gap Rd 30040 770-887-8151
Kenny Foxx, prin. Fax 781-2289
Liberty MS 800/6-8
7465 Wallace Tatum Rd 30040 770-781-4889
Dr. Cindy Styles, prin. Fax 513-3877
North Forsyth HS 1,700/9-12
3635 Coal Mountain Dr 30040 770-781-6637
Nita Giddish, prin. Fax 781-2273
North Forsyth MS 1,000/6-8
3645 Coal Mountain Dr 30040 770-889-0743
Jeff Hunt, prin. Fax 888-1210
Otwell MS 1,000/6-8
605 Tribble Gap Rd 30040 770-887-5248
Jeff Zoul, prin. Fax 888-1214
South Forsyth HS 2,000/9-12
585 Peachtree Pkwy 30041 770-781-2264
Richard Gill, prin. Fax 888-1224
South Forsyth MS 1,400/6-8
2865 Old Atlanta Rd 30041 770-888-3170
Debbie Sarver, prin. Fax 888-3179
Vickery Creek MS 900/6-8
6240 Post Rd 30040 770-667-2580
Connie McCrary, prin. Fax 667-2593

Covenant Christian Academy 200/PK-12
6905 Post Rd 30041 770-674-2990
Johnathan Arnold, hdmstr. Fax 674-2989
Fideles Christian S 100/K-12
1390 Weber Industrial Dr 30041 770-888-6705
Jon Whisenant, dir. Fax 614-6057
Horizon Christian Academy 200/K-12
PO Box 2715 30028 678-947-3583
Garin Berry, admin. Fax 947-0721
Lanier Technical College Post-Sec.
7745 Majors Rd 30041 770-781-6770
Pinecrest Academy 700/PK-12
955 Peachtree Pkwy 30041 770-888-4477
Fax 888-0404

Cusseta, Chattahoochee, Pop. 1,258
Chattahoochee County SD 500/PK-12
26 Merrell St 31805 706-989-3678
Dalton Oliver, supt. Fax 989-3103
www.chattahoochee.k12.ga.us/
Chattahoochee County MSHS 200/6-12
360 Highway 26 31805 706-989-3678
Pam Timms, prin. Fax 989-0649

Cuthbert, Randolph, Pop. 3,592
Randolph County SD 1,700/PK-12
1208 Andrew St, 229-732-2641
Bobby Jenkins, supt. Fax 732-3840
Randolph-Clay HS 500/9-12
RR 3 Box 279, 229-732-2101
Lee Byrd, prin. Fax 732-5633

Randolph-Clay MS 300/6-8
RR 3 Box 279, 229-732-2790
Clifford Cooks, prin. Fax 732-5633

Andrew College Post-Sec.
413 College St, 229-732-2171

Dacula, Gwinnett, Pop. 4,397
Gwinnett County SD
Supt. — See Suwanee
Dacula HS 2,900/9-12
123 Broad St 30019 770-963-6664
Donald Nutt, prin. Fax 338-4665
Dacula MS 2,900/6-8
137 Dacula Rd 30019 770-963-1110
Georgia Barnwell, prin. Fax 338-4632

Hebron Christian Academy 800/K-12
PO Box 1028 30019 770-962-5423
Scott Smith, pres. Fax 339-5683

Dahlonega, Lumpkin, Pop. 4,158
Lumpkin County SD 3,500/PK-12
56 Indian Dr 30533 706-864-3611
Dewey W. Moye, supt. Fax 864-3755
www.lumpkin.k12.ga.us
Lumpkin County HS 1,000/9-12
2001 Indian Dr 30533 706-864-2557
Rudy Hampton, prin. Fax 864-4929
Lumpkin County MS 900/6-8
44 School Dr 30533 706-864-6180
Rick Conner, prin. Fax 864-0199

Hidden Lake Academy 200/7-12
830 Hidden Lake Rd 30533 706-864-4730
Fax 864-9109
North Georgia College & State University Post-Sec.
30597 706-864-1400

Dallas, Paulding, Pop. 6,847
Paulding County SD 20,500/PK-12
3236 Atlanta Hwy 30132 770-443-8000
Trudy Sowar, supt. Fax 443-8089
www.paulding.k12.ga.us
East Paulding HS 1,500/9-12
3320 E Paulding Dr 30157 770-445-5100
Charles Kuss, prin. Fax 445-6357
East Paulding MS 1,000/6-8
2945 Hiram Acworth Hwy 30157 770-443-7000
Gail Davis, prin. Fax 443-0116
Jones MS 1,000/6-8
100 Stadium Dr 30132 770-443-8024
David Viness, prin. Fax 443-8026
Moses MS 1,000/6-8
1066 Old County Farm Rd 30132 770-443-8727
Tracy Bennett, prin. Fax 443-8078
Paulding County HS 1,800/9-12
1297 Villa Rica Hwy 30157 770-443-8008
Jim Gottwald, prin. Fax 443-7030
South Paulding MS 900/6-8
592 Nebo Rd 30157 770-445-8500
Dr. Jinny Farmer, prin. Fax 445-9989
Other Schools – See Douglasville, Hiram, Powder Springs

Dalton, Whitfield, Pop. 30,341
Dalton CSD 8,700/PK-12
100 S Hamilton St 30720 706-278-8766
Dr. Orval Porter, supt. Fax 226-4583
www.daltonpublicschools.com/
Dalton HS 1,500/9-12
1500 Manly St 30720 706-278-8757
Phillip Brown, prin. Fax 226-2430
Dalton MS 1,300/6-8
1250 Cross Plains Trl 30721 706-428-7800
Brian Suits, prin. Fax 428-7850

Whitfield County SD 12,100/PK-12
PO Box 2167 30722 706-217-6780
Dr. Katie Brochu, supt. Fax 278-5042
www.whitfield.k12.ga.us
Eastbrook MS 800/6-8
700 Hill Rd 30721 706-278-6135
Brian Satterfield, prin. Fax 226-9859
New Hope MS 6-8
1325 New Hope Rd 30720 706-673-2295
George Kopcsak, prin. Fax 673-2086
North Whitfield MS 1,000/6-8
3264 Cleveland Rd 30721 706-259-3381
Andrea Bradley, prin. Fax 259-8168
Southeast Whitfield County HS 1,400/9-12
1954 Riverbend Rd 30721 706-226-2753
Alan Long, prin. Fax 278-3433
Valley Point MS 500/6-8
3796 S Dixie Rd 30721 706-277-9662
Britt Adams, prin. Fax 277-7035
Whitfield County Career Academy Vo/Tech
2300 Maddox Chapel Rd NE 30721 706-876-3600
Phillip Brown, prin. Fax 876-3602
Phoenix HS Adult
2818 Airport Rd 30721 706-272-2206
Fred Toney, prin. Fax 272-2200
Other Schools – See Rocky Face, Tunnel Hill

Christian Heritage S 400/K-12
PO Box 912 30722 706-277-1198
Renny Scott, hdmstr. Fax 277-2300
Dalton State College Post-Sec.
213 College Dr 30720 706-272-4436
Pathway Christian Academy 200/PK-12
PO Box 4299 30719 706-279-1396
Debbie Long, prin. Fax 270-8174

Damascus, Early, Pop. 271

Southwest Georgia Academy 300/PK-12
14105 State Road 200, 229-725-4792
Doug Dease, prin. Fax 725-5476

Danielsville, Madison, Pop. 461
Madison County SD 4,600/K-12
PO Box 37 30633 706-795-2191
Keith Cowne, supt. Fax 795-5104
www.madison.k12.ga.us
Madison County HS 1,400/9-12
PO Box 7 30633 706-795-2197
Wayne McIntosh, prin. Fax 795-3116

Madison County MS 1,200/6-8
PO Box 690 30633 706-795-3341
Matt Boggs, prin. Fax 795-5753

Darien, McIntosh, Pop. 1,670
McIntosh County SD 1,600/PK-12
200 Pine St 31305 912-437-6645
Dr. Johnnie Q. Heck, supt. Fax 437-2140
www.mcintosh.k12.ga.us/
McIntosh County Academy 500/9-12
1915 Highway 17 N 31305 912-437-6691
Russell Sowell, prin. Fax 437-3077
McIntosh County MS 500/6-8
500 Green St 31305 912-437-6685
Victoria Bittaker, prin. Fax 437-5676

Dawson, Terrell, Pop. 5,035
Terrell County SD 1,700/PK-12
PO Box 151, 229-995-4425
Robert Aaron, supt. Fax 995-4632
www.terrellcountyschools.net/
Terrell County MSHS 800/6-12
PO Box 151, 229-995-2544
Douglas Bell, prin. Fax 995-4523

Terrell Academy 200/K-12
602 Academy Dr SE, 229-995-4242
William Murdock, hdmstr. Fax 995-6149

Dawsonville, Dawson, Pop. 632
Dawson County SD 3,100/K-12
PO Box 208 30534 706-265-3246
Nicky Gilleland, supt. Fax 265-1226
www.dawson.k12.ga.us
Dawson County HS 800/9-12
1665 Perimeter Rd 30534 706-265-6555
Rick Brown, prin. Fax 265-3936
Dawson County MS 700/6-8
PO Box 688 30534 706-265-2714
Bill Zadernak, prin. Fax 265-1426
Riverview MS 6-8
5126 Highway 9 S 30534 706-216-4849
Janice Darnell, prin. Fax 265-1426

Decatur, DeKalb, Pop. 17,859
DeKalb County SD 92,100/PK-12
3770 N Decatur Rd 30032 678-676-1200
Dr. Crawford Lewis, supt. Fax 676-0785
www.dekalb.k12.ga.us
Bethune MS 1,400/6-8
5200 Covington Hwy 30035 678-875-0302
Terry McMullen, prin. Fax 875-0310
Cedar Grove MS 1,400/6-8
2300 Wildcat Rd 30034 678-874-4202
Agnes Flanagan, prin. Fax 874-4210
Chapel Hill MS 900/6-8
3535 Dogwood Farm Rd 30034 678-676-8502
Carlus Daniel, prin. Fax 676-8510
Columbia HS 1,400/9-12
2106 Columbia Dr 30032 678-874-0802
Dr. Thomas Glanton, prin. Fax 874-0810
Columbia MS 1,400/6-8
3001 Columbia Dr 30034 678-875-0502
Stephanie Amey, prin. Fax 875-0510
DeKalb HS of Technology South Vo/Tech
3303 Panthersville Rd 30034 678-874-4502
Dr. Rick Moore, prin. Fax 874-4510
McNair MS 1,300/6-8
2190 Wallingford Dr 30032 678-874-5102
Merlon Jones, prin. Fax 874-5110
Miller Grove MS 1,300/6-8
2215 Miller Rd 30035 678-676-8902
Triscilla Weaver, prin. Fax 676-8910
Shamrock MS 1,300/6-8
3100 Mount Olive Dr 30033 678-874-7602
Robert Thorpe, prin. Fax 874-7610
Southwest DeKalb HS 1,600/9-12
2863 Kelley Chapel Rd 30034 678-874-1902
John Prince, prin. Fax 874-1910
Towers HS 1,200/9-12
3919 Brookcrest Cir 30032 678-874-2202
Leroy Jenkins, prin. Fax 874-2210
Other Schools – See Atlanta, Avondale Estates, Chamblee, Clarkston, Doraville, Dunwoody, Ellenwood, Lithonia, Stone Mountain, Tucker

Decatur CSD 1,900/PK-12
758 Scott Blvd 30030 404-370-4400
Dr. Phyllis Edwards, supt. Fax 370-4413
www.decatur-city.k12.ga.us
Decatur HS 800/9-12
310 N McDonough St 30030 404-370-4420
Lauri McKain-Fernandez, prin. Fax 370-4434
Renfroe MS 600/6-8
220 W College Ave 30030 404-370-4440
Bruce Roaden, prin. Fax 370-4449

Academe of the Oaks 100/9-12
146 New St 30030 404-405-2173
Fax 377-7178
Agnes Scott College Post-Sec.
141 E College Ave 30030 404-471-6000
Cathedral Academy 300/K-12
4650 Flat Shoals Pkwy 30034 404-243-3656
Vickie Turner, hdmstr. Fax 241-4234
Columbia Theological Seminary Post-Sec.
701 S Columbia Dr 30030 404-378-8821
DeKalb Medical Center Post-Sec.
2701 N Decatur Rd 30033 404-501-5206
DeVry University Post-Sec.
250 N Arcadia Ave 30030 404-292-7900
Georgia Perimeter College Post-Sec.
3251 Panthersville Rd 30034 404-244-5090
Greenforest/McCalep Christian Academy 900/PK-12
3250 Rainbow Dr 30034 404-486-6737
Albert Walker, hdmstr. Fax 486-1127
Green Pastures Christian S 200/PK-12
5455 Flat Shoals Pkwy 30034 770-987-8121
Gloria Locke, admin. Fax 987-7475
Gupton-Jones College of Funeral Service Post-Sec.
5141 Snapfinger Woods Dr 30035 770-593-2257
Omnitech Institute Post-Sec.
4319 Covington Hwy Ste 202 30035 404-284-8121

Demorest, Habersham, Pop. 1,611
Habersham County SD
Supt. — See Clarkesville
Habersham Ninth Grade Academy 9-9
3115 Demorest Mount Airy 30535 706-778-0830
Pam Adams, prin. Fax 778-0848

Piedmont College Post-Sec.
PO Box 10 30535 800-277-7020

Donalsonville, Seminole, Pop. 2,743
Seminole County SD 1,800/PK-12
800 S Woolfork Ave, 229-524-2433
Walter L. Pierce, supt. Fax 524-2212
www.seminole.k12.ga.us
Seminole County MSHS 900/6-12
5582 Highway 39 S, 229-524-5135
Monroe Bonner, prin. Fax 524-5178

Doraville, DeKalb, Pop. 10,029
DeKalb County SD
Supt. — See Decatur
Sequoyah MS 1,000/6-8
3456 Aztec Rd 30340 678-676-7902
Trenton Arnold, prin. Fax 676-7910

Douglas, Coffee, Pop. 10,753
Coffee County SD 7,600/PK-12
PO Box 1290 31534 912-384-2086
Billy Smith, supt. Fax 383-5333
coffee.k12.ga.us
Coffee HS 1,900/9-12
159 Trojan Way 31533 912-384-2094
Greg Tanner, prin. Fax 383-5486
East Coffee MS 700/6-8
1020 Gaskin Ave S 31533 912-384-1342
Nelda Flanders, prin. Fax 383-4160
West Coffee MS 1,200/6-8
1303 Peterson Ave S 31533 912-383-4100
Dr. Elaine Mathis, prin. Fax 383-4124

Citizens Christian Academy 300/K-12
PO Box 1064 31534 912-384-8862
William Rish, hdmstr. Fax 384-8426
South Georgia College Post-Sec.
100 College Park Dr W 31533 912-389-4231

Douglasville, Douglas, Pop. 25,307
Douglas County SD 19,800/PK-12
PO Box 1077 30133 770-651-2000
Donald J. Remillard, supt. Fax 920-4159
www.douglas.k12.ga.us
Alexander HS 1,400/9-12
6500 Alexander Pkwy 30135 770-651-6000
Robert Brown, prin. Fax 651-6003
Chapel Hill HS 1,400/9-12
4899 Chapel Hill Rd 30135 770-651-6200
Nancy Davis, prin. Fax 651-6205
Chapel Hill MS 1,000/6-8
3989 Chapel Hill Rd 30135 770-651-5000
William Foster, prin. Fax 920-4242
Chestnut Log MS 800/6-8
2544 Pope Rd 30135 770-651-5100
Kay Davis, prin. Fax 651-5103
Douglas County HS 1,400/9-12
8705 Campbellton St 30134 770-651-6500
Randy Dye, prin. Fax 651-6504
Fairplay MS 700/6-8
8311 Highway 166 30135 770-651-5300
Monte Beaver, prin. Fax 651-5303
Stewart MS 700/6-8
8138 Malone St 30134 770-651-5400
Dewayne Jackson, prin. Fax 920-4229
Yeager MS 900/6-8
4000 Kings Hwy 30135 770-651-5600
Fax 651-5603
Other Schools – See Lithia Springs

Paulding County SD
Supt. — See Dallas
Austin MS 6-8
3490 Ridge Rd 30134 770-942-0316
Tammy Allen, prin. Fax 942-0548

Harvester Christian Academy 300/PK-12
4241 Central Church Rd 30135 770-942-1583
Jack North, hdmstr. Fax 942-9332
Heirway Christian Academy 200/PK-12
6758 Spring St 30134 770-489-4392
Phyllis Campbell, prin. Fax 489-4318
Inner Harbour S 200/K-12
4685 Dorsett Shoals Rd 30135 770-942-2391
Dr. Penny Honeycutt, prin. Fax 489-0406
Kings Way Christian S 400/PK-12
6456 The Kings Way 30135 770-949-0812
Ray Conway, admin. Fax 949-1045
West Central Technical College Post-Sec.
4600 Timber Ridge Dr 30135 770-947-7200

Dublin, Laurens, Pop. 15,976
Dublin CSD 3,100/PK-12
207 Shamrock Dr 31021 478-272-3440
Dr. Elaine Connell, supt. Fax 272-1249
echalk.dublinirish.org
Dublin HS 900/9-12
1951 Hillcrest Pkwy 31021 478-272-4727
Dr. Gene Nisbet, prin. Fax 277-9829
Dublin MS 800/6-8
1501 N Jefferson St 31021 478-272-8122
Elgin Dixon, prin. Fax 277-9828

Laurens County SD 6,100/PK-12
467 Firetower Rd 31021 478-272-4767
Jerry Hatcher, supt. Fax 277-2619
www.lcboe.net
East Laurens HS 600/9-12
920 US Highway 80 E 31027 478-272-3144
Kelland Waldrep, prin. Fax 274-1032
East Laurens MS 600/6-8
920 US Highway 80 E 31027 478-272-1201
Susan J. Radford, prin. Fax 275-1627
West Laurens HS 1,000/9-12
338 W Laurens School Rd 31021 478-272-1155
Hugh Kight, prin. Fax 275-0643
West Laurens MS 900/6-8
332 W Laurens School Rd 31021 478-272-8452
George Knight, prin. Fax 275-0848

Heart of Georgia Technical Institute Post-Sec.
560 Pinehill Rd 31021 478-275-6590
Trinity Christian S 400/K-12
200 Trinity Rd 31021 478-272-7699
Rick Johnson, prin. Fax 272-7685

Duluth, Gwinnett, Pop. 23,697
Fulton County SD
Supt. — See Atlanta
Northview HS 1,900/9-12
10625 Parsons Rd 30097 770-497-3828
Peter Zervakos, prin. Fax 497-3844
River Trail MS 1,400/6-8
10795 Rogers Cir 30097 770-497-3860
Dawn Melin, prin. Fax 497-3866

Gwinnett County SD
Supt. — See Suwanee
Duluth HS 2,100/9-12
3737 Brock Rd 30096 770-476-5206
Patrick Blenke, prin. Fax 232-3332
Duluth MS 1,200/6-8
3200 Pleasant Hill Rd 30096 770-476-3372
Dr. Kay Harvey, prin. Fax 232-3295
Hull MS 2,000/6-8
1950 Old Peachtree Rd 30097 770-232-3200
Dr. Gwen Tatum, prin. Fax 232-3203
Radloff MS 6-8
3939 Shackleford Rd 30096 678-245-3400
Dr. Patty Heitmuller, prin. Fax 245-3403

DeVry University Post-Sec.
3505 Koger Blvd Ste 170 30096 678-380-9780

Dunwoody, DeKalb, Pop. 34,400
DeKalb County SD
Supt. — See Decatur
DeKalb HS of Technology North Vo/Tech
1995 Womack Rd 30338 678-874-8400
Delores Washington, prin. Fax 874-8410
Dunwoody HS 1,300/9-12
5035 Vermack Rd 30338 678-874-8502
Stacy Stepney, prin. Fax 874-8510

Empire Beauty School Post-Sec.
4719 Ashford-Dunwoody #205 30338 770-672-2448
Weber Jewish Community HS 100/9-12
2012 Womack Rd 30338 770-352-0018
Fax 352-0352

Eastman, Dodge, Pop. 5,422
Dodge County SD 3,500/PK-12
720 College St 31023 478-374-3783
Aubrey H. Corbitt, supt. Fax 374-6697
www.dodge.k12.ga.us
Dodge County HS 1,000/9-12
5911 Oak St 31023 478-374-7711
Susan W. Long, prin. Fax 374-6987
Dodge County MS 800/6-8
1400 Herman Ave 31023 478-374-6492
Jerome Smith, prin. Fax 374-6484

Georgia Aviation Technical College Post-Sec.
71 Airport Rd 31023 478-374-6402

East Point, Fulton, Pop. 37,220
Fulton County SD
Supt. — See Atlanta
Tri-Cities HS 2,000/9-12
2575 Harris St 30344 404-669-8200
Amelia Davis, prin. Fax 669-8158
West MS 1,300/6-8
2376 Headland Dr 30344 404-669-8130
Dan Sims, prin. Fax 669-8121
Woodland MS 800/6-8
2816 Briarwood Blvd 30344 404-346-6420
William Bradley, prin. Fax 346-6527

Atlanta Christian College Post-Sec.
2605 Ben Hill Rd 30344 404-761-8861

Eatonton, Putnam, Pop. 6,917
Putnam County SD 2,600/K-12
158 Old Glenwood Springs Rd 31024 706-485-5381
Dr. Jim Willis, supt. Fax 485-3820
www.putnam.k12.ga.us/boe/
Putnam County HS 700/9-12
140 Sparta Hwy 31024 706-485-9971
Michael Rowland, prin. Fax 485-3128
Putnam County MS 700/6-8
314 S Washington Ave 31024 706-485-8547
Bessie Brown, prin. Fax 485-7090

Gatewood S 400/PK-12
139 Phillips Dr 31024 706-485-8231
Laura Thompson, hdmstr. Fax 485-2455

Edison, Calhoun, Pop. 1,269
Calhoun County SD
Supt. — See Morgan
Calhoun County MSHS 400/6-12
PO Box 366, 229-835-2435
Donald Robinson, prin. Fax 835-3040

Elberton, Elbert, Pop. 4,612
Elbert County SD 3,800/PK-12
50 Laurel Dr 30635 706-213-4000
Samuel Light, supt. Fax 283-6674
www.elbert.k12.ga.us
Elbert County Comprehensive HS 1,100/9-12
600 Abernathy Cir 30635 706-213-4100
Rick Higginbotham, prin. Fax 283-1183
Elbert County MS 900/6-8
1108 Athens Tech Rd 30635 706-213-4200
Paul Garrett, prin. Fax 283-1117

Ellaville, Schley, Pop. 1,662
Schley County SD 1,200/PK-12
PO Box 66 31806 229-937-2405
William Johnson, supt. Fax 937-5180
www.schley.k12.ga.us
Schley County MSHS 500/7-12
PO Box 1350 31806 229-937-0560
Larry Stubbs, prin. Fax 937-0565

Ellenwood, Clayton
DeKalb County SD
Supt. — See Decatur
Cedar Grove HS 1,500/9-12
2360 River Rd 30294 678-874-4002
Ron Davis, prin. Fax 874-4010

Annointed Word Christian S International 100/PK-12
3800 Linecrest Rd 30294 404-241-8200
Betty Evans, admin. Fax 328-9801

Ellijay, Gilmer, Pop. 1,556
Gilmer County SD — 4,000/PK-12
497 Bobcat Trl 30540 — 706-276-5000
Dr. Raiford Cantrell, supt. — Fax 276-5005
www.gilmerschools.com/
Gilmer HS — 1,100/9-12
408 Bobcat Trl 30540 — 706-276-5080
Randal Parson, prin. — Fax 276-5088
Gilmer MS — 900/6-8
1860 S Main St 30540 — 706-276-5030
Nancy Gheesling, prin. — Fax 276-5035

Emerson, Bartow, Pop. 1,130
Bartow County SD
Supt. — See Cartersville
South Central MS — 700/6-8
224 Old Old Alabama Rd SE 30137 — 770-606-5865
Cantey Smith, prin. — Fax 606-3872

Evans, Columbia, Pop. 13,713
Columbia County SD
Supt. — See Appling
Evans HS — 1,700/9-12
4550 Cox Rd 30809 — 706-863-1198
Don Brigdon, prin. — Fax 868-3720
Evans MS — 800/6-8
4318 Washington Rd 30809 — 706-863-2275
Michael Johnson, prin. — Fax 868-2190
Greenbrier HS — 1,700/9-12
5114 Riverwood Pkwy 30809 — 706-650-6040
Dr. Margie Hamilton, prin. — Fax 650-6045
Greenbrier MS — 700/6-8
5120 Riverwood Pkwy 30809 — 706-650-6080
Jackie Creasy, prin. — Fax 650-6085
Lakeside HS — 1,500/9-12
533 Blue Ridge Dr 30809 — 706-863-0027
Jeff Carney, prin. — Fax 868-3721
Lakeside MS — 900/6-8
527 Blue Ridge Dr 30809 — 706-855-6900
Felicia Dumas, prin. — Fax 868-2191
Riverside MS — 900/6-8
1095 Furys Ferry Rd 30809 — 706-868-3712
Don Putnam, prin. — Fax 868-2192

Evans Christian Academy — 100/6-12
562 Old Evans Rd 30809 — 706-364-3565
Freida Lachman, dir. — Fax 868-1557

Fairburn, Fulton, Pop. 6,771
Fulton County SD
Supt. — See Atlanta
Bear Creek MS — 1,300/6-8
7415 Herndon Rd 30213 — 770-969-6080
Dr. Sandra DeShazier, prin. — Fax 306-3584
Creekside HS — 1,600/9-12
7405 Herndon Rd 30213 — 770-306-4300
Michael Robinson, prin. — Fax 306-4313

Arlington Christian S — 400/K-12
4500 Ridge Rd 30213 — 770-964-9871
David Wilson Ph.D., prin. — Fax 306-3630
Landmark Christian Academy — 600/K-12
50 SE Broad St 30213 — 770-306-0647
Matthew Skinner, hdmstr. — Fax 969-6551
Our Lady of Mercy Catholic HS — 300/9-12
861 Evander Holyfield Hwy 30213 — 770-461-2202
JoAnn McPherson, prin. — Fax 461-9353

Fayetteville, Fayette, Pop. 13,455
Fayette County SD — 20,700/PK-12
PO Box 879 30214 — 770-460-3535
Dr. John DeCotis, supt. — Fax 460-8191
www.fcboe.org
Fayette County HS — 2,100/9-12
1 Tiger Trl 30214 — 770-460-3540
Charles Warr, prin. — Fax 460-3410
Fayette MS — 1,000/6-8
450 Grady Ave 30214 — 770-460-3550
Charlene Patterson, prin. — Fax 460-3882
Rising Starr MS — 1,200/6-8
183 Panther Path 30215 — 770-486-2721
Len Patton, prin. — Fax 486-2727
Starr's Mill HS — 1,800/9-12
193 Panther Path 30215 — 770-486-2710
Fax 486-2716
Whitewater HS — 9-12
100 Wildcat Way 30215 — 770-460-3935
Greg Stillions, prin. — Fax 716-3973
Whitewater MS — 1,100/6-8
1533 Highway 85 S 30215 — 770-460-3450
Sandra Kidd, prin. — Fax 460-0362
Fayette Co. Evening HS — Adult
205 LaFayette Ave 30214 — 770-460-3990
Ed Steil, prin. — Fax 460-0482
Other Schools – See Peachtree City, Tyrone

Counterpane S — 100/K-12
PO Box 898 30214 — 770-461-2304
Brenda Erickson, prin. — Fax 460-7016
Fayette Beauty Academy — Post-Sec.
386 Glynn St N 30214 — 770-461-4669
Fayette Christian S — 200/PK-12
152 Longview Rd 30214 — 770-461-3538
Travis Crutchfield, prin. — Fax 460-6013
Grace Christian Academy — 200/PK-12
355 McDonough Rd 30214 — 770-461-0137
Brian Fourman, prin. — Fax 461-1190

Fitzgerald, Ben Hill, Pop. 8,752
Ben Hill County SD — 3,100/K-12
509 W Palm St 31750 — 229-409-5500
Dr. John Key, supt. — Fax 409-5513
www.ben-hill.k12.ga.us
Ben Hill County MS — 800/6-8
134 JC Hunter Rd 31750 — 229-409-5578
Jackie Hall, prin. — Fax 409-5580
Fitzgerald HS — 900/9-12
601 W Cypress St 31750 — 229-409-5530
Mark Wilcox, prin. — Fax 409-5534

East Central Technical College — Post-Sec.
667 Perry House Rd 31750 — 229-468-2000

Flintstone, Walker
Walker County SD
Supt. — See La Fayette
Chattanooga Valley MS — 500/6-8
847 Allgood Rd 30725 — 706-820-0735
Eugene Ward, prin. — Fax 820-0736

Flowery Branch, Hall, Pop. 1,958
Hall County SD
Supt. — See Gainesville
Davis MS — 900/6-8
4335 Falcon Pkwy 30542 — 770-965-3020
Dr. Aaron Turpin, prin. — Fax 965-3025
Flowery Branch HS — 1,000/9-12
4450 Hog Mountain Rd 30542 — 770-967-8000
Dr. Mark Coleman, prin. — Fax 967-1218

Heritage Academy — 200/6-12
3483 Violet St 30542 — 770-536-6900
Jerry Smith, hdmstr. — Fax 536-4496

Folkston, Charlton, Pop. 3,263
Charlton County SD — 2,100/PK-12
500 S 3rd St 31537 — 912-496-2596
Alexander McQueen, supt. — Fax 496-2595
boe.charlton.k12.ga.us/
Charlton County JSHS — 900/7-12
500 Indian Trl 31537 — 912-496-2501
Dr. Drew Sauls, prin. — Fax 496-3732

Forest Park, Clayton, Pop. 21,247
Clayton County SD
Supt. — See Jonesboro
Babb MS — 1,100/6-8
5500 Reynolds Rd 30297 — 404-362-3880
Susan Patrick, prin. — Fax 362-4087
Forest Park HS — 1,600/9-12
5452 Phillips Dr 30297 — 404-362-3890
Delphia Young, prin. — Fax 608-7563
Forest Park MS — 700/6-8
930 Finley Dr 30297 — 404-362-3840
Kevin Booker, prin. — Fax 362-8899

Arnold/Padrick's Univ of Cosmetology — Post-Sec.
4971 Courtney Dr 30297 — 404-361-5641
Beauty College of America — Post-Sec.
1171 Main St 30297 — 404-361-4098

Forsyth, Monroe, Pop. 4,354
Monroe County SD — 4,800/PK-12
PO Box 1308 31029 — 478-994-2031
Scott Cowart, supt. — Fax 994-3364
www.monroe.k12.ga.us
Hubbard MS — 900/6-8
500 Highway 83 S 31029 — 478-994-6803
Steve Edwards, prin. — Fax 994-3061
Persons HS — 1,100/9-12
300 Montpelier Ave 31029 — 478-994-2812
Joe Parlier, prin. — Fax 994-7065
Stephens MS — 900/6-8
66 Thornton Rd 31029 — 478-994-6186
Dr. Mike Hickman, prin. — Fax 994-7061

Monroe Academy — 300/PK-12
433 Highway 41 S 31029 — 478-994-5986
Ted McMichael, hdmstr. — Fax 994-1942

Fort Gaines, Clay, Pop. 1,088
Clay County SD — 300/PK-8
PO Box 219, — 229-768-2232
Dr. Grady Miles, supt. — Fax 768-3654
www.clay.k12.ga.us/
Clay County MS — 100/6-8
200 Hobbs Ln, — 229-768-2234
Terri Marcus, prin. — Fax 768-2363

Fort Oglethorpe, Catoosa, Pop. 7,854
Catoosa County SD
Supt. — See Ringgold
Lakeview-Fort Oglethorpe HS — 1,200/9-12
1850 Battlefield Pkwy 30742 — 706-866-0342
Jerry Ransom, prin. — Fax 861-6645

Fort Valley, Peach, Pop. 8,040
Peach County SD — 4,000/K-12
PO Box 1018 31030 — 478-825-5933
Tommy Daniel, supt. — Fax 825-9970
www.peachschools.org
Fort Valley MS — 600/6-8
712 Peggy Dr 31030 — 478-825-2413
Dr. Quintin Green, prin. — Fax 825-1332
Peach County HS — 1,100/9-12
900 Campus Dr 31030 — 478-825-8258
Claudia Patterson, prin. — Fax 825-2290
Other Schools – See Byron

Fort Valley State University — Post-Sec.
1005 State University Dr 31030 — 478-825-6315

Franklin, Heard, Pop. 886
Heard County SD — 2,100/PK-12
PO Box 1330 30217 — 706-675-3320
Benjamin Hyatt, supt. — Fax 675-3357
www.heard.k12.ga.us/
Heard County Comprehensive HS — 500/9-12
545 Main St 30217 — 706-675-3656
Ronald Furgerson, prin. — Fax 675-8729
Heard County MS — 500/6-8
269 Old Field Rd 30217 — 706-675-9247
Marti Robinson, prin. — Fax 675-9255

Franklin Springs, Franklin, Pop. 750

Emmanuel College — Post-Sec.
PO Box 129 30639 — 800-860-8800

Gainesville, Hall, Pop. 29,806
Gainesville CSD — 5,200/PK-12
508 Oak St 30501 — 770-536-5275
Dr. Steven E. Ballowe, supt. — Fax 287-2004
www.gcssk12.net/
Gainesville HS — 1,200/9-12
830 Century Pl 30501 — 770-536-4441
David Shumake, prin. — Fax 287-2031
Gainesville MS — 1,000/6-8
715 Woodsmill Rd 30501 — 770-534-4237
William Harner, prin. — Fax 287-2022

Hall County SD — 22,400/PK-12
711 Green St NW Ste 100 30501 — 770-534-1080
Dr. Dennis Fordham, supt. — Fax 535-7404
www.hallco.org
Chestatee HS — 1,000/9-12
3005 Sardis Rd 30506 — 770-532-1162
Bill Thompson, prin. — Fax 532-2202
Chestatee MS — 900/6-8
2740 Fran Mar Dr 30506 — 770-297-6270
Pam Osborne, prin. — Fax 297-6275
East Hall HS — 1,000/9-12
3534 E Hall Rd 30507 — 770-536-9921
Mike Gillum, prin. — Fax 535-1184
East Hall MS — 900/6-8
4120 E Hall Rd 30507 — 770-531-9457
Eddie Millwood, prin. — Fax 531-2327
Johnson HS — 1,000/9-12
3305 Poplar Springs Rd 30507 — 770-536-2394
Dr. Sandra Edwards, prin. — Fax 531-3046
Lanier Career Academy — Vo/Tech
2723 Tumbling Creek Rd 30504 — 770-531-2330
Danny Jones, prin.
North Hall HS — 1,100/9-12
4885 Mount Vernon Rd 30506 — 770-983-7331
Gary Brown, prin. — Fax 983-7941
North Hall MS — 800/6-8
4856 Rilla Rd 30506 — 770-983-9749
Raymond Akridge, prin. — Fax 983-9993
South Hall MS — 900/6-8
3215 Poplar Springs Rd 30507 — 770-532-4416
Paula Stubbs, prin. — Fax 531-2348
Hall Co/Gainesville Evening S — Adult
3131 R W Johnson Dr 30507 — 770-531-2330
Susan Johnson, prin. — Fax 450-5978
Other Schools – See Flowery Branch, Oakwood

Brenau Academy — 100/9-12
1 Centennial Cir 30501 — 770-534-6140
Fax 534-6298
Brenau College — Post-Sec.
1 Centennial Cir 30501 — 770-534-6299
Gainesville College — Post-Sec.
PO Box 1358 30503 — 770-718-3639
Interactive College of Technology — Post-Sec.
2323 Browns Bridge Rd 30504 — 678-450-0550
Lakeview Academy — 600/PK-12
796 Lakeview Dr 30501 — 770-532-4383
James Curry Robison, hdmstr. — Fax 536-6142
Riverside Military Academy — 500/6-12
2001 Riverside Dr 30501 — 800-462-2338
Col. Guy Gardner, hdmstr. — Fax 291-3364
Westminster Christian S — 300/PK-12
1397 Thompson Bridge Rd 30501 — 770-534-1081
Craig Bouvier, hdmstr. — Fax 534-1025

Gibson, Glascock, Pop. 713
Glascock County SD — 600/PK-12
PO Box 205 30810 — 706-598-2291
James N. Holton, supt. — Fax 598-2611
Glascock County Consolidated S — 600/PK-12
1230 Panther Way 30810 — 706-598-2121
Sarah Garrett, prin. — Fax 598-2621

Glennville, Tattnall, Pop. 4,859
Tattnall County SD
Supt. — See Reidsville
Glennville MS — 300/6-8
721 E Barnard St 30427 — 912-654-1467
Nick Tatum, prin. — Fax 654-1300

Glenville Christian Academy — 200/K-12
105 Liberty St 30427 — 912-654-3034
Earline Thompson, prin. — Fax 654-3876

Gray, Jones, Pop. 2,053
Jones County SD — 5,200/PK-12
PO Box 519 31032 — 478-986-6580
Jim LeBrun, supt. — Fax 986-1624
www.jones.k12.ga.us/
Califf MS — 700/6-8
110 Maggie Califf St 31032 — 478-986-3046
Alfred Pitts, prin. — Fax 986-1504
Jones County HS — 1,500/9-12
339 Railroad St 31032 — 478-986-5444
John Trimnell, prin. — Fax 986-1589
Other Schools – See Macon

Greensboro, Greene, Pop. 3,318
Greene County SD — 2,300/PK-12
PO Box 209 30642 — 706-453-7688
John Jackson, supt. — Fax 453-9019
www.greene.k12.ga.us
Carson MS — 500/6-8
1010 S Main St 30642 — 706-453-3308
Gus Robinson, prin. — Fax 453-4674
Greene County HS — 600/9-12
1002 S Main St 30642 — 706-453-2271
Jason Doughty, prin. — Fax 453-3311

Greenville, Meriwether, Pop. 893
Meriwether County SD — 4,000/PK-12
PO Box 70 30222 — 706-672-4297
Carol Lane, supt. — Fax 672-1618
www.meriwether.k12.ga.us
Greenville HS — 500/9-12
PO Box 340 30222 — 706-672-4930
Brenda Hudson, prin. — Fax 672-1424
Greenville MS — 400/6-8
PO Box 190 30222 — 706-672-3115
Robert Johnson, prin. — Fax 672-3119
Other Schools – See Manchester

Griffin, Spalding, Pop. 23,460
Griffin-Spalding County SD — 9,800/PK-12
PO Box N 30224 — 770-229-3700
Jesse Bradley, supt. — Fax 229-3708
www.spalding.k12.ga.us
Cowan Road MS — 800/6-8
1185 Cowan Rd 30223 — 770-229-3722
Hoby Davenport, prin. — Fax 227-8583
Flynt MS — 600/6-8
221 Spalding Dr 30223 — 770-229-3739
Eclan David, prin. — Fax 229-3712
Griffin HS — 1,600/9-12
1617 W Poplar St 30224 — 770-229-3752
Dr. Quimby Melton, prin. — Fax 229-3752
Kennedy Road MS — 6-8
280 Kennedy Rd 30223 — 770-229-3760
Brenda James, prin. — Fax 467-4626
Spalding HS — 1,200/9-12
550 Wilson Rd 30224 — 770-229-3775
Darrell Jeffcoat, prin. — Fax 227-6899
Taylor Street MS — 900/6-8
234 E Taylor St 30223 — 770-229-3727
Lindy Pruitt, prin. — Fax 229-3770
Griffin Evening S — Adult
1617 W Poplar St 30224 — 770-467-5015
Christina Wiser, prin.

Grace Academy 100/K-12
PO Box 679 30224 770-467-8220
Lynn Fulop, admin. Fax 467-8869
Griffin Technical College Post-Sec.
501 Varsity Rd 30223 770-228-7366

Grovetown, Columbia, Pop. 6,675
Columbia County SD
Supt. — See Appling
Columbia MS 700/6-8
6000 Columbia Rd 30813 706-541-1252
Dr. Donna Anderson, prin. Fax 541-2742
Grovetown MS 500/6-8
5463 Harlem Grovetown Rd 30813 706-855-2514
Carolyn Fries, prin. Fax 868-3734

Guyton, Effingham, Pop. 1,133
Effingham County SD
Supt. — See Springfield
South Effingham HS 1,200/9-12
1220 Noel C Conaway Rd 31312 912-728-7511
W. Lang Brannen, prin. Fax 728-7529
South Effingham MS 800/6-8
1200 Noel C Conaway Rd 31312 912-728-7500
Dr. Mark Winters, prin. Fax 728-7508

Hahira, Lowndes, Pop. 1,756
Lowndes County SD
Supt. — See Valdosta
Hahira MS 1,200/6-8
PO Box 686 31632 229-794-2838
Kip McLeod, prin. Fax 794-3564

Valwood S 400/PK-12
4830 US Highway 41 N 31632 229-242-8491
Cobb Atkinson, hdmstr. Fax 245-7894

Hamilton, Harris, Pop. 502
Harris County SD 4,400/PK-12
PO Box 388 31811 706-628-4206
Dr. Susan Andrews, supt. Fax 628-5609
www.harris.k12.ga.us
Harris County - Carver MS 1,100/6-8
PO Box 408 31811 706-628-4951
Arnold Jackson, prin. Fax 628-5737
Harris County HS 1,300/9-12
8281 GA Highway 116 31811 706-628-4278
Roger Couch, prin. Fax 628-4335

Hampton, Henry, Pop. 4,458
Clayton County SD
Supt. — See Jonesboro
Lovejoy HS 1,900/9-12
1587 Mcdonough Rd 30228 770-473-2920
Dr. Sam Jackson, prin. Fax 473-2928
Lovejoy MS 1,100/6-8
1588 Lovejoy Rd 30228 770-473-2933
Lee Casey, prin. Fax 603-5777

Henry County SD
Supt. — See Mc Donough
Dutchtown HS 9-12
149 Mitchell Rd 30228 770-515-7510
Dwala Nobles, prin. Fax 515-7515
Dutchtown MS 6-8
155 Mitchell Rd 30228 770-515-7500
Jason Kouns, prin. Fax 515-7505

Harlem, Columbia, Pop. 1,804
Columbia County SD
Supt. — See Appling
Harlem HS 1,000/9-12
1070 Appling Harlem Rd 30814 706-556-5980
Alan Griffin, prin. Fax 556-5986
Harlem MS 400/6-8
375 W Forrest St 30814 706-556-5990
Walker Davis, prin. Fax 556-5961

Hartwell, Hart, Pop. 4,273
Hart County SD 3,500/PK-12
PO Box 696 30643 706-376-5141
Nancy T. Clark, supt. Fax 376-7046
www.hart.k12.ga.us
Hart County HS 1,000/9-12
59 Fifth St 30643 706-376-5461
Dennis Brown, prin. Fax 856-7237
Hart County MS 900/6-8
176 Powell Rd 30643 706-376-5431
Eulin Gibbs, prin. Fax 376-2207

Hawkinsville, Pulaski, Pop. 4,194
Pulaski County SD 1,800/PK-12
206 Mccormick Ave 31036 478-783-7200
Janis Sparrow, supt. Fax 783-7204
www.pulaski.k12.ga.us
Hawkinsville HS 500/9-12
1 Red Devil Dr 31036 478-783-7210
Mary Royal, prin. Fax 783-7251
Pulaski County MS 400/6-8
Unadilla Hwy 31036 478-892-7215
Tony Lester, prin. Fax 783-7297

Hazlehurst, Jeff Davis, Pop. 3,757
Jeff Davis County SD 2,600/PK-12
PO Box 1780 31539 912-375-6700
Dr. Lula Mae Perry, supt. Fax 375-6703
www.jeff-davis.k12.ga.us
Davis HS 700/9-12
156 Collins St 31539 912-375-6760
Ronald Dixon, prin. Fax 375-0945
Davis MS 600/6-8
96 W Jefferson St 31539 912-375-6750
David Stapleton, prin. Fax 375-6756

Hephzibah, Richmond, Pop. 4,084
Richmond County SD
Supt. — See Augusta
Hephzibah Comprehensive HS 1,200/9-12
4558 Brothersville Rd 30815 706-592-2089
Veta New, prin. Fax 592-3975
Hephzibah MS 1,100/6-8
2427 Mims Rd 30815 706-592-4534
Deborah Shepherd, prin. Fax 592-3979
Morgan Road MS 800/6-8
3635 Hiers Blvd 30815 706-796-4992
Janie Norris, prin. Fax 560-3947
Spirit Creek MS 1,000/6-8
115 Dolphin Way 30815 706-592-3987
Sharon McAlevy, prin. Fax 592-3999

Hiawassee, Towns, Pop. 806
Towns County SD 1,200/PK-12
67 Lakeview Cir #C 30546 706-896-2279
Dr. Richard Behrens, supt. Fax 896-2632
www.towns.k12.ga.us
Towns County HS 400/9-12
1400 Highway 76 E 30546 706-896-4131
Roy Perren, prin. Fax 896-6628
Towns County MS 300/6-8
1400 Highway 76 E 30546 706-896-4131
Dr. Marian Sumner, prin. Fax 896-6628
Other Schools – See Blairsville

Hinesville, Liberty, Pop. 29,396
Liberty County SD 11,800/PK-12
110 S Gause St 31313 912-876-2161
Steve E. Wilmoth, supt. Fax 368-6201
www.liberty.k12.ga.us/
Bradwell Institute HS 1,900/9-12
100 Pafford St 31313 912-876-6121
Joni Walker-Seier, prin. Fax 876-6914
Frasier MS 900/6-8
910 Long Frasier Dr 31313 912-877-5367
Tom Alexander, prin. Fax 877-3291
Liberty County HS 1,200/9-12
3216 E Oglethorpe Hwy 31313 912-876-4316
Paula Scott, prin. Fax 876-4303
Snelson Golden MS 1,100/6-8
465 Coates Rd 31313 912-877-3112
Dr. Chris Garretson, prin. Fax 368-5342
Other Schools – See Midway

Hiram, Paulding, Pop. 1,480
Paulding County SD
Supt. — See Dallas
Hiram HS 1,900/9-12
702 Ballentine Dr 30141 770-443-1182
Eddie Fincher, prin. Fax 439-5053

Hogansville, Troup, Pop. 2,751
Troup County SD
Supt. — See La Grange
Callaway HS 700/9-12
221 Whitfield Rd 30230 706-845-2070
Kevin Jones, prin. Fax 845-2071

Homer, Banks, Pop. 1,011
Banks County SD 2,500/PK-12
PO Box 248 30547 706-677-2224
Christopher B. Erwin, supt. Fax 677-2223
www.banks.k12.ga.us
Banks County HS 600/9-12
1486 Historic Homer Hwy # A 30547 706-677-2221
Arthur Wheaton, prin. Fax 677-2688
Banks County MS 600/6-8
712 Thompson St 30547 706-677-2277
Matthew Cooper, prin. Fax 677-5227

Homerville, Clinch, Pop. 2,813
Clinch County SD 1,300/K-12
46 S College St 31634 912-487-5321
Dr. Gayle Hughes, supt. Fax 487-5068
www.clinchcounty.com/
Clinch County HS 500/8-12
863 N Carswell St 31634 912-487-5366
Alvin Henderson, prin. Fax 487-3272

Hoschton, Jackson, Pop. 1,393
Gwinnett County SD
Supt. — See Suwanee
Mill Creek HS 9-12
4400 Braselton Hwy 30548 678-714-5850
Jim Markham, prin. Fax 714-5852
Osborne MS 6-8
4404 Braselton Hwy 30548 770-904-5400
John Campbell, prin. Fax 904-5408

Irwinton, Wilkinson, Pop. 587
Wilkinson County SD 1,700/PK-12
PO Box 206 31042 478-946-5521
Terry Sark, supt. Fax 946-3275
Wilkinson County HS 500/9-12
PO Box 547 31042 478-946-2441
Fax 946-7134
Wilkinson County MS 400/6-8
PO Box 527 31042 478-946-2541
Dr. Aaron Geter, prin. Fax 946-8981

Jackson, Butts, Pop. 4,338
Butts County SD 3,400/K-12
181 N Mulberry St 30233 770-504-2300
Dr. Alan White, supt. Fax 504-2305
www.butts.k12.ga.us
Henderson MS 800/6-8
494 George Tate Dr 30233 770-504-2310
Dr. Mary Jacobs, prin. Fax 504-2315
Jackson HS 1,000/9-12
717 Harkness St 30233 770-504-2340
Duane Kline, prin. Fax 504-2341

Jasper, Pickens, Pop. 2,381
Pickens County SD 4,100/K-12
159 Stegall Dr 30143 706-253-1700
Michael Ballew, supt. Fax 253-1705
www.pickens.k12.ga.us/
Jasper MS 600/6-8
339 W Church St 30143 706-253-1760
Steven McDaniel, prin. Fax 253-1765
Pickens County MS 500/6-8
1802 Refuge Rd 30143 706-253-1830
Chris LeMieux, prin. Fax 253-1835
Pickens HS 1,300/9-12
500 Dragon Dr 30143 706-253-1800
Tommy Qualls, prin. Fax 253-1815

Appalachian Technical College Post-Sec.
100 Campus Dr 30143 706-253-4500

Jefferson, Jackson, Pop. 4,182
Jackson County SD 5,800/PK-12
1660 Winder Hwy 30549 706-367-5151
Dr. Shannon Adams, supt. Fax 367-9457
www.jackson.k12.ga.us
Jackson County Comprehensive HS 1,500/9-12
1668 Winder Hwy 30549 706-367-5003
Dr. Pat Stueck, prin. Fax 367-2146
West Jackson MS 700/6-8
400 Gum Springs Church Rd 30549 706-367-5267
Dr. Russ Chesser, prin. Fax 367-5068
Regional Evening S Adult
441 Gordon St 30549 706-367-2341
Janice Stowe, prin. Fax 367-1647

Other Schools – See Commerce

Jefferson CSD 1,700/PK-12
575 Washington St 30549 706-367-2880
Dr. John Jackson, supt. Fax 367-2291
www.jeffcityschools.org/
Jefferson HS 400/9-12
575 Washington St 30549 706-367-2881
Dr. Kevin Smith, prin. Fax 367-1884
Jefferson MS 400/6-8
635 Old Pendergrass Rd 30549 706-367-2882
Howard McGlennen, prin. Fax 367-5207

Jeffersonville, Twiggs, Pop. 1,242
Twiggs County SD 1,400/PK-12
PO Box 232 31044 478-945-3127
Wanda West, supt. Fax 945-3078
www.twiggs.k12.ga.us
Twiggs County HS 400/9-12
375 Watson Dr 31044 478-945-3112
Walter Stephens, prin. Fax 945-3140
Twiggs County MS 300/7-8
375 Watson Dr 31044 478-945-3113
Perdeola Dwight, prin. Fax 945-3140

Twiggs Academy 200/PK-12
RR 1 Box 1825 31044 478-945-3175

Jesup, Wayne, Pop. 9,424
Wayne County SD 5,200/PK-12
555 Sunset Blvd 31545 912-427-1000
Kendall Keith, supt. Fax 427-1004
www.wayne.k12.ga.us
Puckett MS 600/6-8
475 Durrence Rd 31545 912-427-1061
Denise Voyles, prin. Fax 427-1069
Wayne County HS 1,500/9-12
1 Jacket Dr 31545 912-427-1088
Joe McPipkin, prin. Fax 427-1081
Williams MS 700/6-8
1175 S US Highway 301 31546 912-427-1025
Ronnie Harper, prin. Fax 427-1032

Altamaha Technical College Post-Sec.
1777 W Cherry St 31545 912-427-5800

Jonesboro, Clayton, Pop. 3,818
Clayton County SD 50,400/PK-12
1058 5th Ave 30236 770-473-2700
Dr. Barbara Pulliam, supt. Fax 473-2706
www.clayton.k12.ga.us/
Jonesboro HS 1,600/9-12
7728 Mount Zion Blvd 30236 770-473-2855
Derrick Williams, prin. Fax 603-5177
Jonesboro MS 600/6-8
1308 Arnold St 30236 678-610-4331
Kay Sledge, prin. Fax 610-4347
Kendrick MS 1,400/6-8
7971 Kendrick Rd 30238 770-472-8400
Beverly Garner, prin. Fax 472-8413
Mt. Zion HS 1,800/9-12
2535 Mount Zion Pkwy 30236 770-473-2940
Gary Townsend, prin. Fax 473-2784
Mundy's Mill HS 1,700/9-12
9652 Fayetteville Rd 30238 678-817-3000
Anthony Smith, prin. Fax 817-3007
Mundy's Mill MS 900/6-8
1251 Mundys Mill Rd 30238 770-473-2880
Shyla Ridley, prin. Fax 603-5779
Pointe South MS 1,100/6-8
626 Flint River Rd 30238 770-473-2890
Dr. John Staten, prin. Fax 477-4603
Roberts MS 1,200/6-8
1905 Walt Stephens Rd 30236 678-479-0100
Darrell Herring, prin. Fax 479-0114
Other Schools – See College Park, Forest Park, Hampton, Morrow, Rex, Riverdale

ETI Career Institute Post-Sec.
9500 S Main St 30236 770-477-2799
Georgia Medical Institute Post-Sec.
6431 Tara Blvd 30236 770-994-1900
Mt. Zion Christian Academy 500/PK-12
7102 Mount Zion Blvd 30236 770-478-9842
Dr. Pam Adamson, hdmstr. Fax 478-4817

Kennesaw, Cobb, Pop. 25,816
Cobb County SD
Supt. — See Marietta
Awtrey MS 1,500/6-8
3601 Nowlin Rd NW 30144 770-975-6615
Erin Barnett, prin. Fax 975-6617
Harrison HS 2,200/9-12
4500 Due West Rd NW 30152 678-594-8104
Donald Griggers, prin. Fax 594-8106
Kennesaw Mountain HS 2,800/9-12
1898 Kennesaw Due West Rd 30152 678-594-8190
Sue Gunderman, prin. Fax 594-8192
Lost Mountain MS 1,500/6-8
700 Old Mountain Rd NW 30152 678-594-8224
Susan Wing, prin. Fax 594-8226
McClure MS 6-8
3660 Old Stilesboro Rd NW 30152 770-426-3300
North Cobb HS 2,200/9-12
3400 Highway 293 N 30144 770-975-6685
Gary Boling, prin. Fax 975-6687
Palmer MS 1,300/6-8
690 N Booth Rd NW 30144 770-591-5020
Geraldine Ray, prin. Fax 591-5032
Pine Mountain MS 1,200/6-8
2720 Pine Mountain Cir NW 30152 678-594-8252
Ivia Redmond, prin. Fax 594-8254

Cobb Beauty College Post-Sec.
3096 Cherokee St NW 30144 770-424-6915
Devereux-Georgia Treatment Network Post-Sec.
1291 Stanley Rd NW 30152 800-342-3357
Empire Beauty School Post-Sec.
425 Ernest Barrett Pkwy #H2 30144 770-419-2303
ITT Technical Institute Post-Sec.
1000 Cobb Place Blvd 30144 770-426-3000
Kennesaw State University Post-Sec.
1000 Chastain Rd NW 30144 770-423-6000
Mount Paran Christian S 1,000/PK-12
1275 Stanley Rd NW 30152 770-578-0182
Dr. David Tilley, hdmstr. Fax 977-9284
North Cobb Christian S 900/PK-12
4500 Lakeview Dr NW 30144 770-975-0252
Gary Coker, hdmstr. Fax 975-8446

Shiloh Hills Christian S 600/K-12
260 Hawkins Store Rd NE 30144 770-926-7729
John D. Ward, admin. Fax 926-3762

Kingsland, Camden, Pop. 11,064
Camden County SD 9,700/PK-12
PO Box 1330 31548 912-729-5687
Dr. Ann Proctor, supt. Fax 729-1489
www.camden.k12.ga.us/
Camden County HS 2,700/9-12
PO Box 1450 31548 912-729-7318
Dr. John Tucker, prin. Fax 729-7627
Camden MS 1,300/6-8
1300 Middle School Rd 31548 912-729-3113
Dr. Luther Gibbs, prin. Fax 729-7489
Other Schools – See Saint Marys

Kingston, Bartow, Pop. 665
Bartow County SD
Supt. — See Cartersville
Woodland MS at Euharlee 900/6-8
1061 Euharlee Rd 30145 770-606-5871
Lamar Barnes, prin. Fax 606-2092

La Fayette, Walker, Pop. 6,774
Walker County SD 8,900/PK-12
201 S Duke St 30728 706-638-1240
Roy Sapough, supt. Fax 638-7827
www.walkerschools.org
La Fayette HS 900/9-12
5178 Round Pond Rd 30728 706-638-2342
David Friend, prin. Fax 638-4767
La Fayette MS 1,000/6-8
419 Roadrunner Blvd 30728 706-638-6440
Linda Barker, prin. Fax 638-7616
Other Schools – See Flintstone, Rossville

La Grange, Troup, Pop. 26,424
Troup County SD 12,100/PK-12
PO Box 1228 30241 706-812-7900
Edwin D. Smith, supt. Fax 812-7904
www.troup.org/
Callaway MS 600/6-8
2244 Hammett Rd, 706-845-2080
Thomas Whatley, prin. Fax 845-2081
Gardner-Newman MS 900/6-8
101 Shannon Dr, 706-883-1535
Dr. Martha Richardson, prin. Fax 883-1562
La Grange HS 1,300/9-12
516 N Greenwood St, 706-883-1590
Steve Cole, prin. Fax 812-7976
Long Cane MS 1,100/6-8
326 Long Cane Rd, 706-845-2085
Kim Warner, prin. Fax 845-2086
Troup County Comprehensive HS 1,300/9-12
1920 Hamilton Rd, 706-812-7957
Bill Parsons, prin. Fax 812-7960
West Side Magnet S 500/3-8
301 Forrest Ave, 706-883-1550
Alane Thompson, prin. Fax 883-1563
Other Schools – See Hogansville

Lafayette Christian S 200/PK-12
PO Box 934, 706-881-9423
John Cipolla, hdmstr. Fax 882-2515
La Grange Academy 200/K-12
1501 Vernon Rd, 706-882-8097
Barry Peterson Ph.D., hdmstr. Fax 882-8640
La Grange College Post-Sec.
601 Broad St, 706-880-8000
West Georgia Christian Academy 200/PK-12
1904 Hamilton Rd, 706-884-6575
Stephen Duke, admin. Fax 885-0241
West Georgia Technical College Post-Sec.
303 Fort Dr, 706-845-4323

Lakeland, Lanier, Pop. 2,743
Lanier County SD 1,500/PK-12
PO Box 158 31635 229-482-3966
Eloise Sorrell, supt. Fax 482-3020
www.lanier.k12.ga.us/
Lanier County HS 400/9-12
325 W Patten Ave 31635 229-482-3868
Steve Hankla, prin. Fax 482-3368
Lanier County MS 400/6-8
325 W Patten Ave 31635 229-482-8247
Keith Humphrey, prin. Fax 482-8339

Lakeland Adventist S 50/1-12
842 W Thigpen Ave 31635 229-482-2418

Lawrenceville, Gwinnett, Pop. 26,698
Gwinnett County SD
Supt. — See Suwanee
Central Gwinnett HS 2,300/9-12
564 W Crogan St 30045 770-963-8041
Dr. Valerie Clark, prin. Fax 338-4879
Creekland MS 2,700/6-8
170 Russell Rd 30043 770-338-4700
Dr. Donna Lee, prin. Fax 338-4703
Crews MS 1,300/6-8
1000 Old Snellville Hwy 30044 770-982-6940
Jonathan Patterson, prin. Fax 982-6942
Five Forks MS 1,100/6-8
3250 River Dr 30044 770-972-1506
Dr. Mary Hensien, prin. Fax 736-4547
Maxwell HS of Technology Vo/Tech
990 McElvaney Ln 30044 770-963-6838
Donna Powers, prin. Fax 338-4612
Phoenix HS 700/9-12
501 W Pike St 30045 770-513-6862
Dr. Kevin Tashlein, prin. Fax 513-6864
Richards MS 2,200/6-8
3555 Sugarloaf Pkwy 30044 770-995-7133
Judy Stephens, prin. Fax 338-4791
Sweetwater MS 2,500/6-8
3500 Cruse Rd 30044 770-923-4131
Angela Moton, prin. Fax 931-7077

Aviation Institute of Maintenance Post-Sec.
500 Briscoe Blvd 30045 770-377-5600
Empire Beauty College Post-Sec.
1455 Pleasant Hill Rd #105 30044 770-564-0725
Gwinnett Technical College Post-Sec.
5150 Sugarloaf Pkwy 30043 770-962-7580

Leesburg, Lee, Pop. 2,609
Lee County SD 5,300/PK-12
PO Box 399 31763 229-903-2100
Dr. Lawrence T. Walters, supt. Fax 903-2130
www.lee.k12.ga.us
Lee County HS 1,600/9-12
1 Trojan Way 31763 229-903-2260
Dr. Bill Truby, prin. Fax 903-2292
Lee County MS 1,400/6-8
190 Smithville Rd N 31763 229-903-2140
Gail Melvin, prin. Fax 903-2160

Lexington, Oglethorpe, Pop. 242
Oglethorpe County SD 2,300/PK-12
735 Athens Rd 30648 706-743-8128
Dr. Jeffery C. Welch, supt. Fax 743-3211
www.oglethorpe.k12.ga.us
Oglethorpe County HS 600/9-12
749 Athens Rd 30648 706-743-8124
Phillip Todd, prin. Fax 743-3536
Oglethorpe County MS 600/6-8
757 Athens Rd 30648 706-743-8146
Beverley Levine, prin. Fax 743-3536

Lilburn, Gwinnett, Pop. 11,363
Gwinnett County SD
Supt. — See Suwanee
Berkmar HS 2,600/9-12
405 Pleasant Hill Rd NW 30047 770-921-3636
Kendall Johnson, prin. Fax 806-3715
Berkmar MS 6-8
4355 Lawrenceville Hwy 30047 770-638-2300
Kenney Wells, prin. Fax 638-2309
Lilburn MS 2,200/6-8
4994 Lawrenceville Hwy NW 30047 770-921-1776
James Rayford, prin. Fax 806-3866
Parkview HS 2,600/9-12
998 Cole Rd SW 30047 770-921-2874
Dr. Charles Buchanan, prin. Fax 806-3797
Trickum MS 1,700/6-8
948 Cole Rd SW 30047 770-921-2705
Lynne Davis, prin. Fax 806-3742

Gwinnett College of Business Post-Sec.
4230 Lwrncvll Hwy NW #11 30047 770-381-7200
Killian Hill Christian S 500/K-12
151 Arcado Rd SW 30047 770-921-3224
Paul Williams, prin. Fax 921-9395
Providence Christian Academy 800/K-12
4575 Lawrenceville Hwy NW 30047 770-279-7200
James Vaught, hdmstr. Fax 279-8258

Lincolnton, Lincoln, Pop. 1,621
Lincoln County SD 1,400/PK-12
PO Box 39 30817 706-359-3742
Dr. G. R. Edmunds, supt. Fax 359-7938
www.lincolncountyschools.org
Lincoln County HS 400/9-12
PO Box 580 30817 706-359-3121
Dr. Becky Barden, prin. Fax 359-3552
Lincoln County MS 400/6-8
PO Box 550 30817 706-359-3069
Pam Carmichael, prin. Fax 359-2200

Lindale, Floyd, Pop. 4,187
Floyd County SD
Supt. — See Rome
Pepperell HS 900/9-12
3 Dragon Dr 30147 706-236-1844
Phil Ray, prin. Fax 236-1846
Pepperell MS 800/6-8
200 Hughes Dairy Rd 30147 706-236-1849
Frank Pinson, prin. Fax 802-6776

Lithia Springs, Douglas, Pop. 11,403
Douglas County SD
Supt. — See Douglasville
Lithia Springs HS 1,500/9-12
2520 E County Line Rd 30122 770-651-6700
Larry Ruble, prin. Fax 651-6862
Turner MS 800/6-8
7101 Junior High Dr 30122 770-651-5500
Jean Williams, prin. Fax 651-5503

Colonial Hills Christian S 500/PK-12
7131 Mount Vernon Rd 30122 770-941-6342
Westley Smith, admin. Fax 941-2090
Lithia Christian Academy 200/PK-12
2548 Vulcan Dr 30122 770-941-5406
Lanier Motes, admin. Fax 941-9944

Lithonia, DeKalb, Pop. 2,194
DeKalb County SD
Supt. — See Decatur
King HS 1,700/9-12
3991 Snapfinger Rd 30038 678-874-5402
Sylvester Nelloms, prin. Fax 874-5410
Lithonia HS 9-12
2440 Phillips Rd 30058 678-676-2902
Margie Smith, prin. Fax 676-2910
Lithonia MS 1,600/6-8
2451 Randall Ave 30058 678-875-0702
Patricia May, prin. Fax 875-0710
Miller Grove HS 9-12
2645 DeKalb Medical Pkwy 30058 678-875-1102
Dr. Ralph Simpson, prin. Fax 875-1110
Redan MS 1,300/6-8
1775 Young Rd 30058 678-874-7902
Matthew Priester, prin. Fax 874-7910
Salem MS 1,400/6-8
5333 Salem Rd 30038 678-676-9402
Stanley Mons, prin. Fax 676-9410

Lithonia Adventist Academy 50/K-10
3533 Ragsdale Rd 30038 770-482-0294
Robin Young, prin. Fax 482-6224
Luther Rice University Post-Sec.
3038 Evans Mill Rd 30038 770-484-1204

Locust Grove, Henry, Pop. 2,755
Henry County SD
Supt. — See Mc Donough
Luella HS 1,400/9-12
603 Walker Dr 30248 770-898-9822
George Eckerle, prin. Fax 898-9625
Luella MS 1,400/6-8
2075 Hmpton Locust Grove Rd 30248 678-583-8919
Aaryn Schmuhl, prin. Fax 583-8920

Loganville, Walton, Pop. 7,880
Gwinnett County SD
Supt. — See Suwanee
Grayson HS 2,300/9-12
50 Hope Hollow Rd 30052 770-554-1071
Dr. Keith Chaney, prin. Fax 554-1074
McConnell MS 2,000/6-8
550 Ozora Rd 30052 770-554-1000
Dan Hicks, prin. Fax 554-1003

Walton County SD
Supt. — See Monroe
Loganville HS 1,600/9-12
100 Trident Trl 30052 770-466-4892
Gary Hobbs, prin. Fax 466-5334
Loganville MS 1,400/6-8
152 Clark McCullers Dr 30052 770-466-0713
Eugene Williams, prin. Fax 466-3035
Youth MS 6-8
1804 Highway 81 30052 770-466-6849
Jane Burris, prin. Fax 466-8596

Covenant Christian Academy 300/K-12
3425 Loganville Hwy 30052 770-466-7890
Emmaline McKinnon, prin. Fax 466-2833
Faith Academy 1,100/9-12
2571 Highway 78 30052 770-466-7872
Jacquelyn Griggs, prin. Fax 554-0123
Loganville Christian Academy 400/PK-12
PO Box 867 30052 770-554-9888
Christy Monda, admin. Fax 554-9881

Lookout Mountain, Walker, Pop. 1,577

Covenant College Post-Sec.
14049 Scenic Hwy 30750 706-820-1560

Louisville, Jefferson, Pop. 2,653
Jefferson County SD 3,500/PK-12
PO Box 449 30434 478-625-7626
Carl Bethune, supt. Fax 625-7459
www.jefferson.k12.ga.us
Hi Tech S Vo/Tech
1200 School St 30434 478-625-7764
Teresa Brooks, prin. Fax 625-3120
Jefferson County HS 1,000/9-12
1157 Warrior Trl 30434 478-625-9991
Dr. Molly Howard, prin. Fax 625-8988
Louisville MS 500/6-8
1200 School St 30434 478-625-7764
Samuel Dasher, prin. Fax 625-3120
Other Schools – See Wrens

Jefferson Academy 300/K-12
2264 US Highway 1 N 30434 478-625-8861

Ludowici, Long, Pop. 1,500
Long County SD 1,100/PK-12
PO Box 428 31316 912-545-2367
Dr. Edwin S. Pope, supt. Fax 545-2380
www.long.k12.ga.us/
Long County HS 500/9-12
PO Box 579 31316 912-545-2135
Dr. Dolores Mallard, prin. Fax 545-2136
Walker MS PK-PK, 4-
PO Box 579 31316 912-545-2069
Vicky Wells, prin. Fax 545-2775

Lumpkin, Stewart, Pop. 1,293
Stewart County SD 700/PK-12
PO Box 547 31815 229-838-4329
Henry Moylan, supt. Fax 838-6984
www.stewart.k12.ga.us/
Stewart County MS 100/6-8
PO Box 728 31815 229-838-4532
Calvin Blake, prin. Fax 838-4352
Stewart-Quitman HS 200/9-12
PO Box 706 31815 229-838-4301
Tommy Dopson, prin. Fax 838-4352

Lyons, Toombs, Pop. 4,269
Toombs County SD 2,500/PK-12
117 E Wesley Ave 30436 912-526-3141
Dr. Kendall Brantley, supt. Fax 526-3291
www.toombs.k12.ga.us/
Toombs County HS 700/9-12
600 Lyons Center Rd 30436 912-526-6068
Gail Clark, prin. Fax 526-4612
Toombs County MS 700/6-8
701 Bulldog Rd 30436 912-526-8363
Dr. Roseann Phillips, prin. Fax 526-0240

Toombs Christian Academy 300/PK-12
PO Box 227 30436 912-526-8938
John E. Sharpe, hdmstr. Fax 526-0571

Mableton, Cobb, Pop. 30,600
Cobb County SD
Supt. — See Marietta
Floyd MS 1,000/6-8
4803 Floyd Rd SW 30126 770-819-2453
Lawrence Bynum, prin. Fax 819-2455
Lindley MS 1,400/6-8
50 Veterans Memorial Hwy 30126 770-819-2496
Zinta Perkins, prin. Fax 819-2498
Pebblebrook HS 1,700/9-12
991 Old Alabama Rd SW 30126 770-819-2521
Regina Montgomery, prin. Fax 819-2523

Cumberland Christian Academy 100/6-8
4900 Floyd Rd SW 30126 770-819-6443
Larry Kendrick, hdmstr. Fax 945-0224
Whitefield Academy 600/K-12
1 Whitefield Dr SE 30126 678-305-3000
Timothy Hillen, hdmstr. Fax 305-3010

Mc Donough, Henry, Pop. 3,773
Henry County SD 30,100/PK-12
33 N Zack Hinton Pkwy 30253 770-957-6601
Jack Parish, supt. Fax 914-6178
www.henry.k12.ga.us
Eagle's Landing HS 2,000/9-12
301 Tunis Rd 30253 770-954-9515
Dr. Ethan Hildreth, prin. Fax 914-9789
Eagle's Landing MS 1,500/6-8
295 Tunis Rd 30253 770-914-8189
James Davis, prin. Fax 914-2989

Henry County HS 1,400/9-12
401 E Tomlinson St 30253 770-957-3943
Andy Giddens, prin. Fax 957-0368
Henry County MS 1,400/6-8
166 Holly Smith Dr 30253 770-957-3945
Larry Monk, prin. Fax 957-0368
Ola HS 9-12
357 N Ola Rd, 770-288-3222
Ross Iddings, prin. Fax 288-3230
Ola MS 6-8
353 N Ola Rd, 770-288-2108
Louann Jones, prin. Fax 288-2114
Union Grove HS 1,900/9-12
120 E Lake Rd, 678-583-8502
Rodney Bowler, prin. Fax 583-8850
Union Grove MS 1,500/6-8
210 E Lake Rd, 678-583-8978
Robyn Mullis, prin. Fax 583-8580
Henry County Evening Academy Adult
120 E Lake Rd, 678-583-8856
Vanthony Smith, prin. Fax 583-8850
Other Schools – See Hampton, Locust Grove, Stockbridge

Eagle's Landing Christian Academy 1,200/PK-12
2400 Highway 42 N 30253 770-957-2927
Marshall Chambers, admin. Fax 957-2290

Macon, Bibb, Pop. 95,267

Bibb County SD 24,800/PK-12
484 Mulberry St 31201 478-765-8711
Sharon Patterson, supt. Fax 765-8549
www.bibb.k12.ga.us
Appling MS 600/7-8
1210 Shurling Dr 31211 478-751-6758
Robert Stevenson, prin. Fax 745-4337
Bloomfield MS 6-8
4375 Bloomfield Drive Ext 31206
David Dillard, prin.
Central Magnet HS 1,300/9-12
2155 Napier Ave 31204 478-751-6770
Dr. Erin Weaver, prin. Fax 751-6834
Howard MS 6-8
6600 Forsyth Rd 31201 478-757-5543
Karen Yarbrough, prin. Fax 757-5557
Hutchings HS Vo/Tech
2011 Riverside Dr 31204 478-621-2535
Ron McCall, prin. Fax 621-2742
McEvoy MS 800/7-8
1751 Williamson Rd 31206 478-784-3158
Benjy Morgan, prin. Fax 784-3182
Miller Magnet MS 800/6-8
751 Hendley St 31204 478-751-6766
Tanzy Kilcrease, prin. Fax 751-6829
Northeast Magnet HS 900/9-12
1646 Upper River Rd 31211 478-751-6787
Dr. Sam Scavella, prin. Fax 751-6818
Rutland HS 800/9-12
6250 Skipper Rd 31216 478-784-3120
Jim Finch, prin. Fax 784-5462
Rutland MS 1,000/6-8
6260 Skipper Rd 31216 478-784-3153
Dr. Jerri Hall, prin. Fax 784-6929
Southwest Magnet HS 1,200/9-12
1710 Canterbury Rd 31206 478-784-3122
Tyrone Bacon, prin. Fax 784-5476
Weaver MS 1,100/7-8
2570 Heath Rd 31206 478-471-5804
Dr. Pam Carswell, prin. Fax 471-5806
Westside Magnet HS 1,700/9-12
2851 Heath Rd 31206 478-757-5520
Laura Perkins, prin. Fax 757-5525

Jones County SD
Supt. — See Gray
Clifton Ridge MS 600/6-8
169 Dusty Ln 31211 478-743-5182
Susan Eilers, prin. Fax 743-8282

American Professional Institute Post-Sec.
1990 Riverside Dr 31201 478-746-3243
Central Fellowship Academy 500/PK-12
8460 Hawkinsville Rd 31216 478-788-6909
Truitt Franklin, admin. Fax 788-1614
Central Georgia Technical College Post-Sec.
3300 Macon Tech Dr 31206 478-757-3501
First Presbyterian Day S 1,000/PK-12
5671 Calvin Dr 31210 478-477-6505
Gregg Thompson, hdmstr. Fax 477-2804
Georgia Academy for the Blind Post-Sec.
2895 Vineville Ave 31204 478-751-6083
Gilead Christian Academy 200/PK-12
1931 Rocky Creek Rd 31206 478-788-0606
Brian Gottschall, prin. Fax 788-4382
Macon State College Post-Sec.
100 College Station Dr 31206 478-471-2700
Medical Center of Central Georgia Post-Sec.
777 Hemlock St 31201 478-633-1234
Mercer University in Macon Post-Sec.
1400 Coleman Ave 31207 800-637-2378
Mt. de Sales Academy 600/7-12
851 Orange St 31201 478-751-3240
Katy Prebble, prin. Fax 751-3241
Stratford Academy 900/PK-12
6010 Peake Rd 31220 478-477-8073
David Wahl, hdmstr. Fax 477-0299
Tattnall Square Academy 800/PK-12
111 Trojan Trl 31210 478-477-6760
Barney Hester, hdmstr. Fax 474-7887
Wesleyan College Post-Sec.
4760 Forsyth Rd 31210 800-447-6610
Windsor Academy 300/K-12
4150 Jones Rd 31216 478-781-1621
John Cranford, hdmstr. Fax 781-0757

Mc Rae, Telfair, Pop. 3,041

Telfair County SD 1,700/PK-12
PO Box 240 31055 229-868-5661
Cary Clark, supt. Fax 868-5549
www.telfair.k12.ga.us
Telfair County HS 400/9-12
1900 S 3rd Ave 31055 229-868-6096
Tim Deep, prin. Fax 868-7221
Telfair County MS 400/6-8
101 Highway 280 W 31055 229-868-7465
Coleen McIver, prin. Fax 868-2616

Madison, Morgan, Pop. 3,779

Morgan County SD 3,300/PK-12
1065 East Ave 30650 706-342-0752
Dr. Patricia Stokes, supt. Fax 342-0505
www.morgan.k12.ga.us
Morgan County HS 900/9-12
1231 College Dr 30650 706-342-2336
Dr. Mark Wilson, prin. Fax 342-5046
Morgan County MS 800/6-8
920 Pearl St 30650 706-342-0556
Dr. Ralph Bennett, prin. Fax 342-5048

Manchester, Meriwether, Pop. 3,792

Meriwether County SD
Supt. — See Greenville
Manchester HS 600/9-12
405 N 5th Ave 31816 706-846-8445
Marlowe Hinson, prin. Fax 846-5081
Manchester MS 500/6-8
700 Martin Luther King Jr D 31816 706-846-2846
Edward Boswell, prin. Fax 846-8111

Manor, Ware

Ware County SD
Supt. — See Waycross
Ware County Magnet S 500/K-12
4650 Manor Millwood Rd S 31550 912-287-2338
Dr. Darlene Tanner, prin. Fax 287-2337

Marietta, Cobb, Pop. 61,282

Cobb County SD 93,400/PK-12
514 Glover St SE 30060 770-426-3300
Fred Sanderson, supt. Fax 426-3329
www.cobb.k12.ga.us
Daniell MS 1,000/6-8
2900 Scott Rd 30066 678-594-8048
Merilee Heflin, prin. Fax 594-8050
Dickerson MS 1,500/6-8
855 Woodlawn Dr NE 30068 770-578-2710
Dr. Kevin Daniel, prin. Fax 578-2712
Dodgen MS 800/6-8
1725 Bill Murdock Rd 30062 770-578-2726
James Snell, prin. Fax 578-2728
East Cobb MS 1,400/6-8
380 Holt Rd NE 30068 770-578-2740
Terry Stechmiller, prin. Fax 578-2742
Hightower Trail MS 1,000/6-8
3905 Post Oak Tritt Rd 30062 770-578-7225
Janet Peeler, prin. Fax 578-7227
Kell HS 1,600/9-12
4770 Lee Waters Rd 30066 678-494-7844
Mike Johnson, prin. Fax 494-7846
Lassiter HS 2,300/9-12
2601 Shallowford Rd 30066 678-494-7863
James Carter, prin. Fax 494-7865
Mabry MS 900/6-8
2700 Jims Rd NE 30066 770-928-5546
Dr. Tim Tyson, prin. Fax 928-5548
McCleskey MS 800/6-8
4080 Maybreeze Rd 30066 770-928-5560
Dr. Jerry Dority, prin. Fax 928-5562
Osborne HS 1,800/9-12
2451 Favor Rd SW 30060 770-437-5900
Steven Miletto, prin. Fax 437-5902
Pope HS 1,900/9-12
3001 Hembree Rd NE 30062 770-578-7900
Charlotte Stowers, prin. Fax 578-7902
Simpson MS 900/6-8
3340 Trickum Rd NE 30066 770-971-4711
Sharon Jordan, prin. Fax 971-4507
Smitha MS 1,300/6-8
2025 Powder Springs Rd SW 30064 678-594-8267
Wanda Dukes, prin. Fax 594-8269
Sprayberry HS 1,900/9-12
2525 Sandy Plains Rd 30066 770-578-3200
Susan Galante, prin. Fax 578-3202
Wheeler HS 1,800/9-12
375 Holt Rd NE 30068 770-578-3266
Ed Thayer, prin. Fax 578-3268
Adult Education Center Adult
240 Barber Rd SE 30060 678-594-8011
Tommy Farr, prin. Fax 594-8015
Other Schools – See Acworth, Austell, Kennesaw, Mableton, Powder Springs, Smyrna

Marietta CSD 7,600/K-12
250 Howard St NE 30060 770-422-3500
Dr. Emily Lembeck, supt. Fax 425-4095
www.marietta-city.org
Marietta HS 2,000/9-12
1171 Whitlock Ave SW 30064 770-428-2631
Leigh Colburn, prin. Fax 429-3151
Marietta MS 1,200/7-8
121 Winn St NW 30064 770-422-0311
Tim Jones, prin. Fax 429-3162

Chattahoochee Technical College Post-Sec.
980 S Cobb Dr SE 30060 770-528-4500
Cobb County Christian S 50/PK-12
545 Lorene Dr SW 30060 770-434-1320
Gloria Kelly, admin. Fax 434-1442
Covenant Christian Ministries Academy 200/PK-12
PO Box 4065 30061 770-426-4267
Fax 919-2098
Cumberland Christian Academy 100/9-12
2115 Pair Rd SW 30008 770-819-9942
Larry Kendrick, hdmstr. Fax 945-0224
Dominion Christian HS 300/9-12
4607 Burnt Hickory Rd NW 30064 770-420-2153
Marc Stout, hdmstr. Fax 420-2510
Georgia Medical Institute Post-Sec.
1600 Terrell Rd Ste G 30067 770-428-6303
High-Tech Institute Post-Sec.
1090 Northchase Pky SE #150 30067 770-988-9877
Life University Post-Sec.
1269 Barclay Cir SE 30060 770-426-2600
Roffler Moler Hairstyling College Post-Sec.
1311 Roswell Rd 30062 770-565-3285
Southern Polytech State University Post-Sec.
1100 S Marietta Pkwy SE 30060 770-528-7200
Walker S 1,100/PK-12
700 Cobb Pkwy N 30062 770-427-2689
Donald Robertson, hdmstr. Fax 514-8122

Martinez, Columbia, Pop. 27,700

Augusta Christian S 700/K-12
313 Baston Rd 30907 706-863-2905
Joel Woodcock, hdmstr. Fax 860-6618
Augusta Preparatory Day S 500/PK-12
285 Flowing Wells Rd 30907 706-863-1906
Jack Hall, hdmstr. Fax 863-6198

Metter, Candler, Pop. 4,000

Candler County SD 1,900/PK-12
210 S College St 30439 912-685-5713
Dr. Thomas Bigwood, supt. Fax 685-2076
www.metter.org
Metter HS 500/9-12
RR 3 Box 1500 30439 912-685-2134
Michelle Cliett, prin. Fax 685-2897
Metter MS 400/6-8
431 W Vertia St 30439 912-685-5580
Evelyn Campbell, prin. Fax 685-4970

Midland, Muscogee

Muscogee County SD
Supt. — See Columbus
Midland MS 900/6-8
6990 Warm Springs Rd 31820 706-569-3673
James Wilson, prin. Fax 569-3678

Midway, Liberty, Pop. 1,047

Liberty County SD
Supt. — See Hinesville
Midway MS 900/6-8
425 Edgewater Dr 31320 912-884-6677
Debra Frazier, prin. Fax 884-5944

Milledgeville, Baldwin, Pop. 19,159

Baldwin County SD 5,200/PK-12
PO Box 1188 31059 478-453-4176
C. Trammell, supt. Fax 457-3327
www.baldwin-county-schools.com
Baldwin HS 1,400/9-12
155 GA Highway 49 W 31061 478-453-6429
Lynwood Chandler, prin. Fax 451-3032
Oak Hill MS 1,500/6-8
356 Blandy Rd NW 31061 478-457-3370
Mark Scott, dir. Fax 457-2422
Carver Adult Education Adult
435 E Walton St 31061 478-452-4711
Angela Hudson, prin. Fax 452-7295

Central Georgia Technical College Post-Sec.
54 GA Highway 22 W 31061
Georgia College & State University Post-Sec.
231 W Hancock St 31061 478-445-5350
Georgia Military College Post-Sec.
201 E Greene St 31061 478-445-2700
Milledge Academy 600/PK-12
197 Log Cabin Rd NE 31061 478-452-5570
Larry Prestridge, prin. Fax 452-5000

Millen, Jenkins, Pop. 3,547

Jenkins County SD 1,700/PK-12
PO Box 660 30442 478-982-6000
Hayward Cordy, supt. Fax 982-6002
www.jchs.com/
Jenkins County HS 500/9-12
433 Barney Ave 30442 478-982-4791
Harold Roach, prin. Fax 982-6015
Jenkins County MS 400/6-8
409 Barney Ave 30442 478-982-1063
Dr. Joseph Kirkland, prin. Fax 982-6015

Monroe, Walton, Pop. 11,892

Walton County SD 10,700/PK-12
200 Double Springs Church R 30656 770-266-4417
Dr. Tim Lull, supt. Fax 266-4420
www.walton.k12.ga.us
Carver MS 1,200/6-8
1095 Good Hope Rd 30655 770-267-6000
Sean Callahan, prin. Fax 267-4050
Monroe HS 1,200/9-12
300 Double Springs Church 30656 770-266-4599
Seabrook Royal, prin. Fax 266-4598
Other Schools – See Loganville

Walton Academy 900/PK-12
1 Bulldog Dr 30655 770-267-7578
William Nicholson, hdmstr. Fax 267-4023

Montezuma, Macon, Pop. 4,017

Macon County SD
Supt. — See Oglethorpe
Macon County HS 600/9-12
611 Vienna Rd 31063 478-472-8579
Rickey Edmond, prin. Fax 472-6206
Macon County MS 500/6-8
615 Vienna Rd 31063 478-472-7045
Issiah Ross, prin. Fax 472-2549

Monticello, Jasper, Pop. 2,517

Jasper County SD 2,100/PK-12
1125A Fred Smith St 31064 706-468-6350
Jay L. Brinson, supt. Fax 468-0045
www.jasper.k12.ga.us
Jasper County HS 500/9-12
1289 College St 31064 706-468-2227
Howard Fore, prin. Fax 468-4991
Jasper County MS 500/6-8
1289 College St 31064 706-468-2227
Anne Massengale, prin. Fax 468-4991

Piedmont Academy 300/PK-12
PO Box 231 31064 706-468-8818
James Champion, hdmstr. Fax 468-2409

Morgan, Calhoun, Pop. 1,457

Calhoun County SD 700/PK-12
PO Box 39 39866 229-849-2765
Alvetta Butler, supt. Fax 849-2113
www.calhoun.k12.ga.us/
Other Schools – See Edison

Morganton, Union, Pop. 295

Mountain Area Christian Academy 200/PK-12
PO Box 240 30560 706-374-6222
Howell Teasley, admin. Fax 374-4831

Morrow, Clayton, Pop. 5,034

Clayton County SD
Supt. — See Jonesboro
Morrow HS 1,900/9-12
2299 Old Rex Morrow Rd 30260 404-362-3865
Dr. Morris Blasingame, prin. Fax 362-2044

Morrow MS 1,000/6-8
5968 Maddox Rd 30260 404-362-3860
Greg Curry, prin. Fax 608-2557

Clayton State University Post-Sec.
5900 Lee St 30260 770-961-3400
Interactive College of Technology Post-Sec.
1078 Citizens Pkwy Ste A 30260 770-960-1298
Javelin Technical Training Center Post-Sec.
1396 Southlake Plaza Dr 30260 770-968-9155

Moultrie, Colquitt, Pop. 14,500
Colquitt County SD 8,600/PK-12
PO Box 2708 31776 229-890-6200
Leonard McCoy, supt. Fax 890-6246
www.colquitt.k12.ga.us/
Colquitt County HS 2,200/9-12
1800 Park Ave SE 31768 229-890-6181
Bob Jones, prin. Fax 890-6166
Gray MS 1,000/6-8
812 11th Ave NW 31768 229-890-6189
Nathan Brown, prin. Fax 890-6123
Williams MS 900/6-8
1000 Stadium Dr 31768 229-890-6183
Scott Michie, prin. Fax 890-6258

Moultrie Technical College Post-Sec.
800 Veterans Pkwy N, 229-891-7000

Mount Airy, Habersham, Pop. 669
Habersham County SD
Supt. — See Clarkesville
Habersham Central SHS 1,100/10-12
171 Raider Cir 30563 706-778-7161
Sandra Bennett, prin. Fax 778-1258

Central Heights Christian S 200/PK-12
2664 Highway 197 30563 706-778-3360
Danny Young, prin. Fax 776-2723

Mount Berry, Floyd

Berry College Post-Sec.
2277 Martha Berry Hwy NE 30149 706-232-5374

Mount Vernon, Montgomery, Pop. 2,126
Montgomery County SD 1,300/PK-12
PO Box 315 30445 912-583-2301
Dale Clark, supt. Fax 583-4822
Montgomery County HS 400/9-12
701 Dobbins St 30445 912-583-2296
Luke Smith, prin. Fax 583-4469
Montgomery County MS 300/6-8
701 Dobbins St 30445 912-583-2351
Fax 583-4469

Brewton-Parker College Post-Sec.
Highway 280 30445 800-342-1087

Mount Zion, Carroll, Pop. 1,407
Carroll County SD
Supt. — See Carrollton
Mount Zion MSHS 400/6-12
132 Eagle Dr 30150 770-834-6654
Tracey Barrow, prin. Fax 832-9497

Nahunta, Brantley, Pop. 1,013
Brantley County SD 3,300/PK-12
RR 2 Box 22T 31553 912-462-6176
Greg Jacobs, supt. Fax 462-6731
www.brantley.k12.ga.us/
Brantley County HS 800/9-12
RR 1 Box 4 31553 912-462-5121
Dr. Reba Smith, prin. Fax 462-5123
Brantley County MS 500/7-8
RR 1 Box 4D 31553 912-462-7092
Shelli Tyre, prin. Fax 462-6785

Nashville, Berrien, Pop. 4,760
Berrien County SD 3,100/PK-12
PO Box 625 31639 229-686-2081
Bobby N. Griffin, supt. Fax 686-9002
www.berrien.k12.ga.us
Berrien HS 900/9-12
500 E Smith Ave 31639 229-686-7428
Mike Parker, prin. Fax 686-6251
Berrien MS 800/6-8
800 Tifton Rd 31639 229-686-2021
Dr. Dennis Proctor, prin. Fax 686-6546

Newnan, Coweta, Pop. 20,551
Coweta County SD 19,100/PK-12
PO Box 280 30264 770-254-2801
Blake Bass, supt. Fax 254-2807
www.cowetaschools.org
Arnall MS 1,000/6-8
700 Lora Smith Rd 30265 770-254-2765
Rick Waggoner, prin. Fax 254-2770
Evans MS 800/6-8
1 Evans Dr 30263 770-254-2780
Walter Drake, prin. Fax 254-2783
Madras MS 900/6-8
240 Edgeworth Rd 30263 770-254-2744
Scott Floyd, prin. Fax 304-5928
Newnan HS 1,800/9-12
190 Lagrange St 30263 770-254-2880
Dr. Steve Barker, prin. Fax 254-2797
Northgate HS 1,300/9-12
3220 Fischer Rd 30265 770-463-5585
Dr. Therese Reddekopp, prin. Fax 463-4982
Smokey Road MS 900/6-8
965 Smokey Rd 30263 770-254-2840
Dr. Laurie Jackson, prin. Fax 304-5933
Other Schools – See Senoia, Sharpsburg

Heritage S 400/PK-12
2093 Highway 29 N 30263 770-253-9898
Judith Griffith, hdmstr. Fax 253-4850
Newnan Christian S 200/PK-12
1608 Highway 29 N 30263 770-253-7175
West Central Technical College Post-Sec.
160 Martin Luther King Dr 30263 678-423-2000

Norcross, Gwinnett, Pop. 9,294
Gwinnett County SD
Supt. — See Suwanee
Buchanan HS of Technology Vo/Tech
2595 Beaver Ruin Rd 30071 770-326-8000
Meadowcreek HS 2,100/9-12
4455 Steve Reynolds Blvd 30093 770-381-9680
Dr. Angela Pringle, prin. Fax 806-2230
Norcross HS 2,600/9-12
5300 Spalding Dr 30092 770-448-3674
Mary Anne Charron, prin. Fax 447-2664
Pinckneyville MS 1,300/6-8
5440 W Jones Bridge Rd 30092 770-263-0860
Nancy Martin, prin. Fax 447-2617
Summerour MS 1,100/6-8
585 Mitchell Rd 30071 770-448-3045
Dana Pugh, prin. Fax 417-2476

Ashworth College Post-Sec.
430 Technology Pkwy 30092 770-729-8400
Atlanta Institute of Music Post-Sec.
5985 Financial Dr # 200 30071 770-242-7717
Career Education Institute Post-Sec.
5675 Jimmy Carter Blvd #100 30071 678-966-9411
Georgia Medical Institute Post-Sec.
1750 Beaver Ruin Rd Ste 500 30093 770-921-1085
Greater Atlanta Christian S 1,900/K-12
1575 Indian Trail Rd 30093 770-243-2274
Dr. David L. Fincher, pres. Fax 243-2213
Hopewell Christian Academy 300/PK-12
182 Hunter St 30071 770-903-3387
Horace Buckley, prin. Fax 449-8316
Iverson Business School Post-Sec.
500 Pinnacle Ct 30071 770-446-1333
James Madison High School Post-Sec.
430 Technology Pkwy 30092 770-729-8400
Professional Career Development Inst Post-Sec.
430 Technology Pkwy 30092 770-729-8400
Wesleyan S 1,100/K-12
5405 Spalding Dr 30092 770-448-7640
Zach Young, admin. Fax 448-3699

Oakwood, Hall, Pop. 3,100
Hall County SD
Supt. — See Gainesville
West Hall HS 1,000/9-12
5500 Mcever Rd 30566 770-967-9826
Dr. Jackie Adams, prin. Fax 967-4864
West Hall MS 800/6-8
5470 Mcever Rd 30566 770-967-4871
Dr. Sarah Justus, prin. Fax 967-4874

Lanier Technical College Post-Sec.
2990 Landrum Education Dr 30566 770-531-6300
Maranatha Christian Academy 100/K-12
PO Box 877 30566 770-536-6334

Ocilla, Irwin, Pop. 3,255
Irwin County SD 1,900/PK-12
PO Box 225 31774 229-468-7485
Betty Sue Stripling, supt. Fax 468-7220
www.irwin.k12.ga.us/
Irwin County HS 500/9-12
149 Chieftain Cir 31774 229-468-9421
Bobby Conner, prin. Fax 468-9423
Irwin County MS 400/6-8
149 Chieftain Cir 31774 229-468-5517
Sol Summerlin, prin. Fax 468-3134

Oglethorpe, Macon, Pop. 1,172
Macon County SD 2,300/PK-12
PO Box 488 31068 478-472-8188
Dr. Carolyn Medlock, supt. Fax 472-2042
www.macon.k12.ga.us/
Other Schools – See Montezuma

Oxford, Newton, Pop. 2,040

Oxford College of Emory University Post-Sec.
100 Hamill St 30054 770-784-8888

Peachtree City, Fayette, Pop. 33,010
Fayette County SD
Supt. — See Fayetteville
Booth MS 1,100/6-8
250 S Peachtree Pkwy 30269 770-631-3240
Ted Lombard, prin. Fax 631-3245
McIntosh HS 1,500/9-12
201 Walt Banks Rd 30269 770-631-3232
Tracie Fleming, prin. Fax 631-3278

Pearson, Atkinson, Pop. 1,860
Atkinson County SD 1,700/PK-12
506 E Roberts Ave 31642 912-422-7373
Dr. Joan Wall, supt. Fax 422-7369
www.atkinson.k12.ga.us/
Atkinson County HS 500/8-12
145 Rebel Ln 31642 912-422-3267
Paul Daniel, prin. Fax 422-7889

Pelham, Mitchell, Pop. 3,981
Pelham CSD 1,600/PK-12
188 W Railroad St S 31779 229-294-8715
Dr. Stephen Dunn, supt. Fax 294-2760
Pelham City MS 400/6-8
209 Mathewson Ave SW 31779 229-294-6063
Tom Finland, prin.
Pelham HS 400/9-12
203 Mathewson Ave SW 31779 229-294-8623
Larry Maffit, prin. Fax 294-6069

Pembroke, Bryan, Pop. 2,414
Bryan County SD 6,000/PK-12
66 S Industrial Blvd 31321 912-626-5000
Dr. Sallie Brewer, supt. Fax 653-4386
www.bryan.k12.ga.us/
Bryan County MS 400/6-8
600 Payne Dr 31321 912-626-5050
Deborah Hamm, prin. Fax 653-2705
Bryan County HS 500/9-12
1234 Camellia Dr 31321 912-626-5060
Kay Hughes, prin. Fax 653-2858
Other Schools – See Richmond Hill

Perry, Houston, Pop. 10,566
Houston County SD 22,300/PK-12
PO Box 1850 31069 478-988-6200
Danny Carpenter, supt. Fax 988-6259
www.hcbe.net
Perry HS 1,000/9-12
1307 North Ave 31069 478-988-6298
Dr. Darryl Albritton, prin. Fax 988-6381
Perry MS 900/6-8
495 Perry Pkwy 31069 478-988-6285
Thomas Moore, prin. Fax 988-6345
Other Schools – See Bonaire, Centerville, Warner Robins

Westfield S 700/PK-12
PO Box 2300 31069 478-987-0547
Clint Humphrey, prin. Fax 987-7379

Pinehurst, Dooly, Pop. 367
Dooly County SD
Supt. — See Vienna
Dooly County MS 400/6-8
11949 Highway 41 31070 229-645-3421
Dr. Daniel Sturdivant, prin. Fax 645-3840

Fullington Academy 300/PK-12
PO Box B 31070 229-645-3383
Robert Mooring, hdmstr. Fax 645-3386

Pooler, Chatham, Pop. 8,344
Savannah-Chatham County SD
Supt. — See Savannah
West Chatham MS 1,000/6-8
800 Pine Barren Rd 31322 912-748-3650
Kerry Coursey, prin. Fax 748-3669

Portal, Bulloch, Pop. 584
Bulloch County SD
Supt. — See Statesboro
Portal MSHS 400/6-12
27245 Highway 80 W 30450 912-865-2640
Jimmy Parrish, prin. Fax 865-5659

Powder Springs, Cobb, Pop. 13,760
Cobb County SD
Supt. — See Marietta
Hillgrove HS 9-12
4165 Luther Ward Rd 30127 770-222-2150
Joseph Boland, prin.
Lovinggood MS 6-8
3825 Luther Ward Rd 30127 770-426-3300
McEachern HS 3,200/9-12
2400 New Macland Rd 30127 770-222-3710
Robert Benson, prin. Fax 222-3712
Tapp MS 1,100/6-8
3900 Macedonia Rd 30127 770-222-3758
Denise Magee, prin. Fax 222-3760

Paulding County SD
Supt. — See Dallas
Dobbins MS 1,200/6-8
637 Williams Lake Rd 30127 770-443-4835
Paul Brooksher, prin. Fax 439-1672

Powder Springs Beauty College Post-Sec.
4114 Austell Powder Springs 30127 770-439-9432
Total Learning Center Christian S 300/PK-12
PO Box 13 30127 770-943-2484
Georgia White, prin. Fax 943-9458
Youth Christian S 200/PK-12
4967 Brownsville Rd 30127 770-943-1394
Dennis Willis, prin. Fax 943-0756

Quitman, Brooks, Pop. 4,488
Brooks County SD 2,500/PK-12
PO Box 511 31643 229-263-7531
Debra Folsom, supt. Fax 263-5206
www.brooks.k12.ga.us
Brooks County HS 700/9-12
1081 Barwick Rd 31643 229-263-8923
Howard Akers, prin. Fax 263-7049
Brooks County MS 600/6-8
2171 Moultrie Hwy 31643 229-263-7521
Al Williams, prin. Fax 263-9038

Rabun Gap, Rabun

Rabun Gap-Nacoochee S 300/6-12
339 Nacoochee Dr 30568 706-746-7467
John D. Marshall, hdmstr. Fax 746-2594

Reidsville, Tattnall, Pop. 2,291
Tattnall County SD 3,400/PK-12
146 W Brazell St 30453 912-557-4726
James Turbeville, supt. Fax 557-3036
www.tattnallschools.org/home.asp
Reidsville MS 300/6-8
146 W Brazell St 30453 912-557-3993
Garrett Wilcox, prin. Fax 557-4124
Tattnall County HS 900/9-12
17100 Ga Highway 23 30453 912-557-4374
Bubba Longgrear, prin. Fax 557-4542
Other Schools – See Collins, Glennville

Rex, Clayton
Clayton County SD
Supt. — See Jonesboro
Adamson MS 1,200/6-8
3187 Rex Rd 30273 770-968-2925
Dr. Douglas Hendrix, prin. Fax 968-2949

Richmond Hill, Bryan, Pop. 8,266
Bryan County SD
Supt. — See Pembroke
Richmond Hill HS 1,100/9-12
1 Wildcat Dr 31324 912-459-5151
Charles Spann, prin. Fax 756-4958
Richmond Hill MS 900/6-8
665 Harris Trail Rd 31324 912-459-5130
Helen Herndon, prin. Fax 756-5369

Rincon, Effingham, Pop. 5,598
Effingham County SD
Supt. — See Springfield
Ebenezer MS 800/6-8
1100 Ebenezer Rd 31326 912-754-7757
Elizabeth Helmly, prin. Fax 754-4012

Ringgold, Catoosa, Pop. 2,591
Catoosa County SD 10,000/PK-12
PO Box 130 30736 706-965-2297
Denia Reese, supt. Fax 965-8913
www.catoosa.k12.ga.us
Heritage MS 6-8
4005 Poplar Springs Rd 30736 706-937-3568
Ronnie Bradford, prin. Fax 937-2583
Ringgold HS 1,400/9-12
29 Tiger Trl 30736 706-935-2254
Sharon Vaughn, prin. Fax 965-8910
Ringgold MS 1,300/6-8
217 Tiger Trl 30736 706-935-3381
Lamar Brown, prin. Fax 965-8908
Other Schools – See Fort Oglethorpe, Rossville

Riverdale, Clayton, Pop. 14,880
Clayton County SD
Supt. — See Jonesboro
Riverdale HS 1,900/9-12
160 Roberts Dr 30274 770-473-2905
Dr. Gloria Duncan, prin. Fax 473-2913
Riverdale MS 1,100/6-8
400 Roberts Dr 30274 770-994-4045
Mildred McCoy, prin. Fax 994-4467
Riverdale Vocational HS Vo/Tech
160 Roberts Dr 30274 770-472-3222
Fax 472-3204
Sequoyah MS 6-8
95 Valley Hill Rd SW 30274 770-515-7524
Shauna Heath, prin. Fax 515-7540

Southern Regional Medical Center Post-Sec.
11 Upper Riverdale Rd SW 30274 770-991-8053

Roberta, Crawford, Pop. 771
Crawford County SD 2,100/PK-12
PO Box 8 31078 478-836-3131
Iwanda Dickey, supt. Fax 836-3114
www.crawford.k12.ga.us
Crawford County Comprehensive HS 600/9-12
PO Box 98 31078 478-836-3126
Mike Campbell, prin. Fax 836-4853
Crawford County MS 500/6-8
PO Box 335 31078 478-836-3181
Anthony English, prin. Fax 836-3795

Rochelle, Wilcox, Pop. 1,430
Wilcox County SD
Supt. — See Abbeville
Wilcox County HS 400/9-12
186 7th Ave 31079 229-365-7231
Arney Bryant, prin. Fax 365-7461
Wilcox County MS 300/6-8
114 7th Ave 31079 229-365-2331
Bland Brooks, prin. Fax 365-2641

Rockmart, Polk, Pop. 3,977
Polk County SD
Supt. — See Cedartown
Elm Street MS 700/6-8
100 Morgan Valley Rd 30153 770-684-3151
Greg Christian, prin. Fax 684-1564
Rockmart HS 800/9-12
990 Cartersville Hwy 30153 770-684-5432
Marvin Williams, prin. Fax 684-4768

Coosa Valley Technical College Post-Sec.
466 Brock Rd 30153

Rock Spring, Walker

Northwestern Technical College Post-Sec.
PO Box 569 30739 706-764-3510

Rocky Face, Whitfield
Whitfield County SD
Supt. — See Dalton
West Side MS 600/6-8
580 Lafayette Rd 30740 706-673-2611
Stan Stewart, prin. Fax 673-5349

Rome, Floyd, Pop. 35,303
Floyd County SD 10,400/PK-12
600 Riverside Pkwy NE 30161 706-234-1031
Kelly C. Henson, supt. Fax 236-1824
www.floydboe.net
Armuchee HS 600/9-12
4203 Martha Berry Hwy NW 30165 706-236-1886
Dr. J.C. Burris, prin. Fax 802-6757
Coosa HS 700/9-12
4454 Alabama Hwy NW 30165 706-236-1870
Sam Sprewell, prin. Fax 290-8142
Coosa MS 600/6-8
212 Eagle Dr NW 30165 706-236-1856
Dr. Lisa Landrum, prin. Fax 802-6766
Floyd County Technical HS Vo/Tech
100 Vocational Dr SW 30161 706-236-1860
Kal Oravet, prin. Fax 236-1862
Model HS 600/9-12
3252 Calhoun Rd NE 30161 706-236-1895
Dr. Glenn White, prin. Fax 802-6750
Model MS 500/6-8
164 Barron Rd NE 30161 706-290-8150
David Tucker, prin. Fax 802-6775
Floyd County Transitional Academy Adult
1910 Morrison Campground Rd 30161
706-236-1884
Melinda Strickland, prin. Fax 802-6780
Other Schools – See Armuchee, Lindale

Rome CSD 5,400/PK-12
508 E 2nd St 30161 706-236-5050
Dr. Gayland Cooper, supt. Fax 802-4311
www.rcs.rome.ga.us
Rome HS 1,500/9-12
1000 Veterans Memorial NE 30161 706-235-9653
Dr. J. Tygar Evans, prin. Fax 236-5078
Rome MS 900/7-8
1020 Veterans Memorial NE 30161 706-235-4695
Robert Costley, prin. Fax 234-5903

Coosa Valley Technical Institute Post-Sec.
1 Maurice Culberson Dr SW 30161 706-295-6927
Darlington S 900/PK-12
1014 Cave Spring Rd SW 30161 706-235-6051
Thomas Whitworth, hdmstr. Fax 232-3600
Georgia Highlands College Post-Sec.
PO Box 1864 30162 706-802-5000
Shorter College Post-Sec.
315 Shorter Ave SW 30165 800-868-6980
Unity Christian S 300/PK-12
95 Burton Rd NE 30161 706-292-0700
Glenn Getchell, hdmstr. Fax 292-0772

Rossville, Walker, Pop. 3,406
Catoosa County SD
Supt. — See Ringgold
Lakeview MS 1,200/6-8
416 Cross St 30741 706-866-1040
Bubba Simmons, prin. Fax 861-6644

Walker County SD
Supt. — See La Fayette
Ridgeland HS 1,200/9-12
2478 Happy Valley Rd 30741 706-820-9361
Ron Peck, prin. Fax 820-1342
Rossville MS 600/6-8
1 Bulldog Dr 30741 706-866-2446
Dr. Peggy Norman, prin. Fax 866-1811

Roswell, Fulton, Pop. 78,229
Fulton County SD
Supt. — See Atlanta
Centennial HS 2,100/9-12
9310 Scott Rd 30076 770-650-4230
Scott O'Prey, prin. Fax 650-4250
Crabapple MS 900/6-8
10700 Crabapple Rd 30075 770-552-4520
Dr. Kimothy Jarrett, prin. Fax 552-4524
Elkins Pointe MS 1,000/6-8
11290 Elkins Rd 30076 770-667-2892
Vivian Bankston, prin. Fax 667-2898
Roswell HS 2,200/9-12
11595 King Rd 30075 770-552-4500
Edward Spurka, prin. Fax 552-4509

Blessed Trinity Catholic HS 900/9-12
11320 Woodstock Rd 30075 678-277-9083
Frank Moore, prin. Fax 277-9756
Fellowship Christian S 600/K-12
480 W Crossville Rd 30075 770-993-1650
Donald Wise, prin. Fax 993-9262
North Fulton Beauty College Post-Sec.
408 S Atlanta St Ste 180 30075 770-552-9570

Saint Marys, Camden, Pop. 15,811
Camden County SD
Supt. — See Kingsland
Saint Marys MS 1,000/6-8
205 Martha Dr 31558 912-882-8626
Dr. Jo Beth Bird, prin. Fax 882-5473

Ablaze Academy 50/K-12
300 N Julia St 31558 912-729-6900
Gary Cullins, prin. Fax 576-8944

Saint Simons Island, Glynn, Pop. 12,026

Frederica Academy 400/PK-12
200 Hamilton Rd 31522 912-638-9981
Ellen E. Fleming, hdmstr. Fax 638-1442
Whitefield S 100/PK-12
48 Hampton Point Dr 31522 912-634-8177
Renee Shepherd, admin. Fax 634-2900

Sandersville, Washington, Pop. 5,981
Washington County SD 3,700/PK-12
PO Box 716 31082 478-552-3981
Donna Hinton, supt. Fax 552-3128
www.washington.k12.ga.us/
Elder MS 900/6-8
PO Box 816 31082 478-552-2007
Manzie Broxton, prin. Fax 552-7388
Washington County HS 1,100/9-12
PO Box 1057 31082 478-552-2324
Dewey Carey, prin. Fax 552-3140

Brentwood S 400/PK-12
PO Box 955 31082 478-552-5136
Jackie Holton, prin. Fax 552-2947
Sandersville Technical College Post-Sec.
1189 Deepstep Rd 31082 478-553-2060

Savannah, Chatham, Pop. 127,573
Savannah-Chatham County SD 32,400/PK-12
208 Bull St 31401 912-201-5600
Dr. Thomas Lockamy, supt. Fax 201-5628
www.savannah.chatham.k12.ga.us/
Bartlett MS 800/6-8
207 E Montgomery Xrd 31406 912-961-3500
Robert Lewis, prin. Fax 961-3515
Beach HS 1,300/9-12
3001 Hopkins St 31405 912-201-5330
Deonn Stone, prin. Fax 201-5335
Coastal MS 900/6-8
170 Whitemarsh Island Rd 31410 912-898-3950
Alfred Howard, prin. Fax 898-3951
DeRenne MS 900/6-8
1009 Clinch St 31405 912-201-5900
Marsha Tolbert, prin. Fax 201-5903
Groves HS 1,400/9-12
100 Wheathill Rd 31408 912-965-2520
Cecile Cobb, prin. Fax 965-2564
Hubert MS 500/6-8
768 Grant St 31401 912-201-5235
Dr. Toney Jordan, prin. Fax 201-5238
Jenkins HS 1,700/9-12
1800 E De Renne Ave 31406 912-303-6300
Yolanda Coaxum, prin. Fax 303-6331
Johnson HS 1,200/9-12
3012 Sunset Blvd 31404 912-303-6400
Derrick Muhammad, prin. Fax 303-6418
Myers MS 900/6-8
2025 E 52nd St 31404 912-303-6600
Michael Jones, prin. Fax 303-6601
Savannah Arts Academy 9-12
500 Washington Ave 31405 912-201-5000
Odessa Richards, prin. Fax 201-4160
Savannah HS 1,000/9-12
400 Pennsylvania Ave 31404 912-201-5050
Walter Seabrooks, prin. Fax 201-5055
Shuman MS 700/6-8
415 Goebel Ave 31404 912-201-7500
Dora Myles, prin. Fax 201-7503
Southwest MS 900/6-8
6030 Ogeechee Rd 31419 912-961-3540
Bernadette Ball-Oliver, prin. Fax 961-3548
Tompkins MS 500/6-8
151 Coach Joe Turner St 31408 912-965-6750
Drema Jackson, prin. Fax 965-6768
Windsor Forest HS 1,700/9-12
12419 Largo Dr 31419 912-961-3400
Linda Herman, prin. Fax 961-3422
Adult Education Center Adult
3609 Hopkins St 31405 912-201-5527
Pat Rossiter, prin. Fax 201-5791
Other Schools – See Pooler

Armstrong Atlantic State University Post-Sec.
11935 Abercorn St 31419 800-633-2349

Benedictine Military S 400/9-12
PO Box 13577 31416 912-644-7000
Kelly Burke, prin. Fax 356-3527
Bethesda S 100/1-12
9520 Ferguson Ave 31406 912-351-2055
Irish McCormick, hdmstr. Fax 351-2062
Bible Baptist S 400/PK-12
4700 Skidaway Rd 31404 912-352-3067
Kathryn C. Hodges, admin. Fax 352-9830
Calvary Day S 1,000/PK-12
4625 Waters Ave 31404 912-351-2299
Ralph Finnegan, hdmstr. Fax 351-2280
Chatham Academy 100/1-12
4 Oglethorpe Prfssonal Blvd 31406 912-354-4047
Carolyn Hannaford, prin. Fax 354-4633
Memorial Day S 300/PK-12
6500 Habersham St 31405 912-352-4535
Bill Eaves, hdmstr. Fax 352-4536
Providence Christian S 200/PK-12
4908 Pineland Dr 31405 912-238-5005
David Osborne, hdmstr. Fax 238-8237
St. Andrew's S on the Marsh 400/PK-12
PO Box 30639 31410 912-897-4941
Emeriel Hubbard, hdmstr. Fax 897-4943
St. Vincent Academy 400/9-12
207 E Liberty St 31401 912-236-5508
Sr. Helen Buttimer, prin. Fax 236-7877
Savannah Christian Preparatory S 1,500/PK-12
PO Box 2848 31402 912-234-1653
Roger Yancey, hdmstr. Fax 234-0491
Savannah College of Art & Design Post-Sec.
PO Box 2072 31402 912-525-5000
Savannah Country Day S 1,000/PK-12
824 Stillwood Dr 31419 912-925-8800
Thomas Bonnell, hdmstr. Fax 920-7800
Savannah State University Post-Sec.
3219 College St 31404 912-356-2187
Savannah Technical College Post-Sec.
5717 White Bluff Rd 31405 912-351-6362
South University Post-Sec.
709 Mall Blvd 31406 912-201-8000

Senoia, Coweta, Pop. 2,297
Coweta County SD
Supt. — See Newnan
East Coweta MS 900/6-8
6291 Highway 16 30276 770-599-6607
Derek Pitts, prin. Fax 599-1051

Sharpsburg, Coweta, Pop. 327
Coweta County SD
Supt. — See Newnan
East Coweta HS 2,000/9-12
400 Sharpsburg McCollum Rd 30277 770-254-2850
Kirk Stallings, prin. Fax 254-2857
Lee MS, 370 Willis Rd 30277 6-8
Bob Heaberlin, prin. 770-254-2801

Shellman, Randolph, Pop. 1,094

Randolph Southern S 300/K-12
PO Box 300, 229-679-5324

Siloam, Greene, Pop. 342

Greene Academy 200/PK-12
PO Box 109 30665 706-467-2147
James Prance, hdmstr. Fax 467-2147

Smyrna, Cobb, Pop. 45,610
Cobb County SD
Supt. — See Marietta
Campbell HS 2,100/9-12
5265 Ward St SE 30080 678-842-6850
Kehl Arnson, prin. Fax 842-6852
Campbell MS 1,300/6-8
3295 Atlanta Rd SE 30080 678-842-6873
Lynne Hutnik, prin. Fax 842-6875
Griffin MS 1,000/6-8
4010 King Springs Rd SE 30082 678-842-6917
Darryl York, prin. Fax 842-6919

Atlanta Classical Christian Academy 100/K-12
3110 Sports Ave SE 30080 770-874-8885
Donna Davis, hdmstr. Fax 874-8886
Medix School Post-Sec.
2108 Cobb Pkwy SE 30080 770-980-0002

Snellville, Gwinnett, Pop. 17,961
Gwinnett County SD
Supt. — See Suwanee
Brookwood HS 3,100/9-12
1255 Dogwood Rd 30078 770-972-7642
Jane Stegall, prin. Fax 978-5075
Shiloh HS 2,100/9-12
4210 Shiloh Rd 30039 770-972-8471
Dr. Bill Kruskamp, prin. Fax 736-4345
Shiloh MS 1,600/6-8
4285 Shiloh Rd 30039 770-972-3224
Karen Robinson, prin. Fax 736-4563
Snellville MS 1,800/6-8
3155 Pate Rd 30078 770-972-1530
Linda Boyd, prin. Fax 736-4444
South Gwinnett HS 2,100/9-12
2288 Main St E 30078 770-972-4840
Berry Simmons, prin. Fax 736-4329

Snellville Christian Academy 200/PK-12
PO Box 547 30078 770-979-4966
Laurie Duke, prin. Fax 979-3531

Social Circle, Walton, Pop. 3,722
Social Circle CSD 1,600/PK-12
240B W Hightower Trl 30025 770-464-2731
Dr. Bettye J. Ray, supt. Fax 464-0403
www.scboe.org/
Social Circle HS 400/9-12
154 Alcova Dr 30025 770-464-2611
James Bolton, prin. Fax 464-2612
Social Circle MS 300/6-8
154 Alcova Dr 30025 770-464-1932
Dr. Todd McGhee, prin. Fax 464-2612

Soperton, Treutlen, Pop. 2,769
Treutlen County SD 1,100/K-12
202 3rd St S 30457 912-529-4228
Charles E. Ellington, supt. Fax 529-4226
www.treutlen.k12.ga.us/

Treutlen MSHS
1201 Fowler St 30457 600/6-12
912-529-4536
David L. Avery, prin. Fax 529-6121

Sparks, Cook, Pop. 1,756
Cook County SD
Supt. — See Adel
Cook MS
1000 N Elm St 31647 700/6-8
229-549-5999
Jeff Shealey, prin. Fax 549-5986

Valdosta Technical College Post-Sec.
1001 S Elm St 31647 229-549-7368

Sparta, Hancock, Pop. 1,432
Hancock County SD
PO Box 488 31087 1,500/K-12
706-444-5775
Dr. Awana Leslie, supt. Fax 444-7026
www.hancock.k12.ga.us
Hancock Central MSHS
1311 Highway 15 N 31087 900/6-12
706-444-7009
Stephanie Birdsong, prin. Fax 444-9918

Springfield, Effingham, Pop. 1,971
Effingham County SD
405 N Ash St 31329 9,500/PK-12
912-754-6491
Randy Shearouse, supt. Fax 754-7033
www.effinghamschools.com/
Effingham County HS
1589 GA Highway 119 S 31329 1,400/9-12
912-754-6404
Yancy Ford, prin. Fax 754-6893
Effingham County MS
1290 GA Highway 119 S 31329 600/6-8
912-754-3332
Bobbie Ann Allen, prin. Fax 754-7497
Other Schools – See Guyton, Rincon

Statenville, Echols
Echols County SD
PO Box 207 31648 700/PK-12
229-559-5734
Charles L. Hughes, supt. Fax 559-0484
www.echols.k12.ga.us/
Echols County S
PO Box 40 31648 700/PK-12
229-559-5413
Tim Ragan, prin. Fax 559-0423

Statesboro, Bulloch, Pop. 23,744
Bulloch County SD
150 Williams Rd # A 30458 8,500/PK-12
912-764-6201
Jessie Strickland Ed.D., supt. Fax 764-8436
www.bulloch.k12.ga.us
James MS
18809 US Highway 80 W 30458 600/6-8
912-764-2752
Dr. Daryl Fineran, prin. Fax 489-5916
Langston Chapel MS
156 Langston Chapel Rd 30458 700/6-8
912-681-8779
Elizabeth Williams, prin. Fax 681-6416
Statesboro HS
10 Lester Rd 30458 1,500/9-12
912-489-8751
Marty Waters, prin. Fax 489-5965
Other Schools – See Brooklet, Portal

Bulloch Academy
873 Westside Rd 30458 500/PK-12
912-764-6297
Karolyn Broucek, hdmstr. Fax 764-3165
Georgia Southern University Post-Sec.
PO Box 8024 30460 912-681-5611
Ogeechee Technical College Post-Sec.
1 Joseph E Kennedy Blvd 30458 912-681-5500
Trinity Christian S
571 E Main St 30461 200/K-12
912-489-1375
David Lattner, hdmstr. Fax 764-3136

Stillmore, Emanuel, Pop. 740

Emanuel Academy
PO Box 77 30464 200/K-12
912-562-4405

Stockbridge, Henry, Pop. 11,256
Henry County SD
Supt. — See Mc Donough
Austin Road MS
100 Austin Rd 30281 900/6-8
770-507-5407
Karen Waldon, prin. Fax 507-5413
Stockbridge HS
1151 Old Conyers Rd 30281 1,700/9-12
770-474-8747
Eric Watson, prin. Fax 474-4727
Stockbridge MS
533 Old Conyers Rd 30281 800/6-8
770-474-5710
Vicki Davis, prin. Fax 507-8406

Rockdale County SD
Supt. — See Conyers
Davis MS
3375 E Fairview Rd SW 30281 6-8
770-388-5675
Dr. Wayne Watts, prin.

Community Christian S
2001 Jodeco Rd 30281 800/PK-12
678-432-0191
Dr. Edward Emery, hdmstr. Fax 914-1217
Mt. Vernon Christian S
1738 Fairview Rd 30281 300/PK-12
770-474-1313
John Labor, hdmstr. Fax 474-3010
New Testament Christian Academy
115 Old Conyers Rd 30281 100/PK-12
770-507-5859
Bill Cox, prin. Fax 506-3300

Stone Mountain, DeKalb, Pop. 7,097
DeKalb County SD
Supt. — See Decatur
Freedom MS
505 S Hairston Rd 30088 1,200/6-8
678-874-8702
Paulette Hammonds, prin. Fax 874-8710
Redan HS
5247 Redan Rd 30088 2,000/9-12
678-676-3602
Andrew Tatum, prin. Fax 676-3610
Stephenson HS
701 Stephenson Rd 30087 2,300/9-12
678-676-4202
Morcease Beasley, prin. Fax 676-4210
Stephenson MS
922 Stephenson Rd 30087 1,300/6-8
678-676-4402
Michael Williamson, prin. Fax 676-4410
Stone Mountain HS
4555 Central Dr 30083 1,600/9-12
678-676-6302
Carolyn D. Williams, prin. Fax 676-6310
Stone Mountain MS
5265 Mimosa Dr 30083 1,100/6-8
678-676-4802
Dr. Gloria Dodson, prin. Fax 676-4810

Pro Way Hair School
5684 Memorial Dr 30083 Post-Sec.
770-879-6673

Suches, Union
Union County SD
Supt. — See Blairsville
Woody Gap S
3736 State Highway 60 30572 100/K-12
706-747-2401
Jinjer Taylor, prin. Fax 747-1419

Summerville, Chattooga, Pop. 4,705
Chattooga County SD
33 Middle School Rd 30747 3,200/PK-12
706-857-3447
Mike Poole, supt. Fax 857-3440
www.chattooga.k12.ga.us
Chattooga County HS
989 Highway 114 30747 700/9-12
706-857-2402
Roger Hibbs, prin. Fax 857-2565
Summerville MS
200 Middle School Rd 30747 400/6-8
706-857-2444
Mike Martin, prin. Fax 857-6306

Suwanee, Gwinnett, Pop. 10,562
Gwinnett County SD
437 Old Peachtree Rd NW 30024 128,700/PK-12
678-301-6000
J. Alvin Wilbanks, supt. Fax 301-6030
www.gwinnett.k12.ga.us/
Collins Hill HS
50 Taylor Rd 30024 3,600/9-12
770-682-4100
Glenn McFall, prin. Fax 682-4105
North Gwinnett HS
20 Level Creek Rd 30024 2,800/9-12
770-945-9558
Dr. John Green, prin. Fax 271-5185
Peachtree Ridge HS
1555 Old Peachtree Rd NW 30024 1,900/9-12
678-957-3100
Dr. Steve Flynt, prin.
Other Schools – See Buford, Dacula, Duluth, Hoschton, Lawrenceville, Lilburn, Loganville, Norcross, Snellville

Swainsboro, Emanuel, Pop. 7,063
Emanuel County SD
PO Box 130 30401 4,400/PK-12
478-237-6674
Butch Frye, supt. Fax 237-3404
www.emanuel.k12.ga.us
Swainsboro HS
689 S Main St 30401 1,000/9-12
478-237-2267
Vernon Hardy, prin. Fax 237-3810
Swainsboro MS
200 Tiger Trl 30401 700/6-8
478-237-8047
Wayne Greenway, prin. Fax 237-4295
Other Schools – See Twin City

East Georgia College
131 College Cir 30401 Post-Sec.
478-289-2000
Swainsboro Technical College Post-Sec.
346 Kite Rd 30401 478-289-2200

Sylvania, Screven, Pop. 2,611
Screven County SD
PO Box 1668 30467 3,000/PK-12
912-564-7114
Dr. Whitney Myers, supt. Fax 564-7104
www.screven.k12.ga.us
Screven County HS
PO Box 1688 30467 900/9-12
912-564-7836
Brett Warren, prin. Fax 564-5521
Screven County MS
126 Friendship Rd 30467 800/6-8
912-564-7468
Edwin Lovett, prin. Fax 564-5505

Sylvester, Worth, Pop. 5,903
Worth County SD
504 E Price St 31791 4,100/PK-12
229-776-8600
Dr. Gary L. Russell, supt. Fax 776-8603
www.worth.k12.ga.us
Worth County Comprehensive HS
406 W King St 31791 1,200/9-12
229-776-8625
Barbara Thomas, prin. Fax 777-2075
Worth County MS
1305 N Isabella St 31791 1,100/6-8
229-776-8620
Paul Zimmer, prin. Fax 776-8624

Talbotton, Talbot, Pop. 1,003
Talbot County SD
PO Box 515 31827 200/PK-12
706-665-8528
Robert W. Patrick, supt. Fax 665-3620
www.talbot.k12.ga.us/
Central HS
PO Box 308 31827 200/9-12
706-665-8577
Edward Tymes, prin. Fax 665-3946
Central MS
PO Box 308 31827 6-8
706-665-8578
Edward Tymes, prin. Fax 665-2733

Tallapoosa, Haralson, Pop. 2,956
Haralson County SD
Supt. — See Buchanan
Haralson County Comprehensive HS
1655 Georgia Highway 120 30176 1,000/9-12
770-574-7647
Jim Crocker, prin. Fax 574-7648
Haralson County MS
2633 Georgia Highway 120 30176 900/6-8
770-646-8600
Andy Micacchione, prin. Fax 646-0108

Tallulah Falls, Rabun, Pop. 161

Tallulah Falls S
PO Box 10 30573 200/7-12
706-754-0400
Dr. Kent Anglin, prin. Fax 754-3595

Temple, Paulding, Pop. 3,531
Carroll County SD
Supt. — See Carrollton
Temple HS
589 Sage St 30179 500/9-12
770-562-3218
Mike Angresano, prin. Fax 562-1510
Temple MS
275 Rainey Rd 30179 600/5-8
770-562-6001
Charles Johnson, prin. Fax 562-6002
Villa Rica MS
614 Tumlin Lake Rd 30179 6-8
770-459-0407
James Stocks, prin. Fax 459-5496

Thomaston, Upson, Pop. 9,295
Thomaston-Upson County SD
205 Civic Center Dr 30286 4,700/PK-12
706-647-9621
Dr. Howard Hendley, supt. Fax 647-8705
www.upson.k12.ga.us
Upson-Lee HS
268 Knight Trl 30286 1,400/9-12
706-647-8171
Cleve Hendrix, prin. Fax 647-3708

Upson-Lee MS
101 Holston Dr 30286 1,300/6-8
706-647-6256
Patsy Dean, prin. Fax 647-3631

Flint River Technical College Post-Sec.
1533 Highway 19 S 30286 706-646-6144

Thomasville, Thomas, Pop. 18,233
Thomas County SD
11343 US Highway 319 N 31757 5,000/PK-12
229-225-4380
Dr. Larry Green, supt. Fax 225-5012
www.thomas.k12.ga.us
Thomas County Central HS
4686 US Highway 84 Byp W 31792 1,400/9-12
229-225-5050
Frank Delaney, prin. Fax 227-2422
Thomas County MS
4681 US Highway 84 Byp W 31792 1,800/5-8
229-225-4394
Van Cowart, prin. Fax 225-4378

Thomasville CSD
915 E Jackson St 31792 3,200/PK-12
229-225-2600
Sabrina Boykins-Everett, supt. Fax 226-6997
www.tcitys.org
MacIntyre Park MS
117 Glenwood Dr 31792 700/6-8
229-225-2628
Gene Christie, prin. Fax 225-3502
Thomasville HS
315 S Hansell St 31792 900/9-12
229-225-2634
Dr. Tom McCall, prin. Fax 225-2663

Brookwood S
301 Cardinal Ridge Rd 31792 500/PK-12
229-226-8070
Clauston Jenkins, prin. Fax 227-0326
Southwest Georgia Technical College Post-Sec.
15689 US Highway 19 N 31792 229-225-5096
Thomas University Post-Sec.
1501 Millpond Rd 31792 229-226-1621

Thomson, McDuffie, Pop. 6,782
McDuffie County SD
PO Box 957 30824 4,400/PK-12
706-986-4000
Dr. Mark Petersen, supt. Fax 986-4001
www.mcduffie.k12.ga.us
Thomson HS
PO Box 1077 30824 1,200/9-12
706-986-4200
Rudy Falana, prin. Fax 986-4201
Thomson MS
PO Box 1140 30824 1,000/6-8
706-986-4400
Claude Powell, prin. Fax 986-4496

Tifton, Tift, Pop. 15,862
Tift County SD
PO Box 389 31793 7,500/PK-12
229-387-2400
Dr. John Harper, supt. Fax 386-1020
www.tiftschools.com
Eighth Street MS
700 8th St W 31794 1,200/7-8
229-387-2445
Dr. Ryan Gravitt, prin. Fax 386-1036
Tift County HS
1 Blue Devil Way 31794 1,400/10-12
229-387-2475
Mike Duck, prin. Fax 386-1022
Tift County HS Northeast Campus
3021 Fulwood Rd 31794 600/9-9
229-387-2450
Dr. Willie Miles, prin. Fax 386-1038

Abraham Baldwin Agriculture College Post-Sec.
2802 Moore Hwy 31793 229-391-5000
Moultrie Technical College Post-Sec.
52 Tech Dr 31794 229-391-2600

Tiger, Rabun, Pop. 321
Rabun County SD
Supt. — See Clayton
Rabun County HS
230 Wildcat Hill Dr 30576 600/9-12
706-782-4526
Mark Earnest, prin. Fax 782-7550
Rabun County MS
108 Wildcat Hill Dr 30576 300/7-8
706-782-5470
Kent Woerner, prin. Fax 782-4520

Toccoa, Stephens, Pop. 9,324
Stephens County SD
RR 1 Box 1050 30577 4,400/PK-12
706-886-9415
Gary C. Steppe, supt. Fax 886-3882
www.stephenscountyschools.com
Stephens County HS
6438 White Pine Rd 30577 1,300/9-12
706-886-6825
George Sanders, prin. Fax 886-8765
Stephens County MS
6270 Roselane 30577 1,100/6-8
706-886-2880
Tony Crunkleton, prin. Fax 886-2882

North Georgia Technical College Post-Sec.
8989 GA Highway 17 S 30577 706-779-5591

Toccoa Falls, Stephens

Toccoa Falls College Post-Sec.
PO Box 800899 30598 800-868-3257

Trenton, Dade, Pop. 2,122
Dade County SD
PO Box 188 30752 2,700/PK-12
706-657-4361
Dr. Judy Bean, supt. Fax 657-4572
www.dadecountyschools.org/
Dade County HS
300 Tradition Ln 30752 700/9-12
706-657-7517
Calvin Riddle, prin. Fax 657-4854
Dade MS
250 Pace Dr 30752 600/6-8
706-657-6491
Karen deMarche, prin. Fax 657-3055

Trion, Chattooga, Pop. 2,001
Trion CSD
1255 Pine St 30753 1,300/PK-12
706-734-2363
Dr. Susan Remillard, supt. Fax 734-3397
Trion HS
919 Allgood St 30753 300/9-12
706-734-7316
Dr. Phil Williams, prin. Fax 734-7692
Trion MS
919 Allgood St 30753 300/6-8
706-734-7433
Cindy Anderson, prin. Fax 734-7517

Tucker, DeKalb, Pop. 26,700
DeKalb County SD
Supt. — See Decatur
Tucker HS
5036 Lavista Rd 30084 1,300/9-12
678-874-3702
Scott Butler, prin. Fax 874-3710

Tucker MS 6-8
2160 Idlewood Rd 30084 678-875-0902
Jerry Hogan, prin. Fax 875-0910

Le Cordon Bleu College of Culinary Arts Post-Sec.
1957 Lakeside Pkwy Ste 515 30084 770-938-4711

Tunnel Hill, Whitfield, Pop. 1,220
Whitfield County SD
Supt. — See Dalton
Northwest Whitfield County HS 1,800/9-12
1651 Tunnel Hill Varnell Rd 30755 706-673-6533
Carolyn Towns, prin. Fax 673-7098

Twin City, Emanuel, Pop. 1,760
Emanuel County SD
Supt. — See Swainsboro
Emanuel County Institute 600/6-12
PO Box 218 30471 478-763-2673
Boyd English, prin. Fax 763-3834

Tyrone, Fayette, Pop. 4,783
Fayette County SD
Supt. — See Fayetteville
Flat Rock MS 900/6-8
325 Jenkins Rd 30290 770-969-2830
Oatha Mann, prin. Fax 969-2835
Sandy Creek HS 1,300/9-12
360 Jenkins Rd 30290 770-969-2840
Roy Rabold, prin. Fax 969-2838

Valdosta, Lowndes, Pop. 45,059
Lowndes County SD 9,300/PK-12
PO Box 1227 31603 229-245-2250
Steve Smith, supt. Fax 245-2255
www.lowndes.k12.ga.us
Lowndes HS 2,700/9-12
1112 N Saint Augustine Rd 31601 229-245-2260
Wes Taylor, prin. Fax 245-2468
Lowndes MS 1,100/6-8
2379 Copeland Rd 31601 229-245-2280
Samuel Clemons, prin. Fax 245-2470
Other Schools – See Hahira

Valdosta CSD 7,100/K-12
PO Box 5407 31603 229-333-8500
Sam Allen, supt. Fax 247-7757
www.gocats.org
Newbern MS 800/6-8
2015 E Park Ave 31602 229-333-8566
Dr. Edward Wilson, prin. Fax 245-5655
Valdosta HS 1,900/9-12
3101 N Forrest St 31602 229-333-8540
Brett Stanton, prin. Fax 333-8584
Valdosta MS 900/6-8
110 Burton St 31602 229-333-8555
Martin Roesch, prin. Fax 245-5656

Georgia Christian S 200/PK-12
4359 Dasher Rd 31601 229-559-5131
Open Bible Christian S 400/PK-12
3992 N Oak Street Ext 31605 229-244-6694
Peter D. Smith, prin.
Southland Christian S 200/K-12
2206 E Hill Ave 31601 229-245-8111
Jackie Noble, prin. Fax 245-8189
Valdosta State University Post-Sec.
N Patterson St 31698 229-333-5952
Valdosta Technical College Post-Sec.
4089 Val Tech Rd 31602 229-333-2100

Vidalia, Toombs, Pop. 10,625
Vidalia CSD 2,500/PK-12
301 Adams St 30474 912-537-3088
Tim Smith, supt. Fax 538-0938
www.vidalia-city.k12.ga.us
Trippe MS 500/6-8
2200 McIntosh St 30474 912-537-3813
Gwen Warren, prin. Fax 537-3223
Vidalia HS 700/9-12
1001 North St W 30474 912-537-7931
Mitch Harrington, prin. Fax 537-7508

Southeastern Technical College Post-Sec.
3001 E 1st St 30474 912-538-3100

Vienna, Dooly, Pop. 2,935
Dooly County SD 1,600/PK-12
202 E Cotton St 31092 229-268-4761
Dr. John H. Bembry, supt. Fax 268-6148
www.dooly.k12.ga.us
Dooly County HS 400/9-12
712 N 3rd St 31092 229-268-8181
Randy Ford, prin. Fax 268-1916
Other Schools – See Pinehurst

Villa Rica, Carroll, Pop. 8,087
Carroll County SD
Supt. — See Carrollton
Bay Springs MS 1,100/6-8
122 Bay Springs Rd 30180 770-459-2098
Bruce Tidaback, prin. Fax 459-2097
Villa Rica HS 1,200/9-12
600 Rocky Branch Rd 30180 770-459-5185
Denzil Rogers, prin. Fax 459-2119

Waco, Haralson, Pop. 489

West Central Technical College Post-Sec.
176 Murphy Campus Blvd 30182 770-537-6000

Waleska, Cherokee, Pop. 718

Reinhardt College Post-Sec.
7300 Reinhardt College Cir 30183 770-720-5600

Warm Springs, Meriwether, Pop. 482

Trinity Christian Academy 100/PK-12
PO Box 882 31830 706-655-2080
Angelo DeVivo, admin. Fax 655-2099

Warner Robins, Houston, Pop. 54,264
Houston County SD
Supt. — See Perry
Feagin Mill MS 1,000/6-8
1200 Feagin Mill Rd 31088 478-953-0430
Paige Reaves, prin. Fax 953-0438
Houston County Career & Technology Ctr. Vo/Tech
1311 Corder Rd 31088 478-322-3280
Tim Scott, prin. Fax 322-3294
Houston County HS 2,200/9-12
920 GA Highway 96 31088 478-988-6360
Sheila Beckham, prin. Fax 988-6341
Huntington MS 6-8
206 Wellborn Rd 31088 478-988-7200
Dr. Gwen Taylor, prin.
Northside HS 1,700/9-12
926 Green St 31093 478-929-7858
Dr. J. Robin Hines, prin. Fax 929-7813
Northside MS 700/6-8
500 Johnson Rd 31093 478-929-7845
Ed Mashburn, prin. Fax 929-7124
Warner Robins HS 1,700/9-12
401 S Davis Dr 31088 478-929-7877
Steve Monday, prin. Fax 929-7769
Warner Robins MS 700/6-8
425 Mary Ln 31088 478-929-7832
Dr. Donald Warren, prin. Fax 929-7834

International City Beauty College Post-Sec.
1859 Watson Blvd 31093 478-923-0915
Middle Georgia Technical College Post-Sec.
80 Cohen Walker Dr 31088 478-988-6800

Warrenton, Warren, Pop. 2,016
Warren County SD 900/PK-12
PO Box 228 30828 706-465-3383
Carole Carey, supt. Fax 465-9141
www.warrenschools.com/
Warren County MSHS 400/6-12
1253 Atlanta Hwy 30828 706-465-3742
Dr. Roger Williams, prin. Fax 465-0901

Briarwood Academy 400/PK-12
4859 Thomson Hwy 30828 706-595-5641
John Hammond, hdmstr. Fax 595-0097

Washington, Wilkes, Pop. 4,233
Wilkes County SD 1,700/K-12
313 N Alexander Ave Ste A 30673 706-678-2718
Joyce Williams, supt. Fax 678-3799
www.wilkes.k12.ga.us
Washington-Wilkes Comprehensive HS 500/9-12
304 Gordon St 30673 706-678-2426
Andrew Jackson, prin. Fax 678-2628
Washington-Wilkes MS 400/6-8
304A Gordon St 30673 706-678-7131
Bill Pendrey, prin. Fax 678-3546

Watkinsville, Oconee, Pop. 2,252
Oconee County SD 5,800/PK-12
PO Box 146 30677 706-769-5130
Dr. Thomas Dohrmann, supt. Fax 769-3500
www.oconee.k12.ga.us
Oconee County HS 1,900/9-12
2721 Hog Mountain Rd 30677 706-769-6655
Mark Channell, prin. Fax 769-9499
Oconee County MS 900/6-8
1101 Mars Hill Rd 30677 706-769-3575
Xerona Thomas, prin. Fax 769-3572
Other Schools – See Bogart

Westminster Christian Academy 300/PK-12
1640 New High Shoals Rd 30677 706-769-9372
Dana James, hdmstr. Fax 769-2050

Waycross, Ware, Pop. 15,156
Ware County SD 6,600/PK-12
1301 Bailey St 31501 912-283-8656
Dr. Joseph Barrow, supt. Fax 283-8698
www.ware.k12.ga.us
Ware County HS 1,500/9-12
700 Victory Dr 31503 912-287-2351
Dr. Robert Bussey, prin. Fax 287-2358
Ware County MS 800/6-8
2301 Cherokee St 31503 912-287-2341
Dr. Ken Fields, prin. Fax 287-2353
Waycross MS 600/6-8
700 Central Ave 31501 912-287-2333
Randy Yonz, prin. Fax 287-2352
Other Schools – See Manor

Okefenokee Technical College Post-Sec.
1701 Carswell Ave 31503 912-287-6584
Waycross College Post-Sec.
2100 S Georgia Pkwy W 31503 912-285-6133

Waynesboro, Burke, Pop. 5,865
Burke County SD 4,400/PK-12
789 Perimeter Rd 30830 706-554-5101
C. Douglas Day, supt. Fax 554-8051
www.burke.k12.ga.us
Burke County HS 1,200/9-12
1057 Perimeter Rd 30830 706-554-6691
Chris Henry, prin. Fax 554-8070
Burke County MS 1,200/6-8
356 Southside Dr 30830 706-554-3532
Daphney Ivery, prin. Fax 554-8063

Burke Academy 400/K-12
403 GA Highway 56 S 30830 706-554-4479
Brent Cribb, hdmstr. Fax 554-7582

Winder, Barrow, Pop. 11,654
Barrow County SD 9,800/PK-12
PO Box 767 30680 770-867-4527
Dr. Ron Saunders, supt. Fax 867-4540
www.barrow.k12.ga.us
Apalachee HS 1,200/9-12
940 Haymon Morris Rd 30680 770-586-5111
Dr. Dennis Clarke, prin. Fax 586-5905
Haymon Morris MS 6-8
1008 Haymon Morris Rd 30680 678-963-0602
Dr. Sheila Kahrs, prin.
Russell MS 800/6-8
84 W Midland Ave 30680 770-867-8181
David McGee, prin. Fax 868-1215
Westside MS 900/6-8
PO Box 643 30680 770-307-2972
Dr. Shelia Kahrs, prin. Fax 307-2976
Winder-Barrow HS 1,300/9-12
272 N 5th Ave 30680 770-867-4519
Rob Johnson, prin. Fax 867-6412
Winder-Barrow MS 700/6-8
163 King St 30680 770-867-2116
Mary Beth Deaton, prin. Fax 868-1421
Adult Learning Center Adult
89 E Athens St 30680 770-307-1190
Lisa Maloof, dir. Fax 867-8018

Hope Christian Academy 100/PK-12
8 Pleasant Hll Church Rd SE 30680 770-725-2521

Woodbury, Meriwether, Pop. 1,121

Flint River Academy 300/PK-12
PO Box 247 30293 706-553-2541
Connie Strickland, hdmstr. Fax 553-9777

Woodstock, Cherokee, Pop. 14,889
Cherokee County SD
Supt. — See Canton
Booth MS 1,200/7-8
6550 Putnam Ford Dr 30189 770-926-5707
Rick Townsend, prin. Fax 928-2908
Etowah HS 1,900/9-12
6565 Putnam Ford Dr 30189 770-926-4411
Ron Dunnavant, prin. Fax 926-4157
Woodstock HS 2,200/9-12
2010 Towne Lake Hills S Dr 30189 770-592-3500
Bill Sebring, prin. Fax 592-3509
Woodstock MS 1,200/7-8
2000 Twn Lake Hlls South Dr 30189 770-592-3516
Richard Landolt, prin. Fax 591-8054
Polaris Evening S Adult
2010 Towne Lake Hls S Dr 30189 770-926-1662
Dr. Judy Battles, prin. Fax 592-3509

Cherokee Christian S 400/K-12
3075 Trickum Rd 30188 678-494-5464
Michael Lee, hdmstr. Fax 592-4881

Wrens, Jefferson, Pop. 2,244
Jefferson County SD
Supt. — See Louisville
Wrens MS 300/6-8
101 Griffin St 30833 706-547-6580
Julia Wells, prin. Fax 547-6224

Wrightsville, Johnson, Pop. 3,003
Johnson County SD 1,400/PK-12
PO Box 110 31096 478-864-3302
Dorothy Reynolds, supt. Fax 864-4053
www.johnson.k12.ga.us/
Johnson County HS 400/9-12
210 Trojan Way 31096 478-864-2222
Dr. Michael Akes, prin. Fax 864-4054
Johnson County MS 300/6-8
210 Trojan Way 31096 478-864-2222
Curtis Dixon, prin. Fax 864-4054
Alternative S, 290 Trojan Way 31096 Adult
Willie Greene, prin. 478-864-1760

Young Harris, Towns, Pop. 549

Young Harris College Post-Sec.
PO Box 98 30582 706-379-3111

Zebulon, Pike, Pop. 1,158
Pike County SD 3,000/PK-12
PO Box 386 30295 770-567-8489
Dr. Michael Duncan, supt. Fax 567-8349
www.pike.k12.ga.us/
Pike County HS 800/9-12
PO Box 819 30295 770-567-8770
Charles Garrard, prin. Fax 567-1628
Pike County MS 700/6-8
PO Box 405 30295 770-567-3353
Herbert Hodges, prin. Fax 567-3047

HAWAII

HAWAII DEPARTMENT OF EDUCATION
PO Box 2360, Honolulu 96804-2360
Telephone 808-586-3232
Fax 808-586-3234
Website doe.k12.hi.us

Superintendent of Education   Patricia Hamamoto

HAWAII BOARD OF EDUCATION
PO Box 2360, Honolulu 96804-2360

Chairperson   Randall Yee

PUBLIC, PRIVATE AND CATHOLIC SECONDARY SCHOOLS

Aiea, Honolulu, Pop. 8,906
Hawaii SD
  Supt. — See Honolulu
Aiea HS   1,200/9-12
  98-1276 Ulune St 96701   808-483-7300
  Michael Tokioka, prin.   Fax 483-7303
Aiea IS   700/7-8
  99-600 Kulawea St 96701   808-483-7230
  Tom Kurashige, prin.   Fax 483-7235

Hollywood Beauty College   Post-Sec.
  99-084 Kauhale St Bldg A 96701   808-486-7255

Ewa Beach, Honolulu, Pop. 14,315
Hawaii SD
  Supt. — See Honolulu
Campbell HS   1,900/9-12
  91-980 North Rd 96706   808-689-1200
  Gail Awakuni, prin.   Fax 689-1242
Ilima IS   1,200/7-8
  91-884 Fort Weaver Rd 96706   808-689-1250
  Jon Kitabayashi, prin.   Fax 689-1258

Lanakila Baptist HS   100/7-12
  91-1219 Renton Rd 96706   808-681-3146
  Rick Denham, prin.   Fax 681-0704

Hana, Maui, Pop. 683
Hawaii SD
  Supt. — See Honolulu
Hana S   400/K-12
  PO Box 128 96713   808-248-4815
  Richard Paul, prin.   Fax 248-4819

Hilo, Hawaii, Pop. 40,759
Hawaii SD
  Supt. — See Honolulu
Hilo HS   1,500/9-12
  556 Waianuenue Ave 96720   808-974-4021
  Robert Dircks, prin.   Fax 974-4036
Hilo IS   700/7-8
  587 Waianuenue Ave 96720   808-974-4955
  Elaine Christian, prin.   Fax 974-6184
Waiakea HS   1,300/9-12
  155 W Kawili St 96720   808-974-4888
  Dr. Patricia Nekoba, prin.   Fax 974-4880
Waiakea IS   900/6-8
  200 W Puainako St 96720   808-981-7231
  Maureen Duffy, prin.   Fax 981-7237
Hilo Community S   Adult
  450 Waianuenue Ave # C 96720   808-974-4100
  Leonard Paik, prin.   Fax 974-6170

Hawaii Community College   Post-Sec.
  200 W Kawili St 96720   808-974-7311
St. Joseph JSHS   200/7-12
  1000 Ululani St 96720   808-935-4936
  Sr. Marion Kikukawa, prin.   Fax 969-9019
University of Hawaii at Hilo   Post-Sec.
  200 W Kawili St 96720   808-933-3301

Holualoa, Hawaii, Pop. 3,834

Makua Lani Christian S   100/8-12
  74-4947 Mamalahoa Hwy 96725   808-329-4898
  Thaddea Pitts, prin.   Fax 334-0969

Honokaa, Hawaii, Pop. 2,186
Hawaii SD
  Supt. — See Honolulu
Honoka'a MSHS   800/7-12
  45-527 Pakalana St 96727   808-775-8800
  Natale Gonsalves, prin.   Fax 775-8803

Honolulu, Honolulu, Pop. 378,155
Hawaii SD   179,100/PK-12
  PO Box 2360 96804   808-586-3230
  Patricia Hamamoto, supt.   Fax 586-3234
  doe.k12.hi.us/
Aliamanu MS   900/7-8
  3271 Salt Lake Blvd 96818   808-421-4100
  Robert Eggleston, prin.   Fax 421-4103
Anuenue S   400/K-12
  2528 10th Ave 96816   808-733-8465
  Charles Naumu, prin.   Fax 733-8467
Central MS   600/6-8
  1302 Queen Emma St 96813   808-587-4400
  Melissa Trew, prin.   Fax 587-4409

Dole MS   800/6-8
  1803 Kamehameha IV Rd 96819   808-832-3340
  Myron Monte, prin.   Fax 832-3349
Farrington HS   2,400/9-12
  1564 N King St 96817   808-832-3600
  Catherine Payne, prin.   Fax 832-3587
Jarrett MS   300/6-8
  1903 Palolo Ave 96816   808-733-4888
  Gerald Teramae, prin.   Fax 733-4894
Kaimuki HS   1,300/9-12
  2705 Kaimuki Ave 96816   808-733-4900
  Dennis Manalili, prin.   Fax 733-4929
Kaimuki MS   700/6-8
  631 18th Ave 96816   808-733-4800
  Frank Fernandes, prin.   Fax 733-4810
Kaiser HS   1,000/9-12
  511 Lunalilo Home Rd 96825   808-394-1200
  Larry Kaliloa, prin.   Fax 394-1245
Kalakaua MS   1,000/6-8
  821 Kalihi St 96819   808-832-3130
  Randal Tanaka, prin.   Fax 832-3140
Kalani HS   1,100/9-12
  4680 Kalanianaole Hwy 96821   808-377-7744
  Randiann Porras-Tang, prin.   Fax 377-2483
Kawananakoa MS   800/6-8
  49 Funchal St 96813   808-587-4430
  Sandra Ishihara-Shibata, prin.   Fax 587-4443
McKinley HS   1,900/9-12
  1039 S King St 96814   808-594-0400
  Milton Shishido, prin.   Fax 594-0407
Moanalua HS   2,000/9-12
  2825 Ala Ilima St 96818   808-837-8455
  Darrel Galera, prin.   Fax 831-7919
Moanalua MS   900/7-8
  1289 Mahiole St 96819   808-831-7850
  Caroline Wong, prin.   Fax 831-7859
Niu Valley MS   600/6-8
  310 Halemaumau St 96821   808-377-2440
  John Flynn, prin.   Fax 377-2444
Radford HS   1,300/9-12
  4361 Salt Lake Blvd 96818   808-421-4200
  Robert Stevens, prin.   Fax 421-4210
Roosevelt HS   1,600/9-12
  1120 Nehoa St 96822   808-587-4600
  Dennis Hokama, prin.   Fax 587-4637
Stevenson MS   600/6-8
  1202 Prospect St 96822   808-587-4520
  Burton Amine, prin.   Fax 587-4523
Washington MS   1,000/6-8
  1633 S King St 96826   808-973-0177
  Michael Harano, prin.   Fax 973-0181
Farrington Community S   Adult
  1101 Kalihi St 96819   808-832-3595
  Liberato Viduya, prin.   Fax 832-3588
Kaimuki Community S   Adult
  2705 Kaimuki Ave 96816   808-733-8460
  Richard Matsumoto, prin.   Fax 733-8463
McKinley Community S   Adult
  634 Pensacola St Ste 216 96814   808-594-0540
  Helen Sanpei, prin.   Fax 594-0544
Moanalua/Aiea Community S   Adult
  2825A Ala Ilima St 96818   808-837-8466
  Aileen Hokama, prin.   Fax 837-7926
Other Schools – See Aiea, Ewa Beach, Hana, Hilo,
Honokaa, Hoolehua, Kahuku, Kahului, Kailua, Kailua
Kona, Kaneohe, Kapaa, Kapaau, Kapolei, Keaau,
Kealakekua, Kihei, Lahaina, Lanai City, Laupahoehoe,
Lihue, Makawao, Mililani, Pahala, Pahoa, Pearl City,
Wahiawa, Waialua, Waianae, Wailuku, Waimea,
Waipahu

Academy of the Pacific   200/6-12
  913 Alewa Dr 96817   808-595-6359
  Mollie Sperry, hdmstr.   Fax 595-4235
Argosy University/Hawaii   Post-Sec.
  1001 Bishop St Ste 400 96813   808-536-5555
ASSETS S   400/K-12
  1 Ohana Nui Way 96818   808-423-1356
  Lou Salza, hdmstr.   Fax 422-1920
Babel University Professional School   Post-Sec.
  1720 Ala Moana Blvd Ste A5 96815   808-946-3773
Chaminade University of Honolulu   Post-Sec.
  3140 Waialae Ave 96816   808-735-4711
Christian Academy   300/PK-12
  3400 Moanalua Rd 96819   808-836-0233
  Kenton Werk, prin.   Fax 836-4415
Clayton University   Post-Sec.
  1160 N King St # MSC-106 96817   - -

Damien Memorial S   400/7-12
  1401 Houghtailing St 96817   808-841-0195
  Michael Weaver, prin.   Fax 847-1401
Hawaiian Mission Academy   100/9-12
  1438 Pensacola St 96822   808-536-2207
  Josue Rosado, prin.   Fax 524-3294
Hawaii Baptist Academy   500/7-12
  2429 Pali Hwy 96817   808-595-6301
  Marsha Hirae, prin.   Fax 595-6354
Hawaii Business College   Post-Sec.
  33 S King St Fl 4 96813   808-524-4014
Hawaii Institute of Hair Design   Post-Sec.
  71 S Hotel St 96813   808-533-6596
Hawaii Pacific University   Post-Sec.
  1164 Bishop St 96813   808-544-0200
Hawaii School for the Deaf and the Blind   Post-Sec.
  3440 Leahi Ave 96815
Hawaii Technology Institute   Post-Sec.
  629 Pohukaina St 96813   808-522-2700
Hawaii Theological Seminary   Post-Sec.
  PO Box 861754 96786   808-622-4487
Hawaii Tokai International College   Post-Sec.
  2241 Kapiolani Blvd 96826   808-983-4100
Heald College   Post-Sec.
  1500 Kapiolani Blvd 96814   808-955-1500
Honolulu Community College   Post-Sec.
  874 Dillingham Blvd 96817   808-845-9211
Honolulu Waldorf High S   100/9-12
  1339 Hunakai St 96816   808-735-9311
     Fax 735-5292
Institute of Clinical Acupuncture   Post-Sec.
  1270 Queen Emma St Ste 107 96813   808-521-2288
Iolani S   1,800/K-12
  563 Kamoku St 96826   808-949-5355
  Val Iwashita, hdmstr.   Fax 943-2354
Kamehameha S - Kalapama Campus   3,200/K-12
  2010 Princess Dr 96817   808-842-8211
  Michael Chun, hdmstr.   Fax 842-8411
Kapiolani Community College   Post-Sec.
  4303 Diamond Head Rd 96816   808-734-9111
La Pietra S For Girls   300/6-12
  2933 Poni Moi Rd 96815   808-922-2744
  Nancy White, hdmstr.   Fax 923-4514
Lutheran HS of Hawaii   100/9-12
  1404 University Ave 96822   808-949-5302
  Arthur Gundell, prin.   Fax 947-3701
Maryknoll HS   600/9-12
  1526 Alexander St 96822   808-952-7200
  Betsey Gunderson, prin.   Fax 952-7201
Medical Assisting School of Hawaii   Post-Sec.
  33 S King St Ste 223 96813   808-524-3363
Mid-Pacific Institute   1,100/6-12
  2445 Kaala St 96822   808-973-5000
  Joe Rice, prin.   Fax 973-5099
New York Technical Institute of Hawaii   Post-Sec.
  1375 Dillingham Blvd 96817   808-841-5827
Punahou S   3,700/K-12
  1601 Punahou St 96822   808-944-5711
  Dr. James K. Scott, pres.   Fax 944-5779
Remington College   Post-Sec.
  1111 Bishop St Ste 400 96813   808-942-1000
Sacred Hearts Academy   1,100/PK-12
  3253 Waialae Ave 96816   808-734-5058
  Betty White, prin.   Fax 737-7867
St. Andrew's Priory S   500/K-12
  224 Queen Emma Sq 96813   808-536-6102
  Marilyn Matsunaga, hdmstr.   Fax 538-1035
St. Francis HS   500/6-12
  2707 Pamoa Rd 96822   808-988-4111
  Sr. Joan of Arc Souza, prin.   Fax 988-5497
St. Louis HS   900/4-12
  3142 Waialae Ave 96816   808-739-7777
  Fr. Allen DeLong, prin.   Fax 739-4853
TransPacific Hawaii College   Post-Sec.
  5257 Kalanianaole Hwy 96821   808-377-5402
Travel Institute of the Pacific   Post-Sec.
  1314 S King St Ste 1164 96814   808-591-2708
University of Hawaii at Manoa   Post-Sec.
  2444 Dole St 96822   808-956-8111
Word of Life Academy   500/PK-12
  550 Queen St 96813   808-550-0238
  David Sauceda, prin.   Fax 550-0225
World Medicine Institute   Post-Sec.
  1110 University Ave Ste 308 96826   808-949-1050

Hoolehua, Maui
Hawaii SD
  Supt. — See Honolulu

Moloka'i HS 500/9-12
PO Box 158 96729 808-567-6950
Linda Puleloa, prin. Fax 567-6960
Molokai IS 7-8
PO Box 443 96729 808-567-6950
Gary Zukeran, prin. Fax 567-6960

Kahuku, Honolulu, Pop. 2,063
Hawaii SD
Supt. — See Honolulu
Kahuku JSHS 1,900/7-12
56-490 Kamehameha Hwy 96731 808-293-8950
Lisa DeLong, prin. Fax 293-8960

Kahului, Maui, Pop. 16,889
Hawaii SD
Supt. — See Honolulu
Maui HS 1,700/9-12
660 Lono Ave 96732 808-873-3000
Randy Yamanuha, prin. Fax 873-3010
Maui Waena IS 1,000/6-8
795 Onehee Ave 96732 808-873-3070
Jamie Yap, prin. Fax 873-3066
Maui Community S for Adults Adult
179 Kaahumanu Ave 96732 808-873-3082
Gwen Ueoka, prin. Fax 873-3046

Ka'ahumanu Hou Christian Schools of Maui 200/PK-12
777 Mokulele Hwy 96732 808-871-2477
David Marocco, prin. Fax 871-5668
Maui Community College Post-Sec.
310 W Kaahumanu Ave 96732 808-244-9181

Kailua, Honolulu
Hawaii SD
Supt. — See Honolulu
Kailua HS 1,000/9-12
451 Ulumanu Dr 96734 808-266-7900
Francine Honda, prin. Fax 266-7915
Kailua IS 900/7-8
145 S Kainalu Dr 96734 808-263-1500
Suzanne Mulcahy, prin. Fax 266-7984
Kalaheo HS 1,100/9-12
730 Iliaina St 96734 808-254-7900
James Schlosser, prin. Fax 254-7907
Olomana JSHS 400/7-12
42-471 Kalanianaole Hwy 96734 808-266-7866
August Suehiro, prin. Fax 266-7873
Windward S for Adults Adult
730 Iliaina St 96734 808-254-7955
Gary Takaki, prin. Fax 254-7958

Le Jardin Academy 800/PK-12
917 Kalanianaole Hwy 96734 808-261-0707
Adrian Allan, prin. Fax 262-9339
Redemption Academy 200/PK-12
355 N Kainalu Dr 96734 808-266-2341
Adrian Yuen Ph.D., admin. Fax 266-2342

Kailua Kona, Hawaii, Pop. 45,944
Hawaii SD
Supt. — See Honolulu
Kealakehe HS 1,400/9-12
74-5000 Puohulihuli St 96740 808-327-4300
Wilfred Murakami, prin. Fax 327-4307
Kealakehe IS 1,000/6-8
74-5062 Onipaa St 96740 808-327-4314
Donald Merwin, prin. Fax 327-4315
Kona Community S Adult
74-5000 Puohulihuli St 96740 808-327-4692
Robert Krueger, prin. Fax 327-4693

Hualalai Academy 200/K-12
74-4966 Kealakaa St 96740 808-326-9866
Felicity Johnson, prin. Fax 329-9542

Kamuela, Hawaii, Pop. 5,972

Hawaii Prep Academy 600/K-12
PO Box 428 96743 808-885-7321
Olaf Jorgenson, hdmstr. Fax 881-4003
Parker S 300/K-12
65-1224 Lindsey Rd 96743 808-885-7933
Carl Sturges, prin. Fax 885-6233
Traditional Chinese Medical College HI Post-Sec.
65-1206 Mamalahoa Hwy 96743 808-885-9226

Kaneohe, Honolulu, Pop. 34,970
Hawaii SD
Supt. — See Honolulu
Castle HS 1,800/9-12
45-386 Kaneohe Bay Dr 96744 808-233-5600
Meredith Maeda, prin. Fax 233-5623
King IS 900/7-8
46-155 Kamehameha Hwy 96744 808-233-5727
Cynthia Chun, prin. Fax 233-5747

Christian Education Institute 50/K-12
45-416 Kamehameha Hwy 96744 808-247-8186
Robin Spencer, admin. Fax 234-5753
Golf Academy of Hawaii Post-Sec.
45-550 Kionaole Rd 96744 800-342-7342
Hawaii Pacific University Post-Sec.
45-045 Kamehameha Hwy 96744 808-235-3641
Koolau Baptist Academy 200/PK-12
PO Box 1642 96744 808-233-2900
John Goodale, prin. Fax 233-2903
Windward Community College Post-Sec.
45-720 Keaahala Rd 96744 808-235-7400

Kapaa, Kauai, Pop. 8,149
Hawaii SD
Supt. — See Honolulu
Kapaa HS 1,100/9-12
4695 Mailihuna Rd 96746 808-821-4400
Gilmore Youn, prin. Fax 821-4420
Kapaa MS 700/6-8
4867 Olohena Rd 96746 808-821-4460
Mary Ann Bode, prin. Fax 821-6967

Kapaau, Hawaii, Pop. 1,083
Hawaii SD
Supt. — See Honolulu
Kohala HS 300/9-12
PO Box 279 96755 808-889-7117
Catherine Bratt, prin. Fax 889-7120
Kohala MS 200/6-8
PO Box 777 96755 808-889-7119
Barbara Volhein, prin. Fax 889-7121

Kapolei, Honolulu, Pop. 1,000
Hawaii SD
Supt. — See Honolulu
Kapolei HS 1,900/9-12
91-5007 Kapolei Pkwy 96707 808-692-8200
Alvin Nagasako, prin. Fax 692-8255
Kapolei MS 1,700/6-8
91-5335 Kapolei Pkwy 96707 808-693-7025
Annette Nishikawa, prin. Fax 693-7030

Keaau, Hawaii, Pop. 1,584
Hawaii SD
Supt. — See Honolulu
Kea'au HS 900/9-12
16-725 Keaau Pahoa Rd 96749 808-982-4220
Ann Paulino, prin. Fax 982-4224
Kea'au MS 600/6-8
16-565 Keaau Pahoa Rd 96749 808-982-4200
Jamil Ahmadia, prin. Fax 982-4219

Christian Liberty S 100/PK-12
16-675 Milo St 96749 808-966-8866
Troy Rimel, prin. Fax 966-8866
Kamehameha S - Hawaii Campus 1,000/K-12
16-714 Volcano Rd 96749 808-982-0007
Stan Fortuna, prin. Fax 982-0010

Kealakekua, Hawaii, Pop. 1,453
Hawaii SD
Supt. — See Honolulu
Konawaena HS 900/9-12
81-1043 Konawaena School Rd 96750 808-323-4500
Shawn Suzuki, prin. Fax 323-4515
Konawaena MS 400/6-8
81-1045 Konawaena School Rd 96750 808-323-4566
Nancy Soderberg, prin. Fax 323-4574

Kihei, Maui, Pop. 11,107
Hawaii SD
Supt. — See Honolulu
Lokelani IS 800/6-8
1401 Liloa Dr 96753 808-875-6800
Donna Whitford, prin. Fax 875-6835

Kilauea, Kauai, Pop. 1,685

Kula HS 100/7-12
4551 Kapuna Rd 96754 808-828-0077
David Mireles, hdmstr. Fax 828-0107

Lahaina, Maui, Pop. 9,073
Hawaii SD
Supt. — See Honolulu
Lahaina IS 600/6-8
871 Lahainaluna Rd 96761 808-662-3965
Marsha Nakamura, prin. Fax 662-3968
Lahainaluna HS 1,000/9-12
980 Lahainaluna Rd 96761 808-662-4000
Michael Nakano, prin. Fax 662-3997

Laie, Honolulu, Pop. 5,577

Brigham Young University Post-Sec.
55-220 Kulanui St 96762 808-293-3211

Lanai City, Maui, Pop. 2,400
Hawaii SD
Supt. — See Honolulu
Lanai S 600/K-12
PO Box 630630 96763 808-565-7900
Pierce Myers, prin. Fax 565-7904

Laupahoehoe, Hawaii, Pop. 508
Hawaii SD
Supt. — See Honolulu
Laupahoehoe S 200/K-12
PO Box 189 96764 808-962-2200
Cheryl Merk, prin. Fax 962-2202

Lawai, Kauai, Pop. 1,787

Kahili Adventist S 100/K-12
PO Box 480 96765 808-742-9294
Bud Moon Ph.D., prin. Fax 742-6628

Lihue, Kauai, Pop. 5,536
Hawaii SD
Supt. — See Honolulu
Kamakahelei MS 1,000/6-8
4431 Nuhou St 96766 808-241-3200
Cynthia Metsuoka, prin. Fax 241-3210
Kauai HS 1,300/9-12
3577 Lala Rd 96766 808-274-3160
Linda Tanouye Smith, prin. Fax 274-3170
Kauai Community S for Adults Adult
3607A Lala Rd # P-12 96766 808-274-3390
Eugene Uegawa, prin. Fax 274-3393

Island S 300/PK-12
3-1875 Kaumualii Hwy 96766 808-246-0233
Robert Springer, prin. Fax 245-6053
Kauai Community College Post-Sec.
3-1901 Kaumualii Hwy 96766 808-245-8311

Makawao, Maui, Pop. 5,405
Hawaii SD
Supt. — See Honolulu
Kalama IS 1,100/6-8
120 Makani Rd 96768 808-573-8735
John Costales, prin. Fax 573-8748
Kekaulike HS 1,400/9-12
121 Kula Hwy 96768 808-573-8710
Susan Scofield, prin. Fax 573-2231

Kamehemaha S Maui Campus 1,100/K-12
270 Aapueo Pkwy 96768 808-572-3100
Dr. E. Rodney Chamberlain, hdmstr. Fax 573-7062
Seabury Hall S 400/6-12
480 Olinda Rd 96768 808-572-7235
Joseph J. Schmidt, hdmstr. Fax 572-7196

Mililani, Honolulu, Pop. 28,608
Hawaii SD
Supt. — See Honolulu
Mililani HS 2,300/9-12
95-1200 Meheula Pkwy 96789 808-627-7747
Dr. John Brummel, prin. Fax 627-7375
Mililani MS 1,900/6-8
95-1140 Lehiwa Dr 96789 808-626-7355
Roger Kim, prin. Fax 626-7358

Hanalani S 700/PK-12
94-294 Anania Dr 96789 808-625-0737
Mark Sugimoto, supt. Fax 625-0691

Pahala, Hawaii, Pop. 1,520
Hawaii SD
Supt. — See Honolulu
Ka'u & Pahala S 500/K-12
PO Box 100 96777 808-928-2088
Josephine DeMorales, prin. Fax 928-2092

Pahoa, Hawaii, Pop. 1,027
Hawaii SD
Supt. — See Honolulu
Pahoa JSHS 800/7-12
15-3038 Puna Rd 96778 808-965-2150
Maring Gacusana, prin. Fax 965-2153

Pearl City, Honolulu, Pop. 30,976
Hawaii SD
Supt. — See Honolulu
Highlands IS 1,100/7-8
1460 Hoolaulea St 96782 808-453-6480
Amy Martinson, prin. Fax 453-6484
Pearl City HS 2,000/9-12
2100 Hookiekie St 96782 808-453-6500
Gerald Suyama, prin. Fax 453-6521

Leeward Community College Post-Sec.
96-045 Ala Ike St 96782 808-455-0011
University of Hawaii - West Oahu Post-Sec.
96-129 Ala Ike St 96782 808-454-4700

Wahiawa, Honolulu, Pop. 17,386
Hawaii SD
Supt. — See Honolulu
Leilehua HS 1,800/9-12
1515 California Ave 96786 808-622-6550
Norman Minehira, prin. Fax 622-6554
Wahiawa MS 1,000/6-8
275 Rose St 96786 808-622-6500
Dr. Carol Price, prin. Fax 622-6506
Wheeler MS 600/6-8
2 Wheeler Army Airfield 96786 808-622-6525
Brenda Vierra-Chun, prin. Fax 622-6529
Wahiawa Community S Adult
1515 California Ave 96786 808-622-1634
Leighton Hasegawa, prin. Fax 621-7765

Ho'ala S 100/K-12
1067 California Ave Ste A 96786 808-621-1898
Nancy G. Barry, prin. Fax 622-3615

Waialua, Honolulu, Pop. 3,943
Hawaii SD
Supt. — See Honolulu
Waialua JSHS 800/7-12
67-160 Farrington Hwy 96791 808-637-8200
Valarie Kardash, prin. Fax 637-8209

Waianae, Honolulu, Pop. 8,758
Hawaii SD
Supt. — See Honolulu
Nanakuli JSHS 1,400/7-12
89-980 Nanakuli Ave 96792 808-668-5823
Levi Chang, prin. Fax 668-5828
Waianae HS 1,900/9-12
85-251 Farrington Hwy 96792 808-697-7017
JoAnn Kumasaka, prin. Fax 697-7018
Waianae IS 1,200/7-8
85-626 Farrington Hwy 96792 808-697-7121
John Vannatta, prin. Fax 697-7124

Maili Bible S 100/K-12
87-138 Gilipake St 96792 808-696-3038
Larry Estrella, prin. Fax 696-3060

Wailuku, Maui, Pop. 10,688
Hawaii SD
Supt. — See Honolulu
Baldwin HS 1,700/9-12
1650 Kaahumanu Ave 96793 808-984-5656
Stephen Yamada, prin. Fax 984-5674
Iao IS 800/6-8
1910 Kaohu St 96793 808-984-5610
Catherine Kilborn, prin. Fax 984-5617

St. Anthony JSHS 400/7-12
1618 Lower Main St 96793 808-244-4190
Edwina Wilson-Snyder, prin. Fax 242-8081

Waimea, Kauai, Pop. 7,812
Hawaii SD
Supt. — See Honolulu
Niihau S, PO Box 339 96796 300/K-12
William Arakaki, prin. 808-338-6800
Waimea HS 900/9-12
PO Box 339 96796 808-338-6800
William Arakaki, prin. Fax 338-6807

Waipahu, Honolulu, Pop. 33,108
Hawaii SD
Supt. — See Honolulu
Waipahu HS 2,300/9-12
94-1211 Farrington Hwy 96797 808-675-0222
Patricia Pedersen, prin. Fax 675-0257
Waipahu IS 1,400/7-8
94-455 Farrington Hwy 96797 808-675-0177
Randell Dunn, prin. Fax 675-0181
Waipahu Community S Adult
94-1211 Farrington Hwy 96797 808-675-0254
David Stern, prin. Fax 675-0259

IDAHO

IDAHO DEPARTMENT OF EDUCATION
PO Box 83720, Boise 83720-0003
Telephone 208-332-6800
Fax 208-332-6836
Website http://www.sde.state.id.us
Superintendent of Public Instruction   Marilyn Howard

IDAHO BOARD OF EDUCATION
PO Box 83720, Boise 83720-0003
President   Laird Stone

PUBLIC, PRIVATE AND CATHOLIC SECONDARY SCHOOLS

Aberdeen, Bingham, Pop. 1,839
Aberdeen SD 58 — 700/PK-12
PO Box 610 83210 — 208-397-4113
Chad Struhs, supt. — Fax 397-4114
aberdeen58.org/
Aberdeen HS — 300/9-12
PO Box 610 83210 — 208-397-4152
David Kerns, prin. — Fax 397-4439
Aberdeen MS — 6-8
PO Box 610 83210 — 208-397-3280
Craig Miller, prin. — Fax 397-3281

American Falls, Power, Pop. 3,958
American Falls JSD 381 — 1,600/PK-12
827 Fort Hall Ave 83211 — 208-226-5173
Dr. Ron Bolinger, supt. — Fax 226-5754
www.sd381.k12.id.us
American Falls HS — 500/9-12
2966 S Frontage Rd 83211 — 208-226-2531
Randy Maughan, prin. — Fax 226-5853
Thomas MS — 400/6-8
355 Bannock Ave 83211 — 208-226-5203
Randy Jensen, prin. — Fax 226-5274

Ammon, Bonneville, Pop. 8,623
Bonneville JSD 93
Supt. — See Idaho Falls
Hillcrest HS — 1,200/9-12
2800 Owen St 83406 — 208-525-4429
Scott Miller, prin. — Fax 525-4437

Arco, Butte, Pop. 1,016
Butte County JSD 111 — 600/PK-12
PO Box 89 83213 — 208-527-8235
Dr. Amy Pancheri, supt. — Fax 527-8950
www.buttecountyschools.org
Butte County HS — 200/9-12
PO Box 655 83213 — 208-527-8237
Erik Strom, prin. — Fax 527-8246
Butte County MS — 100/6-8
PO Box 695 83213 — 208-527-3077
Brandon Farris, prin. — Fax 527-4950

Arimo, Bannock, Pop. 335
Marsh Valley JSD 21 — 1,400/PK-12
PO Box 180 83214 — 208-254-3306
Marvin Hansen, supt. — Fax 254-9243
www.marshnet.sd21.k12.id.us
Marsh Valley HS — 400/9-12
12655 S Old Highway 91 83214 — 208-254-3711
Gary Yearsley, prin. — Fax 254-9320
Marsh Valley MS — 200/7-8
12805 S Old Highway 91 83214 — 208-254-3260
Linda Reichardt, prin. — Fax 254-3631

Ashton, Fremont, Pop. 1,129
Fremont County JSD 215
Supt. — See Saint Anthony
North Fremont JSHS — 300/7-12
3581 E 1300 N 83420 — 208-652-7468
David Risenmay, prin. — Fax 652-7784

Bancroft, Caribou, Pop. 366
North Gem SD 149 — 200/PK-12
PO Box 70 83217 — 208-648-7848
Joseph Kren, supt. — Fax 648-7895
sd149.com
North Gem JSHS — 100/7-12
PO Box 70 83217 — 208-648-7848
Joseph Kren, prin. — Fax 648-7895

Blackfoot, Bingham, Pop. 10,646
Blackfoot SD 55 — 3,900/K-12
270 E Bridge St 83221 — 208-785-8800
Dewane Wren, supt. — Fax 785-8809
www.d55.k12.id.us
Blackfoot HS — 1,100/9-12
870 S Fisher Ave 83221 — 208-785-8810
Blaine McInelly, prin. — Fax 785-2329
Mountain View MS — 600/7-8
645 Mitchell Ln 83221 — 208-785-8820
Ryan Wilson, prin. — Fax 785-8823

Snake River SD 52 — 1,900/PK-12
103 S 900 W 83221 — 208-684-3001
Russell Hammond, supt. — Fax 684-3003
www.snakeriver.org
Snake River HS — 600/9-12
922 W Highway 39 83221 — 208-684-3061
Dean Bonney, prin. — Fax 684-3074
Snake River JHS — 300/7-8
918 W Highway 39 83221 — 208-684-3018
Mark Gabrylczyk, prin. — Fax 684-3047

Bliss, Gooding, Pop. 271
Bliss JSD 234 — 200/K-12
PO Box 115 83314 — 208-352-4447
Kevin Lancaster, supt. — Fax 352-4649
www.bliss.k12.id.us
Bliss S — 200/K-12
601 E Highway 30 83314 — 208-352-4445
Kevin Lancaster, prin. — Fax 352-4649

Boise, Ada, Pop. 189,847
ISD of Boise City 1 — 25,400/PK-12
8169 W Victory Rd 83709 — 208-854-4000
Dr. Stan Olson, supt. — Fax 854-4004
www.boiseschools.org
Boise SHS — 1,200/10-12
1010 W Washington St 83702 — 208-854-4270
Ken Anderson, prin. — Fax 854-4271
Borah SHS — 1,400/10-12
6001 Cassia St 83709 — 208-854-4370
Greg Frederick, prin. — Fax 854-4371
Capital SHS — 1,600/10-12
8055 Goddard Rd 83704 — 208-854-4490
Jon Ruzicka, prin. — Fax 854-4491
East JHS — 700/7-9
415 Warm Springs Ave 83712 — 208-854-4730
Bonita Hammer, prin. — Fax 854-4731
Fairmont JHS — 800/7-9
2121 N Cole Rd 83704 — 208-854-4790
Dr. Stacie Curry, prin. — Fax 854-4791
Hillside JHS — 500/7-9
3536 Hill Rd 83703 — 208-854-5120
Marlys Erickson, prin. — Fax 854-5121
Les Bois JHS — 800/7-9
4150 E Grand Forest Dr 83716 — 208-854-5340
Coby Dennis, prin. — Fax 854-5341
North JHS — 800/7-9
1105 N 13th St 83702 — 208-854-5740
Matt Kobe, prin. — Fax 854-5741
Riverglen JHS — 600/7-9
6801 Gary Ln 83714 — 208-854-5910
David Greene, prin. — Fax 854-5914
South JHS — 800/7-9
805 Shoshone St 83705 — 208-854-6110
Dr. Kathleen McCurdy, prin. — Fax 854-6111
Timberline SHS — 1,100/10-12
701 E Boise Ave 83706 — 208-854-6230
Betsy Story, prin. — Fax 854-6232
West JHS — 900/7-9
711 N Curtis Rd 83706 — 208-854-6450
Richard Webb, prin. — Fax 854-6451
Boise Evening S — Adult
6001 Cassia St 83709 — 208-854-6700
Ron Dehlin, prin. — Fax 854-4371

Meridian JSD 2
Supt. — See Meridian
Centennial HS — 1,900/9-12
12400 W Mcmillan Rd 83713 — 208-939-1404
Alta Graham, prin. — Fax 939-1420
Lake Hazel MS — 1,100/6-8
11625 W La Grange St 83709 — 208-362-3703
Kenton Travis, prin. — Fax 362-0258
Scott MS — 1,300/6-8
13600 W Mcmillan Rd 83713 — 208-939-2101
Joe Yochum, prin. — Fax 939-1424

Apollo College Boise — Post-Sec.
1200 N Liberty St 83704 — 208-377-8080
Bishop Kelly HS — 700/9-12
7009 W Franklin Rd 83709 — 208-375-6010
Robert Wehde, prin. — Fax 375-3626

Boise Bible College — Post-Sec.
8695 W Marigold St 83714 — 800-893-7755
Boise Court Reporting Institute — Post-Sec.
1951 S Saturn Way Ste 120 83709 — 208-322-8517
Boise State University — Post-Sec.
1910 University Dr 83725 — 208-426-1011
Covenant Academy — 50/K-12
PO Box 532 83701 — 208-377-2385
David Barrett, admin. — Fax 362-8061
Foundations Academy — 300/K-12
PO Box 2701 83701 — 208-323-3888
David Goodwin, hdmstr. — Fax 672-0522
ITT Technical Institute — Post-Sec.
12302 W Explorer Dr 83713 — 208-322-8844
New Images Academy of Beauty — Post-Sec.
317 E Brookhollow Dr 83706 — 208-375-0190
RiverStone Community S — 200/K-12
5493 Warm Springs Ave 83716 — 208-424-5000
Joe Kennedy, hdmstr. — Fax 424-0033
St. Alphonsus Regional Medical Center — Post-Sec.
1055 N Curtis Rd 83706 — 208-378-2000

Bonners Ferry, Boundary, Pop. 2,647
Boundary County SD 101 — 1,500/PK-12
6577 Main St Ste 101 83805 — 208-267-3146
Dr. Don Bartling, supt. — Fax 267-7217
www.bcsd101.com
Bonners Ferry HS — 500/9-12
6485 Tamarack Ln 83805 — 208-267-3149
Curt-Randall Bayer, prin. — Fax 267-5171
Boundary County MS — 300/6-8
6577 Main St 83805 — 208-267-5852
Dick Behrens, prin. — Fax 267-8099

Bruneau, Owyhee
Bruneau-Grand View JSD 365
Supt. — See Grand View
Rimrock JSHS — 200/7-12
39678 State Highway 78 83604 — 208-834-2260
Phil McCluskey, prin. — Fax 834-2516

Buhl, Twin Falls, Pop. 4,019
Buhl JSD 412 — 1,300/PK-12
920 Main St 83316 — 208-543-6436
Dr. Richard Hill, supt. — Fax 543-6360
www.d412.k12.id.us
Buhl HS — 400/9-12
1 Indian Territory 83316 — 208-543-8262
Gary Moon, prin. — Fax 543-8705
Buhl MS — 300/6-8
525 Sawtooth Ave 83316 — 208-543-8292
Byron Stutzman, prin. — Fax 543-6360

Burley, Cassia, Pop. 9,313
Cassia County JSD 151 — 5,200/PK-12
237 E 19th St 83318 — 208-878-6600
Dr. Michael Chesley, supt. — Fax 878-4231
www.sd151.k12.id.us
Burley JHS — 700/7-9
700 W 16th St 83318 — 208-878-6613
Steve Copmann, prin. — Fax 878-6624
Burley SHS — 700/10-12
2100 Park Ave 83318 — 208-878-6606
Jeff Harrah, prin. — Fax 878-6647
Other Schools – See Declo, Malta, Oakley

Caldwell, Canyon, Pop. 31,041
Caldwell SD 132 — 7,000/K-12
1101 Cleveland Blvd 83605 — 208-455-3300
Dr. Lonnie Barber, supt. — Fax 455-3302
www.caldwellschools.org/
Caldwell HS — 1,100/9-12
3401 S Indiana Ave 83605 — 208-455-3304
Mike Farris, prin. — Fax 455-3256
Jefferson MS — 1,400/6-8
3311 S 10th Ave 83605 — 208-455-3309
Randy Schrader, prin. — Fax 459-6773
Syringa MS — 1,400/6-8
1100 Willow St 83605 — 208-455-3305
Louise Daniels, prin. — Fax 455-3353

Vallivue SD 139 — 4,000/PK-12
5207 S Montana Ave 83607 — 208-454-0445
George Grant, supt. — Fax 454-0293
www.vallivue.org
Vallivue HS — 1,300/9-12
1407 E Homedale Rd 83607 — 208-454-9253
Wyatt Tustin, prin. — Fax 459-7114
Vallivue MS — 700/7-8
16412 S 10th Ave 83607 — 208-454-1426
Rod Lowe, prin. — Fax 454-7846

Albertson College of Idaho — Post-Sec.
2112 Cleveland Blvd 83605 — 208-459-5000
Gem State Academy — 100/9-12
16115 S Montana Ave 83607 — 208-459-1627
Mike Schwartz, prin. — Fax 454-9079

Cambridge, Washington, Pop. 355
Cambridge SD 432 — 200/PK-12
PO Box 39 83610 — 208-257-3321
Dr. Margaret J. Cox, supt. — Fax 257-3323
Cambridge JSHS — 100/7-12
PO Box 39 83610 — 208-257-3311
Angie Lakey-Campbell, prin. — Fax 257-3323

Carey, Blaine, Pop. 527
Blaine County SD 61
Supt. — See Hailey
Carey S — 200/K-12
PO Box 266 83320 — 208-823-4391
John Peck, prin. — Fax 823-4310

Cascade, Valley, Pop. 975
Cascade SD 422 — 400/PK-12
PO Box 291 83611 — 208-382-4227
Elsie Krause, supt. — Fax 382-3797
www.cascadeschools.org
Cascade JSHS — 200/7-12
PO Box 291 83611 — 208-382-4227
Ron Manley, prin. — Fax 382-3797

Castleford, Twin Falls, Pop. 277
Castleford JSD 417 — 300/PK-12
500 W Main St 83321 — 208-537-6511
Kelly Murphey, supt. — Fax 537-6855
www.castlefordschools.com
Castleford S — 300/PK-12
500 W Main St 83321 — 208-537-6511
Andy Wiseman, prin. — Fax 537-6855

Challis, Custer, Pop. 847
Challis JSD 181 — 500/K-12
PO Box 304 83226 — 208-879-4231
Bruce Bradberry Ed.D., supt. — Fax 879-5473
www.d181.k12.id.us/
Challis JSHS — 300/7-12
PO Box 304 83226 — 208-879-2255
Jason Green, prin. — Fax 879-5801

Chubbuck, Bannock, Pop. 10,151

The School of Hairstyling — Post-Sec.
141 E Chubbuck Rd 83202 — 208-232-9170

Clark Fork, Bonner, Pop. 566
Lake Pend Oreille SD 84
Supt. — See Ponderay
Clark Fork JSHS — 100/7-12
PO Box 129 83811 — 208-266-1131
Phil Kemink, prin. — Fax 266-1692

Coeur d Alene, Kootenai, Pop. 36,259
Coeur D'Alene SD 271 — 8,900/PK-12
311 N 10th St 83814 — 208-664-8241
Harry Amend, supt. — Fax 664-1748
www.cdaschools.org
Canfield MS — 800/6-8
1800 E Dalton Ave 83815 — 208-664-9188
Jeff Bengtson, prin. — Fax 769-2951
Coeur D'Alene HS — 1,400/9-12
5530 N 4th St 83815 — 208-667-4507
Randy Russell, prin. — Fax 664-5785
Lake City HS — 1,400/9-12
6101 N Ramsey Rd 83815 — 208-769-0769
John Brumley, prin. — Fax 769-2944
Lakes MS — 700/6-8
930 N 15th St 83814 — 208-667-4544
Chris Hammons, prin. — Fax 769-2982
Woodland MS — 800/6-8
2101 W Saint Michelle 83815 — 208-667-5996
James Lien, prin. — Fax 667-5997
Other Schools – See Post Falls

Lake City Junior Academy — 100/PK-10
111 E Locust Ave 83814 — 208-667-0877
Twila S. Brown, prin. — Fax 665-1462
North Idaho College — Post-Sec.
1000 W Garden Ave 83814 — 208-769-3300
Sage Technical Services — Post-Sec.
2845 W Seltice Way 83814 — 208-765-6346
The Headmasters School of Hair Design — Post-Sec.
317 E Coeur DAlene Lake Dr 83814 — 208-664-0541

Cottonwood, Idaho, Pop. 1,008
Cottonwood JSD 242 — 400/K-12
PO Box 158 83522 — 208-962-3971
Stan Kress, supt. — Fax 962-7780
www.sd242.k12.id.us/District/
Prairie HS — 200/9-12
PO Box 540 83522 — 208-962-3901
Mike Bundy, prin. — Fax 962-7702
Prairie MS — 100/5-8
PO Box 580 83522 — 208-962-3521
David Snodgrass, prin. — Fax 962-3319

Council, Adams, Pop. 765
Council SD 13 — 300/PK-12
PO Box 68 83612 — 208-253-4217
Murray Dalgleish, supt. — Fax 253-4297
www.sd013.k12.id.us
Council JSHS — 200/7-12
PO Box 468 83612 — 208-253-4217
Murray Dalgleish, prin. — Fax 253-4297

Craigmont, Lewis, Pop. 554
Highland JSD 305 — 200/PK-12
PO Box 130 83523 — 208-924-5211
Clair Garrick, supt. — Fax 924-5614
www.sd305.k12.id.us/
Highland JSHS — 100/7-12
PO Box 130 83523 — 208-924-5452
Clair Garrick, prin. — Fax 924-5614

Culdesac, Nez Perce, Pop. 375
Culdesac JSD 342 — 200/PK-12
600 Culdesac Ave 83524 — 208-843-5413
Darrell Olson, supt. — Fax 843-2719
www.culsch.org/
Culdesac S — 200/PK-12
600 Culdesac Ave 83524 — 208-843-5413
Darrell Olson, prin. — Fax 843-2719

Dayton, Franklin, Pop. 447
West Side JSD 202 — 600/PK-12
PO Box 39 83232 — 208-747-3502
Melvin Beutler, supt. — Fax 747-3705
www.wssd.k12.id.us
Lee MS — 100/6-8
PO Box 119 83232 — 208-747-3303
Melvin Beutler, prin. — Fax 747-3637
West Side HS — 200/9-12
PO Box 89 83232 — 208-747-3411
Stanley Bingham, prin. — Fax 747-3990

Deary, Latah, Pop. 534
Whitepine JSD 288
Supt. — See Troy
Deary S — 200/4-12
PO Box 9 83823 — 208-877-1151
Darrah Eggers, prin. — Fax 877-1366

Declo, Cassia, Pop. 336
Cassia County JSD 151
Supt. — See Burley
Declo HS — 300/9-12
505 E Main St 83323 — 208-654-2030
Debra Matsen, prin. — Fax 654-2404
Declo JHS — 300/6-8
205 E Main St 83323 — 208-654-9960
Ronald Knowles, prin. — Fax 654-2070

Dietrich, Lincoln, Pop. 159
Dietrich SD 314 — 200/PK-12
406 N Park St 83324 — 208-544-2158
Ed Simons, supt. — Fax 544-2832
www.sd314.k12.id.us
Dietrich S — 200/PK-12
406 N Park St 83324 — 208-544-2158
Thomas P. Fenelon, prin. — Fax 544-2832

Driggs, Teton, Pop. 1,133
Teton County SD 401 — 1,300/K-12
PO Box 775 83422 — 208-354-2207
Gordon Woolley, supt. — Fax 354-2250
www.d401.k12.id.us
Teton HS — 400/9-12
PO Box 754 83422 — 208-354-2952
Blaine McInelly, prin. — Fax 354-2907
Teton MS — 300/6-8
481 N Main St 83422 — 208-354-2971
Monte Woolstenhulme, prin. — Fax 354-8685

Dubois, Clark, Pop. 623
Clark County SD 161 — 200/PK-12
PO Box 237 83423 — 208-374-5175
Paul Blanford, supt. — Fax 374-5178
Clark County JSHS — 100/7-12
PO Box 237 83423 — 208-374-5215
Paul Blanford, prin. — Fax 374-5234

Eagle, Ada, Pop. 15,253
Meridian JSD 2
Supt. — See Meridian
Eagle HS — 1,900/9-12
574 Park Ln 83616 — 208-939-2189
Terry Beck, prin. — Fax 939-2453
Eagle MS — 1,200/6-8
1000 W Floating Feather Rd 83616 — 208-939-2216
LeAnn Carlsen, prin. — Fax 939-2173

Emmett, Gem, Pop. 5,933
Emmett ISD 221 — 2,900/PK-12
601 E 3rd St 83617 — 208-365-6301
Tom Carlsen, supt. — Fax 365-2961
www.isd221.net
Emmett HS — 700/10-12
721 W 12th St 83617 — 208-365-6323
Steve Beitia, prin. — Fax 365-6100
Emmett JHS — 800/7-9
301 E 4th St 83617 — 208-365-2921
Wade Carter, prin. — Fax 365-2427

Fairfield, Camas, Pop. 399
Camas County SD 121 — 200/K-12
PO Box 370 83327 — 208-764-2625
Ed Marshall, supt. — Fax 764-9218
Camas County HS — 100/9-12
PO Box 370 83327 — 208-764-2472
J.T. Stroder, prin. — Fax 764-9218

Filer, Twin Falls, Pop. 1,690
Filer SD 413 — 1,300/PK-12
700B Stevens St 83328 — 208-326-5981
John Graham, supt. — Fax 326-3350
www.filer.k12.id.us/
Filer HS — 400/9-12
3915 Wildcat Way 83328 — 208-326-5945
Leon Madsen, prin. — Fax 326-3419
Filer MS — 300/6-8
299 Highway 30 83328 — 208-326-5906
Gregory Lanting, prin. — Fax 326-3385

Firth, Bingham, Pop. 418
Firth SD 59 — 900/PK-12
PO Box 69 83236 — 208-346-6815
Dr. Drew Meyer, supt. — Fax 346-6814
www.d59.k12.id.us/
Firth HS — 300/9-12
PO Box 247 83236 — 208-346-6812
Michael Kress, prin. — Fax 346-6987
Firth MS — 300/5-8
410 Roosevelt St 83236 — 208-346-6240
Deanne Dye, prin. — Fax 346-4306

Fruitland, Payette, Pop. 4,116
Fruitland SD 373 — 1,600/PK-12
PO Box A 83619 — 208-452-3595
Alan G. Felgenhauer, supt. — Fax 452-6430
www.fsd.k12.id.us/
Fruitland HS — 400/9-12
PO Box A 83619 — 208-452-4411
Mike Knee, prin. — Fax 452-4485
Fruitland MS — 500/5-8
PO Box A 83619 — 208-452-3350
Diane O'Dell, prin. — Fax 452-4063

Garden Valley, Boise
Garden Valley SD 71 — 300/K-12
PO Box 710 83622 — 208-462-3756
Vic Koshuta, supt. — Fax 462-3570
www.gvsd.net
Garden Valley JSHS — 200/7-12
PO Box 710 83622 — 208-462-3756
Kim Harding, prin. — Fax 462-3570

Genesee, Latah, Pop. 915
Genesee JSD 282 — 300/K-12
PO Box 98 83832 — 208-285-1161
David Neumann, supt. — Fax 285-1495
www.genesee.k12.id.us/
Genesee S — 300/K-12
PO Box 98 83832 — 208-285-1162
Loretta Stowers, prin. — Fax 285-1495

Glenns Ferry, Elmore, Pop. 1,514
Glenns Ferry JSD 192 — 600/PK-12
800 Highway 30 83623 — 208-366-7436
Dr. Kenneth Piippo, supt. — Fax 366-7455
Glenns Ferry HS — 200/9-12
639 N Bannock Ave 83623 — 208-366-7434
Wayne Rush, prin. — Fax 366-2056
Glenns Ferry MS — 100/6-8
639 N Bannock Ave 83623 — 208-366-7438
Connie Wills, prin. — Fax 366-2056

Gooding, Gooding, Pop. 3,323
Gooding JSD 231 — 1,300/PK-12
507 Idaho St 83330 — 208-934-4321
T. Robert Stearns, supt. — Fax 934-4403
www.gooding.k12.id.us/
Gooding HS — 300/9-12
1050 7th Ave W 83330 — 208-934-4831
Gayle Yakovac, prin. — Fax 934-4347
Gooding MS — 300/6-8
1045 7th Ave W 83330 — 208-934-8443
Teresa Jones, prin. — Fax 934-4898

Idaho State School for the Deaf/Blind — Post-Sec.
1450 Main St 83330 — 208-934-4457

Grace, Caribou, Pop. 967
Grace JSD 148 — 500/PK-12
PO Box 347 83241 — 208-425-3984
Ted Taylor, supt. — Fax 425-3809
www.sd148.org/
Grace JSHS — 300/7-12
PO Box 348 83241 — 208-425-3731
Gary Brogan, prin. — Fax 425-3063

Grand View, Owyhee, Pop. 491
Bruneau-Grand View JSD 365 — 400/PK-12
PO Box 310 83624 — 208-834-2253
Vickie Chandler, supt. — Fax 834-2293
Other Schools – See Bruneau

Grangeville, Idaho, Pop. 3,146
Grangeville JSD 241 — 1,500/PK-12
714 Jefferson Ave 83530 — 208-983-0990
Dr. Wayne Davis, supt. — Fax 983-1245
www.jsd241.org/
Grangeville HS — 300/9-12
910 S D St 83530 — 208-983-0580
Gary Stears, prin. — Fax 983-3786
Other Schools – See Kooskia, Riggins

Greenleaf, Canyon, Pop. 874

Greenleaf Friends Academy — 300/PK-12
PO Box 368 83626 — 208-459-6346
Kenneth Sheldon, supt. — Fax 459-7700

Hagerman, Gooding, Pop. 685
Hagerman JSD 233 — 400/K-12
324 N 2nd Ave 83332 — 208-837-4777
Lee Mitchell, supt. — Fax 837-4737
www.hagerman.k12.id.us

Hagerman JSHS 200/7-12
150 Lake St W 83332 208-837-4572
Mark Kress, prin. Fax 837-6502

Hailey, Blaine, Pop. 7,301
Blaine County SD 61 3,500/K-12
118 W Bullion St 83333 208-578-5000
Jim Lewis, supt. Fax 578-5110
www.blaineschools.org/
Wood River HS 900/9-12
950 Fox Acres Rd 83333 208-578-5020
Graham Hume, prin. Fax 578-5120
Wood River MS 700/6-8
900 N 2nd Ave 83333 208-578-5030
Fritz Peters, prin. Fax 578-5130
Other Schools – See Carey

Hansen, Twin Falls, Pop. 984
Hansen SD 415 400/PK-12
550 Main St S 83334 208-423-6387
Dennis Coulter, supt. Fax 423-6808
www.hansen.k12.id.us/
Hansen JSHS 200/7-12
550 Main St S 83334 208-423-5593
Bert Hursh, prin. Fax 423-6808

Harrison, Kootenai, Pop. 270
Kootenai SD 274 300/K-12
13030 E Ogara Rd 83833 208-689-3631
Ron Hill, supt. Fax 689-3641
Kootenai JSHS 100/7-12
13030 E Ogara Rd 83833 208-689-3311
Rich Lund, prin. Fax 689-9072

Hayden, Kootenai, Pop. 10,421

North Idaho Christian S 300/1-12
251 W Miles Ave 83835 208-772-7546
Larry Kay, admin. Fax 762-2749

Hazelton, Jerome, Pop. 703
Valley SD 262 300/PK-12
882 Valley Rd 83335 208-829-5333
Dr. Laural Nelson, supt. Fax 829-5548
valley.sd262.k12.id.us
Valley HS 9-12
882 Valley Rd 83335 208-829-5353
Rod Malone, prin. Fax 829-5548
Valley MS 6-8
882 Valley Rd 83335 208-829-5961
Brian Hardy, prin. Fax 829-5548

Homedale, Owyhee, Pop. 2,590
Homedale JSD 370 1,200/K-12
116 E Owyhee Ave 83628 208-337-4611
Tim Rosandick, supt. Fax 337-4911
www.homedaleschools.org
Homedale HS 300/9-12
203 E Idaho Ave 83628 208-337-4613
Mike Williams, prin. Fax 337-4933
Homedale MS 400/5-8
3437 Johnstone Rd 83628 208-337-5780
Keith Field, prin. Fax 337-5782

Horseshoe Bend, Boise, Pop. 829
Horseshoe Bend SD 73 300/K-12
398 School Dr 83629 208-793-2225
Scott Mutchie, supt. Fax 793-2449
www.hsb-73k12.org
Horseshoe Bend MSHS 200/6-12
398 School Dr 83629 208-793-2225
John Cook, prin. Fax 793-2449

Idaho City, Boise, Pop. 494
Basin SD 72 500/PK-12
PO Box 227 83631 208-392-4183
Frank Gallant, supt. Fax 392-9954
Idaho City MSHS 200/7-12
PO Box 227 83631 208-392-4183
John McFarlane, prin. Fax 392-9954

Idaho Falls, Bonneville, Pop. 51,507
Bonneville JSD 93 8,800/PK-12
3497 N Ammon Rd 83401 208-525-4400
Dr. Charles Shackett, supt. Fax 529-0104
www.d93.k12.id.us
Bonneville HS 1,100/9-12
3165 E Iona Rd 83401 208-525-4406
John Pymm, prin. Fax 525-7014
Rocky Mountain MS 500/7-8
3443 N Ammon Rd 83401 208-525-4403
Shalene French, prin. Fax 525-4469
Sandcreek MS 600/7-8
2955 Owen St 83406 208-525-4416
Lyndon Oswald, prin. Fax 525-4438
Other Schools – See Ammon

Idaho Falls SD 91 9,900/PK-12
690 John Adams Pkwy 83401 208-525-7500
Dr. John Murdoch, supt. Fax 525-7596
www.d91.k12.id.us
Eagle Rock JHS 900/7-9
2020 Pancheri Dr 83402 208-525-7700
Wendy Cavan, prin. Fax 525-7703
Gale JHS 700/7-9
955 Garfield St 83401 208-525-7720
Jim Shank, prin. Fax 525-7724
Idaho Falls SHS 1,200/10-12
601 S Holmes Ave 83401 208-525-7740
Randy Hurley, prin. Fax 525-7768
Skyline SHS 1,100/10-12
1767 Blue Sky Dr 83402 208-525-7770
Trina Caudle, prin. Fax 525-7778
Taylorview JHS 900/7-9
350 Castlerock Ln 83404 208-524-7850
Roberta Crosser, prin. Fax 524-7851

Eastern Idaho Technical College Post-Sec.
1600 S 25th E 83404 208-524-3000

Jerome, Jerome, Pop. 8,039
Jerome JSD 261 2,900/K-12
107 3rd Ave W 83338 208-324-2392
Jim Cobble, supt. Fax 324-7609
www.d261.k12.id.us
Jerome HS 800/9-12
104 Tiger Dr 83338 208-324-8137
Patti O'Dell, prin. Fax 324-1266
Jerome MS 500/7-8
116 3rd Ave W 83338 208-324-8134
Eric Anderson, prin. Fax 324-7458

Kamiah, Lewis, Pop. 1,160
Kamiah JSD 304 500/PK-12
1102 Hill St 83536 208-935-2991
Doug Flaming, supt. Fax 935-4005
www.kamiah.org/
Kamiah HS 200/9-12
711 9th St 83536 208-935-4067
Steve Higgins, prin. Fax 935-4068
Kamiah MS 200/5-8
800 1st St 83536 208-935-4040
Carrie Nygaard, prin. Fax 935-4041

Kellogg, Shoshone, Pop. 2,236
Kellogg JSD 391 1,400/K-12
800 Bunker Ave 83837 208-784-1348
Greg Godwin, supt. Fax 786-3331
www.sd391.k12.id.us
Kellogg HS 400/9-12
2 Jacobs Gulch Rd 83837 208-784-1371
Ralph Lowe, prin. Fax 783-0741
Kellogg MS 400/6-8
810 Bunker Ave 83837 208-784-1311
Sandra Pommerening, prin. Fax 784-0134

Silver Valley Christian Academy 50/PK-12
514 W Brown Ave 83837 208-783-3791
Fax 783-3791

Kendrick, Latah, Pop. 358
Kendrick SD 283 300/PK-12
PO Box 283 83537 208-289-4211
Clark Adamson, supt. Fax 289-4201
Kendrick JSHS 200/7-12
2001 Highway 3 83537 208-289-4202
Jeffrey Cirka, prin. Fax 289-4213

Kimberly, Twin Falls, Pop. 2,700
Kimberly SD 414 1,300/K-12
141 Center St W 83341 208-423-4170
John Garner, supt. Fax 423-6155
www.kimberly.edu/
Kimberly HS 400/9-12
141 Center St W 83341 208-423-4170
Dick Brulotte, prin. Fax 423-5181
Kimberly MS 300/6-8
141 Center St W 83341 208-423-4170
Jeff Jones, prin. Fax 423-6155

Kooskia, Idaho, Pop. 666
Grangeville JSD 241
Supt. — See Grangeville
Clearwater Valley JSHS 200/7-12
PO Box 130 83539 208-926-4511
Fred Woods, prin. Fax 926-4807

Kuna, Ada, Pop. 8,839
Kuna JSD 3 3,700/PK-12
1450 Boise St 83634 208-922-1000
Jay Hummel, supt. Fax 922-5646
www.kunaschools.org
Kuna HS 900/9-12
637 E Deer Flat Rd 83634 208-955-0200
Scott Hill, prin. Fax 922-5646
Kuna MS 900/6-8
1360 Boise St 83634 208-922-1002
Deb McGrath, prin. Fax 922-1030

Lapwai, Nez Perce, Pop. 1,126
Lapwai SD 341 600/PK-12
PO Box 247 83540 208-843-2622
Harold Ott, supt. Fax 843-2910
Lapwai JSHS 300/7-12
PO Box 247 83540 208-843-2241
Bryan Samuels, prin. Fax 843-5289

Leadore, Lemhi, Pop. 88
South Lemhi SD 292 100/K-12
PO Box 119 83464 208-768-2441
Jim Smith, supt. Fax 768-2797
www.leadoreschool.org
Leadore S 100/K-12
PO Box 119 83464 208-768-2441
Jim Smith, prin. Fax 768-2797

Lewiston, Nez Perce, Pop. 30,937
Lewiston ISD 1 4,900/PK-12
3317 12th St 83501 208-748-3000
Dr. Joy C. Rapp, supt. Fax 748-3059
www.lewiston.k12.id.us
Jenifer JHS 600/7-9
1213 16th St 83501 208-748-3300
JoAnne Greear, prin. Fax 748-3349
Lewiston SHS 1,100/10-12
1114 9th Ave 83501 208-748-3100
Dr. Robert Donaldson, prin. Fax 748-3149
Sacajawea JHS 600/7-9
3610 12th St 83501 208-748-3400
Phil Uhlorn, prin. Fax 748-3449

Beacon Christian S 100/K-12
615 Stewart Ave 83501 208-743-8361
Richard Rasmussen, prin. Fax 743-3787
Lewis-Clark State College Post-Sec.
500 8th Ave 83501 208-792-5272
Mr. Leon's School of Hair Design Post-Sec.
205 10th St 83501 208-743-6822
Northwest Childrens Home Education Ctr 100/K-12
PO Box 1288 83501 208-746-8206
Bruce Grimoldby, dir. Fax 746-7482
The Headmasters School of Hair Design Post-Sec.
602 Main St 83501 208-743-1512

Mc Call, Valley, Pop. 2,876
Mc Call-Donnelly SD 421 900/PK-12
120 Idaho St, 208-634-2161
Dr. Terrell Donicht, supt. Fax 634-4075
www.mdsd.org
Mc Call-Donnelly HS 300/9-12
401 N Mission St, 208-634-2218
Tim Thomas, prin. Fax 634-7505
Payette Lakes MS 200/6-8
111 S Samson Trl, 208-634-5994
Susan Buescher, prin. Fax 634-5231

Mackay, Custer, Pop. 531
Mackay JSD 182 200/PK-12
PO Box 390 83251 208-588-2896
Troy Thayne, supt. Fax 588-2269
Mackay JSHS 100/7-12
PO Box 390 83251 208-588-2262
Brandon Farris, prin. Fax 588-2549

Malad City, Oneida, Pop. 2,108
Oneida County SD 351 1,000/PK-12
25 E 50 S Ste A 83252 208-766-4701
Lynn Schow, supt. Fax 766-2930
malad.sd351.k12.id.us
Malad HS 300/9-12
181 Jenkins Ave 83252 208-766-4728
John Cockett, prin. Fax 766-4538
Malad MS 200/6-8
175 Jenkins Ave 83252 208-766-9235
Sheldon Vaughan, prin. Fax 766-9236

Malta, Cassia, Pop. 177
Cassia County JSD 151
Supt. — See Burley
Raft River JSHS 100/7-12
PO Box 68 83342 208-645-2220
Mary Telford, prin. Fax 645-2640

Marsing, Owyhee, Pop. 986
Marsing JSD 363 700/K-12
PO Box 340 83639 208-896-4111
Harold Schockley, supt. Fax 896-4790
www.marsingschools.org/
Marsing HS 200/9-12
PO Box 340 83639 208-896-4111
Chuck Stella, prin. Fax 896-4457
Marsing MS 200/6-8
PO Box 340 83639 208-896-4111
Paul Webster, prin. Fax 896-5128

Melba, Canyon, Pop. 507
Melba JSD 136 700/PK-12
PO Box 185 83641 208-495-1141
Robert Larson, supt. Fax 495-1142
www.melbaschools.org
Melba MSHS 400/6-12
PO Box 185 83641 208-495-2221
Dick Davis, prin. Fax 495-2188

Meridian, Ada, Pop. 41,127
Meridian JSD 2 28,100/PK-12
911 N Meridian Rd 83642 208-855-4500
Dr. Linda Clark, supt. Fax 888-6700
www.meridianschools.org
Lewis & Clark MS 1,100/6-8
4141 E Pine Ave 83642 208-377-1353
Dennis Keogh, prin. Fax 377-3718
Meridian HS 1,500/9-12
1900 W Pine Ave 83642 208-888-4905
Geoff Stands, prin. Fax 888-5273
Meridian MS, 1507 W 8th St 83642 1,500/6-8
Lisa Austin, prin. 208-855-4225
Mountain View HS 1,800/9-12
2000 Millenium Way 83642 208-855-4050
Aaron Maybon, prin. Fax 855-4074
Sawtooth MS 1,000/6-8
3730 N Linder Rd, 208-855-4200
David Moser, prin. Fax 855-4224
Other Schools – See Boise, Eagle

Cole Valley Christian HS 300/7-12
200 E Carlton Ave 83642 208-898-9003
Mark Wood, admin. Fax 898-9016
Northwest Lineman College Post-Sec.
7600 S Meridian Rd 83642 208-888-4817

Middleton, Canyon, Pop. 3,651
Middleton SD 134 2,400/PK-12
5 S 3rd Ave W 83644 208-585-3027
Dr. Rich Bauscher, supt. Fax 585-3028
www.msd134.org
Middleton HS 700/9-12
511 W Main St 83644 208-585-6657
Jim Squibb, prin. Fax 585-3362
Middleton MS 600/6-8
200 S 4th Ave W 83644 208-585-3251
Molly Burger, prin. Fax 585-2098

Midvale, Washington, Pop. 181
Midvale SD 433 — 100/K-12
PO Box 130 83645 — 208-355-2678
James Warren, supt. — Fax 355-2347
www.midvalerangers.org
Midvale S — 100/K-12
PO Box 130 83645 — 208-355-2234
James Warren, prin. — Fax 355-2347

Montpelier, Bear Lake, Pop. 2,636
Bear Lake County SD 33
Supt. — See Paris
Bear Lake HS — 500/9-12
330 Boise St 83254 — 208-847-0294
Alan Schwab, prin. — Fax 847-0144
Bear Lake MS — 300/6-8
633 Washington St 83254 — 208-847-2255
Bruce Belnap, prin. — Fax 847-3626
Clover Creek HS — 9-12
697 Jackson St 83254 — 208-847-2516
Jill Kunz, prin.

Moscow, Latah, Pop. 21,707
Moscow SD 281 — 2,400/PK-12
650 N Cleveland St 83843 — 208-882-1120
Dr. Candis R. Donicht, supt. — Fax 883-4440
www.sd281.k12.id.us
Moscow JHS — 600/7-9
1410 E D St 83843 — 208-882-3577
Dale Kleinert, prin. — Fax 892-1182
Moscow SHS — 600/10-12
402 E 5th St 83843 — 208-882-2591
Robert Celebrezze, prin. — Fax 892-1136

Mr. Leon's School of Hair Design — Post-Sec.
618 S Main St 83843 — 208-882-2923
New Saint Andrews College — Post-Sec.
PO Box 9025 83843 — 208-882-1566
University of Idaho — Post-Sec.
PO Box 444264 83844 — 208-885-6111

Mountain Home, Elmore, Pop. 11,376
Mountain Home SD 193 — 4,600/PK-12
PO Box 1390 83647 — 208-587-2580
Tim McMurtrey, supt. — Fax 587-9896
www.mtnhomesd.org
Mountain Home JHS — 700/8-9
1600 E 6th S 83647 — 208-587-2590
Ernest Elliott, prin. — Fax 587-2597
Mountain Home SHS — 900/10-12
300 S 11th E 83647 — 208-587-2570
Barry Cahill, prin. — Fax 587-2579

Shiloh Christian S — 50/7-12
PO Box 1012 83647 — 208-587-3828
Kristy Blanksma, admin. — Fax 587-7951

Mullan, Shoshone, Pop. 781
Mullan SD 392 — 100/K-12
PO Box 71 83846 — 208-744-1118
Robin Stanley, supt. — Fax 744-1119
www.sd392.k12.id.us
Mullan JSHS — 100/7-12
PO Box 71 83846 — 208-744-1126
Tom Durbin, prin. — Fax 744-1128

Murtaugh, Twin Falls, Pop. 141
Murtaugh JSD 418 — 200/PK-12
PO Box 117 83344 — 208-432-5451
Dennis Osman, supt. — Fax 432-5477
Murtaugh HS — 100/9-12
PO Box 117 83344 — 208-432-5451
Dennis Osman, prin. — Fax 432-5477
Murtaugh MS — 100/6-8
PO Box 117 83344 — 208-432-5451
Dennis Osman, prin. — Fax 432-5477

Nampa, Canyon, Pop. 64,269
Nampa SD 131 — 12,200/PK-12
619 S Canyon St 83686 — 208-468-4600
Gary Larsen, supt. — Fax 468-4638
www.nsd131.org/
Columbia HS — 9-12
301 S Happy Valley Rd 83687 — 208-468-4763
Heath Thomason, prin.
East Valley MS — 800/6-8
4085 E Greenhurst Rd 83686 — 208-468-4760
Terry Adolfson, prin. — Fax 461-4069
Nampa HS — 1,400/9-12
203 Lake Lowell Ave 83686 — 208-465-2760
Byron Holtry, prin. — Fax 465-2741
Skyview HS — 1,700/9-12
1303 E Greenhurst Rd 83686 — 208-468-7820
Matt Crist, prin. — Fax 468-7822
South MS — 900/6-8
229 W Greenhurst Rd 83686 — 208-468-4740
Stuart Vickers, prin. — Fax 465-2779
West MS — 800/6-8
28 S Midland Blvd 83651 — 208-465-2752
Greg Wiles, prin. — Fax 465-2776

Nampa Christian S — 700/PK-12
439 W Orchard Ave 83651 — 208-466-8451
David Claar, supt. — Fax 466-8452
Northwest Nazarene University — Post-Sec.
623 Holly St 83686 — 208-467-8011
Razzle Dazzle College of Hair Design — Post-Sec.
120 Holly St 83686 — 208-465-7660

New Meadows, Adams, Pop. 507
Meadows Valley SD 11 — 200/PK-12
PO Box F 83654 — 208-347-2411
Dr. Terrell L. Donicht, supt. — Fax 347-2624
Meadows Valley S — 200/PK-12
PO Box F 83654 — 208-347-2118
John Preston, prin. — Fax 347-2624

New Plymouth, Payette, Pop. 1,390
New Plymouth SD 372 — 1,000/PK-12
103 SE Avenue 83655 — 208-278-5740
Ryan Kerby, supt. — Fax 278-3069
New Plymouth HS — 300/9-12
207 S Plymouth Ave 83655 — 208-278-5311
Arlo Decker, prin. — Fax 278-5313
New Plymouth MS — 300/6-8
4400 SW 2nd Ave 83655 — 208-278-5788
Darrell Brown, prin. — Fax 278-3773

Nezperce, Lewis, Pop. 515
Nezperce JSD 302 — 200/PK-12
PO Box 279 83543 — 208-937-2551
Terry Erholtz, supt. — Fax 937-2136
www.sd302.k12.id.us/
Nezperce JSHS — 100/7-12
PO Box 279 83543 — 208-937-2551
Skip Wilson, prin. — Fax 937-2136

Notus, Canyon, Pop. 506
Notus SD 135 — 300/K-12
PO Box 256 83656 — 208-459-7442
Joni Cordell, supt. — Fax 455-2439
www.notusschools.k12.id.us/
Notus JSHS — 100/7-12
PO Box 256 83656 — 208-459-4633
Jim Doramus, prin. — Fax 459-6304

Oakley, Cassia, Pop. 662
Cassia County JSD 151
Supt. — See Burley
Oakley JSHS — 200/7-12
PO Box 135 83346 — 208-862-3328
Mark Rose, prin. — Fax 862-3330

Old Town, Bonner, Pop. 204

House of the Lord Christian Academy — 200/PK-12
754 Silver Birch Ln, — 208-437-2184
Michael Croston, admin. — Fax 437-0441

Orofino, Clearwater, Pop. 3,151
Orofino JSD 171 — 1,400/PK-12
PO Box 2259 83544 — 208-476-5593
Dale Durkee, supt. — Fax 476-7293
www.sd171.k12.id.us
Orofino HS — 300/9-12
300 Dunlap Rd 83544 — 208-476-5557
Jerry Nelson, prin. — Fax 476-0147
Orofino JHS — 200/7-8
PO Box 706 83544 — 208-476-4613
Shannon Wilson, prin. — Fax 476-3327
Other Schools – See Weippe

Paris, Bear Lake, Pop. 544
Bear Lake County SD 33 — 1,400/PK-12
PO Box 300 83261 — 208-945-2891
Cliff Walters, supt. — Fax 945-2893
Other Schools – See Montpelier

Parma, Canyon, Pop. 1,803
Parma SD 137 — 1,000/K-12
805 E McConnell Ave 83660 — 208-722-5115
Jim Norton, supt. — Fax 722-7937
www.parmaschools.org
Parma HS — 300/9-12
908 N 8th St 83660 — 208-722-5115
Michael Moore, prin. — Fax 722-7153
Parma MS — 300/6-8
905 E McConnell Ave 83660 — 208-722-5115
Peggy Sharkey, prin. — Fax 722-6913

Paul, Minidoka, Pop. 963
Minidoka County JSD 331
Supt. — See Rupert
West Minico MS — 400/6-8
155 S 600 W 83347 — 208-438-5018
Sandra Miller, prin. — Fax 438-8513

Payette, Payette, Pop. 7,298
Payette JSD 371 — 1,900/PK-12
20 N 12th St 83661 — 208-642-9366
Pauline King, supt. — Fax 642-9006
www.payettesd.k12.id.us
McCain MS — 400/6-8
1215 Center Ave 83661 — 208-642-4122
Sandy Holloway, prin. — Fax 642-6801
Payette HS — 500/9-12
1500 6th Ave S 83661 — 208-642-3327
Sam Nelson, prin. — Fax 642-3368
Payette Night S — Adult
1215 Center Ave 83661 — 208-642-4705
Patrick Townsend, admin. — Fax 642-9006

River of Life Christian S — 100/PK-12
800 17th Ave N 83661 — 208-642-4416
Paul Shover, admin. — Fax 642-4413

Plummer, Benewah, Pop. 974
Plummer/Worley JSD 44 — 500/PK-12
PO Box 130 83851 — 208-686-1621
George W. Olsen, supt. — Fax 686-1019
www.pwsd.com
Lakeside HS — 100/9-12
PO Box 130 83851 — 208-686-1937
James Phillips, prin. — Fax 686-7118
Lakeside MS — 100/6-8
PO Box 130 83851 — 208-686-1627
Judith Sharrett, prin. — Fax 686-7311

Pocatello, Bannock, Pop. 51,009
Pocatello/Chubbuck SD 25 — 11,800/K-12
3115 Pole Line Rd 83201 — 208-232-3563
Carolyn Kennedy, supt. — Fax 235-3280
www.d25.k12.id.us

Century HS — 1,100/9-12
7801 W Diamond Back Dr 83204 — 208-478-6863
Pat Charlton, prin. — Fax 478-6870
Franklin MS — 700/7-8
2271 E Terry St 83201 — 208-233-5590
Francie Stephens, prin. — Fax 233-1024
Hawthorne MS — 500/7-8
1025 W Eldredge Rd 83201 — 208-237-1680
Doug Reader, prin. — Fax 237-1682
Highland HS — 1,400/9-12
1800 Bench Rd 83201 — 208-237-1300
David Ross, prin. — Fax 237-1350
Irving MS — 600/7-8
911 N Grant Ave 83204 — 208-232-3039
James Harrell, prin. — Fax 232-0379
Pocatello HS — 1,100/9-12
325 N Arthur Ave 83204 — 208-233-2056
Don Cotant, prin. — Fax 232-0365

Idaho State University — Post-Sec.
PO Box 8270 83209 — 208-282-0211

Ponderay, Bonner, Pop. 692
Lake Pend Oreille SD 84 — 3,900/PK-12
901 N Triangle Dr 83852 — 208-263-2184
Dick Cvitanich, supt. — Fax 263-5053
www.sd84.k12.id.us
Other Schools – See Clark Fork, Sandpoint

Sandpoint Community Christian S — 100/K-12
477954 Highway 95 83852 — 208-265-8624
Jane Henry, admin. — Fax 263-6504

Post Falls, Kootenai, Pop. 19,984
Coeur D'Alene SD 271
Supt. — See Coeur d Alene
Riverbend Professional Technical Academy — Vo/Tech
525 W Clearwater Loop Rd 83854 — 208-769-5960
Brad Murray, prin.

Post Falls SD 273 — 4,800/K-12
PO Box 40 83877 — 208-773-1658
Jerry Keane, supt. — Fax 773-3218
www.pfsd.com
Post Falls HS — 1,300/9-12
PO Box 40 83877 — 208-773-0581
Steve Smith, prin. — Fax 773-0587
Post Falls MS — 1,200/6-8
PO Box 40 83877 — 208-773-7554
Debbi Davis, prin. — Fax 773-0884
River City MS — 6-8
PO Box 40 83877 — 208-457-0993
Mike Yovetich, prin. — Fax 457-1673

Classical Christian Academy — 100/K-10
3263 E 12th Ave 83854 — 208-777-4400
Dirk Darrow, hdmstr. — Fax 777-2544
Post Falls Christian Academy — 300/K-12
PO Box 2306 83877 — 208-777-0697
Jerry Rogers, admin. — Fax 777-0986

Potlatch, Latah, Pop. 759
Potlatch SD 285 — 600/PK-12
130 6th St 83855 — 208-875-0327
Judy Adamson, supt. — Fax 875-1028
www.potlatchidaho.org
Potlatch JSHS — 300/7-12
130 6th St 83855 — 208-875-1231
Gordon Steinbis, prin. — Fax 875-1028

Preston, Franklin, Pop. 4,845
Preston JSD 201 — 2,400/PK-12
120 E 2nd S 83263 — 208-852-0283
Dr. Barbara Taylor, supt. — Fax 852-3976
www.preston.k12.id.us
Preston HS — 700/9-12
151 E 2nd S 83263 — 208-852-0280
Reid Carlson, prin. — Fax 852-3976
Preston JHS — 500/6-8
450 E Valley View Dr 83263 — 208-852-0751
John Anderson, prin. — Fax 852-3976

Priest River, Bonner, Pop. 1,863
West Bonner County SD 83 — 1,600/PK-12
PO Box 2531 83856 — 208-448-4439
Tony Feldhausen, supt. — Fax 448-4629
www.sd83.k12.id.us
Priest River JHS — 200/7-8
PO Box 519 83856 — 208-448-1118
Gary Go, prin. — Fax 448-1119
Priest River Lamanna HS — 500/9-12
PO Box 549 83856 — 208-448-1211
Ray Stookey, prin. — Fax 448-1212

Rathdrum, Kootenai, Pop. 5,296
Lakeland JSD 272 — 4,200/PK-12
PO Box 39 83858 — 208-687-0431
Charles Kinsey, supt. — Fax 687-1884
www.sd272.k12.id.us
Lakeland JHS — 700/7-9
PO Box 98 83858 — 208-687-0661
John Keating, prin. — Fax 687-1510
Lakeland SHS — 500/10-12
PO Box 69 83858 — 208-687-0181
Conrad Underdahl, prin. — Fax 687-1313
Other Schools – See Spirit Lake

Rexburg, Madison, Pop. 21,862
Madison SD 321 — 4,100/K-12
PO Box 830 83440 — 208-359-3300
Dr. Geoffrey M. Thomas, supt. — Fax 359-3345
www.d321.k12.id.us
Madison JHS — 600/8-9
60 W Main St 83440 — 208-359-3310
Corey Telford, prin. — Fax 359-3352

Madison SHS 1,000/10-12
134 Madison Ave 83440 208-359-3305
Rodger Hampton, prin. Fax 359-3346

Brigham Young University - Idaho Post-Sec.
120 Kimball Building 83460 208-356-2011
Career Beauty College Post-Sec.
57 College Ave 83440 208-356-0222

Richfield, Lincoln, Pop. 429
Richfield SD 316 200/PK-12
555 N Tiger Dr 83349 208-487-2790
Dr. David M. Hocklander, supt. Fax 487-2055
Richfield S 200/PK-12
555 N Tiger Dr 83349 208-487-2790
Mike Smith, prin. Fax 487-2055

Rigby, Jefferson, Pop. 3,035
Jefferson County JSD 251 3,900/PK-12
201 Idaho Ave 83442 208-745-6693
Ron Tolman, supt. Fax 745-0848
www.d251.k12.id.us
Rigby JHS 600/8-9
125 N 1st W 83442 208-745-6674
Sherry Simmons, prin. Fax 745-6675
Rigby SHS 900/10-12
290 N 3800 E 83442 208-745-7704
Mark Neish, prin. Fax 745-7707

Riggins, Idaho, Pop. 404
Grangeville JSD 241
Supt. — See Grangeville
Salmon River JSHS 100/7-12
PO Box 872 83549 208-628-3431
Robin Tellis, prin. Fax 628-3840

Ririe, Jefferson, Pop. 542
Ririe JSD 252 700/PK-12
PO Box 508 83443 208-538-7482
Ron Perrenoud, supt. Fax 538-7363
Ririe HS 200/9-12
PO Box 568 83443 208-538-7311
Charles Barber, prin. Fax 538-7860
Ririe MS 200/5-8
PO Box 548 83443 208-538-5175
Ron Perrenoud, prin. Fax 538-7748

Rockland, Power, Pop. 305
Rockland SD 382 100/K-12
PO Box 119 83271 208-548-2221
James Woodworth, supt. Fax 548-2224
www.rbulldogs.org
Rockland S 100/K-12
PO Box 119 83271 208-548-2221
Dan Ralphs, prin. Fax 548-2224

Rupert, Minidoka, Pop. 5,351
Minidoka County JSD 331 4,300/PK-12
633 Fremont St 83350 208-436-4727
Dr. Scott Rogers, supt. Fax 436-6593
www.sd331.k12.id.us
East Minico MS 600/6-8
1805 H St 83350 208-436-3178
Kevan Vogt, prin. Fax 436-3235
Minico HS 1,200/9-12
292 W 100 S 83350 208-436-4721
Dan Rogers, prin. Fax 436-3266
Other Schools – See Paul

Saint Anthony, Fremont, Pop. 3,375
Fremont County JSD 215 2,600/PK-12
147 N 2nd W 83445 208-624-7542
Dr. Garry Parker, supt. Fax 624-3385
www.sd215.k12.id.us
South Fremont HS 500/9-12
855 N Bridge St 83445 208-624-3416
Larry Bennett, prin. Fax 624-4898
South Fremont JHS 400/6-8
550 N 1st W 83445 208-624-7880
Chester Peterson, prin. Fax 624-4386
Other Schools – See Ashton

Saint Maries, Benewah, Pop. 2,589
Saint Maries JSD 41 1,200/PK-12
PO Box 384 83861 208-245-2579
Dave Cox, supt. Fax 245-3970
www.sd41.k12.id.us/
Saint Maries HS 300/9-12
424 Hells Gulch Rd 83861 208-245-2142
John Cordell, prin. Fax 245-5650

Saint Maries MS 200/6-8
1315 W Jefferson Ave 83861 208-245-3495
Dennis Kachelmier, prin. Fax 245-0506

Salmon, Lemhi, Pop. 3,038
Salmon SD 291 1,100/PK-12
PO Box 790 83467 208-756-4271
Dan Grabowska, supt. Fax 756-6695
www.salmon.k12.id.us/
Salmon HS 300/9-12
PO Box 790 83467 208-756-2415
John Riddle, prin. Fax 756-3484
Salmon MS 300/6-8
PO Box 790 83467 208-756-2207
Gary Pflueger, prin. Fax 756-2099

Sandpoint, Bonner, Pop. 7,378
Lake Pend Oreille SD 84
Supt. — See Ponderay
Sandpoint HS 1,200/9-12
410 S Division Ave 83864 208-263-3034
Becky Kiebert, prin. Fax 263-5321
Sandpoint MS 600/7-8
310 S Division Ave 83864 208-265-4169
Kim Keaton, prin. Fax 263-5525

Shelley, Bingham, Pop. 3,885
Shelley JSD 60 2,000/1-12
545 Seminary Ave 83274 208-357-3411
Bryan Jolley, supt. Fax 357-5741
www.sd60.k12.id.us
Hobbs MS 500/6-8
350 E Pine St 83274 208-357-7667
Joann Montgomery, prin. Fax 357-3003
Shelley HS 600/9-12
570 W Fir St 83274 208-357-7400
Shon Hocker, prin. Fax 357-5585

Shoshone, Lincoln, Pop. 1,488
Shoshone JSD 312 500/PK-12
409 N Apple St 83352 208-886-2338
Mel Wiseman, supt. Fax 886-2038
www.shoshone.k12.id.us
Shoshone JSHS 200/7-12
61 E Highway 24 83352 208-886-2381
Joe Hendrickson, prin. Fax 886-2742

Soda Springs, Caribou, Pop. 3,294
Soda Springs JSD 150 1,000/PK-12
250 E 2nd S 83276 208-547-3371
Dr. Molly Stein, supt. Fax 547-4878
www.sodaschools.org
Soda Springs HS 300/9-12
300 E 1st N 83276 208-547-4308
Michael Button, prin. Fax 547-2629
Tigert MS 200/7-8
250 E 2nd S 83276 208-547-4922
Dr. Molly Stein, prin. Fax 547-2619

Spirit Lake, Kootenai, Pop. 1,431
Lakeland JSD 272
Supt. — See Rathdrum
Timberlake JSHS 700/7-12
PO Box 89869 208-623-6303
Kurt Hoffman, prin. Fax 623-6203

Sugar City, Madison, Pop. 1,352
Sugar-Salem JSD 322 1,300/PK-12
PO Box 150 83448 208-356-8802
Alan Dunn, supt. Fax 356-7237
www.sd322.k12.id.us/
Sugar-Salem HS 400/9-12
1 S Digger Dr 83448 208-356-0274
Jared Jenks, prin. Fax 359-3167
Sugar-Salem JHS 200/7-8
PO Box 180 83448 208-356-4437
Robert Potter, prin. Fax 358-9717

Sun Valley, Blaine, Pop. 1,446

Community S 300/PK-12
PO Box 2118 83353 208-622-3955
Dr. Jon Maksik, hdmstr. Fax 622-3962

Terreton, Jefferson
West Jefferson SD 253 700/PK-12
1256 E 1500 N 83450 208-663-4542
Steven Lambertsen, supt. Fax 663-4543
wjsd.org
West Jefferson HS 200/9-12
1260 E 1500 N 83450 208-663-4391
Richard Hanson, prin. Fax 663-4390

Troy, Latah, Pop. 774
Troy SD 287 300/K-12
PO Box 280 83871 208-835-3791
Donald Armstrong, supt. Fax 835-3790
Troy JSHS 200/7-12
PO Box 280 83871 208-835-2361
Brad Malm, prin. Fax 835-2441

Whitepine JSD 288 300/K-12
502 First Ave 83871 208-877-1408
Daryl Bertelsen, supt. Fax 877-1570
www.sd288.k12.id.us/
Other Schools – See Deary

Twin Falls, Twin Falls, Pop. 36,742
Twin Falls SD 411 6,900/PK-12
201 Main Ave W 83301 208-733-6900
Wiley Dobbs, supt. Fax 733-6987
www.tfsd.k12.id.us
O'Leary JHS 900/7-9
2350 Elizabeth Blvd 83301 208-733-2155
Tom Owens, prin. Fax 733-8666
Stuart JHS 700/7-9
644 Caswell Ave W 83301 208-733-4875
Steve Smith, prin. Fax 733-4949
Twin Falls SHS 1,400/10-12
1615 Filer Ave E 83301 208-733-6551
Ben Allen, prin. Fax 733-8192

College of Southern Idaho Post-Sec.
PO Box 1238 83303 208-733-9554
Lighthouse Christian S 300/PK-12
259 Main Ave E 83301 208-737-1425
Kevin Newbry, prin. Fax 737-4671
Magic Valley Christian S 100/7-12
PO Box 5494 83303 208-733-5999
Diane Davis, supt. Fax 735-0141
Mr. Juan's College of Hair Design Post-Sec.
586 Blue Lakes Blvd N 83301 208-733-7777
Twin Falls Christian Academy 100/K-12
798 Eastland Dr N 83301 208-733-1452
Brent Walker, prin. Fax 734-1417

Wallace, Shoshone, Pop. 887
Wallace SD 393 700/PK-12
405 7th St 83873 208-753-4515
Reid Straabe, supt. Fax 753-4151
www.sd393.k12.id.us
Wallace JSHS 300/7-12
1 Miners Aly 83873 208-753-5315
Gail Harding-Thomas, prin. Fax 753-7105

Weippe, Clearwater, Pop. 386
Orofino JSD 171
Supt. — See Orofino
Timberline JSHS 200/7-12
1150 Highway 11 83553 208-435-4411
Ron Anthony, prin. Fax 435-4846

Weiser, Washington, Pop. 5,386
Weiser SD 431 1,600/PK-12
925 Pioneer Rd 83672 208-414-0616
James Reed, supt. Fax 414-1265
www.sd431.k12.id.us/
Weiser HS 500/9-12
690 W Indianhead Rd 83672 208-414-2595
Kevin Knight, prin. Fax 414-1795
Weiser MS 400/6-8
320 E Galloway Ave 83672 208-414-2620
Larry Goto, prin. Fax 414-2094

Wendell, Gooding, Pop. 2,335
Wendell SD 232 1,100/PK-12
PO Box 300 83355 208-536-2418
Greg Lowe, supt. Fax 536-2629
www.sd232.k12.id.us
Wendell HS 300/9-12
750 E Main St 83355 208-536-2100
Don Fowler, prin. Fax 536-2124
Wendell MS 400/5-8
800 E Main St 83355 208-536-5531
Rob Sauer, prin. Fax 536-5957

Wilder, Canyon, Pop. 1,465
Wilder SD 133 500/K-12
210 A Ave 83676 208-482-6228
Daniel B. Arriola, supt. Fax 482-7019
www.sd133.k12.id.us
Wilder MSHS 200/6-12
210 A Ave 83676 208-482-6228
Joseph Youren, prin. Fax 482-7421

ILLINOIS

ILLINOIS DEPARTMENT OF EDUCATION
100 N 1st St, Springfield 62702-5042
Telephone 866-262-6663
Fax 217-524-8585
Website http://www.isbe.state.il.us

Superintendent of Education   Randy Dunn

ILLINOIS BOARD OF EDUCATION
100 N 1st St, Springfield 62777-0002

Chairperson   Jesse Ruiz

REGIONAL OFFICES OF EDUCATION (ROE)

Adams/Pike ROE
Raymond Scheiter, supt. — 217-277-2080
507 Vermont St, Quincy 62301 — Fax 277-2092
www.wc4.org

Alxndr/Jhnsn/Massac/Pulaski/Union ROE
Janet Ulrich, supt. — 618-634-2292
17 Rustic Campus Dr, Ullin 62992 — Fax 634-2294
www.roe02.k12.il.us/

Bond/Effingham/Fayette ROE
Mark A. Drone, supt. — 618-283-5011
300 S 7th St, Vandalia 62471 — Fax 283-5013
www.fayette.k12.il.us/roeweb/

Boone/Winnebago ROE
Richard Fairgrieves, supt. — 815-636-3060
300 Heart Blvd, Loves Park 61111 — Fax 636-3069
www.4roe.org/

Brown/Cass/Morgan/Scott ROE
Stephen Breese, supt. — 217-243-1804
110 N West St, Jacksonville 62650 — Fax 243-5354
www.roe46.net/

Bureau/Henry/Stark ROE
Bruce Dennison, supt. — 309-936-7890
107 S State St, Atkinson 61235 — Fax 935-6784
www.bhsroe.k12.il.us

Calhoun/Greene/Jersey/Macoupin ROE
Larry Pfeiffer, supt. — 217-854-4016
220 N Broad St, Carlinville 62626 — Fax 854-2032
www.roe40.k12.il.us/

Carroll/Jo Daviess/Stephenson ROE
Marie Stiefel, supt. — 815-947-3810
500 N Rush St, Stockton 61085 — Fax 947-2717
roe8.lth2.k12.il.us/

Champaign/Ford ROE
Judy Pacey, supt. — 217-893-3219
200 S Fredrick St, Rantoul 61866 — Fax 893-0024
www.roe9.k12.il.us/

Christian/Montgomery ROE
Greg Springer, supt. — 217-532-9591
1 Courthouse Sq Rm 202 — Fax 824-2464
Hillsboro 62049
www.montgomery.k12.il.us

Clay/Crawford/Jspr/Lwrnce/Rchlnd ROE
Carol S. Steinman, supt. — 618-392-4631
103 W Main St, Olney 62450 — Fax 392-3993

Clinton/Marion/Washington ROE
David Erlinger, supt. — 618-594-2432
930 Fairfax St Ste B, Carlyle 62231 — Fax 594-7192
www.roe13.k12.il.us/

Clk/Cls/Cumb/Dglas/Edg/Mlt/Shlb ROE
John McNary, supt. — 217-348-0151
730 7th St, Charleston 61920 — Fax 348-0171
www.roe11.k12.il.us/

DeKalb ROE
Gil Morrison, supt. — 815-895-3096
245 W Exchange St Ste 2 — Fax 895-4847
Sycamore 60178

DeWitt/Livingston/McLean ROE
G. Lawrence Daghe, supt. — 309-888-5120
905 N Main St Ste 1, Normal 61761 — Fax 862-0420
www.roe17.k12.il.us/

Dupage ROE
Darlene Ruscitti, supt. — 630-407-5800
421 N County Farm Rd — Fax 682-7773
Wheaton 60187
www.dupage.k12.il.us/

Edwds/Gtn/Hdn/Pope/Sln/Wbsh/Wyn/Wt ROE
Linda Blackman, supt. — 618-253-5581
512 N Main St, Harrisburg 62946 — Fax 252-8472
www.roe20.k12.il.us/

Franklin/Williamson ROE
Barry Kohl, supt. — 618-438-9711
206 Rushing Dr Ste 1, Herrin 62948 — Fax 435-2861
www.roe21.k12.il.us/

Fulton/Schuyler ROE
Alan Coleman, supt. — 309-547-3041
PO Box 307, Lewistown 61542 — Fax 547-3326
www.fulton.k12.il.us/

Grundy/Kendall ROE
Thomas Centowski, supt. — 815-941-3247
1320 Union St, Morris 60450 — Fax 942-5384
www.grundy.k12.il.us/

Hamilton/Jefferson ROE
Paul Cross, supt., 1714 Broadway St — 618-244-8040
Mount Vernon 62864 — Fax 244-8073
www.roe25.com

Hancock/McDonough ROE
Robert Baumann, supt. — 309-837-4821
130 S Lafayette St, Macomb 61455 — Fax 837-2887
mcdonough.k12.il.us/roe26/

Henderson/Mercer/Warren ROE
Glen W. Braden, supt. — 309-734-6822
200 W Broadway, Monmouth 61462 — Fax 734-2452
www.hmwroe27.com

Iroquois/Kankakee ROE
Kathleen Pangle, supt. — 815-937-2950
189 E Court St #600 — Fax 937-2921
Kankakee 60901
www.i-kan.org

Jackson/Perry ROE
Robert L. Koehn, supt. — 618-687-7290
1001 Walnut St — Fax 687-7296
Murphysboro 62966
www.roe30.k12.il.us/

Kane ROE
Dr. Clem Mejia, supt. — 630-232-5955
210 S 6th St, Geneva 60134 — Fax 208-5115
www.kaneroe.org/

Knox ROE
Bonnie Harris, supt. — 309-345-3828
PO Box 430, Galesburg 61402 — Fax 343-2677
www.knox.k12.il.us/knoxcountyroe33/

Lake ROE
Roycealee Wood, supt. — 847-543-7833
800 Lancer Ln Ste E128 — Fax 543-7832
Grayslake 60030
www.lake.k12.il.us/

LaSalle ROE
William Novotney, supt. — 815-434-0780
119 W Madison St, Ottawa 61350 — Fax 434-2453
www.roe35.k12.il.us/

Lee/Ogle ROE
Amy Jo Clemens, supt. — 815-652-2054
7772 S Clinton St, Dixon 61021 — Fax 652-2053

Logan/Mason/Menard ROE
Jean R. Anderson, supt. — 217-732-8388
PO Box 460, Lincoln 62656 — Fax 735-1569
logan.k12.il.us/quickanswers38

Macon/Piatt ROE 39
Richard Shelby, supt. — 217-872-3721
1690 Huston Dr, Decatur 62526 — Fax 872-0239

Madison County ROE
Harry Briggs, supt. — 618-692-6200
PO Box 600, Edwardsville 62025 — Fax 692-7018
www.madison.k12.il.us/

Marshall/Putnam/Woodford ROE
Rolland D. Marshall, supt. — 309-248-8212
PO Box 340, Washburn 61570 — Fax 248-7983
www.roe43.k12.il.us/

McHenry ROE
Gene Goeglein, supt. — 815-334-4475
2200 N Seminary Ave — Fax 338-0475
Woodstock 60098
www.mchenry.k12.il.us/

Monroe-Randolph ROE
Marc Kiehna, supt. — 618-939-5650
107 E Mill St, Waterloo 62298 — Fax 939-5332
www.monroe.k12.il.us/roe45/

Peoria ROE
Gerald Brookhart, supt. — 309-672-6906
211 Fulton St Ste 207, Peoria 61602 — Fax 672-6053
www.peoria.k12.il.us/roe48/

Rock Island ROE
Joseph Vermeire, supt. — 309-736-1111
3430 Avenue Of The Cities — Fax 736-1127
Moline 61265
www.riroe.com/

Saint Clair ROE
Rosella Wamser, supt. — 618-397-8930
500 Wilshire Dr, Belleville 62223 — Fax 397-8928
www.stclair.k12.il.us/

Sangamon ROE
Helen Tolan, supt. — 217-753-6620
200 S 9th St Ste 303 — Fax 535-3166
Springfield 62701
www.roe51.org

Suburban Cook ROE
Robert Ingraffia, supt. — 708-865-9330
10110 Gladstone St — Fax 865-9338
Westchester 60154
www.cook.k12.il.us/

Tazewell ROE
Robin Houchin, supt. — 309-477-2290
PO Box 699, Pekin 61555 — Fax 347-3735
www.tazewell.k12.il.us/quickanswers53

Vermilion ROE
Michael Metzen, supt. — 217-431-2668
200 S College St Ste B — Fax 431-2671
Danville 61832
www.roe54.k12.il.us/

Whiteside ROE
Gary Steinert, supt. — 815-625-1495
1001 W 23rd St, Sterling 61081 — Fax 625-1625
www.wside.k12.il.us/

Will ROE
Richard Duran, supt. — 815-740-8360
302 N Chicago St, Joliet 60432 — Fax 740-4788
www.will.k12.il.us/

PUBLIC, PRIVATE AND CATHOLIC SECONDARY SCHOOLS

Abingdon, Knox, Pop. 3,469
Abingdon CUSD 217 — 800/PK-12
201 W Lower St 61410 — 309-462-2301
Dr. Magie Roberts, supt. — Fax 462-3870
www.abingdon.k12.il.us/
Abingdon HS — 200/9-12
600 W Martin St 61410 — 309-462-2338
Chad Cox, prin. — Fax 462-2492
Abingdon MS — 200/6-8
202 W Snyder St 61410 — 309-462-2336
Stan Adcock, prin. — Fax 462-2207

Addison, DuPage, Pop. 36,767
Addison SD 4 — 3,900/PK-8
222 N JF Kennedy Dr 60101 — 630-628-2500
Dr. Donald Hendricks, supt. — Fax 628-8829
www.asd4.org

Indian Trail JHS — 1,300/6-8
222 N JF Kennedy Dr 60101 — 630-458-2600
Terry Sliva, prin. — Fax 628-2841

DAOES, 301 S Swift Rd 60101
Fred Kane, supt. — 630-620-8770
Technology Center of Dupage — Vo/Tech
301 S Swift Rd 60101 — 630-620-8770
Fred Kane, prin.

DuPage HSD 88
Supt. — See Villa Park
Addison Trail HS — 1,800/9-12
213 N Lombard Rd 60101 — 630-628-3302
Scott Helton, prin. — Fax 628-0177

DeVry University — Post-Sec.
1221 N Swift Rd 60101 — 630-953-1300

Driscoll Catholic HS — 500/9-12
555 N Lombard Rd 60101 — 630-543-6310
Fred Muehleman, prin. — Fax 543-1638

Albion, Edwards, Pop. 1,902
Edwards County CUSD 1 — 1,000/PK-12
37 W Main St 62806 — 618-445-2814
Robert Brutcher, supt. — Fax 445-2272
www.echs.edwrds.k12.il.us/
Edwards County HS — 300/9-12
361 W Main St 62806 — 618-445-2325
Stan Struckmeyer, prin. — Fax 445-3154

Aledo, Mercer, Pop. 3,582
Aledo CUSD 201 — 1,000/PK-12
402 E Main St 61231 — 309-582-2238
Ira Cunningham, supt. — Fax 582-7428
www.aledo.mercer.k12.il.us/unit201

Aledo HS 300/9-12
1500 S College Ave 61231 309-582-2223
Kathy Albert, prin. Fax 582-5920
Aledo JHS 200/6-8
1002 SW 6th St 61231 309-582-2441
Douglas Nelson, prin. Fax 582-2440

Alexander, Morgan
Franklin CUSD 1 400/PK-12
PO Box 140 62601 217-478-3011
Fred Roberts, supt. Fax 478-4921
www.franklinhigh.com
Other Schools – See Franklin

Alexis, Mercer, Pop. 847
United CUSD 304 300/K-12
101 N Holloway St Ofc 2 61412 309-482-3344
Jeffrey Whitsitt, supt. Fax 482-3236
united.k12.il.us/
Other Schools – See Monmouth

Algonquin, McHenry, Pop. 27,569
Community Unit SD 300
Supt. — See Carpentersville
Algonquin MS 500/6-8
520 Longwood Dr 60102 847-658-2545
Peggy Thurow, prin. Fax 658-2547
Jacobs HS 2,000/9-12
2601 Bunker Hill Dr 60102 847-658-2500
Michael Bregy, prin. Fax 658-3203

Consolidated SD 158 4,100/PK-12
650 Academic Dr 60102 847-659-6158
Robert Hammon Ph.D., supt. Fax 659-6122
www.d158.k12.il.us
Heineman MS 6-8
725 Academic Dr 60102 847-659-4300
Jim Stotz, prin. Fax 659-4320
Other Schools – See Huntley, Lake in the Hills

Alsip, Cook, Pop. 19,503
Alsip-Hazelgreen-Oaklawn SD 126 1,700/PK-8
11900 S Kostner Ave 60803 708-389-1900
Robert Berger, supt. Fax 396-3793
www.dist126.k12.il.us
Prairie JHS 400/7-8
11910 S Kostner Ave 60803 708-371-3080
Craig Gwaltney, prin. Fax 396-3798

Atwood Heights SD 125 700/PK-8
12150 S Hamlin Ave 60803 708-371-0080
Dr. Thomas Livingston, supt. Fax 371-7847
Hamlin Upper Grade Center 200/6-8
12150 S Hamlin Ave 60803 708-597-1550
Lisa West, prin. Fax 396-0515

Altamont, Effingham, Pop. 2,271
Altamont CUSD 10 800/PK-12
7 S Ewing St 62411 618-483-6195
Jim Littleford, supt. Fax 483-6303
www.altamont.k12.il.us/
Altamont HS 300/9-12
7 S Ewing St 62411 618-483-6194
Jim Strange, prin. Fax 483-5399

Alton, Madison, Pop. 29,841
Alton CUSD 11 5,300/PK-12
PO Box 9028 62002 618-474-2600
David Elson, supt. Fax 463-2126
www.alton.madison.k12.il.us/
Alton HS, 4200 Humbert Rd 62002 2,200/9-12
Philip Trapani, prin. 618-474-2600
Alton MS 6-8
2200 College Ave 62002 618-474-2700
Henrietta Young, prin. Fax 463-2127

CALC Institute of Technology Post-Sec.
235A E Center Dr 62002 618-474-0616
Marquette HS 300/9-12
219 E 4th St 62002 618-463-0580
Michael Slaughter, prin. Fax 463-0582
Mississippi Valley Christian S 200/PK-12
2009 Seminary St 62002 618-462-1071
Kenneth Jackson, prin. Fax 462-9877
Westminster Christian Academy 100/K-12
1145 College Ave 62002 618-465-1918
Greg Myers, admin. Fax 465-1949

Amboy, Lee, Pop. 2,572
Amboy CUSD 272 1,100/PK-12
11 E Hawley St 61310 815-857-2164
Keith Oates, supt. Fax 857-4434
www.amboy.net/
Amboy HS 300/9-12
11 E Hawley St 61310 815-857-3632
Quintin Shepherd, prin. Fax 857-3631
Amboy JHS 400/5-8
140 S Appleton Ave 61310 815-857-3528
Anne Norris, prin. Fax 857-4603

Anna, Union, Pop. 5,073
Anna CCSD 37 700/K-8
301 S Green St 62906 618-833-6812
Bob Odell, supt. Fax 833-3205
www.anna37.union.k12.il.us/
Anna JHS 300/5-8
301 S Green St 62906 618-833-6415
Ronald Cross, prin. Fax 833-6535

Anna-Jonesboro Community HSD 81 500/9-12
608 S Main St 62906 618-833-8421
William Schildknecht, supt. Fax 833-4239
www.ajchs.union.k12.il.us
Anna-Jonesboro HS 500/9-12
608 S Main St 62906 618-833-8502
James Woodward, prin. Fax 833-5931

Annawan, Henry, Pop. 900
Annawan CUSD 226 500/PK-12
501 W South St 61234 309-935-6781
Joe Buresh, supt. Fax 935-6065
Annawan HS 200/9-12
501 W South St 61234 309-935-6781
Linda Rakestraw, prin. Fax 935-6065

Antioch, Lake, Pop. 10,499
Antioch CCSD 34 2,500/PK-8
800 Main St 60002 847-838-8400
Scott Thompson, supt. Fax 838-8404
www.dist34.lake.k12.il.us
Antioch MS 900/6-8
800 Highview Dr 60002 847-838-8310
J. Eric Skoog, supt. Fax 395-3467

Community HSD 117
Supt. — See Lake Villa
Antioch Community HS 2,200/9-12
1133 Main St 60002 847-395-1421
Michael Nekritz, prin. Fax 395-2435

Arcola, Douglas, Pop. 2,674
Arcola CUSD 306 700/K-12
351 W Washington St 61910 217-268-4963
Reggie Clinton, supt. Fax 268-3809
www.arcola.k12.il.us
Arcola JSHS 300/7-12
351 W Washington St 61910 217-268-4962
Cindy Mills, prin. Fax 268-4483

Argenta, Macon, Pop. 855
Argenta-Oreana CUSD 1 1,000/PK-12
PO Box 440 62501 217-795-2313
David Bottom, supt. Fax 795-2174
www.argenta-oreana.org/
Argenta-Oreana HS 300/9-12
PO Box 469 62501 217-795-4821
Sean German, prin. Fax 795-4550
Argenta-Oreana JHS 200/7-8
PO Box 439 62501 217-795-2163
Steve Johnson, prin. Fax 795-4502

Arlington Heights, Cook, Pop. 75,784
Arlington Heights SD 25 4,800/PK-8
1200 S Dunton Ave 60005 847-758-4900
Dr. Sarah Jerome, supt. Fax 758-4907
www.ahsd25.k12.il.us
South MS 900/6-8
400 S Highland Ave 60005 847-398-4250
Maureen Reilly, prin. Fax 394-6260
Thomas MS 800/6-8
1430 N Belmont Ave 60004 847-398-4260
Thomas O'Rourke, prin. Fax 394-6843

Community Consolidated SD 59 6,400/PK-8
2123 S Arlington Heights Rd 60005 847-593-4300
Dr. Dan Schweers, supt. Fax 593-4300
www.ccsd59.org
Other Schools – See Des Plaines, Elk Grove Village,
Mount Prospect
Township HSD 214 11,900/9-12
2121 S Goebbert Rd 60005 847-718-7600
David Schuler, supt. Fax 718-7609
www.d214.org
Hersey HS 1,900/9-12
1900 E Thomas St 60004 847-718-4800
Tina Cantrell, prin. Fax 718-4817
Other Schools – See Buffalo Grove, Elk Grove Village,
Mount Prospect, Rolling Meadows, Wheeling

Chicago Futabakai Japanese S 700/K-12
2550 N Arlington Heights Rd 60004 847-590-5700
Noboru Hayakawa, prin. Fax 590-9759
Northwest Community Hospital Post-Sec.
800 W Central Rd 60005 847-618-1000
St. Viator HS 1,100/9-12
1213 E Oakton St 60004 847-392-4050
Daniel Lydon, prin. Fax 392-4329

Armstrong, Vermilion
Armstrong Twp. HSD 225 200/9-12
PO Box 37 61812 217-569-2122
Bill Mulvaney, supt. Fax 569-2171
Armstrong HS 200/9-12
PO Box 37 61812 217-569-2122
Bill Mulvaney, prin. Fax 569-2171

Arthur, Douglas, Pop. 2,177
Arthur CUSD 305 500/K-12
301 E Columbia St 61911 217-543-2511
Travis Wilson, supt. Fax 543-2210
www.arthur.k12.il.us
Arthur HS 100/9-12
301 E Columbia St 61911 217-543-2146
David Vieth, prin. Fax 543-2174
Arthur JHS 100/7-8
301 E Columbia St 61911 217-543-2146
David Vieth, prin. Fax 543-2174

Ashland, Cass, Pop. 1,382
A-C Central CUSD 262 500/K-12
PO Box 260 62612 217-476-8112
Lyle Rigdon, supt. Fax 476-8100
cass.k12.il.us/ac-central
A-C Central HS 200/9-12
PO Box 260 62612 217-476-3312
Dan Williams, prin. Fax 476-3730
Other Schools – See Chandlerville

Ashton, Lee, Pop. 1,196
Ashton-Franklin Center CUSD 275 300/K-12
611 Western Ave 61006 815-453-7461
John Zick, supt. Fax 453-7462
www.afcschools.net/index.htm
Ashton-Franklin Center HS 100/9-12
611 Western Ave 61006 815-453-7461
Tommy Harvey, prin. Fax 453-7462
Other Schools – See Franklin Grove

Assumption, Christian, Pop. 1,238
Central A & M CUSD 21 1,100/PK-12
RR 2 Box 12C 62510 217-226-4042
Randall Grigg, supt. Fax 226-4133
www.cam.k12.il.us
Central A & M MS 200/6-8
404 Colegrove St 62510 217-226-4241
Scott Cameron, prin. Fax 226-4442
Other Schools – See Moweaqua

Astoria, Fulton, Pop. 1,164
Astoria CUSD 1 400/PK-12
PO Box 620 61501 309-329-2111
Kirk Abernathy, supt. Fax 329-2214
www.astoria.fulton.k12.il.us
Astoria HS 100/9-12
402 N Jefferson St 61501 309-329-2156
Kirk Abernathy, prin. Fax 329-2246
Astoria JHS 100/6-8
402 N Jefferson St 61501 309-329-2158
Jeannie Goodman, prin. Fax 329-2963

Athens, Menard, Pop. 1,781
Athens CUSD 213 800/PK-12
1 Warrior Way 62613 217-636-8761
Scott Laird, supt. Fax 636-8851
www.athens-213.org
Athens HS 300/9-12
1 Warrior Way 62613 217-636-8314
Dave Root, prin. Fax 636-8851
Athens JHS 200/7-8
1 Warrior Way 62613 217-636-8380
Clay Shoufler, prin. Fax 636-8851

Atwood, Douglas, Pop. 1,267
Atwood-Hammond CUSD 39 500/K-12
PO Box 890 61913 217-578-3111
Kenneth Schwengel, supt. Fax 578-3531
Atwood-Hammond HS 100/9-12
PO Box 890 61913 217-578-2226
Randy Niles, prin. Fax 578-3355

Auburn, Sangamon, Pop. 4,319
Auburn CUSD 10 1,200/PK-12
606 W North St 62615 217-438-6164
Kathryn L. Garrett, supt. Fax 438-6483
sangamon.k12.il.us/auburn/
Auburn HS 300/9-12
511 N 7th St 62615 217-438-6817
Darren Root, prin. Fax 438-6153
Auburn MS 300/5-8
601 N 7th St 62615 217-438-6919
Wayne Jones, prin. Fax 438-3700

Augusta, Hancock, Pop. 631
Southeastern CUSD 337
Supt. — See Bowen
Southeastern HS 200/9-12
PO Box 155 62311 217-392-2125
Todd Fox, prin. Fax 392-2229

Aurora, Kane, Pop. 162,184
Aurora East Unit SD 131 11,400/PK-12
417 5th St 60505 630-299-5550
Michael Radakovich, supt. Fax 299-5500
www.d131.kane.k12.il.us/
Aurora East HS 2,500/9-12
500 Tomcat Ln 60505 630-299-8000
Marin Gonzalez, prin. Fax 299-8199
Cowherd MS 800/6-8
441 N Farnsworth Ave 60505 630-299-5900
Joan Glotzbach, prin. Fax 299-5901
Simmons MS 800/6-8
1130 Sheffer Rd 60505 630-299-4150
Randell Ellison, prin. Fax 299-4151
Waldo MS 900/6-8
56 Jackson St 60505 630-299-8400
Lenore Hernandez, prin. Fax 299-8401
Aurora West Unit SD 129 11,600/PK-12
80 S River St 60506 630-301-5000
Dr. James Rydland, supt. Fax 844-5710
www.sd129.org/
Herget MS, 1550 Deerpath Rd 60506 6-8
Daniel Bridges, prin. 630-301-5006
Jefferson MS 800/6-8
1151 Plum St 60506 630-301-5009
Dr. Sandra Kuzniewski, prin. Fax 844-5711
Washington MS 900/6-8
231 S Constitution Dr 60506 630-301-5017
Deborah Meyer, prin. Fax 844-5712
West Aurora HS 3,100/9-12
1201 W New York St 60506 630-301-5018
John Glimco, prin. Fax 844-4505
Other Schools – See North Aurora

Illinois Math & Science Academy SD 600/10-12
1500 Sullivan Rd 60506 630-907-5000
Stephanie Pace Marshall Ph.D., pres. Fax 907-5062
www.imsa.edu
Illinois Math & Science Academy 600/10-12
1500 Sullivan Rd 60506 630-907-5053
Eric McLaren, prin.

Indian Prairie CUSD 204 24,800/PK-12
780 Shoreline Dr 60504 630-375-3000
Howard Crouse, supt. Fax 375-3009
www.ipsd.org
Granger MS 1,000/6-8
2721 Stonebridge Blvd, 630-375-1010
Mary Kelly, prin. Fax 375-1110
Still MS 1,100/6-8
787 Meadowridge Dr 60504 630-375-3900
Jennifer Nonnemacher, prin. Fax 375-3901
Waubonsie Valley Gold Campus 9-9
1305 Long Grove Dr 60504 630-375-3100
Rudy Keller Ed.D., prin. Fax 375-3101
Waubonsie Valley HS 2,300/10-12
2590 Ogden Ave 60504 630-375-3300
James Schmid, prin. Fax 375-3301
Other Schools – See Naperville

Aurora Central Catholic HS 400/9-12
1255 N Edgelawn Dr 60506 630-907-0095
Rev. F. William Etheredge, admin. Fax 907-1076
Aurora Christian HS 500/6-12
2255 Sullivan Rd 60506 630-892-1551
Paul House, supt. Fax 892-1692
Aurora University Post-Sec.
347 S Gladstone Ave 60506 630-892-6431
Marmion Academy 500/9-12
1000 Butterfield Rd, 60502 630-897-6936
John Milroy, hdmstr. Fax 897-7086

Robert Morris College | Post-Sec.
905 Meridian Lake Dr 60504 | 630-375-8000
Rosary HS | 500/9-12
901 N Edgelawn Dr 60506 | 630-896-0831
Sr. Patricia Burke, prin. | Fax 896-8372

Avon, Fulton, Pop. 886
Avon CUSD 176 | 300/PK-12
320 E Woods St 61415 | 309-465-3708
Alene Reuschel, supt. | Fax 465-9030
www.avonschools.us
Avon HS | 100/9-12
320 E Woods St 61415 | 309-465-3621
Tina Stier, prin. | Fax 465-7194
Avon JHS | 100/6-8
320 E Woods St 61415 | 309-465-3621
Alene Reuschel, prin. | Fax 465-7194

Barrington, Cook, Pop. 10,211
Barrington CUSD 220 | 8,700/PK-12
310 James St 60010 | 847-381-6300
Mary Herrmann, supt. | Fax 381-6337
www.cusd220.org
Barrington HS | 2,700/9-12
616 W Main St 60010 | 847-381-1400
Thomas Leonard, prin. | Fax 304-1847
Barrington MS Prairie Campus | 1,100/6-8
40 E Dundee Rd 60010 | 847-304-3990
Craig Winkelman, prin. | Fax 304-3986
Barrington MS Station Campus | 1,000/6-8
215 Eastern Ave 60010 | 847-381-0464
Donn Mendoza, prin. | Fax 842-1343

Barry, Pike, Pop. 1,324
Barry CUSD 1 | 400/PK-12
401 McDonough St 62312 | 217-335-2323
Dallas Singer, supt. | Fax 335-2211
www.barryschool.net/
Barry HS | 100/9-12
401 McDonough St 62312 | 217-335-2323
Roy Kirkpatrick, prin. | Fax 335-2211
Barry MS | 100/6-8
401 McDonough St 62312 | 217-335-2323
Roy Kirkpatrick, prin. | Fax 335-2211

Bartlett, Cook, Pop. 37,558
SD U-46
Supt. — See Elgin
Bartlett HS | 2,900/9-12
701 W Schick Rd 60103 | 630-372-4700
Diane Longfield, prin. | Fax 372-4682
Eastview MS | 1,200/7-8
321 N Oak Ave 60103 | 630-213-5550
Sherry Hullinger, prin. | Fax 213-5563

Bartonville, Peoria, Pop. 6,154
Limestone Community HSD 310 | 1,100/9-12
4201 Airport Rd 61607 | 309-697-6271
William F. Beach, supt. | Fax 697-9635
www.limestone.k12.il.us
Limestone HS | 1,100/9-12
4201 Airport Rd 61607 | 309-697-6271
Kelly J. Funke, admin. | Fax 697-9635

Oak Grove SD 68 | 500/K-8
4812 Pfeiffer Rd 61607 | 309-697-3367
Marc Devore, supt. | Fax 633-2381
www.oakgrove.peoria.k12.il.us/
Oak Grove West JHS | 200/6-8
6018 W Lancaster Rd 61607 | 309-697-0621
Tim Dotson, prin. | Fax 697-0721

Illinois Welding School | Post-Sec.
5901 Washington St 61607 | 309-633-0379

Batavia, Kane, Pop. 26,328
Batavia Unit SD 101 | 6,000/PK-12
335 W Wilson St 60510 | 630-879-4600
Dr. Jack Barshinger, supt. | Fax 345-7896
www.bps101.net
Batavia HS | 1,700/9-12
1200 Main St 60510 | 630-879-4600
Doug Drexler, prin. | Fax 879-4698
Rotolo MS | 1,500/6-8
1501 S Raddant Rd 60510 | 630-879-4620
Donald McKinney, prin. | Fax 879-4624

Beach Park, Lake, Pop. 11,126
Beach Park CCSD 3 | 2,300/PK-8
11315 W Wadsworth Rd 60099 | 847-599-5070
Dr. Robert Di Virgilio, supt. | Fax 263-2133
www.bpd3.lake.k12.il.us/
Beach Park MS | 1,100/5-8
40667 N Green Bay Rd 60099 | 847-731-6330
Rene Santiago, prin. | Fax 731-2402

Beardstown, Cass, Pop. 5,767
Beardstown CUSD 15 | 1,100/PK-12
101 E 15th St 62618 | 217-323-3099
Robert Bagby, supt. | Fax 323-5190
www.beardstown.com/
Beardstown MSHS | 600/6-12
500 E 15th St 62618 | 217-323-3665
Judy Fitzgerald, prin. | Fax 323-3667

Beecher, Will, Pop. 2,378
Beecher CUSD 200U | 900/K-12
PO Box 338 60401 | 708-946-2266
George Obradovich, supt. | Fax 946-3404
www.beecher.will.k12.il.us
Beecher HS | 300/9-12
PO Box 338 60401 | 708-946-2266
Frank Nardi, prin. | Fax 946-3403
Beecher JHS | 200/6-8
PO Box 308 60401 | 708-946-2202
John Jennings, prin. | Fax 946-3272

Beecher City, Effingham, Pop. 495
Beecher City CUSD 20 | 500/PK-12
PO Box 98 62414 | 618-487-5100
Bruce Owen, supt. | Fax 487-5242
www.bcity.effingham.k12.il.us/
Beecher City JSHS, PO Box 97 62414 | 200/7-12
John Kruger, prin. | 618-487-5117

Belleville, Saint Clair, Pop. 41,209
Belle Valley SD 119 | 900/PK-8
1901 Mascoutah Ave 62220 | 618-234-3445
Pamela S. Floit Ph.D., supt. | Fax 234-7730
www.bellevalley.stclair.k12.il.us
Belle Valley MS South | 400/5-8
1901 Mascoutah Ave 62220 | 618-234-7723
Dr. Tamara Leib, prin. | Fax 234-7980

Belleville SD 118 | 3,600/PK-8
105 W A St 62220 | 618-233-2830
Matt Klosterman, supt. | Fax 233-8355
www.belleville118.stclair.k12.il.us
Central JHS | 400/7-8
1801 Central School Rd 62220 | 618-233-5377
Rocky Horrighs, prin. | Fax 233-5440
West JHS | 400/7-8
840 Royal Heights Rd 62226 | 618-234-8200
Pam Knobeloch, prin. | Fax 234-8220

Belleville Township HSD 201 | 4,800/9-12
2600 W Main St 62226 | 618-222-8241
Dr. Brent Clark, supt. | Fax 233-7586
bths201.org/
Belleville HS East | 2,500/9-12
2555 West Blvd 62221 | 618-222-3700
David Kniepkamp, prin. | Fax 222-3799
Belleville HS West | 2,200/9-12
4063 Frank Scott Pkwy W 62223 | 618-222-7500
Robert Dahm, prin. | Fax 235-2484

Harmony Emge SD 175 | 900/PK-8
7401 Westchester Dr 62223 | 618-397-8444
Greg A. Moats, supt. | Fax 397-8446
www.harmony175.org/
Emge JHS | 400/5-8
7401 Westchester Dr 62223 | 618-397-6557
Andrea Rudanovich, prin. | Fax 397-3011

Whiteside SD 115 | 1,200/PK-8
111 Warrior Way 62221 | 618-239-0000
Peggy K. Burke, supt. | Fax 239-9240
www.whiteside.stclair.k12.il.us/
Whiteside MS | 500/5-8
111 Warrior Way 62221 | 618-239-0000
Ron Trelow, prin. | Fax 239-9240

Althoff Catholic HS | 800/9-12
5401 W Main St 62226 | 618-235-1100
Sr. Jan Renz, prin. | Fax 235-9535
Alvareita's College of Cosmetology | Post-Sec.
5400 W Main St 62226 | 618-257-9193
French Academy | 200/PK-12
219 W Main St 62220 | 618-233-7542
Phillip Paeltz, hdmstr. | Fax 233-0541
St. Elizabeth Hospital | Post-Sec.
211 S 3rd St 62220 | 618-234-2120
Southwestern Illinois College | Post-Sec.
2500 Carlyle Ave 62221 | 618-235-2700

Bellwood, Cook, Pop. 20,121
Bellwood SD 88 | 5,100/PK-8
640 Eastern Ave 60104 | 708-344-9344
Dr. Nichelle Rivers, supt. | Fax 344-9416
www.sd88.org
Roosevelt MS | 1,100/6-8
2500 Oak St 60104 | 708-544-3318
Mark Holder, prin. | Fax 544-0192

Belvidere, Boone, Pop. 22,927
Belvidere CUSD 100 | 7,600/PK-12
1201 5th Ave 61008 | 815-544-0301
Donald Schlomann, supt. | Fax 544-4260
www.district100.com
Belvidere Central MS | 900/6-8
8787 Beloit Rd 61008 | 815-544-0190
Harry Gries, prin. | Fax 544-1128
Belvidere HS | 2,100/9-12
1500 East Ave 61008 | 815-547-6345
Chester Pulaski, prin. | Fax 547-7304
Belvidere South MS | 900/6-8
919 E 6th St 61008 | 815-544-3175
Peter Sloan, prin. | Fax 544-2780

Bement, Piatt, Pop. 1,747
Bement SD 5 | 400/PK-12
201 S Champaign St 61813 | 217-678-4200
Dr. Darrell Stevens, supt. | Fax 678-4251
www.bement.k12.il.us
Bement HS | 100/9-12
201 S Champaign St 61813 | 217-678-4200
Douglas Kepley, prin. | Fax 678-4251
Bement MS | 100/6-8
201 S Champaign St 61813 | 217-678-4200
Elaine Day, prin. | Fax 678-4251

Bensenville, DuPage, Pop. 20,668
Bensenville SD 2 | 2,200/PK-8
210 S Church Rd 60106 | 630-766-5940
Dr. William H. Jordan, supt. | Fax 766-6099
www.bsd2.org
Blackhawk MS | 700/6-8
250 S Church Rd 60106 | 630-766-2601
Michael Robey, prin. | Fax 766-7612

Fenton Community HSD 100 | 1,500/9-12
1000 W Green St 60106 | 630-860-6257
Dr. Alf Logan, supt. | Fax 766-3178
www.fenton100.org
Fenton HS | 1,500/9-12
1000 W Green St 60106 | 630-766-2500
Kathleen Pierce, prin. | Fax 766-3178

Robert Morris College | Post-Sec.
1000 Tower Ln # 200 60106 | 630-787-7800

Benson, Woodford, Pop. 399
Roanoke-Benson CUSD 60
Supt. — See Roanoke
Roanoke-Benson JHS | 200/5-8
PO Box 137 61516 | 309-394-2233
Kris Kahler, prin. | Fax 394-2612

Benton, Franklin, Pop. 6,817
Benton CCSD 47 | 1,000/K-8
308 E Church St 62812 | 618-439-3136
Richard Cook, supt. | Fax 435-4840
www.benton47.frnkln.k12.il.us/
Benton MS | 500/5-8
1000 Forrest St 62812 | 618-438-4011
Jamie Neal, prin. | Fax 435-2152
Benton Consolidated HSD 103 | 700/9-12
511 E Main St 62812 | 618-439-6415
Kelly Stewart, supt. | Fax 438-8091
www.bentonhighschool.org
Benton Consolidated HS | 700/9-12
511 E Main St 62812 | 618-439-3103
Sue Woodfin, prin. | Fax 438-2915

Berkeley, Cook, Pop. 5,148
Berkeley SD 87 | 2,900/PK-8
1200 N Wolf Rd 60163 | 708-449-3350
Dr. Joseph Palermo, supt. | Fax 547-3341
www.berkeley87.org
MacArthur MS | 500/6-8
1310 N Wolf Rd 60163 | 708-449-3185
Dr. Keith Wood, prin. | Fax 649-3780
Other Schools – See Northlake

Berwyn, Cook, Pop. 52,534
Berwyn North SD 98 | 3,100/K-8
6633 16th St 60402 | 708-484-6200
John Belmont, supt. | Fax 795-2482
www.d98.cook.k12.il.us
Lincoln MS | 1,000/6-8
6432 16th St 60402 | 708-795-2475
Gail Quilty-Feijt, prin. | Fax 795-2880
Berwyn South SD 100 | 3,100/K-8
3401 Gunderson Ave 60402 | 708-795-2300
Dr. Patricia A. Wernet, supt. | Fax 795-2317
www.schooldistrict100.org
Freedom MS | 6-8
3016 Ridgeland Ave 60402 | 708-795-5800
Anthony Cundari, prin. | Fax 795-5806
Heritage MS | 800/6-8
6850 31st St 60402 | 708-749-6110
Leslie Hodes, prin. | Fax 749-6124

J. S. Morton HSD 201
Supt. — See Cicero
Morton West HS | 3,400/9-12
2400 Home Ave 60402 | 708-222-5901
John Lucas, prin. | Fax 222-5903

Bethalto, Madison, Pop. 9,649
Bethalto CUSD 8 | 2,800/PK-12
225 James St 62010 | 618-377-7200
J. Steven Harsy, supt. | Fax 377-2845
www.bethalto.org
Civic Memorial HS | 900/9-12
200 School St 62010 | 618-377-7220
John Denton, prin. | Fax 377-7001
Trimpe MS | 700/6-8
910 2nd St 62010 | 618-377-7240
Cindy Blasa, prin. | Fax 377-7218

Bethany, Moultrie, Pop. 1,274
Okaw Valley CUSD 302 | 500/PK-12
PO Box 97 61914 | 217-665-3232
Marilyn Bayley, supt. | Fax 665-3601
www.okawvalley.org
Okaw Valley HS | 100/9-12
PO Box 249 61914 | 217-665-3631
Paula Duis, prin. | Fax 665-3863
Other Schools – See Findlay

Biggsville, Henderson, Pop. 338
West Central CUSD 235 | 600/PK-12
RR 1 Box 72 61418 | 309-627-2371
Ralph Grimm, supt. | Fax 627-2453
West Central HS | 200/9-12
RR 1 Box 72 61418 | 309-627-2377
Karen Rima, prin. | Fax 627-2120
Other Schools – See Stronghurst

Bismarck, Vermilion, Pop. 547
Bismarck-Henning CUSD 1 | 900/K-12
PO Box 350 61814 | 217-759-7261
Randy Hird, supt. | Fax 759-7942
www.bismarck.k12.il.us
Bismarck-Henning HS | 300/9-12
PO Box 350 61814 | 217-759-7291
Rich Decman, prin. | Fax 759-7815
Bismarck-Henning JHS | 300/5-8
PO Box 350 61814 | 217-759-7301
Scott Watson, prin. | Fax 759-7313

Bloomingdale, DuPage, Pop. 21,801
Bloomingdale SD 13 | 1,400/K-8
164 Euclid Ave 60108 | 630-893-9590
Kim Perkins, supt. | Fax 893-1818
www.sd13.org
Westfield MS | 500/6-8
149 Fairfield Way 60108 | 630-529-6211
Earl Overman, prin. | Fax 893-9336

Community Consolidated SD 93 | 4,800/PK-8
230 Covington Dr 60108 | 630-893-9393
Henry Gmitro Ed.D., supt. | Fax 539-3450
www.ccsd93.com
Stratford MS | 900/6-8
251 Butterfield Dr 60108 | 630-980-9898
Tom Doyle, prin. | Fax 980-9914
Other Schools – See Carol Stream

Pivot Point Cosmetology Research Center | Post-Sec.
144C E Lake St 60108 | 847-985-5900

Bloomington, McLean, Pop. 68,507
Bloomington AVC |
PO Box 5187 61702 | 309-829-8671
Tom Frazier, dir. | Fax 828-3546
www.bloomingtonavc.org
Bloomington AVC | Vo/Tech
PO Box 5187 61702 | 309-829-8671
Tom Frazier, dir. | Fax 828-3546

Bloomington SD 87 5,500/K-12
300 E Monroe St 61701 309-827-6031
Robert Nielsen, supt. Fax 827-5717
www.district87.org
Bloomington HS 1,500/9-12
1202 E Locust St 61701 309-828-5201
Cindy Helmers, prin. Fax 829-1078
Bloomington JHS 1,300/6-8
910 N Colton Ave 61701 309-827-0086
Dr. Susan Silvey, prin. Fax 829-0084

Central Catholic HS 300/9-12
1201 Airport Rd 61704 309-661-7000
Joy Allen, prin. Fax 661-7001
Hairmasters Institute of Cosmetology Post-Sec.
506 S McClun St 61701 309-828-1884
Illinois Wesleyan University Post-Sec.
PO Box 2900 61702 309-556-1000

Blue Island, Cook, Pop. 23,175
Community HSD 218
Supt. — See Oak Lawn
Eisenhower HS 1,700/9-12
12700 Sacramento Ave 60406 708-597-6300
Joseph Fowler, prin. Fax 597-9958

Cook County SD 130 3,700/PK-8
12300 Greenwood Ave 60406 708-385-6800
Dr. Michael T. Korsak, supt. Fax 385-8467
www.district130.org/
Kerr MS 400/6-8
12915 Maple Ave 60406 708-385-5959
Gwendolyn DeVries, prin. Fax 371-6812
Veterans Memorial MS 400/6-8
12320 Greenwood Ave 60406 708-489-6630
Anthony C. Smerz, prin. Fax 489-3522
Greenbriar S Adult
12015 Maple Ave 60406 708-385-2915
Dr. Carol Crum, prin. Fax 385-8467
Other Schools – See Crestwood

Cannella School of Hair Design Post-Sec.
12840 Western Ave 60406 708-388-4949
Environmental Technical Institute Post-Sec.
13010 Division St 60406 708-385-0707

Blue Mound, Macon, Pop. 1,061
Meridian CUSD 15 1,100/PK-12
PO Box 347 62513 217-692-2599
Dr. Frank Meyer, supt. Fax 692-2036
www.meridian.k12.il.us
Meridian MS 300/6-8
PO Box 320 62513 217-692-2148
Andrew Pygott, prin. Fax 692-2039
Other Schools – See Macon

Bluffs, Scott, Pop. 740
Scott-Morgan CUSD 2 300/PK-12
PO Box 230 62621 217-754-3351
Dr. Richard Basden, supt. Fax 754-3908
bluffs.scott.k12.il.us
Bluffs HS 100/9-12
PO Box 230 62621 217-754-3815
Carol Kilver, prin. Fax 754-3908
Bluffs JHS 100/6-8
PO Box 230 62621 217-754-3815
Carol Kilver, prin. Fax 754-3908

Bluford, Jefferson, Pop. 766
Webber Twp. HSD 204 200/9-12
PO Box 110 62814 618-732-6121
Dale Colwell, supt. Fax 732-8784
Webber Twp. HS, PO Box 110 62814 200/9-12
Roger Panley, prin. 618-732-6121

Bolingbrook, Will, Pop. 66,151
Valley View CUSD 365-U
Supt. — See Romeoville
Addams MS 900/6-8
905 Lily Cache Ln 60440 630-759-7200
Chris Schaeflein, prin. Fax 759-6362
Bolingbrook HS 2,000/9-12
365 Raider Way 60440 630-759-6400
James Mitchem, prin. Fax 759-2650
Brooks MS 6-8
350 Blair Ln 60440 630-759-6340
Ronald Krause, prin. Fax 759-6360
Humphrey MS 900/6-8
777 Falconridge Way 60440 630-972-9240
John Sparlin, prin. Fax 739-8521

Bourbonnais, Kankakee, Pop. 15,840
Bourbonnais ESD 53 2,600/PK-8
281 W John Casey Rd 60914 815-939-2574
Myron Palomba Ph.D., supt. Fax 939-0481
www.besd53.k12.il.us
Bourbonnais Upper Grade Center 600/7-8
200 W John Casey Rd 60914 815-937-4471
Jon Hodge, prin. Fax 935-7855

Kankakee Area Career Center
4083 N 1000W Rd 60914 815-939-4971
Donald Fay, supt. Fax 939-7598
www.kacc.k12.il.us
Kankakee Area Career Center Vo/Tech
4083 N 1000W Rd 60914 815-939-4971
Tom Hahs, prin. Fax 939-7598

Olivet Nazarene University Post-Sec.
1 University Ave 60914 815-939-5011

Bowen, Hancock, Pop. 513
Southeastern CUSD 337 600/PK-12
PO Box 247 62316 217-842-5236
Michael Owen, supt. Fax 842-5248
www.southeastern337.com/
Southeastern JHS 200/5-8
PO Box 247 62316 217-842-5236
Michael Owen, prin. Fax 842-5248
Other Schools – See Augusta

Bradford, Stark, Pop. 767
Bradford CUSD 1 200/PK-8
115 High St 61421 309-897-2801
John Rosenberry, supt. Fax 897-4451
Bradford JHS, PO Box 400 61421 100/6-8
John Rosenberry, prin. 309-897-4441

Bradley, Kankakee, Pop. 13,386
Bradley SD 61 1,600/PK-8
200 State St 60915 815-933-3371
Scott Goselin, supt. Fax 939-6601
www.besd61.k12.il.us/
Bradley Central MS 500/6-8
260 N Wabash Ave 60915 815-939-3564
Todd Schweizer, prin. Fax 939-6603

Bradley-Bourbonnais Comm. HSD 307 1,800/9-12
700 W North St 60915 815-937-3707
Michael Hogan, supt. Fax 937-0156
www.bbchs.k12.il.us
Bradley-Bourbonnais Community HS 1,800/9-12
700 W North St 60915 815-937-3707
Bill Gamble, prin. Fax 937-0156

Trend Setters College of Cosmetology Post-Sec.
665 W Broadway St 60915 815-932-5049

Braidwood, Will, Pop. 5,790
Reed-Custer CUSD 255U 1,800/K-12
255 Comet Dr 60408 815-458-2307
John Asplund, supt. Fax 458-4106
www.rc255.will.k12.il.us/
Reed-Custer HS 500/9-12
249 Comet Dr 60408 815-458-2166
William Freeman, prin. Fax 458-4138
Reed-Custer MS 400/6-8
407 Comet Dr 60408 815-458-2868
Thomas Greene, prin. Fax 458-4118

Breese, Clinton, Pop. 4,196
Central Community HSD 71 600/9-12
7740 Old US Highway 50 62230 618-526-4578
Kevin R. Meyer, supt. Fax 526-7647
Central Community HS 600/9-12
7740 Old US Highway 50 62230 618-526-4578
B. Jones, prin. Fax 526-7647

Mater Dei HS 600/9-12
900 Mater Dei Dr 62230 618-526-7216
Dennis Litteken, prin. Fax 526-8310

Bridgeport, Lawrence, Pop. 2,167
Red Hill CUSD 10 1,300/PK-12
1250 Judy Ave 62417 618-945-2061
Michael P. Mauzy, supt. Fax 945-7607
www.red.lawrnc.k12.il.us
Red Hill HS 300/9-12
908 Church St 62417 618-945-8221
Kevin Andersen, prin. Fax 945-7151

Bridgeview, Cook, Pop. 15,274

Northwestern Business College Post-Sec.
7725 S Harlem Ave 60455 800-682-9113

Brimfield, Peoria, Pop. 901
Brimfield CUSD 309 700/PK-12
PO Box 238 61517 309-446-3378
Dennis McNamara, supt. Fax 446-3716
peoria.k12.il.us/brimfield309/
Brimfield HS 200/9-12
PO Box 380 61517 309-446-3349
Robert Larson, prin. Fax 446-3716

Broadlands, Champaign, Pop. 307
Heritage CUSD 8 500/PK-12
PO Box 260 61816 217-834-3393
Andrew Larson, supt. Fax 834-3016
www.heritage.k12.il.us
Heritage HS 200/9-12
PO Box 260 61816 217-834-3392
Andrew Larson, prin. Fax 834-3016
Other Schools – See Homer

Brookfield, Cook, Pop. 18,933
Brookfield Lagrange Park SD 95 900/K-8
3524 Maple Ave 60513 708-485-0606
Dr. Douglas Rudig, supt. Fax 485-8066
www.d95.w-cook.k12.il.us
Gross MS 500/5-8
3524 Maple Ave 60513 708-485-0600
Thomas Hurlburt, prin. Fax 485-0638

Brownstown, Fayette, Pop. 700
Brownstown CUSD 201 400/K-12
421 S College Ave 62418 618-427-3355
Doug Slover, supt. Fax 427-3704
Brownstown HS 100/9-12
421 S College Ave 62418 618-427-3839
William Wilson, prin. Fax 427-3704
Brownstown JHS 100/7-8
421 S College Ave 62418 618-427-3839
William Wilson, prin. Fax 427-3704

Brussels, Calhoun, Pop. 143
Brussels CUSD 42 100/K-12
PO Box 128 62013 618-883-2131
Tom Knuckles, supt. Fax 883-2514
Brussels HS 100/7-12
PO Box 128 62013 618-883-2131
Jim Roderick, prin. Fax 883-2514

Buckley, Iroquois, Pop. 579

Christ Lutheran HS 50/9-12
PO Box 8 60918 217-394-2547
Sandy Spitz, prin. Fax 394-2097

Buda, Bureau, Pop. 579
Bureau Valley CUSD 340
Supt. — See Manlius
Bureau Valley South S 300/3-8
PO Box 337 61314 309-895-2037
Susan Zbrozek, prin. Fax 895-2200

Buffalo, Sangamon, Pop. 476
Tri-City CUSD 1 600/PK-12
PO Box 290 62515 217-364-4811
Dr. Jack Magruder, supt. Fax 364-4812
www.tc.sangamon.k12.il.us
Tri-City HS 200/9-12
PO Box 290 62515 217-364-4530
Randall Dwyer, prin. Fax 364-4812
Tri-City JHS 100/6-8
PO Box 290 62515 217-364-4530
Randall Dwyer, prin. Fax 364-4812

Buffalo Grove, Cook, Pop. 43,237
Aptakisic-Tripp CCSD 102 2,300/PK-8
1231 Weiland Rd 60089 847-353-5660
Dr. John Mink, supt. Fax 634-5334
www.dist102.k12.il.us/
Aptakisic JHS 600/7-8
1231 Weiland Rd 60089 847-353-5500
Mark Kuzniewski, prin. Fax 634-5347

Kildeer Countryside CCSD 96 3,500/PK-8
1050 Ivy Hall Ln 60089 847-459-4260
Dr. Thomas Many, supt. Fax 459-2344
www.district96.k12.il.us
Twin Groves MS 700/6-8
2600 N Buffalo Grove Rd 60089 847-821-8946
Marie Schalke, prin. Fax 821-8949
Other Schools – See Long Grove

Township HSD 214
Supt. — See Arlington Heights
Buffalo Grove HS 2,200/9-12
1100 W Dundee Rd 60089 847-718-4000
Patrice Johannes, prin. Fax 718-4122

Wheeling CCSD 21
Supt. — See Wheeling
Cooper MS 700/6-8
1050 Plum Grove Cir 60089 847-520-2750
Dr. Jason Klein, prin. Fax 419-3071

Bunker Hill, Macoupin, Pop. 1,806
Bunker Hill CUSD 8 700/K-12
504 E Warren St 62014 618-585-3116
Mary Rogers, supt. Fax 585-3212
bhschools.org
Bunker Hill HS 200/9-12
314 S Meissner St 62014 618-585-3232
Kevin Blankenship, prin. Fax 585-3241
Meissner JHS 200/6-8
504 E Warren St 62014 618-585-4464
Brad Skertich, prin. Fax 585-3222

Burbank, Cook, Pop. 28,049
Burbank SD 111 2,200/PK-8
7600 Central Ave 60459 708-496-0500
Dr. Thomas R. Long, supt. Fax 496-0510
www.burbank.k12.il.us
Liberty JHS 7-8
5900 W 81st St 60459 708-952-3255
Dr. Mark Schall, prin. Fax 229-0659

Reavis Twp. HSD 220 1,600/9-12
6034 W 77th St 60459 708-599-7200
Dr. James Steyskal, supt. Fax 599-8751
www.rhsd.s-cook.k12.il.us/
Reavis HS 1,600/9-12
6034 W 77th St 60459 708-599-7200
Dr. Bonita Simon, prin. Fax 599-8751

Queen of Peace HS 900/9-12
7659 Linder Ave 60459 708-458-7600
P. Nolan-Fitzgerald, prin. Fax 458-5734
St. Laurence HS 600/9-12
5556 W 77th St 60459 708-458-6900
James Muting, prin. Fax 458-6908

Burlington, Kane, Pop. 477
Central CUSD 301 2,400/PK-12
PO Box 396 60109 847-464-6005
Dr. Bradley J. Hawk, supt. Fax 464-6021
www.burlington.k12.il.us/
Central HS 700/9-12
PO Box 68 60109 847-464-6030
David Olsen, prin. Fax 464-6039
Central MS 600/6-8
PO Box 397 60109 847-464-6000
Lloyd Stover, prin. Fax 464-1709

Burr Ridge, DuPage, Pop. 10,781
Burr Ridge CCSD 180 800/PK-8
15w451 91st St 60527 630-734-6600
Dr. Frank Rink, supt. Fax 325-6450
www.ccsd180.org
Burr Ridge MS 300/5-8
15w451 91st St 60527 630-325-5454
Dr. Debra LeBlanc, prin. Fax 325-6450

Gower SD 62
Supt. — See Willowbrook
Gower MS 400/5-8
7941 S Madison St 60527 630-323-8275
Douglas Wood, prin. Fax 323-2055

Pleasantdale SD 107 800/PK-8
7450 Wolf Rd 60527 708-784-2013
Dr. Mark Fredisdorf, supt. Fax 246-0161
www.d107.org/
Pleasantdale MS 300/5-8
7450 Wolf Rd 60527 708-246-3210
Meg Pokorny, prin. Fax 352-0092

ITT Technical Institute Post-Sec.
7040 High Grove Blvd 60527 630-455-6470
Olympia College Post-Sec.
6880 N Frontage Rd 60527 630-920-1102

Bushnell, McDonough, Pop. 3,150
Bushnell-Prairie City CUSD 170 800/PK-12
845 Walnut St 61422 309-772-9461
David Messersmith, supt. Fax 772-9462
www.bushnell-pc.k12.il.us/

Bushnell-Prairie City HS 200/9-12
845 Walnut St 61422 309-772-2113
Anita Pyle, prin. Fax 772-2104
Bushnell-Prairie City JHS 200/6-8
847 Walnut St 61422 309-772-3123
Raymond Krey, prin.

Byron, Ogle, Pop. 3,292
Byron CUSD 226 1,400/PK-12
696 N Colfax St 61010 815-234-5491
Dr. Margaret Fostiak, supt. Fax 234-4106
leeogle.org/byron/
Byron HS 600/9-12
696 N Colfax St 61010 815-234-5491
Marty Voiles, prin. Fax 234-4106
Byron MS 500/6-8
325 N Colfax St 61010 815-234-5491
Steve Herkert, prin. Fax 234-4225

Cahokia, Saint Clair, Pop. 16,043
Cahokia CUSD 187 4,800/PK-12
1700 Jerome Ln 62206 618-332-3700
Jana Bechtoldt, supt. Fax 332-3706
www.cahokia.stclair.k12.il.us
Cahokia HS 1,200/9-12
800 Range Ln 62206 618-332-3730
Pam Manning, prin. Fax 332-3747
Sauget Academic Center 5-12
1700 Jerome Ln 62206 618-332-3820
Phyllis Jackson, prin. Fax 332-3824
Wirth/Parks MS 1,200/6-8
1900 Mousette Ln 62206 618-332-3722
Tony Brooks, prin. Fax 332-3741

Cairo, Alexander, Pop. 3,462
Cairo Unit SD 1 800/PK-12
2403 Walnut St 62914 618-734-4102
Gary Whitledge, supt. Fax 734-4047
Cairo JSHS 300/7-12
4201 Sycamore St 62914 618-734-2187
Theodis Maltoja, prin. Fax 734-2189

Calumet City, Cook, Pop. 38,688
Calumet City SD 155 1,300/K-8
540 Superior Ave 60409 708-862-7665
Dr. Troy Paraday, supt. Fax 868-7455
www.calumetcity155.org/
Wentworth JHS 500/6-8
560 Superior Ave 60409 708-862-0750
Linda Bozeman, prin. Fax 862-1194

Dolton SD 149 3,700/PK-8
292 Torrence Ave 60409 708-868-7861
Traci Brown, supt. Fax 868-7850
www.schooldistrict149.org
Dirksen MS 1,300/6-8
1650 Pulaski Rd 60409 708-868-2340
Ray Warner, prin. Fax 868-7589

Hoover-Schrum Memorial SD 157 700/PK-8
1255 Superior Ave 60409 708-868-7500
Michael Wierzbicki, supt. Fax 868-7511
www.hsdist157.org
Schrum Memorial MS 300/6-8
485 165th St 60409 708-862-4236
Bennie Knott, prin. Fax 862-4580

Thornton Fractional Township HSD 215 3,100/9-12
1601 Wentworth Ave 60409 708-585-2309
Dr. Robert K. Wilhite, supt. Fax 585-2318
www.tfd215.org/
Center for Academics & Technology Vo/Tech
1605 Wentworth Ave 60409 708-585-2350
Kent Farlow, prin. Fax 585-2356
Thornton Fractional North HS 1,500/9-12
755 Pulaski Rd 60409 708-585-1000
Dwayne Evans, prin. Fax 585-1010
Other Schools – See Lansing

Westwood College Post-Sec.
80 River Oaks Dr Ste D-49 60409 708-832-1988

Calumet Park, Cook, Pop. 8,351
Calumet Public SD 132 1,300/PK-8
1440 W Vermont Ave 60827 708-388-8920
Dr. Doris Hope-Jackson, supt. Fax 388-2138
Calumet MS 400/6-8
1440 W Vermont Ave 60827 708-388-8820
Adrienne Saverson, prin. Fax 388-8557

Cambridge, Henry, Pop. 2,139
Cambridge CUSD 227 600/PK-12
300 S West St 61238 309-937-2144
Steven J. Fink, supt. Fax 937-5128
Cambridge Community HS 200/9-12
300 S West St 61238 309-937-2051
Monte Munsinger, prin. Fax 937-5128
Cambridge JHS 100/7-8
300 S West St 61238 309-937-2051
Monte Munsinger, prin. Fax 937-5128

Campbell Hill, Jackson, Pop. 325
Trico CUSD 176 1,000/K-12
PO Box 220 62916 618-426-1111
Dennis Smith, supt. Fax 426-3625
www.trico176.org
Trico HS 300/9-12
PO Box 336 62916 618-426-1111
Jack Smith, prin. Fax 426-3701
Trico JHS 200/6-8
PO Box 335 62916 618-426-1111
Dennis Smith, prin. Fax 426-3712

Camp Point, Adams, Pop. 1,209
Central CUSD 3 1,000/K-12
2110 Highway 94 N 62320 217-593-7116
Martin Cook, supt. Fax 593-7026
www.cusd3.com/
Central HS 300/9-12
2110 Highway 94 N 62320 217-593-7731
Bill Reed, prin. Fax 593-7025
Central JHS 300/5-8
2110 Highway 94 N 62320 217-593-7741
Pat Heinecke, prin. Fax 593-7028

Canton, Fulton, Pop. 14,970
Canton Union SD 66 2,800/PK-12
20 W Walnut St 61520 309-647-9411
James Lewis, supt. Fax 649-5036
www.cantonusd.org
Canton HS 800/9-12
1001 N Main St 61520 309-647-1820
Robin Tonkin, prin. Fax 649-5039
Ingersoll MS 800/5-8
1605 E Ash St 61520 309-647-6951
Lan Eberle, prin. Fax 647-6959

Graham Hospital Post-Sec.
210 W Walnut St 61520 309-647-4086
LaMonts Intl School of Cosmetology Post-Sec.
60 E Elm St 61520 309-647-4224
Spoon River College Post-Sec.
23235 N County Road 22 61520 309-647-4645

Carbondale, Jackson, Pop. 24,952
Carbondale Community HSD 165 1,200/9-12
330 S Giant City Rd 62902 618-457-4722
Steven Sabens, supt. Fax 457-3353
www.cchs165.jacksn.k12.il.us/
Carbondale Community HS 1,200/9-12
1301 E Walnut St 62901 618-457-3371
Vicky King, prin. Fax 549-1686

Carbondale ESD 95 1,400/PK-8
PO Box 2048 62902 618-457-3591
Dr. Elizabeth Lewin, supt. Fax 457-2043
www.ces95.jacksn.k12.il.us
Carbondale MS 400/6-8
1150 E Grand Ave 62901 618-457-2174
Brad Morris, prin. Fax 457-2176

Brehm Preparatory S 100/6-12
1245 E Grand Ave 62901 618-457-0371
Dr. Richard Collins, dir. Fax 529-1248
Covenant Christian S 100/PK-12
1218 W Freeman St 62901 618-529-3733
Paul Plunkett, prin. Fax 529-3733
Southern Illinois University 62901 Post-Sec.
618-453-2121

Carlinville, Macoupin, Pop. 5,762
Carlinville CUSD 1 1,600/PK-12
18456 Shipman Rd 62626 217-854-9823
Mike Kelly, supt. Fax 854-2777
www.carlinvilleschools.net/
Carlinville HS 500/9-12
829 W Main St 62626 217-854-3104
Pat Drew, prin. Fax 854-5260
Carlinville MS 400/6-8
110 Illinois Ave 62626 217-854-3106
Pat Drew, prin. Fax 854-4503

Blackburn College Post-Sec.
700 College Ave 62626 217-854-3231

Carlyle, Clinton, Pop. 3,424
Carlyle CUSD 1 1,300/PK-12
1400 13th St 62231 618-594-8283
Richard DeFauw, supt. Fax 594-8285
www.carlyle.k12.il.us
Carlyle HS 400/9-12
1461 12th St 62231 618-594-2453
Joe Wilkerson, prin. Fax 594-8286
Carlyle JHS 400/5-8
1631 12th St 62231 618-594-8292
Jim McClaren, prin. Fax 594-8294

Carmi, White, Pop. 5,341
Carmi-White County CUSD 5 1,300/PK-12
301 W Main St 62821 618-382-2341
Dr. Keith Talley, supt. Fax 384-3207
www.carmi.white.k12.il.us
Carmi-White County HS 400/9-12
800 W Main St 62821 618-382-4661
Brad Lee, prin. Fax 382-2453
Carmi-White County MS 300/6-8
205 W Main St 62821 618-382-4631
Terry Gholson, prin. Fax 384-2076

Carol Stream, DuPage, Pop. 40,114
Community Consolidated SD 93
Supt. — See Bloomingdale
Stream MS 900/6-8
283 El Paso Ln 60188 630-462-8940
John Healy, prin. Fax 462-9224

Glenbard Twp. HSD 87
Supt. — See Glen Ellyn
Glenbard North HS 2,900/9-12
990 Kuhn Rd 60188 630-653-7000
Prentiss Lea, prin. Fax 653-7259

Carpentersville, Kane, Pop. 34,815
Community Unit SD 300 18,600/K-12
300 Cleveland Ave 60110 847-426-1300
Dr. Kenneth Arndt, supt. Fax 426-1209
www.d300.kane.k12.il.us
Carpentersville MS 800/7-8
100 Cleveland Ave 60110 847-426-1380
Stephanie Ramstad, prin. Fax 426-1404
Dundee-Crown HS 2,500/9-12
1500 Kings Rd 60110 847-426-1415
Robert Whitehouse, prin. Fax 426-1245
Other Schools – See Algonquin, Dundee, Hampshire

Carrier Mills, Saline, Pop. 1,864
Carrier Mills-Stonefort CUSD 2 600/PK-12
PO Box 217 62917 618-994-2392
Richard Morgan, supt. Fax 994-2929
Carrier Mills HS 200/9-12
PO Box 217 62917 618-994-2392
Richard Morgan, prin. Fax 994-2929

Carrollton, Greene, Pop. 2,552
Carrollton CUSD 1 700/K-12
702 5th St 62016 217-942-5314
Michael Barry, supt. Fax 942-9259
www.c-hawks.org

Carrollton HS 300/9-12
950 3rd St 62016 217-942-6913
Alan Churchman, prin. Fax 942-6835

Carterville, Williamson, Pop. 4,809
Carterville CUSD 5 1,600/PK-12
306 Virginia Ave 62918 618-985-4826
Tim Bleyer, supt. Fax 985-2041
www.c-ville.wilmsn.k12.il.us/
Carterville HS 500/9-12
816 S Division St 62918 618-985-2940
Don Smith, prin. Fax 985-2741
Carterville IS 500/5-8
300 School St 62918 618-985-6411
Keith Liddell, prin. Fax 985-2492

John A. Logan College Post-Sec.
700 Logan College Dr 62918 618-985-3741

Carthage, Hancock, Pop. 2,585
Carthage CUSD 338 800/PK-12
210 S Adams St 62321 217-357-3922
Daniel James, supt. Fax 357-6793
carthageschools.k12.il.us
Carthage HS 300/9-12
210 S Adams St 62321 217-357-2136
Perry Miller, prin. Fax 357-3569
Carthage MS 200/5-8
210 S Adams St 62321 217-357-3914
Vicki Hardy, prin. Fax 357-3755

Cary, McHenry, Pop. 18,121
Cary CCSD 26 3,300/K-8
400 Haber Rd 60013 847-639-7788
Michael Smith, supt. Fax 639-3898
mail.cary26.k12.il.us/
Cary JHS 800/7-8
2109 Crystal Lake Rd 60013 847-639-2148
Linda Coeglein, prin. Fax 516-5507

Community HSD 155
Supt. — See Crystal Lake
Cary-Grove HS 1,800/9-12
2208 3 Oaks Rd 60013 847-639-3825
Sue Popp, prin. Fax 639-3873

Casey, Clark, Pop. 2,943
Casey-Westfield CUSD C4 1,200/PK-12
PO Box 100 62420 217-932-2184
Robert Ehlke, supt. Fax 932-5553
www.cw.k12.il.us/
Casey-Westfield HS 300/9-12
306 E Edgar Ave 62420 217-932-2175
Clyde Frankie, prin. Fax 932-2004
Roosevelt JHS 200/7-8
401 E Main St 62420 217-932-2177
Jo Beard, prin. Fax 932-2753

Catlin, Vermilion, Pop. 2,058
Catlin CUSD 5 600/PK-12
701 1/2 W Vermilion St 61817 217-427-2116
Dr. Guy Banicki, supt. Fax 427-2117
www.catlin.k12.il.us
Catlin HS 200/9-12
701 W Vermilion St 61817 217-427-5331
Kevin Themus, prin. Fax 427-2468

Centralia, Marion, Pop. 13,739
Centralia SD 135 1,500/PK-8
400 S Elm St 62801 618-532-1907
Thomas W. Hawkins, supt. Fax 532-4986
www.ccs135.com
Centralia JHS, 900 S Pine St 62801 500/6-8
Demetria Rogers, prin. 618-533-7130

Centralia Twp. HSD 200 1,100/9-12
1000 E 3rd St 62801 618-532-7391
David Daum, supt. Fax 532-8952
www.centraliahs.org
Centralia HS 1,100/9-12
1000 E 3rd St 62801 618-532-7391
Patricia Collins, prin. Fax 532-8952

Kaskaskia College Post-Sec.
27210 College Rd 62801 618-545-3000

Cerro Gordo, Piatt, Pop. 1,397
Cerro Gordo CUSD 100 600/K-12
PO Box 79 61818 217-763-5221
Ronald Baize, supt. Fax 763-6562
www.cerrogordo.k12.il.us
Cerro Gordo HS 200/9-12
PO Box 79 61818 217-763-2711
Brett Robinson, prin. Fax 763-6562
Cerro Gordo MS 100/6-8
PO Box 79 61818 217-763-6411
Paul Workman, prin. Fax 763-6562

Chadwick, Carroll, Pop. 490
Chadwick-Milledgeville CUSD 399
Supt. — See Milledgeville
Chadwick JHS 100/6-8
PO Box 15 61014 815-684-5191
Roy S Webb, prin. Fax 684-5241

Champaign, Champaign, Pop. 71,958
Champaign CUSD 4 9,400/PK-12
703 S New St 61820 217-351-3800
Arthur R. Culver, supt. Fax 352-3590
www.champaignschools.org/
Centennial HS 1,500/9-12
913 Crescent Dr 61821 217-351-3951
Dr. Judy Wiegand, prin. Fax 351-3730
Central HS 1,300/9-12
610 W University Ave 61820 217-351-3914
William Freyman, prin. Fax 351-3919
Edison MS 700/6-8
306 W Green St 61820 217-351-3790
Joe Williams, prin. Fax 355-2564
Franklin MS 600/6-8
817 N Harris Ave 61820 217-351-3819
Carol Stack, prin. Fax 351-3729
Jefferson MS 800/6-8
1115 Crescent Dr 61821 217-351-3790
Dr. Susan Zola, prin. Fax 351-3754

HS of St. Thomas More 200/9-12
3901 N Mattis Ave 61822 217-352-7210
Tim Millage Ph.D., prin. Fax 352-7213
Judah Christian S 500/PK-12
908 N Prospect Ave 61820 217-359-1701
Daniel Cole, prin. Fax 359-0214
Parkland College Post-Sec.
2400 W Bradley Ave 61821 217-351-2200

Chandlerville, Cass, Pop. 723
A-C Central CUSD 262
Supt. — See Ashland
A-C Central JHS 100/6-8
191 S Bluff St 62627 217-458-2224
Sandra Moody, prin. Fax 458-2223

Channahon, Will, Pop. 10,065
Channahon SD 17 1,600/PK-8
24920 S Sage St 60410 815-467-4315
Lynn Krizic, supt. Fax 467-4343
www.channahon.will.k12.il.us
Channahon JHS 400/7-8
24917 W Sioux Dr 60410 815-467-4314
Matt Swick, prin. Fax 467-2188

Charleston, Coles, Pop. 20,305
Charleston CUSD 1 2,900/PK-12
410 W Polk Ave 61920 217-639-1000
Dr. Gary Niehaus, supt. Fax 639-1005
www.charleston.k12.il.us
Charleston HS 900/9-12
1603 Lincoln Ave 61920 217-639-5000
John Broome, prin. Fax 639-5005
Charleston MS 500/7-8
920 Smith Dr 61920 217-639-6000
Sandy Wilson, prin. Fax 639-6005

Eastern Illinois University Post-Sec.
600 Lincoln Ave 61920 217-581-5000

Chatham, Sangamon, Pop. 9,330
Ball Chatham CUSD 5 4,100/PK-12
201 W Mulberry St 62629 217-483-2416
Dr. Richard Voltz, supt. Fax 483-2940
dist5.bcsd.k12.il.us
Glenwood HS 1,300/9-12
1501 E Plummer Blvd 62629 217-483-2424
Nate Cunningham, prin. Fax 483-5402
Glenwood MS 1,000/6-8
595 Chatham Rd 62629 217-483-2481
Jill Larson, prin. Fax 483-4940

Chester, Randolph, Pop. 7,939
Chester CUSD 139 1,100/PK-12
1940 Swanwick St 62233 618-826-4509
Rebecca Keim, supt. Fax 826-4500
chesteryellowjackets.com
Chester HS 400/9-12
1901 Swanwick St 62233 618-826-2302
Danny Marks, prin. Fax 826-3723

Chicago, Cook, Pop. 2,869,121
City of Chicago SD 299 399,400/PK-12
125 S Clark St 60603 773-553-1000
Arne Duncan, supt. Fax 535-1502
www.cps.k12.il.us/
AASTA 9-12
730 N Pulaski Rd 60624 773-534-6980
Carole Collins Ayanlaja, prin. Fax 534-6805
Academy of Applied Arts Science and Tech 9-12
730 N Pulaski Rd 60624 773-534-6500
Carol Collins-Ayanlaja, prin. Fax 534-6504
Academy of Business Entrepreneurship 9-12
6520 S Wood St 60636 773-535-9150
T. Pannell, prin. Fax 535-9090
Albany Park Multicultural Academy 300/7-8
5039 N Kimball Ave 60625 773-534-5108
Dr. Mary Lee Lasher-Taylor, prin. Fax 534-5178
Allied Health S 9-12
3250 W Monroe St 60624 773-534-6455
Jaquelyn Trainer-Grant, prin. Fax 534-6409
Ames MS 1,000/6-8
1920 N Hamlin Ave 60647 773-534-4970
Lorraine Cruz, prin. Fax 534-4975
Amundsen HS 1,500/9-12
5110 N Damen Ave 60625 773-534-2320
Carlos Munoz, prin. Fax 534-2330
Anderson Community Academy 600/7-8
6315 S Claremont Ave 60636 773-535-9070
Helen Johnson, prin. Fax 535-9478
Arai MS 300/7-8
900 W Wilson Ave 60640 773-534-2610
Barbara Hayes, prin. Fax 534-2589
Armour S 300/4-8
950 W 33rd Pl 60608 773-535-4530
Shelley Cordova, prin. Fax 535-4501
Austin Community Academy HS 1,500/9-12
231 N Pine Ave 60644 773-534-6300
Dr. Tony Scott, prin. Fax 534-6046
BEST Academy 9-9
2719 E 89th St 60617 773-535-6597
Jo Ann Thomas-Woods Ph.D., prin. Fax 535-6598
Best Practices HS 400/9-12
2040 W Adams St 60612 773-534-7610
Clifton Gooden, prin. Fax 534-7601
Big Picture HS 800/9-12
2710 S Dearborn St 60616 773-534-9160
Kothyn Alexander, prin. Fax 534-9223
Big Picture HS at Chavez 50/9-9
4946 S Paulina St 60609 773-535-9219
Alfredo Nambo, prin. Fax 535-9477
Black Magnet S 300/4-8
9101 S Euclid Ave 60617 773-535-6390
Thomas Little, prin. Fax 535-6047
Bogan Computer Tech HS 2,100/9-12
3939 W 79th St 60652 773-535-2180
Robert C. Miller, prin. Fax 535-2165
Bouchet MS 7-8
7401 S Chappel Ave 60649 773-535-0510
Patricia Williams, prin. Fax 535-0559
Bowen HS 700/9-12
2710 E 89th St 60617 773-535-6000
Barbara Strong, prin. Fax 535-6034
Bronzeville Scholastic Institute 9-12
4934 S Wabash Ave 60615 773-535-1150
Dr. Latunja Williams, prin. Fax 535-1228
Brooks College Prep HS 800/9-12
250 E 111th St 60628 773-535-9930
Patricia Nichols, prin. Fax 535-9939
Burnham ES Anthony Branch 4-8
9800 S Torrence Ave 60617 773-535-6526
Dr. Linda Moore, prin. Fax 535-6568
Business Technology HS Vo/Tech
2935 W Polk St 60612 773-534-6900
Obie Laflour, prin. Fax 534-6924
Calumet Career Prep Academy HS Vo/Tech
8131 S May St 60620 773-535-3500
Daya Locke, prin. Fax 535-3526
Canter MS 400/7-8
4959 S Blackstone Ave 60615 773-535-1410
Carolyn Epps, prin. Fax 535-1047
Career/Theme-Focused SLC 9-12
2245 W Jackson Blvd 60612 773-534-7550
Melver Scott, prin. Fax 534-9330
Carver MS 500/4-8
801 E 133rd Pl 60827 773-535-5656
Ida Stewart, prin. Fax 535-5020
Carver Military Academy 800/9-12
13100 S Doty Ave 60827 773-535-5250
John Thomas, prin. Fax 535-5037
Castellanos MS 800/4-8
2524 S Central Park Ave 60623 773-534-1620
Myriam M. Romero, prin. Fax 534-1611
Chicago Academy HS 9-9
3400 N Austin Ave 60634 773-534-0146
Brian Sims, prin. Fax 534-0192
Chicago Agricultural HS 600/9-12
3857 W 111th St 60655 773-535-2500
David Gilligan, prin. Fax 535-2507
Chicago Discovery Academy 400/9-12
2710 E 89th St 60617 773-535-7947
Lynne Nuzzo, prin. Fax 535-6930
Chicago Military Academy 500/9-12
3519 S Giles Ave 60653 773-534-9750
Richard Gray, prin. Fax 534-9760
Chicago Vocational Career Academy Vo/Tech
2100 E 87th St 60617 773-535-6100
Maria Miles, prin. Fax 535-6633
Clark Academic Prep HS 1,100/6-12
5101 W Harrison St 60644 773-534-6250
Annette Gurley, prin. Fax 534-6292
Clemente Community Academy HS 2,300/9-12
1147 N Western Ave 60622 773-534-4000
Fax 534-4012
Collins HS 900/9-12
1313 S Sacramento Dr 60623 773-534-1500
Andrew Denton, prin. Fax 534-1399
CoMETS S 9-12
6520 S Wood St 60636 773-535-9150
Audrey Askins, prin. Fax 535-9090
Community Links HS 9-12
2401 S Marshall Blvd 60623 773-534-1997
Dr. Carlos Azcoitia, prin. Fax 534-0354
Construction Technology HS Vo/Tech
2935 W Polk St 60612 773-534-6900
Michael Dimitroff, prin. Fax 534-6924
Corliss HS 1,100/9-12
821 E 103rd St 60628 773-535-5115
Anthony Spivey, prin. Fax 535-5511
Crane HS 9-12
2245 W Jackson Blvd 60612 773-534-7550
Melver Scott, prin. Fax 534-9330
Crane Technical Preparatory Common S 7-12
2245 W Jackson Blvd 60612 773-534-7550
Melver Scott, prin. Fax 534-7557
Culinary Arts HS 9-12
4747 S Union Ave 60609 773-535-1625
Keith Morris, prin. Fax 535-1581
Culinary Arts HS 9-12
3250 W Monroe St 60624 773-534-6455
Kim Minor, prin. Fax 534-6409
Curie Metro HS 3,000/9-12
4959 S Archer Ave 60632 773-535-2100
Jerryelyn Jones, prin. Fax 535-2049
De La Cruz MS 200/6-8
2317 W 23rd Pl 60608 773-535-4585
Dr. Roy Pletsch, prin. Fax 535-4534
Doolittle MS 400/5-8
535 E 35th St 60616 773-535-1040
Lori Lennix, prin. Fax 535-1034
Douglass Academy 1,100/6-10
543 N Waller Ave 60644 773-534-6176
Dr. Debra Crump, prin. Fax 534-6172
Dunbar Vocational Career Academy Vo/Tech
3000 S King Dr 60616 773-534-9000
Dr. Barbara Hall, prin. Fax 534-9250
Dusable HS 400/10-12
4934 S Wabash Ave 60615 773-535-1100
James Townsend, prin. Fax 535-1004
Dyett Academic Center 600/7-12
555 E 51st St 60615 773-535-1825
Jacquelyn Lemon, prin. Fax 535-1037
Englewood Technical Prep HS 900/9-12
6201 S Stewart Ave 60621 773-535-3600
Diane Jackson, prin. Fax 535-3586
Evergreen Middle Academy 500/6-8
3537 S Paulina St 60609 773-535-4836
Elizabeth Elizondo, prin. Fax 535-4853
EXCEL Academy 9-12
730 N Pulaski Rd 60624 773-534-6560
Marva Whaley-Anobah, prin. Fax 534-6556
FACETS S 9-12
6520 S Wood St 60636 773-535-9150
Jennifer Olson, prin. Fax 535-9090
Farragut Career Academy Vo/Tech
2345 S Christiana Ave 60623 773-534-1300
Edward Guerra, prin. Fax 534-1336
Fenger Academy HS 1,200/9-12
11220 S Wallace St 60628 773-535-5430
William Johnson, prin. Fax 535-5450
Field S 600/4-8
7019 N Ashland Blvd 60626 773-534-2030
Cora Suddoth, prin. Fax 534-2189
Fine and Performing Arts Academy 9-12
1147 N Western Ave 60622 773-534-4000
Fax 534-4012
Foreman HS 1,800/9-12
3235 N Leclaire Ave 60641 773-534-3400
Frank Candioto, prin. Fax 534-3684
Freshman Academy 9-9
4747 S Union Ave 60609 773-535-1625
Theresa White, prin. Fax 535-1581
Freshman Academy 9-9
2100 E 87th St 60617 773-535-6100
JoAnn McCriston, prin. Fax 535-6633
Freshman Academy 9-9
5630 S Rockwell St 60629 773-535-9230
Miguel Davis, prin. Fax 535-9411
Gage Park HS 1,800/9-12
5630 S Rockwell St 60629 773-535-9230
Wilfredo Ortiz, prin. Fax 535-9238
Gallistel Branch MS 6-8
10200 S Avenue J 60617 773-535-6450
Patrick MacMahon, prin. Fax 535-6449
Global Visions Academy 9-9
2710 E 89th St 60617 773-535-6905
Patricia Jones-Hight, prin. Fax 535-6492
Gompers Fine Arts Option MS 500/4-8
12302 S State St 60628 773-535-5475
Melody Seaton, prin. Fax 535-5483
Graphic Design HS 9-12
2935 W Polk St 60612 773-534-6900
Leo Maxie, prin. Fax 534-6924
Grimes S 200/5-8
5450 W 64th Pl 60638 773-535-2364
David Dalton, prin. Fax 535-2366
Hamline S 400/4-8
4747 S Bishop St 60609 773-535-4565
Valerie Brown, prin. Fax 535-4546
Hancock College Prep 800/9-12
4034 W 56th St 60629 773-535-2410
Nancy Apke, prin. Fax 535-2434
Harlan Community Academy HS 900/9-12
9652 S Michigan Ave 60628 773-535-5400
Dr. Gertrude Hill, prin. Fax 535-5061
Harper HS 1,500/9-12
6520 S Wood St 60636 773-535-9150
Dr. Ron Gibbs, prin. Fax 535-9090
Harvey Academic Preparatory S 1,100/8-12
3814 W Iowa St 60651 773-534-6400
Dr. Lona Bibbs, prin. Fax 534-6422
Hirsch Metro HS 600/9-12
7740 S Ingleside Ave 60619 773-535-3100
Joyce Cooper, prin. Fax 535-3240
Hope College Prep HS 1,000/5-12
5515 S Lowe Ave 60621 773-535-3160
Michael Durr, prin. Fax 535-3444
Horticulture HS 9-12
3250 W Adams St 60624 773-534-6455
Carol Williams, prin. Fax 534-6409
Hubbard HS 1,700/9-12
6200 S Hamlin Ave 60629 773-535-2200
Andrew Manno, prin. Fax 535-2218
Hyde Park Academy HS Vo/Tech
6220 S Stony Island Ave 60637 773-535-0880
Stacey McJunkins, prin. Fax 535-0633
Infinity Math/Science Tech HS 9-12
3120 S Kostner Ave 60623 773-535-4225
Martha Irizarry, prin. Fax 535-4270
International Language & Career Academy 9-12
6520 S Wood St 60636 773-535-9150
Tresa Cortesi, prin. Fax 535-9090
Irving Park MS 300/7-8
3815 N Kedvale Ave 60641 773-534-3750
Dr. Carmen Sanchez, prin. Fax 534-3757
Johns Middle Academy 400/4-8
6936 S Hermitage Ave 60636 773-535-9144
Connell McFarland, prin. Fax 535-9499
Jones College Prep HS 700/9-12
606 S State St 60605 773-534-8600
Dr. Donald Fraynd, prin. Fax 534-8625
Journalism Communications & Law Academy 9-12
1147 N Western Ave 60622 773-534-4000
Fax 534-4012
JROTC Service Corps Academy 9-12
730 N Pulaski Rd 60624 773-534-8960
Ferdinand Wipachit, prin. Fax 534-9866
Juarez Community Academy 1,800/9-12
2150 S Laflin St 60608 773-534-7030
Natividad Loredo, prin. Fax 534-7058
Julian HS 1,700/9-12
10330 S Elizabeth St 60643 773-535-5170
William Harris, prin. Fax 535-5230
Kelly HS 2,900/9-12
4136 S California Ave 60632 773-535-4900
Algrid C. Pretkelis, prin. Fax 535-4841
Kelvyn Park HS 2,000/9-12
4343 W Wrightwood Ave 60639 773-534-4200
Dr. Sandra Fontanez-Phelan, prin. Fax 534-4507
Kennedy HS 1,500/9-12
6325 W 56th St 60638 773-535-2325
James Gorecki, prin. Fax 535-2485
Kenwood HS 1,600/9-12
5015 S Blackstone Ave 60615 773-535-1350
Elizabeth Kirby, prin. Fax 535-1360
King HS 900/9-12
4445 S Drexel Blvd 60653 773-535-1180
Dr. Nathaniel Mason, prin. Fax 535-1658
Lake View HS 1,300/9-12
4015 N Ashland Ave 60613 773-534-5440
Scott Feaman, prin. Fax 534-5585
Lane Tech HS Vo/Tech
2501 W Addison St 60618 773-534-5400
Keith Foley, prin. Fax 534-5544
Lincoln Park HS 2,100/9-12
2001 N Orchard St 60614 773-534-8130
Bessie Karvelas, prin. Fax 534-8218
Lindblom College Prep HS 300/8-12
6130 S Wolcott Ave 60636 773-535-9300
Willie Sanders, prin. Fax 535-9314
Lindblom Math/Science Academy 9-12
6130 S Wolcott Ave 60636 773-535-9300
Alan Mather, prin. Fax 535-9314
Logandale MS 6-8
3212 W George St 60618 773-534-5350
Dr. Dennis Sweeney, prin. Fax 534-5349
Lozano Annex 5-8
1501 N Greenview Ave 60622 773-534-4750
Dr. Aurelio Acevedo, prin. Fax 534-4740

Madero MS	400/6-8
3202 W 28th St 60623	773-535-4466
Dr. Rosa Ramirez, prin.	Fax 535-4469
Manley Career Academy	Vo/Tech
2935 W Polk St 60612	773-534-6900
Dr. Katherine Flanagan, prin.	Fax 534-6924
Marshall Metro HS	1,300/9-12
3250 W Adams St 60624	773-534-6455
Dr. Gwendolyn Boyd, prin.	Fax 534-6409
Marshall MS	700/7-8
3900 N Lawndale Ave 60618	773-534-5200
Jose Barillas, prin.	Fax 534-5292
Mather HS	1,900/9-12
5835 N Lincoln Ave 60659	773-534-2350
John Butterfield, prin.	Fax 534-2424
Math Science & Tech Academy	9-12
1147 N Western Ave 60622	773-534-4000
	Fax 534-4012
Medical Careers Academy	9-12
6631 N Bosworth Ave 60626	773-534-2000
Chadra Lang, prin.	Fax 534-2141
Morgan Park JSHS	2,200/7-12
1744 W Pryor Ave 60643	773-535-2550
Dr. Beryl Shingles, prin.	Fax 535-2706
Moses Vines Prep Academy	9-12
730 N Pulaski Rd 60624	773-534-8808
Patricia Woodson, prin.	Fax 534-8945
Multicultural Arts HS	9-12
3120 S Kostner Ave 60623	773-535-4242
Jose Rico, prin.	Fax 535-4273
New Millenium S of Health	9-9
2710 E 89th St 60617	773-535-7650
Dr. Arlana Bedard, prin.	Fax 535-6489
Nia MS	100/4-8
2040 W Adams St 60612	773-534-7494
Michelle Willis, prin.	Fax 534-7497
North-Grand HS	9-12
4338 W Wabansia Ave 60639	773-534-8520
Dr. Asuncion Ayala, prin.	Fax 534-8535
Northside College Prep HS	900/9-12
5501 N Kedzie Ave 60625	773-534-3954
Dr. James Lalley, prin.	Fax 534-3964
Northwest MS	1,100/6-8
5252 W Palmer St 60639	773-534-3250
Marilyn Strojny, prin.	Fax 534-3251
Orr Community Academy HS	800/9-12
730 N Pulaski Rd 60624	773-534-6500
Marva Whaley-Anobah, prin.	Fax 534-6570
Paideia Academy	9-9
6631 N Bosworth Ave 60626	773-534-2000
Peggy Miller-Kramer, prin.	Fax 534-2141
Payton HS	800/9-12
1034 N Wells St 60610	773-534-0034
Gail Ward, prin.	Fax 534-0035
Peace Academy	9-9
6631 N Bosworth Ave 60626	773-534-2000
Margaret Blair, prin.	Fax 534-2141
Perez S	400/3-8
1241 W 19th St 60608	773-534-7650
Sylvia Stamatoglou, prin.	Fax 534-7621
Pershing West MS	4-8
3200 S Calumet Ave 60616	773-534-9240
Cheryl Watkins, prin.	Fax 534-9249
Phillips Academy HS	900/9-12
244 E Pershing Rd 60653	773-535-1603
Euel Bunton, prin.	Fax 535-1605
Phoenix Military Academy	300/9-12
145 S Campbell Ave 60612	773-534-7275
Ferdinand Wipachit, prin.	Fax 534-7273
Prosser Career Academy	Vo/Tech
2148 N Long Ave 60639	773-534-3200
Kenneth Hunter, prin.	Fax 534-3382
Raby S	9-10
3545 W Fulton Blvd 60624	773-534-6755
Janice Jackson, prin.	Fax 534-6938
Richards Career Academy	Vo/Tech
5009 S Laflin St 60609	773-535-4945
Dr. O. Joyce Smith, prin.	Fax 535-4883
Rickover Navy Academy HS	9-12
5900 N Glenwood Ave 60660	773-534-2890
Michael Biela, prin.	Fax 534-2895
Rising Starts Academy	7-8
9000 S Exchange Ave 60617	773-535-6360
Ben Perez, prin.	Fax 535-6303
Robeson HS	1,100/9-12
6835 S Normal Blvd 60621	773-535-3800
James Breashears, prin.	Fax 535-3620
Roosevelt HS	1,600/9-12
3436 W Wilson Ave 60625	773-534-5000
Dr. Alejandra Alvarez, prin.	Fax 534-5044
Sawyer S	900/4-8
5248 S Sawyer Ave 60632	773-535-9275
Gerard Gliege, prin.	Fax 535-9216
Schiller MS	300/4-8
640 W Scott St 60610	773-534-8490
Cynthia Fitzpatrick, prin.	Fax 534-8016
School for Social Justice	9-12
3120 S Kostner Ave 60623	773-535-4300
Rito Martinez, prin.	Fax 535-4271
School of Entrepreneurship	900/9-12
7527 S Constance Ave 60649	773-535-6190
Bill Gerstein, prin.	Fax 535-6960
School of Finance Academy	9-12
4747 S Union Ave 60609	773-535-1625
Joann Scott-Tablo, prin.	Fax 535-1581
School of Finance Academy	9-12
3250 W Adams St 60624	773-534-6455
Tierra Buchanan, prin.	Fax 534-6409
School of Leadership	900/9-12
7527 S Constance Ave 60649	773-535-6190
James Patrick, prin.	Fax 535-6960
School of Technology HS	100/9-9
7529 S Constance Ave 60649	773-535-6180
Dr. Olufemi Adeniji, prin.	Fax 535-6088
School of the Arts	600/9-12
7529 S Constance Ave 60649	773-535-6180
Doug Maclin, prin.	Fax 535-6088
Schurz HS	2,600/9-12
3601 N Milwaukee Ave 60641	773-534-3420
Mary Ann Folino, prin.	Fax 534-3573
Senn HS	1,800/7-12
5900 N Glenwood Ave 60660	773-534-2365
Richard Norman, prin.	Fax 534-2369

Simeon Career Academy	Vo/Tech
8147 S Vincennes Ave 60620	773-535-3200
Leonard Kenebrew, prin.	Fax 535-3465
South Shore Community Academy	400/10-12
7529 S Constance Ave 60649	773-535-6180
Leonard Kenebrew, prin.	Fax 535-6088
Spry Community Links HS	800/9-12
2400 S Marshall Blvd 60623	773-534-1997
Dr. Carlos Azcoitia, prin.	Fax 534-0354
Steinmetz Academic Centre	2,400/9-12
3030 N Mobile Ave 60634	773-534-3030
Dr. Eunice Madon, prin.	Fax 534-3151
Stevenson MS	6-8
4350 W 79th St 60652	773-535-0215
Pamela Rice, prin.	Fax 535-0219
Sullivan HS	1,100/9-12
6631 N Bosworth Ave 60626	773-534-2000
Dr. Joseph Atria, prin.	Fax 534-2141
Taft HS	2,000/7-12
6530 W Bryn Mawr Ave 60631	773-534-1000
Dr. Arthur Tarvardian, prin.	Fax 534-1027
Tilden Career Community HS	1,200/9-12
4747 S Union Ave 60609	773-535-1625
Phyllis Hammond, prin.	Fax 535-1866
Tonti Branch MS	6-8
4950 S Laporte Ave 60638	773-535-2000
Maria Vallejos-Howell, prin.	Fax 535-2474
UPLIFT Community S	6-12
900 W Wilson Ave 60640	773-534-2875
Stephanie Moore, prin.	Fax 534-2876
Vaughn Occupational HS	Vo/Tech
4355 N Linder Ave 60641	773-534-3600
Nancy Mayer, prin.	Fax 534-3631
Von Steuben Metro HS	1,500/9-12
5039 N Kimball Ave 60625	773-534-5100
Clifton Burgess, prin.	Fax 534-5210
Washington HS	1,500/9-12
3535 E 114th St 60617	773-535-5725
Juana Rivera-Vidal, prin.	Fax 535-5038
Wells Community Academy HS	1,100/9-12
936 N Ashland Ave 60622	773-534-7010
Delores Pidgeon, prin.	Fax 534-7078
Westinghouse Career Academy	Vo/Tech
3301 W Franklin Blvd 60624	773-534-6400
Dr. Lona Bibbs, prin.	Fax 534-6422
Williams Preparatory Academy	200/6-8
2710 S Dearborn St 60616	773-534-9235
Bernard Murray, prin.	Fax 534-9236
World Language/Career Academy	9-12
1147 N Western Ave 60622	773-534-4000
	Fax 534-4012
World Language HS	9-12
3120 S Kostner Ave 60623	773-535-4334
Mirtha Quintana-Toomey, prin.	Fax 535-4272
Young Magnet JSHS	2,100/7-12
211 S Laflin St 60607	773-534-7500
Joyce Kenner, prin.	Fax 534-7261
Englewood Evening HS	Adult
6201 S Stewart Ave 60621	773-535-3600
Diane L. Jackson, prin.	Fax 535-3586

Adler School of Professional Psychology	Post-Sec.
65 E Wacker Pl 60601	312-201-5900
Advocate Illinois Masonic	Post-Sec.
836 W Wellington Ave 60657	773-296-8950
Advocate Trinity Hospital	Post-Sec.
2320 E 93rd St 60617	773-978-2000
American Academy of Art	Post-Sec.
332 S Michigan Ave Ste 3 60604	312-461-0600
American Floral Art School	Post-Sec.
634 S Wabash Ave # 210 60605	312-922-9328
American Health Information Management	Post-Sec.
233 N Michigan Ave Ste 2150 60601	312-233-1184
Archbishop Quigley Preparatory Seminary	200/9-12
103 E Chestnut St 60611	312-787-9343
Peter Snieg, prin.	Fax 787-9167
Argosy University/Chicago	Post-Sec.
350 N Orleans St 60654	888-488-7537
Bais Yaakov HS for Girls	100/9-12
3333 W Peterson Ave 60659	773-267-1494
Shulamis Keller, prin.	Fax 267-4798
Brother Rice HS	1,200/9-12
10001 S Pulaski Rd 60655	773-429-4300
James Antos, prin.	Fax 779-5239
Cain's Barber College	Post-Sec.
365 E 51st St 60615	773-536-4441
Cannella School of Hair Design	Post-Sec.
9012 S Commercial Ave 60617	773-221-4700
Cannella School of Hair Design	Post-Sec.
5912 W Roosevelt Rd 60644	773-287-3400
Cannella School of Hair Design	Post-Sec.
4269 S Archer Ave 60632	773-890-0412
Cannella School of Hair Design	Post-Sec.
4217 W North Ave 60639	773-278-4477
Capri Garfield Ridge Sch of Beauty Coll	Post-Sec.
2653 W 63rd St 60629	773-778-8161
Cardean University	Post-Sec.
111 N Canal St Ste 455 60606	866-948-1289
Career College of Chicago	Post-Sec.
11 E Adams St 60603	312-895-6300
Catholic Theological Union	Post-Sec.
5401 S Cornell Ave 60615	773-324-8000
Cheder Lubavitch HS	100/9-12
2754 W Rosemont Ave 60659	773-743-7716
Esther Moscowitz, prin.	Fax 743-7735
Chicago Academy for the Arts	200/9-12
1010 W Chicago Ave 60622	312-421-0202
Pamela Jordan, prin.	Fax 421-3816
Chicago Hope Academy	100/9-12
2189 W Bowler St 60612	312-491-1600
Tina Muzikowski, dir.	Fax 491-1616
Chicago Jesuit Academy	100/5-8
212 S Francisco Ave 60612	773-638-6103
Chicago Sch. of Professional Psychology	Post-Sec.
325 N Wells St 60610	312-329-6600
Chicago School of Massage Therapy	Post-Sec.
17 N State St Fl 5 60602	312-753-7900
Chicago SDA Academy	100/PK-12
7008 S Michigan Ave 60637	773-873-3005
Donaldson Williams, prin.	
Chicago State University	Post-Sec.
9501 S King Dr 60628	773-995-2000

Chicago Theological Seminary	Post-Sec.
5757 S University Ave 60637	773-752-5757
Chicago Waldorf S	400/PK-12
1300 W Loyola Ave 60626	773-465-2662
Mark Lohss, prin.	Fax 465-6648
Chubb Institute	Post-Sec.
25 E Washington St 60602	800-248-2237
College of Office Technology	Post-Sec.
1514 W Division St # 2 60622	773-278-0042
Columbia College	Post-Sec.
600 S Michigan Ave 60605	312-663-1600
Computer Systems Institute	Post-Sec.
318 W Adams St Fl 10 60606	312-346-6774
Cook County Hospital	Post-Sec.
1825 W Harrison St 60612	312-633-8533
Cooking & Hospitality Inst. of Chicago	Post-Sec.
361 W Chestnut St 60610	312-944-0884
Coyne American Institute	Post-Sec.
330 N Green St 60607	800-999-5220
Cristo Rey Jesuit HS	400/9-12
1852 W 22nd Pl 60608	773-890-6800
Patricia Garrity, prin.	Fax 890-6801
De La Salle Institute Main Campus	1,200/9-12
3434 S Michigan Ave 60616	312-842-7355
James Krygier, prin.	Fax 842-5640
De La Salle Institute - West Campus	400/9-12
1040 W 32nd Pl 60608	773-650-6800
Diane Brown, prin.	Fax 650-9722
De Paul University	Post-Sec.
1 E Jackson Blvd 60604	312-362-8000
De Paul University	Post-Sec.
2323 N Seminary Ave 60614	312-362-8000
DeVry University	Post-Sec.
3300 N Campbell Ave 60618	773-929-8500
DeVry University	Post-Sec.
225 W Washington St # 100 60606	312-372-4900
Eagles' Wings Urban Academy	100/PK-12
2447 W Granville Ave 60659	773-743-6345
Cynthia Peterson, admin.	Fax 743-6068
East-West University	Post-Sec.
816 S Michigan Ave 60605	312-939-0111
Erikson Institute	Post-Sec.
420 N Wabash Ave 60611	312-755-2250
Gordon Tech HS	700/9-12
3633 N California Ave 60618	773-539-3600
Edward Howe, prin.	Fax 539-9158
Greater West Town School	Post-Sec.
2021 W Fulton St # 204 60612	312-563-9570
Hales Franciscan HS	400/9-12
4930 S Cottage Grove Ave 60615	773-285-8400
John Young, prin.	Fax 285-7025
Hanna Sacks Girls HS	200/9-12
3021 W Devon Ave 60659	773-338-9222
Hanna Belsky, prin.	Fax 338-2405
Harold S. Washington College	Post-Sec.
30 E Lake St 60601	312-553-5600
Harrington College of Design	Post-Sec.
200 W Madison St 60606	312-939-4975
Harry S. Truman College	Post-Sec.
1145 W Wilson Ave 60640	773-878-1700
Holy Trinity HS	400/9-12
1443 W Division St 60622	773-278-4212
Charlene Szumilas, prin.	Fax 278-0144
Ida Crown Jewish Academy	300/9-12
2828 W Pratt Blvd 60645	773-973-1450
Rabbi Leonard Matanky, prin.	Fax 973-6131
IIT Chicago-Kent College of Law	Post-Sec.
565 W Adams St 60661	312-906-5000
Illinois College of Optometry	Post-Sec.
3241 S Michigan Ave 60616	312-225-1700
Illinois Institute of Technology	Post-Sec.
3300 S Federal St 60616	312-567-3000
Illinois School of Health Careers	Post-Sec.
220 S State St Ste 600 60604	312-913-1230
Institute for Clinical Social Work	Post-Sec.
200 N Michigan Ave Ste 407 60601	312-726-8480
International Academy of Design & Tech	Post-Sec.
1 N State St # 400 60602	312-980-9200
John Marshall Law School	Post-Sec.
315 S Plymouth Ct 60604	312-427-2737
Josephinum HS	200/9-12
1501 N Oakley Blvd 60622	773-276-1261
Sr. Martha Roughan, prin.	Fax 292-3963
Keller Graduate School	Post-Sec.
8501 W Higgins Rd Ste 410 60631	773-695-1000
Kendall College	Post-Sec.
900 N North Branch St 60622	877-588-8860
Kennedy-King College	Post-Sec.
6800 S Wentworth Ave 60621	773-602-5000
Lake Forest Graduate Sch. of Management	Post-Sec.
230 S LaSalle Ste 100 60604	312-435-5330
Latin S of Chicago	1,100/PK-12
59 W North Blvd 60610	312-582-6000
Donald Firke, hdmstr.	Fax 582-6011
Leo HS	300/9-12
7901 S Sangamon St 60620	773-224-9600
Sean Stalling, prin.	Fax 224-3856
Lexington College	Post-Sec.
310 S Peoria St 60607	312-226-6294
Loyola University	Post-Sec.
6525 N Sheridan Rd 60626	773-508-2320
Loyola University - Mundelein College	Post-Sec.
6525 N Sheridan Rd 60626	773-262-8100
Loyola University of Chicago	Post-Sec.
820 N Michigan Ave 60611	312-915-6000
Lubavitch Mesivta of Chicago	100/9-12
2756 W Morse Ave 60645	773-262-0430
Rabbi Moshe Perlstein, dean	Fax 338-2209
Lutheran School of Theology at Chicago	Post-Sec.
1100 E 55th St 60615	773-256-0700
Luther HS North	300/9-12
5700 W Berteau Ave 60634	773-286-3600
Dr. Jeffrey D. Daley, prin.	Fax 286-0304
Luther HS South	300/6-12
3130 W 87th St 60652	773-737-1416
Anthony Rainey, prin.	Fax 737-2882
Lycee Francais de Chicago	400/PK-12
613 W Bittersweet Pl 60613	773-665-0066
Dr. Sylvette Nicolini, prin.	Fax 665-1725
MacCormac College	Post-Sec.
29 E Madison St 60602	312-922-1884
Mac Daniels Beauty School	Post-Sec.
5228 N Clark St 60640	773-561-2376

Malcolm X College Post-Sec.
1900 W Van Buren St 60612 312-850-7031
Maranatha Christian Academy 200/K-12
115 W 108th St 60628 773-264-7702
Betty Millsap, prin. Fax 264-8720
Maria HS 700/9-12
6727 S California Ave 60629 773-925-8686
Sr. Nancy Gannon, prin. Fax 925-8885
Marist HS 1,400/9-12
4200 W 115th St 60655 773-881-5300
Larry Tucker, prin. Fax 881-0595
McCormick Theological Seminary Post-Sec.
5460 S University Ave 60615 800-228-4687
Meadville/Lombard Theological School Post-Sec.
5701 S Woodlawn Ave 60637 773-256-3000
Medical Careers Institute Post-Sec.
116 S Michigan Ave 60603 312-782-9804
Midwest College of Oriental Medicine Post-Sec.
4334 N Hazel St Ste 206 60613 800-593-2320
Moody Bible Institute Post-Sec.
820 N La Salle Dr 60610 800-967-4624
Morgan Park Academy 500/PK-12
2153 W 111th St 60643 773-881-6700
J. William Adams, hdmstr. Fax 881-8409
Mother McAuley Liberal Arts HS 1,600/9-12
3737 W 99th St 60655 773-881-6500
Sr. Rose Wiorek, prin. Fax 881-6562
Mt. Carmel HS 700/9-12
6410 S Dante Ave 60637 773-324-1020
Rev. Carl Markelz, prin. Fax 324-9235
Northeastern Illinois University Post-Sec.
5500 N Saint Louis Ave 60625 773-583-4050
North Park Coll. & Theological Seminary Post-Sec.
3225 W Foster Ave 60625 773-244-6200
North Shore SDA Jr. Academy 100/PK-10
5220 N California Ave 60625 773-769-0733
Helen Bacchus, prin. Fax 769-0928
Northwestern Business College Post-Sec.
4829 N Lipps Ave 60630 773-777-4220
Northwestern Memorial Hospital Post-Sec.
251 E Huron St 60611 312-926-2000
Northwestern University Post-Sec.
303 E Chicago Ave 60611 312-503-6950
Notre Dame HS 500/9-12
3000 N Mango Ave 60634 773-622-9494
Karen Brown, prin. Fax 622-8511
Olive-Harvey College Post-Sec.
10001 S Woodlawn Ave 60628 773-291-6100
Olympia College Post-Sec.
247 S State St Ste 400 60604 312-913-1616
Our Lady of Guadalupe MS 100/6-8
3600 E 96th St 60617 773-768-4021
Robert MacNamara, prin. Fax 768-4165
Our Lady of Tepeyac HS 300/9-12
2228 S Whipple St 60623 773-522-0023
Joni Thompson, prin. Fax 522-0508
Parker S 900/PK-12
330 W Webster Ave 60614 773-353-3000
Daniel B. Frank, prin. Fax 549-4669
Providence-St. Mel S 700/K-12
119 S Central Park Blvd 60624 773-722-4600
Jeanette DiBella, prin. Fax 722-9004
Pyramid Career Institute Post-Sec.
3051 N Lincoln Ave 60657 773-975-9898
Resurrection HS 900/9-12
7500 W Talcott Ave 60631 773-775-6616
Jo Marie Yonkus, prin. Fax 775-0611
Richard J. Daley College Post-Sec.
7500 S Pulaski Rd 60652 773-838-7500
Robert Morris College Post-Sec.
401 S State St 60605 312-935-6800
Roosevelt University Post-Sec.
430 S Michigan Ave 60605 312-341-3500
Rosel School of Cosmetology Post-Sec.
2444 W Devon Ave 60659 773-508-5600
Rush University Post-Sec.
600 S Paulina St # 440 60612 312-942-7120
St. Augustine College Post-Sec.
1333 W Argyle St 60640 773-878-8756
St. Benedict HS 400/9-12
3900 N Leavitt St 60618 773-539-0066
Mary Kay Nickels, prin. Fax 539-3397
St. Francis De Sales HS 300/9-12
10155 S Ewing Ave 60617 773-731-7272
Richard Hawkins, prin. Fax 731-7888
St. Gregory HS 300/9-12
1677 W Bryn Mawr Ave 60660 773-907-2100
Erika Mickelburgh, prin. Fax 907-2120
St. Ignatius College Prep HS 1,200/9-12
1076 W Roosevelt Rd 60608 312-421-5900
Dr. Catherine Karl, prin. Fax 421-7124
St. Mary of Providence School Post-Sec.
4200 N Austin Ave 60634
St. Patrick HS 1,000/9-12
5900 W Belmont Ave 60634 773-282-8844
Dr. Joseph Schmidt, prin. Fax 282-2361
St. Rita of Cascia HS 800/9-12
7740 S Western Ave 60620 773-925-6600
Rev. Thomas R. McCarthy, prin. Fax 925-2451
St. Scholastica Academy 300/9-12
7416 N Ridge Blvd 60645 773-764-5715
Anne Matz, prin. Fax 764-0304
St. Xavier University Post-Sec.
3700 W 103rd St 60655 773-298-3000
San Miguel MS 100/6-8
1949 W 48th St 60609 773-890-1481
Josh Rundle, prin. Fax 254-3382
San Miguel S Gary Comer Campus 50/5-8
819 N Leamington Ave 60651 773-261-8851
Gordon Hannon, prin. Fax 261-8854
School of the Art Institute of Chicago Post-Sec.
37 S Wabash Ave 60603 773-889-5100
SER Business and Technical Institute Post-Sec.
3948 W 26th St Ste 213 60623 773-227-3377
Spanish Coalition for Jobs Post-Sec.
2011 W Pershing Rd 60609 773-247-0707
Spertus College Post-Sec.
618 S Michigan Ave 60605 312-922-9012
Taylor Business Institute Post-Sec.
200 N Michigan Ave Ste 301 60601 312-658-5100
Telshe Yeshiva-Chicago Post-Sec.
3535 W Foster Ave 60625 773-463-7738
Telshe Yeshiva HS 100/9-12
3535 W Foster Ave 60625 773-463-7738
Rabbi Shmuel Adler, dir. Fax 463-2849
The Illinois Institute of Art Post-Sec.
350 N Orleans St Lbby 136 60654 312-280-3500
University of Chicago Post-Sec.
5801 S Ellis Ave 60637 773-702-1234
University of Chicago Lab S 1,700/PK-12
1362 E 59th St 60637 773-702-9450
Dr. David W. Magill, dir. Fax 702-7455
University of Illinois at Chicago Post-Sec.
PO Box 5220 60680 312-996-3000
Univ. of Chicago Hospital/Roosevelt U. Post-Sec.
5841 S Maryland Ave 60637 773-702-6240
VanderCook College of Music Post-Sec.
3140 S Federal St 60616 800-448-2655
Warde S - Holy Name Cathedral 300/5-8
751 N State St 60610 312-466-0700
Susan Sperling, prin. Fax 337-7180
Westwood College Post-Sec.
17 N State St Fl 3 60602 312-739-0850
Westwood College of Technology Post-Sec.
8501 W Higgins Rd Ste 500 60631 847-928-0200
Wilbur Wright College North Post-Sec.
4300 N Narragansett Ave 60634 773-777-7900

Chicago Heights, Cook, Pop. 32,297
Bloom Township HSD 206 3,000/9-12
100 W 10th St 60411 708-755-7010
Glen Giannetti, supt. Fax 755-6859
www.bloomdistrict206.org
Bloom HS 1,500/9-12
101 W 10th St 60411 708-755-1122
Dr. Lenell Navarre, prin. Fax 755-1149
Bloom Trail HS 1,500/9-12
22331 Cottage Grove Ave 60411 708-758-7000
Ronald Ray, prin. Fax 758-8372

Chicago Heights SD 170 3,400/PK-8
30 W 16th St 60411 708-756-4165
Dr. Dorothy Helsel, supt. Fax 756-4164
66.99.25.40/education/district/district.php?sectionid
Washington MS 300/5-8
25 W 16th Pl 60411 708-756-4841
Rhonda Sneed, prin. Fax 756-1008

Flossmoor SD 161 2,600/PK-8
41 E Elmwood Dr 60411 708-647-7000
Dr. Donna C. Joy, supt. Fax 754-2153
www.sd161.org
Other Schools – See Flossmoor

Marian Catholic HS 1,700/9-12
700 Ashland Ave 60411 708-755-7565
Sr. Kathleen Anne Tait, prin. Fax 756-9758
Prairie State College Post-Sec.
202 S Halsted St 60411 708-709-3500

Chicago Ridge, Cook, Pop. 13,900
Chicago Ridge SD 127-5 1,200/PK-8
6135 W 108th St 60415 708-636-2000
Bernard Jumbeck, supt. Fax 636-0916
www.crsd1275.org
Finley JHS 400/6-8
10835 Lombard Ave 60415 708-636-2005
Mary McDonald, prin. Fax 636-0045

Chillicothe, Peoria, Pop. 5,778
Illinois Valley Central Unit SD 321 2,100/PK-12
1300 W Sycamore St 61523 309-274-5418
Dr. David Kinney, supt. Fax 274-5046
www.ivcschools.com/
Chillicothe Elementary Center 500/3-8
914 W Truitt Ave 61523 309-274-6266
Dianne Pointer, prin. Fax 274-2010
Illinois Valley Central HS 700/9-12
1300 W Sycamore St 61523 309-274-5481
Kenton Bergman, prin. Fax 274-8613

Chrisman, Edgar, Pop. 1,287
Edgar County CUSD 6 400/K-12
23231 IL Highway 1 61924 217-269-2513
Norman Tracy, supt. Fax 269-3231
www.chrisman.k12.il.us
Chrisman HS 100/9-12
23231 IL Highway 1 61924 217-269-2823
Terry Furnish, prin. Fax 269-3231
Chrisman-Scottland JHS 100/6-8
23231 IL Highway 1 61924 217-269-3980
Terry Furnish, prin. Fax 269-3231

Christopher, Franklin, Pop. 2,812
Christopher Unit SD 99 800/PK-12
1 Bearcat Dr 62822 618-724-9461
Mark L. Miller, supt. Fax 724-9400
Christopher HS 200/9-12
1 Bearcat Dr 62822 618-724-9461
Forrest Moreland, prin. Fax 724-9400

Cicero, Cook, Pop. 83,029
Cicero SD 99 14,100/K-8
5110 W 24th St 60804 708-863-4856
Dr. Edward F. Aksamit, supt. Fax 652-8105
cicd99.edu/
Unity JHS West 1,300/8-8
2115 S 54th Ave 60804 708-863-8268
Denise Boyle, prin. Fax 656-5652

J. S. Morton HSD 201 6,300/9-12
2423 S Austin Blvd 60804 708-222-5702
Dr. Ben Nowakowski, supt. Fax 222-3087
www.jsmortonhs.com
Morton East HS 2,900/10-12
2423 S Austin Blvd 60804 708-222-5751
Frank Zarate, prin. Fax 222-3090
Morton Freshman Center 9-9
1801 S 55th Ave 60804 708-863-2200
Joseph Gunty, prin. Fax 863-2244
Other Schools – See Berwyn

Morton College Post-Sec.
3801 S Central Ave 60804 708-656-8000

Cisne, Wayne, Pop. 664
North Wayne CUSD 200 500/PK-12
PO Box 235 62823 618-673-2151
Joyce Carson, supt. Fax 673-2152
Cisne HS 100/9-12
PO Box 70 62823 618-673-2154
Penny Arnold, prin. Fax 673-2155
Cisne MS 100/5-8
PO Box 69 62823 618-673-2156
Joyce Carson, prin. Fax 673-2152

Cissna Park, Iroquois, Pop. 783
Cissna Park CUSD 6 400/K-12
PO Box 1 60924 815-457-2171
Dr. Daniel Heinold, supt. Fax 457-3033
www.cissnapark.k12.il.us
Cissna Park HS 100/9-12
PO Box 1 60924 815-457-2171
Jeffrey Maurer, prin. Fax 457-3033
Cissna Park JHS 100/6-8
PO Box 1 60924 815-457-2171
Jeffrey Maurer, prin. Fax 457-3033

Clarendon Hills, DuPage, Pop. 8,235
CCSD 181
Supt. — See Westmont
Clarendon Hills MS 700/6-8
301 Chicago Ave 60514 630-887-4260
David Bendis, prin. Fax 887-4267

Maercker SD 60 1,300/PK-8
5800 Holmes Ave 60514 630-323-2086
Joseph Matula, supt. Fax 323-5541
www.maercker.org
Other Schools – See Willowbrook

Clay City, Clay, Pop. 983
Clay City CUSD 10 400/PK-12
PO Box 542 62824 618-676-1431
William Mauser, supt. Fax 676-1430
www.claycityschools.org
Clay City HS 100/9-12
PO Box 405 62824 618-676-1522
David Mills, prin. Fax 676-1481
Clay City JHS 100/6-8
PO Box 545 62824 618-676-1521
David Mills, prin. Fax 676-1537

Clifton, Iroquois, Pop. 1,284
Central CUSD 4 1,300/PK-12
PO Box 637 60927 815-694-2231
Tonya Evans, supt. Fax 694-2844
www.clifton-u4.k12.il.us/
Central HS 400/9-12
1134 E 3100 North Rd Ste A 60927 815-694-2321
Dr. Arlyn Rabideau, prin. Fax 694-2709
Nash MS 400/5-8
1134 E 3100 North Rd 60927 815-694-2323
Victoria Marquis, prin. Fax 694-2830

Clinton, DeWitt, Pop. 7,336
Clinton CUSD 15 2,000/PK-12
1210 State Route 54 W 61727 217-935-8321
Dr. Jeff Holmes, supt. Fax 935-2300
www.cusd15.k12.il.us/
Clinton HS 600/9-12
Route 54 W 61727 217-935-8337
Ronald Conner, prin. Fax 935-4029
Clinton JHS 500/6-8
701 Illini Dr 61727 217-935-2103
Larry Bethard, prin. Fax 937-1918

Coal City, Grundy, Pop. 4,910
Coal City CUSD 1 1,900/PK-12
100 S Baima St 60416 815-634-2287
Dr. Kent Bugg, supt. Fax 634-8775
www.coalcity.k12.il.us
Coal City HS 600/9-12
655 W Division St 60416 815-634-2396
Susan Rutkowski, prin. Fax 634-2313
Coal City MS 500/6-8
500 S Carbon Hill Rd 60416 815-634-5039
Ken Miller, prin. Fax 634-5049

Cobden, Union, Pop. 1,094
Cobden Unit SD 17 700/PK-12
413 N Appleknocker St 62920 618-893-2313
Karl Sweitzer, supt. Fax 893-4772
www.cobdenappleknockers.com/
Cobden HS 200/9-12
413 N Appleknocker St 62920 618-893-4031
Karl Sweitzer, prin. Fax 893-2138
Cobden JHS 100/7-8
413 N Appleknocker St 62920 618-893-4031
Karl Sweitzer, prin. Fax 893-2138

Colchester, McDonough, Pop. 1,458
West Prairie CUSD 103 800/PK-12
204 S Hun St 62326 309-776-3180
Dr. Terrence Scandrett, supt. Fax 776-3194
www.westprairie.org/
West Prairie MS 200/6-8
600 S Hun St 62326 309-776-3220
John Bushmire, prin. Fax 776-3194
Other Schools – See Sciota

Colfax, McLean, Pop. 996
Ridgeview CUSD 19 600/PK-12
309 N Harrison St 61728 309-723-5111
Dr. Larry Dodds, supt. Fax 723-6395
www.ridgeview19.org
Ridgeview JSHS 400/6-12
202 E Wood St 61728 309-723-2951
Jim Campbell, prin. Fax 723-4851

Collinsville, Madison, Pop. 25,218
Collinsville CUSD 10 4,400/PK-12
201 W Clay St 62234 618-346-6350
Dr. Dennis Craft, supt. Fax 343-3673
www.kahoks.org
Collinsville HS 1,900/9-12
2201 S Morrison Ave 62234 618-346-6320
Dr. Daryl Floit, prin. Fax 346-6341

Collinsville MS   7-8
9801 Collinsville Rd 62234   618-343-2100
Dr. Allen Ellington, prin.   Fax 343-2102

Collinsville Christian Academy   100/K-12
1203 Vandalia St 62234   618-345-4224
Richard Kotras, admin.   Fax 345-6103
Sanford-Brown College   Post-Sec.
1101 Eastport Plaza Dr 62234   618-344-5600

Columbia, Monroe, Pop. 8,545
Columbia CUSD 4   1,700/K-12
100 Parkview Dr 62236   618-281-4772
Leo Sherman, supt.   Fax 281-8081
www.chseagles.com
Columbia HS   500/9-12
100 Parkview Dr 62236   618-281-2532
Sam Keene, prin.   Fax 281-8081
Columbia MS   500/5-8
113 S Rapp Ave 62236   618-281-4993
Roger Chamberlain, prin.   Fax 281-4964

Concord, Morgan, Pop. 173
Triopia CUSD 27   500/PK-12
2204 Concord Arenzville Rd 62631   217-457-2283
Steve McCarty, supt.   Fax 457-2277
www.triopiacusd27.org/education
Triopia JSHS   200/7-12
2204 Concord Arenzville Rd 62631   217-457-2281
Eugene E. Link, prin.   Fax 457-2277

Coulterville, Randolph, Pop. 1,202
Coulterville Unit SD 1   200/K-12
PO Box 396 62237   618-758-2881
Louis Obernuefemann, supt.   Fax 758-2330
www.coulterville1.org/
Coulterville HS   100/9-12
PO Box 396 62237   618-758-2881
Louis Obernuefemann, prin.   Fax 758-2330
Coulterville JHS   100/6-8
PO Box 396 62237   618-758-2881
Louis Obernuefemann, prin.   Fax 758-2330

Country Club Hills, Cook, Pop. 16,339
Bremen Community HSD 228
Supt. — See Midlothian
Hillcrest HS   1,200/9-12
17401 Crawford Ave 60478   708-799-7000
Patricia Welch, prin.   Fax 799-0402

Country Club Hills SD 160   1,600/PK-8
4411 185th Pl 60478   708-957-6200
Charlie T. Kent, supt.   Fax 957-8686
d160.s-cook.k12.il.us/
Southwood MS   600/6-8
18635 Lee St 60478   708-957-6230
Dr. Phyliss Porter, prin.   Fax 799-4033

Cowden, Shelby, Pop. 599
Cowden-Herrick Community USD 3A   500/K-12
PO Box 188 62422   217-783-2126
Lenard Defend, supt.   Fax 783-2126
www.cowden-herrick.k12.il.us/
Cowden-Herrick HS   200/9-12
PO Box 188 62422   217-783-2125
Gary Cadwell, prin.   Fax 783-2124

Crescent City, Iroquois, Pop. 611
Crescent Iroquois CUSD 249   200/K-12
PO Box 190 60928   815-683-2141
Kirt Hendrick, supt.   Fax 683-2219
www.crescent.k12.il.us
Crescent-Iroquois HS   100/9-12
PO Box 10 60928   815-683-2161
Kirt Hendrick, prin.   Fax 683-2163

Crest Hill, Will, Pop. 15,424
Chaney-Monge SD 88   500/PK-8
400 Elsie Ave,   815-722-6673
August Tomac, supt.   Fax 722-7814
Monge JHS   200/6-8
400 Elsie Ave,   815-722-6673
Cathleen Davis, prin.   Fax 722-7814

Crestwood, Cook, Pop. 11,323
Cook County SD 130
Supt. — See Blue Island
Hale MS   400/6-8
5220 135th St 60445   708-385-6690
Linda Battles, prin.   Fax 385-2417

Crete, Will, Pop. 8,313
Crete-Monee CUSD 201U   4,700/PK-12
1500 S Sangamon St 60417   708-367-8300
    Fax 672-2689
www.cm201u.org
Crete-Monee HS   1,500/9-12
760 W Exchange St 60417   708-367-8200
Dr. Robert Meader, prin.   Fax 672-2888
Other Schools – See University Park

Illinois Lutheran HS   100/7-12
1610 Main St 60417   708-672-3262
Joe Archer, prin.   Fax 672-0512

Creve Coeur, Tazewell, Pop. 5,306
Creve Coeur SD 76   700/PK-8
400 N Highland St 61610   309-698-3600
Dr. Jack Wilt, supt.   Fax 698-9827
www.cc76.k12.il.us/
Parkview SD   300/5-8
800 Groveland St 61610   309-698-3610
Brad Bennett, prin.   Fax 698-3902

Crystal Lake, McHenry, Pop. 40,021
Community HSD 155   6,300/9-12
1 Virginia Rd 60014   815-455-8500
Dr. Jill Hawk, supt.   Fax 459-5022
www.d155.org
Crystal Lake Central HS   1,400/9-12
45 W Franklin Ave 60014   815-459-2505
Steve Olson, prin.   Fax 459-2536
Crystal Lake South HS   1,600/9-12
1200 S McHenry Ave 60014   815-455-3860
Marsha Potthoff, prin.   Fax 455-5706

Prairie Ridge HS   1,600/9-12
6000 Dvorak Dr 60012   815-479-0404
Paul Humpa, prin.   Fax 459-8993
Other Schools – See Cary

Crystal Lake CCSD 47   9,000/K-8
300 Commerce Dr 60014   815-459-6070
Ronald Miller, supt.   Fax 459-0263
www.d47schools.org
Beardsley MS   1,200/6-8
515 E Crystal Lake Ave 60014   815-477-5897
Ron Ludwig, prin.   Fax 479-5119
Bernotas MS   900/6-8
170 N Oak St 60014   815-459-9210
Lori Sorensen, prin.   Fax 459-5116
Lundahl MS   1,000/6-8
560 Nash Rd 60014   815-459-5971
Richard Carlstedt, prin.   Fax 479-5113

Prairie Grove CCSD 46   1,000/K-8
3223 IL Route 176 60014   815-459-3023
Mary Fasbender, prin.   Fax 356-0519
www.prairieg.k12.il.us
Prairie Grove JHS   400/6-8
3225 IL Route 176 60014   815-459-3557
Ronald May, prin.   Fax 459-3785

Cosmetology & Spa Institute   Post-Sec.
700 E Terra Cotta Ave 60014   815-385-9663
McHenry County College   Post-Sec.
8900 US Highway 14 60012   815-455-3700

Cuba, Fulton, Pop. 1,385
Fulton County CUSD 3   600/PK-12
PO Box 79 61427   309-785-5021
Dr. Janice Spears, supt.   Fax 785-5432
www.cuba.fulton.k12.il.us
Cuba HS   200/9-12
20325 N State Route 97 61427   309-785-5023
Daryle Coleman, prin.   Fax 785-5102
Cuba MS   100/7-8
20325 N State Route 97 61427   309-785-5023
Daryle Coleman, prin.   Fax 785-5102

Cullom, Livingston, Pop. 548
Tri-Point CUSD 6-J
Supt. — See Kempton
Tri-Point HS   200/9-12
PO Box 316 60929   815-689-2110
Pete Pearson, prin.   Fax 689-2377

Dakota, Stephenson, Pop. 488
Dakota CUSD 201   900/PK-12
400 Campus Dr 61018   815-449-2832
Wanda Herrmann, supt.   Fax 449-2459
www.dakota201.com/
Dakota JSHS   500/7-12
300 Campus Dr 61018   815-449-2812
Debra Keith, prin.   Fax 449-2322

Danville, Vermilion, Pop. 33,106
Danville CCSD 118   6,300/PK-12
516 N Jackson St 61832   217-444-1004
Nanette Mellen, supt.   Fax 444-1021
www.danville.k12.il.us
Danville HS   1,500/9-12
202 E Fairchild St 61832   217-444-1500
Gail Garner, prin.   Fax 444-1529
North Ridge MS   800/6-8
1619 N Jackson St 61832   217-444-3400
Mark Goodwin, prin.   Fax 444-3488
South View MS   700/6-8
133 E 9th St 61832   217-444-1800
Bill Cooper, prin.   Fax 431-5874

Oakwood CUSD 76
Supt. — See Fithian
Oakwood JHS   200/7-8
21600 N 900 East Rd 61834   217-443-2883
Debbie Clow, prin.   Fax 776-2228

VOTEC   200/7-8
15009 Catlin Tilton Rd 61834   217-442-0461
Kay Smoot, supt.   Fax 431-5861
VOTEC   Vo/Tech
15009 Catlin Tilton Rd 61834   217-442-0461
Kay Smoot, prin.   Fax 431-5891

Concept College of Cosmetology   Post-Sec.
2500 Georgetown Rd 61832   217-442-9329
Danville Area Community College   Post-Sec.
2000 E Main St 61832   217-443-3222
First Baptist Christian S   300/PK-12
1211 N Vermilion St 61832   217-442-2434
Robert Lazzell, prin.   Fax 442-8731
Lakeview College of Nursing   Post-Sec.
903 N Logan Ave 61832   217-443-5238
Provena United Samaritans Medical Center   Post-Sec.
812 N Logan Ave 61832   217-443-5201
Schlarman HS   200/9-12
2112 N Vermilion St 61832   217-442-2725
Dr. Raymond Broderick, prin.   Fax 433-2632

Darien, DuPage, Pop. 22,871
Cass SD 63   900/PK-8
8502 Bailey Rd 60561   630-985-2000
Dr. Kerry Foderaro, supt.   Fax 985-0225
www.cassd63.org
Cass JHS   400/5-8
8502 Bailey Rd 60561   630-985-1900
Mark Enright, prin.   Fax 985-2881

Darien SD 61   1,800/PK-8
7414 S Cass Ave 60561   630-968-7505
Warren Johnson, supt.   Fax 968-0872
www.darien61.org
Eisenhower JHS   600/6-8
1410 75th St 60561   630-964-5200
Martin Casey, prin.   Fax 968-8002

Hinsdale Township HSD 86
Supt. — See Hinsdale
Hinsdale South HS   1,800/9-12
7401 Clarendon Hills Rd 60561   630-468-4000
Claudia Geocaris, prin.   Fax 920-8649

Decatur, Macon, Pop. 79,285
Decatur Area Technical Academy
300 E Eldorado St 62523   217-424-3070
John Schultz, supt.
Decatur Area Technical Academy   Vo/Tech
300 E Eldorado St 62523   217-424-3070
John Schultz, prin.
Decatur SD 61   9,100/PK-12
101 W Cerro Gordo St 62523   217-424-3011
Gloria Davis, supt.   Fax 424-3009
www.dps61.org/
Decatur MS   500/7-8
1 Educational Park 62526   217-876-8017
Howard Edwards, prin.   Fax 876-8003
Eisenhower HS   1,200/9-12
1200 S 16th St 62521   217-424-3100
Colleen Legge, prin.   Fax 424-3050
Jefferson MS   500/7-8
4735 E Cantrell St 62521   217-424-3190
Shannen Ray, prin.   Fax 424-3189
MacArthur HS   1,300/9-12
1155 N Fairview Ave 62522   217-424-3156
Dean Schultz, prin.   Fax 424-3167

Decatur Christian S   300/PK-12
3475 N Maple Ave 62526   217-877-5636
Randall Thacker, prin.   Fax 877-7627
Maranatha Christian Academy   100/K-12
555 W Imboden Dr 62521   217-423-2452
Suzanne Hartwig, prin.   Fax 423-2454
Millikin University   Post-Sec.
1184 W Main St 62522   217-424-6211
Mr. John's School of Cosmetology   Post-Sec.
1745 E Eldorado St 62521   217-423-8173
Richland Community College   Post-Sec.
1 College Park 62521   217-875-7200
St. Teresa HS   300/9-12
2710 N Water St 62526   217-875-2431
Joseph McDaniel, prin.   Fax 875-2436

Deerfield, Lake, Pop. 19,232
Deerfield SD 109   3,100/K-8
517 Deerfield Rd 60015   847-945-1844
Dr. Renee Goier, supt.   Fax 945-1853
www.dps109.org
Caruso MS   500/6-8
1801 Montgomery Rd 60015   847-945-8430
Andrew Henrikson, prin.   Fax 945-1963
Shepard MS   500/6-8
440 Grove Ave 60015   847-948-0620
Jay Monier, prin.   Fax 948-8589

Township HSD 113
Supt. — See Highland Park
Deerfield HS   1,700/9-12
1959 Waukegan Rd 60015   224-632-3000
Dr. Al Fleming, prin.   Fax 405-8379

Trinity Evangelical Divinity School   Post-Sec.
2065 Half Day Rd 60015   800-345-8337
Trinity International University   Post-Sec.
2065 Half Day Rd 60015   847-945-8800

DeKalb, DeKalb, Pop. 41,348
De Kalb CUSD 428   9,700/PK-12
901 S 4th St 60115   815-754-2350
Dr. Paul Beilfuss, supt.   Fax 758-6933
dist428.org
De Kalb HS   1,600/9-12
1515 S 4th St 60115   815-754-2100
Lindsey Hall, prin.   Fax 758-0931
Huntley MS   1,200/6-8
821 S 7th St 60115   815-754-2241
Roger Scott, prin.   Fax 758-6062
Rosette MS   1,200/6-8
650 N 1st St 60115   815-754-2226
Craig Bowers, prin.   Fax 758-1097

Northern Illinois University 60115   Post-Sec.
    815-753-1000

De Land, Vermilion, Pop. 467
Deland-Weldon CUSD 57   200/PK-12
304 E IL Route 10 61839   217-736-3311
Gary Brashear, supt.   Fax 736-2654
www.delwel.k12.il.us/
Deland-Weldon HS   100/9-12
304 E IL Route 10 61839   217-664-3314
Gary Brashear, prin.   Fax 736-2654
Other Schools – See Weldon

Delavan, Tazewell, Pop. 1,789
Delavan CUSD 703   500/PK-12
907 Locust St 61734   309-244-8283
Mary Parker, supt.   Fax 244-7696
Delavan HS   200/9-12
907 Locust St 61734   309-244-8285
Andrew Brooks, prin.   Fax 244-8694
Delavan JHS   100/7-8
907 Locust St 61734   309-244-8285
Andrew Brooks, prin.   Fax 244-8694

De Pue, Bureau, Pop. 1,796
De Pue Unit SD 103   400/PK-12
PO Box 800 61322   815-447-2121
Marcia Burress, supt.   Fax 447-2067
De Pue HS   100/9-12
PO Box 800 61322   815-447-2121
Steve Sash, prin.   Fax 447-2067

Des Plaines, Cook, Pop. 56,450
CCSD 62   4,900/PK-8
777 E Algonquin Rd 60016   847-824-1136
Jane Westerhold, supt.   Fax 824-0612
www.d62.org

Algonquin MS   800/6-8
767 E Algonquin Rd   60016   847-824-1205
Martin Wolf, prin.   Fax 824-1270
Chippewa MS   700/6-8
123 N 8th Ave   60016   847-824-1503
Christopher Adkins, prin.   Fax 824-1514

Community Consolidated SD 59
Supt. — See Arlington Heights
Friendship JHS   600/6-8
550 Elizabeth Ln   60018   847-593-4350
Jane Paterala, prin.   Fax 593-7182

East Maine SD 63   3,500/PK-8
10150 Dee Rd   60016   847-299-1900
Dr. Kathleen Williams, supt.   Fax 299-9963
www.emsd63.org
Other Schools – See Niles

Maine Twp. HSD 207
Supt. — See Park Ridge
Maine West HS   2,200/9-12
1755 S Wolf Rd   60018   847-827-6176
Audrey Haugan, prin.   Fax 296-4916

Oakton Community College   Post-Sec.
1600 E Golf Rd   60016   847-635-1600
Willows Academy   200/6-12
1012 E Thacker St   60016   847-824-6900
Tina Verhelst, prin.   Fax 824-7089

Dieterich, Effingham, Pop. 593
Dieterich CUSD 30   500/K-12
PO Box 187   62424   217-925-5249
Dan Niemerg, supt.   Fax 925-5447
www.dieterich.k12.il.us/
Dieterich JSHS   200/7-12
PO Box 187   62424   217-925-5247
Daniel Sarver, prin.   Fax 925-5249

Divernon, Sangamon, Pop. 1,176
Divernon CUSD 13   300/PK-12
PO Box 20   62530   217-628-3414
Mark Spaid, supt.   Fax 628-3814
www.divy.net
Divernon HS   100/9-12
PO Box 20   62530   217-628-3414
Ronald Ervin, prin.   Fax 628-3814

Dixmoor, Cook, Pop. 3,934
West Harvey-Dixmoor SD 147
Supt. — See Harvey
Parks MS   500/6-8
14700 Robey Ave   60426   708-371-9575
Abigail Phillips, prin.   Fax 371-1412

Dixon, Lee, Pop. 15,429
Dixon Unit SD 170   2,300/PK-12
1335 Franklin Grove Rd   61021   815-284-7722
James L. Brown, supt.   Fax 284-8576
www.dps.k12.il.us
Dixon HS   1,000/9-12
300 Lincoln Statue Dr   61021   815-284-7723
Michael Grady, prin.   Fax 284-4297
Reagan MS   1,000/5-8
620 Division St   61021   815-284-7725
Bruce Williams, prin.   Fax 284-1711

Faith Christian S   100/PK-12
7571 S Ridge Rd   61021   815-652-4806
Mark Glenn, supt.   Fax 652-4871
Jack Mabley Development Center   Post-Sec.
1120 Washington Ave   61021   815-288-8300
Sauk Valley Community College   Post-Sec.
173 Illinois Route 2   61021   815-288-5511

Dolton, Cook, Pop. 25,176
Dolton SD 148   3,400/PK-8
PO Box 160   60419   708-841-2290
Dr. Ruby Roberson, supt.   Fax 841-5048
www.district148.net
Roosevelt JHS   500/7-8
111 W 146th St   60419   708-201-2071
Shalonda Randle, prin.   Fax 849-1285

Thornton Twp. HSD 205
Supt. — See South Holland
Thornridge HS   1,800/9-12
15000 Cottage Grove Ave   60419   708-271-4401
Kim Waller, prin.   Fax 271-5028

Dongola, Union, Pop. 803
Dongola School Unit District 66   300/K-12
PO Box 190   62926   618-827-3841
Nancy Dillow, supt.   Fax 827-4641
Dongola HS   100/9-12
PO Box 190   62926   618-827-3524
Jennifer Flowers, prin.   Fax 827-4422
Dongola JHS   50/7-8
PO Box 190   62926   618-827-3524
Jennifer Flowers, prin.   Fax 827-4422

Donovan, Iroquois, Pop. 336
Donovan CUSD 3   500/K-12
PO Box 186   60931   815-486-7397
Jerome Pankey, supt.   Fax 486-7060
www.donovan.k12.il.us/
Donovan HS   200/9-12
PO Box 186   60931   815-486-7395
Scott Strong, prin.   Fax 486-7060
Donovan JHS   100/7-8
PO Box 186   60931   815-486-7395
Scott Strong, prin.   Fax 486-7060

Downers Grove, DuPage, Pop. 49,222
Center Cass SD 66   1,300/PK-8
699 Plainfield Rd   60516   630-783-5000
Dr. Jay Tiede, supt.   Fax 910-0980
www.ccsd66.org/
Lakeview JHS   500/6-8
701 Plainfield Rd   60516   630-985-2700
Paul Windsor, prin.   Fax 985-1545

Community HSD 99   5,400/9-12
6301 Springside Ave   60516   630-795-7100
David Eblen, supt.   Fax 795-7199
www.csd99.org
Downers Grove North HS   2,200/9-12
4436 Main St   60515   630-795-8400
Maria Ward, prin.   Fax 795-8499
Downers Grove South HS   3,200/9-12
1436 Norfolk St   60516   630-795-8500
Mark McDonald, prin.   Fax 795-8599

Downers Grove SD 58   5,100/PK-8
1860 63rd St   60516   630-719-5800
Dale Martin, supt.   Fax 719-9857
www.dg58.dupage.k12.il.us
Herrick MS   600/7-8
4435 Middaugh Ave   60515   630-719-5810
Dr. Mark Manzi, prin.   Fax 719-1628
O'Neill MS   600/7-8
635 59th St   60516   630-719-5815
Matthew Durbala, prin.   Fax 719-1436

Bridge HS   50/8-12
2318 Wisconsin Ave   60515   630-964-1722
Mary Witt, prin.
Marquette Manor Baptist Academy   400/PK-12
333 75th St   60516   630-964-5363
Steven Tompkins, prin.   Fax 964-5385
Midwestern University   Post-Sec.
555 31st St   60515   630-969-4400

Downs, McLean, Pop. 762
Tri-Valley CUSD 3   1,000/PK-12
410 E Washington St   61736   309-378-2351
Brad Cox, supt.   Fax 378-2223
tri-valley.k12.il.us
Tri-Valley HS   300/9-12
503 E Washington St   61736   309-378-2911
Paul Colba, prin.   Fax 378-3202
Tri-Valley MS   400/4-8
505 E Washington St   61736   309-378-3414
Eric Hutt, prin.   Fax 378-3214

Cornerstone Christian Acad of McLean Co.   400/PK-12
22017 E 1200 North Rd   61736   309-662-9900
Becky Shamess, admin.   Fax 662-9904

Dundee, Kane, Pop. 4,494
Community Unit SD 300
Supt. — See Carpentersville
Dundee MS   900/6-8
37w450 IL Route 72   60118   847-426-1485
Kara Vicente, prin.   Fax 426-4008

Hair Professionals Academy   Post-Sec.
825 Village Quarter Rd # B   60118   847-622-7871

Dunlap, Peoria, Pop. 898
Dunlap CUSD 323   2,500/PK-12
PO Box 395   61525   309-243-7716
Jeanne Williamson, supt.   Fax 243-7720
www.dunlapcusd.net
Dunlap HS   800/9-12
PO Box 365   61525   309-243-7751
Lisa Parker, prin.   Fax 243-9565
Dunlap MS   600/6-8
5200 W Cedar Hills Dr   61525   309-243-7778
Thomas Welsh, prin.   Fax 243-1136

Dupo, Saint Clair, Pop. 3,899
Dupo CUSD 196   1,200/PK-12
600 Louisa Ave   62239   618-286-3812
Dr. Michael Koebel, supt.   Fax 286-5554
Dupo HS, 600 Louisa Ave   62239   400/9-12
Dr. Jonathan Heerboth, prin.   618-286-3214
Dupo JHS, 600 Louisa Ave   62239   200/7-8
Dr. Jonathan Heerboth, prin.   618-286-3214

Apostolic Learning Academy   50/K-12
400 Louisa Ave   62239   618-286-4279
Melvin Tucker, dir.   Fax 286-5055

Du Quoin, Perry, Pop. 6,344
Du Quoin CUSD 300   1,500/PK-12
845 E Jackson St   62832   618-542-3856
Gary Kelly, supt.   Fax 542-6614
dqud300.perry.k12.il.us
Du Quoin HS   400/9-12
500 E South St   62832   618-542-4744
Lybrand Beard, prin.   Fax 542-8822
Du Quoin MS   500/5-8
845 E Jackson St   62832   618-542-2646
Aaron Hill, prin.   Fax 542-4373

Christian Fellowship S   100/PK-12
PO Box 227   62832   618-542-6800
Larry Bullock, admin.   Fax 542-6800
DuQuoin Beauty College   Post-Sec.
202 S Washington St   62832   618-542-9777

Durand, Winnebago, Pop. 1,081
Durand CUSD 322   800/K-12
200 W South St   61024   815-248-2171
Greg Stott, supt.   Fax 248-2599
www.durandbulldogs.com
Durand HS   200/9-12
200 W South St   61024   815-248-2171
Jeff Pinker, prin.   Fax 248-2599
Durand JHS   100/7-8
200 W South St   61024   815-248-2171
Kurt Alberstett, prin.   Fax 248-2599

Dwight, Livingston, Pop. 4,388
Dwight Common SD 232   500/PK-8
801 S Franklin St   60420   815-941-6217
Dale Adams, supt.   Fax 584-2950
www.dgs.k12.il.us
Dwight Common MS   6-8
801 S Columbia St   60420   815-941-6120
Mark Pagel, prin.   Fax 584-3771

Dwight Twp. HSD 230   300/9-12
801 S Franklin St   60420   815-941-6217
Dale Adams, supt.   Fax 584-2950
www.dwighthigh.k12.il.us
Dwight HS   300/9-12
801 S Franklin St   60420   815-941-6203
Eric Flohr, prin.   Fax 584-2950

Earlville, LaSalle, Pop. 1,788
Earlville CUSD 9   500/PK-12
PO Box 539   60518   815-246-8371
Patricia Hahto, supt.   Fax 246-8672
Earlville HS   100/9-12
PO Box 539   60518   815-246-8361
Fred Nestler, prin.   Fax 246-8672

East Alton, Madison, Pop. 6,725
East Alton SD 13   1,000/PK-8
210 E Saint Louis Ave   62024   618-433-2150
Michael Gray, supt.   Fax 254-5048
www.eadist13.madison.k12.il.us
East Alton MS   300/6-8
1000 3rd St   62024   618-433-2201
Eric Frankford, prin.   Fax 433-2203

East Dubuque, Jo Daviess, Pop. 1,945
East Dubuque Unit SD 119   600/PK-12
200 Parklane Dr   61025   815-747-2111
Katherine Bryant, supt.   Fax 747-3516
www.edbqhs.org
East Dubuque HS   200/9-12
200 Parklane Dr   61025   815-747-3188
Greg Herbst, prin.   Fax 747-3516

East Moline, Rock Island, Pop. 21,211
East Moline SD 37   2,500/PK-8
836 17th Ave   61244   309-755-4533
Garry Rudish, supt.   Fax 755-6913
www.emsd37.org
Glenview MS   1,100/5-8
3100 7th St   61244   309-755-1919
Jeff Fairweather, prin.   Fax 752-2551

United Township AVC
1275 Avenue of The Cities   61244   309-752-1633
Dr. Barbara Suelter, admin.   Fax 752-1608
uths.revealed.net
United Township Area Career Center   Vo/Tech
1275 Avenue Of The Cities   61244   309-752-1691
Larry Shimmin, dir.

United Township HSD 30   1,800/9-12
1275 Avenue of the Cities   61244   309-752-1633
Barbara L. Suelter Ed.D., supt.   Fax 752-1608
uths.revealed.net/
United Township HS   1,800/9-12
1275 Avenue of the Cities   61244   309-752-1633
Fred Segura, prin.   Fax 752-1608

East Moline Christian S   300/K-12
900 46th Ave   61244   309-796-1485
Rev. James R. Patrick, prin.   Fax 796-1152
La' James College of Hairstyling   Post-Sec.
485 Avenue of the Cities   61244   309-755-1313

Easton, Mason, Pop. 367
Illini Central CUSD 189
Supt. — See Mason City
Illini Central MS   200/6-8
208 N West St   62633   309-562-7251
David Mouser, prin.   Fax 562-7256

East Peoria, Tazewell, Pop. 22,428
East Peoria Community HSD 309   1,100/9-12
1401 E Washington St   61611   309-694-8300
Cliff Cobert, supt.   Fax 694-8322
www.epchs.k12.il.us/
East Peoria Community HS   1,100/9-12
1401 E Washington St   61611   309-694-8300
Paul Whittington, prin.   Fax 694-8322

East Peoria SD 86   1,900/PK-8
601 Taylor St   61611   309-427-5100
Tony Ingold, supt.   Fax 698-1364
www.epd86.org
Central JHS   600/6-8
601 Taylor St   61611   309-427-5200
Joe Sander, prin.   Fax 699-2595

Oehrlein School of Cosmetology   Post-Sec.
100 Meadow Ave   61611   309-699-1561

East Saint Louis, Saint Clair, Pop. 30,995
East St. Louis SD 189   9,600/PK-12
1005 State St   62201   618-646-3000
Theresa Saunders Ed.D., supt.   Fax 583-7186
www.estlouis.stclair.k12.il.us/
Clark MS   700/6-8
3310 State St   62205   618-646-3750
Roland Coleman, prin.   Fax 646-3758
East Saint Louis HS   2,100/9-12
4901 State St   62205   618-646-3700
Terrence Curry, prin.   Fax 646-3708
Lincoln MS   800/6-8
12 S 10th St   62201   618-646-3770
Luberta Allen, prin.   Fax 646-3778
Younge MS   700/6-8
3939 Caseyville Ave   62204   618-646-3760
Vivian Cockrell, prin.   Fax 646-3768

Vee's School of Beauty Culture   Post-Sec.
2701 State St   62205   618-274-1751

Edinburg, Christian, Pop. 1,138
Edinburg CUSD 4   400/PK-12
100 E Martin St   62531   217-623-5603
Susan Dudley, supt.   Fax 623-5604
www.edinburgschools.net
Edinburg HS   100/9-12
100 E Martin St   62531   217-623-5631
Robert Meadows, prin.   Fax 623-5604
Edinburg JHS   100/6-8
100 E Martin St   62531   217-623-5733
Robert Meadows, prin.   Fax 623-5604

Edwardsville, Madison, Pop. 23,600
Edwardsville CUSD 7 — 7,000/PK-12
  708 Saint Louis St 62025 — 618-656-1182
  Dr. Ed Hightower, supt. — Fax 692-7423
  www.ecusd7.org
Edwardsville HS — 2,300/9-12
  6161 Center Grove Rd 62025 — 618-656-7100
  Norm Bohnenstiehl, prin. — Fax 655-1037
Liberty MS — 800/6-8
  1 District Dr 62025 — 618-655-6800
  Dennis Cramsey, prin. — Fax 655-6801
Lincoln MS — 800/6-8
  145 West St 62025 — 618-656-0485
  John Dean, prin. — Fax 659-1268

Alvareita's College of Cosmetology — Post-Sec.
  333 S Kansas St 62025 — 618-656-2593
Metro East Lutheran HS — 200/9-12
  6305 Center Grove Rd 62025 — 618-656-0043
  Daniel S. Kostencki, prin. — Fax 656-3315
Southern Illinois Univ. Edwardsville — Post-Sec.
  62026 — 618-650-2000

Effingham, Effingham, Pop. 12,498
Effingham CUSD 40 — 3,000/PK-12
  PO Box 130 62401 — 217-540-1500
  Daniel Clasby Ph.D., supt. — Fax 540-1510
  www.effingham.k12.il.us
Effingham HS — 900/9-12
  1301 W Grove Ave 62401 — 217-540-1100
  Mike McCollum, prin. — Fax 540-1101
Effingham JHS — 700/6-8
  600 S Henrietta St 62401 — 217-540-1300
  Scott Holst, prin. — Fax 540-1362

St. Anthony of Padua HS — 200/9-12
  PO Box 545 62401 — 217-342-6969
  Marianne Larimer, prin. — Fax 342-6997

Eldorado, Saline, Pop. 4,434
Eldorado CUSD 4 — 1,200/PK-12
  2200 Illinois Ave 62930 — 618-273-6394
  Gary Siebert, supt. — Fax 273-9311
  www.eldorado.k12.il.us/
Eldorado HS — 400/9-12
  2200 Illinois Ave 62930 — 618-273-2881
  Gary Siebert, prin. — Fax 273-8153
Eldorado MS — 300/6-8
  1907 1st St 62930 — 618-273-8056
  Beth Rister, prin. — Fax 273-2943

Elgin, Kane, Pop. 97,117
SD U-46 — 37,100/PK-12
  355 E Chicago St 60120 — 847-888-5000
  Connie L. Neale Ph.D., supt. — Fax 608-4173
  www.u-46.org/
Abbott MS — 800/7-8
  949 Van St 60123 — 847-888-5160
  Greg Schneider, prin. — Fax 608-2740
Elgin HS — 2,300/9-12
  1200 Maroon Dr 60120 — 847-888-5100
  David Smiley, prin. — Fax 888-6997
Ellis MS — 600/7-8
  225 S Liberty St 60120 — 847-888-5151
  Perry Hayes, prin. — Fax 608-2744
Kimball MS — 1,000/7-8
  451 N Mclean Blvd 60123 — 847-888-5290
  Alan Tamburrino, prin. — Fax 608-2749
Larkin HS — 2,600/9-12
  1475 Larkin Ave 60123 — 847-888-5200
  Richard Webb, prin. — Fax 888-6996
Larsen MS — 600/7-8
  665 Dundee Ave 60120 — 847-888-5250
  Alfred Fulton, prin. — Fax 888-7172
Other Schools – See Bartlett, South Elgin, Streamwood

Cannella School of Hair Design — Post-Sec.
  113 W Chicago St 60123 — 847-742-6611
DeVry University — Post-Sec.
  385 Airport Rd 60123 — 847-622-1135
Elgin Academy — 400/K-12
  350 Park St 60120 — 847-695-0300
  John Cooper, prin. — Fax 695-5017
Elgin Community College — Post-Sec.
  1700 Spartan Dr 60123 — 847-697-1000
Fox Valley Lutheran Academy — 50/9-12
  220 Division St 60120 — 847-468-8207
  Janet Zimdahl, prin. — Fax 742-2930
Judson College — Post-Sec.
  1151 N State St 60123 — 847-695-2500
St. Edward Central Catholic HS — 500/9-12
  335 Locust St 60123 — 847-741-7535
  Rev. Max Striedl, prin. — Fax 695-4582
Westminster Christian S — 500/PK-12
  2700 W Highland Ave, — 847-695-0310
  Chad Dirkse, admin. — Fax 695-0135

Elizabeth, Jo Daviess, Pop. 681
Jo Daviess-Carroll AVC
  PO Box 602 61028 — 815-858-2203
   — Fax 858-2316
Jo Daviess-Carroll AVC — Vo/Tech
  PO Box 602 61028 — 815-858-2203
  Donald Lamm, prin. — Fax 858-2316

Elizabethtown, Hardin, Pop. 338
Hardin County CUSD 1 — 700/PK-12
  PO Box 218 62931 — 618-287-2411
  Ernie Fowler, supt. — Fax 287-2421
Hardin County HS — 200/9-12
  RR 2 62931 — 618-287-2141
  Ernie Fowler, prin. — Fax 287-8381
Hardin County JHS — 100/7-8
  RR 2 62931 — 618-287-2141
  Ernie Fowler, prin. — Fax 287-8381

Elk Grove Village, Cook, Pop. 34,666
Community Consolidated SD 59
  Supt. — See Arlington Heights
Grove JHS — 1,000/6-8
  777 W Elk Grove Blvd 60007 — 847-593-4367
  Enza Papeck, prin. — Fax 472-3001

Schaumburg CCSD 54
  Supt. — See Schaumburg
Mead JHS — 700/7-8
  1765 Biesterfield Rd 60007 — 847-357-6000
  Steve Pearce, prin. — Fax 357-6001

Township HSD 214
  Supt. — See Arlington Heights
Elk Grove Village HS — 1,900/9-12
  500 W Elk Grove Blvd 60007 — 847-718-4400
  Frank DeRosa, prin. — Fax 718-4417

Elkville, Jackson, Pop. 966
Elverado CUSD 196 — 500/K-12
  PO Box 130 62932 — 618-568-1152
  Rebecca Canty, supt. — Fax 568-1152
Elverado HS — 100/9-12
  PO Box 217 62932 — 618-568-1104
  Joy Battagliotti, prin. — Fax 568-1551
Other Schools – See Vergennes

Elmhurst, DuPage, Pop. 44,054
Elmhurst SD 205 — 7,400/PK-12
  130 W Madison St 60126 — 630-834-4530
  Dr. Lynn Krizic, supt. — Fax 617-2345
  www.elmhurst.k12.il.us
Bryan MS — 500/6-8
  111 W Butterfield Rd 60126 — 630-617-2350
  Rachel Overton, prin. — Fax 617-2232
Churchville MS — 400/6-8
  155 E Victory Pkwy 60126 — 630-832-8682
  Matthew Haug, prin. — Fax 617-2387
Sandburg MS — 700/6-8
  345 E Saint Charles Rd 60126 — 630-834-4534
  Howard Holbrook, prin. — Fax 617-2380
York Community HS — 2,400/9-12
  355 W Saint Charles Rd 60126 — 630-617-2400
  Diana Smith, prin. — Fax 617-2399

Cannella School of Hair Design — Post-Sec.
  191 N York St 60126 — 630-833-6118
Elmhurst College — Post-Sec.
  190 S Prospect Ave 60126 — 630-279-4100
Immaculate Conception HS — 200/9-12
  217 N Cottage Hill Ave 60126 — 630-530-3460
  Pamela Levar, prin. — Fax 530-2290
Timothy Christian HS — 400/9-12
  1061 S Prospect Ave 60126 — 630-833-7575
  Clyde Rinsema, prin. — Fax 833-9821

Elmwood, Peoria, Pop. 1,868
Elmwood CUSD 322 — 700/PK-12
  301 W Butternut St 61529 — 309-742-8464
  Thomas Kahn, supt. — Fax 742-8812
  www.elmwood.peoria.k12.il.us
Elmwood HS — 200/9-12
  301 W Butternut St 61529 — 309-742-2851
  Ray Driskell, prin. — Fax 742-8093
Elmwood JHS — 100/7-8
  301 W Butternut St 61529 — 309-742-2851
  Ray Driskell, prin. — Fax 742-8093

Elmwood Park, Cook, Pop. 24,876
Elmwood Park CUSD 401 — 3,000/PK-12
  8201 W Fullerton Ave 60707 — 708-583-5830
  Dr. Frank L. McKinzie, supt. — Fax 452-9504
  www.sd401.k12.il.us
Elm MS — 500/7-8
  7607 W Cortland St 60707 — 708-452-3550
  Dr. Paula Hlavacek, prin. — Fax 452-0662
Elmwood Park HS — 900/9-12
  8201 W Fullerton Ave 60707 — 708-583-6211
  James Jennings, prin. — Fax 452-0732

El Paso, Woodford, Pop. 2,727
El Paso-Gridley CUSD 11 — 800/PK-12
  97 W 5th St 61738 — 309-527-4410
  William James, supt. — Fax 527-4040
  www.elpaso375.org/
El Paso-Gridley HS — 300/9-12
  600 N Elm St 61738 — 309-527-4415
  Karen Krug, prin. — Fax 527-4411
Other Schools – See Gridley

Elsah, Jersey, Pop. 641

Principia College 62028 — Post-Sec.
   — 618-374-2131

Erie, Whiteside, Pop. 1,561
Erie CUSD 1 — 700/PK-12
  520 5th Ave 61250 — 309-659-2239
  Michael D. Ryan, supt. — Fax 659-2230
  www.erie1.net
Erie HS — 200/9-12
  435 6th Ave 61250 — 309-659-2239
  Tim McConnell, prin. — Fax 659-2514
Erie MS, 500 5th Ave 61250 — 200/5-8
  Keith Morgan, prin. — 309-659-2239

Eureka, Woodford, Pop. 4,945
Eureka CUSD 140 — 1,600/PK-12
  109 W Cruger Ave 61530 — 309-467-3737
  Dr. Randy K. Crump, supt. — Fax 467-2377
  www.eureka.wodfrd.k12.il.us
Eureka HS — 500/9-12
  200 W Cruger Ave 61530 — 309-467-2361
  Richard Wherley, prin. — Fax 467-2648
Eureka MS — 500/5-8
  2005 S Main St 61530 — 309-467-3771
  Robert Gold, prin. — Fax 467-2052

Eureka College — Post-Sec.
  300 E College Ave 61530 — 309-467-3721

Evanston, Cook, Pop. 74,360
Evanston CCSD 65 — 6,900/PK-8
  1500 McDaniel Ave 60201 — 847-859-8000
  Dr. Hardy Murphy, supt. — Fax 859-8701
  www.district65.net/
Chute MS — 600/6-8
  1400 Oakton St 60202 — 847-859-8600
  James McHolland, prin. — Fax 492-7956

Haven MS — 700/6-8
  2417 Prairie Ave 60201 — 847-859-8200
  Kathleen Roberson, prin. — Fax 492-9983
Nichols MS — 600/6-8
  800 Greenleaf St 60202 — 847-859-8660
  Gordon Hood, prin. — Fax 492-7880

Evanston Twp. HSD 202 — 3,100/9-12
  1600 Dodge Ave 60201 — 847-424-7220
  Dr. Allan Alson, supt. — Fax 492-3872
  www.eths.k12.il.us
Evanston Twp. HS — 3,100/9-12
  1600 Dodge Ave 60201 — 847-424-7200
  Denise Martin, prin. — Fax 492-3872

Garrett Evangelical Theological Seminary — Post-Sec.
  2121 Sheridan Rd 60201 — 847-866-3900
National-Louis University — Post-Sec.
  2840 Sheridan Rd 60201 — 847-475-1100
Northwestern University — Post-Sec.
  1801 Hinman Ave 60208 — 847-491-3741
Pivot Point International — Post-Sec.
  1560 Sherman Ave Ste 700 60201 — 847-866-0500
Roycemore S — 300/PK-12
  640 Lincoln St 60201 — 847-866-6055
  Joseph Becker, hdmstr. — Fax 866-6545
St. Francis Hospital — Post-Sec.
  355 Ridge Ave 60202 — 847-492-4000
Seabury-Western Theological Seminary — Post-Sec.
  2122 Sheridan Rd 60201 — 847-328-9300

Evansville, Randolph, Pop. 705

Christ our Savior Lutheran HS — 100/9-12
  901 Church St 62242 — 618-853-7300
  Sherry L. Prange, prin. — Fax 853-7361

Evergreen Park, Cook, Pop. 20,464
Evergreen Park Community HSD 231 — 900/9-12
  9901 S Kedzie Ave 60805 — 708-424-7400
  Dr. James Gallagher, supt. — Fax 424-7497
  www.evergreenpark.org
Evergreen Park HS — 900/9-12
  9901 S Kedzie Ave 60805 — 708-424-7400
  Dr. Beth Hart, prin. — Fax 424-3045

Evergreen Park ESD 124 — 2,000/K-8
  9400 S Sawyer Ave 60805 — 708-423-0950
  Dr. Craig Fiegel, supt. — Fax 423-4292
  www.d124.org
Central JHS — 500/7-8
  9400 S Sawyer Ave 60805 — 708-424-0148
  Kathleen Hatczel, prin. — Fax 229-8406

Fairbury, Livingston, Pop. 3,940
Fairbury Central CUSD 8
  Supt. — See Forrest
Prairie Central HS — 600/9-12
  411 N 7th St 61739 — 815-692-2355
  Daniel Schmitt, prin. — Fax 692-2438

Fairfield, Wayne, Pop. 5,327
Fairfield Community HSD 225 — 500/9-12
  300 W King St 62837 — 618-842-2649
  David Savage, supt. — Fax 842-4465
  fchs.wayne.k12.il.us
Fairfield Community HS — 500/9-12
  300 W King St 62837 — 618-842-2649
  Diana Zurliene, prin. — Fax 842-5187

Fairfield SD 112 — 600/PK-8
  806 N 1st St 62837 — 618-842-6501
  Rena Talbert, supt. — Fax 842-2932
Center Street S — 400/PK-PK, 4-
  200 W Center St 62837 — 618-842-2679
  Scott Fuhrhop, prin. — Fax 842-4719

Frontier Community College — Post-Sec.
  RR 1 62837 — 618-842-3711

Fairview Heights, Saint Clair, Pop. 15,264
Grant CCSD 110 — 800/PK-8
  10110 Old Lincoln Trl 62208 — 618-398-5577
  Dr. Darrel Hardt, supt. — Fax 398-5578
  www.dist110.com
Grant MS — 300/5-8
  10110 Old Lincoln Trl 62208 — 618-397-2764
  Matt Stines, prin. — Fax 397-7809

Pontiac-William Holliday SD 105 — 600/PK-8
  400 Ashland Dr 62208 — 618-233-2320
  Darrell Sy, supt. — Fax 233-0918
  www.pontiac.stclair.k12.il.us
Pontiac JHS — 200/7-8
  400 Ashland Dr 62208 — 618-233-6004
  Paul Holland, prin. — Fax 233-0918

Farina, Fayette, Pop. 553
South Central CUSD 401
  Supt. — See Kinmundy
South Central HS — 300/9-12
  RR 2 Box 91 62838 — 618-245-3363
  David Scott, prin. — Fax 245-6165

Farmer City, DeWitt, Pop. 2,025
Blue Ridge CUSD 18 — 900/PK-12
  411 N John St 61842 — 309-928-9141
  Jay Harnack, supt. — Fax 928-5478
  www.blueridge18.org
Blue Ridge HS — 300/9-12
  411 N John St 61842 — 309-928-2622
  John Lawrence, prin. — Fax 928-5301
Other Schools – See Mansfield

Farmington, Fulton, Pop. 2,515
Farmington Central CUSD 265 — 400/PK-12
  212 N Lightfoot Rd 61531 — 309-245-1000
  Mark Doan, supt. — Fax 245-9161
  www.dist265.com/
Farmington Central HS — 6-8
  300 N Lightfoot Rd 61531 — 309-245-1000
  Scott Dearman, prin. — Fax 245-9162

Farmington HS
310 N Lightfoot Rd 61531
John Bute, prin.
400/9-12
309-245-1000
Fax 245-9163

Findlay, Shelby, Pop. 698
Okaw Valley CUSD 302
Supt. — See Bethany
Okaw Valley MS
501 W Division 62534
Joel Hackney, prin.
100/6-8
217-756-8521
Fax 756-8599

Fisher, Champaign, Pop. 1,672
Fisher CUSD 1
PO Box 700 61843
Barbara Thompson, supt.
www.fisher.k12.il.us
Fisher JSHS
PO Box 670 61843
Steve Wallick, prin.
600/K-12
217-897-6125
Fax 897-6676

300/7-12
217-897-1225
Fax 897-1708

Fithian, Vermilion, Pop. 531
Oakwood CUSD 76
5834 US Route 150 61844
Keven D. Forney, supt.
www.ltls.org/jxn.html
Oakwood HS
5870 US Route 150 61844
Brenda Ludwig, prin.
Other Schools – See Danville
1,100/PK-12
217-354-4355
Fax 354-2030

300/9-12
217-354-2358
Fax 354-2603

Flanagan, Livingston, Pop. 1,069
Flanagan CUSD 4
PO Box 367 61740
Roger Mitchell, supt.
www.flanagan.k12.il.us/
Flanagan HS
PO Box 367 61740
Jerry W. Farris, prin.
400/PK-12
815-796-2233
Fax 796-2856

200/9-12
815-796-2291
Fax 796-2856

Flora, Clay, Pop. 4,943
Flora CUSD 35
444 S Locust St 62839
Linda Spicer, supt.
www.florail.us/schools.htm
Flora HS
600 S Locust St 62839
Darrell Gummert, prin.
Henson JHS
609 N Stanford Rd 62839
Julie Pearce, prin.
1,500/PK-12
618-662-2412
Fax 662-4587

400/9-12
618-662-8316
Fax 662-2725
400/6-8
618-662-8394
Fax 662-8395

Flossmoor, Cook, Pop. 9,438
Flossmoor SD 161
Supt. — See Chicago Heights
Parker JHS
2810 School St 60422
Dr. Vanessa Atkins, prin.
1,000/6-8
708-647-5400
Fax 799-9207

Homewood-Flossmoor Community HSD 233 2,800/9-12
999 Kedzie Ave 60422
Dr. Laura Murray, supt.
www.hfhighschool.org
Homewood-Flossmoor HS
999 Kedzie Ave 60422
Dr. Von Mansfield, prin.
708-799-3000
Fax 799-9564

2,800/9-12
708-799-3000
Fax 799-9564

Ford Heights, Cook, Pop. 3,382
Ford Heights SD 169
910 Woodlawn Ave 60411
Dr. Willie Davis, supt.
Beck Upper Grade Center
800 E Lincoln Hwy 60411
Jonathan Porter, prin.
900/PK-8
708-758-1370
Fax 758-1372
300/5-8
708-758-1400
Fax 758-0711

Forest Park, Cook, Pop. 15,406
Forest Park SD 91
424 Des Plaines Ave 60130
Dr. Randolph Tinder, supt.
www.forestparkschools.org
Forest Park MS
925 Beloit Ave 60130
Karen Bukowski, prin.
1,100/PK-8
708-366-5700
Fax 366-5761

300/6-8
708-366-5703
Fax 366-2091

Forrest, Livingston, Pop. 1,210
Prairie Central CUSD 8
PO Box 496 61741
Dr. John Capasso, supt.
www.prairiecentral.org
Prairie Central JHS
800 N Wood St 61741
Danny Vaughan, prin.
Other Schools – See Fairbury
2,000/PK-12
815-657-8237
Fax 657-8395

300/7-8
815-657-8660
Fax 657-8677

Forreston, Ogle, Pop. 1,504
Forrestville Valley CUSD 221
PO Box 665 61030
Lowell Taylor, supt.
www.fvdistrict221.org
Forreston HS
PO Box 665 61030
Christopher Shockey, prin.
Forreston MS
PO Box 665 61030
Craig Mathers, prin.
900/PK-12
815-938-2036
Fax 938-9028

300/9-12
815-938-2175
Fax 938-2546
300/6-8
815-938-2195
Fax 938-9028

Fox Lake, Lake, Pop. 9,937
Fox Lake Grade SD 114
Supt. — See Spring Grove
Stanton MS
101 Hawthorne Ln 60020
William Lomas, prin.
300/6-8
847-973-4200
Fax 973-4210

Grant Community HSD 124
285 E Grand Ave 60020
Dr. John Benedetti, supt.
www.grant.lake.k12.il.us/
Grant Community HS
285 E Grand Ave 60020
Dr. Marilyn Howell, prin.
1,400/9-12
847-587-2561
Fax 587-2991

1,400/9-12
847-587-2561
Fax 587-2991

Fox River Grove, McHenry, Pop. 5,059
Fox River Grove SD 3
403 Orchard St 60021
Jacqueline Krause, supt.
www.dist3.org
600/K-8
847-516-5100
Fax 516-9169

Fox River Grove MS
401 Orchard St 60021
Tim Mahaffy, prin.
300/5-8
847-516-5105
Fax 516-5104

Frankfort, Will, Pop. 13,381
Frankfort CCSD 157C
10482 Nebraska St 60423
Dr. Robert J. Madonia, supt.
www.fsd157c.org
Hickory Creek MS
22265 S 80th Ave 60423
Kevin Suchinski, prin.
1,900/PK-8
815-469-5922
Fax 469-8988

700/6-8
815-469-4474
Fax 469-7930

Lincoln-Way Community HSD 210
Supt. — See New Lenox
Lincoln-Way East HS
201 Colorado Ave 60423
Dr. Michael Gardner, prin.
3,200/9-12
815-464-4000
Fax 464-4132

Summit Hill SD 161
21133 S 80th Ave 60423
Keith Pain, supt.
Summit Hill JHS
20130 S Rosewood Dr 60423
Craig Doster, prin.
3,100/PK-8
815-469-9103
Fax 469-9201
800/7-8
815-469-4330
Fax 469-7348

Franklin, Morgan, Pop. 580
Franklin CUSD 1
Supt. — See Alexander
Franklin JSHS
PO Box 199 62638
David Bruno, prin.
200/6-12
217-675-2395
Fax 675-2396

Franklin Grove, Lee, Pop. 1,023
Ashton-Franklin Center CUSD 275
Supt. — See Ashton
Ashton-Franklin Center MS
318 E South St,
Joseph Hilliker, prin.
100/5-8
815-456-2323
Fax 456-3211

Franklin Park, Cook, Pop. 19,060
Franklin Park SD 84
2915 Maple St 60131
David Nemec, supt.
www.d84.org/
Hester JHS
2836 Gustav St 60131
John Kosirog, prin.
1,300/PK-8
847-455-4230
Fax 455-9094

500/6-8
847-455-2150
Fax 455-0945

Leyden HSD 212
3400 Rose St 60131
Dr. Kathryn Robbins, supt.
www.leyden212.org
East Leyden HS
3400 Rose St 60131
Dr. Beth Concannon, prin.
Other Schools – See Northlake
3,500/9-12
847-451-3000
Fax 671-9079

1,900/9-12
847-451-3023
Fax 451-3644

Mannheim SD 83
10401 Grand Ave 60131
Bruce A. Lane Ed.D., supt.
www.d83.org/
Other Schools – See Melrose Park
2,500/K-8
847-455-4413
Fax 451-8290

Freeburg, Saint Clair, Pop. 3,946
Freeburg CCSD 70
408 S Belleville St 62243
Dr. Rob Hawkins, supt.
www.frg70.stclair.k12.il.us
Freeburg ES
408 S Belleville St 62243
Tomi Diefenbach, prin.
800/PK-8
618-539-3188
Fax 539-5795

600/3-8
618-539-3188
Fax 539-6008

Freeburg Community HSD 77
401 S Monroe St 62243
Andrew W. Lehman, supt.
www.fchs77.stclair.k12.il.us
Freeburg HS
401 S Monroe St 62243
Benjamin Howes, prin.
700/9-12
618-539-5533
Fax 539-4887

700/9-12
618-539-5533
Fax 539-4887

Freeport, Stephenson, Pop. 25,867
Freeport SD 145
501 E South St 61032
Dr. Peter Flynn, supt.
www.freeport.k12.il.us
Freeport HS
701 W Moseley St 61032
David Thake, prin.
Freeport JHS
701 W Empire St 61032
Scott Wiley, prin.
4,400/PK-12
815-232-0300
Fax 232-6717

1,400/9-12
815-232-0400
Fax 232-0629
700/7-8
815-232-0500
Fax 232-0536

Aquin Central Catholic HS
1419 S Galena Ave 61032
Kathleen Runte, admin.
Highland Community College
2998 W Pearl City Rd 61032
200/7-12
815-235-3154
Fax 235-3185
Post-Sec.
815-235-6121

Fulton, Whiteside, Pop. 3,856
River Bend CUSD 2
1110 3rd St 61252
Donald D. Mulch, supt.
www.riverbendschools.org
Fulton HS
1207 12th St 61252
Kathleen Schipper, prin.
River Bend MS
415 12th St 61252
James Spielman, prin.
900/K-12
815-589-2711
Fax 589-4630

300/9-12
815-589-3511
Fax 589-3412
200/6-8
815-589-2611
Fax 589-3130

Unity Christian S
711 10th St 61252
Dick Ritzema, prin.
100/7-12
815-589-3912
Fax 589-4430

Gages Lake, Lake, Pop. 8,349
Warren Twp. HSD 121
17962 W Gages Lake Rd 60030
Dr. Philip Sobocinski, supt.
www.wths.net
Other Schools – See Gurnee
1,600/9-12
847-662-1400
Fax 548-0564

Galatia, Saline, Pop. 992
Galatia CUSD 1
200 N Hickory St 62935
Maxine A. Dunn, supt.
Galatia HS
200 N McKinley St 62935
Amy Richey, prin.
Galatia JHS
200 N McKinley St 62935
Amy Richey, prin.
400/K-12
618-268-6371
Fax 268-4949
100/9-12
618-268-4194
Fax 268-4196
100/7-8
618-268-4194
Fax 268-4196

Galena, Jo Daviess, Pop. 3,459
Galena Unit SD 120
1206 Franklin St 61036
Dr. Dennis Dunton, supt.
www.galenaschools.org
Galena HS
1206 Franklin St 61036
Elizabeth Murphy, prin.
Galena MS
1230 Franklin St 61036
Ben Soat, prin.
800/PK-12
815-777-3086
Fax 777-0303

300/9-12
815-777-0917
Fax 777-2089
200/5-8
815-777-2413
Fax 777-4259

Tri-State Christian S
11084 W US Highway 20 61036
Mary Jane Thorne, prin.
200/PK-12
815-777-3800
Fax 777-2991

Galesburg, Knox, Pop. 32,809
Galesburg AVC
1135 W Fremont St 61401
Peggy Miller, supt.
Galesburg AVC
1135 W Fremont St 61401
Peggy Miller, supt.
Galesburg CUSD 205
PO Box 1206 61402
Dr. S. Gene Denisar, supt.
www.galesburg205.org/
Churchill JHS
905 Maple Ave 61401
Bart Arthur, prin.
Galesburg HS
1135 W Fremont St 61401
Diane Hutchins, prin.
Lombard MS
1220 E Knox St 61401
Katy Hasson, prin.
309-343-3733

Vo/Tech
309-343-3733

4,900/PK-12
309-343-1151
Fax 343-7757

600/6-8
309-342-3129
Fax 342-6384
1,400/9-12
309-343-4146
Fax 343-7122
500/6-8
309-342-9171
Fax 342-7135

Carl Sandburg College
2232 S Lake Storey Rd 61401
Knox College
2 E South St 61401
Post-Sec.
309-344-2518
Post-Sec.
309-341-7000

Galt, Whiteside, Pop. 230

Sterling Christian S
PO Box 40 61037
Mick Welding, prin.
100/PK-12
815-625-0309
Fax 625-2658

Galva, Henry, Pop. 2,714
Galva CUSD 224
224 Morgan Rd 61434
James Hochstatter, supt.
cats.k12.il.us
Galva JSHS
224 Morgan Rd 61434
William King, prin.
700/PK-12
309-932-2108
Fax 932-8326

300/7-12
309-932-2151
Fax 932-2152

Gardner, Grundy, Pop. 1,407
Gardner-South Wilmington Twp. HSD 73
PO Box 257 60424
Joseph Ciaccio, supt.
www.gswhs.grundy.k12.il.us
Gardner-South Wilmington Twp. HS
PO Box 257 60424
Chris Becker, prin.
200/9-12
815-237-2176
Fax 237-2842

200/9-12
815-237-2176
Fax 237-2842

Geneseo, Henry, Pop. 6,455
Geneseo CUSD 228
209 S College Ave 61254
Scott Kuffel, supt.
www.dist228.org
Geneseo HS
700 N State St 61254
Mike Haugse, prin.
Geneseo MS
333 E Ogden Ave 61254
Tom Domino, prin.
2,800/PK-12
309-945-0450
Fax 945-0445

900/9-12
309-945-0399
Fax 945-0374
700/6-8
309-945-0599
Fax 945-0580

Geneva, Kane, Pop. 22,236
Geneva CUSD 304
227 N 4th St 60134
Micael A. Jacoby, supt.
www.geneva.k12.il.us/
Geneva Community HS
416 McKinley Ave 60134
Dr. Gregory Fantozzi, prin.
Geneva MS
1415 Viking Dr 60134
Lawrence Bidlack, prin.
5,500/K-12
630-463-3000
Fax 463-3009

1,600/9-12
630-463-3800
Fax 232-9077
1,400/6-8
630-463-3600
Fax 208-7172

Genoa, DeKalb, Pop. 4,561
Genoa-Kingston CUSD 424
980 Park Ave 60135
Scott Wakeley, supt.
www.gkschools.org
Genoa-Kingston HS
980 Park Ave 60135
Don Billington, prin.
Genoa-Kingston MS
941 W Main St 60135
Angelo Lekkas, prin.
1,800/PK-12
815-784-6222
Fax 784-6059

400/9-12
815-784-5111
Fax 784-3124
400/6-8
815-784-5222
Fax 784-4323

Georgetown, Vermilion, Pop. 3,550
Georgetown-Ridge Farm CUSD 4
400 W West St 61846
Kevin Tate, supt.
www.grf.k12.il.us
Georgetown-Ridge Farm HS
500 W Mulberry St 61846
Steve Sliva, prin.
1,300/PK-12
217-662-8488
Fax 662-3402

400/9-12
217-662-6716
Fax 662-3404

Miller JHS
414 W West St 61846
Lisa Gocken, prin.
300/6-8
217-662-6606
Fax 662-6345

Gibson City, Ford, Pop. 3,394
Gibson City-Melvin-Sibley CUSD 5
217 E 17th St 60936
Charles Aubry, supt.
www.gcms.k12.il.us
1,000/K-12
217-784-8296
Fax 784-8558
GCMS HS
815 N Church St 60936
Michael J. Lindy, prin.
300/9-12
217-784-4292
Fax 784-8293
GCMS MS
316 E 19th St 60936
Michael Bleich, prin.
200/6-8
217-784-8731
Fax 784-8726

Gillespie, Macoupin, Pop. 3,306
Gillespie CUSD 7
510 W Elm St 62033
Paul D. Skeans, supt.
www.gillespie.macoupin.k12.il.us/
1,300/PK-12
217-839-2464
Fax 839-3353
Gillespie HS
612 Broadway St 62033
Joe Tieman, prin.
300/9-12
217-839-2114
Fax 839-4302
Gillespie MS, 412 Oregon St 62033
Joe Tieman, prin.
300/6-8
217-839-2116

Gilman, Iroquois, Pop. 1,791
Iroquois West CUSD 10
PO Box 67 60938
Larry Eyre, supt.
www.iwest.k12.il.us/
900/PK-12
815-265-4642
Fax 265-7008
Iroquois West HS
PO Box 67 60938
Kim Hawkins, prin.
300/9-12
815-265-4229
Fax 265-7008
Other Schools – See Onarga

Girard, Macoupin, Pop. 2,247
Girard CUSD 3
525 N 3rd St 62640
Marlene Brady, supt.
www.girardschools.org/
700/PK-12
217-627-2915
Fax 627-3519
Girard HS
525 N 3rd St 62640
Rob Horn, prin.
200/9-12
217-627-2136
Fax 627-3519
Girard MS
525 N 3rd St 62640
Rob Horn, prin.
200/5-8
217-627-2136

Glasford, Peoria, Pop. 1,025
Illini Bluffs CUSD 327
9611 S Hanna City Glsfrd Rd 61533
Randy Stueve, supt.
www.illinibluffs.com
1,000/PK-12
309-389-2231
Fax 389-2251
Illini Bluffs HS
PO Box 320 61533
Kyle Freeman, prin.
300/9-12
309-389-5681
Fax 389-4681
Illini Bluffs MS
212 N Saylor St 61533
Greg Crider, prin.
200/6-8
309-389-3451
Fax 389-3454

Glencoe, Cook, Pop. 8,869
Glencoe SD 35
620 Greenwood Ave 60022
Cathlene Crawford, supt.
www.glencoeschools.org/
1,400/K-8
847-835-7800
Fax 835-7805
Central S
620 Greenwood Ave 60022
Ryan Mollet, prin.
600/5-8
847-835-7600
Fax 835-7605

Glendale Heights, DuPage, Pop. 32,848
Marquardt SD 15
2174 Gladstone Ct Ste C 60139
Dr. Loren D. May, supt.
www.d15.dupage.k12.il.us/
2,700/PK-8
630-295-5450
Fax 295-5455
Marquardt MS
1912 Glen Ellyn Rd 60139
Marie C. Petersen, prin.
800/6-8
630-858-3850
Fax 790-5042

Queen Bee SD 16
1560 Bloomingdale Rd 60139
Dr. James White, supt.
www.queenbee16.org
2,100/PK-8
630-260-6100
Fax 260-6103
Glenside MS
1560 Bloomingdale Rd 60139
Christopher Collins, prin.
700/6-8
630-260-6112
Fax 510-8568

Universal Technical Institute
601 Regency Dr 60139
Post-Sec.
630-529-2662

Glen Ellyn, DuPage, Pop. 27,210
Glen Ellyn CCSD 89
22W600 Butterfield Rd 60137
Dr. John Perdue, supt.
www.ccsd89.org
2,400/PK-8
630-469-8900
Fax 469-8936
Glen Crest MS
725 Sheehan Ave 60137
Dr. Scott Stevens, prin.
900/6-8
630-469-5220
Fax 469-5250

Glen Ellyn SD 41
793 N Main St 60137
Jack K. Barshinger Ed.D., supt.
www.d41.org
3,500/PK-8
630-790-6400
Fax 790-1867
Hadley JHS
240 Hawthorne St 60137
Dr. Christopher Dransoff, prin.
1,100/6-8
630-790-6450
Fax 790-6469

Glenbard Twp. HSD 87
596 Crescent Blvd 60137
Dr. Ronald Smith, supt.
www.glenbard.net
8,900/9-12
630-469-9100
Fax 469-9107
Glenbard South HS
23w200 Butterfield Rd 60137
William Leensvaart, prin.
1,400/9-12
630-469-6500
Fax 469-6572
Glenbard West HS
670 Crescent Blvd 60137
Dr. Pamela Zimmerman, prin.
2,000/9-12
630-469-8600
Fax 469-8615
Other Schools – See Carol Stream, Lombard

College of DuPage
425 22nd St 60137
Post-Sec.
630-942-2800

Glenview, Cook, Pop. 44,818
Glenview CCSD 34
1401 Greenwood Rd 60026
Dr. Gerald Hill, supt.
www.glenview34.org
3,900/K-8
847-998-5000
Fax 998-1629
Attea MS
2500 Chestnut Ave 60026
James Woell, prin.
700/6-8
847-486-7700
Fax 729-6251
Springman MS
2701 Central Rd 60025
Dr. Heather Hopkins, prin.
700/6-8
847-998-5020
Fax 998-4032

Northfield Township HSD 225
1835 Landwehr Rd 60026
Dr. Dave Hales, supt.
www.glenbrook.k12.il.us
4,700/9-12
847-486-4700
Fax 486-4734
Glenbrook South HS
4000 W Lake Ave 60026
Brian Wegley, prin.
2,600/9-12
847-729-2000
Fax 486-4462
Glenbrook Evening HS
4000 W Lake Ave 60026
Steven Von Boeckman, prin.
Adult
847-486-4709
Fax 486-4733
Other Schools – See Northbrook

Immanuel Lutheran S
74 Park Dr 60025
100/PK-10
847-724-0057
Fax 724-1038

Glenwood, Cook, Pop. 8,847
Brookwood SD 167
201 E Glenwood Dyer Rd 60425
Pamela Hollich, supt.
www.brookwood167.org
1,300/PK-8
708-758-5190
Fax 757-2104
Brookwood JHS
201 E Glenwood Lansing Rd 60425
Bethany Lindsay, prin.
300/7-8
708-758-5252
Fax 758-3954

Godfrey, Madison, Pop. 16,571

Alvareita's College of Cosmetology
3048 Godfrey Rd 62035
Post-Sec.
618-466-8952
Lewis & Clark Community College
5800 Godfrey Rd 62035
Post-Sec.
618-466-3411

Golconda, Pope, Pop. 681
Pope County CUSD 1
RR 2 Box 22 62938
Dr. Alice Sutton, supt.
www.pcusd.com/
600/PK-12
618-683-2301
Fax 683-5181
Pope County HS
RR 2 Box 22 62938
Robbie Wright, prin.
200/9-12
618-683-3071
Fax 683-9956

Goreville, Johnson, Pop. 965
Five County Regional Vocational System
Supt. — See Tamms
Five County Regional Vocational Center
201 S Ferne Clyffe 62939
Steve Webb, prin.
Vo/Tech
618-995-9831
Fax 995-9831

Goreville CUSD 1
201 S Ferne Clyffe Rd 62939
Steve Webb, supt.
600/PK-12
618-995-9831
Fax 995-9831
Goreville HS
201 S Ferne Clyffe Rd 62939
Barbara Watkins, prin.
200/9-12
618-995-2142
Fax 995-1188

Granite City, Madison, Pop. 31,294
Granite City CUSD 9
1947 Adams St 62040
Ken Perkins Ed.D., supt.
www.granitecityschools.org
7,800/PK-12
618-451-5800
Fax 451-6135
Coolidge MS
3231 Nameoki Rd 62040
Richard Talley, prin.
1,100/6-8
618-451-5826
Fax 876-5154
Granite City HS
3101 Madison Ave 62040
Jerry McKechan, prin.
2,300/9-12
618-451-5808
Fax 451-6296
Grigsby MS
3801 Cargill Rd 62040
Curt Watters, prin.
800/6-8
618-931-5544
Fax 931-5689

Grant Park, Kankakee, Pop. 1,454
Grant Park CUSD 6
PO Box 549 60940
Dr. Michael Nicholson, supt.
www.grantpark.k12.il.us/
600/K-12
815-465-6013
Fax 465-2505
Grant Park HS
PO Box 549 60940
Robert Gound, prin.
200/9-12
815-465-2181
Fax 465-2505

Granville, Putnam, Pop. 1,409
Putnam County CUSD 535
PO Box 607 61326
Mike Struna, supt.
putnam.k12.il.us/
800/K-12
815-339-2238
Fax 339-6739
Putnam County HS
PO Box 341 61326
Mike Struna, prin.
300/9-12
815-339-6514
Fax 339-2628
Other Schools – See Mc Nabb

Grayslake, Lake, Pop. 21,287
CCSD 46
565 Friederick Rd 60030
Ellen L. Correll, supt.
www.d46.k12.il.us
4,000/PK-8
847-223-3650
Fax 223-3695
Grayslake MS
440 Barron Blvd 60030
Marcus Smith, prin.
800/7-8
847-223-3680
Fax 223-3526

Grayslake Community HSD 127
400 N Lake St 60030
Dr. Catherine Finger, supt.
www.d127.org/
2,100/9-12
847-223-3559
Fax 223-3561
Grayslake Community HS - Central Campus
400 N Lake St 60030
Dr. Randy Davis, prin.
2,100/9-12
847-223-8621
Fax 223-3561
Grayslake Community HS - North Campus
1925 N Route 83 60030
Dr. Kari King, prin.
9-10
847-986-3100
Fax 986-3023

Lake County HS Technology Campus
19525 W Washington St 60030
Linda Jedlicka, dir.
www.techcampus.org
847-223-6681
Fax 223-7363
Lake County HS Technology Campus
19525 W Washington St 60030
Linda Jedlicka, dir.
Vo/Tech
847-223-6681
Fax 223-7363

College of Lake County
19351 W Washington St 60030
Post-Sec.
847-223-6601
Westlake Christian Academy
275 S Lake St 60030
Denise Schlappi, admin.
100/PK-12
847-548-6209
Fax 548-6481

Grayville, White, Pop. 1,673
Grayville CUSD 1
704 W North St 62844
David Jordan, supt.
300/PK-12
618-375-6521
Fax 375-5202
Grayville JSHS
728 W North St 62844
David Jordan, prin.
200/6-12
618-375-7114
Fax 375-6521

Greenfield, Greene, Pop. 1,166
Greenfield CUSD 10
311 Mulberry St 62044
Mike Dickson, supt.
500/K-12
217-368-2447
Fax 368-2724
Greenfield HS
502 East St 62044
Mike Dickson, prin.
200/9-12
217-368-2219
Fax 368-2230

Green Valley, Tazewell, Pop. 705
Midwest Central CUSD 191
Supt. — See Manito
Midwest Central MS
PO Box 219 61534
J. Douglas Cunningham, prin.
300/6-8
309-352-2300
Fax 352-2903

Greenview, Menard, Pop. 832
Greenview CUSD 200
PO Box 320 62642
Gary DePatis, supt.
www.menard.k12.il.us/greenviewhs/welcome.htm
300/K-12
217-968-2295
Fax 968-2297
Greenview JSHS
PO Box 320 62642
Brian Farnsworth, prin.
100/7-12
217-968-2295
Fax 968-2297

Greenville, Bond, Pop. 7,104
Bond County CUSD 2
1008 N Hena St 62246
Dr. Hugh Westbrooks, supt.
www.bccu2.k12.il.us
2,000/PK-12
618-664-0170
Fax 664-5000
Bond City Comm Unit 2 HS
1000 E State Route 140 62246
Andrew Crist, prin.
600/9-12
618-664-1370
Fax 664-4786
Greenville JHS
1200 Junior High Dr 62246
Gary Brauns, prin.
300/6-8
618-664-1226
Fax 664-5071

Greenville Christian Academy
949 Airport Ave 62246
Matthew Mendenhall, admin.
50/K-12
618-664-2175
Fax 664-4350
Greenville College
315 E College Ave 62246
Post-Sec.
618-664-2800

Gridley, McLean, Pop. 1,411
El Paso-Gridley CUSD 11
Supt. — See El Paso
El Paso-Gridley JHS
403 McLean St 61744
Dawn Thompson, prin.
7-8
309-747-2156
Fax 747-2475

Griggsville, Pike, Pop. 1,215
Griggsville-Perry CUSD 4
PO Box 439 62340
Michael Davies, supt.
griggsvilleperry.com
500/PK-12
217-833-2352
Fax 833-2354
Griggsville-Perry HS
PO Box 439 62340
Andrea Allen, prin.
200/9-12
217-833-2352
Fax 833-2354
Other Schools – See Perry

Gurnee, Lake, Pop. 30,396
Gurnee SD 56
900 Kilbourne Rd 60031
Dr. Ben Martindale, supt.
www.d56.lake.k12.il.us/district/
3,000/PK-8
847-336-0800
Fax 336-1110
Viking MS
4460 Old Grand Ave 60031
Patrick Jones, prin.
700/6-8
847-336-2108
Fax 249-0719

Warren Twp. HSD 121
Supt. — See Gages Lake
Warren Twp. HS
500 N OPlaine Rd 60031
Steven Isoya, prin.
9-12
847-662-1400
Fax 599-4848
Warren Twp. HS
34090 N Almond Rd 60031
Dr. Doug Domerocki, prin.
1,600/11-12
847-662-1400
Fax 662-1435

Woodland CCSD 50
1105 N Hunt Club Rd 60031
Joy Swoboda, supt.
www.dist50.net
7,100/PK-8
847-856-3590
Fax 856-0320
Woodland MS
7000 Washington St 60031
Scott Snyder, prin.
2,300/6-8
847-856-3400
Fax 856-3500

DeVry University
1075 Tri State Pkwy Ste 800 60031
Post-Sec.
847-855-2649

Hamilton, Hancock, Pop. 2,895
Hamilton CCSD 328
270 N 10th St 62341
Steven Breckon, supt.
www.hamilton.k12.il.us
700/PK-12
217-847-3315
Fax 847-3915
Hamilton HS
1100 Keokuk St 62341
Dan Oakley, prin.
200/9-12
217-847-3313
Fax 847-3474
Hamilton JHS
270 N 10th St 62341
Dan Oakley, prin.
100/7-8
217-847-3314
Fax 847-3915

Hampshire, Kane, Pop. 3,093
Community Unit SD 300
Supt. — See Carpentersville
Hampshire MSHS 1,700/6-12
560 S State St 60140 847-683-2522
Jim Wallis, prin. Fax 683-1030

Hanover, Jo Daviess, Pop. 827
River Ridge CUSD 210 500/K-12
4141 IL Route 84 S 61041 815-858-9005
Bradley Albrecht, supt. Fax 858-9006
www.riverridge210.org
River Ridge HS 200/9-12
4141 IL Route 84 S 61041 815-858-9005
Thomas Akers, prin. Fax 858-9006
River Ridge MS 100/6-8
4141 IL Route 84 S 61041 815-858-9005
Thomas Akers, prin. Fax 858-9006

Hanover Park, Cook, Pop. 37,643
Keeneyville SD 20 1,700/PK-8
5540 Arlington Dr E 60133 630-894-2250
Dr. Carol Auer, supt. Fax 894-5187
www.esd20.com
Spring Wood MS 600/6-8
5540 Arlington Dr E 60133 630-893-8900
Craig Barringer, prin. Fax 894-9658

Hanover Park College of Beauty Culture Post-Sec.
1166 E Lake St 60133 630-830-6560

Hardin, Calhoun, Pop. 951
Calhoun CUSD 40 600/PK-12
PO Box 387 62047 618-576-2722
Dr. Linda Basden, supt. Fax 576-2641
calhoun.ezl.com
Calhoun HS 200/9-12
PO Box 387 62047 618-576-2229
Carole Crum, prin. Fax 576-8031

Harrisburg, Saline, Pop. 9,638
Harrisburg CUSD 3 2,200/PK-12
40 S Main St 62946 618-253-7637
Ed Bradley, supt. Fax 252-7584
www.hbg.saline.k12.il.us
Harrisburg HS 600/9-12
333 W College St 62946 618-253-7637
Jim Butler, prin. Fax 252-2616
Harrisburg MS 500/6-8
312 Bulldog Blvd 62946 618-253-7107
Kerry Maxam, prin. Fax 253-4114

Southeastern Illinois College Post-Sec.
3575 College Rd 62946 618-252-6376

Hartsburg, Montgomery, Pop. 345
Hartsburg-Emden CUSD 21 300/PK-12
400 W Front St 62643 217-642-5244
Donald Helm, supt. Fax 642-5333
www.logan.k12.il.us/hartem/
Hartsburg-Emden JSHS 200/5-12
400 W Front St 62643 217-642-5244
Dan Savery, prin. Fax 642-5333

Harvard, McHenry, Pop. 8,600
Harvard CUSD 50 2,500/PK-12
1101 N Jefferson St 60033 815-943-4022
Dr. Richard Crosby, supt. Fax 943-4282
www.d50.mchenry.k12.il.us
Harvard HS 600/9-12
1103 N Jefferson St 60033 815-943-6461
Dr. Michelle McReynolds, prin. Fax 943-8506
Harvard JHS 700/5-8
1301 Garfield St 60033 815-943-6466
Linda Heiden, prin. Fax 943-8521

Harvey, Cook, Pop. 29,367
Harvey SD 152 3,100/PK-8
16001 Lincoln Ave 60426 708-333-0300
Dr. Lela Bridges, supt. Fax 333-0349
www.harvey152.org/
Brooks MS 700/7-8
14741 Wallace St 60426 708-333-6390
Maryann West, prin. Fax 333-3177

Thornton Twp. HSD 205
Supt. — See South Holland
Thornton Twp. HS 2,500/9-12
15001 Broadway Ave 60426 708-225-4101
Angelo Armistead, prin.

West Harvey-Dixmoor SD 147 1,700/PK-8
191 W 155th Pl 60426 708-339-9500
Dr. Alex Boyd, supt. Fax 339-9533
www.whd147.org
Other Schools – See Dixmoor

Ingalls Memorial Hospital Post-Sec.
1 Ingalls Dr 60426 708-333-2300

Havana, Mason, Pop. 3,516
Havana CUSD 126 1,200/PK-12
501 S McKinley St 62644 309-543-3384
Dr. Suellen Girard, supt. Fax 543-3385
mason.k12.il.us/havana126
Havana HS 400/9-12
501 S McKinley St 62644 309-543-3337
Scott Kehrberg, prin. Fax 543-6721
Havana JHS 400/5-8
801 E Laurel Ave 62644 309-543-6677
Jerry Wilson, prin. Fax 543-6678

Hawthorn Woods, Lake, Pop. 6,578
Lake Zurich CUSD 95
Supt. — See Lake Zurich
Lake Zurich MS North Campus 700/6-8
95 Hubbard Ln 60047 847-438-2361
Nate Carter, prin. Fax 438-2381

Hazel Crest, Cook, Pop. 14,745
Hazel Crest SD 152-5 1,100/PK-8
1910 170th St 60429 708-335-0790
Dr. Sheila Harrison-Williams, supt. Fax 335-3520
sd1525.org/

Other Schools – See Markham

Hebron, McHenry, Pop. 1,099
Alden Hebron SD 19 500/PK-12
9604 Illinois St 60034 815-648-2886
Kurt Suhr, supt. Fax 648-2339
www.alden-hebron.org
Alden-Hebron HS 100/9-12
9604 Illinois St 60034 815-648-2442
Janet Fredriksen, prin. Fax 648-2339
Alden-Hebron MS 100/6-8
9604 Illinois St 60034 815-648-2442
Delores Swanson, prin. Fax 648-2339

Henry, Marshall, Pop. 2,513
Henry-Senachwine CUSD 5 600/K-12
1023 College St 61537 309-364-3614
Thomas Urban, supt. Fax 364-2990
www.henrysenachwine.org
Henry-Senachwine Consolidated HS 200/9-12
1023 College St 61537 309-364-2829
Michael Miller, prin. Fax 364-2990

Herrin, Williamson, Pop. 11,406
Herrin CUSD 4 2,200/K-12
500 N 10th St 62948 618-988-8024
Mark Collins, supt. Fax 942-6998
www.herrinunit.org
Herrin HS 700/9-12
700 N 10th St 62948 618-942-6606
Terry Ryker, prin. Fax 942-7562
Herrin MS 500/6-8
700 S 14th St 62948 618-942-7461
Steve Robinson, prin. Fax 988-8821

Unity Christian S 200/PK-12
321 N 13th St 62948 618-942-3802
Tracey Mills, prin. Fax 942-7228

Herscher, Kankakee, Pop. 1,565
Herscher CUSD 2 1,900/PK-12
PO Box 504 60941 815-426-2162
William Davison, supt. Fax 426-2872
www.hsd2.k12.il.us
Herscher HS 700/9-12
PO Box 504 60941 815-426-2103
Brian Riegler, prin. Fax 426-2957

Heyworth, McLean, Pop. 2,478
Heyworth CUSD 4 900/PK-12
522 E Main St 61745 309-473-3727
Randall Merker, supt. Fax 473-2220
www.husd4.k12.il.us/
Heyworth HS 400/7-12
308 W Cleveland St 61745 309-473-2322
Jeff Asmus, prin. Fax 473-2323

Hickory Hills, Cook, Pop. 13,752
North Palos SD 117
Supt. — See Palos Hills
Conrady JHS 900/6-8
7950 W 97th St 60457 708-233-4500
Paula Coughlin, prin. Fax 430-8964

Highland, Madison, Pop. 8,739
Highland CUSD 5 2,500/PK-12
PO Box 149 62249 618-654-2106
Marvin Warner, supt. Fax 654-5424
www.highland.madison.k12.il.us/
Highland HS 1,000/9-12
PO Box 149 62249 618-654-7131
Andrew Carmitchel, prin. Fax 654-6548
Highland MS 500/7-8
PO Box 149 62249 618-651-8800
Jeanie Probst, prin. Fax 654-1551

Highland Park, Lake, Pop. 30,897
North Shore SD 112 4,400/PK-8
1936 Green Bay Rd 60035 847-681-6700
Dr. Maureen L. Hager, supt. Fax 266-2379
www.nssd112.org
Edgewood MS 600/6-8
929 Edgewood Rd 60035 847-432-3858
Allison Stein, prin. Fax 432-7326
Elm Place MS 400/6-8
2031 Sheridan Rd 60035 847-432-9217
Michael Lubelfeld, prin. Fax 432-9213
Northwood JHS 400/6-8
945 North Ave 60035 847-432-4770
Steven Hamlin, prin. Fax 432-4886

Township HSD 113 3,500/9-12
1040 Park Ave W 60035 224-765-1000
Dr. Ann Riebock, supt. Fax 926-9326
www.dist113.org
Highland Park HS 1,800/9-12
433 Vine Ave 60035 224-765-2000
John Lorenz, prin. Fax 926-9348
Other Schools – See Deerfield

Hillsboro, Montgomery, Pop. 4,253
Hillsboro CUSD 3 2,000/PK-12
1311 Vandalia Rd 62049 217-532-2942
Donald Burton, supt. Fax 532-3137
www.hillsboroschools.net
Hillsboro HS 600/9-12
522 E Tremont St 62049 217-532-2841
Gary Zerrusen, prin. Fax 532-5179
Hillsboro JHS, 909 Rountree St 62049 500/6-8
David Powell, prin. 217-532-3742

Hillside, Cook, Pop. 8,005
Proviso Township HSD 209
Supt. — See Maywood
Proviso West HS 2,500/9-12
4701 Harrison St 60162 708-449-6400
Alexis Wallace, prin. Fax 449-3636

Hinckley, DeKalb, Pop. 2,048
Hinckley-Big Rock CUSD 429 900/K-12
PO Box 1210 60520 815-286-7575
Glen Littlefield, supt. Fax 286-7577
www.hbr429.org

Hinckley-Big Rock HS 300/9-12
PO Box 1210 60520 815-286-7500
Charles Lawson, prin. Fax 286-7505

Hines, Cook

Edward Hines Veterans Admin. Hospital Post-Sec.
PO Box 5000 60141 708-216-2153

Hinsdale, DuPage, Pop. 17,954
CCSD 181
Supt. — See Westmont
Hinsdale MS 700/6-8
100 S Garfield Ave 60521 630-887-1370
Mary Ticknor, prin. Fax 655-9754
Hinsdale Township HSD 86 4,200/9-12
55th And Grant 60521 630-655-6100
Dr. Nicholas Wahl, supt. Fax 325-9153
www.hinsdale86.org
Hinsdale Central HS 2,400/9-12
55th and Grant 60521 630-570-8000
Dr. James Ferguson, prin. Fax 887-1362
Other Schools – See Darien

Hinsdale Adventist Academy 200/PK-12
631 E Hickory St 60521 630-323-9211
Patricia Williams, prin. Fax 323-9237

Hoffman Estates, Cook, Pop. 50,108
Schaumburg CCSD 54
Supt. — See Schaumburg
Eisenhower JHS 700/7-8
800 Hassell Rd 847-357-5500
Pamela Samson, prin. Fax 357-5501

Township HSD 211
Supt. — See Palatine
Conant HS 2,700/9-12
700 E Cougar Trl 847-755-3600
Timothy Cannon, prin. Fax 755-3623
Hoffman Estates HS 2,200/9-12
1100 W Higgins Rd 847-755-5600
Theresa Busch, prin. Fax 755-5623

American Intercontinental Univ Online Post-Sec.
5550 Prairie Stone Pky #400 60192 847-851-5284

Homer, Champaign, Pop. 1,190
Heritage CUSD 8
Supt. — See Broadlands
Heritage JHS 100/6-8
512 W 1st St 61849 217-896-2421
Chris Kerns, prin. Fax 896-2338

Homer CCSD 33C 2,900/K-8
15733 S Bell Rd, 708-226-7600
William Young, supt. Fax 226-7627
www.homerschools.org
Homer JHS 800/7-8
15711 S Bell Rd, 708-226-7800
Troy Mitchell, prin. Fax 226-7859

Homewood, Cook, Pop. 19,348
Homewood SD 153 3,700/PK-8
18205 Aberdeen St 60430 708-799-5661
Dr. Dale Mitchell, supt. Fax 799-1377
www.homewoodsd153.org/
Hart JHS 800/6-8
18220 Morgan St 60430 708-799-5544
Jeffrey Stawick, prin. Fax 799-8360

Hoopeston, Vermilion, Pop. 5,825
Hoopeston Area CUSD 11 1,300/PK-12
615 E Orange St 60942 217-283-6668
Mark Conolly, supt. Fax 283-5431
www.hoopeston.k12.il.us
Hoopeston Area HS 400/9-12
615 E Orange St 60942 217-283-6662
Hank Hornbeck, prin. Fax 283-5431
Hoopeston Area MS 200/7-8
615 E Orange St 60942 217-283-6664
Hank Hornbeck, prin. Fax 283-7943

Hume, Edgar, Pop. 377
Shiloh CUSD 1 400/PK-12
21751 N 575th St 61932 217-887-2364
James M. Acklin, supt. Fax 887-2448
www.shiloh.k12.il.us
Shiloh JSHS 200/7-12
21751 N 575th St 61932 217-887-2364
Keith Kittell, prin. Fax 887-2562

Huntley, McHenry, Pop. 11,769
Consolidated SD 158
Supt. — See Algonquin
Huntley HS 1,100/9-12
13719 Harmony Rd 60142 847-659-6600
David Johnson, prin. Fax 659-6620

Hutsonville, Crawford, Pop. 618
Hutsonville CUSD 1 400/PK-12
PO Box 218 62433 618-563-4912
Roger Eddy, supt. Fax 563-9122
Hutsonville HS 100/9-12
PO Box 218 62433 618-563-4913
Monte Newlin, prin. Fax 563-9122

Illiopolis, Sangamon, Pop. 892
Sangamon Valley CUSD 9
Supt. — See Niantic
Sangamon Valley MS 100/6-8
341 Matilda St 62539 217-486-2241
Bill Dethrow, prin.

Ina, Jefferson, Pop. 2,432

Rend Lake College Post-Sec.
RR 1 62846 618-437-5321

Ingleside, See Fox Lake
Big Hollow SD 38 1,000/PK-8
34699 N US Highway 12 60041 847-587-2632
Ron Pazanin, supt. Fax 587-2663
www.bighollow.us

Taveirne MS 200/7-8
34699 N US Highway 12 60041 847-587-6800
Henny Sands, prin.

Gavin SD 37 1,100/PK-8
25775 W IL Route 134 60041 847-546-2916
Pamela Rockwood, supt. Fax 546-9584
www.gs37.lake.k12.il.us
Gavin South JHS 500/5-8
25775 W IL Route 134 60041 847-546-9336
Ron Banion, prin. Fax 546-9338

Itasca, DuPage, Pop. 8,382
Itasca SD 10 800/PK-8
200 N Maple St 60143 630-773-1232
Dr. Ken Cull, supt. Fax 773-1342
www.itasca.k12.il.us
Peacock MS 300/6-8
301 E North St 60143 630-773-0335
Reinhard Nickisch, prin. Fax 285-7460

Environmental Technical Institute Post-Sec.
1101 W Thorndale Ave 60143 630-285-9100

Jacksonville, Morgan, Pop. 19,603
Jacksonville SD 117 3,600/PK-12
516 Jordan St 62650 217-243-9411
Lee Hovasse, supt. Fax 243-6844
www.morgan.k12.il.us/jvsd117/index.html
Jacksonville HS 1,200/9-12
1211 N Diamond St 62650 217-243-4384
Ed Wainscott, prin. Fax 245-0445
Turner JHS 600/7-8
664 Lincoln Ave 62650 217-243-3383
Beth Brockschmidt, prin. Fax 243-3459

Illinois College Post-Sec.
1101 W College Ave 62650 217-245-3000
Illinois School for the Deaf Post-Sec.
125 S Webster Ave 62650 217-245-5141
Illinois School for Visually Impaired Post-Sec.
658 E State St 62650 217-479-4400
MacMurray College Post-Sec.
447 E College Ave 62650 217-479-7000
Mr. John's School of Cosmetology & Nails Post-Sec.
1429 S Main St 62650 217-243-1744
Routt HS 100/9-12
500 E College Ave 62650 217-243-8563
Randy Verticchio, prin. Fax 243-7497
Westfair Christian Academy 100/K-12
14 Clarke Dr 62650 217-243-7100
Randy Cooper, prin. Fax 243-2386

Jerseyville, Jersey, Pop. 8,051
Jersey CUSD 100 3,100/PK-12
100 Lincoln Ave 62052 618-498-5561
James Whiteside, supt. Fax 498-5265
www.jersey100.k12.il.us/
Illini MS 600/6-8
1101 S Liberty St 62052 618-498-5527
Cynthia Lindsey, prin. Fax 498-7079
Jersey Community HS 1,000/9-12
801 N State St 62052 618-498-5521
Bonnie Tungett, prin. Fax 498-5332

Johnsburg, McHenry, Pop. 6,003
Johnsburg CUSD 12 2,700/PK-12
2222 Church St 60050 815-385-6916
Dr. Robert Gough, supt. Fax 385-4715
www.jburgd12.k12.il.us
Johnsburg HS 900/9-12
2002 W Ringwood Rd 60050 815-385-9233
Daniel Johnson, prin. Fax 344-0451
Johnsburg JHS 900/5-8
2220 Church St 60050 815-385-6210
Patrick Flynn, prin. Fax 578-2649

Johnston City, Williamson, Pop. 3,487
Johnston City CUSD 1 1,200/PK-12
1103 Monroe Ave 62951 618-983-8021
Gary Schurz, supt. Fax 983-6034
www.jc1.wilmsn.k12.il.us
Johnston City HS 400/9-12
1500 Jefferson Ave 62951 618-983-4700
James Grant, prin. Fax 983-6812

Joliet, Will, Pop. 123,570
Joliet SD 86 10,000/PK-8
420 N Raynor Ave 60435 815-740-3196
Phyllis Wilson Ph.D., supt. Fax 740-6520
www.joliet86.org
Dirksen JHS 600/6-8
203 S Midland Ave 60436 815-729-1566
Kimberly Pfoutz, prin. Fax 744-2346
Gompers JHS 800/6-8
1501 Copperfield Ave 60432 815-727-5276
David Negron, prin. Fax 726-5341
Hufford JHS 1,000/6-8
1125 N Larkin Ave 60435 815-725-3540
Anna White, prin. Fax 744-5974
Washington JHS & Academy 700/6-8
402 Richards St 60433 815-727-5271
Michael Latting, prin. Fax 740-5451

Joliet Twp. HSD 204 5,000/9-12
201 E Jefferson St 60432 815-727-6970
Paul Swanstrom, supt. Fax 727-1277
www.jths.org/
Joliet Central HS 2,700/9-12
201 E Jefferson St 60432 815-727-6740
Craig Spiers, prin. Fax 727-6824
Joliet West HS 2,300/9-12
401 N Larkin Ave 60435 815-727-6940
Cheryl McCarthy, prin. Fax 744-3070

Joliet Catholic Academy 900/9-12
1200 N Larkin Ave 60435 815-741-0500
Jeffrey Budz, prin. Fax 741-9530
Joliet Junior College Post-Sec.
1216 Houbolt Rd 60431 815-729-9020
Professional Choice Hair Design Academy Post-Sec.
2719 W Jefferson St 60435 815-741-8224

Ridgewood Baptist Academy 300/PK-12
1968 Hillcrest Rd 60433 815-726-2121
Brian Keith, prin. Fax 726-2344
University of St. Francis Post-Sec.
500 Wilcox St 60435 815-740-3360

Joppa, Massac, Pop. 414
Joppa-Maple Grove CUSD 38 300/PK-12
PO Box 10 62953 618-543-9023
Catherine Trampe, supt. Fax 543-9264
Joppa JSHS 100/7-12
PO Box 10 62953 618-543-7589
Vickie Artman, prin. Fax 543-9264

Joy, Mercer, Pop. 369
Westmer CUSD 203 600/PK-12
PO Box 436 61260 309-584-4173
Robert Haskell, supt. Fax 584-4115
mercer.k12.il.us/westmer
Westmer HS 200/9-12
PO Box 436 61260 309-584-4174
Andy Siegfried, prin. Fax 584-4257
Westmer JHS 100/6-8
PO Box 436 61260 309-584-4174
Andy Siegfried, prin. Fax 584-4257

Junction, Gallatin, Pop. 135
Gallatin CUSD 7 900/PK-12
5175 Highway 13 62954 618-272-3821
Les Oyler, supt. Fax 272-4101
Gallatin HS 300/9-12
5175 Highway 13 62954 618-272-5141
Lucinda Schmitt, prin. Fax 272-4101
Gallatin JHS 300/5-8
5175 Highway 13 62954 618-272-7341
Tom Mitchell, prin. Fax 272-4101

Justice, Cook, Pop. 12,453
Indian Springs SD 109 2,900/PK-8
7540 S 86th Ave 60458 708-496-8700
Dr. Jon Nebor, supt. Fax 496-8641
www.isd109.org
Wilkins JHS 600/7-8
8001 S 82nd Ave 60458 708-496-8708
William Caron, prin. Fax 728-3114

Kankakee, Kankakee, Pop. 26,995
Kankakee SD 111 5,000/PK-12
240 Warren Ave 60901 815-933-0700
Dr. Brian Ali, supt. Fax 933-9981
www.kankakeeschooldistrict.org
Kankakee HS 1,200/9-12
1200 W Jeffery St 60901 815-933-0740
Fax 933-9149
Kankakee JHS 900/7-8
2250 E Crestwood St 60901 815-933-0730
Mike Rolinitis, prin. Fax 935-7272

Bishop McNamara HS 500/9-12
550 W Brookmont Blvd 60901 815-932-7413
James Laurenti, prin. Fax 932-0926
Grace Baptist Academy 200/K-12
2499 Waldron Rd 60901 815-939-4579
Dwight Ascher, prin. Fax 939-1334
Kankakee Community College Post-Sec.
PO Box 888 60901 815-933-0345
Kankakee Trinity Academy 200/PK-12
410 S Small Ave 60901 815-935-8080
Brad Prairie, prin. Fax 935-0280

Kansas, Edgar, Pop. 832
Kansas CUSD 3 300/PK-12
PO Box 350 61933 217-948-5174
Chris Long, supt. Fax 948-5577
Kansas HS 100/9-12
PO Box 350 61933 217-948-5175
Dwight Stricklin, prin. Fax 948-5577

Kempton, Ford, Pop. 233
Tri-Point CUSD 6-J 600/PK-12
PO Box 128 60946 815-253-6299
Jeffrey L. Fritchtnitch, supt. Fax 253-6298
www.tripoint.k12.il.us
Other Schools – See Cullom, Piper City

Kewanee, Henry, Pop. 12,724
Kewanee CUSD 229 1,800/PK-12
210 Lyle St 61443 309-853-3341
Harold Ford, supt. Fax 852-5504
www.kewaneeschoolsfoundation.org/
Central MS, 215 E Central Blvd 61443 700/4-8
Andy Bullock, prin. 309-853-4290
Kewanee HS 600/9-12
1211 E 3rd St 61443 309-853-3328
Mike Kirkham, prin. Fax 854-0210

Wethersfield CUSD 230 600/PK-12
439 Willard St 61443 309-853-4860
Bill Owens, supt. Fax 856-7976
geese.henry.k12.il.us
Wethersfield JSHS 300/7-12
439 Willard St 61443 309-853-4205
James Peck, prin. Fax 856-7976

Black Hawk College Post-Sec.
1501 State Highway 78 61443 309-852-5671

Kincaid, Christian, Pop. 1,446
South Fork SD 14 400/PK-12
PO Box 20 62540 217-237-4333
Charlotte Davis, supt. Fax 237-4370
South Fork JSHS 200/5-12
PO Box 20 62540 217-237-4333
Charlotte Davis, prin. Fax 237-4370

Kinderhook, Pike, Pop. 239
West Pike CUSD 2 300/PK-12
PO Box 189 62345 217-432-8324
Rodger Hannel, supt. Fax 432-8003
West Pike HS 100/9-12
PO Box 189 62345 217-432-8324
Michael Vaia, prin. Fax 432-8003
West Pike JHS 100/6-8
PO Box 189 62345 217-432-8324
Michael Vaia, prin. Fax 432-8003

Kinmundy, Marion, Pop. 881
South Central CUSD 401 800/PK-12
PO Box 189 62854 618-547-3414
Judy Cole, supt. Fax 547-7790
South Central MS 200/5-8
PO Box 189 62854 618-547-7734
Greg Grinestaff, prin. Fax 547-7790
Other Schools – See Farina

Kirkland, DeKalb, Pop. 1,218
Hiawatha CUSD 426 500/K-12
PO Box 428 60146 815-522-6676
Christine Demory, supt. Fax 522-6619
www.hiawatha426.k12.il.us
Hiawatha HS 300/7-12
PO Box 428 60146 815-522-3335
Ty E. Wolf, prin. Fax 522-3312

Knoxville, Knox, Pop. 3,081
Knoxville CUSD 202 1,100/PK-12
600 E Main St 61448 309-289-2328
Lawrence W. Carlton, supt. Fax 289-9614
bluebullets.knox.k12.il.us/cusd202.htm
Knoxville HS 300/9-12
600 E Main St 61448 309-289-2324
Patrick Callahan, prin. Fax 289-9466
Knoxville JHS 300/5-8
701 E Mill St 61448 309-289-4126
David Summers, prin. Fax 289-4128

Lacon, Marshall, Pop. 1,914
Midland CUSD 7 900/PK-12
206 N High St 61540 309-246-2310
Dean Irlbeck, supt. Fax 246-2311
www.midland-7.org
Other Schools – See Sparland, Varna

Lafox, Kane

Broadview Academy 100/9-12
PO Box 307 60147 630-232-7441
Dr. Randy Siebold, prin. Fax 232-7443

La Grange, Cook, Pop. 15,650
La Grange Highlands SD 106 900/K-8
1750 W Plainfield Rd 60525 708-246-3085
Dr. Arleen Armanetti, supt. Fax 246-0220
www.district106.net
Highlands MS 300/6-8
1850 W Plainfield Rd 60525 708-579-6890
Michael Papierski, prin. Fax 246-0220

La Grange SD 105 1,100/PK-8
1001 S Spring Ave 60525 708-482-2700
James C. Ewing Ed.D., supt. Fax 482-2727
www.d105.net
Gurrie MS 200/7-8
1001 S Spring Ave 60525 708-482-2720
Edmond Hood, prin. Fax 482-2724

Lyons Twp. HSD 204 1,700/9-12
100 S Brainard Ave 60525 708-579-6451
Dennis Kelly, supt. Fax 579-6768
www.lths.net
Lyons Twp. HS North Campus 1,700/11-12
100 S Brainard Ave 60525 708-579-6300
Dave Franson, prin. Fax 579-3187
Other Schools – See Western Springs

La Grange Park, Cook, Pop. 13,062
La Grange SD 102 2,700/PK-8
333 N Park Rd 60526 708-482-2400
Dr. Mark Van Clay, supt. Fax 482-2402
www.dist102.k12.il.us/
Park JHS 600/7-8
325 N Park Rd 60526 708-482-2500
Dr. Laura Schwartz, prin. Fax 352-1170

Nazareth Academy 800/9-12
1209 W Ogden Ave 60526 708-354-0061
Deborah Vondrasek, prin. Fax 354-0109

La Harpe, Hancock, Pop. 1,339
La Harpe CUSD 335 500/PK-12
404 W Main St 61450 217-659-7739
Jo R. Campbell, supt. Fax 659-7730
hancock.k12.il.us/laharpe/
La Harpe HS 100/9-12
404 W Main St 61450 217-659-3713
Lila McKeown, prin. Fax 659-7730
La Harpe JHS 100/6-8
404 W Main St 61450 217-659-7923
Lila McKeown, prin. Fax 659-7730

Lake Bluff, Lake, Pop. 6,170
Lake Bluff ESD 65 1,100/K-8
121 E Sheridan Pl 60044 847-234-9400
Dr. David Vick, supt. Fax 234-6237
www.lbelem.lfc.edu/
Lake Bluff MS 400/6-8
31 E Sheridan Pl 60044 847-234-9407
Michael Donhost, prin. Fax 615-9144

Lake Forest, Lake, Pop. 20,762
Lake Forest Community HSD 115 1,700/9-12
1285 N McKinley Rd 60045 847-234-3600
Dr. Harry Griffith, supt. Fax 582-7797
www.lfhs.org/
Lake Forest HS 1,700/9-12
1285 N McKinley Rd 60045 847-234-3600
Jay Hoffman, prin. Fax 234-7933

Lake Forest SD 67 2,200/PK-8
67 W Deerpath Rd 60045 847-234-6010
Dr. Harry Griffith, supt. Fax 234-2372
www.lfelem.lfc.edu
Deer Path MS 1,000/5-8
155 W Deerpath Rd 60045 847-604-7400
K. Schumacher, prin. Fax 234-2389

Lake Forest Academy 300/9-12
1500 W Kennedy Rd 60045 847-234-3210
John Strudwick, hdmstr. Fax 615-3202

Lake Forest College — Post-Sec.
555 N Sheridan Rd 60045 — 847-234-3100
Lake Forest Graduate Sch. of Management — Post-Sec.
1905 W Field Ct 60045 — 847-234-5005
School of St. Mary MS — 300/4-8
185 E Illinois Rd 60045 — 847-234-0371
Patrick Browne, prin. — Fax 234-9593
Woodlands Academy Sacred Heart — 200/9-12
760 E Westleigh Rd 60045 — 847-234-4300
Madonna Lee Edmunds, prin. — Fax 234-4348

Lake in the Hills, McHenry, Pop. 26,639
Consolidated SD 158
Supt. — See Algonquin
Marlowe MS — 6-8
9625 Haligus Rd, — 847-659-4700
Jake Wakitsch, prin. — Fax 659-4720

Lake Villa, Lake, Pop. 8,089
Community HSD 117 — 2,300/9-12
1625 Deep Lake Rd Ste A 60046 — 847-838-7170
Jay Sabatino Ed.D., supt. — Fax 395-7553
www.d117.org
Lakes Community HS — 9-12
1600 Eagle Way 60046 — 847-838-7100
Dr. Robert Crist, prin. — Fax 395-7553
Other Schools – See Antioch

Lake Villa CCSD 41 — 3,300/PK-8
131 McKinley Ave 60046 — 847-356-2385
Dr. Michael Anderson, supt. — Fax 356-2670
www.district41.org
Palombi MS — 700/7-8
133 McKinley Ave 60046 — 847-356-2118
Mary Jordan, prin. — Fax 356-0833

Lake Zurich, Lake, Pop. 19,170
Lake Zurich CUSD 95 — 6,500/PK-12
400 S Old Rand Rd 60047 — 847-438-2831
Dr. Brian Knutson, supt. — Fax 438-6702
www.lz95.org
Lake Zurich HS — 2,000/9-12
300 Church St 60047 — 847-438-5155
Mike Egan, prin. — Fax 438-5989
Lake Zurich MS South Campus — 900/6-8
435 W Cuba Rd 60047 — 847-540-7070
Dave Gardner, prin. — Fax 540-9438
Other Schools – See Hawthorn Woods

La Moille, Bureau, Pop. 762
La Moille CUSD 303 — 300/K-12
PO Box 470 61330 — 815-638-2018
Colette Sutton, supt. — Fax 638-2392
Allen ES — 100/4-8
PO Box 470 61330 — 815-638-2233
James Brandau, prin. — Fax 638-2886
La Moille HS — 100/9-12
PO Box 440 61330 — 815-638-2144
Colette Sutton, prin. — Fax 638-2392

Lanark, Carroll, Pop. 1,517
Eastland CUSD 308 — 800/PK-12
200 S School St 61046 — 815-493-6301
Mark Hansen, supt. — Fax 493-6303
Eastland HS — 300/9-12
500 S School Dr 61046 — 815-493-6341
Jay Ritchie, prin. — Fax 493-6343
Other Schools – See Shannon

Lansing, Cook, Pop. 27,976
Lansing SD 158 — 2,100/PK-8
18300 Greenbay Ave 60438 — 708-474-6700
Veronda Cottle, supt. — Fax 474-9976
www.d158.net
Memorial JHS — 700/6-8
2721 Ridge Rd 60438 — 708-474-2383
Robert Zimbelman, prin. — Fax 474-9976

Sunnybrook SD 171 — 1,100/PK-8
19266 Burnham Ave 60438 — 708-895-0750
Joseph Majchrowicz Ed.D., supt. — Fax 895-8580
www.sd171.org
Heritage MS — 600/5-8
19250 Burnham Ave 60438 — 708-895-0790
Bruce Christensen, prin. — Fax 895-8580

Thornton Fractional Township HSD 215
Supt. — See Calumet City
Thornton Fractional South HS — 1,600/9-12
18500 Burnham Ave 60438 — 708-585-2000
John Hallberg, prin. — Fax 418-0760

American School — Post-Sec.
2200 E 170th St 60438 — 708-418-2800
Illiana Christian HS — 700/9-12
2261 Indiana Ave 60438 — 708-474-0515
Peter Boonstra, prin. — Fax 474-0581
Luther East HS — 100/9-12
PO Box 404 60438 — 708-895-8441
Dale Cooper, prin. — Fax 895-5220

La Salle, LaSalle, Pop. 9,615
La Salle ESD 122 — 900/PK-8
1165 Saint Vincents Ave 61301 — 815-223-0786
Dr. Joan McGuire, supt. — Fax 223-8740
www.lasalleschools.net/
Lincoln JHS — 200/7-8
1165 Saint Vincents Ave 61301 — 815-223-0933
Jerald Carls, prin. — Fax 223-8740
La Salle-Peru Twp HSD 120 — 1,200/9-12
541 Chartres St 61301 — 815-223-2373
Dr. Craig Carter, supt. — Fax 223-3444
www.lphs.net/
La Salle-Peru Township HS — 1,200/9-12
541 Chartres St 61301 — 815-223-1721
Deb Nelson, prin. — Fax 223-3444

Lasalle-Peru Area Career Center —
6th and Creve Coeur 61301 — 815-223-2454
Mary Stouffer, dir. — Fax 224-5066
Lasalle-Peru Area Career Center — Vo/Tech
6th and Creve Coeur 61301 — 815-223-2454
Mary Stouffer, prin. — Fax 224-5066

Lawrenceville, Lawrence, Pop. 4,597
Lawrence County CUSD 20 — 1,400/PK-12
1802 Cedar St 62439 — 618-943-2326
Michael Sutton, supt. — Fax 943-4092
www.cusd20.com
Lawrenceville HS — 400/9-12
503 8th St 62439 — 618-943-3389
Charles Stegall, prin. — Fax 943-4925
Parkview JHS, 1802 Cedar St 62439 — 300/6-8
Corrie Ray, prin. — 618-943-2327

Lebanon, Saint Clair, Pop. 3,566
Lebanon CUSD 9 — 700/PK-12
200 W Schuetz St 62254 — 618-537-4611
Harry Cavanaugh, supt. — Fax 537-9588
www.lebanon.stclair.k12.il.us
Lebanon HS — 200/9-12
200 W Schuetz St 62254 — 618-537-4423
Leigh Jackson, prin. — Fax 537-9588

McKendree College — Post-Sec.
701 College Rd 62254 — 618-537-6830

Leland, LaSalle, Pop. 947
Leland CUSD 1 — 400/K-12
370 N Main St 60531 — 815-495-3821
Dr. Laurel Walker, supt. — Fax 495-4611
www.leland.lasalle.k12.il.us
Leland HS — 100/9-12
370 N Main St 60531 — 815-495-3231
Dr. Douglas Deschepper, prin. — Fax 495-4611

Lemont, DuPage, Pop. 14,319
Lemont Township HSD 210 — 1,200/9-12
800 Porter St 60439 — 630-257-5838
Dr. Sandra L. Doebert, supt. — Fax 257-7603
lemont.k12.il.us
Lemont HS — 1,200/9-12
800 Porter St 60439 — 630-257-5838
Dr. Thomas Trengove, prin. — Fax 243-0310

Lemont-Bromberek SD 113A — 2,500/PK-8
16100 127th St 60439 — 630-257-2286
Dr. Thomas F. Cusack, supt. — Fax 243-3005
www.sd113a.org/
Old Quarry MS — 900/6-8
16100 127th St 60439 — 630-257-2286
Dawn Pechukas, prin. — Fax 243-3004

Mt. Assisi Academy — 400/9-12
13860 Main St 60439 — 630-257-7844
Sr. Mary Werner, prin. — Fax 257-6362

Lena, Stephenson, Pop. 2,842
Lena Winslow CUSD 202 — 1,100/PK-12
401 Fremont St 61048 — 815-369-3100
John R. Kelley, supt. — Fax 369-3102
www.le-win.net/
Lena-Winslow HS — 400/9-12
516 Fremont St 61048 — 815-369-3115
Dan Todd, prin. — Fax 369-3139
Lena-Winslow JHS — 300/6-8
517 Fremont St 61048 — 815-369-3114
Mark Kuehl, prin. — Fax 369-3162

Le Roy, McLean, Pop. 3,380
Le Roy CUSD 2 — 800/PK-12
600 E Pine St 61752 — 309-962-4211
Edgar A. Coller, supt. — Fax 962-9312
Le Roy HS — 200/9-12
505 E Center St 61752 — 309-962-2911
Gary R. Tipsord, prin. — Fax 962-8421
Le Roy JHS — 100/7-8
505 E Center St 61752 — 309-962-2911
Gary R. Tipsord, prin. — Fax 962-8421

Lewistown, Fulton, Pop. 2,458
Lewistown SD 97 — 800/PK-12
15501 E Avenue L 61542 — 309-547-5826
Daniel Whitsitt, supt. — Fax 547-5235
www.cusd97.fulton.k12.il.us/
Central ES, 15501 E Avenue L 61542 — 300/4-8
Jan Braun, prin. — 309-547-2231
Lewistown Community HS — 200/9-12
15205 N State 100 Hwy 61542 — 309-547-2288
Brad Kenser, prin. — Fax 547-9870

Lexington, McLean, Pop. 1,902
Lexington CUSD 7 — 600/PK-12
PO Box 67 61753 — 309-365-4141
Dr. Brent McArdle, supt. — Fax 365-7381
lexington.k12.il.us
Lexington HS — 200/9-12
PO Box 67 61753 — 309-365-2711
Richard Baker, prin. — Fax 365-5032
Lexington JHS, PO Box 67 61753 — 100/7-8
Richard Baker, prin. — 309-365-2711

Liberty, Adams, Pop. 519
Liberty CUSD 2 — 600/PK-12
505 N Park St 62347 — 217-645-3433
Curtis Simonson, supt. — Fax 645-3241
Liberty HS — 200/9-12
505 N Park St 62347 — 217-645-3433
Jenice Taylor, prin. — Fax 645-3241

Libertyville, Lake, Pop. 21,113
Community HSD 128 — 3,000/9-12
940 W Park Ave 60048 — 847-367-3159
Dr. David Clough, supt. — Fax 816-8533
www.d128.org/
Libertyville HS — 1,800/9-12
708 W Park Ave 60048 — 847-327-7000
Brad Swanson, prin. — Fax 367-2573
Other Schools – See Vernon Hills

Libertyville SD 70 — 2,700/PK-8
1381 Lake St 60048 — 847-362-9695
Dr. Mark Friedman, supt. — Fax 362-3003
www.d70.k12.il.us
Highland MS — 1,000/6-8
310 W Rockland Rd 60048 — 847-362-9020
Sharon Aspinall, prin. — Fax 362-0870

Lincoln, Logan, Pop. 15,039
Lincoln Community HSD 404 — 1,000/9-12
1000 Primm Rd 62656 — 217-732-4131
Dean Langdon, supt. — Fax 735-3963
lchs.k12.il.us/
Lincoln Community HS — 1,000/9-12
1000 Primm Rd 62656 — 217-732-4131
Joyce Hubbard, prin. — Fax 735-3963
Lincoln ESD 27 — 1,300/PK-8
100 S Maple St 62656 — 217-732-2522
Kirby Rodgers, supt. — Fax 732-2198
logan.k12.il.us/les27/
Lincoln JHS — 300/6-8
208 Broadway St 62656 — 217-732-3535
Curtis Nettles, prin. — Fax 732-2198
Lincolnland Technical Education Center —
1000 Primm Rd 62656 — 217-732-4131
Cindy Stover, dir. — Fax 735-3963
Lincolnland Technical Education Center — Vo/Tech
1000 Primm Rd 62656 — 217-732-4131
Cindy Stover, dir. — Fax 735-3963

Lincoln Christian College — Post-Sec.
100 Campus View Dr 62656 — 217-732-3168
Lincoln College — Post-Sec.
300 Keokuk St 62656 — 217-732-3155
Midwest Technical Institute — Post-Sec.
405 Limit St 62656 — 217-735-3105

Lincolnshire, Lake, Pop. 6,398
Adlai E. Stevenson SD 125 — 4,400/9-12
2 Stevenson Dr 60069 — 847-634-4000
Dr. Timothy D. Kanold, supt. — Fax 634-0239
www.district125.k12.il.us
Stevenson HS — 4,400/9-12
1 Stevenson Dr 60069 — 847-634-4000
Dr. Douglas Domeracki, prin. — Fax 634-7309
Lincolnshire-Prairieview SD 103 — 1,700/K-8
1370 N Riverwoods Rd 60069 — 847-295-4030
Larry Fleming, supt. — Fax 295-9196
www.district103.k12.il.us
Wright JHS — 800/5-8
1370 N Riverwoods Rd 60069 — 847-295-1560
Joshua Carpenter, prin. — Fax 295-7136

Keller Graduate School of DeVry Univ. — Post-Sec.
25 Tri State Intl Ste 130 60069 — 847-940-7768

Lincolnwood, Cook, Pop. 12,255
Lincolnwood SD 74 — 1,300/PK-8
6950 N East Prairie Rd 60712 — 847-675-8234
Dr. Donald R. Yeoman, supt. — Fax 675-8244
www.sd74.org
Lincoln Hall MS — 500/6-8
6855 N Crawford Ave 60712 — 847-675-8240
Judy Winer, prin. — Fax 675-8124

Lisle, DuPage, Pop. 21,656
Lisle CUSD 202 — 1,800/PK-12
5211 Center Ave 60532 — 630-493-8000
Dr. J. Peter Lueck, supt. — Fax 971-4054
www.lisle.dupage.k12.il.us/
Lisle HS — 600/9-12
1800 Short St 60532 — 630-493-8300
Ronald Logeman, prin. — Fax 968-0182
Lisle JHS — 400/6-8
5207 Center Ave 60532 — 630-493-8200
Timothy Pociask, prin. — Fax 493-8209

Naperville CUSD 203
Supt. — See Naperville
Kennedy JHS — 1,100/6-8
2929 Green Trails Dr 60532 — 630-420-3220
Donald Perry, prin. — Fax 420-6960

Benedictine University — Post-Sec.
5700 College Rd 60532 — 630-829-6000
Benet Academy — 1,300/9-12
2200 Maple Ave 60532 — 630-719-2782
Stephen A. Marth, prin. — Fax 719-2790
DeVry University — Post-Sec.
6200 Route 53 Ste G-11 60532 — 630-969-6624

Litchfield, Montgomery, Pop. 6,690
Litchfield CUSD 12 — 1,700/PK-12
1702 N State St 62056 — 217-324-2157
Sharon Johnson, supt. — Fax 324-2158
www.litchfield.k12.il.us
Litchfield HS — 500/9-12
1705 N State St 62056 — 217-324-3955
Michael Juenger, prin. — Fax 324-5851
Litchfield MS — 400/6-8
1701 N State St 62056 — 217-324-4668
Mark Hunt, prin. — Fax 324-5693

Tri-County Beauty Academy — Post-Sec.
219 N State St 62056 — 217-324-9062

Lockport, Will, Pop. 19,217
Lockport SD 91 — 700/K-8
808 Adams St 60441 — 815-838-0737
Donna Gray, supt. — Fax 834-4339
www.d91.net/index1.htm
Kelvin Grove MS — 500/4-8
808 Adams St 60441 — 815-838-0737
Zack Ettelbrick, prin. — Fax 834-4339

Lockport Township HSD 205
1323 E 7th St 60441
Dr. Gary Raymond, supt.
www.lths.org
3,300/9-12
815-588-8100
Fax 588-8109

Lockport Township HS Central Campus
1222 S Jefferson St 60441
Peter Sullivan, prin.
9-9
815-588-8200
Fax 588-8209

Lockport Township HS East Campus
1333 E 7th St 60441
K. Brett Gould, prin.
3,300/9-12
815-588-8300
Fax 588-8309

Will County SD 92
708 N State St 60441
Richard Maier, supt.
www.will.k12.il.us
2,100/PK-8
815-838-8031
Fax 838-8080

Oak Prairie JHS
15161 S Gougar Rd,
Mark Murray, prin.
700/6-8
815-836-2724

Lombard, DuPage, Pop. 42,971
Glenbard Twp. HSD 87
Supt. — See Glen Ellyn
Glenbard East HS
1014 S Main St 60148
Maria Ward, prin.
2,600/9-12
630-627-9250
Fax 627-9264

Lombard SD 44
150 W Madison St 60148
James A. Blanche, supt.
www.district44.dupage.k12.il.us/
3,300/PK-8
630-827-4400
Fax 620-3798

Glenn Westlake MS
1514 S Main St 60148
Philip Wieczorek, prin.
1,100/6-8
630-827-4500
Fax 620-3791

Illinois Center for Broadcasting
55 W 22nd St Ste 240 60148
Post-Sec.
630-916-1700

Montini Catholic HS
19W070 16th St 60148
Maryann O'Neill, prin.
700/9-12
630-627-6930
Fax 627-0537

National University of Health Sciences
200 E Roosevelt Rd 60148
Post-Sec.
630-629-2000

Northern Baptist Theological Seminary
660 E Butterfield Rd 60148
Post-Sec.
630-620-2180

London Mills, Fulton, Pop. 439
Spoon River Valley CUSD 4
35265 N IL Route 97 61544
Nancy L. Beem, supt.
www.spoon-river.k12.il.us
400/PK-12
309-778-2204
Fax 778-2655

Spoon River Valley HS
35265 N IL Route 97 61544
Dave Gilliland, prin.
100/9-12
309-778-2201
Fax 778-2655

Spoon River Valley JHS
35265 N IL Route 97 61544
Dave Gilliland, prin.
100/7-8
309-778-2201
Fax 778-2655

Long Grove, Lake, Pop. 7,494
Kildeer Countryside CCSD 96
Supt. — See Buffalo Grove
Woodlawn MS
6362 RFD/Gilmer Rd 60047
Dr. Christine Jakicic, prin.
700/6-8
847-353-8500
Fax 949-8237

Louisville, Clay, Pop. 1,231
North Clay CUSD 25
PO Box C 62858
Monty Aldrich, supt.
700/PK-12
618-665-3358
Fax 665-3358

North Clay Comm. HS
PO Box 220 62858
Carolyn Grahn, prin.
200/9-12
618-665-3102

Love Joy, Saint Clair, Pop. 1,099
Brooklyn Unit SD 188
PO Box 250,
Dr. Raelynn Parks, supt.
300/PK-12
618-271-1028
Fax 271-9108

Lovejoy MS
PO Box 250,
Catherine Calvert, prin.
100/6-8
618-271-1014
Fax 271-9108

Lovejoy Technology Academy
PO Box 250,
Catherine Calvert, prin.
100/9-12
618-271-1014
Fax 271-9108

Loves Park, Winnebago, Pop. 21,660
Harlem Unit SD 122
Supt. — See Machesney Park
Harlem MS
735 Windsor Rd 61111
John Cusimano, prin.
1,300/7-8
815-654-4510
Fax 654-4540

Lovington, Moultrie, Pop. 1,213
Lovington CUSD 303
PO Box 560 61937
Joe Novsek, supt.
www.lovington.k12.il.us/
300/PK-12
217-873-4310
Fax 873-5311

Lovington HS
PO Box 530 61937
100/9-12
217-873-4316
Fax 873-5311

Lyons, Cook, Pop. 10,514
Lyons SD 103
4100 Joliet Ave 60534
Dr. Raymond Lauk, supt.
www.sd103.com/
2,100/K-8
708-783-4100
Fax 780-9725

Washington MS
8101 Ogden Ave 60534
Robert Hildreth, prin.
700/6-8
708-783-4200
Fax 780-9757

Mc Henry, McHenry, Pop. 19,144
Mc Henry CCSD 15
1011 N Green St,
R. Alan Hoffman Ed.D., supt.
www.d15.org
4,600/PK-8
815-385-7210
Fax 344-7121

Mc Henry MS
2120 W Lincoln Rd,
Lori Miscik, prin.
900/6-8
815-385-2522
Fax 578-2101

Parkland S
1802 N Ringwood Rd,
Mike Adams, prin.
700/6-8
815-385-8810
Fax 363-5023

Mc Henry Community HSD 156
4716 W Crystal Lake Rd,
Dr. Phil Hintz, supt.
www.dist156.org
2,300/9-12
815-385-7900
Fax 344-7153

Mc Henry HS-East
1012 N Green St,
Dave Moyer, prin.
1,000/9-12
815-385-1145
Fax 363-8435

Mc Henry HS-West
4724 W Crystal Lake Rd,
Dr. Barbara Johnke, prin.
1,300/9-12
815-385-7077
Fax 363-8651

Montini MS
1405 N Richmond Rd,
Sheila Murphy, prin.
200/4-8
815-385-1022
Fax 363-7536

Machesney Park, Winnebago, Pop. 21,205
Harlem Unit SD 122
8605 N 2nd St 61115
Pascal V. Deluca, supt.
www.harlem.winbgo.k12.il.us
7,900/PK-12
815-654-4500
Fax 654-4600

Harlem HS
1 Huskie Cir 61115
Joe Hazen, prin.
2,300/9-12
815-654-4511
Fax 654-4525

Other Schools – See Loves Park

Mackinaw, Tazewell, Pop. 1,467
Deer Creek-Mackinaw CUSD 701
PO Box 110 61755
Steve Yarnall, supt.
www.deemack.org/
1,200/PK-12
309-359-8965
Fax 359-5291

Deer Creek-Mackinaw HS
PO Box 110 61755
Bill Lamb, prin.
300/9-12
309-359-4421
Fax 359-3125

Mc Leansboro, Hamilton, Pop. 2,713
Hamilton County CUSD 10
PO Box 369 62859
Vince Mitchell, supt.
www.unit10.com
1,200/PK-12
618-643-2328
Fax 643-2015

Hamilton County JSHS
1 Fox Ln 62859
Marty Cox, prin.
600/7-12
618-643-2328
Fax 643-2307

Mc Nabb, Putnam, Pop. 296
Putnam County CUSD 535
Supt. — See Granville
Putnam County JHS
RR 1 Box 17 61335
Sandra Micheletti, prin.
300/5-8
815-882-2116
Fax 882-2118

Macomb, McDonough, Pop. 18,874
Macomb CUSD 185
323 W Jackson St 61455
Dr. Frances Karanovich, supt.
district185.macomb.com/
2,000/PK-12
309-833-4161
Fax 836-2133

Macomb HS
1525 S Johnson St 61455
Michael Sartore, prin.
700/9-12
309-837-2331
Fax 836-1034

Macomb JHS
1525 S Johnson St 61455
Dana Isackson, prin.
300/7-8
309-833-2074
Fax 836-1034

McDonough District Hospital
525 E Grant St 61455
Post-Sec.
309-833-4101

Western Illinois University
1 University Cir 61455
Post-Sec.
309-295-1414

Macon, Macon, Pop. 1,140
Meridian CUSD 15
Supt. — See Blue Mound
Meridian HS
PO Box 380 62544
Jack Blickensderfer, prin.
300/9-12
217-764-5233
Fax 764-5282

Madison, Madison, Pop. 4,445
Madison CUSD 12
1707 4th St 62060
Dr. Sandra Schroeder, supt.
www.schools.lth5.k12.il.us/madison/
1,200/PK-12
618-877-1712
Fax 877-2690

Madison HS
600 Farrish St 62060
Dr. Brian Carey, prin.
200/9-12
618-876-7010
Fax 877-2694

Madison MS
1003 Farrish St 62060
Timothy Miller, prin.
300/PK-PK, 6-
618-876-6409
Fax 877-2693

Mahomet, Champaign, Pop. 5,466
Mahomet-Seymour CUSD 3
PO Box 229 61853
John Alumbaugh, supt.
www.ms.k12.il.us
2,700/PK-12
217-586-4995
Fax 586-5834

Mahomet-Seymour HS
PO Box 1098 61853
Del Ryan, prin.
800/9-12
217-586-4962
Fax 586-6844

Mahomet-Seymour JHS
PO Box 1853 61853
Jeff Starwalt, prin.
600/6-8
217-586-4415
Fax 586-5869

Malta, DeKalb, Pop. 971

Kishwaukee College
21193 Malta Rd 60150
Post-Sec.
815-825-2086

Manhattan, Will, Pop. 3,818
Manhattan SD 114
15606 W Smith Rd 60442
Howard A. Butters, supt.
www.manhattan114.org
1,000/PK-8
815-478-6090
Fax 478-6094

Manhattan JHS
15606 W Smith Rd 60442
Ron Pacheco, prin.
400/6-8
815-478-6090
Fax 478-6094

Christ's Academy
22811 S Cedar Rd 60442
Sharon Meiergerd, prin.
100/PK-12
815-485-2833
Fax 485-2833

Manito, Mason, Pop. 1,724
Midwest Central CUSD 191
1010 S Washington St 61546
Jerry Meyer, supt.
www.midwestcentral.org/
1,200/PK-12
309-968-6868
Fax 968-7916

Midwest Central HS
910 S Washington St 61546
Kathryn Cihlar, prin.
400/9-12
309-968-6766
Fax 968-6340

Other Schools – See Green Valley

Manlius, Bureau, Pop. 348
Bureau Valley CUSD 340
PO Box 289 61338
Dr. Rick Stoecker, supt.
www.bhsroe.k12.il.us/bureauvalley
1,400/PK-12
815-445-3101
Fax 445-2802

Bureau Valley HS
PO Box 289 61338
Terry Gutshall, prin.
500/9-12
815-445-4004
Fax 445-3017

Other Schools – See Buda

Mansfield, Piatt, Pop. 937
Blue Ridge CUSD 18
Supt. — See Farmer City
Blue Ridge JHS
PO Box 69 61854
John Weaver, prin.
100/7-8
217-489-5201
Fax 489-9051

Manteno, Kankakee, Pop. 6,906
Manteno CUSD 5
250 N Poplar St 60950
Michael E. Smith, supt.
www.manteno.k12.il.us
1,900/K-12
815-928-7000
Fax 468-6439

Manteno HS
443 N Maple St 60950
Paul Russert, prin.
500/9-12
815-928-7101
Fax 468-2344

Manteno MS
250 N Poplar St 60950
Scott Horsch, prin.
500/6-8
815-928-7154
Fax 468-8082

Maple Park, Kane, Pop. 1,014
Fox Valley Career Center
47W326 Keslinger Rd 60151
Larry Imel, supt.
www.kaneland.org
630-365-5113
Fax 365-9088

Fox Valley Career Center
47W326 Keslinger Rd 60151
Larry Imel, supt.
Vo/Tech
630-365-5113
Fax 365-9088

Kaneland CUSD 302
47W326 Keslinger Rd 60151
Dr. Charles McCormick, supt.
www.kaneland.org
3,600/PK-12
630-365-5111
Fax 365-9428

Kaneland HS
47W326 Keslinger Rd 60151
Mike Davis, prin.
900/9-12
630-365-5100
Fax 365-8421

Kaneland MS
1N137 Meredith Rd 60151
Richard Burchell, prin.
800/6-8
630-365-3005
Fax 365-5686

Marengo, McHenry, Pop. 6,902
Marengo Community HSD 154
110 Franks Rd 60152
Dr. Dan Bertrand, supt.
www.mchs154.org/
700/9-12
815-568-6511
Fax 568-6510

Marengo HS
110 Franks Rd 60152
Eric Vance, prin.
700/9-12
815-568-6511
Fax 568-6510

Marengo-Union Consolidated ESD 165
816 E Grant Hwy 60152
Dr. Richard Angel, supt.
www.marengo.k12.il.us/
500/PK-8
815-568-8323
Fax 568-8367

Marengo Community MS
816 E Grant Hwy 60152
Phil Grover, prin.
PK-PK, 5-
815-568-5720
Fax 568-7572

Marion, Williamson, Pop. 16,624
Crab Orchard CUSD 3
19189 Cory Bailey St 62959
Derek Hutchins, supt.
400/K-12
618-982-2181
Fax 982-2080

Crab Orchard HS
19189 Cory Bailey Rd 62959
William McSparin, prin.
100/9-12
618-982-2181
Fax 982-2080

Marion CUSD 2
1700 W Cherry St 62959
J. Wade Hudgens, supt.
www.marionunit2.org/
3,900/PK-12
618-993-2321
Fax 997-0943

Marion HS
1501 S Carbon St 62959
Stephen Smith, prin.
1,200/9-12
618-993-8196
Fax 997-8749

Marion JHS
1609 W Main St 62959
Kimberly Brave, prin.
800/6-8
618-997-1317
Fax 997-0477

Marissa, Saint Clair, Pop. 2,096
Marissa CUSD 40
215 North St 62257
Kevin Cogdill, supt.
600/PK-12
618-295-2313
Fax 295-2609

Marissa JSHS
300 School View Dr 62257
Michael Guthrie, prin.
300/7-12
618-295-2393
Fax 295-2276

Markham, Cook, Pop. 12,531
Hazel Crest SD 152-5
Supt. — See Hazel Crest
Frost MS
2206 W 167th St,
Macco Rainey, prin.
400/6-8
708-210-9929
Fax 210-9582

Prairie-Hills ESD 144
3015 W 163rd St,
Dr. I.V. Foster, supt.
phsd144.net/
2,900/PK-8
708-210-2888
Fax 210-9925

Prairie-Hills JHS
3035 W 163rd St,
Tiffany Burnett-Johnson, prin.
700/7-8
708-210-2860
Fax 210-9208

Maroa, Macon, Pop. 1,551
Maroa-Forsyth CUSD 2
PO Box 738 61756
Stephen Stenger, supt.
mfhs1.mfsd.k12.il.us/
1,000/PK-12
217-794-3488
Fax 794-3878

Maroa-Forsyth HS
PO Box 738 61756
Mike Williams, prin.
300/9-12
217-794-3463
Fax 794-5459

Maroa-Forsyth MS
PO Box 738 61756
Kathy Massey, prin.
300/6-8
217-794-5115
Fax 794-3351

Marquette Heights, Tazewell, Pop. 2,822
North Pekin & Marquette Hts SD 102 — 700/PK-8
 51 Yates Rd 61554 — 309-382-2172
 Dr. John Closen, supt. — Fax 382-2122
 www.tazewell.k12.il.us/dist102
Georgetowne MS — 200/6-8
 51 Yates Rd 61554 — 309-382-3456
 Meredith Brooks, prin. — Fax 382-2122

Marshall, Clark, Pop. 3,744
Marshall CUSD 2C — 1,400/PK-12
 503 Pine St 62441 — 217-826-5912
 Dr. Michael Thompson, supt. — Fax 826-5170
 www.marshall.k12.il.us/
Marshall HS — 400/9-12
 806 N 6th St 62441 — 217-826-2395
 John Hasten, prin. — Fax 826-5511
Marshall JHS — 200/7-8
 806 N 6th St 62441 — 217-826-2812
 Richard Manuell, prin. — Fax 826-6065

Martinsville, Clark, Pop. 1,228
Martinsville CUSD 3C — 400/PK-12
 PO Box K 62442 — 217-382-4321
 Jill Rogers, supt. — Fax 382-4183
 www.martinsville.k12.il.us/
Martinsville HS — 100/9-12
 PO Box K 62442 — 217-382-4132
 Ray Schollenbruch, prin. — Fax 382-4761
Martinsville JHS — 100/7-8
 PO Box K 62442 — 217-382-4132
 Ray Schollenbruch, prin. — Fax 382-4761

Mascoutah, Saint Clair, Pop. 5,687
Mascoutah CUSD 19 — 2,800/PK-12
 720 W Harnett St 62258 — 618-566-7414
 Dr. Sam McGowen, supt. — Fax 566-4507
 www.mascoutah19.k12.il.us
Mascoutah HS — 900/9-12
 1313 W Main St 62258 — 618-566-8523
 Mike Scholz, prin. — Fax 566-8693
Mascoutah MS — 600/6-8
 846 N 6th St 62258 — 618-566-2305
 Bob G. Stone, prin. — Fax 566-2307

Mason City, Mason, Pop. 2,521
Illini Central CUSD 189 — 1,000/PK-12
 208 N West St 62664 — 217-482-5180
 Chad Allaman, supt. — Fax 482-3121
 www.mason.k12.il.us/illinicentral189/
Illini Central HS — 300/9-12
 208 N West St 62664 — 217-482-3252
 Patrick Martin, prin. — Fax 482-3323
Other Schools – See Easton

Matteson, Cook, Pop. 14,278
Matteson ESD 162 — 3,000/PK-8
 3625 215th St 60443 — 708-748-0100
 Dr. Blondean Y. Davis, supt. — Fax 748-7302
 www.sd162.org
Huth MS — 600/7-8
 3718 213th Pl 60443 — 708-748-0470
 Ronald Jones, prin. — Fax 503-1119

ITT Technical Institute — Post-Sec.
 600 Holiday Plaza Dr 60443 — 708-747-2571

Mattoon, Coles, Pop. 17,849
Mattoon CUSD 2 — 3,200/K-12
 1701 Charleston Ave 61938 — 217-238-8850
 Larry Lilly, supt. — Fax 238-8855
 www.mattoon.k12.il.us
Mattoon HS — 1,000/9-12
 2521 Walnut Ave 61938 — 217-238-7800
 Ken Reed, prin. — Fax 238-7805
Mattoon MS — 800/6-8
 1200 S 9th St 61938 — 217-238-5800
 Terrie Hudson, prin. — Fax 238-5805
Mattoon Area Adult Education Center — Adult
 1617 Lake Land Blvd 61938 — 217-235-0361
 Mark Nelson, dir. — Fax 258-5286

Lake Land College — Post-Sec.
 5001 Lake Land Blvd 61938 — 217-234-5253

Maywood, Cook, Pop. 26,398
Proviso Township HSD 209 — 4,900/9-12
 807 S 1st Ave 60153 — 708-202-3016
 Dr. Phylistine Murphy, supt.
 www.proviso.w-cook.k12.il.us/
Proviso East HS — 2,300/9-12
 807 S 1st Ave 60153 — 708-344-7000
 Milton Patch, prin. — Fax 344-5942
Other Schools – See Hillside

Loyola University — Post-Sec.
 2160 S 1st Ave 60153 — 708-216-3229
Loyola University Medical Center — Post-Sec.
 2160 S 1st Ave 60153 — 708-216-9000
True Vine Christian Academy — 100/PK-8
 815 Lexington St 60153 — 708-345-8822
 Dr. Gloria Lymon, prin. — Fax 345-5818

Mazon, Grundy, Pop. 898
Mazon-Verona-Kinsman ESD 2C — 300/K-8
 1013 North St 60444 — 815-448-2200
 Dr. Lynn Bertino Neville, supt. — Fax 448-3005
 www.mvkmavericks.org
Mazon-Verona-Kinsman MS — 200/5-8
 1013 North St 60444 — 815-448-2127
 Debra Paulsen, prin. — Fax 448-3005

Melrose Park, Cook, Pop. 23,057
Mannheim SD 83 —
 Supt. — See Franklin Park
Mannheim JHS — 700/6-8
 2600 Hyde Park Ave 60164 — 847-455-5020
 Timothy Daley, prin. — Fax 455-2038

Lincoln Technical Institute — Post-Sec.
 8317 W North Ave 60160 — 708-344-4700

Walther Lutheran HS — 400/9-12
 900 Chicago Ave 60160 — 708-344-0404
 Stephen Zielke, prin. — Fax 344-0525

Mendon, Adams, Pop. 883
CUSD 4 — 800/PK-12
 PO Box 200 62351 — 217-936-2111
 Diane Robertson, supt. — Fax 936-2643
 www.cusd4.com
Unity HS — 200/9-12
 PO Box 200 62351 — 217-936-2116
 William Dorethy, prin. — Fax 936-2643
Unity MS — 200/6-8
 PO Box 200 62351 — 217-936-2727
 Brad Gooding, prin. — Fax 936-2643

Mendota, LaSalle, Pop. 7,178
Mendota CCSD 289 — 1,300/PK-8
 1806 Guiles Ave 61342 — 815-539-7631
 Robert Chinn, supt. — Fax 538-2927
 www.m289.lasalle.k12.il.us/
Northbrook S — 700/PK-PK, 4-
 1804 Guiles Ave 61342 — 815-539-6237
 Cindy Pozzi, prin. — Fax 538-3090
Mendota Township HSD 280 — 600/9-12
 2300 W Main St 61342 — 815-539-7446
 Jeff Prusator, supt. — Fax 539-3103
 mendotahs.org/home.htm
Mendota Township HS — 600/9-12
 2300 W Main St 61342 — 815-539-7446
 Denise Aughenbaugh, prin. — Fax 539-3103

Meredosia, Morgan, Pop. 1,008
Meredosia-Chambersburg CUSD 11 — 300/PK-12
 PO Box 440 62665 — 217-584-1744
 James McCain, supt. — Fax 584-1129
Meredosia-Chambersburg HS — 100/9-12
 PO Box 440 62665 — 217-584-1291
 David Marshall, prin. — Fax 584-1741
Meredosia-Chambersburg JHS — 100/6-8
 PO Box 440 62665 — 217-584-1291
 David Marshall, prin. — Fax 584-1741

Metamora, Woodford, Pop. 2,789
Germantown Hills SD 69 — 800/PK-8
 110 Fandel Rd 61548 — 309-383-2121
 Joe Stieglitz, supt. — Fax 383-2123
 ghills.metamora.k12.il.us
Germantown Hills MS — 500/3-8
 103 Warrior Way 61548 — 309-383-2121
 James B. Dansart, prin. — Fax 383-4739
Metamora Twp. HSD 122 — 900/9-12
 PO Box 109 61548 — 309-367-4151
 Kenneth Maurer, supt. — Fax 367-4351
 mths.metamora.k12.il.us/
Metamora HS — 900/9-12
 PO Box 109 61548 — 309-367-4151
 Greg Christy, prin. — Fax 367-4154

Metropolis, Massac, Pop. 6,368
Massac Unit SD 1 — 2,100/PK-12
 PO Box 530 62960 — 618-524-9376
 William Hatfield, supt. — Fax 524-4432
 www.unit1.massac.k12.il.us/
Massac County HS — 600/9-12
 2841 Old Marion Rd 62960 — 618-524-3440
 Danny Stevens, prin. — Fax 524-3131
Massac JHS — 300/7-8
 PO Box 331 62960 — 618-524-2645
 Lynne Lech, prin. — Fax 524-2765

Midlothian, Cook, Pop. 14,253
Bremen Community HSD 228 — 4,900/9-12
 15233 Pulaski Rd 60445 — 708-389-1175
 Dr. Richard Mitchell, supt. — Fax 389-2552
 www.bhsd228.org
Bremen HS — 1,100/9-12
 15203 Pulaski Rd 60445 — 708-371-3600
 Marcia Mendenhall, prin. — Fax 371-7194
Other Schools – See Country Club Hills, Oak Forest, Tinley Park

Milford, Iroquois, Pop. 1,324
Milford Twp. HSD 233 — 200/9-12
 PO Box 304 60953 — 815-889-5176
 Michael Schmidt, supt. — Fax 889-5221
 www.milford.k12.il.us/
Milford Twp. HS — 200/9-12
 PO Box 257 60953 — 815-889-4184
 Stephen Totheroit, prin. — Fax 889-4871

Millbrook, Kendall, Pop. 288
Newark CCSD 66 —
 Supt. — See Newark
Millbrook JHS — 100/5-8
 PO Box 214 60536 — 630-553-5435
 Richard Sjolund, prin. — Fax 553-1027

Milledgeville, Carroll, Pop. 971
Chadwick-Milledgeville CUSD 399 — 700/PK-12
 PO Box 609 61051 — 815-225-7141
 Terry Bowers, supt. — Fax 225-7847
 www.dist399.net/
Milledgeville HS — 200/9-12
 PO Box 609 61051 — 815-225-7141
 Timothy Schurman, prin. — Fax 225-7847
Other Schools – See Chadwick

Minonk, Woodford, Pop. 2,146
Fieldcrest CUSD 6 — 1,300/PK-12
 1 Dornbush Dr 61760 — 309-432-2177
 Randy Vincent, supt. — Fax 432-3377
 www.fieldcrest.k12.il.us/
Fieldcrest HS — 400/9-12
 1 Dornbush Dr 61760 — 309-432-2529
 William Lapp, prin. — Fax 432-2064
Other Schools – See Toluca, Wenona

Minooka, Grundy, Pop. 4,706
Minooka CCSD 201 — 1,700/PK-8
 333 McEvilly Rd 60447 — 815-467-6121
 J. Michel Morrow, supt. — Fax 467-9544
 www.min201.org/

Minooka JHS — 600/6-8
 333 McEvilly Rd 60447 — 815-467-2136
 Sam Martin, prin. — Fax 467-5087
Minooka Community HSD 111 — 1,500/9-12
 PO Box 827 60447 — 815-467-2557
 Dr. David Middleton, supt. — Fax 467-9733
 www.mchs.net/
Minooka Community HS — 1,500/9-12
 301 S Wabena Ave 60447 — 815-467-2140
 Robert Williams, prin. — Fax 467-2431

Mokena, Will, Pop. 17,172
Mokena SD 159 — 2,400/PK-8
 11244 Willow Crest Ln 60448 — 708-342-4900
 Dr. Gary Bradbury, supt. — Fax 479-3143
 www.mokena159.com
Mokena JHS — 900/6-8
 19815 Kirkstone Way 60448 — 708-342-4870
 Julia Wheaton, prin. — Fax 479-3122

Trend Setters College of Cosmetology — Post-Sec.
 19031 Old LaGrange Rd 60448 — 708-478-6907

Moline, Rock Island, Pop. 43,064
Moline Unit SD 40 — 7,500/PK-12
 1619 11th Ave 61265 — 309-743-1600
 Dr. Cal Lee, supt. — Fax 757-3476
 www.molineschools.org
Deere MS — 600/7-8
 2035 11th St 61265 — 309-743-1622
 William Burrus, prin. — Fax 757-3668
Moline HS — 2,200/9-12
 3600 Avenue Of The Cities 61265 — 309-743-1624
 Gary Koeller, prin. — Fax 757-3667
Wilson MS — 600/7-8
 1301 48th St 61265 — 309-743-1623
 Robert Benson, prin. — Fax 757-3586

Black Hawk College — Post-Sec.
 6600 34th Ave 61265 — 309-796-5000
Brown Mackie College — Post-Sec.
 1527 47th Ave 61265 — 309-762-2100
Quad Cities Christian S — 50/7-12
 2200 5th Ave 61265 — 309-762-3800
 William Olmstead, prin. — Fax 764-2859

Momence, Kankakee, Pop. 3,089
Momence CUSD 1 — 1,300/PK-12
 415 N Dixie Hwy 60954 — 815-472-3501
 Dr. Phillip A. Smith, supt. — Fax 472-3516
 www.momence.k12.il.us
Momence HS — 400/9-12
 101 N Franklin St 60954 — 815-472-6477
 Judith Pappas, prin. — Fax 472-2055
Momence JHS — 400/5-8
 801 W 2nd St 60954 — 815-472-4184
 Michele Keiser, prin. — Fax 472-3517

Monmouth, Warren, Pop. 9,531
Monmouth-Roseville CUSD 238 — 1,500/PK-12
 401 E 2nd Ave 61462 — 309-734-4712
 Martin Payne, supt. — Fax 734-4755
 titans.k12.il.us/district/welcome.htm
Monmouth-Roseville HS — 400/9-12
 325 W 1st Ave 61462 — 309-734-5118
 Jeff Bryan, prin. — Fax 734-2918
Other Schools – See Roseville

United CUSD 304 — 200/7-12
 Supt. — See Alexis
United JSHS, 1905 100th St 61462 — 309-734-9411
 Amy Schmitz, prin.
Yorkwood CUSD 225 — 400/PK-12
 2140 State Highway 135 61462 — 309-734-8514
 Jane Michael, supt. — Fax 734-8515
 www.yorkwood225.net
Yorkwood HS — 100/9-12
 2140 State Highway 135 61462 — 309-734-8511
 Kristen Nelson, prin. — Fax 734-6094
Yorkwood JHS — 100/6-8
 2140 State Highway 135 61462 — 309-734-8511
 Kristen Nelson, prin. — Fax 734-6094

Monmouth College — Post-Sec.
 700 E Broadway 61462 — 309-457-2131

Monticello, Piatt, Pop. 5,184
Monticello CUSD 25 — 1,600/PK-12
 2 Sage Dr 61856 — 217-762-8511
 Dr. Larry McNabb, supt. — Fax 762-8534
 www.sages.us/
Monticello HS — 500/9-12
 1 Sage Dr 61856 — 217-762-8511
 Tip Reedy, prin. — Fax 762-7421
Monticello MS — 400/6-8
 2015 E Washington St 61856 — 217-762-8511
 Jeanne Handley, prin. — Fax 762-7765

Mooseheart, Kane
Mooseheart S — 200/1-12
 255 James J Davis Ave 60539 — 630-906-3646
 Gary Urwiler, supt. — Fax 906-3617

Morris, Grundy, Pop. 12,352
Grundy Area Vocational Center —
 1002 Union St 60450 — 815-942-4390
 David Potts, dir.
 gavc.mornet.org/
Grundy AVC, 1002 Union St 60450 — Vo/Tech
 David Potts, dir. — 815-942-4390

Morris Community HSD 101 — 900/9-12
 1000 Union St 60450 — 815-941-5327
 Steven Fannin, supt. — Fax 941-5407
 www.mchs.grundy.k12.il.us
Morris HS — 900/9-12
 1000 Union St 60450 — 815-942-1294
 Patrick Halloran, prin. — Fax 941-5405

Morris SD 54 — 1,300/PK-8
  54 White Oak Dr 60450 — 815-942-0056
  Barry Green, supt. — Fax 942-0240
  dist54.mornet.org
Shabbona JHS — 500/6-8
  725 School St 60450 — 815-942-3605
  Sheryl Dzuryak, prin. — Fax 941-4531

Nettle Creek CCSD 24 C — 100/K-8
  8820 Scott School Rd 60450 — 815-942-0511
  David Hermann, supt. — Fax 942-9124
Nettle Creek MS — 100/3-8
  8820 Scott School Rd 60450 — 815-942-0511
  David Hermann, prin. — Fax 942-9124

Morrison, Whiteside, Pop. 4,345
Morrison CUSD 6 — 1,200/K-12
  643 Genesee Ave 61270 — 815-772-2064
  Dr. Jody Ware, supt. — Fax 772-4644
  www.morrisonschools.org
Morrison HS — 400/9-12
  643 Genesee Ave 61270 — 815-772-4071
  Janet Ward, prin. — Fax 772-4644
Morrison JHS — 300/6-8
  300 Academic Dr 61270 — 815-772-7264
  Darryl Hogue, prin. — Fax 772-2531

Morrison Institute of Technology — Post-Sec.
  701 Portland Ave 61270 — 815-772-7218

Morrisonville, Christian, Pop. 1,051
Morrisonville CUSD 1 — 300/PK-12
  PO Box 13 62546 — 217-526-4431
  Wesley Wells, supt. — Fax 526-4433
  mohawks.net
Morrisonville HS — 100/9-12
  PO Box 13 62546 — 217-526-4432
  Josh Ebener, prin. — Fax 526-4452
Morrisonville JHS — 100/7-8
  PO Box 13 62546 — 217-526-4432
  Josh Ebener, prin. — Fax 526-4452

Morton, Tazewell, Pop. 15,365
Morton CUSD 709 — 2,700/PK-12
  235 E Jackson St 61550 — 309-263-2581
  Dr. R. Scott Russell, supt. — Fax 266-6320
  www.morton709.org
Morton HS — 900/9-12
  350 N Illinois Ave 61550 — 309-266-7182
  Dennis Johnson, prin. — Fax 263-2168
Morton JHS — 500/7-8
  225 E Jackson St 61550 — 309-266-6522
  Charles Nagel, prin. — Fax 284-5031

Morton Grove, Cook, Pop. 22,705
Golf ESD 67 — 500/K-8
  9401 Waukegan Rd 60053 — 847-966-8200
  Linda Marks, supt. — Fax 966-8290
  www.golf67.net
Golf MS — 300/5-8
  9401 Waukegan Rd 60053 — 847-965-3740
  Keith Westman, prin. — Fax 966-9493

Chicagoland Jewish HS — 100/9-11
  7800 W Lyons St #18 60053 — 847-470-6700
  Roslyn B. Stein, hdmstr. — Fax 324-3701

Mounds, Pulaski, Pop. 1,056
Meridian CUSD 101 — 800/PK-12
  208 Valley Rd 62964 — 618-342-6776
  Dr. Ray Puckett, supt. — Fax 342-6856
  www.mhs101.pulski.k12.il.us
Meridian HS — 200/9-12
  1401 Mounds Rd 62964 — 618-342-6778
  Joseph Rains, prin. — Fax 342-6856

Mount Carmel, Wabash, Pop. 7,772
Wabash CUSD 348 — 1,800/K-12
  218 W 13th St 62863 — 618-262-4181
  Tim Buss, supt. — Fax 262-7912
  www.d348.wabash.k12.il.us
Mount Carmel HS — 600/9-12
  201 N Pear St 62863 — 618-262-5104
  Clyde Leonard, prin. — Fax 262-8781
Mount Carmel MS — 400/6-8
  1520 Poplar St 62863 — 618-262-5699
  Darlene Weir, prin. — Fax 263-9096

Wabash Valley College — Post-Sec.
  2200 College Dr 62863 — 618-262-8641

Mount Carroll, Carroll, Pop. 1,747
West Carroll CUSD 314
  Supt. — See Thomson
West Carroll MS — 100/6-8
  633 S East St 61053 — 815-244-2002
  Jeanette Ashby, prin. — Fax 244-1051

Mount Morris, Ogle, Pop. 3,026
Oregon CUSD 220
  Supt. — See Oregon
Rahn JHS — 400/7-8
  105 W Brayton Rd 61054 — 815-734-6134
  Jeff Fitzpatrick, prin. — Fax 734-7129

Mount Olive, Macoupin, Pop. 2,115
Mt. Olive CUSD 5 — 600/PK-12
  804 W Main St 62069 — 217-999-7831
  Chad Allison, supt. — Fax 999-2150
  www.schools.lth5.k12.il.us/mtolive/
Mount Olive HS, 804 W Main St 62069 — 200/9-12
  Ron Ryan, prin. — 217-999-4231

Mount Prospect, Cook, Pop. 55,784
Community Consolidated SD 59
  Supt. — See Arlington Heights
Holmes JHS — 500/6-8
  1900 W Lonnquist Blvd 60056 — 847-593-4390
  Robert Bohanek, prin. — Fax 593-7386

Mt. Prospect SD 57 — 2,000/K-8
  701 W Gregory St 60056 — 847-394-7300
  Bruce Brown, supt. — Fax 394-7311
  www.dist57.org
Lincoln JHS — 700/6-8
  700 W Lincoln St 60056 — 847-394-7350
  Donald Angelaccio, prin. — Fax 394-7358

River Trails SD 26 — 1,600/PK-8
  1900 E Kensington Rd 60056 — 847-297-4120
  Dr. Terry E. Barker, supt. — Fax 297-4124
  www.rtsd26.org
River Trails MS — 600/6-8
  1000 N Wolf Rd 60056 — 847-298-1750
  Glenn Purpura, prin. — Fax 298-2639

Township HSD 214
  Supt. — See Arlington Heights
Prospect HS — 2,000/9-12
  801 W Kensington Rd 60056 — 847-718-5200
  Karen Rogers, prin. — Fax 718-5216

Christian Life College — Post-Sec.
  400 E Gregory St 60056 — 847-259-1840
ITT Technical Institute — Post-Sec.
  1401 Feehanville Dr 60056 — 847-375-8800

Mount Pulaski, Logan, Pop. 1,643
Mt. Pulaski CUSD 23 — 700/PK-12
  119 N Garden St 62548 — 217-792-7222
  Philip Shelton, supt. — Fax 792-5551
  www.mtpulaski.k12.il.us
Mt. Pulaski HS — 200/9-12
  206 S Spring St 62548 — 217-792-3209
  Russ Galusha, prin. — Fax 792-3248

Mount Sterling, Brown, Pop. 2,037
Brown County CUSD 1 — 700/PK-12
  503 NW Cross St 62353 — 217-773-3359
  Merle Kenady, supt. — Fax 773-2121
  www.bcsd1.net
Brown County HS — 200/9-12
  500 E Main St 62353 — 217-773-3345
  Van Wilson, prin. — Fax 773-2128
Brown County MS — 200/5-8
  504 E Main St 62353 — 217-773-9152
  Marvin Meservey, prin. — Fax 773-9121

Mount Vernon, Jefferson, Pop. 16,486
Mount Vernon Area Vocational Center
  320 S 7th St 62864 — 618-246-5602
  Robert Knutson, dir. — Fax 244-8049
  mtvernonhs.roe25.com
Mount Vernon Area Vocational Center — Vo/Tech
  320 S 7th St 62864 — 618-246-5602
  Robert Knutson, dir. — Fax 244-8049

Mt. Vernon CSD 80 — 1,900/PK-8
  1722 Oakland Ave 62864 — 618-244-8080
  Kevin Settle, supt. — Fax 244-8082
  district.mtv80.org
Casey MS — 500/6-8
  1829 Broadway St 62864 — 618-244-8060
  Karen Copple, prin. — Fax 244-8014

Mt. Vernon Twp. HSD 201 — 1,400/9-12
  320 S 7th St 62864 — 618-244-3700
  Terry Milt, supt. — Fax 244-8047
  www.mvths.org
Mount Vernon HS — 1,400/9-12
  320 S 7th St 62864 — 618-244-3700
  Jerry Pepple, prin. — Fax 244-8047

Mount Zion, Macon, Pop. 4,821
Mt. Zion CUSD 3 — 2,400/PK-12
  455 Elm St 62549 — 217-864-2366
  Kenneth Hendriksen Ph.D., supt. — Fax 864-2200
  www.mtzion.k12.il.us
Mount Zion HS — 800/9-12
  305 S Henderson St 62549 — 217-864-2363
  Greg Bradley, prin. — Fax 864-5815
Mount Zion JHS — 400/7-8
  315 S Henderson St 62549 — 217-864-2369
  Jerry Birkey, prin. — Fax 864-6829

Moweaqua, Christian, Pop. 1,860
Central A & M CUSD 21
  Supt. — See Assumption
Central A & M HS — 300/9-12
  229 E Pine St 62550 — 217-768-3866
  Diana Bandy, prin. — Fax 768-3797

Mulberry Grove, Bond, Pop. 676
Mulberry Grove CUSD 1 — 500/K-12
  801 W Wall St 62262 — 618-326-8812
  Gregory Irwin, supt. — Fax 326-8482
Mulberry Grove HS — 100/9-12
  801 W Wall St 62262 — 618-326-8221
  Michael Gauch, prin. — Fax 326-8482
Mulberry Grove JHS — 100/7-8
  801 W Wall St 62262 — 618-326-8221
  Michael Gauch, prin. — Fax 326-8482

Mundelein, Lake, Pop. 32,251
Diamond Lake SD 76 — 1,300/PK-8
  500 Acorn Ln 60060 — 847-566-9221
  Dr. Roger Prosise, supt. — Fax 566-5689
  www.d76.lake.k12.il.us/
West Oak MS — 600/5-8
  500 Acorn Ln 60060 — 847-566-9220
  Christopher Willeford, prin. — Fax 970-3534

Fremont SD 79 — 1,500/PK-8
  28855 N Fremont Center Rd 60060 — 847-566-0169
  Dr. Rick Taylor, supt. — Fax 566-7280
  www.fremont.lake.k12.il.us
Fremont MS — 900/4-8
  28855 N Fremont Center Rd 60060 — 847-566-9384
  Pam Motsenbocker, prin. — Fax 566-7805

Mundelein Consolidated HSD 120 — 2,100/9-12
  1350 W Hawley St 60060 — 847-949-2200
  Dr. Stan Fields, supt. — Fax 949-0599
  www.mundeleinmustangs.com
Mundelein Consolidated HS — 2,100/9-12
  1350 W Hawley St 60060 — 847-949-2200
  Dr. John Ahlgrim, prin. — Fax 949-0599

Mundelein ESD 75 — 2,200/K-8
  470 N Lake St 60060 — 847-949-2700
  Cynthia Heidorn Ph.D., supt. — Fax 949-2727
  www.district75.org
Sandburg MS — 800/6-8
  855 W Hawley St 60060 — 847-949-2707
  Mark Pilut, prin. — Fax 949-2716

Carmel HS — 1,300/9-12
  1 Carmel Pkwy 60060 — 847-566-3000
  Rev. Robert Carroll, prin. — Fax 566-8465
University of St. Mary of the Lake — Post-Sec.
  1000 E Maple Ave 60060 — 847-566-6401

Murphysboro, Jackson, Pop. 8,509
Murphysboro CUSD 186 — 2,000/PK-12
  819 Walnut St 62966 — 618-684-3781
  Lori James-Gross, supt. — Fax 684-2465
  www.mboro.jacksn.k12.il.us
Murphysboro HS — 800/9-12
  50 Blackwood Dr 62966 — 618-687-2336
  Colleen Doyle, prin. — Fax 687-3532
Murphysboro MS — 500/6-8
  2125 Spruce St 62966 — 618-684-3041
  Larry Lovel, prin. — Fax 687-1042

Murphysboro Christian Academy — 200/PK-12
  805 N 16th St 62966 — 618-684-5083
  Gina Noble, prin. — Fax 687-5614

Naperville, DuPage, Pop. 137,894
Indian Prairie CUSD 204
  Supt. — See Aurora
Crone MS — 1,100/6-8
  4020 111th St 60564 — 630-428-5600
  Stan Gorbatkin, prin. — Fax 428-5601
Gregory MS — 1,000/6-8
  2621 Springdale Cir 60564 — 630-428-6300
  Stephen Severson, prin. — Fax 428-6301
Hill MS — 800/6-8
  1836 Brookdale Rd 60563 — 630-428-6200
  Michael Raczak, prin. — Fax 428-6201
Neuqua Valley Gold Campus — 9-9
  3220 Cedar Glade Dr 60564 — 630-428-6400
  Mark Truckenbrod, prin. — Fax 428-6401
Neuqua Valley HS — 2,500/10-12
  2360 95th St 60564 — 630-428-6000
  Dr. Michael Popp, prin. — Fax 428-6001
Scullen MS — 1,200/6-8
  2815 Mistflower Ln 60564 — 630-428-7000
  Kathleen Kosteck, prin. — Fax 428-7001

Naperville CUSD 203 — 18,900/PK-12
  203 W Hillside Rd 60540 — 630-420-6300
  Dr. Alan Leis, supt. — Fax 420-1066
  www.ncusd203.org/
Jefferson JHS — 900/6-8
  1525 N Loomis St 60563 — 630-420-6307
  Paul Schmidt, prin. — Fax 420-6930
Lincoln JHS — 1,000/6-8
  1320 Olympus Dr 60565 — 630-420-6370
  Dr. Daniel Brace, prin. — Fax 637-4582
Madison JHS — 900/6-8
  1000 River Oak Dr 60565 — 630-420-4257
  Erin Anderson, prin. — Fax 420-6402
Naperville Central HS — 3,000/9-12
  440 Aurora Ave 60540 — 630-420-6420
  Jim Caudill, prin. — Fax 369-6247
Naperville North HS — 3,000/9-12
  899 N Mill St 60563 — 630-420-6484
  Ross Truemper, prin. — Fax 420-4255
Washington JHS — 600/6-8
  201 N Washington St 60540 — 630-420-6390
  Mark Pasztor, prin. — Fax 420-6474
Other Schools – See Lisle

Keller Graduate School — Post-Sec.
  2056 Westings Ave Ste 40 60563 — 630-428-9086
North Central College — Post-Sec.
  30 N Brainard St 60540 — 630-637-5100

Nashville, Washington, Pop. 3,130
Nashville CCSD 49 — 600/PK-8
  750 E Gorman St 62263 — 618-327-4304
  Donald Miller, supt. — Fax 327-4503
  www.county.washington.k12.il.us
Nashville MS — 300/PK-PK, 5-
  750 E Gorman St 62263 — 618-327-3055
  Brent O'Daniell, prin. — Fax 327-4501

Nashville Community HSD 99 — 500/9-12
  1300 S Mill St 62263 — 618-327-8286
  Wendy Davis, supt. — Fax 327-4512
  www.county.washington.k12.il.us
Nashville Comm. HS — 500/9-12
  1300 S Mill St 62263 — 618-327-8286
  Brad Weathers, prin. — Fax 327-4512

Nauvoo, Hancock, Pop. 1,165
Nauvoo-Colusa CUSD 325 — 400/PK-12
  PO Box 308 62354 — 217-453-6451
  Kent Young, supt. — Fax 453-6395
  www.hancock.k12.il.us/nchs325/
Nauvoo-Colusa HS — 200/7-12
  PO Box 308 62354 — 217-453-2231
  Tami Roskamp, prin. — Fax 453-6395
Nauvoo-Colusa JHS — 50/7-8
  PO Box 308 62354 — 217-453-2231
  Tami Roskamp, prin. — Fax 453-6395

Neoga, Cumberland, Pop. 1,809
Neoga CUSD 3 — 900/PK-12
  PO Box 280 62447 — 217-895-2201
  Dr. Debby Poindexter, supt. — Fax 895-3476
  www.neoga.k12.il.us

Neoga HS 300/9-12
PO Box 280 62447 217-895-2205
Benjamin Johnson, prin. Fax 895-3957
Neoga JHS 100/7-8
PO Box 280 62447 217-895-2205
Benjamin Johnson, prin. Fax 895-3957

Newark, Kendall, Pop. 938
Newark CCSD 66 300/K-8
PO Box 686 60541 815-695-5143
John Demay, supt. Fax 695-5776
Other Schools – See Millbrook

Newark Community HSD 18 200/9-12
413 Chicago Rd 60541 815-695-5164
Roger Sanders, supt. Fax 695-5752
www.newarkhs.k12.il.us
Newark Community HS 200/9-12
413 Chicago Rd 60541 815-695-5164
Pauline Berggren, prin. Fax 695-5752

New Athens, Saint Clair, Pop. 2,002
New Athens CUSD 60 600/PK-12
501 Hanft St 62264 618-475-2174
Mike Weaver, supt. Fax 475-2176
www.stclair.k12.il.us
New Athens HS 200/9-12
501 Hanft St 62264 618-475-2173
Dennis Works, prin. Fax 475-2176
New Athens JHS 100/6-8
501 Hanft St 62264 618-475-2172
Jim Marlow, prin. Fax 475-2176

New Berlin, Sangamon, Pop. 1,109
CUSD 16 700/PK-12
PO Box 230 62670 217-488-6111
Valerie Carr, supt. Fax 488-6418
cusd16.k12.il.us
New Berlin HS 200/9-12
PO Box 230 62670 217-488-6012
George Kellner, prin. Fax 488-3207
New Berlin JHS 100/7-8
PO Box 230 62670 217-488-6012
George Kellner, prin. Fax 488-3207

New Lenox, Will, Pop. 21,545
Lincoln-Way Community HSD 210 5,900/9-12
1801 E Lincoln Hwy 60451 815-462-2100
Dr. Lawrence Wyllie, supt. Fax 485-7648
www.lw210.org
Lincoln-Way Central HS 2,600/9-12
1801 E Lincoln Hwy 60451 815-462-2100
Dr. Monica Schmitt, prin. Fax 485-7648
Other Schools – See Frankfort

New Lenox SD 122 5,200/PK-8
102 S Cedar Rd 60451 815-485-2169
Dr. Michael Sass, supt. Fax 485-2236
www.nlsd122.org
Liberty JHS 600/7-8
151 Lenox St 60451 815-462-7951
Lynn Schroeder, prin. Fax 462-0672
Martino JHS 600/7-8
731 E Joliet Hwy 60451 815-485-7593
Del Bitter, prin. Fax 485-9578

Providence Catholic HS 1,100/9-12
1800 W Lincoln Hwy 60451 815-485-2136
Don Sebestyen, prin. Fax 485-2709

Newton, Jasper, Pop. 3,021
Jasper County CUSD 1 1,500/K-12
609 S Lafayette St 62448 618-783-8459
Wayne Savageau, supt. Fax 783-3679
www.cusd1.jasper.k12.il.us
Newton Community HS 600/9-12
201 West End Ave 62448 618-783-2303
Ron Alburtus, prin. Fax 783-3783

Niantic, Macon, Pop. 689
Sangamon Valley CUSD 9 600/PK-12
PO Box 200 62551 217-668-2338
Wayne Honeycutt, supt. Fax 668-2406
Sangamon Valley HS 100/9-12
PO Box 200 62551 217-668-2392
Dan Carie, prin. Fax 668-2406
Other Schools – See Illiopolis

Niles, Cook, Pop. 29,945
East Maine SD 63
Supt. — See Des Plaines
Gemini JHS 800/7-8
8955 N Greenwood Ave 60714 847-827-1181
Scott Herrmann, prin. Fax 827-3499

Park Ridge-Niles CCSD 64
Supt. — See Park Ridge
Emerson MS 800/6-8
8101 N Cumberland Ave 60714 847-318-8110
Victoria Mogil, prin. Fax 318-8122

Niles School of Beauty Culture Post-Sec.
8057 N Milwaukee Ave 60714 847-965-8061
Northridge Preparatory S 300/6-12
8320 W Ballard Rd 60714 847-375-0600
Luke Ferris, prin. Fax 375-0606
Notre Dame HS 800/9-12
7655 W Dempster St 60714 847-965-2900
Steven W. Zeier, prin. Fax 965-2975

Noble, Richland, Pop. 732
West Richland CUSD 2 500/PK-12
PO Box 157 62868 618-723-2334
Don Carlyle, supt. Fax 723-2113
West Richland HS 100/9-12
PO Box 157 62868 618-723-2335
Fax 723-2113
West Richland JHS 100/7-8
PO Box 157 62868 618-723-2335
Fax 723-2113

Nokomis, Montgomery, Pop. 2,315
Nokomis CUSD 22 800/PK-12
511 Oberle St 62075 217-563-7311
Jean M. Chrostoski, supt. Fax 563-2549
www.nokomis.k12.il.us
Nokomis JSHS 400/7-12
511 Oberle St 62075 217-563-2014
Donald Markey, prin. Fax 563-2671

Normal, McLean, Pop. 48,649
ISU Lab SD 1,100/PK-12
Campus Box 5300 61790 309-438-8542
Robert Dean, supt. Fax 438-3813
www.uhigh.ilstu.edu/labschool/
University HS 600/9-12
Campus Box 7100 61790 309-438-8346
Jeff Hill, prin. Fax 438-5198

McLean Co. Unit SD 5 10,900/PK-12
1809 W Hovey Ave 61761 309-452-4476
Dr. Alan Chapman, supt. Fax 452-7418
www.unit5.org
Chiddix JHS 800/6-8
300 S Walnut St 61761 309-452-1191
Timothy Green, prin. Fax 888-6845
Kingsley JHS 1,000/6-8
303 Kingsley St 61761 309-452-4461
Dr. Lynette Mehall, prin. Fax 454-1845
Normal Community HS 1,600/9-12
3900 E Raab Rd 61761 309-728-5000
Dr. Jeanette Nuckolls, prin. Fax 728-5050
Normal Community West HS 1,400/9-12
501 N Parkside Rd 61761 309-888-6060
Thomas Eder, prin. Fax 451-3012
Parkside JHS 900/6-8
101 N Parkside Rd 61761 309-452-8321
Mary Ahillen, prin. Fax 888-6813

Bloomington-Normal School of Radiography Post-Sec.
900 Franklin Ave 61761 309-452-2834
Calvary Baptist Academy 300/K-12
1017 N School St 61761 309-452-7912
Timothy Abney, prin. Fax 451-0033
Heartland Community College Post-Sec.
1500 W Raab Rd 61761 309-827-0500
Illinois State University 61790 Post-Sec.
309-438-2111
Mennonite College of Nursing Post-Sec.
PO Box 5810 61790 309-438-7400

Norridge, Cook, Pop. 14,362
Ridgewood Community HSD 234 800/9-12
7500 W Montrose Ave 60706 708-456-4242
Dr. Robert Lupo, supt. Fax 456-8238
www.ridgenet.org
Ridgewood Community HS 800/9-12
7500 W Montrose Ave 60706 708-456-4242
Kevin Omara, prin. Fax 456-8238

Norris City, White, Pop. 1,043
Norris City-Omaha-Enfield CUSD 3 800/PK-12
PO Box 399 62869 618-378-3222
Michael Phelps, supt. Fax 378-3286
Norris City-Omaha-Enfield HS 300/9-12
PO Box 399 62869 618-378-3312
Cliff Karnes, prin. Fax 378-3364

North Aurora, Kane, Pop. 13,091
Aurora West Unit SD 129
Supt. — See Aurora
Jewel MS 900/6-8
1501 Waterford Rd 60542 630-301-5010
Greg Scalia, prin. Fax 907-3161

Northbrook, Cook, Pop. 34,061
Northbrook ESD 27 1,300/K-8
1250 Sanders Rd 60062 847-498-2610
Dr. David Kroeze, supt. Fax 498-5916
www.northbrook27.k12.il.us/
Wood Oaks JHS 500/6-8
1250 Sanders Rd 60062 847-272-1900
Dr. Jeffrey Schuler, prin. Fax 480-4834

Northbrook SD 28 1,800/K-8
1475 Maple Ave 60062 847-498-7900
Julia James Haley Ph.D., supt. Fax 498-7970
www.northbrook28.net
Northbrook JHS 600/6-8
1475 Maple Ave 60062 847-498-7920
Dr. Peggy J. Hoskin, prin. Fax 656-1712

Northbrook/Glenview SD 30 1,100/K-8
2374 Shermer Rd 60062 847-498-4190
Dr. Linda Vieth, supt. Fax 498-8981
www.district30.k12.il.us
Maple JHS 400/6-8
2370 Shermer Rd 60062 847-400-8900
Steven Waitz, prin. Fax 272-0979

Northfield Township HSD 225
Supt. — See Glenview
Glenbrook North HS 2,100/9-12
2300 Shermer Rd 60062 847-272-6400
Dr. Michael Riggle, prin. Fax 509-2411

West Northfield SD 31 900/K-8
3131 Techny Rd 60062 847-272-6880
Debra Hill, supt. Fax 272-4818
www.dist31.k12.il.us
Field MS 300/6-8
2055 Landwehr Rd 60062 847-272-6884
Robert Machak, prin. Fax 272-1050

Sager Soloman Schechter MS 400/6-8
3210 Dundee Rd 60062 847-412-5700
Linda Schaffzin, prin. Fax 498-5837

North Chicago, Lake, Pop. 36,601
North Chicago SD 187 4,600/PK-12
2000 Lewis Ave 60064 847-689-8150
John F. Barbini Ed.D., supt. Fax 689-6328
www.nchi.lfc.edu/
Neal Math Science Academy 600/7-8
1905 Argonne Dr 60064 847-689-6313
Antoinette Weatherspoon, prin. Fax 689-6332
North Chicago Community HS 900/9-12
1717 17th St 60064 847-578-7400
William King, prin. Fax 689-7473

R. Franklin University of Medicine Post-Sec.
3333 Green Bay Rd 60064 847-578-3000

Northfield, Cook, Pop. 5,491
New Trier Twp. HSD 203
Supt. — See Winnetka
New Trier Twp. HS - Northfield Campus 1,000/9-9
7 Happ Rd 60093 847-446-7000
Jan Borja, prin. Fax 446-4759

Sunset Ridge SD 29 500/K-8
525 Sunset Ridge Rd 60093 847-881-9401
Dr. Howard Bultinck, supt.
www.sunset.k12.il.us
Sunset Ridge MS 300/4-8
525 Sunset Ridge Rd 60093 847-881-9400
Howard Bultinck, prin.

Northlake, Cook, Pop. 11,686
Berkeley SD 87
Supt. — See Berkeley
Northlake MS 400/6-8
202 S Lakewood Ave 60164 708-449-3195
Daniel Sullivan, prin. Fax 547-2548

Leyden HSD 212
Supt. — See Franklin Park
West Leyden HS 1,600/9-12
1000 N Wolf Rd 60164 847-451-3154
Wilford Wagner, prin. Fax 451-3180

Bethel Academy 50/K-12
PO Box 2427 60164 708-865-2855
Louisa Feldman, admin. Fax 865-2870

Oak Brook, DuPage, Pop. 8,847
Butler SD 53 500/K-8
2801 York Rd 60523 630-573-2887
Sandra L. Martin, supt. Fax 573-5374
www.butler53.com
Butler JHS 200/6-8
2801 York Rd 60523 630-573-2760
Edward Condon, prin. Fax 573-1725

Oakbrook Terrace, DuPage, Pop. 2,270

DeVry University Post-Sec.
1 Tower Ln 60181 630-571-1818

Oak Forest, Cook, Pop. 28,229
Arbor Park SD 145 1,400/PK-8
15901 Forest Ave 60452 708-687-8040
Allen J. Jebens, supt. Fax 687-9498
www.arbor145.org/
Arbor Park MS 600/5-8
15900 Oak Ave 60452 708-687-5330
Thomas Savick, prin. Fax 535-4527

Bremen Community HSD 228
Supt. — See Midlothian
Oak Forest HS 1,400/9-12
15201 Central Ave 60452 708-687-0500
David Wilson, prin. Fax 687-0594

Forest Ridge SD 142 1,300/PK-8
15000 Laramie Ave 60452 708-687-3334
Dr. Margaret Longo, supt. Fax 687-2970
www.d142.org
Hille MS 600/6-8
5800 151st St 60452 708-687-2860
Tom Herbert, prin. Fax 687-8569

Capri Oak Forest Coll of Beauty Culture Post-Sec.
15815 Rob Roy Dr 60452 708-687-3020
John Amico's School of Hair Design Post-Sec.
15301 Cicero Ave 60452 708-687-7800

Oakland, Coles, Pop. 971
Oakland CUSD 5 400/K-12
PO Box 200 61943 217-346-2555
Ezra Smithson, supt. Fax 346-2267
www.oak.k12.il.us/
Oakland HS 100/9-12
PO Box 378 61943 217-346-2118
Mike Smith, prin. Fax 346-2267

Oak Lawn, Cook, Pop. 55,136
Community HSD 218 5,100/9-12
10701 Kilpatrick Ave 60453 708-424-2000
Dr. Kevin G. Burns, supt. Fax 424-6389
www.chsd218.org/
Richards HS 1,600/9-12
10601 Central Ave 60453 708-499-2550
Ross Cucio, prin. Fax 499-6941
Other Schools – See Blue Island, Palos Heights

Oak Lawn Community HSD 229 1,700/9-12
9400 Southwest Hwy 60453 708-741-5601
Dr. James J. Briscoe, supt. Fax 424-5297
www.olchs.org
Oak Lawn Community HS 1,700/9-12
9400 Southwest Hwy 60453 708-741-5609
Michael Riordan, prin. Fax 424-5263

Oak Lawn-Hometown SD 123 1,900/PK-8
4201 W 93rd St 60453 708-423-0150
Kathleen McCord, supt. Fax 423-0160
www.d123.org/
Oak Lawn-Hometown MS 6-8
5345 W 99th St 60453 708-499-6400
Andrea Anderson, prin. Fax 499-7684

Ridgeland SD 122 — 2,300/PK-8
6500 W 95th St 60453 — 708-599-5550
Kenneth Jandes, supt.
www.ridgeland122.com
Simmons MS — 500/7-8
6450 W 95th St 60453 — 708-599-8540
Michael Connolly, prin. — Fax 599-8015

Cameo Beauty Academy — Post-Sec.
9714 S Cicero Ave 60453 — 708-636-4660
Fox College — Post-Sec.
4201 W 93rd St 60453 — 708-636-7700
South Side Baptist S — 100/K-12
5220 W 105th St 60453 — 708-425-3435
Robert Burckart, prin. — Fax 425-9016

Oak Park, Cook, Pop. 50,824
Oak Park ESD 97 — 4,900/PK-8
970 Madison St 60302 — 708-524-3000
Dr. Constance Collins, supt. — Fax 524-3019
www.op97.org
Brooks MS — 900/6-8
325 S Kenilworth Ave 60302 — 708-524-3050
Tom Sindelar, prin. — Fax 524-3036
Julian MS — 800/6-8
416 S Ridgeland Ave 60302 — 708-524-3040
Victoria Sharts, prin. — Fax 524-3035

Oak Park-River Forest SD 200 — 3,000/9-12
201 N Scoville Ave 60302 — 708-383-0700
Dr. Susan Bridge, supt. — Fax 434-3917
oprfhs.org
Oak Park-River Forest HS — 3,000/9-12
201 N Scoville Ave 60302 — 708-383-0700
Dr. Susan Bridge, prin. — Fax 434-3917

Fenwick HS — 1,200/9-12
505 Washington Blvd 60302 — 708-386-0127
Dr. James Quaid, prin. — Fax 386-3052
West Suburban College of Nursing — Post-Sec.
3 Erie Ct 60302 — 708-763-6529

Oblong, Crawford, Pop. 1,559
Oblong CUSD 4 — 700/PK-12
PO Box 40 62449 — 618-592-3933
Allen Price, supt. — Fax 592-3427
Oblong HS — 300/9-12
700 S Range St 62449 — 618-592-4235
Fritz Wheeler, prin. — Fax 592-3540

Odin, Marion, Pop. 1,114
Odin Community HSD 700 — 100/9-12
PO Box 250 62870 — 618-775-8266
Norvin Porter, supt. — Fax 775-8268
Odin HS — 100/9-12
PO Box 250 62870 — 618-775-8266
Mike Conlon, prin. — Fax 775-8268

O Fallon, Saint Clair, Pop. 18,600
O'Fallon CCSD 90 — 3,100/PK-8
707 N Smiley St 62269 — 618-632-3666
Dr. Nancy Gibson, supt. — Fax 632-7864
www.ofallon90.net/district/
Fulton JHS — 800/7-8
307 Kyle Rd 62269 — 618-628-0090
Dr. Douglas Wood, prin. — Fax 624-9390

O'Fallon Twp. HSD 203 — 2,200/9-12
600 S Smiley St 62269 — 618-632-3507
Russell Clover, supt. — Fax 632-9730
www.oths.k12.il.us/
O'Fallon HS, 600 S Smiley St 62269 — 2,200/9-12
Stephen Dirnbeck, prin. — 618-632-3507

Shiloh Village SD 85 — 500/PK-8
125 Diamond Ct 62269 — 618-632-7434
Jennifer Filyaw, supt. — Fax 632-8343
Shiloh MS, 1 Wildcat Xing 62269 — 5-8
Robin Becker, prin. — 618-632-7434

Oglesby, LaSalle, Pop. 3,634
Oglesby ESD 125 — 500/PK-8
755 Bennett Ave 61348 — 815-883-9297
Dr. James Boyle, supt. — Fax 883-3568
Washington MS — 200/6-8
212 W Walnut St 61348 — 815-883-3517
Robert Meehan, prin. — Fax 883-3568

Illinois Valley Community College — Post-Sec.
815 N Orlando Smith St 61348 — 815-224-2720

Ohio, Bureau, Pop. 529
Ohio Community HSD 505 — 100/9-12
PO Box 478 61349 — 815-376-2934
Dennis Thompson, supt. — Fax 376-2102
Ohio Community HS — 100/9-12
PO Box 478 61349 — 815-376-4414
Sharon Flesher, prin. — Fax 376-2102

Okawville, Washington, Pop. 1,347
West Washington County CUSD 10 — 700/K-12
PO Box 27 62271 — 618-243-6454
Dr. Dennis Fancher, supt. — Fax 243-6464
www.county.washington.k12.il.us
Okawville JSHS — 400/7-12
400 S Hanover St 62271 — 618-243-5201
Kim Wiley, prin. — Fax 243-6110

Olney, Richland, Pop. 8,575
East Richland CUSD 1 — 2,100/PK-12
1100 E Laurel St 62450 — 618-395-2324
Marilyn J. Holt, supt. — Fax 392-4147
www.east.rchlnd.k12.il.us
East Richland HS — 700/9-12
1200 E Laurel St 62450 — 618-393-2191
Chris Simpson, prin. — Fax 395-1256
East Richland MS — 500/6-8
1099 N Van St 62450 — 618-395-4372
Andy Thomann, prin. — Fax 392-3399

Olney Central College — Post-Sec.
305 N West St 62450 — 618-395-7777

Olympia Fields, Cook, Pop. 4,738
Rich Township HSD 227 — 3,500/9-12
20290 Governors Hwy 60461 — 708-679-5800
Howard Hunigan, supt. — Fax 679-5740
www.rich227.org
Rich Central HS — 1,200/9-12
3600 W 203rd St 60461 — 708-675-5600
John Macon, prin. — Fax 679-5632
Other Schools – See Park Forest, Richton Park

Onarga, Iroquois, Pop. 1,400
Iroquois West CUSD 10
Supt. — See Gilman
Iroquois West MS — 200/6-8
303 N Evergreen St 60955 — 815-268-4355
Vicki Killus, prin. — Fax 265-7008

Oneida, Knox, Pop. 733
ROWVA CUSD 208 — 500/K-12
PO Box 69 61467 — 309-483-3711
Gary Buckingham, supt. — Fax 483-6123
www.rowva.k12.il.us
ROWVA HS — 300/9-12
PO Box 69 61467 — 309-483-6371
Andy Richmond, prin. — Fax 483-8223
ROWVA JHS — 100/7-8
PO Box 69 61467 — 309-483-2803
Chad Wagner, prin. — Fax 483-6378

Opdyke, Jefferson
Opdyke-Belle-Rive CCSD 5 — 200/K-8
PO Box 189 62872 — 618-756-2492
Brenda Lusby, supt. — Fax 756-2792
www.roe25.com/obr/
Opdyke MS — 100/5-8
PO Box 189 62872 — 618-756-2492
Brenda Lusby, prin. — Fax 756-2355

Orangeville, Stephenson, Pop. 762
Orangeville CUSD 203 — 500/PK-12
310 S East St 61060 — 815-789-4450
Randall Otto, supt. — Fax 789-4607
Orangeville HS — 200/9-12
201 S Orange 61060 — 815-789-4289
Michelle Thomas, prin. — Fax 789-4478
Orangeville JHS — 100/7-8
201 S Orange 61060 — 815-789-4289
Michelle Thomas, prin. — Fax 789-4478

Oregon, Ogle, Pop. 4,133
Oregon CUSD 220 — 1,500/PK-12
206 S 10th St 61061 — 815-732-2186
Dr. William Mattingly, supt. — Fax 732-2187
www.ocusd.net
Oregon HS — 600/9-12
210 S 10th St 61061 — 815-732-6241
Jeff Schad, prin. — Fax 732-3361
Other Schools – See Mount Morris

Orion, Henry, Pop. 1,707
Orion CUSD 223 — 1,100/PK-12
PO Box 189 61273 — 309-526-3388
Donald E. Achelpohl, supt. — Fax 526-3711
orionschools.revealed.net/
Orion HS — 400/9-12
PO Box 39 61273 — 309-526-3361
Scott Verstraete, prin. — Fax 526-3854
Orion MS — 300/6-8
PO Box 129 61273 — 309-526-3392
Gary Heard, prin. — Fax 526-3872

Orland Park, Cook, Pop. 54,011
Consolidated HSD 230 — 8,200/9-12
15100 S 94th Ave 60462 — 708-745-5203
Dr. Patrick McMahon, supt. — Fax 349-2105
www.d230.org
Sandburg HS — 3,400/9-12
13300 S La Grange Rd 60462 — 708-671-3100
Debbie Boniface, prin. — Fax 361-9714
Other Schools – See Palos Hills, Tinley Park

Orland SD 135 — 5,900/K-8
15100 S 94th Ave 60462 — 708-364-3306
Dennis Soustek, supt. — Fax 873-6479
www.orland135.org
Century JHS — 1,000/6-8
10801 W 159th St 60467 — 708-364-3500
Cindy Finley, prin. — Fax 349-5840
Jerling JHS — 600/6-8
8851 W 151st St 60462 — 708-364-3700
Steven Cole, prin. — Fax 873-6457
Orland JHS — 600/6-8
14855 West Ave 60462 — 708-364-4200
Linda Kane, prin. — Fax 349-5843

Robert Morris College — Post-Sec.
43 Orland Square Dr 60462 — 708-226-3800

Oswego, Kendall, Pop. 18,521
Oswego CUSD 308 — 9,400/PK-12
4175 State Route 71 60543 — 630-636-3080
Dr. David L. Behlow, supt. — Fax 554-2168
www.oswego308.org
Bednarcick JHS — 500/6-8
3025 Heggs Rd 60543 — 630-636-2500
Janet Stutz, prin. — Fax 922-3278
Oswego East HS — 9-12
1525 Harvey Rd 60543 — 630-636-2200
Ed Howerton, prin. — Fax 554-5830
Oswego HS — 2,400/9-12
4250 State Route 71 60543 — 630-636-2000
Mike Wayne, prin. — Fax 554-7160
Thompson JHS — 1,000/6-8
440 Boulder Hill Pass 60543 — 630-636-2600
Tracy Murphy, prin. — Fax 554-5193
Traughber JHS — 700/6-8
61 Franklin St 60543 — 630-636-2700
Ralph Kober, prin. — Fax 554-5197

Hair Professionals School of Cosmetology — Post-Sec.
PO Box 40 60543 — 630-554-2266

Ottawa, LaSalle, Pop. 18,635
Ottawa ESD 141 — 2,000/PK-8
320 W Main St 61350 — 815-433-1133
Dr. Christine Benson, supt. — Fax 433-1888
www.ottawaelem.lasall.k12.il.us/
Shepherd MS — 500/7-8
701 E McKinley St 61350 — 815-434-7925
Michael Bannister, prin. — Fax 433-9447

Ottawa Twp. HSD 140 — 1,600/9-12
211 E Main St 61350 — 815-433-1323
Thomas Jobst, supt. — Fax 433-1338
www.ottawahigh2.com/
Ottawa Twp. HS — 1,600/9-12
211 E Main St 61350 — 815-433-1323
John Harrison, prin. — Fax 433-1338

Marquette HS — 200/9-12
1000 Paul St 61350 — 815-433-0125
Ron Spandet, prin. — Fax 433-2632

Palatine, Cook, Pop. 66,848
Palatine CCSD 15 — 12,100/PK-8
580 N 1st Bank Dr 60067 — 847-963-3000
Robert A. McKanna, supt. — Fax 963-3200
www.ccsd15.net
Sundling JHS — 700/7-8
1100 N Smith St 60067 — 847-963-3700
Craig Winkelman, prin. — Fax 963-3706
Winston JHS — 7-8
900 E Palatine Rd 60074 — 847-963-7400
Alexandria Leitgeb, prin. — Fax 963-7406
Other Schools – See Rolling Meadows

Township HSD 211 — 13,000/9-12
1750 S Roselle Rd 60067 — 847-755-6600
Roger Thornton, supt. — Fax 755-6810
www.d211.org
Fremd HS — 2,900/9-12
1000 S Quentin Rd 60067 — 847-755-2600
Marina Scott, prin. — Fax 755-2623
Palatine HS — 2,600/9-12
1111 N Rohlwing Rd 60074 — 847-755-1600
Gary Steiger, prin. — Fax 755-1623
Other Schools – See Hoffman Estates, Schaumburg

William Rainey Harper College — Post-Sec.
1200 W Algonquin Rd 60067 — 847-925-6000

Palestine, Crawford, Pop. 1,344
Palestine CUSD 3 — 400/K-12
PO Box 217 62451 — 618-586-2713
Dr. Cal Owens, supt. — Fax 586-2905
Palestine HS — 200/9-12
203 S Washington St 62451 — 618-586-2712
Arlene Lindsay, prin. — Fax 586-5328

Palmyra, Macoupin, Pop. 733
Northwestern CUSD 2 — 400/PK-12
30953 Route 111 62674 — 217-436-2102
Gayle Early, supt. — Fax 436-2701
northwestern.k12.il.us
Northwestern HS — 100/9-12
30889 Route 111 62674 — 217-436-2011
Charles Barlow, prin. — Fax 436-9112
Northwestern JHS — 100/7-8
30889 Route 111 62674 — 217-436-2011
Charles Barlow, prin. — Fax 436-9112

Palos Heights, Cook, Pop. 12,255
Community HSD 218
Supt. — See Oak Lawn
Shepard HS — 1,800/9-12
13049 S Ridgeland Ave 60463 — 708-371-1111
Ty Harting, prin. — Fax 371-7688

Palos Heights SD 128 — 700/PK-8
12809 S McVickers Ave 60463 — 708-597-9040
Dr. Theresa Sak, supt. — Fax 597-9089
www.d128.k12.il.us
Independence JHS — 200/6-8
6610 W Highland Dr 60463 — 708-448-0737
Dr. Kathleen Casey, prin.

Chicago Christian HS — 500/9-12
12001 S Oak Park Ave 60463 — 708-388-7650
Steve Bult, prin. — Fax 388-0154
Trinity Christian College — Post-Sec.
6601 W College Dr 60463 — 708-597-3000

Palos Hills, Cook, Pop. 17,619
Consolidated HSD 230
Supt. — See Orland Park
Stagg HS — 2,300/9-12
8000 W 111th St 60465 — 708-974-7400
Jeff Leach, prin. — Fax 974-0803

North Palos SD 117 — 2,700/PK-8
7825 W 103rd St 60465 — 708-598-5500
Dr. Ken Sorrick, supt. — Fax 598-5539
www.d117.s-cook.k12.il.us/
Other Schools – See Hickory Hills

Hair Professionals Career College — Post-Sec.
10321 S Roberts Rd 60465 — 708-430-1755
Moraine Valley Community College — Post-Sec.
10900 S 88th Ave 60465 — 708-974-4300

Palos Park, Cook, Pop. 4,814
Palos CCSD 118 — 2,000/K-8
8800 W 119th St 60464 — 708-448-4800
Dr. Rosemarie Carroll, supt. — Fax 448-4880
www.palos118.org
Palos South MS — 800/6-8
13100 S 82nd Ave 60464 — 708-448-5900
Donna Clark, prin. — Fax 448-0754

Pana, Christian, Pop. 5,543
Pana CUSD 8 — 1,300/PK-12
PO Box 377 62557 — 217-562-1500
Dr. David Lett, supt. — Fax 562-1501
www.panaschools.com

Pana HS
201 W 8th St 62557
Gayle McRoberts, prin.
500/9-12
217-562-6600
Fax 562-6714
Pana JHS
203 W 8th St 62557
Paul Lauff, prin.
200/7-8
217-562-6500
Fax 562-6712
Pana Adult Center
PO Box 377 62557
Don Kroski, prin.
Adult
217-562-6695
Fax 562-4534

Paris, Edgar, Pop. 8,987
Paris CUSD 4
15601 US Highway 150 61944
Lorraine Bailey, supt.
www.crestwood.k12.il.us
600/PK-12
217-465-5391
Fax 466-1225
Crestwood JHS
15601 US Highway 150 61944
Alan Zuber, prin.
200/6-8
217-465-5391
Fax 466-1225

Paris-Union SD 95
414 S Main St 61944
Connie Sutton, supt.
www.paris95.k12.il.us
1,600/PK-12
217-465-8448
Fax 463-2243
Mayo MS
300 E Wood St 61944
Melanie Ogle, prin.
300/6-8
217-466-3050
Fax 466-3905
Paris HS
309 S Main St 61944
Dave Meister, prin.
700/9-12
217-466-1175
Fax 466-1903

Park Forest, Cook, Pop. 23,560
Park Forest SD 163
242 S Orchard Dr 60466
Dr. Joyce Carmine, supt.
www.sd163.com
2,400/PK-8
708-668-9400
Fax 748-9359
Forest Trail MS
215 Wilson St 60466
Carolyn Stroud, prin.
700/6-8
708-668-9600
Fax 503-2297

Rich Township HSD 227
Supt. — See Olympia Fields
Rich East Campus HS
300 Sauk Trl 60466
Jeff Craig, prin.
1,200/9-12
708-679-6100
Fax 679-7330

Park Ridge, Cook, Pop. 37,460
Maine Twp. HSD 207
1131 S Dee Rd 60068
Dr. Steven Snider, supt.
www.maine207.org
6,800/9-12
847-696-3600
Fax 696-3254
Maine East HS
2601 Dempster St 60068
David Barker, prin.
2,100/9-12
847-825-4484
Fax 825-1636
Maine South HS
1111 S Dee Rd 60068
David Claypool, prin.
Other Schools – See Des Plaines
2,500/9-12
847-825-7711
Fax 825-0677

Park Ridge-Niles CCSD 64
164 S Prospect Ave 60068
Dr. Sally Pryor, supt.
www.d64.org
4,400/PK-8
847-318-4300
Fax 318-4351
Lincoln MS
200 S Lincoln Ave 60068
Jim Blouch, prin.
Other Schools – See Niles
700/6-8
847-318-4215
Fax 318-4210

Patoka, Marion, Pop. 624
Patoka CUSD 100
1220 Kinoka Rd 62875
Travis Roundcount, supt.
www.schools.lth5.k12.il.us/patoka/phs.htm
300/K-12
618-432-5440
Fax 432-5306
Patoka HS
1220 Kinoka Rd 62875
Philip Lark, prin.
100/9-12
618-432-5440
Fax 432-5306
Patoka JHS
1220 Kinoka Rd 62875
Philip Lark, prin.
50/7-8
618-432-5200
Fax 432-5306

Pawnee, Sangamon, Pop. 2,602
Pawnee CUSD 11
810 4th St 62558
Lonny Lemon, supt.
www.pawneeschools.org
700/PK-12
217-625-2471
Fax 625-2251
Pawnee HS
810 4th St 62558
David Roberts, prin.
200/9-12
217-625-2471
Fax 625-2251

Paw Paw, Lee, Pop. 840
Paw Paw CUSD 271
PO Box 508 61353
Robert Priest, supt.
300/K-12
815-627-2841
Fax 627-2971
Paw Paw JSHS, PO Box 37 61353
Galen Noard, prin.
200/5-12
815-627-2671

Paxton, Ford, Pop. 4,486
Paxton-Buckley-Loda CUSD 10
PO Box 50 60957
Clifford McClure, supt.
www.pbl.k12.il.us/hs/lib
1,400/K-12
217-379-3314
Fax 379-2862
Paxton-Buckley-Loda HS
PO Box 50 60957
James Flaherty, prin.
500/9-12
217-379-4331
Fax 379-2491
Paxton-Buckley-Loda JHS
PO Box 50 60957
John Rawdin, prin.
300/6-8
217-379-9202
Fax 379-9169

Payson, Adams, Pop. 1,069
Payson CUSD 1
406 W State St 62360
Rodger Hannel, supt.
adams.k12.il.us/cusd1/
600/PK-12
217-656-3323
Fax 656-4042
Seymour JSHS
420 W Brainard St 62360
John Wallace, prin.
300/7-12
217-656-3355
Fax 656-3584

Pearl City, Stephenson, Pop. 781
Pearl City CUSD 200
PO Box 9 61062
William Faller, supt.
600/PK-12
815-443-2715
Fax 443-2237
Pearl City HS
PO Box 9 61062
Tim Thill, prin.
100/9-12
815-443-2715
Fax 443-2237
Pearl City JHS
PO Box 9 61062
Tim Thill, prin.
100/7-8
815-443-2715
Fax 443-2237

Pecatonica, Winnebago, Pop. 2,081
Pecatonica CUSD 321
PO Box 419 61063
Dr. Charles Norland, supt.
www.pecschools.com/
900/K-12
815-239-1639
Fax 239-2125
Pecatonica Community MS
PO Box 419 61063
Francis Fennell, prin.
300/5-8
815-239-2612
Fax 239-1274
Pecatonica HS
PO Box 419 61063
Thomas Hoffman, prin.
300/9-12
815-239-2611
Fax 239-9128

Pekin, Tazewell, Pop. 33,190
Pekin Community HSD 303
320 Stadium Dr 61554
Paula Davis, supt.
www.pekinhigh.net
2,100/9-12
309-477-4222
Fax 477-4376
Pekin Community HS
1903 Court St 61554
Craig Smock, prin.
2,100/9-12
309-477-4331
Fax 477-4377

Pekin SD 108
501 Washington St 61554
Don White, supt.
www.pekin.net
3,800/PK-8
309-477-4740
Fax 477-4701
Broadmoor JHS
501 Maywood Ave 61554
Jeffrey Nelson, prin.
400/7-8
309-477-4731
Fax 347-7436
Edison JHS, 1400 Earl St 61554
Len Ealey, prin.
400/7-8
309-477-4732

Peoria, Peoria, Pop. 112,907
Norwood ESD 63
6521 W Farmington Rd 61604
James Thomas, prin.
www.norwood63.com/
500/K-8
309-676-3523
Fax 676-6099
Norwood MS
6521 W Farmington Rd 61604
James Thomas, prin.
200/5-8
309-676-3523
Fax 676-6099

Peoria SD 150
3202 N Wisconsin Ave 61603
Ken Hinton, supt.
www.peoria.psd150.org
15,700/PK-12
309-672-6512
Fax 672-6820
Bills MS
6001 N Frostwood Pkwy 61615
Robert Bethel, prin.
300/5-8
309-693-4437
Fax 693-4438
Blaine-Sumner MS
919 S Matthew St 61605
Felix Lobdell, prin.
300/5-8
309-672-6504
Fax 673-6253
Columbia MS
2612 N Bootz Ave 61604
Cindy Janovetz, prin.
300/5-8
309-672-6508
Fax 685-2238
Coolidge HS
2708 W Rohmann Ave 61604
Jorge Carballido, prin.
300/5-8
309-672-6506
Fax 673-7605
Lincoln MS
700 Mary St 61603
Paul Monrad, prin.
400/5-8
309-672-6542
Fax 676-6615
Lindbergh MS
6327 N Sheridan Rd 61614
Mary Davis, prin.
400/5-8
309-693-4427
Fax 693-0499
Loucks-Edison MS
2503 N University St 61604
Gloria Cox, prin.
600/5-8
309-685-5677
Manual HS
811 S Griswold St 61605
William Salzman, prin.
800/9-12
309-672-6600
Fax 672-6605
Peoria HS
1615 N North St 61604
Randy Simmons, prin.
1,000/9-12
309-672-6630
Fax 685-5803
Richwoods HS
6301 N University St 61614
John Meisinger, prin.
1,300/9-12
309-693-4400
Fax 693-4414
Rolling Acres-Edison MS
5617 N Merrimac Ave 61614
Deloris Turner, prin.
300/5-8
309-689-1100
Sterling MS
2315 N Sterling Ave 61604
Tim Delinski, prin.
300/5-8
309-672-6557
Fax 681-8286
Trewyn MS
1419 S Folkers Ave 61605
Carol Penca, prin.
400/5-8
309-672-6500
Fax 673-8537
Von Steuben MS
801 E Forrest Hill Ave 61603
David Obergfel, prin.
400/5-8
309-672-6561
Fax 685-7631
Washington MS
3706 N Grand Blvd 61614
Joan Wojcikewych, prin.
200/5-8
309-672-6563
Fax 672-6564
White MS
304 E Illinois Ave 61603
Scott Montgomery, prin.
300/5-8
309-672-6567
Fax 682-5702
Woodruff HS
1800 NE Perry Ave 61603
Teri Dunn, prin.
1,000/9-12
309-672-6665
Fax 674-8582
Adult Education Center
839 W Moss Ave 61606
Colleen Dries, prin.
Adult
309-672-6702
Adult Education Evening S
839 W Moss Ave 61606
McKinley Moton, prin.
Adult
309-672-6703

Pleasant Valley SD 62
4623 W Red Bud Rd 61604
Allen Johnson, supt.
500/PK-8
309-673-6750
Fax 674-0165
Pleasant Valley MS
3314 W Richwoods Blvd 61604
Sandy Somogyi, prin.
200/5-8
309-679-0634
Fax 679-0652

Bradley University
1501 W Bradley Ave 61625
Post-Sec.
800-447-6460
Illinois Central College
1 College Dr 61635
Post-Sec.
309-694-5011
Methodist College of Nursing
415 NE Saint Mark Ct 61603
Post-Sec.
309-672-5566
Midstate College
411 W Northmoor Rd 61614
Post-Sec.
309-692-4092
Peoria Christian S
3506 N California Ave 61603
Steve Hutton, admin.
900/PK-12
309-686-4500
Fax 686-2569
Peoria Notre Dame HS
5105 N Sheridan Rd 61614
Dr. Patricia A. O'Connell, prin.
1,000/9-12
309-691-8741
Fax 691-0875

St. Francis Medical Center
530 NE Glen Oak Ave 61603
Post-Sec.
309-655-2020
St. Francis Medical Ctr. Coll./Nursing
511 NE Greenleaf St 61603
Post-Sec.
309-655-2596
University of Illinois
PO Box 1649 61656
Post-Sec.
309-438-2181

Peoria Heights, Peoria, Pop. 6,354
Peoria Heights CUSD 325
500 E Glen Ave 61616
Roger Bergia, supt.
www.phcusd325.net
800/PK-12
309-686-8800
Fax 686-8801
Peoria Heights HS
508 E Glen Ave 61616
Rick Simkins, prin.
200/9-12
309-686-8803
Fax 686-8808

Peotone, Will, Pop. 3,673
Peotone CUSD 207U
212 W Wilson St 60468
Kevin Carey, supt.
www.peotoneschools.org
1,800/K-12
708-258-0991
Fax 258-0994
Peotone HS
605 W North St 60468
Doyle Owens, prin.
600/9-12
708-258-3236
Fax 258-6991
Peotone JHS
1 Blue Devil Dr 60468
Greg Oliver, prin.
400/6-8
708-258-3246
Fax 258-6669

Perry, Pike, Pop. 419
Griggsville-Perry CUSD 4
Supt. — See Griggsville
Griggsville-Perry MS
PO Box 98 62362
Andy Stremlau, prin.
100/5-8
217-236-9161
Fax 236-7221

Peru, LaSalle, Pop. 9,817
Peru ESD 124
1325 Park Rd 61354
Mark Cross, supt.
www.perued.net
900/PK-8
815-223-0486
Fax 223-0490
Peru-Washington JHS
1325 Park Rd 61354
Lori Madden, prin.
300/6-8
815-223-0301
Fax 223-0732

St. Bede Academy
Route 6 W 61354
Michelle Mershon, prin.
400/9-12
815-223-3140
Fax 223-8580

Petersburg, Menard, Pop. 2,223
PORTA CUSD 202
PO Box 202 62675
Matthew Bruce, supt.
menard.k12.il.us/porta202/
1,400/PK-12
217-632-3803
Fax 632-3221
PORTA HS
PO Box 202 62675
Darren Hartry, prin.
400/9-12
217-632-3216
Fax 632-5446
PORTA JHS
PO Box 202 62675
Jeff Hill, prin.
200/7-8
217-632-3219
Fax 632-5448

Phoenix, Cook, Pop. 2,121
South Holland SD 151
Supt. — See South Holland
Coolidge MS
15500 7th Ave 60426
Patricia Payne, prin.
500/6-8
708-339-5300
Fax 339-5327

Piasa, Macoupin, Pop. 1,800
Southwestern CUSD 9
PO Box 99 62079
Larry Elsea, supt.
www.piasabirds.net
1,800/PK-12
618-729-3221
Fax 729-3764
Southwestern HS
PO Box 100 62079
Bill Wrenn, prin.
600/9-12
618-729-3211
Fax 729-4276
Southwestern MS
PO Box 70 62079
Virgil Moore, prin.
300/7-8
618-729-3217
Fax 729-9231

Pinckneyville, Perry, Pop. 5,407
Pinckneyville Community HSD 101
600 E Water St 62274
Sandra Jerrells, supt.
500/9-12
618-357-5013
Fax 357-6045
Pinckneyville HS
600 E Water St 62274
Jon Green, prin.
500/9-12
618-357-5013
Fax 357-6045

Pinckneyville SD 50
301 W Mulberry St 62274
Tim O'Leary, supt.
www.p50.perry.k12.il.us/education/components/sectio
nl
600/K-8
618-357-5161
Fax 357-8731
Pinckneyville MS
700 E Water St 62274
Ryan Swan, prin.
400/4-8
618-357-2724

Piper City, Ford, Pop. 756
Tri-Point CUSD 6-J
Supt. — See Kempton
Tri-Point MS
PO Box 158 60959
Jerry Tkachuk, prin.
300/PK-K, 4-8
815-686-2247
Fax 686-2663

Pittsfield, Pike, Pop. 4,544
Pikeland CUSD 10
512 S Madison St 62363
Paula Hawley, supt.
1,400/PK-12
217-285-2147
Fax 285-5059
Pikeland Community S
601 Piper Ln 62363
Daniel Brue, prin.
600/3-8
217-285-9462
Fax 285-9551
Pittsfield HS
201 E Higbee St 62363
Gary Woods, prin.
400/9-12
217-285-6888
Fax 285-9583

Plainfield, Will, Pop. 20,162
Plainfield CCSD 202
15732 S Howard St 60544
Dr. John R. Harper, supt.
www.learningcommunity202.org
18,900/PK-12
815-577-4000
Fax 436-7824
Drauden Point MS
1911 Drauden Rd,
Anthony Manville, prin.
1,300/6-8
815-577-4900
Fax 439-9385
Heritage Grove MS
12450 S Van Dyke Rd,
Stephen Diveley, prin.
1,100/6-8
815-439-4810
Fax 436-4661

Indian Trail MS | 800/6-8
1005 N Eastern Ave 60544 | 815-436-6128
Deborah Livingston, prin. | Fax 436-7536
Jones MS, 15320 W Wallin Dr 60544 | 6-8
Daniel Thorse, prin. | 815-267-3600
Plainfield HS | 2,000/9-12
611 Fort Beggs Dr 60544 | 815-436-3200
Lane Abrell, prin. | Fax 439-2882
Plainfield North HS | 9-12
12005 S 248th Ave, | 815-609-8506
Dr. Peter Pasteris, prin. | Fax 254-6138
Plainfield South HS | 2,500/9-12
7800 Caton Farm Rd, | 815-439-5555
Daniel Goggins, prin. | Fax 436-5108
Timber Ridge MS | 1,200/6-8
2101 S Bronk Rd, | 815-439-3410
Glenna Adams, prin. | Fax 439-3412

Troy CCSD 30 C | 3,500/PK-8
5800 Theodore Dr, | 815-577-6760
Lawrence Wiers, supt. | Fax 577-3795
www.troy30c.org/
Troy MS, 5800 Theodore Dr, | 1,200/6-8
Jeffrey N. Libowitz, prin. | 815-230-9920

Christ Academy | 50/9-12
23756 W 127th St, | 630-922-6084
 | Fax 436-6381

Plano, Kendall, Pop. 5,576
Plano CUSD 88 | 1,400/PK-12
800 S Hale St 60545 | 630-552-8978
William Woody, supt. | Fax 552-8548
www.plano88.org/
Plano HS | 400/9-12
704 W Abe St 60545 | 630-552-3178
Bill Johnson, prin. | Fax 552-7792
Plano MS | 300/6-8
804 S Hale St 60545 | 630-552-3608
Wayne Czyz, prin. | Fax 552-3802

Pleasant Hill, Pike, Pop. 1,012
Pleasant Hill CUSD 3 | 400/PK-12
PO Box 207 62366 | 217-734-2311
Michael Dempsey, supt. | Fax 734-2629
www.phwolves.com/
Pleasant Hill HS | 100/9-12
PO Box 207 62366 | 217-734-2311
James Heafner, prin. | Fax 734-2725

Pleasant Plains, Sangamon, Pop. 758
Pleasant Plains CUSD 8 | 1,300/PK-12
PO Box 20 62677 | 217-626-1041
Maureen Talbert, supt. | Fax 626-1082
ppcusd8.org
Pleasant Plains HS | 400/9-12
PO Box 320 62677 | 217-626-1044
Mike Ward, prin. | Fax 626-1667
Pleasant Plains MS | 400/5-8
2455 N Farmingdale Rd 62677 | 217-626-1061
John Marsaglia, prin. | Fax 626-2272

Polo, Ogle, Pop. 2,485
Polo CUSD 222 | 800/PK-12
100 S Union Ave 61064 | 815-946-3815
Christopher Rademacher, supt. | Fax 946-2493
Aplington MS | 200/6-8
610 E Mason St 61064 | 815-946-2519
Andrew Faivre, prin. | Fax 946-2537
Polo Community HS | 300/9-12
100 S Union Ave 61064 | 815-946-3314
Andy Siegfried, prin. | Fax 946-2493

Pontiac, Livingston, Pop. 11,463
Livingston AVC |
1100 E Indiana Ave 61764 | 815-842-2557
Amy Smith, dir. | Fax 842-1005
pontiac.k12.il.us/lavc/lavc.htm
Livingston AVC | Vo/Tech
1100 E Indiana Ave 61764 | 815-842-2557
Amy Smith, dir. | Fax 842-1005

Pontiac CCSD 429 | 1,300/PK-8
117 W Livingston St 61764 | 815-844-5632
Steve Graham, supt. | Fax 844-5773
www.p429.k12.il.us/
Pontiac JHS | 500/6-8
600 N Morrow St 61764 | 815-842-4343
Judy Donze, prin. | Fax 844-6230

Pontiac Township HSD 90 | 900/9-12
1100 E Indiana Ave 61764 | 815-844-6113
Harlen Cotter, supt. | Fax 844-6116
www.pontiac.k12.il.us
Pontiac HS | 900/9-12
1100 E Indiana Ave 61764 | 815-844-6113
James Drengwitz, prin. | Fax 844-6116

Poplar Grove, Boone, Pop. 2,182
North Boone CUSD 200 | 900/PK-12
17641 Poplar Grove Rd 61065 | 815-765-3322
Michael Houselog, supt. | Fax 765-2053
www.nbcusd.org
North Boone HS | 400/9-12
17823 Poplar Grove Rd 61065 | 815-765-3311
Christine Troller, prin. | Fax 765-3316
North Boone MS | 7-8
17641 Poplar Grove Rd 61065 | 815-765-9274
Kristi Crawford, prin. | Fax 765-9275

Port Byron, Rock Island, Pop. 1,575
Riverdale CUSD 100 | 1,200/PK-12
9624 256th St N 61275 | 309-523-3184
David Bills, supt. | Fax 523-3550
www.riroe.k12.il.us/riroe/riverdale/
Riverdale HS | 400/9-12
9622 256th St N 61275 | 309-523-3181
James Boyd, prin. | Fax 523-2885
Riverdale MS | 300/6-8
9822 256th St N 61275 | 309-523-3131
Ron Jacobs, prin. | Fax 523-3934

Posen, Cook, Pop. 4,869
Posen-Robbins ESD 143-5 | 1,500/PK-8
14025 S Harrison Ave 60469 | 708-388-7200
Gregory Wright, supt. | Fax 388-3868
Other Schools – See Robbins

Princeton, Bureau, Pop. 7,539
Princeton ESD 115 | 1,000/K-8
506 E Dover Rd 61356 | 815-875-3162
Tim Smith, supt. | Fax 875-3101
Logan JHS | 400/6-8
302 W Central Ave 61356 | 815-875-6415
William Gregory, prin. | Fax 872-0034

Princeton HSD 500 | 600/9-12
103 S Euclid Ave 61356 | 815-875-3308
Andrew Bertram, supt. | Fax 875-8525
www.phs-il.org
Princeton HS | 600/9-12
103 S Euclid Ave 61356 | 815-875-3308
Kirk Haring, prin. | Fax 875-8525

Princeton Christian Academy | 100/PK-8
21890 US Highway 34 61356 | 815-875-2933
Marty Kiser, prin. | Fax 875-8113

Princeville, Peoria, Pop. 1,551
Princeville CUSD 326 | 700/PK-12
302 Cordis Ave 61559 | 309-385-2213
Kathryn Hanneken, supt. | Fax 385-1823
www.princeville326.org/
Princeville HS | 200/9-12
302 Cordis Ave 61559 | 309-385-4660
Jim Colyott, prin. | Fax 385-1110

Prophetstown, Whiteside, Pop. 1,970
Prophetstown-Lyndon-Tampico CUSD 3 | 1,000/PK-12
310 W Riverside Dr 61277 | 815-537-5101
Dave Rogers, supt. | Fax 537-5102
wside.k12.il.us/phs/default.htm
Prophetstown HS | 300/9-12
310 W Riverside Dr 61277 | 815-537-5161
Rochelle Streeter, prin. | Fax 537-5102
Other Schools – See Tampico

Prospect Heights, Cook, Pop. 16,807
Prospect Heights SD 23 | 1,500/PK-8
700 N Schoenbeck Rd 60070 | 847-870-3850
Dr. Gregory P. Guarrine, supt. | Fax 870-3896
www.d23.org/
MacArthur MS | 600/6-8
700 N Schoenbeck Rd 60070 | 847-870-3879
Dr. Debra Wilson, prin. | Fax 870-3881

Quincy, Adams, Pop. 39,922
Quincy Area Vocational Technical Center |
219 Baldwin Dr 62301 | 217-224-3775
Ron Baugher, dir. | Fax 221-4800
www.qps.org/qavtc/
Quincy Area Vocational Technical Center | Vo/Tech
219 Baldwin Dr 62301 | 217-224-3775
Ron Baugher, dir. | Fax 221-4800

Quincy SD 172 | 6,800/PK-12
1444 Maine St 62301 | 217-223-8700
Thomas Leahy, supt. | Fax 228-7162
www.qps.org
Quincy JHS | 1,600/7-9
100 S 14th St 62301 | 217-222-3073
Diane Glaub, prin. | Fax 228-7185
Quincy SHS | 1,700/10-12
3322 Maine St 62301 | 217-224-3770
Terry Ellerman, prin. | Fax 228-7149

Blessing Hospital | Post-Sec.
PO Box 7005 62305 | 217-223-8400
Blessing-Rieman College of Nursing | Post-Sec.
PO Box 7005 62305 | 217-228-5520
Gem City College | Post-Sec.
700 State St 62301 | 217-222-0391
John Wood Community College | Post-Sec.
150 S 48th St 62305 | 217-224-6500
Quincy Notre Dame HS | 500/9-12
1400 S 11th St 62301 | 217-223-2479
Raymond Heilmann, prin. | Fax 223-0023
Quincy University | Post-Sec.
1800 College Ave 62301 | 217-222-8020
Vatterott College | Post-Sec.
501 N 3rd St 62301 | 217-224-0600

Ramsey, Fayette, Pop. 1,052
Ramsey CUSD 204 | 500/PK-12
716 W 6th St 62080 | 618-423-2335
Charles Stortzum, supt. | Fax 423-2314
www.ramsey.fayette.k12.il.us/
Ramsey HS | 100/9-12
716 W 6th St 62080 | 618-423-2333
Nick Casey, prin. | Fax 423-2314

Rantoul, Champaign, Pop. 13,009
Rantoul CSD 137 | 2,200/PK-8
400 E Wabash Ave 61866 | 217-893-4171
William Trankina, supt. | Fax 892-4313
www.rcs.k12.il.us/
Eater JHS, 400 E Wabash Ave 61866 | 300/7-8
Mike Penicook, prin. | 217-892-2115

Rantoul Township HSD 193 | 800/9-12
200 S Sheldon St 61866 | 217-892-2151
David Requa, supt. | Fax 892-4442
www.rths.k12.il.us
Rantoul Township HS | 800/9-12
200 S Sheldon St 61866 | 217-892-2151
Scott Amerio, prin. | Fax 892-4442

Raymond, Montgomery, Pop. 925
Panhandle CUSD 2 | 600/PK-12
PO Box 49 62560 | 217-229-4215
Connie Falconer, supt. | Fax 229-4216
Lincolnwood HS | 200/9-12
PO Box 110 62560 | 217-229-4237
Robert Wilson, prin. | Fax 229-3005

Lincolnwood JHS | 100/7-8
PO Box 110 62560 | 217-229-4237
Robert Wilson, prin. | Fax 229-3005

Red Bud, Randolph, Pop. 3,491
Red Bud CUSD 132 | 1,100/PK-12
815 Locust St 62278 | 618-282-3507
John Ingalls, supt. | Fax 282-6151
www.redbud.randolph.k12.il.us/
Red Bud HS | 400/9-12
815 Locust St 62278 | 618-282-3826
Bradley Hall, prin. | Fax 282-6151

Richmond, McHenry, Pop. 1,366
Nippersink SD 2 | 1,600/K-8
PO Box 505 60071 | 815-678-4242
Dr. Paul Hain, supt. | Fax 678-2810
www.nippersinkdistrict2.org
Nippersink MS | 600/6-8
10006 N Main St 60071 | 815-678-7129
Tim Molitor, prin. | Fax 678-7210
Richmond-Burton Community HSD 157 | 700/9-12
PO Box 449 60071 | 815-678-4525
Dan Oest, supt. | Fax 678-4324
www.rbchs.com
Richmond-Burton HS | 700/9-12
PO Box 449 60071 | 815-678-4525
Tom DuBois, prin. | Fax 678-4324

Richton Park, Cook, Pop. 12,883
Rich Township HSD 227 |
Supt. — See Olympia Fields
Rich South Campus HS | 1,100/9-12
5000 Sauk Trl 60471 | 708-679-3000
Roudell Kirkwood, prin. | Fax 679-3168

River Forest, Cook, Pop. 11,483
River Forest SD 90 | 1,400/PK-8
7776 Lake St 60305 | 708-771-8282
Dr. Marlene Kamm, supt. | Fax 771-8291
www.district90.org/
Roosevelt JHS | 700/5-8
7560 Oak Ave 60305 | 708-366-9230
Joanne Trahanas, prin. | Fax 771-8291

Concordia University | Post-Sec.
7400 Augusta St 60305 | 708-771-8300
Dominican University | Post-Sec.
7900 Division St 60305 | 708-366-2490
Trinity HS | 500/9-12
7574 Division St 60305 | 708-771-8383
Michele Whitehead, prin. | Fax 488-2014

River Grove, Cook, Pop. 10,458

Guerin College Preparatory HS | 600/9-12
8001 Belmont Ave 60171 | 708-453-6233
Elizabeth Brown, prin. | Fax 453-6296
Triton College | Post-Sec.
2000 5th Ave 60171 | 708-456-0300

Riverside, Cook, Pop. 8,648
Riverside Brookfield Township HSD 208 | 1,300/9-12
160 Ridgewood Rd 60546 | 708-442-7500
Jack Baldermann, supt. | Fax 447-5570
www.rbhs208.org
Riverside Brookfield Township HS | 1,300/9-12
160 Ridgewood Rd 60546 | 708-442-7500
Jack Baldermann, prin. | Fax 447-5570

Riverside SD 96 | 1,200/PK-8
63 Woodside Rd 60546 | 708-447-5007
Dr. Jonathan Lamberson, supt. | Fax 447-3252
www.district96.org
Hauser JHS | 400/6-8
65 Woodside Rd 60546 | 708-447-3896
Leslie Berman, prin. | Fax 447-5180

Riverton, Sangamon, Pop. 3,140
Riverton CUSD 14 | 1,500/PK-12
PO Box 1010 62561 | 217-629-6009
Tom Mulligan, supt. | Fax 629-6008
sangamon.k12.il.us/riverton/
Riverton HS | 400/9-12
PO Box 560 62561 | 217-629-6003
Bill Lamkey, prin. | Fax 629-6020
Riverton MS | 500/5-8
PO Box 530 62561 | 217-629-6002
Fred Lamkey, prin. | Fax 629-6017

Roanoke, Woodford, Pop. 1,983
Roanoke-Benson CUSD 60 | 600/PK-12
PO Box 320 61561 | 309-923-8921
Lynn Curtis, supt. | Fax 923-7508
www.rb60.com/
Roanoke-Benson HS | 200/9-12
PO Box 320 61561 | 309-923-8401
Mark Zotz, prin. | Fax 923-7508
Other Schools – See Benson

Linn Mennonite Christian S | 50/K-12
1594 County Road 1700 N 61561 | 309-923-5641
Carl Kennell, pres.

Robbins, Cook, Pop. 6,560
Posen-Robbins ESD 143-5 |
Supt. — See Posen
Kellar JHS | 400/6-8
14123 S Lydia Ave 60472 | 708-388-7201
Stacey Hunt, prin. | Fax 388-6177

Robinson, Crawford, Pop. 6,558
Robinson CUSD 2 | 1,700/K-12
PO Box 190 62454 | 618-544-7511
Earl Williams, supt. | Fax 544-9284
www.robinsonschools.com/
Nuttall MS | 400/6-8
400 W Rustic St 62454 | 618-544-8618
Sue Catt, prin. | Fax 544-5304
Robinson HS | 600/9-12
2000 N Cross St 62454 | 618-544-9510
Troy Hickey, prin. | Fax 544-7921

Lincoln Trail College
11220 State Highway 1 62454 — Post-Sec. 618-544-8657

Rochelle, Ogle, Pop. 9,556
Rochelle CCSD 231
444 N 8th St 61068 — 1,800/K-8 815-562-6363
Todd Prusator, supt. — Fax 562-5500
d231.rochelle.net/
Rochelle MS
111 School Ave 61068 — 600/6-8 815-562-7997
Kevin Zilm, prin. — Fax 562-8527
Rochelle Twp. HSD 212
1401 Flagg Rd 61068 — 1,100/9-12 815-562-4161
Douglas Creason, supt. — Fax 562-6693
www.rths.rochelle.net/index.shtml
Rochelle Twp. HS
1401 Flagg Rd 61068 — 1,100/9-12 815-562-4161
Richard Craven, prin. — Fax 562-6693

Rochester, Sangamon, Pop. 2,943
Rochester CUSD 3A
4 Rocket Dr 62563 — 1,900/PK-12 217-498-6210
Dr. Thomas Bertrand, supt. — Fax 498-8045
www.rochester3a.sangamon.k12.il.us
Rochester HS
1 Rocket Dr 62563 — 600/9-12 217-498-9761
Dennis Canny, prin. — Fax 498-9825
Rochester JHS
3 Rocket Dr 62563 — 300/7-8 217-498-9761
Deidre Zobrist, prin. — Fax 498-6204

Rock Falls, Whiteside, Pop. 9,447
Rock Falls ESD 13
602 4th Ave 61071 — 1,000/PK-8 815-626-2604
Jack H. Etnyre, supt. — Fax 626-2627
rfsd13.whitesideroe.org
Rock Falls MS
1701 12th Ave 61071 — 300/6-8 815-626-2626
Jeffrey Brown, prin. — Fax 626-3198
Rock Falls Twp. HSD 301
101 12th Ave 61071 — 700/9-12 815-625-3886
Dr. B. J. Wolf, supt. — Fax 625-3889
Rock Falls Twp. HS
101 12th Ave 61071 — 700/9-12 815-625-3886
Robert Gemeny, prin. — Fax 625-3889

Rockford, Winnebago, Pop. 151,725
Rockford SD 205
201 S Madison St 61104 — 27,400/PK-12 815-966-3101
Dr. Dennis Thompson, supt. — Fax 966-3193
www.rps205.com/
Auburn HS
5110 Auburn St 61101 — 1,700/9-12 815-966-3300
Janice Hawkins, prin. — Fax 966-3911
Eisenhower MS
3525 Spring Creek Rd 61107 — 900/6-8 815-229-2450
Jill Billy, prin. — Fax 229-2456
Flinn MS
2525 Ohio Pkwy 61108 — 900/6-8 815-229-2800
Marcia Strothoff, prin. — Fax 229-2894
Guilford HS
5620 Spring Creek Rd 61114 — 2,000/9-12 815-654-4870
Timothy Kutz, prin. — Fax 654-4901
Jefferson HS
4145 Samuelson Rd 61109 — 1,800/9-12 815-874-9536
Angelina Bua, prin. — Fax 874-2800
Kennedy MS
4664 N Rockton Ave 61103 — 700/6-8 815-654-4880
Theresa Kallstrom, prin. — Fax 654-4874
Lincoln MS
1500 Charles St 61104 — 1,000/6-8 815-229-2400
Michael Valentine, prin. — Fax 229-2420
Rockford East HS
2929 Charles St 61108 — 1,800/9-12 815-229-2100
Peter Paris, prin. — Fax 229-2113
Rockford Environmental Science Academy
1800 Ogilby Rd 61102 — 1,300/6-8 815-489-5509
Keir Rogers, prin. — Fax 966-5360
West MS
1900 N Rockton Ave 61103 — 900/6-8 815-966-3200
Leslie Smith, prin. — Fax 966-3216
Wilson MS
520 N Pierpont Ave 61101 — 500/4-8 815-966-3721
Thomas Schmitt, prin. — Fax 966-8911

Berean Baptist Christian S
5626 Safford Rd 61101 — 300/PK-12 815-962-4841
Douglas E. Swanson, admin. — Fax 962-4851
Boylan Central Catholic HS
4000 Saint Francis Dr 61103 — 1,300/9-12 815-877-0531
Vince McGuire, admin. — Fax 877-2544
Christian Life S
5950 Spring Creek Rd 61114 — 1,100/PK-12 815-877-5749
Dr. R. Jay Nelson, supt. — Fax 877-4358
Educators of Beauty
128 S 5th St 61104 — Post-Sec. 815-969-7030
Keith S
1 Jacoby Pl 61107 — 300/PK-12 815-399-8823
Jon Esler, prin. — Fax 399-2470
North Love Christian S
5301 E Riverside Blvd 61114 — 200/PK-12 815-877-6021
Tom Seeley, prin. — Fax 877-6076
Rockford Business College
730 N Church St 61103 — Post-Sec. 815-965-8616
Rockford Christian S
1401 N Bell School Rd 61107 — 1,100/PK-12 815-399-3465
Randy Taylor, supt. — Fax 391-8004
Rockford College
5050 E State St 61108 — Post-Sec. 815-226-4000
Rockford Lutheran HS
3411 N Alpine Rd 61114 — 600/7-12 815-877-9551
Don Kortze, prin. — Fax 877-4024
Rockford Memorial Hospital
2400 N Rockton Ave 61103 — Post-Sec. 815-971-5000
Rock Valley College
3301 N Mulford Rd 61114 — Post-Sec. 815-654-4250
St. Anthony College of Nursing
5658 E State St 61108 — Post-Sec. 815-395-5100
St. Anthony Medical Center
5666 E State St 61108 — Post-Sec. 815-226-2000

Swedish-American Hospital
1401 E State St 61104 — Post-Sec. 815-968-4400

Rock Island, Rock Island, Pop. 38,857
Rock Island SD 41
2101 6th Ave 61201 — 6,000/PK-12 309-793-5900
Richard Loy, supt. — Fax 793-5905
www.risd41.org/
Edison JHS
4141 9th St 61201 — 400/7-8 309-793-5920
Gary Flecker, prin. — Fax 793-5919
Rock Island HS
1400 25th Ave 61201 — 1,700/9-12 309-793-5950
Terrence Martin, prin. — Fax 793-9866
Washington JHS
3300 18th Ave 61201 — 600/7-8 309-793-5915
Mark Hepner, prin. — Fax 793-5917

Alleman HS
1103 40th St 61201 — 500/9-12 309-786-7793
Colin Letendre, prin. — Fax 786-7834
Augustana College
639 38th St 61201 — Post-Sec. 309-794-7000
Jordan North MS
2825 5 1/2 Ave 61201 — 7-8 309-793-7366
Daniel Lievens, prin.
Trinity College of Nursing
2122 25th Ave 61201 — Post-Sec. 309-779-7700

Rockton, Winnebago, Pop. 5,348
Hononegah Community HSD 207
307 Salem St 61072 — 1,900/9-12 815-624-5010
Dr. Ralph Marshall, supt. — Fax 624-5029
www.hononegah.org
Hononegah Community HS
307 Salem St 61072 — 1,900/9-12 815-624-5005
Judy Rigby, prin. — Fax 624-5025
Rockton SD 140
1050 E Union St 61072 — 1,400/PK-8 815-624-7143
Jean Harezlak, supt. — Fax 624-4640
rockton140.org
Mack MS
11810 Old River Rd 61072 — 500/6-8 815-624-2611
Jay Larson, prin. — Fax 624-5900

Rolling Meadows, Cook, Pop. 24,334
Palatine CCSD 15
Supt. — See Palatine
Plum Grove JHS
2600 Plum Grove Rd 60008 — 800/7-8 847-963-7600
Cheryl Quinn, prin. — Fax 963-7606
Sandburg JHS
2600 Martin Ln 60008 — 700/7-8 847-963-7800
Ed Nelson, prin. — Fax 963-7806

Township HSD 214
Supt. — See Arlington Heights
Rolling Meadows HS
2901 Central Rd 60008 — 1,800/9-12 847-718-5600
Dr. Charles Johns, prin. — Fax 718-5617

Romeoville, Will, Pop. 32,481
Valley View CUSD 365-U
755 Luther Dr 60446 — 15,800/PK-12 815-886-2700
Dr. Phillip Schoffstall, supt. — Fax 886-7294
www.vvsd.org/
Lukancic MS
725 Normantown Rd 60446 — 6-8 815-886-2216
Omar Castillo, prin.
Martinez MS
590 Belmont Dr 60446 — 1,300/6-8 815-886-6100
Kelly Gilbert, prin. — Fax 886-7264
Romeoville HS
100 N Independence Blvd 60446 — 2,400/9-12 815-886-1800
Fax 886-7272

Other Schools – See Bolingbrook

Wilco Area Career Center
500 Wilco Blvd 60446 — 815-838-6941
Katrina Paddick, dir. — Fax 838-1163
www.wilco.k12.il.us
Wilco Area Career Center
500 Wilco Blvd 60446 — Vo/Tech 815-838-6941
Katrinia Paddick, prin. — Fax 838-1163

Lewis University
1 University Pkwy 60446 — Post-Sec. 815-838-0500

Roodhouse, Greene, Pop. 2,229
North Greene Unit SD 3
Supt. — See White Hall
North Greene JHS
403 W North St 62082 — 300/6-8 217-589-4623
Cynthia Carlson, prin. — Fax 589-4028
Roodhouse S
403 W North St 62082 — 400/PK-PK, 4- 217-589-4623
Cynthia Carlson, prin. — Fax 589-4028

Roscoe, Winnebago, Pop. 6,337
Kinnikinnick CCSD 131
5410 Pine Ln 61073 — 2,300/PK-8 815-623-2837
Robert Lauber, supt. — Fax 623-9285
www.kinn131.org
Roscoe MS
6121 Elevator Rd 61073 — 700/6-8 815-623-1884
Julie Cropp, prin. — Fax 623-7604

Roselle, DuPage, Pop. 23,237
Lake Park Community HSD 108
450 Spring Ct 60172 — 1,500/9-12 630-529-4500
Dr. John Butts, supt. — Fax 295-5414
www.lphs.org
Lake Park HS East
600 Medinah Rd 60172 — 1,500/9-12 630-529-4500
Dr. Edward Wardzala, prin. — Fax 295-5212
Lake Park HS West
500 W Bryn Mawr Ave 60172 — 11-12 630-529-4500
Dr. Martin Quinn, prin. — Fax 295-2932

Medinah SD 11
700 E Granville Ave 60172 — 700/K-8 630-893-3737
Dr. Joseph Bailey, supt. — Fax 893-4947
www.medinah.dupage.k12.il.us
Medinah MS
700 E Granville Ave 60172 — 200/6-8 630-893-3838
Dr. Kara Egger, prin. — Fax 893-5198
Roselle SD 12
100 E Walnut St 60172 — 700/K-8 630-529-2091
Dr. Steve Epperson, supt. — Fax 529-2467
www.sd12.k12.il.us/
Roselle MS
500 S Park St 60172 — 300/6-8 630-529-1600
Kathleen Schneiter, prin. — Fax 529-1882

Roseville, McDonough, Pop. 1,043
Monmouth-Roseville CUSD 238
Supt. — See Monmouth
Monmouth-Roseville JHS
200 E Gossett St 61473 — 100/7-8 309-426-2682
Don Farr, prin. — Fax 426-2303

Round Lake, Lake, Pop. 9,333
Round Lake Area SD 116
316 S Rosedale Ct 60073 — 5,400/PK-12 847-270-9000
Dennis Stonewall, supt. — Fax 546-3538
www.rlas.k12.il.org/
Round Lake HS
800 High School Dr 60073 — 1,500/9-12 847-270-9300
Dr. Jeff Brierton, prin. — Fax 546-5872
Round Lake MS, 2000 Lotus Dr 60073 — 7-8 847-270-9400
Paul Flatley, prin.

Roxana, Madison, Pop. 1,524
Roxana CUSD 1
401 Chaffer Ave 62084 — 1,900/PK-12 618-254-7544
David Deets, supt. — Fax 254-7547
www.roxana.k12.il.us
Roxana HS
401 Chaffer Ave 62084 — 600/9-12 618-254-7553
Derek Hacke, prin. — Fax 254-7580
Roxana JHS
401 Chaffer Ave 62084 — 400/6-8 618-254-7561
Laura Montgomery, prin. — Fax 254-8107

Royal, Champaign, Pop. 281
Prairieview CCSD 192
PO Box 27 61871 — 100/K-8 217-583-3300
Victor White, supt. — Fax 583-3391
www.prairieview.k12.il.us
Other Schools – See Thomasboro

Rushville, Schuyler, Pop. 3,144
Schuyler-Industry CUSD 5
740 Maple Ave 62681 — 1,200/PK-12 217-322-4311
R. Mathew Plater, supt. — Fax 322-4398
www.sid5.org
Rushville-Industry HS
730 N Congress St 62681 — 300/9-12 217-322-4316
Donna Sargent, prin. — Fax 322-2844
Schuyler-Industry MS
750 N Congress St 62681 — 400/5-8 217-322-2773
Cindy Ward, prin. — Fax 322-3938

Saint Anne, Kankakee, Pop. 1,188
Saint Anne Community HSD 302
PO Box 630 60964 — 300/9-12 815-427-8141
Kathleen Hickey, supt. — Fax 427-8409
www.sachs.k12.il.us/
Saint Anne Community HS
PO Box 630 60964 — 300/9-12 815-427-8141
Dan Patterson, prin.

Saint Charles, Kane, Pop. 32,010
St. Charles CUSD 303
201 S 7th St 60174 — 12,900/PK-12 630-513-3030
Dr. Barbara Erwin, supt. — Fax 513-5392
www.d303.org
Haines MS
305 S 9th St 60174 — 900/6-8 630-377-4827
Charlie Kyle, prin. — Fax 377-4830
St. Charles East HS
1020 Dunham Rd 60174 — 1,900/9-12 630-584-1100
Bob Miller, prin. — Fax 584-9563
St. Charles North HS
255 Red Gate Rd 60175 — 2,000/9-12 630-443-5700
Kim Zupec, prin. — Fax 443-2769
Thompson MS
705 W Main St 60174 — 900/6-8 630-377-4872
Dr. Pamela Kibbons, prin. — Fax 584-9591
Wredling MS
1200 Dunham Rd 60174 — 1,200/6-8 630-443-3360
Melissa Dockum, prin. — Fax 443-2770

Saint Elmo, Fayette, Pop. 1,408
St. Elmo CUSD 202
1200 N Walnut St 62458 — 500/K-12 618-829-3264
Deborah Philpot, supt. — Fax 829-5161
www.stelmo.org/
Saint Elmo HS
300 W 12th St 62458 — 100/9-12 618-829-3227
Brian Garrard, prin. — Fax 829-5161
Saint Elmo JHS
300 W 12th St 62458 — 100/7-8 618-829-3227
Brian Garrard, prin. — Fax 829-5161

Saint Jacob, Madison, Pop. 897
Triad CUSD 2
Supt. — See Troy
Triad MS
9539 US Highway 40 62281 — 900/6-8 618-644-5511
Dale Sauer, prin. — Fax 644-9435

Saint Joseph, Champaign, Pop. 3,266
St. Joseph-Ogden Community HSD 305
PO Box 890 61873 — 500/9-12 217-469-2586
Dr. Victor E. Zimmerman, supt. — Fax 469-7321
www.sjo.k12.il.us/
St. Joseph-Ogden HS
PO Box 890 61873 — 500/9-12 217-469-2332
Chad Uphoff, prin. — Fax 469-8290

Salem, Marion, Pop. 7,747
Salem Community HSD 600 — 800/9-12
1200 N Broadway Ave 62881 — 618-548-0727
Barbara Smith, supt. — Fax 548-8021
www.salemhigh.com
Salem Community HS — 800/9-12
1200 N Broadway Ave 62881 — 618-548-0727
Brad Detering, prin. — Fax 548-8021

Salem SD 111 — 1,000/K-8
1300 Hawthorn Rd 62881 — 618-548-7702
Mark Cartwright, supt. — Fax 548-7714
www.salem111.com
Salem Franklin Park JHS — 600/4-8
1325 N Franklin St 62881 — 618-548-7704
David Conklin, prin. — Fax 548-7712

Sandoval, Marion, Pop. 1,392
Sandoval CUSD 501 — 600/PK-12
859 W Missouri Ave 62882 — 618-247-3233
Dr. Terry Bethel, supt. — Fax 247-3243
Sandoval HS — 200/9-12
859 W Missouri Ave 62882 — 618-247-3361
Mike Green, prin. — Fax 247-3243
Sandoval JHS — 100/7-8
859 W Missouri Ave 62882 — 618-247-3361
Mike Green, prin. — Fax 247-3243

Sandwich, DeKalb, Pop. 6,820
Indian Valley Vocational Center —
600 Lions Rd 60548 — 815-786-9873
Ron Pieper, dir. — Fax 786-6928
www.indianvalley.org
Indian Valley Vocational Center — Vo/Tech
600 Lions Rd 60548 — 815-786-9873
Ron Pieper, dir. — Fax 786-6928

Sandwich CUSD 430 — 2,500/PK-12
720 Wells St 60548 — 815-786-2187
Rick Schmitt, supt. — Fax 786-6229
www.sandwich430.org
Sandwich Community HS — 800/9-12
515 Lions Rd 60548 — 815-786-2157
Gary Close, prin. — Fax 786-2632
Sandwich MS — 600/6-8
600 Wells St 60548 — 815-786-2138
B.J. Richardson, prin. — Fax 786-6606

Sauk Village, Cook, Pop. 10,550
Community Consolidated SD 168 — 2,700/PK-8
21899 Torrence Ave 60411 — 708-758-1610
Dr. Thomas Ryan, supt. — Fax 758-5929
www.d168.org
Rickover JHS — 600/6-8
22151 Torrence Ave 60411 — 708-758-1900
Rudolph Williams, prin. — Fax 758-1601

Savanna, Carroll, Pop. 3,376
West Carroll CUSD 314
Supt. — See Thomson
West Carroll HS — 200/9-12
500 Cradmoor St 61074 — 815-273-7715
Mary Bush, prin. — Fax 273-7819

Scales Mound, Jo Daviess, Pop. 394
Scales Mound CUSD 211 — 300/PK-12
210 Main St 61075 — 815-845-2215
Dr. Barbara Sloan, supt. — Fax 845-2238
www.scalesmound.net
Scales Mound HS — 100/9-12
210 Main St 61075 — 815-845-2215
Barbara Sloan, prin. — Fax 845-2238
Scales Mound JHS — 100/6-8
210 Main St 61075 — 815-845-2215
Matthew Wiederhott, prin. — Fax 845-2238

Schaumburg, Cook, Pop. 74,342
Schaumburg CCSD 54 — 14,900/PK-8
524 E Schaumburg Rd 60194 — 847-357-5000
Ed Rafferty, supt. — Fax 357-5006
www.sd54.org/
Addams JHS — 800/7-8
700 S Springinsguth Rd 60193 — 847-357-5900
John Schmelzer, prin. — Fax 357-5901
Frost JHS — 700/7-8
320 W Wise Rd 60193 — 847-357-6800
Andrew DuRoss, prin. — Fax 357-6801
Keller JHS — 600/7-8
820 Bode Rd 60194 — 847-357-6500
Stephen Kern, prin. — Fax 357-6501
Other Schools – See Elk Grove Village, Hoffman Estates

Township HSD 211
Supt. — See Palatine
Schaumburg HS — 2,600/9-12
1100 W Schaumburg Rd 60194 — 847-755-4600
Sharon Cross, prin. — Fax 755-4623

Argosy University/Chicago Northwest — Post-Sec.
1000 N Plaza Dr Ste 100 60173 — 847-290-7400
Keller Graduate School — Post-Sec.
1051 Perimeter Dr 60173 — 847-330-0040
Lake Forest Graduate Sch. of Management — Post-Sec.
1295 N Algonquin Rd 60196 — 847-576-1212
Roosevelt University — Post-Sec.
1400 N Roosevelt Blvd 60173 — 847-619-8600
Schaumburg Christian S — 1,300/PK-12
200 N Roselle Rd 60194 — 847-885-3230
James White, prin. — Fax 885-3354
The Illinois Institute of Art — Post-Sec.
1000 N Plaza Dr 60173 — 847-619-3450

Schiller Park, Cook, Pop. 11,657
Schiller Park SD 81 — 1,300/PK-8
4050 Wagner Ave 60176 — 847-671-1816
Dr. Roberta Taylor, supt. — Fax 671-1872
www.sd81.org
Lincoln MS — 400/6-8
4050 Wagner Ave 60176 — 847-678-2916
Brian Minarcik, prin. — Fax 678-4059

Sciota, McDonough, Pop. 56
West Prairie CUSD 103
Supt. — See Colchester

West Prairie HS — 300/9-12
18575 E 800th St 61475 — 309-456-3750
Jeff Bryon, prin. — Fax 456-3997

Seneca, LaSalle, Pop. 2,057
Seneca CCSD 170 — 600/PK-8
174 Oak St 61360 — 815-357-8744
Larry Walker, supt. — Fax 357-1516
www.sgs170.org
Seneca MS South Campus — 300/5-8
410 S Main St 61360 — 815-357-8744
Michael Matteson, prin. — Fax 357-1078
Seneca Township HSD 160 — 500/9-12
PO Box 20 61360 — 815-357-5000
Rodney Engstrom, supt. — Fax 357-5050
www.senecahs.org/
Seneca HS — 500/9-12
PO Box 20 61360 — 815-357-5000
Doug Evans, prin. — Fax 357-1216

Serena, LaSalle
Community Unit SD 2 — 900/K-12
PO Box 107 60549 — 815-496-2850
Daniel P. Joyce, supt. — Fax 496-2987
www.unit2.net/
Serena Community HS — 300/9-12
PO Box 107 60549 — 815-496-2361
Roy E. Smith, prin. — Fax 496-2987

Sesser, Franklin, Pop. 2,122
Sesser-Valier CUSD 196 — 800/PK-12
4626 State Highway 154 62884 — 618-625-5105
Jason Henry, supt. — Fax 625-6696
www.s-v.frnkln.k12.il.us/
Sesser-Valier HS — 200/9-12
4626 State Highway 154 62884 — 618-625-5105
Ron Van Horn, prin. — Fax 625-6696
Sesser-Valier JHS — 200/6-8
4626 State Highway 154 62884 — 618-625-5105
Stephen N. Laur, prin. — Fax 625-6696

Shabbona, DeKalb, Pop. 927
Indian Creek CUSD 425 — 900/K-12
506 S Shabbona Rd 60550 — 815-824-2197
Dr. Bruce Bauer, supt. — Fax 824-2199
www.indiancreekschools.org
Indian Creek HS — 300/9-12
506 S Shabbona Rd 60550 — 815-824-2197
Jim Hammack, prin. — Fax 824-2199
Other Schools – See Waterman

Shannon, Carroll, Pop. 813
Eastland CUSD 308
Supt. — See Lanark
Eastland MS — 300/4-8
601 S Chestnut St 61078 — 815-864-2300
Darcie Feltmeyer, prin. — Fax 864-2281

Shelbyville, Shelby, Pop. 4,805
Shelbyville CUSD 4 — 1,200/PK-12
720 W Main St 62565 — 217-774-4626
Robert Verdun, supt. — Fax 774-2521
shelbyville.k12.il.us/
Moulton MS — 500/4-8
1001 W North 6th St 62565 — 217-774-2169
Jacque Eberspacher, prin. — Fax 774-3042
Shelbyville HS — 400/9-12
1001 W North 6th St 62565 — 217-774-3926
Kevin Ross, prin. — Fax 774-5836

Sparks College — Post-Sec.
131 S Morgan St 62565 — 217-774-5112

Sherrard, Mercer, Pop. 685
Sherrard CUSD 200 — 1,700/PK-12
PO Box 369 61281 — 309-593-4075
Robert Cillum, supt. — Fax 593-4078
www.sherrard.us
Sherrard HS — 600/9-12
4701 176th Ave 61281 — 309-593-2175
Shane Kazubowski, prin. — Fax 593-2775
Sherrard JHS — 300/7-8
4701 176th Ave 61281 — 309-593-2135
Jim Lee, prin. — Fax 593-2143

Sidell, Vermilion, Pop. 607
Jamaica CUSD 12 — 500/PK-12
7087 N 600 East Rd 61876 — 217-288-9306
Mark Janesky, supt. — Fax 288-9306
Jamaica HS — 100/9-12
7087 N 600 East Rd 61876 — 217-288-9392
Mark Janesky, prin.
Jamaica JHS — 100/6-8
7087 N 600 East Rd 61876 — 217-288-9394
Kevin Lipke, prin.

Silvis, Rock Island, Pop. 7,341
Silvis SD 34 — 700/PK-8
1305 5th Ave 61282 — 309-792-9325
Rene Noppe, supt. — Fax 792-8092
www.silvis34.com
Silvis JHS, 1305 5th Ave 61282 — 200/6-8
Ray Bergles, prin. — 309-792-3511

Skokie, Cook, Pop. 63,633
Fairview SD 72 — 300/K-8
7040 Laramie Ave 60077 — 847-929-1050
Dr. Cindy Whittaker, supt. — Fax 929-1060
www.fairview.k12.il.us
Fairview South S — 5-8
7040 Laramie Ave 60077 — 847-929-1048
David Russo, prin. — Fax 929-1058

Niles Township HSD 219 — 4,800/9-12
7700 Gross Point Rd 60077 — 847-626-3000
Neil Codell, supt. — Fax 626-3090
www.niles-hs.k12.il.us
Niles North HS — 2,300/9-12
9800 Lawler Ave 60077 — 847-626-2000
Robert Freeman, prin. — Fax 626-3340
Niles West HS — 2,500/9-12
5701 Oakton St 60077 — 847-626-2500
Dale Vogler, prin. — Fax 626-3700

Skokie SD 68 — 1,600/K-8
9440 Kenton Ave 60076 — 847-676-9000
Dr. Frances McTague, supt. — Fax 676-9232
www.sd68.k12.il.us
Old Orchard JHS — 700/6-8
9310 Kenton Ave 60076 — 847-676-9010
Margaret Clauson, prin. — Fax 676-3827
Skokie SD 69 — 1,400/PK-8
5050 Madison St 60077 — 847-675-7666
Dr. Rebecca L. Nelson, supt. — Fax 675-7675
www.skokie69.k12.il.us
Lincoln JHS — 500/6-8
7839 Lincoln Ave 60077 — 847-676-3545
James Morrison, prin. — Fax 676-3595
Skokie SD 73-5 — 1,100/PK-8
8000 E Prairie Rd 60076 — 847-673-1220
Vicki Gunther, supt. — Fax 673-1565
www.skokie735.k12.il.us/
McCracken MS — 400/6-8
8000 E Prairie Rd 60076 — 847-673-1220
Kate Donegan, prin. — Fax 673-1282

Computer Systems Institute — Post-Sec.
8930 Gross Point Rd 60077 — 847-967-5030
Fasman Yeshiva HS — 200/9-12
7135 Carpenter Rd 60077 — 847-982-2500
Rabbi Moshe Wender, prin. — Fax 674-6381
Hebrew Theological College — Post-Sec.
7135 Carpenter Rd 60077 — 847-982-2500
Knowledge Systems Institute — Post-Sec.
3420 Main St 60076 — 847-679-3135
Olympia College — Post-Sec.
9811 Woods Dr # 200 60077 — 847-470-0277
Ort Technical Institute — Post-Sec.
5440 Fargo Ave 60077 — 847-324-5588

Somonauk, DeKalb, Pop. 1,408
Somonauk CUSD 432 — 1,000/K-8
PO Box 278 60552 — 815-498-2314
M. Susan Workman, supt. — Fax 498-9523
www.somonauk.net/
Somonauk HS — 300/9-12
PO Box 278 60552 — 815-498-2314
David Mantzke, prin. — Fax 498-9841
Somonauk MS — 300/5-8
PO Box 278 60552 — 815-498-1866
Jim Prather, prin. — Fax 498-1647

South Beloit, Winnebago, Pop. 5,435
South Beloit CUSD 320 — 1,100/PK-12
850 Hayes Ave 61080 — 815-389-3478
Michael Duffy, supt. — Fax 389-3477
www.southbeloitschooldistrict.org
South Beloit HS — 200/9-12
245 Prairie Hill Rd 61080 — 815-389-9004
James Miglin, prin. — Fax 389-9268
South Beloit JHS — 200/7-8
840 Blackhawk Blvd 61080 — 815-389-1421
Michael Duffy, prin. — Fax 389-8811

South Elgin, Kane, Pop. 20,229
SD U-46
Supt. — See Elgin
Kenyon Woods MS — 7-8
1515 Raymond St 60177 — 847-289-6685
Sue Welu, prin. — Fax 628-6166
South Elgin HS — 9-12
760 E Main St 60177 — 847-289-3760
Dr. Jean Bowen, prin. — Fax 888-7014

South Holland, Cook, Pop. 22,087
South Holland SD 150 — 1,100/PK-8
848 E 170th St 60473 — 708-339-4240
Dr. Priscilla Palmer, supt. — Fax 339-4244
www.illinois-schools.com/sd150/
McKinley JHS — 400/6-8
16949 Cottage Grove Ave 60473 — 708-339-8500
George Harris, prin.

South Holland SD 151 — 1,500/PK-8
320 E 161st Pl 60473 — 708-339-1516
Dr. Douglas C. Hamilton, supt. — Fax 331-7600
www.shsd151.org
Other Schools – See Phoenix

Thornton Twp. HSD 205 — 6,600/9-12
465 E 170th St 60473 — 708-225-4000
Dr. J. Kamala Buckner, supt. — Fax 225-4004
www.district205.net
Thornwood HS — 2,300/9-12
17101 S Park Ave 60473 — 708-225-4701
Gary Lester, prin. — Fax 225-5033
Other Schools – See Dolton, Harvey

Seton Academy — 300/9-12
16100 Seton Dr 60473 — 708-333-6300
Mary Iannucilli, prin. — Fax 333-1534
South Suburban College of Cook County — Post-Sec.
15800 State St 60473 — 708-596-2000

Sparland, Marshall, Pop. 496
Midland CUSD 7
Supt. — See Lacon
Midland MS — 300/5-8
901 Hilltop Dr 61565 — 309-469-3131
Daniel Mair, prin. — Fax 469-5701

Sparta, Randolph, Pop. 4,434
Sparta CUSD 140 — 1,800/PK-12
203B Dean Ave 62286 — 618-443-5331
Karen Perry, supt. — Fax 443-2023
www.sparta.k12.il.us
Sparta HS — 500/9-12
205 W Hood St 62286 — 618-443-4341
Gregory Jones, prin. — Fax 443-5059
Sparta-Lincoln MS — 500/4-8
203A Dean Ave 62286 — 618-443-5331
Francesca Vallo, prin. — Fax 443-2892

Springfield, Sangamon, Pop. 113,586
Capital Area Career Center
 2201 Toronto Rd, 217-529-5431
 John Bailey, supt. Fax 529-7614
Capital Area Career Center Vo/Tech
 2201 Toronto Rd, 217-529-5431
 Jim Jones, prin. Fax 529-7861

Springfield SD 186 14,500/PK-12
 1900 W Monroe St 62704 217-525-3000
 Dr. Diane Rutledge, supt. Fax 525-3005
 www.springfield.k12.il.us/
Franklin MS 800/6-8
 1200 Outer Park Dr 62704 217-525-3164
 Kristine Huddleston, prin. Fax 525-7937
Grant MS 700/6-8
 1800 W Monroe St 62704 217-525-3170
 Kay Dimon, prin. Fax 525-3390
Jefferson MS 700/6-8
 3001 S Allis St 62703 217-525-3176
 J. Michael Zimmers, prin. Fax 525-3293
Lanphier HS 1,300/9-12
 1300 N 11th St 62702 217-525-3080
 Larry Rowe, prin. Fax 525-3084
Lincoln Magnet MS 300/6-8
 300 S 11th St 62703 217-525-3236
 Margaret Kruger, prin. Fax 525-3294
Springfield HS 1,400/9-12
 101 S Lewis St 62704 217-525-3100
 Chuck Hoots, prin. Fax 525-3122
Springfield Southeast HS 1,400/9-12
 2350 E Ash St 62703 217-525-3130
 Tammie Bolden, prin. Fax 525-3139
Washington MS 600/6-8
 2300 E Jackson St 62703 217-525-3182
 Susan Palmer, prin. Fax 525-3319

Calvary Academy 400/K-12
 1730 W Jefferson St 62702 217-546-9700
 Donna Squires, prin. Fax 546-1926
Lincoln Land Community College Post-Sec.
 5250 Shepherd Rd 62703 217-786-2200
Lutheran HS 200/9-12
 3500 W Washington St, 217-546-6363
 Ralph Nitz, prin. Fax 546-6489
Robert Morris College Post-Sec.
 3101 Montvale Dr 62704 217-793-2500
Sacred Heart-Griffin HS 800/9-12
 1200 W Washington St 62702 217-787-1595
 Sr. Margaret Joanne Grueter, prin. Fax 787-9856
St. John's College Post-Sec.
 421 N 9th St 62702 217-525-5628
St. John's Hospital Post-Sec.
 800 E Carpenter St 62769 217-544-6464
Southern Illinois University Post-Sec.
 PO Box 19621 62794 217-545-8000
Springfield College in Illinois Post-Sec.
 1500 N 5th St 62702 217-525-1420
Undergraduate School of Cosmetology Post-Sec.
 PO Box 195 62705 217-753-8990
University of Illinois at Springfield Post-Sec.
 PO Box 19243 62794 217-206-6600
Ursuline Academy 200/9-12
 1400 N 5th St 62702 217-523-5169
 Dan Manfredo, prin. Fax 523-2131

Spring Grove, McHenry, Pop. 4,715
Fox Lake Grade SD 114 900/PK-8
 29067 W Grass Lake Rd 60081 847-973-4027
 John Donnellan, supt. Fax 973-4010
 www.flgs.lake.k12.il.us
Other Schools – See Fox Lake

Spring Valley, Bureau, Pop. 5,362
Hall HSD 502 400/9-12
 800 W Erie St 61362 815-664-2234
 Leo Johnson, supt. Fax 664-2300
Hall HS 400/9-12
 800 W Erie St 61362 815-664-2100
 Patti Lunn, prin. Fax 664-2300

Spring Valley CCSD 99 700/PK-8
 800 N Richards St 61362 815-664-4242
 Daniel Marenda, supt. Fax 664-2205
Kennedy S 500/PK-PK, 3-
 800 N Richards St 61362 815-664-4601
 Jim Hermes, prin. Fax 664-2205

Stanford, McLean, Pop. 662
Olympia CUSD 16 1,700/PK-12
 903 E 800 North Rd 61774 309-379-6011
 Donald F. Hahn, supt. Fax 379-2328
 www.olympia.org
Olympia HS 700/9-12
 7832 N 100 East Rd 61774 309-379-5911
 Lance Thurman, prin. Fax 379-2583
Olympia MS 400/7-8
 911 E 800 North Rd 61774 309-379-5941
 Steve Wilder, prin. Fax 379-5411

Staunton, Macoupin, Pop. 5,049
Staunton CUSD 6 1,200/PK-12
 801 N Deneen St 62088 618-635-2962
 Kyle Hlafka, supt. Fax 635-2994
 www.staunton.macoupin.k12.il.us/
Staunton HS 400/9-12
 801 N Deneen St 62088 618-635-3838
 Loren Beswick, prin. Fax 635-2834
Staunton JHS 300/6-8
 801 N Deneen St 62088 618-635-3831
 Mark Skertich, prin. Fax 635-4637

Steeleville, Randolph, Pop. 2,033
Steeleville CUSD 138 400/K-12
 701 S Sparta St 62288 618-965-3432
 Stephanie Mulholland, supt. Fax 965-3433
Steeleville HS 100/9-12
 701 S Sparta St 62288 618-965-3432
 Jennifer Hagel, prin. Fax 965-3433

Steger, Cook, Pop. 10,035
Steger SD 194 1,600/PK-8
 3753 Park Ave 60475 708-755-0022
 Jeanne Domink, supt. Fax 755-9512
 www.sd194.org/
Columbia Central MS 400/6-8
 94 Richton Rd 60475 708-755-0021
 Jeff Nelson, prin. Fax 755-1877

St. Liborius S 100/5-8
 3440 Halsted Blvd 60475 708-754-0192
 Mary Jane Bartley, prin. Fax 755-3982

Sterling, Whiteside, Pop. 15,272
Sterling CUSD 5 3,500/PK-12
 410 E Le Fevre Rd 61081 815-626-5050
 Dr. Wil Booker, supt. Fax 622-4113
 www.sterlingschools.org
Challand MS 800/6-8
 1700 6th Ave 61081 815-626-3300
 Suzzette Hesser, prin. Fax 622-4173
Sterling HS 1,100/9-12
 1608 4th Ave 61081 815-625-6800
 Gerald Binder, prin. Fax 622-4157

Whiteside AVC, 1608 5th Ave 61081 900/K-8
 Wilma Hewitt, supt. 815-626-5810
Whiteside AVC, 1608 5th Ave 61081 Vo/Tech
 Wilma Hewitt, prin. 815-626-5810

Educators of Beauty Post-Sec.
 211 E 3rd St 61081 815-625-0247
Newman Central Catholic HS 200/9-12
 1101 W 23rd St 61081 815-625-0500
 Rev. Paul Lipinski, admin. Fax 625-8444

Stillman Valley, Ogle, Pop. 1,072
Meridian CUSD 223 1,800/PK-12
 207 W Main St 61084 815-645-2606
 Robert Prusator, supt. Fax 645-4325
 www.meridian223.org
Meridian JHS 400/6-8
 207 W Main St 61084 815-645-2277
 William Davidson, prin. Fax 645-8181
Stillman Valley HS 500/9-12
 425 S Pine St 61084 815-645-2291
 Michael Nelson, prin. Fax 645-8145

Stockton, Jo Daviess, Pop. 1,882
Stockton CUSD 206 600/PK-12
 500 N Rush St 61085 815-947-3321
 Dr. Kevin Sullivan, supt. Fax 947-2114
 www.stocktonschools.com
Stockton HS 200/9-12
 540 N Rush St 61085 815-947-3323
 Terry Sertle, prin. Fax 947-2673
Stockton MS 100/6-8
 500 N Rush St 61085 815-947-3702
 Brad Fox, prin. Fax 947-2114

Strasburg, Shelby, Pop. 589
Stewardson-Strasburg CUSD 5A 500/PK-12
 RR 1 Box 67 62465 217-682-3355
 Ruth Schneider, supt. Fax 682-3305
 www.sscusd.k12.il.us/
Stewardson-Strasburg HS 100/9-12
 RR 1 Box 67 62465 217-682-3355
 Larry Renshaw, prin. Fax 682-3305

Streamwood, Cook, Pop. 37,477
SD U-46
 Supt. — See Elgin
Canton MS 900/7-8
 1100 Sunset Cir 60107 630-213-5525
 Dr. James Hawkins, prin. Fax 213-5709
Streamwood HS 2,300/9-12
 701 W Schaumburg Rd 60107 630-213-5500
 Oscar Hawthorne, prin. Fax 483-5909
Tefft MS 800/7-8
 1100 Shirley Ave 60107 630-213-5535
 Lavonne Smiley, prin. Fax 213-5646

Streator, LaSalle, Pop. 14,050
Streator ESD 44 1,800/PK-8
 1520 N Bloomington St 61364 815-672-2064
 Dr. Edward Allen, supt. Fax 673-2032
 streator44.il.schoolwebpages.com/
Northlawn JHS 700/6-8
 202 E 1st St 61364 815-672-4558
 Darrick Reiley, prin. Fax 672-8109

Streator Twp. HSD 40 1,000/9-12
 600 N Jefferson St 61364 815-672-0545
 Dr. Hank Boer, supt. Fax 673-3637
Streator Twp. HS 1,000/9-12
 600 N Jefferson St 61364 815-672-0545
 John Gregg, prin. Fax 673-3637

Woodland CUSD 5 500/PK-12
 5800 E 3000 North Rd 61364 815-672-5974
 Douglas Foster, supt. Fax 673-1630
 www.woodland5.org/
Woodland MS 200/9-12
 5800 E 3000 North Rd 61364 815-672-2900
 Dale Farr, prin.

Rhema Christian Academy 50/PK-12
 1634 State Route 23 N 61364 815-672-5751
 Kathy Hawthorne, prin. Fax 672-3451

Stronghurst, Henderson, Pop. 864
West Central CUSD 235
 Supt. — See Biggsville
West Central JHS, PO Box 179 61480 100/6-8
 Jeff Nichols, prin. 309-924-1531

Sugar Grove, Kane, Pop. 6,619

Waubonsee Community College Post-Sec.
 Route 47 at Waubonsee Dr 60554 630-466-7900

Sullivan, Moultrie, Pop. 4,343
Sullivan CUSD 300 1,100/PK-12
 725 N Main St 61951 217-728-8341
 Terry Pearcy, supt. Fax 728-4139
 home.sullivan.k12.il.us/
Sullivan HS 300/9-12
 725 N Main St 61951 217-728-8311
 Stuart Hott, prin. Fax 728-4139
Sullivan MS 300/6-8
 713 N Main St 61951 217-728-8381
 Joe Marks, prin. Fax 728-4139

Summit Argo, Cook, Pop. 9,733
Argo Community HSD 217 1,700/9-12
 7329 W 63rd St 60501 708-728-3200
 Dr. Frank Stout, supt. Fax 728-3155
 www.argo217.k12.il.us/
Argo Comm. HS 1,700/9-12
 7329 W 63rd St 60501 708-728-3200
 Thomas Dixey, prin. Fax 728-3155
Summit SD 104 1,400/PK-8
 6021 S 74th Ave 60501 708-458-0505
 Kevin Cronin, supt. Fax 458-0532
 www.sd104.us
Heritage MS 500/6-8
 6021 S 74th Ave 60501 708-458-7590
 Dennis Lewis, prin. Fax 728-3111

Swansea, Saint Clair, Pop. 11,589
Wolf Branch SD 113 900/K-8
 410 Huntwood Rd 62226 618-277-2100
 Bud Martin, supt. Fax 277-5461
 www.wolfbranchschooldistrict.org/
Wolf Branch MS 300/6-8
 410 Huntwood Rd 62226 618-277-2100
 Jeffrey Burkett, prin. Fax 277-5461

Sycamore, DeKalb, Pop. 13,230
Sycamore CUSD 427 3,100/K-12
 245 W Exchange St 60178 815-899-8100
 Wayne Riesen, supt. Fax 899-8110
 www.syc427.org
Sycamore HS 1,100/9-12
 Spartan Trail 60178 815-899-8131
 Mark Leffler, prin. Fax 899-8166
Sycamore MS 800/6-8
 150 Maplewood Dr 60178 815-899-8171
 Jane Dargatz, prin. Fax 899-8177

Cornerstone Christian Academy 400/PK-12
 355 N Cross St 60178 815-895-8522
 Tom Olmstead, hdmstr. Fax 895-8717
Hair Professionals Career College Post-Sec.
 2245 Gateway Dr 60178 815-756-3596

Table Grove, Knox, Pop. 387
V I T CUSD 2 400/PK-12
 1502 E US Highway 136 61482 309-758-5138
 John Marshall, supt. Fax 758-5298
 vit.k12.il.us
V I T HS 100/9-12
 1500 E US Highway 136 61482 309-758-5136
 Phil Snowden, prin. Fax 758-5126
V I T JHS 100/7-8
 1500 E US Highway 136 61482 309-758-5136
 Phil Snowden, prin. Fax 758-5126

Tamms, Alexander, Pop. 1,178
Egyptian CUSD 5 700/PK-12
 20023 Diswood Rd 62988 618-776-5306
 Linda Davis, supt. Fax 776-5122
 www.egyptianschool.com
Egyptian HS 200/9-12
 20023 Diswood Rd 62988 618-776-5251
 Larry Houston, prin. Fax 776-5122
Egyptian JHS 200/6-8
 20023 Diswood Rd 62988 618-776-5251
 Larry Houston, prin. Fax 776-5122

Five County Regional Vocational System 618-747-2703
 PO Box 70 62988 Fax 747-2872
 Debbie Spomer, supt.
Five County Regional Vocational System Vo/Tech
 PO Box 70 62988 618-747-2703
 Debbie Spomer, prin. Fax 747-2872
Other Schools – See Goreville

Tampico, Whiteside, Pop. 747
Prophetstown-Lyndon-Tampico CUSD 3
 Supt. — See Prophetstown
Tampico MS 200/6-8
 PO Box 189 61283 815-438-3085
 Chad Colmone, prin. Fax 438-3095

Taylor Ridge, Rock Island
Rockridge CUSD 300 1,400/PK-12
 14110 134th Ave W 61284 309-795-1167
 Jack Bambrick, supt. Fax 795-1719
 www.rockridge.k12.il.us
Rockridge HS 400/9-12
 14110 134th Ave W 61284 309-795-1736
 Clayton Naylor, prin. Fax 795-1763
Rockridge JHS 200/7-8
 14110 134th Ave W 61284 309-795-1172
 Jim Widdop, prin. Fax 795-9823

Taylorville, Christian, Pop. 11,296
Taylorville CUSD 3 3,100/PK-12
 512 W Spresser St 62568 217-824-4951
 Dr. Greggory Fuerstenau, supt. Fax 824-5157
 www.taylorvilleschools.com
Taylorville HS 900/9-12
 815 W Springfield Rd 62568 217-824-2268
 Thomas Campbell, prin. Fax 824-3352
Taylorville JHS 800/6-8
 120 E Bidwell St 62568 217-824-4924
 Kirk Kettelkamp, prin. Fax 824-7180

Teutopolis, Effingham, Pop. 1,600
Teutopolis CUSD 50 1,400/PK-12
 PO Box 607 62467 217-857-3535
 Fran Thoele, supt. Fax 857-6265
 www.teutopolisschools.org/

Teutopolis HS 500/9-12
801 W Main St 62467 217-857-3139
Greg Beck, prin. Fax 857-3473
Teutopolis JHS 200/7-8
904 W Water St 62467 217-857-6678
Bill Fritcher, prin. Fax 857-6678

Thomasboro, Champaign, Pop. 1,253
Prairieview CCSD 192
Supt. — See Royal
Prairieview JHS 100/5-8
2499 County Road 2100 E 61878 217-694-4122
Jim Morgan, prin. Fax 694-4123

Thompsonville, Franklin, Pop. 580
Thompsonville Community HSD 112 100/9-12
21191 Shawneetown Rd 62890 618-627-2446
Greg Goins, supt. Fax 627-2446
thompsonville.il.schoolwebpages.com/education/distric
Thompsonville HS 100/9-12
21135 Shawneetown Rd 62890 618-627-2301
Kim Kaytor, prin. Fax 627-2446

Thomson, Carroll, Pop. 549
West Carroll CUSD 314 600/PK-12
801 South St 61285 815-259-2735
Ted Bradshaw, supt. Fax 259-3561
Other Schools – See Mount Carroll, Savanna

Tinley Park, Cook, Pop. 53,792
Bremen Community HSD 228
Supt. — See Midlothian
Tinley Park HS 1,100/9-12
6111 175th St 60477 708-532-1900
John McGraw, prin. Fax 532-4332

CCSD 146 2,400/PK-8
6611 171st St 60477 708-614-4500
Dr. Marion Hoyda, supt. Fax 614-8992
www.district146.org
Central MS 800/6-8
18146 Oak Park Ave 60477 708-614-4510
Deborah Levinson, prin. Fax 614-7271

Consolidated HSD 230
Supt. — See Orland Park
Andrew HS 2,500/9-12
9001 171st St, 708-342-5800
Dr. James Gay, prin. Fax 532-7383

Kirby SD 140 4,200/PK-8
16931 Grissom Dr 60477 708-532-6462
Dr. Michael Byrne, supt. Fax 532-1512
www.ksd140.org
Grissom MS 800/6-8
17000 80th Ave 60477 708-429-3030
Patricia Dwyer, prin. Fax 532-8529
Prairie View MS 1,000/6-8
8500 175th St, 708-532-8540
Joel Martin, prin. Fax 532-8544

Keller Graduate School Post-Sec.
18684 W West Creek Dr 60477 708-342-3300

Toledo, Cumberland, Pop. 1,148
Cumberland CUSD 77 1,000/PK-12
1496 IL Route 121 62468 217-923-3132
Russell Ragon, supt. Fax 923-3132
www.cumberland.k12.il.us/
Cumberland HS 300/9-12
1496 IL Route 121 62468 217-923-3133
Todd Hall, prin. Fax 923-5514
Cumberland JHS 300/6-8
1496 IL Route 121 62468 217-923-3135
Doug Jones, prin. Fax 923-5449

Tolono, Champaign, Pop. 2,741
Tolono CUSD 7 1,400/K-12
PO Box S 61880 217-485-6510
Michael Shonk, supt. Fax 485-3091
www.roe9.k12.il.us/schools/tolono.htm
Unity HS 500/9-12
1127 County Road 800 N 61880 217-485-6230
Phil Morrison, prin.
Unity JHS 200/7-8
1121 County Road 800 N 61880 217-485-6735
Mary Hettinger, prin.

Toluca, Marshall, Pop. 1,298
Fieldcrest CUSD 6
Supt. — See Minonk
Fieldcrest MS West 200/5-8
PO Box 709 61369 815-452-2318
James Demay, prin. Fax 452-2411

Toulon, Stark, Pop. 1,372
Stark County CUSD 100
Supt. — See Wyoming
Stark County HS 300/9-12
PO Box 419 61483 309-286-4451
Michael Domico, prin. Fax 286-3321

Tremont, Tazewell, Pop. 2,009
Tremont CUSD 702 1,000/PK-12
400 W Pearl St 61568 309-925-3461
Donald Beard, supt. Fax 925-5817
Tremont HS 300/9-12
400 W Pearl St 61568 309-925-3823
Jeff Hinman, prin. Fax 925-5817
Tremont JHS 200/6-8
400 W Pearl St 61568 309-925-3823
Jeff Hinman, prin. Fax 925-5817

Trenton, Clinton, Pop. 2,642
Wesclin CUSD 3 1,400/PK-12
10003 State Route 160 62293 618-224-7583
Paul Tockstein, supt. Fax 224-9106
wesclin.k12.il.us
Wesclin HS 400/9-12
10003 State Route 160 62293 618-224-7341
John Isenhower, prin. Fax 224-9106
Wesclin JHS 200/7-8
10003 State Route 160 62293 618-224-7355
John Mullett, prin. Fax 224-9106

Troy, Madison, Pop. 9,069
Triad CUSD 2 4,000/PK-12
PO Box 360 62294 618-667-5400
Dr. Michael Johnson, supt. Fax 667-8854
www.triad.madison.k12.il.us
Triad HS 1,300/9-12
703 E US Highway 40 62294 618-667-5409
Robert Sudhoff, prin. Fax 667-8853
Other Schools – See Saint Jacob

Tuscola, Douglas, Pop. 4,491
Tuscola CUSD 301 1,000/PK-12
409 S Prairie St 61953 217-253-4241
Joe Burgess, supt. Fax 253-4522
www.tuscola.k12.il.us/
East Prairie JHS 300/5-8
409 S Prairie St 61953 217-253-2828
Joseph Yurko, prin. Fax 253-3236
Tuscola HS 300/9-12
500 S Prairie St 61953 217-253-2377
Kyle Ransom, prin. Fax 253-4861

Ullin, Pulaski, Pop. 746
Century CUSD 100 500/PK-12
4721 Shawnee College Rd 62992 618-845-3447
Dr. Paul Franklin, supt. Fax 845-3476
Century HS 100/9-12
4721 Shawnee College Rd 62992 618-845-3518
Terry Moreland, prin. Fax 845-3476
Century MS 100/7-8
4721 Shawnee College Rd 62992 618-845-3518
Terry Moreland, prin. Fax 845-3476

Shawnee Community College Post-Sec.
8364 Shawnee College Rd 62992 618-634-2242

Union, McHenry, Pop. 580

Faith Lutheran HS 50/9-12
PO Box 173 60180 815-338-3547
Robert Schulze, prin. Fax 923-2734

University Park, Will, Pop. 7,658
Crete-Monee CUSD 201U
Supt. — See Crete
Crete-Monee MS 700/7-8
635 Olmstead Ln 60466 708-672-2700
Christian Rivara, prin. Fax 672-2708

Governors State University Post-Sec.
1 University Pkwy 60466 708-534-5000

Urbana, Champaign, Pop. 38,725
Board of Trustees SD 200/9-12
1212 W Springfield Ave 61801 217-333-2870
Kathleen Patton, supt.
University of Illinois HS 200/9-12
1212 W Springfield Ave 61801 217-333-2870
Kathleen Patton, prin.

Urbana SD 116 4,600/PK-12
PO Box 3039 61803 217-384-3636
Dr. Eugene Amberg, supt. Fax 337-4973
www.usd116.org/
Urbana HS 1,300/9-12
1002 S Race St 61801 217-384-3524
Laura Taylor, prin. Fax 384-3532
Urbana MS 1,000/6-8
1201 S Vine St 61801 217-384-3685
Nancy Clinton, prin. Fax 367-3156

Concept College of Cosmetology Post-Sec.
129 N Race St 61801 217-344-7550
Kingswood S 50/K-12
PO Box 834 61803 217-344-5540
Marsh W. Jones, dean Fax 344-5535
Mr. John's School of Cosmetology Post-Sec.
300 S Broadway Ave # 111 61801 217-355-1466
University of Illinois Post-Sec.
901 W Illinois St 61801 217-333-1000

Utica, LaSalle, Pop. 846
Waltham Community CESD 185 100/K-8
946 N 33rd Rd 61373 815-667-4417
Dr. Kristen School, supt. Fax 667-4462
wesd185.org
Waltham S 100/3-8
946 N 33rd Rd 61373 815-667-4417
Cleve Threadgill, prin. Fax 667-4462

Valmeyer, Monroe, Pop. 630
Valmeyer CUSD 3 500/PK-12
300 S Cedar Bluff Dr 62295 618-935-2100
Brian Charron, supt. Fax 935-2108
www.valmeyerk12.org/
Valmeyer HS 100/9-12
300 S Cedar Bluff Dr 62295 618-935-2100
Hattie Doyle, prin.
Valmeyer JHS 100/6-8
300 S Cedar Bluff Dr 62295 618-939-2100
Donna Mueller, prin.

Vandalia, Fayette, Pop. 6,790
Okaw Area Vocational Center
1109 N 8th St 62471 618-283-5150
Darrell Fesser, supt.
Okaw Area Vocational Center Vo/Tech
1109 N 8th St 62471 618-283-5150
Darrell Fesser, prin.

Vandalia CUSD 203 1,800/PK-12
1109 N 8th St 62471 618-283-4525
Garry Krutsinger, supt. Fax 283-4107
www.vcs.fayette.k12.il.us/
Vandalia Community HS 500/9-12
1109 N 8th St 62471 618-283-5155
Rich Well, prin. Fax 283-9855
Vandalia JHS 500/5-8
1011 W Fletcher St 62471 618-283-5151
Rod Grimsley, prin. Fax 283-5165

Varna, Marshall, Pop. 428
Midland CUSD 7
Supt. — See Lacon
Midland HS 300/9-12
1830 IL Rt 17 61375 309-463-2095
Rolf Sivertsen, prin. Fax 463-2630

Vergennes, Jackson, Pop. 333
Elverado CUSD 196
Supt. — See Elkville
Elverado JHS 100/5-8
PO Box 35 62994 618-684-3527
Belinda Conner, prin. Fax 687-3363

Vernon Hills, Lake, Pop. 22,308
Community HSD 128
Supt. — See Libertyville
Vernon Hills HS 1,200/9-12
145 Lakeview Pkwy 60061 847-932-2000
Dr. Ellen Cwick, prin. Fax 932-2049

Hawthorn CCSD 73 5,500/PK-8
841 W End Ct 60061 847-990-4200
Dr. Youssef Yomtoob, supt. Fax 367-3290
www.hawthorn73.org
Hawthorn MS North 1,100/6-8
201 W Hawthorn Pkwy 60061 847-990-4400
John Ahlemeyer, prin. Fax 367-8124
Hawthorn MS South 1,000/6-8
600 Aspen Dr 60061 847-816-8317
Joy Mullaney, prin. Fax 816-9259

Vienna, Johnson, Pop. 1,280
Vienna HSD 133 400/9-12
601 N 1st St 62995 618-658-4461
Dr. Marleis Trover, supt. Fax 658-9727
Vienna HS 400/9-12
601 N 1st St 62995 618-658-3011
Faye Mize, prin. Fax 658-9727

Villa Grove, Douglas, Pop. 2,501
Villa Grove CUSD 302 700/PK-12
400 N Sycamore St 61956 217-832-2261
Dr. Steven N. Poznic, supt. Fax 832-9305
www.vg302.org/education/school/school.php?sectionid=2
Villa Grove HS 300/9-12
400 N Sycamore St 61956 217-832-2321
Mary Pritchard, prin. Fax 832-8450
Villa Grove JHS 100/7-8
400 N Sycamore St 61956 217-832-2261
Sheila Greenwood, prin. Fax 832-9305

Villa Park, DuPage, Pop. 22,891
DuPage County SD 45 3,800/PK-8
255 W Vermont St 60181 630-530-6200
Dr. William Schewe, supt. Fax 530-1624
www.d45.dupage.k12.il.us
Jackson MS 800/6-8
301 W Jackson St 60181 630-530-6240
Tony Palmisano, prin. Fax 530-6271
Jefferson MS 500/6-8
255 W Vermont St 60181 630-530-6230
David Katzin, prin. Fax 993-6348

DuPage HSD 88 4,000/9-12
101 W Highridge Rd 60181 630-530-3980
Dr. Steven K. Humphrey, supt. Fax 832-0198
www.dupage88.net/
Willowbrook HS 2,200/9-12
1250 S Ardmore Ave 60181 630-530-3439
Evelyn Ennsmann, prin. Fax 530-3401
Other Schools – See Addison

Salt Creek SD 48 600/PK-8
1110 S Villa Ave 60181 630-279-8400
Dr. Mary E. Summers, supt. Fax 279-6167
www.saltcreek48.com
Albright MS 300/5-8
1110 S Villa Ave 60181 630-279-6160
Linda Stasko, prin. Fax 279-1614

Islamic Foundation S 700/PK-12
300 W Highridge Rd 60181 630-941-8800
Audrey Zahra Williams, prin. Fax 941-8804
Ms. Robert's Academy of Beauty Culture Post-Sec.
17 E Park Blvd 60181 630-941-3880

Virden, Macoupin, Pop. 3,493
Virden CUSD 4 1,000/PK-12
231 W Fortune St 62690 217-965-4226
James Kirbach, supt. Fax 965-4226
Virden HS 300/9-12
231 W Fortune St 62690 217-965-4127
Ronald Graham, prin. Fax 965-4127
Virden MS 200/6-8
231 W Fortune St 62690 217-965-3942
Ronald Graham, prin. Fax 965-3942

Virginia, Cass, Pop. 1,742
Virginia CUSD 64 400/PK-12
651 S Morgan St 62691 217-452-3085
Lynn Carter, supt. Fax 452-3088
www.go-redbirds.com
Virginia HS 100/9-12
651 S Morgan St 62691 217-452-3087
Karen McCombs, prin. Fax 452-3088
Virginia JHS 100/6-8
651 S Morgan St 62691 217-452-3363
Christine Brinkley, prin. Fax 452-3088

Waltonville, Jefferson, Pop. 423
Waltonville CUSD 1 300/PK-12
804 W Knob St 62894 618-279-7211
Ron Daniels, supt. Fax 279-3291
waltonvilleschools.roe25.com/
Waltonville HS 100/9-12
804 W Knob St 62894 618-279-7211
Ron Daniels, prin. Fax 279-7212

Warren, Jo Daviess, Pop. 1,468
Warren CUSD 205 500/PK-12
311 S Water St 61087 815-745-2653
Karen Sirgany Ph.D., supt. Fax 745-2037
www.205warren.net/
Warren JSHS 200/7-12
311 S Water St 61087 815-745-2641
Barb Pohl, prin. Fax 745-2654

Warrensburg, Macon, Pop. 1,227
Warrensburg-Latham CUSD 11 — 1,200/PK-12
430 W North St 62573 — 217-672-3514
Emmett Aubry, supt. — Fax 672-8468
www.wl.k12.il.us
Warrensburg-Latham HS — 400/9-12
425 W North St 62573 — 217-672-3531
Ken Hatcher, prin. — Fax 672-3770

Warrenville, DuPage, Pop. 13,286
Carmel Montessori Academy — 100/PK-12
3 S 238 State Route 59 60555 — 630-393-2996
Carmen Lafranzo, prin.

Warsaw, Hancock, Pop. 1,689
Warsaw CUSD 316 — 500/PK-12
340 S 11th St 62379 — 217-256-4282
Kim Schilson, supt. — Fax 256-4282
hancock.k12.il.us/whs/
Warsaw JSHS, 340 S 11th St 62379 — 300/6-12
Tom Bertucci, prin. — 217-256-4281

Washburn, Marshall, Pop. 1,111
Lowpoint-Washburn CUSD 21 — 400/PK-12
PO Box 580 61570 — 309-248-7522
Parker Deitrich, supt. — Fax 248-7518
Lowpoint-Washburn JSHS — 200/7-12
PO Box 580 61570 — 309-248-7521
Stan Matheny, prin. — Fax 248-7410

Washington, Tazewell, Pop. 12,040
District 50 Schools — 800/PK-8
304 E Almond Dr 61571 — 309-745-8914
Roger Stevens, supt. — Fax 745-5417
tazewell.k12.il.us/district50/
Manor MS, 1014 School St 61571 — 400/4-8
James Sharp, prin. — 309-745-3921

Washington Community HSD 308 — 1,100/9-12
115 Bondurant St 61571 — 309-444-7704
Dr. James Dunnan, supt. — Fax 444-7451
www.wacohi.net/
Washington Comm HS — 1,100/9-12
115 Bondurant St 61571 — 309-444-7704
Steve Zimmerman, prin. — Fax 444-7451

Washington SD 52 — 800/PK-8
303 Jackson St 61571 — 309-444-4182
Dr. Pat Grisham, supt. — Fax 444-8538
Washington MS — 300/6-8
105 S Spruce St 61571 — 309-444-3361
Diane Orr, prin. — Fax 444-3941

Waterloo, Monroe, Pop. 8,749
Waterloo CUSD 5 — 2,600/PK-12
219 Park St 62298 — 618-939-3453
James Helton, supt. — Fax 939-4578
www.wcusd5.net
Waterloo HS — 900/9-12
200 Bellefontaine Dr 62298 — 618-939-3455
Todd Manning, prin. — Fax 939-5180
Waterloo JHS — 600/6-8
1 Edward Gardner St 62298 — 618-939-3457
Linda Yagge, prin. — Fax 939-1383

Gibault Catholic HS — 400/9-12
501 Columbia Ave 62298 — 618-939-3883
Russell Hart, prin. — Fax 939-7215

Waterman, DeKalb, Pop. 1,218
Indian Creek CUSD 425
Supt. — See Shabbona
Indian Creek MS — 200/6-8
425 S Elm St 60556 — 815-264-7712
Beth Wackerlin, prin. — Fax 264-7826

Watseka, Iroquois, Pop. 5,572
Iroquois County CUSD 9 — 1,200/K-12
109 S 2nd St 60970 — 815-432-4931
Steve Bianchetta, supt. — Fax 432-6889
www.watseka-u9.k12.il.us
Raymond MS — 300/6-8
101 W Mulberry St 60970 — 815-432-2115
James Bunting, prin. — Fax 432-6896
Watseka Community HS — 300/9-12
138 S Belmont Ave 60970 — 815-432-2486
Scott Buchanan, prin. — Fax 432-5578

Wauconda, Lake, Pop. 9,991
Wauconda CUSD 118 — 4,000/PK-12
555 N Main St 60084 — 847-526-7690
Dr. Daniel Coles, supt. — Fax 526-1019
www.cusd118.lake.k12.il.us
Wauconda Community HS — 1,100/9-12
555 N Main St 60084 — 847-526-6611
Daniel Klett, prin. — Fax 487-3595
Wauconda MS — 700/7-8
215 Slocum Lake Rd 60084 — 847-526-2122
David Wilm, prin. — Fax 487-3597

Waukegan, Lake, Pop. 91,452
Waukegan CUSD 60 — 16,100/PK-12
1201 N Sheridan Rd 60085 — 847-336-3100
Dr. Richard B. Olson, supt. — Fax 360-5634
www.waukeganschools.org/
Abbott MS — 800/6-8
1319 Washington St 60085 — 847-360-5487
John Samuelian, prin. — Fax 360-5394
Benny MS — 700/6-8
1401 Montesano Ave 60087 — 847-360-5460
Samuel Taylor, prin. — Fax 360-5395
East MS — 700/6-8
201 N Butrick St 60085 — 847-599-4201
Dr. Cathy Watkins, prin. — Fax 599-4205
Jefferson MS — 800/6-8
600 S Lewis Ave 60085 — 847-360-5473
Dr. Bethel Cager, prin. — Fax 360-5396
Waukegan HS — 2,700/9-12
2325 Brookside Ave 60085 — 847-360-5601
Dr. James Whittington, prin. — Fax 360-5398
Waukegan Ninth Grade Center — 1,100/9-9
1011 Washington St 60085 — 847-263-4765
Bruce Thezan, prin. — Fax 599-4205

Webster MS — 700/6-8
930 New York St 60085 — 847-360-5484
Eugene Head, prin. — Fax 360-5397

Lake County Baptist S — 200/PK-12
1550 W Yorkhouse Rd 60087 — 847-623-7600
Timothy Kowach, prin. — Fax 623-2085
St. Martin de Porres HS — 200/9-12
1 N Genesee St 60085 — 847-623-5500
Sr. Judith Murphy, prin.
Shimer College — Post-Sec.
PO Box 500 60079 — 847-623-8400

Waverly, Morgan, Pop. 1,287
Waverly CUSD 6 — 400/K-12
201 N Miller St 62692 — 217-435-8121
Debra Rust, supt. — Fax 435-3431
www.waverlyscotties.com/
Waverly HS — 100/9-12
201 N Miller St 62692 — 217-435-2211
Debra Rust, prin. — Fax 435-3431

Wayne City, Wayne, Pop. 1,083
Wayne City CUSD 100 — 600/PK-12
PO Box 457 62895 — 618-895-3103
Dr. Peter Andersen, supt. — Fax 895-2331
Wayne City JSHS — 300/7-12
PO Box 427 62895 — 618-895-3103
Myron Caudle, prin. — Fax 895-2331

Weldon, DeWitt, Pop. 434
Deland-Weldon CUSD 57
Supt. — See De Land
Deland-Weldon MS — 50/7-8
2311 N 300 East Rd 61882 — 217-736-2401
Russell Corey, prin. — Fax 736-2654

Wenona, Marshall, Pop. 1,060
Fieldcrest CUSD 6
Supt. — See Minonk
Fieldcrest MS East — 200/5-8
102 W Elm St 61377 — 815-853-4331
John DiMascio, prin. — Fax 853-4786

Westchester, Cook, Pop. 16,680
Westchester SD 92-5 — 1,100/K-8
9981 Canterbury St 60154 — 708-450-2700
Myra Sanders Ph.D., supt. — Fax 450-2718
www.sd925.org
Westchester MS — 400/6-8
1620 Norfolk Ave 60154 — 708-450-2735
Eric Bailey, prin. — Fax 450-2752

St. Joseph HS — 500/9-12
1840 Mayfair Ave 60154 — 708-562-4433
Donna Kiel, prin. — Fax 562-4459

West Chicago, DuPage, Pop. 25,262
Benjamin SD 25 — 900/K-8
28W250 Saint Charles Rd 60185 — 630-876-7800
Joseph Dubec, supt. — Fax 876-3325
www.bendist25.org
Benjamin MS — 400/5-8
28W300 Saint Charles Rd 60185 — 630-876-7820
Andrea Paterala, prin. — Fax 231-3886
Community HSD 94 — 2,100/9-12
326 Joliet St 60185 — 630-876-6200
Dr. Lee Rieck, supt. — Fax 876-6241
www.d94.org
Community HS — 2,100/9-12
326 Joliet St 60185 — 630-876-6200
John W. Highland, prin. — Fax 876-6241

West Chicago ESD 33 — 3,800/PK-8
312 E Forest Ave 60185 — 630-293-6000
Dr. Ed Leman, supt. — Fax 293-6088
www.wegoed33.k12.il.us
West Chicago MS — 800/7-8
238 E Hazel St 60185 — 630-293-6060
Pat Roszowski, prin. — Fax 562-2586

Central Medical Education — Post-Sec.
550 E Washington St 60185 — 630-682-1600
Wheaton Academy — 600/9-12
900 Prince Crossing Rd 60185 — 630-562-7500
Jon Keith, prin. — Fax 231-0842

Western Springs, Cook, Pop. 12,512
Lyons Twp. HSD 204
Supt. — See La Grange
Lyons Twp. HS South Campus — 9-10
4900 Willow Springs Rd 60558 — 708-579-6500
Dave Franson, prin. — Fax 579-9573

Western Springs SD 101 — 1,400/PK-8
4335 Howard Ave 60558 — 708-246-3700
Dr. Brian T. Barnhart, supt. — Fax 482-2581
www.d101.org
McClure JHS — 500/6-8
4225 Wolf Rd 60558 — 708-246-7590
F. Daniel Chick, prin. — Fax 246-4370

West Frankfort, Franklin, Pop. 8,215
Frankfort CUSD 168 — 1,900/PK-12
PO Box 425 62896 — 618-937-2421
George Hopkins, supt. — Fax 932-2025
www.wf168.frnkln.k12.il.us/index.htm
Central JHS — 300/7-8
1500 E 9th St 62896 — 618-937-2444
Linda Varis, prin. — Fax 937-2445
Frankfort Community HS — 600/9-12
601 E Main St 62896 — 618-932-3126
John Hixson, prin. — Fax 932-6515

Westmont, DuPage, Pop. 24,639
CCSD 181 — 4,000/PK-8
1010 Executive Dr Ste 100 60559 — 630-887-1070
Dr. Mary Curley, supt. — Fax 887-1079
www.d181.org/
Other Schools – See Clarendon Hills, Hinsdale

Westmont CUSD 201 — 1,700/PK-12
200 N Linden Ave 60559 — 630-468-8000
Dr. Steven Baule, supt. — Fax 969-9022
www.cusd201.org
Westmont HS — 500/9-12
909 Oakwood Dr 60559 — 630-468-8100
Steven T. Carr, prin. — Fax 654-2758
Westmont JHS — 400/6-8
944 Oakwood Dr 60559 — 630-468-8200
Ronald Fiala, prin. — Fax 654-2203

Westville, Vermilion, Pop. 3,090
Westville CUSD 2 — 1,200/K-12
125 W Ellsworth St 61883 — 217-267-3141
James Owens, prin. — Fax 267-3144
www.westville.k12.il.us
Westville HS, 918 N State St 61883 — 400/9-12
Guy Goodlove, prin. — 217-267-2183
Westville JHS, 412 Moses Ave 61883 — 200/7-8
Greg Lewis, prin. — 217-267-2185

Wheaton, DuPage, Pop. 55,016
Community Unit SD 200 — 14,200/PK-12
130 W Park Ave 60187 — 630-682-2002
Dr. Gary Catalani, supt. — Fax 682-2068
www.cusd200.org
Edison MS — 800/6-8
1125 S Wheaton Ave 60187 — 630-682-2050
David Kanne, prin. — Fax 682-2337
Franklin MS — 700/6-8
211 E Franklin St 60187 — 630-682-2060
Susan Wolfe, prin. — Fax 682-2340
Hubble MS — 1,000/6-8
603 S Main St 60187 — 630-682-2160
Beth Sullivan, prin. — Fax 682-2299
Monroe MS — 900/6-8
1855 Manchester Rd 60187 — 630-682-2285
Wayne Spychala, prin. — Fax 682-2331
Wheaton North HS — 2,200/9-12
1 Falcon Way 60187 — 630-784-7300
Jill Bullo, prin. — Fax 682-2158
Wheaton/Warrenville South HS — 2,400/9-12
1993 Tiger Trl 60187 — 630-784-7200
Dawn Snyder, prin. — Fax 682-2042

Hair Professionals Acad of Cosmetology — Post-Sec.
1145 Butterfield Rd 60187 — 630-653-6630
St. Francis HS — 800/9-12
2130 W Roosevelt Rd 60187 — 630-668-5800
Raeann Huhn, prin. — Fax 668-5893
Wheaton College — Post-Sec.
501 College Ave 60187 — 630-752-5000

Wheeling, Cook, Pop. 35,495
Township HSD 214
Supt. — See Arlington Heights
Wheeling HS — 1,900/9-12
900 S Elmhurst Rd 60090 — 847-718-7000
Dorothy Sievert, prin. — Fax 718-7007
Wheeling CCSD 21 — 7,000/PK-8
999 W Dundee Rd 60090 — 847-537-8270
Dr. Gary E. Mical, supt. — Fax 520-2848
www.d21.k12.il.us
Holmes MS — 900/6-8
221 S Wolf Rd 60090 — 847-520-2790
Thomas Torcheldo, prin. — Fax 419-3073
London MS — 800/6-8
1001 W Dundee Rd 60090 — 847-520-2745
Jim Parker, prin. — Fax 520-2842
Other Schools – See Buffalo Grove

Worsham College of Mortuary Science — Post-Sec.
495 Northgate Pkwy 60090 — 847-808-8444

White Hall, Greene, Pop. 2,622
North Greene Unit SD 3 — 1,200/PK-12
407 N Main St 62092 — 217-374-2842
Vicki VanTuyle, supt. — Fax 374-2849
North Greene HS — 300/9-12
546 N Main St 62092 — 217-374-2131
Jim Roesch, prin. — Fax 374-2132
Other Schools – See Roodhouse

Williamsfield, Knox, Pop. 604
Williamsfield CUSD 210 — 300/PK-12
PO Box 179 61489 — 309-639-2219
Richard Putnam, supt. — Fax 639-2618
www.billtown.org/
Williamsfield HS, PO Box 179 61489 — 100/9-12
Richard Putnam, prin. — 309-639-2216
Williamsfield MS, PO Box 179 61489 — 100/6-8
Pat Hise, prin. — 309-639-2216

Williamsville, Sangamon, Pop. 1,420
Williamsville CUSD 15 — 1,300/PK-12
800 S Walnut St 62693 — 217-566-2014
Randy Harhausen, supt. — Fax 566-2183
www.wcusd15.org/
Williamsville HS — 400/9-12
900 S Walnut St 62693 — 217-566-3361
Rich Spenn, prin. — Fax 566-3792
Williamsville JHS — 300/6-8
500 S Walnut St 62693 — 217-566-3600
Rod McQuality, prin. — Fax 566-2475

Willowbrook, DuPage, Pop. 8,983
Gower SD 62 — 900/K-8
7700 Clarendon Hills Rd 60527 — 630-986-5383
Steve Griesbach, supt. — Fax 323-3074
www.gower.k12.il.us
Other Schools – See Burr Ridge

Maercker SD 60
Supt. — See Clarendon Hills
Westview Hills MS — 400/6-8
630 65th St 60527 — 630-963-1450
Brenda Babinec, prin. — Fax 963-0954

Wilmette, Cook, Pop. 27,266
Avoca SD 37 — 700/K-8
2921 Illinois Rd 60091 — 847-251-3587
Dr. Joseph M. Porto, supt. — Fax 251-7742
www.avoca.k12.il.us

Murphy MS
2921 Illinois Rd 60091
Dr. Deanna Reed, prin.
200/6-8
847-251-3617
Fax 251-4179

Wilmette SD 39
615 Locust Rd 60091
Glenn McGee, supt.
wilmette39.org
3,600/PK-8
847-256-2450
Fax 256-1920

Wilmette JHS
620 Locust Rd 60091
David Palzet, prin.
800/7-8
847-256-7280
Fax 256-0204

Loyola Academy
1100 Laramie Ave 60091
David K. McNulty, prin.
2,000/9-12
847-256-1100
Fax 853-4512

Regina Dominican HS
701 Locust Rd 60091
Kathy Rzany, prin.
400/9-12
847-256-7660
Fax 256-3726

Wilmington, Will, Pop. 5,725
Wilmington CUSD 209U
715 S Joliet St 60481
Anthony Jay Plese, supt.
www.wilmington.will.k12.il.us
1,500/PK-12
815-476-2594
Fax 476-3483

Stevens MS
221 Ryan St 60481
Marty Felesena, prin.
400/6-8
815-476-2189
Fax 476-1941

Wilmington HS
715 S Joliet St 60481
Joseph Hermes, prin.
500/9-12
815-476-2846
Fax 476-3491

Winchester, Scott, Pop. 1,634
Winchester CUSD 1
149 S Elm St 62694
Lawrence Coultas, supt.
700/PK-12
217-742-3175
Fax 742-3312

Winchester HS, 200 W Cross St 62694
Angie Greger, prin.
200/9-12
217-742-3151

Windsor, Shelby, Pop. 1,802
Windsor CUSD 1
PO Box 200 61957
Sharon Keck, supt.
www.windsor.k12.il.us/
500/PK-12
217-459-2636
Fax 459-2661

Windsor JSHS
1424 Minnesota Ave 61957
Don Morgan, prin.
200/7-12
217-459-2636
Fax 459-2794

Winfield, DuPage, Pop. 9,393
Winfield SD 34
0S150 Winfield Rd 60190
Dr. Diane Cody, supt.
www.winfield34.org/
400/PK-8
630-909-4900
Fax 260-2382

Winfield Central S
0S150 Park St 60190
Patti Palagi, prin.
300/3-8
630-909-4960
Fax 933-9236

Winnebago, Winnebago, Pop. 2,990
Winnebago CUSD 323
304 E McNair Rd 61088
Dr. Dennis M. Harezlak, supt.
www.winnebagoschools.org/
1,700/PK-12
815-335-2456
Fax 335-7574

Winnebago HS
200 E McNair Rd 61088
Matthew Zickert, prin.
500/9-12
815-335-2336
Fax 335-7548

Winnebago MS
407 N Elida St 61088
James Burns, prin.
400/6-8
815-335-2364
Fax 335-1437

Winnetka, Cook, Pop. 12,386
New Trier Twp. HSD 203
385 Winnetka Ave 60093
Linda Yonke, supt.
www.newtrier.k12.il.us
4,000/9-12
847-446-7000
Fax 446-0874

New Trier Twp. HS - Winnetka Campus
385 Winnetka Ave 60093
Debbie Stacey, prin.
Other Schools – See Northfield
3,000/10-12
847-446-7000
Fax 446-4759

Winnetka SD 36
1235 Oak St 60093
Dr. Rebecca Vanderbogert, supt.
www.winnetka36.org/
2,100/PK-8
847-446-9400
Fax 446-9408

Washburne MS
515 Hibbard Rd 60093
Daniel Schwartz, prin.
500/7-8
847-446-5892
Fax 446-1380

Hadley School for the Blind
700 Elm St 60093
Post-Sec.
847-446-8111

Music Center of the North Shore
300 Green Bay Rd 60093
Post-Sec.
847-446-3822

North Shore Country Day S
310 Green Bay Rd 60093
Thomas Doar, prin.
400/PK-12
847-446-0674
Fax 446-0675

Winthrop Harbor, Lake, Pop. 6,866
Winthrop Harbor SD 1
500 North Ave 60096
Dr. James Tenbusch, supt.
www.whsd1.org
800/K-8
847-731-3085
Fax 731-3156

North Prairie JHS
500 North Ave 60096
Theodore Brooks, prin.
300/6-8
847-731-3089
Fax 731-3152

Wolf Lake, Union
Shawnee CUSD 84
PO Box 128 62998
Gary Hill, supt.
500/PK-12
618-833-5709
Fax 833-4171

Shawnee HS
PO Box 128 62998
Brent Boren, prin.
100/9-12
618-833-5307
Fax 833-5468

Shawnee JHS
PO Box 128 62998
Brent Boren, prin.
100/6-8
618-833-5307
Fax 833-5468

Wood Dale, DuPage, Pop. 13,451
Wood Dale SD 7
543 N Wood Dale Rd 60191
John Corbett, supt.
www.wd7.org
1,200/PK-8
630-595-9510
Fax 595-5625

Wood Dale JHS
655 N Wood Dale Rd 60191
James Ask, prin.
400/6-8
630-766-6210
Fax 766-1839

Woodhull, Henry, Pop. 813
Alwood CUSD 225
301 E 5th Ave 61490
Shannon Bumann, supt.
www.alwood.net
500/PK-12
309-334-2719
Fax 334-2925

Alwood MSHS
301 E 5th Ave 61490
Scott Petrie, prin.
300/6-12
309-334-2102
Fax 334-2632

Woodlawn, Jefferson, Pop. 635
Woodlawn Community HSD 205
300 N Central St 62898
Alan Estes, supt.
www.roe25.com/woodlawnhs/
200/9-12
618-735-2631
Fax 735-2032

Woodlawn Community HS
300 N Central St 62898
Dave Larkin, prin.
200/9-12
618-735-2631
Fax 735-2032

Woodridge, DuPage, Pop. 33,695
Woodridge SD 68
7925 Janes Ave 60517
Jerome Brendel, supt.
www.woodridge68.org
3,100/PK-8
630-985-7925
Fax 910-2060

Jefferson JHS
7200 Janes Ave 60517
Ron Freed, prin.
700/7-8
630-852-8010
Fax 969-7168

Westwood College
7155 Janes Ave 60517
Post-Sec.
630-434-8244

Wood River, Madison, Pop. 11,121
East Alton-Wood River Community HSD 14
777 N Wood River Ave 62095
John Pearson, supt.
www.eawr.madison.k12.il.us/
700/9-12
618-254-3151
Fax 254-9113

East Alton-Wood River HS
777 N Wood River Ave 62095
Richard Levek, prin.
700/9-12
618-254-3151
Fax 254-9113

Wood River-Hartford ESD 15
501 E Lorena Ave 62095
Michael Loftus, supt.
www.wrh.madison.k12.il.us
900/PK-8
618-254-0607
Fax 254-9048

Lewis-Clark ES
501 E Lorena Ave 62095
Sue Rives, prin.
300/6-8
618-254-4355
Fax 254-7600

Woodstock, McHenry, Pop. 21,103
Woodstock CUSD 200
227 W Judd St 60098
Ellyn A. Wrzeski, supt.
www.d200.mchenry.k12.il.us
5,800/PK-12
815-338-8200
Fax 338-2005

Northwood MS
2121 N Seminary Ave 60098
Robert Hackbart, prin.
800/6-8
815-338-4900
Fax 337-2150

Olson MS
720 W Judd St 60098
Mark Widmer, prin.
600/6-8
815-338-4910
Fax 338-8142

Woodstock HS
501 W South St 60098
Corey Tafoya, prin.
1,800/9-12
815-338-4370
Fax 334-0811

Marian Central Catholic HS
1001 McHenry Ave 60098
Charles Rakers, prin.
700/9-12
815-338-4220
Fax 338-4253

Worth, Cook, Pop. 10,906
Worth SD 127
11218 S Ridgeland Ave 60482
Donna Henningsen, supt.
www.worthschools.org
1,100/PK-8
708-448-2800
Fax 448-6215

Worth JHS
11151 S New England Ave 60482
Dr. Peter Yuska, prin.
400/6-8
708-448-2803
Fax 448-6155

Wyoming, Stark, Pop. 1,395
Stark County CUSD 100
300 Van Buren 61491
Jerry Klooster, supt.
www.bhsroe.k12.il.us/sccu100/
900/PK-12
309-695-6123

Stark County JHS
401 N Galena Ave 61491
Galen Wirth, prin.
Other Schools – See Toulon
200/6-8
309-695-5191
Fax 695-6007

Yorkville, Kendall, Pop. 8,116
Yorkville CUSD 115
PO Box 579 60560
Thomas Engler, supt.
www.yorkville.k12.il.us
2,900/PK-12
630-553-4382
Fax 553-4398

Yorkville HS
797 Game Farm Rd 60560
Frank Bogner, prin.
900/9-12
630-553-4388
Fax 553-4397

Yorkville MS
702 Game Farm Rd 60560
Jeff Szymczak, prin.
400/7-8
630-553-4385
Fax 553-4592

Zeigler, Franklin, Pop. 1,657
Zeigler-Royalton CUSD 188
PO Box 38 62999
George Wilkerson, supt.
600/PK-12
618-596-5841
Fax 596-6789

Zeigler-Royalton HS
PO Box 38 62999
John DeNosky, prin.
200/9-12
618-596-5841
Fax 596-6789

Zeigler-Royalton JHS
PO Box 87 62999
Larry Fillingim, prin.
100/7-8
618-596-2121
Fax 596-2075

Zion, Lake, Pop. 23,814
Zion ESD 6
2200 Bethesda Blvd 60099
Dr. Ronald Wynn, supt.
www.zion6.com
2,900/PK-8
847-872-5455
Fax 746-1280

Central JHS
1716 27th St 60099
Yvonne Brown, prin.
600/7-8
847-746-1431
Fax 746-9750

Zion-Benton Township HSD 126
1 ZB Way 60099
Dr. Bud Marks, supt.
www.zbths.org
2,400/9-12
847-731-9300
Fax 731-4441

Zion-Benton HS
1 ZB Way 60099
Dr. Scott Murphy, prin.
2,400/9-12
847-731-9300
Fax 731-4408

Zion Christian S
1828 Hebron Ave 60099
Scott Leach, prin.
100/K-12
847-872-4088
Fax 872-1032

INDIANA

INDIANA DEPARTMENT OF EDUCATION
Room 229, State House, Indianapolis 46204
Telephone 317-232-6610
Fax 317-232-8004
Website http://www.doe.state.in.us
Superintendent of Public Instruction   Suellen Reed

INDIANA BOARD OF EDUCATION
200 W Washington St Ste 229, Indianapolis 46204-2798
Chairperson   Suellen Reed

EDUCATIONAL SERVICE CENTERS (ESC)

Central Indiana ESC
Tom Pagan, dir., 6321 La Pas Trl   317-387-7100
Indianapolis 46268   Fax 328-7298
www.ciesc.k12.in.us/
East Central ESC
Walter Harrison, dir.   765-825-1247
1601 Indiana Ave   Fax 825-2532
Connersville 47331
www.ecesc.k12.in.us/
Northern Indiana ESC
Jack Davis, dir., 56535 Magnetic Dr   574-254-0111
Mishawaka 46545   Fax 254-0148
www.niesc.k12.in.us/

Northwest Indiana ESC
Dr. Charles Costa, dir.   219-922-0900
2939 41st St, Highland 46322   Fax 922-1246
www.nwiesc.k12.in.us/
Region 8 ESC
Dr. Rodger Smith, dir.   260-439-8800
5122 Homestead Rd   Fax 439-8801
Fort Wayne 46814
www.r8esc.k12.in.us/800/intro.htm
Southern Indiana ESC
J. Scott Turney, dir.   812-482-6641
1102 Tree Lane Dr, Jasper 47546   Fax 482-6652
www.siec.k12.in.us/

Wabash Valley ESC
Larry Rausch, dir., 3061 Benton St   765-463-1589
West Lafayette 47906   Fax 463-1580
www.wviec.k12.in.us/
West Central ESC
David Archer, dir.   765-653-2727
PO Box 21, Greencastle 46135   Fax 653-7897
www.wciesc.k12.in.us/
William E. Wilson ESC
Larry Risk, dir., 11440 Highway 62   812-256-8000
Charlestown 47111   Fax 256-8012
www.wesc.k12.in.us/

PUBLIC, PRIVATE AND CATHOLIC SECONDARY SCHOOLS

Akron, Kosciusko, Pop. 1,044
Tippecanoe Valley SC   2,300/K-12
8343 S State Rd 19 46910   574-353-7741
Daniel V. Kramer, supt.   Fax 353-7743
www.tvsc.k12.in.us
Tippecanoe Valley HS   600/9-12
8345 S State Rd 19 46910   574-353-7031
Mike Overmyer, prin.   Fax 353-1016
Tippecanoe Valley MS   600/6-8
11303 W 800 S 46910   574-353-7353
Earl Richter, prin.   Fax 353-7189

Albion, Noble, Pop. 2,320
Central Noble Community SC   1,500/K-12
200 E Main St 46701   260-636-2175
Dr. Leo Philbin, supt.   Fax 636-7918
www.centralnoble.k12.in.us/
Central Noble HS   400/9-12
302 Cougar Ct 46701   260-636-2117
Jerry Wellman, prin.   Fax 636-2791
Central Noble MS   300/6-8
401 E Highland St 46701   260-636-2279
Brent Wilson, prin.   Fax 636-2461

Alexandria, Madison, Pop. 6,062
Alexandria Community SC   1,700/K-12
202 E Washington St 46001   765-724-4496
John McFarren, supt.   Fax 724-5049
www.alex.k12.in.us
Alexandria MS   400/6-8
308 W 11th St 46001   765-724-4166
Jan Mock, prin.   Fax 724-5045
Alexandria-Monroe HS   500/9-12
1 Burden Ct 46001   765-724-4413
Mike Lee, prin.   Fax 724-5041

Anderson, Madison, Pop. 58,394
Anderson Community SC   9,000/K-12
1229 Lincoln St 46016   765-641-2028
Dr. Timothy D. Long, supt.   Fax 641-2080
www.acsc.net/
Anderson HS   1,500/9-12
4610 Madison Ave 46013   765-641-2037
Philip Nikirk, prin.   Fax 641-2041
East Side MS   800/6-8
2300 Lindberg Rd 46012   765-641-2047
Lucinda McCord, prin.   Fax 641-2050
Ebbertt Education Center   Vo/Tech
325 W 38th St 46013   765-641-2121
Timothy Holbert, prin.   Fax 641-2124
Highland HS   1,500/9-12
2108 E 200 N 46012   765-641-2059
Lennon Brown, prin.   Fax 641-2064
North Side MS   800/6-8
1815 Indiana Ave 46012   765-641-2055
Michael Brandon, prin.   Fax 641-2057
South Side MS   900/6-8
101 W 29th St 46016   765-641-2051
Patrick Fassnatcht, prin.   Fax 641-2053

Frankton-Lapel Community SD   2,300/PK-12
7916 W 300 N 46011   765-734-1261
Ned Speicher, supt.   Fax 734-1129
www.frankton-lapel.org
Other Schools – See Frankton, Lapel

Anderson University   Post-Sec.
1100 E 5th St 46012   765-649-9071
Apex School of Beauty Culture   Post-Sec.
333 Jackson St 46016   765-642-7560
Cross Street Christian S   50/PK-10
2318 W Cross St 46011   765-649-4141
    Fax 649-5953
Indiana Business College   Post-Sec.
140 E 53rd St 46013   765-644-7514
Indiana Christian Academy   300/K-12
432 W 300 N 46012   765-643-7884
William Newton, prin.   Fax 683-4200
Ivy Tech State College   Post-Sec.
104 W 53rd St 46013   765-643-7133
Liberty Christian HS   200/6-12
2323 Columbus Ave 46016   765-644-7774
Dr. Brian Dougherty, supt.   Fax 644-7779

Angola, Steuben, Pop. 7,725
Metro SD of Steuben County   3,000/K-12
400 S Martha St 46703   260-665-2854
Dr. David Goodwin, supt.   Fax 665-9155
www.msdsteuben.k12.in.us
Angola HS   900/9-12
350 S John McBride Ave 46703   260-665-2186
Steve Grill, prin.   Fax 665-7012
Angola MS   700/6-8
1350 E Maumee St 46703   260-665-9581
William Church, prin.   Fax 665-9583

Tri-State University 46703   Post-Sec.
    260-665-4100

Arcadia, Hamilton, Pop. 1,778
Hamilton Heights SC   2,400/PK-12
410 W Main St 46030   317-984-3538
Scott Bryan, supt.   Fax 984-3042
www.hhsc.k12.in.us
Hamilton Heights HS   700/9-12
PO Box 379 46030   317-984-3551
Sterling Boles, prin.   Fax 984-3554
Hamilton Heights MS   700/5-8
PO Box 609 46030   317-984-3588
Chris Walton, prin.   Fax 984-3231

Argos, Marshall, Pop. 1,826
Argos Community SD   700/K-12
410 N 1st St 46501   574-892-5139
Peter O'Rourke, supt.   Fax 892-6527
www.argos.k12.in.us
Argos Community JSHS   300/7-12
500 Yearick St 46501   574-892-5137
Larry Wolfe, prin.   Fax 892-4712

Attica, Fountain, Pop. 3,473
Attica Consolidated SC   1,000/PK-12
205 E Sycamore St 47918   765-762-7000
Dr. Judith Bush, supt.   Fax 762-7007
www.attica.k12.in.us
Attica JSHS   400/7-12
211 E Sycamore St 47918   765-762-7000
Roy Jones, prin.   Fax 762-7017

Auburn, DeKalb, Pop. 12,497
Lakewood Park Christian S   600/PK-12
5555 County Road 29 46706   260-925-1393
Randy Carman, supt.   Fax 925-5010
Reppert School of Auctioneering   Post-Sec.
PO Box 190 46706   800-968-4444

Aurora, Dearborn, Pop. 3,983
South Dearborn Community SC   3,000/PK-12
6109 Squire Pl 47001   812-926-2090
Thomas Book, supt.   Fax 926-4216
www.venus.net/~sdearad1/
South Dearborn HS   1,000/9-12
5770 Highlander Pl 47001   812-926-3772
Robert D. Moorhead, prin.   Fax 926-4162
South Dearborn MS   800/4-8
6098 Squire Pl 47001   812-926-6298
Todd Bowers, prin.   Fax 926-2149

Austin, Scott, Pop. 4,720
Scott County SD 1   1,400/K-12
PO Box 9 47102   812-794-8750
Berley Goodin, supt.   Fax 794-8765
www.scott1.k12.in.us
Austin HS   400/9-12
401 S Highway 31 47102   812-794-8730
Sherman Smith, prin.   Fax 794-8739
Austin MS   300/6-8
401 S Highway 31 47102   812-794-8740
David Deaton, prin.   Fax 794-8739

Avon, Hendricks, Pop. 7,017
Avon Community SC   6,400/K-12
7203 E US Highway 36 46123   317-272-2920
Timothy Ogle, supt.   Fax 272-1704
www.avon.k12.in.us
Avon HS   1,700/9-12
7575 E County Road 150 S 46123   317-272-2586
Rick Adcock, prin.   Fax 272-3100
Avon MS   1,000/7-8
7199 E US Highway 36 46123   317-272-0128
David Leach, prin.   Fax 272-3122

Bainbridge, Putnam, Pop. 753
North Putnam Community SD   1,900/PK-12
300 N Washington St 46105   765-522-6218
Murray Pride, supt.   Fax 522-3562
www.nputnam.k12.in.us
Other Schools – See Roachdale

Batesville, Franklin, Pop. 6,306
Batesville Community SC   1,900/PK-12
626 N Huntersville Rd 47006   812-934-2194
James Freeland, supt.   Fax 933-0833
www.batesville.k12.in.us/
Batesville HS   600/9-12
1 Bulldog Blvd 47006   812-934-4384
Scott Mills, prin.   Fax 934-5964
Batesville MS   500/6-8
201 N Mulberry St 47006   812-934-5175
Orlando Fontanez, prin.   Fax 933-0834

Battle Ground, Tippecanoe, Pop. 1,344
Tippecanoe SC
Supt. — See Lafayette

Battle Ground MS
511 Main St 47920 — 300/6-8 — 765-567-2122
John Louk, prin. — Fax 567-2325

Bedford, Lawrence, Pop. 13,469
North Lawrence Community SD — 5,500/PK-12
460 W St 47421 — 812-279-3521
Dr. Dennis Turner, supt. — Fax 275-1577
www.nlcs.k12.in.us
Bedford MS — 700/6-8
1501 N St 47421 — 812-279-9781
David Schlegel, prin. — Fax 277-3218
Bedford-North Lawrence HS — 1,600/9-12
595 Stars Blvd 47421 — 812-279-9756
Michael Terry, prin. — Fax 279-9304
North Lawrence Vo-Tech Ctr — Vo/Tech
258 BNL Dr 47421 — 812-279-3561
Duane Martin, prin. — Fax 275-1578
Shawswick MS — 300/6-8
71 Shawswick School Rd 47421 — 812-275-6121
Roger Dean, prin. — Fax 275-0543
Other Schools – See Oolitic

Beech Grove, Marion, Pop. 14,457
Beech Grove CSD — 2,400/PK-12
5334 Hornet Ave 46107 — 317-788-4481
Dr. Rex Sager, supt. — Fax 782-4065
www.bgcs.k12.in.us
Beech Grove HS — 700/9-12
5330 Hornet Ave 46107 — 317-786-1447
Harvey Warrner, prin. — Fax 781-2920
Beech Grove MS — 400/7-8
1248 Buffalo St 46107 — 317-784-6649
Thomas Keeley, prin. — Fax 781-2926

St. Francis Hospital Center — Post-Sec.
1600 Albany St 46107 — 317-783-8220

Berne, Adams, Pop. 4,121
South Adams SD — 1,500/K-12
1027 US Highway 27 S 46711 — 260-589-3133
Constance Bailey, supt. — Fax 589-2065
www.southadams.k12.in.us/
South Adams JSHS — 700/7-12
1000 Parkway St 46711 — 260-589-3131
Brent Lehman, prin. — Fax 589-3042

Bicknell, Knox, Pop. 3,288
North Knox SC — 1,500/K-12
PO Box 187 47512 — 812-735-4434
Joe Adams, supt. — Fax 328-6262
www.nknox.k12.in.us
North Knox HS — 500/9-12
10890 N State Road 159 47512 — 812-735-2990
Tim Grove, prin. — Fax 328-2155

Bloomfield, Greene, Pop. 2,520
Bloomfield SD — 1,100/K-12
500 W South St 47424 — 812-384-4507
Ron Hasler, supt. — Fax 384-0172
www.bsd.k12.in.us
Bloomfield JSHS — 500/7-12
501 W Spring St 47424 — 812-384-4550
Greg Parsley, prin. — Fax 384-1422

Eastern Greene SD — 1,400/PK-12
RR 4 Box 351 47424 — 812-825-5722
Randy Barrett, supt. — Fax 825-9413
www.egreene.k12.in.us/
Eastern Greene JSHS — 600/7-12
RR 4 Box 623 47424 — 812-825-5621
David Springer, prin. — Fax 825-6661

Bloomington, Monroe, Pop. 70,642
Monroe County Community SC — 10,700/PK-12
315 E North Dr 47401 — 812-330-7700
Dr. John A. Maloy, supt. — Fax 330-7813
www.mccsc.edu
Batchelor MS — 600/7-8
900 W Gordon Pike 47403 — 812-330-7763
Peggy Chambers, prin. — Fax 330-7766
Bloomington HS North — 1,400/9-12
3901 N Kinser Pike 47404 — 812-330-7724
Jeffry Henderson, prin. — Fax 330-7805
Bloomington HS South — 1,800/9-12
1965 S Walnut St 47401 — 812-330-7714
Mark Fletcher, prin. — Fax 330-7810
Hoosier Hills Career Center — Vo/Tech
3070 N Prow Rd 47404 — 812-330-7730
Edward Brown, dir. — Fax 330-7807
Jackson Creek MS — 700/7-8
3980 S Sare Rd 47401 — 812-330-2451
Donna Noble, prin. — Fax 330-2457
Tri-North MS — 600/7-8
1000 W 15th St 47404 — 812-330-7745
Dr. Gale Hill, prin. — Fax 330-7799

Bloomington Hospital — Post-Sec.
PO Box 1149 47402 — 812-336-6821
Hair Arts Academy — Post-Sec.
933 N Walnut St 47404 — 812-339-1117
Harmony S — 200/K-12
PO Box 1787 47402 — 812-334-8349
Steve Bonchek, dir. — Fax 333-3435
H.O.P.E. Christian Academy — 50/K-12
4100 N Hartstrait Rd 47404 — 812-876-9008
Stacia Kelly, dir. — Fax 935-8176
Indiana University — Post-Sec.
300 N Jordan Ave 47405 — 812-855-4848
Ivy Tech Community College - Bloomington — Post-Sec.
200 Daniels Way 47404 — 812-332-1559
Lighthouse Christian Academy — 300/PK-12
1201 W That Rd 47403 — 812-824-2000
Rayna Amerine, prin. — Fax 824-2017

Bluffton, Wells, Pop. 9,496
Metro SD of Bluffton-Harrison — 1,500/K-12
628 S Bennett St 46714 — 260-824-2620
Thomas Johnson, supt. — Fax 824-6011
www.bhmsd.k12.in.us
Bluffton-Harrison MS — 500/5-8
1500 Stogdill Rd 46714 — 260-824-3536
Jon Bennett, prin. — Fax 824-6011
Bluffton HS — 500/9-12
1 Tiger Trl 46714 — 260-824-3724
Steve Baker, prin. — Fax 824-6011

Community Christian S — 100/PK-12
1225 W Washington St 46714 — 260-824-1203
Vicki Bell, prin. — Fax 824-9572

Boone Grove, Porter
Porter Township SC
Supt. — See Valparaiso
Boone Grove MS — 400/6-8
325 W 550 S 46302 — 219-464-4828
Larry Allen, prin. — Fax 464-4829

Boonville, Warrick, Pop. 6,930
Warrick County SC — 9,100/K-12
300 E Gum St 47601 — 812-897-0400
Brad Schneider, supt. — Fax 897-6033
www.warrick.k12.in.us/
Boonville HS — 800/9-12
300 N 1st St 47601 — 812-897-4701
Mike Whitten, prin. — Fax 897-6061
Boonville JHS — 500/7-8
555 N Yankeetown Rd 47601 — 812-897-1420
William Wilder, prin. — Fax 897-6584
Other Schools – See Lynnville, Newburgh

Borden, Clark, Pop. 810
West Clark Community SC
Supt. — See Sellersburg
Borden JSHS — 300/7-12
301 West St 47106 — 812-967-2087
Lisa Nale, prin. — Fax 967-2086

Bourbon, Marshall, Pop. 1,740
Triton SC — 1,100/K-12
100 Triton Dr 46504 — 574-342-2255
Ted Chittum, supt. — Fax 342-8165
www.triton.k12.in.us/
Triton JSHS — 500/7-12
300 Triton Dr 46504 — 574-342-6505
Michael Chobanov, prin. — Fax 342-8175

Bourbon Christian S — 50/1-12
1325 N Main St 46504 — 574-342-8043
Aaron Yoder, prin. — Fax 342-8145

Brazil, Clay, Pop. 8,166
Clay Community SC
Supt. — See Knightsville
North Clay MS — 1,000/6-8
3 W Knight Dr 47834 — 812-448-1530
Greg Linton, prin. — Fax 442-0608
Northview HS — 1,100/9-12
1 W Knight Dr 47834 — 812-448-2661
Jim Church, prin. — Fax 446-2647

Bremen, Marshall, Pop. 4,593
Bremen Public SD — 1,400/K-12
512 W Grant St 46506 — 574-546-3929
Russ Mikel, supt. — Fax 546-6303
www.bps.k12.in.us
Bremen HS — 500/9-12
511 W Grant St 46506 — 574-546-3511
Bill Mahler, prin. — Fax 546-5477

Bristol, Elkhart, Pop. 1,572

Kessington Christian S — 50/PK-12
19153 County Road 104 46507 — 574-848-4987
Don Dunithan, admin. — Fax 641-2118

Brookville, Franklin, Pop. 2,932
Franklin County Community SC — 3,100/PK-12
1020 Franklin Ave 47012 — 765-647-4128
Dr. William Glentzer, supt. — Fax 647-2417
www.fccsc.k12.in.us
Brookville MS — 500/5-8
9092 Wildcat Ln 47012 — 765-647-6040
Gary Frost, prin. — Fax 647-4960
Franklin County HS — 900/9-12
1 Wildcat Ln 47012 — 765-647-4101
Kim Simonson, prin. — Fax 647-2732

Brownsburg, Hendricks, Pop. 16,956
Brownsburg Community SC — 5,500/K-12
444 E Tilden Dr 46112 — 317-852-5726
Kathleen Corbin, supt. — Fax 852-1015
www.brownsburg.k12.in.us
Brownsburg East MS — 6-8
1250 E Airport Rd 46112 — 317-852-2386
Richard Doss, prin. — Fax 852-1023
Brownsburg HS — 1,700/9-12
1000 S Odell St 46112 — 317-852-2258
Bret Daghe, prin. — Fax 852-1490
Brownsburg West MS — 1,000/6-8
1555 S Odell St 46112 — 317-852-3143
Julie Moster, prin. — Fax 858-4100

Bethesda Christian S — 400/K-12
7950 N County Road 650 E 46112 — 317-852-3101
Dee Tidball, prin. — Fax 852-4301

Brownstown, Jackson, Pop. 3,025
Brownstown Central Community SC — 1,700/PK-12
608 W Commerce St 47220 — 812-358-4271
Roger Bane, supt. — Fax 358-5303
www.btownccs.k12.in.us

Brownstown Central HS — 500/9-12
500 N Elm St 47220 — 812-358-3453
Joseph Sheffer, prin. — Fax 358-5318
Brownstown Central MS — 400/6-8
520 W Walnut St 47220 — 812-358-4947
Peggy Cannon, prin. — Fax 358-3940

Bunker Hill, Miami, Pop. 1,030
Maconaquah SC — 2,400/PK-12
7932 S Strawtown Pike 46914 — 765-689-9131
Carmine Gentile, supt. — Fax 689-0995
www.maconaquah.k12.in.us
Maconaquah HS — 700/9-12
256 E 800 S 46914 — 765-689-9131
David Noonan, prin. — Fax 689-9528
Maconaquah MS — 600/6-8
594 E 800 S 46914 — 765-689-9131
James Callane, prin. — Fax 689-9360

Butler, DeKalb, Pop. 2,726
DeKalb County Eastern Community SD — 1,500/K-12
300 E Washington St 46721 — 260-868-2125
Dr. Jeffrey Stephens, supt. — Fax 868-2562
www.eastsideblazers.net
Eastside JSHS — 700/7-12
603 N Green St 46721 — 260-868-2186
Robert Ruch, prin. — Fax 868-5773

Cambridge City, Wayne, Pop. 2,069
Western Wayne SD
Supt. — See Pershing
Lincoln HS — 400/9-12
215 E Parkway Dr 47327 — 765-478-5916
Dan Sichting, prin. — Fax 478-3262
Lincoln MS — 300/6-8
205 E Parkway Dr 47327 — 765-478-5840
John Engle, prin. — Fax 478-3265

Campbellsburg, Washington, Pop. 579
West Washington SC — 1,000/K-12
9699 W Mount Tabor Rd 47108 — 812-755-4872
Gerald Jackson, supt. — Fax 755-4843
www.wwcs.k12.in.us
West Washington JSHS — 500/7-12
8028 W Batts Rd 47108 — 812-755-4996
Paul Stroud, prin. — Fax 755-4460

Cannelton, Perry, Pop. 1,174
Cannelton CSD — 100/PK-12
125 S 6th St 47520 — 812-547-2637
Marion A. Chapman, supt. — Fax 547-4142
www.cannelton.k12.in.us
Cannelton JSHS — 100/7-12
119 S 3rd St 47520 — 812-547-3296
Sheila Donis, prin. — Fax 547-4142

Carmel, Hamilton, Pop. 43,083
Carmel-Clay SD — 13,400/PK-12
5201 E 131st St 46033 — 317-844-9961
Dr. Barbara Underwood, supt. — Fax 844-9965
www.ccs.k12.in.us
Carmel HS — 3,700/9-12
520 E Main St 46032 — 317-846-7721
John Williams, prin. — Fax 571-4066
Carmel MS — 1,600/6-8
300 S Guilford Rd 46032 — 317-846-7331
Denise Jacobs, prin. — Fax 571-4067
Clay MS — 1,600/6-8
5150 E 126th St 46033 — 317-844-7251
Kent DeKoninck, prin. — Fax 571-4020
Creekside MS — 6-8
3525 W 126th St 46032 — 317-733-6420
Tom Harmas, prin. — Fax 733-6422

Cayuga, Vermillion, Pop. 1,114
North Vermillion Community SC — 800/K-12
5551 N Falcon Dr 47928 — 765-492-4033
Paul Roads, supt. — Fax 492-7001
www.nvc.k12.in.us
North Vermillion JSHS — 400/7-12
5555 N Falcon Dr 47928 — 765-492-3364
Corey Austin, prin. — Fax 492-7006

Cedar Lake, Lake, Pop. 9,509
Hanover Community SC — 1,600/K-12
PO Box 645 46303 — 219-374-3500
Dr. Michael Livovich, supt. — Fax 374-4411
www.hanover.k12.in.us
Hanover Central HS — 500/9-12
10120 W 133rd Ave 46303 — 219-374-3800
Robert McRae, prin. — Fax 374-4408
Hanover Central JHS — 300/7-8
10120 W 133rd Ave 46303 — 219-374-3800
Terry Mucha, prin. — Fax 374-4408

Centerville, Wayne, Pop. 2,436
Centerville-Abington Community SD — 1,700/PK-12
115 W South St 47330 — 765-855-3475
Philip Stevenson, supt. — Fax 855-2524
www.centerville.k12.in.us
Centerville HS — 600/9-12
507 Willow Grove Rd 47330 — 765-855-3481
Tammy Chavis, prin. — Fax 855-3484
Centerville JHS — 200/7-8
509 Willow Grove Rd 47330 — 765-855-5113
Rick Schauss, prin. — Fax 855-5207

Chalmers, White, Pop. 494
Frontier SC — 900/K-12
PO Box 809 47929 — 219-984-5009
Bernard Graser, supt. — Fax 984-5022
www.frontier.k12.in.us
Frontier JSHS — 400/7-12
1 Falcon Dr 47929 — 219-984-5437
Richard Dehne, prin. — Fax 984-5360

Charlestown, Clark, Pop. 5,927
Greater Clark County SD
Supt. — See Jeffersonville

Charlestown HS 600/9-12
1 Pirate Pl 47111 812-256-3328
Dick Johnson, prin. Fax 256-7274
Charlestown MS 500/6-8
8804 High Jackson Rd 47111 812-256-6363
Joyce Traub, prin. Fax 256-7282

Charlottesville, Hancock
Eastern Hancock County Community SC 1,100/PK-12
10370 E County Road 250 N 46117 317-467-0064
Dr. Ellen Welk, supt. Fax 936-5516
www.ehancock.k12.in.us
Eastern Hancock HS 400/9-12
10320 E County Road 250 N 46117 317-936-5595
David Pfaff, prin. Fax 936-5050
Eastern Hancock MS 200/6-8
10380 E County Road 250 N 46117 317-936-5324
David Pfaff, prin. Fax 936-5516

Chesterton, Porter, Pop. 11,139
Duneland SC 5,500/K-12
601 W Morgan Ave 46304 219-983-3605
Dr. Dirk E. Baer, supt. Fax 983-3614
www.duneland.k12.in.us
Chesterton HS 1,800/9-12
2125 S 11th St 46304 219-983-3730
Jim Goetz, prin. Fax 983-3775
Chesterton MS 900/7-8
651 W Morgan Ave 46304 219-983-3776
James Ton, prin. Fax 983-3798

Fairhaven Baptist Academy 200/K-12
86 E Oak Hill Rd 46304 219-926-6636
David Olson, prin. Fax 926-1111

Churubusco, Whitley, Pop. 1,738
Smith-Green Community SD 1,400/PK-12
222 W Tulley St 46723 260-693-2007
David Martin, supt. Fax 693-6434
www.sgcs.k12.in.us/
Churubusco HS 500/9-12
1 Eagle Dr 46723 260-693-2131
David Maugel, prin. Fax 693-3673
Churubusco MS 300/6-8
2 Eagle Dr 46723 260-693-1460
John Davis, prin. Fax 693-1437

Cicero, Hamilton, Pop. 4,347

Indiana Academy 100/9-12
24815 State Road 19 46034 317-984-3575
Perry Pollman, prin. Fax 984-5081

Clarksville, Clark, Pop. 21,237
Clarksville Community SC 1,400/K-12
200 Ettels Ln 47129 812-282-7753
Samuel Gardner, supt. Fax 282-7754
www.ccsc.k12.in.us/
Clarksville HS 400/9-12
800 High School Dr 47129 812-282-8231
Steven Morris, prin. Fax 282-8234
Clarksville MS 400/6-8
101 Ettels Ln 47129 812-282-8235
Pamela Cooper, prin. Fax 280-5004

Our Lady of Providence HS 700/7-12
707 W Highway 131 47129 812-945-2538
Melinda Ernstberger, prin. Fax 945-3460
PJ's College of Cosmetology Post-Sec.
1414 Blackiston Mill Rd 47129 812-282-0459

Clay City, Clay, Pop. 1,019
Clay Community SD
Supt. — See Knightsville
Clay City JSHS 400/7-12
601 Lankford St 47841 812-939-2154
Jeff Bell, prin. Fax 443-2106

Clayton, Hendricks, Pop. 779
Mill Creek Community SC 1,600/PK-12
6631 S County Road 200 W 46118 317-539-9200
Dr. Sherida Brower, supt. Fax 539-9215
www.mccsc.k12.in.us/
Cascade HS 500/9-12
6565 S County Road 200 W 46118 317-539-9315
Todd Gowen, prin. Fax 539-9350
Cascade JHS 200/7-8
6423 S County Road 200 W 46118 317-539-9285
Teresa Godsey, prin. Fax 539-9310

Clinton, Vermillion, Pop. 4,951
South Vermillion Community SC 2,000/K-12
PO Box 387 47842 765-832-2426
Steven E. Miller, supt. Fax 832-7391
www.svcs.k12.in.us
South Vermillion HS 600/9-12
770 Wildcat Dr 47842 765-832-3551
Philip Harrison, prin. Fax 832-3510
South Vermillion MS 500/6-8
950 Wildcat Dr 47842 765-832-7727
Angela Harris, prin. Fax 832-5316

Cloverdale, Putnam, Pop. 2,305
Cloverdale Community SD 1,500/PK-12
310 E Logan St 46120 765-795-4664
Carrie Milner, supt. Fax 795-5166
www.cloverdale.k12.in.us
Cloverdale HS 400/9-12
205 E Market St 46120 765-795-4203
Gary Boyd, prin. Fax 795-4381
Cloverdale MS 500/5-8
312 E Logan St 46120 765-795-2900
Jeff Brookshire, prin. Fax 795-2901

Columbia City, Whitley, Pop. 7,671
Whitley County Consolidated SD 3,500/PK-12
107 N Walnut St 46725 260-244-5772
Dr. Laura Huffman, supt. Fax 244-4099
www.wccs.k12.in.us
Columbia City HS 1,100/9-12
600 N Whitley St 46725 260-244-6136
Steve Doepker, prin. Fax 244-5610
Indian Springs MS 800/6-8
1692 S State Road 9 46725 260-244-5148
Jan Boylen, prin. Fax 244-4710

Columbus, Bartholomew, Pop. 39,058
Bartholomew Consolidated SC 10,600/PK-12
1200 Central Ave 47201 812-376-4220
Dr. John Quick, supt. Fax 376-4486
www.bcsc.k12.in.us
Central MS 800/7-8
725 7th St 47201 812-376-4287
Randy Gratz, prin. Fax 376-4511
Columbus Area Career Connection Vo/Tech
1400 25th St 47201 812-376-4240
Marilyn Metzler, dir. Fax 376-4699
Columbus East HS 1,400/9-12
230 S Marr Rd 47201 812-376-4369
Gary Goshorn, prin. Fax 376-4358
Columbus North HS 1,800/9-12
1400 25th St 47201 812-376-4432
David Clark, prin. Fax 376-4291
Northside MS 900/7-8
1400 27th St 47201 812-376-4405
Charlie McCoy, prin. Fax 376-4479

Columbus Christian S 300/PK-12
3170 Indiana Ave 47201 812-372-3780
Amy Mathis, admin. Fax 372-3878
Columbus Regional Hospital Post-Sec.
2400 17th St 47201 812-376-5439
Indiana Business College Post-Sec.
2222 Poshard Rd 47203 812-379-9000
Ivy Tech Community College - Columbus Post-Sec.
4475 Central Ave 47203 812-372-9925

Connersville, Fayette, Pop. 14,844
Fayette County SC 3,900/PK-12
1401 Spartan Dr 47331 765-825-2178
Fax 825-8060
www.fayette.k12.in.us
Connersville HS 1,100/9-12
1100 Spartan Dr 47331 765-825-1151
Patricia Flowers, prin. Fax 825-0777
Connersville MS 700/7-8
1900 N Grand Ave 47331 765-825-1139
Beth Denham, prin. Fax 827-4346
Whitewater Technical Career Center Vo/Tech
1300 Spartan Dr 47331 765-825-0521
Milton Eley, prin. Fax 827-0836

Temple Christian S 200/PK-12
1382 E State Road 44 47331 765-825-5198
Dr. Stephen Kaiser, prin.

Converse, Miami, Pop. 1,127
Oak Hill United SC 1,200/PK-12
PO Box 550 46919 765-395-3341
Jim Smith, supt. Fax 395-3343
www.ohusc.k12.in.us
Oak Hill HS 500/9-12
7756 W Delphi Pike #27 46919 765-384-4381
Joel Martin, prin. Fax 384-5414
Oak Hill JHS 200/7-8
7760 W Delphi Pike #27 46919 765-384-4385
Greg Perkins, prin. Fax 384-4386

Corydon, Harrison, Pop. 2,720
South Harrison Community SD 3,200/K-12
315 S Harrison Dr 47112 812-738-2168
Dr. Neyland Clark, supt. Fax 738-2158
www.shcsc.k12.in.us/
Corydon Central HS 800/9-12
375 Country Club Rd 47112 812-738-4181
Carole Apple, prin. Fax 738-1145
Corydon Central JHS 400/7-8
377 Country Club Rd 47112 812-738-5750
Mark Black, prin. Fax 738-5752
Other Schools – See Elizabeth

Covington, Fountain, Pop. 2,522
Covington Community SC 1,000/K-12
PO Box 225 47932 765-793-4877
Nate Evans, supt. Fax 793-5209
www.covington.k12.in.us/
Covington Community HS 300/9-12
1017 6th St 47932 765-793-2286
Kirk Booe, prin. Fax 793-5200
Covington MS 200/6-8
514 Railroad St 47932 765-793-4451
Steve Reynolds, prin. Fax 793-5200

Crawfordsville, Montgomery, Pop. 15,201
Crawfordsville Community SD 2,600/PK-12
1000 Fairview Ave 47933 765-362-2342
Kathleen J. Steele, supt. Fax 364-3237
www.cville.k12.in.us
Crawfordsville HS 700/9-12
1 W Athenian Dr 47933 765-362-2340
Greg Hunt, prin. Fax 364-3200
Tuttle MS 600/6-8
612 S Elm St 47933 765-362-2992
Sherri Mitchell, prin. Fax 364-3219

North Montgomery Community SC 2,100/K-12
480 W 580 N 47933 765-359-2112
Dr. Robert Brower, supt. Fax 359-2111
www.nm.k12.in.us/
North Montgomery HS 600/9-12
5945 N US Highway 231 47933 765-362-5140
Terry Russell, prin. Fax 362-6710
Northridge MS 600/6-8
482 W 580 N 47933 765-364-1071
Bruce Hibbard, prin. Fax 362-7985

South Montgomery Community SC
Supt. — See New Market
Southmont HS 600/9-12
6425 S US Highway 231 47933 765-866-0350
Kevin Stewart, prin. Fax 866-2044
Southmont JHS 300/7-8
6425 S US Highway 231 47933 765-866-2023
Mike Sowers, prin. Fax 866-2045

Maranatha Christian S 50/K-12
PO Box 29 47933 765-362-8881
Gloria Stevens, admin. Fax 362-0151
Wabash College Post-Sec.
301 W Wabash Ave 47933 765-361-6100

Crothersville, Jackson, Pop. 1,541
Crothersville Community SD 600/K-12
201 S Preston St 47229 812-793-2601
Dr. Terry Goodin, supt. Fax 793-3004
Crothersville JSHS 300/6-12
109 S Preston St 47229 812-793-2051
Thomas Judd, prin. Fax 793-3004

Crown Point, Lake, Pop. 20,980
Crown Point Community SC 6,200/PK-12
200 E North St 46307 219-663-3371
Fax 662-4304
www.cps.k12.in.us
Crown Point HS 2,000/9-12
1500 S Main St 46307 219-663-4885
Ryan Pitcock, prin. Fax 662-5661
Taft MS 1,000/7-8
1000 S Main St 46307 219-663-1507
Michael Hazen, prin. Fax 662-4349

Culver, Marshall, Pop. 1,525
Culver Community SC 1,200/K-12
PO Box 231 46511 574-842-3364
Brad Schuldt, supt. Fax 842-4615
www.culver.k12.in.us
Culver Community HS 300/9-12
701 School St 46511 574-842-3391
Albert Hanselman, prin. Fax 842-3392
Culver Community MS 200/7-8
1 Cavalier Dr 46511 574-842-5690
George Irvin, prin. Fax 842-5691

Culver Academies 700/9-12
1300 Academy Rd # 156 46511 574-842-7000
John Buxton, hdmstr. Fax 842-8161

Daleville, Delaware, Pop. 1,629
Daleville Community SD 700/K-12
8700 S Bronco Dr 47334 765-378-3329
Paul Garrison, supt. Fax 378-3649
www.daleville.k12.in.us
Daleville JSHS 300/7-12
8400 S Bronco Dr 47334 765-378-3371
John Junco, prin. Fax 378-4076

Danville, Hendricks, Pop. 6,941
Danville Community SC 2,300/PK-12
PO Box 469 46122 317-745-2212
Dr. John McKinney, supt. Fax 745-3924
www.danville.k12.in.us
Danville Community HS 600/9-12
100 Warrior Way 46122 317-745-6431
David Chapman, prin. Fax 745-3908
Danville MS 400/7-8
49 N Wayne St 46122 317-745-5491
Michael Peters, prin. Fax 745-3949

Decatur, Adams, Pop. 9,459
North Adams Community SD 2,300/K-12
PO Box 670 46733 260-724-7146
James Compton, supt. Fax 724-4777
www.nadams.k12.in.us
Bellmont HS 900/9-12
1000 E North Adams Dr 46733 260-724-7121
Adrian Richie, prin. Fax 724-7826
Bellmont MS 500/6-8
1200 E North Adams Dr 46733 260-724-3137
Craig Anderson, prin. Fax 724-4495

Delphi, Carroll, Pop. 3,000
Delphi Community SC 1,700/K-12
501 Armory Rd 46923 765-564-2100
Dr. John Williams, supt. Fax 564-6919
www.delphi.k12.in.us/
Delphi Community HS 500/9-12
501 Armory Rd 46923 765-564-3481
Keith Brakel, prin. Fax 564-3260
Delphi Community MS 400/6-8
501 Armory Rd 46923 765-564-3411
Joanne Allard, prin. Fax 564-2135

Demotte, Jasper, Pop. 3,738

Covenant Christian HS 100/9-12
611 15th St SW 46310 219-987-7651
Clarence Oudman, prin. Fax 987-7652

Denver, Miami, Pop. 530
North Miami Community SD 1,200/K-12
PO Box 218 46926 765-985-3891
Brent Kaufman, supt. Fax 985-3904
www.nmcs.k12.in.us/
North Miami MSHS 600/7-12
570 E 900 N 46926 765-985-2931
Chuck Pavey, prin. Fax 985-2056

Donaldson, Marshall

Ancilla Domini College 46513 Post-Sec.
574-936-8898

Dubois, Dubois
Northeast Dubois County SC — 1,000/K-12
5379 E Main St 47527 — 812-678-2781
Dan Balka, supt. — Fax 678-4418
www.nedubois.k12.in.us
Dubois MS — 300/5-8
4550 N 4th St 47527 — 812-678-2181
Bill Hochgesang, prin. — Fax 678-2282
Northeast Dubois HS — 300/9-12
4711 N Dubois Rd NE 47527 — 812-678-2251
Rick Gladish, prin. — Fax 678-3991

Dugger, Sullivan, Pop. 965
Northeast SC
Supt. — See Hymera
Union JSHS — 200/7-12
7356 E County Road 50 S 47848 — 812-648-2729
Charles Roach, prin. — Fax 648-2594

Dunkirk, Jay, Pop. 2,643
Jay SC
Supt. — See Portland
West Jay MS — 400/6-8
140 E Highland Ave 47336 — 765-768-7648
Mike Crull, prin. — Fax 768-6152

Dyer, Lake, Pop. 14,670
Lake Central SC
Supt. — See Saint John
Kahler MS — 1,100/6-8
600 Joliet St 46311 — 219-865-3535
Scott Graber, prin. — Fax 865-4428

Mid-America Reformed Seminary — Post-Sec.
229 Seminary Dr 46311 — 219-864-2400

East Chicago, Lake, Pop. 31,366
City of East Chicago SD — 6,400/PK-12
210 E Columbus Dr 46312 — 219-391-4100
Dr. John Flores, supt. — Fax 391-4126
www.ecps.org
Block JHS — 500/7-8
2700 Cardinal Dr 46312 — 219-391-4084
Michael Milich, prin. — Fax 391-4282
East Chicago Central HS — 1,400/9-12
1100 W Columbus Dr 46312 — 219-391-4000
Darnell Adell, prin. — Fax 391-4049
West Side JHS — 500/7-8
4001 Indianapolis Blvd 46312 — 219-391-4068
David Allen, prin. — Fax 391-4284

Edinburgh, Johnson, Pop. 4,497
Edinburgh Community SC — 900/K-12
202 Keeley St 46124 — 812-526-2681
Dr. Rebecca Sager, supt. — Fax 526-0271
www.edinburgh.k12.in.us
Edinburgh Community HS — 300/9-12
300 Keeley St 46124 — 812-526-5501
Kevin Rockey, prin. — Fax 526-3439
Edinburgh Community MS — 300/6-8
300 Keeley St 46124 — 812-526-3418
Rich Arkanoff, prin. — Fax 526-3430

Elizabeth, Harrison, Pop. 137
South Harrison Community SD
Supt. — See Corydon
South Central JSHS — 400/7-12
6675 E Highway 11 SE 47117 — 812-969-2941
James Crisp, prin. — Fax 969-3019

Elkhart, Elkhart, Pop. 51,682
Baugo Community SD — 1,800/K-12
29125 County Road 22 46517 — 574-293-8583
Jerry Cook, supt. — Fax 294-2171
www.baugo.com/
Jimtown HS — 500/9-12
59021 County Road 3 46517 — 574-295-2343
Nathan Dean, prin. — Fax 294-2171
Jimtown JHS — 300/7-8
58903 County Road 3 46517 — 574-294-6586
Mike Groh, prin. — Fax 294-8557

Concord Community SD — 4,400/K-12
59040 Minuteman Way 46517 — 574-875-5161
George Dyer, supt. — Fax 875-8762
www.concord.k12.in.us
Concord Community HS — 1,500/9-12
59117 Minuteman Way 46517 — 574-875-6524
Dan Cunningham, prin. — Fax 875-8986
Concord JHS — 800/7-8
24050 County Road 20 46517 — 574-875-5122
Kevin Caird, prin. — Fax 875-1089

Elkhart Community SD — 12,200/PK-12
2720 California Rd 46514 — 574-262-5516
Mark T. Mow, supt. — Fax 262-5733
www.elkhart.k12.in.us
Elkhart Area Career Ctr — Vo/Tech
2424 California Rd 46514 — 574-262-5650
Stephen Barkdull, prin. — Fax 262-5801
Elkhart Central HS — 1,600/9-12
1 Blazer Blvd 46516 — 574-294-4700
Frank Serge, prin. — Fax 295-4712
Elkhart Memorial HS — 1,800/9-12
2608 California Rd 46514 — 574-262-5600
Mark Tobolski, prin. — Fax 262-5625
Moran MS — 700/7-8
200 W Lusher Ave 46517 — 574-295-4805
Levon Johnson, prin. — Fax 295-4807
North Side MS — 700/7-8
300 Lawrence St 46514 — 574-262-5570
Sara Jackowiak, prin. — Fax 262-5573
West Side MS — 700/7-8
101 S Nappanee St 46514 — 574-295-4815
Kristie Stutsman, prin. — Fax 295-4812

Associated Mennonite Biblical Seminaries — Post-Sec.
3003 Benham Ave 46517 — 574-295-3726

Elkhart Christian Academy — 600/PK-12
25943 County Road 22 46517 — 574-293-1609
Dr. Jeffrey Mattner, admin. — Fax 293-3238

Ellettsville, Monroe, Pop. 5,178
Richland-Bean Blossom Community SC — 2,800/PK-12
600 Edgewood Dr 47429 — 812-876-7100
Thomas r. Edington, supt. — Fax 876-7020
www.rbbcsc.k12.in.us/
Edgewood HS — 800/9-12
601 Edgewood Dr 47429 — 812-876-2277
Brad Tucker, prin. — Fax 876-9163
Edgewood JHS — 700/6-8
851 W Edgewood Dr 47429 — 812-876-2005
Larry Sparks, prin. — Fax 876-8985

Elnora, Daviess, Pop. 728
North Daviess County Community SD — 1,100/K-12
5494 E State Road 58 47529 — 812-636-8000
Robert W. Bell, supt. — Fax 636-7546
www.ndaviess.k12.in.us
North Daviess JSHS — 500/7-12
5494 E State Road 58 47529 — 812-636-8000
Jed Jerrels, prin. — Fax 636-7255

Elwood, Madison, Pop. 9,324
Elwood Community SC — 2,000/K-12
1306 N Anderson St 46036 — 765-552-9861
Thomas Austin, supt. — Fax 552-8088
www.elwood.k12.in.us
Elwood Community HS — 600/9-12
1137 N 19th St 46036 — 765-552-9854
Dr. Rocco Fuschetto, prin. — Fax 552-1044
Elwood Community MS — 500/6-8
1207 N 19th St 46036 — 765-552-7378
Jeff Marcuson, prin. — Fax 552-2017
Hinds Career Center — Vo/Tech
1105 N 19th St 46036 — 765-552-9881
James Pearson, prin. — Fax 552-2021

Eminence, Morgan
Eminence Community SC — 500/K-12
PO Box 135 46125 — 765-528-2101
Norman Stockton, supt. — Fax 528-2262
www.eminence.k12.in.us
Eminence JSHS — 300/7-12
PO Box 105 46125 — 765-528-2221
Max Hoke, prin. — Fax 528-2276

Evansville, Vanderburgh, Pop. 117,881
Evansville-Vanderburgh SC — 22,200/PK-12
1 SE 9th St 47708 — 812-435-8477
Dr. Bart McCandless, supt. — Fax 435-8421
www.evsc.k12.in.us/
Bosse HS — 900/9-12
1300 Washington Ave 47714 — 812-477-1661
Robert Adams, prin. — Fax 474-6976
Central HS — 1,300/9-12
5400 N 1st Ave 47710 — 812-435-8292
John Russell, prin. — Fax 435-8515
Evans MS — 500/6-8
837 Tulip Ave 47711 — 812-435-8330
David Smith, prin. — Fax 435-8332
Glenwood MS — 300/6-8
901 Sweetser Ave 47713 — 812-435-8242
Sheila Huff, prin. — Fax 435-8245
Harrison HS — 1,500/9-12
211 Fielding Rd 47715 — 812-477-1046
Janet Leistner, prin. — Fax 474-4118
Harwood MS — 300/6-8
3013 N 1st Ave 47710 — 812-435-8316
Dr. Franzy Fleck, prin. — Fax 435-8517
Helfrich Park MS — 600/6-8
2603 W Maryland St 47712 — 812-435-8246
Timothy McIntosh, prin. — Fax 435-8249
McGary MS — 500/6-8
1535 Joyce Ave 47714 — 812-476-3035
Don Mosbey, prin. — Fax 474-6919
North HS — 1,400/9-12
2319 Stringtown Rd 47711 — 812-435-8283
Brenda Weber, prin. — Fax 435-8349
Oak Hill MS — 700/6-8
7700 Oak Hill Rd 47725 — 812-867-6426
Kenneth Wempe, prin. — Fax 867-4753
Perry Heights MS — 500/6-8
5800 Hogue Rd 47712 — 812-435-8326
Charles Goodman, prin. — Fax 435-8263
Plaza Park MS — 600/6-8
7301 Lincoln Ave 47715 — 812-476-4971
Mary Schweizer, prin. — Fax 474-6922
Reitz HS — 1,400/9-12
350 Dreier Blvd 47712 — 812-435-8206
Christine Settle, prin. — Fax 435-8217
Thomkins MS — 700/6-8
1300 W Mill Rd 47710 — 812-435-8323
Terry Yunker, prin. — Fax 435-8588
Washington MS — 500/6-8
1801 Washington Ave 47714 — 812-477-8983
Rance Ossenberg, prin. — Fax 474-6930

Evansville Day S — 300/PK-12
3400 N Green River Rd 47715 — 812-476-3039
Benjamin Hebebrand, hdmstr. — Fax 476-4061
Evansville Tri-State Beauty College — Post-Sec.
4920 Tippecanoe Dr 47715 — 812-479-6989
Faith Heritage Christian S — 100/K-12
1613 Pollack Ave 47714 — 812-477-7110
Dr. Gregory Pounders, admin. — Fax 477-7121
Indiana Business College — Post-Sec.
4601 Theatre Dr 47715 — 812-476-6000
Ivy Tech Community College - Southwest — Post-Sec.
3501 N 1st Ave 47710 — 812-426-2865
Mater Dei HS — 600/9-12
1300 Harmony Way 47720 — 812-426-2258
Marie Bradley, prin. — Fax 421-5717
Reitz Memorial HS — 800/9-12
1500 Lincoln Ave 47714 — 812-476-4973
Gerry Adams, prin. — Fax 474-2942

Roger's Academy of Hair Design — Post-Sec.
2903 Mount Vernon Ave 47712 — 812-428-4027
University of Evansville — Post-Sec.
1800 Lincoln Ave 47714 — 800-423-8633
University of Southern Indiana — Post-Sec.
8600 University Blvd 47712 — 812-464-8600
Welborn Baptist Hospital — Post-Sec.
401 SE 6th St 47713 — 812-428-8264
Westside Catholic S St. Boniface Campus — 100/4-8
2031 W Michigan St 47712 — 812-422-1014
Dan Gilbert, prin. — Fax 422-1057

Fairland, Shelby, Pop. 1,348
Northwestern Consolidated SC — 1,500/PK-12
4920 W 600 N 46126 — 317-835-7461
Dr. Larry Moore, supt. — Fax 835-4441
www.nwsc.k12.in.us/
Triton Central HS — 500/9-12
4774 W 600 N 46126 — 317-835-3000
Brad Lindsay, prin. — Fax 835-3012
Triton MS — 500/5-8
4740 W 600 N 46126 — 317-835-3006
Mary Giesting, prin. — Fax 835-3008

Fairmount, Grant, Pop. 2,883
Madison-Grant United SC — 1,600/K-12
11580 S E 00 W 46928 — 765-948-4143
Fred Herron, supt. — Fax 948-4150
www.mgargylls.com
Madison-Grant HS — 500/9-12
11700 S E 00 W 46928 — 765-948-4141
Shane Robbins, prin. — Fax 948-4874
Madison-Grant JHS — 300/7-8
11640 S E 00 W 46928 — 765-948-5132
Tom Daniel, prin. — Fax 948-3671

Farmersburg, Sullivan, Pop. 1,213
Northeast SC
Supt. — See Hymera
North Central JSHS — 500/7-12
910 E County Road 975 N 47850 — 812-397-2132
David Scott, prin. — Fax 397-2133

Ferdinand, Dubois, Pop. 2,294
Southeast Dubois County SC — 1,500/K-12
432 E 15th St 47532 — 812-367-1653
Robert Johnson, supt. — Fax 367-1075
www.sedubois.k12.in.us
Forest Park JSHS — 700/7-12
1440 Michigan St 47532 — 812-367-1831
Jeffrey Jessee, prin. — Fax 367-1172

Fishers, Hamilton, Pop. 47,790
Hamilton Southeastern SD — 11,700/PK-12
13485 Cumberland Rd 46038 — 317-594-4100
Dr. Concetta Raimondi, supt. — Fax 594-4109
www.hse.k12.in.us/
Fishers HS — 9-9
13000 Promise Rd 46038 — 317-915-4290
Dr. Scott Syverson, prin. — Fax 915-4299
Fishers JHS — 900/7-8
13257 Cumberland Rd 46038 — 317-594-4150
Brian Cronk, prin. — Fax 594-4159
Hamilton Southeastern HS — 2,600/9-12
13910 E 126th St, — 317-594-4190
Robert Albano, prin. — Fax 594-4199
Hamilton Southeastern JHS — 800/7-8
12001 Olio Rd, — 317-594-4120
Shari Switzer, prin. — Fax 594-4129
Riverside S — 5-8
10910 Eller Rd 46038 — 317-915-4280
Michael Beresford, prin. — Fax 915-4289

Flora, Carroll, Pop. 2,228
Carroll Consolidated SC — 1,200/K-12
2 S 3rd St 46929 — 574-967-4113
John Sayers, supt. — Fax 967-3831
www.carroll.k12.in.us
Carroll JSHS — 600/7-12
2362 E State Road 18 46929 — 574-967-4157
Charles Hucksted, prin. — Fax 967-4027

Floyds Knobs, Floyd
New Albany-Floyd Co. Consolidated SD
Supt. — See New Albany
Floyd Central HS — 1,500/9-12
6575 Old Vincennes Rd 47119 — 812-923-8811
John Marsh, prin. — Fax 923-4010

Fort Branch, Gibson, Pop. 2,334
South Gibson SC — 1,900/K-12
204 W Vine St 47648 — 812-753-4230
Stacey Humbaugh, supt. — Fax 753-4081
www.sgibson.k12.in.us
Gibson Southern HS — 600/9-12
RR 1 Box 496 47648 — 812-753-3011
Jim Isaacs, prin. — Fax 753-3021

Fortville, Hancock, Pop. 3,494
Mt. Vernon Community SC — 3,000/PK-12
1776 W State Road 234 46040 — 317-485-3100
Dr. William Riggs, supt. — Fax 485-3113
www.mvcsc.k12.in.us
Mt. Vernon HS — 800/9-12
8112 N 200 W 46040 — 317-485-3131
Joseph Loomis, prin. — Fax 485-3154
Mt. Vernon MS — 500/7-8
1862 W State Road 234 46040 — 317-485-3160
John Price, prin. — Fax 485-3177

Fort Wayne, Allen, Pop. 219,495
East Allen County SD
Supt. — See New Haven
Harding HS — 600/9-12
6501 Wayne Trce 46816 — 260-446-0240
Neal Brown, prin. — Fax 446-0249
Prince Chapman Academy — 600/6-8
4808 E Paulding Rd 46816 — 260-446-0270
Deborah Watson, prin. — Fax 446-0275

Fort Wayne Community SD   31,200/PK-12
1200 S Clinton St 46802   260-467-1000
Dr. Wendy Robinson, supt.   Fax 467-1980
www.fwcs.k12.in.us
Anthis Career Center   Vo/Tech
1200 Barr St 46802   260-467-1005
Larry Gerardot, prin.   Fax 425-7609
Blackhawk MS   800/6-8
7200 E State Blvd 46815   260-425-7313
Timothy Matthias, prin.   Fax 425-7142
Elmhurst HS   900/9-12
3829 Sandpoint Rd 46809   260-425-7510
Barbara Gentry, prin.   Fax 425-7162
Geyer MS   600/6-8
420 E Paulding Rd 46816   260-467-4300
Mary Lowery, prin.   Fax 467-4364
Jefferson MS   700/6-8
5303 Wheelock Rd 46835   260-425-7374
Michael Morris, prin.   Fax 425-7376
Kekionga MS   700/6-8
2929 Engle Rd 46809   260-425-7378
Dr. Debra Jones, prin.   Fax 425-7381
Lakeside MS   600/6-8
2100 Lake Ave 46805   260-467-8625
Carlton Mable, prin.   Fax 467-8672
Lane MS   600/6-8
4901 Vance Ave 46815   260-425-7386
David Schnelker, prin.   Fax 425-7389
Memorial Park MS   600/6-8
2200 Maumee Ave 46803   260-425-7410
Brian Smith, prin.   Fax 425-7413
Miami MS   600/6-8
8100 Amherst Dr 46819   260-467-8560
Janice Craig, prin.   Fax 467-8606
Northrop HS   2,100/9-12
7001 Coldwater Rd 46825   260-467-2300
Barbara Ahlersmeyer, prin.   Fax 467-2301
North Side HS   1,400/9-12
475 E State Blvd 46805   260-425-7530
Charles DeFord, prin.   Fax 425-7137
Northwood MS   700/6-8
1201 E Washington Center Rd 46825 260-425-7424
Matthew Schiebel, prin.   Fax 425-7175
Portage MS   600/6-8
3521 Taylor St 46802   260-425-7431
Jeff King, prin.   Fax 425-7434
Shawnee MS   800/6-8
1000 E Cook Rd 46825   260-425-7447
Linda McDowell, prin.   Fax 425-7450
Snider HS   2,100/9-12
4600 Fairlawn Pass 46815   260-425-7570
Steve Simmons, prin.   Fax 425-7136
South Side HS   1,400/9-12
3601 S Calhoun St 46807   260-425-7610
Thomas Smith, prin.   Fax 425-7649
Wayne HS   900/9-12
9100 Winchester Rd 46819   260-425-7630
Joselyn Whitticker, prin.   Fax 425-7646
Adult & Continuing Education   Adult
1200 Barr St 46802   260-425-7653
James Davis, admin.

Metro SD of Southwest Allen County   6,300/K-12
4824 Homestead Rd 46814   260-431-2051
Brian Smith, supt.   Fax 431-2099
www.sacs.k12.in.us
Homestead HS   1,900/9-12
4310 Homestead Rd 46814   260-431-2251
Dianne Moake, prin.   Fax 431-2330
Summit MS   800/6-8
4509 Homestead Rd 46814   260-431-2552
Jim Leinker, prin.   Fax 431-2568
Woodside MS   700/6-8
2310 W Hamilton Rd S 46814   260-431-2702
Rick Smith, prin.   Fax 431-2723

Northwest Allen County SD   4,900/PK-12
13119 Coldwater Rd 46845   260-637-3155
Dr. Steven Yager, supt.   Fax 637-8355
www.nacs.k12.in.us/
Carroll 9th Grade Campus   9-9
3905 Carroll Rd 46818   260-637-0064
Kenneth Folks, prin.   Fax 637-5868
Carroll HS   1,100/10-12
3701 Carroll Rd 46818   260-637-3161
Deborah Neumeyer, prin.   Fax 449-4519
Carroll MS   500/6-8
4027 Hathaway Rd 46818   260-637-5159
John Miller, prin.   Fax 637-5478
Maple Creek MS   800/6-8
425 Union Chapel Rd 46845   260-338-0802
Mark Seele, prin.   Fax 338-0369

Bishop Dwenger HS   900/9-12
1300 E Washington Center Rd 46825 260-496-4700
Fred Tone, prin.   Fax 496-4702
Bishop Luers HS   500/9-12
333 E Paulding Rd 46816   260-456-1261
Mary Keefer, prin.   Fax 456-1262
Blackhawk Christian S   800/PK-12
7400 E State Blvd 46815   260-493-7470
Sam Barfell, supt.   Fax 493-7258
Brown Mackie College   Post-Sec.
3000 E Coliseum Blvd 46805   260-484-4400
Canterbury S   300/9-12
3210 Smith Rd 46804   260-436-0746
Jonathan Hancock, hdmstr.   Fax 436-5137
Concordia Lutheran HS   700/9-12
1601 Saint Joe River Dr 46805   260-483-1102
John Marks, prin.   Fax 471-0180
Concordia Theological Seminary   Post-Sec.
6600 N Clinton St 46825   260-452-2100
Fort Wayne School of Radiography   Post-Sec.
700 Broadway 46802   260-425-3990
Indiana Business College   Post-Sec.
6413 N Clinton St 46825   260-471-7667
Indiana Institute of Technology   Post-Sec.
1600 E Washington Blvd 46803   260-422-5561

Indiana Univ-Purdue Univ at Fort Wayne   Post-Sec.
2101 E Coliseum Blvd 46805   260-481-6100
International Business College   Post-Sec.
5699 Coventry Ln 46804   260-459-4500
ITT Technical Institute   Post-Sec.
2810 Dupont Commerce Ct 46825   260-497-6200
Ivy Tech Community College - Northeast   Post-Sec.
3800 N Anthony Blvd 46805   260-482-9171
Keystone S   200/PK-12
1800 Laverne Ave 46805   260-424-4523
Martin Gigler, prin.   Fax 424-4525
Ravenscroft Beauty College   Post-Sec.
6110 Stellhorn Rd 46815   260-486-8868
Rudae's School of Beauty Culture   Post-Sec.
5317 Coldwater Rd 46825   260-483-2466
Taylor University   Post-Sec.
1025 W Rudisill Blvd 46807   260-744-8600
The Masters of Cosmetology College   Post-Sec.
1732 Bluffton Rd 46809   260-747-6667
University of St. Francis   Post-Sec.
2701 Spring St 46808   260-434-3100

Fountain City, Wayne, Pop. 722
Northeastern Wayne SD   1,100/K-12
PO Box 406 47341   765-847-2821
Stephen Bailey, supt.   Fax 847-5355
Northeastern JSHS   600/7-12
7295 N US Highway 27 47341   765-847-2591
Dennis Metzger, prin.   Fax 847-5355

Fowler, Benton, Pop. 2,328
Benton Community SC   2,000/K-12
PO Box 512 47944   765-884-0850
Steven R. Wittenauer, supt.   Fax 884-1614
www.benton.k12.in.us
Other Schools – See Oxford

Francesville, Pulaski, Pop. 880
West Central SC   900/K-12
117 E Montgomery St 47946   219-567-9161
Charles Mellon, supt.   Fax 567-9761
www.west-central.k12.in.us
West Central HS   300/9-12
1852 S US Highway 421 47946   219-567-9119
Don Street, prin.   Fax 567-2597
West Central MS   200/6-8
1850 S US Highway 421 47946   219-567-2534
Kay Beasey, prin.   Fax 567-9535

Frankfort, Clinton, Pop. 16,478
Clinton Prairie SC   1,100/K-12
4431 W State Road 28 46041   765-659-1339
Charles Fink, supt.   Fax 659-5305
www.clintonprairie.com/
Clinton Prairie JSHS   500/7-12
2400 S County Road 450 W 46041   765-659-3305
David R. Larsh, prin.   Fax 659-3205

Frankfort Community SC   3,300/PK-12
50 S Maish Rd 46041   765-654-5585
Dr. Kevin Caress, supt.   Fax 659-6220
www.frankfort.k12.in.us
Frankfort HS   900/9-12
1 S Maish Rd 46041   765-654-8545
Todd Bess, prin.   Fax 654-9224
Frankfort MS   800/6-8
329 N Maish Rd 46041   765-659-3321
Mike McLaughlin, prin.   Fax 659-6260

Franklin, Johnson, Pop. 20,833
Franklin Community SC   4,400/K-12
998 Grizzly Cub Dr 46131   317-738-5800
Dr. William Patterson, supt.   Fax 738-5812
www.fcsc.k12.in.us
Custer Baker MS   1,000/6-8
101 W State Road 44 46131   317-738-5840
Pam Millikan, prin.   Fax 738-5867
Franklin Community HS   1,200/9-12
625 Grizzly Cub Dr 46131   317-738-5700
Leighton Turner, prin.   Fax 738-5703

Franklin College   Post-Sec.
101 Branigin Blvd 46131   317-738-8000

Frankton, Madison, Pop. 1,901
Frankton-Lapel Community SD
Supt. — See Anderson
Frankton JSHS   600/7-12
610 E Clyde St 46044   765-754-7879
Jerry Hoss, prin.   Fax 754-8594

Fremont, Steuben, Pop. 1,691
Fremont Community SD   1,300/K-12
PO Box 665 46737   260-495-5005
Ben Roederer, supt.   Fax 495-9798
fcs.k12.in.us/
Fremont HS   400/9-12
PO Box 655 46737   260-495-9876
Linda Coleman, prin.   Fax 495-1838
Fremont MS   400/5-8
PO Box E 46737   260-495-6100
William Stitt, prin.   Fax 495-7301

French Lick, Orange, Pop. 1,924
Springs Valley Community SC   1,000/K-12
498 S Larry Bird Blvd 47432   812-936-4474
Dr. Robert Haworth, supt.   Fax 936-9392
Springs Valley Comm. JSHS   400/7-12
326 S Larry Bird Blvd 47432   812-936-9984
Todd Pritchett, prin.   Fax 936-9266

Fulton, Fulton, Pop. 323
Caston SC   800/K-12
PO Box 8 46931   574-857-2035
Robert Huffman, supt.   Fax 857-6795
www.caston.k12.in.us/
Caston JSHS   400/7-12
PO Box 128 46931   574-857-3505
Matt Rickett, prin.   Fax 857-6795

Garrett, DeKalb, Pop. 5,762
Garrett-Keyser-Butler Community SD   1,600/K-12
900 E Warfield St 46738   260-357-3185
Alan Middleton, supt.   Fax 357-4565
Garrett HS   500/9-12
801 E Houston St 46738   260-357-4114
Keeman Lobsiger, prin.   Fax 357-5000
Garrett MS   500/5-8
801 E Houston St 46738   260-357-5745
Greg Moe, prin.   Fax 357-3575
Other Schools – See Kendallville

Gary, Lake, Pop. 99,961
Gary Community SC   13,300/PK-12
620 E 10th Pl 46402   219-881-5401
Dr. Mary Steele, supt.   Fax 881-4102
www.garycsc.k12.in.us/
Bailly MS   400/7-8
4621 Georgia St 46409   219-980-6326
Aurelia Weaver, prin.   Fax 981-4463
Emerson Visual Performing Arts JSHS   500/6-12
716 E 7th Ave 46402   219-886-6555
Noah Riley, prin.   Fax 881-4125
Gary Career Center   Vo/Tech
1800 E 35th Ave 46409   219-962-7571
Jerome Hurt, prin.   Fax 962-6269
Pulaski-Dunbar MS   500/7-8
920 E 19th Ave 46407   219-886-6581
Michael Collins, prin.   Fax 881-2057
Roosevelt HS   900/9-12
730 W 25th Ave 46407   219-881-1500
Dr. Leotis Swopes, prin.   Fax 881-1564
Tolleston MS   900/7-8
2700 W 19th Ave 46404   219-977-2145
Lucille Upshaw, prin.   Fax 977-9359
Wallace HS   900/9-12
415 W 45th Ave 46408   219-980-6305
Janice Murray-Minor, prin.   Fax 981-4462
West Side HS   1,200/9-12
900 Gerry St 46406   219-977-2100
Diane Rouse, prin.   Fax 977-2168
Wirt HS   700/9-12
210 N Grand Blvd 46403   219-938-1161
Judy Dunlap, prin.   Fax 938-7544

Lake Ridge SC   2,400/K-12
6111 W Ridge Rd 46408   219-838-1819
Dr. Robert Beach, supt.   Fax 989-7801
www.lakeridgeschools.homestead.com
Calumet HS   600/9-12
3900 Calhoun St 46408   219-838-6990
Leroy Miller, prin.   Fax 989-7849
Lake Ridge MS   500/6-8
3601 W 41st Ave 46408   219-980-0730
Robert Mastej, prin.   Fax 980-0731

Indiana University Northwest   Post-Sec.
3400 Broadway 46408   219-980-6500
Ivy Tech Community College Northwest   Post-Sec.
1440 E 35th Ave 46409   219-981-1111

Gas City, Grant, Pop. 5,910
Mississinewa Community SC   2,200/PK-12
424 E South A St 46933   765-674-8528
Michael Powell, supt.   Fax 674-8529
www.olemiss.k12.in.us/
Baskett MS   500/6-8
125 N Broadway St 46933   765-674-8536
Terry Talbott, prin.   Fax 677-4452
Mississinewa HS   600/9-12
1 Indian Trail Dr 46933   765-674-2248
Lezlie Winter, prin.   Fax 677-4424

Gaston, Delaware, Pop. 992
Wes-Del Community SD   900/K-12
10290 N County Road 600 W 47342 765-358-4006
Steve McColley, supt.   Fax 358-4065
www.wes-del.k12.in.us/
Wes-Del MSHS   500/6-12
10000 N County Road 600 W 47342 765-358-4091
Phillip Gardner, prin.   Fax 358-4065

Georgetown, Floyd, Pop. 2,415
New Albany-Floyd Co. Consolidated SD
Supt. — See New Albany
Highland Hills MS   6-8
3492 Edwardsville Galena Rd 47122 812-923-4014
Gary Hutton, prin.   Fax 923-4031

Goshen, Elkhart, Pop. 29,787
Fairfield Community SD   2,100/K-12
67240 County Road 31 46528   574-831-2188
Thomas Tumey, supt.   Fax 831-5698
www.fairfield.k12.in.us
Fairfield JSHS   900/7-12
67530 US Highway 33 46526   574-831-2184
Philip Hoskins, prin.   Fax 831-2187

Goshen Community SD   5,800/K-12
613 E Purl St 46526   574-533-8631
Bruce Stahly, supt.   Fax 533-2505
www.goshenschools.org/
Goshen HS   1,600/9-12
1 Redskin Rd 46526   574-533-8651
Jim Kirkton, prin.   Fax 534-1567
Goshen MS   1,300/6-8
1216 S Indiana Ave 46526   574-533-0391
Ann Eaton, prin.   Fax 534-3042

Bethany Christian S   300/6-12
2904 S Main St 46526   574-534-2567
Allan Dueck, prin.   Fax 533-0150
Clinton Christian S   100/K-12
61763 County Road 35 46528   574-642-3940
Robert Carroll, prin.   Fax 642-3674
Goshen College   Post-Sec.
1700 S Main St 46526   574-535-7000

Harrison Christian S — 200/1-12
64784 County Road 11 46526 — 574-862-2515
Ruby Wittmer, prin.

Granger, Saint Joseph, Pop. 20,241
Penn-Harris-Madison SC
Supt. — See Mishawaka
Discovery MS — 900/6-8
10050 Brummitt Rd 46530 — 574-674-6010
Sheryll Harper, prin. — Fax 679-4214

Davenport College of Business — Post-Sec.
7121 Grape Rd 46530 — 574-277-8447
Granger Christian S — 200/K-12
52025 Gumwood Rd 46530 — 574-272-5815
Ed Ryan, admin. — Fax 968-2664

Greencastle, Putnam, Pop. 9,987
Area 30 Career Center
1 N Calbert Way Ste A 46135 — 765-653-3515
Michael Walton, supt. — Fax 653-3618
Area 30 Career Center — Vo/Tech
1 N Calbert Way 46135 — 765-653-3515
Lora Wood, prin. — Fax 653-3618

Greencastle Community SC — 2,000/K-12
PO Box 480 46135 — 765-653-9771
Dr. Robert Green, supt. — Fax 653-1282
www.greencastle.k12.in.us
Greencastle HS — 600/9-12
910 E Washington St 46135 — 765-653-9711
Dr. Susan Phillips, prin. — Fax 653-4773
Greencastle MS — 400/6-8
400 Percy L Julian Dr 46135 — 765-653-9774
Shawn Gobert, prin. — Fax 653-5381

South Putnam Community SD — 1,400/K-12
3999 S US Highway 231 46135 — 765-653-3119
Dr. Daniel Schroeder, supt. — Fax 653-7476
www.sputnam.k12.in.us
South Putnam JSHS — 700/7-12
1780 E US Highway 40 46135 — 765-653-3148
Robert Smith, prin. — Fax 653-3149

DePauw University — Post-Sec.
101 E Seminary St 46135 — 765-658-4800

Greenfield, Hancock, Pop. 15,721
Greenfield-Central Community SD — 4,200/PK-12
110 W North St 46140 — 317-462-4434
Dr. Linda Gellert, supt. — Fax 467-4227
gcsc.k12.in.us
Greenfield-Central HS — 1,200/9-12
810 N Broadway St 46140 — 317-462-9211
Steven Bryant, prin. — Fax 467-6723
Greenfield MS — 500/6-8
204 W Park Ave 46140 — 317-462-6827
James Bever, prin. — Fax 467-6730
Other Schools – See Maxwell

Hancock Memorial Hospital — Post-Sec.
801 N State St 46140 — 317-462-0457
PJ's College of Cosmetology — Post-Sec.
1400 W Main St 46140

Greensburg, Decatur, Pop. 10,361
Decatur County Community SD — 2,200/PK-12
1645 W State Road 46 47240 — 812-663-4595
Robert Cupp, supt. — Fax 663-4168
www.decaturco.k12.in.us
North Decatur JSHS — 600/7-12
3172 N State Road 3 47240 — 812-663-4204
Gary Cook, prin. — Fax 663-9606
South Decatur JSHS — 400/7-12
8885 S State Road 3 47240 — 812-591-3330
Bob Hacker, prin. — Fax 591-3331

Greensburg Community SD — 1,800/K-12
504 E Central Ave 47240 — 812-663-4774
Tom Hunter, supt. — Fax 663-5713
www.greensburg.k12.in.us
Greensburg Community HS — 600/9-12
1000 E Central Ave 47240 — 812-663-7176
Phil Chapple, prin. — Fax 663-8911
Greensburg Community JHS — 500/6-8
505 E Central Ave 47240 — 812-663-7523
Garry Moore, prin. — Fax 663-9425

Greentown, Howard, Pop. 2,494
Eastern-Howard SC — 1,300/K-12
221 W Main St Ste 1 46936 — 765-628-3391
Dr. Stephen C. Healy, supt. — Fax 628-5017
www.eastern.k12.in.us
Eastern JSHS — 600/7-12
421 S Harrison St 46936 — 765-628-3333
Ronald Matas, prin. — Fax 628-5021

Greenwood, Johnson, Pop. 39,545
Center Grove Community SC — 7,000/K-12
2929 S Morgantown Rd 46143 — 317-881-9326
Dr. Candace Milhon-Baer, supt. — Fax 881-0241
www.centergrove.k12.in.us
Center Grove HS — 2,100/9-12
2717 S Morgantown Rd 46143 — 317-881-0581
Matt Shockley, prin. — Fax 885-4509
Center Grove MS Central — 800/6-8
4900 W Stones Crossing Rd 46143 — 317-882-9391
Jack Parker, prin. — Fax 885-4534
Center Grove MS North — 900/6-8
202 N Morgantown Rd 46142 — 317-885-8800
Jim Snapp, prin. — Fax 885-3388

Central Nine Career Center SD
1999 US Highway 31 S 46143 — 317-888-4401
Timothy Lavery, supt. — Fax 885-8670
www.central9.k12.in.us
Central Nine Career Center — Vo/Tech
1999 US Highway 31 S 46143 — 317-888-4401
John Strader, prin. — Fax 885-8670

Greenwood Community SC — 3,800/K-12
605 W Smith Valley Rd 46142 — 317-889-4060
David E. Edds, supt. — Fax 889-4068
oak.gws.k12.in.us/
Greenwood Community HS — 1,100/9-12
615 W Smith Valley Rd 46142 — 317-889-4000
James Kaylor, prin. — Fax 889-4039
Greenwood MS — 1,000/6-8
523 S Madison Ave 46142 — 317-889-4040
Vicki Noblitt, prin. — Fax 889-4044

Greenwood Christian Academy — 300/PK-12
PO Box 387 46142 — 317-859-4150
Bruce Peters, hdmstr. — Fax 859-9072

Griffith, Lake, Pop. 16,961
Griffith Public SD — 2,700/K-12
132 N Broad St 46319 — 219-924-4250
Peter N. Morikis, supt. — Fax 922-5933
www.griffith.k12.in.us
Griffith HS — 800/9-12
600 N Wiggs St 46319 — 219-924-4281
William Cope, prin. — Fax 922-5920
Griffith MS — 500/7-8
600 N Raymond St 46319 — 219-924-4280
Terry Mucha, prin. — Fax 922-5927

Hagerstown, Wayne, Pop. 1,719
Nettle Creek SC — 1,300/PK-12
297 E Northmarket St 47346 — 765-489-4543
Joseph Backmeyer, supt. — Fax 489-4914
www.nettlecreek.k12.in.us
Hagerstown JSHS — 600/7-12
701 Baker Rd 47346 — 765-489-4511
Mark Childs, prin. — Fax 489-4333

Hamilton, DeKalb, Pop. 1,224
Hamilton Community SD — 700/K-12
901 S Wayne St 46742 — 260-488-2513
Mark Gould, supt. — Fax 488-2348
www.hamiltoncomm.com/
Hamilton Community JSHS — 300/7-12
903 S Wayne St 46742 — 260-488-2161
Kenneth Webb, prin. — Fax 488-3149

Hamlet, Starke, Pop. 783
Oregon-Davis SC — 800/K-12
5998 N 750 E 46532 — 574-867-2111
William Rentschler, supt. — Fax 867-8191
www.od.k12.in.us
Oregon-Davis JSHS — 300/7-12
5990 N 750 E 46532 — 574-867-4561
Greg Briles, prin. — Fax 867-2481

Hammond, Lake, Pop. 80,547
Hammond CSD — 13,400/PK-12
41 E Williams St 46320 — 219-933-2400
Dr. Walter J. Watkins, supt. — Fax 933-2495
www.hammond.k12.in.us
Area Career Center — Vo/Tech
5727 S Sohl Ave 46320 — 219-933-2428
Audra Peterson, prin. — Fax 933-1680
Eggers MS — 1,000/6-8
5825 Blaine Ave 46320 — 219-933-2449
Barbara Fleming, prin. — Fax 933-1675
Gavit MSHS — 1,700/6-12
1670 175th St 46324 — 219-989-7328
Chuck Hall, prin. — Fax 989-7333
Hammond HS — 800/9-12
5926 S Calumet Ave 46320 — 219-933-2442
Otis Watkins, prin. — Fax 933-1688
Morton HS — 900/9-12
6915 Grand Ave 46323 — 219-989-7316
Theresa Mayerik, prin. — Fax 989-7321
Scott MS — 900/6-8
3635 173rd St 46323 — 219-989-7340
Bobbie Escalante, prin. — Fax 989-7342
Other Schools – See Whiting

Bishop Noll Institute — 1,000/7-12
1519 E Hoffman St 46327 — 219-932-9058
Scott Fech, prin. — Fax 853-1736
Purdue University — Post-Sec.
2200 169th St 46323 — 219-989-2993
St. Margaret Hospital — Post-Sec.
5454 S Hohman Ave 46320 — 219-932-2300
Sawyer College — Post-Sec.
7833 Indianapolis Blvd 46324 — 219-844-0100
Shepherd's Academy — 50/K-12
6518 Grand Ave 46323 — 219-844-8900
Christin Kiesling, prin.

Hanover, Jefferson, Pop. 3,868
Southwestern-Jefferson Co. Cons SC — 1,500/K-12
239 S Main Cross St 47243 — 812-866-6250
Stephen Telfer, supt. — Fax 866-6256
www.swjcs.k12.in.us/
Southwestern MSHS — 800/6-12
167 S Main Cross St 47243 — 812-866-6230
Mike Costlow, prin. — Fax 866-4680

Hanover College — Post-Sec.
PO Box 108 47243 — 812-866-7000

Hartford City, Blackford, Pop. 6,728
Blackford County SD — 2,300/PK-12
668 W 200 S 47348 — 765-348-7550
Gerald Chabot, supt. — Fax 348-7552
www.bcs.k12.in.us
Blackford HS — 700/9-12
2392 N State Road 3 47348 — 765-348-7560
Dr. Sue Neat, prin. — Fax 348-7568
Hartford City MS — 400/6-8
800 W Van Cleve St 47348 — 765-348-7590
Andrew Glentzer, prin. — Fax 348-7593

Hebron, Porter, Pop. 3,541
Metro SD of Boone Township — 800/K-12
307 S Main St 46341 — 219-996-4771
George Letz, supt. — Fax 996-5777
www.hebronschools.k12.in.us/
Hebron HS — 300/9-12
307 S Main St 46341 — 219-996-4771
David Howenstine, prin. — Fax 996-5777
Hebron MS, 307 S Main St 46341 — 6-8
Rick Ankney, prin. — 219-996-4771

Henryville, Clark
West Clark Community SC
Supt. — See Sellersburg
Henryville JSHS — 400/7-12
215 N Ferguson St 47126 — 812-294-1455
Denise H. Bessler, prin. — Fax 294-4276

Highland, Lake, Pop. 23,444
Highland SC — 3,400/K-12
9145 Kennedy Ave 46322 — 219-924-7400
Renner Ventling, supt. — Fax 922-5637
www.highland.k12.in.us
Highland HS — 1,100/9-12
9135 Erie St 46322 — 219-922-5610
James Conway, prin. — Fax 922-5636
Highland MS — 600/7-8
2941 41st St 46322 — 219-922-5620
Kenneth Winston, prin. — Fax 922-5637

Creative Hair Styling Academy — Post-Sec.
2549 Highway Ave 46322 — 219-838-2004

Hobart, Lake, Pop. 26,972
Hobart CSD — 3,600/K-12
32 E 7th St 46342 — 219-942-8885
Dr. John Leach, supt. — Fax 942-0081
www.hobart.k12.in.us
Hobart HS — 1,100/9-12
36 E 8th St 46342 — 219-942-8521
David Spitzer, prin. — Fax 942-3326
Hobart MS — 900/6-8
705 E 4th St 46342 — 219-942-8541
Peter Svetcoff, prin. — Fax 947-7194

River Forest Community SC — 1,400/PK-12
3334 Michigan St 46342 — 219-962-2909
Dr. James Rice, supt. — Fax 962-4951
www.rfcsc.k12.in.us
River Forest HS — 300/9-12
3300 Indiana St 46342 — 219-962-7551
Andrew Wielgus, prin. — Fax 962-8338
River Forest JHS — 200/7-8
3250 Indiana St 46342 — 219-962-7811
Michael Banham, prin. — Fax 962-7554

College of Court Reporting — Post-Sec.
111 W 10th St Ste 111 46342 — 219-942-1459

Hope, Bartholomew, Pop. 2,154
Flat Rock-Hawcreek SC — 1,100/PK-12
PO Box 34 47246 — 812-546-2000
Dr. Phillip Deardorff, supt. — Fax 546-5617
www.flatrock.k12.in.us
Hauser JSHS — 500/7-12
9273 N State Road 9 47246 — 812-546-4421
Tim Stephens, prin. — Fax 546-2005

Howe, Lagrange

Howe Military S — 200/5-12
PO Box 240 46746 — 260-562-2131
Duane Van Orden, supt. — Fax 562-3678

Huntertown, Allen, Pop. 2,335

Heritage Mission S — 50/K-12
1825 W Shoaff Rd 46748 — 260-637-9980
Annette Mains, prin.

Huntingburg, Dubois, Pop. 5,815
Southwest Dubois County SC — 1,900/K-12
PO Box 398 47542 — 812-683-3971
Terry Enlow, supt. — Fax 683-2752
www.swdubois.k12.in.us
Southridge HS — 500/9-12
1110 S Main St 47542 — 812-683-2272
Mike Eineman, prin. — Fax 683-2010
Southridge MS — 500/6-8
1112 S Main St 47542 — 812-683-3372
Al Mihajlovits, prin. — Fax 683-2817

Huntington, Huntington, Pop. 17,163
Huntington County Community SC — 6,300/K-12
1360 Warren Rd 46750 — 260-356-7812
Tracey Shafer, supt. — Fax 358-2216
www.hccsc.k12.in.us
Crestview MS — 600/6-8
1151 W 500 N 46750 — 260-356-6210
Tom Alexander, prin. — Fax 358-2232
Huntington North HS — 2,000/9-12
450 MacGahan St 46750 — 260-356-6104
Ken Kline, prin. — Fax 358-2210
Riverview MS — 600/6-8
2465 Waterworks Rd 46750 — 260-356-0910
Curt Crago, prin. — Fax 358-2243

Huntington College — Post-Sec.
2303 College Ave 46750 — 260-356-6000

Hymera, Sullivan, Pop. 825
Northeast SC — 1,500/PK-12
PO Box 493 47855 — 812-383-5761
Richard Walters, supt. — Fax 383-4591
www.nesc.k12.in.us/
Other Schools – See Dugger, Farmersburg

Indianapolis, Marion, Pop. 783,612
Franklin Twp Community SC 6,900/PK-12
6141 S Franklin Rd 46259 317-862-2411
E. B. Carver, supt. Fax 862-7238
www.ftcsc.k12.in.us
Franklin Central HS 1,700/9-12
6215 S Franklin Rd 46259 317-862-6646
Kevin Koers, prin. Fax 862-7262
Franklin Twp. MS 1,100/7-8
6019 S Franklin Rd 46259 317-862-2446
Leland Thompson, prin. Fax 862-7271

Indianapolis SD 39,800/PK-12
120 E Walnut St 46204 317-226-4000
Dr. Eugene White, supt. Fax 226-4936
www.ips.k12.in.us
Arlington HS 1,600/9-12
4825 N Arlington Ave 46226 317-226-2345
Jacqueline Greenwood, prin. Fax 226-3009
Arsenal Technical HS 2,100/9-12
1500 E Michigan St 46201 317-693-5300
Jerry McLeish, admin. Fax 226-3932
Attucks MS 800/6-8
1140 Dr Mrtn Lthr Kng Jr St 46202 317-226-2800
John DeBoe, prin. Fax 226-3495
Broad Ripple HS 1,500/9-12
1115 Broad Ripple Ave 46220 317-693-5700
Stephen Papesh, prin. Fax 226-3783
Career & Technology Center Vo/Tech
725 N Oriental St 46202 317-693-5430
Luberta Jenkins, prin. Fax 226-3709
Coleman MS 400/6-8
1740 E 30th St 46218 317-226-4110
Mattie Solomon, prin. Fax 226-3589
Donnan MS 900/6-8
1202 E Troy Ave 46203 317-226-4272
Robert Guffin, prin. Fax 226-4355
Douglass MS 300/6-8
2020 Dawson St 46203 317-226-4219
David Newman, prin. Fax 226-4762
Farrington MS 500/6-8
4326 Patricia St 46222 317-226-4261
Yvonne Rambo, prin. Fax 226-4078
Forest Manor MS 500/6-8
4501 E 32nd St 46218 317-226-4363
Karen Dailey, prin. Fax 226-4328
Gambold MS 700/6-8
3725 N Kiel Ave 46224 317-226-4108
Thelma McKenney, prin. Fax 226-3750
Harshman MS 800/6-8
1501 E 10th St 46201 317-226-4101
Linda Casey, prin. Fax 226-3444
Howe Academy 1,700/6-12
4900 Julian Ave 46201 317-693-5590
Anita Silverman, prin. Fax 226-4033
Longfellow MS 400/6-8
510 Laurel St 46203 317-226-4228
Phyllis Barnes, prin. Fax 226-3756
Manual HS 1,500/9-12
2405 Madison Ave 46225 317-226-2200
Richard Grismore, prin. Fax 226-3836
Marshall MS 900/6-8
10101 E 38th St 46235 317-693-5460
Jamyce Banks, prin. Fax 226-3718
McFarland MS 400/6-8
3200 E Raymond St 46203 317-226-4112
Dexter Suggs, prin. Fax 226-3744
Northwest HS 1,500/9-12
5525 W 34th St 46224 317-693-5600
Roy Simpson, prin. Fax 226-3409
Shortridge MS 900/6-8
3401 N Meridian St 46208 317-226-2810
Linda Davis, prin. Fax 226-3725
Sidener MS 300/6-8
2424 Kessler Boulevard E Dr 46220 317-226-4259
James Whisler, prin. Fax 226-3059
Washington Community HS 1,200/6-12
2215 W Washington St 46222 317-693-5555
Keith Burke, prin. Fax 226-3273
Hope Academy/Day Adult HS Adult
1301 E 16th St 46202 317-226-4116
Vickie Nowland, prin. Fax 226-4524

Metro SD of Decatur Township 4,700/K-12
5275 Kentucky Ave 46221 317-856-5265
Donald Stinson, supt. Fax 856-2156
www.msddecatur.k12.in.us
Decatur Central HS 1,500/9-12
5251 Kentucky Ave 46221 317-856-5288
Joe Preda, prin. Fax 856-2157
Decatur MS 900/7-8
5108 S High School Rd 46221 317-856-5274
Mark Anderson, prin. Fax 856-2163

Metro SD of Lawrence Township 16,300/K-12
7601 E 56th St 46226 317-423-8200
Dr. Michael Copper, supt. Fax 543-3534
www.msdlt.k12.in.us
Belzer MS 1,400/6-8
7555 E 56th St 46226 317-545-7411
Ronald Davie, prin. Fax 543-3355
Craig MS 1,400/6-8
6501 Sunnyside Rd 46236 317-823-6805
William Gavaghan, prin. Fax 823-5223
Fall Creek Valley MS 1,300/6-8
9701 E 63rd St 46236 317-823-5490
James Joiner, prin. Fax 823-5497
Lawrence Central HS 2,200/9-12
7300 E 56th St 46226 317-545-5301
Edward Freije, prin. Fax 543-3348
Lawrence North HS 2,700/9-12
7802 Hague Rd 46256 317-849-9455
Lynn Lupold, prin. Fax 576-6406
McKenzie Career Center Vo/Tech
7250 E 75th St 46256 317-576-6420
Barry Norman, prin. Fax 849-2546

Metro SD of Perry Township 11,900/PK-12
6548 Orinoco Ave 46227 317-789-3700
H. Douglas Williams, supt. Fax 789-3709
www.msdpt.k12.in.us
Perry Meridian HS 1,800/9-12
401 W Meridian School Rd 46217 317-789-4400
Anita Silverman, prin. Fax 789-4479
Perry Meridian MS 1,100/7-8
202 W Meridian School Rd 46217 317-789-4100
Dennis Howland, prin. Fax 865-2710
Southport HS 1,700/9-12
971 E Banta Rd 46227 317-789-4800
Barbara Brouwer, prin. Fax 780-4325
Southport MS 1,000/7-8
5715 S Keystone Ave 46227 317-789-4600
Steve Mast, prin. Fax 780-4302

Metro SD of Pike Township 9,700/PK-12
6901 Zionsville Rd 46268 317-293-0393
Nathaniel Jones, supt. Fax 297-7896
www.pike.k12.in.us
Guion Creek MS 900/6-8
4401 W 52nd St 46254 317-293-4549
Ms. Kurt Benjamin, prin. Fax 298-2794
Lincoln MS 900/6-8
5353 W 71st St 46268 317-291-9499
Shelly Haley, prin. Fax 297-1673
New Augusta Public Academy North 800/6-8
6450 Rodebaugh Rd 46268 317-387-4328
Stan Hall, prin. Fax 388-7786
Pike Freshman Center 9-9
6801 Zionsville Rd 46268 317-347-8600
Shawn Smith, prin. Fax 347-8555
Pike HS 1,900/10-12
5401 W 71st St 46268 317-291-5250
Debra Jacobs, prin. Fax 328-7239

Metro SD of Warren Township 11,800/PK-12
975 N Post Rd 46219 317-869-4300
Dr. Peggy Hinckley, supt. Fax 869-4348
www.warren.k12.in.us
Creston MS 1,100/6-8
10925 Prospect St 46239 317-532-6800
Sheri Marcotte, prin. Fax 532-6899
Raymond Park MS 900/6-8
8575 E Raymond St 46239 317-532-8900
Kathy Deck, prin. Fax 532-8999
Stonybrook MS 1,000/6-8
11300 Stonybrook Dr 46229 317-532-8800
Jimmy Meadows, prin. Fax 532-8899
Walker Career Center Vo/Tech
9651 E 21st St 46229 317-532-6150
Lou Anne Schwenn, prin. Fax 532-6199
Warren Central HS 3,300/9-12
9500 E 16th St 46229 317-532-6200
James Burchett, prin. Fax 532-6459

Metro SD of Washington Township 10,000/PK-12
8550 Woodfield Crossing Blv 46240 317-845-9400
Dr. R. Stephen Tegarden, supt. Fax 205-3385
www.msdwt.k12.in.us
Eastwood MS 800/6-8
4401 E 62nd St 46220 317-259-5401
Sylvia Lane, prin. Fax 259-5407
Light Career Center Vo/Tech
1901 E 86th St 46240 317-259-5265
Eldon Horton, prin. Fax 259-5266
North Central HS 3,200/9-12
1801 E 86th St 46240 317-259-5301
C.E. Quandt, prin. Fax 259-5369
Northview MS 1,000/6-8
8401 Westfield Rd 46240 317-259-5421
Nikki Tsangaris, prin. Fax 259-5431
Westlane MS 700/6-8
1301 W 73rd St 46260 317-259-5412
Linda Lawrence, prin. Fax 259-5409

Metro SD of Wayne Township 13,800/PK-12
1220 S High School Rd 46241 317-243-8251
Terry Thompson Ed.D., supt. Fax 243-5744
www.wayne.k12.in.us
Chapel Hill 7th & 8th Grade Center 1,300/7-9
1155 N Girls School Rd 46214 317-241-9285
John Taylor, prin. Fax 243-5728
Davis 9th Grade Center 9-9
1150 N Girls School Rd 46214 317-241-9285
John Taylor, prin.
Davis JHS 1,300/7-9
1155 S High School Rd 46241 317-244-2438
Jeff Hubble, prin. Fax 243-5535
Davis SHS 2,600/10-12
1200 N Girls School Rd 46214 317-244-7691
David Marcotte, prin. Fax 243-5506
Lynhurst 7th & 8th Grade Center 600/7-8
2805 S Lynhurst Dr 46241 317-247-6265
Dan Wilson, prin. Fax 243-5532

A Cut Above Beauty College Post-Sec.
3810 E Southport Rd 46237 317-781-0959
Art Institute of Indianapolis Post-Sec.
3500 Depauw Blvd 46268 317-613-4800
Aviation Institute of Maintenance Post-Sec.
7251 W McCarty St 46241 317-243-4519
Baptist Academy 300/PK-12
2565 Villa Ave 46203 317-788-1587
Barbara Frye, prin. Fax 781-4759
Bishop Silas Chatard HS 800/9-12
5885 Crittenden Ave 46220 317-251-1451
Al Holok, dean Fax 251-3648
Brebeuf Jesuit Prep S 800/9-12
2801 W 86th St 46268 317-524-7149
Andrew F. Noga, prin. Fax 524-7148
Butler University Post-Sec.
4600 Sunset Ave 46208 317-940-8000
Calvary Christian S 200/PK-12
902 Fletcher Ave 46203 317-262-4034
Charles Barcus, prin. Fax 262-4029

Cardinal Ritter HS 400/7-12
3360 W 30th St 46222 317-924-4333
Jo Hoy, prin. Fax 927-7822
Cathedral HS 1,000/9-12
5225 E 56th St 46226 317-542-1481
David Worland, prin. Fax 543-5050
Christian Theological Seminary Post-Sec.
1000 W 42nd St 46208 317-924-1331
Colonial Christian S 300/PK-12
8140 Union Chapel Rd 46240 317-253-0649
Brian Washburn, prin. Fax 254-2840
Community Hospital of Indianapolis Post-Sec.
1500 N Ritter Ave 46219 317-355-5529
Covenant Christian HS 400/9-12
7525 W 21st St 46214 317-390-0202
Brian Hudson, prin. Fax 390-6823
Crossroads Bible College Post-Sec.
601 N Shortridge Rd 46219 317-352-8736
DeVry University Post-Sec.
9100 Keystone Xing Ste 350 46240 317-581-8854
Eagledale Christian S 300/K-12
4950 W 34th St 46224 317-291-4783
Galen Fitzsimmons, prin. Fax 291-7568
Heritage Christian S 1,600/K-12
6401 E 75th St 46250 317-849-3441
Brian Simmons Ed.D., admin. Fax 594-5863
Horizon Christian S 300/PK-12
7702 Indian Lake Rd 46236 317-823-4538
Frank Onorio, admin. Fax 826-2438
Indiana Business College Post-Sec.
5460 Victory Dr Ste 100 46203 317-783-5100
Indiana Business College Post-Sec.
550 E Washington St 46204 800-999-9229
Indiana Business College Northwest Post-Sec.
6300 Technology Dr 46278 317-873-6500
Indianapolis Christian S 100/K-12
620 E 10th St 46202 317-636-4560
Betty Speight, prin. Fax 636-1160
Indiana School for the Deaf Post-Sec.
1200 E 42nd St 46205 317-924-4374
Indiana State School for the Blind Post-Sec.
7725 N College Ave 46240 317-253-1481
Indiana University School of Allied Hlth Post-Sec.
1140 W Michigan St 46202 317-274-4702
Indiana Univ-Purdue Univ at Indianapolis Post-Sec.
355 Lansing St 46202 317-274-5555
Indiana Vocational Technical College Post-Sec.
PO Box 1763 46206 317-921-4882
International Business College Post-Sec.
7205 Shadeland Station Way 46256 317-841-6400
ITT Technical Institute Post-Sec.
9511 Angola Ct 46268 317-875-8640
Ivy Tech Community College Central IN Post-Sec.
1 W 26th St 46208 317-921-4882
Kaye Beauty College Post-Sec.
6346 E 82nd St 46250 317-576-8000
Lincoln Technical Institute Post-Sec.
7225 Winton Dr # 128 46268 800-554-4465
Lutheran HS 300/9-12
5555 S Arlington Ave 46237 317-787-5474
Gary St. Clair, dir. Fax 787-2794
Marian College Post-Sec.
3200 Cold Spring Rd 46222 317-955-6000
Martin University Post-Sec.
PO Box 18567 46218 317-543-3235
MedTech College Post-Sec.
6612 E 75th St Ste 300 46250 317-845-0100
Methodist Hosp/Clarian Health Partners Post-Sec.
PO Box 1367 46206 317-929-5900
Park Tudor S 1,000/PK-12
7200 N College Ave 46240 317-415-2700
Douglas S. Jennings, prin. Fax 254-2714
PJ's College of Cosmetology Post-Sec.
5539 Madison Ave 46227
Professional Careers Institute Post-Sec.
7302 Woodland Dr 46278 317-299-6001
Roncalli HS 1,000/9-12
3300 Prague Rd 46227 317-787-8277
Charles Weisenbach, prin. Fax 788-4095
Scecina Memorial HS 600/9-12
5000 Nowland Ave 46201 317-356-6377
Tom Davis, prin. Fax 322-4287
Summit Academy 100/1-12
3600 W 96th St 46268 317-334-9335
Clair M. Stanley, admin. Fax 334-9335
University of Indianapolis Post-Sec.
1400 E Hanna Ave 46227 317-788-3368

Jasonville, Greene, Pop. 2,482
Metro SD Shakamak 900/K-12
RR 2 Box 42 47438 812-665-3550
Michael Turner, supt. Fax 665-5001
www.shakamak.k12.in.us/
Shakamak JSHS 400/7-12
RR 2 Box 42 47438 812-665-3550
Vanessa Hodge, prin. Fax 665-5001

Jasper, Dubois, Pop. 13,205
Greater Jasper Consolidated SD 3,100/PK-12
1520 Saint Charles St 47546 812-482-1801
Dr. Larry Riggs, supt. Fax 482-3388
www.gjcs.k12.in.us
Jasper HS 1,100/9-12
1600 Saint Charles St 47546 812-482-6050
Jerald Roberts, prin. Fax 634-3971
Jasper MS 700/6-8
3600 N Portersville Rd 47546 812-482-6454
Michael Hile, prin. Fax 482-6457

Jeffersonville, Clark, Pop. 28,025
Greater Clark County SD 10,300/PK-12
2112 Utica Sellersburg Rd 47130 812-283-0701
Dr. Thomas Rohr, supt. Fax 288-4804
www.gcs.k12.in.us
Jeffersonville HS 1,900/9-12
2315 Allison Ln 47130 812-282-6601
William Amerson, prin. Fax 288-4812

Parkview MS   800/6-8
  1600 Brigman Ave 47130   812-288-4844
  Mark Laughner, prin.   Fax 288-2849
River Valley MS   1,000/6-8
  2220 Veterans Pkwy 47130   812-288-4848
  Vicki Lete, prin.   Fax 288-4851
Other Schools – See Charlestown, New Washington

Mid-America College of Funeral Service   Post-Sec.
  3111 Hamburg Pike 47130   812-288-8878

Jonesboro, Grant, Pop. 1,810

King's Academy   100/K-12
  1201 S Water St 46938   765-674-1722
  Tony Miner, prin.   Fax 674-2169

Kendallville, Noble, Pop. 9,682
East Noble SC   3,800/K-12
  702 Dowling St 46755   260-347-2502
  Dr. H. Steve Sprunger, supt.   Fax 347-0111
  www.eastnoble.net
East Noble HS   1,200/9-12
  901 Garden St 46755   260-347-2032
  Ann Linson, prin.   Fax 347-2362
Kendallville Central MS   500/6-8
  401 E Diamond St 46755   260-347-0100
  James Taylor, prin.   Fax 347-7168

Garrett-Keyser-Butler Community SD
  Supt. — See Garrett
Four County Area Voc Coop   Vo/Tech
  1607 E Dowling St 46755   260-349-0250
  Tim Holcomb, prin.   Fax 349-0240

Kentland, Newton, Pop. 1,738
South Newton SC   1,000/PK-12
  110 N 3rd St 47951   219-474-5184
  Ed Corbin, supt.   Fax 474-6966
  www.newton.k12.in.us/
South Newton HS   300/9-12
  13102 S 50 E 47951   219-474-5167
  Carol Kaiser, prin.   Fax 474-6592
South Newton MS   300/6-8
  13100 S 50 E 47951   219-474-5167
  Carol Kaiser, prin.   Fax 474-3624

Knightstown, Henry, Pop. 2,042
C.A. Beard Memorial SC   1,300/K-12
  345 N Adams St 46148   765-345-5101
  Dr. Hal J. Jester, supt.   Fax 345-5103
  www.cabeard.k12.in.us
Knightstown HS   400/9-12
  8149 W US Highway 40 46148   765-345-5153
  James Diagostino, prin.   Fax 345-5103
Knightstown IS   400/5-8
  1 Panther Trl 46148   765-345-5455
  Don Scheumann, prin.   Fax 345-5103

Morton Memorial S   100/1-12
  10892 N State Road 140 46148   765-345-5141
  Patrick Porter, prin.   Fax 345-2063

Knightsville, Clay, Pop. 627
Clay Community SD   4,600/PK-12
  PO Box 169 47857   812-443-4461
  William Schad, supt.   Fax 442-0849
  www.clay.k12.in.us
Other Schools – See Brazil, Clay City

Knox, Starke, Pop. 3,649
Knox Community SC   2,000/K-12
  2 Redskin Trl 46534   574-772-1600
  Kimberly Knott, supt.   Fax 772-1608
  www.knox.k12.in.us
Knox Community HS   600/9-12
  1 Redskin Trl 46534   574-772-1670
  James Condon, prin.   Fax 772-1681
Knox Community MS   500/6-8
  901 S Main St 46534   574-772-1654
  Steve Cronk, prin.   Fax 772-1664

Kokomo, Howard, Pop. 46,154
Kokomo-Center Twp Consolidated SC   7,000/PK-12
  PO Box 2188 46904   765-455-8000
  Dr. Thomas J. Little, supt.   Fax 455-8018
  www.kokomoschools.com
Bon Air MS   400/6-8
  2796 N Apperson Way 46901   765-454-7035
  Chris Lagoni, prin.   Fax 454-7039
Central MS   500/6-8
  303 E Superior St 46901   765-454-7000
  Brian Van Buskirk, prin.   Fax 454-7007
Kokomo Area Career Ctr   Vo/Tech
  2415 S Berkley Rd 46902   765-455-8021
  James Little, dir.   Fax 455-6850
Kokomo HS   1,900/9-12
  2501 S Berkley Rd 46902   765-455-8040
  Harold Canady, prin.   Fax 455-8060
Lafayette Park MS   500/6-8
  923 Korby St 46901   765-454-7065
  Doug Arnold, prin.   Fax 454-7067
Maple Crest MS   400/6-8
  2727 S Washington St 46902   765-455-8085
  Dan Hogan, prin.   Fax 455-8062

Northwestern SC   1,700/K-12
  3075 N Washington St 46901   765-452-3060
  Ryan Snoddy, supt.   Fax 452-3065
  nwsc.k12.in.us
Northwestern HS   600/9-12
  3431 N County Road 400 W 46901   765-454-2332
  Harold Seamon, prin.   Fax 454-2333
Northwestern MS   300/7-8
  3431 N County Road 400 W 46901   765-454-2323
  Brett Davis, prin.   Fax 457-2324

Taylor Community SC   1,500/PK-12
  3750 E County Road 300 S 46902   765-453-3035
  Dr. Ron Mayes, supt.   Fax 455-8531
  www.taylor.k12.in.us
Taylor HS   500/9-12
  3794 E County Road 300 S 46902   765-453-1101
  A.D. Little, prin.   Fax 455-5163
Taylor MS   400/6-8
  3794 E County Road 300 S 46902   765-455-5186
  Steve Townsend, prin.   Fax 455-5157

Indiana University at Kokomo   Post-Sec.
  PO Box 9003 46904   765-453-2000
Ivy Tech Community College - Kokomo   Post-Sec.
  PO Box 1373 46903   765-459-0561
Kokomo Christian S   200/PK-12
  PO Box 2798 46904   765-455-1447
  Suzette Randall, admin.   Fax 864-0944
Rudae's School of Beauty Culture   Post-Sec.
  208 W Jefferson St 46901   765-459-4197
St. Joseph Hospital & Health Center   Post-Sec.
  1907 W Sycamore St 46901   765-452-5611

Kouts, Porter, Pop. 1,737
East Porter County SC   2,000/K-12
  PO Box 370 46347   219-766-2214
  Dr. Ron Gardin, supt.   Fax 766-2885
  www.epcsc.k12.in.us
Kouts MSHS   400/6-12
  PO Box 699 46347   219-766-2231
  Terry Brownell, prin.   Fax 766-3763
Other Schools – See Valparaiso

La Crosse, LaPorte, Pop. 554
Dewey Township SD
  Supt. — See La Porte
La Crosse S   100/K-12
  PO Box 360 46348   219-754-2461
  M. Freeman, prin.   Fax 754-2511

Lafayette, Tippecanoe, Pop. 61,229
Lafayette SC   6,800/K-12
  2300 Cason St 47904   765-771-6000
  Edward Eiler, supt.   Fax 771-6049
  www.lsc.k12.in.us
Jefferson HS   2,100/9-12
  1801 S 18th St 47905   765-772-4700
  Glade Montgomery, prin.   Fax 772-4713
Tecumseh JHS   1,100/7-8
  2101 S 18th St 47905   765-772-4750
  Brett Gruetzmacher, prin.   Fax 772-4763

Tippecanoe SC   10,300/K-12
  21 Elston Rd 47909   765-474-2481
  Richard Wood, supt.   Fax 474-0533
  www.tsc.k12.in.us
East Tipp MS   400/6-8
  7501 E 300 N 47905   765-589-3566
  Linda McTaggart, prin.   Fax 589-3129
McCutcheon HS   1,400/9-12
  4951 US Highway 231 S 47909   765-474-1488
  John Beeker, prin.   Fax 477-9710
Southwestern MS   300/6-8
  2100 W 800 S 47909   765-538-3025
  Marilyn Ferguson, prin.   Fax 538-2877
Wainwright MS   400/6-8
  7501 E 700 S 47905   765-523-2151
  Neal McCutcheon, prin.   Fax 523-2709
Wea Ridge MS   600/6-8
  4410 S 150 E 47909   765-471-2164
  Cory Marshall, prin.   Fax 474-5347
Other Schools – See Battle Ground, West Lafayette

Central Catholic HS   400/7-12
  2410 S 9th St 47909   765-474-2496
  Joe Brettnacher, prin.   Fax 474-8752
First Assembly Christian Academy   100/PK-12
  108 Beck Ln 47909   765-477-5803
  Christopher Johns, prin.   Fax 474-5845
Indiana Business College   Post-Sec.
  2 Executive Dr 47905   765-447-9550
Ivy Tech Community College - Lafayette   Post-Sec.
  PO Box 6299 47903   765-772-9100
Lafayette Beauty Academy   Post-Sec.
  833 Ferry St 47901   765-742-0068
St. Elizabeth School of Nursing   Post-Sec.
  1508 Tippecanoe St 47904   765-423-6400

Lagrange, Lagrange, Pop. 2,949
Lakeland SC   2,300/K-12
  200 S Cherry St 46761   260-499-2400
  Dr. Russell Hodges, supt.   Fax 463-4800
  www.lakeland.k12.in.us
Lakeland HS   700/9-12
  805 E 075 N 46761   260-499-2470
  Patrick Boles, prin.   Fax 463-4058
Lakeland MS   600/6-8
  1055 E 075 N 46761   260-499-2480
  Chris Smith, prin.   Fax 463-2648

Prairie Heights Community SC   1,800/K-12
  305 S 1150 E 46761   260-351-3214
  Paul Thomas, supt.   Fax 351-3614
  www.ph.k12.in.us/
Prairie Heights HS   500/9-12
  245 S 1150 E 46761   260-351-3214
  Pat McLaughlin, prin.   Fax 351-3048
Prairie Heights MS   600/5-8
  395 S 1150 E 46761   260-351-3214
  Brenda Rummel, prin.   Fax 351-2182

Lake Station, Lake, Pop. 13,818
Lake Station Community SD   1,300/PK-12
  2500 Pike St 46405   219-962-1159
  Dan DeHaven, supt.   Fax 962-4011
Edison JSHS   600/6-12
  3304 Parkside Ave 46405   219-962-8531
  Greg Hatch, prin.   Fax 962-2064

Lakeville, Saint Joseph, Pop. 555
Union-North United SC   1,300/K-12
  22601 Tyler Rd 46536   574-784-8141
  Larry Phillips, supt.   Fax 784-2181
  www.unorth.k12.in.us
Laville JSHS   700/7-12
  69969 US Highway 31 46536   574-784-3151
  Jeffery Rehlander, prin.   Fax 784-8695

Lanesville, Harrison, Pop. 618
Lanesville Community SC   600/K-12
  2725 Crestview Ave NE 47136   812-952-2555
  Dr. Phil Partenheimer, supt.   Fax 952-3762
  www.lanesville.k12.in.us/
Lanesville JSHS   300/7-12
  2725 Crestview Ave NE 47136   812-952-2555
  Janet Page, prin.   Fax 952-3762

Lapel, Madison, Pop. 1,862
Frankton-Lapel Community SD
  Supt. — See Anderson
Lapel JSHS   500/7-12
  2883 S State Rd 13 46051   765-534-3137
  Jerry Kemerly, prin.   Fax 534-3883

La Porte, LaPorte, Pop. 21,067
Dewey Township SD   100/K-12
  809 State St 46350   219-326-6808
  Norm Kleist, supt.   Fax 362-3313
  www.lacrosse.k12.in.us/home.htm
Other Schools – See La Crosse

La Porte Community SC   6,300/PK-12
  1921 A St 46350   219-362-7056
  Karen Rice, supt.   Fax 324-9347
  www.lpcsc.k12.in.us
Boston MS   800/6-8
  1000 Harrison St 46350   219-326-6930
  Jim Dermody, prin.   Fax 324-7108
Kesling MS   700/6-8
  306 E 18th St 46350   219-362-7507
  Bill Wilmsen, prin.   Fax 324-5712
La Porte HS   1,900/9-12
  602 F St 46350   219-362-3102
  Greg Handel, prin.   Fax 324-2142

La Lumiere S   100/9-12
  PO Box 5005 46352   219-326-7450
  Michael Kennedy, hdmstr.   Fax 325-3185

Larwill, Whitley, Pop. 281
Whitko Community SC
  Supt. — See Pierceton
Whitko MS   500/6-8
  710 N State Road 5 # 5 46764   260-327-3603
  Jerry Klausing, prin.   Fax 327-3805

Lawrenceburg, Dearborn, Pop. 4,701
Lawrenceburg Community SC   1,300/K-12
  300 Tiger Blvd 47025   812-537-7200
  Dan Kuebler, supt.   Fax 537-0759
  www.lburg.k12.in.us
Greendale MS   300/6-8
  200 Tiger Blvd 47025   812-537-7259
  Karl Galey, prin.   Fax 537-6385
Lawrenceburg HS   500/9-12
  100 Tiger Blvd 47025   812-537-7219
  Mark Wayman, prin.   Fax 537-7221

Lebanon, Boone, Pop. 14,379
Lebanon Community SC   3,400/K-12
  1810 N Grant St 46052   765-482-0380
  Ralph Walker, supt.   Fax 483-3053
  www.leb.k12.in.us/
Lebanon HS   1,000/9-12
  510 Essex Dr 46052   765-482-0400
  Stephen Psikula, prin.   Fax 483-3040
Lebanon MS   800/6-8
  1800 N Grant St 46052   765-482-3400
  Michael Brown, prin.   Fax 483-3049

Leo, Allen
East Allen County SD
  Supt. — See New Haven
Leo JSHS   1,000/7-12
  14600 Amstutz Rd 46765   260-446-0180
  Mark Daniel, prin.   Fax 446-0189

Leopold, Perry
Perry Central Community SC   1,200/PK-12
  18677 Old State Road 37 47551   812-843-5576
  Mary Roberson, supt.   Fax 843-4746
  www.pccs.k12.in.us/
Perry Central JSHS   500/7-12
  18677 Old State Road 37 47551   812-843-5121
  Jack Wright, prin.   Fax 843-4198

Liberty, Union, Pop. 1,959
Union County/College Corner JSD   1,400/K-12
  107 S Layman St 47353   765-458-7471
  Mark Ransford, supt.   Fax 458-5647
  www.uc.k12.in.us/
Union County HS   400/9-12
  410 Patriot Blvd 47353   765-458-5136
  Connie Rosenberger, prin.   Fax 458-6315
Union County MS   400/6-8
  488 State Route 44 E 47353   765-458-7438
  Vicky Snyder, prin.   Fax 458-6041

Ligonier, Noble, Pop. 4,303
West Noble SC   2,500/K-12
  5050 N US Highway 33 46767   260-894-3191
  Dave Speakman, supt.   Fax 894-3260
  westnoble.k12.in.us
West Noble HS   700/9-12
  5094 N US Highway 33 46767   260-894-3191
  Richard Mathew, prin.   Fax 894-4708
West Noble MS   700/5-8
  5194 N US Highway 33 46767   260-894-3196
  William Anders, prin.   Fax 894-4703

Lincoln City, Spencer
North Spencer County SC ... 2,300/PK-12
3720 E State Road 162 47552 ... 812-937-2400
Joan Keller, supt. ... Fax 937-7187
www.nspencer.k12.in.us
Heritage Hills HS ... 900/9-12
3644 E County Road 1600 N 47552 ... 812-937-4472
Dan Scherry, prin. ... Fax 937-4878
Heritage Hills MS ... 400/7-8
PO Box 1777 47552 ... 812-937-4472
Susan Grundhoefer, prin. ... Fax 937-4327

Linton, Greene, Pop. 5,778
Linton-Stockton SC ... 1,400/PK-12
801 1st St NE 47441 ... 812-847-6020
Ronald L. Bush, supt. ... Fax 847-8659
www.lssc.k12.in.us/
Linton-Stockton HS ... 400/9-12
10 H St NE 47441 ... 812-847-6024
Nicholas Karazsia, prin. ... Fax 847-6037
Linton-Stockton JHS ... 300/7-8
109 I St NE 47441 ... 812-847-6022
Jeff Sparks, prin. ... Fax 847-6032

Lizton, Hendricks, Pop. 365
North West Hendricks SD ... 1,600/K-12
PO Box 70 46149 ... 317-994-4100
Larry Rambis, supt. ... Fax 994-5963
www.hendricks.k12.in.us/
Tri-West HS ... 400/9-12
7883 N State Rd 39 46149 ... 317-994-4000
Dolores Mueller, prin. ... Fax 994-5106
Tri-West MS ... 400/6-8
555 W US Highway 136 46149 ... 317-994-4100
Ronald Ward, prin. ... Fax 994-4230

Logansport, Cass, Pop. 19,313
Logansport Community SC ... 4,500/PK-12
2829 George St 46947 ... 574-722-2911
Damon Peigh, supt. ... Fax 722-7634
www.lcsc.k12.in.us
Centrury Career Center ... Vo/Tech
2500 Hopper Dr 46947 ... 574-722-3811
Stephen Hagen, prin. ... Fax 753-7649
Columbia MS ... 400/6-8
1300 N 3rd St 46947 ... 574-753-3797
Kay Scott, prin. ... Fax 753-6159
Lincoln MS ... 600/6-8
2901 Usher St 46947 ... 574-753-7115
Susan Swartz, prin. ... Fax 753-5826
Logansport Community HS ... 1,200/9-12
1 Berry Ln 46947 ... 574-753-0441
Dr. Terry Sargent, prin. ... Fax 753-3688
Landmark Adult Learning Center ... Adult
401 Tanguy St 46947 ... 574-753-6547
Emily Graham, prin. ... Fax 753-4978

Loogootee, Martin, Pop. 2,695
Loogootee Community SC ... 1,100/K-12
PO Box 282 47553 ... 812-295-2595
Larry Weitkamp, supt. ... Fax 295-5595
www.loogootee.k12.in.us/
Loogootee JSHS ... 500/7-12
201 Brooks Ave 47553 ... 812-295-3254
John Mullen, prin. ... Fax 295-5595

Lowell, Lake, Pop. 7,759
Tri-Creek SC ... 3,400/K-12
195 W Oakley Ave 46356 ... 219-696-6661
Dr. Alice A. Neal, supt. ... Fax 696-2150
www.tricreek.k12.in.us
Lowell MS ... 1,100/9-12
2051 E Commercial Ave 46356 ... 219-696-7733
James Koger, prin. ... Fax 696-0042
Lowell HS ... 900/6-8
200 W Oakley Ave 46356 ... 219-696-7701
John Alessia, prin. ... Fax 690-2620

Lowell Christian Academy ... 100/PK-12
PO Box 206 46356 ... 219-696-8094
Deborah Richardson, prin.

Lynn, Randolph, Pop. 1,109
Randolph Southern SC ... 600/K-12
PO Box 385 47355 ... 765-874-1181
Michael Necessary, supt. ... Fax 874-1298
Randolph Southern JSHS ... 300/7-12
PO Box 305 47355 ... 765-874-2541
Michael Manning, prin. ... Fax 874-1298

Lynnville, Warrick, Pop. 804
Warrick County SC
Supt. — See Boonville
Tecumseh JSHS ... 400/7-12
5244 W State Route 68 47619 ... 812-922-3237
Richard Lance, prin. ... Fax 922-3608

Madison, Jefferson, Pop. 12,249
Madison Consolidated SD ... 3,500/K-12
2421 Wilson Ave 47250 ... 812-273-8511
Thomas G. Patterson, supt. ... Fax 273-8516
www.madison.k12.in.us/
Madison Consolidated HS ... 1,000/9-12
743 Clifty Dr 47250 ... 812-265-6672
Jeff Dhonau, prin. ... Fax 265-5689
Madison Consolidated JHS ... 800/6-8
701 8th St 47250 ... 812-265-6756
Michael Robinson, prin. ... Fax 265-5685

Grace Baptist S ... 100/PK-12
920 Montclair St 47250 ... 812-273-4107
Rev. Joel Almaroad, prin. ... Fax 265-5151
Ivy Tech Community College - Southeast ... Post-Sec.
590 Ivy Tech Dr 47250 ... 812-265-2580
King's Daughter's Hospital ... Post-Sec.
PO Box 447 47250 ... 812-265-5211
Shawe Memorial HS ... 200/7-12
201 W State St 47250 ... 812-273-2150
Jerry Bomholt, prin. ... Fax 273-6694

Marengo, Crawford, Pop. 855
Crawford County Community SC ... 1,900/PK-12
5805 E Administration Rd 47140 ... 812-365-2135
Dr. Mark Eastridge, supt. ... Fax 365-2783
www.cccs.k12.in.us/
Crawford County JSHS ... 900/7-12
1130 S State Road 66 47140 ... 812-365-2125
Wayne Apple, prin. ... Fax 365-2127

Marion, Grant, Pop. 30,609
Eastbrook Community SC ... 1,800/K-12
560 S 900 E 46953 ... 765-664-0624
Jerry Harshman, supt. ... Fax 664-0626
www.eastbrook.k12.in.us/
Eastbrook HS ... 600/9-12
560 S 900 E 46953 ... 765-664-1214
Marjorie Green, prin. ... Fax 664-1216
Eastbrook JHS ... 300/7-8
560 S 900 E 46953 ... 765-668-7136
Elizabeth Duckwall, prin. ... Fax 668-7137

Marion Community SD ... 5,200/PK-12
PO Box 2020 46952 ... 765-662-2546
Dr. Andrew M. Nixon, supt. ... Fax 651-2043
www.marion.k12.in.us/
Marion HS ... 1,500/9-12
750 W 26th St 46953 ... 765-664-9051
Jack Gardner, prin. ... Fax 662-0383
Marshall MS ... 700/6-8
720 N Miller Ave 46952 ... 765-664-0507
James Fox, prin. ... Fax 651-2086
McCulloch MS ... 700/6-8
3528 S Nebraska St 46953 ... 765-674-6917
Dr. Michael Shaffer, prin. ... Fax 674-8943
Tucker Career & Technology Center ... Vo/Tech
107 S Pennsylvania St 46952 ... 765-664-9091
Jerry Whitton, prin. ... Fax 651-2048

Indiana Business College ... Post-Sec.
830 N Miller Ave 46952 ... 765-662-7497
Indiana Wesleyan University ... Post-Sec.
4201 S Washington St 46953 ... 765-674-6901
Lakeview Christian S ... 300/PK-12
5318 S Western Ave 46953 ... 765-677-4266
Kelly Brown, prin. ... Fax 677-4269
New Horizons Academy ... 50/7-12
1002 S 930 E 46953 ... 765-668-4009
Eric Saunders, dir. ... Fax 662-1407

Marshall, Parke, Pop. 364
Turkey Run Community SC ... 700/PK-12
1497 E State Road 47 47859 ... 765-597-2750
Dr. Roberta Bowers, supt. ... Fax 597-2755
www.tr.k12.in.us
Turkey Run JSHS ... 300/7-12
1551 E State Road 47 47859 ... 765-597-2700
Pamela Rager, prin. ... Fax 597-2812

Martinsville, Morgan, Pop. 11,614
Metro SD of Martinsville ... 5,400/PK-12
460 S Main St 46151 ... 765-342-6641
Ron Furniss, supt. ... Fax 342-6877
msdadmin.scican.net
Martinsville East MS ... 700/6-8
1459 E Columbus St 46151 ... 765-342-6675
Eric Bowlen, prin. ... Fax 349-5236
Martinsville HS ... 1,500/9-12
1360 E Gray St 46151 ... 765-342-5571
Don Alkire, prin. ... Fax 349-5256
Martinsville West MS ... 700/6-8
109 E Garfield Ave 46151 ... 765-342-6628
Suzie O'Neal, prin. ... Fax 349-5232

Tabernacle Christian S ... 200/K-12
2189 Burton Ln 46151 ... 765-342-0501
Don Nations, prin. ... Fax 342-0502

Maxwell, Hancock
Greenfield-Central Community SD
Supt. — See Greenfield
Maxwell MS ... 500/6-8
102 N Main St 46154 ... 317-326-3121
Harold Olin, prin. ... Fax 326-4711

Medora, Jackson, Pop. 559
Medora Community SC ... 300/K-12
PO Box 369 47260 ... 812-966-2210
Dr. Drew Day, supt. ... Fax 966-2217
www.medorahornets.com
Medora JSHS ... 100/7-12
82 S George 47260 ... 812-966-2201
Paul White, prin. ... Fax 966-2217

Merrillville, Lake, Pop. 30,990
Merrillville Community SC ... 6,500/K-12
6701 Delaware St 46410 ... 219-650-5300
Dr. Tony Lux, supt. ... Fax 650-5320
www.mvsc.k12.in.us
Merrillville HS ... 2,100/9-12
276 E 68th Pl 46410 ... 219-650-5307
Mike Krutz, prin. ... Fax 650-5391
Pierce MS ... 1,100/7-8
199 E 70th Pl 46410 ... 219-650-5308
Paul McKinney, prin. ... Fax 650-5483

Andrean HS ... 800/9-12
5959 Broadway 46410 ... 219-887-5281
Rev. Paul Quanz, prin. ... Fax 981-5072
Brown Mackie College ... Post-Sec.
1000 E 80th Pl Ste 101N 46410 ... 219-769-3321
Davenport University ... Post-Sec.
8200 Georgia St 46410 ... 219-769-5556
DeVry University ... Post-Sec.
1000 E 80th Pl Ste 609 46410 ... 219-736-7440
Merrillville Beauty College ... Post-Sec.
48 W 67th Pl 46410 ... 219-769-2232
Olympia College ... Post-Sec.
707 E 80th Pl Ste 200 46410 ... 219-756-6811

Sawyer College ... Post-Sec.
3803 E Lincoln Hwy 46410 ... 219-947-4555

Michigan City, LaPorte, Pop. 32,335
Michigan City Area SD ... 7,800/PK-12
408 S Carroll Ave 46360 ... 219-873-2000
Michael Harding, supt. ... Fax 873-2072
www.mcas.k12.in.us
Barker MS ... 1,100/6-8
319 Barker Rd 46360 ... 219-873-2057
Peggy Scope, prin. ... Fax 873-3099
Elston MS ... 600/6-8
317 Detroit St 46360 ... 219-873-2035
Karen Robinson, prin. ... Fax 873-2157
Krueger MS ... 1,100/6-8
2001 Springland Ave 46360 ... 219-873-2061
Lisa Emshwiller, prin. ... Fax 873-2063
Michigan City HS ... 1,900/9-12
8466 W Pahs Rd 46360 ... 219-873-2044
Mark Francesconi, prin. ... Fax 873-2055
Smith Area Career Center ... Vo/Tech
817 Lafayette St 46360 ... 219-873-2120
Carolyn Threatt, prin. ... Fax 873-2068

Brown Mackie College ... Post-Sec.
325 E US Highway 20 46360 ... 219-877-3100
Duneland Lutheran HS ... 50/9-12
1237 E Coolspring Ave 46360 ... 219-874-5103
Laurie Rockenseuss, prin. ... Fax 842-4870
Lakeshore Medical Lab Training Programs ... Post-Sec.
402 Franklin St 46360 ... 219-872-7032
Marquette HS ... 200/9-12
306 W 10th St 46360 ... 219-873-1325
John Albert, prin. ... Fax 873-1327

Michigantown, Clinton, Pop. 413
Clinton Central SC ... 1,100/K-12
725 N State Rd 29 46057 ... 765-249-2515
Philip Boley, supt. ... Fax 249-2504
www.clinton.k12.in.us/
Clinton Central JSHS ... 500/7-12
815 N State Rd 29 46057 ... 765-249-2255
Ronald Dunn, prin. ... Fax 249-2504

Middlebury, Elkhart, Pop. 3,035
Middlebury Community SD ... 3,700/K-12
57853 Northridge Dr 46540 ... 574-825-9425
Jim Conner, supt. ... Fax 825-9426
www.mcsin-k12.org/
Heritage MS ... 900/6-8
57697 Northridge Dr Bldg 2 46540 ... 574-825-9951
Mitch Miller, prin. ... Fax 825-9154
Northridge HS ... 1,100/9-12
57697 Northridge Dr Bldg 1 46540 ... 574-825-2142
Steve Lyng, prin. ... Fax 825-1473

Middletown, Henry, Pop. 2,427
Shenandoah SC ... 1,400/K-12
5100 N Raider Rd 47356 ... 765-354-2266
Ron Green, supt. ... Fax 354-2274
www.shenandoah.k12.in.us/
Shenandoah HS ... 400/9-12
7354 W US Highway 36 47356 ... 765-354-6640
Charles Willis, prin. ... Fax 354-3110
Shenandoah MS ... 400/6-8
5156 N Raider Rd 47356 ... 765-354-6638
Greg Allen, prin. ... Fax 354-3120

Milan, Ripley, Pop. 1,811
Milan Community SC ... 1,300/K-12
412 E Carr St 47031 ... 812-654-2365
Donald Swisher, supt. ... Fax 654-2441
www.milan.k12.in.us
Milan HS ... 400/9-12
609 N Warpath Dr 47031 ... 812-654-3096
Michael Parks, prin. ... Fax 654-2368
Milan MS ... 400/5-8
609 N Warpath Dr 47031 ... 812-654-1616
Connie Nobbe, prin. ... Fax 654-2368

Mishawaka, Saint Joseph, Pop. 48,396
Mishawaka CSD ... 5,200/K-12
1402 S Main St 46544 ... 574-254-4500
R. Steven Mills, supt. ... Fax 254-4585
www.mishawaka.k12.in.us
Mishawaka HS ... 1,600/9-12
1202 Lincoln Way E 46544 ... 574-254-7300
George Marzotto, prin. ... Fax 254-7481
Young MS ... 900/7-8
1801 N Main St 46545 ... 574-254-3600
Dan Towner, prin. ... Fax 258-3021

Penn-Harris-Madison SC ... 13,000/K-12
55900 Bittersweet Rd 46545 ... 574-259-7941
Dr. Robert Howard, supt. ... Fax 258-9547
www.phm.k12.in.us
Byrkit HS ... 3,000/9-12
6501 Grape Rd 46545 ... 574-259-2874
Janeen Conway, prin. ... Fax 259-2876
Grissom MS ... 700/6-8
13881 Kern Rd 46544 ... 574-633-4061
Gene Hollenberg, prin. ... Fax 633-2134
Penn HS ... 3,000/9-12
56100 Bittersweet Rd 46545 ... 574-259-7961
Dr. Dave Tydgat, prin. ... Fax 258-9543
Schmucker MS ... 900/6-8
56045 Bittersweet Rd 46545 ... 574-259-5661
Elaine Holmes, prin. ... Fax 259-0807
Other Schools – See Granger

Bais Yaakov of Indiana ... 100/9-12
202 W 7th St 46544 ... 574-257-0689
Miriam Gettinger, prin. ... Fax 255-7553
Bethel College ... Post-Sec.
1001 W McKinley Ave 46545 ... 574-259-8511
First Baptist Christian S ... 200/PK-12
724 N Main St 46545 ... 574-255-3242
Douglas Culp, prin. ... Fax 258-0397

Marian HS 600/9-12
  1311 S Logan St 46544 574-259-5257
  Carl Loesch, prin. Fax 258-7668

Mitchell, Lawrence, Pop. 4,658
Mitchell Community SD 2,100/PK-12
  441 N 8th St 47446 812-849-4481
  John Lantis, supt. Fax 849-2133
  www.mitchell.k12.in.us
Mitchell HS 600/9-12
  1000 W Bishop Blvd 47446 812-849-3663
  Dr. Steve Phillips, prin. Fax 849-5368
Mitchell JHS 500/6-8
  1010 W Bishop Blvd 47446 812-849-3747
  David Branneman, prin. Fax 849-5841

Modoc, Randolph, Pop. 218
Union SC 500/K-12
  PO Box 148 47358 765-853-5464
  Daniel Roach, supt. Fax 853-5070
  www.ecesc.k12.in.us/corporations/unionsch/index.htm
Union JSHS 200/7-12
  PO Box 148 47358 765-853-5421
  Anita Glaze, prin. Fax 853-6057

Monon, White, Pop. 1,687
North White SC 1,000/K-12
  121 W State Road 16 47959 219-253-6618
  Patrick W. McTaggart, supt. Fax 253-6488
  www.nwhite.k12.in.us/
North White HS 300/9-12
  310 E Broadway St 47959 219-253-6638
  Jeff Jones, prin. Fax 253-7004
North White MS 300/6-8
  310 E Broadway St 47959 219-253-7701
  Curt Craig, prin. Fax 253-8462

Monroe, Adams, Pop. 732
Adams Central Community SD 1,200/K-12
  222 W Washington St 46772 260-692-6193
  Michael Pettibone, supt. Fax 692-6198
  www.accs.k12.in.us/
Adams Central HS 400/9-12
  222 W Washington St 46772 260-692-6151
  Bill Hartman, prin. Fax 692-6192
Adams Central MS 300/6-8
  222 W Washington St 46772 260-692-6151
  Aaron McClure, prin. Fax 692-6192

Monroeville, Allen, Pop. 1,275
East Allen County SD
  Supt. — See New Haven
Heritage JSHS 800/7-12
  13608 Monroeville Rd 46773 260-446-0140
  Chris Hissong, prin. Fax 446-0146

Monrovia, Morgan, Pop. 625
Monroe-Gregg SD 900/PK-12
  PO Box 468 46157 317-996-3720
  Paul Kaiser, supt. Fax 996-2977
  www.scican.net/mgsd
Monrovia HS 400/9-12
  PO Box 468 46157 317-996-2259
  Jacob Hagist, prin. Fax 996-3519
Monrovia MS, PO Box 468 46157 6-8
  Bobbie Jo Monahan, prin. 317-996-3768

Montezuma, Parke, Pop. 1,166
Southwest Parke Community SC 1,000/K-12
  4851 S Coxville Rd 47862 765-569-2073
  Leonard R. Orr, supt. Fax 569-0309
  www.swparke.k12.in.us
Riverton Parke JSHS 500/7-12
  4907 S Coxville Rd 47862 765-569-2045
  Dennis Moody, prin. Fax 569-2047

Montgomery, Daviess, Pop. 375
Barr-Reeve Community SD 800/K-12
  PO Box 97 47558 812-486-3220
  Brian Harmon, supt. Fax 486-3509
  www.barr.k12.in.us/
Barr-Reeve JSHS 300/7-12
  PO Box 128 47558 812-486-3265
  Travis Madison, prin. Fax 486-2829

Monticello, White, Pop. 5,548
Twin Lakes SC 2,700/PK-12
  565 S Main St 47960 574-583-7211
  Dr. Thomas Fletcher, supt. Fax 583-8963
  www.twinlakes.k12.in.us/
Roosevelt MS 700/6-8
  721 W Broadway St 47960 574-583-5552
  Scott Clifford, prin. Fax 583-3675
Twin Lakes HS 800/9-12
  300 S 3rd St 47960 574-583-7108
  Robert Cornell, prin. Fax 583-2861

Mooresville, Morgan, Pop. 10,581
Mooresville Consolidated SC 4,300/PK-12
  11 W Carlisle St 46158 317-831-0950
  Curtis Freeman, supt. Fax 831-9202
  www.mcsc.k12.in.us
Hadley MS 700/7-8
  200 W Carlisle St 46158 317-831-9208
  Larry Goldsberry, prin. Fax 831-9249
Mooresville HS 1,300/9-12
  550 N Indiana St 46158 317-831-9203
  Chuck Muston, prin. Fax 831-9206

Morocco, Newton, Pop. 1,090
North Newton SC 1,700/K-12
  PO Box 8 47963 219-285-2228
  Robert Neier, supt. Fax 285-2708
  www.nn.k12.in.us/
North Newton JSHS 800/7-12
  1641 W 250 N 47963 219-285-2252
  Mark Gianfermi, prin. Fax 285-2881

Morristown, Shelby, Pop. 1,174
Shelby Eastern SD
  Supt. — See Shelbyville

Morristown JSHS 500/6-12
  PO Box 260 46161 765-763-1221
  Tim Rayle, prin. Fax 763-7170

Mount Summit, Henry, Pop. 301
Blue River Valley SD 800/PK-12
  PO Box 217 47361 765-836-4816
  Stephen K. Welsh, supt. Fax 836-4817
  www.brv.k12.in.us
Other Schools – See New Castle

Mount Vernon, Posey, Pop. 7,318
Metro SD of Mt. Vernon 2,700/PK-12
  1000 W 4th St 47620 812-838-4471
  Dr. Keith Spurgeon, supt. Fax 833-2078
  www.msdmv.k12.in.us
Mount Vernon HS 900/9-12
  700 Harriett St 47620 812-838-4356
  Steve Riordan, prin. Fax 833-2099
Mount Vernon JHS 700/6-8
  701 Tile Factory Rd 47620 812-833-2077
  Jerry Funkhouser, prin. Fax 833-2083

Muncie, Delaware, Pop. 66,521
Cowan Community SC 700/K-12
  1000 W County Road 600 S 47302 765-289-4866
  Larry D. John, supt. Fax 284-0315
  www.cowan.k12.in.us
Cowan JSHS 300/7-12
  9401 S Nottingham St 47302 765-289-7128
  James Suding, prin. Fax 741-5954

Delaware Community SC 2,900/K-12
  7821 N State Rd 3 47303 765-284-5074
  R. Stephen Gookins, supt. Fax 284-5259
  www.delcomschools.org
Delta HS 900/9-12
  3400 E State Rd 28 47303 765-288-5597
  Gregory Hinshaw, prin. Fax 288-8498
Delta MS 700/6-8
  9800 N County Road 200 E 47303 765-747-0869
  Don Harman, prin. Fax 213-2131

Muncie Community SD 7,600/K-12
  2501 N Oakwood Ave 47304 765-747-5205
  Marlin Creasy Ph.D., supt. Fax 747-5341
  www.muncie.k12.in.us
Muncie Area Career Center Vo/Tech
  2500 N Elgin St 47303 765-747-5250
  Jeff Alexander, dir. Fax 747-5455
Muncie Central HS 1,200/9-12
  801 N Walnut St 47305 765-747-5260
  Dick Daniel, prin. Fax 747-5314
Muncie Southside HS 1,100/9-12
  1601 E 26th St 47302 765-747-5320
  Rebecca Thompson, prin. Fax 747-5325
Northside MS 900/6-8
  2400 W Bethel Ave 47304 765-747-5290
  Dr. Maria Sells, prin. Fax 751-0616
Wilson MS 1,000/6-8
  3100 S Tillotson Ave 47302 765-747-5370
  Dilynn Phelps, prin. Fax 751-0666

University Schools 500/K-12
  2000 W University Ave 47306 765-285-3262
  William Sharp, supt. Fax 285-2166
  www.bsu.edu
Burris Laboratory S 500/K-12
  2000 W University Ave 47306 765-285-8600
  Jay McGee, prin. Fax 285-8620
IN Academy for Science Math & Humanities 11-12
  2121 W University Ave 47306 765-285-7457
  Tracy Cross, prin. Fax 285-2777

Ball Memorial Hospital Post-Sec.
  2401 W University Ave 47303 765-747-3393
Ball State University Post-Sec.
  2000 W University Ave 47306 765-289-1241
Heritage Hall Christian S 300/PK-12
  6401 W River Rd 47304 765-289-6371
  Dennis Ice, prin. Fax 288-9584
Indiana Business College Post-Sec.
  411 W Riggin Rd 47303 765-288-8681
Ivy Tech Community College East Central Post-Sec.
  4301 S Cowan Rd 47302 765-289-2291
PJ's College of Cosmetology Post-Sec.
  2006 N Walnut St 47303

Munster, Lake, Pop. 22,135
Town of Munster SD 4,000/K-12
  8616 Columbia Ave 46321 219-836-9111
  William Pfister, supt. Fax 836-3215
  www.munster.k12.in.us
Munster HS 1,400/9-12
  8808 Columbia Ave 46321 219-836-3200
  Steven L. Tripenfeldas, prin. Fax 836-3203
Wright MS 900/6-8
  8650 Columbia Ave 46321 219-836-6260
  Randolph Harkabus, prin. Fax 836-0501

Nappanee, Elkhart, Pop. 6,762
Wa-Nee Community SD 3,000/K-12
  1300 N Main St 46550 574-773-3131
  Joe Sabo, supt. Fax 773-5593
  www.wanee.k12.in.us/
Northwood HS 800/9-12
  2101 N Main St 46550 574-773-4127
  Louis Bonacorsi, prin. Fax 773-4099
Other Schools – See Wakarusa

South Side Christian S 50/1-12
  901 S Main St 46550 574-773-2566
  Joel Helmuth, prin. Fax 773-4066
United Christian S 100/1-12
  29522 County Road 52 46550 574-773-7505
  Jonathan Hochstetler, prin. Fax 773-7513

Nashville, Brown, Pop. 816
Brown County SC 2,300/PK-12
  PO Box 38 47448 812-988-6601
  Dr. D. Lynn Reed, supt. Fax 988-5403
  www.brownco.k12.in.us
Brown County HS 700/9-12
  PO Box 68 47448 812-988-6606
  Matthew Stark, prin. Fax 988-5422
Brown County JHS 400/7-8
  95 S School House Ln 47448 812-988-6605
  Shane Killinger, prin. Fax 988-5415

New Albany, Floyd, Pop. 36,973
New Albany-Floyd Co. Consolidated SD 9,600/PK-12
  PO Box 1087 47151 812-949-4200
  Dennis Brooks, supt. Fax 949-6900
  www.nafcs.k12.in.us
Hazelwood JHS 700/6-8
  1021 Hazelwood Ave 47150 812-949-4280
  Jacqueline Apple, prin. Fax 949-6962
New Albany HS 2,000/9-12
  1020 Vincennes St 47150 812-949-4272
  Stephen Sipes, prin. Fax 949-6910
Prosser S of Technology Vo/Tech
  4202 Charlestown Rd 47150 812-949-4266
  Alan Taylor, prin. Fax 949-6260
Scribner JHS 600/6-8
  910 Old Vincennes Rd 47150 812-949-4283
  Rhonda Mull, prin. Fax 949-6974
Other Schools – See Floyds Knobs, Georgetown

Christian Academy of Indiana 700/K-12
  1000 Academy Dr 47150 812-944-6200
  Kevin Wilson, prin. Fax 944-6902
Indiana University Southeast Post-Sec.
  4201 Grant Line Rd 47150 812-941-2000

Newburgh, Warrick, Pop. 3,252
Warrick County SC
  Supt. — See Boonville
Castle HS 1,700/9-12
  3344 State Route 261 47630 812-853-3331
  Phil Delong, prin. Fax 853-9886
Castle JHS 900/7-8
  2800 State Route 261 47630 812-853-7347
  Robert Hawkins, prin. Fax 858-1089

ITT Technical Institute Post-Sec.
  10999 Stahl Rd 47630 812-858-1600
Newburgh Christian S 100/PK-12
  7333 Sharon Rd 47630 812-842-0455
  Sharon Dunsworth, admin. Fax 853-3511

New Carlisle, Saint Joseph, Pop. 1,615
New Prairie United SC 2,400/K-12
  5327 N Cougar Rd 46552 574-654-7273
  Duane Wrightson, supt. Fax 654-7274
  www.npusc.k12.in.us
New Prairie HS 600/9-12
  5333 N Cougar Rd 46552 574-654-7271
  Clara Clark, prin. Fax 654-3390
New Prairie JHS 400/7-8
  5331 N Cougar Rd 46552 574-654-3070
  Jim Holifield, prin. Fax 654-7009

New Castle, Henry, Pop. 18,955
Blue River Valley SD
  Supt. — See Mount Summit
Blue River Valley JSHS 400/7-12
  4741 N Hillsboro Rd 47362 765-836-4811
  Ken Howell, prin. Fax 836-3255

New Castle Community SC 3,800/PK-12
  322 Elliott Ave 47362 765-521-7201
  John Newby, supt. Fax 521-7268
  www.nccsc.k12.in.us
New Castle Area Vocational S Vo/Tech
  1407 Walnut St 47362 765-521-7226
  Robert Hobbs, prin. Fax 593-6653
New Castle Chrysler HS 1,000/9-12
  801 Parkview Dr 47362 765-593-6670
  Bruce Gaylor, prin. Fax 593-6696
New Castle MS 600/7-8
  601 Parkview Dr 47362 765-521-7230
  Kellie Stephen, prin. Fax 521-7269

New Harmony, Posey, Pop. 892
New Harmony Town & Twp Cons SD 200/PK-12
  PO Box 396 47631 812-682-4401
  C. G. Epple, supt. Fax 682-3659
  www.nharmony.k12.in.us
New Harmony S 200/PK-12
  PO Box 396 47631 812-682-4401
  Deborah Caudill, prin. Fax 682-3659

New Haven, Allen, Pop. 13,592
East Allen County SD 10,000/PK-12
  1240 State Road 930 E 46774 260-446-0100
  Dr. M. Kay Novotny, supt. Fax 446-0107
  www.eacs.k12.in.us
New Haven HS 900/9-12
  1300 Green Rd 46774 260-446-0220
  Eva Merkel, prin. Fax 446-0228
New Haven MS 600/6-8
  900 Prospect Ave 46774 260-446-0230
  Thelma Green, prin. Fax 446-0236
Other Schools – See Fort Wayne, Leo, Monroeville, Woodburn

New Market, Montgomery, Pop. 656
South Montgomery Community SC 2,100/K-12
  PO Box 8 47965 765-866-0203
  Dr. J. Bret Lewis, supt. Fax 866-0736
  www.southmont.k12.in.us
Other Schools – See Crawfordsville

New Palestine, Hancock, Pop. 1,385
Southern Hancock Co. Community SC | 2,900/PK-12
PO Box 508 46163 | 317-861-4463
James Halik, supt. | Fax 861-2142
cscshc.newpal.k12.in.us/
Doe Creek MS | 700/6-8
PO Box 478 46163 | 317-861-4487
James Voelz, prin. | Fax 861-2136
New Palestine HS | 900/9-12
PO Box 448 46163 | 317-861-4417
Janice Bergeson, prin. | Fax 861-2125

New Washington, Clark
Greater Clark County SD
Supt. — See Jeffersonville
New Washington MSHS | 400/6-12
226 N Highway 62 47162 | 812-293-3368
Ben Ledbetter, prin. | Fax 293-5803

Noblesville, Hamilton, Pop. 33,046
Noblesville SD | 7,100/PK-12
1775 Field Dr 46060 | 317-773-3171
Lynn Lehman, supt. | Fax 773-7845
www.noblesvilleschools.org
Noblesville HS | 1,900/9-12
18111 Cumberland Rd 46060 | 317-773-4680
Annetta Petty, prin. | Fax 776-6289
Noblesville MS | 1,100/7-8
300 N 17th St 46060 | 317-773-0782
Daniel Chapin, prin. | Fax 776-6261

Blessed Theodore Guerin HS | 9-12
15300 N Gray Rd, | 317-582-0120
Keith Marsh, prin. | Fax 582-0140
Kaye Beauty College | Post-Sec.
1111 S 10th St 46060 | 317-773-6189

North Judson, Starke, Pop. 1,884
North Judson-San Pierre SC | 1,500/K-12
801 Campbell Dr 46366 | 574-896-2155
John Heath, supt. | Fax 896-2156
www.njsp.k12.in.us
North Judson JHS | 400/6-8
950 Campbell Dr 46366 | 574-896-2167
Annette Zupin, prin. | Fax 896-3036
North Judson-San Pierre HS | 500/9-12
1 Bluejay Dr 46366 | 574-896-2158
Kelly Shepherd, prin. | Fax 896-3945

North Manchester, Wabash, Pop. 6,064
Manchester Community SD | 1,600/K-12
PO Box 308 46962 | 260-982-7518
Dr. Diana Showalter, supt. | Fax 982-4583
www.mcs.k12.in.us
Manchester HS | 500/9-12
1 Squire Dr 46962 | 260-982-2196
Nancy Alspaugh, prin. | Fax 982-1034
Manchester JHS | 300/7-8
404 W 9th St 46962 | 260-982-8602
Nancy Alspaugh, prin. | Fax 982-1162

Manchester College | Post-Sec.
604 E College Ave 46962 | 260-982-5000

North Vernon, Jennings, Pop. 6,389
Jennings County SC | 5,100/K-12
34 W Main St 47265 | 812-346-4483
Dr. Michael J. Bushong, supt. | Fax 346-4490
www.jcsc.org
Jennings County HS | 1,300/9-12
800 W Walnut St 47265 | 812-346-5588
Kendall Wildey, prin. | Fax 346-4232
Jennings County MS | 900/7-8
820 W Walnut St 47265 | 812-346-4940
Floyd Bowman, prin. | Fax 346-4497

Notre Dame, Saint Joseph, Pop. 10,200

Holy Cross College | Post-Sec.
PO Box 308 46556 | 574-239-8400
St. Mary's College | Post-Sec.
46 Madeliva 46556 | 574-284-4000
University of Notre Dame | Post-Sec.
220 Main Building 46556 | 574-631-5000

Oakland City, Gibson, Pop. 2,587
East Gibson SC | 1,000/PK-12
133 E Morton St 47660 | 812-749-4755
Lynn Blinzinger, supt. | Fax 749-3343
Wood Memorial HS | 300/9-12
943 S Franklin St 47660 | 812-749-4757
Roger Benson, prin. | Fax 749-3512
Wood Memorial JHS | 200/7-8
945A S Franklin St 47660 | 812-749-4715
Mike Brewster, prin. | Fax 749-4988

Oakland City University | Post-Sec.
138 N Lucretia St 47660 | 812-749-4781

Oldenburg, Franklin, Pop. 644

Oldenburg Academy | 200/9-12
PO Box 200 47036 | 812-934-4440
Connie Deardorff, prin. | Fax 934-4838

Oolitic, Lawrence, Pop. 1,127
North Lawrence Community SD
Supt. — See Bedford
Oolitic MS | 400/6-8
903 Hoosier Ave 47451 | 812-275-7551
David Dean, prin. | Fax 277-3219

Oolitic Christian S | 50/PK-12
227 Lafayette Ave 47451 | 812-279-4060
Dennis Gregory, admin. | Fax 279-4749

Orleans, Orange, Pop. 2,303
Orleans Community SD | 800/K-12
173 Marley St 47452 | 812-865-2688
James Terrell, supt. | Fax 865-3428
www.orleans.k12.in.us/
Orleans JSHS | 400/7-12
200 W Wilson St 47452 | 812-865-2688
Gary McClintic, prin. | Fax 865-3532

Osgood, Ripley, Pop. 1,666
Jac-Cen-Del Community SC | 1,000/K-12
723 N Buckeye St 47037 | 812-689-4114
Bill Narwold, supt. | Fax 689-7423
www.jaccendel.k12.in.us/
Jac-Cen-Del JSHS | 500/7-12
4586 N US Highway 421 47037 | 812-689-4643
Raymond Ratledge, prin. | Fax 689-0152

Ossian, Wells, Pop. 2,917
Northern Wells Community SD | 2,600/K-12
PO Box 386 46777 | 260-622-4125
Gina Berridge, supt. | Fax 622-7893
www.nwcs.k12.in.us/
Norwell HS | 800/9-12
1100 E US Highway 224 46777 | 260-543-2213
Greg Mohler, prin. | Fax 543-2591
Norwell MS | 600/6-8
1100 E US Highway 224 46777 | 260-543-2218
Robert Hansbarger, prin. | Fax 543-2510

Oxford, Benton, Pop. 1,232
Benton Community SC
Supt. — See Fowler
Benton Central JSHS | 1,000/7-12
4241 E 300 S 47971 | 765-884-1600
Howard Feuer, prin. | Fax 884-8445

Paoli, Orange, Pop. 3,906
Lost River Career Cooperative SD
610 Elm St 47454 | 812-723-4818
David Embree, supt. | Fax 723-4822
Lost River Career Cooperative S | Vo/Tech
610 Elm St 47454 | 812-723-4818
David Embree, supt. | Fax 723-4822

Paoli Community SC | 1,700/K-12
501 Elm St 47454 | 812-723-4717
Alva Sibbitt, supt. | Fax 723-5100
www.paoli.k12.in.us
Paoli JSHS | 800/7-12
501 Elm St 47454 | 812-723-3905
Jerry Stroud, prin. | Fax 723-4459

Parker City, Randolph, Pop. 1,385
Monroe Central SC | 1,100/K-12
1918 N County Road 1000 W 47368 | 765-468-6868
 | Fax 468-6578
www.monroec.k12.in.us
Monroe Central JSHS | 500/7-12
1878 N County Road 1000 W 47368 | 765-468-7545
Adrian Moulton, prin. | Fax 468-8878

Pekin, Washington, Pop. 1,236
East Washington SC | 1,800/K-12
1050 N Eastern School Rd 47165 | 812-967-3926
Gerald Rose, supt. | Fax 967-5797
www.ewsc.k12.in.us
Eastern HS | 500/9-12
1100 N Eastern School Rd 47165 | 812-967-3931
James Feist, prin. | Fax 967-5767
East Washington MS | 600/5-8
1100 N Eastern School Rd 47165 | 812-967-5000
Linda Luedeman, prin. | Fax 967-5737

Pendleton, Madison, Pop. 3,790
South Madison Community SC | 3,500/K-12
201 S East St 46064 | 765-778-2152
Dr. Thomas Warmke, supt. | Fax 778-8207
www.smadison.k12.in.us
Pendleton Heights HS | 1,000/9-12
1 Arabian Dr 46064 | 765-778-2161
Glen Nelson, prin. | Fax 778-0605
Pendleton Heights MS | 600/7-8
301 S East St 46064 | 765-778-2139
Daniel Joyce, prin. | Fax 778-0557

Pershing, Wayne, Pop. 1,531
Western Wayne SD | 1,200/K-12
PO Box 217 47370 | 765-478-5375
Robert Mahon, supt. | Fax 478-4577
Other Schools – See Cambridge City

Peru, Miami, Pop. 12,897
Peru Community SD | 1,800/PK-12
35 W 3rd St 46970 | 765-473-3081
Thomas McKaig, supt. | Fax 472-5129
www.peru.k12.in.us
Peru HS | 700/9-12
401 N Broadway 46970 | 765-472-3301
Jon Custer, prin. | Fax 472-5148
Peru JHS | 400/7-8
30 Daniel St 46970 | 765-473-3084
Sam Watkins, prin. | Fax 473-4007

Petersburg, Pike, Pop. 2,522
Pike County SC | 2,100/PK-12
907 E Walnut St 47567 | 812-354-8731
D. Thomas, supt. | Fax 354-8733
www.pcsc.k12.in.us
Pike Central HS | 600/9-12
1810 E State Road 56 47567 | 812-354-8478
LeAnne Kelley, prin. | Fax 789-2992
Pike Central MS | 500/6-8
1814 E State Road 56 47567 | 812-354-8478
Calvin Biddle, prin. | Fax 789-2992

Pierceton, Kosciusko, Pop. 685
Whitko Community SC | 2,000/K-12
432 S First St 46562 | 574-594-2658
Jeff Hendrix, supt. | Fax 594-2326
whitko.org
Other Schools – See Larwill, South Whitley

Plainfield, Hendricks, Pop. 21,386
Plainfield Community SC | 4,000/PK-12
985 Longfellow Ln 46168 | 317-839-2578
Dr. Jerry Holifield, supt. | Fax 838-3664
www.plainfield.k12.in.us
Plainfield Community MS | 1,000/6-8
401 Elm Dr 46168 | 317-838-3966
Jerry Goldsberry, prin. | Fax 838-3965
Plainfield HS | 1,200/9-12
709 Stafford Rd 46168 | 317-839-7711
Scott Ollinger, prin. | Fax 838-3671

PJ's College of Cosmetology | Post-Sec.
2026 Stafford Rd 46168

Plymouth, Marshall, Pop. 10,607
Plymouth Community SC | 2,800/PK-12
611 Berkley St 46563 | 574-936-3115
John Hill, supt. | Fax 936-3160
www.plymouth.k12.in.us/
Lincoln JHS | 500/7-8
220 N Liberty St 46563 | 574-936-3113
John McNeil, prin. | Fax 936-3574
Plymouth HS | 1,000/9-12
1 Big Red Dr 46563 | 574-936-2178
Richard Tobias, prin. | Fax 936-4842

Grace Baptist Christian S | 100/PK-12
1830 N Michigan St 46563 | 574-936-3448
Pete Wardlow, prin.

Poneto, Wells, Pop. 236
Southern Wells Community SD | 800/K-12
9120 S 300 W 46781 | 765-728-5537
Neil Potter, supt. | Fax 728-8124
www.swraiders.com
Southern Wells JSHS | 400/7-12
9120 S 300 W 46781 | 765-728-5534
James Schwarzkopf, prin. | Fax 728-8124

Portage, Porter, Pop. 34,915
Portage Township SD | 8,000/PK-12
6240 US Highway 6 46368 | 219-762-6511
Michael Berta, supt. | Fax 762-3263
www.portage.k12.in.us
Fegely MS | 700/6-8
5384 Stone Ave 46368 | 219-763-8150
Rebecca Lyons, prin. | Fax 763-8157
Portage HS | 2,400/9-12
6450 US Highway 6 46368 | 219-764-6026
Caren Swickard, prin. | Fax 764-6062
Willowcreek MS | 1,300/6-8
5962 Central Ave 46368 | 219-763-8090
Michelle Stewart, prin. | Fax 763-8069

Portage Christian S | 300/K-12
3040 Arlene St 46368 | 219-762-8962
Tim Rumley, admin. | Fax 763-9931

Portland, Jay, Pop. 6,297
Jay SC | 3,700/PK-12
404 E Arch St 47371 | 260-726-9341
Barbara Downing, supt. | Fax 726-4959
www.jayschools.k12.in.us
East Jay MS | 500/6-8
225 E Water St 47371 | 260-726-9371
Lee Newman, prin. | Fax 726-2383
Jay County HS | 1,100/9-12
2072 W State Road 67 47371 | 260-726-9306
Dr. Woody Barwick, prin. | Fax 726-9760
Other Schools – See Dunkirk

Poseyville, Posey, Pop. 1,161
Metro SD of North Posey County | 1,500/PK-12
101 N Church St 47633 | 812-874-2243
John Wood, supt. | Fax 874-8806
www.northposey.k12.in.us/
North Posey HS | 500/9-12
5900 High School Rd 47633 | 812-673-4242
Linda J. Crick, prin. | Fax 673-6616
North Posey JHS | 300/7-8
5800 High School Rd 47633 | 812-673-4244
Kevin Sergesketter, prin. | Fax 673-6622

Princeton, Gibson, Pop. 8,512
North Gibson SC | 2,100/K-12
RR 5 Box 49 47670 | 812-385-4851
Dr. John A. Cochren, supt. | Fax 386-1531
www.ngsc.k12.in.us
Princeton Community HS | 600/9-12
RR 5 Box 49 47670 | 812-385-2591
Jon Abbey, prin. | Fax 386-1535
Princeton Community MS | 500/6-8
410 E State St 47670 | 812-385-2020
Dr. Carolyn Cochren, prin. | Fax 386-6746

Ramsey, Harrison
North Harrison Community SC | 2,300/K-12
1260 Highway 64 NW 47166 | 812-347-2407
Monty Schneider, supt. | Fax 347-2870
www.nhcs.k12.in.us
North Harrison HS | 700/9-12
1070 Highway 64 NW 47166 | 812-347-3148
Kelly Simpson, prin. | Fax 347-2875
North Harrison MS | 400/6-8
1180 Highway 64 NW 47166 | 812-347-2421
Jon Howerton, prin. | Fax 347-2835

Rensselaer, Jasper, Pop. 6,167
Rensselaer Central SC | 1,800/PK-12
605 W Grove St 47978 | 219-866-7822
Steven York, supt. | Fax 866-8360
www.rcsc.k12.in.us/
Rensselaer Central HS | 600/9-12
1106 E Grace St 47978 | 219-866-5175
Edward Habrowski, prin. | Fax 866-5135
Rensselaer Central MS | 500/6-8
1106 E Bomber Dr 47978 | 219-866-4661
Gordon Lewis, prin. | Fax 866-2103

St. Joseph's College — Post-Sec.
PO Box 890 47978 — 219-866-6000

Richmond, Wayne, Pop. 38,201
Richmond Community SC — 5,600/K-12
300 Hub Etchison Pkwy 47374 — 765-973-3300
Allen Bourff, supt. — Fax 973-3417
www.rcs.k12.in.us
Richmond HS — 1,600/9-12
380 Hub Etchison Pkwy 47374 — 765-973-3424
Joe Spicer, prin. — Fax 973-3716
Test MS — 400/7-8
33 S 22nd St 47374 — 765-973-3412
Luann Spicer, prin. — Fax 973-3712
Worth MS — 500/7-8
222 NW 7th St 47374 — 765-973-3495
Kathy McCarty, prin. — Fax 973-3703
Find Center — Adult
900 S L St 47374 — 765-973-3486
Susan Hively, prin. — Fax 935-1825

Bethany Theological Seminary — Post-Sec.
615 National Rd W 47374 — 765-983-1800
David Demuth Institute of Cosmetology — Post-Sec.
2 SW 5th St 47374 — 765-935-7964
Earlham Coll. & Earlham Sch. of Religion — Post-Sec.
801 National Rd W 47374 — 765-983-1200
Indiana University East — Post-Sec.
2325 Chester Blvd 47374 — 765-973-8200
Ivy Tech Community College Richmond — Post-Sec.
2325 Chester Blvd 47374 — 765-966-2656
New Creations Christian S — 100/K-12
6412 National Rd E 47374 — 765-935-2790
Tammy Sealy, prin. — Fax 935-3961
PJ's College of Cosmetology — Post-Sec.
115 N 9th St 47374 — 765-962-3005
Reid Hospital & Health Care Services — Post-Sec.
1401 Chester Blvd 47374 — 765-983-3167
Seton Catholic JSHS — 500/7-12
233 S 5th St 47374 — 765-965-6956
Rick Ruhl, prin. — Fax 935-9930

Rising Sun, Ohio, Pop. 2,441
Rising Sun-Ohio County Community SD — 1,000/K-12
110 S Henrietta St 47040 — 812-438-2655
Stephen Patz, supt. — Fax 438-4636
www.risingsunschools.com/
Rising Sun HS — 300/9-12
210 S Henrietta St 47040 — 812-438-2652
Keith Majewski, prin. — Fax 438-2431

Roachdale, Putnam, Pop. 984
North Putnam Community SD
Supt. — See Bainbridge
North Putnam HS — 600/9-12
8869 N County Road 250 E 46172 — 765-522-6282
Alan Zerkel, prin. — Fax 522-2862
North Putnam MS — 400/6-8
8905 N County Road 250 E 46172 — 765-522-2900
Mike Wilcox, prin. — Fax 522-2863

Rochester, Fulton, Pop. 6,407
Rochester Community SC — 2,000/PK-12
PO Box 108 46975 — 574-223-2159
Dr. Debra Howe, supt. — Fax 223-4909
www.rochester.k12.in.us
Rochester Community HS — 600/9-12
PO Box 108 46975 — 574-223-2176
Daniel Ronk, prin. — Fax 223-3401
Rochester Community MS — 500/6-8
PO Box 108 46975 — 574-223-2280
Deborah Carter, prin. — Fax 223-1531

Rockport, Spencer, Pop. 2,116
South Spencer County SC — 1,500/PK-12
321 S 5th St 47635 — 812-649-2591
H. Mike Robinson, supt. — Fax 649-4249
www.sspencer.k12.in.us
South Spencer HS — 400/9-12
1142 N Orchard Rd 47635 — 812-649-9157
Robert Combs, prin. — Fax 649-2214
South Spencer MS — 300/6-8
1298 N Orchard Rd 47635 — 812-649-2203
Gina Scales, prin. — Fax 649-9630

Rockville, Parke, Pop. 2,722
Rockville Community SC — 900/K-12
602 Howard Ave 47872 — 765-569-5582
Gary Storje, supt. — Fax 569-6650
www.rockville.k12.in.us
Rockville JSHS — 400/7-12
506 N Beadle St 47872 — 765-569-5686
Dave Mahurin, prin. — Fax 569-1047

Rossville, Clinton, Pop. 1,514
Rossville Consolidated SD — 600/K-12
PO Box 11 46065 — 765-379-2990
Dr. James Hanna, supt. — Fax 379-3014
www.rossville.k12.in.us/
Rossville HS — 9-12
PO Box 530 46065 — 765-379-2551
Allen Remaly, prin. — Fax 379-2551
Rossville MS — 200/6-8
PO Box 530 46065 — 765-379-2551
Be Ann Younker, prin. — Fax 379-2556

Royal Center, Cass, Pop. 821
Pioneer Regional SC — 1,000/K-12
PO Box 577 46978 — 574-643-2605
Dr. David Bess, supt. — Fax 643-9977
www.pioneer.k12.in.us/
Pioneer JSHS — 500/7-12
PO Box 547 46978 — 574-643-3145
Robert Brock, prin. — Fax 643-2020

Rushville, Rush, Pop. 5,793
Rush County SD — 2,700/PK-12
330 W 8th St 46173 — 765-932-4186
Dr. Edwin Lyskowinsky, supt. — Fax 938-1608
rcs.rushville.k12.in.us/
Rush MS — 500/7-8
1601 N Sexton St 46173 — 765-932-2968
Marla Stevens, prin. — Fax 938-2011
Rushville Consolidated HS — 800/9-12
1201 Lions Path 46173 — 765-932-3901
Garry Watson, prin. — Fax 932-4051

Russiaville, Howard, Pop. 1,159
Western SC — 2,300/K-12
2600 S 600 W 46979 — 765-883-5576
Ronald Wilson, supt. — Fax 883-7946
www.western.k12.in.us
Western HS — 700/9-12
2600 S 600 W 46979 — 765-883-5541
Charles Wolf, prin. — Fax 883-4522
Western MS — 600/6-8
2600 S 600 W 46979 — 765-883-5566
Kyle Barrentine, prin. — Fax 883-4531

Saint John, Lake, Pop. 9,545
Lake Central SC — 8,600/PK-12
8260 Wicker Ave 46373 — 219-365-8507
Janet Emerick, supt. — Fax 365-6406
www.lakecentral.k12.in.us
Lake Central HS — 2,600/9-12
8400 Wicker Ave 46373 — 219-365-8551
Sandra Platt, prin. — Fax 365-7156
Other Schools – See Dyer, Schererville

Saint Leon, Franklin, Pop. 496
Sunman-Dearborn Community SC
Supt. — See Sunman
East Central HS — 1,400/9-12
1 Trojan Ln, Brookville IN 47012 — 812-576-4811
Don Criswell, prin. — Fax 576-2047
Sunman-Dearborn MS — 700/7-8
8356 Schuman Rd, Brookville IN 47012 — 812-576-3500
Mark Watkins, prin. — Fax 576-3506

Saint Mary of the Woods, Vigo

St. Mary-of-the-Woods College — Post-Sec.
1 St Mary of Woods Coll 47876 — 812-535-5151

Saint Meinrad, Spencer

St. Meinrad School of Theology — Post-Sec.
200 Hill Dr 47577 — 812-357-6611

Salem, Washington, Pop. 6,325
Salem Community SD — 2,100/K-12
500 N Harrison St 47167 — 812-883-4437
Dr. Stanley L. Bippus, supt. — Fax 883-1031
www.salemschools.com/
Salem HS — 600/9-12
700 N Harrison St 47167 — 812-883-3904
Jim Ralston, prin. — Fax 883-3905
Salem MS, 1001 N Harrison St 47167 — 500/6-8
Ray Oppel, prin. — 812-883-3808

Schererville, Lake, Pop. 26,142
Lake Central SC
Supt. — See Saint John
Grimmer MS — 1,000/6-8
225 W 77th Ave 46375 — 219-865-6985
Janet Zeck, prin. — Fax 865-4423

Don Roberts Beauty Academy — Post-Sec.
152 E US Highway 30 46375 — 219-864-1600

Scottsburg, Scott, Pop. 5,912
Scott County SD 2 — 2,800/K-12
375 E Mcclain Ave 47170 — 812-752-8946
Robert Hooker, supt. — Fax 752-8951
www.scsd2.k12.in.us/
Scottsburg HS — 700/9-12
500 S Gardner St 47170 — 812-752-8927
Brad Walker, prin. — Fax 752-6207
Scottsburg MS — 700/6-8
425 S 3rd St 47170 — 812-752-8926
Kristin Nass, prin. — Fax 752-8864

Sellersburg, Clark, Pop. 6,140
West Clark Community SC — 3,300/PK-12
601 Renz Ave 47172 — 812-246-3375
Terry Smith, supt. — Fax 246-9731
www.wclark.k12.in.us/IEHome.html
Silver Creek HS — 600/9-12
557 Renz Ave 47172 — 812-246-3391
Michael Crabtree, prin. — Fax 246-8184
Silver Creek MS — 500/6-8
495 N Indiana Ave 47172 — 812-246-4421
Reid Bailey, prin. — Fax 246-7430
Other Schools – See Borden, Henryville

Ivy Tech Community College - Southern — Post-Sec.
8204 Highway 311 47172 — 812-246-3301
Restoration Christian S — 300/PK-12
11515 Highway 31 47172 — 812-246-9271
Sara Hauselman, prin. — Fax 246-0722

Selma, Delaware, Pop. 856
Liberty-Perry Community SC — 1,200/K-12
PO Box 337 47383 — 765-282-5615
James Craig, supt. — Fax 281-3733
www.selma.bsu.edu/
Selma MS — 300/6-8
10501 E County Road 167 S 47383 — 765-288-7242
Alice Mehaffey, prin. — Fax 281-3727
Wapahani HS — 300/9-12
10401 E County Road 167 S 47383 — 765-289-7323
Bryan Rausch, prin. — Fax 281-3724

Seymour, Jackson, Pop. 18,500
Seymour Community SD — 3,800/PK-12
1638 S Walnut St 47274 — 812-522-3340
Dr. Robert Schmielau, supt. — Fax 522-8031
www.scsc.k12.in.us
Seymour HS — 1,200/9-12
1350 W 2nd St 47274 — 812-522-4384
James McCormick, prin. — Fax 523-2347
Seymour MS — 900/6-8
920 N Obrien St 47274 — 812-522-5453
Barbara Bergdoll, prin. — Fax 523-8134

Trinity Lutheran HS — 100/9-12
7120 N County Road 875 E 47274 — 812-524-8547
Joel Landskroener, prin. — Fax 524-8523

Sharpsville, Tipton, Pop. 621
Northern Comm Tipton County SD — 1,000/K-12
4774 N 200 W 46068 — 765-963-2585
Dr. Lee Williford, supt. — Fax 963-3042
www.ncstc.k12.in.us/
Tri Central JSHS — 600/6-12
2115 W 500 N 46068 — 765-963-2560
Dave Driggs, prin. — Fax 963-6844

Shelbyville, Shelby, Pop. 17,853
Blue River Career Programs
801 Saint Joseph St 46176 — 317-392-4191
John Sollman, supt. — Fax 392-5741
www.brcp.net
Blue River Career Ctr — Vo/Tech
801 Saint Joseph St 46176 — 317-392-4191
John Sollman, prin. — Fax 392-5741

Shelby Eastern SD — 1,600/K-12
2451 N 600 E 46176 — 765-544-2246
John Jameson, supt. — Fax 544-2247
www.ses.k12.in.us/
Other Schools – See Morristown, Waldron

Shelbyville Central SD — 3,800/K-12
803 Saint Joseph St 46176 — 317-392-2505
David Adams, supt. — Fax 392-5737
www.shelbycs.org
Shelbyville HS — 1,100/9-12
2003 S Miller St 46176 — 317-398-9731
Tom Zobel, prin. — Fax 392-5709
Shelbyville MS — 900/6-8
1200 W McKay Rd 46176 — 317-392-2551
Denny Ramsey, prin. — Fax 392-5713

Southwestern Cons Shelby County SC — 700/K-12
3406 W 600 S 46176 — 317-729-5746
Cathy Egolf, supt. — Fax 729-5330
www.swshelby.k12.in.us
Southwestern JSHS — 400/7-12
3406 W 600 S 46176 — 317-729-5122
Suzanne Blake, prin. — Fax 729-2424

Sheridan, Hamilton, Pop. 2,664
Marion-Adams SD — 1,100/PK-12
509 E 4th St 46069 — 317-758-4172
Dr. Scott Robison, supt. — Fax 758-6248
www.sheridan.org/school/
Sheridan HS — 400/9-12
24185 Hinesley Rd 46069 — 317-758-4431
Ed Baker, prin. — Fax 758-2406
Sheridan MS, 3030 W 246th St 46069 — 300/6-8
Ed Baker, prin. — 317-758-6780

Shoals, Martin, Pop. 814
Shoals Community SC — 800/PK-12
RR 2 Box 1C 47581 — 812-247-2060
Dr. Anthony Nonte, supt. — Fax 247-2278
shoals.k12.in.us/
Shoals Community JSHS — 400/7-12
RR 2 Box 1A 47581 — 812-247-2090
Stan Mosier, prin. — Fax 247-2056

South Bend, Saint Joseph, Pop. 105,540
South Bend Community SC — 21,100/PK-12
215 S Saint Joseph St 46601 — 574-283-8000
Joan Raymond, supt. — Fax 283-8143
www.sbcsc.k12.in.us
Adams HS — 1,600/9-12
808 S Twyckenham Dr 46615 — 574-283-7700
Thomas Fujimura, prin. — Fax 283-7704
Brown IS — 700/5-8
737 Beale St 46616 — 574-287-9680
Fax 283-5581
Clay HS — 1,600/9-12
19131 Darden Rd 46637 — 574-243-7000
Ruth Warren, prin. — Fax 243-7005
Clay IS — 800/5-8
52900 Lily Rd 46637 — 574-243-7145
James Knight, prin. — Fax 243-7151
Dickinson IS — 700/5-8
4404 Elwood Ave 46628 — 574-283-7625
Dwight Fulce, prin. — Fax 283-7633
Edison IS — 700/5-8
2701 Eisenhower Ave 46615 — 574-283-8900
Sam Schweizer, prin. — Fax 283-8903
Greene IS — 600/5-8
24702 Roosevelt Rd 46614 — 574-283-7900
Lela Warren, prin. — Fax 283-7903
Jackson IS — 800/5-8
5001 Miami St 46614 — 574-231-5600
Margaret Schaller, prin. — Fax 231-5605
Jefferson IS — 500/5-8
528 S Eddy St 46617 — 574-283-8700
James Kapsa, prin. — Fax 283-8703
LaSalle Academy — 600/5-8
2701 Elwood Ave 46628 — 574-283-7500
Janet Scott, prin. — Fax 283-7513
Marshall IS — 600/5-8
1433 Byron Dr 46614 — 574-231-5801
Kristine Simons, prin. — Fax 231-5805
Navarre IS — 700/5-8
4702 Ford St 46619 — 574-283-7345
Derrick White, prin. — Fax 283-7351

Riley HS 1,600/9-12
1902 Fellows St 46613 574-283-8400
Edward Bradford, prin. Fax 283-8405
Washington HS 1,500/9-12
4747 W Washington St 46619 574-283-7200
George McCullough, prin. Fax 283-7205
Adult Education Adult
3206 Sugar Maple Ln 46628 574-283-7505
Anita Brown, admin. Fax 283-7549

Brown Mackie College Post-Sec.
1030 E Jefferson Blvd 46617 574-237-0774
Community Baptist Christian S 300/K-12
5715 Miami St 46614 574-291-3620
Mark French, prin. Fax 291-3648
Indiana University at South Bend Post-Sec.
PO Box 7111 46634 574-237-4111
Ironwood Christian S 50/K-12
4609 S Ironwood Rd 46614 574-231-8006
Kenneth Mendenhall, admin.
Ivy Tech North Central Post-Sec.
220 Dean Johnson Blvd 46601 574-289-7001
Rabbi Naftali Riff Yeshiva HS 50/9-12
3207 High St 46614 574-291-9014
Louis Sandock, admin. Fax 291-9490
St. Joseph HS 800/9-12
1441 N Michigan St 46617 574-233-6137
Susan Richter, prin. Fax 232-3482
Trinity S at Greenlawn 300/7-12
107 S Greenlawn Ave 46617 574-287-5590
Kerry Koller, prin. Fax 236-6628

South Whitley, Whitley, Pop. 1,788
Whitko Community SC
Supt. — See Pierceton
Whitko HS 600/9-12
1 Big Blue Ave 46787 260-723-5146
Parrish Kruger, prin. Fax 723-4724

Speedway, Marion, Pop. 12,793
School Town of Speedway 1,700/K-12
5335 W 25th St 46224 317-244-0236
N. Andrew Wagner, supt. Fax 486-4843
www.speedway.k12.in.us
Speedway HS 500/9-12
5357 W 25th St 46224 317-244-7238
Ray Lawrence, prin. Fax 486-4838
Speedway JHS 300/7-8
5151 W 14th St 46224 317-244-3359
John Dizney, prin. Fax 486-4845

Spencer, Owen, Pop. 2,548
Spencer-Owen Community SD 3,200/PK-12
205 E Hillside Ave 47460 812-829-2233
Marsha Turner-Shear, supt. Fax 829-6614
www.socs.k12.in.us
Owen Valley HS 900/9-12
622 W State Highway 46 47460 812-829-2266
Kimberly Tucker, prin. Fax 829-6605
Owen Valley MS 600/7-8
626 W State Highway 46 47460 812-829-2249
Amy Elkins, prin. Fax 829-6635

Spiceland, Henry, Pop. 776
South Henry SC 800/K-12
6449 S Cemetery Dr 47385 765-987-7882
Dr. John Magers, supt. Fax 987-7589
www.shenry.k12.in.us/
Other Schools – See Straughn

Straughn, Henry, Pop. 251
South Henry SC
Supt. — See Spiceland
Tri JSHS 400/7-12
6972 S State Road 103 47387 765-987-7988
Scott Seibel, prin. Fax 987-8446

Sullivan, Sullivan, Pop. 4,603
Southwest SC 1,900/PK-12
110 N Main St 47882 812-268-6311
Dr. Rita Brodnax, supt. Fax 268-6312
www.swest.k12.in.us/
Sullivan HS 600/9-12
902 N Section St 47882 812-268-6301
George Bauman, prin. Fax 268-6303
Sullivan JHS 200/7-8
820 N Section St 47882 812-268-4000
Keith Brashear, prin. Fax 268-5368

Sunman, Ripley, Pop. 807
Sunman-Dearborn Community SC 4,300/K-12
PO Box 210 47041 812-623-2291
John Roeder, supt. Fax 623-3341
sunmandearborn.k12.in.us
Other Schools – See Saint Leon

Switz City, Greene, Pop. 306
White River Valley SD 900/K-12
PO Box 1470 47465 812-659-1424
Layton Wall, supt. Fax 659-2278
www.wrv.k12.in.us
White River Valley JSHS 400/7-12
PO Box 1470 47465 812-659-2274
Roger Weaver, prin. Fax 659-2278

Syracuse, Kosciusko, Pop. 3,050
Wawasee Community SC 3,500/PK-12
1 Warrior Path Bldg 2 46567 574-457-3188
Dr. Mark Stock, supt. Fax 457-4962
www.wawasee.k12.in.us/
Wawasee HS 1,100/9-12
1 Warrior Path 46567 574-457-3147
Ellen Stevens, prin. Fax 457-4364
Wawasee MS 600/6-8
9850 N State Rd 13 46567 574-457-8839
Anthony Cassel, prin. Fax 457-3575

Tell City, Perry, Pop. 7,684
Tell City-Troy Township SC 1,700/PK-12
837 17th St 47586 812-547-3300
Ronald Etienne, supt. Fax 547-9704
www.tellcity.k12.in.us
Tell City HS 500/9-12
900 12th St 47586 812-547-3131
Dale Stewart, prin. Fax 547-9713
Tell City JHS 400/6-8
3515 Mozart St 47586 812-547-3748
Gary Stath, prin. Fax 547-9737

Terre Haute, Vigo, Pop. 58,096
Vigo County SC 16,300/PK-12
PO Box 3703 47803 812-462-4216
Daniel Tanoos, supt. Fax 462-4379
www.vigoco.k12.in.us
Honey Creek MS 800/6-8
6601 S Carlisle St 47802 812-462-4372
Patrick Sheehan, prin. Fax 462-4367
Otter Creek MS 700/6-8
4801 N Lafayette St 47805 812-462-4391
Mark Kirby, prin. Fax 462-4388
Rose MS 600/6-8
1275 3rd Ave 47807 812-462-4474
Dr. Tammy Roeschlein, prin. Fax 462-4473
Scott MS 600/6-8
1000 Grant St 47802 812-462-4381
Mark Miller, prin. Fax 462-4370
Terre Haute North Vigo HS 2,000/9-12
3434 Maple Ave 47804 812-462-4312
Mick Newport, prin. Fax 462-4204
Terre Haute South Vigo HS 1,800/9-12
3737 S 7th St 47802 812-462-4252
Troy Fears, prin. Fax 462-4408
Wilson MS 800/6-8
301 S 25th St 47803 812-462-4396
Dr. Sharon Pitts, prin. Fax 232-2217
Other Schools – See West Terre Haute

Holy Cross S 100/5-12
PO Box 2316 47802 812-299-1156
Allen Hayne, prin. Fax 298-3162
Indiana Business College Post-Sec.
3175 S 3rd Pl 47802 812-232-4458
Indiana State University 47809 Post-Sec.
812-237-6311
Ivy Tech Community College Wabash Valley Post-Sec.
7999 S US Highway 41 47802 812-299-1121
Rose-Hulman Institute of Technology Post-Sec.
5500 Wabash Ave 47803 812-877-1511
Terre Haute Adventist S 50/K-10
900 S 29th St 47803 812-232-1339
Bev Amlaner, prin.
Terre Haute Christian S 100/K-12
2500 Margaret Ave 47802 812-238-2541
Steven Henry, prin. Fax 234-7610

Thorntown, Boone, Pop. 1,559
Western Boone County Community SD 1,900/PK-12
1201 N State Road 75 46071 765-482-6333
Stephen Sailor, supt. Fax 482-0890
www.bccn.boone.in.us/webo
Western Boone JSHS 900/7-12
1205 N State Road 75 46071 765-482-6143
Rob Ramey, prin. Fax 482-6146

Tipton, Tipton, Pop. 5,229
Tipton Community SC 1,900/K-12
221 N Main St 46072 765-675-2147
Robert Schultz, supt. Fax 675-3857
www.tcsc.k12.in.us
Tipton HS 600/9-12
619 S Main St 46072 765-675-7431
Joe Rushton, prin. Fax 675-9519
Tipton MS 500/6-8
817 S Main St 46072 765-675-7521
Shayne Clark, prin. Fax 675-9027

Topeka, Lagrange, Pop. 1,173
Westview SC 2,200/K-12
1545 S 600 W 46571 260-768-4404
Dr. Randall Zimmerly, supt. Fax 768-7368
www.westview.k12.in.us
Westview JSHS 700/7-12
1635 S 600 W 46571 260-768-4146
Troy Albert, prin. Fax 768-7611

Trafalgar, Johnson, Pop. 895
Nineveh-Hensley-Jackson United SD 1,800/K-12
802 S Indian Creek Dr 46181 317-878-2100
Dr. John Reed, supt. Fax 878-5765
www.nhj.k12.in.us
Indian Creek HS 500/9-12
803 W Indian Creek Dr 46181 317-878-2110
Robert Duke, prin. Fax 878-2112
Indian Creek MS 400/6-8
801 W Indian Creek Dr 46181 317-878-2130
Rodney King, prin. Fax 878-2149

Union City, Randolph, Pop. 3,502
Randolph Eastern SC 1,000/K-12
907 N Plum St 47390 765-964-4994
Cathy Stephen, supt. Fax 964-6590
www.resc.k12.in.us/
Union City Community HS 300/9-12
603 N Walnut St 47390 765-964-4840
Janet Caudle, prin. Fax 964-3775
West Side MS 200/6-8
731 N Plum St 47390 765-964-4830
Amy Dishman, prin. Fax 964-7344

Union Mills, LaPorte
South Central Community SC 800/K-12
9808 S 600 W 46382 219-767-2263
David Geise, supt. Fax 767-2260
www.scentral.k12.in.us/
South Central JSHS 400/7-12
9808 S 600 W 46382 219-767-2266
John Arnett, prin. Fax 767-2260

Upland, Grant, Pop. 3,717

Taylor University Post-Sec.
500 W Reade Ave 46989 765-998-2751

Valparaiso, Porter, Pop. 28,365
East Porter County SC
Supt. — See Kouts
Morgan Twp. MSHS 300/6-12
299 S State Road 49 46383 219-462-5883
Curtis Casbon, prin. Fax 462-4014
Washington Twp. MSHS 400/6-12
381 E State Road 2 46383 219-464-3598
Terry Robbins, prin. Fax 462-3372

Porter Township SC 1,500/K-12
248 S 500 W 46385 219-477-4933
Nicholas Brown, supt. Fax 477-4834
www.ptsc.k12.in.us/
Boone Grove HS 500/9-12
260 S 500 W 46385 219-988-4481
Garry DeRossett, prin. Fax 988-4431
Other Schools – See Boone Grove

Union Township SC 1,600/K-12
599 W 300 N #A 46385 219-759-2531
John Hunter, supt. Fax 759-3250
www.union.k12.in.us
Union Township MS 400/6-8
599 W 300 N 46385 219-759-2561
Jerry Lasky, prin. Fax 759-4359
Wheeler HS 500/9-12
587 W 300 N 46385 219-759-2561
Thomas Taylor, prin. Fax 759-5602

Valparaiso Community SD 6,100/K-12
3801 Campbell St 46385 219-531-3000
Dr. Michael P. Benway, supt. Fax 531-3009
www.valpo.k12.in.us
Franklin MS 800/6-8
605 Campbell St 46385 219-531-3020
Robert Rarick, prin. Fax 531-3026
Jefferson MS 600/6-8
1600 Roosevelt Rd 46383 219-531-3140
Paul Knauff, prin. Fax 531-3146
Porter County Career Ctr Vo/Tech
1005 Franklin St 46383 219-531-3170
Jon Groth, prin. Fax 531-3173
Valparaiso HS 2,000/9-12
2727 N Campbell St 46385 219-531-3070
Patrick Weil, prin. Fax 531-3076

Community College of Indiana-Valparaiso Post-Sec.
2401 Valley Dr 46383 219-464-8514
Don Roberts Beauty School Post-Sec.
1354 Lincoln Way 46383 219-462-5189
Porter Memorial Hospital Post-Sec.
814 Laporte Ave 46383 219-465-4883
Valparaiso University 46383 Post-Sec.
219-464-5000
Victory Christian Academy 200/PK-12
3805 LaPorte Ave 46383 219-548-8803
Joyce Folk, admin. Fax 548-8803

Veedersburg, Fountain, Pop. 2,268
Southeast Fountain SC 1,300/K-12
744 E US Highway 136 47987 765-294-2254
Debra Gilbert, supt. Fax 294-3200
www.sefschools.org/
Fountain Central JSHS 600/7-12
750 E US Highway 136 47987 765-294-2206
Larry Adams, prin. Fax 294-3204

Versailles, Ripley, Pop. 1,781
South Ripley Community SC 1,500/K-12
207 W Tyson St 47042 812-689-6282
Ted Ahaus, supt. Fax 689-6760
www.sripley.k12.in.us/
South Ripley JSHS 800/7-12
1589 S Benham Rd 47042 812-689-5303
Bill Snyder, prin. Fax 689-6715

Southeastern Career SC
901 W US Highway 50 47042 812-689-5253
Brad Street, supt. Fax 689-6977
Southeastern Career Ctr Vo/Tech
901 W US Highway 50 47042 812-689-5253
James Rogers, prin. Fax 689-6977

Vevay, Switzerland, Pop. 1,670
Switzerland County SC 1,600/PK-12
305 W Seminary St 47043 812-427-2611
Tracy Caddell, supt. Fax 427-3695
www.switzerland.k12.in.us
Switzerland County HS 400/9-12
1020 W Main St 47043 812-427-2626
Derek Marshall, prin. Fax 427-3445
Switzerland County MS 400/6-8
1004 W Main St 47043 812-427-3809
Candis Haskell, prin. Fax 427-3807

Vincennes, Knox, Pop. 18,320
South Knox SC 1,100/K-12
6116 E State Rd 61 47591 812-726-4440
Bradley Case, supt. Fax 743-2110
www.sknox.k12.in.us
South Knox MSHS 500/7-12
6136 E State Road 61 47591 812-726-4450
Harry Nolting, prin. Fax 726-4545

Vincennes Community SC 3,000/K-12
300 N 6th St 47591 812-882-4844
Douglas Rose, supt. Fax 885-1427
www.vcsc.k12.in.us
Clark MS 700/6-8
500 Buntin St 47591 812-882-5172
Dennis Query, prin. Fax 885-1419
Lincoln HS 1,000/9-12
3001 Hart St 47591 812-882-8480
David Chapman, prin. Fax 885-1431

Good Samaritan Hospital — Post-Sec.
520 S 7th St 47591 — 812-885-3195
Rivet HS — 200/6-12
210 Barnett St 47591 — 812-882-6215
Dustin Hitt, prin. — Fax 886-1939
Vincennes Beauty College — Post-Sec.
12 S 2nd St 47591 — 812-882-1086
Vincennes University — Post-Sec.
1002 N 1st St 47591 — 800-742-9198

Wabash, Wabash, Pop. 11,380
Heartland Career Center SD — 260-563-7481
79 S 200 W 46992
Gary Sweet, supt. — Fax 563-5544
www.geocities.com/hccin
Heartland Career Ctr — Vo/Tech
79 S 200 W 46992 — 260-563-7481
Mark Hobbs, prin. — Fax 563-5544

Metro SD of Wabash County — 2,600/K-12
204 N 300 W 46992 — 260-563-8050
Dr. Scott Hanback, supt. — Fax 569-6836
www.msdwc.k12.in.us
Northfield JSHS — 600/7-12
154 W 200 N 46992 — 260-563-8050
William Neale, prin. — Fax 569-6839
Southwood JSHS — 600/7-12
564 E State Road 124 46992 — 260-563-8050
Jean Shonkwiler, prin. — Fax 569-6843
Whites JSHS — 100/6-12
5233 S 50 E 46992 — 260-563-1158
Sherman Knight, prin. — Fax 563-8975

Wabash CSD — 1,500/K-12
PO Box 744 46992 — 260-563-2151
Celia Briggs, supt. — Fax 563-2066
www.apaches.k12.in.us
Wabash HS — 400/9-12
580 N Miami St 46992 — 260-563-4131
Stacey Hughes, prin. — Fax 563-6806
Wabash MS — 400/6-8
150 Colerain St 46992 — 260-563-4137
Jim Willey, prin. — Fax 569-9805

Emmanuel Christian S — 100/K-12
129 Southwood Dr 46992 — 260-563-1677
Doug Phillips, prin.

Wakarusa, Elkhart, Pop. 1,619
Wa-Nee Community SD
Supt. — See Nappanee
Northwood MS — 700/6-8
207 N Elkhart St 46573 — 574-862-2710
George Roelandts, prin. — Fax 862-2327

Waldron, Shelby
Shelby Eastern SD
Supt. — See Shelbyville
Waldron JSHS — 400/6-12
PO Box 369 46182 — 765-525-6822
Brian Fehribach, prin. — Fax 525-9727

Walkerton, Saint Joseph, Pop. 2,205
John Glenn SC — 1,700/K-12
101 John Glenn Dr 46574 — 574-586-3129
Richard Reese, supt. — Fax 586-2660
www.jgsc.k12.in.us
Glenn HS — 600/9-12
201 John Glenn Dr 46574 — 574-586-3195
Dan Funston, prin. — Fax 586-3905
Urey MS — 300/7-8
407 Washington St 46574 — 574-586-3184
Janet Carey, prin. — Fax 586-3714

Walton, Cass, Pop. 1,042
Southeastern SC — 1,700/K-12
6422 E State Road 218 46994 — 574-626-2525
Dr. John Bevan, supt. — Fax 626-2751
www.sesc.k12.in.us
Cass JSHS — 800/7-12
6422 E State Road 218 46994 — 574-626-2511
William Isaacs, prin. — Fax 626-2172

Warsaw, Kosciusko, Pop. 12,688
Warsaw Community SC — 6,100/K-12
PO Box 283 46581 — 574-371-5098
Ralph Bailey, supt. — Fax 371-5095
www.warsaw.k12.in.us
Edgewood MS — 500/7-8
900 S Union St 46580 — 574-371-5096
JoElla Smyth, prin. — Fax 371-5010
Lakeview MS — 600/7-8
848 E Smith St 46580 — 574-269-7211
Tom Kline, prin. — Fax 371-5013
Warsaw Community HS — 1,800/9-12
1 Tiger Ln 46580 — 574-371-5099
Dr. Jennifer Brumfield, prin. — Fax 371-5012

Washington, Daviess, Pop. 11,292
Twin Rivers Vocational Area SC
301 E South St 47501 — 812-254-1189
Joyce Memering, supt. — Fax 254-8346
Twin Rivers Vocational S — Vo/Tech
301 E South St 47501 — 812-254-1189
Joyce Memering, prin. — Fax 254-8346

Washington Community SD — 2,500/K-12
301 E South St 47501 — 812-254-5536
Dr. Tom Miller, supt. — Fax 254-8346
www.wcs.k12.in.us
Washington HS — 800/9-12
608 E Walnut St 47501 — 812-254-3860
Gary Puckett, prin. — Fax 254-8374
Washington JHS — 400/7-8
210 NE 6th St 47501 — 812-254-2682
Gary Twomey, prin. — Fax 254-8381

Washington Catholic HS — 200/6-12
201 NE 2nd St 47501 — 812-254-2050
Chad Ballengee, prin. — Fax 254-8746

Waterloo, DeKalb, Pop. 2,209
DeKalb County Central United SC — 4,100/PK-12
3326 County Road 427 46793 — 260-920-1011
Kenneth Fowble, supt. — Fax 837-7767
www.dekalb.k12.in.us
DeKalb HS — 1,200/9-12
3424 County Road 427 46793 — 260-920-1012
David Schnelker, prin. — Fax 837-7841
DeKalb MS — 1,000/6-8
3338 County Road 427 46793 — 260-920-1013
Thomas Sanborn, prin. — Fax 837-7812

Westfield, Hamilton, Pop. 11,182
Westfield Washington SD — 4,700/PK-12
322 W Main St 46074 — 317-867-8000
Mark Keen, supt. — Fax 867-0929
www.wws.k12.in.us
Westfield HS — 1,200/9-12
18250 N Union St 46074 — 317-867-6800
Stacy McGuire, prin. — Fax 867-2909
Westfield MS — 700/7-8
345 W Hoover St 46074 — 317-867-6600
Andrea Martin, prin. — Fax 867-1407

West Lafayette, Tippecanoe, Pop. 29,835
Tippecanoe SC
Supt. — See Lafayette
Harrison HS — 1,500/9-12
5701 N 50 W 47906 — 765-463-3511
Doug Lesley, prin. — Fax 497-9893
Klondike MS — 500/6-8
3307 Klondike Rd 47906 — 765-463-2544
Christine Cannon, prin. — Fax 497-9413

West Lafayette Community SC — 2,000/K-12
1130 N Salisbury St 47906 — 765-746-1641
Iran Floyd, supt. — Fax 746-1644
www.wl.k12.in.us/
West Lafayette JSHS — 1,000/7-12
1105 N Grant St 47906 — 765-746-0400
Dr. Anne Koivo, prin. — Fax 746-0422

Purdue University — Post-Sec.
475 Stadium Mall Dr 47907 — 765-494-4600

West Lebanon, Warren, Pop. 793
Metro SD of Warren County
Supt. — See Williamsport
Seeger Memorial JSHS — 700/7-12
1222 S State Road 263 47991 — 765-893-4445
Ralph Shrader, prin. — Fax 893-8354

West Terre Haute, Vigo, Pop. 2,316
Vigo County SC
Supt. — See Terre Haute
West Vigo HS — 700/9-12
4590 W Sarah Myers Dr 47885 — 812-462-4282
Tom Balitewicz, prin. — Fax 462-4090
West Vigo MS — 600/6-8
4750 W Sarah Myers Dr 47885 — 812-462-4361
Tim Vislosky, prin. — Fax 462-4090

Westville, LaPorte, Pop. 5,266
Metro SD of New Durham Township — 800/K-12
207 E Valparaiso St 46391 — 219-785-2239
Robert Harbart, supt. — Fax 785-4584
Westville JSHS — 300/7-12
207 E Valparaiso St 46391 — 219-785-2531
Robert Harbart, prin. — Fax 785-2990

Purdue University — Post-Sec.
1401 S US Highway 421 46391 — 219-785-5200

Wheatfield, Jasper, Pop. 798
Kankakee Valley SC — 3,200/K-12
PO Box 278 46392 — 219-987-4711
Dr. Glenn Krueger, supt. — Fax 987-4710
www.kv.k12.in.us
Kankakee Valley HS — 1,000/9-12
3923 W State Road 10 46392 — 219-956-3143
Philip Apple, prin. — Fax 956-3143
Kankakee Valley MS — 500/7-8
3923 W State Road 10 46392 — 219-956-3143
William Auker, prin. — Fax 956-3143

Whiteland, Johnson, Pop. 4,202
Clark-Pleasant Community SC — 3,300/K-12
50 Center St 46184 — 317-535-7579
Dr. J.T. Coopman, supt. — Fax 535-4931
www.cpcsc.k12.in.us

Clark Pleasant MS — 600/7-8
222 Tracy St 46184 — 317-535-7121
Sondra Wooton, prin. — Fax 535-2064
Whiteland Community HS — 1,100/9-12
300 Main St 46184 — 317-535-7562
Tom Galovic, prin. — Fax 535-7509

Whiting, Lake, Pop. 4,928
Hammond CSD
Supt. — See Hammond
Clark MSHS — 1,600/6-12
1921 Davis Ave 46394 — 219-659-3522
Dr. Juan Anaya, prin. — Fax 659-1599

Whiting CSD — 900/PK-12
1500 Center St 46394 — 219-659-0656
Dr. Sandra Martinez, supt. — Fax 473-4008
www.whiting.k12.in.us
Whiting HS — 200/9-12
1751 Oliver St 46394 — 219-659-0255
Dirk Flick, prin. — Fax 473-1341
Whiting MS — 200/6-8
1800 New York Ave 46394 — 219-473-1344
Jay Harker, prin. — Fax 473-1341

Calumet College of St. Joseph — Post-Sec.
2400 New York Ave 46394 — 219-473-7770

Williamsport, Warren, Pop. 1,935
Metro SD of Warren County — 1,400/K-12
101 N Monroe St 47993 — 765-762-3364
Terry Roderick, supt. — Fax 762-6623
msdwarco.k12.in.us/
Other Schools – See West Lebanon

Winamac, Pulaski, Pop. 2,447
Eastern Pulaski Community SC — 1,400/K-12
711 School Dr 46996 — 574-946-4010
Robert Klitzman, supt. — Fax 946-4510
www.epulaski.k12.in.us/
Winamac Community HS — 400/9-12
715 School Dr 46996 — 574-946-6151
Rick Defries, prin. — Fax 946-4219
Winamac Community MS — 400/6-8
715 School Dr 46996 — 574-946-6525
Stan Good, prin. — Fax 946-4219

Winchester, Randolph, Pop. 4,889
Randolph Central SC — 1,700/K-12
103 N East St 47394 — 765-584-1401
Philip Wray, supt. — Fax 584-1403
www.rc.k12.in.us
Driver MS — 400/6-8
130 S 100 E 47394 — 765-584-4671
Tim Passmore, prin. — Fax 584-6271
Winchester Community HS — 500/9-12
700 N Union St 47394 — 765-584-8201
Thomas Osborn, prin. — Fax 584-8204

Winona Lake, Kosciusko, Pop. 4,107

Grace College — Post-Sec.
200 Seminary Dr 46590 — 574-372-5100
Grace Theological Seminary — Post-Sec.
200 Seminary Dr 46590 — 574-372-5100
Lakeland Christian Academy — 200/7-12
1093 S 250 E 46590 — 574-267-7265
Joy Lavender, admin. — Fax 267-5687

Wolcott, White, Pop. 954
Tri-County SC — 800/K-12
200 W North St 47995 — 219-279-2418
Dr. Gib Crimmins, supt. — Fax 279-2242
www.trico.k12.in.us
Tri-County MSHS — 500/6-12
11298 W 100 S 47995 — 219-279-2105
Gary Vandergriff, prin. — Fax 279-2108

Woodburn, Allen, Pop. 1,629
East Allen County SD
Supt. — See New Haven
Woodlan JSHS — 700/7-12
17215 Woodburn Rd 46797 — 260-446-0290
Edwin Yoder, prin. — Fax 446-0298

Yorktown, Delaware, Pop. 4,945
Mt. Pleasant Township Community SC — 2,200/K-12
8800 W Smith St 47396 — 765-759-2720
Mary Ann Irwin, supt. — Fax 759-7894
www.yorktown.k12.in.us
Yorktown HS — 700/9-12
1100 S Tiger Dr 47396 — 765-759-2550
Kelly Wittman, prin. — Fax 759-4040
Yorktown MS — 600/6-8
8820 W Smith St 47396 — 765-759-2660
David Sturgeon, prin. — Fax 759-3243

Zionsville, Boone, Pop. 10,336
Zionsville Community SC — 4,200/PK-12
900 Mulberry St 46077 — 317-873-2858
Howard Hull, supt. — Fax 873-8003
www.zcs.k12.in.us
Zionsville Community HS — 1,200/9-12
1000 Mulberry St 46077 — 317-873-3355
Jim Eggers, prin. — Fax 873-8002
Zionsville MS — 1,400/5-8
900 N Ford Rd 46077 — 317-873-2426
Sean Conner, prin. — Fax 733-4001

IOWA

IOWA DEPARTMENT OF EDUCATION
400 E 14th St, Des Moines 50319-0146
Telephone 515-281-5294
Fax 515-242-5988
Website http://www.state.ia.us/educate

Director of Education   Judy Jeffrey

IOWA BOARD OF EDUCATION
400 E 14th St, Des Moines 50319-9000

President   Gene Vincent

AREA EDUCATION AGENCIES (AEA)

AEA 4
Les Douma, admin.   712-722-4378
1382 4th Ave NE   Fax 722-1643
Sioux Center 51250
www.aea4.k12.ia.us
AEA 267
Dean W. Meier, admin.   319-273-8200
3712 Cedar Heights Dr   Fax 273-8229
Cedar Falls 50613
www.aea267.k12.ia.us
Grant Wood AEA 10
Ron Fielder, admin., 4401 6th St SW   319-399-6700
Cedar Rapids 52404   Fax 399-6457
www.aea10.k12.ia.us/
Great River AEA 16
Joe Crozier, admin.   319-753-6561
PO Box 1065, Burlington 52601   Fax 753-1527
www.aea16.k12.ia.us/

Green Valley AEA 14
Connie Maxson, admin.   641-782-8443
1405 N Lincoln St, Creston 50801   Fax 782-4298
www.aea14.k12.ia.us/
Heartland AEA 11
Wayne Rand, admin.   515-270-9030
6500 Corporate Dr   Fax 270-5383
Johnston 50131
www.aea11.k12.ia.us/
Keystone AEA 1
Robert Vittengl, admin.   563-245-1480
1400 2nd St NW, Elkader 52043   Fax 245-1484
www.aea1.k12.ia.us
Loess Hills AEA 13
Glenn Grove, admin.   712-366-0503
PO Box 1109, Council Bluffs 51502   Fax 366-3431
www.aea13.k12.ia.us/

Mississippi Bend AEA 9
Glen Pelecky, admin.   563-359-1371
729 21st St, Bettendorf 52722   Fax 359-5967
www.aea9.k12.ia.us/
Prairie Lakes AEA 8
Kay Forsythe, admin.   515-574-5500
PO Box 1399, Fort Dodge 50501   Fax 574-5508
www.aea8.k12.ia.us/
Southern Prairie AEA 15
Joe Crozier, admin.   641-682-8591
2814 N Court St, Ottumwa 52501   Fax 682-9083
www.aea15.k12.ia.us./
Western Hills AEA 12
Bruce Hopkins, admin.   712-274-6000
1520 Morningside Ave   Fax 274-6123
Sioux City 51106
www.aea12.k12.ia.us/

PUBLIC, PRIVATE AND CATHOLIC SECONDARY SCHOOLS

Ackley, Hardin, Pop. 1,781
AGWSR Community SD   700/K-12
511 State St 50601   641-847-2611
Robert Lehman, supt.   Fax 847-2612
www.ackley.k12.ia.us
AGWSR HS   200/9-12
918 4th Ave 50601   641-847-2633
Joel Bagley, prin.   Fax 847-3345
Other Schools – See Wellsburg

Adair, Guthrie, Pop. 803
Adair-Casey Community SD   400/K-12
3384 Indigo Ave 50002   641-746-2241
James Simmelink, supt.   Fax 746-2243
accs.k12.ia.us
Adair-Casey JSHS   200/7-12
3384 Indigo Ave 50002   641-746-2241
William Umbaugh, prin.   Fax 746-2243

Adel, Dallas, Pop. 3,615
Adel-De Soto-Minburn Community SD   1,300/PK-12
801 Nile Kinnick Dr S 50003   515-993-4283
Tim Hoffman, supt.   Fax 993-4866
www.adel.k12.ia.us
Adel-De Soto-Minburn HS   300/10-12
801 Nile Kinnick Dr S 50003   515-993-4584
Lee Greibel, prin.   Fax 993-3025
Adel-De Soto-Minburn MS   8-9
801 Nile Kinnick Dr S 50003   515-993-3490
Carole Schlapkohl, prin.   Fax 993-1956

Afton, Union, Pop. 877
East Union Community SD   400/K-12
1916 High School Dr 50830   641-347-5215
Steve Clark, supt.   Fax 347-5514
East Union JSHS   300/6-12
1916 High School Dr 50830   641-347-8421
Mark Weis, prin.   Fax 347-5514

Akron, Plymouth, Pop. 1,459
Akron Westfield Community SD   700/PK-12
PO Box 950 51001   712-568-2616
Ron Flynn, supt.   Fax 568-2997
www.akron-westfield.k12.ia.us
Akron Westfield HS   200/9-12
PO Box 950 51001   712-568-2020
Derek Briggs, prin.   Fax 568-2997
Akron Westfield JHS   200/7-8
PO Box 950 51001   712-568-2020
Derek Briggs, prin.   Fax 568-2997
Akron Westfield JHS   200/7-8
PO Box 950 51001   712-568-2020
Cathy Bobier, prin.   Fax 568-2997

Albia, Monroe, Pop. 3,659
Albia Community SD   1,200/K-12
120 Benton Ave E 52531   641-932-5165
Kevin Crall, supt.   Fax 932-5192
www.albia.k12.ia.us
Albia HS   600/7-12
503 B Ave E 52531   641-932-2161
Linda Hoskins, prin.   Fax 932-7069

Alburnett, Linn, Pop. 528
Alburnett Community SD   600/K-12
PO Box 189 52202   319-842-2261
Angel Melendez, supt.   Fax 842-2398
www.alburnett.k12.ia.us
Alburnett JSHS   300/7-12
PO Box 189 52202   319-842-2263
Thomas Stewart, prin.   Fax 842-2398

Algona, Kossuth, Pop. 5,592
Algona Community SD   1,300/PK-12
PO Box 717 50511   515-295-3528
Ross Opsal, supt.   Fax 295-5166
www.algona.k12.ia.us
Algona HS   500/9-12
600 S Hale St 50511   515-295-7207
Bill Fjetland, prin.   Fax 295-9273
Laing MS   300/6-8
213 S Harlan St 50511   515-295-9447
Gregory Stewart, prin.   Fax 295-9448

Bishop Garrigan HS   200/9-12
1224 N Mccoy St 50511   515-295-3521
Michael Stence, prin.   Fax 295-7739

Alleman, Polk, Pop. 426
North Polk Community SD   1,000/K-12
313 NE 141st Ave 50007   515-685-3014
Dr. Ann Curphey, supt.   Fax 685-2002
www.n-polk.k12.ia.us
North Polk JSHS   400/7-12
315 NE 141st Ave 50007   515-685-3528
Gary Fjelland, prin.   Fax 685-3520

Allison, Butler, Pop. 988
Allison-Bristow Community SD   200/K-8
PO Box 428 50602   319-267-2205
Warren Davison, supt.   Fax 267-2926
www.alli-bris.k12.ia.us/
North Butler MS   100/5-8
PO Box 428 50602   319-267-2552
Dan Huff, prin.   Fax 267-2926

Alta, Buena Vista, Pop. 1,857
Alta Community SD   600/PK-12
101 W 5th St 51002   712-200-1010
Dr. Fred Maharry, supt.   Fax 200-1602
www.alta.k12.ia.us
Alta HS   200/9-12
101 W 5th St 51002   712-200-1331
Larry Martin, prin.   Fax 200-1602
Alta MS   200/5-8
1009 S Main St 51002   712-200-1401
Maxine Lampe, prin.   Fax 200-3465

Alton, Sioux, Pop. 1,106
MOC-Floyd Valley Community SD
Supt. — See Orange City
MOC-Floyd Valley MS   300/6-8
1104 5th Ave 51003   712-756-4128
John VandeWeerd, prin.   Fax 756-4100

Ames, Story, Pop. 53,284
Ames Community SD   3,600/K-12
415 Stanton Ave 50014   515-268-6600
W. Ray Richardson, supt.   Fax 268-6633
www.ames.k12.ia.us
Ames HS   1,600/9-12
1921 Ames High Dr 50010   515-817-0600
Michael McGrory, prin.   Fax 817-0601
Ames MS   700/6-8
3915 Mortensen Rd 50014   515-268-2400
Jeff Anderson, prin.   Fax 268-2419

Ames Christian S   100/PK-12
925 S 16th St 50010   515-233-0772
Charles R. Hontz, admin.   Fax 232-0005
Iowa State University 50011   Post-Sec.
515-294-4111
Professional Cosmetology Institute   Post-Sec.
627 Main St 50010   515-232-7250

Anamosa, Jones, Pop. 5,570
Anamosa Community SD   1,300/PK-12
200 S Garnavillo St 52205   319-462-4321
Carol Lensing, supt.   Fax 462-4322
www.anamosa.k12.ia.us
Anamosa HS   400/9-12
209 Sadie St 52205   319-462-3594
Steven Goodall, prin.   Fax 462-2332
West MS   300/6-8
200 S Garnavillo St 52205   319-462-3553
Richard Delagardelle, prin.   Fax 462-4322

Andrew, Jackson, Pop. 450
Andrew Community SD   300/PK-12
PO Box 230 52030   563-672-3221
Kent Hammer, supt.   Fax 672-9750
www.andrew.k12.ia.us
Andrew JSHS   200/7-12
PO Box 230 52030   563-672-3221
William Hamilton, prin.   Fax 672-9750

Anita, Cass, Pop. 1,023
Anita Community SD   300/K-12
1000 Victory Park Rd 50020   712-762-3238
Dan Crozier, supt.   Fax 762-3713
www.anita.k12.ia.us
CAM HS   200/9-12
1000 Victory Park Rd 50020   712-762-3231
Dominic Giegerich, prin.   Fax 762-3713

Ankeny, Polk, Pop. 31,144
Ankeny Community SD   6,700/PK-12
PO Box 189 50021   515-965-9600
Dr. Veronica Stalker, supt.   Fax 965-4234
www.ankeny.k12.ia.us
Ankeny HS   1,300/10-12
1302 N Ankeny Blvd,   515-965-9630
Brenda Colby, prin.   Fax 965-9639
Northview MS   1,000/8-9
1010 NW Prairie Ridge Dr,   515-965-9700
Scott Osborn, prin.   Fax 965-9708

Ankeny Christian Academy 200/PK-12
1604 W 1st St, 515-965-8114
Thomas Michaud, admin. Fax 965-8210
Des Moines Area Community College Post-Sec.
2006 S Ankeny Blvd, 50023 515-964-6200
Faith Baptist Bible College Post-Sec.
1900 NW 4th St, 50023 888-324-8448

Anthon, Woodbury, Pop. 644
Anthon-Oto Community SD 300/K-8
PO Box 705 51004 712-373-5246
Steve Oberg, supt. Fax 373-5326
www.anthon-oto.k12.ia.us/
Anthon-Oto-Maple Valley MS 200/6-8
PO Box 705 51004 712-373-5244
Jane Ellis, prin. Fax 373-5326

Aplington, Butler, Pop. 1,019
Aplington-Parkersburg Community SD
Supt. — See Parkersburg
Aplington/Parkersburg MS 200/6-8
215 10th St 50604 319-347-6621
Jon Thompson, prin. Fax 347-2395

Arlington, Fayette, Pop. 481
Starmont Community SD 800/PK-12
3202 40th St 50606 563-933-4598
Gary Stumberg, supt. Fax 933-2134
www.starmont.k12.ia.us
Starmont HS 300/9-12
3202 40th St 50606 563-933-2218
Fred Kinne, prin. Fax 933-2134
Starmont MS 300/5-8
3202 40th St 50606 563-933-4902
Gerald Hilton, prin. Fax 933-2134

Armstrong, Emmet, Pop. 918
Armstrong-Ringsted Community SD 400/PK-12
PO Box 75 50514 712-868-3550
Robert Busch, supt. Fax 868-3550
www.armstrong.k12.ia.us
Armstrong-Ringsted HS 100/9-12
PO Box 75 50514 712-868-3542
Karl Dearie, prin. Fax 868-3550
Armstrong-Ringsted JHS 100/6-8
PO Box 75 50514 712-864-3590
Karl Dearie, prin. Fax 868-3550

Arnolds Park, Dickinson, Pop. 1,164
Okoboji Community SD
Supt. — See Milford
Okoboji MS 300/5-8
10 Broadway 51331 712-332-5641
David Dorenkamp, prin. Fax 332-7180

Arthur, Ida, Pop. 232
Odebolt-Arthur Community SD
Supt. — See Odebolt
Odebolt-Arthur MS 100/6-8
100 1st Ave 51431 712-668-2767
Danielle Trimble, prin. Fax 668-2631

Atlantic, Cass, Pop. 7,110
Atlantic Community SD 1,500/K-12
1100 Linn St 50022 712-243-4252
Dr. Wendy Prigge, supt. Fax 243-8023
www.atlantic.k12.ia.us/
Atlantic HS 500/9-12
1201 E 14th St 50022 712-243-5358
Roger Herring, prin. Fax 243-8007
Atlantic MS 400/6-8
1100 Linn St 50022 712-243-1330
Todd Roecker, prin. Fax 243-8023

Audubon, Audubon, Pop. 2,274
Audubon Community SD 800/PK-12
800 3rd Ave 50025 712-563-2607
Ron Dobson, supt. Fax 563-3607
www.audubon.k12.ia.us/
Audubon JSHS 400/7-12
800 3rd Ave 50025 712-563-2607
Bonnie Lynam, prin. Fax 563-3607

Aurelia, Cherokee, Pop. 1,013
Aurelia Community SD 300/PK-12
300 Ash St 51005 712-434-2284
Thomas Vint, supt. Fax 434-2053
www.aurelia.k12.ia.us
Aurelia HS 100/9-12
PO Box 367 51005 712-434-5595
David Hickman, prin. Fax 434-2053
Aurelia MS 100/5-8
300 Ash St 51005 712-434-5682
Tom Vint, prin. Fax 434-2053

Avoca, Pottawattamie, Pop. 1,582
A-H-S-T Community SD 600/PK-12
PO Box 158 51521 712-343-6304
Chuck Scott, supt. Fax 343-6915
www.ahst.k12.ia.us
A-H-S-T HS 300/6-12
PO Box 158 51521 712-343-6304
Susie Peterson, prin. Fax 343-6915

Bancroft, Kossuth, Pop. 772
North Kossuth Community SD 400/K-12
PO Box 350 50517 515-885-2464
Mike Landstrum, supt. Fax 885-0041
www.n-kossuth.k12.ia.us
Other Schools – See Swea City

Barnum, Webster, Pop. 195
Manson NW Webster Community SD
Supt. — See Manson
Manson Northwest Webster MS 200/5-8
PO Box 169 50518 515-542-3211
Marlene Johnson, prin. Fax 542-3214

Battle Creek, Ida, Pop. 721
Battle Creek-Ida Grove Community SD
Supt. — See Ida Grove

Battle Creek-Ida Grove MS 200/5-8
600 Chestnut St 51006 712-365-4354
Tony Spradlin, prin. Fax 365-4357

Baxter, Jasper, Pop. 1,073
Baxter Community SD 400/K-12
PO Box 189 50028 641-227-3102
Neil Seales, supt. Fax 227-3217
www.baxter.k12.ia.us
Baxter JSHS 200/7-12
PO Box 189 50028 641-227-3103
Robert Luther, prin. Fax 227-3217

Bedford, Taylor, Pop. 1,576
Bedford Community SD 700/PK-12
PO Box 234 50833 712-523-2656
Joe Drake, supt. Fax 523-3166
www.bedford.k12.ia.us
Bedford MSHS 400/6-12
PO Box 234 50833 712-523-2656
Kim Antisdel-Watson, prin. Fax 523-2308

Belle Plaine, Benton, Pop. 2,879
Belle Plaine Community SD 700/PK-12
1303 2nd Ave 52208 319-444-3611
Mike Milligan, supt. Fax 444-3617
www.belle-plaine.k12.ia.us
Belle Plaine HS 200/9-12
610 13th Ave 52208 319-444-3720
Jodi Bermel, prin. Fax 444-4507
Lincoln JHS 100/7-8
1511 9th Ave 52208 319-444-3631
Christina Jesse, prin. Fax 444-3671

Bellevue, Jackson, Pop. 2,373
Bellevue Community SD 700/PK-12
1601 State St 52031 563-872-4913
Dr. Virgil W. Murray, supt. Fax 872-3216
www.bellevue.k12.ia.us
Bellevue MSHS 400/6-12
1601 State St 52031 563-872-4001
Gary Feuerbach, prin. Fax 872-3216

Marquette HS 100/9-12
502 Franklin St 52031 563-872-3356
James Squiers, prin. Fax 872-3285

Belmond, Wright, Pop. 2,495
Belmond-Klemme Community SD 800/PK-12
411 10th Ave NE 50421 641-444-4300
Dave Sextro, supt. Fax 444-4524
www.belmond-klemme.k12.ia.us
Belmond-Klemme Community JSHS 300/7-12
411 10th Ave NE 50421 641-444-4300
Larry Frakes, prin. Fax 444-4097

Bettendorf, Scott, Pop. 31,456
Bettendorf Community SD 4,400/K-12
3311 Central Ave 52722 563-359-3681
Marty Lucas, supt. Fax 359-3685
www.bettendorf.k12.ia.us
Bettendorf HS 1,500/9-12
3333 18th St 52722 563-332-7001
Jimmy Casas, prin. Fax 332-2326
Bettendorf MS 1,000/6-8
2030 Middle Rd 52722 563-359-3686
Linda Goff, prin. Fax 359-3855

Morning Star Academy 200/PK-10
1426 Tanglefoot Ln 52722 563-359-5700
Cheryl Headley, prin. Fax 359-5737
Rivermont Collegiate 200/PK-12
1821 Sunset Dr 52722 563-359-1366
Rick St. Laurent, hdmstr. Fax 359-7576

Blairsburg, Hamilton, Pop. 228
Northeast Hamilton Community SD 300/K-12
606 Illinois St 50034 515-325-6202
Roark Horn, supt. Fax 325-6235
www.ne-hamilton.k12.ia.us
Northeast Hamilton HS 100/9-12
606 Illinois St 50034 515-325-6234
Patrick Hocking, prin. Fax 325-6235
Northeast Hamilton MS 100/6-8
606 Illinois St 50034 515-325-6234
Patrick Hocking, prin. Fax 325-6235

Blakesburg, Wapello, Pop. 370
Eddyville-Blakesburg Community SD
Supt. — See Eddyville
Eddyville-Blakesburg MS 100/7-8
407 Wilson St 52536 641-938-2203
Lonna McGrath, prin. Fax 938-2613

Bloomfield, Davis, Pop. 2,580
Davis County Community SD 1,400/PK-12
608 S Washington St 52537 641-664-2200
Anne Morgan, supt. Fax 664-2221
www.dcmustangs.com/
Davis County HS 400/9-12
106 N East St 52537 641-664-2200
Ken McKenna, prin. Fax 664-1763
Davis County MS 400/5-8
500 E North St 52537 641-664-2200
Sam Miller, prin. Fax 664-1767

Bode, Humboldt, Pop. 317
Twin Rivers Community SD 200/K-12
PO Box 153 50519 515-379-1526
James Kenton, supt. Fax 379-1645
www.trv.k12.ia.us
Twin Rivers Valley HS 100/9-12
PO Box 153 50519 515-379-1526
Don Hasenkamp, prin. Fax 379-1645

Bonaparte, Van Buren, Pop. 448
Harmony Community SD 500/PK-12
602 8th St 52620 319-592-3600
R. Kelley Rogers, supt. Fax 592-3690
Other Schools – See Farmington

Bondurant, Polk, Pop. 1,991
Bondurant-Farrar Community SD 1,000/PK-12
300 Garfield St SW 50035 515-967-7819
Craig Cochran, supt. Fax 967-7847
www.bondurant.k12.ia.us/
Bondurant-Farrar JSHS 500/7-12
300 Garfield St SW 50035 515-967-3711
Vernon Anderson, prin. Fax 957-9924

Boone, Boone, Pop. 12,807
Boone Community SD 2,100/K-12
500 7th St 50036 515-433-0750
Dr. Theron J. Schutte, supt. Fax 433-0753
boone.k12.ia.us/
Boone HS 900/9-12
500 7th St 50036 515-433-0890
David Kapfer, prin. Fax 433-0989
Boone MS 400/7-8
1640 1st St 50036 515-433-0020
Nate Heying, prin. Fax 433-0026

Des Moines Area Community College Post-Sec.
1125 Hancock Dr 50036 515-432-7203

Britt, Hancock, Pop. 2,019
West Hancock Community SD 600/PK-12
PO Box 128 50423 641-843-3833
Richard Keith, supt. Fax 843-4717
www.whancock.org/
West Hancock HS 200/9-12
PO Box 278 50423 641-843-3863
Ben Muller, prin. Fax 843-4633
Other Schools – See Kanawha

Brooklyn, Poweshiek, Pop. 1,381
Brooklyn-Guernsey-Malcom Community SD 700/PK-12
1090 Jackson St 52211 641-522-7058
Terry McLeod, supt. Fax 522-7211
www.brooklyn.k12.ia.us
Brooklyn-Guernsey-Malcom JSHS 300/7-12
1090 Jackson St 52211 641-522-7058
Rick Radcliffe, prin. Fax 522-7211

Buffalo Center, Winnebago, Pop. 925
North Iowa Community SD 600/PK-12
111 3rd Ave NW 50424 641-562-2921
Larry Hill, supt. Fax 562-2921
www.northiowa.org
North Iowa HS 200/9-12
111 3rd Ave NW 50424 641-562-2525
Daniel Dierks, prin. Fax 562-2921
Other Schools – See Thompson

Burlington, Des Moines, Pop. 25,966
Burlington Community SD 3,600/K-12
1429 West Ave 52601 319-753-6791
Dr. Mike Book, supt. Fax 753-6796
www.burlington.k12.ia.us
Burlington Community HS 1,300/9-12
421 Terrace Dr 52601 319-753-2211
Tom Messinger, prin. Fax 753-6634
Madison MS 300/6-8
2132 Madison Ave 52601 319-753-6253
Mary Settles, prin. Fax 753-6514
Oak Street MS 400/6-8
903 Oak St 52601 319-753-6773
Donita Lynch, prin. Fax 753-0554

Dayton's School of Hair Design Post-Sec.
315 N Main St 52601 319-752-3193
Notre Dame HS 200/7-12
702 S Roosevelt Ave 52601 319-754-8431
Dave Edwards, prin. Fax 752-8690

Burnside, Webster
Southeast Webster-Grand Community SD 600/PK-12
PO Box 49 50521 515-359-2235
Mike Jorgensen, supt. Fax 359-2236
www.se-webster.k12.ia.us
Southeast Webster-Grand HS 300/7-12
PO Box 49 50521 515-359-2235
Launi Dane, prin. Fax 359-2236

Bussey, Marion, Pop. 453
Twin Cedars Community SD 500/PK-12
2204 Highway G71 50044 641-944-5241
Brian VanderSluis, supt. Fax 944-5824
www.twincedars.k12.ia.us
Twin Cedars JSHS 200/7-12
2204 Highway G71 50044 641-944-5243
Dave Roby, prin. Fax 944-5225

Calmar, Winneshiek, Pop. 1,083
South Winneshiek Community SD 600/PK-12
PO Box 430 52132 563-562-3269
Richard Wede, supt. Fax 562-3260
www.s-winneshiek.k12.ia.us
South Winneshiek HS 300/9-12
PO Box 430 52132 563-562-3226
John Grampovnik, prin. Fax 562-3228
Other Schools – See Ossian

C F S Consolidated S 100/6-8
PO Box 815 52132 563-562-3291
Kathryn Schmitt, prin. Fax 562-3292
Northeast Iowa Community College Post-Sec.
PO Box 400 52132 563-562-3263

Camanche, Clinton, Pop. 4,228
Camanche Community SD 1,000/PK-12
PO Box 170 52730 563-259-3000
Thomas Parker, supt. Fax 259-3005
www.camanche.k12.ia.us
Camanche HS 300/9-12
PO Box 170 52730 563-259-3008
Gary DeLacy, prin. Fax 259-3048
Camanche MS 300/5-8
PO Box 170 52730 563-259-3014
Phil Cochran, prin. Fax 259-3031

Carlisle, Warren, Pop. 3,485
Carlisle Community SD — 1,200/PK-12
  430 School St 50047 — 515-989-3589
  Tom Lane, supt. — Fax 989-3075
  www.carlisle.k12.ia.us/
Carlisle HS — 400/9-12
  430 School St 50047 — 515-989-0831
  Michael Anthony, prin. — Fax 989-3075
Carlisle JHS — 7-8
  430 School St 50047 — 515-989-0833
  Diana Whited, prin. — Fax 989-3075

Carroll, Carroll, Pop. 9,986
Carroll Community SD — 1,700/PK-12
  1026 N Adams St 51401 — 712-792-8001
  Rob Cordes, supt. — Fax 792-8008
  www.carroll.k12.ia.us
Carroll HS — 600/9-12
  2809 N Grant Rd 51401 — 712-792-8000
  Steve Haluska, prin. — Fax 792-8118
Carroll MS — 400/6-8
  3203 N Grant Rd 51401 — 712-792-8020
  Jerry Raymond, prin. — Fax 792-8024

Des Moines Area Community College — Post-Sec.
  906 N Grant Rd 51401 — 712-792-1755
Kuemper Catholic HS — 500/9-12
  109 S Clark St 51401 — 712-792-3596
  Penny Miller, prin. — Fax 792-8070

Carson, Pottawattamie, Pop. 696
Riverside Community SD — 700/PK-12
  PO Box 218 51525 — 712-484-2212
  James Sutton, supt. — Fax 484-3957
  www.riverside.k12.ia.us
Riverside Community MS — 200/5-8
  PO Box 218 51525 — 712-484-2291
  Kaylene Kovach, prin. — Fax 484-3957
Other Schools – See Oakland

Cascade, Dubuque, Pop. 1,975
Western Dubuque Community SD
  Supt. — See Farley
Cascade JSHS — 500/7-12
  505 Johnson St NW 52033 — 563-852-3201
  Greg VanderLugt, prin. — Fax 852-7186

Cedar Falls, Black Hawk, Pop. 36,429
Cedar Falls Community SD — 4,200/PK-12
  1002 W 1st St 50613 — 319-553-3000
  Daniel Smith, supt. — Fax 277-0614
  www.cedar-falls.k12.ia.us
Cedar Falls SHS — 1,100/10-12
  1015 Division St 50613 — 319-553-2500
  Rich Powers, prin. — Fax 277-4604
Holmes JHS — 500/7-9
  505 Holmes Dr 50613 — 319-553-2650
  David Welter, prin. — Fax 277-0571
Peet JHS — 500/7-9
  525 E Seerley Blvd 50613 — 319-553-2710
  Mark Farland, prin. — Fax 266-8839

Hamilton College — Post-Sec.
  7009 Nordic Dr 50613 — 319-277-0220
La' James College of Hairstyling — Post-Sec.
  6322 University Ave 50613 — 319-277-2150
University of Northern Iowa — Post-Sec.
  50614 — 319-273-2311
Valley Lutheran HS — 50/9-12
  4520 Rownd St 50613 — 319-266-4565
  Dan Cox, prin. — Fax 266-4054

Cedar Rapids, Linn, Pop. 122,542
Cedar Rapids Community SD — 17,300/PK-12
  346 2nd Ave SW 52404 — 319-558-2000
  David Markward, supt. — Fax 558-2008
  www.cr.k12.ia.us
Franklin MS — 700/6-8
  300 20th St NE 52402 — 319-558-2452
  Colin Williams, prin. — Fax 398-2454
Harding MS — 900/6-8
  4801 Golf St NE 52402 — 319-558-2254
  Randy Krejci, prin. — Fax 378-0671
Jefferson HS — 1,600/9-12
  1243 20th St SW 52404 — 319-558-2435
  Charles McDonnell, prin. — Fax 398-2442
Kennedy HS — 1,700/9-12
  4545 Wenig Rd NE 52402 — 319-558-2251
  Mary Wilcynski, prin. — Fax 294-1118
McKinley MS — 700/6-8
  620 10th St SE 52403 — 319-558-2348
  Connie Tesar, prin. — Fax 398-2347
Metro HS — 500/9-12
  1212 7th St SE 52401 — 319-558-2193
  Kathy Green, prin. — Fax 398-2117
Roosevelt MS — 600/6-8
  300 13th St NW 52405 — 319-558-2153
  Steve Hilby, prin. — Fax 398-2424
Taft MS — 700/6-8
  5200 E Ave NW 52405 — 319-558-2243
  Steve Archibald, prin. — Fax 654-8619
Washington HS — 1,500/9-12
  2205 Forest Dr SE 52403 — 319-558-2161
  Ralph Plagman, prin. — Fax 398-2016

College Community SD — 3,500/K-12
  401 76th Ave SW 52404 — 319-848-5201
  Richard T. Whitehead, supt. — Fax 848-4019
  www.prairiepride.org
Prairie HS — 1,000/9-12
  401 76th Ave SW 52404 — 319-848-5340
  Mark Gronemeyer, prin. — Fax 848-5349
Prairie MS — 800/6-8
  401 76th Ave SW 52404 — 319-848-5310
  Greg Leytem, prin. — Fax 848-5323

American College of Hairstyling — Post-Sec.
  1531 1st Ave SE 52402 — 319-362-1488

Capri College — Post-Sec.
  2945 Williams Pkwy SW 52404 — 319-364-1541
Cedar Valley Christian S — 200/PK-12
  3636 Cottage Grove Ave SE 52403 — 319-366-7462
  Joel DeSousa, prin. — Fax 247-0037
Coe College — Post-Sec.
  1220 1st Ave NE 52402 — 319-399-8000
Hamilton College — Post-Sec.
  3165 Edgewood Pkwy SW 52404 — 319-363-0481
Holy Family - LaSalle MS — 100/6-8
  3700 1st Ave NW 52405 — 319-396-7792
  Rick Louk, prin. — Fax 390-6527
Kirkwood Community College — Post-Sec.
  PO Box 2068 52406 — 319-398-5411
Mercy-St. Luke's Hospital — Post-Sec.
  1026 A Ave NE 52402 — 319-369-7204
Mt. Mercy College — Post-Sec.
  1330 Elmhurst Dr NE 52402 — 319-363-8213
Regis MS — 300/6-8
  735 Prairie Dr NE 52402 — 319-378-0547
  Rick Blackwell, prin. — Fax 247-6099
Xavier HS — 500/9-12
  6300 42nd St NE 52411 — 319-294-6635
  Tom Keating, prin. — Fax 294-6712

Center Point, Linn, Pop. 2,145
Center Point-Urbana Community SD — 1,200/K-12
  PO Box 296 52213 — 319-849-1102
  Alan Marshall, supt. — Fax 849-2312
  www.cen-pt-urb.k12.ia.us
Center Point-Urbana HS — 300/9-12
  PO Box 296 52213 — 319-849-1102
  David Hanneman, prin. — Fax 849-2068
Urbana-Center Point MS — 400/5-8
  PO Box 296 52213 — 319-443-2426
  Brent Winterhof, prin. — Fax 443-2764

Centerville, Appanoose, Pop. 5,814
Centerville Community SD — 1,700/K-12
  PO Box 370 52544 — 641-856-0601
  Richard Turner, supt. — Fax 856-0656
  www.centerville.k12.ia.us
Centerville HS — 500/9-12
  600 CHS Dr 52544 — 641-856-0813
  Bill Messerole, prin. — Fax 856-0809
Howar JHS — 300/7-8
  850 S Park Ave 52544 — 641-856-0760
  Bruce Karpen, prin. — Fax 856-0761

Indian Hills Community College — Post-Sec.
  721 N 1st St 52544 — 641-856-2143

Central City, Linn, Pop. 1,161
Central City Community SD — 500/PK-12
  400 Barber St 52214 — 319-438-6183
  Bill Mertens, supt. — Fax 438-6110
  www.central-city.k12.ia.us
Central City HS — 100/9-12
  400 Barber St 52214 — 319-438-6182
  David Glynn, prin. — Fax 438-6110
Central City MS — 100/6-8
  400 Barber St 52214 — 319-438-6181
  Chad Steckel, prin. — Fax 438-6110

Chariton, Lucas, Pop. 4,590
Chariton Community SD — 1,500/PK-12
  PO Box 738 50049 — 641-774-5967
  Dr. Robert Newsum, supt. — Fax 774-8511
  www.charitonschools.com
Chariton HS — 400/9-12
  501 N Grand St 50049 — 641-774-5066
  Russ Reiter, prin. — Fax 774-8511
Chariton MS — 300/6-8
  1300 N 16th St 50049 — 641-774-5114
  Beth Scott-Thomas, prin. — Fax 774-8511

Charles City, Floyd, Pop. 7,685
Charles City Community SD — 1,500/K-12
  500 N Grand Ave 50616 — 641-257-6500
  Marty Lucas, supt. — Fax 257-6509
  www.charles-city.k12.ia.us
Charles City HS — 600/9-12
  1 Comet Dr 50616 — 641-257-6510
  Shirley Kelly, prin. — Fax 257-1175
Charles City MS — 400/6-8
  500 N Grand Ave 50616 — 641-257-6530
  Ron Hoffman, prin. — Fax 228-9842

Charter Oak, Crawford, Pop. 523
Charter Oak-Ute Community SD — 300/PK-12
  321 Main St 51439 — 712-678-3325
  Rollie Wiebers, supt. — Fax 678-3626
Charter Oak-Ute HS — 100/9-12
  321 Main St 51439 — 712-678-3325
  Rollie Wiebers, prin. — Fax 678-3626
Charter Oak-Ute JHS — 50/7-8
  321 Main St 51439 — 712-678-3325
  Rollie Wiebers, prin. — Fax 678-3626

Cherokee, Cherokee, Pop. 5,158
Cherokee Community SD — 1,200/PK-12
  PO Box 801 51012 — 712-225-6767
  John Chalstrom, supt. — Fax 225-6769
  www.cherokee.k12.ia.us/
Cherokee MS — 400/5-8
  PO Box 801 51012 — 712-225-6750
  Larry Weede, prin. — Fax 225-4841
Washington HS — 400/9-12
  PO Box 801 51012 — 712-225-6755
  Larry Hunecke, prin. — Fax 225-6765

Western Iowa Tech Community College — Post-Sec.
  200 Victory Dr 51012 — 712-225-0238

Churdan, Greene, Pop. 391
Paton-Churdan Community SD — 200/PK-12
  PO Box 157 50050 — 515-389-3111
  Leonard Griffith, supt. — Fax 389-3113
  www.paton-churdan.k12.ia.us

Paton-Churdan JSHS — 100/6-12
  PO Box 157 50050 — 515-389-3111
  Terry Eisenbarth, prin. — Fax 389-3113

Clarence, Cedar, Pop. 1,008
North Cedar Community SD
  Supt. — See Stanwood
North Cedar MS — 300/6-8
  PO Box 310 52216 — 563-452-3179
  Greg Fisher, prin. — Fax 452-3890

Clarinda, Page, Pop. 5,540
Clarinda Community SD — 1,000/PK-12
  PO Box 59 51632 — 712-542-5165
  Paul Honnold, supt. — Fax 542-3802
  www.clarinda.k12.ia.us
Clarinda HS — 400/9-12
  PO Box 59 51632 — 712-542-5167
  Michael Ruffing, prin. — Fax 542-4305
Clarinda MS — 300/5-8
  PO Box 59 51632 — 712-542-2132
  Margaret Nordland, prin. — Fax 542-5949

Iowa Western Community College — Post-Sec.
  923 E Washington St 51632 — 712-542-5117

Clarion, Wright, Pop. 2,856
Clarion-Goldfield Community SD — 1,100/PK-12
  319 3rd Ave NE 50525 — 515-532-3423
  Robert Olson, supt. — Fax 532-2628
  www.clargold.k12.ia.us
Clarion-Goldfield HS — 300/9-12
  1111 Willow Dr 50525 — 515-532-2895
  Dennis March, prin. — Fax 532-2897
Clarion-Goldfield MS — 200/6-8
  300 3rd Ave NE 50525 — 515-532-2412
  Steve Haberman, prin. — Fax 532-2741

Clarksville, Butler, Pop. 1,391
Clarksville Community SD — 400/PK-12
  PO Box 689 50619 — 319-278-4008
  Randall Nichols, supt. — Fax 278-4618
Clarksville JSHS — 200/7-12
  PO Box 689 50619 — 319-278-4273
  Robert Saathoff, prin. — Fax 278-4981

Clear Lake, Cerro Gordo, Pop. 7,977
Clear Lake Community SD — 1,400/K-12
  306 1st Ave N 50428 — 641-357-2181
  Mike Wright, supt. — Fax 357-2182
  www.clearlake.k12.ia.us
Clear Lake HS — 400/9-12
  125 N 20th St 50428 — 641-357-5235
  Jay Mathis, prin. — Fax 357-6218
Clear Lake MS — 300/6-8
  1601 3rd Ave N 50428 — 641-357-6114
  Robert Mondt, prin. — Fax 357-8353

Cleghorn, Cherokee, Pop. 244
Marcus-Meriden-Cleghorn Community SD
  Supt. — See Marcus
Marcus-Meriden-Cleghorn MS — 200/4-8
  PO Box 97 51014 — 712-436-2244
  Bill Sillau, prin. — Fax 436-2695

Clinton, Clinton, Pop. 27,437
Clinton Community SD — 4,300/PK-12
  600 S 4th St 52732 — 563-243-9600
  Randall Clegg, supt. — Fax 243-2415
  www.clinton.k12.ia.us
Clinton HS — 1,200/9-12
  817 8th Ave S 52732 — 563-243-7540
  Karinne Tharaldson, prin. — Fax 243-9612
Lyons MS — 400/6-8
  2810 N 4th St 52732 — 563-242-7858
  Dan Boyd, prin. — Fax 242-6168
Washington MS — 700/6-8
  751 2nd Ave S 52732 — 563-243-0466
  Brian Kenney, prin. — Fax 242-3735

Clinton Community College — Post-Sec.
  1000 Lincoln Blvd 52732 — 563-244-7000
Franciscan University — Post-Sec.
  400 N Bluff Blvd 52732 — 563-242-4023
Prince of Peace Academy College Prep S — 300/K-12
  312 S 4th St 52732 — 563-242-1663
  Nancy Peart, prin. — Fax 243-8272

Clive, Dallas, Pop. 13,671
West Des Moines Community SD
  Supt. — See West Des Moines
Indian Hills JHS — 600/7-8
  9401 Indian Hills Dr 50325 — 515-633-4700
  Shane Christensen, prin. — Fax 633-4799

Colfax, Jasper, Pop. 2,220
Colfax-Mingo Community SD — 800/K-12
  1000 N Walnut St 50054 — 515-674-3646
  Ed Ackerman, supt. — Fax 674-3921
  www.colfax-mingo.k12.ia.us
Colfax-Mingo HS — 300/9-12
  204 N League Rd 50054 — 515-674-4111
  Clayton Hoefs, prin. — Fax 674-4940
Other Schools – See Mingo

College Springs, Page, Pop. 240
South Page Community SD — 300/PK-12
  PO Box 98 51637 — 712-582-3212
  Bill Stattelman, supt. — Fax 582-3217
  www.clarinda.heartland.net
South Page JSHS — 200/6-12
  PO Box 98 51637 — 712-582-3211
  Ron Iles, prin. — Fax 582-3217

Colo, Story, Pop. 881
Colo-Nesco Comm SD
  Supt. — See Mc Callsburg
Colo-Nesco HS — 200/9-12
  PO Box 215 50056 — 641-377-2282
  Steven Buhrow, prin. — Fax 377-2283

Columbus Junction, Louisa, Pop. 1,891
Columbus Community SD — 1,000/PK-12
1210 Colton St 52738 — 319-728-2911
Richard Bridenstine, supt. — Fax 728-8750
www.columbus.k12.ia.us
Columbus Community HS — 300/9-12
1210 Colton St 52738 — 319-728-2231
John Lawrence, prin. — Fax 728-2205
Columbus Community MS — 300/6-8
1210 Colton St 52738 — 319-728-2233
Tony Simmons, prin. — Fax 728-2205

Conrad, Grundy, Pop. 1,036
BCLUW Community SD — 700/K-12
PO Box 670 50621 — 641-366-2819
Mike Ashton, supt. — Fax 366-2175
www.bcluw.k12.ia.us
BCLUW HS — 200/9-12
PO Box 670 50621 — 641-366-2810
Ben Petty, prin. — Fax 366-2951
Other Schools – See Union

Coon Rapids, Carroll, Pop. 1,308
Coon Rapids-Bayard Community SD — 500/PK-12
PO Box 297 50058 — 712-999-2207
Dennis Wentz, supt. — Fax 999-7740
www.crbcrusaders.org
Coon Rapids-Bayard JSHS — 200/7-12
PO Box 297 50058 — 712-999-2208
Shawn Zanders, prin. — Fax 999-7740

Coralville, Johnson, Pop. 16,778
Iowa City Community SD
Supt. — See Iowa City
Northwest JHS — 900/7-8
1507 8th St 52241 — 319-688-1060
Gregg Shoultz, prin. — Fax 339-5728

Corning, Adams, Pop. 1,731
Corning Community SD — 600/K-12
904 8th St 50841 — 641-322-4242
Mike Wells, supt. — Fax 322-5149
www.corning.k12.ia.us
Corning HS — 200/9-12
904 8th St 50841 — 641-322-4245
Kent Jorgensen, prin. — Fax 322-5149
Corning JHS — 100/7-8
10th & Washington 50841 — 641-322-3213
Patty Morris, prin. — Fax 322-4884

Correctionville, Woodbury, Pop. 858
River Valley Community SD — 500/PK-12
PO Box 8 51016 — 712-372-4420
Julie Destiger, supt. — Fax 372-4677
River Valley JSHS — 300/7-12
PO Box 8 51016 — 712-372-4656
John Holbrook, prin. — Fax 372-4784

Corwith, Hancock, Pop. 336
Corwith-Wesley Community SD — 200/K-12
PO Box 220 50430 — 515-583-2304
Jim McDermott, supt. — Fax 583-2030
www.corwith-wesley.k12.ia.us
Corwith-Wesley HS — 100/9-12
PO Box 220 50430 — 515-583-2304
Jim McDermott, prin. — Fax 583-2030

Corydon, Wayne, Pop. 1,553
Wayne Community SD — 600/K-12
102 N Dekalb St 50060 — 641-872-1220
Robert Busch, supt. — Fax 872-2091
www.aea15.k12.ia.us/wayne
Wayne Community HS — 200/9-12
102 N Dekalb St 50060 — 641-872-2184
Dave Daughton, prin. — Fax 872-2091
Wayne Community JHS — 100/7-8
102 N Dekalb St 50060 — 641-872-2184
Shane Brown, prin. — Fax 872-2091

Council Bluffs, Pottawattamie, Pop. 58,656
Council Bluffs Community SD — 9,600/PK-12
12 Scott St 51503 — 712-328-6446
Dr. Richard Christie, supt. — Fax 328-6548
www.cb-schools.org
Jefferson HS — 1,200/9-12
2501 W Broadway 51501 — 712-328-6493
Judy O'Brien, prin. — Fax 328-6497
Kirn JHS — 800/7-8
100 North Ave 51503 — 712-328-6454
Dave Schweitzer, prin. — Fax 328-6554
Lincoln HS — 1,500/9-12
1205 Bonham St 51503 — 712-328-6481
Melanie Shellberg, prin. — Fax 328-6485
Tucker Center for Vocational Education — Vo/Tech
815 N 18th St 51501 — 712-328-6408
Paul Hans, prin. — Fax 328-6425
Wilson JHS — 700/7-8
715 N 21st St 51501 — 712-328-6476
Joel Beyenhof, prin. — Fax 328-6479

Lewis Central Community SD — 2,700/PK-12
1600 E South Omaha Brdge Rd 51503
— 712-366-8202
Mark Schweer, supt. — Fax 366-8315
www.lewiscentral.k12.ia.us
Lewis Central HS — 900/9-12
3504 Harry Langdon Blvd 51503 — 712-366-8222
Doug Radtke, prin. — Fax 366-8340
Lewis Central MS — 600/6-8
3820 Harry Langdon Blvd 51503 — 712-366-8251
Sean Dunphy, prin. — Fax 366-8324

EQ School of Hair Design — Post-Sec.
536 W Broadway 51503 — 712-328-2613
Iowa School for the Deaf — Post-Sec.
3501 Harry Langdon Blvd 51503 — 712-366-0571
Iowa Western Community College — Post-Sec.
2700 College Rd 51503 — 800-432-5852
Jennie Edmundson Memorial Hospital — Post-Sec.
933 E Pierce St 51503 — 712-328-6239

St. Albert HS — 400/7-12
400 Gleason Ave 51503 — 712-328-2316
Jonna Andersen, prin. — Fax 328-8316

Cresco, Howard, Pop. 3,840
Howard-Winneshiek Community SD — 1,500/PK-12
1000 Schroder Dr 52136 — 563-547-2762
Brian Ney, supt. — Fax 547-5973
www.howard-winn.k12.ia.us
Cresco IS — 300/7-8
1000 4th Ave E 52136 — 563-547-2300
Todd Knobloch, prin. — Fax 547-2679
Crestwood HS — 600/9-12
1000 Schroder Dr 52136 — 563-547-2764
Jim Zajicek, prin. — Fax 547-4650

Total Look Sch of Cosmetology & Massage — Post-Sec.
806 3rd St W 52136 — 563-547-3624

Creston, Union, Pop. 7,359
Creston Community SD — 900/PK-12
619 N Maple St 50801 — 641-782-7028
Tim Hood, supt. — Fax 782-7020
www.creston.k12.ia.us/
Creston HS — 500/9-12
601 W Townline St 50801 — 641-782-2116
Todd Wolverton, prin. — Fax 782-9502
Creston MS — 300/6-8
805 Academic Ave 50801 — 641-782-2129
Larry Otten, prin.

Southwestern Community College — Post-Sec.
1501 W Townline St 50801 — 641-782-7081

Crystal Lake, Hancock, Pop. 278
Woden-Crystal Lake Community SD
Supt. — See Woden
Woden-Crystal Lake-Titonka HS — 100/9-12
PO Box 130 50432 — 641-565-3211
M. Rex Heard, prin. — Fax 565-3320

Dallas Center, Dallas, Pop. 1,646
Dallas Center-Grimes Community SD — 1,700/K-12
PO Box 512 50063 — 515-992-3866
Gary Sinclair, supt. — Fax 992-3079
www.dc-grimes.k12.ia.us
Dallas Center-Grimes MS — 400/6-8
PO Box 608 50063 — 515-992-4343
Linda Boettcher, prin. — Fax 992-4076
Other Schools – See Grimes

Danville, Des Moines, Pop. 905
Danville Community SD — 600/K-12
419 S Main St 52623 — 319-392-4223
Stephen McAllister, supt. — Fax 392-8390
www.danville.k12.ia.us/
Danville JSHS — 300/7-12
419 S Main St 52623 — 319-392-4222
Paul Giehl, prin. — Fax 392-8390

Davenport, Scott, Pop. 97,512
Davenport Community SD — 15,700/PK-12
1606 Brady St 52803 — 563-336-5000
Norbert Schuerman, supt. — Fax 336-5080
www.davenport.k12.ia.us
Central HS — 1,400/9-12
1120 N Main St 52803 — 563-323-9900
Tim Wernentin, prin. — Fax 323-3110
North HS — 1,100/9-12
626 W 53rd St 52806 — 563-388-9880
Jane Artman Andrews, prin. — Fax 388-9456
Smart IS — 600/6-8
1934 W 5th St 52802 — 563-323-1837
Trampus Budde, prin. — Fax 323-3093
Sudlow IS — 700/6-8
1414 E Locust St 52803 — 563-326-3502
Bruce Potts, prin. — Fax 326-2248
West HS — 2,200/9-12
3505 W Locust St 52804 — 563-386-5500
Nancy Jacobsen, prin. — Fax 386-5508
Williams IS — 800/6-8
3040 N Division St 52804 — 563-391-6550
Scott McKissick, prin. — Fax 391-0149
Wood IS — 700/6-8
5701 N Division St 52806 — 563-391-6350
Rick Herrig, prin. — Fax 391-4416
Young IS — 300/6-8
1709 N Harrison St 52803 — 563-326-4432
Marianne Corbin, prin. — Fax 326-1165
Other Schools – See Walcott

Assumption HS — 500/9-12
1020 W Central Park Ave 52804 — 563-326-5313
Carmine Draude, prin. — Fax 326-3510
Capri College — Post-Sec.
425 E 59th St 52807 — 563-388-6642
Christ Lutheran HS — 50/9-12
PO Box 1535 52809 — 563-391-2190
Rev. Steven Anderson, admin. — Fax 391-1401
Davenport Barber-Styling College — Post-Sec.
730 E Kimberly Rd 52807 — 563-391-9950
Hamilton Technical College — Post-Sec.
1011 E 53rd St 52807 — 563-386-3570
Kaplan University — Post-Sec.
1801 E Kimberly Rd 52807 — 563-355-3500
La' James College of Hairstyling — Post-Sec.
3802 E 53rd St 52807 — 563-441-7900
Palmer College of Chiropractic — Post-Sec.
1000 Brady St 52803 — 563-884-5000
St. Ambrose University — Post-Sec.
518 W Locust St 52803 — 563-333-6000

Decorah, Winneshiek, Pop. 8,120
Decorah Community SD — 1,700/PK-12
510 Winnebago St 52101 — 563-382-4208
Steven Chambliss, supt. — Fax 387-0753
decorah.k12.ia.us/

Decorah HS — 700/9-12
100 E Claiborne Dr 52101 — 563-382-3643
Kim Sheppard, prin. — Fax 382-3107
Decorah MS — 400/5-8
210 Vernon St 52101 — 563-382-8427
Leona Hoth, prin. — Fax 387-4052

North Wineshiek Community SD — 200/PK-8
3495 N Winn Rd 52101 — 563-735-5411
Tim Dugger, supt. — Fax 735-5430
www.n-winn.k12.ia.us/
North Winneshiek MS — 100/6-8
3495 N Winn Rd 52101 — 563-735-5411
Tim Dugger, prin. — Fax 735-5430

Luther College — Post-Sec.
700 College Dr 52101 — 563-387-2000

Delhi, Delaware, Pop. 458
Maquoketa Valley Community SD — 900/PK-12
PO Box 186 52223 — 563-922-9422
Doug Tuetken, supt. — Fax 922-2160
www.maquoketa-v.k12.ia.us
Maquoketa Valley HS — 300/9-12
PO Box 186 52223 — 563-922-2091
Dave Kuehl, prin. — Fax 922-2160
Maquoketa Valley MS — 200/6-8
PO Box 186 52223 — 563-922-9411
Thomas Gatto, prin. — Fax 922-2160

Denison, Crawford, Pop. 7,420
Denison Community SD — 1,900/K-12
819 N 16th St 51442 — 712-263-2176
Michael Pardun, supt. — Fax 263-5233
www.denison.k12.ia.us
Denison HS — 700/9-12
819 N 16th St 51442 — 712-263-3101
Steve Westerberg, prin. — Fax 263-6009
Denison MS — 400/6-8
1515 Broadway 51442 — 712-263-9393
Patricia Roush, prin. — Fax 263-5418

Denver, Bremer, Pop. 1,604
Denver Community SD — 500/PK-12
PO Box 384 50622 — 319-984-6323
Kathy Gilbert, supt. — Fax 984-5345
www.denver.k12.ia.us
Denver HS — 200/9-12
PO Box 384 50622 — 319-984-5639
Paul Gebel, prin. — Fax 984-5630
Denver MS — 200/6-8
PO Box 384 50622 — 319-984-6041
Joann Butler, prin. — Fax 984-5630

Des Moines, Polk, Pop. 196,093
Des Moines Independent Community SD — 29,400/PK-12
1801 16th St 50314 — 515-242-7911
Dr. Eric Witherspoon, supt. — Fax 242-7579
www.dmps.k12.ia.us
Brody MS — 700/6-8
2501 Park Ave 50321 — 515-242-8443
Randy Gordon, prin. — Fax 244-0927
Callanan MS — 600/6-8
3010 Center St 50312 — 515-242-8101
Kathie Danielson, prin. — Fax 242-8103
East HS — 2,000/9-12
815 E 13th St 50316 — 515-242-7788
Mike Zelenovich, prin. — Fax 242-7958
Goodrell MS — 600/6-8
3300 E 29th St 50317 — 515-242-8444
Dawn Stahly, prin. — Fax 262-8967
Harding MS — 800/6-8
203 E Euclid Ave 50313 — 515-242-8445
Donna Christensen, prin. — Fax 244-3566
Hiatt MS — 600/6-8
1214 E 15th St 50316 — 515-242-7774
Toni Dann, prin. — Fax 242-7789
Hoover HS — 1,200/9-12
4800 Aurora Ave 50310 — 515-242-7300
Connie Cook, prin. — Fax 242-7308
Hoyt MS — 700/6-8
2700 E 42nd St 50317 — 515-242-8446
Billy Jean Stone, prin. — Fax 265-5059
Lincoln HS — 2,200/9-12
2600 SW 9th St 50315 — 515-242-7500
Albert Graziano, prin. — Fax 242-7517
McCombs MS — 700/6-8
201 County Line Rd 50320 — 515-242-8447
Barb Mullahey, prin. — Fax 287-2644
Meredith MS — 800/6-8
4827 Madison Ave 50310 — 515-242-7300
Connie Cook, prin. — Fax 242-8291
Merrill MS — 700/6-8
5301 Grand Ave 50312 — 515-242-8448
Alex Hanna, prin. — Fax 274-1844
North HS — 1,200/9-12
501 Holcomb Ave 50313 — 515-242-7200
Vince Lewis, prin. — Fax 242-7360
Roosevelt HS — 1,600/9-12
4419 Center St 50312 — 515-242-7272
Anita Micich, prin. — Fax 242-7350
Weeks MS — 800/6-8
901 E Park Ave 50315 — 515-242-8449
Susanna Marcucci, prin. — Fax 288-8740

Saydel Community SD — 1,500/PK-12
5740 NE 14th St 50313 — 515-264-0866
Merrill C. Knight, supt. — Fax 264-0869
www.saydel.k12.ia.us
Saydel HS — 400/9-12
5601 NE 7th St 50313 — 515-262-9325
Tracy Hook, prin. — Fax 266-8497
Woodside MS — 400/5-8
5810 NE 14th St 50313 — 515-265-3451
Pam Ewell, prin. — Fax 265-0950

AIB College of Business — Post-Sec.
2500 Fleur Dr 50321 — 515-244-4221

American College of Hairstyling | Post-Sec.
603 E 6th St 50309 | 515-244-0971
Des Moines Area Community College | Post-Sec.
1100 7th St 50314 | 515-244-4226
Des Moines Univ. Osteopathic Medical Ctr | Post-Sec.
3200 Grand Ave 50312 | 515-271-1400
Drake University | Post-Sec.
2507 University Ave 50311 | 515-271-2011
Grand View College | Post-Sec.
1200 Grandview Ave 50316 | 515-263-2800
Grandview Park Baptist S | 400/PK-12
1701 E 33rd St 50317 | 515-265-7579
Dick McWilliams, prin. | Fax 266-9834
Iowa Methodist Medical Center | Post-Sec.
1200 Pleasant St 50309 | 515-241-6201
Iowa School of Beauty | Post-Sec.
3305 70th St 50322 | 515-278-9939
Mercy College of Health Sciences | Post-Sec.
928 6th Ave 50309 | 515-643-3180
Vatterott College | Post-Sec.
6100 Thornton Ave Ste 290 50321 | 515-309-9000

De Witt, Clinton, Pop. 5,128
Central Clinton Community SD | 1,500/K-12
PO Box 110 52742 | 563-659-0700
Dr. Carol Hansen, supt. | Fax 659-0707
www.central-clinton.k12.ia.us
Central HS | 600/9-12
PO Box 110 52742 | 563-659-0715
Brad Oates, prin. | Fax 659-0714
Central MS | 400/6-8
PO Box 110 52742 | 563-659-0735
Steve Haines, prin. | Fax 659-0766

Diagonal, Ringgold, Pop. 310
Diagonal Community SD | 100/PK-12
PO Box 94 50845 | 641-734-5331
Karlene Stephens, supt. | Fax 734-5729
www.diagonal.k12.ia.us
Diagonal JSHS | 100/6-12
PO Box 94 50845 | 641-734-5331
Larry Tepley, prin. | Fax 734-5729

Dike, Grundy, Pop. 1,099
Dike-New Hartford Community SD | 800/PK-12
PO Box D 50624 | 319-989-2552
Lindsey Beecher, supt. | Fax 989-2735
www.dikenh.k12.ia.us
Dike-New Hartford HS | 200/9-12
PO Box D 50624 | 319-989-2485
Michael Williams, prin. | Fax 989-2735
Other Schools – See New Hartford

Donnellson, Lee, Pop. 924
Central Lee Community SD | 1,100/K-12
2642 Highway 218 52625 | 319-835-9510
Chuck Reighard, supt. | Fax 835-3910
www.central-lee.k12.ia.us
Central Lee HS | 400/9-12
2642 Highway 218 52625 | 319-835-5121
Shane Knoche, prin. | Fax 835-5709
Central Lee MS | 300/6-8
2642 Highway 218 52625 | 319-835-5139
Kimberly Kirchner, prin. | Fax 835-5020

Dubuque, Dubuque, Pop. 57,204
Dubuque Community SD | 9,400/PK-12
2300 Chaney Rd 52001 | 563-552-3012
John Burgart, supt. | Fax 552-3014
www.dubuque.k12.ia.us
Dubuque HS | 1,500/9-12
1800 Clarke Dr 52001 | 563-552-5500
Kim Swift, prin. | Fax 552-5502
Hempstead HS | 1,600/9-12
3715 Pennsylvania Ave 52002 | 563-552-5200
David Olson, prin. | Fax 552-5231
Jefferson MS | 800/6-8
1105 Althauser Ave 52001 | 563-552-4700
Phillip Kramer, prin. | Fax 552-4701
Roosevelt MS | 6-8
2001 Radford Rd 52002 | 563-552-5000
Dale Lass, prin. | Fax 552-5001
Washington MS | 900/6-8
51 N Grandview Ave 52001 | 563-552-4800
Mark Burns, prin. | Fax 552-4801

Capri College | Post-Sec.
PO Box 873 52004 | 563-588-2379
Clarke College | Post-Sec.
1550 Clarke Dr 52001 | 563-588-6300
Emmaus Bible College | Post-Sec.
2570 Asbury Rd 52001 | 563-588-8000
Holy Family MS | 400/7-8
1001 Alta Vista St 52001 | 563-582-7236
Kim Hermsen, prin. | Fax 582-7857
Loras College | Post-Sec.
1450 Alta Vista St 52001 | 563-588-7100
University of Dubuque | Post-Sec.
2000 University Ave 52001 | 563-589-3000
University of Dubuque Theological Sem. | Post-Sec.
2000 University Ave 52001 | 800-369-8387
Wahlert HS | 900/9-12
2005 Kane St 52001 | 563-583-9771
Donald Sisler, prin. | Fax 583-9775
Wartburg Theological Seminary | Post-Sec.
333 Wartburg Pl 52003 | 563-589-0200

Dunkerton, Black Hawk, Pop. 774
Dunkerton Community SD | 500/PK-12
509 S Canfield St 50626 | 319-822-4295
Robert Cue, supt. | Fax 822-9456
www.dunkerton.k12.ia.us
Dunkerton HS | 200/7-12
509 S Canfield St 50626 | 319-822-4295
James Moeller, prin. | Fax 822-9456

Dunlap, Harrison, Pop. 1,107
Boyer Valley Community SD | 600/K-12
1102 Iowa Ave 51529 | 712-643-2251
Debra Johnsen, supt. | Fax 643-2279

Boyer Valley MSHS | 300/6-12
1102 Iowa Ave 51529 | 712-643-2258
Chad Straight, prin. | Fax 643-2279

Durant, Cedar, Pop. 1,635
Durant Community SD | 700/K-12
PO Box 607 52747 | 563-785-4432
James Wagner, supt. | Fax 785-4611
www.durant.k12.ia.us
Durant HS | 200/9-12
PO Box 607 52747 | 563-785-4431
Monica Rouse, prin. | Fax 785-6558
Durant MS | 200/5-8
PO Box 607 52747 | 563-785-4433
Rebecca Stineman, prin. | Fax 785-6558

Dyersville, Dubuque, Pop. 4,096

Beckman HS | 500/7-12
1325 9th St SE 52040 | 563-875-7188
Mike Cooper, prin. | Fax 875-7242

Dysart, Tama, Pop. 1,295
Union Community SD
Supt. — See La Porte City
Union MS | 300/6-8
505 West St 52224 | 319-476-5100
Mark Albertsen, prin. | Fax 476-2385

Eagle Grove, Wright, Pop. 3,563
Eagle Grove Community SD | 900/K-12
216 N Commercial Ave 50533 | 515-448-4749
Rodney Montang, supt. | Fax 448-3156
www.eagle-grove.k12.ia.us
Blue MS | 300/5-8
1015 NW 2nd St 50533 | 515-448-4767
Lori Phillips, prin. | Fax 448-5527
Eagle Grove HS | 300/9-12
415 NW 2nd St 50533 | 515-448-5143
Iner Joelson, prin. | Fax 448-3583

Iowa Central Community College | Post-Sec.
316 NW 3rd St 50533 | 515-448-4723

Earlham, Madison, Pop. 1,317
Earlham Community SD | 600/PK-12
PO Box 430 50072 | 515-758-2235
Douglas Latham, supt. | Fax 758-2215
earlham.k12.ia.us/
Earlham HS | 200/9-12
PO Box 430 50072 | 515-758-2214
Jan Fletcher, prin. | Fax 758-2215
Earlham MS | 100/7-8
PO Box 430 50072 | 515-758-2213
Jan Fletcher, prin. | Fax 758-2215

Early, Sac, Pop. 552
Schaller-Crestland Community SD
Supt. — See Schaller
Schaller-Crestland HS | 200/9-12
PO Box 377 50535 | 712-273-5192
Stuart Fuhs, prin. | Fax 273-5120

Eddyville, Mahaska, Pop. 1,065
Eddyville-Blakesburg Community SD | 900/PK-12
1301 Berdan Ext 52553 | 641-969-4226
Dean Cook, supt. | Fax 969-4547
www.ebcsd.com/
Eddyville-Blakesburg HS | 300/9-12
1301 Berdan Ext 52553 | 641-969-4288
Scott Williamson, prin. | Fax 969-4574
Other Schools – See Blakesburg

Edgewood, Clayton, Pop. 912
Edgewood-Colesburg Community SD | 600/PK-12
PO Box 315 52042 | 563-928-6411
Galen Reinsmoen, supt. | Fax 928-6414
www.aea1.k12.ia.us/edge-cole/main.html
Edgewood-Colesburg JSHS | 300/7-12
PO Box 316 52042 | 563-928-6412
Ed Klamfoth, prin. | Fax 928-6414

Eldon, Wapello, Pop. 987
Cardinal Community SD | 700/PK-12
4045 Ashland Rd 52554 | 641-652-7531
Arnie Snook, supt. | Fax 652-3143
www.cardinalcomet.org/
Cardinal MSHS | 400/6-12
4045 Ashland Rd 52554 | 641-652-7531
Dennis Augustine, prin. | Fax 652-3143

Eldora, Hardin, Pop. 2,942
Eldora-New Providence Community SD | 700/K-12
1010 Edgington Ave 50627 | 641-939-5631
Robert Lehman, supt. | Fax 939-3667
www.eldora-np.k12.ia.us
Eldora-New Providence HS | 300/9-12
1800 24th St 50627 | 641-939-3421
Randall Fahr, prin. | Fax 939-3423
Eldora-New Providence MS | 200/5-8
1100 12th Ave 50627 | 641-939-2599
John Zimmerman, prin. | Fax 939-5057

Eldridge, Scott, Pop. 4,995
North Scott Community SD | 3,000/K-12
251 E Iowa St 52748 | 563-285-4819
Tim Dose, supt. | Fax 285-6075
www.north-scott.k12.ia.us
North Scott HS | 1,000/9-12
200 S 1st St 52748 | 563-285-9631
| Fax 285-9308
North Scott JHS | 500/7-8
502 S 5th St 52748 | 563-285-8272
David Griffin, prin. | Fax 285-6045

Pleasant Valley Community SD | 3,200/PK-12
251 E Iowa St 52748 | 563-332-5550
Jim Spelhaug, supt. | Fax 332-4372
www.pleasval.k12.ia.us
Other Schools – See Le Claire, Riverdale

Heritage Christian S | 100/K-12
507 Parkview Dr 52748 | 563-285-9382
Gary Forsee, admin. | Fax 285-9343

Elgin, Fayette, Pop. 662
Valley Community SD | 600/K-12
23493 Canoe Rd 52141 | 563-426-5501
Cathleen Molumby, supt. | Fax 426-5502
www.valley.k12.ia.us
Valley JSHS | 300/7-12
23493 Canoe Rd 52141 | 563-426-5551
David Fox, prin. | Fax 426-5502

Elkader, Clayton, Pop. 1,409
Central Community SD | 600/K-12
PO Box 70 52043 | 563-245-1751
Brian Rodenberg, supt. | Fax 245-1763
www.central.k12.ia.us/
Central Community JSHS | 300/7-12
PO Box 70 52043 | 563-245-1750
Dan Yanda, prin. | Fax 245-1763

Elk Horn, Shelby, Pop. 629
Elk Horn-Kimballton Community SD | 300/PK-12
PO Box 388a 51531 | 712-764-4616
J. Allan Hjelle, supt. | Fax 764-4626
www.elk-horn.k12.ia.us
Elk Horn-Kimballton HS | 100/9-12
PO Box 388a 51531 | 712-764-4606
Casey Berlau, prin. | Fax 764-4626

Emmetsburg, Palo Alto, Pop. 3,759
Emmetsburg Community SD | 700/PK-12
205 King St 50536 | 712-852-3201
John Joynt, supt. | Fax 852-3338
www.emmetsburg.k12.ia.us
Emmetsburg HS | 300/9-12
205 King St 50536 | 712-852-2966
Bill Thompson, prin. | Fax 852-3317
Emmetsburg MS | 200/5-8
1001 Palmer St 50536 | 712-852-2892
Bill Thompson, prin. | Fax 852-3811

Iowa Lakes Community College | Post-Sec.
3200 College Dr 50536 | 712-852-5212

Epworth, Dubuque, Pop. 1,567
Western Dubuque Community SD
Supt. — See Farley
Western Dubuque HS | 700/9-12
PO Box 379 52045 | 563-876-3442
John Hlubek, prin. | Fax 876-5512

Divine Word College Seminary | Post-Sec.
PO Box 380 52045 | 563-876-3353

Essex, Page, Pop. 852
Essex Community SD | 300/K-12
PO Box 299 51638 | 712-379-3117
William Crilly, supt. | Fax 379-3200
Essex JSHS | 100/7-12
PO Box 299 51638 | 712-379-3115
Allen Stuart, prin. | Fax 379-3200

Estherville, Emmet, Pop. 6,566
Estherville Lincoln Central Comm SD | 1,300/PK-12
PO Box 118 51334 | 712-362-2692
Richard J. Magnuson, supt. | Fax 362-2410
www.estherville.k12.ia.us
Estherville Lincoln Central HS | 400/9-12
1520 Central Ave 51334 | 712-362-2659
Susan Bish, prin. | Fax 362-2406
Estherville Lincoln Central MS | 600/3-8
PO Box 118 51334 | 712-362-2335
Michael Peterson, prin. | Fax 362-7822

Iowa Lakes Community College | Post-Sec.
300 S 18th St 51334 | 712-362-7945

Evansdale, Black Hawk, Pop. 4,460
Waterloo Community SD
Supt. — See Waterloo
Bunger MS | 500/6-8
157 S Roosevelt Rd 50707 | 319-433-2550
Brenton Shavers, prin. | Fax 433-2564

Everly, Clay, Pop. 659
Clay Central/Everly Community SD
Supt. — See Royal
Clay Central/Everly HS | 200/9-12
PO Box 110 51338 | 712-834-2227
Charles Kuester, prin. | Fax 834-2193

Exira, Audubon, Pop. 783
Exira Community SD | 300/PK-12
PO Box 335 50076 | 712-268-5555
Charlie Johnson, supt. | Fax 268-2188
www.exira.k12.ia.us
Exira JSHS | 100/7-12
PO Box 335 50076 | 712-268-5318
Allen Zobel, prin. | Fax 268-5319

Fairbank, Buchanan, Pop. 1,043
Wapsie Valley Community SD | 700/K-12
2535 Viking Ave 50629 | 319-638-6711
Dan Peterson, supt. | Fax 638-7061
www.wapsie-valley.k12.ia.us
Wapsie Valley JSHS | 300/7-12
2535 Viking Ave 50629 | 319-638-6711
Chad Garber, prin. | Fax 638-7061

Fairfield, Jefferson, Pop. 9,486
Fairfield Community SD | 1,900/K-12
607 E Broadway Ave 52556 | 641-472-2655
Steven Triplett, supt. | Fax 472-0269
www.fairfieldsfuture.org
Fairfield HS | 600/9-12
605 E Broadway Ave 52556 | 641-472-2059
Thomas Voorhees, prin. | Fax 472-0269

Fairfield MS 500/6-8
404 W Fillmore Ave 52556 641-472-5019
Gary Henry, prin. Fax 472-5301

Fairfield Christian S 50/PK-12
2009 S Main St 52556 641-472-4706
Larry Eklund, prin. Fax 472-4566
Ideal Girls S of Maharishi Vedic City 50/6-12
1661 Highway 1 52556 641-472-7224
Maharishi S of the Age of Enlightenment 200/PK-12
804 N 3rd St 52556 641-472-9400
Ashley Deans Ph.D., hdmstr. Fax 472-1211
Maharishi University of Management Post-Sec.
1000 N 4th St 52557 641-472-7000

Farley, Dubuque, Pop. 1,347
Western Dubuque Community SD 2,700/PK-12
PO Box 279 52046 563-744-3885
Wayne Drexler, supt. Fax 744-3093
www.w-dubuque.k12.ia.us
Drexler MS 400/6-8
PO Box 279 52046 563-744-3371
Tim Showalter, prin. Fax 744-3711
Other Schools – See Cascade, Epworth

Farmington, Van Buren, Pop. 740
Harmony Community SD
Supt. — See Bonaparte
Harmony HS 100/9-12
33727 Route J40 52626 319-592-3192
David Stammeyer, prin. Fax 592-3135
Harmony MS 100/5-8
502 N 4th St 52626 319-878-3814
Diane Fine, prin. Fax 878-3532

Farnhamville, Calhoun, Pop. 407
Prairie Valley Community SD
Supt. — See Gowrie
Prairie Valley MS 200/5-8
3116 Zearing Ave 50538 515-467-5700
Dennis Hammen, prin. Fax 467-5646

Farragut, Fremont, Pop. 488
Farragut Community SD 300/PK-12
PO Box 36 51639 712-385-8131
Jay Lutt, supt. Fax 385-8135
www.farragutschools.org
Farragut JSHS 200/7-12
PO Box 36 51639 712-385-8131
Hilding Sandra, prin. Fax 385-8135

Fayette, Fayette, Pop. 1,275

Upper Iowa University Post-Sec.
PO Box 1857 52142 563-425-5200

Fenton, Kossuth, Pop. 293
Sentral Community SD 200/K-12
PO Box 109 50539 515-889-2261
Arthur Pixler, supt. Fax 889-2264
Sentral JSHS 100/6-12
PO Box 109 50539 515-889-2261
Mary Recker, prin. Fax 889-2264

Fonda, Pocahontas, Pop. 615
Newell-Fonda Community SD
Supt. — See Newell
Newell-Fonda MS 100/6-8
3rd and Howard Sts 50540 712-288-4445
Randall Nielsen, prin. Fax 288-5710

Fontanelle, Adair, Pop. 683
Nodaway Valley Community SD
Supt. — See Greenfield
Nodaway Valley MS 200/6-8
112 S 1st St 50846 641-745-2291
Doug Glackin, prin. Fax 745-3501

Forest City, Winnebago, Pop. 4,246
Forest City Community SD 1,500/PK-12
810 W K St 50436 641-585-2323
Dwight Pierson, supt. Fax 585-5218
www.forestcity.k12.ia.us
Forest City HS 500/9-12
206 W School St 50436 641-585-2324
Ken Baker, prin. Fax 585-3034
Forest City MS 300/6-8
216 W School St 50436 641-585-4772
Timothy G. Kuehl, prin. Fax 585-3432

Forest City Christian S 50/PK-12
305 Walnut St 50436 641-585-3233
Ivon Tokheim, admin. Fax 585-1390
Waldorf College Post-Sec.
106 S 6th St 50436 800-292-1903

Fort Dodge, Webster, Pop. 25,917
Fort Dodge Community SD 4,100/K-12
104 S 17th St 50501 515-576-1161
Linda Brock, supt. Fax 576-1988
www.fort-dodge.k12.ia.us
Fort Dodge HS 1,300/9-12
819 N 25th St 50501 515-955-1770
Rick Kuhlman, prin. Fax 955-3374
Phillips MS 700/7-8
1015 5th Ave N 50501 515-574-5711
Gary Reiners, prin. Fax 576-3160

Iowa Central Community College Post-Sec.
330 Avenue M 50501 515-576-7201
La' James College of Hairstyling Post-Sec.
2604 1st Ave S 50501 515-576-3119
St. Edmond HS 400/6-12
501 N 22nd St 50501 515-955-5850
Chuck Elbert, prin. Fax 955-3569

Fort Madison, Lee, Pop. 10,949
Fort Madison Community SD 2,200/PK-12
PO Box 1423 52627 319-372-7252
Kenneth Marang, supt. Fax 372-7255
www.ft-madison.k12.ia.us
Fort Madison HS 700/9-12
2001 Avenue B 52627 319-372-1862
Bernard Stephenson, prin. Fax 372-1325
Fort Madison MS 500/6-8
1801 Avenue G 52627 319-372-4687
Todd Dirth, prin. Fax 372-0378

Bill Hill's College of Cosmetology Post-Sec.
910 Avenue G 52627 319-372-6248
Holy Trinity HS 200/7-12
2600 Avenue A 52627 319-372-2486
Doris Turner, prin. Fax 372-6310

Fredericksburg, Chickasaw, Pop. 942
Sumner-Fredericksburg SD
Supt. — See Sumner
Sumner-Fredericksburg MS 100/6-8
PO Box 337 50630 563-237-5334
James Hotz, prin. Fax 237-6329

Fremont, Mahaska, Pop. 700
Fremont Community SD 100/PK-8
PO Box 69 52561 641-933-4211
Dean Cook, supt. Fax 933-4123
Fremont MS 50/6-8
PO Box 69 52561 641-933-4211
Angela Livezey, prin. Fax 933-4123

Galva, Ida, Pop. 351
Galva-Holstein Community SD
Supt. — See Holstein
Galva-Holstein MS 200/5-8
207 Noll St 51020 712-282-4213
Mike Richard, prin. Fax 282-4210

Garden Grove, Decatur, Pop. 253
Mormon Trail Community SD
Supt. — See Humeston
Mormon Trail JSHS 100/7-12
PO Box 177 50103 641-443-3425
Francis Newgard, prin. Fax 443-2644

Garnavillo, Clayton, Pop. 768
Clayton Ridge Community SD
Supt. — See Guttenberg
Clayton Ridge MS 200/5-8
PO Box 9 52049 563-964-2321
Ric Olsen, prin. Fax 964-2756

Garner, Hancock, Pop. 2,978
Garner-Hayfield Community SD 900/K-12
PO Box 449 50438 641-923-2718
Tyler Williams, supt. Fax 923-3825
www.garner.k12.ia.us
Garner-Hayfield HS 300/9-12
PO Box 449 50438 641-923-2632
Paul Schoneman, prin. Fax 923-2633
Garner-Hayfield MS 200/6-8
PO Box 449 50438 641-923-2809
Steve Beecher, prin. Fax 923-2031

Garwin, Tama, Pop. 553
GMG Community SD 500/K-12
306 Park St 50632 641-499-2239
Michael Ashton, supt. Fax 499-2159
www.garwin.k12.ia.us
GMG JSHS 200/7-12
306 Park St 50632 641-499-2005
Mark Polich, prin. Fax 499-2552

George, Lyon, Pop. 1,027
George-Little Rock Community SD 500/K-12
PO Box 6 51237 712-475-3311
Joanne C. Smith, supt. Fax 475-3574
www.george-lr.k12.ia.us
George-Little Rock HS 200/9-12
PO Box 6 51237 712-475-3311
Chris Bernard, prin. Fax 475-3574
Other Schools – See Little Rock

Gilbert, Story, Pop. 1,011
Gilbert Community SD 1,000/K-12
103 Mathews Dr 50105 515-232-3740
John Kinley, supt. Fax 232-0099
www.gilbert.k12.ia.us
Gilbert JSHS 500/7-12
103 Mathews Dr 50105 515-232-3738
James Quarnstrom, prin. Fax 232-0099

Gilbertville, Black Hawk, Pop. 718

Don Bosco HS 200/9-12
405 16th Ave 50634 319-296-1692
Matt O'Loughlin, prin. Fax 296-1693

Gilman, Marshall, Pop. 581
East Marshall Community SD 800/K-12
PO Box 159 50106 641-498-7481
Alan Meyer, supt. Fax 498-2035
www.e-marshall.k12.ia.us
East Marshall MS 300/5-8
PO Box 159 50106 641-498-7483
Robert Schelp, prin. Fax 498-2180
Other Schools – See Le Grand

Gilmore City, Humboldt, Pop. 534
Gilmore City-Bradgate Community SD 100/PK-8
402 SE E Ave 50541 515-373-6619
Ron Bollmeyer, supt. Fax 373-6092
www.trv.k12.ia.us
Twin River Valley MS 100/6-8
402 SE E Ave 50541 515-373-6124
Ronald Bollmeyer, prin. Fax 373-6092

Gladbrook, Tama, Pop. 1,018
Gladbrook-Reinbeck Community SD
Supt. — See Reinbeck
Gladbrook-Reinbeck MS 200/6-8
PO Box 370 50635 641-473-2842
Doran Dahms, prin. Fax 473-2913

Glenwood, Mills, Pop. 5,418
Glenwood Community SD 2,000/K-12
103 Central St Ste 300 51534 712-527-9034
Dr. Stan Sibley, supt. Fax 527-4287
www.glenwood.k12.ia.us
Glenwood HS 600/9-12
400 Sivers Rd 51534 712-527-4897
Dave Stickrod, prin. Fax 527-9554
Glenwood MS 300/7-8
111 Lacey St 51534 712-527-4887
Kerry Newman, prin. Fax 527-3411

Glidden, Carroll, Pop. 1,265
Glidden-Ralston Community SD 400/K-12
PO Box 488 51443 712-659-3411
Vicki Lowe, supt. Fax 659-2248
www.glidden-ralston.k12.ia.us
Glidden-Ralston JSHS 200/7-12
PO Box 488 51443 712-659-2205
Kreg Lensch, prin. Fax 659-2248

Goose Lake, Clinton, Pop. 233
Northeast Community SD 800/K-12
PO Box 66 52750 563-577-2249
James Cox, supt. Fax 577-2450
www.northeast.k12.ia.us
Northeast MSHS 400/7-12
PO Box 70 52750 563-577-2249
Joe Jarvis, prin. Fax 577-2248

Gowrie, Webster, Pop. 1,073
Prairie Valley Community SD 800/PK-12
PO Box 49 50543 515-352-3173
James Dick, supt. Fax 352-5573
www.gowrie.k12.ia.us
Prairie Valley HS 300/9-12
PO Box 49 50543 515-352-3142
Marshall Lewis, prin. Fax 352-3143
Other Schools – See Farnhamville

Graettinger, Palo Alto, Pop. 857
Graettinger Community SD 200/K-12
PO Box 58 51342 712-859-3286
Dan Mart, supt. Fax 859-3509
www.graettinger.k12.ia.us
Graettinger/Terril HS 100/9-12
PO Box 58 51342 712-859-3286
Pam Stangeland, prin. Fax 859-3509

Grand Junction, Greene, Pop. 922
East Greene Community SD 400/PK-12
PO Box 377 50107 515-738-5741
G. Mike Harter, supt. Fax 738-5719
www.east-greene.k12.ia.us
Grand Junction JSHS 200/7-12
PO Box 377 50107 515-738-5721
Ron McNeill, prin. Fax 738-5719

Granville, Sioux, Pop. 323

Spalding HS 100/7-12
PO Box 168 51022 712-727-3451
Brad Thiel, prin. Fax 727-3455

Greene, Butler, Pop. 1,071
Greene Community SD 300/PK-12
PO Box 190 50636 641-816-5523
Steve Ward, supt. Fax 816-5921
www.greene.k12.ia.us
North Butler HS 100/9-12
PO Box 190 50636 641-816-5631
Thomas Hamrick, prin. Fax 816-5921

Greenfield, Adair, Pop. 2,008
Nodaway Valley Community SD 800/K-12
410 NW 2nd St 50849 641-743-6127
John Dayton, supt. Fax 343-7173
www.nod-valley.k12.ia.us
Nodaway Valley HS 300/9-12
410 NW 2nd St 50849 641-743-6141
Jeremy Klein, prin. Fax 343-7040
Other Schools – See Fontanelle

Grimes, Polk, Pop. 5,600
Dallas Center-Grimes Community SD
Supt. — See Dallas Center
Dallas Center-Grimes Community HS 400/9-12
3353 240th St 50111 515-986-9747
Mitzi Chizek, prin. Fax 986-9734

Grinnell, Poweshiek, Pop. 9,213
Grinnell-Newburg Community SD 1,800/PK-12
927 4th Ave 50112 641-236-2700
Dr. David Stoakes, supt. Fax 236-2699
www.grinnell.k12.ia.us
Grinnell Community HS 500/9-12
1333 Sunset St 50112 641-236-2720
Linda Smoley, prin. Fax 236-2692
Grinnell Community MS 600/5-8
132 East St S 50112 641-236-2750
Frank Shults, prin. Fax 236-2732

Grinnell College Post-Sec.
PO Box 805 50112 641-269-4000

Griswold, Cass, Pop. 1,005
Griswold Community SD 700/PK-12
PO Box 280 51535 712-778-2152
Darwin Lehmann, supt. Fax 778-4145
www.griswold.k12.ia.us
Griswold MSHS 400/6-12
PO Box 280 51535 712-778-2154
T. J. Dunphy, prin. Fax 778-2161

Grundy Center, Grundy, Pop. 2,589
Grundy Center Community SD — 700/K-12
1301 12th St 50638 — 319-825-5418
John Stevens, supt. — Fax 825-5419
www.grundy-center.k12.ia.us
Grundy Center HS — 300/9-12
1006 M Ave 50638 — 319-825-5449
Steve Vanderpol, prin. — Fax 825-6415
Grundy Center MS — 200/6-8
1006 M Ave 50638 — 319-825-5464
Philip Laube, prin. — Fax 825-6415

Guthrie Center, Guthrie, Pop. 1,654
Guthrie Center Community SD — 600/PK-12
906 School St 50115 — 641-332-2972
Steve Smith, supt. — Fax 332-2973
www.guthrie.k12.ia.us
Guthrie Center HS — 200/9-12
906 School St 50115 — 641-332-2236
Garold Thomas, prin. — Fax 332-2973
Guthrie Center JHS — 100/7-8
906 School St 50115 — 641-332-2974
Brent Meier, prin. — Fax 332-2973

Guttenberg, Clayton, Pop. 1,950
Clayton Ridge Community SD — 600/K-12
PO Box 520 52052 — 563-252-2341
Allen Nelson, supt. — Fax 252-2656
www.guttenberg.k12.ia.us
Clayton Ridge HS — 300/9-12
PO Box 520 52052 — 563-252-2342
James Whalen, prin. — Fax 252-2656
Other Schools – See Garnavillo

Hamburg, Fremont, Pop. 1,236
Hamburg Community SD — 300/PK-12
105 E St 51640 — 712-382-1063
Dr. Paul Sellon, supt. — Fax 382-1211
www.hamburg.k12.ia.us
Hamburg JSHS — 200/7-12
105 E St 51640 — 712-382-2703
Steve Swartout, prin. — Fax 382-1211

Hampton, Franklin, Pop. 4,211
Hampton-Dumont Community SD — 1,100/PK-12
PO Box 336 50441 — 641-456-2175
Leland Morrison, supt. — Fax 456-5750
www.hampton-dumont.k12.ia.us/
Hampton-Dumont HS — 400/9-12
PO Box 336 50441 — 641-456-4893
Trent Grundmeyer, prin. — Fax 456-4569
Hampton-Dumont MS — 300/6-8
PO Box 336 50441 — 641-456-4735
Dave Wempen, prin. — Fax 456-2023

Harlan, Shelby, Pop. 5,165
Harlan Community SD — 1,700/K-12
2102 Durant St 51537 — 712-755-2152
Robert Broomfield, supt. — Fax 755-7312
www.harlan.k12.ia.us
Harlan Community HS — 600/9-12
2102 Durant St 51537 — 712-755-3101
Kent Klinkefus, prin. — Fax 755-7705
Harlan Community MS — 400/6-8
2108 Durant St 51537 — 712-755-3196
Duane Magee, prin. — Fax 755-3699

Hartley, O'Brien, Pop. 1,562
Hartley-Melvin-Sanborn Community SD — 800/PK-12
173 S Central Ave 51346 — 712-928-2022
Lynn Evans, supt. — Fax 928-3607
www.hartley-ms.k12.ia.us
Hartley-Melvin-Sanborn HS — 300/9-12
PO Box 206 51346 — 712-928-3406
Mark Peterson, prin. — Fax 928-2152
Other Schools – See Sanborn

Hastings, Mills, Pop. 223
Nishna Valley Community SD — 300/K-12
58962 380th St 51540 — 712-624-8696
Kurt Kaiser, supt. — Fax 624-9131
www.nishna-valley.k12.ia.us/
Nishna Valley JSHS — 100/7-12
58962 380th St 51540 — 712-624-8696
Deborah Taylor, prin. — Fax 624-9131

Hawarden, Sioux, Pop. 2,428
West Sioux Community SD — 700/K-12
1300 Avenue P 51023 — 712-551-1461
Paul Olson, supt. — Fax 551-1367
www.westsiouxschools.org/
West Sioux HS — 200/9-12
1300 Avenue P 51023 — 712-551-1181
Kim Buryanek, prin. — Fax 551-1514
West Sioux MS — 200/6-8
1300 Avenue P 51023 — 712-551-1022
Paul Olson, prin. — Fax 551-1367

Hinton, Plymouth, Pop. 815
Hinton Community SD — 600/PK-12
PO Box 128 51024 — 712-947-4329
Allen Steen, supt. — Fax 947-4427
www.hintonschool.com/
Hinton HS — 200/9-12
PO Box 128 51024 — 712-947-4328
Susan Martens, prin. — Fax 947-4427
Hinton MS — 200/6-8
PO Box 128 51024 — 712-947-4328
Susan Martens, prin. — Fax 947-4947

Holstein, Ida, Pop. 1,431
Galva-Holstein Community SD — 600/PK-12
PO Box 320 51025 — 712-368-4353
Harold Post, supt. — Fax 368-4843
www.galva-holstein.k12.ia.us/index.htm
Galva-Holstein HS — 200/9-12
PO Box 320 51025 — 712-368-4353
Matt McDonough, prin. — Fax 368-4843
Other Schools – See Galva

Holy Cross, Dubuque, Pop. 341
RHCL Catholic S Holy Cross — 200/4-8
PO Box 368 52053 — 563-870-2405
Dennis Rima, prin. — Fax 870-4101

Hubbard, Hardin, Pop. 861
Hubbard-Radcliffe Community SD — 500/K-12
PO Box 129 50122 — 641-864-2211
Dr. Ron Blakley, supt. — Fax 864-2422
www.hubbard.k12.ia.us
Hubbard-Radcliffe HS — 200/9-12
PO Box 129 50122 — 641-864-2211
Doug Ray, prin. — Fax 864-2422
Other Schools – See Radcliffe

Hudson, Black Hawk, Pop. 2,133
Hudson Community SD — 800/K-12
PO Box 240 50643 — 319-988-3233
David Pappone, supt. — Fax 988-3235
www.hudson.k12.ia.us
Hudson HS — 300/9-12
PO Box 240 50643 — 319-988-4226
Catherine Hicks, prin. — Fax 988-4174
Hudson MS — 300/5-8
PO Box 240 50643 — 319-988-4137
Mark Schlatter, prin. — Fax 988-4137

Hull, Sioux, Pop. 2,041
Boyden-Hull Community SD — 600/K-12
PO Box 678 51239 — 712-439-2711
Steve Grond, supt. — Fax 439-1419
www.boyden-hull.k12.ia.us
Boyden-Hull JSHS — 300/7-12
PO Box 678 51239 — 712-439-2440
Marjorie Wagner, prin. — Fax 439-1419

Western Christian HS — 400/9-12
PO Box 658 51239 — 712-439-1013
Glenn Schaap, prin. — Fax 439-1407

Humboldt, Humboldt, Pop. 4,411
Humboldt Community SD — 1,400/PK-12
1408 9th Ave N 50548 — 515-332-1330
Joyce Judas, supt. — Fax 332-4478
www.humboldt.k12.ia.us
Humboldt HS — 500/9-12
1500 Wildcat Rd 50548 — 515-332-1430
Lori Westhoff, prin. — Fax 332-7150
Humboldt MS — 300/6-8
210 Taft St N 50548 — 515-332-2812
Bob Pattee, prin. — Fax 332-2023

Humeston, Wayne, Pop. 546
Mormon Trail Community SD — 300/PK-12
PO Box 156 50123 — 641-877-2521
Robert McCurdy, supt. — Fax 877-3400
www.mormontrail.k12.ia.us
Other Schools – See Garden Grove

Huxley, Story, Pop. 2,475
Ballard Community SD — 1,100/K-12
PO Box 307 50124 — 515-597-2811
Mike Krumm, supt. — Fax 597-2965
www.ballard.k12.ia.us/
Ballard Community HS — 400/9-12
PO Box 307 50124 — 515-597-2971
John Ronca, prin. — Fax 597-2964
Ballard Community JHS — 200/7-8
PO Box 307 50124 — 515-597-2971
John Ronca, prin. — Fax 597-2764

Ida Grove, Ida, Pop. 2,259
Battle Creek-Ida Grove Community SD — 700/PK-12
301 Moorehead St 51445 — 712-364-3687
Russ Freeman, supt. — Fax 364-3609
www.bc-ig.k12.ia.us
Battle Creek-Ida Grove HS — 300/9-12
900 John Montgomery Dr 51445 — 712-364-3371
Patrick Miller, prin. — Fax 364-4463
Other Schools – See Battle Creek

Independence, Buchanan, Pop. 5,923
Independence Community SD — 1,500/PK-12
1207 1st St W 50644 — 319-334-7400
Devin Embray, supt. — Fax 334-7404
www.independence.k12.ia.us
Independence HS — 500/9-12
1207 1st St W 50644 — 319-334-7405
Karl Kurt, prin. — Fax 334-6096
Independence MS — 400/6-8
1207 1st St W 50644 — 319-334-7415
Meredith Miller, prin. — Fax 334-7418

Indianola, Warren, Pop. 13,205
Indianola Community SD — 3,100/K-12
1304 E 2nd Ave 50125 — 515-961-9500
Michael Teigland, supt. — Fax 961-9505
www.indianola.k12.ia.us
Indianola HS — 1,000/9-12
1304 E 1st Ave 50125 — 515-961-9510
John Monroe, prin. — Fax 961-9519
Indianola MS — 800/6-8
403 S 15th St 50125 — 515-961-9530
Peggy Fillio, prin. — Fax 961-9535

Simpson College — Post-Sec.
701 N C St 50125 — 515-961-6251

Inwood, Lyon, Pop. 871
West Lyon Community SD — 800/PK-12
1787 182nd St 51240 — 712-753-4917
Ralph Herring, supt. — Fax 753-4928
www.west-lyon.k12.ia.us/
West Lyon HS — 300/9-12
1787 182nd St 51240 — 712-753-4917
Doug Jiskoot, prin. — Fax 753-4928
West Lyon JHS — 100/7-8
1787 182nd St 51240 — 712-753-4917
Doug Jiskoot, prin. — Fax 753-4928

Iowa City, Johnson, Pop. 63,807
Iowa City Community SD — 10,700/PK-12
509 S Dubuque St 52240 — 319-688-1000
Dr. Lane Plugge, supt. — Fax 688-1009
www.iccsd.k12.ia.us/
Iowa City HS — 1,500/9-12
1900 Morningside Dr 52245 — 319-688-1040
Mark Hanson, prin. — Fax 339-5705
Southeast JHS — 700/7-8
2501 Bradford Dr 52240 — 319-688-1070
Deb Wretman, prin. — Fax 339-5735
West HS — 1,700/9-12
2901 Melrose Ave 52246 — 319-688-1050
Jerry Arganbright, prin. — Fax 339-5738
Other Schools – See Coralville, North Liberty

La' James College of Hairstyling — Post-Sec.
227 E Market St 52245 — 319-337-2109
Regina HS — 400/7-12
2150 Rochester Ave 52245 — 319-338-5436
Ray Pechous, prin. — Fax 887-3817
University of Iowa — Post-Sec.
107 Calvin Hall 52242 — 319-335-3500

Iowa Falls, Hardin, Pop. 5,106
Iowa Falls Community SD — 1,000/PK-12
710 North St 50126 — 641-648-6400
John Robbins, supt. — Fax 648-6401
www.iowa-falls.k12.ia.us
Iowa Falls HS — 300/9-12
1903 Taylor Ave 50126 — 641-648-6440
Frank Schnoes, prin. — Fax 648-3222
Riverbend MS — 200/7-8
1124 Union St 50126 — 641-648-6430
Jeff Burchfield, prin. — Fax 648-6432

Ellsworth Community College — Post-Sec.
1100 College Ave 50126 — 800-322-9235

Janesville, Bremer, Pop. 822
Janesville Consolidated SD — 300/PK-12
PO Box 478 50647 — 319-987-2581
Robert Weber, supt. — Fax 987-2824
www.janesville.k12.ia.us
Janesville HS — 100/9-12
PO Box 478 50647 — 319-987-2581
Robert Weber, prin. — Fax 987-2824

Jefferson, Greene, Pop. 4,440
Jefferson-Scranton SD — 1,200/PK-12
204 W Madison St 50129 — 515-386-4168
Michael Haluska, supt. — Fax 386-3591
www.jefferson-scranton.k12.ia.us
Jefferson-Scranton HS — 400/9-12
101 Ram Dr 50129 — 515-386-2188
Karen Younie, prin. — Fax 386-2159
Jefferson-Scranton MS — 300/6-8
203 W Harrison St 50129 — 515-386-8126
Scott Johnson, prin. — Fax 386-2142

Jesup, Buchanan, Pop. 2,203
Jesup Community SD — 800/PK-12
PO Box 287 50648 — 319-827-1700
Sarah Pinion, supt. — Fax 827-3905
www.jesup.k12.ia.us
Jesup HS — 300/9-12
PO Box 287 50648 — 319-827-1700
Rodney Chamberlin, prin. — Fax 827-3905
Jesup MS — 200/5-8
PO Box 287 50648 — 319-827-1700
Lisa Loecher, prin. — Fax 827-3905

Jewell, Hamilton, Pop. 1,090
South Hamilton Community SD — 700/PK-12
PO Box 100 50130 — 515-827-5479
Lyle Schwartz, supt. — Fax 827-5368
www.s-hamilton.k12.ia.us
South Hamilton MSHS — 300/7-12
PO Box 100 50130 — 515-827-5418
Steve Gray, prin. — Fax 827-5368

Johnston, Polk, Pop. 10,842
Johnston Community SD — 5,000/PK-12
PO Box 10 50131 — 515-278-0470
K. Richard Sundblad Ph.D., supt. — Fax 278-5884
www.johnston.k12.ia.us
Johnston HS — 900/10-12
PO Box 10 50131 — 515-278-0449
Bruce Hukee, prin. — Fax 276-5795
Johnston MS — 1,300/6-9
PO Box 10 50131 — 515-278-0476
Brian Carico, prin. — Fax 278-0130

La' James College of Hairstyling — Post-Sec.
8805 Chambery Blvd 50131 — 515-278-2208

Kalona, Washington, Pop. 2,415
Mid-Prairie Community SD
Supt. — See Wellman
Mid-Prairie MS — 300/6-8
713 F Ave 52247 — 319-656-2241
Nancy Hurd, prin. — Fax 656-2207

Iowa Mennonite HS — 200/9-12
1421 540th St SW 52247 — 319-656-2073
Wilbur Yoder, prin. — Fax 656-2073

Kanawha, Hancock, Pop. 708
West Hancock Community SD
Supt. — See Britt
West Hancock MS — 200/5-8
PO Box 130 50447 — 641-762-3261
— Fax 762-3263

Keokuk, Lee, Pop. 10,918
Keokuk Community SD — 2,200/K-12
727 Washington St 52632 — 319-524-1402
Jane Babcock, supt. — Fax 524-1114
www.keokuk.k12.ia.us

Keokuk HS
2285 Middle Rd 52632
700/9-12
319-524-2542
Dave Keane, prin.   Fax 524-1784
Keokuk MS
2002 Orleans Ave 52632
600/6-8
319-524-3737
Steven Carman, prin.   Fax 524-1511

Cardinal Stritch HS
2981 Plank Rd 52632
100/7-12
319-524-5450
Mike Ellerman, prin.   Fax 524-5450
Dayton's School of Hair Design   Post-Sec.
23 S 2nd St 52632
319-524-6445
Southeastern Community College   Post-Sec.
PO Box 6007 52632
319-524-3221

Keosauqua, Van Buren, Pop. 1,084
Van Buren Community SD
503 Henry Dr 52565
700/PK-12
319-293-3334
Karen Stinson, supt.   Fax 293-3301
www.van-buren.k12.ia.us
Van Buren Community JSHS
405 4th St 52565
400/7-12
319-293-3183
Kurt Jirak, prin.   Fax 293-3345

Keota, Washington, Pop. 987
Keota Community SD
PO Box 88 52248
400/PK-12
641-636-2189
Dave Harris, supt.   Fax 636-3009
Keota JSHS, PO Box 88 52248   200/7-12
Lisa Brenneman, prin.   641-636-3491

Kingsley, Plymouth, Pop. 1,234
Kingsley-Pierson Community SD
322 Quest Ave 51028
500/K-12
712-378-2861
Scott Bailey, supt.   Fax 378-3729
www.kingsleypierson.com/
Kingsley-Pierson HS
322 Quest Ave 51028
200/9-12
712-378-2861
Randy Wiese, prin.   Fax 378-3729
Other Schools – See Pierson

Knoxville, Marion, Pop. 7,536
Knoxville Community SD
309 W Main St 50138
2,100/PK-12
641-842-6552
Randy Flack, supt.   Fax 842-2109
www.knoxville.k12.ia.us
Knoxville HS
1811 W Madison St 50138
600/9-12
641-842-2173
Kevin Crawford, prin.   Fax 842-2066
Knoxville MS
102 N Lincoln St 50138
500/6-8
641-842-3315
Annette Jauron, prin.   Fax 842-5754

Lake City, Calhoun, Pop. 1,734
Southern Cal Community SD
709 W Main St 51449
600/K-12
712-464-7210
Dwayne Cross, supt.   Fax 464-3724
www.southern-cal.k12.ia.us
Southern Cal MSHS
709 W Main St 51449
300/7-12
712-464-7211
Earl Trachsel, prin.   Fax 464-3724

Lake Mills, Winnebago, Pop. 2,101
Lake Mills Community SD
102 S 4th Ave E 50450
800/PK-12
641-592-0881
Daryl Sherman, supt.   Fax 592-0883
www.lake-mills.k12.ia.us
Lake Mills HS
102 S 4th Ave E 50450
300/9-12
641-592-0893
James Scholbrock, prin.   Fax 592-0883
Lake Mills MS
102 S 4th Ave E 50450
100/7-8
641-592-0894
James Scholbrock, prin.   Fax 592-0883

Lake Park, Dickinson, Pop. 956
Harris-Lake Park Community SD
PO Box 8 51347
300/PK-12
712-832-3809
Tim Christensen, supt.   Fax 832-3812
www.harris-lp.k12.ia.us
Harris-Lake Park MSHS
PO Box 8 51347
200/6-12
712-832-3809
Dennis Peters, prin.   Fax 832-3812

Lake View, Sac, Pop. 1,315
Wall Lake View Auburn SD
PO Box 110 51450
600/PK-12
712-664-5000
Barb Kruthoff, supt.   Fax 664-5021
www.wlva.k12.ia.us
Wall Lake View Auburn HS
PO Box 110 51450
200/9-12
712-664-5001
Kevin Litterer, prin.   Fax 664-5022
Wall Lake View Auburn MS
PO Box 110 51450
100/7-8
712-664-5002
Kevin Litterer, prin.   Fax 664-5022

Lamoni, Decatur, Pop. 2,424
Lamoni Community SD
202 N Walnut St 50140
400/PK-12
641-784-3342
Mike Harrold, supt.   Fax 784-6602
lamoni.k12.ia.us
Lamoni HS
202 N Walnut St 50140
100/9-12
641-784-3351
Daniel Day, prin.   Fax 784-6602
Lamoni MS
202 N Walnut St 50140
100/6-8
641-784-7299
Daniel Day, prin.   Fax 784-6602

Graceland University   Post-Sec.
1 University Pl 50140
641-784-5000

Lansing, Allamakee, Pop. 993
Eastern Allamakee Community SD
696 Main St 52151
500/PK-12
563-538-4202
Wayne Burk, supt.   Fax 538-4202
www.e-allamakee.k12.ia.us/
Kee HS
569 Center St 52151
200/9-12
563-538-4201
Patrick Heiderscheit, prin.   Fax 538-4969

Lansing MS
696 Main St 52151
200/4-8
563-538-4118
Cynthia Lapel, prin.   Fax 538-4202

La Porte City, Black Hawk, Pop. 2,324
Union Community SD
200 Adams St 50651
1,200/K-12
319-342-2674
Neil Mullen, supt.   Fax 342-2393
www.union.k12.ia.us/
Union Community SD
200 Adams St 50651
400/9-12
319-342-2697
Travis Fleshner, prin.   Fax 342-2393
Other Schools – See Dysart

Latimer, Franklin, Pop. 531
CAL Community SD
PO Box 459 50452
200/PK-12
641-579-6087
Stevan Lane, supt.   Fax 579-6408
www.cal.k12.ia.us
CAL HS
PO Box 459 50452
100/9-12
641-579-6086
Amy Karg, prin.   Fax 579-6408

Laurens, Pocahontas, Pop. 1,409
Laurens-Marathon Community SD
300 W Garfield St 50554
400/K-12
712-841-5000
Dan Braunschweig, supt.   Fax 841-5010
www.laurens-marathon.k12.ia.us
Laurens-Marathon HS
300 W Garfield St 50554
200/9-12
712-841-5000
Fred Johnson, prin.   Fax 841-5010
Laurens-Marathon MS
300 W Garfield St 50554
100/6-8
712-841-5000
Fred Johnson, prin.   Fax 841-5010

Lawton, Woodbury, Pop. 694
Lawton-Bronson Community SD
PO Box 128 51030
600/PK-12
712-944-5183
Dr. Robert Morrison, supt.   Fax 944-5568
www.lawton-bronson.k12.ia.us
Lawton JSHS
PO Box 128 51030
300/6-12
712-944-5181
Jeff Thelander, prin.   Fax 944-5568

Le Claire, Scott, Pop. 2,873
Pleasant Valley Community SD
Supt. — See Eldridge
Pleasant Valley JHS
3501 Wisconsin St 52753
500/7-8
563-289-4507
Brian Strusz, prin.   Fax 289-4666

Le Grand, Marshall, Pop. 898
East Marshall Community SD
Supt. — See Gilman
East Marshall HS
PO Box A 50142
200/9-12
641-479-2785
Rex Kozak, prin.   Fax 479-2601

Le Mars, Plymouth, Pop. 9,241
Le Mars Community SD
921 3rd Ave SW 51031
2,200/K-12
712-546-4155
Dr. Todd Wendt, supt.   Fax 546-4157
lemars.k12.ia.us
Le Mars HS
921 3rd Ave SW 51031
700/9-12
712-546-4153
Larry Johnson, prin.   Fax 546-9581
Le Mars MS
977 3rd Ave SW 51031
500/6-8
712-546-7022
Steve Webner, prin.   Fax 546-7024

Gehlen Catholic HS
709 Plymouth St NE 51031
600/7-12
712-546-5126
Jeff Alesch, prin.   Fax 546-9384

Lenox, Taylor, Pop. 1,349
Lenox Community SD
600 S Locust St 50851
400/K-12
641-333-2244
Brad Hohensee, supt.   Fax 333-2247
www.lenox.k12.ia.us
Lenox JSHS
600 S Locust St 50851
200/7-12
641-333-2244
David Henrichs, prin.   Fax 333-2247

Leon, Decatur, Pop. 1,974
Central Decatur Community SD
1201 NE Poplar St 50144
700/PK-12
641-446-4818
Tom Dannen, supt.   Fax 446-7990
www.central-decatur.k12.ia.us/
Central Decatur JSHS
1201 NE Poplar St 50144
400/6-12
641-446-4816
Rob Meier, prin.   Fax 446-7990

Letts, Louisa, Pop. 395
Louisa-Muscatine Community SD
14478 170th St 52754
900/PK-12
319-726-3541
John Dotson, supt.   Fax 726-3334
www.louisa-muscatine.k12.ia.us
Louisa-Muscatine JSHS
14354 170th St 52754
319-726-3421
Gary Verslues, prin.   Fax 726-3649

Liberty Center, Warren
Southeast Warren Community SD
16331 Tyler St 50145
600/PK-12
641-466-3510
Harold Hulleman, supt.   Fax 466-3525
www.se-warren.k12.ia.us
Southeast Warren JSHS
16331 Tyler St 50145
300/7-12
641-466-3331
Terry Gladfelter, prin.   Fax 466-3525

Lineville, Wayne, Pop. 239
Lineville-Clio Community SD
PO Box 98 50147
100/PK-12
641-876-5345
Robert McCurdy, supt.   Fax 876-2805
www.aea15.k12.ia.us
Lineville-Clio JSHS
PO Box 98 50147
100/7-12
641-876-5345
Amy Jackson, prin.   Fax 876-2805

Lisbon, Linn, Pop. 1,935
Lisbon Community SD
PO Box 839 52253
600/PK-12
319-455-2075
Robert Torrence, supt.   Fax 455-2733
www.lisbon.k12.ia.us
Lisbon HS
PO Box 839 52253
200/9-12
319-455-2106
Dan Conner, prin.   Fax 455-3208
Lisbon MS
PO Box 839 52253
100/6-8
319-455-2659
Roger Teeling, prin.   Fax 455-3303

Little Rock, Lyon, Pop. 480
George-Little Rock Community SD
Supt. — See George
George-Little Rock MS
PO Box 247 51243
100/6-8
712-479-2771
Janel Guse, prin.   Fax 479-2770

Logan, Harrison, Pop. 1,498
Logan-Magnolia Community SD
1200 N 2nd Ave 51546
700/PK-12
712-644-2250
James Hammrich, supt.   Fax 644-2934
www.logan.k12.ia.us
Logan-Magnolia JSHS
1200 N 2nd Ave 51546
400/7-12
712-644-2250
Katy Sojka, prin.   Fax 644-2934

Lone Tree, Johnson, Pop. 1,171
Lone Tree Community SD
PO Box 520 52755
400/K-12
319-629-4212
Michael Reeves, supt.   Fax 629-4324
www.lone-tree.k12.ia.us
Lone Tree JSHS
PO Box 520 52755
200/7-12
319-629-4610
Mark Hopkins, prin.   Fax 629-4324

Lost Nation, Clinton, Pop. 479
Midland Community SD
Supt. — See Wyoming
Lost Nation MS
PO Box 217 52254
200/5-8
563-678-2142
Lynn Olson, prin.   Fax 678-2135

Lytton, Calhoun, Pop. 278
Rockwell City-Lytton Community SD
Supt. — See Rockwell City
Rockwell City-Lytton MS
PO Box 49 50561
200/5-8
712-466-2224
Marc DeMoss, prin.   Fax 466-2658

Mc Callsburg, Story, Pop. 269
Colo-Nesco Comm SD
400 Latrobe 50154
600/PK-12
515-434-2302
Gary Pillman, supt.   Fax 434-2302
www.colo-nesco.k12.ia.us
Other Schools – See Colo, Zearing

Mc Gregor, Clayton, Pop. 789
MFL MarMac Community SD
Supt. — See Monona
MFL MarMac MS
PO Box D 52157
400/4-8
563-873-3463
Dave Meyer, prin.   Fax 873-2371

Madrid, Boone, Pop. 2,397
Madrid Community SD
201 N Main St 50156
600/K-12
515-795-3241
Dennis Pelisek, supt.   Fax 795-2121
madrid.k12.ia.us
Madrid HS
599 N Kennedy Ave 50156
200/9-12
515-795-3240
Mark Cosens, prin.   Fax 795-4408
Madrid JHS
599 N Kennedy Ave 50156
100/7-8
515-795-3240
Mark Cosens, prin.   Fax 795-4408

Mallard, Palo Alto, Pop. 285
West Bend - Mallard Community SD
Supt. — See West Bend
West Bend - Mallard MS
PO Box 326 50562
100/6-8
712-425-3452
Ronald Larson, prin.   Fax 425-3413

Malvern, Mills, Pop. 1,336
Malvern Community SD
1505 E 15th St 51551
400/K-12
712-624-8700
Curtis Barclay, supt.   Fax 624-8124
www.malvern.k12.ia.us
Malvern JSHS
1505 E 15th St 51551
200/7-12
712-624-8645
Jim Bonesteel, prin.   Fax 624-8124

Manchester, Delaware, Pop. 5,139
West Delaware County Community SD
601 New St 52057
1,600/PK-12
563-927-3515
Rick Hilbert, supt.   Fax 927-2785
www.w-delaware.k12.ia.us
West Delaware HS
701 New St 52057
700/9-12
563-927-5002
Jon Nordaas, prin.   Fax 927-6222
West Delaware MS
1101 Doctor St 52057
500/5-8
563-927-5004
Fax 927-2785

Manilla, Crawford, Pop. 827
IKM Community SD
PO Box 580 51454
400/K-12
712-654-2852
Jeff Kruse, supt.   Fax 654-9280
www.ikm.k12.ia.us/
IKM Community HS
PO Box 580 51454
200/9-12
712-654-2852
Denise Philipp, prin.   Fax 654-9282
IKM Community JHS
PO Box 580 51454
100/7-8
712-654-9385
Denise Philipp, prin.   Fax 654-9282

Manly, Worth, Pop. 1,341
North Central Community SD
PO Box 190 50456
500/K-12
641-454-2211
Bruce Burton, supt.   Fax 454-2212
www.northcentral.k12.ia.us

North Central JSHS 300/6-12
PO Box 190 50456 641-454-2208
Ken Estes, prin. Fax 454-2212

Manning, Carroll, Pop. 1,453
Manning Community SD 500/PK-12
209 10th St 51455 712-655-3771
Roger Schmiedeskamp, supt. Fax 655-3311
www.manning.k12.ia.us
Manning JSHS 300/7-12
209 10th St 51455 712-655-3781
Brian Wall, prin. Fax 655-3311

Manson, Calhoun, Pop. 1,799
Manson NW Webster Community SD 700/K-12
1227 16th St 50563 712-469-2202
Mark Egli, supt. Fax 469-2298
www.manson-nw.k12.ia.us
Manson Northwest Webster HS 300/9-12
1601 15th St 50563 712-469-2245
Jeff Anliker, prin. Fax 469-3131
Other Schools – See Barnum

Mapleton, Monona, Pop. 1,277
Maple Valley Community SD 500/PK-12
501 S 7th St 51034 712-881-1319
Steve Oberg, supt. Fax 881-1316
www.maple-valley.k12.ia.us
Maple Valley-Anthon Oto HS 300/9-12
410 S 6th St 51034 712-881-1319
Dan Dougherty, prin. Fax 881-1321

Maquoketa, Jackson, Pop. 6,054
Maquoketa Community SD 1,600/PK-12
612 S Vermont St 52060 563-652-4984
Kim P. Huckstadt, supt. Fax 652-6958
www.maquoketa.k12.ia.us
Maquoketa HS 600/9-12
600 Washington St 52060 563-652-2451
William Walters, prin. Fax 652-5324
Maquoketa MS 400/6-8
200 E Locust St 52060 563-652-4956
Autumn Pino, prin. Fax 652-6885

Marcus, Cherokee, Pop. 1,084
Marcus-Meriden-Cleghorn Community SD 600/PK-12
PO Box 667 51035 712-376-4171
Jan Brandhorst, supt. Fax 376-4302
www.marcus-mer-cleg.k12.ia.us
Marcus-Meriden-Cleghorn Community HS 200/9-12
PO Box 667 51035 712-376-4172
Bill Sillau, prin. Fax 376-4302
Other Schools – See Cleghorn

Marengo, Iowa, Pop. 2,536
Iowa Valley Community SD 700/PK-12
359 E Hilton St 52301 319-642-7714
Laurene Lanich, supt. Fax 642-3023
www.iowa-valley.k12.ia.us
Iowa Valley JSHS 300/7-12
359 E Hilton St 52301 319-642-3332
James Bieschke, prin. Fax 642-3023

Marion, Linn, Pop. 28,756
Linn-Mar Community SD 4,800/PK-12
3333 10th St 52302 319-447-3000
Dr. Kathleen Mulholland, supt. Fax 377-9252
www.linnmar.k12.ia.us/
Excelsior MS 900/6-8
3333 10th St 52302 319-447-3130
Marc McCoy, prin. Fax 373-4930
Linn-Mar HS 1,300/9-12
3111 10th St 52302 319-447-3040
Gerald Van Dyke, prin. Fax 377-0486

Marion ISD 2,000/PK-12
PO Box 606 52302 319-377-4691
Nicholas B. Hobbs, supt. Fax 377-4692
www.marion.k12.ia.us/
Marion HS 600/9-12
675 S 15th St 52302 319-377-9891
Gregory Thomas Ph.D., prin. Fax 377-7621
Vernon MS 500/6-8
1301 5th Ave 52302 319-377-9401
Robert Hoyt, prin. Fax 377-7670

Marshalltown, Marshall, Pop. 25,860
Marshalltown Community SD 3,800/K-12
317 Columbus Dr 50158 641-754-1000
Harrison E. Cass, supt. Fax 754-1003
www.marshalltown.k12.ia.us
Marshalltown HS 1,600/9-12
1602 S 2nd Ave 50158 641-754-1130
Bonnie Lowry, prin. Fax 754-1136
Miller MS 400/7-8
125 S 11th St 50158 641-754-1110
Burton Clement, prin. Fax 754-1115

Iowa School of Beauty Post-Sec.
112 Nicholas Dr 50158 641-752-4223
Marshalltown Community College Post-Sec.
3700 S Center St 50158 641-752-7106

Martensdale, Warren, Pop. 463
Martensdale-St. Mary's Community SD 500/K-12
PO Box 350 50160 641-764-2466
Peggy Huisman, supt. Fax 764-2100
www.m-stmarys.k12.ia.us/
Martensdale-St. Mary's JSHS 200/7-12
PO Box 350 50160 641-764-2486
Gary Friday, prin. Fax 764-2100

Mason City, Cerro Gordo, Pop. 28,274
Mason City Community SD 4,200/PK-12
1515 S Pennsylvania Ave 50401 641-421-4400
Keith Sersland, supt. Fax 421-4448
www.masoncityschools.org
Adams MS 500/6-8
29 S Illinois Ave 50401 641-421-4420
Stephen Pottratz, prin. Fax 421-4476

Mason City HS 1,300/9-12
1700 4th St SE 50401 641-421-4431
Douglas Kennedy, prin. Fax 421-4523
Roosevelt MS 500/6-8
303 15th St SE 50401 641-421-4423
Carol Clayton, prin. Fax 421-4489

Hamilton College Post-Sec.
2570 4th St SW 50401 641-423-2530
La' James College of Hairstyling Post-Sec.
24 2nd St NE 50401 641-424-2161
Newman HS 200/9-12
2445 19th St SW 50401 641-423-6939
Mike Kavars, prin. Fax 423-6653
North Iowa Area Community College Post-Sec.
500 College Dr 50401 641-423-1264
North Iowa Christian S 50/K-12
811 N Kentucky Ave 50401 641-423-6440
Janna Voss, admin. Fax 423-6440
North Iowa Mercy Health Center Post-Sec.
1000 4th St SW 50401 641-422-7722
World Wide College of Auctioneering Post-Sec.
PO Box 949 50402 800-423-5242

Massena, Cass, Pop. 414
C & M Community SD 200/K-8
PO Box 7 50853 712-779-2211
James Smelink, supt. Fax 779-3365
www.candm.k12.ia.us
CAM MS 100/6-8
PO Box 7 50853 712-779-2212
Steve Pelzer, prin. Fax 779-3365

Maxwell, Story, Pop. 810
Collins-Maxwell Community SD 500/K-12
400 Metcalf St 50161 515-387-1115
Doug Miller, supt. Fax 387-8842
www.collins-maxwell.k12.ia.us
Collins-Maxwell MSHS 300/6-12
400 Metcalf St 50161 515-387-1115
Kevin Williams, prin. Fax 387-8842

Maynard, Fayette, Pop. 490
West Central Community SD 300/K-12
PO Box 54 50655 563-637-2283
Todd Abrahamson, supt. Fax 637-2294
www.w-central.k12.ia.us/
West Central JSHS 200/7-12
PO Box 54 50655 563-637-2637
John Johnson, prin. Fax 637-2294

Mediapolis, Des Moines, Pop. 1,584
Mediapolis Community SD 900/K-12
PO Box 358 52637 319-394-3237
Fred Whipple, supt. Fax 394-3021
www.mediapolis.k12.ia.us
Mediapolis HS 300/9-12
725 N Northfield St 52637 319-394-3101
Dennis Heiman, prin. Fax 394-9198
Mediapolis MS 200/6-8
725 N Northfield St 52637 319-394-3101
Dennis Heiman, prin. Fax 394-3021

Melcher, Marion, Pop. 1,310
Melcher-Dallas Community SD 400/PK-12
PO Box 489 50163 641-947-2321
Steve Mitchell, supt. Fax 947-2203
www.melcher-dallas.k12.ia.us
Melcher-Dallas HS 100/9-12
PO Box 158 50163 641-947-3731
Ron Juhler, prin. Fax 947-2203
Melcher-Dallas JHS 100/7-8
PO Box 158 50163 641-947-3731
Ron Juhler, prin. Fax 947-2203

Middle Amana, Iowa, Pop. 350
Clear Creek-Amana Community SD
Supt. — See Oxford
Clear Creek-Amana MS 300/6-8
PO Box 70 52307 319-622-3255
Brad Fox, prin. Fax 622-3108

Miles, Jackson, Pop. 458
East Central Community SD 400/K-12
PO Box 367 52064 563-682-7510
James House, supt. Fax 682-7194
www.east-central.k12.ia.us
East Central Community HS 100/9-12
PO Box 367 52064 563-682-7510
Warren Amman, prin. Fax 682-7194
Other Schools – See Sabula

Milford, Dickinson, Pop. 2,466
Okoboji Community SD 900/PK-12
PO Box 147 51351 712-338-4757
Robert Miller, supt. Fax 338-4758
www.okoboji.k12.ia.us
Okoboji HS 300/9-12
PO Box 147 51351 712-338-2446
Michael Schmitz, prin. Fax 338-2550
Other Schools – See Arnolds Park

Mingo, Jasper, Pop. 275
Colfax-Mingo Community SD
Supt. — See Colfax
Colfax-Mingo MS 200/6-8
307 W Mohawk Dr 50168 641-363-4282
Rebecca Maher, prin. Fax 363-3256

Missouri Valley, Harrison, Pop. 2,894
Missouri Valley Community SD 900/PK-12
109 E Michigan St 51555 712-642-2706
Dr. Tom Micek, supt. Fax 642-2456
www.movalley.k12.ia.us
Missouri Valley HS 300/9-12
605 Lincoln Hwy 51555 712-642-4149
Deidre Drees, prin. Fax 642-4624
Missouri Valley MS 200/6-8
607 Lincoln Hwy 51555 712-642-2707
Frank Smith, prin. Fax 642-3738

Mondamin, Harrison, Pop. 414
West Harrison Community SD 500/K-12
410 Pine St 51557 712-646-2231
Richard Gerking, supt. Fax 646-2891
www.w-harrison.k12.ia.us
West Harrison MSHS 300/6-12
410 Pine St 51557 712-646-2231
Christine Snell, prin. Fax 646-2891

Monona, Clayton, Pop. 1,497
MFL MarMac Community SD 1,000/PK-12
PO Box D 52159 563-539-4795
Dale Crozier, supt. Fax 539-4913
www.mflmarmac.k12.ia.us
MFL MarMac HS 400/9-12
PO Box D 52159 563-539-2031
Ed Berry, prin. Fax 539-4913
Other Schools – See Mc Gregor

Monroe, Jasper, Pop. 1,821
PCM Community SD
Supt. — See Prairie City
PCM HS 300/9-12
PO Box 610 50170 641-259-2315
Lee Griebel, prin. Fax 259-2317

Montezuma, Poweshiek, Pop. 1,457
Montezuma Community SD 600/K-12
PO Box 580 50171 641-623-5121
William Cox, supt. Fax 623-5733
www.montezuma.k12.ia.us
Montezuma HS 200/9-12
PO Box 580 50171 641-623-5121
Rhonna Fiihr, prin. Fax 623-5733
Montezuma JHS 100/7-8
PO Box 580 50171 641-623-5121
Rhonna Fiihr, prin. Fax 623-5733

Monticello, Jones, Pop. 3,660
Monticello Community SD 1,100/PK-12
711 N Maple St 52310 319-465-5963
Randy Achenbach, supt. Fax 465-4092
www.monticello.k12.ia.us/
Monticello HS 400/9-12
850 E Oak St 52310 319-465-6597
Joan Young, prin. Fax 465-4253
Monticello MS 300/5-8
217 S Maple St 52310 319-465-3575
William Gilkerson, prin. Fax 465-6959

Moravia, Appanoose, Pop. 723
Moravia Community SD 300/PK-12
505 N Trussell Ave 52571 641-724-0629
Dr. Graham F. Quinn, supt. Fax 724-9858
www.moravia.k12.ia.us
Moravia HS 200/7-12
505 N Trussell Ave 52571 641-724-3241
Kathy Carr, prin. Fax 724-0629

Moulton, Appanoose, Pop. 674
Moulton-Udell Community SD 300/PK-12
305 E 8th St 52572 641-642-3665
Richard Turner, supt. Fax 642-3461
Moulton-Udell JSHS 100/7-12
305 E 8th St 52572 641-642-8131
Randy Alger, prin. Fax 642-3461

Mount Ayr, Ringgold, Pop. 1,803
Mount Ayr Community SD 700/K-12
1001 E Columbus St 50854 641-464-0500
William J. Decker, supt. Fax 464-2325
www.mtayr.k12.ia.us
Mount Ayr JSHS 300/7-12
1001 E Columbus St 50854 641-464-0510
Matt Patton, prin. Fax 464-2325

Mount Pleasant, Henry, Pop. 8,518
Mt. Pleasant Community SD 2,100/PK-12
400 E Madison St 52641 319-385-7750
John Roederer, supt. Fax 385-7788
www.mtpleasantschools.com
Mount Pleasant HS 700/9-12
2104 S Grand Ave 52641 319-385-7700
John Henricksen, prin. Fax 385-7789
Mount Pleasant MS 500/6-8
400 N Adams St 52641 319-385-7730
Darren Hanna, prin. Fax 385-7735

Iowa Wesleyan College Post-Sec.
601 N Main St 52641 319-385-8021
Mount Pleasant Christian S 100/PK-12
1505 E Washington St 52641 319-385-8613
Michael Peters, admin. Fax 385-8415

Mount Vernon, Linn, Pop. 3,905
Mount Vernon Community SD 1,200/PK-12
525 Palisades Rd SW 52314 319-895-8845
Jeff Schwiebert, supt. Fax 895-6185
www.mountvernon.k12.ia.us/
Mount Vernon HS 400/9-12
525 Palisades Rd SW 52314 319-895-8843
Dennis Walsh, prin. Fax 895-6185
Mount Vernon MS 300/6-8
221 1st St NE 52314 319-895-6254
John Krumbholz, prin. Fax 895-8875

Cornell College Post-Sec.
600 1st St NW 52314 319-895-4000

Moville, Woodbury, Pop. 1,642
Woodbury Central Community SD 600/PK-12
PO Box 586 51039 712-873-3128
Thomas Cooper, supt. Fax 873-3162
www.woodbury-central.k12.ia.us
Woodbury Central HS 200/9-12
PO Box 586 51039 712-873-3128
Jerry McPartland, prin. Fax 873-3162
Woodbury Central MS 100/6-8
PO Box 586 51039 712-873-3128
Jerry McPartland, prin. Fax 873-3162

Murray, Clarke, Pop. 761
Murray Community SD 300/PK-12
PO Box 187 50174 641-447-2517
Dr. Dennis Bishop, supt. Fax 447-2313
edu.aea14.k12.ia.us/sch/mu/mu.html
Murray JSHS 200/7-12
PO Box 187 50174 641-447-2517
Ted Nowakowski, prin. Fax 447-2313

Muscatine, Muscatine, Pop. 22,614
Muscatine Community SD 5,200/PK-12
2900 Mulberry Ave 52761 563-263-7223
Thomas Williams, supt. Fax 263-7729
www.muscatine.k12.ia.us
Central MS 600/6-8
901 Cedar St 52761 563-263-7784
Terry Hogenson, prin. Fax 263-0145
Muscatine HS 1,600/9-12
2705 Cedar St 52761 563-263-6141
Robert Weaton, prin. Fax 264-1794
West MS 700/6-8
600 Kindler Ave 52761 563-263-0411
John Lawrence, prin. Fax 263-6645

Muscatine Community College Post-Sec.
152 Colorado St 52761 563-288-6001

Nashua, Chickasaw, Pop. 1,577
Nashua-Plainfield Community SD 700/PK-12
PO Box 569 50658 641-435-4835
Paul Bisgard, supt. Fax 435-4835
www.nashua-plainfield.k12.ia.us
Nashua-Plainfield HS 300/9-12
PO Box 569 50658 641-435-4166
Randall Strabala, prin. Fax 435-4167
Other Schools – See Plainfield

Neola, Pottawattamie, Pop. 820
Tri-Center Community SD 800/PK-12
33980 310th St 51559 712-485-2257
Brett Nanninga, supt. Fax 485-2411
www.tri-center.k12.ia.us
Tri-Center HS 200/9-12
33980 310th St 51559 712-485-2257
Angela Huseman, prin. Fax 485-2411
Tri-Center MS 200/6-8
33980 310th St 51559 712-485-2211
Brian Wedemeyer, prin. Fax 485-2402

Nevada, Story, Pop. 6,676
Nevada Community SD 1,500/PK-12
1035 15th St 50201 515-382-2783
James S. Walker, supt. Fax 382-2836
www.nevada.k12.ia.us
Nevada HS 500/9-12
1001 15th St 50201 515-382-3521
Raphael Murray, prin. Fax 382-2935
Nevada MS 500/5-8
1035 15th St 50201 515-382-2751
Chris Schmidt, prin. Fax 382-2836

Newell, Buena Vista, Pop. 880
Newell-Fonda Community SD 400/K-12
PO Box 297 50568 712-272-3324
Ron Day, supt. Fax 272-4276
www.newell-fonda.k12.ia.us
Newell-Fonda HS 200/9-12
PO Box 297 50568 712-272-3324
Jeff Dicks, prin. Fax 272-4276
Other Schools – See Fonda

New Hampton, Chickasaw, Pop. 3,569
New Hampton Community SD 1,300/PK-12
710 W Main St 50659 641-394-2134
Terry Christie, supt. Fax 394-2662
www.new-hampton.k12.ia.us
New Hampton HS 400/9-12
710 W Main St 50659 641-394-2144
Richard Evans, prin. Fax 394-2921
New Hampton MS 300/5-8
206 W Main St 50659 641-394-2259
Donita Landers, prin. Fax 394-2262

New Hartford, Butler, Pop. 643
Dike-New Hartford Community SD
Supt. — See Dike
Dike-New Hartford JHS 100/7-8
508 Beaver 50660 319-983-2206
Jerold Martinek, prin. Fax 983-2207

New London, Henry, Pop. 1,887
New London Community SD 500/K-12
PO Box 97 52645 319-367-0512
Robert Cardoni, supt.
www.new-london.k12.ia.us
New London JSHS, PO Box 97 52645 300/6-12
Lisa Beames, prin. 319-367-0500

New Sharon, Mahaska, Pop. 1,268
North Mahaska Community SD 500/PK-12
PO Box 89 50207 641-637-2295
Randy Moffit, supt. Fax 637-4559
www.n-mahaska.k12.ia.us
North Mahaska JSHS 300/7-12
PO Box 89 50207 641-637-4187
Douglas Ray, prin. Fax 637-4559

Newton, Jasper, Pop. 15,794
Newton Community SD 3,300/PK-12
807 S 6th Ave W 50208 641-792-5809
Steven McDermott, supt. Fax 792-9159
www.newton.k12.ia.us
Berg MS 500/7-8
1900 N 5th Ave E 50208 641-792-7741
Dave Gallaher, prin. Fax 792-7779
Newton HS 1,000/9-12
800 E 4th St S 50208 641-792-5797
Bill Peters, prin. Fax 792-0005

Des Moines Area Community College Post-Sec.
600 N 2nd Ave W 50208 641-791-3622

Nora Springs, Floyd, Pop. 1,504
Nora Springs-Rock Falls Community SD 500/K-12
PO Box 367 50458 641-749-5301
Todd Lettow, supt. Fax 749-5898
www.norasprings-rockfalls.k12.ia.us
Nora Springs-Rock Falls MSHS 300/6-12
PO Box 367 50458 641-749-5301
Lynn Baldus, prin. Fax 749-5898

North English, Iowa, Pop. 1,010
English Valleys Community SD 500/PK-12
PO Box 490 52316 319-664-3634
Alan Jensen, supt. Fax 664-3636
www.english-valleys.k12.ia.us
English Valleys JSHS 300/7-12
PO Box 490 52316 319-664-3631
Brad Breon, prin. Fax 664-3670

North Liberty, Johnson, Pop. 6,516
Iowa City Community SD
Supt. — See Iowa City
North Central JHS 7-8
180 Forevergreen Rd E 52317 319-688-1210
Willie Barney, prin. Fax 688-1219

Northwood, Worth, Pop. 2,012
Northwood-Kensett Community SD 500/K-12
PO Box 289 50459 641-324-2021
Thomas Nugent, supt. Fax 324-2092
www.nwood-kensett.k12.ia.us
Northwood-Kensett JSHS 300/7-12
PO Box 289 50459 641-324-2142
Keith Fritz, prin. Fax 324-2174

Norwalk, Warren, Pop. 7,794
Norwalk Community SD 2,100/PK-12
906 School Ave 50211 515-981-0676
Dennis Wulf, supt. Fax 981-0559
www.norwalk.k12.ia.us/
Norwalk HS 700/9-12
1201 North Ave 50211 515-981-4201
Dale Barnhill, prin. Fax 981-9875
Norwalk MS 500/6-8
200 Cherry Pkwy 50211 515-981-0435
Mark Crady, prin. Fax 981-0771

Oakland, Pottawattamie, Pop. 1,456
Riverside Community SD
Supt. — See Carson
Riverside Community HS 200/9-12
PO Box 428 51560 712-482-6464
Murray Fenn, prin. Fax 482-3074

Odebolt, Sac, Pop. 1,060
Odebolt-Arthur Community SD 400/PK-12
PO Box 475 51458 712-668-2289
Russ Freeman, supt. Fax 668-2631
showcase.netins.net/web/oahs/
Odebolt-Arthur HS 100/9-12
PO Box 475 51458 712-668-2827
Chuck Foy, prin. Fax 668-2631
Other Schools – See Arthur

Oelwein, Fayette, Pop. 6,498
Oelwein Community SD 1,400/PK-12
307 8th Ave SE 50662 319-283-3536
Jim Patera, supt. Fax 283-4497
www.oelwein.k12.ia.us
Oelwein HS 500/9-12
315 8th Ave SE 50662 319-283-2731
Frank Christenson, prin. Fax 283-1689
Oelwein MS 400/6-8
300 12th Ave SE 50662 319-283-3015
John Amick, prin. Fax 283-4497

Ogden, Boone, Pop. 2,023
Ogden Community SD 900/K-12
PO Box 250 50212 515-275-2894
Bill Roederer, supt. Fax 275-4537
Ogden HS 300/9-12
PO Box 250 50212 515-275-4034
Jerry Wilson, prin. Fax 275-4972
Ogden MS 300/5-8
PO Box 250 50212 515-275-2912
Mike Van Sickle, prin. Fax 275-2908

Olin, Jones, Pop. 703
Olin Consolidated SD 300/K-12
PO Box 320 52320 319-484-2155
Charles Liston, supt. Fax 484-2258
www.olin.k12.ia.us
Olin JSHS 200/7-12
PO Box 320 52320 319-484-2170
Linda Vaughn, prin. Fax 484-2258

Onawa, Monona, Pop. 3,011
West Monona Community SD 700/PK-12
1314 15th St 51040 712-423-2043
John Stanton, supt. Fax 423-3803
www.west-monona.k12.ia.us/
West Monona HS 200/9-12
1314 15th St 51040 712-433-2453
Steve Peiffer, prin. Fax 433-3803
West Monona MS 200/6-8
1314 15th St 51040 712-433-9098
Janet Ryan, prin. Fax 433-1142

Orange City, Sioux, Pop. 5,669
MOC-Floyd Valley Community SD 1,300/PK-12
PO Box 257 51041 712-737-4873
Gary Richardson, supt. Fax 737-8789
www.moc-fv.k12.ia.us/
MOC-Floyd Valley HS 500/9-12
615 8th St SE 51041 712-737-4871
Russ Adams, prin. Fax 737-3933
Other Schools – See Alton

Northwestern College Post-Sec.
101 7th St SW 51041 712-737-7000
Unity Christian HS 300/9-12
216 Michigan Ave SW 51041 712-737-4114
Harlan DeVries, prin. Fax 737-2686

Orient, Adair, Pop. 390
Orient-Macksburg Community SD 300/PK-12
PO Box 129 50858 641-337-5061
Gerald D. Waugh, supt. Fax 337-5013
www.orient-macks.k12.ia.us
Orient-Macksburg JSHS 200/7-12
PO Box 129 50858 641-337-5061
Jennifer Sornson, prin. Fax 337-5591

Osage, Mitchell, Pop. 3,471
Osage Community SD 1,000/PK-12
820 Sawyer Dr 50461 641-732-5381
Stephen Williams, supt. Fax 732-5381
www.osage.k12.ia.us
Osage HS 400/9-12
820 Sawyer Dr 50461 641-732-3102
Steve Nicholson, prin. Fax 732-3456
Osage MS 300/6-8
820 Sawyer Dr 50461 641-732-3127
Ross Grafft, prin. Fax 732-5450

Osceola, Clarke, Pop. 4,730
Clarke Community SD 1,500/K-12
PO Box 535 50213 641-342-4969
Ned Cox, supt. Fax 342-6101
www.clarke.k12.ia.us
Clarke Community HS 500/9-12
800 N Jackson St 50213 641-342-6505
David Walkup, prin. Fax 342-2213
Clarke MS 200/7-8
800 N Jackson St 50213 641-342-4221
Steve Seid, prin. Fax 342-2213

Oskaloosa, Mahaska, Pop. 11,037
Oskaloosa Community SD 1,300/K-12
PO Box 710 52577 641-673-8345
Dr. Carolyn McGaughey, supt. Fax 673-8370
www.oskaloosa.k12.ia.us
Oskaloosa HS, 1816 N 3rd St 52577 800/9-12
Andy Pattee, prin. 641-673-3407
Oskaloosa MS, 1704 N 3rd St 52577 400/6-8
Steve Gray, prin. 641-673-8308

William Penn University Post-Sec.
201 Trueblood Ave 52577 641-673-1001

Ossian, Winneshiek, Pop. 856
South Winneshiek Community SD
Supt. — See Calmar
South Winneshiek MS 100/6-8
PO Box 298 52161 563-532-9365
Charles Ehler, prin. Fax 532-9855

Ottumwa, Wapello, Pop. 24,697
Ottumwa Community SD 4,700/PK-12
422 Mccarroll Dr 52501 641-684-6596
Thomas Rubel, supt. Fax 684-6522
www.ottumwa.k12.ia.us
Evans JHS, 812 Chester Ave 52501 700/7-8
Davis Eidahl, prin. 641-684-6511
Ottumwa HS 1,500/9-12
501 E 2nd St 52501 641-683-4444
Steve Hanson, prin. Fax 682-7528

Indian Hills Community College Post-Sec.
525 Grandview Ave 52501 641-683-5111
Iowa School of Beauty Post-Sec.
609 W 2nd St 52501 641-684-6504
Ottumwa Christian S 100/PK-12
458 N Court St 52501 641-683-9119
Jerry Reed, prin. Fax 683-1084

Oxford, Johnson, Pop. 679
Clear Creek-Amana Community SD 1,300/PK-12
PO Box 487 52322 319-828-4510
Paula Vincent, supt. Fax 828-4743
www.cc-amana.k12.ia.us
Other Schools – See Middle Amana, Tiffin

Packwood, Jefferson, Pop. 220
Pekin Community SD 800/PK-12
1062 Birch Ave 52580 319-695-3707
Dr. Roger Macklem, supt. Fax 695-5130
www.pekincsd.org
Pekin HS 200/9-12
1062 Birch Ave 52580 319-695-3705
Art Sathoff, prin. Fax 661-2353
Pekin MS 200/6-8
1062 Birch Ave 52580 319-695-3707
Dan Maeder, prin. Fax 695-5130

Panora, Guthrie, Pop. 1,161
Panorama Community SD 800/PK-12
PO Box 39 50216 641-755-2317
John Millhollin, supt. Fax 755-3008
www.panorama.k12.ia.us/
Panorama HS 200/9-12
PO Box 39 50216 641-755-2317
Dean Schnoes, prin. Fax 755-3008
Panorama MS 200/6-8
PO Box 39 50216 641-755-2317
Mark Johnston, prin. Fax 755-3008

Parkersburg, Butler, Pop. 1,872
Aplington-Parkersburg Community SD 800/PK-12
610 N Johnson St 50665 319-347-2394
Pat Morgan, supt. Fax 347-2395
www.apl-park.k12.ia.us
Aplington-Parkersburg HS 300/9-12
610 N Johnson St 50665 319-346-1571
Everett Jensen, prin. Fax 346-1012
Other Schools – See Aplington

Paullina, O'Brien, Pop. 1,057
South O'Brien Community SD ... 700/K-12
PO Box 638 51046 ... 712-947-2115
Jerry Nichol, supt. ... Fax 949-2149
www.s-obrien.k12.ia.us
South O'Brien Secondary S ... 400/7-12
PO Box 638 51046 ... 712-949-3454
Danial Hoey, prin. ... Fax 949-3453

Pella, Marion, Pop. 10,107
Pella Community SD ... 2,100/PK-12
PO Box 468 50219 ... 641-628-1111
Mark Wittmer, supt. ... Fax 628-1116
www.pella.k12.ia.us
Pella HS ... 600/9-12
212 E University St 50219 ... 641-628-3870
Mark Lee, prin. ... Fax 628-7402
Pella MS ... 500/6-8
613 E 13th St 50219 ... 641-628-4784
David Versteeg, prin. ... Fax 628-6804

Central College ... Post-Sec.
812 University St 50219 ... 641-628-9000
Pella Christian HS ... 300/9-12
604 Jefferson St 50219 ... 641-628-4440
Darryl De Ruiter, prin. ... Fax 628-3530

Peosta, Dubuque, Pop. 788

Northeast Iowa Community College ... Post-Sec.
RR 1 52068 ... 563-556-5110

Perry, Dallas, Pop. 8,079
Perry Community SD ... 1,700/K-12
1219 Warford St 50220 ... 515-465-4656
Randall J. McCaulley Ed.D., supt. ... Fax 465-2426
www.perry.k12.ia.us/
Perry HS ... 600/9-12
1200 18th St 50220 ... 515-465-3503
Dan Marburger, prin. ... Fax 465-5977
Perry MS ... 400/6-8
1200 18th St 50220 ... 515-465-3531
Shaun Kruger, prin. ... Fax 465-8555

Pierson, Woodbury, Pop. 363
Kingsley-Pierson Community SD
Supt. — See Kingsley
Pierson MS ... 100/7-8
321 4th St 51048 ... 712-375-5939
Randy Wiese, prin. ... Fax 375-5771

Plainfield, Bremer, Pop. 426
Nashua-Plainfield Community SD
Supt. — See Nashua
Nashua-Plainfield MS ... 200/5-8
PO Box 38 50666 ... 319-276-4451
Ron Reusche, prin. ... Fax 276-3541

Pleasantville, Marion, Pop. 1,572
Pleasantville Community SD ... 500/PK-12
415 Jones St 50225 ... 515-848-0555
Dave Isgrig, supt. ... Fax 848-0561
www.pleasantville.k12.ia.us
Pleasantville HS ... 200/9-12
415 Jones St 50225 ... 515-848-0541
Gary Niichel, prin. ... Fax 848-0561
Pleasantville MS ... 6-8
415 Jones St 50225 ... 515-848-0528
Susan Phillips, prin. ... Fax 848-0561

Pocahontas, Pocahontas, Pop. 1,907
Pocahontas Area Community SD ... 600/K-12
202 1st Ave SW 50574 ... 712-335-4311
Joseph Kramer, supt. ... Fax 335-4206
www.pocahontas.k12.ia.us/
Pocahontas Area HS ... 300/9-12
205 2nd Ave NW 50574 ... 712-335-4848
Roger Francis, prin. ... Fax 335-3420
Other Schools – See Rolfe

Pomeroy, Calhoun, Pop. 669
Pomeroy-Palmer Community SD ... 300/K-12
202 E Harrison St 50575 ... 712-468-2268
Larry Kruckenberg, supt. ... Fax 468-2453
www.pom-palm.k12.ia.us
Pomeroy-Palmer Community HS ... 100/7-12
202 E Harrison St 50575 ... 712-468-2268
Dan Grandfield, prin. ... Fax 468-2453

Postville, Allamakee, Pop. 2,244
Postville Community SD ... 600/K-12
PO Box 717 52162 ... 563-864-7651
David Strudthoff, supt. ... Fax 864-7659
www.postville.k12.ia.us
Mott HS ... 200/9-12
PO Box 717 52162 ... 563-864-7651
Michael Mueller, prin. ... Fax 864-7659

Prairie City, Jasper, Pop. 1,371
PCM Community SD ... 1,000/PK-12
PO Box 490 50228 ... 515-994-2685
Kirk Nelson, supt. ... Fax 994-2699
www.pcmonroe.k12.ia.us
PCM MS ... 200/6-8
PO Box 490 50228 ... 515-994-2686
Ron Young, prin. ... Fax 994-2686
Other Schools – See Monroe

Preston, Jackson, Pop. 935
Preston Community SD ... 400/K-12
121 S Mitchell St 52069 ... 563-689-3431
Paul Tobin, supt. ... Fax 689-5823
www.prestonschools.com/
Preston JSHS ... 200/7-12
321 W School St 52069 ... 563-689-4221
David Miller, prin. ... Fax 689-4222

Radcliffe, Hardin, Pop. 582
Hubbard-Radcliffe Community SD
Supt. — See Hubbard

Radcliffe-Hubbard MS ... 100/6-8
PO Box 50230 ... 515-899-2111
James Loonan, prin. ... Fax 899-2116

Redfield, Dallas, Pop. 868
West Central Valley SD
Supt. — See Stuart
West Central Valley MS ... 200/6-8
PO Box B 50233 ... 515-833-2331
Mary Friedman, prin. ... Fax 833-2629

Red Oak, Montgomery, Pop. 5,940
Red Oak Community SD ... 1,200/PK-12
904 N Broad St 51566 ... 712-623-6600
Dr. Kevin Brummer, supt. ... Fax 623-6603
www.redoakschooldistrict.com
Red Oak HS ... 400/9-12
2011 N 8th St 51566 ... 712-623-6610
Terry Weber, prin. ... Fax 623-6613
Red Oak MS ... 300/6-8
308 E Corning St 51566 ... 712-623-6620
Barbara Sims, prin. ... Fax 623-6626

Reinbeck, Grundy, Pop. 1,690
Gladbrook-Reinbeck Community SD ... 800/K-12
300 Cedar St 50669 ... 319-345-2712
Dennis Modlin, supt. ... Fax 345-2242
www.gladbrook-reinbeck.k12.ia.us
Gladbrook-Reinbeck HS ... 300/9-12
600 Blackhawk St 50669 ... 319-345-2921
Mike Studt, prin. ... Fax 345-2242
Other Schools – See Gladbrook

Remsen, Plymouth, Pop. 1,707
Remsen-Union Community SD ... 400/K-12
511 Roosevelt 51050 ... 712-786-1101
Gary Battles, supt. ... Fax 786-1104
Remsen-Union HS ... 100/9-12
511 Roosevelt St 51050 ... 712-786-1101
Kirk Johnson, prin. ... Fax 786-1104
Remsen-Union MS ... 100/6-8
412 Fulton St 51050 ... 712-786-1230
Kirk Johnson, prin. ... Fax 786-1104

St. Marys HS ... 100/9-12
523 Madison St 51050 ... 712-786-1433
Jim Wesselmann, prin. ... Fax 786-2499

Riceville, Howard, Pop. 841
Riceville Community SD ... 400/K-12
912 Woodland Ave 50466 ... 641-985-2288
Christopher Anderson, supt. ... Fax 985-4171
www.riceville.k12.ia.us
Riceville HS ... 100/9-12
912 Woodland Ave 50466 ... 641-985-2288
Rosemary Cameron, prin. ... Fax 985-4001

Riverdale, Scott, Pop. 656
Pleasant Valley Community SD
Supt. — See Eldridge
Pleasant Valley HS ... 1,100/9-12
604 Belmont Rd 52722 ... 563-332-5151
Debbie Menke, prin. ... Fax 332-8525

Scott Community College ... Post-Sec.
500 Belmont Rd 52722 ... 563-441-4000

Riverside, Washington, Pop. 968
Highland Community SD ... 600/PK-12
PO Box B 52327 ... 319-648-3822
Carol Montz, supt. ... Fax 648-4055
www.highland.k12.ia.us
Highland HS ... 200/9-12
PO Box B 52327 ... 319-648-2891
Edward Pundt, prin. ... Fax 648-3310
Highland MS ... 100/6-8
PO Box B 52327 ... 319-648-5018
Shawn Donovan, prin. ... Fax 648-4055

Rockford, Floyd, Pop. 898
Rudd-Rockford-Marble Rock Comm. SD ... 600/PK-12
PO Box 218 50468 ... 641-756-3610
David Herold, supt. ... Fax 756-2369
www.rockford.k12.ia.us
Rockford JSHS ... 300/7-12
PO Box 218 50468 ... 641-756-3813
Rick Dosser, prin. ... Fax 756-2369

Rock Rapids, Lyon, Pop. 2,661
Central Lyon Community SD ... 600/K-12
PO Box 471 51246 ... 712-472-2664
Dave Ackerman, supt. ... Fax 472-3543
www.central-lyon.k12.ia.us
Central Lyon HS ... 200/9-12
PO Box 471 51246 ... 712-472-4051
Curt Busch, prin. ... Fax 472-2115
Central Lyon MS ... 200/6-8
PO Box 471 51246 ... 712-472-4041
Dan Kruse, prin. ... Fax 472-2346

Rock Valley, Sioux, Pop. 2,749
Rock Valley Community SD ... 600/PK-12
1712 20th Ave 51247 ... 712-476-2125
Dennis Mozer, supt. ... Fax 476-2125
www.rvcsd.org
Rock Valley JSHS ... 300/7-12
1712 20th Ave 51247 ... 712-476-2701
David Meylink, prin. ... Fax 476-2125

Netherlands Reformed Christian S ... 300/K-12
712 20th Ave SE 51247 ... 712-476-2821
Harold Schelling, prin. ... Fax 476-5438

Rockwell, Cerro Gordo, Pop. 978
Rockwell-Swaledale Community SD ... 400/PK-12
PO Box 60 50469 ... 641-822-3236
Tom Fey, supt. ... Fax 822-4882
www.rsrebels.org

Rockwell-Swaledale MSHS ... 200/7-12
PO Box 60 50469 ... 641-822-3234
Mark Vervaecke, prin. ... Fax 822-3273

Rockwell City, Calhoun, Pop. 2,133
Rockwell City-Lytton Community SD ... 500/PK-12
1000 Tonawanda St 50579 ... 712-297-7341
Dwayne Cross, supt. ... Fax 297-7320
www.rockwell-city-lytton.k12.ia.us
Rockwell City-Lytton HS ... 200/9-12
1000 Tonawanda St 50579 ... 712-297-8111
Randy Martin, prin. ... Fax 297-7320
Other Schools – See Lytton

Roland, Story, Pop. 1,344
Roland-Story Community SD
Supt. — See Story City
Roland-Story MS ... 400/5-8
206 S Main St 50236 ... 515-388-4348
John Sheahan, prin. ... Fax 388-4435

Rolfe, Pocahontas, Pop. 640
Pocahontas Area Community SD
Supt. — See Pocahontas
Pocohantas Area MS ... 200/6-8
202 1st Ave SW 50581 ... 712-848-3350
Andrew Woiwood, prin. ... Fax 848-3350

Royal, Clay, Pop. 442
Clay Central/Everly Community SD ... 500/PK-12
PO Box 110 51357 ... 712-933-2242
Monte Montgomery, supt. ... Fax 933-2243
www.claycentraleverly.com
Clay Central/Everly MS ... 100/6-8
PO Box 110 51357 ... 712-933-2241
Monte Montgomery, prin. ... Fax 933-2243
Other Schools – See Everly

Runnells, Polk, Pop. 372
Southeast Polk Community SD ... 4,700/PK-12
8379 NE University Ave 50237 ... 515-967-4294
Thomas J. Downs, supt. ... Fax 967-4257
www.se-polk.k12.ia.us/
Southeast Polk HS ... 1,300/9-12
8325 NE University Ave 50237 ... 515-967-6631
Charles Bredlow, prin. ... Fax 967-6450
Southeast Polk JHS ... 800/7-8
8031 NE University Ave 50237 ... 515-967-5509
Glenn Dietzenbach, prin. ... Fax 967-1676

Russell, Lucas, Pop. 572
Russell Community SD ... 200/PK-12
PO Box 487 50238 ... 641-535-2404
Robert McCurdy, supt. ... Fax 535-4181
Russell JSHS ... 100/6-12
PO Box 487 50238 ... 641-535-6105
Sally Johnson, prin. ... Fax 535-4181

Ruthven, Palo Alto, Pop. 706
Ruthven-Ayrshire Community SD ... 300/PK-12
PO Box 159 51358 ... 712-837-5211
Ervin Rowlands, supt. ... Fax 837-5210
www.ruthven.k12.ia.us
Ruthven-Ayrshire JSHS ... 100/7-12
PO Box 159 51358 ... 712-837-5212
Milton Peters, prin. ... Fax 837-5210

Sabula, Jackson, Pop. 674
East Central Community SD
Supt. — See Miles
Sabula MS ... 100/6-8
PO Box 307 52070 ... 563-687-2427
David Sievers, prin. ... Fax 687-2473

Sac City, Sac, Pop. 2,246
Sac Community SD ... 500/PK-12
400 S 16th St 50583 ... 712-662-7030
Ross Opsal, supt. ... Fax 662-6245
sac.k12.ia.us
Sac JSHS ... 300/7-12
300 S 11th St 50583 ... 712-662-3259
Dennis Olhausen, prin. ... Fax 662-4323

Saint Ansgar, Mitchell, Pop. 1,022
St. Ansgar Community SD ... 700/K-12
PO Box 559 50472 ... 641-713-4681
Dwight Widen, supt. ... Fax 713-4042
www.st-ansgar.k12.ia.us
Saint Ansgar HS ... 300/9-12
PO Box 559 50472 ... 641-713-4720
Scott Dryer, prin. ... Fax 713-2449
Saint Ansgar MS ... 200/5-8
PO Box 559 50472 ... 641-713-4040
Scott Dryer, prin. ... Fax 713-4042

Sanborn, O'Brien, Pop. 1,327
Hartley-Melvin-Sanborn Community SD
Supt. — See Hartley
Hartley-Melvin-Sanborn MS ... 300/5-8
PO Box 557 51248 ... 712-930-3281
Dorhout Mark, prin. ... Fax 930-5414

Schaller, Sac, Pop. 732
Schaller-Crestland Community SD ... 500/PK-12
PO Box 249 51053 ... 712-275-4267
Dave Kwikkel, supt. ... Fax 275-4269
www.schaller-crest.k12.ia.us/
Other Schools – See Early

Schleswig, Crawford, Pop. 819
Schleswig Community SD ... 200/K-8
PO Box 250 51461 ... 712-676-3313
Jack Johnson, supt. ... Fax 676-3539
www.schleswig.k12.ia.us
Schleswig MS ... 100/5-8
PO Box 250 51461 ... 712-676-3313
Brian Johnson, prin. ... Fax 676-3539

Sergeant Bluff, Woodbury, Pop. 3,689
Sergeant Bluff-Luton Community SD 1,000/PK-12
PO Box 97 51054 712-943-4338
Rich Caldwell, supt. Fax 943-1131
www.sergeant-bluff.k12.ia.us
Sergeant Bluff-Luton HS 300/9-12
PO Box 97 51054 712-943-5561
Dan Moore, prin. Fax 943-5887
Sergeant Bluff-Luton MS 300/6-8
PO Box 97 51054 712-943-4235
Rod Earleywine, prin. Fax 943-8780

Seymour, Wayne, Pop. 806
Seymour Community SD 300/PK-12
100 S Park Ave 52590 641-898-2291
Dale Weeks, supt. Fax 898-7500
Seymour JSHS 200/7-12
100 S Park Ave 52590 641-898-2291
Dave Lockridge, prin. Fax 898-7500

Sheffield, Franklin, Pop. 954
Sheffield-Chapin Community SD 300/PK-12
PO Box 617 50475 641-892-4160
Tom Fey, supt. Fax 892-4379
www.sheffield-chapin.k12.ia.us
Sheffield-Chapin Community HS 200/9-12
PO Box 617 50475 641-892-4461
Randy Buschbaum, prin. Fax 892-4335

Sheldon, O'Brien, Pop. 4,927
Sheldon Community SD 1,000/PK-12
1700 E 4th St 51201 712-324-2504
Robin Spears, supt. Fax 324-5607
www.sheldon.k12.ia.us
Sheldon HS 400/9-12
1700 E 4th St 51201 712-324-2501
Joe Mueting, prin. Fax 324-5607
Sheldon MS 300/5-8
310 23rd Ave 51201 712-324-4346
Cindy Barwick, prin. Fax 324-4347

Northwest Iowa Community College Post-Sec.
603 W Park St 51201 712-324-5061

Shenandoah, Page, Pop. 5,290
Shenandoah Community SD 1,000/PK-12
304 W Nishna Rd 51601 712-246-1581
Dick Profit, supt. Fax 246-3722
www.shenandoah.k12.ia.us
Shenandoah HS 300/9-12
1000 Mustang Dr 51601 712-246-4727
Chris Heslinga, prin. Fax 246-2842
Shenandoah MS 300/5-8
601 Dr Creighton Cir 51601 712-246-2520
Keith Meyer, prin. Fax 246-6390

Sibley, Osceola, Pop. 2,742
Sibley-Ocheyedan Community SD 900/K-12
120 11th Ave NE 51249 712-754-2533
Jeff Herzberg, supt. Fax 754-2534
www.sibley-ocheyedan.k12.ia.us/
Sibley-Ocheyedan HS 300/9-12
120 11th Ave NE 51249 712-754-3601
Denny Frey, prin.
Sibley-Ocheyedan MS 300/5-8
120 11th Ave NE 51249 712-754-2542
Wayne Miller, prin.

Sidney, Fremont, Pop. 1,221
Sidney Community SD 400/PK-12
PO Box 609 51652 712-374-2141
Gregg Cruickshank, supt. Fax 374-2013
Sidney JSHS 200/7-12
PO Box 609 51652 712-374-2731
Susan Peterson, prin. Fax 374-2013

Sigourney, Keokuk, Pop. 2,210
Sigourney Community SD 700/K-12
107 W Marion St 52591 641-622-2025
David Harris, supt. Fax 622-2319
www.sigourney.k12.ia.us/
Sigourney JSHS 400/7-12
907 E Pleasant Valley St 52591 641-622-2010
Robert Hinrichs, prin. Fax 622-2047

Sioux Center, Sioux, Pop. 6,527
Sioux Center Community SD 900/PK-12
550 9th St NE 51250 712-722-2985
Patrick O'Donnell, supt. Fax 722-2986
www.sioux-center.k12.ia.us
Sioux Center HS 300/9-12
550 9th St NE 51250 712-722-2981
Ray Roseland, prin. Fax 722-2986
Sioux Center MS 300/5-8
550 9th St NE 51250 712-722-3783
Matt Ludwig, prin. Fax 722-2986

Dordt College Post-Sec.
498 4th Ave NE 51250 712-722-6000

Sioux City, Woodbury, Pop. 83,876
Sioux City Community SD 12,500/PK-12
1221 Pierce St 51105 712-279-6667
Larry D. Williams, supt. Fax 279-6690
www.siouxcityschools.org/
East HS 1,300/9-12
5011 Mayhew Ave 51106 712-274-4000
Jeanene Sampson, prin. Fax 274-4670
East MS 1,000/6-8
5401 Lorraine Ave 51106 712-274-4030
Thomas Peterson, prin. Fax 274-4668
North HS 1,400/9-12
4200 Cheyenne Blvd 51104 712-239-7000
Alan Heisterkamp, prin. Fax 239-8270
North MS 6-8
2101 Outer Dr N 51108 712-279-6667
Pete Hathaway, prin. Fax 277-5941
West HS 1,300/9-12
2001 Casselman St 51103 712-279-6772
James Vanderloo, prin. Fax 279-6790
West MS 1,000/6-8
3301 W 19th St 51103 712-279-6813
Cynthia Washinowski, prin. Fax 277-6138

Bishop Heelan HS 700/9-12
1021 Douglas St 51105 712-252-0573
Terry Tomke, prin. Fax 252-4897
Briar Cliff University Post-Sec.
PO Box 2100 51104 712-279-5400
Holy Cross S / Blessed Sacrament Ctr 400/3-8
3030 Jackson St 51104 712-277-4739
Michael Sweeney, prin. Fax 258-3698
Iowa School of Beauty Post-Sec.
2524 Glenn Ave 51106 712-274-9733
Mater Dei S - Nativity Center 400/6-8
4243 Natalia Way 51106 712-274-0268
Marilyn Blum, prin. Fax 274-0377
Mercy Medical Center - Sioux City Post-Sec.
801 5th St 51101 712-279-2018
Morningside College Post-Sec.
1501 Morningside Ave 51106 712-274-5000
St. Luke's College Post-Sec.
2720 Stone Park Blvd 51104 712-279-3149
Siouxland Community Christian S 200/PK-12
6100 Morningside Ave 51106 712-276-4732
Barbara Blanchard, admin. Fax 276-4752
Western Iowa Tech Community College Post-Sec.
PO Box 5199 51102 712-274-6400

Sioux Rapids, Clay, Pop. 709
Sioux Central Community SD 500/PK-12
4440 US Highway 71 50585 712-283-2571
Steve Callison, supt. Fax 283-2285
www.sioux-central.k12.ia.us
Sioux Central JSHS 300/6-12
4440 US Highway 71 50585 712-283-2571
Jeff Scham, prin. Fax 283-2285

Sloan, Woodbury, Pop. 1,031
Westwood Community SD 700/PK-12
1000 Rebel Way 51055 712-428-3355
Kirk Ahrends, supt. Fax 428-3246
www.westwood.k12.ia.us/
Westwood JSHS 300/7-12
1000 Rebel Way 51055 712-428-3303
Gary Schrage, prin. Fax 428-3246

Solon, Johnson, Pop. 1,258
Solon Community SD 1,200/PK-12
301 S Iowa St 52333 319-624-3401
Brad Manard, supt. Fax 624-2518
www.solon.k12.ia.us
Solon HS 300/9-12
600 W 5th St 52333 319-624-3401
Bob Lesan, prin. Fax 624-4091
Solon MS 400/5-8
313 S Iowa St 52333 319-624-3401
Mike Herdliska, prin. Fax 624-2518

Spencer, Clay, Pop. 11,219
Spencer Community SD 2,000/PK-12
PO Box 200 51301 712-262-8950
Greg Ebeling, supt. Fax 262-1116
www.spencer.k12.ia.us
Spencer HS 700/9-12
PO Box 200 51301 712-262-1700
Mike Healy, prin. Fax 262-5704
Spencer MS, PO Box 200 51301 400/7-8
Steve Barber, prin. 712-262-3345

Iowa Lakes Community College Post-Sec.
1900 Grand Ave Ste 8 51301 712-262-7141

Spirit Lake, Dickinson, Pop. 4,444
Spirit Lake Community SD 1,300/K-12
900 20th St 51360 712-336-2820
Tim Grieves, supt. Fax 336-4641
www.spirit-lake.k12.ia.us/
Spirit Lake HS 400/9-12
2701 Hill Ave 51360 712-336-3707
Fred Skretta, prin. Fax 336-3714
Spirit Lake MS 400/5-8
609 28th St 51360 712-336-1370
Steve Ratzlaff, prin. Fax 336-4758

The Faust Institute of Cosmetology Post-Sec.
1543 18th St Ste 15 51360 712-336-3518

Springville, Linn, Pop. 1,036
Springville Community SD 400/K-12
400 Academy St 52336 319-854-6197
Oran Teut, supt. Fax 854-6199
www.springville.k12.ia.us
Springville JSHS 200/6-12
400 Academy St 52336 319-854-6196
Mel Mysak, prin. Fax 854-7891

Stanton, Montgomery, Pop. 700
Stanton Community SD 300/K-12
605 Elliott St 51573 712-829-2162
Judson Ashley, supt. Fax 829-2164
www.stantonschools.com
Stanton JSHS 200/7-12
605 Elliott St 51573 712-829-2162
Jeff Hiser, prin. Fax 829-2164

Stanwood, Cedar, Pop. 674
North Cedar Community SD 1,000/K-12
PO Box 247 52337 563-942-3358
Dr. Gregg Fuerstenau, supt. Fax 942-3596
www.north-cedar.k12.ia.us
North Cedar HS 300/9-12
PO Box 247 52337 563-942-3341
Dain Jeppson, prin. Fax 942-3596
Other Schools – See Clarence

State Center, Marshall, Pop. 1,318
West Marshall Community SD 800/PK-12
PO Box 670 50247 641-483-2660
Ned Sellers, supt. Fax 483-2665
www.w-marshall.k12.ia.us
West Marshall HS 200/9-12
PO Box 670 50247 641-483-2136
James Henrich, prin. Fax 483-2172
West Marshall MS 300/5-8
PO Box 340 50247 641-483-2165
Jeff Barry, prin. Fax 483-9951

Storm Lake, Buena Vista, Pop. 9,973
Storm Lake Community SD 2,100/PK-12
PO Box 638 50588 712-732-8060
Paul Tedesco, supt. Fax 732-8063
www.storm-lake.k12.ia.us
Storm Lake HS 700/9-12
621 Tornado Dr 50588 712-732-8065
Michael Hanna, prin. Fax 732-8068
Storm Lake MS 600/5-8
1811 Hyland Dr 50588 712-732-8080
Ronald Bryan, prin. Fax 732-8084

Buena Vista University Post-Sec.
610 W 4th St 50588 712-749-2235
Iowa Central Community College Post-Sec.
916 Russell St 50588 712-732-2991
St. Mary MSHS 100/6-12
304 Seneca St 50588 712-732-4166
Rose Davis, prin. Fax 732-4590
The Faust Institute of Cosmetology Post-Sec.
PO Box 29 50588 712-732-6571

Story City, Story, Pop. 3,360
Roland-Story Community SD 1,100/PK-12
1009 Story St 50248 515-733-4301
Mike Billings, supt. Fax 733-2131
www.roland-story.k12.ia.us
Roland-Story HS 400/9-12
1009 Story St 50248 515-733-4329
Steve Schlatter, prin. Fax 733-2131
Other Schools – See Roland

Stuart, Guthrie, Pop. 1,741
West Central Valley SD 1,000/PK-12
PO Box 81 50250 515-523-2187
David Rogers, supt. Fax 523-1166
www.studex.k12.ia.us
West Central Valley HS 300/9-12
PO Box 81 50250 515-523-1313
Deborah Wilson, prin. Fax 523-2765
Other Schools – See Redfield

Sully, Jasper, Pop. 895
Lynnville-Sully Community SD 500/K-12
PO Box 210 50251 641-594-4445
Duane Willhite, supt. Fax 594-2770
www.lynnville-sully.k12.ia.us
Lynnville-Sully HS 200/9-12
PO Box 210 50251 641-594-4445
Mike Studt, prin. Fax 594-2770
Lynnville-Sully MS 100/6-8
PO Box 310 50251 641-594-3721
Matt Adams, prin. Fax 594-2770

Sumner, Bremer, Pop. 2,056
Sumner-Fredericksburg SD 700/K-12
PO Box 178 50674 563-578-3341
Rick Pederson, supt. Fax 578-3425
Sumner-Fredericksburg HS 200/9-12
PO Box 178 50674 563-578-3342
Allan Eckelman, prin. Fax 578-3424
Other Schools – See Fredericksburg

Swea City, Kossuth, Pop. 611
North Kossuth Community SD
Supt. — See Bancroft
North Kossuth HS 200/9-12
PO Box 567 50590 515-272-4361
Todd Thompson, prin. Fax 272-4391
North Kossuth MS 100/7-8
PO Box 567 50590 515-272-4361
Todd Thompson, prin. Fax 272-4391

Tabor, Fremont, Pop. 995
Fremont-Mills Community SD 500/PK-12
PO Box 310 51653 712-629-2325
Christopher Herrick, supt. Fax 629-5155
www.fmtabor.k12.ia.us/fm/index.htm
Fremont-Mills MSHS 200/7-12
PO Box 310 51653 712-629-2325
Randall Botts, prin. Fax 629-5155

Tama, Tama, Pop. 2,654
South Tama County Community SD 1,000/PK-12
1702 Harding St 52339 641-484-4811
Larry Molacek, supt. Fax 484-4861
stc.tamatoledo.net/
South Tama County HS 500/9-12
1715 Harding St 52339 641-484-4345
Steve Burr, prin. Fax 484-5152
Other Schools – See Toledo

Terril, Dickinson, Pop. 383
Terril Community SD 100/PK-8
PO Box 128 51364 712-853-6111
Dan Mart, supt. Fax 853-6199
www.terril.k12.ia.us
Terril/Graettinger MS 100/6-8
PO Box 128 51364 712-853-6111
Jared Cecil, prin. Fax 853-6199

Thompson, Winnebago, Pop. 578
North Iowa Community SD
Supt. — See Buffalo Center
North Iowa MS 200/5-8
PO Box 27 50478 641-584-2231
Mike Evans, prin. Fax 584-2230

Thornburg, Keokuk, Pop. 72
Tri-County Community SD ... 300/PK-12
PO Box 17 50255 ... 641-634-2408
Bill Cox, supt. ... Fax 634-2145
www.tri-county.k12.ia.us/
Tri-County HS ... 100/9-12
PO Box 17 50255 ... 641-634-2636
Dennis Phelps, prin. ... Fax 634-2145
Tri-County JHS ... 100/7-8
PO Box 17 50255 ... 641-634-2636
Dennis Phelps, prin. ... Fax 634-2145

Thornton, Cerro Gordo, Pop. 411
Meservey-Thornton Community SD ... 100/5-8
PO Box 150 50479 ... 641-998-2315
Eldon Pyle, supt. ... Fax 998-2196
Meservey-Thornton MS ... 100/5-8
PO Box 150 50479 ... 641-998-2315
Abe Maske, prin. ... Fax 998-2196

Tiffin, Johnson, Pop. 1,415
Clear Creek-Amana Community SD
Supt. — See Oxford
Clear Creek-Amana HS ... 400/9-12
PO Box 199 52340 ... 319-545-2361
Tom McDonald, prin. ... Fax 545-2863

Tipton, Cedar, Pop. 3,147
Tipton Community SD ... 800/K-12
400 E 6th St 52772 ... 563-886-6121
Jeffory Corkery, supt. ... Fax 886-2341
www.tipton.k12.ia.us
Tipton HS ... 300/9-12
400 E 6th St 52772 ... 563-886-6027
Chris Habben, prin. ... Fax 886-2341
Tipton MS ... 200/6-8
400 E 6th St 52772 ... 563-886-6025
Richard Grimoskas, prin. ... Fax 886-2555

Titonka, Kossuth, Pop. 558
Titonka Consolidated SD ... 200/K-8
PO Box 287 50480 ... 515-928-2717
Randy Collins, supt. ... Fax 928-2718
Titonka MS ... 100/6-8
PO Box 287 50480 ... 515-928-2720
Randy Collins, prin. ... Fax 928-2718

Toledo, Tama, Pop. 2,501
South Tama County Community SD
Supt. — See Tama
South Tama County MS ... 400/6-8
201 S Green St 52342 ... 641-484-4121
Steve Cose, prin. ... Fax 484-2699

Traer, Tama, Pop. 1,599
North Tama County Community SD ... 500/K-12
605 Walnut St 50675 ... 319-478-2265
Thomas McDermott, supt. ... Fax 478-2917
www.n-tama.k12.ia.us
North Tama JSHS ... 200/7-12
605 Walnut St 50675 ... 319-478-2911
Irvin Laube, prin. ... Fax 478-2917

Treynor, Pottawattamie, Pop. 946
Treynor Community SD ... 600/K-12
PO Box 369 51575 ... 712-487-3414
Kevin Elwood, supt. ... Fax 487-3332
www.treynor.k12.ia.us
Treynor JSHS ... 300/7-12
PO Box 369 51575 ... 712-487-3804
Joel Bohlken, prin. ... Fax 487-3332

Tripoli, Bremer, Pop. 1,288
Tripoli Community SD ... 500/K-12
209 8th Ave SW 50676 ... 319-882-4201
Robert Longmuir, supt. ... Fax 882-3103
Tripoli JSHS ... 300/6-12
209 8th Ave SW 50676 ... 319-882-4202
Troy Heller, prin. ... Fax 882-3103

Troy Mills, Linn
North Linn Community SD ... 700/K-12
PO Box 200 52344 ... 319-224-3291
Larry G. Boer, supt. ... Fax 224-3727
www.northlinn.k12.ia.us
North Linn HS ... 200/9-12
PO Box 200 52344 ... 319-224-3291
Betty Coleman, prin. ... Fax 224-3232
North Linn MS ... 200/6-8
PO Box 200 52344 ... 319-224-3291
Betty Coleman, prin. ... Fax 224-3232

Truro, Madison, Pop. 454
Interstate 35 Community SD ... 800/PK-12
PO Box 79 50257 ... 641-765-4291
Bill Maske, supt. ... Fax 765-4593
www.i-35.k12.ia.us/
Interstate 35 HS ... 200/9-12
PO Box 79 50257 ... 641-765-4818
Christian Paulson, prin. ... Fax 765-4820
Interstate 35 MS ... 200/5-8
PO Box 200 50257 ... 641-765-4908
Sharon McKimpson, prin. ... Fax 765-4905

Underwood, Pottawattamie, Pop. 733
Underwood Community SD ... 700/PK-12
PO Box 130 51576 ... 712-566-2332
Ed Hawks, supt. ... Fax 566-2070
www.underwood.k12.ia.us
Underwood HS ... 200/9-12
PO Box 130 51576 ... 712-566-2703
Roger Pearson, prin. ... Fax 566-2712
Underwood MS ... 200/6-8
PO Box 130 51576 ... 712-566-2332
J. Lewis Curtis, prin. ... Fax 566-2070

Union, Hardin, Pop. 413
BCLUW Community SD
Supt. — See Conrad
BCLUW MS ... 200/5-8
704 Commercial St 50258 ... 641-486-5371
Dirk Borgman, prin. ... Fax 486-5372

University Park, Mahaska, Pop. 543

Vennard College ... Post-Sec.
PO Box 29 52595 ... 800-686-8391

Urbandale, Polk, Pop. 31,868
Urbandale Community SD ... 3,400/PK-12
6200 Aurora Ave Ste 500W 50322 ... 515-457-5000
Dr. Greg Robinson, supt. ... Fax 457-5018
www.urbandaleschools.com/
Urbandale HS ... 1,200/9-12
7111 Aurora Ave 50322 ... 515-457-6800
Richard Hutchinson, prin. ... Fax 457-6801
Urbandale MS ... 800/6-8
7701 Aurora Ave 50322 ... 515-457-6600
Daniel Meyer, prin. ... Fax 457-6601

Des Moines Christian S ... 800/PK-12
13007 Douglas Pkwy 50323 ... 515-252-2480
Robert Stouffer, admin. ... Fax 251-6911
Hamilton College ... Post-Sec.
4655 121st St 50323 ... 515-727-2100

Van Horne, Benton, Pop. 823
Benton Community SD ... 1,500/PK-12
PO Box 70 52346 ... 319-228-8701
Gary Zittergruen, supt. ... Fax 228-8254
www.benton.k12.ia.us
Benton Community HS ... 500/9-12
PO Box 70 52346 ... 319-228-8701
Bruce Johnson, prin. ... Fax 228-8747
Benton Community MS ... 200/7-8
PO Box 70 52346 ... 319-228-8701
Jo Prusha, prin. ... Fax 228-8747

Van Meter, Dallas, Pop. 907
Van Meter Community SD ... 500/K-12
PO Box 257 50261 ... 515-996-9960
Greg DeTimmerman, supt. ... Fax 996-9954
www.vanmeter.k12.ia.us
Van Meter JSHS ... 200/7-12
PO Box 257 50261 ... 515-996-2221
John Carver, prin. ... Fax 996-2488

Ventura, Cerro Gordo, Pop. 663
Ventura Community SD ... 400/K-12
PO Box 18 50482 ... 641-829-4484
Dan Versteeg, supt. ... Fax 829-3995
www.ventura.k12.ia.us
Ventura JSHS ... 200/7-12
PO Box 18 50482 ... 641-829-4484
Lorene Dykstra, prin. ... Fax 829-3995

Victor, Iowa, Pop. 965
H L V Community SD ... 400/PK-12
PO Box B 52347 ... 319-647-2161
William Lynch, supt. ... Fax 647-2164
www.hlv.k12.ia.us
H L V JSHS ... 200/7-12
PO Box B 52347 ... 319-647-2161
John Long, prin. ... Fax 647-2164

Villisca, Montgomery, Pop. 1,286
Villisca Community SD ... 400/K-12
406 E 3rd St 50864 ... 712-826-2552
Teresa Nook, supt. ... Fax 826-4072
www.villisca.k12.ia.us
Villisca Community JSHS ... 200/6-12
406 E 3rd St 50864 ... 712-826-2552
Lee Haidsiak, prin. ... Fax 826-4072

Vinton, Benton, Pop. 5,210
Vinton-Shellsburg Community SD ... 1,800/K-12
810 W 9th St 52349 ... 319-436-4728
Dr. Randy L. Braden, supt. ... Fax 472-3889
www.vinton-shellsburg.k12.ia.us
Tilford MS ... 500/6-8
308 E 13th St 52349 ... 319-436-4728
Mike Timmermans, prin. ... Fax 472-4014
Washington HS ... 600/9-12
212 W 15th St 52349 ... 319-436-4728
Paul Pedersen, prin. ... Fax 472-5704

Iowa Braille and Sight Saving School ... Post-Sec.
1002 G Ave 52349 ... 319-472-5221

Walcott, Scott, Pop. 1,516
Davenport Community SD
Supt. — See Davenport
Walcott IS ... 400/6-8
545 E James St 52773 ... 563-284-6253
Erica Goldstone, prin. ... Fax 284-5081

Walker, Linn, Pop. 731

Cono Christian S ... 100/PK-12
3269 Quasqueton Ave 52352 ... 319-448-4395
... Fax 448-4397

Walnut, Pottawattamie, Pop. 859
Walnut Community SD ... 300/PK-12
PO Box 528 51577 ... 712-784-2251
Jeff Kruse, supt. ... Fax 784-2177
www.walnut.k12.ia.us
Walnut HS ... 100/9-12
PO Box 528 51577 ... 712-784-3615
Jedd Sherman, prin. ... Fax 784-2177
Walnut MS ... 100/6-8
PO Box 528 51577 ... 712-784-3615
Jedd Sherman, prin. ... Fax 784-2177

Wapello, Louisa, Pop. 2,149
Wapello Community SD ... 800/PK-12
445 N Cedar St 52653 ... 319-523-3641
John Swinton, supt. ... Fax 523-8151
www.wapello.k12.ia.us
Wapello HS ... 200/9-12
501 Buchanan Ave 52653 ... 319-523-3241
Steve Bohlen, prin. ... Fax 523-4408

Wapello JHS ... 100/7-8
501 Buchanan Ave 52653 ... 319-523-8131
Steve Bohlen, prin. ... Fax 523-4408

Washington, Washington, Pop. 7,253
Washington Community SD ... 1,700/PK-12
PO Box 926 52353 ... 319-653-6543
Dave Schmitt, supt. ... Fax 653-5685
www.washington.k12.ia.us/
Washington JHS ... 500/7-9
1111 S Avenue B 52353 ... 319-653-5414
Monte Davis, prin. ... Fax 653-7350
Washington SHS ... 400/10-12
PO Box 271 52353 ... 319-653-2143
Francis Johnston, prin. ... Fax 653-6751

Waterloo, Black Hawk, Pop. 67,054
Waterloo Community SD ... 9,800/PK-12
1516 Washington St 50702 ... 319-433-1800
Dr. Dewitt Jones, supt. ... Fax 433-1886
www.waterloo.k12.ia.us
Central MS ... 800/6-8
1350 Katoski Dr 50701 ... 319-433-2100
Marla Padget, prin. ... Fax 433-2149
East HS ... 1,200/9-12
214 High St 50703 ... 319-433-2400
Mary Jane Meier, prin. ... Fax 433-2498
Hoover MS ... 700/6-8
630 Hillcrest Rd 50701 ... 319-433-2830
Terry Meier, prin. ... Fax 433-2843
Logan MS ... 500/6-8
1515 Logan Ave 50703 ... 319-433-2500
Phillip Anderson, prin. ... Fax 433-2548
West HS ... 1,800/9-12
425 E Ridgeway Ave 50702 ... 319-433-2700
Dr. Gail Moon, prin. ... Fax 433-2749
Other Schools – See Evansdale

Allen College ... Post-Sec.
1825 Logan Ave 50703 ... 319-226-2000
College of Hair Design ... Post-Sec.
722 Water St Ste 201 50703 ... 319-232-9995
Columbus HS ... 600/9-12
3231 W 9th St 50702 ... 319-233-3358
Tom Ulses, prin. ... Fax 235-0733
Covenant Medical Center ... Post-Sec.
3421 W 9th St 50702 ... 319-272-7296
Hawkeye Community College ... Post-Sec.
PO Box 8015 50704 ... 319-296-2320
Walnut Ridge Baptist Academy ... 200/K-12
1307 W Ridgeway Ave 50701 ... 319-235-9309
Kenneth Gould, admin. ... Fax 833-4780

Waucoma, Fayette, Pop. 259
Turkey Valley Community SD ... 600/PK-12
3219 Highway 24 52171 ... 563-776-6011
John Rothlisberger, supt. ... Fax 776-4271
www.turkey-v.k12.ia.us
Turkey Valley JSHS ... 300/7-12
3219 Highway 24 52171 ... 563-776-6011
Joel Weeks, prin. ... Fax 776-4271

Waukee, Dallas, Pop. 7,287
Waukee Community SD ... 3,200/PK-12
560 SE University Ave 50263 ... 515-987-5161
Dr. David Wilkerson, supt. ... Fax 987-2701
www.waukee.k12.ia.us
Prairieview S ... 8-9
655 SE University Ave 50263 ... 515-987-2770
Juley Murphy-Tiernan, prin. ... Fax 987-2789
Waukee HS ... 600/10-12
555 SE University Ave 50263 ... 515-987-5163
Jody Rarigan, prin. ... Fax 987-2784

Waukon, Allamakee, Pop. 4,059
Allamakee Community SD ... 1,500/K-12
1059 3rd Ave NW 52172 ... 563-568-3409
John Speer, supt. ... Fax 568-2677
www.allamakee.k12.ia.us/
Waukon JHS ... 400/7-9
110 5th St NW 52172 ... 563-568-6321
Joe Griffith, prin. ... Fax 568-6410
Waukon SHS ... 400/10-12
1059 3rd Ave NW 52172 ... 563-568-3466
David Ziesmer, prin. ... Fax 568-2677

Waverly, Bremer, Pop. 9,075
Waverly-Shell Rock Community SD ... 2,000/K-12
1415 4th Ave SW 50677 ... 319-352-3630
Jere Vyverberg, supt. ... Fax 352-5676
www.waverly-shellrock.k12.ia.us
Waverly-Shell Rock HS ... 800/9-12
1405 4th Ave SW 50677 ... 319-352-2087
Ken H. Winter, prin. ... Fax 352-2098
Waverly-Shell Rock JHS ... 300/7-8
215 3rd St NW 50677 ... 319-352-3632
Steve Kwikkel, prin. ... Fax 352-5199

Wartburg College ... Post-Sec.
PO Box 1003 50677 ... 319-352-8200

Wayland, Henry, Pop. 948
Waco Community SD ... 500/PK-12
PO Box 158 52654 ... 319-256-6200
Darrell Smith, supt. ... Fax 256-6213
www.wacohs.com
Waco JSHS ... 200/7-12
PO Box 158 52654 ... 319-256-6200
Roger Thornburg, prin. ... Fax 256-6211

Webster City, Hamilton, Pop. 8,106
Webster City Community SD ... 1,700/PK-12
825 Beach St 50595 ... 515-832-9200
Mike Sherwood, supt. ... Fax 832-9204
www.webster-city.k12.ia.us
Webster City HS ... 600/9-12
1001 Lynx Ave 50595 ... 515-832-9210
Larry Hunt, prin. ... Fax 832-9215

Webster City MS   500/5-8
  1101 Des Moines St 50595   515-832-9220
  Becky Hacker-Kluver, prin.   Fax 832-9225

Iowa Central Community College   Post-Sec.
  1725 Beach St 50595   515-832-1632

Wellman, Washington, Pop. 1,455
Mid-Prairie Community SD   1,200/PK-12
  PO Box 150 52356   319-646-6093
  Mark Schneider, supt.   Fax 646-2093
  www.mid-prairie.k12.ia.us
Mid-Prairie HS   300/9-12
  PO Box 150 52356   319-646-6091
  Gerry Beeler, prin.   Fax 646-6097
  Other Schools – See Kalona

Wellsburg, Grundy, Pop. 688
AGWSR Community SD
  Supt. — See Ackley
AGWSR MS   200/6-8
  PO Box 188 50680   641-869-5121
  Robert Hutchcroft, prin.   Fax 869-3426

West Bend, Palo Alto, Pop. 827
West Bend - Mallard Community SD   400/PK-12
  PO Box 247 50597   515-887-7821
  Dr. John Phillips, supt.   Fax 887-7785
  www.west-bend.k12.ia.us
West Bend - Mallard HS   100/9-12
  PO Box 247 50597   515-887-7831
  Samuel Swensen, prin.   Fax 887-7853
  Other Schools – See Mallard

West Branch, Cedar, Pop. 2,297
West Branch Community SD   800/PK-12
  PO Box 637 52358   319-643-7213
  Craig Artist, supt.   Fax 643-7122
  www.west-branch.k12.ia.us
West Branch HS   200/9-12
  PO Box 637 52358   319-643-7216
  Stephen Hennesy, prin.   Fax 643-2415
West Branch MS   200/6-8
  PO Box 637 52358   319-643-5324
  Sara Oswald, prin.   Fax 643-5447

Scattergood Friends S   100/9-12
  1951 Delta Ave 52358   319-643-7600
  Jan Luchini, dir.   Fax 643-7485

West Burlington, Des Moines, Pop. 3,062
West Burlington ISD   700/K-12
  211 Ramsey St 52655   319-752-8747
  James Sleister, supt.   Fax 754-9382
  www.w-burlington.k12.ia.us/
West Burlington HS   200/9-12
  408 W Van Weiss Blvd 52655   319-752-7138
  Ron Teater, prin.   Fax 754-0075
West Burlington JHS   100/7-8
  408 W Van Weiss Blvd 52655   319-752-7138
  Ron Teater, prin.   Fax 754-0075

Southeastern Community College   Post-Sec.
  PO Box 180 52655   319-752-2731

West Des Moines, Polk, Pop. 51,699
West Des Moines Community SD   8,000/PK-12
  3550 Mills Civic Pkwy 50265   515-633-5000
  Thomas Narak, supt.   Fax 633-5099
  www.wdmcs.org
Stilwell JHS   800/7-8
  1601 Vine St 50265   515-633-6000
  Tim Miller, prin.   Fax 633-6099
Valley HS   1,700/10-12
  1140 Valley West Dr 50266   515-633-4000
  Vicky Poole, prin.   Fax 633-4099
Valley Southwoods Freshman HS   700/9-9
  625 S 35th St 50265   515-633-4500
  Lori Diebel, prin.   Fax 633-4599
  Other Schools – See Clive

Dowling Catholic HS   1,200/9-12
  1400 Buffalo Rd 50265   515-222-1045
  Dr. James Dowdle, prin.   Fax 222-1056
Iowa Christian Academy   300/PK-12
  2501 Vine St 50265   515-221-3999
  Donald Beebe, admin.   Fax 225-2387

West Liberty, Muscatine, Pop. 3,462
West Liberty Community SD   1,100/PK-12
  203 E 7th St 52776   319-627-2116
  Rebecca Rodocker, supt.   Fax 627-2963
  www.wl.k12.ia.us
West Liberty HS   400/9-12
  310 W Maxson Ave 52776   319-627-2115
  James Hamilton, prin.   Fax 627-2038
West Liberty MS   500/3-8
  806 N Miller St 52776   319-627-2118
  Vicki Vernon, prin.   Fax 627-2092

West Point, Lee, Pop. 966

Holy Trinity MS   100/6-8
  PO Box 39 52656   319-837-6131
  Daniel Kieler, prin.   Fax 837-8112

Westside, Crawford, Pop. 327
Ar-We-Va Community SD   400/PK-12
  PO Box 108 51467   712-663-4311
  Leonard Griffith, supt.   Fax 663-4313
  www.ar-we-va.k12.ia.us
Westside JSHS   300/6-12
  108 Clinton St 51467   712-663-4312
  Kurt Brosamle, prin.   Fax 663-4313

West Union, Fayette, Pop. 2,492
North Fayette Community SD   900/PK-12
  PO Box 73 52175   563-422-3851
  Ron O'Kones, supt.   Fax 422-3854
  www.n-fayette.k12.ia.us/
North Fayette HS   300/9-12
  PO Box 73 52175   563-422-3852
  Wayne O'Brien, prin.   Fax 422-3854
North Fayette MS   200/6-8
  PO Box 73 52175   563-422-3853
  Kenneth Haught, prin.   Fax 422-3854

Wheatland, Clinton, Pop. 770
Calamus Wheatland Community SD   500/K-12
  PO Box 279 52777   563-374-1292
  Charles Freese, supt.   Fax 374-1080
  www.cal-wheat.k12.ia.us
Calamus/Wheatland JSHS   300/7-12
  PO Box 279 52777   563-374-1292
  Charles Freese, prin.   Fax 374-1080

Whiting, Monona, Pop. 786
Whiting Community SD   200/K-12
  PO Box 295 51063   712-455-2468
  Myron Ballain, supt.   Fax 455-2601
  www.whiting.k12.ia.us/
Whiting JSHS   100/6-12
  PO Box 295 51063   712-455-2468
  William McKelvey, prin.   Fax 455-2601

Williamsburg, Iowa, Pop. 2,710
Williamsburg Community SD   1,100/K-12
  PO Box 120 52361   319-668-1059
  Randy Freeman, supt.   Fax 668-9311
  www.williamsburg.k12.ia.us
Williamsburg JSHS   600/7-12
  PO Box 120 52361   319-668-1050
  Steven Johns, prin.   Fax 668-9311

Wilton, Muscatine, Pop. 2,837
Wilton Community SD   1,000/PK-12
  1002 Cypress St 52778   563-732-2035
  Joe Burnett, supt.   Fax 732-4121
  www.wilton.k12.ia.us
Wilton JSHS   500/7-12
  1002 Cypress St 52778   563-732-2629
  Ken Crawford, prin.   Fax 732-4121

Winfield, Henry, Pop. 1,101
Winfield-Mt. Union Community SD   400/K-12
  PO Box E 52659   319-257-7700
  M. Lynn Ubben, supt.   Fax 257-7714
  www.wmu.k12.ia.us/
Winfield-Mt. Union JSHS   200/7-12
  PO Box E 52659   319-257-7701
  Frederick Probasco, prin.   Fax 257-7703

Winterset, Madison, Pop. 4,738
Winterset Community SD   1,600/PK-12
  PO Box 30 50273   515-462-2718
  Doyle F. Scott Ph.D., supt.   Fax 462-2732
  www.winterset.k12.ia.us
Winterset HS   500/9-12
  624 Husky Dr 50273   515-462-3320
  Greg Criswell, prin.   Fax 462-2178
Winterset JHS   200/7-8
  720 Husky Dr 50273   515-462-3336
  Molly Clark, prin.   Fax 462-2178

Winthrop, Buchanan, Pop. 771
East Buchanan Community SD   500/PK-12
  PO Box 40 50682   319-935-3767
  Dale Greimann, supt.   Fax 935-3749
  www.east-buc.k12.ia.us
East Buchanan HS   200/9-12
  PO Box 40 50682   319-935-3367
  Tom Mossman, prin.   Fax 935-3615
East Buchanan MS   100/6-8
  PO Box 40 50682   319-935-3367
  Tom Mossman, prin.   Fax 935-3615

Woden, Hancock, Pop. 234
Woden-Crystal Lake Community SD   200/K-12
  PO Box 135 50484   641-926-5311
  Susan Lewerke, supt.   Fax 926-5314
  Other Schools – See Crystal Lake

Woodbine, Harrison, Pop. 1,620
Woodbine Community SD   500/PK-12
  501 Weare St 51579   712-647-2411
  Terry Hazard, supt.   Fax 647-2526
Woodbine HS   300/7-12
  501 Weare St 51579   712-647-2227
  Mark Glackin, prin.   Fax 647-2279

Woodward, Dallas, Pop. 1,198
Woodward-Granger Community SD   700/K-12
  306 W 3rd St 50276   515-438-4333
  Jody Gray, supt.   Fax 438-4329
  www.woodward-granger.k12.ia.us
Woodward-Granger HS   200/9-12
  306 W 3rd St 50276   515-438-2115
  Delane Galvin, prin.   Fax 438-4329
Woodward-Granger MS   100/6-8
  306 W 3rd St 50276   515-438-4653
  Delane Galvin, prin.   Fax 438-4329

Wyoming, Jones, Pop. 579
Midland Community SD   600/PK-12
  PO Box 109 52362   563-488-2292
  Al Homandberg, supt.   Fax 488-2253
  www.midland.k12.ia.us
Midland Community HS   200/9-12
  PO Box 109 52362   563-488-2292
  Patti Pace-Tracy, prin.   Fax 488-2253
  Other Schools – See Lost Nation

Zearing, Story, Pop. 580
Colo-Nesco Comm SD
  Supt. — See Mc Callsburg
Colo-Nesco MS   200/5-8
  407 S Center St 50278   641-487-7411
  Andrew Ward, prin.   Fax 487-7414

KANSAS

KANSAS DEPARTMENT OF EDUCATION
120 SE 10th Ave, Topeka 66612-1182
Telephone 785-296-3201
Fax 785-296-7933
Website http://www.ksbe.state.ks.us

Commissioner of Education   Dale Dennis

KANSAS BOARD OF EDUCATION
120 SE 10th Ave, Topeka 66612-1103

PUBLIC, PRIVATE AND CATHOLIC SECONDARY SCHOOLS

Abilene, Dickinson, Pop. 6,456
Abilene USD 435 — 1,500/PK-12
PO Box 639 67410 — 785-263-2630
Dr. Marlin Berry, supt. — Fax 263-7610
www.usd435.k12.ks.us
Abilene HS — 500/9-12
1300 N Cedar St 67410 — 785-263-1260
Dr. Michael Ford, prin. — Fax 263-3327
Abilene MS — 400/6-8
500 NW 14th St 67410 — 785-263-1471
Ron Wilson, prin. — Fax 263-4443

Agra, Phillips, Pop. 290
Eastern Heights USD 324 — 200/K-12
PO Box 209 67621 — 785-638-2255
Randy Lake, supt. — Fax 638-2254
www.usd324.org
Eastern Heights JSHS — 100/6-12
PO Box 209 67621 — 785-638-2244
Troy Stark, prin. — Fax 638-2254

Albert, Barton, Pop. 179
Otis-Bison USD 403 — 200/K-12
RR 1 Box 76A 67511 — 620-923-4661
Jake Befort, supt. — Fax 923-4224
Other Schools – See Bison, Otis

Allen, Lyon, Pop. 213
North Lyon County USD 251
Supt. — See Americus
Northern Heights HS — 200/9-12
1208 Road 345 66833 — 620-528-3521
Doug Boline, prin. — Fax 528-3392

Alma, Wabaunsee, Pop. 760
Mill Creek Valley USD 329 — 400/PK-12
PO Box 157 66401 — 785-765-3394
Larry Jackson, supt. — Fax 765-3624
www.usd329.com/
Wabaunsee HS — 200/9-12
PO Box 218 66401 — 785-765-3315
Dr. Larry Andersen, prin. — Fax 765-3523
Other Schools – See Paxico

Almena, Norton, Pop. 460
Northern Valley USD 212 — 200/PK-12
PO Box 217 67622 — 785-669-2445
Roger Lowry, supt. — Fax 669-2263
www.ruraltel.net/nvalley
Northern Valley HS — 100/9-12
PO Box 217 67622 — 785-669-2445
Roger Lowry, prin. — Fax 669-2263
Other Schools – See Long Island

Altamont, Labette, Pop. 1,068
Labette County USD 506 — 1,700/K-12
PO Box 188 67330 — 620-784-5326
Dennis Wilson, supt. — Fax 784-5879
www.usd506.k12.ks.us
Labette County HS — 600/9-12
PO Box 407 67330 — 620-784-5321
Greg Cartwright, prin. — Fax 784-2682

Alta Vista, Wabaunsee, Pop. 422
Morris County USD 417
Supt. — See Council Grove
Prairie Heights MS — 100/5-8
801 Center St 66834 — 785-499-6313
Cynthia Schrader, prin. — Fax 499-5342

Altoona, Wilson, Pop. 483
Altoona-Midway USD 387
Supt. — See Buffalo
Altoona-Midway MS — 100/6-8
PO Box 128 66710 — 620-568-5725
Orville Walker, prin. — Fax 568-5755

Americus, Lyon, Pop. 944
North Lyon County USD 251 — 600/PK-12
PO Box 527 66835 — 620-443-5116
Steven Mollach, supt. — Fax 443-5659
www.usd251.org/
Other Schools – See Allen

Andale, Sedgwick, Pop. 789
Renwick USD 267 — 2,000/PK-12
PO Box 68 67001 — 316-444-2165
Dr. Dan Peters, supt. — Fax 445-2241
www.usd267.com

Andale HS — 400/9-12
PO Box 28 67001 — 316-444-2607
Stan May, prin. — Fax 445-2501
Other Schools – See Garden Plain

Andover, Butler, Pop. 8,222
Andover USD 385 — 3,400/K-12
1432 N Andover Rd 67002 — 316-733-5017
Mark Evans, supt. — Fax 733-3604
www.usd385.org
Andover Central HS — 600/9-12
603 E Central Ave 67002 — 316-266-8800
Mark Templin, prin. — Fax 266-8840
Andover Central MS — 400/6-8
903 E Central Ave 67002 — 316-266-8845
Doug Baber, prin. — Fax 266-8878
Andover HS — 500/9-12
1744 N Andover Rd 67002 — 316-733-1335
Bob Baier, prin. — Fax 733-3681
Andover MS — 400/6-8
1628 N Andover Rd 67002 — 316-733-5061
Brett White, prin. — Fax 733-3666

Anthony, Harper, Pop. 2,308
Anthony-Harper USD 361 — 1,000/PK-12
PO Box 486 67003 — 620-842-5183
Keith Custer, supt. — Fax 842-5307
www.usd361.k12.ks.us
Chaparral HS — 400/9-12
467 N State Road 14 67003 — 620-842-5155
Al Petz, prin. — Fax 896-2927

Argonia, Sumner, Pop. 509
Argonia USD 359 — 200/PK-12
504 N Pine St 67004 — 620-435-6311
Dr. Julie Dolley, supt. — Fax 435-6623
www.usd359.k12.ks.us/
Argonia JSHS — 100/7-12
504 N Pine St 67004 — 620-435-6611
Jon Mages, prin. — Fax 435-6623

Arkansas City, Cowley, Pop. 11,788
Arkansas City USD 470 — 2,800/PK-12
PO Box 1028 67005 — 620-441-2000
Ron Ballard, supt. — Fax 441-2009
www.arkcity.com
Arkansas City HS — 900/9-12
1200 W Radio Ln 67005 — 620-441-2010
Marci Shearon, prin. — Fax 441-2021
Arkansas City MS — 700/6-8
400 E Kansas Ave 67005 — 620-441-2030
Dr. David Zumwalt, prin. — Fax 441-2036

Ark City Christian Academy — 100/PK-12
PO Box 1181 67005 — 620-442-0022
R. Devin Graves, admin. — Fax 442-0022
Cowley County Community College — Post-Sec.
PO Box 1147 67005 — 620-442-0430

Arma, Crawford, Pop. 1,508
Northeast USD 246 — 600/K-12
PO Box 669 66712 — 620-347-4116
Randl Rivers, supt. — Fax 347-4087
www.usd246.net
Northeast HS — 200/9-12
PO Box 669 66712 — 620-347-4115
Alan Roberts, prin. — Fax 347-4149

Ashland, Clark, Pop. 951
Ashland USD 220 — 200/PK-12
PO Box 187 67831 — 620-635-2220
Jerry Cullen, supt. — Fax 635-2637
www.ashland.k12.ks.us
Ashland HS — 100/9-12
PO Box 187 67831 — 620-635-2814
Bill Day, prin. — Fax 635-2637
Ashland Upper MS — 50/7-8
PO Box 187 67831 — 620-635-2814
Bill Day, prin. — Fax 635-2637

Atchison, Atchison, Pop. 10,111
Atchison USD 409 — 1,600/PK-12
215 N 8th St 66002 — 913-367-4384
Stephen Pummel, supt. — Fax 367-2246
www.usd409.net/

Atchison HS — 500/9-12
1500 Riley St 66002 — 913-367-4162
Forrest Covey, prin. — Fax 367-0415
Atchison MS — 400/6-8
301 N 5th St 66002 — 913-367-5363
James Krone, prin. — Fax 367-1302

Benedictine College — Post-Sec.
1020 N 2nd St 66002 — 913-367-5340
Maur Hill - Mount Academy — 300/9-12
1000 Green St 66002 — 913-367-5482
Sr. Bridget Dickason, prin. — Fax 367-5096
Northeast Kansas Technical College — Post-Sec.
1501 Riley St 66002 — 913-367-6204

Attica, Harper, Pop. 609
Attica USD 511 — 100/K-12
PO Box 415 67009 — 620-254-7661
Troy Piper, supt. — Fax 254-7872
www.attica.net
Attica JSHS — 100/7-12
PO Box 415 67009 — 620-254-7915
Troy Piper, prin. — Fax 254-7872

Atwood, Rawlins, Pop. 1,218
Rawlins County USD 105 — 300/PK-12
205 N 4th St Ste 1 67730 — 785-626-3236
Mark Wolters, supt. — Fax 626-3083
www.usd105.org
Rawlins County JSHS — 200/7-12
100 N 8th St 67730 — 785-626-3289
Kurt Dillon, prin. — Fax 626-1022

Augusta, Butler, Pop. 8,486
Augusta USD 402 — 2,100/PK-12
2345 Greyhound Dr 67010 — 316-775-5484
Jim Lentz, supt. — Fax 775-5035
www.usd402.com
Augusta HS — 700/9-12
2020 Ohio St 67010 — 316-775-5461
Paul Larkin, prin. — Fax 775-3484
Augusta MS — 500/6-8
1001 State St 67010 — 316-775-6383
Eileen Dreiling, prin. — Fax 775-3853

Axtell, Marshall, Pop. 433
Axtell USD 488 — 300/K-12
PO Box N 66403 — 785-736-2304
Larry Geil, supt. — Fax 736-2864
Axtell JSHS — 100/7-12
504 Pine St 66403 — 785-736-2237
Patrick Graham, prin. — Fax 736-2295
Other Schools – See Bern

Baileyville, Nemaha
B & B USD 451 — 200/K-12
PO Box 69 66404 — 785-336-2326
Jerry Turner, supt. — Fax 336-2326
bbh.usd451.k12.ks.us/
Baileyville-St. Benedict JSHS — 100/7-12
PO Box 69 66404 — 785-336-6631
John Vincent, prin. — Fax 336-2835

Baldwin City, Douglas, Pop. 3,637
Baldwin City USD 348 — 1,300/PK-12
PO Box 67 66006 — 785-594-2721
Paul Dorathy, supt. — Fax 594-3408
www.usd348.com/
Baldwin HS — 400/9-12
PO Box 67 66006 — 785-594-2725
Shaun Moseman, prin. — Fax 594-2858
Baldwin JHS — 300/6-8
PO Box 67 66006 — 785-594-2448
Connie Wright, prin. — Fax 594-2449

Baker University — Post-Sec.
PO Box 65 66006 — 785-594-6451

Barnes, Washington, Pop. 144
Barnes USD 223 — 500/PK-12
PO Box 188 66933 — 785-763-4231
Steve Joonas, supt. — Fax 763-4461
www.usd223.org
Other Schools – See Hanover, Linn

Basehor, Leavenworth, Pop. 2,715
Basehor-Linwood USD 458 1,900/PK-12
　PO Box 282　66007 913-724-1396
　Dr. Robert Albers, supt. Fax 724-2709
　www.usd458.org
Basehor-Linwood HS 700/9-12
　PO Box 255　66007 913-724-2266
　Steve Blankenship, prin. Fax 724-2040
Other Schools – See Linwood

Baxter Springs, Cherokee, Pop. 4,344
Baxter Springs USD 508 800/PK-12
　1520 Cleveland Ave　66713 620-856-2375
　Dennis Burke, supt. Fax 856-3943
　www.usd508.org
Baxter Springs HS 300/9-12
　100 N Military Ave　66713 620-856-3366
　Jamie Carlisle, prin. Fax 856-2918
Baxter Springs MS 200/6-8
　1520 Cleveland Ave　66713 620-856-3355
　Mike Cook, prin. Fax 856-3943

Belle Plaine, Sumner, Pop. 1,654
Belle Plaine USD 357 800/PK-12
　PO Box 760　67013 620-488-2288
　Lonn Poage, supt. Fax 488-3517
　www.usd357.k12.ks.us
Belle Plaine HS 300/9-12
　PO Box 8　67013 620-488-2421
　Monte Stewart, prin. Fax 488-3536
Belle Plaine MS 200/6-8
　PO Box 457　67013 620-488-2222
　Mike Couch, prin. Fax 488-3391

Belleville, Republic, Pop. 2,034
Republic County USD 427 500/K-12
　PO Box 469　66935 785-527-5621
　Larry Lysell, supt. Fax 527-5375
Belleville HS 200/9-12
　PO Box 469　66935 785-527-2281
　Daryl Moore, prin. Fax 527-5505
Belleville MS 200/5-8
　PO Box 469　66935 785-527-5669
　Mabel Woodman, prin. Fax 527-5375

Beloit, Mitchell, Pop. 3,869
Beloit USD 273 800/PK-12
　PO Box 547　67420 785-738-3261
　Dr. Joe Harrison, supt. Fax 738-4103
　www.usd273.k12.ks.us/
Beloit JSHS 400/7-12
　PO Box 606　67420 785-738-3593
　Dr. Kelly Arnberger, prin. Fax 738-5566

North Central Kansas Technical College Post-Sec.
　PO Box 507　67420 785-738-2276
St. Johns HS 100/7-12
　209 S Cherry St　67420 785-738-2942
　Martin Hesting, prin. Fax 738-4462

Bennington, Ottawa, Pop. 622
Twin Valley USD 240 600/PK-12
　PO Box 38　67422 785-488-3325
　Richard Harlan, supt. Fax 488-3326
　www.usd240.org
Bennington HS 200/9-12
　PO Box 8　67422 785-488-3321
　Jay Macy, prin. Fax 488-2939
Other Schools – See Tescott

Benton, Butler, Pop. 816
Circle USD 375
　Supt. — See Towanda
Circle MS 300/7-8
　14697 SW 20th St　67017 316-778-1470
　Nita McLean, prin. Fax 778-1749

Bern, Nemaha, Pop. 201
Axtell USD 488
　Supt. — See Axtell
Bern JSHS 100/7-12
　PO Box 144　66408 785-336-3031
　Jim Struber, prin. Fax 336-2507

Bird City, Cheyenne, Pop. 444
Cheylin USD 103 200/K-12
　PO Box 28　67731 785-734-2341
　David Zumbahlen, supt. Fax 734-2489
Cheylin West JSHS 100/7-12
　PO Box 28　67731 785-734-2341
　David Zumbahlen, prin. Fax 734-2489

Bison, Rush, Pop. 221
Otis-Bison USD 403
　Supt. — See Albert
Otis-Bison MS 100/6-8
　PO Box 297　67520 785-356-2611
　Jake Befort, prin. Fax 356-2239

Blue Rapids, Marshall, Pop. 1,061
Valley Heights USD 498
　Supt. — See Waterville
Valley Heights JSHS 200/7-12
　2274 6th Rd　66411 785-363-2508
　Don Potter, prin. Fax 363-2072

Bonner Springs, Wyandotte, Pop. 6,782
Bonner Springs USD 204 2,200/PK-12
　PO Box 435　66012 913-422-5600
　Dr. Robert Van Maren, supt. Fax 422-4193
　www.usd204.k12.ks.us
Bonner Springs HS 700/9-12
　PO Box 216　66012 913-422-5121
　Dr. Jerry Abbott, prin. Fax 422-7284
Clark MS 600/6-8
　PO Box 336　66012 913-422-5115
　Joe DiPonio, prin. Fax 422-1644

Brewster, Thomas, Pop. 274
Brewster USD 314 200/PK-12
　PO Box 220　67732 785-694-2236
　Sherri L. Edmundson, supt. Fax 694-2746
　www.usd314.k12.ks.us
Brewster HS 100/7-12
　PO Box 220　67732 785-694-2236
　Sherri L. Edmundson, prin. Fax 694-2746

Brookville, Saline, Pop. 253
Ell-Saline USD 307 400/K-12
　412 E Anderson Ave　67425 785-225-6813
　Jerry Minneman, supt. Fax 225-6815
　www.ellsaline.org
Ell-Saline HS 100/9-12
　414 E Anderson　67425 785-225-6633
　Steve Williams, prin. Fax 225-6694
Ell-Saline MS 100/7-8
　414 E Anderson　67425 785-225-6633
　Steve Williams, prin. Fax 225-6694

Bucklin, Ford, Pop. 719
Bucklin USD 459 300/K-12
　PO Box 8　67834 620-826-3828
　Terry Marshall, supt. Fax 826-3377
　www.usd459.k12.ks.us/
Bucklin HS 100/9-12
　PO Box 8　67834 620-826-3241
　Darrel Kohlman, prin. Fax 826-9966

Buffalo, Wilson, Pop. 278
Altoona-Midway USD 387 200/K-12
　RR 1 Box 45A　66717 620-537-7721
　Bill Orth, supt. Fax 537-8711
　www.altoonamidway.org/
Altoona-Midway HS 100/9-12
　RR 1 Box 45　66717 620-537-7711
　Doug Reed, prin. Fax 537-2641
Other Schools – See Altoona

Buhler, Reno, Pop. 1,336
Buhler USD 313 2,200/PK-12
　PO Box 320　67522 620-543-2258
　David Brax, supt. Fax 543-2510
　www.buhlerschools.org
Buhler HS 700/9-12
　PO Box 350　67522 620-543-2255
　Mike Berblinger, prin. Fax 543-2853
Other Schools – See Hutchinson

Burden, Cowley, Pop. 557
Central USD 462 300/PK-12
　PO Box 128　67019 620-438-2218
　Marian Hedges, supt. Fax 438-2217
　www.usd462.org
Central JSHS 200/7-12
　PO Box 128　67019 620-438-2215
　Dale Adams, prin. Fax 438-2217

Burlingame, Osage, Pop. 997
Burlingame USD 454 400/PK-12
　100 Bloomquist Dr Ste A　66413 785-654-3328
　Don Blome, supt. Fax 654-3570
　www.usd454.net
Burlingame JSHS 200/7-12
　100 Bloomquist Dr Ste A　66413 785-654-3315
　Tammy Baird, prin. Fax 654-3191

Burlington, Coffey, Pop. 2,764
Burlington USD 244 900/PK-12
　200 S 6th St　66839 620-364-8478
　Dr. Dale Rawson, supt. Fax 364-8548
　www.usd244ks.org
Burlington HS 300/9-12
　830 Cross St　66839 620-364-8672
　Jim Kuhn, prin. Fax 364-8680
Burlington MS 200/6-8
　720 Cross St　66839 620-364-2156
　Tim Martin, prin. Fax 364-8560

Burr Oak, Jewell, Pop. 234
White Rock USD 104
　Supt. — See Esbon
White Rock HS 50/9-12
　PO Box 345　66936 785-647-6361
　William Walker, prin. Fax 647-5391

Burrton, Harvey, Pop. 921
Burrton USD 369 300/K-12
　PO Box 369　67020 620-463-3840
　Drew Harris, supt. Fax 463-2636
　www.burrton.k12.ks.us/
Burrton HS 100/6-12
　PO Box 369　67020 620-463-3820
　John Headrick, prin. Fax 463-2096

Victory Christian Academy 50/7-12
　201 S Victory Rd　67020 620-463-6112
　Bill Cowell, prin. Fax 463-2631

Bushton, Rice, Pop. 298
Lorraine USD 328
　Supt. — See Lorraine
Quivira Heights HS 100/9-12
　500 S Main St　67427 620-562-3597
　Lynn Gales, prin. Fax 562-3248

Caldwell, Sumner, Pop. 1,224
Caldwell USD 360 300/PK-12
　22 N Webb St　67022 620-845-2585
　Jim Reece, supt. Fax 845-2610
　www.usd360.com
Caldwell Secondary S 100/6-12
　21 N Osage St　67022 620-845-2585
　Alan Jamison, prin. Fax 845-2534

Caney, Montgomery, Pop. 2,004
Caney Valley USD 436 900/PK-12
　700 Bullpup Blvd　67333 620-879-9200
　Danny Fulton, supt. Fax 879-9209
　www.caney.com

Caney Valley JSHS 400/7-12
　RR 2 Box 67A　67333 620-879-9220
　Justin Lockwood, prin. Fax 879-9227

Canton, McPherson, Pop. 815
Canton-Galva USD 419 400/PK-12
　PO Box 317　67428 620-628-4901
　Bill Seidl, supt. Fax 628-4380
　www.canton-galva.k12.ks.us
Canton-Galva HS 100/9-12
　PO Box 275　67428 620-628-4401
　Eric Steele, prin. Fax 628-4951
Other Schools – See Galva

Carbondale, Osage, Pop. 1,439
Santa Fe Trail USD 434 1,300/PK-12
　PO Box 310　66414 785-665-7168
　Terry Schmidt, supt. Fax 665-7164
　www.usd434.org
Santa Fe Trail HS 400/9-12
　15701 S California Rd　66414 785-665-7161
　Brian Kraus, prin. Fax 665-7193

Cawker City, Mitchell, Pop. 504
Waconda USD 272 400/K-12
　PO Box 326　67430 785-781-4328
　Jeff Teavis, supt. Fax 781-4318
　www.usd272.org
Lakeside JHS 100/7-8
　PO Box 46　67430 785-781-4911
　Robert Green, prin. Fax 781-4861
Other Schools – See Downs

Cedar Vale, Chautauqua, Pop. 689
Cedar Vale USD 285 200/PK-12
　PO Box 458　67024 620-758-2265
　Dr. Ron Ledford, supt. Fax 758-2647
　www.cvs285.net
Cedar Vale JSHS 100/6-12
　PO Box 458　67024 620-758-2791
　Dennis Myers, prin. Fax 758-2704

Centralia, Nemaha, Pop. 512
Vermillion USD 380
　Supt. — See Vermillion
Centralia JSHS 100/7-12
　PO Box 367　66415 785-857-3324
　John Whetzal, prin. Fax 857-3847

Chanute, Neosho, Pop. 9,053
Chanute USD 413 1,700/K-12
　208 N Lincoln Ave　66720 620-432-2500
　Stephen Parsons, supt. Fax 431-6810
　www.usd413.k12.ks.us
Chanute HS 600/9-12
　400 S Highland Ave　66720 620-432-2510
　Kent Wire, prin. Fax 431-3020
Royster MS 500/6-8
　400 W Main St　66720 620-432-2520
　Brad Miner, prin. Fax 431-7841

Neosho County Community College Post-Sec.
　800 W 14th St　66720 620-431-2820

Chapman, Dickinson, Pop. 1,252
Chapman USD 473 1,000/K-12
　PO Box 249　67431 785-922-6521
　Tony Frieze, supt. Fax 922-6446
　usd473.net
Chapman HS 400/9-12
　PO Box 249　67431 785-922-6561
　Richard Hall, prin. Fax 922-7162
Chapman MS 200/6-8
　PO Box 249　67431 785-922-6555
　Bruce Hurford, prin. Fax 922-6601

Chase, Rice, Pop. 472
Chase-Raymond USD 401 200/K-12
　PO Box 366　67524 620-938-2913
　David Howard, supt. Fax 938-2622
　www.usd401.com/
Chase HS 100/9-12
　PO Box 366　67524 620-938-2923
　David Howard, prin. Fax 938-2456
Raymond JHS 50/7-8
　PO Box 366　67524 620-938-2923
　David Howard, prin. Fax 938-2456

Cheney, Sedgwick, Pop. 1,843
Cheney USD 268 800/K-12
　100 W 6th Ave　67025 316-542-3512
　Brad Neuenswander, supt. Fax 542-0326
　www.cheney268.com
Cheney HS 200/9-12
　100 W 6th Ave　67025 316-542-3113
　Ronald Traxson, prin. Fax 542-3789
Cheney MS 200/6-8
　100 W 6th Ave　67025 316-542-0060
　Amy Wallace, prin. Fax 542-3789

Cherokee, Crawford, Pop. 723
Cherokee USD 247 800/K-12
　PO Box 270　66724 620-457-8350
　Tim Burns, supt. Fax 457-8428
Southeast HS 300/9-12
　PO Box 277　66724 620-457-8365
　Greg Gorman, prin. Fax 457-8389

Cherryvale, Montgomery, Pop. 2,292
Cherryvale USD 447 600/PK-12
　618 E 4th St　67335 620-336-8130
　Randy Wagoner, supt. Fax 336-8133
　www.usd447.org
Cherryvale JSHS 300/7-12
　700 S Carson St　67335 620-336-8100
　George Owens, prin. Fax 336-8110

Chetopa, Labette, Pop. 1,238
Chetopa - St. Paul USD 505 — 500/PK-12
  430 Elm St 67336 — 620-236-7244
  Kim Juenemann, supt. — Fax 236-4271
  www.chetopaschools.org/
Chetopa JSHS — 100/7-12
  430 Elm St 67336 — 620-236-7244
  Kelly Nading, prin. — Fax 236-4271
Other Schools – See Saint Paul

Cimarron, Gray, Pop. 2,036
Cimarron-Ensign USD 102 — 700/K-12
  PO Box 489 67835 — 620-855-7743
  Marc Woofter, supt. — Fax 855-7745
  www.cimarronschools.net
Cimarron JSHS — 300/7-12
  PO Box 489 67835 — 620-855-3323
  Rudy Perez, prin. — Fax 855-3219

Claflin, Barton, Pop. 682
Claflin USD 354 — 300/K-12
  PO Box 346 67525 — 620-587-3878
  Darrell Genereux, supt. — Fax 587-2389
  www.claflin.com
Claflin JSHS — 100/7-12
  PO Box 348 67525 — 620-587-3801
  Danielle Poland, prin. — Fax 587-3677

Clay Center, Clay, Pop. 4,405
Clay Center USD 379 — 1,300/K-12
  PO Box 97 67432 — 785-632-3176
  Michael Folks, supt. — Fax 632-5020
  www.usd379.org/
Clay Center Community HS — 400/9-12
  1630 9th St 67432 — 785-632-2131
  Steve Taylor, prin. — Fax 632-2076
Clay Center Community MS — 300/6-8
  935 Prospect St 67432 — 785-632-3129
  Kristen Ryan, prin. — Fax 632-6013
Other Schools – See Wakefield

Clearwater, Sedgwick, Pop. 2,202
Clearwater USD 264 — 900/PK-12
  PO Box 248 67026 — 620-584-2091
  Kay Highbarger, supt. — Fax 584-6705
  www.usd264.com
Clearwater HS — 400/9-12
  1201 E Ross St 67026 — 620-584-2361
  Steve Meeker, prin. — Fax 584-2083
Clearwater MS — 200/7-8
  140 S 4th St 67026 — 620-584-2036
  Keith Pauly, prin. — Fax 584-2199

Clifton, Washington, Pop. 520
Clifton-Clyde USD 224 — 300/PK-12
  PO Box A 66937 — 785-455-3313
  David Roberts, supt. — Fax 455-3314
Clifton-Clyde MS — 100/4-8
  120 Cloud St 66937 — 785-455-3323
  David Roberts, prin. — Fax 455-3524
Other Schools – See Clyde

Clyde, Cloud, Pop. 721
Clifton-Clyde USD 224
  Supt. — See Clifton
Clifton-Clyde HS — 100/9-12
  616 N High St 66938 — 785-446-3444
  Brenda Scofield, prin. — Fax 446-3458

Coffeyville, Montgomery, Pop. 10,472
Coffeyville USD 445 — 1,400/PK-12
  615 Ellis St 67337 — 620-252-6400
  Robert Morten, supt. — Fax 252-6807
  cvilleschools.com
Field Kindley Memorial HS — 700/9-12
  1110 W 8th St 67337 — 620-252-6410
  Jim Owen, prin. — Fax 252-6818
Roosevelt MS — 300/7-8
  1000 W 8th St 67337 — 620-252-6420
  Alice Morris, prin. — Fax 252-6844

Coffeyville Community College — Post-Sec.
  400 W 11th St 67337 — 620-251-7700

Colby, Thomas, Pop. 5,244
Colby USD 315 — 1,100/K-12
  600 W 3rd St 67701 — 785-460-5000
  Kirk Nielsen, supt. — Fax 460-5050
  www.colbyeagles.org/
Colby HS — 400/9-12
  1890 S Franklin Ave 67701 — 785-460-5300
  Rocky Robbins, prin. — Fax 460-5350
Colby MS — 300/6-8
  750 W 3rd St 67701 — 785-460-5200
  Robb Ross, prin. — Fax 460-5250

Colby Community College — Post-Sec.
  1255 S Range Ave 67701 — 785-462-4690
Heartland Christian S — 100/PK-12
  1995 W 4th St 67701 — 785-460-6419
  Richard Roberts, admin. — Fax 460-8337

Coldwater, Comanche, Pop. 771
Comanche County USD 300 — 300/K-12
  PO Box 721 67029 — 620-582-2181
  Michael Baldwin, supt. — Fax 582-2540
South Central HS — 100/9-12
  PO Box 578 67029 — 620-582-2158
  Michael Baldwin, prin. — Fax 582-2535
Other Schools – See Protection

Colony, Anderson, Pop. 395
Crest USD 479
  Supt. — See Kincaid
Crest HS — 100/9-12
  PO Box 325 66015 — 620-852-3521
  Doug Spillman, prin. — Fax 852-3357

Columbus, Cherokee, Pop. 3,286
Columbus USD 493 — 1,100/PK-12
  802 S Highschool Ave 66725 — 620-429-3661
  Ken Jones, supt. — Fax 429-2673
  www.usd493.com
Central S — 400/4-8
  810 S Highschool Ave 66725 — 620-429-3943
  Bobbi Williams, prin. — Fax 429-2882
Columbus HS — 400/9-12
  124 S Highschool Ave 66725 — 620-429-3821
  Steve Jameson, prin. — Fax 429-3657

Concordia, Cloud, Pop. 5,459
Concordia USD 333 — 1,000/K-12
  217 W 7th St 66901 — 785-243-3518
  Beverly Mortimer, supt. — Fax 243-8883
  www.usd333.com
Concordia JSHS — 600/7-12
  436 W 10th St 66901 — 785-243-2452
  Cheryl Hochhalter, prin. — Fax 243-8805

Cloud County Community College — Post-Sec.
  PO Box 1002 66901 — 785-243-1435

Conway Springs, Sumner, Pop. 1,277
Conway Springs USD 356 — 700/K-12
  110 N Monnet 67031 — 620-456-2961
  Clay Murphy, supt. — Fax 456-3173
  www.usd356.org
Conway Springs HS — 200/9-12
  607 W Saint Louis St 67031 — 620-456-2963
  Brent Davis, prin. — Fax 456-3314
Conway Springs MS — 200/6-8
  112 N Cranmer St 67031 — 620-456-2965
  Vance Williams, prin. — Fax 456-3313

Copeland, Gray, Pop. 339
Copeland USD 476 — 100/PK-8
  PO Box 156 67837 — 620-668-5565
  Donald Grover, supt. — Fax 668-5568
South Gray JHS — 100/6-8
  PO Box 156 67837 — 620-668-5565
  Dick Bixler, prin. — Fax 668-5568

Cottonwood Falls, Chase, Pop. 977
Chase County USD 284 — 500/K-12
  PO Box 569 66845 — 620-273-6303
  Rick Weiss, supt. — Fax 273-6717
  www.usd284.org/
Chase County HS — 200/9-12
  PO Box 400 66845 — 620-273-6354
  Stanley Elliott, prin. — Fax 273-8337
Other Schools – See Strong City

Council Grove, Morris, Pop. 2,275
Morris County USD 417 — 900/PK-12
  17 Wood St 66846 — 620-767-5192
  Diane Miller, supt. — Fax 767-5444
  www.cgrove417.org/
Council Grove HS — 300/9-12
  129 Hockaday St 66846 — 620-767-5149
  Kelly McDiffett, prin. — Fax 767-7280
Other Schools – See Alta Vista

Courtland, Republic, Pop. 302
Pike Valley USD 426
  Supt. — See Scandia
Pike Valley JHS — 100/6-8
  PO Box 320 66939 — 785-374-4221
  Chris Vignery, prin. — Fax 374-4268

Cuba, Republic, Pop. 211
Hillcrest Rural USD 455 — 100/PK-12
  PO Box 167 66940 — 785-729-3816
  Dr. Don Wells, supt. — Fax 729-3352
Hillcrest HS — 50/9-12
  PO Box 167 66940 — 785-729-3333
  Roger Antle, prin. — Fax 729-3692

Cunningham, Kingman, Pop. 490
Cunningham USD 332 — 300/K-12
  PO Box 67 67035 — 620-298-3271
  Melvin Ormiston, supt. — Fax 298-2562
Cunningham HS — 100/9-12
  PO Box 98 67035 — 620-298-2473
  Steve Miller, prin. — Fax 298-5005

Damar, Rooks, Pop. 150
Palco USD 269
  Supt. — See Palco
Damar JHS — 50/6-8
  PO Box 38 67632 — 785-839-4265
  Lisa Gehring, prin. — Fax 839-4278

Deerfield, Kearny, Pop. 900
Deerfield USD 216 — 300/PK-12
  PO Box 274 67838 — 620-426-8516
  Mike Roth, supt. — Fax 426-7890
  www.usd216.org/
Deerfield HS — 100/9-12
  PO Box 274 67838 — 620-426-8401
  Scott Kedrowski, prin. — Fax 426-6903
Deerfield MS — 100/6-8
  PO Box 274 67838 — 620-426-8401
  John Ansley, prin. — Fax 426-6903

Denton, Doniphan, Pop. 185
Midway USD 433 — 100/K-8
  642 Highway 20 E 66017 — 785-359-6526
  Steve Adams, supt. — Fax 359-6522
  www.doniphanwest.org
Doniphan West MS — 100/6-8
  642 Highway 20 E 66017 — 785-359-6526
  Deanna Scherer, prin. — Fax 359-6522

Derby, Sedgwick, Pop. 19,200
Derby USD 260 — 6,500/PK-12
  120 E Washington St 67037 — 316-788-8400
  Craig Wilford, supt. — Fax 788-8449
  www.derbyschools.com

Derby HS — 2,200/9-12
  920 N Rock Rd 67037 — 316-788-8500
  Dr. Kristin Sherwood, prin. — Fax 788-8593
Derby MS — 1,100/7-8
  801 E Madison Ave 67037 — 316-788-8580
  Rod Coykendall, prin. — Fax 788-8062

De Soto, Johnson, Pop. 4,858
De Soto USD 232 — 4,400/PK-12
  35200 W 91st St 66018 — 913-583-8300
  Sharon Zoellner, supt. — Fax 583-8303
  www.usd232.org
De Soto HS — 400/9-12
  35000 W 91st St 66018 — 913-583-8370
  Dave Marford, prin. — Fax 583-8376
Lexington Trails MS — 400/6-8
  8800 Penner Ave 66018 — 913-583-8360
  Mark Schmidt, prin. — Fax 583-8366
Other Schools – See Shawnee

Dexter, Cowley, Pop. 353
Dexter USD 471 — 200/PK-12
  PO Box 97 67038 — 620-876-5415
  Jerry Golden, supt. — Fax 876-5548
  www.usd471.org
Dexter JSHS — 100/7-12
  PO Box 97 67038 — 620-876-5415
  Robert Holmes, prin. — Fax 876-5548

Dighton, Lane, Pop. 1,138
Dighton USD 482 — 300/PK-12
  PO Box 878 67839 — 620-397-2835
  Angela Lawrence, supt. — Fax 397-5932
  www.usd482.k12.ks.us/
Dighton JSHS — 100/7-12
  PO Box 939 67839 — 620-397-5333
  John Levin, prin. — Fax 397-5338

Dodge City, Ford, Pop. 25,568
Dodge City USD 443 — 5,700/K-12
  PO Box 460 67801 — 620-227-1700
  Alan Cunningham, supt. — Fax 227-1695
  www.usd443.org
Dodge City HS — 1,600/9-12
  2201 W Ross Blvd 67801 — 620-227-1611
  Jacque Feist, prin. — Fax 227-1680
Dodge City MS — 800/7-8
  2000 6th Ave 67801 — 620-227-1610
  Carl Helm, prin. — Fax 227-1731

Dodge City Community College — Post-Sec.
  2501 N 14th Ave 67801 — 620-225-1321

Douglass, Butler, Pop. 1,797
Douglass USD 396 — 900/PK-12
  PO Box 158 67039 — 316-747-3300
  James Keller, supt. — Fax 747-3305
  www.usd396.net/
Douglass HS — 300/9-12
  PO Box 158 67039 — 316-747-3310
  Chad Higgins, prin. — Fax 747-3415
Sisk MS — 200/6-8
  PO Box 158 67039 — 316-747-3340
  Robert Swigart, prin. — Fax 747-3346

Downs, Osborne, Pop. 978
Waconda USD 272
  Supt. — See Cawker City
Lakeside HS — 200/9-12
  PO Box 247 67437 — 785-454-3332
  Jim Gierbrecht, prin. — Fax 454-3747

Easton, Leavenworth, Pop. 369
Easton USD 449 — 700/K-12
  32502 Easton Rd 66020 — 913-651-9740
  Dr. Roger Pickerign, supt. — Fax 651-6740
Pleasant Ridge HS — 200/9-12
  32500 Easton Rd 66020 — 913-651-5556
  Andy Metsker, prin. — Fax 651-7797
Pleasant Ridge MS — 200/6-8
  32504 Easton Rd 66020 — 913-651-5522
  Lisa Powers, prin. — Fax 651-0049

Effingham, Atchison, Pop. 585
Atchison County Community USD 377 — 700/PK-12
  PO Box 289 66023 — 913-833-5050
  Stephen Wiseman, supt. — Fax 833-5210
  www.usd377.org/
Atchison County Community HS — 300/9-12
  PO Box 289 66023 — 913-833-2240
  Mark Preut, prin. — Fax 833-2197
Atchison County Community MS — 200/5-8
  PO Box 289 66023 — 913-833-4420
  Tom Sack, prin. — Fax 833-4281

Elbing, Butler, Pop. 209

Berean Academy — 300/K-12
  PO Box 70 67041 — 316-799-2211
  Terry Tilson, supt. — Fax 799-2601

El Dorado, Butler, Pop. 12,686
El Dorado USD 490 — 2,300/PK-12
  124 W Central Ave 67042 — 316-322-4800
  Dr. Tom Biggs, supt. — Fax 322-4801
  www.eldoradoschools.org
El Dorado HS — 600/9-12
  401 Mccollum Rd 67042 — 316-322-4810
  Bret McClendon, prin. — Fax 322-4811
El Dorado MS — 500/6-8
  500 W Central Ave 67042 — 316-322-4820
  Stan Ruff, prin. — Fax 322-4821

Butler Community College — Post-Sec.
  901 S Haverhill Rd 67042 — 316-321-2222

Elkhart, Morton, Pop. 2,120
Elkhart USD 218 — 600/PK-12
   PO Box 999 67950 — 620-697-2195
   Scott Myers, supt. — Fax 697-2607
   www.usd218.org
Elkhart HS — 200/9-12
   PO Box 999 67950 — 620-697-2193
   Rex Richardson, prin. — Fax 697-4415
Elkhart MS — 100/5-8
   PO Box 999 67950 — 620-697-2197
   Rex Toomey, prin. — Fax 697-4828

Ellinwood, Barton, Pop. 2,082
Ellinwood USD 355 — 500/K-12
   300 N Schiller Ave 67526 — 620-564-3226
   Richard Goodschmidt, supt. — Fax 564-2206
   www.usd355.org/
Ellinwood HS — 200/9-12
   210 E 2nd St 67526 — 620-564-3136
   Brian Rowley, prin. — Fax 564-2816
Ellinwood MS — 100/7-8
   210 E 2nd St 67526 — 620-564-3136
   Brian Rowley, prin. — Fax 564-2816

Ellis, Ellis, Pop. 1,827
Ellis USD 388 — 400/K-12
   PO Box 256 67637 — 785-726-4281
   Bernie White, supt. — Fax 726-4677
   www.usd388.k12.ks.us
Ellis HS — 100/9-12
   PO Box 300 67637 — 785-726-3151
   Kyle Hayden, prin. — Fax 726-3169

Ellsworth, Ellsworth, Pop. 2,887
Ellsworth USD 327 — 600/K-12
   PO Box 306 67439 — 785-472-5561
   Doug Moeckel, supt. — Fax 472-5563
   www.usd327.org
Ellsworth HS — 200/9-12
   PO Box 46 67439 — 785-472-4471
   Dale Brungardt, prin. — Fax 472-8109
Other Schools – See Kanopolis

Elwood, Doniphan, Pop. 1,169
Elwood USD 486 — 300/PK-12
   PO Box 368 66024 — 913-365-6735
   Michael Newman, supt. — Fax 365-3503
   www.usd486.org/
Elwood HS — 100/9-12
   PO Box 368 66024 — 913-365-6735
   James Leatherman, prin. — Fax 365-0012

Emporia, Lyon, Pop. 26,666
Emporia USD 253 — 5,100/PK-12
   PO Box 1008 66801 — 620-341-2200
   John Heim, supt. — Fax 341-2205
   www.usd253.org
Emporia HS — 1,600/9-12
   3302 W 18th Ave 66801 — 620-341-2365
   Scott Sheldon, prin. — Fax 341-2376
Emporia MS — 700/7-8
   2300 Graphic Arts Rd 66801 — 620-341-2335
   Steve Ternes, prin. — Fax 341-2341

Emporia State University — Post-Sec.
   1200 Commercial St 66801 — 620-341-1200
Flint Hills Technical College — Post-Sec.
   3301 W 18th Ave 66801 — 620-341-2300

Enterprise, Dickinson, Pop. 823

Enterprise Adventist Academy — 50/9-12
   PO Box 215 67441 — 785-263-8211
    — Fax 263-8368

Erie, Neosho, Pop. 1,178
Erie USD 101 — 800/K-12
   PO Box 137 66733 — 620-244-3264
   Mike Carson, supt. — Fax 244-3664
   www.usd101.com/
Erie HS — 200/9-12
   410 W 3rd St 66733 — 620-244-3287
   Ted Hill, prin. — Fax 244-3290

Esbon, Jewell, Pop. 135
White Rock USD 104 — 100/K-12
   PO Box 19 66941 — 785-725-3222
   William Walker, supt. — Fax 725-3774
White Rock MS — 50/6-8
   PO Box 139 66941 — 785-725-3444
   William Walker, prin. — Fax 725-3774
Other Schools – See Burr Oak

Eskridge, Wabaunsee, Pop. 572
Mission Valley USD 330 — 400/K-12
   PO Box 158 66423 — 785-449-2282
   Chuck Schmidt, supt. — Fax 449-2669
   www.mv330.org
Mission Valley HS — 200/9-12
   12685 Mission Valley Rd 66423 — 785-449-2297
   Braden Anshutz, prin. — Fax 449-2309

Eudora, Douglas, Pop. 4,963
Eudora USD 491 — 1,200/PK-12
   PO Box 500 66025 — 785-542-4910
   Marty Kobza, supt. — Fax 542-4909
   www.eudoraschools.org/
Eudora HS — 400/9-12
   PO Box 712 66025 — 785-542-4980
   Dale Sample, prin. — Fax 542-4990
Eudora MS — 300/6-8
   PO Box 701 66025 — 785-542-4960
   Don Grosdidier, prin. — Fax 542-4970

Eureka, Greenwood, Pop. 2,816
Eureka USD 389 — 800/PK-12
   216 N Main St 67045 — 620-583-5588
   Randy Corn, supt. — Fax 583-8200
   www.389ks.org

Eureka JSHS — 300/7-12
   815 N Jefferson St 67045 — 620-583-7428
   Mike Argabright, prin. — Fax 583-8222

Everest, Brown, Pop. 309
South Brown County USD 430
   Supt. — See Horton
Everest MS — 200/5-8
   713 S 7th St 66424 — 785-548-7536
   Jackie Wenger, prin. — Fax 548-7538

Fort Leavenworth, Leavenworth, Pop. 1,300
Ft. Leavenworth USD 207 — 1,900/PK-9
   207 Education Way 66027 — 913-651-7373
   Deborah Baeuchle, supt. — Fax 758-6010
   www.ftlvn.com
Patton JHS — 400/7-9
   1 Patton Cir 66027 — 913-651-7371
   Dr. Martin Gill, prin. — Fax 758-6097

Fort Riley, Geary, Pop. 112
Geary County USD 475
   Supt. — See Junction City
Fort Riley MS — 600/6-8
   4020 1st Division Rd 66442 — 785-717-4500
   Joseph Handlos, prin. — Fax 717-4501

Fort Scott, Bourbon, Pop. 8,065
Ft. Scott USD 234 — 2,000/PK-12
   424 S Main St 66701 — 620-223-0800
   Dr. Rick Werling, supt. — Fax 223-2760
   www.usd234.org
Fort Scott HS — 600/9-12
   1005 S Main St 66701 — 620-223-0600
   Danny Brown, prin. — Fax 223-5368
Fort Scott MS — 500/6-8
   1105 E 12th St 66701 — 620-223-3262
   Barbara Albright, prin. — Fax 223-8946

Fort Scott Community College — Post-Sec.
   2108 Horton St 66701 — 620-223-2700

Fowler, Meade, Pop. 577
Fowler USD 225 — 200/PK-12
   PO Box 170 67844 — 620-646-5661
   Sam Seybold, supt. — Fax 646-5713
   www.usd225.org/
Fowler HS — 100/7-12
   PO Box 140 67844 — 620-646-5221
   Sam Seybold, prin. — Fax 646-5295

Frankfort, Marshall, Pop. 817
Vermillion USD 380
   Supt. — See Vermillion
Frankfort JSHS — 200/7-12
   PO Box 203 66427 — 785-292-4486
   Rhonda Trimble, prin. — Fax 292-4636

Fredonia, Wilson, Pop. 2,520
Fredonia USD 484 — 800/PK-12
   PO Box 539 66736 — 620-378-4177
   Jim Porter, supt. — Fax 378-4345
   www.fredoniaks.com
Fredonia HS — 300/9-12
   916 Robinson St 66736 — 620-378-4172
   Jim Lambert, prin. — Fax 378-4398
Fredonia MS — 200/6-8
   203 N 8th St 66736 — 620-378-4167
   Laura Fitzmorris, prin. — Fax 378-3635

Frontenac, Crawford, Pop. 3,103
Frontenac USD 249 — 700/PK-12
   208 S Cayuga St 66763 — 620-231-7551
   Gregory Hafner, supt. — Fax 231-2043
   www.frontenac249.k12.ks.us
Frontenac JSHS — 300/7-12
   208 S Cayuga St 66763 — 620-231-7550
   Joe Martin, prin. — Fax 231-2043

Galena, Cherokee, Pop. 3,168
Galena USD 499 — 700/K-12
   702 E 7th St 66739 — 620-783-4499
   Brian Smith, supt. — Fax 783-5547
   www.usd499.org
Galena HS — 200/9-12
   702 E 7th St 66739 — 620-783-4499
   Jeff Eberhart, prin. — Fax 783-1905
Galena MS — 200/6-8
   702 E 7th St 66739 — 620-783-4499
   Danny Albright, prin. — Fax 783-5214

Galva, McPherson, Pop. 730
Canton-Galva USD 419
   Supt. — See Canton
Canton-Galva MS — 200/4-8
   PO Box 96 67443 — 620-654-3321
   Bob Becker, prin. — Fax 654-3335

Garden City, Finney, Pop. 27,216
Garden City USD 457 — 7,400/PK-12
   1205 Fleming St 67846 — 620-276-5100
   Dr. Richard Atha, supt. — Fax 276-5220
   www.gckschools.com
Garden City HS — 2,000/9-12
   1412 N Main St 67846 — 620-276-5170
   James Mireles, prin. — Fax 276-5176
Henderson MS — 600/7-8
   2406 Fleming St 67846 — 620-276-5210
   Lori Peister, prin. — Fax 276-5219
Hubert MS — 600/7-8
   1205 A St 67846 — 620-276-5200
   Gerald Neumann, prin. — Fax 276-5287

Garden City Community College — Post-Sec.
   801 N Campus Dr 67846 — 620-276-7611

Garden Plain, Sedgwick, Pop. 807
Renwick USD 267
   Supt. — See Andale

Garden Plain HS — 200/9-12
   PO Box 128 67050 — 316-531-2272
   Tracy Bourne, prin. — Fax 535-2727

Gardner, Johnson, Pop. 11,670
Gardner Edgerton USD 231 — 3,200/PK-12
   PO Box 97 66030 — 913-856-2000
   Dr. Bill Gilhaus, supt. — Fax 856-7330
   www.usd231.com
Gardner Edgerton HS — 900/9-12
   425 N Waverly Rd 66030 — 913-856-2600
   Dave Webb, prin. — Fax 856-2690
Wheatridge MS — 500/7-8
   318 E Washington St 66030 — 913-856-2900
   Tim Brady, prin. — Fax 856-2980

Garnett, Anderson, Pop. 3,388
Garnett USD 365 — 1,100/K-12
   PO Box 328 66032 — 785-448-6155
   Gordon Myers, supt. — Fax 448-6157
   www.usd365.k12.ks.us
Anderson County JSHS — 500/7-12
   1100 W Highway 31 66032 — 785-448-3115
   G.A. Buie, prin. — Fax 448-6670

Girard, Crawford, Pop. 2,734
Girard USD 248 — 1,100/PK-12
   415 N Summit St 66743 — 620-724-4325
   Gary Snawder, supt. — Fax 724-8446
   www.girard248.org/
Girard HS — 300/9-12
   415 N Summit St 66743 — 620-724-4326
   Blaise Bauer, prin. — Fax 724-6136
Girard MS — 200/6-8
   415 N Summit St 66743 — 620-724-4114
   Randy Heatherly, prin. — Fax 724-4610

Glasco, Cloud, Pop. 509
Southern Cloud USD 334 — 200/K-12
   PO Box 427 67445 — 785-568-2247
   Demitry Evancho, supt. — Fax 568-2298
Glasco HS — 50/9-12
   PO Box 158 67445 — 785-568-2291
   Tom Lynch, prin. — Fax 568-2298
Other Schools – See Miltonvale

Goddard, Sedgwick, Pop. 2,932
Goddard USD 265 — 4,000/K-12
   PO Box 249 67052 — 316-794-4000
   Charles Edmonds, supt. — Fax 794-2222
   www.goddardusd.com
Eisenhower MS — 300/7-8
   PO Box 349 67052 — 316-794-4150
   Jerold Longabaugh, prin. — Fax 794-4063
Goddard HS — 1,200/9-12
   PO Box 189 67052 — 316-794-4100
   Cloyce Spradling, prin. — Fax 794-4130
Goddard MS — 400/7-8
   PO Box 279 67052 — 316-794-4230
   Lisa Hogarty, prin. — Fax 794-4254

Goessel, Marion, Pop. 557
Goessel USD 411 — 300/K-12
   PO Box 68 67053 — 620-367-4601
   John Fast, supt. — Fax 367-4603
   www.usd411.org
Goessel JSHS — 200/7-12
   PO Box 6 67053 — 620-367-2242
   Curt Graves, prin. — Fax 367-2571

Goodland, Sherman, Pop. 4,589
Goodland USD 352 — 900/PK-PK, 1-
   PO Box 509 67735 — 785-899-2397
   Marvin Selby, supt. — Fax 899-8504
   www.usd352.k12.ks.us
Goodland HS — 300/9-12
   PO Box 509 67735 — 785-899-5656
   Harvey Swager, prin. — Fax 899-8517
Grant JHS — 200/7-8
   PO Box 509 67735 — 785-899-7561
   James Mull, prin. — Fax 899-8525

Northwest Kansas Technical College — Post-Sec.
   1209 Harrison St 67735 — 785-899-3641

Grainfield, Gove, Pop. 313
Wheatland USD 292 — 200/PK-12
   PO Box 165 67737 — 785-673-4213
   Gena Stanley, supt. — Fax 673-4234
Wheatland MSHS — 100/7-12
   PO Box 149 67737 — 785-673-4223
   Darrin Herl, prin. — Fax 673-4225

Great Bend, Barton, Pop. 14,927
Great Bend USD 428 — 3,300/PK-12
   201 S Patton Rd 67530 — 620-793-1500
   Dr. Thomas W. Vernon, supt. — Fax 793-1585
   www.usd428.org
Great Bend HS — 1,100/9-12
   2027 Morton St 67530 — 620-793-1521
   Joyce Carter, prin. — Fax 793-1537
Great Bend MS — 500/7-8
   1919 Harrison St 67530 — 620-793-1510
   David Reiser, prin. — Fax 793-1549

Barton County Community College — Post-Sec.
   245 NE 30 Rd 67530 — 620-792-2701

Greensburg, Kiowa, Pop. 1,495
Greensburg USD 422 — 300/PK-12
   401 S Oak St 67054 — 620-723-2145
   Darin Headrick, supt. — Fax 723-2705
Greensburg HS — 100/9-12
   420 S Main St 67054 — 620-723-2164
   Randy Fulton, prin. — Fax 723-2019

Gridley, Coffey, Pop. 370
Le Roy-Gridley USD 245
   Supt. — See Le Roy

Southern Coffey County JHS 100/5-8
  PO Box 426 66852 620-836-2151
  Gary Haehn, prin. Fax 836-4041

Grinnell, Gove, Pop. 314
Grinnell USD 291 100/K-12
  PO Box 68 67738 785-824-3277
  Ken Bockwinkel, supt. Fax 824-3215
Grinnell HS 50/9-12
  PO Box 68 67738 785-824-3277
  Ken Bockwinkel, prin. Fax 824-3215
Grinnell MS 50/6-8
  PO Box 68 67738 785-824-3277
  Ken Bockwinkel, prin. Fax 824-3215

Gypsum, Saline, Pop. 401
Southeast of Saline USD 306 700/K-12
  5056 E Highway K4 67448 785-536-4291
  Robert Goodwin, supt. Fax 536-4247
  www.usd306.k12.ks.us
Southeast Saline JSHS 400/7-12
  5056 E Highway K4 67448 785-536-4286
  Monte Couchman, prin. Fax 536-4292

Haddam, Washington, Pop. 160
North Central USD 221 100/K-12
  1104 Main St 66944 785-778-2910
  Dr. Don L. Wells, supt. Fax 778-2535
  www.northcentralusd221.com
Other Schools – See Morrowville

Halstead, Harvey, Pop. 1,888
Halstead USD 440 700/K-12
  520 W 6th St 67056 316-835-2641
  Dr. Tom Bishard, supt. Fax 835-2305
  www.usd440.com
Halstead HS 200/9-12
  520 W 6th St 67056 316-835-2682
  David Younger, prin. Fax 835-3673
Halstead MS 300/4-8
  221 W 6th St 67056 316-835-2694
  David Younger, prin. Fax 835-2469

Hamilton, Greenwood, Pop. 328
Hamilton USD 390 100/K-12
  2596 W Rd N 66853 620-678-3244
  Richard G. Stapp, supt. Fax 678-3321
  www.hamilton390.net
Hamilton HS 100/7-12
  2596 W Rd N 66853 620-678-3651
  Richard G. Stapp, prin. Fax 678-3321

Hanover, Washington, Pop. 605
Barnes USD 223
  Supt. — See Barnes
Hanover HS 100/9-12
  209 E North St 66945 785-337-2281
  Paul Alexander, prin. Fax 337-2307

Hanston, Hodgeman, Pop. 269
Hanston USD 228 100/K-12
  PO Box 219 67849 620-623-2641
  Ray Patterson, supt. Fax 623-2096
Hanston JSHS 100/7-12
  PO Box 219 67849 620-623-2611
  Mindy Salmans, prin. Fax 623-4488

Hartford, Lyon, Pop. 509
Southern Lyon County USD 252 600/PK-12
  PO Box 278 66854 620-392-5519
  Paul Dorathy, supt. Fax 392-5841
  www.usd252.org/
Hartford JSHS 200/7-12
  PO Box 218 66854 620-392-5515
  Curtis Simons, prin. Fax 392-5960
Other Schools – See Olpe

Haven, Reno, Pop. 1,170
Haven USD 312 1,000/K-12
  PO Box 130 67543 620-465-7727
  Rick White, supt. Fax 465-3595
  www.usd312.k12.ks.us
Haven HS 400/9-12
  PO Box C 67543 620-465-2585
  Terry Fehrenbach, prin. Fax 465-7729
Haven MS 100/7-8
  PO Box B 67543 620-465-2587
  Terry Fehrenback, prin. Fax 465-2588

Haviland, Kiowa, Pop. 596
Haviland USD 474 200/K-12
  PO Box 243 67059 620-862-5256
  Mike Waters, supt. Fax 862-5257
Haviland HS 100/9-12
  PO Box 243 67059 620-862-5217
  Eric Reid, prin. Fax 862-5240

Barclay College Post-Sec.
  PO Box 288 67059 800-862-0226

Hays, Ellis, Pop. 19,915
Hays USD 489 3,100/K-12
  323 W 12th St 67601 785-623-2400
  Fred Kaufman, supt. Fax 623-2409
  www.usd489.com/
Felten MS 500/6-8
  201 E 29th St 67601 785-623-2450
  Craig Pallister, prin. Fax 623-2456
Hays HS 1,100/9-12
  2300 E 13th St 67601 785-623-2600
  Mike Hester, prin. Fax 623-2609
Kennedy MS 300/6-8
  1309 Fort St 67601 785-623-2470
  Lee Keffer, prin. Fax 623-2476

Fort Hays State University Post-Sec.
  600 Park St 67601 785-628-4000
Hays Academy of Hair Design Post-Sec.
  119 W 10th St 67601 785-628-3981

Thomas More Prep-Marion HS 300/9-12
  1701 Hall St 67601 785-625-6577
  Dennis Coakley, prin. Fax 625-3912

Haysville, Sedgwick, Pop. 9,545
Haysville USD 261 4,500/PK-12
  1745 W Grand Ave 67060 316-554-2200
  Dr. John Burke, supt. Fax 554-2230
  www.usd261.com
Haysville MS 1,100/6-8
  900 W Grand Ave 67060 316-554-2251
  Dr. Mike Maurer, prin. Fax 554-2258
Other Schools – See Wichita

Healy, Lane
Healy USD 468 100/K-12
  5006 N Dodge Rd 67850 620-398-2248
  John LaFave, supt. Fax 398-2435
  usd468.k12.ks.us
Healy JSHS 100/7-12
  5006 N Dodge Rd 67850 620-398-2248
  Jim Reece, prin. Fax 398-2435

Herington, Dickinson, Pop. 2,492
Herington USD 487 500/PK-12
  19 N Broadway 67449 785-258-2263
  Scott M. Carter, supt. Fax 258-2982
  www2.teen.k12.ks.us/usd487/
Herington HS 200/9-12
  1401 N D St 67449 785-258-2261
  Bill Ellis, prin. Fax 258-3013
Herington MS 100/6-8
  1317 N D St 67449 785-258-2448
  Bill Ellis, prin. Fax 258-3976

Hesston, Harvey, Pop. 3,614
Hesston USD 460 800/K-12
  PO Box 2000 67062 620-327-4931
  Vern Minor, supt. Fax 327-7157
  www.hesstonschools.org
Hesston HS 300/9-12
  PO Box 2000 67062 620-327-7122
  Larry Thompson, prin. Fax 327-7138
Hesston MS 300/5-8
  PO Box 2000 67062 620-327-7111
  Randy Linton, prin. Fax 327-7115

Hesston College Post-Sec.
  PO Box 3000 67062 620-327-4221

Hiawatha, Brown, Pop. 3,331
Hiawatha USD 415 900/K-12
  PO Box 398 66434 785-742-2266
  John Severin, supt. Fax 742-2301
  www.hiawathaschools.org/
Hiawatha HS 300/9-12
  600 Red Hawk Dr 66434 785-742-3312
  Rick Johnson, prin. Fax 742-7156
Hiawatha MS 300/5-8
  307 S Morrill Ave 66434 785-742-4172
  David Coufal, prin. Fax 742-1744

Highland, Doniphan, Pop. 966
Highland USD 425 200/K-12
  PO Box 8 66035 785-442-3286
  Steve Adams, supt. Fax 442-3289
  www.doniphanwest.org/
Doniphan West HS 100/9-12
  PO Box 8 66035 785-442-3286
  Deborah Strong, prin. Fax 442-3289

Highland Community College Post-Sec.
  PO Box 68 66035 785-442-6000

Hill City, Graham, Pop. 1,511
Hill City USD 281 400/PK-12
  PO Box 309 67642 785-421-2135
  Dr. Patrick Call, supt. Fax 421-5657
  www.usd281.com/
Hill City HS 100/9-12
  PO Box 160 67642 785-421-2117
  Dave Holloway, prin. Fax 421-3029
Longfellow MS 100/6-8
  203 N 2nd Ave 67642 785-421-3451
  Mike Young, prin. Fax 421-6395

Hillsboro, Marion, Pop. 2,839
Durham-Hillsboro-Lehigh USD 410 700/K-12
  812 E A St 67063 620-947-3184
  Gordon Mohn, supt. Fax 947-3263
  www.usd410.net
Hillsboro HS 200/9-12
  500 E Grand Ave 67063 620-947-3991
  Dale Honeck, prin. Fax 947-3251
Hillsboro MS 200/6-8
  400 E Grand Ave 67063 620-947-3297
  Corey Burton, prin. Fax 947-3251

Tabor College Post-Sec.
  400 S Jefferson St 67063 620-947-3121

Hoisington, Barton, Pop. 2,953
Hoisington USD 431 700/PK-12
  106 N Main St 67544 620-653-4134
  Keith Higgins, supt. Fax 653-4073
  www.usd431.net/
Hoisington HS 200/9-12
  218 E 7th St 67544 620-653-2141
  J. B. Elliott, prin. Fax 653-4164
Hoisington MS 100/6-8
  360 W 11th St 67544 620-653-4951
  Dean Andereck, prin. Fax 653-4483

Holcomb, Finney, Pop. 1,936
Holcomb USD 363 800/PK-12
  PO Box 8 67851 620-277-2629
  W.S. Landis, supt. Fax 277-2010
  users.pld.com/holcomb

Holcomb HS 300/9-12
  PO Box 38 67851 620-277-2063
  Bill Bierman, prin. Fax 277-0240
Holcomb MS 200/6-8
  PO Box 89 67851 620-277-2699
  Kristin Ellis, prin. Fax 277-0239

Holton, Jackson, Pop. 3,341
Holton USD 336 1,100/PK-12
  PO Box 352 66436 785-364-3650
  Dr. Brad Rahe, supt. Fax 364-3975
  www.holton.k12.ks.us
Holton HS 300/9-12
  901 New York Ave 66436 785-364-2181
  Alan Bean, prin. Fax 364-5360
Holton MS 200/6-8
  900 Iowa Ave 66436 785-364-2441
  Jay Nelson, prin. Fax 364-5460
North Jackson USD 335 400/PK-12
  12692 266th Rd 66436 785-364-2194
  Jit Milner, supt. Fax 364-4346
  www.jhcobras.net
Jackson Heights HS 100/9-12
  12719 266th Rd 66436 785-364-2195
  Gary Herman, prin. Fax 364-2487

Hope, Dickinson, Pop. 367
Rural Vista USD 481 400/PK-12
  PO Box 217 67451 785-366-7215
  Chris Kleidosty, supt. Fax 366-7217
Hope HS 100/9-12
  PO Box 218 67451 785-366-7221
  Ethan Gruen, prin. Fax 366-7115
Other Schools – See White City

Horton, Brown, Pop. 1,883
South Brown County USD 430 600/PK-12
  522 Central Ave 66439 785-486-2611
  Dr. Steven J. Davies, supt. Fax 486-2496
  usd430.k12.ks.us
Horton HS 200/9-12
  1120 1st Ave E 66439 785-486-2151
  David Norman, prin. Fax 486-2909
Other Schools – See Everest

Howard, Elk, Pop. 786
West Elk USD 282 500/PK-12
  PO Box 607 67349 620-374-2113
  Bert Moore, supt. Fax 374-2414
Howard West Elk JSHS 200/7-12
  PO Box 278 67349 620-374-2147
  John Ireland, prin. Fax 374-2414

Hoxie, Sheridan, Pop. 1,180
Hoxie USD 412 300/PK-12
  PO Box 348 67740 785-675-3258
  Scott Hoyt, supt. Fax 675-2126
  www.hoxie.org/
Hoxie JSHS 200/7-12
  PO Box 989 67740 785-675-3286
  Gary Johnson, prin. Fax 675-2270

Hoyt, Jackson, Pop. 583
Royal Valley USD 337
  Supt. — See Mayetta
Royal Valley HS 300/9-12
  PO Box 128 66440 785-986-6251
  James Holloman, prin. Fax 986-6479

Hugoton, Stevens, Pop. 3,630
Hugoton USD 210 800/PK-12
  205 E 6th St 67951 620-544-4397
  Dr. David Self, supt. Fax 544-7138
  www.usd210.org
Hugoton HS 300/9-12
  215 W 11th St 67951 620-544-4311
  Gardell Schnable, prin. Fax 544-7392
Hugoton MS 200/7-8
  115 W 11th St 67951 620-544-4341
  Ron Keller, prin. Fax 544-4856

Humboldt, Allen, Pop. 1,926
Humboldt USD 258 600/K-12
  801 New York St 66748 620-473-3121
  Robert K. Heigele, supt. Fax 473-2023
  www.usd258.net
Humboldt HS 200/9-12
  1011 Bridge St 66748 620-473-2251
  K.B. Criss, prin. Fax 473-2086
Humboldt MS 100/6-8
  1105 Bridge St 66748 620-473-3348
  K.B. Criss, prin. Fax 473-3141
Humboldt Tech Building Vo/Tech
  1116 New York St 66748 620-473-2251
  K.B. Criss, prin. Fax 473-2086

Hutchinson, Reno, Pop. 40,783
Buhler USD 313
  Supt. — See Buhler
Prairie Hills MS 400/7-8
  3200 Lucille Dr 67502 620-662-6052
  E. Craig Williams, prin. Fax 694-1002
Hutchinson USD 308 4,800/K-12
  PO Box 1908 67504 620-665-4400
  Dr. Wynona Winn, supt. Fax 665-4497
  www.usd308.com/
Hutchinson HS 1,600/9-12
  1401 N Severance St 67501 620-665-4500
  Ronn Roehm, prin. Fax 665-4580
Hutchinson MS 8 300/8-8
  200 W 14th Ave 67501 620-665-4700
  Mike Ellegood, prin. Fax 665-4703
Nickerson USD 309 1,100/K-12
  4501 W 4th Ave 67501 620-663-7141
  Jerry Burch, supt. Fax 663-7148
  www.usd309.k12.ks.us
Reno Valley MS 200/7-8
  1616 Wilshire Dr 67501 620-662-4573
  Julie Wilson, prin. Fax 662-6708

Other Schools – See Nickerson

Central Christian S	300/PK-12
1910 E 30th Ave 67502	620-663-2174
Ralph Vogel, prin.	Fax 663-2176
Hutchinson Community College	Post-Sec.
1300 N Plum St 67501	620-665-3500
Sidney's Hairdressing College	Post-Sec.
916 E 4th Ave 67501	620-662-5481
Trinity HS	200/7-12
1400 E 17th Ave 67501	620-662-5800
Brian Cordel, prin.	Fax 662-1233

Independence, Montgomery, Pop. 9,393
Independence USD 446	2,000/K-12
PO Box 487 67301	620-332-1800
Chuck Schmidt, supt.	Fax 332-1811
www.indyschools.com	
Independence HS	700/9-12
1301 N 10th St 67301	620-332-1815
James Runge, prin.	Fax 332-1831
Independence MS	500/6-8
300 W Locust St 67301	620-332-1836
Patty Clay, prin.	Fax 332-1841

Independence Bible S	100/PK-12
2246 S 10th St 67301	620-331-3781
Matthew Brewer, prin.	Fax 331-3780
Independence Community College	Post-Sec.
PO Box 708 67301	620-331-4100

Ingalls, Gray, Pop. 335
Ingalls USD 477	300/PK-12
PO Box 99 67853	620-335-5136
Dave Novack, supt.	Fax 335-5678
www.ingallsusd477.com/	
Ingalls JSHS	100/7-12
PO Box 99 67853	620-335-5135
Jarrod Stoppel, prin.	Fax 335-5678

Inman, McPherson, Pop. 1,194
Inman USD 448	500/PK-12
PO Box 129 67546	620-585-6424
Kevin Case, supt.	Fax 585-2689
Inman JSHS	200/7-12
PO Box 279 67546	620-585-6441
Scott Friesen, prin.	Fax 585-2797

Iola, Allen, Pop. 6,033
Iola USD 257	1,500/PK-12
408 N Cottonwood St 66749	620-365-4700
Dr. Craig Neuenswander, supt.	Fax 365-4708
www.usd257.org	
Iola HS	500/9-12
300 E Jackson Ave 66749	620-365-4715
David South, prin.	Fax 365-4730
Iola MS	300/6-8
600 East St 66749	620-365-4785
Jack Stanley, prin.	Fax 365-4770

Allen County Community College	Post-Sec.
1801 N Cottonwood St 66749	620-365-5116

Jennings, Decatur, Pop. 135
Prairie Heights USD 295	100/K-12
PO Box 160 67643	785-678-2414
Emery Hart, supt.	Fax 678-2345
www.usd295.k12.ks.us/	
Jennings HS	50/9-12
PO Box 160 67643	785-678-2414
Emery Hart, prin.	Fax 678-2345

Jetmore, Hodgeman, Pop. 933
Jetmore USD 227	300/PK-12
PO Box 100 67854	620-357-8301
Dr. Jim Barrett, supt.	Fax 357-6563
www.jetmorek12.org/	
Jetmore HS	100/9-12
PO Box 100 67854	620-357-8378
Robert Haug, prin.	Fax 357-6563

Jewell, Jewell, Pop. 447
Jewell USD 279	
Supt. — See Randall	
Jewell HS	100/9-12
PO Box 20 66949	785-428-3233
Robert Turner, prin.	Fax 428-3602
Jewell JHS	50/6-8
PO Box 20 66949	785-428-3233
Robert Turner, prin.	Fax 428-3602

Johnson, Stanton, Pop. 1,314
Stanton County USD 452	400/PK-12
PO Box C 67855	620-492-6226
Dr. Lee Tarrant, supt.	Fax 492-1326
users.pld.com/schs/	
Stanton County HS	200/9-12
PO Box C 67855	620-492-6284
Jim Piper, prin.	Fax 492-1326
Stanton County MS	100/6-8
PO Box C 67855	620-492-2223
Carolyn Davidson, prin.	Fax 492-1326

Junction City, Geary, Pop. 17,667
Geary County USD 475	6,400/PK-12
PO Box 370 66441	785-717-4000
Ronald P. Walker, supt.	Fax 717-4003
www.usd475.org/	
Junction City HS	1,600/9-12
900 N Eisenhower Dr 66441	785-717-4200
Stanley Dodds, prin.	Fax 717-4201
Junction City MS	800/6-8
300 W 9th St 66441	785-717-4400
Ferrell Miller, prin.	Fax 717-4401
Other Schools – See Fort Riley	

Barton County Community College	Post-Sec.
540 Grant Ave 66441	785-238-8550

St. Xaviers S	100/K-12
200 N Washington St 66441	785-238-2841
Roger Morris, prin.	Fax 238-5021

Kanopolis, Ellsworth, Pop. 524
Ellsworth USD 327	
Supt. — See Ellsworth	
Kanopolis MS	200/6-8
PO Box 37 67454	785-472-4477
Ken Cravens, prin.	Fax 472-4068

Kansas City, Wyandotte, Pop. 145,757
Kansas City USD 500	20,100/PK-12
625 Minnesota Ave 66101	913-551-3200
Dr. Jill Shackelfor, supt.	Fax 551-3217
www.kckps.org	
Area Technical S	Vo/Tech
2220 N 59th St 66104	913-627-4100
Johnny Stevenson, prin.	Fax 596-5509
Argentine MS	600/6-8
2123 Ruby Ave 66106	913-627-6750
Sabina Gonzales-Hacker, prin.	Fax 627-6783
Arrowhead MS	500/6-8
1715 N 82nd St 66112	913-627-6600
Bernice Cottrell, prin.	Fax 627-6654
Central MS	700/6-8
925 Ivandale St 66101	913-627-6150
James Antos, prin.	Fax 627-6152
Coronado MS	400/6-8
1735 N 64th Ter 66102	913-627-6300
Dr. Judi Duff, prin.	Fax 627-6358
Eisenhower MS	700/6-8
2901 N 72nd St 66109	913-627-6450
Freda Ogburn, prin.	Fax 627-6455
Harmon HS	1,300/9-12
2400 Steele Rd 66106	913-627-7050
Roel Quintanilla, prin.	Fax 627-7185
Northwest MS	600/6-8
2400 N 18th St 66104	913-627-4000
Laurie Boyd, prin.	Fax 627-4052
Rosedale MS	600/6-8
3600 Springfield St 66103	913-627-6900
Lili Englebrick, prin.	Fax 627-6957
Schlagle HS	1,100/9-12
2214 N 59th St 66104	913-627-7500
Douglas Bolden, prin.	Fax 627-7555
Sumner Academy/Arts & Sciences	1,000/8-12
1610 N 8th St 66101	913-627-7200
Mary Viveros, prin.	Fax 627-7205
Washington HS	1,100/9-12
7340 Leavenworth Rd 66109	913-627-7800
Greg Netzer, prin.	Fax 627-7850
West MS	500/6-8
2600 N 44th St 66104	913-627-6000
Shelly Beech, prin.	Fax 627-6053
Wyandotte HS	1,300/9-12
2501 Minnesota Ave 66102	913-627-7650
Walter Thompson, prin.	Fax 627-7700

Piper-Kansas City USD 203	1,300/PK-12
12036 Leavenworth Rd 66109	913-721-2088
John Chapman, supt.	Fax 721-3573
www.piperschools.com/	
Piper HS	400/9-12
4400 N 107th St 66109	913-721-2100
Dr. Bob Runnebaum, prin.	Fax 721-3867
Piper MS	300/6-8
4420 N 107th St 66109	913-721-1144
Laurence Breedlove, prin.	Fax 721-1526

Turner USD 202	3,500/PK-12
800 S 55th St 66106	913-288-4100
Bobby Allen, supt.	Fax 288-3401
www.turnerusd202.org/	
Turner HS	1,100/9-12
2211 S 55th St 66106	913-288-3300
Michelle Sedler, prin.	Fax 288-3301
Turner MS	600/7-8
1312 S 55th St 66106	913-288-4000
William Hatfield, prin.	Fax 288-4001

Bishop Ward HS	500/9-12
708 N 18th St 66102	913-371-1201
Dennis Dorr, prin.	Fax 371-2145
Central Baptist Theological Seminary	Post-Sec.
741 N 31st St 66102	800-677-2287
Cutting Edge Hairstyling Academy	Post-Sec.
4327 State Ave 66102	913-321-0214
Donnelly College	Post-Sec.
608 N 18th St 66102	913-621-8724
Kansas City Christian MS	100/7-8
5500 Woodend Ave 66106	913-722-9955
Kathy Hirleman, prin.	Fax 236-5996
Kansas City Kansas Community College	Post-Sec.
7250 State Ave 66112	913-334-1100
Kansas State School for the Blind	Post-Sec.
1100 State Ave 66102	913-281-3308
Muncie Christian S	200/K-12
3650 N 67th St 66104	913-299-9884
Rex Vincent, admin.	Fax 299-9884
St. John Holy Family MS	50/6-8
515 Ohio Ave 66101	913-371-3923
Jennifer Sears, prin.	Fax 321-5001
University of Kansas Medical Center	Post-Sec.
3901 Rainbow Blvd 66160	913-588-5000

Kensington, Smith, Pop. 492
West Smith County USD 238	200/K-12
PO Box 188 66951	785-476-2218
Jeff Yoxall, supt.	Fax 476-2258
goldbugcountry.com/	
Kensington JSHS	100/7-12
PO Box 188 66951	785-476-2217
Jeff Yoxall, prin.	Fax 476-2210

Kincaid, Anderson, Pop. 180
Crest USD 479	200/K-12
603 E Broad 66039	620-852-3540
Doug Spillman, supt.	Fax 852-3542
www.usd479.net/	
Other Schools – See Colony	

Kingman, Kingman, Pop. 3,270
Kingman-Norwich USD 331	1,200/PK-12
PO Box 416 67068	620-532-3134
Don L. Mason, supt.	Fax 532-3251
www.knusd331.com/	
Kingman HS	300/9-12
260 W Kansas Ave 67068	620-532-3136
Rick Henry, prin.	Fax 532-3027
Other Schools – See Norwich	

Kinsley, Edwards, Pop. 1,551
Kinsley-Offerle USD 347	300/K-12
120 W 8th St 67547	620-659-3646
James Garner, supt.	Fax 659-2669
www.kinsleypublicschools.org/	
Kinsley-Offerle JSHS	200/7-12
716 Colony Ave 67547	620-659-2126
Dr. Walter Autem, prin.	Fax 659-2180

Kiowa, Barber, Pop. 989
South Barber County USD 255	300/K-12
512 Main St 67070	620-825-4115
Bob Hightree, supt.	Fax 825-4145
South Barber HS	100/9-12
1220 N 8th St 67070	620-825-4214
Monty Thompson, prin.	Fax 825-4250

Kismet, Seward, Pop. 511
Kismet-Plains USD 483	
Supt. — See Plains	
Southwestern Heights JSHS	300/6-12
RR 1 Box 24A 67859	620-563-7292
Elton Argo, prin.	Fax 563-7383

La Crosse, Rush, Pop. 1,319
La Crosse USD 395	300/K-12
PO Box 778 67548	785-222-2505
Bill Keeley, supt.	Fax 222-3240
La Crosse HS	100/9-12
PO Box 810 67548	785-222-2528
Kathy Keeley, prin.	Fax 222-3480
La Crosse MS	100/7-8
PO Box 810 67548	785-222-3030
Kathy Keeley, prin.	Fax 222-3480

La Cygne, Linn, Pop. 1,123
Prairie View USD 362	1,000/PK-12
13799 KS Highway 152 66040	913-757-2677
Dotson Bradbury, supt.	Fax 757-4442
www.pv362.org	
Prairie View HS	300/9-12
13731 KS Highway 152 66040	913-757-4447
Alan Jeffery, prin.	Fax 757-4443
Prairie View MS	200/6-8
13667 KS Highway 152 66040	913-757-4447
Lee Jones, prin.	Fax 757-4443

Lakin, Kearny, Pop. 2,343
Lakin USD 215	700/PK-12
1003 W Kingman Ave 67860	620-355-6761
Randall Steinle, supt.	Fax 355-7317
Lakin HS	200/9-12
407 N Campbell St 67860	620-355-6411
Ron Overeem, prin.	Fax 355-6460
Lakin MS	200/5-8
1201 W Kingman Ave 67860	620-355-6973
Tammie Huggard, prin.	Fax 355-8313

Langdon, Reno, Pop. 71
Fairfield USD 310	400/K-12
16115 S Langdon Rd 67583	620-596-2152
Dr. Fred Marten, supt.	Fax 596-2835
www.usd310.k12.ks.us	
Fairfield HS	100/9-12
16115 S Langdon Rd 67583	620-596-2481
Thomas Flax, prin.	Fax 596-2835
Fairfield MS	100/6-8
16115 S Langdon Rd 67583	620-596-2615
Thomas Flax, prin.	Fax 596-2835

Lansing, Leavenworth, Pop. 10,032
Lansing USD 469	1,900/PK-12
613 Holiday Plz 66043	913-727-1100
Dr. Randal Bagby, supt.	Fax 727-1619
usd469.net/	
Lansing HS	700/9-12
220 Lion Ln 66043	913-727-3357
Steve Dike, prin.	Fax 727-2001
Lansing MS	500/6-8
509 Ida St 66043	913-727-1197
Kerry Brungardt, prin.	Fax 727-1349

Larned, Pawnee, Pop. 3,932
Ft. Larned USD 495	1,100/PK-12
120 E 6th St 67550	620-285-3185
Jon Flint, supt.	Fax 285-2973
www.usd495.net	
Larned HS	300/9-12
815 Corse Ave 67550	620-285-2151
Rick Simmoncic, prin.	Fax 285-7148
Larned MS	300/5-8
904 Corse Ave 67550	620-285-8430
Jim Krohn, prin.	Fax 285-8433

Lawrence, Douglas, Pop. 82,120
Lawrence USD 497	10,000/PK-12
110 McDonald Dr 66044	785-832-5000
Randy Weseman, supt.	Fax 832-5016
www.usd497.org	
Lawrence Central JHS	500/7-9
1400 Massachusetts St 66044	785-832-5400
Frank Harwood, prin.	Fax 832-5403

Lawrence Free State HS 1,200/10-12
4700 Overland Dr 66049 785-832-6050
Joe Snyder, prin. Fax 832-6099
Lawrence HS 1,300/10-12
1901 Louisiana St 66046 785-832-5050
Steven Nilhas, prin. Fax 832-5054
Lawrence South JHS 700/7-9
2734 Louisiana St 66046 785-832-5450
Will Fernandez, prin. Fax 832-5453
Lawrence Southwest JHS 700/7-9
2511 Inverness Dr 66047 785-832-5550
Trish Bransky, prin. Fax 832-5554
Lawrence West JHS 600/7-9
2700 Harvard Rd 66049 785-832-5500
Myron Melton, prin. Fax 832-5504

Bishop Seabury Academy 100/7-12
4120 Clinton Pkwy 66047 785-832-1717
Fax 832-1919
Haskell Indian Nations University Post-Sec.
155 Indian Ave Rm 1305 66046 785-749-8404
Pinnacle Career Institute Post-Sec.
1601 W 23rd St Ste 200 66046 800-360-9640
University of Kansas 66045 Post-Sec.
785-864-2700
Veritas Christian S 100/K-12
PO Box 1571 66044 785-749-0083
Dr. Jeffrey L. Barclay, admin. Fax 749-0580

Leavenworth, Leavenworth, Pop. 35,211
Leavenworth USD 453 4,100/PK-12
PO Box 969 66048 913-684-1400
Clay Guthmiller, supt. Fax 684-1407
www.lvksch.org/
Leavenworth HS 1,500/9-12
2012 10th Ave 66048 913-684-1550
John Parker, prin. Fax 684-1555
Leavenworth West MS 400/6-8
1901 Spruce St 66048 913-684-1520
Deborah Lauxman, prin. Fax 684-1523
Warren MS 500/6-8
PO Box 7 66048 913-684-1530
John Parker, prin. Fax 684-1539

Crossroads Christian Academy 50/6-9
PO Box 553 66048 913-680-1411
Susy Winfrey, admin. Fax 680-1411
Immaculata HS 200/9-12
600 Shawnee St 66048 913-682-3900
Mike Connelly, prin. Fax 682-9036
University of Saint Mary Post-Sec.
4100 S 4th St 66048 913-682-5151
Xavier S 200/7-8
721 Osage St 66048 913-682-3135
Ann Connor, prin. Fax 682-5262

Leawood, Johnson, Pop. 28,888
Blue Valley USD 229
Supt. — See Overland Park
Leawood MS 500/6-8
2410 W 123rd St 66209 913-239-5300
Marcia Bone Ed.D., prin. Fax 345-7418
Prairie Star MS 500/6-8
14201 Mission Rd 66224 913-239-5600
Lyn Rantz Ed.D., prin. Fax 685-7620

Lebo, Coffey, Pop. 966
Lebo-Waverly USD 243
Supt. — See Waverly
Lebo HS 200/7-12
PO Box 45 66856 620-256-6341
Todd Barker, prin. Fax 256-6342

Lenexa, Johnson, Pop. 41,995

Brown Mackie College Post-Sec.
9705 Lenexa Dr 66215 913-768-1900
St. James Academy 9-12
24505 Prairie Star Pkwy 66227 913-254-4200
Barbara Burgoon, prin. Fax 254-1892

Leon, Butler, Pop. 646
Bluestem USD 205 700/PK-12
PO Box 8 67074 316-742-3261
Dennis Engels, supt. Fax 742-9265
www.usd205.com
Bluestem HS 200/9-12
PO Box 338 67074 316-742-3281
Neal Weltha, prin. Fax 742-3813
Bluestem MS 100/7-8
625 S Mill Rd 67074 316-742-3263
David Kohls, prin. Fax 742-3748

Leoti, Wichita, Pop. 1,538
Leoti USD 467 500/PK-12
PO Box 967 67861 620-375-4677
Gary Akers, supt. Fax 375-2304
www.leoti.org/
Wichita County HS 100/9-12
800 W Broadway 67861 620-375-2213
Duane Custer, prin. Fax 375-4958
Wichita County JHS 100/6-8
PO Box 908 67861 620-375-2219
John Johnston, prin. Fax 375-2352

Le Roy, Coffey, Pop. 586
Le Roy-Gridley USD 245 300/PK-12
PO Box 278 66857 620-964-2212
Mike Kastle, supt. Fax 964-2413
Southern Coffey County HS 100/9-12
PO Box 188 66857 620-964-2217
Mike Kastle, prin. Fax 964-2413
Other Schools – See Gridley

Lewis, Edwards, Pop. 471
Lewis USD 502 100/PK-12
PO Box 97 67552 620-324-5547
Virgil Ritchie, supt. Fax 324-5297
skyways.lib.ks.us/schools/usd502/index.htm

Lewis HS 100/7-12
PO Box 97 67552 620-324-5541
Virgil Ritchie, prin. Fax 324-5297

Liberal, Seward, Pop. 20,067
Liberal USD 480 4,500/PK-12
PO Box 949 67905 620-604-1010
Vernon Welch, supt. Fax 604-1011
www.usd480.net/
Liberal HS 1,100/9-12
1611 W 2nd St 67901 620-604-1200
Keith Adams, prin. Fax 604-1201
Liberal South MS 300/7-8
950 S Grant Ave 67901 620-604-1300
Brandon Hyde, prin. Fax 604-1301
Liberal West MS 400/7-8
500 N Western Ave 67901 620-604-1400
Khris Thexton, prin. Fax 604-1501

Seward County Community College Post-Sec.
PO Box 1137 67905 620-624-1951
Southwest Kansas Technical School Post-Sec.
PO Box 1599 67905 620-626-3819

Lincoln, Lincoln, Pop. 1,289
Lincoln USD 298 400/PK-12
PO Box 289 67455 785-524-4436
Terry Stratman, supt. Fax 524-3080
www.usd298.com
Lincoln JSHS 200/7-12
PO Box 269 67455 785-524-4193
S. Allen Konicek, prin. Fax 524-5114

Lindsborg, McPherson, Pop. 3,290
Smoky Valley USD 400 1,000/K-12
126 S Main St 67456 785-227-2981
Glen Suppes, supt. Fax 227-2982
www.smokyvalley.org/
Lindsborg MS 200/5-8
401 N Cedar St 67456 785-227-4249
John Denk, prin. Fax 227-3650
Smoky Valley HS 300/9-12
1 Viking Blvd 67456 785-227-2909
Fred VanRanken, prin. Fax 227-2900

Bethany College Post-Sec.
421 N 1st St 67456 785-227-3311

Linn, Washington, Pop. 401
Barnes USD 223
Supt. — See Barnes
Linn HS 100/9-12
300 Parkview St 66953 785-348-5531
Mike Savage, prin. Fax 348-5534

Linwood, Leavenworth, Pop. 380
Basehor-Linwood USD 458
Supt. — See Basehor
Basehor-Linwood MS 300/7-8
PO Box 1 66052 913-724-2323
Michael Boyd, prin. Fax 724-3132

Little River, Rice, Pop. 523
Little River USD 444 300/PK-12
PO Box 218 67457 620-897-6325
Milt Dougherty, supt. Fax 897-6788
www.usd444.com/
Little River HS 100/9-12
PO Box 8 67457 620-897-6201
Lonnie Moser, prin. Fax 897-6203
Little River JHS 100/6-8
PO Box 8 67457 620-897-6201
Lonnie Moser, prin. Fax 897-6203

Logan, Phillips, Pop. 566
Logan USD 326 200/K-12
PO Box 98 67646 785-689-7595
Robert Jackson, supt. Fax 689-7517
www.usd326.k12.ks.us/
Logan HS 100/7-12
PO Box 98 67646 785-689-7574
Robert Jackson, prin. Fax 689-7543

Long Island, Phillips, Pop. 148
Northern Valley USD 212
Supt. — See Almena
Long Island HS 100/5-8
PO Box 98 67647 785-854-7681
Dwight Vallin, prin. Fax 854-7684

Longton, Elk, Pop. 382
Elk Valley USD 283 200/PK-12
PO Box 87 67352 620-642-2811
Art Haibon, supt. Fax 642-6551
www.usd283.org
Elk Valley HS 100/6-12
PO Box 87 67352 620-642-2215
Art Haibon, prin. Fax 642-3361

Lorraine, Ellsworth, Pop. 133
Lorraine USD 328 500/PK-12
PO Box 109 67459 785-472-5241
Roger Robinson, supt. Fax 472-5229
www.usd328.org
Other Schools – See Bushton, Wilson

Lost Springs, Marion, Pop. 70
Centre USD 397 300/PK-12
PO Box 38 66859 785-983-4304
Robert Kiblinger, supt. Fax 983-4352
www.centreschools.com
Centre JSHS 100/7-12
2374 310th St 66859 785-983-4321
Greg Wyatt, prin. Fax 983-4377

Louisburg, Miami, Pop. 2,889
Louisburg USD 416 1,300/PK-12
PO Box 550 66053 913-837-2944
Dr. Rick Doll, supt. Fax 837-5808
www.usd416.org

Louisburg HS 400/9-12
PO Box 399 66053 913-837-2941
Sally Lundblad, prin. Fax 837-5774
Louisburg MS 300/6-8
PO Box 308 66053 913-837-1351
Charles Golladay, prin. Fax 837-1361

Lucas, Russell, Pop. 416
Russell County USD 407
Supt. — See Russell
Lucas-Luray HS 50/9-12
130 N Greeley St 67648 785-525-6244
Phillip Riedel, prin. Fax 525-6245

Lyndon, Osage, Pop. 1,028
Lyndon USD 421 500/PK-12
PO Box 488 66451 785-828-4413
Brian Spencer, supt. Fax 828-3686
Lyndon HS 100/9-12
PO Box 488 66451 785-828-4911
Brad Marcotte, prin. Fax 828-4221

Lyons, Rice, Pop. 3,565
Lyons USD 405 800/PK-12
800 S Workman St 67554 620-257-5196
Anne Lassey, supt. Fax 257-5197
www.usd405.com
Lyons HS 300/9-12
601 E American Rd 67554 620-257-5114
Gary Sechrist, prin. Fax 257-3194
Lyons MS 200/6-8
401 S Douglas Ave 67554 620-257-3961
Glenn Fortmayer, prin. Fax 257-3518

Macksville, Stafford, Pop. 498
Macksville USD 351 300/PK-12
PO Box 487 67557 620-348-3415
Robert Minchew, supt. Fax 348-3217
www.usd351.com
Macksville HS 100/9-12
PO Box 307 67557 620-348-2475
Mike Harvey, prin. Fax 348-3217

Mc Louth, Jefferson, Pop. 785
Mc Louth USD 342 600/K-12
PO Box 40 66054 913-796-2201
Jean Rush, supt. Fax 796-6440
www.mclouth.org
Mc Louth HS 200/9-12
PO Box 40 66054 913-796-6122
John Hamon, prin. Fax 796-6124
Mc Louth MS 100/6-8
PO Box 40 66054 913-796-6122
John Hamon, prin. Fax 796-6124

Mc Pherson, McPherson, Pop. 12,746
Mc Pherson USD 418 2,500/PK-12
514 N Main St 67460 620-241-9400
Randy Watson, supt. Fax 241-9410
www.mcpherson.com/418
Mc Pherson HS 800/9-12
801 E 1st St 67460 620-241-9500
Lew Faust, prin. Fax 241-9506
Mc Pherson MS 600/6-8
700 E Elizabeth St 67460 620-241-9450
John Thissen, prin. Fax 241-9456

Central Christian College of Kansas Post-Sec.
PO Box 1403 67460 620-241-0723
Elyria Christian S 200/K-12
1644 Comanche Rd 67460 620-241-2994
David Case, supt. Fax 241-1238
McPherson College Post-Sec.
PO Box 1402 67460 620-241-0731

Madison, Greenwood, Pop. 822
Madison-Virgil USD 386 300/PK-12
PO Box 398 66860 620-437-2910
Darrel Finch, supt. Fax 437-2916
www.usd386.org/
Madison HS 100/7-12
PO Box 398 66860 620-437-2912
Darrel Finch, prin. Fax 437-2911

Maize, Sedgwick, Pop. 2,042
Maize USD 266 5,900/PK-12
201 S Park St 67101 316-722-0614
Dr. Craig Elliott, supt. Fax 722-8538
www.usd266.com
Maize HS 1,700/9-12
11600 W 45th St N 67101 316-722-0441
Teresa Ott, prin. Fax 722-6214
Other Schools – See Wichita

Manhattan, Riley, Pop. 44,733
Manhattan-Ogden USD 383 5,100/PK-12
2031 Poyntz Ave 66502 785-587-2000
Dr. Robert Shannon, supt. Fax 587-2006
www.usd383.org
Anthony MS 400/7-8
2501 Browning Ave 66502 785-587-2890
Vickie Kline, prin. Fax 587-2899
Eisenhower MS 300/7-8
800 Walters Dr 66502 785-587-2880
Greg Hoyt, prin. Fax 587-2888
Manhattan HS West/East Campus 1,800/9-12
2100 Poyntz Ave 66502 785-587-2100
Terry McCarty, prin. Fax 587-2132

American Institute of Baking Post-Sec.
PO Box 3999 66505 785-537-4750
Crum's Beauty College Post-Sec.
512 Poyntz Ave 66502 785-776-4794
Flint Hills Christian S 200/PK-12
3905 Green Valley Rd 66502 785-776-2223
Warren Holmes, admin. Fax 776-3016
Kansas State University 66506 Post-Sec.
785-532-6250
Manhattan Christian College Post-Sec.
1415 Anderson Ave 66502 785-539-3571

Mankato, Jewell, Pop. 880
Mankato USD 278 — 200/K-12
  301 N West St 66956 — 785-378-3102
  William Walker, supt. — Fax 378-3438
  www.usd278.org/
Mankato JSHS — 100/7-12
  301 N West St 66956 — 785-378-3126
  Allen Walter, prin. — Fax 378-3530

Marion, Marion, Pop. 2,058
Marion-Florence USD 408 — 600/K-12
  101 N Thorp St 66861 — 620-382-2117
  Lee Leiker, supt. — Fax 382-2118
  www.usd408.com
Marion HS — 200/9-12
  701 E Main St 66861 — 620-382-2168
  Ken Arnhold, prin. — Fax 382-6021
Marion MS — 100/7-8
  125 S Lincoln St 66861 — 620-382-6070
  Tod Gordon, prin. — Fax 382-6073

Marysville, Marshall, Pop. 3,133
Marysville USD 364 — 700/PK-12
  211 S 10th St 66508 — 785-562-5308
  Doug Powers, supt. — Fax 562-5309
  www.marysvilleschools.org
Marysville HS — 400/9-12
  1111 Walnut St 66508 — 785-562-5386
  John Waugh, prin. — Fax 562-5390
Marysville JHS — 7-8
  1005 Walnut St 66508 — 785-562-5356
  Cindy Scarbrough, prin. — Fax 562-5390

Mayetta, Jackson, Pop. 336
Royal Valley USD 337 — 900/PK-12
  PO Box 219 66509 — 785-966-2246
  John A. Rundle, supt. — Fax 966-2400
  www.rv337.com/
Royal Valley MS — 300/5-8
  PO Box 189 66509 — 785-966-2251
  Dr. Don DeKeyser, prin. — Fax 966-2833
Other Schools – See Hoyt

Meade, Meade, Pop. 1,658
Meade USD 226 — 500/PK-12
  PO Box 400 67864 — 620-873-2081
  Robert Herbig, supt. — Fax 873-2201
Meade HS — 200/9-12
  PO Box 400 67864 — 620-873-2981
  Jack Pavlovich, prin. — Fax 873-2201

Medicine Lodge, Barber, Pop. 2,067
Barber County North USD 254 — 600/PK-12
  PO Box 288 67104 — 620-886-3370
  Suzanne Germes, supt. — Fax 886-3640
  www.usd254.org/
Medicine Lodge HS — 200/9-12
  400 W Eldorado Ave 67104 — 620-886-5667
  Mike Hubka, prin. — Fax 886-3053
Medicine Lodge MS — 200/6-8
  100 BH Born Blvd 67104 — 620-886-5644
  Mark Buck, prin. — Fax 886-3082

Melvern, Osage, Pop. 426
Marais Des Cygnes Valley USD 456 — 300/K-12
  PO Box 158 66510 — 785-549-3521
  Ted Vannocker, supt. — Fax 549-3659
  www.usd456.org
Marais Des Cygnes Valley HS — 100/9-12
  PO Box 158 66510 — 785-549-3313
  Ted Vannocker, prin. — Fax 549-3576
Other Schools – See Quenemo

Meriden, Jefferson, Pop. 691
Jefferson West USD 340 — 1,000/PK-12
  PO Box 267 66512 — 785-484-3444
  Dr. Rob Little, supt. — Fax 484-3148
Jefferson West HS — 400/9-12
  PO Box 268 66512 — 785-484-3331
  Ed West, prin. — Fax 484-2021
Jefferson West MS — 200/6-8
  PO Box 410 66512 — 785-484-2900
  William Scott, prin. — Fax 484-2904

Miltonvale, Cloud, Pop. 491
Southern Cloud USD 334
  Supt. — See Glasco
Miltonvale HS — 100/7-12
  PO Box 394 67466 — 785-427-3250
  Roger Perkins, prin. — Fax 427-3181

Minneapolis, Ottawa, Pop. 2,044
North Ottawa County USD 239 — 600/K-12
  PO Box 257 67467 — 785-392-2167
  Dr. Larry Combs, supt. — Fax 392-3038
  www.usd239.org/
Minneapolis JSHS — 300/7-12
  PO Box 317 67467 — 785-392-2113
  Greg Brown, prin. — Fax 392-2275

Minneola, Clark, Pop. 702
Minneola USD 219 — 300/K-12
  PO Box 157 67865 — 620-885-4372
  Mark Walker, supt. — Fax 885-4509
Minneola HS — 100/9-12
  PO Box 157 67865 — 620-885-4611
  Steve Meneley, prin. — Fax 885-4509

Montezuma, Gray, Pop. 974
Montezuma USD 371 — 200/PK-12
  PO Box 355 67867 — 620-846-2293
  Dr. Donald Grover, supt. — Fax 846-2294
  www.sghs.musd371.k12.ks.us/
South Gray HS — 50/9-12
  PO Box 355 67867 — 620-846-2281
  Tim Skinner, prin. — Fax 846-2181

Moran, Allen, Pop. 550
Marmaton Valley USD 256 — 400/K-12
  128 W Oak St 66755 — 620-237-4250
  Darrel Kellerman, supt. — Fax 237-8872

Marmaton Valley HS — 200/7-12
  128 W Oak St 66755 — 620-237-4251
  Maurice Strecker, prin. — Fax 237-8872

Morrowville, Washington, Pop. 160
North Central USD 221
  Supt. — See Haddam
North Central JSHS — 100/6-12
  221 N Morton St 66958 — 785-265-3585
  Bill Heinen, prin. — Fax 265-4541

Moscow, Stevens, Pop. 247
Moscow USD 209 — 200/K-12
  PO Box 158 67952 — 620-598-2205
  Larry Philippi, supt. — Fax 598-2233
  moscowschools.us/
Moscow HS — 100/6-12
  PO Box 160 67952 — 620-598-2250
  Stuart Moore, prin. — Fax 598-2233

Mound City, Linn, Pop. 817
Jayhawk USD 346 — 600/PK-12
  PO Box 278 66056 — 913-795-2247
  James Knox, supt. — Fax 795-2185
  www.usd346.k12.ks.us/
Jayhawk-Linn JSHS — 300/7-12
  PO Box D 66056 — 913-795-2224
  Rex Bollinger, prin. — Fax 795-2406

Moundridge, McPherson, Pop. 1,645
Moundridge USD 423 — 400/K-12
  PO Box K 67107 — 620-345-8611
  Rustin Clark, supt. — Fax 345-8617
  www.usd423.org
Moundridge HS — 100/9-12
  PO Box 610 67107 — 620-345-2816
  Clark Wedel, prin. — Fax 345-5218
Moundridge MS — 100/5-8
  PO Box 607 67107 — 620-345-2826
  Vance Unrau, prin. — Fax 345-5307

Mullinville, Kiowa, Pop. 271
Mullinville USD 424 — 50/PK-8
  PO Box 6 67109 — 620-548-2521
  John Jones, supt. — Fax 548-2515
  www.mullinville.org
Mullinville JHS — 50/7-8
  PO Box 6 67109 — 620-548-2217
  John Jones, prin. — Fax 548-2278

Mulvane, Sedgwick, Pop. 5,536
Mulvane USD 263 — 1,900/PK-12
  PO Box 130 67110 — 316-777-1102
  Donna Augustine-Shaw, supt. — Fax 777-1103
  www.usd263.com
Mulvane HS — 600/9-12
  1900 N Rock Rd 67110 — 316-777-1183
  Steve Rader, prin. — Fax 777-2228
Mulvane MS — 300/7-8
  915 Westview Dr 67110 — 316-777-2022
  Traci Becker, prin. — Fax 777-4967

Natoma, Osborne, Pop. 337
Paradise USD 399 — 200/PK-12
  PO Box 100 67651 — 785-885-4843
  Aaron Homburg, supt. — Fax 885-4523
  www.usd399.com/
Natoma HS — 100/7-12
  PO Box 100 67651 — 785-885-4849
  Adam McDaniel, prin. — Fax 885-4523
Paradise JHS — 7-8
  PO Box 10 67651 — 785-885-4849
  Aaron Homburg, prin. — Fax 885-4523

Neodesha, Wilson, Pop. 2,734
Neodesha USD 461 — 800/PK-12
  PO Box 88 66757 — 620-325-2610
  Daryl Pruter, supt. — Fax 325-2368
  www.neodesha.com/neodesha/district.html
Neodesha JSHS — 400/7-12
  1000 N 8th St 66757 — 620-325-3015
  Terence Wilson, prin. — Fax 325-2382

Ness City, Ness, Pop. 1,403
Ness City USD 303 — 300/PK-12
  414 E Chestnut St 67560 — 785-798-2210
  Randall Jansonius, supt. — Fax 798-3581
  www.nesscityschools.org
Ness City JSHS — 100/7-12
  200 N 5th St 67560 — 785-798-3991
  George Staten, prin. — Fax 798-3064

Newton, Harvey, Pop. 17,977
Newton USD 373 — 3,600/PK-12
  308 E 1st St 67114 — 316-284-6200
  Dr. John Morton, supt. — Fax 284-6207
  www.newton.k12.ks.us
Chisholm MS — 400/6-8
  900 E 1st St 67114 — 316-284-6260
  Cesar Pena, prin. — Fax 284-6267
Newton HS — 1,100/9-12
  900 W 12th St 67114 — 316-284-6280
  Ken Rickard, prin. — Fax 284-6288
Santa Fe MS — 400/6-8
  130 W Broadway St 67114 — 316-284-6270
  Victoria Adame, prin. — Fax 284-6596

Newton Christian HS — 50/9-12
  224 NW 60th St 67114 — 316-283-3858
  Roger Ericksten, prin. — Fax 283-3858

Nickerson, Reno, Pop. 1,183
Nickerson USD 309
  Supt. — See Hutchinson
Nickerson HS — 300/9-12
  305 S Nickerson St 67561 — 620-422-3215
  Kevin Abbott, prin. — Fax 422-3229

North Newton, McPherson, Pop. 1,563

Bethel College — Post-Sec.
  300 E 27th St 67117 — 316-283-2500

Norton, Norton, Pop. 2,901
Norton USD 211 — 700/PK-12
  105 E Waverly St 67654 — 785-877-3386
  Greg Mann, supt. — Fax 877-2030
Norton Community HS — 200/9-12
  513 W Wilberforce St 67654 — 785-877-3338
  Lary Stull, prin. — Fax 877-6940
Norton JHS — 100/7-8
  706 Jones Ave 67654 — 785-877-5851
  Larry Mills, prin. — Fax 877-3771

Nortonville, Jefferson, Pop. 605
Jefferson County North USD 339
  Supt. — See Winchester
Jefferson County North MS — 6-8
  100 Charger Ln 66060 — 913-886-3870
  Gary Bedigrew, prin. — Fax 886-6280

Norwich, Kingman, Pop. 535
Kingman-Norwich USD 331
  Supt. — See Kingman
Norwich HS — 100/9-12
  209 Parkway St 67118 — 620-478-2235
  Lanny Hower, prin. — Fax 478-2879

Oakley, Logan, Pop. 2,030
Oakley USD 274 — 500/PK-12
  208 E 2nd St 67748 — 785-672-4588
  Bill Steiner, supt. — Fax 672-3044
Oakley HS — 200/9-12
  118 W 7th St 67748 — 785-672-3241
  Fred Teeter, prin. — Fax 672-3743
Oakley MS — 100/6-8
  611 Center Ave 67748 — 785-672-3820
  Robert Sattler, prin. — Fax 672-3010

Oberlin, Decatur, Pop. 1,884
Oberlin USD 294 — 500/PK-12
  131 E Commercial St 67749 — 785-475-3805
  Kelly Glodt, supt. — Fax 475-3076
  www.usd294.org
Decatur Community JSHS — 200/7-12
  605 E Commercial St 67749 — 785-475-2231
  Charles Haag, prin. — Fax 475-2802

Olathe, Johnson, Pop. 105,274
Olathe USD 233 — 22,600/PK-12
  PO Box 2000 66063 — 913-780-7000
  Dr. Patricia All, supt. — Fax 780-8007
  www.olatheschools.com/
California Trail JHS — 800/7-9
  13775 W 133rd St 66062 — 913-780-7220
  Larry Katzif, prin. — Fax 780-7229
Chisholm Trail JHS — 600/7-9
  16700 W 159th St 66062 — 913-780-7240
  Bill Weber, prin. — Fax 780-7249
Frontier Trail JHS — 800/7-9
  15300 W 143rd St 66062 — 913-780-7210
  Jim McMullen, prin. — Fax 780-7216
Indian Trail JHS — 500/7-9
  1440 E 151st St 66062 — 913-780-7230
  Tracy Maring, prin. — Fax 780-7234
Olathe East SHS — 1,400/10-12
  14545 W 127th St 66062 — 913-780-7120
  Dr. Tom Barry, prin. — Fax 780-7137
Olathe North SHS — 1,100/10-12
  600 E Prairie St 66061 — 913-780-7140
  Dr. Connie Heinen, prin. — Fax 780-7837
Olathe Northwest SHS — 800/10-12
  21300 College Blvd 66061 — 913-780-7150
  Dr. Gwen Poss, prin. — Fax 780-7159
Olathe South SHS — 1,500/10-12
  1640 E 151st St 66062 — 913-780-7160
  Phil Clark, prin. — Fax 780-7170
Oregon Trail JHS — 700/7-9
  1800 W Dennis Ave 66061 — 913-780-7250
  Steve Massey, prin. — Fax 780-7256
Pioneer Trail JHS — 600/7-9
  15100 W 127th St 66062 — 913-780-7270
  Kim Gillespie, prin. — Fax 780-7278
Prairie Trail JHS — 7-9
  21600 W 107th St 66061 — 913-780-7280
  Stacey Yurkovich, prin. — Fax 780-7289
Santa Fe Trail JHS — 1,000/7-9
  1100 N Ridgeview Rd 66061 — 913-780-7290
  Heather Oliva-Martinez, prin. — Fax 780-7296

Kansas School for the Deaf — Post-Sec.
  450 E Park St 66061 — 913-791-0573
Metro Academy — 400/6-12
  17550 W 159th St 66062 — 913-648-6894
  Robin Sullivan, admin.
Mid-America Nazarene University — Post-Sec.
  2030 E College Way 66062 — 913-782-3750
Superior School of Hairdressing — Post-Sec.
  1215 E Santa Fe St 66061 — 913-782-4004

Olpe, Lyon, Pop. 513
Southern Lyon County USD 252
  Supt. — See Hartford
Olpe HS — 200/7-12
  PO Box 206 66865 — 620-475-3223
  Shari Hatfield, prin. — Fax 475-3951

Onaga, Pottawatomie, Pop. 687
Onaga-Havensville-Wheaton USD 322 — 400/PK-12
  PO Box 60 66521 — 785-889-4614
  Greg Markowitz, supt. — Fax 889-4662
  www.usd322.org
Onaga HS — 100/9-12
  500 High St 66521 — 785-889-4251
  Greg Markowitz, prin. — Fax 889-4944

Osage City, Osage, Pop. 2,954
Osage City USD 420 — 700/K-12
520 Main St 66523 — 785-528-3176
David Carriger, supt. — Fax 528-3932
www.usd420.org
Osage City HS — 200/9-12
515 Ellinwood St 66523 — 785-528-3172
Troy Hutton, prin. — Fax 528-2980

Osawatomie, Miami, Pop. 4,595
Osawatomie USD 367 — 1,100/PK-12
1200 Trojan Dr 66064 — 913-755-4172
Robert Cook, supt. — Fax 755-2031
Osawatomie HS — 400/9-12
1200 Trojan Dr 66064 — 913-755-2191
Doug Chisam, prin. — Fax 755-2645
Osawatomie MS — 300/6-8
428 Pacific Ave 66064 — 913-755-4155
Dan Welch, prin. — Fax 755-2197

Osborne, Osborne, Pop. 1,497
Osborne County USD 392 — 400/PK-12
234 N 3rd St Ste B 67473 — 785-346-2145
Daniel Newman, supt. — Fax 346-2448
www.usd392.k12.ks.us
Osborne JSHS — 200/7-12
219 N 2nd St 67473 — 785-346-2143
Tom Conway, prin. — Fax 346-2331

Oskaloosa, Jefferson, Pop. 1,157
Oskaloosa USD 341 — 600/PK-12
404 Park St 66066 — 785-863-2539
Dr. Loren Lutes, supt. — Fax 863-3080
www.usd341.org
Oskaloosa HS — 200/9-12
404 Park St 66066 — 785-863-2281
Brad Reed, prin. — Fax 863-3106
Oskaloosa MS — 200/6-8
404 Park St 66066 — 785-863-3237
Darren Shupe, prin. — Fax 863-9247

Oswego, Labette, Pop. 1,989
Oswego USD 504 — 500/PK-12
PO Box 129 67356 — 620-795-2126
Terry Karlin, supt. — Fax 795-4871
Oswego HS — 100/9-12
1501 Tomahawk Trl 67356 — 620-795-2125
Rod Wittmer, prin. — Fax 795-2130
Oswego MS — 100/6-8
410 Kansas St 67356 — 620-795-4724
Mikel Ward, prin. — Fax 795-4799

Otis, Rush, Pop. 316
Otis-Bison USD 403
Supt. — See Albert
Otis-Bison HS — 100/9-12
PO Box 257 67565 — 785-387-2337
Mark Goodheart, prin. — Fax 387-2557

Ottawa, Franklin, Pop. 12,031
Ottawa USD 290 — 2,400/K-12
123 W 4th St 66067 — 785-229-8010
Dean Katt, supt. — Fax 229-8019
www.usd290.org
Career Technology Educational Coop — Vo/Tech
908 W 11th St 66067 — 785-229-8020
Justin Henry, prin. — Fax 229-8029
Ottawa HS — 800/9-12
1120 S Ash St 66067 — 785-229-8020
Justin Henry, prin. — Fax 229-8029
Ottawa MS — 600/6-8
1230 S Ash St 66067 — 785-229-8030
Randy Oliver, prin. — Fax 229-8039

Bethel Christian Academy — 50/PK-12
3755 Nevada Rd 66067 — 785-242-1226
Donita Callahan, prin. — Fax 242-1226
Ottawa University — Post-Sec.
1001 S Cedar St 66067 — 785-242-5200

Overland Park, Johnson, Pop. 160,368
Blue Valley USD 229 — 18,700/PK-12
PO Box 23901 66283 — 913-239-4000
Tom Trigg Ed.D., supt. — Fax 239-4150
www.bluevalleyk12.org
Blue Valley MS — 500/6-8
5001 W 163rd Ter, — 913-239-5100
Roxana Rogers, prin. — Fax 681-4159
Blue Valley North HS — 1,500/9-12
12200 Lamar Ave 66209 — 913-239-3000
Carter Burns Ed.D., prin. — Fax 345-7338
Blue Valley Northwest HS — 1,500/9-12
13260 Switzer Rd 66213 — 913-239-3400
Amy Murphy Ed.D., prin. — Fax 681-7045
Blue Valley West HS — 1,300/9-12
16200 Antioch Rd, — 913-239-3700
John Laurie Ph.D., prin. — Fax 402-3025
Harmony MS — 700/6-8
10101 W 141st St 66221 — 913-239-5200
Sheila Albers, prin. — Fax 681-4811
Lakewood MS — 300/6-8
6601 Edgewater Dr 66223 — 913-239-5800
Scott Currier, prin. — Fax 681-4726
Overland Trail MS — 600/6-8
6201 W 133rd St 66209 — 913-239-5400
Jessica Dain Ed.D., prin. — Fax 681-4432
Oxford MS — 500/6-8
12500 Switzer Rd 66213 — 913-239-5500
Jan Draper, prin. — Fax 681-4502
Other Schools – See Leawood, Stilwell

College of Hair Design — Post-Sec.
10324 Mastin St 66212 — 913-492-4114
Hyman Brand Hebrew Academy — 300/K-12
5801 W 115th St 66211 — 913-327-8150
Adam Holden, hdmstr. — Fax 327-8180
Johnson County Community College — Post-Sec.
12345 College Blvd 66210 — 913-469-8500

LaBaron Hairdressing Academy — Post-Sec.
8119 Robinson St 66204 — 913-642-0077
Overland Christian S — 100/PK-12
7401 Metcalf Ave 66204 — 913-722-0272
Greg Blake, prin. — Fax 722-2135
St. Thomas Aquinas HS — 1,300/9-12
11411 Pflumm Rd 66215 — 913-345-1411
Dr. Bill Ford, pres. — Fax 345-2319
Westminster Christian HS — 100/9-12
9333 W 95th St 66221 — 913-685-2322
William Fischer, prin. — Fax 685-9822
Wright Business School — Post-Sec.
8951 Metcalf Ave 66212 — 913-385-7700

Oxford, Sumner, Pop. 1,134
Oxford USD 358 — 400/PK-12
PO Box 937 67119 — 620-455-2227
Charles Coblentz, supt. — Fax 455-3680
www.usd358.com
Oxford JSHS — 200/7-12
PO Box 970 67119 — 620-455-2410
Lindell Franz, prin. — Fax 455-3741

Palco, Rooks, Pop. 235
Palco USD 269 — 200/PK-12
PO Box B 67657 — 785-737-4635
David Miller, supt. — Fax 737-4636
www.usd269.k12.ks.us/
Palco HS — 50/9-12
PO Box 29 67657 — 785-737-4645
David Miller, prin. — Fax 737-4646
Other Schools – See Damar

Paola, Miami, Pop. 5,065
Paola USD 368 — 2,100/PK-12
PO Box 268 66071 — 913-294-3646
Rod Allen, supt. — Fax 294-3623
www.usd368.org/
Paola HS — 700/9-12
401 Angela Dr 66071 — 913-294-4367
Jerry Henn, prin. — Fax 294-3497
Paola MS — 500/6-8
405 N Hospital Dr 66071 — 913-294-3726
Cynthia Goering, prin. — Fax 294-3044

Parsons, Labette, Pop. 11,296
Parsons USD 503 — 1,600/PK-12
PO Box 1056 67357 — 620-421-5950
Dr. Deborah Perbeck, supt. — Fax 421-5954
www.vikingnet.net
Parsons HS — 600/9-12
3030 Morton Ave 67357 — 620-421-3660
Marty Anderson, prin. — Fax 423-8816
Parsons MS — 400/6-8
2719 Main St 67357 — 620-421-4190
Terry Smith, prin. — Fax 423-8822

Labette Community College — Post-Sec.
200 S 14th St 67357 — 620-421-6700

Paxico, Wabaunsee, Pop. 213
Mill Creek Valley USD 329
Supt. — See Alma
Mill Creek Valley JHS — 100/7-8
PO Box 128 66526 — 785-636-5353
Daniel Wagner, prin. — Fax 636-5116

Peabody, Marion, Pop. 1,354
Peabody-Burns USD 398 — 400/PK-12
506 N Elm St 66866 — 620-983-2198
Thomas Alstrom, supt. — Fax 983-2247
Peabody-Burns JSHS — 200/7-12
810 N Sycamore St 66866 — 620-983-2196
Mary Brown, prin. — Fax 983-2773

Perry, Jefferson, Pop. 898
Perry USD 343 — 1,000/PK-12
PO Box 729 66073 — 785-597-5138
Steve Johnston, supt. — Fax 597-2254
www.usd343.org/
Perry-Lecompton HS — 300/9-12
PO Box 18 66073 — 785-597-5124
Al Ferrell, prin. — Fax 597-5177
Perry-Lecompton MS — 300/5-8
PO Box 31 66073 — 785-597-5159
Armin Landis, prin. — Fax 597-5014

Phillipsburg, Phillips, Pop. 2,510
Phillipsburg USD 325 — 600/PK-12
240 S 7th St 67661 — 785-543-5281
Kent Otte, supt. — Fax 543-2271
www.usd235.com
Phillipsburg HS — 200/9-12
410 S 7th St 67661 — 785-543-5251
Brian Boeve, prin. — Fax 543-6305
Phillipsburg MS — 200/5-8
647 7th St 67661 — 785-543-5114
Rick Riffel, prin. — Fax 543-2934

Pittsburg, Crawford, Pop. 19,276
Pittsburg USD 250 — 2,500/K-12
PO Box 75 66762 — 620-235-3100
Gary Price, supt. — Fax 235-3106
www.usd250.org
Pittsburg HS — 800/9-12
1978 E 4th St 66762 — 620-235-3200
Mike Philpot, prin. — Fax 235-3210
Pittsburg MS — 600/6-8
1310 N Broadway St 66762 — 620-235-3240
Cory Gibson, prin. — Fax 235-3248

Pittsburg State University — Post-Sec.
1701 S Broadway St 66762 — 620-231-7000
St. Mary's Colgan HS — 200/7-12
212 E 9th St 66762 — 620-231-4690
Dr. Bill Dickey, prin. — Fax 231-0690

Plains, Meade, Pop. 1,180
Kismet-Plains USD 483 — 700/PK-12
PO Box 760 67869 — 620-563-7103
Larrell Cook, supt. — Fax 563-7348
www.usd483.net
Other Schools – See Kismet

Plainville, Rooks, Pop. 1,917
Plainville USD 270 — 400/PK-12
111 W Mill St 67663 — 785-434-4678
Dr. Harry Austin, supt. — Fax 434-7404
Plainville HS — 200/9-12
202 SE Cardinal Ave 67663 — 785-434-4547
Cherie Nicholson, prin. — Fax 434-4689

Pleasanton, Linn, Pop. 1,381
Pleasanton USD 344 — 400/K-12
PO Box 480 66075 — 913-352-8534
Tim Conrad, supt. — Fax 352-6588
www.usd344.org/
Pleasanton HS — 200/7-12
PO Box 480 66075 — 913-352-8701
David Schmidt, prin. — Fax 352-6588

Pomona, Franklin, Pop. 952
West Franklin USD 287 — 900/PK-12
510 E Franklin St 66076 — 785-566-3396
Dr. Susan Myers, supt. — Fax 566-8325
www.usd287.org
Pomona HS — 200/9-12
511 E Franklin St 66076 — 785-566-3392
Royce Powelson, prin. — Fax 566-8454
Other Schools – See Williamsburg

Prairie Village, Johnson, Pop. 21,729

Kansas City Christian HS — 200/9-12
4801 W 79th St 66208 — 913-648-5227
E. Allan Chugg, prin. — Fax 648-5269

Pratt, Pratt, Pop. 6,422
Pratt USD 382 — 1,200/PK-12
401 N Ninnescah St 67124 — 620-672-4500
Dr. Glen Davis, supt. — Fax 672-4509
www.usd382.com
Liberty MS — 300/6-8
300 S Iuka St 67124 — 620-672-4530
Mike McDermeit, prin. — Fax 672-4539
Pratt HS — 400/9-12
401 S Hamilton St 67124 — 620-672-4540
Tim Kuhn, prin. — Fax 672-4549

Skyline USD 438 — 300/K-12
20269 W US Highway 54 67124 — 620-672-5651
Mike Sanders, supt. — Fax 672-9377
www.usd438.k12.ks.us
Skyline HS — 100/9-12
20269 W US Highway 54 67124 — 620-672-5651
Herb McPherson, prin. — Fax 672-9377

Pratt Community College — Post-Sec.
Hwy 61 67124 — 620-672-5641

Pretty Prairie, Reno, Pop. 598
Pretty Prairie USD 311 — 300/K-12
PO Box 218 67570 — 620-459-6241
A.C. Boland, supt. — Fax 459-6810
www.usd311.com
Pretty Prairie HS — 100/9-12
PO Box 326 67570 — 620-459-6313
Brad Wade, prin. — Fax 459-6935
Pretty Prairie MS — 100/5-8
PO Box 326 67570 — 620-459-6911
Brad Wade, prin. — Fax 459-6729

Protection, Comanche, Pop. 540
Comanche County USD 300
Supt. — See Coldwater
South Central MS — 100/6-8
PO Box 38 67127 — 620-622-4545
Matt Jellison, prin. — Fax 622-4844

Quenemo, Osage, Pop. 461
Marais Des Cygnes Valley USD 456
Supt. — See Melvern
Marais Des Cygnes Valley MS — 100/4-8
PO Box 139 66528 — 785-759-3512
Twila Wollenberg, prin. — Fax 759-3515

Quinter, Gove, Pop. 901
Quinter USD 293 — 400/PK-12
PO Box 540 67752 — 785-754-2470
Allaire Homburg, supt. — Fax 754-3365
www.quinterhs.org
Quinter JSHS — 200/7-12
PO Box 459 67752 — 785-754-3660
Gary Feldkamp, prin. — Fax 754-3905

Randall, Jewell, Pop. 77
Jewell USD 279 — 200/K-12
PO Box 96 66963 — 785-739-2216
Ron Kelley, supt. — Fax 739-2219
Other Schools – See Jewell

Randolph, Riley, Pop. 174
Blue Valley USD 384 — 200/K-12
PO Box 98 66554 — 785-293-5256
Brady Burton, supt. — Fax 293-5607
www.usd384.k12.ks.us/home.html
Blue Valley HS — 100/9-12
PO Box 68 66554 — 785-293-5255
Tim Winter, prin. — Fax 293-5372
Randolph MS — 100/5-8
PO Box 38 66554 — 785-293-5253
Tim Winter, prin. — Fax 293-4405

Ransom, Ness, Pop. 307
Western Plains USD 106 — 100/PK-12
311 W Ogden St 67572 — 785-398-2535
James Frank, supt. — Fax 398-2492
www.usd106.k12.ks.us/

Western Plains HS — 50/9-12
PO Box 218 67572 — 785-731-2352
Jon Nuttle, prin. — Fax 731-2235

Rexford, Thomas, Pop. 155
Golden Plains USD 316
Supt. — See Selden
Golden Plains HS — 100/9-12
PO Box 100 67753 — 785-687-3265
Dr. Roger Baskerville, prin. — Fax 687-2285
Golden Plains MS — 100/6-8
PO Box 100 67753 — 785-687-3265
Dr. Roger Baskerville, prin. — Fax 687-2285

Richmond, Franklin, Pop. 518
Central Heights USD 288 — 600/K-12
3521 Ellis Rd 66080 — 785-869-3455
Deanne Alexander, supt. — Fax 869-2675
www.usd288.k12.ks.us
Central Heights JSHS — 300/7-12
3521 Ellis Rd 66080 — 785-869-3555
Tom Horstick, prin. — Fax 869-2675

Riley, Riley, Pop. 884
Riley County USD 378 — 700/PK-12
PO Box 326 66531 — 785-485-4000
Brad Starnes, supt. — Fax 485-2860
www.usd378.org/
Riley County HS — 200/9-12
PO Box 38 66531 — 785-485-4020
Steve Mies, prin. — Fax 485-2426

Riverton, Cherokee
Riverton USD 404 — 800/K-12
PO Box 290 66770 — 620-848-3386
David L. Walters, supt. — Fax 848-9853
www.usd404.org/
Riverton HS — 200/9-12
PO Box 290 66770 — 620-848-3388
Todd Berry, prin. — Fax 848-3609
Riverton MS — 200/6-8
PO Box 260 66770 — 620-848-3355
Becky Murray, prin. — Fax 848-3609

Roeland Park, Johnson, Pop. 7,075

Bishop Miege HS — 800/9-12
5041 Reinhardt Dr 66205 — 913-262-2700
Stan Herbic, prin. — Fax 262-2752

Rolla, Morton, Pop. 456
Rolla USD 217 — 200/PK-12
PO Box 167 67954 — 620-593-4344
Gregg Dunkelberger, supt. — Fax 593-4250
www.usd217.org
Rolla HS — 100/6-12
PO Box 167 67954 — 620-593-4345
Gary Bane, prin. — Fax 593-4204

Rosalia, Butler
Flinthills USD 492 — 300/K-12
PO Box 188 67132 — 620-476-2237
Dr. Phil Mahan, supt. — Fax 476-2253
www.usd492.org/
Flinthills MSHS — 200/7-12
PO Box 188 67132 — 620-476-2215
Bob Diepenbrock, prin. — Fax 476-2244

Rose Hill, Butler, Pop. 3,710
Rose Hill USD 394 — 1,800/PK-12
104 N Rose Hill Rd 67133 — 316-776-3300
Randal Chickadonz, supt. — Fax 776-3309
www.usd394.com
Rose Hill HS — 600/9-12
104 N Rose Hill Rd 67133 — 316-776-3360
Stephen Gammer, prin. — Fax 776-3378
Rose Hill MS — 500/6-8
104 N Rose Hill Rd 67133 — 316-776-3320
Kay Walker, prin. — Fax 776-3319

Rossville, Shawnee, Pop. 1,001
Kaw Valley USD 321
Supt. — See Saint Marys
Rossville HS — 200/7-12
PO Box 68 66533 — 785-584-6193
John Johnson, prin. — Fax 584-6379

Rozel, Pawnee, Pop. 172
Pawnee Heights USD 496 — 200/K-12
PO Box 98 67574 — 620-527-4212
Raymond Patterson, supt. — Fax 527-4213
www.usd496.net/
Pawnee Heights HS — 100/9-12
PO Box 97 67574 — 620-527-4211
Dan Binder, prin. — Fax 527-4215

Russell, Russell, Pop. 4,404
Russell County USD 407 — 1,000/K-12
802 N Main St 67665 — 785-483-2173
David Couch, supt. — Fax 483-2175
www.usd407.org/usd/links.html
Ruppenthal MS — 200/6-8
400 N Elm St 67665 — 785-483-3174
Duane Adams, prin. — Fax 483-5386
Russell HS — 300/9-12
565 E State St 67665 — 785-483-5631
Larry Bernard, prin. — Fax 483-5636
Other Schools – See Lucas

Sabetha, Nemaha, Pop. 2,559
Sabetha USD 441 — 1,000/PK-12
107 Oregon St 66534 — 785-284-2175
Dennis Stones, supt. — Fax 284-3739
sabetha441.k12.ks.us
Sabetha HS — 300/9-12
1011 S US Old Highway 75 66534 — 785-284-2155
Todd Evans, prin. — Fax 284-2600
Sabetha MS — 200/6-8
751 Blue Jay Dr 66534 — 785-284-2151
Thomas Palmer, prin. — Fax 284-0061
Other Schools – See Wetmore

Saint Francis, Cheyenne, Pop. 1,390
St. Francis USD 297 — 400/K-12
PO Box 1110 67756 — 785-332-8182
Carl Werner, supt. — Fax 332-8177
www.usd297.k12.ks.us
Saint Francis JSHS — 200/7-12
PO Box 1110 67756 — 785-332-8153
Scott Carmichael, prin. — Fax 332-8177

Saint George, Pottawatomie, Pop. 457
Rock Creek USD 323
Supt. — See Westmoreland
Rock Creek JSHS — 400/7-12
9355 Flush Rd 66535 — 785-494-8591
Dennis Post, prin. — Fax 494-8595

Saint John, Stafford, Pop. 1,249
St. John-Hudson USD 350 — 400/K-12
406 N Monroe St 67576 — 620-549-3564
Dr. James Kenworthy, supt. — Fax 549-3964
www.usd350.com/
Saint John JSHS — 200/7-12
505 N Broadway St 67576 — 620-549-3277
Mike Burgan, prin. — Fax 549-3279

Saint Marys, Pottawatomie, Pop. 2,253
Kaw Valley USD 321 — 1,000/PK-12
411 W Lasley St 66536 — 785-437-2254
Martin Stessman, supt. — Fax 437-3155
www.kawvalley.k12.ks.us/
Saint Marys HS — 200/7-12
601 E Lasley St 66536 — 785-437-6257
Eric Steele, prin. — Fax 437-3460
Other Schools – See Rossville

Saint Paul, Neosho, Pop. 657
Chetopa - St. Paul USD 505
Supt. — See Chetopa
Saint Paul HS — 100/7-12
1st & Washington 66771 — 620-449-2245
Felix Diskin, prin. — Fax 449-8960

Salina, Saline, Pop. 45,833
Salina USD 305 — 7,600/PK-12
PO Box 797 67402 — 785-309-4700
Dr. Robert Winter, supt. — Fax 309-4737
www.usd305.com
Lakewood MS — 900/6-8
1135 E Lakewood Cir 67401 — 785-309-4000
Reuben Montoy, prin. — Fax 309-4001
Salina Area Technical S — Vo/Tech
2562 Centennial Rd # A 67401 — 785-309-3100
Duane Custer, prin. — Fax 309-3101
Salina Central HS — 1,100/9-12
650 E Crawford St 67401 — 785-309-3500
Stan Vaughn, prin. — Fax 309-3501
Salina South HS — 1,100/9-12
730 E Magnolia Rd 67401 — 785-309-3700
Myron Graber, prin. — Fax 309-3701
Salina South MS — 900/6-8
2040 S 4th St 67401 — 785-309-3900
Mike Lowers, prin. — Fax 309-3901

Academy of Hair Design — Post-Sec.
115 S 5th St 67401 — 785-825-8155
Brown Mackie College — Post-Sec.
2106 S 9th St 67401 — 785-825-5422
Kansas State University — Post-Sec.
2310 Centennial Rd 67401 — 785-826-2600
Kansas Wesleyan University — Post-Sec.
100 E Claflin Ave 67401 — 785-827-5541
Sacred Heart HS — 200/7-12
234 E Cloud St 67401 — 785-827-4422
John Krajicek, prin. — Fax 827-8648
St. Johns Military S — 100/7-12
PO Box 5020 67402 — 785-823-7231
Doug Randolph, prin. — Fax 823-7236
Salina Area Vocational Technical School — Post-Sec.
2562 Centennial Rd 67401 — 785-309-3100

Satanta, Haskell, Pop. 1,197
Satanta USD 507 — 400/PK-12
PO Box 279 67870 — 620-649-2234
Ardith Dunn, supt. — Fax 649-2668
www.usd507.org
Satanta JSHS — 200/7-12
PO Box 69 67870 — 620-649-2611
Ron Levan, prin. — Fax 649-2668

Scandia, Republic, Pop. 387
Pike Valley USD 426 — 300/PK-12
PO Box 291 66966 — 785-335-2206
Gary Kraus, supt. — Fax 335-2219
www.pikevalley.com/
Pike Valley HS — 100/9-12
PO Box 339 66966 — 785-335-2294
Gary Kraus, prin. — Fax 335-2386
Other Schools – See Courtland

Scott City, Scott, Pop. 3,640
Scott County USD 466 — 900/PK-12
PO Box 288 67871 — 620-872-7600
Dean Katt, supt. — Fax 872-7609
www.usd466.com/
Scott City HS — 300/9-12
712 Main St 67871 — 620-872-7620
Eric Swanson, prin. — Fax 872-7629
Scott City MS — 300/5-8
809 W 9th St 67871 — 620-872-7640
Neal George, prin. — Fax 872-7649

Sedan, Chautauqua, Pop. 1,288
Chautauqua County USD 286 — 400/PK-12
302 N Sherman 67361 — 620-725-3187
Scott Hills, supt. — Fax 725-5642
www.usd286-sedan-ks.org
Sedan HS — 200/7-12
416 E Elm St 67361 — 620-725-3186
Mike Todd, prin. — Fax 725-3188

Sedgwick, Harvey, Pop. 1,637
Sedgwick USD 439 — 500/K-12
PO Box K 67135 — 316-772-5783
Michael Hull, supt. — Fax 772-0274
www.usd439.k12.ks.us
Sedgwick HS — 100/9-12
PO Box K 67135 — 316-772-5155
Kevin Stucky, prin. — Fax 772-0334

Selden, Sheridan, Pop. 190
Golden Plains USD 316 — 200/K-12
PO Box 199 67757 — 785-386-4559
Dr. Roger Baskerville, supt. — Fax 386-4562
usd316.k12.ks.us/
Other Schools – See Rexford

Seneca, Nemaha, Pop. 2,084
Nemaha Valley USD 442 — 500/K-12
318 Main St 66538 — 785-336-6101
Brian Harris, supt. — Fax 336-2268
www.usd442.org
Nemaha Valley HS — 200/9-12
214 N 11th St 66538 — 785-336-3557
Patrick McKernan, prin. — Fax 336-3672

Sharon Springs, Wallace, Pop. 762
Wallace County USD 241 — 200/K-12
521 N Main St 67758 — 785-852-4252
Susan Scherling, supt. — Fax 852-4603
www.usd241.org/
Wallace County HS — 100/9-12
521 N Main St 67758 — 785-852-4240
Bruce Bolen, prin. — Fax 852-4603

Shawnee, Johnson, Pop. 54,093
De Soto USD 232
Supt. — See De Soto
Mill Valley HS — 800/9-12
5900 Monticello Rd 66226 — 913-422-4351
Dr. Joe Novak, prin. — Fax 422-4039
Monticello Trails MS — 700/6-8
6100 Monticello Rd 66226 — 913-422-1100
Tobie Waldeck, prin. — Fax 422-4990

Cutting Edge Hairstyling Academy — Post-Sec.
12148 Shawnee Mission Pkwy 66216 — 913-962-0076
Maranatha Academy — 400/4-12
6826 Lackman Rd 66217 — 913-631-0637
Boyd Beck, prin. — Fax 631-0899
Midland Adventist Academy — 200/K-12
6915 Maurer Rd 66217 — 913-268-7400
Gary Kruger, prin. — Fax 268-4968

Shawnee Mission, See Merriam
Shawnee Mission USD 512 — 28,700/PK-12
7235 Antioch Rd 66204 — 913-993-6200
Marjorie Kaplan Ph.D., supt. — Fax 993-6247
www.smsd.org
Antioch MS — 500/7-8
8200 W 71st St 66204 — 913-993-0000
Dr. Kevin Peters, prin. — Fax 993-0199
Broadmoor Technical Center — Vo/Tech
6701 W 83rd St 66204 — 913-993-9700
Dr. Scott Sherman, prin. — Fax 993-9799
Hocker Grove MS — 600/7-8
10400 Johnson Dr 66203 — 913-993-0200
Debbie Pfortmiller, prin. — Fax 993-0399
Indian Hills MS — 500/7-8
6400 Mission Rd 66208 — 913-993-0400
Carla Allen, prin. — Fax 993-0599
Indian Woods MS — 800/7-8
9700 Woodson Dr 66207 — 913-993-0600
Jim Wink, prin. — Fax 993-0799
Mission Valley MS — 600/7-8
8500 Mission Rd 66206 — 913-993-0800
Dr. Susie Ostmeyer, prin. — Fax 993-0999
Shawnee Mission East HS — 2,100/9-12
7500 Mission Rd 66208 — 913-993-6600
Dr. Angelo Cocolis, prin. — Fax 993-6899
Shawnee Mission North HS — 2,000/9-12
7401 Johnson Dr 66202 — 913-993-6900
Tony Lake, prin. — Fax 993-7099
Shawnee Mission Northwest HS — 1,900/9-12
12701 W 67th St 66216 — 913-993-7200
Dr. William Harrington, prin. — Fax 993-7499
Shawnee Mission South HS — 1,700/9-12
5800 W 107th St 66207 — 913-993-7500
Dr. Joe Gilhaus, prin. — Fax 993-7799
Shawnee Mission West HS — 2,000/9-12
8800 W 85th St 66212 — 913-993-7800
Dr. Charles McLean, prin. — Fax 993-8099
Trailridge MS — 600/7-8
7500 Quivira Rd 66216 — 913-993-1000
Dr. Larry King, prin. — Fax 993-1199
Westridge MS — 1,000/7-8
9300 Nieman Rd 66214 — 913-993-1200
Janice Jackson, prin. — Fax 993-1399

Silver Lake, Shawnee, Pop. 1,340
Silver Lake USD 372 — 700/PK-12
PO Box 39 66539 — 785-582-4026
Dr. Steven Pegram, supt. — Fax 582-5259
www.silverlakeeagles.org
Silver Lake JSHS — 300/7-12
PO Box 39 66539 — 785-582-4639
Larry Winter, prin. — Fax 582-4265

Smith Center, Smith, Pop. 1,773
Smith Center USD 237 — 500/PK-12
PO Box 329 66967 — 785-282-6665
Ron Meitler, supt. — Fax 282-6518
www.usd237.com
Smith Center JSHS — 200/7-12
PO Box 329 66967 — 785-282-6609
Greg Koelsch, prin. — Fax 282-5206

Solomon, Dickinson, Pop. 1,063
Solomon USD 393 — 400/K-12
  113 E 7th St 67480 — 785-655-2541
  Dr. Jim Day, supt. — Fax 655-2505
  www.solomon393.k12.ks.us
Solomon JSHS — 200/7-12
  409 N Pine St 67480 — 785-655-2551
  Bob Warkentine, prin. — Fax 655-3011

South Haven, Sumner, Pop. 379
South Haven USD 509 — 200/PK-12
  PO Box 229 67140 — 620-892-5216
  John Showman, supt. — Fax 892-5814
  www.usd509.org/
South Haven JSHS — 100/6-12
  PO Box 229 67140 — 620-892-5215
  Kim White, prin. — Fax 892-5814

Spearville, Ford, Pop. 843
Spearville USD 381 — 400/K-12
  PO Box 338 67876 — 620-385-2676
  Mark Littell, supt. — Fax 385-2614
Spearville JSHS — 200/6-12
  PO Box 158 67876 — 620-385-2631
  David Jackson, prin. — Fax 385-2641

Spring Hill, Johnson, Pop. 3,745
Spring Hill USD 230 — 1,000/K-12
  101 E South St 66083 — 913-592-7200
  Dr. Barton L. Goering, supt. — Fax 592-7270
  www.usd230.org
Spring Hill HS — 500/9-12
  217th St & Bronco Blvd 66083 — 913-592-7299
  Dr. Wayne Burke, prin. — Fax 592-5424
Spring Hill MS — 400/6-8
  300 E South St 66083 — 913-592-7288
  Stephen Fleer, prin. — Fax 592-7225

Stafford, Stafford, Pop. 1,097
Stafford USD 349 — 300/PK-12
  PO Box 400 67578 — 620-234-5243
  Dr. Mary Jo Taylor, supt. — Fax 234-6986
  www.stafford349.com
Stafford MSHS — 200/7-12
  PO Box 370 67578 — 620-234-5248
  John Wyrick, prin. — Fax 234-6041

Sterling, Rice, Pop. 2,568
Sterling USD 376 — 500/PK-12
  PO Box 188 67579 — 620-278-3621
  Fred Dierksen, supt. — Fax 278-3882
  www.usd376.com
Sterling HS — 200/9-12
  308 E Washington Ave 67579 — 620-278-2171
  Gregg Errebo, prin. — Fax 278-3237
Sterling JHS — 100/7-8
  412 N 5th St 67579 — 620-278-3646
  Gregg Errebo, prin. — Fax 278-3673

Sterling College — Post-Sec.
  125 W Cooper St 67579 — 620-278-2173

Stilwell, Johnson
Blue Valley USD 229
  Supt. — See Overland Park
Blue Valley HS — 1,200/9-12
  6001 W 159th St 66085 — 913-239-4800
  Scott Bacon, prin. — Fax 681-4254
Pleasant Ridge MS — 800/6-8
  9000 W 165th St 66085 — 913-239-5700
  Diana Tate, prin. — Fax 681-7111

Stockton, Rooks, Pop. 1,477
Stockton USD 271 — 400/PK-12
  211 Main St 67669 — 785-425-6360
  Jim Hickel, supt. — Fax 425-6923
  www.usd271.k12.ks.us/
Stockton HS — 100/9-12
  211 Main St 67669 — 785-425-6784
  Keith Hall, prin. — Fax 425-6200

Strong City, Chase, Pop. 598
Chase County USD 284
  Supt. — See Cottonwood Falls
Chase County MS — 100/5-8
  PO Box 279 66869 — 620-273-6676
  Jerry Pittman, prin. — Fax 273-6690

Sublette, Haskell, Pop. 1,576
Sublette USD 374 — 400/PK-12
  PO Box 670 67877 — 620-675-2277
  Rex Bruce, supt. — Fax 675-2652
  www.usd374.org/
Sublette MSHS — 200/7-12
  PO Box 460 67877 — 620-675-2232
  Mike Simmons, prin. — Fax 675-8347

Crosswalk Christian S — 50/PK-12
  PO Box 730 67877 — 620-675-2283
  Kristi Walter, prin.

Sylvan Grove, Lincoln, Pop. 310
Sylvan Grove USD 299 — 200/K-12
  PO Box 308 67481 — 785-526-7175
  Jude Stecklein, supt. — Fax 526-7182
  www.usd299.k12.ks.us/
Sylvan Unified JSHS — 100/7-12
  PO Box 308 67481 — 785-526-7175
  Byron Marshall, prin. — Fax 526-7182

Syracuse, Hamilton, Pop. 1,848
Syracuse USD 494 — 500/PK-12
  PO Box 1187 67878 — 620-384-7872
  Joan Friend, supt. — Fax 384-7692
  www.syracuse.k12.ks.us
Syracuse JSHS — 200/7-12
  PO Box 1187 67878 — 620-384-7446
  Paul Zuzelski, prin. — Fax 384-6686

Tecumseh, Shawnee
Shawnee Heights USD 450 — 2,800/PK-12
  4401 SE Shawnee Heights Rd 66542 — 785-379-5800
  Martin Stessman, supt. — Fax 379-5810
  www.snh450.k12.ks.us/
Shawnee Heights HS — 9-10
  4141 SE Shawnee Heights Rd 66542 — 785-379-5860
  Matthew Hirsch, prin. — Fax 379-5869
Shawnee Heights MS — 600/7-8
  4335 SE Shawnee Heights Rd 66542 — 785-379-5830
  Cleo Gardner, prin. — Fax 379-5848
Shawnee Heights SHS — 500/11-12
  4201 SE Shawnee Heights Rd 66542 — 785-379-5880
  Warren Watson, prin. — Fax 379-5889

Tescott, Ottawa, Pop. 340
Twin Valley USD 240
  Supt. — See Bennington
Tescott HS — 100/9-12
  PO Box 196 67484 — 785-283-4385
  David Zlab, prin. — Fax 283-4347

Tipton, Mitchell, Pop. 243

Tipton Catholic JSHS — 50/7-12
  PO Box 146 67485 — 785-373-5835
  Gery Hake, prin. — Fax 373-5637

Tonganoxie, Leavenworth, Pop. 3,317
Tonganoxie USD 464 — 1,500/K-12
  PO Box 199 66086 — 913-845-2153
  Dr. Richard Erickson, supt. — Fax 845-3629
  www.tong464.k12.ks.us
Tonganoxie JHS — 400/7-9
  PO Box 980 66086 — 913-845-2627
  Steve Woolf, prin. — Fax 845-2734
Tonganoxie SHS — 400/10-12
  PO Box 179 66086 — 913-845-2654
  Tatia Shelton, prin. — Fax 845-3716

Topeka, Shawnee, Pop. 122,008
Auburn-Washburn USD 437 — 5,200/PK-12
  5928 SW 53rd St 66610 — 785-339-4000
  Dr. Brenda S. Dietrich, supt. — Fax 339-4025
  www.usd437.net
Washburn Rural HS — 1,600/9-12
  5900 SW 61st St 66619 — 785-339-4100
  William Edwards, prin. — Fax 339-4125
Washburn Rural MS — 800/7-8
  5620 SW 61st St 66619 — 785-339-4300
  Gerald Meier, prin. — Fax 339-4325

Seaman USD 345 — 3,300/PK-12
  901 NW Lyman Rd 66608 — 785-575-8600
  Mike Mathes, supt. — Fax 575-8620
  www.usd345.com/
Logan JHS — 400/7-9
  1124 NW Lyman Rd 66608 — 785-575-8700
  Kathleen Sooter, prin. — Fax 575-8703
Northern Hills JHS — 400/7-9
  5620 NW Topeka Blvd 66617 — 785-286-8400
  Robert Horton, prin. — Fax 286-8403
Seaman SHS — 800/10-12
  4850 NW Rochester Rd 66617 — 785-286-8300
  Ron Vinduska, prin. — Fax 286-8320

Topeka USD 501 — 13,600/PK-12
  624 SW 24th St 66611 — 785-295-3000
  Tony Sawyer, supt. — Fax 575-6161
  www.topeka.k12.ks.us
Chase MS — 500/6-8
  2250 NE State St 66616 — 785-295-3840
  Teresa Songs, prin. — Fax 575-6632
Eisenhower MS — 400/6-8
  3305 SE Minnesota Ave 66605 — 785-274-6160
  Steven Roberts, prin. — Fax 274-4603
French MS — 600/6-8
  5257 SW 33rd St 66614 — 785-438-4150
  Vicki Weseman, prin. — Fax 271-3609
Highland Park HS — 1,000/9-12
  2424 SE California Ave 66605 — 785-274-6000
  Dale Cushinberry, prin. — Fax 274-4896
Jardine MS — 600/6-8
  2600 SW 33rd St 66611 — 785-274-6330
  Jeanne Vawter, prin. — Fax 274-4768
Kaw Area Technical S — Vo/Tech
  5724 SW Huntoon St 66604 — 785-273-7141
  Richard Hoffman, dir. — Fax 273-7080
Landon MS — 400/6-8
  731 SW Fairlawn Rd 66606 — 785-438-4220
  Robert Cronkhite, prin. — Fax 271-3737
Robinson MS — 500/6-8
  1125 SW 14th St 66604 — 785-295-3770
  Tammy Austin, prin. — Fax 575-6720
Topeka HS — 1,900/9-12
  800 SW 10th Ave 66612 — 785-295-3150
  Dr. Linda Wiley, prin. — Fax 575-6255
Topeka West HS — 1,100/9-12
  2001 SW Fairlawn Rd 66604 — 785-438-4000
  Dr. Stan Wagstaff, prin. — Fax 271-3497
Adult Education Center — Adult
  5724 SW Huntoon St 66604 — 785-228-6406
  Mary Ann Wittman, coord. — Fax 273-7080

American Academy of Hair Design — Post-Sec.
  901 SW 37th St 66611 — 785-267-5800
Baker University School of Nursing — Post-Sec.
  1500 SW 10th Ave 66604 — 888-866-4242
Bryan Career College — Post-Sec.
  1527 SW Fairlawn Rd 66604 — 785-272-0889
Community College of Cosmetology — Post-Sec.
  3602 SW Topeka Blvd 66611 — 785-267-7701
Hayden HS — 600/9-12
  401 SW Gage Blvd 66606 — 785-272-5210
  Mark Madsen, prin. — Fax 272-2975
Heritage Christian S — 200/PK-12
  3102 NW Topeka Blvd 66617 — 785-286-0427
  Aletha Rogers, prin. — Fax 286-9898

KAW Area Technical School — Post-Sec.
  5724 SW Huntoon St 66604 — 785-273-7140
Washburn University — Post-Sec.
  1700 SW College Ave 66621 — 785-231-1010
WTI Topeka Campus — Post-Sec.
  3712 SW Burlingame Cir 66609 — 785-354-4568

Towanda, Butler, Pop. 1,338
Circle USD 375 — 1,300/K-12
  PO Box 9 67144 — 316-541-2577
  Eliese Holt, supt. — Fax 536-2249
  www.usd375.org
Circle HS — 500/9-12
  PO Box 158 67144 — 316-541-2277
  Al Sersland, prin. — Fax 541-2115
Other Schools – See Benton

Tribune, Greeley, Pop. 765
Greeley County USD 200 — 300/PK-12
  400 W Lawrence St 67879 — 620-376-4211
  Bill Wilson, supt. — Fax 376-2465
  www.tribuneschools.org
Greeley County HS — 100/7-12
  400 W Lawrence St 67879 — 620-376-4265
  Dale Herl, prin. — Fax 376-2465

Troy, Doniphan, Pop. 1,032
Troy USD 429 — 400/PK-12
  PO Box 190 66087 — 785-985-3950
  Dr. Doug Huxman, supt. — Fax 985-3688
  www.troyusd.org/
Troy MSHS — 200/7-12
  PO Box 160 66087 — 785-985-3533
  Don Cash, prin. — Fax 985-3885

Tyro, Montgomery, Pop. 223

Tyro Community Christian S — 200/K-12
  PO Box 308 67364 — 620-289-4450
  Terry Byrd, prin. — Fax 289-4459

Udall, Cowley, Pop. 789
Udall USD 463 — 200/PK-12
  PO Box 386 67146 — 620-782-3355
  Loren Feldkamp, supt. — Fax 782-9690
  www.usd463.org/
Udall HS — 100/9-12
  PO Box 356 67146 — 620-782-3623
  Grady Sewell, prin. — Fax 782-9689
Udall MS — 6-8
  PO Box 356 67146 — 620-782-3623
  Grady Sewell, prin. — Fax 782-9689

Ulysses, Grant, Pop. 5,790
Ulysses USD 214 — 1,700/PK-12
  111 S Baughman St 67880 — 620-356-3655
  Bill Hall, supt. — Fax 356-5181
  www.ulysses.org
Kepley MS — 400/6-8
  113 N Colorado St 67880 — 620-356-3025
  Juan Perez, prin. — Fax 356-3024
Ulysses HS — 500/9-12
  501 N Mccall St 67880 — 620-356-1380
  Rodger Hilton, prin. — Fax 356-5566

Uniontown, Bourbon, Pop. 281
Uniontown USD 235 — 500/PK-12
  401 5th St 66779 — 620-756-4302
  Randy Rockhold, supt. — Fax 756-4492
  www.usd235.org/
Uniontown HS — 200/7-12
  601 5th St 66779 — 620-756-4301
  Tracy Smith, prin. — Fax 756-4340

Valley Center, Sedgwick, Pop. 5,167
Valley Center USD 262 — 2,300/PK-12
  PO Box 157 67147 — 316-755-7100
  Mike Meier, supt. — Fax 755-7102
  www.usd262.net
Valley Center HS — 800/9-12
  800 N Meridian Ave 67147 — 316-755-7130
  Louise Herrington, prin. — Fax 755-7134
Valley Center MS — 600/6-8
  737 N Meridian Ave 67147 — 316-755-7160
  Paul Schultz, prin. — Fax 755-7164

Valley Falls, Jefferson, Pop. 1,217
Valley Falls USD 338 — 400/K-12
  700 Oak St 66088 — 785-945-3214
  David Grove, supt. — Fax 945-3215
  www.usd338.com
Valley Falls HS — 100/9-12
  601 Elm St 66088 — 785-945-3229
  Robert Davies, prin. — Fax 945-3220

Vermillion, Marshall, Pop. 101
Vermillion USD 380 — 600/PK-12
  PO Box 107 66544 — 785-382-6216
  Elizabeth Reust, supt. — Fax 382-6213
  www.usd380.com
Other Schools – See Centralia, Frankfort

Victoria, Ellis, Pop. 1,181
Victoria USD 432 — 300/K-12
  PO Box 139 67671 — 785-735-9212
  Linda Kenne, supt. — Fax 735-9229
Victoria HS — 100/9-12
  PO Box 20 67671 — 785-735-9211
  Mike Kreller, prin. — Fax 735-9216

Wakeeney, Trego, Pop. 1,800
WaKeeney USD 208 — 400/PK-12
  527 Russell Ave 67672 — 785-743-2145
  Robert Scheib, supt. — Fax 743-2071
  www.wakeeney.com/schools/
Trego Community HS — 100/9-12
  1200 Russell Ave 67672 — 785-743-2061
  Daryl Stegman, prin. — Fax 743-2449

Wakefield, Clay, Pop. 854
Clay Center USD 379
  Supt. — See Clay Center

Wakefield HS 100/9-12
PO Box 40 67487 785-461-5437
Penny Hargrove, prin. Fax 461-5892

Wamego, Pottawatomie, Pop. 4,237
Wamego USD 320 1,300/PK-12
510 E US Highway 24 66547 785-456-7643
Doug Conwell, supt. Fax 456-8125
www.usd320.com
Wamego HS 500/9-12
801 Lincoln St 66547 785-456-2214
Donna Workman, prin. Fax 456-7382
Wamego MS 300/6-8
1701 Kaw Valley Rd 66547 785-456-7682
Larry Doll, prin. Fax 456-2944

Washington, Washington, Pop. 1,168
Washington USD 222 300/PK-12
PO Box 275 66968 785-325-2261
Michael Stegman, supt. Fax 325-2771
www.usd222.org
Washington JSHS 200/7-12
PO Box 275 66968 785-325-2261
Phil Wilson, prin. Fax 325-2138

Waterville, Marshall, Pop. 646
Valley Heights USD 498 400/K-12
PO Box 89 66548 785-363-2398
John Bergkamp, supt. Fax 363-2269
www.valleyheights.org/
Other Schools – See Blue Rapids

Wathena, Doniphan, Pop. 1,331
Wathena USD 406 400/PK-12
PO Box 38 66090 785-989-4427
Mike Newman, supt. Fax 989-4680
Wathena HS 200/7-12
PO Box 38 66090 785-989-4426
Robert Blair, prin. Fax 989-3317

Waverly, Coffey, Pop. 573
Lebo-Waverly USD 243 600/PK-12
PO Box 457 66871 785-733-2651
Allen Pokorny, supt. Fax 733-2707
www.usd243ks.org/
Waverly HS 100/7-12
PO Box 8 66871 785-733-2561
Karl Hamm, prin. Fax 733-2756
Other Schools – See Lebo

Wellington, Sumner, Pop. 8,299
Wellington USD 353 1,800/K-12
PO Box 648 67152 620-326-4300
Dr. Allen Hillen, supt. Fax 326-4304
www.usd353.com/
Wellington HS 600/9-12
1700 E 16th St 67152 620-326-4310
Dale Liston, prin. Fax 326-4383
Wellington MS 400/6-8
605 N A St 67152 620-326-4320
Jerry Hodson, prin. Fax 326-4390

Wellsville, Franklin, Pop. 1,595
Wellsville USD 289 800/PK-12
602 Walnut St 66092 785-883-2388
Denise O'Dea, supt. Fax 883-4453
www.wellsville-usd289.org
Wellsville HS 200/9-12
602 Walnut St 66092 785-883-2057
Sheldon Pokorney, prin. Fax 883-2294
Wellsville MS 200/6-8
602 Walnut St 66092 785-883-4350
Mitchell Lubin, prin. Fax 883-2260

Weskan, Wallace
Weskan USD 242 100/PK-12
PO Box 155 67762 785-943-5222
Mike Nulton, supt. Fax 943-5303
Weskan JSHS 100/7-12
PO Box 155 67762 785-943-5222
Mike Nulton, prin. Fax 943-5303

Westmoreland, Pottawatomie, Pop. 637
Rock Creek USD 323 700/PK-12
PO Box 70 66549 785-457-3732
Darrel Stufflebeam, supt. Fax 457-3701
www.rockcreekschools.org
Other Schools – See Saint George

Wetmore, Nemaha, Pop. 357
Sabetha USD 441
Supt. — See Sabetha
Wetmore HS 100/9-12
PO Box AB 66550 785-866-2860
Timothy Weis, prin. Fax 866-5450

White City, Morris, Pop. 497
Rural Vista USD 481
Supt. — See Hope
White City HS 100/9-12
PO Box 8 66872 785-349-2211
Sid Tanner, prin. Fax 349-2138

Whitewater, Butler, Pop. 636
Remington-Whitewater USD 206 500/K-12
PO Box 243 67154 316-799-2115
Jim Johnson, supt. Fax 799-2307
remington.ks.schoolwebpages.com
Remington HS 200/9-12
8850 NW Meadowlark Rd 67154 316-799-2123
James Regier, prin. Fax 799-2943
Remington MS 100/6-8
PO Box 99 67154 316-799-2131
Bruce Krase, prin. Fax 799-2581

Wichita, Sedgwick, Pop. 354,617
Haysville USD 261
Supt. — See Haysville
Haysville Campus HS 1,300/9-12
2100 W 55th St S 67217 316-554-2236
Myron Regier, prin. Fax 554-2241

Maize USD 266
Supt. — See Maize
Maize South MS 1,000/7-8
3701 N Tyler Rd 67205 316-722-0421
John Blazek, prin. Fax 722-4077

Wichita USD 259 45,300/PK-12
201 N Water St 67202 316-973-4000
Winston Brooks, supt. Fax 973-4595
www.usd259.com
Allison Traditional Magnet MS 500/6-8
221 S Seneca St 67213 316-973-4800
Dr. Deborah Laudermilk, prin. Fax 973-4810
Brooks Technology & Arts Magnet MS 700/6-8
3802 E 27th St N 67220 316-973-6450
Charles Williams, prin. Fax 973-6581
Coleman MS 600/6-8
1544 N Governeour Rd 67206 316-973-6600
Stephanie Stovall, prin. Fax 973-6699
Curtis MS 800/6-8
1031 S Edgemoor St 67218 316-973-7350
Keith Wilson, prin. Fax 973-7410
Hadley MS 800/6-8
1101 Dougherty St 67212 316-973-7800
Dr. Shelly Martin, prin. Fax 973-7737
Hamilton MS 500/6-8
1407 S Broadway St 67211 316-973-5350
Robert Garner, prin. Fax 973-5360
Jardine MS Magnet 600/6-8
3550 Ross Pkwy 67210 316-973-4300
Rod Sprague, prin. Fax 973-4310
Marshall MS 500/6-8
1510 N Payne St 67203 316-973-9000
Mark Jollife, prin. Fax 973-9010
Mayberry Magnet MS 600/6-8
207 S Sheridan St 67213 316-973-5800
Terrell Davis, prin. Fax 973-5808
Mead MS 600/6-8
2601 E Skinner St 67211 316-973-8500
Linda Mathur, prin. Fax 973-8503
Pleasant Valley MS 600/6-8
2220 W 29th St N 67204 316-973-8000
Charles Wakefield, prin. Fax 973-8008
Robinson MS 700/6-8
328 N Oliver St 67208 316-973-8600
Judy Rapp, prin. Fax 973-8625
Stucky MS 700/6-8
4545 N Broadview Cir 67220 316-973-8400
Dr. Ken Jantz, prin. Fax 973-8410
Truesdell MS 1,000/6-8
2464 S Glenn Ave 67217 316-973-3900
Fred Lichtenfelt, prin. Fax 973-3904
Wichita East HS 2,300/9-12
2301 E Douglas Ave 67211 316-973-7200
Ken Thiessen, prin. Fax 973-7224
Wichita Heights HS 1,500/9-12
5301 N Hillside St 67219 316-973-1400
Mark Christian, prin. Fax 973-1410
Wichita North HS 1,600/9-12
1437 N Rochester St 67203 316-973-6300
Denise Wren, prin. Fax 973-6190
Wichita Northwest HS 1,500/9-12
1220 N Tyler Rd 67212 316-973-6000
Jim McNiece, prin. Fax 973-6070
Wichita Southeast HS 2,000/9-12
903 S Edgemoor St 67218 316-973-2700
Leroy Parks, prin. Fax 973-2755
Wichita South HS 1,700/9-12
701 W 33rd St S 67217 316-973-5450
Bruce Deterding, prin. Fax 973-5519
Wichita West HS 1,400/9-12
820 S Osage St 67213 316-973-3600
Lori Doyle, prin. Fax 973-3657
Wilbur MS 1,000/6-8
340 N Tyler Rd 67212 316-973-1100
Cherie Crain, prin. Fax 973-1110

Bishop Carroll HS 900/9-12
8101 W Central Ave 67212 316-722-2390
Leticia Nielsen, prin. Fax 722-6670
Calvary Christian S 100/PK-12
3003 E Kellogg Dr 67211 316-652-0773
Carol Page, admin. Fax 618-0375
Classic College of Hair Design Post-Sec.
1675 S Rock Rd Ste 101 67207 316-681-2288
Friends University Post-Sec.
2100 W University Ave 67213 316-295-5000
Independent S 800/K-12
8317 E Douglas Ave 67207 316-686-0152
Fax 686-3918
Kapaun Mt. Carmel HS 800/9-12
8506 E Central Ave 67206 316-634-0315
Dr. Dennis McGuire, prin. Fax 636-2437
Midway Christian S 50/K-12
5135 S Broadway St 67216 316-522-2099
Ernie Hough, prin. Fax 524-4238
Newman University Post-Sec.
3100 W McCormick St 67213 316-942-4291
Old Town Barber & Beauty College Post-Sec.
1207 E Douglas Ave 67211 316-264-4891
Trinity Academy HS 200/9-12
12345 E 21st St N 67206 316-634-0909
David Swank, hdmstr. Fax 634-0928
Vatterott College Post-Sec.
3639 N Comotara St 67226 316-634-0066
Vernon's Kansas School of Cosmetology Post-Sec.
2531 S Seneca St 67217 316-265-2629
Wichita Adventist Christian Academy 100/K-10
2725 S Osage St 67217 316-267-9472
Sharon Burton, prin.
Wichita Area Technical College Post-Sec.
2021 S Eisenhower St 67209 316-677-1550
Wichita Area Technical College Post-Sec.
324 N Emporia St 67202 316-833-4664
Wichita Area Technical College Post-Sec.
301 S Grove St 67211 316-677-9282
Wichita Collegiate S 1,000/PK-12
9115 E 13th St N 67206 316-634-0433
Tom Davis, hdmstr. Fax 634-0598
Wichita State University Post-Sec.
1845 Fairmount St 67260 316-978-3456
Wichita Technical Institute Post-Sec.
2051 S Meridian Ave 67213 316-943-2241
Xenon International Sch of Hair Design Post-Sec.
3804 W Douglas Ave 67203 316-943-5516

Williamsburg, Franklin, Pop. 370
West Franklin USD 287
Supt. — See Pomona
Williamsburg HS 100/9-12
PO Box 7 66095 785-746-5777
Susan Wildeman, prin. Fax 746-5250

Wilson, Ellsworth, Pop. 765
Lorraine USD 328
Supt. — See Lorraine
Wilson JSHS 100/7-12
PO Box 220 67490 785-658-2202
Brian Smith, prin. Fax 658-2205

Winchester, Jefferson, Pop. 579
Jefferson County North USD 339 400/K-12
310 5th St 66097 913-774-2000
Timothy Marshall, supt. Fax 774-2027
www.usd339.net
Jefferson County North HS 200/9-12
302 5th St 66097 913-774-8515
Michael Hess, prin. Fax 774-8535
Other Schools – See Nortonville

Winfield, Cowley, Pop. 12,016
Winfield USD 465 2,700/PK-12
920 Millington St 67156 620-221-5100
Marvin Estes, supt. Fax 221-0508
www.usd465.com
Winfield HS 900/9-12
300 N Viking Blvd 67156 620-221-5160
David Reiser, prin. Fax 221-5165
Winfield MS 600/6-8
400 E 9th Ave 67156 620-221-5130
Dennis Gerber, prin. Fax 221-5147

Southwestern College Post-Sec.
100 College St 67156 620-229-6000

Winona, Logan, Pop. 212
Triplains USD 275 100/PK-12
PO Box 97 67764 785-846-7869
David Porter, supt. Fax 846-7767
usd275.k12.ks.us/
Winona HS 50/9-12
PO Box 97 67764 785-846-7496
David Porter, prin. Fax 846-7767

Yates Center, Woodson, Pop. 1,520
Woodson USD 366 500/PK-12
PO Box 160 66783 620-625-8804
Rusty Arnold, supt. Fax 625-8806
www.usd366.net
Yates Center HS 200/9-12
PO Box 160 66783 620-625-8820
Raymond Harvey, prin. Fax 625-8850

KENTUCKY

KENTUCKY DEPARTMENT OF EDUCATION
500 Mero St, Frankfort 40601-1987
Telephone 502-564-4770
Fax 502-564-5680
Website http://www.education.ky.gov
Commissioner of Education   Gene Wilhoit

KENTUCKY BOARD OF EDUCATION
500 Mero St Ste 1, Frankfort 40601-1957
Chairperson   Keith Travis

PUBLIC, PRIVATE AND CATHOLIC SECONDARY SCHOOLS

Albany, Clinton, Pop. 2,255
Clinton County SD | 1,600/K-12
RR 4 Box 100 42602 | 606-387-6480
Mickey McFall, supt. | Fax 387-5437
www.clinton.k12.ky.us
Clinton County HS | 500/9-12
RR 4 Box 35 42602 | 606-387-5569
David Warinner, prin. | Fax 387-8659
Clinton County MS | 500/5-8
RR 4 Box 90 42602 | 606-387-6466
Jimmy Brown, prin. | Fax 387-6469

Kentucky Tech System
Supt. — None
Clinton County Area Technology Center | Vo/Tech
RR 4 Box 40 42602 | 606-387-6448
Farris Pierce, prin. | Fax 387-4035

Alexandria, Campbell, Pop. 8,206
Campbell County SD | 3,900/K-12
101 Orchard Ln 41001 | 859-635-2173
Anthony Strong, supt. | Fax 448-2439
www.campbellcountyschools.org/
Campbell County HS | 1,500/9-12
909 Camel Xing 41001 | 859-635-4161
Ginger Webb, prin. | Fax 448-4886
Campbell County MS | 1,100/6-8
8000 Alexandria Pike 41001 | 859-635-6077
Dave Sandlin, prin. | Fax 448-4863

Kentucky Tech System
Supt. — None
McCormick Area Technology Center | Vo/Tech
50 Orchard Ln 41001 | 859-635-4101
Joseph Amann, prin. | Fax 635-2766

Bishop Brossart HS | 400/9-12
4 Grove St 41001 | 859-635-2108
Thomas Seither, prin. | Fax 635-2135

Ashland, Boyd, Pop. 21,491
Ashland ISD | 3,200/K-12
PO Box 3000 41105 | 606-327-2706
Phil Eason, supt. | Fax 327-2705
www.ashland.k12.ky.us/
Blazer HS | 1,000/9-12
1500 Blazer Blvd 41102 | 606-327-6040
Andy Ballash, prin. | Fax 324-0517
Verity MS | 500/7-8
2800 Kansas St 41102 | 606-327-2727
Richard Oppenheimer, prin. | Fax 327-2765

Boyd County SD | 3,500/PK-12
1104 Bob McCullough Dr 41102 | 606-928-4141
Howard Osborne, supt. | Fax 928-4771
www.boyd.k12.ky.us
Boyd County Career & Technical Center | Vo/Tech
12300 Midland Trail Rd 41102 | 606-928-7120
Loretta Dixon, dir. | Fax 928-6432
Boyd County HS | 1,000/9-12
12307 Midland Trail Rd 41102 | 606-928-7100
Rhonda Salisbury, prin. | Fax 928-1312
Boyd County MS | 700/6-8
1226 Summitt Rd 41102 | 606-928-9547
Bill Boblett, prin. | Fax 928-2067
Other Schools – See Rush

Fairview ISD | 700/PK-12
2127 Main St W 41102 | 606-324-3877
Billy Musick, supt. | Fax 324-2288
www.fairview.k12.ky.us
Fairview HS | 400/6-12
2123 Main St W 41102 | 606-324-9226
Brad Greene, prin. | Fax 325-1486

Ashland Community and Technical College | Post-Sec.
1400 College Dr 41101 | 606-329-2999
Rose Hill Christian S | 300/PK-12
1001 Winslow Rd 41102 | 606-329-1957
Dr. Randy Douglas, prin. | Fax 324-6420

Augusta, Bracken, Pop. 1,222
Augusta ISD | 300/K-12
307 Bracken St 41002 | 606-756-2545
John Cordle, supt. | Fax 756-2149
www.augusta.k12.ky.us
Augusta JSHS | 200/6-12
207 Bracken St 41002 | 606-756-2105
Lisa McCane, prin. | Fax 756-3000

Barbourville, Knox, Pop. 3,493
Barbourville ISD | 600/PK-12
PO Box 520 40906 | 606-546-3120
Larry Warren, supt. | Fax 546-3452
www.barbourvilleind.com
Barbourville JSHS | 300/7-12
PO Box 520 40906 | 606-546-3129
Paul Middleton, prin. | Fax 546-3337

Kentucky Tech System
Supt. — None
Knox County Area Technology Center | Vo/Tech
210 Wall St 40906 | 606-546-5320
Stacy Imel, prin. | Fax 546-3818

Knox County SD | 4,700/PK-12
200 Daniel Boone Dr 40906 | 606-546-3157
Michael Jones, supt. | Fax 546-2819
www.knox.k12.ky.us/
Knox Central HS | 900/9-12
311 N Main St 40906 | 606-546-9253
Allen Storie, prin. | Fax 546-5684
Other Schools – See Corbin

Union College | Post-Sec.
310 College St 40906 | 606-546-4151

Bardstown, Nelson, Pop. 10,458
Bardstown ISD | 1,700/PK-12
308 N 5th St 40004 | 502-331-8800
Brent Holsclaw, supt. | Fax 331-8830
www.btown.k12.ky.us
Bardstown HS | 500/9-12
400 N 5th St 40004 | 502-331-8802
Thomas Hamilton, prin. | Fax 331-8832
Bardstown MS | 500/6-8
410 N 5th St 40004 | 502-331-8803
Bob Blackmon, prin. | Fax 331-8833

Kentucky Tech System
Supt. — None
Nelson County Area Technology Center | Vo/Tech
1060 Bloomfield Rd 40004 | 502-348-9096
Ron Woods, prin. | Fax 348-9097

Nelson County SD | 4,400/PK-12
PO Box 2277 40004 | 502-349-7000
Janice Lantz, supt. | Fax 349-7004
www.nelson.k12.ky.us
Nelson County HS | 1,500/9-12
1070 Bloomfield Rd 40004 | 502-349-7010
Sara Wilson, prin. | Fax 349-7017
Old Kentucky Home MS | 500/6-8
301 Wildcat Ln 40004 | 502-349-7040
Ryan Clark, prin. | Fax 349-7042
Other Schools – See Bloomfield

Bethlehem HS | 300/9-12
309 W Stephen Foster Ave 40004 | 502-348-8594
Paul Schum, prin. | Fax 349-1247

Bardwell, Carlisle, Pop. 796
Carlisle County SD | 800/PK-12
4557 State Route 1377 42023 | 270-628-3800
Danny Brown, supt. | Fax 628-5477
www.carlisle.k12.ky.us/
Carlisle County HS | 200/9-12
4557 State Route 1377 42023 | 270-628-3800
Kelli Edging, prin. | Fax 628-3837
Carlisle County MS | 200/6-8
4557 State Route 1377 42023 | 270-628-3800
Jackie Ballard, prin. | Fax 628-3974

Barlow, Ballard, Pop. 705
Ballard County SD | 1,500/PK-12
3465 Paducah Rd 42024 | 270-665-8400
Edward Adami, supt. | Fax 665-9844
www.ballard.k12.ky.us
Ballard County MS | 300/6-8
3561 Paducah Rd 42024 | 270-665-8400
Casey Allen, prin. | Fax 665-5153
Ballard Memorial HS | 400/9-12
3561 Paducah Rd 42024 | 270-665-8400
Donald Shively, prin. | Fax 665-5312
Ballard Technical & Career Center | Vo/Tech
11 Vocational School Rd 42024 | 270-665-8400
Dana Rohrer, prin. | Fax 665-5006

Beattyville, Lee, Pop. 1,178
Kentucky Tech System
Supt. — None
Lee County Area Technology Center | Vo/Tech
PO Box B 41311 | 606-464-5018
Jerry Hollon, prin. | Fax 464-0663
Lee County SD | 1,300/K-12
PO Box 668 41311 | 606-464-5000
Frank Kincaid, supt. | Fax 464-5009
www.lee.k12.ky.us
Lee County HS | 400/9-12
PO Box J 41311 | 606-464-5005
James Evans, prin. | Fax 464-5014
Lee County MS | 300/6-8
PO Box N 41311 | 606-464-5010
Alice Sipple, prin. | Fax 464-5011

Bedford, Trimble, Pop. 719
Trimble County SD | 1,600/K-12
PO Box 275 40006 | 502-255-3201
Marcia Haney-Dunaway, supt. | Fax 255-5105
www.trimble.k12.ky.us/
Trimble County HS | 400/9-12
1029 Highway 421 N 40006 | 502-255-7781
Rebecca Moore, prin. | Fax 255-5126
Trimble County MS | 600/6-8
116 Wentworth Ave 40006 | 502-255-7361
Mike Genton, prin. | Fax 255-5102

Belfry, Pike
Kentucky Tech System
Supt. — None
Belfry Area Technology Center | Vo/Tech
PO Box 280 41514 | 606-353-4951
Annette Harris-Ward, prin. | Fax 353-0868
Pike County SD
Supt. — See Pikeville
Belfry HS | 600/9-12
PO Box 160 41514 | 606-237-3900
Rod Varney, prin. | Fax 237-5119
Belfry MS | 6-8
PO Box 850 41514 | 606-353-7239
James Hurley, prin. | Fax 353-0530

Bellevue, Campbell, Pop. 6,138
Bellevue ISD | 900/PK-12
219 Center St 41073 | 859-261-2108
Wayne Starnes, supt. | Fax 261-1708
www.bellevue.k12.ky.us
Bellevue HS | 400/7-12
201 Center St 41073 | 859-261-2980
Mike Wills, prin. | Fax 261-1825

Benton, Marshall, Pop. 4,165
Marshall County SD | 4,600/PK-12
86 High School Rd 42025 | 270-527-8628
Steve Knight, supt. | Fax 527-0804
www.marshall.k12.ky.us
Benton MS | 200/6-8
906 Joe Creason Dr 42025 | 270-527-9991
Kern Cothran, prin. | Fax 527-9992
Marshall County HS | 1,400/9-12
416 High School Rd 42025 | 270-527-1453
Trent Lovett, prin. | Fax 527-0578

Marshall County Technical Center	Vo/Tech
341 High School Rd 42025	270-527-8648
Lewis Mathis, prin.	Fax 527-1920
South Marshall MS	300/6-8
85 Sid Darnall Rd 42025	270-527-3828
Russell Buchanan, prin.	Fax 527-7616
Other Schools – See Calvert City	

Christian Fellowship S	200/PK-12
PO Box 610 42025	270-527-8377
Bill Rowley, prin.	Fax 527-2872

Berea, Madison, Pop. 11,259

Berea ISD	1,000/PK-12
3 Pirate Pkwy 40403	859-986-8446
Gary Conkin, supt.	Fax 986-1839
www.berea.k12.ky.us	
Berea Community HS	300/9-12
1 Pirate Pkwy 40403	859-986-4911
John Masters, prin.	Fax 986-4640
Berea Community MS	200/6-8
1 Pirate Pkwy 40403	859-986-4911
John Masters, prin.	Fax 986-4640

Madison County SD	
Supt. — See Richmond	
Foley MS	800/6-8
211 Glades Rd 40403	859-986-8473
Arno Norwell, prin.	Fax 986-3362
Madison Southern HS	900/9-12
213 Glades Rd 40403	859-986-8424
Hubert Broaddus, prin.	Fax 986-3092

Berea College 40404	Post-Sec.
	859-985-3000

Betsy Layne, Floyd

Floyd County SD	
Supt. — See Prestonsburg	
Betsy Layne HS	500/9-12
PO Box 437 41605	606-478-9138
Sean Ousley, prin.	Fax 478-3805

Beverly, Bell

Red Bird Mission S	300/K-12
15420 S Highway 66 40913	606-598-2416
Robert Ferguson, prin.	Fax 598-7314

Bloomfield, Nelson, Pop. 856

Nelson County SD	
Supt. — See Bardstown	
Bloomfield MS	500/6-8
96 Arnold Ln 40008	502-349-7201
Glenn Spalding, prin.	Fax 349-7203

Booneville, Owsley, Pop. 109

Owsley County SD	800/K-12
PO Box 340 41314	606-593-6363
Stephen Jackson, supt.	Fax 593-6368
Owsley County JSHS	400/7-12
PO Box 310 41314	606-593-5185
Teresa Barrett, prin.	Fax 593-6312

Bowling Green, Warren, Pop. 50,663

Bowling Green ISD	3,400/PK-12
1211 Center St 42101	270-746-2200
Dr. John Settle, supt.	Fax 746-2205
www.b-g.k12.ky.us	
Bowling Green HS	1,000/9-12
1801 Rockingham Ave 42104	270-746-2300
Gary Fields, prin.	Fax 746-2305
Bowling Green JHS	900/6-8
900 Campbell Ln 42104	270-746-2290
Dr. Penny Masden, prin.	Fax 746-2295

Warren County SD	11,100/PK-12
PO Box 51810 42102	270-781-5150
Dale Brown, supt.	Fax 781-2392
www.warren.k12.ky.us/	
Drakes Creek MS	700/7-8
704 Cypress Wood Ln 42104	270-843-0165
David Hutchison, prin.	Fax 782-6138
Greenwood HS	1,300/9-12
5065 Scottsville Rd 42104	270-842-3627
Mark Davis, prin.	Fax 842-2037
Moss MS	600/7-8
2565 Russellville Rd 42101	270-843-0166
Tom Renick, prin.	Fax 843-8512
Warren Central HS	1,100/9-12
559 Morgantown Rd 42101	270-842-7302
Kathy Goff, prin.	Fax 781-5115
Warren East HS	800/9-12
6867 Louisville Rd 42101	270-781-1277
Bailey Norris, prin.	Fax 843-2610
Warren East MS	400/7-8
7031 Louisville Rd 42101	270-843-0181
Beverly Dillard, prin.	Fax 781-8565

Bowling Green Christian Academy	200/PK-12
1730 Destiny Ln 42104	270-782-9552
Jim Cox, dir.	Fax 782-9585
Bowling Green Technical College	Post-Sec.
1845 Loop Ave 42101	270-746-7461
Bowling Green Technical College	Post-Sec.
1127 Morgantown Rd 42101	270-746-7807
Draughons Junior College	Post-Sec.
2421 Fitzgerald Industrial 42101	270-843-6750
PJs College of Cosmetology	Post-Sec.
1901 Russellville Rd Ste 10 42101	270-846-6444
Western Kentucky University	Post-Sec.
1 Big Red Way 42101	270-745-0111

Brandenburg, Meade, Pop. 2,158

Kentucky Tech System	
Supt. — None	
Meade County Area Technology Center	Vo/Tech
110 Greer St 40108	270-422-3955
Faye Campbell, prin.	Fax 422-3307

Meade County SD	4,600/PK-12
PO Box 337 40108	270-422-7500
Mitch Crump, supt.	Fax 422-5494
www.meade.k12.ky.us	
Meade County HS	1,500/9-12
938 Old State Rd 40108	270-422-7515
William Adams, prin.	Fax 422-3928
Pepper MS	800/7-8
1055 Old Ekron Rd 40108	270-422-7530
David Dailey, prin.	Fax 422-5515

Brooksville, Bracken, Pop. 601

Bracken County SD	1,200/K-12
348 W Miami St 41004	606-735-2523
Tony Johnson, supt.	Fax 735-3640
www.bracken.k12.ky.us	
Bracken County HS	400/9-12
PO Box 128 41004	606-735-3153
Martha Hall, prin.	Fax 735-2549
Bracken County MS	400/5-8
167 Parsley Dr 41004	606-735-3425
Leah Jefferson, prin.	Fax 735-2057

Brownsville, Edmonson, Pop. 933

Edmonson County SD	1,700/K-12
PO Box 129 42210	270-597-2101
Patrick Waddell, supt.	Fax 597-2103
www.edmonson.k12.ky.us	
Edmonson County HS	600/9-12
220 Wild Cat Way 42210	270-597-2151
Gary Meredith, prin.	Fax 597-2962
Edmonson County MS	300/7-8
210 Wild Cat Way 42210	270-597-2932
Ricky Houchin, prin.	Fax 597-2182

Buckhorn, Perry, Pop. 144

Perry County SD	
Supt. — See Hazard	
Buckhorn HS	200/9-12
18392 KY Highway 28 41721	606-398-7176
Harvey Colwell, prin.	Fax 398-7930

Buckner, Oldham

Kentucky Tech System	
Supt. — None	
Oldham County Area Technology Center	Vo/Tech
PO Box 127 40010	502-222-0131
Michael Denny, prin.	Fax 222-8195

Oldham County SD	10,100/PK-12
PO Box 218 40010	502-222-8880
Paul Upchurch, supt.	Fax 222-8885
www.oldham.k12.ky.us	
Oldham County HS	1,200/9-12
PO Box 187 40010	502-222-9461
Dave Weedman, prin.	Fax 222-0558
Oldham County MS	1,000/6-8
PO Box 157 40010	502-222-1451
Chris Kraft, prin.	Fax 222-5178
Other Schools – See Crestwood, Goshen	

Burgin, Mercer, Pop. 880

Burgin ISD	400/K-12
PO Box B 40310	859-748-4000
Richard Webb, supt.	Fax 748-4010
www.burgin.k12.ky.us	
Burgin HS	200/6-12
PO Box B 40310	859-748-5282
Martha Collier, prin.	Fax 748-4002

Burkesville, Cumberland, Pop. 1,765

Cumberland County SD	1,100/K-12
PO Box 420 42717	270-864-3377
John L. Hurt, supt.	Fax 864-5803
www.cland.k12.ky.us	
Cumberland County HS	300/9-12
PO Box 380 42717	270-864-3451
Kay Graham-Bright, prin.	Fax 864-1284
Cumberland County MS	300/6-8
PO Box 70 42717	270-864-5818
Glen Murphy, prin.	Fax 864-2590

Burlington, Boone, Pop. 6,070

Boone County SD	
Supt. — See Florence	
Camp Ernst MS	6-8
6515 Camp Ernst Rd 41005	859-534-4000
Eric McArtor, prin.	Fax 534-4001

Burna, Livingston

Livingston County SD	
Supt. — See Smithland	
Livingston County MS	300/7-8
PO Box 109 42028	270-988-3263
Larry McGregor, prin.	Fax 988-2518

Butler, Pendleton, Pop. 626

Pendleton County SD	
Supt. — See Falmouth	
Sharp MS	700/6-8
35 Wright Rd 41006	859-472-7000
Jeff Aulick, prin.	Fax 472-7011

Cadiz, Trigg, Pop. 2,443

Trigg County SD	2,000/K-12
202 Main St 42211	270-522-6075
Tim McGinnis, supt.	Fax 522-7782
www.trigg.k12.ky.us/	

Trigg County HS	600/9-12
203 Main St 42211	270-522-2200
Sharon Knight, prin.	Fax 522-2224
Trigg County MS	700/5-8
206 Lafayette St 42211	270-522-2210
Wendell Benningfield, prin.	Fax 522-2203

Calhoun, McLean, Pop. 812

McLean County SD	1,500/K-12
PO Box 245 42327	270-273-5257
William Melloy, supt.	Fax 273-5259
www.mclean.k12.ky.us	
McLean County HS	500/9-12
1859 State Route 136 E 42327	270-273-5278
Tommy Burrough, prin.	Fax 273-5208
McLean County MS	400/6-8
1901 State Route 136 E 42327	270-273-5191
Tres Settle, prin.	Fax 273-9876

Calvert City, Marshall, Pop. 2,723

Marshall County SD	
Supt. — See Benton	
North Marshall MS	600/6-8
3111 US Highway 95 42029	270-395-7108
Kent Barlow, prin.	Fax 395-5449

Campbellsville, Taylor, Pop. 10,689

Campbellsville ISD	1,200/PK-12
136 S Columbia Ave 42718	270-465-4162
Diane Woods-Ayers, supt.	Fax 465-3918
www.cville.k12.ky.us/	
Campbellsville HS	400/9-12
230 W Main St 42718	270-465-8774
Greg Chick, prin.	Fax 789-4007
Campbellsville MS	400/5-8
315 Roberts Rd 42718	270-465-5121
Chris Kidwell, prin.	Fax 789-3718

Taylor County SD	2,500/K-12
1209 E Broadway St 42718	270-465-5371
Gary Seaborne, supt.	Fax 789-3954
www.taylor.k12.ky.us	
Taylor County HS	800/9-12
300 Ingram Ave 42718	270-465-4431
Gaylon Yarberry, prin.	Fax 465-5731
Taylor County MS	600/6-8
1207 E Broadway St 42718	270-465-2877
Cherry Harvey, prin.	Fax 789-1753

Campbellsville University	Post-Sec.
1 University Dr 42718	270-789-5000

Campton, Wolfe, Pop. 405

Wolfe County SD	1,300/PK-12
PO Box 160 41301	606-668-8002
Stephen Butcher, supt.	Fax 668-8050
www.wolfe.k12.ky.us	
Wolfe County HS	400/9-12
PO Box 790 41301	606-668-8202
Deatrah Barnett, prin.	Fax 668-8250
Wolfe County MS	300/6-8
PO Box 460 41301	606-668-8152
Wilma Terrill, prin.	Fax 668-8100

Carlisle, Nicholas, Pop. 2,002

Nicholas County SD	1,100/K-12
395 W Main St 40311	859-289-3770
Gregory Reid, supt.	Fax 289-3777
www.nicholas.k12.ky.us/	
Nicholas County HS	300/9-12
103 School Dr 40311	859-289-3780
Doug Bechanon, prin.	Fax 289-6429

Carrollton, Carroll, Pop. 3,802

Carroll County SD	1,800/K-12
813 Hawkins St 41008	502-732-7070
Carroll Yager, supt.	Fax 732-7073
www.carroll.k12.ky.us	
Carroll County HS	500/9-12
1706 Highland Ave 41008	502-732-7075
Curt Hahn, prin.	Fax 732-7012
Carroll County MS	500/6-8
408 5th St 41008	502-732-7080
Bill Hogan, prin.	Fax 732-7107

Kentucky Tech System	
Supt. — None	
Carroll County Area Technology Center	Vo/Tech
1704 Highland Ave 41008	502-732-4479
Jennifer Stafford, prin.	Fax 732-4837

Christian Academy of Carrollton	200/PK-12
1703 Easterday Rd 41008	502-732-4734
Katie Matson, admin.	Fax 732-4732

Catlettsburg, Boyd, Pop. 1,908

Calvary Christian S	100/PK-12
17839 Bear Creek Rd 41129	606-929-5599
Denise Wallace, dir.	Fax 928-9219

Cave City, Barren, Pop. 1,920

Caverna ISD	800/PK-12
1102 N Dixie Hwy 42127	270-773-2530
Samuel Dick, supt.	Fax 773-2524
www.caverna.k12.ky.us	
Other Schools – See Horse Cave	

Cecilia, Hardin

Hardin County SD	
Supt. — See Elizabethtown	
Central Hardin HS	1,500/9-12
3040 Leitchfield Rd 42724	270-737-6800
Ron Ortiz, prin.	Fax 765-3889

West Hardin MS — 600/6-8
10471 Leitchfield Rd 42724 — 270-862-3924
James Roe, prin. — Fax 862-3647

Clinton, Hickman, Pop. 1,387
Hickman County SD — 800/PK-12
416 N Waterfield Dr 42031 — 270-653-2341
Steve Bayko, supt. — Fax 653-6007
www.hickman.k12.ky.us
Hickman County HS — 400/7-12
301 Cresap St 42031 — 270-653-4044
Richard Brazell, prin. — Fax 653-3200

Cloverport, Breckinridge, Pop. 1,248
Cloverport ISD — 300/PK-12
PO Box 37 40111 — 270-788-3910
J. Scaggs, supt. — Fax 788-6290
www.cport.k12.ky.us
Fraize HS — 100/9-12
101 4th St 40111 — 270-788-3388
David Buchele, prin. — Fax 788-6640
Fraize MS — 100/6-8
101 4th St 40111 — 270-788-3388
David Buchele, prin. — Fax 788-6640

Columbia, Adair, Pop. 4,152
Adair County SD — 1,800/PK-12
1204 Greensburg St 42728 — 270-384-2476
Darrell Treece, supt. — Fax 384-5841
www.adair.k12.ky.us
Adair County HS — 700/9-12
526 Indian Dr 42728 — 270-384-2751
Troy Young, prin. — Fax 384-6900
Adair County MS — 300/7-8
322 General John Adair Dr 42728 — 270-384-5308
Alma Rich, prin. — Fax 384-2168

Lindsey Wilson College — Post-Sec.
210 Lindsey Wilson St 42728 — 270-384-8100

Corbin, Whitley, Pop. 7,932
Corbin ISD — 2,400/K-12
108 Roy Kidd Ave 40701 — 606-528-1303
Ed McNeel, supt. — Fax 523-1747
www.corbinschools.org
Corbin East S — 300/1-2
529 Master St 40701 — 606-528-4080
Dalene McBurney, prin. — Fax 523-3614
Corbin HS — 600/9-12
1901 Snyder St 40701 — 606-528-3902
Joyce Phillips, prin. — Fax 523-3627
Corbin MS — 500/6-8
706 S Kentucky Ave 40701 — 606-523-3619
Dave Cox, prin. — Fax 523-3621

Kentucky Tech System
Supt. — None
Corbin Area Technology Center — Vo/Tech
1909 Snyder St 40701 — 606-528-5338
Ron Partin, prin. — Fax 528-0532

Knox County SD
Supt. — See Barbourville
Lynn Camp JSHS — 600/6-12
100 N KY 830 40701 — 606-528-5429
Roger Jackson, prin. — Fax 528-4750

Covington, Kenton, Pop. 42,687
Covington ISD — 3,800/PK-12
25 E 7th St 41011 — 859-392-1000
Jack Moreland, supt. — Fax 292-5916
www.covington.k12.ky.us
Chapman Vocational Education Ctr — Vo/Tech
25th & Madison 41014 — 859-655-9545
Mark Raleigh, prin. — Fax 581-7124
Holmes HS — 1,000/9-12
2500 Madison Ave 41014 — 859-655-9545
Ray Finke, prin. — Fax 581-7259
Holmes JHS — 200/8-8
2500 Madison Ave 41014 — 859-655-9545
Ray Finke, prin. — Fax 581-7153
Covington Adult HS — Adult
14 W Southern Ave #20 41015 — 859-292-5864
Robert Ryan, prin. — Fax 292-5866

Kenton County SD
Supt. — See Fort Wright
Scott HS — 1,200/9-12
5400 Old Taylor Mill Rd 41015 — 859-356-3146
Clay Dawson, prin. — Fax 356-5516

Calvary Christian S — 700/PK-12
5955 Taylor Mill Rd 41015 — 859-356-9201
Donald James, admin. — Fax 356-8962
Covington Catholic HS — 500/9-12
1600 Dixie Hwy 41011 — 859-491-2247
Michael Clines, prin. — Fax 448-2242
Covington Latin HS — 200/8-12
21 E 11th St 41011 — 859-291-7044
Andrew Barczak, prin. — Fax 291-1939
Holy Cross HS — 400/9-12
3617 Church St 41015 — 859-431-1335
Clay Eifert, prin. — Fax 655-2184
Notre Dame Academy — 600/9-12
1699 Hilton Dr 41011 — 859-261-4300
Sr. Elaine Marie Winter, prin. — Fax 292-7722

Crestview Hills, Kenton, Pop. 3,232

Thomas More College — Post-Sec.
333 Thomas More Pkwy 41017 — 859-341-5800

Crestwood, Oldham, Pop. 2,095
Oldham County SD
Supt. — See Buckner

East Oldham MS — 6-8
1201 E Highway 22 40014 — 502-222-8480
Lynda Redmon, prin. — Fax 222-8489
South Oldham HS — 1,000/9-12
5900 Highway 329 Byp 40014 — 502-241-6681
Barbara Fendley, prin. — Fax 241-0955
South Oldham MS — 800/6-8
6403 W Highway 146 40014 — 502-241-0320
Rob Clayton, prin. — Fax 241-1438

Trend Setter's Academy of Beauty Culture — Post-Sec.
6539 W Highway 22 40014

Cumberland, Harlan, Pop. 2,380
Harlan County SD
Supt. — See Harlan
Cumberland HS — 300/9-12
600 Redskin Dr 40823 — 606-589-4625
Ed Clem, prin. — Fax 589-2312

Southeast Kentucky Community/Tech Coll — Post-Sec.
300 College Rd 40823 — 606-589-2145

Cynthiana, Harrison, Pop. 6,260
Harrison County SD — 3,100/K-12
324 Webster Ave 41031 — 859-234-7110
Dr. Roy Woodward, supt. — Fax 234-8164
www.harrison.k12.ky.us
Harrison County HS — 1,000/9-12
320 Webster Ave 41031 — 859-234-7117
Robert Barr, prin. — Fax 234-0115
Harrison County MS — 800/6-8
269 Education Dr 41031 — 859-234-7123
Michael McIntire, prin. — Fax 234-8385

Kentucky Tech System
Supt. — None
Harrison County Area Technology Center — Vo/Tech
327 Webster Ave 41031 — 859-234-5286
John Hodge, prin. — Fax 234-0658

Danville, Boyle, Pop. 15,294
Boyle County SD — 2,700/K-12
352 N Danville Byp 40422 — 859-236-6634
Steve Burkich, supt. — Fax 236-8624
www.boyle.k12.ky.us
Boyle County HS — 900/9-12
1637 Perryville Rd 40422 — 859-236-5047
Elmer Thomas, prin. — Fax 236-7820
Boyle County MS — 700/6-8
1651 Perryville Rd 40422 — 859-236-4212
Mike LaFavers, prin. — Fax 236-9596
Danville ISD — 1,700/K-12
152 E Martin L King Blvd 40422 — 859-238-1300
Robert Rowland, supt. — Fax 238-1330
www.danville.k12.ky.us
Bate MS — 500/6-8
460 Stanford Ave 40422 — 859-238-1305
Michael Godbey, prin. — Fax 238-1343
Danville HS — 500/9-12
203 E Lexington Ave 40422 — 859-238-1308
Joseph Payne, prin. — Fax 238-1338

Central Kentucky Technical College — Post-Sec.
59 Corporate Dr 40422 — 859-239-7030
Centre College — Post-Sec.
600 W Walnut St 40422 — 859-238-5200
Kentucky School for the Deaf — Post-Sec.
S 2nd St 40422 — 859-239-7017
National College of Business & Tech. — Post-Sec.
115 E Lexington Ave 40422 — 859-236-6991

Dawson Springs, Hopkins, Pop. 2,978
Dawson Springs ISD — 700/PK-12
118 E Arcadia Ave 42408 — 270-797-3811
Alexis Seymore, supt. — Fax 797-5201
www.dsprings.k12.ky.us/
Dawson Springs HS — 200/9-12
317 Eli St 42408 — 270-797-2957
Teresa Ashby, prin. — Fax 797-5201
Dawson Springs MS — 200/5-8
317 Eli St 42408 — 270-797-2991
Renee Miller, prin. — Fax 797-5201

Dayton, Campbell, Pop. 5,677
Dayton ISD — 1,000/K-12
200 Clay St 41074 — 859-491-6565
Gary Rye, supt. — Fax 292-3995
www.dayton.k12.ky.us
Dayton HS — 500/7-12
200 Greendevil Ln 41074 — 859-292-7486
Dan Ridder, prin. — Fax 261-1606

Dixon, Webster, Pop. 604
Kentucky Tech System
Supt. — None
Webster County Area Technology Center — Vo/Tech
PO Box 230 42409 — 270-639-5035
Tom Sisk, prin. — Fax 639-5545

Webster County SD — 1,900/PK-12
28 State Route 1340 42409 — 270-639-5083
James Kemp, supt. — Fax 639-0111
www.webster.k12.ky.us
Webster County HS — 600/9-12
1922 US Highway 41A S 42409 — 270-639-5092
Carolyn Nolen, prin. — Fax 639-0128

Dry Ridge, Grant, Pop. 2,068
Grant County SD
Supt. — See Williamstown
Grant County HS — 1,100/9-12
715 Warsaw Rd 41035 — 859-824-9739
Tracey Glass-Lamb, prin. — Fax 824-9756

Grant County MS — 900/6-8
305 School Rd 41035 — 859-824-7161
Ronald Livingood, prin. — Fax 824-7163

Eastern, Floyd
Floyd County SD
Supt. — See Prestonsburg
Allen Central HS — 400/9-12
PO Box 139 41622 — 606-358-9543
Lorena Hall, prin. — Fax 358-9247
Allen Central MS — 300/6-8
PO Box 193 41622 — 606-358-0110
Davida Bickford, prin. — Fax 358-0112

Eddyville, Lyon, Pop. 2,353
Lyon County SD — 1,000/K-12
217 Jenkins Rd 42038 — 270-388-9715
Dr. Lee Gold, supt. — Fax 388-4962
www.lyon.k12.ky.us
Lyon County HS — 300/9-12
209 Fairview Ave 42038 — 270-388-9715
Carroll Wadlington, prin. — Fax 388-2296
Lyon County MS — 300/6-8
111 W Fairview Ave 42038 — 270-388-9715
Victor Zimmerman, prin. — Fax 388-0517

Edgewood, Kenton, Pop. 9,188
Kenton County SD
Supt. — See Fort Wright
Dixie Heights HS — 1,200/9-12
3010 Dixie Hwy 41017 — 859-341-7650
Kimberly Banta, prin. — Fax 341-2531
Turkey Foot MS — 700/6-8
3230 Turkeyfoot Rd 41017 — 859-341-0216
Tom Arnzen, prin. — Fax 341-7217

Gateway Community & Technical College — Post-Sec.
790 Thomas More Pkwy 41017 — 859-442-4150
St. Elizabeth Medical Center — Post-Sec.
1 Medical Village Dr 41017 — 859-344-2170

Edmonton, Metcalfe, Pop. 1,578
Metcalfe County SD — 1,600/K-12
1007 W Stockton St 42129 — 270-432-3171
Patricia Hurt, supt. — Fax 432-3170
www.metcalfe.k12.ky.us
Metcalfe County HS — 500/9-12
208 Randolph St 42129 — 270-432-2481
Dorothy McCubbin, prin. — Fax 432-2714
Metcalfe County MS — 300/7-8
100 Hornet Ave 42129 — 270-432-3359
Mike Vaught, prin. — Fax 432-5828

Elizabethtown, Hardin, Pop. 23,239
Elizabethtown ISD — 2,300/K-12
219 Helm St 42701 — 270-765-6146
Gary French, supt. — Fax 765-2158
www.etown.k12.ky.us
Elizabethtown HS — 700/9-12
620 N Mulberry St 42701 — 270-769-3381
Nathan Huggins, prin. — Fax 769-2539
Stone MS — 600/6-8
323 Morningside Dr 42701 — 270-769-6343
Beth Mather, prin. — Fax 769-6749

Hardin County SD — 12,700/PK-12
65 W A Jenkins Rd 42701 — 270-769-8800
Richard Hughes Ed.D., supt. — Fax 769-8888
www.hardin.k12.ky.us
Bluegrass MS — 700/6-8
170 W A Jenkins Rd 42701 — 270-765-2658
Brenda Pirtle, prin. — Fax 737-0450
Hardin HS — 1,200/9-12
384 W A Jenkins Rd 42701 — 270-769-8906
Bryan Todd, prin. — Fax 769-8996
Other Schools – See Cecilia, Glendale, Radcliff, Vine Grove

Elizabethtown Beauty School — Post-Sec.
308 N Miles St 42701 — 270-765-2118
Elizabethtown Community College — Post-Sec.
600 College Street Rd 42701 — 270-769-2371
Elizabethtown Technical College — Post-Sec.
620 College Street Rd 42701 — 270-766-5133
Trend Setter's Academy of Beauty Culture — Post-Sec.
622B Westport Rd 42701 — 270-765-5243

Elkton, Todd, Pop. 1,964
Todd County SD — 1,900/PK-12
804 S Main St 42220 — 270-265-2436
David Eakles, supt. — Fax 265-5414
www.todd.k12.ky.us
Todd County Central HS — 500/9-12
806 S Main St 42220 — 270-265-2506
Bruce Voth, prin. — Fax 265-9408
Todd County MS — 500/6-8
515 W Main St 42220 — 270-265-2511
Bruce Gray, prin. — Fax 265-9414

Eminence, Henry, Pop. 2,242
Eminence ISD — 400/PK-12
291 W Broadway St 40019 — 502-845-4788
David Baird, supt. — Fax 845-2339
www.eminence.k12.ky.us
Eminence HS — 200/9-12
PO Box 146 40019 — 502-845-5427
Steve Frommeyer, prin. — Fax 845-1310
Eminence MS — 5-8
PO Box 146 40019 — 502-845-5427
Steve Frommeyer, prin. — Fax 845-1310

Erlanger, Kenton, Pop. 16,826
Erlanger-Elsmere ISD   2,200/K-12
    500 Graves Ave 41018   859-727-2009
    Michael D. Sander, supt.   Fax 727-5653
    www.erlanger.k12.ky.us
Lloyd HS   600/9-12
    450 Bartlett Ave 41018   859-727-1555
    John Riehemann, prin.   Fax 727-5912
Tichenor MS   500/6-8
    305 Bartlett Ave 41018   859-727-2255
    Carl Schwierjohann, prin.   Fax 342-2425

St. Henry HS   900/9-12
    3755 Scheben Dr 41018   859-525-0255
    David Otte, prin.   Fax 525-5855

Evarts, Harlan, Pop. 1,068
Harlan County SD
    Supt. — See Harlan
Evarts HS   400/9-12
    PO Box 9 40828   606-837-2502
    Bob Howard, prin.   Fax 837-3411

Fairdale, Jefferson, Pop. 6,563
Jefferson County SD
    Supt. — See Louisville
Fairdale HS Magnet Career Academy   800/9-12
    1001 Fairdale Rd 40118   502-485-8248
    Linda Brown, prin.   Fax 485-8761

Falmouth, Pendleton, Pop. 2,103
Pendleton County SD   2,800/PK-12
    2525 US Highway 27 N 41040   859-654-6911
    J. Robert Yost, supt.   Fax 654-6143
    www.pendleton.k12.ky.us
Pendleton County HS   900/9-12
    2359 US Highway 27 N 41040   859-654-3355
    John White, prin.   Fax 654-4235
Other Schools – See Butler

Fern Creek, Jefferson, Pop. 16,406
Jefferson County SD
    Supt. — See Louisville
Fern Creek Traditional HS   1,200/9-12
    9115 Fern Creek Rd 40291   502-485-8251
    Tito Castillo, prin.   Fax 485-8032

Flemingsburg, Fleming, Pop. 3,097
Fleming County SD   2,500/K-12
    211 W Water St 41041   606-845-5851
    Kelley F. Crain, supt.   Fax 849-3158
    www.fleming.k12.ky.us/
Fleming County HS   800/9-12
    1658 Elizaville Rd 41041   606-845-6601
    Brad Sorrell, prin.   Fax 845-3102
Simons MS   400/7-8
    242 W Water St 41041   606-845-9331
    Thomas Price, prin.   Fax 849-2309

Florence, Boone, Pop. 24,689
Boone County SD   15,100/K-12
    8330 US Highway 42 41042   859-283-1003
    Bryan Blavatt, supt.   Fax 282-3312
    www.boone.k12.ky.us/
Boone County HS   1,400/9-12
    7056 Burlington Pike 41042   859-282-5655
    Peggy Brooks, prin.   Fax 282-5653
Jones MS   700/6-8
    8000 Spruce Dr 41042   859-282-4610
    Steve Sorrell, prin.   Fax 282-2364
Ockerman MS   800/6-8
    8300 US Highway 42 41042   859-282-3240
    David Claggett, prin.   Fax 282-3242
Other Schools – See Burlington, Hebron, Union

Beckfield College   Post-Sec.
    16 Spiral Dr 41042   859-371-9393
Hair Design School   Post-Sec.
    7285 Turfway Rd 41042   859-283-2690
Heritage Academy   400/K-12
    7216 US Highway 42 41042   859-525-0213
    Howard Davis, admin.   Fax 525-0650
Interactive College of Technology
    11 Spiral Dr Ste 8 41042   859-282-8989
National College of Business & Tech.   Post-Sec.
    7627 Ewing Blvd 41042   859-525-6510
Southwestern College of Business   Post-Sec.
    8095 Connector Dr 41042   859-282-9999

Fort Knox, Hardin, Pop. 21,495

Sullivan University   Post-Sec.
    PO Box 998 40121   502-942-8500

Fort Mitchell, Kenton, Pop. 7,822
Beechwood ISD   900/K-12
    50 Beechwood Rd 41017   859-331-3250
    Dr. Fred Bassett, supt.   Fax 331-7528
    www.beechwood.k12.ky.us
Beechwood JSHS   500/7-12
    54 Beechwood Rd 41017   859-331-1220
    Glen Miller, prin.   Fax 426-3744

Kentucky Tech System
    Supt. — None
Patton Area Technology Center   Vo/Tech
    3234 Turkeyfoot Rd 41017   859-341-2266
    Ray Stanley, prin.   Fax 341-6486

Brown Mackie College   Post-Sec.
    309 Buttermilk Pike 41017   859-341-5627

Fort Thomas, Campbell, Pop. 16,019
Fort Thomas ISD   2,300/K-12
    28 N Fort Thomas Ave 41075   859-781-3333
    Larry Stinson, supt.   Fax 442-4015
    www.ft-thomas.k12.ky.us/
Highlands HS   800/9-12
    2400 Memorial Pkwy 41075   859-781-5900
    Elgin Emmons, prin.   Fax 442-4221
Highlands MS   600/6-8
    2350 Memorial Pkwy 41075   859-781-5900
    Mary Adams, prin.   Fax 442-4210

Fort Wright, Kenton, Pop. 5,580
Kenton County SD   12,600/PK-12
    1055 Eaton Dr 41017   859-344-8888
    Tim Hanner, supt.   Fax 344-1531
    www.kenton.k12.ky.us/
Other Schools – See Covington, Edgewood,
    Independence, Taylor Mill

Frankfort, Franklin, Pop. 27,408
Frankfort ISD   800/PK-12
    309 Shelby St Ste 201 40601   502-875-8661
    Dr. Judith M. Lucarelli, supt.   Fax 875-8663
    www.frankfort.k12.ky.us
Frankfort HS   300/9-12
    328 Shelby St 40601   502-875-8655
    Paul Christy, prin.   Fax 875-8657

Franklin County SD   5,800/PK-12
    916 E Main St 40601   502-695-6700
    Monte Chance, supt.   Fax 695-6708
    www.franklin.k12.ky.us/
Bondurant MS   600/6-8
    Bondurant Dr 40601   502-875-8440
    Greg Gaby, prin.   Fax 875-8442
Elkhorn MS   700/6-8
    1060 E Main St 40601   502-695-6740
    Bob Bell, prin.   Fax 695-6745
Franklin Co. Career & Technical Center   Vo/Tech
    1106 E Main St 40601   502-695-6790
    Karen Schneider, prin.   Fax 695-6791
Franklin County HS   900/9-12
    1100 E Main St 40601   502-695-6750
    Sharon Collett, prin.   Fax 695-6755
Western Hills HS   700/9-12
    100 Doctors Dr 40601   502-875-8400
    Dennis Hancock, prin.   Fax 227-4568

J & M Academy of Cosmetology   Post-Sec.
    110A Brighton Park Blvd 40601   502-695-8001
Kentucky State University   Post-Sec.
    400 E Main St 40601   502-597-6000

Franklin, Simpson, Pop. 8,009
Simpson County SD   2,600/PK-12
    PO Box 467 42135   270-586-8877
    James Flynn, supt.   Fax 586-2011
    www.simpson.k12.ky.us
Franklin Simpson HS   800/9-12
    PO Box 389 42135   270-586-3273
    Lowell Hammers, prin.   Fax 586-2021
Franklin Simpson MS   500/6-8
    PO Box 637 42135   270-586-4401
    Monte Cassady, prin.   Fax 586-2048

Frenchburg, Menifee, Pop. 554
Menifee County SD   1,100/K-12
    PO Box 110 40322   606-768-8002
    Charles Mitchell, supt.   Fax 768-8050
    www.menifee.k12.ky.us
Menifee County HS   300/9-12
    119 Indian Creek Rd 40322   606-768-8102
    Elaine Brown, prin.   Fax 768-8200
Menifee County MS   300/6-8
    59 Indian Creek Rd 40322   606-768-8252
    Benny Patrick, prin.   Fax 768-8300

Fulton, Fulton, Pop. 2,636
Fulton ISD   500/K-12
    313 Main St 42041   270-472-1553
    Dianne Owen, supt.   Fax 472-6921
    www.fulton-ind.k12.ky.us
Fulton City HS   200/7-12
    700 Stephen Beale Dr 42041   270-472-1741
    Wayne Benningfield, prin.   Fax 472-6135

Georgetown, Scott, Pop. 19,438
Scott County SD   6,300/PK-12
    PO Box 578 40324   502-863-3663
    Dallas Blankenship, supt.   Fax 863-5367
    www.scott.k12.ky.us
Georgetown MS   600/6-8
    730 S Hamilton St 40324   502-863-3805
    Tommy Hurt, prin.   Fax 867-1372
Ninth Grade Center   500/9-9
    1072 Cardinal Dr 40324   502-863-4635
    Betty Hughes, prin.   Fax 868-0515
Scott County MS   900/6-8
    1036 Cardinal Dr 40324   502-863-7202
    Jennifer Sutton, prin.   Fax 863-7452
Scott County SHS   1,200/10-12
    1080 Cardinal Dr 40324   502-863-4131
    Chip Southworth, prin.   Fax 867-0544

Georgetown College   Post-Sec.
    400 E College St 40324   502-863-8011

Glasgow, Barren, Pop. 13,614
Barren County SD   4,000/PK-12
    202 W Washington St 42141   270-651-3787
    Jerry Ralston, supt.   Fax 651-8836
    www.trojan2000.org

Barren County HS   1,200/9-12
    507 Trojan Trl 42141   270-651-6315
    Keith Hale, prin.   Fax 651-9211
Barren County MS   600/7-8
    555 Trojan Trl 42141   270-651-4909
    Cortni Crews, prin.   Fax 651-5137

Glasgow ISD   1,700/K-12
    PO Box 1239 42142   270-651-6757
    Dr. Fred P. Carter, supt.   Fax 651-9791
    www.glasgow.k12.ky.us
Glasgow HS   500/9-12
    1601 Columbia Ave 42141   270-651-8801
    Tommy Elliott, prin.   Fax 651-5189
Glasgow MS   500/6-8
    105 Scottie Dr 42141   270-651-2256
    Randy Wilkinson, prin.   Fax 651-3090

Kentucky Tech System
    Supt. — None
Barren County Area Technology Center   Vo/Tech
    491 Trojan Trl 42141   270-651-2196
    Hal Toms, prin.   Fax 651-2197

Bowling Green Technical College   Post-Sec.
    129 State Ave 42141   270-651-5373
Glasgow Christian Academy   200/PK-12
    600 Cavalry Dr 42141   270-651-7729
    Melinda Campbell, admin.   Fax 651-6811
PJs College of Cosmetology   Post-Sec.
    124 S Public Sq 42141   270-651-6553

Glendale, Hardin
Hardin County SD
    Supt. — See Elizabethtown
East Hardin MS   600/6-8
    129 College St 42740   270-369-7370
    Paul Connelly, prin.   Fax 369-6380

Goshen, Oldham, Pop. 935
Oldham County SD
    Supt. — See Buckner
North Oldham HS   600/9-12
    1815 S Highway 1793 40026   502-228-0158
    Lisa Jarrett, prin.   Fax 228-7735
North Oldham MS   800/5-8
    1801 S Highway 1793 40026   502-228-9998
    Rob Smith, prin.   Fax 228-0985

Grayson, Carter, Pop. 3,980
Carter County SD   4,700/PK-12
    228 S Carol Malone Blvd 41143   606-474-6696
    Larry Prichard, supt.   Fax 474-6125
    www.carter.k12.ky.us
East Carter County HS   600/9-12
    405 Hitchins Rd 41143   606-474-5714
    Ada Steele, prin.   Fax 475-9200
East Carter MS   600/6-8
    520 Robert and Mary St 41143   606-474-5156
    Shannon Wilburn, prin.   Fax 474-4027
Other Schools – See Olive Hill

Carter Christian Academy   100/PK-12
    PO Box 490 41143   606-475-1919
    Pat Collier, admin.   Fax 475-1433
Kentucky Christian University   Post-Sec.
    100 Academic Pkwy 41143   606-474-3000

Greensburg, Green, Pop. 2,443
Green County SD   1,700/K-12
    PO Box 369 42743   270-932-5231
    Marshall Lowe, supt.   Fax 932-3624
    www.green.k12.ky.us
Green County HS   500/9-12
    PO Box 227 42743   270-932-7481
    Michael Tucker, prin.   Fax 932-3214
Green County MS   400/6-8
    PO Box 176 42743   270-932-7773
    Timothy Deaton, prin.   Fax 932-7617

Kentucky Tech System
    Supt. — None
Green County Area Technology Center   Vo/Tech
    PO Box 167 42743   270-932-4263
    Rick Atwell, prin.   Fax 932-3072

Greenup, Greenup, Pop. 1,173
Greenup County SD   3,000/K-12
    45 Musketeer Dr 41144   606-473-9819
    John Younce, supt.   Fax 473-5710
    www.greenup.k12.ky.us/
Greenup County HS   900/9-12
    196 Musketeer Dr 41144   606-473-9812
    Matt Baker, prin.   Fax 473-7854
Other Schools – See South Shore, Wurtland

Kentucky Tech System
    Supt. — None
Greenup County Area Technology Center   Vo/Tech
    146 Musketeer Dr 41144   606-473-9344
    Marsha Martin, prin.   Fax 473-9177

Greenville, Muhlenberg, Pop. 4,315
Kentucky Tech System
    Supt. — None
Muhlenberg County Area Technology Center   Vo/Tech
    201 Airport Rd 42345   270-338-1271
    Andrew Swansey, prin.   Fax 338-6802

Muhlenberg County SD
    Supt. — See Powderly
Muhlenberg County Career HS   Vo/Tech
    3875 St Rt 181 N 42345   270-338-5460
    Jim Price, prin.   Fax 377-0581

Muhlenberg North HS | 800/9-12
501 Robert L Draper Way 42345 | 270-338-0040
Mark Eades, prin. | Fax 338-2442
Muhlenberg North MS | 700/6-8
1000 N Main St 42345 | 270-338-3550
Robby Davis, prin. | Fax 338-2911
Muhlenberg South HS | 700/9-12
2900 State Route 176 42345 | 270-338-9409
Micky Strader, prin. | Fax 338-9710
Muhlenberg South MS | 500/6-8
200 Pritchett Dr 42345 | 270-338-4650
Ed McCarraher, prin. | Fax 338-0151

Muhlenberg Job Corps Center | Post-Sec.
3875 Highway 181 N 42345 | 270-338-5460

Hardinsburg, Breckinridge, Pop. 2,393
Breckinridge County SD | 2,600/PK-12
PO Box 148 40143 | 270-756-3000
Evelyn Neely, supt. | Fax 756-6888
www.breck.k12.ky.us/
Other Schools – See Harned

Harlan, Harlan, Pop. 1,945
Harlan County SD | 4,700/PK-12
251 Ball Park Rd 40831 | 606-573-4330
Timothy Saylor, supt. | Fax 573-5767
www.harlan.k12.ky.us/
Cawood HS | 700/9-12
279 Ball Park Rd 40831 | 606-573-5029
Michael Ashurst, prin. | Fax 573-2424
Other Schools – See Cumberland, Evarts

Harlan ISD | 900/K-12
420 E Central St 40831 | 606-573-8700
David Johnson, supt. | Fax 573-8711
www.harlan-ind.k12.ky.us
Harlan MSHS | 500/5-12
420 E Central St 40831 | 606-573-8750
Sheila Smith, prin. | Fax 573-8753

Jenny Lea Academy of Cosmetology | Post-Sec.
114 N Cumberland Ave 40831 | 606-573-4276

Harned, Breckinridge
Breckinridge County SD
Supt. — See Hardinsburg
Breckinridge County HS | 800/9-12
PO Box 130 40144 | 270-756-3080
Dale Butler, prin. | Fax 756-3081
Breckinridge County MS | 600/6-8
PO Box 39 40144 | 270-756-3060
Kathy Gedling, prin. | Fax 756-3061

Kentucky Tech System
Supt. — None
Breckinridge County Area Technology Ctr. | Vo/Tech
PO Box 68 40144 | 270-756-2138
Wayne Spencer, prin. | Fax 756-2878

Harrodsburg, Mercer, Pop. 8,085
Harrodsburg ISD | 900/PK-12
371 E Lexington St 40330 | 859-734-8400
Dr. H.M. Snodgrass, supt. | Fax 734-8404
www.hburg.k12.ky.us
Harrodsburg HS | 200/9-12
441 E Lexington St 40330 | 859-734-8420
Wade Stanfield, prin. | Fax 734-8425
Harrodsburg MS | 200/6-8
443 E Lexington St 40330 | 859-734-8415
Terry Gordon, prin. | Fax 734-8425

Kentucky Tech System
Supt. — None
Harrodsburg Area Technology Center | Vo/Tech
PO Box 628 40330 | 859-734-9329
Duane Flora, prin. | Fax 734-3613

Mercer County SD | 2,200/K-12
961 Moberly Rd 40330 | 859-734-4364
Bruce Johnson, supt. | Fax 734-4852
www.mercer.k12.ky.us
King MS | 700/5-8
1101 Moberly Rd 40330 | 859-734-4364
Jennifer Miller, prin. | Fax 734-0811
Mercer County HS | 700/9-12
937 Moberly Rd 40330 | 859-734-4364
Terry Yates, prin. | Fax 734-6364

Hartford, Ohio, Pop. 2,603
Kentucky Tech System
Supt. — None
Ohio County Area Technology Center | Vo/Tech
1406 S Main St 42347 | 270-274-9612
Brad Sisk, prin. | Fax 274-9633

Ohio County SD | 3,900/PK-12
PO Box 70 42347 | 270-298-3249
Soretta Ralph, supt. | Fax 298-3886
www.ohio.k12.ky.us
Ohio County HS | 1,200/9-12
1400 S Main St 42347 | 270-274-3366
John Stofer, prin. | Fax 274-9482
Ohio County MS | 600/7-8
1404 S Main St 42347 | 270-274-7893
Dr. Rebecca Stobaugh, prin. | Fax 274-7320

Hawesville, Hancock, Pop. 961
Hancock County SD | 1,000/K-12
83 State Route 271 N 42348 | 270-927-6914
Mike Gray, supt. | Fax 927-6916
www.hancock.k12.ky.us
Other Schools – See Lewisport

Hazard, Perry, Pop. 4,745
Hazard ISD | 800/K-12
325 Broadway St 41701 | 606-436-3911
Sandra Johnson, supt. | Fax 436-2742
www.hazard.k12.ky.us
Eversole MS | 300/5-8
601 Broadway St 41701 | 606-436-4721
John Quillen, prin. | Fax 439-3726
Hazard HS | 300/9-12
157 Bulldog Ln 41701 | 606-439-1318
Donald Mobelini, prin. | Fax 439-2285

Knott County SD
Supt. — See Hindman
Cordia HS | 100/7-12
6060 Lotts Creek Rd 41701 | 606-785-4457
Mildred Faye Gayheart, prin. | Fax 785-4669
Perry County SD | 4,400/K-12
315 Park Ave 41701 | 606-439-5814
John Paul Amis, supt. | Fax 439-2512
www.perry.k12.ky.us/
Perry County Central HS | 1,000/9-12
305 Park Ave 41701 | 606-439-5888
Estill Neace, prin. | Fax 439-2825
Other Schools – See Buckhorn

Hazard Community & Technical College | Post-Sec.
1 Community College Dr 41701 | 606-436-5721

Hebron, Boone
Boone County SD
Supt. — See Florence
Conner HS | 1,400/9-12
3310 Cougar Path 41048 | 859-334-4400
Michael Blevins, prin. | Fax 334-4406
Conner MS | 1,200/6-8
3300 Cougar Path 41048 | 859-334-4410
Linda Viox, prin. | Fax 334-4435

Kentucky Tech System
Supt. — None
Boone County Area Technology Center | Vo/Tech
3320 Cougar Path 41048 | 859-689-7855
Al Tucker, prin. | Fax 689-7828

Henderson, Henderson, Pop. 27,468
Henderson County SD | 6,700/K-12
1805 2nd St 42420 | 270-831-5000
Dr. Thomas Richey, supt. | Fax 831-5009
www.henderson.k12.ky.us
Henderson County Area Technology Center | Vo/Tech
2440 Zion Rd 42420 | 270-831-8850
Victor Doty, prin. | Fax 831-8853
Henderson County HS | 2,200/9-12
2424 Zion Rd 42420 | 270-831-8800
Bruce Swanson, prin. | Fax 831-8870
Henderson County North MS | 900/6-8
1707 2nd St 42420 | 270-831-5060
Scottie Long, prin. | Fax 831-5064
Henderson County South MS | 700/6-8
800 S Alves St 42420 | 270-831-5050
Dane Ferguson, prin. | Fax 831-5058

Henderson Community College | Post-Sec.
2660 S Green St 42420 | 270-827-1867
Pat Wilson Beauty College | Post-Sec.
326 N Main St 42420 | 270-826-5195

Hickman, Fulton, Pop. 2,442
Fulton County SD | 700/PK-12
2780 Moscow Ave 42050 | 270-236-3923
Dr. Charles Holliday, supt. | Fax 236-2184
www.fulton.k12.ky.us
Fulton County HS | 200/9-12
2740 Moscow Ave 42050 | 270-236-3904
Gary Meredith, prin. | Fax 236-9004
Fulton County MS | 200/6-8
2770 Moscow Ave 42050 | 270-236-3923
David L. Caldwell, prin. | Fax 236-4708

Kentucky Tech System
Supt. — None
Fulton County Area Technology Center | Vo/Tech
2720 Moscow Ave 42050 | 270-236-2517
Tom Pyron, prin. | Fax 236-9395

Highland Heights, Campbell, Pop. 6,472

Gateway Community & Technical College | Post-Sec.
90 Campbell Dr 41076 | 859-442-4108

Hi Hat, Floyd
Floyd County SD
Supt. — See Prestonsburg
South Floyd HS | 400/9-12
299 Mt Raider Dr # 101 41636 | 606-452-9600
Keith Henry, prin. | Fax 452-2155
South Floyd MS | 200/7-8
299 Mt Raider Dr # 102 41636 | 606-452-9607
Zenith Hall, prin. | Fax 452-4810

Hindman, Knott, Pop. 771
Kentucky Tech System
Supt. — None
Knott County Area Technology Center | Vo/Tech
1996 Highway 160 S 41822 | 606-785-5350
Patrick Goodin, prin. | Fax 785-5445

Knott County SD | 2,500/PK-12
PO Box 869 41822 | 606-785-3153
Harold Combs, supt. | Fax 785-0800
www.knott.k12.ky.us
Knott County Central HS | 700/9-12
PO Box 819 41822 | 606-785-3166
Bobby Pollard, prin. | Fax 785-3169

Other Schools – See Hazard

Hodgenville, Larue, Pop. 2,787
LaRue County SD | 2,300/K-12
PO Box 39 42748 | 270-358-4111
Sam Sanders, supt. | Fax 358-3053
www.larue.k12.ky.us
LaRue County HS | 700/9-12
925 S Lincoln Blvd 42748 | 270-358-2210
Paul Mullins, prin. | Fax 358-9469
LaRue County MS | 400/7-8
911 S Lincoln Blvd 42748 | 270-358-3196
Lori Indalecio, prin. | Fax 358-9088

Hopkinsville, Christian, Pop. 28,678
Christian County SD | 8,900/K-12
PO Box 609 42241 | 270-887-1300
Robert C. Lovingood, supt. | Fax 887-1316
www.christian.k12.ky.us
Career & Technical Center | Vo/Tech
705 N Elm St 42240 | 270-887-1228
Michelle Dillard, prin. | Fax 887-1242
Christian County HS | 1,300/9-12
220 Glass Ave 42240 | 270-887-1100
Kathy Hancock, prin. | Fax 887-1294
Christian County MS | 800/6-8
210 Glass Ave 42240 | 270-887-1130
Larry Cavanah, prin. | Fax 887-1189
Hopkinsville HS | 1,000/9-12
430 Koffman Dr 42240 | 270-887-1200
Jay Buckley, prin. | Fax 887-1118
Hopkinsville MS | 600/6-8
434 Koffman Dr 42240 | 270-887-1230
Mark Page, prin. | Fax 887-1234
North Drive MS | 600/6-8
831 North Dr 42240 | 270-887-1250
Mike Beck, prin. | Fax 887-1287

Brown Mackie College | Post-Sec.
4001 Fort Campbell Blvd 42240 | 270-886-1302
Heritage Christian Academy | 400/PK-12
8349 Eagle Way Bypass 42240 | 270-885-2417
Linda Garris, hdmstr. | Fax 885-0094
Hopkinsville Community College | Post-Sec.
PO Box 2100 42241 | 270-886-3921
University Heights Academy | 300/K-12
1300 Academy Dr 42240 | 270-886-0254
Pam Nunn, prin. | Fax 886-2716

Horse Cave, Hart, Pop. 2,272
Caverna ISD
Supt. — See Cave City
Caverna HS | 200/9-12
2276 S Dixie St 42749 | 270-773-2828
Pat Waddell, prin. | Fax 773-2825
Caverna MS | 200/6-8
2276 S Dixie St 42749 | 270-773-2828
Nathan E. Wyatt, prin. | Fax 773-2825

Hyden, Leslie, Pop. 200
Kentucky Tech System
Supt. — None
Leslie County Area Technology Center | Vo/Tech
PO Box 902 41749 | 606-672-2859
Larry Sparks, prin. | Fax 672-4943

Leslie County SD | 2,100/K-12
PO Box 949 41749 | 606-672-2397
Thomas Sizemore, supt. | Fax 672-4224
www.leslie.k12.ky.us
Leslie County HS | 600/9-12
PO Box 970 41749 | 606-672-2337
O. Shepherd, prin. | Fax 672-2858
Leslie County MS | 400/7-8
PO Box 965 41749 | 606-672-5580
Dana Coots, prin. | Fax 672-2858

Frontier School of Midwifery | Post-Sec.
PO Box 528 41749 | 606-672-2312

Independence, Kenton, Pop. 17,070
Kenton County SD
Supt. — See Fort Wright
Kenton HS | 1,300/9-12
11132 Madison Pike 41051 | 859-363-4100
Richard Culross, prin. | Fax 363-4101
Summit View MS | 800/6-8
5002 Madison Pike 41051 | 859-363-4800
David Johnstone, prin. | Fax 363-4804
Twenhofel MS | 800/6-8
11800 Taylor Mill Rd 41051 | 859-356-5559
Cheryl Jones, prin. | Fax 356-1137

Community Christian Academy | 200/PK-12
11875 Taylor Mill Rd 41051 | 859-356-7990
Tara Bates, prin. | Fax 356-7991

Inez, Martin, Pop. 456
Kentucky Tech System
Supt. — None
Martin County Area Technology Center | Vo/Tech
HC 68 Box 2177 41224 | 606-298-3879
Charles Six, prin. | Fax 298-7240

Martin County SD | 2,200/PK-12
PO Box 366 41224 | 606-298-3572
Mark Blackburn, supt. | Fax 298-4427
www.martin.k12.ky.us
Clark HS | 600/9-12
HC 63 Box 810 41224 | 606-298-3591
Patricia Elliott, prin. | Fax 298-5148
Inez MS | 400/6-8
PO Box 5001 41224 | 606-298-3045
Greg Cornette, prin. | Fax 298-7314
Other Schools – See Warfield

Irvine, Estill, Pop. 2,748
Estill County SD — 2,400/PK-12
PO Box 930 40336 — 606-723-2181
Bert Hensley, supt. — Fax 723-6029
www.estill.k12.ky.us
Estill County HS — 700/9-12
2675 Winchester Rd 40336 — 606-723-3537
Blain Click, prin. — Fax 723-4894
Estill County MS — 600/6-8
2805 Winchester Rd 40336 — 606-723-5136
Chesteen Robbins, prin. — Fax 723-2041

Jackson, Breathitt, Pop. 2,407
Breathitt County SD — 2,200/PK-12
PO Box 750 41339 — 606-666-2491
Arch Turner, supt. — Fax 666-2493
www.breathitt.k12.ky.us
Breathitt County HS — 600/9-12
2307 Bobcat Ln 41339 — 606-666-7511
Derek McKnight, prin. — Fax 666-7765
Sebastian MS — 400/7-8
244 L B J Rd 41339 — 606-666-8894
Tim Bobrowski, prin. — Fax 666-5336

Jackson ISD — 600/PK-12
940 Highland Ave 41339 — 606-666-4979
Timothy Spencer, supt. — Fax 666-4350
www.jackson-ind.k12.ky.us
Jackson City S — 600/PK-12
940 Highland Ave 41339 — 606-666-5164
James Yount, prin. — Fax 666-2555

Kentucky Tech System
Supt. — None
Breathitt County Area Technology Center — Vo/Tech
PO Box 786 41339 — 606-666-5153
Margaret Gross, prin. — Fax 666-5394

Oakdale Christian Academy — 50/7-12
5801 Beattyville Rd 41339 — 606-666-5422
Daniel Fisher, prin. — Fax 666-5422

Jamestown, Russell, Pop. 1,666
Russell County SD — 2,800/K-12
PO Box 440 42629 — 270-343-3191
Scott Pierce, supt. — Fax 343-3072
www.russell.k12.ky.us/
Other Schools – See Russell Springs

Jeffersontown, Jefferson, Pop. 26,331
Jefferson County SD
Supt. — See Louisville
Jeffersontown HS Magnet Career Academy — 900/9-12
9600 Old Six Mile Ln 40299 — 502-485-8275
Marsha Dohn, prin. — Fax 485-8832

Jenkins, Letcher, Pop. 2,321
Jenkins ISD — 600/PK-12
PO Box 74 41537 — 606-832-2183
John Shook, supt. — Fax 832-2181
www.jenkins.k12.ky.us
Jenkins MSHS — 200/7-12
PO Box 552 41537 — 606-832-2184
Teresa Bentley, prin. — Fax 832-4238

Lancaster, Garrard, Pop. 4,014
Garrard County SD — 2,400/PK-12
322 W Maple Ave 40444 — 859-792-3018
Ray Woolsey, supt. — Fax 792-4733
www.garrard.k12.ky.us/
Garrard County HS — 700/9-12
304 W Maple Ave 40444 — 859-792-2146
Kevin Stull, prin. — Fax 792-4352
Garrard MS — 600/6-8
324 W Maple Ave 40444 — 859-792-2108
Cindy Rogers, prin. — Fax 792-9618

Kentucky Tech System
Supt. — None
Garrard County Area Technology Center — Vo/Tech
306 W Maple Ave 40444 — 859-792-2144
James Alford, prin. — Fax 792-4058

Lawrenceburg, Anderson, Pop. 9,246
Anderson County SD — 3,700/PK-12
103 N Main St 40342 — 502-839-3406
Kim Shaw, supt. — Fax 839-2501
www.anderson.k12.ky.us
Anderson County HS — 1,000/9-12
1 Bearcat Dr 40342 — 502-839-5118
Ray Woodyard, prin. — Fax 839-3486
Anderson County MS — 900/6-8
200 Mustang Trl 40342 — 502-839-9261
Steve Carmichael, prin. — Fax 839-2534

Central Kentucky Technical College — Post-Sec.
1500 Bypass N 40342 — 502-839-8488
Christian Academy of Lawrenceburg — 100/PK-12
PO Box 498 40342 — 502-839-9992
James Everett, admin. — Fax 839-3728

Lebanon, Marion, Pop. 5,821
Kentucky Tech System
Supt. — None
Marion County Area Technology Center — Vo/Tech
721 E Main St 40033 — 270-692-3155
Howard Carey, prin. — Fax 692-1357

Marion County SD — 3,000/PK-12
755 E Main St 40033 — 270-692-3721
Roger Marcum, supt. — Fax 692-1899
www.marion.k12.ky.us
Lebanon MS — 400/6-8
200 Corporate Dr 40033 — 270-692-3441
Daniel Imes, prin. — Fax 692-0266

Marion County HS — 900/9-12
735 E Main St 40033 — 270-692-6066
Taylora Brown, prin. — Fax 692-6248
St. Charles MS — 300/6-8
1155 Highway 327 40033 — 270-692-4578
John A. Brady, prin. — Fax 692-1176

Leitchfield, Grayson, Pop. 6,263
Grayson County SD — 4,100/PK-12
PO Box 4009 42755 — 270-259-4011
Teddy White, supt. — Fax 259-4756
www.grayson.k12.ky.us
Grayson County HS — 1,200/9-12
340 School House Rd 42754 — 270-259-4078
Michael Huffman, prin. — Fax 259-6131
Grayson County MS — 1,000/6-8
726 John Hill Taylor Dr 42754 — 270-259-4175
Bill Embry, prin. — Fax 259-5875
Grayson County Technology Center — Vo/Tech
252 School House Rd 42754 — 270-259-3195
Cynthia Smith, prin. — Fax 259-8082

Lewisport, Hancock, Pop. 1,628
Hancock County SD
Supt. — See Hawesville
Hancock County HS — 400/9-12
80 State Route 271 S 42351 — 270-927-6953
Rick Lasley, prin. — Fax 927-8677
Hancock County MS — 400/6-8
100 State Route 271 S 42351 — 270-927-6712
Gina Biever, prin. — Fax 927-6712

Lexington, Fayette, Pop. 263,618
Fayette County SD — 33,100/PK-12
701 E Main St 40502 — 859-381-4000
Stu Silberman, supt. — Fax 381-4106
www.fayette.k12.ky.us/
Beaumont MS — 1,100/6-8
2080 Georgian Way 40504 — 859-381-3094
Dr. Thomas Mowery, prin. — Fax 381-3109
Bryan Station HS — 1,400/9-12
1866 Edgewood Dr 40505 — 859-381-3308
Gladys Peoples, prin. — Fax 381-3330
Bryan Station Magnet MS — 700/6-8
1865 Wickland Dr 40505 — 859-381-3288
Jim Thomas, prin. — Fax 293-3292
Clark MS — 900/6-8
3341 Clays Mill Rd 40503 — 859-381-3036
Lisa Goodin, prin. — Fax 381-3037
Clay HS — 1,800/9-12
2100 Fontaine Rd 40502 — 859-381-3423
John Nochta, prin. — Fax 381-3430
Crawford MS — 900/6-8
1813 Charleston Dr 40505 — 859-381-3370
Joyce Florence, prin. — Fax 381-3378
Dunbar HS — 2,200/9-12
1600 Man O War Blvd 40513 — 859-381-3546
Anthony Orr, prin. — Fax 381-3560
Eastside Technical Center — Vo/Tech
2208 Liberty Rd 40509 — 859-381-3740
Joe Norman, prin. — Fax 381-3747
Hayes MS — 500/6-8
260 Richardson Pl 40509 — 859-381-4195
Sherri Heise, prin. — Fax 381-4937
Lafayette HS — 1,900/9-12
400 Reed Ln 40503 — 859-381-3474
Mike McKenzie, prin. — Fax 381-3487
Leestown Math Science & Tech MS — 600/6-8
2010 Leestown Rd 40511 — 859-381-3181
Ezra Farris, prin.
Lexington Traditional Magnet MS — 500/6-8
350 N Limestone 40508 — 859-381-3192
Charlotte Jernigan, prin. — Fax 252-6795
Morton MS — 800/6-8
1225 Tates Creek Rd 40502 — 859-381-3533
Jock Gum, prin. — Fax 381-3536
School for Creative and Performing Arts — 300/4-8
400 Lafayette Pkwy 40503 — 859-381-3332
M. Cunninghamn-Amos, prin. — Fax 381-3334
Southern MS — 800/6-8
400 Wilson Downing Rd 40517 — 859-381-3582
Jane Dreidame, prin. — Fax 381-3588
Southside Technical Center — Vo/Tech
1784 Harrodsburg Rd 40504 — 859-381-3603
James Hardin, prin. — Fax 381-3807
Tates Creek HS — 1,700/9-12
1111 Centre Pkwy 40517 — 859-381-3620
Sam Meaux, prin. — Fax 381-3635
Tates Creek MS — 700/6-8
1105 Centre Pkwy 40517 — 859-381-3052
Earl Stivers, prin. — Fax 381-3053
Winburn MS — 700/6-8
1060 Winburn Dr 40511 — 859-381-3967
Tina Stevenson, prin. — Fax 381-3971

Blue Grass Baptist S — 200/K-12
3743 Red River Dr 40517 — 859-272-1217
Guy Causey, prin. — Fax 273-8658
Bluegrass Community & Technical College — Post-Sec.
470 Cooper Dr 40506 — 859-246-6200
Central Kentucky Technical College — Post-Sec.
308 Vo Tech Rd 40511 — 859-246-2400
Kaufman Beauty School — Post-Sec.
701 E High St 40502 — 859-266-2024
Lexington Beauty College — Post-Sec.
90 Southport Dr 40503 — 859-278-7483
Lexington Catholic HS — 700/9-12
2250 Clays Mill Rd 40503 — 859-277-7183
Sally Stevens, prin. — Fax 276-5086
Lexington Christian Academy HS — 400/9-12
450 W Reynolds Rd 40503 — 859-422-5701
Dr. Ollie Gibbs, hdmstr. — Fax 224-0456

Lexington Christian Academy JHS — 200/7-8
450 W Reynolds Rd 40503 — 859-477-5702
John Eckelbarger, prin. — Fax 422-5792
Lexington Theological Seminary — Post-Sec.
631 S Limestone 40508 — 859-252-0361
National College of Business & Tech. — Post-Sec.
628 E Main St 40508 — 859-253-0621
Pathology and Cytology Laboratories — Post-Sec.
290 Big Run Rd 40503 — 859-278-9513
St. Joseph's Hospital — Post-Sec.
1 Saint Joseph Dr 40504 — 859-278-3436
Sayre S — 600/PK-12
194 N Limestone 40507 — 859-254-1361
Clayton Chambliss, prin. — Fax 231-0508
Spencerian College — Post-Sec.
1575 Winchester Rd 40505 — 859-223-9608
Sullivan University — Post-Sec.
2355 Harrodsburg Rd 40504 — 800-467-6281
Transylvania University — Post-Sec.
300 N Broadway 40508 — 859-233-8300
University of Kentucky 40506 — Post-Sec.
— 859-257-9000
Univ. of Kentucky Chandler Medical Ctr. — Post-Sec.
103 Administration Plz A311 40536 — 859-323-5126

Liberty, Casey, Pop. 1,871
Casey County SD — 2,400/PK-12
1922 N US Highway 127 42539 — 606-787-6941
Linda Hatter, supt. — Fax 787-5231
www.casey.k12.ky.us
Casey County HS — 700/9-12
1841 E KY 70 42539 — 606-787-6151
Tim Goodlett, prin. — Fax 787-8654
Casey County MS — 400/7-8
1673 E KY 70 42539 — 606-787-6769
Terri Price, prin. — Fax 787-5337

Kentucky Tech System
Supt. — None
Casey County Area Technology Center — Vo/Tech
1723 E KY 70 42539 — 606-787-6241
David Horseman, prin. — Fax 787-6243

Lick Creek, Pike, Pop. 221
Pike County SD
Supt. — See Pikeville
East Ridge HS — 800/9-12
19471 Lick Mountain Rd 41540 — 606-835-2811
Ralph Kilgore, prin. — Fax 835-2899

Lily, Laurel

Cornerstone Christian S — 100/PK-12
PO Box 810 40740 — 606-526-8893
Matthew Webb, prin. — Fax 526-8801

London, Laurel, Pop. 7,653
Laurel County SD — 8,700/K-12
275 S Laurel Rd 40744 — 606-862-4600
James Francis, supt. — Fax 862-4601
www.laurel.k12.ky.us
North Laurel HS — 1,100/9-12
1300 E Hal Rogers Pkwy 40741 — 606-862-4699
Sheila Hibbard, prin. — Fax 862-4700
North Laurel MS — 900/6-8
101 Johnson Rd 40741 — 606-862-4715
David Hensley, prin. — Fax 862-4717
South Laurel HS — 1,300/9-12
201 S Laurel Rd 40744 — 606-862-4727
Jeff Jackson, prin. — Fax 862-4728
South Laurel MS — 1,200/6-8
223 S Laurel Rd 40744 — 606-862-4745
Jeff Reed, prin. — Fax 862-4746

Lost Creek, Breathitt

Riverside Christian S — 100/K-12
10812 Highway 15 S 41348 — 606-666-2359
Beverly Burroughs, prin. — Fax 666-5211

Louisa, Lawrence, Pop. 2,007
Lawrence County SD — 2,600/PK-12
50 Bulldog Ln 41230 — 606-638-9671
Jeffery May, supt. — Fax 638-0128
www.lawrence.k12.ky.us
Lawrence County HS — 800/9-12
100 Bulldog Ln 41230 — 606-638-9676
Cassandra Webb, prin. — Fax 638-3227
Louisa MS — 500/6-8
9 Bulldog Ln 41230 — 606-638-4090
Thomas Gibson, prin. — Fax 638-4865

Louisville, Jefferson, Pop. 248,762
Jefferson County SD — 89,600/PK-12
PO Box 34020 40232 — 502-485-3011
Stephen Daeschner Ph.D., supt. — Fax 485-3991
www.jefferson.k12.ky.us
Atherton HS — 900/9-12
3000 Dundee Rd 40205 — 502-485-8202
John Hudson, prin. — Fax 485-8985
Ballard HS — 1,700/9-12
6000 Brownsboro Rd 40222 — 502-485-8206
James Jury, prin. — Fax 485-8856
Barret MS — 700/6-8
2561 Grinstead Dr 40206 — 502-485-8207
Tom Wortham, prin. — Fax 485-8579
Brown S — 1,500/K-12
546 S 1st St 40202 — 502-485-8216
Ruth Jarrell, prin. — Fax 485-8741
Butler HS — 1,600/9-12
2222 Crums Ln 40216 — 502-485-8220
Stephen Bocko, prin. — Fax 485-8517
Carrithers MS — 700/6-8
4320 Billtown Rd 40299 — 502-485-8224
Pat Gausepohl, prin. — Fax 485-8394

Central HS Magnet Career Academy 1,000/9-12
  1130 W Chestnut St 40203 502-485-8226
  Dan Withers, prin. Fax 485-7034
Conway MS 900/6-8
  6300 Terry Rd 40258 502-485-8233
  Debra Mercer, prin. Fax 485-8076
Doss HS Magnet Career Academy 1,000/9-12
  7601 Saint Andrews Church 40214 502-485-8239
  Glenn Baete, prin. Fax 485-8080
DuPont Manual HS 1,800/9-12
  120 W Lee St 40208 502-485-8241
  Beverly Keepers, prin. Fax 485-8035
Farnsley MS 1,000/6-8
  3400 Lees Ln 40216 502-485-8242
  Rob Stephenson, prin. Fax 485-8663
Highland MS 1,000/6-8
  1700 Norris Pl 40205 502-485-8266
  Steven Heckman, prin. Fax 485-8831
Iroquois HS Magnet Career Academy 1,100/9-12
  4615 Taylor Blvd 40215 502-485-8269
  Brian Shumate, prin. Fax 485-8033
Iroquois MS 700/6-8
  5650 Southern Pkwy 40214 502-485-8270
  Betty Graham, prin. Fax 485-8380
Jefferson County HS 700/9-12
  900 S Floyd St 40203 502-485-3173
  Buell Snyder, prin. Fax 485-3671
Jefferson County Traditional MS 900/6-8
  1418 Morton Ave 40204 502-485-8272
  Mark Rose, prin. Fax 485-8635
Jefferson MS 1,100/6-8
  1501 Rangeland Rd 40219 502-485-8273
  Janice McDowell, prin. Fax 485-8045
Johnson Traditional MS 900/6-8
  2509 Wilson Ave 40210 502-485-8277
  Beverly Johnson, prin. Fax 485-8679
Kammerer MS 900/6-8
  7315 Wesboro Rd 40222 502-485-8279
  Patricia Parker, prin. Fax 485-8618
Kennedy Metro MS 100/1-8
  4515 Taylorsville Rd 40220 502-485-6950
  David Mike, prin. Fax 491-7290
Knight MS 600/6-8
  9803 Blue Lick Rd 40229 502-485-8287
  Kenneth Black, prin. Fax 485-8073
Lassiter MS 700/6-8
  8200 Candleworth Dr 40214 502-485-8288
  Andrea Jackson, prin. Fax 485-8373
Louisville Male HS 1,600/9-12
  4409 Preston Hwy 40213 502-485-8292
  David Wilson, prin. Fax 485-8770
Meyzeek MS 1,100/6-8
  828 S Jackson St 40203 502-485-8299
  Keith Look, prin. Fax 485-8641
Moore Traditional HS 600/9-12
  6415 Outer Loop 40228 502-485-8304
  Edward Weber, prin. Fax 485-8168
Moore Traditional MS 1,000/6-8
  6415 Outer Loop 40228 502-485-8219
  Diana Drake-Hicks, prin. Fax 485-8913
Myers MS 900/6-8
  3741 Pulliam Dr 40218 502-485-8305
  William Bennett, prin. Fax 485-8157
Newburg MS 1,100/6-8
  4901 Exeter Ave 40218 502-485-8306
  Dianna Drake-Hicks, prin. Fax 485-8883
Noe MS 1,200/6-8
  121 W Lee St 40208 502-485-8307
  Kathleen Sayre, prin. Fax 485-8056
Pleasure Ridge Park HS Magnet Academy 1,800/9-12
  5901 Greenwood Rd 40258 502-485-8311
  David Johnson, prin. Fax 485-8093
Seneca HS Magnet Career Academy 1,700/9-12
  3510 Goldsmith Ln 40220 502-485-8323
  Mary Greenlee, prin. Fax 485-8174
Shawnee HS Magnet Career Academy 600/9-12
  4018 W Market St 40212 502-485-8326
  Mernia Hill, prin. Fax 485-8738
Southern HS Magnet Career Academy 1,400/9-12
  8620 Preston Hwy 40219 502-485-8330
  Jerry Keepers, prin. Fax 485-8029
Southern Leadership Academy 700/6-8
  4530 Bellevue Ave 40215 502-485-8331
  Anita Jones, prin. Fax 485-8381
Waggener Traditional HS 1,000/9-12
  330 S Hubbards Ln 40207 502-485-8340
  Candace Conway, prin. Fax 485-8140
Western Math Science Tech Magnet HS 700/9-12
  2501 Rockford Ln 40216 502-485-8344
  Louis Hughley, prin. Fax 485-8969
Western MS 600/6-8
  2201 W Main St 40212 502-485-8345
  Beth Johnson, prin. Fax 485-8047
Westport MS and Fine Arts Academy 1,100/6-8
  8100 Westport Rd 40222 502-485-8346
  Jan Calvert, prin. Fax 485-8590
Youth Performing Arts JSHS 7-12
  1517 S 2nd St 40208 502-485-8355
  Beverly Keepers, prin. Fax 485-8808
Other Schools – See Fairdale, Fern Creek,
  Jeffersontown, Middletown, Valley Station

Academy of Our Lady of Mercy 400/9-12
  1176 E Broadway 40204 502-584-4273
  Julie Crone, prin. Fax 584-9651
Assumption HS 1,000/9-12
  2170 Tyler Ln 40205 502-458-9551
  Mary Ann Steutermann, prin. Fax 454-8411
Bellarmine University Post-Sec.
  2001 Newburg Rd 40205 502-452-8000

Beth Haven Christian S 500/PK-12
  5515 Johnsontown Rd 40272 502-937-3516
  Amy Rogers, prin. Fax 937-3364
Brown Cancer Center Post-Sec.
  529 S Jackson St 40202 502-588-6905
Brown Mackie College Post-Sec.
  300 High Rise Dr 40213 502-968-7191
Christian Academy of Louisville 1,700/K-12
  700 S English Station Rd 40245 502-244-3225
  William McKinley, supt. Fax 244-1824
Covenant Classical Academy 50/K-12
  13902 Factory Ln 40245 502-243-0404
  R. Lance Harris, hdmstr. Fax 243-0404
Daymar College Post-Sec.
  4400 Brckenridge Ln #415 40218 502-495-1040
Decker College Post-Sec.
  10830 Penion Dr 40299 502-266-6676
DeSales HS 300/9-12
  425 W Kenwood Dr 40214 502-368-6519
  Tim Keogh, prin. Fax 366-6172
Donta School of Beauty Culture Post-Sec.
  515 W Oak St 40203 502-583-1018
Embry-Riddle Aeronautical University Post-Sec.
  300 High Rise Dr Ste 392 40213 502-942-0625
Evangel Christian S 300/K-12
  5400 Minor Ln 40219 502-968-7744
  Roger Hoagland, prin. Fax 968-8414
Galen College of Nursing Post-Sec.
  1031 Zorn Ave Ste 400 40207 502-582-2305
Hair Design School Post-Sec.
  1049 Bardstown Rd 40204 502-459-8150
Hair Design School Post-Sec.
  4160 Bardstown Rd 40218 502-491-0077
Holy Cross HS 400/9-12
  5144 Dixie Hwy 40216 502-447-4363
  Sr. Maryann Tarquinio, prin. Fax 448-1062
ITT Technical Institute Post-Sec.
  10509 Timberwood Cir 40223 502-327-7424
Jefferson Community & Technical College Post-Sec.
  109 E Broadway 40202 502-584-0181
Jefferson Technical College Post-Sec.
  727 W Chestnut St 40203 502-213-4290
Kentucky Country Day S 800/K-12
  4100 Springdale Rd 40241 502-423-0440
  Brad Lyman, hdmstr. Fax 423-0445
Kentucky School for the Blind Post-Sec.
  1867 Frankfort Ave 40206
Louisville Collegiate S 700/K-12
  2427 Glenmary Ave 40204 502-479-0340
  Michael Collins, prin. Fax 454-8549
Louisville Jr. Academy 50/1-10
  2988 Newburg Rd 40205 502-452-2965
  Brent Ruckle, prin. Fax 452-2965
Louisville Presbyterian Seminary Post-Sec.
  1044 Alta Vista Rd 40205 502-895-3411
Louisville Technical Institute Post-Sec.
  3901 Atkinson Square Dr 40218 800-844-6528
National College of Business & Tech. Post-Sec.
  4205 Dixie Hwy 40216 502-447-7634
On Fire Christian Academy 100/K-12
  5627 New Cut Rd 40214 502-368-0080
  Kristine Salvo, admin. Fax 368-0088
Pitt Academy 50/PK-12
  6010 Preston Hwy 40219 502-966-6979
  Sherry Downey, prin. Fax 962-8878
Portland Christian JSHS 100/7-12
  2500 Portland Ave 40212 502-778-6114
  Timothy Morrow, prin. Fax 772-7027
Presentation Academy 400/9-12
  861 S 4th St 40203 502-583-5935
  Barbara Wine, prin. Fax 583-1342
Sacred Heart Academy 800/9-12
  3175 Lexington Rd 40206 502-897-6097
  Dr. Beverly McAuliffe, prin. Fax 896-3935
St. Francis HS 100/9-12
  233 W Broadway 40202 502-736-1000
  Alexandra Thurstone, prin. Fax 736-1049
St. Xavier HS 1,500/9-12
  1609 Poplar Level Rd 40217 502-637-4712
  Nelson Nunn, prin. Fax 634-2171
School of Hair Design Post-Sec.
  5120 Dixie Hwy 40216 502-447-0111
Southern Baptist Theological Seminary Post-Sec.
  2825 Lexington Rd 40280 502-897-4011
Spalding University Post-Sec.
  851 S 4th St 40203 502-585-9911
Spencerian College Post-Sec.
  4627 Dixie Hwy 40216 502-447-1000
Sullivan University Post-Sec.
  3101 Bardstown Rd 40205 800-844-1354
The Hair Design School Post-Sec.
  151 Chenoweth Ln 40207 502-897-9401
Trend Setter's Academy of Beauty Culture Post-Sec.
  7283 Dixie Hwy 40258 502-937-6816
Trinity HS 1,400/9-12
  4011 Shelbyville Rd 40207 502-895-9427
  Daniel Zoeller, prin. Fax 895-6837
University of Louisville Post-Sec.
  2301 S 3rd St 40208 502-852-5555
Ursuline S for Performing Arts 500/K-12
  3105 Lexington Rd 40206 502-897-1816
  Anna Jo Paul, dir.
Valor Traditional Academy 100/K-12
  11501 Schlatter Rd 40291 502-239-3345
  Diane Seel, prin. Fax 239-3344
Walden S 300/K-12
  4238 Westport Rd 40207 502-893-0433
  Linda VanHouten, prin. Fax 895-8668
Whitefield Academy 700/PK-12
  7711 Fegenbush Ln 40228 502-239-2509
  Robert Hensley, hdmstr. Fax 239-3144

Ludlow, Kenton, Pop. 4,283

Ludlow ISD 1,000/K-12
  525 Elm St 41016 859-261-8210
  Elizabeth Grause, supt. Fax 291-6811
  www.ludlow.k12.ky.us
Ludlow HS 300/9-12
  515 Elm St 41016 859-261-8211
  Michael Borchers, prin. Fax 655-7536
Ludlow MS 300/6-8
  150 Adela Ave 41016 859-655-7500
  David Rust, prin. Fax 655-7536

Mc Kee, Jackson, Pop. 969

Jackson County SD 2,300/PK-12
  PO Box 217 40447 606-287-7181
  Ralph Hoskins, supt. Fax 287-8469
  www.jackson.k12.ky.us
Jackson County HS 600/9-12
  PO Box 427 40447 606-287-7155
  Steve Caroll, prin. Fax 287-7123
Jackson County MS 600/6-8
  PO Box 1329 40447 606-287-8351
  Keith Bingham, prin. Fax 287-8360

Kentucky Tech System
  Supt. — None
Jackson Area Technology Center Vo/Tech
  PO Box 1509 40447 606-287-2163
  Alonzo Moore, prin. Fax 287-7538

Madisonville, Hopkins, Pop. 19,321

Hopkins County SD 7,000/PK-12
  320 S Seminary St 42431 270-825-6000
  James Stevens, supt. Fax 825-6062
  www.hopkins.k12.ky.us
Browning Springs MS 500/6-8
  357 W Arch St 42431 270-825-6006
  Darrell Wilson, prin. Fax 825-6009
Hopkins County Central HS 1,000/9-12
  6625 Hopkinsville Rd 42431 270-825-6133
  Susanne Wolford, prin. Fax 825-6135
Madison MS 500/6-8
  510 Brown Rd 42431 270-825-6160
  Steve Gilliam, prin. Fax 825-6016
Madisonville North Hopkins HS 1,100/9-12
  4515 Hanson Rd 42431 270-825-6017
  Chad Burgett, prin. Fax 825-6045
Other Schools – See Nortonville

Madisonville Community College Post-Sec.
  2000 College Dr 42431 270-821-2250

Manchester, Clay, Pop. 1,668

Clay County SD 3,800/PK-12
  128 Richmond Rd 40962 606-598-2168
  Douglas Adams, supt. Fax 598-7829
  www.clay.k12.ky.us
Clay County HS 1,100/9-12
  415 Clay County High Rd 40962 606-598-3737
  Michael White, prin. Fax 598-8976
Clay County MS 700/7-8
  239 Richmond Rd 40962 606-598-1810
  Wayne Napier, prin. Fax 598-1230

Kentucky Tech System
  Supt. — None
Clay County Area Technology Center Vo/Tech
  1097 N Highway 11 40962 606-598-2194
  Eugene Hensley, prin. Fax 598-4201

Southeast School of Cosmetology Post-Sec.
  PO Box 493 40962 606-598-7901

Marion, Crittenden, Pop. 3,087

Crittenden County SD 1,300/K-12
  601 W Elm St 42064 270-965-3525
  John Belt, supt. Fax 965-9064
  www.crittenden.k12.ky.us
Crittenden County HS 400/9-12
  519 1/2 W Gum St 42064 270-965-2248
  Karen Nasseri, prin. Fax 965-2797
Crittenden County MS 300/6-8
  519 W Gum St 42064 270-965-5221
  Vince Clark, prin. Fax 965-5082

Martin, Floyd, Pop. 636

Kentucky Tech System
  Supt. — None
Floyd County Area Technology Center Vo/Tech
  HC 79 Box 205 41649 606-285-3088
  Lenville Martin, prin. Fax 285-0274

Piarist S 100/9-12
  PO Box 870 41649 606-285-3950
  Rev. Thomas Carroll, prin. Fax 285-3950

Mayfield, Graves, Pop. 10,228

Graves County SD 4,500/K-12
  2290 State Route 121 N 42066 270-328-2656
  Brady Link, supt. Fax 328-1561
  www.graves.k12.ky.us
Graves County HS 1,300/9-12
  1107 W Housman St 42066 270-674-6242
  Ward Bushart, prin. Fax 247-8540
Graves County MS 700/7-8
  625 Jimtown Rd 42066 270-674-4890
  Rim Watson, prin. Fax 251-3693

Kentucky Tech System
  Supt. — None
Mayfield/Graves County Area Tech Center Vo/Tech
  710 Douthitt St 42066 270-247-4710
  Roger Pierce, prin. Fax 247-4721

Mayfield ISD   900/PK-12
709 S 8th St 42066   270-247-3868
Lonnie Burgett, supt.   Fax 247-3854
www.mayfield.k12.ky.us
Mayfield HS   400/9-12
700 Douthitt St 42066   270-247-4461
Anthony Hatchell, prin.   Fax 247-9624
Mayfield MS   400/6-8
112 W College St 42066   270-247-7521
Joey Henderson, prin.   Fax 247-8297

Mid-Continent University   Post-Sec.
99 E Powell Rd 42066   270-247-8521
Northside Baptist Christian S   100/PK-12
711 N 12th St 42066   270-247-0516
Jan Lewis, prin.   Fax 247-7125

Maysville, Mason, Pop. 8,941
Kentucky Tech System
Supt. — None
Mason County Area Technology Center   Vo/Tech
646 Kenton Station Rd 41056   606-759-7101
Judson Pate, prin.   Fax 759-7568

Mason County SD   2,700/PK-12
PO Box 130 41056   606-564-5563
Tim Moore, supt.   Fax 564-5392
www.mason.k12.ky.us/
Mason County HS   800/9-12
1320 US Highway 68 41056   606-564-3393
Steven Appelman, prin.   Fax 564-5360
Mason County MS   600/6-8
420 Chenault Dr 41056   606-564-6748
Betsy Cook, prin.   Fax 564-5958

Maysville Community & Technical College   Post-Sec.
1755 US Highway 68 41056   606-759-7141
St. Patrick S   300/1-12
318 Limestone St 41056   606-564-5949
    Fax 564-8795

Middlesboro, Bell, Pop. 10,858
Middlesboro ISD   1,800/K-12
PO Box 959 40965   606-242-8800
Darryl Wilder, supt.   Fax 248-8805
www.mboro.k12.ky.us
Middlesboro HS   600/9-12
4404 Cumberland Ave 40965   606-242-8820
Ed Jones, prin.   Fax 242-8825
Middlesboro MS   400/6-8
4400 Cumberland Ave 40965   606-242-8880
Steve Spangler, prin.   Fax 242-8885

Collins School of Cosmetology   Post-Sec.
111 W Chester Ave 40965   606-248-3602

Middletown, Jefferson, Pop. 6,005
Jefferson County SD
Supt. — See Louisville
Crosby MS   1,100/6-8
303 Gatehouse Ln 40243   502-485-8235
Kirk Lattimore, prin.   Fax 485-8424
Eastern HS   1,800/9-12
12400 Old Shelbyville Rd 40243   502-485-8243
James Sexton, prin.   Fax 485-3883

Midway, Woodford, Pop. 1,591

Midway College   Post-Sec.
512 E Stephens St 40347   800-755-0031

Millersburg, Bourbon, Pop. 833

Millersburg Military Academy   50/6-12
PO Box 278 40348   859-484-3352
Mark Sifford, prin.   Fax 484-3342

Monticello, Wayne, Pop. 6,053
Kentucky Tech System
Supt. — None
Wayne County Area Technology Center   Vo/Tech
150 Cardinal Way 42633   606-348-8424
Danny Guffey, prin.   Fax 348-5090

Monticello ISD   800/PK-12
132 College St 42633   606-348-5311
Donnie Robison, supt.   Fax 348-3664
www.monticello.k12.ky.us/
Monticello HS   200/9-12
135 Cave St 42633   606-348-5312
Johnny Chaplin, prin.   Fax 348-3039
Monticello MS   200/6-8
135 Cave St 42633   606-348-5312
Johnny Chaplin, prin.   Fax 348-3039
Wayne County SD   2,500/PK-12
534 Albany Rd 42633   606-348-8484
John Dalton, supt.   Fax 348-0734
www.wayne.k12.ky.us
Lloyd MS   400/7-8
314 Albany Rd 42633   606-348-6691
Robert Wixson, prin.   Fax 348-5495
Wayne County HS   700/9-12
2 Kenny Davis Blvd 42633   606-348-5575
Peggy Shearer, prin.   Fax 348-3458

Morehead, Rowan, Pop. 7,627
Rowan County SD   2,900/PK-12
121 E 2nd St 40351   606-784-8928
Marvin Moore, supt.   Fax 783-1011
www.rowan.k12.ky.us
Rowan County MS   800/6-8
415 W Sun St 40351   606-784-8911
Tresia Swain, prin.   Fax 784-5579

Rowan County SHS   900/9-12
499 Viking Dr 40351   606-784-8956
Mark Murray, prin.   Fax 784-1067

Lakeside Christian Academy   200/PK-12
2535 US Highway 60 W 40351   606-784-2751
Tammy McKinney, admin.   Fax 784-0056
Morehead State University   Post-Sec.
100 Admissions Center 40351   606-783-2000
Rowan Technical College   Post-Sec.
609 Viking Dr 40351   606-783-1538

Morganfield, Union, Pop. 3,481
Union County SD   2,300/PK-12
510 S Mart St 42437   270-389-1694
Dr. Gerald L. Novak, supt.   Fax 389-9806
www.union.k12.ky.us/
Clements Victory Technical HS   Vo/Tech
2302 US Highway 60 E 42437   270-389-2419
Claudia Stocking, prin.   Fax 389-9383
Union County HS   700/9-12
4464 US Highway 60 W 42437   270-389-1454
Matt Ciecorka, prin.   Fax 389-2715
Union County MS   500/6-8
4465 US Highway 60 W 42437   270-389-0224
Jon Farley, prin.   Fax 389-0245

Earle C. Clements Job Corps Center   Post-Sec.
2302 US Highway 60 E 42437   270-389-5310

Morgantown, Butler, Pop. 2,545
Butler County SD   1,800/PK-12
PO Box 339 42261   270-526-5624
Larry Woods, supt.   Fax 526-5625
www.butler.k12.ky.us/
Butler Co. Area Vocational/Technical S   Vo/Tech
799 Veterans Way 42261   270-526-2223
Eric Keeling, prin.
Butler County HS   600/9-12
PO Box 248 42261   270-526-2204
Mike Elmore, prin.   Fax 526-2268
Butler County MS   500/6-8
PO Box 10 42261   270-526-5647
Hazel Short, prin.   Fax 526-3238

Mount Olivet, Robertson, Pop. 294
Robertson County SD   400/K-12
PO Box 108 41064   606-724-5431
Charles Brown, supt.   Fax 724-5921
school.robertson.k12.ky.us
Deming JSHS   200/7-12
PO Box 168 41064   606-724-5421
Jeremy McCloud, prin.   Fax 724-5225

Mount Sterling, Montgomery, Pop. 6,033
Kentucky Tech System
Supt. — None
Montgomery County Area Technology Ctr   Vo/Tech
682 Woodford Dr 40353   859-498-1103
Michael Kindred, prin.   Fax 498-5960

Montgomery County SD   4,100/PK-12
700 Woodford Dr 40353   859-497-8760
Daniel Freeman, supt.   Fax 497-8780
www.montgomery.k12.ky.us
McNabb MS   1,000/6-8
3570 Indian Mound Dr 40353   859-497-8770
Dean Cvit Kovic, prin.   Fax 497-9683
Montgomery County HS   1,100/9-12
724 Woodford Dr 40353   859-497-8765
Shannon White, prin.   Fax 497-8705

Nu-Tek Academy of Beauty   Post-Sec.
153 Evans Dr 40353   859-498-4460

Mount Vernon, Rockcastle, Pop. 2,589
Kentucky Tech System
Supt. — None
Rockcastle County Area Technology Center   Vo/Tech
PO Box 275 40456   606-256-4346
Ralph Baker, prin.   Fax 256-4337

Rockcastle County SD   2,900/PK-12
245 Richmond St 40456   606-256-2125
Larry Hammond, supt.   Fax 256-2126
www.rockcastle.k12.ky.us
Rockcastle County HS   800/9-12
PO Box 1410 40456   606-256-4816
John Hale, prin.   Fax 256-3755
Rockcastle County MS   800/6-8
PO Box 1730 40456   606-256-5118
Jason S. Coguer, prin.   Fax 256-2622

Cumberland Technical College   Post-Sec.
PO Box 275 40456   606-256-4346

Mount Washington, Bullitt, Pop. 8,605
Bullitt County SD
Supt. — See Shepherdsville
Bullitt East HS   900/9-12
11450 Highway 44 E 40047   502-538-7322
David Marshall, prin.   Fax 538-8368
Eastside MS   6-8
6925 Highway 44 E 40047   502-538-3767
Bonita Franklin, prin.   Fax 538-0659
Mt. Washington MS   800/6-8
269 Water St 40047   502-538-4227
Denise Allen, prin.   Fax 955-9530

Munfordville, Hart, Pop. 1,581
Hart County SD   3,100/PK-12
511 W Union St 42765   270-524-2631
Rickey Line, supt.   Fax 524-2634
www.hart.k12.ky.us/

Hart County HS   700/9-12
1014 S Dixie Hwy 42765   270-524-9341
Chris Mueller, prin.   Fax 524-3251

Murray, Calloway, Pop. 15,311
Calloway County SD   3,000/PK-12
PO Box 800 42071   270-762-7300
Steve Hoskins, supt.   Fax 762-7310
www.calloway.k12.ky.us
Calloway County HS   900/9-12
2108 College Farm Rd 42071   270-762-7375
Yvette Pyle, prin.   Fax 762-7380
Calloway County MS   700/6-8
2112 College Farm Rd 42071   270-762-7355
Tawnya Hunter, prin.   Fax 762-7360
Kentucky Tech System
Supt. — None
Murray/Calloway County Area Tech Center   Vo/Tech
1800 Sycamore St 42071   270-753-1870
Dennis Harper, prin.   Fax 759-9656
Murray ISD   1,700/K-12
208 S 13th St 42071   270-753-4363
Bob Rogers, supt.   Fax 759-4906
www.murray.k12.ky.us/
Murray HS   500/9-12
501 Doran Rd 42071   270-753-5202
Teresa Speed, prin.   Fax 753-8391
Murray MS   700/4-8
801 Main St 42071   270-753-5125
Lou Carter, prin.   Fax 753-9039

Ezell's Cosmetology School   Post-Sec.
PO Box 1431 42071   270-753-4723
Murray State University   Post-Sec.
PO Box 9 42071   270-762-3011

New Castle, Henry, Pop. 919
Henry County SD   2,100/K-12
326 S Main St 40050   502-845-8600
Tim Abrams, supt.   Fax 845-8601
www.henry.k12.ky.us
Henry County HS   600/9-12
1120 Eminence Rd 40050   502-845-8670
Graham Wied, prin.   Fax 845-8671
Henry County MS   500/6-8
1124 Eminence Rd 40050   502-845-8660
Steve Swank, prin.   Fax 845-8661

Newport, Campbell, Pop. 16,243
Newport ISD   2,300/K-12
301 E 8th St 41071   859-292-3004
Michael Brandt, supt.   Fax 292-3073
www.newport.k12.ky.us
Newport HS   600/9-12
900 E 6th St 41071   859-292-3023
Scott Draud, prin.   Fax 292-8340
Newport MS   500/6-8
30 W 8th St 41071   859-292-3017
David Upchurch, prin.   Fax 292-3049

Brighton Center   Post-Sec.
601 Washington Ave 41071   859-491-8303
Daymar College - Northern Kentucky   Post-Sec.
76 Carothers Rd 41071   859-291-0800
Holy Trinity JHS   100/6-8
40 Chesapeake Ave 41071   859-292-0487
Sr. Mary Ruth Lubbers, prin.   Fax 292-0487
Newport Central Catholic HS   400/9-12
13 Carothers Rd 41071   859-292-0001
Robert Noll, prin.   Fax 292-0656
Northern Kentucky University 41099   Post-Sec.
    859-572-5100

Nicholasville, Jessamine, Pop. 22,251
Jessamine County SD   6,800/PK-12
871 Wilmore Rd 40356   859-885-4179
Lu Young, supt.   Fax 887-4811
www.jessamine.k12.ky.us
East Jessamine HS   900/9-12
815 Sulphur Well Pike 40356   859-885-7240
Janet Granada, prin.   Fax 881-0161
East Jessamine MS   900/6-8
851 Wilmore Rd 40356   859-885-5561
Bill Pickett, prin.   Fax 887-1797
West Jessamine HS   900/9-12
2101 Wilmore Rd 40356   859-887-2421
Al Crout, prin.   Fax 887-8854
West Jessamine MS   800/6-8
1400 Wilmore Rd 40356   859-885-2244
Terry Meckstroth, prin.   Fax 885-8078

Barrett & Company School of Hair Design   Post-Sec.
973 Kimberly Sq 40356   859-885-9136

Nortonville, Hopkins, Pop. 1,259
Hopkins County SD
Supt. — See Madisonville
South Hopkins MS   500/6-8
9140 Hopkinsville Rd 42442   270-825-6125
Stuart Fitch, prin.   Fax 825-6085

Olive Hill, Carter, Pop. 1,794
Carter County SD
Supt. — See Grayson
Carter County Career & Technical Center   Vo/Tech
15 Grahn Rd 41164   606-286-4022
Jack Lowe, prin.   Fax 286-6333
West Carter County HS   600/9-12
PO Box 1479 41164   606-286-2481
Rebecca Corsetti, prin.   Fax 286-8026
West Carter County MS   600/6-8
PO Box 1510 41164   606-286-5354
Sherry Horsley, prin.   Fax 286-8556

Oneida, Clay

Oneida Baptist Institute 300/K-12
PO Box 67 40972 606-847-4111
Dan Stockton, prin. Fax 847-4496

Owensboro, Daviess, Pop. 54,312

Daviess County SD 10,300/PK-12
PO Box 21510 42304 270-852-7000
Thomas Shelton, supt. Fax 852-7030
www.daviess.k12.ky.us/
Apollo HS 1,400/9-12
2280 Tamarack Rd 42301 270-852-7100
Tom Purcell, prin. Fax 852-7110
Burns MS 800/6-8
4610 Goetz Dr 42301 270-852-7400
Mark Owens, prin. Fax 852-7410
College View MS 800/6-8
5061 New Hartford Rd 42303 270-852-7500
Joe Mason, prin. Fax 852-7510
Daviess County HS 1,600/9-12
4255 New Hartford Rd 42303 270-852-7300
Matthew Constant, prin. Fax 852-7310
Daviess County MS 800/6-8
1415 E 4th St 42303 270-852-7600
Gates Settle, prin. Fax 852-7610

Kentucky Tech System
Supt. — None
Daviess County State Vo-Tech S Vo/Tech
1901 Southeastern Pkwy 42303 270-686-4400

Owensboro ISD 3,900/PK-12
PO Box 249 42302 270-686-1000
Dr. Larry D. Vick, supt. Fax 684-5756
www.owensboro.k12.ky.us
Owensboro HS 1,000/9-12
1800 Frederica St 42301 270-686-1110
Anita Burnette, prin. Fax 686-1019
Owensboro MS 600/7-8
1300 Booth Ave 42301 270-686-1130
Janice Eaves, prin. Fax 686-1173

Brescia University Post-Sec.
717 Frederica St 42301 270-685-3131
Daymar College Post-Sec.
3361 Buckland Sq 42301 270-926-4040
Kentucky Wesleyan College Post-Sec.
3000 Frederica St 42301 270-926-3111
Mr. Jim's Beauty College Post-Sec.
1240 Carter Rd 42301 270-684-3505
Owensboro Catholic HS 600/9-12
1524 W Parrish Ave 42301 270-684-3215
Harold Staples, prin. Fax 684-7050
Owensboro Catholic MS 300/7-8
2540 Christie Pl 42301 270-683-0480
James Duffy, prin. Fax 683-0495
Owensboro Community & Technical College Post-Sec.
1501 Frederica St 42301 270-687-7255
Owensboro Community & Technical College Post-Sec.
4800 New Hartford Rd 42303 270-686-4400
Owensboro Mercy Health System Post-Sec.
811 E Parrish Ave 42303 270-688-2100

Owenton, Owen, Pop. 1,453

Owen County SD 1,700/K-12
1600 Highway 22 E 40359 502-484-3934
Mark Cleveland, supt. Fax 484-9095
www.owen.k12.ky.us
Bowling MS 500/6-8
1960 Highway 22 E 40359 502-484-5701
Jo Ella Wallace, prin. Fax 484-3044
Owen County HS 600/9-12
2340 Highway 22 E 40359 502-484-5509
Tim Hitzfield, prin. Fax 484-0444

Owingsville, Bath, Pop. 1,515

Bath County SD 2,300/PK-12
405 W Main St 40360 606-674-6314
Nancy Hutchinson, supt. Fax 674-2647
www.bath.k12.ky.us
Bath County HS 500/9-12
645 Chenault Dr 40360 606-674-6325
Paul Prater, prin. Fax 674-9188
Bath County MS 500/6-8
432 W Main St 40360 606-674-8165
Lloyd Sartin, prin. Fax 674-2676

Paducah, McCracken, Pop. 25,565

Kentucky Tech System
Supt. — None
Paducah Area Technology Center Vo/Tech
2400 Adams St 42003 270-443-6592
Don Rowlett, prin. Fax 442-6233

McCracken County SD 6,700/PK-12
435 Berger Rd 42003 270-538-4000
M. Tim Heller, supt. Fax 538-4001
www.mccracken.k12.ky.us
Lone Oak HS 800/9-12
225 John E Robinson Dr 42001 270-538-4150
Donna Wear, prin. Fax 538-4151
Lone Oak MS 600/6-8
300 Cumberland Ave 42001 270-538-4130
Larry Hopper, prin. Fax 538-4131
Reidland HS 500/9-12
5349 Old Benton Rd 42003 270-538-4210
Glen Ringstaff, prin. Fax 538-4211
Reidland MS 500/6-8
5347 Benton Rd 42003 270-538-4190
Scott Pullen, prin. Fax 538-4191
Other Schools – See West Paducah

Paducah ISD 2,900/PK-12
PO Box 2550 42002 270-444-5600
R.J. Greene, supt. Fax 444-5607
www.paducah.k12.ky.us
Paducah MS 700/6-8
342 Lone Oak Rd 42001 270-444-5710
Tim Huddleston, prin. Fax 444-5709
Paducah Tilghman HS 800/9-12
2400 Washington St 42003 270-444-5650
Arthur Davis, prin. Fax 444-5659

Community Christian Academy 400/K-12
3230 Buckner Ln 42001 270-575-0025
Clara Downs, admin. Fax 443-2230
Paducah Technical College Post-Sec.
509 S 30th St 42001 800-995-4438
St. Mary HS 200/9-12
1243 Elmdale Rd 42003 270-442-1681
Rosann Whiting, prin. Fax 442-7920
St. Mary MS 200/6-8
1243 Elmdale Rd 42003 270-442-1681
Rosann Whiting, prin. Fax 442-7920
West Kentucky Comm. & Technical College Post-Sec.
PO Box 7380 42002 270-554-9200

Paintsville, Johnson, Pop. 4,031

Johnson County SD 3,600/PK-12
253 N Mayo Trl 41240 606-789-2530
Orville Hamilton, supt. Fax 789-2506
www.johnson.k12.ky.us
Johnson Central HS 1,000/9-12
257 N Mayo Trl 41240 606-789-2500
Steve Whitaker, prin. Fax 789-2547
Johnson County MS 600/7-8
251 N Mayo Trl 41240 606-789-4133
Tim Adams, prin. Fax 789-4135

Paintsville ISD 700/K-12
305 2nd St 41240 606-789-2654
Coy Samons, supt. Fax 789-7412
www.paintsville.k12.ky.us
Paintsville MSHS, 225 2nd St 41240 400/7-12
David Bolen, prin. 606-789-2656

Mayo Technical College Post-Sec.
513 3rd St 41240 606-789-5321

Paris, Bourbon, Pop. 9,271

Bourbon County SD 2,700/PK-12
3343 Lexington Rd 40361 859-987-2180
Lana Fryman, supt. Fax 987-2182
www.bourbon.k12.ky.us/boco/
Bourbon County HS 800/9-12
3343 Lexington Rd 40361 859-987-2185
Travis Huber, prin. Fax 987-5850
Bourbon County MS 600/6-8
3343 Lexington Rd 40361 859-987-2185
Larry Tapp, prin. Fax 987-5854

Paris ISD 700/K-12
310 W 7th St 40361 859-987-2160
Janice Cox Blackburn, supt. Fax 987-6749
www.paris.k12.ky.us
Paris HS 200/9-12
308 W 7th St 40361 859-987-2168
Vicki Grigson, prin. Fax 987-2132
Paris MS 200/5-8
304 W 7th St 40361 859-987-2163
Travis Earlywine, prin. Fax 987-2164

Park Hills, Kenton, Pop. 2,880

Gateway Community & Technical College Post-Sec.
1025 Amsterdam Rd 41011 859-292-3930
Maysville Community College Post-Sec.
1401 Dixie Hwy 41011

Phelps, Pike, Pop. 1,298

Pike County SD
Supt. — See Pikeville
Phelps JSHS 400/7-12
PO Box 925 41553 606-456-3482
Andy Dotson, prin. Fax 456-8988

Pikeville, Pike, Pop. 6,286

Kentucky Tech System
Supt. — None
Millard Area Technology Center Vo/Tech
7925 Millard Hwy 41501 606-437-6059
Jim Bob Hamilton, prin. Fax 437-0502

Pike County SD 9,400/PK-12
PO Box 3097 41502 606-433-9000
Frank Welch, supt. Fax 432-3321
www.pike.k12.ky.us
Millard MS 500/4-8
8015 Millard Hwy 41501 606-432-3380
Tommy Thornsbury, prin. Fax 433-9677
Pike County Central HS 700/9-12
100 Winners Circle Dr 41501 606-432-4352
Eddie McCoy, prin. Fax 432-7733
Shelby Valley HS 600/9-12
125 Douglas Park 41501 606-639-0033
Forrest Dale Johnson, prin. Fax 639-2074
Other Schools – See Belfry, Lick Creek, Phelps, Virgie

Pikeville ISD 1,200/K-12
401 N Mayo Trl 41501 606-432-8161
Jerry Green, supt. Fax 432-2119
www.pikeville.k12.ky.us/
Pikeville JSHS 600/7-12
120 Championship Dr 41501 606-432-0185
Jon Stratton, prin. Fax 432-2022

East Kentucky Beauty College Post-Sec.
5333 N Mayo Trl 41501 606-432-3627
Methodist Hospital of Kentucky Post-Sec.
911 S Mayo Rd 41501 606-437-3500
National College of Business & Tech. Post-Sec.
288 S Mayo Trl # 2 41501 606-432-5477
Pikeville College Post-Sec.
147 Sycamore St 41501 606-218-5250

Pine Knot, McCreary, Pop. 1,549

McCreary County SD
Supt. — See Stearns
Pine Knot Career Institute Vo/Tech
PO Box 1990 42635 606-354-2176
Nathan Nevels, coord. Fax 354-2170

Pineville, Bell, Pop. 2,060

Bell County SD 3,100/PK-12
PO Box 340 40977 606-337-7051
George Thompson, supt. Fax 337-1412
www.bellcountyschools.bell.k12.ky.us
Bell County HS 900/9-12
RR 1 Box 88 40977 606-337-7061
Jeff Saylor, prin. Fax 337-0867

Kentucky Tech System
Supt. — None
Bell County Area Technology Center Vo/Tech
RR 7 Box 199A 40977 606-337-3094
Barney Judd, prin. Fax 337-9053
Pineville ISD 600/PK-12
401 W Virginia Ave 40977 606-337-5701
Michael White, supt. Fax 337-9983
www.pineville.k12.ky.us
Pineville JSHS 300/7-12
401 W Virginia Ave 40977 606-337-2361
Paula Goodin, prin. Fax 337-3720

Clear Creek Baptist Bible College Post-Sec.
300 Clear Creek Rd 40977 606-337-3196

Pippa Passes, Knott, Pop. 294

Alice Lloyd College Post-Sec.
100 Purpose Rd 41844 606-368-2101
Buchanan S 200/K-12
100 Purpose Rd 41844 606-368-6108
Yvon Allen, prin. Fax 368-6216

Powderly, Muhlenberg, Pop. 851

Muhlenberg County SD 4,600/K-12
510 W Main St 42367 270-338-2871
Dale Todd, supt. Fax 338-0529
www.mberg.k12.ky.us
Other Schools – See Greenville

Prestonsburg, Floyd, Pop. 3,677

Floyd County SD 6,700/K-12
106 N Front Ave 41653 606-886-2354
Dr. Paul W. Fanning, supt. Fax 886-8862
www.floyd.kyschools.us
Adams MS 400/6-8
2520 S Lake Dr 41653 606-886-2671
Jack Goodman, prin. Fax 886-7026
Prestonsburg HS 600/9-12
825 Blackcat Blvd 41653 606-886-2252
Ted George, prin. Fax 886-1745
Other Schools – See Betsy Layne, Eastern, Hi Hat

Carl D. Perkins Job Corps Center Post-Sec.
478 Meadows Br 41653 606-886-1037
Prestonsburg Community College Post-Sec.
110 Bert T Combs Dr 41653 606-886-3863

Princeton, Caldwell, Pop. 6,394

Caldwell County SD 1,800/PK-12
PO Box 229 42445 270-365-8000
Carrell Boyd, supt. Fax 365-5742
www.caldwell.k12.ky.us/
Caldwell County HS 600/9-12
350 Beckner Ln 42445 270-365-8010
James Schmidt, prin. Fax 365-9742
Caldwell County MS 500/6-8
440 Beckner Ln 42445 270-365-8020
Will Brown, prin. Fax 365-9573

Kentucky Tech System
Supt. — None
Caldwell County Area Technology Center Vo/Tech
130 Vocational School Rd 42445 270-365-5563
Arthur Dunn, prin. Fax 365-5609

Providence, Webster, Pop. 3,544

Providence ISD 400/K-12
302 W Main St 42450 270-667-7007
Edwina Sheffield, supt. Fax 667-7606
www.providence.k12.ky.us
Providence HS 100/9-12
301 Cedar St 42450 270-667-7065
James Robinson, prin. Fax 667-7952

Raceland, Greenup, Pop. 2,388

Raceland-Worthington ISD 900/K-12
600 Rams Blvd 41169 606-836-2144
John Stephens, supt. Fax 833-5807
www.raceland.k12.ky.us
Raceland-Worthington HS 400/7-12
500 Rams Blvd 41169 606-836-8221
Marilyn Lamblin, prin. Fax 494-2341

Radcliff, Hardin, Pop. 21,894

Hardin County SD
Supt. — See Elizabethtown

North Hardin HS | 1,400/9-12
801 S Logsdon Pkwy 40160 | 270-351-3167
Bill Dennison, prin. | Fax 352-4512
Radcliff MS | 500/6-8
1145 S Dixie Blvd 40160 | 270-351-1171
Alvin Garrison, prin. | Fax 352-5193

Hair Design School | Post-Sec.
640 Knox Blvd 40160 | 270-351-4473
North Hardin Christian S | 300/PK-12
1298 Rogersville Rd 40160 | 270-351-7700
A. Paige Hardin, prin. | Fax 351-7757

Richmond, Madison, Pop. 29,080
Kentucky Tech System
Supt. — None
Madison County Area Technology Center | Vo/Tech
PO Box 809 40476 | 859-624-4520
Douglas West, prin. | Fax 624-9659

Madison County SD | 9,800/PK-12
PO Box 768 40476 | 859-624-4500
Billy Michael Caudill, supt. | Fax 624-4508
www.madison.k12.ky.us/
Madison Central HS | 1,400/9-12
705 N 2nd St 40475 | 859-624-4505
Gina Lakes, prin. | Fax 623-3925
Madison MS | 700/6-8
101 Summit St 40475 | 859-624-4550
Brad Winkler, prin. | Fax 624-4543
Model Laboratory HS | 200/9-12
521 Lancaster Ave 40475 | 859-622-3766
James Dantic, prin. | Fax 622-6658
Model Laboratory MS | 500/6-8
521 Lancaster Ave 40475 | 859-622-3766
James Dantic, prin. | Fax 622-6658
Moores MS | 700/6-8
1143 Berea Rd 40475 | 859-624-4545
Franklin Thomas, prin. | Fax 624-4534
Other Schools – See Berea

Eastern Kentucky University | Post-Sec.
521 Lancaster Ave 40475 | 859-622-1000
National College of Business & Tech. | Post-Sec.
139 S Killarney Ln 40475 | 859-623-8956

Rush, Boyd
Boyd County SD
Supt. — See Ashland
Ramey-Estep HS | 100/7-12
2901 Pigeon Roost Rd 41168 | 606-928-5801
Elizabeth Brewster, prin. | Fax 928-5574

Russell, Greenup, Pop. 3,574
Kentucky Tech System
Supt. — None
Russell Area Technology Center | Vo/Tech
705 Red Devil Ln 41169 | 606-836-1256
Keith Parsons, prin. | Fax 836-3784

Russell ISD | 2,100/PK-12
409 Belfonte St 41169 | 606-836-9679
Dr. Susan E. Compton, supt. | Fax 836-2865
www.russell-ind.k12.ky.us
Russell HS | 700/9-12
709 Red Devil Ln 41169 | 606-836-9658
Sean Howard, prin. | Fax 836-9650
Russell MS | 500/6-8
707 Red Devil Ln 41169 | 606-836-8135
Mary Robinson, prin. | Fax 836-0614

Russell Springs, Russell, Pop. 2,464
Kentucky Tech System
Supt. — None
Lake Cumberland Area Technology Center | Vo/Tech
PO Box 599 42642 | 270-866-6175
Chester Taylor, prin. | Fax 866-2424

Russell County SD
Supt. — See Jamestown
Russell County HS | 800/9-12
2166 S Highway 127 42642 | 270-866-3341
Darren Gossage, prin. | Fax 866-8830
Russell County MS | 500/7-8
2258 S Highway 127 42642 | 270-866-2224
Kenneth Pickett, prin. | Fax 866-8679

Russellville, Logan, Pop. 7,202
Kentucky Tech System
Supt. — None
Russellville Area Technology Center | Vo/Tech
1103 W 9th St 42276 | 270-726-8432
Don Evans, prin. | Fax 726-6303

Logan County SD | 3,300/PK-12
PO Box 417 42276 | 270-726-2436
Marshall Kemp, supt. | Fax 726-8892
www.logan.k12.ky.us
Logan County HS | 900/9-12
2200 Bowling Green Rd 42276 | 270-726-8454
Bob Nylin, prin. | Fax 726-1108

Russellville ISD | 1,200/PK-12
355 S Summer St 42276 | 270-726-8405
Ray Hammers, supt. | Fax 726-4036
www.rville.k12.ky.us/district/
Russellville HS | 400/9-12
1101 W 9th St 42276 | 270-726-8421
Jennifer Kelley, prin. | Fax 726-3685
Russellville MS | 400/5-8
210 E 7th St 42276 | 270-726-8428
Dee Guffy, prin. | Fax 726-8888

Saint Catharine, Washington

St. Catharine College | Post-Sec.
2375 Bardstown Rd 40061 | 800-599-2000

Salyersville, Magoffin, Pop. 1,587
Magoffin County SD | 2,200/K-12
PO Box 109 41465 | 606-349-6117
Donald F. Cecil, supt. | Fax 349-3417
www.magoffin.k12.ky.us/
Magoffin County HS | 700/9-12
201 Hornet Dr 41465 | 606-349-2011
Tony Skaggs, prin. | Fax 349-5345
Whitaker MS | 400/7-8
221 Hornet Dr 41465 | 606-349-5190
Johnnie Johnson, prin. | Fax 349-5139

Sandy Hook, Elliott, Pop. 690
Elliott County SD | 1,200/K-12
PO Box 767 41171 | 606-738-8002
John Williams, supt. | Fax 738-8050
www.elliott.k12.ky.us/
Elliott County JSHS | 500/7-12
PO Box 687 41171 | 606-738-8052
Larry Salyer, prin. | Fax 738-8000

Infinite Possibilities Christian Academy | 50/7-12
PO Box 86 41171 | 606-738-6417
Dr. Virginia Cornett, admin. | Fax 738-4310

Scottsville, Allen, Pop. 4,413
Allen County SD | 3,000/PK-12
238 Bowling Green Rd 42164 | 270-237-3181
Larry Williams, supt. | Fax 237-3898
www.allen.k12.ky.us
Allen County Scottsville HS | 900/9-12
1545 Bowling Green Rd 42164 | 270-622-4119
Greg Dunn, prin. | Fax 622-5882
Allen County Technical Center | Vo/Tech
1501 Bowling Green Rd 42164 | 270-622-4711
William Cooper, prin. | Fax 622-7006
Bazzell MS | 700/6-8
201 New Gallatin Rd 42164 | 270-622-7140
Rick Fisher, prin. | Fax 622-4649

Shelbyville, Shelby, Pop. 10,390
Kentucky Tech System
Supt. — None
Shelby County Area Technology Center | Vo/Tech
230 Rocket Ln 40065 | 502-633-6554
Deborah Anderson, prin. | Fax 633-4212

Shelby County SD | 5,500/PK-12
PO Box 159 40066 | 502-633-2375
Elaine Farris, supt. | Fax 633-1988
www.shelby.kyschools.us
Shelby County East MS | 600/6-8
600 Rocket Ln 40065 | 502-633-1478
Anthony Sieg, prin. | Fax 633-6981
Shelby County HS | 1,500/9-12
PO Box 69 40066 | 502-633-2344
Gary Kidwell, prin. | Fax 647-0238
Shelby County West MS | 700/6-8
100 Warrior Way 40065 | 502-633-4869
Kymberly Rice, prin. | Fax 647-4525

Cornerstone Christian Academy | 200/K-12
3850 Frankfort Rd 40065 | 502-633-4070
Matt Maxwell, prin. | Fax 633-4605

Shepherdsville, Bullitt, Pop. 8,600
Bullitt County SD | 11,100/PK-12
1040 Highway 44 E 40165 | 502-543-2271
Michael Eberbaugh, supt. | Fax 543-3608
www.bullitt.k12.ky.us/
Bernheim MS | 500/6-8
700 Audubon Dr 40165 | 502-543-7614
Julie Buckner, prin. | Fax 543-8295
Bullitt Central HS | 1,200/9-12
1330 Highway 44 E 40165 | 502-543-7021
Karen Hayden, prin. | Fax 543-1797
Bullitt Lick MS | 700/6-8
555 W Blue Lick Rd 40165 | 502-543-6806
Scott Hrebicik, prin. | Fax 543-1685
Hebron MS | 800/6-8
3300 E Hebron Ln 40165 | 502-957-3540
Charles Higdon, prin. | Fax 957-6014
North Bullitt HS | 900/9-12
3200 E Hebron Ln 40165 | 502-957-2186
Greg Schultz, prin. | Fax 957-6762
Zoneton MS | 6-8
PO Box 1229 40165 | 502-955-7067
Harley Wise, prin. | Fax 955-7027
Other Schools – See Mount Washington

Kentucky Tech System
Supt. — None
Bullitt County Area Technology Center | Vo/Tech
395 High School Dr 40165 | 502-543-7018
Linda Sosnin, prin. | Fax 543-1691

Silver Grove, Campbell, Pop. 1,181
Silver Grove ISD | 300/PK-12
PO Box 400 41085 | 859-441-3894
Danny Montgomery, supt. | Fax 441-4299
www.s-g.k12.ky.us
Silver Grove S | 300/PK-12
PO Box 400 41085 | 859-441-3873
Patrick Tucker, prin. | Fax 441-4299

Smithland, Livingston, Pop. 392
Livingston County SD | 900/PK-12
PO Box 219 42081 | 270-928-2111
Jack Monroe, supt. | Fax 928-2112
www.livingston.k12.ky.us/

Livingston Central HS | 400/9-12
PO Box 369 42081 | 270-928-2065
Michael Riley, prin. | Fax 928-2066
Other Schools – See Burna

Somerset, Pulaski, Pop. 11,786
Pulaski County SD | 7,200/K-12
PO Box 1055 42502 | 606-679-1123
Tim Eaton, supt. | Fax 679-1438
www.pulaski.net
Northern MS | 800/6-8
650 Oak Leaf Ln 42503 | 606-678-5230
Angela Murphy, prin. | Fax 678-2729
Pulaski County HS | 1,000/9-12
511 E University Dr 42503 | 606-679-1574
Robert Bowers, prin. | Fax 677-2771
Southern MS | 1,000/6-8
200 Enterprise Dr 42501 | 606-679-6855
Troy Dotson, prin. | Fax 679-2270
Southwestern HS | 1,100/9-12
1765 WTLO Rd 42503 | 606-678-9000
Boyd Randolph, prin. | Fax 678-9277

Somerset ISD | 1,500/PK-12
305 College St 42501 | 606-679-4451
Wilson Leonard Sears, supt. | Fax 678-0864
www.somerset.k12.ky.us
Meece MS | 500/5-8
210 Barnett St 42501 | 606-678-5821
Cloyd Bumgardner, prin. | Fax 678-2934
Somerset HS | 500/9-12
301 College St 42501 | 606-678-4721
Jeff Perkins, prin. | Fax 677-0087

Somerset Christian S | 200/K-12
PO Box 3330 42564 | 606-451-1600
Guy Crubaugh, prin. | Fax 677-9850
Somerset Community College | Post-Sec.
808 Monticello St 42501 | 606-679-8501

S Portsmouth, Greenup

Harvest Christian Academy | 100/K-12
PO Box 398 41174 | 606-932-3007
John Bower, prin. | Fax 932-2240

South Shore, Greenup, Pop. 1,225
Greenup County SD
Supt. — See Greenup
McKell MS | 400/6-8
129 Bulldog Ln 41175 | 606-932-3221
Donald Harrison, prin. | Fax 932-9844

Springfield, Washington, Pop. 2,739
Washington County SD | 1,800/PK-12
120 Mackville Hl 40069 | 859-336-5470
Larry Graves, supt. | Fax 336-5480
www.washington.k12.ky.us
Washington County HS | 600/9-12
601 Lincoln Park Rd 40069 | 859-336-5475
Eugene Smith, prin. | Fax 336-5983
Washington County MS | 200/6-8
603 Lincoln Park Rd 40069 | 859-336-5475
Stacy Hall, prin.

Stanford, Lincoln, Pop. 3,423
Kentucky Tech System
Supt. — None
Lincoln County Area Technology Center | Vo/Tech
422 Education Way 40484 | 606-365-8500
Richard Kazsuk, prin. | Fax 365-8504

Lincoln County SD | 3,700/PK-12
PO Box 265 40484 | 606-365-2124
Dr. Teresa Wallace, supt. | Fax 365-1660
www.lincoln.k12.ky.us
Fort Logan HS | 100/9-12
305 Danville Ave 40484 | 606-365-1333
Scott Montgomery, prin. | Fax 365-4020
Lincoln County HS | 1,100/9-12
60 Education Way 40484 | 606-365-9111
Ty Howard, prin. | Fax 365-1750
Lincoln County MS | 700/7-8
285 Education Way 40484 | 606-365-8400
Pam Hart, prin. | Fax 365-8600

Stanton, Powell, Pop. 3,026
Powell County SD | 2,500/PK-12
PO Box 430 40380 | 606-663-3300
Lonnie Morris, supt. | Fax 663-3303
www.powell.k12.ky.us/
Powell County HS | 700/9-12
700 W College Ave 40380 | 606-663-3320
Lance Smith, prin. | Fax 663-3406
Powell County MS | 600/6-8
PO Box 400 40380 | 606-663-3308
Karen Rose, prin. | Fax 663-3307

Stearns, McCreary, Pop. 1,550
McCreary County SD | 2,500/PK-12
120 Raider Way 42647 | 606-376-2591
Ray Ball, supt. | Fax 376-5584
www.mccreary.k12.ky.us
McCreary Central HS | 900/9-12
400 Raider Way 42647 | 606-376-5051
David Cothron, prin. | Fax 376-3005
McCreary County MS | 300/7-8
180 Raider Way 42647 | 606-376-5081
Aaron Anderson, prin. | Fax 376-9580
Other Schools – See Pine Knot

Taylor Mill, Kenton, Pop. 6,866
Kenton County SD
Supt. — See Fort Wright

Woodland MS 800/6-8
5399 Old Taylor Mill Rd   41015 859-356-7300
Charles Ladwig, prin. Fax 356-7595

Taylorsville, Spencer, Pop. 1,107
Spencer County SD 2,300/PK-12
207 W Main St   40071 502-477-3250
R. Larry Holt, supt. Fax 477-3259
www.spencer.k12.ky.us
Spencer County HS 600/9-12
520 Taylorsville Rd   40071 502-477-3255
Robert DeHoag, prin. Fax 477-3212
Spencer County MS 500/6-8
PO Box 250   40071 502-477-3260
Dena Kent, prin. Fax 477-6796

Tompkinsville, Monroe, Pop. 2,654
Kentucky Tech System
Supt. — None
Monroe County Area Technology Center Vo/Tech
PO Box 338   42167 270-487-8261
Larry Carter, prin. Fax 487-0094

Monroe County SD 2,000/PK-12
PO Box 10   42167 270-487-5456
George Wilson, supt. Fax 487-5571
www.monroe.k12.ky.us
Monroe County HS 600/9-12
755 Old Mulkey Rd   42167 270-487-6217
Phillip Bartley, prin. Fax 487-8274
Monroe County MS 500/6-8
600 S Main St   42167 270-487-9624
Kevin Cloyd, prin. Fax 487-9534

Union, Boone, Pop. 3,135
Boone County SD
Supt. — See Florence
Gray MS 1,000/6-8
10400 US Highway 42   41091 859-384-5333
Tom Hummel, prin. Fax 384-5318
Ryle HS 1,300/9-12
10379 US Highway 42   41091 859-384-5300
Randall Cooper, prin. Fax 384-5312

Valley Station, Jefferson, Pop. 22,840
Jefferson County SD
Supt. — See Louisville
Frost MS 400/6-8
13700 Sandray Blvd   40272 502-485-8256
Dwight Hoskins, prin. Fax 485-8453
Stuart MS 1,300/6-8
4601 Valley Station Rd   40272 502-485-8334
Jennifer Colley, prin. Fax 485-8713
Valley Traditional HS 900/9-12
10200 Dixie Hwy   40272 502-485-8339
Greg Sheeley, prin. Fax 485-8666

Vanceburg, Lewis, Pop. 1,680
Lewis County SD 2,400/K-12
PO Box 159   41179 606-796-2811
Maurice Reeder, supt. Fax 796-3081
www.lewis.k12.ky.us
Lewis County HS 700/9-12
PO Box 99   41179 606-796-2823
Jamie Weddington, prin. Fax 796-3066
Lewis County MS 500/6-8
PO Box 69   41179 606-796-6228
Larry Riley, prin. Fax 796-6255
Meade Vocational Education Center Vo/Tech
PO Box 130   41179 606-796-6106
Stanley Allen, prin. Fax 796-9739

Vancleve, Breathitt

Kentucky Mountain Bible College Post-Sec.
PO Box 10   41385 800-879-5622
Mt. Carmel HS 100/8-12
PO Box 2   41385 606-666-5008
John Mills, prin. Fax 666-4612

Versailles, Woodford, Pop. 7,487
Woodford County SD 3,600/PK-12
330 Pisgah Rd   40383 859-873-4701
Paul Stahler, supt. Fax 873-1614
www.woodford.k12.ky.us
Woodford County HS 1,200/9-12
180 Frankfort St   40383 859-873-5434
Rob Akers, prin. Fax 873-7731
Woodford County MS 700/6-8
100 School House Rd   40383 859-873-4721
Stephanie Koontz, prin. Fax 873-4436

Villa Hills, Kenton, Pop. 7,919

Villa Madonna Academy 200/9-12
2500 Amsterdam Rd   41017 859-331-6333
Pamela McQueen, prin. Fax 331-8615

Vine Grove, Hardin, Pop. 4,066
Hardin County SD
Supt. — See Elizabethtown
Alton MS 700/6-8
100 Country Club Rd   40175 270-877-2135
Jama Bennett, prin. Fax 877-6297

Virgie, Pike
Pike County SD
Supt. — See Pikeville
Virgie MS 300/6-8
PO Box 310   41572 606-639-2774
Danny Osborne, prin. Fax 639-4086

Walton, Boone, Pop. 2,598
Walton-Verona SD 1,100/PK-12
16 School Rd   41094 859-485-4181
Bill Boyle, supt. Fax 485-1810
www.w-v.k12.ky.us
Walton-Verona JSHS 500/7-12
30 School Rd   41094 859-485-7721
Mark Krummen, prin. Fax 485-7739

Warfield, Martin, Pop. 279
Martin County SD
Supt. — See Inez
Warfield MS 200/6-8
PO Box 378   41267 606-395-5900
Robbie Fletcher, prin. Fax 395-5902

Warsaw, Gallatin, Pop. 1,808
Gallatin County SD 1,500/PK-12
PO Box 147   41095 859-567-2828
Dorothy B. Perkins, supt. Fax 567-4528
www.gallatin.k12.ky.us
Gallatin County HS 400/9-12
PO Box 146   41095 859-567-7901
Roxann Booth, prin. Fax 567-8222
Gallatin County MS 400/6-8
PO Box 149   41095 859-567-5791
Amy Sutler, prin. Fax 567-6107

West Liberty, Morgan, Pop. 3,344
Kentucky Tech System
Supt. — None
Morgan County Area Technology Center Vo/Tech
PO Box 249   41472 606-743-8452
Robert Martin, prin. Fax 743-8500

Morgan County SD 2,200/K-12
PO Box 489   41472 606-743-8002
Joe Dan Gold, supt. Fax 743-8050
www.morgancountyschools.com/
Morgan County HS 700/9-12
PO Box 606   41472 606-743-8052
Addison Whitt, prin. Fax 743-8100
Morgan County MS 500/6-8
PO Box 580   41472 606-743-8102
Darren Sparkman, prin. Fax 743-8150

West Paducah, McCracken
McCracken County SD
Supt. — See Paducah
Heath HS 600/9-12
4330 Metropolis Lake Rd   42086 270-538-4090
Russ Tilford, prin. Fax 538-4091
Heath MS 500/6-8
4336 Metropolis Lake Rd   42086 270-538-4070
Greg Webb, prin. Fax 538-4071

Whitesburg, Letcher, Pop. 1,542
Kentucky Tech System
Supt. — None
Letcher County Area Technology Center Vo/Tech
185 Circle Dr   41858 606-633-5053
Barbara Ison, prin. Fax 633-8084

Letcher County SD 3,000/PK-12
224 Parks St   41858 606-633-4455
Anna C. Craft, supt. Fax 633-4724
www.letcher.k12.ky.us/
Letcher County Central HS 600/9-12
38 College Dr   41858 606-633-2339
Stephen Boggs, prin. Fax 633-2447
Whitesburg MS 200/6-8
366 Parks St   41858 606-633-2761
Marcia Caudill, prin. Fax 633-4137

Jenny Lea Academy of Cosmetology Post-Sec.
74 Parkway Plaza Loop   41858 606-573-4276

Whitesville, Daviess, Pop. 599

Trinity HS 100/9-12
10510 Main Cross St   42378 270-233-5184
Bill Hagan, prin. Fax 233-9293

Williamsburg, Whitley, Pop. 5,033
Whitley County SD 4,500/PK-12
300 Main St   40769 606-549-7000
Lonnie Anderson, supt. Fax 549-7006
www.whitley.k12.ky.us/
Whitley County HS 1,200/9-12
350 Boulevard Of Champions   40769 606-549-7025
Scott Paul, prin. Fax 549-7035
Whitley County MS 700/7-8
351 Boulevard Of Champions   40769 606-549-7050
Rich Prewitt, prin. Fax 549-7055

Williamsburg ISD 800/PK-12
1000 Main St   40769 606-549-6044
Dennis Byrd, supt. Fax 549-6076
www.wburg.k12.ky.us
Williamsburg S 700/PK-12
1000 Main St   40769 606-549-6044
Joy Mack, prin. Fax 549-6076

University of the Cumberlands Post-Sec.
6178 College Station Dr   40769 606-549-2200

Williamstown, Grant, Pop. 3,362
Grant County SD 3,700/K-12
820 Arnie Risen Blvd   41097 859-824-3323
Donald W. Martin, supt. Fax 824-3508
www.grant.k12.ky.us/
Other Schools – See Dry Ridge

Williamstown ISD 800/PK-12
300 Helton St   41097 859-824-7144
Charles Wilson, supt. Fax 824-3237
www.wtown.k12.ky.us
Williamstown JSHS 400/6-12
300 Helton St   41097 859-824-4421
Brad Winkler, prin. Fax 824-4736

Wilmore, Jessamine, Pop. 5,818

Asbury College Post-Sec.
1 Macklem Dr   40390 859-858-3511
Asbury Theological Seminary Post-Sec.
204 N Lexington Ave   40390 800-227-2879

Winchester, Clark, Pop. 16,378
Clark County SD 5,200/K-12
1600 W Lexington Ave   40391 859-744-4545
Bob Lee, supt. Fax 745-3935
www.clark.k12.ky.us
Clark HS 1,500/9-12
620 Boone Ave   40391 859-744-6111
Gordon Parido, prin. Fax 745-2418
Clark MS 700/6-8
1 Educational Plz   40391 859-744-0427
Pamela Whitesides, prin. Fax 745-3907
Conkwright MS 500/6-8
360 Mount Sterling Rd   40391 859-744-8433
Becke Cleaver, prin. Fax 745-2027

Kentucky Tech System
Supt. — None
Clark County Area Technology Center Vo/Tech
PO Box 727   40392 859-744-1250
Joe Norman, prin. Fax 744-9979

Motif Beauty Academy Post-Sec.
23 W Lexington Ave   40391 859-745-5886
Winchester Christian Academy 100/6-12
PO Box 617   40392 859-745-6026
Pam McDaniels, prin. Fax 744-5830

Wurtland, Greenup, Pop. 1,043
Greenup County SD
Supt. — See Greenup
Wurtland MS 400/6-8
700 Center St   41144 606-836-1023
Tracy Claxon, prin. Fax 836-3939

LOUISIANA

LOUISIANA DEPARTMENT OF EDUCATION
PO Box 94064, Baton Rouge 70804-9064
Telephone 225-342-3602
Fax 225-342-7316
Website http://www.doe.state.la.us

Superintendent of Education   Cecil Picard

LOUISIANA BOARD OF EDUCATION
PO Box 94064, Baton Rouge 70804-9064

President   Linda Johnson

PUBLIC, PRIVATE AND CATHOLIC SECONDARY SCHOOLS

Abbeville, Vermilion, Pop. 11,698
Vermilion Parish SD — 8,600/PK-12
  PO Box 520 70511 — 337-893-3973
  Joseph D. Hebert, supt. — Fax 898-0939
  www.vrml.k12.la.us
Abbeville HS — 800/9-12
  1305 Wildcat Dr 70510 — 337-893-1874
  Ralph Thibobeaux, prin. — Fax 893-0935
Williams MS — 700/6-8
  1105 Prairie Ave 70510 — 337-893-3943
  Mikal Stall, prin. — Fax 893-5190
Other Schools – See Erath, Gueydan, Kaplan, Maurice

Harvest Time Christian Academy — 100/K-10
  103 Robert Wells Rd 70510 — 337-892-6722
  Brett Darby, prin. — Fax 898-3365
Louisiana Technical College - Gulf Area — Post-Sec.
  PO Box 878 70511 — 337-893-4984
Vermilion Catholic HS — 200/9-12
  425 Park Ave 70510 — 337-893-6636
  Gerard Richard, prin. — Fax 898-0394

Albany, Livingston, Pop. 956
Livingston Parish SD
  Supt. — See Livingston
Albany HS — 500/9-12
  PO Box 1090 70711 — 225-567-9319
  Bruce Chaffin, prin. — Fax 567-9162
Albany MS — 400/6-8
  PO Box 1210 70711 — 225-567-5231
  Melvin Wild, prin. — Fax 567-9177

Alexandria, Rapides, Pop. 45,649
Rapides Parish SD — 22,200/PK-12
  PO Box 1230 71309 — 318-487-0888
  Gary L. Jones, supt. — Fax 449-3167
  www.rapides.k12.la.us
Alexandria HS — 1,000/9-12
  800 Ola St 71303 — 318-448-8234
  Joe Moreau, prin. — Fax 487-9994
Alexandria MS — 600/6-8
  122 Maryland Ave 71301 — 318-445-5343
  M. Vercher, prin. — Fax 442-8650
Bolton HS — 700/9-12
  2101 Vance Ave 71301 — 318-448-3628
  William Higgins, prin. — Fax 448-4329
Brame MS — 800/6-8
  4800 Dawn St 71303 — 318-443-3688
  Walter Fall, prin. — Fax 442-3966
Peabody Magnet HS — 700/9-12
  2727 Jones Ave 71302 — 318-448-3457
  Lee Dotson, prin. — Fax 487-0771
Smith MS — 600/6-8
  3100 Jones Ave 71302 — 318-445-6241
  Linda Young, prin. — Fax 445-9255
Other Schools – See Ball, Deville, Glenmora, Hineston, Lecompte, Lena, Pineville, Tioga

Alexandria Academy of Beauty — Post-Sec.
  2305 Rapides Ave 71301 — 318-442-7715
Grace Christian S — 500/PK-12
  4900 Jackson Street Ext 71303 — 318-445-8735
  Kay Blackburn, prin. — Fax 443-1034
Holy Savior Menard HS — 400/7-12
  4603 Coliseum Blvd 71303 — 318-445-8233
  Ronald Roy, prin. — Fax 448-8170
Louisiana State University at Alexandria — Post-Sec.
  8100 Highway 71 S 71302 — 318-445-3672
Louisiana Technical College - Alexandria — Post-Sec.
  PO Box 5698 71307 — 318-487-5439
Rapides Regional Medical Center — Post-Sec.
  PO Box 30101 71301 — 318-473-3150

Amite, Tangipahoa, Pop. 4,390
Tangipahoa Parish SD — 17,600/PK-12
  59656 Puleston Rd 70422 — 985-748-2502
  Louis Joseph, supt. — Fax 748-8587
  www.tangischools.org
Amite HS — 500/9-12
  403 S Laurel St 70422 — 985-748-9301
  Lucille Morris, prin. — Fax 748-2814

West Side MS — 600/5-8
  401 W Oak St 70422 — 985-748-9073
  Jo Fairburn, prin. — Fax 748-9225
Other Schools – See Hammond, Independence, Kentwood, Loranger, Ponchatoula, Tickfaw

Oak Forest Academy — 400/PK-12
  600 Walnut St 70422 — 985-748-4222
  Sam Bella, prin. — Fax 748-4320

Anacoco, Vernon, Pop. 818
Vernon Parish SD
  Supt. — See Leesville
Anacoco JSHS — 400/7-12
  4740 Port Arthur Ave 71403 — 337-239-3039
  Norman Beason, prin. — Fax 239-0243

Angie, Washington, Pop. 236
Washington Parish SD
  Supt. — See Franklinton
Angie JHS — 200/6-8
  64433 Dixon St 70426 — 985-986-3105
  Randy Branch, prin. — Fax 986-5515

Arcadia, Bienville, Pop. 2,898
Bienville Parish SD — 2,500/PK-12
  PO Box 418 71001 — 318-263-9416
  William Britt, supt. — Fax 263-3100
  www.bienvilleschools.com
Arcadia JSHS — 200/7-12
  967 Daniel St 71001 — 318-263-2264
  William Wysinger, prin. — Fax 263-9703
Other Schools – See Bienville, Castor, Gibsland, Ringgold, Saline

Arnaudville, Saint Landry, Pop. 1,393
St. Landry Parish SD
  Supt. — See Opelousas
Beau Chene HS — 800/9-12
  7076 Highway 93 70512 — 337-662-5815
  Robert Lanclos, prin. — Fax 662-3688

Athens, Claiborne, Pop. 254
Claiborne Parish SD
  Supt. — See Homer
Athens S — 300/PK-12
  15520 Highway 9 71003 — 318-258-3241
  Craig Roberson, prin. — Fax 258-6160

Mount Olive Christian S — 100/PK-12
  15349 Highway 9 71003 — 318-258-5661

Atlanta, Winn, Pop. 146
Winn Parish SD
  Supt. — See Winnfield
Atlanta S — 300/PK-12
  118 School Rd 71404 — 318-628-4613
  Susan Horne, prin. — Fax 628-4247

Avondale, Jefferson, Pop. 5,813
Jefferson Parish SD
  Supt. — See Marrero
Ford MS — 600/6-8
  435 S Jamie Blvd 70094 — 504-436-2474
  Allen Hayes, prin. — Fax 436-0604

Baker, East Baton Rouge, Pop. 13,552
Baker City SD — 1,500/PK-12
  PO Box 680 70704 — 225-774-5795
  C. Lester Klotz, supt. — Fax 774-5797
  www.bakerschools.org
Baker HS — 600/9-12
  3200 Groom Rd 70714 — 225-775-1259
  Earl Langlois, prin. — Fax 775-4011
Baker MS — 500/6-8
  5903 Groom Rd 70714 — 225-775-9750
  Ernest Morris, prin. — Fax 775-9753

Bethany Christian S — 400/K-12
  13855 Plank Rd 70714 — 225-774-0133
  Carolyn DeSalvo, prin. — Fax 774-0163

Central Private S — 700/PK-12
  12801 Centerra Ct 70714 — 225-261-3341
  Kyle Achord, prin. — Fax 261-3490

Baldwin, Saint Mary, Pop. 2,682
St. Mary Parish SD
  Supt. — See Centerville
Boudreau MS — 400/6-8
  PO Box 120 70514 — 337-924-7990
  Steven Guillory, prin. — Fax 924-7999
West St. Mary HS — 500/9-12
  PO Box 120 70514 — 337-924-7990
  Steven Guillory, prin. — Fax 924-7999

Ball, Rapides, Pop. 3,682
Rapides Parish SD
  Supt. — See Alexandria
Tioga JHS — 500/7-8
  1150 Tioga Rd 71405 — 318-640-9412
  John Grimes, prin. — Fax 640-0126

Basile, Evangeline, Pop. 2,377
Evangeline Parish SD
  Supt. — See Ville Platte
Basile JSHS — 400/5-12
  PO Box 666 70515 — 337-432-5012
  Georgeanna Courville, prin. — Fax 432-6414

Bastrop, Morehouse, Pop. 12,763
Morehouse Parish SD — 5,200/PK-12
  PO Box 872 71221 — 318-281-5784
  Richard Hartley, supt. — Fax 283-3456
  www.mpsb.us/
Bastrop HS — 900/9-12
  402 Highland Ave 71220 — 318-281-0194
  Thomas Thrower, prin. — Fax 281-0457
Career Center — 100/9-9
  1607 Martin L King S 71220 — 318-281-1407
  Ralph Davenport, prin. — Fax 283-3460
Morehouse JHS — 500/7-8
  1001 W Madison Ave 71220 — 318-281-0776
  Howard Loche, prin. — Fax 283-1846
Other Schools – See Mer Rouge

Bastrop Beauty School #1 — Post-Sec.
  117 S Vine St 71220 — 318-281-8652
Louisiana Technical College - Bastrop — Post-Sec.
  PO Box 1120 71221 — 318-283-0836
Mt. Zion Christian Academy — 50/K-12
  14413 Old Bonita Rd 71220 — 318-281-7784
Prairie View Academy — 300/PK-12
  9942 Edwin St 71220 — 318-281-7044
  Edward Bain, prin. — Fax 281-4113

Baton Rouge, East Baton Rouge, Pop. 225,090
East Baton Rouge Parish SD — 44,500/PK-12
  PO Box 2950 70821 — 225-922-5400
  Charlotte D. Placide, supt. — Fax 922-5411
  www.ebrschools.org/
Baton Rouge HS — 1,200/9-12
  2825 Government St 70806 — 225-383-0520
  Nanette Greer, prin. — Fax 344-3066
Belaire HS — 900/9-12
  12121 Tams Dr 70815 — 225-272-1860
  Robert Webb, prin. — Fax 272-3782
Broadmoor HS — 1,000/9-12
  10100 Goodwood Blvd 70815 — 225-926-1420
  Daryl Glueck, prin. — Fax 928-5472
Broadmoor MS — 800/6-8
  1225 Sharp Rd 70815 — 225-272-0540
  Rebel Ellerbee, prin. — Fax 272-0195
Capitol HS — 600/9-12
  1000 N 23rd St 70802 — 225-383-0353
  Linda Lewis, prin. — Fax 387-1635
Capitol MS — 500/6-8
  5100 Greenwell Springs Rd 70806 — 225-231-9292
  Katie Blunschi, prin. — Fax 344-0424
Central HS — 1,100/9-12
  10200 E Brookside Dr 70818 — 225-261-3438
  Ronnie Devall, prin. — Fax 261-3501
Central MS — 800/6-8
  11526 Sullivan Rd 70818 — 225-261-2237
  Larry Causey, prin. — Fax 261-9973

Crestworth MS | 500/6-8
10650 Avenue F 70807 | 225-775-6845
Nancy McKay, prin. | Fax 775-0051
Glasgow MS | 600/6-8
1676 Glasgow Ave 70808 | 225-925-2942
Nellwyn Vordenbaumn-East, prin. | Fax 928-3565
Glen Oaks HS | 700/9-12
6650 Cedar Grove Dr 70812 | 225-356-4306
Wilbert August, prin. | Fax 359-6782
Glen Oaks MS | 600/6-8
5300 Monarch Ave 70811 | 225-357-3790
Thelemese Porter, prin. | Fax 357-1841
Istrouma Magnet HS | 700/9-12
3730 Winbourne Ave 70805 | 225-355-7701
Elisha Jackson, prin. | Fax 359-9807
Kenilworth MS | 600/6-8
7600 Boone Ave 70808 | 225-766-8111
Viola Jackson, prin. | Fax 767-9061
Lee HS | 700/9-12
1105 Lee Dr 70808 | 225-383-7744
David Phillips, prin. | Fax 346-8196
McKinley HS | 700/9-12
800 E Mckinley St 70802 | 225-344-7696
Armond Brown, prin. | Fax 387-5435
McKinley Magnet MS | 600/6-8
4200 Gus Young Ave 70802 | 225-388-0089
Joyce Green-Graham, prin. | Fax 387-1434
Park Forest MS | 800/6-8
3760 Aletha Dr 70814 | 225-275-6650
Adam Smith, prin. | Fax 275-3058
Prescott MS | 600/6-8
4055 Prescott Rd 70805 | 225-357-6481
Elida Bera, prin. | Fax 355-2672
Scotlandville Magnet HS | 900/9-12
9870 Scotland Ave 70807 | 225-775-3715
Mary McManus, prin. | Fax 775-1205
Sherwood MS | 800/6-8
1020 Marlbrook Dr 70815 | 225-272-3090
Phyllis Crawford, prin. | Fax 273-9459
Southeast MS | 800/6-8
15000 S Harrells Ferry Rd 70816 | 225-753-5930
Shelly Colvin, prin. | Fax 756-8601
Southern University Lab S | 500/PK-12
PO Box 9414 70813 | 225-771-3490
Sheila Lewis, dir. | Fax 771-2782
Tara HS | 1,100/9-12
9002 Whitehall Ave 70806 | 225-927-6100
Luanne Estess, prin. | Fax 928-0122
University Lab S | 900/K-12
Louisiana State Univ 70803 | 225-578-3221
Dr. Edward Greene, prin. | Fax 578-3326
Westdale MS | 700/6-8
5650 Claycut Rd 70806 | 225-924-1308
Sherry Brock, prin. | Fax 926-9929
Woodlawn HS | 1,100/9-12
15755 Jefferson Hwy 70817 | 225-753-1200
John McCann, prin. | Fax 751-9269
Other Schools – See Pride

Recovery SD, PO Box 94064 70804 | 17,100/PK-12
Leroy Helire, dir. | 877-453-2721
www.nolapublicschools.net/
Other Schools – See New Orleans

Baton Rouge Community College | Post-Sec.
5310 Florida Blvd 70806 | 225-216-8040
Baton Rouge General Medical Center | Post-Sec.
PO Box 2511 70821 | 225-387-7767
Baton Rouge School of Computers | Post-Sec.
10425 Plaza Americana Dr 70816 | 225-923-2525
Calvary Christian S | 200/PK-12
9611 Siegen Ln 70810 | 225-766-7008
Dr. Wendell Douglas, prin. | Fax 767-3271
Camelot College | Post-Sec.
2618 Wooddale Blvd # A 70805 | 225-928-3005
Catholic HS | 800/8-12
855 Hearthstone Dr 70806 | 225-383-0397
Br. Barry Landry, prin. | Fax 383-0381
Christian Life Academy | 700/PK-12
2037 Quail Dr 70808 | 225-769-6760
Larry Perdue, prin. | Fax 769-8068
Court Reporting Institute of Louisiana | Post-Sec.
12090 S Harrells Ferry Rd 70816 | 225-292-1950
Delta College of Arts & Technology | Post-Sec.
7380 Exchange Pl 70806 | 225-928-7770
Diesel Driving Academy | Post-Sec.
8067 Airline Hwy 70815 | 225-929-9990
D-Jay's School of Beauty Arts & Sciences | Post-Sec.
5131 Government St 70806 | 225-926-2530
Domestic Health Care Institute | Post-Sec.
4826 Jamestown Ave 70808 | 225-925-5312
Dunham S | 600/K-12
11111 Roy Emerson Dr 70810 | 225-767-7097
Episcopal S of Baton Rouge | 1,100/PK-12
3200 Woodland Ridge Blvd 70816 | 225-753-3180
Kay Betts, hdmstr. | Fax 756-0926
Family Christian Academy | 200/K-12
PO Box 262550 70826 | 225-768-3026
Dave Smith, admin. | Fax 768-3213
Gables Academy | 100/3-12
15333 Jefferson Hwy 70817 | 225-752-9231
Hosanna Christian Academy | 500/K-12
8850 Goodwood Blvd 70806 | 225-926-4885
David Hand, admin. | Fax 926-8458
ITI Technical College | Post-Sec.
13944 Airline Hwy 70817 | 225-752-4233
Jehovah-Jireh Christian Academy | 200/PK-12
1771 N Lobdell Ave 70806 | 225-932-2357
Jones Creek Adventist Academy | 100/K-12
4363 Jones Creek Rd 70817 | 225-751-8219
| Fax 751-3404
Lockworks Academie of Hairdressing | Post-Sec.
2834 S Sherwood Forest Blvd 70816 | 225-295-1435

Louisiana New School Academy | 100/PK-12
1900 North Blvd 70806 | 225-381-7238
Louisiana School/Visually Impaired | Post-Sec.
PO Box 4328 70821
Louisiana State School for the Deaf | Post-Sec.
PO Box 3074 70821
Louisiana State University & A & M Coll. | Post-Sec.
Louisiana State Univ 70803 | 225-388-3202
Louisiana Technical College-Baton Rouge | Post-Sec.
3250 N Acadian Thruway E 70805 | 225-359-9204
Medical Training College | Post-Sec.
10525 Plaza Americana Dr 70816 | 225-926-5820
MedVance Institute | Post-Sec.
9255 Interline Ave 70809 | 225-248-1015
Millerville Academy | 200/PK-12
1615 Millerville Rd 70816 | 225-272-0164
Virginia Phacker, prin. | Fax 272-0196
Our Lady of the Lake College | Post-Sec.
7434 Perkins Rd 70808 | 225-768-1700
Our Lady of the Lake Medical Center | Post-Sec.
5000 Hennessy Blvd 70808 | 225-769-7799
Parkview Baptist S | 1,700/K-12
PO Box 45212 70895 | 225-291-2500
Kenneth Payne, supt. | Fax 293-4135
Redemptorist HS | 700/7-12
4000 Saint Gerard Ave 70805 | 225-357-0936
John Fabre, prin. | Fax 357-4555
Remington College | Post-Sec.
10551 Coursey Blvd 70816 | 225-922-3990
Runnels S | 900/PK-12
17255 S Harrells Ferry Rd 70816 | 225-751-5712
Dr. L. K. Runnels, prin. | Fax 753-0276
St. Josephs Academy | 800/9-12
3015 Broussard St 70808 | 225-383-7207
Linda Harvison, prin. | Fax 344-5714
St. Michael the Archangel HS | 700/9-12
PO Box 86110 70879 | 225-753-9782
Joseph Wray, prin. | Fax 753-0605
Southern University A&M College | Post-Sec.
Southern University 70813 | 225-771-4500
Starkey Academy | 300/K-12
10510 Joor Rd 70818 | 225-261-1390
Rick Truax, prin. | Fax 261-9399

Bell City, Calcasieu
Calcasieu Parish SD
Supt. — See Lake Charles
Bell City S | 500/K-12
PO Box 100 70630 | 337-622-3210
Reinette Guillory, prin. | Fax 622-3595

Belle Chasse, Plaquemines, Pop. 8,512
Plaquemines Parish SD
Supt. — See Port Sulphur
Belle Chasse HS | 700/9-12
8346 Highway 23 70037 | 504-394-2810
Monica Wertz, prin. | Fax 393-1182
Belle Chasse MS | 700/5-8
13476 Highway 23 70037 | 504-656-2315
Joe Williamson, prin. | Fax 656-2401

Belle Rose, Assumption
Assumption Parish SD
Supt. — See Napoleonville
Belle Rose MS | 200/5-8
PO Box 229 70341 | 225-473-8917
Stacy Garrison, prin. | Fax 473-8429

Benton, Bossier, Pop. 2,922
Bossier Parish SD | 18,500/PK-12
PO Box 2000 71006 | 318-549-5000
Kenneth Kruithof, supt. | Fax 549-5044
www.bossierschools.org
Benton HS | 600/9-12
6136 Highway 3 71006 | 318-549-5240
Scott Smith, prin. | Fax 549-5252
Benton MS | 700/5-8
6140 Highway 3 71006 | 318-549-5310
Dwayne Slack, prin. | Fax 549-5323
Other Schools – See Bossier City, Elm Grove, Haughton, Plain Dealing, Shreveport

Bernice, Union, Pop. 1,777
Union Parish SD
Supt. — See Farmerville
Bernice S | 500/K-12
PO Box 570 71222 | 318-285-7606
Jackuline Hill, prin. | Fax 285-5006

Berwick, Saint Mary, Pop. 4,350
St. Mary Parish SD
Supt. — See Centerville
Berwick HS | 500/9-12
700 Pattie Dr 70342 | 985-384-8450
Buffy Fegenbush, prin. | Fax 384-8505
Berwick JHS | 400/6-8
3955 Highway 182 70342 | 985-384-5664
Thomas D. Bourgeois, prin. | Fax 384-5663

Bienville, Bienville, Pop. 255
Bienville Parish SD
Supt. — See Arcadia
Bienville S | 100/K-12
PO Box 212 71008 | 318-385-7591
Billy Rogers, prin. | Fax 385-7750

Bogalusa, Washington, Pop. 12,949
Bogalusa City SD | 2,600/PK-12
PO Box 310 70429 | 985-735-1392
Jerry O. Payne, supt. | Fax 732-7510
www.bogalusaschools.org/
Bogalusa HS | 800/9-12
PO Box 580 70429 | 985-735-8161
Bill Murray, prin. | Fax 735-9768
Bogalusa JHS | 600/6-8
1403 North Ave 70427 | 985-732-3706
| Fax 735-6430

Louisiana Technical College - Sullivan | Post-Sec.
1710 Sullivan Dr 70427 | 985-732-6640

Boothville, Plaquemines, Pop. 2,743
Plaquemines Parish SD
Supt. — See Port Sulphur
Boothville-Venice S | 500/PK-12
1 Oiler Dr 70038 | 985-534-7520
Laverne Maynor, prin. | Fax 534-7328

Bossier City, Bossier, Pop. 58,111
Bossier Parish SD
Supt. — See Benton
Airline HS | 1,400/9-12
2801 Airline Dr 71111 | 318-549-5080
Kim Gaspard, prin. | Fax 549-5093
Bossier HS | 700/9-12
777 Bearkat Dr 71111 | 318-549-6680
David Thrash, prin. | Fax 549-6693
Cope MS | 600/6-8
4814 Shed Rd 71111 | 318-549-5380
Judy Grooms, prin. | Fax 549-5393
Greenacres MS | 700/6-8
2220 Airline Dr 71111 | 318-549-6210
Kathy Bouck, prin. | Fax 549-6223
Parkway HS | 1,000/9-12
4301 Panther Dr 71112 | 318-549-6910
Joe Huffman, prin. | Fax 549-6922
Rusheon MS | 800/6-8
2401 Old Minden Rd 71112 | 318-549-6610
Giselle Bryant, prin. | Fax 549-6623
Adult Learning Center | Adult
415 Monroe St 71111 | 318-549-6839
Jerry Allen, prin. | Fax 549-6842

Bossier Parish Community College | Post-Sec.
6220 E Texas St 71111 | 318-678-6000
Pat Goins Benton Road Beauty School | Post-Sec.
1701 Old Minden Rd Ste 36 71111 | 318-746-7674

Bourg, Terrebonne
Terrebonne Parish SD
Supt. — See Houma
South Terrebone HS | 1,100/9-12
3879 Highway 24 70343 | 985-868-7850
Kenneth Delcambre, prin. | Fax 868-1691

Boutte, Saint Charles, Pop. 2,702
St. Charles Parish SD
Supt. — See Luling
Hahnville HS | 1,400/9-12
200 Tiger Dr 70039 | 985-758-7537
Barbara Fuselier, prin. | Fax 758-9876

Braithwaite, Plaquemines
Plaquemines Parish SD
Supt. — See Port Sulphur
Phoenix HS | 100/9-12
13073 Highway 15 70040 | 985-333-4573
John Barthelemy, prin. | Fax 333-4395

Breaux Bridge, Saint Martin, Pop. 7,505
St. Martin Parish SD
Supt. — See Saint Martinville
Breaux Bridge HS | 900/9-12
1015B Breaux Bridge Sr High 70517 | 337-332-3131
Ronnie Dore, prin. | Fax 332-4058
Breaux Bridge JHS | 300/7-8
100 Martin St 70517 | 337-332-2844
Marie Romagosa, prin. | Fax 332-4831

Broussard, Lafayette, Pop. 6,314
Lafayette Parish SD
Supt. — See Lafayette
Broussard MS | 600/5-8
1325 S Morgan Ave 70518 | 337-837-9031
Keisha Hawkins, prin. | Fax 837-1057

Episcopal S of Acadiana | 500/PK-12
1557 Smede Hwy 70518 | 337-365-1416
Lynn Blevins, hdmstr. | Fax 367-9841

Brusly, West Baton Rouge, Pop. 2,000
West Baton Rouge Parish SD
Supt. — See Port Allen
Brusly HS | 500/9-12
630 Frontage Rd 70719 | 225-749-2815
Walt Lemoine, prin. | Fax 749-8563
Brusly MS | 400/6-8
601 N Kirkland St 70719 | 225-749-3123
Elaine Strauss, prin. | Fax 749-8570

Bunkie, Avoyelles, Pop. 4,535
Avoyelles Parish SD
Supt. — See Marksville
Bunkie HS | 500/9-12
435 Evergreen St 71322 | 318-346-6216
Mary Wilson, prin. | Fax 346-9611
Bunkie MS | 300/7-8
205 S Cottonwood St 71322 | 318-346-7227
Althea Dupar, prin. | Fax 346-6964

Buras, Plaquemines, Pop. 3,702
Plaquemines Parish SD
Supt. — See Port Sulphur
Buras HS | 300/9-12
1 Wildcat Dr 70041 | 985-657-9435
Stanley Gaudet, prin. | Fax 657-6272
Buras MS | 300/6-8
34158 Highway 11 70041 | 985-657-7721
Brian Briggs, prin. | Fax 657-7740

Calhoun, Ouachita
Ouachita Parish SD
Supt. — See Monroe

Calhoun MS
191 Highway 80 E 71225 — 500/6-8, 318-644-5840
Don Coker, prin. — Fax 644-5418

Calvin, Winn, Pop. 230
Winn Parish SD
Supt. — See Winnfield
Calvin S
PO Box 80 71410 — 300/PK-12, 318-727-8784
Rodney Shelton, prin. — Fax 727-9224

Cameron, Cameron, Pop. 2,041
Cameron Parish SD
PO Box 1548 70631 — 1,800/PK-12, 337-775-5784
Douglas L. Chance, supt. — Fax 775-5097
www.camsch.org
Johnson Bayou S
6304 Gulf Beach Hwy 70631 — 200/K-12, 337-569-2138
Gene Reynolds, prin. — Fax 569-2673
Other Schools – See Grand Chenier, Hackberry, Lake
Charles

Campti, Natchitoches, Pop. 1,058
Natchitoches Parish SD
Supt. — See Natchitoches
Lakeview JSHS
7305 Highway 9 71411 — 600/7-12, 318-476-3360
Terry Williams, prin. — Fax 476-2851

Carencro, Lafayette, Pop. 6,022
Lafayette Parish SD
Supt. — See Lafayette
Carencro MS
4301 N University Ave 70520 — 800/6-8, 337-896-6127
Louella Riggs Cook, prin. — Fax 896-7620

Castor, Bienville, Pop. 215
Bienville Parish SD
Supt. — See Arcadia
Castor S
PO Box 69 71016 — 400/PK-12, 318-544-7271
Pat Boyd, prin. — Fax 544-9077

Cecilia, Saint Martin, Pop. 1,374
St. Martin Parish SD
Supt. — See Saint Martinville
Cecilia HS
PO Box 360 70521 — 600/9-12, 337-667-6221
Anthony Polotzola, prin. — Fax 667-6795
Cecilia JHS
PO Box 129 70521 — 400/7-8, 337-667-6226
Allen Blanchard, prin. — Fax 667-7352

Centerville, Saint Mary
St. Mary Parish SD
PO Box 170 70522 — 10,100/PK-12, 337-836-9661
Dr. Donald Aguillard, supt. — Fax 836-5461
www.stmary.k12.la.us
Centerville S
PO Box 59 70522 — 600/PK-12, 337-836-5103
Mike Galler, prin. — Fax 836-9594
Other Schools – See Baldwin, Berwick, Franklin, Morgan
City, Patterson

Chalmette, Saint Bernard, Pop. 32,100
St. Bernard Parish SD
200 E Saint Bernard Hwy 70043 — 3,000/PK-12, 504-301-2000
Doris Voitier, supt. — Fax 301-2010
www.stbernard.k12.la.us
Chalmette HS
1100 E Judge Perez Dr 70043 — 1,500/7-12, 504-301-2600
Wayne Warner, prin. — Fax 301-2610

Nunez Community College
3700 La Fontaine St 70043 — Post-Sec., 504-680-2240

Chataignier, Evangeline, Pop. 375
Evangeline Parish SD
Supt. — See Ville Platte
Chataignier ES
PO Box 189 70524 — 200/4-8, 337-885-3173
Janice Soileau, prin. — Fax 885-2236

Chauvin, Terrebonne, Pop. 3,375
Terrebonne Parish SD
Supt. — See Houma
Lacache MS
5266 Highway 56 70344 — 500/5-8, 985-594-3945
Anita Landry, prin. — Fax 594-4128

Choudrant, Lincoln, Pop. 578
Lincoln Parish SD
Supt. — See Ruston
Choudrant HS
PO Box 220 71227 — 300/7-12, 318-768-2542
Doug Postel, prin. — Fax 768-4182

Church Point, Acadia, Pop. 4,704
Acadia Parish SD
Supt. — See Crowley
Church Point HS
305 E Lougarre St 70525 — 500/9-12, 337-684-5472
Lee Ward Bellard, prin. — Fax 684-5137
Church Point MS
340 W Martin Luther King Dr 70525 — 300/6-8, 337-684-6381
Paul Derousselle, prin. — Fax 684-0123

Clinton, East Feliciana, Pop. 1,958
East Feliciana Parish SD
PO Box 397 70722 — 2,400/PK-12, 225-683-8277
Glen Brady Ph.D., supt. — Fax 683-3320
www.efpsb.k12.la.us
Clinton HS
PO Box 426 70722 — 300/9-12, 225-683-3321
Dave Carter, prin. — Fax 683-5115
Clinton MS
12126 Liberty St 70722 — 300/6-8, 225-683-5267
Shirley Cupit, prin. — Fax 683-9592
Other Schools – See Jackson

Silliman Institute
PO Box 946 70722 — 500/PK-12, 225-683-5383
Marvin Holland, hdmstr. — Fax 683-6728

Colfax, Grant, Pop. 1,641
Grant Parish SD
PO Box 208 71417 — 3,600/PK-12, 318-627-3274
Sheila S. Jackson, supt. — Fax 627-5931
www.gpsb.org/
Other Schools – See Dry Prong, Georgetown,
Montgomery

Columbia, Caldwell, Pop. 469
Caldwell Parish SD
PO Box 1019 71418 — 1,800/PK-12, 318-649-2689
John Sartin, supt. — Fax 649-0636
Caldwell Parish HS
163 Spartan Dr 71418 — 500/9-12, 318-649-2750
Sherry Jones, prin. — Fax 649-0021
Caldwell Parish JHS
114 Trojan Dr 71418 — 300/7-8, 318-649-2340
Harrell Tucker, prin. — Fax 649-2341

Converse, Sabine, Pop. 403
Sabine Parish SD
Supt. — See Many
Converse S
PO Box 10 71419 — 500/K-12, 318-567-2673
Larry Patrick, prin. — Fax 567-3400

Cottonport, Avoyelles, Pop. 2,274

Louisiana Technical College - Avoyelles — Post-Sec.
508 Choupique Ln 71327 — 318-876-2401

Cotton Valley, Webster, Pop. 1,166
Webster Parish SD
Supt. — See Minden
Cotton Valley S
PO Box 457 71018 — 300/PK-12, 318-832-4716
Ronnie Rhymes, prin. — Fax 832-5273

Coushatta, Red River, Pop. 2,228
Red River Parish SD
PO Box 1369 71019 — 1,600/PK-12, 318-932-4081
Kay Easley, supt. — Fax 932-4367
www.rrbulldogs.com/
Red River HS
915 E Carrol St 71019 — 400/9-12, 318-932-4913
William Edward Wilson, prin. — Fax 932-5334
Red River JHS
915 E Carrol St 71019 — 200/7-8, 318-932-5265
Diane L. Newton, prin. — Fax 932-9052

Riverdale Academy — 300/PK-12
RR 1 Box 104 71019 — 318-932-5876

Covington, Saint Tammany, Pop. 8,769
St. Tammany Parish SD
PO Box 940 70434 — 34,800/PK-12, 985-892-2276
Gayle G. Sloan, supt. — Fax 898-3267
www.stpsb.org
Covington HS
73030 Lion Dr 70433 — 1,600/9-12, 985-892-3422
Danny Guillory, prin. — Fax 875-9699
Pitcher JHS
415 S Jefferson Ave 70433 — 300/7-8, 985-892-3021
Jay Gaines, prin. — Fax 892-1188
Other Schools – See Folsom, Madisonville, Mandeville,
Pearl River, Slidell

Aveda Institute — Post-Sec.
1355 Polders Ln 70433 — 985-892-9953
Delta College — Post-Sec.
19231 6th Ave 70433 — 985-892-6651
Northlake Christian S — 700/PK-12
70104 Wolverine Dr 70433 — 985-892-2683
David Diamond, hdmstr. — Fax 893-4363
St. Paul's HS — 700/8-12
PO Box 928 70434 — 985-892-3200
Br. Raymond Bulliard, prin. — Fax 892-4048
St. Scholastica Academy — 700/8-12
PO Box 1210 70434 — 985-892-2540
Mary Kathryn Villere, prin. — Fax 893-5256

Crowley, Acadia, Pop. 13,940
Acadia Parish SD
PO Box 309 70527 — 9,700/PK-12, 337-783-3664
John E. Bourque, supt. — Fax 783-3761
www.acadia.k12.la.us/
Crowley HS
263 Hensgens Rd 70526 — 700/9-12, 337-783-5313
Steve Duplechin, prin. — Fax 783-7796
Crowley MS
401 W Northern Ave 70526 — 600/6-8, 337-783-5305
Antoinette Pete, prin. — Fax 783-5338
Other Schools – See Church Point, Iota, Midland, Rayne

Louisiana Technical College - Acadian — Post-Sec.
1933 W Hutchinson Ave 70526 — 337-788-7521
Northside Christian S — 300/K-12
811 E Northern Ave 70526 — 337-783-3620
Rev. Randy Trahan, prin. — Fax 788-3461
Notre Dame HS — 500/9-12
910 N Eastern Ave 70526 — 337-783-3519
Cindy Istre, prin. — Fax 788-2115

Cut Off, Lafourche, Pop. 5,325
Lafourche Parish SD
Supt. — See Thibodaux
Larose-Cut Off MS
13356 W Main St 70345 — 600/6-8, 985-693-3273
Matthew Hodson, prin. — Fax 693-3270

Delcambre, Vermilion, Pop. 2,155
Iberia Parish SD
Supt. — See New Iberia
Delcambre JSHS
601 W Main St 70528 — 500/6-12, 337-685-2595
Cory Bourque, prin. — Fax 685-6099

Delhi, Richland, Pop. 3,112
Richland Parish SD
Supt. — See Rayville
Delhi HS
413 Main St 71232 — 200/9-12, 318-878-2235
Milton Linder, prin. — Fax 878-8967
Delhi MS
106 Toombs St 71232 — 300/5-8, 318-878-3748
Floyd McDade, prin. — Fax 878-3749

Denham Springs, Livingston, Pop. 9,204
Livingston Parish SD
Supt. — See Livingston
Denham Springs Freshman HS
940 N Range Ave 70726 — 600/9-9, 225-665-7890
Patty Dumiller, prin. — Fax 665-1865
Denham Springs JHS
401 Hatchell Ln 70726 — 900/6-8, 225-665-8898
Jennifer Barclay, prin. — Fax 665-8601
Denham Springs SHS
1000 N Range Ave 70726 — 1,300/10-12, 225-665-8851
Harold Wax, prin. — Fax 665-4082
Live Oak HS
35086 Hwy 16 70706 — 800/9-12, 225-665-8858
John Curtis, prin. — Fax 665-8850
Southside JHS
PO Box 907 70727 — 800/6-8, 225-664-4221
Alan E. Murphy, prin. — Fax 664-3307

Community Christian Academy — 100/PK-12
400 N River Rd 70726 — 225-665-5696
Denham Springs Beauty College — Post-Sec.
923 Florida Ave SE 70726 — 225-665-6188

Dequincy, Calcasieu, Pop. 3,310
Calcasieu Parish SD
Supt. — See Lake Charles
Dequincy HS
207 N Overton St 70633 — 300/9-12, 337-786-5251
Craig Neal, prin. — Fax 786-7668
Dequincy MS
1603 W 4th St 70633 — 300/6-8, 337-786-3000
Billy Kellogg, prin. — Fax 786-5778

Deridder, Beauregard, Pop. 11,103
Beauregard Parish SD
PO Box 938 70634 — 6,000/PK-12, 337-463-5551
Myrna Cooley, supt. — Fax 463-6735
www.beau.k12.la.us/
Beauregard Vocational Center — Vo/Tech
PO Box 1090 70634 — 337-462-2784
Robert Treme, prin.
Deridder HS — 700/9-12
PO Box 1090 70634 — 337-463-3266
Robert Treme, prin. — Fax 463-9358
Deridder JHS — 700/6-8
415 N Frusha Dr 70634 — 337-463-9083
Kim Hayes, prin. — Fax 463-7696
East Beauregard HS — 500/6-12
5364 Highway 113 70634 — 337-328-7512
Tim Cooley, prin. — Fax 328-8132
Other Schools – See Fields, Longville, Merryville, Singer

Beckwith Christian S — 100/PK-12
5525 Highway 27 70634 — 337-462-7006

Destrehan, Saint Charles, Pop. 8,031
St. Charles Parish SD
Supt. — See Luling
Destrehan HS
1 Wildcat Ln 70047 — 1,400/9-12, 985-764-9946
Lorel Gonzales, prin. — Fax 764-9948
Hurst MS
170 Rd Runner Ln 70047 — 500/7-8, 985-764-6367
Stephen Weber, prin. — Fax 764-2678

Deville, Rapides, Pop. 1,113
Rapides Parish SD
Supt. — See Alexandria
Buckeye JSHS
PO Box 439 71328 — 800/7-12, 318-466-5678
Carol Passmore, prin. — Fax 466-9269

Dodson, Winn, Pop. 347
Winn Parish SD
Supt. — See Winnfield
Dodson S
PO Box 97 71422 — 400/PK-12, 318-628-2172
Robin Potts, prin. — Fax 628-7515

Donaldsonville, Ascension, Pop. 7,552
Ascension Parish SD
PO Box 189 70346 — 14,600/PK-12, 225-473-7981
Donald Songy, supt. — Fax 473-8058
www.apsb.org
Donaldsonville HS
100 Tiger Dr 70346 — 600/7-12, 225-474-2730
Ronald Rabalais, prin. — Fax 473-4496
Other Schools – See Geismar, Gonzales, Prairieville,
Saint Amant

Ascension Catholic HS — 200/9-12
311 Saint Vincent St 70346 — 225-473-9227
Mark Shamburger, prin. — Fax 473-9235

Downsville, Union, Pop. 117
Union Parish SD
Supt. — See Farmerville

Downsville S 500/K-12
PO Box 8 71234 318-982-5318
Curtis Williams, prin. Fax 982-5737

Doyline, Webster, Pop. 829
Webster Parish SD
Supt. — See Minden
Doyline JSHS 300/6-12
PO Box 657 71023 318-745-2118
Johnny Rowland, prin. Fax 745-3695

Dry Prong, Grant, Pop. 421
Grant Parish SD
Supt. — See Colfax
Dry Prong JHS 500/7-8
PO Box 147 71423 318-899-5697
Ben LaGrone, prin. Fax 899-7364
Grant HS 700/9-12
17779 Highway 167 71423 318-899-3331
Randy Crawford, prin. Fax 899-5724
Grant Academy Adult
17771 Highway 167 71423 318-899-3999
Norman Garlington, prin. Fax 899-5555

Dubach, Lincoln, Pop. 811
Lincoln Parish SD
Supt. — See Ruston
Dubach HS 100/7-12
PO Box 159 71235 318-777-3470
Donna Doss, prin. Fax 777-8409

Duson, Lafayette, Pop. 1,657
Lafayette Parish SD
Supt. — See Lafayette
Judice MS 500/6-8
2645 S Fieldspan Rd 70529 337-984-1250
Martha P. Broussard, prin. Fax 988-3693

Edgard, Saint John the Baptist, Pop. 2,753
St. John The Baptist Parish SD
Supt. — See Reserve
West St. John HS 300/8-12
PO Box 66 70049 985-497-3271
Elton Oubre, prin. Fax 497-5009

Elizabeth, Allen, Pop. 578
Allen Parish SD
Supt. — See Oberlin
Elizabeth S 300/PK-12
PO Box 580 70638 318-634-5341
Michael Stainback, prin. Fax 634-5218

Elm Grove, Bossier
Bossier Parish SD
Supt. — See Benton
Elm Grove MS 800/6-8
PO Box 108 71051 318-549-6500
Robert Marlow, prin. Fax 549-6513

Elton, Jefferson Davis, Pop. 1,244
Jefferson Davis Parish SD
Supt. — See Jennings
Elton JSHS 300/6-12
902 2nd St 70532 337-584-2991
David Troutman, prin. Fax 584-2244

Epps, West Carroll, Pop. 1,149
West Carroll Parish SD
Supt. — See Oak Grove
Epps S 300/K-12
PO Box 277 71237 318-926-3624
Edwin Guchereau, prin. Fax 926-5655

Erath, Vermilion, Pop. 2,181
Vermilion Parish SD
Supt. — See Abbeville
Erath HS 500/9-12
808 S Broadway St 70533 337-937-8451
Francis Touchet, prin. Fax 937-5109
Erath MS 700/4-8
800 S Broadway St 70533 337-937-4441
Lynn Moss, prin. Fax 937-5125

Eunice, Saint Landry, Pop. 11,586
St. Landry Parish SD
Supt. — See Opelousas
Eunice Career & Technical Education Ctr. Vo/Tech
421 S 10th St 70535 337-457-8686
Mike Corrigan, prin. Fax 457-0307
Eunice HS 800/9-12
301 S Bobcat Dr 70535 337-457-3011
Margaret Leger, prin. Fax 457-3720
Eunice JHS 500/7-8
751 W Oak Ave 70535 337-457-7386
Edward Brown, prin. Fax 457-1764
Eunice Adult Education Adult
PO Box 1486 70535 337-457-7428
George Fisher, prin.

Louisiana Academy of Beauty Post-Sec.
550 E Laurel Ave 70535 337-457-7627
Louisiana State University at Eunice Post-Sec.
PO Box 1129 70535 337-457-7311
St. Edmund HS 300/7-12
351 W Magnolia Ave 70535 337-457-3777
Beth Christ, prin. Fax 457-2510

Evans, Vernon
Vernon Parish SD
Supt. — See Leesville
Evans S 400/PK-12
PO Box 69 70639 337-286-5289
William Carver, prin. Fax 286-9298

Farmerville, Union, Pop. 3,776
Union Parish SD 2,900/PK-12
PO Box 308 71241 318-368-9715
Judy Mabry, supt. Fax 368-3311
www.unionparishschools.org/

Farmerville HS 400/9-12
300 Anthony St 71241 318-368-2661
Johnny Mance, prin. Fax 368-2229
Farmerville JHS 300/6-8
606 Bernice St 71241 318-368-9235
Andy Allred, prin. Fax 368-1989
Other Schools – See Bernice, Downsville, Marion,
Spearsville

Louisiana Tech. Coll. - North Central Post-Sec.
PO Box 548 71241 318-368-3179

Ferriday, Concordia, Pop. 3,615
Concordia Parish SD
Supt. — See Vidalia
Ferriday HS 300/9-12
801 Ee Wallace Blvd N 71334 318-757-8626
Debra Harris, prin. Fax 757-0763
Ferriday JHS 300/6-8
201 Martin Luther King Blvd 71334 318-757-8695
Dorothy Parker, prin. Fax 757-8696

Huntington S 200/K-12
300 Lynwood Dr 71334 318-757-4515
Louisiana Tech. College - Shelby Jackson Post-Sec.
PO Box 1465 71334 318-757-6501

Fields, Beauregard
Beauregard Parish SD
Supt. — See Deridder
Hyatt S 200/K-12
6249 Highway 109 70653 337-786-6722
Mac Spikes, prin. Fax 786-8833

Florien, Sabine, Pop. 691
Sabine Parish SD
Supt. — See Many
Florien HS 300/7-12
PO Box 70 71429 318-586-3681
Eddie Jones, prin. Fax 586-4818

Folsom, Saint Tammany, Pop. 603
St. Tammany Parish SD
Supt. — See Covington
Folsom JHS 200/6-8
83055 Hay Hollow Rd 70437 985-796-3724
Sharon Garrett, prin. Fax 796-3701

Forest, West Carroll, Pop. 272
West Carroll Parish SD
Supt. — See Oak Grove
Forest S 400/K-12
PO Box 368 71242 318-428-3672
Richard M. Strong, prin. Fax 428-8875

Franklin, Saint Mary, Pop. 8,059
St. Mary Parish SD
Supt. — See Centerville
Franklin HS 500/9-12
1401 Cynthia St 70538 337-828-0143
Ray Francis, prin. Fax 828-0184
Franklin JHS 400/6-8
525 Morris St 70538 337-828-0855
Tybus Burdett, prin. Fax 828-5095
Franklin Adult Education Learning Center Adult
1706 Main St 70538 337-828-0121
Jody Charpentier, prin. Fax 828-0196

Hanson Memorial HS 300/6-12
903 Anderson St 70538 337-828-3487
Sherri Higdon, prin. Fax 828-0787

Franklinton, Washington, Pop. 3,641
Washington Parish SD 4,800/PK-12
PO Box 587 70438 985-839-3436
Gary Fowler, supt. Fax 839-5464
www.wpsb.org
Franklinton HS 600/9-12
1 Demon Cir 70438 985-839-6781
Beverly Young, prin. Fax 839-9830
Franklinton JHS 500/6-8
617 Main St 70438 985-839-3501
Pauline Bankston, prin. Fax 839-6912
Franklinton Vo Career Ctr Vo/Tech
616 T W Barker Dr 70438 985-839-6218
Robert Johnson, prin. Fax 839-5464
Pine S 700/PK-12
27164 Highway 62 70438 985-848-5243
Geary Mckenzie, prin. Fax 848-9433
Other Schools – See Angie, Mount Hermon, Varnado

Bowling Green S 500/PK-12
700 Varnado St 70438 985-839-5317
Lewis Murray, admin. Fax 839-5668

French Settlement, Livingston, Pop. 1,009
Livingston Parish SD
Supt. — See Livingston
French Settlement JSHS 400/7-12
15875 LA Highway 16 70733 225-698-3561
Daniel Amond, prin. Fax 698-6458

Galliano, Lafourche, Pop. 4,294
Lafourche Parish SD
Supt. — See Thibodaux
South Lafourche HS 1,300/9-12
PO Box 160 70354 985-632-5721
Mary Curole, prin. Fax 632-6723

Geismar, Ascension
Ascension Parish SD
Supt. — See Donaldsonville
Dutchtown HS 1,100/9-12
13165 Highway 73 70734 225-621-8250
David Alexander, prin. Fax 677-8191

Dutchtown MS 700/6-8
13078 Highway 73 70734 225-621-2355
Doug Walker, prin. Fax 621-2351

Georgetown, Grant, Pop. 303
Grant Parish SD
Supt. — See Colfax
Georgetown S 300/PK-12
PO Box 99 71432 318-827-5306
William Norris Ph.D., prin. Fax 827-9481

Gibsland, Bienville, Pop. 1,091
Bienville Parish SD
Supt. — See Arcadia
Gibsland-Coleman S 300/K-12
PO Box 70 71028 318-843-6247
Kenneth Gipson, prin. Fax 843-9804

Glenmora, Rapides, Pop. 1,551
Rapides Parish SD
Supt. — See Alexandria
Glenmora JSHS 300/7-12
PO Box 697 71433 318-748-8145
Dr. Emily Rutherford, prin. Fax 748-8146
Plainview S 300/PK-12
PO Box 698 71433 318-634-5944
Sonia Rasmussen, prin. Fax 634-5389

Golden Meadow, Lafourche, Pop. 2,151
Lafourche Parish SD
Supt. — See Thibodaux
Golden Meadow MS 500/6-8
630 S Bayou Dr 70357 985-475-7314
Lonnie Rousse, prin. Fax 475-6623

Gonzales, Ascension, Pop. 8,339
Ascension Parish SD
Supt. — See Donaldsonville
East Ascension HS 1,000/9-12
612 E Worthy St 70737 225-621-2400
Randy Watts, prin. Fax 621-2397
Gonzales MS 600/6-8
1502 W Orice Roth Rd 70737 225-621-2505
Charles Barbera, prin. Fax 621-2509

Ascension College Post-Sec.
320 E Ascension St 70737 225-647-6609
Faith Academy 400/K-10
10469 Airline Hwy 70737 225-644-3110
John Craig Wascom, admin. Fax 647-2368

Grambling, Lincoln, Pop. 4,371
Lincoln Parish SD
Supt. — See Ruston
Grambling State University Lab. HS 100/9-12
407 Central Ave 71245 318-274-6153
Dr. Larry Lewis, prin. Fax 274-3215
Grambling State University MS 100/6-8
407 Central Ave 71245 318-274-6531
Dr. Vicki Brown, prin. Fax 274-3360

Grambling State University Post-Sec.
PO Box 864 71245 318-274-3811

Grand Cane, DeSoto, Pop. 193

Central S 200/K-12
PO Box 71 71032 318-858-3319

Grand Chenier, Cameron
Cameron Parish SD
Supt. — See Cameron
South Cameron JSHS 300/8-12
753 Oak Grove Hwy 70643 337-542-4628
Dale Skinner, prin. Fax 542-4419

Grand Coteau, Saint Landry, Pop. 1,036

Academy of the Sacred Heart 400/PK-12
PO Box 310 70541 337-662-5275
Mary Burns, hdmstr. Fax 662-3011

Grand Isle, Jefferson, Pop. 1,563
Jefferson Parish SD
Supt. — See Marrero
Grand Isle S 200/PK-12
PO Box 995 70358 504-522-8015
Richard Augustin, prin. Fax 787-3878

Grant, Allen
Allen Parish SD
Supt. — See Oberlin
Fairview S 400/PK-12
PO Box 216 70644 318-634-5354
Gary Lockhart, prin. Fax 634-5357

Gray, Terrebonne, Pop. 4,260
Terrebonne Parish SD
Supt. — See Houma
Bourgeois HS 1,200/9-12
1 Reservation Ct 70359 985-872-3277
Nason Authement, prin. Fax 872-3270

Greensburg, Saint Helena, Pop. 604
St. Helena Parish SD 1,300/PK-12
PO Box 540 70441 225-222-4349
J. Wayne Meadows, supt. Fax 222-4937
www.sthpk-12.net
St. Helena Central HS 400/9-12
14340 Highway 37 70441 225-222-4402
Gary Porter, prin. Fax 222-6986
St. Helena Central MS 400/5-8
PO Box 1240 70441 225-222-6291
Kathran Randolph, prin. Fax 222-6780

Louisiana Tech. Coll. - Florida Parishes Post-Sec.
PO Box 1300 70441 225-222-4251

Gretna, Jefferson, Pop. 17,180
Jefferson Parish SD
Supt. — See Marrero
Gretna MS 800/6-8
910 Gretna Blvd 70053 504-366-0120
Elizabeth A. Davis, prin. Fax 366-8807
Livaudais MS 800/6-8
925 Lamar Ave 70056 504-393-7544
Luther McClain, prin. Fax 393-9610

Archbishop Blenk HS 600/8-12
17 Gretna Blvd 70053 504-367-2626
David Pooley, prin. Fax 367-7128
Believer's Life Christian Academy 400/PK-12
501 Lapalco Blvd 70056 504-348-4685
Dr. Wendell Douglas, admin. Fax 340-6611
Gretna Career College Training Institute Post-Sec.
1415 Whitney Ave 70053 504-366-5409
Moler Beauty College Post-Sec.
59 Westbank Expy 70053 504-362-1999
School of Urban Missions Post-Sec.
511 Westbank Expressway 70053 504-362-3634

Gueydan, Vermilion, Pop. 1,594
Vermilion Parish SD
Supt. — See Abbeville
Gueydan HS 300/6-12
901 Main St 70542 337-536-6938
Luddy Herpin, prin. Fax 536-7000

Hackberry, Cameron, Pop. 1,664
Cameron Parish SD
Supt. — See Cameron
Hackberry S 300/K-12
1390 School St 70645 337-762-3305
Austin Labove, prin. Fax 762-3304

Hammond, Tangipahoa, Pop. 17,715
Tangipahoa Parish SD
Supt. — See Amite
Hammond HS 1,200/9-12
45168 River Rd 70401 985-345-7235
Gwen Myers, prin. Fax 345-5252
Hammond JHS 500/7-8
111 J W Davis Dr 70403 985-345-2654
Janice Williams, prin. Fax 542-4215
Tangipahoa Parish Magnet HS 100/9-12
411 E Crystal St 70401 985-542-5634
Dale Brouillette, prin. Fax 542-9987

Louisiana Technical College - Hammond Post-Sec.
PO Box 489 70404 985-543-4120
North Oaks Medical Center Post-Sec.
15790 Medical Arts Dr 70403 985-543-6600
St. Thomas Aquinas HS 300/9-12
14520 Voss Dr 70401 985-542-7662
Jose Becerra, prin. Fax 542-4010
Southeastern Louisiana University Post-Sec.
PO Box 784 70404 985-549-2000

Harrisonburg, Catahoula, Pop. 734
Catahoula Parish SD 1,800/PK-12
PO Box 290 71340 318-744-5727
Ronald Lofton, supt. Fax 744-9221
catahoula.nls.k12.la.us/
Harrisonburg HS 100/9-12
800 Bushley St 71340 318-744-5273
Malcolm Terry, prin. Fax 744-2098
Other Schools – See Jonesville, Sicily Island

Harvey, Jefferson, Pop. 21,222
Jefferson Parish SD
Supt. — See Marrero
Cox HS 1,100/8-11
2200 Lapalco Blvd 70058 504-367-6388
Darvell Edwards, prin. Fax 367-3176
West Jefferson HS 1,500/9-12
2200 8th St 70058 504-368-6055
Lale Geer, prin. Fax 368-0535

Louisiana Tech. Coll. - West Jefferson Post-Sec.
475 Manhattan Blvd 70058 504-361-6464
St. Rosalie MS 400/6-8
2115 Oakmere Dr 70058 504-348-9330
Mary Wenzel, prin. Fax 348-9331

Haughton, Bossier, Pop. 2,802
Bossier Parish SD
Supt. — See Benton
Haughton HS 1,000/9-12
210 E Mckinley Ave 71037 318-549-5450
Gene Couvillion, prin. Fax 549-5470
Haughton MS 900/6-8
3955 Elm St 71037 318-549-5560
Susan Salter, prin. Fax 549-5573

Haynesville, Claiborne, Pop. 2,561
Claiborne Parish SD
Supt. — See Homer
Haynesville JSHS 400/5-12
9930 Highway 79 71038 318-624-0905
William Kennedy, prin. Fax 624-2488

Claiborne Academy 200/K-12
6741 Highway 79 71038 318-927-2747

Hineston, Rapides
Rapides Parish SD
Supt. — See Alexandria
Oak Hill HS 300/7-12
PO Box 269 71438 318-793-2014
Eugene Alford, prin. Fax 793-8589

Holden, Livingston
Livingston Parish SD
Supt. — See Livingston
Holden S 600/K-12
30120 LA 441 Hwy 70744 225-567-9367
Linda Pittman, prin. Fax 567-5248

Homer, Claiborne, Pop. 3,604
Claiborne Parish SD 2,700/PK-12
PO Box 600 71040 318-927-3502
James Scriber, supt. Fax 927-9184
Homer HS 300/9-12
1008 N Main St 71040 318-927-2985
Dwight Mitchell, prin. Fax 927-4733
Homer JHS 300/6-8
1009 Pearl St 71040 318-927-2826
Keith Beard, prin. Fax 927-4376
Other Schools – See Athens, Haynesville, Lisbon, Summerfield

Hornbeck, Vernon, Pop. 421
Vernon Parish SD
Supt. — See Leesville
Hornbeck S 500/PK-12
PO Box 9 71439 318-565-4440
Joey Whiddon, prin. Fax 565-4136

Houma, Terrebonne, Pop. 32,025
Terrebonne Parish SD 19,300/PK-12
PO Box 5097 70361 985-876-7400
Ed Richard, supt. Fax 872-1411
www.tpsd.org
Ellender Memorial HS 1,100/9-12
3012 Patriot Dr 70363 985-868-7903
Marilyn Schwartz, prin. Fax 868-3503
Evergreen JHS 1,100/7-9
5000 W Main St 70360 985-876-2606
M. Torbert, prin. Fax 868-4395
Grand Caillou MS 600/4-8
3933 Grand Caillou Rd 70363 985-879-3001
Judy Gaspard, prin. Fax 879-3009
Houma JHS 1,100/7-9
315 Saint Charles St 70360 985-872-1511
Tom Soudelier, prin. Fax 872-5121
Oaklawn JHS 600/7-8
2215 Acadian Dr 70363 985-872-3904
Demetria Maryland, prin. Fax 917-1917
Terrebonne HS 900/9-12
7318 Main St 70360 985-879-3377
Graham Douglas, prin. Fax 223-2270
Terrebonne Vo-Tech HS Vo/Tech
3051 Patriot Dr 70363 985-851-1163
Marcel Fournier, prin. Fax 876-1364
Bayou Cane Adult Education Adult
6484 W Main St 70360 985-876-3180
K. Brown, coord. Fax 876-0411
Other Schools – See Bourg, Chauvin, Gray, Montegut

Houma Christian S 400/K-12
109 Valhi Blvd 70360 985-851-7423
Michael Carlos, prin. Fax 872-4958
L.E. Fletcher Technical Community Coll. Post-Sec.
PO Box 5033 70361 985-857-3655
Omega Institute of Cosmetology Post-Sec.
229 S Hollywood Rd 70360 985-876-9334
South Louisiana Beauty College Post-Sec.
300 Howard Ave 70363 985-873-8978
Vandebilt Catholic HS 900/8-12
209 S Hollywood Rd 70360 985-876-2551
Jim Reiss, prin. Fax 868-9774

Independence, Saint Helena, Pop. 1,711
Tangipahoa Parish SD
Supt. — See Amite
Independence HS 500/9-12
270 Tiger Ave 70443 985-878-9436
Ron Genco, prin. Fax 878-4831
Independence MS 500/4-8
PO Box 97 70443 985-878-4376
Malcolm Mizell, prin. Fax 878-4848

Iota, Acadia, Pop. 1,388
Acadia Parish SD
Supt. — See Crowley
Iota HS 400/9-12
456 S 5th St 70543 337-779-2534
Ronald Doguet, prin. Fax 779-2872
Iota MS 200/6-8
426 S 5th St 70543 337-779-2536
Debra Seibert, prin. Fax 779-2594

Iowa, Calcasieu, Pop. 2,628
Calcasieu Parish SD
Supt. — See Lake Charles
Iowa HS 500/9-12
PO Box 1460 70647 337-582-3561
David Butler, prin. Fax 582-7477

Jackson, East Feliciana, Pop. 3,896
East Feliciana Parish SD
Supt. — See Clinton
Jackson HS 300/9-12
3501 Highway 10 70748 225-634-5931
Joseph Jones, prin. Fax 634-3207
Jackson MS 200/6-8
3503 Highway 10 70748 225-634-5932
Sharon Jones, prin. Fax 634-5955

Louisiana Technical College - Folkes Post-Sec.
3337 Highway 10 70748 225-634-2636

Jeanerette, Iberia, Pop. 5,955
Iberia Parish SD
Supt. — See New Iberia
Jeanerette HS 400/9-12
8217 E Old Spanish Trl 70544 337-276-6038
Raymond Marceaux, prin. Fax 276-5016
Jeanerette MS 200/7-8
609 Pellerin Rd 70544 337-276-4320
Frederick Magee, prin. Fax 276-7064

Jefferson, Jefferson, Pop. 14,521
Jefferson Parish SD
Supt. — See Marrero
Riverdale HS 1,000/9-12
240 Riverdale Dr 70121 504-833-7288
Connie Tiliakos, prin. Fax 837-5401
Riverdale MS 600/6-8
3900 Jefferson Hwy 70121 504-828-2706
Randy Bennett, prin. Fax 833-5125

Jena, LaSalle, Pop. 2,925
LaSalle Parish SD 2,700/PK-12
PO Box 90 71342 318-992-2161
Roy Breithaupt, supt. Fax 992-8457
www.lasallepsb.com
Jena HS 500/9-12
PO Box 89 71342 318-992-5195
Scott Windham, prin. Fax 992-4797
Jena JHS 200/7-8
PO Box 920 71342 318-992-5815
June Fowler, prin. Fax 992-6392
Other Schools – See Olla, Urania

Jennings, Jefferson Davis, Pop. 10,712
Jefferson Davis Parish SD 5,000/PK-12
PO Box 640 70546 337-824-1834
Tommy Lee Smith, supt. Fax 824-9737
webserver.jeffersondavis.org/topmain.htm
Hathaway S 500/K-12
4040 Pine Island Hwy 70546 337-824-4452
Mona Miller, prin. Fax 824-2769
Jennings HS 600/9-12
PO Box 1090 70546 337-824-0642
James McKeivier, prin. Fax 824-5585
Other Schools – See Elton, Lacassine, Lake Arthur, Roanoke, Welsh

---

Bethel Christian S 200/K-12
PO Box 729 70546 337-824-0020
Sheila Reed, admin. Fax 824-0579
Louisiana Technical College - M. Smith Post-Sec.
1230 N Main St 70546 337-824-4811

Jonesboro, Jackson, Pop. 3,808
Jackson Parish SD 1,900/PK-12
PO Box 705 71251 318-259-4456
William Gary Black, supt. Fax 259-2527
www.jpsb.us/
Jonesboro-Hodge HS 500/7-12
225 Pershing Hwy 71251 318-259-4138
Bertha Robinson, prin. Fax 259-2701
Weston S 500/PK-12
213 Highway 505 71251 318-259-7313
Wayne Alford, prin. Fax 259-1056
Other Schools – See Quitman

Jonesville, Catahoula, Pop. 2,369
Catahoula Parish SD
Supt. — See Harrisonburg
Block HS 300/8-12
300 Division St 71343 318-339-7996
Donald Money, prin. Fax 339-7901
Central S 100/K-12
244 Larto Bayou Rd 71343 318-339-7574
Andrea Cruse, prin. Fax 339-7925

Kaplan, Vermilion, Pop. 5,104
Vermilion Parish SD
Supt. — See Abbeville
Kaplan HS 500/9-12
200 E Pirate Ln 70548 337-643-6385
David Dupuis, prin. Fax 643-3543
Rost MS 500/5-8
112 W 6th St 70548 337-643-8545
Samuel Hinckley, prin. Fax 643-7013

Kenner, Jefferson, Pop. 70,202
Jefferson Parish SD
Supt. — See Marrero
Bonnabel HS 1,700/9-12
2801 Bruin Dr 70065 504-443-4564
Ray Ferrand, prin. Fax 443-3401
Roosevelt MS 700/6-8
3315 Maine Ave 70065 504-443-1361
Robert Simmons, prin. Fax 443-3425

Herzing College Post-Sec.
2400 Veterans Memorial #410 70062 504-733-0074
John Jay Kenner Academy Post-Sec.
2844 Tennessee Ave 70062 504-467-2951
Moler Beauty College Post-Sec.
1919 Veterans Blvd #100 70062 504-467-1888
Southwest University Post-Sec.
2200 Veterans Blvd 70062 504-468-2900

Kentwood, Tangipahoa, Pop. 2,174
Tangipahoa Parish SD
Supt. — See Amite
Kentwood JSHS 300/7-12
PO Box 88 70444 985-229-2881
Ginger Francois, prin. Fax 229-6031
Sumner JSHS 700/7-12
15841 Highway 440 70444 985-229-8805
John Alston, prin. Fax 229-2043

Kilbourne, West Carroll, Pop. 433
West Carroll Parish SD
Supt. — See Oak Grove
Kilbourne S 300/K-12
PO Box 339 71253 318-428-3721
Shelton Kavalir, prin. Fax 428-3860

Kinder, Allen, Pop. 2,129
Allen Parish SD
Supt. — See Oberlin

Kinder HS 300/9-12
145 Highway 383 70648 337-738-2886
Joseph Kent Reed, prin. Fax 738-5665
Kinder MS 300/6-8
PO Box 610 70648 337-738-3223
Tracey Odom, prin. Fax 738-3425

Labadieville, Assumption, Pop. 1,821
Assumption Parish SD
Supt. — See Napoleonville
Labadieville MS 500/5-8
PO Box 127 70372 985-526-4227
Susan Harrison, prin. Fax 526-4163

Lacassine, Jefferson Davis
Jefferson Davis Parish SD
Supt. — See Jennings
Lacassine S 500/PK-12
PO Box 50 70650 337-588-4206
Brian Lejeune, prin. Fax 588-4283

Lafayette, Lafayette, Pop. 111,667
Lafayette Parish SD 29,700/PK-12
PO Box 2158 70502 337-236-6800
Dr. James Easton, supt. Fax 233-0977
www.lft.k12.la.us
Acadiana HS 1,800/9-12
315 Rue De Belier 70506 337-984-2646
Janet Hiatt, prin. Fax 984-0769
Acadian MS 500/5-8
4201 Moss St 70507 337-233-2496
Linda Nance, prin. Fax 235-6711
Alleman MS 800/5-8
600 Roselawn Blvd 70503 337-984-7210
Rubye Hilliard, prin. Fax 984-7212
Breaux MS 800/6-8
1400 S Orange St 70501 337-234-2313
Loretta Caldwell, prin. Fax 234-1915
Carencro HS 1,400/9-12
721 W Butcher Switch Rd 70507 337-896-6192
Annette Rath, prin. Fax 896-7592
Comeaux HS 1,800/9-12
100 W Bluebird St 70508 337-984-8395
Joseph Craig, prin. Fax 984-1112
Lafayette HS 2,000/9-12
3000 W Congress St 70506 337-984-5284
Dr. Patrick Leonard, prin. Fax 984-0153
Lafayette MS 400/6-8
1301 W University Ave 70506 337-234-4032
Rick Poulan, prin. Fax 235-4971
Martin MS 800/5-8
401 Broadmoor Blvd 70503 337-984-9796
Bobby Badeaux, prin. Fax 984-9968
Moss MS 700/5-8
805 Teurlings Dr 70501 337-289-1994
Kenneth Douet, prin. Fax 289-1997
Northside HS 1,000/9-12
301 Dunand St 70501 337-232-0681
Carlton Handy, prin. Fax 235-5443
Smith Career Center Vo/Tech
200 18th St 70501 337-233-2026
Carol Vital, prin. Fax 237-6351
Other Schools – See Broussard, Carencro, Duson, Scott, Youngsville

Blue Cliff College Post-Sec.
100 Asma Blvd Ste 350 70508 337-269-0620
Cosmetology Training Center Post-Sec.
2516 Johnston St 70503 337-237-6868
Lafayette General Medical Center Post-Sec.
PO Box 52009 70505 337-261-7381
Lockworks Academie of Hairdressing Post-Sec.
2922 Johnston St 70503 337-233-0511
Louisiana Technical College - Lafayette Post-Sec.
1101 Bertrand Dr 70506 337-262-5962
Remington College Post-Sec.
303 Rue Louis XIV # 8 70508 337-981-4010
Ronnie & Dorman's School of Hair Design Post-Sec.
2002 Johnston St 70503 337-232-1806
St. Thomas More HS 1,000/9-12
450 E Farrel Rd 70508 337-988-3700
Raymond Simon, prin. Fax 988-2911
South Louisiana Community College Post-Sec.
320 Devalcourt St 70506 337-521-8896
Teurlings Catholic HS 600/9-12
139 Teurlings Dr 70501 337-235-5711
Michael Boyer, prin. Fax 234-8057
Unitech Training Academy Post-Sec.
3605 Ambassador Caffery Pky 70503 337-988-6764
University Medical Center Post-Sec.
2390 W Congress St 70506 337-261-6004
University of Louisiana at Lafayette Post-Sec.
PO Box 44548 70504 337-482-1000

Lafitte, Jefferson, Pop. 1,507
Jefferson Parish SD
Supt. — See Marrero
Fisher MSHS 500/7-12
2529 Jean Lafitte Blvd 70067 504-689-3665
George Hebert, prin. Fax 689-7556

Lake Arthur, Jefferson Davis, Pop. 2,916
Jefferson Davis Parish SD
Supt. — See Jennings
Lake Arthur JSHS 400/7-12
4374 Tiger Ln 70549 337-774-5152
Bridget Thomas, prin. Fax 774-2522

Lake Charles, Calcasieu, Pop. 70,735
Calcasieu Parish SD 31,300/PK-12
PO Box 800 70602 337-491-1600
Wayne Savoy, supt. Fax 437-1293
www.cpsb.org
Barbe HS 1,800/9-12
2200 W Mcneese St 70605 337-478-3626
Charles Adkins, prin. Fax 474-6782

Calcasieu Career Center Vo/Tech
1120 W 18th St 70601 337-491-1720
Thail Pete, prin. Fax 491-1727
Houston HS 1,100/9-12
880 Sam Houston Jones Pkwy 70611 337-855-3528
Douglas McCullor, prin. Fax 855-3235
LaGrange HS 1,000/9-12
3420 Louisiana Ave 70607 337-477-4571
Bobby Jack Thompson, prin. Fax 477-1565
Lake Charles/Boston HS 400/9-12
1509 Enterprise Blvd 70601 337-436-9594
Solomon Cannon, prin. Fax 436-6532
Molo Magnet MS 500/6-8
2300 Medora St 70601 337-433-6785
James Wilson, prin. Fax 439-0787
Moss Bluff MS 800/6-8
297 Park Rd 70611 337-217-3351
John Duhon, prin. Fax 217-8026
Oak Park MS 500/6-8
2200 Oak Park Blvd 70601 337-478-3310
Martin Guillory, prin. Fax 474-0753
Reynaud MS 300/6-8
745 S Shattuck St 70601 337-436-5729
Ellaweena Woods, prin. Fax 491-0963
T & I Vocational Center Vo/Tech
736 E College St 70607 337-491-1736
George Albers, prin. Fax 474-7553
Washington-Marion Magnet HS 700/9-12
2802 Pineview St 70615 337-433-5892
Merculus Chretien, prin. Fax 436-7829
Welsh MS 1,300/6-8
1500 W Mcneese St 70605 337-477-8959
M.L. Sarver, prin. Fax 474-0519
White MS 700/6-8
1000 E McNeese St 70607 337-477-1648
Charles Allen, prin. Fax 478-7899
Adult & Continuing Education Adult
1015 6th Ave 70601 337-491-1781
Jerry Adams, prin. Fax 491-1782
Other Schools – See Bell City, Dequincy, Iowa, Starks, Sulphur, Vinton, Westlake

Cameron Parish SD
Supt. — See Cameron
Grand Lake S 600/K-12
1039 Highway 384 70607 337-598-2231
David Duhon, prin. Fax 598-2961

Delta School of Business and Technology Post-Sec.
517 Broad St 70601 337-439-5765
Demmon School of Beauty Post-Sec.
1222 Ryan St 70601 337-439-9265
Hamilton Christian Academy 400/PK-12
1415 8th St 70601 337-439-1178
Dr. Wayne McEntire, prin. Fax 433-1877
Lake Charles Memorial Hospital Post-Sec.
1701 Oak Park Blvd 70601 337-494-3200
Lakewood Christian Academy 100/PK-12
2520 W Sale Rd 70605 337-477-0531
Ray Hoffpauir, prin. Fax 477-0572
McNeese State University Post-Sec.
4100 Ryan St 70605 337-475-5000
St. Louis HS 600/9-12
1620 Bank St 70601 337-436-7275
William Simon, prin. Fax 436-6792
St. Patrick's Hospital Post-Sec.
524 S Ryan St 70601 337-491-7730
Sowela Technical Community College Post-Sec.
PO Box 16950 70616 337-491-2698
Stage One - The Hair School Post-Sec.
209 W College St 70605 337-474-0533

Lake Providence, East Carroll, Pop. 4,751
East Carroll Parish SD 1,500/PK-12
PO Box 71254 318-559-2222
Dr. Voleria Millikin, supt. Fax 559-3864
e-carrollschools.org
Lake Providence HS 300/9-12
602 Mrtin Luther King Jr Dr 71254 318-559-1984
Rosie Armstrong, prin. Fax 559-5380
Lake Providence JHS 300/6-8
1205 Gould Blvd 71254 318-559-2520
Janice Harris, prin. Fax 559-0679
Monticello S 200/K-12
1046 Highway 577 71254 318-552-6366
Phil Jackson, prin. Fax 552-7658

Briarfield Academy 200/K-12
301 Riddle Ln 71254 318-559-2360
Louisiana Technical College - Tallulah Post-Sec.
PO Box 368 71254 318-559-0239

Laplace, Saint John the Baptist, Pop. 24,194

St. Charles Catholic HS 400/9-12
100 Dominican Rd 70068 985-652-3809
Andrew Cupit, prin. Fax 652-2609

Lecompte, Rapides, Pop. 1,340
Rapides Parish SD
Supt. — See Alexandria
Rapides HS 300/9-12
PO Box 770 71346 318-776-9371
Deborah Coe, prin. Fax 776-5844
Raymond MS 200/5-8
PO Box 429 71346 318-776-5489
Dr. Karl Carpenter, prin. Fax 776-9459

Leesville, Vernon, Pop. 6,432
Vernon Parish SD 9,900/PK-12
201 Belview Rd 71446 337-239-3401
Cynthia Gillespie, supt. Fax 238-5777
www.vpsb.k12.la.us

Hicks S 300/PK-12
1296 Hicks School Rd 71446 337-239-6045
Randy Lansdale, prin. Fax 239-6149
Leesville HS 900/9-12
502 Berry Ave 71446 337-239-3464
James Williams, prin. Fax 239-2485
Leesville JHS 600/7-8
480 Berry Ave 71446 337-239-3874
Roger Rolon, prin. Fax 238-4113
Pickering JSHS 500/7-12
497 Lebleu Rd 71446 337-537-1555
Barbara Barnickel, prin. Fax 537-3019
Other Schools – See Anacoco, Evans, Hornbeck, Pitkin, Rosepine, Simpson

Louisiana Technical College-Lamar Salter Post-Sec.
15014 Lake Charles Hwy 71446 337-537-3135

Lena, Rapides
Rapides Parish SD
Supt. — See Alexandria
Northwood S 800/PK-12
8830 Highway 1 N 71447 318-793-8021
Donald Welch, prin. Fax 793-8503

Lisbon, Claiborne, Pop. 155
Claiborne Parish SD
Supt. — See Homer
Pineview S 200/PK-12
430 Hebron Rd 71048 318-353-6334
Sandra Boston, prin. Fax 353-6568

Livingston, Livingston, Pop. 1,432
Livingston Parish SD 21,700/PK-12
PO Box 1130 70754 225-686-7044
Randy Pope, supt. Fax 686-3052
www.lpsb.org
Doyle JSHS 400/7-12
PO Box 160 70754 225-686-2318
Tony Terry, prin. Fax 686-2701
Other Schools – See Albany, Denham Springs, French Settlement, Holden, Maurepas, Springfield, Walker, Watson

Livonia, Pointe Coupee, Pop. 1,343
Pointe Coupee Parish SD
Supt. — See New Roads
Livonia HS 600/7-12
PO Box 549 70755 225-637-2532
Major Swindler, prin. Fax 637-3024

Lockport, Lafourche, Pop. 2,611
Lafourche Parish SD
Supt. — See Thibodaux
Lockport MS 400/6-8
720 Main St 70374 985-532-2597
Robert Rome, prin. Fax 532-2833

Logansport, DeSoto, Pop. 1,647
De Soto Parish SD
Supt. — See Mansfield
Logansport HS 300/7-12
PO Box 549 71049 318-697-4338
Lillie Giles, prin. Fax 697-6507
Stanley S 400/PK-12
14323 Highway 84 71049 318-697-2664
Carolyn Phillips, prin. Fax 697-5984

Longville, Beauregard
Beauregard Parish SD
Supt. — See Deridder
South Beauregard JSHS 600/6-12
151 Longville Church Rd 70652 337-725-3536
Marlin Ramsey, prin. Fax 725-6222

Loranger, Tangipahoa
Tangipahoa Parish SD
Supt. — See Amite
Loranger HS 500/9-12
PO Box 560 70446 985-878-6271
Billie J. Theriot, prin. Fax 878-4975
Loranger MS 700/4-8
PO Box 469 70446 985-878-9455
Melissa Stilley, prin. Fax 878-4907

Loreauville, Iberia, Pop. 955
Iberia Parish SD
Supt. — See New Iberia
Loreauville JSHS 400/7-12
PO Box 446 70552 337-229-4701
Carole M. Judice, prin. Fax 229-4275

Luling, Saint Charles, Pop. 2,803
St. Charles Parish SD 9,100/PK-12
13855 River Rd 70070 985-785-6289
Dr. Rodney Lafon, supt. Fax 785-1025
www.stcharles.k12.la.us
Smith MS, 281 Sugarland Pkwy 70070 6-8
Dianne Powell, prin. 985-785-6289
Other Schools – See Boutte, Destrehan, Paradis, Saint Rose

Lutcher, Saint James, Pop. 3,632
St. James Parish SD 4,200/PK-12
PO Box 338 70071 225-869-5375
P. Edward Cancienne, supt. Fax 869-8845
www.stjames.k12.la.us
Career & Technology Center Vo/Tech
1410 Buddy Whitney St 70071 225-869-3902
Josehine Oubre, prin. Fax 869-7935
Lutcher HS 1,000/7-12
PO Box 489 70071 225-869-5741
Eugene Hoover, prin. Fax 869-8872
Other Schools – See Saint James, Vacherie

Madisonville, Saint Tammany, Pop. 709
St. Tammany Parish SD
Supt. — See Covington

Madisonville JHS | 400/4-8
PO Box 850 70447 | 985-845-3355
Fran Shea, prin. | Fax 845-9018

Mamou, Evangeline, Pop. 3,438
Evangeline Parish SD
Supt. — See Ville Platte
Mamou JSHS | 600/5-12
1008 7th St 70554 | 337-468-5793
Paula Diane Fontenot, prin. | Fax 468-2220

Mandeville, Saint Tammany, Pop. 11,476
St. Tammany Parish SD
Supt. — See Covington
Fontainebleau HS | 2,100/9-12
100 Bulldog Dr 70471 | 985-892-7112
Johnny Vitrano, prin. | Fax 892-9894
Fontainebleau JHS | 1,200/7-8
100 Hurricane Aly 70471 | 985-875-7501
Dr. Tim Schneider, prin. | Fax 875-7650
Mandeville HS | 1,600/9-12
1 Skipper Dr 70471 | 985-626-5225
Bruce Bundy, prin. | Fax 626-5298
Mandeville JHS | 700/7-8
639 Carondelet St 70448 | 985-626-4428
Mary Ann Cucchiara, prin. | Fax 674-0401
Monteleone JHS | 7-8
63000 Blue Martin Dr 70448 | 985-951-8088
Donna Addison, prin.

Mangham, Richland, Pop. 572
Richland Parish SD
Supt. — See Rayville
Mangham HS | 200/9-12
PO Box 348 71259 | 318-248-2485
Althan Smith, prin. | Fax 248-2406
Mangham JHS | 200/6-8
810 McConnel St 71259 | 318-248-2729
Connie Williams, prin. | Fax 248-2931

Mansfield, DeSoto, Pop. 5,486
De Soto Parish SD | 4,900/PK-12
201 Crosby St 71052 | 318-872-2836
Walter Lee, supt. | Fax 872-1324
www.desoto.k12.la.us
Mansfield HS | 500/9-12
401 Kings Hwy 71052 | 318-872-0793
David Rougeau, prin. | Fax 872-2223
Mansfield MS | 400/6-8
1915 McArthur Dr 71052 | 318-872-1309
Clint Fuller, prin. | Fax 872-1319
Other Schools – See Logansport, Pelican, Stonewall

Louisiana Technical College - Mansfield | Post-Sec.
PO Box 1236 71052 | 318-872-2243

Mansura, Avoyelles, Pop. 1,574
Avoyelles Parish SD
Supt. — See Marksville
Mansura MS | 300/7-8
1869 Saint Jean St 71350 | 318-964-2332
Allen Wanersdorfer, prin. | Fax 964-2110

Many, Sabine, Pop. 2,808
Sabine Parish SD | 4,000/PK-12
PO Box 1079 71449 | 318-256-9228
Dorman Jackson, supt. | Fax 256-0105
www.sabine.k12.la.us
Many HS | 300/9-12
100 Tiger Dr 71449 | 318-256-2114
Wayne Chance, prin. | Fax 256-0492
Many JHS | 500/4-8
1801 Natchitoches Hwy 71449 | 318-256-3573
Madeline Owens, prin. | Fax 256-9619
Other Schools – See Converse, Florien, Negreet, Noble, Pleasant Hill, Zwolle

Louisiana Technical Coll.-Sabine Valley | Post-Sec.
PO Box 790 71449 | 318-256-4101

Marion, Union, Pop. 808
Union Parish SD
Supt. — See Farmerville
Marion S | 200/PK-12
PO Box 67 71260 | 318-292-4410
Nikki Cranford, prin. | Fax 292-4422

Marksville, Avoyelles, Pop. 5,695
Avoyelles Parish SD | 6,800/PK-12
221 Tunica Dr W 71351 | 318-253-5982
Dr. Ronald Mayeux, supt. | Fax 253-5178
avoyellespsb.com
Marksville HS | 600/9-12
407 W Bontemps St 71351 | 318-253-9356
Charles Jones, prin. | Fax 253-4256
Marksville MS | 300/7-8
152 Schoolhouse Rd 71351 | 318-253-8952
Mary Speer, prin. | Fax 253-9955
Other Schools – See Bunkie, Mansura, Moreauville

Marrero, Jefferson, Pop. 36,100
Jefferson Parish SD | 50,300/PK-12
2500 Bent Tree Ln 70072 | 504-349-7600
Diane Roussel, supt. | Fax 349-7960
www.jppss.k12.la.us
Cullier Career Center | Vo/Tech
1429 Ames Blvd Ste B 70072 | 504-340-6963
Rita Foster, prin. | Fax 341-1022
Ehret HS | 2,800/9-12
4300 Patriot St 70072 | 504-340-7651
Clothilde Cobert, prin. | Fax 340-7295
Ellender MS | 1,100/6-8
4501 E Ames Blvd 70072 | 504-341-9469
Frank Rawle, prin. | Fax 348-0054
Higgins HS | 1,700/9-12
7201 Lapalco Blvd 70072 | 504-341-2273
Carolyn H. Van Norman, prin. | Fax 341-8110

Marrero MS | 1,000/6-8
4100 7th St 70072 | 504-341-5842
Earline Bridges, prin. | Fax 341-0004
Truman MS | 900/6-8
5417 Ehret Rd 70072 | 504-341-0961
Tommy Ory, prin. | Fax 347-4497
Other Schools – See Avondale, Grand Isle, Gretna, Harvey, Jefferson, Kenner, Lafitte, Metairie, New Orleans, Westwego

Archbishop Shaw HS | 500/8-12
1000 Barataria Blvd 70072 | 504-340-6727
Rev. Michael Conway, prin. | Fax 347-9883
Immaculata HS | 400/9-12
537 Avenue D 70072 | 504-341-6217
Sr. Maria Colombo, prin. | Fax 341-6229

Maurepas, Livingston
Livingston Parish SD
Supt. — See Livingston
Maurepas S | 400/K-12
PO Box 39 70449 | 225-695-6111
Steve Vampran, prin. | Fax 695-3265

Maurice, Vermilion, Pop. 650
Vermilion Parish SD
Supt. — See Abbeville
North Vermilion HS | 800/7-12
11609 LA Highway 699 70555 | 337-898-1491
Michael Guilbeaux, prin. | Fax 893-8684

Meraux, Saint Bernard, Pop. 8,849

Archbishop Hannan HS | 500/8-12
2501 Archbishop Hannan Blvd 70075 | 504-279-1921
John Serio, prin. | Fax 279-0200

Mer Rouge, Morehouse, Pop. 695
Morehouse Parish SD
Supt. — See Bastrop
Delta JSHS | 300/6-12
PO Box 162 71261 | 318-647-3443
Calvin Dismuke, prin. | Fax 647-5631

Merryville, Beauregard, Pop. 1,131
Beauregard Parish SD
Supt. — See Deridder
Merryville S | 500/K-12
7061 Highway 110 W 70653 | 337-825-8046
Michael Kay, prin. | Fax 825-6443

Metairie, Jefferson, Pop. 145,500
Jefferson Parish SD
Supt. — See Marrero
Adams MS | 800/6-8
5525 Henican Pl 70003 | 504-887-5240
Cheryl Milam, prin. | Fax 887-0173
Bunche MS | 500/6-8
8101 Simon St 70003 | 504-737-3132
D. Dumas, prin. | Fax 737-7606
East Jefferson HS | 1,000/9-12
400 Phlox Ave 70001 | 504-888-7171
James Kytle, prin. | Fax 888-2072
Harris MS | 700/6-8
911 Elise Ave 70003 | 504-733-0867
Otis Guichet, prin. | Fax 733-0953
Haynes MS | 500/6-8
1416 Metairie Rd 70005 | 504-837-8300
Jerome Helmstetter, prin. | Fax 837-2110
King HS | 1,500/9-12
4301 Grace King Pl 70002 | 504-888-7334
Alexander Tiliakos, prin. | Fax 888-2082
Meisler MS | 1,200/6-8
3700 Cleary Ave 70002 | 504-888-5832
Glenn Fallon, prin. | Fax 888-5855

Archbishop Chapelle HS | 1,100/8-12
8800 Veterans Memorial Blvd 70003 | 504-467-3105
Mary Beth Drez, prin. | Fax 466-3191
Archbishop Rummel HS | 1,300/8-12
PO Box 663 70004 | 504-834-5592
Michael Begg, prin. | Fax 832-4016
Blue Cliff College | Post-Sec.
3501 Severn Ave Ste 20 70002 | 504-456-3141
Crescent City Baptist S | 400/PK-12
4828 Utica St 70006 | 504-885-4700
Bill Rigsby, prin. | Fax 885-4703
Ecole Classique S | 500/PK-12
5236 Glendale St 70006 | 504-887-3507
Sal Federico, hdmstr. | Fax 887-8140
Heritage Academy | 100/9-12
2900 Wytchwood Dr 70003 | 504-887-7111
Holy Rosary HS | 100/9-12
2525 Maine Ave 70003 | 504-464-4747
Wiley Ates, prin. | Fax 464-5745
Louisiana Technical College - Jefferson | Post-Sec.
5200 Blair St 70001 | 504-736-7074
Lutheran HS | 200/9-12
3864 17th St 70002 | 504-455-4062
Ron Royuk, prin. | Fax 455-4453
Metairie Park Country Day S | 700/K-12
300 Park Rd 70005 | 504-837-5204
David Drinkwater, prin. | Fax 837-0015
Remington College | Post-Sec.
321 Veterans Memorial Blvd 70005 | 504-831-8889
Ridgewood Prepatory S | 400/PK-12
201 Pasadena Ave 70001 | 504-835-2545
M. J. Montgomery, prin. | Fax 837-1864
St. Martin's Episcopal S | 800/PK-12
5309 Airline Dr 70003 | 504-733-0353
Chris Proctor, hdmstr. | Fax 736-8802

Midland, Acadia
Acadia Parish SD
Supt. — See Crowley

Midland JSHS | 300/8-12
735 S Crocker St 70559 | 337-783-3310
John Briley, prin. | Fax 783-3332

Minden, Webster, Pop. 13,313
Webster Parish SD | 7,200/PK-12
PO Box 520 71058 | 318-377-7052
Wayne Williams, supt. | Fax 377-4114
www.webster.k12.la.us/
Minden HS | 800/9-12
PO Box 838 71058 | 318-377-2766
Morris Busby, prin. | Fax 377-9274
Webster JHS | 500/7-8
700 E Union St 71055 | 318-377-3847
Elena Black, prin. | Fax 377-1943
Other Schools – See Cotton Valley, Doyline, Sarepta, Shongaloo, Sibley, Springhill

Glenbrook S | 300/K-12
1674 Country Club Cir 71055 | 318-377-2135
Darden Gladney, admin. | Fax 377-0578
Louisiana Technical Coll. - NW Louisiana | Post-Sec.
PO Box 835 71058 | 318-371-3035

Monroe, Ouachita, Pop. 52,163
Monroe City SD | 9,400/PK-12
PO Box 4180 71211 | 318-325-0601
Dr. James Dupree, supt. | Fax 323-2864
monroe.k12.la.us/mcs/
Carroll Magnet HS | 700/9-12
PO Box 5040 71211 | 318-387-8441
Donald Green, prin. | Fax 325-6305
Carroll Magnet JHS | 400/7-8
2913 Renwick St 71201 | 318-322-1683
Jimmy Jones, prin. | Fax 322-0833
King MS | 700/6-8
3716 Nutland Rd 71202 | 318-387-1825
Debbie Blue, prin. | Fax 325-4285
Lee JHS | 600/7-8
1600 N 19th St 71201 | 318-323-1143
Tammie McDaniels, prin. | Fax 325-5236
Neville HS | 800/9-12
600 Forsythe Ave 71201 | 318-323-2237
Brent Vidrine, prin. | Fax 387-8774
Wossman HS | 700/9-12
1600 Arizona Ave 71202 | 318-387-2932
Sam Moore, prin. | Fax 322-1378
Ouachita Parish SD | 17,900/PK-12
PO Box 1642 71212 | 318-388-2204
Dr. Robert Webber, supt. | Fax 338-5320
www.opsb.net
Ouachita JHS | 700/7-8
5500 Blanks St 71203 | 318-345-5100
Marsha Dell Baker, prin. | Fax 345-3308
Ouachita Parish HS | 1,100/9-12
681 Highway 594 71203 | 318-343-2769
Todd Guice, prin. | Fax 343-9594
Richwood HS | 400/9-12
5901 Highway 165 Byp 71202 | 318-361-0467
Anthony Killian, prin. | Fax 361-9810
Richwood JHS | 7-8
5901 Highway 165 Byp 71202 | 318-651-0200
Tereatha Chisley, prin. | Fax 398-9825
Sterlington HS | 400/7-12
233 Keystone Rd 71203 | 318-665-2725
Ross Davis, prin. | Fax 665-2727
Other Schools – See Calhoun, West Monroe

Career Technical College | Post-Sec.
2319 Louisville Ave 71201 | 318-323-2889
Cloyd's Beauty School #2 | Post-Sec.
1311 Winnsboro Rd 71202 | 318-322-5314
Cloyd's Beauty School #3 | Post-Sec.
2514 Ferrand St 71201 | 318-322-5314
Excelsior Christian S | 200/PK-12
3220 Highway 165 71202 | 318-387-7333
Dr. Robert Sheridan, prin. | Fax 387-7330
Ouachita Christian S | 800/PK-12
7065 Highway 165 N 71203 | 318-325-6000
William Stokes, hdmstr. | Fax 387-7000
Pat Goins Beauty School | Post-Sec.
3138 Louisville Ave 71201 | 318-322-0796
River Oaks S | 300/PK-12
600 Hideaway Rd 71203 | 318-343-4185
Dr. William Middleton, prin. | Fax 343-1107
St. Francis Medical Center | Post-Sec.
PO Box 1901 71210 | 318-327-4141
St. Frederick HS | 400/7-12
3300 Westminister Ave 71201 | 318-323-9636
Jennifer Malone, prin. | Fax 323-7456
University of Louisiana at Monroe | Post-Sec.
700 University Ave 71209 | 318-342-1000

Montegut, Terrebonne, Pop. 1,784
Terrebonne Parish SD
Supt. — See Houma
Montegut MS | 600/5-8
138 Dolphin St 70377 | 985-594-5886
Catherine Telford, prin. | Fax 594-9666

Monterey, Concordia
Concordia Parish SD
Supt. — See Vidalia
Monterey S | 400/PK-12
PO Box 127 71354 | 318-386-2214
Neeva Sibley, prin. | Fax 386-7356

Montgomery, Grant, Pop. 795
Grant Parish SD
Supt. — See Colfax
Montgomery HS | 300/7-12
PO Box 428 71454 | 318-646-2879
Vickey Dubois, prin. | Fax 646-3926

Moreauville, Avoyelles, Pop. 931
Avoyelles Parish SD
  Supt. — See Marksville
Avoyelles HS   500/9-12
  287 Main St 71355   318-985-2361
  Bruce Juneau, prin.   Fax 985-2786

Morgan City, Saint Mary, Pop. 12,282
St. Mary Parish SD
  Supt. — See Centerville
Morgan City HS   700/9-12
  2400 Tiger Dr 70380   985-384-1754
  Peter Boudreaux, prin.   Fax 384-7054
Morgan City JHS   400/7-8
  911 Marguerite St 70380   985-384-5922
  Kenneth Holmes, prin.   Fax 385-4170
Morgan City Adult Education   Adult
  PO Box 830 70381   985-385-0502
  Vincent Holcomb, coord.

Central Catholic HS   200/7-12
  2100 Cedar St 70380   985-385-5372
  Vic Bonnaffee, prin.   Fax 385-3444
Immanuel Christian S   200/PK-12
  901 Fig St 70380   985-385-2129
  Gwen Ross, admin.   Fax 385-3041
Louisiana Tech. Coll. - Young Memorial   Post-Sec.
  PO Box 2148 70381   985-380-2436

Morganza, Pointe Coupee, Pop. 635
Pointe Coupee Parish SD
  Supt. — See New Roads
Pointe Coupee Central HS   700/7-12
  8434 Pointe Coupee Rd 70759   225-638-3085
  Larry Oliver, prin.   Fax 638-9595

Mount Hermon, Washington
Washington Parish SD
  Supt. — See Franklinton
Mount Hermon S   500/PK-12
  36119 Highway 38 70450   985-877-4642
  Ruth Stoudenmier, prin.   Fax 877-4710

Napoleonville, Assumption, Pop. 699
Assumption Parish SD   4,100/PK-12
  4901 Highway 308 70390   985-369-7251
  Earl Martinez, supt.   Fax 369-2530
  www.assumption.k12.la.us
Assumption HS   1,100/9-12
  PO Box 830 70390   985-369-2956
  Joey Comeaux, prin.   Fax 369-6252
Napoleonville MS   400/5-8
  4847 Highway 1 70390   985-369-6587
  Craig Stephens, prin.   Fax 369-6595
Other Schools – See Belle Rose, Labadieville

Natchitoches, Natchitoches, Pop. 18,113
Natchitoches Parish SD   6,700/PK-12
  310 Royal St 71457   318-352-2358
  Elwanda Murphy, supt.   Fax 352-8138
  www.nat.k12.la.us/
Natchitoches Central HS   1,300/9-12
  6513 Highway 1 Byp 71457   318-352-2211
  Ronald Waites, prin.   Fax 357-8837
Natchitoches JHS   400/7-8
  1621 Welch St 71457   318-357-9410
  Mona Bamburg, prin.   Fax 357-8677
NSU Middle Lab S   200/6-8
  NSU Campus 71497   318-357-4509
  Drew Moore, prin.   Fax 357-4260
Other Schools – See Campti

Louisiana Technical College-Natchitoches   Post-Sec.
  PO Box 657 71458   318-357-3162
Northwestern State University   Post-Sec.
  College Ave 71497   318-357-6361
St. Mary's S   500/PK-12
  PO Box 2070 71457   318-352-8394
  Mark Shamburger, prin.   Fax 352-5798

Negreet, Sabine
Sabine Parish SD
  Supt. — See Many
Negreet S   400/PK-12
  PO Box 14 71460   318-256-2349
  Dan Salter, prin.   Fax 256-5868

Newellton, Tensas, Pop. 1,389
Tensas Parish SD
  Supt. — See Saint Joseph
Newellton JSHS   200/7-12
  400 Verona St 71357   318-467-5109
  Don Barton, prin.   Fax 467-5108

New Iberia, Iberia, Pop. 32,502
Iberia Parish SD   14,200/PK-12
  PO Box 200 70562   337-365-2341
  E. Baudry, supt.   Fax 365-6996
  www.iberia.k12.la.us
Anderson Street MS   500/7-8
  1059 Anderson St 70560   337-365-3932
    Fax 367-8285
Belle Place MS   500/7-8
  4110 Loreauville Rd 70563   337-364-2141
  Bertha Myers, prin.   Fax 365-9463
Iberia MS   700/7-8
  613 Weeks Island Rd 70560   337-364-3927
  Michael Bonin, prin.   Fax 365-9681
Iberia Parish Career Center   Vo/Tech
  618 Recreation Dr 70560   337-365-7231
  Nathan Cormier, prin.   Fax 367-0875
New Iberia HS   1,600/9-12
  1301 E Admiral Doyle Dr 70560   337-369-6412
  Jean Reaux, prin.   Fax 364-6920
Westgate HS   1,200/9-12
  2305 Jefferson Island Rd 70560   337-365-2431
  James Gray, prin.   Fax 364-3487

Other Schools – See Delcambre, Jeanerette, Loreauville

Assembly Christian S   300/K-12
  4219 E Admiral Doyle Dr 70560   337-364-4340
  Armand Prentiss, prin.   Fax 364-8310
Catholic HS   900/4-12
  1301 Delasalle Dr 70560   337-364-5116
  Dr. Timothy Uhl, prin.   Fax 364-5041
Highland Baptist Christian S   400/PK-12
  708 Angers St 70563   337-364-2273
  Janie Lamothe, admin.   Fax 369-6303
Louisiana Technical College - Teche Area   Post-Sec.
  PO Box 11057 70562   337-373-0011
Neill Institute   Post-Sec.
  1301A W Saint Peter St 70560   337-365-6570
Vortex Helicopters   Post-Sec.
  PO Box 9789 70562   228-864-7357

New Orleans, Orleans, Pop. 469,032
Jefferson Parish SD
  Supt. — See Marrero
Taylor S for Science & Tech   7-9
  822 S Clearview Pkwy 70123   504-736-1873
  Kristy Haber, prin.   Fax 736-1856

Orleans Parish SD   10,400/PK-12
  401 Nashville Ave 70115   504-304-5686
  Anthony Amato, supt.   Fax 304-6286
  www.nops.k12.la.us/
McDonogh 35 HS   1,300/7-12
  1331 Kerlerec St 70116   504-942-3592
  Philip White, prin.   Fax 945-0677
McMain Magnet JSHS   1,300/7-12
  5712 S Claiborne Ave 70125   504-862-5117
  Bridgitte Frick, prin.   Fax 862-5123
New Orleans Science and Math HS   700/9-12
  5625 Loyola Ave 70124   504-324-7061
Orleans Parish PM S   7-12
  5712 S Claiborne Ave 70125   504-239-3685
  Tyrone Casby, prin.

Recovery SD
  Supt. — See Baton Rouge
Clark HS   500/9-12
  1301 N Derbigny St 70116   504-827-4519
  Tracy Guillory, prin.   Fax 827-4537
Cohen HS   800/9-12
  3520 Dryades St 70115   877-453-2721
Douglass HS   800/9-12
  3820 Saint Claude Ave 70117   877-453-2721
McDonogh HS   1,200/9-12
  2426 Esplanade Ave 70119   877-453-2721
Rabouin HS   Vo/Tech
  737 Carondelet St 70130   877-453-2721
Reed S   1,700/K-12
  5316 Michoud Blvd 70129   877-453-2721
Washington HS   500/9-12
  1201 S Roman St 70125   877-453-2721

Academy of the Sacred Heart   200/5-8
  4521 Saint Charles Ave 70115   504-891-1943
  Sr. Cynthia Vives, prin.   Fax 891-2755
Academy of the Sacred Heart   300/9-12
  4521 Saint Charles Ave 70115   504-891-1943
  Sr. Lynne Lieux, prin.   Fax 891-9744
Bishop McManus Academy   200/PK-12
  8801 Chef Menteur Hwy 70127   504-390-4858
  Tammy McManus, admin.   Fax 324-0268
Bishop Perry MS   100/5-8
  1941 Dauphine St 70116   504-943-3734
  Rev. David Theroux, prin.   Fax 943-1320
Brother Martin HS   1,500/8-12
  4401 Elysian Fields Ave 70122   504-283-1561
  Gerald Tullier, prin.   Fax 286-8462
Bryman College   Post-Sec.
  824 Elmwood Park Blvd # 110 70123   504-733-7117
Cabrini HS   400/8-12
  1400 Moss St 70119   504-483-8695
  Yvonne Hrapmann, prin.   Fax 483-8671
Cameron College   Post-Sec.
  PO Box 19288 70119   504-821-5881
Charity-Delgado School of Nursing   Post-Sec.
  450 S Claiborne Ave 70112   504-568-6483
Culinary Institute of New Orleans   Post-Sec.
  2100 Saint Charles Ave 70130   504-525-2433
De La Salle HS   700/8-12
  5300 Saint Charles Ave 70115   504-895-5717
  Gina Hall, prin.   Fax 895-1300
Delgado Community College   Post-Sec.
  615 City Park Ave 70119   504-483-4114
Desire Street Academy   200/7-12
  PO Box 26966 70186   504-945-5548
Dillard University   Post-Sec.
  2601 Gentilly Blvd 70122   504-816-4670
Eastern College of Health Vocations   Post-Sec.
  201 Evans Rd 70123   504-885-3353
Faith Christian Academy   300/K-12
  13123 I 10 Service Rd 70128   504-248-1120
Holy Cross HS   900/5-12
  4950 Dauphine St 70117   504-942-3100
  Dr. Joseph H. Murry, prin.   Fax 943-7676
Jesuit HS   1,400/8-12
  4133 Banks St 70119   504-486-6631
  Michael Giambelluca, prin.   Fax 483-3942
John Jay Beauty College   Post-Sec.
  540 Robert E Lee Blvd 70124   504-282-8128
Louisiana State University   Post-Sec.
  1100 Florida Ave 70119   504-948-8530
Louisiana State Univ. Health Sci. Center   Post-Sec.
  433 Bolivar St 70112   504-568-4808
Loyola University New Orleans   Post-Sec.
  6363 Saint Charles Ave 70118   504-865-2011
Marian Central MS   400/6-8
  2221 Mendez St 70122   504-288-1411
  Emily M. Paul, prin.   Fax 286-0209

McGehee S   400/PK-12
  2343 Prytania St 70130   504-561-1224
  Eileen Powers, prin.   Fax 525-7910
Medical Center of Louisiana/Charity Cmps   Post-Sec.
  1532 Tulane Ave 70112   504-568-2311
Moler Beauty College   Post-Sec.
  3968 Old Gentilly Rd 70126   504-282-2539
Moler Beauty College   Post-Sec.
  2940 Canal St 70119   504-821-8842
Mt. Carmel Academy   1,300/9-12
  7027 Milne Blvd 70124   504-288-7626
  Sr. Camille Anne Campbell, prin.   Fax 288-7629
Newcomb College of Tulane University   Post-Sec.
  1229 Broadway St 70118   504-865-5594
Newman S   900/PK-12
  1903 Jefferson Ave 70115   504-899-5641
  Thomas Price, hdmstr.   Fax 896-8597
New Orleans Baptist Theological Seminary   Post-Sec.
  3939 Gentilly Blvd 70126   504-282-4455
New Orleans Job Corps Center   Post-Sec.
  3801 Hollygrove St 70118   504-486-0641
New Orleans School of Urban Missions   Post-Sec.
  PO Box 53344 70153   800-385-6364
Notre Dame Seminary   Post-Sec.
  2901 S Carrollton Ave 70118   504-866-7426
Ochsner School of Allied Health Sciences   Post-Sec.
  1516 Jefferson Hwy 70121   504-842-3267
Our Lady of Holy Cross College   Post-Sec.
  4123 Woodland Dr 70131   504-394-7744
Redeemer-Seton HS   300/9-12
  1453 Crescent Dr 70122   504-288-1494
  Joan Johnson, prin.   Fax 288-1499
St. Augustine HS   700/7-12
  2600 A P Tureaud Ave 70119   504-944-2424
  Rev. Raphael Velazquez, prin.   Fax 947-7712
St. Marys Academy   600/7-12
  6905 Chef Menteur Hwy 70126   504-245-0200
  Sr. Jennie Jones, prin.   Fax 245-8732
St. Marys Dominican HS   1,100/8-12
  7701 Walmsley Ave 70125   504-865-9401
  Dr. Nancy Autin, prin.   Fax 866-5958
Southern University in New Orleans   Post-Sec.
  6400 Press Dr 70126   504-286-5000
Stevenson's Academy of Hair Design   Post-Sec.
  2039 Lapeyrouse St 70116   504-945-2312
Stevenson's Academy of Hair Design   Post-Sec.
  401 Opelousas Ave 70114   504-368-6377
Touro Infirmary   Post-Sec.
  1401 Foucher St 70115   504-897-8244
Tulane University   Post-Sec.
  6823 Saint Charles Ave 70118   504-865-4000
University of New Orleans 70148   Post-Sec.
    504-280-6000
Ursuline Academy HS   400/9-12
  2635 State St 70118   504-861-9150
  Nancy Hernandez, prin.   Fax 861-7392
William Carey College   Post-Sec.
  3939 Gentilly Blvd # 309 70126   504-865-1502
Xavier University   Post-Sec.
  1 Drexel Dr 70125   504-486-7411
Xavier University Prep HS   400/9-12
  5116 Magazine St 70115   504-899-6061
  Carolyn Oubre, prin.   Fax 891-8766

New Roads, Pointe Coupee, Pop. 4,876
Pointe Coupee Parish SD   2,800/PK-12
  PO Box 579 70760   225-638-8674
  Dr. Daniel Raws, supt.   Fax 638-3904
Other Schools – See Livonia, Morganza

Catholic HS of Pte. Coupee   600/7-12
  504 4th St W 70760   225-638-3469
  Marsha Langlois, prin.   Fax 638-6471
False River Academy   600/PK-12
  201 Major Pkwy 70760   225-638-3783
  Kenneth LeBeau, prin.   Fax 638-8555
Louisiana Technical College - Jumonville   Post-Sec.
  605 Hospital Rd 70760   225-342-3070

Noble, Sabine, Pop. 263
Sabine Parish SD
  Supt. — See Many
Ebarb S   400/PK-12
  5340 Highway 482 71462   318-645-9402
  Victor Sepulvado, prin.   Fax 645-4689

Oakdale, Allen, Pop. 7,992
Allen Parish SD
  Supt. — See Oberlin
Oakdale HS   300/9-12
  101 S 13th St 71463   318-335-2338
  Danny Hindmon, prin.   Fax 335-3257
Oakdale JHS   400/5-8
  124 S 13th St 71463   318-335-1558
  Linda Thompson, prin.   Fax 335-4690

Louisiana Technical College - Oakdale   Post-Sec.
  PO Box EM 71463   318-335-3944

Oak Grove, West Carroll, Pop. 2,126
West Carroll Parish SD   2,400/PK-12
  314 E Main St 71263   318-428-2378
  Jerry Dosher, supt.   Fax 428-3775
  www.wcpsb.com
Oak Grove JSHS   400/7-12
  501 W Main St 71263   318-428-2308
  Mark Bowman, prin.   Fax 428-2311
Other Schools – See Epps, Forest, Kilbourne

Oberlin, Allen, Pop. 1,859
Allen Parish SD   4,200/PK-12
  PO Box C 70655   337-639-4311
  Michael Doucet, supt.   Fax 639-2346
  www.allen.k12.la.us

Oberlin HS
　PO Box D　70655　300/7-12
　Peter LeBas, prin.　337-639-4341
　　　　Fax 639-2508
Other Schools – See Elizabeth, Grant, Kinder, Oakdale,
　Reeves

Covenant Christian S　100/PK-12
　PO Box H　70655　337-639-9227
　William Currie, prin.　Fax 639-4465

Olla, LaSalle, Pop. 1,375
LaSalle Parish SD
　Supt. — See Jena
LaSalle HS　200/9-12
　PO Box 458　71465　318-495-5165
　Ronda Richardson, prin.　Fax 495-5503

Opelousas, Saint Landry, Pop. 22,753
St. Landry Parish SD　15,600/PK-12
　PO Box 310　70571　337-948-3657
　Lanny Moreau, supt.　Fax 942-0204
　www.slp.k12.la.us
Northwest HS　500/8-12
　3746 Highway 104　70570　337-543-2255
　Raymond Cassimere, prin.　Fax 543-8796
Opelousas HS　1,100/9-12
　PO Box 1269　70571　337-942-5634
　Rodney Johnson, prin.　Fax 942-6219
Opelousas JHS　600/7-8
　PO Box 130　70571　337-942-4957
　Ryan Hooks, prin.　Fax 942-2659
St. Landry Accelerated Transition S　50/7-8
　152 Violet Dr　70570　337-948-4763
　Walter Phythian, prin.　Fax 948-9792
St. Landry Adult Education　Adult
　PO Box 660　70571　337-948-8525
　Evavattae Green, prin.
Other Schools – See Arnaudville, Eunice, Port Barre,
　Washington

Acadiana Preparatory S　200/PK-12
　1592 E Prudhomme St　70570　337-948-6551
　John Doyel, prin.　Fax 948-1006
Louisiana Technical College - T H Harris　Post-Sec.
　332 E South St　70570　337-948-0239
Opelousas Catholic S　700/K-12
　428 E Prudhomme St　70570　337-942-5404
　Perry Fontenot, prin.　Fax 942-5922
Opelousas School of Cosmetology　Post-Sec.
　529 E Vine St　70570　337-942-6147
Westminster Christian Academy　600/PK-12
　186 Westminster Dr　70570　337-948-8607
　William A. Thompson, supt.　Fax 948-8983

Paradis, Saint Charles
St. Charles Parish SD
　Supt. — See Luling
Martin MS　600/7-8
　434 South St　70080　985-758-7579
　Erin Raiford, prin.　Fax 758-7570

Parks, Saint Martin, Pop. 536
St. Martin Parish SD
　Supt. — See Saint Martinville
Parks MS　400/5-8
　1010A Saint Louis Dr　70582　337-845-4753
　Roger Wiltz, prin.　Fax 845-5532

Patterson, Saint Mary, Pop. 5,156
St. Mary Parish SD
　Supt. — See Centerville
Patterson HS　500/9-12
　2525 Main St　70392　985-395-2675
　Michael Brocato, prin.　Fax 395-5453
Patterson JHS　700/4-8
　1101 1st St　70392　985-395-6772
　Molly Stadalis, prin.　Fax 395-6773

Pearl River, Saint Tammany, Pop. 1,932
St. Tammany Parish SD
　Supt. — See Covington
Creekside JHS　500/6-8
　65434 Highway 41　70452　985-863-5882
　Lisa Virga, prin.　Fax 863-7658
Pearl River HS　600/9-12
　39110 Taylor St　70452　985-863-2591
　Michael Winkler, prin.　Fax 863-5934

Pelican, DeSoto
De Soto Parish SD
　Supt. — See Mansfield
Pelican All Saints S　200/PK-12
　200 All Saints Rd　71063　318-755-2318
　Toras Hill, prin.　Fax 755-2066

Pine Prairie, Evangeline, Pop. 1,160
Evangeline Parish SD
　Supt. — See Ville Platte
Pine Prairie S　800/PK-12
　PO Box 200　70576　337-599-2300
　Marvelyn Harris, prin.　Fax 599-2003

Pineville, Rapides, Pop. 13,858
Rapides Parish SD
　Supt. — See Alexandria
Pineville HS　1,100/8-12
　1511 Line St　71360　318-442-8990
　Dewayne Lemoine, prin.　Fax 487-1984
Pineville JHS　600/7-8
　501 Edgewood Dr　71360　318-640-0512
　Columbus Goodman, prin.　Fax 640-9692
Slocum Learning Center　Adult
　901 Crepe Myrtle St　71360　318-445-7185
　David Phillips, prin.

Louisiana College　Post-Sec.
　PO Box 560　71359　318-487-7011

Pineville Beauty School　Post-Sec.
　1008 Main St　71360　318-445-1040

Pitkin, Vernon
Vernon Parish SD
　Supt. — See Leesville
Pitkin S　600/PK-12
　PO Box 307　70656　318-358-3121
　Roger Willis, prin.　Fax 358-3580

Plain Dealing, Bossier, Pop. 1,049
Bossier Parish SD
　Supt. — See Benton
Plain Dealing HS　100/9-12
　300 E Vance St　71064　318-326-7700
　Aubrey Sayes, prin.　Fax 326-7713
Plain Dealing MS　100/6-8
　279 Vance St　71064　318-326-7780
　Aubrey Sayes, prin.　Fax 326-7788

Plain Dealing Academy　100/PK-12
　200 Garrett St　71064　318-326-5823

Plaquemine, Iberville, Pop. 6,894
Iberville Parish SD　4,200/PK-12
　PO Box 151　70765　225-687-4341
　Martin Bera, supt.　Fax 687-5408
　www.ipsb.net
Gay MS　500/5-8
　PO Box 717　70765　225-687-6845
　Dianna Outlaw, prin.　Fax 687-6826
Plaquemine HS　700/9-12
　PO Box 326　70765　225-687-6367
　Russell Plasczyk, prin.　Fax 687-4422
Other Schools – See Rosedale, Saint Gabriel, White
　Castle

Louisiana Technical College - Westside　Post-Sec.
　59125 Bayou Rd　70764　225-687-6392
St. John HS　200/9-12
　24250 Regina St　70764　225-687-3056
　Perry Le Grange, prin.　Fax 687-3530

Plaucheville, Avoyelles, Pop. 278

St. Joseph S　400/PK-12
　PO Box 59　71362　318-922-3401
　Michael DeCook, prin.　Fax 922-3776

Pleasant Hill, Sabine, Pop. 711
Sabine Parish SD
　Supt. — See Many
Pleasant Hill S　300/PK-12
　PO Box 8　71065　318-796-3670
　Curt Nix, prin.　Fax 796-2644

Ponchatoula, Tangipahoa, Pop. 5,450
Tangipahoa Parish SD
　Supt. — See Amite
Ponchatoula HS　1,400/9-12
　19452 Highway 22　70454　985-386-3514
　Cynthia Foster, prin.　Fax 386-0011
Ponchatoula JHS　700/7-8
　315 E Oak St　70454　985-370-5322
　Vic Bender, prin.　Fax 370-5327

Port Allen, West Baton Rouge, Pop. 5,150
West Baton Rouge Parish SD　3,500/PK-12
　3761 Rosedale Rd　70767　225-343-8309
　David Corona, supt.　Fax 387-2101
　www.wbrschools.net
Devall MS　300/4-8
　11851 N River Rd　70767　225-627-4268
　John Currier, prin.　Fax 627-9252
Port Allen HS　500/9-12
　3553 Rosedale Rd　70767　225-383-1107
　Warren LeJeune, prin.　Fax 344-6312
Port Allen MS　300/5-8
　610 Rosedale Rd　70767　225-383-5777
　JoAnn Grimes, prin.　Fax 383-8811
Other Schools – See Brusly

Port Barre, Saint Landry, Pop. 2,290
St. Landry Parish SD
　Supt. — See Opelousas
Port Barre MS　400/5-8
　PO Box 69　70577　337-585-7256
　William Edgar Duplechain, prin.　Fax 585-2290
Port Barre MSHS　700/5-12
　PO Box 69　70577　337-585-7256
　William Duplechain, prin.　Fax 585-2290

Port Sulphur, Plaquemines, Pop. 3,523
Plaquemines Parish SD　3,600/PK-12
　PO Box 70　70083　985-564-2743
　James Hoyle, supt.　Fax 564-9100
　www.ppsb.org/
Port Sulphur HS　200/9-12
　164 School Rd　70083　985-564-2423
　Terri Ancar, prin.　Fax 564-2842
Other Schools – See Belle Chasse, Boothville,
　Braithwaite, Buras

Prairieville, Ascension
Ascension Parish SD
　Supt. — See Donaldsonville
Galvez MS　700/5-8
　42018 Highway 933　70769　225-621-2424
　Linda Embry, prin.　Fax 621-2434
Prairieville MS　500/5-8
　16200 Highway 930　70769　225-621-2340
　Diane Gautreau, prin.　Fax 673-4883

Pride, East Baton Rouge
East Baton Rouge Parish SD
　Supt. — See Baton Rouge

Northeast JSHS　700/7-12
　13700 Pride Port Hudson Rd　70770　225-654-5808
　Jessie LeBlanc, prin.　Fax 654-5591

Quitman, Jackson, Pop. 167
Jackson Parish SD
　Supt. — See Jonesboro
Quitman S　500/PK-12
　PO Box 38　71268　318-259-2698
　Steve Shovan, prin.　Fax 259-1139

Raceland, Lafourche, Pop. 5,564
Lafourche Parish SD
　Supt. — See Thibodaux
Central Lafourche HS　1,400/9-12
　4820 Highway 1　70394　985-532-3319
　Blaine Degruise, prin.　Fax 532-3822
Raceland MS　800/6-8
　PO Box C　70394　985-537-6528
　Ann Danos, prin.　Fax 537-5182
Opportunity Place　Adult
　196 Johnny Dufrene Dr　70394　985-532-3114
　　　　Fax 532-6112

Rayne, Acadia, Pop. 8,537
Acadia Parish SD
　Supt. — See Crowley
Armstrong MS　500/6-8
　700 Martin Luther King Blvd　70578　337-334-3377
　Marshall Thibodeaux, prin.　Fax 334-2681
Rayne HS　600/9-12
　1016 N Polk St　70578　337-334-3691
　Bobby Hamlin, prin.　Fax 334-5568

Rayville, Richland, Pop. 4,116
Richland Parish SD　3,900/PK-12
　PO Box 599　71269　318-728-5964
　Cathy Stockton, supt.　Fax 728-6366
　www.richland.k12.la.us
Rayville HS　500/9-12
　193 Highway 3048　71269　318-728-3296
　Dr. Georgia Ineichen, prin.　Fax 728-5652
Rayville JHS　300/6-8
　225 Highway 3048　71269　318-728-3618
　Tony Guirlando, prin.　Fax 728-9374
Other Schools – See Delhi, Mangham

Riverfield Academy　400/PK-12
　115 Wood St　71269　318-728-3281
　Marie Miller, prin.　Fax 728-3285

Reeves, Allen, Pop. 210
Allen Parish SD
　Supt. — See Oberlin
Reeves S　300/PK-12
　PO Box 100　70658　337-666-2414
　Donald Bennett, prin.　Fax 666-2812

Reserve, Saint John the Baptist, Pop. 8,847
St. John The Baptist Parish SD　6,400/PK-12
　PO Box AL　70084　985-536-1106
　Michael K. Coburn, supt.　Fax 536-1109
　www.stjohn.k12.la.us
East St. John HS　1,300/9-12
　1 Wildcat Dr　70084　985-536-4226
　Debbie Schum, prin.　Fax 536-4286
Other Schools – See Edgard

Louisiana Tech. Coll. - River Parishes　Post-Sec.
　PO Box AQ　70084　985-536-4418
Reserve Christian S　300/PK-12
　PO Box AA　70084　985-536-2418
　Rod Aguillard, prin.　Fax 479-3135
Riverside Academy　700/PK-12
　332 Railroad Ave　70084　985-536-4246
　Heidi Tomeny-Duhe, prin.　Fax 536-2127

Ringgold, Bienville, Pop. 1,592
Bienville Parish SD
　Supt. — See Arcadia
Ringgold JSHS　300/7-12
　4044 Bienville Rd # B　71068　318-894-2271
　William Davis, prin.　Fax 894-4444

River Ridge, Jefferson, Pop. 14,800

Curtis Christian S　600/PK-12
　10125 Jefferson Hwy　70123　504-737-4621
　John Curtis, prin.　Fax 737-7326

Roanoke, Jefferson Davis
Jefferson Davis Parish SD
　Supt. — See Jennings
Welsh-Roanoke JHS　200/6-8
　PO Box 9　70581　337-753-2317
　Kenneth Lasserre, prin.　Fax 753-2245

Rosedale, Iberville, Pop. 739
Iberville Parish SD
　Supt. — See Plaquemine
North Iberville S　500/PK-12
　PO Box 200　70772　225-625-2522
　Wyvetta Parker, prin.　Fax 625-2559

Rosepine, Vernon, Pop. 1,386
Vernon Parish SD
　Supt. — See Leesville
Rosepine JSHS　400/7-12
　PO Box 369　70659　337-463-6079
　Steve Thomas, prin.　Fax 462-6132

Ruston, Lincoln, Pop. 20,634
Lincoln Parish SD　6,300/PK-12
　410 S Farmerville St　71270　318-255-1430
　Danny Bell, supt.　Fax 255-3203
　www.lincolnschools.org/

Lincoln Parish Career Academy Vo/Tech
1428 Arlington St 71270 318-254-2096
Foster Harris, prin. Fax 254-1247
Ruston HS 1,200/9-12
900 Bearcat Dr 71270 318-255-0807
Kenny Henderson, prin. Fax 251-2202
Ruston JHS 600/7-8
481 Tarbutton Rd 71270 318-251-1601
Tim Nutt, prin. Fax 254-5235
Other Schools – See Choudrant, Dubach, Grambling, Simsboro

Bethel Christian S 100/K-12
2901 Winona Dr 71270 318-255-1112
Cedar Creek S 700/PK-12
2400 Cedar Creek Dr 71270 318-255-7707
Connie Bradford, prin. Fax 251-2846
Louisiana Technical College - Ruston Post-Sec.
PO Box 1070 71273 318-251-4145
Louisiana Tech University Post-Sec.
PO Box 3168 71272 318-257-0211
Pat Goins Ruston Beauty School Post-Sec.
213 W Alabama Ave 71270 318-255-2717

Saint Amant, Ascension
Ascension Parish SD
Supt. — See Donaldsonville
Saint Amant HS 1,300/9-12
12035 Highway 431 70774 225-621-2565
Doug Moreau, prin. Fax 621-2573
Saint Amant MS 600/5-8
44317 Highway 429 70774 225-621-2600
Brenda Holmes, prin. Fax 621-2593

Saint Benedict, Saint Tammany

St. Joseph Seminary College 70457 Post-Sec.
985-892-1800

Saint Francisville, West Feliciana, Pop. 1,672
West Feliciana Parish SD 2,400/PK-12
PO Box 1910 70775 225-635-3891
Lloyd Lindsey, supt. Fax 635-0108
www.wfpsb.org
West Feliciana HS 600/9-12
PO Box 580 70775 225-635-4561
Michael Thornhill, prin. Fax 635-5588
West Feliciana MS 500/6-8
PO Box 690 70775 225-635-3898
Al Lemoine, prin. Fax 635-6925

Saint Gabriel, Iberville, Pop. 5,527
Iberville Parish SD
Supt. — See Plaquemine
East Iberville S 500/PK-12
3285 Highway 75 70776 225-642-5410
Lionel Johnson, prin. Fax 642-9607

Saint James, Saint James
St. James Parish SD
Supt. — See Lutcher
Saint James HS 700/7-12
PO Box 101 70086 225-265-3911
Harry Francois, prin. Fax 265-2455

Saint Joseph, Tensas, Pop. 1,222
Tensas Parish SD 500/PK-12
PO Box 318 71366 318-766-3269
Carol Johnson, supt. Fax 766-3634
www.tensas.k12.la.us/
Davidson HS 200/7-12
720 Plank Rd 71366 318-766-3585
Noah Johnson, prin. Fax 766-7988
Other Schools – See Newellton

Tensas Academy 200/PK-12
PO Box 555 71366 318-766-4384
Bonnie Adcock, prin. Fax 766-3559

Saint Martinville, Saint Martin, Pop. 6,993
St. Martin Parish SD 8,600/PK-12
PO Box 859 70582 337-394-6261
E.R. Valerie Haaga, supt. Fax 394-6387
www.stmartin.k12.la.us
St. Martinville HS 900/9-12
762 N Main St 70582 337-394-3135
Michael Kreamer, prin. Fax 394-9702
St. Martinville JHS 300/7-8
7190 Main Hwy 70582 337-394-4764
James Skipper, prin. Fax 394-9619
Other Schools – See Breaux Bridge, Cecilia, Parks

Louisiana Technical College - Evangeline Post-Sec.
PO Box 68 70582 337-394-6466

Saint Rose, Saint Charles, Pop. 6,259
St. Charles Parish SD
Supt. — See Luling
Cammon MS 300/6-8
234 Pirate Dr 70087 504-467-4536
Sylvia Zeno, prin. Fax 468-3873

ITT Technical Institute Post-Sec.
140 James Dr E 70087 504-463-0338

Saline, Bienville, Pop. 290
Bienville Parish SD
Supt. — See Arcadia
Saline S 300/PK-12
PO Box 129 71070 318-576-3215
Tony Hough, prin. Fax 576-9068

Sarepta, Webster, Pop. 914
Webster Parish SD
Supt. — See Minden

Sarepta S 500/K-12
6041 Highway 2 71071 318-847-4301
William Franklin, prin. Fax 847-4891

Scott, Lafayette, Pop. 7,885
Lafayette Parish SD
Supt. — See Lafayette
Scott MS 900/5-8
PO Box 427 70583 337-235-9698
Ron LeBlanc, prin. Fax 235-9805

Shongaloo, Webster, Pop. 158
Webster Parish SD
Supt. — See Minden
Shongaloo S 300/K-12
229 Highway Alt 2 71072 318-846-2541
Cynthia Hair, prin. Fax 846-2891

Shreveport, Caddo, Pop. 198,364
Bossier Parish SD
Supt. — See Benton
Bossier Parish Technical S Vo/Tech
2010 N Market St 71107 318-676-7811
Carol Johnston, prin. Fax 676-7805

Caddo Parish SD 42,800/PK-12
PO Box 32000 71130 318-603-6300
Ollie Tyler, supt. Fax 631-5241
www.caddo.k12.la.us/
Bethune MS 700/6-8
4331 Henry St 71109 318-636-6336
Perry Daniel, prin. Fax 636-6812
Bickham MS 700/6-8
7240 Old Mooringsport Rd 71107 318-929-4106
James Windham, prin. Fax 929-2416
Broadmoor MS Laboratory 700/6-8
441 Atlantic Ave 71105 318-861-2403
Kimberly Brun, prin. Fax 865-4142
Byrd HS 2,000/9-12
3201 Line Ave 71104 318-869-2567
Jerry Badgley, prin. Fax 869-2253
Caddo Career/Tech Center Vo/Tech
5950 Union Ave 71108 318-636-5150
Gayle Flowers, prin. Fax 621-9138
Caddo Middle Career & Tech Center Vo/Tech
6310 Clift Ave 71106 318-868-2753
Curtis Hooks, prin. Fax 868-2755
Caddo Parish Magnet HS 1,100/9-12
1601 Viking Dr 71101 318-221-2501
Mary Rounds, prin. Fax 227-1393
Caddo Parish Magnet MS 1,200/6-8
7635 Cornelious Ln 71106 318-868-6588
Kay Robinson, prin. Fax 865-6125
Captain Shreve HS 1,100/9-12
6115 E Kings Hwy 71105 318-865-7137
Dr. Sandra McCalla, prin. Fax 865-5041
Clark MS 800/6-8
351 Hearne Ave 71103 318-425-8742
Lewis McCulloch, prin. Fax 425-1151
Fair Park HS 700/9-12
3222 Greenwood Rd 71109 318-635-8181
Bruce Daigle, prin. Fax 631-1982
Green Oaks HS 500/9-12
2550 Thomas E Howard Dr 71107 318-425-3411
Cleveland White, prin. Fax 425-3414
Huntington HS 1,300/9-12
6801 Rasberry Ln 71129 318-687-6655
Jerry Davis, prin. Fax 687-0943
Linear MS 500/6-8
1845 Linear St 71107 318-221-1589
Ronald King, prin. Fax 221-0130
Linwood MS 800/6-8
401 W 70th St 71106 318-861-2401
Monica Jenkins-Moore, prin. Fax 865-1036
Northwood HS 900/9-12
5939 Old Mooringsport Rd 71107 318-929-3513
Louis Cook, prin. Fax 929-7498
Ridgewood MS 800/6-8
2001 Ridgewood Dr 71118 318-686-0383
Dr. Gerald Burrow, prin. Fax 686-0390
Southwood HS 1,700/9-12
9000 Walker Rd 71118 318-686-9512
Kenneth Wood, prin. Fax 687-7588
Washington HS 500/9-12
2104 Milam St 71103 318-222-2186
Dr. Curly White, prin. Fax 226-0628
Woodlawn HS 800/9-12
7340 Wyngate Blvd 71106 318-686-3161
Carter Bedford, prin. Fax 687-6787
Youree Drive MS 1,000/6-8
6008 Youree Dr 71105 318-868-5324
Arleen Hague, prin. Fax 861-5086
Hamilton Terrace Learning Center Adult
1105 Louisiana Ave 71101 318-221-4506
John Baldwin, prin. Fax 424-7864
Other Schools – See Vivian

American School of Business Post-Sec.
702 Professional Dr N 71105 318-798-3333
Ayers Institute Post-Sec.
3010 Knight St Ste 300 71105 318-868-3000
Blue Cliff College Post-Sec.
200 N Thomas Dr # A 71107 318-425-7941
Calvary Baptist Academy 900/PK-12
9333 Linwood Ave 71106 318-687-4923
Rhonda Honea, prin. Fax 687-4925
Centenary College of Louisiana Post-Sec.
PO Box 41188 71134 318-869-5011
Diesel Driving Academy Post-Sec.
PO Box 36949 71133 318-636-6300
Evangel Christian Academy 600/K-12
7425 Broadacres Rd 71129 318-688-7061
Linda Bass, prin. Fax 688-7322
Guy's Shreveport Academy of Cosmetology Post-Sec.
1141 Shreveport Barksdale 71105 318-865-5591

Louisiana State University Post-Sec.
1 University Pl 71115 318-797-5000
Louisiana Tech. Coll.-Shreveport-Bossier Post-Sec.
PO Box 78527 71137 318-676-7811
Loyola College Prep S 400/9-12
921 Jordan St 71101 318-221-2675
G. Frank Israel, prin. Fax 221-2678
Northwestern State University Post-Sec.
1800 Line Ave 71101 318-677-3100
Overton Brooks VA Medical Center Post-Sec.
510 E Stoner Ave 71101 318-424-6037
Pat Goins Shreveport Beauty School Post-Sec.
6363 Hearne Ave Ste 106 71108 318-631-1833
Shreveport Job Corps Center Post-Sec.
2815 Lillian St 71109 318-227-9331
Southern University at Shreveport Post-Sec.
3050 M L King Dr 71107 318-674-3300
University Christian Prep S 200/PK-12
4800 Old Mooringsport Rd 71107 318-221-2697
Carmen Heflen, prin. Fax 221-2790

Sibley, Webster, Pop. 1,082
Webster Parish SD
Supt. — See Minden
Lakeside JSHS 400/7-12
9090 Highway 371 71073 318-377-2133
Beverly Smith, prin. Fax 382-0733

Sicily Island, Catahoula, Pop. 432
Catahoula Parish SD
Supt. — See Harrisonburg
Martin JHS 100/5-8
PO Box 338 71368 318-389-5651
Phyllis Parker, prin. Fax 389-5651
Sicily Island HS 100/9-12
PO Box 128 71368 318-389-5337
Marguerita Krause, prin. Fax 389-5309

Simpson, Vernon, Pop. 547
Vernon Parish SD
Supt. — See Leesville
Simpson S 400/PK-12
PO Box 8 71474 337-383-7810
David Lewis, prin. Fax 383-7816

Simsboro, Lincoln, Pop. 686
Lincoln Parish SD
Supt. — See Ruston
Simsboro S 600/K-12
1 Tiger Dr 71275 318-247-6265
Barbara Kirkland, prin. Fax 247-6276

Singer, Beauregard
Beauregard Parish SD
Supt. — See Deridder
Singer S 300/K-12
153 Highway 110 E 70660 337-463-5908
Dennis Burk, prin. Fax 463-0199

Slidell, Saint Tammany, Pop. 26,947
St. Tammany Parish SD
Supt. — See Covington
Boyet JHS 700/7-8
59295 Rebel Dr 70461 985-643-3775
Mitchell Stubbs, prin. Fax 643-9470
Clearwood JHS 600/4-8
130 Clearwood Dr 70458 985-641-8200
Alan Bennett, prin. Fax 641-7122
Northshore HS 1,500/9-12
100 Panther Dr 70461 985-649-6400
Dr. Michael Peterson, prin. Fax 649-3613
St. Tammany JHS 600/6-8
701 Cleveland Ave 70458 985-643-1592
Hannah Rucker, prin. Fax 643-5873
Salmen HS 900/9-12
4040 Berkley St 70458 985-643-7359
Byron Williams, prin. Fax 645-8776
Slidell HS 1,900/9-12
1 Tiger Dr 70458 985-643-2992
William Percy, prin. Fax 649-6853
Slidell JHS 1,000/6-8
333 Pennsylvania Ave 70458 985-641-5914
Brennan McCurley, prin. Fax 641-6397

Academy of Creative Hair Design Post-Sec.
3805 Pontchartrain Dr #16 70458 985-643-2614
First Baptist Christian S 300/1-12
4141 Pontchartrain Dr 70458 985-643-3725
John Jay Slidell Beauty College Post-Sec.
3144 Pontchartrain Dr 70458 985-643-0677
Louisiana Technical College - Slidell Post-Sec.
PO Box 827 70459 985-646-6430
Pope John Paul II HS 400/9-12
1901 Jaguar Dr 70461 985-649-0914
Richard Berkowitz, prin. Fax 649-5494

Sorrento, Ascension, Pop. 1,292

Louisiana Technical College - Ascension Post-Sec.
9697 Airline Hwy 70778 225-675-5398
River Parishes Community College Post-Sec.
PO Box 310 70778 225-675-8270

Spearsville, Union, Pop. 153
Union Parish SD
Supt. — See Farmerville
Spearsville S 400/K-12
PO Box 18 71277 318-778-3752
Frankie Futch, prin. Fax 778-3269

Springfield, Livingston, Pop. 396
Livingston Parish SD
Supt. — See Livingston
Springfield HS 300/9-12
PO Box 39 70462 225-294-3256
Edward Foster, prin. Fax 294-4800

Springfield MS | 400/4-8
PO Box 40 70462 | 225-294-3306
Steve Parrill, prin. | Fax 294-3307

Springhill, Webster, Pop. 5,246
Webster Parish SD
Supt. — See Minden
Springhill JSHS | 500/7-12
507 W Church St 71075 | 318-539-2563
Melanie Jacobs, prin. | Fax 539-2569

Starks, Calcasieu
Calcasieu Parish SD
Supt. — See Lake Charles
Starks S | 400/PK-12
PO Box 69 70661 | 337-743-5341
Vickie Poole, prin. | Fax 743-5458

Stonewall, DeSoto, Pop. 1,857
De Soto Parish SD
Supt. — See Mansfield
North DeSoto HS | 400/9-12
PO Box 430 71078 | 318-925-6917
Bart Weaver, prin. | Fax 925-1940
North DeSoto MS | 500/4-8
PO Box 310 71078 | 318-925-4520
Keith Simmons, prin. | Fax 925-4719

Sulphur, Calcasieu, Pop. 19,901
Calcasieu Parish SD
Supt. — See Lake Charles
LeBlanc MS | 400/6-8
1100 N Crocker St 70663 | 337-527-5296
Thomas Finnie, prin. | Fax 527-5297
Lewis MS | 700/6-8
1752 Cypress St 70663 | 337-527-6178
Tony Dougherty, prin. | Fax 528-3773
Sulphur 9th Grade Campus | 9-9
600 Willow Ave 70663 | 337-527-9100
Charles Hansen, prin. | Fax 527-6779
Sulphur SHS | 1,300/10-12
100 Sycamore St 70663 | 337-527-6679
Keith Bonin, prin. | Fax 528-3209

Parkview Baptist S | 100/K-12
1623 Picard Rd 70663 | 337-527-7089

Summerfield, Claiborne
Claiborne Parish SD
Supt. — See Homer
Summerfield S | 300/PK-12
PO Box 158 71079 | 318-927-3621
D'Arcy Stevens, prin. | Fax 927-9160

Tallulah, Madison, Pop. 8,715
Madison Parish SD | 1,900/PK-12
PO Box 1620 71284 | 318-574-3616
Michael Johnson, supt. | Fax 574-3667
www.madisonpsb.org/
Madison HS | 300/9-12
800 Wyche St 71282 | 318-574-3529
Will Rogers, prin. | Fax 574-5943
Madison MS | 300/6-8
900 W Askew St 71282 | 318-574-0933
Dennis Redden, prin. | Fax 574-9919

Louisiana Technical College - Tallulah | Post-Sec.
PO Box 1740 71284 | 318-574-4820
Tallulah Academy-Delta Christian S | 300/K-12
700 Wood St 71282 | 318-574-2606
Dr. David Bass, prin. | Fax 574-3390

Thibodaux, Lafourche, Pop. 14,463
Lafourche Parish SD | 15,500/PK-12
PO Box 879 70302 | 985-446-5631
Jo Ann Matthews, supt. | Fax 435-4683
www.lafourche.k12.la.us
East Thibodaux MS | 600/6-8
802 E 7th St 70301 | 985-446-5616
Dan Landry, prin. | Fax 446-5610
Sixth Ward MS | 300/6-8
PO Box 1236 70302 | 985-633-2449
Marla Tabor, prin. | Fax 633-7373
Thibodaux HS | 1,500/9-12
1355 Tiger Dr 70301 | 985-447-4071
Shelba Harlan, prin. | Fax 447-4077
West Thibodaux MS | 500/6-8
1111 E 12th St 70301 | 985-446-6889
Edmond Adams, prin. | Fax 447-1777
Other Schools – See Cut Off, Galliano, Golden Meadow, Lockport, Raceland

Louisiana Technical College - LaFourche | Post-Sec.
1425 Tiger Dr 70301 | 985-447-0924
Nicholls State University | Post-Sec.
University Station 70310 | 985-446-8111
White HS | 800/8-12
555 Cardinal Dr 70301 | 985-446-8486
David Boudreaux, prin. | Fax 448-1275

Tickfaw, Tangipahoa, Pop. 624
Tangipahoa Parish SD
Supt. — See Amite
Nesom MS | 500/6-8
PO Box 280 70466 | 985-345-2166
Maureen Terese, prin. | Fax 345-3731

Tioga, Rapides
Rapides Parish SD
Supt. — See Alexandria
Tioga HS | 900/9-12
PO Box 1030 71477 | 318-640-9661
Kim Hutchinson, prin. | Fax 640-1986

Urania, LaSalle, Pop. 688
LaSalle Parish SD
Supt. — See Jena
LaSalle JHS | 200/6-8
PO Box 520 71480 | 318-495-3474
Steve Long, prin. | Fax 495-3478

Vacherie, Saint James, Pop. 2,354
St. James Parish SD
Supt. — See Lutcher
Science & Math Academy | 7-12
PO Box 482 70090 | 225-265-3042
Elvis Cavalier, coord. | Fax 265-7093

Varnado, Washington, Pop. 339
Washington Parish SD
Supt. — See Franklinton
Varnado HS | 200/9-12
25543 Washington St, Angie LA 70426
 | 985-732-2025
Emma Jean Ross, prin. | Fax 732-5198

Vidalia, Concordia, Pop. 4,349
Concordia Parish SD | 3,800/PK-12
PO Box 950 71373 | 318-336-4226
Kerry Laster Ph.D., supt. | Fax 336-5875
cpsbla.us
Vidalia HS | 400/9-12
2201 Murray Dr 71373 | 318-336-6231
Rick Brown, prin. | Fax 336-6233
Vidalia JHS | 400/6-8
210 Gillespie St 71373 | 318-336-6227
Paul Nelson, prin. | Fax 336-6229
Other Schools – See Ferriday, Monterey

Vidalia Beauty School | Post-Sec.
208 Westside Dr 71373 | 318-336-2377

Ville Platte, Evangeline, Pop. 8,297
Evangeline Parish SD | 5,500/PK-12
1123 Te Mamou Rd 70586 | 337-363-6651
Rayford J. Fontenot, supt. | Fax 363-8086
www.epsb.com
Bayou Chicot ES | 300/4-8
4576 US Highway 167 N 70586 | 337-461-2687
Shirley Tezenor, prin. | Fax 461-2601
Ville Platte JSHS | 800/5-12
210 W Cotton St 70586 | 337-363-3387
Peggy Edwards, prin. | Fax 363-7274
Other Schools – See Basile, Chataignier, Mamou, Pine Prairie

Christian Heritage Academy | 200/PK-12
607 Prosper St 70586 | 337-363-7690
Rev. Jeff Piker, supt. | Fax 363-7699
Louisiana Tech. Coll.-Charles B Coreil | Post-Sec.
1124 Vocational Dr 70586 | 337-363-2197
Sacred Heart HS | 300/9-12
114 Trojan Ln 70586 | 337-363-1475
Andrew Ducote, admin. | Fax 363-0348

Vinton, Calcasieu, Pop. 3,215
Calcasieu Parish SD
Supt. — See Lake Charles
Vinton HS | 300/9-12
1603 Grace Ave 70668 | 337-589-7223
Mitch Manuel, prin. | Fax 589-7612
Vinton MS | 200/6-8
900 Horridge St 70668 | 337-589-7567
Stephen Hardy, prin. | Fax 589-7587

Vivian, Caddo, Pop. 3,915
Caddo Parish SD
Supt. — See Shreveport
North Caddo HS | 400/9-12
201 Airport Dr 71082 | 318-375-3258
Ken Cochran, prin. | Fax 222-8430

Walker, Livingston, Pop. 5,317
Livingston Parish SD
Supt. — See Livingston
Walker HS | 1,200/9-12
PO Box 249 70785 | 225-664-4825
Steve Long, prin. | Fax 664-4321
Walker JHS, PO Box 219 70785 | 400/6-8
Homer Wentzel, prin. | 225-665-8970
Westside JHS | 600/6-8
12615 Burgess Ave 70785 | 225-665-8259
Kevin Pope, prin. | Fax 665-8283

Washington, Saint Landry, Pop. 1,064
St. Landry Parish SD
Supt. — See Opelousas
North Central HS | 200/9-12
6579 Highway 10 70589 | 337-623-4239
John Murphy, prin. | Fax 623-5360
Washington Career & Technical Education | Vo/Tech
PO Box 430 70589 | 337-826-7360
Andrew Leon, prin. | Fax 826-5264

Watson, Livingston
Livingston Parish SD
Supt. — See Livingston
Live Oak MS | 800/6-8
PO Box 470 70786 | 225-664-3211
Patricia McCumsey, prin. | Fax 664-1551

Welsh, Jefferson Davis, Pop. 3,313
Jefferson Davis Parish SD
Supt. — See Jennings
Welsh HS | 300/9-12
306 Bourgeois St 70591 | 337-734-2361
Patrick Deshotel, prin. | Fax 734-4149

Westlake, Calcasieu, Pop. 4,603
Calcasieu Parish SD
Supt. — See Lake Charles
Arnett MS | 400/6-8
400 Sulphur Ave 70669 | 337-436-9657
Vance Richmond, prin. | Fax 436-5745
Westlake HS | 500/9-12
1000 Garden Dr 70669 | 337-433-6866
Steve Powers, prin. | Fax 433-8088
Westlake HS T & I | Vo/Tech
2307 Jones St 70669 | 337-439-6373
Larry Singer, prin. | Fax 433-6308

West Monroe, Ouachita, Pop. 13,018
Ouachita Parish SD
Supt. — See Monroe
Good Hope MS | 700/6-8
400 Good Hope Rd 71291 | 318-396-9693
Twainna Calhoun, prin. | Fax 397-5110
Riser MS | 600/6-8
100 Price Dr 71292 | 318-387-0567
George Barefield, prin. | Fax 387-9072
West Monroe HS | 2,000/9-12
201 Riggs St 71291 | 318-323-3771
Shere Lynne May, prin. | Fax 388-4594
West Ouachita HS | 1,000/9-12
4061 Caples Rd 71292 | 318-249-2117
Mickey Merritt, prin. | Fax 249-4774
West Ridge MS | 600/6-8
6977 Cypress St 71291 | 318-397-8444
James Aulds, prin. | Fax 397-9376
Woodlawn MS | 300/6-8
175 Woodlawn School Rd 71292 | 318-325-1574
Charles Dykes, prin. | Fax 325-9858

Claiborne Christian S | 300/PK-12
334 Laird St 71291 | 318-396-7968
Elizabeth Rigdon, prin. | Fax 397-0567
Cloyd's Beauty School #1 | Post-Sec.
603 Natchitoches St 71291 | 318-322-5314
Louisiana Tech. Coll. Delta-Ouachita | Post-Sec.
609 Vocational Pkwy 71292 | 318-397-6100
Northeast Baptist S | 100/PK-12
102 Wilson St 71291 | 318-325-2077

Westwego, Jefferson, Pop. 10,526
Jefferson Parish SD
Supt. — See Marrero
Worley MS | 600/6-8
801 Spartan Ln 70094 | 504-348-4964
Joseph Fonseca, prin. | Fax 348-7057

White Castle, Iberville, Pop. 1,887
Iberville Parish SD
Supt. — See Plaquemine
White Castle HS | 300/7-12
32695 Graham St 70788 | 225-545-3621
Wayne Rodrigue, prin. | Fax 545-2964

Winnfield, Winn, Pop. 5,484
Winn Parish SD | 2,800/PK-12
PO Box 430 71483 | 318-628-6936
Steve Bartlett, supt. | Fax 628-2582
www.winnpsb.org
Winnfield HS | 500/9-12
PO Box 968 71483 | 318-628-3506
Karen Griffin, prin. | Fax 628-3417
Winnfield MS | 400/6-8
685 Thomas Mill Rd 71483 | 318-628-2765
Kaye Kieffer, prin. | Fax 628-1838
Other Schools – See Atlanta, Calvin, Dodson

Louisiana Technical College - Huey Long | Post-Sec.
303 S Jones St 71483 | 318-628-3815

Winnsboro, Franklin, Pop. 5,149
Franklin Parish SD | 2,800/PK-12
7293 Prairie Rd 71295 | 318-435-9046
Dr. Lanny Johnson, supt. | Fax 435-3392
www.franklin.k12.la.us
Franklin Parish HS | 500/9-12
1600 Glover Dr 71295 | 318-435-5676
John Brown, prin. | Fax 435-6493

Franklin Academy | 300/K-12
2110 Loop Rd 71295 | 318-435-9520
Pete Lewis, prin. | Fax 435-9508
Louisiana Technical College-NE Louisiana | Post-Sec.
1710 Warren St 71295 | 318-435-2163

Youngsville, Lafayette, Pop. 4,717
Lafayette Parish SD
Supt. — See Lafayette
Youngsville MS | 600/5-8
PO Box 1049 70592 | 337-856-5961
Darrel Combs, prin. | Fax 856-9945

Zachary, East Baton Rouge, Pop. 11,791
Zachary Community SD | 3,200/PK-12
4656 Main St 70791 | 225-658-4969
H. Warren Drake, supt. | Fax 658-5261
www.zacharyschools.org
Northwestern MS | 800/6-8
5200 E Central Ave 70791 | 225-654-9201
Debby Brian, prin. | Fax 658-2025
Zachary HS | 1,000/9-12
4100 Bronco Ln 70791 | 225-654-2776
Kevin Lemoine, prin. | Fax 658-0010

Zwolle, Sabine, Pop. 1,748
Sabine Parish SD
Supt. — See Many
Zwolle JSHS | 300/7-12
PO Box 188 71486 | 318-645-6104
Chad Crow, prin. | Fax 645-4830

MAINE

MAINE DEPARTMENT OF EDUCATION
State House Station #23, Augusta 04333
Telephone 207-624-6600
Fax 207-624-6700
Website http://www.maine.gov/education/index.shtml
Commissioner of Education   Susan A. Gendron

MAINE BOARD OF EDUCATION
State House Station #23, Augusta 04333
Chairperson   James Carignan

PUBLIC, PRIVATE AND CATHOLIC SECONDARY SCHOOLS

Ashland, Aroostook
MSAD 32 — 400/K-12
PO Box 289 04732 — 207-435-3661
Roland Caron, supt. — Fax 435-8421
Ashland Community JSHS — 200/6-12
PO Box 369 04732 — 207-435-3481
David Keaton, prin. — Fax 435-6417

Auburn, Androscoggin, Pop. 23,313
Auburn SD — 3,900/K-12
PO Box 800 04212 — 207-784-6431
Barbara Eretzian, supt. — Fax 784-2969
www.auburnschl.edu
Auburn MS — 600/7-8
38 Falcon Dr 04210 — 207-784-1356
Kathleen Fuller-Cutler, prin. — Fax 784-1359
Little HS — 1,100/9-12
77 Harris St 04210 — 207-783-8528
James Miller, prin. — Fax 784-9243

Central Maine Community College — Post-Sec.
1250 Turner St 04210 — 207-755-5100
St. Dominic Regional HS — 300/9-12
121 Gracelawn Rd 04210 — 207-782-6911
G. Michael Welch, prin. — Fax 795-6439

Augusta, Kennebec, Pop. 18,618
Augusta SD — 2,700/PK-12
40 Pierce Dr Ste 3 04330 — 207-626-2468
Cornelia Brown, supt. — Fax 626-2444
www.augustaschools.org/
Capitol Area Technical Center — Vo/Tech
40 Pierce Dr 04330 — 207-626-2475
Scott Phair, prin. — Fax 626-2498
Cony HS — 900/9-12
120 Cony St 04330 — 207-626-2460
James Anastasio, prin. — Fax 626-2541
Hodgkins MS, 17 Malta St 04330 — 400/7-8
Jeffrey Boston, prin. — 207-626-2490

University of Maine — Post-Sec.
46 University Dr 04330 — 207-621-3000

Baileyville, Washington
Union SD 107 — 600/K-12
PO Box 580 04694 — 207-427-6913
Barry McLaughlin, supt. — Fax 427-3166
Woodland JSHS — 300/7-12
14 First Ave 04694 — 207-427-3325
Patricia Metta, prin. — Fax 427-3950

Bangor, Penobscot, Pop. 31,550
Applied Technology Region
Supt. — None
United Technologies Center-Region 4 — Vo/Tech
200 Hogan Rd 04401 — 207-942-5296
Greg Miller, prin. — Fax 942-0776

Bangor SD — 4,100/K-12
73 Harlow St 04401 — 207-992-4150
Robert Ervin, supt. — Fax 992-4163
www.bangorschools.net
Bangor HS — 1,500/9-12
885 Broadway 04401 — 207-941-6200
Norris Nickerson, prin. — Fax 941-6212
Cohen MS — 500/6-8
304 Garland St 04401 — 207-941-6230
Richard Cookson, prin. — Fax 941-6235
Doughty MS — 500/6-8
143 5th St 04401 — 207-941-6220
Robert MacDonald, prin. — Fax 947-7606

All Saints S - St. John Campus — 300/4-8
PO Box 1749 04402 — 207-942-0955
Marcia Diamond, prin. — Fax 942-2398
Bangor Christian S — 400/PK-12
1476 Broadway 04401 — 207-947-7356
Jim Chasse, prin. — Fax 262-9528
Bangor Theological Seminary — Post-Sec.
PO Box 411 04402 — 207-942-6781

Bapst Memorial HS — 500/9-12
100 Broadway 04401 — 207-947-0313
Fax 941-2474
Beal College — Post-Sec.
99 Farm Rd 04401 — 207-947-4591
Eastern Maine Community College — Post-Sec.
354 Hogan Rd 04401 — 207-974-4600
Eastern Maine Medical Center — Post-Sec.
489 State St 04401 — 207-973-7051
Husson College — Post-Sec.
1 College Cir 04401 — 207-941-7000
New England School of Communications — Post-Sec.
1 College Cir 04401 — 207-941-7176
Pierre's School of Cosmetology — Post-Sec.
635 Broadway 04401 — 207-942-0039

Bar Harbor, Hancock, Pop. 2,768

College of the Atlantic — Post-Sec.
105 Eden St 04609 — 207-288-5015

Bar Mills, York
MSAD 6 — 4,000/K-12
PO Box 38 04004 — 207-929-3831
Suzanne Lukas, supt. — Fax 929-5955
www.sad6.k12.me.us
Other Schools – See Buxton, Standish

Bath, Sagadahoc, Pop. 9,322
Bath SD — 1,600/K-12
39 Andrews Rd 04530 — 207-443-6601
Martha Witham, supt. — Fax 443-8295
www.bathpublicschools.com
Bath MS — 400/6-8
6 Old Brunswick Rd 04530 — 207-443-8270
Lawrence Dyer, prin. — Fax 443-8273
Bath Regional Vocational Center — Vo/Tech
800 High St 04530 — 207-443-8257
Merton Dearnley, prin. — Fax 443-8256
Morse HS — 800/9-12
826 High St 04530 — 207-443-8250
Ricque Finucane, prin. — Fax 443-8268

Hyde S — 200/9-12
616 High St 04530 — 207-443-5584
Fax 443-1450

Belfast, Waldo, Pop. 6,808
MSAD 34 — 1,800/K-12
PO Box 363 04915 — 207-338-1960
M. Robbins Young, supt. — Fax 338-4597
www.sad34.net
Belfast Area HS — 600/9-12
98 Waldo Ave 04915 — 207-338-1790
Harris Arthers, prin. — Fax 338-6713
Howard MS — 500/6-8
173 Lincolnville Ave 04915 — 207-338-3320
Kimberly Buckheit, prin. — Fax 338-5588

Berwick, York
MSAD 60
Supt. — See North Berwick
Noble MS — 500/7-8
46 Cranberry Meadow Rd 03901 — 207-698-1320
Daniel Baker, prin. — Fax 698-4400

Bethel, Oxford
MSAD 44 — 1,100/K-12
21 Philbrook St 04217 — 207-824-2185
David W. Murphy Ed.D., supt. — Fax 824-2725
ths.sad44.org/sad44
Telstar HS — 300/9-12
284 Walkers Mills Rd 04217 — 207-824-2136
Shawn Lambert, prin. — Fax 824-7130
Telstar MS — 300/6-8
284 Walkers Mills Rd 04217 — 207-824-2136
Russell Tornrose, prin. — Fax 824-0496

Gould Academy — 200/9-12
PO Box 860 04217 — 207-824-7700
Fax 824-7728

Biddeford, York, Pop. 21,685
Biddeford SD — 3,000/PK-12
PO Box 1865 04005 — 207-282-8280
Sarah-Jane Poli, supt. — Fax 284-7956
www.biddschools.org
Biddeford HS — 1,000/9-12
20 Maplewood Ave 04005 — 207-282-1596
Bernard Binette, prin. — Fax 282-8275
Biddeford MS — 700/6-8
335 Hill St 04005 — 207-282-5957
Marie Shields, prin. — Fax 282-7983
Biddeford Regional Center of Tech — Vo/Tech
10 Maplewood Ave 04005 — 207-282-1501
Ronald Gagnon, prin. — Fax 282-7986

University of New England — Post-Sec.
11 Hills Beach Rd 04005 — 207-283-0171

Bingham, Somerset, Pop. 1,071
MSAD 13 — 300/K-12
PO Box 649 04920 — 207-672-5502
N. Kenneth Smith, supt. — Fax 672-5502
www.sad13.k12.me.us/
Upper Kennebec Valley JSHS — 200/7-12
PO Box 669 04920 — 207-672-3300
Juliana Richard, prin. — Fax 672-4485

Blue Hill, Hancock

Stevens Academy — 300/9-12
23 Union St 04614 — 207-374-2808
Jo Ann Douglass, hdmstr. — Fax 374-2982

Boothbay Harbor, Lincoln, Pop. 1,267
Boothbay-Boothbay Harbor Community SD — 800/K-12
51 Emery Ln 04538 — 207-633-2874
Eileen King, supt. — Fax 633-5458
Boothbay Region HS — 300/9-12
236 Townsend Ave 04538 — 207-633-2421
John Tourtillotte, prin. — Fax 633-7129

Brewer, Penobscot, Pop. 9,075
Brewer SD — 1,600/K-12
49 Capri St 04412 — 207-989-3160
Daniel Lee, supt. — Fax 989-8622
www.breweredu.org/
Brewer HS — 900/9-12
79 Parkway S 04412 — 207-989-4140
Brad Fox, prin. — Fax 989-8659
Brewer MS — 300/6-8
5 Somerset St 04412 — 207-989-8640
William Leithiser, prin. — Fax 989-8635

Bridgton, Cumberland, Pop. 2,195
MSAD 61 — 2,200/K-12
900 Portland Rd 04009 — 207-647-3048
Frank Gorham, supt. — Fax 647-5682
www.sad61.k12.me.us/
Other Schools – See Naples

Brunswick, Cumberland, Pop. 14,683
Applied Technology Region
Supt. — None
Maine Vocational Region 10 — Vo/Tech
68 Church Rd 04011 — 207-729-6622
Shirley Hartwell, prin. — Fax 721-0907

Brunswick SD — 3,400/K-12
35 Union St 04011 — 207-319-1900
James Ashe, supt. — Fax 725-1700
www.brunswick.k12.me.us/
Brunswick HS — 1,200/9-12
116 Maquoit Rd 04011 — 207-319-1910
Bruce Cook, prin. — Fax 798-5515
Brunswick JHS — 700/6-8
65 Columbia Ave 04011 — 207-319-1930
John Paige, prin. — Fax 721-0602

Bowdoin College 04011 — Post-Sec.
207-725-3000

235

Buckfield, Oxford
MSAD 39 700/PK-12
PO Box 190 04220 207-336-2666
Richard Colpitts, supt. Fax 336-2417
www.sad39.k12.me.us
Buckfield JSHS 300/7-12
160 Morrill St 04220 207-336-2151
Donald Reiter, prin. Fax 336-2460

Bucksport, Hancock, Pop. 2,989
Bucksport SD 1,100/K-12
PO Box 1519 04416 207-469-7311
Marc Curtis, supt. Fax 469-6640
www.bucksportschools.com/
Bucksport HS 500/9-12
PO Box 400 04416 207-469-6650
Thomas Sullivan, prin. Fax 469-2081
Bucksport MS 300/5-8
PO Box 910 04416 207-469-6647
Thomas Jandreau, prin. Fax 469-2068

Buxton, York
MSAD 6
Supt. — See Bar Mills
Bonny Eagle MS 900/6-8
92 Sokokis Trl 04093 207-929-3833
Ansel Stevens, prin. Fax 929-9181

Living Waters Christian S 100/PK-12
PO Box 566 04093 207-727-4499
Robert Nelson, prin. Fax 727-4422

Calais, Washington, Pop. 3,363
Union SD 106 800/PK-12
32 Blue Devil Hl 04619 207-454-7561
James Underwood, supt. Fax 454-2516
Calais MSHS 400/7-12
34 Blue Devil Hl Ste 2 04619 207-454-2591
Jeanne Bishop, prin. Fax 454-0306
Saint Croix Regional Tech Center Vo/Tech
34 Blue Devil Hl Ste 1 04619 207-454-2581
Robert Moholland, lead tchr. Fax 454-2597

Washington County Community College Post-Sec.
1 College Dr 04619 207-454-1000

Camden, Knox, Pop. 4,022
Five Towns Community SD 700/9-12
PO Box 1267 04843 207-236-3358
Patricia Hopkins, supt. Fax 236-7810
www.fivetowns.net
Other Schools – See Rockport

MSAD 28 800/K-8
PO Box 1267 04843 207-236-3358
Patricia Hopkins, supt. Fax 236-7810
www.fivetowns.net
Camden-Rockport MS 400/5-8
34 Knowlton St 04843 207-236-7805
G. Sandford Nevens, prin. Fax 236-7815

Cape Elizabeth, Cumberland, Pop. 8,854
Cape Elizabeth SD 1,800/K-12
PO Box 6267 04107 207-799-2217
Alan Hawkins, supt. Fax 799-2914
www.cape.k12.me.us
Cape Elizabeth HS 500/9-12
345 Ocean House Rd 04107 207-799-3309
Jeffrey Shedd, prin. Fax 767-8050
Cape Elizabeth MS 600/5-8
14 Scott Dyer Rd 04107 207-799-8176
Steven Connolly, prin. Fax 767-0832

Caribou, Aroostook, Pop. 8,308
Caribou SD 1,700/PK-12
628 Main St 04736 207-496-6311
Franklin McElwain, supt. Fax 498-3261
www.caribouschools.org
Caribou HS 600/9-12
308 Sweden St 04736 207-493-4260
Susan Foren-Lamoreau, prin. Fax 493-4244
Caribou MS 500/5-8
21 Glenn St 04736 207-493-4240
Susan White, prin. Fax 493-4243
Caribou Regional Technology Center Vo/Tech
308 Sweden St #1 04736 207-493-4270
Lynn McNeal, prin. Fax 493-4242

Pierre's School of Cosmetology Post-Sec.
30 Skyway Dr 04736 207-498-6067

Carmel, Penobscot
MSAD 23 700/PK-8
PO Box 208 04419 207-848-5173
John Backus, supt. Fax 848-5196
www.sad23.k12.me.us
Caravel MS 300/6-8
520 Irish Rd 04419 207-848-3615
Rhonda Sperrey, prin. Fax 848-0884

Carabaset Vly, Franklin

Carrabassett Valley Academy 100/8-12
3197 Carrabassett Dr, 207-237-2250
Fax 237-2213

Castine, Hancock

Maine Maritime Academy Post-Sec.
Battle Ave 04420 207-326-4311

Corinth, Penobscot
MSAD 64 1,300/K-12
408 Main St 04427 207-285-3334
Leonard Ney, supt. Fax 285-4343
msad64.dcix.net
Central HS 400/9-12
PO Box 370 04427 207-285-3326
Garry Spencer, prin. Fax 285-4342
Central MS 400/5-8
PO Box 19 04427 207-285-3177
Martin Gray, prin. Fax 285-4350

Cornish, York

Ossipee Valley Christian S 100/K-12
1890 North Rd 04020 207-793-4005
Susan Smith, admin. Fax 793-2904

Cumberland Center, Cumberland, Pop. 1,890
MSAD 51 2,500/PK-12
PO Box 6A 04021 207-829-4800
Robert Hasson, supt. Fax 829-4802
www.msad51.org
Greely HS 700/9-12
303 Main St 04021 207-829-4805
Christopher Mosca, prin. Fax 829-2256
Greely MS 600/6-8
351 Tuttle Rd 04021 207-829-4815
Kim Brandt, prin. Fax 829-4819

Danforth, Washington
MSAD 14 200/PK-12
31A Houlton Rd 04424 207-448-2882
William Dobbins, supt. Fax 448-7235
East Grand S 200/PK-12
31 Houlton Rd 04424 207-448-2260
David Apgar, prin. Fax 448-7880

Deer Isle, Hancock
Deer Isle - Stonington Community SD
Supt. — See Sargentville
Deer Isle - Stonington HS 200/9-12
251 N Deer Isle Rd 04627 207-348-2303
Penny Wendell, prin. Fax 348-2304

Dexter, Penobscot, Pop. 2,650
MSAD 46 1,100/K-12
10 Spring St 04930 207-924-5262
Kevin Jordan, supt. Fax 924-7660
www.msad46.org
Dexter MS 300/5-8
62 Abbott Hill Rd 04930 207-924-5571
Juliana Richard, prin. Fax 924-7668
Dexter Regional HS 400/9-12
12 Abbott Hill Rd 04930 207-924-5536
Stephen Bell, prin. Fax 924-7673
Tri-County Regional Technology Center Vo/Tech
14 Abbott Hill Rd 04930 207-924-7670
Nicholas Vafiades, prin. Fax 924-5539

Dixfield, Oxford, Pop. 1,300
MSAD 21 900/K-12
145 Weld St 04224 207-562-7254
Thomas Ward Ed.D., supt. Fax 562-7059
www.sad21.k12.me.us
Dirigo HS 300/9-12
145 Weld St 04224 207-562-4251
Daniel Hart, prin. Fax 562-6074
Dirigo MS 200/5-8
45 Middle School Dr 04224 207-562-7552
Celena Ranger, prin. Fax 562-8329

Dover Foxcroft, Piscataquis, Pop. 3,077
MSAD 68 700/K-8
69 High St 04426 207-564-2421
John Dirnbauer, supt. Fax 564-3487
www.sad68.com/
Se Do Mo Cha MS 300/5-8
63 Harrison Ave 04426 207-564-8376
Jay Robinson, prin. Fax 564-6531

Foxcroft Academy 500/9-12
975 W Main St 04426 207-564-8351
Fax 564-8394

Dyer Brook, Aroostook
Southern Aroostook Community SD 400/K-12
922 Dyer Brook Rd, 207-757-8223
Terry Comeau, supt. Fax 757-8257
www.sacs.csd109.k12.me.us/
Southern Aroostook Community S 400/K-12
922 Dyer Brook Rd, 207-757-8206
Jon Porter, prin. Fax 757-8257

East Holden, Penobscot
MSAD 63
Supt. — See Holden
Holbrook MS 300/5-8
202 Kidder Hill Rd 04429 207-843-7769
Gary Conyar, prin. Fax 843-4328

East Machias, Washington

Washington Academy 300/9-12
PO Box 190 04630 207-255-8301
Fax 255-8303

East Millinocket, Penobscot, Pop. 2,075
Union SD 113 600/K-12
45 North St Ste 2 04430 207-746-3500
Sara Alberts, supt. Fax 746-3516
Schenck HS 200/9-12
45 North St 04430 207-746-3511
Pamela Hamilton, prin. Fax 746-3516
Other Schools – See Medway

Easton, Aroostook
Easton SD 200/PK-12
PO Box 126 04740 207-488-7700
Franklin D. Keenan, supt. Fax 488-2840
Easton JSHS 100/7-12
PO Box 66 04740 207-488-7702
Ralph Conroy, prin. Fax 488-7707

Eastport, Washington, Pop. 1,594
Union SD 104 600/PK-12
102 High St 04631 207-853-2567
Arthur Wittine, supt. Fax 853-6260
Shead HS 200/9-12
89 High St 04631 207-853-6254
Terry Lux, prin. Fax 853-2919

Eliot, York
MSAD 35 2,700/PK-12
64 Depot Rd 03903 207-439-2438
Gerald Clockedile, supt. Fax 439-2531
www.msad35.net/
Marshwood JHS 700/6-8
626 Dow Hwy 03903 207-439-1399
Valerie McKenny, prin. Fax 439-3504
Other Schools – See South Berwick

Ellsworth, Hancock, Pop. 6,784
Ellsworth SD 1,300/K-12
PO Box 4906 04605 207-667-8136
Frank Hackett, supt. Fax 667-6493
www.ellsworth.k12.me.us/
Ellsworth HS 600/9-12
299 State St 04605 207-667-4722
William Connors, prin. Fax 667-5027
Ellsworth MS 300/6-8
20 Forrest Ave 04605 207-667-6494
James Newett, prin. Fax 667-6496
Hancock County Tech Center Vo/Tech
112 Boggy Brook Rd 04605 207-667-9729
Richard Thomas, prin. Fax 667-7138

Fairfield, Kennebec, Pop. 2,794
MSAD 49 2,700/PK-12
8 School St 04937 207-453-4200
Dean Baker, supt. Fax 453-4208
www.sad49.k12.me.us/
Lawrence HS 900/9-12
9 School St 04937 207-453-4200
Pamela Swett, prin. Fax 453-4219
Lawrence JHS 500/7-8
7 School St 04937 207-453-4200
Robert Riley, prin. Fax 453-4214

Kennebec Valley Community College Post-Sec.
92 Western Ave 04937 207-453-5000

Falmouth, Cumberland, Pop. 7,610
Falmouth SD 2,200/K-12
51 Woodville Rd 04105 207-781-3200
George Entwistle, supt. Fax 781-5711
www.falmouthschools.org
Falmouth HS 600/9-12
74 Woodville Rd 04105 207-781-7429
Allyn Hutton, prin. Fax 781-3985
Falmouth MS 700/5-8
52 Woodville Rd 04105 207-781-3740
Jeffrey Rodman, prin. Fax 781-7423

Governor Baxter School for the Deaf Post-Sec.
Mackworth Island 04105 207-781-3165

Farmingdale, Kennebec, Pop. 2,070
MSAD 16
Supt. — See Hallowell
Hall-Dale HS 400/9-12
97 Maple St 04344 207-622-6211
Stephen MacDougall, prin. Fax 626-0355
Hall-Dale MS 300/6-8
111 Maple St 04344 207-622-4162
Steven Lavoie, prin. Fax 622-7515

Farmington, Franklin, Pop. 4,197
MSAD 9
Supt. — See New Sharon
Foster Reg Applied Tech Center Vo/Tech
173 Seamon Rd 04938 207-778-3562
Glenn Kapiloff, prin. Fax 778-3562
Mt. Blue HS 900/9-12
129 Seamon Rd 04938 207-778-3561
Joseph Moore, prin. Fax 778-3564
Mt. Blue MS 400/7-8
269 Middle St 04938 207-778-3511
Gary Oswald, prin. Fax 778-5810

University of Maine Post-Sec.
246 Main St 04938 207-778-7000

Fort Fairfield, Aroostook, Pop. 1,729
MSAD 20 700/PK-12
28 High School Dr #B 04742 207-473-4455
Jeannette Condon, supt. Fax 473-4095
Fort Fairfield MSHS 400/6-12
28 High School Dr #A 04742 207-472-3271
Mark Jenkins, prin. Fax 472-3281

Fort Kent, Aroostook, Pop. 2,123
MSAD 27 1,200/PK-12
23 W Main St Ste 101 04743 207-834-3189
Sandra Bernstein, supt. Fax 834-3395
www.sad27.k12.me.us/
Fort Kent Community HS 400/9-12
84 Pleasant St 04743 207-834-5540
Timothy Doak, prin. Fax 834-2723

University of Maine Post-Sec.
23 University Dr 04743 207-834-7500

Freeport, Cumberland, Pop. 1,829
Freeport SD | 1,300/PK-12
17 West St 04032 | 207-865-0928
Elaine Tomaszewski, supt. | Fax 865-2855
www.freeportschooldistrict.com/
Freeport HS | 500/9-12
30 Holbrook St 04032 | 207-865-4706
Thomas Edwards, prin. | Fax 865-2900
Freeport MS | 300/6-8
19 Kendall Ln 04032 | 207-865-6051
Kathleen Marquis-Girard, prin. | Fax 865-2902

Maine Classical S | 100/K-12
PO Box 243 04032 | 207-865-6820
Kristofer Anderson, pres. | Fax 865-6820
Pine Tree Academy | 100/PK-12
67 Pownal Rd 04032 | 207-865-4747
 | Fax 865-1768

Frenchville, Aroostook
MSAD 33 | 300/PK-12
PO Box 9 04745 | 207-543-7334
Fern Desjardins, supt. | Fax 543-6242
www.msad33.org
St. John Valley Tech Center | Vo/Tech
PO Box 509 04745 | 207-543-6606
Conrad Cyr, prin. | Fax 543-6115
Other Schools – See Saint Agatha

Fryeburg, Oxford, Pop. 1,580
MSAD 72 | 900/K-12
124 Portland St 04037 | 207-935-2600
Gary MacDonald, supt. | Fax 935-3787
www.msad72.k12.me.us/
Ockett MS | 400/6-8
25 Molly Ockett Dr 04037 | 207-935-2401
Sharon Burnell, prin. | Fax 935-4470

Fryeburg Academy | 700/9-12
745 Main St 04037 | 207-935-2001
 | Fax 935-4292

Gardiner, Kennebec, Pop. 6,209
MSAD 11 | 2,400/PK-12
150 Highland Ave 04345 | 207-582-5346
Paul Knowles, supt. | Fax 582-8305
www.sad11.k12.me.us
Gardiner Area HS | 800/9-12
40 W Hill Rd 04345 | 207-582-3150
Chad Kempton, prin. | Fax 582-0434
Gardiner Regional MS | 600/6-8
161 Cobbossee Ave 04345 | 207-582-1326
Arthur Warren, prin. | Fax 582-6823

Gorham, Cumberland, Pop. 3,618
Gorham SD | 2,800/K-12
381 Main St 04038 | 207-222-1000
Theodore Sharpe, supt. | Fax 839-5003
www.gorhamschools.org/
Gorham HS | 800/9-12
41 Morrill Ave 04038 | 207-222-1100
John Drisko, prin. | Fax 839-7742
Gorham MS | 700/6-8
106 Weeks Rd 04038 | 207-222-1220
Dennis Duquette, prin. | Fax 839-4092

Gray, Cumberland
MSAD 15 | 2,100/K-12
14 Shaker Rd 04039 | 207-657-3335
Victoria Burns, supt. | Fax 657-2040
www.msad15.org/
Gray-New Gloucester HS | 700/9-12
10 Libby Hill Rd 04039 | 207-657-3323
Paul Penna, prin. | Fax 657-3329
Gray-New Gloucester MS | 500/6-8
31 Libby Hill Rd 04039 | 207-657-4994
Peter Cook, prin. | Fax 657-5219

Greenville, Piscataquis, Pop. 1,601
Union SD 60 | 300/K-12
PO Box 100 04441 | 207-695-3708
Dr. Steven M. Pound, supt. | Fax 695-3709
Greenville MSHS | 200/6-12
PO Box 100 04441 | 207-695-2666
Cory Smith, prin. | Fax 695-4614

Guilford, Piscataquis, Pop. 1,082
MSAD 4 | 900/PK-12
25 Campus Dr # 2 04443 | 207-876-3444
Paul Stearns, supt. | Fax 876-3446
www.sad4.com/
Piscataquis Community HS | 300/9-12
9 Campus Dr 04443 | 207-876-4625
Jeffrey Aronson, prin. | Fax 876-4628
Piscataquis Community MS | 300/4-8
25 Campus Dr # 1 04443 | 207-876-4301
Gregory Bellemare, prin. | Fax 876-4291

Hallowell, Kennebec, Pop. 2,467
MSAD 16 | 1,000/K-12
7 Reed St 04347 | 207-622-6351
Don Siviski, supt. | Fax 622-7866
www.halldale.org/
Other Schools – See Farmingdale

Hampden, Penobscot, Pop. 3,895
MSAD 22 | 2,300/PK-12
24 Main Rd N 04444 | 207-862-3255
Richard Lyons, supt. | Fax 862-2789
www.sad22.us/
Hampden Academy | 800/9-12
1 Main Rd N 04444 | 207-862-3791
Ruey Yehle, prin. | Fax 862-4577
Reeds Brook MS | 400/6-8
28A Main Rd S 04444 | 207-862-3540
Thomas Ingraham, prin. | Fax 862-3551
Other Schools – See Winterport

Harrington, Washington
MSAD 37 | 800/K-12
PO Box 79 04643 | 207-483-2734
Deborah Stewart, supt. | Fax 483-6051
www.sad37.com
Narraguagus HS | 300/9-12
RR 1 Box 489 04643 | 207-483-2746
Nancy Melhorn, prin. | Fax 483-2771

Hartland, Somerset, Pop. 1,038
MSAD 48
Supt. — See Newport
Somerset Valley MS | 300/5-8
45 Blake St 04943 | 207-938-4770
Don Roux, prin. | Fax 938-2114

Hebron, Oxford

Hebron Academy | 200/6-12
PO Box 309 04238 | 207-966-2100
 | Fax 966-1111

Hermon, See Bangor
Hermon SD | 1,100/PK-12
31 Billings Rd 04401 | 207-848-4000
Patricia Duran, supt. | Fax 848-5226
www.hermon.net
Hermon HS | 500/9-12
2415 Route 2 04401 | 207-848-4000
Brian Walsh, prin. | Fax 848-5591
Hermon MS | 300/5-8
29 Billings Rd 04401 | 207-848-4000
Brian Carpenter, prin. | Fax 848-2163

Hinckley, Somerset

Averill HS / Alfond MS | 100/5-12
PO Box 159 04944 | 207-238-4200
 | Fax 238-4207

Hiram, Oxford
MSAD 55 | 1,300/K-12
62 Brownfield Rd 04041 | 207-625-8683
Sylvia Pease, supt. | Fax 625-8153
www.sad55.k12.me.us/
Sacopee Valley JSHS | 500/8-12
115 S Hiram Rd 04041 | 207-625-3208
Joseph Findlay, prin. | Fax 625-7869

Holden, Penobscot
MSAD 63 | 600/K-8
202 Kidder Hill Rd 04429 | 207-843-7851
Louise Regan, supt. | Fax 843-7295
Other Schools – See East Holden

Houlton, Aroostook, Pop. 5,627
Applied Technology Region
Supt. — None
Region 2 School of Applied Tech | Vo/Tech
PO Box 307 04730 | 207-532-9541
Michael Howard, prin. | Fax 532-6975

MSAD 29 | 1,300/PK-12
PO Box 190 04730 | 207-532-6555
Stephen Fitzpatrick, supt. | Fax 532-6481
www.sad29.k12.me.us/
Houlton HS | 400/9-12
7 Bird St 04730 | 207-532-6551
Martin Bouchard, prin. | Fax 532-6282
Houlton JHS | 200/7-8
7 Bird St 04730 | 207-532-6551
Martin Bouchard, prin. | Fax 532-6282

MSAD 70 | 600/PK-12
175 Hodgdon Mills Rd 04730 | 207-532-3015
Robert McDaniel, supt. | Fax 532-2679
www.msad70.net/
Hodgdon HS | 200/9-12
175 Hodgdon Mills Rd 04730 | 207-532-2413
Clark Rafford, prin. | Fax 532-4043

Greater Houlton Christian Academy | 200/PK-12
27 School St 04730 | 207-532-0736
Mark B. Jago, hdmstr. | Fax 532-9553

Howland, Penobscot, Pop. 1,304
MSAD 31 | 700/K-12
PO Box 326 04448 | 207-732-3112
Jerry White, supt. | Fax 732-3390
Hichborn MS | 200/6-8
PO Box 406 04448 | 207-732-3113
Carol Marcinkus, prin. | Fax 732-4085
Penobscot Valley HS | 200/9-12
PO Box 328 04448 | 207-732-3111
Carol Marcinkus, prin. | Fax 732-5500

Islesboro, Waldo
Islesboro SD | 100/K-12
PO Box 118 04848 | 207-734-6723
Donald Kanicki, supt. | Fax 734-8159
Islesboro Central S | 100/K-12
PO Box 118 04848 | 207-734-2251
Michael Wright, prin. | Fax 734-8159

Jackman, Somerset
MSAD 12 | 200/K-12
PO Box 239 04945 | 207-668-7749
Richard Curtis, supt. | Fax 668-4482
www.sad12.com/
Forest Hills Consolidated S | 200/K-12
PO Box 239 04945 | 207-668-5291
Richard Curtis, prin. | Fax 668-4482

Jay, Franklin
Jay SD | 900/K-12
5 Tiger Dr 04239 | 207-897-3936
Robert Wall, supt. | Fax 897-5431

Jay HS | 300/9-12
33 Community Dr 04239 | 207-897-4336
John Robinson, prin. | Fax 897-9313
Jay MS | 300/5-8
23 Community Dr 04239 | 207-897-4319
Scott Albert, prin. | Fax 897-3513

Jonesport, Washington
Moosabec Community SD | 100/9-12
127 Snare Creek Ln 04649 | 207-497-2154
Colleen Haskell, supt. | Fax 497-2703
Jonesport-Beals HS | 100/9-12
180 Snare Creek Ln 04649 | 207-497-5454
Colleen Haskell, prin. | Fax 497-3004

Kennebunk, York, Pop. 4,206
MSAD 71 | 2,000/PK-12
87 Fletcher St 04043 | 207-985-1100
Thomas Farrell, supt. | Fax 985-1104
www.msad71.net
Kennebunk HS | 900/9-12
89 Fletcher St 04043 | 207-985-1110
Nelson Beaudoin, prin. | Fax 985-1350
Kennebunk MS | 600/6-8
60 Thompson Rd 04043 | 207-467-8004
Frances Farr, prin. | Fax 467-9059

Heartwood College of Art | Post-Sec.
123 York St 04043 | 207-985-0985

Kennebunkport, York, Pop. 1,100

Landing School of Boatbuilding & Design | Post-Sec.
PO Box 1490 04046 | 207-985-7976

Kents Hill, Kennebec

Kents Hill S | 200/9-12
PO Box 257 04349 | 207-685-4914
 | Fax 685-9529

Kittery, York, Pop. 5,151
Kittery SD | 1,200/K-12
200 Rogers Rd 03904 | 207-439-6819
Larry Littlefield, supt. | Fax 439-5407
www.kitteryschools.org/
Shapleigh MS | 300/6-8
43 Stevenson Rd 03904 | 207-439-2572
Gregory Goodness, prin. | Fax 439-9958
Traip Academy | 300/9-12
12 Williams Ave 03904 | 207-439-1121
Patricia Garnis, prin. | Fax 439-3789

Lee, Penobscot
MSAD 30 | 100/K-8
31 Winn Rd 04455 | 207-738-2665
Frederick Woodman, supt. | Fax 738-2010
www.msad30.org/
Mt. Jefferson JHS | 100/6-8
61 Winn Rd 04455 | 207-738-2866
 | Fax 738-3817

Lee Academy | 200/9-12
4 Winn Rd 04455 | 207-738-2252
Bruce Lindberg, prin. | Fax 738-3257

Lewiston, Androscoggin, Pop. 35,922
Lewiston SD | 4,500/K-12
36 Oak St 04240 | 207-795-4100
Leon Levesque, supt. | Fax 753-6413
www.lewiston.k12.me.us/
Lewiston HS | 1,400/9-12
156 East Ave 04240 | 207-795-4190
Wilfred LeBlanc, prin. | Fax 795-4119
Lewiston MS | 700/7-8
75 Central Ave 04240 | 207-795-4180
Maureen Lachapelle, prin. | Fax 753-1789
Lewiston Regional Technical Center | Vo/Tech
156 East Ave 04240 | 207-795-4144
Donald Cannan Ed.D., prin. | Fax 795-4147

Andover College | Post-Sec.
475 Lisbon St 04240 | 800-639-3110
Bates College | Post-Sec.
1 Bates College 04240 | 207-786-6000
Central Maine Christian Academy | 100/PK-12
390 Main St 04240 | 207-777-0007
Patricia St. Hilaire, prin. | Fax 777-0007
Central Maine Medical Center | Post-Sec.
300 Main St 04240 | 207-795-2840
Mr. Bernard's School of Hair Fashion | Post-Sec.
PO Box 1163 04243 | 207-783-7765
Vineyard Christian S | 100/PK-12
9 Foss Rd 04240 | 207-784-9500
Ruth Handler, dir. | Fax 777-3076

Limestone, Aroostook, Pop. 1,245
Limestone SD | 300/K-12
97 High St 04750 | 207-325-4888
Frank McElwain, supt. | Fax 325-4969
Limestone S | 300/K-12
93 High St 04750 | 207-325-4742
Ryan Enman, prin. | Fax 325-4780

Maine School of Science & Mathematics | 10-12
95 High St 04750 | 207-325-3303
Walter Warner, supt. | Fax 325-3340
www.mssm.org/
Maine School of Science & Mathematics | 10-12
95 High St 04750 | 207-325-3303
Catherine Bowker, dean | Fax 325-3340

Lincoln, Penobscot, Pop. 3,399
Applied Technology Region
Supt. — None

North Penobscot Tech-Region 3 — Vo/Tech
35 W Broadway 04457 — 207-794-3004
Alan Dickey, prin. — Fax 794-8049

MSAD 67 — 1,300/PK-12
PO Box 250 04457 — 207-794-6500
Omar Norton, supt. — Fax 794-2600
www.sad67.k12.me.us/
Mattanawcook Academy — 400/9-12
33 Reed Dr 04457 — 207-794-6711
James Boothby, prin. — Fax 794-3205
Mattanawcook JHS — 400/5-8
45 School St 04457 — 207-794-8935
David Theoharides, prin. — Fax 794-2601

Lisbon Falls, Androscoggin, Pop. 4,674
Union SD 30 — 1,400/K-12
4 Campus St 04252 — 207-353-6711
Shannon Welsh Ed.D., supt. — Fax 353-3032
www.union30.org/
Lisbon HS — 400/9-12
591 Lisbon St 04252 — 207-353-3030
Kenneth Healey, prin. — Fax 353-7908
Sugg MS — 300/7-8
567 Lisbon St 04252 — 207-353-3055
Richard Green, prin. — Fax 353-3053

Litchfield, Kennebec, Pop. 275
Supt. — See Wales
Ricker MS — 300/3-8
573 Richmond Rd 04350 — 207-268-4136
Aurelie Bush, prin. — Fax 268-4318

Livermore Falls, Androscoggin, Pop. 1,935
MSAD 36 — 1,000/K-12
9 Cedar St 04254 — 207-897-6722
Terry Despres, supt. — Fax 897-2362
www.sad36.org/
Livermore Falls HS — 300/9-12
25 Cedar St 04254 — 207-897-3428
Roderick Wright, prin. — Fax 897-2254
Livermore Falls MS — 300/6-8
1 Highland Ave 04254 — 207-897-2121
— Fax 897-9377

Lubec, Washington
MSAD 19 — 200/K-12
44 South St 04652 — 207-733-5573
Michael Buckley, supt. — Fax 733-2004
Lubec Consolidated S — 200/K-12
44 South St 04652 — 207-733-5591
Lovina Wormell, prin. — Fax 733-2004

Machias, Washington, Pop. 1,773
Union SD 102 — 700/K-12
Outer Court St 04654 — 207-255-6585
Scott Porter, supt. — Fax 255-8054
Coastal Washington City Inst of Tech — Vo/Tech
RR 1 Box 12A 04654 — 207-255-6585
Scott Porter, prin. — Fax 255-8054
Machias Memorial HS — 100/9-12
109 Court St 04654 — 207-255-3812
Timothy Reynolds, prin. — Fax 255-3093

University of Maine — Post-Sec.
9 OBrien Ave 04654 — 207-255-1200

Madawaska, Aroostook, Pop. 3,653
Madawaska SD — 800/PK-12
328 Saint Thomas St Ste 201 04756 — 207-728-3346
Carlton Dubois, supt. — Fax 728-7823
Madawaska MSHS — 400/6-12
135 7th Ave 04756 — 207-728-3371
Conrad Cyr, prin. — Fax 728-3636

Madison, Somerset, Pop. 2,956
MSAD 59 — 1,000/PK-12
55 Weston Ave 04950 — 207-696-3323
Sandra MacArthur, supt. — Fax 696-5631
www.sad59.k12.me.us/
Madison Area Memorial HS — 300/9-12
486 Main St 04950 — 207-696-3395
Colin Campbell, prin. — Fax 696-5644
Madison JHS — 300/5-8
205 Main St 04950 — 207-696-3381
Bonnie Levesque, prin. — Fax 696-5640

Mars Hill, Aroostook, Pop. 1,717
MSAD 42 — 500/PK-12
PO Box 1006 04758 — 207-425-3771
Roger Shaw, supt. — Fax 429-8461
www.cahs.sad42.k12.me.us/
Central Aroostook JSHS — 200/7-12
PO Box 310 04758 — 207-425-2811
Kevin Grass, prin. — Fax 429-8460

Medway, Penobscot
Union SD 113
Supt. — See East Millinocket
Medway MS — 200/5-8
PO Box 608 04460 — 207-746-3470
Kevin Towle, prin. — Fax 746-5930

Mexico, Oxford, Pop. 2,302
Applied Technology Region
Supt. — None
School of Applied Tech-Region 9 — Vo/Tech
377 River Rd 04257 — 207-364-3764
David Driscoll, prin. — Fax 364-2074

MSAD 43 — 1,500/K-12
3 Recreation Dr 04257 — 207-364-7896
James Hodgkins, supt. — Fax 364-5609
valnet.mtvalleyhs.sad43.k12.me.us
Mountain Valley MS — 400/6-8
58 Highland Ter 04257 — 207-364-7926
Charles Lever, prin. — Fax 364-5608

Other Schools – See Rumford

Millinocket, Penobscot, Pop. 6,922
Millinocket SD — 800/K-12
45 North St Ste 2 04462 — 207-723-6400
Sara Alberts, supt. — Fax 723-6410
Millinocket MS — 200/6-8
199 State St 04462 — 207-723-6415
Paige Coville, prin. — Fax 723-6437
Stearns HS — 300/9-12
199 State St 04462 — 207-723-6430
Paul MacDonald, prin. — Fax 723-6437

Milo, Piscataquis, Pop. 2,129
MSAD 41 — 900/K-12
37 W Main St 04463 — 207-943-7317
Shirley Wright, supt. — Fax 943-5314
msad41.us/
Penquis Valley HS — 400/7-12
48 Penquis Loop 04463 — 207-943-7346
Scott Gordon, prin. — Fax 943-5333

Monmouth, Kennebec
Monmouth SD — 800/K-12
PO Box 460 04259 — 207-933-3062
Stephen Cottrell, supt. — Fax 933-3061
www.monmouthschools.org/
Monmouth Academy — 300/9-12
96 Academy Rd 04259 — 207-933-4416
Michael Burnham, prin. — Fax 933-7222
Monmouth MS — 300/4-8
PO Box 240 04259 — 207-933-9002
Stephen Philbrook, prin. — Fax 933-7252

Mount Desert, Hancock
Mt. Desert Community SD — 700/9-12
PO Box 60 04660 — 207-288-5049
Robert Liebow, supt. — Fax 288-5071
www.u98.k12.me.us
Mt. Desert Island HS — 700/9-12
PO Box 180 04660 — 207-288-5011
Sally Leighton, prin. — Fax 288-0692

Naples, Cumberland
MSAD 61
Supt. — See Bridgton
Lake Region HS — 800/9-12
1877 Roosevelt Trl 04055 — 207-693-6221
Roger Lowell, prin. — Fax 693-4591
Lake Region MS — 400/7-8
204 Kansas Rd 04055 — 207-647-8403
Charles Lomonte, prin. — Fax 647-0991
Lake Region Vocational Center — Vo/Tech
1879 Roosevelt Trl 04055 — 207-693-3864
Rosie Schacht, prin. — Fax 693-3864

Newcastle, Lincoln

Lincoln Academy — 600/9-12
81 Academy Hl 04553 — 207-563-3596
— Fax 563-1067

Newport, Penobscot, Pop. 1,843
MSAD 48 — 2,100/PK-12
PO Box 40 04953 — 207-368-5091
William Braun, supt. — Fax 368-2192
www.msad48.org
Nokomis Regional HS — 800/9-12
PO Box 100 04953 — 207-368-4354
Arnold Shorey, prin. — Fax 368-3276
Sebasticook Valley MS — 300/5-8
337 Williams Rd 04953 — 207-368-4592
Fredrick Johnston, prin. — Fax 368-4598
Other Schools – See Hartland

New Sharon, Franklin
MSAD 9 — 2,800/K-12
11 School Ln 04955 — 207-778-6571
Michael Cormier, supt. — Fax 778-4160
www.msad9.com
Other Schools – See Farmington

New Vineyard, Franklin

Open Bible Baptist Christian S — 50/PK-12
PO Box 242 04956 — 207-778-9065
Herman Ellis, prin. — Fax 778-9065

Norridgewock, Somerset, Pop. 1,496

Riverview Memorial S — 50/K-10
201 Mercer Rd 04957 — 207-634-2641
— Fax 634-5812

North Anson, Somerset
MSAD 74 — 800/K-12
56 N Main St 04958 — 207-635-2727
Regina Campbell Ed.D., supt. — Fax 635-3599
www.sad74.k12.me.us:16080/district/
Carrabec HS — 300/9-12
PO Box 20 04958 — 207-635-2296
Kenneth Coville, prin. — Fax 635-2217

North Berwick, York, Pop. 1,568
MSAD 60 — 3,200/K-12
PO Box 819 03906 — 207-676-2234
Paul J. Andrade, supt. — Fax 676-3229
www.sad60.k12.me.us
Noble HS — 1,100/9-12
388 Somersworth Rd 03906 — 207-676-2843
Christian Elkington, prin. — Fax 676-2842
Other Schools – See Berwick

North Bridgton, Cumberland

Bridgton Academy — 200/12-12
PO Box 292 04057 — 207-647-3322
— Fax 647-8513

North Haven, Knox
MSAD 7 — 100/PK-12
RR 1 Box 699 04853 — 207-867-4707
Thomas Marx, supt. — Fax 867-4438
nhcsxserve.sad7.k12.me.us/
North Haven Community S — 100/PK-12
RR 1 Box 699 04853 — 207-867-4707
A. Barney Hallowell, prin. — Fax 867-4438

Norway, Oxford, Pop. 3,023
Applied Technology Region
Supt. — None
Oxford Hills Tech-Region 11 — Vo/Tech
PO Box 313 04268 — 207-743-7756
David Mason, prin. — Fax 743-0667

Oakland, Kennebec, Pop. 3,510
MSAD 47 — 2,700/PK-12
41 Heath St 04963 — 207-465-7384
James Morse Ed.D., supt. — Fax 465-9130
www.msad47.org/
Messalonskee HS — 900/9-12
131 Messalonskee High Dr 04963 — 207-465-7381
Lori Putnam, prin. — Fax 465-9151
Messalonskee MS — 600/6-8
33 School Bus Dr 04963 — 207-465-2167
Mark Hatch, prin. — Fax 465-9683

Old Orchard Beach, York, Pop. 7,789
Old Orchard Beach SD — 1,100/PK-12
28 Jameson Hill Rd 04064 — 207-934-5751
Eric Matthews, supt. — Fax 934-1917
Loranger MS — 400/4-8
148 Saco Ave 04064 — 207-934-2361
James Boisvert, prin. — Fax 934-3712
Old Orchard Beach HS — 400/9-12
40 E Emerson Cummings Blvd 04064 — 207-934-4461
Richard DiFusco, prin. — Fax 934-3705

Old Town, Penobscot, Pop. 8,127
Old Town SD — 1,600/K-12
156 Oak St 04468 — 207-827-7171
David Walker, supt. — Fax 827-3922
www.otsd.org/
Leonard MS — 300/6-8
156 Oak St 04468 — 207-827-3900
John Keane, prin. — Fax 827-3922
Old Town HS — 800/9-12
203 Stillwater Ave 04468 — 207-827-3910
Joseph Gallant, prin. — Fax 827-3918

Orono, Penobscot, Pop. 9,789
Union SD 87 — 1,000/K-12
18 Goodridge Dr 04473 — 207-866-5521
Kelly Clenchy, supt. — Fax 866-7111
www.orono.u87.k12.me.us/
Orono HS — 400/9-12
14 Goodridge Dr 04473 — 207-866-4916
Cathryn Knox, prin. — Fax 866-7116
Orono MS — 200/6-8
14 Goodridge Dr 04473 — 207-866-2350
Robert Lucy, prin. — Fax 866-7111

University of Maine 04469 — Post-Sec.
— 207-581-1110

Orrington, Penobscot

Calvary Chapel Christian S — 200/PK-12
154 River Rd 04474 — 207-991-9684
— Fax 989-0687

Oxford, Oxford, Pop. 1,284
MSAD 17 — 3,800/K-12
1570 Main St Ste 11 04270 — 207-743-8972
Mark Eastman Ed.D., supt. — Fax 743-2878
www.sad17.k12.me.us/
Other Schools – See South Paris

Phillips, Franklin
MSAD 58 — 1,000/PK-12
1401 Rangeley Rd 04966 — 207-639-2086
Quenten Clark, supt. — Fax 639-4139
www.sad58.k12.me.us/
Other Schools – See Strong

Pittsfield, Somerset, Pop. 3,222
MSAD 53 — 800/PK-8
PO Box 488 04967 — 207-487-5107
Michael A. Gallagher, supt. — Fax 487-6310
Warsaw MS — 400/5-8
27 School St 04967 — 207-487-5145
Scott White, prin. — Fax 487-4511

Maine Central Institute — 500/9-12
125 S Main St 04967 — 207-487-3355
— Fax 487-3512

Poland, Androscoggin
Union SD 29 — 1,800/K-12
1146 Maine St 04274 — 207-998-2753
Nina Schlikin, supt. — Fax 998-2727
www.poland-hs.u29.k12.me.us/union29/union29.html
Poland Regional HS — 600/9-12
1457 Maine St 04274 — 207-998-5400
William Doughty, prin. — Fax 998-5060
Whittier MS — 100/7-8
1457 Maine St 04274 — 207-998-5400
William Doughty, prin. — Fax 998-5060

Portland, Cumberland, Pop. 63,635
Portland SD — 7,500/K-12
196 Allen Ave 04103 — 207-874-8100
Mary Jo O'Connor, supt. — Fax 874-8199
www.portlandschools.org

Casco Bay HS | 9-12
196 Allen Ave 04103 | 207-874-8160
Derek Pierce, prin. | Fax 797-5437
Deering HS | 1,400/9-12
370 Stevens Ave 04103 | 207-874-8260
Kenneth Kunin, prin. | Fax 874-8153
King MS | 500/6-8
92 Deering Ave 04102 | 207-874-8140
Michael McCarthy, prin. | Fax 874-8290
Lincoln MS | 600/6-8
522 Stevens Ave 04103 | 207-874-8145
Kathleen Rossi, prin. | Fax 874-8288
Moore MS | 600/6-8
171 Auburn St 04103 | 207-874-8150
Stephen Rogers, prin. | Fax 874-8272
Portland Arts & Technology HS | Vo/Tech
196 Allen Ave 04103 | 207-874-8165
| Fax 874-8170
Portland HS | 1,200/9-12
284 Cumberland Ave 04101 | 207-874-8250
Michael Johnson, prin. | Fax 874-8248

Andover College | Post-Sec.
901 Washington Ave 04103 | 800-639-3110
Cheverus HS | 400/9-12
267 Ocean Ave 04103 | 207-774-6238
John Mullen, prin. | Fax 828-0207
Headhunter Institute | Post-Sec.
1041 Brighton Ave 04102 | 207-772-2591
Maine College of Art | Post-Sec.
97 Spring St 04101 | 207-775-3052
McAuley HS | 300/9-12
631 Stevens Ave 04103 | 207-797-3802
Sr. Edward Mary Kelleher, prin. | Fax 797-3804
Mercy Hospital | Post-Sec.
144 State St 04101 | 207-879-3000
Pierre's School of Cosmetology | Post-Sec.
319 Marginal Way 04101 | 207-774-9413
University of Southern Maine | Post-Sec.
PO Box 9300 04104 | 207-780-4141
Waynflete S | 500/PK-12
360 Spring St 04102 | 207-774-5721
| Fax 772-4782
Westbrook College | Post-Sec.
716 Stevens Ave 04103 | 207-797-7261

Presque Isle, Aroostook, Pop. 9,449
MSAD 1 | 1,800/PK-12
PO Box 1118 04769 | 207-764-4101
Gehrig Johnson, supt. | Fax 764-4103
www.sad1.org/
Presque Isle HS | 600/9-12
16 Griffin St 04769 | 207-764-0121
Eric Waddell, prin. | Fax 764-7720
Presque Isle MS | 300/6-8
569 Skyway St 04769 | 207-764-4474
Larry Fox, prin. | Fax 764-3078
Presque Isle Regional Tech Center | Vo/Tech
79 Blake St 04769 | 207-764-1356
Gene McLuskey, prin. | Fax 764-8107

Northern Maine Community College | Post-Sec.
33 Edgemont Dr 04769 | 207-768-2700
University of Maine at Presque Isle | Post-Sec.
181 Main St 04769 | 207-768-9400

Rangeley, Franklin
Union SD 37 | 200/K-12
PO Box 97 04970 | 207-864-3313
Philip Richardson, supt. | Fax 864-2451
Rangeley Lakes Regional S | 200/K-12
PO Box 97 04970 | 207-864-3311
| Fax 864-2451

Raymond, Cumberland
Raymond SD | 600/K-8
434 Webbs Mills Rd 04071 | 207-655-8666
Sandra S. Caldwell, supt. | Fax 655-8663
www.raymondmaine.org/schools/District/default.htm
Jordan-Small MS | 300/5-8
423 Webbs Mills Rd 04071 | 207-655-4743
| Fax 655-6952

Readfield, Kennebec
Maranacook Community SD | 900/6-12
45 Millard Harrison Dr 04355 | 207-685-3336
Richard A. Abramson, supt. | Fax 685-4703
169.244.33.66/~union_42/
Maranacook Community HS | 500/9-12
2250 Millard Harrison Dr 04355 | 207-685-4923
Janet Lori Putnam, prin. | Fax 685-9597
Maranacook Community MS | 400/6-8
2100 Millard Harrison Dr 04355 | 207-685-3128
Mary Callan, prin. | Fax 685-9876

Richmond, Sagadahoc, Pop. 1,775
Richmond SD | 600/PK-12
PO Box 190 04357 | 207-737-2221
Denison Gallaudet Ph.D., supt. | Fax 737-8707
www.richmond.k12.me.us/
Richmond HS | 200/9-12
132 Main St 04357 | 207-737-4348
Deborah Smith Fisk, prin. | Fax 737-8707
Richmond MS | 200/6-8
132 Main St 04357 | 207-737-8655
Ralph Peterson, prin. | Fax 737-8741

Rockland, Knox, Pop. 7,613
Applied Technology Region
Supt. — None
Mid-Coast School of Tech-Region 8 | Vo/Tech
1 Main St 04841 | 207-594-2161
W. Tim Hathorne, prin. | Fax 594-7506

MSAD 5 | 1,500/K-12
28 Lincoln St 04841 | 207-596-6620
Dennis Howard, supt. | Fax 596-2004
www.msad5.org
Rockland District HS | 500/9-12
400 Broadway 04841 | 207-596-2010
Michael Gundel, prin. | Fax 596-2028
Rockland District MS | 300/6-8
30 Broadway 04841 | 207-596-2020
Deborah Folsom, prin. | Fax 596-2026

Rockport, Knox
Five Towns Community SD
Supt. — See Camden
Camden Hills Regional HS | 700/9-12
25 Keelson Dr 04856 | 207-236-7800
Nick Ithomitis, prin. | Fax 236-7813

Rumford, Oxford, Pop. 5,419
MSAD 43
Supt. — See Mexico
Mountain Valley HS | 600/9-12
799 Hancock St 04276 | 207-364-4547
Matthew Gilbert, prin. | Fax 364-3436

Sabattus, Androscoggin
Oak Hill Community SD | 600/9-12
PO Box 220 04280 | 207-375-4273
Paul Malinski, supt. | Fax 375-2522
Other Schools – See Wales

Union SD 44
Supt. — See Wales
Sabattus Central S | 3-8
40 Ball Park Rd 04280 | 207-375-6961
Beverly Coursey, prin. | Fax 375-8871

Saco, York, Pop. 17,876
Union SD 7 | 2,200/K-8
90 Beach St 04072 | 207-284-4505
Michael LaFortune, supt. | Fax 284-5951
www.saco.org
Saco MS | 800/6-8
40 Buxton Rd 04072 | 207-282-4181
Richard Talbot, prin. | Fax 286-1807

Thornton Academy | 1,100/9-12
438 Main St 04072 | 207-282-3361
| Fax 282-3508

Saint Agatha, Aroostook
MSAD 33
Supt. — See Frenchville
Wisdom MSHS | 200/7-12
PO Box 69 04772 | 207-543-7717
Tammy LeBlanc, prin. | Fax 543-6316

Sanford, York, Pop. 10,296
Sanford SD | 3,700/K-12
917 Main St Ste 200 04073 | 207-324-2810
John Turcotte, supt. | Fax 324-5742
www.sanford.org
Sanford HS | 1,300/9-12
52 Sanford High Blvd 04073 | 207-324-4050
Allan Young, prin. | Fax 490-5152
Sanford JHS | 700/7-8
708 Main St 04073 | 207-324-3114
Becky Brink, prin. | Fax 490-5139
Sanford Regional Vocational Center | Vo/Tech
52 Sanford High Blvd 04073 | 207-324-2942
Deborah Guimont, prin. | Fax 324-2957

Pierre's School of Cosmetology | Post-Sec.
913 Main St 04073 | 207-490-1274

Sargentville, Hancock
Deer Isle - Stonington Community SD | 500/K-12
RR 1 Box 27A 04673 | 207-359-8400
Robert Webster, supt. | Fax 359-8451
Other Schools – See Deer Isle

Scarborough, Cumberland, Pop. 2,586
Scarborough SD | 3,200/K-12
PO Box 370 04070 | 207-730-4100
David Doyle, supt. | Fax 730-4104
www.scarborough.k12.me.us
Scarborough HS | 900/9-12
20 Gorham Rd 04074 | 207-730-5000
Andrew Dolloff, prin. | Fax 730-5007
Scarborough MS | 800/6-8
44 Gorham Rd 04074 | 207-730-4800
Jo Anne Sizemore, prin. | Fax 730-4804

Searsport, Waldo, Pop. 1,151
MSAD 56 | 800/K-12
6 Mortland Rd 04974 | 207-548-6643
Mary Szwec, supt. | Fax 548-2310
www.msad56.org/
Searsport District HS | 300/9-12
24 Mortland Rd 04974 | 207-548-2313
Gregg Palmer, prin. | Fax 548-2354
Searsport District MS | 200/6-8
26 Mortland Rd 04974 | 207-548-2311
Brian Corrigan, prin. | Fax 548-2352

Sherman Station, Penobscot
MSAD 25 | 400/K-12
PO Box 20 04777 | 207-365-4272
| Fax 365-4334

Other Schools – See Stacyville

Skowhegan, Somerset, Pop. 6,990
MSAD 54 | 2,900/K-12
196 W Front St 04976 | 207-474-9508
Brent Colbry, supt. | Fax 474-7422
www.msad54.org/

Skowhegan Area HS | 1,000/9-12
61 Academy Cir 04976 | 207-474-5511
Gilbert Eaton, prin. | Fax 474-0992
Skowhegan Area MS | 500/7-8
155 Academy Cir 04976 | 207-474-3339
John Krasnavage, prin. | Fax 474-9588
Skowhegan Regional Vocational Center | Vo/Tech
61 Academy Cir 04976 | 207-474-2151
Raymond Arbour, prin. | Fax 858-4879

South Berwick, York
MSAD 35
Supt. — See Eliot
Marshwood HS | 900/9-12
260 Dow Hwy 03908 | 207-384-4500
Paul Mehlhorn, prin. | Fax 384-2151

Berwick Academy | 600/K-12
31 Academy St 03908 | 207-384-2164
Richard Ridgway, prin. | Fax 384-3332

South China, Kennebec
Union SD 52
Supt. — See Winslow
China MS | 300/5-8
773 Lakeview Dr 04358 | 207-445-2065
Brenda Beale, prin. | Fax 445-3278

Crown Regional S | 50/1-12
9 Legion Memorial Dr 04358 | 207-445-5614
Earl Weigett, prin. | Fax 445-5627
Erskine Academy | 700/9-12
309 Windsor Rd 04358 | 207-445-2962
Donald Poulin, hdmstr. | Fax 445-5520

South Paris, Oxford, Pop. 2,320
MSAD 17
Supt. — See Oxford
Oxford Hills Comprehensive HS | 1,300/9-12
256 Main St 04281 | 207-743-8914
Theodore Moccia, prin. | Fax 743-5326
Oxford Hills MS | 600/7-8
100 Pine St 04281 | 207-743-5946
Harold Small, prin. | Fax 743-8048

Oxford Hills Christian Academy | 100/K-12
PO Box 318 04281 | 207-743-5970
Stephen Holbrook, admin. | Fax 743-9082

South Portland, Cumberland, Pop. 23,553
South Portland SD | 3,200/K-12
130 Wescott Rd 04106 | 207-871-0555
Wendy Houlihan, supt. | Fax 871-0559
www.spsd.org
Mahoney MS | 300/6-8
240 Ocean St 04106 | 207-799-7386
Kathy Germani, prin. | Fax 767-7731
Memorial MS | 400/6-8
120 Wescott Rd 04106 | 207-773-5629
Megan Welter, prin. | Fax 772-4597
South Portland HS | 1,100/9-12
637 Highland Ave 04106 | 207-767-3266
Jeanne Crocker, prin. | Fax 767-7713

Greater Portland Christian S | 200/K-12
1338 Broadway 04106 | 207-767-5123
Mary Willink, prin. | Fax 767-5124
Maine Medical Center | Post-Sec.
SMTC Fort Rd 04106 | 207-767-9589
Southern Maine Community College | Post-Sec.
2 Fort Rd 04106 | 207-741-5500

Stacyville, Penobscot
MSAD 25
Supt. — See Sherman Station
Katahdin MSHS | 200/7-12
PO Box 50 | 207-365-4218
Rae Bates, prin. | Fax 365-6011

Standish, Cumberland
MSAD 6
Supt. — See Bar Mills
Bonny Eagle HS | 1,200/9-12
700 Saco Rd 04084 | 207-929-3840
Sheila Jepson, prin. | Fax 929-9147

St. Joseph's College of Maine | Post-Sec.
278 Whites Bridge Rd 04084 | 207-892-6766

Strong, Franklin
MSAD 58
Supt. — See Phillips
Mt. Abram Regional HS | 300/9-12
RR 1 Box 760 04983 | 207-678-2701
Jeanne Tucker, prin. | Fax 678-2668

Sullivan, Hancock
Flanders Bay Community SD | 300/9-12
2165 US Hwy 1 Ste 3 04664 | 207-422-3522
Donald LaPlante, supt. | Fax 422-9568
Sumner Memorial HS | 300/9-12
2456 US Hwy 1 04664 | 207-422-3510
Michael Eastman, prin. | Fax 422-6463

Thomaston, Knox, Pop. 2,445
MSAD 50 | 1,000/K-12
12 Star St 04861 | 207-354-2555
Judith Harvey, supt. | Fax 354-2564
www.sad50.k12.me.us
Georges Valley HS | 300/9-12
47 Valley St 04861 | 207-354-2502
Neal Guyer, prin. | Fax 354-2369
Thomaston MS | 200/5-8
65 Watts Ln 04861 | 207-354-6353
Mary-Alice McLean, prin. | Fax 354-6238

Thorndike, Waldo
MSAD 3
  Supt. — See Unity
Mt. View HS   500/9-12
  577 Mount View Rd 04986   207-568-3255
  Lynda Letteney, prin.   Fax 568-7550
Mt. View JHS   300/7-8
  575 Mount View Rd 04986   207-568-7561
  Osmond Crowley, prin.   Fax 568-7590

Topsham, Sagadahoc, Pop. 6,147
MSAD 75   3,400/K-12
  50 Republic Ave 04086   207-729-9961
  J. Michael Wilhelm Ed.D., supt. Fax 725-9354
  www.link75.org/
Mt. Ararat HS   1,100/9-12
  73 Eagles Way 04086   207-729-2951
  Craig King, prin.   Fax 729-2953
Mt. Ararat MS   800/6-8
  66 Republic Ave 04086   207-729-2950
  Brenda Brown, prin.   Fax 729-2964

Trenton, Hancock

Life Christian Academy   100/PK-12
  171 Bar Harbor Rd 04605   207-667-8622
  Renee Clark, admin.   Fax 664-0238

Turner, Androscoggin
MSAD 52   2,200/PK-12
  486 Turner Ctr Rd 04282   207-225-3795
  Thomas Hanson, supt.   Fax 225-5608
  www.msad52.k12.me.us/
Leavitt Area HS   700/9-12
  21 Matthews Way 04282   207-225-3533
  Patrick Hartnett, prin.   Fax 225-3978
Tripp MS   400/7-8
  65 Matthews Way 04282   207-225-3261
  Cathy McCue, prin.   Fax 225-2102

Unity, Waldo
MSAD 3   1,600/K-12
  74 School St 04988   207-948-6136
  Wayne Enman, supt.   Fax 948-2678
  www.mvhs.sad3.k12.me.us
  Other Schools – See Thorndike

Unity College   Post-Sec.
  HC 78 Box 1 04988   207-948-3131

Van Buren, Aroostook, Pop. 2,759
MSAD 24   500/PK-12
  110 School Dr 04785   207-868-2746
  Clayton Belanger, supt.   Fax 868-5420
Van Buren District HS   200/7-12
  169 Main St 04785   207-868-5274
                        Fax 868-3537
Van Buren Regional Technology Center Vo/Tech
  169 Main St 04785   207-868-2746
  Clayton Belanger, prin.   Fax 868-5420

Vinalhaven, Knox
MSAD 8   200/K-12
  RR 1 Box 112 04863   207-863-4800
  George Joseph, supt.   Fax 863-4572
Vinalhaven S   200/K-12
  RR 1 Box 112 04863   207-863-4800
  Mike Felton, prin.   Fax 863-4572

Waldo, See Belfast
Applied Technology Region
  Supt. — None
Waldo County Tech Center-Region 7   Vo/Tech
  1022 Waterville Rd 04915   207-342-5231
  Paul Cochrane, prin.   Fax 342-4070

Waldoboro, Lincoln, Pop. 1,420
MSAD 40
  Supt. — See Warren
Gray MS   200/7-8
  PO Box 326 04572   207-832-2106
  Ben Vail, prin.   Fax 832-2108
Medomak Valley HS   700/9-12
  320 Manktown Rd 04572   207-832-5389
  Robert Strong, prin.   Fax 832-2280

Wales, Androscoggin
Oak Hill Community SD
  Supt. — See Sabattus

Oak Hill HS   600/9-12
  PO Box 400 04280   207-375-4950
  Patricia Doyle, prin.   Fax 375-4048
Union SD 44   800/K-8
  971 Gardiner Rd 04280   207-375-4273
  Paul Malinski, supt.   Fax 375-2522
  www.schoolunion44.org/index.html
  Other Schools – See Litchfield, Sabattus

Warren, Knox
MSAD 40   2,100/K-12
  44 School St 04864   207-273-4070
  Pamela Carnahan, supt.   Fax 273-4143
  shakespeare.mvhs.sad40.k12.me.us
  Other Schools – See Waldoboro

Washburn, Aroostook
MSAD 45   400/PK-12
  33 School St 04786   207-455-8301
  Brooke Clenchy, supt.   Fax 455-8217
  www.msad45.net/
Washburn District HS   100/9-12
  1359 Main St 04786   207-455-4501
  Robert Doar, prin.   Fax 455-4509

Waterboro, York
MSAD 57   3,700/PK-12
  PO Box 499 04087   207-247-3221
  Lynda Green, supt.   Fax 247-3477
  fc.sad57.k12.me.us/
Massabesic HS   1,200/9-12
  88 West Rd 04087   207-247-3141
  Deborah Mitchell, prin.   Fax 247-3146
Massabesic JHS   600/7-8
  PO Box 460 04087   207-247-6121
  Mark Fisher, prin.   Fax 247-8621

Waterville, Kennebec, Pop. 15,758
Waterville SD   2,000/K-12
  25 Messalonskee Ave 04901 207-873-4281
  Eric Haley, supt.   Fax 872-5531
  www.wtvl.k12.me.us
Mid Maine Technical Center   Vo/Tech
  3 Brooklyn Ave 04901   207-873-0102
  Mark Powers, prin.   Fax 873-7057
Waterville HS   600/9-12
  1 Brooklyn Ave 04901   207-873-2751
  Chris Hollingsworth, prin.   Fax 873-7058
Waterville JHS   500/6-8
  120 W River Rd 04901   207-873-2144
  Peter Thiboutot, prin.   Fax 873-5752

Colby College   Post-Sec.
  150 Mayflower Hill Dr 04901 207-872-3000
Pierre's School of Cosmetology   Post-Sec.
  251 Kennedy Memorial Dr 04901 207-873-0682
Temple Academy   100/PK-12
  60 W River Rd 04901   207-873-5325
  Elise Rossignol, prin.   Fax 872-2084
Thomas College   Post-Sec.
  180 W River Rd 04901   207-859-1110

Wells, York
Wells-Ogunquit Community SD   1,500/K-12
  PO Box 09490   207-646-8331
  Edward McDonough, supt.   Fax 646-0314
Wells HS   500/9-12
  PO Box 579 04090   207-646-7011
  Milton Teagus, prin.   Fax 646-4842
Wells JHS   500/5-8
  PO Box 310 04090   207-646-5142
  Christopher Chessie, prin.   Fax 646-2899

York County Community College Post-Sec.
  PO Box 529 04090   207-646-9282

Westbrook, Cumberland, Pop. 16,051
Westbrook SD   2,700/K-12
  117 Stroudwater St 04092   207-854-0800
  Stan Sawyer, supt.   Fax 854-0809
  www.westbrookschools.org
Wescott JHS   600/6-8
  426 Bridge St 04092   207-854-0830
  Brian Mazjanis, prin.   Fax 854-0858
Westbrook HS   800/9-12
  125 Stroudwater St 04092   207-854-0810
  Marc Gousse, prin.   Fax 854-0812

Westbrook Regional Technology Center Vo/Tech
  125 Stroudwater St 04092   207-854-0820
  Todd Fields, dir.   Fax 854-0822

Windham, Cumberland, Pop. 13,020
Windham SD   2,800/K-12
  228 Windham Center Rd 04062 207-892-1800
  Sanford Prince, supt.   Fax 892-1805
  www.windham.k12.me.us
Windham HS   900/9-12
  406 Gray Rd 04062   207-892-1810
  Deborah McAfee, prin.   Fax 892-1813
Windham MS   700/6-8
  408 Gray Rd 04062   207-892-1820
  Harold Shortsleeve, prin.   Fax 892-1826

Windham Christian Academy   100/PK-12
  1051 Roosevelt Trl 04062   207-892-2244
  Roy Mickelson, prin.   Fax 893-1289

Winslow, Kennebec, Pop. 5,436
Union SD 52   2,600/K-12
  20 Dean St 04901   207-872-1960
  Elaine Miller, supt.   Fax 859-2405
  www.su52.com
Winslow HS   600/9-12
  20 Danielson St 04901   207-872-1990
  Douglas Carville, prin.   Fax 872-1993
Winslow JHS   300/6-8
  6 Danielson St 04901   207-872-1973
  Hugh Riordan, prin.   Fax 872-1977
  Other Schools – See South China

Winterport, Waldo, Pop. 1,274
MSAD 22
  Supt. — See Hampden
Wagner MS   200/6-8
  PO Box 739 04496   207-223-4309
  Dale Williams, prin.   Fax 223-4325

Winthrop, Kennebec, Pop. 2,819
Winthrop SD   1,000/PK-12
  17A Highland Ave 04364   207-377-2296
  Terry Despres, supt.   Fax 377-3915
  www.winthrop.k12.me.us
Winthrop HS   300/9-12
  211 Rambler Rd 04364   207-377-2228
  Kevin Harrington, prin.   Fax 377-7486
Winthrop MS   200/6-8
  400 Rambler Rd 04364   207-377-2249
  Karen Criss, prin.   Fax 377-3667

Wiscasset, Lincoln, Pop. 1,233
Wiscasset SD   900/K-12
  214 Gardiner Rd 04578   207-882-6303
  Jay Readinger, supt.   Fax 882-4077
  www.wiscasset.k12.me.us
Wiscasset HS   400/9-12
  272 Gardiner Rd 04578   207-882-7722
  Susan Poppish, prin.   Fax 882-8251
Wiscasset MS   300/6-8
  83 Federal St 04578   207-882-7767
  Linda Bleile, prin.   Fax 882-8279

Yarmouth, Cumberland, Pop. 3,338
Yarmouth SD   1,400/K-12
  101 McCartney St 04096   207-846-5586
  Ken Murphy Ed.D., supt.   Fax 846-2339
  www.yarmouth.k12.me.us
Harrison MS   500/5-8
  220 McCartney St 04096   207-846-2499
  Bruce Brann, prin.   Fax 846-2489
Yarmouth HS   500/9-12
  286 W Elm St 04096   207-846-5535
  Edward Hall, prin.   Fax 846-2326

North Yarmouth Academy   300/6-12
  148 Main St 04096   207-846-9051
                        Fax 846-8829

York, York, Pop. 9,818
York SD   2,200/K-12
  469 US Route 1 03909   207-363-3403
  Henry Scipione, supt.   Fax 363-5602
  www.yorkschools.org/
York HS   700/9-12
  1 Robert Stevens Dr 03909   207-363-3621
  Robert Stevens, prin.   Fax 363-1809
York MS   700/5-8
  30 Organug Rd 03909   207-363-4214
  Stephen Bishop, prin.   Fax 363-1815

MARYLAND

MARYLAND DEPARTMENT OF EDUCATION
200 W Baltimore St, Baltimore 21201-2502
Telephone 410-767-0600
Fax 410-333-6033
Website http://www.marylandpublicschools.org
Superintendent of Schools   Nancy Grasmick

MARYLAND BOARD OF EDUCATION
200 W Baltimore St, Baltimore 21201-2502
President   Edward Root

PUBLIC, PRIVATE AND CATHOLIC SECONDARY SCHOOLS

Aberdeen, Harford, Pop. 14,184
Harford County SD
  Supt. — See Bel Air
Aberdeen HS 1,200/9-12
  251 Paradise Rd 21001 410-273-5500
  Thomas M. Szerensits, prin. ..... Fax 273-5587
Aberdeen MS 1,300/6-8
  111 Mount Royal Ave 21001 410-273-5510
  Gladys Pace, prin. ..... Fax 273-5542

Accident, Garrett, Pop. 348
Garrett County SD
  Supt. — See Oakland
Northern Garrett County HS 500/9-12
  86 Pride Pkwy 21520 301-746-8668
  Gary Reichenbecher, prin. ..... Fax 746-8942
Northern MS 500/6-8
  371 Pride Pkwy 21520 301-746-8165
  William T. Carlson, prin. ..... Fax 746-8865
Northern Evening HS ..... Adult
  86 Pride Pkwy 21520 301-746-8668
  Gary Reichenbecher, prin.

Accokeek, Prince George's, Pop. 4,477
Prince George's County SD
  Supt. — See Upper Marlboro
Burroughs MS 800/6-8
  14400 Berry Rd 20607 301-203-3200
  George Covington, prin. ..... Fax 203-3207

Beddow HS 100/7-12
  501 Bryan Point Rd 20607 301-292-1968
  ..... Fax 292-2095

Adelphi, Prince George's, Pop. 13,524
Prince George's County SD
  Supt. — See Upper Marlboro
Buck Lodge MS 900/6-8
  2611 Buck Lodge Rd 20783 301-431-6290
  Constance Gibb, prin. ..... Fax 445-8404

Hope Christian Academy 50/PK-12
  2601 Powder Mill Rd 20783 301-434-7800
  Robyn Watts, dir. ..... Fax 879-7005

Annapolis, Anne Arundel, Pop. 36,178
Anne Arundel County SD 77,800/PK-12
  2644 Riva Rd 21401 410-222-5000
  Eric J. Smith Ed.D., supt. ..... Fax 222-5602
  www.aacps.org/
Annapolis HS 1,700/9-12
  2700 Riva Rd 21401 410-266-5240
  Donald Lilley, prin. ..... Fax 266-5644
Annapolis MS 500/6-8
  1399 Forest Dr 21403 410-267-8658
  Carolyn Burton-Page, prin. ..... Fax 267-8924
Bates MS 600/6-8
  701 Chase St 21401 410-263-0270
  Diane Bragdon, prin. ..... Fax 263-0295
Broadneck HS 2,200/9-12
  1265 Green Holly Dr, ... 410-757-1300
  Lucinda Hudson, prin. ..... Fax 757-5621
Other Schools – See Arnold, Baltimore, Crofton,
  Edgewater, Fort Meade, Gambrills, Glen Burnie,
  Harwood, Linthicum Heights, Lothian, Millersville,
  Odenton, Pasadena, Severn, Severna Park

Annapolis Area Christian S 1,000/PK-12
  716 Bestgate Rd 21401 410-266-8251
  Larry Kooi, supt. ..... Fax 573-6866
Key S 700/PK-12
  534 Hillsmere Dr 21403 410-263-9231
  Marcella Yedid, hdmstr. ..... Fax 280-5516
St. John's College ..... Post-Sec.
  PO Box 2800 21404 410-263-2371
St. Mary HS 600/9-12
  113 Duke Of Gloucester St 21401 410-263-3294
  Dr. Charles Reiter, prin. ..... Fax 269-7843
United States Naval Academy ..... Post-Sec.
  121 Blake Rd 21402 410-293-1000

Arnold, Anne Arundel, Pop. 20,261
Anne Arundel County SD
  Supt. — See Annapolis

Magothy River MS 700/6-8
  241 Peninsula Farm Rd 21012 410-544-0926
  Charles Dunlap, prin. ..... Fax 544-1867
Severn River MS 900/6-8
  241 Peninsula Farm Rd 21012 410-544-0922
  Patrick Bathras, prin.

Anne Arundel Community College ..... Post-Sec.
  101 College Pkwy 21012 410-647-7100

Baltimore, Baltimore, Pop. 628,670
Anne Arundel County SD
  Supt. — See Annapolis
Brooklyn Park MS 600/6-8
  200 Hammonds Ln 21225 410-636-2967
  Raymond Bibeault, prin.

Baltimore CSD 86,200/PK-12
  200 E North Ave 21202 410-396-8700
  Dr. Bonnie Copeland, admin. ..... Fax 396-8898
  www.bcps.k12.md.us
Academy for College & Career Exploration 9-12
  2500 E Northern Pkwy 21214 410-396-7607
  Christopher Maher, prin. ..... Fax 426-6750
Baltimore City College HS 1,400/9-12
  3220 The Alameda 21218 410-396-6557
  Tim Dawson, prin. ..... Fax 243-0669
Baltimore Freedom Academy 600/9-12
  101 S Caroline St 21231 443-984-2737
  Tisha Edwards, prin. ..... Fax 675-5205
Baltimore Polytechnic Institute ..... Vo/Tech
  1400 W Cold Spring Ln 21209 410-396-7026
  Dr. Barney Wilson, prin. ..... Fax 235-5027
Baltimore S for the Arts 300/9-12
  712 Cathedral St 21201 410-396-1185
  Leslie Shepard, prin. ..... Fax 539-1430
Banks HS 700/9-12
  2500 E Northern Pkwy 21214 443-984-1541
  Anthony Harold, prin. ..... Fax 254-7455
Calverton MS 1,000/6-8
  1100 Whitmore Ave 21216 410-396-0581
  Marjorie Miles, prin. ..... Fax 545-7849
Canton MS 500/6-8
  801 S Highland Ave 21224 410-558-3879
  Ara Shishmanian, prin. ..... Fax 558-3879
Carver Voc-Tech HS ..... Vo/Tech
  2201 Presstman St 21216 410-396-0553
  Michael Plitt, prin. ..... Fax 396-0059
Central Career Academy at Briscoe ..... Vo/Tech
  900 Druid Hill Ave 21201 410-396-0771
  Marva Randolph, prin. ..... Fax 396-0317
Chinquapin MS 900/6-8
  900 Woodbourne Ave 21212 410-396-6424
  Deborah King, prin. ..... Fax 396-0381
Diggs-Johnson MS 300/8-9
  1300 Herkimer St 21223 410-396-1572
  Camille Smith, prin. ..... Fax 385-0340
Digital Harbor HS 900/9-12
  1100 Covington St 21230 443-984-1256
  Brian Eyer, prin. ..... Fax 539-7270
Douglass HS 1,300/9-12
  2301 Gwynns Falls Pkwy 21217 410-396-7821
  Isabelle Grant, prin. ..... Fax 523-7557
Dunbar HS 700/9-12
  1400 Orleans St 21231 410-396-9478
  Roger Shaw, prin. ..... Fax 545-7526
Dunbar MS 500/6-8
  500 N Caroline St 21205 410-396-9296
  Betty Donaldson, prin. ..... Fax 396-2954
Edmondson-Westside HS 1,100/9-12
  501 N Athol Ave 21229 410-396-0685
  Delphine Lee, prin. ..... Fax 545-7715
Entrepreneur Academy 9-12
  2000 Edgewood St 21216 410-396-0722
  Rose Hamm, prin.
Fallstaff MS 400/6-8
  3801 Fallstaff Rd 21215 410-396-0682
  Faith Hibbert, prin. ..... Fax 545-1737
Forest Park S 1,500/PK-12
  3701 Eldorado Ave 21207 410-396-0753
  Loretta Breese, prin. ..... Fax 396-0143
Franklin JHS 400/6-8
  1201 Cambria St 21225 410-396-1373
  Paul Llufrio, prin. ..... Fax 396-8434

Garrison MS 800/6-8
  3910 Barrington Rd 21207 410-396-0735
  Isiah Hemphill, prin. ..... Fax 545-7861
Hamilton MS 900/6-8
  5609 Sefton Ave 21214 410-396-6370
  Christine Connor, prin. ..... Fax 396-6561
Harbor City East HS 600/9-12
  2555 Harford Rd 21218 410-396-6241
  ..... Fax 396-7170
Harlem Park MS 800/6-8
  1500 Harlem Ave 21217 410-396-0612
  Teresa Lance, prin. ..... Fax 669-5815
Heritage HS 800/9-12
  2801 Saint Lo Dr 21213 410-396-6637
  Karen Lawrence, prin. ..... Fax 467-5560
Homeland Academy 2,000/9-12
  2000 Edgewood St 21216 410-396-0721
  Maisha Washington, prin. ..... Fax 945-2712
Lemmel MS 1,000/6-8
  2801 N Dukeland St 21216 410-396-0664
  Vera Holly, prin. ..... Fax 225-9457
Lewis HS, 6401 Pioneer Dr 21214 9-12
  Jean Ragin, prin. 410-545-1783
Liberal Arts Academy 9-12
  2000 Edgewood St 21216 410-396-0723
  Lamarge Wyatt, prin.
Lombard MS 600/6-8
  1601 E Lombard St 21231 410-396-9261
  Gwen Taliferro, prin. ..... Fax 396-9039
Maritime Academy 9-12
  3711 Clifton Ave 21216 410-396-0630
  Marco Clark, prin.
Marshall HS 600/9-12
  5000 Truesdale Rd 21206 410-396-1997
  Russell Williams, prin.
Marshall MS 800/6-8
  5001 Sinclair Ln 21206 410-396-9103
  Richard Greene, prin. ..... Fax 396-6153
Mergenthaler Vo-Tech HS ..... Vo/Tech
  3500 Hillen Rd 21218 410-396-6496
  Dr. Irby Miller, prin. ..... Fax 243-5354
New Era Academy 600/9-12
  2700 Seamon Ave 21225 443-984-2415
  John Davis, prin. ..... Fax 355-1130
Northeast MS 700/6-8
  5001 Moravia Rd 21206 410-396-9218
  Paul Dunford, prin. ..... Fax 396-1680
Northwestern HS 1,300/9-12
  6900 Park Heights Ave 21215 410-396-0646
  Sharon Kanter, prin. ..... Fax 396-0866
Paquin S 500/PK-PK, 1-
  2200 Sinclair Ln 21213 410-396-9399
  Rosetta Stith, prin. ..... Fax 522-2229
Patterson HS 1,900/9-12
  100 Kane St 21224 410-396-9276
  Laura D'Anna, prin. ..... Fax 633-0179
Pimlico MS 900/6-8
  3500 W Northern Pkwy 21215 410-396-0806
  Brenda Abrams, prin. ..... Fax 396-0580
Poole MS 500/6-8
  1300 W 36th St 21211 410-396-6456
  Diane Brown, prin. ..... Fax 396-7009
Renaissance Academy 9-12
  200 Font Hill Ave 21223 443-984-3164
  Karl Perry, prin.
Savage Institute of Visual Arts 9-12
  200 Font Hill Ave 21223 443-984-2833
  April Peters, prin.
Southeast MS 500/6-8
  6820 Fait Ave 21224 410-396-9291
  Barbara Sparrow, prin. ..... Fax 284-4947
Southern HS 600/9-12
  1100 Covington St 21230 410-396-1500
  Catherine Gomes, admin. ..... Fax 539-8331
Southwestern HS 1,600/9-12
  200 Font Hill Ave 21223 410-396-1422
  Darline Lyles, prin. ..... Fax 396-0209
Talent Development S 9-12
  1500 Harlem Ave 21217 443-984-2744
  Jeffrey Robinson, prin.
Thomas Medical Arts Academy 9-12
  200 Font Hill Ave 21223 410-396-1420
  Starletta Jackson, prin.

Upton S 200/K-12
811 W Lanvale St 21217 410-396-0775
Idalyn Hauss, prin. Fax 225-9005
Washington MS 700/6-8
1301 McCulloh St 21217 410-396-7734
Lynette Harris, prin. Fax 396-0552
W.E.B. Dubois HS 700/9-12
2201 Pinewood Ave 21214 410-396-6435
Delores Berry, prin. Fax 254-5936
West Baltimore MS 1,200/6-8
201 N Bend Rd 21229 410-396-0700
Toni Worthington, prin. Fax 396-7700
Western HS 900/9-12
4600 Falls Rd 21209 410-396-7040
Landa McLaurin, prin. Fax 396-7492
Winston MS 600/6-8
1101 Winston Ave 21212 410-396-6356
Eldon Thomas, prin. Fax 532-6584

Baltimore County SD
Supt. — See Towson
Arbutus MS 900/6-8
5525 Shelbourne Rd 21227 410-887-1402
Margaret Sholl, prin. Fax 536-1164
Carver Center for Arts & Technology Vo/Tech
938 York Rd 21204 410-887-2775
Joseph Freed, prin. Fax 769-9114
Catonsville HS 1,500/9-12
421 Bloomsbury Ave 21228 410-887-0808
Robert Tomback, prin. Fax 747-9473
Chesapeake HS 1,000/9-12
1801 Turkey Point Rd 21221 410-887-0100
David Lloyd, prin. Fax 682-3426
Deep Creek MS 900/6-8
1000 S Marlyn Ave 21221 410-887-0112
Maria Lowry, prin. Fax 391-6534
Dumbarton MS 900/6-8
300 Dumbarton Rd 21212 410-887-3176
Nancy Fink, prin. Fax 887-3176
Dundalk HS 1,400/9-12
1901 Delvale Ave 21222 410-887-7023
Margaret Johnson, prin. Fax 887-7025
Dundalk MS 600/6-8
7400 Dunmanway 21222 410-887-7018
Thomas Shouldice, prin. Fax 887-7284
Eastern Technical HS Vo/Tech
1100 Mace Ave 21221 410-887-0190
Patrick McCusker, prin. Fax 887-0424
Golden Ring MS 900/6-8
6700 Kenwood Ave 21237 410-887-0130
John S. Bowden, prin. Fax 682-6750
Holabird MS 800/6-8
1701 Delvale Ave 21222 410-887-7049
Susan Melton, prin. Fax 887-7275
Kenwood HS 1,800/9-12
501 Stemmers Run Rd 21221 410-887-0153
Paul D. Martin, prin. Fax 887-6382
Lansdowne HS Business & Finance 1,200/9-12
3800 Hollins Ferry Rd 21227 410-887-1415
Thomas DeHart, prin. Fax 887-1461
Lansdowne MS 800/6-8
2400 Lansdowne Rd 21227 410-887-1411
Kiki Geis, prin. Fax 887-7405
Loch Raven HS 1,000/9-12
1212 Cowpens Ave 21286 410-887-3525
Jacqueline Lamp, prin. Fax 887-5898
Loch Raven Technical Academy 1,000/6-8
8101 Lasalle Rd 21286 410-887-3518
Linda Wilson, prin. Fax 821-6398
Meadowood Education Center 100/6-8
1849 Gwynn Oak Ave 21207 410-887-6888
C. Anthony Thompson, prin. Fax 887-6889
Middle River MS 900/6-8
800 Middle River Rd 21220 410-887-0165
Donna Vlachos, prin. Fax 887-0167
Milford Mill Academy 1,400/9-12
3800 Washington Ave 21244 410-887-0660
Nathaniel Gibson, prin. Fax 887-0605
Old Court MS 1,100/6-8
4627 Old Court Rd 21208 410-887-0742
I. Lynette Woodley, prin. Fax 887-0670
Overlea HS 1,200/9-12
5401 Kenwood Ave 21206 410-887-5241
James Thanner, prin. Fax 661-0174
Parkville HS & Center of Technology 2,000/9-12
2600 Putty Hill Ave 21234 410-887-5257
Kevin Harahan, prin. Fax 668-7503
Parkville MS 1,200/6-8
8711 Avondale Rd 21234 410-887-5250
Stephen Edgar, prin. Fax 887-5315
Patapsco HS 1,600/9-12
8100 Wise Ave 21222 410-887-7060
Edmund L. Mitzel, prin. Fax 887-7062
Perry Hall HS 2,300/9-12
4601 Ebenezer Rd 21236 410-887-5108
Brian Gonzalez, prin. Fax 887-5116
Perry Hall MS 1,500/6-8
4300 Ebenezer Rd 21236 410-887-5100
Allen Zink, prin. Fax 887-5152
Pikesville HS 1,100/9-12
7621 Labyrinth Rd 21208 410-887-1217
Dorothy Hardin, prin. Fax 486-8436
Pikesville MS 1,200/6-8
7701 7 Mile Ln 21208 410-887-1207
Ilene Swirnow, prin. Fax 887-1259
Pine Grove MS 1,200/6-8
9200 Old Harford Rd 21234 410-887-5270
Jack Wilson, prin. Fax 668-5237
Sollers Point Technical HS Vo/Tech
325 Sollers Point Rd 21222 410-887-7075
Diane Young, prin. Fax 887-7238
Southwest Academy 1,300/6-8
6200 Johnnycake Rd 21207 410-887-0825
B. Maria Hopewell, prin. Fax 887-0829
Sparrows Point HS 800/9-12
7400 N Point Rd 21219 410-887-7517
Robert Santa Croce, prin. Fax 887-7533
Sparrows Point MS 600/6-8
7400 N Point Rd 21219 410-887-7524
John T. Foley, prin. Fax 477-6953
Stemmers Run MS 1,000/6-8
201 Stemmers Run Rd 21221 410-887-0177
John Ward, prin. Fax 918-1787
Stricker MS 900/6-8
7855 Trappe Rd 21222 410-887-7038
Deborah Klaus, prin. Fax 285-1864
Sudbrook Magnet MS 1,000/6-8
4300 Bedford Rd 21208 410-887-6720
Sharon E. Robbins, prin. Fax 887-6737
Towson HS Law/Public Policy 1,500/9-12
69 Cedar Ave 21286 410-887-3608
Jane Barranger, prin. Fax 583-1375
Western S of Technology Vo/Tech
100 Kenwood Ave 21228 410-887-0840
E. Donald Weglein, prin. Fax 887-1024
Woodlawn HS 2,000/9-12
1801 Woodlawn Dr 21207 410-887-1309
Daric V. Jackson, prin. Fax 887-1324
Woodlawn MS 900/6-8
3033 Saint Lukes Ln 21207 410-887-1304
Brian W. Scriven, prin. Fax 298-4352

All-State Career School Post-Sec.
2200 Broening Hwy Ste 160 21224 410-631-1818
Archbishop Curley HS 700/9-12
3701 Sinclair Ln 21213 410-485-5000
Barry Brownlee, prin. Fax 483-2545
Arlington Baptist S 400/K-12
3030 N Rolling Rd 21244 410-655-9300
Roger Salomon, admin. Fax 496-3901
Bais Hamedrash & Mesivta S of Baltimore 100/9-12
6823 Old Pimlico Rd 21209 410-486-0006
Sholom Salfer, prin. Fax 602-9738
Baltimore Actors Theatre Conservatory 50/K-12
300 Dumbarton Rd 21212 410-337-8519
Dr. Walter Anderson, hdmstr. Fax 337-8582
Baltimore City Community College Post-Sec.
2901 Liberty Heights Ave 21215 410-462-8000
Baltimore Hebrew University Post-Sec.
5800 Park Heights Ave 21215 410-578-6900
Baltimore International College Post-Sec.
17 Commerce St 21202 410-752-4710
Baltimore School of Massage Post-Sec.
6401 Dogwood Rd 21207 410-944-8855
Baltimore Studio of Hair Design Post-Sec.
318 N Howard St 21201 410-539-1935
Beren HS 200/9-12
400 Mount Wilson Ln 21208 410-484-7200
Jacob Schuchman, prin. Fax 484-3060
Beth Tfiloh Community S 1,100/PK-12
3300 Old Court Rd 21208 410-486-1905
Z. Schorr, dir. Fax 415-6348
Boys Latin S of Maryland 600/K-12
822 W Lake Ave 21210 410-377-5192
Dr. H. Mebane Turner, hdmstr. Fax 377-4312
Broadcasting Institute of Maryland Post-Sec.
7200 Harford Rd 21234 410-254-2770
Bryn Mawr S 900/PK-12
109 W Melrose Ave 21210 410-323-8800
Maureen Walsh, hdmstr. Fax 377-8963
Calvert Hall College HS 1,100/9-12
8102 La Salle Rd 21286 410-825-4266
Louis Heidrick, prin. Fax 825-6826
Cardinal Gibbons S 400/6-12
3225 Wilkens Ave 21229 410-644-1770
Philip Forte, prin. Fax 525-3757
Catholic HS of Baltimore 300/9-12
2800 Edison Hwy 21213 410-732-6200
Keith Harmeyer, prin. Fax 732-7639
College of Notre Dame of Maryland Post-Sec.
4701 N Charles St 21210 410-435-0100
Community College of Baltimore County Post-Sec.
7200 Sollers Point Rd 21222 410-282-6700
Community College of Baltimore County Post-Sec.
7201 Rossville Blvd 21237 410-682-6000
Coppin State University Post-Sec.
2500 W North Ave 21216 410-951-3000
Empire Beauty School Post-Sec.
5633 Reisterstown Rd 21215 410-358-4500
Forbush S 300/PK-12
6501 N Charles St 21204 410-938-4400
James Truscello, dir. Fax 938-4421
Friends S of Baltimore 1,000/PK-12
5114 N Charles St 21210 410-649-3200
Matthew Micciche, hdmstr. Fax 649-3213
Gilman S 1,000/PK-12
5407 Roland Ave 21210 410-323-3800
Jon McGill, prin. Fax 532-6513
Goucher College Post-Sec.
1021 Dulaney Valley Rd 21204 410-337-6000
Greater Baltimore Medical Center Post-Sec.
6701 N Charles St 21204 410-828-2121
Harrison Career Institute Post-Sec.
1040 Park Ave 21201 410-962-0303
Institute of Notre Dame 400/9-12
901 N Aisquith St 21202 410-522-7800
Anne Seeley, prin. Fax 522-7810
Johns Hopkins University Post-Sec.
600 N Wolfe St 21287 410-955-3182
Johns Hopkins University Post-Sec.
3400 N Charles St 21218 410-516-8000
Kingdom Academy 200/K-12
7000B Rossville Blvd 21237 410-391-8000
Lori Meehan, admin. Fax 390-3090
Loyola College Post-Sec.
4501 N Charles St 21210 410-617-2000
Maryland Beauty Academy of Essex Post-Sec.
505 Eastern Blvd 21221 410-686-4477
Maryland General Hospital Post-Sec.
827 Linden Ave 21201 410-995-8600
Maryland Institute College of Art Post-Sec.
1300 W Mount Royal Ave 21217 410-669-9200
Maryland School for the Blind Post-Sec.
3501 Taylor Ave 21236
Mercy HS 500/9-12
1300 E Northern Pkwy 21239 410-433-8880
Sr. Carol Wheeler, prin. Fax 323-8816
Mercy Hospital Post-Sec.
301 Saint Paul St 21202 410-332-9202
Morgan State University Post-Sec.
1700 E Cold Spring Ln 21251 443-885-3333
Mother Seton Academy 100/6-8
724 S Ann St 21231 410-563-2833
Sr. Eileen Clinton, prin. Fax 563-7353
Mt. St. Joseph HS 1,100/9-12
4403 Frederick Ave 21229 410-644-3300
Barry Fitzpatrick, prin. Fax 646-6221
Mt. Zion Baptist Christian S 300/PK-12
2000 E Belvedere Ave 21239 410-426-2309
Shawn Floyd, prin. Fax 426-5412
National Technological University Post-Sec.
1001 Fleet St 21202 410-843-6401
Ner Israel Rabbinical College Post-Sec.
400 Mount Wilson Ln 21208 410-484-7200
New All Saints S 200/5-8
3510 Eldorado Ave 21207 410-664-9433
Henry Fortier, prin. Fax 664-9434
North American Trade Schools Post-Sec.
6901 Security Blvd Ste 16 21244 410-298-4844
Our Lady of Mt. Carmel HS 300/9-12
1706 Old Eastern Ave 21221 410-686-1023
Kathleen Sipes, prin. Fax 686-2361
Peabody Institute Johns Hopkins Univ. Post-Sec.
1 E Mount Vernon Pl 21202 410-659-8150
Purpose & Potential Christian Arts Acad 100/PK-12
5814 Harford Rd 21214 410-444-2899
Patricia Matthews, admin. Fax 444-1434
Rabbi Steinberg S 300/6-12
6300 Smith Ave 21209 443-548-7700
Rabbi Naftoli Hexter, prin. Fax 548-0347
Roland Park Country S 700/K-12
5204 Roland Ave 21210 410-323-5500
Jean Brune, hdmstr. Fax 323-2164
St. Frances Academy 300/9-12
501 E Chase St 21202 410-539-5794
Sr. Marcia Hall, prin. Fax 685-2650
St. Ignatius Loyola Academy 100/6-8
740 N Calvert St 21202 410-539-8268
Jeffrey Sindler, prin. Fax 539-4821
St. Mary's Seminary & University Post-Sec.
5400 Roland Ave 21210 410-864-4000
Seton Keough HS 500/9-12
1201 S Caton Ave 21227 410-646-4444
Dr. Curtis Turner, prin. Fax 573-0107
Sisters Academy of Baltimore 5-8
146 2nd Ave 21227 410-242-1212
Sr. Debra Liesen, prin. Fax 242-5104
Sojourner-Douglass College Post-Sec.
500 N Caroline St 21205 410-276-0306
Talmudical Academy 600/K-12
4445 Old Court Rd 21208 410-484-6600
Rabbi Teichman, prin. Fax 484-5717
TESST College of Technology Post-Sec.
1520 S Caton Ave 21227 410-644-6400
Union Memorial Hospital Post-Sec.
201 E University Pkwy 21218 410-554-2739
University of Baltimore Post-Sec.
1420 N Charles St 21201 410-837-4200
University of Maryland Post-Sec.
520 W Lombard St 21201 410-706-3100
University of Maryland Post-Sec.
1000 Hilltop Cir 21250 410-455-1000
Yeshivas Lev Shlomo 200/9-12
7201 Park Heights Ave 21208 410-764-6500
Rabbi Menachem Braun, prin. Fax 764-8871
Yeshivat Rambam/Maimonides Academy 300/PK-12
6300 Park Heights Ave 21215 410-358-6091
Dr. Rita Shloush, admin. Fax 358-4229

Bel Air, Harford, Pop. 9,948

Harford County SD 39,500/PK-12
102 S Hickory Ave 21014 410-838-7300
Jacqueline Haas, supt. Fax 893-2478
www.hcps.org/
Bel Air HS 1,600/9-12
100 Heighe St 21014 410-638-4600
Joseph Voshkuhl, prin. Fax 638-4604
Bel Air MS 1,500/6-8
99 Idlewild St 21014 410-638-4140
Nancy Reynolds, prin. Fax 638-4144
Harford Technical HS Vo/Tech
200 Thomas Run Rd 21015 410-638-3804
Charles Hagan, prin. Fax 638-3820
Southampton MS 1,500/6-8
1200 Moores Mill Rd 21014 410-638-4150
Barb Canavan, prin. Fax 638-4305
Wright HS 1,800/9-12
1301 N Fountain Green Rd 21015 410-638-4110
William Ekey, prin. Fax 638-4114
Other Schools – See Aberdeen, Edgewood, Fallston, Havre de Grace, Joppa, Pylesville

---

Carroll S 900/9-12
703 E Churchville Rd 21014 410-838-8333
Paul G. Barker, prin. Fax 836-8514
Harford Community College Post-Sec.
401 Thomas Run Rd 21015 410-836-4000
Harford Lutheran S 100/6-10
1515 Emmorton Rd 21014 410-399-9646
Ruth Heilman, prin. Fax 399-9645
International Beauty School Post-Sec.
227 Archer St 21014 410-838-0845
John Carroll HS 800/9-12
703 E Churchville Rd 21014 410-879-2480
Paul Barker, prin. Fax 836-8514

Beltsville, Prince George's, Pop. 14,476

Prince George's County SD
Supt. — See Upper Marlboro
High Point HS 2,300/9-12
3601 Powder Mill Rd 20705 301-572-6400
Scott Smith, prin. Fax 572-6481

King MS 900/7-8
4545 Ammendale Rd 20705 301-572-0650
Robin Wiltison, prin. Fax 572-0668

TESST Technology Institute Post-Sec.
4600 Powder Mill Rd Ste 500 20705 301-937-8448

Berlin, Worcester, Pop. 3,742
Worcester County SD
Supt. — See Newark
Decatur HS 1,400/9-12
9913 Seahawk Rd 21811 410-641-2171
Louis Taylor, prin. Fax 641-1135
Decatur MS 700/7-8
9815 Seahawk Rd 21811 410-641-2846
Mel Ross, prin. Fax 641-3274

Worcester Preparatory S 600/PK-12
PO Box 1006 21811 410-641-3575
Dr. Barry W. Tull, hdmstr. Fax 641-3586
Wor-Wic Community College Post-Sec.
10452 Old Ocean City Blvd 7 21811 410-641-4134

Bethesda, Montgomery, Pop. 55,277
Montgomery County SD
Supt. — See Rockville
Bethesda-Chevy Chase HS 1,600/9-12
4301 E West Hwy 20814 240-497-6300
Sean Bulson, prin. Fax 497-6306
Johnson HS 1,900/9-12
6400 Rock Spring Dr 20814 301-571-6900
Dr. Christopher Garran, prin. Fax 571-6916
North Bethesda MS 700/6-8
8935 Bradmoor Dr 20817 301-571-3883
Alton E. Sumner, prin. Fax 571-3881
Pyle MS 1,300/6-8
6311 Wilson Ln 20817 301-320-6540
Michael Zarchin, prin. Fax 320-6647
Westland MS 1,000/6-8
5511 Massachusetts Ave 20816 301-320-6515
Dr. Ursula Hermann, prin. Fax 320-7054
Whitman HS 1,900/9-12
7100 Whittier Blvd 20817 301-320-6600
Dr. Alan Goodwin, prin. Fax 320-6594

DeVry University Post-Sec.
4550 Montgomery Ave Ste 100 20814 301-652-8477
Holton-Arms S 700/3-12
7303 River Rd 20817 301-365-5300
Diana Beebe, prin. Fax 365-6085
Landon S 700/3-12
6101 Wilson Ln 20817 301-320-3200
David Armstrong, prin. Fax 320-2787
Lycee Rochambeau 1,100/K-12
9600 Forest Rd 20814 301-530-8260
Martine Quelen, prin. Fax 564-5779
Stone Ridge S of the Sacred Heart 800/PK-12
9101 Rockville Pike 20814 301-657-4322
Sr. Anne Dyer, hdmstr. Fax 657-4393
Washington Waldorf S 300/PK-12
4800 Sangamore Rd 20816 301-229-6107
Natalie Adams, chrpsn. Fax 229-9379

Bladensburg, Prince George's, Pop. 7,911
Prince George's County SD
Supt. — See Upper Marlboro
Bladensburg HS 1,700/9-12
4200 57th Ave 20710 301-887-6700
Madeline Blanding, prin. Fax 887-6710

Elizabeth Seton HS 500/9-12
5715 Emerson St 20710 301-864-4532
Sharon Pasterick, prin. Fax 864-8946

Boonsboro, Washington, Pop. 2,841
Washington County SD
Supt. — See Hagerstown
Boonsboro HS 900/9-12
10 Campus Ave 21713 301-766-8022
Martin Green, prin. Fax 791-4138
Boonsboro MS 800/6-8
1 J H Wade Dr 21713 301-766-8038
Renee Foose, prin. Fax 432-2644

Bowie, Prince George's, Pop. 53,660
Prince George's County SD
Supt. — See Upper Marlboro
Bowie HS 2,700/9-12
15200 Annapolis Rd 20715 301-805-2600
John Birckhead, prin. Fax 805-2619
Tall Oaks Vocational HS Vo/Tech
2112 Church Rd 20721 301-390-0230
Larry McCray, prin. Fax 390-0228
Tasker MS 1,500/7-8
4901 Collington Rd 20715 301-805-2660
Karen Coley, prin. Fax 805-2663

Belair Baptist Christian Academy 100/K-12
PO Box 796 20718 301-262-0578
Gary Kohl, admin.
Bowie State University Post-Sec.
14000 Jericho Park Rd 20715 301-464-3000

Brandywine, Prince George's, Pop. 1,406
Prince George's County SD
Supt. — See Upper Marlboro
Gwynn Park HS 1,500/9-12
13800 Brandywine Rd 20613 301-372-0140
W. Garrow King, prin. Fax 372-0149
Gwynn Park MS 800/7-8
8000 Dyson Rd 20613 301-372-0120
Laura Danner, prin. Fax 372-0119

Brooklandville, Baltimore

Maryvale Prep HS 400/6-12
11300 Falls Rd 21022 410-252-3366
Sr. Shawn Marie Maguire, hdmstr. Fax 252-3740

Park S 900/PK-12
PO Box 8200 21022 410-339-7070
David Jackson, hdmstr. Fax 339-4125
St. Paul's S for Boys 900/PK-12
PO Box 8100 21022 410-825-4400
Thomas J. Reid, hdmstr. Fax 427-0390
St. Paul's S for Girls 500/K-12
PO Box 8100 21022 410-823-6323
Michael Eanes, hdmstr. Fax 828-7238

Brunswick, Frederick, Pop. 5,122
Frederick County SD
Supt. — See Frederick
Brunswick HS 900/9-12
101 Cummings Dr 21716 240-236-8600
Kristi Mitchell, prin. Fax 236-8601
Brunswick MS 600/6-8
301 Cummings Dr 21716 240-236-5400
Arthur Fairweather, prin. Fax 236-5401

Burtonsville, Montgomery, Pop. 5,853
Montgomery County SD
Supt. — See Rockville
Banneker MS 1,100/6-8
14800 Perrywood Dr 20866 301-989-5747
Samuel A. Rivera, prin. Fax 879-1032
Paint Branch HS 1,800/9-12
14121 Old Columbia Pike 20866 301-989-5600
Jeanette E. Dixon, prin. Fax 989-5609

California, Saint Mary's, Pop. 7,626

Blades School of Hair Design Post-Sec.
PO Box 226 20619 301-862-9797

Callaway, Saint Mary's

King's Christian Academy 300/K-12
20738 Point Lookout Rd 20620 301-994-3080
Sarah Patterson, admin. Fax 994-3087

Cambridge, Dorchester, Pop. 10,781
Dorchester County SD 4,800/PK-12
PO Box 619 21613 410-228-4747
Fred Hildenbrand, supt. Fax 228-1847
www.dcps.k12.md.us
Cambridge-South Dorchester HS 900/9-12
2475 Cambridge Beltway 21613 410-228-9224
Tom Gebert, prin. Fax 228-0724
Dorchester County School of Technology Vo/Tech
2465 Cambridge Beltway 21613 410-228-3457
John Hurley, prin. Fax 221-9601
Maces Lane MS 700/6-8
1101 Maces Ln 21613 410-228-2111
James Bell, prin. Fax 221-5278
Other Schools – See Hurlock

Countryside Christian S 200/PK-12
5333 Austin Rd 21613 410-228-0574
Timothy Oakes, prin. Fax 221-8659

Camp Springs, Prince George's, Pop. 16,392

Progressive Christian Academy 400/PK-12
5408 Brinkley Rd 20748 301-449-3160

Capitol Heights, Prince George's, Pop. 4,274
Prince George's County SD
Supt. — See Upper Marlboro
Central HS 1,200/9-12
200 Cabin Branch Rd 20743 301-499-7080
Fletcher James, prin. Fax 499-7087
Fairmont Heights HS 1,100/9-12
1401 Nye St 20743 301-925-1360
Peggy Nicholson, prin. Fax 925-1371
Walker Mill MS 700/7-8
800 Karen Blvd 20743 301-808-4055
Douglas Jones, prin. Fax 808-4039

Maple Springs Baptist Bible Coll. & Sem. Post-Sec.
4130 Belt Rd 20743 301-736-3631

Catonsville, Baltimore, Pop. 39,820
Baltimore County SD
Supt. — See Towson
Catonsville MS 600/6-8
2301 Edmondson Ave 21228 410-887-0803
Deborah Bittner, prin. Fax 887-1036

Community College of Baltimore County Post-Sec.
800 S Rolling Rd 21228 410-455-6050
Mt. de Sales Academy 500/9-12
700 Academy Rd 21228 410-744-8498
Sr. Elizabeth Allen, prin. Fax 747-5105

Centreville, Queen Anne's, Pop. 2,353
Queen Anne's County SD 7,500/PK-12
202 Chesterfield Ave 21617 410-758-2403
Dr. Bernard Sadusky, supt. Fax 758-8200
www.boe.qacps.k12.md.us
Centreville MS 600/6-8
231 Ruthsburg Rd 21617 410-758-0883
Sue Stein, prin. Fax 758-4447
Queen Anne's County HS 1,100/9-12
125 Ruthsburg Rd 21617 410-758-0500
Richard McNeil, prin. Fax 758-4454
Other Schools – See Stevensville, Sudlersville

Gunston Day S 100/9-12
PO Box 200 21617 410-758-0620
Fax 758-0628

Chesapeake City, Cecil, Pop. 783
Cecil County SD
Supt. — See Elkton
Bohemia Manor HS 700/9-12
2755 Augustine Herman Hwy 21915 410-885-2075
Randy Sheaffer, prin. Fax 885-2485

Bohemia Manor MS 500/6-8
2757 Augustine Herman Hwy 21915 410-885-2095
Berkeley Orr, prin. Fax 885-2485

Chestertown, Kent, Pop. 4,678
Kent County SD 2,600/PK-12
215 Washington Ave 21620 410-778-1595
Anthony Pack, supt. Fax 778-6193
www.kent.k12.md.us
Chestertown MS 400/5-8
402 E Campus Ave 21620 410-778-1771
John Schrecongost, prin. Fax 778-6541
Other Schools – See Galena, Rock Hall, Worton

Washington College Post-Sec.
300 Washington Ave 21620 410-778-2800

Clarksburg, Montgomery
Montgomery County SD
Supt. — See Rockville
Rocky Hill MS 800/6-8
22401 Brick Haven Way 20871 301-353-8282
Steven Whiting, prin. Fax 601-3197

Clarksville, Howard
Howard County SD
Supt. — See Ellicott City
Clarksville MS 700/6-8
6535 Trotter Rd 21029 410-313-7057
JoAnn Hutchens, prin. Fax 313-7061
River Hill HS 1,600/9-12
12101 State Route 108 21029 410-313-7120
William Ryan, prin. Fax 313-7406

Clear Spring, Washington, Pop. 450
Washington County SD
Supt. — See Hagerstown
Clear Spring HS 500/9-12
12630 Broadfording Rd 21722 301-766-8082
Michael Shockey, prin. Fax 842-0082
Clear Spring MS 500/6-8
12628 Broadfording Rd 21722 301-766-8094
Paul Engle, prin. Fax 842-3826

Clinton, Prince George's, Pop. 19,987
Prince George's County SD
Supt. — See Upper Marlboro
Decatur MS 800/7-8
8200 Pinewood Dr 20735 301-449-4950
Rudolph Saunders, prin. Fax 449-2105
Surrattsville HS 1,300/9-12
6101 Garden Dr 20735 301-599-2453
Alice Swift-Howard, prin. Fax 599-2565

Grace Brethren Christian S 800/PK-12
6501 Surratts Rd 20735 301-868-1600
George Hornickel, dir. Fax 868-9475

Cockeysville, Baltimore, Pop. 18,668
Baltimore County SD
Supt. — See Towson
Cockeysville MS 800/6-8
10401 Greenside Dr 21030 410-887-7626
Philip Taylor, prin. Fax 887-7628

College Park, Prince George's, Pop. 25,329

University of Maryland 20742 Post-Sec.
301-405-1000
University of Maryland Post-Sec.
Univ Blvd And Adelphi Rd 20742 301-985-7000

Colmar Manor, Prince George's, Pop. 1,299

New Covenant Christian Academy 50/PK-12
3805 Lawrence St 20722 301-277-2596
Dr. Cleola Spears, prin. Fax 277-9303

Colora, Cecil

West Nottingham Academy 200/9-12
1079 Firetower Rd 21917 410-658-5556
John Watson, hdmstr. Fax 658-6790

Columbia, Howard, Pop. 88,254
Howard County SD
Supt. — See Ellicott City
Atholton HS 1,200/9-12
6520 Freetown Rd 21044 410-313-7065
Marcia Leonard, prin. Fax 313-7078
Hammond HS 1,300/9-12
8800 Guilford Rd 21046 410-313-7615
Dr. Sylvia Patillo, prin. Fax 313-7632
Harper's Choice MS 600/6-8
5450 Beaverkill Rd 21044 410-313-6929
C. Stephen Wallis, prin. Fax 313-5612
Long Reach HS 1,600/9-12
6101 Old Dobbin Ln 21045 410-313-7117
Edmund Evans, prin. Fax 313-7422
Oakland Mills HS 1,100/9-12
9410 Kilimanjaro Rd 21045 410-313-6945
Frank Eastham, prin. Fax 313-6948
Oakland Mills MS 500/6-8
9540 Kilimanjaro Rd 21045 410-313-6937
Yvonne Smith, prin. Fax 313-7447
Wilde Lake HS 1,400/9-12
5460 Trumpeter Rd 21044 410-313-6965
Restia Whitaker, prin. Fax 313-6972
Wilde Lake MS 600/6-8
10481 Cross Fox Ln 21044 410-313-6957
Scott Conroy, prin. Fax 313-6963

Atholton Adventist S 200/K-10
6520 Martin Rd 21044 301-596-5593
Marilynn Peeke, prin. Fax 997-0367
Columbia Center Post-Sec.
6740 Alexander Bell Dr 21046 410-290-1777
Howard Community College Post-Sec.
10901 Little Patuxent Pkwy 21044 410-772-4800

Lincoln Technical Institute — Post-Sec.
9325 Snowden River Pkwy 21046 — 410-290-7100

Cresaptown, Allegany, Pop. 4,586
Allegany County SD
Supt. — See Cumberland
Center for Career & Technical Education — Vo/Tech
14211 McMullen Hwy SW 21502 — 301-729-6486
Deborah Bittinger, prin. — Fax 729-0661
Evening HS — Adult
14211 McMullen Hwy SW 21502 — 301-729-6486
Robert Hunter, prin.

Calvary Christian Academy — 300/PK-12
PO Box 5154 21505 — 301-729-0791
Geoff Wheeler, prin. — Fax 729-1648

Crisfield, Somerset, Pop. 2,780
Somerset County SD
Supt. — See Westover
Crisfield 8-9 Academy — 8-9
210 N Somerset Ave 21817 — 410-968-0150
Monique Ward, prin. — Fax 968-1178
Crisfield HS — 200/10-12
210 N Somerset Ave 21817 — 410-968-0150
Debra Josenhens, prin. — Fax 968-1178

Crofton, Anne Arundel, Pop. 12,781
Anne Arundel County SD
Supt. — See Annapolis
Crofton MS — 1,000/6-8
2301 Davidsonville Rd 21114 — 410-793-0280
Sharon Hansen, prin. — Fax 793-0295

Crownsville, Anne Arundel, Pop. 1,514

Indian Creek S — 500/PK-10
680 Evergreen Rd 21032 — 410-923-3660
Anne C. Chambers, hdmstr. — Fax 923-3884

Cumberland, Allegany, Pop. 20,833
Allegany County SD — 10,600/PK-12
PO Box 1724 21501 — 301-759-2000
Dr. William J. AuMiller, supt. — Fax 759-2039
www.boe.allconet.org
Allegany HS — 800/9-12
616 Sedgwick St 21502 — 301-777-8110
Michael S. Calhoun, prin. — Fax 759-2534
Braddock MS — 700/6-8
909 Holland St 21502 — 301-777-7990
Danny R. Carter, prin. — Fax 777-9741
Ft. Hill HS — 1,000/9-12
500 Greenway Ave 21502 — 301-777-2570
Stephen Lewis, prin. — Fax 777-2572
Washington MS — 800/6-8
200 N Massachusetts Ave 21502 — 301-777-5360
Harry Smith, prin. — Fax 777-8452
Other Schools – See Cresaptown, Frostburg, Lonaconing, Mount Savage, Westernport

---

Allegany College of Maryland — Post-Sec.
12401 Willowbrook Rd 21502 — 301-784-5000
Bishop Walsh S — 300/PK-12
700 Bishop Walsh Rd 21502 — 301-724-5360
Sr. Phyllis McNally, prin. — Fax 722-0555
International Beauty School — Post-Sec.
214 Paca St 21502 — 301-777-3020

Damascus, Montgomery, Pop. 9,817
Montgomery County SD
Supt. — See Rockville
Baker MS — 500/7-8
25400 Oak Dr 20872 — 301-253-7010
Louise Worthington, prin. — Fax 253-7020
Damascus HS — 1,900/9-12
25921 Ridge Rd 20872 — 301-253-7030
Robert G. Domergue, prin. — Fax 253-7036

Darlington, Harford

Harford Friends S, PO Box 208 21034 — 200/PK-12
Jonathan Huxtable, prin. — 410-457-5099

Denton, Caroline, Pop. 2,996
Caroline County SD — 5,400/PK-12
204 Franklin St 21629 — 410-479-1460
Dr. Edward W. Shirley, supt. — Fax 479-0108
cl.k12.md.us
Lockerman MS — 900/6-8
410 Lockerman St 21629 — 410-479-2760
Dale Brown, prin. — Fax 479-3594
Other Schools – See Federalsburg, Ridgely

Wesleyan Christian S — 200/PK-12
PO Box 118 21629 — 410-479-2292
L.A. Drummond, admin. — Fax 479-3294

District Heights, Prince George's, Pop. 6,168
Prince George's County SD
Supt. — See Upper Marlboro
Suitland HS — 2,700/9-12
5200 Silver Hill Rd 20747 — 301-817-0500
Mark Fossett, prin. — Fax 817-0515

Easton, Talbot, Pop. 12,503
Talbot County SD — 4,100/PK-12
PO Box 1029 21601 — 410-822-0330
K. Salmon, supt. — Fax 820-4260
www.tcps.k12.md.us
Easton HS — 1,100/9-12
723 Mecklenburg Ave 21601 — 410-822-4180
Dr. Timothy Thurber, prin. — Fax 819-5814
Easton MS — 900/6-8
201 Peach Blossom Ln 21601 — 410-822-2910
Marcia Sprankle, prin. — Fax 822-7210
Other Schools – See Saint Michaels

Chesapeake Christian S — 200/PK-12
1009 N Washington St 21601 — 410-822-7600
Horace Ward, admin. — Fax 819-6974
SS. Peter & Paul HS — 800/9-12
900 High St 21601 — 410-822-2275
James Nemeth, prin. — Fax 822-1767

Edgewater, Anne Arundel
Anne Arundel County SD
Supt. — See Annapolis
Center of Applied Technology-South — Vo/Tech
211 Central Ave E 21037 — 410-956-5900
Ronald Alberico, prin. — Fax 956-5905
Central MS — 1,000/6-8
221 Central Ave E 21037 — 410-956-5800
O. Jenkins, prin. — Fax 956-1266
South River HS — 2,000/9-12
201 Central Ave E 21037 — 410-956-5600
James Hamilton, prin. — Fax 956-5137
South River Evening HS — Adult
201 Central Ave E 21037 — 410-956-0462
Rosaria Jablonski, prin.

Edgewood, Harford, Pop. 23,903
Harford County SD
Supt. — See Bel Air
Edgewood HS — 1,300/9-12
2415 Willoughby Beach Rd 21040 — 410-612-1500
Joseph Schmitz, prin. — Fax 612-1585
Edgewood MS — 1,300/6-8
2311 Willoughby Beach Rd 21040 — 410-612-1518
Wayne Perry, prin. — Fax 612-1523

Eldersburg, Carroll, Pop. 9,720

St. Stephen's Classical Christian Acad — 100/K-12
2275 Liberty Rd 21784 — 410-795-1249
Christopher Jorgensen, hdmstr. — Fax 795-8820

Elkridge, Howard, Pop. 12,953
Howard County SD
Supt. — See Ellicott City
Elkridge Landing MS — 700/6-8
7085 Montgomery Rd 21075 — 410-313-5040
Thomas Saunders, prin. — Fax 313-5045
Mayfield Woods MS — 600/6-8
7950 Red Barn Way 21075 — 410-313-5022
Susan Griffith, prin. — Fax 313-5029

Elkton, Cecil, Pop. 13,586
Cecil County SD — 16,300/PK-12
201 Booth St 21921 — 410-996-5400
Dr. Carl Roberts, supt. — Fax 996-5454
www.ccps.org
Cherry Hill MS — 500/6-8
2535 Singerly Rd 21921 — 410-996-5020
Elizabeth Cronin, prin. — Fax 996-5435
Elkton HS — 1,000/9-12
110 James St 21921 — 410-996-5000
Vincent Cariello, prin. — Fax 996-5646
Elkton MS — 600/6-8
615 North St 21921 — 410-996-5010
Robert Gerard, prin. — Fax 996-5639
Other Schools – See Chesapeake City, North East, Perryville, Rising Sun

---

Elkton Christian S — 500/PK-12
144 Appleton Rd 21921 — 410-398-6444
Dr. Gary Frasier, admin. — Fax 392-0397

Ellicott City, Howard, Pop. 56,397
Howard County SD — 49,000/PK-12
10910 State Route 108 21042 — 410-313-6600
Dr. Sydney Cousin, supt. — Fax 313-6833
www.howard.k12.md.us
Bonnie Branch MS — 700/6-8
4979 Ilchester Rd 21043 — 410-313-2580
Kathryn McKinley, prin. — Fax 313-2586
Burleigh Manor MS — 600/6-8
4200 Centennial Ln 21042 — 410-313-2507
Steve Gibson, prin. — Fax 313-2513
Centennial HS — 1,500/9-12
4300 Centennial Ln 21042 — 410-313-2856
Scott Pfeifer, prin. — Fax 313-2891
Dunloggin MS — 500/6-8
9129 Northfield Rd 21042 — 410-313-2831
Cher Jones, prin. — Fax 313-2530
Ellicott Mills MS — 500/6-8
4445 Montgomery Rd 21043 — 410-313-2839
Michael Goins, prin. — Fax 313-2845
Folly Quarter MS — 700/6-8
13500 Triadelphia Rd 21042 — 410-313-1506
Carl Perkins, prin. — Fax 313-1509
Howard HS — 1,200/9-12
8700 Old Annapolis Rd 21043 — 410-313-2867
Gina Massella, prin. — Fax 313-2870
Mt. Hebron HS — 1,600/9-12
9440 Old Frederick Rd 21042 — 410-313-2880
Veronica Bohn, prin. — Fax 313-2543
Patapsco MS — 700/6-8
8885 Old Frederick Rd 21043 — 410-313-2848
Carol Mohsberg, prin. — Fax 313-2852
Other Schools – See Clarksville, Columbia, Elkridge, Fulton, Glenelg, Glenwood, Jessup, Laurel, Marriottsville

---

Glenelg Country S — 700/PK-12
12793 Folly Quarter Rd 21042 — 410-531-8600
Ryland Chapman, hdmstr. — Fax 531-1882

Emmitsburg, Frederick, Pop. 2,421

Mt. St. Mary's University — Post-Sec.
16300 Old Emmitsburg Rd 21727 — 301-447-6122

Fallston, Harford, Pop. 5,730
Harford County SD
Supt. — See Bel Air
Fallston HS — 1,700/9-12
2301 Carrs Mill Rd 21047 — 410-638-4120
Kevin Fleming, prin. — Fax 638-4125
Fallston MS — 1,200/6-8
2303 Carrs Mill Rd 21047 — 410-638-4129
Mary Blome, prin. — Fax 638-4237

James Run Christian Academy — 50/9-12
2022 Fallston Rd 21047 — 410-877-1576
R. Michael Robbins, prin. — Fax 877-8738

Federalsburg, Caroline, Pop. 2,603
Caroline County SD
Supt. — See Denton
Richardson HS — 600/9-12
25320 Richardson Rd 21632 — 410-754-5575
Roger Eareckson, prin. — Fax 754-3497
Richardson MS — 500/6-8
25390 Richardson Rd 21632 — 410-754-5263
Michael J. Iseman, prin. — Fax 754-5695

Forestville, Prince George's, Pop. 16,731
Prince George's County SD
Supt. — See Upper Marlboro
Forestville HS — 900/9-12
7001 Beltz Dr 20747 — 301-817-0400
Eric Lyles, prin. — Fax 817-0416
Jackson MS — 1,000/7-8
3500 Regency Pkwy 20747 — 301-817-0310
Trevor Christopher, prin. — Fax 817-0339

Bishop McNamara HS — 800/9-12
6800 Marlboro Pike 20747 — 301-735-8401
Marco Clark, prin. — Fax 735-0934

Fort Meade, Anne Arundel, Pop. 12,509
Anne Arundel County SD
Supt. — See Annapolis
MacArthur MS — 1,100/6-8
3500 Rockenbach Rd 20755 — 410-674-0032
Reginald Farrare, prin. — Fax 674-8021
Meade HS — 1,800/9-12
1100 Clark Rd 20755 — 410-674-7710
Joan Valentine, prin. — Fax 551-8210
Meade MS — 900/6-8
1103 26th St 20755 — 410-674-2355
M. Jacques Smith, prin. — Fax 674-2612

Fort Washington, Prince George's, Pop. 24,032
Prince George's County SD
Supt. — See Upper Marlboro
Friendly HS — 1,500/9-12
10000 Allentown Rd 20744 — 301-449-4900
Edward Ryans, prin. — Fax 449-4911
Gourdine MS — 500/7-8
8700 Allentown Rd 20744 — 301-449-4940
Leatriz Covington, prin. — Fax 449-4948
Oxon Hill MS — 700/7-8
9570 Fort Foote Rd 20744 — 301-749-4270
Tricia Dixson, prin. — Fax 749-4286

Frederick, Frederick, Pop. 56,128
Frederick County SD — 38,100/PK-12
115 E Church St 21701 — 301-644-5000
Dr. Linda Burgee, supt. — Fax 696-6848
www.fcps.org
Ballenger Creek MS — 1,200/6-8
5525 Ballenger Creek Pike 21703 — 240-236-5700
Mita Badshah, prin. — Fax 236-5701
Career and Technology Center — Vo/Tech
7922 Opossumtown Pike 21702 — 240-236-8500
Gregory Solberg, prin. — Fax 236-8501
Crestwood MS — 6-8
7100 Foxcroft Dr 21703 — 240-566-9000
Kathleen M. Hartsock, prin. — Fax 566-9001
Frederick HS — 1,500/9-12
650 Carroll Pkwy 21701 — 240-236-7000
Denise Fargo-Devine, prin. — Fax 236-7015
Johnson HS — 1,900/9-12
1501 N Market St 21701 — 240-236-8200
Marlene Tarr, prin. — Fax 236-8201
Johnson MS — 700/6-8
1799 Schifferstadt Blvd 21701 — 240-236-4900
Michelle Concepcion, prin. — Fax 236-4901
Linganore HS — 1,500/9-12
12013 Old Annapolis Rd 21701 — 240-236-7800
Margaret Lyburn, prin. — Fax 236-7801
Monocacy MS — 600/6-8
8009 Opossumtown Pike 21702 — 240-236-4700
Everett Warren, prin. — Fax 236-4701
Tuscarora HS — 700/9-12
5312 Ballenger Creek Pike 21703 — 240-236-6400
Jay Berno, prin. — Fax 236-6401
West Frederick MS — 900/6-8
515 W Patrick St 21701 — 240-236-4000
Dr. Paulette Shockey, prin. — Fax 236-4050
Other Schools – See Brunswick, Ijamsville, Middletown, New Market, Thurmont, Walkersville

---

ABI - AccuTech Business Institute — Post-Sec.
5310 Spectrum Dr # A 21703 — 301-694-0211
Frederick Community College — Post-Sec.
7932 Opossumtown Pike 21702 — 301-846-2400
Hood College — Post-Sec.
401 Rosemont Ave 21701 — 301-663-3131
Maryland School for the Deaf — Post-Sec.
PO Box 250 21705
New Life Christian S — 200/K-12
5909 Jefferson Pike 21703 — 301-663-8418
Paul Kemp, prin. — Fax 698-1583
St. John's Literary Institute — 300/9-12
889 Butterfly Ln 21703 — 301-662-4210
Robert Boyer, prin. — Fax 662-5166

Frostburg, Allegany, Pop. 8,107
Allegany County SD
Supt. — See Cumberland

Beall JSHS 900/7-12
331 E Main St 21532 301-689-3377
Greg Smith, prin. Fax 689-8709

Frostburg State University 21532 Post-Sec.
301-687-4000

Fulton, Howard
Howard County SD
Supt. — See Ellicott City
Lime Kiln MS 500/6-8
11650 Scaggsville Rd 20759 410-880-5988
Brenda Thomas, prin. Fax 880-5996
Reservoir HS 1,200/9-12
11550 Scaggsville Rd 20759 410-888-8850
Adrianne Kaufman, prin. Fax 888-8849

Gaithersburg, Montgomery, Pop. 57,365
Montgomery County SD
Supt. — See Rockville
Forest Oak MS 1,000/6-8
651 Saybrooke Oaks Blvd 20877 301-670-8242
John Burley, prin. Fax 840-5322
Gaithersburg HS 2,100/9-12
314 S Frederick Ave 20877 301-840-4700
Darryl Williams, prin. Fax 840-4707
Gaithersburg MS 500/7-8
2 Teachers Way 20877 301-840-4554
Thelma Smith, prin. Fax 840-4570
Lakelands Park MS 6-8
1200 Main St 20878 301-670-1400
Joseph Sacco, prin. Fax 670-1418
Montgomery Village MS 700/6-8
19300 Watkins Mill Rd 20886 301-840-4660
Eric Davis, prin. Fax 840-6388
Quince Orchard HS 1,900/9-12
15800 Quince Orchard Rd 20878 301-840-4686
Daniel Shea, prin. Fax 840-4699
Ridgeview MS 700/7-8
16600 Raven Rock Dr 20878 301-840-4770
Dr. Carol Levine, prin. Fax 840-4679
Watkins Mill HS 2,000/9-12
10301 Apple Ridge Rd 20886 301-840-3959
Peter J. Cahill, prin. Fax 840-3980

Aesthetics Institutes of Cosmetology Post-Sec.
15958 Shady Grove Rd Unit C 20877 301-330-9252
Covenant Life S 800/K-12
7501 Muncaster Mill Rd 20877 301-869-4500
Greg Somerville, admin. Fax 948-4920
Sodexho Marriott Healthcare Mid-Atlantic Post-Sec.
9801 Washingtonian Blvd 20878 301-987-4127

Galena, Kent, Pop. 433
Kent County SD
Supt. — See Chestertown
Galena MS 200/5-8
114 S Main St 21635 410-648-5132
Gayle Gill, prin. Fax 648-6881

Gambrills, Anne Arundel
Anne Arundel County SD
Supt. — See Annapolis
Arundel HS 2,000/9-12
1001 Annapolis Rd 21054 410-674-6500
Sharon Stratton, prin. Fax 672-3711

Germantown, Montgomery, Pop. 55,419
Montgomery County SD
Supt. — See Rockville
Clemente MS 900/6-8
18808 Waring Station Rd 20874 301-601-0344
Shawn Joseph, prin. Fax 601-0370
King MS 1,000/6-8
13737 Wisteria Dr 20874 301-353-8080
William Gregory, prin. Fax 601-0399
Kingsview MS 1,300/6-8
18909 Kingsview Rd 20874 301-601-4611
Dennis G. Queen, prin. Fax 601-4610
Neelsville MS 800/6-8
11700 Neelsville Church Rd 20876 301-353-8064
Dollye McClain, prin. Fax 353-8094
Northwest HS 1,800/9-12
13501 Richter Farm Rd 20874 301-601-4660
Sylvia K. Morrison, prin. Fax 601-4662
Seneca Valley HS 1,600/9-12
19401 Crystal Rock Dr 20874 301-353-8000
Suzanne Maxey, prin. Fax 353-8004

Montgomery College Post-Sec.
20200 Observation Dr 20876 301-353-7818

Glen Burnie, Anne Arundel, Pop. 38,922
Anne Arundel County SD
Supt. — See Annapolis
Corkran MS 800/6-8
7600 Quarterfield Rd 21061 410-222-6493
Debbie Montgomery, prin.
Glen Burnie HS 2,100/9-12
7550 Baltimore Annapolis Bl 21060 410-761-8950
Sam Salamy, prin. Fax 761-3711
Marley MS 900/6-8
7730 Baltimore Annapolis Bl 21060 410-761-0934
Susan Cassidy, prin. Fax 761-0736
North County HS 2,100/9-12
10 1st Ave E 21061 410-222-6970
Patricia Plitt, prin. Fax 222-6976
Glen Burnie Evening HS Adult
7505 Baltimore Annapolis Bl 21060 410-761-3664
Nelson Horine, prin.

Glencoe, Baltimore

Oldfields S 200/8-12
1500 Glencoe Rd 21152 410-472-4800
George Swope, hdmstr. Fax 472-3141

Glenelg, Howard
Howard County SD
Supt. — See Ellicott City
Glenelg HS 1,200/9-12
14025 Burntwoods Rd 21737 410-313-5528
Karl Schindler, prin. Fax 313-5540

Glenwood, Howard
Howard County SD
Supt. — See Ellicott City
Glenwood MS 600/6-8
2680 State Route 97 21738 410-313-5520
Richard Wilson, prin. Fax 313-5534

Cornerstone Academy of Glenwood 50/1-12
3060 State Route 97 21738 410-489-5775
Carol Parent, admin. Fax 489-5776

Great Mills, Saint Mary's
St. Mary's County SD
Supt. — See Leonardtown
Great Mills HS 1,600/9-12
21130 Great Mills Rd 20634 301-863-4001
Tracey Heibel, prin. Fax 863-4006

Greenbelt, Prince George's, Pop. 22,096
Prince George's County SD
Supt. — See Upper Marlboro
Greenbelt MS 700/7-8
8950 Edmonston Rd 20770 301-513-5040
Judy Austin, prin. Fax 513-5097
Roosevelt HS 2,800/9-12
7601 Hanover Pkwy 20770 301-513-5400
Sylvester Conyers, prin. Fax 513-5047

Hagerstown, Washington, Pop. 36,953
Washington County SD 20,200/PK-12
PO Box 730 21741 301-766-2800
Dr. Elizabeth Morgan, supt. Fax 766-2829
www.wcboe.k12.md.us
Hicks MS 700/6-8
1321 S Potomac St 21740 301-766-8110
Roger Stenersen, prin. Fax 766-8116
Northern MS 800/5-8
701 Northern Ave 21742 301-766-8258
Barbara Rice, prin. Fax 797-5887
North Hagerstown HS 1,200/9-12
1200 Pennsylvania Ave 21742 301-766-8238
Valerie Novak, prin. Fax 733-3158
South Hagerstown HS 1,100/9-12
1101 S Potomac St 21740 301-766-8369
Rick Akers, prin. Fax 766-8474
Washington Co. Job Development Center Vo/Tech
1350 Marshall St 21740 301-766-8451
Francis Murray, prin. Fax 824-2035
Washington County Technical HS Vo/Tech
50 W Oak Ridge Dr 21740 301-766-8050
Jeff Stouffer, prin. Fax 797-9743
Western Heights MS 700/5-8
1300 Marshall St 21740 301-766-8403
Jennifer Ruppenthal, prin. Fax 766-8540
Evening HS Adult
1151 S Potomac St 21740 301-766-8460
Robert Beard, coord. Fax 766-8471
Other Schools – See Boonsboro, Clear Spring, Hancock,
Smithsburg, Williamsport

Award Beauty School Post-Sec.
26 E Antietam St 21740 301-733-4520
Broadfording Christian Academy 300/K-12
13535 Broadfording Church 21740 301-797-8886
Rick Burkett, prin. Fax 797-3155
Grace Academy 400/PK-12
13321 Cearfoss Pike 21740 301-733-2033
Rev. N. Lynn Wakefield, admin. Fax 733-4706
Hagerstown Business College Post-Sec.
18618 Crestwood Dr 21742 301-739-2670
Hagerstown Community College Post-Sec.
11400 Robinwood Dr 21742 301-790-2800
Heritage Academy 300/PK-12
12215 Walnut Pt W 21740 301-582-2600
Harold Miles, prin. Fax 582-2603
Highland View Academy 50/9-12
10100 Academy Dr 21740 301-739-8480
Fax 733-4770
Paradise Mennonite S 200/1-10
19308 Air View Rd 21742 301-733-1368
Lester Showalter, prin.
St. Maria Goretti HS 200/9-12
1535 Oak Hill Ave 21742 301-739-4266
Christopher Siedor, prin. Fax 739-4261

Halethorpe, Baltimore

Good Shepherd S 100/8-12
4100 Maple Ave 21227 410-247-2770

Hampstead, Carroll, Pop. 5,336
Carroll County SD
Supt. — See Westminster
North Carroll HS 1,600/9-12
1400 Panther Dr 21074 410-751-3450
Kimberly Dolch, prin. Fax 751-3457
North Carroll MS 700/6-8
2401 Hanover Pike 21074 410-751-3440
Carl Snook, prin. Fax 751-3464
Shiloh MS 800/6-8
3675 Willow St 21074 410-386-4570
James Carver, prin. Fax 386-4579

Hancock, Washington, Pop. 1,699
Washington County SD
Supt. — See Hagerstown
Hancock MSHS 400/6-12
289 W Main St 21750 301-766-8186
Warren Barrett, prin. Fax 678-7218

Harwood, Anne Arundel
Anne Arundel County SD
Supt. — See Annapolis
Southern HS 1,500/8-12
4400 Solomons Island Rd 20776 410-867-7100
Jason Dykstra, prin. Fax 867-7100

Havre de Grace, Harford, Pop. 11,398
Harford County SD
Supt. — See Bel Air
Havre De Grace HS 700/9-12
700 Congress Ave 21078 410-939-6600
Wayne Thibeault, prin. Fax 939-6667
Havre De Grace MS 700/6-8
401 Lewis Ln 21078 410-939-6608
Glenn Jensen, prin. Fax 939-6613

Helen, Saint Mary's
St. Mary's County SD
Supt. — See Leonardtown
Brent MS 900/6-8
29675 Point Lookout Rd 20635 301-884-4635
Ryan Hitchman, prin. Fax 884-8937

Huntingtown, Calvert
Calvert County SD
Supt. — See Prince Frederick
Huntington HS 9-12
4125 Solomons Island Rd 20639 410-414-7036
Robert Dredger, prin. Fax 535-4633
Plum Point MS 800/6-8
1475 Plum Point Rd 20639 410-535-7400
Mary Friedman, prin. Fax 535-7413

Calverton S 400/PK-12
300 Calverton School Rd 20639 410-535-0216
Daniel Hildebrand, hdmstr. Fax 535-6934

Hurlock, Dorchester, Pop. 1,865
Dorchester County SD
Supt. — See Cambridge
North Dorchester HS 600/9-12
5875 Cloverdale Rd 21643 410-943-4511
Vaughn Evans, prin. Fax 943-3499
North Dorchester MS 500/6-8
5745 Cloverdale Rd 21643 410-943-3322
Dana Goodman, prin. Fax 943-3797

Hyattsville, Prince George's, Pop. 15,161
Prince George's County SD
Supt. — See Upper Marlboro
Hyattsville MS 800/7-8
6001 42nd Ave 20781 301-209-5830
Gail Dorsey, prin. Fax 209-5849
Northwestern HS 2,600/9-12
7000 Adelphi Rd 20782 301-985-1820
Jerome Thomas, prin. Fax 985-1833
Orem MS 1,000/7-8
6100 Editors Park Dr 20782 301-853-0840
Kenneth Calvin, prin. Fax 853-0839
Northwestern Evening HS Adult
7000 Adelphi Rd # B220 20782 301-985-1460
Diane Baker, prin. Fax 985-5749

De Matha Catholic HS 900/9-12
4313 Madison St 20781 301-864-3666
Dr. Daniel McMahon, prin. Fax 864-0248
Washington United Christian Academy 100/PK-12
PO Box 5417 20782 301-807-9397
Saramma Moses, admin. Fax 559-6942

Ijamsville, Frederick, Pop. 350
Frederick County SD
Supt. — See Frederick
Oakdale MS 500/6-8
9840 Old National Pike 21754 240-236-5500
Neal Case, prin. Fax 236-5501
Urbana HS 1,500/9-12
3471 Campus Dr 21754 240-236-7600
Dr. George Seaton, prin. Fax 236-7601
Windsor Knolls MS 1,000/6-8
11150 Windsor Rd 21754 240-236-5000
Tracey Lucas, prin. Fax 236-5001

Indian Head, Charles, Pop. 3,440
Charles County SD
Supt. — See La Plata
Henson MS 900/6-8
3535 Livingston Rd 20640 301-375-8550
Ronald Stup, prin. Fax 375-9216
Lackey HS 1,500/9-12
3000 Chicamuxen Rd 20640 301-753-1753
Curry Werkheiser, prin. Fax 743-9076
Smallwood MS 700/6-8
4990 Indian Head Hwy 20640 301-743-5422
Cynthia Warren, prin. Fax 753-8421

Jessup, Howard, Pop. 6,537
Howard County SD
Supt. — See Ellicott City
Patuxent Valley MS 700/6-8
9151 Vollmerhausen Rd 20794 410-880-5840
Sterlind Burke, prin. Fax 880-5846

Joppa, Harford, Pop. 11,084
Harford County SD
Supt. — See Bel Air
Joppatowne HS 1,000/9-12
555 Joppa Farm Rd 21085 410-612-1510
Macon Tucker, prin. Fax 612-1528
Magnolia MS 900/6-8
299 Fort Hoyle Rd 21085 410-612-1525
Joseph Mascari, prin. Fax 612-1598

Chesapeake Christian S 100/K-12
900 Trimble Rd 21085 410-676-8815
Lisa Gordon, admin. Fax 679-8825

Kensington, Montgomery, Pop. 1,920
Montgomery County SD
Supt. — See Rockville
Einstein HS 1,800/9-12
11135 Newport Mill Rd 20895 301-929-2200
James Fernandez, prin. Fax 649-8279
Newport Mill MS 700/6-8
11311 Newport Mill Rd 20895 301-929-2244
Nelson McLeod, prin. Fax 929-2274

Academy of the Holy Cross 500/9-12
4920 Strathmore Ave 20895 301-942-2100
Sr. Katherine Kase, prin. Fax 929-6440

Kingsville, Baltimore, Pop. 3,550

Open Bible Christian Academy 100/PK-12
13 Open Bible Way 21087 410-593-9940
William Trautman, hdmstr. Fax 593-9942

Landover, Prince George's, Pop. 5,052
Prince George's County SD
Supt. — See Upper Marlboro
Gholson MS 900/7-8
900 Nalley Rd 20785 301-883-8390
Teri Hudson, prin. Fax 883-8394
Kenmoor MS 800/7-8
2500 Kenmoor Dr 20785 301-925-2300
Diana Mitchell, prin. Fax 925-2317

Jericho Christian Academy 300/K-12
8500 Jericho City Dr 20785 301-333-9400
Dr. J. Yvonne Parker, prin. Fax 333-0521
Ultrasound Diagnostic School Post-Sec.
8401 Corporate Dr Ste 500 20785 301-588-0786

Lanham Seabrook, Prince George's, Pop. 16,792
Prince George's County SD
Supt. — See Upper Marlboro
DuVal HS 1,100/9-12
9880 Good Luck Rd 20706 301-918-8600
Thomas Anderson, prin. Fax 918-8606
Johnson MS 800/7-8
5401 Barker Pl 20706 301-918-8680
Ronald Curtis, prin. Fax 918-8688

Capital Bible Seminary Post-Sec.
6511 Princess Garden Pkwy 20706 301-552-1400
Lanham Christian S 300/K-12
8400 Good Luck Rd 20706 301-552-9102
Gene Pinkard, hdmstr. Fax 552-2021
Washington Bible College Post-Sec.
6511 Princess Garden Pkwy 20706 301-552-1400

La Plata, Charles, Pop. 7,590
Charles County SD 25,700/PK-12
PO Box 2770 20646 301-932-6610
James E. Richmond, supt. Fax 932-6651
www.ccboe.com
La Plata HS 1,600/9-12
6035 Radio Station Rd 20646 301-934-1100
Garth Bowling, prin. Fax 934-5657
Somers MS 1,100/6-8
300 Willow Ln 20646 301-934-4663
Joseph Warfield, prin. Fax 934-2982
Other Schools – See Indian Head, Newburg, Pomfret, Waldorf

College of Southern Maryland Post-Sec.
PO Box 910 20646 301-934-2251

Largo, Prince George's, Pop. 9,475

Prince George's Community College Post-Sec.
301 Largo Rd 20774 301-336-6000

Laurel, Prince George's, Pop. 20,653
Howard County SD
Supt. — See Ellicott City
Hammond MS 600/6-8
8110 Aladdin Dr 20723 410-880-5830
Kerry McGowan, prin. Fax 880-5837
Murray Hill MS 600/6-8
9989 Winter Sun Rd 20723 410-880-5897
Carolyn Jameson, prin. Fax 880-5938

Prince George's County SD
Supt. — See Upper Marlboro
Eisenhower MS 900/6-8
13725 Briarwood Dr 20708 301-497-3620
Charoscar Coleman, prin. Fax 497-3637
Laurel HS 2,200/9-12
8000 Cherry Ln 20707 301-497-2050
Dwayne Jones, prin. Fax 497-2068

Capitol College Post-Sec.
11301 Springfield Rd 20708 800-950-1992
St. Vincent Pallotti HS 400/9-12
113 Saint Marys Pl 20707 301-725-3228
Stephen Edmonds, prin. Fax 776-4343
Tai Sophia Insitute Post-Sec.
7750 Montpelier Rd 20723 800-735-2968

Leonardtown, Saint Mary's, Pop. 1,965
St. Mary's County SD 16,300/PK-12
PO Box 641 20650 301-475-5511
Dr. Michael Martirano, supt. Fax 475-4262
www.smcps.org/
Forrest Career & Technology Center Vo/Tech
24005 Point Lookout Rd 20650 301-475-0242
Robert Taylor, prin. Fax 475-0245
Leonardtown HS 1,600/9-12
23995 Point Lookout Rd 20650 301-475-0200
James Smith, prin. Fax 475-0204
Leonardtown MS 1,000/6-8
24015 Point Lookout Rd 20650 301-475-0230
Charlottis Woodley, prin. Fax 475-0237
Other Schools – See Great Mills, Helen, Lexington Park, Morganza

Leonard Hall Naval Academy 100/6-12
PO Box 507 20650 301-475-8029
Suzanne Wisnieski, prin. Fax 475-8518
St. Mary's Ryken HS 600/9-12
22600 Camp Calvert Rd 20650 301-475-2814
Mary Joy Hurlburt, prin. Fax 475-7972

Lexington Park, Saint Mary's, Pop. 9,943
St. Mary's County SD
Supt. — See Leonardtown
Esperanza MS 900/6-8
22790 Maple Rd 20653 301-863-4016
Jill Snyder-Mills, prin. Fax 863-4020
Spring Ridge MS 900/6-8
19856 Three Notch Rd 20653 301-863-4031
Maureen Montgomery, prin. Fax 863-4035

Linthicum Heights, Anne Arundel, Pop. 2,980
Anne Arundel County SD
Supt. — See Annapolis
Lindale MS, 415 Andover Rd 21090 1,100/6-8
George Lindley, prin. 410-691-4344

Lonaconing, Allegany, Pop. 1,164
Allegany County SD
Supt. — See Cumberland
Westmar HS 400/9-12
16915 Lwr Georges Crk Rd SW 21539301-463-5751
Wayne Nicol, prin. Fax 463-2231

Lothian, Anne Arundel
Anne Arundel County SD
Supt. — See Annapolis
Southern MS 900/6-8
5235 Solomons Island Rd 20711 410-867-2084
Mary Ann Buckley, prin.

Lusby, Calvert
Calvert County SD
Supt. — See Prince Frederick
Mill Creek MS 700/6-8
12200 Margaret Taylor Rd 20657 410-535-7824
Darrel Prioleau, prin. Fax 257-7829
Patuxent HS 1,700/9-12
12485 Rousby Hall Rd 20657 410-535-7865
Nancy Highsmith, prin. Fax 535-7875
Southern MS 700/6-8
9615 H G Trueman Rd 20657 410-535-7877
Larry Butler, prin. Fax 535-7879

Lutherville, Baltimore, Pop. 16,442
Baltimore County SD
Supt. — See Towson
Ridgely MS 1,000/6-8
121 E Ridgely Rd 21093 410-887-7650
Susan Evans, prin. Fax 887-7834

Mc Henry, Garrett

Garrett College Post-Sec.
PO Box 151 21541 301-387-3000

Mardela Springs, Wicomico, Pop. 356
Wicomico County SD
Supt. — See Salisbury
Mardela MSHS 700/6-12
24940 Delmar Rd 21837 410-677-5142
Dr. Daniel Pyle, prin. Fax 677-5166

Marriottsville, Howard
Howard County SD
Supt. — See Ellicott City
Marriotts Ridge HS 1,200/9-12
12100 Woodford Dr 21104 410-313-5568
Pat Saunderson, prin.
Mount View MS 700/6-8
12101 Woodford Dr 21104 410-313-5545
James Evans, prin. Fax 313-5551

Chapelgate Christian Academy 500/6-12
2600 Marriottsville Rd 21104 410-442-5888
Robin Van Ness, hdmstr. Fax 442-5820

Middletown, Frederick, Pop. 2,805
Frederick County SD
Supt. — See Frederick
Middletown HS 1,300/9-12
200 Schoolhouse Dr 21769 240-236-7400
Kathleen Schlappal, prin. Fax 236-7450
Middletown MS 1,000/6-8
100 High St 21769 240-236-4200
Donna Faith, prin. Fax 236-4250

Millersville, Anne Arundel
Anne Arundel County SD
Supt. — See Annapolis
Old Mill HS 2,400/9-12
600 Patriot Ln 21108 410-969-9010
Kathy Kubic, prin. Fax 969-1620
Old Mill MS North 900/6-8
610 Patriot Ln 21108 410-969-5950
Sean McElhaney, prin.
Old Mill MS South 900/6-8
620 Patriot Ln 21108 410-969-7000
Catherine Gilbert, prin.

Strayer University Post-Sec.
1520 Jabez Run Ste 100 21108 410-923-4500

Mitchellville, Prince George's, Pop. 12,593
Prince George's County SD
Supt. — See Upper Marlboro
Just MS 1,000/7-8
1300 Campus Way N 20721 301-808-4040
Marian White-Hood, prin. Fax 808-5050

Monkton, Baltimore
Baltimore County SD
Supt. — See Towson
Hereford MS 1,000/6-8
712 Corbett Rd 21111 410-887-7902
Cathryn Walrod, prin. Fax 887-7904

Montgomery Village, Montgomery, Pop. 38,051

Ets Chaiyim S 100/K-12
20300 Pleasant Ridge Dr 20886 301-216-9592
Daniel Switzer, prin. Fax 216-9594

Morganza, Saint Mary's
St. Mary's County SD
Supt. — See Leonardtown
Chopticon HS 1,600/9-12
25390 Colton Point Rd 20660 301-475-0215
Joseph North, prin. Fax 475-0222

Mount Airy, Carroll, Pop. 7,904
Carroll County SD
Supt. — See Westminster
Mount Airy MS 600/6-8
102 Watersville Rd 21771 301-751-3554
Virginia Savell, prin. Fax 795-1756

Mount Savage, Allegany
Allegany County SD
Supt. — See Cumberland
Mount Savage S 1,200/PK-12
13201 New School Rd NW 21545 301-264-3220
Gary Llewellyn, prin. Fax 264-4015

Newark, Worcester
Worcester County SD 6,700/PK-12
6270 Worcester Hwy 21841 410-632-5000
Jon Andes, supt. Fax 632-0364
www.worcester.k12.md.us
Worcester Career & Technology Center Vo/Tech
6268 Worcester Hwy 21841 410-632-5050
Jane Pruitt, prin. Fax 632-5059
Other Schools – See Berlin, Pocomoke City, Snow Hill

Newburg, Charles
Charles County SD
Supt. — See La Plata
Piccowaxen MS 500/6-8
12834 Rock Point Rd 20664 301-934-1977
Kenneth Schroeck, prin. Fax 934-1628

New Carrollton, Prince George's, Pop. 13,043
Prince George's County SD
Supt. — See Upper Marlboro
Carroll MS 900/7-8
6130 Lamont Dr 20784 301-918-8640
Eric Wood, prin. Fax 918-8646

Hair Academy Post-Sec.
8435 Annapolis Rd 20784 301-459-2509

New Market, Frederick, Pop. 452
Frederick County SD
Supt. — See Frederick
New Market MS 900/6-8
125 W Main St 21774 240-236-4600
Daniel Lippy, prin. Fax 236-4650

New Windsor, Carroll, Pop. 1,331
Carroll County SD
Supt. — See Westminster
New Windsor MS 500/6-8
1000 Green Valley Rd 21776 410-751-3355
Donald Bell, prin. Fax 751-3358

North Bethesda, Montgomery, Pop. 38,610

Georgetown Preparatory S 400/9-12
10900 Rockville Pike 20852 301-493-5000
Edward Kowalchick, hdmstr. Fax 493-5905

North East, Cecil, Pop. 2,753
Cecil County SD
Supt. — See Elkton
Cecil County S of Technology Vo/Tech
900 N East Rd 21901 410-996-6250
Lewis Erbe, prin. Fax 996-6256
North East HS 1,100/9-12
300 Irishtown Rd 21901 410-996-6200
Terill Stammler, prin. Fax 996-6264
North East MS 800/6-8
200 E Cecil Ave 21901 410-996-6210
Kevin Daughtery, prin. Fax 996-6236
Rising Sun HS 1,100/9-12
100 Tiger Dr 21901 410-658-9115
George Larson, prin. Fax 658-9121

Cecil Community College Post-Sec.
1 Seahawk Dr 21901 410-287-6060
Tome S 400/K-12
581 S Maryland Ave 21901 410-287-2050
Dr. F. Darcy Williams, hdmstr. Fax 287-8999

Oakland, Garrett, Pop. 1,936
Garrett County SD 4,800/PK-12
40 S 2nd St 21550 301-334-8900
Wendell Teets, supt. Fax 334-8916
www.ga.k12.md.us/
Southern Garrett County HS 800/9-12
345 Oakland Dr 21550 301-334-9447
Tom Woods, prin. Fax 334-0962
Southern MS 700/6-8
605 Harvey Winters Dr 21550 301-334-8881
John Rickman, prin. Fax 334-2315
Southern Evening HS Adult
345 Oakland Dr 21550 301-334-9447
Thomas Woods, prin.
Other Schools – See Accident

Mountaintop Adventist S 50/K-10
16335 Garrett Hwy 21550 301-387-9532
Marie Schuberthan, prin. Fax 387-5799

Ocean City, Worcester, Pop. 7,142

Ocean City Christian S 100/K-12
12637A Ocean Gtwy 21842 410-213-7595
Dwayne Purnell, admin. Fax 213-8001

Odenton, Anne Arundel, Pop. 12,833
Anne Arundel County SD
Supt. — See Annapolis
Arundel MS 1,000/6-8
1179 Hammond Ln 21113 410-674-6900
Paul Strickler, prin. Fax 674-6593

Olney, Montgomery, Pop. 23,019
Montgomery County SD
Supt. — See Rockville
Farquhar MS 700/6-8
16915 Batchellors Forest Rd 20832 301-924-3100
Scott Murphy, prin. Fax 924-3152
Parks MS 1,000/6-8
19200 Olney Mill Rd 20832 301-924-3180
Sarah Pinkney-Murkey, prin. Fax 924-3288

Owings, Calvert
Calvert County SD
Supt. — See Prince Frederick
Northern HS 1,800/9-12
2950 Chaneyville Rd 20736 410-257-1519
George Miller, prin. Fax 257-1530
Northern MS 800/6-8
2954 Chaneyville Rd 20736 410-257-1622
Karen Burnett, prin. Fax 257-1623
Windy Hill MS 800/6-8
9560 Boyds Turn Rd 20736 410-257-1560
Ed Cassidy, prin. Fax 257-1556

Owings Mills, Baltimore, Pop. 9,474
Baltimore County SD
Supt. — See Towson
New Town HS 1,000/9-12
4931 New Town Blvd 21117 410-887-1614
Margaret Spicer, prin. Fax 654-8897
Owings Mills HS 1,300/9-12
124 S Tollgate Rd 21117 410-887-1700
Diane Garbarino, prin. Fax 581-1713

Bais Yaakov Girls S 1,300/K-12
11111 Park Heights Ave 21117 410-363-3300
Ari Flamm, dir. Fax 363-3231
Empire Beauty School Post-Sec.
9616 Reisterstown Rd Ste 105 21117 800-575-5983
Garrison Forest S 600/PK-12
300 Garrison Forest Rd 21117 410-363-1500
G. Peter O'Neill, hdmstr. Fax 363-8441
ITT Technical Institute Post-Sec.
11301 Red Run Blvd 21117 443-394-7115
McDonogh S 1,300/K-12
PO Box 380 21117 410-363-0600
W. Dixon, prin. Fax 581-4777

Oxon Hill, Prince George's, Pop. 35,355
Prince George's County SD
Supt. — See Upper Marlboro
Oxon Hill HS 2,500/9-12
6701 Leyte Dr 20745 301-749-4300
Gordon Libby, prin. Fax 749-4320
Potomac HS 1,000/9-12
5211 Boydell Ave 20745 301-702-3900
Sandra Nelson, prin. Fax 702-3886

Parkton, Baltimore
Baltimore County SD
Supt. — See Towson
Hereford HS 1,300/9-12
17301 York Rd 21120 410-887-1905
John Bereska, prin. Fax 887-1944

Pasadena, Anne Arundel, Pop. 10,012
Anne Arundel County SD
Supt. — See Annapolis
Chesapeake Bay MS 1,800/6-8
4804 Mountain Rd 21122 410-437-2400
Gary Williams, prin. Fax 437-9920
Chesapeake HS 1,900/9-12
4798 Mountain Rd 21122 410-255-9600
Harry Calender, prin. Fax 360-4365
Fox MS, 7922 Outing Ave 21122 800/6-8
Kevin Dennehy, prin. 410-437-5512
Northeast HS 1,500/9-12
1121 Duvall Hwy 21122 410-437-6400
George Kispert, prin. Fax 437-7012

Perry Hall, Baltimore, Pop. 22,723

Perry Hall Christian S 300/K-12
3919 Schroeder Ave 21128 410-256-4886
Cathy Tarbart, admin. Fax 256-5451

Perryville, Cecil, Pop. 3,705
Cecil County SD
Supt. — See Elkton
Perryville HS 1,000/9-12
1696 Perryville Rd 21903 410-996-6000
Peter Callahan, prin. Fax 996-6027
Perryville MS 700/6-8
850 Aiken Ave 21903 410-996-6010
R. Joseph Buckley, prin. Fax 996-6048

Pocomoke City, Worcester, Pop. 4,147
Worcester County SD
Supt. — See Newark
Pocomoke HS 400/9-12
1817 Old Virginia Rd 21851 410-632-5180
Ty Mills, prin. Fax 632-5189
Pocomoke MS 500/4-8
800 8th St 21851 410-632-5150
Caroline Bloxom, prin. Fax 632-5159

Pomfret, Charles
Charles County SD
Supt. — See La Plata
McDonough HS 1,400/9-12
7165 Marshall Corner Rd 20675 301-934-2944
Jervie Petty, prin. Fax 753-8408

Poolesville, Montgomery, Pop. 5,423
Montgomery County SD
Supt. — See Rockville
Poole MS 500/6-8
17014 Tom Fox Ave 20837 301-972-7979
Richard Bishop, prin. Fax 972-7982
Poolesville JSHS 1,300/7-12
17501 W Willard Rd 20837 301-972-7900
Deena Levine, prin. Fax 972-7943

Port Deposit, Cecil, Pop. 672

Lighthouse Christian Academy 200/K-12
7 Pleasant View Church Rd 21904 410-378-3279
Fax 658-3004

Potomac, Montgomery, Pop. 44,822
Montgomery County SD
Supt. — See Rockville
Cabin John MS 1,000/6-8
10701 Gainsborough Rd 20854 301-469-1150
Paulette Smith, prin. Fax 469-1003
Churchill HS 2,100/9-12
11300 Gainsborough Rd 20854 301-469-1200
Dr. Joan Benz, prin. Fax 469-1208

Bullis S 600/3-12
10601 Falls Rd 20854 301-299-8500
Thomas Farquhar, hdmstr. Fax 299-9050
Connelly Holy Child S 400/6-12
9029 Bradley Blvd 20854 301-365-0955
Maureen Appel, hdmstr. Fax 365-0981
German S Washington DC 600/K-12
8617 Chateau Dr 20854 301-365-4400
Klaus-Dieter Bloch, prin. Fax 365-3905
Heights S 500/3-12
10400 Seven Locks Rd 20854 301-365-4300
Alvaro de Vicente, hdmstr. Fax 365-4303
McLean S of Maryland 500/K-12
8224 Lochinver Ln 20854 301-299-8277
Darlene Pierro, hdmstr. Fax 299-1639
Muslim Community S 100/PK-12
7917 Montrose Rd 20854 301-340-6713
Dr. Mahboobeh Ayat, prin. Fax 340-7339
St. Andrew's Episcopal S 500/6-12
8804 Postoak Rd 20854 301-983-5200
Robert F. Kosasky, hdmstr. Fax 983-4710

Prince Frederick, Calvert, Pop. 1,885
Calvert County SD 17,300/PK-12
1305 Dares Beach Rd 20678 410-535-1700
Jack Smith, supt. Fax 535-7476
www.calvertnet.k12.md.us
Calvert Career Ctr Vo/Tech
330 Dorsey Rd 20678 410-535-7450
Barbara McKimmie, prin. Fax 535-7418
Calvert HS 1,800/9-12
600 Dares Beach Rd 20678 410-535-7333
Susan Johnson, prin. Fax 535-7200
Calvert MS 500/6-8
435 Solomons Island Rd N 20678 410-535-7355
Bruce Hutchinson, prin. Fax 535-7356
Other Schools – See Huntingtown, Lusby, Owings

Princess Anne, Somerset, Pop. 2,388
Somerset County SD
Supt. — See Westover
Washington 8-9 Academy 200/8-9
10902 Old Princess Anne Rd 21853 410-651-0480
Deborah Dean, prin. Fax 651-0235
Washington HS 300/10-12
10902 Old Princess Anne Rd 21853 410-651-0480
Keith O'Neal, prin. Fax 651-0235

University of Maryland Eastern Shore Post-Sec.
11868 Academic Oval 21853 410-651-2200

Pylesville, Harford
Harford County SD
Supt. — See Bel Air
North Harford HS 1,400/9-12
211 Pylesville Rd 21132 410-638-3650
David Thomas, prin. Fax 638-3666
North Harford MS 1,200/6-8
112 Pylesville Rd 21132 410-638-3658
Dr. Bruce Kovacs, prin. Fax 638-3669

Randallstown, Baltimore, Pop. 30,870
Baltimore County SD
Supt. — See Towson
Deer Park Magnet MS 1,300/6-8
9830 Winands Rd 21133 410-887-0726
Penelope Martin, prin. Fax 887-0704
Randallstown HS 1,500/9-12
4000 Offutt Rd 21133 410-887-0748
Thomas Evans, prin. Fax 887-0759

Sojourner Christian Academy 50/5-12
9980 Liberty Rd 21133
Myra Harris, prin.

Reisterstown, Baltimore, Pop. 19,314
Baltimore County SD
Supt. — See Towson
Franklin HS 1,500/9-12
12000 Reisterstown Rd 21136 410-887-1119
Dean Terry, prin. Fax 833-4434
Franklin MS 1,400/6-8
10 Cockeys Mill Rd 21136 410-887-1114
Lynn Wolf, prin. Fax 517-2548

Maryland Beauty Academy Post-Sec.
152 Chartley Dr 21136 410-517-0442
More S 200/6-12
12039 Reisterstown Rd 21136 410-526-5000
Mark Waldman, pres. Fax 526-7631

Ridgely, Caroline, Pop. 1,346
Caroline County SD
Supt. — See Denton
Caroline Career & Technical Ctr Vo/Tech
10855 Central Ave 21660 410-479-0100
Theresa Stafford, prin. Fax 479-1308
North Caroline HS 1,000/9-12
10990 River Rd 21660 410-479-2332
Brian Spiering, prin. Fax 479-2743

Benedictine S 100/K-12
14299 Benedictine Ln 21660 410-634-2112
Fax 634-2640

Rising Sun, Cecil, Pop. 1,766
Cecil County SD
Supt. — See Elkton
Rising Sun MS 700/6-8
289 Pearl St 21911 410-658-5535
Diana Rudolph, prin. Fax 658-9173

Riverdale, Prince George's, Pop. 5,120
Prince George's County SD
Supt. — See Upper Marlboro
Parkdale HS 2,300/9-12
6001 Good Luck Rd 20737 301-513-5700
Donald Horrigan, prin. Fax 513-5209
Wirt MS 800/7-8
62nd Pl & Tuckerman St 20737 301-985-1720
Helen King, prin. Fax 985-1440

Rock Hall, Kent, Pop. 2,321
Kent County SD
Supt. — See Chestertown
Rock Hall MS 200/5-8
21203 E Sharp St 21661 410-639-2279
Virginia Newlin, prin. Fax 639-2998

Rockville, Montgomery, Pop. 55,213
Montgomery County SD 138,900/PK-12
850 Hungerford Dr 20850 301-279-3000
Jerry D. Weast Ed.D., supt. Fax 279-3221
www.mcps.k12.md.us/
Frost MS 1,200/6-8
9201 Scott Dr 20850 301-279-3949
Dr. Joey N. Jones, prin. Fax 279-3956
Hoover MS 1,100/6-8
8810 Postoak Rd 20854 301-469-1010
Billie Jean Bensen, prin. Fax 469-1013
Magruder HS 2,200/9-12
5939 Muncaster Mill Rd 20855 301-840-4600
Dr. Andrel Ghelman, prin. Fax 840-4617
Montgomery HS 1,800/9-12
250 Richard Montgomery Dr 20852 301-279-8400
E. Moreno Carrasco, prin. Fax 279-8428
Parkland MS 1,200/6-8
4610 W Frankfort Dr 20853 301-460-2180
Kevin Hobbs, prin. Fax 460-9624
Redland MS 900/6-8
6505 Muncaster Mill Rd 20855 301-840-4680
Carol A. Weiss, prin. Fax 840-4688
Rockville HS 1,200/9-12
2100 Baltimore Rd 20851 301-517-8105
Dr. Debra Munk, prin. Fax 517-8288
Tilden MS 500/7-8
11211 Old Georgetown Rd 20852 301-230-5930
Karen Rabin, prin. Fax 230-5991
West MS 1,100/6-8
651 Great Falls Rd 20850 301-279-3979
Nanette Poirier, prin. Fax 517-8216
Wood MS 1,000/6-8
14615 Bauer Dr 20853 301-460-2150
David Brubaker, prin. Fax 460-2159
Wootton HS 2,200/9-12
2100 Wootton Pkwy 20850 301-279-8550
Dr. Michael J. Doran, prin. Fax 279-8569
Other Schools – See Bethesda, Burtonsville, Clarksburg, Damascus, Gaithersburg, Germantown, Kensington, Olney, Poolesville, Potomac, Sandy Spring, Silver Spring

Berman Hebrew Academy 800/PK-12
13300 Arctic Ave 20853 301-962-9400
Rabbi William Altshul, hdmstr. Fax 962-3991
Montgomery College Post-Sec.
51 Mannakee St 20850 301-279-5000
Montrose Christian S 400/PK-12
5100 Randolph Rd 20852 301-770-5335
Tracy Mohr, hdmstr. Fax 881-7345
Smith Jewish Day S 700/7-12
11710 Hunters Ln 20852 301-881-1400
Roz Landy, prin. Fax 230-1986
Strayer University Post-Sec.
4 Research Pl Ste 100 20850 301-548-5500

Saint James, Washington

St. James S 200/8-12
17641 College Rd 21781 301-733-9330
Rev. D. Stuart Dunnan, hdmstr. Fax 739-1310

Saint Marys City, Saint Mary's, Pop. 3,200

St. Mary's College of Maryland Post-Sec.
18952 E Fisher Rd 20686 301-862-0200

Saint Michaels, Talbot, Pop. 1,139
Talbot County SD
Supt. — See Easton
Saint Michaels JSHS 400/7-12
200 Seymour Ave 21663 410-745-2852
Frank Hagen, prin. Fax 745-9939

Salisbury, Wicomico, Pop. 25,247
Wicomico County SD 14,500/PK-12
PO Box 1538 21802 410-677-4400
Dr. Charlene C. Boston, supt. Fax 677-4444
www.wcboe.org
Bennett HS 1,400/9-12
300 E College Ave 21804 410-677-5141
Clayton J. Belgie, prin. Fax 677-5126
Bennett MS 1,000/6-8
200 E College Ave 21804 410-677-5140
C. Michael Johnson, prin. Fax 677-5133
Parkside HS 1,100/9-12
1015 Beaglin Park Dr 21804 410-677-5143
Steven Grudis, prin. Fax 677-5104
Salisbury MS 900/6-8
607 Morris St 21801 410-677-5149
Cathy Townsend, prin. Fax 677-5122
Wicomico HS 1,200/9-12
201 Long Ave 21804 410-677-5146
Lorenzo Hughes, prin. Fax 677-5151
Wicomico MS 800/6-8
635 E Main St 21804 410-677-5145
Kimberly D. Miles, prin. Fax 677-5197
Evening HS Adult
PO Box 1538 21802 410-677-4537
Andrew Turner, coord. Fax 677-4418
Other Schools – See Mardela Springs

Agape Christian Academy 50/PK-12
208 Tilghman Rd 21804 410-546-5664
Cynthia Smith, admin. Fax 219-7914
Del-Mar-Va Beauty Academy Post-Sec.
111 Milford St 21804 410-742-7929
Salisbury Christian S 600/PK-12
807 Parker Rd 21804 410-546-0661
Jim Fox, hdmstr. Fax 546-4674
Salisbury S 500/PK-12
6279 Hobbs Rd 21804 410-742-4464
James G. Landi, hdmstr. Fax 546-2310
Salisbury University Post-Sec.
1101 Camden Ave 21801 410-543-6000
Wor-Wic Community College Post-Sec.
32000 Campus Dr 21804 410-334-2800

Sandy Spring, Montgomery, Pop. 3,092
Montgomery County SD
Supt. — See Rockville
Sherwood HS 2,100/9-12
300 Olney Sandy Spring Rd 20860 301-924-3200
John Yore, prin. Fax 924-3220

Sandy Spring Friends S 500/PK-12
16923 Norwood Rd 20860 301-774-7455
Ken Smith, hdmstr. Fax 924-1115

Severn, Anne Arundel, Pop. 24,499
Anne Arundel County SD
Supt. — See Annapolis
Center of Applied Technology-North Vo/Tech
800 Stevenson Rd 21144 410-969-3100
John Hammond, prin. Fax 360-4364

Archbishop Spalding HS 900/9-12
8080 New Cut Rd 21144 410-969-9105
Kathleen Mahar, prin. Fax 969-1026
Calvary Chapel Christian Academy 100/PK-12
8064 New Cut Rd 21144 410-969-5101
Barbara Fridy, prin. Fax 969-7729

Severna Park, Anne Arundel, Pop. 28,507
Anne Arundel County SD
Supt. — See Annapolis
Severna Park HS 1,800/9-12
60 Robinson Rd 21146 410-544-0900
William Myers, prin. Fax 647-2978
Severna Park MS 1,300/6-8
450 Jumpers Hole Rd 21146 410-647-7900
Sharon Morell, prin. Fax 315-8006
Severna Park Evening HS Adult
60 Robinson Rd 21146 410-544-0182
John France, prin.

Severn S 600/6-12
201 Water St 21146 410-647-7700
William Creeden, hdmstr. Fax 544-9455

Silver Spring, Montgomery, Pop. 76,540
Montgomery County SD
Supt. — See Rockville
Argyle MS 600/6-8
2400 Bel Pre Rd 20906 301-460-2400
Debra Mugge, prin. Fax 460-2423
Belt MS, 12601 Dalewood Dr 20906 6-8
Alison Serino, prin. 301-929-2050
Blair HS 3,300/9-12
51 University Blvd E 20901 301-649-2800
Phillip Gainous, prin. Fax 649-2830
Blake HS 1,800/9-12
300 Norwood Rd 20905 301-879-1300
Carole C. Goodman, prin. Fax 879-1306
Briggs-Chaney MS 800/6-8
1901 Rainbow Dr 20905 301-989-6000
Kimberly Johnson, prin. Fax 989-6020
Eastern MS 900/6-8
300 University Blvd E 20901 301-650-6650
Charlotte C. Boucher, prin. Fax 650-6657
Edison HS of Technology Vo/Tech
12501 Dalewood Dr 20906 301-929-2175
Carlos Hamlin, prin. Fax 929-2177
Kennedy HS 1,600/9-12
1901 Randolph Rd 20902 301-929-2100
Fred H. Lowenbach, prin. Fax 929-2124
Key MS 900/6-8
910 Schindler Dr 20903 301-431-7630
Eric Minus, prin. Fax 431-7639
Lee MS 700/6-8
11800 Monticello Ave 20902 301-649-8100
Mary Beth Waits, prin. Fax 649-8110
Loiederman MS 6-8
12701 Goodhill Rd 20906 301-929-2282
Alison Serino, prin. Fax 962-5993
Northwood HS 9-12
919 University Blvd W 20901 301-649-8088
Henry Johnson, prin.
Silver Spring International MS 900/6-8
313 Wayne Ave 20910 301-650-6544
Victoria Parcan, prin. Fax 649-8005
Sligo MS 700/6-8
1401 Dennis Ave 20902 301-649-8121
Doreen Brandes, prin. Fax 649-8145
Springbrook HS 2,000/9-12
201 Valley Brook Dr 20904 301-989-5700
Michael Durso, prin. Fax 622-1875
Takoma Park MS 1,000/6-8
7611 Piney Branch Rd 20910 301-650-6444
Jean Haven, prin. Fax 230-5924
Wheaton HS 1,500/9-12
12601 Dalewood Dr 20906 301-929-2050
Dr. George Arlotto, prin. Fax 929-2081
White Oak MS 900/6-8
12201 New Hampshire Ave 20904 301-989-5780
Dr. Carol Dahlberg, prin. Fax 989-5696

Adventist HealthCare Health Careers Ctr Post-Sec.
501 Sligo Ave 20910 301-585-7006
Barrie S 400/PK-12
13500 Layhill Rd 20906 301-576-2800
Tim Trautman, hdmstr. Fax 576-2803
Everest Institute Post-Sec.
8757 Georgia Ave Ste 650 20910 301-495-4400
Forcey Christian MS 100/6-8
12625 Galway Dr 20904 301-572-6607
Ezekiel Wharton, admin. Fax 572-2652
Griggs International Academy Post-Sec.
PO Box 4437 20914 301-680-6570
Griggs University Post-Sec.
PO Box 4437 20914 301-680-6570
Holy Cross Hospital Post-Sec.
1500 Forest Glen Rd 20910 301-905-1216
Montgomery Beauty School Post-Sec.
8736 Arliss St 20901 301-459-2509
National Labor College Post-Sec.
1000 New Hampshire Ave 20903 301-431-6400
Newport S 100/PK-12
12101 Tech Rd 20904 301-942-4550
Fax 949-2654
School of Art & Design @ Montgomery Coll Post-Sec.
10500 Georgia Ave 20902 301-649-4454
Spencerville Adventist Academy 300/K-12
15930 Good Hope Rd 20905 301-421-9101
Brian Kittleson, prin. Fax 421-0007
Thornton Friends S 50/6-8
11612 New Hampshire Ave 20904 301-622-9033
Michael DeHart, hdmstr. Fax 622-4786
Thornton Friends S 100/9-12
13925 New Hampshire Ave 20904 301-384-0320
Michael DeHart, hdmstr. Fax 236-9481
Washington Christian Academy 200/6-12
13421 Georgia Ave 20906 301-649-1070
Larry Danner, hdmstr. Fax 649-9863
Yeshiva College of the Nations Capital Post-Sec.
1216 Arcola Ave 20902 301-593-2534
Yeshiva of Greater Washington - Boys Div 100/7-12
1216 Arcola Ave 20902 301-649-7077
Rabbi Dovid Niman, prin. Fax 649-7053
Yeshiva of Greater Washington - Girls 200/7-12
2010 Linden Ln 20910 301-962-5111
Sima Jacoby, prin. Fax 962-8372

Smithsburg, Washington, Pop. 2,594
Washington County SD
Supt. — See Hagerstown
Smithsburg HS 800/9-12
66 N Main St 21783 301-766-8337
Melvin Whitfield, prin. Fax 824-2617
Smithsburg MS 700/6-8
68 N Main St 21783 301-766-8353
Dee Shumaker, prin. Fax 824-5147

Snow Hill, Worcester, Pop. 2,386
Worcester County SD
Supt. — See Newark
Snow Hill HS 400/9-12
305 S Church St 21863 410-632-5270
Mark Record, prin. Fax 632-5279
Snow Hill MS 500/4-8
5719 Coulbourne Ln 21863 410-632-5240
Tom Davis, prin. Fax 632-5249

Springdale, Prince George's
Prince George's County SD
Supt. — See Upper Marlboro
Flowers HS 2,500/9-12
10001 Ardwick Ardmore Rd 20774 301-636-8000
Helene Nobles-Jones, prin. Fax 636-8008

Stevenson, Baltimore

St. Timothy's S 100/9-12
8400 Greenspring Ave 21153 410-486-7400
Fax 486-1167
Villa Julie College Post-Sec.
1525 Greenspring Valley Rd 21153 410-486-7000

Stevensville, Queen Anne's, Pop. 1,862
Queen Anne's County SD
Supt. — See Centreville
Kent Island HS 1,200/9-12
900 Love Point Rd 21666 410-604-2070
Joanna Tolson, prin. Fax 604-2089
Stevensville MS 800/6-8
610 Main St 21666 410-643-3194
Denise Hershberger, prin. Fax 643-3046

Sudlersville, Queen Anne's, Pop. 388
Queen Anne's County SD
Supt. — See Centreville
Sudlersville MS 400/6-8
PO Box D 21668 410-438-3151
Kevin Kintop, prin. Fax 438-3151

Eastern Shore Junior Academy 50/PK-10
407 Dudley Corners Rd 21668 410-438-3288
Lowell Litten, prin. Fax 438-3778

Suitland, Prince George's, Pop. 33,515
Prince George's County SD
Supt. — See Upper Marlboro
Drew-Freeman MS 1,000/6-8
2600 Brooks Dr 20746 301-817-0900
Joyce Edwards, prin. Fax 817-0915

Gods Church International Christian S 100/K-12
4650 Suitland Rd 20746 301-568-6200
Nettie Nichols, prin. Fax 568-6299
New Creation Academy of Hair Design Post-Sec.
3930 Bexley Pl 20746 301-899-9100

Sykesville, Carroll, Pop. 4,373
Carroll County SD
Supt. — See Westminster
Century HS 1,200/9-12
355 Ronsdale Rd 21784 410-386-4400
Andrew Cockley, prin. Fax 386-4413
Liberty HS 1,100/9-12
5855 Bartholow Rd 21784 410-751-3560
Florence Oliver, prin. Fax 795-8103
Oklahoma Road MS 900/6-8
6300 Oklahoma Rd 21784 410-751-3600
Catherine Hood, prin. Fax 552-0719
South Carroll HS 1,100/9-12
1300 W Old Liberty Rd 21784 410-751-3575
George Phillips, prin. Fax 795-8516
Sykesville MS 900/6-8
7301 Springfield Ave 21784 410-751-3545
Thomas Eckenrode, prin. Fax 795-9081

Takoma Park, Montgomery, Pop. 17,717

Columbia Union College Post-Sec.
7600 Flower Ave 20912 301-891-4000
Montgomery College Post-Sec.
7600 Takoma Ave 20912 301-650-1300
Takoma Academy 300/9-12
8120 Carroll Ave 20912 301-434-4700
C. Dunbar Henri, prin. Fax 434-4814
Washington Adventist Hospital Post-Sec.
7600 Carroll Ave 20912 301-891-7600

Taneytown, Carroll, Pop. 5,335
Carroll County SD
Supt. — See Westminster
Northwest MS 600/6-8
99 Kings Dr 21787 410-751-3270
Dana Falls, prin. Fax 751-3275

Temple Hills, Prince George's, Pop. 6,865
Prince George's County SD
Supt. — See Upper Marlboro
Crossland HS 1,700/9-12
6901 Temple Hill Rd 20748 301-449-4800
Charles Thomas, prin. Fax 449-4801
Marshall MS 700/7-8
4909 Brinkley Rd 20748 301-702-7540
Raynah Adams, prin. Fax 702-7555
Shugart MS 800/6-8
2000 Callaway St 20748 301-702-3950
Ms. Curtis Smalls, prin. Fax 702-3957
Stoddert MS 800/6-8
2501 Olson St 20748 301-702-7500
Rudyard Wallace, prin. Fax 702-7515
Crossland Evening HS Adult
6901 Temple Hill Rd 20748 301-449-4994
Ernest Caldwell, prin. Fax 449-2126

Thurmont, Frederick, Pop. 5,890
Frederick County SD
Supt. — See Frederick
Catoctin HS 1,000/9-12
14745 Sabillasville Rd 21788 240-236-8100
Jack Newkirk, prin. Fax 236-8101
Thurmont MS 700/6-8
408 E Main St 21788 240-236-5100
Barbara Keiling, prin. Fax 236-5101

Timonium, See Lutherville
Baltimore County SD
Supt. — See Towson
Dulaney JSHS 2,200/8-12
255 E Padonia Rd 21093 410-887-7633
Lyle Patzkowsky, prin. Fax 666-8915

R. Paul Academy of Cosmetology Arts/Sci Post-Sec.
1811 York Rd Ste B 21093 410-252-4481

Towson, Baltimore, Pop. 51,793
Baltimore County SD 109,200/PK-12
6901 N Charles St 21204 410-887-4281
Dr. Joe Hairston, supt. Fax 887-4309
www.bcps.org
Other Schools – See Baltimore, Catonsville, Cockeysville, Lutherville, Monkton, Owings Mills, Parkton, Randallstown, Reisterstown, Timonium

Baltimore Lutheran HS | 500/6-12
1145 Concordia Dr 21286 | 410-825-2323
Randal C. Gast, prin. | Fax 825-2506
Loyola Blakefield HS | 1,000/6-12
PO Box 6819 21285 | 410-823-0601
Rev. Thomas Pesci, pres. | Fax 823-5277
Medix School | Post-Sec.
700 York Rd 21204 | 410-337-5155
Notre Dame Preparatory S | 700/6-12
815 Hampton Ln 21286 | 410-825-6202
Clare Pitz, prin. | Fax 832-2625
TESST College of Technology | Post-Sec.
803 Glen Eagles Ct 21286 | 410-296-5350
Towson Catholic HS | 300/9-12
114 Ware Ave 21204 | 410-427-4900
Susan Banks, prin. | Fax 427-4995
Towson State University | Post-Sec.
8000 York Rd 21252 | 410-830-2000

Union Bridge, Carroll, Pop. 1,018
Carroll County SD
Supt. — See Westminster
Key HS | 1,200/9-12
3825 Bark Hill Rd 21791 | 410-751-3320
Randy Clark, prin. | Fax 751-3325

Upper Marlboro, Prince George's, Pop. 674
Prince George's County SD | 129,700/PK-12
14201 School Ln 20772 | 301-952-6000
Howard Burnett, admin. | Fax 952-1383
www.pgcps.org
Croom Vocational HS | Vo/Tech
8520 Duvall Rd 20772 | 301-952-7750
Sherrill Lilly, prin. | Fax 952-7758
Douglass HS | 1,700/9-12
8000 Croom Rd 20772 | 301-952-2400
Monica Goldson, prin. | Fax 627-3377
Kettering MS | 700/7-8
65 Herrington Dr 20774 | 301-808-4060
Legaunt Jones, prin. | Fax 808-5920
Largo HS | 1,800/9-12
505 Largo Rd 20774 | 301-808-8880
Richmond Myrick, prin. | Fax 808-4066
Madison MS | 900/7-8
7300 Woodyard Rd 20772 | 301-599-2422
Mark King, prin. | Fax 599-2562
Wise JHS | 7-8
12650 Brooke Ln 20772 | 301-952-6000
Other Schools – See Accokeek, Adelphi, Beltsville, Bladensburg, Bowie, Brandywine, Capitol Heights, Clinton, District Heights, Forestville, Fort Washington, Greenbelt, Hyattsville, Landover, Lanham Seabrook, Laurel, Mitchellville, New Carrollton, Oxon Hill, Riverdale, Springdale, Suitland, Temple Hills

Capitol Christian Academy | 300/PK-12
610 Largo Rd 20774 | 301-336-2200
Gary O'Neill, admin. | Fax 336-6704
Clinton Christian S | 700/PK-12
6707 Woodyard Rd 20772 | 301-599-9600
Lisa Duey, admin. | Fax 599-9603
Queen Anne S | 300/6-12
14111 Oak Grove Rd 20774 | 301-249-5000
J. Temple Blackwood, hdmstr. | Fax 249-3838

Riverdale Baptist S | 1,100/PK-12
1133 Largo Rd 20774 | 301-249-7000
Terry Zink, admin. | Fax 249-3425

Waldorf, Charles, Pop. 15,058
Charles County SD
Supt. — See La Plata
Hanson MS | 1,000/6-8
12350 Vivian Adams Dr 20601 | 301-645-4520
Stephanie Wesolowski, prin. | Fax 870-1182
Mattawoman MS | 1,100/6-8
10145 Berry Rd 20603 | 301-645-7708
William Wise Ed.D., prin. | Fax 638-0043
Stoddert MS | 800/6-8
2040 Saint Thomas Dr 20602 | 301-645-1334
Sylvia Lawson, prin. | Fax 870-1183
Stone HS | 2,000/9-12
3785 Leonardtown Rd 20601 | 301-645-2601
Heath Morrison, prin. | Fax 932-4278
Westlake HS | 1,700/9-12
3300 Middletown Rd 20603 | 301-645-8857
Chrystal Benson, prin. | Fax 932-8583

Aaron's Academy of Beauty | Post-Sec.
340 Post Office Rd 20602 | 301-645-3681
Grace Brethren Christian S | 600/PK-12
13000 Zekiah Dr 20601 | 301-645-0406
Lloyd C. Chadwick, dir. | Fax 645-7463

Walkersville, Frederick, Pop. 5,517
Frederick County SD
Supt. — See Frederick
Walkersville HS | 1,200/9-12
81 W Frederick St 21793 | 240-236-7200
Rebecca Koontz, prin. | Fax 236-7250
Walkersville MS | 1,000/6-8
55 W Frederick St 21793 | 240-236-4400
Larkin Hohnke, prin. | Fax 236-4401
Evening HS | Adult
44 W Frederick St 21793 | 240-236-8450
Richard Ramsburg, prin. | Fax 236-8451

Westernport, Allegany, Pop. 2,037
Allegany County SD
Supt. — See Cumberland
Westmar MS | 300/6-8
400 Philos Ave 21562 | 301-359-3046
Martin E. Crump, prin. | Fax 359-8049

Westminster, Carroll, Pop. 17,403
Carroll County SD | 28,900/PK-12
125 N Court St 21157 | 410-751-3000
Charles Ecker, supt. | Fax 751-3003
www.carrollk12.org/
Carroll County Career & Tech Center | Vo/Tech
1229 Washington Rd 21157 | 410-751-3669
Catherine Engel, prin. | Fax 751-3677
Westminster East MS | 800/6-8
121 Longwell Ave 21157 | 410-751-3656
Jeffrey Alisauckas, prin.
Westminster HS | 2,000/9-12
1225 Washington Rd 21157 | 410-751-3630
John Seaman, prin. | Fax 751-3640
Westminster West MS | 1,100/6-8
60 Monroe St 21157 | 410-751-3661
Thomas Hill, prin.

Winters Mill HS | 1,100/9-12
560 Gorsuch Rd 21157 | 410-386-1500
Sherri-Le Bream, prin. | Fax 386-1513
Carroll County Evening HS | Adult
125 N Court St 21157 | 410-751-3000
Other Schools – See Hampstead, Mount Airy, New Windsor, Sykesville, Taneytown, Union Bridge

Carroll Christian S | 300/PK-12
550 Baltimore Blvd 21157 | 410-876-3838
David Rifenberick Ph.D., admin. | Fax 876-7766
Carroll Community College | Post-Sec.
1601 Washington Rd 21157 | 410-386-8000
McDaniel College | Post-Sec.
2 College Hl 21157 | 410-848-7000

Westover, Somerset
Somerset County SD | 2,500/PK-12
7982A Crisfield Hwy 21871 | 410-651-1616
Karen-Lee Brofee, supt. | Fax 651-2931
www.somerset.k12.md.us
Tawes Technology & Career Center | Vo/Tech
7982 Crisfield Hwy 21871 | 410-651-2285
Jim Webster, prin. | Fax 651-3154
Other Schools – See Crisfield, Princess Anne

Holly Grove Christian S | 500/K-12
7317 Mennonite Church Rd 21871 | 410-957-0222
Stacey Johnson, prin. | Fax 957-4250

Wheaton, Montgomery

American Beauty Academy | Post-Sec.
2518 University Blvd W 20902 | 301-949-3000
Our Lady of Good Counsel HS | 1,100/9-12
11601 Georgia Ave 20902 | 301-942-1155
John Graham, prin. | Fax 942-3656

White Plains, Charles, Pop. 3,560

Southern Maryland Christian Academy | 400/PK-12
PO Box 1668 20695 | 301-870-2550
Colleen Gaines, prin. | Fax 934-2855

Williamsport, Washington, Pop. 1,914
Washington County SD
Supt. — See Hagerstown
Springfield MS | 800/6-8
334 Sunset Ave 21795 | 301-766-8389
David Reeder, prin. | Fax 766-8401
Williamsport HS | 900/9-12
5 S Clifton Dr 21795 | 301-766-8423
John Davidson, prin. | Fax 223-9610

Gateway Christian Academy | 100/PK-12
PO Box 590 21795 | 301-582-4595
Greg Prytherch, prin. | Fax 223-5972

Worton, Kent
Kent County SD
Supt. — See Chestertown
Kent County HS | 800/9-12
25301 Lambs Meadow Rd 21678 | 410-778-4540
Ed Silver, prin. | Fax 778-3802

Wye Mills, Talbot

Chesapeake College | Post-Sec.
PO Box 8 21679 | 410-822-5400

MASSACHUSETTS

MASSACHUSETTS DEPARTMENT OF EDUCATION
350 Main St, Malden 02148-5089
Telephone 781-388-3000
Fax 781-388-3392
Website http://www.doe.mass.edu
Commissioner of Education   David Driscoll

MASSACHUSETTS BOARD OF EDUCATION
350 Main St, Malden 02148-5089
Chairperson   James Peyser

PUBLIC, PRIVATE AND CATHOLIC SECONDARY SCHOOLS

Abington, Plymouth, Pop. 13,817
Abington SD — 2,500/PK-12
  1 Ralph Hamlin Ln 02351 — 781-982-2150
  John Aherne, supt. — Fax 982-2157
  www.abington.k12.ma.us
Abington HS — 600/9-12
  201 Gliniewicz Way 02351 — 781-982-2160
  Teresa Sullivan, prin. — Fax 982-0061
Frolio JHS — 400/7-8
  1071 Washington St 02351 — 781-982-2170
  Felicia Moschella, prin. — Fax 982-2173

Acton, Middlesex
Acton-Boxborough Regional SD — 2,600/7-12
  16 Charter Rd 01720 — 978-264-4700
  William Ryan, supt. — Fax 263-8409
  ab.mec.edu
Acton-Boxborough Regional HS — 1,700/9-12
  36 Charter Rd 01720 — 978-264-4700
  Stephen Donovan, prin. — Fax 266-2521
Grey JHS — 900/7-8
  16 Charter Rd 01720 — 978-264-4700
  Craig Hardimon, prin. — Fax 266-2535

Acushnet, Bristol, Pop. 3,170
Acushnet SD — 1,100/K-8
  708 Middle Rd 02743 — 508-998-0260
  Dr. Coral M. Grout, supt. — Fax 998-0262
  www.acushnetschools.net
Ford MS — 600/5-8
  708 Middle Rd 02743 — 508-998-0265
  Stephen Donovan, prin. — Fax 998-7316

Adams, Berkshire, Pop. 6,356
Adams-Cheshire Regional SD
  Supt. — See Cheshire
Adams Memorial MS — 400/6-8
  30 Columbia St 01220 — 413-743-0554
  Kimberly Roberts-Morandi, prin. — Fax 743-8424

Agawam, Hampden, Pop. 28,528
Agawam SD
  Supt. — See Feeding Hills
Agawam HS — 1,200/9-12
  760 Cooper St 01001 — 413-821-0521
  Dr. Linda J. Prystupa, prin. — Fax 821-0536

Amesbury, Essex, Pop. 12,109
Amesbury SD — 2,700/PK-12
  10 Congress St 01913 — 978-388-0507
  Charles L. Chaurette, supt. — Fax 388-8315
  www.ci.amesbury.ma.us
Amesbury HS — 800/9-12
  5 Highland St 01913 — 978-388-4800
  Leslie Murray, prin. — Fax 388-3393
Amesbury MS — 900/5-8
  220 Main St 01913 — 978-388-0515
  Michael Curry, prin. — Fax 388-1626

Amherst, Hampshire, Pop. 17,824
Amherst-Pelham SD — 2,000/7-12
  170 Chestnut St 01002 — 413-362-1810
  Jere Hochman, supt. — Fax 549-9811
  www.arps.org/
Amherst Regional HS — 1,400/9-12
  21 Matoon St 01002 — 413-362-1700
  Mark Jackson, prin. — Fax 549-9704
Amherst Regional MS — 700/7-8
  170 Chestnut St 01002 — 413-362-1850
  Mary Cavalier, prin. — Fax 549-9812

Amherst College — Post-Sec.
  PO Box 5000 01002 — 413-542-2000
Hampshire College — Post-Sec.
  893 West St 01002 — 413-549-4600
University of Massachusetts 01003 — Post-Sec.
  413-545-0111

Andover, Essex, Pop. 8,242
Andover SD — 5,900/PK-12
  36 Bartlet St 01810 — 978-623-8501
  Claudia Bach Ed.D., supt. — Fax 623-8505
  www.aps1.net
Andover HS — 1,700/9-12
  100 Shawsheen Rd 01810 — 978-623-8632
  Peter Anderson, prin. — Fax 623-8636

Andover West MS — 500/6-8
  98 Shawsheen Rd 01810 — 978-623-8700
  Marilyn Holmes, prin. — Fax 623-8718
Doherty MS — 600/6-8
  50 Bartlet St 01810 — 978-623-8750
  Bruce Maki, prin. — Fax 623-8770
Wood Hill MS — 400/6-8
  11 Cross St 01810 — 978-623-8925
  Patrick Bucco, prin. — Fax 623-8929

Greater Lawrence SD
  57 River Rd 01810 — 978-686-0194
  Frank Vacirca, supt. — Fax 687-6209
  www.glts.tec.ma.us
Greater Lawrence Technical S — Vo/Tech
  57 River Rd 01810 — 978-686-0194
  Marybeth Sullivan, prin. — Fax 687-6209

Massachusetts School of Law at Andover — Post-Sec.
  500 Federal St 01810 — 978-681-0800
Phillips Academy — 1,100/9-12
  180 Main St 01810 — 978-749-4000
  Barbara Chase, hdmstr. — Fax 749-4526

Arlington, Middlesex, Pop. 42,000
Arlington SD — 4,300/K-12
  869 Massachusetts Ave 02476 — 781-316-3502
  Nate Levenson, supt. — Fax 316-3509
  www.arlington.k12.ma.us
Arlington HS — 1,100/9-12
  869 Massachusetts Ave 02476 — 781-316-3593
  Charles Skidmore, prin. — Fax 316-3504
Ottoson MS — 1,000/6-8
  63 Acton St 02476 — 781-316-3744
  Stavroula Bouris, prin. — Fax 641-5436

Arlington Catholic HS — 700/9-12
  16 Medford St 02474 — 781-646-7770
  Stephen Biagioni, prin. — Fax 648-8345

Ashburnham, Worcester
Ashburnham-Westminster Regional SD
  Supt. — See Westminster
Oakmont Regional HS — 700/9-12
  9 Oakmont Dr 01430 — 978-827-5907
  Donald Lawrence, prin. — Fax 827-1413
Overlook MS — 600/6-8
  10 Oakmont Dr 01430 — 978-827-1425
  John Sunderland, prin. — Fax 827-1423

Cushing Academy — 400/9-12
  PO Box 8000 01430 — 978-827-7000
  Dr. Jim Tracy, hdmstr. — Fax 827-7500

Ashland, Middlesex, Pop. 12,066
Ashland SD — 2,600/PK-12
  90 Concord St 01721 — 508-881-0150
  Dr. Richard Hoffmann, supt. — Fax 881-0161
  www.ashlandhs.org
Ashland HS — 600/9-12
  87 W Union St 01721 — 508-881-0177
  Michael Tempesta, prin. — Fax 881-0186
Ashland MS — 400/7-8
  87 W Union St 01721 — 508-881-0167
  Kevin Carney, prin. — Fax 881-0169

Athol, Worcester, Pop. 8,732
Athol-Royalston SD — 2,300/PK-12
  PO Box 968 01331 — 978-249-2400
  Anthony Polito, supt. — Fax 249-2402
  www.athol-royalstonschools.org
Athol HS — 600/9-12
  2363 Main St 01331 — 978-249-2435
  Kent Strong, prin. — Fax 249-7217
Athol-Royalston MS — 500/6-8
  1062 Pleasant St 01331 — 978-249-2430
  Christopher Collins, prin. — Fax 249-0055
Bigelow S — 100/PK-12
  129 Allen St 01331 — 978-249-2403
  Patricia Byrnes, prin. — Fax 249-7210

Attleboro, Bristol, Pop. 43,502
Attleboro SD — 6,500/PK-12
  100 Rathbun Willard Dr 02703 — 508-222-0012
  Joel Lovering, supt. — Fax 223-1577
  www.attleboroschools.com

Attleboro HS — 1,900/9-12
  100 Rathbun Willard Dr 02703 — 508-222-5150
  Jacqueline A. Proulx, prin. — Fax 223-1579
Attleboro Vo-Tech HS — Vo/Tech
  100 Rathbun Willard Dr 02703 — 508-222-5150
   — Fax 223-1509
Brennan MS — 700/5-8
  320 Rathbun Willard Dr 02703 — 508-222-6260
  Richard L. George, prin. — Fax 223-1555
Coelho MS — 600/5-8
  99 Brown St 02703 — 508-761-7551
  Carol Martin, prin. — Fax 223-1595
Wamsutta MS — 700/5-8
  300 Locust St 02703 — 508-223-1540
  David Sutherland, prin. — Fax 226-2087

Bishop Feehan HS — 800/9-12
  70 Holcott Dr 02703 — 508-226-6223
  Christopher Servant, prin. — Fax 226-7696

Auburn, Worcester, Pop. 15,005
Auburn SD — 2,300/K-12
  5 West St 01501 — 508-832-7755
  Dr. Helene Skrzyniarz, supt. — Fax 832-7757
  www.auburnpublicschools.com/
Auburn HS — 600/9-12
  99 Auburn St 01501 — 508-832-7711
  Casey Handfield, prin. — Fax 832-7710
Auburn MS — 600/6-8
  10 Swanson Rd 01501 — 508-832-7722
  Ann O'Leary-Ortiz, prin. — Fax 832-8655

Auburndale, See Newton

Lasell College — Post-Sec.
  1844 Commonwealth Ave 02466 — 617-243-2225

Avon, Norfolk, Pop. 4,558
Avon SD — 700/PK-12
  Patrick Clark Dr 02322 — 508-588-0230
  Margaret Frieswyk, supt. — Fax 559-1081
  avon.k12.ma.us/
Avon MSHS — 300/7-12
  287 W Main St 02322 — 508-583-4822
  Ronald B. Seely, prin. — Fax 588-5501

Ayer, Middlesex, Pop. 2,889
Ayer SD — 1,400/PK-12
  141 Washington St 01432 — 978-772-8600
  Dr. Lore Nielson, supt. — Fax 772-7444
  www.ayer.mec.edu/
Ayer HS — 400/9-12
  141 Washington St 01432 — 978-772-8600
  Don Parker, prin. — Fax 772-8615
Ayer MS — 400/5-8
  141 Washington St 01432 — 978-772-8600
  Lyn Lawrence, prin. — Fax 772-8643

Babson Park, Norfolk

Babson College — Post-Sec.
  PO Box 57310 02457 — 781-235-1200

Baldwinville, Worcester, Pop. 1,795
Narragansett Regional SD — 1,600/PK-12
  462 Baldwinville Rd 01436 — 978-939-5661
  Stephen Hemman Ed.D., supt. — Fax 939-5179
  www.nrsd.org/
Narragansett MS — 500/5-8
  460 Baldwinville Rd 01436 — 978-393-5928
  Rob Rouleau, prin. — Fax 939-8422
Narragansett Regional HS — 500/9-12
  464 Baldwinville Rd 01436 — 978-939-5388
  John Jasinski, prin. — Fax 939-5723

Barnstable, Barnstable, Pop. 48,854

Trinity Christian Academy — 100/PK-12
  979 Mary Dunn Rd 02630 — 508-790-0114
  Frederick Caldwell, hdmstr. — Fax 790-1293

Barre, Worcester, Pop. 1,094
Quabbin SD — 3,200/PK-12
  PO Box 667 01005 — 978-355-4668
  Maureen Marshall, supt. — Fax 355-6756
  www.quabbin.k12.ma.us

Quabbin Regional MSHS | 1,600/7-12
PO Box 429 01005 | 978-355-4651
Bernard Audette, prin. | Fax 355-0163

Bedford, Middlesex, Pop. 12,996
Bedford SD | 2,200/K-12
97 McMahon Rd 01730 | 781-275-7588
Maureen Lacroix, supt. | Fax 275-1332
www.bedford.k12.ma.us
Bedford HS | 700/9-12
9 Mudge Way 01730 | 781-275-1700
Jonathon Sills, prin. | Fax 275-6664
Glenn MS | 500/6-8
99 McMahon Rd 01730 | 781-275-3201
Tom Campbell, prin. | Fax 275-7632

East Coast Aero Tech School | Post-Sec.
150 Hanscom Dr 01730 | 781-274-8448
Middlesex Community College | Post-Sec.
210 Springs Rd 01730 | 781-280-3200

Belchertown, Hampshire, Pop. 2,339
Belchertown SD | 1,800/PK-12
PO Box 841 01007 | 413-323-0456
Richard Pazasis, supt. | Fax 323-0448
www.belchertownps.org
Belchertown HS | 700/9-12
142 Old Springfield Rd 01007 | 413-323-9419
Christine Parzych, prin. | Fax 323-9406
Jabish MS | 7-8
62 N Washington St 01007 | 413-323-0433
Thomas Ruscio, prin. | Fax 323-0450

Bellingham, Norfolk, Pop. 4,535
Bellingham SD | 2,700/PK-12
60 Harpin St 02019 | 508-883-1706
T.C. Mattock Ed.D., supt. | Fax 883-0180
www.bellingham.k12.ma.us
Bellingham HS | 800/9-12
60 Blackstone St 02019 | 508-966-3761
Peter Badalament, prin. | Fax 966-4183
Memorial MS | 900/5-8
130 Blackstone St 02019 | 508-883-2330
Elaine D'Alfonso, prin. | Fax 883-2037

Belmont, Middlesex, Pop. 24,720
Belmont SD | 3,700/K-12
644 Pleasant St 02478 | 617-484-2642
Peter Holland, supt. | Fax 484-2365
www.belmont.k12.ma.us
Belmont HS | 1,100/9-12
221 Concord Ave 02478 | 617-484-4700
Jonathan Landman, prin. | Fax 484-0080
Chenery MS | 1,200/5-8
95 Washington St 02478 | 617-484-3900
Deborah Alexander, prin. | Fax 484-3676

Belmont Hill S | 400/7-12
350 Prospect St 02478 | 617-484-4410
Richard Melvoin, prin. | Fax 484-4688
Waldorf HS of Massachusetts Bay | 100/9-12
132 Lexington St 02478 | 617-489-6600
| Fax 489-6619

Berkley, Bristol
Berkley SD | 900/K-8
21 N Main St 02779 | 508-822-5220
Robert James Ed.D., supt. | Fax 823-1772
Berkley MS | 400/5-8
21 N Main St 02779 | 508-884-9434
T. Ross Edminster, prin. | Fax 823-1772

Beverly, Essex, Pop. 40,255
Beverly SD | 4,000/PK-12
502 Cabot St 01915 | 978-921-6100
James Hayes Ed.D., supt. | Fax 922-6597
www.beverlyschools.org/index2.shtm
Beverly HS | 1,300/9-12
100 Sohier Rd 01915 | 978-921-6132
Dr. Carla Scuzzarella, prin. | Fax 927-9460
Briscoe MS | 600/6-8
7 Sohier Rd 01915 | 978-921-6103
Matthew Poska, prin. | Fax 927-7781

Endicott College | Post-Sec.
376 Hale St 01915 | 978-927-0585
Montserrat College of Art | Post-Sec.
PO Box 26 01915 | 800-836-0487
Waring S | 100/6-12
35 Standley St 01915 | 978-927-8793

Billerica, Middlesex, Pop. 37,609
Billerica SD | 6,300/K-12
365 Boston Rd 01821 | 978-436-9500
Robert Calabrese, supt. | Fax 436-9595
www.billerica.mec.edu
Billerica Memorial HS | 1,500/9-12
35 River St 01821 | 978-436-9300
Richard Safier, prin. | Fax 436-9393
Locke MS | 700/6-8
110 Allen Rd 01821 | 978-436-9420
Alexander Infanger, prin. | Fax 436-9424
Marshall MS | 900/6-8
15 Floyd St 01821 | 978-436-9440
Roland Boucher, prin. | Fax 439-1242

Shawsheen Valley Vocational Technical SD
100 Cook St 01821 | 978-667-2111
Charles Lyons, supt.
www.shawsheen.tec.ma.us
Shawsheen Valley Technical HS | Vo/Tech
100 Cook St 01821 | 978-667-2111
Robert Cunningham, prin. | Fax 663-6272

Blackstone, Worcester, Pop. 8,023
Blackstone-Millville Regional SD | 2,300/PK-12
175 Lincoln St 01504 | 508-883-4400
Everett B. Campbell, supt. | Fax 883-9892
www.bmrsd.net

Blackstone-Millville Regional HS | 600/9-12
175 Lincoln St 01504 | 508-876-0117
Richard Porter, prin. | Fax 883-9892
Hartnett MS | 600/6-8
35 Federal St 01504 | 508-876-0193
Kimberly Shaver-Hood, prin. | Fax 876-0198

Bolton, Worcester
Nashoba Regional SD | 3,100/PK-12
50 Mechanic St 01740 | 978-779-0539
Michael Wood Ed.D., supt. | Fax 779-5537
www.nrsd.net
Nashoba Regional HS | 800/9-12
12 Green Rd 01740 | 978-779-2257
John Smith, prin. | Fax 779-2854
Other Schools – See Lancaster, Stow

Boston, Suffolk, Pop. 581,616
Boston SD | 58,900/PK-12
26 Court St 02108 | 617-635-9000
| Fax 635-9059
www.bostonpublicschools.org/
Boston Latin S | 2,400/7-12
78 Avenue Louis Pasteur 02115 | 617-635-8895
Cornelia Kelley, hdmstr. | Fax 635-7883
English HS | 1,300/9-12
144 McBride St 02130 | 617-635-8979
Jose Duarte, hdmstr. | Fax 635-8988
Quincy Upper S | 700/6-12
152 Arlington St 02116 | 617-635-8940
Bak Fun Wong, prin. | Fax 635-1524
Snowden International HS | 400/9-12
150 Newbury St 02116 | 617-635-9989
Gloria Coulter, hdmstr. | Fax 635-9996
Other Schools – See Brighton, Charlestown, Dorchester, East Boston, Hyde Park, Jamaica Plain, Mattapan, Roslindale, Roxbury, Roxbury Crossing, South Boston, West Roxbury

Bay State College | Post-Sec.
122 Commonwealth Ave 02116 | 617-217-9000
Benjamin Franklin Inst. of Technology | Post-Sec.
41 Berkeley St 02116 | 617-423-4630
Berklee College of Music | Post-Sec.
1140 Boylston St 02215 | 617-266-1400
Beth Israel Healthcare | Post-Sec.
330 Brookline Ave 02215 | 617-667-2539
Blaine The Beauty Career School | Post-Sec.
30 West St 02111 | 617-266-2661
Boston Architectural Center | Post-Sec.
320 Newbury St 02115 | 617-262-5000
Boston Baptist College | Post-Sec.
950 Metropolitan Ave 02136 | 617-364-3510
Boston Conservatory | Post-Sec.
8 Fenway 02215 | 617-536-6340
Boston University | Post-Sec.
121 Bay State Rd 02215 | 617-353-2000
Boston University Academy | 200/9-12
1 University Rd 02215 | 617-353-9000
James Berkman, hdmstr. | Fax 353-8999
Boston University Medical Center | Post-Sec.
100 E Newton St 02118 | 617-638-5300
Brigham and Women's Hospital | Post-Sec.
75 Francis St 02115 | 617-732-7493
Bunker Hill Community College | Post-Sec.
250 Rutherford Ave 02129 | 617-228-2000
Butera School of Art | Post-Sec.
111 Beacon St 02116 | 617-536-4623
Cathedral HS | 200/9-12
74 Union Park St 02118 | 617-542-2325
Christol Murch, prin. | Fax 542-1745
Children's Hospital | Post-Sec.
300 Longwood Ave 02115 | 617-355-6433
Commonwealth S | 100/9-12
151 Commonwealth Ave 02116 | 617-266-7525
| Fax 266-5769
Emerson College | Post-Sec.
120 Boylston St 02116 | 617-824-8600
Emmanuel College | Post-Sec.
400 Fenway 02115 | 617-277-9340
Fisher College | Post-Sec.
118 Beacon St 02116 | 617-236-8800
Gibbs College of Boston | Post-Sec.
126 Newbury St 02116 | 617-578-7100
Learning Institute for Beauty Sciences | Post-Sec.
867 Boylston St 02116 | 617-424-6565
Massachusetts College of Art | Post-Sec.
621 Huntington Ave 02115 | 617-232-1555
MA College of Pharmacy & Health Sciences | Post-Sec.
179 Longwood Ave 02115 | 617-732-2800
Massachusetts School Professional Psych. | Post-Sec.
221 Rivermoor St 02132 | 617-327-6777
MGH Institute of Health Professions | Post-Sec.
36 1st Ave 02129 | 617-726-3140
New England College of Finance | Post-Sec.
10 High St Ste 204 02110 | 617-951-2350
New England College of Optometry | Post-Sec.
424 Beacon St 02115 | 800-824-5526
New England Conservatory of Music | Post-Sec.
290 Huntington Ave 02115 | 617-585-1100
New England School of Art & Design | Post-Sec.
75 Arlington St 02116 | 617-573-8785
New England School of Law | Post-Sec.
154 Stuart St 02116 | 617-451-0010
New England School of Photography | Post-Sec.
537 Commonwealth Ave 02215 | 617-437-1868
Newman Preparatory S | 300/9-12
247 Marlborough St 02116 | 617-267-4530
J. Harry Lynch, prin. | Fax 267-7070
North Bennet Street School | Post-Sec.
39 N Bennet St 02113 | 617-227-0155
Northeastern University | Post-Sec.
360 Huntington Ave 02115 | 617-373-2000
Richmond University London England | Post-Sec.
343 Congress St Ste 3100 02210 | 617-450-5617
School of the Museum of Fine Arts | Post-Sec.
230 Fenway 02115 | 617-267-6100
Simmons College | Post-Sec.
300 Fenway 02115 | 617-521-2000

Suffolk University | Post-Sec.
8 Ashburton Pl 02108 | 617-573-8460
The Art Inst. of Boston at Leslie Univ. | Post-Sec.
700 Beacon St 02215 | 617-262-1223
Tufts University | Post-Sec.
136 Harrison Ave 02111 | 617-636-7000
University of Massachusetts Boston | Post-Sec.
100 William T Mrrissey Blvd 02125 | 617-287-5000
Urban College of Boston | Post-Sec.
178 Tremont St 02111 | 617-292-4723
Veterans Administration Medical Center | Post-Sec.
150 S Huntington Ave 02130 | 617-232-9500
Wentworth Institute of Technology | Post-Sec.
550 Huntington Ave 02115 | 617-442-9010
Wheelock College | Post-Sec.
200 Riverway 02215 | 617-734-5200
Winsor S | 400/5-12
103 Pilgrim Rd 02215 | 617-735-9500
Rachel Friis Stettler, prin. | Fax 739-5519

Bourne, Barnstable, Pop. 1,284
Bourne SD | 2,500/K-12
36 Sandwich Rd 02532 | 508-759-0660
Edmond LaFleur, supt. | Fax 759-1107
bourne.k12.ma.us
Bourne HS | 600/9-12
75 Waterhouse Rd 02532 | 508-759-0670
Ronald McCarthy, prin. | Fax 759-0677
Bourne MS | 800/5-8
77 Waterhouse Rd 02532 | 508-759-0690
Ernest Frias, prin. | Fax 759-0695

Upper Cape Cod Vo-Tech SD
220 Sandwich Rd 02532 | 508-759-7711
Barry Motta, supt. | Fax 759-7208
Upper Cape Cod Regional Technical S | Vo/Tech
220 Sandwich Rd 02532 | 508-759-7711
Kevin Farr, prin. | Fax 759-7208

Boylston, Worcester
Berlin-Boylston SD | 500/7-12
215 Main St 01505 | 508-869-2837
Dr. Marcia Lukon, supt. | Fax 869-0023
www.mec.edu/bbps
Tahanto Regional MS | 500/7-12
1001 Main St 01505 | 508-869-2333
Carol Bryngelson, prin. | Fax 869-0175

Bradford, See Haverhill

Bradford Christian Academy | 100/6-12
97 Oxford Ave 01835 | 978-373-7900
Larry George, hdmstr. | Fax 373-7911

Braintree, Norfolk, Pop. 33,800
Braintree SD | 4,900/K-12
348 Pond St 02184 | 781-380-0130
Dr. Peter Kurzberg, supt. | Fax 380-0146
www.braintreepublicschools.com
Braintree HS | 1,400/9-12
128 Town St 02184 | 781-848-4000
William Farrington, prin. | Fax 380-0116
East MS | 700/6-8
305 River St 02184 | 781-380-0170
Michael Connelly, prin. | Fax 848-4522
South MS | 600/6-8
232 Peach St 02184 | 781-380-0160
Edward McDonough, prin. | Fax 380-0164

Archbishop Williams HS | 500/9-12
80 Independence Ave 02184 | 781-843-3636
Mary Lou Sadowski, prin. | Fax 843-3782
Marino Montessori S | 100/6-9
59 Albee Dr 02184 | 617-590-8882
Thayer Academy | 700/6-12
745 Washington St 02184 | 781-843-3580
William Koskores, hdmstr. | Fax 380-8785

Bridgewater, Plymouth, Pop. 7,242
Bridgewater-Raynham Regional SD
Supt. — See Raynham
Bridgewater-Raynham Regional HS | 1,600/9-12
166 Mount Prospect St 02324 | 508-697-6902
Jeffrey Granatino, prin. | Fax 279-2110
Williams MS | 1,200/5-8
200 South St 02324 | 508-697-6968
Howard Gilmore, prin. | Fax 697-6775

Bridgewater State College 02325 | Post-Sec.
| 508-697-1237

Brighton, See Boston
Boston SD
Supt. — See Boston
Boston Community Leadership Academy | 400/9-12
20 Warren St 02135 | 617-635-8937
Nicole Bahnam, hdmstr. | Fax 635-8942
Brighton HS | 1,300/9-12
25 Warren St 02135 | 617-635-9873
Toby Romer, hdmstr. | Fax 635-9892
Edison MS | 700/6-8
60 Glenmont Rd 02135 | 617-635-8436
Eliot Stern, prin. | Fax 635-8446

Bryman Institute | Post-Sec.
1505 Commonwealth Ave 02135 | 617-783-9955
Margolis Mesivta of Greater Boston | 100/9-12
34 Sparhawk St 02135 | 617-779-0166
Aerial Blumberg, prin. | Fax 779-0166
Mt. St. Joseph Academy | 300/9-12
617 Cambridge St 02135 | 617-254-8383
Kathleen Fraser, prin. | Fax 254-0240

Brockton, Plymouth, Pop. 95,090
Brockton SD | 16,100/PK-12
43 Crescent St 02301 | 508-580-7000
Basan Nembirkow, supt. | Fax 580-7587
www.brocktonpublicschools.com

Brockton HS | 4,200/9-12
700 Belmont St 02301 | 508-580-7633
Susan Szachowicz, prin. | Fax 580-7600
East JHS | 700/7-8
464 Centre St 02302 | 508-580-7351
Donald Burrill, prin. | Fax 580-7090
North JHS | 700/7-8
108 Oak St 02301 | 508-580-7371
Patrick Hart, prin. | Fax 580-7088
South JHS | 700/7-8
105 Keith Ave 02301 | 508-580-7311
Kenneth Cardone, prin. | Fax 580-7089
West JHS | 700/7-8
271 West St 02301 | 508-580-7381
Michael Smith, prin. | Fax 580-7307
Paine S, 211 Crescent St 02302 | Adult
Linda Faria-Braun, admin. | 508-580-7475

Ailano School of Aesthetics | Post-Sec.
553 Forest Ave 02301 | 508-587-3883
Ailano School of Cosmetology | Post-Sec.
PO Box 4740 02303 | 508-583-5433
Brockton Hospital | Post-Sec.
680 Centre St 02302 | 508-941-7044
Cardinal Spellman HS | 500/9-12
738 Court St 02302 | 508-583-6875
Sr. Thomasine Knowlton, prin. | Fax 580-1977
Computer-Ed Business Institute | Post-Sec.
375 Westgate Dr 02301 | 508-941-0730
LaBaron Hairdressing Academy | Post-Sec.
240 Liberty St 02301 | 508-583-1700
Massasoit Community College | Post-Sec.
1 Massasoit Blvd 02302 | 508-588-9100

Brookline, Norfolk, Pop. 57,600
Brookline SD | 5,900/PK-12
333 Washington St 02445 | 617-730-2403
Dr. William Lupini, supt. | Fax 730-2108
www.brookline.mec.edu
Brookline HS | 1,900/9-12
115 Greenough St 02445 | 617-713-5000
Robert Weintraub, prin. | Fax 713-5005

Boston Graduate Sch for Psychoanalysis | Post-Sec.
1583 Beacon St 02446 | 617-277-3915
Boston Trinity Academy | 100/6-12
1187 Beacon St 02446 | 617-975-0080
Timothy Wiens, hdmstr. | Fax 975-0083
Dexter S | 400/PK-12
20 Newton St 02445 | 617-522-5544
William Phinney, prin. | Fax 522-8166
Hellenic College/Holy Cross Sch Theology | Post-Sec.
50 Goddard Ave 02445 | 617-731-3500
Maimonides S | 700/K-12
34 Philbrick Rd 02445 | 617-232-4452
Joshua Wolff, dir. | Fax 566-2061
Newbury College | Post-Sec.
129 Fisher Ave 02445 | 617-730-7000
New England Hebrew Academy | 200/PK-12
PO Box 514 02446 | 617-731-5330
Rabbi Chaim Ciment, dir. | Fax 277-0752
New England Institute of Art | Post-Sec.
10 Brookline Pl 02445 | 617-739-1700
Southfield S | 200/PK-12
10 Newton St 02445 | 617-522-6980

Burlington, Middlesex, Pop. 23,302
Burlington SD | 3,500/K-12
123 Cambridge St 01803 | 781-270-1800
Dr. James L. Picone, supt. | Fax 270-1773
www.burlington.mec.edu
Burlington HS | 900/9-12
123 Cambridge St 01803 | 781-270-1800
Linda Hayes, prin. | Fax 229-4893
Simonds MS | 900/6-8
144 Winn St 01803 | 781-270-1782
Richard Connors, prin. | Fax 270-1654

Open Bible Academy | 100/K-12
3 Winn St 01803 | 781-272-2074

Buzzards Bay, Barnstable, Pop. 3,250

Massachusetts Maritime Academy | Post-Sec.
101 Academy Dr 02532 | 508-830-5000

Byfield, Essex
Triton Regional SD | 3,600/PK-12
112 Elm St 01922 | 978-465-2397
Sandra Halloran, supt. | Fax 465-8599
www.trsd.net
Triton Regional HS | 1,000/9-12
112 Elm St 01922 | 978-462-8171
Robert C. Manseau, prin. | Fax 465-6868
Triton Regional MS | 500/7-8
112 Elm St 01922 | 978-463-5845
Peter Gadd, prin. | Fax 465-6868

Dummer Academy | 400/9-12
1 Elm St 01922 | 978-465-1763
John Doggett, hdmstr. | Fax 463-9896

Cambridge, Middlesex, Pop. 101,587
Cambridge SD | 6,300/K-12
159 Thorndike St 02141 | 617-349-6494
Dr. Thomas Fowler-Finn, supt. | Fax 349-6496
www.cpsd.us
Cambridge Rindge & Latin HS | 1,900/9-12
459 Broadway 02138 | 617-349-6632
Dr. Sybil Knight, prin. | Fax 349-6749

Boston Archdiocesan Choir S | 50/5-8
29 Mount Auburn St 02138 | 617-868-8658
Sr. Kathleen Berube, prin. | Fax 354-7092
Buckingham Browne & Nichols HS | 400/9-12
80 Gerrys Landing Rd 02138 | 617-547-6100
Rebecca Upham, hdmstr. | Fax 576-1139

Buckingham Browne & Nichols MS | 200/7-8
80 Sparks St 02138 | 617-800-2336
Rebecca Upham, hdmstr. | Fax 491-5159
Cambridge College | Post-Sec.
1000 Massachusetts Ave 02138 | 617-868-1000
Cambridge School of Culinary Arts | Post-Sec.
2020 Massachusetts Ave 02140 | 617-354-2020
Ecole Bilingue S of Boston | 500/PK-12
45 Matignon Rd 02140 | 617-499-1451
 | Fax 499-1454
Episcopal Divinity School | Post-Sec.
99 Brattle St 02138 | 617-868-3450
Harvard University | Post-Sec.
8 Garden St 02138 | 617-495-1000
Hult International Business School | Post-Sec.
1 Education St 02141 | 617-746-1990
Lesley University | Post-Sec.
29 Everett St 02138 | 617-349-8800
Longy School of Music | Post-Sec.
1 Follen St 02138 | 617-876-0956
Massachusetts Institute of Technology | Post-Sec.
77 Massachusetts Ave 02139 | 617-253-1000
Matignon HS | 600/9-12
1 Matignon Rd 02140 | 617-876-1212
Donald Dabenigno, prin. | Fax 661-3905
North Cambridge Catholic HS | 200/9-12
40 Norris St 02140 | 617-876-6068
Robert McCarthy, prin. | Fax 576-1898
Weston Jesuit School of Theology | Post-Sec.
3 Phillips Pl 02138 | 617-492-1960

Canton, Norfolk, Pop. 18,530
Blue Hills Vocational SD |
800 Randolph St 02021 | 781-828-5800
Kenneth M. Rocke, supt. | Fax 828-0794
www.bluehills.org
Blue Hills Regional Technical S | Vo/Tech
800 Randolph St 02021 | 781-828-5800
Kenneth M. Rocke, prin. | Fax 828-0794

Canton SD | 3,000/PK-12
960 Washington St 02021 | 781-821-5060
Irene Sherry Kaplan Ed.D., supt. | Fax 575-6500
www.cantonma.org
Canton HS | 800/9-12
900 Washington St 02021 | 781-821-5050
Edward Mulvey, prin. | Fax 821-5052
Galvin MS | 700/6-8
55 Pecunit St 02021 | 781-821-5070
Thomas LaLiberte, prin. | Fax 575-6509

Bay State School of Technology | Post-Sec.
225 Turnpike St 02021 | 781-828-3434

Carver, Plymouth
Carver SD | 2,100/PK-12
3 Carver Square Blvd 02330 | 508-866-6160
Dr. Patricia B. Grenier, supt. | Fax 866-2920
www.carver.org
Carver HS | 600/9-12
60 S Meadow Rd 02330 | 508-866-6140
Kathleen Spencer, prin. | Fax 866-5639
Carver MS | 500/6-8
60 S Meadow Rd 02330 | 508-866-6130
Daniel Daly, prin. | Fax 866-6880

Charlemont, Franklin

Academy at Charlemont | 100/5-12
Mohawk Trail 01339 | 413-339-4912
 | Fax 339-4324

Charlestown, See Boston
Boston SD
Supt. — See Boston
Charlestown HS | 1,300/9-12
240 Medford St 02129 | 617-635-9914
Michael Fung, hdmstr. | Fax 635-9928
Edwards MS | 500/6-8
28 Walker St 02129 | 617-635-8516
Michael Sabin, prin. | Fax 635-8522

RETS Electronic School | Post-Sec.
570 Rutherford Ave 02129 | 800-739-8700

Charlton, Worcester
Dudley-Charlton Regional SD
Supt. — See Dudley
Charlton MS | 800/5-8
2 Oxford Rd 01507 | 508-248-1423
Kathryn Tucker, prin. | Fax 248-1418
Southern Worcester Co. Reg Vocational SD
57 Old Muggett Hill Rd 01507 | 508-248-5971
Steven Mondor, supt. | Fax 248-4747
www.baypath.tec.ma.us
Bay Path Regional Vo Tech HS | Vo/Tech
57 Old Muggett Hill Rd 01507 | 508-248-5971
Steven Mondor, prin. | Fax 248-4747

Chatham, Barnstable, Pop. 1,916
Chatham SD | 700/PK-12
425 Crowell Rd 02633 | 508-945-5130
Mary Ann Lanzo, supt. | Fax 945-5133
www.chatham.k12.ma.us
Chatham HS | 200/9-12
425 Crowell Rd 02633 | 508-945-5140
Paul Mangelinkx, prin. | Fax 945-5110
Chatham MS | 200/5-8
425 Crowell Rd 02633 | 508-945-5148
Rosemary Williams, prin. | Fax 945-5143

Chelmsford, Middlesex, Pop. 33,858
Chelmsford SD
Supt. — See North Chelmsford
McCarthy MS | 1,000/5-8
250 North Rd 01824 | 978-251-5122
Curt Bates, prin. | Fax 251-5130
Parker MS | 800/5-8
75 Graniteville Rd 01824 | 978-251-5133
Richard O'Donnell, prin. | Fax 251-5140

Chelsea, Suffolk, Pop. 34,106
Chelsea SD | 6,100/PK-12
500 Broadway 02150 | 617-889-8415
Thomas S. Kingston, supt. | Fax 889-8361
chelseaschools.com
Browne S | 5-8
180 Walnut St 02150 | 617-889-8652
Cove Davis, prin. | Fax 889-8459
Chelsea HS | 1,300/9-12
299 Everett Ave 02150 | 617-889-8418
Morton Orlov, prin. | Fax 889-8468
Clark Avenue S | 1,200/5-8
8 Clark Ave 02150 | 617-889-7540
Linda Breau, prin. | Fax 889-7539
Wright S | 1,100/5-8
180 Walnut St 02150 | 617-889-8467
Donna Covino, prin. | Fax 889-8463

Cheshire, Berkshire
Adams-Cheshire Regional SD | 1,800/PK-12
125 Savoy Rd 01225 | 413-743-2939
Alfred Skrocki, supt. | Fax 743-4135
www.acrsd.net
Hoosac Valley HS | 500/9-12
125 Savoy Rd 01225 | 413-743-5200
Henry Duval, prin. | Fax 743-8420
Other Schools – See Adams

Chestnut Hill, See Newton

Beaver Country Day S | 400/6-12
791 Hammond St 02467 | 617-738-2700
Peter Hutton, prin. | Fax 738-2701
Boston College | Post-Sec.
140 Commonwealth Ave 02467 | 617-552-8000
Brimmer and May S | 400/PK-12
69 Middlesex Rd 02467 | 617-566-7462
Anne Reenstierna, hdmstr. | Fax 734-5147
Pine Manor College | Post-Sec.
400 Heath St 02467 | 617-731-7000

Chicopee, Hampden, Pop. 54,992
Chicopee SD | 7,500/PK-12
180 Broadway St 01020 | 413-594-3410
Richard W. Rege, supt. | Fax 594-3552
www.chicopee.mec.edu/
Bellamy MS | 900/6-8
314 Pendleton Ave 01020 | 413-594-3527
Paul Radwanski, prin. | Fax 594-1838
Chicopee Comprehensive HS | 1,200/9-12
617 Montgomery St 01020 | 413-594-3534
Stanley Kozikowski, prin. | Fax 594-3492
Chicopee HS | 1,000/9-12
820 Front St 01020 | 413-594-3437
Roland Joyal, prin. | Fax 594-3500
Fairview MS | 900/6-8
26 Memorial Ave 01020 | 413-594-3501
Michele Partyka, prin. | Fax 594-3509

Elms College | Post-Sec.
291 Springfield St 01013 | 413-594-2761
Porter and Chester Institute | Post-Sec.
134 Dulong Cir 01022 | 413-593-3339

Clinton, Worcester, Pop. 7,943
Clinton SD | 1,900/K-12
150 School St 01510 | 978-365-4200
Gerald M. Gaw, supt. | Fax 365-5037
clinton.k12.ma.us
Clinton HS | 700/8-12
200 W Boylston St 01510 | 978-365-4208
James Hastings, prin. | Fax 365-4219

Cohasset, Norfolk, Pop. 7,075
Cohasset SD | 1,400/K-12
143 Pond St 02025 | 781-383-6111
Denise Walsh Ed.D., supt. | Fax 383-6507
www.cohassetk12.org
Cohasset MSHS | 700/6-12
143 Pond St 02025 | 781-383-6100
Joel Antolini, prin. | Fax 383-6556

Concord, Middlesex, Pop. 4,700
Concord SD | 2,000/K-8
120 Meriam Rd 01742 | 978-318-1500
Brenda D Finn Ed.D., supt. | Fax 318-1537
www.colonial.net
Concord MS | 700/6-8
835 Old Marlboro Rd 01742 | 978-318-1380
Arthur Unobskey, prin. | Fax 318-1392

Concord-Carlisle SD | 1,200/9-12
120 Meriam Rd 01742 | 978-318-1500
Brenda Finn, supt. | Fax 318-1537
www.colonial.net
Concord-Carlisle HS | 1,200/9-12
500 Walden St 01742 | 978-318-1400
Arthur Dulong, prin. | Fax 318-1435

Concord Academy | 300/9-12
166 Main St 01742 | 978-402-2200
Jacob Dresden, hdmstr. | Fax 402-2210
Fenn S | 300/4-9
516 Monument St 01742 | 978-369-5800
Gerard Ward, hdmstr. | Fax 371-7520
Middlesex S | 400/9-12
PO Box 9122 01742 | 978-369-2550
Kathleen Carroll Giles, hdmstr. | Fax 369-3846

Conway, Franklin

Conway School of Landscape Design | Post-Sec.
PO Box 179 01341 | 413-369-4044

Dalton, Berkshire, Pop. 7,155
Central Berkshire Regional SD | 2,300/PK-12
PO Box 299 01227 | 413-684-0320
Donna Harlan, supt. | Fax 684-1520
www.cbrsd.org

Nessacus Regional MS 600/6-8
35 Fox Rd 01226 413-684-0780
Gerard Dery, prin. Fax 684-4214
Wahconah Regional HS 800/9-12
150 Old Windsor Rd 01226 413-684-1330
James Conro, prin. Fax 684-5032

Danvers, Essex, Pop. 24,174
Danvers SD 3,600/K-12
64 Cabot Rd 01923 978-777-4539
Betty G. Allen Ph.D., supt. Fax 777-8931
www.danvers.mec.edu
Danvers HS 1,000/9-12
60 Cabot Rd 01923 978-777-8925
Eileen Erwin, prin. Fax 777-8931
Holten-Richmond MS 900/6-8
57 Conant St 01923 978-774-8590
Michael Cali, prin. Fax 762-8686

North Shore Community College Post-Sec.
1 Ferncroft Rd 01923 978-762-4000
St. Johns Prep S 1,000/9-12
72 Spring St 01923 978-774-1050
Edward Hardiman Ph.D., prin. Fax 774-5767

Dedham, Norfolk, Pop. 23,782
Dedham SD 3,000/PK-12
PO Box 246 02027 781-326-5622
Antonio Fernandes, supt. Fax 320-0193
www.dedham.k12.ma.us
Dedham HS 1,000/8-12
140 Whiting Ave 02026 781-326-4773
Alan Winrow, prin. Fax 320-8126

Noble And Greenough S 500/7-12
10 Campus Dr 02026 781-326-3700
Robert Henderson, hdmstr. Fax 320-8118
Ursuline Academy 400/7-12
85 Lowder St 02026 781-326-6161
Sr. Mercedes Videira, prin. Fax 326-4898

Deerfield, Franklin

Deerfield Academy 600/9-12
7 Boyden Ln 01342 413-772-0241
Eric Widmer, prin. Fax 772-1100
Eaglebrook S 300/6-9
Pine Nook Rd 01342 413-774-7411
Fax 772-2394

Dighton, Bristol
Bristol County Agricultural SD
135 Center St 02715 508-669-6744
Russell James, supt. Fax 669-6747
www.bristolaggie.mec.edu/
Bristol County Agricultural HS Vo/Tech
135 Center St 02715 508-669-6744
Krista Paynton, prin. Fax 669-6747

Dighton-Rehoboth Regional SD
Supt. — See North Dighton
Dighton MS 400/5-8
1250R Somerset Ave 02715 508-669-4200
Paul Swett, prin. Fax 669-4210

Dorchester, See Boston
Boston SD
Supt. — See Boston
Academy of Public Service 300/9-12
9 Peacevale Rd 02124 617-635-8910
Zachary Robbins, hdmstr. Fax 635-7825
Boston Latin Academy 1,600/7-12
205 Townsend St 02121 617-635-9957
Maria Garcia-Aaronson, hdmstr. Fax 635-6696
Burke HS 900/9-12
60 Washington St 02121 617-635-9837
Carol Moore, hdmstr. Fax 635-9852
Cleveland MS 600/6-8
11 Charles St 02122 617-635-8631
Kennietha Jones, prin. Fax 635-6413
Harbor S 300/6-8
294 Bowdoin St 02122 617-635-6365
Amy Marx, dir. Fax 635-6367
King MS 400/6-8
77 Lawrence Ave 02121 617-635-8212
Audrey Leung-Tat, prin. Fax 635-9356
McCormack MS 700/6-8
315 Mount Vernon St 02125 617-635-8657
Jane King, prin. Fax 635-9788
New Boston MS 700/6-8
270 Columbia Rd 02121 617-635-1650
Debra Socia, prin. Fax 635-1637
Noonan Business Academy 600/9-12
9 Peacevale Rd 02124 617-635-9730
John Leonard, hdmstr. Fax 635-7888
Wilson MS 600/6-8
18 Croftland Ave 02124 617-635-8827
Claudette Mulligan-Gates, prin. Fax 635-6414

Boston College HS 1,200/9-12
150 William T Mrrissey Blvd 02125 617-474-5115
Stephen Hughes, prin. Fax 474-5105
Caritas Laboure College Post-Sec.
2120 Dorchester Ave 02124 617-296-8300
Epiphany S 100/5-8
154 Centre St 02124 617-326-0425
Fax 326-0424
Seaton Academy 9-12
2220 Dorchester Ave 02124 617-296-1087
Maureen White Ed.D., prin. Fax 296-1089

Douglas, Worcester
Douglas SD 1,600/PK-12
21 Davis St 01516 508-476-7001
Robert Melican, supt. Fax 476-3719
www.douglas.k12.ma.us/
Douglas MSHS 400/8-12
33 Davis St 01516 508-476-4100
Brett Kustigian, prin. Fax 476-7310

Dover, Norfolk, Pop. 2,163
Dover-Sherborn SD 1,000/6-12
157 Farm St 02030 508-785-0036
Perry Davis, supt. Fax 785-2239
www.doversherborn.org
Dover-Sherborn Regional HS 500/9-12
9 Junction St 02030 508-785-0624
Denise Lonergan, prin. Fax 785-8141
Dover-Sherborn Regional MS 500/6-8
155 Farm St 02030 508-785-0635
Paul Berkel, prin. Fax 785-0796

Dracut, Middlesex, Pop. 25,594
Dracut SD 4,300/PK-12
2063 Lakeview Ave 01826 978-957-2660
Elaine Espindle, supt. Fax 957-2682
www.dracut.k12.ma.us
Dracut HS 1,100/9-12
1540 Lakeview Ave 01826 978-957-1500
Patricia Power, prin. Fax 957-9717
Lakeview JHS 800/7-8
1570 Lakeview Ave 01826 978-957-3330
Theresa Rogers, prin. Fax 957-4075

Dudley, Worcester, Pop. 3,700
Dudley-Charlton Regional SD 4,300/PK-12
68 Dudley Oxford Rd 01571 508-943-6888
Sean Gilrein, supt. Fax 943-1077
www.dc-regional.k12.ma.us/
Dudley MS 600/5-8
70 Dudley Oxford Rd 01571 508-943-2224
Gregg Desto, prin. Fax 949-0722
Shepherd Hill Regional HS 1,100/9-12
68 Dudley Oxford Rd 01571 508-943-6700
Timothy M. Schur, prin. Fax 943-5956
Other Schools – See Charlton

Nichols College 01571 Post-Sec.
508-943-1560

Duxbury, Plymouth, Pop. 1,637
Duxbury SD 3,200/K-12
130 Saint George St 02332 781-934-7600
Eileen Williams, supt. Fax 934-7644
www.duxbury.k12.ma.us
Duxbury HS 1,000/9-12
130 Saint George St 02332 781-934-7650
John E. McCarthy, prin. Fax 934-7617
Duxbury MS 800/6-8
130 Saint George St 02332 781-934-7640
Jeffrey Knight, prin. Fax 934-7608

East Boston, See Boston
Boston SD
Supt. — See Boston
East Boston HS 1,500/9-12
86 White St 02128 617-635-9896
Michael Rubin, hdmstr. Fax 635-9726
Umana/Barnes MS 800/6-8
312 Border St 02128 617-635-8481
Dr. Jose Salgado, prin. Fax 635-9595

Savio Prep HS 200/9-12
165 Byron St 02128 617-567-2710
James McHugh, prin. Fax 569-6883

East Bridgewater, Plymouth, Pop. 11,104
East Bridgewater SD 2,400/PK-12
11 Plymouth St 02333 508-378-8200
Margaret H. Strojny Ph.D., supt. Fax 378-8225
www.ebps.net
East Bridgewater HS 700/9-12
11 Plymouth St 02333 508-378-8214
Anthony Sarno, prin. Fax 378-8226
Mitchell MS 1,000/4-8
435 Central St 02333 508-378-8209
Allen Duarte, prin. Fax 378-8228

East Falmouth, Barnstable, Pop. 5,577
Falmouth SD 4,400/PK-12
340 Teaticket Hwy 02536 508-548-0151
Dennis Richards, supt. Fax 457-9032
www.falmouth.k12.ma.us
Other Schools – See Falmouth

Easthampton, Hampshire, Pop. 16,340
Easthampton SD 1,600/PK-12
50 Payson Ave 01027 413-529-1500
Deborah Carter, supt. Fax 529-1567
www.easthampton.k12.ma.us
Easthampton HS 400/9-12
70 Williston Ave 01027 413-529-1585
Jeffrey Sealander, prin. Fax 529-1591
White Brook MS 600/5-8
200 Park St 01027 413-529-1530
Julie Salzman, prin. Fax 529-1534

Williston Northampton S 500/7-12
19 Payson Ave 01027 413-529-3000
Brian Wright, hdmstr. Fax 527-9494

East Longmeadow, Hampden, Pop. 13,367
East Longmeadow SD 2,700/K-12
180 Maple St 01028 413-525-5450
Dr. Edward Costa, supt. Fax 525-5456
www.eastlongmeadow.org
Birchland Park MS 700/6-8
50 Hanward Hl 01028 413-525-5480
Kathleen Hill, prin. Fax 525-5320
East Longmeadow HS 900/9-12
180 Maple St 01028 413-525-5460
Richard Freccero, prin. Fax 525-5496

Baptist Village Academy 100/PK-12
50 Parker St 01028 413-525-1153
Timothy Sheranko, prin. Fax 525-9991

East Sandwich, Barnstable, Pop. 3,171
Sandwich SD
Supt. — See Sandwich

Sandwich HS 1,200/9-12
365 Quaker Meeting House Rd 02537 508-888-4900
Ellin Booras, prin. Fax 833-8392

East Taunton, See Taunton
Taunton SD
Supt. — See Taunton
Martin MS 800/5-8
131 Caswell St 02718 508-821-1250
Christopher Baralta, prin. Fax 821-1273

East Walpole, Norfolk, Pop. 3,800
Walpole SD
Supt. — See Walpole
Bird MS 500/6-8
625 Washington St 02032 508-660-7226
Sandra J. Esmond, prin. Fax 660-7229

East Weymouth, Norfolk
Weymouth SD
Supt. — See Weymouth
Adams IS 2,200/5-8
89 Middle St 02189 781-335-1100
Zeffro Gianetti, prin. Fax 340-2544
Chapman MS 5-8
1051 Commercial St 02189 781-337-4500
Sheila Fisher, prin. Fax 340-2594

Everett, Middlesex, Pop. 37,540
Everett SD 5,400/PK-12
121 Vine St 02149 617-389-7950
Frederick Foresteire, supt. Fax 394-2408
www.everett.k12.ma.us/
Everett HS 1,700/9-12
548 Broadway 02149 617-394-2490
Thomas J. Stella, prin. Fax 389-5841

Pope John XXIII Central HS 400/9-12
888 Broadway 02149 617-389-0240
William Fitzgerald Ph.D., prin. Fax 389-2201

Fairhaven, Bristol, Pop. 16,132
Fairhaven SD 2,200/K-12
128 Washington St 02719 508-979-4000
Dr. Robert Baldwin, supt. Fax 979-4149
www.fairhavenps.org/
Fairhaven HS 700/9-12
12 Huttleston Ave 02719 508-979-4052
Jean Cote, prin. Fax 979-4140
Hastings MS 600/6-8
30 School St 02719 508-979-4063
Dr. Ann Dargon, prin. Fax 979-4068

Fall River, Bristol, Pop. 92,760
Fall River SD 14,900/PK-12
417 Rock St 02720 508-675-8420
Richard D. Pavao, supt. Fax 675-8462
www.fallriver.k12.ma.us/
Durfee HS 2,900/9-12
360 Elsbree St 02720 508-675-8130
Donald Rebello, prin. Fax 675-8186
Kuss MS 600/6-8
290 Rock St 02720 508-675-8335
Robert Hassan, prin. Fax 675-1984
Lord MS 700/6-8
151 Amity St 02721 508-675-8208
Kurt Peterson, lead tchr. Fax 675-8253
Morton MS 800/6-8
376 President Ave 02720 508-675-8340
James Murano, prin. Fax 675-8414
Talbot MS 800/6-8
124 Melrose St 02723 508-675-8350
Karol G. Coffin, prin. Fax 675-8356

Greater Fall River SD
251 Stonehaven Rd 02723 508-678-2891
Rogerio Ramos, supt. Fax 679-6423
www.diman.mec.edu
Diman Regional Vocational Technical HS Vo/Tech
251 Stonehaven Rd 02723 508-678-2891
Brian S. Bentley, prin. Fax 679-6423

Bishop Connolly HS 400/9-12
373 Elsbree St 02720 508-676-1071
Paul Cartier, prin. Fax 676-8594
Bristol Community College Post-Sec.
777 Elsbree St 02720 508-678-2811
East Gate Christian Academy 100/PK-12
397 Bay St 02724 508-730-1735
Dr. Ronald Bernier, hdmstr. Fax 674-6166
Rob Roy Academy Fall River Campus Post-Sec.
260 S Main St 02721 508-672-4751

Falmouth, Barnstable, Pop. 4,047
Falmouth SD
Supt. — See East Falmouth
Falmouth HS 1,300/9-12
874 Gifford Street Ext 02540 508-540-2200
Paul Cali, prin. Fax 548-7515
Lawrence MS 800/7-8
113 Lakeview Ave 02540 508-548-0606
Douglas White, prin. Fax 457-9778

Falmouth Academy 200/7-12
7 Highfield Dr 02540 508-457-9696
David Faus, hdmstr. Fax 457-4112
National Grad. Sch. Quality Systems Mgmt Post-Sec.
186 Jones Rd 02540 508-457-1313

Feeding Hills, Hampden, Pop. 5,450
Agawam SD 4,200/K-12
1305 Springfield Ste 1 01030 413-821-0548
Mary A. Czajkowski Ed.D., supt. Fax 789-1835
www.agawampublicschools.org
Agawam JHS 700/7-8
1305 Springfield St #2 01030 413-821-0561
Kevin Littlefield, prin. Fax 786-4240
Other Schools – See Agawam

Fiskdale, Worcester, Pop. 2,189
Tantasqua SD 1,500/7-12
320 Brookfield Rd 01518 508-347-3077
Kathleen H. Reynolds, supt. Fax 347-2697
www.tantasqua.org
Tantasqua Regional HS 900/9-12
319 Brookfield Rd 01518 508-347-9301
James White, prin. Fax 347-1049
Tantasqua Regional JHS 600/7-8
320 Brookfield Rd 01518 508-347-7381
Theodore Friend, prin. Fax 347-3994
Tantasqua Regional Tech HS Vo/Tech
319 Brookfield Rd 01518 508-347-3045
Timothy Prouty, prin. Fax 347-1049

Fitchburg, Worcester, Pop. 39,948
Fitchburg SD 6,700/PK-12
376 South St 01420 978-345-3200
Andre Ravenelle, supt. Fax 348-2305
www.fitchburg.k12.ma.us
Academy MS 1,000/5-8
98 Academy St 01420 978-343-2146
Steven Silverman, prin. Fax 348-2323
Brown Arts Vision S 700/5-8
62 Academy St 01420 978-345-3278
Theresa Mayer, prin. Fax 348-2316
Fitchburg HS 1,500/9-12
140 Arnhow Farm Rd 01420 978-345-3240
Rich Masciarelli, prin. Fax 348-2303
Memorial MS 1,100/5-8
615 Rollstone St 01420 978-345-3295
Francis Thomas, prin. Fax 343-2121

Montachusett Regional Vo/Tech HSD
1050 Westminster St 01420 978-345-9200
James Culkeen, supt. Fax 345-9165
www.montytech.net
Montachusett Reg Vocational Technical HS Vo/Tech
1050 Westminster St 01420 978-345-9200
Donald Cranson, prin. Fax 348-1176

Fitchburg State College Post-Sec.
160 Pearl St 01420 978-345-2151
Henri's School of Hair Design Post-Sec.
PO Box 2244 01420 978-342-6061
Notre Dame HS 100/7-12
151 South St 01420 978-343-7635
Jeffrey Hammond, prin. Fax 343-6579
St. Bernards HS 500/9-12
45 Harvard St 01420 978-342-3212
James Conry, admin. Fax 345-8067

Florence, See Northampton
Northampton SD
Supt. — See Northampton
Kennedy MS 700/6-8
100 Bridge Rd 01062 413-587-1489
Lesley Wilson, prin. Fax 587-1495

Foxboro, Norfolk, Pop. 5,706
Foxboro SD 2,900/PK-12
60 South St 02035 508-543-1660
Kathleen Tyrell, supt. Fax 543-4793
www.foxborough.k12.ma.us
Ahern MS 900/5-8
111 Mechanic St 02035 508-543-1610
Susan Abrams, prin. Fax 543-1613
Foxboro HS 800/9-12
120 South St 02035 508-543-1616
Jeffrey Theodoss, prin. Fax 543-1670

Framingham, Middlesex, Pop. 67,300
Framingham SD 7,900/PK-12
14 Vernon St Ste 201 01701 508-626-9117
Dr. Christopher H. Martes, supt. Fax 626-9119
www.framingham.k12.ma.us
Cameron MS 500/6-8
215 Elm St 01701 508-879-2290
Judith Kelly, prin. Fax 788-3560
Framingham HS 2,100/9-12
115 A St 01701 508-620-4963
Michael Welch, prin. Fax 877-6603
Fuller MS 700/6-8
31 Flagg Dr 01702 508-620-4956
Juan Rodriguez, prin. Fax 628-1308
Walsh MS 600/6-8
301 Brook St 01701 508-626-9180
Jay Cummings, prin. Fax 626-9167

South Middlesex Vocational Tech. SD
750 Winter St 01702 508-416-2100
Peter D. Dewar, supt. Fax 416-2342
www.jpkeefehs.org
Keefe Technical HS Vo/Tech
750 Winter St 01702 508-416-2100
Karl Lord, prin. Fax 416-2342

Blaine The Beauty Career School Post-Sec.
624 Worcester Rd 01702 508-370-3700
Blaine The Beauty Career School Post-Sec.
624 Worcester Rd 01702 580-370-7447
Framingham State College Post-Sec.
PO Box 101 01704 508-620-1220
Marian HS 300/9-12
273 Union Ave 01702 508-875-7646
Sr. Catherine Clifford, prin. Fax 875-0838

Franklin, Norfolk, Pop. 30,175
Franklin SD 5,800/PK-12
355 E Central St 02038 508-541-5243
David Crisafulli, supt. Fax 533-0321
www.franklin.k12.ma.us
Franklin HS 1,400/9-12
218 Oak St 02038 508-528-5600
Dennis Wilkinson, prin. Fax 541-2107
Mann MS 800/6-8
224 Oak St 02038 508-553-0322
Anne Bergen, prin. Fax 541-7071
Remington MS 600/6-8
628 Washington St 02038 508-541-2130
Timothy Farmer, prin. Fax 541-2124
Sullivan MS 6-8
500 Lincoln St 02038 508-553-0322
Beth Wittcoff, prin. Fax 542-2109

Tri-County SD
147 Pond St 02038 508-528-5400
John Jones, supt. Fax 528-6074
www.tri-county.tc
Tri-County Regional Vo-Tech HS Vo/Tech
147 Pond St 02038 508-528-5400
Barbara Renzoni, prin. Fax 528-6074

Dean College Post-Sec.
99 Main St 02038 508-541-1900

Gardner, Worcester, Pop. 21,049
Gardner SD 3,300/PK-12
130 Elm St 01440 978-632-1000
Carol Daring Ph.D., supt. Fax 632-1164
www.gardnerk12.org
Gardner HS 1,000/9-12
200 Catherine St 01440 978-632-1600
Michael Baldassarre, prin. Fax 630-4040
Gardner MS 800/6-8
297 Catherine St 01440 978-632-1603
Mitchel Aho, prin. Fax 632-4234

Mt. Wachusett Community College Post-Sec.
444 Green St 01440 978-632-6600

Georgetown, Essex
Georgetown SD 1,600/PK-12
51 North St 01833 978-352-5777
Larry Borin, supt. Fax 352-5778
www.georgetown.k12.ma.us
Georgetown MSHS 700/6-12
11 Winter St 01833 978-352-5790
Peter Lucia, prin. Fax 352-5798

Gloucester, Essex, Pop. 30,730
Gloucester SD 4,000/PK-12
6 School House Rd 01930 978-281-9800
Christopher Farmer, supt. Fax 281-9899
www.gloucesterschools.com/GPS_WEBSITE/district/sch_co
Gloucester HS 1,300/9-12
32 Leslie O Johnson Rd 01930 978-281-9870
Joseph Sullivan, prin. Fax 281-9733
O'Maley MS 900/6-8
32 Cherry St 01930 978-281-9850
Michael Tracy, prin. Fax 281-9890

Grafton, Worcester
Grafton SD 2,900/PK-12
30 Providence Rd 01519 508-839-5421
Joseph Connors Ph.D., supt. Fax 839-7618
www.grafton.k12.ma.us
Grafton Memorial HS 500/9-12
24 Providence Rd 01519 508-839-5425
James Pignataro, prin. Fax 839-8544
Grafton MS 600/6-8
60 North St 01519 508-839-5420
Richard Lind, prin. Fax 839-8528

Granby, Hampshire, Pop. 1,327
Granby SD 1,100/PK-12
387 E State St 01033 413-467-7193
Patricia A. Stevens, supt. Fax 467-3909
www.the-spa.com/ghs/
Granby JSHS 500/7-12
385 E State St 01033 413-467-7105
Mary McDowell, prin. Fax 467-3909

Holyoke Catholic HS 400/9-12
66 School St 01033 413-467-2477
Sr. Cornelia Roy, prin. Fax 467-2012

Great Barrington, Berkshire, Pop. 2,810
Berkshire Hills SD
Supt. — See Stockbridge
Monument Mountain Regional HS 600/9-12
600 Stockbridge Rd 01230 413-528-3346
Marianne Young, prin. Fax 528-9267
Monument Valley Regional MS 5-8
313 Monument Valley Rd 01230 413-644-2300
Jane Furey, prin. Fax 274-2394

Dewey Academy 50/10-12
389 Main St 01230 413-528-9800
Great Barrington Waldorf HS 50/9-12
454 Main St 01230 413-528-8833
Stephen Sagarin, admin. Fax 528-5132
Simon's Rock College of Bard Post-Sec.
80 Alford Rd 01230 413-528-0771

Greenfield, Franklin, Pop. 14,016
Greenfield SD 2,100/PK-12
141 Davis St 01301 413-772-1311
Joseph Ruscio, supt. Fax 774-7940
gpsk12.org
Greenfield HS 600/9-12
1 Lenox Ave 01301 413-772-1350
Nancy Athas, prin. Fax 774-6204
Greenfield MS 500/6-8
195 Federal St 01301 413-772-1360
Karen Cubino, prin. Fax 772-1367

Greenfield Community College Post-Sec.
1 College Dr 01301 413-775-1000
Stoneleigh-Burnham S 200/7-12
574 Bernardston Rd 01301 413-774-2711
Martha Shepardson-Killam, hdmstr. Fax 772-2602

Groton, Middlesex, Pop. 1,044
Groton Dunstable Regional SD 2,700/PK-12
PO Box 729 01450 978-448-5505
Alan Genovese, supt. Fax 448-9402
www.gdrsd.org
Groton Dunstable Regional HS 700/9-12
PO Box 730 01450 978-448-6362
Joseph Dillon, prin. Fax 448-0390
Groton Dunstable Regional MS 800/5-8
PO Box 727 01450 978-448-6155
Beth Raucci, prin. Fax 448-1201

Groton S 400/8-12
PO Box 991 01450 978-448-3363
Richard B. Commons, hdmstr. Fax 448-3100
Lawrence Academy 400/9-12
PO Box 992 01450 978-448-6535
D. Scott Wiggins, hdmstr. Fax 448-9208

Hadley, Hampshire
Hadley SD 600/PK-12
125 Russell St 01035 413-586-0822
Dr. Nicholas Young, supt. Fax 582-6453
www.hadleyschools.org
Hopkins Academy 300/7-12
131 Russell St 01035 413-584-1106
William Mahoney, prin. Fax 582-6455

Hartsbrook S 300/PK-12
193 Bay Rd 01035 413-586-1908
Jacqui Defelice, dir. Fax 586-9438

Hampden, Hampden
Hampden-Wilbraham SD
Supt. — See Wilbraham
Burgess MS 300/5-8
85 Wilbraham Rd 01036 413-566-8950
Noel Pixley, prin. Fax 566-2163

Hanover, Plymouth, Pop. 11,912
Hanover SD 2,800/PK-12
188 Broadway 02339 781-878-0786
Mary Ann Jackman, supt. Fax 871-3374
www.hanoverschools.org
Hanover HS 700/9-12
287 Cedar St 02339 781-878-5450
Edwin Walsh, prin. Fax 871-0590
Hanover MS 900/5-8
45 Whiting St 02339 781-871-1122
Edward Lee, prin. Fax 871-8792

South Shore Regional SD
476 Webster St 02339 781-878-8822
John Kosko, supt. Fax 982-0281
www.ssvotech.org
South Shore Vocational Technical HS Vo/Tech
476 Webster St 02339 781-878-8822
Charles Homer, prin. Fax 982-0281

Hanscom AFB, See Bedford
Lincoln SD
Supt. — See Lincoln
Hanscom MS 300/4-8
Ent Rd 01731 781-274-0050
Barry Hopping, prin. Fax 274-7329

Hanson, Plymouth, Pop. 2,188
Whitman-Hanson SD
Supt. — See Whitman
Hanson MS 500/6-8
111 Liberty St 02341 781-618-7575
Paul Carroll, prin. Fax 618-8815

Hardwick, Worcester

Eagle Hill S 200/8-12
242 Old Petersham Rd 01037 413-477-6000
Peter J. McDonald, hdmstr. Fax 477-6837

Harvard, Worcester
Harvard SD 1,200/K-12
39 Mass Ave 01451 978-456-4140
Dr. Thomas Jefferson, supt. Fax 456-8592
www.psharvard.org
Bromfield S 700/6-12
14 Mass Ave 01451 978-456-4152
Tom Hall, prin. Fax 456-3013

Harwich, Barnstable
Cape Cod Regional Technical HSD
351 Pleasant Lake Ave 02645 508-432-4500
F. Carroll, supt. Fax 432-7916
capetech.us
Cape Cod Regional Technical HS Vo/Tech
351 Pleasant Lake Ave 02645 508-432-4500
William N. Fisher, prin. Fax 432-7916

Harwich SD 1,500/K-12
81 Oak St 02645 508-430-7200
Rosemary Joseph, supt. Fax 430-7205
www.harwich.edu
Harwich HS 400/9-12
75 Oak St 02645 508-430-7207
Kevin Turner, prin. Fax 430-7223
Harwich MS 400/6-8
204 Sisson Rd 02645 508-430-7212
Mary Childress, prin. Fax 430-7230

Hatfield, Hampshire, Pop. 1,234
Hatfield SD 500/PK-12
34 School St 01038 413-247-5641
Patrice Dardenne, supt. Fax 247-0201
Smith Academy 200/7-12
34 School St 01038 413-247-5641
Scott A. Goldman, prin. Fax 247-0201

Hathorne, Essex
Essex Agricultural & Technical HSD
PO Box 362 01937 978-774-0050
Helen Hegarty, supt. Fax 774-6530
www.agtech.org
Essex Agricultural & Technical HS Vo/Tech
PO Box 362 01937 978-774-0050
Helen Hegarty, prin. Fax 774-6530

Haverhill, Essex, Pop. 60,326
Haverhill SD — 8,000/PK-12
4 Summer St 01830 — 978-374-3400
Gerard Quatrale Ed.D., supt. — Fax 374-3422
www.haverhill-ma.com
Consentino MS — 700/6-8
685 Washington St 01832 — 978-374-5775
James Scully, prin. — Fax 374-3442
Haverhill HS — 1,900/9-12
137 Monument St 01832 — 978-374-5700
Joseph McMilleon, prin. — Fax 374-5705
Hunking MS — 500/6-8
98 Winchester St 01835 — 978-374-5787
Larry Marino, prin. — Fax 372-5890
Nettle MS — 500/6-8
150 Boardman St 01830 — 978-374-5792
Gerald Kayo, prin. — Fax 374-3441
Whittier MS — 500/6-8
256 Concord St 01830 — 978-374-5782
Albert Powers, prin. — Fax 372-5999

Whittier Vocational SD
115 Amesbury Line Rd 01830 — 978-373-4101
Karen Sarkisian, supt. — Fax 521-0260
Whittier Regional Vocational HS — Vo/Tech
115 Amesbury Line Rd 01830 — 978-373-4101
Scott Williams, prin. — Fax 521-0260

Northern Essex Community College — Post-Sec.
100 Elliott St 01830 — 978-556-3000

Hingham, Plymouth, Pop. 5,454
Hingham SD — 3,600/PK-12
220 Central St 02043 — 781-741-1500
Dorothy Galo, supt. — Fax 749-7457
www.hinghamschools.com/
Hingham HS — 1,000/9-12
17 Union St 02043 — 781-741-1560
Paula Girouard McCann, prin. — Fax 741-1515
Hingham MS — 900/6-8
1103 Main St 02043 — 781-741-1550
Roger Boddie, prin. — Fax 749-6297

Notre Dame Academy — 500/9-12
1073 Main St 02043 — 781-749-5930
Sr. Janice Carmen, prin. — Fax 749-8366

Holbrook, Norfolk, Pop. 11,041
Holbrook SD — 1,400/K-12
227 Plymouth St 02343 — 781-767-1226
Susan E. Martin, supt. — Fax 767-1312
www.holbrook.k12.ma.us/
Holbrook JSHS — 600/7-12
245 S Franklin St 02343 — 781-767-4616
Edward Dunn, prin. — Fax 767-2697

Holden, Worcester, Pop. 14,628
Wachusett Regional SD
Supt. — See Jefferson
Mountview MS — 700/6-8
270 Shrewsbury St 01520 — 508-829-5577
John Sullivan, prin. — Fax 829-3711
Wachusett Regional HS — 1,800/9-12
1401 Main St 01520 — 508-829-6771
Hal Lane, prin. — Fax 829-4895

Holliston, Middlesex, Pop. 12,926
Holliston SD — 3,100/PK-12
370 Hollis St 01746 — 508-429-0654
Bradford L. Jackson, supt. — Fax 429-0653
www.holliston.mec.edu
Adams MS — 800/6-8
323 Woodland St 01746 — 508-429-0657
Maureen Szal, prin. — Fax 429-0690
Holliston HS — 900/9-12
370 Hollis St 01746 — 508-429-0677
Mary E. Canty, prin. — Fax 429-8225

Holyoke, Hampden, Pop. 40,015
Holyoke SD — 7,400/PK-12
57 Suffolk St 01040 — 413-534-2005
Dr. Eduardo B. Carballo, supt. — Fax 534-2297
www.hps.holyoke.ma.us
Dean Vocational Technical HS — Vo/Tech
1045 Main St 01040 — 413-534-2071
Victor Zwirko, prin. — Fax 536-9694
Holyoke HS — 1,300/9-12
500 Beech St 01040 — 413-534-2020
David Dupont, prin. — Fax 534-2098
Lynch MS — 400/6-8
1575 Northampton St 01040 — 413-534-2050
Paul Hyry, prin. — Fax 532-8443
Peck MS — 800/6-8
1916 Northampton St 01040 — 413-534-2040
Teresa Pudlo, prin. — Fax 532-8563

Holyoke Community College — Post-Sec.
303 Homestead Ave 01040 — 413-538-7000

Hopedale, Worcester, Pop. 3,961
Hopedale SD — 1,100/PK-12
25 Adin St 01747 — 508-634-2220
Dr. Patricia C. Ruane, supt. — Fax 478-1471
www.hopedale.k12.ma.us
Hopedale JSHS — 500/7-12
25 Adin St 01747 — 508-634-2217
Dennis Breen, prin. — Fax 478-5698

Hopkinton, Middlesex, Pop. 2,305
Hopkinton SD — 3,300/K-12
88A Hayden Rowe St 01748 — 508-497-9800
John E. Phelan Ed.D., supt. — Fax 435-5110
www.hopkinton.k12.ma.us
Hopkinton HS — 800/9-12
90 Hayden Rowe St 01748 — 508-497-9820
Dorothy Gould, prin. — Fax 497-9829
Hopkinton MS — 800/6-8
88 Hayden Rowe St 01748 — 508-497-9830
William Lynch Ed.D., prin. — Fax 497-9803

Hudson, Middlesex, Pop. 14,267
Hudson SD — 2,700/K-12
155 Apsley St 01749 — 978-567-6100
Sheldon Berman, supt. — Fax 567-6103
www.hudson.k12.ma.us
Hudson JSHS — 1,000/8-12
69 Brigham St 01749 — 978-567-6250
John Stapelfeld, prin. — Fax 567-6285

Hudson Catholic HS — 100/9-12
198 Main St 01749 — 978-562-6701
Caroline Flynn, prin. — Fax 567-0755

Hull, Plymouth, Pop. 10,466
Hull SD — 1,300/PK-12
7 Hadasah Way 02045 — 781-925-0771
Dr. Paula DeLaney, supt. — Fax 925-0615
www.town.hull.ma.us
Hull HS — 400/9-12
180 Main St 02045 — 781-925-3000
Robert Neeley, prin. — Fax 925-3071
Memorial MS — 300/6-8
81 Central Ave 02045 — 781-925-2040
Bruce Berman, prin. — Fax 925-8002

Huntington, Hampshire
Gateway SD — 1,500/PK-12
12 Littleville Rd 01050 — 413-685-1000
Dr. David B. Hopson, supt. — Fax 667-8739
www.grsd.org
Gateway Regional HS — 400/9-12
12 Littleville Rd 01050 — 413-685-1100
Kathleen McSweeney, prin. — Fax 667-5593
Gateway Regional MS — 400/5-8
12 Littleville Rd 01050 — 413-685-1200
Peter Curro, prin. — Fax 667-5669

Hyannis, Barnstable, Pop. 14,120
Barnstable SD — 5,100/PK-12
PO Box 955 02601 — 508-790-9802
Thomas McDonald, supt. — Fax 790-6454
www.barnstable.k12.ma.us/
Barnstable HS — 2,000/9-12
744 W Main St 02601 — 508-790-6445
Patricia Graves, prin. — Fax 790-6430
Barnstable MS — 1,100/7-8
895 Falmouth Rd 02601 — 508-790-6460
Donald Bidgood, prin. — Fax 790-6435

Blaine The Beauty Career School — Post-Sec.
18 Center St 02601 — 508-771-1680
St. Francis Xavier Prep S — 200/5-8
33 Cross St 02601 — 508-771-7200
Robert Deburro, hdmstr. — Fax 771-7233

Hyde Park, See Boston
Boston SD
Supt. — See Boston
Community Academy of Science & Health — 9-12
655 Metropolitan Ave 02136 — 617-635-8950
Linda Cabral, prin. — Fax 635-8948
Engineering S — 9-12
655 Metropolitan Ave 02136 — 617-635-6425
Mweusi Willingham, prin. — Fax 635-7698
Hyde Park HS — 1,200/9-12
655 Metropolitan Ave 02136 — 617-635-8948
Linda Cabral, hdmstr. — Fax 635-9724
Rogers MS — 600/6-8
15 Everett St 02136 — 617-635-8700
Michael McCarthy, prin. — Fax 635-8708
Social Justice Academy — 9-12
655 Metropolitan Ave 02136 — 617-635-6969
Winston Cox, prin. — Fax 635-9780

Ipswich, Essex, Pop. 4,132
Ipswich SD — 2,100/PK-12
1 Lord Sq 01938 — 978-356-2935
Richard Korb, supt. — Fax 356-0445
www.ipswichschools.org
Ipswich HS — 600/9-12
136 High St 01938 — 978-356-3137
Barry Cahill, prin. — Fax 356-3720
Ipswich MS — 500/6-8
130 High St 01938 — 978-356-3535
Cheryl Forster, prin. — Fax 412-8169

Jamaica Plain, See Boston
Boston SD
Supt. — See Boston
Curley MS — 700/6-8
493 Centre St 02130 — 617-635-8176
Gerardo Martinez, prin. — Fax 635-8184

Jefferson, Worcester
Wachusett Regional SD — 7,000/PK-12
1745 Main St 01522 — 508-829-1670
Thomas Pandiscio Ed.D., supt. — Fax 829-1680
www.wrsd.net
Other Schools – See Holden, Rutland, Sterling

Kingston, Plymouth, Pop. 4,774
Silver Lake Regional SD — 2,900/7-12
250 Pembroke St 02364 — 781-585-4313
Dana Parker, supt. — Fax 585-2994
www.silverlake.mec.edu
Silver Lake Regional HS — 1,800/9-12
260 Pembroke St 02364 — 781-585-3844
Richard Kelley, prin. — Fax 585-6544
Silver Lake Regional MS — 1,100/7-8
256 Pembroke St 02364 — 781-582-3555
Jeffrey Lucove, prin. — Fax 582-3599

Sacred Heart HS — 800/7-12
399 Bishops Hwy 02364 — 781-585-7511
John Enos, prin. — Fax 585-1249

Lakeville, Plymouth
Freetown-Lakeville SD — 1,600/4-12
98 Howland Rd 02347 — 508-923-2000
Dr. Stephen Furtado, supt. — Fax 923-9960
www.freelake.mec.edu/

Apponequet Regional HS — 900/9-12
100 Howland Rd 02347 — 508-947-2660
Gary Lincoln, prin. — Fax 946-2350
Freetown-Lakeville MS — 800/6-8
96 Howland Rd 02347 — 508-923-3516
James Hunt, prin. — Fax 946-2050

Lancaster, Worcester
Nashoba Regional SD
Supt. — See Bolton
Burbank MS — 300/6-8
1 Hollywood Dr 01523 — 978-365-4558
Patrick Perkins, prin. — Fax 365-6882

Lawrence, Essex, Pop. 72,492
Lawrence SD — 11,600/PK-12
255 Essex St 01840 — 978-975-5900
Wilfredo T. Laboy Ed.D., supt. — Fax 975-5904
www.lawrence.k12.ma.us
Arlington MS — 5-8
150 Arlington St 01841 — 978-975-5926
Juan Rodriguez, prin. — Fax 975-4004
Lawrence HS — 2,500/9-12
233 Haverhill St 01840 — 978-975-2750
Thomas D. Sharkey Ed.D., prin. — Fax 685-0807
Leonard MS — 400/6-8
60 Allen St 01840 — 978-975-5962
Mary Frangipane, prin. — Fax 975-7965
South Lawrence East MS — 5-8
165 Crawford St 01843 — 978-975-5970
Dina Hickey, prin. — Fax 975-2780
Adult Learning Center — Adult
243 S Broadway 01843 — 978-975-5917
Samaria Tavares Hash, admin. — Fax 975-6070

Blessed Stephen Bellesini Academy — 100/5-8
94 Bradford St 01840 — 978-989-0004
Julie DeFillippo, dir. — Fax 989-9404
Central Catholic HS — 900/9-12
300 Hampshire St 01841 — 978-682-0260
David DeFillippo, prin. — Fax 685-2707

Lee, Berkshire, Pop. 2,020
Lee SD — 900/K-12
310 Greylock St 01238 — 413-243-0276
Jason P. McCandless, supt. — Fax 243-4995
www.lee.k12.ma.us/
Lee MSHS — 500/7-12
300 Greylock St 01238 — 413-243-2787
Kerry Burke, prin. — Fax 243-4105

Frontline Church S — 50/PK-12
160 High St 01238 — 413-243-2673
Stephen Capello, prin. — Fax 243-3920

Leicester, Worcester, Pop. 10,191
Leicester SD — 1,900/PK-12
1078 Main St 01524 — 508-892-7040
Michael Dubrule, supt. — Fax 892-7043
www.leicester.k12.ma.us/
Leicester HS — 600/9-12
174 Paxton St 01524 — 508-892-7030
Thomas Lauder, prin. — Fax 892-7034
Leicester MS — 500/6-8
70 Winslow Ave 01524 — 508-892-7055
Paul Belsito, prin. — Fax 892-7047

Lenox, Berkshire, Pop. 1,687
Lenox SD — 800/PK-12
6 Walker St 01240 — 413-637-5550
William Coan, supt. — Fax 637-5559
www.lenoxps.org
Lenox Memorial HS — 500/6-12
197 East St 01240 — 413-637-5560
Bruce Walker, prin. — Fax 637-5564

Berkshire Christian S — 100/PK-12
PO Box 1980 01240 — 413-637-2474
Matthew Kinnaman, hdmstr. — Fax 637-8336

Leominster, Worcester, Pop. 42,000
Leominster SD — 5,600/PK-12
24 Church St 01453 — 978-534-7700
Marilyn Fratturelli, supt. — Fax 534-7775
www.leominster.mec.edu/
Leominster Center Technical Education — Vo/Tech
122 Granite St 01453 — 978-534-7735
George Luoto, prin. — Fax 534-7934
Leominster HS — 1,200/9-12
122 Granite St 01453 — 978-534-7715
Dr. William Hart, prin. — Fax 537-1765
Samoset MS — 600/5-8
100 DeCicco Dr 01453 — 978-534-7725
Elizabeth Schaper, prin. — Fax 466-8603
Sky View MS — 700/5-8
500 Kennedy Way 01453 — 978-534-7780
Donald Lacharite, prin. — Fax 840-8600
Southeast MS — 600/5-8
95 Viscoloid Ave 01453 — 978-534-7751
Elizabeth Pratt, prin. — Fax 466-8603

Lexington, Middlesex, Pop. 30,600
Lexington SD — 6,200/PK-12
1557 Massachusetts Ave 02420 — 781-861-2550
Paul Ash Ph.D., supt. — Fax 863-5829
lps.lexingtonma.org
Clarke MS — 800/6-8
17 Stedman Rd 02421 — 781-861-2450
Pamela Houlares, prin. — Fax 674-2043
Diamond MS — 800/6-8
99 Hancock St 02420 — 781-861-2460
Joanne Hennessy, prin. — Fax 861-2470
Lexington HS — 1,800/9-12
251 Waltham St 02421 — 781-861-2320
Dr. Michael Jones, prin. — Fax 861-2440

Minuteman Voc Tech SD
758 Marrett Rd 02421 781-861-6500
William Callahan, supt. Fax 863-1747
www.minuteman.org
Minuteman Regional HS Vo/Tech
758 Marrett Rd 02421 781-861-6500
James Amara, prin. Fax 863-1747

Lexington Christian Academy 300/6-12
48 Bartlett Ave 02420 781-862-7850
Dr. J. Barry Koops, hdmstr. Fax 863-8503
Sodexho Marriott Services Post-Sec.
PO Box 9196 02420 800-926-7429

Lincoln, Middlesex, Pop. 2,850
Lincoln SD 1,300/K-8
Ballfield Rd 01773 781-259-9409
Michael Brandmeyer, supt. Fax 259-9246
www.lincnet.org/
Other Schools – See Hanscom AFB

Littleton, Middlesex, Pop. 2,867
Littleton SD 1,600/PK-12
PO Box 1486 01460 978-486-8951
Paul Livingston, supt. Fax 486-9581
www.littletonps.org/
Littleton HS 400/9-12
56 King St 01460 978-952-2555
John Buckey, prin. Fax 486-0758
Littleton MS 400/6-8
55 Russell St 01460 978-486-8938
Kevin Moran, prin. Fax 952-4547

Longmeadow, Hampden, Pop. 15,467
Longmeadow SD 3,400/PK-12
127 Grassy Gutter Rd 01106 413-565-4200
E. Jahn Hart, supt. Fax 565-4215
www.longmeadow.k12.ma.us/
Glenbrook MS 400/6-8
110 Cambridge Cir 01106 413-565-4250
Michael Sullivan, prin. Fax 565-4277
Longmeadow HS 1,000/9-12
95 Grassy Gutter Rd 01106 413-565-4220
Lawrence Berte, prin. Fax 565-4233
Williams MS 400/6-8
410 Williams St 01106 413-565-4260
Mary Sedran, prin. Fax 565-4254

Bay Path College Post-Sec.
588 Longmeadow St 01106 413-565-1000

Lowell, Middlesex, Pop. 104,351
Lowell SD 15,100/PK-12
155 Merrimack St 01852 978-937-7604
Dr. Karla Brooks Baehr, supt. Fax 446-7436
www.lowell.k12.ma.us/
Bartlett MS 500/5-8
79 Wannalancit St 01854 978-937-8968
Grace Wai, prin. Fax 441-3745
Butler MS 600/5-8
1140 Gorham St 01852 978-937-8973
Eilish A. Connaughton, prin. Fax 937-2819
Daley MS 900/5-8
150 Fleming St 01851 978-937-8981
Liam Skinner, prin. Fax 937-7610
Lowell HS 2,600/10-12
50 Father Morissette Blvd 01852 978-937-8900
William Samaras, hdmstr. Fax 937-8902
Lowell HS Freshman Academy 1,300/9-9
43 French St 01852 978-441-3707
Jim DeProfio, prin. Fax 441-3706
Robinson MS 600/5-8
110 June St 01850 978-937-8974
Marianne Bond, prin. Fax 937-8988
Rogers MS 700/5-8
43 Highland St 01852 978-937-7675
Timothy McGillicuddy, prin. Fax 937-7609
Stoklosa MS, 560 Broadway St 01854 5-8
Jackie Travers, prin. 978-937-7604
Sullivan MS 700/5-8
150 Draper St 01852 978-937-8993
Edith LaBran, prin. Fax 937-3278
Wang MS 700/5-8
365 W Meadow Rd 01854 978-937-7683
Gayle Feeney, prin. Fax 937-7680
Adult Basic Education Program Adult
408 Merrimack St 01854 978-937-8989
Fred Abisi, dir. Fax 458-9007

Blaine The Beauty Career School Post-Sec.
231 Central St 01852 978-459-9959
Community Christian Academy 200/PK-12
105R Princeton Blvd 01851 978-453-4738
Rev. Raffoul Najem, admin. Fax 453-1506
Lowell Academy Hairstyling Institute Post-Sec.
136 Central St 01852 978-453-3235
Lowell Catholic HS 200/9-12
530 Stevens St 01851 978-452-1794
Maryellen DeMarco, prin. Fax 452-5646
Middlesex Community College Post-Sec.
33 Kearney Sq 01852 978-656-3213
University of Massachusetts Lowell Post-Sec.
1 University Ave 01854 978-934-4000

Ludlow, Hampden, Pop. 18,820
Ludlow SD 3,100/PK-12
63 Chestnut St 01056 413-583-8372
Theresa Kane Ed.D., supt. Fax 583-5666
www.ludlowps.org
Baird MS 800/6-8
1 Rooney Rd 01056 413-583-5685
Donna Hogan, prin. Fax 583-5636
Ludlow HS 1,000/9-12
500 Chapin St 01056 413-589-9001
Gordon Smith, prin. Fax 583-5637

Jolie Hair and Beauty Academy Post-Sec.
44 Sewall St 01056 413-589-0747

Lunenburg, Worcester, Pop. 1,694
Lunenburg SD 1,400/PK-12
1033 Massachusetts Ave 01462 978-582-4100
Loxi Jo Calmes, supt. Fax 582-4103
Lunenburg HS 600/9-12
1079 Massachusetts Ave 01462 978-582-4115
Michael Barney, prin. Fax 582-4153
Turkey Hill MS 400/6-8
129 Northfield Rd 01462 978-582-4110
Keith Hochstein, prin. Fax 582-4109

Twin City Christian S 300/PK-12
194 Electric Ave 01462 978-582-4901
Gregory Arnold, prin. Fax 582-4978

Lynn, Essex, Pop. 89,571
Lynn SD 13,300/PK-12
90 Commercial St 01905 781-593-1680
Nicholas P. Kostan, supt. Fax 477-7487
www.lynnschools.org/
Breed MS 1,000/6-8
90 OCallaghan Way 01905 781-477-7330
James Ridley, prin. Fax 581-6985
Career Development Center Vo/Tech
33 N Common St 01902 781-268-3000
Rhonda Cormier, prin.
Classical HS 1,500/9-12
235 OCallaghan Way 01905 781-477-7404
Warren White, prin. Fax 477-7212
English HS 1,600/9-12
50 Goodridge St 01902 781-477-7366
Andrew M. Fila, prin. Fax 477-7365
Lynn Vocational Technical Institute Vo/Tech
80 Neptune Blvd 01902 781-477-7420
Brian Coughlin, prin. Fax 477-7415
Marshall MS 900/6-8
19 Porter St 01902 781-477-7360
Anita Rassias, prin. Fax 477-7355
Pickering MS 700/6-8
70 Conomo Ave 01904 781-477-7440
Patricia A. Barton, prin. Fax 477-7202

St. Mary JSHS 500/7-12
35 Tremont St 01902 781-595-7885
Carl DiMaiti, prin. Fax 595-4471

Lynnfield, Essex, Pop. 11,274
Lynnfield SD 2,000/PK-12
55 Summer St 01940 781-334-5800
Richard Palermo, supt. Fax 334-5802
www.shore.net/~schoolhq
Lynnfield HS 500/9-12
275 Essex St 01940 781-334-5820
Robert Hassett, prin. Fax 334-7207
Lynnfield MS 700/5-8
505 Main St 01940 781-334-5810
Stephen Ralston, prin. Fax 334-7203

Malden, Middlesex, Pop. 55,816
Malden SD 6,100/PK-12
200 Pleasant St 02148 781-397-7204
Joan Connolly, supt. Fax 397-7276
www.malden.mec.edu
Malden HS 1,600/9-12
77 Salem St 02148 781-397-7223
Dana Brown, prin. Fax 397-7224

Blaine The Beauty Career School Post-Sec.
347 Pleasant St 02148 781-397-7400
Learning Institute for Beauty Sciences Post-Sec.
384 Main St 02148 781-324-3400
Malden Catholic HS 500/9-12
99 Crystal St 02148 781-322-3098
Thomas Arria, hdmstr. Fax 397-0573
New England Hair Academy Post-Sec.
110 Florence St Ste 203 02148 781-324-6799

Manchester, Essex, Pop. 5,286
Manchester Essex Regional SD 1,200/K-12
36 Lincoln St 01944 978-526-4919
Robert Shaps, supt. Fax 526-7585
www.mersd.org
Manchester Essex Regional MSHS 500/7-12
36 Lincoln St 01944 978-526-4412
Peter Sack, prin. Fax 526-2044

Mansfield, Bristol, Pop. 7,170
Mansfield SD 4,700/K-12
2 Park Row 02048 508-261-7500
John Moretti, supt. Fax 261-7509
www.mansfieldschools.com
Mansfield HS 1,100/9-12
250 East St 02048 508-261-7540
Brenda Hodges, prin. Fax 339-0259
Qualters MS 1,100/6-8
240 East St 02048 508-261-7530
David Thomson, prin. Fax 261-7535

Marblehead, Essex, Pop. 19,971
Marblehead SD 3,000/K-12
9 Widger Rd 01945 781-639-3141
Dr. Philip Devaux, supt. Fax 639-3149
www.marblehead.com/schools
Marblehead HS 900/9-12
2 Humphrey St 01945 781-639-3100
John Ziergiebel, prin. Fax 639-3105
Marblehead Veterans MS 900/7-8
217 Pleasant St 01945 781-639-3120
Libby Moore, prin. Fax 639-3130

Marion, Plymouth, Pop. 1,426

Tabor Academy 500/9-12
66 Spring St 02738 508-748-2000
Jay Stroud, hdmstr. Fax 291-6666

Marlborough, Middlesex, Pop. 37,980
Assabet Valley SD
215 Fitchburg St 01752 508-485-9430
Eugene Carlo, supt. Fax 460-3472
www.assabettech.com
Assabet Valley Regional Technicall HS Vo/Tech
215 Fitchburg St 01752 508-485-9430
Mary Jo Nawrocki, prin. Fax 460-3472
Marlborough SD 4,900/PK-12
17 Washington St 01752 508-460-3509
Rose Marie Boniface, supt. Fax 485-1142
www.marlborough.k12.ma.us
Marlborough HS 1,600/8-12
431 Bolton St 01752 508-460-3500
Mary Carlson, prin. Fax 460-3501

Hillside S 100/5-9
404 Robin Hill St 01752 508-485-2824
David Beecher, hdmstr. Fax 485-4420

Marshfield, Plymouth, Pop. 4,002
Marshfield SD 4,600/PK-12
76 S River St 02050 781-834-5000
Middleton McGoodwin Ed.D., supt. Fax 834-5070
marshfield.ma.schoolwebpages.com/
Furnace Brook MS 1,000/6-8
500 Furnace St 02050 781-834-5020
Alfred Makein, prin. Fax 834-5899
Marshfield HS 1,300/9-12
167 Forest St 02050 781-834-5050
Robert Keuther, prin. Fax 834-5040

Mashpee, Barnstable
Mashpee SD 2,100/K-12
150 Old Barnstable Rd # A 02649 508-539-1500
Ann Bradshaw, supt. Fax 477-5805
www.mashpee.k12.ma.us
Mashpee HS 1,000/7-12
500 Old Barnstable Rd 02649 508-539-3600
Ira Brown, prin. Fax 539-3607

Mattapan, See Boston
Boston SD
Supt. — See Boston
Lewenberg MS 500/6-8
20 Outlook Rd 02126 617-635-8623
Myrtlene Mayfield, prin. Fax 635-9947
Mildred Avenue MS 700/6-8
5 Mildred Ave 02126 617-635-1645
Shirley Allen, prin. Fax 635-1641

Mattapoisett, Plymouth, Pop. 2,949
Old Rochester Regional SD 1,200/7-12
135 Marion Rd 02739 508-758-2772
William R. Cooper, supt. Fax 758-2802
www.oldrochester.org
Old Rochester Regional HS 700/9-12
135 Marion Rd 02739 508-758-3745
Bruce Clarke, prin. Fax 758-3167
Old Rochester Regional JHS 500/7-8
133 Marion Rd 02739 508-758-4928
Simonne J. Conlon, prin. Fax 758-6021

Maynard, Middlesex, Pop. 10,325
Maynard SD 1,400/PK-12
12 Bancroft St 01754 978-897-2222
Dr. Mark R. Masterson, supt. Fax 897-4610
web.maynard.ma.us/schools/
Fowler MS 600/4-8
3 Tiger Dr 01754 978-897-6700
Robert Brooks, prin. Fax 897-5737
Maynard HS 300/9-12
1 Tiger Dr 01754 978-897-8891
John Lent, prin. Fax 897-6089

Medfield, Norfolk, Pop. 5,985
Medfield SD 3,000/PK-12
459 Main St Fl 3 02052 508-359-2302
Robert Maguire, supt. Fax 359-9829
www.medfield.net
Blake MS 700/6-8
24 Pound St 02052 508-359-2396
Margaret Mongiello, prin. Fax 359-0134
Medfield HS 800/9-12
88R South St 02052 508-359-8385
Andrew W. Keough, prin. Fax 359-2963

Medford, Middlesex, Pop. 54,734
Medford SD 4,400/PK-12
489 Winthrop St 02155 781-393-2442
Roy Belson, supt. Fax 393-2322
www.medford.k12.ma.us
Andrews MS 600/6-8
3000 Mystic Valley Pkwy 02155 781-393-2228
Alan Levy, prin. Fax 395-8128
McGlynn MS 600/6-8
3004 Mystic Valley Pkwy 02155 781-393-2333
James Deveney, prin. Fax 393-5462
Medford HS 1,200/9-12
489 Winthrop St 02155 781-393-2301
Paul Krueger, prin. Fax 395-1468
Medford Vo-Tech HS Vo/Tech
489 Winthrop St 02155 781-393-2260
William Mahoney, prin. Fax 395-1468

Lawrence Memorial/Regis College Post-Sec.
170 Governors Ave 02155 781-306-6600
St. Clement S 200/K-12
579 Boston Ave 02155 617-393-5600
Robert Chervier, prin. Fax 396-3230
The Elizabeth Grady School of Esthetics Post-Sec.
222 Boston Ave 02155 781-391-9380
Tufts University Post-Sec.
520 Boston Ave 02155 617-628-5000

Medway, Norfolk, Pop. 9,931
Medway SD 2,900/PK-12
45 Holliston St 02053 508-533-3222
Dr. Richard Grandmont, supt. Fax 533-3226
www.medwayschools.org

Medway HS 800/9-12
88 Summer St 02053 508-533-3227
Richard Pearson, prin. Fax 533-3246
Medway MS 900/5-8
45 Holliston St 02053 508-533-3230
Joanne Senier-LaBarre, prin. Fax 533-3257

Melrose, Middlesex, Pop. 26,784
Melrose SD 3,300/PK-12
360 Lynn Fells Pkwy 02176 781-662-2000
R. Leblanc-Considine, supt. Fax 979-2285
www.melroseschools.com
Melrose HS 1,000/9-12
360 Lynn Fells Pkwy 02176 781-979-2202
Dan Burke, prin. Fax 979-2205
Melrose MS 800/6-8
350 Lynn Fells Pkwy 02176 781-979-2102
Thomas Brow, prin. Fax 979-2104

Mendon, Worcester
Mendon-Upton Regional SD 2,600/PK-12
PO Box 5 01756 508-634-1585
Paul Daigle, supt. Fax 634-1582
mu-regional.k12.ma.us
Other Schools – See Upton

Methuen, Essex, Pop. 44,850
Methuen SD 7,200/PK-12
10 Ditson Pl 01844 978-681-1317
Charles P. Littlefield Ed.D., supt. Fax 794-4749
www.methuen.k12.ma.us
Methuen HS 1,900/9-12
1 Ranger Rd 01844 978-681-1360
Arthur Nicholson, prin. Fax 681-1397

Fellowship Christian Academy 200/PK-12
1 Fellowship Way 01844 978-686-9373
Presentation of Mary Academy 200/9-12
209 Lawrence St 01844 978-682-9391
Rose Maria Redman, prin. Fax 975-3595

Middleboro, Plymouth, Pop. 6,837
Middleborough SD 3,700/PK-12
30 Forest St 02346 508-946-2000
Robert Sullivan, supt. Fax 946-2004
www.middleboro.k12.ma.us
Middleboro HS 900/9-12
71 E Grove St 02346 508-946-2010
Katherine Flaherty, prin. Fax 946-8852
Nichols MS 900/6-8
112 Tiger Dr 02346 508-946-2020
Scott Kellett, prin. Fax 946-2019

Bay State College Post-Sec.
71 E Grove St 02346 508-946-5559

Middleton, Essex, Pop. 4,921
North Shore Regional Vocational SD 978-762-0001
PO Box 806 01949 Fax 777-8403
Amelia O'Malley, supt.
www.nsths.mec.edu
North Shore Regional Vocational HS Vo/Tech
PO Box 806 01949 978-762-0001
Richard McLaughlin, prin. Fax 762-4589

Milford, Worcester, Pop. 23,339
Milford SD 4,200/PK-12
31 W Fountain St 01757 508-478-1100
Thomas J. Davoren, supt. Fax 478-1459
www.milford.ma.us/schools.htm
Milford HS 1,100/9-12
31 W Fountain St 01757 508-478-1110
John Brucato, prin. Fax 478-1460
Milford MS East 300/8-8
45 Main St 01757 508-478-1170
Joseph Pfeil, prin. Fax 634-2381

Millbury, Worcester, Pop. 12,228
Millbury SD 2,000/PK-12
12 Martin St 01527 508-865-9501
David Roach, supt. Fax 865-0888
www.millbury.k12.ma.us
Millbury Memorial JSHS 900/7-12
12 Martin St 01527 508-865-5841
Anne Steele, prin. Fax 865-0888

Millis, Norfolk, Pop. 4,081
Millis SD 1,300/PK-12
245 Plain St 02054 508-376-7000
Peter Sanchioni, supt. Fax 376-7020
www.millis.k12.ma.us/
Millis HS 300/9-12
245 Plain St 02054 508-376-7010
Linda McCann, prin. Fax 376-7020
Millis MS 400/5-8
245 Plain St 02054 508-376-7014
Andrew Zitoli, prin. Fax 376-7020

Milton, Norfolk, Pop. 27,000
Milton SD 3,500/PK-12
25 Gile Rd 02186 617-696-4808
Magdalene Giffune, supt. Fax 696-5099
www.edline.net/pages/Milton_Public_Schools
Milton HS 900/9-12
25 Gile Rd 02186 617-696-4470
John Drottar, prin. Fax 696-5038
Pierce MS 900/6-8
451 Central Ave 02186 617-696-4568
John Phelan, prin. Fax 698-2238

Curry College Post-Sec.
1071 Blue Hill Ave 02186 617-333-0500
Fontbonne Academy 500/9-12
930 Brook Rd 02186 617-696-3241
Mary Ellen Barnes, prin. Fax 696-7688
Milton Academy 1,000/K-12
170 Centre St 02186 617-898-1798
Robin Robertson, hdmstr. Fax 898-1700

Monson, Hampden, Pop. 2,101
Monson SD 1,500/PK-12
PO Box 159 01057 413-267-4150
Carol A. Woodbury, supt. Fax 267-9168
www.monsonschools.com
Granite Valley MS 500/5-8
21 Thompson St 01057 413-267-4155
Patricia Clem, prin. Fax 267-4624
Monson HS 400/9-12
55 Margaret St 01057 413-267-4589
James Peters, prin. Fax 267-4157

Montague, Franklin
Gill-Montague SD
Supt. — See Turners Falls
Great Falls MS 300/7-8
224 Turnpike Rd 01351 413-863-3188
Jeffrey Kenney, prin. Fax 863-3189
Turners Falls HS 400/9-12
222 Turnpike Rd 01351 413-863-9341
Robert B. Morrill, prin. Fax 863-3189

Nantucket, Nantucket, Pop. 3,069
Nantucket SD 1,100/K-12
10 Surfside Rd 02554 508-228-7285
Alan Myers, supt. Fax 325-5318
www.npsk.org
Nantucket HS 400/9-12
10 Surfside Rd 02554 508-228-7280
George Kelly, prin. Fax 325-5318
Peirce MS 300/6-8
10 Surfside Rd 02554 508-228-7283
Lyndell Kalman, prin. Fax 325-7597

Natick, Middlesex, Pop. 30,700
Natick SD 4,600/PK-12
13 E Central St 01760 508-647-6500
James Connolly, supt. Fax 647-6506
www.natick.k12.ma.us
Kennedy MS 600/5-8
165 Mill St 01760 508-647-6650
Rosemary Vickery, prin. Fax 647-6658
Natick HS 1,200/9-12
15 West St 01760 508-647-6600
John Hughes, prin. Fax 651-7372
Wilson MS 800/5-8
22 Rutledge Rd 01760 508-647-6670
Ruth Evans, prin. Fax 647-6678

Montrose S 100/6-12
45 E Central St 01760 508-650-6925
Dr. Karen Bohlin, prin. Fax 650-6926
Walnut Hill S 300/9-12
12 Highland St 01760 508-650-5020
Stephanie Perrin, hdmstr. Fax 653-9593

Needham, Norfolk, Pop. 29,200
Needham SD 4,700/PK-12
1330 Highland Ave 02492 781-455-0400
Daniel Gutekanst, supt. Fax 455-0417
www.needham.k12.ma.us/
Pollard MS 1,100/6-8
200 Harris Ave 02492 781-455-0480
Glenn Brand, prin. Fax 455-0413
Other Schools – See Needham Heights

Franklin W. Olin College of Engineering Post-Sec.
Olin Way 02492 781-292-2300
Haddad MS 200/6-8
110 May St 02492 781-449-0133
Jane Abel, prin. Fax 449-8096
St. Sebastians Country Day S 300/7-12
1191 Greendale Ave 02492 781-449-5200
William Burke, hdmstr. Fax 449-5630

Needham Heights, Norfolk
Needham SD
Supt. — See Needham
Needham HS 1,400/9-12
609 Webster St 02494 781-455-0800
Paul Richards, prin. Fax 449-5111

New Bedford, Bristol, Pop. 94,112
Greater New Bedford Reg Vo/Tech HSD
1121 Ashley Blvd 02745 508-998-3321
Michael Shea, supt. Fax 995-7268
www.gnbvt.edu
Greater New Bedford Reg. Vo Tech HS Vo/Tech
1121 Ashley Blvd 02745 508-998-3321
Luis Lopes, prin. Fax 995-7268

New Bedford SD 14,300/PK-12
455 County St 02740 508-997-4511
Michael Longo, supt. Fax 997-0298
www.newbedford.k12.ma.us/
Keith MS, 70 Hathaway Blvd 02740 800/7-8
Joaquim Costa, prin. 508-997-4511
New Bedford HS 3,300/9-12
230 Hathaway Blvd 02740 508-997-4511
Donald Vasconcelles, prin.
Normandin MS 1,300/6-8
81 Felton St 02745 508-997-4511
Jeanne Bonneau, prin. Fax 995-6975
Roosevelt MS, 119 Frederick St 02744 1,000/6-8
Brian Abdallah, prin. 508-997-4511

LaBaron Hairdressing Academy Post-Sec.
281 Union St 02740 508-996-6611
Nazarene Christian Academy 200/PK-12
764 Hathaway Rd 02740 508-992-7944
Susan Helm, prin. Fax 994-1457
Rob Roy Academy Post-Sec.
1872 Acushnet Ave 02746 508-995-8711
St. Luke's Hospital Post-Sec.
101 Page St 02740 508-997-1525

Newburyport, Essex, Pop. 17,499
Newburyport SD 2,300/K-12
70 Low St 01950 978-465-4457
Mary Murray, supt. Fax 462-3495
www.newburyport.k12.ma.us/

Newburyport HS 800/9-12
241 High St 01950 978-465-4440
James Lee, prin. Fax 465-2198
Nock MS 700/5-8
70 Low St 01950 978-465-4447
Jayne Rotsko, prin. Fax 465-4074

Newton, Middlesex, Pop. 84,323
Newton SD
Supt. — See Newtonville
Bigelow MS 500/6-8
42 Vernon St 02458 617-552-7800
Todd Harrison, prin. Fax 552-7752
Oak Hill MS 600/6-8
130 Wheeler Rd 02459 617-559-9200
Henry Van Putten, prin. Fax 552-5547

Boston College Post-Sec.
885 Centre St 02459 617-552-4350
Hebrew College Post-Sec.
160 Herrick Rd 02459 617-559-8610
Mt. Alvernia HS 200/7-12
790 Centre St 02458 617-969-2260
Kathleen Kent, prin. Fax 969-4246
Newton Country Day S 300/5-12
785 Centre St 02458 617-244-4246
Sr. Barbara Rogers, prin. Fax 965-5313
Trinity Catholic HS 200/9-12
575 Washington St 02458 617-244-1841
Kelly Surapaneni, prin. Fax 796-9175

Newton Center, See Newton
Newton SD
Supt. — See Newtonville
Brown MS 800/6-8
125 Meadowbrook Rd 02459 617-552-7409
John Jordan, prin. Fax 552-7729
Newton South HS 1,500/9-12
140 Brandeis Rd 02459 617-559-6700
Brenda Keegan, prin. Fax 559-6701

Andover Newton Theological School Post-Sec.
210 Herrick Rd 02459 800-864-2687
Bais Yaakov of Boston HS 50/9-12
561 Ward St 02459 617-965-7547
Rabbi Tsvi Yehuda Levin, prin. Fax 965-0345
Mt. Ida College Post-Sec.
777 Dedham St 02459 617-969-7000
Solomon Schechter S of Greater Boston 300/4-8
125 Wells Ave 02459 617-928-9100
Arnold Zar-Kessler, dir. Fax 964-9401

Newtonville, See Newton
Newton SD 11,400/PK-12
100 Walnut St 02460 617-559-6100
Dr. Jeffrey Young, supt. Fax 559-6101
www.newton.mec.edu/
Day MS 800/6-8
21 Minot Pl 02460 617-559-9100
Gina Healy, prin. Fax 559-9103
Newton North HS 2,100/9-12
360 Lowell Ave 02460 617-559-6200
Jennifer Huntington, prin. Fax 559-6204
Other Schools – See Newton, Newton Center

Norfolk, Norfolk
King Philip SD 1,900/7-12
18 King St 02056 508-520-7991
Richard J. Robbat, supt. Fax 520-2044
www.kingphilip.org
King Philip Regional MS North 800/7-8
18 King St 02056 508-541-7324
William A. Rice, prin. Fax 541-3467
Other Schools – See Wrentham

North Adams, Berkshire, Pop. 14,334
North Adams SD 2,100/PK-12
191 E Main St 01247 413-662-3225
James E. Montepare, supt. Fax 662-3212
www.northadamsschools.com
Conte MS 500/6-8
24 N Church St 01247 413-662-3200
Diane Ryczek, prin. Fax 662-3212
Drury HS 600/9-12
1130 S Church St 01247 413-662-3240
John Solari, prin. Fax 662-3239

Northern Berkshire Vocational SD
70 Hodges Crossroads 01247 413-663-5383
James Brosnan, supt. Fax 664-9424
www.mccanntech.org
McCann Technical S Vo/Tech
70 Hodges Crossroads 01247 413-663-5383
Gary Rivers, prin. Fax 664-9424

C.H. McCann Technical School Post-Sec.
70 Hodges Crossroads 01247 413-663-5383
Massachusetts College of Liberal Arts Post-Sec.
375 Church St 01247 413-662-5000

Northampton, Hampshire, Pop. 29,287
Northampton SD 2,900/K-12
212 Main St 01060 413-587-1331
Isabelina Babcock, supt. Fax 587-1318
www.nps.northampton.ma.us
Northampton HS 900/9-12
380 Elm St 01060 413-587-1346
Beth Singer, prin. Fax 587-1374
Other Schools – See Florence

Northampton-Smith SD
80 Locust St 01060 413-587-1414
Frank Llamas, supt. Fax 587-1405
Smith Vocational & Agricultural HS Vo/Tech
80 Locust St 01060 413-587-1414
Veronica Carroll, prin. Fax 587-1406

Smith College 01063 Post-Sec.
413-584-2700

North Andover, Essex, Pop. 22,792
North Andover SD 4,100/K-12
43 High St 01845 978-794-1503
Harry K. Harutunian, supt. Fax 794-0231
www.nandover.mec.edu
North Andover HS 1,200/9-12
430 Osgood St 01845 978-794-1711
Susan Nicholson, prin. Fax 794-1505
North Andover MS 1,100/6-8
495 Main St 01845 978-794-1870
Joan McQuade, prin. Fax 794-3619

Brooks S 400/9-12
1160 Great Pond Rd 01845 978-686-6101
Lawrence Becker, prin. Fax 725-6215
Merrimack College Post-Sec.
315 Turnpike St 01845 978-683-7111

North Attleboro, Bristol, Pop. 16,178
North Attleborough SD 4,700/PK-12
6 Morse St 02760 508-643-2100
Richard A. Smith, supt. Fax 643-2110
www.naschools.net
North Attleboro HS 1,200/9-12
1 Wilson W Whitty Way 02760 508-643-2115
Robert Gay, prin. Fax 643-2173
North Attleboro MS 1,200/6-8
564 Landry Ave 02760 508-643-2130
Victoria Ekk, prin. Fax 643-2134

Northborough, Worcester, Pop. 5,761
Northborough-Southborough SD 4,400/PK-12
44 Bearfoot Rd 01532 508-351-7000
Rosemary Joseph, supt. Fax 351-7049
www.nsboro.k12.ma.us/
Algonquin Regional HS 1,200/9-12
79 Bartlett St 01532 508-351-7010
Edward Gallagher, prin. Fax 393-9226
Melican MS 700/6-8
145 Lincoln St 01532 508-351-7020
Patricia Montimurro, prin. Fax 351-7006
Other Schools – See Southborough

North Brookfield, Worcester, Pop. 2,635
North Brookfield SD 800/K-12
10 High School Dr 01535 508-867-9821
Erin Nosek, supt. Fax 867-8148
www.northbrookfield.k12.ma.us
North Brookfield JSHS 300/7-12
10 High School Dr 01535 508-867-7131
Fax 867-3496

North Chelmsford, Middlesex
Chelmsford SD 5,800/PK-12
190 Richardson Rd 01863 978-251-5100
Richard Moser Ph.D., supt. Fax 251-5110
www.chelmsford.k12.ma.us/
Chelmsford HS 1,700/9-12
200 Richardson Rd 01863 978-251-5111
W. Allen Thomas, prin. Fax 251-5117
Other Schools – See Chelmsford

North Dartmouth, Bristol, Pop. 8,000
Dartmouth SD
Supt. — See South Dartmouth
Dartmouth MS 1,100/6-8
366 Slocum Rd 02747 508-997-9333
Stephen Pettey, prin. Fax 999-7720

Bishop Stang HS 600/9-12
500 Slocum Rd 02747 508-996-5602
Theresa Dougall, pres. Fax 994-6756
Southern New England School of Law Post-Sec.
333 Faunce Corner Rd 02747 508-998-9600
University of Massachusetts Dartmouth Post-Sec.
285 Old Westport Rd 02747 508-999-8000

North Dighton, Bristol
Dighton-Rehoboth Regional SD 3,300/K-12
2700 Regional Rd 02764 508-252-5000
Dr. Francis Connor, supt. Fax 252-5024
www.drregional.org/
Dighton-Rehoboth Regional HS 1,000/9-12
2700 Regional Rd 02764 508-252-5025
Trent Danella, prin. Fax 252-5110
Other Schools – See Dighton, Rehoboth

North Eastham, Barnstable, Pop. 1,570
Nauset SD
Supt. — See Orleans
Nauset Regional HS 1,100/9-12
100 Cable Rd 02651 508-255-1505
Thomas Conrad, prin. Fax 255-9701

North Easton, Bristol, Pop. 4,400
Easton SD 3,800/PK-12
PO Box 359 02356 508-230-3200
Dr. William Simmons, supt. Fax 238-3563
www.easton.k12.ma.us/
Ames HS 800/10-12
100 Lothrop St 02356 508-230-3210
Wesley Paul, prin. Fax 238-7325
Easton JHS 900/7-9
98 Columbus Ave 02356 508-230-3222
John P. Giuggio, prin. Fax 230-0198

Stonehill College Post-Sec.
320 Washington St 02357 508-565-1373

Northfield, Franklin, Pop. 1,322
Pioneer Valley SD 1,100/PK-12
97 F Sumner Turner Rd 01360 413-498-2911
Kevin Courtney, supt. Fax 498-0045
www.pioneervalley.k12.ma.us
Pioneer Valley Regional JSHS 500/7-12
97 F Sumner Turner Rd 01360 413-498-2931
Cheryl McDaniel-Thomas, prin. Fax 498-0184

Northfield Mt. Hermon S 700/9-12
206 Main St 01360 413-498-3000
Thomas Sturtevant, hdmstr. Fax 498-3170

North Quincy, See Quincy
Quincy SD
Supt. — See Quincy
Atlantic MS 500/6-8
86 Hollis Ave 02171 617-984-8727
Laura Bogan, prin. Fax 984-8646
North Quincy HS 1,500/9-12
316 Hancock St 02171 617-984-8744
Louis Ioanilli, prin. Fax 984-8647

North Reading, Middlesex, Pop. 12,002
North Reading SD 2,600/K-12
19 Sherman Rd 01864 978-664-7810
David Troughton, supt. Fax 664-0252
North Reading HS 700/9-12
191 Park St 01864 978-664-7800
Jon Bernard, prin. Fax 664-7826
North Reading MS 600/6-8
19 Sherman Rd 01864 978-664-7806
Richard C. Hodges, prin. Fax 276-0687

Norton, Bristol, Pop. 1,899
Norton SD 3,200/PK-12
64 W Main St 02766 508-285-0100
Lincoln DeMoura, supt. Fax 285-0199
www.norton.mec.edu
Norton HS 700/9-12
66 W Main St 02766 508-285-0160
Susan Carney, prin. Fax 285-0164
Norton MS 800/6-8
215 W Main St 02766 508-285-0140
Roger Parent, prin. Fax 286-9457

New Testament Christian S 200/PK-12
PO Box AJ 02766 508-285-9771
Lynne Brennan, prin. Fax 285-6775
Wheaton College Post-Sec.
26 E Main St 02766 800-394-6003

Norwell, Plymouth
Norwell SD 2,000/PK-12
322 Main St 02061 781-659-8800
Donald J. Beaudette Ed.D., supt. Fax 659-8805
www.norwellschools.org
Norwell HS 600/9-12
18 South St 02061 781-659-8810
Andrea Keating, prin. Fax 659-1824
Norwell MS 500/6-8
328 Main St 02061 781-659-8814
Rodrigo Borgueta, prin. Fax 659-8822

Norwood, Norfolk, Pop. 28,500
Norwood SD 3,500/PK-12
PO Box 67 02062 781-762-6804
Dr. Edward P. Quigley, supt. Fax 762-0229
www.norwood.k12.ma.us/
Coakley MS 900/6-8
PO Box 67 02062 781-762-7880
Margery Tessier, prin. Fax 255-5630
Norwood HS 1,100/9-12
PO Box 67 02062 781-769-2333
George Usevich, prin. Fax 762-0826

FINE Mortuary College Post-Sec.
150 Kerry Pl 02062 781-762-1211
ITT Technical Institute Post-Sec.
333 Boston Providence Tpke 02062 781-278-0708
Universal Technical Institute Post-Sec.
1 Upland Rd 02062 781-948-2030

Oak Bluffs, Dukes
Martha's Vineyard SD
Supt. — See Vineyard Haven
Martha's Vineyard Regional HS 800/9-12
PO Box 1385 02557 508-693-1033
Margaret Regan, prin. Fax 693-1891

Orange, Franklin, Pop. 3,791
Ralph C. Mahar Regional SD 700/7-12
PO Box 680 01364 978-544-2920
Eileen Perkins, supt. Fax 544-8383
www.rcmahar.org
Mahar Regional HS 700/7-12
PO Box 680 01364 978-544-2542
Francis Zak, prin. Fax 544-8383

Orleans, Barnstable, Pop. 1,699
Nauset SD 1,800/6-12
78 Eldridge Park Way 02653 508-255-8800
Michael Gradone, supt. Fax 240-2351
www.nausetschools.org
Nauset Regional MS 700/6-8
70 S Orleans Rd 02653 508-255-0016
Greg Baecker, prin. Fax 240-1105
Other Schools – See North Eastham

Osterville, Barnstable, Pop. 2,911

Cape Cod Academy 400/K-12
PO Box 469 02655 508-428-5400
Thomas Evans, prin. Fax 428-0701

Oxford, Worcester, Pop. 5,969
Oxford SD 2,200/PK-12
5 Sigourney St 01540 508-987-6050
Ernest Boss, supt. Fax 987-6054
www.oxps.org
Oxford HS 600/9-12
495 Main St 01540 508-987-6081
David Grenier, prin. Fax 987-6083
Oxford MS 700/5-8
497 Main St 01540 508-987-6074
Katherine Hackett, prin. Fax 987-2588

Palmer, Hampden, Pop. 4,069
Palmer SD 2,000/K-12
24 Converse St 01069 413-283-2650
Dr. Linda Denault, supt. Fax 283-2655
www.palmerschools.org
Palmer HS 700/8-12
4105 Main St 01069 413-283-6511
James Conro, prin. Fax 283-3476
Pathfinder Vocational-Technical SD
240 Sykes St 01069 413-283-9701
Gerald Paist, supt. Fax 284-0032
www.pathfindertech.org/
Pathfinder Reg Vocational Technical HS Vo/Tech
240 Sykes St 01069 413-283-9701
Mark Condon, prin. Fax 284-0032

Paxton, Worcester

Anna Maria College Post-Sec.
50 Sunset Ln 01612 508-849-3360

Peabody, Essex, Pop. 49,759
Peabody SD 6,200/PK-12
21 Johnson St 01960 978-536-6500
Nadine Binkley, supt. Fax 536-6504
www.peabody.k12.ma.us/
Higgins MS 1,500/6-8
1 King St 01960 978-536-4800
Melissa Matarazzo, prin. Fax 536-4810
Peabody Veterans Memorial HS 1,900/9-12
485 Lowell St 01960 978-536-4500
Patrick Larkin, prin. Fax 535-9578

Bishop Fenwick HS 900/9-12
99 Margin St 01960 978-531-8200
David Marion, prin. Fax 531-2483

Pembroke, Plymouth
Pembroke SD 1,800/K-12
72 Pilgrim Rd 02359 781-829-1178
Dr. Patricia Randall, supt. Fax 826-1182
www.pembroke.mec.edu
Pembroke Community MS 7-8
559 School St 02359 781-293-8627
Steven LaMarche, prin. Fax 294-0916
Pembroke HS 9-12
80 Learning Ln 02359 781-293-9281
Ruth Lynch, prin. Fax 293-2812

Pepperell, Middlesex, Pop. 2,350
North Middlesex SD
Supt. — See Townsend
Nissitissit MS 600/6-8
33 Chase Ave 01463 978-433-0114
Michael Tikonoff, prin. Fax 433-0118

Pittsfield, Berkshire, Pop. 44,779
Pittsfield SD 6,500/PK-12
269 1st St 01201 413-499-9512
Dr. Katherine Darlington, supt. Fax 448-2643
www.pittsfield.net/
Herberg MS 800/6-8
501 Pomeroy Ave 01201 413-448-9640
Christopher Jacoby, prin. Fax 448-9644
Pittsfield HS 900/9-12
300 East St 01201 413-499-9535
Howard Eberwein, prin. Fax 443-7216
Reid MS 700/6-8
950 North St 01201 413-448-9620
Linda Carrier, prin. Fax 443-1587
Taconic HS 1,000/9-12
96 Valentine Rd 01201 413-448-9600
Douglas McNally, prin. Fax 499-4835

Berkshire Community College Post-Sec.
1350 West St 01201 413-499-4660
Berkshire Medical Center Post-Sec.
725 North St 01201 413-447-2144
Mildred Elley Business School Post-Sec.
505 East St 01201 413-499-8618
Miss Hall's S 100/9-12
PO Box 1166 01202 413-443-6401
Fax 448-2994
St. Joseph Central HS 200/8-12
22 Maplewood Ave 01201 413-447-9121
Margaret Downing, prin. Fax 443-7020

Plymouth, Plymouth, Pop. 7,258
Plymouth SD 8,700/PK-12
253 S Meadow Rd 02360 508-830-4300
Barry Haskell, supt. Fax 746-1873
www.plymouthschools.com
Plymouth Community IS 1,400/5-8
117 Long Pond Rd 02360 508-830-4450
Dr. Fred Sarke, prin. Fax 830-4464
Plymouth North HS 1,100/9-12
41 Obery St 02360 508-830-4400
John Siever, prin. Fax 830-4420
Plymouth South HS 900/9-12
490 Long Pond Rd 02360 508-224-7512
Patricia Connors, prin. Fax 224-6765
Plymouth South MS 900/5-8
488 Long Pond Rd 02360 508-224-2725
Anna Stompleski, prin. Fax 224-5660
Plymouth South Technical S Vo/Tech
490 Long Pond Rd 02360 508-224-7512
Patricia Connors, prin. Fax 224-9532

Prides Crossing, See Beverly

Landmark S 500/2-12
PO Box 227 01965 978-236-3010
Robert Broudo, hdmstr. Fax 921-0361

Provincetown, Barnstable, Pop. 3,374
Provincetown SD 300/PK-12
2 Mayflower Ln 02657 508-487-5000
Janice Lachowetz, supt. Fax 487-5098
www.provincetown.k12.ma.us
Provincetown JSHS 200/7-12
12 Winslow St 02657 508-487-5040
Edward Boxer, prin. Fax 487-5089

Quincy, Norfolk, Pop. 89,059
Quincy SD | 8,700/PK-12
70 Coddington St 02169 | 617-984-8700
Dr. Richard DeCristofaro, supt. | Fax 984-8806
www.quincypublicschools.com
Broad Meadows MS | 400/6-8
50 Calvin Rd 02169 | 617-984-8723
Colleen Roberts, prin. | Fax 984-8834
Center for Technical Education | Vo/Tech
107 Woodward Ave 02169 | 617-984-8731
Emily Lebo, prin. | Fax 984-8601
Central MS | 600/6-8
1012 Hancock St 02169 | 617-984-8725
Jennifer Fay, prin. | Fax 984-8661
Point Webster MS | 300/6-8
60 Lancaster St 02169 | 617-984-6600
James McGuire, prin. | Fax 984-6609
Quincy HS | 1,400/9-12
52 Coddington St 02169 | 617-984-8751
Frank Santoro, prin. | Fax 984-8643
Sterling MS | 300/6-8
444 Granite St 02169 | 617-984-8729
Earl Metzler, prin. | Fax 984-8640
Other Schools – See North Quincy

Eastern Nazarene College | Post-Sec.
23 E Elm Ave 02170 | 617-773-6350
Mansfield Beauty School | Post-Sec.
200 Parkingway St 02169 | 617-479-1090
MA Sch. of Barbering & Mens Hairstyling | Post-Sec.
1585 Hancock St 02169 | 617-770-4444
Quincy College | Post-Sec.
34 Coddington St 02169 | 617-984-1600
Rhodec International | Post-Sec.
59 Coddington St Ste 104 02169 | 617-472-4942
Woodward S for Girls | 100/6-12
1102 Hancock St 02169 | 617-773-5610

Randolph, Norfolk, Pop. 31,200
Randolph SD | 3,600/PK-12
40 Highland Ave 02368 | 781-961-6205
Dr. Richard H. Silverman, supt. | Fax 961-6295
www.randolph.mec.edu/
Randolph Community MS | 800/7-8
225 High St 02368 | 781-961-6243
John Sheehan, prin. | Fax 961-6286
Randolph HS | 1,000/9-12
70 Memorial Pkwy 02368 | 781-961-6220
Robert Johnson, prin. | Fax 961-6235

Raynham, Bristol, Pop. 2,100
Bridgewater-Raynham Regional SD | 6,000/PK-12
777 Pleasant St 02767 | 508-824-2730
Robert McIntyre, supt. | Fax 824-2746
www.bridge-rayn.org
Raynham MS | 700/5-8
420 Titicut Rd 02767 | 508-997-0504
Paul Grueter, prin. | Fax 977-0659
Other Schools – See Bridgewater

Reading, Middlesex, Pop. 22,539
Reading SD | 4,200/K-12
82 Oakland Rd 01867 | 781-944-5800
Patrick A. Schettini Ph.D., supt. | Fax 942-9149
reading.k12.ma.us
Coolidge MS | 500/6-8
89 Birch Meadow Dr 01867 | 781-942-9158
John Doherty, prin. | Fax 942-9118
Parker MS | 500/6-8
45 Temple St 01867 | 781-944-1236
Linda Darisse, prin. | Fax 942-9008
Reading Memorial HS | 1,200/9-12
62 Oakland Rd 01867 | 781-944-8200
Joseph Finigan, prin. | Fax 942-5435

Austin Preparatory S | 700/6-12
101 Willow St 01867 | 781-944-4900
Paul Moran, prin. | Fax 944-7530

Rehoboth, Bristol
Dighton-Rehoboth Regional SD
Supt. — See North Dighton
Beckwith MS | 700/5-8
330R Winthrop St 02769 | 508-252-5080
Anthony Ferreira, prin. | Fax 252-5082

Revere, Suffolk, Pop. 47,002
Revere SD | 4,900/PK-12
101 School St 02151 | 781-286-8226
Dr. Paul Dakin, supt. | Fax 286-8221
www.revereps.mec.edu
Garfield Magnet MS | 6-8
176 Garfield Ave 02151 | 781-286-8298
Patricia Massa, prin. | Fax 286-8128
Revere HS | 1,400/9-12
101 School St 02151 | 781-286-8222
David Deruosi, prin. | Fax 286-8378
Seacoast MSHS | 200/7-12
101 School St 02151 | 781-485-2715
Thomas Misci, prin. | Fax 485-2718

Rochester, Plymouth
Old Colony Reg Vocational Technical HSD
476 North Ave 02770 | 508-763-8011
David Ferreira, supt. | Fax 763-9821
www.oldcolony.tec.ma.us
Old Colony Reg Vocational Tech HS | Vo/Tech
476 North Ave 02770 | 508-763-8011
David Ferreira, prin. | Fax 763-9821

Rockland, Plymouth, Pop. 16,123
Rockland SD | 3,000/K-12
34 Mackinlay Way 02370 | 781-878-3893
James A. Kerrigan, supt. | Fax 982-1483
www.rockland.mec.edu/
Rockland HS | 800/9-12
52 Mackinlay Way 02370 | 781-871-0541
Stephen Sangster, prin. | Fax 878-0158
Rogers MS | 700/6-8
100 Taunton Ave 02370 | 781-878-4341
Paul Stanish, prin. | Fax 871-8448

Master's Academy | 100/K-12
525 Beech St 02370 | 781-871-8214
Dr. Omar Adams, hdmstr. | Fax 871-8721

Rockport, Essex, Pop. 5,448
Rockport SD | 1,000/K-12
24 Jerdens Ln 01966 | 978-546-1200
Rosemary A. Ditullio Ph.D., supt. | Fax 546-1205
rockport.k12.ma.us
Rockport HS | 300/9-12
24 Jerdens Ln 01966 | 978-546-1234
Charles Symonds, prin. | Fax 546-1205
Rockport MS | 300/6-8
26 Jerdens Ln 01966 | 978-546-1250
Charles Symonds, prin. | Fax 546-1205

Roslindale, See Boston
Boston SD
Supt. — See Boston
Irving MS | 800/6-8
105 Cummins Hwy 02131 | 617-635-8072
James Watson, prin. | Fax 635-9363

Roxbury, See Boston
Boston SD
Supt. — See Boston
Dearborn MS | 400/6-8
35 Greenville St 02119 | 617-635-8412
Teresa Soares-Pena, prin. | Fax 635-8419
Lewis MS | 300/6-8
131 Walnut Ave 02119 | 617-635-8137
Ronald Spratling, prin. | Fax 635-6341
O'Bryant HS of Mathematics & Science | 1,300/7-12
55 Malcolm X Blvd 02120 | 617-635-9932
Joel Stembridge, hdmstr. | Fax 635-7769
Timilty MS | 700/6-8
205 Roxbury St 02119 | 617-635-8109
Valeria Lowe-Barehmi, prin. | Fax 635-8115
Boston Adult Technical Academy | Adult
75 Malcolm X Blvd 02120 | 617-635-1542
Rachel Bonkovsky, dir. | Fax 635-6362

Roxbury Crossing, See Boston
Boston SD
Supt. — See Boston
Madison Park Technical Vocational HS | Vo/Tech
75 Malcolm X Blvd 02120 | 617-635-8970
Charles McAfee, hdmstr. | Fax 635-9831

Roxbury Community College | Post-Sec.
1234 Columbus Ave 02120 | 617-427-0060

Rutland, Worcester, Pop. 2,145
Wachusett Regional SD
Supt. — See Jefferson
Central Tree MS | 500/5-8
281 Main St 01543 | 508-886-0073
C. Erik, prin. | Fax 886-0141

Devereux Center in Massachusetts | Post-Sec.
PO Box 219 01543 | 508-886-4746

Salem, Essex, Pop. 42,067
Salem SD | 4,900/PK-12
29 Highland Ave 01970 | 978-740-1212
Dr. Lawrence Callahan, supt. | Fax 740-3083
www.salem.k12.ma.us/
Collins MS | 1,000/6-8
29 Highland Ave 01970 | 978-740-1191
Mary Manning, prin. | Fax 740-1183
Salem HS | 1,300/9-12
77 Wilson St 01970 | 978-740-1123
Ann Papagiotas, prin. | Fax 740-1110

Salem State College | Post-Sec.
352 Lafayette St 01970 | 978-741-6000

Sandwich, Barnstable, Pop. 2,998
Sandwich SD | 4,100/K-12
16 Dewey Ave 02563 | 508-888-1054
Nancy Young, supt. | Fax 833-8023
www.sandwich.k12.ma.us
Other Schools – See East Sandwich

Saugus, Essex, Pop. 26,200
Saugus SD | 3,300/PK-12
23 Main St 01906 | 781-231-5000
Keith Manville, supt. | Fax 233-9424
www.mec.edu/saugus/
Belmonte MS | 800/6-8
25 Dow St 01906 | 781-231-5052
Charles Naso, prin. | Fax 233-5665
Saugus HS | 900/9-12
1 Pierce Memorial Dr 01906 | 781-231-5027
Joseph Diorio, prin. | Fax 231-5030

Scituate, Plymouth, Pop. 5,180
Scituate SD | 3,100/K-12
606 Chief Justice Cushing 02066 | 781-545-8759
Mark Mason, supt. | Fax 545-6291
www.scituate.k12.ma.us/
Gates IS | 500/7-8
327 First Parish Rd 02066 | 781-545-8760
Richard Blake, prin. | Fax 545-8767
Scituate HS | 800/9-12
606 Chief Justice Cushing 02066 | 781-545-8750
Donna Nuzzo-Mueller, prin. | Fax 545-8758

Seekonk, Bristol, Pop. 13,046
Seekonk SD | 2,300/PK-12
69 School St 02771 | 508-336-7711
Dr. Raleigh C. Buchanan, supt. | Fax 336-2264
www.seekonk.k12.ma.us
Hurley MS | 600/6-8
650 Newman Ave 02771 | 508-761-7570
Dennis Fernandes, prin. | Fax 336-9630
Seekonk HS | 700/9-12
261 Arcade Ave 02771 | 508-336-7272
Marcia McGovern, prin. | Fax 336-8535

Sharon, Norfolk, Pop. 5,893
Sharon SD | 3,500/K-12
1 School St 02067 | 781-784-1570
Claire W. Jackson Ph.D., supt. | Fax 784-1573
www.sharon.k12.ma.us
Sharon HS | 1,100/9-12
181 Pond St 02067 | 781-784-1554
Dr. George Anthony, prin. | Fax 784-1550
Sharon MS | 800/6-8
75 Mountain St 02067 | 781-784-1560
Kevin O'Rourke, prin. | Fax 784-8432

Chabad Day S | 100/PK-12
162 N Main St 02067 | 781-784-4269
Sara Wolosow, prin. | Fax 634-0485

Sheffield, Berkshire
Southern Berkshire Regional SD | 1,000/PK-12
PO Box 339 01257 | 413-229-8778
Valerie Spriggs, supt. | Fax 229-2913
sbrsd.org
Mount Everett Regional HS | 400/7-12
PO Box 326 01257 | 413-229-8734
Glenn Devoti, prin. | Fax 229-2044

Berkshire S | 400/9-12
245 N Undermountain Rd 01257 | 413-229-8511
Michael Maher, hdmstr. | Fax 229-1010

Shelburne Falls, Franklin, Pop. 1,996
Mohawk Trail SD | 1,500/PK-12
24 Ashfield Rd 01370 | 413-625-0192
Michael Buoniconti, supt. | Fax 625-0196
www.mtrsd.k12.ma.us/
Mohawk Trail Regional HS | 800/7-12
26 Ashfield Rd 01370 | 413-625-9811
Philip Dzialo, prin. | Fax 625-6652

Shirley, Middlesex, Pop. 1,559
Shirley SD | 800/PK-8
34 Lancaster Rd 01464 | 978-425-2630
Thomas Scott, supt. | Fax 425-2640
Shirley MS | 300/5-8
1 Hospital Rd 01464 | 978-425-2630
Daniel Schauben-Fuerst, prin. | Fax 425-0474

Shrewsbury, Worcester, Pop. 25,900
Shrewsbury SD | 4,700/K-12
100 Maple Ave 01545 | 508-841-8400
Dr. Anthony J. Bent, supt. | Fax 841-8490
www.ci.shrewsbury.ma.us
Oak MS | 6-8
45 Oak St 01545 | 508-841-1200
Stephen Lobban, prin. | Fax 841-1223
Shrewsbury HS | 1,300/9-12
64 Holden St 01545 | 508-841-8800
Daniel Gutekanst, prin. | Fax 841-8858

St. John's HS | 1,100/9-12
378 Main St 01545 | 508-842-8934
Michael W. Welch, admin. | Fax 842-3670

Somerset, Bristol, Pop. 17,655
Somerset SD | 2,800/K-12
580 Whetstone Hill Rd 02726 | 508-324-3100
Richard Medeiros, supt. | Fax 324-3107
www.musictown.mec.edu
Somerset HS | 1,000/9-12
270 Grandview Ave 02726 | 508-324-3115
Robert Pineault, prin. | Fax 324-3104
Somerset MS | 700/6-8
1141 Brayton Ave 02726 | 508-324-3140
Elizabeth Ponte, prin. | Fax 324-3145

Somerville, Middlesex, Pop. 76,296
Somerville SD | 5,100/PK-12
181 Washington St 02143 | 617-625-6600
Dr. Albert F. Argenziano, supt. | Fax 625-4731
www.somerville.k12.ma.us
Lincoln Park Community S at Edgerly | 200/5-8
8 Bonair St 02145 | 617-625-6600
John O'Meara, prin.
Somerville HS | 1,700/9-12
81 Highland Ave 02143 | 617-625-6600
Thomas Galligani, prin. | Fax 629-4763

Computer-Ed Business Institute | Post-Sec.
5 Middlesex Ave 02145 | 781-933-7681

Southborough, Worcester
Northborough-Southborough SD
Supt. — See Northborough
Trottier MS | 500/6-8
49 Parkerville Rd 01772 | 508-485-2400
Linda Murdock, prin. | Fax 481-1506

St. Marks S | 300/9-12
PO Box 9105 01772 | 508-786-6000
Elsa Hill, hdmstr. | Fax 786-6109

South Boston, See Boston
Boston SD
Supt. — See Boston
Excel HS | 600/9-12
95 G St 02127 | 617-635-9870
Ligia Noriega, hdmstr. | Fax 635-9711
Gavin MS | 700/6-8
215 Dorchester St 02127 | 617-635-8817
Alexander Mathews, prin. | Fax 635-8826
Monument HS | 400/9-12
95 G St 02127 | 617-635-9865
Jonathan Pizzi, hdmstr. | Fax 635-9711

Southbridge, Worcester, Pop. 13,631
Southbridge SD | 2,500/K-12
41 Elm St 01550 | 508-764-5414
Dale Hanley, supt. | Fax 764-8325
www.southbridge.k12.ma.us/

Southbridge HS 600/9-12
25 Cole Ave 01550 508-764-5450
Sheila Haskins, prin. Fax 764-5479
Wells JHS 600/6-8
82 Marcy St 01550 508-764-5440
Lillian M. Talbot, prin. Fax 764-5496

South Dartmouth, Bristol, Pop. 9,850
Dartmouth SD 4,300/PK-12
8 Bush St 02748 508-997-3391
Stephen Russell, supt. Fax 991-4184
www.dartmouth.mec.edu
Dartmouth HS 1,300/9-12
555 Bakerville Rd 02748 508-961-2700
Donna Dimery, prin. Fax 910-1410
Other Schools – See North Dartmouth

South Deerfield, Franklin, Pop. 1,906
Frontier Regional SD 700/7-12
219 Christian Ln 01373 413-665-1155
Regina H. Nash Ed.D., supt. Fax 665-8506
Frontier Regional JSHS 700/7-12
113 N Main St 01373 413-665-2118
Donald Skroski, prin. Fax 665-1518

South Dennis, Barnstable, Pop. 3,559
Dennis-Yarmouth SD
Supt. — See South Yarmouth
Wixon MS 600/4-8
901 Route 134 02660 508-398-7695
Lisa McMahon, prin. Fax 398-7608

South Easton, Bristol
Southeastern Regional Voc Tech SD
250 Foundry St 02375 508-238-4374
James Hager, supt. Fax 230-3779
www.sersd.org
Southeastern Regional Vo-Tech HS Vo/Tech
250 Foundry St 02375 508-238-4371
Jerome Burke, prin. Fax 238-4318

Southeastern Technical Institute Post-Sec.
250 Foundry St 02375 508-238-1860

South Hadley, Hampshire, Pop. 5,400
South Hadley SD 2,300/PK-12
116 Main St 01075 413-538-5060
Gus Sayer, supt. Fax 532-6284
www.shschools.com
Smith MS 800/5-8
100 Mosier St 01075 413-538-5074
Melodie Goodwin, prin. Fax 532-5302
South Hadley HS 700/9-12
153 Newton St 01075 413-538-5063
Daniel T. Smith, prin. Fax 532-6538

Mt. Holyoke College Post-Sec.
50 College St 01075 413-538-2000
Valley Christian S, 36 Hadley St 01075 100/PK-12
Carol Whiteley, prin. 413-533-8545

South Hamilton, Essex, Pop. 2,750
Hamilton-Wenham SD
Supt. — See Wenham
Hamilton-Wenham Regional HS 700/9-12
775 Bay Rd 01982 978-468-5300
Robert Krol, prin. Fax 468-0241
Miles River MS 500/6-8
787 Bay Rd 01982 978-468-5320
Janice Desantis, prin. Fax 468-8454

Gordon-Conwell Theological Seminary Post-Sec.
130 Essex St 01982 978-468-7111
Pingree S 300/9-12
537 Highland St 01982 978-468-4415
Peter M. Cowen, hdmstr. Fax 468-3758

South Lancaster, Worcester, Pop. 1,772

Atlantic Union College Post-Sec.
PO Box 1000 01561 978-368-2000
South Lancaster Academy 100/9-12
PO Box 1129 01561 978-368-8544
Allyson Cram, prin. Fax 365-2244

Southwick, Hampden
Southwick-Tolland SD 1,900/PK-12
86 Powder Mill Rd 01077 413-569-5391
Thomas Witham, supt. Fax 569-1711
www.strsd.southwick.ma.us/
Powder Mill MS 600/5-8
94 Powder Mill Rd 01077 413-569-5951
Ronald Peloquin, prin. Fax 569-1710
Southwick HS 600/9-12
93 Feeding Hills Rd 01077 413-569-6171
Michael J. Camerota, prin. Fax 569-1723

South Yarmouth, Barnstable, Pop. 10,358
Dennis-Yarmouth SD 4,100/K-12
296 Station Ave 02664 508-398-7600
Dan Cabral, supt. Fax 398-7622
www.dy-regional.k12.ma.us/
Dennis-Yarmouth Regional HS 1,100/9-12
210 Station Ave 02664 508-398-7630
Kenneth Jenks, prin. Fax 398-7602
Other Schools – See South Dennis, West Yarmouth

Spencer, Worcester, Pop. 6,306
Spencer-East Brookfield SD 1,900/PK-12
306 Main St 01562 508-885-8500
Ralph Hicks Ed.D., supt. Fax 885-8504
www.ultranet.com/~seb
Knox Trail JHS 400/7-8
73 Ash St 01562 508-885-8550
John Williams, prin. Fax 885-8557
Prouty HS 600/9-12
302 Main St 01562 508-885-8505
Kevin Wells, prin. Fax 885-8511

Springfield, Hampden, Pop. 152,157
Springfield SD 24,500/PK-12
PO Box 1410 01102 413-787-7100
Dr. Joseph P. Burke, supt. Fax 787-7211
www.sps.springfield.ma.us
Chestnut Accelerated MS 1,200/6-8
355 Plainfield St 01107 413-750-2333
Lydia Martinez, prin. Fax 750-2351
Duggan MS 900/6-8
1015 Wilbraham Rd 01109 413-787-7410
Jonathan Swan, prin. Fax 750-2209
Forest Park MS 900/6-8
46 Oakland St 01108 413-787-7420
Carol Fazio, prin. Fax 787-7419
Kennedy MS 700/6-8
1385 Berkshire Ave 01151 413-787-7510
Frances Cameron, prin. Fax 787-7561
Kiley MS 1,100/6-8
180 Cooley St 01128 413-787-7240
Catherine McCarthy, prin. Fax 787-7247
Putnam Vocational Technical HS Vo/Tech
1300 State St 01109 413-787-7424
Kevin McCaskill, prin. Fax 787-7330
Springfield Central HS 1,800/9-12
1840 Roosevelt Ave 01109 413-787-7085
Richard Stoddard, prin. Fax 787-7040
HS of Commerce 1,700/9-12
415 State St 01105 413-787-7220
Ann Henry, prin. Fax 787-7041
Springfield HS of Science-Tech 1,900/9-12
1250 State St 01109 413-750-2000
Karen Lott, prin. Fax 750-2047
Van Sickle MS 1,100/6-8
1170 Carew St 01104 413-750-2887
Cheryl DeSpirt-Lambert, prin. Fax 750-2972

American International College Post-Sec.
1000 State St 01109 413-737-7000
Cathedral HS 1,000/9-12
260 Surrey Rd 01118 413-782-5285
John Miller, prin. Fax 782-5065
MacDuffie S 200/6-12
1 Ames Hill Dr 01105 413-734-4971
Kathryn Gibson, prin. Fax 734-6693
Mansfield Beauty School Post-Sec.
266 Bridge St 01103 413-788-7575
Pioneer Valley Christian S 300/PK-12
965 Plumtree Rd 01119 413-782-8031
Timothy Duff, hdmstr. Fax 782-8033
Springfield College Post-Sec.
263 Alden St 01109 413-748-3000
Springfield Technical Community College Post-Sec.
1 Armory Sq 01105 413-781-7822
Ultrasound Diagnostic School Post-Sec.
365 Cadwell Dr 01104 413-739-4700
Western New England College Post-Sec.
1215 Wilbraham Rd 01119 413-782-3111

Sterling, Worcester
Wachusett Regional SD
Supt. — See Jefferson
Chocksett MS 500/5-8
40 Boutelle Rd 01564 978-422-6552
Marguerite Snow, prin. Fax 422-7720

Stockbridge, Berkshire
Berkshire Hills SD 600/PK-12
207 Pleasant St 01262 413-274-6400
Donna Moyer, supt. Fax 274-6407
www.bhrsd.org
Other Schools – See Great Barrington

Berkshire Country Day S 300/PK-12
55 Interlaken Rd 01262 413-637-0755
Robert Peterson, hdmstr. Fax 637-8927
DeSisto S 100/8-12
PO Box 369 01262 413-298-3776

Stoneham, Middlesex, Pop. 22,203
Stoneham SD 3,000/PK-12
149 Franklin St 02180 781-279-3826
Joseph Connelly, supt. Fax 279-3818
Stoneham HS 900/9-12
149 Franklin St 02180 781-279-3810
Thomas Ryan, prin. Fax 279-2070
Stoneham MS 700/6-8
101 Central St 02180 781-279-3840
Christine McMenimen, prin. Fax 279-3843

Edgewood/Greater Boston Academy 100/PK-12
108 Pond St 02180 781-665-9053
Fax 665-3264

Stoughton, Norfolk, Pop. 27,500
Stoughton SD 4,100/PK-12
232 Pearl St 02072 781-344-4000
Claire McCarthy, supt. Fax 344-6417
www.stoughtonschools.org/
O'Donnell MS 1,000/6-8
211 Cushing St 02072 781-344-7002
Wayne R. Hester, prin. Fax 297-5263
Stoughton HS 1,300/9-12
232 Pearl St 02072 781-344-7001
Philip Iacobacci, prin. Fax 341-6041

Stow, Middlesex
Nashoba Regional SD
Supt. — See Bolton
Hale MS 300/6-8
55 Hartley Rd 01775 978-897-4788
Margaret Morgan, prin. Fax 897-3631

Sudbury, Middlesex
Lincoln-Sudbury SD 1,400/9-12
390 Lincoln Rd 01776 978-443-9961
John Ritchie, supt. Fax 443-8824
www.lsrhs.net/
Lincoln-Sudbury Regional HS 1,400/9-12
390 Lincoln Rd 01776 978-443-9961
John Ritchie, prin. Fax 443-8824

Sudbury SD 3,000/K-8
40 Fairbank Rd 01776 978-443-1058
John Brackett, supt. Fax 443-9001
www.sudbury.k12.ma.us
Curtis MS 1,000/6-8
22 Pratts Mill Rd 01776 978-443-1071
Kathryn J. Codianne, prin. Fax 443-1098

Sutton, Worcester
Sutton SD 1,700/PK-12
383 Boston Rd 01590 508-581-1600
Cecilia DiBella, supt. Fax 865-6463
Sutton HS 400/9-12
Boston Rd 01590 508-581-1640
Gail Van Buren, prin. Fax 917-0063
Sutton MS 400/6-8
409 Boston Rd 01590 508-581-1630
William Harper, prin. Fax 865-6463

Swampscott, Essex, Pop. 13,650
Swampscott SD 2,400/K-12
207 Forest Ave 01907 781-596-8800
Matthew Malone Ed.D., supt. Fax 598-4379
swampscottk12ma.us/
Swampscott HS 800/9-12
207 Forest Ave 01907 781-596-8830
Steve O'Brien Ed.D., prin. Fax 598-4379
Swampscott MS 600/6-8
71 Greenwood Ave 01907 781-596-8820
Ronald Landman Ed.D., prin. Fax 593-2126

Marian Court College Post-Sec.
35 Littles Point Rd 01907 781-595-6768

Swansea, Bristol
Swansea SD 2,100/K-12
1 Gardners Neck Rd 02777 508-675-1195
Stephen C. Flanagan, supt. Fax 672-1040
www.swanseaschools.org
Case HS, 70 School St 02777 600/9-12
Brian McCann, prin. 508-675-7483
Case JHS, 195 Main St 02777 500/6-8
Chris Stanton, prin. 508-675-0116

New England Christian Academy 300/PK-12
271 Sharps Lot Rd 02777 508-676-3011
Dr. Gary Morris, prin. Fax 646-0392

Taunton, Bristol, Pop. 56,781
Bristol-Plymouth Regional-Tech SD
940 County St 02780 508-823-5151
John Avery, supt. Fax 880-7287
www.bptech.org
Bristol-Plymouth Regional Technical S Vo/Tech
940 County St 02780 508-823-5151
Richard Gross, prin. Fax 822-2687

Taunton SD 8,400/PK-12
50 Williams St 02780 508-821-1100
Donald Cleary, supt. Fax 821-1177
www.tauntonschools.org
Friedman MS 900/5-8
500 Norton Ave 02780 508-821-1493
John Cabral, prin. Fax 821-3185
Mulcahey MS 500/5-8
28 Clifford St 02780 508-821-1255
Dr. Anthony Azar, prin. Fax 821-1360
Parker MS 500/5-8
50 Williams St 02780 508-821-1112
Raymond O'Malley, prin. Fax 821-1361
Taunton HS 2,000/9-12
50 Williams St 02780 508-821-1101
Matt Mattos, prin. Fax 821-1362
Other Schools – See East Taunton

Coyle & Cassidy HS 700/9-12
2 Hamilton St 02780 508-823-6164
Dr. Mary Pat Tranter, prin. Fax 823-2530
Rob Roy Academy Taunton Campus Post-Sec.
1 School St 02780 508-822-1405
Taunton Catholic MS 300/5-8
61 Summer St 02780 508-822-0491
Margaret Menear, prin. Fax 824-0469

Tewksbury, Middlesex, Pop. 11,000
Tewksbury SD 4,800/PK-12
139 Pleasant St 01876 978-640-7800
Christine McGrath, supt. Fax 640-7804
www.mec.edu/tewksbury/
Tewksbury Memorial HS 1,100/9-12
320 Pleasant St 01876 978-640-7825
Gerald Ferris, prin. Fax 640-7829
Wynn MS 800/7-8
1 Griffin Way 01876 978-640-7846
John Donoghue, prin. Fax 640-7850

Electrology Institute of New England Post-Sec.
1501 Main St Ste 50 01876 800-548-6339

Topsfield, Essex, Pop. 2,711
Masconomet SD 2,000/7-12
20 Endicott Rd 01983 978-887-2323
Claire Sheff Kohn, supt. Fax 887-3573
www.masconomet.org
Masconomet Regional HS 1,300/9-12
20 Endicott Rd 01983 978-887-2323
Pamela Culver, prin. Fax 887-7243
Masconomet Regional MS 700/7-8
20 Endicott Rd 01983 978-887-2323
Catherine Cullinane, prin. Fax 887-1991

Townsend, Middlesex, Pop. 1,164
North Middlesex SD 4,800/PK-12
23 Main St 01469 978-597-8713
James McCormick, supt. Fax 597-6534
nmiddlesex.mec.edu
Hawthorne Brook MS 600/6-8
64 Brookline St 01469 978-597-6914
Pamela Miller, prin. Fax 597-5261

North Middlesex Regional HS 1,200/9-12
19 Main St 01469 978-597-8721
James O'Shea, prin. Fax 597-0350
Other Schools – See Pepperell

Turners Falls, Franklin, Pop. 4,731
Franklin County Technical SD
82 Industrial Blvd 01376 413-863-9561
Dr. Steven Johnson, supt. Fax 863-2816
www.fcts.org
Franklin County Technical HS Vo/Tech
82 Industrial Blvd 01376 413-863-9561
Paul Cohen, prin. Fax 863-2816

Gill-Montague SD 1,300/PK-12
35 Crocker Ave 01376 413-863-9324
Sue M. Gee, supt. Fax 863-4560
www.gmrsd.k14.mass.edu
Other Schools – See Montague

Edwards Academy 100/K-12
251 Millers Falls Rd 01376 413-863-3700
Alfred Popp, hdmstr. Fax 863-8170
Hallmark Institute of Photography Post-Sec.
PO Box 308 01376 413-863-2478

Tyngsboro, Middlesex
Greater Lowell Technical HSD
250 Pawtucket Blvd 01879 978-441-4800
James M. Cassin, supt. Fax 441-5353
www.gltech.org
Greater Lowell Technical HS Vo/Tech
250 Pawtucket Blvd 01879 978-441-4807
Mary Jo Santoro, prin. Fax 441-5353

Tyngsborough SD 2,300/PK-12
50 Norris Rd 01879 978-649-7488
David Hawkins, supt. Fax 649-7199
Tyngsborough HS 600/9-12
36 Norris Rd 01879 978-649-7571
Donald Ciampa, prin. Fax 649-4210
Tyngsboro MS 500/6-8
50 Norris Rd 01879 978-649-3115
Stephen Coughlan, prin. Fax 649-8673

Academy of Notre Dame HS 300/9-12
180 Middlesex Rd 01879 978-649-7611
Sr. Mary Farren, prin. Fax 649-2909

Upton, Worcester, Pop. 2,347
Blackstone Valley Regional Vo/Tech SD
65 Pleasant St 01568 508-529-7758
Michael Fitzpatrick, supt. Fax 529-3079
www.valleytech.k12.ma.us
Blackstone Valley Regional Vo-Tech HS Vo/Tech
65 Pleasant St 01568 508-529-7758
Richard Brennan, prin. Fax 839-2403

Mendon-Upton Regional SD
Supt. — See Mendon
Nipmuc Regional HS 800/8-12
90 Pleasant St 01568 508-529-2130
Joan Scribner, prin. Fax 529-2129

Uxbridge, Worcester, Pop. 3,400
Uxbridge SD 2,100/K-12
62 Capron St 01569 508-278-8648
Daniel J. Stefanilo, supt. Fax 278-8612
uxbridge.mec.edu
Uxbridge HS 500/9-12
62 Capron St 01569 508-278-8636
George Zini, prin. Fax 278-8627
Whitin MS 800/5-8
120 Granite St 01569 508-278-8640
Howard Boyaj, prin. Fax 278-8639

Vineyard Haven, Dukes, Pop. 1,762
Martha's Vineyard SD 800/9-12
4 Pine St 02568 508-693-2007
Dr. James Weiss, supt. Fax 693-3190
www.mv.k12.ma.us
Other Schools – See Oak Bluffs

Wakefield, Middlesex, Pop. 24,825
Northeast Metro Vocational SD
100 Hemlock Rd 01880 781-246-0810
Patricia R. Cronin, supt. Fax 246-4919
northeastmetrotech.com
Northeast Metro Regional Vocational HS Vo/Tech
100 Hemlock Rd 01880 781-246-0810
John Crowley, prin. Fax 246-4919

Wakefield SD 3,400/K-12
60 Farm St 01880 781-246-6400
Dr. Maynard Suffredini, supt. Fax 245-9164
www.wakefield.k12.ma.us/
Galvin JHS 1,100/5-8
525 Main St 01880 781-246-6410
Paula Mullen, prin. Fax 224-5009
Wakefield Memorial HS 1,000/9-12
60 Farm St 01880 781-246-6440
Fax 246-4714

Our Lady of Nazareth Academy 100/9-12
14 Winship Dr 01880 781-245-5210
Maria Melendez Ph.D., prin. Fax 245-6648

Walpole, Norfolk, Pop. 5,495
Norfolk County Agricultural SD
400 Main St 02081 508-668-0268
Angela Avery, supt. Fax 668-0612
www.norfolkaggie.org
Norfolk County Agricultural HS Vo/Tech
400 Main St 02081 508-668-0268
Gail Murphy, prin. Fax 668-0612

Walpole SD 4,100/PK-12
135 School St 02081 508-660-7200
Kathleen A. Smith, supt. Fax 668-1167
www.walpole.ma.us
Johnson MS 500/6-8
111 Robbins Rd 02081 508-660-7242
Jean Krim, prin. Fax 660-7240
Walpole HS 1,000/9-12
275 Common St 02081 508-660-7257
Frank Sambuceti, prin. Fax 850-7958
Other Schools – See East Walpole

Waltham, Middlesex, Pop. 58,894
Waltham SD 4,700/PK-12
617 Lexington St 02452 781-314-5440
Dr. Susan I. Parrella, supt. Fax 314-5411
www.city.waltham.ma.us/SCHOOL/WebPage/tofc.htm
Kennedy MS 500/6-8
510 Moody St 02453 781-314-5560
John Cawley, prin. Fax 314-5571
McDevitt MS 600/6-8
75 Church St 02452 781-314-5590
Brad Morgan, prin. Fax 314-5601
Waltham HS 1,500/9-12
617 Lexington St 02452 781-314-5440
John Graceffa, prin. Fax 647-0309

Bentley College Post-Sec.
175 Forest St 02452 781-891-2000
Blaine The Beauty Career School Post-Sec.
314 Moody St 02453 781-899-1500
Brandeis University Post-Sec.
415 South St 02453 781-736-3500
Center for Digital Imaging Arts at BU Post-Sec.
282 Moody St 02453 800-808-2342
Chapel Hill-Chauncy Hall S 200/9-12
785 Beaver St 02452 781-894-2644
Siri Akal Khalsa, hdmstr. Fax 894-8768

Ware, Hampshire, Pop. 6,533
Ware SD 1,200/K-12
PO Box 240 01082 413-967-4271
Richard B. Holzman, supt. Fax 967-9580
www.ware.k12.ma.us
Ware JSHS 400/8-12
237 West St 01082 413-967-6234
Richard Seveney, prin. Fax 967-9053

Wareham, Plymouth, Pop. 19,232
Wareham SD 3,500/PK-12
54 Marion Rd 02571 508-291-3500
James D. Collins, supt. Fax 291-3578
www.wareham.mec.edu/district/
Wareham HS 1,000/9-12
7 Viking Dr 02571 508-291-3510
John Amaral, prin. Fax 291-3577
Wareham MS 900/6-8
4 Viking Dr 02571 508-291-3550
Glenn Brand, prin. Fax 291-3538

Warren, Worcester, Pop. 1,516
Quaboag Regional SD 1,500/PK-12
PO Box 1538 01083 413-436-9256
Carol Jacobs, supt. Fax 436-9738
www.quaboag.org
Quaboag Regional MSHS 700/7-12
PO Box 909 01083 413-436-5991
Charles Collins, prin. Fax 436-9636

Watertown, Middlesex, Pop. 32,915
Watertown SD 2,400/K-12
30 Common St 02472 617-926-7700
Dr. Steven A. Hiersche, supt. Fax 923-1234
www.watertown.k12.ma.us
Watertown HS 700/9-12
50 Columbia St 02472 617-926-7760
Michael Noftsker, prin. Fax 926-7723
Watertown MS 600/6-8
68 Waverley Ave 02472 617-926-7783
James Carter, prin. Fax 926-5407

New England School of Acupuncture Post-Sec.
40 Belmont St 02472 617-926-1788
Perkins School for the Blind Post-Sec.
175 N Beacon St 02472 617-924-3434

Wayland, Middlesex, Pop. 2,500
Wayland SD 3,000/K-12
PO Box 408 01778 508-358-3774
Gary Burton, supt. Fax 358-7708
www.wayland.k12.ma.us
Wayland HS 900/9-12
264 Old Connecticut Path 01778 508-358-3705
Charles Ruopp, prin. Fax 358-8082
Wayland MS 700/6-8
201 Main St 01778 508-655-6670
Charlie Schlegel, prin. Fax 655-2548

Webster, Worcester, Pop. 11,849
Webster SD 1,200/K-12
PO Box 430 01570 508-943-0104
Vincent Simone Ed.D., supt. Fax 949-2364
Bartlett JSHS 800/7-12
52 Lake Pkwy 01570 508-943-8552
Michael Hackenson, prin. Fax 949-8274

Wellesley, Norfolk, Pop. 26,600
Wellesley SD 4,200/K-12
40 Kingsbury St 02481 781-446-6210
Matthew King, supt. Fax 446-6207
www.wellesley.mec.edu/
Wellesley HS 1,100/9-12
50 Rice St 02481 781-446-6290
Rena Mirkin, prin. Fax 237-6004
Wellesley MS 900/6-8
50 Kingsbury St 02481 781-446-6235
John D'Auria, prin. Fax 239-1206

Dana Hall S 500/6-12
45 Dana Rd 02482 781-235-3010
Blair Jenkins, prin. Fax 235-6491

Massachusetts Bay Community College Post-Sec.
50 Oakland St 02481 781-239-3000
Wellesley College Post-Sec.
106 Central St 02481 781-235-0320

Wendell, Franklin

Lake Grove School-Maple Valley Post-Sec.
PO Box 767 01379 888-585-9007

Wenham, Essex, Pop. 4,212
Hamilton-Wenham SD 2,200/K-12
5 School St 01984 978-468-5310
Dr. Marinel D. McGrath, supt. Fax 468-7889
www.hw-regional.k12.ma.us
Other Schools – See South Hamilton

Gordon College Post-Sec.
255 Grapevine Rd 01984 978-927-2300

West Barnstable, Barnstable, Pop. 1,508

Cape Cod Community College Post-Sec.
2240 Iyannough Rd 02668 508-362-2131

Westborough, Worcester, Pop. 3,917
Westborough SD 3,500/PK-12
PO Box 1152 01581 508-836-7700
Dr. Anne Towle, supt. Fax 836-7704
www.westborough.org
Gibbons MS 600/7-8
20 Fisher St 01581 508-836-7740
Dr. David Fredette, prin. Fax 836-7744
Westborough HS 1,000/9-12
90 W Main St 01581 508-836-7720
John Pierce, prin. Fax 836-7723

West Boylston, Worcester, Pop. 6,611
West Boylston SD 1,100/K-12
125 Crescent St 01583 508-835-2917
Thomas J. Kane, supt. Fax 835-8992
www.wbschools.com
West Boylston S 700/6-12
125 Crescent St 01583 508-835-4475
Francine Bullock, prin. Fax 835-8992

West Bridgewater, Plymouth
West Bridgewater SD 1,000/PK-12
2 Spring St 02379 508-894-1230
Dr. Robert H. White, supt. Fax 894-1232
wbridgewaterschools.com
West Bridgewater JSHS 400/7-12
155 W Center St 02379 508-894-1220
Lew Klaiman, prin. Fax 894-1226

New England Baptist Academy 200/K-12
560 N Main St 02379 508-584-5188
Rev. Joseph Coppola, prin. Fax 584-7555

Westfield, Hampden, Pop. 40,560
Westfield SD 6,000/PK-12
22 Ashley St 01085 413-572-6403
Dr. Thomas McDowell, supt. Fax 572-6518
www.k12.westfield.ma.us/
North MS 800/6-8
350 Southampton Rd 01085 413-572-6441
Ronald Rix, prin. Fax 572-1669
Parkside Academy 5-8
22 Ashley St 01085 413-562-7421
Joseph Dupelle, prin. Fax 572-6355
South MS 700/6-8
30 W Silver St 01085 413-568-1900
F. Dennis Fahey, prin. Fax 572-4892
Westfield HS 1,600/9-12
177 Montgomery Rd 01085 413-572-6466
Raymond Broderick, prin. Fax 572-6346
Westfield Vocational Technical HS Vo/Tech
33 Smith Ave 01085 413-572-6533
Steven Pippin, prin. Fax 572-6542

St. Marys HS 100/9-12
27 Bartlett St 01085 413-568-5692
Paul Romani, prin. Fax 562-3501
Westfield State College Post-Sec.
PO Box 1630 01086 413-572-5300

Westford, Middlesex
Nashoba Valley Technical SD
100 Littleton Rd 01886 978-692-4711
Judith Klimkiewicz, supt. Fax 392-0570
Nashoba Valley Technical HS Vo/Tech
100 Littleton Rd 01886 978-692-4711
Victor Kiloski, prin. Fax 392-0570

Westford SD 5,000/K-12
23 Depot St 01886 978-692-5560
Stephen C. Foster, supt. Fax 692-4842
www.westford.mec.edu/schools
Blanchard MS 600/6-8
14 West St 01886 978-692-5582
Suzanne McGrail, prin. Fax 692-5598
Stony Brook S 600/6-8
9 Farmers Way 01886 978-692-2708
Joan Barry, prin. Fax 692-5391
Westford Academy 1,400/9-12
30 Patten St 01886 978-692-5570
Ellen Parker, prin. Fax 692-5567

Westhampton, Hampshire
Hampshire SD 800/7-12
19 Stage Rd 01027 413-527-7200
Dr. Barbara Ripa, supt. Fax 529-9497
Hampshire Regional JSHS 800/7-12
19 Stage Rd 01027 413-527-7680
James Connolly, prin. Fax 527-1831

Westminster, Worcester
Ashburnham-Westminster Regional SD 2,400/PK-12
11 Oakmont Ave 01473 978-827-1434
Mr. Michael Zapantis, supt. Fax 827-5969
www.awrsd.org

Other Schools – See Ashburnham

West Newbury, Essex
Pentucket SD 3,500/PK-12
22 Main St 01985 978-363-2280
William Compton Ed.D., supt. Fax 363-1165
www.prsd.org
Pentucket Regional HS 900/9-12
24 Main St 01985 978-363-5507
Arlene Townes, prin. Fax 363-2730
Pentucket Regional MS 600/7-8
20 Main St 01985 978-363-2957
Renzo Binaghi, prin. Fax 363-2720

Weston, Middlesex, Pop. 10,200
Weston SD 2,400/PK-12
89 Wellesley St 02493 781-529-8080
Alan Oliff, supt. Fax 529-8097
www.westonschools.org/
Weston HS 700/9-12
444 Wellesley St 02493 781-529-8030
Robert Desaulniers, prin. Fax 529-8043
Weston MS 600/6-8
456 Wellesley St 02493 781-529-8060
John Gibbons, prin. Fax 529-8072

Blessed John XXIII National Seminary Post-Sec.
558 South Ave 02493 781-899-5500
Cambridge S of Weston 300/9-12
45 Georgian Rd 02493 781-642-8600
Jane Moulding, hdmstr. Fax 398-8344
Regis College Post-Sec.
235 Wellesley St 02493 781-768-2000
Rivers S 400/6-12
333 Winter St 02493 781-235-9300
Thomas Olverson, hdmstr. Fax 239-3614

Westport, Bristol, Pop. 13,852
Westport Community SD 1,900/PK-12
17 Main Rd 02790 508-636-1137
Dr. Linda L. Galton, supt. Fax 636-1146
www.westportschools.org
Westport HS 500/9-12
19 Main Rd 02790 508-636-1050
Johanna Riley, prin. Fax 636-1053
Westport MS 600/5-8
400 Old County Rd 02790 508-636-1090
James Gibney, prin. Fax 636-7413

West Roxbury, See Boston
Boston SD
Supt. — See Boston
Brook Farm Business & Service Academy 9-12
1205 VFW Pkwy 02132 617-635-6956
Edmund Donnelly, prin. Fax 635-7894
Media Communications Technology HS 9-12
1205 VFW Pkwy 02132 617-635-8935
Sung-Joon Pai, prin. Fax 635-7912
Parkway Academy of Technology & Health 9-12
1205 VFW Pkwy 02132 617-635-6732
Barbara Ferrer, prin. Fax 635-8917
Urban Science Academy 9-12
1205 VFW Pkwy 02132 617-635-8930
Rasheed Meadows, prin. Fax 635-7895
West Roxbury Education Complex 1,300/9-12
1205 VFW Pkwy 02132 617-635-8917
Donald Pellegrini, hdmstr. Fax 635-7997

Catholic Memorial HS 700/7-12
235 Baker St 02132 617-469-8000
Richard Chisholm, prin. Fax 325-0888
Roxbury Latin S 300/7-12
101 Saint Theresa Ave 02132 617-325-4920
Kerry P. Brennan, hdmstr. Fax 325-3585

West Springfield, Hampden, Pop. 27,953
West Springfield SD 4,000/PK-12
26 Central St 01089 413-263-3290
Dr. Suzanne Marotta, supt. Fax 739-8748
www.wsps.org
West Springfield HS 1,200/9-12
425 Piper Rd 01089 413-263-3400
Anne McKenzie, prin. Fax 781-4836
West Springfield MS 1,000/6-8
31 Middle School Dr 01089 413-263-3406
Thomas McNulty, prin. Fax 781-0965

Kay Harvey Hairdressing Academy Post-Sec.
11 Central St 01089 413-732-7117

Westwood, Norfolk, Pop. 12,557
Westwood SD 2,600/PK-12
220 Nahatan St 02090 781-326-7500
Fax 326-8154
www.westwood.k12.ma.us
Thurston MS 700/6-8
850 High St 02090 781-326-7500
Fax 326-2709
Westwood HS 700/9-12
200 Nahatan St 02090 781-326-7500
Emily Parks, prin. Fax 461-8561

Xaverian Brothers HS 700/9-12
800 Clapboardtree St 02090 781-326-6392
Br. Daniel Skala, hdmstr. Fax 320-0458

West Yarmouth, Barnstable, Pop. 5,409
Dennis-Yarmouth SD
Supt. — See South Yarmouth
Mattacheese MS 700/6-8
440 Higgins Crowell Rd 02673 508-778-7979
Emily Mezzetti, prin. Fax 778-7987

Weymouth, Norfolk, Pop. 53,900
Weymouth SD 6,400/K-12
111 Middle St 02189 781-335-1460
Joseph Rull, supt. Fax 335-8777
www.weymouth.ma.us/schools/index.asp
Weymouth HS 1,600/9-12
1 Wildcat Way 02190 781-337-7500
Marilyn Slattery, prin. Fax 340-2568
Other Schools – See East Weymouth

South Shore Christian Academy 300/PK-12
45 Broad St 02188 781-331-4340
Dr. John Seel, admin. Fax 331-9956

Whitinsville, Worcester, Pop. 5,639
Northbridge SD 2,500/PK-12
87 Linwood Ave 01588 508-234-8156
Paul Soojian, supt. Fax 234-8469
www.northbridge.k12.ma.us
Northbridge HS 700/9-12
427 Linwood Ave 01588 508-234-6221
Christine Johnson, prin. Fax 234-0802
Northbridge MS 800/5-8
171 Linwood Ave 01588 508-234-8718
Michael Gauthier, prin.

Whitinsville Christian S 600/K-12
279 Linwood Ave 01588 508-234-8211
Lance Engbers, hdmstr. Fax 234-8212

Whitman, Plymouth, Pop. 13,240
Whitman-Hanson SD 4,300/PK-12
600 Franklin St 02382 781-618-7411
John F. McEwan Ed.D., supt. Fax 618-7498
www.whrsd.k12.ma.us
Whitman-Hanson Regional HS 1,200/9-12
600 Franklin St 02382 781-618-7020
Pamela A. Gould, prin. Fax 618-7099
Whitman MS 600/6-8
77 Corthell Ave 02382 781-781-7035
George Ferro, prin. Fax 781-7091
Other Schools – See Hanson

Wilbraham, Hampden, Pop. 3,352
Hampden-Wilbraham SD 3,800/PK-12
621 Main St 01095 413-596-3884
Dr. Paul Gagliarducci, supt. Fax 599-1328
www.hwrsd.org
Minnechaug Regional HS 1,300/9-12
621 Main St 01095 413-596-9011
Martin O'Shea, prin. Fax 596-8907
Wilbraham MS 500/7-8
466 Stony Hill Rd 01095 413-596-9061
Stephen Hale, prin. Fax 596-9382
Other Schools – See Hampden

Wilbraham & Monson Academy 400/6-12
423 Main St 01095 413-596-6811
Rodney LaBrecque, hdmstr. Fax 596-2448

Williamstown, Berkshire, Pop. 4,791
Mount Greylock Regional SD 800/7-12
1781 Cold Spring Rd 01267 413-458-9582
Dr. William Travis, supt. Fax 458-2856
www.mgrhs.org
Mount Greylock Regional JSHS 800/7-12
1781 Cold Spring Rd 01267 413-458-9582
Ellen Kaiser, prin. Fax 458-2856

Buxton S 100/9-12
291 South St 01267 413-458-3919
Fax 458-9427
Williams College 01267 Post-Sec.
413-597-3131

Wilmington, Middlesex, Pop. 17,654
Wilmington SD 3,800/PK-12
161 Church St 01887 978-694-6000
William H. McAlduff, supt. Fax 694-6005
www.wilmington.k12.ma.us
Wilmington HS 900/9-12
159 Church St 01887 978-694-6060
Eric Tracy, prin. Fax 694-6074
Wilmington MS 900/6-8
25 Carter Ln 01887 978-694-6080
Frank Orlando, prin. Fax 694-6085

Winchendon, Worcester, Pop. 4,316
Winchendon SD 1,800/PK-12
175 Grove St 01475 978-297-0031
Peter Azar Ed.D., supt. Fax 297-5250
www.winchendonk12.org
Murdock MSHS 800/7-12
3 Memorial Dr 01475 978-297-1256
Patricia Washburn, prin. Fax 297-0509

Winchendon S 200/8-12
172 Ash St 01475 978-297-1223
J. William Labelle, hdmstr. Fax 297-0911

Winchester, Middlesex, Pop. 20,267
Winchester SD 3,600/PK-12
154 Horn Pond Brook Rd 01890 781-721-7004
V. James Marini, supt. Fax 721-0016
www.winchester.k12.ma.us
McCall MS 900/6-8
458 Main St 01890 781-721-7026
Evander French, prin. Fax 721-1235
Winchester HS 900/9-12
80 Skillings Rd 01890 781-721-7020
Thomas Gwin, prin. Fax 721-1366

Winthrop, Suffolk, Pop. 18,127
Winthrop SD 1,500/K-12
45 Pauline St 02152 617-846-5500
Dr. Steven Jenkins, supt. Fax 539-0891
www.winthrop.k12.ma.us
Winthrop HS 600/9-12
400 Main St 02152 617-846-5500
Stephen Chrabaszcz, prin. Fax 539-0535
Winthrop MS 500/6-8
151 Pauline St 02152 617-846-5507
Zoe Haskell, prin. Fax 539-0891

Woburn, Middlesex, Pop. 37,809
Woburn SD 4,600/K-12
55 Locust St 01801 781-937-8233
Carl Batchelder Ed.D., supt. Fax 937-3805
woburnpublicschools.com/
Joyce JHS 500/6-8
55 Locust St 01801 781-937-8233
W. Spencer Mullin Ph.D., prin. Fax 932-0668
Kennedy JHS 600/6-8
33 Middle St 01801 781-937-8230
Carl Nelson, prin. Fax 937-8223
Woburn HS 1,400/9-12
88 Montvale Ave 01801 781-937-8210
Robert Norton, prin. Fax 937-8216

Catherine Hinds Institute of Esthetics Post-Sec.
300 Wildwood Ave 01801 781-935-3344
ITT Technical Institute Post-Sec.
10 Forbes Rd 01801 781-937-8324

Woods Hole, Barnstable

Woods Hole Oceanographic Institution Post-Sec.
86 Water St 02543 508-457-2000

Worcester, Worcester, Pop. 175,706
Worcester SD 24,100/PK-12
20 Irving St 01609 508-799-3116
James A. Caradonio Ed.D., supt. Fax 799-3119
www.wpsweb.com/default2.asp
Accelerated Learning Lab S 800/PK-12
15 Claremont St 01610 508-799-3077
Jane Grady, prin. Fax 799-8202
Burncoat HS 1,300/9-12
179 Burncoat St 01606 508-799-3300
John Bierfeldt, prin. Fax 799-8206
Burncoat MS 700/7-8
135 Burncoat St 01606 508-799-3390
Lisa A. Houlihan, prin. Fax 799-8207
Doherty Memorial HS 1,500/9-12
299 Highland St 01602 508-799-3270
Sally Maloney, prin. Fax 799-3276
Forest Grove MS 1,000/7-8
495 Grove St 01605 508-799-3420
Maureen McCullough, prin. Fax 799-8218
North HS 1,200/9-12
150 Harrington Way 01604 508-799-3370
David Elworthy, prin. Fax 799-8252
South Community HS 1,400/9-12
170 Apricot St 01603 508-799-3325
Maureen R. Ciccone, prin. Fax 799-8242
Sullivan MS 1,100/7-8
140 Apricot St 01603 508-799-3350
Robert Jennings, prin. Fax 799-8244
University Park Campus S 200/7-12
12 Freeland St 01603 508-799-3591
June Eressy, coord. Fax 799-8159
Worcester East MS 800/7-8
420 Grafton St 01604 508-799-3430
Rose M. Dawkins, prin. Fax 799-8251
Worcester Vocational HS Vo/Tech
2 Grove St 01605 508-799-1980
Francis P. Canali, prin. Fax 799-1933

Assumption College Post-Sec.
500 Salisbury St 01609 508-767-7000
Bancroft S 600/K-12
110 Shore Dr 01605 508-853-2640
Scott Reisinger, hdmstr. Fax 853-7824
Bancroft School of Massage Therapy Post-Sec.
333 Shrewsbury St 01604 508-757-7923
Becker College Post-Sec.
61 Sever St 01609 508-791-9241
Clark University Post-Sec.
950 Main St 01610 508-793-7711
College of the Holy Cross Post-Sec.
1 College St 01610 508-793-2011
First Assembly Christian Academy 200/PK-12
30 Tyler Prentice Rd 01605 508-853-8641
April Graziano, prin. Fax 853-2169
Hair in Motion Beauty Academy Post-Sec.
73 Hamilton St 01604 508-756-6060
Holy Name Central Catholic HS 900/7-12
144 Granite St 01604 508-753-6371
Mary Riordan, admin. Fax 831-1287
Notre Dame Academy 300/9-12
425 Salisbury St 01609 508-757-6200
Sr. Ann Morrison, prin. Fax 757-7200
Quinsigamond Community College Post-Sec.
670 W Boylston St 01606 508-853-2300
Rob Roy Academy Post-Sec.
150 Pleasant St 01609 508-799-2111
St. Mary HS 100/7-12
50 Richland St 01610 508-753-1170
Rev. Thaddeus Stachura, prin. Fax 795-0560
St. Peter-Marian Central HS 1,100/7-12
781 Grove St 01605 508-852-5555
Matthew Sturgis, prin. Fax 852-7238
Salter School Post-Sec.
155 Ararat St 01606 508-853-1074
University of Massachusetts at Worcester Post-Sec.
55 Lake Ave N 01655 508-856-8989
Worcester Academy 600/6-12
81 Providence St 01604 508-754-5302
Dexter Morse, hdmstr. Fax 752-2382
Worcester Polytechnic Institute Post-Sec.
100 Institute Rd 01609 508-831-5000
Worcester State College Post-Sec.
486 Chandler St 01602 508-929-8000
Yeshiva Achei Tmimim Academy 100/PK-12
22 Newton Ave 01602 508-752-0904
Rabbi Hershel Fogelman, dean Fax 799-7413

Wrentham, Norfolk
King Philip SD
Supt. — See Norfolk
King Philip Regional HS 1,100/9-12
201 Franklin St 02093 508-384-1000
Elaine Hanson, prin. Fax 384-1006

MICHIGAN

MICHIGAN DEPARTMENT OF EDUCATION
608 W Allegan St, Lansing 48933-1524
Telephone 517-373-3324
Fax 517-335-4565
Website http://www.michigan.gov/mde
Superintendent of Public Instruction   Michael Flanagan

MICHIGAN BOARD OF EDUCATION
608 W Allegan St, Lansing 48933-1524
President   Kathleen N. Straus

INTERMEDIATE SCHOOL DISTRICTS (ISD)

Allegan County ISD
Robert Brenner, supt.   269-673-2161
310 Thomas St, Allegan 49010   Fax 673-2361
www.alleganisd.org
Alpena/Montmorency/Alcona ESD
Thomas Lanway, supt.   989-354-3101
2118 US Highway 23 S   Fax 356-3385
Alpena 49707
www.amaesd.k12.mi.us
Barry ISD
James A. Hund, supt.   269-945-9545
535 W Woodlawn Ave   Fax 945-2575
Hastings 49058
www.barryisd.org
Bay-Arenac ISD
Michael R. Dewey, supt.   989-686-4410
4228 2 Mile Rd, Bay City 48706   Fax 667-3286
www.baisd.net
Berrien County ISD
Jeffrey Siegel, supt.   269-471-7725
711 Saint Joseph Ave   Fax 471-2941
Berrien Springs 49103
www.remc11.k12.mi.us/bcisd
Branch ISD
Michael Beckwith, supt.   517-279-5730
370 Morse St, Coldwater 49036   Fax 279-5766
www.branch-isd.org
Calhoun ISD
Christopher Wigent, supt.   269-781-5141
17111 G Dr N, Marshall 49068   Fax 781-7071
www.calhounisd.org
Charlevoix/Emmet ISD
Mark Eckhardt, supt.   231-547-9947
8568 Mercer Rd, Charlevoix 49720 Fax 547-5621
www.charemisd.org
Cheboygan/Otsego/Presque Isle ISD
Mary Vratanina, supt.   231-238-9394
6065 Learning Ln   Fax 238-8551
Indian River 49749
www.copesd.k12.mi.us
Clare-Gladwin RESD
Doug Dodge, supt.   989-386-3851
4041 E Mannsiding Rd   Fax 386-3238
Clare 48617
www.cgresd.net/
Clinton County RESA
Lawrence Lloyd, supt.   989-224-6831
1013 S US Highway 27 Ste A   Fax 224-9574
Saint Johns 48879
www.ccresa.org
C.O.O.R. ISD
Robert Jones, supt.   989-275-9555
PO Box 827, Roscommon 48653   Fax 275-5881
www.coorisd.k12.mi.us
Copper Country ISD
Dennis Harbour, supt.   906-482-4250
PO Box 270, Hancock 49930   Fax 482-1931
www.copperisd.org
Delta/Schoolcraft ISD
Michael Koster, supt.   906-786-9300
2525 3rd Ave S, Escanaba 49829   Fax 786-9318
dsisd.k12.mi.us
Dickinson/Iron ISD
Johanna Ostwald, supt.   906-779-2690
1074 Pyle Dr, Kingsford 49802   Fax 779-2669
www.diisd.org
Eastern UP ISD
Peter Everson, supt., PO Box 883 906-632-3373
Sault Sainte Marie 49783   Fax 632-1125
www.eup.k12.mi.us
Eaton ISD
Albert Widner, supt.   517-543-5500
1790 Packard Hwy   Fax 543-6633
Charlotte 48813
www.eaton.k12.mi.us/
Genesee ISD
Thomas Svitkovich Ed.D., supt.   810-591-4400
2413 W Maple Ave, Flint 48507   Fax 591-7570
www.geneseeisd.org

Gogebic/Ontonagon ISD
Bruce Mayle, supt.   906-575-3438
PO Box 218, Bergland 49910   Fax 575-3373
www.goisd.k12.mi.us
Gratiot/Isabella RESD
Michael Matlosz, supt.   989-875-5101
PO Box 310, Ithaca 48847   Fax 875-7531
www.edzone.net/giresd/
Hillsdale ISD
Robert W. Henthorne, supt.   517-437-0990
310 W Bacon St, Hillsdale 49242 Fax 439-4388
www.hillsdale-isd.org
Huron ISD
Janet Richards, supt.   989-269-6406
711 E Soper Rd, Bad Axe 48413   Fax 269-9218
www.hisd.k12.mi.us
Ingham ISD
Stanley Kogut, supt.   517-676-1051
2630 W Howell Rd, Mason 48854   Fax 676-1277
www.inghamisd.org
Ionia County ISD
George Hubbard, supt.   616-527-4900
2191 Harwood Rd, Ionia 48846   Fax 527-4731
www.ionia-isd.k12.mi.us
Iosco RESA
Thomas Caldwell, supt.   989-362-3006
27 N Rempert Rd   Fax 362-9076
Tawas City 48763
www.iresa.k12.mi.us
Jackson County ISD
John M. Graves, supt.   517-768-5200
6700 Browns Lake Rd   Fax 787-2026
Jackson 49201
www.jcisd.org
Kalamazoo RESA
W. Craig Misner, supt.   269-385-1500
1819 E Milham Ave   Fax 381-9423
Kalamazoo 49002
www.kresa.org
Kent ISD
Michael S. Weiler, supt.   616-364-1333
2930 Knapp St NE   Fax 364-1488
Grand Rapids 49525
www.kentisd.org
Lapeer County ISD
Joseph Keena, supt.   810-664-5917
1996 W Oregon St, Lapeer 48446   Fax 664-1011
www.lcisd.k12.mi.us
Lenawee ISD
Stephen Krusich, supt.   517-265-2119
4107 N Adrian Hwy, Adrian 49221 Fax 265-7405
scnc.lisd.k12.mi.us
Lewis Cass ISD
John Ostrowski, supt.   269-445-3891
61682 Dailey Rd, Cassopolis 49031 Fax 445-2981
www.lewcass.k12.mi.us
Livingston ESA
Sally Vaughn, supt.   517-546-5550
1425 W Grand River Ave   Fax 546-7047
Howell 48843
www.lesa.k12.mi.us
Macomb ISD
Michael DeVault, supt.   586-228-3300
44001 Garfield Rd   Fax 286-1523
Clinton Township 48038
www.misd.net
Manistee ISD
Charlene Myers, supt.   231-723-4264
772 E Parkdale Ave   Fax 398-3036
Manistee 49660
www.manistee.org
Marquette-Alger RESA
June Schaefer, supt.   906-226-5100
321 E Ohio St, Marquette 49855   Fax 226-5134
www.maresa.k12.mi.us

Mason/Lake ISD
Jeanne Oakes, supt.   231-757-3716
2130 W US Highway 10   Fax 757-2406
Ludington 49431
www.mlisd.k12.mi.us
Mecosta-Osceola ISD
Curtis Finch, supt., 15760 190th Ave 231-796-3543
Big Rapids 49307   Fax 796-3300
www.moisd.org
Menominee ISD
Lawrence Godwin, supt.   906-863-5665
1201 41st Ave, Menominee 49858   Fax 863-7776
www.mc-isd.org
Midland County ESA
Clark Volz, supt.   989-631-5890
3917 Jefferson Ave, Midland 48640 Fax 631-4361
www.mcesa.k12.mi.us
Monroe County ISD
Donald Spencer, supt.   734-242-5799
1101 S Raisinville Rd   Fax 242-0567
Monroe 48161
misd.k12.mi.us/
Montcalm Area ISD
George P. Stamas, supt.   989-831-5261
PO Box 367, Stanton 48888   Fax 831-8727
www.maisd.com
Muskegon Area ISD
Dr. Michael H. Bozym, supt.   231-777-2637
630 Harvey St, Muskegon 49442   Fax 773-3498
www.muskegonisd.org
Newaygo County RESA
Robert E. DeVries, supt.   231-924-0381
4747 W 48th St, Fremont 49412   Fax 924-8910
www.ncresa.org/
Oakland ISD
Vickie Markavitch, supt.   248-209-2000
2111 Pontiac Lake Rd   Fax 209-2206
Waterford 48328
www.oakland.k12.mi.us
Oceana ISD
Jeanne Oakes, supt.   231-873-5651
844 S Griswold St, Hart 49420   Fax 873-5779
oceanaisd.com
Ottawa Area ISD
Karen McPhee, supt.   616-738-8940
13565 Port Sheldon St   Fax 738-8946
Holland 49424
www.oaisd.org
Saginaw ISD
Richard Lane, supt.   989-399-7473
6235 Gratiot Rd, Saginaw   Fax 793-1571
www.sisd.cc/
St. Clair RESA
Dan DeGrow, supt.   810-364-8990
PO Box 1500, Marysville 48040   Fax 364-7474
www.sccresa.org/
St. Joseph County ISD
Dr. Jay Newman, supt.   269-467-5400
62445 Shimmel Rd   Fax 467-4309
Centreville 49032
www.sjcisd.org
Sanilac ISD
Tony Parker, supt.   810-648-4700
175 E Aitken Rd, Peck 48466   Fax 648-5784
www.sanilac.k12.mi.us
Shiawassee RESD
John E. Hagel, supt.   989-743-3471
1025 N Shiawassee St   Fax 743-6477
Corunna 48817
sresd.k12.mi.us/
Traverse Bay Area ISD
Michael Kenney, supt.   231-922-6200
PO Box 6020, Traverse City 49696 Fax 922-6270
www.tbaisd.k12.mi.us
Tuscola ISD
Carol Socha, supt.   989-673-2144
1385 Cleaver Rd, Caro 48723   Fax 673-5366
www.tisd.k12.mi.us

Van Buren ISD
Jeffrey Mills, supt.   269-674-8091
490 S Paw Paw St   Fax 674-8030
Lawrence 49064
www.vbisd.org/

Washtenaw ISD
William Miller, supt.   734-994-8100
PO Box 1406, Ann Arbor 48106   Fax 994-2203

Wayne RESA
Marlene Davis, supt.   734-334-1300
PO Box 807, Wayne 48184   Fax 334-1760
www.resa.net
Wexford/Missaukee ISD
Scott Crosby, supt.   231-876-2260
9907 E 13th St, Cadillac 49601   Fax 876-2272
www.wmisd.org

PUBLIC, PRIVATE AND CATHOLIC SECONDARY SCHOOLS

Ada, Kent
Forest Hills SD
Supt. — See Grand Rapids
Central MS   700/7-8
5810 Ada Dr SE 49301   616-493-8750
Nancy Flink, prin.   Fax 493-8764
Eastern MSHS   2,100/7-12
2200 Pettis Ave NE 49301   616-493-8830
Linda LaBerteaux, prin.   Fax 493-8839

Addison, Lenawee, Pop. 619
Addison Community SD   1,200/K-12
219 N Comstock St 49220   517-547-6123
Richard Naughton, supt.   Fax 547-3838
scnc.addison.k12.mi.us
Addison HS   400/9-12
219 N Comstock St 49220   517-547-6121
Gayle Dodson, prin.   Fax 547-3838
Addison MS   300/6-8
219 N Comstock St 49220   517-547-6125
Kevin Ohrman, prin.   Fax 547-3838

Adrian, Lenawee, Pop. 22,054
Adrian SD   3,200/K-12
227 N Winter St 49221   517-263-2115
Lindle Cochran, supt.   Fax 265-5381
www.adrian.k12.mi.us
Adrian HS   1,200/9-12
785 Riverside Ave 49221   517-263-2181
Gerald Burg, prin.   Fax 263-0814
Adrian MS 7-8   300/7-8
615 Springbrook Ave 49221   517-263-0543
Mike Perez, prin.   Fax 265-5984

Lenawee ISD
4107 N Adrian Hwy 49221   517-265-2119
Stephen Krusich, supt.   Fax 265-7405
scnc.lisd.k12.mi.us
LISD Vocational-Technical Center   Vo/Tech
1372 N Main St 49221   517-263-2108
Larry Schroeder, prin.   Fax 263-9433

Madison SD   1,400/PK-12
3498 Treat Hwy 49221   517-263-0741
James Hartley, supt.   Fax 265-5635
www.madison.k12.mi.us
Madison HS   400/9-12
3498 Treat Hwy 49221   517-263-0742
Connie Ries, prin.   Fax 265-1848
Madison MS   300/6-8
3498 Treat Hwy 49221   517-263-0743
Brad Anschuetz, prin.   Fax 265-5635

Adrian College   Post-Sec.
110 S Madison St 49221   517-265-5161
Berean Baptist Academy   100/K-12
751 W Maumee St 49221   517-263-5050
Justin Raymond, prin.   Fax 266-2491
Fiser's College of Cosmetology   Post-Sec.
329 1/2 E Maumee St 49221   517-264-2199
Jackson Community College   Post-Sec.
1376 N Main St 49221   517-265-5515
Jackson Community College   Post-Sec.
2651 W Cadmus Rd 49221   517-263-1351
Lenawee Christian S   600/PK-12
111 Wolf Creek Hwy 49221   517-265-7590
Wesley Willis, supt.   Fax 265-6558
Siena Heights University   Post-Sec.
1247 E Siena Heights Dr 49221   517-263-0731

Alanson, Emmet, Pop. 807
Littlefield SD   400/K-12
7400 North St 49706   231-548-2261
Bently Laser, supt.   Fax 548-2132
Littlefield S   400/K-12
7400 North St 49706   231-548-2261
Edward Cole, prin.   Fax 548-2165

Alba, Antrim
Alba SD   200/PK-12
PO Box 10 49611   231-584-2000
Jeffery DiRosa, supt.   Fax 584-2001
www.torchlake.com/albaschool/
Alba S   200/PK-12
PO Box 10 49611   231-584-2000
Jeffrey DiRosa, prin.   Fax 584-2001

Albion, Calhoun, Pop. 9,130
Albion SD   1,700/PK-12
1418 Cooper St 49224   517-629-9166
Mario Morrow, supt.   Fax 629-8209
www.albion.k12.mi.us
Albion HS   500/9-12
225 E Watson St 49224   517-629-9421
Debra Swartz, prin.   Fax 630-3305
Washington Gardner MS   500/6-8
401 E Michigan Ave 49224   517-629-9448
Julie Cummins, prin.   Fax 629-8257

Albion College   Post-Sec.
611 E Porter St 49224   517-629-1000

Algonac, Saint Clair, Pop. 4,602
Algonac Community SD   2,400/K-12
1216 Saint Clair Blvd 48001   810-794-9364
Dennis Guiser, supt.   Fax 794-0040
www.algonac.k12.mi.us
Algonac HS   700/9-12
5200 Taft Rd 48001   810-794-4911
Michael Sharrow, prin.   Fax 794-8876
Algonquin JHS   600/6-8
9185 Marsh Rd 48001   810-794-9317
Andrew Rogers, prin.   Fax 794-8872

Allegan, Allegan, Pop. 4,909
Allegan SD   2,900/PK-12
550 5th St 49010   269-673-5431
Kevin Harness, supt.   Fax 673-5463
www.alleganpublicschools.org/
Allegan HS   900/9-12
1560 M 40 N 49010   269-673-7002
Jim Mallard, prin.   Fax 686-2486
White MS   700/6-8
3300 115th Ave 49010   269-673-2241
George Mohr, prin.   Fax 686-0309

Allendale, Ottawa, Pop. 6,950
Allendale SD   1,200/PK-12
6561 Lake Michigan Dr 49401   616-892-5570
Catherine Ceglarek, supt.   Fax 895-6690
www.allendale.k12.mi.us
Allendale HS   500/9-12
10760 68th Ave 49401   616-892-5585
Steve Scholten, prin.   Fax 895-4280
Allendale MS   600/5-8
6561 Lake Michigan Dr 49401   616-892-5595
Rocky Thompson, prin.   Fax 895-9111

Grand Valley State University   Post-Sec.
1 Campus Dr 49401   616-895-6611

Allen Park, Wayne, Pop. 28,762
Allen Park SD   3,600/K-12
9601 Vine Ave 48101   313-928-4467
R. Douglas Pretty, supt.   Fax 928-4511
www.apps.k12.mi.us
Allen Park HS   1,100/9-12
18401 Champaign Rd 48101   313-383-7517
Janet McBurney, prin.   Fax 386-3688
Allen Park MS   900/6-8
8401 Vine Ave 48101   313-928-6152
Michael Dawson, prin.   Fax 383-5372

Cabrini HS   300/K-12
15305 Wick Rd 48101   313-388-0110
Cheryl Szczodrowski, prin.   Fax 388-1876
Inter City Baptist S   300/K-12
4700 Allen Rd 48101   313-928-6900
James Hubbard, prin.   Fax 928-7310

Alma, Gratiot, Pop. 9,330
Alma SD   2,200/PK-12
1500 Pine Ave 48801   989-463-3111
Don Pavlik, supt.   Fax 466-2943
www.almaschools.net
Alma HS   500/9-12
1500 Pine Ave 48801   989-463-3111
Donald Everhart, prin.   Fax 463-2176
Alma MS   600/6-8
1700 N Pine 48801   989-463-3111
Carolyn Studley, prin.   Fax 466-7612
Alma Adult Education   Adult
300 Republic Ave 48801   989-463-3111
Kathy Johnston, prin.   Fax 466-6814

Gratiot/Isabella RESD
Supt. — See Ithaca
Gratiot Technical Education Center   Vo/Tech
327 E Center St 48801   989-466-4832
Fax 466-9734

Alma College   Post-Sec.
614 W Superior St 48801   989-463-7111

Almont, Lapeer, Pop. 2,841
Almont Community SD   1,300/K-12
401 Church St 48003   810-798-8561
Steven Zott, supt.   Fax 798-2367
www.almont.k12.mi.us
Almont HS   500/9-12
4701 Howland Rd 48003   810-798-8595
R. Robert Watt, prin.   Fax 798-7011
Almont MS   6-8
4624 Kidder Rd 48003   810-798-3578
Dr. Tina Kerr, prin.   Fax 798-3549

Alpena, Alpena, Pop. 10,951
Alpena SD   5,000/K-12
2373 Gordon Rd 49707   989-358-5040
David J. Werner, supt.   Fax 358-5041
www.alpenaschools.com
Alpena HS   1,700/9-12
3303 S 3rd Ave 49707   989-358-5200
Claudia Werner, prin.   Fax 358-5205
Thunder Bay JHS   900/7-8
3500 S 3rd Ave 49707   989-358-5400
Joyce McCoy, prin.   Fax 358-5499

ACES/Oxbow Adult/Alternative/Comm Educ   Adult
700 Pinecrest St 49707   989-358-5170
Patrick Timmons, prin.   Fax 358-5175

Alpena Community College   Post-Sec.
666 Johnson St 49707   989-356-9021

Ann Arbor, Washtenaw, Pop. 114,498
Ann Arbor SD   16,600/PK-12
PO Box 1188 48106   734-994-2200
Dr. George Fornero, supt.   Fax 994-2414
www.aaps.k12.mi.us/
Clague JHS   700/6-8
2616 Nixon Rd 48105   734-994-1976
Michael Hecker, prin.   Fax 994-1645
Community HS   500/9-12
401 N Division St 48104   734-994-2025
Judith Conger, dean   Fax 994-0042
Forsyth JHS   700/6-8
1655 Newport Rd 48103   734-994-1985
Janet Schwamb, prin.   Fax 994-5749
Huron HS   2,100/9-12
2727 Fuller Rd 48105   734-994-2043
Arthur Williams, prin.   Fax 994-2048
Pioneer HS   2,700/9-12
601 W Stadium Blvd 48103   734-994-2126
Louis Young, prin.   Fax 994-2198
Scarlett JHS   600/6-8
3300 Lorraine St 48108   734-971-1694
Benjamin Edmondson, prin.   Fax 971-1274
Slauson JHS   800/6-8
1019 W Washington St 48103   734-994-2005
Patricia Rose, prin.   Fax 994-1681
Tappan JHS   800/6-8
2251 E Stadium Blvd 48104   734-994-2016
Gary Court, prin.   Fax 997-1873
Stone S   Adult
2800 Stone School Rd 48104   734-971-2665
Gayl Dybdahl, prin.   Fax 971-7759

Cleary University - Washtenaw Campus   Post-Sec.
3601 Plymouth Rd 48105   734-332-4477
Concordia University   Post-Sec.
4090 Geddes Rd 48105   734-995-7300
Father Gabriel Richard HS   200/9-12
4333 Whitehall Dr 48105   734-662-0496
Brian P. Wolcott, prin.   Fax 662-4133
Greenhills S   500/6-12
850 Greenhills Dr 48105   734-769-4010
Peter Fayroian, prin.   Fax 769-5029
Ross Medical Education Center   Post-Sec.
4741 Washtenaw Ave 48108   734-434-7320
Steiner S of Ann Arbor   100/9-12
2230 Pontiac Trl 48105   734-669-9394
Sara Lambert, admin.   Fax 669-9396
University of Michigan-Ann Arbor   Post-Sec.
1220 Student Activities Bld 48109   734-764-1817
University of Michigan-Ann Arbor   Post-Sec.
400 N Ingalls St 48109   734-764-7188
Washtenaw Community College   Post-Sec.
PO Box D-1 48106   734-973-3300

Armada, Macomb, Pop. 1,636
Armada Area SD   2,300/PK-12
74500 Burk St 48005   586-784-4512
Arnold Kummerow, supt.   Fax 784-4268
www.macomb.k12.mi.us/armada
Armada HS   600/9-12
23655 Armada Center Rd 48005   586-784-9156
Lillian Demas, prin.   Fax 784-9592
Armada MS   500/6-8
23550 Armada Center Rd 48005   586-784-9105
William Zebelian, prin.   Fax 784-8650

Ashley, Gratiot, Pop. 525
Ashley Community SD   400/K-12
PO Box 6 48806   989-847-4000
Roger A. Keck, supt.   Fax 847-3500
www.bearnet.net
Ashley JSHS   200/7-12
PO Box 6 48806   989-847-2514
Tom Saylor, prin.   Fax 847-4204

Athens, Calhoun, Pop. 1,074
Athens Area SD   800/K-12
300 E Holcomb St 49011   269-729-5427
Dr. Randall Davis, supt.   Fax 729-9610
www.athensk12.org
Athens HS   300/9-12
300 E Holcomb St 49011   269-729-5414
Joseph Chambers, prin.   Fax 729-9616
Athens MS   300/5-8
515 E Williams St 49011   269-729-5421
Richard Franklin, prin.   Fax 729-9613

Factoryville Christian S   50/PK-12
33650 Factoryville Rd 49011   269-729-4203
Rev. Fred Goebert, admin.   Fax 729-4182

Atlanta, Montmorency
Atlanta Community SD   400/K-12
PO Box 619 48709   989-785-4877
James Mouch, supt.   Fax 785-2611
www.atlanta.k12.mi.us

Atlanta JSHS 200/7-12
PO Box 619 49709 989-785-4842
Derrel Kent, prin. Fax 785-2617

Attica, Lapeer
Lapeer County ISD
Supt. — See Lapeer
Lapeer County ISD Education Center Vo/Tech
690 N Lake Pleasant Rd 48412 810-664-1124
Dorothy Oppenheiser, prin. Fax 724-7600

Auburn, Bay, Pop. 1,989
Bay City SD
Supt. — See Bay City
Western HS 1,400/9-12
500 W Midland Rd 48611 989-662-4481
Oren Lusher, prin. Fax 662-4413
Western MS 900/6-8
500 W Midland Rd 48611 989-662-4489
Paula Weiss, prin. Fax 662-0185

Auburn Hills, Oakland, Pop. 20,471
Avondale SD 3,800/PK-12
2940 Waukegan St 48326 248-537-6000
George Heitsch, supt. Fax 537-6005
www.avondale.k12.mi.us
Avondale HS 1,100/9-12
2800 Waukegan St 48326 248-537-6100
Fred Cromie, prin. Fax 537-6105
Other Schools – See Rochester Hills

Auburn Hills Christian S 200/K-12
PO Box 4386 48321 248-373-3399
Scott Wickson, prin. Fax 373-2001
Baker College of Auburn Hills Post-Sec.
1500 University Dr 48326 248-340-0600
Oakland Christian S 500/K-12
3075 Shimmons Rd 48326 248-373-2700
Randall Speck, admin. Fax 373-9255

Au Gres, Arenac, Pop. 1,001
Au Gres-Sims SD 500/K-12
PO Box 648 48703 989-876-7150
Robert Colby, supt. Fax 876-6752
www.ags-schools.org
Au Gres-Sims JSHS 300/6-12
PO Box 648 48703 989-876-7157
Gary Iwinski, prin. Fax 876-6860

Augusta, Kalamazoo, Pop. 873
Galesburg-Augusta Community SD
Supt. — See Galesburg
Galesburg-Augusta MS 300/6-8
750 W Van Buren St 49012 269-484-2020
Christopher Hurley, prin. Fax 731-4138

Bad Axe, Huron, Pop. 3,332
Bad Axe SD 1,400/K-12
760 S Van Dyke Rd 48413 989-269-9938
James L. Wencel, supt. Fax 269-2739
hatchet.badaxe.k12.mi.us/newsite/
Bad Axe HS 400/9-12
200 N Barrie Rd 48413 989-269-9593
Wayne Brady, prin. Fax 269-6947
Bad Axe JHS 300/6-8
750 S Van Dyke Rd 48413 989-269-2735
Virginia Lounsbury, prin. Fax 269-9001

Huron ISD
711 E Soper Rd 48413 989-269-6406
Janet Richards, supt. Fax 269-9218
www.hisd.k12.mi.us
Huron Area Technical Center Vo/Tech
1160 S Van Dyke Rd 48413 989-269-9284
Michael Moorman, prin. Fax 269-2844

Great Lakes College Post-Sec.
150 Nugent Rd 48413 989-755-3444

Baldwin, Lake, Pop. 1,108
Baldwin Community SD 800/K-12
525 4th St 49304 231-745-4791
Randall Howes, supt. Fax 745-3240
www.baldwin.k12.mi.us
Baldwin JSHS 400/6-12
525 4th St 49304 231-745-4683
Faith Thomas-Jones, prin. Fax 745-2898

Bangor, Van Buren, Pop. 1,907
Bangor SD 1,500/K-12
801 W Arlington St 49013 269-427-6800
Ronald D. Davis, supt. Fax 427-8274
www.bangorvikings.org
Bangor Career Academy Vo/Tech
799 W Arlington St 49013 269-427-6839
Lynn Johnson, prin. Fax 427-8274
Bangor HS 400/9-12
801 W Arlington St 49013 269-427-6844
Jeff Melvin, prin. Fax 427-8274
Bangor MS 400/6-8
803 W Arlington St 49013 269-427-6824
Jim Greydanus, prin. Fax 427-8274

Baraga, Baraga, Pop. 1,268
Baraga Area SD 500/K-12
PO Box 428 49908 906-353-6664
Norman McKindles, supt. Fax 353-7454
www.baragaschools.org
Baraga JSHS 300/7-12
PO Box 428 49908 906-353-6661
Jeff Gulan, prin. Fax 353-6662

Bath, Clinton
Bath Community SD 1,000/K-12
PO Box 310 48808 517-641-6721
Dr. Therese Peterson, supt. Fax 641-6958
www.bath.k12.mi.us
Bath HS 300/9-12
PO Box 159 48808 517-641-6724
Bart Rypstra, prin. Fax 641-7046

Bath MS 300/6-8
PO Box 148 48808 517-641-6781
Ray Freeze, prin. Fax 641-4996

Battle Creek, Calhoun, Pop. 53,827
Battle Creek SD 6,900/PK-12
3 Van Buren St W 49017 269-965-9500
Dr. Charles Coleman, supt. Fax 965-9474
www.battlecreekpublicschools.org
Battle Creek Central HS 1,700/9-12
100 Van Buren St W 49017 269-965-9526
Bruce Barney, prin. Fax 660-5864
Calhoun Area Technology Center Vo/Tech
475 Roosevelt Ave E 49017 269-968-2271
Gene Niedzwiecki, prin. Fax 968-4344
Kellogg MS 600/6-8
60 Van Buren St W 49017 269-965-9655
Bobbi Morehead, prin. Fax 965-9789
Northwestern MS 500/6-8
176 Limit St 49017 269-965-9607
Scott Millin, prin. Fax 965-9525
South Hill Academy 300/6-12
50 Spencer St 49014 269-965-9671
Maurice Ware, prin. Fax 965-9682
Southwestern MS 300/6-8
390 Washington Ave S 49015 269-965-9625
Gus Calbert, prin. Fax 965-9698
Springfield MS 400/5-8
1023 Avenue A 49015 269-965-9640
Jane Berger, prin. Fax 962-2486
Adult Education Center Adult
77 Capital Ave NE 49017 269-965-9515
Sharlie Jones, prin. Fax 965-9545

Harper Creek Community SD 2,400/K-12
201 Crosby Dr 49014 269-979-1136
John Severson, supt. Fax 660-1190
www.harpercreek.net
Harper Creek HS 800/9-12
12677 Beadle Lake Rd 49014 269-979-1121
Steve Guerra, prin. Fax 441-2206
Harper Creek MS 600/5-8
7454 B Dr N 49014 269-979-1131
Gary Garland, prin. Fax 979-4613

Lakeview SD 3,100/K-12
15 Arbor St 49015 269-565-2400
Cindy S. Ruble, supt. Fax 565-2428
www.lakeviewspartans.org
Lakeview HS 1,100/9-12
15060 Helmer Rd S 49015 269-565-3700
Steve Skalka, prin. Fax 565-3708
Lakeview MS 900/5-8
300 28th St S 49015 269-565-3900
Jim Owen, prin. Fax 565-3908

Pennfield SD 1,900/K-12
8587 Pennfield Rd 49017 269-961-9781
Dale Kimball, supt. Fax 961-9799
www.pennfield.k12.mi.us
Pennfield Dunlap MS 500/6-8
8587 Pennfield Rd 49017 269-961-9784
Don Hepner, prin. Fax 961-9799
Pennfield HS 600/9-12
8587 Pennfield Rd 49017 269-961-9770
Barry Duckham, prin. Fax 961-9799

Battle Creek SDA Academy 200/PK-12
480 Parkway Dr 49017 269-965-1278
Kevin Kossick, prin. Fax 965-3250
Calhoun Christian S 100/PK-12
PO Box 872 49016 269-979-4166
Carrie Krontz, admin. Fax 979-4166
Davenport College of Business Post-Sec.
200 Van Buren St W 49017 269-968-6105
Kambly School/Developmentally Impaired Post-Sec.
1003 North Ave 49017
Kellogg Community College Post-Sec.
450 North Ave 49017 269-965-3931
St. Philip Catholic Central HS 200/9-12
20 Cherry St 49017 269-963-4503
Marcy Arnson, prin. Fax 963-5590
St. Philip MS 100/6-8
20 Cherry St 49017 269-963-4935
Marcy Arnson, prin. Fax 963-5590
Wright Beauty Academy Post-Sec.
492 Capital Ave SW 49015 269-964-4016

Bay City, Bay, Pop. 35,428
Bangor Township SD 2,500/K-12
3520 Old Kawkawlin Rd 48706 989-684-8121
Michael Andress, supt. Fax 684-6000
www.bangorschools.org
Glenn HS 900/9-12
3201 Kiesel Rd 48706 989-684-7510
Patti Smith, prin. Fax 684-1545
McAuliffe MS 600/6-8
3281 Kiesel Rd 48706 989-686-7640
Barbara Bibbee, prin. Fax 684-7633
Bay City SD 9,100/K-12
910 N Walnut St 48706 989-686-9700
Carolyn Wierda, supt. Fax 686-1047
www.bcschools.net
Central HS 1,700/9-12
1624 Columbus Ave 48708 989-893-9541
Tim Marciniak, prin. Fax 893-0333
Handy MS 1,200/6-8
601 Blend St 48706 989-684-1723
Carla Derocher, prin. Fax 684-1960
Other Schools – See Auburn

All Saints HS 200/9-12
217 S Monroe St 48708 989-892-2533
Fax 892-7188
Bayshire Beauty Academy Post-Sec.
917 Saginaw St 48708 989-894-2431
Great Lakes College Post-Sec.
3930 Traxler Ct 48706 989-686-1572

Holy Family MS 200/6-8
2307 S Monroe St #200 48708 989-892-8332
Barbara Rakowski, prin. Fax 892-8727

Bear Lake, Manistee, Pop. 338
Bear Lake SD 400/K-12
PO Box 188 49614 231-864-3133
Gregory Webster, supt. Fax 864-3434
www.bearlake.k12.mi.us
Bear Lake Secondary S 200/6-12
PO Box 188 49614 231-864-3133
Michael Matesich, prin. Fax 864-3434

Beaver Island, Charlevoix
Beaver Island Community SD 100/K-12
PO Box 235 49782 231-448-2744
Kathleen McNamara, supt. Fax 448-2919
www.beaverisland.k12.mi.us
Beaver Island Community S 100/K-12
PO Box 235 49782 231-448-2744
Kathleen McNamara, prin. Fax 448-2919

Beaverton, Gladwin, Pop. 1,127
Beaverton Rural SD 1,700/K-12
PO Box 529 48612 989-246-3000
Joan Cashin, supt. Fax 435-7631
www.brs.cgresd.net
Beaverton HS 600/9-12
3090 Crockett Rd 48612 989-246-3010
Jeffrey M. Budge, prin. Fax 246-3366
Beaverton MS 600/4-8
440 S Ross St 48612 989-246-3020
Gregory Paxton, prin. Fax 246-3420

Belding, Ionia, Pop. 5,852
Belding Area SD 1,700/PK-12
1975 Orchard St 48809 616-794-4700
Charles Barker, supt. Fax 794-4730
www.bas-k12.org/
Belding HS 700/9-12
850 Hall St 48809 616-794-4900
Aaron West, prin. Fax 794-4956
Belding MS 600/6-8
410 Ionia St 48809 616-794-4400
John Deiter, prin. Fax 794-4420

Bellaire, Antrim, Pop. 1,157
Bellaire SD 600/K-12
204 W Forrest Home Ave 49615 231-533-8141
Ronald Nurnberger, supt. Fax 533-6797
www.bellaire.k12.mi.us
Bellaire JSHS 400/6-12
204 W Forrest Home Ave 49615 231-533-8015
Scott Morgan, prin. Fax 533-8244

Belleville, Wayne, Pop. 3,944
Van Buren SD 6,100/K-12
555 W Columbia Ave 48111 734-697-9123
Pete L. Lazaroff, supt. Fax 697-6385
www.resa.net/vanburen
Belleville HS 1,900/9-12
501 W Columbia Ave 48111 734-697-9133
Kevin Kelly, prin. Fax 697-6551
North MS 800/6-8
47097 McBride Ave 48111 734-697-9171
Dianne Tilson, prin. Fax 697-6573
South MS 700/6-8
45201 Owen St 48111 734-697-8711
Michelle Herring, prin. Fax 697-6576

Michigan Institute of Aeronautics Post-Sec.
47884 D St 48111 734-483-3758

Bellevue, Eaton, Pop. 1,357
Bellevue Community SD 900/K-12
201 West St 49021 269-763-9432
David Blossom, supt. Fax 763-3101
www.bellevue-schools.com/
Bellevue HS 300/9-12
575 Love Hwy 49021 269-763-9413
David Blossom, prin. Fax 763-3955
Bellevue MS 300/5-8
904 W Capital Ave 49021 269-763-9401
Andrea Nessel, prin. Fax 763-3266

Benton Harbor, Berrien, Pop. 11,010
Benton Harbor Area SD 4,600/PK-12
PO Box 1107 49023 269-605-1000
Paula Dawning, supt. Fax 605-1043
www.bhas.org
Benton Harbor HS 1,300/9-12
870 Colfax Ave 49022 269-605-1200
Dimtric Roseboro, prin. Fax 605-0761
Fair Plain Renaissance MS 400/6-8
120 E Napier Ave 49022 269-605-0658
Layne Hunt, prin. Fax 605-1403
Hull MS 500/6-8
1716 Territorial Rd 49022 269-605-1500
Kevin Simmons, prin. Fax 605-1503
McCord Renaissance MS 300/6-8
465 S Mccord St 49022 269-605-1600
Joseph Payton, prin. Fax 605-1603

Lake Michigan College Post-Sec.
2755 E Napier Ave 49022 269-927-8100

Benzonia, Benzie, Pop. 483
Benzie County Central SD 2,000/K-12
9222 Homestead Rd 49616 231-882-9654
David Micinski, supt. Fax 882-9121
www.benzie.k12.mi.us
Benzie Central HS 600/9-12
PO Box 240 49616 231-882-4497
Peter Olson, prin. Fax 882-5699
Benzie Central JHS 300/7-8
930 Homestead Rd 49616 231-882-4498
David Clasen, prin. Fax 882-7627

Berkley, Oakland, Pop. 15,239
Berkley SD — 4,400/PK-12
2211 Oakshire Ave 48072 — 248-837-8000
Tresa Zumsteg Ph.D., supt. — Fax 544-5835
www.berkley.k12.mi.us
Anderson MS — 600/6-8
3205 Catalpa Dr 48072 — 248-837-8200
Steve Frank, prin. — Fax 546-0696
Berkley HS — 1,400/9-12
2325 Catalpa Dr 48072 — 248-837-8100
Derrick Lopez, prin. — Fax 544-5860
Other Schools – See Oak Park

Berrien Springs, Berrien, Pop. 1,810
Berrien Springs SD — 1,600/PK-12
1 Sylvester Ave 49103 — 269-471-2891
Robert Irvin, supt. — Fax 471-2590
www.homeoftheshamrocks.org
Berrien Springs HS — 500/9-12
1 Sylvester Ave 49103 — 269-471-1748
Todd Wiedemann, prin. — Fax 471-1511
Berrien Springs MS — 400/6-8
1 Sylvester Ave 49103 — 269-471-2796
Ryan Pesce, prin. — Fax 471-2590

Andrews Academy — 300/9-12
8833 Garland Ave 49104 — 269-471-3138
Allan Chase, prin. — Fax 471-6368
Andrews University 49104 — Post-Sec.
269-471-7771

Bessemer, Gogebic, Pop. 2,029
Bessemer City SD — 600/PK-12
301 E Sellar St 49911 — 906-667-0802
Al Gaiss, supt. — Fax 667-0318
www.bessemerareaschools.org
Johnston JSHS — 300/7-12
100 W Lead St 49911 — 906-667-0413
Jim Partanen, prin. — Fax 667-0320

Beverly Hills, Oakland, Pop. 10,210
Birmingham SD
Supt. — See Birmingham
Berkshire MS — 800/6-8
21707 W 14 Mile Rd 48025 — 248-203-4702
Jim Moll, prin. — Fax 203-4802
Groves HS — 1,400/9-12
20500 W 13 Mile Rd 48025 — 248-203-3530
Fred Procter, prin. — Fax 203-3636

Detroit Country Day MS Hillview Campus — 400/6-8
22400 Hillview Ln 48025 — 248-646-7985
Gerald T. Hanson, hdmstr.
Detroit Country Day S 13 Mile Campus — 1,500/9-12
22305 W 13 Mile Rd 48025 — 248-646-7717
Gerald T. Hanson, hdmstr. — Fax 646-2458

Big Rapids, Mecosta, Pop. 10,797
Big Rapids SD — 2,200/PK-12
21034 15 Mile Rd 49307 — 231-796-2627
Thomas Langdon, supt. — Fax 592-0639
www.brps.k12.mi.us
Big Rapids HS — 700/9-12
21175 15 Mile Rd 49307 — 231-796-7651
Tim Haist, prin. — Fax 592-8505
Big Rapids MS — 500/6-8
500 N Warren Ave 49307 — 231-796-9965
Russ Greenleaf, prin. — Fax 592-3494

Mecosta-Osceola ISD — 231-796-3543
15760 190th Ave 49307 — Fax 796-3300
Curtis Finch, supt.
www.moisd.org
Mecosta-Osceola Career Center — Vo/Tech
15830 190th Ave 49307 — 231-796-5805
Fax 796-0262

Ferris State University — Post-Sec.
901 S State St 49307 — 231-591-2000

Birch Run, Saginaw, Pop. 1,754
Birch Run Area SD — 1,900/K-12
12400 Church St 48415 — 989-624-9307
Wayne S. Wright, supt. — Fax 624-5081
www.birchrun.k12.mi.us
Birch Run HS — 600/9-12
12450 Church St 48415 — 989-624-9392
Tricia Murphy-Alderman, prin. — Fax 624-8502
Greene MS — 600/5-8
8225 Main St 48415 — 989-624-5821
Doug Rowley, prin. — Fax 624-8507

Birmingham, Oakland, Pop. 19,161
Birmingham SD — 7,900/PK-12
550 W Merrill St 48009 — 248-203-3000
Dr. John Hoeffler, supt. — Fax 203-3007
www.birmingham.k12.mi.us
Derby MS — 700/6-8
1300 Derby Rd 48009 — 248-203-5003
Deborah Hubbell, prin. — Fax 203-4948
Seaholm HS — 1,100/9-12
2436 W Lincoln St 48009 — 248-203-3707
Terry Piper, prin. — Fax 203-3706
Other Schools – See Beverly Hills, Bloomfield Hills

Eton Academy — 200/1-12
1755 E Melton Rd 48009 — 248-642-1150
Peter Pullen, hdmstr. — Fax 642-3670
Roeper S — 300/6-12
1051 Oakland Ave 48009 — 248-203-7300
Randall Dunn, hdmstr. — Fax 642-8619

Blanchard, Isabella
Montabella Community SD
Supt. — See Edmore
Montabella HS — 300/9-12
1456 N County Line Rd 49310 — 989-427-5175
Ron Pincumbe, prin. — Fax 427-5107

Montabella MS — 400/5-8
1324 E North County Line Rd 49310 — 989-427-5414
Ronald Farrell, prin. — Fax 427-5602

Blissfield, Lenawee, Pop. 3,258
Blissfield Community SD — 1,400/K-12
630 S Lane St 49228 — 517-486-2205
Paul Palka, supt. — Fax 486-5701
www.blissfield.k12.mi.us
Blissfield HS — 500/9-12
630 S Lane St 49228 — 517-486-2148
Jerry Johnson, prin. — Fax 486-4749
Blissfield MS — 400/6-8
1305 Beamer Rd 49228 — 517-486-4420
Bette Kohler, prin. — Fax 486-4758

Bloomfield Hills, Oakland, Pop. 3,880
Birmingham SD
Supt. — See Birmingham
Birmingham Covington S — 600/3-8
1525 Covington Rd 48301 — 248-203-4425
Dale Truding, prin. — Fax 203-4433

Bloomfield Hills SD — 6,000/K-12
4175 Andover Rd 48302 — 248-341-5400
Steven A. Gaynor, supt. — Fax 341-5449
www.bloomfield.org
Andover HS — 900/9-12
4200 Andover Rd, — 248-341-5600
Heidi Kattula, prin. — Fax 341-5699
Bloomfield Hills MS — 500/6-8
4200 Quarton Rd, — 248-341-6000
Kaarin Averill, prin. — Fax 341-6099
East Hills MS — 600/6-8
2800 Kensington Rd, — 248-341-6200
Arnold Jahnke, prin. — Fax 341-6299
International Academy — 100/9-12
1020 E Square Lake Rd, — 248-341-5900
Bert Okma, prin. — Fax 341-5959
Lahser HS — 1,000/9-12
3456 Lahser Rd, — 248-341-5700
Charlie Hollerith, prin. — Fax 341-5899
Other Schools – See West Bloomfield

Academy of the Sacred Heart — 500/PK-12
1250 Kensington Rd 48304 — 248-646-8900
Sr. Bridget Bearss, prin. — Fax 646-4143
Brother Rice HS — 700/9-12
7101 Lahser Rd 48301 — 248-647-2526
John Birney, prin. — Fax 647-8170
Cranbrook Academy of Art — Post-Sec.
PO Box 801 48303 — 248-645-3300
Cranbrook S — 1,600/PK-12
39221 Woodward Ave 48304 — 248-645-3300
Arlyce Seibert, prin. — Fax 645-3524
Marian HS — 600/9-12
7225 Lahser Rd 48301 — 248-644-1750
Sr. Kathleen Budesky, prin. — Fax 644-6107
Oakland Community College — Post-Sec.
2480 Opdyke Rd 48304 — 248-341-2000

Bloomingdale, Van Buren, Pop. 516
Bloomingdale SD — 1,100/K-12
PO Box 217 49026 — 269-521-3900
Dale Schreuder, supt. — Fax 521-3907
www.remc11.k12.mi.us/blooming
Bloomingdale HS — 400/9-12
PO Box 217 49026 — 269-521-3910
Allan Thorbjornsen, prin. — Fax 521-3915
Bloomingdale MS — 6-8
PO Box 217 49026 — 269-521-3950
Sheryl Griffin, prin. — Fax 521-3958

Boyne City, Charlevoix, Pop. 3,367
Boyne City SD — 1,200/K-12
321 S Park St 49712 — 231-439-8190
James D. Cooper, supt. — Fax 439-8195
www.boyne.k12.mi.us
Boyne City HS — 400/9-12
1035 Boyne Ave 49712 — 231-439-8100
Karen Jarema, prin. — Fax 439-8194
Boyne City MS — 400/5-8
1025 Boyne Ave 49712 — 231-439-8200
Mindy Porter, prin. — Fax 439-8233

Boyne Falls, Charlevoix, Pop. 361
Boyne Falls SD — 300/K-12
PO Box 356 49713 — 231-549-2211
Gary Urman, supt. — Fax 549-2922
www.boynefalls.org
Boyne Falls S — 300/K-12
PO Box 356 49713 — 231-549-2212
William Aten, prin. — Fax 549-2922

Breckenridge, Gratiot, Pop. 1,330
Breckenridge Community SD — 1,000/K-12
PO Box 217 48615 — 989-842-3182
Dennis Hagey, supt. — Fax 842-3625
breck.edzone.net/
Breckenridge HS — 300/9-12
PO Box 217 48615 — 989-842-3182
Dean Havelka, prin. — Fax 842-3186
Breckenridge MS — 300/6-8
PO Box 217 48615 — 989-842-3182
Sheila Pilmore, prin. — Fax 842-3186

Brethren, Manistee
Kaleva-Norman-Dickson SD — 1,000/K-12
PO Box 36 49619 — 231-477-5353
Gregory Webster, supt. — Fax 477-5240
www.knd.k12.mi.us
Brethren HS — 300/9-12
PO Box 36 49619 — 231-477-5355
Wayne Bernier, prin. — Fax 477-5242
Brethren MS — 200/7-8
PO Box 36 49619 — 231-477-5354
Wayne Bernier, prin. — Fax 477-5351

Bridgeport, Saginaw, Pop. 8,569
Bridgeport-Spaulding Community SD — 1,400/PK-12
PO Box 657 48722 — 989-777-1770
Desmon Daniel, supt. — Fax 777-4720
www.bscs.k12.mi.us
Bridgeport HS — 700/9-12
4691 Bearcat Blvd 48722 — 989-777-3100
Andrew Kowalczyk, prin. — Fax 777-6910
Bridgeport-Spaulding MS — 7-8
4221 Bearcat Blvd 48722 — 989-777-0440
David Hurst, prin. — Fax 777-2284

Bridgeport Baptist Academy — 100/K-12
PO Box 249 48722 — 989-777-6811
William Swain, prin. — Fax 777-7376

Bridgman, Berrien, Pop. 2,433
Bridgman SD — 1,000/K-12
9964 Gast Rd 49106 — 269-466-0271
Kevin Ivers, supt. — Fax 466-0221
www.bridgmanschools.com
Bridgman HS — 400/9-12
9964 Gast Rd 49106 — 269-465-6848
Mike Shuler, prin. — Fax 466-0355
Reed MS — 300/5-8
10254 California 49106 — 269-465-5410
Patrick Weckel, prin. — Fax 466-0393

Brighton, Livingston, Pop. 7,029
Brighton Area SD — 7,200/K-12
125 S Church St 48116 — 810-299-4000
Dave Pruneau, supt. — Fax 299-4092
bas.k12.mi.us/
Brighton HS — 2,300/9-12
7878 Brighton Rd 48116 — 810-299-4100
Ken Hamman, prin. — Fax 299-4111
Maltby MS — 800/6-8
4740 Bauer Rd 48116 — 810-299-3600
Marcia Tomasko, prin. — Fax 299-3610
Scranton MS — 900/6-8
8415 Maltby Rd 48116 — 810-299-3700
Henry Vecchioni, prin. — Fax 299-3710

Ross Medical Education Center — Post-Sec.
5757 Whitmore Lake Rd #800 48116 — 810-227-0160

Brimley, Chippewa
Brimley Area SD — 500/K-12
7134 S M 221 49715 — 906-248-3219
Alan Kantola, supt. — Fax 248-3220
www.eup.k12.mi.us/brimley/
Brimley HS — 200/7-12
7134 S M 221 49715 — 906-248-3218
Brian Reattoir, prin. — Fax 248-5339

Bay Mills Community College — Post-Sec.
12214 W Lakeshore Dr 49715 — 906-248-3354

Britton, Lenawee, Pop. 685
Britton-Macon Area SD — 500/K-12
201 College Ave 49229 — 517-451-4581
Robert Tebo, supt. — Fax 451-8595
Britton-Macon S — 500/K-12
201 College Ave 49229 — 517-451-4581
Randy Salisbury, prin. — Fax 451-8595

Bronson, Branch, Pop. 2,367
Bronson Community SD — 1,300/K-12
215 W Chicago St 49028 — 517-369-3257
Bob Walter, supt. — Fax 369-2802
www.bronson.k12.mi.us
Bronson JSHS — 700/7-12
450 E Grant St 49028 — 517-369-3230
Sean McNatt, prin. — Fax 369-3506

Brooklyn, Jackson, Pop. 1,220
Columbia SD — 1,800/K-12
11775 Hewitt Rd 49230 — 517-592-6641
Brent Beamish, supt. — Fax 592-8090
columbiaschooldistrict.org
Columbia Central HS — 500/9-12
11775 Hewitt Rd 49230 — 517-592-6634
David Slusher, prin. — Fax 592-8909
Columbia MS — 500/6-8
321 School St 49230 — 517-592-2181
Greg Meschke, prin. — Fax 592-3447

Brown City, Sanilac, Pop. 1,325
Brown City Community SD — 1,100/K-12
PO Box 160 48416 — 810-346-2781
Jerry Steigerwald, supt. — Fax 346-3762
www.bc.k12.mi.us
Brown City JSHS — 500/7-12
PO Box 160 48416 — 810-346-2781
Scott Roper, prin. — Fax 346-2381

Brownstown, See Flat Rock
Woodhaven-Brownstown SD — 5,100/K-12
24975 Van Horn Rd 48134 — 734-783-3300
Barbara Lott, supt. — Fax 783-3316
www.woodhaven.k12.mi.us
Woodhaven HS — 1,100/10-12
24787 Van Horn Rd 48134 — 734-783-3333
Michael Vogel, prin. — Fax 783-3342
Other Schools – See Woodhaven

Buchanan, Berrien, Pop. 4,579
Buchanan Community SD — 1,700/PK-12
401 W Chicago St 49107 — 269-695-8401
David Casey, supt. — Fax 695-8450
www.buchananschools.com
Buchanan HS — 500/9-12
401 W Chicago St 49107 — 269-695-8403
Richard Gregg, prin. — Fax 695-8414
Buchanan MS — 400/6-8
610 W 4th St 49107 — 269-695-8406
Joseph Malbouef, prin. — Fax 695-8459

Buckley, Wexford, Pop. 556
Buckley Community SD — 400/K-12
  PO Box 38 49620 — 231-269-3325
  Chet Janik, supt. — Fax 269-3833
  www.buckleyschools.com
Buckley Community S — 400/K-12
  PO Box 38 49620 — 231-269-3325
  Chet Janik, prin. — Fax 269-3833

Burr Oak, Saint Joseph, Pop. 777
Burr Oak Community SD — 300/K-12
  PO Box 337 49030 — 269-489-2213
  Terry Conklin, supt. — Fax 489-5198
  www.remc12.k12.mi.us/burr-oak/
Burr Oak HS — 200/7-12
  PO Box 337 49030 — 269-489-5534
  Terry Conklin, prin. — Fax 489-5198

Burton, Genesee, Pop. 30,890
Atherton Community SD — 1,100/K-12
  3354 S Genesee Rd 48519 — 810-591-9182
  Mark Madden, supt. — Fax 591-1926
  www.athertonschools.com
Atherton HS — 300/9-12
  3354 S Genesee Rd 48519 — 810-591-9184
  Robert Belous, prin. — Fax 591-9180
Atherton MS — 400/4-8
  3444 S Genesee Rd 48519 — 810-591-0604
  Trevor Alward, prin. — Fax 591-9456

Bendle SD — 1,700/PK-12
  2283 E Scottwood Ave 48529 — 810-591-2501
  John Angle, supt. — Fax 591-2210
  www.bendleschools.org
Bendle HS — 400/9-12
  2294 E Bristol Rd 48529 — 810-591-5103
  William Parish, prin. — Fax 591-2510
Bendle MS — 300/6-8
  4093 Barnes Ave 48529 — 810-591-3385
  Scott Williams, prin. — Fax 591-2540

Bentley Community SD — 1,000/K-12
  1170 N Belsay Rd 48509 — 810-591-9100
  John E. Schantz, supt. — Fax 591-9102
Bentley HS — 300/9-12
  1150 N Belsay Rd 48509 — 810-591-5811
  Richard Cunningham, prin. — Fax 591-9158
Bentley MS — 400/5-8
  1180 N Belsay Rd 48509 — 810-591-9040
  Folke Boman, prin. — Fax 591-9166

Faithway Christian S — 200/PK-12
  1225 S Center Rd 48509 — 810-743-0055
  Doug Littrell, admin. — Fax 743-0033
Genesee Christian S — 400/PK-12
  1223 S Belsay Rd 48509 — 810-743-3108
  Jerry Kramer, prin. — Fax 743-3230
St. Thomas More Academy — 100/K-12
  6456 E Bristol Rd 48519 — 810-742-2411
  Dan Le Blanc, prin. — Fax 742-4803
Valley Christian Academy — 200/PK-12
  3266 S Genesee Rd 48519 — 810-742-4500
  Kris Davidson, prin. — Fax 742-4537

Byron, Shiawassee, Pop. 580
Byron Area SD — 1,300/K-12
  312 W Maple St 48418 — 810-266-4881
  Dr. Mark E. Miller, supt. — Fax 266-5723
  www.byron.k12.mi.us
Byron HS — 400/9-12
  312 W Maple St 48418 — 810-266-4620
  Tom Dykstra, prin. — Fax 266-5010
Byron MS — 300/6-8
  312 W Maple St 48418 — 810-266-4422
  Terry Evanish, prin. — Fax 266-4151

Byron Center, Kent
Byron Center SD — 3,300/K-12
  8542 Byron Center Ave SW 49315 — 616-878-6100
  Howard Napp, supt. — Fax 878-6120
  www.bcpsk12.net
Byron Center HS — 900/9-12
  8500 Burlingame Ave SW 49315 — 616-878-6600
  Karl Nelson, prin. — Fax 878-6620
Byron Center West MS — 500/7-8
  8654 Homerich Ave SW 49315 — 616-878-6500
  Mike Spahr, prin. — Fax 878-6520

Wayland UNSD — 3,100/K-12
  500 100th St SW 49315 — 269-792-2181
  Eivor Swan, supt. — Fax 792-4322
  www.wayland.k12.mi.us
Other Schools – See Wayland

Zion Christian S — 100/PK-12
  7555 Byron Center Ave SW 49315 — 616-878-9472
  Tom Kwekel, prin. — Fax 878-9473

Cadillac, Wexford, Pop. 10,131
Cadillac Area SD — 3,200/K-12
  421 S Mitchell St 49601 — 231-876-5000
  Paul Liabenow, supt. — Fax 876-5021
  www.vikingnet.org
Cadillac JHS — 600/8-9
  500 Chestnut St 49601 — 231-876-5700
  Dave Champion, prin. — Fax 876-5721
Cadillac SHS — 800/10-12
  400 Linden St 49601 — 231-876-5800
  William Chilman, prin. — Fax 876-5821

Wexford/Missaukee ISD —
  9907 E 13th St 49601 — 231-876-2260
  Scott Crosby, supt. — Fax 876-2272
  www.wmisd.org
Wexford-Missaukee Area Career Tech — Vo/Tech
  9901 E 13th St 49601 — 231-876-2200
   — Fax 876-2212

Baker College of Cadillac — Post-Sec.
  9600 E 13th St 49601 — 231-876-3100
Cadillac Heritage Christian S — 100/PK-12
  1706 Wright St 49601 — 231-775-4272
  William Goodwill, admin. — Fax 775-2999

Caledonia, Kent, Pop. 1,156
Caledonia Community SD — 3,400/PK-12
  9753 Duncan Lake Ave SE 49316 — 616-891-8185
  Jerry Phillips, supt. — Fax 891-9253
  www.caledonia.k12.mi.us
Caledonia HS — 1,000/9-12
  9050 Kraft Ave SE 49316 — 616-891-8129
  Jim Glazier, prin. — Fax 891-7038
Duncan Lake MS — 6-8
  9757 Duncan Lake Ave SE 49316 — 616-891-1380
  Cheryl Davis, prin. — Fax 891-0833
Kraft Meadows MS — 800/6-8
  9230 Kraft Ave SE 49316 — 616-891-8649
  Brian Leatherman, prin. — Fax 891-7013

Dutton Christian S — 100/6-8
  6729 Hanna Lake Ave SE 49316 — 616-698-8660
   — Fax 698-2281

Calumet, Houghton, Pop. 831
Calumet Laurium Keweenaw SD — 1,500/K-12
  57070 Mine St 49913 — 906-337-0311
  Darryl Pierce, supt. — Fax 337-1406
  www.clk.k12.mi.us
Calumet HS — 500/9-12
  57070 Mine St 49913 — 906-337-0311
  Robert Barrette, prin. — Fax 337-5405
Washington MS — 400/6-8
  57070 Mine St 49913 — 906-337-0311
  Michael Steber, prin. — Fax 337-5406

Camden, Hillsdale, Pop. 550
Camden-Frontier SD — 600/K-12
  4971 W Montgomery Rd 49232 — 517-368-5991
  Will Schantl, supt. — Fax 368-5959
Camden Frontier HS — 200/9-12
  4971 W Montgomery Rd 49232 — 517-368-5255
  Reed Kimball, prin. — Fax 368-5950
Camden Frontier MS — 100/7-8
  4971 W Montgomery Rd 49232 — 517-368-5255
  Reed Kimball, prin. — Fax 368-5950

Canton, Wayne, Pop. 81,500
Plymouth-Canton Community SD
  Supt. — See Plymouth
Canton HS — 2,100/9-12
  8415 N Canton Center Rd 48187 — 734-416-2850
  Dr. Cassandra Smith, prin. — Fax 416-7531
Discovery MS — 900/6-8
  45083 Hanford Rd 48187 — 734-416-2880
  Roche LaVictor, prin. — Fax 416-2895
Plymouth HS — 2,000/9-12
  8400 N Beck Rd 48187 — 734-582-5500
  Dr. Michael Bee, prin. — Fax 582-5555
Salem HS — 2,200/9-12
  46181 Joy Rd 48187 — 734-416-7800
  Gerald Ostoin, prin. — Fax 416-7791

Agape Christian Academy — 200/PK-12
  PO Box 87770 48187 — 734-394-0357
  Daniel Watkins, prin. — Fax 394-0206
Plymouth Christian Academy — 800/PK-12
  43065 Joy Rd 48187 — 734-459-3505
  Dr. Marilyn Meell, hdmstr. — Fax 459-9997

Capac, Saint Clair, Pop. 2,193
Capac Community SD — 1,900/PK-12
  403 N Glassford St 48014 — 810-395-4321
  Jerry Jennex, supt. — Fax 395-4858
  www.capac.k12.mi.us
Capac JSHS — 700/8-12
  541 N Glassford St 48014 — 810-395-3800
  Michael Mrozinski, prin. — Fax 395-2427

Carleton, Monroe, Pop. 2,711
Airport Community SD — 3,400/PK-12
  11270 Grafton Rd 48117 — 734-654-2414
  Larry Audet, supt. — Fax 654-3424
  www.airport.k12.mi.us
Airport HS — 1,000/9-12
  11330 Grafton Rd 48117 — 734-654-6208
  Robert Matkovic, prin. — Fax 654-3005
Wagar MS — 900/6-8
  11200 Grafton Rd 48117 — 734-654-6205
  Mark Arnold, prin. — Fax 654-0057

Carney, Menominee, Pop. 222
Carney-Nadeau SD — 300/K-12
  PO Box 68 49812 — 906-639-2000
  Kenneth Linder, supt. — Fax 639-2176
  www.cnps.us
Carney-Nadeau S — 300/K-12
  PO Box 68 49812 — 906-639-2171
  Ken Linder, prin. — Fax 639-2176

Caro, Tuscola, Pop. 4,188
Caro Community SD — 2,100/K-12
  301 N Hooper St 48723 — 989-673-3166
  Neil Beckwith, supt. — Fax 673-6248
  www.caro.k12.mi.us
Caro HS — 700/9-12
  301 N Hooper St 48723 — 989-673-3165
  Gary Mohr, prin. — Fax 673-8707
Caro MS — 500/6-8
  301 N Hooper St 48723 — 989-673-3167
  JoAnn Nordstrom, prin. — Fax 673-1225

Tuscola ISD —
  1385 Cleaver Rd 48723 — 989-673-2144
  Carol Socha, supt. — Fax 673-5366
  www.tisd.k12.mi.us
Tuscola Technology Center — Vo/Tech
  1401 Cleaver Rd 48723 — 989-673-5300
  Steve Ley, prin. — Fax 673-4228

Great Lakes College — Post-Sec.
  1231 Cleaver Rd 48723 — 989-673-5857

Carrollton, Saginaw, Pop. 6,521
Carrollton SD
  Supt. — See Saginaw
Carrollton HS — 400/9-12
  PO Box 548 48724 — 989-753-3433
  Traci Smith, prin. — Fax 754-1041
Carrollton MS — 400/6-8
  PO Box 517 48724 — 989-753-9704
  Tiffany Peterson, prin. — Fax 754-1470

Carson City, Montcalm, Pop. 1,190
Carson City-Crystal Area SD — 1,200/K-12
  PO Box 780 48811 — 989-584-3138
  Robert Swanson, supt. — Fax 584-3539
  www.carsoncity.k12.mi.us
Carson City HS — 400/9-12
  PO Box 780 48811 — 989-584-3175
  Beth Robb, prin. — Fax 584-3043
Carson City MS — 300/6-8
  PO Box 780 48811 — 989-584-3903
  Charles Larkins, prin. — Fax 584-3259

Fellowship Baptist Academy — 100/PK-12
  8070 S Bloomer St 48811 — 989-584-6430
  Kevin McAlvey, prin. — Fax 584-6716

Carsonville, Sanilac, Pop. 494
Carsonville-Port Sanilac SD — 600/K-12
  100 N Goetze Rd 48419 — 810-657-9393
  Harold Titus, supt. — Fax 657-9060
  www.carsport.k12.mi.us
Carsonville-Port Sanilac JSHS — 300/7-12
  100 N Goetze Rd 48419 — 810-657-9394
  Ann Binienda, prin. — Fax 657-9431

Caseville, Huron, Pop. 895
Caseville SD — 300/K-12
  PO Box 1068 48725 — 989-856-2940
  Dr. Dan Tighe, supt. — Fax 856-3095
  www.caseville.k12.mi.us
Caseville JSHS — 200/7-12
  PO Box 1068 48725 — 989-856-2111
  Ken Ewald, prin. — Fax 856-8641

Cass City, Tuscola, Pop. 2,604
Cass City SD — 1,400/PK-12
  4868 Seeger St 48726 — 989-872-2200
  Kenneth Micklash, supt. — Fax 872-5015
  www.casscity.k12.mi.us
Cass City HS — 500/9-12
  4868 Seeger St 48726 — 989-872-2148
  Jon Good, prin. — Fax 872-5015
Cass City MS — 500/5-8
  4805 Ale St 48726 — 989-872-4397
  Jeff Hartel, prin. — Fax 872-2990

Cassopolis, Cass, Pop. 1,831
Cassopolis SD — 1,200/K-12
  PO Box 98 49031 — 269-445-0500
  Gregory Weatherspoon, supt. — Fax 445-0505
  www.cassopolis.k12.mi.us
Beatty JSHS — 500/7-12
  PO Box 98 49031 — 269-445-0540
  Rusty Stitt, prin. — Fax 445-3112

Cedar Lake, Montcalm

Great Lakes Adventist Academy — 200/9-12
  PO Box 68 48812 — 989-427-5181
  Raymond Davis, prin. — Fax 427-5027

Cedar Springs, Kent, Pop. 3,184
Cedar Springs SD — 3,600/PK-12
  204 E Muskegon St 49319 — 616-696-1204
  Andrew Booth, supt. — Fax 696-3755
  www.csredhawks.org
Cedar Springs HS — 1,000/9-12
  204 E Muskegon St 49319 — 616-696-1200
  Karl Pilar, prin. — Fax 696-4016
Cedar Springs MS — 600/7-8
  204 E Muskegon St 49319 — 616-696-9100
  Bill VanHorn, prin. — Fax 696-3109

Cedarville, Mackinac
Les Cheneaux Community SD — 400/K-12
  PO Box 366 49719 — 906-484-2256
  Rod Goehmann, supt. — Fax 484-2072
  eup.k12.mi.us/les_cheneaux
Cedarville MSHS — 200/6-12
  PO Box 366 49719 — 906-484-2256
  Randy Schaedig, prin. — Fax 484-2403

Center Line, Macomb, Pop. 8,370
Center Line SD — 3,000/PK-12
  26400 Arsenal 48015 — 586-510-2000
  Judith P. Pritchett, supt. — Fax 510-2019
  www.clps.org
Center Line HS — 900/9-12
  26300 Arsenal 48015 — 586-510-2100
  Michael Dodge, prin. — Fax 510-2119
Wolfe MS — 700/6-8
  8640 McKinley 48015 — 586-510-2300
  Amy Maruca, prin. — Fax 510-2319

Central Lake, Antrim, Pop. 998
Central Lake SD — 500/K-12
  PO Box 128 49622 — 231-544-3141
  Augusta Bishop, supt. — Fax 544-2903
  clps.k12.mi.us

Central Lake JSHS | 300/6-12
PO Box 128 49622 | 231-544-3341
Mike Linton, prin. | Fax 544-2903

Centreville, Saint Joseph, Pop. 1,570
Centreville SD | 1,000/K-12
PO Box 158 49032 | 269-467-5220
William Miller, supt. | Fax 467-5226
cpschools.org
Centreville HS | 300/9-12
PO Box 158 49032 | 269-467-5210
Mike Morris, prin. | Fax 467-5214
Centreville MS | 100/7-8
PO Box 158 49032 | 269-467-5205
Barbara Lester, prin. | Fax 467-4864

Glen Oaks Community College | Post-Sec.
62249 Shimmel Rd 49032 | 269-467-9945

Charlevoix, Charlevoix, Pop. 2,851
Charlevoix SD | 1,400/K-12
208 W Clinton St 49720 | 231-547-3200
John J. Sturock, supt. | Fax 547-0556
www.rayder.net
Charlevoix HS | 500/9-12
05200 Marion Center Rd 49720 | 231-547-3222
Gary Grundman, prin. | Fax 547-3245
Charlevoix MS | 400/5-8
108 E Garfield Ave 49720 | 231-547-3206
Keith Haske, prin. | Fax 547-3244

Charlotte, Eaton, Pop. 8,795
Charlotte SD | 3,300/K-12
378 State St 48813 | 517-541-5100
Carl Ellinger, supt. | Fax 541-5105
www.charlottenet.org
Charlotte HS | 1,000/9-12
378 State St 48813 | 517-541-5600
Leland Wheaton, prin. | Fax 541-5605
Charlotte MS | 1,100/5-8
1068 Carlisle Hwy 48813 | 517-541-5700
Christopher Rugh, prin. | Fax 541-5705

Chassell, Houghton
Chassell Township SD | 300/K-12
PO Box 140 49916 | 906-523-4691
James Frantti, supt. | Fax 523-4969
www.cts.k12.mi.us/
Chassell Township S | 300/K-12
PO Box 140 49916 | 906-523-4491
George Stockero, prin. | Fax 523-4969

Cheboygan, Cheboygan, Pop. 5,290
Cheboygan Area SD | 1,600/K-12
905 W Lincoln Ave 49721 | 231-627-4436
Paul L. Ellinger, supt. | Fax 627-9105
cheboygan.k12.mi.us/
Cheboygan HS | 700/9-12
801 W Lincoln Ave 49721 | 231-627-7191
Randy Johnson, prin. | Fax 627-2430
Cheboygan MS | 600/6-8
905 W Lincoln Ave 49721 | 231-627-7103
Mark Dombroski, prin. | Fax 627-4151

Chelsea, Washtenaw, Pop. 4,586
Chelsea SD | 2,900/K-12
500 Washington St 48118 | 734-433-2200
David K. Killips, supt. | Fax 433-2218
www.chelsea.k12.mi.us
Beach MS | 500/7-8
445 Mayer Dr 48118 | 734-433-2202
Andrew Ingall, prin. | Fax 433-2212
Chelsea HS | 1,100/9-12
740 N Freer Rd 48118 | 734-433-2201
Ronald Mead, prin. | Fax 433-2211

Chesaning, Saginaw, Pop. 2,482
Chesaning UNSD | 2,000/K-12
PO Box 95 48616 | 989-845-7020
Kathy Stewart, supt. | Fax 845-3722
www.chesaningschools.net
Chesaning MS | 700/5-8
431 N 4th St 48616 | 989-845-7040
Michael McGough, prin. | Fax 845-5335
Chesaning Union HS | 700/9-12
850 N 4th St 48616 | 989-845-2040
David Lewis, prin. | Fax 845-2117

Chesterfield, Macomb
L'Anse Creuse SD
Supt. — See Harrison Township
L'Anse Creuse MS East | 800/6-8
30300 Hickey Rd 48051 | 586-493-5200
Erick Alsup, prin. | Fax 493-5205

Clare, Clare, Pop. 3,219
Clare SD | 1,500/PK-12
201 E State St 48617 | 989-386-9945
John Leppanen, supt. | Fax 386-6055
www.clare.k12.mi.us/
Clare HS | 500/9-12
306 Schoolcrest Ave 48617 | 989-386-7789
Kim Kolbe, prin. | Fax 386-1236
Clare MS | 500/5-8
209 E State St 48617 | 989-386-9979
Steve Newkirk, prin. | Fax 386-4008

Clarkston, Oakland, Pop. 980
Clarkston Community SD | 7,800/PK-12
6389 Clarkston Rd 48346 | 248-623-5400
Albert Roberts, supt. | Fax 623-5450
ww2.clarkston.k12.mi.us/
Clarkston HS | 2,400/9-12
6093 Flemings Lake Rd 48346 | 248-623-3600
Jan Meagher, prin. | Fax 623-3535
Clarkston JHS | 1,200/6-8
6595 Middle Lake Rd 48346 | 248-623-5600
Shawn Ryan, prin. | Fax 623-5680
Sashabaw MS | 800/6-8
5565 Pine Knob Rd 48346 | 248-623-4200
Linda Foran, prin. | Fax 623-4205

Oakland ISD
Supt. — See Waterford
Oakland Technical Campus NW | Vo/Tech
8211 Big Lake Rd 48346 | 248-922-5800
Chuck Locklear, prin. | Fax 922-5805

Springfield Christian Academy | 100/K-12
8585 Dixie Hwy 48348 | 248-625-9760
Patrick Wagner, dir. | Fax 625-9640

Clawson, Oakland, Pop. 12,447
Clawson SD | 1,400/K-12
626 Phillips Ave 48017 | 248-655-4411
James Nolan, supt. | Fax 655-4422
www.clawson.k12.mi.us
Clawson HS | 400/9-12
101 John M Ave 48017 | 248-655-4200
Daveda Colbert, prin. | Fax 655-4205
Clawson MS | 300/6-8
150 John M Ave 48017 | 248-655-4250
John Dickinson, prin. | Fax 655-4251

Academy of Court Reporting | Post-Sec.
1330 W 14 Mile St 48017 | 248-353-4880

Climax, Kalamazoo, Pop. 767
Climax-Scotts Community SD | 700/K-12
372 S Main St 49034 | 269-746-2400
Dr. Geoffrey Balkam, supt. | Fax 746-4374
www.remc12.k12.mi.us/climax-scotts/
Climax-Scotts JSHS | 400/7-12
372 S Main St 49034 | 269-746-2300
 | Fax 746-4142

Clinton, Lenawee, Pop. 2,373
Clinton Community SD | 1,200/K-12
341 E Michigan Ave 49236 | 517-456-6501
David Pray, supt. | Fax 456-4324
www.clinton.k12.mi.us/
Clinton HS | 400/9-12
340 E Michigan Ave 49236 | 517-456-6511
Timothy Wilson, prin. | Fax 456-2042
Clinton MS | 300/6-8
100 E Franklin St 49236 | 517-456-6507
Donald Dunham, prin. | Fax 456-4997

Clinton Township, Macomb, Pop. 95,648
Chippewa Valley SD | 13,800/K-12
19120 Cass Ave 48038 | 586-723-2000
Mark Deldin, supt. | Fax 723-2001
www.chippewavalleyschools.org
Algonquin MS | 600/6-8
19150 Briarwood Ln 48036 | 586-723-3000
Dan Martini, prin. | Fax 723-3501
Chippewa Valley HS | 2,000/9-12
18300 19 Mile Rd 48038 | 586-723-2300
Dr. Jerry Davisson, prin. | Fax 723-2301
Seneca MS | 1,200/6-8
42755 Romeo Plank Rd 48038 | 586-723-3900
Susan Grenier, prin. | Fax 723-3901
Wyandot MS | 600/6-8
39490 Garfield Rd 48038 | 586-723-4200
Darleen Sims, prin. | Fax 723-4201
Other Schools – See Macomb

Clintondale Community SD | 2,700/PK-12
35100 Little Mack Ave 48035 | 586-791-6300
George Sassin, supt. | Fax 790-7643
www.clintondale.k12.mi.us
Clintondale HS | 800/9-12
35200 Little Mack Ave 48035 | 586-791-6300
Gregory Green, prin. | Fax 790-7645
Clintondale MS | 700/6-8
35300 Little Mack Ave 48035 | 586-791-6300
Michael Gray, prin. | Fax 790-7642

L'Anse Creuse SD
Supt. — See Harrison Township
Pankow Center | Vo/Tech
24600 F V Pankow Blvd 48036 | 586-783-6570
Gerald Hope, prin. | Fax 783-6577

Baker College of Clinton Township | Post-Sec.
34950 Little Mack Ave 48035 | 586-791-6610
Faith Christian S | 200/K-12
23130 Remick Dr 48036 | 586-783-9630
Matt Fenton, prin. | Fax 783-9628
Macomb Community College | Post-Sec.
44575 Garfield Rd 48038 | 586-445-7999

Clio, Genesee, Pop. 2,638
Clio SD | 3,600/PK-12
430 N Mill St 48420 | 810-591-0500
Fay Latture, supt. | Fax 591-0140
www.clioschools.org
Carter MS | 1,200/5-8
300 Upland Dr 48420 | 810-591-0503
Carole Chapman, prin. | Fax 591-8148
Clio HS | 1,100/9-12
1 Mustang Dr 48420 | 810-591-1359
Keith Smith, prin. | Fax 591-8169

Coldwater, Branch, Pop. 10,731
Branch ISD
370 Morse St 49036 | 517-279-5730
Michael Beckwith, supt. | Fax 279-5766
www.branch-isd.org
Branch Area Career Center | Vo/Tech
366 Morse St 49036 | 517-279-5721
Michael Hoffner, prin. | Fax 279-5777

Coldwater Community SD | 3,200/PK-12
401 Sauk River Dr 49036 | 517-279-5910
Milli Haug, supt. | Fax 279-7651
www.coldwater.k12.mi.us/
Coldwater HS | 1,000/9-12
275 N Fremont St 49036 | 517-279-5930
John Heistan, prin. | Fax 278-2475

Legg MS | 800/6-8
175 Green St 49036 | 517-279-5940
Ron Drzewicki, prin. | Fax 279-5945

School of Creative Hair Design | Post-Sec.
470 Marshall St 49036 | 517-279-2355

Coleman, Midland, Pop. 1,284
Coleman Community SD | 1,000/K-12
PO Box 522 48618 | 989-465-6060
Al Roeseler, supt. | Fax 465-9853
www.colemanschools.net
Coleman HS | 300/9-12
4951 N Lewis Rd 48618 | 989-465-6171
Loren Partlo, prin. | Fax 465-9222
Coleman MS | 300/6-8
991 E Railway St 48618 | 989-465-6177
Mary Pitchford, prin. | Fax 465-9855

Coloma, Berrien, Pop. 1,554
Coloma Community SD | 2,200/PK-12
PO Box 550 49038 | 269-468-2424
Terry Ann Boguth, supt. | Fax 468-2440
www.ccs.coloma.org
Coloma JHS | 300/8-9
PO Box 550 49038 | 269-468-2405
Peter Olsen, prin. | Fax 468-2428
Coloma SHS | 500/10-12
PO Box 550 49038 | 269-468-2400
John Brown, prin. | Fax 468-2423

Colon, Saint Joseph, Pop. 1,196
Colon Community SD | 800/K-12
400 Dallas St 49040 | 269-432-3442
Lloyd Kirby, supt. | Fax 432-2577
www.colonschools.org
Colon JHS | 400/7-12
400 Dallas St 49040 | 269-432-3231
Jill Groenendyk, prin. | Fax 432-9851

Commerce Township, Oakland, Pop. 26,955
Huron Valley SD
Supt. — See Highland
Oak Valley MS | 700/6-8
4200 White Oak Trl 48382 | 248-684-8101
Scott Lindberg, prin. | Fax 684-8105

Walled Lake Consolidated SD
Supt. — See Walled Lake
Central HS | 1,600/9-12
1600 E Oakley Park Rd 48390 | 248-956-4700
Dr. David Barry, prin. | Fax 956-4705
Northern HS | 1,500/9-12
6000 Bogie Lake Rd 48382 | 248-956-5300
John Toma, prin. | Fax 956-5305
Smart MS | 1,000/6-8
8500 Commerce Rd 48382 | 248-956-3500
Moe Kouris, prin. | Fax 956-3505

Comstock Park, Kent, Pop. 6,530
Comstock Park SD | 2,200/PK-12
PO Box 800 49321 | 616-254-5001
Dwight Anderson, supt. | Fax 784-5404
www.cppschools.com
Comstock Park HS | 700/9-12
PO Box 900 49321 | 616-254-5200
John Kraus, prin. | Fax 785-9835
Mill Creek MS | 500/6-8
PO Box 850 49321 | 616-254-5100
August Harju, prin. | Fax 785-2464

Concord, Jackson, Pop. 1,114
Concord Community SD | 900/K-12
PO Box 338 49237 | 517-524-8850
 | Fax 524-8613

www.ccs.k12.mi.us
Concord HS | 300/9-12
PO Box 338 49237 | 517-524-8384
Michael Corey, prin. | Fax 524-6196
Concord MS | 300/6-8
PO Box 338 49237 | 517-524-8854
Dave Kubel, prin. | Fax 524-7324

Constantine, Saint Joseph, Pop. 2,135
Constantine SD | 1,600/K-12
664 Canaris St 49042 | 269-435-8900
Norman L. Taylor, supt. | Fax 435-8980
www.constps.org
Constantine HS | 500/9-12
1 Falcon Dr 49042 | 269-435-8920
Tim Staffen, prin. | Fax 435-8981
Constantine MS | 400/6-8
260 W 6th St 49042 | 269-435-8940
Seth Parker, prin. | Fax 435-8982

Cooks, Schoolcraft
Big Bay de Noc SD | 300/K-12
8928 00.25 Rd 49817 | 906-644-2773
Terry Brooks, supt. | Fax 644-2615
www.dsisd.k12.mi.us/bigbay
Big Bay de Noc S | 300/K-12
8928 00.25 Rd 49817 | 906-644-2773
Julie Peterson, prin. | Fax 644-2615

Coopersville, Ottawa, Pop. 4,090
Coopersville Area SD | 2,300/K-12
198 East St 49404 | 616-997-3200
Kevin O'Neill, supt. | Fax 997-3214
www.coopersvillebroncos.org/
Coopersville JHS | 600/6-8
198 East St 49404 | 616-997-3400
Tom Fox, prin. | Fax 997-3414
Coopersville SHS | 800/9-12
198 East St 49404 | 616-997-3500
Ron Veldman, prin. | Fax 997-3514

Corunna, Shiawassee, Pop. 3,389
Corunna SD | 2,300/K-12
124 N Shiawassee St 48817 | 989-743-6338
John Smith, supt. | Fax 743-4474
corunna.k12.mi.us

Corunna HS | 700/9-12
417 E King St 48817 | 989-743-3441
Kelly Smith, prin. | Fax 743-5901
Corunna MS | 600/6-8
400 N Comstock St 48817 | 989-743-3441
John Fattal, prin. | Fax 743-8761

Covert, Van Buren
Covert SD | 700/K-12
35323 M 140 Hwy 49043 | 269-764-3701
Dr. Stephanie Burrage, supt. | Fax 764-8598
www.covertps.org
Covert HS | 200/9-12
35323 M 140 Hwy 49043 | 269-764-3730
Leadraine Roby, prin. | Fax 764-8598
Covert MS | 100/7-8
35323 M 140 Hwy 49043 | 269-764-3730
Leadriane Roby, prin. | Fax 764-8598

Croswell, Sanilac, Pop. 2,439
Croswell-Lexington SD | 2,500/PK-12
5407 Peck Rd 48422 | 810-679-1000
Charles Smith, supt. | Fax 679-1005
www.cros-lex.k12.mi.us
Croswell-Lexington HS | 800/9-12
5461 Peck Rd 48422 | 810-679-1500
William Jedele, prin. | Fax 679-1505
Croswell-Lexington MS | 600/6-8
5485 Peck Rd 48422 | 810-679-1400
Dale Ann Ogden, prin. | Fax 679-1405

Crystal Falls, Iron, Pop. 1,726
Forest Park SD | 300/K-12
801 Forest Pkwy 49920 | 906-875-6761
Tom Jayne, supt. | Fax 875-4660
www.fptrojans.org
Forest Park JSHS | 300/7-12
801 Forest Pkwy 49920 | 906-875-6869
Mark Johnson, prin. | Fax 875-4660

Custer, Mason, Pop. 319
Mason County Eastern SD | 600/K-12
18 S Main St 49405 | 231-757-3733
Michael Oakes, supt. | Fax 757-9671
mceschools.com
Mason County Eastern JSHS | 400/6-12
18 S Main St 49405 | 231-757-3733
Scott Sherman, prin. | Fax 757-9671

Dansville, Ingham, Pop. 432
Dansville SD | 900/K-12
PO Box 187 48819 | 517-623-6120
Michael V. Simeck, supt. | Fax 623-6719
dansville.org
Dansville HS | 300/9-12
PO Box 187 48819 | 517-623-6120
John Chandler, prin. | Fax 623-0127
Dansville MS | 200/6-8
PO Box 13 48819 | 517-623-6120
David O. Sheathelm, prin. | Fax 623-6719

Davison, Genesee, Pop. 5,443
Davison Community SD | 5,200/9-12
PO Box 319 48423 | 810-591-0801
R. Clay Perkins, supt. | Fax 591-7813
www.davison.k12.mi.us
Davison HS | 1,400/9-12
1250 N Oak Rd 48423 | 810-591-3531
Kevin Brown, prin. | Fax 591-3555
Davison MS | 800/7-8
600 S Dayton St 48423 | 810-591-0848
Shelly Fenner-Krasny, prin. | Fax 591-2754

Faith Baptist S | 400/K-12
7306 E Atherton Rd 48423 | 810-653-9661
Larry Nagengast, prin. | Fax 658-0087

Dearborn, Wayne, Pop. 96,670
Dearborn SD | 17,900/PK-12
18700 Audette St 48124 | 313-827-3020
Dr. John Artis, supt. | Fax 827-3137
www.dearbornschools.org
Bryant MS | 800/6-8
460 N Vernon St 48128 | 313-827-2900
Marc Zigterman, prin. | Fax 827-2905
Dearborn HS | 1,600/9-12
19501 Outer Dr 48124 | 313-827-1600
Gail Shenkman, prin. | Fax 827-1605
Ford HS | 1,500/9-12
20601 Rotunda Dr 48124 | 313-827-1500
Gerald Dodd, prin. | Fax 827-1505
Fordson HS | 2,200/9-12
13800 Ford Rd 48126 | 313-827-1400
Imad Fadlallah, prin. | Fax 827-1405
Salina IS | 800/4-8
2623 Salina St 48120 | 313-827-6600
Glenn Maleyko, prin. | Fax 827-6605
Smith MS | 800/6-8
23851 Yale St 48124 | 313-827-2800
Hassane Jaafar, prin. | Fax 827-2805
Stout MS | 900/6-8
18500 Oakwood Blvd 48124 | 313-827-4600
Julia Maconochie, prin. | Fax 827-4605
Woodworth MS | 900/6-8
4951 Ternes St 48126 | 313-827-7100
Troy Patterson, prin. | Fax 827-7105

American Islamic Academy | 400/K-12
6409 Schaefer Rd 48126 | 313-945-6504
Michele Jarrait, prin. | Fax 945-1976
Davenport University - Eastern Region | Post-Sec.
4801 Oakman Blvd 48126 | 313-581-4400
Divine Child HS | 900/9-12
1001 N Silvery Ln 48128 | 313-562-1990
Rev. John Kiselica, prin. | Fax 562-9361
Henry Ford Community College | Post-Sec.
5101 Evergreen Rd 48128 | 313-845-9615
National Institute of Technology | Post-Sec.
23400 Michigan Ave Ste 200 48124 | 313-562-4228

University of Michigan-Dearborn | Post-Sec.
4901 Evergreen Rd 48128 | 313-593-5000

Dearborn Heights, Wayne, Pop. 57,373
Crestwood SD | 3,600/PK-12
1501 N Beech Daly Rd 48127 | 313-278-0903
Joseph Pius, supt. | Fax 278-4774
csdm.k12.mi.us
Crestwood HS | 1,100/9-12
1501 N Beech Daly Rd 48127 | 313-278-7475
James Baker, prin. | Fax 792-0205
Riverside MS | 1,100/5-8
25900 W Warren St 48127 | 313-792-0201
Jennifer McFarlane, prin. | Fax 792-0201

Dearborn Heights SD 7 | 3,000/K-12
20629 Annapolis St 48125 | 313-278-1900
Jeffrey Bartold, supt. | Fax 278-1413
www.resa.net/district7
Annapolis HS | 800/9-12
4650 Clippert St 48125 | 313-278-9870
Dan Scott, prin. | Fax 278-1238
Best JHS | 800/6-8
22201 Powers Ave 48125 | 313-278-6200
Jon Znamierowski, prin. | Fax 278-2470
Westwood Community SD | 2,000/K-12
3335 S Beech Daly St 48125 | 313-565-1900
Dr. Ernando F. Minghine, supt. | Fax 565-3162
www.westwood.k12.mi.us
Robichaud JSHS | 1,000/7-12
3601 Janet St 48125 | 313-565-8850
Pamela Harris, prin. | Fax 565-0304

Decatur, Van Buren, Pop. 1,882
Decatur SD | 1,200/PK-12
110 Cedar St 49045 | 269-423-6800
Dr. Elizabeth Godwin, supt. | Fax 423-6849
www.raiderpride.org/
Decatur HS | 300/9-12
110 Cedar St 49045 | 269-423-6850
Rick Bushor, prin. | Fax 423-6899
Decatur MS | 400/5-8
405 N Phelps St 49045 | 269-423-6900
Larry Smith, prin. | Fax 423-6949

Deckerville, Sanilac, Pop. 932
Deckerville Community SD | 800/K-12
2633 Black River St 48427 | 810-376-3615
Alan Broughton, supt. | Fax 376-3115
www.deckerville.k12.mi.us
Deckerville HS | 400/7-12
2633 Black River St 48427 | 810-376-3875
Donald Schelke, prin. | Fax 376-3115

Deerfield, Lenawee, Pop. 979
Deerfield SD | 400/K-12
PO Box 217 49238 | 517-447-3215
Larry Shilling, supt. | Fax 447-3282
deerfield.schoolwebpages.com
Deerfield S | 400/K-12
PO Box 217 49238 | 517-447-3015
Dr. Lana Callihan, prin. | Fax 447-3282

Delton, Barry
Delton Kellogg SD | 1,900/K-12
327 N Grove St 49046 | 269-623-9200
Ronald Archer, supt. | Fax 623-9269
www.dkschools.org/
Delton Kellogg HS | 600/9-12
327 N Grove St 49046 | 269-623-9226
Paul Blacken, prin. | Fax 623-9292
Delton Kellogg MS | 600/5-8
6325 Delton Rd 49046 | 269-623-9229
Brooke Ballee, prin. | Fax 623-9259

De Tour Village, Chippewa, Pop. 421
De Tour Area SD | 200/K-12
PO Box 429 49725 | 906-297-2421
Joe Powers, supt. | Fax 297-3403
eup.k12.mi.us/detour/index.html
De Tour JSHS | 100/7-12
PO Box 429 49725 | 906-297-2011
Angela Reed, prin. | Fax 297-3403

Detroit, Wayne, Pop. 911,402
Detroit SD | 152,800/PK-12
7321 2nd Ave 48202 | 313-873-7450
William Coleman, supt. | Fax 873-7433
www.detroitk12.org
Beaubien S | 1,000/7-9
19701 Wyoming St 48221 | 313-494-7250
Belinda Raines, prin. | Fax 494-7241
Breithaupt Vocational Education | Vo/Tech
9300 Hubbell St 48228 | 313-866-9550
Vanessa Spencer, prin. | Fax 866-9605
Cass Technical HS | Vo/Tech
2421 2nd Ave 48201 | 313-263-2000
George Cohen, prin. | Fax 263-2001
Central S | 1,900/PK-12
2425 Tuxedo St 48206 | 313-252-3000
Anthony Womack, prin. | Fax 866-0969
Cerveny MS | 700/6-8
15850 Strathmoor St 48227 | 313-866-9600
Gladys Stoner, prin. | Fax 866-9626
Chadsey HS | 1,300/6-12
5335 Martin St 48210 | 313-596-3690
Shirley Hightower, prin. | Fax 596-7686
Cleveland MS | 1,000/6-8
13322 Conant St 48212 | 313-866-3500
Garnet Green, prin. | Fax 866-3592
Clippert Academy | 400/5-8
1981 McKinstry St 48209 | 313-849-5009
Brenda Feggins, prin. | Fax 849-5740
Cody HS | 2,000/9-12
18445 Cathedral St 48228 | 313-866-9200
Ronnie Phillips, prin. | Fax 866-9266
Coffey MS | 500/6-8
17210 Cambridge Ave 48235 | 313-852-0582
Gerald Craft, prin. | Fax 852-0589

Columbus MS | 800/6-8
18025 Brock St 48205 | 313-866-2070
Alvin Wood, prin. | Fax 866-2098
Communications & Media Arts HS | 500/9-12
14771 Mansfield St 48227 | 313-866-9300
Kim Gray, prin. | Fax 866-9304
Cooley HS | 2,000/4-12
15055 Hubbell St 48227 | 313-866-9400
Thomas Woodhouse, prin. | Fax 866-9422
Crockett HS, 8950 Saint Cyril St 48213 | 9-12
Brenda Belcher, prin. | 313-494-1805
Crockett Tech S | Vo/Tech
571 Mack Ave 48201 | 313-494-1805
Barbara Eason, prin. | Fax 494-0992
Davis Aerospace Technical HS | Vo/Tech
10200 Erwin St 48234 | 313-866-5401
Alsce Johnson, prin. | Fax 866-5408
Denby Technical & Preparatory HS | Vo/Tech
12800 Kelly Rd 48224 | 313-866-7200
Diane Fisher, prin. | Fax 866-2038
Detroit HS for Fine & Performing Arts | 500/9-12
123 Selden St 48201 | 313-494-6000
Denise Davis-Cotton, prin. | Fax 494-2129
Drew MS | 1,000/6-8
9600 Wyoming St 48204 | 313-873-6880
Sallie Polk, prin. | Fax 873-0114
Earhart MS | 700/6-8
1000 Scotten St 48209 | 313-849-3945
Gerald Vasquez, prin. | Fax 849-4746
Ellington Conservatory of Music/Art | 800/5-8
8030 E Outer Dr 48213 | 313-866-2860
Stanley Waldon, prin. | Fax 866-2866
Farwell MS | 800/6-8
19955 Fenelon St 48234 | 313-866-3700
Delores Johnson, prin. | Fax 866-3632
Finney HS | 2,200/6-12
17200 Southampton St 48224 | 313-417-8800
Alvin Ward, prin. | Fax 417-8816
Ford HS | 1,800/9-12
20000 Evergreen Rd 48219 | 313-494-7567
Terry Truvillion, prin. | Fax 494-7565
Golightly Career and Technical Center | Vo/Tech
900 Dickerson St 48215 | 313-822-8820
Laura Royster, prin. | Fax 866-3131
Hally Magnet S | 600/6-8
2585 Grove St 48221 | 313-494-3939
Hattie Cason, prin. | Fax 494-7089
Heilmann Park MS | 1,100/6-8
19035 Crusade St 48205 | 313-866-7233
Cheryl Harshaw, prin. | Fax 866-7329
Hutchins MS | 600/6-8
8820 Woodrow Wilson St 48206 | 313-873-2777
Virginia Clay, prin. | Fax 873-1068
International Academy | 200/4-8
8401 Woodward Ave 48202 | 313-596-3690
Beverly Hibbler, prin. | Fax 873-3088
Kettering HS | 1,700/8-12
6101 Van Dyke St 48213 | 313-866-5336
Willie Howard, prin. | Fax 852-9615
King HS | 2,100/6-12
3200 E Lafayette St 48207 | 313-494-7373
Paul Gray, prin. | Fax 494-7359
Lessenger MS | 1,100/3-8
8401 Trinity St 48228 | 313-945-1330
Eric George, prin. | Fax 945-1557
MacKenzie HS | 2,200/5-12
9275 Wyoming St 48204 | 313-873-9900
Bernard Bonam, prin. | Fax 873-9930
McMichael MS | 500/5-8
6050 Linwood St 48208 | 313-596-3502
Deborah Hunter-Harvill, prin. | Fax 596-3500
McNair MS | 900/6-8
4180 Marlborough St 48215 | 313-417-8898
John White, prin. | Fax 417-8796
Miller MS | 800/3-9
2322 Dubois St 48207 | 313-494-2642
Pierre Hendrix, prin. | Fax 494-7351
Mumford HS | 2,100/8-12
17525 Wyoming St 48221 | 313-494-7064
Linda S. Spight, prin. | Fax 494-7124
Munger MS | 700/5-8
5525 Martin St 48210 | 313-596-3565
Sharon Robinson, prin. | Fax 596-3561
Murphy JHS | 700/6-8
23901 Fenkell St 48223 | 313-494-7585
Anthony Jones, prin. | Fax 494-7550
Murray-Wright HS | 1,600/9-12
2001 W Warren Ave 48208 | 313-596-3555
Grady Jones, prin. | Fax 596-3552
New MS Academy East | 200/6-8
17201 Annott St 48205 | 313-866-2072
Debra Jenkins, prin. | Fax 866-2074
Northern S | 2,000/PK-12
9026 Woodward Ave 48202 | 313-873-1250
Marvin Youmans, prin. | Fax 873-1290
Northwestern S | 1,500/8-12
2200 W Grand Blvd 48208 | 313-596-0700
Patricia Pickett, prin. | Fax 596-0710
Osborn HS | 2,200/8-12
11600 E 7 Mile Rd 48205 | 313-866-0343
Matthew Dixon, prin. | Fax 866-0356
Pershing HS | 2,200/8-12
18875 Ryan Rd 48234 | 313-866-7700
Lisa Phillips, prin. | Fax 866-3296
Phoenix Multicultural Academy | 700/5-8
7735 Lane St 48209 | 313-849-2419
Anna Rodriguez, prin. | Fax 849-1170
Post MS | 700/6-8
8200 Midland St 48238 | 313-494-7322
Yolanda Hebert, prin. | Fax 494-7326
Randolph Career and Technical Center | Vo/Tech
17101 Hubbell St 48235 | 313-494-7100
Joseph W. Smith, prin. | Fax 494-7114
Redford HS | 2,100/7-12
21431 Grand River Ave 48219 | 313-494-7500
Thurman Stephens, prin. | Fax 494-7511

Renaissance HS 900/9-12
6565 W Outer Dr 48235 313-494-7212
Deborah Harley, prin. Fax 494-7243
Robinson MS 600/6-8
13000 Essex Ave 48215 313-866-5500
Sharon Lee, prin. Fax 866-5580
Ruddiman MS 600/6-8
7350 Southfield Fwy 48228 313-271-0120
Anthony Huston, prin. Fax 271-0979
Scott S 6-8
18400 Hoover St 48205 313-866-6700
Beverly Butler, prin. Fax 866-2693
Southeastern HS 2,200/6-12
3030 Fairview St 48214 313-866-4500
Brenda Gatlin, prin. Fax 866-5555
Southwestern HS 800/9-12
6921 W Fort St 48209 313-849-4521
Robert Hodge, prin. Fax 849-4734
Taft MS 700/6-8
19501 Berg Rd 48219 313-494-7577
Naomi Lewis, prin. Fax 494-7538
University MS 400/6-8
2001 Myrtle St 48208 313-596-3780
Gerlma Johnson, prin. Fax 596-3783
Washington Careers Center Vo/Tech
13000 Dequindre St 48212 313-252-3059
Julia Purkett, prin. Fax 866-0671
Webber MS 600/3-8
4700 Tireman St 48204 313-596-4750
Diane Goins, prin. Fax 596-4748
Western International HS 1,600/8-12
1500 Scotten St 48209 313-849-4758
Rebecca Luna, prin. Fax 849-4695
Other Schools – See Redford

College for Creative Studies Post-Sec.
201 E Kirby St 48202 313-664-7400
Cornerstone S 200/6-8
6861 E Nevada St 48234 313-892-1860
Dennis Wrosch, prin. Fax 892-1861
Detroit Health Department Post-Sec.
1151 Taylor St 48202 313-876-4090
Detroit Urban Lutheran S 300/K-12
8181 Greenfield Rd 48228 313-582-9900
R. David Siefker, prin. Fax 582-0817
DMC University Laboratories Post-Sec.
4201 Saint Antoine St 48201 313-745-3053
East Bethlehem Lutheran S 100/K-12
3510 E Outer Dr 48234 313-892-2671
Carlyn Roth, prin. Fax 892-1754
East Catholic HS 100/9-12
7320 Saint Anthony Pl 48213 313-921-9650
Sr. Jolene VanHandel, prin. Fax 921-8905
Grace Hospital Post-Sec.
6071 W Outer Dr 48235 313-966-3525
Harper Hospital Post-Sec.
3990 John R St 48201 313-745-9375
Henry Ford Hospital Post-Sec.
2799 W Grand Blvd 48202 313-876-1257
Lewis College of Business Post-Sec.
17370 Meyers Rd 48235 313-862-6300
Loyola HS 100/9-12
15325 Pinehurst St 48238 313-861-2407
DeLisa Jones, prin. Fax 861-4718
Marygrove College Post-Sec.
8425 W McNichols Rd 48221 313-927-1200
Michigan Barber School Post-Sec.
8988 Grand River Ave # 90 48204 313-894-2300
National Institute of Technology Post-Sec.
300 River Place Dr Ste 1000 48207 313-567-5350
Our Lady of Guadalupe MS 5-8
4330 Central St 48210 313-849-2965
Meghan Evoy, prin. Fax 849-3144
Sacred Heart Major Seminary Post-Sec.
2701 W Chicago 48206 313-883-8500
St. John's Hospital Post-Sec.
22101 Moross Rd 48236 313-343-7531
SER Business and Technical Institute Post-Sec.
9301 Michigan Ave 48210 313-846-2240
University of Detroit/Jesuit HS 900/7-12
8400 S Cambridge Ave 48221 313-862-5400
Susan Rowe, prin. Fax 927-2330
University of Detroit-Mercy Post-Sec.
PO Box 19900 48219 313-993-1000
Wayne County Community College Post-Sec.
801 W Fort St 48226 313-496-2500
Wayne State University Post-Sec.
5980 Cass Ave 48202 313-577-2424

De Witt, Clinton, Pop. 4,499
DeWitt SD 2,800/K-12
PO Box 800, 517-668-3000
Tina Templin, supt. Fax 668-3018
www.dewitt.edzone.net
DeWitt JHS 500/7-8
PO Box 800, 517-668-3200
Neil Hufnagel, prin. Fax 668-3255
Other Schools – See Lansing

Dexter, Washtenaw, Pop. 2,913
Dexter Community SD 3,500/K-12
7714 Ann Arbor St 48130 734-424-4100
Evelynn Shirk, supt. Fax 424-4112
www.dexter.k12.mi.us
Dexter HS 1,000/9-12
2200 N Parker Rd 48130 734-424-4240
Kit Moran, prin. Fax 424-2747
Mill Creek MS 500/7-8
7305 Dexter Ann Arbor Rd 48130 734-424-4150
Jami Bronson, prin. Fax 424-4159

Dollar Bay, Houghton
Dollar Bay-Tamarack City SD 300/K-12
PO Box 371 49922 906-482-5800
Jan Quarless, supt. Fax 487-5931
www.dollarbay.k12.mi.us
Dollar Bay JSHS 100/7-12
PO Box 371 49922 906-482-5812
William Tarbox, prin. Fax 487-5940

Douglas, Allegan, Pop. 1,197
Saugatuck SD 800/PK-12
PO Box 818 49406 269-857-1444
Timothy Wood, supt. Fax 857-1448
www.saugatuck.k12.mi.us
Other Schools – See Saugatuck

Dowagiac, Cass, Pop. 5,857
Dowagiac UNSD 2,700/PK-12
206 Main St 49047 269-782-4400
Peg Stowers, supt. Fax 782-3152
www.dowagiacschools.org
Dowagiac MS 400/7-8
57072 Riverside Dr 49047 269-782-4440
Michael Frazier, prin. Fax 782-4449
Union HS 700/9-12
701 W Prairie Ronde St 49047 269-782-4420
Paul Hartsig, prin. Fax 782-9518

Southwestern Michigan College Post-Sec.
58900 Cherry Grove Rd 49047 269-782-1000

Dryden, Lapeer, Pop. 814
Dryden Community SD 800/K-12
3866 Rochester Rd 48428 810-796-9534
Thomas J. Goulette, supt. Fax 796-3698
www.dryden.k12.mi.us
Dryden JSHS 400/7-12
3866 Rochester Rd 48428 810-796-2266
Ruth Fox, prin. Fax 796-2510

Dundee, Monroe, Pop. 3,583
Dundee Community SD 1,700/PK-12
420 Ypsilanti St 48131 734-529-2350
Robert Black, supt. Fax 529-5606
www.dundee.k12.mi.us
Dundee HS 500/9-12
130 Viking Dr 48131 734-529-7008
Jacqueline Schultz, prin. Fax 529-7053
Dundee MS 500/5-8
420 Ypsilanti St 48131 734-529-2350
Fax 529-5606

Durand, Shiawassee, Pop. 3,888
Durand Area SD 1,700/PK-12
310 N Saginaw St 48429 989-288-2681
Dr. Jan Amsterburg, supt. Fax 288-3553
durand.k12.mi.us/
Durand Area HS 600/9-12
9575 E Monroe Rd 48429 989-288-2684
Lyle Thomas, prin. Fax 288-2986
Durand MS 500/6-8
9550 E Lansing Rd 48429 989-288-3435
Adam Neisler, prin. Fax 288-5563

East China, Saint Clair, Pop. 3,216
East China SD 5,500/K-12
1585 Meisner Rd 48054 810-676-1018
Rodney Green, supt. Fax 676-1037
www.ecsd.us
Other Schools – See Marine City, Saint Clair

East Jordan, Charlevoix, Pop. 2,418
East Jordan SD 1,300/K-12
PO Box 399 49727 231-536-0053
Robert Hansen, supt. Fax 536-3310
www.ejps.org/
East Jordan HS 400/9-12
PO Box 399 49727 231-536-2259
Tammy Jackson, prin. Fax 536-3536
East Jordan MS 300/6-8
PO Box 399 49727 231-536-2823
Michael Haynes, prin. Fax 536-0051

East Lansing, Ingham, Pop. 47,245
East Lansing SD 3,500/K-12
841 Timberlane St Ste A 48823 517-333-7420
David Chapin, supt. Fax 333-7470
www.elps.k12.mi.us
East Lansing HS 1,200/9-12
509 Burcham Dr 48823 517-333-7539
Paula Steele, prin. Fax 333-7513
MacDonald MS 600/7-8
1601 Burcham Dr 48823 517-333-7600
Debra Auge, prin. Fax 333-5098

Career Quest Learning Center Post-Sec.
5000 Northwind Dr Ste 120 48823 517-318-3330
Douglas J Educational Center Post-Sec.
333 Albert Ave Ste 110 48823 517-333-9656
Lakeside Christian S 100/PK-12
7868 E M 78 48823 517-339-1037
Treila Jill Friar, dir. Fax 339-0103
MI State Univ. - Detroit College of Law Post-Sec.
316 DCLMSU and Bus Lib Bldg 48824
517-432-0222
Michigan State University Post-Sec.
450 Administration Bldg 48824 517-355-1855

Eastpointe, Macomb, Pop. 33,394
East Detroit SD 5,900/K-12
15115 Deerfield Ave 48021 586-445-4400
Bruce Kefgen, supt. Fax 445-4427
www.eastdetroit.org
East Detroit HS 1,700/9-12
15501 Couzens Ave 48021 586-445-4455
Paul Szymanski, prin. Fax 445-4522
Kelly MS 800/6-8
24701 Kelly Rd 48021 586-445-4570
Ira Hamden, prin. Fax 445-4582
Oakwood MS 700/6-8
14825 Nehls Ave 48021 586-445-4600
Sam Ellis, prin. Fax 445-4612
Kellwood S Adult
19200 Stephens Dr 48021 586-445-4451
Robin White, admin. Fax 445-4450

Eaton Rapids, Eaton, Pop. 5,320
Eaton Rapids SD 3,100/K-12
501 King St 48827 517-663-8155
William DeFrance, supt. Fax 663-2236
www.erps.k12.mi.us
Eaton Rapids HS 1,000/9-12
800 State St 48827 517-663-2231
David Johnson, prin. Fax 663-0616
Eaton Rapids MS 500/7-8
815 Greyhound Dr 48827 517-663-8151
Stephen Dembowski, prin. Fax 663-0625

Eau Claire, Berrien, Pop. 646
Eau Claire SD 800/K-12
PO Box 398 49111 269-461-6947
D. Stefan Jaggi, supt. Fax 461-0089
www.eau-claire.k12.mi.us
Eau Claire HS 300/9-12
7450 Hochberger Rd 49111 269-461-6997
Mark Costello, prin. Fax 461-0065
Eau Claire MS 7-8
7450 Hochberger Rd 49111 269-461-0083
Chris Porter, prin. Fax 461-0065

Eben Junction, Alger
Superior Central SD 400/K-12
PO Box 148 49825 906-439-5531
Mary Kay Wanska, supt. Fax 439-5734
s-c.maresa.k12.mi.us
Superior Central S 400/K-12
PO Box 148 49825 906-439-5532
Loren Vannest, prin. Fax 439-5234

Ecorse, Wayne, Pop. 11,046
Ecorse SD 1,300/K-12
4024 W Jefferson Ave 48229 313-294-4750
Emma Epps, supt. Fax 294-4769
www.resa.net/ecorse/
Ecorse Community HS 500/8-12
27385 W Outer Dr 48229 313-294-4700
Stan Childress, prin. Fax 294-4709

Edmore, Montcalm, Pop. 1,251
Montabella Community SD 1,100/PK-12
PO Box 349 48829 989-427-5148
Scott Crosby, supt. Fax 427-3828
www.montabella.com
Other Schools – See Blanchard

Edwardsburg, Cass, Pop. 1,133
Edwardsburg SD 2,300/K-12
69410 Section St 49112 269-663-3055
Sherman Ostrander, supt. Fax 663-6485
www.remc11.k12.mi.us/edward
Edwardsburg HS 700/9-12
69410 Section St 49112 269-663-1044
David Zech, prin. Fax 663-8915
Edwardsburg MS 500/6-8
69410 Section St 49112 269-663-1031
Anthony Koontz, prin. Fax 663-8638

Elk Rapids, Antrim, Pop. 1,728
Elk Rapids SD 1,500/K-12
707 E 3rd St 49629 231-264-8692
Jon Hoover, supt. Fax 264-6538
www.erschools.com
Cherryland MS 400/6-8
707 E 3rd St 49629 231-264-8991
Terry Morris, prin. Fax 264-9370
Elk Rapids HS 500/9-12
308 Meguzee Pt 49629 231-264-8108
Steven Gallagher, prin. Fax 264-0895

Ellsworth, Antrim, Pop. 471
Ellsworth Community SD 300/K-12
9467 Park St 49729 231-588-2544
James Emery, supt. Fax 588-6183
www.ellsworth.k12.mi.us/
Ellsworth Community S 300/K-12
9467 Park St 49729 231-588-2544
Michelle Fox, prin. Fax 588-6183

Elsie, Clinton, Pop. 1,016
Ovid-Elsie Area SD 1,500/K-12
8989 E Colony Rd 48831 989-834-2271
Wayne Petroelje, supt. Fax 862-5887
www.oe.k12.mi.us/
Ovid-Elsie HS 500/9-12
8989 E Colony Rd 48831 989-834-2271
Kirk Baese, prin. Fax 862-4463
Ovid-Elsie MS 300/7-8
8989 E Colony Rd 48831 989-834-2271
Jerry Goosen, prin. Fax 862-4463

Engadine, Mackinac
Engadine Consolidated SD 300/K-12
W13920 Melville St 49827 906-477-6313
James Wilcoxen, supt. Fax 477-6643
www.eup.k12.mi.us/engadine
Engadine JSHS 100/7-12
W13920 Melville St 49827 906-477-6449
Stu Hobbs, prin. Fax 477-6643

Erie, Monroe
Mason Consolidated SD 1,500/PK-12
2400 Mason Eagles Dr 48133 734-848-5475
Marlene Mills, supt. Fax 848-2516
scnc.eriemason.k12.mi.us/
Mason HS 500/9-12
2400 Mason Eagles Dr 48133 734-848-5755
Thomas McGarry, prin. Fax 848-5425
Mason MS 400/6-8
2260 Samaria Rd 48133 734-848-4944
Tom McGarry, prin. Fax 848-0035

Escanaba, Delta, Pop. 12,778
Escanaba Area SD 2,900/K-12
1500 Ludington St 49829 906-786-5411
Thomas Smith, supt. Fax 786-0106
www.escanabaschool.com

Escanaba HS 1,200/9-12
500 S Lincoln Rd 49829 906-786-6521
Gerald Kulbertis, prin. Fax 786-2166
Escanaba MS 500/7-8
1500 Ludington St 49829 906-786-7462
Catherine Johnson, prin. Fax 786-5958

Bay de Noc Community College Post-Sec.
2001 N Lincoln Rd 49829 906-786-5802
U.P. Academy of Hair Design Post-Sec.
1619 Ludington St 49829 906-786-5750

Essexville, Bay, Pop. 3,653
Essexville-Hampton SD 1,900/K-12
303 Pine St 48732 989-894-9700
Corinne Netzley, supt. Fax 894-9705
www.e-hps.net
Cramer JHS 500/6-8
313 Pine St 48732 989-894-9740
Connie Hamilton, prin. Fax 894-9720
Garber HS 600/9-12
213 Pine St 48732 989-894-9710
Doug Trombley, prin. Fax 894-9730

Evart, Osceola, Pop. 1,720
Evart SD 1,300/K-12
PO Box 917 49631 231-734-5594
Howard Hyde, supt. Fax 734-2931
www.evart.k12.mi.us/
Evart HS 400/9-12
6221 95th Ave 49631 231-734-5551
Scott Bogner, prin. Fax 734-4156
Evart MS 400/5-8
321 N Hemlock St 49631 231-734-4222
Alan Kullman, prin. Fax 734-2931

Ewen, Ontonagon
Ewen-Trout Creek SD 200/K-12
14312 Airport Rd 49925 906-988-2350
Catherine Shamion, supt. Fax 988-2549
www.etc.k12.mi.us/
Ewen-Trout Creek JSHS 200/7-12
14312 Airport Rd 49925 906-988-2365
Lee Lindberg, prin. Fax 988-2864

Fairgrove, Tuscola, Pop. 619
Akron-Fairgrove SD 400/K-12
PO Box 217 48733 989-693-6163
Joe Candela, supt. Fax 693-6560
www.a-f.k12.mi.us
Akron-Fairgrove JSHS 200/7-12
PO Box 217 48733 989-693-6112
John Amend, prin. Fax 693-6160

Fair Haven, Saint Clair, Pop. 1,505
Anchor Bay SD
Supt. — See New Baltimore
Anchor Bay HS 1,800/9-12
6319 County Line Rd 48023 586-648-2525
Judy Stefanac, prin. Fax 716-8306

Fairview, Oscoda
Fairview Area SD 400/K-12
1879 E Miller Rd 48621 989-848-7000
Bruce Nelson, supt. Fax 848-7070
www.fairview.k12.mi.us
Fairview JSHS 200/7-12
1879 E Miller Rd 48621 989-848-7050
Raymond Poellet, prin. Fax 848-7073

Farmington, Oakland, Pop. 10,168
Farmington SD 11,900/PK-12
32500 Shiawassee Rd 48336 248-489-3349
Susan Zurralec, supt. Fax 489-3348
www.farmington.k12.mi.us
Farmington HS 1,400/9-12
32000 Shiawassee Rd 48336 248-489-3455
John Barrett, prin. Fax 489-3474
Other Schools – See Farmington Hills

Mercy HS 1,000/9-12
29300 W 11 Mile Rd 48336 248-476-8020
Caroline Witte, prin. Fax 476-3691

Farmington Hills, Oakland, Pop. 80,874
Farmington SD
Supt. — See Farmington
Dunckel MS 700/6-8
32800 W 12 Mile Rd 48334 248-489-3577
Allen Archer, prin. Fax 489-3590
East MS 800/6-8
25000 Middlebelt Rd 48336 248-489-3601
Ken Sanders, prin. Fax 489-3606
Harrison HS 1,100/9-12
29995 W 12 Mile Rd 48334 248-489-3499
Jim Myers, prin. Fax 489-3514
North Farmington HS 1,400/9-12
32900 W 13 Mile Rd 48334 248-785-2005
Richard Jones, prin. Fax 855-2060
Power MS 800/6-8
34740 Rhonswood St 48335 248-489-3622
Robert Kovar, prin. Fax 489-3628
Warner MS 600/6-8
30303 W 14 Mile Rd 48334 248-785-2030
Mildred Crawley Taylor, prin. Fax 855-2831
Farmington Community S Adult
30415 Shiawassee Rd 48336 248-489-3333
Pat Karas, prin. Fax 489-3380

Center for Humanistic Studies Post-Sec.
26811 Orchard Lake Rd 48334 248-476-1122
Oakland Community College Post-Sec.
27055 Orchard Lake Rd 48334 248-522-3400

Farwell, Clare, Pop. 860
Farwell Area SD 1,600/K-12
371 E Main St 48622 989-588-9917
David Peterson, supt. Fax 588-6440

Farwell HS 500/9-12
399 E Michigan St 48622 989-588-9913
Phyllis Hall, prin. Fax 588-6041
Farwell MS 500/5-8
500 E Ohio St 48622 989-588-9915
Catheryn Gross, prin. Fax 588-3337

Fennville, Allegan, Pop. 1,471
Fennville SD 1,100/K-12
5 Memorial Dr 49408 269-561-7331
Mark Dobias, supt. Fax 561-5792
www.accn.org/~fps/index.html
Fennville HS 400/9-12
4 Memorial Dr 49408 269-561-7241
Amber Lugten, prin. Fax 561-6901
Fennville MS 400/6-8
1 Memorial Dr 49408 269-561-7341
Jody Martin, prin. Fax 561-2143
Pearl Alternative & Adult Education Ctr. Adult
1779 56th St 49408 269-561-2343
Dave Coffindaffer, dir. Fax 561-5108

Fenton, Genesee, Pop. 11,832
Fenton Area SD 3,600/K-12
3100 Owen Rd 48430 810-591-4701
Peggy Yates, supt. Fax 591-4705
www.fenton.k12.mi.us
Fenton HS 1,200/9-12
3200 W Shiawassee Ave 48430 810-591-2600
Mark Suchowski, prin. Fax 591-2605
Schmidt MS 600/7-8
3255 Donaldson Dr 48430 810-591-7700
Kevin Cornell, prin. Fax 591-7705

Lake Fenton Community SD 1,100/K-12
11425 Torrey Rd 48430 810-591-4141
Ralph Coaster, supt. Fax 591-9866
lake-fenton.k12.mi.us
Lake Fenton MS 6-8
11425 Torrey Rd 48430 810-591-2209
Nancy Harrison, prin. Fax 591-8475
Other Schools – See Linden

Charles Stewart Mott Community College Post-Sec.
2100 W Thompson Rd 48430 810-762-0200

Ferndale, Oakland, Pop. 21,693
Ferndale SD 3,500/PK-12
2920 Burdette St 48220 248-586-8652
Gary Meier, supt. Fax 586-8655
www.ferndaleschools.org
Ferndale HS 1,100/9-12
881 Pinecrest Dr 48220 248-548-8621
Herb Ivory, prin. Fax 586-8620
Ferndale MS 600/7-8
725 Pinecrest Dr 48220 248-586-8830
Dawn Warren, prin. Fax 586-8834
University HS Vo/Tech
1244 Paxton St 48220 248-586-8846
George Tomey, prin. Fax 586-8857
Taft Education Center Adult
427 Allen St 48220 248-586-8916
Fran Foote, dir. Fax 586-8909
Other Schools – See Oak Park

Virginia Farrell Beauty School Post-Sec.
22925 Woodward Ave 48220 248-398-4647

Fife Lake, Grand Traverse, Pop. 466
Forest Area Community SD 700/K-12
7741 Shippy Rd SW 49633 231-369-4191
Matthew A. Cairy, supt. Fax 369-4153
www.forestarea.k12.mi.us
Forest Area HS 200/9-12
7661 W Shippy Rd SW 49633 231-369-2884
Charles Schwarz, prin. Fax 369-3646
Forest Area MS 100/6-8
7661 W Shippy Rd SW 49633 231-369-2867
Charles Schwarz, prin. Fax 369-3618

Flat Rock, Wayne, Pop. 9,056
Flat Rock Community SD 1,800/K-12
PO Box 130 48134 734-782-2451
Charlene Coulson Ed.D., supt. Fax 782-9665
www.flatrockschools.org
Flat Rock HS 500/9-12
28100 Aspen Dr 48134 734-782-1270
Mary Ann Perttunen, prin. Fax 782-2509
Simpson MS 400/6-8
24900 Meadows Ave 48134 734-782-2453
Kit Hoekstra, prin. Fax 782-0812

Flint, Genesee, Pop. 120,292
Beecher Community SD 1,600/PK-12
1020 W Coldwater Rd 48505 810-591-9200
Forrest Gunderson, supt. Fax 591-5755
www.beecherschools.org
Other Schools – See Mount Morris

Carman-Ainsworth SD 5,300/K-12
G3475 W Court St 48532 810-591-3700
William Haley, supt. Fax 591-3323
www.carman.k12.mi.us
Carman-Ainsworth HS 1,600/9-12
1300 N Linden Rd 48532 810-591-3240
Steve Tunnicliff, prin. Fax 591-3215
Carman-Ainsworth MS 1,100/6-8
1409 W Maple Ave 48507 810-591-3500
Kevin Summey, prin. Fax 591-3594

Flint SD 18,600/PK-12
923 E Kearsley St 48503 810-760-1000
Ira Rutherford, supt. Fax 760-6790
www.flintschools.org
Central HS 1,500/9-12
601 Crapo St 48503 810-760-1042
Corinne Edwards, prin. Fax 760-7671
Flint Southwestern Academy 1,400/7-12
1420 W 12th St 48507 810-760-1400
Thomas Hill, prin. Fax 760-7772

Genessee Area Skill Ctr Vo/Tech
G5081 Torrey Rd 48507 810-760-1444
Doug Weir, dir. Fax 760-7759
Holmes MS 600/7-8
6602 Oxley Dr 48504 810-760-1620
Cheryl Adkins, prin. Fax 760-5346
Longfellow MS 600/6-8
1255 N Chevrolet Ave 48504 810-760-1336
LaVern Bond, prin. Fax 760-6857
Northern HS 1,300/9-12
G3284 Mackin Rd 48504 810-760-1740
Clyde Bell, prin. Fax 760-5009
Northwestern Preparatory Academy 800/7-12
G2138 W Carpenter Rd 48505 810-760-1780
Cheryl Tate, prin. Fax 760-6809
Whittier MS 700/6-8
701 Crapo St 48503 810-760-1175
Elnora Crutchfield, prin. Fax 760-5175
Mott Adult HS Adult
2421 Corunna Rd 48503 810-760-7723
George Barker, prin. Fax 760-1945

Kearsley Community SD 3,900/PK-12
4396 Underhill Dr 48506 810-591-8000
Jeffry Morgan, supt. Fax 591-8421
www.kearsley.k12.mi.us
Armstrong MS 900/6-8
6161 Hopkins Rd 48506 810-591-9929
Patti Yorks, prin. Fax 591-9944
Kearsley HS 1,100/9-12
4302 Underhill Dr 48506 810-591-8000
Kevin Walworth, prin. Fax 591-9883

Westwood Heights SD 1,300/PK-12
3484 N Jennings Rd 48504 810-591-0870
Jerri Lynn Williams, supt. Fax 591-0898
www.hamadyhawks.net
Hamady HS 300/9-12
3223 W Carpenter Rd 48504 810-591-0890
Keely Mounger, prin. Fax 591-5140
Hamady MS 200/7-8
3223 W Carpenter Rd 48504 810-591-0895
Gary Fant, prin. Fax 591-5140

Baker College of Flint Post-Sec.
1050 W Bristol Rd 48507 810-767-4000
Charles Stewart Mott Community College Post-Sec.
1401 E Court St 48503 810-762-0200
Flint Institute of Barbering Post-Sec.
3214 Flushing Rd 48504 810-232-4711
Hurley Medical Center Post-Sec.
701 W 8th Ave 48503 810-257-9237
Kettering University Post-Sec.
1700 W 3rd Ave 48504 810-762-9500
Michigan School for the Blind Post-Sec.
1301 W Court St 48503 810-257-1400
Mr. David's School of Cosmetolgy Post-Sec.
3600 S Dort Hwy 48507 810-742-9010
Powers HS 900/9-12
G2040 W Carpenter Rd 48505 810-591-4741
Thomas Furnas, prin. Fax 591-1794
Ross Medical Education Center Post-Sec.
1036 Gilbert St 48532 810-230-1100
University of Michigan-Flint Post-Sec.
303 E Kearsley St 48502 810-762-3000

Flushing, Genesee, Pop. 8,197
Flushing Community SD 4,100/PK-12
522 N McKinley Rd 48433 810-591-1180
Barbara Goebel, supt. Fax 591-0656
www.flushing.k12.mi.us
Flushing HS 1,400/9-12
5039 Deland Rd 48433 810-591-3770
Gary Whitmire, prin. Fax 591-0693
Flushing MS 700/7-8
8100 Carpenter Rd 48433 810-591-2800
Rita Brust, prin. Fax 591-0148

Sharps Academy of Hairstyling Post-Sec.
115 E Main St 48433 810-659-3348

Fort Gratiot, Saint Clair, Pop. 8,968
Port Huron Area SD
Supt. — See Port Huron
Fort Gratiot MS 700/6-8
3985 Keewahdin Rd 48059 810-984-6544
Debra Ladensack, prin. Fax 385-1624

Fowler, Clinton, Pop. 1,092
Fowler SD 500/PK-12
PO Box 408 48835 989-593-2296
Scott Koenigsknecht, supt. Fax 593-2125
www.fps.k12.mi.us
Fowler HS 200/9-12
PO Box 407 48835 989-593-2250
Daymond Grifka, prin. Fax 593-2358

Most Holy Trinity MS 100/4-8
11144 W Kent St 48835 989-593-2616
Martha Maier, prin. Fax 593-2801

Fowlerville, Livingston, Pop. 3,119
Fowlerville Community SD 3,100/K-12
PO Box 769 48836 517-223-6000
Ed Alverson, supt. Fax 223-6022
www.fvl.k12.mi.us
Fowlerville HS 700/10-12
7677 W Sharpe Rd 48836 517-223-6002
Wayne Roedel, prin. Fax 223-6065
Fowlerville JHS 800/7-9
700 N Grand Ave 48836 517-223-6003
Tom Tannar, prin. Fax 223-6199

Frankenmuth, Saginaw, Pop. 4,804
Frankenmuth SD 1,300/K-12
941 E Genesee St 48734 989-652-9958
Michael Murphy, supt. Fax 652-9780
www.frankenmuth.k12.mi.us/

Frankenmuth HS   600/9-12
525 E Genesee St 48734   989-652-9955
Donald Zoller, prin.   Fax 652-7253
Rittmueller MS   300/5-8
965 E Genesee St 48734   989-652-6119
Martin Mattlin, prin.   Fax 652-2921

Frankfort, Benzie, Pop. 1,502
Frankfort-Elberta Area SD   600/K-12
534 11th St 49635   231-352-4641
Thomas Stobie, supt.   Fax 352-5066
www.frankfort.k12.mi.us
Frankfort JSHS   300/7-12
534 11th St 49635   231-352-4781
Matt Stapleton, prin.   Fax 352-6501

Fraser, Macomb, Pop. 15,120
Fraser SD   4,700/PK-12
33466 Garfield Rd 48026   586-293-5100
Richard Repicky, supt.   Fax 293-0480
www.macomb.k12.mi.us/fraser/schfras.htm
Fraser HS   1,500/9-12
34270 Garfield Rd 48026   586-879-2000
Dr. David Richards, prin.   Fax 293-1953
Richards MS   800/7-8
33500 Garfield Rd 48026   586-294-5720
Jeffrey Wood, prin.   Fax 294-1678

Freeland, Saginaw, Pop. 1,421
Freeland Community SD   1,400/K-12
710 Powley Dr 48623   989-695-5527
Allen Veenkant, supt.   Fax 695-5789
www.freeland.k12.mi.us
Freeland HS   500/9-12
8250 Webster Rd 48623   989-695-2586
Bernard Maxwell, prin.   Fax 695-8022
Freeland MS   7-8
8250 Webster Rd 48623   989-692-4032
Christopher Arrington, prin.   Fax 692-4034

Free Soil, Mason, Pop. 179
Freesoil Community SD   200/K-12
8480 N Democrat St 49411   231-464-5651
Steven Rybicki, supt.   Fax 464-5337
Freesoil Community JSHS   100/7-12
8480 N Democrat St 49411   231-464-5651
Steven Rybicki, prin.   Fax 464-5337

Fremont, Newaygo, Pop. 4,252
Fremont SD   2,600/K-12
220 W Pine St 49412   231-924-2350
John D. Kingsnorth Ph.D., supt.   Fax 924-5264
www.fremont.net
Fremont HS   800/9-12
204 E Main St 49412   231-924-5300
Thomas Palmer, prin.   Fax 924-9262
Fremont MS   600/6-8
500 W Woodrow St 49412   231-924-0230
Carolyn Hummel, prin.   Fax 924-9149

Newaygo County RESA
4747 W 48th St 49412   231-924-0381
Robert E. DeVries, supt.   Fax 924-8910
www.ncresa.org/
Newaygo County Career-Tech Center   Vo/Tech
4645 W 48th St 49412   231-924-0380
Kirk Wyers, dir.

Providence Christian HS   100/9-12
5479 W 72nd St 49412   231-924-9780
Sue Tameling, admin.   Fax 924-1676

Fruitport, Muskegon, Pop. 1,094
Fruitport Community SD   3,100/PK-12
3255 Pontaluna Rd 49415   231-865-4100
Nicholas Ceglarek, supt.   Fax 865-3393
www.fruitport.k12.mi.us
Fruitport HS   1,000/9-12
357 N 6th Ave 49415   231-865-3101
Patti Bralier, prin.   Fax 865-6351
Fruitport MS   800/6-8
3113 Pontaluna Rd 49415   231-865-3128
James Reinhart, prin.   Fax 865-4086

Calvary Christian S   300/PK-12
5873 Kendra Rd 49415   231-865-2141
Tom Kapanka, admin.   Fax 865-8730

Galesburg, Kalamazoo, Pop. 1,982
Galesburg-Augusta Community SD   1,300/PK-12
1076 N 37th St 49053   269-484-2000
Eric Palmu, supt.   Fax 484-2001
www.gacsnet.org
Galesburg-Augusta HS   400/9-12
1076 N 37th St 49053   269-484-2010
Todd Reynolds, prin.   Fax 484-2011
Other Schools – See Augusta

Galien, Berrien, Pop. 579
Galien Township SD   400/PK-8
PO Box 248 49113   269-545-3364
Marilyn Tilmann, supt.   Fax 545-2483
www.remc11.k12.mi.us./galien
Galien MS   100/6-8
PO Box 248 49113   269-545-3365
Marilyn Tilmann, prin.   Fax 545-0103

Garden City, Wayne, Pop. 29,547
Garden City SD   5,000/K-12
1333 Radcliff St 48135   734-762-8300
Richard Witkowski, supt.   Fax 762-8530
www.resa.net/gardencity/index.html
Garden City HS   1,500/9-12
6500 Middlebelt Rd 48135   734-762-8500
Jerry Perttunen, prin.   Fax 762-8531
Garden City MS   800/7-8
1851 Radcliff St 48135   734-762-8400
Brian Sumner, prin.   Fax 763-8533

Cambridge Center   Adult
28901 Cambridge St 48135   734-762-8430
Jack Pelon, prin.   Fax 762-8534

United Christian S   100/PK-12
29205 Florence St 48135   734-522-6487
Roger Stombaugh, prin.   Fax 522-3020

Gaylord, Otsego, Pop. 3,741
Gaylord Community SD   3,700/K-12
615 S Elm Ave 49735   989-705-3080
Carl Hilling, supt.   Fax 732-6029
www.gaylordschools.com
Gaylord HS   1,100/9-12
90 Livingston Blvd 49735   989-731-0969
Lori Pearson, prin.   Fax 731-2585
Gaylord MS   600/7-8
600 E 5th St 49735   989-731-0848
Gerald Belanger, prin.   Fax 732-2632

Grace Baptist Christian S   100/PK-12
PO Box 177 49734   989-731-1221
Robert Perrotti, prin.   Fax 731-1122
St. Mary Cathedral S   400/PK-12
321 N Otsego Ave 49735   989-732-5801
Tom Saporito, prin.   Fax 732-2085

Genesee, Genesee
Genesee SD   1,000/PK-12
PO Box 220 48437   810-591-1650
Mark Hilt, supt.   Fax 591-1646
www.genesee.k12.mi.us
Genesee JSHS   500/7-12
7347 N Genesee Rd 48437   810-591-1450
Richard Carsten, prin.   Fax 591-0302

Gibraltar, Wayne, Pop. 4,704
Gibraltar SD
Supt. — See Woodhaven
Carlson HS   900/9-12
30550 W Jefferson Ave 48173   734-379-7100
William Stevenson, prin.   Fax 379-5444
Shumate MS   800/6-8
30550 W Jefferson Ave 48173   734-379-7600
Brad Coon, prin.   Fax 379-2370

Gladstone, Delta, Pop. 5,290
Gladstone Area SD   1,600/K-12
400 S 10th St 49837   906-428-2417
William Pistulka, supt.   Fax 789-8457
www.gladstoneschools.com
Gladstone HS   600/9-12
2100 M-35 49837   906-428-9200
Jay Kulbertis, prin.   Fax 789-8312
Gladstone MS   400/6-8
300 S 10th St 49837   906-428-2295
Bill Slough, prin.   Fax 789-8404

Gladwin, Gladwin, Pop. 3,036
Gladwin Community SD   2,000/K-12
1206 N Spring St 48624   989-426-9255
Rick W. Seebeck, supt.   Fax 426-5981
www.gcsnet.org
Gladwin HS   700/9-12
1400 N Spring St 48624   989-426-7341
Bill Shellenbarger, prin.   Fax 426-6031
Gladwin JHS   500/6-8
401 N Bowery Ave 48624   989-426-3808
Clair Wetmore, prin.   Fax 426-6038

Skeels Northern Christian S   100/PK-12
3956 N M 18 48624   989-426-2054
Rick Lopez, admin.   Fax 426-2054

Glen Arbor, Leelanau

Leelanau S   100/9-12
1 Old Homestead Rd 49636   231-334-5800
Richard Odell, pres.   Fax 334-5898

Gobles, Van Buren, Pop. 813
Gobles SD   900/K-12
PO Box 412 49055   269-628-5618
Scott Dunsmore, supt.   Fax 628-5306
www.gobles.org/
Gobles HS   300/9-12
PO Box 412 49055   269-628-2113
Corey Harbaugh, prin.   Fax 628-2748
Gobles MS   7-8
PO Box 412 49055   269-628-5680
Chris Miller, prin.   Fax 628-2748

Gobles Jr. Academy   50/1-10
32110 6th Ave 49055   269-628-2704
Thomas Coffee, prin.   Fax 628-7314

Goodrich, Genesee, Pop. 1,440
Goodrich Area SD   2,100/K-12
8029 Gale Rd 48438   810-591-2250
Kimberly A. Hart, supt.   Fax 591-2550
www.goodrich.k12.mi.us/
Goodrich HS   700/9-12
8029 Gale Rd 48438   810-591-2251
David St. Aubin, prin.   Fax 591-2234
Goodrich MS   500/6-8
7480 Gale Rd 48438   810-591-4210
Jerry Lawrason Ph.D., prin.   Fax 636-7879

Grand Blanc, Genesee, Pop. 8,018
Grand Blanc Community SD   5,400/PK-12
11920 S Saginaw St 48439   810-591-6000
Dr. Michael Newton, supt.   Fax 591-6018
www.grandblancschools.org
Grand Blanc HS   1,600/10-12
12500 Holly Rd 48439   810-591-6638
Jennifer Hammond, prin.   Fax 591-6693
Grand Blanc HS West   600/9-9
1 Jewett Trl 48439   810-591-6350
   Fax 591-6400

Grand Blanc MS East   6-8
6100 Perry Rd 48439   810-591-9632
Clarence Garner, prin.
Grand Blanc MS West   6-8
1515 E Reid Rd 48439   810-591-0556
Jeff Neall, prin.

Sharps Academy of Hairstyling   Post-Sec.
8166 Holly Rd 48439   810-695-6742

Grand Haven, Ottawa, Pop. 10,842
Grand Haven Area SD   6,000/PK-12
1415 S Beechtree St 49417   616-850-5015
Keith Konarska, supt.   Fax 850-5010
www.ghaps.org
Grand Haven HS   2,000/9-12
17001 Ferris St 49417   616-850-6000
Scott Grimes, prin.   Fax 850-6010
Lakeshore MS   600/6-8
900 Cutler St 49417   616-850-6500
Julia Houle, prin.   Fax 850-6510
White Pines MS   800/6-8
1400 S Griffin St 49417   616-850-6300
Mike Shelton, prin.   Fax 850-6310

Grand Ledge, Eaton, Pop. 7,816
Grand Ledge SD   5,400/PK-12
220 Lamson St 48837   517-627-3241
Marsha Wells, supt.   Fax 627-1767
www.glps.k12.mi.us/
Beagle MS   600/6-8
600 W South St 48837   517-627-4274
Charles Phillips, prin.   Fax 622-1752
Grand Ledge HS   1,700/9-12
820 Spring St 48837   517-627-5194
Richard Pochert, prin.   Fax 627-2591
Hayes MS   800/6-8
12620 Nixon Rd 48837   517-627-5080
Jill Mangrum, prin.   Fax 622-1922

Grand Marais, Alger
Burt Township SD   100/K-12
PO Box 338 49839   906-494-2543
Thomas Scaife, supt.   Fax 494-2522
Burt Township S   100/K-12
PO Box 338 49839   906-494-2521
Thomas Scaife, prin.   Fax 494-2522

Grand Rapids, Kent, Pop. 195,601
East Grand Rapids SD   2,900/K-12
2915 Hall St SE 49506   616-235-3535
Dr. James Morse, supt.   Fax 235-6730
www.egrps.org/
East Grand Rapids HS   1,000/9-12
2211 Lake Dr SE 49506   616-235-7555
Patrick Cwayna, prin.   Fax 235-7592
East Grand Rapids MS   700/6-8
2425 Lake Dr SE 49506   616-235-7551
J. Peter Stuursma, prin.   Fax 235-7587

Forest Hills SD   11,900/K-12
6590 Cascade Rd SE 49546   616-493-8800
J. Michael Washburn, supt.   Fax 493-8560
www.fhps.k12.mi.us
Forest Hills Central HS   1,400/9-12
5901 Hall St SE 49546   616-493-8700
Terry Urquhart, prin.   Fax 493-8721
Forest Hills Northern HS   1,400/9-12
3801 Leonard St NE 49525   616-493-8600
Tom VanderWoude, prin.   Fax 493-8644
Northern Hills MS   700/7-8
3775 Leonard St NE 49525   616-493-8650
Nancy Susterka, prin.   Fax 493-8686
Other Schools – See Ada

Grand Rapids SD   19,000/PK-12
PO Box 117 49501   616-819-2000
Bert Bleke, supt.   Fax 819-2104
www.grps.k12.mi.us
Burton MS   700/6-8
2133 Buchanan Ave SW 49507   616-819-2269
Jesus Solis, prin.   Fax 819-2282
Central HS   1,000/9-12
421 Fountain St NE 49503   616-819-2310
Ed Shalhoup, prin.   Fax 819-2369
Creston HS   1,000/9-12
1720 Plainfield Ave NE 49505   616-819-2424
Kurt Johnson, prin.   Fax 819-2427
Harrison MS   400/6-8
1440 Davis Ave NW 49504   616-819-2570
Gary Barton, prin.   Fax 819-2571
Kent Vocational Options   Vo/Tech
864 Crahen Ave NE 49525   616-819-2740
Karen Truax, prin.   Fax 819-2741
Madison MS   6-8
1050 Iroquois Dr SE 49506   616-819-2640
Steve Kadau, prin.   Fax 819-2660
Northeast MS   500/6-8
1400 Fuller Ave NE 49505   616-819-2818
Jackie Bell, prin.   Fax 819-2844
Ottawa Hills HS   1,200/9-12
2055 Rosewood Ave SE 49506   616-819-2900
Martha Williams, prin.   Fax 819-2877
Riverside MS   400/7-8
265 Eleanor St NE 49505   616-819-2969
Michelle Ghareeb, prin.   Fax 819-2981
Union HS   1,300/9-12
1800 Tremont Blvd NW 49504   616-819-3160
Janice Johnson, prin.   Fax 819-3205
Westwood MS   500/7-8
1525 Mount Mercy Dr NW 49504   616-819-3300
Raul Ysasi, prin.   Fax 819-3301

Kelloggsville SD   2,000/PK-12
242 52nd St SE 49548   616-538-7460
Samuel Wright, supt.   Fax 530-8194
www.kelloggsville.k12.mi.us
Kelloggsville HS   500/9-12
23 Jean St SW 49548   616-532-1570
Mike Fine, prin.   Fax 532-7780

Kelloggsville MS 500/6-8
4650 Division Ave S 49548 616-532-1575
Scott Gunn, prin. Fax 532-1579

Kenowa Hills SD 3,700/K-12
2325 4 Mile Rd NW 49544 616-784-2511
James Gillette, supt. Fax 784-8323
khps.org
Kenowa Hills HS 1,200/9-12
3825 Hendershot Ave NW 49544 616-784-2400
Peggy Mathis, prin. Fax 647-0149
Kenowa Hills MS 600/7-8
3950 Hendershot Ave NW 49544 616-785-3225
Ruth Posthumus, prin. Fax 784-2404

Kent ISD
2930 Knapp St NE 49525 616-364-1333
Michael S. Weiler, supt. Fax 364-1488
www.kentisd.org
Kent Career/Technical Center Vo/Tech
1655 E Beltline Ave NE 49525 616-364-8421
Rick Briggs, prin. Fax 364-9140

Northview SD 3,300/PK-12
4365 Hunsberger Ave NE 49525 616-363-6861
Michael Stearns, supt. Fax 363-9609
www.nvps.net
Crossroads MS 500/7-8
4400 Ambrose Ave NE 49525 616-361-3430
F. Andrew Scogg, prin. Fax 363-7868
Northview HS 1,200/9-12
4451 Hunsberger Ave NE 49525 616-363-4857
Mark Thomas, prin. Fax 361-3494

———————

Aquinas College Post-Sec.
1607 Robinson Rd SE 49506 800-678-9593
Calvin College Post-Sec.
3201 Burton St SE 49546 616-957-6000
Calvin Theological Seminary Post-Sec.
3233 Burton St SE 49546 616-957-6036
Catholic Central HS 900/9-12
319 Sheldon Blvd SE 49503 616-233-5801
Steve Passinault, prin. Fax 459-0257
Chic University of Cosmetology Post-Sec.
1735 4 Mile Rd NE 49525 616-363-9853
Chic University of Cosmetology Post-Sec.
455 Standale Plz NW 49544 616-735-9680
Cornerstone University Post-Sec.
1001 E Beltline Ave NE 49525 616-949-5300
Covenant Christian HS 300/10-12
1401 Ferndale Ave SW, 616-453-5048
Richard Noorman, prin. Fax 453-4277
Cutlerville Christian MS 200/6-8
67 68th St SW 49548 616-455-3860
Jim VanDyken, prin. Fax 455-1960
Davenport University Post-Sec.
415 Fulton St E 49503 616-451-3511
Grace Bible College Post-Sec.
PO Box 910 49509 800-968-1887
Grand Rapids Christian HS 1,100/9-12
2300 Plymouth Ave SE 49506 616-574-5500
Jim Primus, prin. Fax 241-3141
Grand Rapids Community College Post-Sec.
143 Bostwick Ave NE 49503 616-234-4000
Grand Rapids MS 500/7-8
1875 Rosewood Ave SE 49506 616-574-6350
Mary Broene, prin. Fax 574-6316
Grand Rapids SDA Academy 200/K-12
1151 Oakleigh Rd NW 49504 616-791-9797
Debra Barr, prin. Fax 791-7242
ITT Technical Institute Post-Sec.
4020 Sparks Dr SE 49546 616-956-1060
Kendall College of Art & Design Post-Sec.
17 Fountain St NW 49503 616-451-2787
Kent Career/Technical Center Vo/Tech
1655 E Beltline Ave NE 49525 616-364-8421
North Hills Classical Academy 100/K-12
2777 Knapp St NE 49525 616-365-0525
Peter VandeBrake, hdmstr. Fax 365-3683
NorthPointe Christian HS 400/7-12
3101 Leonard St NE 49525 616-942-0350
Randy Fleenor, prin. Fax 942-4647
Olympia Career Training Institute Post-Sec.
1750 Woodworth St NE 49525 616-364-8464
Plymouth Christian HS 200/7-12
965 Plymouth Ave NE 49505 616-454-9481
Laura Ash, prin. Fax 454-7243
Reformed Bible College Post-Sec.
3333 E Beltline Ave NE 49525 616-222-3000
Ross Medical Education Center Post-Sec.
2035 28th St SE Ste O 49508 616-243-3070
South Christian HS 800/9-12
160 68th St SW 49548 616-455-3210
Larry Plaisier, prin. Fax 455-8840
Spectrum Health Post-Sec.
100 Michigan St NE 49503 616-391-1605
Taratuta School of Truck Driving Post-Sec.
2215 Oak Indstrl Dr NE #212 49505 616-742-9000
West Catholic HS 600/9-12
1801 Bristol Ave NW 49504 616-233-5900
Stan Spetoskey, prin. Fax 453-4320

Grandville, Kent, Pop. 16,622
Grandville SD 8,700/K-12
3131 Barrett Ave SW 49418 616-254-6550
Ronald Caniff, supt. Fax 254-6557
www.grandville.k12.mi.us
Grandville HS 1,900/9-12
4700 Canal Ave SW 49418 616-254-6430
Randy Morris, prin. Fax 254-6462
Grandville MS 900/7-8
3535 Wilson Ave SW 49418 616-254-6610
Theresa Waterbury, prin. Fax 254-6613

———————

Calvin Christian HS 500/9-12
3750 Ivanrest Ave SW 49418 616-538-0990
Barbara Engbers, prin. Fax 538-9930

Calvin Christian MS 200/7-8
3740 Ivanrest Ave SW 49418 616-531-7400
John Kramer, prin. Fax 531-7402

Grant, Newaygo, Pop. 885
Grant SD 2,400/PK-12
148 Elder St 49327 231-834-5621
Thomas Cutler, supt. Fax 834-7146
www.grantps.net
Grant HS 700/9-12
331 E State Rd 49327 231-834-5622
Tom Szocinski, prin. Fax 834-8043
Grant JHS 700/5-8
96 E 120th St 49327 231-834-5910
Lance Jones, prin. Fax 834-9029

Grass Lake, Jackson, Pop. 1,106
Grass Lake Community SD 1,100/K-12
990 Grass Lake Rd 49240 517-522-8491
Brad Hamilton, supt. Fax 522-8195
www.grasslakeschools.com
Grass Lake HS 300/9-12
11500 Warrior Trl 49240 517-522-8495
Kathy Pecora, prin. Fax 522-5490
Grass Lake MS 300/5-8
1000 Grass Lake Rd 49240 517-522-8494
Douglas Moeckel, prin. Fax 522-4775

Grayling, Crawford, Pop. 1,960
Crawford AuSable SD 2,000/PK-12
403 E Michigan Ave 49738 989-344-3500
Fax 348-6822

casdk12.net
Grayling HS 700/9-12
1135 N Old 27 49738 989-344-3532
Doniel Pummell, prin. Fax 348-7799
Grayling MS 500/6-8
500 Spruce St 49738 989-344-3550
Jeffrey Branch, prin. Fax 348-7045

Greenville, Montcalm, Pop. 8,193
Greenville SD 3,800/K-12
1414 Chase St 48838 616-754-3686
Terance Lunger, supt. Fax 754-5374
www.greenville.k12.mi.us
Greenville HS 1,200/9-12
111 N Hillcrest St 48838 616-754-3681
Harold Deines, prin. Fax 754-1994
Greenville MS 1,000/6-8
1321 Chase St 48838 616-754-9361
Diane Brissette, prin. Fax 754-2901

Grosse Ile, Wayne, Pop. 9,781
Grosse Ile Township SD 2,000/K-12
23276 E River Rd 48138 734-362-2555
Dena Dardzinski, supt. Fax 362-2594
www.gischools.org/
Grosse Ile HS 700/9-12
7800 Grays Dr 48138 734-362-2400
Delores Elswick, prin. Fax 362-2496
Grosse Ile MS 500/6-8
23270 E River Rd 48138 734-362-2500
Cynthia Taylor, prin. Fax 362-2596

Grosse Pointe, Wayne, Pop. 5,563
Grosse Pointe SD 8,800/K-12
389 Saint Clair St 48230 313-432-3000
Dr. C. Suzanne Klein, supt. Fax 432-3002
www.gpschools.org
Brownell MS 700/6-8
260 Chalfonte Ave 48236 313-432-3900
Dr. Michael Dib, prin. Fax 432-3902
Grosse Pointe North HS 1,500/9-12
707 Vernier Rd 48236 313-432-3200
Tim Bearden, prin. Fax 432-3202
Grosse Pointe South HS 1,600/9-12
11 Grosse Pointe Blvd 48236 313-432-3500
Al Diver, prin. Fax 432-3502
Parcells MS 700/6-8
20600 Mack Ave 48236 313-432-4600
Mark Mulholland, prin. Fax 432-4602
Pierce MS 600/6-8
15430 Kercheval St 48230 313-432-4700
Gary Buslepp, prin. Fax 432-4702

———————

Detroit Institute of Ophthalmology Post-Sec.
15415 E Jefferson Ave 48230 313-824-4710
University Liggett S 700/PK-12
1045 Cook St 48236 313-884-4444
Matthew H. Hanley, prin. Fax 884-1775
University Liggett S 200/6-8
850 Briar Cliff Dr 48236 313-886-4220
Lynne Myavec, prin. Fax 417-8002

Gwinn, Marquette, Pop. 2,370
Gwinn Area SD 1,400/K-12
50 W State Highway M35 49841 906-346-9283
Steven E. Peffers, supt. Fax 346-3616
www.gwinn.k12.mi.us
Gwinn HS 400/9-12
50 W State Highway M35 49841 906-346-9247
Kevin Luokkala, prin. Fax 346-0300
Gwinn MS 200/7-8
135 W Granite St 49841 906-346-5914
Kimberly Van Drese, prin. Fax 346-6213

Hale, Iosco
Hale Area SD 800/K-12
200 W Main St 48739 989-728-7661
Rhonda Provoast, supt. Fax 728-2406
Hale HS 300/9-12
415 E Main St 48739 989-728-2861
Maxine Yetter, prin. Fax 728-7101
Hale MS 300/5-8
311 N Washington St 48739 989-728-3551
Denis Fitzgerald, prin. Fax 728-9551

Hamilton, Allegan
Hamilton Community SD 2,500/K-12
4815 136th Ave 49419 269-751-5148
James Kos, supt. Fax 751-7116
www.hamiltonschools.us
Hamilton HS 800/9-12
4911 136th Ave 49419 269-751-5185
Doug Braschler, prin. Fax 751-7670
Hamilton MS 600/6-8
4845 136th Ave 49419 269-751-4436
Scott Smith, prin. Fax 751-8560

Hamtramck, Wayne, Pop. 22,437
Hamtramck SD 3,600/PK-12
PO Box 12012 48212 313-872-9270
Felix Chow, supt. Fax 872-8679
www.hamtramck.k12.mi.us
Hamtramck HS 1,000/9-12
11410 Charest St 48212 313-892-7505
Patrick Victor, prin. Fax 892-1990
Kosciuszko MS 900/6-8
2333 Burger St 48212 313-365-4625
Dennis Kemp, prin. Fax 365-4760

Hancock, Houghton, Pop. 4,313
Hancock SD 1,000/K-12
417 Quincy St 49930 906-487-5925
John Vaara, supt. Fax 487-5216
www.hancock.k12.mi.us
Hancock Central HS 300/9-12
501 Campus Dr 49930 906-483-2540
John Sanregret, prin. Fax 483-2539
Hancock MS 200/6-8
417 Quincy St 49930 906-487-5923
Monica Healy, prin. Fax 487-5924

———————

Finlandia University Post-Sec.
601 Quincy St 49930 906-482-5300

Harbor Beach, Huron, Pop. 1,761
Harbor Beach Community SD 700/K-12
402 S 5th St 48441 989-479-3261
Ron Kraft, supt. Fax 479-9881
www.harborbeach.k12.mi.us/
Harbor Beach HS 300/9-12
402 S 5th St 48441 989-479-3261
Doug Hassler, prin. Fax 479-9881
Harbor Beach MS 200/5-8
402 S 5th St 48441 989-479-3261
Denise Kish, prin. Fax 479-9881

Harbor Springs, Emmet, Pop. 1,573
Harbor Springs SD 1,100/K-12
800 State Rd 49740 231-526-4545
Dr. David Larson, supt. Fax 526-4544
www.harborps.org
Harbor Springs HS 400/9-12
327 E Bluff Dr 49740 231-526-4800
Susan Jacobs, prin. Fax 526-8010
Harbor Springs MS 300/6-8
800 State Rd 49740 231-526-4700
Scott Cochran, prin. Fax 526-4760

———————

Harbor Light Christian S 100/PK-12
8333 Clayton Rd 49740 231-347-7859
Joseph Fox, prin. Fax 347-7703

Harper Woods, Wayne, Pop. 13,952
Harper Woods SD 1,000/K-12
20225 Beaconsfield St 48225 313-839-1296
Daniel Danosky, supt. Fax 839-1249
www.hwschools.org
Harper Woods HS 400/9-12
20225 Beaconsfield St 48225 313-839-7400
Peter Newman, prin. Fax 839-4360
Harper Woods MS 7-8
20225 Beaconsfield St 48225 313-839-7400
Peter Newman, prin. Fax 839-4360

———————

Regina HS 700/9-12
20200 Kelly Rd 48225 313-526-0220
Sr. M. Leanne Leszczynski, prin. Fax 526-5850

Harris, Menominee
Bark River-Harris SD 700/K-12
PO Box 350 49845 906-466-9981
Thomas G. Bartol, supt. Fax 466-2925
www.dsisd.k12.mi.us/barkriver
Bark River-Harris JSHS 300/7-12
PO Box 350 49845 906-466-5321
Lawrence Wanic, prin. Fax 466-2925

Harrison, Clare, Pop. 2,098
Harrison Community SD 1,800/K-12
PO Box 529 48625 989-539-7871
Christopher L. Rundle, supt. Fax 539-7491
www.cgresd.net/hcs
Harrison HS 700/9-12
PO Box 529 48625 989-539-7417
Thomas House, prin. Fax 539-4319
Harrison MS 500/6-8
PO Box 529 48625 989-539-7194
Ronald Wilson, prin. Fax 539-0460

———————

Mid-Michigan Community College Post-Sec.
1375 S Clare Ave 48625 989-386-6622

Harrison Township, Macomb, Pop. 24,685
L'Anse Creuse SD 11,000/PK-12
36727 Jefferson Ave 48045 586-783-6300
Dr. DiAnne Pellerin, supt. Fax 783-6310
www.lc-ps.org
L'Anse Creuse HS 1,700/9-12
38495 LAnse Creuse St 48045 586-783-6400
Patrick Mulcahy, prin. Fax 783-6408
L'Anse Creuse MS Central 700/6-8
38000 Reimold St 48045 586-783-6430
Patricia Rabenburg, prin. Fax 783-6437

L'Anse Creuse MS South | 600/6-8
34641 Jefferson Ave 48045 | 586-493-5620
Greg Dixon, prin. | Fax 493-5625
Other Schools – See Chesterfield, Clinton Township,
Macomb, Mount Clemens

Hart, Oceana, Pop. 1,986
Hart SD | 1,300/PK-12
301 Johnson St W 49420 | 231-873-6214
Peter Moss, supt. | Fax 873-6244
www.hart.k12.mi.us
Hart HS | 400/9-12
300 Johnson St W 49420 | 231-873-5691
Randy Nesbit, prin. | Fax 873-0586
Hart MS | 300/6-8
308 Johnson St W 49420 | 231-873-6320
Phillip Espinoza, prin. | Fax 873-0245

Hartford, Van Buren, Pop. 2,472
Hartford SD | 1,400/K-12
115 School St Unit B 49057 | 269-621-7000
Gary Pardike, supt. | Fax 621-3887
www.hartford-schools.org
Hartford HS | 400/9-12
115 School St Unit A 49057 | 269-621-7100
Kenneth Kent, prin. | Fax 621-7160
Hartford MS | 300/6-8
141 School St 49057 | 269-621-7200
John Visser, prin. | Fax 621-7260

Hartland, Livingston
Hartland Consolidated SD
Supt. — See Howell
Hartland HS | 1,600/9-12
10635 Dunham Rd 48353 | 810-746-2200
Chuck Hughes, prin. | Fax 746-2201
Hartland MS | 900/7-8
3250 Hartland Rd 48353 | 810-746-2400
Steve Livingway, prin. | Fax 746-2401

Haslett, Ingham, Pop. 10,230
Haslett SD | 2,800/K-12
5593 Franklin St 48840 | 517-339-8242
Michael Duda, supt. | Fax 339-1360
www.haslett.k12.mi.us/
Haslett HS | 900/9-12
5450 Marsh Rd 48840 | 517-339-8249
Bart Wegenke, prin. | Fax 339-7353
Haslett MS | 700/6-8
1535 Franklin St 48840 | 517-339-8233
Andy Pridgeon, prin. | Fax 339-4837

Hastings, Barry, Pop. 7,122
Hastings Area SD | 3,400/PK-12
232 W Grand St 49058 | 269-948-4400
Christopher Cooley, supt. | Fax 948-4425
www.hassk12.org
Hastings HS | 1,000/9-12
520 W South St 49058 | 269-948-4409
Timothy Johnston, prin. | Fax 948-8081
Hastings MS | 800/6-8
232 W Grand St 49058 | 269-948-4404
Michael Karasinski, prin. | Fax 945-6101

Barry County Christian S | 100/PK-12
2999 McKeown Rd 49058 | 269-948-2151
Ken Oosterhouse, admin. | Fax 948-2795

Hazel Park, Oakland, Pop. 18,549
Hazel Park SD | 3,500/PK-12
23136 Hughes Ave 48030 | 248-542-3910
Victor C. Mayo Ed.D., supt. | Fax 544-5443
www.hazelpark.k12.mi.us/
Hazel Park HS | 1,200/9-12
23400 Hughes Ave 48030 | 248-541-5216
Don Vogt, prin. | Fax 544-5389
Hazel Park JHS | 50/7-8
22770 Highland Ave 48030 | 248-658-2300
Douglas Esler, prin.
Hazel Park Adult S | Adult
420 W 9 Mile Rd 48030 | 248-544-5388
Gary Tweddle, prin.

Hemlock, Saginaw, Pop. 1,601
Hemlock SD | 1,400/K-12
PO Box 260 48626 | 989-642-5282
Rudy Godefroidt, supt. | Fax 642-2773
www.hemlock.k12.mi.us
Hemlock HS, PO Box 260 48626 | 500/9-12
Rudy Godefroidt, prin. | 989-642-5287
Hemlock MS, PO Box 260 48626 | 300/6-8
Terry Keyser, prin. | 989-642-5253

Hesperia, Oceana, Pop. 980
Hesperia Community SD | 1,100/K-12
PO Box 338 49421 | 231-854-6185
Jack Mansfield, supt. | Fax 854-1586
www.hesp.net
Hesperia HS | 300/9-12
PO Box 338 49421 | 231-854-6385
D. Robert Hellenga, prin. | Fax 854-6070
Hesperia MS | 400/5-8
PO Box 338 49421 | 231-854-6475
David Bukala, prin. | Fax 854-6096

Hickory Corners, Kalamazoo
Gull Lake Community SD
Supt. — See Richland
Gull Lake MS | 500/7-8
9500 N 40th St 49060 | 269-671-5135
Craig Bartholomew, prin. | Fax 671-4077

Highland, Oakland
Huron Valley SD | 10,600/PK-12
2390 S Milford Rd 48357 | 248-684-8000
Jackie Johnston, supt. | Fax 684-8235
www.huronvalley.k12.mi.us
Highland MS | 700/6-8
305 N John St 48357 | 248-684-8080
Marty Lindberg, prin. | Fax 684-8186

Milford HS | 1,900/9-12
2380 S Milford Rd 48357 | 248-684-8091
Michael Krystyniak, prin. | Fax 684-8094
Other Schools – See Commerce Township, Milford,
White Lake

Highland Hills Christian S | 100/K-12
179 Woodruff Lake Rd 48357 | 248-887-0698
Dr. Mario Chadinha, prin. | Fax 887-3825

Highland Park, Wayne, Pop. 16,044
Highland Park SD | 2,800/PK-12
20 Bartlett St 48203 | 313-957-3000
Arthur Carter Ed.D., supt. | Fax 868-4950
www.resa.net/highlandpark/index.htm
Highland Park Career Acad/Adult Ed | Vo/Tech
Glendale at 2nd Ave 48203 | 313-957-3007
Belvin Liles, dir. | Fax 852-0206
Highland Park Community HS | 700/9-12
15900 Woodward Ave 48203 | 313-957-3002
Samuel Craig, prin. | Fax 868-0483

Hillman, Montmorency, Pop. 693
Hillman Community SD | 600/K-12
PO Box 518 49746 | 989-742-2908
Thomas Harmon, supt. | Fax 742-4509
hillman.amaesd.k12.mi.us
Hillman JSHS | 300/7-12
PO Box 518 49746 | 989-742-4538
Jack Richards, prin. | Fax 742-4536

Hillsdale, Hillsdale, Pop. 8,070
Hillsdale Community SD | 1,800/PK-12
30 S Norwood Ave 49242 | 517-437-4401
Richard Ames, supt. | Fax 439-4194
www.hillsdaleschools.org
Davis MS | 400/6-8
30 N West St 49242 | 517-439-4326
Jackie Wickham, prin. | Fax 437-1195
Hillsdale HS | 500/9-12
30 S Norwood Ave 49242 | 517-439-4320
Douglas Willer, prin. | Fax 437-0377

Hillsdale ISD
310 W Bacon St 49242 | 517-437-0990
Robert W. Henthorne, supt. | Fax 439-4388
www.hillsdale-isd.org
Workforce Development & Tech Center | Vo/Tech
279 Industrial Dr 49242 | 517-437-3729
Kevin Leonard, dir. | Fax 437-3743

Hillsdale Academy | 200/K-12
1 Academy Ln 49242 | 517-439-8644
Kenneth Calvert, prin. | Fax 607-2794
Hillsdale Beauty College | Post-Sec.
64 Waldron St 49242 | 517-437-4670
Hillsdale College | Post-Sec.
33 E College St 49242 | 517-437-7341
Jackson Community College | Post-Sec.
PO Box 712 49242 | 517-437-3343

Holland, Ottawa, Pop. 34,666
Holland SD | 5,300/PK-12
156 W 11th St 49423 | 616-494-2000
Frank Garcia, supt. | Fax 392-8225
www.holland.k12.mi.us
East MS | 600/6-8
373 E 24th St 49423 | 616-494-2425
Nery Garcia, prin. | Fax 355-0674
Holland HS | 1,600/9-12
600 Van Raalte Ave 49423 | 616-494-2200
Dave Kail, prin. | Fax 393-7534
West MS | 600/6-8
500 W 24th St 49423 | 616-494-2350
Kathryn Curry, prin. | Fax 393-7544

Ottawa Area ISD
13565 Port Sheldon St 49424 | 616-738-8940
Karen McPhee, supt. | Fax 738-8946
www.oaisd.org
Careerline Tech Center | Vo/Tech
13663 Port Sheldon St 49424 | 616-738-8950
Dale Henderson, dir.

West Ottawa SD | 9,300/K-12
1138 136th Ave 49424 | 616-738-5700
Rosemary Ervine, supt. | Fax 738-5792
www.westottawa.net
Harbor Lights S | 1,900/6-8
1024 136th Ave 49424 | 616-738-6700
Jeri Start, prin. | Fax 738-6791
Macatawa Bay MS | 1,900/6-8
3700 140th Ave 49424 | 616-786-2000
Greg Wieman, prin. | Fax 786-2091
West Ottawa HS | 1,800/9-12
3685 Butternut Dr 49424 | 616-786-1000
| Fax 786-1091

Calvary Baptist S | 200/PK-12
518 Plasman Ave 49423 | 616-396-4494
Paul L. Davis, admin. | Fax 396-0326
Holland Christian HS | 900/9-12
950 Ottawa Ave 49423 | 616-820-2905
Troy Stahl, prin. | Fax 820-2910
Hope College | Post-Sec.
PO Box 9000 49422 | 616-395-7000
North Shore Christian MS | 200/6-8
556 Butternut Dr 49424 | 616-820-4055
Gary Dewey, prin. | Fax 820-4060
South Shore Christian MS | 200/6-8
850 Ottawa Ave 49423 | 616-820-3205
Mark Van Dyke, prin. | Fax 820-3210
Western Theological Seminary | Post-Sec.
101 E 13th St 49423 | 616-392-8555

Holly, Oakland, Pop. 6,233
Holly Area SD | 4,000/K-12
111 College St 48442 | 248-328-3100
R. Kent Barnes, supt. | Fax 328-3145
www.hollyareaschools.com
Holly HS | 1,300/9-12
6161 E Holly Rd 48442 | 248-328-3200
David Nuss, prin. | Fax 328-3297
Sherman MS | 700/7-8
14470 N Holly Rd 48442 | 248-328-3400
Anne Doriean, prin. | Fax 328-3404

Adelphian Jr. Academy | 50/1-10
PO Box 208 48442 | 248-634-9481
Sunimal Kulasekere, prin. | Fax 634-9222

Holt, Ingham, Pop. 11,744
Holt SD | 6,000/K-12
5780 W Holt Rd 48842 | 517-694-0401
Thomas Davis, supt. | Fax 694-1335
holt.k12.mi.us
Holt JHS | 1,000/7-8
1784 Aurelius Rd 48842 | 517-694-7117
Johnny Scott, prin. | Fax 694-3535
Holt SHS | 1,300/10-12
5885 W Holt Rd 48842 | 517-694-2162
Brian Templin, prin. | Fax 699-3451
9th Grade Campus | 500/9-9
5780 Holt Rd 48842 | 517-694-4370
Nick Johnson, prin. | Fax 694-8362

Capitol City Baptist S | 200/K-12
5100 Willoughby Rd 48842 | 517-694-6122
Brian Ogle, prin. | Fax 694-3344
St. Matthew Lutheran S | 100/K-12
2418 Aurelius Rd 48842 | 517-694-3182
George Lemke, admin. | Fax 694-6371

Holton, Muskegon
Holton SD | 1,100/K-12
PO Box 159 49425 | 231-821-1700
John Fazer, supt. | Fax 821-1724
www.remc4.k12.mi.us/holton/
Holton HS | 300/9-12
PO Box 159 49425 | 231-821-1725
Troycie Nichols, prin. | Fax 821-1774
Holton MS | 400/5-8
PO Box 159 49425 | 231-821-1775
Ken Haggart, prin. | Fax 821-1824

Homer, Calhoun, Pop. 1,823
Homer Community SD | 1,000/K-12
403 S Hillsdale St 49245 | 517-568-4461
Brent Holcomb, supt. | Fax 568-4468
www.remc12.k12.mi.us/homer
Homer HS | 400/9-12
403 S Hillsdale St 49245 | 517-568-4464
Tom Salow, prin. | Fax 568-7125
Homer MS | 300/5-8
403 S Hillsdale St 49245 | 517-568-4456
Scott Salow, prin. | Fax 568-4468

Hopkins, Allegan, Pop. 577
Hopkins SD | 1,400/K-12
PO Box 278 49328 | 269-793-7261
Thomas Martin, supt. | Fax 793-3154
www.hpsvikings.org
Hopkins HS | 500/9-12
333 S Clark St 49328 | 269-793-7616
Steven Anderson, prin. | Fax 793-7085
Hopkins MS | 300/6-8
215 S Clark St 49328 | 269-793-7407
Ken Szczepanski, prin. | Fax 793-4086

Horton, Jackson
Hanover-Horton SD | 1,400/K-12
PO Box 60 49246 | 517-563-0100
Linda Brian, supt. | Fax 563-0150
hhsd.k12.mi.us
Hanover-Horton HS | 500/9-12
10000 Moscow Rd 49246 | 517-563-0101
Rod Hardy, prin. | Fax 563-0155
Hanover-Horton MS | 400/6-8
10000 Moscow Rd 49246 | 517-563-0102
Denise Dennison, prin. | Fax 563-0160

Houghton, Houghton, Pop. 7,134
Houghton-Portage Township SD | 1,300/K-12
1603 Gundlach Rd 49931 | 906-482-0451
William Polkinghorne, supt. | Fax 487-9764
www.houghton.k12.mi.us/
Houghton Central HS | 500/9-12
1603 Gundlach Rd 49931 | 906-482-0450
Kathryn Simila, prin. | Fax 487-5218
Houghton MS | 300/6-8
1603 Gundlach Rd 49931 | 906-482-4871
James Luoma, prin. | Fax 483-2566

Michigan Technological University | Post-Sec.
1400 Townsend Dr 49931 | 906-487-1885

Houghton Lake, Roscommon, Pop. 3,353
Houghton Lake Community SD | 2,000/K-12
6001 W Houghton Lake Dr 48629 | 989-366-2000
Greg McMillan, supt. | Fax 366-2070
www.hlcs.k12.mi.us
Houghton Lake HS | 700/9-12
4433 W Houghton Lake Dr 48629 | 989-366-2006
Jack Kramer, prin. | Fax 366-2071
Houghton Lake MS | 500/6-8
4441 W Houghton Lake Dr 48629 | 989-366-2017
Mary Jo Dismang, prin. | Fax 366-2078

Houghton Lake Institute of Cosmetology | Post-Sec.
PO Box 669 48629 | - -

Howard City, Montcalm, Pop. 1,611
Tri County Area SD
Supt. — See Sand Lake

Tri County HS 700/9-12
21338 Kendaville Rd 49329 231-937-4338
Mark Simons, prin. Fax 937-5684
Tri County MS 600/6-8
21350 Kendaville Rd 49329 231-937-4318
Kurt Mabie, prin. Fax 937-6319

Howell, Livingston, Pop. 9,603
Hartland Consolidated SD 5,200/K-12
9525 E Highland Rd 48843 810-746-2100
Janet Sifferman, supt. Fax 746-2101
hartland.k12.mi.us
Other Schools – See Hartland

Howell SD 7,500/K-12
411 N Highlander Way 48843 517-548-6234
W. Charles Breiner, supt. Fax 548-6229
www.howellschools.com
Highlander Way MS 900/6-8
511 N Highlander Way 48843 517-548-6252
Ann Anderson, prin. Fax 545-1455
Howell HS 1,700/10-12
1200 W Grand River Ave 48843 517-548-6206
Marge Hamill, prin. Fax 545-1496
Howell HS Freshman Campus 9-9
1400 W Grand River Ave 48843 517-548-6267
Larry Cowger, prin. Fax 545-1439
Three Fires MS 1,000/6-8
4125 Crooked Lake Rd 48843 517-548-6387
Sue Muntz, prin. Fax 548-7524

Cleary University - Livingston Campus Post-Sec.
3750 Cleary College Dr 48843 517-548-3670
Howell College of Cosmetology Post-Sec.
1800 Dorr Rd 48843 517-546-4155

Hudson, Lenawee, Pop. 2,428
Hudson Area SD 1,100/K-12
781 N Maple Grove Ave 49247 517-448-8912
Kathryn Malnar Ed.D., supt. Fax 448-8570
www.hudson.k12.mi.us
Hudson Area HS 300/9-12
771 N Maple Grove Ave 49247 517-448-8912
Mike Osborne, prin. Fax 448-8975
Hudson MS 300/6-8
771 N Maple Grove Ave 49247 517-445-8912
Mike Osborne, prin. Fax 448-5702

Hudsonville, Ottawa, Pop. 7,175
Hudsonville SD 4,800/PK-12
3886 Van Buren St 49426 616-669-1740
Roxanne DeWeerd, supt. Fax 669-4878
www.hudsonville.k12.mi.us
Baldwin Street MS 700/6-8
3835 Baldwin St 49426 616-669-7750
David Powers, prin. Fax 669-7755
Hudsonville Freshman Campus S 400/9-9
5535 School Ave 49426 616-669-1510
Curt McDowell, prin. Fax 669-4895
Hudsonville SHS 1,100/10-12
5037 32nd Ave 49426 616-669-1500
Dave Feenstra, prin. Fax 669-4891
Riley Street MS 400/6-8
2745 Riley St 49426 616-669-1740
Mike Cooke, prin. Fax 896-1925

Freedom Baptist S 400/PK-12
6340 Autumn Dr 49426 616-669-2270
Philip B. Hayes, prin. Fax 669-2410
Unity Christian HS 800/9-12
3487 Oak St 49426 616-669-1820
Jack Postma, prin. Fax 669-5760

Ida, Monroe
Ida SD 1,700/K-12
3145 Prairie St 48140 734-269-3110
Marv Dick, supt. Fax 269-2294
www.idaschools.org
Ida HS 600/9-12
3145 Prairie St 48140 734-269-3485
Cathy Griffith, prin. Fax 269-3495
Ida MS 500/5-8
3145 Prairie St 48140 734-269-2220
Sheldon Wiens, prin. Fax 269-2576

Imlay City, Lapeer, Pop. 3,852
Imlay City Community SD 2,300/PK-12
PO Box 128 48444 810-724-9861
Timothy Edwards Ph.D., supt. Fax 724-4307
www.imlay.k12.mi.us/
Imlay City HS 700/9-12
1001 Norlin Dr 48444 810-724-9810
Gary Richards, prin. Fax 724-9897
Imlay City MS 500/6-8
495 W 1st St 48444 810-724-9811
Laurie Lee, prin. Fax 724-9896

Indian River, Cheboygan
Inland Lakes SD 1,100/K-12
5243 S Straits Hwy 49749 231-238-6868
Dale Rieger, supt. Fax 238-4181
www.inlandlakes.org
Inland Lakes HS 400/9-12
5243 S Straits Hwy 49749 231-238-6868
Donald Killingbeck, prin. Fax 238-7240
Inland Lakes MS 300/5-8
5243 S Straits Hwy 49749 231-238-6868
Matthew Hirsh, prin. Fax 238-4872

Inkster, Wayne, Pop. 29,478
Inkster SD 1,300/PK-12
29115 Carlysle St 48141 734-722-5310
Thomas Maridada, admin. Fax 722-2150
www.inksterschools.org/
Blanchette MS 600/6-8
1771 Henry Ruff Rd 48141 734-326-7041
Darryl Love, prin. Fax 722-5402

Inkster HS 300/9-12
3250 Middlebelt Rd 48141 734-326-8519
Nick Edwards, prin. Fax 467-9698

Peterson-Warren Academy 100/K-12
PO Box 888 48141 313-565-5808
Juanita Martin, prin. Fax 565-7784

Interlochen, Grand Traverse

Interlochen Arts Academy 500/9-12
PO Box 199 49643 231-276-7200
Timothy Wade, prin. Fax 276-7885

Ionia, Ionia, Pop. 12,124
Ionia SD 3,200/K-12
250 E Tuttle Rd 48846 616-527-9280
Patricia Batista, supt. Fax 527-8846
www.ionia.k12.mi.us
Heartlands Institute of Technology Vo/Tech
250 E Tuttle Rd 48846 616-527-6540
Anne Sharkey-Scott, prin. Fax 527-6670
Ionia HS 1,000/9-12
250 E Tuttle Rd 48846 616-527-0600
Benjamin Kirby, prin. Fax 527-8057
Ionia MS 800/6-8
438 Union St 48846 616-527-0040
Cheri Meier, prin. Fax 527-3380

Iron Mountain, Dickinson, Pop. 7,973
Iron Mountain SD 1,300/PK-12
PO Box 280 49801 906-779-2600
Dennis Chartier, supt. Fax 779-2676
www.imschools.org
Central MS 300/6-8
PO Box 280 49801 906-779-2620
Robert Strang, prin. Fax 779-2634
Iron Mountain HS 400/9-12
PO Box 280 49801 906-779-2610
Maryann Boddy, prin. Fax 779-2638
North Dickinson County SD 400/K-12
W6588 State Highway M69 49831 906-542-9281
Claude Siders, supt. Fax 542-6950
www.go-nordics.com
North Dickinson S 400/K-12
W6588 State Highway M69 49831 906-542-9281
Dan Nurmi, prin. Fax 542-6950

Iron River, Iron, Pop. 3,265
West Iron County SD 1,200/PK-12
601 Garfield Ave 49935 906-265-9218
Timothy Peruzzi, supt. Fax 265-9736
www.westiron.org
West Iron County HS 400/9-12
701 Garfield Ave 49935 906-265-5184
Christopher Thomson, prin. Fax 265-2294
West Iron County MS 400/5-8
612 W Adams St 49935 906-265-0016
Michael Berutti, prin. Fax 265-3402

Ironwood, Gogebic, Pop. 5,953
Ironwood Area SD 900/PK-12
650 E Ayer St 49938 906-932-0200
James Rayner, supt. Fax 932-9915
www.ironwood.k12.mi.us/
Wright MSHS 700/6-12
650 E Ayer St 49938 906-932-0932
Tim Kolesar, prin. Fax 932-9915

Gogebic Community College Post-Sec.
E4946 Jackson Rd 49938 906-932-4231

Ishpeming, Marquette, Pop. 6,535
Ishpeming SD 1 1,000/PK-12
319 E Division St 49849 906-485-5501
Stephen Piereson, supt. Fax 485-1422
www.ishpemingschools.com
Ishpeming HS 300/9-12
319 E Division St 49849 906-485-1066
Brian Sarvello, prin.
Phelps IS, 700 E North St 49849 300/5-8
Charleen Willey, prin. 906-486-4438

NICE Community SD 1,300/K-12
300 S Westwood Dr 49849 906-485-1021
Henry Bothwell, prin. Fax 485-4095
www.nice.k12.mi.us/
Aspen Ridge MS 300/6-8
350 Aspen Ridge School Rd 49849 906-485-3176
Dennis Tasson, prin. Fax 485-3182
Westwood HS 400/9-12
300 S Westwood Dr 49849 906-485-1023
David Boase, prin. Fax 485-1530

Ithaca, Gratiot, Pop. 3,099
Gratiot/Isabella RESD
PO Box 310 48847 989-875-5101
Michael Matlosz, supt. Fax 875-7531
www.edzone.net/giresd/
Other Schools – See Alma

Ithaca SD 1,200/K-12
710 N Union St 48847 989-875-3700
Charles Schnetzler, supt. Fax 875-4538
www.edzone.net/~ithaca
Ithaca HS 400/9-12
710 N Union St 48847 989-875-3373
Tom Neuenfeldt, prin. Fax 875-2500
Ithaca MS 7-8
710 N Union St 48847 989-875-3373
Keith Wing, prin. Fax 875-2500

Jackson, Jackson, Pop. 35,152
East Jackson SD 1,600/K-12
1404 N Sutton Rd 49202 517-764-2090
Bruce Van Eyck, supt. Fax 764-6033
scnc.ejs.k12.mi.us/

East Jackson HS 500/9-12
1566 N Sutton Rd 49202 517-764-1700
Kevin Herendeen, prin. Fax 764-6083
East Jackson MS 400/6-8
4340 Walz Rd 49201 517-764-6010
Heather Jacobs, prin. Fax 764-6081
Jackson County ISD
6700 Browns Lake Rd 49201 517-768-5200
John M. Graves, supt. Fax 787-2026
www.jcisd.org
Jackson Area Career Center Vo/Tech
6800 Browns Lake Rd 49201 517-768-5200
Denise Belt, prin. Fax 787-2844
Jackson SD 7,500/PK-12
522 Wildwood Ave 49201 517-841-2200
Daniel Evans, supt. Fax 789-8056
jps.k12.mi.us/~jps/
Firth MS 100/6-9
205 Seymour Ave 49202 517-841-3870
Robert Smoots, prin. Fax 768-5904
Jackson HS 1,800/9-12
544 Wildwood Ave 49201 517-841-3700
Pam Fitzgerald, prin. Fax 768-5910
Parkside MS 1,100/7-8
2400 4th St 49203 517-841-2300
David Kiesel, prin. Fax 768-5668
Northwest Community SD 3,700/PK-12
4000 Van Horn Rd 49201 517-569-2247
Emily Kress, supt. Fax 569-2395
www.nsd.k12.mi.us
Kidder MS 900/6-8
6700 Rives Junction Rd 49201 517-569-2247
Dan Brooks, prin. Fax 569-2931
Northwest HS 1,000/9-12
4200 Van Horn Rd 49201 517-569-2247
Erik Bergh, prin. Fax 569-2398
Vandercook Lake SD 1,400/K-12
1000 E Golf Ave 49203 517-782-9044
Anthony Hollow, supt. Fax 788-3690
scnc.vandy.k12.mi.us
Vandercook Lake JSHS 700/6-12
1000 E Golf Ave 49203 517-782-8167
Mark Schonhard, prin. Fax 782-3730

Western SD
Supt. — See Parma
Western Options Ctr & Adult & Comm Educ Adult
3950 Catherine St 49203 517-841-8700
Deborah Batchelder, prin. Fax 841-8807

Baker College of Jackson Post-Sec.
2800 Springport Rd 49202 517-789-6123
Jackson Catholic MS 300/7-8
915 Cooper St 49202 517-784-3385
Ronald Niedzwiecki, prin. Fax 782-7883
Jackson Christian HS 200/6-12
4200 Lowe Rd 49203 517-783-2658
Bob Stanton, prin. Fax 783-4235
Jackson Community College Post-Sec.
2111 Emmons Rd 49201 517-787-0800
Jackson Community College Post-Sec.
3610 Wildwood Ave 49202 517-787-7012
Lumen Christi HS 600/9-12
3483 Spring Arbor Rd 49203 517-787-0630
Rev. Thomas Rieden, prin. Fax 787-1066

Jenison, Ottawa, Pop. 17,882
Jenison SD 4,600/PK-12
8375 20th Ave 49428 616-457-8890
Thomas TenBrink, supt. Fax 457-8898
www.jpsonline.org/
Jenison HS 1,600/9-12
2140 Bauer Rd 49428 616-457-3400
Mark Dievendorf, prin. Fax 457-4070
Jenison JHS 800/7-8
8295 20th Ave 49428 616-457-1402
Donna Bergeon, prin. Fax 457-8090

Johannesburg, Otsego
Johannesburg-Lewiston Area SD 900/K-12
10854 M 32 E 49751 989-732-1773
James Hilgendorf, supt. Fax 732-6556
www.jlas.org
Johannesburg-Lewiston HS 200/9-12
10854 M 32 E 49751 989-731-4420
Will Kearney, prin. Fax 732-6556

Jonesville, Hillsdale, Pop. 2,332
Jonesville Community SD 1,300/PK-12
202 Wright St 49250 517-849-9075
Dr. Richard Paul, supt. Fax 849-2434
www.jonesvilleschools.org
Jonesville HS 400/9-12
460 Adrian Rd 49250 517-849-9934
Chellie Broesamle, prin. Fax 849-2755
Jonesville MS 300/6-8
401 E Chicago St 49250 517-849-3210
Penny Snyder, prin. Fax 849-3213

Kalamazoo, Kalamazoo, Pop. 75,312
Comstock SD 2,500/K-12
3010 Gull Rd 49048 269-388-9461
Dr. David Hutton, supt. Fax 388-9481
www.comstockps.org
Comstock HS 800/9-12
2107 N 26th St 49048 269-388-9400
Donald Eastman, prin. Fax 388-9464
Comstock Northeast MS 700/6-8
1423 N 28th St 49048 269-388-9433
Jay Birchmeier, prin. Fax 388-9664
Adult Education Adult
3010 Gull Rd 49048 269-388-9477
Steve Symons, prin. Fax 388-9491

Kalamazoo RESA
1819 E Milham Ave 49002 — 269-385-1500
W. Craig Misner, supt. — Fax 381-9423
www.kresa.org
Young Adult Program — Adult
422 E South St 49007 — 269-488-9601
Jane Bilicki, prin. — Fax 488-9613

Kalamazoo SD — 10,300/K-12
1220 Howard St 49008 — 269-337-0100
Janice M. Brown Ed.D., supt. — Fax 337-0149
www.kalamazoopublicschools.com
Central HS — 1,400/9-12
2432 N Drake Rd 49006 — 269-337-0300
Carl Myles, prin. — Fax 337-0391
Hillside MS — 600/7-8
1941 Alamo Ave 49006 — 269-337-0570
Timon Kendall, prin. — Fax 337-1618
Maple Magnet MS — 600/6-8
922 W Maple St 49008 — 269-337-0730
Deborah Johnston, prin. — Fax 337-1633
Milwood MS — 600/6-8
2916 Konkle St 49001 — 269-337-0670
Kevin Campbell, prin. — Fax 337-1628
Norrix HS — 1,300/9-12
606 E Kilgore Rd 49001 — 269-337-0200
David LaPrairie, prin. — Fax 337-1617

Parchment SD
Supt. — See Parchment
Barclay Hills Education Center — Adult
1125 E Mosel Ave 49004 — 269-488-1470
April Goodwin, prin. — Fax 488-1480

Davenport University — Post-Sec.
4123 W Main St 49006 — 269-552-3308
Heritage Christian Academy — 300/K-12
6312 Quail Run Dr 49009 — 269-372-1400
James Wessing, admin. — Fax 372-6018
Kalamazoo Christian HS — 500/9-12
2121 Stadium Dr 49008 — 269-381-2250
Thomas Kamp, prin. — Fax 381-0319
Kalamazoo Christian MS — 300/6-8
3333 S Westnedge Ave 49008 — 269-343-3645
Jeff Blamer, prin. — Fax 343-4649
Kalamazoo College — Post-Sec.
1200 Academy St 49006 — 269-337-7000
Kalamazoo Jr. Academy — 100/K-10
1601 Nichols Rd 49006 — 269-342-8943
Robert Adams, prin.
Kalamazoo Valley Community College — Post-Sec.
PO Box 4070 49003 — 269-372-5000
Msgr. Hackett HS — 500/9-12
1000 W Kilgore Rd 49008 — 269-381-2646
Tim Eastman, prin. — Fax 381-3919
Olympia Career Training Institute — Post-Sec.
5177 W Main St 49009 — 269-381-9616
Reformed Heritage Christian S — 100/K-12
700 Fletcher Ave 49006 — 269-383-0505
Lynelle Schreuder, admin. — Fax 383-2381
Western Michigan University 49008 — Post-Sec.
— 269-387-1000
West Michigan Coll of Barbering & Beauty — Post-Sec.
3026 Lovers Ln 49001 — 269-381-4424

Kalkaska, Kalkaska, Pop. 2,250
Kalkaska SD — 1,800/K-12
PO Box 580 49646 — 231-258-9109
Dan McKenzie, supt. — Fax 258-4474
www.kpschools.com/
Kalkaska HS — 600/9-12
PO Box 580 49646 — 231-258-9167
Dale Kasza, prin. — Fax 258-5188
Kalkaska MS — 400/6-8
PO Box 580 49646 — 231-258-4040
Diane Swoverland, prin. — Fax 258-3576

Kent City, Kent, Pop. 1,057
Kent City Community SD — 1,100/K-12
200 N Clover St 49330 — 616-678-7714
Gregory Pratt, supt. — Fax 678-4320
www.kent-city.k12.mi.us
Kent City HS — 500/9-12
351 N Main St 49330 — 616-678-4210
Fred Groenke, prin. — Fax 678-4371
Kent City MS — 6-8
285 N Main St 49330 — 616-678-4214
— Fax 678-5099

Algoma Christian S — 300/PK-12
PO Box 220 49330 — 616-678-7480
F. Michael Carlon, prin. — Fax 678-7484

Kentwood, Kent, Pop. 46,487
Kentwood SD — 9,000/PK-12
5820 Eastern Ave SE 49508 — 616-455-4400
Mary Leiker, supt. — Fax 455-4476
www.kentwoodps.org
Crestwood MS — 600/6-8
2674 44th St SE 49512 — 616-455-1200
Merl Siefken, prin. — Fax 455-2338
East Kentwood Freshman Campus HS — 800/9-9
6170 Valley Lane Dr SE 49508 — 616-698-9292
John Brillhart, prin. — Fax 698-0313
East Kentwood HS — 1,900/10-12
6230 Kalamazoo Ave SE 49508 — 616-698-6700
Joe Beel, prin. — Fax 698-2384
Pinewood MS — 800/6-8
2100 60th St SE 49508 — 616-455-1224
John Keenoy, prin. — Fax 455-2054
Valleywood MS — 600/6-8
1110 50th St SE 49508 — 616-538-7670
Michael Zoerhoff, prin. — Fax 538-9301
Kentwood Community Education — Adult
28 60th St SE 49548 — 616-261-6166
Brian O'Hara, prin. — Fax 261-6170

West Michigan Lutheran HS — 100/9-12
1934 52nd St SE 49508 — 616-455-2200
John Engelbrecht, prin. — Fax 455-2211

Kimball, Saint Clair, Pop. 7,247

New Life Christian Academy — 200/PK-12
5517 Griswold Rd 48074 — 810-367-3770
Lee Ann Shimmel, admin. — Fax 367-2249

Kinde, Huron, Pop. 518
North Huron SD — 600/K-12
21 Main St 48445 — 989-874-4100
Maryann Thompson, supt. — Fax 874-4109
www.nhuron.org
North Huron JSHS — 300/7-12
21 Main St 48445 — 989-874-4101
Elizabeth Loegel, prin. — Fax 874-4129

Kingsford, Dickinson, Pop. 5,435
Breitung Township SD — 2,000/K-12
2000 W Pyle Dr 49802 — 906-779-2650
Douglas Massignan, supt. — Fax 779-9017
www.kingsford.org
Kingsford HS — 700/9-12
431 Hamilton Ave 49802 — 906-779-2670
Robert Usitalo, prin. — Fax 779-2883
Kingsford MS — 500/6-8
445 Hamilton Ave 49802 — 906-779-2680
Craig Allen, prin. — Fax 774-1354

Dickinson/Iron ISD — 906-779-2690
1074 Pyle Dr 49802
Johanna Ostwald, supt. — Fax 779-2669
www.diisd.org
Dickinson-Iron Tech Educ Center — Vo/Tech
300 North Blvd 49802 — 906-779-2697
Paul Bonsall, prin. — Fax 779-2087

Kingsley, Grand Traverse, Pop. 1,522
Kingsley Area SD — 1,500/K-12
PO Box 580 49649 — 231-263-5262
Lynn Gullekson, supt. — Fax 263-5282
www.kingsley.k12.mi.us/
Kingsley HS — 400/9-12
PO Box 580 49649 — 231-263-5262
Terry Street, prin. — Fax 263-2630
Kingsley MS — 500/5-8
PO Box 580 49649 — 231-263-5262
Ken Knudsen, prin. — Fax 263-4623

Kingston, Tuscola, Pop. 441
Kingston Community SD — 700/PK-12
5790 State St 48741 — 989-683-2294
George Bednorek, supt. — Fax 683-2644
www.kingston.k12.mi.us
Kingston JSHS — 300/7-12
5790 State St 48741 — 989-683-2550
Joseph Murphy, prin. — Fax 683-2644

Kinross, Chippewa

Maplewood Baptist Academy — 100/K-12
255 W M-80 49752 — 906-495-5200
Tim Rader, prin. — Fax 495-7433

Laingsburg, Shiawassee, Pop. 1,208
Laingsburg Community SD — 1,200/PK-12
205 S Woodhull Rd 48848 — 517-651-2705
Richard Dunham, supt. — Fax 651-9075
laingsburg.k12.mi.us
Laingsburg HS — 400/9-12
8008 Woodbury Rd 48848 — 517-651-5091
Mike Foster, prin. — Fax 651-9621
Laingsburg MS — 300/6-8
112 High St 48848 — 517-651-5034
Gregory Kingdon, prin. — Fax 651-2613

Lake City, Missaukee, Pop. 937
Lake City Area SD — 1,200/K-12
PO Box 900 49651 — 231-839-4333
Harry E. Ashton, supt. — Fax 839-5219
www.lakecityschools.net
Lake City HS — 400/9-12
PO Box 900 49651 — 231-839-4331
Judy Baase, prin. — Fax 839-6031
Lake City MS — 300/6-8
PO Box 900 49651 — 231-839-7163
Dave Swanson, prin. — Fax 839-6042

Lake Leelanau, Leelanau

St. Mary S — 200/PK-12
PO Box 340 49653 — 231-256-9636
Chris Smith, prin. — Fax 256-7239

Lake Linden, Houghton, Pop. 1,074
Lake Linden-Hubbell SD — 600/K-12
601 Calumet St 49945 — 906-296-6211
Randall Roberts, supt. — Fax 296-0943
www.lakelinden.k12.mi.us
Lake Linden Hubbell JSHS — 300/7-12
601 Calumet St 49945 — 906-296-6681
Craig Sundblad, prin. — Fax 296-0219

Lake Odessa, Ionia, Pop. 2,278
Lakewood SD — 2,500/K-12
639 Jordan Lake St 48849 — 616-374-8043
Gunnard Johnson, supt. — Fax 374-8858
www.lakewood.k12.mi.us
Lakewood HS — 800/9-12
7223 Velte Rd 48849 — 616-374-8868
Michael O'Mara, prin. — Fax 374-1468
Other Schools – See Woodland

Lake Orion, Oakland, Pop. 2,730
Lake Orion Community SD — 7,400/PK-12
315 N Lapeer St 48362 — 248-693-5413
Christine Lehman, prin. — Fax 693-5466
www.lakeorion.k12.mi.us/

Lake Orion Community HS — 2,100/9-12
495 E Scripps Rd 48360 — 248-693-5420
Todd Dunckley, prin. — Fax 693-5459
Scripps MS — 600/6-8
385 E Scripps Rd 48360 — 248-693-5440
Dan Haas, prin. — Fax 693-5301
Waldon MS — 600/6-8
2509 Waldon Rd 48360 — 248-391-1100
Heidi Kast, prin. — Fax 391-5452
Other Schools – See Oakland

Lake Orion Baptist S — 100/K-12
255 E Scripps Rd 48360 — 248-693-6203
Dennis Quattlebaum, prin. — Fax 693-6177

Lakeview, Montcalm, Pop. 1,116
Lakeview Community SD — 1,800/PK-12
123 5th St 48850 — 989-352-6226
J. Mark Parsons, supt. — Fax 352-8245
www.lakeviewschools.net
Lakeview HS — 600/9-12
9800 Youngman Rd 48850 — 989-352-7221
Michael Travis, prin. — Fax 352-6320
Lakeview MS — 400/6-8
516 Washington St 48850 — 989-352-8016
Robert Ivan, prin. — Fax 352-6710

L Anse, Baraga, Pop. 2,147
L'Anse Area SD — 800/K-12
201 N 4th St 49946 — 906-524-6121
Ray Pasquali, supt. — Fax 524-6001
www.laschools.k12.mi.us
L'Anse HS — 200/9-12
201 N 4th St 49946 — 906-524-6122
Henry Moore, prin. — Fax 524-6231
L'Anse MS — 200/6-8
201 N 4th St 49946 — 906-524-5390
Robert Willman, prin. — Fax 524-0345

Lansing, Ingham, Pop. 118,379
DeWitt SD
Supt. — See De Witt
DeWitt HS — 800/9-12
3100 W Clark Rd 48906 — 517-668-3100
Michael Foster, prin. — Fax 668-3155

Lansing SD — 15,800/PK-12
519 W Kalamazoo St 48933 — 517-325-6000
Dr. E. Sharon Banks, supt. — Fax 325-6028
lsd.k12.mi.us
Eastern HS — 1,500/9-12
220 N Pennsylvania Ave 48912 — 517-325-6500
Pam Backus-Diggs, prin. — Fax 325-7341
Everett HS — 1,600/9-12
3900 Stabler St 48910 — 517-325-6600
Dale Glynn, prin. — Fax 325-6626
Gardner MS — 1,000/6-8
333 Dahlia Dr 48911 — 517-325-6540
Norm Gear, prin. — Fax 325-6256
Hill Vocational Center — Vo/Tech
5815 Wise Rd 48911 — 517-325-6900
Cordell Henderson, prin. — Fax 325-6344
Otto MS — 800/6-8
500 E Thomas St 48906 — 517-325-6570
Rod Doig, prin. — Fax 374-6587
Pattengill MS — 700/6-8
1017 Jerome St 48912 — 517-325-6640
Donna Pohl, prin. — Fax 325-6665
Rich MS — 800/6-8
2600 Hampden Dr 48911 — 517-325-6670
Sam Davis, prin. — Fax 325-6465
Riddle MS — 200/6-8
221 Huron St 48915 — 517-325-6868
Betty Javoroski, prin. — Fax 325-7314
Sexton HS — 1,100/9-12
102 Mcpherson Ave 48915 — 517-325-6700
Broderick Williams, prin. — Fax 325-7284

Waverly SD — 3,200/PK-12
515 Snow Rd 48917 — 517-321-7265
Thomas J. Pillar, supt. — Fax 321-8577
www.waverly.k12.mi.us
Waverly HS — 1,100/9-12
160 Snow Rd 48917 — 517-323-3831
David Percival, prin. — Fax 323-7714
Waverly MS — 600/7-8
620 Snow Rd 48917 — 517-321-7240
Vincent Perkins, prin. — Fax 321-5789

Davenport College of Business — Post-Sec.
220 E Kalamazoo St 48933 — 517-484-2600
Educational Inst./American Hotel-Lodging — Post-Sec.
2113 N High St 48906 — 800-344-3320
Greater Lansing Adventist S — 100/K-10
5330 W St Joe Hwy 48917 — 517-321-5565
Chad Bernard, prin. — Fax 321-5580
Great Lakes Christian College — Post-Sec.
6211 W Willow Hwy 48917 — 517-321-0242
Lansing Catholic Central HS — 500/9-12
501 Marshall St 48912 — 517-267-2100
Thomas Maloney, prin. — Fax 267-2135
Lansing Christian HS — 300/6-12
3405 Belle Chase Way 48911 — 517-882-5777
Audrey Castelbuono, prin. — Fax 272-9567
Lansing Community College — Post-Sec.
419 N Capitol Ave 48933 — 517-483-1620
New Covenant Christian S — 200/K-12
PO Box 80707 48908 — 517-323-8903
Jim Ryckman, prin. — Fax 323-0421
Ross Medical Education Center — Post-Sec.
913 W Holmes Rd Ste 260 48910 — 517-887-0180
Thomas M. Cooley Law School — Post-Sec.
PO Box 13038 48901 — 517-371-5140

Lapeer, Lapeer, Pop. 9,343
Lapeer Community SD — 7,300/PK-12
1025 W Nepessing St 48446 — 810-667-2401
Debbie Thompson, supt. — Fax 667-2411
www.lapeerschools.org

Lapeer East HS 1,400/8-12
933 S Saginaw St 48446 810-667-2418
Kelly Paige, prin. Fax 667-2422
Lapeer West HS 1,500/8-12
170 Millville Rd 48446 810-667-2423
Kevin Walters, prin. Fax 667-2428

Lapeer County ISD
1996 W Oregon St 48446 810-664-5917
Joseph Keena, supt. Fax 664-1011
www.lcisd.k12.mi.us
Other Schools – See Attica

Health Enrichment Center Post-Sec.
204 E Nepessing St 48446 810-667-9453

Lathrup Village, Oakland, Pop. 4,220
Southfield SD
Supt. — See Southfield
Lathrup HS 1,600/9-12
19301 W 12 Mile Rd 48076 248-746-7204
Marcia Whitaker, prin. Fax 746-7488

Lawrence, Van Buren, Pop. 1,046
Lawrence SD 800/PK-12
650 W Saint Joseph St 49064 269-674-8233
Richard Stoll, supt. Fax 674-8206
www.lawrenceschools.cc
Lawrence JSHS 400/7-12
650 W Saint Joseph St 49064 269-674-8232
John Overley, prin. Fax 674-8206

Van Buren ISD
490 S Paw Paw St 49064 269-674-8091
Jeffrey Mills, supt. Fax 674-8030
www.vbisd.org/
Van Buren Technology Center Vo/Tech
250 South St 49064 269-674-8091
Sue Conklin, prin. Fax 674-8954

Lawton, Van Buren, Pop. 1,854
Lawton Community SD 1,100/PK-12
101 Primary Way 49065 269-624-7900
Joseph Trimboli, supt. Fax 624-6489
www.lawtoncs.org
Lawton HS 300/9-12
101 Blue Pride Dr 49065 269-624-7800
Tammy Wilson, prin. Fax 624-6554
Lawton MS 300/6-8
100 Blue Pride Dr 49065 269-624-7600
Tim Cerven, prin. Fax 624-5206

Leland, Leelanau
Leland SD 400/K-12
PO Box 498 49654 231-256-9857
Michael Hartigan, supt. Fax 256-9844
mail.leland.k12.mi.us
Leland S 400/K-12
PO Box 498 49654 231-256-9857
Terry Breen, prin. Fax 256-9844

Le Roy, Osceola, Pop. 263
Pine River Area SD 1,300/K-12
17445 Pine River Rd 49655 231-829-3141
Jim Ganger, supt. Fax 829-4410
www.pineriver.k12.mi.us
Pine River Area HS 500/9-12
17445 Pine River Rd 49655 231-829-3841
Barb Parmenter, prin. Fax 829-4410
Pine River MS 300/6-8
17445 Pine River Rd 49655 231-829-4064
Barb Parmenter, prin. Fax 829-4410

Leslie, Ingham, Pop. 2,009
Leslie SD 1,400/K-12
432 N Main St 49251 517-589-8200
Robert Howe, supt. Fax 589-5340
scnc.leslie.k12.mi.us/~schools/
Leslie HS 500/9-12
4141 Hull Rd 49251 517-589-8294
Jeff Manthei, prin. Fax 589-5720
Leslie MS 400/5-8
400 Kimball St 49251 517-589-8218
Rick Samulak, prin. Fax 589-5714

Lincoln, Alcona, Pop. 354
Alcona Community SD 1,000/K-12
PO Box 249 48742 989-736-6212
Shawn Thornton, supt. Fax 736-6261
Alcona HS 300/9-12
PO Box 249 48742 989-736-8534
Jim Watts, prin. Fax 736-8495
Alcona MS 300/6-8
PO Box 249 48742 989-736-8534
Terrence Allison, prin. Fax 736-3184

Lincoln Park, Wayne, Pop. 39,131
Lincoln Park SD 5,200/K-12
1650 Champaign Rd 48146 313-389-0200
Randall H. Kite, supt. Fax 389-1322
www.resa.net/lincolnpark
Lincoln Park HS 1,400/9-12
1701 Champaign Rd 48146 313-389-0234
Dr. Kathy Evans, prin. Fax 383-5738
Lincoln Park MS 900/7-8
2800 Lafayette Blvd 48146 313-389-0757
Betty Diener, prin. Fax 389-0761

Linden, Genesee, Pop. 3,201
Lake Fenton Community SD
Supt. — See Fenton
Lake Fenton HS 500/9-12
4070 Lahring Rd 48451 810-591-9405
Julie Williams, prin. Fax 591-9495

Linden Community SD 3,000/K-12
7205 Silver Lake Rd 48451 810-591-0980
Elizabeth Leonard, prin. Fax 591-5587
www.lindenschools.org
Linden HS 900/9-12
7201 Silver Lake Rd 48451 810-591-0410
Brian Boudreau, prin. Fax 591-8014
Linden MS 700/6-8
325 Stan Eaton Dr 48451 810-591-8180
Julie Brown, prin. Fax 591-4377

Litchfield, Hillsdale, Pop. 1,447
Litchfield Community SD 500/K-12
210 Williams St 49252 517-542-2388
Clair Dean, supt. Fax 542-2580
www.litchfieldschools.com/
Litchfield JSHS, 210 Williams St 49252 300/6-12
Clair Dean, prin. 517-542-2386

Livonia, Wayne, Pop. 99,487
Clarenceville SD 2,000/PK-12
20210 Middlebelt Rd 48152 248-473-8900
Cheryl M. Leach, supt. Fax 476-5460
www.clarenceville.k12.mi.us
Clarenceville HS 600/9-12
20155 Middlebelt Rd 48152 248-473-8926
Paul Shepich, prin. Fax 476-8051
Clarenceville MS 500/6-8
20210 Middlebelt Rd 48152 248-473-8915
Kathleen Guntzviller, prin. Fax 473-2073

Livonia SD 17,700/PK-12
15125 Farmington Rd 48154 734-744-2500
Randy A. Liepa, supt. Fax 744-2569
www.livonia.k12.mi.us
Churchill HS 2,200/9-12
8900 Newburgh Rd 48150 734-744-2650
R. Joseph Anderson, prin. Fax 744-2652
Emerson MS 700/7-8
29100 W Chicago St 48150 734-744-2665
Thomas Tobe, prin. Fax 744-2667
Franklin HS 1,700/9-12
31000 Joy Rd 48150 734-744-2655
Daniel Willenborg, prin. Fax 744-2657
Frost MS 800/7-8
14041 Stark Rd 48154 734-744-2670
Christina Berry, prin. Fax 744-2672
Holmes MS 600/7-8
16200 Newburgh Rd 48154 734-744-2675
Dorothy Chomicz, prin. Fax 744-2677
Livonia Career/Technical Center Vo/Tech
8985 Newburgh Rd 48150 734-744-2816
Dr. Janet Haas, prin. Fax 744-2817
Riley MS 700/7-8
15555 Henry Ruff St 48154 734-744-2680
Eric Stromberg, prin. Fax 744-2682
Stevenson HS 2,200/9-12
33500 6 Mile Rd 48152 734-744-2660
Steven Archibald, prin. Fax 744-2662
Other Schools – See Westland

Ladywood HS 500/9-12
14680 Newburgh Rd 48154 734-591-1544
Sr. Mary Smith, prin. Fax 591-4214
Madonna University Post-Sec.
36600 Schoolcraft St 48150 734-432-5300
Schoolcraft College Post-Sec.
18600 Haggerty Rd 48152 734-462-4400
Virginia Farrell Beauty School Post-Sec.
33425 5 Mile Rd 48154 734-427-3970

Lowell, Kent, Pop. 4,121
Lowell Area SD 3,900/K-12
300 High St 49331 616-987-2500
Shari Jo Miller, supt. Fax 987-2511
www.lowellschools.com/
Lowell HS 1,300/9-12
11700 Vergennes St 49331 616-987-2900
Scott Vashaw, prin. Fax 987-2911
Lowell MS 900/6-8
750 Foreman St 49331 616-987-2800
Linda Warren, prin. Fax 987-2811

Ludington, Mason, Pop. 8,303
Ludington Area SD 2,500/K-12
809 E Tinkham Ave 49431 231-845-7303
Cal DeKuiper, supt. Fax 843-4930
www.lasd.net
DeJonge JHS 400/7-8
706 E Tinkham Ave 49431 231-845-3810
Mark Boon, prin. Fax 845-3814
Ludington HS 800/9-12
508 N Washington Ave 49431 231-845-3880
Mark Boon, prin. Fax 845-3881
Mason/Lake ISD
2130 W US Highway 10 49431 231-757-3716
Jeanne Oakes, supt. Fax 757-2406
www.mlisd.k12.mi.us
Other Schools – See Scottville

Mc Bain, Missaukee, Pop. 747
McBain Rural Agricultural SD 1,100/PK-12
107 E Maple St 49657 231-825-2165
Daniel Bachman, supt. Fax 825-2119
www.mcbain.k12.mi.us
Mc Bain HS 400/9-12
107 E Maple St 49657 231-825-2412
Phillip Christensen, prin. Fax 825-2119
Mc Bain MS 300/6-8
107 E Maple St 49657 231-825-8041
Gail Loeks, prin. Fax 825-2119

Northern Michigan Christian S 400/PK-12
128 S Martin St 49657 231-825-2492
Jim Hofman, prin. Fax 825-2371

Mackinac Island, Mackinac, Pop. 500
Mackinac Island SD 100/K-12
PO Box 340 49757 906-847-3377
Jack Dehring, supt. Fax 847-3773
mackinac.eup.k12.mi.us
Mackinac Island S 100/K-12
PO Box 340 49757 906-847-3377
Jack Dehring, supt. Fax 847-3773

Mackinaw City, Cheboygan, Pop. 854
Mackinaw City SD 100/K-12
609 W Central Ave 49701 231-436-8211
Jeffrey Curth, supt. Fax 436-5434
www.mackcity.k12.mi.us
Mackinaw City JSHS 100/7-12
609 W Central Ave 49701 231-436-8211
Vince LaCavera, prin.

Macomb, Macomb, Pop. 22,714
Chippewa Valley SD
Supt. — See Clinton Township
Dakota HS 2,100/9-12
21051 21 Mile Rd 48044 586-723-2702
Tom Heethius, prin. Fax 723-2701
Iroquois MS 900/6-8
48301 Romeo Plank Rd 48044 586-723-3700
James Capoferi, prin. Fax 723-3701

L'Anse Creuse SD
Supt. — See Harrison Township
L'Anse Creuse HS - North 1,700/9-12
23700 21 Mile Rd 48042 586-493-5270
David Jackson, prin. Fax 493-5275
L'Anse Creuse MS North 600/6-8
46201 Fairchild Rd 48042 586-493-5260
John Da Via, prin. Fax 493-5265

Lutheran HS North 600/9-12
16825 24 Mile Rd 48042 586-781-9151
Steven Buuck, prin. Fax 781-8673

Madison Heights, Oakland, Pop. 30,463
Lamphere SD 2,300/K-12
31201 Dorchester Ave 48071 248-589-1990
Marsha Pando, supt. Fax 589-2618
www.lamphere.k12.mi.us
Lamphere HS 700/9-12
610 W 13 Mile Rd 48071 248-589-3943
Ed Okuniewski, prin. Fax 589-0240
Page MS 600/6-8
29615 Tawas St 48071 248-589-3428
Douglas Kelley, prin. Fax 545-1870

Madison SD 2,700/PK-12
25421 Alger St 48071 248-399-7800
Dr. William Harrison, supt. Fax 399-2229
www.madisonschools.k12.mi.us/
Madison HS 600/9-12
915 E 11 Mile Rd 48071 248-548-1800
Robert Crowell, prin. Fax 548-9758
Wilkinson MS 300/7-8
26524 John R Rd 48071 248-399-0455
Fred Agemy, prin. Fax 399-1965

Bishop Foley HS 500/9-12
32000 Campbell Rd 48071 248-585-1210
Joanne Molnar, prin. Fax 585-3667
Dorsey Business School Post-Sec.
30821 Barrington St 48071 248-588-9660
Mr. Bela's School of Cosmetology Post-Sec.
29475 John R Rd 48071 248-543-4333

Mancelona, Antrim, Pop. 1,401
Mancelona SD 1,200/K-12
PO Box 739 49659 231-587-9764
Matthew J. Miller, supt. Fax 587-9500
mancelonaschools.org/
Mancelona HS 400/9-12
PO Box 739 49659 231-587-8551
John Smith, prin. Fax 587-5401
Mancelona MS 400/5-8
PO Box 739 49659 231-587-9869
Diana Kelly, prin. Fax 587-0615

Manchester, Washtenaw, Pop. 2,232
Manchester Community SD 1,300/K-12
410 City Rd 48158 734-428-9711
David Oegema Ph.D., supt. Fax 428-9188
www.mcs.k12.mi.us
Manchester HS 400/9-12
20500 Dutch Dr 48158 734-428-7333
John Eisley, prin. Fax 428-0178
Manchester MS 400/5-8
710 City Rd 48158 734-428-7442
Jack Corey, prin. Fax 428-9264

Manistee, Manistee, Pop. 6,711
Manistee Area SD 1,600/K-12
550 Maple St 49660 231-723-3521
Robert Olsen, supt. Fax 723-1507
www.honoredstudents.org
Manistee HS 600/9-12
525 12th St 49660 231-723-2549
Andy Huber, prin. Fax 398-9277
Manistee MS 400/6-8
550 Maple St 49660 231-723-3271
Matt Kieffer, prin. Fax 723-5879

Manistee Catholic Central S 200/PK-12
1200 US Highway 31 S 49660 231-723-2529
Karen Tetsworth, prin. Fax 723-0669

Manistique, Schoolcraft, Pop. 3,481
Manistique Area SD 500/K-12
100 N Cedar St 49854 906-341-4300
Esther Mudge, supt. Fax 341-2374
www.manistique.k12.mi.us

Manistique HS
100 N Cedar St 49854 — 400/9-12
906-341-4300
Butch Yurk, prin. — Fax 341-8473
Manistique MS — 6-8
100 N Cedar St 49854
906-341-4300
Jason Lockwood, prin. — Fax 341-8473

Manton, Wexford, Pop. 1,224
Manton Consolidated SD — 1,000/K-12
105 5th St 49663
231-824-6411
Lon D. Schneider, supt. — Fax 824-4101
www.manton.k12.mi.us
Manton HS — 300/9-12
105 5th St 49663
231-824-6411
Bradley Jacobs, prin. — Fax 824-6114
Manton MS — 300/5-8
105 5th St 49663
231-824-6401
Sue Murchie, prin. — Fax 824-4121

Maple City, Leelanau
Glen Lake Community SD — 900/K-12
3375 W Burdickville Rd 49664
231-334-3061
Tom Harwood, supt. — Fax 334-6255
www.glenlake.k12.mi.us
Glen Lake JSHS — 500/6-12
3375 W Burdickville Rd 49664
231-334-3061
Dennis Furton, prin. — Fax 334-6295

Marcellus, Cass, Pop. 1,116
Marcellus Community SD — 1,000/K-12
PO Box 48 49067
269-646-7655
Mary Cooper, supt. — Fax 646-2700
www.marcelluscs.org/
Marcellus HS — 300/9-12
PO Box 48 49067
269-646-5081
William Markovich, prin. — Fax 646-5021
Marcellus MS — 300/5-8
PO Box 48 49067
269-646-3158
Mary McCrumb, prin. — Fax 646-2438

Howardsville Christian S — 200/K-12
53441 Bent Rd 49067
269-646-9367
David Sponable, admin. — Fax 646-7006

Marine City, Saint Clair, Pop. 4,500
East China SD
Supt. — See East China
Marine City HS — 800/9-12
1085 Ward St 48039
810-676-1900
William Jedele, prin. — Fax 676-1925
Marine City MS — 600/6-8
6373 King Rd 48039
810-676-1201
Michael Alley, prin. — Fax 676-1225

Cardinal Mooney College Prep S — 200/9-12
660 S Water St 48039
810-765-8825
Sr. Karen Lietz, prin. — Fax 765-7164

Marion, Osceola, Pop. 839
Marion SD — 700/K-12
PO Box O 49665
231-743-2486
Charles Chase, supt. — Fax 743-2890
marion.k12.mi.us
Marion JSHS — 400/7-12
PO Box O 49665
231-743-2836
Larry Johnson, prin. — Fax 743-9622

Marlette, Sanilac, Pop. 2,086
Marlette Community SD — 1,400/K-12
6230 Euclid St 48453
989-635-7425
Duane Lange, supt. — Fax 635-7103
www.marlette.k12.mi.us
Marlette HS — 500/9-12
3051 Moore St 48453
989-635-4930
Dale Moore, prin. — Fax 635-5300
Marlette MS — 500/4-8
6230 Euclid St 48453
989-635-7427
Michael Distelrath, prin. — Fax 635-7103

Marquette, Marquette, Pop. 20,704
Marquette Area SD — 3,600/K-12
1201 W Fair Ave 49855
906-225-5320
Jon Harrwig, supt. — Fax 225-5340
www.mapsnet.org
Bothwell MS — 800/6-8
1200 Tierney St 49855
906-225-4262
Sara Norton, prin. — Fax 225-4229
Marquette HS — 1,300/9-12
1203 W Fair Ave 49855
906-225-4254
Robert Anthony, prin. — Fax 225-5370

Father Marquette MS — 200/5-8
414 W College Ave 49855
906-226-7912
Karen Ogles, prin. — Fax 225-9962
Marquette General Hospital — Post-Sec.
420 W Magnetic St 49855
906-225-3434
Northern Michigan University — Post-Sec.
1401 Presque Isle Ave 49855
906-227-1000

Marshall, Calhoun, Pop. 7,295
Marshall SD — 2,500/K-12
100 E Green St 49068
269-781-1250
Dr. Joyce K. Phillips, supt. — Fax 789-1813
www.marshall.k12.mi.us
Marshall HS — 900/9-12
701 N Marshall Ave 49068
269-781-1252
Ronald Behrenwald, prin. — Fax 781-5304
Marshall MS — 800/5-8
100 E Green St 49068
269-781-1250
Michael Miles, prin. — Fax 781-7757

Martin, Allegan, Pop. 424
Martin SD — 700/K-12
PO Box 241 49070
269-672-7194
D.G. Alexander, supt. — Fax 672-7116
www.martin.k12.mi.us
Martin MSHS — 400/6-12
PO Box 241 49070
269-672-5555
Dirk Weedreyer, prin. — Fax 672-9263

East Martin Christian HS — 50/9-12
518 118th Ave 49070
269-672-7673
George E. Fennema, prin. — Fax 672-7826

Marysville, Saint Clair, Pop. 9,833
Marysville SD — 2,700/K-12
1111 Delaware Ave 48040
810-364-7731
John Silveri, supt. — Fax 364-3150
www.marysville.k12.mi.us/mps/
Marysville HS — 900/9-12
1325 Michigan Ave 48040
810-364-7161
Bill Farnsworth, prin. — Fax 364-8878
Marysville IS — 600/6-8
400 Collard Dr 48040
810-364-6336
John Sazehn, prin. — Fax 364-4456

St. Clair RESA — 500/
PO Box 1500 48040
810-364-8990
Dan DeGrow, supt. — Fax 364-7474
www.sccresa.org/
St. Clair Technical Education Center — Vo/Tech
PO Box 1500 48040
810-364-8990
Frederic Stanley, prin. — Fax 364-8139

Mason, Ingham, Pop. 7,831
Ingham ISD — 500/
2630 W Howell Rd 48854
517-676-1051
Stanley Kogut, supt. — Fax 676-1277
www.inghamisd.org
Capital Area Career Center — Vo/Tech
611 Hagadorn Rd 48854
517-244-1330
Jim Menapace, prin. — Fax 676-3602

Mason SD — 3,200/K-12
118 W Oak St 48854
517-676-2484
James C. Harvey, supt. — Fax 676-6058
scnc.mason.k12.mi.us
Mason HS — 1,100/9-12
1001 S Barnes St 48854
517-676-9055
Lance Delbridge, prin. — Fax 244-6412
Mason MS — 800/6-8
235 Temple St 48854
517-676-6514
Daniel McConeghy, prin. — Fax 676-0287

Mattawan, Van Buren, Pop. 2,755
Mattawan Consolidated SD — 3,500/K-12
56720 Murray St 49071
269-668-3361
James Weeldreyer, supt. — Fax 668-2372
www.mattawan.k12.mi.us
Mattawan HS — 1,100/9-12
56720 Murray St 49071
269-668-3361
Colin Ripmaster, prin. — Fax 668-8245
Mattawan MS — 900/6-8
56720 Murray St 49071
269-668-3361
Jan Hall, prin. — Fax 668-3188

Mayville, Tuscola, Pop. 1,028
Mayville Community SD — 1,100/PK-12
6250 Fulton St 48744
989-843-6115
Bob Smith, supt. — Fax 843-6988
www.mayville.k12.mi.us
Mayville HS — 400/9-12
6250 Fulton St 48744
989-843-6115
Rhonda Blackburn, prin. — Fax 843-7208
Mayville MS — 300/6-8
6210 Fulton St 48744
989-843-6115
John LaGraff, prin. — Fax 843-7209

Melvindale, Wayne, Pop. 10,601
Melvindale-Northern Allen Park SD — 1,800/K-12
18530 Prospect St 48122
313-389-3300
Cora Kelly, supt. — Fax 389-3312
www.melnap.k12.mi.us
Melvindale HS — 700/9-12
18656 Prospect St 48122
313-389-3320
Russell Pickell, prin. — Fax 389-2072
Strong MS — 700/6-8
3303 Oakwood Blvd 48122
313-389-3330
Mark Kavorkian, prin. — Fax 389-2077

Mendon, Saint Joseph, Pop. 925
Mendon Community SD — 600/K-12
148 Kirby Rd 49072
269-496-8491
Charles Frisbie, supt. — Fax 496-8234
www.mendonschools.org
Mendon HS — 200/9-12
148 Kirby Rd 49072
269-496-8491
Jay Peterson, prin. — Fax 496-8234
Mendon MS — 6-8
148 Kirby Rd 49072
269-496-8491
Jay Peterson, prin. — Fax 496-8234

Menominee, Menominee, Pop. 8,851
Menominee Area SD — 1,500/PK-12
1230 13th St 49858
906-863-9951
Dr. Carol Swingle, supt. — Fax 863-1171
www.menominee.k12.mi.us/
Menominee HS — 700/9-12
2101 18th St 49858
906-863-7814
Paul Schneider, prin. — Fax 863-8883
Menominee JHS — 300/7-8
2101 18th St 49858
906-863-9929
Randy Verkerke, prin. — Fax 863-8883

Merrill, Saginaw, Pop. 773
Merrill Community SD — 900/PK-12
PO Box 488 48637
989-643-7261
John Searles, supt. — Fax 643-5570
www.astihosted.com/mcsddcp/
Merrill HS — 300/9-12
PO Box 488 48637
989-643-7231
Gary Smith, prin. — Fax 643-7942
Merrill MS — 200/6-8
PO Box 488 48637
989-643-7247
Michael Thayer, prin. — Fax 643-5971

Mesick, Wexford, Pop. 451
Mesick Consolidated SD — 900/K-12
PO Box 275 49668
231-885-1200
Dennis Stratton, supt. — Fax 885-1234
www.mesick.org

Mesick HS
PO Box 275 49668 — 300/9-12
231-885-1201
Mark Krell, prin. — Fax 885-2554
Mesick MS — 300/5-8
PO Box 275 49668
231-885-1207
Deann Jenkins, prin. — Fax 885-2544

Michigan Center, Jackson, Pop. 4,863
Michigan Center SD — 1,500/PK-12
400 S State St 49254
517-764-5778
Mark Haag, supt. — Fax 764-5790
scnc.mcps.k12.mi.us
Michigan Center JSHS — 700/7-12
400 S State St 49254
517-764-1440
Tom Claus, prin. — Fax 764-3346

Middleton, Gratiot
Fulton SD — 800/PK-12
8060 Ely Hwy 48856
989-236-7300
Charles Seguna, supt. — Fax 236-7660
www.fulton.edzone.net
Fulton HS — 200/9-12
8060 Ely Hwy 48856
989-236-7232
Chuck Mungall, prin. — Fax 236-7628
Fulton MS — 200/7-8
8060 Ely Hwy 48856
989-236-7232
Terry Maier, prin. — Fax 236-7628

Middleville, Barry, Pop. 2,802
Thornapple-Kellogg SD — 2,900/PK-12
10051 Green Lake Rd 49333
269-795-3313
Kevin Konarska, supt. — Fax 795-5401
www.tk.k12.mi.us
Thornapple-Kellogg HS — 900/9-12
3885 Bender Rd 49333
269-795-3394
Ellen Zack, prin. — Fax 795-5492
Thornapple-Kellogg MS — 700/6-8
10375 Green Lake Rd 49333
269-795-3349
Jon Washburn, prin. — Fax 795-5455

Midland, Midland, Pop. 42,175
Bullock Creek SD — 1,800/K-12
1420 S Badour Rd 48640
989-631-9022
John M. Hill, supt. — Fax 631-2882
www.bcreek.k12.mi.us
Bullock Creek HS — 700/9-12
1420 S Badour Rd 48640
989-631-2340
Charles Schwedler, prin. — Fax 631-2882
Bullock Creek MS — 500/6-8
644 S Badour Rd 48640
989-631-9260
Craig Carmoney, prin. — Fax 832-4018

Midland SD — 9,600/K-12
600 E Carpenter St 48640
989-923-5001
Dr. Gary Hughes, supt. — Fax 923-5003
www.mps.k12.mi.us
Central MS — 600/6-8
305 E Reardon St 48640
989-923-5571
Paula Geller, prin. — Fax 923-5518
Dow HS — 1,400/9-12
3901 N Saginaw Rd 48640
989-923-5382
Janice Goodall, prin. — Fax 923-5301
Jefferson MS — 900/6-8
800 W Chapel Ln 48640
989-923-5873
Ray Fryar, prin. — Fax 923-5800
Midland HS — 1,700/9-12
1301 Eastlawn Dr 48642
989-923-5181
Michael Frazee, prin. — Fax 923-5100
Northeast MS — 900/6-8
1305 E Sugnet Rd 48642
989-923-5772
Margaret Lee, prin. — Fax 923-5780

Calvary Baptist Academy — 400/PK-12
6100 Perrine Rd 48640
989-832-3341
Michael Reece, prin. — Fax 832-7443
Davenport University - Central Region — Post-Sec.
3555 E Patrick Rd 48642
989-835-5588
Midland Christian S — 100/K-12
4417 W Wackerly St 48640
989-835-9881
William Spicer, prin. — Fax 835-5201
Northwood University — Post-Sec.
4000 Whiting Dr 48640
800-457-7878

Milan, Monroe, Pop. 4,977
Milan Area SD — 2,200/K-12
100 Big Red Dr 48160
734-439-5050
Dennis McComb, supt. — Fax 439-5083
www.milanareaschools.org/
Milan HS — 700/9-12
200 Big Red Dr 48160
734-439-5000
Ron Reed, prin. — Fax 439-5084
Milan MS — 500/6-8
920 North St 48160
734-439-5200
William Brown, prin. — Fax 439-5288

Milford, Oakland, Pop. 6,319
Huron Valley SD
Supt. — See Highland
Muir MS — 600/6-8
425 George St 48381
248-684-8060
Gayle Lizzet, prin. — Fax 684-8068

West Highland Christian Academy — 100/K-12
1116 S Hickory Ridge Rd 48380
248-887-6698
Eunice Sanford, admin. — Fax 887-4645

Millington, Tuscola, Pop. 1,115
Millington Community SD — 1,600/K-12
8655 Gleason Rd 48746
989-871-5227
Lawrence R. Kroswek, supt. — Fax 871-5260
www.mcsdistrict.com
Meachum JHS — 600/5-8
8537 Gleason Rd 48746
989-871-5269
Michael Carmean, prin. — Fax 871-5249
Millington HS — 500/9-12
8780 Dean Rd 48746
989-871-5221
Thomas Frampton, prin. — Fax 871-5244

Mio, Oscoda, Pop. 1,886
Mio-AuSable SD 700/K-12
1110 W 8th St 48647 989-826-2400
Linda Fuchs, supt. Fax 826-2415
www.mio.k12.mi.us
Mio-AuSable HS 300/9-12
1110 W 8th St 48647 989-826-2481
James Gendernalik, prin. Fax 826-2416
Mio-AuSable MS 7-8
1110 W 8th St 48647 989-826-2481
James Gendernalik, prin. Fax 826-2416

Monroe, Monroe, Pop. 21,630
Jefferson SD 2,200/PK-12
2400 N Dixie Hwy 48162 734-289-5550
Timothy Fitzpatrick, supt. Fax 289-5574
www.jefferson.k12.mi.us/
Jefferson HS 800/9-12
5707 Williams Rd 48162 734-289-5555
Wanda Owsley, prin. Fax 289-5595
Jefferson MS 500/PK-PK, 7-
5102 N Stoney Creek Rd 48162 734-289-5565
Stephen Kinsland, prin. Fax 289-5596

Monroe SD 6,900/K-12
PO Box 733 48161 734-265-3000
David Taylor, supt. Fax 265-3001
www.monroe.k12.mi.us
Cantrick MS 600/6-8
1008 Riverview Ave 48162 734-265-3800
Jeffrey LaRoux, prin. Fax 265-3801
Monroe HS 2,200/9-12
901 Herr Rd 48161 734-265-3400
Ralph Carducci, prin. Fax 265-3401
Monroe MS 1,100/6-8
503 Washington St 48161 734-265-4000
Gary Griffin, prin. Fax 265-4001

Meadow Montessori S 200/PK-12
1670 S Raisinville Rd 48161 734-241-9496
Catharine Calder, hdmstr. Fax 241-0829
Michigan College of Beauty Post-Sec.
15232 1/2 S Dixie Hwy 48161 734-241-8877
Monroe County Community College Post-Sec.
1555 S Raisinville Rd 48161 734-242-7300
St. Mary Catholic HS 500/9-12
108 W Elm Ave 48162 734-241-0663
Beth Dusseau, prin. Fax 241-9042

Montague, Muskegon, Pop. 2,347
Montague Area SD 1,500/PK-12
4882 Stanton Blvd 49437 231-893-1515
James Booth, supt. Fax 894-6586
www.montague.k12.mi.us
Chisholm MS 400/6-8
4700 Stanton Blvd 49437 231-894-5617
Gary Beaudoin, prin. Fax 894-5728
Montague HS 500/9-12
4900 Stanton Blvd 49437 231-894-2661
Kevin Kruger, prin. Fax 893-0609

Montrose, Genesee, Pop. 1,559
Montrose Community SD 1,700/PK-12
PO Box 3129 48457 810-591-7267
Mark Kleinhans, supt. Fax 591-7268
www.montrose.k12.mi.us
Hill-McCloy HS 500/9-12
PO Box 3129 48457 810-591-7267
James Ply, prin. Fax 591-7281
Kuehn-Haven MS 500/5-8
PO Box 3129 48457 810-591-7267
Edward Graham, prin. Fax 591-7282

Morenci, Lenawee, Pop. 2,352
Morenci Area SD 900/K-12
500 Page St 49256 517-458-7501
Kyle Griffith, supt. Fax 458-7821
www.morenci.k12.mi.us
Morenci HS 300/9-12
788 Coomer St 49256 517-458-7502
Nate Parker, prin. Fax 458-7146
Morenci MS 300/5-8
304 Page St 49256 517-458-7506
Kay Johnson, prin. Fax 458-3379

Morley, Mecosta, Pop. 498
Morley-Stanwood Community SD 1,600/K-12
4700 Northland Dr 49336 231-856-4392
Linda L.H. Myers, supt. Fax 856-4180
morleystanwood.org
Morley-Stanwood HS 400/9-12
4700 Northland Dr 49336 231-856-4444
Dennis Szczerowski, prin. Fax 856-7012
Morley-Stanwood MS 500/5-8
4808 Northland Dr 49336 231-856-4550
Terry Baker, prin. Fax 856-0136

Morrice, Shiawassee, Pop. 887
Morrice Area SD 700/K-12
691 Purdy Ln 48857 517-625-3142
Bruce Burger, supt. Fax 625-3866
www.morrice.k12.mi.us
Morrice JSHS 300/7-12
691 Purdy Ln 48857 517-625-3143
Lee J. Turner, prin. Fax 625-8935

Mount Clemens, Macomb, Pop. 17,111
L'Anse Creuse SD
Supt. — See Harrison Township
L'Anse Creuse/Mt Clemens Adult Educ Ctr. Adult
33 N River Rd 48043 586-783-6420
Michelle Irwin, prin. Fax 783-6423

Mount Clemens Community SD 3,700/PK-12
167 Cass Ave 48043 586-469-6100
Dr. T.C. Wallace, supt. Fax 469-5569
www.mtcps.org
Mount Clemens HS 700/9-12
155 Cass Ave 48043 586-461-3400
Nelson Jackson, prin. Fax 469-7058

Mount Clemens MS 500/7-8
161 Cass Ave 48043 586-461-3300
Paul Reeves, prin. Fax 469-7066

Mount Morris, Genesee, Pop. 3,351
Beecher Community SD
Supt. — See Flint
Beecher HS 500/9-12
6255 Neff Rd 48458 810-591-9220
Sean Richmond, admin. Fax 591-6911
Beecher MS 400/7-8
6255 Neff Rd 48458 810-591-9220
Sean Richmond, admin. Fax 591-6911
Riley Adult Education Adult
1149 W Klein St 48458 810-591-9219
D. Cassidy, coord. Fax 591-5617

Mount Morris Consolidated SD 2,800/K-12
12356 Walter St 48458 810-591-8760
Lisa Hagel, supt. Fax 591-7469
www.mtmorrisschools.org
Johnson HS 800/9-12
8041 Neff Rd 48458 810-591-2370
John Ploof, prin. Fax 591-3410
Mount Morris JHS 500/7-8
12356 Walter St 48458 810-591-7100
Richard Fedchenko, prin. Fax 591-7105

Mount Pleasant, Isabella, Pop. 25,687
Beal City SD 700/PK-12
3117 Elias Rd 48858 989-644-3901
Robert J. Kjolhede, supt. Fax 644-5847
www.edzone.net\bealcity
Beal City JSHS 300/7-12
3117 Elias Rd 48858 989-644-3944
Jeffrey Jackson, prin. Fax 644-5847

Mount Pleasant SD 4,200/K-12
720 N Kinney Ave 48858 989-775-2300
Gary Allen, supt. Fax 775-2309
www.mtpleasant.edzone.net
Mount Pleasant HS 1,200/9-12
1155 S Elizabeth St 48858 989-775-2200
Jeffrey Thoenes, prin. Fax 773-0631
Mt. Pleasant Vocational Education Ctr Vo/Tech
1155 S Elizabeth St 48858 989-775-2210
Michael Pung, prin. Fax 775-2215
West IS 600/7-8
440 S Bradley St 48858 989-775-2220
Luke Stafanovsky, prin. Fax 775-2229
Mount Pleasant Comm. & Adult Ed. Adult
1651 S Bamber Rd 48858 989-775-2370
Mary Murphy, prin. Fax 773-7840

Central Michigan University Post-Sec.
100 Warriner Hall 48859 989-774-4000
M.J. Murphy Beauty College Post-Sec.
201 W Broadway 48858 989-772-2339
Mt. Pleasant Christian Academy 100/K-12
1802 E High St 48858 989-773-9082
Terry Carlson, admin. Fax 772-7468
Sacred Heart Academy 300/7-12
316 E Michigan St 48858 989-772-1457
Denny Starnes, prin. Fax 772-1707
Saginaw Chippewa Tribal College Post-Sec.
2274 Enterprise Dr 48858 989-775-4123

Munising, Alger, Pop. 2,470
Munising SD 900/K-12
411 Elm Ave 49862 906-387-2251
Barbara Hase, supt. Fax 387-5416
www.mps-up.com
Munising MSHS 500/7-12
810 State Highway M28 W 49862 906-387-2103
Peter Kelto, prin. Fax 387-5686

Muskegon, Muskegon, Pop. 39,825
Muskegon Area ISD
630 Harvey St 49442 231-777-2637
Dr. Michael H. Bozym, supt. Fax 773-3498
www.muskegonisd.org
Muskegon Area Career Tech Center Vo/Tech
200 Harvey St 49442 231-767-3600
Mike Carpenter, prin. Fax 767-2692

Muskegon SD 5,300/PK-12
349 W Webster Ave 49440 231-720-2000
Joseph Schulze, supt. Fax 720-2050
www.muskegon.k12.mi.us/
Bunker JHS 800/6-8
2312 Denmark St 49441 231-720-2300
Bradley Perkins, prin. Fax 720-2325
Muskegon HS 1,500/9-12
80 W Southern Ave 49441 231-720-2800
Dr. Kent Nolen, prin. Fax 720-2811
Steele JHS 600/6-8
1150 Amity Ave 49442 231-720-3000
Arthur Duren, prin. Fax 720-3025

Oakridge SD 2,000/PK-12
275 S Wolf Lake Rd 49442 231-788-7100
Thomas Paniucki, supt. Fax 788-7114
www.oakridgeschools.org
Oakridge HS 600/9-12
5493 Hall Rd 49442 231-788-7300
Dave Mieras, prin. Fax 788-7314
Oakridge MS 300/7-8
251 S Wolf Lake Rd 49442 231-788-7400
Wayne Brown, prin. Fax 788-7414

Orchard View SD 2,600/PK-12
35 S Sheridan Dr 49442 231-760-1300
B. Jack VanderWall, supt. Fax 760-1323
www.orchardview.org
Orchard View HS 700/9-12
2310 Marquette Ave 49442 231-760-1400
Jerry Walter, prin. Fax 760-1407
Orchard View MS 700/6-8
35 S Sheridan Dr 49442 231-760-1500
Jim Nielsen, prin. Fax 760-1506

Reeths-Puffer SD
Supt. — See North Muskegon
Reeths-Puffer HS 1,300/9-12
1545 Roberts Rd 49445 231-744-1647
Daniel Beckeman, prin. Fax 744-4796

Baker College of Muskegon Post-Sec.
1903 Marquette Ave 49442 231-777-5200
Muskegon Catholic Central HS 300/9-12
1145 W Laketon Ave 49441 231-755-2201
Robert Bridges, prin. Fax 755-8615
Muskegon Catholic Central MS 200/6-8
1145 W Laketon Ave 49441 231-759-0180
Michael Devitt, prin. Fax 755-2415
Muskegon Community College Post-Sec.
221 S Quarterline Rd 49442 231-773-9131
Ross Medical Education Center Post-Sec.
950 W Norton Ave 49441 231-730-9531
Western Michigan Christian HS 200/9-12
455 E Ellis Rd 49441 231-779-9644
David VerMerris, prin. Fax 798-9018

Muskegon Heights, Muskegon, Pop. 11,817
Muskegon Heights SD 2,300/PK-12
2603 Leahy St 49444 231-830-3200
Dana Bryant Ph.D., supt. Fax 830-3560
www.remc4.k12.mi.us/muskegon-hts/
Muskegon Heights HS 600/9-12
2441 Sanford St 49444 231-830-3700
Danny Smith, prin. Fax 830-3534
Muskegon Heights MS 300/7-8
55 E Sherman Blvd 49444 231-830-3600
Reedell Holmes, prin. Fax 830-3572

Napoleon, Jackson, Pop. 1,332
Napoleon Community SD 1,700/K-12
PO Box 308 49261 517-536-8667
James Graham, supt. Fax 536-8006
scnc.ncs.k12.mi.us/
Napoleon HS 500/9-12
PO Box 308 49261 517-536-8667
Barb Nugent, prin. Fax 536-8007
Napoleon MS 400/6-8
PO Box 308 49261 517-536-8667
Shelley Jusick, prin. Fax 536-8005

Negaunee, Marquette, Pop. 4,483
Negaunee SD 1,500/K-12
101 S Pioneer Ave 49866 906-475-4157
Jim Derocher, supt. Fax 475-5107
www.negaunee.k12.mi.us/
Negaunee HS 500/9-12
500 W Arch St 49866 906-475-7861
Robert Bonetti, prin. Fax 475-7989
Negaunee MS 400/6-8
102 W Case St 49866 906-475-7866
Bob Trebilcock, prin. Fax 475-6408

Newaygo, Newaygo, Pop. 1,688
Newaygo SD 1,900/K-12
PO Box 820 49337 231-652-6984
Larry Lethorn, supt. Fax 652-6505
www.newaygo.net
Newaygo HS 600/9-12
PO Box 820 49337 231-652-1646
Joel Lantz, prin. Fax 652-3500
Newaygo MS 500/6-8
PO Box 820 49337 231-652-1285
Maureen Phillips, prin. Fax 652-9704

New Baltimore, Macomb, Pop. 9,749
Anchor Bay SD 6,500/K-12
52801 Ashley Dr 48047 586-725-2861
Leonard A. Woodside, supt. Fax 725-0290
www.anchorbay.misd.net
Anchor Bay MS North 700/6-8
52805 Ashley Dr 48047 586-725-7373
Tim Brisbois, prin. Fax 725-6760
Anchor Bay MS South 800/6-8
48650 Sugarbush Rd 48047 586-949-4510
Douglas Glassford, prin. Fax 949-4739
Other Schools – See Fair Haven

Newberry, Luce, Pop. 1,679
Tahquamenon Area SD 1,100/PK-12
700 Newberry Ave 49868 906-293-3226
Roderick Martin, supt. Fax 293-3709
eup.k12.mi.us/tahquamenon
Newberry HS 300/9-12
700 Newberry Ave 49868 906-293-3243
Tonya Perry, prin.
Newberry MS 300/6-8
700 Newberry Ave 49868 906-293-5197
Dennis Peacock, prin.

New Boston, Wayne
Huron SD 2,100/K-12
32044 Huron River Dr 48164 734-782-2441
Thomas Hosler, supt. Fax 783-0338
www.huronschools.org
Huron HS 700/9-12
32044 Huron River Dr 48164 734-782-1436
Rod Hopper, prin. Fax 783-1534
Renton JHS 500/6-8
31578 Huron River Dr 48164 734-782-2483
Kurt Mrocko, prin. Fax 783-0327

New Buffalo, Berrien, Pop. 2,201
New Buffalo Area SD 700/K-12
1112 E Clay St 49117 269-469-6010
Michael Lindley, supt. Fax 469-3315
www.nbas.org
New Buffalo HS 200/9-12
1112 E Clay St 49117 269-469-6001
Ronald Hart, prin. Fax 469-6017
New Buffalo MS 200/6-8
1112 E Clay St 49117 269-469-6003
William Welling, prin. Fax 469-6017

New Haven, Macomb, Pop. 4,231
New Haven Community SD — 1,100/PK-12
  PO Box 482000 48048 — 586-749-5123
  Dr. James Avery, supt. — Fax 749-6307
  newhaven.misd.net/
New Haven HS — 400/9-12
  PO Box 482000 48048 — 586-749-5104
  Denise Robbins, prin. — Fax 749-8460
Other Schools – See Ray

New Lothrop, Shiawassee, Pop. 597
New Lothrop Area SD — 800/PK-12
  PO Box 339 48460 — 810-638-5091
  John Strycker, supt. — Fax 638-7277
  www.newlothrop.k12.mi.us
New Lothrop JSHS — 400/7-12
  PO Box 339 48460 — 810-638-5054
  James Dohm, prin. — Fax 638-5057

Newport, Monroe

Lutheran HS South — 50/9-12
  8290 N Telegraph Rd 48166 — 734-586-8832
  Steven Garrabrandt, prin. — Fax 586-2478

Niles, Berrien, Pop. 11,906
Brandywine SD — 1,600/K-12
  1830 S 3rd St 49120 — 269-684-7150
  Gary Rider, supt. — Fax 684-8998
  www.remc11.k12.mi.us/brandy/
Brandywine MSHS — 700/7-12
  1700 Bell Rd 49120 — 269-683-4800
  Christine Banaszak, prin. — Fax 683-1186

Niles Community SD — 3,600/PK-12
  111 Spruce St 49120 — 269-683-0732
  Douglas Law, supt. — Fax 684-6337
  www.nilesschools.org
Niles HS — 1,000/9-12
  1441 Eagle St 49120 — 269-683-2894
  James Knoll, prin. — Fax 684-9516
Ring Lardner MS — 700/7-8
  801 N 17th St 49120 — 269-683-6610
  Douglas Langmeyer, prin. — Fax 684-9524
Niles Adult Education — Adult
  111 Spruce St 49120 — 269-684-4480
  Richard Klemm, dir. — Fax 684-9548

North Adams, Hillsdale, Pop. 508
North Adams-Jerome SD — 600/K-12
  4555 Knowles Rd 49262 — 517-287-4214
  Christopher Voisin, supt. — Fax 287-4722
  www.najps.org
North Adams-Jerome JSHS — 300/7-12
  4555 Knowles Rd 49262 — 517-287-4214
  Carl Christenson, prin. — Fax 287-4722

North Branch, Lapeer, Pop. 1,008
North Branch Area SD — 2,700/K-12
  PO Box 3620 48461 — 810-688-3570
  Alan Piwinski, supt. — Fax 688-4344
  northbranchschools.lapeer.org/
North Branch HS — 800/9-12
  PO Box 3620 48461 — 810-688-3001
  Mark Hiltunen, prin. — Fax 688-8057
North Branch MS — 400/7-8
  PO Box 3620 48461 — 810-688-4431
  John Sherman, prin. — Fax 688-4344

Wesleyan Christian Acad of North Branch — 200/PK-12
  6674 Rogers Dr 48461 — 810-688-2575
  Larry Curell, supt. — Fax 688-3635

North Muskegon, Muskegon, Pop. 4,023
North Muskegon SD — 900/K-12
  1600 Mills Ave 49445 — 231-719-4100
  Mr. John L. Weaver, supt. — Fax 744-0739
  www.nmps.k12.mi.us
North Muskegon HS — 300/9-12
  1507 Mills Ave 49445 — 231-719-4110
  James VanBergen, prin. — Fax 744-0739
North Muskegon MS — 200/6-8
  1507 Mills Ave 49445 — 231-719-4110
  James VanBergen, prin. — Fax 744-0739

Reeths-Puffer SD — 4,100/PK-12
  991 W Giles Rd 49445 — 231-744-4736
  Stephen Cousins, supt. — Fax 744-9497
  www.reeths-puffer.org/
Reeths-Puffer MS — 700/7-8
  1911 W Giles Rd 49445 — 231-744-4721
  Steve Edwards, prin. — Fax 744-6049
Other Schools – See Muskegon

Northport, Leelanau, Pop. 652
Northport SD — 200/K-12
  PO Box 188 49670 — 231-386-5153
  Ty Wessell, supt. — Fax 386-9838
Northport S — 200/K-12
  PO Box 188 49670 — 231-386-5154
  Ty Wessell, prin. — Fax 386-9838

Northville, Oakland, Pop. 6,405
Northville SD — 6,100/K-12
  501 W Main St 48167 — 248-349-3400
  Leonard Rezmierski, supt. — Fax 347-6928
  www.northville.k12.mi.us/
Hillside MS — 800/6-8
  775 N Center St 48167 — 248-344-8493
  James Cracraft, prin. — Fax 334-8480
Meads Mill MS — 700/6-8
  16700 Franklin Rd, — 248-344-8435
  Sue Meyer, prin. — Fax 334-1830
Northville HS — 1,800/9-12
  45700 6 Mile Rd, — 248-344-8420
  Dennis Colligan, prin. — Fax 344-8497

Norton Shores, Muskegon, Pop. 23,193
Mona Shores SD — 4,200/K-12
  3374 Mccracken St 49441 — 231-780-4751
  Terry Babbitt, supt. — Fax 780-2099
  www.monashores.net
Mona Shores HS — 1,400/9-12
  1121 Seminole Rd 49441 — 231-780-4711
  Dennis Vanderstelt, prin. — Fax 780-3634
Mona Shores MS — 1,000/6-8
  1700 Woodside Rd 49441 — 231-759-8506
  Scott Levandoski, prin. — Fax 755-0514

Norway, Dickinson, Pop. 2,896
Norway-Vulcan Area SD — 300/PK-12
  300 Section St 49870 — 906-563-9552
  Randall Van Gasse, supt. — Fax 563-5169
  www.norway.k12.mi.us
Norway HS — 300/9-12
  300 Section St 49870 — 906-563-9542
  Donald Byczek, prin. — Fax 563-8708
Vulcan MS, 300 Section St 49870 — 5-8
  Andrew Hongisto, prin. — 906-563-9563

Novi, Oakland, Pop. 50,786
Novi Community SD — 6,100/K-12
  25345 Taft Rd 48374 — 248-449-1200
  Peter Dion, supt. — Fax 449-1219
  www.novi.k12.mi.us
Novi HS — 1,800/9-12
  24062 Taft Rd 48375 — 248-449-1500
  John Lawrence, prin. — Fax 449-1519
Novi MS — 1,000/7-8
  49000 W 11 Mile Rd 48374 — 248-449-1600
  Milan Obrenovich, prin. — Fax 449-1619

Catholic Central HS — 1,100/9-12
  27225 Wixom Rd 48374 — 248-596-3810
  Rev. Richard Ranalletti, prin. — Fax 596-3811
Franklin Road Christian S — 300/K-12
  40800 W 13 Mile Rd 48377 — 248-668-7100
  Rev. Timothy Gambino, supt. — Fax 668-7101
Novi Christian S — 200/K-12
  45301 W 11 Mile Rd 48375 — 248-349-9441
  Dr. Gary Elfner, admin. — Fax 349-3481

Oakland, Oakland
Lake Orion Community SD
  Supt. — See Lake Orion
Oakview MS — 600/6-8
  917 Lake George Rd 48363 — 248-693-0321
  Alice Seppanen, prin. — Fax 693-5419

Oak Park, Oakland, Pop. 29,146
Berkley SD
  Supt. — See Berkley
Norup MS — 600/3-8
  14450 Manhattan St 48237 — 248-837-8300
  Barbara Kirschenheiter, prin. — Fax 547-5558

Ferndale SD
  Supt. — See Ferndale
Center for Advanced Studies & the Arts — 11-12
  23561 Rosewood St 48237 — 248-586-8860
  Bill James, prin. — Fax 548-8863
Ferndale Adult & Community Education — Adult
  22001 Republic St 48237 — 248-586-8900
  Fran Foote Ph.D., dir. — Fax 586-8882
Oak Park SD — 3,900/PK-12
  13900 Granzon St 48237 — 248-691-8400
  Sandra Harris, supt. — Fax 691-8405
  www.oakparkschools.org
Oak Park HS — 1,400/9-12
  13701 Oak Park Blvd 48237 — 248-691-8412
  Dr. Joann Wright, prin. — Fax 691-8492
Roosevelt MS — 1,000/6-8
  23261 Scotia Rd 48237 — 248-691-8449
  Shirley Lusby, prin. — Fax 691-8509

Beth Jacob School for Girls — 400/K-12
  14390 W 10 Mile Rd 48237 — 248-544-9070
  Shulamis Rubinfeld, prin. — Fax 544-4662
Michigan Jewish Institute — Post-Sec.
  25401 Coolidge Hwy 48237 — 248-414-6900
Oholei Yosef Yitzchak Lubavich S — 100/K-12
  14000 W 9 Mile Rd 48237 — 248-541-6022
  Rabbi B. Stein, prin.
Yeshiva Gedolah HS — 100/9-12
  24600 Greenfield Rd 48237 — 248-968-3360
  David Wayntraub, prin. — Fax 968-8613
Yeshiva Gedolah Rabbinical College — Post-Sec.
  24600 Greenfield Rd 48237 — 248-968-3360

Okemos, Ingham, Pop. 20,216
Okemos SD — 4,300/K-12
  4406 Okemos Rd 48864 — 517-349-1418
  Lee Gerard Ph.D., supt. — Fax 349-6235
  okemos.k12.mi.us/
Chippewa MS — 500/6-8
  4000 Okemos Rd 48864 — 517-349-4460
  Thomas Tweedy, prin. — Fax 347-9824
Kinawa MS — 500/6-8
  1900 Kinawa Dr 48864 — 517-349-9220
  Barbara Hoevel, prin. — Fax 347-4189
Okemos HS — 1,400/9-12
  2800 Jolly Rd 48864 — 517-351-7900
  John Lanzetta, prin. — Fax 351-2850

Olivet, Eaton, Pop. 1,714
Olivet Community SD — 1,300/K-12
  255 1st St 49076 — 269-749-9129
  David Campbell, supt. — Fax 749-9701
  www.olivetschools.org
Olivet HS — 400/9-12
  255 1st St 49076 — 269-749-9571
  Randall VanDyke, prin. — Fax 749-4560
Olivet MS — 500/4-8
  255 1st St 49076 — 269-749-9953
  M. Bensinger, prin. — Fax 749-9701

Olivet College — Post-Sec.
  300 S Main St 49076 — 269-749-7000

Onaway, Presque Isle, Pop. 974
Onaway Area SD — 700/K-12
  PO Box 307 49765 — 989-733-4970
  Bob Szymoniak, supt. — Fax 733-8612
  onaway.mi.schoolwebpages.com/
Onaway HS — 200/9-12
  PO Box 307 49765 — 989-733-4800
  Matt Lukshaitis, prin. — Fax 733-4889
Onaway MS — 100/6-8
  PO Box 307 49765 — 989-733-4850
  Matt Lukshaitis, prin. — Fax 733-4899

Onekama, Manistee, Pop. 643
Onekama Consolidated SD — 500/K-12
  5016 Main St 49675 — 231-889-4251
  Lee Sandy, supt. — Fax 889-3720
  www.onekama.k12.mi.us
Onekama MSHS — 300/6-12
  5016 Main St 49675 — 231-889-5521
  Gina Hagen, prin. — Fax 889-9567

Onsted, Lenawee, Pop. 920
Onsted Community SD — 1,800/K-12
  PO Box 220 49265 — 517-467-2174
  Robert Herrera, supt. — Fax 467-2026
  www.onsted.k12.mi.us
Onsted HS — 500/9-12
  PO Box 220 49265 — 517-467-2171
  Dave Lauer, prin. — Fax 467-6910
Onsted MS — 500/6-8
  PO Box 220 49265 — 517-467-2168
  Kelly Coffin, prin. — Fax 467-6907

Ontonagon, Ontonagon, Pop. 1,696
Ontonagon Area SD — 700/K-12
  301 Greenland Rd 49953 — 906-884-4963
  Louis Gregory, supt. — Fax 884-2057
  www.oasd.k12.mi.us
Ontonagon JSHS — 300/7-12
  701 Parker Ave 49953 — 906-884-4433
  John Shiner, prin. — Fax 884-2742

Orchard Lake, Oakland

St. Marys Preparatory HS — 500/9-12
  3535 Indian Trl 48324 — 248-683-0530
  James Glowacki, prin. — Fax 683-1740
SS. Cyril and Methodius Seminary — Post-Sec.
  3535 Indian Trl 48324 — 248-683-0310

Ortonville, Oakland, Pop. 1,526
Brandon SD — 3,700/K-12
  1025 S Ortonville Rd 48462 — 248-627-1800
  Thomas Miller, supt. — Fax 627-4533
  www.brandon.k12.mi.us
Brandon HS — 1,100/9-12
  1025 S Ortonville Rd 48462 — 248-627-1820
  Dr. Michael Ferguson, prin. — Fax 627-5628
Brandon MS — 600/7-8
  609 S Ortonville Rd 48462 — 248-627-1830
  Dr. William Snyder, prin. — Fax 627-7201

Oscoda, Iosco, Pop. 1,061
Oscoda Area SD — 1,700/PK-12
  3550 E River Rd 48750 — 989-739-2033
  Christine Beardsley, supt. — Fax 739-2325
  www.oscodaschools.org
Oscoda Area HS — 600/9-12
  3550 E River Rd 48750 — 989-739-9121
  Rexford G. Hart, prin. — Fax 739-1688
Richardson S — 700/3-8
  3630 E River Rd 48750 — 989-739-9173
  Charles Negro, prin. — Fax 739-2510

Otisville, Genesee, Pop. 867
Lakeville Community SD — 1,800/K-12
  11107 Washburn Rd 48463 — 810-591-6525
  James Richardson, supt. — Fax 591-6538
  www.lakeville.k12.mi.us/
Lakeville HS — 700/9-12
  11107 Washburn Rd 48463 — 810-591-4051
  Dennis Grunden, prin. — Fax 591-6522
Lakeville MS — 500/6-8
  11107 Washburn Rd 48463 — 810-591-3945
  Aaron Moran, prin. — Fax 591-6632

Otsego, Allegan, Pop. 3,944
Otsego SD — 2,300/PK-12
  313 W Allegan St 49078 — 269-692-6066
  Dennis M. Patzer, supt. — Fax 692-6074
  www.otsegobulldogs.org
Otsego HS — 700/9-12
  540 Washington St 49078 — 269-692-6166
  Herve Dardis, prin. — Fax 692-6188
Otsego MS — 500/6-8
  538 Washington St 49078 — 269-692-6199
  Bill Houseman, prin. — Fax 692-6203

Ostego Baptist Academy — 100/PK-12
  247 E Allegan St 49078 — 269-694-6738
  James Millward, supt.

Ottawa Lake, Monroe
Whiteford Agricultural SD — 800/PK-12
  6655 Consear Rd 49267 — 734-856-1443
  Craig Haugen, supt. — Fax 854-6463
  scnc.whiteford.k12.mi.us
Whiteford HS — 300/9-12
  6655 Consear Rd 49267 — 734-856-1443
  Jeff Humason, prin. — Fax 856-2564
Whiteford MS — 200/6-8
  6655 Consear Rd 49267 — 734-856-1443
  Jeff Humason, prin. — Fax 856-2564

Owendale, Huron, Pop. 285
Owendale-Gagetown Area SD | 200/K-12
7166 E Main St 48754 | 989-678-4261
Dana Compton, supt. | Fax 678-4284
www.owengage.org/
Owendale-Gagetown JSHS | 100/6-12
7166 E Main St 48754 | 989-678-4141
Dana Compton, prin. | Fax 678-0920

Owosso, Shiawassee, Pop. 15,471
Owosso SD | 4,000/K-12
PO Box 340 48867 | 989-723-8131
Gary Bredahl, supt. | Fax 723-7777
www.owosso.k12.mi.us
Owosso HS | 1,300/9-12
765 E North St 48867 | 989-723-8231
Marci Williams, prin. | Fax 729-5600
Owosso MS | 600/7-8
219 N Water St 48867 | 989-723-3460
Greg Gray, prin. | Fax 729-5760

Baker College of Owosso | Post-Sec.
1020 S Washington St 48867 | 989-729-3300

Oxford, Oakland, Pop. 3,568
Oxford Area Community SD | 3,900/K-12
105 Pontiac Rd 48371 | 248-969-5000
Virginia Brennan-Kyro, supt. | Fax 969-5016
www.oxford.k12.mi.us
Oxford HS | 1,200/9-12
745 N Oxford Rd 48371 | 248-969-5100
Mike Schweig, prin. | Fax 969-5145
Oxford MS | 900/6-8
1420 E Lakeville Rd 48371 | 248-969-1800
Dr. Karen Sage, prin. | Fax 969-1840

Painesdale, Houghton
Adams Township SD | 500/K-12
PO Box 37 49955 | 906-482-0599
Dan Sternhagen, supt. | Fax 487-5999
www.adams.k12.mi.us
Jeffers JSHS | 200/7-12
PO Box 37 49955 | 906-482-0580
Janice Maierle, prin. | Fax 487-5999

Paradise, Chippewa
Whitefish Township SD | 100/K-12
PO Box 58 49768 | 906-492-3353
Patrick Rowley, supt. | Fax 492-3254
www.eup.k12.mi.us/whitefish
Whitefish Township S | 100/K-12
PO Box 58 49768 | 906-492-3353
Patrick Rowley, prin. | Fax 492-3254

Parchment, Kalamazoo, Pop. 1,881
Parchment SD | 1,900/K-12
520 N Orient St 49004 | 269-488-1050
Michael O'Connor, supt. | Fax 488-1060
www.parchmentschools.org
Parchment HS | 600/9-12
1916 E G Ave 49004 | 269-488-1100
Scott Karaptian, prin. | Fax 488-1110
Parchment MS | 400/6-8
307 N Riverview Dr 49004 | 269-488-1200
George Stamas, prin. | Fax 488-1210
Other Schools – See Kalamazoo

Parma, Jackson, Pop. 890
Western SD | 2,600/K-12
1400 S Dearing Rd 49269 | 517-841-8100
William Coale Ph.D., supt. | Fax 841-8801
www.westernschools.org/
Western HS | 800/9-12
1400 S Dearing Rd 49269 | 517-841-8200
Brent Cryderman, prin. | Fax 841-8802
Western MS | 700/6-8
1400 S Dearing Rd 49269 | 517-841-8300
Amy Potts, prin. | Fax 841-8803
Other Schools – See Jackson

Paw Paw, Van Buren, Pop. 3,380
Paw Paw SD | 2,200/K-12
119 Johnson Rd 49079 | 269-657-8800
Mark Bielang, supt. | Fax 657-7292
www.ppps.org
Paw Paw HS | 700/9-12
30609 E Red Arrow Hwy 49079 | 269-657-8840
Diana Davis, prin. | Fax 655-0009
Paw Paw MS | 500/6-8
313 W Michigan Ave 49079 | 269-657-8870
Donald Barnhouse, prin. | Fax 657-5011

Peck, Sanilac, Pop. 590
Peck Community SD | 600/K-12
222 Lapeer St 48466 | 810-378-5171
David M. Bush, supt. | Fax 378-5116
www.peck.k12.mi.us
Peck JSHS, 222 Lapeer St 48466 | 300/7-12
Willard Roles, prin. | 810-378-5501

Sanilac ISD |
175 E Aitken Rd 48466 | 810-648-4700
Tony Parker, supt. | Fax 648-5784
www.sanilac.k12.mi.us
Sanilac Career Center | Vo/Tech
175 E Aitken Rd 48466 | 810-648-4700
Deborah Wild, dir. | Fax 648-4834

Pellston, Emmet, Pop. 791
Pellston SD | 700/K-12
172 Park St 49769 | 231-539-8682
William Tebbe, supt. | Fax 539-8838
www.icebox.k12.mi.us
Pellston HS | 300/9-12
172 Park St 49769 | 231-539-8801
Teresa Emery, prin. | Fax 539-8110
Pellston MS | 200/6-8
172 Park St 49769 | 231-539-8801
Anthony Basanese, prin. | Fax 539-8110

Pentwater, Oceana, Pop. 966
Pentwater SD | 300/K-12
600 Park St 49449 | 231-869-4100
Tim Rossler, supt. | Fax 869-4535
www.pentwater.k12.mi.us
Pentwater S | 300/K-12
600 Park St 49449 | 231-869-4100
Ronald J. Huffman, prin. | Fax 869-4535

Perry, Shiawassee, Pop. 2,044
Perry SD | 2,000/PK-12
PO Box 900 48872 | 517-625-3100
Jacklyn Hurd, supt. | Fax 625-6256
www.perry.k12.mi.us
Perry HS | 600/9-12
2555 W Britton Rd 48872 | 517-625-3104
Steven Liestenfeltz, prin. | Fax 625-0012
Perry MS | 500/6-8
2775 W Britton Rd 48872 | 517-625-6196
Dan Hare, prin. | Fax 625-0120

Petersburg, Monroe, Pop. 1,146
Summerfield SD | 900/K-12
17555 Ida West Rd 49270 | 734-279-1035
John Hewitt, supt. | Fax 279-1448
www.summerfield.k12.mi.us
Summerfield HS | 300/9-12
17555 Ida West Rd 49270 | 734-279-1012
Scott Leach, prin. | Fax 279-1018
Summerfield S | 100/7-8
232 E Elm St 49270 | 734-279-1013
Jodi Bucher, prin. | Fax 279-1017

Petoskey, Emmet, Pop. 6,154
Petoskey SD | 3,100/K-12
PO Box 247 49770 | 231-348-2100
John Scholten, supt. | Fax 348-2342
www.petoskeyschools.org
Petoskey HS | 1,100/9-12
1500 Hill St 49770 | 231-348-2160
David Snyder, prin. | Fax 348-2214
Petoskey MS | 700/6-8
801 Northmen Dr 49770 | 231-348-2150
David Gracy, prin. | Fax 348-2234

North Central Michigan College | Post-Sec.
1515 Howard St 49770 | 231-348-6600

Pewamo, Ionia, Pop. 559
Pewamo-Westphalia SD | 600/PK-12
5101 S Clintonia Rd 48873 | 989-587-5100
Ronald A. Simon, supt. | Fax 587-5120
www.pw.k12.mi.us
Pewamo-Westphalia JHSH | 400/7-12
5101 S Clintonia Rd 48873 | 989-587-5105
Michelle Sharp, prin. | Fax 587-3550

Pickford, Chippewa
Pickford SD | 400/K-12
PO Box 278 49774 | 906-647-6285
Keith Krahnke, supt. | Fax 647-3706
pickford.eup.k12.mi.us/
Pickford HS | 100/9-12
PO Box 278 49774 | 906-647-4028
Neil Harrison, prin. | Fax 647-3706

Pigeon, Huron, Pop. 1,160
Elkton-Pigeon-Bay Port Laker SD | 1,100/K-12
6136 Pigeon Rd 48755 | 989-453-4600
John F. Raab, supt. | Fax 453-4609
www.lakerschools.org/
Laker HS | 400/9-12
6136 Pigeon Rd 48755 | 989-453-4600
Lisa Dicamillo, prin. | Fax 453-4615
Laker MS | 300/6-8
6136 Pigeon Rd 48755 | 989-453-4600
Lisa DiCamillo, prin. | Fax 453-4609

Pinckney, Livingston, Pop. 2,409
Pinckney Community SD | 200/K-12
2130 E MI 36 48169 | 810-225-3900
Daniel Danosky, supt. | Fax 225-3905
www.pcs.k12.mi.us
Pathfinder S | 50/7-8
2100 E MI 36 48169 | 810-225-5200
Richard Todd, prin. | Fax 225-5205
Pinckney Community HS | 100/9-12
10255 Dexter Pinckney Rd 48169 | 810-225-5500
James Darga, prin. | Fax 225-5505

Pinconning, Bay, Pop. 1,354
Pinconning Area SD | 1,900/K-12
605 W 5th St 48650 | 989-879-4556
Darren Kroczaleski, supt. | Fax 879-4705
www.pasd.org/
Pinconning Area HS | 600/9-12
605 W 5th St 48650 | 989-879-2311
Mike Vieau, prin. | Fax 879-7258
Pinconning Area MS | 300/7-8
605 W 5th St 48650 | 989-879-2311
Dan Byrne, prin. | Fax 879-7258

Pittsford, Hillsdale
Pittsford Area SD | 700/K-12
9304 Hamilton Rd 49271 | 517-523-3481
Richard S. Satterlee, supt. | Fax 523-3467
scnc.pas.k12.mi.us
Pittsford JSHS | 300/7-12
9304 Hamilton Rd 49271 | 517-523-3481
Charles Pelham, prin. | Fax 523-2059

Freedom Farm Christian S | 100/K-12
9400 E Beecher Rd 49271 | 517-523-3426
Timothy Neinas, prin. | Fax 523-3427

Plainwell, Allegan, Pop. 3,986
Plainwell Community SD | 2,900/PK-12
600 North Dr 49080 | 269-685-5823
Daniel Heckman, supt. | Fax 685-1108
www.plainwellschools.org

Plainwell HS | 800/9-12
684 Starr Rd 49080 | 269-685-9554
Sue Wakefield, prin. | Fax 685-9064
Plainwell MS | 700/6-8
720 Brigham St 49080 | 269-685-5813
William Willett, prin. | Fax 685-2099

Plymouth, Wayne, Pop. 8,870
Plymouth-Canton Community SD | 18,500/K-12
454 S Harvey St 48170 | 734-416-2700
Dr. James Ryan, supt. | Fax 416-4932
www.pccs.k12.mi.us
Central MS | 700/6-8
650 Church St 48170 | 734-416-2990
Joyce Johnson, prin. | Fax 416-7699
East MS | 800/6-8
1042 S Mill St 48170 | 734-416-4950
Marsha Hoff, prin. | Fax 416-4949
Pioneer MS | 700/6-8
46081 Ann Arbor Rd W 48170 | 734-416-2770
Philip Freeman, prin. | Fax 416-7569
West MS | 800/6-8
44401 W Ann Arbor Trl 48170 | 734-416-7550
Ellison Franklin, prin. | Fax 416-7648
Other Schools – See Canton

Metropolitan SDA Jr Academy | 50/K-10
15585 N Haggerty Rd 48170 | 734-420-4044
David Tripp, prin. | Fax 420-3710
Michigan Theological Seminary | Post-Sec.
41550 E Ann Arbor Trl 48170 | 734-207-9581

Pontiac, Oakland, Pop. 67,152
Oakland ISD
Supt. — See Waterford
Joblink Career Center | Vo/Tech
1847 N Perry St 48340 | 248-276-9470
Roland Hill, dir. | Fax 276-9471
Oakland Technical Campus NE | Vo/Tech
1371 N Perry St 48340 | 248-451-2700
Roosevelt Daniel, dean | Fax 451-2720

Pontiac SD | 10,700/K-12
47200 Woodward Ave 48342 | 248-451-6800
Mildred Mason Ph.D., supt. | Fax 451-6890
www.pontiac.k12.mi.us
Jefferson MS | 600/6-8
600 Motor St 48341 | 248-451-7600
Wendy Fitzpatrick, prin. | Fax 451-7631
Lincoln MS | 600/6-8
131 Hillside Dr 48342 | 248-451-7650
Gloria Hill, prin. | Fax 451-7670
Madison MS | 800/6-8
1275 N Perry St 48340 | 248-451-8010
Arlee Ewing, prin. | Fax 451-8034
Pontiac Central HS | 1,400/9-12
300 W Huron St 48341 | 248-451-7100
Derrick Coleman, prin. | Fax 451-7181
Pontiac Northern HS | 1,600/9-12
1051 Arlene Ave 48340 | 248-451-7300
Joanne Battle, prin. | Fax 451-7321
Washington MS | 600/6-8
710 Menominee Rd 48341 | 248-451-7740
Billie Fair, prin. | Fax 451-7761
Bethune South Campus | Adult
154 Lake St 48341 | 248-451-8060
Janice Hall, prin. | Fax 451-8063

Marist Academy | 300/6-8
1300 Giddings Rd 48340 | 248-373-5371
Sandra Favrow, prin. | Fax 373-4707
Notre Dame Preparatory HS | 800/9-12
1300 Giddings Rd 48340 | 248-373-5300
Rev. Joseph Hindelang, prin. | Fax 373-8024
Oakland County Health Division | Post-Sec.
1200 N Telegraph Rd 48341 | 248-858-1832

Portage, Kalamazoo, Pop. 45,679
Portage SD | 8,900/K-12
8111 S Westnedge Ave 49002 | 269-323-5000
Pete McFarlane, supt. | Fax 323-5001
www.portageps.org
Northern HS | 1,400/9-12
1000 Idaho Ave 49024 | 269-323-5400
Jim French, prin. | Fax 323-5490
North MS | 600/6-8
5808 Oregon Ave 49024 | 269-323-5700
Celeste Shelton-Harris, prin. | Fax 323-5790
Portage Central HS | 1,500/9-12
8135 S Westnedge Ave 49002 | 269-323-5200
Eric Alburtus, prin. | Fax 323-5290
Portage Central MS | 700/6-8
8305 S Westnedge Ave 49002 | 269-323-5600
David Babcock, prin. | Fax 323-5690
West MS | 700/6-8
7145 Moorsbridge Rd 49024 | 269-323-5800
Larry Killips, prin. | Fax 323-5890

Chic University of Cosmetology | Post-Sec.
6091 Constitution Blvd 49024 | 269-329-3333
Wright Beauty Academy | Post-Sec.
6666 Lovers Ln 49002 | 269-321-8708

Port Hope, Huron, Pop. 298
Port Hope Community SD | 100/K-12
7840 Portland Rd 48468 | 989-428-4151
Scott Belt, supt. | Fax 428-4153
www.porthope.k12.mi.us
Port Hope S | 100/K-12
7840 Portland Rd 48468 | 989-428-4151
Michael Bowman, prin. | Fax 428-4153

Port Huron, Saint Clair, Pop. 31,747
Port Huron Area SD | 12,100/PK-12
PO Box 5013 48061 | 810-984-3101
Michael Jones, supt. | Fax 984-6606
www.port-huron.k12.mi.us

Central MS 800/6-8
200 32nd St 48060 810-984-6533
Terry Stoneburner, prin. Fax 989-2709
Chippewa MS 700/6-8
2800 Chippewa Trl 48060 810-984-6539
Lisa Duman, prin. Fax 989-2712
Holland Woods MS 500/6-8
1617 Holland Ave 48060 810-984-6548
Cheryl Rogers, prin. Fax 989-2713
Port Huron HS 1,800/9-12
2215 Court St 48060 810-984-2611
H. Ronald Wollen, prin. Fax 984-6559
Port Huron Northern HS 1,700/9-12
1799 Krafft Rd 48060 810-984-2671
Craig Dahlke, prin. Fax 984-2747
Port Huron Adult Ed Programs Adult
1320 Washington Ave 48060 810-984-6552
Gloria Henry, prin.
Other Schools – See Fort Gratiot

Baker College of Port Huron Post-Sec.
3403 Lapeer Rd 48060 810-985-7000
McCormick Catholic Academy 100/6-8
2865 Henry St 48060 810-985-9599
Deborah Krueger, prin. Fax 985-9686
Port Huron Hospital Post-Sec.
1001 Kearney St 48060 810-987-5000
Ross Medical Education Center Post-Sec.
3568 Pine Grove Ave 48060 810-982-0454
St. Clair County Community College Post-Sec.
323 Erie St 48060 810-984-3881

Portland, Ionia, Pop. 3,786
Portland SD 2,000/K-12
1100 Ionia Rd 48875 517-647-4161
Charles Dumas, supt. Fax 647-2975
www.portlandk12.org
Portland HS 600/9-12
1100 Ionia Rd 48875 517-647-2981
David Bouck, prin. Fax 647-1791
Portland MS 500/6-8
745 Storz St 48875 517-647-2985
Bill Carlton, prin. Fax 647-2820

St. Patrick HS 100/9-12
122 N West St 48875 517-647-7551
Sr. Patricia Kidder, prin. Fax 647-4545

Posen, Presque Isle, Pop. 284
Posen Consolidated SD 9 300/K-12
PO Box 187 49776 989-766-2573
Dennis Stratton, supt. Fax 766-2519
www.posen.k12.mi.us
Posen Consolidated JSHS 200/7-12
PO Box 187 49776 989-766-2471
Clifford Kelly, prin. Fax 766-2519

Potterville, Eaton, Pop. 2,221
Potterville SD 900/K-12
420 N High St 48876 517-645-2662
Fax 645-0092
www.pps.k12.mi.us/
Potterville HS 300/9-12
422 N High St 48876 517-645-7609
Linda Wigginton, prin. Fax 645-0177
Potterville MS 300/5-8
424 N High St 48876 517-645-4777
Michelle Goodwin, prin. Fax 645-0091

Powers, Menominee, Pop. 427
North Central Area SD 500/PK-12
PO Box 601 49874 906-497-5821
Kenneth Groh, supt. Fax 497-5066
www.ncajets.org
North Central JSHS 200/7-12
PO Box 601 49874 906-497-5226
Randall Platti, prin. Fax 497-5066

Prescott, Ogemaw, Pop. 287
Whittemore-Prescott Area SD
Supt. — See Whittemore
Whittemore-Prescott JHS 200/7-8
PO Box 100 48756 989-873-4986
Dorothy Miller, prin. Fax 873-6096

Quincy, Branch, Pop. 1,655
Quincy Community SD 1,200/PK-12
1 Educational Pkwy 49082 517-639-7141
Joseph Lopez, supt. Fax 639-4273
www.quincyschools.org
Quincy HS 500/9-12
18 Colfax St 49082 517-639-9245
William Milnes, prin. Fax 639-3701
Quincy MS 400/6-8
32 Fulton St 49082 517-639-4201
David Spalding, prin. Fax 639-3701

Rapid River, Delta
Rapid River SD 300/K-12
PO Box 68 49878 906-474-6411
Terri Mileski, supt. Fax 474-9903
Rapid River JSHS 300/6-12
PO Box 68 49878 906-474-6411
Karen Lundquist, prin. Fax 474-9883

Ravenna, Muskegon, Pop. 1,231
Ravenna SD 1,100/K-12
12322 Stafford St 49451 231-853-2231
David Paulsen, supt. Fax 853-2193
www.ravenna.k12.mi.us
Ravenna HS 400/9-12
2766 S Ravenna Rd 49451 231-853-2218
Karen Barker, prin. Fax 853-6981
Ravenna MS 300/6-8
2700 S Ravenna Rd 49451 231-853-2268
Dale Overbeek, prin. Fax 853-2629

Ray, Macomb
New Haven Community SD
Supt. — See New Haven
New Haven MS 300/6-8
24125 26 Mile Rd 48096 586-749-3401
David Rayes, prin. Fax 749-8338

Reading, Hillsdale, Pop. 1,118
Reading Community SD 1,000/K-12
519 W Elm St 49274 517-283-2166
Robert Luchenbill, supt. Fax 283-3519
www.rcsk12.org
Owens JSHS 500/7-12
301 Chestnut St 49274 517-283-2142
Rick Bailey, prin. Fax 283-3758

Redford, Wayne, Pop. 51,100
Detroit SD
Supt. — See Detroit
Ann Arbor Trail MS 500/6-8
7635 Chatham 48239 313-274-8560
Deborah Ferguson, prin. Fax 274-8074

Redford Union SD 4,500/PK-12
18499 Beech Daly Rd 48240 313-242-6000
Brian Motter, supt. Fax 242-6025
www.redfordu.k12.mi.us
Hilbert MS 900/6-8
26440 Puritan 48239 313-242-4000
Susan Shelton, prin. Fax 242-4005
Redford Union HS 1,300/9-12
17711 Kinloch 48240 313-242-4200
Diane Scott, prin. Fax 242-4205
Pearson Education Center Adult
19990 Beech Daly Rd 48240 313-242-6100
Karen Moran, dir. Fax 242-6105

South Redford SD 3,400/K-12
26141 Schoolcraft 48239 313-535-4000
William F. Weber Ph.D., supt. Fax 535-6121
southredford.net
Pierce MS 800/6-8
25605 Orangelawn 48239 313-937-8880
Michael White, prin. Fax 937-9486
Thurston HS 1,100/9-12
26255 Schoolcraft 48239 313-535-4000
William Zolkowski, prin. Fax 592-0740

Ross Medical Education Center Post-Sec.
9327 Telegraph Rd 48239 313-794-6448

Reed City, Osceola, Pop. 2,409
Reed City Area SD 1,600/K-12
829 S Chestnut St 49677 231-832-2201
Steven B. Westhoff, supt. Fax 832-2202
www.reedcity.k12.mi.us
Reed City HS 600/9-12
225 W Church Ave 49677 231-832-2224
Tom Antioho, prin. Fax 832-2501
Reed City MS 500/6-8
233 W Church Ave 49677 231-832-6174
Tim Webster, prin. Fax 832-6180

Reese, Tuscola, Pop. 1,372
Reese SD 1,100/PK-12
PO Box 389 48757 989-868-9864
Storm Lairson, supt. Fax 868-9570
www.reese.k12.mi.us/
Reese HS 400/9-12
PO Box 389 48757 989-868-4191
Ryle Kiser, prin. Fax 868-4091
Reese MS 300/5-8
PO Box 389 48757 989-868-4157
Brian Wiskur, prin. Fax 868-1609

Remus, Mecosta
Chippewa Hills SD 2,600/PK-12
3226 Arthur Rd 49340 989-967-2000
Cheryl Hahnenberg, supt. Fax 967-2009
www.chsd.us
Chippewa Hills HS 800/9-12
3226 Arthur Rd 49340 989-967-2100
John Zolynsky, prin. Fax 967-2109
Chippewa Hills IS 600/6-8
3102 Arthur Rd 49340 989-967-2200
Bob Grover, prin. Fax 967-2209

Republic, Marquette
Republic-Michigamme SD 200/K-12
RR 1 Box 201A 49879 906-376-2277
Vicki Holsworth, supt. Fax 376-8299
www.republicmichigamme.maisd.k12.mi.us
Republic-Michigamme S 200/K-12
RR 1 Box 201A 49879 906-376-2277
Vicki Holsworth, prin. Fax 376-8299

Richland, Kalamazoo, Pop. 669
Gull Lake Community SD 3,000/K-12
11775 E D Ave 49083 269-629-5880
Rich Ramsey, supt. Fax 629-5527
www.gulllakecs.org
Gull Lake HS 1,000/9-12
9550 M 89 49083 269-629-5803
James Corstange, prin. Fax 629-3077
Other Schools – See Hickory Corners

Richmond, Macomb, Pop. 5,371
Richmond Community SD 2,000/PK-12
68931 S Main St 48062 586-727-3565
Patrick Bird, supt. Fax 727-2098
www.richmond.misd.net/
Richmond HS 700/9-12
35320 Division Rd 48062 586-727-3225
Patrick Olsen, prin. Fax 727-9072
Richmond MS 600/5-8
35250 Division Rd 48062 586-727-7552
Timm Kelly, prin. Fax 727-2545

Riley, Saint Clair
Memphis Community SD 1,100/K-12
34110 Bordman Rd 48041 810-392-2151
Dr. David Symington, supt. Fax 392-3614
www.memphis.k12.mi.us
Memphis HS 300/9-12
34130 Bordman Rd 48041 810-392-2186
Sharon Manthey, prin. Fax 392-2083
Memphis JHS 300/6-8
34130 Bordman Rd 48041 810-392-2131
Kenneth Reygaert, prin. Fax 392-2513

River Rouge, Wayne, Pop. 9,495
River Rouge SD 2,300/PK-12
1460 Coolidge Hwy 48218 313-297-9600
Marie Miller, supt. Fax 842-8790
www.resa.net/riverrouge/index.htm
River Rouge HS 1,000/8-12
1460 Coolidge Hwy 48218 313-297-9600
Rosa Benford, prin. Fax 297-7322

Riverview, Wayne, Pop. 13,026
Riverview Community SD 2,600/K-12
13425 Colvin St, 734-285-9660
Roger Allen, supt. Fax 285-9822
www.wcresa.k12.mi.us/riverview
Riverview HS 900/9-12
12431 Longsdorf St, 734-285-7361
Charles Pike, prin. Fax 785-6598
Seitz MS 700/6-8
17800 Kennebec St, 734-285-2043
Fred Keier, prin. Fax 285-6649

Detroit Business Institute Post-Sec.
19100 Fort St, 734-479-0660
Richard HS 500/9-12
15325 Pennsylvania Rd, 734-284-1875
Br. James Rottenbucher, prin. Fax 284-9304

Rochester, Oakland, Pop. 11,021
Rochester Community SD 14,200/K-12
501 W University Dr 48307 248-726-3000
Dave Pruneau, supt. Fax 726-3105
www.rochester.k12.mi.us/
Hart MS 1,000/6-8
6500 Sheldon Rd 48306 248-726-4500
Cheryl Tocco, prin. Fax 726-4505
Reuther JHS 700/6-8
1430 E Auburn Rd 48307 248-726-4700
Dave Hurst, prin. Fax 726-4705
Stony Creek HS 1,300/9-12
575 Tienken Rd 48306 248-726-5700
Dan Hickey, prin. Fax 726-5705
Van Hoosen JHS 800/6-8
1339 N Adams Rd 48306 248-726-4900
Stephen Cook, prin. Fax 726-4905
Other Schools – See Rochester Hills

Lutheran HS Northwest 300/9-12
1000 Bagley Ave 48309 248-852-6677
Paul Looker, prin. Fax 852-2667
Oakland University Post-Sec.
2200 N Squirrel Rd 48309 248-370-2100
Rochester Hills Christian S 300/PK-12
3300 S Livernois Rd 48307 248-852-0585
Karen Patton, prin. Fax 852-4757

Rochester Hills, Oakland, Pop. 68,754
Avondale SD
Supt. — See Auburn Hills
Avondale MS 600/7-8
1445 W Auburn Rd 48309 248-537-6300
Todd Robinson, prin. Fax 537-6305

Rochester Community SD
Supt. — See Rochester
Adams HS 1,400/9-12
3200 W Tienken Rd 48306 248-726-5200
Diann Flack, prin. Fax 726-5205
Rochester HS 1,700/9-12
180 S Livernois Rd 48307 248-726-5400
Wendy Shepard, prin. Fax 726-5405
West JHS 900/6-8
500 Old Perch Rd 48309 248-726-5000
Mike Dillon, prin. Fax 726-5005

Holy Family Regional S - South Campus 500/4-8
2633 John R Rd 48307 248-299-3798
Sr. Karen Hawver, prin. Fax 299-3843
Rochester College Post-Sec.
800 W Avon Rd 48307 248-218-2000
Waldorf Institute of the Great Lakes 100/9-12
3976 S Livernois Rd 48307 248-299-2680
Fax 299-2682

Rock, Delta
Mid-Peninsula SD 300/K-12
5055 Saint Nicholas 31st Rd 49880 906-359-4387
David Gadomski, supt. Fax 359-4167
www.dsisd.k12.mi.us/midpen
Mid-Peninsula S 300/K-12
5055 Saint Nicholas 31st Rd 49880 906-359-4390
Michael Loy, prin. Fax 359-4113

Rockford, Kent, Pop. 4,832
Rockford SD 7,700/PK-12
350 N Main St 49341 616-863-6320
Michael Shibler Ph.D., supt. Fax 866-1911
www.rockfordschools.org
East Rockford MS 900/6-8
8615 9 Mile Rd NE 49341 616-863-6140
Dan Warren, prin. Fax 863-6565
North Rockford MS 900/6-8
397 E Division St 49341 616-863-6300
Lisa Weidenfeller, prin. Fax 866-5998
Rockford Freshman Center 600/9-9
4500 Kroes St NE 49341 616-863-6348
Douglas VanderJagt, prin. Fax 866-7134
Rockford HS 1,800/10-12
4100 Kroes St NE 49341 616-863-6030
Daniel Zang, prin. Fax 866-5997

Rogers City, Presque Isle, Pop. 3,236
Rogers City Area SD · 700/K-12
251 W Huron Ave 49779 · 989-734-9100
Paul Mancine, supt. · Fax 734-7428
www.rcas.k12.mi.us
Rogers City JSHS · 500/6-12
1033 W Huron Ave 49779 · 989-734-9170
Deborah Jones, prin. · Fax 734-2969

Romeo, Macomb, Pop. 3,791
Romeo Community SD · 5,500/K-12
316 N Main St 48065 · 586-752-0200
Joseph Beck, supt. · Fax 752-0228
www.romeo.k12.mi.us
Romeo HS · 1,700/9-12
11091 32 Mile Rd 48065 · 586-752-0300
Gavin Johnson, prin. · Fax 752-0402
Romeo MS · 700/6-8
297 Prospect St 48065 · 586-752-0240
Sam Argiri, prin. · Fax 752-0256
Other Schools – See Washington

Romulus, Wayne, Pop. 23,709
Romulus Community SD · 4,000/PK-12
36540 Grant St 48174 · 734-532-1600
Joel Carr, supt. · Fax 532-1611
www.romulus.net/
Romulus HS · 1,100/9-12
9650 Wayne Rd 48174 · 734-532-1000
Daniel Hurst, prin. · Fax 532-1001
Romulus JHS · 700/7-8
37300 Wick Rd 48174 · 734-532-1700
Phyllis Adkins, prin. · Fax 532-1701

Roscommon, Roscommon, Pop. 1,133
Gerrish-Higgins SD · 1,800/K-12
PO Box 825 48653 · 989-275-6600
Donald Mick, supt. · Fax 275-6608
www.ghsd.k12.mi.us/
Roscommon HS · 600/9-12
PO Box 825 48653 · 989-275-6675
Daniel Scow, prin. · Fax 275-6681
Roscommon MS · 600/5-8
PO Box 825 48653 · 989-275-6640
Ron Alden, prin. · Fax 275-6609

Kirtland Community College · Post-Sec.
10775 N Saint Helen Rd 48653 · 989-275-5000

Rose City, Ogemaw, Pop. 719
West Branch-Rose City Area SD
Supt. — See West Branch
Rose City MS · 400/5-8
PO Box 407 48654 · 989-343-2280
Shelly Fales, prin. · Fax 343-2299

Roseville, Macomb, Pop. 47,925
Roseville Community SD · 6,200/K-12
18975 Church St 48066 · 586-445-5505
John Kment, supt. · Fax 771-1772
www.rcs.misd.net
Eastland JHS · 600/7-9
18700 Frank St 48066 · 586-445-5702
Mark Blaszkowski, prin. · Fax 445-5721
Roseville HS · 1,300/10-12
17855 Common Rd 48066 · 586-445-5542
Peter Hedemark, prin. · Fax 445-5654
Roseville JHS · 1,000/7-9
16250 Martin Rd 48066 · 586-445-5605
Paul Schummer, prin. · Fax 445-5620

Dorsey Business School · Post-Sec.
31542 Gratiot Ave 48066 · 586-296-3225

Royal Oak, Oakland, Pop. 58,650
Oakland ISD
Supt. — See Waterford
Oakland Technical Campus SE · Vo/Tech
5055 Delemere Ave 48073 · 248-288-4020
Bonnie Crowson, dean · Fax 288-4071

Royal Oak SD · 6,300/PK-12
1123 Lexington Blvd 48073 · 248-435-8400
Thomas Moline, supt. · Fax 435-6170
royaloakschools.com
Addams MS · 700/6-8
2222 W Webster Rd 48073 · 248-288-3100
Cecilia Boyer, prin. · Fax 288-3144
Dondero HS · 900/9-12
709 N Washington Ave 48067 · 248-541-7100
Bridget Schipper, prin. · Fax 541-0408
Keller MS · 700/6-8
1505 N Campbell Rd 48067 · 248-542-6500
George Guzzio, prin. · Fax 542-9227
Kimball HS · 1,300/9-12
1500 Lexington Blvd 48073 · 248-435-8500
Thomas Neville, prin. · Fax 288-8733

David Pressley School of Cosmetology · Post-Sec.
1127 S Washington Ave 48067 · 248-548-5090
Oakland Community College · Post-Sec.
739 S Washington Ave 48067 · 248-246-2400
Shrine Academy · 100/7-8
3500 W 13 Mile Rd 48073 · 248-549-2928
Gabrielle Erken, prin. · Fax 549-2953
Shrine HS · 300/9-12
3500 W 13 Mile Rd 48073 · 248-549-2925
Gabrielle Erken, prin. · Fax 549-2953
William Beaumont Hospital · Post-Sec.
3601 W 13 Mile Rd 48073 · 248-551-0681

Rudyard, Chippewa
Rudyard Area SD · 1,100/K-12
PO Box 246 49780 · 906-478-3771
Nancy Berkompas, supt. · Fax 478-3912
eup.k12.mi.us/rudyard/index.html
Rudyard HS · 300/9-12
PO Box 246 49780 · 906-478-3471
Richard Guimond, prin. · Fax 478-4101

Rudyard MS, PO Box 246 49780 · 300/6-8
Richard Smith, prin. · 906-478-3710

Saginaw, Saginaw, Pop. 59,235
Buena Vista SD · 1,200/PK-12
PO Box 14829 48601 · 989-755-2184
Deborah T. Clarke, supt. · Fax 755-2187
www.bvsd.org
Buena Vista HS · 400/9-12
PO Box 14829 48601 · 989-754-1493
Nathaniel McClain, prin. · Fax 758-0915
Ricker MS · 400/5-8
PO Box 14829 48601 · 989-753-6438
Theresa Doyle, prin. · Fax 753-4953
Carrollton SD · 1,100/K-12
3211 Carla Dr 48604 · 989-754-1475
Craig Douglas, supt. · Fax 754-1470
www2.carrollton.k12.mi.us/
Carrollton Omni Adult Education · Adult
479 Shattuck Rd 48604 · 989-753-3478
Mary Beth Handeyside, prin. · Fax 754-1470
Other Schools – See Carrollton

Saginaw SD · 11,500/PK-12
550 Millard St 48607 · 989-399-6500
Gerald D. Dawkins, supt. · Fax 399-6635
www.spsd.net
Central MS · 600/6-8
1010 Hoyt Ave 48607 · 989-399-5300
Glenda Richardson, prin. · Fax 399-5315
Hill HS · 1,400/9-12
3115 Mackinaw St 48602 · 989-399-5800
Kathleen Andros, prin. · Fax 399-5815
North MS · 600/6-8
1101 N Bond St 48602 · 989-399-5400
Ostranda Lane, prin. · Fax 399-5415
Saginaw Arts & Sciences Academy · 400/6-12
200 Congress Ave 48602 · 989-399-5500
Janet Nash, prin. · Fax 399-5515
Saginaw Career Complex · Vo/Tech
2102 Weiss St 48602 · 989-399-6150
Julie Walker, prin. · Fax 399-6165
Saginaw HS · 1,000/9-12
3100 Webber St 48601 · 989-399-6000
Clifford Davis, prin. · Fax 399-6015
South MS · 800/6-8
224 N Elm St 48602 · 989-399-5600
Craig McCane, prin. · Fax 399-5615
Webber MS · 600/6-8
2600 Prescott Ave 48601 · 989-399-5700
Billy Erwin, prin. · Fax 399-5715

Saginaw Township Community SD · 4,900/PK-12
PO Box 6278 48608 · 989-399-8044
Jerry Seese Ed.D., supt. · Fax 797-1801
stcs.org
Heritage HS · 1,600/9-12
3465 N Center Rd 48603 · 989-799-5790
Michael Newman, prin. · Fax 799-5159
White Pine MS · 1,100/6-8
505 N Center Rd, · 989-797-1814
Bonnie Eaves, prin. · Fax 797-1859

Swan Valley SD · 1,700/PK-12
8380 OHern Rd 48609 · 989-921-3701
Richard Syrek, supt. · Fax 921-3705
www.swanvalley.k12.mi.us
Swan Valley HS · 600/9-12
8400 OHern Rd 48609 · 989-921-2401
Mat McRae, prin. · Fax 921-2405
Swan Valley MS · 400/6-8
453 Van Wormer Rd 48609 · 989-921-2601
Karsten Schlenter, prin. · Fax 921-2605

Community Baptist Christian S · 200/PK-12
8331 Gratiot Rd 48609 · 989-781-2340
Vicki Torrey, prin. · Fax 781-1344
Davenport University · Post-Sec.
5300 Bay Rd 48604 · 989-799-7800
Grace Christian S · 100/PK-12
4619 Mackinaw Rd 48603 · 989-793-2129
Jeffrey Howe, prin. · Fax 793-2125
Michigan Lutheran Seminary · 300/9-12
2777 Hardin St 48602 · 989-793-1041
Paul Prange, pres. · Fax 793-4213
Nouvel Catholic Central HS · 500/9-12
2555 Wieneke Rd 48603 · 989-791-4330
Ron Szewczyk, prin. · Fax 797-6610
Ross Medical Education Center · Post-Sec.
4054 Bay Rd 48603 · 989-793-9800
St. Mary's Medical Center · Post-Sec.
830 S Jefferson Ave 48601 · 989-776-8176
Valley Lutheran HS · 300/9-12
3560 McCarty Rd 48603 · 989-790-1676
John M. Brandt, prin. · Fax 790-1680

Saint Charles, Saginaw, Pop. 2,169
St. Charles Community SD · 1,200/K-12
891 W Walnut St 48655 · 989-865-9961
Michael Wallace, supt. · Fax 865-6185
www.stccs.org
Saint Charles HS · 400/9-12
881 W Walnut St 48655 · 989-865-9991
Heather Ballien, prin. · Fax 865-8185
Thurston MS · 300/6-8
893 W Walnut St 48655 · 989-865-9927
Patricia Sowle, prin. · Fax 865-2429

Saint Clair, Saint Clair, Pop. 5,881
East China SD
Supt. — See East China
Saint Clair HS · 1,000/9-12
2200 Clinton Ave 48079 · 810-676-1700
Ronald Miller, prin. · Fax 676-1725
Saint Clair MS · 700/6-8
4335 Yankee Rd 48079 · 810-676-1800
Kevin Miller, prin. · Fax 676-1825

Saint Clair Shores, Macomb, Pop. 61,896
Lake Shore SD · 3,200/K-12
28850 Harper Ave 48081 · 586-285-8480
Brian Annable, supt. · Fax 285-8463
www.lakeshoreschools.org
Kennedy MS · 800/6-8
23101 Masonic Blvd 48082 · 586-285-8800
Gordon Kennedy, prin. · Fax 285-8804
Lake Shore HS · 1,100/9-12
22980 E 13 Mile Rd 48082 · 586-285-8900
Betty Sands, prin. · Fax 285-8904

Lakeview SD · 2,900/K-12
20300 Statler St 48081 · 586-445-4000
Sandra Feeley Myrand, supt. · Fax 445-4029
www.lakeview.misd.net
Jefferson MS · 700/6-8
27900 Rockwood St 48081 · 586-445-4130
Fred Zielke, prin. · Fax 445-4041
Lakeview HS · 1,100/9-12
21100 E 11 Mile Rd 48081 · 586-445-4045
Robert duBois, prin. · Fax 445-4072

South Lake SD · 2,200/K-12
23101 Stadium Dr 48080 · 586-445-1600
William C. Putney, supt. · Fax 445-4202
www.solake.org
South Lake HS · 900/9-12
21900 E 9 Mile Rd 48080 · 586-435-1400
Louis Steigerwald, prin. · Fax 445-4243
South Lake MS · 400/7-8
21621 California St 48080 · 586-435-1300
Richard Norsigian, prin. · Fax 778-3151

Virginia Farrell Beauty School · Post-Sec.
23620 Harper Ave 48080 · 586-775-6640

Saint Ignace, Mackinac, Pop. 2,535
St. Ignace Area SD · 700/K-12
840 Portage St 49781 · 906-643-8145
Mike Springsteen, supt. · Fax 643-0247
www.eup.k12.mi.us/st_ignace
Lasalle HS · 300/8-12
850 W Portage St 49781 · 906-643-8800
Donald Gustafson, prin. · Fax 643-7696

Saint Johns, Clinton, Pop. 7,513
Saint Johns SD · 3,100/K-12
PO Box 230 48879 · 989-227-4050
Robert Kudwa, supt. · Fax 227-4099
www.stjohns.edzone.net
Saint Johns HS · 1,100/9-12
501 W Sickles St 48879 · 989-227-4000
Mark Palmer, prin. · Fax 227-4199
Saint Johns MS · 800/6-8
900 W Townsend Rd 48879 · 989-227-4300
Dennis Toth, prin. · Fax 227-4399

Saint Joseph, Berrien, Pop. 8,656
St. Joseph SD · 2,600/K-12
2214 S State St 49085 · 269-926-3100
Carole Schmidt Ph.D., supt. · Fax 926-3103
www.remc11.k12.mi.us/stjoe/
St. Joseph HS · 1,000/9-12
2521 Stadium Dr 49085 · 269-926-3200
Jeffrey Runser, prin. · Fax 926-3203
Upton MS · 700/6-8
800 Maiden Ln 49085 · 269-926-3400
Allen Skibbe, prin. · Fax 926-3403

Lake Michigan Catholic HS · 200/9-12
915 Pleasant St 49085 · 269-983-2511
John Berlin, prin. · Fax 983-0883
Lake Michigan Catholic MS · 100/6-8
915 Pleasant St 49085 · 269-983-2511
John Berlin, prin. · Fax 983-0883
Michigan Lutheran HS · 100/9-12
615 E Marquette Woods Rd 49085 · 269-429-7861
Michael Butzow, prin. · Fax 429-4428
Twin City Beauty College · Post-Sec.
2600 Lincoln Ave 49085 · 269-428-2900

Saint Louis, Gratiot, Pop. 5,445
St. Louis SD · 1,200/PK-12
113 E Saginaw St 48880 · 989-681-2545
Robert Lange, supt. · Fax 681-5894
www.edzone.net/~stlouis
Nurnberger MS · 300/6-8
312 Union St 48880 · 989-681-5155
George Herrington, prin. · Fax 681-4658
St. Louis HS · 400/9-12
113 E Saginaw St 48880 · 989-681-2500
Tom Steere, prin. · Fax 681-4535

Saline, Washtenaw, Pop. 8,704
Saline Area SD · 5,200/PK-12
200 N Ann Arbor St 48176 · 734-429-8000
Dr. Beverley Geltner, supt. · Fax 429-8010
www.salineschools.com
Saline HS · 1,700/9-12
1300 Campus Pkwy 48176 · 734-429-8030
Jean Durst, prin. · Fax 429-8036
Saline MS · 900/7-8
7190 N Maple Rd 48176 · 734-429-8070
Nic Cooper, prin. · Fax 429-8076

Washtenaw Christian Academy · 200/PK-12
7200 Moon Rd 48176 · 734-429-7733
Amanda Cousino, prin. · Fax 944-8343

Sand Creek, Lenawee
Sand Creek Community SD · 1,000/K-12
6850 Sand Creek Hwy 49279 · 517-436-3108
Don Barnes, supt. · Fax 436-3143
scnc.sandcreek.k12.mi.us
Sand Creek JSHS · 500/7-12
6518 Sand Creek Hwy 49279 · 517-436-3124
Steven Laundra, prin. · Fax 436-3193

Sand Lake, Montcalm, Pop. 505
Tri County Area SD 2,300/K-12
PO Box 79 49343 616-636-5454
James K. Scholten M.A., supt. Fax 636-5677
www.tricountyschools.com
Other Schools – See Howard City

Sandusky, Sanilac, Pop. 2,705
Sandusky Community SD 1,400/K-12
191 Pine Tree Ln 48471 810-648-3400
Timothy A. Lentz, supt. Fax 648-5113
www.sandusky.k12.mi.us
Sandusky HS 400/9-12
191 Pine Tree Ln 48471 810-648-3401
Mike Phillips, prin. Fax 648-3148
Sandusky MS 400/5-8
395 S Sandusky Rd 48471 810-648-3300
Fred Hicks, prin. Fax 648-5221

Sanford, Midland, Pop. 945
Meridian SD 1,600/PK-12
3361 N M 30 48657 989-687-3200
William Newkirk, supt. Fax 687-3222
www.merps.k12.mi.us
Meridian HS 400/9-12
3303 N M 30 48657 989-687-3300
Dennis Stine, prin. Fax 687-3309
Meridian JHS 400/6-8
3475 N M 30 48657 989-687-3360
William Chilman, prin. Fax 687-3364

Saranac, Ionia, Pop. 1,321
Saranac Community SD 1,200/K-12
88 Pleasant St 48881 616-642-1400
Bruce Chadwick, supt. Fax 642-1405
www.saranac.k12.mi.us
Harker MS 300/6-8
234 Weeks Rd 48881 616-642-1300
Randy Masterson, prin. Fax 642-1305
Saranac HS 400/9-12
150 Pleasant St 48881 616-642-1100
Ron Fales, prin. Fax 642-1105

Saugatuck, Allegan, Pop. 1,037
Saugatuck SD
Supt. — See Douglas
Saugatuck MSHS 400/6-12
401 Elizabeth St 49453 269-857-2133
Timothy Travis, prin. Fax 857-6145

Sault Sainte Marie, Chippewa, Pop. 15,300
Sault Sainte Marie Area SD 2,500/PK-12
876 Marquette Ave 49783 906-635-6609
Daniel Reattoir Ed.D., supt. Fax 635-6642
www.eup.k12.mi.us/sault/
Sault Area Career Center Vo/Tech
904 Marquette Ave 49783 906-635-6652
Gary Deuman, prin. Fax 635-6641
Sault Sainte Marie Area HS 1,000/9-12
904 Marquette Ave 49783 906-635-6605
John Sherry, prin. Fax 635-6641
Sault Sainte Marie MS 700/6-8
684 Marquette Ave 49783 906-635-6604
Tom Stabile, prin. Fax 635-3841

Lake Superior State University Post-Sec.
1000 College Dr 49783 906-632-6841

Schoolcraft, Kalamazoo, Pop. 1,549
Schoolcraft Community SD 1,200/K-12
629 E Clay St 49087 269-488-7390
Douglas Knobloch, supt. Fax 488-7391
www.remc12.k12.mi.us/schoolcraft/
Schoolcraft HS 400/9-12
629 E Clay St 49087 269-488-7350
John Kolassa, prin. Fax 488-7364
Schoolcraft MS 200/7-8
629 E Clay St 49087 269-488-7300
Douglas Maltby, prin. Fax 488-7303

Scottville, Mason, Pop. 1,262
Mason County Central SD 1,600/PK-12
300 W Broadway St 49454 231-757-3713
Charles Sandro, supt. Fax 757-5716
www.mccschools.com
Mason County Central HS 500/9-12
300 W Broadway St 49454 231-757-4748
Jack Murchie, prin. Fax 757-9084
Mason County Central MS 500/5-8
310 W Beryl St 49454 231-757-3724
Jeff Mount, prin. Fax 757-4820
Community Education Consortium Adult
300 W Broadway St 49454 231-757-3471
Christy Christmas, prin. Fax 757-5716

Mason/Lake ISD
Supt. — See Ludington
Mason-Lake Int SD Career Technical Educ Vo/Tech
3000 N Stiles Rd 49454 231-845-6211
Michael Robinson, admin. Fax 845-7227

West Shore Community College Post-Sec.
PO Box 277 49454 231-845-6211

Sebewaing, Huron, Pop. 1,898
Unionville-Sebewaing SD 1,000/K-12
2203 Wildner Rd 48759 989-883-2360
John Walker, supt. Fax 883-9021
www.usa.k12.mi.us
Unionville-Sebewaing HS 400/9-12
2203 Wildner Rd 48759 989-883-2534
Michael Harris, prin. Fax 883-9739
Unionville-Sebewaing MS 300/5-8
2203 Wildner Rd 48759 989-883-3140
Mark Gainforth, prin. Fax 883-9469

Shelby, Oceana, Pop. 1,971
Shelby SD 1,700/PK-12
525 N State St 49455 231-861-5211
Dana McGrew, supt. Fax 861-5416
hs.shelby.k12.mi.us/main/
Shelby HS 500/9-12
641 N State St 49455 231-861-4452
Fran Schamber, prin. Fax 861-6867
Shelby MS 400/6-8
525 N State St 49455 231-861-4521
Vaughn White, prin. Fax 861-0415

Shelby Township, Macomb, Pop. 69,500
Utica Community SD
Supt. — See Sterling Heights
Eisenhower SHS 2,000/10-12
6500 25 Mile Rd 48316 586-797-1300
Robert Van Camp, prin. Fax 797-1301
Malow JHS 1,300/7-9
6400 25 Mile Rd 48316 586-797-3500
Robert Hock, prin. Fax 797-3501
Shelby JHS 1,200/7-9
51700 Van Dyke Ave 48316 586-797-3700
Patricia Gonser, prin. Fax 797-3701

Shepherd, Isabella, Pop. 1,427
Shepherd SD 1,700/K-12
PO Box 219 48883 989-828-5520
Fax 828-5679
www.edzone.net/~shepherd
Shepherd HS 500/9-12
100 E Hall St 48883 989-828-6601
Nate Bootz, prin. Fax 828-5452
Shepherd MS 400/6-8
150 E Hall St 48883 989-828-6605
Claire Bunker, prin. Fax 828-6578

Sidney, Montcalm
Montcalm Area ISD
Supt. — See Stanton
Montcalm Area Career Center Vo/Tech
1550 W Sidney Rd 48885 989-328-6621
Paula Fortino, prin. Fax 328-2000

Montcalm Community College Post-Sec.
2800 College Dr 48885 989-328-2111

Southfield, Oakland, Pop. 77,488
Southfield SD 10,200/PK-12
24661 Lahser Rd 48033 248-746-8500
Beverley Geltner, supt. Fax 746-8540
www.southfield.k12.mi.us
Birney MS 900/6-8
27225 Evergreen Rd 48076 248-746-8800
Sterling Russell, prin. Fax 352-0709
Levey MS 800/6-8
25300 W 9 Mile Rd, 248-746-8740
Kelly Dean, prin. Fax 746-8718
Southfield HS 1,600/9-12
24675 Lahser Rd, 248-746-8601
Anthony Muhammad, prin. Fax 746-8773
Thompson MS 600/6-8
16300 Lincoln Dr 48076 248-746-7400
Josha Talison, prin. Fax 746-7493
Other Schools – See Lathrup Village

Akiva Hebrew Day S 300/PK-12
21100 W 12 Mile Rd 48076 248-386-1625
Rabbi Yigal Tsaidi, prin. Fax 386-1632
Detroit Business Institute Post-Sec.
23077 Greenfield Rd #LL28 48075 248-552-6300
Lawrence Technological University Post-Sec.
21000 W 10 Mile Rd 48075 248-204-4000
Lawton School Post-Sec.
20755 Greenfield Rd Ste 300 48075 248-569-7787
National Institute of Technology Post-Sec.
26111 Evergreen Rd Ste 201 48076 248-799-9933
Northwestern Technological Institute Post-Sec.
24567 Northwestern Hwy #200 48075 248-358-4006
Oakland Community College Post-Sec.
22322 Rutland Ave 48075 248-233-2700
Providence Hospital Post-Sec.
16001 W 9 Mile Rd 48075 248-424-3000
Southfield Christian S 700/K-12
28650 Lahser Rd 48034 248-357-3660
Phil Ackley, prin. Fax 357-5271
Specs Howard School of Broadcast Arts Post-Sec.
19900 W 9 Mile Rd 48075 248-358-9000
Yeshivas Darchei Torah S 300/K-12
21550 W 12 Mile Rd 48076 248-948-1080
Sara Kahn, prin. Fax 948-1825

Southgate, Wayne, Pop. 30,064
Southgate Community SD 5,000/K-12
13201 Trenton Rd 48195 734-246-4600
David Peden, supt. Fax 283-6791
www.southgateschools.com
Anderson HS 1,100/10-12
15475 Leroy St 48195 734-246-4611
Michael Kell, prin. Fax 246-7840
Davidson MS 800/8-9
15800 Trenton Rd 48195 734-246-4628
Marilyn Svaluto, prin. Fax 246-7280
Asher Adult & Community Education Adult
14101 Leroy St 48195 734-246-4633
Judy Cock, dir. Fax 246-7244

Dorsey Business School Post-Sec.
15755 Northline Rd 48195 734-285-5400

South Haven, Van Buren, Pop. 5,075
South Haven SD 2,100/PK-12
554 Green St 49090 269-637-0520
J. David Myers, supt. Fax 637-3025
www.shps.org
Baseline MS 600/6-8
7357 Baseline Rd 49090 269-637-0530
John Weiss, prin. Fax 639-8009

Mohr HS 800/9-12
600 Elkenburg St 49090 269-637-0500
Dene Hadden, prin. Fax 637-0516

South Lyon, Oakland, Pop. 10,895
South Lyon Community SD 7,000/K-12
345 S Warren St 48178 248-573-8127
William Pearson, supt. Fax 437-8686
www.slcs.us
Centennial MS 700/6-8
62500 9 Mile Rd 48178 248-573-8600
David Phillips, prin. Fax 573-8611
Millennium MS 900/6-8
61526 9 Mile Rd 48178 248-573-8200
Ronald Webber, prin. Fax 573-8231
South Lyon HS 1,900/9-12
1000 N Lafayette St 48178 248-573-8150
Larry Jackson, prin. Fax 437-0233

Sparta, Kent, Pop. 4,102
Sparta Area SD 2,800/PK-12
465 S Union St 49345 616-887-8253
Randy Neelis, supt. Fax 887-9958
www.spartaschools.org
Sparta HS 900/9-12
480 S State St 49345 616-887-8213
Kent Swinson, prin. Fax 887-1264
Sparta MS 800/5-8
240 Glenn St 49345 616-887-8211
Joel Stoner, prin. Fax 887-1080

Spring Arbor, Jackson, Pop. 2,010

Spring Arbor University Post-Sec.
106 N Main St 49283 517-750-1200

Spring Lake, Ottawa, Pop. 2,427
Spring Lake SD 2,200/PK-12
345 Hammond St 49456 616-846-5500
Larry Mason, supt. Fax 846-9830
www.spring-lake.k12.mi.us
Spring Lake HS 800/9-12
16140 148th Ave 49456 616-846-5501
Mike Gilchrist, prin. Fax 847-5855
Spring Lake MS 300/7-8
345 Hammond St 49456 616-846-5502
Ron Schneider, prin. Fax 847-7913

Springport, Jackson, Pop. 687
Springport SD 1,100/K-12
PO Box 100 49284 517-857-3495
Roland Pakonen, supt. Fax 857-4179
scnc.sps.k12.mi.us/
Springport HS 400/9-12
PO Box 100 49284 517-857-3475
Chris Kregal, prin. Fax 857-3251
Springport MS 300/6-8
PO Box 100 49284 517-857-3445
Tanya Overweg, prin. Fax 857-3453

Standish, Arenac, Pop. 2,072
Standish-Sterling Community SD 1,900/PK-12
3789 Wyatt Rd 48658 989-846-3670
Claude Inch, supt. Fax 846-7890
www.standish-sterling.org
Standish-Sterling Central HS 600/9-12
2401 Grove Street Rd 48658 989-846-3660
Mark Williams, prin. Fax 846-3666
Standish-Sterling MS 600/5-8
3789 Wyatt Rd 48658 989-846-4526
Beverly Skinner, prin. Fax 846-4529

Stanton, Montcalm, Pop. 1,519
Central Montcalm SD 2,100/PK-12
PO Box 9 48888 989-831-5243
Roger Thelen, supt. Fax 831-5580
www.qualityschool.org
Central Montcalm HS 600/9-12
1480 S Sheridan Rd 48888 989-831-2100
Jerry Winkler, prin. Fax 831-2110
Central Montcalm MS 400/7-8
1480 Sheridan Rd SW 48888 989-831-2200
Sandy SanMiguel, prin. Fax 831-2210
Central Montcalm Adult/Community Educ Adult
618 W Main St 48888 989-831-7902
Kathryn Betts, prin. Fax 831-7862

Montcalm Area ISD
PO Box 367 48888 989-831-5261
George P. Stamas, supt. Fax 831-8727
www.maisd.com
Other Schools – See Sidney

Stephenson, Menominee, Pop. 848
Stephenson Area SD 800/K-12
PO Box 509 49887 906-753-2221
Michael Gaunt, supt. Fax 753-4676
www.stephenson.k12.mi.us
Stephenson JSHS 400/7-12
PO Box 529 49887 906-753-2222
Roger J. Cole, prin. Fax 753-2326

Sterling Heights, Macomb, Pop. 126,182
Utica Community SD 28,700/PK-12
11303 Greendale Dr 48312 586-797-1000
Joan Sergent, supt. Fax 797-1001
www.macomb.k12.mi.us/utica/schutic.htm
Bemis JHS 1,000/7-8
12500 19 Mile Rd 48313 586-797-2500
Joyce Spade, prin. Fax 797-2501
Davis JHS 900/7-9
11311 Plumbrook Rd 48312 586-797-2700
Robert McBroom, prin. Fax 797-2701
Ford HS 1,800/9-12
11911 Clinton River Rd 48313 586-797-1600
Gloria Bawol, prin. Fax 797-1601
Heritage JHS 600/7-9
37400 Dodge Park Rd 48312 586-797-3100
Linda Hall, prin. Fax 797-3101

Jeanette JHS 1,000/7-9
40400 Gulliver Dr 48310 586-797-3300
Robyn Thompson, prin. Fax 797-3301
Stevenson SHS 1,700/10-12
39701 Dodge Park Rd 48313 586-797-1900
Jerry Willis, prin. Fax 797-1901
Other Schools – See Shelby Township, Utica

Warren Consolidated SD
Supt. — See Warren
Career Prep Center Vo/Tech
12200 15 Mile Rd 48312 586-825-2800
Frank Antonucci, prin. Fax 698-4519
Carleton JHS 600/6-8
8900 15 Mile Rd 48312 586-825-2590
Stephen Bigelow, prin. Fax 698-4286
Flynn JHS 600/6-8
2899 Fox Hill Dr 48310 586-825-2900
Thomas Cassidy, prin. Fax 698-4304
Grissom JHS 800/6-8
35701 Ryan Rd 48310 586-825-2560
Susan Nye, prin. Fax 698-4313
Sterling Heights HS 1,600/9-12
12901 15 Mile Rd 48312 586-825-2700
Todd Biederwolf, prin. Fax 698-4253

Bethesda Christian S 300/PK-12
14500 Metropolitan Pkwy 48312 586-446-9900
Sandra Ondra, prin. Fax 446-9904
Sterling Christian S 200/PK-12
33380 Ryan Rd 48310 586-268-5420
Tony Bryson, prin. Fax 795-0929

Stevensville, Berrien, Pop. 1,192
Lakeshore SD 2,900/PK-12
5771 Cleveland Ave 49127 269-428-1400
Donald Frank, supt. Fax 428-1574
www.lakeshoreschools.k12.mi.us
Lakeshore HS 1,000/9-12
5771 Cleveland Ave 49127 269-428-1402
William Scaletta, prin. Fax 428-1572
Lakeshore MS 700/6-8
1459 W John Beers Rd 49127 269-428-1408
William Shepard, prin. Fax 428-1571

Stockbridge, Ingham, Pop. 1,292
Stockbridge Community SD 1,600/K-12
305 W Elizabeth St 49285 517-851-7188
Bruce Brown, supt. Fax 851-8334
scs.k12.mi.us/
Stockbridge HS 500/9-12
416 N Clinton St 49285 517-851-7770
Karl Heidrich, prin. Fax 851-9446
Stockbridge MS 400/6-8
305 W Elizabeth St 49285 517-851-8149
Brian Thompson, prin. Fax 851-8334

Sturgis, Saint Joseph, Pop. 11,127
Sturgis SD 2,900/K-12
107 W West St 49091 269-659-1500
Robert Olsen, supt. Fax 659-1584
sturgis.k12.mi.us
Sturgis HS 900/9-12
216 Vinewood Ave 49091 269-659-1515
Wayne Stitt, prin. Fax 659-1532
Sturgis MS 700/6-8
1400 E Lafayette St 49091 269-659-1550
Eric Anderson, prin. Fax 659-1553
Community/Adult S Adult
107 W West St 49091 269-659-1540
Cheryl Locey, prin. Fax 659-1584

Lake Area Christian S 100/PK-12
63590 Borgert Rd 49091 269-651-5135
Dean Miller, admin. Fax 651-8648

Suttons Bay, Leelanau, Pop. 590
Suttons Bay SD 1,100/K-12
PO Box 367 49682 231-271-8604
Tom Harwood, supt. Fax 271-8691
www.suttonsbay.k12.mi.us
Suttons Bay HS 400/9-12
PO Box 367 49682 231-271-8603
Susan Rummel, prin. Fax 271-8690
Suttons Bay MS 200/6-8
PO Box 367 49682 231-271-8602
Kathleen Maisonville, prin. Fax 271-8689

Swartz Creek, Genesee, Pop. 5,247
Swartz Creek Community SD 4,400/K-12
8354 Cappy Ln 48473 810-591-2381
Dr. Jeff Pratt, supt. Fax 591-2784
www.swartzcreek.org
Swartz Creek HS 1,300/9-12
1 Dragon Dr 48473 810-591-1801
Michael Vanderlip, prin. Fax 591-1895
Swartz Creek MS 1,000/6-8
8230 Crapo St 48473 810-591-1705
Kevin Klaeren, prin. Fax 591-1712

Tawas City, Iosco, Pop. 1,961
Iosco RESA
27 N Rempert Rd 48763 989-362-3006
Thomas Caldwell, supt. Fax 362-9076
www.iresa.k12.mi.us
Career & Technical Education Center Vo/Tech
27 N Rempert Rd 48763 989-362-3006
James O'Farrell, dir. Fax 362-6905

Tawas Area SD 1,500/K-12
245 M 55 W 48763 989-984-2250
Jerry W. Youngs, supt. Fax 984-2253
www.tawas.net
Tawas Area HS 500/9-12
255 M 55 W 48763 989-984-2100
James Kiblinger, prin. Fax 984-2106
Tawas Area MS 300/7-8
255 M 55 W 48763 989-984-2150
William Grusecki, prin. Fax 984-2165

Taylor, Wayne, Pop. 65,589
Taylor SD 10,400/PK-12
23033 Northline Rd 48180 734-374-1200
Lee Lewis, supt. Fax 287-6083
www.taylorschools.net/
Brake MS 600/7-8
13500 Pine St 48180 734-374-1227
Lynn Wilk, prin. Fax 374-1577
Career Center HS Vo/Tech
9601 Westlake St 48180 313-295-5757
Terry Turner, prin.
Hoover MS 600/7-8
27101 Beverly Rd 48180 313-295-5775
Teresa Winnie, prin. Fax 295-8354
Kennedy HS 1,400/9-12
13505 Kennedy Dr 48180 734-374-1229
Wayne Hamilton, prin. Fax 374-1676
Truman HS 1,800/9-12
11211 Beech Daly Rd 48180 734-946-6551
Ronald Vespremi, prin. Fax 946-6590
West MS 700/7-8
10575 William St 48180 313-295-5783
Michael Wiltse, prin. Fax 291-2203

Baptist Park S 200/PK-12
12501 Telegraph Rd 48180 734-287-2720
Roger Cook, admin. Fax 287-2184
Light and Life Christian S 200/PK-12
8900 Pardee Rd 48180 313-292-1660
Rev. George Kennedy, admin. Fax 292-0489
Oakwood Jr. Academy 100/K-10
26300 Goddard Rd 48180 313-291-6790
Lynnette Jefferson, prin. Fax 291-3713
Taylortown School of Beauty Post-Sec.
23129 Ecorse Rd 48180 313-291-2177

Tecumseh, Lenawee, Pop. 8,751
Tecumseh SD 3,400/K-12
212 N Ottawa St 49286 517-424-7318
Michael McAran, supt. Fax 423-3847
tps.k12.mi.us
Tecumseh HS 1,100/9-12
760 Brown St 49286 517-423-6008
Robert Scheick, prin. Fax 423-9644
Tecumseh MS 1,100/5-8
307 N Maumee St 49286 517-423-1105
Rick Hilderley, prin. Fax 423-1300

Tekonsha, Calhoun, Pop. 699
Tekonsha SD 400/K-12
245 S Elm St 49092 517-767-4121
Donald Vernon, supt. Fax 767-3465
www.tekonsha.k12.mi.us
Tekonsha MSHS 200/6-12
245 S Elm St 49092 517-767-4121
Joe Huepenbecker, prin. Fax 767-3465

Temperance, Monroe, Pop. 6,542
Bedford SD 5,400/K-12
1623 W Sterns Rd 48182 734-850-6000
Jon White, supt. Fax 850-6099
www.bedford.k12.mi.us
Bedford HS 1,800/9-12
8285 Jackman Rd 48182 734-850-6100
Dennis Caldwell, prin. Fax 850-6199
Bedford JHS 900/7-8
8405 Jackman Rd 48182 734-850-6200
Mary L. Zaums, prin. Fax 850-6299

State Line Christian S 400/K-12
6320 Lewis Ave 48182 734-847-6774
John Morrissey, prin. Fax 847-4968

Three Oaks, Berrien, Pop. 1,791
River Valley SD 1,000/K-12
15480 Three Oaks Rd 49128 269-756-9541
Chester Sanders, supt. Fax 756-6631
www.rivervalleyschools.org/
River Valley HS 600/7-12
15480 Three Oaks Rd 49128 269-756-9541
Jose Vera, prin. Fax 756-3007

Three Rivers, Saint Joseph, Pop. 7,172
Three Rivers Community SD 2,800/K-12
851 6th Avenue Rd 49093 269-279-1100
Roger Rathburn, supt. Fax 279-5584
www.trschools.org
Three Rivers HS 900/9-12
700 6th Ave 49093 269-279-1120
Dan Ryan, prin. Fax 273-8014
Three Rivers MS 700/6-8
1101 Jefferson St 49093 269-279-1130
Gloria Wimbley, prin. Fax 279-1139
Three Rivers Adult & Community Education Adult
416 Washington St 49093 269-279-9581
Lois Millet, dir. Fax 279-1160

Traverse City, Grand Traverse, Pop. 14,466
Traverse Bay Area ISD
PO Box 6020 49696 231-922-6200
Michael Kenney, supt. Fax 922-6270
www.tbaisd.k12.mi.us
TBA Career Tech Center Vo/Tech
880 Parsons Rd 49686 231-922-6273
Fax 922-6364

Traverse City Area SD 10,600/PK-12
PO Box 32 49685 231-933-1725
Jim Feil, supt. Fax 933-1726
www.tcaps.net
Traverse City Central SHS 1,300/10-12
PO Box 32 49685 231-933-3500
Michael Murray, prin. Fax 933-3506
Traverse City East JHS 1,200/6-9
PO Box 32 49685 231-933-7300
Glenn Solowiej, prin. Fax 933-6998
Traverse City West JHS 1,500/7-9
PO Box 32 49685 231-933-8200
Pam Alfieri, prin. Fax 933-8205

Traverse City West SHS 1,400/10-12
PO Box 32 49685 231-933-7500
Joe Tibaldi, prin. Fax 933-7506

Munson Medical Center Post-Sec.
1105 6th St 49684 231-935-6501
Northwestern Michigan College Post-Sec.
1701 E Front St 49686 231-922-1000
St. Elizabeth Ann Seton MS 300/6-8
1601 3 Mile Rd N 49686 231-932-4810
Patrick Cleland, prin. Fax 932-4814
St. Francis HS 300/9-12
123 E 11th St 49684 231-946-8038
Robert Bridges, prin. Fax 946-1878
Traverse City Christian S 100/7-12
753 Emerson Rd 49686 231-929-1747
K. Patrick Rode Ph.D., prin. Fax 929-1831

Trenton, Wayne, Pop. 19,619
Trenton SD 3,100/K-12
2603 Charlton Rd 48183 734-676-8600
Dr. John Savel, supt. Fax 676-4851
www.resa.net/trenton/
Arthurs MS 700/6-8
4000 Marian Dr 48183 734-676-8700
Stephanie Spurr, prin. Fax 676-7364
Trenton HS 1,100/9-12
2601 Charlton Rd 48183 734-692-4530
Michael Doyle, prin. Fax 692-4615

Troy, Oakland, Pop. 81,071
Troy SD 11,900/PK-12
4400 Livernois Rd 48098 248-823-4000
Dr. Janet Jopke, supt. Fax 823-4013
www.troy.k12.mi.us
Athens HS 2,000/9-12
4333 John R Rd 48085 248-823-2900
Dr. Catherine Cost, prin. Fax 823-2913
Baker MS 600/6-8
1291 Torpey Dr 48083 248-823-4600
Larry Hahn, prin. Fax 823-4613
Boulan Park MS 800/6-8
3570 Northfield Pkwy 48084 248-823-4900
Jo Kwasny, prin. Fax 823-4913
Larson MS 800/6-8
2222 E Long Lake Rd 48085 248-823-4800
Dennis Seppanen, prin. Fax 823-4813
Smith MS 800/6-8
5835 Donaldson Dr 48085 248-823-4700
Stuart Redpath, prin. Fax 823-4713
Troy HS 2,000/9-12
4777 Northfield Pkwy 48098 248-823-2700
Marj Dziatczak, prin. Fax 823-2713

Bethany Christian S 300/PK-12
2601 John R Rd 48083 248-689-4821
Robert McIlwaine, prin. Fax 689-3441
Carnegie Institute Post-Sec.
550 Stephenson Hwy Ste 100 48083 248-589-1078
Christian Leadership Academy 100/K-12
3668B Livernois Rd 48083 248-457-1510
George Kelly, hdmstr. Fax 457-1520
ITT Technical Institute Post-Sec.
1522 E Big Beaver Rd 48083 248-524-1800
Michigan College of Beauty Post-Sec.
3498 Rochester Rd 48083 248-528-0303
Walsh Coll. Accountancy & Bus. Admin. Post-Sec.
PO Box 7006 48007 248-689-8282

Twining, Arenac, Pop. 187
Arenac Eastern SD 400/PK-12
PO Box 98 48766 989-867-4234
Rocky Aldrich, supt. Fax 867-4241
www.arenaceastern.org
Arenac Eastern S 400/PK-12
PO Box 98 48766 989-867-4234
Rick Green, prin. Fax 867-4241

Ubly, Sanilac, Pop. 843
Ubly Community SD 900/K-12
2020 Union St 48475 989-658-8202
Hal Hooks, supt. Fax 658-2361
bearcat.ubly.k12.mi.us/
Ubly HS 300/9-12
2020 Union St 48475 989-658-8554
Frederick Ligrow, prin. Fax 658-2072

Union City, Branch, Pop. 1,767
Union City Community SD 1,300/K-12
430 Saint Joseph St 49094 517-741-8091
Martin Chard, supt. Fax 741-5205
www.ucschools.net/
Union City HS 400/9-12
430 Saint Joseph St 49094 517-741-8561
Michael Furnas, prin. Fax 741-3772
Union City MS 400/5-8
435 Saint Joseph St 49094 517-741-5381
Ronna Steel, prin. Fax 741-8513

University Center, Bay

Delta College 48710 Post-Sec.
989-686-9093
Saginaw Valley State University Post-Sec.
7400 Bay Rd 48710 989-790-4000

Utica, Macomb, Pop. 4,655
Utica Community SD
Supt. — See Sterling Heights
Eppler JHS 700/7-9
45461 Brownell St 48317 586-797-2900
Juliet Patterson, prin. Fax 797-2901
Utica SHS 1,500/10-12
47255 Shelby Rd 48317 586-797-2200
Janet Jones, prin. Fax 797-2201

Vanderbilt, Otsego, Pop. 595

Vanderbilt Area SD   200/K-12
947 Donovan St   49795   989-983-4121
Jeffrey Liedel, supt.   Fax 983-4571
www.vanderbilt.k12.mi.us
Vanderbilt Area S   200/K-12
947 Donovan St   49795   989-983-2561
Jeffrey Liedel, prin.   Fax 983-3051

Vassar, Tuscola, Pop. 2,774

Vassar SD   1,600/K-12
220 Athletic St   48768   989-823-8535
R. Middlin, supt.   Fax 823-7823
www.vassar.k12.mi.us
Vassar HS, 220 Athletic St   48768   500/9-12
Paul Wojno, prin.   989-823-8534
Vassar MS, 220 Athletic St   48768   200/7-8
Phil Marcy, prin.   989-823-8533

Juniata Christian S   200/K-12
5656 Washburn Rd   48768   989-843-5326
Dean Bryan, prin.

Vermontville, Eaton, Pop. 792

Maple Valley SD   2,300/PK-12
11090 Nashville Hwy   49096   517-852-9699
Kim L. Kramer, supt.   Fax 852-5076
scnc.mvs.k12.mi.us
Maple Valley JSHS   800/7-12
11090 Nashville Hwy   49096   517-852-9275
Todd Gonser, prin.   Fax 852-2283

Vestaburg, Montcalm

Vestaburg Community SD   800/K-12
7188 Avenue B   48891   989-268-5353
Donald Myers, supt.   Fax 268-5852
www.vcs-k12.net
Vestaburg HS   200/9-12
7188 Avenue B   48891   989-268-5343
Michael Joslyn, prin.   Fax 268-5246
Vestaburg MS   200/6-8
7188 Avenue B   48891   989-268-5883
Judy Shimunek, prin.   Fax 268-5898

Vicksburg, Kalamazoo, Pop. 2,249

Vicksburg Community SD   2,700/PK-12
PO Box 158   49097   269-321-1000
Charles Glaes, supt.   Fax 321-1055
www.vicksburg-community-schools.org
Vicksburg HS   900/9-12
501 E Highway St   49097   269-321-1100
Rob Kuhlman, prin.   Fax 321-1155
Vicksburg MS   700/6-8
348 E Prairie St   49097   269-321-1300
Greg Tibbetts, prin.   Fax 321-1355

Wakefield, Gogebic, Pop. 2,022

Wakefield-Marenisco SD   300/K-12
715 Putnam St   49968   906-224-9421
Richard Bouvette, supt.   Fax 224-1771
www.wakefield.k12.mi.us
Wakefield-Marenisco S   300/K-12
715 Putnam St   49968   906-224-7211
Carrie Nyman, prin.   Fax 224-1771

Waldron, Hillsdale, Pop. 584

Waldron Area SD   400/K-12
13380 Waldron Rd   49288   517-286-6251
John McGonigle, supt.   Fax 286-6254
scnc.waldron.k12.mi.us
Waldron HS   100/9-12
13380 Waldron Rd   49288   517-286-6251
John McGonigle, prin.   Fax 286-6254
Waldron MS   100/6-8
13380 Waldron Rd   49288   517-286-6251
Sandra Schantl, prin.   Fax 286-6254

Walkerville, Oceana, Pop. 263

Walkerville SD   400/PK-12
PO Box 68   49459   231-873-4850
Ronald Stoneman, supt.   Fax 873-5861
www.walkerville.k12.mi.us
Walkerville JSHS   200/7-12
PO Box 68   49459   231-873-3652
Jeffrey Forner, prin.   Fax 873-5615

Walled Lake, Oakland, Pop. 6,776

Walled Lake Consolidated SD   15,400/PK-12
850 Ladd Rd Bldg D   48390   248-956-2000
James R. Geisler Ph.D., supt.   Fax 956-2123
www.walledlake.k12.mi.us
Walled Lake MS   900/6-8
46720 W Pontiac Trl   48390   248-956-2900
Karen Jacobson, prin.   Fax 956-2905
Western HS   1,600/9-12
600 Beck Rd   48390   248-956-4400
Lawrence Barlow, prin.   Fax 956-4405
Other Schools – See Commerce Township, West
Bloomfield, Wixom

Warren, Macomb, Pop. 136,016

Fitzgerald SD   3,300/PK-12
23200 Ryan Rd   48091   586-757-1750
Janette Brill, supt.   Fax 758-0991
www.fitz.k12.mi.us
Chatterton MS   800/6-8
24333 Ryan Rd   48091   586-757-6650
Marcia Keast, prin.   Fax 758-0928
Fitzgerald HS   1,000/9-12
23200 Ryan Rd   48091   586-757-7070
Laurie Fournier, prin.   Fax 757-5536

Van Dyke SD   4,100/K-12
23500 Mac Arthur Blvd   48089   586-758-8333
Kathleen Spaulding, supt.   Fax 758-8332
www.macomb.k12.mi.us/vandyke
Lincoln HS   1,000/9-12
22900 Federal Ave   48089   586-758-8306
Robert Blair, prin.   Fax 758-8304

Lincoln MS   700/7-8
22500 Federal Ave   48089   586-758-8320
Alena Zachery, prin.   Fax 758-8322
Warren Consolidated SD   16,400/K-12
31300 Anita Dr   48093   586-825-2400
Dr. James Clor, supt.   Fax 698-4116
www.wcs.k12.mi.us/
Beer MS   700/6-8
3200 Martin Rd   48092   586-558-3352
Annette Lauria, prin.   Fax 698-4277
Carter MS   800/6-8
12000 Masonic Blvd   48093   586-825-2620
Doug Babcock, prin.   Fax 698-4295
Cousino HS   1,600/9-12
30333 Hoover Rd   48093   586-574-3100
Gregory Bishop, prin.   Fax 698-4204
Warren-Mott HS   1,600/9-12
3131 E 12 Mile Rd   48092   586-574-3250
Brad Martin, prin.   Fax 698-4226
Other Schools – See Sterling Heights

Warren Woods SD   3,100/K-12
27100 Schoenherr Rd   48088   586-439-4400
Robert Livernois Ph.D., supt.   Fax 445-4004
warrenwoods.misd.net
Warren Woods MS   700/6-8
13400 E 12 Mile Rd   48088   586-439-4403
Daniel Gilbertson, prin.   Fax 574-9830
Warren Woods Tower HS   1,000/9-12
27900 Bunert Rd   48088   586-439-4402
Dr. Robert Livernois, prin.   Fax 445-8013

Davenport University - Warren   Post-Sec.
27650 Dequindre St   48092   586-558-8700
De La Salle Collegiate HS   800/9-12
14600 Common Rd   48088   586-778-2207
Patrick Adams, prin.   Fax 778-5118
Immaculate Conception Ukranian HS   100/9-12
29400 Westbrook Ave   48092   586-574-0510
Michaeline Weigle, prin.   Fax 574-2723
Macomb Christian S   300/PK-12
28501 Lorraine Ave   48093   586-751-8980
Beverly Edwards, prin.   Fax 751-7946
Macomb Community College   Post-Sec.
14500 E 12 Mile Rd   48088   586-445-7000
Ross Medical Education Center   Post-Sec.
27120 Dequindre Rd   48092   586-574-0830
Zoe Christian S   400/PK-12
13900 Masonic Blvd   48088   586-415-7555
Richard Mallino, admin.   Fax 415-0449

Washington, Macomb

Romeo Community SD
Supt. — See Romeo
Powell MS   700/6-8
62100 Jewell Rd   48094   586-752-0270
Jeffrey LaPerriere, prin.   Fax 752-0276

Waterford, Oakland, Pop. 74,500

Oakland ISD
2111 Pontiac Lake Rd   48328   248-209-2000
Vickie Markavitch, supt.   Fax 209-2206
www.oakland.k12.mi.us
Oakland Science Math & Technology Ctr   Vo/Tech
1480 Scott Lake Rd   48328   248-209-2399
   Fax 209-2390
Other Schools – See Clarkston, Pontiac, Royal Oak,
Wixom
Waterford SD   11,100/K-12
1150 Scott Lake Rd   48328   248-666-4000
Dr. Thomas Tattan, supt.   Fax 666-2558
www.waterford.k12.mi.us
Crary MS   800/6-8
501 N Cass Lake Rd   48328   248-682-9300
Lynn Kosinski, prin.   Fax 682-0220
Kettering HS   1,400/9-12
2800 Kettering Dr   48329   248-673-1261
Josh Wenning, prin.   Fax 673-1778
Mason MS   900/6-8
3835 W Walton Blvd   48329   248-674-2281
Cheryl Ellsworth, prin.   Fax 673-3718
Mott HS   1,800/9-12
1151 Scott Lake Rd   48328   248-674-4134
Raymond Nester, prin.   Fax 674-2825
Pierce MS   1,000/6-8
5145 Hatchery Rd   48329   248-674-0331
Yvonne Dixon, prin.   Fax 674-4222

Michigan College of Beauty   Post-Sec.
5620 Dixie Hwy   48329   248-623-9494
Mt. Zion Christian S   200/K-12
3200 Beacham Dr   48329   248-334-0488
Thomas Kocik, prin.   Fax 334-0465
Oakland Community College   Post-Sec.
7350 Cooley Lake Rd   48327   248-942-3100
Our Lady of the Lakes HS   200/9-12
5495 Dixie Hwy   48329   248-623-0340
Thomas Oppat, prin.   Fax 623-7536
Our Lady of the Lakes MS   200/6-8
5501 Dixie Hwy   48329   248-623-2201
Kathleen Lewis, prin.   Fax 623-2274
Waterford Christian Academy   200/PK-12
220 N Cass Lake Rd   48328   248-682-8112
James C. Slayton, admin.   Fax 682-3414

Watersmeet, Gogebic

Watersmeet Township SD   200/K-12
PO Box 217   49969   906-358-4500
George R. Peterson, supt.   Fax 358-4713
www.watersmeet.k12.mi.us/
Watersmeet Township S   200/K-12
PO Box 217   49969   906-358-4555
George R. Peterson, prin.   Fax 358-3036

Watervliet, Berrien, Pop. 1,802

Watervliet SD   1,400/K-12
450 E Red Arrow Hwy   49098   269-463-5566
Robert Gabel, supt.   Fax 463-6809
www.watervliet.k12.mi.us/
Watervliet HS   400/9-12
450 E Red Arrow Hwy   49098   269-463-4221
Greg Chisek, prin.   Fax 463-6809
Watervliet MS   400/6-8
450 E Red Arrow Hwy   49098   269-463-0342
Dave Armstrong, prin.   Fax 463-0325

Grace Christian S   200/K-12
325 N M 140   49098   269-463-5545
John Davis, admin.   Fax 463-5739

Wayland, Allegan, Pop. 3,976

Wayland UNSD
Supt. — See Byron Center
Wayland HS   1,000/9-12
870 E Superior St   49348   269-792-2254
Thomas Cutler, prin.   Fax 792-1101
Wayland Union MS   600/7-8
701 Wildcat Dr   49348   269-792-2306
Mike Haverdink, prin.   Fax 792-1102

Wayne, Wayne, Pop. 18,934

Wayne-Westland Community SD
Supt. — See Westland
Franklin MS   800/6-8
33555 Annapolis St   48184   734-419-2400
Darlene Scott, prin.   Fax 595-2401
Wayne Memorial HS   2,000/9-12
3001 4th St   48184   734-419-2200
John Albrecht, prin.   Fax 595-2227

Dorsey Business School   Post-Sec.
34841 Veterans Plz   48184   734-595-1540
Oakwood - Hospital Annapolis Center   Post-Sec.
33155 Annapolis St   48184   734-467-4000

Webberville, Ingham, Pop. 1,531

Webberville Community SD   600/K-12
313 E Grand River Rd   48892   517-521-3422
William C. Skilling, supt.   Fax 521-4139
www.webbervilleschools.org
Webberville JSHS   300/7-12
309 E Grand River Rd   48892   517-521-3447
Brian Friddle, prin.   Fax 521-4740

West Bloomfield, Oakland, Pop. 67,200

Bloomfield Hills SD
Supt. — See Bloomfield Hills
West Hills MS   400/6-8
2601 Lone Pine Rd   48323   248-341-6100
Edward Bretzlaff, prin.   Fax 341-6199

Walled Lake Consolidated SD
Supt. — See Walled Lake
Walnut Creek MS   800/6-8
7601 Walnut Lake Rd   48323   248-956-2400
Joan Heinz, prin.   Fax 956-2405

West Bloomfield SD   6,800/K-12
5810 Commerce Rd   48324   248-865-6420
Dr. Gary Faber, supt.   Fax 865-6481
www.westbloomfield.k12.mi.us/
Abbott MS   800/6-8
3380 Orchard Lake Rd   48324   248-865-3670
Amy Hughes, prin.   Fax 865-3671
Orchard Lake MS   800/6-8
6000 Orchard Lake Rd   48322   248-865-4480
Sonja James, prin.   Fax 865-4481
West Bloomfield HS   2,000/9-12
4925 Orchard Lake Rd   48323   248-865-6720
Bob Pyles, prin.   Fax 865-6721

Jewish Academy of Metropolitan Detroit   200/9-12
6600 W Maple Rd   48322   248-592-5263
Rabbi Lee Buckman, prin.   Fax 592-0022

West Branch, Ogemaw, Pop. 1,916

West Branch-Rose City Area SD   2,600/K-12
PO Box 308   48661   989-343-2000
David L. Marston, supt.   Fax 343-2006
www.wbrc.k12.mi.us/
Ogemaw Heights HS   900/9-12
PO Box 308   48661   989-343-2020
David Walby, prin.   Fax 343-2130
Surline MS   600/5-8
PO Box 308   48661   989-343-2140
Larry DeAugustine, prin.   Fax 343-2239
Other Schools – See Rose City

Ogemaw Hills Christian S   100/K-12
2106 S Gray Rd   48661   989-345-2084
LeAnne Gormong, admin.   Fax 345-2094

Westland, Wayne, Pop. 85,707

Livonia SD
Supt. — See Livonia
Western Wayne Skill Center - Ford   Vo/Tech
8075 Ritz Ave   48185   734-744-2810
Alphonse DiPaolo, prin.   Fax 744-2811

Wayne-Westland Community SD   14,000/PK-12
36745 Marquette St   48185   734-419-2000
Dr. Gregory Baracy, supt.   Fax 595-2123
www.wwcsd.net/
Adams MS   800/6-8
33705 Palmer Rd   48186   734-419-2380
David Ingham, prin.   Fax 595-2374
Ford Career-Technical Center   Vo/Tech
36455 Marquette St   48185   734-419-2100
Ginny Kowalski, prin.   Fax 595-2127
Glenn HS   2,100/9-12
36105 Marquette St   48185   734-419-2300
Joan Sedik, prin.   Fax 595-2338

Marshall MS 1,000/6-8
35100 Bay View St 48186 734-419-2277
Robert Van Valkenburg Ph.D., prin. Fax 595-2588
Stevenson MS 800/6-8
38501 Palmer Rd 48186 734-419-2350
Ginny O'Brien, prin. Fax 595-2692
Tinkham Adult and Community Education Adult
450 S Venoy Rd 48186 734-419-2427
Tim Dziobak, prin. Fax 595-2439
Other Schools – See Wayne

Huron Valley Lutheran HS 100/9-12
33740 Cowan Rd 48185 734-525-0160
Daniel Schultz, prin. Fax 525-6717
Lutheran HS Westland 200/9-12
33300 Cowan Rd 48185 734-422-2090
Steven Schwecke, prin. Fax 422-8566
Virginia Farrell Beauty School Post-Sec.
34580 Ford Rd 48185 734-729-9220
Westland Christian Academy 500/K-12
34033 Palmer Rd 48186 734-326-3581
Carol Enersen, admin. Fax 326-3352

White Cloud, Newaygo, Pop. 1,431
White Cloud SD 1,500/PK-12
PO Box 1003 49349 231-689-6820
Ethan Ebenstein, supt. Fax 689-3210
www.whitecloud.net
White Cloud HS 500/9-12
PO Box 1000 49349 231-689-1707
Tom Cameron, prin. Fax 689-3349
White Cloud MS 400/6-8
PO Box 1001 49349 231-689-2181
Tom Cameron, prin. Fax 689-3339

Whitehall, Muskegon, Pop. 2,808
Whitehall SD 2,100/PK-12
541 E Slocum St 49461 231-893-1005
Darlene Dongvillo, supt. Fax 894-6450
www.whitehall.k12.mi.us
Whitehall HS 700/9-12
3100 White Lake Dr 49461 231-893-1020
John VanLoon, prin. Fax 893-2923
Whitehall MS 500/6-8
401 S Elizabeth St 49461 231-893-1030
Dale McKenzie, prin. Fax 894-6844

White Lake, Oakland, Pop. 22,608
Huron Valley SD
Supt. — See Highland
Lakeland HS 1,400/9-12
1630 Bogie Lake Rd 48383 248-676-8320
Bob Behnke, prin. Fax 676-8381
White Lake MS 700/6-8
1450 Bogie Lake Rd 48383 248-684-8004
Paul Gmelin, prin. Fax 676-8437

White Pigeon, Saint Joseph, Pop. 1,619
White Pigeon Community SD 800/K-12
410 Prairie Ave 49099 269-483-7676
Marvin Schneider, supt. Fax 483-2256
www.wpcschools.org
White Pigeon HS 300/9-12
410 Prairie Ave 49099 269-483-7679
Patrick West, prin. Fax 483-8742
White Pigeon MS 7-8
410 Prairie Ave 49099 269-483-7679
Patrick West, prin. Fax 483-2256

Whitmore Lake, Washtenaw, Pop. 3,251
Whitmore Lake SD 1,300/K-12
8845 Main St 48189 734-449-4464
Scott Menzel, supt. Fax 449-5336
www.wlps.net/
Whitmore Lake HS 400/9-12
8877 Main St 48189 734-449-4461
Tom DeKeyser, prin. Fax 449-5576
Whitmore Lake MS 400/5-8
8845 Main St 48189 734-449-4715
Mary Anne Waters, prin. Fax 449-1042

Whittemore, Iosco, Pop. 466
Whittemore-Prescott Area SD 1,400/K-12
PO Box 250 48770 989-756-2500
Ted Matuszak, supt. Fax 756-2278
www.wpas.net/
Whittemore-Prescott Area HS 400/9-12
PO Box 280 48770 989-756-2501
Scott Reynolds, prin. Fax 756-3363
Other Schools – See Prescott

Williamston, Ingham, Pop. 3,784
Williamston Community SD 2,100/PK-12
418 Highland St 48895 517-655-4361
Joel Raddatz, supt. Fax 655-7500
www.wmston.k12.mi.us
Williamston HS 700/9-12
3939 Vanneter Rd 48895 517-655-2142
Randal Bowles, prin. Fax 655-7501
Williamston MS 500/6-8
3845 Vanneter Rd 48895 517-655-4668
Brian DeRath, prin. Fax 655-7502

Wilson, Menominee, Pop. 1,391

Wilson Jr. Academy 50/1-10
N13925 County Road 551 49896 906-639-2566
Martin Cunningham, prin. Fax 639-2566

Wixom, Oakland, Pop. 13,548
Oakland ISD
Supt. — See Waterford
Oakland Technical Campus SW Vo/Tech
1000 Beck Rd 48393 248-668-5600
Allen Beckner, dean Fax 668-5670

Walled Lake Consolidated SD
Supt. — See Walled Lake
Banks MS 900/6-8
1760 Charms Rd 48393 248-956-2200
Mark Hess, prin. Fax 956-2205

Wolverine, Cheboygan, Pop. 356
Wolverine Community SD 300/K-12
PO Box 219 49799 231-525-8201
Susan Denise, supt. Fax 525-8591
www.wolverine.k12.mi.us
Wolverine HS 100/7-12
PO Box 219 49799 231-525-9050
Gary Phillips, prin. Fax 525-8251

Woodhaven, Wayne, Pop. 12,802
Gibraltar SD 3,300/PK-12
19370 Vreeland Rd 48183 734-692-4000
Eric Federico, supt. Fax 692-7577
resa.net/gibraltar
Other Schools – See Gibraltar

Woodhaven-Brownstown SD
Supt. — See Brownstown
Henry MS 900/8-9
24825 Hall Rd 48183 734-362-6100
Molly Mazei, prin. Fax 362-3045

Woodland, Barry, Pop. 496
Lakewood SD
Supt. — See Lake Odessa
Lakewood MS 600/6-8
8699 Brown Rd 48897 616-374-2400
David Nisbet, prin. Fax 374-2424

Wyandotte, Wayne, Pop. 27,432
Wyandotte SD 4,300/K-12
639 Oak St 48192 734-759-5000
Dr. Patricia Cole, supt. Fax 759-5009
www.wyandotte.org
Roosevelt HS 1,400/9-12
540 Eureka Rd 48192 734-759-5000
Mary McFarlane, prin. Fax 759-5009
Wilson MS 700/7-8
1275 15th St 48192 734-759-5300
Thomas Kell, prin. Fax 759-5309

Our Lady of Mt. Carmel HS 100/9-12
2609 10th St 48192 734-284-7311
Sr. Mary Van Camp, prin. Fax 284-8566

Wyoming, Kent, Pop. 70,205
Godfrey-Lee SD 1,400/K-12
963 Joosten St SW 49509 616-241-4722
Jack Wallington, supt. Fax 241-4707
www.remc8.k12.mi.us/godfrey
Lee HS 400/9-12
1335 Lee St SW 49509 616-452-3296
David Britten, prin. Fax 241-4677
Lee MS 300/6-8
1335 Lee St SW 49509 616-452-3298
David Britten, prin. Fax 241-4677

Godwin Heights SD 2,100/PK-12
15 36th St SW 49548 616-252-2090
Valdis Gailitis, supt. Fax 252-2232
www.godwinschools.org
Godwin Heights HS 700/9-12
50 35th St SW 49548 616-252-2050
Jonathan Whan, prin. Fax 252-2067
Godwin Heights MS 500/6-8
111 36th St SE 49548 616-252-2070
Nkenge Bergan, prin. Fax 252-2075

Wyoming SD 5,100/K-12
3575 Gladiola Ave SW, 616-530-7550
Jon A. Felske, supt. Fax 530-7557
www.wyoming.k12.mi.us
Jackson Park MS 600/6-8
1331 33rd St SW 49509 616-530-7540
Kirk Bloomquist, prin. Fax 249-7659
Newhall MS 600/6-8
1840 38th St SW, 616-530-7590
Adrian Lamar, prin. Fax 249-7673
Rogers HS 800/9-12
1350 Prairie Pkwy SW 49509 616-530-7580
Gary Karasinski, prin. Fax 530-7589
Wyoming Park HS 800/9-12
2125 Wrenwood St SW, 616-530-7560
Stewart Schofield, prin. Fax 249-7649

Potter's House HS 100/9-12
2500 Newport St SW, 616-249-8050
John Walcott, admin. Fax 249-8555
Tri-Unity Christian HS 200/7-12
2104 44th St SW, 616-532-6766
Tom Aldrich, prin. Fax 532-8701

Yale, Saint Clair, Pop. 2,005
Yale SD 2,300/K-12
198 School Dr 48097 810-387-4274
Ralph Darin, supt. Fax 387-4418
www.yale.k12.mi.us
Yale HS 700/9-12
247 School Dr 48097 810-387-3231
Kenneth Nicholl, prin. Fax 387-9108
Yale JHS 500/6-8
198 School Dr 48097 810-387-3231
Joseph Haynes, prin. Fax 387-9207

Ypsilanti, Washtenaw, Pop. 22,492
Lincoln Consolidated SD 5,900/PK-12
8970 Whittaker Rd 48197 734-484-7000
Fred Williams, supt. Fax 484-1212
lincoln.k12.mi.us
Lincoln HS 1,400/9-12
7425 Willis Rd 48197 734-484-7004
Derrick Coleman, prin. Fax 484-7012
Lincoln MS 1,200/6-8
8744 Whittaker Rd 48197 734-484-7033
Lynn Cleary, prin. Fax 484-7088

Willow Run Community SD 2,700/PK-12
2171 E Michigan Ave 48198 734-481-8200
Ron Ciranna, supt. Fax 481-8151
wrcs.k12.mi.us
Willow Run HS 700/9-12
235 Spencer Ln 48198 734-961-6015
Dr. Walter Jenkins, prin. Fax 481-8185
Willow Run MS 500/6-8
235 Spencer Ln 48198 734-961-6162
Melvin Anglin, prin. Fax 481-8170
Adult Education Adult
181 Oregon St 48198 734-961-6454
Karyn Goven, prin. Fax 482-3550

Ypsilanti SD 4,200/PK-12
1885 Packard Rd 48197 734-714-1218
Dr. James Hawkins, supt. Fax 714-1220
www.ypsd.org
East MS 500/6-8
510 Emerick St 48198 734-714-1400
Janice Sturdivant, prin. Fax 714-1423
Regional Career Technical Center Vo/Tech
2095 Packard Rd 48197 734-714-1276
Bob Wilkinson, prin. Fax 714-1274
West MS 600/6-8
105 N Mansfield St 48197 734-714-1300
Monica Merritt, prin. Fax 714-1303
Ypsilanti HS 1,200/9-12
2095 Packard Rd 48197 734-714-1000
Layne Hunt, prin. Fax 714-1029

Ave Maria College Post-Sec.
300 W Forest Ave 48197 734-337-4545
Calvary Christian Academy 200/K-12
1007 Ecorse Rd 48198 734-482-1990
Fax 484-5118
Eastern Michigan University 48197 Post-Sec.
734-487-1849

Zeeland, Ottawa, Pop. 5,645
Zeeland SD 5,700/PK-12
PO Box 110 49464 616-748-3000
Gary L. Feenstra, supt. Fax 748-3035
www.zeeland.k12.mi.us
Cityside MS 600/6-8
320 E Main Ave 49464 616-748-3200
Jon Voss, prin. Fax 748-3210
Creekside MS 500/6-8
179 W Roosevelt Ave 49464 616-748-3300
Greg Eding, prin. Fax 748-3325
Zeeland East HS 1,600/9-12
3333 96th Ave 49464 616-748-3100
Nate Robrahn, prin. Fax 748-3198
Zeeland West HS 800/9-12
3390 100th Ave 49464 616-748-4500
Colleen Johnson, prin. Fax 748-4505

MINNESOTA

MN DEPARTMENT OF EDUCATION
1500 Highway 36 W, Roseville 55113-4035
Telephone 651-582-8200
Website cfl.state.mn.us

Commissioner of Education   Alice Seagren

PUBLIC, PRIVATE AND CATHOLIC SECONDARY SCHOOLS

Ada, Norman, Pop. 1,601
Ada-Borup SD 2854 — 500/PK-12
  604 W Thorpe Ave 56510 — 218-784-5310
  Ollen Church, supt. — Fax 784-2237
  www.ada.k12.mn.us
Ada-Borup JSHS — 300/7-12
  604 W Thorpe Ave 56510 — 218-784-5300
  Michael Kolness, prin. — Fax 784-3475

Adams, Mower, Pop. 787
Southland SD 500 — 700/K-12
  PO Box 351 55909 — 507-582-3283
  Gary Kuphal, supt. — Fax 582-7813
  www.isd500.k12.mn.us
Southland HS — 300/9-12
  PO Box 351 55909 — 507-582-3568
  Jon Ellerbusch, prin. — Fax 582-7813
Southland MS — 200/6-8
  PO Box 351 55909 — 507-582-3568
  Jon Ellerbusch, prin. — Fax 582-7813

Adrian, Nobles, Pop. 1,230
Adrian SD 511 — 700/PK-12
  PO Box 40 56110 — 507-483-2266
  Roger Graff, supt. — Fax 483-2342
  www.adrianschool.net
Adrian HS — 200/9-12
  PO Box 40 56110 — 507-483-2232
  Roger Graff, prin. — Fax 483-2375
Adrian MS — 200/6-8
  PO Box 40 56110 — 507-483-2232
  Roger Graff, prin. — Fax 483-2375

Aitkin, Aitkin, Pop. 2,013
Aitkin SD 1 — 1,300/PK-12
  306 2nd St NW 56431 — 218-927-2115
  Bernie Novak, supt. — Fax 927-4234
  www.aitkin.k12.mn.us
Aitkin HS — 600/7-12
  306 2nd St NW 56431 — 218-927-2115
  Steven Wilkowski, prin. — Fax 927-4234

Albany, Stearns, Pop. 1,896
Albany SD 745 — 1,600/PK-12
  PO Box 330 56307 — 320-845-2171
  John Tritabaugh, supt. — Fax 845-4017
  www.albany.k12.mn.us
Albany HS — 500/9-12
  PO Box 330 56307 — 320-845-2171
  Tim Wege, prin. — Fax 845-4017
Albany JHS — 300/7-8
  PO Box 330 56307 — 320-845-2171
  Charles Griffith, prin. — Fax 845-4017

Alberta, Stevens, Pop. 142
Chokio-Alberta SD 771
  Supt. — See Chokio
Chokio-Alberta JSHS — 100/7-12
  PO Box 96 56207 — 320-324-7141
  Paul Brownlow, prin. — Fax 324-7143

Albert Lea, Freeborn, Pop. 17,886
Albert Lea SD 241 — 3,500/K-12
  211 W Richway Dr 56007 — 507-379-4800
  David Prescott, supt. — Fax 379-4898
  albertlea.k12.mn.us
Albert Lea HS — 1,200/9-12
  2000 Tiger Ln 56007 — 507-379-5340
  Alan Root, prin. — Fax 379-5498
Southwest MS — 600/7-8
  1601 W Front St 56007 — 507-379-5240
  Marsha Langseth, prin. — Fax 379-5338

Riverland Community College — Post-Sec.
  2200 Riverland Dr 56007 — 507-373-0656

Albertville, Wright, Pop. 5,236
St. Michael-Albertville SD 885 — 4,800/PK-12
  11343 50th St NE 55301 — 763-497-3180
  Dr. Marcia Ziegler, supt. — Fax 497-6588
  www.stma.k12.mn.us
St Michael-Albertville HS — 1,000/9-12
  11343 50th St NE 55301 — 763-497-2192
  Mark Minkler, prin. — Fax 497-6590
Other Schools – See Saint Michael

Alden, Freeborn, Pop. 638
Alden-Conger ISD 242 — 400/K-12
  PO Box 99 56009 — 507-874-3240
  Joe Guanella, supt. — Fax 874-2747
  www.alden-conger.org
Alden-Conger HS — 300/6-12
  PO Box 99 56009 — 507-874-3240
  Paul Ragatz, dean — Fax 874-2747

Alexandria, Douglas, Pop. 9,746
Alexandria SD 206 — 4,100/K-12
  PO Box 308 56308 — 320-762-2141
  Dr. Ric Dressen, supt. — Fax 762-2765
  www.alexandria.k12.mn.us
Discovery JHS — 1,100/7-9
  510 McKay Ave N 56308 — 320-762-7900
  Chad Duwenhoegger, prin. — Fax 762-8347
Jefferson SHS — 1,100/10-12
  1401 Jefferson St 56308 — 320-762-2142
  Joseph Hill, prin. — Fax 762-7749

Alexandria Technical College — Post-Sec.
  1601 Jefferson St 56308 — 320-762-0221

Amboy, Blue Earth, Pop. 555
Maple River SD 2135
  Supt. — See Mapleton
Maple River West MS — 200/6-8
  PO Box 70 56010 — 507-674-3046
  Marcene Kluender, prin. — Fax 674-3079

Andover, Anoka, Pop. 28,938
Anoka-Hennepin SD 11
  Supt. — See Coon Rapids
Andover HS — 1,400/9-12
  2115 Andover Blvd NW 55304 — 763-506-8400
  Dan Dehnicke, prin. — Fax 767-3575
Oak View MS — 1,200/6-8
  15400 Hanson Blvd NW 55304 — 763-506-5600
  Diane Steffen, prin. — Fax 506-5603

Meadow Creek Christian S — 800/PK-12
  3037 Bunker Lake Blvd NW 55304 — 763-427-4595
  Wendall Harris, supt. — Fax 427-3398

Annandale, Wright, Pop. 2,866
Annandale SD 876 — 1,800/K-12
  PO Box 190 55302 — 320-274-5602
  Steve Niklaus, supt. — Fax 274-5978
  www.annandale.k12.mn.us
Annandale HS — 600/9-12
  PO Box 190 55302 — 320-274-8208
  Richard Ofstedal, prin. — Fax 274-2316
Annandale MS — 600/5-8
  PO Box 190 55302 — 320-274-8226
  Dean Jennissen, prin. — Fax 274-5978

Anoka, Anoka, Pop. 17,858
Anoka-Hennepin SD 11
  Supt. — See Coon Rapids
Anoka HS — 2,500/9-12
  3939 7th Ave 55303 — 763-506-6200
  Terry Abram, prin. — Fax 506-6203
Moore MS — 1,000/6-8
  1523 5th Ave 55303 — 763-506-5000
  Kathy Baufield, prin. — Fax 506-5003
Sandburg MS — 900/6-8
  1902 2nd Ave 55303 — 763-506-6000
  Mary Wolverton, prin. — Fax 506-6003
Secondary Technical Education Program — Vo/Tech
  1355 W Highway 10 55303 — 763-433-4000
  Ginny Karbowski, dir.

Anoka Technical College — Post-Sec.
  1355 W Highway 10 55303 — 763-576-4700

Apple Valley, Dakota, Pop. 48,938
Rosemount-Apple Valley-Eagan ISD 196
  Supt. — See Rosemount
Apple Valley HS — 2,300/9-12
  14450 Hayes Rd 55124 — 952-431-8200
  Steve Degenaar, prin. — Fax 431-8744
Eastview HS — 2,200/9-12
  6200 140th St W 55124 — 952-431-8900
  Richard Dewey, prin. — Fax 431-8911
Falcon Ridge MS — 1,300/6-8
  12900 Johnny Cake Ridge Rd 55124 — 952-431-8760
  Noel Mehus, prin. — Fax 431-8770
School of Enviromental Studies — 500/11-12
  12155 Johnny Cake Ridge Rd 55124 — 952-431-8750
  Dan Bodette, prin. — Fax 431-8755
Scott Highlands MS — 900/6-8
  14011 Pilot Knob Rd 55124 — 952-423-7581
  Daniel Wilharber, prin. — Fax 423-7601
Valley MS — 1,200/6-8
  900 Garden View Dr 55124 — 952-431-8300
  Dave McKeag, prin. — Fax 431-8313

Arden Hills, Ramsey, Pop. 9,952
Mounds View SD 621
  Supt. — See Shoreview

Mounds View HS — 1,900/9-12
  1900 Lake Valentine Rd 55112 — 651-633-4031
  Julie Wikelius, prin. — Fax 639-6063

Arlington, Sibley, Pop. 2,070
Sibley East SD 2310 — 1,300/PK-12
  PO Box 1000 55307 — 507-964-2292
  John Langenbrunner, supt. — Fax 964-8245
  www.sibleyeast.org/
Sibley East SHS — 300/10-12
  PO Box 1000 55307 — 507-964-8235
  James Swanson, prin. — Fax 964-8245
Other Schools – See Gaylord

Ashby, Grant, Pop. 462
Ashby SD 261 — 300/K-12
  PO Box 30 56309 — 218-747-2257
  Allan Jensen, supt. — Fax 747-2289
  www.ashby.k12.mn.us
Ashby JSHS — 100/7-12
  PO Box 30 56309 — 218-747-2257
  Roger Jansen, prin. — Fax 747-2289

Country Bible Christian Academy — 50/PK-12
  27871 140th Ave 56309 — 218-685-4026
  Thomas Aul, admin. — Fax 685-6712

Aurora, Saint Louis, Pop. 1,805
Mesabi East SD 2711 — 900/PK-12
  601 N 1st St W 55705 — 218-229-3321
  Gene Paulson, supt. — Fax 229-3736
  www.mesabieast.k12.mn.us/
Mesabi East JSHS — 500/7-12
  601 N 1st St W 55705 — 218-229-3321
  Jorma Rahkola, prin. — Fax 229-3736

Austin, Mower, Pop. 23,466
Austin SD 492 — 3,600/K-12
  401 3rd Ave NW 55912 — 507-433-0966
  Dr. Candace Raskin, supt. — Fax 433-0950
  www.austin.k12.mn.us
Austin HS — 1,200/9-12
  301 3rd St NW 55912 — 507-433-0401
  Bradley Bergstrom, prin. — Fax 433-0403
Ellis MS — 900/6-8
  1700 4th Ave SE 55912 — 507-433-8800
  Katie Berglund, prin. — Fax 433-7330

Pacelli HS — 100/9-12
  311 4th St NW 55912 — 507-437-3278
  Norm Blaser, prin. — Fax 433-5693
Riverland Community College — Post-Sec.
  1900 8th Ave NW 55912 — 507-433-0600

Babbitt, Saint Louis, Pop. 1,653
St. Louis County SD 2142
  Supt. — See Virginia
Babbitt JSHS — 200/7-12
  30 South Dr 55706 — 218-827-3101
  Steve Reznicek, prin. — Fax 827-3103

Badger, Roseau, Pop. 467
Badger SD 676 — 200/PK-12
  PO Box 68 56714 — 218-528-3201
  Gwen Borgen, supt. — Fax 528-3366
  www.badger.k12.mn.us
Badger JSHS — 100/7-12
  PO Box 68 56714 — 218-528-3201
  Gwen Borgen, prin. — Fax 528-3366

Bagley, Clearwater, Pop. 1,218
Bagley SD 162 — 1,100/PK-12
  202 Bagley Ave NW 56621 — 218-694-6184
  Gary Bratvold, supt. — Fax 694-3221
  www.bagley.k12.mn.us/
Bagley JSHS — 500/7-12
  1130 Main Ave N 56621 — 218-694-3120
  Steve Cairns, prin. — Fax 694-3225

Barnesville, Clay, Pop. 2,245
Barnesville SD 146 — 800/K-12
  PO Box 189 56514 — 218-354-2217
  Phil Jensen, supt. — Fax 354-7260
  barnesville.k12.mn.us/
Barnesville JSHS — 400/7-12
  PO Box 189 56514 — 218-354-2228
  Bryan Strand, prin. — Fax 354-2305

Barnum, Carlton, Pop. 565
Barnum SD 91 — 700/PK-12
  3675 County Road 140 55707 — 218-389-6978
  David Bottem, supt. — Fax 389-3259
  www.barnum.k12.mn.us

Barnum JSHS   300/7-12
   3675 County Road 140   55707   218-389-3273
   William Crandall, prin.   Fax 389-3259

Barrett, Grant, Pop. 351
  West Central Area SD 2342   800/PK-12
   301 County Road 2   56311   320-528-2650
   Gerald Ness, supt.   Fax 528-2279
   www.westcentralareaschools.net
  West Central Area Secondary S   400/7-12
   301 County Road 2   56311   320-528-2520
   Nels Onstad, prin.   Fax 528-2609

Battle Lake, Otter Tail, Pop. 782
  Battle Lake SD 542   500/K-12
   402 Summit St W   56515   218-864-5215
   Rick Bleichner, supt.   Fax 864-8651
  Battle Lake JSHS   300/7-12
   402 Summit St W   56515   218-864-5215
   Jeff Drake, prin.   Fax 864-8651

Baudette, Lake of the Woods, Pop. 1,044
  Lake of the Woods SD 390   700/PK-12
   PO Box 310   56623   218-634-2735
   Connie Nelson, supt.   Fax 634-2467
   www.blw.k12.mn.us/
  Lake of the Woods JSHS   400/7-12
   PO Box 310   56623   218-634-2510
   Mark Nohner, prin.   Fax 634-2750

Baxter, Crow Wing, Pop. 6,733
  Brainerd SD 181
   Supt. — See Brainerd
  Forestview MS   1,000/5-8
   12149 Knollwood Dr   56425   218-822-6900
   Carol Pasanen, prin.   Fax 822-6238

  Lake Region Christian S   200/PK-12
   7398 Fairview Rd   56425   218-828-1226
   Mark Monroe, prin.   Fax 828-1643

Becker, Sherburne, Pop. 3,263
  Becker SD 726   2,500/PK-12
   12000 Hancock St SE   55308   763-261-4502
   Steven Dooley, supt.   Fax 261-4559
   www.becker.k12.mn.us
  Becker HS   700/9-12
   12000 Hancock St SE   55308   763-261-4501
   David Lund, prin.   Fax 261-4559
  Becker MS   600/6-8
   12000 Hancock St SE   55308   763-261-6300
   Nancy Helmer, prin.   Fax 261-6306

Belgrade, Stearns, Pop. 743
  Belgrade-Brooten-Elrosa SD 2364   800/PK-12
   PO Box 339   56312   320-254-8213
   Robert Dell, supt.   Fax 254-3785
  Belgrade-Brooten-Elrosa JSHS   400/7-12
   PO Box 339   56312   320-254-8211
   Brian Gauer, prin.   Fax 254-3784

Belle Plaine, Scott, Pop. 4,032
  Belle Plaine SD 716   1,400/PK-12
   220 S Market St   56011   952-873-2400
   Kelly D. Smith, supt.   Fax 873-6909
   belleplaine.k12.mn.us
  Belle Plaine HS   400/9-12
   220 S Market St   56011   952-873-2403
   Lowell Hoffman, prin.   Fax 873-6909
  Belle Plaine JHS   200/7-8
   130 S Willow St   56011   952-873-2402
   Matthew Hillman, dean   Fax 873-3314

Bellingham, Lac qui Parle, Pop. 197
  Bellingham SD 371   100/K-12
   522 1st St   56212   320-568-2118
   Ray Seiler, supt.   Fax 568-2230
  Bellingham HS   50/7-12
   522 1st St   56212   320-588-2118
   Ray Seiler, prin.   Fax 588-2230

Bemidji, Beltrami, Pop. 12,724
  Bemidji SD 31   4,500/K-12
   3300 Gillett Dr NW   56601   218-333-3100
   Dr. James Hess, supt.   Fax 333-3129
   www.bemidji.k12.mn.us
  Bemidji HS   1,500/9-12
   3300 Gillett Dr NW   56601   218-444-1600
   Richard Anderson, prin.   Fax 444-1630
  Bemidji MS   1,100/6-8
   3300 Gillett Dr NW   56601   218-333-3215
   James Wheeler, prin.   Fax 333-3333

  Bemidji State University   Post-Sec.
   1500 Birchmont Dr NE   56601   218-755-2000
  Northwest Technical College   Post-Sec.
   905 Grant Ave SE   56601   218-755-4270
  Oak Hills Christian College   Post-Sec.
   1600 Oak Hills Rd SW   56601   888-751-8670

Benson, Swift, Pop. 3,279
  Benson SD 777   1,100/PK-12
   1400 Montana Ave   56215   320-843-2710
   Carl Remmers, supt.   Fax 843-2262
   benson.k12.mn.us
  Benson JSHS   500/7-12
   1400 Montana Ave   56215   320-843-2710
   Lee Westrum, prin.   Fax 843-2262

Bertha, Todd, Pop. 450
  Bertha-Hewitt SD 786   500/PK-12
   PO Box 8   56437   218-924-2500
   Larry Werder, supt.   Fax 924-3252
  Bertha JSHS   200/7-12
   PO Box 8   56437   218-924-2500
   Robert Sieling, prin.   Fax 924-3252

Bigfork, Itasca, Pop. 462
  Grand Rapids SD 318
   Supt. — See Grand Rapids
  Bigfork JSHS   100/7-12
   PO Box 228   56628   218-743-3444
   Scott Patrow, prin.   Fax 743-3443

Big Lake, Sherburne, Pop. 7,796
  Big Lake SD 727   3,200/PK-12
   PO Box 407   55309   763-262-2536
   Jonathan Miller, supt.   Fax 262-2539
   www.biglake.k12.mn.us
  Big Lake HS   800/9-12
   PO Box 749   55309   763-262-2547
   Mark Canton, prin.   Fax 262-2543
  Big Lake MS   800/6-8
   PO Box 720   55309   763-262-2567
   Glenn Evans, prin.   Fax 262-2563

Birchdale, Koochiching
  South Koochiching-Rainy River SD 363
   Supt. — See Northome
  Indus JSHS   100/7-12
   8560 Highway 11   56629   218-634-2425
   Wade Pilloud, prin.   Fax 634-1334

Bird Island, Renville, Pop. 1,186
  BOLD SD 2534   800/K-12
   PO Box 460   55310   320-365-4060
   Dr. Michael Funk, supt.   Fax 365-3515
   boldschools.govoffice.com/
  Other Schools – See Olivia

Blackduck, Beltrami, Pop. 748
  Blackduck SD 32   800/PK-12
   PO Box 550   56630   218-835-5200
   Robert G. Doetsch, supt.   Fax 835-4491
   www.blackduck.k12.mn.us
  Blackduck HS   400/7-12
   PO Box 550   56630   218-835-5210
   Wendy Templin, prin.   Fax 835-4491

Blaine, Anoka, Pop. 50,425
  Anoka-Hennepin SD 11
   Supt. — See Coon Rapids
  Blaine HS   2,900/9-12
   12555 University Ave NE   55434   763-506-6500
   Norm Hande, prin.   Fax 506-6503
  Roosevelt MS   1,200/6-8
   650 NE Main St   55434   763-506-5800
   Greg Blodgett, prin.   Fax 506-5803

  Spring Lake Park SD 16
   Supt. — See Spring Lake Park
  Westwood MS   1,000/6-8
   711 91st Ave NE   55434   763-784-8625
   Paula Hoff, prin.   Fax 786-7815

  Regency Beauty Academy   Post-Sec.
   40 County Road 10 NE   55434   763-784-9102

Blooming Prairie, Steele, Pop. 1,960
  Blooming Prairie SD 756   800/PK-12
   202 4th Ave NW   55917   507-583-4426
   Barry Olson, supt.   Fax 583-7952
   www.blossoms.k12.mn.us
  Blooming Prairie JSHS   400/7-12
   202 4th Ave NW   55917   507-583-4426
   Barry Olson, prin.   Fax 583-7952

Bloomington, Hennepin, Pop. 83,080
  Bloomington SD 271   10,500/K-12
   1350 W 106th St   55431   952-681-6400
   Dr. Gary Prest, supt.   Fax 681-6401
   www.bloomington.k12.mn.us
  Jefferson HS   1,700/9-12
   4001 W 102nd St   55437   952-806-7600
   Steve Hill, prin.   Fax 806-7601
  Kennedy HS   1,800/9-12
   9701 Nicollet Ave S   55420   952-681-5000
   Ron Simmons, prin.   Fax 681-5001
  Oak Grove MS   800/6-8
   1300 W 106th St   55431   952-681-6600
   Ray Knoss, prin.   Fax 681-6601
  Olson MS   900/6-8
   4551 W 102nd St   55437   952-806-8600
   Dr. Judith Johnson, prin.   Fax 806-8601
  Valley View MS   800/6-8
   8900 Portland Ave S   55420   952-681-5800
   Dr. Debra Fincham, prin.   Fax 681-5801

  Academy College   Post-Sec.
   1101 E 78th St   55420   952-851-0066
  Bethany Academy   300/K-12
   4300 W 98th St   55437   952-831-8686
   Jesse Hinrichs, supt.   Fax 831-9568
  Concordia Academy - Bloomington   500/9-12
   8201 Park Ave S   55420   952-854-0224
   Lynn Henry, prin.   Fax 854-8527
  National American University   Post-Sec.
   112 W Market   55425   952-883-0439
  Normandale Community College   Post-Sec.
   9700 France Ave S   55431   952-832-6000
  Northwestern Health Sciences University   Post-Sec.
   2501 W 84th St   55431   952-888-4777
  Scot Lewis School of Cosmetology   Post-Sec.
   9749 Lyndale Ave S   55420   952-881-8662
  Trinity S at River Ridge   400/7-12
   2300 E 88th St   55420   952-854-0008
   William Wacker, prin.   Fax 854-3232

Blue Earth, Faribault, Pop. 3,519
  Blue Earth Area ISD 2860   1,400/K-12
   315 E 6th St   56013   507-526-3188
   Dale Brandsoy, supt.   Fax 526-2432
   www.blueearth.k12.mn.us

  Blue Earth Area MS   200/7-8
   315 E 6th St   56013   507-526-3115
   Melissa McGuire, prin.   Fax 526-2432
  Blue Earth HS   500/9-12
   1125 N Highway 169   56013   507-526-3201
   Jack Eustice, prin.   Fax 526-3260

Bovey, Itasca, Pop. 659
  Greenway SD 316
   Supt. — See Coleraine
  Connor-Jasper MS   400/5-8
   PO Box 40   55709   218-245-2661
   Dennis Perreault, prin.   Fax 245-3483

Braham, Isanti, Pop. 1,374
  Braham SD 314   900/K-12
   PO Box 488   55006   320-396-3313
   Nicholas Waldoch, supt.   Fax 396-3068
   www.braham.k12.mn.us
  Braham Area JSHS   400/7-12
   PO Box 488   55006   320-396-4444
   Kurt Kahlenbeck, prin.   Fax 396-3068

Brainerd, Crow Wing, Pop. 13,722
  Brainerd SD 181   5,000/PK-12
   804 Oak St   56401   218-822-6900
   Gerald Walseth, supt.   Fax 822-6901
   www.brainerd.k12.mn.us
  Brainerd HS South Campus   9-9
   400 Quince St   56401   218-828-5200
   William Severson, prin.   Fax 828-5201
  Brainerd SHS   1,600/10-12
   702 S 5th St   56401   218-824-6200
   Erich Heise, prin.   Fax 824-6325
  Other Schools – See Baxter

  Central Lakes College   Post-Sec.
   501 W College Dr   56401   218-855-8000

Brandon, Douglas, Pop. 426
  Brandon SD 207   300/PK-12
   PO Box 185   56315   320-524-2263
   Mark Westby, supt.   Fax 524-2228
   www.brandon.k12.mn.us
  Brandon HS   200/7-12
   PO Box 185   56315   320-524-2263
   Tom Trisko, prin.   Fax 524-2228

Breckenridge, Wilkin, Pop. 3,458
  Breckenridge SD 846   900/PK-12
   710 13th St N   56520   218-643-2694
   David Pace, supt.   Fax 643-5229
   www.breckenridge.k12.mn.us
  Breckenridge HS   300/9-12
   710 13th St N   56520   218-643-2694
   Daniel Bettin, prin.   Fax 643-5229
  Breckenridge MS   200/6-8
   810 Beede Ave   56520   218-643-6681
   Donald Schill, prin.   Fax 643-5021

Brooklyn Center, Hennepin, Pop. 28,362
  Brooklyn Center SD 286   1,700/PK-12
   6500 Humboldt Ave N   55430   763-561-2120
      Fax 560-2647

   www.brookcntr.k12.mn.us/index
  Brooklyn Center JSHS   800/7-12
   6500 Humboldt Ave N   55430   763-561-2120
   E. Rudy Ross, prin.   Fax 561-1062

  Brown College   Post-Sec.
   6860 Shingle Creek Pkwy   55430   763-566-2279
  Minnesota School of Business   Post-Sec.
   5910 Shingle Creek Pky #200   55430   763-566-7777
  National American University   Post-Sec.
   6120 Earle Brown Dr Ste 100   55430   763-560-8377

Brooklyn Park, Hennepin, Pop. 67,781
  Osseo SD 279
   Supt. — See Maple Grove
  Brooklyn JHS   1,100/7-9
   7377 Noble Ave N   55443   763-569-7700
   Rob Mendolia, prin.   Fax 569-7707
  North View JHS   1,200/7-9
   5869 69th Ave N   55429   763-585-7200
   Dr. McCauley, prin.   Fax 585-7210
  Park Center SHS   1,500/10-12
   7300 Brooklyn Blvd   55443   763-569-7600
   Kelli Parpart, prin.   Fax 569-7606

  Hennepin Technical College   Post-Sec.
   9000 Brooklyn Blvd   55445   763-488-2500
  North Hennepin Community College   Post-Sec.
   7411 85th Ave N   55445   763-424-0702

Browerville, Todd, Pop. 724
  Browerville SD 787   500/PK-12
   PO Box 185   56438   320-594-2272
   Larry Werder, supt.   Fax 594-8105
   www.browerville.k12.mn.us/
  Browerville JSHS   300/7-12
   PO Box 185   56438   320-594-2272
   Robert Schaefer, prin.   Fax 594-8105

Browns Valley, Traverse, Pop. 647
  Browns Valley SD 801   200/PK-8
   PO Box 56   56219   320-695-2103
   Dale Gilje, supt.   Fax 695-2868
  Browns Valley MS   100/5-8
   PO Box N   56219   320-695-2103
   Brenda Reed, prin.   Fax 695-2868

Brownton, McLeod, Pop. 804
  McLeod West SD 2887   500/K-12
   PO Box 99   55312   320-328-5214
   Thomas Hiebert, supt.   Fax 328-5216
   mcleod.k12.mn.us

McLeod West HS | 200/7-12
PO Box 99 55312 | 320-328-5214
| Fax 328-5216

Buffalo, Wright, Pop. 12,486
Buffalo SD 877 | 5,200/K-12
214 1st Ave NE 55313 | 763-682-5200
Jim Bauck, supt. | Fax 682-8785
www.buffalo.k12.mn.us
Buffalo Community MS | 1,200/6-8
1300 Highway 25 N 55313 | 763-682-8200
Julie Swaggert, prin. | Fax 682-8209
Buffalo HS | 1,700/9-12
877 Bison Blvd 55313 | 763-682-8100
Nicholas Miller, prin. | Fax 682-8118

Burnsville, Dakota, Pop. 59,805
Burnsville-Eagan-Savage ISD 191 | 11,000/K-12
100 River Ridge Ct 55337 | 952-707-2000
Benjamin Kanninen, supt. | Fax 707-2002
www.isd191.org
Burnsville SHS | 2,400/10-12
600 Highway 13 E 55337 | 952-707-2100
Kay Joyce, prin. | Fax 707-2102
Metcalf JHS | 800/7-9
2250 Diffley Rd 55337 | 952-707-2400
Kelly Ronn, prin. | Fax 707-2402
Nicollet JHS | 900/7-9
400 E 134th St 55337 | 952-707-2600
Sue Slater, prin. | Fax 707-2602
Other Schools – See Savage

Oliver Thein Beauty College | Post-Sec.
150 Cobblestone Ln 55337 | 612-435-3882

Butterfield, Watonwan, Pop. 549
Butterfield SD 836 | 200/K-12
PO Box 189 56120 | 507-956-2771
Lisa Shellum, supt. | Fax 956-3431
Butterfield JSHS | 100/7-12
PO Box 189 56120 | 507-956-2771
Lisa Shellum, prin. | Fax 956-3431

Byron, Olmsted, Pop. 3,531
Byron SD 531 | 1,600/PK-12
501 10th Ave NE 55920 | 507-775-2383
Wendy Shannon Ph.D., supt. | Fax 775-2385
bears.byron.k12.mn.us
Byron HS | 600/8-12
601 4th St NW 55920 | 507-775-2301
Michael Duffy, prin. | Fax 775-2303

Caledonia, Houston, Pop. 2,967
Caledonia SD 299 | 900/PK-12
511 W Main St 55921 | 507-725-3389
Michael Moriarty, supt. | Fax 725-3558
www.cps.k12.mn.us/
Caledonia Area HS | 400/9-12
825 N Warrior Ave 55921 | 507-725-3316
Ronald Helmers, prin. | Fax 725-3319
Caledonia Area MS | 200/6-8
825 N Warrior Ave 55921 | 507-725-3316
Brian Doty, prin. | Fax 725-3319

Cambridge, Isanti, Pop. 6,382
Cambridge-Isanti SD 911 | 4,800/PK-12
315 7th Ln NE 55008 | 763-689-6188
Bruce Novak, supt. | Fax 689-6200
www.cambridge.k12.mn.us
Cambridge-Isanti HS | 1,600/9-12
430 8th Ave NW 55008 | 763-689-6066
Mitchell Clausen, prin. | Fax 689-6060
Cambridge MS | 800/5-8
31374 Xylite St NE 55008 | 763-552-6300
Charlie Burroughs, prin. | Fax 552-6399
Minnesota Center S | 100/6-8
201 Centennial Dr 55008 | 763-691-8661
Timothy Truebenbach, prin. | Fax 691-8677
Other Schools – See Isanti

Anoka-Ramsey Community College | Post-Sec.
300 Polk St S 55008 | 763-689-7000
Cambridge Christian S | 200/K-12
2211 Main St S 55008 | 763-689-3806
Sarah Newton, admin. | Fax 689-3807

Campbell, Wilkin, Pop. 236
Campbell-Tintah SD 852 | 100/PK-12
PO Box 8 56522 | 218-630-5311
Joel Young, supt. | Fax 630-5881
www.angelfire.com/home/ctschool
Campbell-Tintah S | 100/PK-12
PO Box 8 56522 | 218-630-5311
Joel Young, prin. | Fax 630-5881

Canby, Yellow Medicine, Pop. 1,838
Canby SD 891 | 600/PK-12
307 1st St W 56220 | 507-223-2001
Loren Hacker, supt. | Fax 223-2011
www.canbymn.org/
Canby JSHS | 400/7-12
307 1st St W 56220 | 507-223-2002
Robert Slaba, prin. | Fax 223-2012

Minnesota West Community & Tech College | Post-Sec.
1011 1st St W 56220 | 800-658-2535

Cannon Falls, Goodhue, Pop. 3,881
Cannon Falls SD 252 | 1,400/PK-12
820 Minnesota St E 55009 | 507-263-3331
Todd Sesker, supt. | Fax 263-2555
www.cannonfallsschools.com
Cannon Falls HS | 700/7-12
820 Minnesota St E 55009 | 507-263-3331
Steve Fredrickson, prin. | Fax 263-2515

Carlton, Carlton, Pop. 798
Carlton SD 93 | 700/PK-12
PO Box 310 55718 | 218-384-4225
Scott Hoch, supt. | Fax 384-3543
www.carlton.k12.mn.us
Carlton JSHS | 400/7-12
PO Box 310 55718 | 218-384-4226
Dave Battaglia, prin. | Fax 384-3607

Cass Lake, Cass, Pop. 842
Cass Lake-Bena SD 115 | 1,000/PK-12
208 Central Ave NW 56633 | 218-335-2204
Todd Chessmore, supt. | Fax 335-2614
www.clbs.k12.mn.us
Cass Lake-Bena HS | 200/9-12
15308 State Highway 371 NW 56633 | 218-335-2203
Patti Muckala, prin. | Fax 335-7649
Cass Lake-Bena MS | 300/5-8
15314 State Highway 371 NW 56633 | 218-335-7851
Steve Novak, prin. | Fax 335-1194

Center City, Chisago, Pop. 569

Hazelden Graduate School | Post-Sec.
PO Box 11 55428 | 651-213-4175

Champlin, Hennepin, Pop. 23,003
Anoka-Hennepin SD 11
Supt. — See Coon Rapids
Champlin Park HS | 3,100/9-12
6025 109th Ave N 55316 | 763-506-6800
Rhoda Mhirpiri, prin. | Fax 506-6803
Jackson MS | 2,300/6-8
6000 109th Ave N 55316 | 763-506-5200
Larry Siedow, prin. | Fax 506-5203

Chaska, Carver, Pop. 20,654
Chaska SD 112 | 7,900/K-12
11 Peavey Rd 55318 | 952-556-6100
David Jennings, supt. | Fax 556-6109
www.district112.org
Chaska MS East | 1,000/6-8
1600 Park Ridge Dr 55318 | 952-556-7600
James Bach, prin. | Fax 556-7609
Chaska MS West | 900/6-8
140 Engler Blvd 55318 | 952-556-7400
Sheryl Hough, prin. | Fax 556-7409
Chaska SHS | 1,700/10-12
545 Pioneer Trl 55318 | 952-556-7100
Paul McMahan, prin. | Fax 556-7109
Pioneer Ridge Freshman Center | 600/9-9
1085 Pioneer Trl 55318 | 952-556-7800
Dennis Baldus, prin. | Fax 556-7809

Southwest Christian HS | 200/9-12
103 Peavey Rd 55318 | 952-556-0040
Dr. Paul Norby, admin. | Fax 556-5567

Chatfield, Fillmore, Pop. 2,430
Chatfield SD 227 | 900/PK-12
205 Union St NE 55923 | 507-867-4210
Philip Minkkinen, supt. | Fax 867-3147
www.chatfieldpublicschools.net
Chosen Valley JSHS | 400/7-12
205 Union St NE 55923 | 507-867-4210
Randy Paulson, prin. | Fax 867-3147

Chisago City, Chisago, Pop. 2,928

Chisago Lakes Baptist Academy | 100/K-12
9387 Wyoming Trl 55013 | 651-257-4587

Chisholm, Saint Louis, Pop. 4,822
Chisholm SD 695 | 800/PK-12
300 3rd Ave SW 55719 | 218-254-5726
James Varichak, supt. | Fax 254-3741
www.chisholm.k12.mn.us
Chisholm HS | 400/7-12
301 4th St SW 55719 | 218-254-5726
Jerry Lawrence, prin. | Fax 254-3741

Chokio, Stevens, Pop. 446
Chokio-Alberta SD 771 | 200/K-12
PO Box 68 56221 | 320-324-7131
Paul Brownlow, supt. | Fax 324-2731
Other Schools – See Alberta

Circle Pines, Anoka, Pop. 4,774
Centennial SD 12 | 6,900/K-12
4707 North Rd 55014 | 763-792-6000
Dr. Roger Worner, supt. | Fax 792-6050
www.isd12.org
Centennial HS | 2,100/9-12
4757 North Rd 55014 | 763-792-5000
Tom Breuning, prin. | Fax 792-5050
Other Schools – See Lino Lakes

Clara City, Chippewa, Pop. 1,359
MACCRAY SD 2180 | 800/K-12
PO Box 690 56222 | 320-847-2154
Dr. Gary Spawn, supt. | Fax 847-3239
www.maccray.k12.mn.us/
MACCRAY HS | 300/9-12
PO Box 690 56222 | 320-847-2478
Gary Sims, prin. | Fax 847-3239
MACCRAY JHS | 100/7-8
PO Box 690 56222 | 320-847-3525
Gary Sims, prin. | Fax 847-5220

Clearbrook, Clearwater, Pop. 540
Clearbrook-Gonvick ISD 2311 | 500/K-12
16770 Clearwater Lake Rd 56634 | 218-776-3112
Diane Lehse, supt. | Fax 776-3117
www.cgbearzone.com
Clearbrook-Gonvick JSHS | 300/7-12
16770 Clearwater Lake Rd 56634 | 218-776-3112
Lon Burgess, prin. | Fax 776-3117

Cleveland, LeSueur, Pop. 710
Cleveland ISD 391 | 400/PK-12
PO Box 310 56017 | 507-931-5953
Brian Phillips, supt. | Fax 931-9088
cleveland.k12.mn.us/district.php3
Cleveland S | 400/PK-12
PO Box 310 56017 | 507-931-5953
Brian Phillips, prin. | Fax 931-9088

Climax, Polk, Pop. 242
Climax-Shelly ID 592 | 100/PK-12
PO Box 67 56523 | 218-857-2385
Norman Baumbarn, supt. | Fax 857-3544
www.climax.k12.mn.us
Climax HS | 100/7-12
PO Box 67 56523 | 218-857-2395
Shirley Moger, prin. | Fax 857-3544

Clinton, Big Stone, Pop. 438
Clinton-Graceville-Beardsley SD 2888 | 400/K-12
PO Box 361 56225 | 320-325-5282
Mary Smidt, supt. | Fax 325-5509
www.graceville.k12.mn.us
Other Schools – See Graceville

Cloquet, Carlton, Pop. 11,407
Cloquet SD 94 | 2,200/PK-12
302 14th St 55720 | 218-879-6721
Kenneth Scarbrough, supt. | Fax 879-6724
www.cloquet.k12.mn.us
Cloquet HS | 700/9-12
1000 18th St 55720 | 218-879-3393
Warren Peterson, prin. | Fax 879-6494
Cloquet MS | 500/6-8
509 Carlton Ave 55720 | 218-879-3328
Tom Brenner, prin. | Fax 879-4175

Cloquet Christian Academy | 100/K-12
1705 Wilson Ave 55720 | 218-879-2536
Jason Peterson, admin. | Fax 879-8889
Fond du Lac Tribal Community College | Post-Sec.
2101 14th St 55720 | 218-879-0800

Cokato, Wright, Pop. 2,761
Dassel-Cokato SD 466 | 2,200/PK-12
PO Box 1700 55321 | 320-286-4100
Don Hainlen, supt. | Fax 286-4101
www.dc.k12.mn.us
Dassel-Cokato HS | 700/9-12
PO Box 1600 55321 | 320-286-4100
Paul Thomas, prin. | Fax 286-4201
Dassel-Cokato MS | 700/5-8
PO Box 1500 55321 | 320-286-4100
Jeff Powers, prin. | Fax 286-4176

Cold Spring, Stearns, Pop. 3,301
Rocori SD 750 | 2,400/PK-12
534 5th Ave N 56320 | 320-685-4901
Scott R. Staska, supt. | Fax 685-4906
www.rocori.k12.mn.us/
Rocori HS | 800/9-12
534 5th Ave N 56320 | 320-685-8683
Terry Bizal, prin. | Fax 685-4906
Rocori MS | 400/7-8
533 Main St 56320 | 320-685-3296
Cheryl Schmidt, prin. | Fax 685-3474

Coleraine, Itasca, Pop. 1,062
Greenway SD 316 | 1,300/PK-12
PO Box 195 55722 | 218-245-1566
Rodney Thompson, supt. | Fax 245-6507
www.greenway.k12.mn.us/
Greenway HS | 400/9-12
PO Box 520 55722 | 218-245-1287
Dan Adams, prin. | Fax 245-2397
Other Schools – See Bovey

Collegeville, Stearns

St. Johns Preparatory S | 300/7-12
PO Box 4000 56321 | 320-363-3315
Fr. Gordan Tavis, prin. | Fax 363-3513
St. John's University | Post-Sec.
PO Box 7155 56321 | 320-363-2011

Columbia Heights, Anoka, Pop. 18,428
Columbia Heights SD 13 | 2,900/K-12
1440 49th Ave NE 55421 | 763-528-4500
Dr. Nancy Kaldor, supt. | Fax 571-9203
www.colheights.k12.mn.us
Central MS | 700/6-8
900 49th Ave NE 55421 | 763-586-4701
Brian Espe, prin. | Fax 528-4707
Columbia Heights HS | 900/9-12
1400 49th Ave NE 55421 | 763-528-4600
Matt Schoen, prin. | Fax 571-9267

Comfrey, Brown, Pop. 363
Comfrey SD 81 | 200/K-12
305 Ochre St W 56019 | 507-877-3491
Wayne Olson, supt. | Fax 877-3492
comfreyed.org
Comfrey JSHS | 100/7-12
305 Ochre St W 56019 | 507-877-3491
Wayne Olson, prin. | Fax 877-3492

Cook, Saint Louis, Pop. 609
St. Louis County SD 2142
Supt. — See Virginia
Cook JSHS | 300/7-12
306 E Vermilion Blvd 55723 | 218-666-5221
Kevin Abrahamson, prin. | Fax 666-5223

Coon Rapids, Anoka, Pop. 62,310
Anoka-Hennepin SD 11 — 40,400/PK-12
11299 Hanson Blvd NW 55433 — 763-506-1000
Dr. Roger Giroux, supt. — Fax 506-1003
www.anoka.k12.mn.us
Coon Rapids HS — 2,700/9-12
2340 Northdale Blvd NW 55433 — 763-506-7100
Charles Achter, prin. — Fax 506-7103
Coon Rapids MS — 1,600/6-8
11600 Raven St NW 55433 — 763-506-4800
Michelle Langenfeld, prin. — Fax 506-4803
Northdale MS — 1,500/6-8
11301 Dogwood St NW 55448 — 763-506-5400
Laurie Jacklitch, prin. — Fax 506-5403
Other Schools – See Andover, Anoka, Blaine, Champlin

Anoka-Ramsey Community College — Post-Sec.
11200 Mississippi Blvd NW 55433 — 763-427-2600

Cottage Grove, Washington, Pop. 31,800
South Washington County SD 833 — 15,400/K-12
7362 E Point Douglas Rd S 55016 — 651-458-6300
Tom Nelson, supt. — Fax 458-6318
www.sowashco.k12.mn.us
Cottage Grove JHS — 1,100/7-9
9775 Indian Blvd S 55016 — 651-768-6800
Elise Block, prin. — Fax 768-6828
Park SHS — 1,700/10-12
8040 80th St S 55016 — 651-768-3700
Walter Lyszak, prin. — Fax 768-3705
Other Schools – See Saint Paul Park, Woodbury

Cotton, Saint Louis
St. Louis County SD 2142
Supt. — See Virginia
Cotton JSHS — 100/7-12
PO Box 187 55724 — 218-482-3232
Sidney Simonson, prin. — Fax 482-3233

Cottonwood, Lyon, Pop. 1,132
Lakeview SD 2167 — 600/K-12
PO Box 107 56229 — 507-423-5164
Wayne Kazmierczak, supt. — Fax 423-5568
www.lakeview2167.com
Lakeview HS — 300/7-12
PO Box 107 56229 — 507-423-5166

Cromwell, Carlton, Pop. 193
Cromwell-Wright SD 95 — 300/PK-12
PO Box 7 55726 — 218-644-3737
Herbert Hilinski, supt. — Fax 644-3992
www.cromwellwright.k12.mn.us
Cromwell-Wright JSHS — 100/7-12
PO Box 7 55726 — 218-644-3716
Joan Bloemendaal-Gruett, prin. — Fax 644-3992

Crookston, Polk, Pop. 7,939
Crookston SD 593 — 1,300/K-12
402 Fisher Ave #593 56716 — 218-281-5313
Ralph Christofferson, supt. — Fax 281-3505
www.crookston.k12.mn.us
Crookston HS — 600/8-12
402 Fisher Ave 56716 — 218-281-2144
Richard Koop, prin. — Fax 281-4709

University of Minnesota — Post-Sec.
2900 University Ave 56716 — 218-281-6510

Crosby, Crow Wing, Pop. 2,275
Crosby-Ironton SD 182 — 1,400/PK-12
711 Poplar St 56441 — 218-545-8801
Linda Lawrie, supt. — Fax 545-8836
www.ci.k12.mn.us
Crosby-Ironton JSHS — 700/7-12
711 Poplar St 56441 — 218-545-8802
Jim Christenson, prin. — Fax 545-8835

Dawson, Lac qui Parle, Pop. 1,504
Dawson-Boyd SD 378 — 600/PK-12
848 Chestnut St 56232 — 320-769-2955
Brad Madsen, supt. — Fax 769-4502
dawsonboydschools.org/
Dawson-Boyd JSHS — 300/7-12
848 Chestnut St 56232 — 320-769-2955
Keri Bergson, prin. — Fax 769-4502

Deer River, Itasca, Pop. 940
Deer River SD 317 — 1,000/PK-12
PO Box 307 56636 — 218-246-2420
Mark Adams, supt. — Fax 246-8948
www.deerriver.k12.mn.us/
Deer River JSHS — 500/7-12
PO Box 307 56636 — 218-246-8241
Matthew Grose, prin. — Fax 246-8717

Delano, Wright, Pop. 4,152
Delano SD 879 — 1,900/PK-12
700 Elm Ave E 55328 — 763-972-3365
John Sweet, supt. — Fax 972-6706
www.delano.k12.mn.us
Delano HS — 600/9-12
700 Elm Ave E 55328 — 763-972-3365
Dr. Bruce Locklear, prin. — Fax 972-6706
Delano MS — 600/5-8
700 Elm Ave E 55328 — 763-972-3365
Richard Rominski, prin. — Fax 972-6706

Detroit Lakes, Becker, Pop. 7,652
Detroit Lakes SD 22 — 2,700/PK-12
PO Box 766 56502 — 218-847-9271
Mark Adams, supt. — Fax 847-9273
www.detroitlakes.com
Detroit Lakes HS — 900/9-12
1301 Roosevelt Ave 56501 — 218-847-4491
Steven Morben, prin. — Fax 846-1797

Detroit Lakes MS — 700/6-8
510 11th Ave 56501 — 218-847-9228
Michael Suckert, prin. — Fax 847-0057

MN State Community & Technical College — Post-Sec.
900 Highway 34 E 56501 — 800-492-4836

Dilworth, Clay, Pop. 3,092
Dilworth-Glyndon-Felton SD 2164 — 1,400/PK-12
PO Box 188 56529 — 218-287-2371
Bernie Lipp, supt. — Fax 287-2709
www.dgf.k12.mn.us
Dilworth-Glyndon-Felton JHS — 200/7-8
PO Box 188 56529 — 218-287-2148
Colleen Houglum, prin. — Fax 287-2709
Other Schools – See Glyndon

Dodge Center, Dodge, Pop. 2,372
Triton SD 2125 — 1,100/K-12
813 W Highway St 55927 — 507-374-2192
Robert Kelly, supt. — Fax 374-6524
www.triton.k12.mn.us/
Triton HS — 400/9-12
813 W Highway St 55927 — 507-374-6305
Brett Joyce, prin. — Fax 374-2447
Other Schools – See West Concord

Duluth, Saint Louis, Pop. 85,734
Duluth SD 709 — 10,500/PK-12
215 N 1st Ave E 55802 — 218-336-8752
Keith Dixon, supt. — Fax 336-8773
www.duluth.k12.mn.us
Central HS — 1,100/9-12
800 E Central Entrance 55811 — 218-733-2130
Lisa Mitchell-Krocak, prin. — Fax 733-2153
Denfeld HS — 1,200/9-12
4405 W 4th St 55807 — 218-628-4863
Ed Crawford, prin. — Fax 628-4870
East HS — 1,400/9-12
2900 E 4th St 55812 — 218-728-7426
Laurie Knapp, prin. — Fax 728-7439
Morgan Park MS — 500/6-8
1243 88th Ave W 55808 — 218-626-4512
— Fax 626-4520
Ordean MS — 700/6-8
301 N 40th Ave E 55804 — 218-525-0810
Jerry Maki, prin. — Fax 525-0815
Secondary Technical S — Vo/Tech
802 E Central Entrance 55811 — 218-336-8975
Jim Arndt, admin. — Fax 336-8979
Woodland MS — 800/6-8
201 Clover St 55812 — 218-728-7456
Bonnie Wolden, prin. — Fax 728-7460
Area Learning Center — Adult
215 N 1st Ave E 55802 — 218-336-8790
Beth Tamminen, admin. — Fax 336-8791

College of Saint Scholastica — Post-Sec.
1200 Kenwood Ave 55811 — 218-723-6000
Cosmetology Careers Unlimited - Duluth — Post-Sec.
121 W Superior St 55802 — 218-722-7484
Duluth Business University — Post-Sec.
4724 Mike Colalillo Dr 55807 — 218-722-3361
Lake Superior College — Post-Sec.
2101 Trinity Rd 55811 — 218-733-7600
Lakeview Christian Academy — 300/PK-12
155 W Central Entrance 55811 — 218-723-8844
Don Chamberlain, admin. — Fax 722-7850
Marshall S — 500/5-12
1215 Rice Lake Rd 55811 — 218-727-7266
Marlene David, hdmstr. — Fax 727-1569
University of Minnesota — Post-Sec.
10 University Dr 55812 — 218-726-8000

Eagan, Dakota, Pop. 64,006
Rosemount-Apple Valley-Eagan ISD 196
Supt. — See Rosemount
Black Hawk MS — 1,100/6-8
1540 Deerwood Dr 55122 — 651-683-8521
Richard Wendorff, prin. — Fax 683-8527
Dakota Hills MS — 1,400/6-8
4183 Braddock Trl 55123 — 651-683-6800
Steven Troen, prin. — Fax 683-6858
Eagan HS — 2,300/9-12
4185 Braddock Trl 55123 — 651-683-6900
Polly Reikowaki, prin. — Fax 683-6910

Argosy University/Twin Cities — Post-Sec.
1515 Central Pkwy 55121 — 651-846-2882
Rasmussen College — Post-Sec.
3500 Federal Dr 55122 — 651-687-9000

Eagle Bend, Todd, Pop. 591
Eagle Valley SD 2759 — 400/PK-12
PO Box 299 56446 — 218-738-6442
Dale Svaren, supt. — Fax 738-6493
www.evps.k12.mn.us
Eagle Valley JSHS — 200/7-12
PO Box 299 56446 — 218-738-6442
Richard Lundgren, prin. — Fax 738-6493

East Grand Forks, Polk, Pop. 7,562
East Grand Forks SD 595 — 1,800/PK-12
PO Box 151 56721 — 218-773-3494
Walt Aanenson, supt. — Fax 773-7408
www.egf.k12.mn.us/
Central MS — 400/6-8
PO Box 151 56721 — 218-773-1141
Robert Simonson, prin. — Fax 773-9112
East Grand Forks HS — 600/9-12
PO Box 151 56721 — 218-773-2405
Steven Heyd, prin. — Fax 773-3070

Northland Community & Technical College — Post-Sec.
2022 Central Ave NE 56721 — 800-451-3441

Sacred Heart HS — 200/7-12
122 3rd St NW 56721 — 218-773-0230
Phillip Meyer, prin. — Fax 773-7042

Eden Prairie, Hennepin, Pop. 59,470
Eden Prairie SD 272 — 10,200/K-12
8100 School Rd 55344 — 952-975-7000
Melissa Krull Ph.D., supt. — Fax 975-7012
www.edenpr.org
Central MS — 1,600/7-8
8025 School Rd 55344 — 952-975-7300
Joe Epping, prin. — Fax 975-7320
Eden Prairie HS — 3,400/9-12
17185 Valley View Rd 55346 — 952-975-8000
Conn McCartan, prin. — Fax 975-8020

International School of Minnesota — 600/PK-12
6385 Beach Rd 55344 — 952-918-1800
Susan Berg, dir. — Fax 918-1801
NTI-School of CAD Technology — Post-Sec.
11995 Singletree Ln 55344 — 952-944-0080
Rasmussen College — Post-Sec.
7905 Golden Triangle # 100 55344 — 952-545-2000

Eden Valley, Meeker, Pop. 914
Eden Valley-Watkins SD 463 — 800/PK-12
298 Brooks St N 55329 — 320-453-6310
Larry Peterson, supt. — Fax 453-5600
www.evw.k12.mn.us
Eden Valley Secondary S — 400/7-12
298 Brooks St N 55329 — 320-453-2900
Bruce Kiehn, prin. — Fax 453-5600

Edgerton, Pipestone, Pop. 1,004
Edgerton SD 581 — 300/PK-12
PO Box 28 56128 — 507-442-7881
Leroy Domagala, supt. — Fax 442-8541
edgertonpublic.com
Edgerton JSHS — 100/7-12
PO Box 28 56128 — 507-442-7881
Gene Miller, prin. — Fax 442-8541

Southwest Minnesota Christian HS — 100/9-12
550 Elizabeth St W 56128 — 507-442-4471
Paul Bootsma, prin. — Fax 442-5801

Edina, Hennepin, Pop. 46,656
Edina SD 273 — 7,200/K-12
5701 Normandale Rd 55424 — 952-848-3900
Ken Dragseth, supt. — Fax 848-3901
www.edina.k12.mn.us
Edina SHS — 1,600/10-12
6754 Valley View Rd 55439 — 952-848-3800
Aldo Sicoli, prin. — Fax 848-3801
South View MS — 1,100/6-9
4725 S View Ln 55424 — 952-848-3700
Trevor Johnson, prin. — Fax 848-3701
Valley View MS — 1,200/6-9
6750 Valley View Rd 55439 — 952-848-3500
Shawn Dudley, prin. — Fax 848-3501

Elgin, Wabasha, Pop. 872
Elgin-Millville SD 806 — 500/PK-12
PO Box 364 55932 — 507-876-2493
Gordy Gellrink, supt. — Fax 876-2110
www.elgin.k12.mn.us/
Elgin JSHS — 300/7-12
PO Box 364 55932 — 507-876-2521
Clark Olstad, prin. — Fax 876-2110

Elk River, Sherburne, Pop. 18,783
Elk River Area SD 728 — 10,800/PK-12
815 Highway 10 55330 — 763-241-3400
Mark Bezek, supt. — Fax 241-3407
www.elkriver.k12.mn.us
Elk River Area HS — 2,000/9-12
900 School St NW 55330 — 763-241-3434
James Voight, prin. — Fax 241-3421
Salk JHS — 600/6-8
11970 Highland Rd NW 55330 — 763-241-3455
Ric Lange, prin. — Fax 241-3456
Vandenberg JHS — 600/6-8
948 Proctor Ave NW 55330 — 763-241-3450
Clair Olson, prin. — Fax 241-3451
Other Schools – See Rogers, Zimmerman

Rivers Christian Academy — 300/PK-12
829 School St NW 55330 — 763-441-6594
Kenneth Mitchell, prin. — Fax 441-2150

Ellsworth, Nobles, Pop. 528
Ellsworth SD 514 — 200/PK-12
PO Box 8 56129 — 507-967-2242
George Berndt, supt. — Fax 967-2588
Ellsworth S — 200/PK-12
PO Box 8 56129 — 507-967-2151
George Berndt, supt. — Fax 967-2588

Ely, Saint Louis, Pop. 3,714
Ely SD 696 — 700/PK-12
600 E Harvey St 55731 — 218-365-6166
Thomas W. Bruels, supt. — Fax 365-6138
www.ely.k12.mn.us
Memorial JSHS — 400/7-12
600 E Harvey St 55731 — 218-365-6166
Joselyn Murphy, prin. — Fax 365-6138

Vermillion Community College — Post-Sec.
1900 E Camp St 55731 — 800-475-6666

Erskine, Polk, Pop. 420
Win-E-Mac SD 2609 — 600/K-12
23130 345th St SE 56535 — 218-687-2236
Dan Parent, supt. — Fax 563-2902

Win-E-Mac JSHS 300/7-12
23130 345th St SE 56535 218-687-2236
Kevin McKeever, prin. Fax 563-2902

Esko, Carlton
Esko SD 99 1,100/PK-12
PO Box 10 55733 218-879-2969
Curt Tryggestad, supt. Fax 879-7490
www.esko.k12.mn.us/
Lincoln JSHS 500/7-12
PO Box 10 55733 218-879-4673
Randy Bowen, prin. Fax 879-7490

Evansville, Douglas, Pop. 547
Evansville SD 208 200/PK-12
PO Box 40 56326 218-948-2241
Allan Jensen, supt. Fax 948-2441
www.evansville.k12.mn.us/
Evansville JSHS 100/7-12
PO Box 40 56326 218-948-2241
Allen Jensen, prin. Fax 948-2441

Eveleth, Saint Louis, Pop. 3,742
Eveleth-Gilbert SD 2154 1,400/PK-12
801 Jones St 55734 218-744-7701
Michael Lang, supt. Fax 744-4381
isd2154.k12.mn.us
Eveleth-Gilbert SHS 300/10-12
801 Jones St 55734 218-744-7707
Deborah Hilde, prin. Fax 744-4381
Other Schools – See Gilbert

Mesabi Range Community & Technical Coll. Post-Sec.
PO Box 648 55734 218-744-3302

Excelsior, Hennepin, Pop. 2,314
Minnetonka SD 276
Supt. — See Minnetonka
Minnetonka West MS 1,000/6-8
6421 Hazeltine Blvd 55331 952-401-5300
Bill Jacobson, prin. Fax 401-5350

Eyota, Olmsted, Pop. 1,660
Dover-Eyota SD 533 1,100/PK-12
615 South Ave 55934 507-545-2125
Bruce Klaehn, supt. Fax 545-2349
www.desch.org
Dover-Eyota JSHS 500/7-12
615 South Ave 55934 507-545-2631
Donald Johnson, prin. Fax 545-2218

Fairfax, Renville, Pop. 1,293
GFW SD 2365
Supt. — See Gibbon
GFW MS 300/5-8
PO Box 489 55332 507-426-7251
Ralph Fairchild, prin. Fax 426-7425

Prairie Lutheran MS 50/5-8
PO Box 130 55332 507-426-7755
Macord Johnson, prin. Fax 426-8372

Fairmont, Martin, Pop. 10,666
Fairmont Area SD 2752 1,800/K-12
115 S Park St 56031 507-238-4234
Harlow Hanson, supt. Fax 235-4050
fairmont.k12.mn.us
Fairmont JSHS 900/7-12
900 Johnson St 56031 507-238-4411
Lynn Manske, prin. Fax 238-4070

Faribault, Rice, Pop. 21,814
Faribault SD 656 3,900/PK-12
PO Box 618 55021 507-333-6016
Gwendolyn Jackson, supt. Fax 333-6077
www.faribault.k12.mn.us/
Faribault HS 1,300/9-12
330 9th Ave SW 55021 507-333-6100
Lyle Turtle, prin. Fax 333-6248
Faribault MS 900/6-8
704 17th St SW 55021 507-333-6300
Jill Louters, prin. Fax 333-6400

Bethlehem Academy 200/7-12
105 3rd Ave SW 55021 507-334-3948
Bette Blaisdell, prin. Fax 334-3949
Minnesota School for the Deaf Post-Sec.
PO Box 308 55021
Riverland Technical College Post-Sec.
1225 3rd St SW 55021 800-422-0391
Shattuck/St. Marys S 300/6-12
PO Box 218 55021 507-333-1500
Nick Stoneman, hdmstr. Fax 333-1595

Farmington, Dakota, Pop. 16,060
Farmington SD 192 5,200/K-12
421 Walnut St 55024 651-463-5000
Dr. Bradley Meeks, supt. Fax 463-5010
www.farmington.k12.mn.us
Farmington MS West 800/8-9
4200 208th St W 55024 651-460-1500
Christine Weymouth, prin. Fax 460-1510
Farmington SHS 900/10-12
800 Denmark Ave 55024 651-460-1400
Monica Kittock-Sargent, prin. Fax 460-1410

Christian Life S 200/PK-12
6300 212th St W 55024 651-463-4545
Pastor Darin Kindle, admin. Fax 463-8353

Fergus Falls, Otter Tail, Pop. 14,033
Fergus Falls SD 544 2,800/K-12
4B East Dr 56537 218-998-0544
Mark Bezek, supt. Fax 998-3952
www.fergusfalls.k12.mn.us
Fergus Falls HS 900/9-12
518 Friberg Ave 56537 218-736-6971
Greg Winter, prin. Fax 998-3946
Fergus Falls MS 900/5-8
601 Randolph Ave 56537 218-998-0544
Dean Monke, prin. Fax 998-3943

Hillcrest Lutheran Academy 200/7-12
610 Hillcrest Dr 56537 218-739-3371
Jeff Isaac, prin. Fax 739-3372
MN State Community & Technical College Post-Sec.
1414 College Way 56537 218-739-7500

Fertile, Polk, Pop. 876
Fertile-Beltrami SD 599 600/PK-12
PO Box 648 56540 218-945-6933
Don Blaeser, supt. Fax 945-6934
fertilebeltrami.k12.mn.us/FBSchool/Home/home.htm
Fertile-Beltrami JSHS 300/7-12
PO Box 648 56540 218-945-6953
Brian Clarke, prin. Fax 945-6934

Finlayson, Pine, Pop. 316
East Central SD 2580 900/PK-12
61085 State Highway 23 55735 320-245-2289
Todd McCormick, supt. Fax 245-5453
www.eastcentral.k12.mn.us
Other Schools – See Sandstone

Fisher, Polk, Pop. 419
Fisher SD 600 300/K-12
313 Park Ave 56723 218-891-4105
Randy Bruer, supt. Fax 891-4251
www.fisher.k12.mn.us
Fisher JSHS 200/7-12
313 Park Ave 56723 218-891-4905
Erik Erie, prin. Fax 891-4251

Floodwood, Saint Louis, Pop. 496
Floodwood SD 698 500/PK-12
PO Box 287 55736 218-476-2285
Palmer Anderson, supt. Fax 476-2813
www.floodwood.k12.mn.us/
Floodwood JSHS 200/7-12
PO Box 287 55736 218-476-2285
Laverne Hakly, prin. Fax 476-2813

Foley, Benton, Pop. 2,404
Foley SD 51 1,700/PK-12
PO Box 297 56329 320-968-7175
Dr. Fred Nolan, supt. Fax 968-8608
foley.k12.mn.us
Foley HS 600/9-12
PO Box 397 56329 320-968-7246
Alan Niemann, prin. Fax 968-8456
Foley MS 600/4-8
PO Box 297 56329 320-968-6251
Sandra Backowski, prin. Fax 968-8608

Forest Lake, Washington, Pop. 15,942
Forest Lake SD 831 7,400/K-12
6100 210th St N 55025 651-982-8100
Lynn Steenblock, supt. Fax 982-8114
www.forestlake.k12.mn.us
Century JHS 1,100/7-9
21395 Goodview Ave N 55025 651-982-8600
Dr. Benjamin Lewis, prin. Fax 982-8690
Forest Lake SHS 1,800/10-12
6101 Scandia Trl N 55025 651-982-8400
Dr. Steve Massey, prin. Fax 982-8428
Southwest JHS 800/7-9
943 9th Ave SW 55025 651-982-8700
Marc Peterson, prin. Fax 982-8798

Foreston, Mille Lacs, Pop. 445

Faith Christian S 100/K-12
11818 160th Ave 56330 320-294-5501
Randy Peterson, admin. Fax 294-5197

Fosston, Polk, Pop. 1,527
Fosston SD 601 700/PK-12
301 1st St E 56542 218-435-6335
Dale Salberg, supt. Fax 435-1663
www.fosston.k12.mn.us
Fosston JSHS 300/7-12
301 1st St E 56542 218-435-1909
Thomas Sedler, prin. Fax 435-6340

Frazee, Becker, Pop. 1,393
Frazee-Vergas SD 23 1,200/PK-12
PO Box 186 56544 218-334-3181
Deron Stender, supt. Fax 334-3182
www.frazee.k12.mn.us/
Frazee JSHS 600/7-12
PO Box 186 56544 218-334-3181
Terry Karger, prin. Fax 334-4696

Fridley, Anoka, Pop. 27,169
Fridley SD 14 2,400/K-12
6000 Moore Lake Dr W 55432 763-502-5000
Mark Robertson, supt. Fax 502-5040
www.fridley.k12.mn.us
Fridley HS 800/9-12
6000 Moore Lake Dr W 55432 763-502-5600
Dr. Dave Webb, prin. Fax 502-5640
Fridley MS 800/5-8
6100 Moore Lake Dr W 55432 763-502-5400
Margaret Leibfried, prin. Fax 502-5440

Totino-Grace HS 1,100/9-12
1350 Gardena Ave NE 55432 763-571-9116
Julie Michels, prin. Fax 571-9118

Fulda, Murray, Pop. 1,251
Fulda SD 505 500/PK-12
410 College Ave N 56131 507-425-2514
John Widvey, supt. Fax 425-2001
www.fps.mntm.org
Fulda JSHS 300/7-12
410 College Ave N 56131 507-425-2516
Luther Onken, prin. Fax 425-2001

Gaylord, Sibley, Pop. 2,237
Sibley East SD 2310
Supt. — See Arlington
Sibley East JHS 300/7-9
PO Box 356 55334 507-237-3315
Steve Harter, prin. Fax 237-3300

Gibbon, Sibley, Pop. 788
GFW SD 2365 900/PK-12
323 E 11th St 55335 507-834-9813
Stephen Malone, supt. Fax 834-6264
www.gfw.k12.mn.us
Other Schools – See Fairfax, Winthrop

Gilbert, Saint Louis, Pop. 1,797
Eveleth-Gilbert SD 2154
Supt. — See Eveleth
Eveleth-Gilbert JHS 300/7-9
Summit St 55741 218-741-7773
Jan Mesich, prin. Fax 741-7504

Glencoe, McLeod, Pop. 5,534
Glencoe-Silver Lake SD 2859 1,300/PK-12
1621 16th St E 55336 320-864-2491
John Hornung, supt. Fax 864-6320
www.gsl.k12.mn.us
Glencoe-Silver Lake HS 200/9-12
1825 16th St E 55336 320-864-2400
Scot Kerbaugh, prin. Fax 864-6475
Lincoln JHS 300/7-8
1621 16th St E 55336 320-864-2455
Chris Sonju, prin. Fax 864-2475

Glenville, Freeborn, Pop. 704
Glenville-Emmons SD 2886 400/K-12
PO Box 38 56036 507-448-2889
David Olson, supt. Fax 448-2836
www.geschools.com
Glenville-Emmons JSHS 200/7-12
230 5th St SE 56036 507-448-2889
David Olson, prin. Fax 448-2836

Glenwood, Pope, Pop. 2,451
Minnewaska SD 2149 800/PK-12
25122 State Highway 28 56334 320-239-4800
Keith Redfield, supt. Fax 239-1362
www.minnewaska.k12.mn.us
Minnewaska Area HS 500/9-12
25122 State Highway 28 56334 320-239-4800
Lyle Katzenmeyer, prin. Fax 239-1362
Minnewaska Area MS 5-8
25122 State Highway 28 56334 320-239-4800
Pat Falk, prin. Fax 239-1362

Glyndon, Clay, Pop. 1,134
Dilworth-Glyndon-Felton SD 2164
Supt. — See Dilworth
Dilworth-Glyndon-Felton HS 400/9-12
513 Parke Ave S 56547 218-498-2263
Tom Gravel, prin. Fax 498-2488

Golden Valley, Hennepin, Pop. 20,505
Robbinsdale SD 281
Supt. — See New Hope
Sandburg MS 1,400/6-8
2400 Sandburg Ln 55427 763-504-8200
Tom Henderlite, prin. Fax 504-8231

Goodhue, Goodhue, Pop. 874
Goodhue SD 253 600/PK-12
PO Box 128 55027 651-923-4447
Robert Bangston, supt. Fax 923-4083
www.goodhue.net
Goodhue JSHS 300/7-12
PO Box 128 55027 651-923-4447
Mark Roubinek, prin. Fax 923-4083

Goodridge, Pennington, Pop. 106
Goodridge SD 561 200/K-12
PO Box 195 56725 218-378-4133
Galen Clow, supt. Fax 378-4142
www.goodridge.k12.mn.us
Goodridge JSHS 100/7-12
PO Box 195 56725 218-378-4133
Elden Winge, prin. Fax 378-4142

Graceville, Big Stone, Pop. 585
Clinton-Graceville-Beardsley SD 2888
Supt. — See Clinton
Clinton-Graceville-Beardsley HS 200/7-12
PO Box 398 56240 320-748-7233
Randy Bergquist, prin. Fax 748-7159

Granada, Martin, Pop. 306
Granada-Huntley-East Chain SD 2536 300/PK-12
PO Box 17 56039 507-447-2211
Randy Grupe, supt. Fax 447-2214
www.ghec.k12.mn.us
Granada - Huntley - East Chain JSHS 200/7-12
PO Box 17 56039 507-447-2211
Robert Grant, prin. Fax 447-2214

Grand Marais, Cook, Pop. 1,427
Cook County SD 166 600/K-12
101 W 5th St 55604 218-387-2271
Charles Futterer, supt. Fax 387-1093
www.cookcountyschools.org/
Cook County MSHS 400/6-12
101 W 5th St 55604 218-387-2273
John Engelking, prin. Fax 387-9746

Grand Meadow, Mower, Pop. 947
Grand Meadow SD 495 — 300/K-12
PO Box 68 55936 — 507-754-5318
Joseph Brown, supt. — Fax 754-5608
www.gm.k12.mn.us/
Grand Meadow HS — 100/9-12
PO Box 68 55936 — 507-754-5310
David Stadum, prin. — Fax 754-5608
Grand Meadow MS — 100/5-8
PO Box 68 55936 — 507-754-5310
David Stadium, prin. — Fax 754-5608

Grand Rapids, Itasca, Pop. 7,764
Grand Rapids SD 318 — 3,800/K-12
820 NW 1st Ave 55744 — 218-327-5700
Joe Silko, supt. — Fax 327-5702
www.isd318.org
Elkington MS — 800/6-8
1000 NE 8th Ave 55744 — 218-327-5800
Len Rothlisberger, prin. — Fax 327-5801
Grand Rapids HS — 1,300/9-12
800 NW Conifer Dr 55744 — 218-327-5760
Jim Smokrovich, prin. — Fax 327-5761
Other Schools – See Bigfork

Itasca Community College — Post-Sec.
1851 E US Highway 169 55744 — 218-327-4460

Granite Falls, Yellow Medicine, Pop. 2,991
Yellow Medicine East SD 2190 — 1,100/K-12
450 9th Ave 56241 — 320-564-4081
Dwayne Strand, supt. — Fax 564-4781
www.yme.k12.mn.us
Yellow Medicine East JSHS — 600/7-12
450 9th Ave 56241 — 320-564-4083
Karen Norell, prin. — Fax 564-4782

Minnesota West Community & Tech College — Post-Sec.
1593 11th Ave 56241 — 800-657-3247

Greenbush, Roseau, Pop. 763
Greenbush-Middle River SD 2683 — 500/PK-12
PO Box 70 56726 — 218-782-2231
Ron Ruud, supt. — Fax 782-3141
www.middleriver.k12.mn.us/
Greenbush-Middle River HS — 100/9-12
PO Box 70 56726 — 218-782-2232
Eldon Sparby, prin. — Fax 782-2165
Other Schools – See Middle River

Grove City, Meeker, Pop. 618
ACGC SD 2396 — 900/PK-12
27250 Minnesota Highway 4 56243 — 320-857-2271
Pamela Kyllingstad, supt. — Fax 857-2989
acgc.k12.mn.us
ACGC JSHS — 400/5-12
27250 Minnesota Highway 4 56243 — 320-857-2276
Sherri Broderius, prin. — Fax 857-2937

Grygla, Marshall, Pop. 233
Grygla SD 447 — 200/PK-12
PO Box 18 56727 — 218-294-6155
Galen Clow, supt. — Fax 294-6766
Grygla JSHS — 100/7-12
PO Box 18 56727 — 218-294-6155
Patti Johnson, prin. — Fax 294-6766

Hallock, Kittson, Pop. 1,125
Kittson Central SD 2171 — 500/PK-12
PO Box 670 56728 — 218-843-3682
Bruce Jensen, supt. — Fax 843-2856
kittson.k12.mn.us
Kittson Central HS — 200/7-12
PO Box 670 56728 — 218-843-3682
Terry Ogorek, prin. — Fax 843-2856

Halstad, Norman, Pop. 597
Norman County West SD 2527
Supt. — See Hendrum
Norman County West JSHS — 200/7-12
PO Box 328 56548 — 218-456-2151
Caline Olson, prin. — Fax 456-2193

Hancock, Stevens, Pop. 700
Hancock SD 768 — 200/K-12
PO Box 367 56244 — 320-392-5622
Jerry Martinson, supt. — Fax 392-5156
Hancock JSHS — 100/7-12
PO Box 367 56244 — 320-392-5622
Jerry Martinson, prin. — Fax 392-5156

Harmony, Fillmore, Pop. 1,136
Fillmore Central SD 2198 — 700/PK-12
PO Box 599 55939 — 507-886-6464
Myrna Luehmann, supt. — Fax 886-6642
www.isd2198.k12.mn.us/
Fillmore Central HS — 200/9-12
PO Box 599 55939 — 507-886-6464
Heath Olstad, prin. — Fax 886-6642
Other Schools – See Preston

Hastings, Dakota, Pop. 19,705
Hastings SD 200 — 5,000/K-12
1000 11th St W 55033 — 651-437-6111
Tim Collins, supt. — Fax 437-1928
www.hastings.k12.mn.us
Hastings HS — 1,800/9-12
200 General Sieben Dr 55033 — 651-480-0205
Mike Johnson, prin. — Fax 480-8128
Hastings MS — 1,200/6-8
1000 11th St W 55033 — 651-438-0705
Mark Zuzek, prin. — Fax 438-0707

Hawley, Clay, Pop. 1,855
Hawley SD 150 — 1,100/K-12
PO Box 608 56549 — 218-483-4647
Phil Jensen, supt. — Fax 483-4802
www.hawley.k12.mn.us/

Hawley JSHS — 400/7-12
PO Box 608 56549 — 218-483-3555
Mike Martin, prin. — Fax 483-4802
Spring Prairie S — 300/K-12
PO Box 608 56549 — 218-483-3316
Wayne LePard, prin. — Fax 483-4638

Hayfield, Dodge, Pop. 1,383
Hayfield SD 203 — 900/PK-12
9 6th Ave SE 55940 — 507-477-3235
Ron Evjen, supt. — Fax 477-3230
hayfield.k12.mn.us
Hayfield JSHS — 400/7-12
9 6th Ave SE 55940 — 507-477-3235
Brandon Macrafic, prin. — Fax 477-3230

Hector, Renville, Pop. 1,143
Buffalo Lake-Hector SD 2159 — 600/PK-12
PO Box 307 55342 — 320-848-2233
Dr. Rick Clark, supt. — Fax 848-2401
blh.k12.mn.us
Buffalo Lake-Hector JSHS — 300/6-12
PO Box 307 55342 — 320-848-2233
Cory Klabunde, prin. — Fax 848-2401

Hendrum, Norman, Pop. 308
Norman County West SD 2527 — 400/PK-12
PO Box 39 56550 — 218-861-5800
Caline Olson, supt. — Fax 861-6223
www.ncw.k12.mn.us
Other Schools – See Halstad

Henning, Otter Tail, Pop. 788
Henning SD 545 — 400/PK-12
500 School Ave 56551 — 218-583-2927
Deborah Wanek, supt. — Fax 583-2312
www.henning.k12.mn.us
Henning JSHS — 200/7-12
500 School Ave 56551 — 218-583-2927
Deborah Wanek, prin. — Fax 583-2312

Herman, Grant, Pop. 441
Herman-Norcross SD 264 — 100/K-12
PO Box 288 56248 — 320-677-2291
Tom Knoll, supt. — Fax 677-2412
herman.mn.schoolwebpages.com
Herman JSHS — 100/7-12
PO Box 288 56248 — 320-677-2291
Steve Wymore, prin. — Fax 677-2412

Hermantown, Saint Louis, Pop. 8,367
Hermantown SD 700 — 2,000/K-12
4307 Ugstad Rd 55811 — 218-729-9313
Brad Johnson, supt. — Fax 729-9315
www.hermantown.k12.mn.us
Hermantown HS — 600/9-12
4335 Hawk Circle Dr 55811 — 218-729-8874
Lois Backscheider, prin. — Fax 729-0180
Hermantown MS — 800/4-8
4289 Ugstad Rd 55811 — 218-729-6690
David Radovich, prin. — Fax 729-9890

Hibbing, Saint Louis, Pop. 16,851
Hibbing SD 701 — 2,600/K-12
800 E 21st St 55746 — 218-263-4850
Robert Belluzzo, supt. — Fax 262-0494
www.hibbing.k12.mn.us
Hibbing HS — 1,400/7-12
800 E 21st St 55746 — 218-263-0400
Mike Raich, prin. — Fax 262-5137

Cosmetology Careers Unlimited - Hibbing — Post-Sec.
110 E Howard St 55746 — 218-263-8354
Hibbing Community College — Post-Sec.
1515 E 25th St 55746 — 218-262-7200

Hill City, Aitkin, Pop. 472
Hill City SD 2 — 400/PK-12
500 Ione Ave 55748 — 218-697-2394
Scott Vedbraaten, supt. — Fax 697-2594
www.hillcity.k12.mn.us/
Hill City JSHS — 200/7-12
500 Ione Ave 55748 — 218-697-2394
Dean Yocum, prin. — Fax 697-2594

Hills, Rock, Pop. 597
Hills-Beaver Creek SD 671 — 300/PK-12
PO Box 547 56138 — 507-962-3240
David Deragisch, supt. — Fax 962-3238
www.hbcpatriots.com
Hills-Beaver Creek JSHS — 100/7-12
PO Box 547 56138 — 507-962-3240
David Deragisch, prin. — Fax 962-3238

Hinckley, Pine, Pop. 1,358
Hinckley-Finlayson SD 2165 — 1,100/PK-12
PO Box 308 55037 — 320-384-6277
Jack Almos, supt. — Fax 384-6135
www.hf.k12.mn.us/
Hinckley-Finlayson HS — 500/7-12
PO Box 308 55037 — 320-384-6132
Mark Roubinek, prin. — Fax 384-6135

Holdingford, Stearns, Pop. 729
Holdingford SD 738 — 1,100/PK-12
PO Box 250 56340 — 320-746-2196
Roger Carlson, supt. — Fax 746-2274
www.holdingford.k12.mn.us
Holdingford JSHS — 500/7-12
PO Box 250 56340 — 320-746-2221
Patrick Vandrovec, prin. — Fax 746-9959

Hopkins, Hennepin, Pop. 17,127
Hopkins SD 270 — 8,000/K-12
1001 Highway 7 55305 — 952-988-4000
Michael Kremer, supt. — Fax 988-4020
www.hopkins.k12.mn.us
Other Schools – See Minnetonka

Adler Graduate School — Post-Sec.
1001 Highway 7 # 311 55305 — 952-988-4170
Blake S — 1,300/PK-12
110 Blake Rd S 55343 — 952-988-3400
John Gulla, hdmstr. — Fax 988-3455

Houston, Winona, Pop. 1,011
Houston SD 294 — 800/PK-12
306 W Elm St 55943 — 507-896-5323
Kim Ross, supt. — Fax 896-3452
houston.k12.mn.us
Houston JSHS — 200/7-12
306 W Elm St 55943 — 507-896-5323
Todd Lundberg, prin. — Fax 896-4665

Howard Lake, Wright, Pop. 1,922
Howard Lake-Waverly-Winsted SD 2687 — 1,000/PK-12
PO Box 708 55349 — 320-543-3521
George Ladd, supt. — Fax 543-3590
www.hlww.k12.mn.us
Howard Lake MS — 200/6-8
PO Box 708 55349 — 320-543-3501
Dean Wessman, prin. — Fax 543-3590
Howard Lake-Waverly-Winsted HS — 300/9-12
PO Box 708 55349 — 320-543-3471
Michael Day, prin. — Fax 543-3590

Hutchinson, McLeod, Pop. 13,451
Hutchinson SD 423 — 3,100/PK-12
30 Glen St NW 55350 — 320-587-2860
Dan Vanoverbeke, supt. — Fax 587-4590
www.hutch.k12.mn.us
Hutchinson HS — 1,000/9-12
1200 Roberts Rd SW 55350 — 320-587-2151
Ron Johnson, prin. — Fax 587-8217
Hutchinson MS — 700/6-8
1365 S Grade Rd SW 55350 — 320-587-2854
Catherine Gillach, prin. — Fax 587-2857

Maplewood Academy — 100/9-12
700 Main St N 55350 — 320-587-2830
Steve Sherman, prin. — Fax 587-5649
Ridgewater College-Hutchinson Campus — Post-Sec.
2 Century Ave SE 55350 — 320-587-3636

International Falls, Koochiching, Pop. 6,454
International Falls SD 361 — 1,300/1-12
1515 11th St 56649 — 218-283-8468
Don Langan, supt. — Fax 283-8104
www.isd361.k12.mn.us
Falls HS — 700/7-12
1515 11th St 56649 — 218-283-2571
Tim Everson, prin. — Fax 283-2384

Rainy River Community College — Post-Sec.
1501 Highway 71 56649 — 218-285-7722

Inver Grove Heights, Dakota, Pop. 31,281
Inver Grove Heights Community SD 199 — 3,700/K-12
2990 80th St E 55076 — 651-306-7800
Dr. Deirdre Wells, supt. — Fax 306-7295
www.invergrove.k12.mn.us
Inver Grove Heights MS — 900/6-8
8167 Cahill Ave 55076 — 651-306-7200
Joshua Alexander, prin. — Fax 306-7152
Simley HS — 1,200/9-12
2920 80th St E 55076 — 651-306-7000
Richard Ehlers, prin. — Fax 306-7016

Inver Hills Community College — Post-Sec.
2500 80th St E 55076 — 651-450-8500

Iron, Saint Louis, Pop. 135
St. Louis County SD 2142
Supt. — See Virginia
Cherry JSHS — 200/7-12
3943 Tamminen Rd 55751 — 218-258-8991
John Metsa, prin. — Fax 258-8993

Isanti, Isanti, Pop. 4,186
Cambridge-Isanti SD 911
Supt. — See Cambridge
Isanti MS — 600/6-8
201 Centennial Dr 55040 — 763-691-8661
Timothy Truebenbach, prin. — Fax 691-8662

Isle, Mille Lacs, Pop. 807
Isle SD 473 — 700/K-12
PO Box 25 56342 — 320-676-3146
Allen Ralston, supt. — Fax 676-3966
www.isle.k12.mn.us
Isle JSHS — 300/7-12
PO Box 25 56342 — 320-676-3101
Jeff Searles, dean — Fax 676-3966

Ivanhoe, Lincoln, Pop. 641
Ivanhoe SD 403 — 200/7-12
PO Box 9 56142 — 507-694-1540
Dick Orcutt, supt. — Fax 694-1125
www.lincolnhi.org
Lincoln HS — 200/7-12
PO Box 9 56142 — 507-694-1540
David Vik, prin. — Fax 694-1125

Jackson, Jackson, Pop. 3,464
Jackson County Central SD 2895 — 1,200/PK-12
PO Box 119 56143 — 507-847-3608
Gery Arndt, supt. — Fax 847-3078
www.jccschools.com/
Jackson County Central HS — 400/9-12
PO Box 119 56143 — 507-847-5310
Jim Hirman, prin. — Fax 847-3078
Other Schools – See Lakefield

Minnesota West Community & Tech College — Post-Sec.
PO Box 269 56143 — 800-658-2522

Janesville, Waseca, Pop. 2,111
Janesville-Waldorf-Pemberton SD 2835   600/PK-12
  PO Box 389 56048   507-234-5478
  Tami Sens, supt.   Fax 234-5796
Janesville-Waldorf-Pemberton HS   300/7-12
  PO Box 389 56048   507-234-5796
  Michael Meihak, prin.   Fax 234-5135

Jordan, Scott, Pop. 4,731
Jordan SD 717   1,500/PK-12
  500 Sunset Dr 55352   952-492-6200
  Larry Kauzlarich, supt.   Fax 492-4445
  www.jordan.k12.mn.us
Jordan HS   500/9-12
  600 Sunset Dr 55352   952-492-4400
  Mark Ruggeberg, prin.   Fax 492-4425
Jordan MS   400/5-8
  500 Sunset Dr 55352   952-492-2332
  Lance Chambers, prin.   Fax 492-4450

Karlstad, Kittson, Pop. 750
Tri-County SD 2358   300/PK-12
  PO Box 178 56732   218-436-2261
  Ron Ruud, supt.   Fax 436-2263
  www.tricounty.k12.mn.us
Tri-County HS   100/7-12
  PO Box 178 56732   218-436-2374
  Dave Sorgaard, prin.   Fax 436-3422

Kasson, Dodge, Pop. 5,030
Kasson-Mantorville SD 204   1,900/PK-12
  101 16th St NE 55944   507-634-1100
  Peter Grant, supt.   Fax 634-6661
  www.komets.k12.mn.us
Kasson-Mantorville HS   500/9-12
  101 16th St NE 55944   507-634-2961
  Jerry Reker, prin.   Fax 634-4745
Kasson-Mantorville MS   300/7-8
  105 16th St NE 55944   507-634-4030
  Alan Hodge, prin.   Fax 634-6485

Kelliher, Beltrami, Pop. 304
Kelliher SD 36   300/PK-12
  PO Box 259 56650   218-647-8286
  Terry Bartness, supt.   Fax 647-8660
Kelliher JSHS   200/6-12
  PO Box 259 56650   218-647-8286
  Shelly DeJean, dean   Fax 647-8660

Kenyon, Goodhue, Pop. 1,657
Kenyon-Wanamingo SD 2172
  Supt. — See Wanamingo
Kenyon-Wanamingo HS   300/9-12
  400 6th St 55946   507-789-6186
  Donna Judson, prin.   Fax 789-6188
Kenyon-Wanamingo MS   300/5-8
  400 6th St 55946   507-789-6186
  Patrick Walsh, prin.   Fax 789-6188

Kerkhoven, Kandiyohi, Pop. 735
Kerkhoven-Murdock-Sunburg SD 775   600/PK-12
  PO Box 168 56252   320-264-1411
  Martin Heidelberger, supt.   Fax 264-1410
  www.kms.k12.mn.us
Kerkhoven JSHS   300/7-12
  PO Box 168 56252   320-264-1412
  Michael Coquyt, prin.   Fax 264-1410

Kiester, Faribault, Pop. 525
United South Central SD 2134
  Supt. — See Wells
United South Central MS   300/5-8
  PO Box 300 56051   507-294-3206
  Tracy Frank, prin.   Fax 294-3215

Kimball, Stearns, Pop. 639
Kimball SD 739   800/PK-12
  PO Box 368 55353   320-398-5585
  Scott Thielman, supt.   Fax 398-5595
  www.kimball.k12.mn.us/
Kimball JSHS   400/7-12
  PO Box 368 55353   320-398-7700
  Scott Thielman, prin.   Fax 398-7733

La Crescent, Houston, Pop. 5,066
La Crescent-Hokah SD 300   1,500/PK-12
  703 S 11th St 55947   507-895-4484
  David Krenz, supt.   Fax 895-8560
  www.isd300.k12.mn.us
La Crescent MSHS   1,000/6-12
  1301 Lancer Dr 55947   507-895-4481
  Rick Wolter, prin.   Fax 895-4490

Lake Benton, Lincoln, Pop. 687
Lake Benton SD 404   200/K-12
  PO Box 158 56149   507-368-4236
  William Delaney, supt.   Fax 368-4347
  www.lakebentonschool.org/
Lake Benton JSHS   100/7-12
  PO Box 158 56149   507-368-4241
  William Delaney, prin.   Fax 368-4347

Lake City, Wabasha, Pop. 5,238
Lake City SD 813   1,400/PK-12
  PO Box 454 55041   651-345-2198
  Jerry Jensen, supt.   Fax 345-3709
  www.lake-city.k12.mn.us
Lincoln JSHS   700/7-12
  PO Box 454 55041   651-345-4553
  Thomas Boe, prin.   Fax 345-3709

Lake Crystal, Blue Earth, Pop. 2,490
Lake Crystal Wellcome Memorial SD 2071   800/PK-12
  PO Box 160 56055   507-726-2323
  Les Norman, supt.   Fax 726-2334
  www.isd2071.k12.mn.us

Lake Crystal Wellcome Memorial JSHS   400/7-12
  PO Box 160 56055   507-726-2110
  Linda Isebrand, prin.   Fax 726-2283

Lake Elmo, Washington, Pop. 7,714
Stillwater Area SD 834
  Supt. — See Stillwater
Oak-Land JHS   1,000/7-9
  820 Manning Ave N 55042   651-351-8500
  Derek Berg, prin.   Fax 351-8505

Lakefield, Jackson, Pop. 1,701
Jackson County Central SD 2895
  Supt. — See Jackson
Jackson County Central MS   300/6-8
  PO Box 338 56150   507-662-6625
  Kari Schultz, prin.   Fax 662-5083

Sioux Valley Lutheran HS   50/9-12
  72957 400th Ave 56150   507-839-3517
      Fax 839-3516

Lake Park, Becker, Pop. 821
Lake Park-Audubon ISD 2889   700/K-12
  PO Box 479 56554   218-238-5914
  Dale Hogie, supt.   Fax 238-5643
  www.lakeparkaudubon.org
Lake Park-Audubon JSHS   300/7-12
  PO Box 479 56554   218-238-5916
  Kevin Ricke, prin.   Fax 238-6828

Lakeville, Dakota, Pop. 47,805
Lakeville Area SD 194   9,100/K-12
  8670 210th St W 55044   952-469-7100
  Gary Amoroso, supt.   Fax 469-6054
  www.isd194.k12.mn.us
Century MS, 18610 Ipava Ave 55044   600/6-8
  Catherine Gillach, prin.   952-232-2300
Kenwood Trail JHS   700/6-8
  19455 Kenwood Trl 55044   952-232-3800
  Jerry Pederson, prin.
Lakeville North HS   2,300/9-12
  19600 Ipava Ave 55044   952-232-3600
  Julia Espe, prin.   Fax 469-3367
McGuire JHS   700/6-8
  21220 Holyoke Ave 55044   952-232-2200
  Craig Menozzi, prin.

Lamberton, Redwood, Pop. 819
Red Rock Central SD 2884   500/PK-12
  PO Box 278 56152   507-752-7361
  Dr. John Brennan, supt.   Fax 752-6133
  www.rrcnet.org
Red Rock Central HS   300/6-12
  PO Box 278 56152   507-752-7361
  Bruce Olson, admin.   Fax 752-6133

Lancaster, Kittson, Pop. 341
Lancaster SD 356   200/PK-12
  PO Box 217 56735   218-762-5400
  Phillip Dyrud, supt.   Fax 762-5512
  www.lancaster.k12.mn.us/
Lancaster JSHS   100/7-12
  PO Box 217 56735   218-762-5400
  Bradley Homstad, prin.   Fax 762-5512

Lanesboro, Fillmore, Pop. 775
Lanesboro SD 229   400/PK-12
  100 Kirkwood St E 55949   507-467-2229
  Jeff Boggs, supt.   Fax 467-3026
Lanesboro JSHS   200/7-12
  100 Kirkwood St E 55949   507-467-2229
  Brett Clarke, prin.   Fax 467-3026

Laporte, Hubbard, Pop. 146
Laporte SD 306   300/PK-12
  315 Main St W 56461   218-224-2288
  Jeff Peura, supt.   Fax 224-2905
  laporte.k12.mn.us
Laporte JSHS   200/7-12
  315 Main St W 56461   218-224-2288
  Harvey Johnson, prin.   Fax 224-2905

Le Center, LeSueur, Pop. 2,306
Le Center SD 392   700/K-12
  150 W Tyrone St 56057   507-357-6802
  Tony Boyer, supt.   Fax 357-4825
  lc.k12.mn.us
Le Center JSHS   300/7-12
  150 W Tyrone St 56057   507-357-6802
  Terry Ronayne, prin.   Fax 357-4825

Le Roy, Mower, Pop. 919
Le Roy SD 499   400/PK-12
  PO Box 1000 55951   507-324-5743
  Arnold Prince, supt.   Fax 324-5149
  www.leroy.k12.mn.us
Le Roy-Ostrander JSHS   200/7-12
  PO Box 1000 55951   507-324-5741
  Steven Sallee, prin.   Fax 324-5149

Lester Prairie, McLeod, Pop. 1,431
Lester Prairie SD 424   500/K-12
  PO Box 158 55354   320-395-2521
  Joseph Miller, supt.   Fax 395-4204
  www.lp.k12.mn.us
Lester Prairie JSHS   300/7-12
  PO Box 158 55354   320-395-3001
  Joe Miller, prin.   Fax 395-4204

Le Sueur, LeSueur, Pop. 4,220
Le Sueur-Henderson SD 2397   1,300/PK-12
  115 1/2 N 5th St #200 56058   507-665-8828
  David Johnson, supt.   Fax 665-6858
  www.isd2397.k12.mn.us
Le Sueur-Henderson MSHS   700/7-12
  901 Ferry St 56058   507-665-3305
  Kevin Enerson, prin.   Fax 665-6012

Lewiston, Winona, Pop. 1,496
Lewiston-Altura SD 857   800/PK-12
  PO Box 741 55952   507-523-2191
  Bruce Montplaisir, supt.   Fax 523-3460
  www.lewalt.k12.mn.us
Lewiston-Altura JSHS   400/7-12
  PO Box 741 55952   507-523-2191
  Lance Zellmann, prin.   Fax 523-3460

Lindstrom, Chisago, Pop. 3,519
Chisago Lakes SD 2144   3,600/PK-12
  13750 Lake Blvd 55045   651-213-2000
  Michael McLoughlin, supt.   Fax 213-2050
  www.chisagolakes.k12.mn.us
Chisago Lakes HS   1,200/9-12
  13750 Lake Blvd 55045   651-213-2500
  Dave Ertl, prin.   Fax 213-2550
Chisago Lakes MS   800/6-8
  13750 Lake Blvd 55045   651-213-2400
  John Menard, prin.   Fax 213-2051

Lino Lakes, Anoka, Pop. 18,795
Centennial SD 12
  Supt. — See Circle Pines
Centennial MS   1,800/6-8
  399 Elm St 55014   763-792-5400
  Jerry Meschke, prin.   Fax 792-5450

Litchfield, Meeker, Pop. 6,685
Litchfield SD 465   1,900/PK-12
  114 N Holcombe Ave Ste 100 55355   320-693-2444
  William Wold, supt.   Fax 593-6528
  www.litchfield.k12.mn.us
Litchfield HS   700/9-12
  901 N Gilman Ave 55355   320-693-2424
  Chris Bates, prin.   Fax 593-3308
Litchfield MS   400/6-8
  340 E 10th St 55355   320-693-2441
  Patrick Devine, prin.   Fax 593-3485

Little Canada, Ramsey, Pop. 9,738
Roseville Area SD 623
  Supt. — See Roseville
Roseville Area MS   900/7-8
  15 County Road B2 E 55117   651-482-5280
  Juanita Hoskins, prin.   Fax 482-5299

Little Falls, Morrison, Pop. 7,848
Little Falls SD 482   2,900/K-12
  1001 5th Ave SE 56345   320-632-2002
  Dr. Bruce Anderson, supt.   Fax 632-2010
  www.lfalls.k12.mn.us
Little Falls Community HS   1,100/9-12
  1001 5th Ave SE 56345   320-616-2200
  Bob Just, prin.   Fax 616-2210
Little Falls Community MS   700/6-8
  1000 1st Ave NE 56345   320-616-4200
  Maxine Strege, prin.   Fax 616-4210

Mary of Lourdes MS   100/5-8
  205 3rd St NW 56345   320-632-6742
  Maria Heymans-Becker, prin.   Fax 632-3556

Littlefork, Koochiching, Pop. 690
Littlefork-Big Falls SD 362   300/PK-12
  700 Main St 56653   218-278-6614
  Bryan Kehoe, supt.   Fax 278-6615
  www.isd362.k12.mn.us
Littlefork-Big Falls S   300/PK-12
  700 Main St 56653   218-278-6614
  Bryan Kehoe, prin.   Fax 278-6615

Long Lake, Hennepin, Pop. 1,838
Orono SD 278   2,500/K-12
  PO Box 46 55356   952-449-8300
  Dr. Karen Orcutt, supt.   Fax 449-8399
  www.orono.k12.mn.us
Orono HS   800/9-12
  PO Box 26 55356   952-449-8400
  Dane Benson, prin.   Fax 449-8449
Orono MS   600/6-8
  PO Box 16 55356   952-449-8450
  Pat Wroten, prin.   Fax 449-8453

Long Prairie, Todd, Pop. 2,967
Long Prairie-Grey Eagle SD 2753   1,400/PK-12
  205 2nd St S 56347   320-732-2194
  Donald Hansen, supt.   Fax 732-3791
  www.lpge.k12.mn.us/
Long Prairie-Grey Eagle HS   500/9-12
  510 9th St NE 56347   320-732-2194
  Karrie Boser, prin.   Fax 732-6470
Long Prairie MS   300/6-8
  205 2nd St S 56347   320-732-2194
  Paul Weinzierl, prin.   Fax 732-2844

Luverne, Rock, Pop. 4,531
Luverne SD 2184   1,400/PK-12
  709 N Kniss Ave 56156   507-283-8088
  Gary Fisher, supt.   Fax 283-9681
  www.isd2184.net/
Luverne HS   400/9-12
  709 N Kniss Ave 56156   507-283-4491
  Donna Judson, prin.   Fax 283-9681
Luverne MS   300/6-8
  709 N Kniss Ave 56156   507-283-4491
  Donna Judson, prin.   Fax 283-9681

Lyle, Mower, Pop. 570
Lyle SD 497   300/K-12
  700 E 2nd St 55953   507-325-4144
  Jerry Reshetar, supt.   Fax 325-4611
  www.lyle.k12.mn.us
Lyle HS   200/7-12
  700 E 2nd St 55953   507-325-2201
  Royce Helmbrecht, prin.   Fax 325-4611

Mabel, Fillmore, Pop. 755
Mabel-Canton SD 238 400/PK-12
PO Box 337 55954 507-493-5423
James Busta, supt. Fax 493-5425
www.mabelcanton.k12.mn.us/
Mabel-Canton JSHS 200/7-12
PO Box 337 55954 507-493-5422
Kay Dahle, prin. Fax 493-5425

Mc Gregor, Aitkin, Pop. 405
Mc Gregor SD 4 500/PK-12
PO Box 160, 218-768-2111
Lynette Maas, supt. Fax 768-3901
www.mcgregor.k12.mn.us
Mc Gregor JSHS 300/7-12
PO Box 160, 218-768-2111
Paul Grams, prin. Fax 768-3802

Madelia, Watonwan, Pop. 2,301
Madelia SD 837 600/PK-12
320 Buck Ave SE 56062 507-642-3232
Norm Miller, supt. Fax 642-3622
Madelia JSHS 300/7-12
320 Buck Ave SE 56062 507-642-3232
Allan Beyer, prin. Fax 642-3622

Madison, Lac qui Parle, Pop. 1,721
Lac Qui Parle Valley SD 2853 1,100/PK-12
2860 291st Ave 56256 320-752-4200
Robert Munsterman, supt. Fax 752-4401
www.lqpv.org/
Lac Qui Parle Valley JSHS 600/7-12
2860 291st Ave 56256 320-752-4200
Jon Fulton, prin. Fax 752-4401

Mahnomen, Mahnomen, Pop. 1,177
Mahnomen 432 800/PK-12
PO Box 319 56557 218-935-2211
Jerry Nesland, supt. Fax 935-5921
Mahnomen JSHS 400/7-12
PO Box 319 56557 218-935-2213
Jack Stronstad, prin. Fax 935-5921

Mahtomedi, Washington, Pop. 8,076
Mahtomedi SD 832 3,000/K-12
1520 Mahtomedi Ave 55115 651-407-2000
Dr. Mark Wolak, supt. Fax 407-2025
www.mahtomedi.k12.mn.us
Mahtomedi HS 1,100/9-12
8000 75th St N 55115 651-407-2100
Fax 407-2125
Mahtomedi MS 800/6-8
8100 75th St N 55115 651-407-2200
Dr. Sharon Zweber, prin. Fax 407-2225

Mankato, Blue Earth, Pop. 33,925
Mankato SD 77 7,700/K-12
PO Box 8741 56002 507-387-1868
E.R. Waltman, supt. Fax 387-4257
www.isd77.k12.mn.us
Mankato East HS 1,000/9-12
2600 Hoffman Rd 56001 507-387-5671
Donald Poplau, prin. Fax 387-7927
Mankato East JHS 500/7-8
2600 Hoffman Rd 56001 507-345-6625
Rich Dahman, prin. Fax 387-2890
Mankato West HS 1,200/9-12
1351 S Riverfront Dr 56001 507-387-3461
Bruce Borchers, prin. Fax 345-1502
Other Schools – See North Mankato

Bethany Lutheran College Post-Sec.
700 Luther Dr 56001 507-344-7000
Fitzgerald MS 200/6-8
110 N 5th St 56001 507-388-9344
Kim Meyer, prin. Fax 388-2750
Immanuel Lutheran S 100/K-12
421 N 2nd St 56001 507-345-3027
Karl Olmanson, prin. Fax 345-1562
Loyola HS 200/9-12
145 Good Counsel Dr 56001 507-388-2997
Shelley Schultz, prin. Fax 388-3081
Minnesota State University Mankato Post-Sec.
PO Box 8400 56002 507-389-2463
Rasmussen College Post-Sec.
501 Holly Ln 56001 507-625-6556
Sr. Rosalind Gefre School
416 S Front St 56001 507-344-0220

Maple Grove, Hennepin, Pop. 57,172
Osseo SD 279 21,500/PK-12
11200 93rd Ave N 55369 763-391-7000
James Smith, supt. Fax 391-7070
www.district279.org
Maple Grove JHS 1,600/7-9
7000 Hemlock Ln N 55369 763-315-7600
Laurel Anderson, prin. Fax 315-7601
Maple Grove SHS 1,800/10-12
9800 Fernbrook Ln N 55369 763-391-8700
Wendy Loberg, prin. Fax 391-8701
Other Schools – See Brooklyn Park, Osseo

Heritage Christian Academy 500/PK-12
15655 Bass Lake Rd 55311 763-463-2200
Rodney Nelson, pres. Fax 463-2299

Maple Lake, Wright, Pop. 1,735
Maple Lake SD 881 900/PK-12
PO Box 760 55358 320-963-3171
Mark Redemske, supt. Fax 963-3170
www.maplelake.k12.mn.us
Maple Lake JSHS 500/7-12
PO Box 820 55358 320-963-3171
Mary James, prin. Fax 963-3170

Mapleton, Blue Earth, Pop. 1,670
Maple River SD 2135 1,300/PK-12
PO Box 515 56065 507-524-3918
Wayne Gilman, supt. Fax 524-4882
www.isd2135.k12.mn.us/
Maple River HS 400/9-12
PO Box 515 56065 507-524-3918
Dan Anderson, prin. Fax 524-4919
Other Schools – See Amboy, Minnesota Lake

Maplewood, Ramsey, Pop. 35,945
North St. Paul-Maplewood-Oakdale SD 622
Supt. — See North Saint Paul
Glenn MS 900/6-8
1560 County Road B E 55109 651-748-6300
Nancy Weinand, prin. Fax 748-6391
Maplewood MS 900/6-8
2410 Holloway Ave E 55109 651-748-6500
Ruthanne Strohn, prin. Fax 748-6591

Hill-Murray HS 900/9-12
2625 Larpenteur Ave E 55109 651-777-1376
Dr. Susan Paul, prin. Fax 748-2444

Marshall, Lyon, Pop. 12,545
Marshall SD 413 2,200/PK-12
400 Tiger Dr 56258 507-537-6924
Klint Willert, supt. Fax 537-6931
www.swmn.org
Marshall HS 900/9-12
400 Tiger Dr 56258 507-537-6920
Wade McKittrick, prin. Fax 537-6933
Marshall MS 300/7-8
207 N 4th St 56258 507-537-6938
Doug Deragisch, prin. Fax 537-6942

Southwest Minnesota State University Post-Sec.
1501 State St 56258 507-537-7678

Mayer, Carver, Pop. 776

Mayer Lutheran HS 300/9-12
305 5th St NE 55360 952-657-2251
Tim Bierbaum, prin. Fax 657-2344

Mazeppa, Wabasha, Pop. 791
Zumbrota-Mazeppa SD 2805 1,200/PK-12
PO Box 222 55956 507-843-4080
Roger Rueckert, supt. Fax 843-4086
www.zmschools.us/
Zumbrota-Mazeppa MS 300/5-8
425 Chestnut St NE 55956 507-843-2165
Richard Meyerhofer, prin. Fax 843-5853
Other Schools – See Zumbrota

Medford, Steele, Pop. 1,078
Medford SD 763 700/PK-12
750 2nd Ave SE 55049 507-451-5250
Gary Hanson, supt. Fax 451-6474
www.medford.k12.mn.us/
Medford JSHS 300/7-12
750 2nd Ave SE 55049 507-451-5250
Keith Kottke, prin. Fax 451-6474

Melrose, Stearns, Pop. 3,186
Melrose SD 740 1,100/PK-12
546 N 5th Ave E 56352 320-256-4224
Kevin Wellen, supt. Fax 256-4311
www.melrose.k12.mn.us
Melrose HS 600/9-12
546 N 5th Ave E 56352 320-256-4224
Chad Doetkott, prin. Fax 256-4311
Melrose MS 6-8
566 N 5th Ave E 56352 320-256-4224
Tim Truebenbach, prin. Fax 256-4311

Menahga, Wadena, Pop. 1,212
Menahga SD 821 700/PK-12
PO Box 160 56464 218-564-4141
Fred Seybert, supt. Fax 564-5401
www.menahga.k12.mn.us
Menahga JSHS 300/7-12
PO Box 160 56464 218-564-4141
Mary Merchant, prin. Fax 564-5401

Mendota Heights, Dakota, Pop. 11,343
West St. Paul-Mendota Hts-Eagan SD 197 4,700/K-12
1897 Delaware Ave 55118 651-681-2300
Jay Haugen, supt. Fax 681-9102
isd197.org
Friendly Hills MS 700/5-8
701 Mendota Heights Rd 55120 651-905-4100
Susan Larkin, prin. Fax 905-4101
Sibley HS 1,500/9-12
1897 Delaware Ave 55118 651-681-2350
Helen Fisk, prin. Fax 405-2461
Other Schools – See West Saint Paul

Brown College Post-Sec.
1440 Northland Dr 55120 651-905-3400
Convent of the Visitation S 600/PK-12
2455 Visitation Dr 55120 651-683-1700
Fax 454-7144
Le Cordon Bleu College of Culinary Arts Post-Sec.
1408 Northland Dr Ste 102 55120 651-675-4700
St. Thomas Academy 700/7-12
949 Mendota Heights Rd 55120 651-454-4570
Thomas Mich Ph.D., hdmstr. Fax 454-4574

Middle River, Marshall, Pop. 313
Greenbush-Middle River SD 2683
Supt. — See Greenbush
Greenbush-Middle River JHS 100/6-8
PO Box 130 56737 218-222-3310
Sharon Schultz, prin. Fax 222-3314

Milaca, Mille Lacs, Pop. 2,820
Milaca SD 912 1,900/PK-12
500 Highway 23 W 56353 320-982-7210
Dr. Barbra Zakrajsek, supt. Fax 982-7179
www.milaca.k12.mn.us
Milaca HS 1,000/7-12
500 Highway 23 W 56353 320-982-7206
Richard Rhoades, prin. Fax 983-3566

Minneapolis, Hennepin, Pop. 373,188
Minneapolis SD 1 38,200/PK-12
807 Broadway St NE 55413 612-668-0000
Thandiwe Peebles, supt. Fax 668-0195
www.mpls.k12.mn.us
Afrocentric Academy 600/6-8
1501 Aldrich Ave N 55411 612-668-2600
Tiffanie Brooks, admin. Fax 668-2610
Anthony MS 700/6-8
5757 Irving Ave S 55419 612-668-3240
Jackie Hanson, prin. Fax 668-3250
Anwatin MS 700/6-8
256 Upton Ave S 55405 612-668-2450
Beth Russell, prin. Fax 668-2460
Edison HS 1,300/9-12
700 22nd Ave NE 55418 612-668-1300
Larry Lucio, prin. Fax 668-1320
Field MS 500/5-8
4645 4th Ave S 55419 612-668-3640
Erin Glynn, prin. Fax 668-3661
Folwell MS 600/6-8
3611 20th Ave S 55407 612-668-4550
Carla Steinbach, prin. Fax 668-4560
Henry HS 1,600/9-12
4320 Newton Ave N 55412 612-668-2000
Gary Kociemba, prin. Fax 668-1993
Lake Harriet Upper ES 500/3-8
4912 Vincent Ave S 55410 612-668-3310
Marsha Seltz, prin. Fax 668-3320
Northeast MS 600/6-8
2955 Hayes St NE 55418 612-668-1500
Ben Perry, prin. Fax 668-1510
North HS 1,200/9-12
1500 James Ave N 55411 612-668-1700
Michael Favor, prin. Fax 668-1770
Olson MS 700/6-8
1607 51st Ave N 55430 612-668-1640
Barbara Muir, prin. Fax 668-1650
Roosevelt HS 1,400/9-12
4029 28th Ave S 55406 612-668-4800
Bruce Gilman, prin. Fax 668-4810
Sanford MS 400/6-8
3524 42nd Ave S 55406 612-668-4900
Meredith Davis, prin. Fax 668-4910
South HS 1,900/9-12
3131 19th Ave S 55407 612-668-4300
Linda Nelson, prin. Fax 668-4310
Southwest HS 1,600/9-12
3414 W 47th St 55410 612-668-3030
Bill Smith, prin. Fax 668-3080
Washburn HS 1,300/9-12
201 W 49th St 55419 612-668-3400
Steve Couture, prin. Fax 668-3410
P M HS Adult
1501 Aldrich Ave N 55411 612-668-2612
Jackie Sowell-Davis, prin. Fax 668-2617

Wayzata SD 284 9,700/PK-12
210 County Road 101 N 55447 952-745-5000
Bob Ostlund, supt. Fax 745-5091
www.wayzata.k12.mn.us
Other Schools – See Plymouth, Wayzata

Art Institutes International Minnesota Post-Sec.
15 S 9th St 55402 612-332-3361
Art Instruction Schools Post-Sec.
3400 Technology Dr 55418 612-362-5000
Augsburg College Post-Sec.
2211 Riverside Ave 55454 612-330-1000
Aveda College Post-Sec.
400 Central Ave SE 55414 612-378-7404
Bais Yaakov HS of the Twin Cities 50/9-12
4221 Sunset Blvd 55416 952-915-9117
Sarah Gibber, prin. Fax 915-9116
Blake S - Northrup Campus 400/9-12
511 Kenwood Pkwy 55403 952-988-3700
Marc Bogursky, prin. Fax 988-3705
Breck S 1,200/PK-12
123 Ottawa Ave N 55422 763-381-8100
Samuel Salas, hdmstr. Fax 381-8288
Capella University Post-Sec.
225 S 6th St 9th Floor 55402 888-227-3552
De La Salle HS 600/9-12
1 De La Salle Dr 55401 612-676-7600
Barry Lieske, prin. Fax 362-9641
Dunwoody College of Technology Post-Sec.
818 Dunwoody Blvd 55403 612-374-5800
Hennepin County Medical Center Post-Sec.
701 Park Ave 55415 612-347-2352
Herzing College Post-Sec.
5700 W Broadway Ave 55428 763-535-3000
Maranatha Christian Academy 800/PK-12
4021 Thomas Ave N 55412 612-588-2850
Brian Sullivan, admin. Fax 588-7854
Minneapolis College of Art & Design Post-Sec.
2501 Stevens Ave 55404 612-874-3700
Minneapolis Community and Tech College Post-Sec.
1501 Hennepin Ave 55403 612-341-7000
Minneapolis School of Massage & Bodywork Post-Sec.
81 Lowry Ave NE 55418 612-788-8907
Minneapolis VA Medical Center Post-Sec.
1 Veterans Dr 55417 612-725-2000
Minnehaha Academy 500/9-12
3100 W River Pkwy 55406 612-729-8321
Nancy Johnson, prin. Fax 728-7787

North Central University — Post-Sec.
910 Elliot Ave 55404 — 612-332-3491
North Memorial Medical Center — Post-Sec.
3300 Oakdale Ave N 55422 — 763-520-5200
St. Mary's Campus Coll. of St. Catherine — Post-Sec.
2500 S 6th St 55454 — 612-332-5521
St. Mary's University of Minnesota — Post-Sec.
2500 Park Ave 55404 — 866-437-2788
San Miguel MS — 200/6-8
3800 Pleasant Ave 55409 — 612-870-1109
Sr. Mary Willette, prin. — Fax 870-1224
Summit Academy OIC — Post-Sec.
935 Olson Memorial Hwy 55405 — 612-377-0150
University of Minnesota — Post-Sec.
231 Pillsbury Dr SE 55455 — 612-625-5000
Walden University — Post-Sec.
155 5th Ave S Ste 100 55401 — 612-338-7224
Woodcrest Baptist Academy — 100/K-12
6875 University Ave NE 55432 — 763-571-6409

Minneota, Lyon, Pop. 1,396
Minneota SD 414 — 500/K-12
PO Box 98 56264 — 507-872-6532
John Kraker, supt. — Fax 872-5172
www.minneotaschools.org/
Minneota JSHS — 300/7-12
PO Box 98 56264 — 507-872-6175
— Fax 872-6494

Minnesota Lake, Faribault, Pop. 671
Maple River SD 2135
Supt. — See Mapleton
Maple River East MS — 100/6-8
PO Box 218 56068 — 507-462-3348
James Bisel, prin. — Fax 462-3219

Minnetonka, Hennepin, Pop. 50,690
Hopkins SD 270
Supt. — See Hopkins
Hopkins HS — 2,000/10-12
2400 Lindbergh Dr 55305 — 952-988-4500
Ronald Chall, prin. — Fax 988-4716
Hopkins North JHS — 1,000/7-9
10700 Cedar Lake Rd 55305 — 952-988-4800
Patrice Schmidt, prin. — Fax 988-4869
Hopkins West JHS — 1,000/7-9
3830 Baker Rd 55305 — 952-988-4400
Terry Wolfson, prin. — Fax 988-4477

Minnetonka SD 276 — 7,600/K-12
5621 County Rd 101 55345 — 952-401-5000
Dennis Peterson, supt. — Fax 401-5083
www.minnetonka.k12.mn.us
Minnetonka East MS — 900/6-8
17000 Lake Street Ext 55345 — 952-401-5200
Pete Dymit, prin. — Fax 401-5268
Minnetonka HS — 2,400/9-12
18301 Highway 7 55345 — 952-401-5700
David Adney, prin. — Fax 401-5709
Other Schools – See Excelsior

Minnetonka Christian Academy — 200/K-12
3500 Williston Rd 55345 — 952-935-4497
Dawn Campanello, prin. — Fax 935-4498

Minnetrista, Hennepin, Pop. 4,849
Westonka SD 277 — 2,200/K-12
5901 Sunnyfield Rd E 55364 — 952-491-8000
Gene Zulk, supt. — Fax 491-8012
www.westonka.k12.mn.us
Other Schools – See Mound

Montevideo, Chippewa, Pop. 5,383
Montevideo SD 129 — 1,500/PK-12
2001 William Ave 56265 — 320-269-8833
David Baukol, supt. — Fax 269-8834
www.montevideoschools.com
Montevideo HS — 500/9-12
1501 William Ave 56265 — 320-269-6446
Bruce Bergeson, prin. — Fax 269-6446
Montevideo MS — 500/5-8
2001 William Ave 56265 — 320-269-6431
Gary Radke, prin. — Fax 269-8834

Montgomery, LeSueur, Pop. 2,869
Montgomery-Lonsdale SD 394 — 1,100/PK-12
101 2nd St NE 56069 — 507-364-8100
Ray Farwell, supt. — Fax 364-8103
www.montlonsdale.k12.mn.us
Montgomery-Lonsdale HS — 500/7-12
101 2nd St NE 56069 — 507-364-8111
Michael Bergevin, prin. — Fax 364-8103

Monticello, Wright, Pop. 9,648
Monticello SD 882 — 3,800/PK-12
302 Washington St 55362 — 763-271-0300
James Johnson, supt. — Fax 271-0313
www.monticello.k12.mn.us
Monticello HS — 1,100/9-12
5225 School Blvd 55362 — 763-271-0350
Doug Standke, prin. — Fax 271-0359
Monticello MS — 900/6-8
800 E Broadway St 55362 — 763-271-0500
Jeff Scherber, prin. — Fax 271-0510

Moorhead, Clay, Pop. 32,786
Moorhead SD 152 — 3,900/K-12
2410 14th St S 56560 — 218-284-3330
Dr. Larry Nybladh, supt. — Fax 284-3332
www.moorhead.k12.mn.us
Horizon MS — 1,000/6-8
3601 12th Ave S 56560 — 218-284-7300
Colleen Tupper, prin. — Fax 284-7333
Moorhead HS — 1,700/9-12
2300 4th Ave S 56560 — 218-284-2300
Eugene Boyle, prin. — Fax 284-2333

Concordia College — Post-Sec.
901 8th St S 56562 — 218-299-4000
MN State Community & Technical College — Post-Sec.
1900 28th Ave S 56560 — 800-426-5603
Minnesota State University Moorhead — Post-Sec.
1104 7th Ave S 56563 — 218-236-2011
Park Christian S — 500/PK-12
300 17th St N 56560 — 218-236-0500
Terinne Berg, admin. — Fax 236-7301
Rita's Moorhead Beauty College — Post-Sec.
17 4th St S 56560 — 218-236-7201

Moose Lake, Carlton, Pop. 2,371
Moose Lake SD 97 — 800/K-12
PO Box 489 55767 — 218-485-4435
Timothy Caroline, supt. — Fax 485-8110
Moose Lake JSHS — 400/7-12
PO Box 489 55767 — 218-485-4622
Robert Indihar, prin. — Fax 485-8681

Mora, Kanabec, Pop. 3,457
Mora SD 332 — 1,900/PK-12
400 Maple Ave E 55051 — 320-679-6200
Howard Caldwell, supt. — Fax 679-6209
www.mora.k12.mn.us
Mora HS — 900/7-12
400 Maple Ave E 55051 — 320-679-6220
Mark Antonson, prin. — Fax 679-6238

Morgan, Redwood, Pop. 863
Cedar Mountain SD 2754 — 400/K-12
PO Box 188 56266 — 507-249-5990
Robert Tews, supt. — Fax 249-3149
Cedar Mountain JSHS — 200/7-12
PO Box 188 56266 — 507-249-5888
Stephanie Perry, prin. — Fax 249-3149

Morris, Stevens, Pop. 5,161
Morris SD 769 — 1,000/PK-12
201 S Columbia Ave 56267 — 320-589-4840
Scott Monson, supt. — Fax 589-3203
www.morris.k12.mn.us
Morris Area JSHS — 600/7-12
201 S Columbia Ave 56267 — 320-589-4400
George Morrow, prin. — Fax 589-3203

University of Minnesota — Post-Sec.
600 E 4th St 56267 — 320-589-2211

Morristown, Rice, Pop. 1,013
Waterville-Elysian-Morristown SD 2143
Supt. — See Waterville
Waterville-Elysian-Morristown JHS — 100/7-8
PO Box 278 55052 — 507-685-4222
Bernardine Sautter, prin. — Fax 685-2420

Cannon Valley Lutheran HS — 50/9-12
PO Box 346 55052 — 507-685-2636
Douglas Mierow, admin. — Fax 685-4502

Motley, Morrison, Pop. 641
Staples-Motley ISD 2170
Supt. — See Staples
Motley-Staples MS — 400/6-8
PO Box 68 56466 — 218-352-6170
Jim Hofer, prin. — Fax 352-6508

Mound, Hennepin, Pop. 9,376
Westonka SD 277
Supt. — See Minnetrista
Mound-Westonka HS — 900/8-12
5905 Sunnyfield Rd E 55364 — 952-491-8100
Keith Randklev, prin. — Fax 491-8103

Mounds View, Ramsey, Pop. 12,696
Mounds View SD 621
Supt. — See Shoreview
Edgewood MS — 600/6-8
5100 Edgewood Dr 55112 — 763-784-2010
Penny Howard, prin. — Fax 639-6253

Mountain Iron, Saint Louis, Pop. 2,976
Mountain Iron-Buhl SD 712 — 600/PK-12
5529 Emerald Ave 55768 — 218-735-8271
Loren Sauter, supt. — Fax 735-8244
Mountain Iron-Buhl JSHS — 300/7-12
PO Box 537 55768 — 218-735-8277
Don Stahl, prin. — Fax 735-8217

Mountain Lake, Cottonwood, Pop. 2,048
Mountain Lake SD 173 — 500/PK-12
PO Box 400 56159 — 507-427-2325
William Strom, supt. — Fax 427-3047
www.mountainlake.k12.mn.us
Mountain Lake JSHS — 200/7-12
PO Box 400 56159 — 507-427-2325
William Strom, prin. — Fax 427-3047

Mountain Lake Christian S — 100/PK-12
710 11th Ave 56159 — 507-427-2010
Chad Schneider, admin. — Fax 427-3123

Nashwauk, Itasca, Pop. 912
Nashwauk-Keewatin SD 319 — 700/PK-12
400 2nd St 55769 — 218-885-2705
John Klarich, supt. — Fax 885-2905
Nashwauk JSHS — 300/7-12
400 2nd St 55769 — 218-885-1280
Robert Bestul, prin. — Fax 885-2910

Nevis, Hubbard, Pop. 368
Nevis SD 308 — 600/PK-12
PO Box 138 56467 — 218-652-3500
Steven Rassier, supt. — Fax 652-3505
www.nevis.k12.mn.us

Nevis JSHS — 300/7-12
PO Box 138 56467 — 218-652-3500
Jodi Sandmeyer, prin. — Fax 652-3505

New Brighton, Ramsey, Pop. 21,751
Mounds View SD 621
Supt. — See Shoreview
Highview MS — 800/6-8
2300 7th St NW 55112 — 651-633-8144
Mona Fadness, prin. — Fax 639-6273
Irondale HS — 1,500/9-12
2425 Long Lake Rd 55112 — 651-786-5200
Colleen Wambach, prin. — Fax 639-6043

United Theological Seminary/Twin Cities — Post-Sec.
3000 5th St NW 55112 — 651-255-6107

Newfolden, Marshall, Pop. 346
Marshall County Central SD 441 — 400/K-12
PO Box 189 56738 — 218-874-8530
Ronald Paggen, supt. — Fax 874-8581
Central JSHS — 200/7-12
PO Box 189 56738 — 218-874-7225
Bryan Thygeson, prin. — Fax 874-8581

New Hope, Hennepin, Pop. 20,317
Robbinsdale SD 281 — 13,300/K-12
4148 Winnetka Ave N 55427 — 763-504-8000
Stan F. Mack, supt. — Fax 504-8979
www.rdale.k12.mn.us
Robbinsdale Cooper HS — 2,100/9-12
8230 47th Ave N 55428 — 763-504-8500
Jeff McGonigal, prin. — Fax 504-8531
Other Schools – See Golden Valley, Plymouth,
Robbinsdale

New London, Kandiyohi, Pop. 1,102
New London-Spicer SD 345 — 1,600/K-12
PO Box 430 56273 — 320-354-2252
Paul Carlson, supt. — Fax 354-9001
nls.k12.mn.us
New London-Spicer HS — 600/9-12
PO Box 430 56273 — 320-354-2252
Kevin Acquard, prin. — Fax 354-9001
New London-Spicer MS — 600/5-8
PO Box 430 56273 — 320-354-2252
Rick Swenson, prin. — Fax 354-4244

New Prague, Scott, Pop. 5,391
New Prague Area SD 721 — 2,900/PK-12
111 Main St W 56071 — 952-758-1700
Dr. Frances Poplau, supt. — Fax 758-1799
www.np.k12.mn.us
New Prague HS — 900/9-12
221 12th St NE 56071 — 952-758-1200
Tom Doig, prin. — Fax 758-1299
New Prague MS — 700/6-8
721 Central Ave N 56071 — 952-758-1400
Tim Dittberner, prin. — Fax 758-1499

New Richland, Waseca, Pop. 1,168
NRHEG SD 2168 — 1,000/PK-12
PO Box 427 56072 — 507-465-3205
Richard Lorenz, supt. — Fax 465-8633
NRHEG HS — 300/9-12
PO Box 427 56072 — 507-465-3205
Paul Sparby, prin. — Fax 465-8633

New Ulm, Brown, Pop. 13,401
New Ulm SD 88 — 2,400/PK-12
400 S Payne St 56073 — 507-359-8401
Harold Remme, supt. — Fax 359-8406
www.newulm.k12.mn.us/
New Ulm HS — 900/9-12
414 S Payne St 56073 — 507-359-8420
Mark Bergmann, prin. — Fax 359-8432
New Ulm MS — 400/7-8
15 N State St 56073 — 507-359-8480
Steve Weber, prin. — Fax 359-7012

Cathedral HS — 200/9-12
600 N Washington St 56073 — 507-354-4511
Jason Olson, prin. — Fax 354-5711
Holy Trinity MS — 200/5-8
515 N State St 56073 — 507-354-4311
Randy Althoff, prin. — Fax 354-7071
Martin Luther College — Post-Sec.
1995 Luther Ct 56073 — 507-354-8221
Minnesota Valley Lutheran HS — 300/9-12
45638 561st Ave 56073 — 507-354-6851
Tim Plath, prin. — Fax 354-6854

New York Mills, Otter Tail, Pop. 1,189
New York Mills SD 553 — 800/PK-12
PO Box 218 56567 — 218-385-4201
Todd Cameron, supt. — Fax 385-2551
www.nymills.k12.mn.us
New York Mills JSHS — 400/7-12
PO Box 218 56567 — 218-385-4211
Matthew Aker, prin. — Fax 385-2551

Nicollet, Nicollet, Pop. 972
Nicollet SD 507 — 300/K-12
PO Box 108 56074 — 507-232-3411
Todd Meyer, supt. — Fax 232-3536
isd507.k12.mn.us
Nicollet S — 300/K-12
PO Box 108 56074 — 507-232-3448
Todd Meyer, prin. — Fax 232-3536

North Branch, Chisago, Pop. 9,457
North Branch SD 138 — 2,700/PK-12
PO Box 370 55056 — 651-674-1000
Rodney Reisnouer, supt. — Fax 674-1010
www.northbranch.k12.mn.us

North Branch HS 1,100/9-12
38175 Grand Ave 55056 651-674-1500
Brad Windschill, prin. Fax 674-1510
North Branch MS 900/6-8
38431 Lincoln Trl 55056 651-674-1300
Todd Tetzlaff, prin. Fax 674-1310

Northfield, Rice, Pop. 18,187
Northfield SD 659 3,600/PK-12
1400 Division St S 55057 507-663-0629
L. Chris Richardson Ph.D., supt. Fax 663-0611
www.nfld.k12.mn.us
Northfield HS 1,300/9-12
1400 Division St S 55057 507-663-0630
Joel Leer, prin. Fax 645-3455
Northfield MS 900/6-8
2200 Division St S 55057 507-663-0650
Burt Bemmels, prin. Fax 663-0660

Carleton College Post-Sec.
1 N College St 55057 507-646-4000
Laura Baker School Post-Sec.
211 Oak St 55057 507-645-8866
St. Olaf College Post-Sec.
1500 Saint Olaf Ave 55057 507-646-2222

North Mankato, Nicollet, Pop. 12,248
Mankato SD 77
Supt. — See Mankato
Dakota Meadows JHS 600/7-8
1900 Howard Dr 56003 507-387-5077
Shane Baier, prin. Fax 387-1119

South Central College Post-Sec.
1920 Lee Blvd 56003 507-389-7200

Northome, Koochiching, Pop. 222
South Koochiching-Rainy River SD 363 400/K-12
PO Box 465 56661 218-897-5275
Dr. Jerry Struss, supt. Fax 897-5280
www.northome.k12.mn.us
Northome JSHS 100/7-12
PO Box 465 56661 218-897-5275
Shannon Avenson, prin. Fax 897-5280
Other Schools – See Birchdale

Northrop, Martin, Pop. 250

Martin Luther HS 100/9-12
PO Box 228 56075 507-436-5249

North Saint Paul, Ramsey, Pop. 12,568
North St. Paul-Maplewood-Oakdale SD 622 11,100/K-12
2520 12th Ave E 55109 651-748-7410
Patricia Phillips, supt. Fax 748-7413
www.isd622.org/
North HS 2,000/9-12
2416 11th Ave E 55109 651-748-6000
Greg Nelson, prin. Fax 748-6091
Other Schools – See Maplewood, Oakdale

Norwood Young America, Carver, Pop. 3,176
Central ISD 108 1,000/PK-12
PO Box 247 55368 952-467-7000
Brian Corlett, supt. Fax 467-7003
www.central.k12.mn.us
Central HS 400/9-12
PO Box 247 55368 952-467-7100
Ron Brand, prin. Fax 467-7103
Central MS 200/6-8
PO Box 247 55368 952-467-7200
Kevin Starr, prin. Fax 467-7203

Oakdale, Washington, Pop. 27,673
North St. Paul-Maplewood-Oakdale SD 622
Supt. — See North Saint Paul
Skyview Community MS 900/6-8
1100 Heron Ave N 55128 651-702-8000
Thomas Harrold, prin. Fax 702-8091
Tartan HS 1,800/9-12
828 Greenway Ave N 55128 651-702-8600
John Bezek, prin. Fax 702-8799

Globe College Post-Sec.
7166 10th St N 55128 651-730-5100

Ogilvie, Kanabec, Pop. 483
Ogilvie SD 333 700/K-12
333 School Dr 56358 320-272-5000
Tom Rich, supt. Fax 272-5072
www.ogilvie.k12.mn.us
Ogilvie HS 400/7-12
333 School Dr 56358 320-272-5000
Jeffrey Ehlenz, prin. Fax 272-5072

Okabena, Jackson, Pop. 180
Heron Lake-Okabena SD 330 300/PK-12
PO Box 97 56161 507-853-4507
Becky Cselovszki, supt. Fax 853-4642
www.ssc.mntm.org
Southwest Star Concept S 200/7-12
PO Box 97 56161 507-853-4507
Becky Cselovszki, prin. Fax 853-4642

Oklee, Red Lake, Pop. 387
Oklee SD 627 200/K-12
PO Box 100 56742 218-796-5136
James Guetter, supt. Fax 796-5139
Oklee S 200/K-12
PO Box 100 56742 218-796-5136
Fax 796-5139

Olivia, Renville, Pop. 2,524
BOLD SD 2534
Supt. — See Bird Island

BOLD JSHS 500/7-12
701 9th St S 56277 320-523-1031
Alan Erickson, prin. Fax 523-5410

Onamia, Mille Lacs, Pop. 888
Onamia SD 480 700/K-12
35465 125th Ave 56359 320-532-4174
John Varner, supt. Fax 532-4658
www.onamia.k12.mn.us
Onamia JSHS 400/7-12
35465 125th Ave 56359 320-532-4174
Dennis Hitzemann, prin. Fax 532-4658

Orr, Saint Louis, Pop. 246
St. Louis County SD 2142
Supt. — See Virginia
Orr JSHS 100/7-12
PO Box 307 55771 218-757-3225
Sidney Simonson, prin. Fax 757-3666

Ortonville, Big Stone, Pop. 2,096
Ortonville SD 62 600/PK-12
200 Trojan Dr 56278 320-839-6181
Jeffrey Taylor, supt. Fax 839-3708
Ortonville S 600/PK-12
200 Trojan Dr 56278 320-839-6183
Joel Stattelman, prin. Fax 839-2499

Osakis, Douglas, Pop. 1,570
Osakis SD 213 700/PK-12
PO Box X 56360 320-859-2191
Gregg Allen, supt. Fax 859-2835
Osakis JSHS 400/7-12
PO Box X 56360 320-859-2192
Tim Roggenbuck, prin. Fax 859-2835

Osseo, Hennepin, Pop. 2,517
Osseo SD 279
Supt. — See Maple Grove
Osseo JHS 1,300/7-9
10223 93rd Ave N 55369 763-391-8800
Willie Johnson, prin. Fax 391-8801
Osseo SHS 1,700/10-12
317 2nd Ave NW 55369 763-391-8500
Bob Perdaems, prin. Fax 391-8501

Owatonna, Steele, Pop. 23,333
Owatonna SD 761 4,800/K-12
515 W Bridge St 55060 507-444-8600
Tom Tapper, supt. Fax 444-8688
www.owatonna.k12.mn.us/
Owatonna HS 1,700/9-12
333 E School St 55060 507-444-8810
Don Johnson, prin. Fax 444-8999
Owatonna JHS 800/7-8
500 15th St NE 55060 507-444-8710
Kyle DeKam, prin. Fax 444-8799

Owatonna Christian S 200/PK-12
265 26th St NE 55060 507-451-3495
Pillsbury Baptist Bible College Post-Sec.
315 S Grove Ave 55060 507-451-2710

Parkers Prairie, Otter Tail, Pop. 1,024
Parkers Prairie SD 547 600/PK-12
PO Box 46 56361 218-338-6011
Michael Martin, supt. Fax 338-4077
Parkers Prairie JSHS 300/7-12
PO Box 46 56361 218-338-6011
Connie Wenker, prin. Fax 338-4077

Park Rapids, Hubbard, Pop. 3,392
Park Rapids SD 309 1,700/PK-12
301 Huntsinger Ave 56470 218-237-6500
Glenn Chiodo, supt. Fax 237-6519
www.parkrapids.k12.mn.us
Century MS 500/5-8
501 Helten Ave 56470 218-237-6300
Bruce Gravalin, prin. Fax 237-6349
Park Rapids Area HS 600/9-12
401 Huntsinger Ave 56470 218-237-6400
Al Judson, prin. Fax 237-6401

Paynesville, Stearns, Pop. 2,301
Paynesville SD 741 1,100/PK-12
217 W Mill St 56362 320-243-7525
Todd Burlingame, supt. Fax 243-3410
Paynesville HS 400/9-12
795 W Highway 23 56362 320-243-3761
Lorie Floura, prin. Fax 243-4534
Paynesville MS 300/6-8
801 W Highway 23 56362 320-243-3724
John Janotta, prin. Fax 243-4534

Pelican Rapids, Otter Tail, Pop. 2,443
Pelican Rapids SD 548 1,200/PK-12
PO Box 642 56572 218-863-5910
Kent Baldry, supt. Fax 863-5915
Pelican Rapids JSHS 600/7-12
PO Box 642 56572 218-863-5910
Glenn Moerke, prin. Fax 863-5915

Pequot Lakes, Crow Wing, Pop. 974
Pequot Lakes SD 186 1,400/PK-12
PO Box 368 56472 218-568-4996
Percy Lingen, supt. Fax 568-5259
www.pequotlakes.com
Pequot Lakes HS 400/9-12
PO Box 368 56472 218-568-9210
John McDonald, prin. Fax 568-9250
Pequot Lakes MS 400/6-8
PO Box 368 56472 218-568-9357
Randy Hansen, prin. Fax 568-5259

Perham, Otter Tail, Pop. 2,718
Perham-Dent SD 1,600/PK-12
200 5th St SE 56573 218-346-4501
Tamara Uselman, supt. Fax 346-4506
www.perham.k12.mn.us
Perham HS 600/9-12
200 5th St SE 56573 218-346-6500
John Rutten, prin. Fax 346-6504
Prairie Wind MS 500/5-8
480 Coney St 56573 218-346-1700
Kitty Krueger, prin. Fax 346-1704

Peterson, Fillmore, Pop. 223
Rushford-Peterson SD 239
Supt. — See Rushford
Rushford-Peterson MS 200/6-8
PO Box 8 55962 507-875-2238
Jeffrey Miller, prin. Fax 875-2316

Pierz, Morrison, Pop. 1,296
Pierz SD 484 1,000/PK-12
112 Kamnic St 56364 320-468-6458
George Weber, supt. Fax 468-6408
www.pierz.k12.mn.us
Healy JSHS 500/7-12
112 Kamnic St 56364 320-468-6458
Paul Demorett, prin. Fax 468-6577

Pillager, Cass, Pop. 470
Pillager SD 116 800/PK-12
323 E 2nd St 56473 218-746-3772
Chuck Arns, supt. Fax 746-4236
www.pillager.k12.mn.us/
Pillager JSHS 400/7-12
323 E 2nd St 56473 218-746-3557
Scott Doss, prin. Fax 746-3406

Pine City, Pine, Pop. 3,212
Pine City SD 578 1,700/K-12
1400 Main St S 55063 320-629-4000
Darwin Bostic, supt. Fax 629-4070
www.pinecity.k12.mn.us
Pine City JSHS 900/7-12
1400 Main St S 55063 320-629-4112
George Johnson, prin. Fax 629-4105

Pine Technical College Post-Sec.
900 4th St SE 55063 320-629-5100

Pine Island, Goodhue, Pop. 2,943
Pine Island SD 255 1,200/K-12
PO Box 398 55963 507-356-8326
Brian Grenell, supt. Fax 356-8827
www.pineisland.k12.mn.us
Pine Island HS 400/9-12
PO Box 398 55963 507-356-8326
Kevin Cardille, prin. Fax 356-8827
Pine Island MS 400/5-8
PO Box 398 55963 507-356-2488
Darren Overton, prin. Fax 356-8827

Pine River, Cass, Pop. 954
Pine River-Backus SD 2174 1,000/PK-12
PO Box 610 56474 218-587-4720
Catherine Bettino, supt. Fax 587-4120
www.prbackus.k12.mn.us
Pine River-Backus HS 500/7-12
PO Box 610 56474 218-587-4425
Allen Ralston, prin. Fax 587-3108

Pipestone, Pipestone, Pop. 4,297
Pipestone Area SD 2689 1,400/PK-12
1401 7th St SW 56164 507-825-5861
Jim Lentz, supt. Fax 825-6718
pas.k12.mn.us
Pipestone HS 400/9-12
1401 7th St SW 56164 507-825-5861
Ray Staatz, prin. Fax 825-6729
Pipestone MS 400/5-8
1401 7th St SW 56164 507-825-5861
Ray Staatz, prin. Fax 825-6729

Minnesota West Community & Tech College Post-Sec.
1314 N Hiawatha Ave 56164 507-825-5471

Plainview, Wabasha, Pop. 3,245
Plainview SD 810 1,200/PK-12
500 W Broadway 55964 507-534-3651
Eric Bartleson, supt. Fax 534-3907
www.plainview.k12.mn.us/
Plainview JSHS 600/7-12
500 W Broadway 55964 507-534-3128
Bill Ihrke, prin. Fax 534-3907

Plymouth, Hennepin, Pop. 69,164
Robbinsdale SD 281
Supt. — See New Hope
Plymouth MS 1,200/6-8
10011 36th Ave N 55441 763-504-7100
Susan Manikowski, prin. Fax 504-7131
Robbinsdale Armstrong HS 2,300/9-12
10635 36th Ave N 55441 763-504-8800
David Dahl, prin. Fax 504-8831

Wayzata SD 284
Supt. — See Minneapolis
Wayzata Central MS 800/6-8
305 Vicksburg Ln N 55447 763-745-6000
Steven Root, prin. Fax 745-6091
Wayzata East MS 700/6-8
12000 Ridgemount Ave W 55441 763-745-6200
Michael Trewick, prin. Fax 745-6291
Wayzata HS 3,100/9-12
4955 Peony Ln N, 763-745-6600
Craig Paul, prin. Fax 745-6691

Providence Academy | 200/PK-12
15100 Schmidt Lake Rd, | 763-258-2500
Dr. Todd Flanders, hdmstr. | Fax 258-2501
Scot Lewis Beauty School | Post-Sec.
4124 Lancaster Ln N 55441 | 763-551-0562
West Lutheran HS | 200/9-12
3350 Harbor Ln N 55447 | 763-509-9378
Merlin Meitner, prin. | Fax 509-0861

Preston, Fillmore, Pop. 1,402
Fillmore Central SD 2198
Supt. — See Harmony
Fillmore Central MS | 200/5-8
PO Box 50 55965 | 507-765-3843
Brenda Lentz, prin. | Fax 765-3636

Princeton, Mille Lacs, Pop. 4,437
Princeton SD 477 | 3,400/PK-12
706 1st St 55371 | 763-389-2422
Mark Sleeper, supt. | Fax 389-9142
www.princeton.k12.mn.us
Princeton HS | 1,100/9-12
807 8th Ave S 55371 | 763-389-4101
Peter Olson, prin. | Fax 389-5816
Princeton MS | 800/6-8
1100 4th Ave N 55371 | 763-389-6705
Richard Lahn, prin. | Fax 389-6737

Prinsburg, Kandiyohi, Pop. 457

Central Minnesota Christian S | 400/PK-12
PO Box 98 56281 | 320-978-8700
Rodney DeBoer, prin. | Fax 978-6797

Prior Lake, Scott, Pop. 20,038
Prior Lake - Savage Area SD 719 | 5,500/K-12
PO Box 539 55372 | 952-226-0000
Dr. Tom Westerhaus, supt. | Fax 226-0049
www.priorlake-savage.k12.mn.us
Hidden Oaks MS | 800/7-8
PO Box 539 55372 | 952-226-0700
Dr. Corey Lunn, prin. | Fax 226-0749
Other Schools – See Savage

Proctor, Saint Louis, Pop. 2,776
Proctor SD 704 | 1,900/PK-12
131 9th Ave 55810 | 218-628-4934
Diane Rauschenfels, supt. | Fax 628-4937
www.proctor.k12.mn.us
Jedlicka MS | 500/6-8
131 9th Ave 55810 | 218-628-4926
Kim Juntunen, prin. | Fax 628-4932
Proctor HS | 600/9-12
131 9th Ave 55810 | 218-628-4926
Nancy Olson, prin. | Fax 628-4931

Randolph, Dakota, Pop. 325
Randolph SD 195 | 500/PK-12
PO Box 38 55065 | 507-263-2151
Donald Pressnall, supt. | Fax 645-5950
www.randolph.k12.mn.us
Randolph JSHS | 200/7-12
PO Box 38 55065 | 507-263-2151
Michael Kelley, prin. | Fax 645-5950

Redlake, Beltrami, Pop. 1,068
Red Lake SD 38 | 1,400/PK-12
PO Box 499 56671 | 218-679-3353
Stuart Desjarlait, supt. | Fax 679-2321
www.paulbunyan.net/rlschools/
Red Lake HS | 400/9-12
PO Box 499 56671 | 218-679-3733
Chris Dunshee, prin. | Fax 679-2717
Red Lake MS | 300/6-8
PO Box 499 56671 | 218-679-2700
Gregory Ferrin, prin. | Fax 679-2733

Red Lake Falls, Red Lake, Pop. 1,594
Red Lake Falls SD 630 | 400/PK-12
PO Box 399 56750 | 218-253-2139
Alan Foley, supt. | Fax 253-2135
LaFayette JSHS | 200/7-12
PO Box 399 56750 | 218-253-2163
Mike Verdun, prin. | Fax 253-4480

Red Wing, Goodhue, Pop. 16,020
Red Wing SD 256 | 2,900/K-12
2451 Eagle Ridge Dr 55066 | 651-385-4500
Stan Slessor, supt. | Fax 385-4510
www.redwing.k12.mn.us
Red Wing HS | 1,100/9-12
2451 Eagle Ridge Dr 55066 | 651-385-4600
Jim Pohl, prin. | Fax 385-4610
Twin Bluff MS | 700/6-8
2120 Twin Bluff Rd 55066 | 651-385-4530
Nancy Glasenapp, prin. | Fax 385-4540

Minnesota State College Southeast Tech. | Post-Sec.
308 Pioneer Rd 55066 | 800-657-4849

Redwood Falls, Redwood, Pop. 5,339
Redwood Area SD 2897 | 1,500/PK-12
100 George Ramseth Dr 56283 | 507-644-3531
Rick Ellingworth, supt. | Fax 644-3057
redwood.mntm.org
Redwood Valley HS | 500/9-12
100 George Ramseth Dr 56283 | 507-644-3511
Don Yrjo, prin. | Fax 644-3057
Redwood Valley MS | 500/5-8
100 George Ramseth Dr 56283 | 507-644-3521
Wade Mathers, prin. | Fax 644-3057

Remer, Cass, Pop. 378
Northland Community SD 118 | 500/PK-12
316 Main St E Rm 200 56672 | 218-566-2351
Mike Doro, supt. | Fax 566-3199
www.isd118.k12.mn.us

Northland HS | 300/7-12
316 Main St E Rm 300 56672 | 218-566-2352
Joe Akre, prin. | Fax 566-3199

Renville, Renville, Pop. 1,288
Renville County West SD 2890 | 700/K-12
PO Box 338 56284 | 320-329-8362
Doug Conboy, supt. | Fax 329-3271
www.rcw.k12.mn.us
Renville County West HS | 400/7-12
PO Box 338 56284 | 320-329-8368
Lance Bagstad, prin. | Fax 329-8191

Richfield, Hennepin, Pop. 34,079
Richfield SD 280 | 4,000/K-12
7001 Harriet Ave 55423 | 612-798-6000
Barbara Devlin, supt. | Fax 798-6057
www.richfield.k12.mn.us
Richfield HS | 1,400/9-12
7001 Harriet Ave 55423 | 612-798-6100
Dr. Jill Johnson, prin. | Fax 798-6127
Richfield JHS | 900/6-8
7461 Oliver Ave S 55423 | 612-798-6400
Susan Sommerfeld, prin. | Fax 798-6427

Academy of Holy Angels | 900/9-12
6600 Nicollet Ave 55423 | 612-798-2600
Heidi Foley, prin. | Fax 798-2610
Blessed Trinity S | 200/4-8
6720 Nicollet Ave 55423 | 612-869-5200
Kim Doyle, prin. | Fax 767-2191
Minnesota School of Business | Post-Sec.
1401 W 76th St Ste 500 55423 | 612-861-2000

Robbinsdale, Hennepin, Pop. 13,668
Robbinsdale SD 281
Supt. — See New Hope
Robbinsdale HS | 700/6-8
3730 Toledo Ave N 55422 | 763-504-4800
Christopher Holden, prin. | Fax 504-4831

Rochester, Olmsted, Pop. 92,507
Rochester ISD 535 | 16,000/PK-12
615 7th St SW 55902 | 507-285-8551
Jerry Williams, supt. | Fax 281-6020
www.rochester.k12.mn.us
Adams MS | 1,100/6-8
1525 31st St NW 55901 | 507-285-8840
Richard Jones, prin. | Fax 285-8481
Century HS | 1,800/9-12
2525 Viola Rd NE 55906 | 507-287-7150
Chuck Briscoe, prin. | Fax 285-8595
Friedell MS | 400/6-8
1200 S Broadway 55904 | 507-287-1480
Monica Bowler, prin. | Fax 287-1490
Kellogg MS | 1,000/6-8
503 17th St NE 55906 | 507-285-8701
Dwight Jennings, prin. | Fax 287-1586
Marshall HS | 1,700/9-12
1510 14th St NW 55901 | 507-285-8693
Richard Stirn, prin. | Fax 281-7312
Mayo HS | 1,800/9-12
1420 11th Ave SE 55904 | 507-285-8819
John Frederikson, prin. | Fax 285-8792
Willow Creek MS | 1,100/6-8
2425 11th Ave SE 55904 | 507-285-8876
Fay Sandven, prin. | Fax 285-8606
Hawthorne Adult Literacy Center | Adult
700 4th Ave SE 55904 | 507-287-2642
Julie Nigon, admin. | Fax 287-2643

Crossroads College | Post-Sec.
920 Mayowood Rd SW 55902 | 507-288-4563
Faith Christian S | 100/K-12
4016 28th St SE 55904 | 507-289-8094
Tony Haddad, admin. | Fax 529-4017
Lourdes HS | 600/9-12
621 W Center St 55902 | 507-289-3991
Dennis Nigon, prin. | Fax 289-4008
Mayo School of Health Sciences | Post-Sec.
200 1st Ave SW 55905 | 507-284-3678
Rochester Community & Technical College | Post-Sec.
851 30th Ave SE 55904 | 507-285-7210
Rochester Community & Technical College | Post-Sec.
1926 Collegeview Rd E 55904 | 800-247-1296
St. Mary's/Mayo Medical Center | Post-Sec.
1216 2nd St NW 55902 | 507-255-5221
Schaeffer Academy | 400/K-12
2700 Schaeffer Ln NE 55906 | 507-286-1050
Keith Phillips, hdmstr. | Fax 282-3823
Sr. Rosalind Gefre School of Massage | Post-Sec.
300 Elton Hills Dr NW 55901 | 507-286-8608
University of Minnesota Rochester | Post-Sec.
855 30th Ave SE 55904 | 507-280-2838
Victory Academy | 100/K-12
606 36th Ave SE 55904 | 507-289-3834

Rockford, Wright, Pop. 3,880
Rockford SD 883 | 1,800/PK-12
PO Box 9 55373 | 763-477-9165
Michael J. Smith, supt. | Fax 477-5833
www.rockford.k12.mn.us
Rockford HS | 600/9-12
PO Box 70 55373 | 763-477-5846
Eric Williams, prin. | Fax 477-6123
Rockford MS | 400/6-8
PO Box 189 55373 | 763-477-5831
Marie Flanary, prin. | Fax 477-5832

Rogers, Hennepin, Pop. 5,934
Elk River Area SD 728
Supt. — See Elk River
Rogers HS | 900/9-12
21000 141st Ave N 55374 | 763-274-3140
Roman Pierskalla, prin. | Fax 274-3141

Rogers JHS | 800/6-8
20855 141st Ave N 55374 | 763-241-3550
Nancy Elsmore, prin. | Fax 241-3518

Roseau, Roseau, Pop. 2,740
Roseau SD 682 | 1,500/PK-12
509 3rd St NE 56751 | 218-463-1471
Larry Guggisberg, supt. | Fax 463-3243
www.roseau.k12.mn.us/
Roseau JSHS | 700/7-12
509 3rd St NE 56751 | 218-463-2770
Terry Gotziaman, prin. | Fax 463-3658

Rosemount, Dakota, Pop. 16,974
Rosemount-Apple Valley-Eagan ISD 196 | 28,200/K-12
14445 Diamond Path W 55068 | 651-423-7700
John D. Currie, supt. | Fax 423-7614
www.district196.org
Rosemount HS | 1,900/9-12
3335 142nd St W 55068 | 651-423-7501
Gregory Clausen, prin. | Fax 423-7511
Rosemount MS | 1,000/6-8
3135 143rd St W 55068 | 651-423-7570
Mary Thompson, prin. | Fax 423-7664
Other Schools – See Apple Valley, Eagan

Dakota Co. Technical College | Post-Sec.
1300 145th St E 55068 | 651-423-8000
First Baptist Secondary S | 100/7-12
14400 Diamond Path W 55068 | 651-423-2271

Roseville, Ramsey, Pop. 33,105
Roseville Area SD 623 | 6,300/K-12
1251 County Road B2 W 55113 | 651-635-1600
John Thein, supt. | Fax 635-1659
www.isd623.org
Roseville Area HS | 2,100/9-12
1240 County Road B2 W 55113 | 651-635-1660
Connie Nicholson, prin. | Fax 635-1699
Other Schools – See Little Canada

American Academy of Acupuncture | Post-Sec.
1925 W County Rd B2 55113 | 651-631-0204
Concordia Academy | 500/9-12
2400 Dale St N 55113 | 651-484-8429
Tim Bermer, admin. | Fax 484-0594
Minneapolis Business College | Post-Sec.
1711 County Road B W 55113 | 651-636-7406
National American University | Post-Sec.
1550 Highway 36 W 55113 | 651-644-1265
North Heights Christian Academy | 300/K-12
2701 Rice St 55113 | 651-484-7825
Jeffrey Taylor, prin. | Fax 484-8636

Rothsay, Wilkin, Pop. 502
Rothsay SD 850 | 200/K-12
123 2nd St NW 56579 | 218-867-2117
Mary Donohue Stetz, supt. | Fax 867-2376
www.rothsay.k12.mn.us
Rothsay S | 200/K-12
123 2nd St NW 56579 | 218-867-2116
Mary Donohue Stetz, prin. | Fax 867-2376

Round Lake, Nobles, Pop. 416
Round Lake SD 516 | 200/7-12
445 Harrison St 56167 | 507-945-8123
John Cselovszki, supt. | Fax 945-8124
www.svrlb.mntm.org
Round Lake JSHS | 200/7-12
445 Harrison St 56167 | 507-945-8123
John Cselovszki, prin. | Fax 945-8124

Royalton, Morrison, Pop. 868
Royalton SD 485 | 700/PK-12
PO Box 5 56373 | 320-584-5531
John Franzoia, supt. | Fax 584-5218
www.royalton.k12.mn.us
Royalton JSHS | 400/7-12
PO Box 5 56373 | 320-584-5531
Lee Obermiller, prin. | Fax 584-5218

Rush City, Chisago, Pop. 2,469
Rush City SD 139 | 1,000/K-12
PO Box 566 55069 | 320-358-4855
Vern Koepp, supt. | Fax 358-1351
www.rushcity.k12.mn.us
Rush City HS | 500/7-12
PO Box 566 55069 | 320-358-4795
Mark Saari, prin. | Fax 358-1261

Rushford, Fillmore, Pop. 1,754
Rushford-Peterson SD 239 | 700/PK-12
PO Box 627 55971 | 507-864-7785
Jeffrey Miller, supt. | Fax 864-2085
www.r-pschools.com
Rushford-Peterson HS | 200/9-12
PO Box 627 55971 | 507-864-7786
Brad Johnson, prin. | Fax 864-2085
Other Schools – See Peterson

Russell, Lyon, Pop. 350
Russell SD 418 | 100/6-8
PO Box 310 56169 | 507-823-4371
Bruce Houck, supt. | Fax 823-4657
R T R MS | 100/6-8
PO Box 310 56169 | 507-823-4371
Jim Burns, admin. | Fax 823-4657

Saginaw, Saint Louis
St. Louis County SD 2142
Supt. — See Virginia
Albrook JSHS | 200/7-12
7427 Seville Rd 55779 | 218-729-8322
Gary Friedlieb, prin. | Fax 729-8808

Saint Anthony, Hennepin, Pop. 7,915
St. Anthony-New Brighton SD 282 — 1,600/PK-12
  3303 33rd Ave NE 55418 — 612-706-1000
  Robert Duncan, supt. — Fax 706-1020
  www.stanthony.k12.mn.us
Saint Anthony MS — 400/6-8
  3303 33rd Ave NE 55418 — 612-706-1030
  Shirley Gregoire, prin. — Fax 706-1040
Saint Anthony Village HS — 600/9-12
  3303 33rd Ave NE 55418 — 612-706-1100
  Thomas Keith, prin. — Fax 706-1020

Saint Bonifacius, Hennepin, Pop. 2,310

Crown College — Post-Sec.
  8700 College View Dr 55375 — 952-446-4100

Saint Charles, Winona, Pop. 3,393
St. Charles SD 858 — 1,100/PK-12
  600 E 6th St 55972 — 507-932-4423
  Thomas Ames, supt. — Fax 932-4700
  www.scschools.net
Saint Charles HS — 500/7-12
  600 E 6th St 55972 — 507-932-4420
  Henry Welle, prin. — Fax 932-4700

Saint Clair, Blue Earth, Pop. 813
St. Clair SD 75 — 700/PK-12
  PO Box 99 56080 — 507-245-3501
  Rick Linnell, supt. — Fax 245-3517
  www.isd75.k12.mn.us/
Saint Clair JSHS — 300/7-12
  PO Box 99 56080 — 507-245-3027
  Alan Fitterer, prin. — Fax 245-3690

Saint Cloud, Stearns, Pop. 59,458
St. Cloud Area SD 742 — 7,800/PK-12
  1000 44th Ave N 56303 — 320-253-9333
  Bruce Watkins, supt. — Fax 529-4343
  www.isd742.org
Apollo HS — 1,400/9-12
  1000 44th Ave N 56303 — 320-253-1600
  Pat Mullen, prin. — Fax 253-8475
North JHS — 700/7-8
  1212 29th Ave N 56303 — 320-251-2159
  Dave Earp, prin. — Fax 251-7350
South JHS — 800/7-8
  1120 15th Ave S 56301 — 320-251-1322
  Dave Earp, prin. — Fax 251-2911
Technical HS — Vo/Tech
  233 12th Ave S 56301 — 320-252-2231
  Roger Ziemann, prin. — Fax 252-0257

Cathedral HS & John XXIII MS — 500/7-12
  PO Box 1579 56302 — 320-251-3421
  Lynn Grewing, prin. — Fax 253-5576
Model College of Hair Design — Post-Sec.
  201 8th Ave S 56301 — 320-253-4222
Rasmussen College — Post-Sec.
  226 Park Ave S 56301 — 320-251-5600
Saint Cloud Christian S — 300/K-12
  PO Box 1002 56302 — 320-252-8182
  MaryJo Froemming, admin. — Fax 656-9678
St. Cloud Hospital — Post-Sec.
  1406 6th Ave N 56303 — 320-255-5666
St. Cloud Regency Beauty Academy — Post-Sec.
  110 2nd St S 56387 — 320-251-0500
St. Cloud State University — Post-Sec.
  720 4th Ave S 56301 — 877-654-7278
St. Cloud Technical College — Post-Sec.
  1540 Northway Dr 56303 — 320-252-0101
SS. Peter Paul & Michael MS — 300/5-8
  1215 11th Ave N 56303 — 320-251-5295
  Mary Opatz, prin. — Fax 251-5295

Saint Francis, Anoka, Pop. 6,449
St. Francis SD 15 — 5,700/K-12
  4115 Ambassador Blvd NW 55070 — 763-753-7040
  Edward Saxton, supt. — Fax 753-4693
  www.stfrancis.k12.mn.us
Saint Francis HS — 1,800/9-12
  3325 Bridge St NW 55070 — 763-213-1500
  Paul Neubauer, prin. — Fax 213-1693
Saint Francis MS — 1,000/6-8
  23026 Ambassador Blvd NW 55070 — 763-213-8500
  Dale Johnson, prin. — Fax 753-3821

Saint James, Watonwan, Pop. 4,592
St. James SD 840 — 1,300/PK-12
  500 8th Ave S 56081 — 507-375-5974
  Dr. Keith Togstad, supt. — Fax 375-7143
  www.stjames.k12.mn.us
St. James JSHS — 500/8-12
  500 8th Ave S 56081 — 507-375-3381
  Bruce Aamot, prin. — Fax 375-4371

Saint Joseph, Stearns, Pop. 5,089

College of Saint Benedict — Post-Sec.
  37 College Ave S 56374 — 320-363-5011

Saint Louis Park, Hennepin, Pop. 44,114
St. Louis Park SD 283 — 3,800/K-12
  6425 W 33rd St 55426 — 952-928-6000
  Debra Bowers, supt. — Fax 928-6020
  www.slpschools.org
St. Louis Park HS — 1,300/9-12
  6425 W 33rd St 55426 — 952-928-6100
  Robert Laney, prin. — Fax 928-6113
St. Louis Park JHS — 600/7-8
  2025 Texas Ave S 55426 — 952-928-6300
  Les Bork, prin. — Fax 928-6383

Benilde-St. Margarets HS — 1,200/7-12
  2501 Highway 100 S 55416 — 952-927-4176
  Stacy Furness, prin. — Fax 920-8889

Groves Academy — 200/1-12
  3200 Highway 100 S 55416 — 952-920-6377
  John Alexander, hdmstr. — Fax 920-2068
Health System Minnesota/Methodist Hosp. — Post-Sec.
  6500 Excelsior Blvd 55426 — 952-993-3601
High-Tech Institute — Post-Sec.
  5100 Gamble Dr Ste 200 55416 — 763-560-9700

Saint Michael, Wright, Pop. 12,850
St. Michael-Albertville SD 885
  Supt. — See Albertville
St. Michael-Albertville MS — 900/6-8
  4862 Naber Ave NE 55376 — 763-497-2655
  Jennifer Kelly, prin. — Fax 497-6591

Saint Paul, Ramsey, Pop. 280,404
St. Paul SD 625 — 39,600/PK-12
  360 Colborne St 55102 — 651-293-8100
  Dr. Meria Carstarphen, supt. — Fax 290-8331
  www.spps.org
Arlington HS — 1,900/9-12
  1495 Rice St 55117 — 651-293-6900
  Patty Murphy, prin. — Fax 293-6904
Battle Creek MS — 700/7-8
  2121 N Park Dr 55119 — 651-293-8960
  Peter Christensen, prin. — Fax 293-8866
Central HS — 2,100/9-12
  275 Lexington Pkwy N 55104 — 651-632-6000
  Mary Mackbee, prin. — Fax 293-5433
Cleveland Quality MS — 500/7-8
  1000 Walsh St 55106 — 651-293-8880
  Jill Gebeke, prin. — Fax 293-8888
Como Park HS — 1,400/9-12
  740 Rose Ave W 55117 — 651-293-8800
  Dan Mesick, prin. — Fax 293-8806
Harding HS — 2,100/9-12
  1540 6th St E 55106 — 651-793-4700
  Todd Hochman, prin. — Fax 293-8912
Hazel Park MS — 800/7-8
  1140 White Bear Ave N 55106 — 651-293-8920
  Nadya Parker, prin. — Fax 228-3609
Highland Park HS — 1,400/9-12
  1015 Snelling Ave S 55116 — 651-293-8940
  Omoyefe Agbamu, prin. — Fax 293-8939
Highland Park JHS — 900/7-8
  975 Snelling Ave S 55116 — 651-293-8950
  Theresa Battle, prin. — Fax 293-8953
Humboldt HS — 900/9-12
  30 Baker St E 55107 — 651-293-8600
  John Bianchi, prin. — Fax 293-8605
Humboldt JHS — 500/7-8
  640 Humboldt Ave 55107 — 651-293-8630
  Mary Williams, prin. — Fax 293-6660
International Academy / LEAP — 500/7-12
  631 Albert St N 55104 — 651-228-7706
  Rose Santos, prin. — Fax 292-7981
Johnson HS — 1,700/9-12
  1349 Arcade St 55106 — 651-293-8890
  Kay Arndt, prin. — Fax 293-8895
Murray JHS — 800/7-8
  2200 Buford Ave 55108 — 651-293-8740
  Winston Tucker, prin. — Fax 293-8742
Ramsey JHS — 800/7-8
  1700 Summit Ave 55105 — 651-293-8860
  Bruce Maeda, prin. — Fax 298-1587
Washington Technology Magnet MS — 800/6-8
  1041 Marion St 55117 — 651-293-8830
  Mike McCollor, prin. — Fax 228-4331
Evening HS — Adult
  275 Lexington Pkwy N 55104 — 651-632-6015
  Peter Atakpu, prin. — Fax 632-6036
Hubbs Center for Lifelong Learning — Adult
  1030 University Ave W 55104 — 651-290-4822
   — Fax 290-4785

Other Schools – See Woodbury

Bethel College — Post-Sec.
  3900 Bethel Dr 55112 — 651-638-6400
Bethel Seminary — Post-Sec.
  3949 Bethel Dr 55112 — 651-638-6180
Christ's Household of Faith S — 200/K-12
  355 Marshall Ave 55102 — 651-265-3400
  Vernon R. Harms, prin. — Fax 227-9813
College of Saint Catherine — Post-Sec.
  2004 Randolph Ave 55105 — 651-690-6000
College of Saint Scholastica — Post-Sec.
  340 Cedar St 55101 — 651-298-1015
College of Visual Arts — Post-Sec.
  344 Summit Ave 55102 — 800-224-1536
Concordia University-St. Paul — Post-Sec.
  275 Syndicate St N 55104 — 651-641-8278
Cretin-Derham Hall HS — 1,200/9-12
  550 Albert St S 55116 — 651-690-2443
  Laurie Jennrich, prin. — Fax 696-3394
E Metro Opportunities Industrialization — Post-Sec.
  1919 University Ave W # 500 55104 — 651-291-5088
Faith Baptist Christian S — 100/K-12
  1365 Westminster St, — 651-771-5568
Hamline University — Post-Sec.
  1536 Hewitt Ave 55104 — 651-523-2800
Luther Seminary — Post-Sec.
  2481 Como Ave 55108 — 800-588-4373
Macalester College — Post-Sec.
  1600 Grand Ave 55105 — 651-696-6000
McNally Smith College of Music — Post-Sec.
  19 Exchange St E 55101 — 651-291-0177
Metropolitan State University — Post-Sec.
  700 7th St E 55106 — 651-793-1300
Mounds Park Academy — 700/PK-12
  2051 Larpenteur Ave E 55109 — 651-777-2555
  Michael Downs, hdmstr. — Fax 777-8633
Northwestern College — Post-Sec.
  3003 Snelling Ave N 55113 — 651-631-5100

St. Agnes HS — 300/9-12
  530 Lafond Ave 55103 — 651-228-1161
  Jeff Brengman, hdmstr. — Fax 228-1158
St. Bernard S — 300/PK-12
  170 Rose Ave W 55117 — 651-489-1338
  Jeffrey Lenzmeier, prin. — Fax 488-9466
St. Paul Academy & Summit S — 1,000/6-12
  1712 Randolph Ave 55105 — 651-698-2451
  Bryn Roberts, hdmstr. — Fax 698-6787
St. Paul College — Post-Sec.
  235 Marshall Ave 55102 — 651-846-1600
Scot Lewis School — Post-Sec.
  1905 Suburban Ave 55119 — 651-209-6930
University of St. Thomas — Post-Sec.
  2115 Summit Ave 55105 — 651-962-5000
William Mitchell College of Law — Post-Sec.
  875 Summit Ave 55105 — 651-227-9171

Saint Paul Park, Washington, Pop. 5,028
South Washington County SD 833
  Supt. — See Cottage Grove
Oltman JHS — 700/7-9
  1020 3rd St 55071 — 651-768-3500
  Aaron Harper, prin. — Fax 768-3555

Saint Peter, Nicollet, Pop. 10,162
Saint Peter SD — 1,800/K-12
  100 Lincoln Dr 56082 — 507-934-5703
  Jeffrey Olson, supt. — Fax 934-2805
  www.stpeterschools.org
Saint Peter HS — 600/9-12
  100 Lincoln Dr 56082 — 507-934-4210
  Paul Peterson, prin. — Fax 934-4783
Saint Peter MS — 300/7-8
  100 Lincoln Dr 56082 — 507-934-4210
  Laurie Burg, prin. — Fax 934-4783

Gustavus Adolphus College — Post-Sec.
  800 W College Ave 56082 — 507-933-8000

Sandstone, Pine, Pop. 2,481
East Central SD 2580
  Supt. — See Finlayson
East Central Secondary S — 400/6-12
  214 Eagle Dr 55072 — 320-245-2216
  F Joseph Giesen, prin. — Fax 245-2448

Sartell, Stearns, Pop. 11,854
Sartell-St Stephen SD 748 — 3,600/PK-12
  212 3rd Ave N 56377 — 320-656-3715
  Dr. Dale Gasser, supt. — Fax 656-3765
  www.sartell.k12.mn.us
Sartell HS — 800/9-12
  748 7th Ave N 56377 — 320-656-0748
  Brenda Steve, prin. — Fax 656-5296
Sartell MS — 900/5-8
  627 3rd Ave N 56377 — 320-253-2200
  Michael Spanier, prin. — Fax 253-1403

Sauk Centre, Stearns, Pop. 4,001
Sauk Centre SD 743 — 1,200/PK-12
  903 State Rd 56378 — 320-352-2284
  Dan Brooks, supt. — Fax 352-3404
  www.isd743.k12.mn.us/
Sauk Centre JHS — 300/7-9
  903 State Rd 56378 — 320-352-2258
  Belinda Selfors, prin. — Fax 352-3404
Sauk Centre SHS — 400/10-12
  903 State Rd 56378 — 320-352-2258
  Cory Larson, prin. — Fax 352-3404

Sauk Rapids, Benton, Pop. 11,620
Sauk Rapids-Rice SD 47 — 4,100/PK-12
  1833 Osauka Rd 56379 — 320-253-4703
  Greg Vandal, supt. — Fax 255-1914
  www.isd47.org
Sauk Rapids-Rice HS — 1,200/9-12
  1835 Osauka Rd 56379 — 320-253-4700
  Erich Martens, prin. — Fax 258-1717
Sauk Rapids-Rice MS — 800/6-8
  901 1st St S 56379 — 320-654-9073
  Larry Stracke, prin. — Fax 259-8909
Hillside ECFE & ABE — Adult
  30 4th Ave S 56379 — 320-255-8910
  Deborah Campbell, dir. — Fax 258-1197

Sr. Rosalind Gefre School — Post-Sec.
  1007 Industrial Dr S 56379 — 320-259-6185

Savage, Scott, Pop. 25,202
Burnsville-Eagan-Savage ISD 191
  Supt. — See Burnsville
Eagle Ridge JHS — 900/7-9
  13955 Glendale Rd 55378 — 952-707-2800
  David Helke, prin. — Fax 707-2802

Prior Lake - Savage Area SD 719
  Supt. — See Prior Lake
Prior Lake HS — 1,600/9-12
  7575 150th St W 55378 — 952-226-8600
  Dr. Craig Olson, prin. — Fax 226-8649

Sebeka, Wadena, Pop. 693
Sebeka SD 820 — 600/PK-12
  PO Box 249 56477 — 218-837-5101
  Joe Merseth, supt. — Fax 837-5967
  www.sebeka.com
Sebeka JSHS — 300/7-12
  PO Box 249 56477 — 218-837-5101
  Dave Fjeldheim, prin. — Fax 837-5967

Shakopee, Scott, Pop. 26,681
Shakopee SD 720 — 4,800/K-12
  505 Holmes St S 55379 — 952-496-5006
  Jon McBroom, supt. — Fax 445-8446
  www.shakopee.k12.mn.us

Shakopee JHS
1137 Marschall Rd 55379
1,100/7-9
952-496-5752
Chris Lindholm, prin.
Fax 496-5792
Shakopee SHS
200 10th Ave E 55379
1,000/10-12
952-496-5152
James Murphy, prin.
Fax 445-3268

Sherburn, Martin, Pop. 1,065
Martin County West SD 2448
Supt. — See Welcome
Martin County West HS
16 W 5th St 56171
300/9-12
507-764-4671
David Traetow, prin.
Fax 764-4691

Shoreview, Ramsey, Pop. 27,105
Mounds View SD 621
9,500/K-12
350 Highway 96 W 55126
651-636-3650
Dr. Janet Witthuhn, supt.
Fax 639-6103
www.moundsviewschools.org
Chippewa MS
1,200/6-8
5000 Hodgson Rd 55126
651-483-6635
Patrick Fox, prin.
Fax 639-6233
Other Schools – See Arden Hills, Mounds View, New Brighton

Silver Bay, Lake, Pop. 2,037
Lake Superior SD 381
Supt. — See Two Harbors
Kelly JSHS, 137 Banks Blvd 55614
300/7-12
George Starkovich, prin.
218-226-4437

Slayton, Murray, Pop. 2,015
Murray County Central SD 2169
900/PK-12
2420 28th St 56172
507-836-6183
Steve Jones, supt.
Fax 836-6375
Murray County Central JSHS
400/7-12
2420 28th St 56172
507-836-6184
Steve Jones, prin.
Fax 836-6375

Sleepy Eye, Brown, Pop. 3,416
Sleepy Eye SD 84
700/PK-12
400 4th Ave SW 56085
507-794-7903
Jay Haugen, supt.
Fax 794-5404
Sleepy Eye JSHS
300/7-12
400 4th Ave SW 56085
507-794-7904
Elia Bruggeman, prin.
Fax 794-5404

St. Mary JSHS
300/7-12
104 Saint Marys St NW 56085
507-794-4121
Jerry Neubauer, prin.
Fax 794-4841

South Saint Paul, Dakota, Pop. 19,787
South St. Paul SD 6
3,400/PK-12
104 5th Ave S 55075
651-457-9400
Dr. Dana Babbitt, supt.
Fax 457-9485
www.sspps.org
South Saint Paul HS
1,700/7-12
700 2nd St N 55075
651-457-9408
H. Butch Moening, prin.
Fax 457-9455

Springfield, Brown, Pop. 2,177
Springfield SD 85
700/PK-12
12 Burns Ave 56087
507-723-4283
Luther Heller, supt.
Fax 723-6407
www.springfield.mntm.org/
Springfield JSHS
400/7-12
12 Burns Ave 56087
507-723-4288
Karen Strasser, prin.
Fax 723-4447

Spring Grove, Houston, Pop. 1,296
Spring Grove SD 297
400/K-12
PO Box 626 55974
507-498-3221
James Busta, supt.
Fax 498-3470
Spring Grove JSHS
200/7-12
PO Box 626 55974
507-498-3223
Nancy Gulbranson, prin.
Fax 498-3470

Spring Lake Park, Anoka, Pop. 6,806
Spring Lake Park SD 16
3,300/K-12
8000 Highway 65 NE 55432
763-786-5570
Don Helmstetter, supt.
Fax 784-7838
www.springlakeparkschools.org
Spring Lake Park HS
1,200/9-12
8001 Able St NE 55432
763-786-5571
Glenn Martin, prin.
Fax 786-2661
Other Schools – See Blaine

Spring Valley, Fillmore, Pop. 2,527
Kingsland SD 2137
Supt. — See Wykoff
Kingsland HS
300/9-12
705 N Section Ave 55975
507-346-7276
Darrin Strosahl, prin.
Fax 346-7278

Staples, Todd, Pop. 3,042
Staples-Motley ISD 2170
1,500/PK-12
202 Pleasant Ave NE 56479
218-894-2430
Fax 894-1828
Staples-Motley HS
500/9-12
401 Centennial Ln 56479
218-894-2431
Dean Ogg, prin.
Fax 894-2434
Other Schools – See Motley

Central Lakes College
Post-Sec.
1830 Airport Rd 56479
218-894-5100

Stephen, Marshall, Pop. 684
Stephen-Argyle Central SD 2856
400/PK-12
PO Box 68 56757
218-478-3315
Chris Mills, supt.
Fax 478-3537
Stephen JSHS
200/7-12
PO Box 68 56757
218-478-3314
Mark Koulik, prin.
Fax 478-3537

Stewartville, Olmsted, Pop. 5,522
Stewartville SD 534
1,800/PK-12
500 4th St SW 55976
507-533-1438
Dr. David Thompson, supt.
Fax 533-4012
ssd.k12.mn.us
Stewartville HS
600/9-12
500 4th St SW 55976
507-533-1600
Bruce Hoff, prin.
Fax 533-4143
Stewartville MS
400/6-8
500 4th St SW 55976
507-533-1666
Bruce Hoff, prin.
Fax 533-1021

Stillwater, Washington, Pop. 16,734
Stillwater Area SD 834
8,800/K-12
1875 Greeley St S 55082
651-351-8301
Keith Ryskoski, supt.
Fax 351-8380
www.stillwater.k12.mn.us
Stillwater Area SHS
2,200/10-12
5701 Stillwater Blvd N 55082
651-351-8040
Chris Lennox, prin.
Fax 351-8049
Stillwater JHS
1,200/7-9
523 Marsh St W 55082
651-351-6905
Richard Wippler, prin.
Fax 351-6999
Other Schools – See Lake Elmo

Swanville, Morrison, Pop. 352
Swanville SD 486
400/PK-12
PO Box 98 56382
320-547-2431
Gene Harthan, supt.
Fax 547-2576
www.swanville.k12.mn.us
Swanville JSHS
200/7-12
PO Box 98 56382
320-547-2431
Dennis Saurer, prin.
Fax 547-2576

Thief River Falls, Pennington, Pop. 8,427
Thief River Falls SD 564
2,100/PK-12
230 Labree Ave S 56701
218-681-8711
Irv Peterson, supt.
Fax 681-3252
trf.k12.mn.us
Franklin MS
500/6-8
300 Spruce Ave S 56701
218-681-8813
Bob Wayne, prin.
Fax 681-4771
Lincoln HS
700/9-12
101 Knight Ave S 56701
218-681-7432
Tom Hunt, prin.
Fax 681-4510

Northland Community & Technical College
Post-Sec.
Highway 1 E 56701
800-628-9918

Tower, Saint Louis, Pop. 469
St. Louis County SD 2142
Supt. — See Virginia
Tower-Soudan JSHS
200/7-12
PO Box 469 55790
218-753-4040
Sidney Simonson, prin.
Fax 753-6461

Tracy, Lyon, Pop. 2,145
Tracy SD 417
800/PK-12
934 Pine St 56175
507-629-5500
David A. Marlette, supt.
Fax 629-5507
tracy.k12.mn.us
Tracy JSHS
500/7-12
934 Pine St 56175
507-629-5500
Chad Anderson, prin.
Fax 629-5507

Trimont, Martin, Pop. 727
Martin County West SD 2448
Supt. — See Welcome
Martin County West JHS
200/7-8
PO Box 408 56176
507-639-2081
Allison Schmidt, prin.
Fax 639-2091

Truman, Martin, Pop. 1,217
Truman SD 458
400/K-12
PO Box 276 56088
507-776-2111
Paul Sundholm, supt.
Fax 776-3379
www.truman.k12.mn.us
Truman JSHS
200/7-12
PO Box 276 56088
507-776-2111
Dustin Bosshart, prin.
Fax 776-3379

Twin Valley, Norman, Pop. 834
Norman County East SD 2215
400/PK-12
PO Box 420 56584
218-584-5151
Larry Swanson, supt.
Fax 584-5170
nce.k12.mn.us/
Norman County East HS
200/7-12
PO Box 420 56584
218-584-5151
Gregory Lund, prin.
Fax 584-5170

Two Harbors, Lake, Pop. 3,561
Lake Superior SD 381
1,400/PK-12
1640 Highway 2 55616
218-834-8201
Sheldon Johnson, supt.
Fax 834-8239
www.isd381.k12.mn.us/
Two Harbors JSHS
600/7-12
1640 Highway 2 Ste 100 55616
218-834-8201
Robert Nyberg, prin.
Fax 834-8239
Other Schools – See Silver Bay

Tyler, Lincoln, Pop. 1,154
Tyler SD 409
200/9-12
PO Box 659 56178
507-247-5913
Bruce Houck, supt.
Fax 247-3876
www.rtrschools.org
Russell-Tyler-Ruthton HS
200/9-12
PO Box 659 56178
507-247-5911
Tim Christensen, prin.
Fax 247-3876

Ulen, Clay, Pop. 536
Ulen-Hitterdal SD 914
300/K-12
PO Box 389 56585
218-596-8853
Allen H. Zenor, supt.
Fax 596-8610
www.ulenhitterdal.k12.mn.us
Ulen-Hitterdal JSHS
100/7-12
PO Box 389 56585
218-596-8853
Kent Henrickson, prin.
Fax 596-8610

Underwood, Otter Tail, Pop. 329
Underwood SD 550
500/K-12
100 Southern Ave E 56586
218-826-6101
Gary Sletten, supt.
Fax 826-6310
www.underwood.k12.mn.us
Underwood JSHS
200/7-12
100 Southern Ave E 56586
218-826-6102
John Hamann, prin.
Fax 826-6310

Upsala, Morrison, Pop. 417
Upsala SD 487
400/PK-12
PO Box 190 56384
320-573-2174
Gene Harthan, supt.
Fax 573-2173
Upsala JSHS
200/7-12
PO Box 190 56384
320-573-2176
Dave Piasecki, prin.
Fax 573-2173

Verndale, Wadena, Pop. 569
Verndale SD 818
500/PK-12
411 SW Brown St 56481
218-445-5184
James Madsen, supt.
Fax 445-5185
Verndale JSHS
200/7-12
411 SW Brown St 56481
218-445-5184
Dean Krogstad, prin.
Fax 445-5185

Vesta, Redwood, Pop. 326
Wabasso SD 640
Supt. — See Wabasso
Vesta JSHS
100/7-12
320 Centre St W 56292
507-342-7111
Ted Suss, prin.
Fax 347-7111

Victoria, Carver, Pop. 5,176

Holy Family HS
100/9-12
8101 Kochia Ln 55386
952-443-4659
Kathie Brown, prin.
Fax 443-1822

Virginia, Saint Louis, Pop. 8,888
St. Louis County SD 2142
2,400/PK-12
1701 N 9th Ave 55792
218-749-8130
Charles Rick, supt.
Fax 749-8133
www.isd2142.k12.mn.us/
Other Schools – See Babbitt, Cook, Cotton, Iron, Orr, Saginaw, Tower

Virginia SD 706
1,800/PK-12
411 S 5th Ave 55792
218-742-3901
Phillip Johnson, supt.
Fax 742-3960
www.virginia.k12.mn.us/
Virginia Secondary S
800/7-12
411 S 5th Ave 55792
218-742-3916
Michael Krebsbach, prin.

Mesabi Range Community & Technical Coll.
Post-Sec.
1001 Chestnut St W 55792
218-749-7700

Wabasha, Wabasha, Pop. 2,597
Wabasha-Kellogg SD 811
700/PK-12
2113 Hiawatha Dr E 55981
651-565-3559
Jim Freihammer, supt.
Fax 565-2769
www.wabasha-kellogg.k12.mn.us/
Wabasha-Kellogg JSHS
400/7-12
2113 Hiawatha Dr E 55981
651-565-3559
Jon Stern, prin.
Fax 565-2769

Wabasso, Redwood, Pop. 666
Wabasso SD 640
500/PK-12
PO Box 69 56293
507-342-5114
Ted Suss, supt.
Fax 342-5203
www.wabassoschool.com
Wabasso JSHS
200/7-12
PO Box 69 56293
507-342-5114
Ted Suss, prin.
Fax 342-5203
Other Schools – See Vesta

Waconia, Carver, Pop. 7,986
Waconia SD 110
2,400/PK-12
24 S Walnut St 55387
952-442-0600
Jerry Kjergaard, supt.
Fax 442-0609
www.waconia.k12.mn.us
Clearwater MS
700/5-8
1650 Community Dr 55387
952-442-0650
Peter Gustafson, prin.
Fax 442-0659
Waconia HS
700/9-12
1400 Community Dr 55387
952-442-0670
Mark Fredericksen, prin.
Fax 442-0679

Wadena, Wadena, Pop. 4,175
Wadena-Deer Creek SD 2155
1,100/PK-12
PO Box 151 56482
218-632-2155
Jerome Enget, supt.
Fax 632-2199
www.wdc2155.k12.mn.us
Wadena-Deer Creek HS
700/7-12
PO Box 151 56482
218-632-2300
Tim Bjorge, prin.
Fax 632-2399

MN State Community & Technical College
Post-Sec.
PO Box 566 56482
800-247-2007

Walker, Cass, Pop. 1,125
Walker-Hackensack-Akeley SD 113
1,000/PK-12
PO Box 4000 56484
218-547-1311
Jeff Lindstrom, supt.
Fax 547-4298
www.wha.k12.mn.us
Walker-Hackensack-Akeley HS
300/9-12
PO Box 4000 56484
218-547-4210
Peggy Novak, prin.
Fax 547-4297
Walker-Hackensack-Akeley MS
300/6-8
PO Box 4000 56484
218-547-5321
Peggy Novak, prin.
Fax 547-5333

Walnut Grove, Redwood, Pop. 568
Westbrook-Walnut Grove SD 2898
Supt. — See Westbrook
Westbrook-Walnut Grove MS
200/5-8
PO Box 278 56180
507-859-2141
Paul Olson, prin.
Fax 859-2329

Wanamingo, Goodhue, Pop. 1,029
Kenyon-Wanamingo SD 2172 — 900/PK-12
225 3rd Ave 55983 — 507-824-2211
Jeff Evert, supt. — Fax 824-2212
Other Schools – See Kenyon

Warren, Marshall, Pop. 1,650
Warren-Alvarado-Oslo SD 2176 — 600/PK-12
224 E Bridge Ave 56762 — 218-745-5393
Dr. Ken Henry, supt. — Fax 745-5886
www.wao.k12.mn.us
Warren-Alvarado-Oslo JSHS — 300/7-12
224 E Bridge Ave 56762 — 218-745-4646
Seann Dikkers, prin. — Fax 745-7658

Warroad, Roseau, Pop. 1,684
Warroad SD 690 — 1,600/PK-12
510 Cedar Ave NW 56763 — 218-386-1472
— Fax 386-1909
www.warroad.k12.mn.us
Warroad HS — 500/9-12
510 Cedar Ave NW 56763 — 218-386-1820
William Kirkeby, prin. — Fax 386-1909
Warroad MS — 400/4-8
510 Cedar Ave NW 56763 — 218-386-1877
Craig Oftedahl, prin. — Fax 386-2179

Waseca, Waseca, Pop. 9,576
Waseca SD 829 — 2,100/PK-12
501 Elm Ave E 56093 — 507-835-2500
James Schmitt, supt. — Fax 835-1161
www.waseca.k12.mn.us
Waseca HS — 800/9-12
1717 2nd St NW 56093 — 507-835-5470
Jeanne Swanson, prin. — Fax 835-1724
Waseca JHS — 400/7-8
400 19th Ave NW 56093 — 507-835-1048
Bill Bunkers, prin. — Fax 835-1063

Watertown, Carver, Pop. 3,608
Watertown-Mayer SD 111 — 1,500/PK-12
1001 Highway 25 Shls NW 55388 — 952-955-0200
Karsten Anderson, supt. — Fax 955-0215
www.wm.k12.mn.us/
Watertown-Mayer HS — 500/9-12
1001 Highway 25 Shls NW 55388 — 952-955-0240
Scott Gengler, prin. — Fax 955-0251
Watertown-Mayer MS — 500/5-8
1001 Highway 25 Shls NW 55388 — 952-955-0210
Scott Alger, dean — Fax 955-0215

Waterville, LeSueur, Pop. 1,882
Waterville-Elysian-Morristown SD 2143 — 1,200/PK-12
500 Paquin St E 56096 — 507-362-4432
Joel Whitehurst, supt. — Fax 362-4561
www.wem.k12.mn.us/
Waterville-Elysian-Morristown HS — 300/9-12
500 Paquin St E 56096 — 507-362-4431
John Kaplan, prin. — Fax 362-4561
Other Schools – See Morristown

Waubun, Mahnomen, Pop. 395
Waubun SD 435 — 600/PK-12
PO Box 98 56589 — 218-473-6171
Boyd Bradbury, supt. — Fax 473-6191
Waubun JSHS — 300/7-12
PO Box 98 56589 — 218-473-6173
Helen Kennedy, prin. — Fax 473-6190

Wayzata, Hennepin, Pop. 4,032
Wayzata SD 284
Supt. — See Minneapolis
Wayzata West MS — 700/6-8
149 Barry Ave N 55391 — 952-745-6400
Alice Woog, prin. — Fax 745-6491

Welcome, Martin, Pop. 696
Martin County West SD 2448 — 900/K-12
PO Box 268 56181 — 507-728-8276
Randy Grupe, supt. — Fax 728-8278
www.martin.k12.mn.us
Other Schools – See Sherburn, Trimont

Wells, Faribault, Pop. 2,434
United South Central SD 2134 — 1,000/PK-12
250 2nd Ave SW 56097 — 507-553-3134
Robert Stuerman, supt. — Fax 553-5929
www.usc.k12.mn.us
United South Central HS — 400/9-12
250 2nd Ave SW 56097 — 507-553-5819
Rick Herman, prin. — Fax 553-5929
Other Schools – See Kiester

Westbrook, Cottonwood, Pop. 780
Westbrook-Walnut Grove SD 2898 — 500/PK-12
PO Box 129 56183 — 507-274-5450
Loy Woelber, supt. — Fax 274-6113
Westbrook-Walnut Grove HS — 200/9-12
PO Box 128 56183 — 507-274-5450
William Richards, prin. — Fax 858-2329
Other Schools – See Walnut Grove

West Concord, Dodge, Pop. 822
Triton SD 2125
Supt. — See Dodge Center
Triton MS — 200/6-8
PO Box 38 55985 — 507-527-2211
Craig Schlichting, prin. — Fax 527-2213

West Saint Paul, Dakota, Pop. 19,070
West St. Paul-Mendota Hts-Eagan SD 197
Supt. — See Mendota Heights
Heritage MS — 800/5-8
121 Butler Ave W 55118 — 651-905-4000
Chris Hiti, prin. — Fax 905-4001

St. Croix Lutheran HS — 300/9-12
1200 Oakdale Ave 55118 — 651-455-1521
Richard Gibson, prin. — Fax 451-3968
Sr. Rosalind Gefre School of Massage — Post-Sec.
149 Thompson Ave Ste 150 55118 — 651-554-3013

Wheaton, Traverse, Pop. 1,531
Wheaton SD 803 — 500/PK-12
1700 3rd Ave S 56296 — 320-563-8283
Shawn Hogan, supt. — Fax 563-4218
www.wheaton.k12.mn.us
Wheaton JSHS — 300/6-12
1700 3rd Ave S 56296 — 320-563-8282
Kurt Kahlenbeck, prin. — Fax 563-4218

White Bear Lake, Ramsey, Pop. 24,388
White Bear Lake Area SD 624 — 7,700/PK-12
4855 Bloom Ave 55110 — 651-407-7500
Dr. Theodore Blaesing, supt. — Fax 407-7566
www.whitebear.k12.mn.us
Central MS — 1,100/6-8
4857 Bloom Ave 55110 — 651-653-2888
Noel Schmidt, prin. — Fax 653-2885
Sunrise Park MS — 50/6-8
2399 Cedar Ave 55110 — 651-653-2700
Kathy Baker, prin. — Fax 653-2716
White Bear Lake Area HS North Campus — 1,400/9-10
5040 Bald Eagle Ave 55110 — 651-653-2920
Dr. Jill Thelen, prin. — Fax 653-2630
White Bear Lake Area HS South Campus — 1,400/11-12
3551 McKnight Rd N 55110 — 651-773-6200
Larry Denucci, prin. — Fax 773-6215

Century College — Post-Sec.
3300 Century Ave N 55110 — 651-779-3200

Willmar, Kandiyohi, Pop. 18,303
Willmar SD 347 — 4,100/K-12
611 5th St SW 56201 — 320-231-8500
Kathryn Leedom, supt. — Fax 231-1061
www.willmar.k12.mn.us
Willmar HS — 1,300/9-12
2701 30th St NE 56201 — 320-231-8300
Rob Anderson, prin. — Fax 231-8460
Willmar JHS — 600/7-8
201 Willmar Ave SE 56201 — 320-214-6000
Mike Prunty, prin. — Fax 235-1254

Rice Memorial Hospital — Post-Sec.
301 Becker Ave SW 56201 — 320-231-4530
Ridgewater College-Willmar Campus — Post-Sec.
PO Box 1097 56201 — 320-235-5114

Willow River, Pine, Pop. 334
Willow River SD 577 — 500/PK-12
PO Box 66 55795 — 218-372-3131
Steve Wymore, supt. — Fax 372-3132
Willow River JSHS — 200/7-12
PO Box 66 55795 — 218-372-3131
Steve Wymore, prin. — Fax 372-3132

Windom, Cottonwood, Pop. 4,499
Windom SD 177 — 1,000/K-12
PO Box C177 56101 — 507-831-6901
Douglas Froke, supt. — Fax 831-6919
www.windom.k12.mn.us
Windom Area HS — 400/9-12
PO Box C177 56101 — 507-831-6910
Douglas Froke, prin. — Fax 831-6909
Windom MS — 300/5-8
PO Box C177 56101 — 507-831-6910
Tom Farrell, prin. — Fax 831-6909

Winona, Winona, Pop. 26,641
Winona Area SD 861 — 3,900/K-12
903 Gilmore Ave 55987 — 507-494-0861
Paul Durand, supt. — Fax 494-0863
www.winona.k12.mn.us
Winona HS — 1,400/9-12
901 Gilmore Ave 55987 — 507-494-1504
Nancy Wondrasch, prin. — Fax 494-1501
Winona MS — 1,300/5-8
1570 Homer Rd 55987 — 507-494-1000
Sharon Suchla, prin. — Fax 494-1002

Cotter HS — 400/9-12
1115 W Broadway St 55987 — 507-453-5802
Sandra Blank, prin. — Fax 453-5006
Cotter JHS — 200/7-8
101 E Wabasha St 55987 — 507-453-5366
Dave Forney, prin. — Fax 453-5806
Hope Lutheran HS — 50/9-12
253 Liberty St 55987 — 507-474-7799
— Fax 452-8992
Minnesota State College Southeast Tech. — Post-Sec.
PO Box 409 55987 — 507-453-2700
Minnesota State College Southeast Tech. — Post-Sec.
110 Galewski Dr 55987 — 507-453-2630
St. Mary's University of Minnesota — Post-Sec.
700 Terrace Hts Ste 2 55987 — 507-452-4430
Winona State University — Post-Sec.
PO Box 5838 55987 — 507-457-5000

Winsted, McLeod, Pop. 2,279

Holy Trinity S — 400/PK-12
PO Box 38 55395 — 320-485-2182
Tony Kielkuckl, prin. — Fax 485-4283

Winthrop, Sibley, Pop. 1,323
GFW SD 2365
Supt. — See Gibbon
GFW HS — 300/9-12
PO Box 1001 55396 — 507-647-5382
Jeff Bertrang, prin. — Fax 647-4329

Woodbury, Washington, Pop. 49,415
South Washington County SD 833
Supt. — See Cottage Grove
Lake JHS — 1,000/7-9
3133 Pioneer Dr 55125 — 651-768-6400
Sandra Nielson, prin. — Fax 768-6428
Woodbury JHS — 800/7-9
1425 School Dr 55125 — 651-768-4500
Dennis Roos, prin. — Fax 768-4567
Woodbury SHS — 1,700/10-12
2665 Woodlane Dr 55125 — 651-768-4400
Linda Plante, prin. — Fax 768-4412

St. Paul SD 625
Supt. — See Saint Paul
Crosswinds MS — 400/6-8
600 Weir Dr 55125 — 651-379-2600
Anne Anderson, prin. — Fax 379-2690

New Life Academy — 600/PK-12
6758 Bailey Rd 55129 — 651-459-4121
Dr. Aaron Gonzalez, admin. — Fax 459-6194

Worthington, Nobles, Pop. 11,192
Worthington SD 518 — 2,300/K-12
1117 Marine Ave 56187 — 507-372-2172
John Landgaard, supt. — Fax 372-2174
www.isd518.net
Worthington HS — 700/9-12
1211 Clary St 56187 — 507-376-6121
Bruce Blatti, prin. — Fax 372-4304
Worthington MS — 500/6-8
1401 N Crailsheim Rd 56187 — 507-376-4174
Jeff Britten, prin. — Fax 372-1424

Minnesota West Community & Tech College — Post-Sec.
1450 Collegeway 56187 — 507-372-2107

Wrenshall, Carlton, Pop. 333
Wrenshall SD 100 — 400/PK-12
PO Box 68 55797 — 218-384-4274
Shawn Northey, supt. — Fax 384-4293
Wrenshall JSHS — 200/7-12
PO Box 68 55797 — 218-384-4274
Mary Georgesen, prin. — Fax 384-4293

Wykoff, Fillmore, Pop. 453
Kingsland SD 2137 — 900/PK-12
201 Bartlett St W 55990 — 507-352-4341
Larry Thompkins, supt. — Fax 352-6071
www.kingsland.k12.mn.us
Kingsland MS — 200/6-8
PO Box 96 55990 — 507-352-2731
Jim Hecimovich, prin. — Fax 352-6071
Other Schools – See Spring Valley

Zimmerman, Sherburne, Pop. 3,679
Elk River Area SD 728
Supt. — See Elk River
Zimmerman JSHS — 1,000/6-12
25900 4th St W 55398 — 763-241-3505
Mike Elsmore, prin. — Fax 241-3506

Zumbrota, Goodhue, Pop. 2,941
Zumbrota-Mazeppa SD 2805
Supt. — See Mazeppa
Zumbrota-Mazeppa HS — 400/9-12
705 Mill St 55992 — 507-732-7395
Erick Enger, prin. — Fax 732-4511

MISSISSIPPI

MISSISSIPPI DEPARTMENT OF EDUCATION
PO Box 771, Jackson 39205-0771
Telephone 601-359-3513
Fax 601-359-3242
Website http://www.mde.k12.ms.us

Superintendent of Education   Hank Bounds

MISSISSIPPI BOARD OF EDUCATION
PO Box 771, Jackson 39205-0771

Chairperson   Rosetta Richard

PUBLIC, PRIVATE AND CATHOLIC SECONDARY SCHOOLS

Aberdeen, Monroe, Pop. 6,278
Aberdeen SD   1,600/PK-12
  PO Box 607 39730   662-369-4682
  Lavon Reed, supt.   Fax 369-0987
  www.aberdeen.k12.ms.us
Aberdeen HS   500/9-12
  PO Box 607 39730   662-369-8933
  Natoya Jones, prin.   Fax 369-6004
Shivers JHS   200/7-8
  PO Box 607 39730   662-369-6241
  James Swindell, prin.   Fax 369-3207

Monroe County SD
  Supt. — See Amory
Monroe County Technical Center   Vo/Tech
  50057 Airport Rd 39730   662-369-7845
  Billy Loague, prin.   Fax 369-9607

Ackerman, Choctaw, Pop. 1,655
Choctaw County SD   1,800/PK-12
  PO Box 398 39735   662-285-4022
  Dr. Arlene Amos, supt.   Fax 285-4049
  www.choctaw.k12.ms.us/
Ackerman JSHS   500/7-12
  PO Box 296 39735   662-285-4101
  Ronda Huffman, prin.   Fax 285-4099
Choctaw County Career & Technology Ctr   Vo/Tech
  PO Box 775 39735   662-285-4152
  Freddie King, prin.   Fax 285-4199
Other Schools – See Weir

Amory, Monroe, Pop. 6,800
Amory SSD   1,800/K-12
  PO Box 330 38821   662-256-5991
  Jim Sappington, supt.   Fax 256-6302
  www.amoryschools.com/
Amory HS   500/9-12
  PO Box 330 38821   662-256-5753
  David Poss, prin.   Fax 256-5754
Amory MS   500/6-8
  700 2nd Ave N 38821   662-256-5658
  Cheryl Moore, prin.   Fax 256-6304
Amory Vocational Center   Vo/Tech
  PO Box 330 38821   662-256-7601
  Leigh Todd, prin.   Fax 256-1649

Monroe County SD   2,600/K-12
  PO Box 209 38821   662-257-2176
  Jimmy Dahlem, supt.   Fax 257-2181
  www.monroe.k12.ms.us
Hatley S   1,000/K-12
  60186 Hatley Rd 38821   662-256-4563
  Van Pearson, prin.   Fax 256-5626
Other Schools – See Aberdeen, Hamilton, Smithville

Anguilla, Sharkey, Pop. 859
South Delta SD
  Supt. — See Rolling Fork
South Delta MS   300/6-8
  PO Box 487 38721   662-873-6535
  Beverly Wilson, prin.   Fax 873-6073

Arcola, Washington, Pop. 540
Hollandale SD
  Supt. — See Hollandale
Chambers MS   200/7-8
  PO Box 396 38722   662-827-2438
  Angela Johnson, prin.   Fax 827-7168

Deer Creek S   200/K-12
  PO Box 376 38722   662-827-5165
  F. E. Allegrezza, admin.   Fax 827-5128

Ashland, Benton, Pop. 559
Benton County SD   1,300/K-12
  PO Box 247 38603   662-224-6252
  Ron Wilkerson, supt.   Fax 224-3607
  www.benton.k12.ms.us
Ashland MSHS   400/6-12
  PO Box 187 38603   662-224-6247
  John Henry Bostick, prin.   Fax 224-3614
Benton Co. Regional Vocational Center   Vo/Tech
  PO Box 754 38603   662-224-3108
  Belinda Massengill, prin.   Fax 224-3629
Other Schools – See Hickory Flat

Avon, Washington
Western Line SD   2,000/PK-12
  PO Box 50 38723   662-335-7186
  Larry Green, supt.   Fax 378-2285
  www.westernline.k12.ms.us/

Riverside HS   500/7-12
  PO Box 80 38723   662-335-4527
  Michael Mcneece, prin.   Fax 334-1797
Other Schools – See Greenville

Baldwyn, Lee, Pop. 3,332
Baldwyn SD   1,000/K-12
  107 W Main St 38824   662-365-1000
  Harvey G. Brooks, supt.   Fax 365-1003
  baldwyn.ms.schoolwebpages.com/
Baldwyn HS   300/9-12
  512 N Fourth St 38824   662-365-1020
  Ronnie Hill, prin.   Fax 365-1028
Baldwyn MS   300/5-8
  452 N Fourth St 38824   662-365-1015
  Ronnie Hill, prin.   Fax 365-1029

Bassfield, Jefferson Davis, Pop. 295
Jefferson Davis County SD
  Supt. — See Prentiss
Bassfield JSHS   400/7-12
  PO Box 370 39421   601-943-5391
  L.C. Firle, prin.   Fax 943-5790

Batesville, Panola, Pop. 7,598
South Panola SD   4,500/K-12
  209 Boothe St 38606   662-563-9361
  Dr. Keith Shaffer, supt.   Fax 563-6077
  www.southpanola.k12.ms.us
Batesville JHS   1,000/6-8
  507 Tiger Dr 38606   662-563-4503
  Darrell Tucker, prin.   Fax 563-6038
South Panola HS   1,200/9-12
  601 Tiger Dr 38606   662-563-4756
  Dr. Gearl Loden, prin.   Fax 563-8993

Batesville Job Corps Center   Post-Sec.
  821 Highway 51 S 38606   662-563-4656
North Delta S   500/PK-12
  330 Green Wave Ln 38606   662-563-4536
  Herman Coats, admin.   Fax 563-5690

Bay Saint Louis, Hancock, Pop. 9,433
Bay St. Louis-Waveland SD   2,200/K-12
  201 Carroll Ave 39520   228-467-6621
  Kim Stasny, supt.   Fax 466-4895
  www.bwsd.org/
Bay HS   600/9-12
  750 Blue Meadow Rd 39520   228-467-6611
  Marca Alexander, prin.   Fax 466-0883
Bay-Waveland MS   600/6-8
  600 Pine St 39520   228-463-0315
  Carolyn Barcelona, prin.   Fax 467-5872

Our Lady Academy   200/7-12
  222 S Beach Blvd 39520   228-467-7048
  Sr. Jackie Howard, prin.   Fax 467-1666
St. Stanislaus College Prep S   500/6-12
  304 S Beach Blvd 39520   228-467-9057
  Br. Ronald Hingle, prin.   Fax 466-2972

Bay Springs, Jasper, Pop. 2,178
West Jasper Consolidated SD   1,800/PK-12
  PO Box 610 39422   601-764-2280
  Kaye Dyess, supt.   Fax 764-4490
  www2.mde.k12.ms.us/3112/
Bay Springs HS   300/9-12
  PO Box 389 39422   601-764-4151
  Larry W. Callahan, prin.   Fax 764-6445
Bay Springs MS   400/5-8
  PO Box 587 39422   601-764-3378
  George Duke, prin.   Fax 764-2329
Other Schools – See Heidelberg, Stringer

Sylva-Bay Academy   300/K-12
  PO Box J 39422   601-764-2157
  Dr. Lavahn Moss, hdmstr.   Fax 764-6755

Belmont, Tishomingo, Pop. 1,945
Tishomingo Co. Special Municipal SSD
  Supt. — See Iuka
Belmont S   1,000/K-12
  PO Box 250 38827   662-454-7924
  Malcolm Kuykendall, prin.   Fax 454-7611

Belzoni, Humphreys, Pop. 2,568
Humphreys County SD   1,900/K-12
  PO Box 678 39038   662-247-6000
  Joyce McNair, supt.   Fax 247-6004

Humphreys County HS   500/9-12
  PO Box 658 39038   662-247-6040
  Jimmie Washington, prin.   Fax 247-6044
Humphreys County Vocational Center   Vo/Tech
  PO Box 672 39038   662-247-6030
  Jimmy Hurst, prin.   Fax 247-6034
Humphreys JHS   300/7-8
  610 Cohn St 39038   662-247-6050
  Barbara Williams, prin.   Fax 247-6054

Humphreys Academy   300/1-12
  PO Box 179 39038   662-247-1572
  Mac W. Abernathy, admin.   Fax 247-2776

Benoit, Bolivar, Pop. 599
Benoit SD   300/PK-12
  PO Box 189 38725   662-742-3287
  Dr. Suzanne Hawley, supt.   Fax 742-3149
  www.benoit.k12.ms.us/
Brooks S   300/PK-12
  PO Box 8 38725   662-742-3257
  Brenda Hopson, prin.   Fax 742-3498

Benton, Yazoo

Benton Academy   500/K-12
  PO Box 308 39039   662-673-9722
  Jamie Carr, admin.   Fax 673-9090

Biloxi, Harrison, Pop. 48,972
Biloxi Public SD   5,800/K-12
  PO Box 168 39533   228-374-1810
  Paul Tisdale, supt.   Fax 436-5171
  www.biloxischools.net
Biloxi JHS   1,000/8-9
  1424 Father Ryan Ave 39530   228-435-1421
  Murray Killebrew, prin.   Fax 435-1426
Biloxi SHS   1,100/10-12
  1845 Richard Dr 39532   228-435-6105
  Pamela Manners, prin.   Fax 435-6353
Career Technology Center   Vo/Tech
  1845 Richard Dr 39532   228-435-6318
  Glenn Dedeaux, prin.   Fax 435-6318

Mercy Cross HS   400/7-12
  390 Crusaders Dr 39530   228-374-4145
  Bobby Trosclair, prin.   Fax 374-8119

Blue Mountain, Tippah, Pop. 673
South Tippah SD
  Supt. — See Ripley
Blue Mountain S   300/K-12
  PO Box 97 38610   662-685-4706
  Eddie Conner, prin.   Fax 685-4706

Blue Mountain College   Post-Sec.
  PO Box 160 38610   662-685-4771

Blue Springs, Union, Pop. 147
Union County SD
  Supt. — See New Albany
East Union S   800/K-12
  1548 Highway 9 S 38828   662-534-6920
  Walter Moore, prin.   Fax 534-6941

Bogue Chitto, Lincoln, Pop. 689
Lincoln County SD
  Supt. — See Brookhaven
Bogue Chitto S   500/K-12
  385 Monticello St 39629   601-734-2723
  Bill McGehee, prin.   Fax 734-6020

Booneville, Prentiss, Pop. 8,619
Booneville SD   1,400/K-12
  PO Box 358 38829   662-728-5445
  Larry Morgan, supt.   Fax 728-4940
  www.booneville.k12.ms.us
Booneville HS   400/9-12
  300B W George E Allen Dr 38829   662-728-2953
  Rickey J. Neaves, prin.   Fax 728-2953
Booneville MS   400/5-8
  300A W George E Allen Dr 38829   662-728-5843
  Rickey J. Neaves, prin.   Fax 728-2427

Prentiss County SD   2,300/K-12
  PO Box 179 38829   662-728-4911
  Kenneth Chism, supt.   Fax 728-2000
  www2.mde.k12.ms.us/5900/index.html
Jumpertown S   300/K-12
  717 Highway 4 W 38829   662-728-6378
  Anthony Michael, prin.   Fax 728-9420

Prentiss County Vocational Technical S Vo/Tech
302 W George E Allen Dr 38829
Linda Sweeney, dir. 662-728-9259
Fax 728-9259
Thrasher S 500/K-12
167 County Road 1040 38829 662-728-5233
Cathy Trimble, prin. Fax 728-8107
Other Schools – See New Site, Wheeler

Northeast Mississippi Community College Post-Sec.
101 Cunningham Blvd 38829 662-728-7751

Brandon, Rankin, Pop. 18,065
Rankin County SD 14,700/K-12
PO Box 1359 39043 601-825-5590
Dr. Lynn Weathersby, supt. Fax 825-2618
www.rcsd.ms/
Brandon HS 1,200/9-12
3090 Highway 18 39042 601-825-2261
George Gilreath, prin. Fax 591-1037
Brandon MS 1,000/6-8
200 School Rd 39042 601-825-5998
Buddy Bailey, prin. Fax 825-8402
Northwest HS 1,200/9-12
5805 Highway 25 39047 601-992-2242
Jean Massey, prin. Fax 992-6005
Northwest MS 1,100/6-8
1 Paw Print Pl 39047 601-992-1329
Jacob McEwen, prin. Fax 992-1347
Other Schools – See Florence, Pelahatchie, Puckett, Richland, Sandhill

Brookhaven, Lincoln, Pop. 9,810
Brookhaven SD 3,200/PK-12
326 E Court St 39601 601-833-6661
Lea Barrett Ed.D., supt. Fax 833-4154
www.telapex.com/~bschool/index.html
Alexander JHS 500/7-8
713 Beauregard St 39601 601-833-7549
Johnny Waller, prin. Fax 835-5467
Brookhaven HS 700/9-12
443 E Monticello St 39601 601-833-4498
Susan Chapman, prin. Fax 823-3792
Brookhaven Technical Center Vo/Tech
325 E Court St 39601 601-833-8335
Don Coleman, dir. Fax 835-3985

Lincoln County SD 2,800/K-12
PO Box 826 39602 601-835-0011
Terry M. Brister, supt. Fax 833-3030
lcsd.k12.ms.us/
Enterprise S 700/K-12
1601 Highway 583 SE 39601 601-833-7284
Shannon Eubanks, prin. Fax 835-1261
Star S 900/K-12
1880 Highway 550 NW 39601 601-833-3473
Wayne Rogers, prin. Fax 833-1254
West Lincoln S 600/K-12
948 Jackson Liberty Dr SW 39601 601-833-4600
Jason Case, prin. Fax 833-9909
Other Schools – See Bogue Chitto

Brookhaven Academy 500/K-12
PO Box 3339 39603 601-833-4041
Dr. Miller Hammill, hdmstr. Fax 833-1846

Brooklyn, Forrest
Forrest County Agricultural HSD
215 Old Highway 49 E 39425
Kyle Nobles, supt. 601-582-4102
Fax 545-9483
Forrest County Agricultural HS Vo/Tech
215 Old Highway 49 E 39425 601-582-4741
Karen Norwood, prin. Fax 582-9031

Bruce, Calhoun, Pop. 2,055
Calhoun County SD
Supt. — See Pittsboro
Bruce HS 400/7-12
PO Box 248 38915 662-983-3350
Rickie Vaughn, prin. Fax 983-3356

Byhalia, Marshall, Pop. 717
Marshall County SD
Supt. — See Holly Springs
Byhalia HS 500/9-12
PO Box 346 38611 662-838-2206
Brian Taylor, prin. Fax 838-2218
Henry JHS 5-8
172 Highway 309 N 38611 662-838-2591
Kerry Reid, prin. Fax 838-5141

Caledonia, Monroe, Pop. 998
Lowndes County SD
Supt. — See Columbus
Caledonia HS 500/9-12
111 Confederate Dr 39740 662-356-2001
Mike Putnam, prin. Fax 356-2036
Caledonia MS 500/6-8
105 Confederate Dr 39740 662-356-2042
Karen Pittman, prin. Fax 356-2045

Calhoun City, Calhoun, Pop. 1,835
Calhoun County SD
Supt. — See Pittsboro
Calhoun City HS 400/6-12
PO Box 559 38916 662-628-5112
Dale Hays, prin. Fax 628-6240

Calhoun Academy 400/PK-12
PO Box C 38916 662-412-2087
Mike Haynie, admin. Fax 412-2081

Camden, Madison
Madison County SD
Supt. — See Flora
Jackson HS 400/9-12
2000 Loring Rd 39045 662-468-2531
Reginal Barnes, prin. Fax 468-3430

Canton, Madison, Pop. 12,856
Canton SD 3,300/K-12
403 Lincoln St 39046 601-859-4110
Dwight Luckett, supt. Fax 859-4023
www.cantonpublicschooldistrict.com/
Canton Career Center Vo/Tech
487 N Union Street Ext 39046 601-859-3984
Michael Myrick, prin. Fax 859-1115

Canton HS 900/9-12
634 Finney Rd 39046 601-859-5325
Cleveland Anderson, prin. Fax 859-2554
Nichols MS 800/6-8
529 Mace St 39046 601-859-3741
Roosevelt Greenwood, prin. Fax 859-6561

Madison County SD
Supt. — See Flora
Madison County Vocational Complex Vo/Tech
1633 W Peace St 39046 601-859-6847
Mike Thomas, dir. Fax 859-0372
Northeast Madison MS 300/6-8
820 Sulphur Springs Rd 39046 601-855-2406
Dr. Earnest Ward, prin. Fax 859-7615

Canton Academy 300/K-12
PO Box 116 39046 601-859-5231
David Glasgow, prin. Fax 859-5232

Carriere, Pearl River
Pearl River County SD 2,100/K-12
7306 Highway 11 39426 601-798-7744
Dennis Penton, supt. Fax 798-3527
www.prc.k12.ms.us/
Pearl River Central HS 700/9-12
7407 Highway 11 39426 601-798-1986
Loren Harris, prin. Fax 799-0068
Pearl River Central JHS 700/6-8
7391 Highway 11 39426 601-798-5654
Joseph White Ed.D., prin. Fax 798-2822

Carrollton, Carroll, Pop. 398
Carroll County SD 1,100/K-12
PO Box 256 38917 662-237-9276
Billy Joe Ferguson, supt. Fax 237-9703
www.ccs.k12.ms.us/
Other Schools – See North Carrollton

Carroll Academy 400/K-12
PO Box 226 38917 662-237-6858
Cameron Wright, admin. Fax 237-9231

Carson, Jefferson Davis
Jefferson Davis County SD
Supt. — See Prentiss
Davis County Voc-Tech Center Vo/Tech
PO Box 70 39427 601-792-5005
Dr. Thomas Johnson, prin. Fax 792-2511

Carthage, Leake, Pop. 4,642
Leake County SD 3,200/K-12
PO Box 478 39051 601-267-4579
Melanie H. Hartley, supt. Fax 267-5283
www.leakesd.k12.ms.us
Carthage HS 400/9-12
704 N Jordan St 39051 601-267-7713
J.B. Norwood, prin. Fax 267-3738
Carthage JHS 400/6-8
801 Martin Luther King Dr 39051 601-267-8909
Haywood Hannah, prin. Fax 267-5902
Edinburg S 500/K-12
673 Mars Hill Rd 39051 601-267-7137
Rebecca Marble, prin. Fax 267-3007
Leake County Vo-Tech Ctr Vo/Tech
703 N West St 39051 601-267-8442
Monte Ladner, prin. Fax 267-5150
Thomastown S 400/K-12
7100 Highway 429 39051 601-267-7896
Calvin Melton, prin. Fax 298-1295
Other Schools – See Walnut Grove

Academy of Hair Design #7 Post-Sec.
215 Highway 35 N 39051 601-267-8031
J & J Hair Design College Post-Sec.
116 E Franklin St 39051 601-267-3678

Centreville, Wilkinson, Pop. 1,614
Wilkinson County SD
Supt. — See Woodville
Winans MS 400/6-8
PO Box 610 39631 601-645-0008
Robert Williams, prin. Fax 645-0170

Centreville Academy 400/K-12
PO Box 70 39631 601-645-5912
Lea E. Hurst, prin. Fax 645-5940

Charleston, Tallahatchie, Pop. 2,102
East Tallahatchie Consolidated SD 1,600/K-12
411 E Chestnut St 38921 662-647-5524
William Tribble, supt. Fax 647-3720
www2.mde.k12.ms.us/6811/
Charleston HS 400/9-12
411 E Chestnut St 38921 662-647-5359
Ellis Smith, prin. Fax 647-3724
Charleston MS 700/4-8
411 E Chestnut St 38921 662-647-5486
Glinda Hardy, prin. Fax 647-2396
East Tallahatchie Vocational Ctr Vo/Tech
411 E Chestnut St 38921 662-647-5359
Barbara Herod-Hence, prin. Fax 647-3724

Strider Academy 200/K-12
3698 MS Highway 32 Central 38921 662-647-5833
Joe Bradshaw, prin. Fax 647-5702

Clarksdale, Coahoma, Pop. 19,833
Clarksdale Municipal SD 3,200/K-12
PO Box 1088 38614 662-627-8500
Dr. Wilma Wade, supt. Fax 627-8542
www.cdps.k12.ms.us/
Clarksdale HS 700/9-12
PO Box 1088 38614 662-627-8530
Olenza Mc Bride, prin. Fax 627-8549
Higgins MS 300/6-8
PO Box 1088 38614 662-627-8550
W. Donald Clark, prin. Fax 627-8543
Keen Vocational Center Vo/Tech
PO Box 1088 38614 662-627-8580
Jim Cobbs, prin. Fax 627-8582
Oakhurst MS 300/6-8
PO Box 1088 38614 662-627-8560
Linda Downing, prin. Fax 627-8512

Coahoma County Agricultural SD
3240 Friars Point Rd 38614 662-624-9424
Dr. Vivian Presley, supt. Fax 624-4315
www2.mde.k12.ms.us/1402
Coahoma Agricultural HS Vo/Tech
3240 Friars Point Rd 38614 662-621-4160
John Brown, prin. Fax 624-8045

Coahoma County SD 1,900/K-12
1555 Lee Dr 38614 662-624-5448
Pauline Rhoads, supt. Fax 624-5512
www.coahoma.k12.ms.us
Coahoma County JSHS 600/7-12
1535 Lee Dr 38614 662-627-7378
Roosevelt Ramsey, prin. Fax 627-9731

Coahoma Community College Post-Sec.
3240 Friars Point Rd 38614 662-627-2571
Lee Academy 500/K-12
415 Lee Dr 38614 662-627-7891
Ricky Weiss, prin. Fax 627-7896

Cleveland, Bolivar, Pop. 13,184
Cleveland SD 3,100/PK-12
305 Merritt Dr 38732 662-843-3529
Montrell Greene Ph.D., supt. Fax 843-9731
www.cleveland.k12.ms.us/
Cleveland Career Development & Tech Ctr. Vo/Tech
601 3rd St 38732 662-843-8818
Judy Stevenson, dir. Fax 843-0308
Cleveland HS 500/9-12
300 W Sunflower Rd 38732 662-843-2460
Arthur Holbrook, prin. Fax 843-2455
East Side HS 400/9-12
601 Lucy Seaberry Blvd 38732 662-843-2338
Charles Brady, prin. Fax 843-1900
Green JHS 300/7-8
205 N Bolivar Ave 38732 662-843-2456
Robert Montesi, prin. Fax 843-6820
Smith MS 300/7-8
715 S Martin Luther King Dr 38732 662-843-4355
Lisa Bramuchi, prin. Fax 843-7334

Bayou Academy 400/PK-12
PO Box 417 38732 662-843-3708
Robert Foust, admin. Fax 843-9618
Delta State University Post-Sec.
Hwy 8 W 38733 662-846-3000

Clinton, Hinds, Pop. 24,207
Clinton SD 4,900/K-12
PO Box 300 39060 601-924-7533
Tommie Henderson, supt. Fax 924-6345
www.clintonpublicschools.com
Clinton Career Complex Vo/Tech
713 Lakeview Dr 39056 601-924-0247
Margera Harris, prin. Fax 924-1168
Clinton HS 900/10-12
401 Arrow Dr 39056 601-924-5656
James Reeves, prin. Fax 924-4622
Clinton JHS 900/7-8
711 Lakeview Dr 39056 601-924-0619
Anthony Goins, prin. Fax 924-7703
Sumner Hill JHS 400/9-9
400 W Northside Dr 39056 601-924-5510
Willie McInnis, prin. Fax 924-4182

Mississippi College Post-Sec.
PO Box 4086 39058 601-925-3000
Mount Salus Christian S 100/K-12
PO Box 240 39060 601-924-6652
Phyllis Hurley, admin. Fax 924-3377

Coffeeville, Yalobusha, Pop. 935
Coffeeville SD 700/K-12
16849 Okahoma St 38922 662-675-8941
Eddie Anderson, supt. Fax 675-5004
www2.mde.k12.ms.us/8111/index.htm
Coffeeville HS 200/8-12
16849 Okahoma St 38922 662-675-8904
Michael Moore, prin. Fax 675-8905

Coldwater, Tate, Pop. 1,632
Tate County SD
Supt. — See Senatobia
Coldwater HS 400/7-12
671 West St 38618 662-622-5511
Lakimberly Gallagher, prin. Fax 622-7601
Senatobia/Tate Vocational-Technical Ctr Vo/Tech
165 W Central Ave 38618 662-622-5149
Richard Hartley, prin. Fax 622-7005

Collins, Covington, Pop. 2,743
Covington County SD 3,400/K-12
PO Box 1269 39428 601-765-4457
Isaac Sanford, supt. Fax 765-4102
www.cov.k12.ms.us/
Collins HS 500/9-12
PO Box 1479 39428 601-765-3203
Charles Lewis, prin. Fax 765-4116
Collins MS 500/5-8
PO Box 757 39428 601-765-4908
Kevin Jackson, prin. Fax 765-4100
Covington County Vocational Ctr Vo/Tech
PO Box 1268 39428 601-765-8253
Cecil Easterling, prin. Fax 765-6360
Other Schools – See Mount Olive, Seminary

Collinsville, Lauderdale, Pop. 1,364
Lauderdale County SD
Supt. — See Meridian
West Lauderdale S 1,200/5-12
9916 W Lauderdale Rd 39325 601-737-2277
Mike Ethridge, prin. Fax 737-2377

Columbia, Marion, Pop. 6,344
Columbia SD 1,500/K-12
613 Bryan Ave 39429 601-736-2366
Dr. Marietta James, supt. Fax 736-2653
www.columbiaschools.org
Columbia HS 500/9-12
1009 Broad St 39429 601-736-5334
Sheila Burbridge, prin. Fax 731-1068
Jefferson MS 400/6-8
611 Owens St 39429 601-736-2786
Raymond Powell, prin. Fax 731-3762

Marion County SD 2,400/PK-12
600 Broad St 39429 601-736-7193
Craig Robbins, supt. Fax 736-6274
www.marion.k12.ms.us/
East Marion JSHS 500/7-12
527 E Marion School Rd 39429 601-736-5100
Karl Mann, prin. Fax 736-8215
Loftin Career and Technology Ctr Vo/Tech
1140 Highway 13 S 39429 601-736-6095
Ron Fortenberry, prin. Fax 731-2077
Other Schools – See Foxworth

Columbia Academy 400/K-12
1548 Highway 98 E 39429 601-736-6418
H. Tom Porter, hdmstr. Fax 736-0098

Columbus, Lowndes, Pop. 24,959
Columbus Municipal SD 5,100/K-12
PO Box 1308 39703 662-241-7400
Dr. Lester Beason, supt. Fax 241-7453
www.columbuscityschools.org/
Columbus HS 1,300/9-12
215 Hemlock St 39702 662-241-7200
Lanell Kellum, prin. Fax 241-7205
Lee MS 900/7-8
1815 Military Rd 39701 662-241-7300
Robert Keenum, prin. Fax 241-7305
McKellar Vocational Center Vo/Tech
810 N Browder St 39702 662-241-7290
LaNell Kellum, prin. Fax 241-7293

Lowndes County SD 5,300/K-12
1053 Highway 45 S 39701 662-244-5000
Michael Halford, supt. Fax 244-5043
www.lowndes.k12.ms.us/
New Hope HS 800/9-12
3419 New Hope Rd 39702 662-244-4701
Bobby Eiland, prin. Fax 244-4725
New Hope MS 700/6-8
462 Center Rd 39702 662-244-4740
Joe York, prin. Fax 244-4758
West Lowndes HS 200/9-12
644 S Frontage Rd 39701 662-328-1369
Roosevelt Bridges, prin. Fax 327-3353
West Lowndes MS 200/6-8
1380 Motley Rd 39701 662-244-5060
Robert Smith, prin. Fax 327-4857
Other Schools – See Caledonia

Heritage Academy 700/K-12
625 Magnolia Ln 39705 662-327-5272
Termie Land, admin. Fax 327-2226
Mississippi University for Women Post-Sec.
1100 College St Unit W1613 39701 662-329-7106

Como, Panola, Pop. 1,311
North Panola Consolidated SD
Supt. — See Sardis
Como MS 300/7-8
202 Lewers St 38619 662-526-5938
Rodney Flowers, prin. Fax 526-5990
North Panola Career & Technical Center Vo/Tech
601 Railroad St 38619 662-526-5804
Dorothy Jones, prin. Fax 526-0160

Corinth, Alcorn, Pop. 14,083
Alcorn SD 3,700/K-12
PO Box 1420 38835 662-286-5591
Mike Wamsley, supt. Fax 286-7713
www.alcorn.k12.ms.us
Alcorn County Vocational Complex Vo/Tech
2101 Norman Rd 38834 662-286-7727
Edward M. Settle, prin. Fax 286-5674
Biggersville JSHS 200/7-12
571 Highway 45 38834 662-286-3542
Gary Johnson, prin. Fax 286-3023
Kossuth HS 400/9-12
15 County Road 604 38834 662-286-3653
Stan Platt, prin. Fax 286-3507
Kossuth MS 500/5-8
17 County Road 604 38834 662-286-7093
Fred Jackson, prin. Fax 286-6837
Other Schools – See Glen

Corinth SD 1,800/K-12
1204 N Harper Rd 38834 662-287-2425
Edward Lee Childress, supt. Fax 286-1885
www.corinth.k12.ms.us
Corinth HS 500/9-12
1310 N Harper Rd 38834 662-286-1000
Wayne Henry, prin. Fax 286-1003
Corinth JHS 300/7-8
1000 E 5th St 38834 662-286-1261
Brian Knippers, prin. Fax 287-0296

ICS The Wright Beauty College Post-Sec.
2077 Highway 72 E Anx 38834 662-287-0944

Crawford, Oktibbeha, Pop. 650
Oktibbeha County SD
Supt. — See Starkville
East Oktibbeha County HS 200/7-12
1780 Moor High Rd 39743 662-272-5660
Clifford Reynolds, prin. Fax 272-5231

Crystal Springs, Copiah, Pop. 5,841
Copiah County SD
Supt. — See Hazlehurst
Crystal Springs HS 500/9-12
201 Newton St 39059 601-892-4791
Angela Jones, prin. Fax 892-2071
Crystal Springs MS 800/4-8
2092 S Pat Harrison Dr 39059 601-892-2722
Lee Payton, prin. Fax 892-9949

Mississippi Job Corps Center Post-Sec.
PO Box 817 39059 601-892-3348

Decatur, Newton, Pop. 1,432
Newton County SD 1,800/K-12
PO Box 97 39327 601-635-2317
Billy Pierce, supt. Fax 635-4025
www.newton.k12.ms.us
Newton Co. Career and Technical Center Vo/Tech
PO Box 742 39327 601-635-4138
Wayne McDill, prin. Fax 635-4024
Newton County HS 800/6-12
PO Box 278 39327 601-635-2718
Rodney Tadlock, prin. Fax 635-4045

East Central Community College Post-Sec.
PO Box 129 39327 601-635-2111
Newton County Academy 200/K-12
PO Box 25 39327 601-635-2756
Mike Tucker, admin. Fax 635-3525

De Kalb, Kemper, Pop. 945
Kemper County SD 1,300/PK-12
PO Box 219 39328 601-743-2657
June Wright, supt. Fax 743-9297
kemper.k12.ms.us/
Kemper County HS 500/7-12
PO Box 429 39328 601-743-5292
Melvin Willis, prin. Fax 743-5952
Stennis Vocational Complex Vo/Tech
PO Box 88 39328 601-743-5226
Jackqueline Pollock, prin. Fax 743-2351

Kemper Academy 300/K-12
PO Box 459 39328 601-743-2232
Pete McCleskey, admin. Fax 743-9627

D Iberville, Harrison, Pop. 7,868
Harrison County SD
Supt. — See Gulfport
D'Iberville HS 900/9-12
3320 Warrior Dr, 228-392-2678
Elmer Mullins, prin. Fax 396-3446
D'Iberville MS 600/5-8
10000 Gorenflo Rd, 228-392-1746
Annette Luther, prin. Fax 392-9948

Drew, Sunflower, Pop. 2,287
Drew SD 600/K-12
286 W Park Ave 38737 662-745-6657
Dennis Silas, supt. Fax 745-6630
www2.mde.k12.ms.us/6720/
Drew HS 200/9-12
288 Green Ave 38737 662-745-8586
Sammie Armstrong, prin. Fax 745-6630
Hunter MS 200/5-8
10 Swoope Rd 38737 662-745-8940
Sam Evans, prin. Fax 745-6630

North Sunflower Academy 200/K-12
148 Academy Rd 38737 662-756-2547
Charlie Francis, admin. Fax 756-2580

Durant, Holmes, Pop. 2,886
Durant SD 600/K-12
PO Box 669 39063 662-653-3175
Glennie Carlisle, supt. Fax 653-6151
Durant HS 300/7-12
PO Box 669 39063 662-653-3429
Elizabeth Terrell, prin. Fax 653-3472

Holmes County SD
Supt. — See Lexington
Williams-Sullivan S 500/K-12
14494 Highway 51 39063 662-653-6262
Sandra Winston, prin. Fax 653-6519

Ecru, Pontotoc, Pop. 989
Pontotoc County SD
Supt. — See Pontotoc
North Pontotoc HS 400/9-12
8324 Highway 15 N 38841 662-489-5612
Roger Smith, prin. Fax 489-7068
North Pontotoc MS 400/6-8
8324 Highway 15 N 38841 662-489-2479
Libby Young, prin. Fax 489-2985

Ellisville, Jones, Pop. 3,442
Jones County SD 7,800/K-12
5204 Highway 11 N 39437 601-649-5201
Thomas Prine, supt. Fax 649-1613
www.jones.k12.ms.us/
South Jones JSHS 1,000/7-12
313 Anderson St 39437 601-477-8452
Richard Shoemake, prin. Fax 477-3505
Other Schools – See Laurel

Jones County Junior College Post-Sec.
900 S Court St 39437 601-477-4000

Enterprise, Clarke, Pop. 457
Enterprise SD 800/K-12
503 S River Rd 39330 601-659-7965
Arthur McMillan, supt. Fax 659-3254
www.esd.k12.ms.us/
Enterprise HS 200/9-12
503 S River Rd 39330 601-659-4435
Mike Weathers, prin. Fax 659-3254
Enterprise MS 400/4-8
105 Short St 39330 601-659-7722
Pamela Himebrook, prin. Fax 659-7722

Ethel, Attala, Pop. 448
Attala County SD
Supt. — See Kosciusko
Ethel JSHS 300/7-12
PO Box 340 39067 662-674-5673
Roger Hill, prin. Fax 674-5817

Eupora, Webster, Pop. 2,261
Webster County SD 1,800/K-12
212 W Clark Ave 39744 662-258-5921
Jimmy Pittman, supt. Fax 258-3134
www.webster.k12.ms.us/
Eupora HS 500/7-12
404 W Fox Ave 39744 662-258-4041
James Mason, prin. Fax 258-4716
Webster County Career & Technology Ctr Vo/Tech
102 Hall Rd 39744 662-258-8206
Jack Treloar, prin. Fax 258-6728
Other Schools – See Maben

Falkner, Tippah, Pop. 207
North Tippah SD
Supt. — See Tiplersville
Falkner JSHS 300/7-12
PO Box 139 38629 662-837-7892
Kurt Kutrip, prin. Fax 837-8800

Fayette, Jefferson, Pop. 2,169
Jefferson County SD 1,500/K-12
PO Box 157 39069 601-786-3721
John E. Dickey, supt. Fax 786-8441
Jefferson County HS 500/9-12
2277 Main St 39069 601-786-3919
Barbara Lewis, prin. Fax 786-6002
Jefferson County MS 500/5-8
468 Highway 33 39069 601-786-3900
Inder Mitchell, prin. Fax 786-2273
Jefferson County Vocational Center Vo/Tech
205 Industrial Park Rd 39069 601-786-3642
David Perry, prin. Fax 786-2271

Flora, Madison, Pop. 1,527
Madison County SD 9,800/K-12
PO Box 159 39071 601-879-3025
Michael Kent, supt. Fax 879-3039
www.madison.k12.ms.us
East Flora MS 100/6-8
PO Box J 39071 601-879-3809
William Carter, prin. Fax 879-3158
Other Schools – See Camden, Canton, Madison, Ridgeland

Tri-County Academy 200/K-12
PO Box K 39071 601-879-8517
Keith Lockhart, prin. Fax 879-3373

Florence, Rankin, Pop. 2,718
Rankin County SD
Supt. — See Brandon
Florence HS 600/9-12
232 Highway 469 N 39073 601-845-2205
Tony Martin, prin. Fax 845-3752
Florence MS 500/6-8
PO Box 159 39073 601-845-2862
Beverly Weathersby, prin. Fax 845-2114
McLaurin JSHS 500/7-12
130 Tiger Dr 39073 601-845-2247
Bill Lenington, prin. Fax 845-1170

Wesley College Post-Sec.
PO Box 1070 39073 800-748-9972

Flowood, Rankin, Pop. 6,260

University Christian S 200/K-12
1240 Luckney Rd 39232 601-992-5333
Pam Ulrich, admin. Fax 992-5320

Forest, Scott, Pop. 5,970
Forest Municipal SD 1,600/K-12
325 Cleveland St 39074 601-469-3250
Skip Lathem, supt. Fax 469-3101
www2.mde.k12.ms.us/6220/
Forest HS 400/9-12
511 Cleveland St 39074 601-469-3255
Billy Wilbanks, prin. Fax 469-8250
Hawkins MS 500/5-8
803 E Oak St 39074 601-469-1474
Phylis Campbell, prin. Fax 469-8251

Scott County SD 4,100/K-12
100 E First St 39074 601-469-3861
Frank McCurdy, supt. Fax 469-3874
www.scott.k12.ms.us
Forest/Scott County Career & Tech Ctr Vo/Tech
521 Cleveland St 39074 601-469-2913
Chuck Wade, prin. Fax 469-2917
Scott Central S 900/K-12
2415 Old Jackson Rd 39074 601-469-4883
Gene Bright, prin. Fax 469-3746
Other Schools – See Lake, Morton, Sebastopol

Foxworth, Marion
Marion County SD
Supt. — See Columbia
West Marion HS 300/9-12
2 W Marion St 39483 601-736-6381
Bryan Hoda, prin. Fax 731-7937
West Marion JHS 200/7-8
2 W Marion St 39483 601-736-6381
Craig Wise, prin. Fax 731-7937

French Camp, Choctaw, Pop. 389

French Camp Academy 200/9-12
1 Fine Pl 39745 662-547-6113
John Cockrell, prin. Fax 547-6302

Fulton, Itawamba, Pop. 3,935
Itawamba County SD 3,200/PK-12
605 S Cummings St 38843 662-862-2159
F. G. Wiygul, supt. Fax 862-4713
www.itawamba.k12.ms.us/
Itawamba Agricultural HS 600/9-12
11900 Highway 25 S 38843 662-862-3104
Michael Nanney, prin. Fax 862-5494
Itawamba County Vocational Center Vo/Tech
PO Box 548 38843 662-862-3137
Gary Hamm, prin. Fax 862-3138
Other Schools – See Mantachie, Tremont

Itawamba Community College Post-Sec.
602 W Hill St 38843 662-862-8000

Gallman, Copiah

Copiah Academy 500/K-12
PO Box 125 39077 601-892-3770
Carol Rigby, prin. Fax 892-6222

Gautier, Jackson, Pop. 16,753
Pascagoula SD
Supt. — See Pascagoula
Gautier HS 800/9-12
4307 Gautier Vancleave Rd 39553 228-522-8783
Bernard Rogers, prin. Fax 522-8788
Gautier MS 700/6-8
1920 Graveline Rd 39553 228-522-8806
Emily Sims, prin. Fax 522-8813

Mississippi Gulf Coast Community College Post-Sec.
39553 228-497-9602

Georgetown, Copiah, Pop. 344

Union Academy | 200/K-12
1110 Mary St 39078 | 601-858-2255
David Langston, admin. | Fax 858-2256

Glen, Alcorn, Pop. 292

Alcorn SD
Supt. — See Corinth
Alcorn Central HS | 500/9-12
8 County Road 254 38846 | 662-286-8720
Rivers Stroup, prin. | Fax 286-8720
Alcorn Central MS | 500/5-8
8A County Road 254 38846 | 662-286-3674
Dr. Stephanie Clausel, prin. | Fax 286-6712

Goodman, Madison, Pop. 1,201

Holmes Community College | Post-Sec.
PO Box 369 39079 | 662-472-2312

Greenville, Washington, Pop. 39,521

Greenville SD | 7,200/PK-12
PO Box 1619 38702 | 662-334-7000
| Fax 334-7021
www.gvillepublicschools.com/
Coleman MS | 600/7-8
400 Highway 1 N 38701 | 662-334-7036
Linda Felton, prin. | Fax 334-7040
Greenville Technical Center | Vo/Tech
PO Box 4620 38704 | 662-334-7171
Sherry E. Jackson, prin. | Fax 334-2848
Greenville-Weston HS - Greenville Campus | 1,600/9-12
419 E Robertshaw St 38701 | 662-334-7062
Carey Spears, prin. | Fax 334-7060
Greenville-Weston HS Weston Campus | 9-12
901 Archer Rd 38701 | 662-334-7080
Carey Spears, prin. | Fax 334-7091
Solomon MS | 600/7-8
556 Bowman Blvd 38701 | 662-334-7050
Michael McNeece, prin. | Fax 334-7053

Western Line SD
Supt. — See Avon
O'Bannon HS | 400/7-12
PO Box 5816 38704 | 662-335-2637
Willie Goins, prin. | Fax 334-1689

Delta Beauty College | Post-Sec.
697 Delta Pl 38701 | 662-332-0587
Greenville Christian S | 400/K-12
PO Box 4398 38704 | 662-332-0946
Donald Murphy, admin. | Fax 332-0948
St. Joseph HS | 300/7-12
700 Golf St 38701 | 662-378-9711
Alan Powers, prin. | Fax 378-3496
Washington S | 800/K-12
1605 E Reed Rd 38703 | 662-334-4096
Rodney Brown, hdmstr. | Fax 332-0434

Greenwood, LeFlore, Pop. 17,594

Greenwood SD | 3,400/PK-12
401 Howard St 38930 | 662-453-4231
Dr. Leslie Daniels, supt. | Fax 455-7409
www.greenwood.k12.ms.us/
Greenwood Career and Technical Ctr | Vo/Tech
616 Sycamore Ave 38930 | 662-455-7414
Kirby Love, prin. | Fax 455-8979
Greenwood HS | 700/9-12
1209 Garrard Ave 38930 | 662-455-7450
Percy Powell, prin. | Fax 455-7468
Greenwood MS | 500/7-8
1200 Garrard Ave 38930 | 662-455-3661
Lorita Harris, prin. | Fax 455-5559

Leflore County SD | 3,000/K-12
1901 Highway 82 W 38930 | 662-453-8566
Cedell Pulley, supt. | Fax 459-7265
www.leflorecountyschools.org
East MS | 400/4-8
208 Meadowbrook Rd 38930 | 662-453-9182
Annie Johnson, prin. | Fax 451-7734
Elzy HS | 600/7-12
604 Elzy Ave 38930 | 662-453-3394
Byron Haynes, prin. | Fax 459-7266
Leflore County Vocational Center | Vo/Tech
PO Box 1158 38935 | 662-453-7706
Charles Streeter, prin. | Fax 453-7733
Other Schools – See Itta Bena

Pillow Academy | 900/K-12
69601 Highway 82 W 38930 | 662-453-1266
Russell Robertson, hdmstr. | Fax 455-6484

Grenada, Grenada, Pop. 14,649

Grenada SD | 4,500/K-12
PO Box 1940 38902 | 662-226-1606
Dr. Buddy Pender, supt. | Fax 226-7994
www.gsd.k12.ms.us/
Grenada HS | 1,100/9-12
1875 Fairground Rd 38901 | 662-226-8844
Dr. Thomas Taylor, prin. | Fax 227-6109
Grenada MS | 1,200/6-8
28 Jones Rd 38901 | 662-226-5135
Dr. Carole White, prin. | Fax 227-6106
Grenada Vocational Complex | Vo/Tech
2035 Jackson Ave 38901 | 662-226-5969
Don Connerley, prin. | Fax 226-5992

Academy of Hair Design #1 | Post-Sec.
2003B Commerce St 38901 | 662-226-2462
Kirk Academy | 600/K-12
PO Box 1008 38902 | 662-226-2791
Allen O. Smithers, admin. | Fax 226-2791

Gulfport, Harrison, Pop. 71,810

Gulfport SD | 6,000/K-12
2001 Pass Rd 39501 | 228-865-4600
Glen East, supt. | Fax 865-4718
www.gulfportschools.k12.ms.us/
Bayou View MS | 800/6-8
212 43rd St 39507 | 228-865-4633
Jerry Morgan, prin. | Fax 867-1967
Gulfport Central HS | 700/6-8
1310 42nd Ave 39501 | 228-870-1035
Eddie Peasant, prin. | Fax 870-1041

Gulfport HS | 1,600/9-12
100 Perry St 39507 | 228-896-7525
Michael Lindsey, prin. | Fax 896-6867
Gulfport Vocational Annex S | Vo/Tech
100 Perry St 39507 | 228-896-6011
David Fava, prin. | Fax 896-7686

Harrison County SD | 12,500/K-12
11072 Highway 49 39503 | 228-539-6500
Henry Arledge, supt. | Fax 539-6507
www.harrison.k12.ms.us/DesktopDefault.aspx
Harrison Central 9th Grade S | 700/9-9
10453 Klein Rd 39503 | 228-832-6711
Rebecca Moore, prin. | Fax 832-0940
Harrison Central SHS | 1,500/10-12
15600 School Rd 39503 | 228-832-2610
James Cater, prin. | Fax 832-7433
Harrison County Vocational Complex | Vo/Tech
15600 School Rd 39503 | 228-832-6652
Larry Thrash, prin. | Fax 539-5965
North Gulfport MS | 1,000/7-8
4715 Illinois Ave 39501 | 228-864-8944
Charles Dubra, prin. | Fax 863-7326
Other Schools – See D Iberville

Blue Cliff College | Post-Sec.
2200 25th Ave 39501 | 228-896-9727
Chris' Beauty College | Post-Sec.
1265 Pass Rd 39501 | 228-864-2920
Gulfport Job Corps Center | Vo/Tech
3300 20th St 39501 | 228-864-9691
Mississippi Gulf Coast Community College | Post-Sec.
39507 | 228-896-3355
St. John HS | 400/7-12
620 Pass Rd 39501 | 228-863-8141
Dr. Bill Heath, prin. | Fax 864-2788
William Carey College | Post-Sec.
1856 Beach Dr 39507 | 228-867-9201

Guntown, Lee, Pop. 1,205

Lee County SD
Supt. — See Tupelo
Guntown MS | 600/6-8
PO Box 8 38849 | 662-348-8801
Phil Ferguson, prin. | Fax 348-8810

Hamilton, Monroe

Monroe County SD
Supt. — See Amory
Hamilton S | 700/K-12
40201 Hamilton Rd 39746 | 662-343-8307
Mark Howell, prin. | Fax 343-5813

Hattiesburg, Forrest, Pop. 46,664

Forrest County SD | 2,400/K-12
PO Box 1977 39403 | 601-545-6055
Kay H. Clay Ed.D., supt. | Fax 545-6054
www.forrest.k12.ms.us/
North Forrest JSHS | 400/7-12
693 Eatonville Rd 39401 | 601-545-9304
Brian Freeman, prin. | Fax 545-9318

Hattiesburg SD | 4,700/K-12
PO Box 1569 39403 | 601-582-5078
Annie Wimbish Ed.D., supt. | Fax 582-6666
www.hpsd.k12.ms.us/
Burger MS | 700/7-8
174 W S F Tatum Blvd 39401 | 601-582-0536
Joann Wynn, prin. | Fax 582-0572
Hattiesburg HS | 900/10-12
301 Hutchinson Ave 39401 | 601-544-0811
Yvonne Bryant, prin. | Fax 582-2524
9th Grade Academy | 400/9-9
301 Hutchinson Ave 39401 | 601-544-0811
Yvonne Bryant, prin. | Fax 583-7325

Lamar County SD
Supt. — See Purvis
Oak Grove HS | 1,100/9-12
5198 Old Highway 11 39402 | 601-264-7232
Wayne Folks, prin. | Fax 264-7234
Oak Grove MS | 900/6-8
2543 Old Highway 24 39402 | 601-264-4634
Ben Burnett, prin. | Fax 264-0160

Academy of Hair Design #6 | Post-Sec.
5912 US Highway 49 39401 | 601-583-1290
Antonelli College | Post-Sec.
1500 N 31st Ave 39401 | 601-583-4100
Forrest General Hospital | Post-Sec.
6051 U S Highway 49 39401 | 601-288-4201
Hattiesburg Radiology Group | Post-Sec.
5000 W 4th St 39402 | 601-288-4241
Presbyterian Christian HS | 300/7-12
221 Bonhomie Rd 39401 | 601-582-4956
Chip Jones, prin. | Fax 582-4960
Sacred Heart S | 400/PK-10
608 Southern Ave 39401 | 601-583-8683
Dr. Maribeth Andereck, prin. | Fax 583-8684
University of Southern Mississippi | Post-Sec.
PO Box 5165 39406 | 601-266-5000
William Carey College | Post-Sec.
498 Tuscan Ave 39401 | 800-962-5991

Hazlehurst, Copiah, Pop. 4,373

Copiah County SD | 2,900/PK-12
254 W Gallatin St 39083 | 601-894-1341
Rickey Clopton, supt. | Fax 894-2634
www.copiahcounty.org/School%20District.htm
Other Schools – See Crystal Springs, Wesson

Hazlehurst CSD | 1,000/PK-12
119 Robert McDaniel Dr 39083 | 601-894-1152
Henry Dorsey, supt. | Fax 894-3170
Hazlehurst HS | 500/9-12
101 S Haley St 39083 | 601-894-2489
Marvin Davis, prin. | Fax 894-2033
Hazlehurst MS | 500/5-8
112 School Dr 39083 | 601-894-3463
James Holloway, prin. | Fax 894-2629

Heidelberg, Jasper, Pop. 823

East Jasper Consolidated SD | 1,200/K-12
PO Box E 39439 | 601-787-3281
Dr. Beverly Bullard, supt. | Fax 787-3410
www.eastjasper.k12.ms.us

Heidelberg JSHS | 500/7-12
PO Box M 39439 | 601-787-3414
Dr. Odessa Borten, prin. | Fax 787-3416

West Jasper Consolidated SD
Supt. — See Bay Springs
Jasper County Career Development Ctr | Vo/Tech
2419 Highway 528 39439 | 601-787-4753
Stephen Sullivan, prin. | Fax 787-2060

Heidelberg Academy | 200/K-12
PO Box Q 39439 | 601-787-4589
W.E. Faggert, hdmstr. | Fax 787-3371

Hernando, DeSoto, Pop. 8,344

DeSoto County SD | 23,700/K-12
5 E South St 38632 | 662-429-5271
Milton Kuykendall, supt. | Fax 429-4198
www.desoto.k12.ms.us/
Hernando HS | 1,000/9-12
805 Dilworth Ln 38632 | 662-429-4170
Freddie Joseph, prin. | Fax 449-1100
Hernando MS | 800/6-8
700 Dilworth Ln 38632 | 662-429-4154
Jerry Darnell, prin. | Fax 429-4189
Other Schools – See Horn Lake, Lake Cormorant, Olive
Branch, Southaven

Hickory Flat, Benton, Pop. 540

Benton County SD
Supt. — See Ashland
Hickory Flat S | 500/K-12
1005 Spruce St 38633 | 662-333-7731
Gerald Clark, prin. | Fax 333-4127

Hollandale, Washington, Pop. 3,248

Hollandale SD | 1,000/K-12
PO Box 128 38748 | 662-827-2276
Willie Amos, supt. | Fax 827-5261
www2.mde.k12.ms.us/7611/
Simmons HS | 300/9-12
PO Box 428 38748 | 662-827-2228
Roger Liddell, prin. | Fax 827-2231
Other Schools – See Arcola

Holly Springs, Marshall, Pop. 7,924

Holly Springs SD | 1,800/K-12
840 Highway 178 E 38635 | 662-252-2183
Dr. Cynthia Gentry, supt. | Fax 252-7718
www.hssd.k12.ms.us
Holly Springs HS | 800/K-12
165 N Walthall St 38635 | 662-252-4371
Adams Andrews, prin. | Fax 252-7720
Holly Springs Vocational S | Vo/Tech
410 E Falconer Ave 38635 | 662-252-2071
Bob Bigham, prin. | Fax 252-7719

Marshall County SD | 3,300/K-12
158 E College Ave 38635 | 662-252-4271
Dan Ranolph, supt. | Fax 252-5129
www.mde.k12.ms.us/Districts/Marshall.htm
Byers S | 800/K-12
4178 Highway 72 38635 | 662-851-7826
Gary Hannah, prin. | Fax 851-4027
Other Schools – See Byhalia, Potts Camp

Marshall Academy | 500/K-12
100 Academy Dr 38635 | 662-252-3449
Tommy C. Gunn, admin. | Fax 252-4510
Rust College | Post-Sec.
150 Rust Ave 38635 | 662-252-8000

Horn Lake, DeSoto, Pop. 15,146

DeSoto County SD
Supt. — See Hernando
Horn Lake HS | 1,400/9-12
3360 Church Rd 38637 | 662-393-5273
Jim Ferguson, prin. | Fax 393-5275
Horn Lake MS | 1,400/6-8
6585 Horn Lake Rd 38637 | 662-393-7443
Van Alexander, prin. | Fax 342-5039

Houlka, Chickasaw, Pop. 553

Chickasaw County SD | 500/PK-12
PO Box 480 38850 | 662-568-3333
Kathy Davis, supt. | Fax 568-2993
chickasaw.k12.ms.us/
Houlka S | 500/PK-12
PO Box 277 38850 | 662-568-2772
William W. Cotton, prin. | Fax 568-7931

Houston, Chickasaw, Pop. 3,982

Houston SD | 1,900/K-12
PO Box 351 38851 | 662-456-3332
Steve Coker, supt. | Fax 456-5259
www.houston.k12.ms.us
Houston HS | 500/9-12
PO Box 568 38851 | 662-456-3320
Rick Allen, prin. | Fax 456-3527
Houston MS | 500/6-8
PO Box 192 38851 | 662-456-5174
Burnell McDonald, prin. | Fax 456-2254
Houston Vocational Center | Vo/Tech
PO Box 608 38851 | 662-456-3748
Beverly James, prin. | Fax 456-5172

Independence, Tate

Tate County SD
Supt. — See Senatobia
Independence HS | 700/7-12
PO Box 159 38638 | 662-233-4691
Al Reed, prin. | Fax 233-2214

Indianola, Sunflower, Pop. 11,562

Indianola SD | 2,700/K-12
702 Highway 82 E 38751 | 662-887-2654
Dr. Auwilda M. Polk, supt. | Fax 887-7042
www2.mde.k12.ms.us/6721/
Gentry HS | 600/10-12
801 BB King Rd 38751 | 662-887-2433
Peirce McIntosh, prin. | Fax 887-7410
Merritt MS | 500/6-8
705 Kinlock Rd 38751 | 662-887-1449
Clifford Wilson, prin. | Fax 887-5247
Pennington JHS | 200/9-9
701 Chapman St 38751 | 662-887-1852
Sam Brock, prin. | Fax 887-5453

Sunflower County SD | 1,900/K-12
PO Box 70 38751 | 662-887-4919
Thomas Edwards, supt. | Fax 887-7051
www2.mde.k12.ms.us/6700/scsd.html
Other Schools – See Moorhead, Ruleville

Indianola Academy | 500/PK-12
PO Box 967 38751 | 662-887-2025
Dr. Virgil Strickland, hdmstr. | Fax 887-3117

Itta Bena, LeFlore, Pop. 2,085
Leflore County SD
Supt. — See Greenwood
Leflore County HS | 500/7-12
PO Box 564 38941 | 662-254-7762
Charles Ollie, prin. | Fax 254-7530

Mississippi Valley State University | Post-Sec.
14000 Highway 82 W # 7222 38941 | 662-254-9041

Iuka, Tishomingo, Pop. 2,977
Tishomingo Co. Special Municipal SSD | 3,200/K-12
1620 Paul Edmondson Dr 38852 | 662-423-3206
John B. Moore, supt. | Fax 423-7313
www.tishomingo.k12.ms.us
Iuka MS | 400/5-8
507 W Quitman St 38852 | 662-423-3316
Jimmy Smith, prin. | Fax 423-2426
Tishomingo County HS | 600/9-12
701 Highway 72 38852 | 662-423-7300
Terry King, prin. | Fax 423-7307
Other Schools – See Belmont, Tishomingo

Jackson, Hinds, Pop. 179,599
Jackson SD | 30,900/PK-12
PO Box 2338 39225 | 601-960-8700
Earl Watkins Ph.D., supt. | Fax 960-8713
www.jackson.k12.ms.us
Bailey Magnet JSHS | 1,000/7-12
1900 N State St 39202 | 601-960-5343
Dr. Dorothy Terry, prin. | Fax 592-2496
Blackburn MS | 500/6-8
1311 W Pearl St 39203 | 601-960-5329
Bobby Brown, prin. | Fax 360-2601
Brinkley MS | 500/6-8
3535 Albermarle Rd 39213 | 601-987-3573
Robert Jackson, prin. | Fax 987-3746
Callaway HS | 900/9-12
601 Beasley Rd 39206 | 601-987-3535
Clinton Johnson, prin. | Fax 987-3729
Chastain MS | 1,000/6-8
4650 Manhattan Rd 39206 | 601-987-3550
Michael Ellis, prin. | Fax 987-4930
Forest Hill HS | 1,000/9-12
2607 Raymond Rd 39212 | 601-371-4313
Norm Chappell, prin. | Fax 371-4379
Hardy MS | 700/6-8
545 Ellis Ave 39209 | 601-960-5362
Nehru Brown, prin. | Fax 360-2686
Hill HS | 1,000/9-12
2185 Fortune St 39204 | 601-960-5354
Lydia Haynes, prin. | Fax 360-2625
Jackson Career Development Center | Vo/Tech
2703 First Ave 39209 | 601-960-5322
Isaac Norwood, prin. | Fax 960-5411
Lanier HS | 900/9-12
833 Maple St 39203 | 601-960-5369
Stanley Blackmon, prin. | Fax 960-4047
Murrah HS | 1,100/9-12
1400 Murrah Dr 39202 | 601-960-5380
Dr. Roy Brookshire, prin. | Fax 360-2622
Northwest Jackson MS | 700/6-8
7020 Medgar Evers Blvd 39213 | 601-987-3609
Dr. Edward Buck, prin. | Fax 987-4975
Peeples MS | 900/6-8
290 Treehaven Dr 39212 | 601-371-4345
Dr. Kay McClure, prin. | Fax 371-4722
Powell MS | 900/6-8
3655 Livingston Rd 39213 | 601-987-3580
Dr. Freddrick Murray, prin. | Fax 987-3583
Provine HS | 1,000/9-12
2400 Robinson St 39209 | 601-960-5393
Tex Red, prin. | Fax 360-2606
Rowan MS | 300/6-8
136 E Ash St 39202 | 601-960-5349
Calvin Lockett, prin. | Fax 960-4046
Siwell Road MS | 800/6-8
1983 N Siwell Rd 39209 | 601-923-2550
Dr. Josephine Kelly, prin. | Fax 923-2570
Whitten MS | 700/6-8
210 Daniel Lake Blvd 39212 | 601-371-4309
Marvin Grayer, prin. | Fax 371-4728
Wingfield HS | 900/9-12
1985 Scanlon Dr 39204 | 601-371-4350
Dr. William Sellers, prin. | Fax 371-4734

Academy of Hair Design #3 | Post-Sec.
1815 Terry Rd 39204 | 601-372-9800
Antonelli College | Post-Sec.
2323 Lakeland Dr 39232 | 601-362-9991
Belhaven College | Post-Sec.
1500 Peachtree St 39202 | 601-968-5927
Christ Missionary & Industrial S | 200/PK-12
3910 Main St 39213 | 601-366-6413
Education Center S | 200/1-12
4080 Old Canton Rd 39216 | 601-982-2812
Lynn Macon, prin. | Fax 982-2827
Hillcrest Christian S | 700/K-12
4060 S Siwell Rd 39212 | 601-372-0149
Robert Welch, hdmstr. | Fax 371-8061
Hinds Community College | Post-Sec.
1750 Chadwick Dr 39204 | 601-372-6507
Jackson Academy | 1,500/PK-12
PO Box 14978 39236 | 601-362-9676
Peter Jernberg, prin. | Fax 364-5722
Jackson Preparatory S | 800/7-12
PO Box 4940 39296 | 601-939-8611
Susan Lindsay, hdmstr. | Fax 936-4068
Jackson State University | Post-Sec.
1440 J R Lynch St 39217 | 601-979-2100
Magnolia College of Cosmetology | Post-Sec.
4725 I-55 N 39206 | 601-362-6940
Millsaps College | Post-Sec.
PO Box 15495 39210 | 601-974-1000
Mississippi Baptist Medical Center | Post-Sec.
1225 N State St 39202 | 601-968-5130

Mississippi College | Post-Sec.
151 E Griffith St 39201 | 601-353-3907
Mississippi School for the Blind | Post-Sec.
1252 Eastover Dr 39211 | 601-984-8000
Mississippi School for the Deaf | Post-Sec.
1253 Eastover Dr 39211 | 601-984-8001
Reformed Theological Seminary | Post-Sec.
5422 Clinton Blvd 39209 | 601-923-1600
St. Dominic-Jackson Memorial Hospital | Post-Sec.
969 Lakeland Dr 39216 | 601-364-6935
Traxler School of Hair | Post-Sec.
2845 Suncrest Dr 39212 | 601-371-3253
University of Mississippi Medical Center | Post-Sec.
2500 N State St 39216 | 601-984-1010
Virginia College | Post-Sec.
5360 I 55 N 39211 | 601-977-0960
Wesley Biblical Seminary | Post-Sec.
PO Box 9938 39286 | 601-957-1314

Kilmichael, Montgomery, Pop. 765
Montgomery County SD
Supt. — See Winona
Montgomery County HS | 200/7-12
PO Box 278 39747 | 662-262-5535
Lewis Zeigler, prin. | Fax 262-4218

Kiln, Hancock, Pop. 1,262
Hancock County SD | 4,200/K-12
17304 Highway 603 39556 | 228-255-0376
David Kopf, supt. | Fax 255-0378
www.hancock.k12.ms.us
Hancock HS | 1,100/9-12
7084 Stennis Airport Rd 39556 | 228-467-2251
Donnie Gholston, prin. | Fax 467-2689
Hancock MS | 1,000/6-8
7070 Stennis Airport Rd 39556 | 228-467-1889
Denise Wilkinson, prin. | Fax 467-2812
Hancock Vocational Technical Center | Vo/Tech
7180 Stennis Airport Rd 39556 | 228-467-3568
Rick Saucier, prin. | Fax 466-4944

Kosciusko, Attala, Pop. 7,351
Attala County SD | 1,300/PK-12
100 Courthouse 39090 | 662-289-2801
Curtis Burrell, supt. | Fax 289-2804
www2.mde.k12.ms.us/0400/
Kosciusko-Attala County Voc Complex | Vo/Tech
450 Highway 12 E 39090 | 662-289-2689
Tony Holder, prin. | Fax 289-2701
Other Schools – See Ethel, Mc Adams

Kosciusko SSD | 2,000/K-12
206 S Huntington St 39090 | 662-289-4771
Dr. David Sistrunk, supt. | Fax 289-1177
Kosciusko HS | 600/9-12
206 S Huntington St 39090 | 662-289-2424
Jonathan Carnes, prin. | Fax 289-8767
Kosciusko JHS | 500/6-8
206 S Huntington St 39090 | 662-289-3737
Tony McGee, prin. | Fax 289-5388

Magnolia Bible College | Post-Sec.
PO Box 1109 39090 | 662-289-2896

Lake, Newton, Pop. 404
Scott County SD
Supt. — See Forest
Lake Attendance Center | 800/K-12
24442 Highway 80 39092 | 601-775-3248
Randy Martin, prin. | Fax 775-3861
Lake MS | 300/4-8
1770 E Scott Rd 39092 | 601-775-3614
Kathy Myers, prin. | Fax 775-8830

Lake Cormorant, DeSoto
DeSoto County SD
Supt. — See Hernando
Lake Cormorant MS | 5-8
3203 Wilson Mill Rd 38641 | 662-895-3434
Rhonda Guice, prin.

Laurel, Jones, Pop. 18,044
Jones County SD
Supt. — See Ellisville
Fatherree Voc-Tech Center | Vo/Tech
2409 Moose Dr 39440 | 601-425-2378
Bruce Strickland, prin. | Fax 425-2349
Northeast Jones JSHS | 1,000/7-12
68 Northeast Dr 39443 | 601-425-2347
A. Dwain Strickland, prin. | Fax 649-1736
West Jones JSHS | 1,300/7-12
254 Springhill Rd 39443 | 601-729-8144
Mark Herrington, prin. | Fax 729-8148

Laurel SD | 3,100/PK-12
PO Box 288 39441 | 601-649-6391
Dr. Glenn McGee, supt. | Fax 649-6398
www.laurelschools.com
Jones MS | 500/7-8
1125 N 5th Ave 39440 | 601-428-5312
Cecelia Luter, prin. | Fax 426-6775
Laurel HS | 700/9-12
1100 W 12th St 39440 | 601-649-4145
Carolyn Stone, prin. | Fax 426-2347
Laurel Vocational Technical Center | Vo/Tech
1100 W 11th St 39440 | 601-649-4144
Lydia Sanders, prin. | Fax 428-1390

Laurel Christian S | 400/PK-12
PO Box 8425 39441 | 601-649-3999
Rick Bartley, hdmstr. | Fax 649-1027
Mississippi College of Beauty Culture | Post-Sec.
732 Sawmill Rd 39440 | 601-428-7127
Southeastern Baptist College | Post-Sec.
4229 Highway 15 N 39440 | 601-426-6346

Leakesville, Greene, Pop. 1,011
Greene County SD | 2,000/K-12
PO Box 1329 39451 | 601-394-2364
Richard Fleming, supt. | Fax 394-5542
www.greene.k12.ms.us/
Greene County HS | 500/9-12
4336 High School Rd 39451 | 601-394-5290
Mike Chatham, prin. | Fax 394-4878
Greene County Vo-Tech Complex | Vo/Tech
173 Vocational Technical Rd 39451 | 601-394-2973
Bobby Walley, prin. | Fax 394-5953

Leakesville JHS | 400/5-8
PO Box 1479 39451 | 601-394-2495
Debbie McLeod, prin. | Fax 394-5690

Learned, Hinds, Pop. 47

Rebul Academy | 300/PK-12
5257 Learned Rd 39154 | 601-885-6802
Paul Kirchharr, admin. | Fax 885-9550

Leland, Washington, Pop. 5,234
Leland SD | 1,000/K-12
408 4th St 38756 | 662-686-5000
Johnnye M. Breland, supt. | Fax 686-5029
www2.mde.k12.ms.us/7612/
Leland HS | 300/9-12
403 E 3rd St 38756 | 662-686-5020
Cynthia Johnson, prin. | Fax 686-5027
Leland School Park MS | 300/5-8
200 Milam St 38756 | 662-686-5017
Glenda Triplett-Jackson, prin. | Fax 686-5042
Leland Vo Complex | Vo/Tech
S Deer Creek Dr 38756 | 662-686-5025
Johnny Tucker, prin. | Fax 686-5024

Lexington, Holmes, Pop. 1,963
Holmes County SD | 3,500/K-12
PO Box 630 39095 | 662-834-2175
Stephen Bailey, supt. | Fax 834-9060
holmes.k12.ms.us
Holmes County Vocational Center | Vo/Tech
PO Box 390 39095 | 662-834-3052
Frank Kimes, prin. | Fax 834-3053
Marshall S | 1,000/K-12
12572 Highway 12 39095 | 662-235-5113
George Jackson, prin. | Fax 235-5551
McClain HS | 800/6-12
PO Box 270 39095 | 662-834-2172
Dr. Percy Washington, prin. | Fax 834-2709
Other Schools – See Durant

Central Holmes Christian S | 300/K-12
PO Box 279 39095 | 662-834-3011
Terry Cox, admin. | Fax 834-1011

Liberty, Amite, Pop. 675
Amite County SD | 1,400/K-12
PO Box 378 39645 | 601-657-4361
Charles E. Kirkfield, supt. | Fax 657-4291
www.amite.k12.ms.us/
Amite County HS | 300/9-12
PO Box 328 39645 | 601-657-8920
Charlie Floyd, prin. | Fax 657-4044
Amite County Vocational Educational S | Vo/Tech
PO Box 770 39645 | 601-657-8081
Augustus Russ, prin. | Fax 657-8098

Amite School Center | 300/K-12
PO Box 354 39645 | 601-657-8896
J. Walt Gaston, hdmstr. | Fax 657-4642

Long Beach, Harrison, Pop. 16,938
Long Beach SSD | 3,300/K-12
19148 Commission Rd 39560 | 228-864-1146
Carrolyn Hamilton, supt. | Fax 863-3196
www.lbsd.k12.ms.us
Long Beach HS | 1,100/9-12
300 E Old Pass Rd 39560 | 228-863-6945
Susan Whiten, prin. | Fax 864-8661
Long Beach MS | 800/6-8
204 N Cleveland Ave 39560 | 228-864-3370
Mary Jean Harvey, prin. | Fax 867-1789

University of Southern Mississippi | Post-Sec.
730 E Beach Blvd 39560 | 228-865-4500

Lorman, Jefferson

Alcorn State University | Post-Sec.
PO Box 359 39096 | 601-877-6147

Louisville, Winston, Pop. 6,831
Louisville Municipal SD | 2,900/K-12
PO Box 909 39339 | 662-773-3411
Harry D. Kemp, supt. | Fax 773-4013
louisville.k12.ms.us/
Eiland MS | 300/7-8
508 Camille Ave 39339 | 662-773-9001
Leevel Yarbrough, prin. | Fax 773-4016
Louisville HS | 600/9-12
200 Ivy Ave 39339 | 662-773-3431
Ken McMullan, prin. | Fax 773-4017
Waiya S | 500/K-12
13937 Highway 397 39339 | 662-773-6770
Janie Hailey-Tarlton, prin. | Fax 773-6764
Winston-Louisville Vocational Center | Vo/Tech
204 Ivy Ave 39339 | 662-773-6152
Dr. Clyde Lindley, prin. | Fax 773-9572
Other Schools – See Noxapater

Grace Christian S | 200/PK-12
173 McLeod Rd 39339 | 662-773-8524
Thomas Dickson, hdmstr. | Fax 773-4308
Winston Academy | 400/K-12
PO Box 545 39339 | 662-773-3569
Farrell Rigby, prin. | Fax 773-8373

Lucedale, George, Pop. 2,750
George County SD | 4,000/K-12
5152 Main St 39452 | 601-947-6993
Donnie Howell, supt. | Fax 947-8805
www.george.k12.ms.us
George County HS | 1,000/9-12
9284 Highway 63 S 39452 | 601-947-3116
Paul Wallace, prin. | Fax 947-1076
George County MS | 1,000/6-8
330 Church St 39452 | 601-947-3106
Patsy Horn, prin. | Fax 947-6004

Lumberton, Lamar, Pop. 2,345
Lumberton SD | 900/K-12
PO Box 551 39455 | 601-796-2441
John Ladner, supt. | Fax 796-2051
www.lumberton.k12.ms.us/
Lumberton HS | 200/9-12
PO Box 551 39455 | 601-796-2451
Dennis Holder, prin. | Fax 796-7907

Bass Memorial Academy 100/9-12
6433 U S Highway 11 39455 601-794-8561
Fax 794-8881

Maben, Webster, Pop. 784
Oktibbeha County SD
Supt. — See Starkville
West Oktibbeha County HS 200/7-12
PO Box 506 39750 662-263-8106
Helen Kennard, prin. Fax 263-5440

Webster County SD
Supt. — See Eupora
East Webster HS 300/7-12
RR 2 Box 468 39750 662-263-5321
Bill Brand, prin. Fax 263-4518

Mc Adams, Attala
Attala County SD
Supt. — See Kosciusko
Mc Adams JSHS 300/7-12
PO Box 127 39107 662-289-3838
Bryan Weaver, prin. Fax 289-7181

Mc Comb, Pike, Pop. 11,957
McComb SD 2,800/K-12
PO Box 868, 601-684-4661
Pat Cooper, supt. Fax 249-4732
www.mccomb.k12.ms.us
Business & Technology Complex Vo/Tech
1003 Virginia Ave, 601-684-5288
Betty Wilson, prin. Fax 249-2454
Denman JHS 500/7-8
1211 Louisiana Ave, 601-684-2387
Ruby Husband, prin. Fax 249-3564
Mc Comb HS 700/9-12
310 7th St, 601-684-5678
Levander German, prin. Fax 249-4737

Parklane Academy 800/K-12
1115 Parklane St, 601-684-7841
Billy Swindle, admin. Fax 684-4166
SW Mississippi Regional Medical Center Post-Sec.
PO Box 1307, 601-249-1807

Macon, Noxubee, Pop. 2,373
Noxubee County SD 2,200/PK-12
PO Box 540 39341 662-726-4527
Kevin Jones Ed.D., supt. Fax 726-2809
www.noxcnty.k12.ms.us
Liddell MS 600/5-8
PO Box 229 39341 662-726-4880
Louise Tate, prin. Fax 726-5044
Noxubee County HS 600/9-12
PO Box 490 39341 662-726-4428
Royce Stevens, prin. Fax 726-5048
Noxubee County Vocational Center Vo/Tech
PO Box 387 39341 662-726-4225
Annie Snow, dir. Fax 726-2804

Central Academy 300/K-12
PO Box 231 39341 662-726-4817
Brach White, prin. Fax 726-9711

Madden, Leake

Leake Academy 500/PK-12
PO Box 128 39109 601-267-4461
Jerry Crowe, hdmstr. Fax 267-6933

Madison, Madison, Pop. 15,869
Madison County SD
Supt. — See Flora
Madison Central HS 1,700/9-12
1417 Highland Colony Pkwy 39110 601-856-7121
Edith Mitchell, prin. Fax 898-5006
Madison MS 1,300/6-8
1365 Mannsdale Rd 39110 601-605-4171
Ron Morrison, prin. Fax 853-2254
Scott S 9-9
200 Crawford St 39110 601-605-0054
Ted Poore, prin. Fax 898-5017

Madison-Ridgeland Academy 900/K-12
7601 Old Canton Rd 39110 601-856-4455
Tommy Thompson, hdmstr. Fax 853-3835
St. Joseph Catholic S 300/7-12
PO Box 2027 39130 601-898-4800
William Heller, prin. Fax 898-4689

Magee, Simpson, Pop. 4,169
Simpson County SD
Supt. — See Mendenhall
Magee HS 500/9-12
501 Choctaw St E 39111 601-849-2263
George Huffman, prin. Fax 849-2144
Magee MS 600/5-8
300 1st St NE 39111 601-849-3334
Terrell Luckey, prin. Fax 849-6130

Magnolia, Pike, Pop. 2,047
South Pike SD 2,100/K-12
250 W Myrtle St 39652 601-783-3742
Dr. Ann Mitchell, supt. Fax 783-6733
www.spike.k12.ms.us/
South Pike HS 500/9-12
205 W Myrtle St 39652 601-783-2312
Alonzell Dillon, prin. Fax 783-4179
South Pike MS 300/7-8
275 W Myrtle St 39652 601-783-2574
Joe Leavy, prin. Fax 783-2272
South Pike Vo Ctr Vo/Tech
252 W Bay St 39652 601-783-5832
Brenda Jackson, prin. Fax 783-3491

Mantachie, Itawamba, Pop. 1,120
Itawamba County SD
Supt. — See Fulton
Mantachie S 500/7-12
PO Box 38 38855 662-282-4276
Scott Blackley, prin. Fax 282-4270

Marks, Quitman, Pop. 1,940
Quitman County SD 1,600/K-12
PO Box E 38646 662-326-5451
Valmadge Towner, supt. Fax 326-3694
www2.mde.k12.ms.us/6000/

Palmer JSHS 500/8-12
PO Box 350 38646 662-326-5191
Edgar Holman, prin. Fax 326-8918
Quitman County Vocational S Vo/Tech
PO Box 117 38646 662-326-8427
Charles Phipps, prin. Fax 326-8430

Delta Academy 300/PK-12
PO Box 70 38646 662-326-8164
Hoyte Carothers, admin. Fax 326-3201

Meadville, Franklin, Pop. 507
Franklin County SD 1,500/PK-12
PO Box 605 39653 601-384-2340
Lona Thomas, supt. Fax 384-2393
www2.mde.k12.ms.us/1900/index.htm
Franklin County Vo-Tech Ctr Vo/Tech
PO Box 155 39653 601-384-5889
Jack Hollingsworth, prin. Fax 384-5578
Franklin HS 400/9-12
PO Box 666 39653 601-384-2965
Marion Bilbo, prin. Fax 384-2498
Franklin JHS 400/6-8
236 Edison St S 39653 601-384-2441
Marshall Bankston, prin. Fax 384-2085

Mendenhall, Simpson, Pop. 2,526
Simpson County SD 4,300/K-12
111 Education Ln 39114 601-847-1562
Jack McAlpin, supt. Fax 847-8003
www2.mde.k12.ms.us/6400/index.htm
Mendenhall HS 600/9-12
207 Circle Dr 39114 601-847-2411
Roosevelt Oatis, prin. Fax 847-8002
Mendenhall JHS 600/5-8
733 Dixie Ave 39114 601-847-2296
Onnie Sue Lee, prin. Fax 847-7175
Simpson County Technical Center Vo/Tech
3415 Simpson Highway 49 39114 601-847-4000
Dr. Kay Berry, prin. Fax 847-8011
Other Schools – See Magee

Simpson County Academy 600/K-12
124 Academy Cir 39114 601-847-1395
Jane C. Hubbard, prin. Fax 847-1338

Meridian, Lauderdale, Pop. 39,559
Lauderdale County SD 6,300/K-12
PO Box 5498 39302 601-693-1683
David Little, supt. Fax 485-1748
www.lauderdale.k12.ms.us
Clarkdale S 900/K-12
7000 Highway 145 39301 601-693-4463
Jan Miller, prin. Fax 483-6329
Northeast Lauderdale HS 600/9-12
702 Briarwood Rd 39305 601-679-8523
Rob Calcote, prin. Fax 679-7515
Northeast MS 700/5-8
7763 Highway 39 39305 601-483-3532
Richard Kelly, prin. Fax 485-0846
Southeast HS 400/9-12
2362 Long Creek Rd 39301 601-483-5501
Billy Burnham, prin. Fax 483-6347
Southeast MS 500/5-8
2535 Old Highway 19 SE 39301 601-485-5751
Kenny Neal, prin. Fax 485-2302
Other Schools – See Collinsville

Meridian SD 6,200/K-12
PO Box 31 39302 601-483-6271
Sylvia Autry, supt. Fax 484-4917
www.mpsd.k12.ms.us
Collins Vocational Center Vo/Tech
PO Box 31 39302 601-483-3331
Lisa Barfield, prin. Fax 484-5173
Griffin JHS 400/8-9
2814 Davis St 39301 601-484-4073
Vickey Hood, prin. Fax 484-4090
Meridian SHS 1,100/10-12
2320 32nd St 39305 601-482-3191
R.D. Harris, prin. Fax 483-5502
Northwest JHS 500/8-9
4400 32nd St 39307 601-484-4094
Patrick Ross, prin. Fax 484-5180

Calvary Christian S 100/K-12
PO Box 4238 39304 601-483-2305
Perry Miller, admin. Fax 482-5376
Final Touch Beauty School Post-Sec.
5700 N Hills St 39307 601-485-7733
Lamar S 600/K-12
544 Lindley Rd 39305 601-482-1345
John Stephens, admin. Fax 482-7202
Meridian Community College Post-Sec.
910 Highway 19 N 39307 601-483-8241
Pentecostal Christian Academy 50/PK-12
PO Box 1390 39302 601-693-7375
Fred Summerville, supt. Fax 693-7347

Mississippi State, Oktibbeha, Pop. 12,400

Mississippi State University Post-Sec.
PO Box J 39762 662-325-2323

Mize, Smith, Pop. 278
Smith County SD
Supt. — See Raleigh
Mize S 800/K-12
PO Box 187 39116 601-733-2242
David Burris, prin. Fax 733-2243

Monticello, Lawrence, Pop. 1,726
Lawrence County SD 2,400/K-12
346 Thomas E Jolly Dr W 39654 601-587-2506
Russell Caudill, supt. Fax 587-2221
www.lawrence.k12.ms.us
Lawrence County HS 600/9-12
PO Box 488 39654 601-587-4910
Daryl Scoggin, prin. Fax 587-5001
Lawrence County Vo-Tech Ctr Vo/Tech
PO Box 578 39654 601-587-9346
P. Darrell Turner, prin. Fax 587-2980
Paige MS 500/5-8
PO Box 489 39654 601-587-2128
Tamm Fairburn, prin. Fax 587-7178

Mooreville, Lee
Lee County SD
Supt. — See Tupelo
Mooreville HS 400/9-12
PO Box 60 38857 662-842-6859
Robert Smith, prin. Fax 841-5988
Mooreville MS 6-8
PO Box 60 38857 662-680-4894
Craig Cherry, prin. Fax 680-4896

Moorhead, Sunflower, Pop. 2,429
Sunflower County SD
Supt. — See Indianola
Moorhead MS 200/6-8
PO Box 749 38761 662-246-5680
Verna Ransom, prin. Fax 246-5080

Mississippi Delta Community College Post-Sec.
PO Box 668 38761 662-246-6322

Morton, Scott, Pop. 3,426
Scott County SD
Supt. — See Forest
Jack Upper MS 500/5-8
PO Box 500 39117 601-732-6977
Tina Thomas, prin. Fax 732-2242
Morton HS 400/9-12
238 E Fourth Ave 39117 601-732-6210
Sarah Richardson, prin. Fax 732-8086

Moss Point, Jackson, Pop. 15,327
Jackson County SD
Supt. — See Vancleave
East Central HS 700/9-12
21700 Slider Rd 39562 228-588-7000
Tim Anderson, prin. Fax 588-7045
East Central MS 700/6-8
5404 Hurley Wade Rd 39562 228-588-7009
R. L. Watson, prin. Fax 588-7043

Moss Point SD 3,800/PK-12
4924 Church St 39563 228-475-0691
Dr. Rachel Carpenter, supt. Fax 474-5002
www.mp.k12.ms.us/
Magnolia JHS 300/7-8
4924 Church St 39563 228-475-1429
Kim Staley, prin. Fax 474-3397
Moss Point HS 1,200/9-12
4924 Church St 39563 228-475-5721
Tommy Molden, prin. Fax 474-3305
Moss Point Vocational Center Vo/Tech
4924 Church St 39563 228-474-1455
Dr. Senita Walker, prin. Fax 474-1458

Mound Bayou, Bolivar, Pop. 2,055
Mound Bayou SD 700/K-12
201 Green St 38762 662-741-2555
William Crockett, supt. Fax 741-2726
www2.mde.k12.ms.us/0616/MBPS.htm
Kennedy Memorial HS 300/7-12
204 N Edwards Ave 38762 662-741-2510
Dr. I.D. Thompson, prin. Fax 741-2246

Mount Olive, Covington, Pop. 899
Covington County SD
Supt. — See Collins
Mt. Olive S 500/K-12
PO Box 309 39119 601-797-3914
Dwight Yates, prin. Fax 797-3980

Myrtle, Union, Pop. 420
Union County SD
Supt. — See New Albany
Myrtle S 700/K-12
PO Box 40 38650 662-988-2416
Vince Jordan, prin. Fax 988-2000
West Union S 600/K-12
1610 State Road 30 W 38650 662-534-4982
Paul Correro, prin. Fax 534-6745

Natchez, Adams, Pop. 17,621
Natchez-Adams SD 3,200/PK-12
10 Homochitto St 39120 601-445-2800
Dr. Anthony L. Morris, supt. Fax 445-2818
www.natchez.k12.ms.us/
Fallin Career & Technology Center Vo/Tech
315 Sgt Prentiss Dr 39120 601-445-2902
Linda Grafton, prin. Fax 445-2967
Lewis MS 700/7-8
1221 N Dr ML King Jr St 39120 601-445-2927
Bettye Bell, prin. Fax 445-2966
Natchez HS 1,200/9-12
319 Sgt Prentiss Dr 39120 601-445-2863
James Loftin, prin. Fax 445-3014

Adams County Christian S 700/PK-12
300 Chinquapin Ln 39120 601-442-1422
John R. Gray, admin. Fax 442-1477
Cathedral Unit S 700/PK-12
701 N Dr ML King Jr St 39120 601-442-2531
Patrick Sanguinetti, prin. Fax 442-0960
Copiah-Lincoln Community College Post-Sec.
11 Copiah Lincoln Circle 39120 601-442-9111
Trinity Episcopal Day S 400/PK-12
1 Mallan G Morgan Dr 39120 601-442-5424
Dr. Delecia Seay Carey, hdmstr. Fax 442-3216

Nettleton, Itawamba, Pop. 1,942
Nettleton SD 1,400/K-12
PO Box 409 38858 662-963-2151
James Malone, supt. Fax 963-7407
www.nettletonschools.com/
Nettleton HS 400/9-12
PO Box 409 38858 662-963-2306
Russell Taylor, prin. Fax 963-7410
Nettleton MS 600/4-8
PO Box 409 38858 662-963-7406
Van Ross, prin. Fax 963-7407

New Albany, Union, Pop. 7,796
New Albany SD 2,000/K-12
301 State Highway 15 N 38652 662-534-1800
Charles E. Garrett Ed.D., supt. Fax 534-3608
www.newalbany.k12.ms.us
New Albany HS 500/9-12
201 State Highway 15 N 38652 662-534-1805
Jay Foster, prin. Fax 534-1817

New Albany MS 500/6-8
400 Apple St 38652 662-534-1820
Robert Merritt, prin. Fax 534-1819
New Albany Vocational Complex Vo/Tech
PO Box 771 38652 662-534-1810
Jackie Ford, prin. Fax 534-1811

Union County SD 2,700/K-12
PO Box 939 38652 662-534-1960
John F. Weeden, supt. Fax 534-1961
www.union.k12.ms.us
Ingomar S 600/K-12
1384 County Road 101 38652 662-534-2680
Roger Browning, prin. Fax 534-5463
Other Schools – See Blue Springs, Myrtle

New Augusta, Perry, Pop. 703
Perry County SD 1,400/K-12
PO Box 137 39462 601-964-3211
Gregory S. Dearman, supt. Fax 964-8204
www.perry.k12.ms.us/
Perry Central HS 300/9-12
PO Box 139 39462 601-964-3235
Richard Burge, prin. Fax 964-8273
Perry County Vocational Tech Center Vo/Tech
PO Box 139 39462 601-964-8282
Rex Buckhaults, prin. Fax 964-8562

New Site, Prentiss
Prentiss County SD
Supt. — See Booneville
New Site HS 300/9-12
1020 Highway 4 E 38859 662-728-5205
Luke Ledbetter, prin. Fax 728-1965

Newton, Newton, Pop. 3,665
Newton Municipal SD 1,000/K-12
205 School St 39345 601-683-2451
Mina Bryan, supt. Fax 683-7131
www.nmsd.k12.ms.us
Newton HS 200/9-12
201 W First St 39345 601-683-2232
Dr. Bill Shaw, prin. Fax 683-6808
Newton Municipal Career Center Vo/Tech
203 W First St 39345 601-683-6338
Tanya Walker, prin. Fax 683-2283
Pilate MS 300/5-8
531 E Church St 39345 601-683-3926
Dr. Virginia Young, prin. Fax 683-7139

North Carrollton, Carroll, Pop. 482
Carroll County SD
Supt. — See Carrollton
George JSHS 500/7-12
PO Box 398 38947 662-237-4701
Cory Blaylock, prin. Fax 237-4522

Noxapater, Winston, Pop. 418
Louisville Municipal SD
Supt. — See Louisville
Noxapater S 400/K-12
220 W Alice St 39346 662-724-4241
James Brooks, prin. Fax 724-4240

Ocean Springs, Jackson, Pop. 17,443
Jackson County SD
Supt. — See Vancleave
St. Martin HS 1,600/7-12
10800 Yellow Jacket Rd 39564 228-875-8418
Toriano Holloway, prin. Fax 875-8426

Ocean Springs SD 5,200/K-12
PO Box 7002 39566 228-875-7706
Robert Hirsch, supt. Fax 875-7708
www.ossd.k12.ms.us
Keys Technology Center Vo/Tech
PO Box 7002 39566 228-872-3411
Jan Griffin, dir. Fax 872-0011
Ocean Springs HS 1,600/9-12
PO Box 7002 39566 228-875-0333
David Baggett, prin. Fax 872-0023
Ocean Springs MS 1,400/6-8
PO Box 7002 39566 228-872-6210
Dr. Scherrine Davenport, prin. Fax 872-9850

Day Spa Career College Post-Sec.
3900 Bienville Blvd 39564 228-875-4809

Okolona, Chickasaw, Pop. 2,949
Okolona SSD 800/K-12
PO Box 510 38860 662-447-2353
Eddie Prather, supt. Fax 447-9955
okolona.k12.ms.us/
Okolona JSHS 400/7-12
PO Box 510 38860 662-447-2362
Paul Dobbs, prin. Fax 447-3306
Okolona Vocational Complex Vo/Tech
605 N Church St 38860 662-447-3331
Amy Anderson, prin.

Olive Branch, DeSoto, Pop. 24,938
DeSoto County SD
Supt. — See Hernando
Center Hill MSHS 6-10
13250 Kirk Rd 38654
George Loper, prin.
Lewisburg MSHS 6-10
1755 Craft Rd 38654
James Brady, prin.
Olive Branch HS 1,700/9-12
9366 E Sandidge Rd 38654 662-893-3344
Kyle Brigance, prin. Fax 895-3667
Olive Branch MS 1,500/6-8
6530 Blocker St 38654 662-895-4610
Danny Freeze, prin. Fax 895-7358

Oxford, Lafayette, Pop. 12,761
Lafayette County SD 2,100/K-12
100 Commodore Dr 38655 662-234-3271
W. Michael Foster, supt. Fax 236-3019
www.lafayette.k12.ms.us
Lafayette HS 500/9-12
160 Commodore Dr 38655 662-234-3614
Adam Pugh, prin. Fax 234-3856
Lafayette MS 700/5-8
102 Commodore Dr 38655 662-234-1664
Joe Hendrix, prin. Fax 232-8736

Oxford/Lafayette School of Applied Tech Vo/Tech
1904 Highway 7 S 38655 662-234-9469
Dr. Gary Druckemiller, prin. Fax 236-2496

Oxford SD 3,100/PK-12
224 Bramlett Blvd 38655 662-234-3541
Jerry Webb Ed.D., supt. Fax 232-2862
www.oxford.k12.ms.us
Oxford HS 800/9-12
222 Bramlett Blvd 38655 662-234-1562
William Hovious, prin. Fax 236-7941
Oxford MS 500/7-8
501 Mrtin Luther King Jr Dr 38655 662-234-2288
Martha Shotts, prin. Fax 234-0235

Pascagoula, Jackson, Pop. 25,865
Pascagoula SD 7,400/K-12
PO Box 250 39568 228-938-6491
Wayne Rodolfich, supt. Fax 938-6528
psd.k12.ms.us/
Applied Technology Center Vo/Tech
2602 Market St 39567 228-938-6579
Ms. Pat Taylor, dir. Fax 938-6597
Colmer MS 600/6-8
3112 Eden St 39581 228-938-6473
Nick Overby, prin. Fax 938-6593
Lott MS 500/6-8
2234 Pascagoula St 39567 228-938-6465
Debra Sivori, prin. Fax 938-6463
Pascagoula HS 1,200/9-12
1716 Tucker Ave 39567 228-938-6443
Cindy Jackson, prin. Fax 938-6445
Other Schools – See Gautier

Resurrection Catholic HS 200/7-12
520 Watts Ave 39567 228-762-3353
Darnell Cuevas, prin. Fax 769-1226

Pass Christian, Harrison, Pop. 6,599
Pass Christian SD 1,900/K-12
257 Davis Ave 39571 228-452-7271
Sue Matheson Ed.D., supt. Fax 452-7121
www.passchristianschools.com/
Pass Christian HS 500/9-12
720 W North St 39571 228-452-2008
Cathy Broadway, prin. Fax 452-7340
Pass Christian MS 500/6-8
270 W Second St 39571 228-452-4653
Ronald Storey, prin. Fax 452-7375

Pearl, Rankin, Pop. 22,824
Pearl SD 3,600/K-12
PO Box 5750 39288 601-932-7916
Dr. Stan Miller, supt. Fax 932-7929
www.pearl.k12.ms.us/
Pearl HS 900/9-12
500 Pirates Cv 39208 601-932-7931
John Buchanan, prin. Fax 932-7992
Pearl JHS 900/6-8
200 Mary Ann Dr 39208 601-932-7952
Tracy Adcock, prin. Fax 932-7998

Academy of Hair Design #4 Post-Sec.
3167 Highway 80 E 39208 601-939-4441

Pelahatchie, Rankin, Pop. 1,477
Rankin County SD
Supt. — See Brandon
Pelahatchie JSHS 300/7-12
PO Box 569 39145 601-854-8135
Brad Peets, prin. Fax 854-8638

East Rankin Academy 700/PK-12
PO Box 509 39145 601-854-5691
Robert Gates, hdmstr. Fax 854-5893

Perkinston, Stone

Mississippi Gulf Coast Community College Post-Sec.
PO Box 609 39573 601-928-5211

Petal, Forrest, Pop. 7,687
Petal SSD 3,600/K-12
PO Box 523 39465 601-545-3002
James Hutto, supt. Fax 584-4700
www.petalschools.com
Petal HS 1,000/9-12
1145 Highway 42 39465 601-583-3538
Jack Linton, prin. Fax 545-1229
Petal MS 900/6-8
203 Highway 42 39465 601-584-6301
Michael Hogan, prin. Fax 584-4716

Pheba, Clay

Hebron Christian S 200/K-12
6230 Henryville Rd 39755 662-494-7513
Sam Pearson, prin. Fax 494-1002

Philadelphia, Neshoba, Pop. 7,277
Neshoba County SD 2,900/K-12
PO Box 338 39350 601-656-3752
V.C. Manning, supt. Fax 656-3789
www.neshoba.k12.ms.us/
Neshoba Central HS 800/9-12
1125 Golf Course Rd 39350 601-656-6004
Joey Blount, prin. Fax 656-6004
Neshoba Central MS 700/6-8
1000 Saint Francis Dr 39350 601-656-4636
Harry Bates, prin. Fax 389-2989

Philadelphia SD 1,100/K-12
248 Byrd Ave N 39350 601-656-2955
Dr. Britt Dickens, supt. Fax 656-3141
www.philadelphia.k12.ms.us/
Philadelphia HS 300/9-12
248 Byrd Ave N 39350 601-656-2672
Bobby Luke, prin. Fax 656-0015
Philadelphia MS 100/7-8
248 Byrd Ave N 39350 601-656-6439
Ben Johnson, prin. Fax 656-5328

Picayune, Pearl River, Pop. 10,641
Picayune SD 3,500/K-12
706 Goodyear Blvd 39466 601-798-3230
Dr. Penny Wallin, supt. Fax 798-1742
www.pcu.k12.ms.us/

Picayune JHS 600/7-8
702 Goodyear Blvd 39466 601-798-5449
Dean Shaw, prin. Fax 799-4715
Picayune Memorial HS 1,100/9-12
800 Fifth Ave 39466 601-798-1380
D. Herndon, prin. Fax 798-4705
PMHS Career & Technology Center Vo/Tech
600 Goodyear Blvd 39466 601-798-7601
Elizabeth Pope, prin. Fax 799-4711

Piney Woods, Rankin

Piney Woods S 200/9-12
PO Box 100 39148 601-845-2214
Sekufele Lewanika, hdmstr. Fax 845-2604

Pittsboro, Calhoun, Pop. 209
Calhoun County SD 2,500/PK-12
PO Box 58 38951 662-412-3152
Beth Hardin, supt. Fax 412-3157
www2.mde.k12.ms.us/0700/
Other Schools – See Bruce, Calhoun City, Vardaman

Plantersville, Lee, Pop. 1,173
Lee County SD
Supt. — See Tupelo
Plantersville MS 100/5-8
PO Box 129 38862 662-842-4690
Kenneth Jones, prin. Fax 791-0491

Pontotoc, Pontotoc, Pop. 5,636
Pontotoc CSD 2,200/K-12
140 Education Dr 38863 662-489-3336
Conwell Duke, supt. Fax 489-7932
www.pontotoc.k12.ms.us
Pontotoc HS 600/9-12
123 N Main St 38863 662-489-1275
Keith Davis, prin. Fax 489-5255
Pontotoc JHS 700/5-8
132 N Main St 38863 662-489-8360
Cristie Hooker, prin. Fax 489-8947

Pontotoc County SD 3,000/K-12
285 Highway 15 S 38863 662-489-3932
John Simmons, supt. Fax 489-3922
www.pcsd.k12.ms.us/
Pontotoc Ridge Career & Tech Center Vo/Tech
354 Ridge Dr 38863 662-489-1826
Phil Ryan, prin. Fax 489-0704
South Pontotoc HS 400/9-12
1523 S Pontotoc Rd 38863 662-489-5925
Kenny Roberts, prin. Fax 489-8598
South Pontotoc MS 300/6-8
1523 S Pontotoc Rd 38863 662-489-3476
Scotty Collins, prin. Fax 489-6252
Other Schools – See Ecru

Poplarville, Pearl River, Pop. 2,664
Poplarville SSD 2,000/PK-12
804 S Julia St 39470 601-795-8477
Gylde Fitzpatrick, supt. Fax 795-0712
poplarville.k12.ms.us/web/home.asp
Poplarville Career Development Center Vo/Tech
9 Career Center Cir 39470 601-795-8343
Donnis Stringfellow, prin. Fax 795-1353
Poplarville HS 500/9-12
1 Hornet Dr 39470 601-795-8424
Carl Merritt, prin. Fax 795-1345
Poplarville MS 500/6-8
6 Spirit Dr 39470 601-795-1350
Leah Stevens, prin. Fax 795-1351

Pearl River Community College Post-Sec.
Station A 39470 601-795-6801

Port Gibson, Claiborne, Pop. 1,748
Claiborne County SD 1,500/K-12
PO Box 337 39150 601-437-4232
Annie Kilcrease Ph.D., supt. Fax 437-4409
Clairborne Co. Voc Educational Complex Vo/Tech
PO Box 47 39150 601-437-3800
Janice Reed, prin. Fax 437-3801
Port Gibson HS 500/9-12
159 Old Highway 18 39150 601-437-4190
Nathaniel Martin, prin. Fax 437-4409
Port Gibson MS 400/6-8
159 Old Highway 18 39150 601-437-4251
Earl Taylor, prin. Fax 437-3099

Chamberlain-Hunt Academy 100/7-12
124 Mccomb Ave 39150 601-437-4291
A. Shane Blanton, pres. Fax 437-4313

Potts Camp, Marshall, Pop. 510
Marshall County SD
Supt. — See Holly Springs
Potts Camp S 500/4-12
PO Box 697 38659 662-333-6354
Ken Basil, prin. Fax 333-7023

Prentiss, Jefferson Davis, Pop. 1,074
Jefferson Davis County SD 2,200/K-12
PO Box 1197 39474 601-792-4267
Dennis Fortenberry, supt. Fax 792-2251
www.jeffersondavis.k12.ms.us
Prentiss JSHS 600/6-12
PO Box 1168 39474 601-792-4646
Audie Reese McCormick, prin. Fax 792-8149
Other Schools – See Bassfield, Carson

Prentiss Christian S 400/K-12
PO Box 1287 39474 601-792-8549
Danny Quick, prin. Fax 792-2560

Puckett, Rankin, Pop. 364
Rankin County SD
Supt. — See Brandon
Puckett Attendance Center 300/7-12
PO Box 40 39151 601-825-5742
Scott Parham, prin. Fax 825-9838

Purvis, Lamar, Pop. 2,308
Lamar County SD 6,400/K-12
PO Box 609 39475 601-794-1030
Glenn Swan, supt. Fax 794-1012
www.lamar.k12.ms.us

Lamar County Vo-Tech Ctr | Vo/Tech
41 College Dr 39475 | 601-794-8298
Bruce Hankins, prin. | Fax 794-1026
Purvis HS | 500/9-12
PO Box 1089 39475 | 601-794-2708
C.H. Bryant, prin. | Fax 794-2150
Purvis MS | 500/5-8
PO Box 1089 39475 | 601-794-2708
Linda Greer, prin. | Fax 794-2150
Other Schools – See Hattiesburg, Sumrall

Lamar Christian S | 300/K-12
PO Box 880 39475 | 601-794-0016
Louis M. Nicolosi, admin. | Fax 794-3726

Quitman, Clarke, Pop. 2,407
Quitman SD | 2,300/K-12
104 E Franklin St 39355 | 601-776-2186
Dr. Pam Compton, supt. | Fax 776-1051
www.qsd.k12.ms.us
Clarke County Vocational Center | Vo/Tech
910 N Archusa Ave 39355 | 601-776-5219
Willie Plummer, prin. | Fax 776-5219
Quitman HS | 600/9-12
210 S Jackson Ave 39355 | 601-776-3341
Charlie Parkerson, prin. | Fax 776-6136
Quitman JHS | 600/6-8
501 W Lynda St 39355 | 601-776-6243
Shannon Sudbury, prin. | Fax 776-1288

Raleigh, Smith, Pop. 1,223
Smith County SD | 2,900/K-12
PO Box 308 39153 | 601-782-4296
Warren Woodrow, supt. | Fax 782-9895
www2.mde.k12.ms.us/6500
Raleigh JSHS | 600/7-12
RR 1 Box 500 39153 | 601-782-4261
Jay Gilbert, prin. | Fax 782-4359
Smith County Vocational Complex | Vo/Tech
PO Box 37 39153 | 601-782-4211
Dan King, prin. | Fax 782-9842
Other Schools – See Mize, Taylorsville

Raymond, Hinds, Pop. 1,758
Hinds County SD | 6,700/K-12
13192 Highway 18 39154 | 601-857-5222
Dr. Stephen Handley, supt. | Fax 857-8548
www.hinds.k12.ms.us/
Carver MS | 500/6-8
417 Palestine St 39154 | 601-857-5006
Lana Clark, prin. | Fax 857-4935
Hinds County Career Center | Vo/Tech
PO Box 789 39154 | 601-857-5536
Sammy White, prin. | Fax 857-2212
Raymond HS | 500/9-12
14050 Highway 18 39154 | 601-857-8016
John Neal, prin. | Fax 857-2007
Other Schools – See Terry

Central Hinds Academy | 400/K-12
2894 Raymond Bolton Rd 39154 | 601-857-5568
Steven Harrell, hdmstr. | Fax 857-5082
Hinds Community College | Post-Sec.
PO Box 1100 39154 | 601-857-5261

Richland, Rankin, Pop. 6,447
Rankin County SD
Supt. — See Brandon
Richland HS | 700/7-12
1202 Highway 49 S 39218 | 601-939-5144
Stanley Shows, prin. | Fax 939-7631

Richton, Greene, Pop. 1,037
Richton SD | 700/K-12
PO Box 568 39476 | 601-788-6581
Bruce Weigle, supt. | Fax 788-9391
Richton JSHS | 300/7-12
PO Box 568 39476 | 601-788-9608
Lana McIlwain, prin. | Fax 788-6390

Ridgeland, Madison, Pop. 21,435
Madison County SD
Supt. — See Flora
Olde Towne MS | 700/6-8
210 Sunnybrook Rd 39157 | 601-898-8730
Allen Lawrence, prin. | Fax 853-8108
Ridgeland HS | 800/9-12
586 Sunnybrook Rd 39157 | 601-898-5023
Lee Boozer, prin. | Fax 853-8656

St. Andrew's Episcopal S | 1,200/PK-12
370 Old Agency Rd 39157 | 601-853-6000
Steve Blanchard, hdmstr. | Fax 853-6001

Ripley, Tippah, Pop. 5,509
South Tippah SD | 2,700/K-12
PO Box 439 38663 | 662-837-7156
Dr. Wardell Herring, supt. | Fax 837-1362
ww2.dixie-net.com/Ripley-HS/
North South Tippah County Vo-Tech Ctr | Vo/Tech
PO Box 533 38663 | 662-837-9798
Howard Newby, prin. | Fax 837-8833
Pine Grove S | 600/K-12
3510A County Road 600 38663 | 662-837-7789
William Witt, prin. | Fax 837-8179
Ripley HS | 500/9-12
720 S Clayton St 38663 | 662-837-7583
Lynn McGee, prin. | Fax 837-0118
Ripley MS | 600/5-8
718 S Clayton St 38663 | 662-837-7959
James Storey, prin. | Fax 837-0251
Other Schools – See Blue Mountain

Foster's Cosmetology College | Post-Sec.
PO Box 66 38663 | 662-837-9334

Rolling Fork, Sharkey, Pop. 2,343
South Delta SD | 1,300/PK-12
PO Box 219 39159 | 662-873-4302
Georgia C. Russell, supt. | Fax 873-4198
South Delta HS | 400/9-12
303 Parkway Ave 39159 | 662-873-4308
Harold Arrington, prin. | Fax 873-6106
South Delta Vocational Ctr | Vo/Tech
285 Maple St 39159 | 662-873-2029
James Tankson, prin. | Fax 873-4194
Other Schools – See Anguilla

Sharkey Issaquena Academy | 300/K-12
272 Academy Dr 39159 | 662-873-4241
Linda Sherwood Dick, admin. | Fax 873-4637

Rosedale, Bolivar, Pop. 2,427
West Bolivar SD | 1,200/K-12
PO Box 189 38769 | 662-759-3525
Henry Phillips, supt. | Fax 759-6795
www.wbsd.k12.ms.us/
Barnes Vocational Center | Vo/Tech
500 Bradford St 38769 | 662-759-3791
Arthur Holmes, prin. | Fax 759-6795
West Bolivar HS | 300/9-12
498 Bradford St 38769 | 662-759-3346
Simon Carter, prin. | Fax 759-6795
West Bolivar MS | 400/5-8
1307 Highway 1 38769 | 662-759-3743
Larry Johnson, prin. | Fax 759-6795

Ruleville, Sunflower, Pop. 3,030
Sunflower County SD
Supt. — See Indianola
Ruleville Central HS | 300/9-12
360 L F Packer Dr 38771 | 662-756-4757
James Johnson, prin. | Fax 756-0052
Ruleville MS | 300/6-8
PO Box 129 38771 | 662-756-4698
Dr. Viola Williams, prin. | Fax 756-4902

Saltillo, Lee, Pop. 3,426
Lee County SD
Supt. — See Tupelo
Saltillo HS | 600/9-12
PO Box 460 38866 | 662-869-5466
Keith Steele, prin. | Fax 869-7229

Sandhill, Rankin
Rankin County SD
Supt. — See Brandon
Pisgah HS | 300/7-12
PO Box 70 39161 | 601-829-1138
Norman Session, prin. | Fax 829-1753

Sardis, Panola, Pop. 2,045
North Panola Consolidated SD | 1,700/K-12
PO Box 334 38666 | 662-487-2305
Robert L. Massey, supt. | Fax 487-2050
npanola.k12.ms.us/
North Panola HS | 400/9-12
PO Box 278 38666 | 662-487-1070
Lucinda Carter, prin. | Fax 487-2052
Other Schools – See Como

Scooba, Kemper, Pop. 608

East Mississippi Community College | Post-Sec.
PO Box 158 39358 | 662-476-8442

Sebastopol, Scott, Pop. 230
Scott County SD
Supt. — See Forest
Sebastopol Attendance Center | 600/K-12
PO Box 86 39359 | 601-625-8654
Charles Brown, prin. | Fax 625-9426

Seminary, Covington, Pop. 345
Covington County SD
Supt. — See Collins
Seminary S | 1,100/K-12
PO Box 34 39479 | 601-722-3220
Robert Walker, prin. | Fax 722-3972

Senatobia, Tate, Pop. 6,667
Senatobia Municipal SD | 1,700/K-12
104 McKie St 38668 | 662-562-4897
Mike Flynn, supt. | Fax 562-4996
www.senatobia.k12.ms.us/
Senatobia JSHS | 800/7-12
221 Warrior Dr 38668 | 662-562-4230
Jerry Barrett, prin. | Fax 562-6659

Tate County SD | 2,900/K-12
107 Court St 38668 | 662-562-5861
Gary Walker, supt. | Fax 562-8516
www.tcsd.k12.ms.us/
Other Schools – See Coldwater, Independence

J & J Hair Design College | Post-Sec.
562 W Main St Ste B 38668 | 662-562-8010
Magnolia Heights S | 600/K-12
1 Chiefs Dr 38668 | 662-562-4491
Dr. Marvin Lishman, admin. | Fax 562-0386
Northwest Mississippi Community College | Post-Sec.
4975 Highway 51 N 38668 | 662-562-3200

Shannon, Lee, Pop. 1,697
Lee County SD
Supt. — See Tupelo
Shannon JSHS | 800/7-12
PO Box 8 38868 | 662-767-9566
Mike Scott, prin. | Fax 767-2847

Shaw, Bolivar, Pop. 2,288
Shaw SD | 700/K-12
200 Jefferson Ave 38773 | 662-754-2611
Charles Barron, supt. | Fax 754-2612
www2.mde.k12.ms.us/0615/shdhot.htm
Shaw HS | 300/8-12
PO Box 510 38773 | 662-754-2611
John Sullivan, prin. | Fax 754-4418

Shelby, Bolivar, Pop. 2,802
North Bolivar SD | 900/K-12
PO Box 38774 | 662-398-4000
Ronzy Humphrey, supt. | Fax 398-7884
www.nbsd.k12.ms.us/
Broad Street HS | 300/8-12
PO Box 149 38774 | 662-398-4040
Frederick Ford, prin. | Fax 398-5900

Smithville, Monroe, Pop. 878
Monroe County SD
Supt. — See Amory
Smithville S | 700/K-12
PO Box 149 38870 | 662-651-4276
Sam Wilson, prin. | Fax 651-4163

Southaven, DeSoto, Pop. 34,760
DeSoto County SD
Supt. — See Hernando
Desoto Central HS | 1,000/9-12
2911 Central Pkwy 38672 | 662-536-3612
Charlie Tipton, prin. | Fax 536-3623
Desoto Central MS | 900/6-8
2611 Central Pkwy 38672 | 662-349-6660
William McCulley, prin. | Fax 349-1045
DeSoto County Vocational Complex | Vo/Tech
847 Rasco Rd 38671 | 662-393-6211
Phillip Sublett, prin. | Fax 393-5708
Southaven HS | 1,400/9-12
899 Rasco Rd 38671 | 662-393-9300
Jeff Gilder, prin. | Fax 342-1393
Southaven MS | 1,200/6-8
175 Rasco Rd 38671 | 662-280-0422
Mike McCoy, prin. | Fax 280-3613

Northwest Mississippi Community College | Post-Sec.
5197 WE Ross Pkwy 38671 | 662-342-1570
Southern Baptist Educational Center | 1,200/PK-12
7400 Getwell Rd 38672 | 662-349-3096
David Manley, pres. | Fax 349-4962

Starkville, Oktibbeha, Pop. 22,419
Oktibbeha County SD | 800/K-12
105 N Dr Douglas L Conner D 39759 | 662-323-1472
Walter Conley, supt. | Fax 323-9614
www.oktibbeha.k12.ms.us
Other Schools – See Crawford, Maben

Starkville SD | 4,200/PK-12
401 Greensboro St 39759 | 662-324-4050
Dr. Phillip Burchfield, supt. | Fax 324-4068
www.starkville.k12.ms.us
Armstrong JHS | 700/7-8
303 McKee St 39759 | 662-324-4070
Bob Fuller, prin. | Fax 324-4075
Millsaps Career & Tech Center | Vo/Tech
803 Louisville St 39759 | 662-324-4170
James Stidham, prin. | Fax 324-4103
Starkville HS | 1,100/9-12
603 Yellow Jacket Dr 39759 | 662-324-4130
Kathi Wilson, prin. | Fax 324-4128

Starkville Academy | 800/K-12
505 Academy Rd 39759 | 662-323-7814
Sammy Henderson, admin. | Fax 323-5480
Starkville Christian S | 100/K-12
303 Lynn Ln 39759 | 662-323-7453
Rev. Randall Witbeck, prin. | Fax 323-7571

Steens, Lowndes

Immanuel Center for Christian Education | 300/PK-12
6405 Military Rd 39766 | 662-328-7888
Bob Williford, admin. | Fax 328-7750

Stringer, Jasper
West Jasper Consolidated SD
Supt. — See Bay Springs
Stringer S | 700/K-12
PO Box 68 39481 | 601-428-5508
Margaret Pollard, prin. | Fax 426-6760

Summit, Pike, Pop. 1,400
North Pike SD | 1,800/K-12
1036 Jaguar Trl 39666 | 601-276-2216
Dr. Ben Cox, supt. | Fax 276-3666
North Pike HS | 400/9-12
1022 Jaguar Trl 39666 | 601-276-2175
Darryl Brock, prin. | Fax 276-2720
North Pike MS | 600/5-8
2034 Highway 44 NE 39666 | 601-684-3283
Carl Felder, prin. | Fax 684-3269

Southwest Mississippi Community College | Post-Sec.
39666 | 601-276-2001

Sumrall, Lamar, Pop. 1,085
Lamar County SD
Supt. — See Purvis
Sumrall JSHS | 700/6-12
PO Box 187 39482 | 601-758-4730
Larry Easterling, prin. | Fax 758-0512

Taylorsville, Smith, Pop. 1,281
Smith County SD
Supt. — See Raleigh
Taylorsville S | 800/K-12
PO Box 8 39168 | 601-785-6942
Jeff Duvall, prin. | Fax 785-9711

Terry, Hinds, Pop. 672
Hinds County SD
Supt. — See Raymond
Byram MS | 800/6-8
2009 Byram Bulldog Blvd 39170 | 601-372-4597
David Campbell, prin. | Fax 346-2383
Terry HS | 1,000/9-12
235 W Beasley St 39170 | 601-878-5905
Dr. Bill Sellers, prin. | Fax 878-2782

Tiplersville, Tippah, Pop. 393
North Tippah SD | 1,300/K-12
PO Box 65 38674 | 662-223-4384
Junior Wooten, supt. | Fax 223-5379
Other Schools – See Falkner, Walnut

Tishomingo, Tishomingo, Pop. 310
Tishomingo Co. Special Municipal SSD
Supt. — See Iuka
Tishomingo County Vo-Tech Complex | Vo/Tech
PO Box 890 38873 | 662-438-6689
Gary Taylor, prin. | Fax 438-6777

Tougaloo, Hinds

Tougaloo College | Post-Sec.
500 W County Line Rd 39174 | 601-977-7700

Tremont, Itawamba, Pop. 393
Itawamba County SD
Supt. — See Fulton
Tremont Attendance Center | 300/K-12
PO Box 9 38876 | 662-652-3391
Jerry Wiygul, prin. | Fax 652-3994

Tunica, Tunica, Pop. 1,067
Tunica County SD — 2,100/PK-12
 PO Box 758 38676 — 662-363-2811
 Jerry Gentry, supt. — Fax 363-3061
 www2.mde.k12.ms.us/7200/tunica%20county%20schoolwebsite2.htm
Rosa Fort HS — 700/8-12
 PO Box 997 38676 — 662-363-1343
 Larry Ball, prin. — Fax 363-4222
Tunica Vo-Tech Center — Vo/Tech
 2400 Old Highway 61 N 38676 — 662-363-2051
 Dorothy Dunn, prin. — Fax 363-2052

Tunica Institute of Learning S — 200/K-12
 PO Box 966 38676 — 662-363-1051
 Jeff King, prin. — Fax 363-2037

Tupelo, Lee, Pop. 35,297
Lee County SD — 4,500/K-12
 1280 College View St 38804 — 662-841-9144
 John Green, supt. — Fax 680-6012
 www.lcs.k12.ms.us
 Other Schools – See Guntown, Mooreville, Plantersville, Saltillo, Shannon

Tupelo SD — 7,100/PK-12
 PO Box 557 38802 — 662-841-8850
 Dr. Randy McCoy, supt. — Fax 841-8887
 www.tupeloschools.com/
Tupelo HS — 1,800/9-12
 4125 Cliff Gookin Blvd 38801 — 662-841-8970
 Mac Curlee, prin. — Fax 841-8987
Tupelo HS Career Center — Vo/Tech
 4125 Cliff Gookin Blvd 38801 — 662-841-8990
 M.D. Cameron, prin. — Fax 840-8799
Tupelo MS — 1,100/7-8
 1009 Varsity Dr 38801 — 662-840-8780
 Linda Clifton, prin. — Fax 840-1831

Creations College of Cosmetology — Post-Sec.
 PO Box 2635 38803 — 662-844-9264
Mississippi University for Women-Tupelo — Post-Sec.
 1918 Briar Ridge Rd 38804 — 662-844-0284
North Mississippi Medical Center — Post-Sec.
 830 S Gloster St 38801 — 662-841-3136
Tupelo Christian Academy — 100/K-12
 PO Box 167 38802 — 662-791-7731
 — Fax 791-7735

Tylertown, Walthall, Pop. 1,873
Walthall County SD — 2,200/K-12
 814A Morse Ave 39667 — 601-876-3401
 Greg Ellzey, supt. — Fax 876-6982
 www.wcsd.k12.ms.us/
Dexter S — 300/K-12
 927 Highway 48 E 39667 — 601-876-3985
 Jerry Pigott, prin. — Fax 876-5410
Salem S — 500/K-12
 881 Highway 27 N 39667 — 601-876-2580
 Charles Boyd, prin. — Fax 876-4155
Tylertown JSHS — 700/7-12
 204 High School Rd 39667 — 601-876-3370
 Cynthia Magee, prin. — Fax 876-3122
Walthall County Career & Tech Center — Vo/Tech
 803 Ball Ave 39667 — 601-222-1500
 Wade Carney, prin. — Fax 222-1506

Union, Newton, Pop. 2,058
Union SD — 200/K-12
 208 Peachtree St 39365 — 601-774-9579
 Don Brantley, supt. — Fax 774-5796
 www.unioncity.k12.ms.us/
Union HS — 200/9-12
 101 Forest St 39365 — 601-774-8257
 Joey Ezelle, prin. — Fax 774-9600
Union MS — 5-8
 115 James St 39365 — 601-774-5303
 Brett Rigby, prin. — Fax 774-9607

University, See Oxford

University of Mississippi 38677 — Post-Sec.
 — 662-232-7226

Utica, Hinds, Pop. 932
Hinds County Agricultural SD —
 PO Box 1089 39175 — 601-885-7047
 Dr. Clyde Muse, supt. — Fax 885-2676
Hinds County Agricultural HS — Vo/Tech
 PO Box 1089 39175 — 601-885-7083
 Robert Strong, prin. — Fax 885-2676

Vancleave, Jackson, Pop. 3,214
Jackson County SD — 8,800/K-12
 12210 Colonel Vickrey Rd 39565 — 228-826-1757
 Rucks H. Robinson Ed.D., supt. — Fax 826-3393
 www.jcsd.k12.ms.us/
Jackson County Technology Center — Vo/Tech
 12425 Highway 57 39565 — 228-826-5944
 Judy Moore, prin. — Fax 826-4209
Vancleave HS — 600/9-12
 12424 Highway 57 39565 — 228-826-4701
 Todd Knight, prin. — Fax 826-5066
Vancleave MS — 600/6-8
 4725 Bull Dog Ln 39565 — 228-826-5902
 Joe Hubal, prin. — Fax 826-1421
 Other Schools – See Moss Point, Ocean Springs

Vardaman, Calhoun, Pop. 1,038
Calhoun County SD —
 Supt. — See Pittsboro

Vardaman HS — 300/7-12
 PO Box 193 38878 — 662-682-7574
 Gregg Pepper, prin. — Fax 682-7743

Vicksburg, Warren, Pop. 26,005
Vicksburg Warren SD — 8,600/PK-12
 1500 Mission 66 39180 — 601-638-5122
 Dr. James Price, supt. — Fax 631-2819
 www.vwsd.k12.ms.us
Vicksburg HS — 1,100/9-12
 3701 Drummond St 39180 — 601-636-2914
 Charlie Tolliver, prin. — Fax 631-2885
Vicksburg JHS — 700/7-8
 1533 Baldwin Ferry Rd 39180 — 601-636-1966
 Dr. Edward Wiggins, prin. — Fax 631-2830
Warren Central HS — 1,000/9-12
 1000 Highway 27 39180 — 601-638-3372
 Edwin Douglas, prin. — Fax 631-2937
Warren Central JHS — 700/7-8
 1630 Baldwin Ferry Rd 39180 — 601-638-3981
 Pam Wilbanks, prin. — Fax 631-2839

All Saints' Episcopal S — 100/8-12
 2717 Confederate Ave 39180 — 601-636-5266
 Fr. William Martin, hdmstr. — Fax 636-8987
Campus Preparatory Christian S — 200/K-12
 219 Baptist Dr 39180 — 601-631-0014
 Vickey White, admin. — Fax 631-0659
Hinds Community College — Post-Sec.
 755 Highway 27 39180 — 601-638-0600
Porters Chapel Academy — 200/K-12
 3460 Porters Chapel Rd 39180 — 601-638-3733
 Gwen Reiber Ed.D., admin. — Fax 638-6311
St. Aloysius HS — 400/7-12
 1900 Grove St 39183 — 601-636-2256
 Michele Townsend, prin. — Fax 631-0430

Walnut, Tippah, Pop. 750
North Tippah SD —
 Supt. — See Tiplersville
Walnut S — 500/K-12
 PO Box 240 38683 — 662-223-6471
 Bo Seago, prin. — Fax 223-5275

Walnut Grove, Leake, Pop. 1,011
Leake County SD —
 Supt. — See Carthage
South Leake HS — 300/7-12
 PO Box 159 39189 — 601-253-2393
 James Chambers, prin. — Fax 253-0100

Water Valley, Yalobusha, Pop. 3,763
Water Valley SD — 1,300/K-12
 PO Box 788 38965 — 662-473-1203
 Sammy Higdon, supt. — Fax 473-1225
 www.wvsd.k12.ms.us/
Water Valley JSHS — 500/7-12
 PO Box 647 38965 — 662-473-2468
 Glenn Kitchens, prin. — Fax 473-1444

Waynesboro, Wayne, Pop. 5,133
Wayne County SD — 3,800/K-12
 810 Chickasawhay St 39367 — 601-735-4871
 R.P. Staten, supt. — Fax 735-4872
 www.mde.k12.ms.us/districts/wayne.htm
Wayne County HS — 1,000/9-12
 1325 Azalea Dr 39367 — 601-735-2851
 Al Smith, prin. — Fax 735-1389
Wayne County Vocational Center — Vo/Tech
 800 Collins St 39367 — 601-735-5036
 Bobby Jones, prin. — Fax 735-6326
Waynesboro MS — 600/5-8
 155 Wayne St 39367 — 601-735-3159
 DeJuan Walley, prin. — Fax 735-6316

Wayne Academy — 200/K-12
 PO Box 308 39367 — 601-735-2921
 Allen Stevens, admin. — Fax 735-2117

Webb, Tallahatchie, Pop. 551
West Tallahatchie SD — 1,200/K-12
 PO Box 129 38966 — 662-375-9291
 Howard H. Hollins, supt. — Fax 375-9294
 www2.mde.k12.ms.us/6812/index.htm
West Tallahatchie JSHS — 500/7-12
 PO Box 130 38966 — 662-375-8829
 Iva Houston, prin. — Fax 375-7402

Weir, Choctaw, Pop. 546
Choctaw County SD —
 Supt. — See Ackerman
Weir S — 500/PK-12
 PO Box 98 39772 — 662-547-7062
 Glen Beard, prin. — Fax 547-7074

Wesson, Copiah, Pop. 1,696
Copiah County SD —
 Supt. — See Hazlehurst
Wesson S — 1,000/K-12
 1048 Grove St 39191 — 601-643-2221
 Billy Britt, prin. — Fax 643-2458

Copiah-Lincoln Community College — Post-Sec.
 PO Box 457 39191 — 601-643-5101

West, Holmes, Pop. 204

East Holmes Academy — 300/K-12
 PO Box 247 39192 — 662-967-2226
 David Drake, hdmstr. — Fax 967-2264

West Point, Clay, Pop. 11,858
West Point SD — 3,500/PK-12
 PO Box 656 39773 — 662-494-4242
 Steve Montgomery, supt. — Fax 494-8605
 www.westpoint.k12.ms.us/
Fifth Street JHS — 600/7-8
 PO Box 776 39773 — 662-494-2191
 Alvin Taylor, prin. — Fax 494-2432
West Point Career and Technology Center — Vo/Tech
 PO Box 1136 39773 — 662-494-6176
 Rob Smith, prin. — Fax 495-2426
West Point HS — 1,000/9-12
 PO Box 616 39773 — 662-494-5083
 Tim Fowler, prin. — Fax 494-0969

Gibson's Barber & Beauty College — Post-Sec.
 PO Box 990 39773 — 662-494-5444
Mary Holmes College — Post-Sec.
 PO Box 1257 39773 — 662-494-6820
Oak Hill Academy — 600/K-12
 800 N Eshman Ave 39773 — 662-494-5043
 Jack Henderson, prin. — Fax 494-0487

Wheeler, Prentiss
Prentiss County SD —
 Supt. — See Booneville
Wheeler S — 500/K-12
 PO Box 98 38880 — 662-365-2629
 Todd Swinney, prin. — Fax 365-2535

Wiggins, Stone, Pop. 4,213
Stone County SD — 2,600/K-12
 214 Critz St N 39577 — 601-928-7247
 James Morrison, supt. — Fax 928-5122
 stoneweb.stone.k12.ms.us
Stone HS — 700/9-12
 400 Border Ave E 39577 — 601-928-5492
 Wendy Rogers, prin. — Fax 928-6874
Stone MS — 600/6-8
 532 Central Ave E 39577 — 601-928-4876
 Vicky Compston, prin. — Fax 928-6440

Winona, Montgomery, Pop. 5,086
Montgomery County SD — 400/K-12
 PO Box 687 38967 — 662-283-4533
 Sammie McCaskill, supt. — Fax 283-4584
 www.mcsd.k12.ms.us
 Other Schools – See Kilmichael

Winona SD — 1,200/K-12
 218 Fairground St 38967 — 662-283-3731
 Bernard Taylor, supt. — Fax 283-1003
 www2.mde.k12.ms.us/4920/wps.html
Dulin Career and Technical Ctr — Vo/Tech
 300 N Applegate St 38967 — 662-283-3601
 Dwight Lollar, prin. — Fax 283-9807
Winona HS — 600/7-12
 301 Fairground St 38967 — 662-283-1244
 Harold Holiman, prin. — Fax 283-4267

Winona Christian S — 200/PK-12
 1014 S Applegate St 38967 — 662-283-1169
 Rick Hammarstrom, admin. — Fax 283-3333

Woodville, Wilkinson, Pop. 1,170
Wilkinson County SD — 1,700/K-12
 PO Box 785 39669 — 601-888-3582
 Mildred McGhee, supt. — Fax 888-3133
 www2.mde.k12.ms.us/7900
King Vocational Complex — Vo/Tech
 PO Box 1193 39669 — 601-888-4394
 Gwendolyn Vanderson, prin. — Fax 888-4740
Wilkinson County HS — 400/9-12
 522 Pinckneyville Rd 39669 — 601-888-4228
 Donnie Hollins, prin. — Fax 888-4736
 Other Schools – See Centreville

Wilkinson County Christian Academy — 300/K-12
 PO Box 977 39669 — 601-888-4313
 Carrie Cupit, admin. — Fax 888-3588

Yazoo City, Yazoo, Pop. 12,098
Yazoo City Municipal SD — 3,000/PK-12
 1133 Calhoun Ave 39194 — 662-746-2125
 Rebecca Turner-Berry, supt. — Fax 746-9210
 www.yazoocity.k12.ms.us/
Woolfolk MS — 1,000/5-8
 209 E Fifth St 39194 — 662-746-2904
 Paula Smith, prin. — Fax 746-8609
Yazoo City HS — 600/9-12
 1825 Dr Mrtn Lthr Kng Jr Dr 39194 — 662-746-2378
 John Wallace, prin. — Fax 746-3779
Yazoo City Vocational Center — Vo/Tech
 1825 Dr Mrtn Lthr Kng Jr Dr 39194 — 662-746-7642
 Patricia Hall, prin. — Fax 746-0991

Yazoo County SD — 1,800/K-12
 PO Box 1088 39194 — 662-746-4672
 John Smith, supt. — Fax 746-9270
 www.yazoo.k12.ms.us
Yazoo County HS — 500/9-12
 6789 Highway 49 Frontage Rd 39194 — 662-746-1492
 Phillip Chisolm, prin. — Fax 746-1593
Yazoo County JHS — 300/7-8
 6781 Highway 49 Frontage Rd 39194 — 662-746-1596
 Ray Mathis, prin. — Fax 746-1616

Manchester Academy — 500/K-12
 2132 Gordon Ave 39194 — 662-746-5913
 Mike Nutt, hdmstr. — Fax 746-5108

MISSOURI

MISSOURI DEPARTMENT OF EDUCATION
PO Box 480, Jefferson City 65102-0480
Telephone 573-751-4212
Fax 573-751-1179
Website http://www.dese.mo.gov
Commissioner of Education   D. Kent King

MISSOURI BOARD OF EDUCATION
PO Box 480, Jefferson City 65102-0480
President   Peter Herschend

PUBLIC, PRIVATE AND CATHOLIC SECONDARY SCHOOLS

Adrian, Bates, Pop. 1,819
Adrian R-III SD | 700/K-12
PO Box 98 64720 | 816-297-2710
Doug Hedrick, supt. | Fax 297-2980
www.adrian.k12.mo.us/
Adrian JSHS | 300/7-12
PO Box 98 64720 | 816-297-4460
John Beaman, prin. | Fax 297-2980

Advance, Stoddard, Pop. 1,217
Advance R-IV SD | 500/K-12
PO Box 370 63730 | 573-722-3581
Michael Redman, supt. | Fax 722-9886
www.advance.k12.mo.us/default.asp
Advance JSHS | 300/7-12
PO Box 370 63730 | 573-722-3584
C.A. Counts, prin. | Fax 722-5479

Albany, Gentry, Pop. 1,846
Albany R-III SD | 500/PK-12
101 W Jefferson St 64402 | 660-726-3911
Harry Wheeler, supt. | Fax 726-5841
www.albany.k12.mo.us
Albany HS | 200/9-12
101 W Jefferson St 64402 | 660-726-3912
Michael Adkins, prin. | Fax 726-5841
Albany MS | 100/6-8
101 W Jefferson St 64402 | 660-726-3912
Michael Adkins, prin. | Fax 726-5841

Alma, Lafayette, Pop. 386
Santa Fe R-X SD | 400/K-12
PO Box 197 64001 | 660-674-2238
Dr. Douglas Wright, supt. | Fax 674-2239
schoolweb.missouri.edu/santafe.k12.mo.us
Santa Fe HS | 200/7-12
PO Box 197 64001 | 660-674-2236
Tom Burton, prin. | Fax 674-2760

Alton, Oregon, Pop. 647
Alton R-IV SD | 800/K-12
RR 2 Box 2180 65606 | 417-778-7216
Sheila Wheeler, supt. | Fax 778-6394
schoolweb.missouri.edu/alton.k12.mo.us
Alton HS | 400/7-12
RR 2 Box 2180 65606 | 417-778-7215
Dave McQuerter, prin. | Fax 778-7851

Amoret, Bates, Pop. 216
Miami R-I SD | 200/K-12
RR 1 Box 418 64722 | 660-267-3480
Verlin Tyler, supt. | Fax 267-3630
www.miami-eagles.k12.mo.us/
Miami JSHS | 100/7-12
RR 1 Box 418 64722 | 660-267-3484
Garry J. Dunn, prin. | Fax 267-3630

Anderson, McDonald, Pop. 1,835
McDonald County R-I SD | 3,400/PK-12
100 Mustang Dr 64831 | 417-845-3321
Randall Smith, supt. | Fax 845-6972
www.mcdonaldco.k12.mo.us/
Anderson JHS | 7-8
100 Red Bird Ln 64831 | 417-845-3488
Ted Snodgrass, prin. | Fax 845-7406
McDonald County HS | 1,000/9-12
100 Mustang Dr 64831 | 417-845-3322
Stephen Buckingham, prin. | Fax 845-8467

Annapolis, Iron, Pop. 295
South Iron County R-I SD | 500/PK-12
PO Box 218 63620 | 573-598-4241
M. Homer Lewis, supt. | Fax 598-4210
www.schoolweb.missouri.edu/southiron.k12.mo.us/
South Iron JSHS | 200/7-12
PO Box 218 63620 | 573-598-4241
Brad Crocker, prin. | Fax 598-4210

Appleton City, Saint Clair, Pop. 1,309
Appleton City R-II SD | 400/K-12
PO Box 126 64724 | 660-476-2161
Bob Elder, supt. | Fax 476-5564
appletoncity.k12.mo.us/
Appleton City HS | 200/7-12
PO Box 126 64724 | 660-476-2118
Terry Mayfield, prin. | Fax 476-5564

Archie, Cass, Pop. 899
Archie R-V SD | 600/PK-12
PO Box 106 64725 | 816-293-5312
Dr. Forrest Bollow, supt. | Fax 293-5712
Archie JSHS | 300/6-12
PO Box 106 64725 | 816-293-5312
Rick Stark, prin. | Fax 293-5712

Arnold, Jefferson, Pop. 20,070
Fox C-6 SD | 11,600/PK-12
745 Jeffco Blvd 63010 | 636-296-8000
Dr. Dianne Brown, supt. | Fax 282-5170
www.fox.k12.mo.us
Fox HS | 1,800/9-12
751 Jeffco Blvd 63010 | 636-296-5210
Dr. Kevin Rossiter, prin. | Fax 282-6980
Fox MS | 500/7-8
743 Jeffco Blvd 63010 | 636-296-5077
Laura Gabler, prin. | Fax 282-5171
Ridgewood MS | 500/7-8
1401 Ridgewood School Rd 63010 | 636-282-1459
Kristen Pelster, prin. | Fax 282-5193
Other Schools – See Imperial

Holy Child MS | 100/6-8
2322 Tenbrook Rd 63010 | 636-296-1544
Joann Coyle, prin. | Fax 296-7823
ITT Technical Institute | Post-Sec.
1930 Meyer Drury Dr 63010 | 636-464-6600

Ash Grove, Greene, Pop. 1,446
Ash Grove R-IV SD | 900/K-12
100 N Maple Ln 65604 | 417-751-2534
Richard Harris, supt. | Fax 751-2283
www.ashgrove.k12.mo.us/
Ash Grove JSHS | 400/7-12
100 N Maple Ln 65604 | 417-751-2330
Don Christensen, prin. | Fax 751-2889

Ashland, Boone, Pop. 2,234
Southern Boone County R-I SD | 1,300/K-12
PO Box 16510 | 573-657-2147
Susan Gauzy, supt. | Fax 657-5513
schoolweb.missouri.edu/ashland.k12.mo.us/
Southern Boone County HS | 400/9-12
PO Box 168 65010 | 573-657-2144
Johnny Thompson, prin. | Fax 657-9035
Southern Boone County MS | 300/6-8
PO Box 168 65010 | 573-657-2146
Gerald Hocker, prin. | Fax 657-5513

Atlanta, Macon, Pop. 448
Atlanta C-3 SD | 200/K-12
PO Box 367 63530 | 660-239-4212
William Perkins, supt. | Fax 239-4205
www.atlanta.k12.mo.us/
Atlanta JSHS | 100/7-12
PO Box 367 63530 | 660-239-4211
Steve Coulson, prin. | Fax 239-4205

Aurora, Lawrence, Pop. 7,121
Aurora R-VIII SD | 2,100/PK-12
409 W Locust St 65605 | 417-678-3373
Dr. Dale Slagle, supt. | Fax 678-4043
www.hdnet.k12.mo.us
Aurora HS | 600/9-12
101 S Roosevelt Ave 65605 | 417-678-3355
Alana Pharis, prin. | Fax 678-2905
Robinson JHS | 300/7-8
1044 S Lincoln Ave 65605 | 417-678-3630
Jana Wilson, prin. | Fax 678-4043

Ava, Douglas, Pop. 3,037
Ava R-I SD | 1,600/PK-12
PO Box 338 65608 | 417-683-4717
Andrew Underwood, supt. | Fax 683-6329
www.avaschools.k12.mo.us/
Ava HS | 500/9-12
PO Box 338 65608 | 417-683-5747
Jason Dial, prin. | Fax 683-2306
Ava MS | 500/5-8
PO Box 338 65608 | 417-683-3835
Clayton King, prin. | Fax 683-9101

Ava Victory Academy | 200/PK-12
PO Box 314 65608 | 417-683-6630
Valerie Stanton, supt. | Fax 683-1402
Teen Harvest | 50/1-12
HC 71 Box 352 65608 | 417-683-1080
Paul Neighbour, admin. | Fax 683-1080

Bakersfield, Ozark, Pop. 284
Bakersfield R-IV SD | 500/PK-12
PO Box 38 65609 | 417-284-7333
Jackie Estes, supt. | Fax 284-7335
Bakersfield JSHS | 200/6-12
PO Box 38 65609 | 417-284-3744
Greg Jackson, prin. | Fax 284-7335

Ballwin, Saint Louis, Pop. 31,006
Parkway C-2 SD
Supt. — See Chesterfield
Parkway South HS | 2,100/9-12
801 Hanna Rd 63021 | 314-415-7700
Gary Mazzola, prin. | Fax 415-7712
Parkway Southwest MS | 800/6-8
701 Wren Ave 63021 | 314-415-7300
Chelsea Watson, prin. | Fax 415-7334
Parkway West HS | 1,600/9-12
14653 Clayton Rd 63011 | 314-415-7500
Beth Plunkett, prin. | Fax 415-7534

Rockwood R-VI SD
Supt. — See Eureka
Crestview MS | 1,200/6-8
16025 Clayton Rd 63011 | 636-207-2520
James Wipke, prin. | Fax 207-2529
Lafayette HS | 2,100/9-12
17050 Clayton Rd 63011 | 636-458-7200
Larry Schmidt, prin. | Fax 458-7219
Selvidge MS | 700/6-8
235 New Ballwin Rd 63021 | 636-207-2622
Sean Stryhal, prin. | Fax 207-2632

Grabber School of Hair Design | Post-Sec.
14557 Manchester Rd 63011 | 636-227-4440

Barnard, Nodaway, Pop. 253
South Nodaway County R-IV SD | 200/PK-12
209 Morehouse St 64423 | 660-652-3221
Terry Hutchings, supt. | Fax 652-3411
missouri.ihigh.com/southnodaway
South Nodaway JSHS | 100/7-12
209 Morehouse St 64423 | 660-652-3727
Kyle Collins, prin. | Fax 652-3411

Bell City, Stoddard, Pop. 454
Bell City R-II SD | 300/K-12
25254 Walnut St 63735 | 573-733-4444
Rhonda Niemczyk, supt. | Fax 733-4114
Bell City JSHS | 200/7-12
25254 Walnut St 63735 | 573-733-4444
Matthew Asher, prin. | Fax 733-4114

Belle, Maries, Pop. 1,329
Maries County R-II SD | 800/PK-12
PO Box 819 65013 | 573-859-3800
Dr. Ted Spessard, supt. | Fax 859-3883
Belle HS | 300/9-12
PO Box 819 65013 | 573-859-6114
Thomas Keller, prin. | Fax 859-3883
Other Schools – See Bland

Belton, Cass, Pop. 23,575
Belton SD 124 | 5,100/PK-12
110 W Walnut St 64012 | 816-348-1000
Dr. Kenneth Southwick, supt. | Fax 348-1068
www.beltonschools.org
Belton HS Freshman Center | 400/9-9
801 W North Ave 64012 | 816-348-1726
Bob Poisal, prin. | Fax 348-1727
Belton SHS | 1,000/10-12
107 Pirate Pkwy 64012 | 816-348-1036
Virgil Poisal, prin. | Fax 348-1516
Yeokum MS | 800/7-8
613 Mill St 64012 | 816-348-1042
Jeff Mehlenbacher, prin. | Fax 348-1534

Heartland Family S   200/PK-12
810 S Cedar St 64012   816-331-1000
David L. Baker, hdmstr.   Fax 322-2782

Benton, Scott, Pop. 730
Scott County R-IV SD   1,000/K-12
4035 State Highway 77 63736   573-545-3887
Don Moore, supt.   Fax 545-3929
kelly.k12.mo.us/
Kelly HS   300/9-12
4035 State Highway 77 63736   573-545-3541
Tom Hulshof, prin.   Fax 545-4485
Scott County MS   300/6-8
4035 State Highway 77 63736   573-545-3541
Mark Kiehne, prin.   Fax 545-4386

Stage One The Hair Academy   Post-Sec.
547 County Highway 250 63736   573-335-5078

Berkeley, Saint Louis, Pop. 9,867
Ferguson-Florissant R-II SD
Supt. — See Florissant
Berkeley MS   500/7-8
8300 Frost Ave 63134   314-524-3883
Winston Rogers, prin.   Fax 521-4826

Bernie, Stoddard, Pop. 1,801
Bernie R-XIII SD   600/PK-12
516 W Main Ave 63822   573-293-5333
Robin Ritchie, supt.   Fax 293-5731
www.bernie.k12.mo.us
Bernie JSHS   200/7-12
516 W Main Ave 63822   573-293-5334
Scott Mercer, prin.   Fax 293-5731

Bethany, Harrison, Pop. 3,065
South Harrison County R-II SD   900/PK-12
PO Box 445 64424   660-425-8044
Richard Smith, supt.   Fax 425-7050
www.shr2.k12.mo.us
North Central Career Center   Vo/Tech
PO Box 445 64424   660-425-2196
Larry Linthacum, dir.   Fax 425-2197
South Harrison County R-II HS   400/7-12
PO Box 445 64424   660-425-8051
Dennis Eastin, prin.   Fax 425-7447

Bevier, Macon, Pop. 724
Bevier C-4 SD   300/K-12
400 Bloomington St 63532   660-773-6611
Joan Patrick, supt.   Fax 773-6964
Bevier JSHS   100/7-12
400 Bloomington St 63532   660-773-5213
Kenneth Kelso, prin.   Fax 773-6964

Billings, Christian, Pop. 1,137
Billings R-IV SD   400/K-12
118 W Mount Vernon Rd 65610   417-744-2623
Cynthia Brandt, supt.   Fax 744-4545
www.billings.k12.mo.us
Billings HS   200/7-12
118 W Mount Vernon Rd 65610   417-744-2551
Jim Millsap, prin.   Fax 744-2720

Bismarck, Saint Francois, Pop. 1,516
Bismarck R-V SD   600/K-12
PO Box 257 63624   573-734-6111
Dr. Damon Gamble, supt.   Fax 734-2957
schoolweb.missouri.edu/bismarck.k12.mo.us
Bismarck JSHS   300/7-12
PO Box 257 63624   573-734-6111
Ray Politte, prin.   Fax 734-2957

Black, Reynolds
Lesterville R-IV SD
Supt. — See Lesterville
Lesterville Ranch Campus   100/K-12
RR 1 Box 127 63625   573-269-4207
Mary T. Balderas, prin.   Fax 269-4277

Bland, Gasconade, Pop. 570
Maries County R-II SD
Supt. — See Belle
Maries County MS   200/6-8
PO Box 10 65014   573-646-3912
Dwane Smith, prin.   Fax 646-3148

Bloomfield, Stoddard, Pop. 1,898
Bloomfield R-XIV SD   800/PK-12
PO Box 650 63825   573-568-4564
Dr. Sheila Perry, supt.   Fax 568-4565
bloomfield.k12.mo.us/
Bloomfield HS   200/9-12
PO Box 650 63825   573-568-2146
Toni Hill, prin.   Fax 568-2147

Blue Eye, Stone, Pop. 137
Blue Eye R-V SD   700/K-12
PO Box 105 65611   417-779-5332
Dan Ray, supt.   Fax 779-2151
www.blueeye.k12.mo.us
Blue Eye HS   200/9-12
PO Box 105 65611   417-779-5331
Ben Johnson, prin.   Fax 779-2151
Blue Eye MS   300/5-8
PO Box 38 65611   417-779-4299
Craig Linson, prin.   Fax 779-4526

Blue Springs, Jackson, Pop. 49,398
Blue Springs R-IV SD   13,100/K-12
1801 NW Vesper St 64015   816-224-1300
Dr. Paul Kinder, supt.   Fax 224-1310
www.bluesprings-schools.net
Blue Springs Freshman Center   1,000/9-9
2103 NW Vesper St 64015   816-224-1325
Dan Anderson, prin.   Fax 224-1344
Blue Springs HS   1,600/10-12
2000 NW Ashton Dr 64015   816-224-3459
David Adams, prin.   Fax 229-1025

Blue Springs South HS   1,300/10-12
1200 SE Adams Dairy Rd 64014   816-224-1315
Keith Maxey, prin.   Fax 224-1324
Brittany Hill MS   900/6-8
2701 NW 1st St 64014   816-224-1700
Lee Holstrom, prin.   Fax 224-1704
Moreland Ridge MS   900/6-8
900 SW Bishop Dr 64015   816-224-1800
Kevin Grover, prin.   Fax 224-1805
Sunny Vale MS   700/6-8
3930 S R D Mize Rd 64015   816-224-1330
Beverly Leonard, prin.   Fax 224-1309
Other Schools – See Lees Summit

House of Heavilin Beauty College   Post-Sec.
2000 SW State Route 7 64014   816-229-9000
Plaza Heights Christian Academy   200/PK-12
1500 SW Clark Rd 64015   816-228-0670
Michael Hart, admin.   Fax 229-4092

Bolivar, Polk, Pop. 9,598
Bolivar R-I SD   2,400/K-12
524 W Madison St 65613   417-326-5291
Leonard Zanatta, supt.   Fax 326-3562
www.bolivar.k12.mo.us/
Bolivar HS   700/9-12
1401 Highway D 65613   417-326-5228
J. Collins, prin.   Fax 326-4325
Bolivar MS   600/6-8
604 W Jackson St 65613   417-326-3811
Kevin Lowery, prin.   Fax 326-8277

Southwest Baptist University   Post-Sec.
1600 University Ave 65613   417-328-5281

Bonne Terre, Saint Francois, Pop. 4,696
North St. Francois County R-I SD   3,200/PK-12
300 Berry Rd 63628   573-358-2247
Dr. Terry Gibbons, supt.   Fax 358-2377
www.ncsd.k12.mo.us
North St. Francois County HS   1,000/9-12
7151 Raider Rd 63628   573-358-8890
Ron McCutchen, prin.   Fax 358-0021
Unitec Career Center   Vo/Tech
7163 Raider Rd 63628   573-358-2271
Steve Noble, prin.   Fax 358-3577
Other Schools – See Desloge

Boonville, Cooper, Pop. 8,399
Boonville R-I SD   1,500/PK-12
736 Main St 65233   660-882-7474
Dr. Greg Gettings, supt.   Fax 882-5721
www.boonville.k12.mo.us/
Boonslick Technical Education Center   Vo/Tech
1694 W Ashley Rd 65233   660-882-5306
Joyce Schuster, dir.   Fax 882-3269
Boonville HS   500/9-12
1690A W Ashley Rd 65233   660-882-7426
Jay M. Webster, prin.   Fax 882-3368
Elliott MS   400/6-8
700 Main St 65233   660-882-6649
Ono Monachino, prin.   Fax 882-8646

Bosworth, Carroll, Pop. 382
Bosworth R-V SD   200/PK-12
102 E Eldridge St 64623   660-534-7311
Linda Specie, supt.   Fax 534-7409
Bosworth JSHS   100/7-12
102 E Eldridge St 64623   660-534-7311
Linda Specie, prin.   Fax 534-7409

Bourbon, Crawford, Pop. 1,380
Crawford County R-I SD   1,100/K-12
1444 S Old Highway 66 65441   573-732-4426
Christopher Gaines, supt.   Fax 732-4545
warhawks.k12.mo.us/
Bourbon HS   300/9-12
1500 S Old Highway 66 65441   573-732-5615
Tom Wales, prin.   Fax 732-4407
Bourbon MS   400/5-8
363 Jost St 65441   573-732-4424
Michael Whittaker, prin.   Fax 732-4424

Bowling Green, Pike, Pop. 5,228
Bowling Green R-I SD   1,400/K-12
700 W Adams St 63334   573-324-5441
Frank Berlin, supt.   Fax 324-2439
www.bgschools.k12.mo.us
Bowling Green HS   500/9-12
700 W Adams St 63334   573-324-5341
Kent Hufty, prin.   Fax 324-3011
Bowling Green MS   400/6-8
700 W Adams St 63334   573-324-2181
Jeff Swartz, prin.   Fax 324-2439

Bradleyville, Taney, Pop. 100
Bradleyville R-I SD   200/K-12
PO Box 20 65614   417-796-2288
Joe Combs, supt.   Fax 796-2289
Bradleyville JSHS   100/7-12
PO Box 20 65614   417-796-2288
Robert Comer, prin.   Fax 796-2289

Branson, Taney, Pop. 6,231
Branson R-IV SD   3,300/K-12
400 Cedar Ridge Dr 65616   417-334-6541
Dr. Doug Hayter, supt.   Fax 334-6619
www.branson.k12.mo.us
Branson HS   1,000/9-12
935 Buchanan Rd 65616   417-334-6511
Chip Arnette, prin.   Fax 332-3212
Branson JHS   500/7-8
263 Buccaneer Dr 65616   417-334-3087
Brad Swofford, prin.   Fax 336-3913

Brashear, Adair, Pop. 274
Adair County R-II SD   300/K-12
205 W Dewey St 63533   660-323-5272
Diane Bradley, supt.   Fax 323-5250
brashear.k12.mo.us

Adair County R-II JSHS   100/7-12
205 W Dewey St 63533   660-323-5272
Richard Johnson, prin.   Fax 323-5250

Braymer, Caldwell, Pop. 951
Braymer C-4 SD   400/PK-12
400 Bobcat Ave 64624   660-645-2284
Paula Sprouse, supt.   Fax 645-2780
www.brayc4.k12.mo.us/
Braymer JSHS   200/7-12
400 Bobcat Ave 64624   660-645-2284
Gwenda Barton, prin.   Fax 645-2780

Breckenridge, Caldwell, Pop. 465
Breckenridge R-I SD   100/K-12
400 W Colfax St 64625   660-644-5715
Lachrissa Smith, supt.   Fax 644-5710
www.breckenridgeschool.org/
Breckenridge JSHS   50/7-12
400 W Colfax St 64625   660-644-5715
Lachrissa Smith, prin.   Fax 644-5710

Brentwood, Saint Louis, Pop. 7,519
Brentwood SD   900/K-12
90 Yorkshire Lane Ct 63144   314-962-4507
Charles Penberthy, supt.   Fax 962-7302
www.brentwood.k12.mo.us
Brentwood HS   300/9-12
2221 High School Dr 63144   314-962-3837
David Faulkner, prin.   Fax 963-3166
Brentwood MS   200/6-8
9127 White Ave 63144   314-962-8238
Julie Sperry, prin.   Fax 968-8724

Brighton, Polk
Pleasant Hope R-VI SD
Supt. — See Pleasant Hope
Pleasant Hope Ranch S   100/6-12
5545 N Highway 13 65617   417-376-3000
Vera Ker, prin.   Fax 376-3575

Bronaugh, Vernon, Pop. 243
Bronaugh R-VII SD   200/PK-12
527 E 6th St 64728   417-922-3211
Patricia Phillips, supt.   Fax 922-3308
www.bronaugh.k12.mo.us/
Bronaugh JSHS   100/7-12
527 E 6th St 64728   417-922-3211
Tim Judd, prin.   Fax 922-3308

Brookfield, Linn, Pop. 4,633
Brookfield R-III SD   1,300/PK-12
124A N Pershing Dr 64628   660-258-7443
Dr. Paul Barger, supt.   Fax 258-4711
www.brookfield.k12.mo.us
Brookfield Area Career Center   Vo/Tech
122 N Pershing Dr 64628   660-258-2682
Bob Brinkley, prin.   Fax 258-3875
Brookfield HS   400/9-12
124 N Pershing Dr 64628   660-258-7242
Bob Brinkley, prin.   Fax 258-2871
Brookfield MS   300/6-8
126 N Pershing Dr 64628   660-258-7335
Melinda Wilbeck, prin.   Fax 258-2190

Broseley, Butler
Twin Rivers R-X SD   1,000/K-12
PO Box 146 63932   573-328-4321
Andy Arbeitman, supt.   Fax 328-1070
www.semo.net/schools/TwinRivers/
Twin Rivers HS   300/9-12
PO Box 146 63932   573-328-4730
Jerry Stockton, prin.   Fax 328-1511

Brunswick, Chariton, Pop. 907
Brunswick R-II SD   300/PK-12
1008 County Rd 65236   660-548-3550
Dr. Bill Page, supt.   Fax 548-3029
schoolweb.missouri.edu/brunswick.k12.mo.us/
Brunswick JSHS   100/7-12
1008 County Rd 65236   660-548-3771
David Figg, prin.   Fax 548-3072

Bucklin, Linn, Pop. 505
Bucklin R-II SD   200/K-12
26832 Highway 129 64631   660-695-3555
Rick Roberts, supt.   Fax 695-3345
www.bucklin.k12.mo.us/
Bucklin R-II S   200/K-12
26832 Highway 129 64631   660-695-3225
Rick Roberts, prin.   Fax 695-3345

Buffalo, Dallas, Pop. 2,851
Dallas County R-I SD   2,000/PK-12
309 W Commercial St 65622   417-345-2222
Gary Arthaud, supt.   Fax 345-8446
www.dallasr1.k12.mo.us/
Buffalo HS   600/9-12
500 W Main St 65622   417-345-2223
Shawn Randles, prin.   Fax 345-8495
Buffalo MS   600/5-8
1001 Truman 65622   417-345-2335
Sandra Goss, prin.   Fax 345-5968
Other Schools – See Louisburg

Bunceton, Cooper, Pop. 354
Cooper County R-IV SD   200/K-12
PO Box 110 65237   660-427-5347
Mary Battles, supt.   Fax 427-5348
bunceton.k12.mo.us
Bunceton JSHS   100/7-12
PO Box 110 65237   660-427-5415
Connie Kunze, prin.   Fax 427-5348

Bunker, Reynolds, Pop. 427
Bunker R-III SD   300/K-12
PO Box 365 63629   573-689-2507
Clint Johnston, supt.   Fax 689-2011
Bunker JSHS   100/7-12
PO Box 365 63629   573-689-2211
Ken Cook, prin.   Fax 689-2011

Burlington Junction, Nodaway, Pop. 622
West Nodaway R-I SD — 400/PK-12
PO Box 260 64428 — 660-725-4613
Terry W. Buholt, supt. — Fax 725-4300
West Nodaway JSHS — 200/7-12
PO Box 260 64428 — 660-725-3317
Malcolm Buckner, prin. — Fax 725-4300

Butler, Bates, Pop. 4,214
Ballard R-II SD — 200/K-12
RR 1 Box 497 64730 — 816-297-2656
Gary Layton, supt. — Fax 297-4002
Ballard JSHS — 100/7-12
RR 1 Box 497 64730 — 816-297-2656
John Siebeneck, prin. — Fax 297-4002

Butler R-V SD — 1,100/PK-12
420 S Fulton St 64730 — 660-679-0653
Sterling Green, supt. — Fax 679-6626
www.butlerschools.org
Butler JSHS — 500/7-12
420 S Fulton St 64730 — 660-679-6121
Greg Sewell, prin. — Fax 679-6626

Cabool, Texas, Pop. 2,120
Cabool R-IV SD — 900/PK-12
PO Box 65689 — 417-962-3153
Wesley Davis, supt. — Fax 962-5043
www.cabool.k12.mo.us/index.html
Cabool HS — 300/9-12
PO Box 613 65689 — 417-962-3153
Jon Turner, prin. — Fax 962-5663
Cabool MS — 300/5-8
PO Box 613 65689 — 417-962-3153
Mary Holder, prin. — Fax 962-5043

Cadet, Washington
Kingston SD K-14 — 900/K-12
10047 Diamond Rd 63630 — 573-438-4982
Gary Milner, supt. — Fax 438-8813
www.kingston.k12.mo.us/
Kingston HS — 300/9-12
10047 Diamond Rd 63630 — 573-438-4982
Dale Van Deven, prin. — Fax 438-1212
Kingston MS — 200/6-8
10047 Diamond Rd 63630 — 573-438-4982
Glenda Milner, prin. — Fax 438-1212

Cainsville, Harrison, Pop. 368
Cainsville R-I SD — 100/PK-12
PO Box 108 64632 — 660-893-5213
Donald Wilburn, supt. — Fax 893-5713
Cainsville JSHS — 100/7-12
PO Box 108 64632 — 660-893-5214
Donald Wilburn, prin. — Fax 893-5713

Cairo, Randolph, Pop. 299
Northeast Randolph County R-IV SD — 400/K-12
301 W Martin St 65239 — 660-263-2788
Marge Gibson, supt. — Fax 263-5735
Northeast JSHS — 200/6-12
301 W Martin St 65239 — 660-263-2788
Greg Taylor, prin. — Fax 263-5735

Caledonia, Washington, Pop. 158
Valley R-VI SD — 500/K-12
1 Viking Dr 63631 — 573-779-3446
John Yount, supt. — Fax 779-3505
www.valley.k12.mo.us/
Valley JSHS — 200/7-12
1 Viking Dr 63631 — 573-779-3515
Rick W. Radford, prin. — Fax 779-3346

Calhoun, Henry, Pop. 500
Calhoun R-VIII SD — 200/PK-12
409 S College St 65323 — 660-694-3422
Mark Pottorff, supt. — Fax 694-3501
Calhoun JSHS — 100/7-12
200 W 7th St 65323 — 660-694-3412
John Crane, prin. — Fax 694-3333

California, Moniteau, Pop. 4,054
Moniteau County R-I SD — 1,300/K-12
1501 W Buchanan St 65018 — 573-796-2145
Mary Wood, supt. — Fax 796-4503
www.californiak12.org/
California HS — 400/9-12
1501 W Buchanan St 65018 — 573-796-4911
Brenda VanGilder, prin. — Fax 796-4503
California MS — 300/6-8
211 S Owen St 65018 — 573-796-2146
Scott Jarvis, prin. — Fax 796-8257

Camdenton, Camden, Pop. 2,949
Camdenton R-III SD — 4,000/PK-12
PO Box 1409 65020 — 573-346-9213
Ronald Hendricks, supt. — Fax 346-9211
camdenton.k12.mo.us/
Camdenton HS — 1,300/9-12
PO Box 1409 65020 — 573-346-9232
Dr. Brian Henry, prin. — Fax 346-9238
Camdenton MS — 700/7-8
PO Box 1409 65020 — 573-346-9257
Bill Ray, prin. — Fax 346-9288
Lake Career & Technical Center — Vo/Tech
PO Box 1409 65020 — 573-346-9260
Dr. Gail White, dir. — Fax 346-9284

Cameron, Clinton, Pop. 9,908
Cameron R-I SD — 1,800/PK-12
105 E 5th St 64429 — 816-632-2170
Ronald White, supt. — Fax 632-2612
www.cameron.k12.mo.us
Cameron HS — 500/9-12
1022 S Chestnut St 64429 — 816-632-2129
Don Gerber, prin. — Fax 632-1634
Cameron MS — 500/5-8
915 Park Ave 64429 — 816-632-2185
Dwight Sanders, prin. — Fax 632-3752

Campbell, Dunklin, Pop. 1,863
Campbell R-II SD — 700/PK-12
801 S State Route 53 63933 — 573-246-2133
Darrell Wilburn, supt. — Fax 246-3212
www.campbell.k12.mo.us
Campbell JSHS — 300/7-12
801 S State Route 53 63933 — 573-246-2576
Jay Thornton, prin. — Fax 246-2890

Canton, Lewis, Pop. 2,495
Canton R-V SD — 600/PK-12
200 S 4th St 63435 — 573-288-5216
David Tramel, supt. — Fax 288-5442
canton.k12.mo.us/
Canton JSHS — 300/7-12
200 S 4th St 63435 — 573-288-5216
Andy Turgeon, prin. — Fax 288-5442

Culver-Stockton College — Post-Sec.
1 College Hl 63435 — 573-288-5221

Cape Girardeau, Cape Girardeau, Pop. 35,741
Cape Girardeau SD 63 — 4,100/PK-12
301 N Clark St 63701 — 573-335-1867
Mark Bowles, supt. — Fax 335-1820
cape.k12.mo.us
Cape Girardeau Career & Technology Ctr. — Vo/Tech
1080 S Silver Springs Rd 63703 — 573-334-0826
Rich Payne, dir. — Fax 334-5930
Central HS — 1,300/9-12
1000 S Silver Springs Rd 63703 — 573-335-8228
Dr. Mike Cowan, prin. — Fax 334-1114
Central JHS — 700/7-8
205 Caruthers St 63701 — 573-334-2923
Roy Merideth, prin. — Fax 335-7173

Cape Girardeau Career & Technical School — Post-Sec.
1080 S Silver Springs Rd 63703 — 573-334-0826
Eagle Ridge Christian S — 200/PK-12
4210 State Highway K 63701 — 573-339-1335
Janice Margrabe, admin. — Fax 339-1390
Metro Business College — Post-Sec.
1732 N Kingshighway St 63701 — 573-334-9181
Notre Dame Regional HS — 500/9-12
265 Notre Dame Dr 63701 — 573-335-6772
Br. David Migliorino, prin. — Fax 335-3458
Southeast MO Hospital College of Nursing — Post-Sec.
2001 William St # 2 63703 — 573-334-6825
Southeast Missouri State University — Post-Sec.
1 University St 63701 — 573-651-2000

Cardwell, Dunklin, Pop. 761
Southland C-9 SD — 400/PK-12
500 S Main St 63829 — 573-654-3574
Raymond Lasley, supt. — Fax 654-3575
Southland JSHS — 200/7-12
500 S Main St 63829 — 573-654-3531
Ted Wilkerson, prin. — Fax 654-3534

Carl Junction, Jasper, Pop. 5,860
Carl Junction R-I SD — 2,800/K-12
PO Box 4 64834 — 417-649-7026
Phillip Cook, supt. — Fax 649-6594
www.cj.k12.mo.us
Carl Junction HS — 800/9-12
PO Box 4 64834 — 417-649-7081
Rita McClary, prin. — Fax 649-5791
Carl Junction JHS — 400/7-8
PO Box 4 64834 — 417-649-7246
Debra Elbrader, prin. — Fax 649-0022

Carrollton, Carroll, Pop. 4,010
Carrollton R-VII SD — 1,000/PK-12
300 E 9th St 64633 — 660-542-2769
Donald Reynolds, supt. — Fax 542-3416
Carrollton Area Career Center — Vo/Tech
305 E 10th St 64633 — 660-542-0000
Scott Bradley, dir. — Fax 542-0600
Carrollton HS — 300/9-12
300 E 9th St 64633 — 660-542-1276
Robert O. Kottman, prin. — Fax 542-1903
Carrollton JHS — 200/7-8
300 E 9th St 64633 — 660-542-3472
Brent Dobbins, prin. — Fax 542-3169

Carthage, Jasper, Pop. 12,892
Carthage R-IX SD — 3,600/PK-12
710 Lyon St 64836 — 417-359-7000
Gary Reed, supt. — Fax 359-7004
www.carthage.k12.mo.us
Carthage JHS — 800/7-9
827 E Centennial Ave 64836 — 417-359-7050
Ron Wallace, prin. — Fax 359-7057
Carthage SHS — 800/10-12
714 S Main St 64836 — 417-359-7020
Phil Lewis, prin. — Fax 359-7037
Carthage Technical Center — Vo/Tech
609 S River St 64836 — 417-359-7026
Eddie Stephens, prin. — Fax 359-7098

Caruthersville, Pemiscot, Pop. 6,564
Caruthersville SD 18 — 1,700/PK-12
1711 Ward Ave 63830 — 573-333-6100
Nick Thiele, supt. — Fax 333-6108
www.caruthersville.k12.mo.us/
Caruthersville HS — 400/9-12
1708 Ward Ave 63830 — 573-333-6110
Mike Wallace, prin. — Fax 333-6117
Caruthersville MS — 400/6-8
1705 Ward Ave 63830 — 573-333-6120
Jimmie Jean Bullington, prin. — Fax 333-1835

Cassville, Barry, Pop. 3,012
Cassville R-IV SD — 2,100/PK-12
1501 Main St 65625 — 417-847-2221
Jim Orrell, supt. — Fax 847-4009
wildcats.cassville.k12.mo.us/

Cassville HS — 600/9-12
1501 Main St 65625 — 417-847-3137
Brad F. Hanson, prin. — Fax 847-5111
Cassville MS — 500/6-8
1501 Main St 65625 — 417-847-3136
Eric White, prin. — Fax 847-3156

Cedar Hill, Jefferson, Pop. 1,966
Northwest R-I SD
Supt. — See High Ridge
Northwest HS — 2,200/9-12
6005 Cedar Hill Rd 63016 — 636-274-0555
James Knirr, prin. — Fax 274-2076

Center, Ralls, Pop. 636
Ralls County R-II SD — 700/K-12
21622 Highway 19 63436 — 573-267-3397
Deanette Jarman, supt. — Fax 267-3538
schoolweb.missouri.edu/rallsr2.k12.mo.us
Twain HS — 300/9-12
21622 Highway 19 63436 — 573-267-3397
Paul Mensching, prin. — Fax 267-3538
Twain JHS — 200/6-8
21622 Highway 19 63436 — 573-267-3397
Cheryl Mack, prin. — Fax 267-3538

Centerview, Johnson, Pop. 256
Johnson County R-VII SD — 700/PK-12
92 NW State Route 58 64019 — 660-656-3316
Dr. Craig Eaton, supt. — Fax 656-3316
crs.k12.mo.us
Crest Ridge HS — 200/9-12
92 NW State Route 58 64019 — 660-656-3391
John Hays, prin. — Fax 656-3316
Crest Ridge MS — 200/6-8
92 NW State Route 58 64019 — 660-656-3843
Rebecca Gudde, prin. — Fax 656-3316

Centralia, Boone, Pop. 3,768
Centralia R-VI SD — 1,400/PK-12
635 S Jefferson St 65240 — 573-682-3561
Glenn Brown Ed.D., supt. — Fax 682-2181
www.centralia.k12.mo.us
Boren MS — 400/5-8
110 N Jefferson St 65240 — 573-682-2617
Philip Gooding, prin. — Fax 682-1500
Centralia HS — 400/9-12
849 S Jefferson St 65240 — 573-682-3508
Darin Ford, prin. — Fax 682-2749

Sunnydale Adventist Academy — 100/9-12
6818 Audrain Rd 9139 65240 — 573-682-2164
— Fax 682-3136

Chadwick, Christian
Chadwick R-I SD — 200/K-12
7090 State Highway 125 S 65629 — 417-634-2669
Dr. Gordon Logsdon, supt. — Fax 634-2668
Chadwick JSHS — 100/7-12
7090 State Highway 125 S 65629 — 417-634-3588
Mary Holder, prin. — Fax 634-2668

Chaffee, Scott, Pop. 3,000
Chaffee R-II SD — 600/PK-12
517 W Yoakum Ave 63740 — 573-887-3532
Dr. Arnold Bell, supt. — Fax 887-3926
schoolweb.missouri.edu/chaffeeRII.k12.mo.us
Chaffee JSHS — 300/7-12
517 W Yoakum Ave 63740 — 573-887-3226
Neil S. Glass, prin. — Fax 887-3926

Chamois, Osage, Pop. 460
Osage County R-I SD — 200/K-12
614 S Poplar St 65024 — 573-763-5666
Thomas Allen, supt. — Fax 763-5686
www.chamois.k12.mo.us
Chamois HS — 100/7-12
614 S Poplar St 65024 — 573-763-5393
Brad Strobel, prin. — Fax 763-5686

Charleston, Mississippi, Pop. 5,855
Charleston R-I SD — 1,200/K-12
PO Box 39 63834 — 573-683-3776
Kevin Miller, supt. — Fax 683-2909
charleston.k12.mo.us/
Charleston HS — 400/9-12
PO Box 39 63834 — 573-683-3761
David Wilson, prin. — Fax 683-2909
Charleston MS — 300/6-8
PO Box 39 63834 — 573-683-3346
Pamela Ferrell, prin. — Fax 683-2909

Chesterfield, Saint Louis, Pop. 47,067
Parkway C-2 SD — 19,500/PK-12
455 N Woods Mill Rd 63017 — 314-415-8100
Robert Malito Ph.D., supt. — Fax 415-8009
www.pkwy.k12.mo.us/index.cfm
Parkway Central HS — 1,400/9-12
369 N Woods Mill Rd 63017 — 314-415-7900
Tim Gannon, prin. — Fax 415-7913
Parkway Central MS — 1,000/6-8
471 N Woods Mill Rd 63017 — 314-415-7800
Lauretta Holloway, prin. — Fax 415-7834
Parkway West MS — 1,100/6-8
2312 Baxter Rd 63017 — 314-415-7400
Linda Lelonek, prin. — Fax 415-7409
Other Schools — See Ballwin, Creve Coeur, Manchester

Rockwood R-VI SD
Supt. — See Eureka
Marquette HS — 2,100/9-12
2351 Clarkson Rd 63017 — 636-537-4300
Dr. Paige Muench, prin. — Fax 537-4319

Chesterfield Day S — 500/PK-12
1100 White Rd 63017 — 314-469-6622
Marianne Kearney, prin. — Fax 469-7889
Gateway Academy — 200/PK-12
17815 Wild Horse Creek Rd 63005 — 636-519-9099
Larry Hofstetter, dir. — Fax 519-1621

Logan College of Chiropractic — Post-Sec.
1851 Schoettler Rd 63017 — 636-227-2100
St. Joseph's Institute for the Deaf — Post-Sec.
1809 Clarkson Rd 63017 — 636-532-3211
Westwood Jr. Academy — 50/PK-10
16601 Wild Horse Creek Rd 63005 — 636-519-8222
Fax 519-8221

Chilhowee, Johnson, Pop. 338
Chilhowee R-IV SD — 100/K-12
PO Box 98 64733 — 660-678-2511
Andy Henley, supt. — Fax 678-5711
www.chilhowee.k12.mo.us
Chilhowee JSHS — 100/7-12
PO Box 98 64733 — 660-678-4511
Renee Gregory, prin. — Fax 678-5711

Chillicothe, Livingston, Pop. 8,791
Chillicothe R-II SD — 2,000/K-12
PO Box 530 64601 — 660-646-4566
Dale Wallace, supt. — Fax 646-6508
www.chillicotheschools.org/
Chillicothe HS — 700/9-12
2801 Hornet Rd 64601 — 660-646-0700
Thomas Anderson, prin. — Fax 646-7106
Chillicothe MS — 500/6-8
1529 Calhoun St 64601 — 660-646-1916
Bryan Prewitt, prin. — Fax 646-5065
Grand River Tech S — Vo/Tech
1200 Fair St 64601 — 660-646-3414
Ron Wolf, prin. — Fax 646-3568

Chillicothe Beauty Academy — Post-Sec.
505 Elm St 64601 — 660-646-4198

Clarksville, Pike, Pop. 498
Pike County R-III SD — 700/PK-12
28176 Highway WW 63336 — 573-242-3546
Paul Terpening, supt. — Fax 485-2393
www.clopton.k12.mo.us
Clopton JSHS — 300/7-12
28176 Highway WW 63336 — 573-242-3546
Timothy Reller, prin. — Fax 485-2393
Other Schools – See Eolia

Clarkton, Dunklin, Pop. 1,293
Clarkton C-4 SD — 400/PK-12
PO Box 637 63837 — 573-448-3712
Philip Harrison, supt. — Fax 448-5182
www.clarkton.k12.mo.us
Clarkton JSHS — 200/7-12
PO Box 637 63837 — 573-448-3120
Merlyn Johnson, prin. — Fax 448-3226

Clayton, Saint Louis, Pop. 15,974
Clayton SD — 2,700/PK-12
2 Mark Twain Cir 63105 — 314-854-6000
Dr. Don Senti, supt. — Fax 854-6096
www.clayton.k12.mo.us
Clayton HS — 900/9-12
1 Mark Twain Cir 63105 — 314-854-6600
Dr. Louise Losos, prin. — Fax 854-6793
Wydown MS — 600/6-8
6500 Wydown Blvd 63105 — 314-854-6400
Mary Ann Goldberg, prin. — Fax 854-6491

Cleveland, Cass, Pop. 636
Midway R-I SD — 600/K-12
5801 State Route 2 64734 — 816-250-2994
Paul Fregeau, supt. — Fax 899-2823
www.midway.k12.mo.us
Midway JSHS — 300/7-12
5801 State Route 2 64734 — 816-250-2994
Robert Weltsch, prin. — Fax 899-2823

Clever, Christian, Pop. 1,176
Clever R-V SD — 700/K-12
103 S Public Ave 65631 — 417-743-4800
Richard Henson, supt. — Fax 743-4802
www.clever.k12.mo.us
Clever HS — 200/9-12
401 Inman St 65631 — 417-743-4830
Robert Parker, prin. — Fax 743-4832
Clever MS — 200/5-8
103 S Public Ave 65631 — 417-743-4820
Benjy Fenske, prin. — Fax 743-4802

Clifton Hill, Randolph, Pop. 127
Westran R-I SD
Supt. — See Huntsville
Westran MS — 200/6-8
622 Harlan St 65244 — 660-261-4511
Steven Spotts, prin. — Fax 261-4292

Climax Springs, Camden, Pop. 83
Climax Springs R-IV SD — 200/PK-12
119 Nort Dr 65324 — 573-347-3905
Daniel Slack, supt. — Fax 347-9931
csprings.k12.mo.us/
Climax Springs JSHS — 100/7-12
119 Nort Dr 65324 — 573-347-2351
Gregery Caine, prin. — Fax 347-2394

Clinton, Henry, Pop. 9,349
Clinton SD 124 — 2,200/PK-12
701 S 8th St 64735 — 660-885-2237
William Biggerstaff, supt. — Fax 885-7033
clinton.k12.mo.us
Clinton HS — 700/9-12
701 S 8th St 64735 — 660-885-2247
Frank Dahman, prin. — Fax 885-2012
Clinton MS — 500/6-8
701 S 8th St 64735 — 660-885-3353
Andy Ford, prin. — Fax 885-4826
Clinton Technical S — Vo/Tech
701 S 8th St 64735 — 660-885-6101
Richard Wells, dir. — Fax 885-6789

Cole Camp, Benton, Pop. 1,045
Cole Camp R-I SD — 800/K-12
500 S Keeney St 65325 — 660-668-4427
Dr. Jerry Cochran, supt. — Fax 668-4703
Cole Camp HS — 300/9-12
500 S Keeney St 65325 — 660-668-3751
Perry Gorrell, prin. — Fax 668-4703
Cole Camp MS — 200/6-8
500 S Keeney St 65325 — 660-668-3502
Tyler Clark, prin. — Fax 668-4703

Columbia, Boone, Pop. 88,534
Columbia SD 93 — 16,400/PK-12
1818 W Worley St 65203 — 573-214-3400
Dr. Phyllis Chase, supt. — Fax 214-3401
www.columbia.k12.mo.us/
Columbia Area Career Ctr — Vo/Tech
4203 S Providence Rd 65203 — 573-214-3800
Dr. Arden Boyer-Stephens, dir. — Fax 214-3801
Hickman SHS — 2,000/10-12
1104 N Providence Rd 65203 — 573-214-3000
Michael Jeffers, prin. — Fax 214-3057
Jefferson JHS — 800/8-9
713 Rogers St 65201 — 573-214-3210
Nyle Klinginsmith, prin. — Fax 214-3211
Oakland JHS — 800/8-9
3405 Oakland Pl 65202 — 573-214-3220
Dr. Kimberly Presko, prin. — Fax 214-3221
Rock Bridge SHS — 1,500/10-12
4303 S Providence Rd 65203 — 573-214-3100
Andy Kohl, prin. — Fax 214-3109
West JHS — 1,000/8-9
401 Clinkscales Rd 65203 — 573-214-3230
Dr. Sandra Logan, prin. — Fax 214-3231

Christian Fellowship S — 300/K-12
4600 Christian Fellowshp Rd 65203 — 573-445-8565
Scott Williams, prin. — Fax 445-8564
Columbia Beauty Academy — Post-Sec.
1729 W Broadway Ste 5 65203 — 573-445-6611
Columbia College — Post-Sec.
1001 Rogers St 65201 — 800-231-2391
Jerry's School of Hairstyling — Post-Sec.
1001 Royal Birkdale Dr 65203 — 573-449-7527
Stephens College — Post-Sec.
PO Box 2121 65215 — 573-442-2211
University of Missouri — Post-Sec.
228 Jesse Hall 65211 — 573-882-2121

Conception, Nodaway

Conception Seminary College 64433 — Post-Sec.
660-944-2886

Conception Junction, Nodaway, Pop. 199
Jefferson C-123 SD — 200/PK-12
37614 US Highway 136 64434 — 660-944-2316
Rob Dowis, supt. — Fax 944-2315
www.jc123.k12.mo.us/
Jefferson JSHS — 100/7-12
37614 US Highway 136 64434 — 660-944-2316
Tim Jermain, prin. — Fax 944-2315

Concordia, Lafayette, Pop. 2,384
Concordia R-II SD — 600/PK-12
PO Box 879 64020 — 660-463-7235
Mary Beth Scherer, supt. — Fax 463-1326
www.concordia.k12.mo.us
Concordia JSHS — 200/7-12
PO Box 879 64020 — 660-463-2246
Mike Trautman, prin. — Fax 463-4081

St. Paul Lutheran HS — 100/9-12
PO Box 719 64020 — 660-463-2238
Fax 463-7621

Conway, Laclede, Pop. 748
Laclede County R-I SD — 800/PK-12
726 W Jefferson Ave 65632 — 417-589-2951
Larry Clinefelter, supt. — Fax 589-3202
Conway HS — 300/9-12
726 W Jefferson Ave 65632 — 417-589-2941
Sondra Caffey, prin. — Fax 589-2500
Conway JHS — 100/7-8
726 W Jefferson Ave 65632 — 417-589-8247
Cindy Hawkins, prin. — Fax 589-2500

Cooter, Pemiscot, Pop. 441
Cooter R-IV SD — 300/K-12
PO Box 218 63839 — 573-695-3312
William Crowder, supt. — Fax 695-3073
Cooter JSHS — 100/7-12
PO Box 218 63839 — 573-695-4972
Frank Killian, prin. — Fax 695-3073

Craig, Holt, Pop. 298
Craig R-III SD — 100/K-12
402 N Ward St 64437 — 660-683-5351
Hershel Ferguson, supt. — Fax 683-5769
www.schoolweb.missouri.edu/craigr3.k12.mo.us
Craig JSHS — 100/7-12
402 N Ward St 64437 — 660-683-5431
Terry Petersen, prin. — Fax 683-5769

Crane, Stone, Pop. 1,418
Crane R-III SD — 700/K-12
PO Box 405 65633 — 417-723-5300
Tyler Laney, supt. — Fax 723-5551
www.crane.k12.mo.us
Crane HS — 200/9-12
PO Box 405 65633 — 417-723-5383
Bill Redus, prin. — Fax 723-5551
Crane MS — 200/5-8
PO Box 405 65633 — 417-723-8177
Karla Edwards, prin. — Fax 723-5551

Creighton, Cass, Pop. 336
Sherwood-Cass R-VIII SD — 900/PK-12
PO Box 98 64739 — 660-499-2239
Freddie Doherty, supt. — Fax 499-2624
sherwood.k12.mo.us
Sherwood HS — 300/9-12
PO Box 98 64739 — 660-499-2239
Stephen Fox, prin. — Fax 499-2258
Sherwood MS — 200/6-8
PO Box 98 64739 — 660-499-2203
Tim Komer, prin. — Fax 499-2585

Creve Coeur, Saint Louis, Pop. 16,718
Parkway C-2 SD
Supt. — See Chesterfield
Parkway Northeast MS — 1,100/6-8
181 Coeur De Ville Dr 63141 — 314-415-7100
Kim Brandon, prin. — Fax 415-7113
Parkway North HS — 1,300/9-12
12860 Fee Fee Rd, Saint Louis MO 63146 — 314-415-7600
Jenny Marquart, prin. — Fax 415-7634

Crocker, Pulaski, Pop. 1,042
Crocker R-II SD — 600/PK-12
PO Box 488 65452 — 573-736-5000
Dr. Jim Bogle, supt. — Fax 736-5924
www.crocker.k12.mo.us/
Crocker JSHS — 300/7-12
PO Box 488 65452 — 573-736-5000
Wayne Juliano, prin. — Fax 736-2801

Crystal City, Jefferson, Pop. 4,421
Crystal City SD 47 — 600/PK-12
1100 Mississippi Ave 63019 — 636-937-4411
Ronald Swafford, supt. — Fax 937-2512
www.crystal.k12.mo.us/
Crystal City HS — 300/9-12
1100 Mississippi Ave 63019 — 636-937-2005
Tammy Ridgeway, prin. — Fax 937-2512

Cuba, Crawford, Pop. 3,351
Crawford County R-II SD — 1,400/K-12
1 Wildcat Pride Dr 65453 — 573-885-2534
Waymon W. Boast, supt. — Fax 885-3900
www.cuba.k12.mo.us/
Cuba HS — 400/9-12
1 Wildcat Pride Dr 65453 — 573-885-2534
Tony Hermann, prin. — Fax 885-7726
Cuba MS — 400/5-8
1 Wildcat Pride Dr 65453 — 573-885-2534
J.W. Brandt, prin. — Fax 885-6278

Dadeville, Dade, Pop. 222
Dadeville R-II SD — 200/K-12
PO Box 188 65635 — 417-995-2201
Nancy Brannon, supt. — Fax 995-2110
Dadeville JSHS — 100/7-12
PO Box 188 65635 — 417-995-2201
Matt Bushey, prin. — Fax 995-2110

Dearborn, Platte, Pop. 541
North Platte County R-I SD — 700/PK-12
212 W 6th St 64439 — 816-450-3511
Dr. Francis Moran, supt. — Fax 992-8727
www.nplatte.k12.mo.us/
North Platte HS — 200/9-12
212 W 6th St 64439 — 816-450-3344
John Green, prin. — Fax 992-8955
North Platte JHS — 100/7-8
212 W 6th St 64439 — 816-450-3350
Roger Giger, prin. — Fax 992-3665

Deepwater, Saint Clair, Pop. 502
Lakeland R-III SD — 500/PK-12
12530 Lakeland School Dr 64740 — 417-644-2223
Dr. Kenneth Wilson, supt. — Fax 644-2316
www.lakelandschools.com/index.html
Lakeland JSHS — 200/7-12
12530 Lakeland School Dr 64740 — 417-644-2223
Jeff Osner, prin. — Fax 644-2316

Deering, Pemiscot, Pop. 130
Delta C-7 SD — 300/K-12
PO Box 297 63840 — 573-757-6648
James Williams, supt. — Fax 757-9691
www.schoolweb.missouri.edu/deltac7.k12.mo.us/
Delta C-7 JSHS — 100/7-12
PO Box 297 63840 — 573-757-6611
Kenny Copley, prin. — Fax 757-9691

De Kalb, Buchanan, Pop. 258
Buchanan County R-IV SD — 400/K-12
702 Main St 64440 — 816-685-3160
Lane Novinger, supt. — Fax 685-3203
De Kalb JSHS — 200/7-12
702 Main St 64440 — 816-685-3211
Travis A. Dittemore, prin. — Fax 685-3156

Delta, Cape Girardeau, Pop. 527
Delta R-V SD — 300/PK-12
PO Box 787 63744 — 573-794-2500
Tom Allen, supt. — Fax 794-2504
Delta JSHS — 200/7-12
PO Box 787 63744 — 573-794-2511
Nathan Crowden, prin. — Fax 794-2504

Desloge, Saint Francois, Pop. 4,938
North St. Francois County R-I SD
Supt. — See Bonne Terre
North County MS — 600/7-8
406 E Chestnut St 63601 — 573-431-6700
Larry Kekec, prin. — Fax 431-5203

Mineral Area College — Post-Sec.
PO Box 1000 63601 — 573-431-4593

De Soto, Jefferson, Pop. 6,501
Desoto SD 73 2,800/K-12
221 S 3rd St 63020 636-586-1000
Terry Noble, supt. Fax 586-1009
www.desoto.k12.mo.us
De Soto HS 900/9-12
815 Amvets Dr 63020 636-586-1050
Brent Norton, prin. Fax 586-1059
De Soto JHS 500/7-8
731 Amvets Dr 63020 636-586-1030
Brian Tharp, prin. Fax 586-1039

Dexter, Stoddard, Pop. 7,374
Dexter R-XI SD 2,100/PK-12
1031 Brown Pilot Ln 63841 573-614-1000
Dr. Kenneth Jackson, supt. Fax 614-1002
dexter.k12.mo.us/
Dexter HS 600/9-12
1101 W Grant St 63841 573-614-1030
Bryce Matthews, prin. Fax 614-1032
Hill MS 500/6-8
1107 Brown Pilot Ln 63841 573-614-1010
Dr. Kimberly Flowers, prin. Fax 614-1012

Diamond, Newton, Pop. 825
Diamond R-IV SD 800/K-12
PO Box 68 64840 417-325-5186
Mark Mayo, supt. Fax 325-5338
www.diamondwildcats.org/
Diamond HS 200/9-12
PO Box 68 64840 417-325-5188
Patricia Wilson, prin. Fax 325-5331
Diamond MS 300/5-8
PO Box 68 64840 417-325-5336
Danny DeWitt, prin. Fax 325-5333

Dixon, Pulaski, Pop. 1,610
Dixon R-I SD 1,100/PK-12
PO Box A 65459 573-759-7163
Barry Morrow, supt. Fax 759-2506
www.dixonr1.yhti.net/
Dixon HS 400/9-12
PO Box A 65459 573-759-7119
Jeff Koonce, prin. Fax 759-3625
Dixon MS 300/6-8
PO Box A 65459 573-759-7139
Jim Brown, prin. Fax 759-6627

Doniphan, Ripley, Pop. 1,909
Doniphan R-I SD 1,700/PK-12
309 Pine St 63935 573-996-3819
Kevin Sandlin, supt. Fax 996-5865
www.doniphanr1.k12.mo.us
Current River Vocational S Vo/Tech
301 E Spring St 63935 573-996-2915
John Wesemann, prin. Fax 996-7838
Doniphan HS 500/9-12
5 Ball Park Rd 63935 573-996-3312
Gini Barnett, prin. Fax 996-3739
Doniphan MS 400/6-8
651 E Summit St 63935 573-996-3614
Donald Sanders, prin. Fax 996-4525

Dora, Ozark
Dora R-III SD 300/PK-12
PO Box 14 65637 417-261-2346
Chris Berger, supt. Fax 261-2673
www.dora.org
Dora JSHS 200/7-12
PO Box 14 65637 417-261-2263
Rick Luna, prin. Fax 261-2673

Drexel, Bates, Pop. 1,098
Drexel R-IV SD 400/K-12
PO Box 860 64742 816-657-4715
Patricia Yocum, supt. Fax 657-4798
Drexel HS 200/7-12
PO Box 860 64742 816-619-2287
Gerald D. Whalen, prin. Fax 657-4798

Eagleville, Harrison, Pop. 324
North Harrison R-III SD 200/PK-12
12023 Fir St 64442 660-867-5222
Nancy J. Parman, supt. Fax 867-5263
North Harrison County JSHS 100/7-12
12023 Fir St 64442 660-867-5221
Mark Fletcher, prin. Fax 867-5263

Earth City, Saint Louis

ITT Technical Institute Post-Sec.
3640 Corporate Trail Dr 63045 314-298-7800
Midwest Institute - Earth City Post-Sec.
4260 Shoreline Dr 63045 314-344-3334

Easton, Buchanan, Pop. 258
East Buchanan County C-1 SD
Supt. — See Gower
East Buchanan MS 200/6-8
301 N County Park Rd 64443 816-473-2451
Cindy Rumpf, prin. Fax 473-2604

East Prairie, Mississippi, Pop. 3,134
East Prairie R-II SD 1,200/PK-12
304 E Walnut St 63845 573-649-3562
Scott Downing, supt. Fax 649-5455
www.eprairie.k12.mo.us
East Prairie HS 300/9-12
304 E Walnut St 63845 573-649-3564
Steve Douglas, prin. Fax 649-3208
East Prairie JHS 200/7-8
210 E Washington St 63845 573-649-9368
Eva Chance, prin. Fax 649-9370

Edina, Knox, Pop. 1,207
Knox County R-I SD 600/PK-12
RR 3 Box 59 63537 660-397-2228
Terry Robertson, supt. Fax 397-3998
www.knox.k12.mo.us/
Knox County JSHS 300/7-12
RR 3 Box 59 63537 660-397-2231
D.J. Leverton, prin. Fax 397-3282

Eldon, Miller, Pop. 4,892
Eldon R-I SD 2,000/PK-12
110 S Oak St 65026 573-392-8000
Dr. C.J. Huff, supt. Fax 392-8080
www.eldon.k12.mo.us/
Eldon Career Center Vo/Tech
112 S Pine St 65026 573-392-8060
Matt Davis, dir. Fax 392-9154
Eldon HS 600/9-12
101 S Pine St 65026 573-392-8010
Leane McNay, prin. Fax 392-5057
Eldon MS 300/7-8
1400 N Grand Ave 65026 573-392-8020
Chris Miller, prin. Fax 392-9151

El Dorado Springs, Cedar, Pop. 3,761
El Dorado Springs R-II SD 1,300/PK-12
901 S Grand Ave 64744 417-876-3112
Greg Koetting, supt. Fax 876-2128
El Dorado Springs HS 400/9-12
901 S Grand Ave 64744 417-876-3112
David Copeland, prin. Fax 876-2128
El Dorado Springs MS 300/6-8
901 S Grand Ave 64744 417-876-3112
David Hedrick, prin. Fax 876-2128

El Dorado Christian S 200/PK-12
1600 S Ohio St 64744 417-876-2201
Kathy Davis, prin. Fax 876-4913

Ellington, Reynolds, Pop. 1,022
Southern Reynolds County R-II SD 600/PK-12
1 School St 63638 573-663-3591
Dawna Burrow, supt. Fax 663-2412
www.ellington.k12.mo.us/
Southern Reynolds County HS 300/7-12
1 School St 63638 573-663-2291
Paulette Crouthers, prin. Fax 663-2155

Ellsinore, Carter, Pop. 364
East Carter County R-II SD 800/PK-12
24 S Herren Ave 63937 573-322-5625
Tim Hager, supt. Fax 322-8586
www.ecarter.k12.mo.us
East Carter County R-II HS 400/7-12
24 S Herren Ave 63937 573-322-5653
Barry Stahl, prin. Fax 322-5720

Elsberry, Lincoln, Pop. 2,253
Elsberry R-II SD 900/K-12
PO Box 106 63343 573-898-5554
Larry Flanagan, supt. Fax 898-3140
schoolweb.missouri.edu/elsberry.k12.mo.us/
Cannon MS 300/5-8
PO Box 106 63343 573-898-5554
Ken Youmans, prin. Fax 898-5825
Elsberry HS 300/9-12
PO Box 106 63343 573-898-5554
Errol Spratt, prin. Fax 898-9132

Eminence, Shannon, Pop. 542
Eminence R-I SD 300/PK-12
PO Box 730 65466 573-226-3251
Donna Depee, supt. Fax 226-3250
eminence.echalk.com/
Eminence JSHS 200/7-12
PO Box 730 65466 573-226-3252
Garry Cutts, prin. Fax 226-3211

Eolia, Pike, Pop. 443
Pike County R-III SD
Supt. — See Clarksville
Pike-Lincoln Technical Center Vo/Tech
PO Box 38 63344 573-485-2900
Krista Flowers, dir. Fax 485-2388

Essex, Stoddard, Pop. 529
Richland R-I SD 400/K-12
PO Box 8 63846 573-283-5332
Ken Latham, supt. Fax 283-5798
www.richland.k12.mo.us/
Richland JSHS 200/7-12
PO Box 8 63846 573-283-5332
Brenda Campbell, prin. Fax 283-5798

Eugene, Cole, Pop. 159
Cole County R-V SD 700/K-12
PO Box 78 65032 573-498-4000
Mark Blythe, supt. Fax 498-4090
www.coler-v.k12.mo.us/
Eugene JSHS 400/7-12
PO Box 78 65032 573-498-4001
Rob Ferguson, prin. Fax 498-4091

Eureka, Saint Louis, Pop. 8,575
Rockwood R-VI SD 22,900/PK-12
111 E North St 63025 636-938-2200
Dr. Craig H. Larson, supt. Fax 938-2251
www.rockwood.k12.mo.us
Eureka HS 1,400/9-12
4525 Highway 109 63025 636-938-2400
Dr. Kevin Keltner, prin. Fax 938-2411
Other Schools – See Ballwin, Chesterfield, Fenton, Glencoe

Everton, Dade, Pop. 321
Everton R-III SD 200/K-12
211 School St 65646 417-535-2221
Chuck Adams, supt. Fax 535-4105
Everton JSHS 100/7-12
211 School St 65646 417-535-2221
Terry Winton, prin. Fax 535-4105

Ewing, Lewis, Pop. 454
Lewis County C-1 SD 1,000/PK-12
PO Box 366 63440 573-209-3217
Jacqueline Ebeling, supt. Fax 209-3318
www.lewis.k12.mo.us
Highland JSHS 500/7-12
PO Box 366 63440 573-209-3215
Paul Sulser, prin. Fax 209-3469

Excelsior Springs, Clay, Pop. 11,226
Excelsior Springs SD 40 3,300/PK-12
PO Box 248 64024 816-630-9200
James Horton, supt. Fax 630-9203
estigers.k12.mo.us
Excelsior Springs Career Ctr Vo/Tech
PO Box 248 64024 816-630-9240
Don Roberts, dir. Fax 630-9245
Excelsior Springs HS 900/9-12
PO Box 248 64024 816-630-9210
Alan Bunch, prin. Fax 630-9227
Excelsior Springs MS 700/6-8
PO Box 248 64024 816-630-9230
William Bielefeld, prin. Fax 630-9236
Excelsior Springs Technical HS Vo/Tech
PO Box 248 64024 816-630-5501
Tom Mayfield, prin. Fax 637-1806

Martinez School of Cosmetology Post-Sec.
248 1/2 E Broadway St 64024 816-630-3900

Exeter, Barry, Pop. 715
Exeter R-VI SD 300/K-12
RR 1 Box 509 65647 417-835-2922
Larry Wood, supt. Fax 835-3201
www.exeter.k12.mo.us/
Exeter HS 100/9-12
RR 1 Box 509 65647 417-835-3745
Robert Taylor, prin. Fax 835-3201

Fairfax, Atchison, Pop. 631
Fairfax R-III SD 200/PK-12
500 E Main St 64446 660-686-2421
Ed Defenbaugh, supt. Fax 686-2848
www.fairfaxk12mo.us/
Fairfax JSHS 100/7-12
500 E Main St 64446 660-686-2851
Dustin Barnes, prin. Fax 686-3436

Fair Grove, Greene, Pop. 1,260
Fair Grove R-X SD 1,100/K-12
PO Box 367 65648 417-759-2233
Gene Rice, supt. Fax 759-7150
www.fairgrove.k12.mo.us
Fair Grove HS 300/9-12
PO Box 367 65648 417-759-2554
David Hunter, prin. Fax 759-7685
Fair Grove MS 300/6-8
PO Box 367 65648 417-759-2556
Charity Rael, prin. Fax 759-9053

Fair Play, Polk, Pop. 432
Fair Play R-II SD 400/K-12
PO Box 1020 65649 417-654-2231
Renee Sagaser, supt. Fax 654-2800
www.fairplay.k12.mo.us/
Fair Play JSHS 200/7-12
PO Box 1020 65649 417-654-2232
Danny Cantrell, prin. Fax 654-2232

Farmington, Saint Francois, Pop. 14,335
Farmington R-VII SD 3,900/PK-12
PO Box 570 63640 573-701-1300
Dr. W. L. Sanders, supt. Fax 701-1309
www.farmington.k12.mo.us
Farmington HS 1,200/9-12
1 Black Knight Dr 63640 573-701-1310
Dr. David Waters, prin. Fax 701-1329
Farmington MS 600/7-8
506 S Fleming St 63640 573-701-1330
Dorothy Winslow, prin. Fax 701-1339

Mineral Area Regional Medical Center Post-Sec.
1212 Weber Rd 63640 573-756-4581
Missouri Beauty Academy Post-Sec.
222 E Columbia St 63640 573-756-2730

Faucett, Buchanan
Mid-Buchanan County R-V SD 700/K-12
3221 State Route H SE 64448 816-238-1646
John James, supt. Fax 238-4150
www.midbuchanan.k12.mo.us
Mid-Buchanan JSHS 400/7-12
3221 State Route H SE 64448 816-238-1646
Bob Pierce, prin. Fax 238-2484

Fayette, Howard, Pop. 2,724
Fayette R-III SD 800/PK-12
705 Lucky St 65248 660-248-2153
Darryl Pannier, supt. Fax 248-3702
www.fayette.k12.mo.us/
Clark MS 200/6-8
704 Lucky St 65248 660-248-3800
Lisa Templeton, prin. Fax 248-2610
Fayette HS 200/9-12
510 N Cleveland St 65248 660-248-2124
Darren Rapert, prin. Fax 248-2120

Central Methodist University Post-Sec.
411 Central Methodist Sq 65248 660-248-3391

Fenton, Saint Louis, Pop. 4,340
Rockwood R-VI SD
Supt. — See Eureka
Rockwood South MS 1,000/6-8
1628 Hawkins Rd 63026 636-861-7723
Dr. Karen Seiber, prin. Fax 861-7730
Rockwood Summit HS 1,400/9-12
1780 Hawkins Rd 63026 636-861-7700
Dale Menke, prin. Fax 861-7717

Allied College - South
  645 Gravois Bluffs Blvd 63026   Post-Sec.
                         800-502-2627
St. Louis College of Health Careers   Post-Sec.
  1297 N Highway Dr 63026   636-529-0000
Sanford-Brown College   Post-Sec.
  1345 Smizer Mill Rd 63026   636-349-4900

Festus, Jefferson, Pop. 9,938
Festus R-VI SD   2,800/K-12
  1515 Midmeadow Ln 63028   636-937-4920
  Robert Taylor, supt.   Fax 937-8525
  www.csd.org/festus
Festus HS   800/9-12
  501 Westwind Dr 63028   636-937-5410
  Gregory Roman, prin.   Fax 937-8048
Festus MS   400/7-8
  1717 W Main St 63028   636-937-5417
  Gregory Lentz, prin.   Fax 937-4171

Jefferson County R-VII SD   700/PK-8
  1250 Dooling Hollow Rd 63028   636-937-9188
  Michael Parnell, supt.   Fax 937-9189
Danby-Rush Tower MS   300/6-8
  1250 Dooling Hollow Rd 63028   636-937-9188
  Kim Weik, prin.   Fax 937-9189

St. Pius X HS   400/9-12
  1030 Saint Pius Dr 63028   636-931-7488
  Norma Overberg, prin.   Fax 931-7487

Florissant, Saint Louis, Pop. 51,018
Ferguson-Florissant R-II SD   13,500/PK-12
  1005 Waterford Dr 63033   314-506-9000
  Jeffrey Spiegel, supt.   Fax 506-9010
  www.fergflor.org/
Cross Keys MS   900/7-8
  14205 Cougar Dr 63033   314-506-9700
  David Watkins, prin.   Fax 506-9701
McCluer HS   1,600/9-12
  1896 S New Florissant Rd 63031   314-506-9400
  Nicole Whitesell, prin.   Fax 506-9401
McCluer North HS   1,500/9-12
  705 Waterford Dr 63033   314-506-9200
  Dr. Hopper, prin.   Fax 506-9201
Other Schools – See Berkeley, Saint Louis

Hazelwood SD   18,000/K-12
  15955 New Halls Ferry Rd 63031   314-953-5000
  Chris L. Wright Ph.D., supt.   Fax 953-5085
  www.hazelwoodschools.org/
Hazelwood Central HS   2,500/9-12
  15875 New Halls Ferry Rd 63031   314-953-5400
  Frank Smith, prin.   Fax 953-5413
Hazelwood MS   1,100/7-8
  1605 Shackelford Rd 63031   314-953-5500
  Darrell Strong, prin.   Fax 953-5513
Other Schools – See Hazelwood, Saint Louis

Special SD of St. Louis County
  Supt. — See Saint Louis
North County Technical S   Vo/Tech
  1700 Derhake Rd 63033   314-989-7600
  Mike Powers, prin.   Fax 989-7665

Missouri Sch. of Barbering & Hairstyling   Post-Sec.
  1125 N US Highway 67 63031   314-839-0310
North County Christian S   500/PK-12
  845 Dunn Rd 63031   314-972-6227
  Ken Rankin, admin.   Fax 972-6220
St. Louis Christian College   Post-Sec.
  1360 Grandview Dr 63033   314-837-6777

Fordland, Webster, Pop. 720
Fordland R-III SD   600/PK-12
  PO Box 55 65652   417-738-2296
  William H. Marcus, supt.   Fax 767-4483
  www.fordland.k12.mo.us
Fordland HS   200/9-12
  PO Box 118 65652   417-738-2212
  Brian Wilson, prin.   Fax 767-2240
Fordland MS   200/6-8
  PO Box 55 65652   417-738-2119
  Judy Kindall, prin.   Fax 767-4483

Forsyth, Taney, Pop. 1,659
Forsyth R-III SD   1,100/PK-12
  PO Box 187 65653   417-546-6384
  Dr. Tom Darnell, supt.   Fax 546-2204
  www.forsythr3.k12.mo.us/
Forsyth HS   400/9-12
  PO Box 187 65653   417-546-6383
  Bruce Simpson, prin.   Fax 546-5987
Forsyth MS   400/5-8
  PO Box 187 65653   417-546-6382
  Ben Bilyeu, prin.   Fax 546-6943

Fort Leonard Wood, Pulaski, Pop. 15,863
Waynesville R-VI SD
  Supt. — See Waynesville
Wood MS   600/6-8
  7076 Pulaski Ave 65473   573-329-2311
  Jess Grizzell, prin.   Fax 329-2827

Lincoln University   Post-Sec.
  Truman Educ Center Bldg 499 65473 573-681-5421

Fredericktown, Madison, Pop. 3,854
Fredericktown R-I SD   2,000/PK-12
  803 E Highway 72 63645   573-783-2570
  Dr. Kelly Burlison, supt.   Fax 783-7045
  fredericktown.k12.mo.us/
Fredericktown HS   700/9-12
  805 E Highway 72 63645   573-783-3628
  John K. Gibbs, prin.   Fax 783-8224
Fredericktown MS   500/6-8
  501 Park Dr 63645   573-783-6555
  Chadd Starkey, prin.   Fax 783-8079

Fulton, Callaway, Pop. 12,315
Fulton SD 58   2,300/PK-12
  2 Hornet Dr 65251   573-642-2206
  Dr. Mark Enderle, supt.   Fax 642-1444
  www.fulton.k12.mo.us/
Fulton HS   800/9-12
  1 Hornet Dr 65251   573-642-2023
  Teresa Arms, prin.   Fax 592-7401
Fulton MS   600/6-8
  403 E 10th St 65251   573-642-7221
  Jeffrey Wright, prin.   Fax 642-6282

Missouri School for the Deaf   Post-Sec.
  505 E 5th St 65251   573-592-4000
Westminister College   Post-Sec.
  501 Westminster Ave 65251   573-642-3361
William Woods University   Post-Sec.
  1 University Ave 65251   573-642-2251

Gainesville, Ozark, Pop. 610
Gainesville R-V SD   700/PK-12
  HC 3 Box 170 65655   417-679-4260
  Bill Looney, supt.   Fax 679-4270
Gainesville HS   400/7-12
  160 Bulldog Dr 65655   417-679-4200
  Joe Donley, prin.   Fax 679-4270

Galena, Stone, Pop. 469
Galena R-II SD   500/PK-12
  PO Box 286 65656   417-357-6027
  Allen Meyer, supt.   Fax 357-8444
Galena JSHS   200/7-12
  PO Box 286 65656   417-357-6618
  Gary Hill, prin.   Fax 357-8444

Gallatin, Daviess, Pop. 1,754
Gallatin R-V SD   600/PK-12
  602 S Olive St 64640   660-663-2171
  James Ruse, supt.   Fax 663-2559
  gallatin.k12.mo.us
Gallatin JSHS   300/7-12
  602 S Olive St 64640   660-663-2171
  Charles Burrell, prin.   Fax 663-2559

Galt, Grundy, Pop. 274
Grundy County R-V SD   200/K-12
  PO Box 6 64641   660-673-6511
  Robert Deaver, supt.   Fax 673-6523
Grundy County JSHS   100/7-12
  PO Box 6 64641   660-673-6511
  Randy Huffman, prin.   Fax 673-6523

Garden City, Cass, Pop. 1,627

Training Center Christian S   100/PK-12
  PO Box 200 64747   816-773-8367
  Judy Williams, admin.   Fax 862-6052

Gideon, New Madrid, Pop. 1,059
Gideon SD 37   400/K-12
  PO Box 227 63848   573-448-3911
  Dr. David Hollingshead, supt.   Fax 448-5197
  gideon.k12.mo.us/
Gideon JSHS   200/7-12
  PO Box 227 63848   573-448-3471
  Keenan Buchanan, prin.   Fax 448-3868

Gilman City, Daviess, Pop. 379
Gilman City R-IV SD   200/PK-12
  PO Box 45 64642   660-876-5221
  David Cross, supt.   Fax 876-5553
Gilman City JSHS   100/7-12
  PO Box 45 64642   660-876-5221
  Jason Tolen, prin.   Fax 876-5553

Gladstone, Clay, Pop. 27,089

Paris II Educational Center   Post-Sec.
  6840 N Oak Trfy 64118   816-468-6666

Glasgow, Howard, Pop. 1,212
Howard County R-II SD   300/PK-12
  860 Randolph St 65254   660-338-2012
  Michael Reynolds, supt.   Fax 338-2610
  www.glasgow.k12.mo.us/
Glasgow JSHS   200/7-12
  860 Randolph St 65254   660-338-2012
  Michael Reynolds, prin.   Fax 338-2610

Glencoe, Saint Louis
Rockwood R-VI SD
  Supt. — See Eureka
LaSalle Springs MS   800/6-8
  3300 Highway 109 63038   636-938-2425
  Scott Francin, prin.   Fax 938-2434
Rockwood Valley MS   800/6-8
  1220 Babler Park Dr 63038   636-458-7324
  Katie Reboulet, prin.   Fax 458-7325
Wildwood MS   800/6-8
  17401 Manchester Rd 63038   636-458-7360
  Dr. Gregory Batenhorst, prin.   Fax 458-7372

Golden City, Barton, Pop. 915
Golden City R-III SD   300/PK-12
  1208 Walnut St 64748   417-537-4900
  Susan Whittle, supt.   Fax 537-8717
Golden City JSHS   100/7-12
  1208 Walnut St 64748   417-537-8311
  Larry Malle, prin.   Fax 537-8717

Gower, Buchanan, Pop. 1,431
East Buchanan County C-1 SD   700/K-12
  100 Smith St 64454   816-424-6466
  Charles Nance, supt.   Fax 424-3511
  www.ebsk12.com/
East Buchanan HS   200/9-12
  100 Smith St 64454   816-424-6460
  Scott Antle, prin.   Fax 424-6410
Other Schools – See Easton

Graham, Nodaway, Pop. 189
Nodaway-Holt R-VII SD   300/PK-12
  318 S Taylor St 64455   660-939-2137
  Bruce Skoglund, supt.   Fax 939-2200
  www.asde.com/~nodholt/
Nodaway-Holt HS   100/7-12
  318 S Taylor St 64455   660-939-2135
  Corbet Wilson, prin.   Fax 939-2201

Grain Valley, Jackson, Pop. 6,991
Grain Valley R-V SD   3,100/K-12
  PO Box 304 64029   816-847-5006
  Dr. Chris Small, supt.   Fax 229-4831
  www.grainvalley.k12.mo.us
Grain Valley HS   600/9-12
  PO Box 304 64029   816-847-5000
  Mike Witt, prin.   Fax 847-5002
Grain Valley MS   500/6-8
  PO Box 304 64029   816-229-3499
  Theresa Nelson, prin.   Fax 847-5017

Granby, Newton, Pop. 2,164
East Newton County R-VI SD   1,600/K-12
  22808 E Highway 86 64844   417-472-6231
  Tanya Vest, supt.   Fax 472-3500
  www.enr6.k12.mo.us
East Newton HS   500/9-12
  22876 E Highway 86 64844   417-472-6238
  Todd McCrackin, prin.   Fax 472-7129

Grandview, Jackson, Pop. 25,210
Grandview C-4 SD   3,800/PK-12
  724 Main St 64030   816-316-5000
  Dr. John Martin, supt.   Fax 316-5050
  www.csd4.k12.mo.us
Grandview HS   1,300/9-12
  2300 High Grove Rd 64030   816-316-5800
  Ted Vernon, prin.   Fax 316-5898
Grandview MS   600/6-8
  12650 Manchester Ave 64030   816-316-5600
  Cynthia Johnson, prin.   Fax 316-5699
Other Schools – See Kansas City

Grandview Christian S   200/K-12
  12340 Grandview Rd 64030   816-767-8630
  Bill Tudor, prin.   Fax 763-5029
House of Heavilin Beauty College   Post-Sec.
  12020 Blue Ridge Ext 64030   816-767-8000

Grant City, Worth, Pop. 871
Worth County R-III SD   400/K-12
  RR 3 Box 107 64456   660-564-3389
  Dr. Linda Gray Smith, supt.   Fax 564-2193
  wc.k12.mo.us/index.html
Worth County JSHS   200/7-12
  RR 3 Box 107 64456   660-564-2218
  Dale Healy, prin.   Fax 564-2193

Green City, Sullivan, Pop. 668
Green City R-I SD   400/PK-12
  301 Northeast St 63545   660-874-4127
  Charlotte Baker, supt.   Fax 874-4515
  www.greencity.k12.mo.us/
Green City JSHS   200/7-12
  301 Northeast St 63545   660-874-4127
  Donnie Campbell, prin.   Fax 874-5010

Greenfield, Dade, Pop. 1,319
Greenfield R-IV SD   500/K-12
  410 College St 65661   417-637-5321
  David Hardage, supt.   Fax 637-5805
  greenfield.k12.mo.us/
Greenfield JSHS   200/7-12
  410 College St 65661   417-637-5328
  Michael Redlich, prin.   Fax 637-5805

Green Ridge, Pettis, Pop. 436
Green Ridge R-VIII SD   400/K-12
  PO Box 70 65332   660-527-3315
  Tim Lenz, supt.   Fax 527-3299
  greenridge.k12.mo.us
Green Ridge JSHS   200/7-12
  PO Box 70 65332   660-527-3315
  Ty Payne, prin.   Fax 527-3299

Greenville, Wayne, Pop. 444
Greenville R-II SD   900/PK-12
  PO Box 320 63944   573-224-3844
  Jim Morrison, supt.   Fax 224-3412
Greenville HS   300/9-12
  PO Box 320 63944   573-224-3618
  Todd Porter, prin.   Fax 224-3580
Greenville JHS   200/7-8
  PO Box 320 63944   573-224-3833
  Rick Rainwater, prin.   Fax 224-3580

Hale, Carroll, Pop. 471
Hale R-I SD   200/PK-12
  PO Box 248 64643   660-565-2417
  Michael Spears, supt.   Fax 565-2418
Hale JSHS   100/7-12
  PO Box 248 64643   660-565-2417
  Michael Spears, prin.   Fax 565-2418

Half Way, Polk, Pop. 188
Halfway R-III SD   300/K-12
  2150 Highway 32 65663   417-445-2351
  Jon Oetinger, supt.   Fax 445-2026
  www.halfwayschools.org
Halfway JSHS   100/7-12
  2150 Highway 32 65663   417-445-2211
  Shane Dublin, prin.   Fax 445-2026

Hallsville, Boone, Pop. 988
Hallsville R-IV SD   1,200/PK-12
  421 E Highway 124 65255   573-696-5512
  Thomas Baugh, supt.   Fax 696-3606
  hallsville.schools.missouri.org
Hallsville HS   300/9-12
  421 E Highway 124 65255   573-696-5512
  Paul Dodson, prin.   Fax 696-1482

Hallsville MS | 400/5-8
421 E Highway 124 65255 | 573-696-5512
Christopher Crane, prin. | Fax 696-7238

Hamilton, Caldwell, Pop. 1,820
Hamilton R-II SD | 700/PK-12
PO Box 128 64644 | 816-583-2134
Stephen Yost, supt. | Fax 583-2139
Hamilton MS | 200/5-8
PO Box 128 64644 | 816-583-2173
Troy Ford, prin. | Fax 583-2686
Penney HS | 300/9-12
PO Box 128 64644 | 816-583-2136
Tim Schieber, prin. | Fax 583-2319

Hannibal, Marion, Pop. 17,577
Hannibal SD 60 | 3,600/PK-12
4650 McMasters Ave 63401 | 573-221-1258
Dr. Jill Janes, supt. | Fax 221-2994
www.hannibal.k12.mo.us
Hannibal Career & Technical Center | Vo/Tech
4550 McMasters Ave 63401 | 573-221-4430
Roger McGregor, dir. | Fax 221-7971
Hannibal HS | 1,100/9-12
4500 Mcmasters Ave 63401 | 573-221-2733
Darin Powell, prin. | Fax 221-9511
Hannibal MS | 900/6-8
4700 Mcmasters Ave 63401 | 573-221-5840
Kenneth Treaster, prin. | Fax 221-7779

Hannibal Area Voc. Technical School | Post-Sec.
4550 McMasters Ave 63401 | 573-221-4430
Hannibal-LaGrange College | Post-Sec.
2800 Palmyra Rd 63401 | 573-221-3675

Hardin, Ray, Pop. 602
Hardin-Central C-2 SD | 200/K-12
PO Box 548 64035 | 660-398-4394
Steven Andes, supt. | Fax 398-4396
www.hardincentral.k12.mo.us/phpnuke/
Hardin-Central JSHS | 100/7-12
PO Box 548 64035 | 660-398-4394
Dean Hays, prin. | Fax 398-4396

Harrisburg, Boone, Pop. 187
Harrisburg R-VIII SD | 600/K-12
1000 S Harris 65256 | 573-875-5604
Richard K. Davis, supt. | Fax 875-8877
harrisburg.k12.mo.us
Harrisburg JSHS | 300/7-12
801 S Harris St 65256 | 573-875-5602
Janice Rehak, prin. | Fax 443-1559

Harrisonville, Cass, Pop. 9,418
Harrisonville R-IX SD | 2,600/PK-12
503 S Lexington St 64701 | 816-380-2727
Todd E. White, supt. | Fax 380-3134
www.harrisonvilleschools.org/
Cass Career Center | Vo/Tech
1600 E Elm St 64701 | 816-380-3253
James Spencer, dir. | Fax 380-4534
Harrisonville HS | 800/9-12
1504 E Elm St 64701 | 816-380-3273
Kelly Harris, prin. | Fax 380-5853
Harrisonville MS | 500/6-8
601 S Highland Dr 64701 | 816-380-7654
Debra Schuler, prin. | Fax 884-5733

Harrisonville Christian S West Campus | 100/5-8
1202 S Commercial St 64701 | 816-380-6499
Al Sancken, admin. | Fax 380-6489

Hartville, Wright, Pop. 602
Hartville R-II SD | 800/PK-12
PO Box 460 65667 | 417-741-7676
John Link, supt. | Fax 741-7746
schoolweb.missouri.edu/hartville.k12.mo.us/
Hartville JSHS | 400/7-12
PO Box 460 65667 | 417-741-7676
Scott Keith, prin. | Fax 741-7746

Hayti, Pemiscot, Pop. 3,130
Hayti R-II SD | 900/K-12
PO Box 469 63851 | 573-359-6500
Thomas Tucker, supt. | Fax 359-6502
www.edline.net/pages/hhs
Hayti HS | 400/7-12
PO Box 469 63851 | 573-359-6503
David Gilmore, prin. | Fax 359-6504

Pemiscot County Special SD | 573-359-0021
1317 State Highway 84 63851 | Fax 359-6525
Sandra Manley, supt.
Pemiscot County Vocational S | Vo/Tech
1317 State Highway 84 63851 | 573-359-2601
James White, dir. | Fax 359-1317

Hazelwood, Saint Louis, Pop. 25,848
Hazelwood SD
Supt. — See Florissant
Hazelwood West HS | 1,700/9-12
1 Wildcat Ln 63042 | 314-953-5800
Ingrid Clark-Jackson, prin. | Fax 953-5813
Hazelwood West MS | 7-8
1 Wildcat Ln 63042 | 314-953-5800
Ingrid Clark-Jackson, prin. | Fax 953-5813

Sanford-Brown College | Post-Sec.
75 Village Square Shop Ctr 63042 | 314-731-5200

Herculaneum, Jefferson, Pop. 3,162
Dunklin R-V SD | 1,400/PK-12
PO Box 306 63048 | 636-479-5200
Dr. Victor Buehler, supt. | Fax 479-6208
www.dunklin.k12.mo.us/
Herculaneum HS | 500/9-12
1 Blackcat Dr 63048 | 636-479-5200
Doug Lawyer, prin. | Fax 479-4479

Senn-Thomas MS | 400/5-8
200 Senn Tomas Dr 63048 | 636-479-5200
D.J. Goodwin, prin. | Fax 479-7219

Hermann, Gasconade, Pop. 2,698
Gasconade County R-I SD | 1,100/K-12
164 State Highway 100 W 65041 | 573-486-2116
Mark Leech, supt. | Fax 486-3032
www.hermann.k12.mo.us
Hermann HS | 400/9-12
164 State Highway 100 W 65041 | 573-486-5425
Gary Menke, prin. | Fax 486-3058
Hermann MS | 400/4-8
164 State Highway 100 W 65041 | 573-486-3121
Mark Brooks, prin. | Fax 486-5106

Hermitage, Hickory, Pop. 493
Hermitage R-IV SD | 300/K-12
PO Box 327 65668 | 417-745-6418
Shelly Aubuchon, supt. | Fax 745-6475
Hermitage HS | 100/9-12
PO Box 327 65668 | 417-745-6417
Ed Vest, prin. | Fax 745-6475
Hermitage MS | 50/7-8
PO Box 327 65668 | 417-745-6417
Ed Vest, prin. | Fax 745-6475

Higbee, Randolph, Pop. 642
Higbee R-VIII SD | 200/K-12
PO Box 128 65257 | 660-456-7277
Ted Rathburn, supt. | Fax 456-7278
Higbee JSHS | 100/7-12
PO Box 128 65257 | 660-456-7206
Karl Jansen, prin. | Fax 456-7207

Higginsville, Lafayette, Pop. 4,655
Lafayette County C-1 SD | 1,100/PK-12
805 W 31st St 64037 | 660-584-3631
Donald Quick, supt. | Fax 584-2622
huskers.k12.mo.us
Lafayette County HS | 400/9-12
807a W 31st St 64037 | 660-584-3661
Joseph Mintner, prin. | Fax 584-8666
Lafayette County MS | 300/6-8
807b W 31st St 64037 | 660-584-7161
Ray Sutherland, prin. | Fax 584-8666

High Ridge, Jefferson, Pop. 4,423
Northwest R-I SD | 7,400/K-12
2843 Community Ln 63049 | 636-677-3473
Dr. John Urkevich, supt. | Fax 677-5480
www.nwr1.k12.mo.us/
Other Schools – See Cedar Hill, House Springs

Hillsboro, Jefferson, Pop. 1,680
Grandview R-II SD | 900/K-12
11470 Highway C 63050 | 636-944-3941
Dr. Michael Brown, supt. | Fax 944-5239
schoolweb.missouri.edu/grandviewr2
Grandview HS | 300/9-12
11470 Highway C 63050 | 636-944-3390
Maurice Creason, prin. | Fax 944-3515
Grandview MS | 200/6-8
11470 Highway C 63050 | 636-944-3931
James Keeling, prin. | Fax 944-5239

Hillsboro R-III SD | 3,600/K-12
20 Hawk Dr 63050 | 636-789-0060
Dr. Shelton Smith, supt. | Fax 789-3216
www.hillsboro.k12.mo.us/
Hillsboro HS | 1,100/9-12
123 Leon Hall Pkwy 63050 | 636-789-0010
Cheryl Aylesworth, prin. | Fax 789-3211
Hillsboro JHS | 600/7-8
12 Hawk Dr 63050 | 636-789-0020
Terry Edwards, prin. | Fax 789-3212

Christian Outreach S | 100/PK-12
4450 Outreach Dr 63050 | 636-789-3411
John Speropoulos, prin. | Fax 789-2585
Jefferson College | Post-Sec.
1000 Viking Dr 63050 | 636-797-3000

Holcomb, Dunklin, Pop. 693
Holcomb R-III SD | 600/PK-12
PO Box 190 63852 | 573-792-3113
James Gore, supt. | Fax 792-3118
holcomb.k12.mo.us/
Holcomb JSHS | 200/7-12
PO Box 190 63852 | 573-792-3362
Scottie Blackburn, prin. | Fax 792-3631

Holden, Johnson, Pop. 2,555
Holden R-III SD | 1,400/PK-12
1612 S Main St 64040 | 816-732-5568
Scott Slava, supt. | Fax 732-4336
schoolweb.missouri.edu/holden.k12.mo.us/
Holden HS | 400/9-12
1901 S Main St 64040 | 816-732-5523
Matt Lindsey, prin. | Fax 732-4142
Holden MS | 400/6-8
301 Eagle Dr 64040 | 816-732-4125
Greg Montgomery, prin. | Fax 732-2009

Hollister, Taney, Pop. 3,884
Hollister R-V SD | 1,200/PK-12
1798 State Highway BB 65672 | 417-332-0130
Brett Reese, supt. | Fax 334-2663
www.hollister.k12.mo.us/
Hollister HS | 300/9-12
2112 State Highway BB 65672 | 417-334-6119
Dan Vandiver, prin. | Fax 334-2663
Hollister MS | 400/5-8
1798 State Highway BB 65672 | 417-337-9313
Craig Carson, prin. | Fax 336-5263

New Life Academy | 100/K-12
PO Box 380 65673 | 417-334-7084
Dr. Neil Smith, hdmstr. | Fax 334-1794

Hopkins, Nodaway, Pop. 568
North Nodaway County R-VI SD | 300/PK-12
PO Box 260 64461 | 660-778-3411
Joan Bolon, supt. | Fax 778-3210
www.nnr6.k12.mo.us/
North Nodaway County JSHS | 100/6-12
PO Box 260 64461 | 660-778-3315
Charles McKee, prin. | Fax 778-3210

Hornersville, Dunklin, Pop. 675
Senath-Hornersville C-8 SD
Supt. — See Senath
Senath-Hornersville MS | 300/5-8
601 School St 63855 | 573-737-2455
Jason Skelton, prin. | Fax 737-2456

House Springs, Jefferson
Northwest R-I SD
Supt. — See High Ridge
Northwest Valley MS | 1,300/7-8
PO Box 500 63051 | 636-671-3470
Kevin Carl, prin. | Fax 671-1535

Houston, Texas, Pop. 1,969
Houston R-I SD | 1,100/PK-12
423 W Pine St 65483 | 417-967-3024
Clinton Waters, supt. | Fax 967-4887
www.houston.k12.mo.us
Houston HS | 400/9-12
423 W Pine St 65483 | 417-967-3024
Audrey Kell, prin. | Fax 967-3669
Houston MS | 200/6-8
423 W Pine St 65483 | 417-967-3024
Charlie Malam, prin. | Fax 967-5481

Hughesville, Pettis, Pop. 176
Pettis County R-V SD | 400/K-12
16215 Highway H 65334 | 660-827-0772
Amy Fagg, supt. | Fax 827-0772
Northwest JSHS | 200/7-12
16215 Highway H 65334 | 660-827-0774
Brett Hieronymus, prin. | Fax 827-0772

Humansville, Polk, Pop. 970
Humansville R-IV SD | 400/K-12
300 N Oak St 65674 | 417-754-2535
Shannon Vanderburg, supt. | Fax 754-8565
www.humansville.k12.mo.us/
Humansville HS | 200/7-12
300 N Oak St 65674 | 417-754-2219
Tammy Highley, prin. | Fax 754-8565

Hume, Bates, Pop. 344
Hume R-VIII SD | 100/PK-12
PO Box 402 64752 | 660-643-7411
Ryan Huff, supt. | Fax 643-7506
Hume JSHS | 100/6-12
PO Box 402 64752 | 660-643-7411
Ryan Huff, prin. | Fax 643-7506

Huntsville, Randolph, Pop. 1,599
Westran R-I SD | 800/PK-12
210 W Depot St 65259 | 660-277-4429
Kelly Shelby, supt. | Fax 277-4420
westran.k12.mo.us/
Westran HS | 200/9-12
601 Hornet Ln 65259 | 660-277-4415
Mike Nagel, prin. | Fax 277-4644
Other Schools – See Clifton Hill

Hurley, Stone, Pop. 163
Hurley R-I SD | 300/K-12
PO Box 248 65675 | 417-369-3271
Doug Arnold, supt. | Fax 369-2212
schoolweb.missouri.edu/hurley.k12.mo.us/
Hurley JSHS | 100/7-12
PO Box 248 65675 | 417-369-3271
Lisa May, prin. | Fax 369-2212

Iberia, Miller, Pop. 661
Iberia R-V SD | 800/PK-12
PO Box 156 65486 | 573-793-6818
James M. McLeod, supt. | Fax 793-6821
www.iberia.k12.mo.us
Iberia HS | 300/7-12
PO Box 156 65486 | 573-793-2228
Don Fields, prin. | Fax 793-2946

PowerHouse Christian Academy | 50/PK-12
PO Box 95 65486 | 573-793-3325
Thomas Nelson, admin.

Imperial, Jefferson, Pop. 4,156
Fox C-6 SD
Supt. — See Arnold
Seckman HS | 1,600/9-12
2800 Seckman Rd 63052 | 636-282-1485
Don Grimshaw, prin. | Fax 282-5177
Seckman MS | 800/7-8
2840 Seckman Rd 63052 | 636-296-5707
David R. Black, prin. | Fax 296-5707

Windsor C-1 SD | 2,500/PK-12
6208 US Highway 61/67 63052 | 636-464-4400
Dr. Rudy Duran, supt. | Fax 464-4454
www.windsor.k12.mo.us/district/
Windsor HS | 900/9-12
6208 US Highway 61/67 63052 | 636-464-4429
Michael Steinkamp, prin. | Fax 464-4456
Windsor MS | 800/6-8
6208 US Highway 61/67 63052 | 636-464-4417
Ernie Perkins, prin. | Fax 464-4473

Independence, Jackson, Pop. 112,079
Fort Osage R-I SD | 4,700/K-12
2101 N Twyman Rd 64058 | 816-650-7000
Larry E. Ewing, supt. | Fax 650-3888
www.fortosage.net
Career & Technology Center | Vo/Tech
2101 N Twyman Rd 64058 | 816-650-7180
Mike Pantleo, prin. | Fax 650-7195

Ft. Osage HS 1,400/9-12
2101 N Twyman Rd 64058 816-650-7030
Steven Scott, prin. Fax 650-7088
Osage Trail MS 800/7-8
2101 N Twyman Rd 64058 816-650-7151
Karen Blessing, prin. Fax 650-7152

Independence SD 30 13,800/PK-12
218 N Pleasant St 64050 816-521-2700
Dr. Jim Hinson, supt. Fax 521-2999
www.indep.k12.mo.us
Bingham MS 1,800/6-8
1716 S Speck Rd 64057 816-796-4850
Charles Garner, prin. Fax 796-4880
Bridger MS 1,800/6-8
18200 E State Route 78 64057 816-796-4800
Belinda Woodson, prin. Fax 796-4812
Chrisman HS 1,700/9-12
1223 N Noland Rd 64050 816-521-2720
Jason Dial, prin. Fax 521-2729
Pioneer MS 1,800/6-8
1656 S Speck Rd 64057 816-796-4885
Elizabeth Savidge, prin. Fax 796-4899
Truman HS 1,700/9-12
3301 S Noland Rd 64055 816-521-2710
Kristel Barr, prin. Fax 521-2913

Kansas City SD 33
Supt. — See Kansas City
Nowlin MS 700/6-8
2800 S Hardy Ave 64052 816-418-4125
Belinda Woodson, prin. Fax 418-4145
Van Horn HS 1,000/9-12
1109 S Arlington Ave 64053 816-418-4000
Dr. Mary Long, prin. Fax 418-4021

Blur River Community College Post-Sec.
20301 E State Route 78 64057 816-220-6550
Englewood Christian Academy 300/PK-12
10628 E Winner Rd 64052 816-254-8313
Brian A. Ross, admin. Fax 254-7065
Graceland University Post-Sec.
1401 W Truman Rd 64050 816-833-0524
Independence College of Cosmetology Post-Sec.
815 W 23rd St S 64055 816-252-4247
National American University Post-Sec.
3620 Arrowhead Ave 64057 816-353-4554
St. Mary Bundschu Memorial HS 200/9-12
622 N Main St 64050 816-252-8733
Trudy Jonas, prin. Fax 252-2780

Ironton, Iron, Pop. 1,377
Arcadia Valley R-II SD 1,100/PK-12
750 Park Dr 63650 573-546-9700
Clifford Carver, supt. Fax 546-7314
www.av.k12.mo.us
Arcadia Valley Career Tech Vo/Tech
650 Park Dr 63650 573-546-9700
Dave Ruhman, prin. Fax 546-6956
Arcadia Valley HS 400/9-12
520 Park Dr 63650 573-546-9700
Lance Sprenkel, prin. Fax 546-3934
Arcadia Valley MS 400/5-8
550 Park Dr 63650 573-546-9700
Eddie Dunivan, prin. Fax 546-7304

Jackson, Cape Girardeau, Pop. 12,477
Jackson R-II SD 4,600/K-12
614 E Adams St 63755 573-243-9501
Ron Anderson, supt. Fax 243-9503
www.jackson.k12.mo.us
Hawkins JHS 800/8-9
210 N West Ln 63755 573-243-9533
Cory Crosnoe, prin. Fax 243-9584
Jackson SHS 1,200/10-12
315 S Missouri St 63755 573-243-9513
Richard McClard, prin. Fax 243-9524

Saxony Lutheran HS 100/9-12
2004 Saxony Ln 63755 573-204-7555
Fax 204-7445

Jameson, Daviess, Pop. 121
North Daviess R-III SD 100/PK-12
413 E 2nd St 64647 660-828-4123
Todd Willhite, supt. Fax 828-4122
www.ndaviess.k12.mo.us
North Daviess JSHS 100/7-12
413 E 2nd St 64647 660-828-4123
Kristi Critten, prin. Fax 828-4122

Jamesport, Daviess, Pop. 507
Tri-County R-VII SD 200/PK-12
904 W Auberry Grv 64648 660-684-6118
Mary Kish, supt. Fax 684-6218
Tri-County JSHS 100/7-12
904 W Auberry Grv 64648 660-684-6116
Robert Evans, prin. Fax 684-6218

Jamestown, Moniteau, Pop. 391
Moniteau County C-1 SD 200/K-12
222 School St 65046 660-849-2141
James Deeken, supt. Fax 849-2600
Moniteau County JSHS 100/7-12
222 School St 65046 660-849-2141
Kevin Kohler, prin. Fax 849-2600

Jasper, Jasper, Pop. 1,034
Jasper County R-V SD 500/K-12
201 W Mercer St 64755 417-394-2416
Kathy Fall, supt. Fax 394-2394
www.jasper.k12.mo.us/
Jasper County JSHS 300/7-12
201 W Mercer St 64755 417-394-2511
Bill Hodge, prin. Fax 394-2394

Jefferson City, Cole, Pop. 37,550
Blair Oaks R-II SD 600/K-12
6124 Falcon Ln 65101 573-636-2020
Dr. James Jones, supt. Fax 636-2202
www.blairoaks.k12.mo.us
Blair Oaks JSHS 400/7-12
6124 Falcon Ln 65101 573-635-8514
Vince Matlick, prin. Fax 635-6327

Jefferson City SD 8,200/PK-12
315 E Dunklin St 65101 573-659-3000
Bert Kimble, supt. Fax 659-3044
www.jcps.k12.mo.us
Jefferson City HS 1,800/10-12
609 Union St 65101 573-659-3050
Richard Pemberton, prin. Fax 659-3153
Jefferson MS 1,000/6-8
1201 Fairgrounds Rd 65109 573-659-3250
Roberta Hubbs, prin. Fax 659-3259
Lewis and Clark MS 1,000/6-8
325 Lewis and Clark Dr 65101 573-659-3200
Robert Steffes, prin. Fax 659-3209
Nichols Career Center Vo/Tech
605 Union St 65101 573-659-3100
Mike Kriegshauser, prin. Fax 659-3154
Simonsen Ninth Grade Center 700/9-9
501 E Miller St 65101 573-659-3125
Rhonda Key, prin. Fax 659-7362

Helias HS 900/9-12
1305 Swifts Hwy 65109 573-635-6139
Rev. Jean Dietrich, prin. Fax 635-5615
Lincoln University Post-Sec.
820 Chestnut St 65101 573-681-5000
Merrell Univ of Beauty Arts & Science Post-Sec.
1101R SW Boulevard 65109 573-635-4433
Metro Business College Post-Sec.
1407 Southwest Blvd 65109 573-635-6600
Nichols Career Center Post-Sec.
605 Union St 65101 573-659-3100

Jennings, Saint Louis, Pop. 15,160
Jennings SD 3,300/PK-12
2559 Dorwood Dr 63136 314-653-8000
Dr. Terry Stewart, supt. Fax 653-8030
www.jenningsk12.net/index.html
Jennings HS 800/9-12
8850 Cozens Ave 63136 314-653-8100
Clarence Holman, prin. Fax 653-8102
Jennings JHS 500/7-8
8831 Cozens Ave 63136 314-653-8150
Sam Gilkey, prin. Fax 653-8168

Joplin, Jasper, Pop. 46,373
Joplin R-VIII SD 7,400/PK-12
PO Box 128 64802 417-625-5200
Dr. Jim Simpson, supt. Fax 625-5210
www.joplin.k12.mo.us
Franklin Tech S Vo/Tech
PO Box 128 64802 417-625-5260
David Rockers, dir. Fax 625-5266
Joplin HS 2,000/9-12
PO Box 128 64802 417-625-5230
Dr. Kerry Sachetta, prin. Fax 625-5238
Memorial MS 800/6-8
PO Box 128 64802 417-625-5250
Stephen Gilbreth, prin. Fax 625-5256
North MS 500/6-8
PO Box 128 64802 417-625-5270
Barbara D. Cox, prin. Fax 625-5273
South MS 500/6-8
PO Box 128 64802 417-625-5280
Ron Mitchell, prin. Fax 625-5284

Class Act I School of Cosmetology Post-Sec.
512 Main St 64801 417-781-7070
College Heights Christian S 600/PK-12
4311 Newman Rd 64801 417-782-4114
Dirk Pearce, prin. Fax 659-9092
Franklin Technology - MSSU Post-Sec.
3950 Newman Rd 64801 417-659-4400
Jefferson Independent Day S 300/PK-12
3401 Newman Rd 64801 417-781-5124
Leonard Kupersmith, prin. Fax 781-1949
McAuley Catholic HS 100/9-12
930 S Pearl Ave 64801 417-624-9320
Gene Koester, prin. Fax 626-8334
Messenger College Post-Sec.
300 E 50th St 64804 417-624-7070
Missouri Southern State University Post-Sec.
3950 Newman Rd 64801 417-625-9300
New Dimensions School of Hair Design Post-Sec.
705 Illinois Ave Ste 12 64801 417-782-2875
Ozark Christian College Post-Sec.
1111 N Main St 64801 417-624-2518
St. John's Regional Medical Center Post-Sec.
2727 Mc Clelland Blvd 64804 417-781-2727
St. Peter MS 100/6-8
802 Byers Ave 64801 417-624-5605
Greg Emory, prin. Fax 624-6254
Vatterott College Post-Sec.
809 Illinois Ave 64801 417-781-5633
Wichita Technical Institute Post-Sec.
1531 E 32nd St 64804 417-206-9115

Kahoka, Clark, Pop. 2,218
Clark County R-I SD 1,100/PK-12
427 W Chestnut St 63445 660-727-2377
Dr. Randy Sheriff, supt. Fax 727-2035
Clark County HS 400/9-12
680 E Main St 63445 660-727-2205
Ritchie Kracht, prin. Fax 727-2245
Clark County MS 300/6-8
384 N Jefferson St 63445 660-727-3319
Jason Church, prin. Fax 727-2035

Shiloh Christian S 50/K-12
RR 1 Box 68A 63445 573-853-4346
Christina Shoup, prin. Fax 588-7730

Kaiser, Miller, Pop. 485
School of the Osage R-II SD
Supt. — See Lake Ozark
Osage HS 500/9-12
PO Box 198 65047 573-348-0115
Dr. Mark Fickie, prin. Fax 348-9774

Kansas City, Jackson, Pop. 442,768
Center SD 58 2,700/PK-12
8701 Holmes Rd 64131 816-349-3300
Dr. Robert Bartman, supt. Fax 349-3431
www.center.k12.mo.us
Center HS 800/9-12
8715 Holmes Rd 64131 816-349-3330
Harold Hawkins, prin. Fax 349-3427
Center MS 600/6-8
326 E 103rd St 64114 816-612-4000
Linda Williams, prin. Fax 612-4053

Grandview C-4 SD
Supt. — See Grandview
Martin City MS 6-8
201 E 133rd St 64145 816-316-5700
Dr. Barbara Schell, prin. Fax 316-5751

Hickman Mills C-I SD 7,200/K-12
9000 Old Santa Fe Rd 64138 816-316-7000
Dr. Marge Williams, supt. Fax 316-7020
www.hickmanmills.org
Ervin JHS 900/6-8
10530 Greenwood Rd 64134 816-316-7600
Angie McConico, prin. Fax 316-7601
Hickman Mills HS 1,200/9-12
9010 Old Santa Fe Rd 64138 816-316-7300
Bill Sculley, prin. Fax 316-8009
Ruskin HS 900/9-12
7000 E 111th St #46 64134 816-316-7400
Jim Tinsley, prin. Fax 316-7475
Smith-Hale JHS 900/6-8
8925 Longview Rd 64134 816-316-7700
Jan Davis, prin. Fax 316-7704

Kansas City SD 33 30,400/PK-12
1211 McGee St 64106 816-418-7000
Dr. Bernard Taylor, supt. Fax 418-7631
www.kcmsd.net
Central HS 1,000/9-12
3221 Indiana Ave 64128 816-418-2000
William McClendon, prin. Fax 418-2027
Central Magnet MS 500/6-8
3611 E Linwood Blvd 64128 816-418-2100
Jeanette Pointer-Shelby, prin. Fax 418-2115
Kansas City MS of the Arts 600/6-8
4848 Woodland Ave 64110 816-418-2400
Charles Dorch, prin. Fax 418-2415
King MS 500/6-8
4201 Indiana Ave 64130 816-418-2475
Archie Brown, prin. Fax 418-2480
Lincoln College Prep HS 600/9-12
2111 Woodland Ave 64108 816-418-3000
Regina Ellis, prin. Fax 418-3015
Lincoln College Prep MS 6-8
2012 E 23rd St 64127 816-418-3525
Kenneth Holstine, prin. Fax 418-3530
Manual Career & Tech Center Vo/Tech
1215 E Truman Rd 64106 816-418-5207
Tom Levin, prin. Fax 418-5215
Manual East Campus Career & Tech Center Vo/Tech
1924 Van Brunt Blvd 64127 816-418-3131
Fax 418-1389
Northeast HS 1,200/9-12
415 Van Brunt Blvd 64124 816-418-3300
Vicki Murillo, prin. Fax 418-3310
Northeast MS 800/6-8
4904 Independence Ave 64124 816-418-3400
T. Allen McClain, prin. Fax 418-3410
Paseo Academy of Performing Arts 700/9-12
4747 Flora Ave 64110 816-418-2275
Dr. Juanita Hempstead, prin. Fax 418-2300
Rogers MS 600/6-8
6400 E 23rd St 64129 816-418-4770
Arlene Penner, prin. Fax 418-4803
Southeast HS 800/9-12
3500 E Meyer Blvd 64132 816-418-1075
Fax 418-1080
Westport HS 800/9-12
315 E 39th St 64111 816-418-6100
Connie Espinoza, prin. Fax 418-6185
Westport MS 6-8
300 E 39th St 64111 816-418-6200
Derald Davis, prin. Fax 418-6262
Other Schools – See Independence

North Kansas City SD 74
Supt. — See North Kansas City
Antioch MS 900/6-8
2100 NE 65th St 64118 816-413-6200
Robert Russell, prin. Fax 413-6205
Career & Technical Education Vo/Tech
1950 NE 46th St 64116 816-413-5056
Leigh Anne Knight, dir. Fax 413-5215
Eastgate MS 700/6-8
4700 NE Parvin Rd 64117 816-413-5800
Daniel Clemens, prin. Fax 413-5805
Maple Park MS 800/6-8
5300 N Bennington Ave 64119 816-413-5700
Charlotte Sands, prin. Fax 413-5705
New Mark MS 900/6-8
515 NE 106th St 64155 816-413-6300
Robert Winter, prin. Fax 413-6305
Northgate MS 700/6-8
2117 NE 48th St 64118 816-413-6100
Steve St. Louis, prin. Fax 413-6105

Oak Park HS 1,900/9-12
825 NE 79th Ter 64118 816-413-5300
John Kreuger, prin. Fax 413-5305
Winnetonka HS 1,700/9-12
5815 NE 48th St 64119 816-413-5500
Dr. Harold Condra, prin. Fax 413-5505

Park Hill SD 9,400/K-12
7703 NW Barry Rd 64153 816-359-4000
Dr. Dennis Fisher, supt. Fax 359-4049
www.parkhill.k12.mo.us
Congress MS 800/7-8
8150 N Congress Ave 64152 816-359-4230
Dr. Timothy Todd, prin. Fax 359-4219
Lakeview MS 800/7-8
6720 NW 64th St 64151 816-359-4220
Jim Dunn, prin. Fax 359-4229
Park Hill HS 1,400/9-12
7701 NW Barry Rd 64153 816-359-4110
J Bradford Kincheloe, prin. Fax 359-4119
Park Hill South HS 1,500/9-12
4500 NW River Park Dr 64150 816-359-4120
Dale Longenecker, prin. Fax 359-4129

Raytown C-2 SD
Supt. — See Raytown
Raytown MS 1,100/6-8
4900 Pittman Rd 64133 816-268-7360
Dr. Georgetta May, prin. Fax 268-7365

ARAMARK Healthcare Support Services SW Post-Sec.
1000 Carondelet Dr 64114 816-943-2146
Archbishop O'Hara HS 600/9-12
9001 James A Reed Rd 64138 816-763-4800
Walter Bowman, prin. Fax 763-0156
Aviation Institute of Maintenance Post-Sec.
3130 Terrace St 64111 816-753-9920
Avila University Post-Sec.
11901 Wornall Rd 64145 816-942-8400
Barstow S 600/PK-12
11511 State Line Rd 64114 816-942-3255
Art Atkison, hdmstr. Fax 942-3227
Blue Ridge Christian S 300/K-12
8524 Blue Ridge Blvd 64138 816-358-0950
John Yallaly, prin. Fax 358-1138
Calvary Bible College & Theological Sem Post-Sec.
15800 Calvary Rd 64147 816-322-0110
Cleveland Chiropractic College Post-Sec.
6401 Rockhill Rd 64131 816-501-0100
Concorde Career College Post-Sec.
3239 Broadway St 64111 816-531-5223
Cristos Academy 50/9-12
11000 Ruskin Way 64134 816-966-8877
Eric Smith, admin. Fax 966-2018
DeVry University Post-Sec.
11224 Holmes Rd 64131 816-941-0430
DeVry University Post-Sec.
1100 Main St Ste 118 64105 816-221-1300
Grantham University Post-Sec.
7200 NW 86th St Ste M 64153 800-955-2527
Heritage College Post-Sec.
534 E 99th St 64131 816-942-5474
High-Tech Institute Post-Sec.
9001 State Line Rd 64114 816-444-4300
House of Heavilin Beauty College Post-Sec.
5720 Troost Ave 64110 816-523-2471
ITT Technical Institute Post-Sec.
9150 E 41st Ter 64133 816-276-1400
Kansas City Academy 100/6-12
7933 Main St 64114 816-444-5225
Mary Statz, prin. Fax 444-8354
Kansas City Art Institute Post-Sec.
4415 Warwick Blvd 64111 800-522-5224
KC Univ. of Medicine and Biosciences Post-Sec.
1750 Independence Ave 64106 816-283-2000
Keller Graduate School Post-Sec.
10401 Holmes Rd Ste 310 64131 816-941-0367
Lutheran HS 100/9-12
12411 Wornall Rd 64145 816-241-5478
Chris Domsch, prin. Fax 876-2069
Maple Woods Community College Post-Sec.
2601 NE Barry Rd 64156 816-437-3000
Midwestern Baptist Theological Seminary Post-Sec.
5001 N Oak Trfy 64118 816-414-3700
Nazarene Theological Seminary Post-Sec.
1700 E Meyer Blvd 64131 816-333-6254
Notre Dame De Sion HS 400/9-12
10631 Wornall Rd 64114 816-942-3282
Michelle Olson, prin. Fax 942-4052
Pembroke Hill S 1,200/PK-12
400 W 51st St 64112 816-936-1200
Dr. Richard Hibschman, hdmstr. Fax 936-1208
Pembroke Hill S - Ward Pkwy Campus 100/6-12
5121 State Line Rd 64112 816-936-1500
Fax 936-1509
Penn Valley Community College Post-Sec.
3201 Southwest Traffic Way 64111 816-759-4000
Pinnacle Career Institute Post-Sec.
1001 E 101st Ter Ste 325 64131 800-614-0900
Research College of Nursing Post-Sec.
2525 E Meyer Blvd 64132 816-995-2800
Research Medical Center Post-Sec.
2316 E Meyer Blvd 64132 816-276-4101
Rockhurst HS 900/9-12
9301 State Line Rd 64114 816-363-2036
Larry Ruby, prin. Fax 363-3764
Rockhurst University Post-Sec.
1100 Rockhurst Rd 64110 816-501-4000
St. Luke's College Post-Sec.
8320 Ward Pkwy Ste 300 64114 816-932-2367
St. Paul School of Theology Post-Sec.
5123 E Truman Rd 64127 816-483-9600
St. Pius X HS 300/9-12
1500 NE 42nd Ter 64116 816-453-3450
Joseph Monachino, prin. Fax 452-7082
St. Teresa Academy 500/9-12
5600 Main St 64113 816-523-3522
Nancy Hand, prin. Fax 523-0232

Truman Medical Center Post-Sec.
2301 Holmes St 64108 816-556-3153
University of Missouri Post-Sec.
5100 Rockhill Rd 64110 816-235-1000
Vatterott College Post-Sec.
8955 E 38th Ter 64129 816-861-1000

Kearney, Clay, Pop. 6,573
Kearney R-I SD 4,300/K-12
1002 S Jefferson St 64060 816-628-4116
Dr. Chris Belcher, supt. Fax 628-4074
www.kearney.k12.mo.us
Kearney HS 1,000/9-12
715 E 19th St 64060 816-628-4585
Daryl Rinne, prin. Fax 628-3383
Summit Ridge MS 900/6-8
2215 S Campus St 64060 816-628-2650
Randy Wepler, prin. Fax 628-1938

Kennett, Dunklin, Pop. 11,072
Kennett SD 39 2,200/PK-12
510 College Ave 63857 573-717-1100
Jerry Noble, supt. Fax 717-1016
www.kennett.k12.mo.us
Kennett Career & Technology Center Vo/Tech
1400 W Washington St 63857 573-717-1123
Doug Irvin, dir. Fax 717-1386
Kennett HS 500/9-12
1400 W Washington St 63857 573-717-1120
Edward Siebenhuener, prin. Fax 717-1128
Kennett MS 500/6-8
510 College Ave 63857 573-717-1105
Ward Billings, prin. Fax 717-1106

Keytesville, Chariton, Pop. 523
Keytesville R-III SD 200/PK-12
27247 Highway 5 65261 660-288-3767
Paul Vossler, supt. Fax 288-3110
schoolweb.missouri.edu/keytesville.k-12.mo.us
Keytesville JSHS 100/7-12
27247 Highway 5 65261 660-288-3767
Rena Roth, prin. Fax 288-3110

King City, Gentry, Pop. 950
King City R-I SD 400/PK-12
PO Box 189 64463 660-535-4319
Kendall Ebersold, supt. Fax 535-4765
www.kingcity.k12.mo.us
King City JSHS 200/7-12
PO Box 189 64463 660-535-4319
John Silkett, prin. Fax 535-4765

Kingdom City, Callaway, Pop. 128
North Callaway County R-I SD 1,300/K-12
2690 US Highway 54 65262 573-386-2214
Dr. Roy Moss, supt. Fax 386-2169
northcallaway.k12.mo.us/
North Callaway HS 400/9-12
2700 US Highway 54 65262 573-386-2211
Carol Green, prin. Fax 386-2403

Kingsville, Johnson, Pop. 263
Kingsville R-I SD 300/K-12
PO Box 7 64061 816-597-3422
Kevin Coleman, supt. Fax 597-3702
www.kingsville.k12.mo.us/
Kingsville JSHS 100/7-12
PO Box 7 64061 816-597-3422
Lorna Warren, prin. Fax 597-3702

Kirbyville, Taney, Pop. 144
Kirbyville R-VI SD 300/K-8
6225 E State Highway 76 65679 417-337-8913
Jerry Parrett, supt. Fax 348-0794
www.kirbyville.k12.mo.us/
Kirbyville MS 200/4-8
6225 E State Highway 76 65679 417-348-0444
Matt Dean, prin. Fax 348-0525

Kirksville, Adair, Pop. 17,157
Kirksville R-III SD 2,500/PK-12
1901 E Hamilton St 63501 660-665-7774
Dr. Eugene Croarkin, supt. Fax 665-3281
www.kirksville.k12.mo.us
Kirksville Area Technical Center Vo/Tech
1103 Cottage Grove Pl 63501 660-665-2865
Teresa Jones, dir. Fax 626-1477
Kirksville HS 800/9-12
1300 Cottage Grove Pl 63501 660-665-4631
Patrick Williams, prin. Fax 626-1439
Kirksville MS 600/6-8
1515 Cottage Grove Pl 63501 660-665-3793
Mike Bartig, prin. Fax 626-1418

Kirksville Coll. of Osteopathic Medicine Post-Sec.
800 W Jefferson St 63501 660-626-2237
School of Health Management Post-Sec.
800 W Jefferson St 63501 660-626-2237
Truman State University Post-Sec.
100 E Normal St 63501 660-785-4000

Kirkwood, Saint Louis, Pop. 27,294
Kirkwood R-VII SD 5,100/K-12
11289 Manchester Rd 63122 314-213-6101
David Damerall, supt. Fax 984-0002
www.kirkwood.k12.mo.us
Kirkwood HS 1,800/9-12
801 W Essex Ave 63122 314-213-6110
David Holley, prin. Fax 984-4412
Nipher MS 600/6-8
700 S Kirkwood Rd 63122 314-213-6180
Carol Migneron, prin. Fax 213-6178
North Kirkwood MS 600/6-8
11287 Manchester Rd 63122 314-213-6170
Jeanette Tendai, prin. Fax 213-6177

St. Louis Community College Post-Sec.
11333 Big Bend Rd 63122 314-984-7500

Ursuline Academy 600/9-12
341 S Sappington Rd 63122 314-966-4556
Dr. Patricia Hensley, prin. Fax 966-4662

Knob Noster, Johnson, Pop. 2,652
Knob Noster R-VIII SD 1,700/PK-12
401 E Wimer St 65336 660-563-3186
Dr. Margret Anderson, supt. Fax 563-3026
knobnoster.k12.mo.us/
Knob Noster HS 500/9-12
504 S Washington Ave 65336 660-563-2283
Richard Miller, prin. Fax 563-3384
Knob Noster MS 400/6-8
211 E Wimer St 65336 660-563-2260
Peter Greene, prin. Fax 563-3274

Koshkonong, Oregon, Pop. 203
Oregon-Howell R-III SD 300/K-12
PO Box 398 65692 417-867-5601
Steve Morgan, supt. Fax 867-3757
koshkonong.k12.mo.us/
Koshkonong JSHS 200/7-12
PO Box 398 65692 417-867-5601
Jeanie White, prin. Fax 867-3757

Laddonia, Audrain, Pop. 599
Community R-VI SD 400/K-12
35063 Highway BB 63352 573-492-6223
Dr. Carrie Eidson, supt. Fax 492-6268
www.community.k12.mo.us/
Community HS 200/6-12
35063 Highway BB 63352 573-492-6222
Jacob Moss, prin. Fax 492-6407

Lake Ozark, Camden, Pop. 1,725
School of the Osage R-II SD 1,700/PK-12
PO Box 1960 65049 573-365-4091
Dr. Mary Ann Johnson, supt. Fax 365-5748
www.osage.k12.mo.us
Osage JHS 300/7-8
PO Box 1960 65049 573-365-5343
Tony Slack, prin. Fax 365-3761
Other Schools – See Kaiser

Lamar, Barton, Pop. 4,538
Lamar R-I SD 1,400/PK-12
202 W 7th St 64759 417-682-3527
Mike Resa, supt. Fax 682-6013
www.lamar.k12.mo.us
Lamar Area Vocational S Vo/Tech
202 W 7th St 64759 417-682-3384
Karl Morey, dir. Fax 682-3420
Lamar HS 400/9-12
202 W 7th St 64759 417-682-5571
Kevin Baldwin, prin. Fax 681-0328
Lamar MS 300/6-8
202 W 7th St 64759 417-682-3548
Alan Ray, prin. Fax 682-3420

La Monte, Pettis, Pop. 1,042
La Monte R-IV SD 400/PK-12
301 S Washington St 65337 660-347-5439
Joan Twidwell, supt. Fax 347-5467
La Monte JSHS 200/7-12
301 S Washington St 65337 660-347-5439
Kevin Kultgen, prin. Fax 347-5467

La Plata, Macon, Pop. 1,447
La Plata R-II SD 400/K-12
201 W Moore St 63549 660-332-7001
Thomas Ward, supt. Fax 332-7929
laplata.k12.mo.us
La Plata JSHS 200/7-12
201 W Moore St 63549 660-332-7001
Steve Safley, prin. Fax 332-7656

Laquey, Pulaski
Laquey R-V SD 800/PK-12
PO Box 130 65534 573-765-3716
Bob Boulware, supt. Fax 765-4052
www.laquey.k12.mo.us/
Laquey R-V HS 200/9-12
PO Box 130 65534 573-765-4051
Gary Houchens, prin. Fax 765-5608
Laquey R-V MS 200/5-8
PO Box 130 65534 573-765-3129
Jerry Stenson, prin. Fax 765-3129

Lathrop, Clinton, Pop. 2,216
Lathrop R-II SD 900/K-12
700 East St 64465 816-528-7500
Dr. Chris Blackburn, supt. Fax 528-7514
schoolweb.missouri.edu/lathrop.k12.mo.us
Lathrop HS 300/9-12
612 Center St 64465 816-528-7600
Tod Winterboer, prin. Fax 528-7637
Lathrop MS 200/6-8
700 Center St 64465 816-528-7700
Chris Fine, prin. Fax 528-7759

Lawson, Ray, Pop. 2,387
Lawson R-XIV SD 1,400/PK-12
PO Box 157 64062 816-580-7277
S. Craig Barker, supt. Fax 296-7723
schoolweb.missouri.edu/lawson.k12.mo.us/
Central MS 400/5-8
PO Box 157 64062 816-580-7279
Pat Penning, prin. Fax 296-3164
Lawson HS 400/9-12
PO Box 157 64062 816-580-7270
Don Edwards, prin. Fax 296-3048

Leadwood, Saint Francois, Pop. 1,145
West St. Francois County R-IV SD 1,000/PK-12
1124 Main St 63653 573-562-7535
Stacy Stevens, supt. Fax 562-7510
westco.k12.mo.us
West County MS 300/6-8
1124 Main St 63653 573-562-7544
Kevin Coffman, prin. Fax 562-7510
Other Schools – See Park Hills

Lebanon, Laclede, Pop. 12,628
Lebanon R-III SD — 4,700/PK-12
  321 S Jefferson Ave 65536 — 417-532-9141
  Dr. Duane Widhalm, supt. — Fax 532-9492
  www.lebanon.k12.mo.us
Lebanon HS — 1,400/9-12
  777 Brice St 65536 — 417-532-9144
  Robert Smith, prin. — Fax 532-3386
Lebanon JHS — 700/7-8
  500 N Adams Ave 65536 — 417-532-9121
  Pat Bauer, prin. — Fax 533-3805
Lebanon Tech & Career Center — Vo/Tech
  Hwy 64 Bypass 65536 — 417-532-5494
  Gail Holcomb, prin. — Fax 532-4510

Lees Summit, Jackson, Pop. 74,948
Blue Springs R-IV SD
  Supt. — See Blue Springs
Delta Woods MS — 600/6-8
  4401 NE Lakewood Way 64064 — 816-795-5830
  Steve Cook, prin. — Fax 795-5839

Lee's Summit R-VII SD — 16,100/PK-12
  600 SE Miller St 64063 — 816-986-1000
  Dr. David McGehee, supt. — Fax 986-1170
  www.leesummit.k12.mo.us
Campbell MS — 1,100/7-8
  1201 NE Colbern Rd 64086 — 816-986-3175
  Dr. Vicki Porter, prin. — Fax 986-3245
Lee's Summit HS — 2,600/9-12
  400 SE Blue Pkwy 64063 — 816-986-2000
  John Faulkenberry, prin. — Fax 986-2095
Lee's Summit North HS — 2,100/9-12
  901 NE Douglas St 64086 — 816-986-3000
  Dr. Dave Ulrich, prin. — Fax 986-3170
Lee's Summit West HS — 9-12
  2600 SW Ward Rd 64082 — 816-986-4000
  Dr. Cindy Bateman, prin. — Fax 986-4115
Pleasant Lea MS — 900/7-8
  630 SW Persels Rd 64081 — 816-986-1175
  Janette Cooley, prin. — Fax 986-1225
Summit Lakes MS — 600/7-8
  3500 SW Windemere Dr 64082 — 816-986-1375
  Dr. Don Andrews, prin. — Fax 986-1435
Summit Technical Academy — Vo/Tech
  777 NW Blue Pkwy 64086 — 816-524-3366
  Bob White, prin. — Fax 524-1436

Lee's Summit Community Christian S — 700/PK-12
  1450 SW Jefferson St 64081 — 816-524-0185
  Linda Harrelson, admin. — Fax 524-4105
Longview Community College — Post-Sec.
  500 SW Longview Rd 64081 — 816-672-2000

Leeton, Johnson, Pop. 627
Leeton R-X SD — 400/PK-12
  500 N Main St 64761 — 660-653-2301
  Dr. William Nicely, supt. — Fax 653-4315
  www.leeton.k12.mo.us/
Leeton HS — 100/9-12
  500 N Main St 64761 — 660-653-4314
  Jeff Curley, prin. — Fax 653-4315
Leeton MS — 100/6-8
  500 N Main St 64761 — 660-653-4314
  Jeff Curley, prin. — Fax 653-4315

Leopold, Bollinger
Leopold R-III SD — 200/K-12
  PO Box 39 63760 — 573-238-2211
  Derek Urhahn, supt. — Fax 238-9868
  schoolweb.missouri.edu/leopold.k12.mo.us/
Leopold JSHS — 100/7-12
  PO Box 39 63760 — 573-238-2211
  Keenan Kinder, prin. — Fax 283-9868

Lesterville, Reynolds
Lesterville R-IV SD — 300/PK-12
  PO Box 120 63654 — 573-637-2201
  Earlene Fox, supt. — Fax 637-2279
Lesterville JSHS — 100/7-12
  PO Box 120 63654 — 573-637-2201
  Keith Groom, prin. — Fax 637-2279
Other Schools – See Black

Lexington, Lafayette, Pop. 4,667
Lexington R-V SD — 1,300/PK-12
  100 S 13th St 64067 — 660-259-4369
  James F. Judd, supt. — Fax 259-4992
  www.lexington.k12.mo.us
Lexington HS — 300/9-12
  2309 Aull Ln 64067 — 660-259-4391
  Jerry Mitchell, prin. — Fax 259-2166
Lexington MS — 400/5-8
  1111 S 24th St 64067 — 660-259-4611
  Al Voelker, prin. — Fax 259-2538
Lex La-Ray Tech Ctr — Vo/Tech
  2323 High School Dr 64067 — 660-259-2264
  Brandon Russell, prin. — Fax 259-6262

Wentworth Military Academy — Post-Sec.
  1880 Washington Ave 64067 — 660-259-2221
Wentworth Military Academy — 300/7-12
  1880 Washington Ave 64067 — 660-259-2221

Liberal, Barton, Pop. 808
Liberal R-II SD — 500/K-12
  PO Box 38 64762 — 417-843-5115
  William Harvey, supt. — Fax 843-6698
Liberal HS — 200/9-12
  PO Box 38 64762 — 417-843-2125
  Danny R. Decker, prin. — Fax 843-2403
Liberal MS — 100/6-8
  PO Box 38 64762 — 417-843-6033
  Margaret Gillard, prin. — Fax 843-2403

Liberty, Clay, Pop. 27,982
Liberty SD 53 — 7,900/PK-12
  650 Conistor Ln 64068 — 816-736-5300
  Dr. W. Scott Taveau, supt. — Fax 736-5306
  www.liberty.k12.mo.us
Liberty JHS — 1,200/8-9
  600 W Kansas St 64068 — 816-736-5380
  Scott Carr, prin. — Fax 736-5384
Liberty SHS — 1,600/10-12
  200 Blue Jay Dr 64068 — 816-736-5340
  Dr. Martin Jacobs, prin. — Fax 736-5345
South Valley JHS — 8-9
  800 Midjay Dr 64068 — 816-736-7300
  Dr. Brad Armstrong, prin. — Fax 736-7301

William Jewell College — Post-Sec.
  500 College Hl 64068 — 816-781-7700

Licking, Texas, Pop. 2,572
Licking R-VIII SD — 900/PK-12
  PO Box 179 65542 — 573-674-2911
  Dr. John Hood, supt. — Fax 674-4064
Licking JSHS — 500/7-12
  PO Box 149 65542 — 573-674-2711
  Stephen Denbow, prin. — Fax 674-4064

Lincoln, Benton, Pop. 1,064
Lincoln R-II SD — 600/K-12
  PO Box 39 65338 — 660-547-3514
  Michael Ringen, supt. — Fax 547-3729
Lincoln JSHS — 300/7-12
  PO Box 39 65338 — 660-547-3514
  Alan Bancroft, prin. — Fax 547-3729

Linn, Osage, Pop. 1,399
Osage County R-II SD — 700/PK-12
  1212 E Main St 65051 — 573-897-4200
  Nancy Gillespie, supt. — Fax 897-3768
  www.linn.k12.mo.us
Linn JSHS — 400/7-12
  1212 E Main St 65051 — 573-897-4216
  Jo Ellen Hicks, prin. — Fax 897-4570

Linn State Technical College — Post-Sec.
  1 Technology Dr 65051 — 573-897-3603

Lockwood, Dade, Pop. 969
Lockwood R-I SD — 300/K-12
  400 W 4th St 65682 — 417-232-4513
  Bill Rogers, supt. — Fax 232-4187
  www.lockwood.k12.mo.us/
Lockwood HS — 100/9-12
  400 W 4th St 65682 — 417-232-4513
  Dennis Cornish, prin. — Fax 232-4187

Lone Jack, Jackson, Pop. 557
Lone Jack C-6 SD — 500/K-12
  201 W Lne Jack Lees Smmt Rd 64070 — 816-697-3539
  Ronald Davies, supt. — Fax 697-8869
  www.lonejackc6.net
Lone Jack JSHS — 300/7-12
  313 S Bynum Rd 64070 — 816-697-2215
  Scott Stewart, prin. — Fax 566-3128

Louisburg, Dallas, Pop. 149
Dallas County R-I SD
  Supt. — See Buffalo
Dallas County Career Center — Vo/Tech
  PO Box 100 65685 — 417-752-3491
  Alex Kyser, prin. — Fax 752-3493

Louisiana, Pike, Pop. 3,808
Louisiana R-II SD — 800/K-12
  3321 Georgia St 63353 — 573-754-4261
  Dan Jones, supt. — Fax 754-4319
  www.schoolweb.missouri.edu/louisiana.k12.mo.us
Louisiana HS — 200/9-12
  3321 Georgia St 63353 — 573-754-6181
  Calvin Jesberg, prin. — Fax 754-5964
Louisiana MS — 200/6-8
  3321 Georgia St 63353 — 573-754-5340
  Chuck Tophinke, prin. — Fax 754-5377

Ludlow, Livingston, Pop. 198
Southwest Livingston County R-I SD — 200/K-12
  4944 Highway DD 64656 — 660-738-4433
  John Locker, supt. — Fax 738-4441
  www.southwestr1.org/
Southwest Livingston County JSHS — 100/7-12
  4944 Highway DD 64656 — 660-738-4433
  Jennie D. Thorne, prin. — Fax 738-4441

Macks Creek, Camden, Pop. 278
Macks Creek R-V SD — 400/PK-12
  245 State Rd N 65786 — 573-363-5909
  Alan Stauffacher, supt. — Fax 363-0127
Macks Creek JSHS — 200/7-12
  245 State Rd N 65786 — 573-363-5911
  Brent Yates, prin. — Fax 363-5981

Macon, Macon, Pop. 5,438
Macon County R-I SD — 1,400/PK-12
  702 N Missouri St 63552 — 660-385-5719
  Debbie Livingston, supt. — Fax 385-7179
  www.macon.k12.mo.us/
Macon Area Vocational Technical S — Vo/Tech
  702 N Missouri St 63552 — 660-385-2158
  Mickey E. Briscoe, dir. — Fax 385-3667
Macon County HS — 400/9-12
  702 N Missouri St 63552 — 660-385-5748
  Dwight E. Tietsort, prin. — Fax 385-2746
Macon County MS — 300/6-8
  702 N Missouri St 63552 — 660-385-2189
  Dustin Fanning, prin. — Fax 385-7230

Madison, Monroe, Pop. 570
Madison C-3 SD — 300/PK-12
  309 S Thomas St 65263 — 660-291-5115
  John Ross, supt. — Fax 291-5006
  www.schoolweb.missouri.edu/madisonc3.k12.mo.us/

Madison JSHS — 200/7-12
  309 S Thomas St 65263 — 660-291-4515
  Warren Salmons, prin. — Fax 291-5006

Malden, Dunklin, Pop. 4,659
Malden R-I SD — 1,100/K-12
  407 Highway J 63863 — 573-276-5794
  Kenneth Cook, supt. — Fax 276-5796
  www.malden.k12.mo.us/
Malden JSHS — 500/7-12
  407 Highway J 63863 — 573-276-4546
  Robert Wilson, prin. — Fax 276-4548

Malta Bend, Saline, Pop. 239
Malta Bend R-V SD — 100/K-12
  PO Box 10 65339 — 660-595-2371
  Ryan Nowlin, supt. — Fax 595-2430
Malta Bend JSHS — 100/6-12
  PO Box 10 65339 — 660-595-2371
  Ryan Nowlin, prin. — Fax 595-2430

Manchester, Saint Louis, Pop. 19,106
Parkway C-2 SD
  Supt. — See Chesterfield
Parkway South MS — 700/6-8
  760 Woods Mill Rd 63011 — 314-415-7200
  Craig Fenner, prin. — Fax 415-7213

Kennedy HS — 500/9-12
  500 Woods Mill Rd 63011 — 636-227-5900
  Christine Bolesta, prin. — Fax 227-0298

Mansfield, Wright, Pop. 1,342
Mansfield R-IV SD — 700/PK-12
  316 W Ohio St 65704 — 417-924-8458
  Arlene Magnin, supt. — Fax 924-3427
  www.mansfieldschool.net/
Mansfield HS — 200/9-12
  315 W Ohio St 65704 — 417-924-3236
  Randy Short, prin. — Fax 924-8789
Mansfield JHS — 100/7-8
  316 W Ohio St 65704 — 417-924-8625
  Randy Short, prin. — Fax 924-8789

Maplewood, Saint Louis, Pop. 8,972
Maplewood Richmond Heights SD — 1,000/PK-12
  7539 Manchester Rd 63143 — 314-644-4400
  Dr. Linda Henke, supt. — Fax 781-3160
Maplewood Richmond Heights HS — 300/9-12
  7539 Manchester Rd 63143 — 314-644-4401
  S. Patrick McEvoy, prin. — Fax 644-3681
Other Schools – See Saint Louis

Marble Hill, Bollinger, Pop. 1,505
Woodland R-IV SD — 900/K-12
  RR 3 Box 3210 63764 — 573-238-3343
  Dennis Parham, supt. — Fax 238-2153
  www.woodland.k12.mo.us/
Woodland JSHS — 400/7-12
  RR 3 Box 3210 63764 — 573-238-2663
  Jennings Wilkinson, prin. — Fax 238-0186

New Salem Baptist Academy — 100/PK-12
  HC 64 Box 4220 63764 — 573-238-2643
  Tim Willis, admin. — Fax 238-1107

Marceline, Linn, Pop. 2,466
Marceline R-V SD — 700/PK-12
  400 E Santa Fe Ave 64658 — 660-376-3371
  Ed Schoenfelt, supt. — Fax 376-6001
  www.marceline.k12.mo.us
Marceline HS — 200/9-12
  314 E Santa Fe Ave 64658 — 660-376-2411
  Gabe Edgar, prin. — Fax 376-6016
Marceline MS — 200/6-8
  314 E Santa Fe Ave 64658 — 660-376-2411
  Gabe Edgar, prin. — Fax 376-6016

Marionville, Lawrence, Pop. 2,140
Marionville R-IX SD — 800/K-12
  PO Box 409 65705 — 417-258-7755
  Larry Brown, supt. — Fax 258-2564
  www.marionville.us/
Marionville JSHS — 300/7-12
  PO Box 409 65705 — 417-258-2521
  Mark Marler, prin. — Fax 258-5625

Marquand, Madison, Pop. 250
Marquand-Zion R-VI SD — 200/K-12
  PO Box A 63655 — 573-783-3388
  Duane Schindler, supt. — Fax 783-3067
Marquand-Zion JSHS — 100/7-12
  PO Box A 63655 — 573-783-3388
  Pamela Moyers, prin. — Fax 783-3067

Marshall, Saline, Pop. 12,017
Marshall SD — 2,400/K-12
  860 W Vest St 65340 — 660-886-7414
  Dr. Robert Gordon, supt. — Fax 886-5641
  www.marshallschools.com/
Bueker MS — 800/5-8
  565 S Odell Ave 65340 — 660-886-6833
  Lance Tobin, prin. — Fax 886-7529
Marshall HS — 900/9-12
  805 S Miami Ave 65340 — 660-886-2244
  Glenn Miller, prin. — Fax 886-2669
Saline County Career Ctr — Vo/Tech
  900 W Vest St 65340 — 660-886-6958
  Dr. Greg Nolting, dir. — Fax 886-3092

Missouri Valley College — Post-Sec.
  500 E College St 65340 — 660-831-4000

Marshfield, Webster, Pop. 6,291
Marshfield R-I SD — 2,900/PK-12
  114 Commercial St 65706 — 417-859-2120
  Michael Wutke, supt. — Fax 859-2193
  www.mr1.k12.mo.us/

Marshfield HS | 900/9-12
370 State Highway DD 65706 | 417-859-2120
Jan Hibbs, prin. | Fax 859-7756
Marshfield JHS | 700/6-8
660 N Locust St 65706 | 417-859-2120
Alan Thomas, prin. | Fax 859-4970

Maryland Heights, Saint Louis, Pop. 25,583
Pattonville R-III SD
Supt. — See Saint Ann
Pattonville HS | 2,000/9-12
2497 Creve Coeur Mill Rd 63043 | 314-213-8051
Jeff Marion, prin. | Fax 213-8651
Pattonville Hts MS | 600/6-8
195 Fee Fee Rd 63043 | 314-213-8033
Scot Mosher, prin. | Fax 213-8633

Allied College - North | Post-Sec.
13723 Riverport Dr Ste 103 63043 | 866-501-1291

Maryville, Nodaway, Pop. 10,622
Maryville R-II SD | 1,500/PK-12
1429 S Munn Ave 64468 | 660-562-3255
Vickie Miller, supt. | Fax 562-4113
www.maryville.k12.mo.us/
Maryville HS | 500/9-12
1503 S Munn Ave 64468 | 660-562-3511
Ronald Landherr, prin. | Fax 562-4822
Maryville MS | 400/5-8
525 W South Hills Dr 64468 | 660-562-3244
Kevin Pitts, prin. | Fax 562-4130
Northwest Technical S | Vo/Tech
1515 S Munn Ave 64468 | 660-562-3022
Mike Jordan, dir. | Fax 562-2010

Northwest Missouri State University | Post-Sec.
800 University Dr 64468 | 660-562-1212

Maysville, DeKalb, Pop. 1,160
Maysville R-I SD | 700/K-12
PO Box 68 64469 | 816-449-2308
Ronald McElwain, supt. | Fax 449-5678
maysville.k12.mo.us/
Maysville JSHS | 300/7-12
PO Box 68 64469 | 816-449-2154
Paul Niece, prin. | Fax 449-5610

Meadville, Linn, Pop. 452
Meadville R-IV SD | 300/PK-12
PO Box 217 64659 | 660-938-4111
Kenneth Dudley, supt. | Fax 938-4100
Meadville JSHS | 100/7-12
PO Box 217 64659 | 660-938-4112
Ron Holcer, prin. | Fax 938-4100

Memphis, Scotland, Pop. 2,004
Scotland County R-I SD | 700/PK-12
RR 3 Box 19A 63555 | 660-465-8531
David Shalley, supt. | Fax 465-8636
scotland.k12.mo.us/
Scotland County JSHS | 300/7-12
RR 3 Box 19A 63555 | 660-465-8901
Kenneth Cross, prin. | Fax 465-7715

Mendon, Chariton, Pop. 203
Northwestern R-I SD | 200/PK-12
PO Box 43 64660 | 660-272-3201
William Jones, supt. | Fax 272-3419
Northwestern HS | 100/9-12
PO Box 43 64660 | 660-272-3201
Ron Garber, prin. | Fax 272-3738
Northwestern MS | 100/5-8
PO Box 43 64660 | 660-272-3201
Ron Garber, prin. | Fax 272-3738

Mercer, Mercer, Pop. 327
North Mercer County R-III SD | 200/PK-12
PO Box 648 64661 | 660-382-4214
Dan Owens, supt. | Fax 382-4239
www.northmercer.k12.mo.us
Mercer JSHS | 100/7-12
PO Box 648 64661 | 660-382-4214
Stacy Snyder, prin. | Fax 382-4239

Mexico, Audrain, Pop. 10,956
Mexico SD 59 | 2,400/K-12
920 S Jefferson St 65265 | 573-581-3773
T. Lloyd Little, supt. | Fax 581-4410
www.mexicoschools.net/
Hart Mexico Area Vo Tech S | Vo/Tech
905 N Wade St 65265 | 573-581-5684
Duane Bennett, dir. | Fax 581-7084
Mexico HS | 800/9-12
639 N Wade St 65265 | 573-581-4296
Gregory Baber, prin. | Fax 581-3788
Mexico JHS | 600/6-8
1200 W Boulevard St 65265 | 573-581-4664
Nancy A. Goedeke, prin. | Fax 581-8440

Missouri Military Academy | 200/6-12
204 Grand Ave 65265 | 573-581-1776
Ronald Kelly, prin. | Fax 581-0081

Milan, Sullivan, Pop. 1,902
Milan C-2 SD | 700/PK-12
373 S Market St 63556 | 660-265-4414
Bill Lewis, supt. | Fax 265-4315
Milan JSHS | 300/7-12
373 S Market St 63556 | 660-265-4415
Mark Forster, prin. | Fax 265-4315

Miller, Lawrence, Pop. 778
Miller R-II SD | 600/K-12
110 W 6th St 65707 | 417-452-3515
Dr. Anthony Rossetti, supt. | Fax 452-2709
Miller JSHS | 300/7-12
110 W 6th St 65707 | 417-452-3271
David Geurin, prin. | Fax 452-3936

Moberly, Randolph, Pop. 13,733
Moberly SD | 2,400/PK-12
926 Kwix Rd 65270 | 660-269-2600
Robert Bach, supt. | Fax 269-2611
moberly.k12.mo.us/
Moberly Area Technical Center | Vo/Tech
1625 Gratz Brown St 65270 | 660-269-2690
Lester Abel, dir. | Fax 269-2692
Moberly HS | 700/9-12
1625 Gratz Brown St 65270 | 660-269-2660
Mike Barner, prin. | Fax 263-5977
Moberly MS | 500/6-8
920 Kwix Rd 65270 | 660-269-2680
Aaron Vitt, prin. | Fax 269-8519

Central Christian College of the Bible | Post-Sec.
911 E Urbandale Dr 65270 | 888-263-3900
Maranatha SDA S | 50/5-8
1400 E McKinsey St 65270 | 660-263-8600
Moberly Area Community College | Post-Sec.
101 College Ave 65270 | 660-263-4110

Mokane, Callaway, Pop. 192
South Callaway County R-II SD | 1,000/PK-12
10135 State Road C 65059 | 573-676-5225
Dr. Nick Boren, supt. | Fax 676-5134
www.sc.k12.mo.us
South Callaway HS | 300/9-12
10135 State Road C 65059 | 573-676-5211
Troy Clawson, prin. | Fax 676-5132
South Callaway MS | 300/5-8
10135 State Road C 65059 | 573-676-5216
Michael R. Auer, prin. | Fax 676-5347

Monett, Barry, Pop. 7,735
Monett R-I SD | 2,000/PK-12
800 E Scott St 65708 | 417-235-7422
Dr. Charles Cudney, supt. | Fax 235-1415
hs1.monett.k12.mo.us/
Monett HS | 600/9-12
1 David Sippy Dr 65708 | 417-235-5445
David Steward, prin. | Fax 235-7884
Monett MS | 300/7-8
700 9th St 65708 | 417-235-6228
John Jungmann, prin. | Fax 235-3278
Southwest Area Career Center | Vo/Tech
711 9th St 65708 | 417-235-7022
Ted Dorton, dir. | Fax 235-8270

Monroe City, Monroe, Pop. 2,602
Monroe City R-I SD | 800/PK-12
401 US Highway 24/36 E 63456 | 573-735-4631
Dr. Kirk Eidson, supt. | Fax 735-2413
www.monroe.k12.mo.us
Monroe City MS | 200/5-8
430 N Washington St 63456 | 573-735-4742
Fred Cochrane, prin. | Fax 735-2413
Monroe City R-I HS | 300/9-12
401 US Highway 24/36 E 63456 | 573-735-4626
James Redmon, prin. | Fax 735-2413

Montgomery City, Montgomery, Pop. 2,483
Montgomery County R-II SD | 1,400/PK-12
418 N Highway 19 63361 | 573-564-2278
Donald Francis, supt. | Fax 564-6182
www.mc-wildcats.org/
Montgomery County MS | 300/6-8
418 N Highway 19 63361 | 573-564-2253
Steven Weinhold, prin. | Fax 564-6182
Montomery County HS | 500/9-12
394 N Highway 19 63361 | 573-564-2213
James Luetjen, prin. | Fax 564-3516

Montrose, Henry, Pop. 426
Montrose R-XIV SD | 100/K-12
PO Box 175 64770 | 660-693-4812
Kevin Gwaltney, supt. | Fax 693-4594
Montrose HS | 50/9-12
PO Box 175 64770 | 660-693-4812
Kevin Gwaltney, prin. | Fax 693-4594

Morrisville, Polk, Pop. 354
Marion C. Early R-V SD | 700/K-12
PO Box 96 65710 | 417-376-2255
Dr. Ron McIntire, supt. | Fax 376-3243
mcearly.k12.mo.us
Early JSHS | 400/6-12
PO Box 96 65710 | 417-376-2216
Mark Summers, prin. | Fax 376-3243

Mound City, Holt, Pop. 1,131
Mound City R-II SD | 300/PK-12
PO Box 247 64470 | 660-442-3737
Ken Eaton, supt. | Fax 442-5941
Mound City HS | 100/7-12
PO Box 247 64470 | 660-442-5429
Jason Eggers, prin. | Fax 442-5941

Mountain Grove, Wright, Pop. 4,563
Mountain Grove R-III SD | 1,500/K-12
PO Box 806 65711 | 417-926-3177
Bridget Williams, supt. | Fax 926-3177
www.mgr3.k12.mo.us
Mountain Grove HS | 500/9-12
PO Box 806 65711 | 417-926-3177
Marcie Stumpff, prin. | Fax 926-1702
Mountain Grove MS | 400/6-8
PO Box 806 65711 | 417-926-3177
J.T. Hale, prin. | Fax 926-1673
Ozark Mountain Technical Center | Vo/Tech
PO Box 806 65711 | 417-926-3177
Earl Crofford, dir. | Fax 926-6858

Mountain View, Howell, Pop. 2,451
Mountain View-Birch Tree R-III SD | 1,400/PK-12
PO Box 464 65548 | 417-934-5404
Jerry Nicholson, supt. | Fax 934-5404
mvbt.k12.mo.us/

Liberty HS | 400/9-12
PO Box 464 65548 | 417-934-2020
Steven Richards, prin. | Fax 934-5404
Liberty MS | 200/7-8
PO Box 464 65548 | 417-934-2020
Walt Belcher, prin. | Fax 934-5404

Mount Vernon, Lawrence, Pop. 4,227
Mt. Vernon R-V SD | 1,600/K-12
731 S Landrum St 65712 | 417-466-7573
Dan Breeden, supt. | Fax 466-7058
Mount Vernon HS | 500/9-12
400 W Highway 174 65712 | 417-466-7526
Russ Cruzan, prin. | Fax 466-4307
Mount Vernon MS | 500/5-8
731 S Landrum St 65712 | 417-466-3137
Robert Senninger, prin. | Fax 466-7058

Myrtle, Oregon
Couch R-I SD | 300/PK-12
RR 1 Box 1187 65778 | 417-938-4211
Rolla Fraley, supt. | Fax 938-4267
Couch JSHS | 200/7-12
RR 1 Box 1187 65778 | 417-938-4212
Tom Bull, prin. | Fax 938-4267

Naylor, Ripley, Pop. 608
Naylor R-I SD | 400/K-12
RR 2 Box 512 63953 | 573-399-2505
Stephen Cookson, supt. | Fax 399-2874
schoolweb.missouri.edu/naylor.k12.mo.us/
Naylor JSHS | 200/7-12
RR 2 Box 512 63953 | 573-399-2506
Terry Arnold, prin. | Fax 399-2388

Neelyville, Butler, Pop. 494
Neelyville R-IV SD | 700/PK-12
PO Box 8 63954 | 573-989-3813
Larry Graves, supt. | Fax 989-3434
neelyville.k12.mo.us/
Neelyville JSHS | 300/7-12
PO Box 8 63954 | 573-989-3815
Brad Hagood, prin. | Fax 989-6322

Neosho, Newton, Pop. 10,714
Neosho R-V SD | 4,500/PK-12
511 S Neosho Blvd 64850 | 417-451-8600
Dr. Richard Page, supt. | Fax 451-8604
www.neosho.k12.mo.us
Neosho HS | 1,200/9-12
511 S Neosho Blvd 64850 | 417-451-8670
Charles Blaney, prin. | Fax 451-8605
Neosho JHS | 300/8-8
511 S Neosho Blvd 64850 | 417-451-8660
Jennifer Cryer, prin. | Fax 451-8687

Crowder College | Post-Sec.
601 Laclede Ave 64850 | 417-451-3223
Neosho Beauty College | Post-Sec.
116 N Wood St 64850 | 417-451-7216
Ozark Christian Academy | 100/K-12
PO Box 786 64850 | 417-451-1100
Joyce Prichoda, prin. | Fax 451-9902

Nevada, Vernon, Pop. 8,411
Nevada R-V SD | 2,600/PK-12
800 W Hickory St 64772 | 417-448-2000
Dr. Ted Davis, supt. | Fax 448-2006
www.nevada.k12.mo.us
Nevada HS | 800/9-12
800 W Hickory St 64772 | 417-448-2020
Chance Wistrom, prin. | Fax 448-2039
Nevada MS | 600/6-8
900 N Olive St 64772 | 417-448-2040
Steve Beckett, prin. | Fax 448-2048
Nevada Regional Tech-Center | Vo/Tech
900 W Ashland St 64772 | 417-448-2090
Sean Smith, dir. | Fax 448-2092

Calvary Christian S | 100/K-12
113 W Arch St 64772 | 417-667-4200
Cottey College | Post-Sec.
1000 W Austin Blvd 64772 | 417-667-8181

New Bloomfield, Callaway, Pop. 646
New Bloomfield R-III SD | 700/K-12
PO Box 188 65063 | 573-491-3700
Dr. James Botts, supt. | Fax 491-3772
www.callaway.k12.mo.us
New Bloomfield JSHS | 300/7-12
PO Box 188 65063 | 573-491-3700
Julie Trammell, prin. | Fax 491-3696

Newburg, Phelps, Pop. 481
Newburg R-II SD | 500/PK-12
PO Box C 65550 | 573-762-2211
Dr. Steve Bounds, supt. | Fax 762-2512
www.rollanet.org/~wolf
Newburg JSHS | 200/7-12
PO Box C 65550 | 573-762-2331
Steve Guffey, prin. | Fax 762-2512

New Cambria, Macon, Pop. 220
Macon County R-IV SD | 200/K-12
PO Box 70 63558 | 660-226-5615
Ron Garber, supt. | Fax 226-5618
schoolweb.missouri.edu/maconr4.k12.mo.us/
Macon County JSHS | 100/7-12
PO Box 70 63558 | 660-226-5615
Carol Burstert, prin. | Fax 226-5618

New Franklin, Howard, Pop. 1,104
New Franklin R-I SD | 400/PK-12
412 W Broadway 65274 | 660-848-2141
Dr. Jeanie Gordon, supt. | Fax 848-2226
www.nfranklin.k12.mo.us/
New Franklin MSHS | 200/6-12
412 W Broadway 65274 | 660-848-2314
David Haggard, prin. | Fax 848-3071

New Haven, Franklin, Pop. 1,895
New Haven SD 500/K-12
100 Park Dr 63068 573-237-3231
Kyle Kruse, supt. Fax 237-5959
New Haven HS 200/9-12
100 Park Dr 63068 573-237-2629
Timothy Strobel, prin. Fax 237-5959
New Haven MS 100/6-8
100 Park Dr 63068 573-237-2900
Dennis Carey, prin. Fax 237-5959

New Madrid, New Madrid, Pop. 3,223
New Madrid County R-I SD 1,900/PK-12
310 US Highway 61 63869 573-688-2161
Bill Nance, supt. Fax 688-2169
Central HS 500/9-12
310 US Highway 61 63869 573-688-2165
John Garner, prin. Fax 688-2169
Central MS 400/6-8
308 US Highway 61 63869 573-688-2176
Thomas Drummond, prin. Fax 688-2245
New Madrid R-I Tech Skills Center Vo/Tech
310 US Highway 61 63869 573-688-2161
Lance Tollison, dir. Fax 688-2169

Newtown, Sullivan, Pop. 204
Newtown-Harris R-III SD 100/K-12
PO Box 128 64667 660-794-2245
W. Anderson, supt. Fax 794-2730
www.nhtigers.k12.mo.us
Newtown-Harris JSHS 100/7-12
PO Box 128 64667 660-794-2245
Misty Foster, prin. Fax 794-2730

Niangua, Webster, Pop. 469
Niangua R-V SD 300/PK-12
301 Rumsey St 65713 417-473-6101
Andy Adams, supt. Fax 473-6124
schoolweb.missouri.edu/niangua.k12.mo.us
Niangua JSHS 100/7-12
301 Rumsey St 65713 417-473-6101
Perry Dobson, prin. Fax 473-6124

Nixa, Christian, Pop. 13,906
Nixa R-II SD 4,200/PK-12
205 North St 65714 417-875-5400
Dr. Stephen Kleinsmith, supt. Fax 725-7405
www.nixa.k12.mo.us
Nixa HS 1,200/9-12
514 S Nicholas Rd 65714 417-724-3500
Mark Overstreet, prin. Fax 724-3515
Nixa JHS 700/7-8
205 North St 65714 417-875-5430
Mark McGehee, prin. Fax 875-5426

Norborne, Carroll, Pop. 795
Norborne R-VIII SD 200/K-12
PO Box 192 64668 660-593-3319
Douglas Carpenter, supt. Fax 593-3657
www.schoolweb.missouri.edu/norborne.k12.mo.us/index.html
Norborne HS 100/7-12
PO Box 192 64668 660-593-3319
Wade Schroeder, prin. Fax 593-3657

Normandy, Saint Louis, Pop. 5,139
Normandy SD
Supt. — See Saint Louis
Normandy MS 900/7-8
7855 Natural Bridge Rd 63121 314-493-0500
Todd Williams, prin. Fax 493-0560

North Kansas City, Clay, Pop. 4,728
North Kansas City SD 74 17,300/PK-12
2000 NE 46th St 64116 816-413-5000
Dr. Thomas Cummings, supt. Fax 413-5005
www.nkcsd.k12.mo.us
North Kansas City HS 1,700/9-12
620 E 23rd Ave 64116 816-413-5900
Dr. Dan Wartick, prin. Fax 413-5905
Other Schools – See Kansas City

Colorado Technical University Post-Sec.
520 E 19th Ave 64116 816-472-7400
North Kansas City Hospital Post-Sec.
2800 Clay Edwards Dr 64116 816-691-2000

Norwood, Wright, Pop. 573
Norwood R-I SD 400/K-12
675 N Hawk St 65717 417-746-4101
Don Forrest, supt. Fax 746-9950
www.norwood.k12.mo.us/
Norwood HS 200/9-12
675 N Hawk St 65717 417-746-4101
Marcella Swatosh, prin. Fax 746-9950
Norwood MS 100/5-8
675 N Hawk St 65717 417-746-4101
Fred Vanbibber, prin. Fax 746-4804

Novinger, Adair, Pop. 526
Adair County R-I SD 300/PK-12
PO Box B 63559 660-488-6411
William Lake, supt. Fax 488-5400
www.novinger.k12.mo.us
Adair County JSHS 200/7-12
PO Box B 63559 660-488-6411
Scott Wyant, prin. Fax 488-5400

Oak Grove, Jackson, Pop. 6,943
Oak Grove R-VI SD 2,000/PK-12
1305 Salem St 64075 816-690-4156
Dr. James Haley, supt. Fax 690-3031
www.oakgrove.k12.mo.us
Oak Grove HS 600/9-12
605 SE 12th St 64075 816-690-4152
Randall McClain, prin. Fax 690-5666
Oak Grove MS 500/6-8
401 SE 12th St 64075 816-690-4154
Lacee B. Sell, prin. Fax 690-3976

Oak Ridge, Cape Girardeau, Pop. 202
Oak Ridge R-VI SD 400/K-12
PO Box 10 63769 573-266-3218
Dr. Gerald Landewee, supt. Fax 266-0133
www.showme.net/ork/
Oak Ridge JSHS 200/7-12
PO Box 10 63769 573-266-3630
Allan Horrell, prin. Fax 266-0133

Odessa, Lafayette, Pop. 4,846
Odessa R-VII SD 2,300/K-12
701 S 3rd St 64076 816-633-5316
Sandra Sloan, supt. Fax 633-8582
www.odessa.k12.mo.us/
Odessa HS 800/9-12
713 S 3rd St 64076 816-633-5533
Peter Rorvig, prin. Fax 633-7506
Odessa MS 800/5-8
607 S 5th St 64076 816-633-1500
Sherry Billings, prin. Fax 633-7101

O Fallon, Saint Charles, Pop. 59,678
Ft. Zumwalt R-II SD 18,100/K-12
110 Virgil St 63366 636-272-6620
Dr. Bernard J. DuBray, supt. Fax 980-1946
www.fzschools.org
Ft. Zumwalt North HS 1,200/9-12
1230 Tom Ginnever Ave 63366 636-272-4447
Betty Whitlock, prin. Fax 272-6124
Ft. Zumwalt North MS 1,100/6-8
210 Virgil St 63366 636-281-2356
Dr. Larry Lusch, prin. Fax 281-0005
Ft. Zumwalt West HS 2,300/9-12
1251 Turtle Creek Dr 63366 636-281-4030
Neil Berry, prin. Fax 281-0202
Ft. Zumwalt West MS 1,100/6-8
150 Waterford Crossing Dr, 636-272-6690
Lori Jessen, prin. Fax 272-6361
Other Schools – See Saint Peters

Christian HS 300/7-12
1145 Tom Ginnever Ave 63366 636-978-1680
H. Eric Pipkin, prin. Fax 978-5024
St. Dominic HS 700/9-12
31 Saint Dominic Dr 63366 636-240-8303
Cathy Fetter, prin. Fax 240-9884

Oran, Scott, Pop. 1,247
Oran R-III SD 400/K-12
PO Box 250 63771 573-262-2330
Mitchell Wood, supt. Fax 262-2330
www.oran.k12.mo.us
Oran JSHS 200/7-12
PO Box 250 63771 573-262-3345
Travis Spane, prin. Fax 262-2289

Oregon, Holt, Pop. 908
South Holt County R-I SD 400/K-12
201 S Barbour St 64473 660-446-2282
Linda Blum, supt. Fax 446-2312
www.southholtr1.com
South Holt County JSHS 200/7-12
201 S Barbour St 64473 660-446-3454
Mike Leach, prin. Fax 446-2312

Orrick, Ray, Pop. 875
Orrick R-XI SD 500/K-12
100 Kirkham St 64077 816-770-0094
Marcus Stucker, supt. Fax 496-2306
www.orrick.k12.mo.us
Orrick JSHS 200/7-12
100 Kirkham St 64077 816-770-3327
Rick Wrisinger, prin. Fax 496-3829

Osborn, DeKalb, Pop. 448
Osborn R-0 SD 200/K-12
275 Clinton Ave 64474 816-675-2217
Gaylon Whitmer, supt. Fax 675-2222
schoolweb.missouri.edu/osborn.k12.mo.us/
Osborn JSHS 100/7-12
275 Clinton Ave 64474 816-675-2217
Mike Trosper, prin. Fax 675-2222

Osceola, Saint Clair, Pop. 822
Osceola SD 600/PK-12
76 SE Highway WW 64776 417-646-8143
Aron Bennett, supt. Fax 646-8075
www.osceola.k12.mo.us
Osceola JSHS 300/7-12
76 SE Highway WW 64776 417-646-8144
Herb Collins, prin. Fax 646-8549

Otterville, Cooper, Pop. 483
Otterville R-VI SD 300/K-12
PO Box 177 65348 660-366-4391
Fax 366-4293
Otterville JSHS 100/7-12
PO Box 177 65348 660-366-4621
Jean Carton, prin. Fax 366-4293

Overland, Saint Louis, Pop. 16,438
Ritenour SD
Supt. — See Saint Louis
Ritenour HS 1,800/9-12
9100 Saint Charles Rock Rd 63114 314-493-6105
Rhonda Haniford, prin. Fax 429-6725
Ritenour MS 800/6-8
2500 Marshall Ave 63114 314-493-6250
Suzanne Johnson, prin. Fax 429-6726

Owensville, Gasconade, Pop. 2,519
Gasconade County R-II SD 2,000/K-12
PO Box 65066 65066 573-437-2177
Dr. Sally Knight, supt. Fax 437-5808
owensville.k12.mo.us
Owensville HS 600/9-12
PO Box 536 65066 573-437-2174
Levy Robert, prin. Fax 437-7174
Owensville MS 500/6-8
PO Box 536 65066 573-437-2172
Teresa Ragan, prin. Fax 437-6704

Ozark, Christian, Pop. 13,070
Ozark R-VI SD 3,900/K-12
PO Box 166 65721 417-581-7694
Dr. Gordon Pace, supt. Fax 581-0562
www.ozark.k12.mo.us
Ozark HS 1,100/9-12
PO Box 166 65721 417-582-5901
Mark Wheeler, prin. Fax 582-5944
Ozark JHS 700/7-8
PO Box 166 65721 417-582-4701
Kevin Patterson, prin. Fax 582-4714

Pacific, Franklin, Pop. 5,702
Meramec Valley R-III SD 3,600/PK-12
126 N Payne St 63069 636-271-1400
Randy George, supt. Fax 271-1406
www.mvr3.k12.mo.us/
Pacific HS 1,100/9-12
425 Indian Warpath Dr 63069 636-627-1414
Ellen Sachs, prin. Fax 257-8340
Riverbend MS 8-8
2085 Highway N 63069 636-271-1481
Gary Peck, prin. Fax 271-8080

Palmyra, Marion, Pop. 3,476
Palmyra R-I SD 1,100/K-12
PO Box 151 63461 573-769-2066
Eric Churchwell, supt. Fax 769-4218
schoolweb.missouri.edu/palmyra.k12.mo.us
Palmyra HS 400/9-12
PO Box 151 63461 573-769-2067
Kevin Hillman, prin. Fax 769-4218
Palmyra MS 300/5-8
PO Box 151 63461 573-769-2174
Mary Scholl, prin. Fax 769-4227

Paris, Monroe, Pop. 1,494
Paris R-II SD 600/PK-12
740 Cleveland St 65275 660-327-4112
Jim Masters, supt. Fax 327-4290
paris.k12.mo.us/site/
Paris HS 200/9-12
25686 Business Highway 24 65275 660-327-4111
Richard Reading, prin. Fax 327-6220
Paris JHS 100/7-8
25678 Business Highway 24 65275 660-327-4563
Sally Eales, prin. Fax 327-4782

Park Hills, Saint Francois, Pop. 8,322
Central R-III SD 1,900/PK-12
200 High St 63601 573-431-2616
Dr. David Stevens, supt. Fax 431-2107
www.centralr3.org
Central HS 500/9-12
116 Rebel Dr 63601 573-431-1211
Brad Coleman, prin. Fax 431-0700
Central MS 500/6-8
801 Columbia St 63601 573-431-1322
Mike Harlow, prin. Fax 431-5393

West St. Francois County R-IV SD
Supt. — See Leadwood
West County HS 300/9-12
768 Highway M 63601 573-562-7521
Eric Moyers, prin. Fax 562-7510

Parkville, Platte, Pop. 4,892

Park University Post-Sec.
8700 NW River Park Dr 64152 816-741-2000

Patton, Bollinger
Meadow Heights R-II SD 600/K-12
RR 1 Box 2365 63662 573-866-0060
Victor Martin, supt. Fax 866-3240
Meadow Heights JSHS 300/7-12
RR 1 Box 2365 63662 573-866-2924
Mitchell Nanney, prin. Fax 866-2219

Pattonsburg, Daviess, Pop. 242
Pattonsburg R-II SD 200/PK-12
PO Box 200 64670 660-367-2111
Wendell Burns, supt. Fax 367-4205
Pattonsburg JSHS 100/7-12
PO Box 200 64670 660-367-2111
Chris Gannan, prin. Fax 367-4205

Peculiar, Cass, Pop. 3,331
Raymore-Peculiar R-II SD 4,500/PK-12
PO Box 366 64078 816-779-3300
David McGehee, supt. Fax 779-3380
www.raypec.k12.mo.us
Raymore-Peculiar Freshman Center 9-9
PO Box 366 64078 816-779-3400
Eric Arnold, prin. Fax 779-3410
Raymore-Peculiar MS 800/7-8
PO Box 366 64078 816-779-6865
Bill Scully, prin. Fax 779-4202
Raymore-Peculiar SHS 1,100/10-12
PO Box 366 64078 816-779-6656
Susan Mize, prin. Fax 779-6725

Perryville, Perry, Pop. 7,777
Perry County SD 32 2,200/K-12
326 College St 63775 573-547-7500
Beverly Schonhoff, supt. Fax 547-8572
www.perryville.k12.mo.us
Perry County MS 700/5-8
326 College St 63775 573-547-7500
Velda Haertling, prin. Fax 547-1962
Perryville Area Career Center Vo/Tech
326 College St 63775 573-547-7500
David Toney, dir. Fax 517-0396
Perryville HS 800/9-12
326 College St 63775 573-547-7500
Dr. Steven E. Wolf, prin. Fax 517-0592

St. Vincent JSHS 300/7-12
210 S Waters St 63775 573-547-2560
Lisa Best, prin. Fax 547-4191

Philadelphia, Marion
Marion County R-II SD | 200/PK-12
PO Box 100 63463 | 573-439-5913
Dianna Hoenes, supt. | Fax 439-5914
Marion County JSHS | 100/7-12
PO Box 100 63463 | 573-439-5913
Eric Spratt, prin. | Fax 439-5914

Piedmont, Wayne, Pop. 1,956
Clearwater R-I SD | 1,200/PK-12
RR 4 Box 1004 63957 | 573-223-7426
Blane Keel, supt. | Fax 223-2932
Clearwater HS | 400/9-12
RR 4 Box 1004 63957 | 573-223-4524
Paul D'Amico, prin. | Fax 223-3208
Clearwater MS | 400/5-8
RR 4 Box 1004 63957 | 573-223-7724
Samuel Holmes, prin. | Fax 223-3117

Pierce City, Lawrence, Pop. 1,401
Pierce City R-VI SD | 700/PK-12
300 N Myrtle St 65723 | 417-476-2555
Lois Klatt, supt. | Fax 476-5213
schoolweb.missouri.edu/piercecity.k12.mo.us/
Pierce City HS | 200/9-12
300 N Myrtle St 65723 | 417-476-2515
Russell Moreland, prin. | Fax 476-3516
Pierce City MS | 200/6-8
300 N Myrtle St 65723 | 417-476-2842
Gayla DeGraffenreid, prin. | Fax 476-5405

Pilot Grove, Cooper, Pop. 735
Pilot Grove C-4 SD | 300/PK-12
107 School St 65276 | 660-834-6915
Dr. Carol Maher, supt. | Fax 834-6925
www.schoolweb.missouri.edu/pilotgrovec4.k12.mo.us/
Pilot Grove HS | 100/9-12
107 School St 65276 | 660-834-4415
Mike Scott, prin. | Fax 834-4401
Pilot Grove MS | 100/6-8
107 School St 65276 | 660-834-4415
Mike Scott, prin. | Fax 834-4401

Plato, Texas, Pop. 64
Plato R-V SD | 500/PK-12
PO Box A 65552 | 417-458-3333
V. Leon Slape, supt. | Fax 458-4706
www.plato.k12.mo.us/
Plato JSHS | 300/6-12
PO Box A 65552 | 417-458-4980
Charles Crain, prin. | Fax 458-4706

Platte City, Platte, Pop. 4,836
Platte County R-III SD | 2,400/PK-12
PO Box 1400 64079 | 816-858-5420
Dr. Mark Harpst, supt. | Fax 858-5593
pcr3pirates.org
Northland Career Center | Vo/Tech
PO Box 1400 64079 | 816-858-5505
Cheryl Hill, dir. | Fax 858-3278
Platte City MS | 400/6-8
PO Box 1400 64079 | 816-858-2036
Terry Hart, prin. | Fax 858-3748
Platte County HS | 700/9-12
PO Box 1400 64079 | 816-858-2822
Craig Robinson, prin. | Fax 858-5140

Plattsburg, Clinton, Pop. 2,448
Clinton County R-III SD | 800/K-12
PO Box 287 64477 | 816-539-2183
W. M. Lord, supt. | Fax 539-2412
ccr3.k12.mo.us
Clinton County R-III MS | 200/6-8
PO Box 287 64477 | 816-539-3920
Ronald Hay, prin. | Fax 539-2412
Plattsburg HS | 300/9-12
PO Box 287 64477 | 816-539-2184
Kenneth Tongue, prin. | Fax 539-3315

Pleasant Hill, Cass, Pop. 6,176
Pleasant Hill R-III SD | 2,100/PK-12
301 N McKissock St 64080 | 816-540-3161
Dr. Wesley Townsend, supt. | Fax 540-5135
www.pleasanthillschools.com
Pleasant Hill HS | 700/9-12
1 Rooster Way 64080 | 816-540-3111
Tim Ryan, prin. | Fax 987-6084
Pleasant Hill MS | 500/6-8
1301 E Myrtle St 64080 | 816-540-2149
Gary Hancock, prin. | Fax 987-2017

Pleasant Hope, Polk, Pop. 557
Pleasant Hope R-VI SD | 900/K-12
PO Box 387 65725 | 417-267-2850
Bob Biggs, supt. | Fax 267-4373
www.phr6.com
Pleasant Hope HS | 300/9-12
PO Box 387 65725 | 417-267-2271
Gary Jenkins, prin. | Fax 267-5007
Pleasant Hope MS | 300/5-8
PO Box 387 65725 | 417-267-7701
Bill Redinger, prin. | Fax 267-9221
Other Schools – See Brighton

Point Lookout, Taney

College of the Ozarks 65726 | Post-Sec.
| 417-334-6411

Polo, Caldwell, Pop. 596
Polo R-VII SD | 400/K-12
300 W School St 64671 | 660-354-2326
Robert Newhart, supt. | Fax 354-2910
polo.k12.mo.us/
Polo HS | 100/9-12
300 W School St 64671 | 660-354-2524
Jason T. Snodgrass, prin. | Fax 354-2738
Polo MS | 100/5-8
300 W School St 64671 | 660-354-2200
Beverly Deis, prin. | Fax 354-3162

Poplar Bluff, Butler, Pop. 16,583
Poplar Bluff R-I SD | 4,900/PK-12
1110 N Westwood Blvd 63901 | 573-785-7751
Randy Winston, supt. | Fax 785-0336
www.r1schools.org
Poplar Bluff HS | 1,300/9-12
1300 Victory Ln 63901 | 573-785-6471
Scot Young, prin. | Fax 785-6471
Poplar Bluff JHS | 800/7-8
550 N Westwood Blvd 63901 | 573-785-5602
Bob Case, prin. | Fax 785-5602
Technical Career Center | Vo/Tech
3203 Oak Grove Rd 63901 | 573-785-2248
Jean Winston, prin. | Fax 785-4168

Three Rivers Community College | Post-Sec.
2080 Three Rivers Blvd 63901 | 573-840-9600

Portageville, New Madrid, Pop. 3,186
Portageville SD | 800/PK-12
904 King Ave 63873 | 573-379-3855
Kerwin Urhahn, supt. | Fax 379-5817
portageville.k12.mo.us
Portageville HS | 300/9-12
904 King Ave 63873 | 573-379-3819
Jason Aycock, prin. | Fax 379-3159
Portageville MS | 300/5-8
902 King Ave 63873 | 573-379-3853
Judy Scherer, prin. | Fax 379-3159

Potosi, Washington, Pop. 2,687
Potosi R-III SD | 2,200/1-12
400 N Mine St 63664 | 573-438-5485
Randy Davis, supt. | Fax 438-5487
www.potosi.k12.mo.us
Evans MS | 400/7-8
303 S Lead St 63664 | 573-438-2101
Don Young, prin. | Fax 438-4635
Potosi HS | 800/9-12
1 Trojan Dr 63664 | 573-438-2156
Rhonda Phares, prin. | Fax 438-2269

Prairie Home, Cooper, Pop. 225
Prairie Home R-V SD | 200/K-12
PO Box 105 65068 | 660-841-5296
Dr. Larry Davis, supt. | Fax 841-5513
Prairie Home JSHS | 100/7-12
PO Box 105 65068 | 660-841-5296
Robert Glenn, prin. | Fax 841-5513

Princeton, Mercer, Pop. 979
Princeton R-V SD | 400/K-12
1008 E Coleman St 64673 | 660-748-3211
Alan Hamilton, supt. | Fax 748-3212
www.tigertown.k12.mo.us/
Princeton JSHS | 200/7-12
1008 E Coleman St 64673 | 660-748-3490
George Scurlock, prin. | Fax 748-3212

Purdin, Linn, Pop. 217
Linn County R-I SD | 300/PK-12
PO Box 130 64674 | 660-244-5035
John Brinkley, supt. | Fax 244-5025
www.linnr1.k12.mo.us
Linn County JSHS | 100/7-12
PO Box 130 64674 | 660-244-5035
Ryan Livingston, prin. | Fax 244-5242

Purdy, Barry, Pop. 1,110
Purdy R-II SD | 700/K-12
PO Box 248 65734 | 417-442-3216
Jerry Lingo, supt. | Fax 442-3963
purdy.k12.mo.us/
Purdy HS | 200/9-12
PO Box 248 65734 | 417-442-3215
Robert Vice, prin. | Fax 442-3963
Purdy MS | 200/6-8
PO Box 248 65734 | 417-442-7066
Janet McComick, prin. | Fax 442-3963

Puxico, Stoddard, Pop. 1,142
Puxico R-VIII SD | 900/K-12
481 N Bedford St 63960 | 573-222-3762
Jerry Hobbs, supt. | Fax 222-3137
www.puxico.k12.mo.us
Mingo/Puxico Technical HS | Vo/Tech
481 N Bedford St 63960 | 573-222-2675
William Pogue, prin. | Fax 222-3137
Puxico JSHS | 400/7-12
481 N Bedford St 63960 | 573-222-3175
Kyle Dare, prin. | Fax 222-2375

Queen City, Schuyler, Pop. 638
Schuyler County R-I SD | 700/PK-12
PO Box 351 63561 | 660-766-2204
Marty Albertson, supt. | Fax 766-2400
schuyler.k12.mo.us
Schuyler County R-I HS | 200/9-12
PO Box 100 63561 | 660-766-2424
Alan Kerr, prin. | Fax 766-2646
Schuyler County R-I MS | 100/7-8
PO Box 248 63561 | 660-766-2296
Pam Barnett, prin. | Fax 766-2400

Ravenwood, Nodaway, Pop. 448
Northeast Nodaway County R-V SD | 300/PK-12
PO Box 206 64479 | 660-937-3112
James Farmer, supt. | Fax 937-3110
www.nen.k12.mo.us
Northeast Nodaway HS | 100/7-12
PO Box 206 64479 | 660-937-3125
Tracy Bottoms, prin. | Fax 937-3110

Raytown, Jackson, Pop. 29,747
Raytown C-2 SD | 9,100/PK-12
6608 Raytown Rd 64133 | 816-268-7000
Dr. Dale Houck, supt. | Fax 268-7019
www.raytownschools.org/
Herndon Career Center | Vo/Tech
11501 E State Route 350 64138 | 816-268-7140
Dr. Brian Mann, dir. | Fax 268-7149

Raytown HS | 1,400/9-12
6019 Blue Ridge Blvd 64133 | 816-268-7300
Steven T. Shelton, prin. | Fax 268-7315
Raytown South HS | 1,300/9-12
8211 Sterling Ave 64138 | 816-268-7330
Dr. Kevin Overfelt, prin. | Fax 268-7345
Raytown South MS | 1,000/6-8
8401 E 83rd St 64138 | 816-268-7380
Randy Thomas, prin. | Fax 268-7385
Other Schools – See Kansas City

Cedarvale Junior Academy | 50/PK-10
9933 E 56th St 64133 | 816-353-4828
S. Smith, prin.

Reeds Spring, Stone, Pop. 507
Reeds Spring R-IV SD | 2,200/PK-12
22595 Main St 65737 | 417-272-8173
Angie Besendorfer, supt. | Fax 272-8656
www.wolves.k12.mo.us
Gibson Technical Center | Vo/Tech
386 W State Highway 76 65737 | 417-272-3271
Don York, prin. | Fax 272-1529
Reeds Spring HS | 600/9-12
20277 State Highway 413 65737 | 417-272-8171
Jim Chandler, prin. | Fax 272-1481
Reeds Spring MS | 300/7-8
21016 Main St 65737 | 417-272-8245
Mendy Moss, prin. | Fax 272-8490

Republic, Greene, Pop. 9,680
Republic R-III SD | 3,500/PK-12
518 N Hampton Ave 65738 | 417-732-3605
Dr. Pam Hedgpeth, supt. | Fax 732-3609
www.republic.k12.mo.us/
Republic HS | 900/9-12
1 Tiger Dr 65738 | 417-732-3650
Vickie Neal, prin. | Fax 732-3659
Republic MS | 500/7-8
518 N Hampton Ave 65738 | 417-732-3640
Pat Mithelavage, prin. | Fax 732-3649

Rich Hill, Bates, Pop. 1,494
Rich Hill R-IV SD | 500/K-12
703 N 3rd St 64779 | 417-395-2418
Garry Pirch, supt. | Fax 395-2407
www.richhill.k12.mo.us/
Rich Hill HS | 200/7-12
703 N 3rd St 64779 | 417-395-4191
Leonard Tourtillott, prin. | Fax 395-2407

Richland, Pulaski, Pop. 1,831
Richland R-IV SD | 700/PK-12
714 E Jefferson Ave 65556 | 573-765-3241
Dr. Terry Wolfe, supt. | Fax 765-5552
schoolweb.missouri.edu/richlandr4.k12.mo.us/
Richland HS | 200/9-12
714 E Jefferson Ave 65556 | 573-765-3711
Doug Smith, prin. | Fax 765-5552
Richland JHS | 100/7-8
714 E Jefferson Ave 65556 | 573-765-3711
Joe Ridgeway, prin. | Fax 765-5552

Richmond, Ray, Pop. 6,078
Richmond R-XVI SD | 1,200/PK-12
749 Driskill Dr 64085 | 816-776-6912
Jim Robins, supt. | Fax 776-5554
richmond.k12.mo.us
Richmond HS | 500/9-12
451 E South St 64085 | 816-776-2226
Karen Southwick, prin. | Fax 776-8748
Richmond MS | 400/6-8
715 S Wellington St 64085 | 816-776-5841
Damon Kizzire, prin. | Fax 776-2788

Ridgeway, Harrison, Pop. 529
Ridgeway R-V SD | 100/PK-12
305 Main St 64481 | 660-872-6813
Troy Gregory, supt. | Fax 872-6230
Ridgeway JSHS | 50/7-12
305 Main St 64481 | 660-872-6813
Joe Shelton, prin. | Fax 872-6230

Risco, New Madrid, Pop. 380
Risco R-II SD | 200/K-12
PO Box 17 63874 | 573-396-5568
Stan Templeton, supt. | Fax 396-5503
Risco JSHS | 100/7-12
PO Box 17 63874 | 573-396-5568
Jeanie Johnston, prin. | Fax 396-5503

Rock Port, Atchison, Pop. 1,359
Rock Port R-II SD | 400/K-12
600 S Nebraska St 64482 | 660-744-6298
Richard Baldwin, supt. | Fax 744-5539
Rock Port JSHS | 200/7-12
600 S Nebraska St 64482 | 660-744-6296
Douglas Miller, prin. | Fax 744-5539

Rogersville, Greene, Pop. 1,744
Logan-Rogersville R-VIII SD | 1,900/PK-12
100 E Front St 65742 | 417-753-2891
Dr. Richard A. Markley, supt. | Fax 753-3063
Logan-Rogersville HS | 600/9-12
4700 S State Highway 125 65742 | 417-753-2813
Jeremy Tucker, prin. | Fax 753-3960
Logan-Rogersville MS | 500/6-8
8225 E Farm Road 174 65742 | 417-753-2896
Richard McPheeters, prin. | Fax 753-3182

Rolla, Phelps, Pop. 17,266
Rolla SD 31 | 4,100/PK-12
500A Forum Dr 65401 | 573-458-0100
Terry Adams, supt. | Fax 458-0105
rolla.k12.mo.us
Rolla JHS | 700/8-9
1360 Soest Rd 65401 | 573-458-0130
Stephen Laub, prin. | Fax 458-0135
Rolla SHS | 1,100/10-12
900 Bulldog Run 65401 | 573-458-0140
Roger Berkbuegler, prin. | Fax 458-0145

Rolla Technical Center | Vo/Tech
500 Forum Dr 65401 | 573-458-0160
Janece Martin, dir. | Fax 458-0164
Rolla Technical Institute | Vo/Tech
1304 E 10th St 65401 | 573-458-0150
Floyd Baker, dir. | Fax 458-0155

Metro Business College | Post-Sec.
1202 E State Route 72 65401 | 573-364-8464
Salem College of Hairstyling | Post-Sec.
1051 Kingshighway St Ste 1 65401 | 573-368-3136
University of Missouri | Post-Sec.
102 Parker 65409 | 573-341-4164

Rosendale, Andrew, Pop. 181
North Andrew County R-VI SD | 400/K-12
9120 Highway 48 64483 | 816-567-2965
Jim Shultz, supt. | Fax 567-2096
schoolweb.missouri.edu/nandrew.k12.mo.us/
North Andrew HS | 100/9-12
9120 Highway 48 64483 | 816-567-2525
Shannon Nolte, prin. | Fax 567-2096
North Andrew MS | 100/6-8
9120 Highway 48 64483 | 816-567-2527
Shannon Nolte, prin. | Fax 567-2096

Russellville, Cole, Pop. 737
Cole County R-I SD | 800/PK-12
PO Box 427 65074 | 573-782-3534
Richard Morelock, supt. | Fax 782-3545
www.cole.k12.mo.us
Cole County R-I MS | 200/6-8
PO Box 430 65074 | 573-782-4915
Matt Abernathy, prin. | Fax 782-3775
Russellville HS | 200/9-12
PO Box 427 65074 | 573-782-3973
Zach Templeton, prin. | Fax 782-3262

Saint Albans, Franklin

Chesterfield Day S | 100/PK-12
PO Box 78 63073 | 636-458-6688
Marianne Kearney, hdmstr. | Fax 458-6660

Saint Ann, Saint Louis, Pop. 13,408
Pattonville R-III SD | 6,000/K-12
11097 Saint Charles Rock Rd 63074 | 314-213-8500
Hugh Kinney, supt. | Fax 213-8601
www.psdr3.org
Holman MS | 700/6-8
11055 Saint Charles Rock Rd 63074 | 314-213-8032
Jim Schwab, prin. | Fax 213-8632
Other Schools – See Maryland Heights

Ritenour SD
Supt. — See Saint Louis
Hoech MS | 800/6-8
3312 Ashby Rd 63074 | 314-493-6200
Tim Streicher, prin. | Fax 426-3837

Patsy & Rob's Academy of Beauty | Post-Sec.
18 Northwest Plz 63074 | 314-298-8808
Vatterott College | Post-Sec.
3925 Industrial Dr 63074 | 800-345-6018

Saint Charles, Saint Charles, Pop. 61,253
Francis Howell R-III SD | 20,800/PK-12
4545 Central School Rd 63304 | 636-851-4000
Renee Schuster, supt. | Fax 851-4093
www.fhsd.k12.mo.us
Barnwell MS | 900/6-8
1035 Jungs Station Rd 63303 | 636-851-4100
David Eckhoff, prin. | Fax 851-4095
Hollenbeck MS | 800/6-8
4555 Central School Rd 63304 | 636-851-5400
Woody Borgschulte, prin. | Fax 851-4132
Howell Central HS | 2,200/9-12
5199 Highway N 63304 | 636-851-4600
Jack Ameis, prin. | Fax 851-4111
Howell HS | 1,700/9-12
7001 S Highway 94 63304 | 636-851-4700
Chris Geiner, prin. | Fax 851-4116
Howell North HS | 2,100/9-12
2549 Hackmann Rd 63303 | 636-851-4900
Darlene Jones, prin. | Fax 851-4123
Howell Union HS | 2,000/9-12
1405 Highway D 63304 | 636-851-5000
Mike Hylen, prin. | Fax 851-4127
Saeger MS | 900/6-8
5201 Highway N 63304 | 636-851-5600
Brian Schick, prin. | Fax 851-4138
Other Schools – See Weldon Spring

St. Charles County R-V SD | 1,200/K-12
2165 Highway V 63301 | 636-250-5000
Daniel G. Dozier, supt. | Fax 250-5444
www.ofsd.k12.mo.us
Orchard Farm HS | 400/9-12
2165 Highway V 63301 | 636-250-5400
Tim McInnis, prin. | Fax 250-5425
Orchard Farm MS | 300/6-8
2165 Highway V 63301 | 636-250-5300
Marcia Cummins, prin. | Fax 250-5306

St. Charles R-VI SD | 5,900/K-12
1025 Country Club Rd 63303 | 636-443-4000
Dr. James Cale, supt. | Fax 443-4001
www.stcharles.k12.mo.us
Hardin MS | 700/6-8
1950 Elm St 63301 | 636-443-4300
Michael Ebert, prin. | Fax 443-4301
Jefferson MS | 700/6-8
2660 Zumbehl Rd 63301 | 636-443-4400
Gerry Kettenbach, prin. | Fax 443-4401
Lewis & Clark Career Center | Vo/Tech
2400 Zumbehl Rd 63301 | 636-443-4950
Kathy Frederking, prin. | Fax 443-4951

St. Charles HS | 1,000/9-12
725 N Kingshighway St 63301 | 636-443-4100
Jerry Cook, prin. | Fax 443-4101
St. Charles West HS | 1,000/9-12
3601 Droste Rd 63301 | 636-443-4200
Kim Fitterling, prin. | Fax 443-4201

Duchesne HS | 700/9-12
2550 Elm St 63301 | 636-946-6767
Rev. Kenneth Brown, prin. | Fax 946-6267
Lewis & Clark Career Center | Post-Sec.
2400 Zumbehl Rd 63301 | 636-443-4950
Lindenwood University | Post-Sec.
209 S Kingshighway St 63301 | 636-949-2000
SS. Elizabeth & Robert MS | 200/6-8
1424 S 1st Capitol Dr 63303 | 636-946-1474
Marlene DiMaggio, prin. | Fax 946-6014

Saint Clair, Franklin, Pop. 4,420
St. Clair R-XIII SD | 2,400/K-12
905 Bardot St 63077 | 636-629-3500
Michael D. Murphy, supt. | Fax 629-4466
stclair.k12.mo.us/
Saint Clair HS | 900/9-12
1015 School Dr 63077 | 636-629-3500
Bradley Ellis, prin. | Fax 629-1979
Saint Clair JHS, 925 School Dr 63077 | 500/6-8
Kevin Goddard, prin. | 636-629-3500

Sainte Genevieve, Sainte Genevieve, Pop. 4,666
St. Genevieve County R-II SD | 2,100/K-12
375 N 5th St 63670 | 573-883-4500
Mikel Stewart, supt. | Fax 883-5957
www.stegen.k12.mo.us
Sainte Genevieve HS | 700/9-12
715 Washington St 63670 | 573-883-4500
Charles Crouther, prin. | Fax 883-5957
Sainte Genevieve MS | 600/6-8
211 N 5th St 63670 | 573-883-4500
John Boyd, prin. | Fax 883-5957

Valle Catholic HS | 200/9-12
40 N 4th St 63670 | 573-883-7496
Sara Menard, prin. | Fax 883-9142

Saint Elizabeth, Miller, Pop. 300
St. Elizabeth R-IV SD | 300/PK-12
PO Box 68 65075 | 573-493-2246
Sid Doerhoff, supt. | Fax 493-2380
www.schoolweb.missouri.edu/st.elizabeth.k12.mo.us
Saint Elizabeth JSHS | 100/7-12
PO Box 68 65075 | 573-493-2246
Leroy Heckemeyer, prin. | Fax 493-2380

Saint James, Phelps, Pop. 3,941
St. James R-I SD | 1,800/PK-12
101 E Scioto St 65559 | 573-265-3261
Joy Tucker, supt. | Fax 265-6126
www.stjames.k12.mo.us/
St. James HS | 700/9-12
101 E Scioto St 65559 | 573-265-3262
Charles West, prin. | Fax 265-3652
St. James MS | 500/6-8
1 Tiger Dr 65559 | 573-265-7484
Jim Harris, prin. | Fax 265-6302

Saint Joseph, Buchanan, Pop. 72,663
St. Joseph SD | 11,800/PK-12
925 Felix St 64501 | 816-671-4000
Melody Smith, supt. | Fax 671-4470
www.sjsd.k12.mo.us
Benton HS | 900/9-12
5655 S 4th St 64504 | 816-671-4030
Rick German, prin. | Fax 671-4036
Bode MS | 500/7-8
720 N Noyes Blvd 64506 | 816-671-4050
Roberta Dias, prin. | Fax 671-4473
Central HS | 1,700/9-12
2602 Edmond St 64501 | 816-671-4080
Marlie Williams, prin. | Fax 671-4474
Hillyard Technical Center | Vo/Tech
3434 Faraon St 64506 | 816-671-4170
Regenia Briggs, dir. | Fax 671-4479
Lafayette HS | 900/9-12
412 E Highland Ave 64505 | 816-671-4220
Dr. Tyran Sumy, prin. | Fax 671-4480
Robidoux MS | 400/7-8
4212 Saint Joseph Ave 64505 | 816-671-4350
Mike Buckler, prin. | Fax 671-4487
Spring Garden MS | 500/7-8
5802 S 22nd St 64503 | 816-671-4380
Lara Gilpin, prin. | Fax 671-4489
Truman MS | 500/7-8
3227 Olive St #45 64507 | 816-671-4400
Beery Johnson, prin. | Fax 671-4491

Bishop Le Blond HS | 300/9-12
3529 Frederick Ave 64506 | 816-279-1629
Janet Wilcox, prin. | Fax 279-5488
Missouri Western State College | Post-Sec.
4525 Downs Dr 64507 | 816-271-4200
St. Joseph Christian S | 300/PK-12
5401B Gene Field Rd 64506 | 816-279-3760
Rich Fox, prin. | Fax 279-4574
Vatterott College | Post-Sec.
3131 Frederick Ave 64506 | 816-364-5399

Saint Louis, Saint Louis, Pop. 332,223
Affton SD 101 | 2,500/K-12
8701 Mackenzie Rd 63123 | 314-638-8770
Dr. Don Francis, supt. | Fax 631-2548
www.affton.k12.mo.us
Affton HS | 800/9-12
8309 Mackenzie Rd 63123 | 314-638-6330
Jeff Morris, prin. | Fax 633-5990
Rogers MS | 600/6-8
7550 Mackenzie Rd 63123 | 314-351-9679
Jeff Remelius, prin. | Fax 351-6381

Bayless SD | 1,600/PK-12
4530 Weber Rd 63123 | 314-631-2244
Maureen Clancy-May, supt. | Fax 544-6315
csd.org/schools/bayless/baylesshome.html#bsd
Bayless HS | 500/9-12
4532 Weber Rd 63123 | 314-544-6342
Denise Swanger, prin. | Fax 544-6315
Bayless JHS | 300/7-8
4532 Weber Rd 63123 | 314-544-6306
Ron Tucker, prin. | Fax 544-6315

Ferguson-Florissant R-II SD
Supt. — See Florissant
Ferguson HS | 800/7-8
70 January Ave 63135 | 314-506-9600
Susan Kelly, prin. | Fax 506-9601
McCluer South - Berkeley HS | 500/9-12
201 Brotherton Ln 63135 | 314-506-9800
Vernon Mitchell, prin. | Fax 506-9801

Hancock Place SD | 1,800/PK-12
9101 S Broadway 63125 | 314-544-1300
Dr. Ed Stewart, supt. | Fax 631-3752
hancock.k12.mo.us
Hancock HS | 500/9-12
229 W Ripa Ave 63125 | 314-544-1200
Jason Naucke, prin. | Fax 544-6427
Hancock Place MS | 500/6-8
243 W Ripa Ave 63125 | 314-544-6423
Scott Wilkerson, prin. | Fax 544-6470

Hazelwood SD
Supt. — See Florissant
Hazelwood East HS | 1,900/9-12
11300 Dunn Rd 63138 | 314-953-5600
Mark Martin, prin. | Fax 953-5613
Kirby MS | 1,300/7-8
1865 Dunn Rd 63138 | 314-953-5700
Dr. Richard Bass, prin. | Fax 953-5713

Ladue SD | 3,200/PK-12
9703 Conway Rd 63124 | 314-994-7080
David Benson, supt. | Fax 994-0441
www.ladue.k12.mo.us
Ladue MS | 800/6-8
9701 Conway Rd 63124 | 314-993-3900
Cathy Richter, prin. | Fax 997-8736
Watkins HS | 1,100/9-12
1201 S Warson Rd 63124 | 314-993-6447
Joseph Powers, prin. | Fax 994-1467

Lindbergh R-VIII SD | 5,400/K-12
4900 S Lindbergh Blvd 63126 | 314-729-2480
Dr. James Sandfort, supt. | Fax 729-2482
www.lindbergh.k12.mo.us
Lindbergh HS | 1,800/9-12
4900 S Lindbergh Blvd 63126 | 314-729-2410
Dr. Ron Helms, prin. | Fax 729-2412
Sperreng MS | 1,300/6-8
12111 Tesson Ferry Rd 63128 | 314-729-2420
Dr. Jennifer Tiller, prin. | Fax 729-2422

Maplewood Richmond Heights SD
Supt. — See Maplewood
Maplewood Richmond Heights MS | 200/7-8
7539 Manchester Rd 63143 | 314-644-4406
Charles J. Pearson, prin. | Fax 781-4629

Mehlville R-IX SD | 11,700/K-12
3120 Lemay Ferry Rd 63125 | 314-467-5000
Dr. Jerry Chambers, supt. | Fax 467-5099
www.mehlvilleschooldistrict.com/
Bernard MS | 800/6-8
1054 Forder Rd 63129 | 314-467-6600
Michele Condon, prin. | Fax 467-6699
Buerkle MS | 700/6-8
623 Buckley Rd 63125 | 314-467-6800
Scott Hayes, prin. | Fax 467-6899
Mehlville HS | 2,000/9-12
3200 Lemay Ferry Rd 63125 | 314-467-6000
Vincent Viviano, prin. | Fax 467-6099
Oakville HS | 2,100/9-12
5557 Milburn Rd 63129 | 314-467-7000
William Scheffler, prin. | Fax 467-7099
Oakville MS | 700/6-8
5950 Telegraph Rd 63129 | 314-467-7400
Mike Salsman, prin. | Fax 467-7499
Washington MS | 700/6-8
5165 Ambs Rd 63128 | 314-467-7600
Robert Linderer, prin. | Fax 467-7699

Normandy SD | 5,500/PK-12
3855 Lucas and Hunt Rd 63121 | 314-493-0400
Connie Calloway, supt. | Fax 493-0475
www.normandy.k12.mo.us
Normandy HS | 1,300/9-12
6701 Saint Charles Rock Rd 63133 | 314-493-0600
Carl Hudson, prin. | Fax 493-0668
Other Schools – See Normandy

Ritenour SD | 6,200/K-12
2420 Woodson Rd 63114 | 314-493-6010
Paul Doerrer, supt. | Fax 426-7144
www.ritenour.k12.mo.us
Other Schools – See Overland, Saint Ann

Riverview Gardens SD | 7,900/K-12
1370 Northumberland Dr 63137 | 314-869-2505
Dr. Henry P. Williams, supt. | Fax 869-6354
www.rgsd.org
Riverview Gardens Central MS | 900/7-8
9800 Patricia Barkalow Dr 63137 | 314-869-2600
Gloria Ross, prin. | Fax 388-6028
Riverview Gardens HS | 1,900/9-12
1218 Shepley Dr 63137 | 314-869-4700
Marshall Peeples, prin. | Fax 388-6020
Westview MS | 500/7-8
1950 Nemnich Rd 63136 | 314-867-0410
Nolen Ross, prin. | Fax 388-6055

Special SD of St. Louis County 10-12
12110 Clayton Rd 63131 314-989-8100
Dr. Peter Kachris, supt. Fax 989-8440
ssd.k12.mo.us
South County Technical HS Vo/Tech
12721 W Watson Rd 63127 314-989-7400
Dave Baker, prin. Fax 989-7503
Other Schools – See Florissant

St. Louis City SD 36,800/PK-12
801 N 11th St 63101 314-231-3720
Dr. Creg Williams, supt. Fax 345-2661
www.slps.org/
Beaumont HS 1,400/9-12
3836 Natural Bridge Ave 63107 314-533-2410
Travis Brown, prin. Fax 535-0786
Blewett MS 500/6-8
1927 Cass Ave 63106 314-231-7738
Annie Chambers, prin. Fax 231-0073
Blow MS Community Education Center 300/6-8
516 Loughborough Ave 63111 314-353-1349
Dr. James L. Lange, prin. Fax 353-9048
Bunche International Studies MS 300/6-8
3125 S Kingshighway Blvd 63139 314-772-1779
Carol Howard, prin. Fax 772-1715
Busch/Academic-Athletic Academy 300/6-8
5910 Clifton Ave 63109 314-352-1043
William C. Bullerdick, prin. Fax 352-3685
Carnahan MS 500/6-8
4041 S Broadway 63118 314-457-0582
Doris Johnson, prin. Fax 457-9741
Carr Lane Visual & Performing Art MS 600/6-8
1004 N Jefferson Ave 63106 314-231-0413
Melba Davis, prin. Fax 241-1213
Central Visual and Performing Arts HS 500/9-12
3125 S Kingshighway Blvd 63139 314-771-2772
Dr. Stanley Engram, prin. Fax 771-0135
Cleveland NJROTC Academy 1,000/9-12
4352 Louisiana Ave 63111 314-832-0933
Julius Penn, prin. Fax 832-0246
Community Access Job Training Vo/Tech
4915 Donovan Ave 63109 314-481-4095
Dr. Roland Werner, prin. Fax 481-4220
Compton-Drew ILC MS 500/6-8
5130 Oakland Ave 63110 314-652-9282
Andrea Walker, prin. Fax 652-9371
Fanning MS Community Education Center 300/6-8
3417 Grace Ave 63116 314-772-1038
Diane M. Bowles, prin. Fax 772-0437
Gateway HS 1,400/9-12
5101 McRee Ave 63110 314-776-3300
Shepard Pittman, prin. Fax 776-8267
Gateway MS 600/6-8
1200 N Jefferson Ave 63106 314-241-2295
Mulugheta Teferi, prin. Fax 241-7698
Humboldt MS 400/6-8
2516 S 9th St 63104 314-772-5566
Georgia L. Calhoun, prin. Fax 772-3180
Langston MS 400/6-8
5511 Wabada Ave 63112 314-383-2908
Carol Barnes, prin. Fax 385-4632
Long MS Community Education Center 500/6-8
5028 Morganford Rd 63116 314-481-3440
Alva Blue, prin. Fax 481-7329
L'Ouverture MS 400/6-8
3021 Hickory St 63104 314-664-3579
Juanita Jones, prin. Fax 664-7955
McKinley Classical Jr. Academy 400/6-8
2156 Russell Blvd 63104 314-773-0027
Brenda Smith, prin. Fax 771-9749
Metro HS 200/9-12
4015 McPherson Ave 63108 314-534-3894
Wilfred D. Moore, prin. Fax 531-4894
Miller Career Academy Vo/Tech
1000 N Grand Blvd 63106 314-371-0394
Stephen Warmack, prin. Fax 371-1311
Northwest MS 700/6-8
5140 Riverview Blvd 63120 314-385-4774
Valerie Carter, prin. Fax 389-3566
Pruitt Military Academy 300/6-8
1212 N 22nd St 63106 314-231-1443
Herbert Buie, prin. Fax 231-4895
Roosevelt HS 1,600/9-12
3230 Hartford St 63118 314-776-6040
Sylvia Shead, prin. Fax 776-0152
Soldan International Studies HS 900/9-12
918 Union Blvd 63108 314-367-9222
Thomas Cason, prin. Fax 367-1898
Stevens MS Community Education Center 300/6-8
1033 Whittier St 63113 314-533-8550
Laura Washington, prin. Fax 533-0306
Stowe MS 500/6-8
5750 Lotus Ave 63112 314-382-7310
Vernice Hicks, prin. Fax 382-4277
Sumner Magnet HS 1,100/9-12
4248 Cottage Ave 63113 314-371-1048
George Edwards, prin. Fax 531-9852
Turner MS 300/6-8
2615 Billups Ave 63113 314-535-8482
Yolanda Austin, prin. Fax 535-0196
Vashon HS 1,400/9-12
3035 Cass Ave 63106 314-533-9487
Calvin Starks, prin. Fax 533-7540
Webster MS 300/6-8
2127 N 11th St 63106 314-231-9196
Rose Mary Johnson, prin. Fax 231-3927
Yeatman MS Community Education Center 500/6-8
4265 Athlone Ave 63115 314-261-8132
Valerie Taylor, prin. Fax 389-4613
Washington Education Center Adult
2030 S Vandeventer Ave 63110 314-771-4041
Annette Hayes, prin. Fax 771-4053

University City SD 5,700/PK-12
8136 Groby Rd 63130 314-290-4000
Dr. James Victory, supt. Fax 725-7692
www.ucityschools.org
Other Schools – See University City

Webster Groves SD
Supt. — See Webster Groves
Hixson MS 700/7-8
630 S Elm Ave 63119 314-963-6450
Dr. Mary Stefanus, prin. Fax 918-4624

Wellston SD 600/PK-12
6574 Saint Louis Ave 63121 314-290-7900
Dr. Charles Brown, supt. Fax 290-7905
www.wellston.k12.mo.us
Bishop MS 200/5-8
6310 Wellsmar Ave 63133 314-290-7600
Robert Hudson, prin. Fax 290-7605
Eskridge HS 100/9-12
1200 Sutter Ave 63133 314-290-7800
Henry Anderson, prin. Fax 290-7805

Aquinas Institute of Theology Post-Sec.
3642 Lindell Blvd 63108 314-658-3882
Bais Yaakov HS of St. Louis 50/9-12
700 North and South Rd 63130 314-863-9230
Dr. William H. Solomon, prin. Fax 863-3856
Barnes-Jewish College of Nursing Post-Sec.
306 S Kingshighway Blvd 63110 314-454-7055
Bishop DuBourg HS 900/9-12
5850 Eichelberger St 63109 314-832-3030
Bridget Timoney, prin. Fax 832-0529
Block Yeshiva HS 100/9-12
1146 N Warson Rd 63132 314-872-8701
Rabbi Gabriel Munk, prin. Fax 872-8703
Burroughs S 600/7-12
755 S Price Rd 63124 314-993-4040
Keith Shahan, hdmstr. Fax 993-6458
Cardinal Ritter College Prep HS 200/9-12
701 N Spring Ave 63108 314-446-5500
Carmele Hall, prin. Fax 446-5570
Central Institute for the Deaf Post-Sec.
818 S Euclid Ave 63110 314-652-3200
Chaminade College Preparatory S 900/6-12
425 S Lindbergh Blvd 63131 314-993-4400
Rev. Ralph Siefert, pres. Fax 993-4403
Christian Brothers College HS 900/9-12
1850 De La Salle Dr 63141 314-985-6100
Br. David Poos, prin. Fax 985-6115
Churchill S 100/2-10
1035 Price School Ln 63124 314-997-4343
Fax 997-2760
Clayton University Post-Sec.
11939 Manchester Rd # 123 63131 636-825-6305
Concordia Lutheran MS 50/6-8
3630 Ohio Ave 63118 314-865-1144
Fax 772-4210
Concordia Seminary Post-Sec.
801 De Mun Ave 63105 314-721-5934
Cor Jesu Academy 500/9-12
10230 Gravois Rd 63123 314-842-1546
Sr. Sheila O'Neill, prin. Fax 842-6061
Covenant Theological Seminary Post-Sec.
12330 Conway Rd 63141 800-264-8064
Crossroads S 200/7-12
500 De Baliviere Ave 63112 314-367-8085
William Handmaker, prin. Fax 367-9711
Deaconess College of Nursing Post-Sec.
6150 Oakland Ave 63139 314-768-3044
De LaSalle MS 100/6-8
4145 Kennerly Ave 63113 314-531-9820
Mark Cosenza, prin. Fax 531-4820
De Smet Jesuit HS 1,200/9-12
233 N New Ballas Rd 63141 314-567-3500
Dr. Gregory Densberger, prin. Fax 567-1519
DeVry University Post-Sec.
1801 Park 270 Dr Ste 260 63146 314-542-4222
DVA Medical Center Post-Sec.
1 Jefferson Barracks Rd 63125 314-894-6631
Elaine Steven Beauty College Post-Sec.
10420 W Florissant Ave 63136 314-868-8196
Fontbonne University Post-Sec.
6800 Wydown Blvd 63105 314-889-1419
Harris-Stowe State University Post-Sec.
3026 Laclede Ave 63103 314-340-3300
Hickey College Post-Sec.
940 Westport Plz 63146 314-434-2212
IHM Health Studies Center Post-Sec.
2500 Abbott Pl 63143 314-768-1234
IHM Health Studies Center Post-Sec.
3663 Lindell Blvd 63108 314-768-1000
Incarnate Word Academy 500/9-12
2788 Normandy Dr 63121 314-725-5850
Dr. Randy Mikolas, prin. Fax 725-2308
Jefferson S 100/7-12
4100 S Lindbergh Blvd 63127 314-843-4151
Fax 843-3527
Keller Graduate School Post-Sec.
1010 Market St Ste 550 63101 314-588-0066
Kenrick School of Theology Post-Sec.
5200 Glennon Dr 63119 314-792-6100
Life Christian S 300/PK-12
13001 Gravois Rd 63127 314-842-1781
Jay McCurry, prin. Fax 843-2731
Logos S 100/7-12
9137 Old Bonhomme Rd 63132 314-997-7002
Fax 997-6848
Loyola Academy 300/6-8
3854 Washington Blvd 63108 314-531-9091
Frank Corley, prin. Fax 531-3603
Lutheran HS North 400/9-12
5401 Lucas and Hunt Rd 63121 314-389-3100
Tim Hipenbecker, prin. Fax 389-3103
Lutheran HS South 600/9-12
9515 Tesson Ferry Rd 63123 314-631-1400
Paul Buetow, prin. Fax 631-7762
Lutheran School of Nursing Post-Sec.
3547 S Jefferson Ave 63118 314-577-5850
Marian MS 200/5-8
3112 Meramec St 63118 314-351-7674
Sr. Rosalie Wisniewski, prin. Fax 351-5496

Mary Institute/St. Louis Country Day S 1,200/PK-12
101 N Warson Rd 63124 314-993-5100
Matt Gossage, prin. Fax 995-7470
Maryville University of St. Louis Post-Sec.
13550 Conway Rd 63141 314-529-9300
Midwest Institute for Medical Assistants Post-Sec.
10910 Manchester Rd 63122 314-965-8363
Missouri Baptist University Post-Sec.
1 College Park Dr 63141 314-434-1115
Missouri College Post-Sec.
10121 Manchester Rd 63122 314-821-7700
Missouri School for the Blind Post-Sec.
3815 Magnolia Ave 63110 314-776-4320
Missouri Tech Post-Sec.
1167 Corporate Lake Dr 63132 314-569-3600
National Academy of Beauty Arts Post-Sec.
157 Concord Plz 63128 314-842-3616
Nerinx Hall HS 600/9-12
530 E Lockwood Ave 63119 314-968-1505
Jane Kosash, prin. Fax 968-0604
Notre Dame HS 500/9-12
320 E Ripa Ave 63125 314-544-1015
Sr. Michelle Emmerich, prin. Fax 544-8003
Parks College of St. Louis University Post-Sec.
221 N Grand Blvd # 119 63103 314-977-2500
Patricia Stevens College Post-Sec.
330 N 4th St Ste 306 63102 314-421-0949
Principia S 600/PK-12
13201 Clayton Rd 63131 314-434-2100
Peter Stevens, hdmstr. Fax 275-3583
Ranken Technical College Post-Sec.
4431 Finney Ave 63113 314-371-0236
Rosati-Kain HS 400/9-12
4389 Lindell Blvd 63108 314-533-8513
Sr. Joan Andert, prin. Fax 533-1618
St. Elizabeth Academy 200/9-12
3401 Arsenal St 63118 314-771-5134
Susan Geldmacher, prin. Fax 771-3528
St. John's Mercy Medical Center Post-Sec.
615 S New Ballas Rd 63141 314-569-6182
St. John the Baptist Prep HS 400/9-12
5021 Adkins Ave 63116 314-351-5604
Dr. John Kosash, prin. Fax 351-3050
St. John Vianney HS 800/9-12
1311 S Kirkwood Rd 63122 314-965-4853
Larry Keller, prin. Fax 965-1950
St. Joseph Academy 600/9-12
2307 S Lindbergh Blvd 63131 314-965-7205
Nancy Repking, prin. Fax 965-9114
St. Louis College of Health Careers Post-Sec.
909 S Taylor Ave 63110 314-652-0300
St. Louis College of Pharmacy Post-Sec.
4588 Parkview Pl 63110 314-367-8700
St. Louis Community College Post-Sec.
3400 Pershall Rd 63135 314-595-4200
St. Louis Community College Post-Sec.
5600 Oakland Ave 63110 314-644-9100
St. Louis Hair Academy Post-Sec.
3701 Kossuth Ave 63107 314-533-3125
St. Louis Priory S 400/7-12
500 S Mason Rd 63141 314-434-3690
Rev. Michael Brunner, hdmstr. Fax 576-7088
St. Louis University Post-Sec.
221 N Grand Blvd 63103 314-977-2222
St. Louis University HS 1,000/9-12
4970 Oakland Ave 63110 314-531-0330
Dr. Mary Schenkenberg, prin. Fax 531-8446
St. Mary's HS 500/9-12
4701 S Grand Blvd 63111 314-481-8400
Kevin Hacker, prin. Fax 481-3670
Tower Grove Christian S 400/K-12
4257 Magnolia Ave 63110 314-776-6473
Jim Kerr, prin. Fax 776-4867
Trinity Catholic HS 500/9-12
1720 Redman Rd 63138 314-741-1333
Kirk Boschert, prin. Fax 741-1335
University of Missouri Post-Sec.
1 University Blvd 63121 314-516-5000
Vatterott College Post-Sec.
12970 Maurer Industrial Dr 63127 314-843-4200
Villa Duchesne HS 300/9-12
801 S Spoede Rd 63131 314-432-2021
Dr. Patty Fagin, prin. Fax 432-7713
Villa Duchesne JHS 100/7-8
801 S Spoede Rd 63131 314-432-2021
Dr. Patty Fagin, prin. Fax 432-7713
Visitation Academy HS 300/9-12
3020 N Ballas Rd 63131 314-625-9100
Matthew Walsh, prin. Fax 432-5354
Visitation Academy JHS 100/7-8
3020 N Ballas Rd 63131 314-625-9123
Matthew J. Walsh, prin. Fax 432-7210
Washington University in St. Louis Post-Sec.
1 Brookings Dr 63130 314-935-5000
Webster University Post-Sec.
470 E Lockwood Ave 63119 314-968-6900
Westminster Christian Academy 800/7-12
10900 Ladue Rd 63141 314-997-2900
James Marsh, hdmstr. Fax 997-2903
Whitfield S 500/6-12
175 S Mason Rd 63141 314-434-5141
Ruth Greathouse, prin. Fax 434-6193

Saint Peters, Saint Charles, Pop. 53,397

Ft. Zumwalt R-II SD
Supt. — See O Fallon
DuBray MS 1,000/6-8
100 DuBray Dr 63376 636-279-7979
Mike Anderson, prin. Fax 278-4749
Ft. Zumwalt South HS 2,200/9-12
8050 Mexico Rd 63376 636-978-1212
Dr. Graham Weir, prin. Fax 980-1745
Ft. Zumwalt South MS 1,100/6-8
300 Knaust Rd 63376 636-281-0776
Paul Myers, prin. Fax 281-0006

Abbott Acad of Cosmetology Arts/Sciences — Post-Sec.
  2101 Parkway Dr 63376 — 636-447-0100
Lutheran HS of St. Charles County — 400/9-12
  5100 Mexico Rd 63376 — 636-928-5100
  Larry Marty, prin. — Fax 928-8451
St. Charles Community College — Post-Sec.
  4601 Mid Rivers Mall Dr 63376 — 636-922-8000
Sanford-Brown College — Post-Sec.
  100 Richmond Center Blvd 63376 — 888-793-2433

Salem, Dent, Pop. 4,743
Salem R-80 SD — 1,500/K-12
  1400 Tiger Pride Dr 65560 — 573-729-6642
  Steve Bryant, supt. — Fax 729-8493
  www.salem.k12.mo.us/
Salem JHS — 400/7-9
  1400 Tiger Pride Dr 65560 — 573-729-4261
  Larry Maxwell, prin. — Fax 729-2720
Salem SHS — 500/10-12
  1400 Tiger Pride Dr 65560 — 573-729-2222
  Jane Reeves, prin. — Fax 729-7408

Salisbury, Chariton, Pop. 1,663
Salisbury R-IV SD — 500/K-12
  PO Box 314 65281 — 660-388-6699
  Dr. Roger Dorson, supt. — Fax 388-6753
Salisbury JSHS — 300/6-12
  PO Box 314 65281 — 660-388-6442
  Bob Fuka, prin. — Fax 388-5651

Sarcoxie, Jasper, Pop. 1,347
Sarcoxie R-II SD — 800/K-12
  PO Box 310 64862 — 417-548-3134
  Charles Price, supt. — Fax 548-6165
Sarcoxie JSHS — 400/6-12
  PO Box 310 64862 — 417-548-2153
  John Ihm, prin. — Fax 548-6165

Savannah, Andrew, Pop. 4,887
Savannah R-III SD — 2,400/K-12
  PO Box 151 64485 — 816-324-3144
  Donald Lawrence, supt. — Fax 324-5594
  www.savannah.k12.mo.us
Savannah HS — 700/9-12
  701 State Rte E 64485 — 816-324-3128
  Steve Kellepouris, prin. — Fax 324-6536
Savannah MS — 500/6-8
  701 W Chestnut St 64485 — 816-324-3126
  Leisa Blair, prin. — Fax 324-6397

Scott City, Scott, Pop. 4,570
Scott City R-I SD — 1,000/K-12
  3000 Main St 63780 — 573-264-2381
  Diann Bradshaw, supt. — Fax 264-2206
  scschools.k12.mo.us/
Scott City HS — 300/9-12
  3000 Main St 63780 — 573-264-2138
  Kerry Thompson, prin. — Fax 264-2206
Scott City MS — 300/6-8
  3000 Main St 63780 — 573-264-2139
  Paul Sharp, prin. — Fax 264-2206

Sedalia, Pettis, Pop. 20,048
Sedalia SD 200 — 4,500/PK-12
  2806 Matthew Dr 65301 — 660-829-6450
  Marvin Ebersold, supt. — Fax 827-8938
  sedalia.k12.mo.us
Sedalia MS — 1,000/6-8
  2205 S Ingram Ave 65301 — 660-829-6500
  Martin White, prin. — Fax 827-6112
Smith-Cotton HS — 1,300/9-12
  312 E Broadway Blvd 65301 — 660-829-6300
  Todd Whitney, prin. — Fax 829-6409

American College of Hair Design — Post-Sec.
  125 Duke Rd 65301 — 660-827-3295
Sacred Heart HS — 100/9-12
  416 W 3rd St 65301 — 660-827-3800
  Dr. Mark Register, admin. — Fax 827-3806
State Fair Community College — Post-Sec.
  3201 W 16th St 65301 — 660-530-5800

Senath, Dunklin, Pop. 1,632
Senath-Hornersville C-8 SD — 800/K-12
  PO Box 370 63876 — 573-738-2669
  Yancy Poorman, supt. — Fax 738-9845
  www.shs.k12.mo.us/
Senath-Hornersville HS — 200/9-12
  PO Box 370 63876 — 573-738-2661
  Kim Campbell, prin. — Fax 738-3481
Other Schools – See Hornersville

Seneca, Newton, Pop. 2,161
Seneca R-VII SD — 1,700/K-12
  PO Box 469 64865 — 417-776-3426
  Joe Layton, supt. — Fax 776-2177
  schoolweb.missouri.edu/seneca.k12.mo.us/
Seneca HS — 600/9-12
  PO Box 469 64865 — 417-776-3926
  Ronald Wallace, prin. — Fax 776-1878
Wells MS — 400/6-8
  PO Box 469 64865 — 417-776-3911
  John Whitehead, prin. — Fax 776-2673

Seymour, Webster, Pop. 1,905
Seymour R-II SD — 1,000/PK-12
  416 E Clinton Ave 65746 — 417-935-2287
  Frank Rowles, supt. — Fax 935-4060
  schoolweb.missouri.edu/seymour.k12.mo.us/
Seymour HS — 300/9-12
  625 E Clinton Ave 65746 — 417-935-4508
  Bruce Denney, prin. — Fax 935-4539
Seymour MS — 200/6-8
  501 E Clinton Ave 65746 — 417-935-4626
  Brian Bell, prin. — Fax 935-2848

Shelbina, Shelby, Pop. 1,891
Shelby County R-IV SD — 800/PK-12
  4154 Highway 36 63468 — 573-588-4961
  Timothy Hadfield, supt. — Fax 588-2490
  www.cardinals.k12.mo.us
South Shelby JSHS — 400/6-12
  4154 Highway 36 63468 — 573-588-4163
  Brett Thompson, prin. — Fax 588-2490

Shelbyville, Shelby, Pop. 681
North Shelby SD — 400/PK-12
  3071 Highway 15 63469 — 573-633-2410
  Larry Smoot, supt. — Fax 633-2138
  schoolweb.missouri.edu/nshelby.k12.mo.us
North Shelby JSHS — 200/7-12
  3071 Highway 15 63469 — 573-633-2410
  Kimala Gaines, prin. — Fax 633-2138

Sheldon, Vernon, Pop. 526
Sheldon R-VIII SD — 200/K-12
  PO Box 68 64784 — 417-884-5113
  Phyllis Sprenkle, supt. — Fax 884-5331
  www.sheldon.k12.mo.us
Sheldon JSHS — 100/7-12
  PO Box 68 64784 — 417-884-5111
  Connie Estes, prin. — Fax 884-5331

Sikeston, Scott, Pop. 16,960
Scott County Central SD — 400/PK-12
  20794 US Highway 61 63801 — 573-471-2686
  Joel Holland, supt. — Fax 471-2686
  scottcentral.k12.mo.us
Scott County Central JSHS — 200/7-12
  20794 US Highway 61 63801 — 573-471-2001
  Gary Francis, prin. — Fax 471-2004

Sikeston R-6 SD — 3,900/K-12
  1002 Virginia St 63801 — 573-472-2581
  Stephen Borgsmiller, supt. — Fax 472-2584
  www.sikeston.k12.mo.us
Sikeston Career & Technology Center — Vo/Tech
  1002 Virginia St 63801 — 573-471-5442
  Laura Hendley, dir. — Fax 472-8861
Sikeston JHS — 600/8-9
  1002 Virginia St 63801 — 573-471-0792
  Andy Comstock, prin. — Fax 471-0793
Sikeston SHS — 800/10-12
  1002 Virginia St 63801 — 573-472-8850
  Tom Williams, prin. — Fax 472-8857

Silex, Lincoln, Pop. 219
Silex R-I SD — 300/K-12
  PO Box 46 63377 — 573-384-5227
  Rick Pierson, supt. — Fax 384-5996
  schoolweb.missouri.edu/silex.k12.mo.us/
Silex JSHS — 200/7-12
  PO Box 46 63377 — 573-384-5227
  Bruce Werkmeister, prin. — Fax 384-5996

Slater, Saline, Pop. 1,950
Slater SD — 500/PK-12
  515 Elm St 65349 — 660-529-2278
  Paul Vaillancourt, supt. — Fax 529-2279
Slater HS — 200/9-12
  515 Elm St 65349 — 660-529-3133
  Paul Crews, prin. — Fax 529-2279

Smithton, Pettis, Pop. 495
Smithton R-VI SD — 600/K-12
  505 S Myrtle Ave 65350 — 660-343-5316
  Bill Hadlow, supt. — Fax 343-5389
  smithton.k12.mo.us
Smithton JSHS — 300/7-12
  505 S Myrtle Ave 65350 — 660-343-5318
  Barbara Bancroft, prin. — Fax 343-5389

Smithville, Clay, Pop. 6,206
Smithville R-II SD — 1,900/PK-12
  645 S Commercial Ave 64089 — 816-532-0406
  Dr. Robert Leachman, supt. — Fax 532-4192
  www.smithville.k12.mo.us/
Smithville HS — 500/9-12
  645 S Commercial Ave 64089 — 816-532-0405
  Wayne Krueger, prin. — Fax 532-4193
Smithville MS — 500/6-8
  675 S Commercial Ave 64089 — 816-532-1122
  Susan Hurst, prin. — Fax 532-3210

Sparta, Christian, Pop. 1,207
Sparta R-III SD — 700/PK-12
  PO Box 160 65753 — 417-634-4284
  Jeff Hyatt, supt. — Fax 634-3156
  www.sparta.k12.mo.us
Sparta HS — 200/9-12
  PO Box 160 65753 — 417-634-3224
  Teresa McKenzie, prin. — Fax 634-3156
Sparta MS — 200/6-8
  PO Box 160 65753 — 417-634-5518
  Joy Finney, prin. — Fax 634-3156

Spokane, Christian
Spokane R-VII SD — 700/PK-12
  345 Highlandville Rd 65754 — 417-443-2200
  Dr. Mickie Harris, supt. — Fax 443-2205
  www.spokane.k12.mo.us
Spokane HS — 200/9-12
  PO Box 218 65754 — 417-443-3502
  Daryl Bernskoetter, prin. — Fax 443-2205
Spokane MS — 200/6-8
  PO Box 218 65754 — 417-443-3506
  Pamila Rowe, prin. — Fax 443-2069

Springfield, Greene, Pop. 150,867
Springfield R-XII SD — 24,200/PK-12
  940 N Jefferson Ave 65802 — 417-523-0000
  Dr. Norman Ridder, supt. — Fax 523-0196
  sps.k12.mo.us/
Carver MS — 800/6-8
  3325 W Battlefield St 65807 — 417-888-2510
  Dr. Dan O'Reilly, prin. — Fax 888-2514

Central HS — 1,400/6-12
  423 E Central St 65802 — 417-523-9600
  Everett Isaacs, prin. — Fax 523-9695
Cherokee MS — 1,000/6-8
  420 E Farm Rd 182 65810 — 417-523-7200
  David Schmitz, prin. — Fax 523-7295
Glendale HS — 1,500/9-12
  2727 S Ingram Mill Rd 65804 — 417-523-8900
  Gary Prouty, prin. — Fax 523-8995
Hickory Hills MS — 600/6-8
  3429 E Trafficway St 65802 — 417-523-7100
  Kelly Allison, prin. — Fax 523-7195
Hillcrest HS — 1,200/9-12
  3319 N Grant Ave 65803 — 417-523-8000
  Justin Herrell, prin. — Fax 523-8095
Jarrett MS — 600/6-8
  840 S Jefferson Ave 65806 — 417-523-6600
  Dr. Nathaniel Quinn, prin. — Fax 523-2163
Kickapoo HS — 1,800/9-12
  3710 S Jefferson Ave 65807 — 417-523-8500
  Douglas Bloch, prin. — Fax 523-8595
Parkview HS — 1,500/9-12
  516 W Meadowmere St 65807 — 417-523-9200
  Judy Brunner, prin. — Fax 523-2337
Pershing MS — 800/6-8
  2120 S Ventura Ave 65804 — 417-523-2400
  Dr. Kim Finch, prin. — Fax 523-2495
Pipkin MS — 600/6-8
  1215 N Boonville Ave 65802 — 417-523-6000
  Dr. Sharri Harwick, prin. — Fax 523-6195
Pleasant View MS — 400/6-8
  2210 E State Highway AA 65803 — 417-523-2100
  Dr. Ronald Snodgrass, prin. — Fax 523-2395
Reed MS — 600/6-8
  2000 N Lyon Ave 65803 — 417-523-6300
  Leslie Ford, prin. — Fax 523-6395
Study MS — 500/6-8
  2343 W Olive St 65802 — 417-523-6400
  James T. Rush, prin. — Fax 523-6495

Assemblies of God Theological Seminary — Post-Sec.
  1435 N Glenstone Ave 65802 — 417-268-1000
Baptist Bible College — Post-Sec.
  628 E Kearney St 65803 — 800-228-5754
Bryan College — Post-Sec.
  237 S Florence Ave 65806 — 417-862-5700
Central Bible College — Post-Sec.
  3000 N Grant Ave 65803 — 800-831-4222
Cox College of Nursing & Health Sciences — Post-Sec.
  1423 N Jefferson Ave 65802 — 417-269-3401
Drury University — Post-Sec.
  900 N Benton Ave 65802 — 417-873-7879
Evangel University — Post-Sec.
  1111 N Glenstone Ave 65802 — 417-865-2811
Forest Inst./Professional Psychology — Post-Sec.
  1322 S Campbell Ave 65807 — 417-831-7902
Global University — Post-Sec.
  1211 S Glenstone Ave 65804 — 417-862-9533
Greenwood Laboratory S — 400/K-12
  901 S National Ave, — 417-836-5124
  Dr. Janice Duncan, dir. — Fax 836-8449
Missouri College of Cosmetology North — Post-Sec.
  2555 W Kearney St 65803 — 417-866-2786
Missouri State University — Post-Sec.
  901 S National Ave, 65897 — 417-836-5000
New Covenant Academy — 400/PK-12
  3304 S Cox Ave 65807 — 417-887-9848
  Tim Siebert, pres. — Fax 887-2419
Ozarks Technical Community College — Post-Sec.
  PO Box 5958 65801 — 417-895-7000
Professional Massage Training Center — Post-Sec.
  229 E Commercial St 65803 — 417-863-7682
St. John's Regional Health Center — Post-Sec.
  1235 E Cherokee St 65804 — 417-885-2845
St. John's School of Nursing — Post-Sec.
  4431 S Fremont Ave 65804 — 417-885-2098
Southwest Baptist University — Post-Sec.
  4431 S Fremont Ave 65804 — 417-841-5046
Springfield Catholic HS — 300/9-12
  2340 S Eastgate Ave 65809 — 417-887-8817
  Dean Crayton, prin. — Fax 885-1165
Springfield College — Post-Sec.
  1010 W Sunshine St 65807 — 417-864-7220
Springfield SDA S — 50/5-8
  704 S Belview Ave 65802 — 417-862-0833
Vatterott College — Post-Sec.
  3850 S Campbell Ave 65807 — 417-831-8116

Stanberry, Gentry, Pop. 1,199
Stanberry R-II SD — 300/PK-12
  610 N Park St 64489 — 660-783-2136
  Dr. Bruce Johnson, supt. — Fax 783-2177
  www.sr2.k12.mo.us/
Stanberry JSHS — 200/7-12
  610 N Park St 64489 — 660-783-2163
  Gregory Dias, prin. — Fax 783-2177

Steele, Pemiscot, Pop. 2,197
South Pemiscot County R-V SD — 800/K-12
  611 Beasley Rd 63877 — 573-695-4426
  Mitchell Fisher, supt. — Fax 695-4427
  southpem.k12.mo.us/
South Pemiscot HS — 300/7-12
  611 Beasley Rd 63877 — 573-695-3342
  Brandon Jones, prin. — Fax 695-7461

Steelville, Crawford, Pop. 1,445
Steelville R-III SD — 1,000/PK-12
  PO Box 339 65565 — 573-775-2175
  Harvey Richards, supt. — Fax 775-2179
  steelville.k12.mo.us
Steelville HS — 300/9-12
  PO Box 339 65565 — 573-775-2144
  Kurt Keller, prin. — Fax 775-5050
Steelville MS — 300/5-8
  PO Box 339 65565 — 573-775-2176
  Nancy Obermiller, prin. — Fax 775-2591

Stet, Carroll
Stet R-XV SD — 100/K-12
  18760 Cardinal Rd 64680 — 660-484-3122
  Fred Weibling, supt. — Fax 484-3124
Stet JSHS — 50/7-12
  18760 Cardinal Rd 64680 — 660-484-3122
  Steven Street, prin. — Fax 484-3124

Stewartsville, DeKalb, Pop. 746
Stewartsville C-2 SD — 300/K-12
  902 Buchanan St 64490 — 816-669-3792
  Steve Davisson, supt. — Fax 669-8125
  www.geocities.com/stewartsvillec2/index.html
Stewartsville JSHS — 200/7-12
  902 Buchanan St 64490 — 816-669-3258
  John Reed, prin. — Fax 669-8125

Stockton, Cedar, Pop. 1,954
Stockton R-I SD — 1,100/K-12
  PO Box 190 65785 — 417-276-5143
  Dr. Vicki Sandberg, supt. — Fax 276-3765
  www.schoolweb.missouri.edu/stockton.k12.mo.us/
Stockton HS — 300/9-12
  PO Box 190 65785 — 417-276-5141
  John French, prin. — Fax 276-6389
Stockton MS — 300/5-8
  PO Box 190 65785 — 417-276-6161
  Travis Shaw, prin. — Fax 276-4909

Stoutland, Camden, Pop. 181
Stoutland R-II SD — 500/PK-12
  7584 State Road T 65567 — 417-286-3984
  Geanine Bloch, supt. — Fax 286-3153
  www.schoolweb.missouri.edu/stoutland/
Stoutland JSHS — 300/7-12
  7584 State Road T 65567 — 417-286-3711
  B. Steven Burns, prin. — Fax 286-3981

Stover, Morgan, Pop. 1,000
Morgan County R-I SD — 700/PK-12
  701 N Oak St 65078 — 573-377-2217
  Jackie Wilkerson, supt. — Fax 377-2211
  schoolweb.missouri.edu/stover.k12.mo.us/
Morgan County R-I HS — 200/9-12
  701 N Oak St 65078 — 573-377-2218
  Daniel Jordan, prin. — Fax 377-2211
Morgan County R-I MS — 300/5-8
  701 N Oak St 65078 — 573-377-4284
  Janice Gerken, prin. — Fax 377-4441

Strafford, Greene, Pop. 1,884
Strafford R-VI SD — 1,100/PK-12
  201 W McCabe St 65757 — 417-736-7000
  John Collins, supt. — Fax 736-7016
  straffordschools.net
Strafford HS — 300/9-12
  201 W Mccabe St 65757 — 417-736-7000
  LaVeda Berry, prin. — Fax 736-7020
Strafford MS — 300/6-8
  201 W McCabe St 65757 — 417-736-7000
  Shane Pierce, prin. — Fax 736-7019

Sturgeon, Boone, Pop. 941
Sturgeon R-V SD — 500/K-12
  210 W Patton St 65284 — 573-687-3515
  Stan Ingraham, supt. — Fax 687-2116
  www.sturgeon.k12.mo.us/
Sturgeon HS — 200/9-12
  210 W Patton St 65284 — 573-687-3512
  Gina Mills, prin. — Fax 687-3441
Sturgeon MS — 200/5-8
  210 W Patton St 65284 — 573-687-2155
  Jeff Carr, prin. — Fax 687-1226

Sullivan, Franklin, Pop. 6,486
Sullivan SD — 2,200/PK-12
  138 Taylor St 63080 — 573-468-5171
  Dr. James Thornsberry, supt. — Fax 468-7720
  www.eagles.k12.mo.us
Sullivan HS — 700/9-12
  1073 E Vine St 63080 — 573-468-5181
  Jennifer Schmidt, prin. — Fax 860-3524
Sullivan MS — 500/6-8
  1156 Elmont Rd 63080 — 573-468-5191
  Terri Parks, prin. — Fax 860-2326

Summersville, Texas, Pop. 541
Summersville R-II SD — 500/K-12
  PO Box 198 65571 — 417-932-4045
  Charlie Taylor, supt. — Fax 932-5360
  www.summersville.k12.mo.us/
Summersville JSHS — 300/7-12
  PO Box 198 65571 — 417-932-4929
  Mark Hampton, prin. — Fax 932-5360

Sweet Springs, Saline, Pop. 1,546
Sweet Springs R-VII SD — 400/K-12
  105 Main St 65351 — 660-335-4860
  Boyd Jones, supt. — Fax 335-4378
  sweetsprings.k12.mo.us/
Sweet Springs JSHS — 200/7-12
  105 Main St 65351 — 660-335-6341
  Rex Roberts, prin. — Fax 335-6379

Tarkio, Atchison, Pop. 1,883
Tarkio R-I SD — 600/K-12
  312 S 11th St 64491 — 660-736-4161
  Robert Bruner, supt. — Fax 736-4546
  www.tarkio.k12.mo.us
Tarkio JSHS — 200/7-12
  312 S 11th St 64491 — 660-736-4118
  Bill Fox, prin. — Fax 736-4546

Thayer, Oregon, Pop. 2,133
Thayer R-II SD — 600/PK-12
  401 E Walnut St 65791 — 417-264-7261
  Bill Garrison, supt. — Fax 264-4608
  thayer.k12.mo.us/
Thayer JSHS — 300/7-12
  401 E Walnut St 65791 — 417-264-7261
  Kevin Hedden, prin. — Fax 264-4608

Theodosia, Ozark, Pop. 245
Lutie R-VI SD — 200/K-12
  HC 4 Box 4775 65761 — 417-273-4274
  Christopher Felmlee, supt. — Fax 273-4171
  www.schoolweb.missouri.edu/lutie.k12.mo.us
Lutie JSHS — 100/7-12
  HC 4 Box 4775 65761 — 417-273-4150
  Cindy McKee, prin. — Fax 273-4171

Tina, Carroll, Pop. 193
Tina-Avalon R-II SD — 200/PK-12
  11896 Highway 65 64682 — 660-622-4211
  Dorothy Benson, supt. — Fax 622-4210
  tinaavalon.k12.mo.us/
Tina-Avalon JSHS — 100/7-12
  11896 Highway 65 64682 — 660-622-4212
  David Garber, prin. — Fax 622-4210

Tipton, Moniteau, Pop. 3,197
Moniteau County R-VI SD — 600/K-12
  305 US Highway 50 E 65081 — 660-433-5520
  Paul Wootten, supt. — Fax 433-5241
  tipton.k12.mo.us/
Tipton HS — 300/7-12
  305 US Highway 50 E 65081 — 660-433-5529
  Alfred Norman, prin. — Fax 433-2419

Trenton, Grundy, Pop. 6,123
Trenton R-IX SD — 1,200/K-12
  1607 Normal St 64683 — 660-359-3994
  Craig Noah, supt. — Fax 359-3995
Trenton HS — 400/9-12
  1415 Oklahoma Ave 64683 — 660-359-2291
  Becky Albrecht, prin. — Fax 359-4073
Trenton MS — 400/5-8
  1417 Oklahoma Ave 64683 — 660-359-4328
  Toni Cox, prin. — Fax 359-6554

———

North Central Missouri College — Post-Sec.
  1301 Main St 64683 — 660-359-3948

Troy, Lincoln, Pop. 8,317
Troy R-III SD — 4,900/K-12
  951 W College St 63379 — 636-462-6098
  Terry Morrow, supt. — Fax 528-2411
  www.troy.k12.mo.us
Buchanan HS — 1,600/9-12
  1190 Old Cap Au Gris Rd 63379 — 636-528-4618
  Stephen Hunter, prin. — Fax 528-5164
Troy MS — 800/7-8
  713 W College St 63379 — 636-528-7057
  Mary Ingmire, prin. — Fax 528-2199

Tuscumbia, Miller, Pop. 220
Miller County R-III SD — 300/K-12
  PO Box 1 65082 — 573-369-2375
  Nancy Henke, supt. — Fax 369-2833
  www.tuscumbialions.com/
Tuscumbia HS — 100/9-12
  PO Box 1 65082 — 573-369-2375
  Lyle Holzbierlein, prin. — Fax 369-2833

Union, Franklin, Pop. 8,421
Union R-XI SD — 2,900/K-12
  PO Box 440 63084 — 636-583-8626
  Dr. VeAnn Tilson, supt. — Fax 583-2403
  union.k12.mo.us
Union HS — 1,000/9-12
  PO Box 440 63084 — 636-583-2513
  Dennis Lottman, prin. — Fax 583-4203
Union MS — 500/7-8
  PO Box 440 63084 — 636-583-5855
  Shirlie Wright, prin. — Fax 583-6156

———

East Central College — Post-Sec.
  1964 Prairie Dell Rd 63084 — 636-583-5193

Union Star, DeKalb, Pop. 415
Union Star R-II SD — 100/K-12
  6132 NW State Route Z 64494 — 816-593-2294
  Steve Thompson, supt. — Fax 593-4427
Union Star JSHS — 100/7-12
  6132 NW State Route Z 64494 — 816-593-2294
  Clinton Fine, prin. — Fax 593-4427

Unionville, Putnam, Pop. 1,984
Putnam County R-I SD — 800/PK-12
  803 S 20th St 63565 — 660-947-3361
  Heath Halley, supt. — Fax 947-2912
  www.nemr.net/~midgets
Putnam County HS — 200/9-12
  803 S 20th St 63565 — 660-947-2481
  Jeremy Watt, prin. — Fax 947-2912
Putnam County MS — 200/6-8
  802 S 18th St 63565 — 660-947-3237
  Barbara Hodges, prin. — Fax 947-2912

University City, Saint Louis, Pop. 37,757
University City SD
  Supt. — See Saint Louis
Brittany Woods MS — 600/7-8
  8125 Groby Rd 63130 — 314-290-4280
  Bernadette White, prin. — Fax 997-1786
University City HS — 1,100/9-12
  7401 Balson Ave 63130 — 314-290-4100
  Dr. Elizabeth Bender, prin. — Fax 290-4120

Urbana, Hickory, Pop. 417
Hickory County R-I SD — 500/K-12
  RR 1 Box 838 65767 — 417-993-4241
  Mark Beem, supt. — Fax 993-4269
  hickorycountyschools.net/
Skyline HS — 200/9-12
  RR 1 Box 838 65767 — 417-993-4226
  Randall Dougherty, prin. — Fax 993-5947
Skyline MS — 5-8
  RR 1 Box 838 65767 — 417-993-4254
  Daniel Roberts, prin. — Fax 993-5948

Valley Park, Saint Louis, Pop. 6,382
Valley Park SD — 1,200/PK-12
  1 Main St 63088 — 636-923-3500
  Laura Kinder, supt. — Fax 861-1002
  www.vp.k12.mo.us
Valley Park HS — 300/9-12
  1 Main St 63088 — 636-923-3500
  Randall Fidler, prin. — Fax 225-0542
Valley Park MS — 200/6-8
  1 Main St 63088 — 636-923-3500
  Tad Savage, prin. — Fax 225-1529

Van Buren, Carter, Pop. 833
Van Buren R-I SD — 600/PK-12
  PO Box 550 63965 — 573-323-4281
  Dr. Jeffrey Lindsey, supt. — Fax 323-4297
  schoolweb.missouri.edu/vanburen.k12.mo.us
Van Buren JSHS — 300/6-12
  PO Box 550 63965 — 573-323-4295
  Mark Wood, prin. — Fax 323-4295

Vandalia, Audrain, Pop. 4,097
Van-Far R-I SD — 600/K-12
  2200 W US Highway 54 63382 — 573-594-6111
  Kevin Freeman, supt. — Fax 594-2878
  www.vf.k12.mo.us
Van-Far JSHS — 300/7-12
  2200 W US Highway 54 63382 — 573-594-6442
  Lyndel Whittle, prin. — Fax 594-3054

Verona, Lawrence, Pop. 722
Verona R-VII SD — 400/K-12
  PO Box 7 65769 — 417-498-2274
  Dr. Robert Abeln, supt. — Fax 498-6590
  schoolweb.missouri.edu/verona.k12.mo.us/
Verona JSHS — 200/7-12
  PO Box 7 65769 — 417-498-6775
  Dr. Dennis Sloan, prin. — Fax 498-6590

Versailles, Morgan, Pop. 2,631
Morgan County R-II SD — 1,600/PK-12
  913 W Newton St 65084 — 573-378-4231
  Jeffery Carter, supt. — Fax 378-5714
  www.mcr2.k12.mo.us/
Morgan County HS — 500/9-12
  913 W Newton St 65084 — 573-378-4697
  Tom Andreas, prin. — Fax 378-2704
Morgan County MS — 400/6-8
  913 W Newton St 65084 — 573-378-5432
  Matt Unger, prin. — Fax 378-6610

Viburnum, Iron, Pop. 812
Iron County C-4 SD — 500/K-12
  PO Box 368 65566 — 573-244-5422
  Clay Whitener, supt. — Fax 244-3410
Viburnum JSHS — 200/7-12
  PO Box 368 65566 — 573-244-5521
  Doug Ruck, prin. — Fax 244-3410

Vienna, Maries, Pop. 620
Maries County R-I SD — 600/K-12
  PO Box 218 65582 — 573-422-3304
  Richard Spacek, supt. — Fax 422-3185
Vienna HS — 300/7-12
  PO Box 218 65582 — 573-422-3363
  Daryl Bernskoetter, prin. — Fax 422-3185

Villa Ridge, Franklin, Pop. 1,865

———

Crosspoint Christian S — 100/K-12
  PO Box 100 63089 — 636-742-5380
  Diane Beumer, prin. — Fax 742-5917

Walker, Vernon, Pop. 275
Northeast Vernon County R-I SD — 200/PK-12
  216 E Leslie Ave 64790 — 417-465-2221
  Charles Naas, supt. — Fax 465-2388
Northeast Vernon County R-I HS — 100/7-12
  216 E Leslie Ave 64790 — 417-465-2221
  Monte Padgett, prin. — Fax 465-2388

Walnut Grove, Greene, Pop. 632
Walnut Grove R-V SD — 300/K-12
  PO Box 187 65770 — 417-788-2543
  Marty Witt, supt. — Fax 788-1254
Walnut Grove JSHS — 200/7-12
  PO Box 187 65770 — 417-788-2544
  Darin Meinders, prin. — Fax 788-1254

Wardell, Pemiscot, Pop. 268
North Pemiscot County R-I SD — 400/K-12
  PO Box 38 63879 — 573-628-3471
  Keith Henke, supt. — Fax 628-3472
North Pemiscot County JSHS — 200/6-12
  PO Box 38 63879 — 573-628-3465
  Terry Hamilton, prin. — Fax 628-3418

Warrensburg, Johnson, Pop. 17,075
Warrensburg R-VI SD — 3,200/K-12
  PO Box 638 64093 — 660-747-7823
  Deborah Orr, supt. — Fax 747-9615
  warrensburg.k12.mo.us
Warrensburg Area Career Center — Vo/Tech
  205 S Ridgeview Dr 64093 — 660-747-2283
  Dan Gordon, prin. — Fax 747-3778
Warrensburg HS — 1,000/9-12
  1411 S Ridgeview Dr 64093 — 660-747-2262
  Simone Dillingham, prin. — Fax 747-8731
Warrensburg MS — 800/6-8
  640 E Gay St 64093 — 660-747-5612
  Jim Elliott, prin. — Fax 747-8779

———

Central Missouri State University — Post-Sec.
  64093 — 660-543-4111

Warrenton, Warren, Pop. 6,016
Warren County R-III SD — 2,700/K-12
  302 Kuhl Ave 63383 — 636-456-6901
  Dr. John Long, supt. — Fax 456-7687
  www.warrencor3.org

Black Hawk MS 700/6-8
302 Kuhl Ave 63383 636-456-6903
Barbara Crowell, prin. Fax 456-1445
Warren County R-III HS 900/9-12
803 Pinckney St 63383 636-456-6902
David Buck, prin. Fax 456-5771

Warsaw, Benton, Pop. 2,139
Warsaw R-IX SD 1,500/PK-12
PO Box 248 65355 660-438-7120
Michael Stevenson, supt. Fax 438-3749
www.warsaw.k12.mo.us/
Boise MS 300/6-8
PO Box 1750 65355 660-438-9079
Brent Depee, prin. Fax 438-3749
Warsaw HS 500/9-12
PO Box 248 65355 660-438-7351
Brent Depee, prin. Fax 438-3749

Washburn, Barry, Pop. 455
Southwest R-V SD 900/PK-12
PO Box 297 65772 417-826-5410
Richard Asbill, supt. Fax 826-5603
www.swr5.k12.mo.us
Southwest HS 200/9-12
PO Box 297 65772 417-826-5413
Vicki Enyart, prin. Fax 826-5603
Southwest MS 300/5-8
PO Box 297 65772 417-826-5050
Ben Abramovitz, prin. Fax 826-5603

Washington, Franklin, Pop. 13,608
Washington SD 4,100/PK-12
PO Box 357 63090 636-239-2727
Scott Huddleston, supt. Fax 239-3315
www.washington.k12.mo.us
Four Rivers Career Center Vo/Tech
550 Blue Jay Dr 63090 636-239-7777
Steve Matyas, prin. Fax 239-0791
Washington HS 1,400/9-12
600 Blue Jay Dr 63090 636-239-4717
Richard Riggs, prin. Fax 390-4157
Washington MS 600/7-8
401 E 14th St 63090 636-239-4783
Dr. Richard Martin, prin. Fax 239-4252

St. Francis Borgia Regional HS 700/9-12
1000 Borgia Dr 63090 636-239-7871
George Wingbermuehle, prin. Fax 239-1198

Waynesville, Pulaski, Pop. 3,572
Waynesville R-VI SD 5,100/K-12
200 Fleetwood Dr 65583 573-774-6497
Dr. Ed Musgrove, supt. Fax 774-6491
waynesville.k12.mo.us
Waynesville HS 1,400/9-12
200 GW Ln 65583 573-774-6401
Allen Voth, prin. Fax 774-2393
Waynesville MS 700/6-8
1001 Historic 66 W 65583 573-774-6198
Joe Petrich, prin. Fax 774-6089
Waynesville Technical Academy Vo/Tech
810 Roosevelt St 65583 573-774-6106
Dr. Bob Chapman, dir. Fax 774-3355
Other Schools – See Fort Leonard Wood

Central College of Cosmetology Post-Sec.
PO Box 463 65583 573-336-3888

Weaubleau, Hickory, Pop. 517
Weaubleau R-III SD 500/PK-12
509 N Center St 65774 417-428-3317
Stephen Pharr, supt. Fax 428-3521
www.weaubleau.k12.mo.us
Weaubleau HS 200/7-12
509 N Center St 65774 417-428-3368
Christopher Ford, prin. Fax 428-3004

Webb City, Jasper, Pop. 10,251
Webb City R-VII SD 3,900/PK-12
411 N Madison St 64870 417-673-6000
Ronald Lankford, supt. Fax 673-6007
www.wccards.k12.mo.us/
Webb City HS 1,100/9-12
621 N Madison St 64870 417-673-6010
Stephen Gollhofer, prin. Fax 673-6017
Webb City JHS 600/7-8
807 W 1st St 64870 417-673-6030
Trey Moeller, prin. Fax 673-6037

Webster Groves, Saint Louis, Pop. 23,164
Webster Groves SD 4,200/K-12
400 E Lockwood Ave 63119 314-961-1233
Dr. Brent Underwood, supt. Fax 918-4023
www.webster.k12.mo.us
Webster Groves HS 1,400/9-12
100 Selma Ave 63119 314-963-6400
Dr. Jon D. Clark, prin. Fax 963-6483

Other Schools – See Saint Louis

Eden Theological Seminary Post-Sec.
475 E Lockwood Ave 63119 314-961-3627

Weldon Spring, Saint Charles, Pop. 5,283
Francis Howell R-III SD
Supt. — See Saint Charles
Bryan MS 1,000/6-8
605 Independence Rd 63304 636-477-3060
Sue Hartman, prin. Fax 477-3075
Howell MS 800/6-8
825 OFallon Rd 63304 636-851-4800
Amy Johnston, prin. Fax 851-4121

Wellington, Lafayette, Pop. 784
Wellington-Napoleon R-IX SD 400/K-12
PO Box 280 64097 816-934-2531
Jeffrey Sumy, supt. Fax 934-8649
www.well-nap.k12.mo.us/
Wellington-Napoleon JSHS 200/7-12
PO Box 280 64097 816-240-2621
Kenneth Holland, prin. Fax 934-8649

Wellsville, Montgomery, Pop. 1,401
Wellsville-Middletown R-I SD 500/PK-12
900 Burlington St 63384 573-684-2428
Kerry Hesse, supt. Fax 684-2018
wmr1.k12.mo.us/
Wellsville JSHS 300/6-12
900 Burlington St 63384 573-684-2017
Dan Wiebers, prin. Fax 684-2018

Wentzville, Saint Charles, Pop. 12,253
Wentzville R-IV SD 7,800/K-12
1 Campus Dr 63385 636-327-3800
Dr. Tom Byrnes, supt. Fax 327-8611
www.wentzville.k12.mo.us
Holt HS 1,200/9-12
600 Campus Dr 63385 636-327-3876
John Waters, prin. Fax 327-3953
Timberland HS 1,000/9-12
559 E Highway N 63385 636-327-3988
Ed Liliensiek, prin. Fax 327-3922
Wentzville MS 1,000/6-8
405 Campus Dr 63385 636-327-3815
Kim Bertram, prin. Fax 327-3954
Wentzville South MS 900/6-8
561 E Highway N 63385 636-327-3928
Jennifer Waters, prin. Fax 327-3955

Midwest Theological Seminary Post-Sec.
PO Box 365 63385 636-327-4645

Weston, Platte, Pop. 1,649
West Platte County R-II SD 700/K-12
1103 Washington St 64098 816-640-2236
Kyle B. Stephenson, supt. Fax 386-2104
schoolweb.missouri.edu/wprii.k12.mo.us/index.htm
West Platte County JSHS 300/7-12
1103 Washington St 64098 816-640-2292
Stanley Coulson, prin. Fax 386-2293

Westphalia, Osage, Pop. 320
Osage County R-III SD 800/PK-12
PO Box 37 65085 573-455-2375
Archie Derboven, supt. Fax 455-9884
www.fatima.k12.mo.us/
Fatima JSHS 500/7-12
PO Box 37 65085 573-455-2550
Daniel Ramsey, prin. Fax 455-9884

West Plains, Howell, Pop. 10,930
Richards R-V SD 400/K-8
3461 County Rd 1710 65775 417-256-5239
Jerry Premer, supt. Fax 256-3314
Richards MS 100/6-8
3461 County Road 1710 65775 417-256-5239
Reta House, prin. Fax 256-3314

West Plains R-VII SD 2,500/K-12
613 W 1st St 65775 417-256-6150
Karla Eslinger, supt. Fax 256-8616
wphs.k12.mo.us/
South Central Career Center Vo/Tech
610 E Olden St 65775 417-256-6150
Rodney Wood, dir. Fax 256-5786
West Plains HS 1,200/9-12
602 E Olden St 65775 417-256-6150
Ronald Estes, prin. Fax 256-8908
West Plains MS 600/5-8
730 E Olden St 65775 417-256-6150
Fred Czerwonka, prin. Fax 256-8907

Missouri State University - West Plains Post-Sec.
128 Garfield Ave 65775 417-255-7255

Wheatland, Hickory, Pop. 388
Wheatland R-II SD 300/K-12
PO Box 68 65779 417-282-6433
Eric Cooley, supt. Fax 282-5733
www.wheatlandschool.com/
Wheatland JSHS 200/7-12
PO Box 68 65779 417-282-5833
Matt Gunter, prin. Fax 282-5733

Wheaton, Barry, Pop. 717
Wheaton R-III SD 400/K-12
PO Box 249 64874 417-652-3914
Jim Cummins, supt. Fax 652-7355
Wheaton JSHS 200/7-12
PO Box 249 64874 417-652-7249
Lance Massey, prin. Fax 652-7355

Willard, Greene, Pop. 3,253
Willard R-II SD 3,400/K-12
460 Kime St 65781 417-742-2584
Dr. Kent Medlin, supt. Fax 742-2586
www.willard.k12.mo.us/
Willard HS 1,000/9-12
205 Miller Rd 65781 417-742-3524
Don Tuck, prin. Fax 742-3667
Willard MS 800/6-8
407 Farmer Rd 65781 417-742-2588
Amy Sims, prin. Fax 742-3505

Willow Springs, Howell, Pop. 2,080
Willow Springs R-IV SD 1,400/PK-12
215 W 4th St 65793 417-469-3260
Don Hamby, supt. Fax 469-5127
www.willowspringsschool.com/
Willow Springs HS 400/9-12
215 W 4th St 65793 417-469-2114
Derrick Hutsell, prin. Fax 469-2507
Willow Springs MS 400/5-8
215 W 4th St 65793 417-469-3211
Malcolm Gum, prin. Fax 469-1229

Windsor, Henry, Pop. 3,258
Henry County R-I SD 700/PK-12
210 North St 65360 660-647-3533
Mary Elsensohn, supt. Fax 647-2711
Windsor JSHS 300/7-12
210 North St 65360 660-647-3106
Kyle Powell, prin. Fax 647-3218

Winfield, Lincoln, Pop. 800
Winfield R-IV SD 1,600/K-12
701 W Elm St 63389 636-668-8188
Dr. Richard Staley, supt. Fax 668-8641
schoolweb.missouri.edu/winfield.k12.mo.us/
Winfield HS 500/9-12
701 W Elm St 63389 636-668-8130
Thomas D. Challender, prin. Fax 566-6455
Winfield MS 400/6-8
701 W Elm St 63389 636-668-8001
James D. Hale, prin. Fax 668-6044

Winona, Shannon, Pop. 1,298
Winona R-III SD 600/PK-12
PO Box 248 65588 573-325-8101
Scott Lindsey, supt. Fax 325-8447
Winona HS 200/9-12
PO Box 248 65588 573-325-8101
Donald Wakefield, prin. Fax 325-4700

Winston, Daviess, Pop. 247
Winston R-VI SD 200/PK-12
PO Box 38 64689 660-749-5456
Lisa Bielby, supt. Fax 749-5432
Winston JSHS 100/7-12
PO Box 38 64689 660-749-5456
Jerry Steele, prin. Fax 749-5432

Wright City, Warren, Pop. 1,941
Wright City R-II SD 1,400/PK-12
PO Box 198 63390 636-745-7200
Dr. Mark Porter, supt. Fax 745-3613
www.wrightcity.k12.mo.us/
Wright City HS 400/9-12
PO Box 198 63390 636-745-7500
Mike Dorband, prin. Fax 745-7518
Wright City MS 500/5-8
PO Box 198 63390 636-745-7300
Richard Lagemann, prin. Fax 745-7304

Zalma, Bollinger, Pop. 95
Zalma R-V SD 300/K-12
HC 2 Box 184 63787 573-722-5504
Darryl Sauer, supt. Fax 722-9870
Zalma JSHS 100/7-12
HC 2 Box 184 63787 573-722-3320
Gerard Vandeven, prin. Fax 722-9870

MONTANA

MONTANA OFFICE OF PUBLIC INSTRUCTION
PO Box 202501, Helena 59620-2501
Telephone 406-444-3095
Fax 406-444-2893
Website http://www.opi.state.mt.us

State Superintendent of Public Instruction   Linda McCulloch

MONTANA BOARD OF EDUCATION
PO Box 202501, Helena 59620-2501

Chairperson   Kirk Miller

COUNTY SUPERINTENDENTS OF SCHOOLS

Beaverhead County Office of Education
  Dorothy Donovan, supt.   406-683-3737
  2 S Pacific St, Dillon 59725   Fax 683-3769
Big Horn County Office of Education
  Gary Hickey, supt.   406-665-9820
  PO Box 908, Hardin 59034   Fax 665-9738
Blaine County Office of Education
  Carol Elliot, supt.   406-357-3270
  PO Box 819, Chinook 59523   Fax 357-2199
Broadwater County Office of Education
  Judy Gillespie, supt.   406-266-3443
  515 Broadway St, Townsend 59644   Fax 266-3674
Carbon County Office of Education
  Jerry Scott, supt.   406-446-1301
  PO Box 116, Red Lodge 59068   Fax 446-9155
Carter County Office of Education
  Carole Carey, supt.   406-775-8721
  PO Box 352, Ekalaka 59324   Fax 775-8703
Cascade County Office of Education
  Jess Anderson, supt.   406-454-6776
  325 2nd Ave N, Great Falls 59401   Fax 454-6778
Chouteau County Office of Education
  L. Stollfuss, supt.   406-622-3242
  PO Box 459, Fort Benton 59442   Fax 622-3028
Custer County Office of Education
  Ellen Zook, supt.   406-874-3421
  1010 Main St, Miles City 59301   Fax 874-3452
Daniels County Office of Education
  Patricia McDonnell, supt.   406-487-2651
  PO Box 67, Scobey 59263   Fax 487-5432
Dawson County Office of Education
  Martha Young, supt.   406-377-3963
  207 W Bell St, Glendive 59330   Fax 377-2022
Deer Lodge County Office of Education
  Michael O'Rourke, supt.   406-563-9178
  Courthouse, Anaconda 59711   Fax 563-4001
Fallon County Office of Education
  Marlene Ferrell, supt.   406-778-7127
  PO Box 1117, Baker 59313   Fax 778-3431
Fergus County Office of Education
  Shirley Barrick, supt.   406-538-3136
  712 W Main St, Lewistown 59457   Fax 538-2819
Flathead County Office of Education
  Donna Maddux, supt.   406-758-5720
  800 S Main St, Kalispell 59901   Fax 758-5850
Gallatin County Office of Education
  Mary Ellen Fitzgerald, supt.   406-582-3090
  311 W Main St Rm 107   Fax 582-3093
  Bozeman 59715
  www.gallatin.mt.gov/schools/index.htm
Garfield County Office of Education
  Karla Christensen, supt.   406-557-6115
  PO Box 28, Jordan 59337   Fax 557-2625
Glacier County Office of Education
  Jetta Johnson, supt.   406-873-2295
  1210 E Main St, Cut Bank 59427   Fax 873-9103
Golden Valley County Office of Education
  Sharon Carpenter, supt.   406-568-2342
  107 Kemp St, Ryegate 59074   Fax 568-2598

Granite County Office of Education
  Jo Ann Husbyn, supt.   406-859-3831
  PO Box 520, Philipsburg 59858   Fax 859-3817
Hill County Office of Education
  Shirley Isbell, supt.   406-265-5481
  315 4th St, Havre 59501   Fax 265-5487
Jefferson County Office of Education
  Garry Bauer, supt.   406-225-4114
  PO Box H, Boulder 59632   Fax 225-4149
Judith Basin County Office of Education
  Julie Peevey, supt.   406-566-2277
  PO Box 307, Stanford 59479   Fax 566-2211
Lake County Office of Education
  Joyce Decker Wegner, supt.   406-883-7262
  106 4th Ave E, Polson 59860   Fax 883-7283
  www.lakecounty-mt.org/schools
Lewis & Clark County Office of Education
  Marsha Davis, supt.   406-447-8344
  PO Box 1725, Helena 59624   Fax 447-8370
Liberty County Office of Education
  Rachel Ghekiere, supt.   406-759-5216
  PO Box 684, Chester 59522   Fax 759-5996
Lincoln County Office of Education
  Ron Higgins, supt.   406-293-7781
  418 Mineral Ave, Libby 59923   Fax 293-9794
Madison County Office of Education
  Judi Osborn, supt.   406-843-4217
  PO Box 247, Virginia City 59755   Fax 843-5261
McCone County Office of Education
  Jackie Becker, supt.   406-485-3590
  PO Box 180, Circle 59215   Fax 485-2689
Meagher County Office of Education
  Susan Beley, supt., PO Box 354   406-547-3612
  White Sulphur Springs 59645   Fax 547-3388
Mineral County Office of Education
  Billye Ann Bricker, supt.   406-822-3534
  PO Box 100, Superior 59872   Fax 822-3579
Missoula County Office of Education
  Rachel Vielleux, supt.   406-258-4860
  438 W Spruce St, Missoula 59802   Fax 258-4731
Musselshell County Office of Education
  Kathryn Pfister, supt.   406-323-1470
  506 Main St, Roundup 59072   Fax 323-3303
Park County Office of Education
  Rodney Olson, supt.   406-222-4148
  414 E Callender St   Fax 222-4199
  Livingston 59047
Petroleum County Office of Education
  Stephanie Downs, supt.   406-429-5551
  PO Box 226, Winnett 59087   Fax 429-6328
Phillips County Office of Education
  Vivian Taylor, supt.   406-654-2010
  PO Box 138, Malta 59538   Fax 654-1213
Pondera County Office of Education
  Jo Stone, supt.   406-278-4055
  Courthouse, Conrad 59425   Fax 278-4070
Powder River County Office of Education
  Charlotte Miller, supt.   406-436-2488
  PO Box 300, Broadus 59317   Fax 436-2151

Powell County Office of Education
  Jules Waber, supt.   406-846-3680
  409 Missouri Ave   Fax 846-2784
  Deer Lodge 59722
Prairie County Office of Education
  Cindy Bond, supt.   406-635-5577
  PO Box 566, Terry 59349   Fax 635-5576
Ravalli County Office of Education
  Ernie Jean, supt.   406-375-2007
  PO Box 5017, Hamilton 59840   Fax 375-6351
Richland County Office of Education
  Gail Anne Staffanson, supt.   406-433-1608
  201 W Main St, Sidney 59270   Fax 433-3731
Roosevelt County Office of Education
  Pat Stennes, supt.   406-653-6266
  400 2nd Ave S, Wolf Point 59201   Fax 653-6203
Rosebud County Office of Education
  Sharyn Thomas, supt.   406-356-2537
  PO Box 407, Forsyth 59327   Fax 356-2537
Sanders County Office of Education
  Kathy McEldery, supt.   406-826-4288
  PO Box 519, Plains 59859   Fax 826-4288
Sheridan County Office of Education
  Milton Hovland, supt.   406-765-3403
  100 W Laurel Ave   Fax 765-2609
  Plentywood 59254
Silver Bow County Office of Education
  Edward Heard, supt.   406-497-6215
  155 W Granite St, Butte 59701   Fax 497-6328
Stillwater County Office of Education
  Barbara Campbell, supt.   406-322-8057
  PO Box 1139, Columbus 59019   Fax 322-8007
Sweet Grass County Office of Education
  Linda DeCock, supt.   406-932-5147
  PO Box 1310, Big Timber 59011   Fax 932-5112
Teton County Office of Education
  John Maloney, supt.   406-466-2907
  PO Box 610, Choteau 59422   Fax 466-2138
Toole County Office of Education
  Boyd Jackson, supt.   406-424-8329
  226 1st St S, Shelby 59474   Fax 424-8321
Treasure County Office of Education
  Kathleen Thomas, supt.   406-342-5545
  PO Box 429, Hysham 59038   Fax 342-5445
Valley County Office of Education
  Lynne Nyquist, supt.   406-228-6226
  501 Court Sq Ste 2   Fax 228-9027
  Glasgow 59230
Wheatland County Office of Education
  Susan Beley, supt.   406-632-4816
  PO Box 637, Harlowton 59036   Fax 632-4880
Wibaux County Office of Education
  Patricia Zinda, supt.   406-796-2481
  PO Box 291, Wibaux 59353   Fax 796-2625
Yellowstone County Office of Education
  A.J. Micheletti, supt.   406-256-6933
  PO Box 35022, Billings 59107   Fax 256-6930
  www.co.yellowstone.mt.us

PUBLIC, PRIVATE AND CATHOLIC SECONDARY SCHOOLS

Absarokee, Stillwater, Pop. 1,067
Absarokee SD   400/K-12
  327 S Woodard Ave 59001   406-328-4583
  David Huether, supt.   Fax 328-4077
  www.absarokee.k12.mt.us/
Absarokee HS   100/9-12
  327 S Woodard Ave 59001   406-328-4583
  Kevin Smith, prin.   Fax 328-4077
Absarokee MS   100/7-8
  327 S Woodard Ave 59001   406-328-4583
  Kevin Smith, prin.   Fax 328-4077

Alberton, Mineral, Pop. 393
Alberton SD 2   200/K-12
  PO Box 330 59820   406-722-4413
  James Baldwin, supt.   Fax 722-3040
Alberton HS   100/9-12
  PO Box 330 59820   406-722-3381
  Carl Dehne, prin.   Fax 722-3040

Alberton MS   50/7-8
  PO Box 330 59820   406-722-4413
  Carl Dehne, prin.   Fax 722-3040

Anaconda, Deer Lodge, Pop. 10,093
Anaconda SD 10   1,400/PK-12
  400 Main St 59711   406-563-6361
  James Whealon, supt.   Fax 563-6333
Anaconda HS   500/9-12
  5th & Main 59711   406-563-5269
  Walt Hansen, prin.   Fax 563-5260
Moodry JHS   300/7-8
  3rd & Cherry 59711   406-563-6242
  Sue Meredith, prin.   Fax 563-6242

Arlee, Lake, Pop. 489
Arlee SD JT & 8   500/PK-12
  PO Box 37 59821   406-726-3216
  Gordon Friberg, supt.   Fax 726-3940
  www.arlee.k12.mt.us/

Arlee HS   100/9-12
  PO Box 37 59821   406-726-3216
  Richard Bachmeier, prin.   Fax 726-3940
Arlee JHS   100/7-8
  PO Box 37 59821   406-726-3216
  Richard Bachmeier, prin.   Fax 726-3940

Ashland, Rosebud, Pop. 484
Ashland ESD 32J   100/PK-8
  PO Box 17 59003   406-784-2568
  Dale Bernard, supt.   Fax 784-6138
Ashland MS   50/5-8
  PO Box 17 59003   406-784-2568
  Dale Bernard, prin.   Fax 784-6138

St. Labre Catholic Indian HS   200/9-12
  1 Mission Rd 59004   406-784-4500
  Augie Lopez, prin.   Fax 784-4565

St. Labre Catholic Indian S — 200/6-8
　1 Mission Rd　59004 — 406-784-4500
　Scott Gion, prin. — Fax 784-4565

Augusta, Lewis and Clark
Augusta SD 45 — 100/PK-12
　PO Box 307　59410 — 406-562-3384
　Russ Bean, supt. — Fax 562-3898
Augusta HS — 50/9-12
　PO Box 307　59410 — 406-562-3384
　Russ Bean, prin. — Fax 562-3898
Augusta MS — 50/7-8
　PO Box 307　59410 — 406-562-3384
　Russ Bean, prin. — Fax 562-3898

Bainville, Roosevelt, Pop. 150
Bainville SD — 100/K-12
　PO Box 177　59212 — 406-769-2321
　Brock Carpenter, supt. — Fax 769-3291
Bainville HS — 50/9-12
　PO Box 177　59212 — 406-769-2321
　Paula Schledewitz, prin. — Fax 769-3291
Bainville MS — 50/7-8
　PO Box 177　59212 — 406-769-2321
　Paula Schledewitz, prin. — Fax 769-3291

Baker, Fallon, Pop. 1,647
Baker SD 12 — 400/PK-12
　PO Box 659　59313 — 406-778-3574
　Ron Meredith, supt. — Fax 778-2785
　www.baker.k12.mt.us/
Baker HS — 200/9-12
　1015 S 3rd W　59313 — 406-778-3329
　Don Schillinger, prin. — Fax 778-2785
Baker JHS — 100/7-8
　PO Box 659　59313 — 406-778-3329
　David Breitbach, prin. — Fax 778-2785

Belfry, Carbon
Belfry SD 3 — 100/PK-12
　PO Box 210　59008 — 406-664-3319
　Martha Young, supt. — Fax 664-3274
Belfry HS — 50/9-12
　PO Box 210　59008 — 406-664-3319
　Martha Young, prin. — Fax 664-3274
Belfry MS — 50/7-8
　PO Box 210　59008 — 406-664-3319
　Martha Young, prin. — Fax 664-3274

Belgrade, Gallatin, Pop. 6,816
Belgrade SD 44 — 2,500/PK-12
　PO Box 166　59714 — 406-388-6951
　Herbert Benz, supt. — Fax 388-0122
　www.belgrade.k12.mt.us
Belgrade HS — 700/9-12
　303 N Hoffman St　59714 — 406-388-4224
　Lee Hazelbaker, prin. — Fax 388-4633
Belgrade MS — 400/7-8
　410 Triple Crown St　59714 — 406-388-1309
　Kevin McNelis, prin. — Fax 388-8894

Belt, Cascade, Pop. 615
Belt SD 29 — 300/PK-12
　PO Box 197　59412 — 406-277-3351
　Calvin Johnson, supt. — Fax 277-4466
Belt HS — 100/9-12
　PO Box 197　59412 — 406-277-3351
　Craig Cummings, prin. — Fax 277-4466
Belt MS — 100/7-8
　PO Box 197　59412 — 406-277-3351
　Craig Cummings, prin. — Fax 277-4466

Bigfork, Flathead
Bigfork SD 38 — 900/PK-12
　PO Box 188　59911 — 406-837-7400
　Russell Kinzer, supt. — Fax 837-7407
Bigfork HS — 400/9-12
　PO Box 188　59911 — 406-837-7420
　Thom Peck, prin. — Fax 837-7245
Bigfork MS — 100/7-8
　PO Box 188　59911 — 406-837-7412
　Wayne Loeffler, prin. — Fax 837-7438

Swan River ESD 4 — 200/K-8
　1205 Swan Hwy　59911 — 406-837-4528
　 — Fax 837-4055
Swan River MS — 50/7-8
　1205 Swan Hwy　59911 — 406-837-4528
　Peter Loyda, prin. — Fax 837-4688

Big Sandy, Chouteau, Pop. 658
Big Sandy SD 11 — 200/PK-12
　PO Box 570　59520 — 406-378-2501
　Edward Ray, supt. — Fax 378-2275
Big Sandy HS — 100/9-12
　PO Box 570　59520 — 406-378-2502
　Edward Ray, prin. — Fax 378-2275
Big Sandy JHS — 50/7-8
　PO Box 570　59520 — 406-378-2502
　Bill Edwards, prin. — Fax 378-2275

Big Timber, Sweet Grass, Pop. 1,695
Big Timber ESD 1 — 400/PK-8
　PO Box 887　59011 — 406-932-5939
　Gary Harkness, supt. — Fax 932-4069
　www.bigtimber-gs.k12.mt.us
Big Timber MS — 100/7-8
　PO Box 887　59011 — 406-932-5939
　Mark Ketcham, prin. — Fax 932-4069

Sweet Grass County HSD — 200/9-12
　PO Box 886　59011 — 406-932-5993
　Alvin Buerkle, supt. — Fax 932-5982
Sweet Grass County HS — 200/9-12
　PO Box 886　59011 — 406-932-5993
　Kip Ryan, prin. — Fax 932-5982

Billings, Yellowstone, Pop. 95,220
Billings SD 2 — 15,900/PK-12
　415 N 30th St　59101 — 406-247-3780
　Rod Svee, supt. — Fax 247-3882
　www.billings.k12.mt.us

Billings 9th Grade Academy — 9-9
　415 N 30th St　59101 — 406-237-9316
　John English, prin.
Billings HS — 1,800/9-12
　425 Grand Ave　59101 — 406-247-2100
　C. Scott Anderson, prin. — Fax 255-3521
Billings West HS — 2,100/9-12
　2201 Saint Johns Ave　59102 — 406-655-1400
　Dennis Sulser, prin. — Fax 655-3100
Career Center — Vo/Tech
　3723 Central Ave　59102 — 406-655-3070
　Charles McGahan, prin.
Castle Rock MS — 700/7-8
　1441 Governors Blvd　59105 — 406-237-6600
　Randy Morrison, prin. — Fax 254-1116
James MS — 600/7-8
　1200 30th St W　59102 — 406-655-3124
　Kip Farnum, prin. — Fax 655-3129
Lewis & Clark MS — 600/7-8
　1315 Lewis Ave　59102 — 406-255-3720
　Steve Pomroy, prin. — Fax 255-3723
Riverside MS — 500/7-8
　3700 Madison Ave　59101 — 406-255-3740
　Lewis Anderson, prin. — Fax 255-3534
Skyview HS — 1,600/9-12
　1775 High Sierra Blvd　59105 — 406-247-2300
　Bob Whalen, prin. — Fax 255-3507
Adult & Basic Education — Adult
　415 N 30th St　59101 — 406-247-3703
　Woodrow Jensen, prin. — Fax 247-3799

Canyon Creek ESD 4 — 200/PK-8
　3139 Duck Creek Rd　59101 — 406-656-4471
　Stephanie Long, supt. — Fax 655-1031
　www.canyoncreek.k12.mt.us/
Canyon Creek MS — 100/7-8
　3139 Duck Creek Rd　59101 — 406-656-4471
　Stephanie Long, prin. — Fax 655-1031

Elder Grove ESD 8 — 300/K-8
　1532 S 64th St W　59106 — 406-656-2893
　Rob McDonald, supt. — Fax 656-4346
Elder Grove MS — 100/7-8
　1532 S 64th St W　59106 — 406-656-2893
　Monica Pugh, prin. — Fax 651-1987

Elysian ESD 23 — 100/PK-8
　6416 Elysian Rd　59101 — 406-656-4101
　 — Fax 656-9941
Elysian MS — 50/7-8
　6416 Elysian Rd　59101 — 406-656-4101
　Brenda Koch, prin. — Fax 656-9941

Lockwood ESD 26 — 1,200/PK-8
　1932 US Highway 87 E　59101 — 406-252-6022
　Eileen Johnson, supt. — Fax 259-2502
　www.lockwood.k12.mt.us/
Lockwood MS — 400/6-8
　1932 US Highway 87 E　59101 — 406-259-0154
　Mike Sullivan, prin. — Fax 259-2502

Billings Central Catholic HS — 300/9-12
　3 Broadwater Ave　59101 — 406-245-6651
　Sheldon Hanser, prin. — Fax 259-3124
Billings Christian S — 100/K-12
　4525 Grand Ave　59106 — 406-656-9484
　Paul Waggoner, prin. — Fax 655-4880
College of Coiffure Art — Post-Sec.
　1423 Wyoming Ave　59102 — 406-656-9114
Montana State University - Billings — Post-Sec.
　1500 University Dr　59101 — 406-657-2011
MSU Billings College of Technology — Post-Sec.
　3803 Central Ave　59102 — 406-656-4445
Rocky Mountain College — Post-Sec.
　1511 Poly Dr　59102 — 406-657-1000
Sage Technical Commerical Driving School — Post-Sec.
　3044 Hesper Rd　59102 — 800-545-4546
St. Francis Upper S — 200/6-8
　205 N 32nd St　59101 — 406-259-5037
　Jim Stanton, prin. — Fax 259-7981
St. Vincent's Hospital & Health Center — Post-Sec.
　PO Box 35200　59107 — 406-657-7102

Bonner, Missoula, Pop. 1,669
Potomac ESD 11 — 100/PK-8
　29750 Potomac Rd　59823 — 406-244-5581
　 — Fax 244-5840
Potomac MS — 50/7-8
　29750 Potomac Rd　59823 — 406-244-5581
　Roland Dierken, lead tchr. — Fax 244-5840

Boulder, Jefferson, Pop. 1,363
Boulder SD 7 — 200/PK-8
　PO Box 176　59632 — 406-225-3740
　Robert Klein, supt. — Fax 225-3289
Boulder MS — 100/7-8
　PO Box 176　59632 — 406-225-3316
　Donna Minard, prin. — Fax 225-9218

Jefferson HSD 1 — 300/9-12
　PO Box 176　59632 — 406-225-3740
　Robert Klein, supt. — Fax 225-3289
Jefferson HS — 300/9-12
　PO Box 176　59632 — 406-225-3317
　T.J. Eyer, prin. — Fax 225-3289

Box Elder, Hill
Box Elder SD — 400/PK-12
　PO Box 205　59521 — 406-352-4195
　Robert Heppner, supt. — Fax 352-3830
Box Elder HS — 100/9-12
　PO Box 205　59521 — 406-352-4195
　Mark Irvin, prin. — Fax 352-3830
Box Elder MS — 100/7-8
　PO Box 205　59521 — 406-352-4195
　Mark Irvin, prin. — Fax 352-3830

Rocky Boy ESD 87J — 400/PK-12
　RR 1 Box 620　59521 — 406-395-4291
　Sandra Murie, supt. — Fax 395-4829
Rocky Boy HS — 100/9-12
　RR 1 Box 620　59521 — 406-395-4270
　Voyd St. Pierre, prin. — Fax 395-4829
Rocky Boy MS — 100/7-8
　RR 1 Box 620　59521 — 406-395-4270
　Josephine Corcoran, prin. — Fax 395-4829

Stone Child College — Post-Sec.
　PO Box 1082　59521 — 406-395-4313

Bozeman, Gallatin, Pop. 30,753
Anderson ESD 41 — 200/PK-8
　10040 Cottonwood Rd　59718 — 406-587-1305
　Terry Vanderpan, supt. — Fax 587-2501
　www.theandersonschool.org/
Anderson MS — 50/7-8
　10040 Cottonwood Rd　59718 — 406-587-1305
　Will Schofield, prin. — Fax 587-2501
Bozeman SD 7 — 5,100/PK-12
　PO Box 520　59771 — 406-522-6001
　Dr. Michael Redburn, supt. — Fax 522-6065
　www.bozeman.k12.mt.us/
Bozeman HS — 1,800/9-12
　205 N 11th Ave　59715 — 406-522-6200
　Godfrey Saunders, prin. — Fax 522-6222
Chief Joseph MS — 500/6-8
　309 N 11th Ave　59715 — 406-522-6300
　Diane Cashell, prin. — Fax 522-6306
Sacajawea MS — 600/6-8
　3525 S 3rd Rd　59715 — 406-522-6470
　Diana McDonough, prin. — Fax 522-6474
LaMotte ESD 43 — 100/PK-8
　841 Bear Canyon Rd　59715 — 406-586-2838
　 — Fax 586-8626
　www.lamotteschool.com
LaMotte MS — 50/7-8
　841 Bear Canyon Rd　59715 — 406-586-2838
　LeeAnn Burke, prin. — Fax 585-2636
Monforton ESD 27 — 200/PK-8
　6001 Monforton School Rd　59718 — 406-586-1557
　Lynne Scalia, supt. — Fax 587-5049
Monforton MS — 100/7-8
　6001 Monforton School Rd　59718 — 406-586-1557
　Lynne Scalia, prin. — Fax 587-5049

Academy of Cosmetology — Post-Sec.
　133 W Mendenhall St　59715 — 406-587-1265
Headwaters Academy — 50/6-9
　418 W Garfield St　59715 — 406-585-9997
Heritage Christian S — 200/PK-12
　4310 Durston Rd　59718 — 406-587-9311
　Mathew Henry, admin. — Fax 587-1838
Montana State University - Bozeman — Post-Sec.
　103 Culbertson Hall　59715 — 406-994-2452
Mt. Ellis Academy — 100/9-12
　3641 Bozeman Trail Rd　59715 — 406-587-5178
　 — Fax 587-5170
Petra Academy — 100/K-12
　100 Discovery Dr Ste 101　59718 — 406-582-8165
　Louise Turner, prin. — Fax 556-8777

Brady, Pondera
Dutton/Brady SD 28
　Supt. — See Dutton
Dutton/Brady MS — 50/7-8
　309 2nd Ave NE　59416 — 406-753-2522
　James Mepham, prin. — Fax 753-2270

Bridger, Carbon, Pop. 759
Bridger SD 2 — 200/PK-12
　PO Box 467　59014 — 406-662-3533
　John Ballard, supt. — Fax 662-3076
　www.bridger.k12.mt.us
Bridger HS — 100/9-12
　PO Box 467　59014 — 406-662-3533
　John Ballard, prin. — Fax 662-3076
Bridger MS — 50/7-8
　PO Box 467　59014 — 406-662-3588
　John Ballard, prin. — Fax 662-3520

Broadus, Powder River, Pop. 446
Broadus SD 79J — 400/K-12
　PO Box 500　59317 — 406-436-2658
　Richard Cameron, supt. — Fax 436-2660
Broadus MS — 100/7-8
　PO Box 500　59317 — 406-436-2658
　Jim Hansen, prin. — Fax 436-2660
Powder River County District HS — 100/9-12
　PO Box 500　59317 — 406-436-2658
　Jim Hansen, prin. — Fax 436-2660

Broadview, Yellowstone, Pop. 150
Broadview SD 21-J — 100/K-12
　PO Box 147　59015 — 406-667-2337
　Rey Busch, supt. — Fax 667-2195
Broadview HS — 50/9-12
　PO Box 147　59015 — 406-667-2337
　Rey Busch, prin. — Fax 667-2195

Brockton, Roosevelt, Pop. 241
Brockton SD 55 — 200/PK-12
　PO Box 198　59213 — 406-786-3195
　Sherry Westergard, supt. — Fax 786-3121
　www.brockton.k12.mt.us/
Brockton HS — 100/9-12
　PO Box 198　59213 — 406-786-3313
　Jim Dillon, prin. — Fax 786-3377
Gilligan MS — 50/7-8
　PO Box 198　59213 — 406-786-3311
　Jim Dillon, prin. — Fax 786-3377

Browning, Glacier, Pop. 1,066
Browning SD 9 — 1,900/PK-12
PO Box 610 59417 — 406-338-2715
Mary Johnson, supt. — Fax 338-3200
www.bps.k12.mt.us/
Browning HS — 600/9-12
PO Box 610 59417 — 406-338-2745
Janet Guardipee, prin. — Fax 338-2844
Browning MS — 300/6-8
PO Box 610 59417 — 406-338-2725
Willie Sharp, prin. — Fax 338-5320

Blackfeet Community College — Post-Sec.
PO Box 819 59417 — 406-338-5441

Butte, Silver Bow, Pop. 32,716
Butte SD 1 — 4,400/K-12
111 N Montana St 59701 — 406-533-2501
Chuck Uggetti, supt. — Fax 533-2525
www.butte.k12.mt.us
Butte HS — 1,500/9-12
401 S Wyoming St 59701 — 406-533-2200
John Metz, prin. — Fax 533-2220
East MS — 800/7-8
2600 Grand Ave 59701 — 406-533-2600
Larry Driscoll, prin. — Fax 496-2670

Butte Academy of Beauty Culture — Post-Sec.
303 W Park St 59701 — 406-723-8565
Butte Central Catholic HS — 200/9-12
9 S Idaho St 59701 — 406-782-6761
Tim Norbeck, prin. — Fax 723-3873
Montana Tech College of Technology — Post-Sec.
25 Basin Creek Rd 59701 — 406-496-3701
Montana Tech of the University of MT — Post-Sec.
1300 W Park St 59701 — 406-496-4101

Cascade, Cascade, Pop. 800
Cascade SD — 400/PK-12
PO Box 529 59421 — 406-468-9383
Kenneth Kelly, supt. — Fax 468-2212
www.cascade.k12.mt.us
Cascade HS — 100/9-12
321 Central Ave W 59421 — 406-468-2267
Dave Marzolf, prin. — Fax 468-2212
Cascade MS — 100/7-8
321 Central Ave W 59421 — 406-468-2267
Dave Marzolf, prin. — Fax 468-2212

Charlo, Lake, Pop. 358
Charlo SD 7-J — 300/PK-12
PO Box 10 59824 — 406-644-2207
Wes Young, supt. — Fax 644-2400
www.charlo.k12.mt.us/
Charlo HS — 100/9-12
PO Box 10 59824 — 406-644-2206
Steve Love, prin. — Fax 644-2400
Charlo MS — 100/7-8
PO Box 10 59824 — 406-644-2206
Clair Rasmussen, prin. — Fax 644-2401

Chester, Liberty, Pop. 833
Chester Joplin Inverness SD 48 1J — 300/PK-12
PO Box 550 59522 — 406-759-5108
Dollyann Willcutt, supt. — Fax 759-5867
www.chester.k12.mt.us/
Chester Joplin Inverness HS — 100/9-12
PO Box 550 59522 — 406-759-5108
Pam Graff, prin. — Fax 759-5867
Chester Joplin Inverness MS — 50/7-8
PO Box 550 59522 — 406-759-5108
Pam Graff, prin. — Fax 759-5867

Chinook, Blaine, Pop. 1,325
Chinook SD 10 — 400/PK-12
PO Box 1059 59523 — 406-357-2628
Jay Eslick, supt. — Fax 357-2238
Chinook HS — 200/9-12
PO Box 1059 59523 — 406-357-2236
Matt Molyneaux, prin. — Fax 357-2238
Chinook MS — 100/7-8
PO Box 1059 59523 — 406-357-2237
Matt Molyneaux, prin. — Fax 357-2238

Choteau, Teton, Pop. 1,776
Choteau SD 1 — 500/PK-12
204 7th Ave NW 59422 — 406-466-5303
Kent Kultgen, supt. — Fax 466-5305
Choteau HS — 200/9-12
204 7th Ave NW 59422 — 406-466-5303
Neal Wedum, prin. — Fax 466-5305
Choteau MS — 100/7-8
204 7th Ave NW 59422 — 406-466-5303
Neal Wedum, prin. — Fax 466-5305

Circle, McCone, Pop. 593
Circle SD 1 — 300/K-12
PO Box 99 59215 — 406-485-2545
Mike Radakovich, supt. — Fax 485-2332
Circle HS — 100/9-12
PO Box 99 59215 — 406-485-3600
Ken Larson, prin. — Fax 485-2332
Redwater MS — 50/7-8
PO Box 99 59215 — 406-485-2140
Ken Larson, prin. — Fax 485-2332

Clancy, Jefferson
Clancy ESD 1 — 300/PK-8
PO Box 209 59634 — 406-933-5575
Robert Klein, supt. — Fax 933-5715
www.clancy.k12.mt.us/
Clancy MS — 100/7-8
PO Box 209 59634 — 406-933-5575
Bruce Dunkle, prin. — Fax 933-5715

Montana City ESD 27 — 400/PK-8
11 McClellan Creek Rd 59634 — 406-442-6779
Tony Kloker, supt. — Fax 443-8875
Montana City MS — 100/6-8
11 McClellan Creek Rd 59634 — 406-442-6779
Kathy Kidder, prin. — Fax 443-8875

Clinton, Missoula
Clinton ESD 32 — 200/K-8
PO Box 250 59825 — 406-825-3113
Mark Latrielle, supt. — Fax 825-3114
Clinton MS — 50/7-8
PO Box 250 59825 — 406-825-3113
Kelly Benson, prin. — Fax 825-3114

Clyde Park, Park, Pop. 333
Shields Valley SD J12
Supt. — See Wilsall
Shields Valley HS — 100/9-12
PO Box 40 59018 — 406-686-4621
Ryan Boettcher, prin. — Fax 686-4937

Colstrip, Rosebud, Pop. 2,382
Colstrip SD 19 — 700/PK-12
PO Box 159 59323 — 406-748-4699
Harry Cheff, supt. — Fax 748-2268
www.colstrip.k12.mt.us/
Brattin MS — 200/6-8
216 Olive Dr 59323 — 406-748-4699
Dinny Bennett, prin. — Fax 748-3143
Colstrip HS — 300/9-12
5000 Pine Butte Dr 59323 — 406-748-4699
Dennis Davenport, prin. — Fax 748-2517

Columbia Falls, Flathead, Pop. 3,963
Columbia Falls SD 6 — 2,500/PK-12
PO Box 1259 59912 — 406-892-6550
Michael Nicosia, supt. — Fax 892-6552
www.sd6.k12.mt.us
Columbia Falls HS — 800/9-12
PO Box 1259 59912 — 406-892-6500
Terri Burghardt, prin. — Fax 892-6583
Columbia Falls JHS — 500/7-8
PO Box 1259 59912 — 406-892-6530
Dave Wick, prin. — Fax 892-6528

Deer Park ESD 2 — 100/K-8
2105 Middle Rd 59912 — 406-892-5388
— Fax 892-3504
Deer Park MS — 50/7-8
2105 Middle Rd 59912 — 406-892-5388
Kim Anderson, prin. — Fax 892-3504

Columbus, Stillwater, Pop. 1,890
Columbus SD 6 — 600/PK-12
433 N 3rd St 59019 — 406-322-5373
Allan Sipes, supt. — Fax 322-5028
www.columbus.k12.mt.us/
Columbus HS — 200/9-12
433 N 3rd St 59019 — 406-322-5373
George McKay, prin. — Fax 322-5028
Columbus MS — 200/6-8
415 N 3rd St 59019 — 406-322-5375
Ron Osborne, prin. — Fax 322-5376

Condon, Missoula
Swan Valley ESD 33 — 50/PK-8
6423 Highway 83 59826 — 406-754-2320
— Fax 754-2627
Swan Valley MS — 50/7-8
6423 Highway 83 59826 — 406-754-2320
Shirley Webb, prin. — Fax 754-2627

Conrad, Pondera, Pop. 2,657
Conrad SD 10 — 700/PK-12
215 S Maryland St 59425 — 406-278-5521
Kurt Hilyard, supt. — Fax 278-3630
www.montana.com/conrad/
Conrad HS — 200/9-12
308 S Illinois St 59425 — 406-278-3285
Orlen Zempel, prin. — Fax 278-3806
Utterback MS — 100/7-8
24 2nd Ave SW 59425 — 406-278-3227
Craig Barringer, prin. — Fax 271-2680

Corvallis, Ravalli
Corvallis SD 1 — 1,400/PK-12
PO Box 700 59828 — 406-961-4211
Daniel Sybrant, supt. — Fax 961-5144
www.corvallis.k12.mt.us
Corvallis HS — 500/9-12
PO Box 700 59828 — 406-961-3201
Sarah Schumacher, prin. — Fax 961-4894
Corvallis JHS — 300/7-8
PO Box 700 59828 — 406-961-3007
Thomas Miller, prin. — Fax 961-5144

Crow Agency, Big Horn, Pop. 1,446

Little Big Horn College 59022 — Post-Sec.
406-638-3104

Culbertson, Roosevelt, Pop. 708
Culbertson SD — 200/PK-12
PO Box 459 59218 — 406-787-6246
Larry Crowder, supt. — Fax 787-6244
culbertsonschool.k12.mt.us
Culbertson HS — 100/9-12
PO Box 459 59218 — 406-787-6241
Jerry Waagen, prin. — Fax 787-6244
Culbertson MS — 50/7-8
PO Box 459 59218 — 406-787-6241
Jerry Waagen, prin. — Fax 787-6244

Custer, Yellowstone
Custer SD 15 — 100/K-12
PO Box 69 59024 — 406-856-4117
Garret Franks, supt. — Fax 856-4206
Custer HS — 50/9-12
PO Box 69 59024 — 406-856-4117
Garret Franks, prin. — Fax 856-4206

Custer MS — 50/7-8
PO Box 69 59024 — 406-856-4117
Garret Franks, prin. — Fax 856-4206

Cut Bank, Glacier, Pop. 3,096
Cut Bank SD 15 — 1,200/PK-12
101 3rd Ave SE 59427 — 406-873-2229
Wade Johnson, supt. — Fax 873-4691
www.cutbank.k12.mt.us
Cut Bank HS — 300/9-12
101 3rd Ave SE 59427 — 406-873-5629
Karen Underwood, prin. — Fax 873-4691
Cut Bank JHS — 200/7-8
101 3rd Ave SE 59427 — 406-873-4421
Don Paulson, prin. — Fax 873-4691

Darby, Ravalli, Pop. 785
Darby SD 9 — 500/PK-12
209 School Dr 59829 — 406-821-3841
Bruce Wallace, supt. — Fax 821-4977
www.darby.k12.mt.us/
Darby HS — 200/9-12
209 School Dr 59829 — 406-821-3252
Loyd Rennaker, prin. — Fax 821-4904
Darby MS — 100/7-8
209 School Dr 59829 — 406-821-3252
Loyd Rennaker, prin. — Fax 821-4904

Deer Lodge, Powell, Pop. 3,324
Deer Lodge ESD 1 — 500/PK-8
444 Montana Ave 59722 — 406-846-1553
Tom Cotton, supt. — Fax 846-1599
Duvall MS — 100/7-8
444 Montana Ave 59722 — 406-846-1684
Rick Chrisman, prin. — Fax 846-1599

Powell County HSD — 300/9-12
709 Missouri Ave 59722 — 406-846-2757
Rick Duncan, supt. — Fax 846-2759
pchs.dl.k12.mt.us
Powell County HS — 300/9-12
709 Missouri Ave 59722 — 406-846-2757
Terry Mosier, prin. — Fax 846-2759

Denton, Fergus, Pop. 293
Denton SD 84 — 100/PK-12
PO Box 1048 59430 — 406-567-2370
Bill Phillips, supt. — Fax 567-2559
Denton HS — 100/9-12
PO Box 1048 59430 — 406-567-2370
Bill Phillips, prin. — Fax 567-2559
Denton JHS — 50/7-8
PO Box 1048 59430 — 406-567-2370
Bill Phillips, prin. — Fax 567-2559

Dillon, Beaverhead, Pop. 4,035
Beaverhead County HSD — 400/9-12
104 N Pacific St 59725 — 406-683-2361
Fred Chouinard, supt. — Fax 683-5263
Beaverhead County HS — 400/9-12
104 N Pacific St 59725 — 406-683-2361
Gary Haverfield, prin. — Fax 683-5263

Dillon ESD 10 — 700/PK-8
225 E Reeder St 59725 — 406-683-4311
Melinda Berkram, supt. — Fax 683-4312
www.dillonelem.k12.mt.us/
Dillon MS — 200/6-8
14 Cottom Dr 59725 — 406-683-2368
Randy Shipman, prin. — Fax 683-2369

University of Montana - Western — Post-Sec.
710 S Atlantic St 59725 — 406-683-7011

Dixon, Sanders
Dixon ESD 9 — 100/PK-8
PO Box 10 59831 — 406-246-3566
— Fax 246-3379
Dixon MS — 50/7-8
PO Box 10 59831 — 406-246-3566
Mark Faroni, prin. — Fax 246-3379

Dodson, Phillips, Pop. 113
Dodson SD — 100/PK-12
PO Box 278 59524 — 406-383-4362
Les Wells, supt. — Fax 383-4489
Dodson HS — 50/9-12
PO Box 278 59524 — 406-383-4362
Rod Simpson, prin. — Fax 383-4489
Dodson MS — 50/7-8
PO Box 278 59524 — 406-383-4362
Rod Simpson, prin. — Fax 383-4489

Drummond, Granite, Pop. 327
Drummond SD 11 — 200/K-12
PO Box 349 59832 — 406-288-3281
Paula Johnston, supt. — Fax 288-3299
Drummond HS — 100/9-12
PO Box 349 59832 — 406-288-3281
Paula Johnston, prin. — Fax 288-3299
Drummond MS — 50/7-8
PO Box 349 59832 — 406-288-3283
Kitty Logan, prin. — Fax 288-3299

Dutton, Teton, Pop. 385
Dutton/Brady SD 28 — 100/PK-12
101 2nd St NE 59433 — 406-476-3424
Tim Tharp, supt. — Fax 476-3342
Dutton/Brady HS — 50/9-12
101 2nd St NE 59433 — 406-476-3424
Jim Mepham, prin. — Fax 476-3342
Other Schools – See Brady

East Helena, Lewis and Clark, Pop. 1,682
East Helena ESD 9 — 1,000/PK-8
PO Box 1280 59635 — 406-227-7700
Ron Whitmoyer, supt. — Fax 227-5534
www.ehps.k12.mt.us
East Valley MS — 400/6-8
PO Box 1280 59635 — 406-227-7740
Dan Rispens, prin. — Fax 227-9730

Ekalaka, Carter, Pop. 401
Carter County HSD | 100/9-12
PO Box 458 59324 | 406-775-8767
Wade Northrup, supt. | Fax 775-8766
Carter County HS | 100/9-12
PO Box 458 59324 | 406-775-8767
Wade Northrop, prin. | Fax 775-8766

Ekalaka ESD 15 | 100/PK-8
PO Box 458 59324 | 406-775-8767
Wade Northrup, supt. | Fax 775-8766
Ekalaka MS | 50/7-8
PO Box 458 59324 | 406-775-8767
Wade Northrop, prin. | Fax 775-8766

Ennis, Madison, Pop. 884
Ennis SD 52 | 400/PK-12
PO Box 517 59729 | 406-682-4258
Douglas Walsh, supt. | Fax 682-7751
Ennis HS | 100/9-12
PO Box 517 59729 | 406-682-4258
Greg Fitzgerald, prin. | Fax 682-7751
Ennis MS | 100/7-8
PO Box 517 59729 | 406-682-4237
Brian Hilton, prin. | Fax 682-7751

Eureka, Lincoln, Pop. 1,009
Eureka SD 13 | 900/PK-12
PO Box 2000 59917 | 406-297-5637
Gary Blaz, supt. | Fax 297-2644
www.eureka.k12.mt.us/
Eureka MS | 100/7-8
PO Box 2000 59917 | 406-297-5603
Rod Schmidt, prin. | Fax 297-5653
Lincoln County HS | 400/9-12
PO Box 2000 59917 | 406-297-5702
Alan Robbins, prin. | Fax 297-5714

Fairfield, Teton, Pop. 652
Fairfield SD 21 | 300/PK-12
PO Box 399 59436 | 406-467-2103
Mark Anderson, supt. | Fax 467-2554
www.fairfield.k12.mt.us/
Fairfield HS | 100/9-12
PO Box 399 59436 | 406-467-2528
Les Meyer, prin. | Fax 467-2554
Fairfield MS | 50/7-8
PO Box 399 59436 | 406-467-2425
Matt Genger, prin. | Fax 467-2554

Greenfield ESD 75 | 100/PK-8
590 2nd Rd NE 59436 | 406-467-2433
 | Fax 467-3138
Greenfield MS | 50/7-8
590 2nd Rd NE 59436 | 406-467-2433
Loren Sasser, prin. | Fax 467-3138

Fairview, Richland, Pop. 671
Fairview SD | 200/PK-12
PO Box 467 59221 | 406-742-5265
Matt Schriver, supt. | Fax 742-3336
www.fairview.k12.mt.us/
Fairview HS | 100/9-12
PO Box 467 59221 | 406-742-5265
Luke Kloker, prin. | Fax 742-8265
Fairview MS | 50/7-8
PO Box 467 59221 | 406-742-5265
Luke Kloker, prin. | Fax 742-8265

Flaxville, Daniels, Pop. 83
Flaxville SD 3 | 50/PK-12
PO Box 89 59222 | 406-474-2211
Loren Dunk, supt. | Fax 474-2242
Flaxville HS | 50/9-12
PO Box 89 59222 | 406-474-2211
Loren Dunk, prin. | Fax 474-2242
Flaxville MS | 50/7-8
PO Box 89 59222 | 406-474-2211
Loren Dunk, prin. | Fax 474-2242

Florence, Ravalli
Florence-Carlton SD 15-6 | 900/PK-12
5602 Old US Highway 93 59833 | 406-273-6751
John McGee, supt. | Fax 273-2802
www.florence.k12.mt.us
Florence-Carlton HS | 300/9-12
5602 Old US Highway 93 59833 | 406-273-6301
Rebecca Stapert, prin. | Fax 273-2643
Florence-Carlton MS | 200/7-8
5602 Old US Highway 93 59833 | 406-273-0587
Ed Norman, prin. | Fax 273-0545

Forsyth, Rosebud, Pop. 1,914
Forsyth SD 4 | 400/PK-12
PO Box 319 59327 | 406-346-2796
David Shreeve, supt. | Fax 346-7455
Forsyth HS | 100/9-12
PO Box 319 59327 | 406-346-2796
Doug Roberts, prin. | Fax 346-9219
Forsyth MS | 100/7-8
PO Box 319 59327 | 406-346-2796
Doug Roberts, prin. | Fax 346-9219

Fort Benton, Chouteau, Pop. 1,502
Ft. Benton SD 1 | 400/PK-12
PO Box 399 59442 | 406-622-5691
Robert Anderson, supt. | Fax 622-5691
www.fortbenton.k12.mt.us/
Fort Benton HS | 100/9-12
PO Box 399 59442 | 406-622-3213
Jim Howard, prin. | Fax 622-5691
Fort Benton JHS | 100/7-8
PO Box 399 59442 | 406-622-3213
Jim Howard, prin. | Fax 622-5691

Frazer, Valley, Pop. 403
Frazer SD 2 | 100/K-12
PO Box 488 59225 | 406-695-2241
Richard Whitesell, supt. | Fax 695-2243

Frazer HS | 50/9-12
PO Box 488 59225 | 406-695-2241
Richard Whitesell, prin. | Fax 695-2243
Frazer MS | 50/7-8
PO Box 488 59225 | 406-695-2241
Richard Whitesell, prin. | Fax 695-2243

Lustre Christian HS | 50/9-12
294 Lustre Rd 59225 | 406-392-5735
Al Leland, supt. | Fax 392-5765

Frenchtown, Missoula
Frenchtown SD 40 | 1,200/PK-12
PO Box 117 59834 | 406-626-2600
Dr. Peggy Anderson, supt. | Fax 626-2605
www.frenchtown.k12.mt.us
Frenchtown HS | 400/9-12
PO Box 117 59834 | 406-626-2670
Jon Fimmel, prin. | Fax 626-2676
Frenchtown MS | 200/7-8
PO Box 117 59834 | 406-626-2650
Rory Wershaar, prin. | Fax 626-2605

Froid, Roosevelt, Pop. 191
Froid SD | 100/K-12
PO Box 218 59226 | 406-766-2343
Roger Britton, supt. | Fax 766-2206
Froid HS | 50/9-12
PO Box 218 59226 | 406-766-2342
Roger Britton, prin. | Fax 766-2206
Froid MS | 50/7-8
PO Box 218 59226 | 406-766-2342
Roger Britton, prin. | Fax 766-2206

Fromberg, Carbon, Pop. 498
Fromberg SD 30 | 200/PK-12
PO Box 189 59029 | 406-668-7611
Ed Combs, supt. | Fax 668-7602
Fromberg HS | 100/9-12
PO Box 189 59029 | 406-668-7611
Ed Combs, prin. | Fax 668-7602
Fromberg MS | 50/7-8
PO Box 189 59029 | 406-668-7755
Ed Combs, prin. | Fax 668-7602

Gallatin Gateway, Gallatin
Gallatin Gateway ESD 35 | 100/PK-8
PO Box 265 59730 | 406-763-4415
Kim DeBruycker, supt. | Fax 763-4886
Gallatin Gateway MS | 50/7-8
PO Box 265 59730 | 406-763-4415
Kim DeBruycker, prin. | Fax 763-4886

Ophir ESD 72 | 100/PK-8
45465 Gallatin Rd 59730 | 406-995-4281
AnneMarie Mistretta, supt. | Fax 995-2161
Ophir MS | 50/7-8
45465 Gallatin Rd 59730 | 406-995-4281
AnneMarie Mistretta, prin. | Fax 995-2161

Gardiner, Park
Gardiner SD 7 | 200/PK-12
510 Stone St 59030 | 406-848-7261
Leland Stocker, supt. | Fax 848-9489
Gardiner HS | 100/9-12
510 Stone St 59030 | 406-848-7261
Ken Ballagh, prin. | Fax 848-9489
Gardiner MS | 50/7-8
510 Stone St 59030 | 406-848-7563
Ken Ballagh, prin. | Fax 848-9489

Geraldine, Chouteau, Pop. 266
Geraldine SD 44 | 100/PK-12
PO Box 347 59446 | 406-737-4311
Rodney Simpson, supt. | Fax 737-4478
Geraldine HS | 50/9-12
PO Box 347 59446 | 406-737-4371
Rodney Simpson, prin. | Fax 737-4478
Geraldine MS | 50/7-8
PO Box 347 59446 | 406-737-4371
Rodney Simpson, prin. | Fax 737-4478

Geyser, Judith Basin
Geyser SD 58 | 100/PK-12
PO Box 70 59447 | 406-735-4368
Tobin Novasio, supt. | Fax 735-4452
Geyser HS | 50/9-12
PO Box 70 59447 | 406-735-4368
Tobin Novasio, prin. | Fax 735-4452
Geyser MS | 50/7-8
PO Box 70 59447 | 406-735-4368
Tobin Novasio, prin. | Fax 735-4452

Gildford, Hill
North Star SD 99 | 100/PK-12
PO Box 250 59525 | 406-355-4481
Terry Grant, supt. | Fax 355-4532
Other Facilities – See Rudyard

Glasgow, Valley, Pop. 3,122
Glasgow SD 1-A | 900/PK-12
PO Box 28 59230 | 406-228-2406
Glenn Hageman, supt. | Fax 228-2407
www.glasgow.k12.mt.us/
Glasgow HS | 200/9-12
PO Box 28 59230 | 406-228-2485
Margaret Markle, prin. | Fax 228-4061
Glasgow MS | 100/7-8
PO Box 28 59230 | 406-228-2485
Margaret Markle, prin. | Fax 228-4061

Glendive, Dawson, Pop. 4,717
Glendive SD | 1,300/PK-12
PO Box 701 59330 | 406-377-5293
Jim Germann, supt. | Fax 377-6212
Dawson County HS | 400/9-12
PO Box 701 59330 | 406-377-5265
Bruce Clausen, prin. | Fax 377-8206
Washington MS | 400/5-8
PO Box 701 59330 | 406-377-2356
Ross Farber, prin. | Fax 377-2357

Dawson Community College | Post-Sec.
PO Box 421 59330 | 406-377-3396

Grass Range, Fergus, Pop. 148
Grass Range SD 27 | 100/PK-12
PO Box 58 59032 | 406-428-2122
Debbie Clausen, supt. | Fax 428-2235
Grass Range HS | 50/9-12
PO Box 58 59032 | 406-428-2341
Debbie Clausen, prin. | Fax 428-2235
Grass Range MS | 50/7-8
PO Box 58 59032 | 406-428-2122
Debbie Clausen, prin. | Fax 428-2235

Great Falls, Cascade, Pop. 56,155
Great Falls SD 1 | 13,900/PK-12
PO Box 2429 59403 | 406-268-6001
Dr. W. Bryan Dunn, supt. | Fax 268-6002
www.gfps.k12.mt.us
East MS | 600/7-8
4040 Central Ave 59405 | 406-268-6500
Shelly Fagenstrom, prin. | Fax 268-6524
Great Falls HS | 1,900/9-12
1900 2nd Ave S 59405 | 406-268-6250
Fred Anderson, prin. | Fax 268-6256
North MS | 600/7-8
2601 8th St NE 59404 | 406-268-6525
Tom Maguire, prin. | Fax 268-6575
Russell HS | 1,700/9-12
228 17th Ave NW 59404 | 406-268-6100
Dick Kloppel, prin. | Fax 268-6109

Benefits Health Care-West Campus | Post-Sec.
PO Box 5013 59403 | 406-727-3333
Dahl's College of Beauty | Post-Sec.
718 Central Ave 59401 | 406-454-3453
Foothills Community Christian S | 200/PK-12
2210 5th Ave N 59401 | 406-452-5276
Ted Clark, admin. | Fax 452-8606
Great Falls Central Catholic HS | 100/9-12
121 23rd St S 59401 | 406-791-5940
Hugh Smith, prin. | Fax 454-5942
Montana School for the Deaf and Blind | Post-Sec.
3911 Central Ave 59405 | 406-771-6000
Montana State Univ Great Falls College | Post-Sec.
2100 16th Ave S 59405 | 406-771-4300
University of Great Falls | Post-Sec.
1301 20th St S 59405 | 406-761-8210

Hamilton, Ravalli, Pop. 4,163
Hamilton SD 3 | 1,600/PK-12
217 Daly Ave 59840 | 406-363-2280
John Matt, supt. | Fax 363-1843
www.hsd3.org
Hamilton HS | 600/9-12
327 Fairgrounds Rd 59840 | 406-375-6060
Kevin Conwell, prin. | Fax 375-6076
Hamilton MS | 400/6-8
209 S 5th St 59840 | 406-363-2121
Kelly Benson, prin. | Fax 363-7032

Hardin, Big Horn, Pop. 3,448
Hardin SD 17-H | 1,700/PK-12
RR 1 Box 1001 59034 | 406-665-1304
Albert Peterson, supt. | Fax 665-2784
www.hardin.k12.mt.us
Hardin HS | 500/9-12
702 N Terry Ave 59034 | 406-665-6300
Keith Campbell, prin. | Fax 665-1909
Hardin MS | 400/6-8
611 5th St W 59034 | 406-665-6350
Don Gilbertson, prin. | Fax 665-1409

Harlem, Blaine, Pop. 828
Harlem SD 12 | 600/PK-12
PO Box 339 59526 | 406-353-2289
Neil Terhune, supt. | Fax 353-2674
Harlem HS | 200/9-12
PO Box 339 59526 | 406-353-2287
Nancy Coleman, prin. | Fax 353-2674
Harlem MS | 100/7-8
PO Box 339 59526 | 406-353-2287
Nancy Coleman, prin. | Fax 353-2674

Fort Belknap College | Post-Sec.
PO Box 159 59526 | 406-353-2607

Harlowton, Wheatland, Pop. 977
Harlowton SD 16 | 400/PK-12
PO Box 288 59036 | 406-632-4822
Andrew Begger, supt. | Fax 632-4416
Harlowton HS | 100/9-12
304 Division St 59036 | 406-632-4324
Gregg Wasson, prin. | Fax 632-4416
Hillcrest MS | 100/7-8
304 Division St 59036 | 406-632-4361
Gregg Wasson, prin. | Fax 632-4416

Harrison, Madison
Harrison SD 23 | 100/PK-12
PO Box 7 59735 | 406-685-3428
Dan Rask, supt. | Fax 685-3430
Harrison HS | 100/9-12
PO Box 7 59735 | 406-685-3428
Darren Strauch, prin. | Fax 685-3430
Harrison MS | 50/7-8
PO Box 7 59735 | 406-685-3471
Darren Strauch, prin. | Fax 685-3430

Havre, Hill, Pop. 9,448
Havre SD | 2,000/PK-12
PO Box 7791 59501 | 406-265-4356
Kirk Miller, supt. | Fax 265-8460
www.havre.k12.mt.us/
Havre HS | 700/9-12
PO Box 7791 59501 | 406-265-6731
Jim Donovan, prin. | Fax 265-3217

Havre MS 500/6-8
1441 11th St W 59501 406-265-9613
Vance Blatter, prin. Fax 265-4414

Anchor Academy 100/7-12
24247 Base Rd 59501 406-394-4454
Dennis McElwrath, hdmstr. Fax 394-4457
Montana State University Northern Post-Sec.
PO Box 7751 59501 406-265-3700

Hays, Blaine, Pop. 333
Hays-Lodge Pole SD 50 200/PK-12
PO Box 110 59527 406-673-3120
James Anderson, supt. Fax 673-3294
Hays-Lodge Pole HS 100/9-12
PO Box 110 59527 406-673-3120
Fax 673-3415
Hays-Lodge Pole MS 100/7-8
PO Box 110 59527 406-673-3120
Fax 673-3415

Heart Butte, Pondera, Pop. 499
Heart Butte SD 1 200/PK-12
PO Box 259 59448 406-338-2211
Richard Richardson, supt. Fax 338-5832
Heart Butte HS 100/9-12
PO Box 259 59448 406-338-3344
Leonard Guardipee, prin. Fax 338-2088
Heart Butte MS 50/7-8
PO Box 259 59448 406-338-2200
Leonard Guardipee, prin. Fax 338-2088

Helena, Lewis and Clark, Pop. 26,718
Helena SD 1 8,100/K-12
55 S Rodney St 59601 406-324-2001
Dr. Bruce Messinger, supt. Fax 324-2035
www.helena.k12.mt.us/
Anderson MS 1,100/6-8
1200 Knight St 59601 406-324-2800
Bruce Campbell, prin. Fax 324-2801
Capital HS 1,400/9-12
100 Valley Dr 59601 406-324-2500
Randy Carlson, prin. Fax 324-2501
Helena HS 1,700/9-12
1300 Billings Ave 59601 406-324-2200
Donald Wood-Foucar, prin. Fax 324-2201
Helena MS 700/6-8
1025 N Rodney St 59601 406-324-1000
Tom Lipp, prin. Fax 324-1001

Carroll College Post-Sec.
1601 N Benton Ave 59625 406-447-4300
Helena College of Tech of the Univ of MT Post-Sec.
1115 N Roberts St 59601 406-444-6800

Highwood, Chouteau
Highwood SD 28 100/PK-12
160 West St S 59450 406-733-2081
Tim Bronk, supt. Fax 733-2671
Highwood HS 50/9-12
160 West St S 59450 406-733-2081
Tim Bronk, prin. Fax 733-2671
Highwood MS 50/6-8
160 West St S 59450 406-733-2081
Tim Bronk, prin. Fax 733-2671

Hinsdale, Valley
Hinsdale SD 100/PK-12
PO Box 398 59241 406-364-2314
Stephen Henderson, supt. Fax 364-2205
Hinsdale HS 50/9-12
PO Box 398 59241 406-364-2314
Stephen Henderson, prin. Fax 364-2205
Hinsdale MS 50/7-8
PO Box 398 59241 406-364-2314
Don Johnson, prin. Fax 364-2205

Hobson, Judith Basin, Pop. 231
Hobson SD 25 100/PK-12
PO Box 410 59452 406-423-5483
Dale Shupe, supt. Fax 423-5260
www.hobson.k12.mt.us/
Hobson HS 50/9-12
PO Box 410 59452 406-423-5483
Dale Shupe, prin. Fax 423-5260
Hobson MS 50/7-8
PO Box 410 59452 406-423-5483
Dale Shupe, prin. Fax 423-5260

Hot Springs, Sanders, Pop. 531
Hot Springs SD 14J 200/PK-12
PO Box 1005 59845 406-741-3285
Larry Markuson, supt. Fax 741-3287
Hot Springs HS 100/9-12
PO Box 1005 59845 406-741-2962
Larry Markuson, prin. Fax 741-3287
Hot Springs MS 50/7-8
PO Box 1005 59845 406-741-2962
Larry Markuson, prin. Fax 741-3287

Hysham, Treasure, Pop. 281
Hysham SD 1 100/PK-12
PO Box 272 59038 406-342-5237
Jon Pehrson, supt. Fax 342-5257
www.hysham.k12.mt.us/
Hysham HS 50/9-12
PO Box 272 59038 406-342-5237
Jon Pehrson, prin. Fax 342-5257
Hysham MS 50/7-8
PO Box 272 59038 406-342-5237
Jon Pehrson, prin. Fax 342-5257

Joliet, Carbon, Pop. 586
Joliet SD 7 400/PK-12
PO Box 590 59041 406-962-2200
Les Cabot, supt. Fax 962-3958
Joliet HS 100/9-12
PO Box 590 59041 406-962-3541
Marilyn Vukonich, prin. Fax 962-3958

Joliet MS 100/7-8
PO Box 590 59041 406-962-3541
Marilyn Vukonich, prin. Fax 962-3958

Jordan, Garfield, Pop. 353
Jordan SD 1 200/PK-12
PO Box 409 59337 406-557-2259
Jennifer O'Connor, supt. Fax 557-2778
Garfield County HS 100/9-12
PO Box 409 59337 406-557-2259
Jennifer O'Connor, prin. Fax 557-2778
Jordan MS 50/7-8
PO Box 409 59337 406-557-2716
Jennifer O'Connor, prin. Fax 557-2778

Judith Gap, Wheatland, Pop. 153
Judith Gap SD 21J 100/PK-12
PO Box 67 59453 406-473-2211
Don Amundson, supt. Fax 473-2250
Judith Gap HS 50/9-12
PO Box 67 59453 406-473-2211
Don Amundson, prin. Fax 473-2250
Judith Gap MS 50/7-8
PO Box 67 59453 406-473-2211
Don Amundson, prin. Fax 473-2250

Kalispell, Flathead, Pop. 16,391
Cayuse Prairie ESD 10 200/K-8
897 Lake Blaine Rd 59901 406-756-4560
Fax 756-4570
Cayuse Prairie MS 50/7-8
897 Lake Blaine Rd 59901 406-756-4560
Rick Nadeau, prin. Fax 756-4570

Evergreen ESD 50 700/PK-8
18 W Evergreen Dr 59901 406-751-1111
Joel Voytoski, supt. Fax 752-2307
Evergreen JHS 100/7-8
18 W Evergreen Dr 59901 406-751-1131
Ted Tiegs, prin. Fax 751-1134

Fair-Mont-Egan ESD 3 200/PK-8
797 Fairmont Rd 59901 406-755-7072
Fax 755-7077
Fair-Mont-Egan MS 50/7-8
797 Fairmont Rd 59901 406-755-7072
Christine Anthony, prin. Fax 755-7077

Helena Flats ESD 15 200/K-8
1000 Helena Flats Rd 59901 406-257-2301
Paul Jenkins, supt. Fax 257-2304
Helena Flats MS 100/7-8
1000 Helena Flats Rd 59901 406-257-2301
Paul Jenkins, prin. Fax 257-2304

Kalispell SD 5 4,300/PK-12
233 1st Ave E 59901 406-751-3434
Dr. Darlene Schottle, supt. Fax 751-3416
www.sd5.k12.mt.us
Flathead SHS 1,800/10-12
644 4th Ave W 59901 406-751-3500
Callie Langohr, prin. Fax 751-3505
Kalispell JHS 400/8-9
205 Northwest Ln 59901 406-751-3800
Barry Grace, prin. Fax 751-3805

Smith Valley ESD 89 200/PK-8
600 Batavia Ln 59901 406-756-4535
Fax 756-4534
Smith Valley MS 50/7-8
600 Batavia Ln 59901 406-756-4535
Harold Welling, prin. Fax 756-4534

West Valley ESD 1 300/PK-8
2290 Farm To Market Rd 59901 406-755-7239
Todd Fiske, supt. Fax 755-7300
West Valley MS 100/6-8
2290 Farm to Market Rd 59901 406-755-7239
Todd Fiske, prin. Fax 755-7300

Flathead Valley Community College Post-Sec.
777 Grandview Dr 59901 406-756-3822
Stillwater Christian S 300/K-12
1251 Willow Glen Dr 59901 406-752-4400
Daniel Makowski, supt. Fax 755-4061

Kila, Flathead
Kila ESD 20 100/PK-8
PO Box 40 59920 406-257-2428
Fax 755-6663
Kila MS 50/7-8
PO Box 40 59920 406-257-2428
Renee Boisseau, prin. Fax 755-6663

Lambert, Richland
Lambert SD 86 100/PK-12
PO Box 260 59243 406-774-3333
Ron Gebhardt, supt. Fax 774-3335
www.midrivers.com/~ihs/
Lambert HS 50/9-12
PO Box 260 59243 406-774-3333
Ron Gebhardt, prin. Fax 774-3335
Lambert MS 50/7-8
PO Box 260 59243 406-774-3333
Ron Gebhardt, prin. Fax 774-3335

Lame Deer, Rosebud, Pop. 1,918
Lame Deer SD 6 600/PK-12
PO Box 96 59043 406-477-6305
Gary Scott, supt. Fax 477-6535
www.lamedeer.k12.mt.us/
Lame Deer HS 200/9-12
PO Box 96 59043 406-477-8900
Brian Bradley, prin. Fax 477-8906
Lame Deer MS 100/7-8
PO Box 96 59043 406-477-8900
Don Christman, prin. Fax 477-8840

Chief Dull Knife College Post-Sec.
PO Box 98 59043 406-477-6215

Laurel, Yellowstone, Pop. 6,292
Laurel SD 7 1,700/PK-12
410 Colorado Ave 59044 406-628-8623
Josh Middleton, supt. Fax 628-8625
www.laurel.k12.mt.us
Laurel HS 600/9-12
203 E 8th St 59044 406-628-7911
Doug Neihart, prin. Fax 628-3558
Laurel MS 400/6-8
410 Colorado Ave 59044 406-628-6919
Linda Filpula, prin. Fax 628-3350

Lavina, Golden Valley, Pop. 210
Lavina SD 100/PK-12
PO Box 290 59046 406-636-2143
Rhonda Russell, supt. Fax 636-4911
Lavina HS 50/9-12
PO Box 290 59046 406-636-2143
Loren Osler, prin. Fax 636-4911
Lavina MS 50/7-8
PO Box 290 59046 406-636-2143
Loren Osler, prin. Fax 636-4911

Lewistown, Fergus, Pop. 5,923
Lewistown SD 1 1,400/PK-12
215 7th Ave S 59457 406-538-8777
Charles Brown, supt. Fax 538-7292
www.lewistown.k12.mt.us
Fergus HS 500/9-12
1001 Casino Creek Dr 59457 406-538-2321
Scott Dubbs, prin. Fax 538-3835
Lewistown MS 200/7-8
914 W Main St 59457 406-538-5419
Pat Hould, prin. Fax 538-2300

Libby, Lincoln, Pop. 2,606
Libby SD 4 1,500/PK-12
724 Louisiana Ave 59923 406-293-8811
K. Maki, supt. Fax 293-8812
www.libby.org/plummer/lps/
Libby HS 600/9-12
150 Education Way 59923 406-293-8802
Rik Rewerts, prin. Fax 293-3927
Libby MS 500/5-8
101 Ski Rd 59923 406-293-2763
Ron Goodman, prin. Fax 293-2862

Kootenai Valley Christian S 100/PK-12
1024 Montana Ave 59923 406-293-2303
Mike Wickstrom, admin. Fax 293-2303

Lima, Beaverhead, Pop. 231
Lima SD 12 100/PK-12
PO Box 186 59739 406-276-3571
Tim Dehl, supt. Fax 276-3495
Lima HS 50/9-12
PO Box 186 59739 406-276-3571
Tim Dehl, prin. Fax 276-3495
Lima MS 50/7-8
PO Box 186 59739 406-276-3571
Tim Dehl, prin. Fax 276-3495

Lincoln, Lewis and Clark
Lincoln SD 38 200/PK-12
PO Box 39 59639 406-362-4201
Kathy Heisler, supt. Fax 362-4030
Lincoln HS 100/9-12
PO Box 39 59639 406-362-4201
Carla Anderson, prin. Fax 362-4030
Lincoln MS 50/7-8
PO Box 39 59639 406-362-4201
Carla Anderson, prin. Fax 362-4030

Livingston, Park, Pop. 7,073
Livingston SD 4 1,500/PK-12
132 S B St 59047 406-222-0861
Andrew Anderson, supt. Fax 222-7323
www.livingston.k12.mt.us
Park HS 600/9-12
102 View Vista Dr 59047 406-222-0448
Eric Messerli, prin. Fax 222-9404
Sleeping Giant MS 300/6-8
301 View Vista Dr 59047 406-222-3292
Tena Versland, prin. Fax 222-3512

Pine Creek ESD 19 50/K-8
2575 E River Rd 59047 406-222-0059
Fax 222-0059
Pine Creek MS 50/7-8
2575 E River Rd 59047 406-222-0059
Leah Shannon-Beye, lead tchr. Fax 222-0059

Lodge Grass, Big Horn, Pop. 518
Lodge Grass SD 27 500/PK-12
PO Box 810 59050 406-639-2304
Doug Woods, supt. Fax 639-2388
www.lodgegrass.k12.mt.us/
Lodge Grass HS 200/9-12
PO Box 810 59050 406-639-2385
John Small, prin. Fax 639-2066
Lodge Grass MS 100/7-8
PO Box 810 59050 406-639-2333
Kenneth Deputee, prin. Fax 639-2388

Lolo, Missoula, Pop. 2,746
Lolo ESD 7 600/PK-8
11395 US Highway 93 S 59847 406-273-0451
Michael Magone, supt. Fax 273-2628
www.lolo.k12.mt.us/
Lolo MS 200/6-8
11395 US Highway 93 S 59847 406-273-6141
Dave Hansen, prin. Fax 273-2628

Woodman ESD 18 50/K-8
18470 Lolo Creek Rd 59847 406-273-6770
Fax 273-6659
Woodman MS 50/7-8
18470 Lolo Creek Rd 59847 406-273-6770
Louise Rhode, prin. Fax 273-6659

Malta, Phillips, Pop. 1,974
Malta SD   900/K-12
   PO Box 670   59538   406-654-1871
   Kris Kuehn, supt.   Fax 654-2226
   www.montanavision.net/~maltahs
Malta HS   200/9-12
   South 9th St W   59538   406-654-2002
   John Roberts, prin.   Fax 654-2226
Malta JHS   100/7-8
   South 9th St W   59538   406-654-2225
   John Roberts, prin.   Fax 654-2226

Manhattan, Gallatin, Pop. 1,447
Manhattan SD 3   500/PK-12
   PO Box 425   59741   406-284-6460
   Jerry Pease, supt.   Fax 284-6853
Manhattan HS   200/9-12
   PO Box 425   59741   406-284-3341
   Bob Moore, prin.   Fax 284-6853
Manhattan MS   100/7-8
   PO Box 425   59741   406-284-3250
   Scott Schumacher, prin.   Fax 284-6853

Manhattan Christian S   400/PK-12
   8000 Churchill Rd   59741   406-282-7261
   Randall VanDyk, admin.   Fax 282-7701

Marion, Flathead
Marion ESD 54   100/K-8
   205 Gopher Ln   59925   406-854-2333
      Fax 854-2690
Marion MS   50/7-8
   205 Gopher Ln   59925   406-854-2333
   Kris Ryan, prin.   Fax 854-2690

Medicine Lake, Sheridan, Pop. 239
Medicine Lake SD 7   100/K-12
   PO Box 265   59247   406-789-2211
   David Kloker, supt.   Fax 789-2213
Medicine Lake HS   50/9-12
   PO Box 265   59247   406-789-2211
   David Kloker, prin.   Fax 789-2213
Medicine Lake MS   50/7-8
   PO Box 265   59247   406-789-2211
   David Kloker, prin.   Fax 789-2213

Melstone, Musselshell, Pop. 136
Melstone SD   100/PK-12
   PO Box 97   59054   406-358-2352
   Chad Johnson, supt.   Fax 358-2346
Melstone HS   50/9-12
   PO Box 97   59054   406-358-2352
   Chad Johnson, prin.   Fax 358-2346
Melstone MS   50/7-8
   PO Box 97   59054   406-358-2352
   Chad Johnson, prin.   Fax 358-2346

Miles City, Custer, Pop. 8,242
Miles City SD 1   1,700/PK-12
   1604 Main St   59301   406-234-3840
   Jack Regan, supt.   Fax 234-3147
   garfieldweb.com/milescity/
Custer County District HS   600/9-12
   20 S Center Ave   59301   406-234-4920
   Rick Powell, prin.   Fax 234-4923
Washington MS   300/7-8
   210 N 9th St   59301   406-234-2084
   Doug Ellingson, prin.   Fax 234-7403

Miles Community College   Post-Sec.
   2715 Dickinson St   59301   406-234-3031

Missoula, Missoula, Pop. 60,722
Bonner ESD 14   400/PK-8
   9045 Highway 200   59802   406-258-6151
   Doug Ardiana, supt.   Fax 258-6153
   www.bonner.k12.mt.us
Bonner MS   100/7-8
   9045 Highway 200   59802   406-258-6151
   Doug Ardiana, prin.   Fax 258-6153
DeSmet ESD 20   100/PK-8
   6355 Padre Ln   59808   406-549-4994
      Fax 549-4994
DeSmet MS   50/7-8
   6355 Padre Ln   59808   406-549-4994
   Rose Woodford, prin.   Fax 549-4994
Hellgate ESD 4   1,200/PK-8
   2385 Flynn Ln   59808   406-728-5626
   Dr. Doug Reisig, supt.   Fax 728-5636
   www.hellgate.k12.mt.us
Hellgate MS   400/6-8
   2385 Flynn Ln   59808   406-721-2452
   Nancy Singleton, prin.   Fax 728-0967
Missoula SD 1   8,800/K-12
   215 S 6th St W   59801   406-728-2400
   Jim Clark, supt.   Fax 542-4009
   www.mcps.k12.mt.us
Big Sky HS   1,400/9-12
   3100 South Ave W   59804   406-728-2401
   Paul Johnson, prin.   Fax 549-4616
Hellgate HS   1,300/9-12
   900 S Higgins Ave   59801   406-728-2402
   Jane Bennett, prin.   Fax 728-2496
Meadow Hill MS   400/6-8
   4210 S Reserve St   59803   406-542-4045
   Nick Carter, prin.   Fax 721-4418
Porter MS   500/6-8
   2510 Central Ave W   59804   406-542-4060
   Gail Chandler, prin.   Fax 542-4098
Sentinel HS   1,200/9-12
   901 South Ave W   59801   406-728-2403
   Rob Watson, prin.   Fax 329-5959
Washington MS   500/6-8
   645 W Central Ave   59801   406-542-4085
   Robert Gearheart, prin.   Fax 721-7346
Other Schools – See Seeley Lake

Target Range ESD 23   400/PK-8
   4095 South Ave W   59804   406-549-9239
   Bill Coulter, supt.   Fax 728-8841
   www.target.k12.mt.us
Target Range MS   100/7-8
   4095 South Ave W   59804   406-549-9239
   Bill Coulter, prin.   Fax 728-8841

Loyola Sacred Heart HS   200/9-12
   320 Edith St   59801   406-549-6101
   Jeremy Beck, prin.   Fax 542-1432
Modern Beauty School   Post-Sec.
   2700 Paxson St Ste G   59801   406-721-1800
St. Patrick Hospital   Post-Sec.
   PO Box 4587   59806   406-543-7271
University of Montana   59812   Post-Sec.
      406-243-0211
Univ of Montana Missoula College of Tech   Post-Sec.
   909 South Ave W   59801   406-243-7882

Moore, Fergus, Pop. 186
Moore SD 44   100/PK-12
   509 Highland Ave   59464   406-374-2231
   David Lloyd, supt.   Fax 374-2490
Moore HS   50/9-12
   509 Highland Ave   59464   406-374-2231
   David Lloyd, prin.   Fax 374-2490
Moore MS   50/7-8
   509 Highland Ave   59464   406-374-2231
   David Lloyd, prin.   Fax 374-2490

Nashua, Valley, Pop. 312
Nashua SD 13E   100/K-12
   PO Box 170   59248   406-746-3411
   Arlene Bigby, supt.   Fax 746-3458
Nashua HS   50/9-12
   PO Box 170   59248   406-746-3411
   Arlene Bigby, prin.   Fax 746-3458
Nashua MS   50/7-8
   PO Box 170   59248   406-746-3411
   Arlene Bigby, prin.   Fax 746-3458

Noxon, Sanders
Noxon SD 10   200/K-12
   300 Noxon Ave   59853   406-847-2442
   Jackie Veto, supt.   Fax 847-2232
Noxon HS   100/9-12
   300 Noxon Ave   59853   406-847-2442
   Kelly Moore, prin.   Fax 847-2232
Noxon MS   50/7-8
   300 Noxon Ave   59853   406-847-2442
   Kelly Moore, prin.   Fax 847-2232

Opheim, Valley, Pop. 105
Opheim SD 9D   100/PK-12
   PO Box 108   59250   406-762-3214
   Leroy Nelson, supt.   Fax 762-3348
Opheim HS   50/9-12
   PO Box 108   59250   406-762-3214
   Leroy Nelson, prin.   Fax 762-3348
Opheim MS   50/7-8
   PO Box 108   59250   406-762-3214
   Leroy Nelson, prin.   Fax 762-3348

Pablo, Lake, Pop. 1,298

Salish Kootenai College   Post-Sec.
   PO Box 70   59855   406-675-4800

Park City, Stillwater
Park City SD 5   300/PK-12
   PO Box 278   59063   406-633-2406
   Dick Webb, supt.   Fax 633-2913
Park City HS   100/9-12
   PO Box 278   59063   406-633-2350
   Thomas Gauthier, prin.   Fax 633-2913
Park City MS   100/7-8
   PO Box 278   59063   406-633-2350
   Thomas Gauthier, prin.   Fax 633-2913

Peerless, Daniels
Peerless SD 2   50/PK-12
   PO Box 475   59253   406-893-4377
   Terry Puckett, supt.   Fax 893-4399
Peerless HS   50/9-12
   PO Box 475   59253   406-893-4377
   Terry Puckett, prin.   Fax 893-4399
Peerless MS   50/7-8
   PO Box 475   59253   406-893-4377
   Terry Puckett, prin.   Fax 893-4399

Philipsburg, Granite, Pop. 939
Philipsburg SD 1   200/PK-12
   PO Box 400   59858   406-859-3232
   Mike Cutler, supt.   Fax 859-3674
Granite HS   100/9-12
   PO Box 400   59858   406-859-3232
   Mike Cutler, prin.   Fax 859-3674
Philipsburg MS   50/7-8
   PO Box 400   59858   406-859-3232
   Sue Johnson, prin.   Fax 859-3674

Plains, Sanders, Pop. 1,169
Plains SD 1   500/PK-12
   PO Box 549   59859   406-826-3666
   Richard Magera, supt.   Fax 826-4439
Plains HS   200/9-12
   PO Box 549   59859   406-826-3666
   Larry McDonald, prin.   Fax 826-4439
Plains MS   100/7-8
   PO Box 549   59859   406-826-3666
   Larry McDonald, prin.   Fax 826-4439

Plentywood, Sheridan, Pop. 1,855
Plentywood SD 20   400/PK-12
   100 E Laurel Ave   59254   406-765-1803
   Joe Bennett, supt.   Fax 765-1195
   www.plentywood.k12.mt.us/

Plentywood HS   100/9-12
   100 E Laurel Ave   59254   406-765-1803
   Rob Pedersen, prin.   Fax 765-1195
Plentywood MS   100/7-8
   100 E Laurel Ave   59254   406-765-1803
   Rob Pedersen, prin.   Fax 765-1195

Plevna, Fallon, Pop. 131
Plevna SD 55   100/K-12
   PO Box 158   59344   406-772-5666
   Jule Walker, supt.   Fax 772-5548
Plevna HS   50/9-12
   PO Box 158   59344   406-772-5666
   Jule Walker, prin.   Fax 772-5548
Plevna MS   50/7-8
   PO Box 158   59344   406-772-5666
   Jule Walker, prin.   Fax 772-5548

Polson, Lake, Pop. 4,497
Polson SD 23   1,600/PK-12
   111 4th Ave E   59860   406-883-6355
   Sue McCormick, supt.   Fax 883-6345
   www.polson.k12.mt.us
Polson HS   500/9-12
   111 4th Ave E   59860   406-883-6351
   Rixon Rafter, prin.   Fax 883-6330
Polson MS   300/7-8
   111 4th Ave E   59860   406-883-6335
   Brian Adams, prin.   Fax 883-6334

Poplar, Roosevelt, Pop. 899
Poplar SD 9   900/PK-12
   PO Box 458   59255   406-768-3408
   Ivan Small, supt.   Fax 768-5510
   www.poplar.k12.mt.us/
Poplar HS   300/9-12
   PO Box 458   59255   406-768-3408
   Julanne Gauger, prin.   Fax 768-5510
Poplar JHS   200/7-8
   PO Box 458   59255   406-768-3408
   Diana Knudson, prin.   Fax 768-5510

Fort Peck Community College   Post-Sec.
   PO Box 398   59255   406-768-5551

Power, Teton
Power SD 30   100/K-12
   PO Box 155   59468   406-463-2251
   Ward Fifield, supt.   Fax 463-2360
   www.power.k12.mt.us/
Power HS   50/9-12
   PO Box 155   59468   406-463-2251
   Jon Konen, prin.   Fax 463-2360
Power MS   50/7-8
   PO Box 155   59468   406-463-2251
   Jon Konen, prin.   Fax 463-2360

Pray, Park
Arrowhead ESD 75   100/PK-8
   PO Box 37   59065   406-333-4359
   Adam Galvin, supt.   Fax 333-4975
   www.arrowheadschool.net
Arrowhead MS   50/7-8
   PO Box 37   59065   406-333-4359
   Adam Galvin, prin.   Fax 333-4975

Pryor, Big Horn, Pop. 654
Pryor SD   100/K-12
   PO Box 229   59066   406-259-7329
   Luke Enemy Hunter, supt.   Fax 245-8938
Plenty Coups HS   100/9-12
   PO Box 229   59066   406-259-7329
   Dell Fritzler, prin.   Fax 245-8938
Pryor MS   50/7-8
   PO Box 229   59066   406-259-7329
   Dell Fritzler, prin.   Fax 245-8938

Ramsay, Silver Bow
Ramsay ESD 3   100/K-8
   PO Box 105   59748   406-782-5470
      Fax 723-8905
Ramsay MS   50/7-8
   PO Box 105   59748   406-782-5470
   Rosemary Garvey, prin.   Fax 723-8905

Rapelje, Stillwater
Rapelje SD 32   100/K-12
   PO Box 89   59067   406-663-2215
   Jerry Thompson, supt.   Fax 663-2299
Rapelje HS   50/9-12
   PO Box 89   59067   406-663-2215
   Jerry Thompson, prin.   Fax 663-2299
Rapelje MS   50/7-8
   PO Box 89   59067   406-663-2215
   Jerry Thompson, prin.   Fax 663-2299

Red Lodge, Carbon, Pop. 2,273
Red Lodge SD 1   500/PK-12
   PO Box 1090   59068   406-446-1804
   Mark Brajcich, supt.   Fax 446-2037
Red Lodge HS   200/9-12
   PO Box 1090   59068   406-446-1903
   Rex Ternan, prin.   Fax 446-3953
Red Lodge MS   100/7-8
   PO Box 1090   59068   406-446-2110
   Tina Lynch, prin.   Fax 446-3975

Reedpoint, Stillwater
Reedpoint SD 9-9   100/K-12
   PO Box 338,   406-326-2245
   Tim Dolphay, supt.   Fax 326-2339
   www.reedpoint.k12.mt.us/
Reedpoint HS   50/9-12
   PO Box 338,   406-326-2245
   Tim Dolphay, prin.   Fax 326-2339
Reedpoint MS   50/7-8
   PO Box 338,   406-326-2225
   Tim Dolphay, prin.   Fax 326-2339

Richey, Dawson, Pop. 180
Richey SD
 PO Box 60 59259   100/K-12
 Brad Moore, supt.   406-773-5680
    Fax 773-5554
Richey HS
 PO Box 60 59259   50/9-12
 Brad Moore, prin.   406-773-5523
    Fax 773-5554
Richey MS
 PO Box 60 59259   50/7-8
 Brad Moore, prin.   406-773-5680
    Fax 773-5554

Roberts, Carbon
Roberts SD 5
 PO Box 78 59070   200/K-12
 Jeff Bermes, supt.   406-445-2421
    Fax 445-2506
Roberts HS
 PO Box 78 59070   100/9-12
 Jeff Bermes, prin.   406-445-2421
    Fax 445-2506
Roberts MS
 PO Box 78 59070   50/7-8
 Jeff Bermes, prin.   406-445-2421
    Fax 445-2506

Ronan, Lake, Pop. 1,900
Ronan SD 30
 PO Box R 59864   1,400/PK-12
 Andrew Holmlund, supt.   406-676-3390
 www.ronank12.edu/   Fax 676-3392
Ronan HS
 PO Box R 59864   400/9-12
 Tom Stack, prin.   406-676-3390
    Fax 676-3330
Ronan MS
 PO Box R 59864   400/6-8
 Andrea Johnson, prin.   406-676-3390
    Fax 676-2852

Rosebud, Rosebud
Rosebud SD 12
 PO Box 38 59347   100/PK-12
 Dan Lantis, supt.   406-347-5353
    Fax 347-5544
Rosebud HS
 601 Main St 59347   50/9-12
 Dan Lantis, prin.   406-347-5353
    Fax 347-5544
Rosebud MS
 PO Box 38 59347   50/7-8
 Dan Lantis, prin.   406-347-5353
    Fax 347-5544

Roundup, Musselshell, Pop. 1,910
Roundup SD 55
 700 3rd St W 59072   600/K-12
 William Schlepp, supt.   406-323-1507
    Fax 323-1927
Roundup HS
 525 6th Ave W 59072   200/9-12
 Chad Sealey, prin.   406-323-2402
    Fax 323-1583
Roundup MS
 525 6th Ave W 59072   100/7-8
 Chad Sealey, prin.   406-323-2402
    Fax 323-1583

Roy, Fergus
Roy SD 74
 PO Box 9 59471   100/K-12
 Dustin Sturm, supt.   406-464-2511
    Fax 464-2561
Roy HS
 PO Box 9 59471   50/9-12
 Dustin Sturm, prin.   406-464-2511
    Fax 464-2561
Roy MS
 PO Box 9 59471   50/7-8
 Dustin Sturm, prin.   406-464-2511
    Fax 464-2561

Rudyard, Hill
North Star SD 99
 Supt. — See Gildford
North Star HS
 PO Box 129 59540   100/9-12
 Terry Grant, prin.   406-355-4481
    Fax 355-4532
North Star MS
 105 3rd Ave NE 59540   50/7-8
 Terry Grant, prin.   406-355-4481
    Fax 355-4532

Ryegate, Golden Valley, Pop. 271
Ryegate SD 1
 PO Box 129 59074   100/K-12
 Robert Rooley, supt.   406-568-2211
    Fax 568-2528
Ryegate HS
 PO Box 129 59074   50/9-12
 Robert Rooley, prin.   406-568-2211
    Fax 568-2528
Ryegate MS
 PO Box 129 59074   50/7-8
 Robert Pooley, prin.   406-568-2211
    Fax 568-2528

Saco, Phillips, Pop. 206
Saco SD
 PO Box 298 59261   100/PK-12
 Glen Monson, supt.   406-527-3531
    Fax 527-3479
Saco HS
 PO Box 298 59261   50/9-12
 Tanya Funk, prin.   406-527-3531
    Fax 527-3479
Saco MS
 PO Box 298 59261   50/7-8
 Tanya Funk, prin.   406-527-3531
    Fax 527-3479

Saint Ignatius, Lake, Pop. 796
St. Ignatius SD 28
 PO Box 1540 59865   500/PK-12
 Dr. Tim Skinner, supt.   406-745-4420
    Fax 745-4421
St. Ignatius HS
 PO Box 1540 59865   200/9-12
 Jason Sargent, prin.   406-745-3811
    Fax 745-4060
St. Ignatius MS
 PO Box 1540 59865   100/6-8
 Jason Sargent, prin.   406-745-3811
    Fax 745-4060

Saint Regis, Mineral
Saint Regis SD 1
 PO Box K 59866   200/PK-12
 Becky Aaring, supt.   406-649-2427
 www.stregis.k12.mt.us/   Fax 649-2788
Saint Regis HS
 PO Box K 59866   100/9-12
 Don Almquist, prin.   406-649-2311
    Fax 649-2788
Saint Regis MS
 PO Box K 59866   50/7-8
 Don Almquist, prin.   406-649-2311
    Fax 649-2788

Sand Coulee, Cascade
Centerville SD 5
 PO Box 100 59472   300/PK-12
 Mike Meyer, supt.   406-736-5167
 www.centerville.k12.mt.us/   Fax 736-5210
Centerville HS, PO Box 100 59472   100/9-12
 Matthew McCale, prin.   406-736-5167
Centerville MS, PO Box 100 59472   50/7-8
 Matthew McCale, prin.   406-736-5167

Savage, Richland
Savage SD 7J
 PO Box 110 59262   100/K-12
 John McNeil, supt.   406-776-2317
    Fax 776-2260
Savage HS
 PO Box 110 59262   100/9-12
 John McNeil, prin.   406-776-2317
    Fax 776-2419
Savage MS
 PO Box 110 59262   50/7-8
 John McNeil, prin.   406-776-2317
    Fax 776-2419

Scobey, Daniels, Pop. 1,047
Scobey SD 1
 PO Box 10 59263   200/K-12
 Dave Selvig, supt.   406-487-2202
    Fax 487-2204
Scobey HS
 205 2nd Ave E 59263   100/9-12
 George Rider, prin.   406-487-2202
    Fax 487-2204
Scobey MS
 205 2nd Ave E 59263   50/7-8
 George Rider, prin.   406-487-2202
    Fax 487-2204

Seeley Lake, Missoula
Missoula SD 1
 Supt. — See Missoula
Seeley-Swan HS
 PO Box 416 59868   200/9-12
 Robert Holden, prin.   406-677-2224
    Fax 677-2949
Seeley Lake ESD 34
 PO Box 840 59868   200/PK-8
 Thomas Korst, supt.   406-677-2265
    Fax 677-2264
Seeley MS
 PO Box 840 59868   100/7-8
 Thomas Korst, prin.   406-677-2265
    Fax 677-2264

Shelby, Toole, Pop. 3,306
Shelby SD 14
 1010 Oilfield Ave 59474   500/PK-12
 Tom Rogers, supt.   406-434-2622
 www.shelby.k12.mt.us/   Fax 434-2959
Shelby HS
 1001 Valley St 59474   200/9-12
 Shawn Clark, prin.   406-424-8910
    Fax 434-7273
Shelby MS
 1001 Valley St 59474   100/7-8
 Shawn Clark, prin.   406-424-8910
    Fax 434-7273

Shepherd, Yellowstone
Shepherd SD 37
 PO Box 8 59079   900/PK-12
 Robert Barnes, supt.   406-373-5461
 www.shepherd.k12.mt.us/   Fax 373-5284
Shepherd HS
 PO Box 8 59079   300/9-12
 Kenneth Poepping, prin.   406-373-5300
    Fax 373-5342
Shepherd MS
 PO Box 8 59079   200/7-8
 Matt Torix, prin.   406-373-5873
    Fax 373-5648

Sheridan, Madison, Pop. 670
Sheridan SD 5
 PO Box 586 59749   200/PK-12
 Tony Graham, supt.   406-842-5302
 www.sheridan.k12.mt.us/   Fax 842-5391
Sheridan HS
 PO Box 586 59749   100/9-12
 Jory Thompson, prin.   406-842-5401
    Fax 842-5856
Sheridan MS
 PO Box 586 59749   50/7-8
 Tony Graham, prin.   406-842-5302
    Fax 842-5391

Sidney, Richland, Pop. 4,512
Sidney SD
 200 3rd Ave SE 59270   1,200/PK-12
 Doug Sullivan, supt.   406-433-4080
 www.sidneyps.com   Fax 433-4358
Sidney HS
 1012 4th Ave SE 59270   400/9-12
 Dan Farr, prin.   406-433-2330
    Fax 433-2481
Sidney JHS
 415 S Central Ave 59270   200/7-8
 Rollie Sullivan, prin.   406-433-4050
    Fax 433-4052

Simms, Cascade
Sun River Valley ESD 55
 PO Box 380 59477   400/PK-12
 Elaine Forrest, supt.   406-264-5111
    Fax 264-5188
Simms HS
 PO Box 380 59477   100/9-12
 Steve Jones, prin.   406-264-5110
    Fax 264-5189
Other Schools – See Sun River

Somers, Flathead
Somers ESD 29
 PO Box 159 59932   500/PK-8
 Teri Wing, supt.   406-857-3661
 www.somersdist29.org   Fax 857-3144
Somers MS
 PO Box 159 59932   200/6-8
 Lori Schieffer, prin.   406-857-3661
    Fax 857-3144

Stanford, Judith Basin, Pop. 429
Stanford SD 12
 PO Box 506 59479   100/PK-12
 Scott Chauvet, supt.   406-566-2265
    Fax 566-2772
Stanford HS
 PO Box 506 59479   100/9-12
 Scott Chauvet, prin.   406-566-2265
    Fax 566-2772

Stanford MS   50/7-8
 PO Box 506 59479   406-566-2265
 Scott Chauvet, prin.   Fax 566-2772

Stevensville, Ravalli, Pop. 1,784
Lone Rock ESD 13
 1112 Three Mile Creek Rd 59870   300/PK-8
 Michael Williams, supt.   406-777-3314
    Fax 777-2770
Lone Rock MS
 1112 Three Mile Creek Rd 59870   100/7-8
 Marjorie Johnson, prin.   406-777-3314
    Fax 777-2770
Stevensville SD 2
 300 Park St 59870   1,100/PK-12
 Dennis Kimzey, supt.   406-777-5481
 www.stevensville.k12.mt.us/   Fax 777-1381
Stevensville HS
 300 Park St 59870   500/9-12
 Jim Notaro, prin.   406-777-5481
    Fax 777-5291
Stevensville JHS
 300 Park St 59870   200/7-8
 Bob Connors, prin.   406-777-5533
    Fax 777-5291

Sunburst, Toole, Pop. 413
Sunburst SD 2
 PO Box 710 59482   300/PK-12
 John Hvidsten, supt.   406-937-2811
    Fax 937-2828
Sunburst HS
 PO Box 710 59482   100/9-12
 John Hvidsten, prin.   406-937-2811
    Fax 937-2828
Sunburst MS
 PO Box 710 59482   50/7-8
 Brian Barrows, prin.   406-937-2816
    Fax 937-4444

Sun River, Cascade
Sun River Valley ESD 55
 Supt. — See Simms
Sun River MS
 301 Largent St 59483   100/6-8
 Rick Danelson, prin.   406-264-5330
    Fax 264-5333

Superior, Mineral, Pop. 886
Superior SD 3
 PO Box 400 59872   400/K-12
 Bill Woodford, supt.   406-822-3600
 www.sd3.k12.mt.us/   Fax 822-3601
Superior HS
 PO Box 400 59872   100/9-12
 Allan Labbe, prin.   406-822-4851
    Fax 822-4396
Superior MS
 PO Box 400 59872   100/7-8
 Allan Labbe, prin.   406-822-4851
    Fax 822-4396

Terry, Prairie, Pop. 589
Terry SD 5
 PO Box 187 59349   200/PK-12
 Dale Kimmet, supt.   406-635-5533
 www.terry.k12.mt.us/   Fax 635-5705
Terry HS
 PO Box 187 59349   100/9-12
 Dale Kimmet, prin.   406-635-5533
    Fax 635-5705
Terry MS
 PO Box 187 59349   50/7-8
 Dale Kimmet, prin.   406-635-5595
    Fax 635-5705

Thompson Falls, Sanders, Pop. 1,323
Thompson Falls SD 2
 PO Box 129 59873   600/K-12
 Jerry Pauli, supt.   406-827-3323
    Fax 827-3020
Thompson Falls HS
 PO Box 129 59873   300/9-12
 Don Jensen, prin.   406-827-3561
    Fax 827-9463
Thompson Falls MS
 PO Box 129 59873   100/7-8
 Tom Holleran, prin.   406-827-3593
    Fax 827-0306

Three Forks, Gallatin, Pop. 1,823
Three Forks SD J-24
 212 E Neal St 59752   600/K-12
 John Overstreet, supt.   406-285-3216
    Fax 285-3216
Three Forks HS
 210 E Neal St 59752   200/9-12
 Tom Blakely, prin.   406-285-3503
    Fax 285-3503
Three Forks MS
 210 E Neal St 59752   100/7-8
 Tom Blakely, prin.   406-285-3503
    Fax 285-3503

Townsend, Broadwater, Pop. 1,914
Townsend SD 1
 201 N Spruce St 59644   700/PK-12
 Brian Patrick, supt.   406-266-5512
    Fax 266-4957
Broadwater HS
 201 N Spruce St 59644   200/9-12
 Rob Hankins, prin.   406-266-3455
    Fax 266-3448
Townsend MS
 201 N Spruce St 59644   100/7-8
 Brad Racht, prin.   406-266-4983
    Fax 266-4966

Trout Creek, Sanders
Trout Creek ESD 6
 85 Pine St 59874   100/PK-8
    406-827-3629
    Fax 827-4185
Trout MS
 85 Pine St 59874   50/7-8
 Diana Kauers, prin.   406-827-3629
    Fax 827-4185

Troy, Lincoln, Pop. 963
Troy SD 1
 PO Box 867 59935   500/K-12
 Brady Selle, supt.   406-295-4606
    Fax 295-4802
Troy HS
 PO Box 867 59935   200/9-12
 Rodney Smith, prin.   406-295-4520
    Fax 295-5371
Troy MS
 PO Box 867 59935   100/7-8
 Rodney Smith, prin.   406-295-4520
    Fax 295-5371

Turner, Blaine
Turner SD 43
 PO Box 40 59542   100/PK-12
 Gordon Hahn, supt.   406-379-2315
    Fax 379-2398

Turner HS
    PO Box 40 59542
    Gordon Hahn, prin.
50/9-12
406-379-2219
Fax 379-2398

Turner MS
    PO Box 40 59542
    Gordon Hahn, prin.
50/7-8
406-379-2219
Fax 379-2398

Twin Bridges, Madison, Pop. 405
Twin Bridges SD 7
    PO Box 419 59754
    David Whitesell, supt.
    www.twinbridges.k12.mt.us
200/K-12
406-684-5657
Fax 684-5458

Twin Bridges HS
    PO Box 419 59754
    David Whitesell, prin.
100/9-12
406-684-5657
Fax 684-5458

Twin Bridges MS
    PO Box 419 59754
    Douglas Denson, prin.
50/7-8
406-684-5613
Fax 684-5458

Ulm, Cascade
Ulm ESD 85
    PO Box 189 59485
100/PK-8
406-866-3313
Fax 866-3209

Ulm MS
    PO Box 189 59485
    Lauri Ingebritson, prin.
50/7-8
406-866-3313
Fax 866-3209

Valier, Pondera, Pop. 476
Valier SD 18
    PO Box 528 59486
    Matt Genger, supt.
200/PK-12
406-279-3613
Fax 279-3764

Valier HS
    PO Box 528 59486
    Matt Genger, prin.
100/9-12
406-279-3613
Fax 279-3764

Valier MS
    PO Box 528 59486
    Matt Genger, prin.
50/7-8
406-279-3314
Fax 279-3510

Vaughn, Cascade
Vaughn ESD 74
    480 Central Ave 59487
100/PK-8
406-965-2231
Fax 965-3703

Vaughn MS
    480 Central Ave 59487
    Jack O'Connor, prin.
50/7-8
406-965-2231
Fax 965-3703

Victor, Ravalli
Victor SD 7
    425 4th Ave 59875
    Orville Getz, supt.
    www.victor.k12.mt.us/
300/PK-12
406-642-3221
Fax 642-3446

Victor HS
    425 4th Ave 59875
    Danny Johnston, prin.
100/9-12
406-642-3221
Fax 642-3446

Victor MS
    425 4th Ave 59875
    Danny Johnston, prin.
100/6-8
406-642-3221
Fax 642-3446

Westby, Sheridan, Pop. 153
Westby SD 3
    PO Box 109 59275
    Wayne Koterba, supt.
    www.westbyschool.k12.mt.us/
50/PK-12
406-385-2258
Fax 385-2430

Westby HS
    PO Box 109 59275
    Wayne Koterba, prin.
50/9-12
406-385-2258
Fax 385-2430

Westby MS
    PO Box 109 59275
    Wayne Koterba, prin.
50/7-8
406-385-2225
Fax 385-2430

West Yellowstone, Gallatin, Pop. 1,213
West Yellowstone SD 69
    PO Box 460 59758
    Donna Purcell, supt.
200/K-12
406-646-7617
Fax 646-7232

West Yellowstone HS
    PO Box 460 59758
    Mike Maples, prin.
100/9-12
406-646-7617
Fax 646-7232

West Yellowstone MS
    PO Box 460 59758
    Mike Maples, prin.
50/7-8
406-646-7617
Fax 646-7232

Whitefish, Flathead, Pop. 5,784
Olney-Bissell ESD 58
    5955 Farm To Market Rd 59937
100/PK-8
406-862-2828
Fax 862-2838

Bissell MS
    5955 Farm to Market Rd 59937
    Lona Everett, prin.
50/7-8
406-862-2828
Fax 862-2838

Whitefish SD 44
    600 2nd St E 59937
    Jerry House, supt.
    www.wfps.k12.mt.us
1,900/PK-12
406-862-8640
Fax 862-1507

Whitefish-Central JHS
    600 2nd St E 59937
    Kim Anderson, prin.
300/7-8
406-862-8650
Fax 862-8664

Whitefish HS
    1143 4th St 59937
    Kent Paulson, prin.
700/9-12
406-862-8600
Fax 862-2586

Whitehall, Jefferson, Pop. 1,100
Whitehall SD 4-47
    PO Box 1109 59759
    Randy Cline, supt.
500/PK-12
406-287-3455
Fax 287-3843

Whitehall HS
    PO Box 1109 59759
    Patrick Audet, prin.
200/9-12
406-287-3862
Fax 287-3843

Whitehall JHS
    PO Box 1109 59759
    Luann Metcalf, prin.
100/7-8
406-287-3882
Fax 287-5508

White Sulphur Springs, Meagher, Pop. 1,010
White Sulphur Springs SD 8
    PO Box C 59645
    Cal Moore, supt.
    www.whitesulphur.k12.mt.us/
100/PK-12
406-547-3751
Fax 547-3922

White Sulphur Springs HS
    PO Box C 59645
    Andy Lind, prin.
100/9-12
406-547-3351
Fax 547-2407

White Sulphur Springs MS
    PO Box C 59645
    Andy Lind, prin.
50/7-8
406-547-3351
Fax 547-2407

Whitewater, Phillips
Whitewater SD
    PO Box 46 59544
    Darin Cummings, supt.
100/PK-12
406-674-5418
Fax 674-5460

Whitewater HS
    PO Box 46 59544
    Darin Cummings, prin.
50/9-12
406-674-5417
Fax 674-5460

Whitewater MS
    PO Box 46 59544
    Darin Cummings, prin.
50/7-8
406-674-5417
Fax 674-5460

Wibaux, Wibaux, Pop. 520
Wibaux SD 6
    RR 1 Box 2073 59353
    Kirby Eisenhauer, supt.
200/PK-12
406-796-2474
Fax 796-2259

Wibaux HS
    RR 1 Box 2073 59353
    Kirby Eisenhauer, prin.
100/9-12
406-795-2474
Fax 795-2259

Wibaux JHS
    RR 1 Box 2073 59353
    Janet Huisman, prin.
50/7-8
406-796-2474
Fax 796-2259

Willow Creek, Gallatin
Willow Creek SD
    PO Box 189 59760
    Russ McKenna, supt.
    www.willowcreek.k12.mt.us/
100/PK-12
406-285-6991
Fax 285-6923

Willow Creek HS
    PO Box 189 59760
    Russ McKenna, prin.
50/9-12
406-285-6991
Fax 285-6923

Willow Creek MS
    PO Box 189 59760
50/7-8
406-285-6991
Fax 285-6923

Wilsall, Park
Shields Valley SD J12
    PO Box 131 59086
    Jason Butcher, supt.
300/PK-12
406-578-2535
Fax 578-2176

Shields Valley MS
    PO Box 131 59086
    Ryan Boettcher, prin.
    Other Schools – See Clyde Park
100/7-8
406-578-2535
Fax 578-2176

Winifred, Fergus, Pop. 151
Winifred SD 115
    PO Box 109 59489
    Stephanie Wooderchak, supt.
100/PK-12
406-462-5349
Fax 462-5477

Winifred HS
    PO Box 109 59489
    Stephanie Wooderchak, prin.
50/9-12
406-462-5420
Fax 462-5477

Winifred MS
    PO Box 109 59489
    Stephanie Wooderchak, prin.
50/7-8
406-462-5349
Fax 462-5477

Winnett, Petroleum, Pop. 183
Winnett SD
    PO Box 167 59087
    Dr. Clay Dunlap, supt.
100/PK-12
406-429-2251
Fax 429-7631

Winnett HS
    PO Box 167 59087
    Dr. Clay Dunlap, prin.
50/9-12
406-429-2251
Fax 429-7631

Winnett MS
    PO Box 167 59087
    Clay Dunlap, prin.
50/7-8
406-429-2251
Fax 429-7631

Wolf Point, Roosevelt, Pop. 2,619
Frontier ESD 3
    HC 31 Box 3043 59201
    Justin Jimison, supt.
200/PK-8
406-653-2501
Fax 653-2508

Frontier MS
    HC 31 Box 3043 59201
    Leland Roundy, prin.
50/7-8
406-653-2501
Fax 653-2508

Wolf Point SD 45
    220 4th Ave S 59201
    Paul Huber, supt.
    wolfpoint.k12.mt.us/
900/PK-12
406-653-2361
Fax 653-1881

Wolf Point HS
    213 6th Ave S 59201
    Joseph Paine, prin.
300/9-12
406-653-1200
Fax 653-3104

Wolf Point JHS
    213 6th Ave S 59201
100/7-8
406-653-1200
Fax 653-3104

Worden, Yellowstone
Huntley Project SD 24
    1477 Ash St 59088
    David Mahon, supt.
    www.huntley.k12.mt.us/
800/PK-12
406-967-2540
Fax 967-2547

Huntley Project HS
    1477 Ash St 59088
    Tynie Mader, prin.
300/9-12
406-967-2540
Fax 967-2589

Huntley Project MS
    1477 Ash St 59088
    Frank Hollowell, prin.
100/7-8
406-967-2540
Fax 967-3054

Wyola, Big Horn
Wyola ESD 29
    PO Box 66 59089
    Wanda Johnston, supt.
50/PK-8
406-343-2722
Fax 343-5901

Wyola MS
    PO Box 66 59089
7-8
406-343-2722
Fax 343-5901

NEBRASKA

NEBRASKA DEPARTMENT OF EDUCATION
PO Box 94987, Lincoln 68509-4987
Telephone 402-471-2295
Fax 402-471-0117
Website http://www.nde.state.ne.us

Commissioner of Education   Doug Christensen

NEBRASKA BOARD OF EDUCATION
PO Box 94987, Lincoln 68509-4987

President   Fred Meyer

EDUCATIONAL SERVICE UNITS (ESU)

ESU 1
Robert H. Uhing, admin.   402-287-2061
211 10th St, Wakefield 68784   Fax 287-2065
www.esu1.org/
ESU 2
Michael Ough, admin.   402-721-7710
PO Box 649, Fremont 68026   Fax 721-7712
www.esu2.org/
ESU 3
Gil Kettlehut, admin.   402-597-4800
6949 S 110th St, La Vista 68128   Fax 597-4811
www2.esu3.org/esu3/
ESU 4
Jon Fisher, admin.   402-274-4354
PO Box 310, Auburn 68305   Fax 274-4356
www.esu4.org/
ESU 5
Al Schneider, admin.   402-223-5277
900 W Court St, Beatrice 68310   Fax 223-5279
www.esu5.org/
ESU 6
Donald L. Fritz, admin.   402-761-3341
PO Box 748, Milford 68405   Fax 761-3279
www.esu6.org/

ESU 7
Norman Ronell, admin.   402-564-5753
2657 44th Ave, Columbus 68601   Fax 563-1121
gilligan.esu7.org/
ESU 8
Randall Peck, admin.   402-887-5041
PO Box 89, Neligh 68756   Fax 887-4604
www.esu8.org/
ESU 9
Calvin Loughran, admin.   402-463-5611
PO Box 2047, Hastings 68902   Fax 463-9555
www.esu9.org/
ESU 10
Wayne Bell, admin.   308-237-5927
PO Box 850, Kearney 68848   Fax 237-5920
www.esu10.org/
ESU 11
Ron Karr, admin.   308-995-6585
PO Box 858, Holdrege 68949   Fax 995-6587
www.esu11.org/
ESU 13
Terry Miller, admin.   308-635-3696
4215 Avenue I, Scottsbluff 69361   Fax 635-0680
www.esu13.org/

ESU 14
H. Mark Hardy, admin.   308-254-4677
PO Box 77, Sidney 69162   Fax 254-5371
ESU 15
Brent McMurtrey, admin.   308-334-5160
PO Box 398, Trenton 69044   Fax 334-5581
www.esu15.org
ESU 16
, PO Box 915, Ogallala 69153   308-284-8481
www.esu16.org/   Fax 284-8483
ESU 17
, PO Box 227, Ainsworth 69210   402-387-1420
www.esu17.org/   Fax 387-1028
ESU 18
David Myers, admin.   402-436-1610
PO Box 82889, Lincoln 68501   Fax 436-1620
www.lps.org/
ESU 19
, 3215 Cuming St, Omaha 68131   402-557-2020
www.ops.org/   Fax 557-2019

PUBLIC, PRIVATE AND CATHOLIC SECONDARY SCHOOLS

Adams, Gage, Pop. 481
Freeman SD   300/K-12
PO Box 259 68301   402-988-2525
John Brazell, supt.   Fax 988-3475
www.freemanpublicschools.org/
Freeman JSHS   100/7-12
PO Box 259 68301   402-988-2525
Bob Michl, prin.   Fax 988-3475

Ainsworth, Brown, Pop. 1,817
Ainsworth SD   500/K-12
PO Box 65 69210   402-387-2333
Darrell Peterson, supt.   Fax 387-0525
www.esu17.k12.ne.us/~advcomp/
Ainsworth HS   200/9-12
PO Box 65 69210   402-387-2082
Harvey J. Wewel, prin.   Fax 387-0525
Ainsworth MS   100/6-8
PO Box 65 69210   402-387-2082
Harvey Wewel, prin.   Fax 387-0525

Albion, Boone, Pop. 1,711
Boone Central SD   600/K-12
PO Box 391 68620   402-395-2134
Larry Lambert, supt.   Fax 395-2137
www.boonecentral.esu7.org/
Boone Central HS   300/9-12
PO Box 391 68620   402-395-2134
Darrell Barnes, prin.   Fax 395-2137
Other Schools – See Petersburg

Allen, Dixon, Pop. 397
Allen SD   200/K-12
PO Box 190 68710   402-635-2484
Don Schmidt, supt.   Fax 635-2331
allenweb.esu1.org/
Allen JSHS   100/7-12
PO Box 190 68710   402-635-2484
Monty Miller, prin.   Fax 635-2331

Alliance, Box Butte, Pop. 8,579
Alliance SD   2,100/K-12
1604 Sweetwater Ave 69301   308-762-5475
Larry Ross, supt.   Fax 762-8249
www.aps.k12.ne.us
Alliance HS   600/9-12
100 W 14th St 69301   308-762-3359
Deron Dolfi, prin.   Fax 762-3359
Alliance MS   400/6-8
1100 Laramie Ave 69301   308-762-3079
Rita Moravek, prin.   Fax 762-7302

Alma, Harlan, Pop. 1,174
Alma SD   300/K-12
PO Box 170 68920   308-928-2131
Donald A. Ferguson, supt.   Fax 928-2763
www.esu11.k12.ne.us/alma/home
Alma JSHS   200/7-12
PO Box 170 68920   308-928-2131
Paul Joseph, prin.   Fax 928-2763

Amherst, Buffalo, Pop. 279
Amherst SD   300/K-12
PO Box 8 68812   308-826-3131
Ted W. Classen, supt.   Fax 826-4865
userweb.esu10.org/~amherst/
Amherst JSHS   100/7-12
PO Box 8 68812   308-826-3131
Roger Thomsen, prin.   Fax 826-4865

Ansley, Custer, Pop. 500
Ansley SD   200/K-12
PO Box 370 68814   308-935-1121
Larry Humphrey, supt.   Fax 935-9103
Ansley JSHS   100/7-12
PO Box 370 68814   308-935-1121
Lance C. Bristol, prin.   Fax 935-9103

Arapahoe, Furnas, Pop. 995
Arapahoe SD   300/K-12
PO Box 360 68922   308-962-5458
Damon McDonald, supt.   Fax 962-7481
www.esu11.org/arapahoe/fp.html
Arapahoe HS   200/7-12
PO Box 360 68922   308-962-5458
Daren Hatch, prin.   Fax 962-7481

Arcadia, Valley, Pop. 350
Arcadia SD   100/K-12
PO Box 248 68815   308-789-6522
Larry Humphrey, supt.   Fax 789-6214
Arcadia JSHS   100/7-12
PO Box 248 68815   308-789-6522
                                       Fax 789-6214

Arlington, Washington, Pop. 1,222
Arlington SD   600/K-12
PO Box 580 68002   402-478-4173
Steve Schneider, supt.   Fax 478-4176
www.esu3.org/districts/arlington/aps.htm
Arlington JSHS   300/7-12
PO Box 580 68002   402-478-4171
Lynn Johnson, prin.   Fax 478-4176

Arnold, Custer, Pop. 624
Arnold SD   200/K-12
PO Box 399 69120   308-848-2226
Robert Brown, supt.   Fax 848-2201

Arnold JSHS   100/7-12
PO Box 399 69120   308-848-2226
Michael Harvey, prin.   Fax 848-2201

Arthur, Arthur, Pop. 130
Arthur County HSD   50/7-12
PO Box 145 69121   308-764-2253
John R. Frates, supt.   Fax 764-2206
Arthur County JSHS   50/7-12
PO Box 145 69121   308-764-2253
                                       Fax 764-2206

Ashland, Saunders, Pop. 2,380
Ashland-Greenwood SD   800/PK-12
1200 Boyd St 68003   402-944-2128
Craig Pease, supt.   Fax 944-3310
www.agps.org/
Ashland-Greenwood HS   200/9-12
1200 Boyd St 68003   402-944-2114
Ray Bentzen, prin.   Fax 944-2116
Ashland-Greenwood MS   100/7-8
1200 Boyd St 68003   402-944-2114
Ray Bentzen, prin.   Fax 944-2116

Atkinson, Holt, Pop. 1,188
West Holt RHSD   200/9-12
PO Box 457 68713   402-925-2890
William McAllister, supt.   Fax 925-2177
West Holt Rural HS   200/9-12
PO Box 457 68713   402-925-2890
Kevin L. Young, prin.   Fax 925-2177

Auburn, Nemaha, Pop. 3,125
Auburn SD   900/K-12
820 Central Ave Ste 1 68305   402-274-4830
Charles Chevalier, supt.   Fax 274-5227
www.auburnpublicschools.org/
Auburn JSHS   400/7-12
1829 Central Ave 68305   402-274-4328
Nancy Fuller, prin.   Fax 274-5434

Aurora, Hamilton, Pop. 4,247
Aurora SD   1,300/K-12
300 L St 68818   402-694-6923
Larry Ramaekers, supt.   Fax 694-5097
www.esu9.org
Aurora MS   300/7-9
300 L St 68818   402-694-6915
Kenneth Thiele, prin.   Fax 694-3815
Aurora SHS   300/10-12
300 L St 68818   402-694-6968
Douglas Kittle, prin.   Fax 694-2573

Axtell, Kearney, Pop. 721
Axtell Community SD   300/K-12
PO Box 97 68924   308-743-2414
Thomas Sandberg, supt.   Fax 743-2417
www.esu11.org/axtell/INDEX.HTM
Axtell JSHS   100/7-12
PO Box 97 68924   308-743-2415
Douglas Hinze, prin.   Fax 743-2417

Bancroft, Cuming, Pop. 502
Bancroft-Rosalie SD   300/K-12
PO Box 129 68004   402-648-3337
Jon Cerny, supt.   Fax 648-3338
www.bancroft-rosalie.org/
Bancroft HS   100/9-12
PO Box 129 68004   402-648-3336
Mike Sjuts, prin.   Fax 648-3338
Bancroft JHS   100/7-8
PO Box 129 68004   402-648-3336
Mike Sjuts, prin.   Fax 648-3338

Bartlett, Wheeler, Pop. 116
Wheeler Central SD   100/K-12
PO Box 68 68622   308-654-3273
Dan Hoesly, supt.   Fax 654-3237
Wheeler Central JSHS   100/7-12
PO Box 68 68622   308-654-3273
Dan Hoesly, prin.   Fax 654-3237

Bartley, Red Willow, Pop. 350
Southwest SD 179   300/K-12
PO Box 187 69020   308-692-3223
David Hendricks, supt.   Fax 692-3221
www.southwest.k12.ne.us/home
Southwest MS   50/6-8
PO Box 187 69020   308-692-3223
Don Hosick, prin.   Fax 692-3351
Other Schools – See Indianola

Bassett, Rock, Pop. 681
Rock County HSD   100/9-12
PO Box 448 68714   402-684-3411
David D. Wade, supt.   Fax 684-3671
Rock County HS   100/9-12
PO Box 448 68714   402-684-3411
Steve Camp, prin.   Fax 684-3671

Battle Creek, Madison, Pop. 1,168
Battle Creek SD   400/K-12
PO Box 190 68715   402-675-6905
Jay Bellar, supt.   Fax 675-1038
bcps.esu8.org/
Battle Creek JSHS   300/7-12
PO Box 190 68715   402-675-3705
Mark Lenihan, prin.   Fax 675-1038

Bayard, Morrill, Pop. 1,193
Bayard SD   500/K-12
PO Box 607 69334   308-586-1700
Allen D. Gross, supt.   Fax 586-1638
Bayard JSHS   200/7-12
PO Box 607 69334   308-586-1700
Robert C. Gregory, prin.   Fax 586-1638

Beatrice, Gage, Pop. 12,945
Beatrice SD   2,300/PK-12
320 N 5th St 68310   402-223-1515
Dale Kruse, supt.   Fax 223-1509
Beatrice HS   800/9-12
600 Orange Blvd 68310   402-223-1515
Jason Sutter, prin.   Fax 223-1510
Beatrice MS   500/6-8
215 N 5th St 68310   402-223-1545
Randy Schlueter, prin.   Fax 223-1547

Joseph's College of Beauty   Post-Sec.
618 Court St 68310   402-223-3588
Southeast Community College   Post-Sec.
4771 W Scott Rd 68310   402-228-3468

Bellevue, Sarpy, Pop. 46,734
Bellevue SD   8,900/PK-12
1600 Highway 370 68005   402-293-4000
John Deegan, supt.   Fax 293-5002
www.bellevuepublicschools.org
Bellevue East HS   1,400/9-12
1401 High School Dr 68005   402-293-4150
Daniel Larson, prin.   Fax 293-4259
Bellevue Mission MS   700/7-8
2202 Washington St 68005   402-293-4260
Larry Murry, prin.   Fax 293-4350
Bellevue West HS   1,400/9-12
1501 Thurston Ave 68123   402-293-4040
Kevin Rohlfs, prin.   Fax 293-4149
Fontenelle MS   700/7-8
701 Kayleen Dr 68005   402-293-4360
Alicia Richards, prin.   Fax 293-4450

Bellevue University   Post-Sec.
1000 Galvin Rd S 68005   402-293-3700

Benedict, York, Pop. 274
Cross County Community SD
Supt. — See Stromsburg
Cross County MS - Benedict   100/5-8
PO Box 135 68316   402-732-6677
Ron Nickel, prin.   Fax 732-6678

Benkelman, Dundy, Pop. 962
Dundy County SD   300/PK-12
PO Box 586 69021   308-423-2738
Dallas Watkins, supt.   Fax 423-2711
Dundy County HS   100/9-12
PO Box 586 69021   308-423-2738
Jim Kent, prin.   Fax 423-2711

Bennington, Douglas, Pop. 916
Bennington SD   600/K-12
11620 N 156th St 68007   402-238-3044
Terry Haack, supt.   Fax 238-2185
www.benningtonschools.org/

Bennington JSHS   300/7-12
11620 N 156th St 68007   402-238-2447
Stan Turner, prin.   Fax 238-2950

Bertrand, Phelps, Pop. 814
Bertrand SD   300/K-12
PO Box 278 68927   308-472-3427
Dr. Greg Barnes, supt.   Fax 472-3429
www.esu11.org/bertrand/home2.html
Bertrand JSHS   100/7-12
PO Box 278 68927   308-472-3427
Michael Williams, prin.   Fax 472-3429

Big Springs, Deuel, Pop. 410
South Platte SD   200/K-12
PO Box 457 69122   308-889-3622
David J. Spencer, supt.   Fax 889-3523
southplatte.ne.schoolwebpages.com/
South Platte HS   100/7-12
PO Box 457 69122   308-889-3622
Jane Brown, prin.   Fax 889-3523

Blair, Washington, Pop. 7,798
Blair Community SD   2,300/PK-12
PO Box 288 68008   402-426-2610
Steven P. Shanahan, supt.   Fax 426-3110
www.esu3.org/districts/Blair/Dist/
Blair HS   700/9-12
PO Box 288 68008   402-426-4941
Thomas Anderson, prin.   Fax 426-4949
Otte Blair MS   600/6-8
PO Box 288 68008   402-426-3678
James Sides, prin.   Fax 426-1788

Dana College   Post-Sec.
2848 College Dr 68008   402-426-9000

Bloomfield, Knox, Pop. 1,075
Bloomfield SD   200/PK-12
PO Box 308 68718   402-373-4800
John W. Post, supt.   Fax 373-2712
bloomfield.esu1.org/
Bloomfield JSHS   100/7-12
PO Box 308 68718   402-373-4800
John W. Post, prin.   Fax 373-2712

Blue Hill, Webster, Pop. 829
Blue Hill SD   400/K-12
PO Box 217 68930   402-756-2085
Kendall L. Steffensen, supt.   Fax 756-2086
www.bluehillschools.org/
Blue Hill JSHS   200/7-12
PO Box 217 68930   402-756-3043
Rodney Olson, prin.   Fax 756-3044

Boys Town, Douglas, Pop. 869

Boys Town HS   400/9-12
13803 Flanagan Blvd 68010   402-498-1800
Robert Gehringer, prin.   Fax 498-1797

Bradshaw, York, Pop. 329
Heartland Community SD
Supt. — See Henderson
Heartland Community JHS   100/7-8
PO Box 98 68319   402-736-4353
Blaine Friesen, prin.   Fax 736-4602

Brady, Lincoln, Pop. 367
Brady SD   200/K-12
PO Box 68 69123   308-584-3317
Patrick W. Cullen, supt.   Fax 584-3725
athena.esu16.org/bradyschool/index.htm
Brady JSHS   100/7-12
PO Box 68 69123   308-584-3317
Patrick W. Cullen, prin.   Fax 584-3725

Brainard, Butler, Pop. 353
East Butler SD   300/K-12
PO Box 36 68626   402-545-2081
Gary Gustafson, supt.   Fax 545-2023
www.ebutler.esu7.org/eastbutler.html
Brainard JSHS   200/7-12
PO Box 36 68626   402-545-2081
Gerald Reinsch, prin.   Fax 545-2023

Bridgeport, Morrill, Pop. 1,536
Bridgeport SD 63   500/K-12
PO Box 430 69336   308-262-1470
Randall R. Butcher, supt.   Fax 262-0520
www.bridgeportschools.org/
Bridgeport JSHS   200/7-12
PO Box 430 69336   308-262-0346
Dan Hadden, prin.   Fax 262-0444

Broken Bow, Custer, Pop. 3,385
Broken Bow SD   900/K-12
323 N 7th Ave 68822   308-872-6821
Timothy B. Shafer, supt.   Fax 872-2751
Broken Bow HS   300/9-12
323 N 7th Ave 68822   308-872-2475
Francis Patch, prin.   Fax 872-2528
Broken Bow MS   200/6-8
322 N 9th Ave 68822   308-872-6441
Edward Lowe, prin.   Fax 872-2751

Bruning, Thayer, Pop. 275
Bruning-Davenport USD
Supt. — See Davenport
Bruning-Davenport HS   100/9-12
PO Box 70 68322   402-353-4685
Trudy Clark, prin.   Fax 353-4445

Burwell, Garfield, Pop. 1,082
Burwell HSD   200/7-12
PO Box 670 68823   308-346-4150
Daniel Bird, supt.   Fax 346-5430
Burwell JSHS   200/7-12
PO Box 670 68823   308-346-4150
David Owen, prin.   Fax 346-5430

Butte, Boyd, Pop. 353
West Boyd USD   300/K-12
PO Box 139 68722   402-775-2040
Russell Lechtenberg, supt.   Fax 775-2041
Butte JSHS   100/7-12
PO Box 139 68722   402-775-2201
Russell Lechtenberg, prin.   Fax 775-2204
Other Schools – See Spencer

Cairo, Hall, Pop. 786
Centura SD   600/PK-12
PO Box 430 68824   308-485-4258
David Schley, supt.   Fax 485-4780
Centura JSHS   300/7-12
PO Box 430 68824   308-485-4258
Gary Monter, prin.   Fax 485-4780

Callaway, Custer, Pop. 630
Callaway SD   200/K-12
PO Box 188 68825   308-836-2272
Patrick Osmond, supt.   Fax 836-2771
Callaway JSHS   100/7-12
PO Box 188 68825   308-836-2272
David Weber, prin.   Fax 836-2771

Cambridge, Furnas, Pop. 1,014
Cambridge SD   300/K-12
PO Box 100 69022   308-697-3322
Ronald Streit, supt.   Fax 697-4880
www.esu11.org/cambridge/
Cambridge HS   100/9-12
PO Box 100 69022   308-697-3322
Don Keyser, prin.   Fax 697-4880

Cedar Bluffs, Saunders, Pop. 612
Cedar Bluffs SD   300/PK-12
PO Box 66 68015   402-628-2060
Jeffrey R. Walburn, supt.   Fax 628-2005
www.cedarbluffsschools.org/
Cedar Bluffs JSHS   200/7-12
PO Box 66 68015   402-628-2080
Daniel Cleveland, prin.   Fax 628-2108

Cedar Rapids, Boone, Pop. 382
Cedar Rapids SD   200/K-12
PO Box 218 68627   308-358-0640
Amy Dickey, supt.   Fax 358-0211
Cedar Rapids JSHS   100/7-12
PO Box 218 68627   308-358-0640
James T. Widdifield, prin.   Fax 358-0211

Central City, Merrick, Pop. 2,946
Central City SD   800/PK-12
PO Box 57 68826   308-946-3055
Jeffrey D. West, supt.   Fax 946-3149
Central City HS   300/9-12
PO Box 57 68826   308-946-3086
Shawn McDiffett, prin.   Fax 946-2954
Central City MS   300/5-8
PO Box 57 68826   308-946-3056
Thomas McGuire, prin.   Fax 946-2124

Nebraska Christian S   200/PK-12
1847 Inskip Ave 68826   308-946-3836
Scott Johnson, prin.   Fax 946-3837

Chadron, Dawes, Pop. 5,598
Chadron SD   900/K-12
602 E 10th St 69337   308-432-0700
Sherlock V. Himing, supt.   Fax 432-0702
www.chadronschools.org/
Chadron HS   300/9-12
901 Cedar St 69337   308-432-0707
Stephen Osborn, prin.   Fax 432-0723
Chadron MS   200/5-8
551 E 6th St 69337   308-432-0708
Richard Moore, prin.   Fax 432-0720

Pine Ridge Job Corps
Supt. — None
Pine Ridge Job Corps   Vo/Tech
15710 Highway 385 69337   308-432-3316
Brian Kizer, prin.   Fax 432-4145

Chadron State College   Post-Sec.
1000 Main St 69337   308-432-6000

Chambers, Holt, Pop. 319
Chambers SD   200/K-12
PO Box 218 68725   402-482-5233
Robert Hanger, supt.   Fax 482-5234
chambers.esu8.org/
Chambers JSHS   100/7-12
PO Box 218 68725   402-482-5233
Fred Hansen, prin.   Fax 482-5234

Chappell, Deuel, Pop. 959
Creek Valley SD   200/K-12
PO Box 608 69129   308-874-2911
Paul J. Calvert, supt.   Fax 874-2602
Creek Valley HS   100/7-12
PO Box 608 69129   308-874-3310
Brent Christensen, prin.   Fax 874-2604
Other Schools – See Lodgepole

Clarks, Merrick, Pop. 349
High Plains Community SD
Supt. — See Polk
High Plains MS   100/6-8
PO Box 205 68628   308-548-2216
Karyee LeSuer, prin.   Fax 548-2120

Clarkson, Colfax, Pop. 681
Clarkson SD   300/K-12
PO Box 140 68629   402-892-3454
Daniel C. Polk, supt.   Fax 892-3455
teachers.esu7.org/clarkson/
Clarkson JSHS   200/7-12
PO Box 140 68629   402-892-3454
Rich Lemburg, prin.   Fax 892-3455

Clay Center, Clay, Pop. 839
Clay Center SD | 200/PK-12
  PO Box 125 68933 | 402-762-3561
  Lee Sayer, supt. | Fax 762-3200
  www.esu9.org/%7Ecc/home.html
Clay Center JSHS | 100/7-12
  PO Box 125 68933 | 402-762-3561
  Jim Bovee, prin. | Fax 762-3200

Clearwater, Antelope, Pop. 370
Nebraska USD 1
  Supt. — See Royal
Clearwater JSHS | 100/7-12
  PO Box 38 68726 | 402-485-2505
  Jeff Hoesing, prin. | Fax 485-2634

Cody, Cherry, Pop. 147
Cody-Kilgore SD | 200/K-12
  PO Box 216 69211 | 402-823-4190
  Larry Sweley, supt. | Fax 823-4275
Cody-Kilgore JSHS | 100/7-12
  PO Box 216 69211 | 402-823-4190
  Kathleen Fullerton, prin. | Fax 823-4275

Coleridge, Cedar, Pop. 510
Coleridge Community SD | 200/K-12
  PO Box 37 68727 | 402-283-4844
  Daniel J. Hoesing, supt. | Fax 283-4230
  coleridge.esu1.org/
Coleridge JSHS | 100/7-12
  PO Box 37 68727 | 402-283-4844
  Craig Frerichs, prin. | Fax 283-4230

Columbus, Platte, Pop. 20,880
Columbus SD | 3,500/K-12
  PO Box 947 68602 | 402-563-7000
  Paul Hillyer, supt. | Fax 563-7005
  www.columbuspublicschools.org
Columbus HS | 1,200/9-12
  PO Box 947 68602 | 402-563-7050
  Amy Romshek, prin. | Fax 563-7058
Columbus MS | 800/6-8
  PO Box 947 68602 | 402-563-7060
  Douglas Kluth, prin. | Fax 563-7068

Lakeview CSD | 800/K-12
  3744 83rd St 68601 | 402-563-2345
  Kurt Harrison, supt. | Fax 564-5209
Lakeview HS | 300/9-12
  3744 83rd St 68601 | 402-563-2345
  Robert Arp, prin. | Fax 564-5209

Central Community College | Post-Sec.
  PO Box 1027 68602 | 402-564-7132
Scotus Central Catholic JSHS | 400/7-12
  1554 18th Ave 68601 | 402-564-7165
  Wayne Morfeld, prin. | Fax 564-6004

Cook, Johnson, Pop. 310
Nemaha Valley SD | 200/K-12
  PO Box 255 68329 | 402-864-4171
  Jack Moles, supt. | Fax 864-2074
Cook JSHS | 100/7-12
  PO Box 255 68329 | 402-864-4171
  Kirk Gottschalk, prin. | Fax 864-2074

Cozad, Dawson, Pop. 4,229
Cozad CSD | 1,000/K-12
  PO Box 268 69130 | 308-784-2745
  John Grinde, supt. | Fax 784-2728
Cozad HS | 300/9-12
  PO Box 268 69130 | 308-784-2744
  Phill Parker, prin. | Fax 784-2728
Cozad MS | 200/6-8
  1810 Meridian Ave 69130 | 308-784-2746
  Todd Hilyard, prin. | Fax 784-2606

Crawford, Dawes, Pop. 1,071
Crawford SD | 300/PK-12
  908 5th St 69339 | 308-665-1537
  Merrell Nelsen, supt. | Fax 665-1483
Crawford JSHS | 100/7-12
  908 5th St 69339 | 308-665-1531
  Troy Lurz, prin. | Fax 665-1483

Creighton, Knox, Pop. 1,219
Creighton SD | 400/K-12
  PO Box 10 68729 | 402-358-3663
  Fred Boelter, supt. | Fax 358-3804
  creighton.esu1.org/
Creighton Community JSHS | 300/7-12
  PO Box 10 68729 | 402-358-3663
  Jeff Jensen, prin. | Fax 358-3804

Crete, Saline, Pop. 6,321
Crete SD | 1,200/PK-12
  920 Linden Ave 68333 | 402-826-5855
  John Fero, supt. | Fax 826-5120
  www.creteschools.org/
Crete HS | 500/9-12
  1500 E 15th St 68333 | 402-826-5811
  Timothy Conway, prin. | Fax 826-2701
Crete MS | 6-8
  1700 Glenwood Ave 68333 | 402-826-5844
  Marcus Everts, prin. | Fax 826-7789

Doane College | Post-Sec.
  1014 Boswell Ave 68333 | 402-826-2161

Crofton, Knox, Pop. 723
Crofton Community SD | 400/K-12
  PO Box 429 68730 | 402-388-2440
  Randall Anderson, supt. | Fax 388-4265
  www.croftonschools.com/
Crofton JSHS | 300/7-12
  PO Box 429 68730 | 402-388-2440
  Todd Strom, prin. | Fax 388-4265

Curtis, Frontier, Pop. 770
Medicine Valley SD | 300/K-12
  PO Box 9 69025 | 308-367-4106
  Barry H. Limoges, supt. | Fax 367-4108
  www.mvraiders.org
Medicine Valley JSHS | 200/7-12
  PO Box 9 69025 | 308-367-4106
  Steven Gleisberg, prin. | Fax 367-4108

Nebraska Coll of Technical Agriculture | Post-Sec.
  RR 3 Box 23A 69025 | 308-367-4124

Dalton, Cheyenne, Pop. 329
Leyton SD | 200/K-12
  PO Box 297 69131 | 308-377-2303
  James M. Calder, supt. | Fax 377-2304
Leyton HS | 100/9-12
  PO Box 297 69131 | 308-377-2303
  Sue E. Kandel, prin. | Fax 377-2304

Davenport, Thayer, Pop. 310
Bruning-Davenport USD | 200/K-12
  PO Box 68335 | 402-364-2225
  Loren Pokorny, supt. | Fax 364-2477
Bruning-Davenport MS | 50/7-8
  PO Box 68335 | 402-364-2225
  Trudy Clark, prin. | Fax 364-2477
Other Schools – See Bruning

David City, Butler, Pop. 2,618
David City SD | 700/PK-12
  750 D St 68632 | 402-367-4590
  Jerry Phillips, supt. | Fax 367-3479
  www.davidcitypublicschools.org/
David City JSHS | 300/7-12
  750 D St 68632 | 402-367-3187
  Tom Jahde, prin. | Fax 367-3479

Aquinas HS | 300/6-12
  PO Box 149 68632 | 402-367-3175
  David McMahon, prin. | Fax 367-3176

Daykin, Jefferson, Pop. 173
Meridian SD | 200/K-12
  PO Box 190 68338 | 402-446-7265
  Stephen Deger, supt. | Fax 446-7246
Meridian JSHS | 100/7-12
  PO Box 190 68338 | 402-446-7265
  Kenneth Stauss, prin. | Fax 446-7246

Deshler, Thayer, Pop. 817
Deshler SD | 300/K-12
  PO Box 547 68340 | 402-365-7272
  Larry Wilbeck, supt. | Fax 365-7560
Deshler JSHS | 200/7-12
  PO Box 547 68340 | 402-365-7272
  Jack Waite, prin. | Fax 365-7560

De Witt, Saline, Pop. 577
Tri County SD | 500/K-12
  72520 Highway 103 68341 | 402-683-2015
  Timothy Dewaard, supt. | Fax 683-2116
Tri County JSHS | 300/7-12
  72520 Highway 103 68341 | 402-683-2015
  Dennis Shipp, prin. | Fax 683-2116

Dodge, Dodge, Pop. 682
Dodge CSD | 200/K-12
  209 N Ash St 68633 | 402-693-2207
  Thomas Reeser, supt. | Fax 693-2209
  dodge.esu2.org/
Dodge JSHS | 100/7-12
  209 N Ash St 68633 | 402-693-2207
  Danny J. Schiefelbein, prin. | Fax 693-2209

Doniphan, Hall, Pop. 764
Doniphan-Trumbull SD | 500/K-12
  PO Box 300 68832 | 402-845-2282
  Del Prindle, supt. | Fax 845-6688
Doniphan-Trumbull JSHS | 200/7-12
  PO Box 300 68832 | 402-845-6531
  Alois Meier, prin. | Fax 845-6688

Dorchester, Saline, Pop. 626
Dorchester SD | 200/K-12
  PO Box 7 68343 | 402-946-2781
  Alan Ehlers, supt. | Fax 946-6271
Dorchester JSHS | 100/7-12
  PO Box 7 68343 | 402-946-2781
  Terrence Gautreaux, prin. | Fax 946-6271

Dunning, Blaine, Pop. 99
Sandhills SD | 200/K-12
  PO Box 460 68833 | 308-538-2224
  Alberta Moore, supt. | Fax 538-2228
Dunning JSHS | 100/7-12
  PO Box 460 68833 | 308-538-2224
   | Fax 538-2228

Elba, Howard, Pop. 243
Elba SD | 100/K-12
  PO Box 100 68835 | 308-863-2228
  Michael Gillming, supt. | Fax 863-2329
Elba JSHS | 100/7-12
  PO Box 100 68835 | 308-863-2228
  Joelene Dredge, prin. | Fax 863-2329

Elgin, Antelope, Pop. 706
Elgin SD | 200/K-12
  PO Box 399 68636 | 402-843-2455
  Gayla Fredrickson, supt. | Fax 843-2475
  teachers.esu8.org/wpdesign/
Elgin HS | 100/9-12
  PO Box 399 68636 | 402-843-2457
  Corey Fisher, prin. | Fax 843-2475

Pope John XXIII Central Catholic HS | 100/7-12
  PO Box 179 68636 | 402-843-5325
  Jason Heitz, prin. | Fax 843-2297

Elkhorn, Douglas, Pop. 7,869
Elkhorn SD | 3,300/PK-12
  PO Box 439 68022 | 402-289-2579
  Roger Breed, supt. | Fax 289-2585
  www.elkhorn.esu3.org/
Elkhorn HS | 900/9-12
  PO Box 439 68022 | 402-289-4239
  Bary J. Habrock, prin. | Fax 289-4383
Elkhorn MS | 400/6-8
  PO Box 439 68022 | 402-289-2428
  Michael Tomjack, prin. | Fax 289-2585
Other Schools – See Omaha

Mt. Michael Benedictine HS | 200/9-12
  22520 Mount Michael Rd 68022 | 402-289-2541
  Tom Ridder, prin. | Fax 289-4539

Elm Creek, Buffalo, Pop. 884
Elm Creek SD | 400/K-12
  PO Box 490 68836 | 308-856-4300
  Larry Babcock, supt. | Fax 856-4907
Elm Creek JSHS | 200/7-12
  PO Box 490 68836 | 308-856-4300
  Gary Brouillette, prin. | Fax 856-4907

Elwood, Gosper, Pop. 739
Elwood SD | 300/K-12
  PO Box 107 68937 | 308-785-2491
  Richard D. Einspahr, supt. | Fax 785-2322
  www.esu11.org/elwood/elwhome.html
Elwood JSHS | 200/7-12
  PO Box 107 68937 | 308-785-2491
  Jon S. Davis, prin. | Fax 785-2322

Emerson, Dakota, Pop. 817
Emerson-Hubbard SD | 300/K-12
  PO Box 9 68733 | 402-695-2621
  Thomas Becker, supt. | Fax 695-2622
Emerson-Hubbard JSHS | 200/7-12
  PO Box 9 68733 | 402-695-2636
  Ed Stansberry, prin. | Fax 695-2622

Eustis, Frontier, Pop. 432
Eustis-Farnham SD | 300/K-12
  PO Box 9 69028 | 308-486-3991
  Carl Dietz, supt. | Fax 486-5350
  www.esu11.org/eustis/home.htm
Eustis-Farnham HS | 100/7-12
  PO Box 9 69028 | 308-486-3991
  Kyle Hemmerling, prin. | Fax 486-5350

Ewing, Holt, Pop. 418
Ewing SD | 100/K-12
  PO Box 98 68735 | 402-626-7235
  John Brickner, supt. | Fax 626-7236
  www.esu8.org/~ewing/homepage.html
Ewing JSHS | 100/7-12
  PO Box 98 68735 | 402-626-7235
  Greg A. Appleby, prin. | Fax 626-7236

Exeter, Fillmore, Pop. 685
Exeter-Milligan SD | 300/PK-12
  PO Box 139 68351 | 402-266-5911
  Thomas Sharp, supt. | Fax 266-4811
Exeter-Milligan JSHS | 200/7-12
  PO Box 139 68351 | 402-266-5911
  Lindley Schlueter, prin. | Fax 266-4811

Fairbury, Jefferson, Pop. 4,112
Fairbury SD | 1,000/PK-12
  703 K St 68352 | 402-729-6104
  Frederick J. Helmink, supt. | Fax 729-6392
Fairbury JSHS | 500/7-12
  1501 9th St 68352 | 402-729-6116
  Jeff Vetter, prin. | Fax 729-6275

Fairfield, Clay, Pop. 455
South Central Nebraska Unified SD | 1,100/PK-12
  30671 Highway 14 68938 | 402-726-2151
  Kent Miller, supt. | Fax 726-2208
Sandy Creek JSHS | 200/7-12
  30671 Highway 14 68938 | 402-726-2151
  Jason Searle, prin. | Fax 726-2208
Other Schools – See Nelson, Superior

Fairmont, Fillmore, Pop. 667
Fillmore Central SD
  Supt. — See Geneva
Fillmore Central MS | 200/5-8
  PO Box 157 68354 | 402-268-3411
  Brian Tonniges, prin. | Fax 268-3491

Falls City, Richardson, Pop. 4,375
Falls City SD | 900/PK-12
  PO Box 129 68355 | 402-245-2825
  Dr. Jon Habben, supt. | Fax 245-2022
Falls City HS | 300/9-12
  1400 Fulton St 68355 | 402-245-2116
  Arlan Andreesen, prin. | Fax 245-5050
Falls City MS | 200/6-8
  PO Box 129 68355 | 402-245-3455
  Rick Johnson, prin. | Fax 245-2022

Sacred Heart S | 300/K-12
  1820 Fulton St 68355 | 402-245-4151
  Doug Goltz, prin. | Fax 245-5217

Firth, Lancaster, Pop. 616
Norris SD 160 | 1,700/PK-12
  25211 S 68th St 68358 | 402-791-0000
  Roy Baker, supt. | Fax 791-0025
  www.norris160.org
Norris HS | 500/9-12
  25211 S 68th St 68358 | 402-791-0010
  John Skretta, prin. | Fax 791-0025
Norris MS | 400/6-8
  25211 S 68th St 68358 | 402-791-0020
  Barry Stark, prin. | Fax 791-0025

Fort Calhoun, Washington, Pop. 906
Fort Calhoun SD — 600/K-12
PO Box 430 68023 — 402-468-5592
Gerald M Beach, supt. — Fax 468-5593
www.ftc.esu3.org/
Fort Calhoun JSHS — 300/7-12
PO Box 430 68023 — 402-468-5591
Donald Johnson, prin. — Fax 468-5593

Franklin, Franklin, Pop. 990
Franklin SD — 300/K-12
1001 M St 68939 — 308-425-6283
Mike Lucas, supt. — Fax 425-6553
www.esu11.org/franklin/franklin.home.html
Franklin JSHS — 200/7-12
1001 M St 68939 — 308-425-6283
— Fax 425-6553

Fremont, Dodge, Pop. 25,198
Fremont SD — 4,500/K-12
957 N Pierce St 68025 — 402-727-3000
Stephen Sexton, supt. — Fax 727-3002
www.fpsweb.org
Fremont HS — 1,300/9-12
1750 N Lincoln Ave 68025 — 402-727-3050
Joe Sajevic, prin. — Fax 727-3033
Fremont MS — 1,000/6-8
540 Johnson Rd 68025 — 402-727-3100
Gale Hamilton, prin. — Fax 727-3963

Archbishop Bergan JSHS — 200/6-12
545 E 4th St 68025 — 402-721-9683
Ron Beacom, prin. — Fax 721-5366
Bahner College of Hairstyling — Post-Sec.
1660 N Grant St 68025 — 402-721-6500
Midland Lutheran College — Post-Sec.
900 N Clarkson St 68025 — 402-721-5480

Friend, Saline, Pop. 1,176
Friend SD — 300/K-12
PO Box 67 68359 — 402-947-2781
Chris Effken, supt. — Fax 947-2026
Friend JSHS — 200/7-12
PO Box 67 68359 — 402-947-2781
James Moore, prin. — Fax 947-2026

Fullerton, Nance, Pop. 1,287
Fullerton SD — 400/K-12
PO Box 520 68638 — 308-536-2431
Jeffrey Anderson, supt. — Fax 536-2432
Fullerton HS — 100/9-12
PO Box 520 68638 — 308-536-2431
Pat Larsen, prin. — Fax 536-2432

Geneva, Fillmore, Pop. 2,164
Fillmore Central SD — 600/K-12
1410 L St 68361 — 402-759-4955
Mark Norvell, supt. — Fax 759-4038
www.fcps.esu6.org/
Fillmore Central HS — 200/9-12
1410 L St 68361 — 402-759-3141
James Rose, prin. — Fax 759-4038
Other Schools – See Fairmont

Geneva North SD — 100/K-12
855 N 1st St 68361 — 402-759-3164
— Fax 759-4804
Geneva North HS — 100/9-12
855 N 1st St 68361 — 402-759-3164
Richard Wehland, prin. — Fax 759-4804

Genoa, Nance, Pop. 905
Twin River SD — 500/K-12
PO Box 640 68640 — 402-993-2274
Donald Q. Graff, supt. — Fax 993-7718
www.esu7.org/~trweb/
Twin River JSHS at Genoa — 300/7-12
PO Box 640 68640 — 402-993-2911
— Fax 993-7718

Gering, Scotts Bluff, Pop. 7,832
Gering SD — 1,900/PK-12
1800 8th St 69341 — 308-436-3125
Don Hague, supt. — Fax 436-4301
www.geringschools.net
Gering JHS — 400/7-9
800 Q St 69341 — 308-436-3123
Maurie Deines, prin. — Fax 436-6010
Gering SHS — 500/10-12
1500 U St 69341 — 308-436-3121
Eldon Hubbard, prin. — Fax 436-4214

Gibbon, Buffalo, Pop. 1,792
Gibbon SD — 500/K-12
PO Box 790 68840 — 308-468-6555
Larry Witt, supt. — Fax 468-5164
Gibbon JSHS — 300/7-12
PO Box 790 68840 — 308-468-5721
Julie Schnitzler, prin. — Fax 468-5164

Giltner, Hamilton, Pop. 397
Giltner SD — 200/K-12
PO Box 160 68841 — 402-849-2238
Kenneth Mahlin, supt. — Fax 849-2440
Giltner JSHS — 100/7-12
PO Box 160 68841 — 402-849-2238
Douglas Bandemer, prin. — Fax 849-2440

Gordon, Sheridan, Pop. 1,630
Gordon-Rushville HSD — 200/9-12
PO Box 530 69343 — 308-282-1322
William Tuma, supt. — Fax 282-2207
Gordon-Rushville HS — 200/9-12
PO Box 530 69343 — 308-282-1322
Robert Drews, prin. — Fax 282-2207

Gordon-Rushville SD — 400/K-8
PO Box 530 69343 — 308-282-0216
William C. Tuma, supt. — Fax 282-1512
Other Schools – See Rushville

Gothenburg, Dawson, Pop. 3,631
Gothenburg SD — 800/K-12
1322 Avenue I 69138 — 308-537-3651
Michael Teahon, supt. — Fax 537-3965
Gothenburg JSHS — 400/7-12
1322 Avenue I 69138 — 308-537-3651
Randy Evans, prin. — Fax 537-3965

Grand Island, Hall, Pop. 43,771
Grand Island SD — 7,800/PK-12
PO Box 4904 68802 — 308-385-5900
Dr. Steve Joel, supt. — Fax 385-5949
www.gi.esu10.k12.ne.us/
Barr MS — 700/6-8
602 W Stolley Park Rd 68801 — 308-385-5875
Conda Allen, prin. — Fax 385-5875
Grand Island HS — 1,900/9-12
2124 N Lafayette Ave 68803 — 308-385-5950
Kenton Mann, prin. — Fax 385-5966
Walnut MS — 800/6-8
1600 N Custer Ave 68803 — 308-385-5990
Vikki Deuel, prin. — Fax 385-5992
Westridge MS — 300/6-8
1812 Mansfield Rd 68803 — 308-385-5886
Dan Brosz, prin. — Fax 385-5003

Northwest HSD — 700/9-12
2710 N North Rd 68803 — 308-385-6398
Bill L. Mowinkel, supt. — Fax 385-6393
Northwest HS — 700/9-12
2710 N North Rd 68803 — 308-385-6398
Doyle E. Denney, prin. — Fax 385-6393

Central Catholic HS — 500/6-12
1200 Ruby Ave 68803 — 308-384-2440
John Golka, prin. — Fax 389-3274
Central Community College — Post-Sec.
PO Box 4903 68802 — 308-398-4222
Grand Island Christian S — 100/PK-12
1804 W State St 68803 — 308-384-2755
Tim Salcedo, prin. — Fax 389-3286
Heartland Lutheran HS — 100/9-12
3900 W Husker Hwy 68803 — 308-385-3900
Fred Chandler, dir. — Fax 381-7415
Joseph's College of Beauty — Post-Sec.
305 W 3rd St 68801 — 308-381-8848

Grant, Perkins, Pop. 1,158
Perkins County SD — 300/K-12
PO Box 829 69140 — 308-352-4735
Kirk Russell, supt. — Fax 352-4769
www.pcs.k12.ne.us/
Perkins County HS — 100/9-12
PO Box 829 69140 — 308-352-4735
Dean Friedel, prin. — Fax 352-4769

Greeley, Greeley, Pop. 511
Greeley-Wolbach SD — 200/PK-12
PO Box 160 68842 — 308-428-3145
Gene Haddix, supt. — Fax 428-5395
Greeley-Wolbach HS — 50/9-12
PO Box 160 68842 — 308-428-3145
Todd Beck, prin. — Fax 428-5395
Other Schools – See Wolbach

Gretna, Sarpy, Pop. 3,924
Gretna SD — 1,700/K-12
11717 S 216th St 68028 — 402-332-3265
Kevin Riley, supt. — Fax 332-5833
gretna.esu3.org/
Gretna HS — 500/9-12
11335 S 204th St 68028 — 402-332-3936
Kirk Eledge, prin. — Fax 332-4119
Gretna MS — 400/6-8
11705 S 216th St 68028 — 402-332-3048
Rex Anderson, prin. — Fax 332-2931

Hampton, Hamilton, Pop. 437
Hampton SD — 100/K-12
458 5th St 68843 — 402-725-3117
Russ Hoppner, supt. — Fax 725-3334
www.esu9.org/%7Ehampton/
Hampton JSHS — 100/7-12
458 5th St 68843 — 402-725-3116
Gerald Eickhoff, prin. — Fax 725-3334

Harrisburg, Banner
Banner County SD — 200/K-12
PO Box 5 69345 — 308-436-5263
Lana Sides, supt. — Fax 436-5252
schools.esu13.org/bannercounty/
Banner County JSHS — 100/7-12
PO Box 5 69345 — 308-436-5263
Gerald Wallace, prin. — Fax 436-5252

Harrison, Sioux, Pop. 281
Sioux County HSD — 50/9-12
PO Box 38 69346 — 308-668-2415
William A. Porter, supt. — Fax 668-2260
siouxco.panesu.org/
Sioux County SD — 50/9-12
PO Box 38 69346 — 308-668-2415
William A. Porter, prin. — Fax 668-2260

Hartington, Cedar, Pop. 1,606
Hartington SD — 300/K-12
PO Box 75 68739 — 402-254-3947
Scott Swisher, supt. — Fax 254-3945
hartington.esu1.org/
Hartington JSHS — 200/7-12
PO Box 75 68739 — 402-254-3947
Timothy Koehler, prin. — Fax 254-3945

Cedar Catholic HS — 100/7-12
PO Box 15 68739 — 402-254-3906
Mike McCabe, prin. — Fax 254-3976

Harvard, Clay, Pop. 969
Harvard SD — 300/K-12
PO Box 100 68944 — 402-772-2171
Larry Turnquist, supt. — Fax 772-2204
Harvard JSHS — 100/7-12
PO Box 100 68944 — 402-772-2171
Brent Williamson, prin. — Fax 772-2204

Hastings, Adams, Pop. 23,536
Adams Central RHSD — 500/7-12
PO Box 1088 68902 — 402-463-3285
Melvin R. Crowe, supt. — Fax 463-6344
Adams Central JSHS — 500/7-12
PO Box 1088 68902 — 402-463-3285
David Barrett, prin. — Fax 463-6344

Hastings SD — 3,300/PK-12
714 W 5th St 68901 — 402-461-7500
Gene Cosby, supt. — Fax 461-7509
www1.hastings.esu9.k12.ne.us/
Hastings HS — 1,000/9-12
1100 W 14th St 68901 — 402-461-7550
Jay Opperman, prin. — Fax 461-7535
Hastings MS — 500/7-8
505 N Hastings Ave 68901 — 402-461-7520
Jeffrey Schneider, prin. — Fax 461-7650

Central Community College — Post-Sec.
PO Box 1024 68902 — 402-463-9811
Hastings College — Post-Sec.
PO Box 269 68902 — 402-463-2402
Joseph's College of Beauty — Post-Sec.
828 W 2nd St 68901 — 402-463-1357
Mary Lanning Memorial Hospital — Post-Sec.
715 N Saint Joseph Ave 68901 — 402-463-4521
St. Cecilia MSHS — 300/6-12
521 N Kansas Ave 68901 — 402-462-2105
Marie Butler, prin. — Fax 462-2106

Hayes Center, Hayes, Pop. 248
Hayes Center SD — 200/K-12
PO Box 8 69032 — 308-286-3341
Thomas M. McMahon, supt. — Fax 286-3330
Hayes Center JSHS — 100/7-12
PO Box 8 69032 — 308-286-3341
Kathryn A. Repass, prin. — Fax 286-3330

Hay Springs, Sheridan, Pop. 602
Hay Springs SD — 100/K-12
PO Box 280 69347 — 308-638-4434
Ernest Griffiths, supt. — Fax 638-7500
www.hshawks.com/
Hay Springs JSHS — 100/6-12
PO Box 280 69347 — 308-638-4434
Ernest Griffiths, prin. — Fax 638-7500

Hebron, Thayer, Pop. 1,469
Thayer Central Community SD — 400/K-12
PO Box 9 68370 — 402-768-6117
Dan Jantzen, supt. — Fax 768-6110
www.tccs.esu6.org/
Thayer Central HS — 200/7-12
PO Box 9 68370 — 402-768-6117
Tom W. Kiburz, prin. — Fax 768-6110

Hemingford, Box Butte, Pop. 946
Hemingford SD — 400/K-12
PO Box 217 69348 — 308-487-3328
Casper Q. Ningen, supt. — Fax 487-5215
www.hemingfordschools.org/
Hemingford JSHS — 200/7-12
PO Box 217 69348 — 308-487-3328
Peggy Thayer, prin. — Fax 487-5215

Henderson, York, Pop. 999
Heartland Community SD — 300/K-12
PO Box 626 68371 — 402-723-4434
Norman Yoder, supt. — Fax 723-4431
www.heartlandschools.org/
Heartland Community HS — 100/9-12
PO Box 626 68371 — 402-723-4434
Blaine Friesen, prin. — Fax 723-4431
Other Schools – See Bradshaw

Hershey, Lincoln, Pop. 561
Hershey SD — 400/K-12
PO Box 369 69143 — 308-368-5574
Michael J. Cunning, supt. — Fax 368-5570
Hershey JSHS — 200/7-12
PO Box 369 69143 — 308-368-5573
Richard Elsasser, prin. — Fax 368-5570

Hildreth, Franklin, Pop. 356
Wilcox-Hildreth SD
Supt. — See Wilcox
Wilcox-Hildreth MS — 100/6-8
PO Box 157 68947 — 308-938-3825
Roger Boyer, prin. — Fax 938-5335

Holdrege, Phelps, Pop. 5,521
Holdrege SD — 1,000/K-12
PO Box 2002 68949 — 308-995-8663
Cynthia Wendell, supt. — Fax 995-6956
www.thedusters.org/
Holdrege HS — 400/9-12
PO Box 2002 68949 — 308-995-6558
Richard Meyer, prin. — Fax 995-8662
Holdrege MS — 300/5-8
PO Box 2002 68949 — 308-995-5421
Russell Baker, prin. — Fax 995-4970

Homer, Dakota, Pop. 603
Homer Community SD — 400/PK-12
PO Box 340 68030 — 402-698-2377
Bruce Johnson, supt. — Fax 698-2379
homerweb.esu1.org/
Homer JSHS — 200/7-12
PO Box 340 68030 — 402-698-2377
Randy Primer, prin. — Fax 698-2379

Hooper, Dodge, Pop. 799
Logan View SD — 900/K-12
2163 County Road G 68031 — 402-654-3317
Jeffrey E. Edwards, supt. — Fax 654-3699
Logan View SD — 400/7-12
2163 County Road G 68031 — 402-654-3317
Kolin Haecker, prin. — Fax 654-3699

Howells, Colfax, Pop. 631
Howells SD — 200/K-12
PO Box 159 68641 — 402-986-1621
Thomas Reeser, supt. — Fax 986-1261
Howells JSHS — 200/7-12
PO Box 159 68641 — 402-986-1621
Dan Martin, prin. — Fax 986-1261

Humboldt, Richardson, Pop. 885
Humboldt & Table Rock Steinauer USD 2007 300/PK-12
PO Box 31 68376 — 402-862-2235
Clinton Kimbrough, supt. — Fax 862-3135
www.humboldt.esu6.org
Humboldt & Table Rock Steinauer HS — 100/9-12
PO Box 31 68376 — 402-862-2235
Laurie Kimbrough, prin. — Fax 862-3135
Other Schools – See Table Rock

Humphrey, Platte, Pop. 761
Humphrey SD — 200/PK-12
PO Box 278 68642 — 402-923-1230
Greg Sjuts, supt. — Fax 923-1235
www.humphrey.esu7.org/
Humphrey JSHS — 100/7-12
PO Box 278 68642 — 402-923-1230
Russell Flamig, prin. — Fax 923-1235

St. Francis S — 300/K-12
300 S 7th St #277 68642 — 402-923-0818
Darron Artl, prin. — Fax 923-1590

Hyannis, Grant, Pop. 267
Hyannis HSD — 100/7-12
PO Box 286 69350 — 308-458-2202
Raymond M. Davis, supt. — Fax 458-2227
Hyannis JSHS — 100/7-12
PO Box 286 69350 — 308-458-2202
Dennis R. Wilbur, prin. — Fax 458-2227

Imperial, Chase, Pop. 1,969
Chase County SD — 600/K-12
PO Box 577 69033 — 308-882-4304
Matthew Fisher, supt. — Fax 882-5629
Chase County HS — 200/9-12
PO Box 577 69033 — 308-882-4304
Bruce Vires, prin. — Fax 882-5629

Indianola, Red Willow, Pop. 622
Southwest SD 179
Supt. — See Bartley
Southwest HS — 100/9-12
39145 Road 718 69034 — 308-364-2202
Cory Grint, prin. — Fax 364-2265

Johnson, Nemaha, Pop. 261
Johnson-Brock SD — 200/K-12
PO Box 186 68378 — 402-868-5235
Warren P. Barnell, supt. — Fax 868-4785
manila.esu4.org/JohnsonBrock/
Johnson JSHS — 100/7-12
PO Box 186 68378 — 402-868-5235
Jacquelyn Kelsay, prin. — Fax 868-4785

Kearney, Buffalo, Pop. 28,211
Kearney SD — 5,800/K-12
310 W 24th St 68845 — 308-698-8000
Kenneth Anderson, supt. — Fax 698-8001
userweb.esu10.org/~kearney/
Horizon MS — 400/7-8
915 W 35th St 68845 — 308-698-8120
Kipp Peterson, prin. — Fax 698-8143
Kearney HS — 1,400/9-12
3610 6th Ave 68845 — 308-698-8060
Steve Wickham, prin. — Fax 698-8061
Sunrise MS — 400/7-8
4611 Avenue N 68847 — 308-698-8150
Lance Fuller, prin. — Fax 698-8152

Kearney West HSD — 200/7-12
2802 30th Ave 68845 — 308-338-2011
Timothy Odea, supt. — Fax 865-5323
www.esu10.org/~westkrny/wkhshome.htm
Kearney West HS — 200/7-12
2802 30th Ave 68845 — 308-338-2011
Anthony Kleidosty, prin. — Fax 865-5323

Joseph's of Kearney Sch of Hair Design — Post-Sec.
2213 Central Ave 68847 — 308-234-6594
Kearney Catholic HS — 300/6-12
PO Box 1866 68848 — 308-234-2610
Terrence Torson, prin. — Fax 234-4986
University of Nebraska at Kearney — Post-Sec.
905 W 25th St 68845 — 308-865-8526

Kenesaw, Adams, Pop. 853
Kenesaw SD — 300/K-12
PO Box 129 68956 — 402-752-3215
William J Troshynski, supt. — Fax 752-3579
www.esu9.org/~kenesaw/
Kenesaw JSHS — 100/7-12
PO Box 129 68956 — 402-752-3215
Robby Thompson, prin. — Fax 752-3579

Kimball, Kimball, Pop. 2,396
Kimball SD — 600/K-12
816 E 3rd St 69145 — 308-235-2188
Jerry Williams, supt. — Fax 235-3269
Kimball JSHS — 300/7-12
901 S Nadine St 69145 — 308-235-4861
Chad L. Denker, prin. — Fax 235-4128

Laurel, Cedar, Pop. 939
Laurel-Concord SD — 400/K-12
PO Box 8 68745 — 402-256-3133
Daniel Hoesing, supt. — Fax 256-9465
www.laurel.esu1.org
Laurel-Concord JSHS — 200/7-12
PO Box 8 68745 — 402-256-3731
Leslie Owen, prin. — Fax 256-9465

La Vista, Sarpy, Pop. 13,895
Papillion-La Vista SD
Supt. — See Papillion
La Vista JHS — 1,000/7-9
7900 Edgewood Blvd 68128 — 402-898-0436
Thomas Furby, prin. — Fax 898-0442

Leigh, Colfax, Pop. 435
Leigh Community SD — 200/K-12
PO Box 98 68643 — 402-487-2228
Grant Norgaard, supt. — Fax 487-3341
www.esu7.org/~leiweb/leigh.html
Leigh JSHS — 100/7-12
PO Box 98 68643 — 402-487-2228
Steven Borer, prin. — Fax 487-2607

Lewellen, Garden, Pop. 268
Garden County SD
Supt. — See Oshkosh
Garden County JHS — 50/5-8
PO Box 268 69147 — 308-778-5561
Paula J Sissel, prin. — Fax 778-5568

Lewiston, Pawnee, Pop. 81
Lewiston SD — 200/K-12
PO Box 74 68380 — 402-865-4675
Dr. Bruce McCoy, supt. — Fax 865-4875
Lewiston JSHS — 100/7-12
PO Box 74 68380 — 402-865-4675
Dan Parks, prin. — Fax 865-4875

Lexington, Dawson, Pop. 10,113
Lexington SD — 2,800/PK-12
PO Box 890 68850 — 308-324-4681
Richard Eisenhauer Ed.D., supt. — Fax 324-2528
www.lex.esu10.org/
Lexington HS — 800/9-12
705 W 13th St 68850 — 308-324-4691
David Gordon, prin. — Fax 324-7224
Lexington MS — 700/6-8
1100 N Washington St 68850 — 308-324-2349
Dean Tickle, prin. — Fax 324-6612

Lincoln, Lancaster, Pop. 235,594
Lincoln SD — 31,800/PK-12
PO Box 82889 68501 — 402-436-1000
E. Susan Gourley Ph.D., supt. — Fax 436-1620
www.lps.org/
Culler MS — 600/6-8
5201 Vine St 68504 — 402-436-1210
John Zetterman, prin. — Fax 436-1226
Dawes MS — 500/6-8
5130 Colfax Ave 68504 — 402-436-1211
Dave Knudsen, prin. — Fax 436-1234
Goodrich MS — 700/6-8
4600 Lewis Ave 68521 — 402-436-1213
Michael Henninger, prin. — Fax 436-1259
Irving MS — 700/6-8
2745 S 22nd St 68502 — 402-436-1214
Hugh McDermott, prin. — Fax 436-1266
Lefler MS — 600/6-8
1100 S 48th St 68510 — 402-436-1215
Kelly Schrad, prin. — Fax 436-1278
Lincoln East HS — 1,600/9-12
1000 S 70th St 68510 — 402-436-1302
Dr. Mary Lehmanowsky, prin. — Fax 436-1325
Lincoln HS — 2,000/9-12
2229 J St 68510 — 402-436-1301
Dr. Michael Wortman, prin. — Fax 436-1540
Lincoln Northeast HS — 1,700/9-12
2635 N 63rd St 68507 — 402-436-1303
Kurt Glathar, prin. — Fax 436-1345
Lincoln Northstar HS — 1,200/9-12
5801 N 33rd St 68504 — 402-436-1305
Dr. Nancy Becker, prin. — Fax 436-1054
Lincoln Southeast HS — 1,700/9-12
2930 S 37th St 68506 — 402-436-1304
Dr. Patrick Hunter-Pirtle, prin. — Fax 436-1357
Lincoln Southwest HS — 1,500/9-12
7001 S 14th St 68512 — 402-436-1306
Jerry Wilks, prin. — Fax 436-1085
Lux MS — 900/6-8
7800 High St 68506 — 402-436-1220
William Bucher, prin. — Fax 436-1309
Mickle MS — 700/6-8
2500 N 67th St 68507 — 402-436-1216
John Neal, prin. — Fax 436-1287
North Star MS — 200/6-8
5801 N 33rd St 68504 — 402-436-1305
Dr. Nancy Becker, prin. — Fax 436-1054
Park MS — 700/6-8
855 S 8th St 68508 — 402-436-1212
Dr. Terry Neddenriep, prin. — Fax 436-1247
Pound MS — 700/6-8
4740 S 45th St 68516 — 402-436-1217
Dr. Christopher Deibler, prin. — Fax 436-1205
Scott MS — 900/6-8
2200 Pine Lake Rd 68512 — 402-436-1218
Dr. Linda Hix, prin. — Fax 436-1283

Bryan LGH College of Health Science — Post-Sec.
5035 Everett St 68506 — 402-481-8697
College of Hair Design — Post-Sec.
304 S 11th St 68508 — 402-477-4040
College View Academy — 100/K-12
5240 Calvert St 68506 — 402-483-1181
David Branum, prin. — Fax 483-5574
Hamilton College - Lincoln Campus — Post-Sec.
PO Box 82826 68501 — 402-474-5315

Joseph's College of Beauty — Post-Sec.
2637 O St 68510 — 402-435-2333
Lincoln Christian JSHS — 300/7-12
5801 S 84th St 68516 — 402-488-8888
Dave Pauli, supt. — Fax 488-6617
Lincoln Lutheran JSHS — 400/6-12
1100 N 56th St 68504 — 402-467-5404
Scott Ernstmeyer, prin. — Fax 467-5405
Lincoln Pius X HS — 1,000/9-12
6000 A St 68510 — 402-488-0931
Thomas Seib, prin. — Fax 488-1061
Myotherapy Institute — Post-Sec.
6020 S 58th St 68516 — 402-421-7410
Nebraska Wesleyan University — Post-Sec.
5000 Saint Paul Ave 68504 — 402-466-2371
Parkview Christian S — 100/1-12
4400 N 1st St 68521 — 402-474-5820
Dr. David Myers, supt. — Fax 474-5830
Southeast Community College — Post-Sec.
8800 O St 68520 — 402-437-2500
Union College — Post-Sec.
3800 S 48th St 68506 — 402-488-2331
University of Nebraska — Post-Sec.
14th & R Sts 68588 — 402-472-7211

Lindsay, Platte, Pop. 269
Holy Family S — 200/1-12
PO Box 158 68644 — 402-428-3455
Nathan Vitosh, prin. — Fax 428-3231

Litchfield, Sherman, Pop. 264
Litchfield SD — 100/K-12
PO Box 167 68852 — 308-446-2244
Michael Gillming, supt. — Fax 446-2244
Litchfield JSHS — 100/7-12
PO Box 167 68852 — 308-446-2244
Brad Stithem, prin. — Fax 446-2244

Lodgepole, Cheyenne, Pop. 353
Creek Valley SD
Supt. — See Chappell
Creek Valley MS — 5-8
PO Box 158 69149 — 308-483-5252
Dennis O'Connor, prin. — Fax 483-5251

Loomis, Phelps, Pop. 387
Loomis SD — 200/K-12
PO Box 250 68958 — 308-876-2111
Keith Fagot, supt. — Fax 876-2372
teachers.esu11.org/sarehart/
Loomis JSHS — 100/7-12
PO Box 250 68958 — 308-876-2111
— Fax 876-2372

Louisville, Cass, Pop. 1,061
Louisville SD — 500/K-12
PO Box 489 68037 — 402-234-3585
Edward D. Kasl, supt. — Fax 234-2141
Louisville HS — 200/9-12
PO Box 489 68037 — 402-234-3585
Cindy Osterloh, prin. — Fax 234-2141
Louisville MS — 100/6-8
PO Box 489 68037 — 402-234-3585
Cindy Osterloh, prin. — Fax 234-2141

Loup City, Sherman, Pop. 929
Loup City SD — 300/K-12
PO Box 628 68853 — 308-745-0120
Caroline B. Winchester, supt. — Fax 745-0130
Loup City HS — 100/9-12
PO Box 628 68853 — 308-745-0548
Nicholas R. Hodge, prin. — Fax 745-0130

Lynch, Boyd, Pop. 250
Lynch SD — 100/K-12
PO Box 98 68746 — 402-569-2081
Nelson Dahl, supt. — Fax 569-2091
Lynch JSHS — 100/7-12
PO Box 98 68746 — 402-569-2081
Nelson Dahl, prin. — Fax 569-2091

Lyons, Burt, Pop. 923
Lyons-Decatur Northeast SD — 400/K-12
PO Box 526 68038 — 402-687-2363
Fred Hansen, supt. — Fax 687-2472
www.lyonsdecaturschools.org/
Northeast JSHS — 200/7-12
PO Box 526 68038 — 402-687-2349
Douglas Smith, prin. — Fax 687-2472

Mc Cook, Red Willow, Pop. 7,926
Mc Cook SD — 1,500/K-12
700 W 7th St 69001 — 308-345-2510
Donald Marchant, supt. — Fax 345-2511
www.mc.esu15.k12.ne.us
Mc Cook JHS — 300/7-9
800 W 7th St 69001 — 308-345-6940
Dennis Berry, prin. — Fax 345-6941
Mc Cook SHS — 300/10-12
600 W 7th St 69001 — 308-345-5422
Jerome Smith, prin. — Fax 345-5477

Mid-Plains Community College — Post-Sec.
1205 E 3rd St 69001 — 800-658-4348

Mc Cool Junction, York, Pop. 388
Mc Cool Junction SD — 200/K-12
PO Box 278 68401 — 402-724-2231
Curtis Cogswell, supt. — Fax 724-2232
Mc Cool Junction JSHS — 100/7-12
PO Box 278 68401 — 402-724-2231
Grant E. Fisher, prin. — Fax 724-2232

Macy, Thurston, Pop. 836
UMO N HO N Nation SD — 400/PK-12
PO Box 280 68039 — 402-837-5622
Morris Bates, supt. — Fax 837-5245
macyweb.esu1.org/

UMO N HO N Nation HS   100/9-12
   PO Box 280   68039   402-837-5222
   David Friedli, prin.   Fax 837-5245
UMO N HO N Nation MS   100/6-8
   PO Box 280   68039   402-837-5622
   Mary Beth Wilson, prin.   Fax 837-5245

Nebraska Indian Community College   Post-Sec.
   PO Box 428   68039   402-837-5078

Madison, Madison, Pop. 2,344
Madison SD   600/K-12
   PO Box 450   68748   402-454-3336
   David Melick, supt.   Fax 454-2238
Madison HS   200/9-12
   PO Box 450   68748   402-454-3336
   Steve Borer, prin.   Fax 454-2238
Madison MS   100/6-8
   PO Box 450   68748   402-454-3336
   Steve Borer, prin.   Fax 454-2238

Malcolm, Lancaster, Pop. 435
Malcolm SD   500/K-12
   10004 NW 112th St   68402   402-796-2151
   Gene Neddenriep, supt.   Fax 796-2178
   www.malcolmschools.esu6.org/
Malcolm JSHS   200/7-12
   10002 NW 112th St   68402   402-796-2151
   Earl Nannen, prin.   Fax 796-2189

Maxwell, Lincoln, Pop. 317
Maxwell SD   300/PK-12
   PO Box 188   69151   308-582-4585
   Charles Hervert, supt.   Fax 582-4584
   userweb.esu16.org/~maxwell/home.html
Maxwell JSHS   100/7-12
   PO Box 188   69151   308-582-4585
   Aubrey Boucher, prin.   Fax 582-4584

Maywood, Frontier, Pop. 310
Maywood SD   200/K-12
   PO Box 46   69038   308-362-4223
   Barry Limoges, supt.   Fax 362-4454
   webquests.esu16.org:8080/Maywood/
Maywood JSHS   100/7-12
   PO Box 46   69038   308-362-4223
   Jeffrey Koehler, prin.   Fax 362-4454

Mead, Saunders, Pop. 604
Mead SD   300/K-12
   PO Box 158   68041   402-624-2745
   George Robertson, supt.   Fax 624-2001
Mead JSHS   200/7-12
   PO Box 158   68041   402-624-3435
   Cliff Owen, prin.   Fax 624-2001

Merna, Custer, Pop. 387
Anselmo-Merna SD   300/K-12
   PO Box 68   68856   308-643-2224
   Richard Schlesselman, supt.   Fax 643-2243
Merna JSHS   100/7-12
   PO Box 68   68856   308-643-2224
   Sue McNeil, prin.   Fax 643-2243

Milford, Seward, Pop. 2,067
Milford SD   800/PK-12
   PO Box C   68405   402-761-3321
   Kevin Wingard, supt.   Fax 761-3322
   www.milfordpublicschools.org/
Milford JSHS   300/7-12
   PO Box C   68405   402-761-2525
   Tod J. Meyer, prin.   Fax 761-2663

Southeast Community College   Post-Sec.
   600 State St   68405   402-761-2131

Minatare, Scotts Bluff, Pop. 792
Minatare SD   200/K-12
   PO Box 425   69356   308-783-1232
   Charles J. Bunner, supt.   Fax 783-2982
Minatare JSHS   100/7-12
   PO Box 425   69356   308-783-1733
   Michael W. Halley, prin.   Fax 783-2982

Minden, Kearney, Pop. 2,952
Minden SD   900/PK-12
   PO Box 301   68959   308-832-2440
   Scott Maline, supt.   Fax 832-2567
Jones MS   300/4-8
   PO Box 301   68959   308-832-2338
   John Osgood, prin.   Fax 832-3236
Minden HS   300/9-12
   PO Box 301   68959   308-832-2254
   Steve Sampy, prin.   Fax 832-1892

Mitchell, Scotts Bluff, Pop. 1,804
Mitchell SD   600/K-12
   1819 19th Ave   69357   308-623-1707
   Kent Halley, supt.   Fax 623-1330
   www.mpstigers.net
Mitchell JSHS   300/7-12
   1819 19th Ave   69357   308-623-1707
   Troy Unzicker, prin.   Fax 623-1330

Morrill, Scotts Bluff, Pop. 936
Morrill SD   500/K-12
   PO Box 486   69358   308-247-2149
   Roy Ingram, supt.   Fax 247-2196
Morrill JSHS   200/7-12
   PO Box 486   69358   308-247-2149
   Kenton McLellan, prin.   Fax 247-2196

Mullen, Hooker, Pop. 456
Mullen SD   200/K-12
   PO Box 127   69152   308-546-2223
   Charles R. Hafer, supt.   Fax 546-2209
   athena.esu16.org/mps/index.html
Mullen JSHS   100/7-12
   PO Box 127   69152   308-546-2223
   Joel R. Ruybalid, prin.   Fax 546-2209

Murdock, Cass, Pop. 272
Elmwood-Murdock SD   400/K-12
   PO Box 407   68407   402-867-2341
   Daniel Novak, supt.   Fax 867-2009
   www.elm.esu3.org/index.htm
Elmwood-Murdock JSHS   200/7-12
   PO Box 407   68407   402-867-2341
   Tim Allemang, prin.   Fax 867-2009

Murray, Cass, Pop. 491
Conestoga SD   700/K-12
   PO Box 184   68409   402-235-2992
   Mark Sievering, supt.   Fax 227-2992
   www.conestogacougars.org/
Conestoga JSHS   300/7-12
   PO Box 40   68409   402-235-2271
   Randall Reinke, prin.   Fax 235-2421

Nebraska City, Otoe, Pop. 7,113
Nebraska City SD   1,300/PK-12
   215 N 12th St   68410   402-873-6033
   Keith Rohwer, supt.   Fax 873-6030
   www.nebcity.esu6.org
Nebraska City HS   500/9-12
   141 Steinhart Park Rd   68410   402-873-3360
   Mark Adler, prin.   Fax 873-3831
Nebraska City MS   300/6-8
   909 1st Corso   68410   402-873-5591
   Jenny M Powell, prin.   Fax 873-5641

Lourdes Central S   200/6-12
   412 2nd Ave   68410   402-873-6154
   Fr. Mark Tasler, prin.   Fax 873-3154
Nebraska School for Visually Handicapped   Post-Sec.
   10th St & 10th Ave   68410

Neligh, Antelope, Pop. 1,591
Neligh-Oakdale SD   400/K-12
   PO Box 149   68756   402-887-4166
   Glen Morgan, supt.   Fax 887-5322
Neligh-Oakdale JSHS   200/7-12
   PO Box 149   68756   402-887-4166
   George Loofe, prin.   Fax 887-5322

Nelson, Nuckolls, Pop. 557
South Central Nebraska Unified SD
   Supt. — See Fairfield
Lawrence/Nelson JSHS   100/7-12
   PO Box 368   68961   402-225-3371
   Steven W. Senff, prin.   Fax 225-5431

Newcastle, Dixon, Pop. 287
Newcastle SD   200/K-12
   PO Box 187   68757   402-355-2231
   Vicki Caldwell, supt.   Fax 355-2635
   newcastle.esu1.org/
Newcastle JSHS   100/7-12
   PO Box 187   68757   402-355-2231
   Scott Cole, prin.   Fax 355-2635

Newman Grove, Madison, Pop. 788
Newman Grove SD   300/K-12
   PO Box 370   68758   402-447-2721
   James E. Koontz, supt.   Fax 447-2445
Newman Grove JSHS   200/7-12
   PO Box 370   68758   402-447-6294
      Fax 447-2445

Niobrara, Knox, Pop. 370
Niobrara SD   200/K-12
   PO Box 310   68760   402-857-3323
   David D. Hamm, supt.   Fax 857-3877
Niobrara JSHS   100/5-12
   PO Box 310   68760   402-857-3322
   Margaret Sandoz, prin.   Fax 857-3716

Santee SD   100/K-12
   206 Frazier Ave E   68760   402-857-2741
   Bruce Blanchard, supt.   Fax 857-2743
   santeeweb.esu1.org/
Santee HS   50/9-12
   206 Frazier Ave E   68760   402-857-2741
   Vincent Hurley, prin.   Fax 857-2743

Norfolk, Madison, Pop. 24,061
Norfolk SD   4,200/PK-12
   PO Box 139   68702   402-644-2500
   Randy Nelson, supt.   Fax 644-2506
   www.norfolkpublicschools.org/
Norfolk JHS   700/8-9
   PO Box 139   68702   402-644-2516
   David Wright, prin.   Fax 644-2519
Norfolk SHS   1,100/10-12
   PO Box 139   68702   402-644-2529
   Stephen Morton, prin.   Fax 644-2538

Joseph's College of Beauty   Post-Sec.
   202 Madison Ave   68701   402-371-3358
Lutheran HS Northeast   100/9-12
   PO Box 2454   68702   402-379-3040
   Paul Leckband, prin.   Fax 379-8340
Nebraska Christian College   Post-Sec.
   1800 Syracuse Ave   68701   402-379-5000
Norfolk Catholic HS   400/7-12
   2300 Madison Ave   68701   402-371-2784
   Jeff Bellar, prin.   Fax 379-2929
Northeast Community College   Post-Sec.
   PO Box 469   68702   402-371-2020

North Bend, Dodge, Pop. 1,199
North Bend Central SD   500/K-12
   PO Box 160   68649   402-652-3268
   James Havelka, supt.   Fax 652-8348
   northbend.esu2.org/
North Bend Central JSHS   300/7-12
   PO Box 160   68649   402-652-3268
   Randall McIntyre, prin.   Fax 652-8348

North Platte, Lincoln, Pop. 23,924
North Platte SD   3,900/K-12
   PO Box 1557   69103   308-696-3301
   Paul R. Brochtrup, supt.   Fax 535-5300
   www.nppsd.org
Adams MS   700/6-8
   1200 Mcdonald Rd   69101   308-535-7112
   Matt Irish, prin.   Fax 535-5309
Madison MS   200/6-8
   1400 N Madison Ave   69101   308-535-7126
   David Carpenter, prin.   Fax 535-5303
North Platte HS   1,300/9-12
   1220 W 2nd St   69101   308-535-7105
      Fax 535-7111

Mid-Plains Community College   Post-Sec.
   601 W State Farm Rd   69101   800-658-4308
Mid-Plains Community College   Post-Sec.
   1101 Halligan Dr   69101   800-658-4308
North Platte Beauty Academy   Post-Sec.
   107 W 6th St   69101   308-532-4664
St. Patrick HS   200/7-12
   PO Box 970   69103   308-532-1874
   Mark Stillstead, admin.   Fax 532-8015

Oakland, Burt, Pop. 1,310
Oakland Craig SD   500/K-12
   309 N Davis Ave   68045   402-685-5661
   David Jones, supt.   Fax 685-5697
   ocknights.esu2.org/
Oakland Craig HS   200/9-12
   309 N Davis Ave   68045   402-685-5661
   Michael Apple, prin.   Fax 685-5697
Oakland Craig JHS   100/7-8
   309 N Davis Ave   68045   402-685-5661
   Michael Apple, prin.   Fax 685-5697

Odell, Gage, Pop. 340
Diller-Odell SD   300/K-12
   PO Box 188   68415   402-766-4171
   David Schindler, supt.   Fax 766-4211
   www.dillerodell.org/
Diller-Odell JSHS   200/7-12
   PO Box 188   68415   402-766-4171
   Darrell Vitosh, prin.   Fax 766-4211

Ogallala, Keith, Pop. 4,773
Ogallala SD   1,500/PK-12
   205 E 6th St   69153   308-284-4060
   Tucker Lillis, supt.   Fax 284-3981
   www.opsd.org/
Ogallala HS   400/9-12
   602 E G St   69153   308-284-4029
   Daniel Chromy, prin.   Fax 284-3869
Ogallala MS   300/6-8
   205 E 6th St   69153   308-284-4478
   George Clear, prin.   Fax 284-8129

Omaha, Douglas, Pop. 404,267
Elkhorn SD
   Supt. — See Elkhorn
Elkhorn Ridge MS   400/6-8
   17880 Marcy St   68118   402-334-9302
   Kevin Riggert, prin.   Fax 289-2585
Millard SD   19,500/PK-12
   5606 S 147th St   68137   402-895-8200
   Dr. Keith Lutz, supt.   Fax 895-8448
   www.mpsomaha.org
Andersen MS   800/6-8
   15404 Adams St   68137   402-895-8440
   Jeff Alfrey, prin.   Fax 895-8410
Beadle MS   600/6-8
   18201 Jefferson St   68135   402-894-6100
   Nancy Johnston, prin.   Fax 894-6140
Kiewit MS   1,000/6-8
   15650 Howard St   68118   402-691-1470
   Philip Koch, prin.   Fax 691-1490
Millard Central MS   900/6-8
   12801 L St   68137   402-895-8225
   Dr. Jim Sutfin, prin.   Fax 895-8574
Millard North HS   2,300/9-12
   1010 S 144th St   68154   402-691-1365
   Dr. Rick Werkheiser, prin.   Fax 691-1336
Millard North MS   600/6-8
   2828 S 139th St   68144   402-691-1280
   Dr. Gary Barta, prin.   Fax 691-1275
Millard South HS   1,900/9-12
   14905 Q St   68137   402-895-8268
   Jon Lopez, prin.   Fax 894-6160
Millard West HS   1,800/9-12
   5710 S 176th Ave   68135   402-894-6000
   Dr. Richard Kolowski, prin.   Fax 894-6060
Russell MS   800/6-8
   5304 S 172nd St   68135   402-895-8500
   Brian Begley, prin.   Fax 895-8368
Omaha SD   44,500/PK-12
   3215 Cuming St   68131   402-557-2222
   John Mackiel, supt.   Fax 557-2019
   www.ops.org
Benson HS   1,400/9-12
   5120 Maple St   68104   402-557-3000
   Lisa Dale, prin.   Fax 557-3039
Beveridge Magnet MS   800/7-8
   1616 S 120th St   68144   402-557-4000
   Cara Riggs, prin.   Fax 557-4009
Bryan HS   1,400/9-12
   4700 Giles Rd   68157   402-557-3100
   Dave Collins, prin.   Fax 557-3139
Bryan MS   900/7-8
   8210 S 42nd St   68147   402-557-4100
   Susan Colvin, prin.   Fax 557-4129
Buffet Magnet ES   5-8
   14101 Larimore Ave   68164   402-561-6160
   Dr. ReNae Kehrberg, prin.   Fax 561-6170
Burke HS   2,000/9-12
   12200 Burke St   68154   402-557-3200
   Dr. Connie Eichhorn, prin.   Fax 557-3239

Career Center | Vo/Tech
3230 Burt St 68131 | 402-557-3700
Dr. Gloria Aden, prin. | Fax 557-3709
Central HS | 2,400/9-12
124 N 20th St 68102 | 402-557-3300
Jerry Bexten, prin. | Fax 557-3339
Hale MS | 500/7-8
6143 Whitmore St 68152 | 402-557-4200
M. Patricia Nedley, prin. | Fax 557-4229
King Science MS | 500/5-8
3720 Florence Blvd 68110 | 402-557-3720
Dr. Deborah Frison, prin. | Fax 557-4459
Lewis & Clark MS | 700/7-8
6901 Burt St 68132 | 402-557-4300
Dr. Lisa Sterba, prin. | Fax 557-4309
Marrs Magnet Center | 700/5-8
5619 S 19th St 68107 | 402-557-4400
Pamela Cohn, prin. | Fax 557-4429
McMillan Magnet MS | 800/7-8
3802 Redick Ave 68112 | 402-557-4500
Gregory Emmel, prin. | Fax 557-4509
Monroe MS | 900/7-8
5105 Bedford Ave 68104 | 402-557-4600
Herman Colvin, prin. | Fax 557-4609
Morton MS | 800/7-8
4606 Terrace Dr 68134 | 402-557-4700
Ivory Woods, prin. | Fax 557-4709
Norris MS | 1,000/7-8
2235 S 46th St 68106 | 402-557-4800
Burrell Williams, prin. | Fax 557-4809
Omaha North HS | 1,800/9-12
4410 N 36th St 68111 | 402-557-3400
Gene Haynes, prin. | Fax 557-3439
Omaha Northwest HS | 1,800/9-12
8204 Crown Point Ave 68134 | 402-557-3500
Bernice Nared, prin. | Fax 557-3539
Omaha South HS | 1,700/9-12
4519 S 24th St 68107 | 402-557-3600
Nancy Faber, prin. | Fax 557-3639

Westside Community SD | 5,800/PK-12
909 S 76th St 68114 | 402-390-2100
Kenneth Bird, supt. | Fax 390-2120
www.westside66.org/
Westside HS | 1,800/9-12
8701 Pacific St 68114 | 402-343-2600
John Crook, prin. | Fax 343-2608
Westside MS | 1,000/7-8
8601 Arbor St 68124 | 402-390-6464
Eric G. Weber, prin. | Fax 390-6454

Assumption/Guadalupe S | 100/3-8
5602 S 22nd St 68107 | 402-734-4504
Cheryl Castle, prin. | Fax 734-4505
Bishop Clarkson Memorial Hospital | Post-Sec.
4350 Dewey Ave 68105 | 402-552-3203
Brownell-Talbot S | 500/PK-12
400 N Happy Hollow Blvd 68132 | 402-556-3772
Diane Desler, prin. | Fax 553-2994
Capitol School of Hairstyling - West | Post-Sec.
2819 S 125th Ave Ste 268 68144 | 402-333-3329
Clarkson College | Post-Sec.
101 S 42nd St 68131 | 402-552-3100
College of Saint Mary | Post-Sec.
7000 Mercy Rd 68106 | 402-399-2400
Concordia Lutheran JSHS | 200/7-12
15656 Fort St 68116 | 402-445-4000
Matthew Korte, prin. | Fax 965-9310
Creighton Preparatory S | 1,000/9-12
7400 Western Ave 68114 | 402-393-1190
John Naatz, prin. | Fax 343-1889
Creighton University | Post-Sec.
2500 California Plz 68178 | 402-280-2700
Duchesne Academy | 300/9-12
3601 Burt St 68131 | 402-558-3800
Laura Hickman, prin. | Fax 558-0051
Grace University | Post-Sec.
1311 S 9th St 68108 | 402-449-2800
Gross HS | 600/9-12
7700 S 43rd St 68147 | 402-734-2000
Dr. Dorothy Ostrowski, prin. | Fax 734-4270
Hamilton College | Post-Sec.
3350 N 90th St 68134 | 402-572-8500
Immanuel Medical Center | Post-Sec.
6901 N 72nd St 68122 | 402-572-2270
ITT Technical Institute | Post-Sec.
9814 M St 68127 | 402-331-2900
Jesuit MS | 100/4-8
2311 N 22nd St 68110 | 402-346-4464
Anthony Connelly, prin. | Fax 341-1817
Madonna S | 50/K-12
6402 N 71st St 68104 | 402-556-1883
Steven Slater, prin. | Fax 556-7332
Marian HS | 700/9-12
7400 Military Ave 68134 | 402-571-2618
Elizabeth Kish, hdmstr. | Fax 571-1952
Mercy HS | 300/9-12
1501 S 48th St 68106 | 402-553-9424
Carolyn Jaworski, prin. | Fax 553-0394
Metropolitan Community College | Post-Sec.
30th & Fort Sts 68111 | 402-449-8300
Metropolitan Community College | Post-Sec.
204th & Dodge St 68103 | 402-457-2000
Metropolitan Community College | Post-Sec.
PO Box 3777 68103 | 402-449-8400
Nebraska Methodist College | Post-Sec.
720 N 87th St 68114 | 402-354-7200
Omaha Christian Academy | 300/PK-12
5612 L St 68117 | 402-399-9565
Timothy Koehn, supt. | Fax 399-0248
Omaha School of Massage Therapy | Post-Sec.
9748 Park Dr 68127 | 402-331-3694
Roncalli HS | 300/9-12
6401 Sorensen Pkwy 68152 | 402-571-7670
Curt Feilmeier, prin. | Fax 571-3216

Skutt Catholic HS | 700/9-12
3131 S 156th St 68130 | 402-333-0818
Patrick J. Slattery, prin. | Fax 333-1790
The Creative Center | Post-Sec.
10850 Emmet St 68164 | 402-898-1000
University of Nebraska at Omaha | Post-Sec.
60th And Dodge St 68182 | 402-554-2800
University of Nebraska Medical Center | Post-Sec.
987020 Nebraska Medical Ctr 68198 | 402-559-4200
Vatterott College | Post-Sec.
11818 I St 68137 | 402-891-9411
Xenon Intl School of Hair Design | Post-Sec.
8516 Park Dr 68127 | 402-393-2933

O Neill, Holt, Pop. 3,721
O'Neill SD | 900/K-12
PO Box 230, | 402-336-3775
Amy Shane, supt. | Fax 336-4890
O'Neill JSHS | 400/7-12
PO Box 230, | 402-336-1544
Steven Brosz, prin. | Fax 336-1105

St. Mary S | 200/PK-12
326 E Benton St, | 402-336-2664
Candy Conradt, prin. | Fax 336-2055

Orchard, Antelope, Pop. 372
Nebraska USD 1
Supt. — See Royal
Orchard JSHS | 100/7-12
PO Box 269 68764 | 402-893-3215
Dale Martin, prin. | Fax 893-2065

Ord, Valley, Pop. 2,220
Ord SD | 500/K-12
PO Box 199 68862 | 308-728-5013
Max Kroger, supt. | Fax 728-5108
Ord JSHS | 300/7-12
PO Box 199 68862 | 308-728-3241
Gerain Spatz, prin. | Fax 728-5108

Osceola, Polk, Pop. 915
Osceola SD | 300/K-12
PO Box 198 68651 | 402-747-3121
Kenneth Heinz, supt. | Fax 747-3041
www.esu7.org/~oweb/osceola.html
Osceola JSHS | 100/9-12
PO Box 198 68651 | 402-747-3121
Russ Gade, prin. | Fax 747-3041
Osceola MS | 50/7-8
PO Box 198 68651 | 402-747-3121
Russ Gade, prin. | Fax 747-3041

Oshkosh, Garden, Pop. 839
Garden County HSD | 100/9-12
PO Box 230 69154 | 308-772-3242
Lewis Gellett, supt. | Fax 772-3039
Garden County HS | 100/9-12
PO Box 230 69154 | 308-772-3242
Dave Barker, prin. | Fax 772-3039

Garden County SD | 100/K-8
PO Box 230 69154 | 308-772-3336
Lewis Gellett, supt. | Fax 772-4059
Other Schools – See Lewellen

Osmond, Pierce, Pop. 769
Osmond SD | 300/K-12
PO Box 458 68765 | 402-748-3777
Ted Hillman, supt. | Fax 748-3210
Osmond JSHS | 200/7-12
PO Box 458 68765 | 402-748-3777
Randy Jochum, prin. | Fax 748-3210

Overton, Dawson, Pop. 654
Overton SD | 300/PK-12
PO Box 310 68863 | 308-987-2424
Mark A. Aten, supt. | Fax 987-2349
Overton JSHS | 200/7-12
PO Box 310 68863 | 308-987-2424
Mitch Kubicek, prin. | Fax 987-2349

Oxford, Furnas, Pop. 849
Southern Valley SD | 500/K-12
43739 Highway 89 68967 | 308-868-2222
Chuck Lambert, supt. | Fax 868-2223
teachers.esu11.org/sovalley/
Southern Valley JSHS | 300/7-12
43739 Highway 89 68967 | 308-868-2222
Brent Hollinger, prin. | Fax 868-2223

Palmer, Merrick, Pop. 456
Palmer SD | 200/K-12
PO Box 248 68864 | 308-894-3065
Shawn A. Scott, supt. | Fax 894-8245
www.palmer.esu7.org/school/school.html
Palmer JSHS | 100/7-12
PO Box 248 68864 | 308-894-3065
Shawn A. Scott, prin. | Fax 894-8245

Palmyra, Otoe, Pop. 546
Palmyra SD | 500/K-12
PO Box 130 68418 | 402-780-5327
Clyde Childers, supt. | Fax 780-5328
Palmyra JSHS | 200/7-12
PO Box 130 68418 | 402-780-5327
David Bottrell, prin. | Fax 780-5328

Papillion, Sarpy, Pop. 17,829
Papillion-La Vista SD | 8,400/PK-12
420 S Washington St 68046 | 402-537-9998
Harlan Metschke, supt. | Fax 537-6216
www.paplv.esu3.org
Papillion JHS | 1,000/7-9
423 S Washington St 68046 | 402-898-0424
John A McGill, prin. | Fax 898-0430
Papillion-Lavista SHS | 1,300/10-12
402 E Centennial Rd 68046 | 402-898-0400
James Glover, prin. | Fax 898-0415

Papillion-La Vista South HS | 700/10-12
10799 Highway 370 68046 | 402-829-4600
Enid A. Schonewise, prin. | Fax 827-1330
Other Schools – See La Vista

Pawnee City, Pawnee, Pop. 966
Pawnee City SD | 300/K-12
PO Box 393 68420 | 402-852-2988
Wayne Kohler, supt. | Fax 852-2993
Pawnee City JSHS | 100/7-12
PO Box 393 68420 | 402-852-2988
Robert West, prin. | Fax 852-2993

Paxton, Keith, Pop. 561
Paxton Consolidated SD | 200/K-12
PO Box 368 69155 | 308-239-4283
Delbert F. Dack, supt. | Fax 239-4359
userweb.esu16.org/~ppaxton/school.html
Paxton JSHS | 100/7-12
PO Box 368 69155 | 308-239-4283
Sheri M. Chittenden, prin. | Fax 239-4359

Pender, Thurston, Pop. 1,135
Pender SD | 400/K-12
PO Box 629 68047 | 402-385-3244
Joe Sherwood, supt. | Fax 385-3342
Pender JSHS | 200/7-12
PO Box 629 68047 | 402-385-3244
Carol Hilker, prin. | Fax 385-3342

Peru, Nemaha, Pop. 846

Peru State College | Post-Sec.
PO Box 10 68421 | 402-872-3815

Petersburg, Boone, Pop. 345
Boone Central SD
Supt. — See Albion
Boone Central MS | 100/7-8
PO Box 240 68652 | 402-386-5302
Mary Thieman, prin. | Fax 386-5464

Pierce, Pierce, Pop. 1,750
Pierce SD | 700/K-12
201 N Sunset St 68767 | 402-329-4677
Daniel Navrkal, supt. | Fax 329-4678
Pierce JSHS | 400/7-12
201 N Sunset St 68767 | 402-329-6217
Mark Brahmer, prin. | Fax 329-4678

Pilger, Stanton, Pop. 375
Wisner-Pilger SD
Supt. — See Wisner
Wisner-Pilger MS | 100/7-8
PO Box 325 68768 | 402-396-3566
David Ludwig, prin. | Fax 529-3477

Plainview, Pierce, Pop. 1,314
Plainview SD | 400/K-12
PO Box 638 68769 | 402-582-4993
Donovan Betterman, supt. | Fax 582-4665
Plainview JSHS | 200/7-12
PO Box 638 68769 | 402-582-4991
Randall Klooz, prin. | Fax 582-4665

Plattsmouth, Cass, Pop. 7,031
Plattsmouth SD | 1,600/K-12
1916 E Highway 34 68048 | 402-296-3322
Renee Jacobson, supt. | Fax 296-3342
www.plattsmouthschools.org/
Plattsmouth HS | 500/9-12
1916 E Highway 34 68048 | 402-296-3322
Connie Heinen, prin. | Fax 296-3342
Plattsmouth MS | 500/5-8
1724 8th Ave 68048 | 402-296-3174
Mark Smith, prin. | Fax 296-2910

Pleasanton, Buffalo, Pop. 350
Pleasanton SD | 200/K-12
PO Box 190 68866 | 308-388-2041
Ronald Wymore, supt. | Fax 388-5502
Pleasanton JSHS | 100/7-12
PO Box 190 68866 | 308-388-2041
Ronald Wymore, prin. | Fax 388-5502

Polk, Polk, Pop. 306
High Plains Community SD | 300/K-12
PO Box 29 68654 | 402-765-2271
Dennis Gray, supt. | Fax 765-3332
High Plains HS | 100/9-12
PO Box 29 68654 | 402-765-3331
Cletus Arasmith, prin. | Fax 765-3332
Other Schools – See Clarks

Ponca, Dixon, Pop. 1,033
Ponca SD | 400/K-12
PO Box 568 68770 | 402-755-2241
Philip Wineland, supt. | Fax 755-2992
poncaweb.esu1.org/PHS.htm
Ponca JSHS | 200/7-12
PO Box 568 68770 | 402-755-2241
Michelle Rinas, prin. | Fax 755-2992

Potter, Cheyenne, Pop. 415
Potter-Dix SD | 200/K-12
PO Box 189 69156 | 308-879-4434
Kevin Thomas, supt. | Fax 879-4566
www.pdcoyotes.com
Potter-Dix HS | 100/7-12
PO Box 189 69156 | 308-879-4434
Mike Mitchell, prin. | Fax 879-4566

Prague, Saunders, Pop. 331
Prague SD | 100/K-12
PO Box 98 68050 | 402-663-4388
Gene L. Burton, supt. | Fax 663-4312
Prague JSHS | 100/7-12
PO Box 98 68050 | 402-663-4388
Raymond Collins, prin. | Fax 663-4312

Ralston, Douglas, Pop. 6,241
Ralston SD — 3,000/PK-12
8545 Park Dr 68127 — 402-331-4700
Virginia Moon, supt. — Fax 331-4843
www.ralstonschools.org/
Ralston HS — 900/9-12
8969 Park Dr 68127 — 402-331-7373
Greg Shepard, prin. — Fax 331-7345
Ralston MS — 500/7-8
8202 Lakeview St 68127 — 402-331-4701
Kathleen Krzycki, prin. — Fax 331-5376

Randolph, Cedar, Pop. 908
Randolph SD 45 — 400/K-12
PO Box 755 68771 — 402-337-0252
Tedsen Hillman, supt. — Fax 337-0235
www.randolphpublic.org/
Randolph JSHS — 200/7-12
PO Box 755 68771 — 402-337-0252
Steven Rinehart, prin. — Fax 337-0235

Ravenna, Buffalo, Pop. 1,308
Ravenna SD — 500/K-12
PO Box 8400 68869 — 308-452-3249
Dwaine Uttecht, supt. — Fax 452-3172
Ravenna JSHS — 200/7-12
PO Box 8400 68869 — 308-452-3249
Devon Huebert, prin. — Fax 452-3172

Raymond, Lancaster, Pop. 192
Raymond Central SD — 700/K-12
1800 W Agnew Rd 68428 — 402-785-2615
Thomas Rother, supt. — Fax 785-2097
www.rcentral.org
Raymond JSHS — 400/7-12
1800 W Agnew Rd 68428 — 402-785-2685
Ivan Dixon, prin. — Fax 785-2097

Red Cloud, Webster, Pop. 1,062
Red Cloud SD — 300/K-12
121 W 7th Ave 68970 — 402-746-2818
Joan Reznicek, supt. — Fax 746-2817
www.esu9.org/%7Eredcloud/
Red Cloud JSHS — 100/7-12
121 W 7th Ave 68970 — 402-746-2818
Joan M Reznicek, prin. — Fax 746-2817

Rising City, Butler, Pop. 386
Rising City SD — 200/PK-12
PO Box 160 68658 — 402-542-2216
Daniel Alberts, supt. — Fax 542-2265
Rising City JSHS — 100/7-12
PO Box 160 68658 — 402-542-2216
Daniel J. Alberts, prin. — Fax 542-2265

Roseland, Adams, Pop. 237
Silver Lake SD — 300/K-12
PO Box 8 68973 — 402-756-6611
Gale McDonald, supt. — Fax 756-6613
Silver Lake JSHS — 100/7-12
PO Box 8 68973 — 402-756-6611
Kenneth Mahoney, prin. — Fax 756-6613

Royal, Antelope, Pop. 72
Nebraska USD 1 — 600/K-12
PO Box 98 68773 — 402-893-2068
William A. Kuester, supt. — Fax 893-9949
neunified1.esu8.org/
Other Schools – See Clearwater, Orchard, Verdigre

Rushville, Sheridan, Pop. 926
Gordon-Rushville SD
Supt. — See Gordon
Gordon-Rushville MS — 100/6-8
PO Box 590 69360 — 308-327-2448
William Paul, prin. — Fax 327-2504

Saint Edward, Boone, Pop. 757
Saint Edward SD — 200/K-12
PO Box C 68660 — 402-678-2282
Dr. Rodger Lenhard, supt. — Fax 678-2284
Saint Edward JSHS — 100/7-12
PO Box C 68660 — 402-678-2282
Dr. Rodger Lenhard, prin. — Fax 678-2284

Saint Paul, Howard, Pop. 2,257
Saint Paul SD — 700/K-12
PO Box 325 68873 — 308-754-4433
Douglas Ackles, supt. — Fax 754-5374
Saint Paul JSHS — 300/7-12
PO Box 325 68873 — 308-754-4433
John Weitzel, prin. — Fax 754-5374

Sargent, Custer, Pop. 624
Sargent SD — 200/K-12
PO Box 366 68874 — 308-527-4119
Robert Brown, supt. — Fax 527-3332
Sargent JSHS — 100/7-12
PO Box 366 68874 — 308-527-4119
Donald Seifried, prin. — Fax 527-3332

Schuyler, Colfax, Pop. 5,381
Schuyler Central HSD — 400/9-12
401 Adam St 68661 — 402-352-3527
Robin Stevens, supt. — Fax 352-5552
Schuyler Central HS — 400/9-12
401 Adam St 68661 — 402-352-3527
Joyce Baumert, prin. — Fax 352-5552

Scotia, Greeley, Pop. 297
North Loup Scotia SD — 200/K-12
PO Box 307 68875 — 308-245-3201
Gene Haddix, supt. — Fax 245-9133
Scotia JSHS — 100/7-12
PO Box 307 68875 — 308-245-3201
Richard Johnson, prin. — Fax 245-9133

Scottsbluff, Scotts Bluff, Pop. 14,774
Scottsbluff SD — 2,900/PK-12
2601 Broadway 69361 — 308-635-6200
Gary L. Reynolds, supt. — Fax 635-6217
www.sbps.net/

Bluffs MS — 600/6-8
23rd & Broadway 69361 — 308-635-6270
James Schmucker, prin. — Fax 635-6271
Scottsbluff HS — 900/9-12
313 E 27th St 69361 — 308-635-6230
Charles Nighswonger, prin. — Fax 635-6240

Regional West Medical Center — Post-Sec.
4021 Avenue B 69361 — 308-635-3711
Western Nebraska Community College — Post-Sec.
1601 E 27th St 69361 — 308-635-3606

Scribner, Dodge, Pop. 942
Scribner-Snyder SD — 500/PK-12
PO Box L 68057 — 402-664-2567
Richard A. Alt, supt. — Fax 664-2708
www.sstrojans.esu2.org/
Scribner-Snyder JSHS — 100/7-12
PO Box L 68057 — 402-664-2567
Alfred Ivey, prin. — Fax 664-2708

Seward, Seward, Pop. 6,752
Seward SD — 1,300/PK-12
410 South St 68434 — 402-643-2941
Marlene Uhing, supt. — Fax 643-4986
www.sewardpublicschools.org
Seward HS — 500/9-12
532 Northern Heights Dr 68434 — 402-643-2988
Ronald Lamberty, prin. — Fax 643-2599
Seward MS — 400/5-8
237 S 3rd St 68434 — 402-643-2986
Steven P. Schrad, prin. — Fax 643-6686

Concordia University — Post-Sec.
800 N Columbia Ave 68434 — 402-643-3651

Shelby, Polk, Pop. 662
Shelby SD — 300/K-12
PO Box 218 68662 — 402-527-5946
Larry C. Stick, supt. — Fax 527-5133
shelby.esu7.org
Shelby JSHS — 100/7-12
PO Box 218 68662 — 402-527-5946
Keith Jurrens, prin. — Fax 527-5133

Shelton, Buffalo, Pop. 1,142
Shelton SD — 400/K-12
PO Box 610 68876 — 308-647-6742
Earnest Hall, supt. — Fax 647-5233
Shelton JSHS — 200/7-12
PO Box 610 68876 — 308-647-5459
Gale R. Dunkhas, prin. — Fax 647-5233

Platte Valley Academy — 50/1-12
19338 W Campus Dr 68876 — 308-647-5151
Charles Castle, prin. — Fax 647-5368

Shickley, Fillmore, Pop. 361
Shickley SD — 100/K-12
PO Box 407 68436 — 402-627-3375
Paul D. Sheffield, supt. — Fax 627-2003
Shickley JSHS — 100/7-12
PO Box 407 68436 — 402-627-3375
— Fax 627-2003

Sidney, Cheyenne, Pop. 6,443
Sidney SD — 1,700/PK-12
2103 King St 69162 — 308-254-5855
John Hakonson, supt. — Fax 254-5756
www.sidneyraiders.com/
Sidney HS — 400/9-12
1122 19th Ave 69162 — 308-254-5893
Todd Rhodes, prin. — Fax 254-5992
Sidney MS — 200/7-8
1122 19th Ave 69162 — 308-254-5853
Jill Finkey, prin. — Fax 254-5854

Western Nebraska Community College — Post-Sec.
69162 — 800-221-9682

South Sioux City, Dakota, Pop. 12,030
South Sioux City SD — 3,200/K-12
PO Box 158 68776 — 402-494-2425
Steve Rector, supt. — Fax 494-3916
www.sioux.esu1.org
South Sioux City MS — 800/7-9
3625 G St 68776 — 402-494-3061
John Laughhunn, prin. — Fax 494-8427
South Sioux City SHS — 700/10-12
3301 G St 68776 — 402-494-2433
Patrick Nauroth, prin. — Fax 494-2464

Spalding, Greeley, Pop. 520
Spalding SD — 100/K-12
PO Box 220 68665 — 308-497-2431
Benje Hookstra, supt. — Fax 497-2141
Spalding JSHS — 100/7-12
PO Box 220 68665 — 308-497-2431
Benje Hookstra, prin. — Fax 497-2141

Spalding Academy — 100/K-12
PO Box 310 68665 — 308-497-2103
Kevin Kirwan, prin. — Fax 497-2105

Spencer, Boyd, Pop. 518
West Boyd USD
Supt. — See Butte
Spencer-Naper HS — 100/7-12
PO Box 10 68777 — 402-589-1333
Michael Sanne, prin. — Fax 589-1142

Springfield, Sarpy, Pop. 1,482
South Sarpy SD 46 — 1,000/K-12
14801 S 108th St 68059 — 402-592-1300
Richard Hindalong, supt. — Fax 597-8551
www.sarpy46.org/
Platteview Central JHS — 200/7-8
14801 S 108th St 68059 — 402-339-5052
Ralph Glock, prin. — Fax 339-3166

Platteview HS — 300/9-12
14801 S 108th St 68059 — 402-339-3606
Scott Shepard, prin. — Fax 339-3751

Springview, Keya Paha, Pop. 235
Keya Paha County HSD — 50/9-12
PO Box 219 68778 — 402-497-3501
Katherine Meink, supt. — Fax 497-4321
Keya Paha County HS — 50/9-12
PO Box 219 68778 — 402-497-3501
Katherine Meink, supt. — Fax 497-4321

Stanton, Stanton, Pop. 1,645
Stanton Community SD — 500/K-12
PO Box 749 68779 — 402-439-2233
Michael Sieh, supt. — Fax 439-2270
www.esu8.org/~stanton/highschool/home.html
Stanton MSHS — 200/7-12
PO Box 749 68779 — 402-439-2250
Chris Stogdill, prin. — Fax 439-2270

Stapleton, Logan, Pop. 277
Stapleton SD — 200/PK-12
PO Box 128 69163 — 308-636-2252
Daniel Hutchison, supt. — Fax 636-2618
Stapleton JSHS — 100/7-12
PO Box 128 69163 — 308-636-2252
Craig D. Marshall, prin. — Fax 636-2618

Stella, Richardson, Pop. 212
SE Nebraska Consolidated SD — 200/K-12
RR 1 Box 1C 68442 — 402-883-2600
Michael R. Montgomery, supt. — Fax 883-2020
SE Nebraska Cons HS — 100/7-12
RR 1 Box 1C 68442 — 402-883-2400
Michael R. Montgomery, prin. — Fax 883-2020

Sterling, Johnson, Pop. 497
Sterling SD — 200/K-12
PO Box 39 68443 — 402-866-4761
James Duval, supt. — Fax 866-4771
Sterling JSHS — 100/7-12
PO Box 39 68443 — 402-866-4761
Gregory Peterson, prin. — Fax 866-4771

Stromsburg, Polk, Pop. 1,179
Cross County Community SD — 400/K-12
PO Box 525 68666 — 402-764-2156
Rady Page, supt. — Fax 764-2156
Cross County HS - Stromsburg — 100/9-12
PO Box 525 68666 — 402-764-5521
Evan Wieseman, prin. — Fax 764-8294
Other Schools – See Benedict

Stuart, Holt, Pop. 597
Stuart SD — 200/K-12
PO Box 99 68780 — 402-924-3302
Robert J. Hanzlik, supt. — Fax 924-3676
Stuart JSHS — 100/7-12
PO Box 99 68780 — 402-924-3302
Robert J. Hanzlik, prin. — Fax 924-3676

Sumner, Dawson, Pop. 236
Sumner-Eddyville-Miller SD — 200/K-12
PO Box 126 68878 — 308-752-2925
Dennis Chipman, supt. — Fax 752-2600
SEM JSHS — 100/7-12
PO Box 126 68878 — 308-752-2925
James Langin, prin. — Fax 752-2600

Superior, Nuckolls, Pop. 1,946
South Central Nebraska Unified SD
Supt. — See Fairfield
Superior JSHS — 200/7-12
PO Box 288 68978 — 402-879-3257
Robert Cook, prin. — Fax 879-3022

Sutherland, Lincoln, Pop. 1,189
Sutherland SD — 400/PK-12
PO Box 217 69165 — 308-386-4656
Michael Cunning, supt. — Fax 386-2426
userweb.esu16.org/~shs/
Sutherland JSHS — 200/7-12
PO Box 217 69165 — 308-386-4656
Brian Maschmann, prin. — Fax 386-2426

Sutton, Clay, Pop. 1,429
Sutton SD — 400/PK-12
PO Box 590 68979 — 402-773-5569
Larry Weaver, supt. — Fax 773-5578
Sutton JSHS — 200/7-12
PO Box 590 68979 — 402-773-4303
Elizabeth Ericson, prin. — Fax 773-5578

Syracuse, Otoe, Pop. 1,812
Syracuse-Dunbar-Avoca SD — 600/K-12
PO Box P 68446 — 402-269-2383
Bradley Buller, supt. — Fax 269-2224
Syracuse JSHS — 300/7-12
PO Box P 68446 — 402-269-2381
Joy Stilmock, prin. — Fax 269-3028

Table Rock, Pawnee, Pop. 251
Humboldt & Table Rock Steinauer USD 2007
Supt. — See Humboldt
Humboldt & Table Rock Steinauer MS — 100/5-8
PO Box F 68447 — 402-839-2085
Don Day, prin. — Fax 839-2088

Taylor, Loup, Pop. 211
Loup County SD — 100/K-12
PO Box 170 68879 — 308-942-6115
Wayne Ruppert, supt. — Fax 942-6248
Loup County JSHS — 100/7-12
PO Box 170 68879 — 308-942-6115
Ken Sheets, prin. — Fax 942-6248

Tecumseh, Johnson, Pop. 1,707
Tecumseh SD — 400/K-12
PO Box 338 68450 — 402-335-3320
Randall Marymee, supt. — Fax 335-3346

Tecumseh JSHS 200/7-12
PO Box 338 68450 402-335-3328
Richard Lester, prin. Fax 335-3346

Tekamah, Burt, Pop. 1,842
Tekamah-Herman SD 600/PK-12
112 N 13th St 68061 402-374-2157
Kevin Nolan, supt. Fax 374-2155
www.tekamah.esu2.org/
Tekamah JSHS 300/7-12
112 N 13th St 68061 402-374-2156
Daniel Gross, prin. Fax 374-2155

Thedford, Thomas, Pop. 193
Thedford RHSD 100/7-12
PO Box 248 69166 308-645-2230
Bevin Brown, supt. Fax 645-2618
webquests.esu16.org:8080/ttrojans/
Thedford Rural JSHS 100/7-12
PO Box 248 69166 308-645-2230
Gary Klahn, prin. Fax 645-2618

Tilden, Madison, Pop. 1,083
Elkhorn Valley SD 400/K-12
PO Box 430 68781 402-368-5301
Ken Navratil, supt. Fax 368-5338
www.esu8.org/~falcon/ev.html
Elkhorn Valley JSHS 200/7-12
PO Box 430 68781 402-368-5301
Beth Johnsen, prin. Fax 368-5338

Trenton, Hitchcock, Pop. 488
Hitchcock County USD 300/K-12
PO Box 69044 308-334-5575
Cynthia Huff, supt. Fax 334-5381
Hitchcock County HS 100/7-12
PO Box 368 69044 308-334-5575
John Varilek, prin. Fax 334-5381

Tryon, McPherson
McPherson County HSD 50/9-12
PO Box 38 69167 308-587-2262
France Blanchard, supt. Fax 587-2571
userweb.esu16.org/~mchs/
McPherson County HS 50/9-12
PO Box 38 69167 308-587-2262
Fax 587-2571

Utica, Seward, Pop. 835
Centennial SD 600/PK-12
PO Box 187 68456 402-534-2291
Brian Maher, supt. Fax 534-2291
www.centennialpublic.org/
Centennial JSHS 300/7-12
PO Box 187 68456 402-534-2321
Ryan Ruhl, prin. Fax 534-2291

Valentine, Cherry, Pop. 2,784
Valentine CSD 400/K-8
239 N Wood St 69201 402-376-3367
Jamie Isom, supt. Fax 376-3386
Valentine MS 200/6-8
239 N Wood St 69201 402-376-3367
Ron Billings, prin. Fax 376-3386

Valentine Rural HSD 300/9-12
431 N Green St 69201 402-376-2730
Jamie S. Isom, supt. Fax 376-2736
www.vhs.esu17.org
Valentine Rural HS 300/9-12
431 N Green St 69201 402-376-2730
Dave Renning, prin. Fax 376-2736

Valley, Douglas, Pop. 1,823
Douglas County West Community SD 500/K-12
PO Box 378 68064 402-359-2583
Robert Albers, supt. Fax 359-4371
www.dcwest.org/
Douglas County West HS 200/9-12
PO Box 378 68064 402-359-2121
JoAnn Stevens, prin. Fax 359-4371
Other Schools – See Waterloo

Verdigre, Knox, Pop. 501
Nebraska USD 1
Supt. — See Royal
Verdigre JSHS 100/7-12
204 2nd St 68783 402-668-2275
Michael Zulkoski, prin. Fax 668-2276

Waco, York, Pop. 255

Nebraska Lutheran HS 100/9-12
203 Kendall St 68460 402-728-5236
Charron Craig, prin. Fax 728-5433

Wahoo, Saunders, Pop. 4,010
Wahoo SD 900/PK-12
2201 N Locust St 68066 402-443-3051
Edward Rastovski, supt. Fax 443-4731
www.wahooschools.org/
Wahoo HS 300/9-12
2201 N Locust St 68066 402-443-4332
Rick Swearengin, prin. Fax 443-4731
Wahoo MS 200/6-8
2201 N Locust St 68066 402-443-3101
Timothy A. Farley, prin. Fax 443-4731

Bishop Neumann Central HS 300/7-12
202 S Linden St 68066 402-443-4151
Rev. Troy Schweiger, prin. Fax 443-5551

Wakefield, Dixon, Pop. 1,336
Wakefield SD 500/K-12
PO Box 330 68784 402-287-2012
Michael Moody, supt. Fax 287-2014
www.wakefieldschools.org/
Wakefield JSHS 200/7-12
PO Box 330 68784 402-287-2012
Bill Heimann, prin. Fax 287-2014

Wallace, Lincoln, Pop. 320
Wallace SD 65 R 200/K-12
PO Box 127 69169 308-387-4323
Wendel L. Cass, supt. Fax 387-4322
Wallace JSHS 100/7-12
PO Box 127 69169 308-387-4323
Larry Seger, prin. Fax 387-4322

Walthill, Thurston, Pop. 893
Walthill SD 200/K-12
PO Box 3C 68067 402-846-5432
Larry Frost, supt. Fax 846-5029
walthweb.esu1.org/
Walthill JSHS 100/7-12
PO Box 3C 68067 402-846-5432
Henry Eggert, prin. Fax 846-5029

Waterloo, Douglas, Pop. 474
Douglas County West Community SD
Supt. — See Valley
Douglas County West MS 100/5-8
PO Box 328 68069 402-779-2646
Mitch Mollring, prin. Fax 779-2534

Wauneta, Chase, Pop. 608
Wauneta-Palisade SD 300/K-12
PO Box 368 69045 308-394-5700
Charles Isom, supt. Fax 394-5962
www.geocities.com/wauneta.geo
Wauneta-Palisade HS 100/9-12
PO Box 368 69045 308-394-5650
Rod Ready, prin. Fax 394-5962
Wauneta Palisade JHS 50/7-8
PO Box 368 69045 308-394-5650
Rod Ready, prin. Fax 394-5962

Wausa, Knox, Pop. 603
Wausa SD 200/K-12
PO Box 159 68786 402-586-2255
Robert C. Marks Ed.D., supt. Fax 586-2406
wausaweb.esu1.org/
Wausa JSHS 100/7-12
PO Box 159 68786 402-586-2255
Fax 586-2406

Waverly, Lancaster, Pop. 2,598
Waverly SD 1,300/K-12
PO Box 426 68462 402-786-2321
Dan Ernst, supt. Fax 786-2799
www.dist145.esu6.org/
Waverly HS 600/9-12
PO Box 426 68462 402-786-2765
Philip Warrick, prin. Fax 786-2760
Waverly MS 400/6-8
PO Box 426 68462 402-786-2348
Phillip Picquet, prin. Fax 786-2760

Wayne, Wayne, Pop. 5,391
Wayne SD 900/K-12
611 W 7th St 68787 402-375-3150
Joseph Reinert, supt. Fax 375-5251
Wayne HS 300/9-12
611 W 7th St 68787 402-375-3150
Mark E. Hanson, prin. Fax 375-5251
Wayne MS 300/5-8
611 W 7th St 68787 402-375-2230
Timothy Krupicka, prin. Fax 375-2342

Wayne State College Post-Sec.
1111 Main St 68787 402-375-7000

Weeping Water, Cass, Pop. 1,130
Weeping Water SD 400/K-12
PO Box 206 68463 402-267-2445
Brian Gregg, supt. Fax 267-5217
www.weepingwaterps.org/
Weeping Water JSHS 200/7-12
PO Box 206 68463 402-267-4265
Keith Leckron, prin. Fax 267-5217

West Point, Cuming, Pop. 3,545
West Point SD 700/PK-12
PO Box 188 68788 402-372-5860
Theodore De Turk, supt. Fax 372-5458
www.wpcadets.org/
West Point-Beemer JSHS 400/7-12
PO Box 188 68788 402-372-5546
Stephen Grizzle, prin. Fax 372-2252

Central Catholic HS 200/9-12
419 E Decatur St 68788 402-372-5326
Ken Hajek, prin. Fax 372-5327

Wilber, Saline, Pop. 1,790
Wilber-Clatonia SD 500/K-12
PO Box 487 68465 402-821-2266
David D Rokusek, supt. Fax 821-3013
Wilber-Clatonia JSHS 300/7-12
PO Box 487 68465 402-821-2508
Ronald Oltman, prin. Fax 821-3013

Wilcox, Kearney, Pop. 359
Wilcox-Hildreth SD 300/K-12
PO Box 190 68982 308-478-5265
Roger Boyer, supt. Fax 478-5260
www.esu11.org/wilcohildr/home.htm
Wilcox-Hildreth HS 100/9-12
PO Box 190 68982 308-478-5265
Victor Young, prin. Fax 478-5260
Other Schools – See Hildreth

Winnebago, Thurston, Pop. 779
Winnebago SD 400/K-12
PO Box KK 68071 402-878-2224
Fred Williams, supt. Fax 878-2472
winnebago.esu1.org/
Winnebago JSHS 200/7-12
PO Box KK 68071 402-878-2224
Fax 878-2472

Little Priest Tribal College Post-Sec.
PO Box 720 68071 402-878-2380

Winside, Wayne, Pop. 444
Winside SD 300/K-12
PO Box 158 68790 402-286-4466
Donavon Leighton, supt. Fax 286-4466
winside.esu1.org/
Winside JSHS 100/7-12
PO Box 158 68790 402-286-4465
Jeffrey Messersmith, prin. Fax 286-4466

Wisner, Cuming, Pop. 1,222
Wisner-Pilger SD 500/K-12
PO Box 580 68791 402-529-3249
Alan Harms, supt. Fax 529-3477
www.wisnerpilger.org/
Wisner HS 200/9-12
PO Box 580 68791 402-529-3249
Christopher Uttecht, prin. Fax 529-3477
Other Schools – See Pilger

Wolbach, Greeley, Pop. 276
Greeley-Wolbach SD
Supt. — See Greeley
Greeley-Wolbach JHS 7-8
PO Box 67 68882 308-246-5232
Todd Beck, prin. Fax 246-5234

Wood River, Hall, Pop. 1,202
Wood River RHSD 300/7-12
PO Box 518 68883 308-583-2249
Tom Moore, supt. Fax 583-2395
Wood River Rural JSHS 300/7-12
PO Box 518 68883 308-583-2249
David Barrett, prin. Fax 583-2395

Wymore, Gage, Pop. 1,629
Southern SD 1 500/K-12
PO Box 237 68466 402-645-3326
William Shimeall, supt. Fax 645-8049
www.southernschools.org/
Southern JSHS 200/7-12
PO Box 237 68466 402-645-3326
Steven Whitwer, prin. Fax 645-8049

Wynot, Cedar, Pop. 178
Wynot SD 200/K-12
PO Box 157 68792 402-357-2121
John Werner, supt. Fax 357-2524
Wynot HS 100/9-12
PO Box 157 68792 402-357-2121
Richard Higgins, prin. Fax 357-2524
Wynot MS 50/5-8
PO Box 157 68792 402-357-2121
Richard Higgins, prin. Fax 357-2524

York, York, Pop. 7,873
York SD 1,300/K-12
2918 N Delaware Ave 68467 402-362-6655
Terrence Kenealy, supt. Fax 362-6943
york.ne.schoolwebpages.com
York HS 500/9-12
1005 Duke Dr 68467 402-362-6655
Dan Endorf, prin. Fax 362-2994
York MS 300/6-8
1200 N East Ave 68467 402-362-6655
Richard Moses, prin. Fax 362-6831

York College Post-Sec.
912 Kiplinger Ave 68467 402-363-5600

Yutan, Saunders, Pop. 1,199
Yutan SD 500/K-12
1200 2nd St 68073 402-625-2243
Kevin Johnson, supt. Fax 625-2812
Yutan JSHS 200/7-12
1200 2nd St 68073 402-625-2241
Dan Schnoes, prin. Fax 625-2812

NEVADA

NEVADA DEPARTMENT OF EDUCATION
700 E Fifth St, Carson City 89701-5096
Telephone 775-687-9200
Fax 775-687-9101
Website http://www.doe.nv.gov/

Superintendent of Instruction   Keith Rheault

NEVADA BOARD OF EDUCATION
700 E Fifth St, Carson City 89701-5096

President   John Gwaltney

PUBLIC, PRIVATE AND CATHOLIC SECONDARY SCHOOLS

Alamo, Lincoln
Lincoln County SD
Supt. — See Panaca
Pahranagat Valley HS — 100/9-12
PO Box 298 89001 — 775-725-3321
Steven Hansen, prin. — Fax 725-3334
Pahranagat Valley MS — 100/6-8
PO Box 539 89001 — 775-725-3601
Randal Allen, prin. — Fax 725-3358

Austin, Lander
Lander County SD
Supt. — See Battle Mountain
Austin JSHS — 100/6-12
PO Box 160 89310 — 775-964-2467
Toby Melver, prin. — Fax 964-1206

Battle Mountain, Lander, Pop. 3,542
Lander County SD — 1,300/K-12
PO Box 1300 89820 — 775-635-2886
Curtis Jordan, supt. — Fax 635-5347
www.lander.k12.nv.us
Battle Mountain HS — 400/9-12
PO Box 1330 89820 — 775-635-5436
Amy Kester, prin. — Fax 635-5459
Battle Mountain JHS — 200/7-8
PO Box 1360 89820 — 775-635-2415
Lorraine Sparks, prin. — Fax 635-6118
Other Schools – See Austin

Beatty, Nye, Pop. 1,623
Nye County SD
Supt. — See Tonopah
Beatty HS — 100/9-12
PO Box 806 89003 — 775-553-2595
Nancy Hein, prin. — Fax 553-2887

Boulder City, Clark, Pop. 15,314
Clark County SD
Supt. — See Las Vegas
Boulder City HS — 800/9-12
1101 5th St 89005 — 702-799-8200
Jeanne M. Donadio, prin. — Fax 799-8230
Garrett MS — 600/6-8
1200 Avenue G 89005 — 702-799-8290
Jamey Lynn Hood, prin. — Fax 799-8252

Carlin, Elko, Pop. 2,060
Elko County SD
Supt. — See Elko
Carlin S — 800/K-12
PO Box 730 89822 — 775-754-6317
Norm Mahlberg, prin. — Fax 754-2175

Carson City, Carson City, Pop. 54,311
Carson City SD — 8,600/K-12
PO Box 603 89702 — 775-283-2000
Dr. Mary Pierczynski, supt. — Fax 283-2090
www.carsoncityschools.com
Carson HS — 2,600/9-12
1111 N Saliman Rd 89701 — 775-283-1600
Fred Perdomo, prin. — Fax 283-1790
Carson MS — 1,200/6-8
1140 W King St 89703 — 775-283-2800
Sam Santillo, prin. — Fax 283-2890
Eagle Valley MS — 1,000/6-8
4151 E Fifth St 89701 — 775-283-2600
F. Mariani, prin. — Fax 283-2690

Capital Christian S — 300/PK-12
1600 Snyder Ave 89701 — 775-883-3009
Keith Squires, prin. — Fax 883-3012
Carson City Beauty Academy — Post-Sec.
2531 N Carson St 89706 — 775-885-9853
Western Nevada Community College — Post-Sec.
2201 W College Pkwy 89703 — 775-445-3000

Dayton, Lyon, Pop. 2,217
Lyon County SD
Supt. — See Yerington
Dayton HS — 600/9-12
335 Dayton Valley Rd 89403 — 775-246-6240
Teri White, prin. — Fax 246-6245
Dayton IS — 500/6-8
315 Dayton Valley Rd 89403 — 775-246-6250
Neal Freitas, prin. — Fax 246-6253

Dyer, Esmeralda

Deep Springs College — Post-Sec.
HC 72 Box 45001 89010 — 760-872-2000

Elko, Elko, Pop. 16,075
Elko County SD — 12,000/K-12
PO Box 1012 89803 — 775-738-5196
Antoinette Cavanaugh, supt. — Fax 738-5857
www.elko.k12.nv.us
Elko HS — 1,200/9-12
987 College Ave 89801 — 775-738-7281
Mike Altenburg, prin. — Fax 738-9616
Elko JHS — 700/7-8
777 Country Club Dr 89801 — 775-738-7236
Mollie Kuhn, prin. — Fax 753-3876
Adult HS — Adult
PO Box 1012 89803 — 775-753-2233
Susan Jones, prin. — Fax 753-2257
Other Schools – See Carlin, Jackpot, Owyhee, Spring
Creek, Wells, West Wendover

Great Basin College — Post-Sec.
1500 College Pkwy 89801 — 800-343-2724

Ely, White Pine, Pop. 3,691
White Pine County SD — 1,400/K-12
1135 Avenue C 89301 — 775-289-4851
Bob Dolezal, supt. — Fax 289-3999
www.whitepine.k12.nv.us
White Pine County HS — 400/9-12
1800 Bobcat Dr 89301 — 775-289-4811
Adam Young, prin. — Fax 289-1542
White Pine County MS — 300/6-8
844 Aultman St 89301 — 775-289-4841
Aaron Hansen, prin. — Fax 289-1565
Other Schools – See Lund

Eureka, Eureka
Eureka County SD — 200/K-12
PO Box 249 89316 — 775-237-5373
Ben Zunino, supt. — Fax 237-5014
www.eureka.k12.nv.us
Eureka County JSHS — 100/7-12
PO Box 237 89316 — 775-237-5361
Ken Fujii, prin. — Fax 237-5113

Fallon, Churchill, Pop. 7,748
Churchill County SD — 4,400/K-12
545 E Richards St 89406 — 775-423-5184
Dr. Carolyn Ross, supt. — Fax 423-2959
www.churchill.k12.nv.us
Churchill County HS — 1,300/9-12
1222 S Taylor St 89406 — 775-423-2181
John Riley, prin. — Fax 423-8968
Churchill County JHS — 700/7-8
650 S Maine St 89406 — 775-423-7701
Judy Pratt, prin. — Fax 423-8010
Lahontan Valley HS — 9-12
690 S Maine St 89406 — 775-423-6322
Keith Boone, prin. — Fax 423-6364

Fernley, Lyon, Pop. 10,047
Lyon County SD
Supt. — See Yerington
Fernley HS — 700/9-12
1300 US Highway 95A S 89408 — 775-575-3400
Sue Segura, prin. — Fax 575-3406
Fernley IS — 700/5-8
320 US Highway 95A S 89408 — 775-575-3390
Jeff Freeman, prin. — Fax 575-3394
Fernley Adult Education Center — Adult
1300 US Highway 95A S 89408 — 775-575-3409
Kathleen Jameson, prin. — Fax 575-3399

Gabbs, Nye, Pop. 947
Nye County SD
Supt. — See Tonopah
Gabbs S — 400/K-12
PO Box 147 89409 — 775-285-2692
Selway Mulkey, prin. — Fax 285-2381

Gardnerville, Douglas, Pop. 2,177
Douglas County SD
Supt. — See Minden

Carson Valley MS — 900/7-9
PO Box 157 89410 — 775-782-2265
Marty Swisher, prin. — Fax 782-7341
Pau-Wa-Lu MS — 800/7-9
PO Box 157 89410 — 775-265-6100
Robbin Pedrett, prin. — Fax 265-1653

Gerlach, Washoe
Washoe County SD
Supt. — See Reno
Gerlach MSHS — 100/6-12
555 East Sunset Blvd 89412 — 775-557-2326
Carol Kaufmann, prin. — Fax 557-2587

Hawthorne, Mineral, Pop. 4,162
Mineral County SD — 800/K-12
PO Box 1540 89415 — 775-945-2403
Steven Cook, supt. — Fax 945-3709
gohawthorne.com
Hawthorne MS — 300/4-8
PO Box 1060 89415 — 775-945-2411
Hugh Qualls, prin. — Fax 945-1003
Mineral County HS — 300/7-12
PO Box 938 89415 — 775-945-3332
Margaret Ruybalid, prin. — Fax 945-3371

Henderson, Clark, Pop. 214,852
Clark County SD
Supt. — See Las Vegas
Basic HS — 2,100/9-12
400 Palo Verde Dr 89015 — 702-799-8000
Susan Segal, prin. — Fax 799-8966
Brown JHS — 1,400/6-8
307 Cannes St 89015 — 702-799-8900
Andre Long, prin. — Fax 799-3511
Community College HS South — 900/9-12
700 College Dr, — 702-651-3080
Dennis Birr, prin. — Fax 651-3075
Coronado HS — 2,300/9-12
1001 Coronado Center Dr 89052 — 702-799-6800
Lee Koelliker, prin. — Fax 799-6839
Foothill HS — 2,000/9-12
800 College Dr, — 702-799-3500
Gretchen K. Crehan, prin. — Fax 799-3524
Greenspun JHS — 1,600/6-8
140 N Valle Verde Dr 89074 — 702-799-0920
Elizabeth Howe, prin. — Fax 799-0765
Green Valley HS — 3,000/9-12
460 N Arroyo Grande Blvd 89014 — 702-799-0950
Jeffrey Horn, prin. — Fax 799-0717
Liberty HS — 1,100/9-12
3700 Liberty Heights Ave 89052 — 702-799-2270
Kelly Bucherie, prin. — Fax 799-6858
Mannion MS — 6-8
155 Paradise Hills Dr E, — 702-799-3020
David W. Erbach, prin. — Fax 799-3501
Miller MS — 1,500/6-8
2400 Cozy Hill Cir 89052 — 702-799-2260
Tamathy Larnerd, prin. — Fax 799-1309
Webb MS — 6-8
2200 Reunion Ave 89052 — 702-799-1305
William Skorkowsky, prin. — Fax 799-1310
White MS — 1,800/6-8
1661 Galleria Dr 89014 — 702-799-0777
Kim Grytdahl, prin. — Fax 799-7690

Art Institute of Las Vegas — Post-Sec.
2350 Corporate Cir 89074 — 702-369-9944
DeVry University — Post-Sec.
2490 Paseo Verde Pkwy #150 89074 — 702-933-9700
ITT Technical Institute — Post-Sec.
168 N Gibson Rd 89014 — 702-558-5404
Lake Mead Christian Academy — 500/K-12
540 E Lake Mead Pkwy 89015 — 702-565-5831
Gayle Sue Blakeley, admin. — Fax 566-6206
Las Vegas College — Post-Sec.
170 N Stephanie St Ste 145 89074 — 702-368-6200
Touro Univ. Coll. / Osteopathic Medicine — Post-Sec.
874 American Pacific Dr 89014 — 702-856-3262
Warren-Walker Green Valley Academy — 300/5-12
1165 Sandy Ridge Ave 89052 — 702-616-3027
Ron Bennett, hdmstr. — Fax 616-2065

Incline Village, Washoe, Pop. 7,119
Washoe County SD
Supt. — See Reno
Incline HS — 400/9-12
PO Box 6860 89450 — 775-832-4260
John Clark, prin. — Fax 832-4208
Incline MS — 300/6-8
931 Southwood Blvd 89451 — 775-832-4220
Harry Haaser, prin. — Fax 832-4210

Sierra Nevada College-Lake Tahoe — Post-Sec.
999 Tahoe Blvd 89451 — 800-332-8666

Indian Springs, Clark, Pop. 1,164
Clark County SD
Supt. — See Las Vegas
Indian Springs HS — 100/9-12
PO Box 1088 89018 — 702-382-8011
Katherine Christensen, prin. — Fax 879-3142
Indian Springs MS — 100/6-8
400 Sky Rd 89018 — 702-382-8011
Katherine Christensen, prin. — Fax 879-3142

Jackpot, Elko
Elko County SD
Supt. — See Elko
Jackpot S — 700/K-12
PO Box 463 89825 — 775-755-2374
Brian Messmer, prin. — Fax 755-2291

Las Vegas, Clark, Pop. 517,017
Clark County SD — 263,500/PK-12
2832 E Flamingo Rd 89121 — 702-799-5310
Walt Rulffes, supt. — Fax 799-5505
www.ccsd.net/
Advance Technologies Academy — Vo/Tech
2501 Vegas Dr 89106 — 702-799-7870
Karen Diamond, prin. — Fax 799-0656
Arbor View HS — 9-12
7500 Whispering Sands Dr 89131 — 702-799-6669
Patrick Hayden, prin.
Bailey MS — 6-8
2500 N Hollywood Blvd 89156 — 702-799-4811
Karen Stansfield-Paquett, prin. — Fax 799-4807
Becker MS — 1,500/6-8
9151 Pinewood Hills Dr 89134 — 702-799-4460
Karen L. West, prin. — Fax 799-4470
Bonanza HS — 2,700/9-12
6665 Del Rey Ave 89146 — 702-799-4000
Dawn L. Shupe, prin. — Fax 799-4078
Brinley MS — 1,200/6-8
2480 Maverick St 89108 — 702-799-4550
Rosalind Gibson, prin. — Fax 799-4549
Cadwallader MS — 1,100/6-8
7775 Elkhorn Rd 89131 — 702-799-6692
Kathryn Singer, prin. — Fax 799-4536
Canarelli MS — 1,200/6-8
7808 S Torrey Pines Dr 89139 — 702-799-1340
Kristy Keller, prin. — Fax 799-5715
Cannon JHS — 1,100/6-8
5850 Euclid St 89120 — 702-799-5600
Elmer Manzanares, prin. — Fax 799-5644
Cashman MS — 1,200/6-8
4622 W Desert Inn Rd 89102 — 702-799-5880
Joy J. Lea, prin. — Fax 799-5947
Centennial HS — 2,900/9-12
10200 Centennial Pkwy 89149 — 702-799-3440
Gerald Velasquez, prin. — Fax 799-3443
Chaparral HS — 2,700/9-12
3850 Annie Oakley Dr 89121 — 702-799-7580
Penny R. Elliott, prin. — Fax 799-0776
Cimarron-Memorial HS — 2,800/9-12
2301 N Tenaya Way 89128 — 702-799-4400
Janice Rowland, prin. — Fax 799-4425
Clark HS — 2,600/9-12
4291 Pennwood Ave 89102 — 702-799-5800
Ronnie Smith, prin. — Fax 799-5813
Community College HS West — 1,000/9-12
6375 W Charleston Blvd 89146 — 702-651-5030
Dennis Birr, prin. — Fax 651-5035
Cortney JHS — 1,700/6-8
5301 E Hacienda Ave 89122 — 702-799-2400
Teresa Holden, prin. — Fax 799-2407
Del Sol HS — 9-12
3100 E Patrick Ln 89120 — 702-799-6830
John A. Barlow, prin. — Fax 799-2235
Desert Pines HS — 2,800/9-12
3800 Harris Ave 89110 — 702-799-2196
— Fax 799-2198
Durango HS — 2,600/9-12
7100 W Dewey Dr 89113 — 702-799-5850
Mark Gums, prin. — Fax 799-5855
Eldorado HS — 2,700/9-12
1139 Linn Ln 89110 — 702-799-7200
Richard Carranza, prin. — Fax 799-7255
Fertitta MS — 1,200/6-8
9905 W Mesa Vista Ave 89148 — 702-799-1900
Patricia LaMonica, prin. — Fax 799-5688
Fremont MS — 1,500/6-8
1100 E Saint Louis Ave 89104 — 702-799-5558
Ben Montoya, prin. — Fax 799-5566
Garside JHS — 1,500/6-8
300 S Torrey Pines Dr 89107 — 702-799-4245
Stephanie Wong, prin. — Fax 799-4296
Gibson MS — 1,200/6-8
3900 W Washington Ave 89107 — 702-799-4700
Trent Day, prin. — Fax 799-4705
Guinn MS — 1,100/6-8
4150 S Torrey Pines Dr 89103 — 702-799-5900
Georgia Taton, prin. — Fax 799-5905
Harney MS — 1,700/6-8
1580 S Hollywood Blvd 89142 — 702-799-3240
Grant A. Hanevold, prin. — Fax 799-3286
Hyde Park MS — 1,700/6-8
900 Hinson St 89107 — 702-799-4260
James Kuzma, prin. — Fax 799-0348

Johnson JHS — 1,500/6-8
7701 Ducharme Ave 89145 — 702-799-4480
Terry Ann Sobrero, prin. — Fax 799-4497
Keller MS — 1,800/6-8
301 Fogg St 89110 — 702-799-3220
April Key, prin. — Fax 799-3226
Knudson MS — 1,400/6-8
2400 Atlantic St 89104 — 702-799-7470
Northey Henderson, prin. — Fax 799-0157
Las Vegas Academy HS — 1,400/9-12
315 S 7th St 89101 — 702-799-7800
Stephen T. Clark, prin. — Fax 799-7948
Las Vegas HS — 3,300/9-12
6500 E Sahara Ave 89142 — 702-799-0180
Patrice Johnson, prin. — Fax 799-0192
Lawrence JHS — 1,600/6-8
4410 S Juliano Rd 89147 — 702-799-2540
Kathryn Mead, prin. — Fax 799-2563
Leavitt MS — 1,700/6-8
4701 Quadrel St 89129 — 702-799-4699
Shanna Mack, prin. — Fax 799-4528
Lied MS — 1,600/6-8
5350 W Tropical Pkwy 89130 — 702-799-4620
Taylor Powers, prin. — Fax 799-4626
Mack MS — 6-8
4250 Karen Ave 89121 — 702-799-2005
Joseph Murphy, prin. — Fax 799-2412
Martin MS — 1,400/6-8
2800 Stewart Ave 89101 — 702-799-7922
Regina J. Adams, prin. — Fax 799-7959
Molasky MS — 1,500/6-8
7801 W Gilmore Ave 89129 — 702-799-3400
Bart Mangino, prin. — Fax 799-3407
Monaco MS — 1,700/6-8
1870 N Lamont St 89115 — 702-799-3670
Russ Reinhart, prin. — Fax 799-3202
O'Callaghan MS — 1,900/6-8
1450 Radwick Dr 89110 — 702-799-7340
Susan Echols, prin. — Fax 799-8870
Orr MS — 1,200/6-8
1562 E Katie Ave 89119 — 702-799-5573
George Leavens, prin. — Fax 799-0297
Palo Verde HS — 3,500/9-12
333 S Pavilion Center Dr 89144 — 702-799-1450
Daniel Phillips, prin. — Fax 799-1455
Robison MS — 1,500/6-8
825 Marion Dr 89110 — 702-799-7300
Arnold Sanchez, prin. — Fax 799-7302
Rogich MS — 1,300/6-8
235 N Pavilion Center Dr 89144 — 702-799-6040
Lynda Pearson, prin. — Fax 799-6094
Saville MS — 6-8
8101 N Torrey Pines Dr 89131 — 702-799-3460
Kathy A. Kulas, prin. — Fax 799-4511
Sawyer MS — 1,600/6-8
5450 Redwood St 89118 — 702-799-5980
Kim Friel, prin. — Fax 799-5969
Schofield MS — 1,600/6-8
8625 Spencer St 89123 — 702-799-2290
Elizabeth C. Angelcor, prin. — Fax 799-5717
Shadow Ridge HS — 2,000/9-12
5050 Brent Ln 89131 — 702-799-6699
Thomas Barberini, prin. — Fax 799-4698
Sierra Vista HS — 2,700/9-12
8100 W Robindale Rd 89113 — 702-799-6820
Emil T. Wozniak, prin. — Fax 799-6847
Silverado HS — 3,000/9-12
1650 Silver Hawk Ave 89123 — 702-799-5790
Mark Coleman, prin. — Fax 799-5744
Silvestri JHS — 1,800/6-8
1055 E Silverado Ranch Blvd, — 702-799-2240
Debbie Brockett, prin. — Fax 799-2247
Southern Nevada Vocational Technical Ctr — Vo/Tech
5710 Mountain Vista St 89120 — 702-799-7500
Richard Arguello, prin. — Fax 799-0896
Spring Valley HS — 9-12
3750 S Buffalo Dr 89147 — 702-799-2580
Robert A. Gerye, prin. — Fax 799-1288
Tarkanian MS — 6-8
5800 W Pyle Ave 89141 — 702-799-6801
Brenda Larsen-Mitchell, prin. — Fax 799-6805
Valley HS — 2,900/9-12
2839 Burnham Ave, — 702-799-5450
Ron Montoya, prin. — Fax 799-1074
Von Tobel MS — 1,400/6-8
2436 N Pecos Rd 89115 — 702-799-7280
Jessie Phee, prin. — Fax 799-7286
Western HS — 2,200/9-12
4601 W Bonanza Rd 89107 — 702-799-4080
Lillie Pearl Morgan, prin. — Fax 799-4104
West MS — 1,200/6-8
2050 Saphire Stone Ave 89106 — 702-799-3120
Jimmie Jones, prin. — Fax 799-3126
Woodbury MS — 1,100/6-8
3875 E Harmon Ave 89121 — 702-799-7660
Greg Snelling, prin. — Fax 799-0805
Desert Rose Adult HS — Adult
1251 Robin St 89106 — 702-799-6240
Sandra Ransel, prin. — Fax 799-6260
Other Schools – See Boulder City, Henderson, Indian Springs, Laughlin, Logandale, Mesquite, North Las Vegas, Overton, Sandy Valley

Academy of Hair Design — Post-Sec.
4445 W Charleston Blvd 89102 — 702-878-1185
Aces-Full Academy for Casino Dealers — Post-Sec.
557 E Sahara Ave Ste 220 89104 — 702-369-1194
American Career Institute — Post-Sec.
2340 Paseo Del Prado #D-208 89102 — 702-222-3522
Associated Pathologist Laboratories — Post-Sec.
4230 Burnham Ave 89119 — 702-733-7866
Bishop Gorman HS — 1,100/9-12
1801 S Maryland Pkwy 89104 — 702-732-1945
Dr. Paul Sullivan, prin. — Fax 732-2856
Calvary Chapel Christian S — 500/K-12
7175 W Oquendo Rd 89113 — 702-248-8879
John Weaver, admin. — Fax 220-7461

Dahan Institute of Massage Studies — Post-Sec.
10381 Starthistle Ln 89135 — 702-434-1338
Faith Lutheran JSHS — 1,200/6-12
2015 S Hualapai Way 89117 — 702-804-4400
Kevin Dunning, dir. — Fax 804-4488
Gateway Christian Academy — 50/PK-12
1900 N Gateway Rd 89115 — 702-452-7111
Ginny Proffitt, prin. — Fax 438-2781
Heritage College — Post-Sec.
3315 Spring Mountain Rd 89102 — 702-368-2338
High-Tech Institute — Post-Sec.
2320 S Rancho Dr 89102 — 702-385-6700
Las Vegas Junior Academy — 100/K-10
6059 W Oakey Blvd 89146 — 702-871-7208
Janet Block, prin. — Fax 364-5456
Le Cordon Bleu College of Culinary Arts — Post-Sec.
1451 Center Crossing Rd 89144 — 702-365-7690
Marinello School of Beauty — Post-Sec.
5001 E Bonanza Rd Ste 110 89110 — 702-796-6200
Meadows S — 800/K-12
8601 Scholar Ln 89128 — 702-254-1610
William Richardson, hdmstr. — Fax 254-2452
Mountain View Christian S — 700/PK-12
3900 E Bonanza Rd 89110 — 702-452-1300
Crystal McClanahan, prin. — Fax 452-0499
Paradise Christian Academy — 200/PK-12
2525 Emerson Ave 89121 — 702-732-8256
Teena Oglesby, admin. — Fax 732-8515
PCI Dealers School — Post-Sec.
920 S Valley View Blvd 89107 — 702-877-4724
Pima Medical Institute — Post-Sec.
3333 E Flamingo Rd 89121 — 702-458-7650
Southern Nevada Univ of Cosmetology — Post-Sec.
3430 E Tropicana Ave 89121 — 702-458-6333
Trinity Christian S — 300/PK-12
950 E Sahara Ave 89104 — 702-735-5778
Thurban Warrick, prin. — Fax 731-0961
University Baptist Academy — 50/K-12
1490 E University Ave 89119 — 702-732-3385
Elizabeth Scafani, prin.
University of Nevada Las Vegas — Post-Sec.
4505 S Maryland Pkwy 89154 — 800-334-8658

Laughlin, Clark, Pop. 4,791
Clark County SD
Supt. — See Las Vegas
Laughlin MSHS — 400/6-12
1900 Cougar Dr 89029 — 702-298-1996
Richard Edwards, prin. — Fax 298-5493

Logandale, Clark
Clark County SD
Supt. — See Las Vegas
Moapa Valley HS — 600/9-12
2400 St Joseph St 89021 — 702-397-2611
Sheri L. Hales-Davies, prin. — Fax 397-2892

Lovelock, Pershing, Pop. 1,898
Pershing County SD — 800/K-12
PO Box 389 89419 — 775-273-7819
Daniel Fox, supt. — Fax 273-2668
www.pershing.k12.nv.us
Pershing County HS — 300/9-12
PO Box 990 89419 — 775-273-2625
Charles Safford, prin. — Fax 273-2163
Pershing County MS — 100/7-8
PO Box 1020 89419 — 775-273-1200
Charles Safford, prin. — Fax 273-3191

Lund, White Pine
White Pine County SD
Supt. — See Ely
Lund JSHS — 100/7-12
PO Box 129 89317 — 775-238-5200
Alan Hedges, prin. — Fax 238-0208

Mc Dermitt, Humboldt, Pop. 373
Humboldt County SD
Supt. — See Winnemucca
Mc Dermitt JSHS — 100/7-12
PO Box 98 89421 — 775-532-8761
John Moddrell, prin. — Fax 532-8017

Mesquite, Clark, Pop. 11,780
Clark County SD
Supt. — See Las Vegas
Hughes MS — 500/6-8
550 Hafen Ln 89027 — 702-346-3250
Clifford Hughes, prin. — Fax 346-3095
Virgin Valley HS — 600/9-12
820 Valley View Dr 89027 — 702-346-2780
M. DeLos Perkins, prin. — Fax 346-7265

Minden, Douglas, Pop. 1,441
Douglas County SD — 7,100/K-12
PO Box 1888 89423 — 775-782-5134
John Soderman, supt. — Fax 782-3162
dcsd.k12.nv.us
Douglas HS — 1,500/10-12
PO Box 1888 89423 — 775-782-5136
Mark VanVoorst, prin. — Fax 782-7039
Other Schools – See Gardnerville, Zephyr Cove

Sierra Lutheran HS — 50/9-12
1617 Water St Ste S 89423 — 775-782-0060
Debbie Conner, admin. — Fax 782-0454

North Las Vegas, Clark, Pop. 144,502
Clark County SD
Supt. — See Las Vegas
Area Tech Trade Ctr — Vo/Tech
444 W Brooks Ave 89030 — 702-799-8300
Cynthia Morris, prin. — Fax 799-8371
Bridger MS — 1,400/6-8
2505 N Bruce St 89030 — 702-799-7185
Milana Winter, prin. — Fax 799-7074
Canyon Springs HS — 9-12
350 E Alexander Rd 89032 — 702-799-1870
Ronan Matthew, prin. — Fax 799-1876

Cheyenne HS | 2,900/9-12
3200 W Alexander Rd 89032 | 702-799-4830
Jeffrey Geihs, prin. | Fax 799-4856
Community College HS East | 1,000/9-12
3200 E Cheyenne Ave 89030 | 702-651-4071
Dennis Birr, prin. | Fax 651-4627
Cram MS | 2,100/6-8
1900 W Deer Springs Way 89084 | 702-799-7020
Jeri Plunkett, prin. | Fax 799-8346
Findlay MS | 6-8
333 W Tropical Pkwy 89031 | 702-799-3160
David Bechtel, prin. | Fax 799-3169
Johnston MS | 6-8
2855 Lawrence St, | 702-799-7001
Kenneth Fowler, prin. | Fax 799-7010
Legacy HS | 9-12
150 W Deer Springs Way 89084 | 702-799-1777
Tammy Malich, prin. | Fax 799-1701
Mojave HS | 2,800/9-12
5302 Goldfield St 89031 | 702-799-0432
Charity Varnado, prin. | Fax 799-0437
Rancho HS | 3,300/9-12
1900 Searles Ave 89030 | 702-799-7000
Robert Chesto, prin. | Fax 799-8316
Sedway MS | 1,900/6-8
3465 Engelstad St 89032 | 702-799-3880
Evans Rutledge, prin. | Fax 799-1785
Smith MS | 1,100/6-8
1301 E Tonopah Ave 89030 | 702-799-7080
Neddy Alvarez, prin. | Fax 799-7195
Swainston MS | 1,600/6-8
3500 W Gilmore Ave 89032 | 702-799-4860
Bevelyn Smothers, prin. | Fax 799-4806

American Institute of Technology | Post-Sec.
4610 Vandenberg Dr Ste A, | 702-644-1234
Community College of Southern Nevada | Post-Sec.
3200 E Cheyenne Ave 89030 | 702-651-4000

Overton, Clark
Clark County SD
Supt. — See Las Vegas
Lyon MS | 400/6-8
179 S Anderson 89040 | 702-397-8610
David Wilson, prin. | Fax 397-2754

Owyhee, Elko, Pop. 908
Elko County SD
Supt. — See Elko
Owyhee S | 700/K-12
PO Box 100 89832 | 775-757-3400
Gwen Anne Thacker, prin. | Fax 757-3663

Pahrump, Nye, Pop. 7,424
Nye County SD
Supt. — See Tonopah
Clarke MS | 1,000/6-8
4201 N Blagg Rd 89060 | 775-727-5546
Jeff Wales, prin. | Fax 727-7104
Pahrump Valley HS | 1,000/9-12
501 E Calvada Blvd 89048 | 775-727-7737
Kent Roberts, prin. | Fax 727-7722

New Hope Christian Academy | 100/PK-12
781 West St 89048 | 775-751-1867
Julie Schmidt, admin. | Fax 751-3387

Panaca, Lincoln
Lincoln County SD | 1,000/K-12
PO Box 118 89042 | 775-728-4471
Clark M. Hardy, supt. | Fax 728-4435
www.lincoln.k12.nv.us
Lincoln County HS | 200/9-12
PO Box 268 89042 | 775-728-4481
Craig Babcock, prin. | Fax 728-4484
Meadow Valley MS | 100/7-8
PO Box 567 89042 | 775-728-4655
Marty Soderborg, prin. | Fax 728-4302
Other Schools – See Alamo

Reno, Washoe, Pop. 193,882
Washoe County SD | 60,400/K-12
PO Box 30425 89520 | 775-348-0200
Paul Dugan, supt. | Fax 348-0304
www.washoe.k12.nv.us
Billinghurst MS | 1,200/7-8
6685 Chesterfield Ln 89523 | 775-746-5870
Ken Cervantes, prin. | Fax 746-5875
Clayton MS | 700/7-8
1295 Wyoming Ave 89503 | 775-746-5860
Daniel Garfinkle, prin. | Fax 746-5864
Cold Springs MS | 6-8
18235 Cody Ct 89506 | 775-348-0200
Roberta Duval, prin.
Damonte Ranch MSHS | 1,200/7-12
10500 Rio Wrangler Pkwy, | 775-851-5656
Denise Hausauer, prin. | Fax 851-5663
Galena HS | 1,700/9-12
3600 Butch Cassidy Dr 89511 | 775-851-5630
Rick Borba, prin. | Fax 851-5607
Hare Occupational Center | Vo/Tech
350 Hunter Lake Dr 89509 | 775-857-4947
Michele Lewis, admin.

Hug HS | 1,200/9-12
2880 Sutro St 89512 | 775-333-5300
Andrew Kelley, prin. | Fax 333-5312
McQueen HS | 1,900/9-12
6055 Lancer St 89523 | 775-746-5880
John Carlson, prin. | Fax 747-6883
North Valleys HS | 2,000/9-12
1470 E Golden Valley Rd 89506 | 775-677-5499
Cinda Gifford, prin. | Fax 677-5497
O'Brien MS | 1,200/7-8
10500 Stead Blvd 89506 | 775-677-5420
Scott Grange, prin. | Fax 677-5423
Pine MS | 900/7-8
4800 Neil Rd 89502 | 775-689-2550
Bryn Lapenta, prin. | Fax 689-2539
Regional Technical Institute | Vo/Tech
380 Edison Way 89502 | 775-861-4418
Michele Lewis, prin. | Fax 861-4415
Reno HS | 1,800/9-12
395 Booth St 89509 | 775-333-5050
Bob Sullivan, prin. | Fax 333-5058
Swope MS | 800/7-8
901 Keele Dr 89509 | 775-333-5330
Dr. Michele Collins, prin. | Fax 333-5083
TMCC Magnet SHS | 200/11-12
7000 Dandini Blvd 89512 | 775-674-7660
Susan Mayes-Smith, prin. | Fax 674-7931
Traner MS | 600/7-8
1700 Carville Dr 89512 | 775-333-5130
Mike Bumgartner, prin. | Fax 333-5135
Vaughn MS | 800/7-8
1200 Bresson Ave 89502 | 775-333-5160
Ginny Knowles, prin. | Fax 333-5118
Washoe MSHS | 500/7-12
777 W 2nd St 89503 | 775-333-5150
Heather Murray, prin. | Fax 333-5122
Wooster HS | 1,500/9-12
1331 E Plumb Ln 89502 | 775-333-5100
Jess Castillo, prin. | Fax 333-5108
Other Schools – See Gerlach, Incline Village, Sparks

Bishop Manogue HS | 600/9-12
110 Bishop Manogue Dr 89511 | 775-336-6000
Tim Petersen, prin. | Fax 336-6015
Career College of Northern Nevada | Post-Sec.
1195 Corporate Blvd Ste A 89502 | 775-856-2266
Church Academy | 100/K-12
1205 N McCarran Blvd 89512 | 775-329-5848
Ron Poe, prin. | Fax 329-3360
Morrison University | Post-Sec.
10315 Professional Cir #201, | 775-850-0700
Reno Tahoe Job Training Academy | Post-Sec.
130B E Plumb Ln 89502 | 775-329-5665
Sierra Nevada HS | 500/9-12
5005 Echo Ave 89506 | 775-789-0948
Dr. Joseph Reading, prin. | Fax 789-1091
Silver State Adventist S | 100/K-10
PO Box 11950 89510 | 775-322-0714
 | Fax 322-8064
Truckee Meadows Community College | Post-Sec.
7000 Dandini Blvd 89512 | 775-673-7000
University of Nevada 89557 | Post-Sec.
 | 775-784-1110

Round Mountain, Nye
Nye County SD
Supt. — See Tonopah
Round Mountain JSHS | 200/6-12
PO Box 1427 89045 | 775-377-2690
Barbara Floto, prin. | Fax 377-1239

Sandy Valley, Clark
Clark County SD
Supt. — See Las Vegas
Sandy Valley MS | 100/6-8
HC 31 Box 111 89019 | 702-723-5344
Marilyn Miks, prin. | Fax 723-5251

Silver Springs, Lyon, Pop. 2,253
Lyon County SD
Supt. — See Yerington
Silver Stage HS | 400/9-12
3755 W Spruce Ave 89429 | 775-577-5071
Patrick Peters, prin. | Fax 577-5079
Silver Stage MS | 500/5-8
3800 W Spruce Ave 89429 | 775-577-5050
Connie Jackson, prin. | Fax 577-5053

Smith, Lyon, Pop. 1,033
Lyon County SD
Supt. — See Yerington
Smith Valley JSHS | 100/7-12
20 Day Ln 89430 | 775-465-2332
Keri Pommerening, prin. | Fax 465-2681

Sparks, Washoe, Pop. 77,295
Washoe County SD
Supt. — See Reno
Dilworth MS | 700/7-8
255 Prater Way 89431 | 775-353-5740
Ken Cervantes, prin. | Fax 353-5584
Mendive MS | 1,200/7-8
1900 Whitewood Dr 89434 | 775-353-5990
Juliana Annand, prin. | Fax 353-5994

Reed HS | 2,300/9-12
1350 Baring Blvd 89434 | 775-353-5700
Mary Vesco, prin. | Fax 353-5708
Shaw MS | 7-8
600 Eagle Canyon Dr, | 775-425-7777
Dave Fullenwider, prin.
Spanish Springs HS | 1,800/9-12
1065 Eagle Canyon Dr, | 775-425-7733
Ross Gregory, prin. | Fax 425-7735
Sparks HS | 1,200/9-12
820 15th St 89431 | 775-353-5550
Nancy Sanger, prin. | Fax 353-5514
Sparks MS | 900/7-8
2275 18th St 89431 | 775-353-5770
Jay Polish, prin. | Fax 353-5585

Excel Christian S | 100/K-12
740 Baring Blvd 89434 | 775-356-9995
Bonnie Krupa, admin. | Fax 356-9527
Legacy Christian HS | 100/7-12
816 Holman Way 89431 | 775-358-1112
Gregory Root, admin. | Fax 358-5030
Reno Christian Academy | 200/K-12
2100 El Rancho Dr 89431 | 775-331-0909
Kim Troop, admin. | Fax 331-5358

Spring Creek, Elko, Pop. 5,866
Elko County SD
Supt. — See Elko
Spring Creek HS | 900/9-12
14550 Lamoille Hwy 89815 | 775-753-5575
Betty Fobes, prin. | Fax 753-5956
Spring Creek MS | 700/6-8
14650 Lamoille Hwy 89815 | 775-777-1688
Keith Walz, prin. | Fax 777-1738

Tonopah, Nye, Pop. 3,616
Nye County SD | 5,700/K-12
PO Box 113 89049 | 775-482-6258
Dr. William Roberts, supt. | Fax 482-8573
www.nye.k12.nv.us
Tonopah HS | 100/9-12
PO Box 1349 89049 | 775-482-3698
Patsy Jensen, prin. | Fax 482-3935
Other Schools – See Beatty, Gabbs, Pahrump, Round Mountain

Virginia City, Storey
Storey County SD | 500/K-12
PO Box C 89440 | 775-847-0983
Dr. Robert Slaby, supt. | Fax 847-0989
www.storey.k12.nv.us
Virginia City HS | 100/9-12
PO Box C 89440 | 775-847-0992
Patrick Beckwith, prin. | Fax 847-0994
Virginia City MS | 100/6-8
PO Box C 89440 | 775-847-0980
Todd Hess, prin. | Fax 847-0913

Wells, Elko, Pop. 1,281
Elko County SD
Supt. — See Elko
Wells S | 700/K-12
PO Box 338 89835 | 775-752-3837
Jack French, prin. | Fax 752-2470

West Wendover, Elko, Pop. 4,857
Elko County SD
Supt. — See Elko
West Wendover JSHS | 400/7-12
PO Box 3830 89883 | 775-664-3940
Craig Hill, prin. | Fax 664-3944

Winnemucca, Humboldt, Pop. 6,570
Humboldt County SD | 3,700/K-12
310 E 4th St 89445 | 775-623-8100
Charlotte Petersen, supt. | Fax 623-8102
www.humboldt.k12.nv.us
Lowry HS | 1,000/9-12
5375 Kluncy Canyon Rd 89445 | 775-623-8130
Kirk Brower, prin. | Fax 623-8185
Winnemucca JHS | 500/7-8
451 Reinhart St 89445 | 775-623-8120
Ray Garrison, prin. | Fax 623-8208
Other Schools – See Mc Dermitt

Yerington, Lyon, Pop. 3,127
Lyon County SD | 7,700/K-12
25 E Goldfield Ave 89447 | 775-463-6800
Nat Lommori, supt. | Fax 463-6808
lyon.k12.nv.us
Yerington HS | 500/9-12
114 Pearl St 89447 | 775-463-6822
Keith Savage, prin. | Fax 463-6828
Yerington IS | 500/5-8
215 Pearl St 89447 | 775-463-6833
Harriet Hasbrouck, prin. | Fax 463-6840
Other Schools – See Dayton, Fernley, Silver Springs, Smith

Zephyr Cove, Douglas, Pop. 1,434
Douglas County SD
Supt. — See Minden
Kingsbury MS | 200/6-8
PO Box 648 89448 | 775-588-6281
Nancy Rollston, prin. | Fax 588-8893
Whittell HS | 200/9-12
PO Box 677 89448 | 775-588-2446
Janie Gray, prin. | Fax 588-2443

NEW HAMPSHIRE

NEW HAMPSHIRE DEPT. OF EDUCATION
101 Pleasant St, Concord 03301-3852
Telephone 603-271-3494
Fax 603-271-1953
Website http://www.ed.state.nh.us

Commissioner of Education   Lyonel Tracy

NEW HAMPSHIRE BOARD OF EDUCATION
101 Pleasant St, Concord 03301-3852

Chairperson   David Ruedig

SCHOOL ADMINISTRATIVE UNITS (SAU)

SAU 1
Keith Burke, supt., 106 Hancock Rd — 603-924-3336
Peterborough 03458 — Fax 924-6707
www.conval.edu/

SAU 2
Dr. Phillip McCormack, supt. — 603-279-7947
103 Main St, Meredith 03253 — Fax 279-3044
www.sau2.k12.nh.us/

SAU 3
John Moulis, supt. — 603-752-6500
183 Hillside Ave, Berlin 03570 — Fax 752-2528
www.sau3.org/

SAU 4
Marie Ross, supt. — 603-744-5555
20 N Main St, Bristol 03222 — Fax 744-6659
www.newfound.k12.nh.us

SAU 5
Norman Couture, supt. — 603-868-5100
36 Coe Dr, Durham 03824 — Fax 868-6668
www.orcsd.org

SAU 6
Jacqueline Guillette, supt. — 603-543-4200
165 Broad St, Claremont 03743 — Fax 543-4244
www.sau6.k12.nh.us/

SAU 7
Robert Mills, supt. — 603-237-5571
21 Academy St, Colebrook 03576 — Fax 237-5126

SAU 8
Dr. Christine Rath, supt. — 603-225-0811
16 Rumford St, Concord 03301 — Fax 226-2187
www.concord.k12.nh.us

SAU 9
Dr. Carl Nelson, supt. — 603-356-5533
19 Pine St, North Conway 03860 — Fax 356-5144

SAU 10
Dr. John Moody, supt. — 603-432-1210
18 S Main St, Derry 03038 — Fax 432-1264
www.derry.k12.nh.us

SAU 11
Dr. John O'Connor, supt. — 603-516-6800
288 Central Ave, Dover 03820 — Fax 516-6809
www.dover.k12.nh.us/

SAU 12
Dr. Nathan Greenberg, supt. — 603-432-6920
268 Mammoth Rd — Fax 425-1049
Londonderry 03053

SAU 13
Dr. Gwen Poirer, supt. — 603-539-2610
626 Plains Rd, Silver Lake 03875 — Fax 539-9064

SAU 14
Barbara Munsey, supt. — 603-679-5402
213 Main St, Epping 03042 — Fax 679-1237

SAU 15
Armand LaSelva, supt. — 603-622-3731
90 Farmer Rd, Hooksett 03106 — Fax 669-4352

SAU 16
Dr. Arthur Hanson, supt. — 603-775-8653
24 Front St, Exeter 03833 — Fax 775-8673
www.sau16.org/

SAU 17
James O'N eil, supt. — 603-642-3688
178 Main St, Kingston 03848 — Fax 642-7885

SAU 18
Dr. Robert McKenney, supt. — 603-934-3108
119 Central St, Franklin 03235 — Fax 934-3462

SAU 19
Dr. Darrell Lockwood, supt. — 603-497-4818
11 School St, Goffstown 03045 — Fax 497-8425
www.goffstown.k12.nh.us

SAU 20
Patrick Low, supt. — 603-466-3632
123 Main St, Gorham 03581 — Fax 466-3870
www.sau20.org/

SAU 21
James F. Gaylord, supt. — 603-926-8992
2 Alumni Dr, Hampton 03842 — Fax 926-5157
www.sau21.k12.nh.us

SAU 23
Bruce Labs, supt. — 603-787-2113
2975 Dartmouth College Hwy — Fax 787-2118
North Haverhill 03774
www.sau23.k12.nh.us

SAU 24
Dr. Christine Tyrie, supt. — 603-428-3269
PO Box 2417, Henniker 03242 — Fax 428-3850

SAU 25
Ann Remus, supt. — 603-472-3755
103 County Rd, Bedford 03110 — Fax 472-2567
www.sau25.net/

SAU 26
Marjorie Chiafery, supt. — 603-424-6200
36 McElwain St, Merrimack 03054 — Fax 424-6229
www.merrimack.k12.nh.us

SAU 27
Catherine M. Hamblett, supt. — 603-578-3570
1 Highlander Ct, Litchfield 03052 — Fax 886-1267

SAU 28
Dr. Elaine Cutler, supt. — 603-425-1976
PO Box 510, Windham 03087 — Fax 425-1719

SAU 29
Michele Munson, supt. — 603-357-9002
34 West St, Keene 03431 — Fax 357-9012

SAU 30
Robert Champlin, supt. — 603-524-5710
PO Box 309, Laconia 03247 — Fax 528-8442

SAU 31
Kathleen Murphy, supt. — 603-659-5020
186A Main St, Newmarket 03857 — Fax 659-5022

SAU 32
Russell W. Collins, supt. — 603-469-3442
92 Bonner Rd, Meriden 03770 — Fax 469-3985

SAU 33
David Sandmann, supt. — 603-895-4299
43 Harriman Hill Rd — Fax 895-0147
Raymond 03077
www.raymond.k12.nh.us

SAU 34
Dr. Barbara Baker, supt. — 603-464-4466
PO Box 2190, Deering 03244 — Fax 464-4053

SAU 35
Donald Johnson, supt. — 603-444-3925
32 Main St, Littleton 03561 — Fax 444-6299
www.sau35.k12.nh.us

SAU 36
Dr. Dean Cascadden, supt. — 603-837-9363
14 King Sq, Whitefield 03598 — Fax 837-2326
www.sau36.org

SAU 37
Dr. Michael Ludwell, supt. — 603-624-6300
286 Commercial St — Fax 644-0357
Manchester 03101
www.mansd.org

SAU 38
Dr. Kenneth Dassau, supt. — 603-352-6955
600 Old Homestead Hwy — Fax 358-6708
East Swanzey 03446
www.mrsd.org/

SAU 39
Howard P. Coulter, supt. — 603-673-2690
PO Box 849, Amherst 03031 — Fax 672-1786
www.sprise.com/

SAU 40
Robert Suprenant, supt. — 603-673-2202
100 West St, Milford 03055 — Fax 672-8221

SAU 41
Richard Pike, supt. — 603-465-7118
PO Box 1588, Hollis 03049 — Fax 465-3933
www.sau41.k12.nh.us

SAU 42
Julia Earl, supt. — 603-594-4300
PO Box 687, Nashua 03061 — Fax 594-4350
www.nashua.edu

SAU 43
William J. Mealey, supt. — 603-863-3540
9 Depot St Ste 2, Newport 03773 — Fax 863-5368

SAU 44
Judy McGann, supt. — 603-942-1290
569 1st NH Tpke — Fax 942-1295
Northwood 03261

SAU 45
Michael Lancor, supt., PO Box 419 — 603-476-5247
Moultonborough 03254 — Fax 476-8009
www.moultonborough.k12.nh.us

SAU 46
Dr. Michael Martin, supt. — 603-753-6561
105 Community Dr — Fax 753-6023
Penacook 03303

SAU 47
James O'Neill, supt. — 603-532-8100
10 Main St, Jaffrey 03452 — Fax 532-8164
www.sau47.k12.nh.us

SAU 48
Mark Halloran, supt. — 603-536-1254
47 Old Ward Bridge Rd — Fax 536-3545
Plymouth 03264
www.sau48.k12.nh.us/

SAU 49
John Robertson, supt. — 603-569-1658
PO Box 190, Wolfeboro Falls 03896 — Fax 569-6983
www.govwentworth.k12.nh.us

SAU 50
Dr. George Cushing, supt. — 603-422-9572
48 Post Rd, Greenland 03840 — Fax 422-9575
www.sau50.k12.nh.us/

SAU 51
Dr. Owen Conway, supt. — 603-435-5526
175 Barnstead Rd Unit 3 — Fax 435-5331
Pittsfield 03263
www.barnstead.k12.nh.us

SAU 52
Dr. Robert Lister, supt. — 603-431-5080
50 Clough Dr, Portsmouth 03801 — Fax 431-6753
www.cityofportsmouth.com/school/

SAU 53
Thomas Haley, supt. — 603-485-5188
267 Pembroke St, Pembroke 03275 — Fax 485-9529
www.sau53.org

SAU 54
Michael Hopkins, supt. — 603-332-3678
150 Wakefield St Ste 8 — Fax 335-7367
Rochester 03867
www.rochesterschools.com

SAU 55
Dr. Douglas McDonald, supt. — 603-382-6119
30 Greenough Rd, Plaistow 03865 — Fax 382-3334

SAU 56
Karen Soule, supt. — 603-692-4450
51 W High St, Somersworth 03878 — Fax 692-9100

SAU 57
Michael Dalahanty, supt. — 603-893-7040
38 Geremonty Dr, Salem 03079 — Fax 893-7080

SAU 58
Sherwood Fluery, supt. — 603-636-1437
15 Preble St, Groveton 03582 — Fax 636-6102

SAU 59
Donald Parks, supt. — 603-286-4116
433 W Main St, Northfield 03276 — Fax 286-7402
www.winnisquam.k12.nh.us/Sau/index.htm

SAU 60
Joseph Della Badia, supt. — 603-826-7756
PO Box 600, Charlestown 03603 — Fax 826-4430

SAU 61
Brian Blake, supt. — 603-755-2627
356 Main St, Farmington 03835 — Fax 755-2060

SAU 62
Barbara Tremblay, supt. — 603-632-5563
PO Box 789, Enfield 03748 — Fax 632-4181
mascoma.k12.nh.us

SAU 63
Francine Fullam, supt. — 603-878-1026
659 Turnpike Rd # 120 — Fax 878-3871
New Ipswich 03071

SAU 64
William Lander, supt. — 603-473-2326
39 Main St, Union 03887 — Fax 473-2218
www.sau64.k12.nh.us

SAU 65
Thomas Brennan, supt. — 603-526-2051
190 Main St, New London 03257 — Fax 526-2145

SAU 66
Dr. Richard Ayers, supt. — 603-746-5186
204 Maple St, Contoocook 03229 — Fax 746-5714

SAU 67
Kathleen Holt, supt. — 603-224-4728
32 White Rock Hill Rd, Bow 03304 — Fax 224-4111

SAU 68
Michael Cosgriff, supt. — 603-745-2051
PO Box 846, Lincoln 03251 — Fax 745-2352
www.lin-wood.k12.nh.us

SAU 70
Wayne Gersen, supt. — 603-643-6050
45 Lyme Rd, Hanover 03755 — Fax 643-3073
members.valley.net/~SAU70/SAU70HOME.html

SAU 71
Dr. John Handfield, supt. — 603-863-2420
29 School Rd, Lempster 03605 — Fax 863-2451

SAU 72
Normand Tanguay, supt. — 603-875-7890
PO Box 120, Alton 03809 — Fax 875-0391
www.alton.k12.nh.us

SAU 73
Dr. Paul P. DeMinico, supt. — 603-527-9215
47 Cherry Valley Rd, Gilford 03249 — Fax 527-9216

SAU 74
Michael Morgan, supt. — 603-664-2715
41 Province Ln, Barrington 03825 — Fax 664-2609
www.barrington.k12.nh.us

SAU 75
John Moses, supt. — 603-863-9689
PO Box 287, Grantham 03753 — Fax 863-9684

SAU 76
Dr. Gordon Schnare, supt. — 603-795-4431
PO Box 117, Lyme 03768 — Fax 795-9407

SAU 77
Karen Stewart, admin. — 603-638-2800
PO Box 130, Monroe 03771 — Fax 638-2031

SAU 78
Noelle Vitt, supt. 603-353-2170
PO Box 153, Orford 03777 Fax 353-2189
SAU 79
Dr. Harry Fensom, supt. 603-267-9097
PO Box 309, Gilmanton 03237 Fax 267-9498

SAU 80
W. Michael Cozort, supt. 603-267-9223
58 School St, Belmont 03220 Fax 267-9225
www.shaker.k12.nh.us

SAU 81
Philip Bell, supt. 603-886-1235
20 Library St, Hudson 03051
SAU 88
Michael Harris, supt. 603-448-1634
PO Box 488, Lebanon 03766 Fax 448-0602
www.lebanon.k12.nh.us

PUBLIC, PRIVATE AND CATHOLIC SECONDARY SCHOOLS

Allenstown, Merrimack
Allenstown SD
Supt. — See Pembroke
Dupont MS 300/5-8
10 School St 03275 603-485-4474
Betsey Stebbins, prin. Fax 485-1806

Alstead, Cheshire
Fall Mountain Regional SD
Supt. — See Charlestown
Fall Mountain Regional Vocational Center Vo/Tech
RR 1 Box 89 03602 603-835-6319
Heidi Gove, prin. Fax 835-6254
Vilas MS 100/5-8
PO Box 670 03602 603-835-6351
Carol Bennett, prin. Fax 835-2052

Alton, Belknap
Prospect Mountain SD 100/9-12
PO Box 120 03809 603-875-8600
Normand Tanguay, supt.
Prospect Mountain HS 100/9-12
PO Box 1620 03809 603-875-3800
Russell Holden, prin. Fax 875-8200

Amherst, Hillsborough
Amherst SD 1,700/K-8
PO Box 849 03031 603-673-2690
Howard P. Colter, supt. Fax 672-1786
www.sprise.com
Amherst MS 900/5-8
PO Box 966 03031 603-673-8944
Porter Dodge, prin. Fax 673-6774

Souhegan Cooperative SD 1,000/9-12
PO Box 849 03031 603-673-2690
Howard Colter, supt. Fax 672-1786
Souhegan Coop. HS 1,000/9-12
PO Box 1152 03031 603-673-9940
Scott Prescott, prin. Fax 673-0318

Andover, Merrimack

Proctor Academy 300/9-12
PO Box 500 03216 603-735-6000
Mike Henryques, hdmstr. Fax 735-6284

Antrim, Hillsborough, Pop. 1,325
Contoocook Valley SD
Supt. — See Peterborough
Great Brook MS 400/5-8
16 School St 03440 603-588-6630
Richard Nannicelli, prin. Fax 588-3207

Barrington, Strafford
Barrington SD 900/PK-8
41 Province Ln 03825 603-664-2715
Michael Morgan, supt. Fax 664-2609
www.barrington.k12.nh.us
Barrington MS 400/5-8
20 Haley Dr 03825 603-664-2127
Peter Warburton, prin. Fax 664-5275

Good Shepherd S 200/K-12
37 Province Ln 03825 603-664-2742
Elizabeth Shortle, prin. Fax 664-7196

Bedford, Hillsborough
Bedford SD 2,900/PK-8
103 County Rd 03110 603-472-3755
Ann Remus, supt. Fax 472-2567
www.sau.25.net
McKelvie MS 900/6-8
108 Liberty Hill Rd 03110 603-472-3951
Jan Raudonis, prin. Fax 472-4503

Michael's School of Hair Design Post-Sec.
73 S River Rd Ste 26 03110 603-668-4300
Mount Zion Christian S 200/K-12
469 S River Rd 03110 603-606-7930
Robert Carter, hdmstr. Fax 606-7935

Belmont, Belknap
Shaker Regional SD 1,500/PK-12
58 School St 03220 603-267-9223
W. Michael Cozort, supt. Fax 267-9225
www.shaker.k12.nh.us
Belmont HS 500/9-12
255 Seavey Rd 03220 603-267-6525
Marcia Hayward, prin. Fax 267-5962
Belmont MS 500/5-8
38 School St 03220 603-267-9220
Robert Gadomski, prin. Fax 267-9221

Berlin, Coos, Pop. 10,122
Berlin SD 2,400/1-12
183 Hillside Ave 03570 603-752-6500
John Moulis, supt. Fax 752-2528
www.sau3.org/
Berlin HS 600/9-12
550 Willard St 03570 603-752-4122
Gary K. Bisson, prin. Fax 752-8566
Berlin JHS 300/7-8
200 State St 03570 603-752-5311
Beverly A. Dupont, prin. Fax 752-8580
Berlin Reg Voc Ctr Vo/Tech
550 Willard St 03570 603-752-4122
Roland Pinette, prin. Fax 752-8566

New Hampshire Community Tech College Post-Sec.
2020 Riverside Dr 03570 603-752-1113

Bethlehem, Grafton
Profile SD 300/7-12
691 Profile Rd 03574 603-444-3925
Donald Johnson, supt. Fax 444-6299
Profile HS 200/9-12
691 Profile Rd 03574 603-823-7411
Richard Larcom, prin. Fax 823-7490
Profile JHS 100/7-8
691 Profile Rd 03574 603-823-7411
Richard Larcom, prin. Fax 823-7490
Other Schools – See Littleton

White Mountain S 100/9-12
371 W Farm Rd 03574 603-444-2928
Alan T. Popp, hdmstr. Fax 444-1258

Bow, Merrimack
Bow SD 1,800/PK-12
32 White Rock Hill Rd 03304 603-224-4728
Kathleen Holt, supt. Fax 224-4111
www.bownet.org
Bow HS 600/9-12
32 White Rock Hill Rd 03304 603-228-2210
George Edwards, prin. Fax 228-2212
Bow Memorial S 600/5-8
20 Bow Center Rd 03304 603-225-3212
Kirk Spofford, prin. Fax 228-2228

Brentwood, Rockingham

Lighthouse Christian Academy 100/K-12
263 Route 125 03833 603-642-3756
Cheryl Jenkins, admin. Fax 642-7845

Bristol, Grafton, Pop. 1,483
Newfound Area SD 1,500/PK-12
20 N Main St 03222 603-744-5555
Marie Ross, supt. Fax 744-6659
www.newfound.k12.nh.us
Newfound Memorial MS 400/6-8
155 N Main St 03222 603-744-8162
Eric Chase, prin. Fax 744-8037
Newfound Regional HS 500/9-12
150 Newfound Rd 03222 603-744-6006
Michael O'Malley, prin. Fax 744-2526

Canaan, Grafton
Mascoma Valley Regional SD
Supt. — See Enfield
Indian River MS 500/5-8
45 Royal Rd 03741 603-632-4357
Dorothy Campbell, prin. Fax 632-4262
Mascoma Valley Regional HS 500/9-12
27 Royal Rd 03741 603-632-4308
Patrick Andrew, prin. Fax 632-5419

Cardigan Mountain S 200/6-9
62 Alumni Dr 03741 603-523-4321
Thomas Needham, hdmstr. Fax 523-7227

Candia, Rockingham

Remington HS 50/7-12
PO Box 62 03034 603-483-5664
Jeffrey Philbrick, hdmstr. Fax 483-4811

Charlestown, Sullivan, Pop. 1,173
Fall Mountain Regional SD 1,900/PK-12
PO Box 600 03603 603-826-7756
Joseph Della Badia, supt. Fax 826-4430
www.fall-mountain.k12.nh.us
Charlestown MS 200/6-8
PO Box 325 03603 603-826-7711
Dianne Hicks, prin. Fax 826-3102
Other Schools – See Alstead, Langdon, Walpole

Chester, Rockingham

Chester College of New England Post-Sec.
40 Chester St 03036 603-887-4401

Claremont, Sullivan, Pop. 13,355
Claremont SD 2,000/PK-12
165 Broad St 03743 603-543-4200
Jacqueline E. Guillette, supt. Fax 543-4244
www.sau6.k12.nh.us
Claremont MS 500/6-8
107 South St 03743 603-543-4250
Donald Hart, prin. Fax 543-4289
Stevens HS 700/9-12
175 Broad St 03743 603-543-4220
Leo Couture, prin. Fax 543-4220
Sugar River Valley Regional Ctr West Vo/Tech
111 South St 03743 603-543-4291
Jill Edson, prin.

New Hampshire Community Tech College Post-Sec.
1 College Dr 03743 603-542-7744

Colebrook, Coos
Colebrook SD 500/K-12
21 Academy St 03576 603-237-5571
Robert Mills, supt. Fax 237-5126
www.colebrook.k12.nh.us/
Colebrook Academy 200/9-12
13 Academy St 03576 603-237-4280
Priscilla McGuire, prin. Fax 237-5717

Pittsburg SD 200/K-12
21 Academy St 03576 603-237-5571
Robert Mills, supt. Fax 237-5126
Other Schools – See Pittsburg

Concord, Merrimack, Pop. 41,823
Concord SD 5,400/PK-12
16 Rumford St 03301 603-225-0811
Dr. Christine Rath, supt. Fax 226-2187
www.concord.k12.nh.us
Concord HS 1,800/9-12
170 Warren St 03301 603-225-0800
Gene Connolly, prin. Fax 223-2054
Concord Regional Technical Center Vo/Tech
170 Warren St 03301 603-225-0800
Donna Nelson, prin. Fax 225-0826
Rundlett MS 1,300/6-8
144 South St 03301 603-225-0865
George Rogers, prin. Fax 226-3288

Merrimack Valley SD 2,800/PK-12
105 Community Dr 03303 603-753-6561
Michael Martin, supt. Fax 753-6023
www.mv.k12.nh.us
Other Schools – See Penacook

Bishop Brady HS 500/9-12
25 Columbus Ave 03301 603-224-7418
Jean Barker, prin. Fax 228-6664
Concord Academy of Hair Design Post-Sec.
20 S Main St 03301 603-224-2211
Franklin Pierce College Post-Sec.
5 Chenell Dr 03301 603-228-1155
Franklin Pierce Law Center Post-Sec.
2 White St 03301 603-228-9217
Granite State College Post-Sec.
8 Old Suncook Rd 03301 603-228-3000
Hesser College Post-Sec.
25 Hall St 03301 603-225-9200
New Hampshire Technical Institute Post-Sec.
11 Institute Dr 03301 603-271-6484
St. Paul's S 500/9-12
325 Pleasant St 03301 603-229-4600
William Matthews, prin. Fax 229-4892
Trinity Christian S 300/K-12
80 Clinton St 03301 603-225-5410
Peter Flint, prin. Fax 225-3235

Contoocook, Merrimack, Pop. 1,334
Hopkinton SD 1,000/PK-12
204 Maple St 03229 603-746-5186
Dr. Richard Ayers, supt. Fax 746-5714
www.hopkintonschools.org/
Hopkinton HS 400/9-12
297 Park Ave 03229 603-746-4167
Steven Chamberlin, prin. Fax 746-5109
Hopkinton MS 200/7-8
297 Park Ave 03229 603-746-4167
Steven Chamberlin, prin. Fax 746-5109

Conway, Carroll, Pop. 1,604
Conway SD
Supt. — See North Conway
Kennett HS 1,000/9-12
176 Main St 03818 603-447-6364
John Loynd, prin. Fax 447-6842
Kennett MS 400/7-8
176 Main St 03818 603-447-5408
Kevin M. Richard, prin. Fax 447-6842
Mt. Washington Career & Technical Center Vo/Tech
176 Main St 03818 603-447-5209
Neal Moylan, prin. Fax 447-6842

Deering, Hillsborough
Hillsboro-Deering Cooperative SD 1,400/PK-12
2300 2nd NH Tpke 03244 603-464-4466
Dr. Barbara Baker, supt. Fax 464-4053
Other Schools – See Hillsborough

Derry, Rockingham, Pop. 20,446
Derry Cooperative SD 7,400/PK-PK, 1-
18 S Main St 03038 603-432-1210
Dr. John Moody, supt. Fax 432-1264
www.derry.k12.nh.us
Hood Memorial MS 900/6-8
5 Hood Rd 03038 603-432-1224
Austin Garofalo, prin. Fax 432-1227
Pinkerton Academy 3,300/9-12
5 Pinkerton St 03038 603-437-5200
Mary A. Anderson, prin. Fax 432-5328
West Running Brook MS 800/6-8
1 W Running Brook Ln 03038 603-432-1250
Mary Ann Krikorian, prin. Fax 432-1243

Calvary Christian S 300/K-12
145 Hampstead Rd 03038 603-434-1501
Dr. Judy Buck, prin. Fax 437-8096

Dover, Strafford, Pop. 28,216
Dover SD 4,000/K-12
288 Central Ave 03820 603-516-6800
Dr. John O'Connor, supt. Fax 516-6809
www.dover.k12.nh.us
Dover HS 1,600/9-12
25 Alumni Dr 03820 603-516-6900
Christopher George, prin. Fax 516-6926
Dover MS 1,100/5-8
16 Daley Dr 03820 603-516-7200
Lawrence DeYoung, prin. Fax 516-5747
Dover Reg Vocational Center Vo/Tech
25 Alumni Dr 03820 603-516-6976
Kenneth Latchaw, dir. Fax 516-6926

McIntosh College Post-Sec.
23 Cataract Ave 03820 603-742-1234
Portsmouth Christian Academy 800/PK-12
20 Seaborne Dr 03820 603-742-3617
Dr. David Thompson, hdmstr. Fax 750-0490
St. Thomas Aquinas HS 700/9-12
197 Dover Point Rd 03820 603-742-3206
Jeffrey Quinn, prin. Fax 749-7822

Dublin, Cheshire

Dublin Christian Academy 100/K-12
PO Box 521 03444 603-563-8505
Kevin Moody, prin. Fax 563-8008
Dublin S 100/9-12
PO Box 522 03444 603-563-8584
Christopher Horgan, prin. Fax 563-7121

Durham, Strafford, Pop. 9,236

Oyster River Cooperative SD 2,200/K-12
36 Coe Dr 03824 603-868-5100
Norman Couture, supt. Fax 868-6668
www.orcsd.org
Oyster River HS 700/9-12
55 Coe Dr 03824 603-868-2375
Richard Gremlitz, prin. Fax 868-2049
Oyster River MS 700/5-8
1 Coe Dr 03824 603-868-2155
Marcia Ross, prin. Fax 868-3469

University of New Hampshire 03824 Post-Sec.
603-862-1234

East Swanzey, Cheshire

Hinsdale SD 700/PK-12
600 Old Homestead Hwy 03446 603-352-6955
Dr. Kenneth Dassau, supt. Fax 358-6708
www.mrsd.org
Other Schools – See Hinsdale

Monadnock Regional SD 2,400/PK-12
600 Old Homestead Hwy 03446 603-352-6955
Dr. Kenneth Dassau, supt. Fax 358-6708
www.mrsd.org
Monadnock Regional HS 900/9-12
580 Old Homestead Hwy 03446 603-352-6575
Joseph Smith, prin. Fax 355-1209
Monadnock Regional JHS 400/7-8
580 Old Homestead Hwy 03446 603-352-6575
Matthew Young, prin. Fax 355-1209

Winchester SD 500/PK-8
600 Old Homestead Hwy 03446 603-352-6955
Dr. Kenneth Dassau, supt. Fax 358-6708
www.mrsd.org
Other Schools – See Winchester

Enfield, Grafton, Pop. 1,560

Mascoma Valley Regional SD 1,500/PK-12
PO Box 789 03748 603-632-5563
Barbara Tremblay, supt. Fax 632-4181
Other Schools – See Canaan

Epping, Rockingham, Pop. 1,384

Epping SD 1,100/PK-12
213 Main St 03042 603-679-5402
Barbara Munsey, supt. Fax 679-1237
www.sau14.k12.nh.us/
Epping MS 300/6-8
21 Prospect St 03042 603-679-5472
Gary Tirone, prin. Fax 679-2966
Epping MSHS 400/9-12
21 Prospect St 03042 603-679-5472
Dixie Tremblay, prin. Fax 679-2966

Exeter, Rockingham, Pop. 9,556

Exeter SD 4,500/PK-12
24 Front St 03833 603-775-8653
Dr. Arthur Hanson, supt. Fax 775-8673
www.sau16.org/
Exeter Area HS 1,600/9-12
30 Linden St 03833 603-775-8400
Victor Sokul, prin. Fax 775-8989
Seacoast School of Tech Vo/Tech
40 Linden St 03833 603-775-8461
Nancy Pierce, prin. Fax 778-0459
Other Schools – See Stratham

Phillips Exeter Academy 1,000/9-12
20 Main St 03833 603-772-4311
Tyler Tingley, prin. Fax 777-4399

Farmington, Strafford, Pop. 3,567

Farmington SD 1,500/PK-12
356 Main St 03835 603-755-2627
Brian Blake, supt. Fax 755-2060
www.sau61.com/
Farmington HS 500/9-12
1 Thayer Dr 03835 603-755-2811
G. Lee, prin. Fax 755-3252
Wilson Memorial MS 600/4-8
12 Memorial Dr 03835 603-755-2181
Clayton Lewis, prin. Fax 755-9473

Franklin, Merrimack, Pop. 8,613

Franklin SD 1,400/K-12
119 Central St 03235 603-934-3108
Dr. Robert A. McKenney, supt. Fax 934-3462
www.franklin.k12.nh.us/
Franklin HS 500/9-12
115 Central St 03235 603-934-5441
Robert Braman, prin. Fax 934-7445
Franklin MS 400/5-8
200 Sanborn St 03235 603-934-5828
James Friel, prin. Fax 934-2432

Gilford, Belknap

Gilford SD 1,400/K-12
47 Cherry Valley Rd 03249 603-527-9215
Dr. Paul P. DeMinico, supt. Fax 527-9216
www.sau.gilford.k12.nh.us
Gilford HS 500/9-12
88 Alvah Wilson Rd 03249 603-524-7135
Kenneth Wiswell, prin. Fax 524-3867
Gilford MS 400/5-8
72 Alvah Wilson Rd 03249 603-527-2460
James G. Kemmerer, prin. Fax 527-2461

Goffstown, Hillsborough, Pop. 14,621

Goffstown SD 3,100/PK-12
11 School St 03045 603-497-4818
Dr. Darrell Lockwood, supt. Fax 497-8425
www.goffstown.k12.nh.us
Goffstown Area HS 1,300/9-12
27 Wallace Rd 03045 603-497-4841
Frank McBride, prin. Fax 497-5257
Mountain View MS 1,100/5-8
41 Lauren Ln 03045 603-497-8288
Rose Colby, prin. Fax 497-4987

Gorham, Coos, Pop. 1,910

Gorham SD 600/K-12
123 Main St 03581 603-466-3632
Steven Welford, supt. Fax 466-3870
Gorham HS 200/9-12
120 Main St 03581 603-466-2776
Keith F. Parent, prin. Fax 466-3111
Gorham MS 100/6-8
120 Main St 03581 603-466-2776
Keith Parent, prin. Fax 466-3111

Greenland, Rockingham

Rye SD 600/PK-8
48 Post Rd 03840 603-422-9572
Dr. George Cushing, supt. Fax 422-9575
Other Schools – See Rye

Groveton, Coos, Pop. 1,255

Northumberland SD 500/K-12
8 Preble St 03582 603-636-1437
Sherwood Fluery, supt. Fax 636-6102
Groveton HS 200/9-12
65 State St 03582 603-636-1619
Pierre Couture, prin. Fax 636-9752
Groveton MS 100/7-8
65 State St 03582 603-636-1619
Pierre Couture, prin. Fax 636-9752

Stratford SD 200/K-12
8 Preble St 03582 603-636-1437
Sherwood Fluery, supt. Fax 636-6102
Other Schools – See North Stratford

Hampstead, Rockingham

Hampstead SD
Supt. — See Plaistow
Hampstead MS 600/5-8
26 School St 03841 603-329-6743
Richard Taft, prin. Fax 329-4120

Hampton, Rockingham, Pop. 7,989

Hampton SD 1,500/PK-8
2 Alumni Dr 03842 603-926-8992
James Gaylord, supt. Fax 926-5157
www.sau21.k12.nh.us
Hampton Academy JHS 500/6-8
29 Academy Ave 03842 603-926-2000
Manfred Muscara, prin. Fax 926-1855

Seabrook SD 900/PK-8
2 Alumni Dr 03842 603-926-8992
James F. Gaylord, supt. Fax 926-5157
www.sau21.k12.nh.us
Other Schools – See Seabrook

Winnacunnet Cooperative SD 1,200/9-12
2 Alumni Dr 03842 603-926-8992
James F. Gaylord, supt. Fax 926-5157
www.sau21.k12.nh.us
Winnacunnet HS 1,200/9-12
1 Alumni Dr 03842 603-926-3395
Randall Zito, prin. Fax 926-7824

Hanover, Grafton, Pop. 6,538

Hanover SD 1,700/K-12
45 Lyme Rd 03755 603-643-6050
Wayne Gersen, supt. Fax 643-3073
Hanover HS 700/9-12
41 Lebanon St 03755 603-643-3431
Deborah Gillespie, prin. Fax 643-0661
Richmond MS 400/6-8
63 Lyme Rd 03755 603-643-6040
Susan Finer, prin. Fax 643-0662

Dartmouth College 03755 Post-Sec.
603-646-1110

Henniker, Merrimack, Pop. 1,693

John Stark Regional SD 900/9-12
PO Box 2417 03242 603-428-3269
Dr. Christine Tyrie, supt. Fax 428-3850
Other Schools – See Weare

Weare SD 1,300/PK-8
PO Box 2417 03242 603-428-3269
Dr. Christine Tyrie, supt. Fax 428-3850
sau24.k12.nh.us
Other Schools – See Weare

New England College Post-Sec.
26 Bridge St 03242 603-428-2211

Hillsborough, Hillsborough, Pop. 1,826

Hillsboro-Deering Cooperative SD
Supt. — See Deering
Hillsboro-Deering HS 500/9-12
12 Hillcat Dr 03244 603-464-1130
Jon Ingraham, prin. Fax 464-4028
Hillsboro-Deering MS 400/6-8
6 Hillcat Dr 03244 603-464-1120
Linda Raines, prin. Fax 464-5759

Hinsdale, Cheshire, Pop. 1,718

Hinsdale SD
Supt. — See East Swanzey
Hinsdale HS 200/9-12
PO Box 46 03451 603-336-5984
John Hartnett, prin. Fax 336-7497
Hinsdale JHS 100/7-8
PO Box 46 03451 603-336-5984
John Harnett, prin. Fax 336-7497

Hollis, Hillsborough

Hollis/Brookline Cooperative SD 1,200/7-12
PO Box 1588 03049 603-465-7118
Richard Pike, supt. Fax 465-3933
www.sau41.k12.nh.us
Hollis/Brookline HS 800/9-12
24 Cavalier Ct 03049 603-465-2269
Timothy Kelley, prin. Fax 465-2485
Hollis/Brookline MS 400/7-8
25 Main St 03049 603-465-2223
Patricia Goyette, prin. Fax 465-7523

Hooksett, Merrimack, Pop. 2,573

Hooksett SD 1,400/PK-8
90 Farmer Rd 03106 603-622-3731
Armand LaSelva, supt. Fax 669-4352

Cawley MS 500/6-8
89 Whitehall Rd 03106 603-485-9959
Ronald L. Pedro, prin. Fax 485-5291

Southern New Hampshire University Post-Sec.
2500 N River Rd 03106 603-668-2211

Hudson, Hillsborough, Pop. 7,626

Hudson SD 4,100/PK-12
20 Library St 03051 603-886-1235
Philip Bell, supt. Fax 886-1236
www.sau81.org/
Alvirne HS 1,400/9-12
200 Derry Rd 03051 603-886-1260
Bryan Lane, prin. Fax 595-1525
Hudson Memorial MS 1,100/6-8
1 Memorial Dr 03051 603-886-1240
Susan Nadeau, prin. Fax 883-1252
Palmer Vocational Tech Center Vo/Tech
200 Derry Rd 03051 603-886-1260
Jane Parkin, dir.

Continental Academie of Hair Design Post-Sec.
PO Box 370 03051 603-889-1614

Jaffrey, Cheshire, Pop. 2,558

Jaffrey-Rindge Cooperative SD 1,700/PK-12
10 Main St 03452 603-532-8100
James O'Neill, supt. Fax 532-8164
www.sau47.k12.nh.us
Conant HS 500/9-12
3 Conant Way 03452 603-532-8131
Lawrence Murphy, prin. Fax 532-8102
Jaffrey-Rindge MS 400/6-8
1 Conant Way 03452 603-532-8122
Thomas Fitzgerald, prin. Fax 532-8124

Keene, Cheshire, Pop. 22,780

Keene SD 3,800/PK-12
34 West St 03431 603-357-9002
Michele Munson, supt. Fax 357-9012
www.sau29.k12.nh.us/
Cheshire Ctr of Applied Science & Tech Vo/Tech
43 Arch St 03431 603-352-0640
Wayne Cotton, prin.
Keene HS 1,800/9-12
43 Arch St 03431 603-352-0640
William Marston, prin. Fax 357-1512
Keene MS 800/6-8
17 Washington St 03431 603-357-9023
Dorothy Frazier, prin. Fax 357-9045

Antioch University New England Post-Sec.
40 Avon St 03431 603-357-3122
Franklin Pierce College Post-Sec.
17 Bradco St 03431 603-357-0079
Keene Beauty Academy Post-Sec.
800 Park Ave 03431 603-357-3736
Keene State College Post-Sec.
229 Main St 03435 603-352-1909

Kingston, Rockingham

Sanborn Regional SD 1,800/PK-12
178 Main St 03848 603-642-3688
James O'Neil, supt. Fax 642-7885
sanborn.k12.nh.us
Sanborn Regional HS 600/9-12
13 Church St 03848 603-642-3341
Gail Sudduth, prin. Fax 642-6947
Other Schools – See Newton

Laconia, Belknap, Pop. 17,134

Laconia SD 2,500/PK-12
PO Box 309 03247 603-524-5710
Robert Champlin, supt. Fax 528-8442
www.laconia.k12.nh.us
Huot Technical Center Vo/Tech
345 Union Ave 03246 603-528-8693
Scott Davis, prin.
Laconia HS 800/9-12
345 Union Ave 03246 603-524-3350
Jonathan Freeman, prin. Fax 528-8683
Memorial MS 600/6-8
150 Mcgrath St 03246 603-524-4632
James McCollum, prin. Fax 528-8675

Empire Beauty School Post-Sec.
556 Main St 03246 603-524-8777
Laconia Christian S 100/PK-12
1386 Meredith Center Rd 03246 603-524-3250
Rick Duba, prin. Fax 524-3285
New Hampshire Technical College Post-Sec.
379 Belmont Rd 03246 603-524-3207

Langdon, Sullivan

Fall Mountain Regional SD
Supt. — See Charlestown
Fall Mountain Regional HS 700/9-12
134 FMRHS Rd 03602 603-835-6318
Thomas Ferenc, prin. Fax 835-6254

Lebanon, Grafton, Pop. 12,792

Lebanon SD 2,000/PK-12
PO Box 488 03766 603-448-1634
Michael Harris, supt. Fax 448-0602
www.lebanon.k12.nh.us
Lebanon HS 700/9-12
195 Hanover St 03766 603-448-2055
James Nourse, prin. Fax 448-0605
Lebanon JHS 300/7-8
75 Bank St 03766 603-448-3056
Anne Evensen, prin. Fax 448-0616

Upper Valley Teacher Institute Post-Sec.
1 Court St Ste 210 03766 603-448-6507

Lincoln, Grafton

Lincoln-Woodstock Cooperative SD 400/K-12
PO Box 846 03251 603-745-2051
Michael Cosgriff, supt. Fax 745-2352
www.lin-wood.k12.nh.us
Lin-Wood S 400/K-12
PO Box 97 03251 603-745-2214
Robert Nelson, prin. Fax 745-6797

Lisbon, Grafton, Pop. 1,246
Lisbon Regional SD — 400/K-12
25 Highland Ave 03585 — 603-444-3925
Donald Johnson, supt. — Fax 444-6299
www.lisbon.k12.nh.us/
Lisbon Regional HS — 200/9-12
24 Highland Ave 03585 — 603-838-5506
Richard Toner, prin. — Fax 838-5012
Lisbon Regional MS — 100/6-8
24 Highland Ave 03585 — 603-838-5506
Richard Toner, prin. — Fax 838-5012

Litchfield, Hillsborough
Litchfield SD — 1,700/PK-12
1 Highlander Ct 03052 — 603-578-3570
Catherine Hamblett, supt. — Fax 886-1236
Campbell HS — 500/9-12
1 Highlander Ct 03052 — 603-546-0300
William Marston, prin. — Fax 546-0310
Litchfield MS — 600/5-8
19 McElwain Dr 03052 — 603-424-0566
Martin Schlichter, prin. — Fax 424-1296

Tabernacle Christian S — 200/K-12
242 Derry Rd 03052 — 603-883-6310
Harold McGrath, prin. — Fax 883-2413

Littleton, Grafton, Pop. 4,633
Littleton SD — 900/K-12
32 Main St 03561 — 603-444-3925
Donald Johnson, supt. — Fax 444-6299
www.sau35.k12.nh.us
Bronson JHS — 200/7-8
96 School St 03561 — 603-444-3361
George Brodeur, prin. — Fax 444-3009
Littleton HS — 300/9-12
105 School St 03561 — 603-444-5601
Alan Smith, prin. — Fax 444-3009

Profile SD
Supt. — See Bethlehem
Gallen Regional Vocational Center — Vo/Tech
105 School St 03561 — 603-444-5186
Forrest Goodwin, prin.

Londonderry, Rockingham, Pop. 10,114
Londonderry SD — 5,600/PK-12
268 Mammoth Rd 03053 — 603-432-6920
Dr. Nathan Greenberg, supt. — Fax 425-1049
www.londonderry.org
Londonderry HS — 1,700/9-12
295 Mammoth Rd 03053 — 603-432-6941
James Elefante, prin. — Fax 425-1022
Londonderry MS — 1,400/6-8
313 Mammoth Rd 03053 — 603-432-6925
Andrew Corey, prin. — Fax 432-0714

Manchester, Hillsborough, Pop. 108,871
Manchester SD — 17,400/PK-12
286 Commercial St 03101 — 603-624-6300
Michael Ludwell Ph.D., supt. — Fax 624-6337
www.mansd.org
Hillside MS — 1,000/6-8
112 Reservoir Ave 03104 — 603-624-6352
Steven Donohue, prin. — Fax 628-6049
Manchester Central HS — 2,400/9-12
207 Lowell St 03104 — 603-624-6363
John Rist, prin. — Fax 624-6376
Manchester Memorial HS — 2,100/9-12
1 Crusader Way 03103 — 603-624-6378
Arthur Adamakos, prin. — Fax 628-6009
Manchester School of Tech — Vo/Tech
530 S Porter St 03103 — 603-624-6490
James Stopa, prin. — Fax 628-6146
Manchester West HS — 2,100/9-12
9 Notre Dame Ave 03102 — 603-624-6384
Janice Thompson, prin. — Fax 628-6153
McLaughlin MS — 800/6-8
290 S Mammoth Rd 03109 — 603-628-6247
Barry Albert, prin. — Fax 628-6274
Parkside MS — 800/6-8
75 Parkside Ave 03102 — 603-624-6356
Dawn Smith-Michaud, prin. — Fax 624-6355
Southside MS — 1,000/6-8
140 S Jewett St 03103 — 603-624-6359
Mark Willis, prin. — Fax 624-6361

Continental Academie of Hair Design — Post-Sec.
228 Maple St 03103 — 603-622-5851
Derryfield S — 400/6-12
2108 River Rd 03104 — 603-669-4524
Randle Richardson, prin. — Fax 625-9715
Franklin Pierce College — Post-Sec.
670 N Commercial St Ste 206 03101 — - -
Hesser College — Post-Sec.
3 Sundial Ave 03103 — 603-668-6660
Jolicoeur S — 100/1-12
1 Mammoth Rd 03109 — 603-621-3599
Noel J. Sullivan, prin. — Fax 623-6940
New England EMS Institute — Post-Sec.
1 Elliot Way 03103 — 603-628-2220
New Hampshire Community Tech College — Post-Sec.
1066 Front St 03102 — 603-668-6706
St. Anselm College — Post-Sec.
100 Saint Anselms Dr 03102 — 603-641-7000
St. Joseph Regional JHS — 300/7-8
460 Pine St 03104 — 603-624-4811
Sr. Barbara McLean, prin. — Fax 624-6670
Trinity HS — 400/9-12
581 Bridge St 03104 — 603-668-2910
Denis Mailloux, prin. — Fax 668-2913
University of New Hampshire — Post-Sec.
400 Commercial St 03101 — 603-668-0700

Meredith, Belknap, Pop. 1,654
Inter-Lakes Cooperative SD — 1,300/PK-12
103 Main St Ste 2 03253 — 603-279-7947
Dr. Phillip McCormack, supt. — Fax 279-3044
inter-lakes.k12.nh.us
Inter-Lakes HS — 400/9-12
1 Laker Ln 03253 — 603-279-6162
Patricia Kennelly, prin. — Fax 279-5302
Inter-Lakes MS — 400/5-8
1 Laker Ln 03253 — 603-279-6162
Everett Bennett, prin. — Fax 279-6344

Meriden, Sullivan

Kimball Union Academy — 300/9-12
PO Box 188 03770 — 603-469-2000
Michael J. Schafer, hdmstr. — Fax 469-2040

Merrimack, Hillsborough, Pop. 22,156
Merrimack SD — 3,900/1-12
36 McElwain St 03054 — 603-424-6200
Marjorie Chiafery, supt. — Fax 424-6229
www.merrimack.k12.nh.us
Merrimack HS — 1,600/9-12
38 Mcelwain St 03054 — 603-424-6204
Kenneth Johnson, prin. — Fax 424-6230
Merrimack MS — 7-8
31 Madeline Bennett Ln 03054 — 603-424-6289
Thomas Levesque, prin. — Fax 423-1109

South Merrimack Christian Academy — 300/K-12
517 Boston Post Rd 03054 — 603-880-6832
Brian Burbach, prin. — Fax 598-7085
Thomas More College of Liberal Arts — Post-Sec.
6 Manchester St 03054 — 603-880-8308

Milford, Hillsborough, Pop. 8,015
Milford SD — 2,500/PK-12
100 West St 03055 — 603-673-2202
Robert Suprenant, supt. — Fax 673-2202
www.milfordschools.net
Milford Applied Technology Center — Vo/Tech
100 West St 03055 — 603-673-4201
Rosie Deloge, prin. — Fax 673-4201
Milford HS — 900/9-12
100 West St 03055 — 603-673-4201
Bradford Craven, prin. — Fax 673-4201
Milford MS — 800/5-8
33 Osgood Rd 03055 — 603-673-5221
Anthony DeMarco, prin. — Fax 673-5221

Milford Christian Academy — 100/1-12
273 Elm St 03055 — 603-673-9324
Marsha Dandermey, dir. — Fax 672-4539

Milton, Strafford
Milton SD
Supt. — See Union
Nute HS — 200/9-12
PO Box 337 03851 — 603-652-4591
John T. Parkhurst, prin. — Fax 652-9926
Nute JHS — 100/7-8
PO Box 337 03851 — 603-652-4591
John T. Parkhurst, prin. — Fax 652-9926

Moultonborough, Carroll
Moultonborough SD — 700/PK-12
PO Box 419 03254 — 603-476-5247
Michael Lancor, supt. — Fax 476-8009
www.moultonborough.k12.nh.us
Moultonborough Academy — 100/7-8
PO Box 228 03254 — 603-476-5517
Andrew Coppinger, prin. — Fax 476-5153
Moultonborough Academy — 200/9-12
PO Box 228 03254 — 603-476-5517
Andrew Coppinger, prin. — Fax 476-5153

Nashua, Hillsborough, Pop. 87,285
Nashua SD — 14,200/PK-12
PO Box 687 03061 — 603-594-4300
Julia Earl, supt. — Fax 594-4350
www.nashua.edu
Academy of Learning & Technology — 600/6-10
47 Grand Ave 03060 — 603-594-4326
Patricia Place, prin.
Elm Street JHS — 1,000/6-8
117 Elm St 03060 — 603-594-4322
Pauline Caron, prin. — Fax 594-4370
Fairgrounds JHS — 700/6-8
27 Cleveland St 03060 — 603-594-4393
Michael Hogan, prin. — Fax 594-4355
Nashua HS North — 2,000/11-12
10 Chuck Druding Dr 03063 — 603-589-6400
R. Patrick Corbin, prin. — Fax 589-6449
Nashua HS South — 3,300/9-12
36 Riverside Dr 03062 — 603-594-4311
Jennifer Seusing, prin. — Fax 594-4373
Pennichuck JHS — 600/6-8
207 Manchester St 03064 — 603-594-4308
Paul F. Asbell, prin. — Fax 594-4413

Bishop Guertin HS — 800/9-12
194 Lund Rd 03060 — 603-889-4107
Linda Brodeur, prin. — Fax 889-0701
Daniel Webster College — Post-Sec.
20 University Dr 03063 — 603-577-6000
Hesser College — Post-Sec.
410 Amherst St 03063 — 603-883-0404
Nashua Catholic Regional JHS — 300/7-8
6 Bartlett Ave 03064 — 603-882-7011
Sandra Clay-Hillyard, prin. — Fax 594-8955
Nashua Christian Academy — 300/K-12
34 Franklin St 03064 — 603-889-8892
Christine Urban, admin. — Fax 883-0061
New Hampshire Community Tech College — Post-Sec.
505 Amherst St 03063 — 603-882-6923
Rivier College — Post-Sec.
420 S Main St 03060 — 603-888-1311

New Hampton, Belknap

New Hampton S — 300/9-12
PO Box 579 03256 — 603-677-3400
Andrew Menke, hdmstr. — Fax 677-3480

New Ipswich, Hillsborough
Mascenic Regional SD — 1,400/PK-12
659 Turnpike Rd # 120 03071 — 603-878-1026
Francine Fullam, supt. — Fax 878-2657
www.mascenic.com/
Boynton MS — 500/5-8
500 Turnpike Rd 03071 — 603-878-4800
Thomas Starratt, prin. — Fax 878-0525
Mascenic Regional HS — 400/9-12
175 Turnpike Rd 03071 — 603-878-1113
Craig Mueller, prin. — Fax 878-3344

Wilton-Lyndeboro Cooperative SD — 400/7-12
659 Turnpike Rd # 120 03071 — 603-878-1026
Francine Fullam, supt. — Fax 878-2657
Other Schools – See Wilton

New London, Merrimack
Kearsarge Regional Cooperative SD — 2,100/K-12
169 Main St 03257 — 603-526-2051
Thomas Brennan, supt. — Fax 526-2145
www.kearsarge.k12.nh.us/
Kearsarge Regional MS — 500/6-8
114 Cougar Ct 03257 — 603-526-6415
Donald R. West, prin. — Fax 526-2934
Other Schools – See North Sutton

Colby-Sawyer College — Post-Sec.
100 Main St 03257 — 603-526-3000

Newmarket, Rockingham, Pop. 4,917
Newmarket SD — 1,100/PK-12
186 Main St 03857 — 603-659-5020
Kathleen Murphy, supt. — Fax 659-5022
Newmarket Central JSHS — 600/6-12
213 S Main St 03857 — 603-659-3271
Deborah Brooks, prin. — Fax 659-5304

Newport, Sullivan, Pop. 3,772
Newport SD — 1,300/K-12
9 Depot St Ste 2 03773 — 603-863-3540
William J. Mealey, supt. — Fax 863-5368
Newport HS — 400/9-12
245 N Main St 03773 — 603-863-2414
Barry Connell, prin. — Fax 863-0887
Newport MS — 300/6-8
245 N Main St 03773 — 603-863-2414
Barry Connell, prin. — Fax 863-0887
Sugar River Valley Reg Voc Ctr — Vo/Tech
243 N Main St 03773 — 603-863-3759
Cathryn Baird, prin.

Sunapee SD — 500/K-12
9 Depot St Ste 2 03773 — 603-863-3540
William J. Mealey, supt. — Fax 863-5368
Other Schools – See Sunapee

Newton, Rockingham
Sanborn Regional SD
Supt. — See Kingston
Sanborn Regional MS — 500/6-8
31 W Main St #A 03858 — 603-382-6226
Kathleen Laureti, prin. — Fax 382-9771

North Conway, Carroll, Pop. 2,032
Conway SD — 2,200/K-12
19 Pine St 03860 — 603-356-5533
Dr. Carl Nelson, supt. — Fax 356-5144
www.kennett.k12.nh.us
Other Schools – See Conway

Northfield, Merrimack
Winnisquam Regional SD — 1,800/PK-12
433 W Main St 03276 — 603-286-4116
Donald Parks, supt. — Fax 286-7402
www.winnisquam.k12.nh.us
Other Schools – See Tilton

North Haverhill, Grafton
Haverhill Cooperative SD — 800/PK-12
2975 Dartmouth College Hwy 03774 — 603-787-2113
Bruce C. Labs, supt. — Fax 787-2118
www.sau23.k12.nh.us
Haverhill Cooperative MS — 300/4-8
175 Morrill Dr 03774 — 603-787-2100
Brent L. Walker, prin. — Fax 787-6117
Other Schools – See Woodsville

North Stratford, Coos
Stratford SD
Supt. — See Groveton
Stratford HS — 100/9-12
19 School St 03590 — 603-922-3387
Georgia Caron, prin. — Fax 922-3303

North Sutton, Merrimack
Kearsarge Regional Cooperative SD
Supt. — See New London
Kearsage Regional HS — 700/9-12
PO Box 182 03260 — 603-927-4261
Carlton J. Fitzgerald, prin. — Fax 927-4453

Northwood, Rockingham
Northwood SD — 1,200/K-12
569 1st NH Tpke 03261 — 603-942-1290
Judy McGann, supt. — Fax 942-1295
www.northwood.k12.nh.us/
Coe Brown Academy — 700/9-12
907 1st NH Tpke 03261 — 603-942-5531
David Smith, prin. — Fax 942-7537

Orford, Grafton
Rivendell Interstate SD — 600/K-12
PO Box 153 03777 — 603-353-2170
Noelle Vitt, supt. — Fax 353-2189
www.rivendellschool.org
Rivendell Academy — 300/6-12
RR 1 Box 82b 03777 — 603-353-4321
Dr. Carol Fritz, prin. — Fax 353-4414

Pelham, Hillsborough
Pelham SD
Supt. — See Windham
Pelham HS — 600/9-12
85 Marsh Rd 03076 — 603-635-2115
Dr. Dorothy Mohr, prin. — Fax 635-3994
Pelham Memorial MS — 600/6-8
59 Marsh Rd 03076 — 603-635-2321
Catherine A. Pinsonneaut, prin. — Fax 635-2369

Pembroke, Merrimack, Pop. 6,561
Allenstown SD — 500/K-8
267 Pembroke St 03275 — 603-485-5188
Thomas Haley, supt. — Fax 485-9529
www.sau53.org
Other Schools – See Allenstown

Pembroke SD — 1,900/K-12
267 Pembroke St 03275 — 603-485-5188
Thomas Haley, supt. — Fax 485-9529
www.sau53.org
Pembroke Academy — 1,000/9-12
209 Academy Rd 03275 — 603-485-7881
Michael A. Reardon, prin. — Fax 485-1824
Three Rivers MS — 400/5-8
243 Academy Rd 03275 — 603-485-9539
Deborah Bulkley, prin. — Fax 485-1829

Penacook, See Concord
Merrimack Valley SD
  Supt. — See Concord
Merrimack Valley HS   900/9-12
  106 Village St 03303   603-753-4311
  Michael Jette, prin.   Fax 753-6423
Merrimack Valley MS   600/6-8
  14 Allen St 03303   603-753-6336
  Mary R. Estee, prin.   Fax 753-8107

Peterborough, Hillsborough, Pop. 2,685
Contoocook Valley SD   3,100/PK-12
  106 Hancock Rd 03458   603-924-3336
  Keith R. Burke, supt.   Fax 924-6707
  www.conval.edu
Applied Technology Center Region 14   Vo/Tech
  182 Hancock Rd 03458   603-371-0310
  Chester Bowles, prin.   Fax 924-9176
ConVal Regional HS   1,200/9-12
  184 Hancock Rd 03458   603-924-3869
  Susan Dell, prin.   Fax 924-9176
South Meadow MS   500/5-8
  108 Hancock Rd 03458   603-924-7105
  Richard Dunning, prin.   Fax 924-2064
Other Schools – See Antrim

Pittsburg, Coos
Pittsburg SD
  Supt. — See Colebrook
Pittsburg HS   100/9-12
  12 School St 03592   603-538-6536
  James Shallow, prin.   Fax 538-6996

Pittsfield, Merrimack, Pop. 1,717
Pittsfield SD   800/PK-12
  175 Barnstead Rd Unit 3 03263   603-435-5526
  Dr. Owen Conway, supt.   Fax 435-5331
Pittsfield HS   300/9-12
  23 Oneida St 03263   603-435-6701
  Karen Erlandson, prin.   Fax 435-7087
Pittsfield MS   100/7-8
  23 Oneida St 03263   603-435-6701
  Karen Erlandson, prin.   Fax 435-7087

Plainfield, Sullivan

Runnemede S   100/K-12
  PO Box 120 03781   603-675-2634
      Fax 675-2040

Plaistow, Rockingham
Hampstead SD   1,100/PK-PK, 1-
  30 Greenough Rd 03865   603-382-6119
  Dr. Douglas McDonald, supt.   Fax 382-3334
  www.hampstead.k12.nh.us
Other Schools – See Hampstead

Timberlane Regional SD   4,500/PK-12
  30 Greenough Rd 03865   603-382-6119
  Dr. Douglas McDonald, supt.   Fax 382-3334
  www.timberlane.net/
Timberlane Regional HS   1,400/9-12
  36 Greenough Rd 03865   603-382-6541
  Charles R. Coker, prin.   Fax 382-8086
Timberlane Regional MS   1,200/6-8
  44 Greenough Rd 03865   603-382-7131
  Gilbert Johanson, prin.   Fax 382-2781

Plymouth, Grafton, Pop. 3,967
Pemi-Baker Regional HSD   900/9-12
  47 Old Ward Bridge Rd 03264   603-536-1254
  John True, supt.   Fax 536-3545
Plymouth Regional HS   900/9-12
  86 Old Ward Bridge Rd 03264   603-536-1444
  Bruce Parsons, prin.   Fax 536-9086
Plymouth Regional Technical Center   Vo/Tech
  86 Old Ward Bridge Rd 03264   603-536-1444
  Dr. Gwen Blair, prin.

Calvary Christian S   100/K-12
  115 Yeaton Rd 03264   603-536-4022
  Richard Anderson, prin.   Fax 536-9896
Holderness S   300/9-12
  PO Box 1879 03264   603-536-1257
  Phillip Peck, hdmstr.   Fax 536-1267
Plymouth State University   Post-Sec.
  17 High St 03264   603-535-5000

Portsmouth, Rockingham, Pop. 21,002
Portsmouth SD   2,800/PK-12
  50 Clough Dr 03801   603-431-5080
  Dr. Robert Lister, supt.   Fax 431-6753
  www.portsmouth.k12.nh.us
Portsmouth HS   1,100/9-12
  50 Alumni Cir 03801   603-436-7100
  Forrest S. Ransdell, prin.   Fax 427-2320
Portsmouth MS   500/6-8
  155 Parrott Ave 03801   603-436-5781
  John Stokel, prin.   Fax 427-2326
Region Center 19 Vocational S   Vo/Tech
  50 Alumni Cir 03801   603-436-7100
  Pamela MacArtney, prin.   Fax 427-2320

Franklin Pierce College   Post-Sec.
  73 Corporate Dr 03801   603-433-2000
Hesser College   Post-Sec.
  170 Commerce Way 03801   603-436-5300
Portsmouth Beauty School of Hair Design   Post-Sec.
  140 Congress St 03801   603-436-7775

Raymond, Rockingham, Pop. 2,516
Raymond SD   1,600/PK-12
  43 Harriman Hill Rd 03077   603-895-4299
  David Sandmann, supt.   Fax 895-0147
  www.raymond.k12.nh.us
Gove MS   500/5-8
  1 Stephen Batchelder Pkwy 03077   603-895-3394
  Caesar Meledandri, prin.   Fax 895-9856
Raymond HS   600/9-12
  45 Harriman Hill Rd 03077   603-895-6616
  Michael Shore, prin.   Fax 895-1582

Rindge, Cheshire

Franklin Pierce College   Post-Sec.
  20 College Rd 03461   800-437-0048
Hampshire Country S   50/3-12
  122 Hampshire Rd 03461   603-899-3325
  William Dickerman, hdmstr.   Fax 899-6521
Meeting S   50/9-12
  120 Thomas Rd 03461   603-899-3366
  Jacqueline Stillwell, prin.   Fax 899-6216

Rochester, Strafford, Pop. 29,654
Rochester SD   4,800/PK-12
  150 Wakefield St Ste 8 03867   603-332-3678
  Michael Hopkins, supt.   Fax 335-7367
  www.rochesterschools.com
Creteau Regional Technology Center   Vo/Tech
  140 Wakefield St 03867   603-335-7351
  Richard Towne, prin.   Fax 335-7353
Rochester MS   1,100/6-8
  47 Brock St 03867   603-332-4090
  Walter Helliesen, prin.   Fax 332-9384
Spaulding HS   1,600/9-12
  130 Wakefield St 03867   603-332-0757
  Robert Pedersen, prin.   Fax 330-0251

Rye, Rockingham
Rye SD
  Supt. — See Greenland
Rye JHS   200/6-8
  501 Washington Rd 03870   603-964-5591
  Janice Yost, prin.   Fax 964-3881

Salem, Rockingham, Pop. 27,400
Salem SD   5,300/PK-12
  38 Geremonty Dr 03079   603-893-7040
  Michael Delahanty, supt.   Fax 893-7080
  www.salemschooldistrictnh.com
Salem HS   2,200/9-12
  44 Geremonty Dr 03079   603-893-7069
  William Hagen, prin.   Fax 893-7087
Salem Regional Vocational Center   Vo/Tech
  44 Geremonty Dr 03079   603-893-7073
  Robert Pariseau, prin.
Woodbury MS, 206 Main St 03079   1,200/6-8
  Deborah Jordan-Connell, prin.   603-893-7055

Hesser College   Post-Sec.
  11 Manor Pkwy 03079   603-898-3480

Sanbornton, Belknap

Sant Bani S   200/K-12
  19 Ashram Rd 03269   603-934-4240
  Kent Bicknell, prin.   Fax 934-2970

Seabrook, Rockingham
Seabrook SD
  Supt. — See Hampton
Seabrook MS   400/5-8
  236 Walton Rd 03874   603-474-9221
  Stanley Shupe, prin.   Fax 474-3504

Somersworth, Strafford, Pop. 11,786
Somersworth SD   1,800/PK-12
  51 W High St 03878   603-692-4450
  Dr. Charles Ott, supt.   Fax 692-9100
Somersworth HS   600/9-12
  11 Memorial Dr 03878   603-692-2431
  Brian Flanagan, prin.   Fax 692-7326
Somersworth MS   600/5-8
  7 Memorial Dr 03878   603-692-2126
  Paul Maskwa, prin.   Fax 692-9101
Somersworth Regional Vocational Center   Vo/Tech
  18 Cemetery Rd 03878   603-692-2242
  Barney Share, dir.   Fax 692-9116

Empire Beauty School   Post-Sec.
  362 Route 108 03878   603-692-1515
Tri-City Christian Academy   300/K-12
  150 W High St 03878   603-692-2093
  Paul Edgar, prin.   Fax 692-6305

South Tamworth, Carroll

Community S   50/4-12
  1164 Bunker Hill Rd 03883   603-323-7000
  Martha R. Carlson, dir.   Fax 323-8240

Stratham, Rockingham
Exeter SD
  Supt. — See Exeter
Cooperative MS   1,400/6-8
  100 Academic Way 03885   603-775-8700
  Thomas O'Malley, prin.   Fax 775-0151

New Hampshire Community Tech College   Post-Sec.
  277 Portsmouth Ave 03885   603-772-1194

Sunapee, Sullivan
Sunapee SD
  Supt. — See Newport
Sunapee HS   200/9-12
  10 North Rd 03782   603-763-5615
  Sean Moynihan, prin.   Fax 763-3055
Sunapee MS   100/6-8
  10 North Rd 03782   603-763-5615
  Sean Moynihan, prin.   Fax 763-3055

Mount Royal Academy   100/K-12
  26 Seven Hearths Ln 03782   603-763-9010
  David Thibault, prin.   Fax 763-5390

Tilton, Belknap, Pop. 3,081
Winnisquam Regional SD
  Supt. — See Northfield
Winnisquam Ag. Educ. Center   Vo/Tech
  435 W Main St 03276   603-286-4531
  Janet Rosequist, dir.

Winnisquam Regional HS   500/9-12
  435 W Main St 03276   603-286-4531
  Judith Farr, prin.   Fax 286-2006
Winnisquam Regional MS   500/6-8
  76 Winter St 03276   603-286-7143
  Thomas Croteau, prin.   Fax 286-7410

Tilton S   200/9-12
  30 School St 03276   603-286-4342
  James Clements, hdmstr.   Fax 286-3137

Union, Carroll
Milton SD   700/K-12
  39 Main St 03887   603-473-2326
  William Lander, supt.   Fax 473-2218
Other Schools – See Milton

Walpole, Cheshire, Pop. 3,304
Fall Mountain Regional SD
  Supt. — See Charlestown
Walpole MS   200/5-8
  PO Box 549 03608   603-756-4728
  Samuel Jacobs, prin.   Fax 756-3343

Warner, Merrimack

Magdalen College   Post-Sec.
  511 Kearsarge Mountain Rd 03278   603-456-2656

Weare, Hillsborough
John Stark Regional SD
  Supt. — See Henniker
Stark Regional HS   900/9-12
  618 N Stark Hwy 03281   603-529-7675
  Arthur Aaronson, prin.   Fax 529-4646

Weare SD
  Supt. — See Henniker
Weare MS   600/5-8
  16 East Rd 03281   603-529-7555
  David Pabst, prin.   Fax 529-7555

Westmoreland, Cheshire

Pioneer Junior Academy   50/1-12
  13 Mount Gilboa Rd 03467   603-399-4803
  Brianna Perry, prin.   Fax 399-4803

Whitefield, Coos, Pop. 1,041
White Mountains Regional SD   1,700/PK-12
  14 King Sq 03598   603-837-9363
  Dr. Dean Cascadden, supt.   Fax 837-2326
  www.sau36.org
Whitefield Reg Voc Ctr   Vo/Tech
  PO Box 338 03598   603-837-2528
  Lori Lane, prin.   Fax 837-9161
White Mountains Regional HS   400/9-12
  PO Box 338 03598   603-837-2528
  Robert Sampson, prin.   Fax 837-3811

Wilton, Hillsborough, Pop. 1,165
Wilton-Lyndeboro Cooperative SD
  Supt. — See New Ipswich
Wilton-Lyndeborough HS   200/9-12
  PO Box 255 03086   603-654-6123
  Trevor Ebel, prin.   Fax 654-2104
Wilton-Lyndeborough MS   100/7-8
  PO Box 255 03086   603-654-6123
  Trevor Ebel, prin.   Fax 654-2104

Center for Anthroposophy   100/9-12
  PO Box 545 03086   603-654-2566
  Milan Daler, admin.   Fax 654-5258
High Mowing S   100/9-12
  222 Isaac Frye Hwy 03086   603-654-2391
  Virginia Buhr, admin.   Fax 654-6588

Winchester, Cheshire, Pop. 1,735
Winchester SD
  Supt. — See East Swanzey
Thayer JHS   200/6-8
  PO Box 7 03470   603-239-4381
  David Funkhouser, prin.   Fax 239-4457

Windham, Rockingham
Pelham SD   2,000/1-12
  PO Box 510 03087   603-425-1976
  Dr. Elaine Cutler, supt.   Fax 425-1719
  www.pelhamsd.org
Other Schools – See Pelham

Windham SD   1,600/PK-PK, 1-
  PO Box 510 03087   603-425-1976
  Dr. Elaine Cutler, supt.   Fax 425-1719
  www.windhamsd.org
Windham MS   600/6-8
  112 Lowell Rd 03087   603-893-2636
  Stephen Plocharczyk, prin.   Fax 870-9007

Wolfeboro, Carroll, Pop. 2,783
Governor Wentworth Regional SD   3,100/PK-12
  26 Bay St 03894   603-569-1658
  John Robertson, supt.   Fax 569-6983
  www.govwentworth.k12.nh.us
Kingswood Regional HS   1,000/9-12
  396 S Main St 03894   603-569-2055
  Paul MacMillan, prin.   Fax 569-8104
Kingswood Regional MS   500/7-8
  404 S Main St 03894   603-569-3689
  Kirkland O. Ross, prin.   Fax 569-8113
Region 9 Vocational Technical Center   Vo/Tech
  384 S Main St 03894   603-569-4361
  Stephen Guyer, prin.   Fax 569-8657

Brewster Academy   400/9-12
  80 Academy Dr 03894   603-569-1600
  Dr. Michael E. Cooper, hdmstr.   Fax 569-7272

Woodsville, Grafton, Pop. 1,122
Haverhill Cooperative SD
  Supt. — See North Haverhill
Woodsville HS   300/9-12
  9 High St 03785   603-747-2781
  Brian Desilets, prin.   Fax 747-2766

NEW JERSEY

NEW JERSEY DEPARTMENT OF EDUCATION
100 River View Plz #CN500, Trenton 08611-3418
Telephone 609-292-4469
Fax 609-777-4099
Website http://www.state.nj.us/education
Commissioner of Education   Lucille Davy

NEW JERSEY BOARD OF EDUCATION
100 River View Plz #CN500, Trenton 08611-3418
President   Arnold Hyndman

COUNTY SUPERINTENDENTS OF SCHOOLS

Atlantic County Office of Education
  Dr. Daniel Loggi, supt.   609-625-0004
  6260 Old Harding Hwy   Fax 625-6539
  Mays Landing 08330
  www.aclink.org/education/homepage.asp
Bergen County Office of Education
  Dr. Aaron Graham, supt.   201-336-6875
  1 Bergen County Plz #350   Fax 336-6880
  Hackensack 07601
Burlington County Office of Education
  Walter Keiss, supt.   609-265-5060
  PO Box 6000, Mount Holly 08060 Fax 265-5932
  www.state.nj.us
Camden County Office of Education
  Dr. Paul Stephenson, supt.   856-401-2400
  509 Lakeland Rd   Fax 401-2410
  Blackwood 08012
Cape May County Office of Education
  Dr. Albert Monillas, supt.   609-465-1283
  4 Moore Rd   Fax 465-2094
  Cape May Court House
Cumberland County Office of Education
  Dr. Daniel Mastrobuono, supt.   856-451-0211
  19 Landis Ave, Bridgeton 08302 Fax 455-9523

Essex County Office of Education
  Anthony Marino, supt.   973-395-4677
  7 Glenwood Ave Ste 404   Fax 395-4696
  East Orange 07017
Gloucester County Office of Education
  Dr. H. Mark Stanwood, supt.   856-468-6500
  1492 Tanyard Rd, Sewell 08080   Fax 468-9115
  www.co.gloucester.nj.us/education/index.htm
Hudson County Office of Education
  Robert Osak, supt.   201-319-3850
  595 Newark Ave, Jersey City 07306 Fax 319-3650
Hunterdon County Office of Education
  Frank Dragotta, supt.   908-788-1414
  PO Box 2900, Flemington 08822   Fax 788-1457
Mercer County Office of Education
  Michael Klavon, supt.   609-588-5884
  1075 Old Trenton Rd   Fax 588-5849
  Trenton 08690
Middlesex County Office of Education
  Dr. Patrick Piegari, supt.   732-249-2900
  1501 Livingston Ave   Fax 296-0683
  North Brunswick 08902
Monmouth County Office of Education
  Eugenia Lawson, supt.   732-431-7816
  PO Box 1264, Freehold 07728   Fax 577-0679

Morris County Office of Education
  Dr. Thomas Kane, supt.   973-285-8332
  30 Schuyler Pl, Morristown 07960 Fax 285-8341
Ocean County Office of Education
  Dr. Bruce Greenfield, supt.   732-929-2078
  212 Washington St   Fax 506-5336
  Toms River 08753
Passaic County Office of Education
  Dr. Judith Weiss, supt.   973-569-2110
  501 River St, Paterson 07524   Fax 754-0241
Salem County Office of Education
  Michael Elwell, supt.   856-339-8611
  94 Market St, Salem 08079   Fax 935-6290
Somerset County Office of Education
  David Livingston, supt.   908-541-5700
  PO Box 3000, Somerville 08876   Fax 722-6902
Sussex County Office of Education
  Barry Worman, supt.   973-579-6996
  262 White Lake Rd, Sparta 07871 Fax 579-6476
  www.sussex.nj.us/
Union County Office of Education
  Dr. Carmen Centuolo, supt.   908-654-9860
  300 North Ave E, Westfield 07090 Fax 654-9869
Warren County Office of Education
  William King, supt.   908-475-6326
  537 Oxford St, Belvidere 07823 Fax 475-6394
  www.warrennet.org/wcdoe/

PUBLIC, PRIVATE AND CATHOLIC SECONDARY SCHOOLS

Aberdeen, Monmouth, Pop. 17,038
Matawan-Aberdeen Regional SD   3,000/K-12
  1 Crest Way 07747   732-290-2705
  Bruce M. Quinn, supt.   Fax 290-0751
  www.marsd.k12.nj.us
Matawan Regional HS   1,000/9-12
  450 Atlantic Ave 07747   732-290-2800
  Dr. Christine Robbins, prin.   Fax 566-2404
Other Schools – See Cliffwood

Monmouth County Vocational SD
  Supt. — See Freehold
Aberdeen Vocational S   Vo/Tech
  450 Atlantic Ave 07747   732-566-5599
  James Johnson, prin.   Fax 566-2392

Absecon, Atlantic, Pop. 7,835
Absecon CSD   900/K-8
  800 Irelan Ave 08201   609-641-5375
  James A. Giaquinto, supt.   Fax 641-8692
  www.absconschools.org
Attales MS   400/5-8
  800 Irelan Ave 08201   609-641-5375
  Karen Woods, prin.   Fax 641-8692

Holy Spirit HS   900/9-12
  500 S New Rd 08201   609-646-3000
  Fr. Joseph Perreault, prin.   Fax 646-1770

Adelphia, Monmouth

Talmudical Academy of New Jersey   Post-Sec.
  Route 524 07710   732-431-1600
Talmudical Academy of NJ   50/9-12
  PO Box 7 07710   732-431-1600
  Mendy Nestlebaum, prin.   Fax 431-3951

Allendale, Bergen, Pop. 6,775
Allendale SD   1,000/K-8
  100 Brookside Ave 07401   201-327-2020
  Jerilyn M. Caprio Ed.D., supt.   Fax 825-6553
  www.allendaleschoolsnj.com
Brookside MS   600/4-8
  100 Brookside Ave 07401   201-327-2021
  Bruce Winkelstein, prin.   Fax 825-6553

Northern Highlands Regional HSD   1,200/9-12
  298 Hillside Ave 07401   201-327-8700
  Dr. Robert McGuire, supt.   Fax 327-5274
  www.northernhighlands.org
Northern Highlands Regional HS   1,200/9-12
  298 Hillside Ave 07401   201-327-8700
  John Keenan, prin.   Fax 327-3370

Allentown, Monmouth, Pop. 1,859
Upper Freehold Regional SD   2,000/PK-12
  27 High St 08501   609-259-7292
  Robert Connelly, supt.   Fax 259-0881
  www.ufrsd.net

Allentown HS   900/9-12
  27 High St 08501   609-259-2160
  Christopher Nagy, prin.   Fax 259-0390

Annandale, Hunterdon, Pop. 1,074
Hunterdon Co Vocational SD
  Supt. – See Flemington
North Hunterdon Vocational S   Vo/Tech
  1445 State Route 31 S 08801   908-735-6774
  Kim Metz, prin.

North Hunterdon/Vorhees Regional HSD 2,700/9-12
  1445 State Route 31 S 08801   908-735-2846
  Dr. Charles Shaddow, supt.   Fax 735-6914
  www.nhvweb.net
North Hunterdon HS   1,500/9-12
  1445 State Route 31 S 08801   908-735-5191
  Michael Hughes, prin.   Fax 735-5191
Other Schools – See Glen Gardner

Asbury, Hunterdon
Bethlehem Township SD   600/K-8
  940 Iron Bridge Rd 08802   908-537-4044
  Dr. Mario Barbiere, supt.   Fax 537-7224
  www.btschools.org
Hoppock MS   300/5-8
  280 Asbury West Portal Rd 08802   908-479-6336
  Edward Keegan, prin.   Fax 479-1021

Asbury Park, Monmouth, Pop. 16,693
Asbury Park SD   2,700/PK-12
  407 Lake Ave 07712   732-776-2606
  Dr. Antonio N. Lewis, supt.   Fax 774-8067
  www.asburypark.k12.nj.us
Asbury Park HS   600/9-12
  1003 Sunset Ave 07712   732-776-2638
  Dr. Linda Palumbo, prin.   Fax 776-3119
Asbury Park MS   700/6-8
  1200 Bangs Ave 07712   732-776-2559
  Frank Vanalesti, prin.   Fax 776-7503
Asbury Evening HS   Adult
  523 Lake Ave 07712   732-776-2666
  Bernadette Williams, prin.   Fax 776-2667

Monmouth County Vocational SD
  Supt. — See Freehold
Culinary Education Center   Vo/Tech
  101 Drury Ln 07712   732-988-3299
  Michael Sirianni, prin.   Fax 776-8096

Atco, Camden
Winslow Township SD   7,200/PK-12
  30 Cooper Folly Rd 08004   856-767-2850
  Dr. Michael Schreiner, supt.
  www.winslow-schools.com
Winslow Twp. HS   1,600/9-12
  200 Coopers Folly Rd 08004   856-767-1850
  Jesse King, prin.

Winslow Twp. MS   1,300/7-9
  200 Coopers Folly Rd 08004   856-767-7222
  Dr. Mary Alimenti, prin.

Atlantic City, Atlantic, Pop. 40,385
Atlantic City SD   6,800/PK-12
  1300 Atlantic Ave 08401   609-343-7200
  Fredrick Nickles, supt.   Fax 345-3268
  www.acboe.org/
Atlantic City HS   2,600/9-12
  1400 N Albany Ave 08401   609-343-7300
  Oscar Torres, prin.   Fax 343-7345
Atlantic City Evening HS   Adult
  1400 N Albany Ave 08401   609-343-7300
  George Cullingford, admin.   Fax 343-7345

Audubon, Camden, Pop. 9,118
Audubon SD   1,600/K-12
  350 Edgewood Ave 08106   856-547-1325
  Mary Ann Reede, supt.   Fax 546-5853
  www.audubon.k12.nj.us/
Audubon JSHS   900/7-12
  350 Edgewood Ave 08106   856-547-7695
  Donald Borden, prin.   Fax 547-4073

Avenel, Middlesex, Pop. 15,504
Woodbridge Township SD
  Supt. — See Woodbridge
Avenel MS   700/6-8
  85 Woodbine Ave 07001   732-396-7020
  Gary Kuzniak, prin.   Fax 574-0573

Barnegat, Ocean, Pop. 1,160
Barnegat Township SD   2,100/K-12
  550 Barnegat Blvd N 08005   609-698-5800
  Dr. Thomas C. McMahon, supt.   Fax 698-6608
  www.bts.k12.nj.us
Barnegat HS   9-12
  180 Bengal Blvd 08005   609-660-7510
  Joseph Saxton, prin.   Fax 660-7598
Brackman MS   800/6-8
  600 Barnegat Blvd N 08005   609-698-5880
  Stephen Nichol, prin.   Fax 698-7965

Barrington, Camden, Pop. 7,072
Barrington Borough SD   600/K-8
  311 Reading Ave 08007   856-547-8467
  Dr. Loyola Garcia, supt.   Fax 547-5533
  www.ccts-ettc.org/barrington
Woodland MS   300/4-8
  1 School Ln 08007   856-547-8402
  Patricia Moore, prin.   Fax 522-1248

Basking Ridge, Somerset, Pop. 4,000
Bernards Township SD   4,900/K-12
  101 Peachtree Rd 07920   908-204-2600
  Dr. Valerie A. Goger, supt.   Fax 766-7641
  www.bernardsboe.com/

Annin MS
70 Quincy Rd 07920 — 1,200/6-8 — 908-204-2610
Frank Howlett, prin. — Fax 204-0244
Ridge HS — 1,300/9-12
268 S Finley Ave 07920 — 908-204-2585
Richard Stotler, prin. — Fax 204-2582

Bayonne, Hudson, Pop. 60,905
Bayonne SD — 7,900/PK-12
669 Avenue A 07002 — 201-858-5817
Dr. Patricia L. McGeehan, supt. — Fax 858-6289
www.bhs.bboed.org/
Bayonne HS — 2,100/9-12
667 Avenue A 07002 — 201-858-5900
Richard Baccarella, prin. — Fax 858-6263
Public S 14 — 200/4-8
101 W 23rd St 07002 — 201-858-6281
Janice Lo Re, prin. — Fax 436-5079
ACC Evening HS — Adult
Avenue A & 28th St 07002 — 201-858-5851
Monica Flynn, dir.

Hudson County Vocational SD
Supt. — See North Bergen
Hudson County AVTS - Bayonne — Vo/Tech
Ave A & 28th St 07002 — 201-854-2107
Joseph Sirangelo, prin.

Bayonne Hospital School of Nursing — Post-Sec.
29 E 29th St 07002 — 201-339-9656
Holy Family Academy — 300/9-12
239 Avenue A 07002 — 201-339-7341
Sr. Mary Ford, prin. — Fax 339-9295
Marist HS — 400/9-12
1241 Kennedy Blvd 07002 — 201-437-4544
Br. Stephen Schlitte, prin. — Fax 437-6013
Yeshiva Gedola of Bayonne — 100/9-12
735 Avenue C 07002 — 201-339-7187
Shmuel Horowitz, prin. — Fax 339-8339

Bayville, Ocean
Central Regional SD — 2,300/7-12
509 Forest Hills Pkwy 08721 — 732-269-1100
David Trethaway, supt. — Fax 269-7723
www.centralreg.k12.nj.us
Central Regional HS — 1,500/9-12
509 Forest Hills Pkwy 08721 — 732-269-1100
Bruce Orsino, prin. — Fax 269-7723
Central Regional MS — 800/7-8
509 Forest Hills Pkwy 08721 — 732-269-1100
T. Parlapanides, prin. — Fax 269-7723

Beachwood, Ocean, Pop. 10,712
Toms River Regional SD
Supt. — See Toms River
Toms River IS South — 6-8
1675 Pinewald Rd 08722 — 732-818-8570
Paul Gluck, prin.

Belleville, Essex, Pop. 36,300
Belleville SD — 4,400/K-12
102 Passaic Ave 07109 — 973-450-3500
Dr. Edward Kliszus, supt. — Fax 450-3504
www.belleville.k12.nj.us/
Belleville HS — 1,600/9-12
100 Passaic Ave 07109 — 973-450-3500
Joseph Patrillo, prin. — Fax 450-4021
Belleville MS — 700/7-8
279 Washington Ave 07109 — 973-450-3532
Dr. Marilyn McGrath, prin.

Bellmawr, Camden, Pop. 11,261
Bellmawr Borough SD — 900/K-8
256 Anderson Ave 08031 — 856-931-3620
Deborah Monahan Ph.D., supt. — Fax 931-9326
bellmawrschools.org
Bell Oaks SD — 400/5-8
256 Anderson Ave 08031 — 856-931-6273
Anthony Farinelli, prin.

Belmar, Monmouth, Pop. 5,975

St. Rose HS — 600/9-12
607 7th Ave 07719 — 732-681-2858
Dr. Michele Campbell, prin. — Fax 280-2745

Belvidere, Warren, Pop. 2,777
Belvidere SD — 900/K-12
809 Oxford St 07823 — 908-475-6600
Dr. Jean Atkin Gool, supt. — Fax 475-6619
www.belvideresd.org
Belvidere HS — 500/9-12
809 Oxford St 07823 — 908-475-4025
Dirk Swaneveld, prin. — Fax 475-1685
Oxford Street MS — 200/4-8
807 Oxford St 07823 — 908-475-4001
Karl Rice, prin. — Fax 475-6619

Bergenfield, Bergen, Pop. 26,181
Bergenfield SD — 3,700/K-12
100 S Prospect Ave 07621 — 201-385-8202
Dr. Michael Kuchar, supt. — Fax 385-3718
www.bergenfield.org/
Bergenfield HS — 1,100/9-12
80 S Prospect Ave 07621 — 201-385-8600
Hank Sinatra, prin. — Fax 439-0978
Brown MS — 900/6-8
130 S Washington Ave 07621 — 201-385-8847
Steven Kaminsky, prin. — Fax 385-0219

Berkeley Heights, Union, Pop. 11,980
Berkeley Heights SD — 2,700/PK-12
345 Plainfield Ave 07922 — 908-464-1718
Judith Rattner, supt. — Fax 464-7673
www.bhs.k12.nj.us
Columbia MS — 600/6-8
345 Plainfield Ave 07922 — 908-464-1600
John Dennis, prin. — Fax 464-7673
Livingston HS — 900/9-12
175 Watchung Blvd 07922 — 908-464-3100
John Farinella, prin. — Fax 464-7508

Bernardsville, Somerset, Pop. 7,559
Somerset Hills SD — 1,900/K-12
25 Olcott Ave 07924 — 908-204-1930
Peter Miller, supt. — Fax 953-0567
www.shsd.org/index.htm
Bernards HS — 700/9-12
25 Olcott Ave 07924 — 908-630-3001
Dr. Lynn Caravello, prin. — Fax 766-8223

Bernardsville MS — 500/5-8
141 Seney Dr 07924 — 908-204-1916
Dr. Lynn Kratz, prin. — Fax 953-2184

Blackwood, Camden, Pop. 5,120
Black Horse Pike Regional SD — 3,500/9-12
580 Erial Rd 08012 — 856-227-4106
Ralph E. Ross, supt. — Fax 227-6835
www.bhprsd.org
Highland HS — 1,000/9-12
450 Erial Rd 08012 — 856-227-4100
Frank Palatucci, prin. — Fax 227-3619
Other Schools – See Erial, Runnemede

Gloucester Township SD — 7,800/K-8
17 Erial Rd 08012 — 856-227-1400
Thomas Seddon, supt. — Fax 228-1422
www.gloucestertownshipschools.org/
Glen Landing MS — 900/6-8
85 Little Gloucester Rd 08012 — 856-227-3534
Alan Gansert, prin.
Lewis MS, 875 Erial Rd 08012 — 800/6-8
Constance Bauer, prin. — 856-227-8400
Other Schools – See Sicklerville

Camden County College — Post-Sec.
PO Box 200 08012 — 856-227-7200
Helene Fuld School of Nursing — Post-Sec.
PO Box 1669 08012 — 856-374-0100
Pennco Tech — Post-Sec.
PO Box 1427 08012 — 856-232-0310

Blairstown, Warren
North Warren Regional SD — 1,000/7-12
PO Box 410 07825 — 908-362-9342
Dr. John Toleno, supt. — Fax 362-8744
www.northwarren.org
North Warren Regional JSHS — 1,000/7-12
PO Box 410 07825 — 908-362-8211
G. Kennedy Greene, prin. — Fax 362-7353

Blair Academy — 400/9-12
PO Box 600 07825 — 908-362-6121
T. Chandler Hardwick, hdmstr. — Fax 362-5157

Bloomfield, Essex, Pop. 48,200
Bloomfield Township SD — 5,900/PK-12
155 Broad St 07003 — 973-680-8555
Thomas Dowd, supt. — Fax 680-0263
www.bloomfield.k12.nj.us
Bloomfield HS — 1,900/9-12
160 Broad St 07003 — 973-680-8600
Pasquale Orsini, prin. — Fax 680-8684
Bloomfield MS — 1,000/7-8
60 Huck Rd 07003 — 973-680-8620
Patricia Pelikan, prin. — Fax 338-6523

Essex County Vocational SD
Supt. — See Verona
Essex County Vocational HS-Bloomfield — Vo/Tech
209 Franklin St 07003 — 973-429-8893
Eric Love, prin. — Fax 429-7330

Bloomfield College — Post-Sec.
467 Franklin St 07003 — 973-748-9000
Concorde School of Hair Design — Post-Sec.
9 Ward St 07003 — 973-680-0099

Bloomingdale, Passaic, Pop. 7,693
Bloomingdale SD — 700/K-8
31 Captolene Ave 07403 — 973-838-3282
Thomas W. Comiciotto, supt. — Fax 838-8188
www.bloomingdale.k12.nj.us
Bergen MS — 300/5-8
225 Glenwild Ave 07403 — 973-838-4835
Daniel C. French, prin. — Fax 283-1893

Bogota, Bergen, Pop. 8,181
Bogota SD — 1,000/K-12
1 Henry C Luthin Pl 07603 — 201-441-4800
Jose R. Negron, supt. — Fax 489-5759
Bogota JSHS — 500/7-12
2 Henry C Luthin Pl 07603 — 201-441-4809
Arnold Oftedal, prin. — Fax 441-4849

Boonton, Morris, Pop. 8,427
Boonton SD — 1,300/K-12
434 Lathrop Ave 07005 — 973-335-3994
Mario Cardinale, supt. — Fax 335-8281
www.boonton.org/schools/schools/index.htm
Boonton HS — 600/9-12
306 Lathrop Ave 07005 — 973-335-9700
Augustus Modla, prin. — Fax 402-5135
Boonton MS — 100/7-8
306 Lathrop Ave 07005 — 973-335-9700
Carl Cucchiara, prin. — Fax 402-5135

Bordentown, Burlington, Pop. 4,013
Bordentown Regional SD — 2,100/K-12
48 Dunns Mill Rd 08505 — 609-298-0025
John Polomano, supt. — Fax 298-2515
www.bordentown.k12.nj.us
Bordentown Regional HS — 700/9-12
50 Dunns Mill Rd 08505 — 609-298-0025
Frederick D'Antoni, prin. — Fax 291-0347
McFarland JHS — 300/7-8
87 Crosswicks St 08505 — 609-298-0674
Dr. Norine Gerepka-Bachalis, prin. — Fax 291-1929

Bound Brook, Somerset, Pop. 10,151
Bound Brook Borough SD — 1,600/PK-12
W 2nd St LaMonte Building 08805 — 732-652-7920
Dr. Edward Hoffman, supt. — Fax 271-9097
www.bbrook.k12.nj.us
Bound Brook MSHS — 700/7-12
111 W Union Ave 08805 — 732-652-7950
Dr. Daniel Gallagher, prin. — Fax 356-6445

Branchburg, Somerset
Branchburg Township SD — 1,900/K-8
240 Baird Rd 08876 — 908-722-3335
Walter Oberwanowicz, supt. — Fax 526-6144
www.branchburg.k12.nj.us
Branchburg Central MS — 600/6-8
220 Baird Rd 08876 — 908-526-1415
William Feldman, prin. — Fax 526-7486

Brick, Ocean, Pop. 78,300
Brick Township SD — 11,200/PK-12
101 Hendrickson Ave 08724 — 732-785-3000
Dr. Thomas Seidenberger, supt. — Fax 840-9089
www.brickschools.org/
Brick Township HS — 1,800/9-12
346 Chambersbridge Rd 08723 — 732-262-2500
Dennis Filippone, prin. — Fax 920-5907
Brick Township Memorial HS — 1,900/9-12
2001 Lanes Mill Rd 08724 — 732-785-3090
Robert Anderson, prin. — Fax 458-2748
Lake Riviera MS — 1,200/6-8
171 Beaverson Blvd 08723 — 732-262-2600
Susan McNamara, prin. — Fax 477-0392
Veteran's Memorial MS — 1,500/6-8
105 Hendrickson Ave 08724 — 732-785-3030
John VanDerslice, prin. — Fax 458-9777

Ocean County Vocational SD
Supt. — See Toms River
Ocean County Voc-Tech S - Brick — Vo/Tech
350 Chambersbridge Rd 08723 — 732-920-0050
Vern Beadle, prin. — Fax 920-0108

Capri Institute of Hair Design — Post-Sec.
268 Brick Blvd 08723 — 732-920-3600

Bridgeton, Cumberland, Pop. 22,785
Bridgeton SD — 2,800/PK-12
PO Box 657 08302 — 856-455-8030
Dr. H. Victor Gilson, supt. — Fax 451-0815
www.bridgeton.k12.nj.us/
Bridgeton HS — 900/9-12
111 N West Ave 08302 — 856-455-8030
Lynn Williams, prin. — Fax 455-0486
Broad Street MS — 300/6-8
251 W Broad St 08302 — 856-455-8030
J. Michael Coyne, prin. — Fax 453-7684
Adult Learning Center — Adult
111 N West Ave 08302 — 856-455-8030
Sam Hull, prin. — Fax 455-4217

Cumberland County Vocational SD
601 Bridgeton Ave 08302 — 856-451-9000
Darlene Barber, supt. — Fax 451-8487
www.cumberland.tec.nj.us
Cumberland County Technical Educ. Center — Vo/Tech
601 Bridgeton Ave 08302 — 856-451-9000
Robert Riccio, prin. — Fax 451-8487

Fairfield Township SD — 500/PK-8
13 Ramah Rd 08302 — 856-451-1128
Thomas Smith, supt. — Fax 455-2666
www.fairfield.k12.nj.us
Fairfield Township MS — 200/5-8
1112 Bridgeton Millville Pk 08302 — 856-451-2164
John Klug, prin. — Fax 451-8155

Cumberland Co. Tech. Education Center — Post-Sec.
601 Bridgeton Ave 08302 — 856-451-9000

Bridgewater, Somerset, Pop. 36,400
Bridgewater-Raritan Regional SD — 8,500/PK-12
PO Box 6030 08807 — 908-685-2777
Dr. Walter Mahler, supt. — Fax 231-8496
www.brrsd.k12.nj.us
Bridgewater-Raritan HS — 2,400/9-12
PO Box 6569 08807 — 908-231-8660
Dr. James Riccobono, prin. — Fax 231-0467
Bridgewater-Raritan MS — 2,100/6-8
PO Box 6933 08807 — 908-231-8661
Nancy Mahoney, prin. — Fax 575-0847

Somerset County Vocational SD
PO Box 6350 08807 — 908-526-8900
Michael Maddaluna, supt. — Fax 704-0784
www.scti.org
Somerset County Vo-Tech HS — Vo/Tech
PO Box 6350 08807 — 908-526-8900
Edmund Jones, prin. — Fax 704-0784
Somerset County Adult Tech Inst — Adult
PO Box 6350 08807 — 908-526-8900
Joseph Malone, dir. — Fax 526-9494

Brigantine, Atlantic, Pop. 12,631
Brigantine CSD — 1,100/K-8
PO Box 947 08203 — 609-266-7671
Robert Previti, supt. — Fax 266-4748
www.brigantine.atlnet.org
Brigantine North MS — 500/5-8
PO Box 947 08203 — 609-266-3603
William Gussie, prin. — Fax 266-7062

Brookside, Morris
Mendham Township SD — 900/K-8
W Main St 07926 — 973-543-7107
Christine Johnson, supt. — Fax 543-5537
www.mendhamtwp.org
Mendham Twp. MS — 400/5-8
16 Washington Valley Rd 07926 — 973-543-2505
Stephen Geisel, prin. — Fax 543-0701

Budd Lake, Morris, Pop. 7,272
Mount Olive Township SD — 4,500/K-12
89 US Highway 46 07828 — 973-691-4008
Rosalie S. Lamonte Ph.D., supt. — Fax 691-4022
www.mtoliveboe.org
Mount Olive MS — 1,000/6-8
160 Wolfe Rd 07828 — 973-691-4006
Dr. Tracey Severns, prin. — Fax 691-4029
Other Schools – See Flanders

Buena, Atlantic, Pop. 3,832
Buena Regional SD — 2,400/K-12
PO Box 309 08310 — 856-697-0800
Diane DeGiacomo, supt. — Fax 697-4963
www.buena.k12.nj.us/
Buena Regional HS — 1,000/9-12
125 E Weymouth Rd 08310 — 856-697-2400
Ken Soboloski, prin. — Fax 697-4701
Other Schools – See Minotola

Burlington, Burlington, Pop. 9,809
Burlington CSD — 1,800/PK-12
518 Locust Ave 08016 — 609-387-5874
Dr. Edward Gola, supt. — Fax 386-6971
www.burlington-nj.net

Burlington City JSHS | 900/7-12
100 Blue Devil Way 08016 | 609-387-5800
Julian Jenkins, prin. | Fax 387-4287

Burlington Township SD | 4,100/PK-12
PO Box 428 08016 | 609-387-3955
Christopher Manno, supt. | Fax 239-2192
www.burltwpsch.org/
Burlington Twp. HS | 1,000/9-12
610 Fountain Ave 08016 | 609-387-1713
William Stonis, prin. | Fax 387-0439
Hopkins MS | 600/7-8
700 Jacksonville Rd 08016 | 609-387-3774
Lawrence Penny, prin. | Fax 239-0883

Institute of Logistical Management | Post-Sec.
PO Box 427 08016 | 609-747-1515
Life Center Academy | 400/PK-12
2045 Columbus Rd 08016 | 609-499-2100
Robert H. Newman, prin. | Fax 499-4905
St. Mary's Hall/Doane Academy | 200/PK-12
350 Riverbank 08016 | 609-386-3500
John F. McGee, hdmstr. | Fax 386-5878

Butler, Morris, Pop. 8,099
Butler SD | 1,100/K-12
38 Bartholdi Ave 07405 | 973-492-2032
Dr. Rene Rovtar, supt. | Fax 492-1016
www.morris.k12.nj.us/butler
Butler HS | 500/9-12
38 Bartholdi Ave 07405 | 973-492-2000
William Hanisch, prin. | Fax 492-8672
Butler MS | 300/5-8
34 Pearl Pl 07405 | 973-492-2079
Andrea Vladichak, prin. | Fax 492-9774

Morris County Vocational SD
Supt. — See Denville
Academy for Law & Public Safety | Vo/Tech
Bartholdi Ave 07405 | 973-492-2000
William Hanisch, prin.

Caldwell, Essex, Pop. 7,620
Caldwell-West Caldwell SD
Supt. — See West Caldwell
Cleveland JHS | 600/6-8
36 Academy Rd 07006 | 973-228-9115
Casey Shorter, prin.

Caldwell College | Post-Sec.
9 Ryerson Ave 07006 | 973-618-3000
Mt. St. Dominic Academy | 300/9-12
3 Ryerson Ave 07006 | 973-226-0660
Sr. Frances Sullivan, prin. | Fax 226-2693

Califon, Hunterdon, Pop. 1,060
Lebanon Township SD | 800/K-8
70 Bunnvale Rd 07830 | 908-638-4521
Judith Burd, supt. | Fax 638-5511
www.lebtwpk8.org
Woodglen MS | 400/5-8
70 Bunnvale Rd 07830 | 908-638-4111
Michael Rubright, prin. | Fax 638-8418

Tewksbury Township SD | 300/PK-8
173 County Road 517 07830 | 908-439-2101
Dr. Gayle M. Carrick, supt. | Fax 439-2655
www.tewksburyschools.org
Old Turnpike MS | 300/5-8
171 County Road 517 07830 | 908-439-2010
William Petrick, prin. | Fax 439-3160

Camden, Camden, Pop. 80,089
Camden CSD | 14,500/PK-12
201 N Front St 08102 | 856-966-2040
Annette Knox, supt. | Fax 966-2138
www.camden.k12.nj.us
Brimm Medical Arts HS | Vo/Tech
1626 Copewood St 08103 | 856-966-2500
Joseph Carruth, prin. | Fax 966-2489
Camden HS | 1,000/9-12
1700 Park Blvd 08103 | 856-966-5100
Betty Herring, prin. | Fax 966-4756
Creative & Performing Arts HS | 9-12
Filmore & Carl Miller Blvd 08104 | 856-966-8955
Davida Coe, prin. | Fax 964-9759
East Camden MS | 600/5-8
3064 Stevens St 08105 | 856-966-5111
Patricia Kenny, prin. | Fax 964-9791
Hatch MS | 400/6-8
1875 Park Blvd 08103 | 856-966-5122
Calvin Gunning, prin. | Fax 964-0778
Morgan Village MS | 500/5-8
1000 Morgan Blvd 08104 | 856-966-5330
Louis Mason, prin. | Fax 964-8443
Pyne Poynt MS | 500/4-8
800 Erie St 08102 | 856-966-5360
Daniel Edwards, prin. | Fax 964-8462
Veterans Memorial MS | 500/5-8
26th & Hayes 08105 | 856-966-5090
Patricia Cook, prin. | Fax 541-5141
Wilson HS | 1,200/9-12
3100 Federal St 08105 | 856-966-5300
Mary Edwards, prin. | Fax 966-4755
Riggs Adult Education S | Adult
1656 Kaighns Ave 08103 | 856-966-5223
John Randall, prin. | Fax 541-8671

Cooper Hospital/Univ Medical Center | Post-Sec.
1 Cooper Plz # 217 08103 | 856-342-2416
Our Lady of Lourdes School of Nursing | Post-Sec.
1600 Haddon Ave 08103 | 856-757-3729
Rowan University | Post-Sec.
200 N Broadway 08102 | 856-757-2857
Rutgers-The State University of N.J. | Post-Sec.
311 N 5th St 08102 | 856-225-6026
San Miguel S | 50/6-8
836 S 4th St 08103 | 856-342-6707
Lenee Johnson, prin. | Fax 342-6708
West Jersey Health System | Post-Sec.
1000 Atlantic Ave 08104 | 856-342-4600

Cape May, Cape May, Pop. 3,923
Lower Cap May Regional SD | 1,800/7-12
687 Route 9 08204 | 609-884-3475
Jack Pfizenmayer, supt. | Fax 884-7067
lcmrschool.org/lcmr/index.htm

Lower Cape May Regional HS | 1,100/9-12
687 Route 9 08204 | 609-884-3475
Joe Castellucci, prin. | Fax 884-0546
Teitelman MS | 700/7-8
687 Route 9 08204 | 609-884-3475
Eugene Sole, prin. | Fax 884-4311

Cape May Court House, Cape May, Pop. 4,426
Cape May County Vo-Tech SD
188 Crest Haven Rd, | 609-465-2161
William E. Desmond, supt. | Fax 465-3069
www.capemaytech.com
Cape May County Tech HS | Vo/Tech
188 Crest Haven Rd, | 609-465-2161
Robert Matthies, prin.
Cape May County Tech Evening HS | Adult
188 Crest Haven Rd, | 609-465-2161
George Miller, prin.

Dennis Township SD | 500/PK-8
601 Hagen Rd, | 609-861-0549
George Papp, supt. | Fax 861-1833
dennis.capemayschools.com/
Other Schools – See Dennisville

Middle Township SD | 2,900/PK-12
216 S Main St, | 609-465-1800
Michael Kopakowski, supt. | Fax 465-7058
middle.capemayschools.com/
Middle Twp. HS | 1,100/9-12
300 E Atlantic Ave, | 609-465-1852
David Salvo, prin. | Fax 465-3415
Middle Twp. MS 4 | 600/6-8
300 E Pacific Ave, | 609-465-1834
Amos Kraybill, prin. | Fax 465-5524

Burdette Tomlin Memorial Hospital | Post-Sec.
2 Stone Harbor Blvd, | 609-463-2180
Cape Christian Academy | 200/PK-12
10 Oyster Rd, | 609-465-4132
James Patterson, admin. | Fax 465-0170
Cape May County Technical Institute | Post-Sec.
188 Crest Haven Rd, | 609-465-2161

Carlstadt, Bergen, Pop. 5,994
Carlstadt SD | 500/PK-8
550 Washington St 07072 | 201-939-6502
Frank Legato, supt. | Fax 939-5710
www.carlstadt.org
Washington MS | 300/3-8
325 3rd St 07072 | 201-939-6506
Lawrence Giblin, prin. | Fax 939-8371

Carneys Point, Salem, Pop. 7,686
Penns Grove-Carneys Point Regional SD
Supt. — See Penns Grove
Penns Grove HS | 600/9-12
334 Harding Hwy 08069 | 856-299-6300
Dr. Paul Rufino, prin. | Fax 299-5192

Salem Community College | Post-Sec.
460 Hollywood Ave 08069 | 856-299-2100

Carteret, Middlesex, Pop. 21,653
Carteret Borough SD | 3,800/PK-12
599 Roosevelt Ave 07008 | 732-541-8960
Kevin Ahearn, supt. | Fax 541-7028
www.carteretschools.org
Carteret HS | 1,000/9-12
199 Washington Ave 07008 | 732-541-8960
Dennis Siddons, prin. | Fax 969-4004
Carteret MS | 900/6-8
300 Carteret Ave 07008 | 732-541-8960
Eugene Barrett, prin. | Fax 541-0483

Cedar Grove, Essex, Pop. 12,053
Cedar Grove Township SD | 1,400/K-12
520 Pompton Ave 07009 | 973-239-1550
Dr. Eugene Polles, supt. | Fax 239-2994
www.cedargrove.k12.nj.us
Cedar Grove HS | 400/9-12
90 Rugby Rd 07009 | 973-239-6400
Judith Nappi, prin. | Fax 857-9833
Cedar Grove Memorial MS | 500/5-8
500 Ridge Rd 07009 | 973-239-2646
Lawrence Neugebauer, prin. | Fax 239-2003

Chatham, Morris, Pop. 8,440
School District of the Chathams | 3,100/K-12
58 Meyersville Rd 07928 | 973-635-5656
James O'Neill, supt. | Fax 701-0146
www.chatham-nj.org/coin
Chatham HS | 800/9-12
255 Lafayette Ave 07928 | 973-635-9075
Michael LaSusa, prin. | Fax 635-8670
Chatham MS | 700/6-8
480 Main St 07928 | 973-635-7200
Kenneth Wark, prin. | Fax 635-7190

Cherry Hill, Camden, Pop. 70,100
Cherry Hill Township SD | 10,900/K-12
45 Ranoldo Ter 08034 | 856-429-5600
Dr. Morton Sherman, supt. | Fax 354-1864
www.cherryhill.k12.nj.us/
Beck MS | 600/7-8
936 Cropwell Rd 08003 | 856-424-4505
Dr. Dennis Perry, prin. | Fax 424-8602
Carusi MS | 900/6-8
315 Roosevelt Dr 08002 | 856-667-1220
Brian Betze, prin. | Fax 779-0613
Cherry Hill HS - East | 2,100/9-12
1750 Kresson Rd 08003 | 856-424-2222
John O'Breza, prin. | Fax 424-0637
Cherry Hill HS - West | 1,600/9-12
2101 Chapel Ave W 08002 | 856-663-8006
George Munyan, prin. | Fax 663-5746
Rosa International MS | 800/6-8
485 Browning Ln 08003 | 856-616-8787
Ed Canzanese, prin.

Camden Catholic HS | 800/9-12
300 Cuthbert Rd 08002 | 856-663-2247
Thomas Kiely, prin. | Fax 661-0632
Chubb Institute | Post-Sec.
2100 Route 38 08002 | 856-988-9880
Empire Beauty School | Post-Sec.
2100 State Highway #38 08002 | 856-667-8887
Harris School of Business | Post-Sec.
1 Mall Dr Ste 700 08002 | 856-662-5300

Kings Christian S | 400/PK-12
5 Carnegie Plz 08003 | 856-489-6720
Jonathan Nazigian, prin. | Fax 489-6727
Living Faith Christian Academy | 200/K-10
202 Park Blvd 08002 | 856-665-5507
Gail Foster, prin. | Fax 665-5601

Chester, Morris, Pop. 1,655
Chester Township SD | 1,300/K-8
415 State Route 24 07930 | 908-879-7383
Michael Roth, supt. | Fax 879-8669
www.chester-nj.org
Black River MS | 400/6-8
Route 513 07930 | 908-879-6363
Robert Mullen, prin. | Fax 879-9085

West Morris Regional HSD | 2,400/9-12
10 S Four Bridges Rd 07930 | 908-879-6404
Anthony di Battista, supt. | Fax 879-8861
www.wmrhsd.org
West Morris Central HS | 1,300/9-12
259 Bartley Naughright Rd 07930 | 908-879-5212
Michael Reilly, prin. | Fax 879-2741
Other Schools – See Mendham

Cinnaminson, Burlington, Pop. 14,583
Cinnaminson Township SD | 2,400/K-12
PO Box 224 08077 | 856-829-7600
Salvatore Illuzzi, supt. | Fax 786-9618
www.cinnaminson.com
Cinnaminson HS | 900/9-12
1197 Riverton Rd 08077 | 856-829-7770
Michael Zank, prin. | Fax 829-7777
Cinnaminson MS | 600/6-8
312 N Fork Landing Rd 08077 | 856-786-8012
Gay Moceri, prin. | Fax 786-1860

Clark, Union, Pop. 14,629
Clark Township SD | 2,300/K-12
365 Westfield Ave 07066 | 732-574-9600
Dr. Brian Zychowski, supt. | Fax 382-5957
www.clarkschools.org
Johnson Regional HS | 900/9-12
365 Westfield Ave 07066 | 732-382-0910
Robert Taylor, prin. | Fax 382-5957
Kumpf MS | 500/6-8
59 Mildred Ter 07066 | 732-381-0400
James Carovillano, prin. | Fax 381-0262

Mother Seton Regional HS | 400/9-12
Valley Rd 07066 | 732-382-1952
Sr. Regina Martin, prin. | Fax 382-4725

Clarksburg, Monmouth
Millstone Township SD | 1,700/K-8
18 Schoolhouse Rd 08510 | 732-446-0890
Dr. William Setaro, supt. | Fax 792-2948
www.millstone.k12.nj.us
Millstone Township MS | 800/5-8
308 Millstone Rd 08510 | 732-446-6802
Daniel Bland, prin. | Fax 792-9754

Clayton, Gloucester, Pop. 7,157
Clayton SD | 1,100/PK-12
300 W Chestnut St 08312 | 856-881-8700
Dr. Catherine Hills, supt. | Fax 863-8196
www.clayton.k12.nj.us
Clayton MSHS | 500/7-12
350 E Clinton St 08312 | 856-881-8701
Cleve Bryan, prin. | Fax 863-0808

Cliffside Park, Bergen, Pop. 22,892
Cliffside Park SD | 2,300/K-12
525 Palisade Ave 07010 | 201-313-2310
Robert J. Paladino, supt. | Fax 943-7050
www.cliffsidepark.edu
Cliffside Park HS | 1,000/9-12
64 Riverview Ave 07010 | 201-313-2370
Michael Romagnino, prin. | Fax 313-7961

Cliffwood, Monmouth, Pop. 1,500
Matawan-Aberdeen Regional SD
Supt. — See Aberdeen
Matawan Aberdeen MS | 1,000/6-8
469 Matawan Ave 07721 | 732-290-2600
Walter Uszenski, prin. | Fax 566-1183

Clifton, Passaic, Pop. 79,823
Clifton SD, PO Box 2209 07015 | 9,700/K-12
Michael Rice Ph.D., supt. | 973-470-2260
www.clifton.k12.nj.us
Clifton HS | 3,200/9-12
333 Colfax Ave 07013 | 973-470-2312
William Cannici, prin. | Fax 458-9290
Columbus MS | 1,200/6-8
350 Piaget Ave 07011 | 973-470-2360
Dr. Robert Valente, prin. | Fax 470-2365
Wilson MS | 1,200/6-8
1400 Van Houten Ave 07013 | 973-470-2350
William Hahn, prin. | Fax 470-2607

Capri Institute of Hair Design | Post-Sec.
1595 Main Ave 07011 | 973-772-4610
KeySkills Learning | Post-Sec.
50 Mount Prospect Ave 07013 | 973-778-8136

Collingswood, Camden, Pop. 14,220
Collingswood Borough SD | 2,000/K-12
200 Lees Ave 08108 | 856-962-5732
James Bathurst, supt. | Fax 962-5723
collingswood.k12.nj.us
Collingswood HS | 900/9-12
424 W Collings Ave 08108 | 856-962-5701
Charles Earling, prin. | Fax 962-5565
Collingswood MS | 300/7-8
414 W Collings Ave 08108 | 856-962-5702
John McMullin, prin. | Fax 962-5751

Colonia, Middlesex, Pop. 18,238
Woodbridge Township SD
Supt. — See Woodbridge
Colonia HS | 1,300/9-12
180 East St 07067 | 732-499-6500
Robert McLaughlin, prin. | Fax 574-2575
Colonia MS | 600/6-8
100 Delaware Ave 07067 | 732-396-7000
Gregg Miller, prin. | Fax 574-0772

Colts Neck, Monmouth
Colts Neck Township SD — 1,500/K-8
70 Conover Rd 07722 — 732-946-0055
Dr. Richard Fitzpatrick, supt. — Fax 946-4792
www.coltsneckschools.org
Cedar Drive MS — 600/6-8
73 Cedar Dr 07722 — 732-946-0055
Joan Kilcommons, prin. — Fax 462-4108

Freehold Regional HSD
Supt. — See Englishtown
Colts Neck HS — 1,400/9-12
59 Five Points Rd 07722 — 732-761-0190
R. McChesney, prin. — Fax 761-0193

Columbus, Burlington
Northern Burlington County Regional SD — 1,900/7-12
160 Mansfield Rd E 08022 — 609-298-3900
Dr. James Sarruda, supt. — Fax 291-8279
www.nburlington.com
Northern Burlington County Regional HS — 1,200/9-12
160 Mansfield Rd E 08022 — 609-298-3900
Eric C. Barnett, prin. — Fax 291-8279
Northern Burlington County Regional JHS — 700/7-8
160 Mansfield Rd E 08022 — 609-298-3900
Denise Dunham, prin.

Convent Station, Morris

Academy of St. Elizabeth — 300/9-12
PO Box 297 07961 — 973-605-3200
Sr. Patricia Costello, prin.

Cranford, Union, Pop. 22,624
Cranford Township SD — 3,400/K-12
132 Thomas St 07016 — 908-709-6202
Dr. Lawrence S. Feinsod, supt. — Fax 272-7735
www.cranfordschools.org
Cranford HS — 1,000/9-12
201 W End Pl 07016 — 908-709-6272
Carol Grossi, prin. — Fax 276-6552
Orange Avenue S — 700/3-8
901 Orange Ave 07016 — 908-709-6257
Kathleen Gorski, prin. — Fax 272-3025

Union County College — Post-Sec.
1033 Springfield Ave 07016 — 908-709-7000

Creamridge, Monmouth

New Jersey United Christian Academy — 50/8-12
73 Holmes Mill Rd 08514 — 609-738-2121
Donna Torres, prin. — Fax 738-2151

Cresskill, Bergen, Pop. 7,896
Cresskill SD — 1,500/K-12
1 Lincoln Dr 07626 — 201-567-5919
Dr. Charles Khoury, supt. — Fax 567-7976
www.cresskillboe.k12.nj.us
Cresskill JSHS — 700/7-12
1 Lincoln Dr 07626 — 201-567-5479
Peter Eftychiou, prin. — Fax 567-0028

Delanco, Burlington, Pop. 3,316
Delanco Township SD — 400/K-8
411 Walnut St 08075 — 856-461-0859
Michael Livengood, supt. — Fax 461-6903
www.delanco.com
Walnut Street MS — 100/6-8
411 Walnut St 08075 — 856-461-0874
Dorothy Mongo, prin. — Fax 461-6903

Delran, Burlington, Pop. 13,178
Delran Township SD — 2,500/K-12
52 Hartford Rd 08075 — 856-461-6800
Dr. George Sharp, supt. — Fax 461-6125
www.delran.k12.nj.us
Delran HS — 700/9-12
50 Hartford Rd 08075 — 856-461-6100
John Fricke, prin. — Fax 764-6177
Delran MS — 600/6-8
905 S Chester Ave 08075 — 856-461-8822
James Duda, prin. — Fax 461-0311

Harrison Career Institute — Post-Sec.
4000 Route 130 08075 — 856-764-8933
Holy Cross HS — 800/9-12
5035 Route 130 08075 — 856-461-5400
Joseph Lemme, prin. — Fax 764-0806

Demarest, Bergen, Pop. 4,910
Demarest SD — 700/K-8
568 Piermont Rd 07627 — 201-768-6060
Lawrence V. Hughes, supt. — Fax 767-9122
www.nvnet.org
Demarest MS — 300/5-8
568 Piermont Rd 07627 — 201-768-6061
Michael Fox, prin. — Fax 768-9122

Northern Valley Regional SD — 2,300/9-12
162 Knickerbocker Rd 07627 — 201-768-2200
Dr. Jan A. Furman, supt. — Fax 768-7356
www.nvnet.org/nvhs/
Northern Valley Regional HS — 1,100/9-12
150 Knickerbocker Rd 07627 — 201-768-3200
Bruce Sabatini, prin. — Fax 768-5438
Other Schools – See Old Tappan

Academy of the Holy Angels — 500/9-12
315 Hillside Ave 07627 — 201-768-7822
Jennifer Moran, prin. — Fax 768-6933

Dennisville, Cape May
Dennis Township SD
Supt. — See Cape May Court House
Dennis Township MS — 6-8
165 Academy Rd 08214 — 609-861-2821
James DiCarlo, prin. — Fax 861-5229

Denville, Morris, Pop. 13,812
Denville Township SD — 1,800/K-8
501 Openaki Rd 07834 — 973-366-1001
John Sakala, supt. — Fax 366-2481
www.denville.org
Valleyview MS — 600/6-8
320 Diamond Spring Rd 07834 — 973-627-7050
George Deamer, prin. — Fax 627-0632

Morris County Vocational SD
400 E Main St 07834 — 973-627-4600
James Rogers, supt. — Fax 627-4958
www.mcvts.org
Academy for Visual & Performing Arts — Vo/Tech
400 E Main St 07834 — 973-335-9700
Vito D'Alconzo, prin.
Morris County School of Technology — Vo/Tech
400 E Main St 07834 — 973-627-4600
Thomas Barnard, prin. — Fax 627-4958
Other Schools – See Butler, Rockaway

Morris Catholic HS — 400/9-12
200 Morris Ave 07834 — 973-627-6674
Dr. Jeanne Gradone, prin. — Fax 627-4351

Deptford, Gloucester
Deptford Township SD — 3,700/PK-12
2022 Good Intent Rd 08096 — 856-232-2700
Marie R. Louis, supt. — Fax 227-7473
www.deptford.k12.nj.us/
Deptford Twp. HS — 1,200/9-12
575 Fox Run Rd 08096 — 856-232-2713
Gary Swenson, prin. — Fax 374-9145
Other Schools – See Sewell

Harrison Career Institute — Post-Sec.
1450 Clements Bridge Rd 08096 — 856-384-2888

Dover, Morris, Pop. 18,372
Dover Town SD — 2,700/PK-12
100 Grace St 07801 — 973-989-2000
Charles P. DeLorenzo, supt. — Fax 989-1662
www.dover-nj.org
Dover HS — 800/9-12
100 Grace St 07801 — 973-989-2010
Paul DiRupo, prin. — Fax 989-1662
East Dover MS — 400/7-8
302 E McFarlan St 07801 — 973-989-2040
Kathleen Casiano, prin. — Fax 361-2117

Dover Business College — Post-Sec.
15 E Blackwell St 07801 — 973-285-8400
Joe Kubert Sch of Cartoon & Graphic Arts — Post-Sec.
37 Myrtle Ave 07801 — 973-361-1327

Dumont, Bergen, Pop. 17,523
Dumont SD — 2,600/K-12
25 Depew St 07628 — 201-387-3082
Dr. James Montesano, supt. — Fax 387-0259
www.dumontnj.org
Dumont HS — 800/9-12
101 New Milford Ave 07628 — 201-387-3060
Maria Poidomani, prin. — Fax 387-8461

Dunellen, Middlesex, Pop. 7,008
Dunellen SD — 1,100/K-12
High & Lehigh Sts 08812 — 732-968-3226
Dr. Joyce F. Baynes, supt. — Fax 968-3513
www.dunellenschools.org/
Dunellen HS — 300/9-12
411 First St 08812 — 732-968-0885
Pio Pennisi, prin. — Fax 968-3138
Lincoln MS, Lincoln Ave 08812 — 200/7-8
Pio Pennisi, prin. — 732-968-0885

Eastampton, Burlington
Eastampton Township SD — 800/K-8
1 Student Dr 08060 — 609-267-9172
Susan Mintz, supt. — Fax 261-3338
www.eastampton.k12.nj.us
Eastampton Township MS — 500/4-8
1 Student Dr 08060 — 609-267-9172
Robert Krastek, prin. — Fax 261-3338

East Brunswick, Middlesex, Pop. 47,400
East Brunswick Township SD — 8,700/PK-12
760 State Route 18 08816 — 732-613-6705
Dr. JoAnn Magistro, supt. — Fax 698-9871
www.ebnet.org
Churchill JHS — 1,500/8-9
18 Norton Rd 08816 — 732-613-6800
Mark Sutor, prin. — Fax 257-0087
East Brunswick SHS — 2,100/10-12
380 Cranbury Rd 08816 — 732-613-6904
Robert Murphy, prin. — Fax 254-1938

Middlesex County Vo-Tech HSD —
PO Box 1070 08816 — 732-257-3300
Dr. Karen McCloud-Hjazeh, supt. — Fax 651-0618
www.mcvts.net
East Brunswick Vocational HS — Vo/Tech
PO Box 1070 08816 — 732-254-8700
Paul LaPilusa, prin. — Fax 613-9608
Adult HS - East Brunswick — Adult
112 Rues Ln 08816 — 732-257-3300
Judy Alexander, contact — Fax 613-9608
Other Schools – See Edison, Perth Amboy, Piscataway, Woodbridge

East Hanover, Morris, Pop. 9,926
East Hanover Township SD — 1,100/K-8
20 School Ave 07936 — 973-887-2112
Larry Santos, supt. — Fax 887-2773
www.easthanoverschools.org/
East Hanover MS — 400/6-8
477 Ridgedale Ave 07936 — 973-887-8810
Robert Allen, prin. — Fax 887-5079

Hanover Park Regional HSD — 1,400/9-12
75 Mount Pleasant Ave 07936 — 973-887-0320
Dr. John W. Adamus, supt. — Fax 887-9247
Hanover Park HS — 800/9-12
63 Mount Pleasant Ave 07936 — 973-887-0300
Edward Franko, prin. — Fax 515-7680
Other Schools – See Whippany

East Orange, Essex, Pop. 69,212
East Orange SD — 10,600/PK-12
715 Park Ave 07017 — 973-266-5760
Laval S. Wilson, supt. — Fax 678-4865
www.eastorange.k12.nj.us
Costley MS — 600/6-8
116 Hamilton St 07017 — 973-266-5660
Amaila Trono, prin. — Fax 266-2956
East Orange Campus 9 HS — 500/9-9
34 N Walnut St 07017 — 973-266-5800
Dr. Nicholas Del Tufo, prin. — Fax 266-2954

East Orange Campus HS — 1,800/10-12
340 Prospect St 07017 — 973-266-7360
Dr. Kelvin Harris, prin. — Fax 266-7368
Healy MS — 600/6-8
116 Hamilton St 07017 — 973-266-5670
Janis Burchell, prin. — Fax 675-5094
Sojourner Truth MS — 600/6-8
116 Hamilton St 07017 — 973-266-5665
Vincent Stallings, prin. — Fax 395-3586
Tyson JSHS — 700/6-12
161 Elmwood Ave 07018 — 973-266-5970
Laura Trimmings, prin. — Fax 414-0154
Edmonson Comm. Education Ctr. — Adult
74 Halsted St 07018 — 973-266-5640
Arlene King, dir. — Fax 266-2890

Ahlus Sunnah S — 300/PK-12
215 N Oraton Pkwy 07017 — 973-672-4124
Umar Abdallah, prin. — Fax 672-3919
Best Care Training Institute — Post-Sec.
68 S Harrison St 07017 — 973-673-3900
Joy's School of Hair Design — Post-Sec.
44 Glenwood Ave 07017 — 973-673-4141

East Rutherford, Bergen, Pop. 8,697
Carlstadt-East Rutherford Regional HSD — 500/9-12
120 Paterson Ave 07073 — 201-935-4155
Dr. Sam Feldman, supt. — Fax 935-5639
www.bectonhs.org
Becton Regional HS — 500/9-12
120 Paterson Ave 07073 — 201-935-3007
James Jencarelli, prin. — Fax 935-5639

East Windsor, Mercer, Pop. 22,353
East Windsor Regional SD
Supt. — See Hightstown
Kreps MS, 5 Kent Ln 08520 — 1,100/6-8
Virginia Kearns, prin. — 609-443-7767

Eatontown, Monmouth, Pop. 14,124
Eatontown SD — 1,200/K-8
215 Broad St 07724 — 732-542-1310
Jean E Hoover, supt. — Fax 542-1700
www.eatontown.com
Memorial MS — 300/7-8
7 Grant Ave 07724 — 732-542-5013
Ron Danielson, prin. — Fax 389-1364

Monmouth-Ocean Ed. Serv. Comm. SD
Supt. — See Tinton Falls
Monmouth Adult Education Commission — Adult
2 Meridian Rd 07724 — 732-389-5555
Elizabeth Dalessio, prin.

Edgewater Park, Burlington, Pop. 8,388
Edgewater Park Township SD — 800/K-8
25 Washington Ave 08010 — 609-877-2124
Scott Streckbein, supt. — Fax 877-3941
www.edgewaterpark.k12.nj.us
Ridgeway MS, 300 Delanco Rd 08010 — 400/5-8
Dennis Corbett, prin. — 609-871-3434

Edison, Middlesex, Pop. 99,500
Edison Township SD — 13,100/K-12
312 Pierson Ave 08837 — 732-452-4900
Dr. Vincent J. Capraro, supt. — Fax 452-4993
www.edison.k12.nj.us
Adams MS — 700/6-8
1081 New Dover Rd 08820 — 732-452-2920
Daniel Donnelly, prin. — Fax 452-2922
Edison HS — 1,900/9-12
50 Boulevard Of Eagles 08817 — 732-650-5200
Joseph Kovacs, prin. — Fax 650-5259
Hoover MS — 800/6-8
174 Jackson Ave 08837 — 732-452-2940
Nicholas Romanetz, prin. — Fax 452-2949
Jefferson MS — 700/6-8
450 Division St 08817 — 732-650-5290
Joseph Drew, prin. — Fax 652-5295
Stevens HS — 2,200/9-12
855 Grove Ave 08820 — 732-452-2800
Wilson MS — 800/6-8
50 Woodrow Wilson Dr 08820 — 732-452-2870
Daniel Donnelly, prin. — Fax 452-2876

Middlesex County Vo-Tech HSD
Supt. — See East Brunswick
Academy of Science and Technology — Vo/Tech
100 Technology Dr 08837 — 732-452-2600
Glenn Methner, prin. — Fax 906-8421

Abundant Life Christian Academy — 50/K-12
2195 Woodbridge Ave 08817 — 732-985-6717
Priscilla Walsh, prin. — Fax 985-2394
Bishop George AHR HS — 900/9-12
1 Tingley Ln 08820 — 732-549-1108
Sr. Donna Trukowski, prin. — Fax 494-2229
Cittone Institute — Post-Sec.
1697 Oak Tree Rd 08820 — 732-548-8798
Middlesex County College — Post-Sec.
2600 Woodbridge Ave 08837 — 732-548-6000
Rabbi Jacob Joseph School — Post-Sec.
1 Plainfield Ave 08817 — 732-985-6533
Rabbi Jacob Joseph S — 100/9-12
1 Plainfield Ave 08817 — 732-985-6533
Yitzchok Weintraub, dir. — Fax 985-6553
Wardlaw-Hartridge S — 400/PK-12
1295 Inman Ave 08820 — 908-754-1882
Fax 754-4922

Egg Harbor City, Atlantic, Pop. 4,486
Egg Harbor City SD — 500/PK-8
527 Philadelphia Ave 08215 — 609-965-1034
John Gilly, supt. — Fax 965-6719
www.ehcs.k12.nj.us
Rittenberg MS — 200/5-8
528 Philadelphia Ave 08215 — 609-965-1034
Jack Griffith, prin. — Fax 965-4742

Pilgrim Academy — 400/K-12
PO Box 322 08215 — 609-965-2866
Dr. Hubert Hartzler, hdmstr. — Fax 965-3379

Egg Harbor Township, Atlantic
Egg Harbor Township SD
Supt. — See Pleasantville

Egg Harbor Township HS
24 High School Dr 08234
Kim Gruccio, prin.
Egg Harbor Township MS
4034 Fernwood Ave 08234
Mildred Peretti, prin.
1,800/9-12
609-653-0100
Fax 927-8844
1,000/7-8
609-383-3355
Fax 383-0628

Atlantic Christian S
391 Zion Rd 08234
Joseph Sanelli, admin.
Star Technical Institute
3003 Englsh Crk Ave #212 08234
Trocki Hebrew Academy
6814 Black Horse Pike 08234
Rabbi Joslit, prin.
500/PK-12
609-653-1199
Fax 653-1435
Post-Sec.
609-407-2999
300/PK-12
609-383-8484
Fax 383-1114

Elizabeth, Union, Pop. 123,215
Elizabeth SD
500 N Broad St 07208
Pablo Munoz, supt.
www.elizabeth.k12.nj.us
Battin MS
300 S Broad St 07202
Aaron Goldblatt, prin.
Cleveland MS
436 1st Ave 07206
Deborah Dixon, prin.
Elizabeth HS
600 Pearl St 07202
Ann Marie Remus, prin.
Hamilton MS
310 Cherry St 07208
Marianela Martin, prin.
Holmes MS
436 1st Ave 07206
Michael Scarpato, prin.
McAuliffe MS
300 S Broad St 07202
Jacqueline Jennings, prin.
Reilly MS
425 Grier Ave 07202
Deborah DeMattia, prin.
19,400/PK-12
908-436-5010
Fax 436-5037

500/6-8
908-436-6300
Fax 436-6293
500/6-8
908-436-6011
Fax 436-6012
5,100/9-12
908-436-6855
Fax 436-6850
900/6-8
908-436-6100
Fax 436-6082
500/6-8
908-436-6070
Fax 436-6052
500/6-8
908-436-6340
Fax 436-6328
200/7-8
908-436-6180
Fax 436-6173

Benedictine Academy
840 N Broad St 07208
Sr. Germaine Fritz, prin.
Bruriah HS for Girls
35 North Ave 07208
Chaya Newman, prin.
Drake College of Business
125 Broad St 07201
Elizabeth General Medical Center School
925 E Jersey St 07201
Jewish Educational Center
330 Elmora Ave 07208
Rav Elazar M. Teitz, dean
St. Mary of the Assumption HS
237 S Broad St 07202
Janet Malko, prin.
St. Patrick Academy
227 Court St 07206
Joseph Picaro, prin.
St. Patrick HS
221 Court St 07206
Joseph Picaro, prin.
Trinity Christian Academy
417 Pennington St 07202
Kathleen Salardino, prin.
Union County College
12 W Jersey St 07201
200/9-12
908-352-0670
Fax 352-0698
400/7-12
908-355-4850
Fax 351-5420
Post-Sec.
908-352-5509
Post-Sec.
908-965-7390
1,000/PK-12
908-355-4850
Fax 289-5245
300/9-12
908-352-4350
Fax 352-2359
200/5-8
908-351-2188
Fax 351-6086
200/9-12
908-353-5220
Fax 629-1123
200/PK-12
908-352-9725
Fax 352-3970
Post-Sec.
908-965-6000

Elmwood Park, Bergen, Pop. 18,964
Elmwood Park SD
465 Boulevard 07407
Joseph Casapulla, supt.
www.epps.org/
Memorial HS
375 River Dr 07407
Richard Tomko, prin.
Memorial MS
375 River Dr 07407
Lawrence DeSantis, prin.
2,000/K-12
201-794-2979
Fax 703-9337

600/9-12
201-794-2933
Fax 797-1405
500/6-8
201-794-2823
Fax 791-3438

Elwood, Atlantic, Pop. 1,487
Mullica Township SD
PO Box 318 08217
Dr. David Dunlevy, supt.
www.mullica.k12.nj.us
Mullica Township MS
PO Box 318 08217
Kevin Dugan, prin.
700/K-8
609-561-3868
Fax 561-7133

400/5-8
609-561-3868
Fax 561-7133

Emerson, Bergen, Pop. 7,284
Emerson SD
131 Main St 07630
Dr. Vincent Taffaro, supt.
www.emerson.k12.nj.us
Emerson JSHS
131 Main St 07630
1,100/PK-12
201-599-4178
Fax 599-4160

400/7-12
201-262-4447
Fax 262-1041

Englewood, Bergen, Pop. 26,106
Englewood CSD
12 Tenafly Rd 07631
Carol A. Lisa, supt.
www.epsd.org
Dismus MS
325 Tryon Ave 07631
Peter Elbert, prin.
Liberty S
12 Tenafly Rd 07631
Joseph Bell, prin.
Morrow HS
274 Knickerbocker Rd 07631
Dr. Paula Valenti, prin.
2,400/PK-12
201-862-6000
Fax 569-6099

600/6-8
201-862-6025
Fax 833-9103
9-12
201-862-6249
Fax 871-5931
800/9-12
201-862-6049
Fax 833-9620

Dwight-Englewood S
315 E Palisade Ave 07631

Englewood Hospital & Medical Center
350 Engle St 07631
Yeshiva Ohr Simcha of Englewood
101 W Forest Ave 07631
Rabbi Yosef Strassfeld, prin.
1,000/PK-12
201-569-9500
Fax 569-6350
Post-Sec.
201-894-3002
100/9-12
201-816-1800
Fax 567-6013

Englewood Cliffs, Bergen, Pop. 5,564
Englewood Cliffs SD
143 Charlotte Pl 07632
Philomena T. Pezzano Ed.D., supt.
www.englewoodcliffs.org
Upper S
143 Charlotte Pl 07632
Joseph Spano, prin.
400/K-8
201-567-7292
Fax 567-2738

300/3-8
201-567-6151
Fax 541-8672

St. Peter's College 07632
Post-Sec.
201-568-7730

Englishtown, Monmouth, Pop. 1,788
Freehold Regional HSD
11 Pine St 07726
James Wasser, supt.
www.frhsd.com
Other Schools – See Colts Neck, Farmingdale, Freehold, Manalapan, Marlboro
10,800/9-12
732-792-7300
Fax 446-9126

Manalapan-Englishtown Regional SD
54 Main St 07726
Maureen Lally Ed.D., supt.
www.mers.k12.nj.us
Other Schools – See Manalapan
5,400/K-8
732-786-2500
Fax 786-2542

Erial, Camden, Pop. 2,500
Black Horse Pike Regional SD
Supt. — See Blackwood
Timber Creek Regional HS
501 Jarvis Rd 08081
Mae Robinson, prin.
1,100/9-12
856-232-9703
Fax 232-5267

Divers Academy International
1500 Liberty Pl 08081
Post-Sec.
800-238-3483

Ewing, Mercer, Pop. 36,000
Ewing Township SD
1331 Lower Ferry Rd 08618
Raymond Broach Ed.D., supt.
www.ewing.k12.nj.us
Ewing HS
900 Parkway Ave 08618
Dr. Rodney Logan, prin.
Fisher MS
1325 Lower Ferry Rd 08618
Darrell Jackson, prin.
3,600/K-12
609-538-9800
Fax 538-0041

1,200/9-12
609-538-9800
Fax 882-8172
900/6-8
609-538-9800
Fax 637-9753

College of New Jersey
PO Box 7718 08628
Harrison Career Institute
1001 Spruce St Ste 7 08638
Mercer Christian Academy
2015 Pennington Rd 08618
Gregg Garman, hdmstr.
Villa Victoria Academy - Upper
376 W Upper Ferry Rd 08628
Sr. Mary Ann Gecina, prin.
Post-Sec.
609-771-1855
Post-Sec.
609-656-4303
200/PK-12
609-882-7300
Fax 883-2816
100/7-12
609-882-1700
Fax 882-8421

Fairfield, Essex, Pop. 7,615

StenoTech Career Institute
20 Just Rd 07004
The Institute for Health Education
7 Spielman Rd 07004
Post-Sec.
973-882-4875
Post-Sec.
973-808-1666

Fair Haven, Monmouth, Pop. 5,949
Fair Haven Borough SD
224 Hance Rd 07704
William Presutti, supt.
www.fairhaven.edu
Knollwood MS
224 Hance Rd 07704
Thomas Famulary, prin.
1,000/PK-8
732-747-2294
Fax 747-7441

600/4-8
732-747-0320
Fax 747-7441

Fair Lawn, Bergen, Pop. 31,585
Fair Lawn SD
37-01 Fair Lawn Ave 07410
Bruce Watson, supt.
www.fairlawnschools.org/
Fair Lawn HS
14-00 Berdan Ave 07410
James Marcella, prin.
Jefferson MS
35-01 Morlot Ave 07410
Dr. John Dunay, prin.
Memorial MS
12-00 1st St 07410
Kenneth Bratspies, prin.
4,600/K-12
201-794-5500
Fax 797-9296

1,500/9-12
201-794-5455
Fax 794-8107
700/6-8
201-703-2240
Fax 475-9185
400/6-8
201-794-5470
Fax 703-2237

Artistic Academy of Hair Design
21 Broadway 07410
Post-Sec.
201-794-3502

Far Hills, Somerset, Pop. 903

School of the Hills
3545 US Highway 206 07931
Lynn Guretse, admin.
50/PK-10
908-781-5535
Fax 781-6773

Farmingdale, Monmouth, Pop. 1,576
Freehold Regional HSD
Supt. — See Englishtown
Howell HS
405 Squankum Yellowbrook Rd 07727
Zina Duerbig, prin.
1,700/9-12
732-919-2131
Fax 919-1964

Howell Township SD
200 Squankum Yellowbrook Rd 07727
Dr. Enid Golden, supt.
www.howell.k12.nj.us
Howell Township MS North
501 Squankum Yellowbrook Rd 07727
Joe Isola, prin.
Other Schools – See Freehold, Howell
7,000/K-8
732-751-2480
Fax 919-1060

1,300/6-8
732-919-0095
Fax 919-1008

Flanders, Morris, Pop. 1,200
Mount Olive Township SD
Supt. — See Budd Lake
Mount Olive HS
18 Corey Rd 07836
Kevin Stansberry, prin.
1,300/9-12
973-927-2208
Fax 927-2204

Flemington, Hunterdon, Pop. 4,234
Flemington-Raritan Regional SD
50 Court St 08822
Jack Farr, supt.
www.frsd.k12.nj.us/
3,400/K-8
908-284-7561
Fax 284-7514

Reading-Fleming MS
50 Court St 08822
Kathleen Suchorsky, prin.
1,200/6-8
908-284-7504

Hunterdon Central Regional HSD
84 State Route 31 08822
Dr. LeRoy Seitz, supt.
www.hcrhs.k12.nj.us
Hunterdon Central Regional HS
84 State Route 31 08822
Peter Karycki, prin.
2,800/9-12
908-782-5727
Fax 788-6745
2,800/9-12
908-284-7155
Fax 284-7313

Hunterdon Co Vocational SD
8 Bartles Corner Rd Ste 2 08822
Richard Van Gulik, supt.
Hunterdon County Polytech S
8 Bartles Corner Rd Ste 2 08822
Richard Van Gulik, prin.
Hunterdon County Vocational S
84 State Route 31 08822
Dan Kerr, prin.
Hunterdon County Vocational S - Bartles
8 Bartles Corner Rd 08822
Dan Kerr, prin.
Other Schools – See Annandale, Glen Gardner
908-788-1119
Fax 788-1457
Vo/Tech
908-788-1119

Vo/Tech
908-284-1444
Fax 284-9824
Vo/Tech
908-806-3855

Hunterdon Christian Academy
116 Main St 08822
Shannon Nusser, supt.
100/K-12
908-782-9700
Fax 782-4857

Florence, Burlington, Pop. 8,564
Florence Township SD
201 Cedar St 08518
Dr. Louis G. Talarico, supt.
www.florence.k12.nj.us
Florence Township Memorial HS
500 E Front St 08518
Stephen Falcone, prin.
Florence Township MS
250 Pine St 08518
Stephen Falcone, prin.
1,500/PK-K
609-499-4600
Fax 499-9679

400/9-12
609-499-4620
Fax 499-3424
400/6-8
609-499-4647
Fax 499-8356

Florham Park, Morris, Pop. 12,508
Florham Park Borough SD
PO Box 39 07932
Dr. William Ronzitti, supt.
www.fpks.org
Ridgedale MS
71 Ridgedale Ave 07932
Mark Majeski, prin.
900/K-8
973-822-3880
Fax 822-0716

300/6-8
973-822-3855
Fax 822-7963

Fords, Middlesex, Pop. 14,392
Woodbridge Township SD
Supt. — See Woodbridge
Fords MS, 100 Fanning St 08863
Cynthia Lagunovich, prin.
600/6-8
732-417-5400

Forked River, Ocean, Pop. 4,243
Lacey Township SD
Supt. — See Lanoka Harbor
Lacey Twp. MS
660 Denton Ave 08731
Paul Berkowicz, prin.
1,200/6-8
609-242-2100

Fort Lee, Bergen, Pop. 37,139
Ft. Lee SD
255 Whiteman St 07024
Joanne Calabro, supt.
www.fortlee-boe.net
Cole MS
467 Stillwell Ave 07024
Rosemarie Giacomelli, prin.
Fort Lee HS
3000 Lemoine Ave 07024
Jay Berman, prin.
3,300/K-12
201-585-4610
Fax 585-0691

600/7-8
201-585-4660
Fax 585-1688
1,000/9-12
201-585-4675
Fax 585-2296

Franklin Lakes, Bergen, Pop. 11,142
Franklin Lakes SD
490 Pulis Ave 07417
Roger Bayersdorfer, supt.
www.franklinlakes.k12.nj.us/
Franklin Avenue MS
755 Franklin Ave 07417
Georgiann Gongora, prin.
1,300/K-8
201-891-1856
Fax 891-9333

400/6-8
201-891-0202
Fax 848-5190

Ramapo Indian Hills Regional HSD
Supt. — See Oakland
Ramapo HS
331 George St 07417
Dr. Michael Jordan, prin.
1,200/9-12
201-891-1500
Fax 891-6844

Franklinville, Gloucester
Delsea Regional SD
PO Box 405 08322
Frank Borelli, supt.
www.delsea.k12.nj.us
Delsea Regional HS
PO Box 405 08322
Joseph Sottosanti, prin.
Delsea Regional MS
PO Box 405 08322
Piera Gravenor, prin.
1,900/7-12
856-694-0100
Fax 694-4417

1,300/9-12
856-694-0100
Fax 694-2046
600/7-8
856-694-0100
Fax 694-4417

Freehold, Monmouth, Pop. 11,465
Freehold Borough SD
280 Park Ave 07728
Philip Meara, supt.
www.freeholdboro.k12.nj.us
Freehold IS
280 Park Ave 07728
Nelson Ribon, prin.
1,300/PK-8
732-761-2100
Fax 462-8954

400/6-8
732-761-2156
Fax 761-2181

Freehold Regional HSD
Supt. — See Englishtown
Freehold Borough HS
2 Robertsville Rd 07728
Linda Jewell, prin.
Freehold Twp. HS
281 Elton Adelphia Rd 07728
Elizabeth Higley, prin.
Freehold Evening HS
2 Robertsville Rd 07728
Sam Grove, prin.
1,200/9-12
732-431-8360
Fax 577-8228
2,000/9-12
732-431-8460
Fax 780-5314
Adult
732-431-8589

Freehold Township SD 4,300/PK-8
384 W Main St 07728 732-866-8400
William Setaro Ed.D., supt. Fax 761-1809
www.freeholdtwp.k12.nj.us/
Barkalow MS 700/6-8
498 Stillwells Corner Rd 07728 732-431-4403
John Soviero, prin. Fax 294-5560
Eisenhower MS 800/6-8
279 Burlington Rd 07728 732-431-3910
Dianne Brethauer, prin. Fax 294-7180

Howell Township SD
Supt. — See Farmingdale
Memorial MS 6-8
458 Adelphia Rd 07728 732-919-1085
Chuck Welsh, prin. Fax 751-0325

Monmouth County Vocational SD
PO Box 5033 07728 732-431-7942
Brian McAndrew Ed.D., supt. Fax 409-6736
www.mcvsd.org
Biotechnology HS Vo/Tech
5000 Kozloski Rd 07728 732-431-6443
Linda Eno, prin. Fax 409-6736
Freehold Vocational S Vo/Tech
21 Robertsville Rd 07728 732-462-7570
James Johnson, prin. Fax 294-0569
Monmouth County Career Center Vo/Tech
1000 Kozloski Rd 07728 732-431-3773
Anthony Schaible, prin. Fax 409-7292
Other Schools – See Aberdeen, Asbury Park, Hazlet, Highlands, Keyport, Lincroft, Long Branch, Middletown, Neptune, Wall

Frenchtown, Hunterdon, Pop. 1,520
Delaware Valley Regional HSD 900/9-12
19 Senator Stout Rd 08825 908-996-2131
Martin Matula, supt. Fax 996-4527
www.dvrhs.org
Delaware Valley Reg. HS 900/9-12
19 Senator Stout Rd 08825 908-996-2131
Brian Fogelson, prin. Fax 996-6653

Galloway, Atlantic
Galloway Township SD 3,500/K-8
101 S Reeds Rd 08205 609-748-1250
Douglas Groff, supt. Fax 748-1796
www.gtps.k12.nj.us
Galloway Township MS 900/7-8
100 S Reeds Rd 08205 609-748-1250
Dr. Donald Gross, prin.

Greater Egg Harbor Regional HSD
Supt. — See Mays Landing
Absegami HS 2,100/9-12
201 S Wrangleboro Rd 08205 609-652-1372
Raymond Dolton, prin. Fax 652-0139

Garfield, Bergen, Pop. 29,701
Garfield SD 4,200/PK-12
125 Outwater Ln 07026 973-340-5000
Nicholas Perrapato, supt. Fax 340-4620
www.garfield.k12.nj.us/
Garfield HS 1,100/9-12
125 Outwater Ln 07026 973-340-5010
Doug Petrie, prin. Fax 546-8430
Jefferson MS 600/7-8
62 Alpine St 07026 973-340-5039
Marilyn Martorano, prin. Fax 340-1963

Gibbstown, Gloucester, Pop. 3,902
Greenwich Township SD 500/PK-8
415 Swedesboro Rd 08027 856-224-4920
Francine Marteski Ed.D., supt. Fax 224-5761
www.greenwich.k12.nj.us
Nehaunsey MS 200/5-8
415 Swedesboro Rd 08027 856-224-4920
Suzanne Gibson, prin. Fax 224-5765

Gillette, Morris
Long Hill Township SD 1,000/K-8
759 Valley Rd 07933 908-647-1200
Arthur DiBenedetto, supt. Fax 647-7818
www.longhill.org
Other Schools – See Stirling

Gladstone, Somerset, Pop. 2,086

Gill St. Bernard's S 600/PK-12
PO Box 604 07934 908-234-1611
Fax 234-1715

Glassboro, Gloucester, Pop. 19,094
Glassboro SD 2,300/PK-12
560 Joseph Bowe Memorial Bl 08028 856-881-0123
Michael Gorman, supt. Fax 881-0884
www.glassboro.k12.nj.us
Glassboro HS 700/9-12
550 Joseph L Bowe Blvd 08028 856-881-2200
Santina Haldeman, prin. Fax 307-1189
Glassboro IS 400/7-8
202 Delsea Dr N 08028 856-881-2313
Marianne Carver, prin. Fax 881-3751

Rowan University Post-Sec.
201 Mullica Hill Rd 08028 856-256-4000

Glen Gardner, Hunterdon, Pop. 1,991
Hunterdon Co Vocational SD
Supt. — See Flemington
Voorhees Vocational S Vo/Tech
256 County Road 513 08826 908-638-5226
Kim Metz, prin.

North Hunterdon/Vorhees Regional HSD
Supt. — See Annandale
Voorhees HS 1,200/9-12
256 County Road 513 08826 908-638-6116
David Steffan, prin. Fax 638-8689

Glen Ridge, Essex, Pop. 7,166
Glen Ridge SD 1,700/PK-12
12 High St 07028 973-429-8302
Daniel Fishbein Ed.D., supt. Fax 429-5750
glenridge.org
Glen Ridge HS 700/7-12
200 Ridgewood Ave 07028 973-429-8303
Kenneth Rota, prin. Fax 429-3531

Glen Rock, Bergen, Pop. 11,502
Glen Rock SD 2,300/K-12
620 Harristown Rd 07452 201-445-7700
George Connelly, supt. Fax 389-5019
www.glenrocknj.org/
Glen Rock HS 600/9-12
600 Harristown Rd 07452 201-445-7700
James McCarthy, prin. Fax 389-5015
Glen Rock MS 600/6-8
400 Hamilton Ave 07452 201-445-7700
Edward Thompson, prin. Fax 389-5042

Gloucester City, Camden, Pop. 11,435
Gloucester City SD 2,100/PK-12
520 Cumberland St 08030 856-456-9394
Dr. Mary T. Stansky, supt. Fax 742-8815
www.gcsd.k12.nj.us
Gloucester City JSHS 900/7-12
1300 Market St 08030 856-456-7000
Jack Don, prin. Fax 456-2348
Gloucester City Adult HS Adult
520 Cumberland St 08030 856-456-3374
George Henry, prin. Fax 742-8570

Gloucester Catholic HS 700/9-12
333 Ridgeway St 08030 856-456-4400
John Colman, prin. Fax 456-3599
P.B. Cosmetology Education Centre Post-Sec.
110 Monmouth St 08030 856-456-4927

Great Meadows, Warren, Pop. 1,108
Great Meadows Reg SD 1,200/K-8
PO Box 74 07838 908-637-6576
James Alercia, supt. Fax 637-6356
www.gmrsd.com
Great Meadows Regional MS 400/6-8
273 US Highway 46 07838 908-637-4584
Mark Ippolito, prin. Fax 637-4492

Green Brook, Somerset
Green Brook Township SD 900/K-8
132 Jefferson Ave 08812 732-968-7734
Stephanie Bilenker, supt. Fax 968-1869
www.greenbrooktps.org
Green Brook MS 500/4-8
132 Jefferson Ave 08812 732-968-1051
Linda Pollard, prin. Fax 968-7582

Hackensack, Bergen, Pop. 43,493
Bergen County Vocational SD
Supt. — See Paramus
Bergen Academies Vo/Tech
200 Hackensack Ave 07601 201-343-6000
Patricia Cosgrove, prin. Fax 343-8884
Evening Vocational Technical HS Vo/Tech
200 Hackensack Ave 07601 201-343-6000
Fax 996-0062

Hackensack SD 5,000/PK-12
355 State St 07601 201-646-7830
Dr. Joseph Montesano, supt. Fax 646-7827
www.hackensackelementary.org
Hackensack HS 1,700/9-12
135 1st St 07601 201-646-7900
Mark Porto, prin. Fax 646-7922
Hackensack MS 700/7-8
360 Union St 07601 201-646-7842
Andrea Parchment, prin. Fax 646-7840

Academy of Massage Therapy Post-Sec.
321 Main St 07601 201-568-3220
American Business Academy Post-Sec.
66 Moore St 07601 201-488-9400
Fairleigh Dickinson University Post-Sec.
150 Kotte Pl 07601 201-692-2675
Hackensack Univ Medical Center Post-Sec.
30 Prospect Ave 07601 201-996-2000
Parisian Academy Post-Sec.
362 State St 07601 201-487-2203

Hackettstown, Warren, Pop. 9,366
Hackettstown SD 1,900/K-12
PO Box 465 07840 908-850-6500
Robert Gratz, supt. Fax 850-4985
www.hackettstown.org
Hackettstown HS 900/9-12
701 Warren St 07840 908-852-8150
Christina Steffner, prin. Fax 852-6214
Hackettstown MS 400/5-8
500 Washington St 07840 908-852-8554
Michael Meyer, prin. Fax 850-6544

Centenary College Post-Sec.
400 Jefferson St 07840 908-852-1400

Haddonfield, Camden, Pop. 11,616
Haddonfield Borough SD 2,200/K-12
1 Lincoln Ave 08033 856-429-4130
Joseph O'Brien Ed.D., supt. Fax 354-2179
www.haddonfield.k12.nj.us
Haddonfield Memorial HS 800/9-12
401 Kings Hwy E 08033 856-429-3960
Priscilla Vimislik, prin. Fax 795-8910
Haddonfield MS 500/6-8
5 Lincoln Ave 08033 856-429-5851
Alan Fegley, prin. Fax 429-2006

Pope Paul VI HS 1,200/9-12
901 Hopkins Rd 08033 856-858-4900
Sr. Marianne McCann, prin. Fax 858-6832

Haddon Heights, Camden, Pop. 7,495
Haddon Heights SD 1,200/K-12
300 2nd Ave 08035 856-547-1412
Dr. Nancy Hacker, supt. Fax 547-3868
hhsd.k12.nj.us
Haddon Heights JSHS 800/7-12
301 2nd Ave 08035 856-547-1920
David Sandowich, prin. Fax 547-6808

Baptist S 400/K-12
Third & Station Ave 08035 856-547-2996
Lynn Conahan, admin. Fax 547-6584

Haledon, Passaic, Pop. 8,408
Passaic County Manchester Regional HSD 800/9-12
70 Church St 07508 973-389-2820
Dr. Raymond Kwak, supt. Fax 956-8805
www.mrhs.net
Manchester Regional HS 800/9-12
70 Church St 07508 973-389-2820
Tim Smithhart, prin. Fax 956-8805

Hamburg, Sussex, Pop. 3,495
Wallkill Valley Regional SD 900/9-12
10 Grumm Rd 07419 973-827-4100
Joseph DiPasquale, supt. Fax 827-8318
www.wallkill.k12.nj.us
Wallkill Valley Regional HS 900/9-12
10 Grumm Rd 07419 973-827-4100
Joseph DiPasquale, prin. Fax 827-8318

Hamilton, Mercer
Hamilton Township SD 12,600/K-12
90 Park Ave 08690 609-631-4100
Neil Bencivengo, supt. Fax 631-4103
www.hamilton.k12.nj.us
Crockett MS 900/6-8
2631 Kuser Rd 08691 609-631-4149
Barbara Panfili, prin. Fax 631-4116
Grice MS 1,000/6-8
901 Whitehorse Hamilton Sq 08610 609-631-4152
David Innocenzi, prin. Fax 631-4119
Hamilton East-Steinert HS 1,600/9-12
2900 Klockner Rd 08690 609-631-4150
Michael Gilbert, prin. Fax 631-4117
Hamilton North-Nottingham HS 1,300/9-12
1055 Klockner Rd 08619 609-631-4161
Neal Campeas, prin. Fax 631-4129
Hamilton West-Watson HS 1,300/9-12
2720 S Clinton Ave 08610 609-631-4168
David McWilliam, prin. Fax 631-4137
Reynolds MS 1,200/6-8
2145 Yrdvl Hamilton Squ Rd 08690 609-631-4162
Joseph Slavin, prin. Fax 631-4130
Accredited Evening HS Adult
90 Park Ave 08690 609-890-3600
Dr. Lois Braender, prin. Fax 631-4106

Trenton Catholic Academy 300/9-12
175 Leonard Ave 08610 609-586-3705
Susan Kuk, prin. Fax 586-6584

Hammonton, Atlantic, Pop. 12,994
Hammonton SD 2,900/PK-12
PO Box 631 08037 609-567-7000
Mary Lou DeFrancisco, supt. Fax 561-3567
www.hammontonps.org/
Hammonton HS 1,200/9-12
566 Old Forks Rd 08037 609-567-7000
James Donoghue, prin. Fax 567-2021
Hammonton MS 800/6-8
75 N Liberty St 08037 609-567-7007
Gene Miller, prin. Fax 561-3974

St. Joseph HS 200/9-12
328 Vine St 08037 609-561-8700
James J. Cavalieri, prin. Fax 561-8701

Harrison, Hudson, Pop. 14,262
Harrison SD, 430 William St 07029 1,900/K-12
Anthony Comprelli, supt. 973-483-4627
www.harrison.k12.nj.us
Harrison HS 700/9-12
1 N 5th St 07029 973-482-5050
Ronald Shields, prin. Fax 482-3625
Washington MS 300/6-8
223 Hamilton St 07029 973-483-2285
Susan B. Green, prin.

Hasbrouck Heights, Bergen, Pop. 11,636
Hasbrouck Heights SD 1,500/K-12
379 Boulevard 07604 201-393-8145
Joseph C. Luongo, supt. Fax 288-0289
www.hhschools.org
Hasbrouck Heights HS 400/9-12
365 Boulevard 07604 201-288-3971
Peter O'Hare, prin. Fax 288-2083
Hasbrouck Heights MS 400/6-8
365 Boulevard 07604 201-393-8190
Edward Bolcar, prin. Fax 288-2083

Hawthorne, Passaic, Pop. 18,363
Hawthorne SD 2,200/PK-12
PO Box 2 07507 973-427-1300
Dr. Richard Spirito, supt. Fax 427-1757
www.hawthorne.k12.nj.us
Hawthorne HS 600/9-12
160 Parmelee Ave 07506 973-423-6415
Dr. David Browne, prin. Fax 423-6422
Lincoln MS 600/6-8
230 Hawthorne Ave 07506 973-423-6460
Douglas Alexander, prin. Fax 427-5393

Hawthorne Christian Academy 500/K-12
2000 State Rt 208 07506 973-423-3331
Donald J.Klingen, hdmstr. Fax 238-1718
Roman Academy of Beauty Culture Post-Sec.
431 Lafayette Ave 07506 973-423-2223

Hazlet, Monmouth, Pop. 21,976
Hazlet Township SD 3,300/K-12
421 Middle Rd 07730 732-264-8402
Renae LaPrete, supt. Fax 264-1599
www.hazlet.org
Hazlet MS 600/7-8
1639 Union Ave 07730 732-264-0940
John DeGenito, prin. Fax 264-0571
Raritan HS 1,000/9-12
419 Middle Rd 07730 732-264-8411
Colleen Rafter, prin. Fax 264-3214

Monmouth County Vocational SD
Supt. — See Freehold
Hazlet Vocational S Vo/Tech
417 Middle Rd 07730 732-264-4995
James Johnson, prin. Fax 264-3846

Hibernia, Morris, Pop. 200
Rockaway Township SD 2,700/K-8
PO Box 500 07842 973-627-8200
Dr. Arthur Travlos, supt. Fax 627-7968
www.morris.k12.nj.us/rocktwp

Other Schools – See Rockaway

High Bridge, Hunterdon, Pop. 3,816
High Bridge SD — 400/K-8
50 Thomas St 08829 — 908-638-4103
Dr. Patricia Ash, supt. — Fax 638-4211
www.hbschools.org
High Bridge MS — 200/6-8
50 Thomas St 08829 — 908-638-4101
Patricia Ash, prin. — Fax 638-4211

Highland Park, Middlesex, Pop. 14,221
Highland Park SD — 1,600/PK-12
435 Mansfield St 08904 — 732-572-6990
David Ottaviano, supt. — Fax 393-1174
www.highlandpark.k12.nj.us
Highland Park MSHS — 700/7-12
102 N 5th Ave 08904 — 732-572-2400
Roy Knapp, prin. — Fax 819-7041

Highlands, Monmouth, Pop. 5,367
Henry Hudson Regional SD — 500/7-12
1 Grand Tour 07732 — 732-872-0900
Brian Zychowski, supt. — Fax 708-1409
www.henryhudsonreg.k12.nj.us/
Hudson Regional JSHS — 500/7-12
1 Grand Tour 07732 — 732-872-0900
Brian Zychowski, prin. — Fax 708-1409

Monmouth County Vocational SD
Supt. — See Freehold
Marine Academy of Science & Technology — Vo/Tech
Building 305 07732 — 732-291-0995
Paul Christopher, prin. — Fax 291-9367

Hightstown, Mercer, Pop. 5,311
East Windsor Regional SD — 4,600/K-12
384 Stockton St 08520 — 609-443-7704
Ronald E. Bolandi, supt. — Fax 443-8040
www.eastwindsorregionalschools.com/
Hightstown HS — 1,300/9-12
25 Leshin Ln 08520 — 609-443-7738
John Ward, prin. — Fax 443-7880
Other Schools – See East Windsor

Peddie S — 500/9-12
PO Box A 08520 — 609-490-7500
John Green, hdmstr. — Fax 944-7912

Hillsborough, Somerset
Hillsborough Township SD — 11,400/K-12
379 S Branch Rd 08844 — 908-369-0030
Karen Lake, supt. — Fax 369-8286
www.hillsborough.k12.nj.us
Hillsborough HS — 2,200/9-12
466 Raider Blvd 08844 — 908-874-4200
George D. Poye, prin. — Fax 874-3762
Hillsborough MS — 1,800/6-8
260 Triangle Rd 08844 — 908-874-3420
Joseph Trybulski, prin. — Fax 874-3492

Hillsdale, Bergen, Pop. 10,090
Hillsdale SD — 1,300/K-8
32 Ruckman Rd 07642 — 201-664-0282
Anthony DeNorchia, supt. — Fax 664-9049
www.hillsdaleschools.com
White MS — 600/5-8
120 Magnolia Ave 07642 — 201-664-0286
Noreen Hajinlian, prin. — Fax 664-2715

Pascack Valley Regional HSD
Supt. — See Montvale
Pascack Valley HS — 1,000/9-12
200 Piermont Ave 07642 — 201-358-7060
Barbara Sapienza, prin. — Fax 358-7102

Hillside, Union, Pop. 21,044
Hillside Township SD — 3,100/K-12
195 Virginia St 07205 — 908-352-7664
Raymond Bandlow Ph.D., supt. — Fax 282-5831
www.hillsidek12.org
Hillside HS — 1,000/9-12
1085 Liberty Ave 07205 — 908-352-7664
Eva Marie Raleigh, prin. — Fax 352-4246
Krumbiegel MS — 500/7-8
145 Hillside Ave 07205 — 908-352-7664
Martin Dickerson, prin. — Fax 282-5840

Hoboken, Hudson, Pop. 39,482
Hoboken SD, 1115 Clinton St 07030 — 1,900/PK-12
Patrick Gagliardi, supt. — 201-356-3601
www.hoboken.k12.nj.us
Brandt MS, 215 9th St 07030 — 300/5-8
Stacy Michaelides, prin. — 201-356-3691
DeMarest MS, 158 4th St 07030 — 300/5-8
Elizabeth Falco, prin. — 201-356-3741
Hoboken HS — 700/9-12
9th & Clinton St 07030 — 201-356-3701
Patrick Gagliardi, prin. — Fax 656-4549

Academy of the Sacred Heart — 100/9-12
713 Washington St 07030 — 201-659-7139
Sr. Jacqueline Carey, prin. — Fax 659-8027
Hudson S — 200/5-12
601 Park Ave 07030 — 201-659-8335
— Fax 222-3669
Stevens Institute of Technology — Post-Sec.
Castle Point on Hudson 07030 — 201-216-5100

Holmdel, Monmouth
Holmdel Township SD — 3,600/K-12
PO Box 407 07733 — 732-946-1800
Dr. Maureen E. Flaherty, supt. — Fax 946-1875
www.holmdelschools.org
Holmdel HS — 1,200/9-12
36 Crawfords Corner Rd 07733 — 732-946-1832
Cheryl Swider, prin. — Fax 946-0093
Satz IS — 600/7-8
24 Crawfords Corner Rd 07733 — 732-946-1808
Arthur Howard, prin. — Fax 834-0089

St. John Vianney HS — 1,000/9-12
540 Line Rd 07733 — 732-739-0800
Joseph Deroba, prin. — Fax 739-0824

Hopatcong, Sussex, Pop. 16,097
Hopatcong Borough SD — 2,600/K-12
PO Box 1029 07843 — 973-398-8801
Dr. Wayne Threlkeld, supt. — Fax 398-1961
www.hopatcongschools.org/

Hopatcong HS — 800/9-12
PO Box 1029 07843 — 973-398-8803
Emil Binotto, prin. — Fax 398-9048
Hopatcong MS — 600/6-8
PO Box 1029 07843 — 973-398-8804
Theresa Williams, prin. — Fax 398-4184

Howell, Monmouth
Howell Township SD
Supt. — See Farmingdale
Howell Township MS South — 1,200/6-8
1 Kuzminski Way 07731 — 732-836-1327
Thomas Feaster, prin. — Fax 836-0698

Lakewood Preparatory S — 200/K-12
152 Lanes Mill Rd 07731 — 732-364-2812
— Fax 364-4004

Irvington, Essex, Pop. 60,600
Irvington Township SD — 7,700/K-12
1 University Pl 07111 — 973-399-6800
Ethel Davion, supt. — Fax 372-3724
www.irvington.k12.nj.us
Irvington HS — 1,600/9-12
1253 Clinton Ave 07111 — 973-399-6897
Neely Hackett, prin. — Fax 399-3484
Union Avenue MS — 800/6-8
427 Union Ave 07111 — 973-399-6885
Albert Joy, prin. — Fax 371-0957
University MS — 700/6-8
255 Myrtle Ave 07111 — 973-399-6880
— Fax 351-1025
Irvington Adult HS — Adult
1 University Pl 07111 — 973-399-1083
Shakuur Sabuur, prin.

Iselin, Middlesex, Pop. 16,141
Woodbridge Township SD
Supt. — See Woodbridge
Iselin MS, 900 Woodruff St 08830 — 700/6-8
Jacqueline Miller, prin. — 732-602-8450
Kennedy Memorial HS — 1,000/9-12
200 Washington Ave 08830 — 732-602-8650
Michael Cilento, prin. — Fax 634-1112

Ultrasound Diagnostic School — Post-Sec.
675 US Route 1 2nd Flr 08830 — 732-634-1131

Jackson, Ocean, Pop. 800
Jackson Township SD — 9,200/K-12
151 Don Connor Blvd 08527 — 732-833-4600
Thomas Gialanella, supt. — Fax 833-4609
www.jacksonsd.org
Goetz MS — 1,300/6-8
835 Patterson Rd 08527 — 732-833-4610
Faith Lessig, prin. — Fax 833-4749
Jackson Liberty HS — 9-12
125 N Hope Chapel Rd 08527 — 732-833-4700
Maureen Butler, prin. — Fax 833-7099
Jackson Memorial HS — 2,700/9-12
101 Don Connor Blvd 08527 — 732-833-4621
Anthony Gaita, prin. — Fax 833-4629
McAuliffe MS — 900/6-8
35 Hope Chapel Rd 08527 — 732-833-4701
Kevin Dieugenio, prin. — Fax 833-4729
Jackson Adult HS — Adult
101 Don Connor Blvd 08527 — 732-833-4638
Laura Wheaton, dir. — Fax 833-4629

Ocean County Vocational SD
Supt. — See Toms River
Ocean County Voc-Tech S - Jackson — Vo/Tech
850 Toms River Rd 08527 — 732-928-3830
Thomas McInerney, prin. — Fax 928-0490

Jamesburg, Middlesex, Pop. 6,477
Jamesburg SD — 600/PK-8
13 Augusta St 08831 — 732-521-0303
Shirley Ann Bzdewka, supt. — Fax 521-1267
www.jamesburg.org
Breckwedel MS — 200/6-8
13 Augusta St 08831 — 732-521-0640
Shirley Ann Bzdewka, prin. — Fax 521-1267

Yeshiva Tiferes Naftoli of Central NJ — 100/9-12
3059 Englishtown Rd 08831 — 732-446-5841
Rabbi Asa Minkowich, prin.

Jersey City, Hudson, Pop. 239,097
Hudson County Vocational SD
Supt. — See North Bergen
Explore 2000 — Vo/Tech
525 Montgomery St 07302 — 201-369-5560
Charles Matthews, prin.
Hudson Co. AVTS Jersey City Vo-Tech Ctr — Vo/Tech
525 Montgomery St 07302 — 201-631-6302
Barbara Mendolla, prin.

Jersey CSD — 25,700/PK-12
346 Claremont Ave 07305 — 201-915-6202
Dr. Charles T. Epps, supt.
www.jcboe.org/
Dickinson HS — 2,600/9-12
2 Palisade Ave 07306 — 201-714-4400
James Burke, prin. — Fax 792-2292
Ferris HS — 1,200/9-12
35 Colgate St 07302 — 201-915-6660
Nicole Hazel, prin. — Fax 333-2060
Infante MS — 100/8-8
3055 John F Kennedy Blvd 07306 — 201-714-4370
Mary Louf, prin. — Fax 659-7711
Lincoln HS — 600/9-12
60 Crescent Ave 07304 — 201-915-6700
Dr. Michael Winds, prin. — Fax 435-4493
McNair Academic HS — 500/9-12
123 Coles St 07302 — 201-418-7618
Robert Roggenstein, prin. — Fax 792-1498
Nolan MS — 500/6-8
88 Gates Ave 07305 — 201-915-6570
Anna Ortiz-Rivas, prin. — Fax 369-3749
Snyder HS — 800/9-12
239 Bergen Ave 07305 — 201-915-6600
Ellen Ruane, coord. — Fax 946-1562
Adult Education Center — Adult
299 Sip Ave 07306 — 201-217-7883
Margaret DiNardo, coord. — Fax 395-9215
Adult Evening HS — Adult
2 Palisade Ave 07306 — 201-714-4440
Margaret DiNardo, coord.

Academy of St. Aloysius — 200/9-12
2495 John F Kennedy Blvd 07304 — 201-433-8877
Tara Brunt, prin. — Fax 433-8839
Christ Hospital School of Nursing — Post-Sec.
176 Palisade Ave 07306 — 201-795-8360
Chubb Institute — Post-Sec.
40 Journal Sq 07306 — 201-876-3800
Harrison Career Institute — Post-Sec.
600 Pavonia Ave 07306 — 201-222-1700
Hudson Area School of Radiologic Tech. — Post-Sec.
176 Palisade Ave 07306 — 201-795-8246
Hudson Catholic HS — 600/9-12
790 Bergen Ave 07306 — 201-332-5970
Dr. Paul Ward, prin. — Fax 332-6373
Hudson County Community College — Post-Sec.
25 Journal Sq 07306 — 201-656-2020
Micro Tech Training Center — Post-Sec.
3000 John F Kennedy Blvd 07306 — 201-216-9901
Natural Motion Institute of Hair Design — Post-Sec.
2800 Kennedy Blvd 07306 — 201-659-0303
New Jersey City University — Post-Sec.
2039 John F Kennedy Blvd 07305 — 201-200-6000
New Jersey School of Locksmithing — Post-Sec.
392 Summit Ave 07306 — 201-963-9688
Resurrection S — 200/4-8
189 Brunswick St 07302 — 201-653-1699
Sr. Eleanor Uhl, prin. — Fax 418-9019
St. Aloysius HS — 400/9-12
721 W Side Ave 07306 — 201-435-9240
Thomas Gentile, prin. — Fax 435-2115
St. Anthony HS — 200/9-12
175 8th St 07302 — 201-653-5143
Edward Santana, prin. — Fax 653-8120
St. Dominic Academy — 500/9-12
2572 John F Kennedy Blvd 07304 — 201-434-5938
Sr. Vivean Jennings, prin. — Fax 434-2603
St. Francis Hospital — Post-Sec.
1 McWilliams Pl 07302 — 201-795-7001
St. Mary HS — 300/9-12
209 3rd St 07302 — 201-656-8008
Beatriz Esteban-Messina, prin. — Fax 653-4518
St. Peter Prep S — 1,000/9-12
144 Grand St 07302 — 201-434-4400
Kevin Cuddihy, prin. — Fax 547-2341
St. Peter's College — Post-Sec.
2627 John F Kennedy Blvd 07306 — 201-915-9000

Keansburg, Monmouth, Pop. 10,746
Keansburg Borough SD — 2,000/PK-12
100 Palmer Pl 07734 — 732-787-2007
Barbara Trzeszkowski, supt. — Fax 495-6714
www.keansburg.k12.nj.us
Bolger MS — 600/5-8
100 Palmer Pl 07734 — 732-787-2007
Nicholas Eremita, prin. — Fax 495-7906
Keansburg HS — 500/9-12
140 Port Monmouth Rd 07734 — 732-787-2007
Thomas Normile, prin. — Fax 495-5401

Kearny, Hudson, Pop. 39,853
Kearny SD — 4,900/PK-12
100 Davis Ave 07032 — 201-955-5021
Robert Mooney, supt. — Fax 955-0544
www.kearnyschools.com/
Kearny HS — 1,500/9-12
336 Devon St 07032 — 201-955-5048
Frank Digesere, prin. — Fax 998-9653

Kearny Christian Academy — 100/PK-12
172 Midland Ave 07032 — 201-998-0788
Jane Botelho, admin. — Fax 998-1102

Kenilworth, Union, Pop. 7,736
Kenilworth SD — 1,300/PK-12
426 Boulevard 07033 — 908-276-1644
Dr. Lloyd Leschuk, supt. — Fax 276-7598
www.kenilworthschools.com
Brearley JSHS — 700/7-12
401 Monroe Ave 07033 — 908-931-9696
Charles Capello, prin. — Fax 931-1618

Capri Institute of Hair Design — Post-Sec.
660 N Michigan Ave 07033 — 908-964-1330

Keyport, Monmouth, Pop. 7,504
Keyport Borough SD — 1,100/PK-12
335 Broad St 07735 — 732-264-2840
John Dumford, supt. — Fax 888-3343
www.keyportschools.org/Keyport
Keyport JSHS — 500/8-12
351 Broad St 07735 — 732-264-0902
Miguel Hernandez, prin. — Fax 888-3342

Monmouth County Vocational SD
Supt. — See Freehold
Keyport Vocational S — Vo/Tech
280 Atlantic St 07735 — 732-739-0592
James Johnson, prin. — Fax 739-1470

Kinnelon, Morris, Pop. 9,475
Kinnelon Borough SD — 2,100/K-12
109 Kiel Ave 07405 — 973-838-1418
James Opiekun, supt. — Fax 838-5527
www.kinnelonpublicschools.org/
Kinnelon HS — 600/9-12
121 Kinnelon Rd 07405 — 973-838-5500
Sharon Toriello, prin. — Fax 838-0261
Miller MS — 500/6-8
117 Kiel Ave 07405 — 973-838-5250
John P. Hynes, prin. — Fax 838-3998

Lake Hopatcong, Morris, Pop. 3,000
Jefferson Township SD — 3,500/K-12
28 Bowling Green Pkwy 07849 — 973-663-5780
Gary Bowen, supt. — Fax 663-2790
www.jefftwp.org
Other Schools – See Oak Ridge

Lakehurst, Ocean, Pop. 2,582
Ocean County Vocational SD
Supt. — See Toms River
Ocean County Voc-Tech S - Navy Lakehurst — Vo/Tech
PO Box 1125 08733 — 732-657-4000
Karen Homiek, prin. — Fax 657-4500

Lakewood, Ocean, Pop. 38,800
Lakewood Township SD 5,200/PK-12
655 Princeton Ave 08701 732-905-3633
Edward W. Luick, supt. Fax 364-1657
www.lakewood.k12.nj.us/
Lakewood HS 1,300/9-12
855 Somerset Ave 08701 732-905-3502
Fax 905-0895
Lakewood MS 700/7-8
755 Somerset Ave 08701 732-905-3600
Fax 905-3695
Evening HS, 655 Princeton Ave 08701 Adult
David Weintraub, prin. 732-905-3600

Bais Kaila Torah Prep HS 200/9-12
PO Box 952 08701 732-370-4300
Naomi Weitzner, prin. Fax 367-0389
Bais Shaindel HS 50/9-12
685 River Ave 08701 732-363-7074
Devorah Eckstein, prin. Fax 363-3399
Bais Yaakov HS 50/9-12
277 James St 08701 732-370-8200
Ettil Yagod, prin. Fax 370-2076
Beth Medrash Govoha Post-Sec.
617 6th St 08701 732-367-1060
Calvary Academy 300/PK-12
1133 E County Line Rd 08701 732-363-3633
Melissa Payne, hdmstr. Fax 363-7337
Georgian Court University Post-Sec.
900 Lakewood Ave 08701 732-364-2200
Lakewood Cheder S Bais Faga 1,200/3-8
350 Courtney Rd 08701 732-363-5070
Suri Jacobovitch, prin. Fax 370-1195
Mesivta Keren HaTorah 100/9-12
120 2nd St 08701 732-942-7300
Rabbi Moshe Rabinowitz, prin. Fax 363-4222
Mesivta Keser Torah 100/9-12
455 14th St 08701 732-681-5656
Rev. David Heinemann, prin. Fax 681-7171
Mesivta of Lakewood 50/9-12
415 6th St 08701 732-905-8370
Fax 363-9052
Star Technical Institute Post-Sec.
1255 Highway 70 Ste 12N 08701 732-901-9710
Yeshiva Bais Aharon 100/9-12
1430 14th St 08701 732-367-7604
Binyomin Schulgasser, admin. Fax 367-1777
Yeshiva Ohr Chodosh 50/9-12
PO Box 826 08701 732-364-7062
Rabbi Chesky Schonfeld, dir. Fax 364-1754
Yeshivas Bais Pinchos 50/9-12
1951 New Central Ave 08701 732-367-2880
Rabbi Yaakov Licht, prin. Fax 364-5258

Lambertville, Hunterdon, Pop. 3,880
South Hunterdon Regional HSD 300/7-12
301 Mt Airy Harbourton Rd 08530 609-397-1888
Lisa Brady, supt. Fax 397-2366
www.shrhs.org
South Hunterdon Regional HS 300/7-12
301 Mt Airy Harbourton Rd 08530 609-397-2060
Donald Woodring, prin. Fax 397-2366

Lanoka Harbor, Ocean
Lacey Township SD 6,500/K-12
PO Box 216 08734 609-971-2002
Richard Starodub, supt. Fax 242-9406
www.lacey.k12.nj.us
Lacey Twp. HS 1,500/9-12
PO Box 206 08734 609-971-2020
William Zylinski, prin. Fax 242-0873
Other Schools – See Forked River

Laurel Springs, Camden, Pop. 1,957

Empire Beauty School Post-Sec.
1305 Blackwood Clementon Rd 08021
856-435-8100

Lawrenceville, Mercer, Pop. 6,446
Lawrence Township SD 3,600/K-12
2565 Princeton Pike 08648 609-671-5500
Dr. Thomas Butler, supt. Fax 883-4225
www.ltps.org
Lawrence HS 1,300/9-12
2525 Princeton Pike 08648 609-671-5510
Donald Proffit, prin. Fax 771-4095
Lawrence MS 500/7-8
2455 Princeton Ave 08648 609-671-5520
Andrew Zuckerman, prin. Fax 637-0768

Empire Beauty School Post-Sec.
1719 Brunswick Ave 08648 609-392-4545
Lawrenceville S 800/9-12
PO Box 6008 08648 609-896-0400
Elizabeth Duffy, hdmstr. Fax 895-2161
Notre Dame HS 1,300/9-12
601 Lawrenceville Rd 08648 609-882-7900
Mary Liz Ivins, prin. Fax 882-5723
Rider University Post-Sec.
2083 Lawrenceville Rd 08648 609-896-5000

Lebanon, Hunterdon, Pop. 1,162
Clinton Township SD 1,600/PK-8
PO Box 362 08833 908-236-7235
Dr. Elizabeth Nastus, supt. Fax 236-6358
www.ctsd.k12.nj.us
Round Valley MS 500/6-8
128 Cokesbury Rd 08833 908-236-6341
Gerard Dalton, prin. Fax 236-2847

Leonardo, Monmouth, Pop. 3,788
Middletown Township SD
Supt. — See Middletown
Bayshore MS 700/6-8
36 Leonardville Rd 07737 732-291-1380
Carol Force, prin.

Leonia, Bergen, Pop. 8,888
Leonia SD 1,600/K-12
570 Grand Ave 07605 201-947-0230
Dr. Bernard Josefsberg, supt. Fax 947-4782
www.leoniaschools.org
Leonia HS 500/9-12
100 Christie Heights St 07605 201-461-7441
Edward Bertolini, prin. Fax 461-8957
Leonia MS 400/6-8
500 Broad Ave 07605 201-461-9100
Maureen Willis, prin. Fax 461-1510

Lincoln Park, Morris, Pop. 10,870
Lincoln Park Borough SD 1,000/K-8
92 Ryerson Rd 07035 973-696-5500
Dr. Joyce J. Valenza, supt. Fax 696-9273
www.lincolnparkboe.org
Lincoln Park MS 400/5-8
90 Ryerson Rd 07035 973-696-5520
Marilyn Castellano, prin. Fax 872-8930

Craig Upper S 100/9-12
200 Comly Rd 07035 973-305-8085
David Blanchard, hdmstr. Fax 305-8086

Lincroft, Monmouth, Pop. 6,193
Monmouth County Vocational SD
Supt. — See Freehold
High Technology HS Vo/Tech
PO Box 119 07738 732-842-8444
Daniel Simon, prin. Fax 219-9418

Brookdale Community College Post-Sec.
765 Newman Springs Rd 07738 732-842-1900
Christian Brothers Academy 900/9-12
850 Newman Springs Rd 07738 732-747-1959
Br. Stephen Olert, prin. Fax 747-1643

Linden, Union, Pop. 39,877
Linden SD 5,900/PK-12
2 E Gibbons St 07036 908-486-2800
Joseph Martino, supt. Fax 486-6331
www.linden.k12.nj.us
Linden HS 1,800/9-12
121 W Saint Georges Ave 07036 908-486-5432
Barry Black, prin. Fax 486-3242
McManus MS 800/6-8
300 Edgewood Rd 07036 908-486-7751
Denise Cleary, prin. Fax 486-8968
Soehl MS 600/6-8
300 E Henry St 07036 908-486-0550
Joseph Picaro, prin. Fax 486-3478
Linden Adult Evening S Adult
121 W Saint Georges Ave 07036 908-486-2212
Jean Forstenhausler, contact Fax 925-4427

Micropower Computer Institute Post-Sec.
1203 W Saint Georges Ave 07036 908-587-9070
Victory Christian Academy 100/PK-12
2301 Grier Ave 07036 908-925-7920

Lindenwold, Camden, Pop. 17,377
Lindenwold SD 2,000/PK-12
1017 E Linden Ave 08021 856-784-4071
Geraldine Carroll, supt. Fax 435-5887
lindenwold.k12.nj.us
Lindenwold HS 500/9-12
801 Egg Harbor Rd 08021 856-741-0320
Dr. Scott Oswald, prin. Fax 741-0350
Lindenwold MS 600/5-8
40 White Horse Ave 08021 856-346-3330
J. Scott Strong, prin. Fax 346-0554

Linwood, Atlantic, Pop. 7,370
Linwood SD 1,000/K-8
51 Belhaven Ave 08221 609-926-6703
Thomas A. Baruffi Ed.D., supt. Fax 926-6705
www.linwoodschools.org/
Belhaven MS 500/5-8
51 Belhaven Ave 08221 609-926-6700
Frank Rudnesky Ed.D., prin. Fax 926-6705

Mainland Regional HSD 1,600/9-12
1301 Oak Ave 08221 609-927-2461
Dr. Russell J. Dever, supt. Fax 927-1942
www.mainlandregional.net
Mainland Regional HS 1,600/9-12
1301 Oak Ave 08221 609-927-4151
Dr. Robert Blake, prin. Fax 927-1942

Little Egg Harbor Township, Ocean, Pop. 13,333
Pinelands Regional SD 1,900/7-12
520 Nugentown Rd 08087 609-296-3106
Dr. Detlef Kern, supt. Fax 294-9519
www.pinelandsregional.org/
Pinelands Regional HS 800/10-12
565 Nugentown Rd 08087 609-296-3106
Thomas Procopio, prin. Fax 296-6905
Pinelands Regional JHS 1,000/7-9
590 Nugentown Rd 08087 609-296-3106
Lawrence Mesarick, prin. Fax 296-2626

Little Falls, Passaic, Pop. 11,294
Little Falls Township SD 800/K-8
560 Main St 07424 973-256-1034
Bruce deLyon, supt. Fax 256-6542
www.lfnjschools.org/
Little Falls MS 1 400/5-8
32 Stevens Ave 07424 973-256-1037
Raymond Mead, prin. Fax 785-4857

Passaic Valley Regional HSD 1 1,000/9-12
160 E Main St 07424 973-890-2560
Dr. Viktor Joganow, supt. Fax 890-0512
www.pvhs.k12.nj.us
Passaic Valley Regional HS 1,000/9-12
160 E Main St 07424 973-890-2500
Dr. Viktor Joganow, prin. Fax 890-0512

Little Ferry, Bergen, Pop. 10,799
Little Ferry SD 900/PK-8
130 Liberty St 07643 201-641-6192
Frank R. Scarafile, supt. Fax 641-6604
www.littleferry.k12.nj.us
Memorial MS 400/5-8
130 Liberty St 07643 201-641-6186
Kathy Brennan, prin. Fax 641-3245

Little Silver, Monmouth, Pop. 6,123
Little Silver Borough SD 800/K-8
124 Willow Dr 07739 732-741-2188
Marjorie Heller, supt. Fax 741-3644
www.littlesilverschools.org/lss
Markham Place MS 400/5-8
95 Markham Pl 07739 732-741-7112
Don Merce, prin. Fax 741-3562

Red Bank Regional HSD 1,000/9-12
101 Ridge Rd 07739 732-842-8000
Edward Westervelt, supt. Fax 842-8504
www.redbankregional.k12.nj.us
Red Bank Regional HS 1,000/9-12
101 Ridge Rd 07739 732-842-8000
C. Arthur Albrizio, prin. Fax 842-8504

Livingston, Essex, Pop. 27,500
Livingston Township SD 5,000/K-12
11 Foxcroft Dr 07039 973-535-8000
Brad Draeger, supt. Fax 535-1254
www.livingston.org
Heritage MS 800/7-8
20 Foxcroft Dr 07039 973-535-8000
Pat Boland, prin. Fax 597-9492
Livingston HS 1,500/9-12
30 Robert H Harp Dr 07039 973-535-8000
Pam Clause-McGroarty, prin. Fax 994-4297

Gibbs College Post-Sec.
630 W Mount Pleasant Ave 07039 973-744-2010
Kushner Hebrew Academy 800/PK-12
110 S Orange Ave 07039 973-597-1115
Susan Dworken, hdmstr. Fax 597-3363
Newark Academy 500/6-12
91 S Orange Ave 07039 973-992-7000
Elizabeth Riegelman, prin. Fax 992-8962
St. Barnabas Medical Center Post-Sec.
94 Old Short Hills Rd 07039 973-533-5628

Lodi, Bergen, Pop. 24,182
Lodi SD 3,200/PK-12
8 Hunter St 07644 973-778-4620
Frank Quatrone, supt. Fax 778-6393
www.lodi.k12.nj.us
Jefferson MS 700/6-8
75 1st St 07644 973-478-8662
Robert Sciolaro, prin. Fax 478-0358
Lodi HS 800/9-12
99 Putnam St 07644 973-478-6100
Daniel Cody, prin. Fax 478-4012

Felician College Post-Sec.
262 S Main St 07644 973-559-6000
Immaculate Conception HS 200/9-12
258 S Main St 07644 973-773-2400
Sr. Mary Alicia Adametz, prin. Fax 614-0893

Long Branch, Monmouth, Pop. 31,523
Long Branch SD 4,200/PK-12
540 Broadway 07740 732-571-2868
Joseph Ferraina, supt. Fax 229-0797
www.longbranch.k12.nj.us
Long Branch HS 1,100/9-12
391 Westwood Ave 07740 732-229-7300
James Simonelli, prin. Fax 229-2825
Long Branch MS 900/6-8
364 Indiana Ave 07740 732-229-5533
John Perri, prin. Fax 229-4898

Monmouth County Vocational SD
Supt. — See Freehold
Adult Technical Center Vo/Tech
255 W End Ave 07740 732-229-3019
Assunta Paulisko, prin. Fax 229-5727

Ilan HS 50/9-12
82 Norwood Ave 07740 732-870-2800
Raizi Chechik, hdmstr. Fax 870-0885
Monmouth Medical Center Post-Sec.
300 2nd Ave 07740 732-222-5200

Long Valley, Morris, Pop. 1,744
Washington Township SD 2,800/K-8
53 W Mill Rd 07853 908-876-4172
Gerald Vernotica Ed.D., supt. Fax 876-9392
www.wtschools.org
Long Valley MS N, 51 W Mill Rd 07853 1,300/5-8
Dr. Kevin Walsh, prin. 908-876-3434

Lumberton, Burlington
Lumberton Township SD 1,600/K-8
33 Municipal Dr 08048 609-267-1406
Frank Logandro, supt. Fax 267-0002
www.lumberton.k12.nj.us/
Lumberton MS 600/6-8
30 Dimsdale Dr 08048 609-265-0123
Patricia Hutchinson, prin. Fax 265-0476

Lyndhurst, Bergen, Pop. 18,262
Lyndhurst Township SD 2,100/PK-12
1050 Wall St W Ste 645 07071 201-438-5683
Joseph Abate, supt. Fax 896-2118
Lyndhurst HS 600/9-12
400 Weart Ave 07071 201-896-2100
Anita Pescevich, prin. Fax 896-2088

Madison, Morris, Pop. 15,352
Madison SD 2,200/PK-12
359 Woodland Rd 07940 973-593-3100
Richard Noonan, supt. Fax 301-2170
www.madisonpublicschools.org
Madison HS 700/9-12
170 Ridgedale Ave 07940 973-593-3117
Greg Robertson, prin. Fax 593-3141
Madison JHS 400/7-8
285 Main St 07940 973-593-3149
Ann Marie Hodges, prin. Fax 966-1908

Drew University Post-Sec.
36 Madison Ave 07940 973-408-3000
Fairleigh Dickinson University Post-Sec.
285 Madison Ave 07940 800-338-8803

Mahwah, Bergen, Pop. 17,905
Mahwah Township SD 3,200/PK-12
60 Ridge Rd 07430 201-882-2400
Charles Montesano, supt. Fax 529-1287
www.mahwah.k12.nj.us
Mahwah HS 800/9-12
50 Ridge Rd 07430 201-882-2300
John Pascale, prin. Fax 512-0949
Ramapo Ridge MS 800/6-8
150 Ridge Rd 07430 201-882-2380
Brian Miller, prin. Fax 529-6790

Lincoln Technical Institute — Post-Sec.
70 McKee Dr 07430 — 201-529-1414
National Tax Training School — Post-Sec.
PO Box 767 07430 — 201-684-0828
Ramapo College of New Jersey — Post-Sec.
505 Ramapo Valley Rd 07430 — 201-684-7500

Manahawkin, Ocean, Pop. 1,594
Southern Regional SD — 2,300/7-12
105 Cedar Bridge Rd 08050 — 609-597-9481
James Kerfoot, supt. — Fax 978-0298
www.srsd.net
Southern Regional HS — 9-10
600 N Main St 08050 — 609-597-9481
Dr. Christopher Traficante, prin. — Fax 978-5375
Southern Regional HS — 1,300/11-12
90 Cedar Bridge Rd 08050 — 609-597-9481
Eric Wilhelm, prin. — Fax 978-5357
Southern Regional MS — 1,000/7-8
75 Cedar Bridge Rd 08050 — 609-597-9481
Eric Wilhelm, prin. — Fax 978-8209
Adult Evening HS — Adult
105 Cedar Bridge Rd 08050 — 609-597-9481
Jan Kristbergs, prin. — Fax 978-5352

Manalapan, Monmouth
Freehold Regional HSD
Supt. — See Englishtown
Manalapan HS — 2,200/9-12
30 Church Ln 07726 — 732-792-7200
— Fax 446-4981

Manalapan-Englishtown Regional SD
Supt. — See Englishtown
Manalapan-Englishtown MS — 1,300/7-8
155 Millhurst Rd 07726 — 732-786-2650
Robert Williams, prin. — Fax 786-2660

Manasquan, Monmouth, Pop. 6,413
Manasquan SD — 1,700/K-12
169 Broad St 08736 — 732-528-8800
Carole Morris, supt. — Fax 223-6286
www.manasquanboe.org/
Manasquan HS — 1,100/9-12
167 Broad St 08736 — 732-528-8820
Cary McCormack, prin. — Fax 528-0316

Manchester, Ocean
Manchester Township SD
Supt. — See Whiting
Manchester Township HS — 1,100/9-12
101 S Colonial Dr 08759 — 732-657-2121
David Walling, prin. — Fax 657-2781
Manchester Township MS — 800/6-8
2759 Ridgeway Rd 08759 — 732-657-1717
Thomas Baxter, prin. — Fax 657-0326

Manville, Somerset, Pop. 10,401
Manville Borough SD — 1,200/PK-PK, 1-
410 Brooks Blvd 08835 — 908-231-8545
Dr. Donald Burkhardt, supt. — Fax 704-0510
www.manvilleschools.org
Batcho IS, 100 N 13th Ave 08835 — 300/6-8
Dr. James Brunn, prin. — 908-231-8521
Manville HS — 400/9-12
1100 Brooks Blvd 08835 — 908-231-6806
Dr. Rodney J. Logan, prin. — Fax 231-8543

Maple Shade, Burlington, Pop. 19,211
Maple Shade Township SD — 2,000/K-12
170 Frederick Ave 08052 — 856-779-1750
Cheryl Smith, supt. — Fax 779-1054
www.mapleshade.org/
Maple Shade JSHS — 900/7-12
180 Frederick Ave 08052 — 856-779-2880
Raymond Marini, prin. — Fax 779-8849

Maplewood, Essex, Pop. 21,756
South Orange-Maplewood SD — 6,100/K-12
525 Academy St 07040 — 973-762-5600
Peter Horoschak, supt. — Fax 378-9464
www.somsd.k12.nj.us
Columbia HS — 2,000/9-12
17 Parker Ave 07040 — 973-378-5266
Renee Pollack, prin. — Fax 378-5234
Maplewood MS — 700/6-8
7 Burnett St 07040 — 973-378-7660
Kristopher Harrison, prin. — Fax 378-5247
Other Schools – See South Orange

Margate City, Atlantic, Pop. 8,328
Margate City SD — 600/K-8
8103 Winchester Ave 08402 — 609-822-1686
Dominick Potena, supt. — Fax 822-3399
www.margateschools.org
Tighe MS — 200/6-8
7804 Amherst Ave 08402 — 609-822-2353
James Rhoads, prin. — Fax 822-8456

Marlboro, Monmouth
Freehold Regional HSD
Supt. — See Englishtown
Marlboro HS — 2,200/9-12
95 N Main St 07746 — 732-671-8393
James Mullevey, prin. — Fax 972-6615

Marlboro Township SD — 5,800/PK-8
1980 Township Dr 07746 — 732-972-2000
Dr. David Abbott, supt. — Fax 972-2003
www.marlboro.k12.nj.us
Marlboro MS — 1,200/6-8
355 County Road 520 07746 — 732-972-2100
Patricia Nieliwocki, prin. — Fax 972-6765
Other Schools – See Morganville

Marlton, Burlington, Pop. 10,228
Evesham Township SD — 5,100/K-8
25 S Maple Ave 08053 — 856-983-1800
Patricia Lucas, supt. — Fax 983-2939
www.evesham.k12.nj.us
Demasi MS — 700/6-8
199 Evesboro Medford Rd 08053 — 856-988-0777
Virginia Grossman, prin.
Marlton MS — 1,100/6-8
150 Tomlinson Mill Rd 08053 — 856-988-0684
Gary Hoffman, prin.

Lenape Regional HSD
Supt. — See Shamong Township
Cherokee HS North — 2,300/9-12
120 Tomlinson Mill Rd 08053 — 856-983-5140
Linda Roher, prin. — Fax 596-6495

Rizzieri Aveda School — Post-Sec.
6001 Lincoln Dr W 08053 — 856-988-8600

Martinsville, Somerset

Pingry S — 1,000/K-12
PO Box 366 08836 — 908-647-5555
Nathaniel Conard, prin. — Fax 647-3703

Matawan, Monmouth, Pop. 8,873
Old Bridge Township SD — 7,300/K-12
4207 County Road 516 07747 — 732-290-3976
Dr. Simon Bosco, supt. — Fax 441-3816
www.oldbridgeadmin.org
Old Bridge HS — 9-12
4209 County Road 516 07747 — 732-290-3900
Dr. James Hickey, prin. — Fax 566-1263
Other Schools – See Old Bridge

Mays Landing, Atlantic, Pop. 2,090
Atlantic County Vocational SD
5080 Atlantic Ave 08330 — 609-625-2249
Dr. Philip Guenther, supt. — Fax 625-2876
www.acitech.org
Atlantic County Institute of Technology — Vo/Tech
5080 Atlantic Ave 08330 — 609-625-2249
Ronald DeFelice, prin. — Fax 625-0707
Atlantic County Adult Education — Adult
5080 Atlantic Ave 08330 — 609-625-2249
Maryann Sakamoto, prin. — Fax 625-8622
Greater Egg Harbor Regional HSD — 3,600/9-12
1824 Dr Dennis Foreman Dr 08330 — 609-625-1456
Adam Pfeffer Ed.D., supt. — Fax 625-0045
www.gehrhsd.org/
Oakcrest HS — 1,500/9-12
1824 Dr Dennis Foreman Dr 08330 — 609-909-2600
Anthony Mongelluzzo, prin. — Fax 625-0872
Other Schools – See Galloway
Hamilton Township SD — 2,800/PK-8
1876 Dr Dennis Foreman Dr 08330 — 609-476-6300
Frederickc Donatucci, supt. — Fax 625-4847
www.hamiltonschools.org
Davies MS — 700/7-8
1876 Dr Dennis Foreman Dr 08330 — 609-625-6600
Michael Muldoon, prin. — Fax 625-2267

Atlantic Cape Community College — Post-Sec.
5100 Black Horse Pike 08330 — 609-343-4900
Atlantic Co. Vocational Technical School — Post-Sec.
5080 Atlantic Ave 08330 — 609-625-2249

Maywood, Bergen, Pop. 9,494
Maywood SD — 800/PK-8
452 Maywood Ave 07607 — 201-845-9114
Dr. Robert Otinsky, supt. — Fax 845-7146
www.maywoodschools.org
Maywood Avenue S — 500/PK-K, 4-8
452 Maywood Ave 07607 — 201-845-9110
Raymond Bauer, prin. — Fax 291-1917

Medford, Burlington
Burlington County Inst. of Technology
Supt. — See Mount Holly
Burlington Co. Institute of Technology — Vo/Tech
10 Hawkin Rd 08055 — 609-654-0200
Joseph Porter, prin. — Fax 654-1081

Lenape Regional HSD
Supt. — See Shamong Township
Lenape HS — 2,000/9-12
235 Hartford Rd 08055 — 609-654-5111
Barry Croll, prin. — Fax 953-6779
Shawnee HS — 1,700/9-12
600 Tabernacle Rd 08055 — 609-654-7544
Charles Fleischman, prin. — Fax 654-5509

Medford Township SD — 2,400/K-8
128 Route 70 Ste 1 08055 — 609-654-6416
Joseph J. Del Rossi Ed.D., supt. — Fax 654-7436
www.medford.k12.nj.us/
Medford Township Memorial MS — 700/7-8
55 Mill St 08055 – Phillip Petru, prin. — 609-654-7707

Medford Lakes, Burlington, Pop. 4,205
Medford Lakes Borough SD — 500/PK-8
135 Mudjekeewis Trl 08055 — 609-654-0991
Diane Bacher, supt. — Fax 654-7629
www.medford-lakes.k12.nj.us
Neeta S — 400/3-8
44 Neeta Trl 08055 — 609-654-5155
Karen Rockhill, prin. — Fax 953-8258

Mendham, Morris, Pop. 5,130
Mendham Borough SD — 700/PK-8
12 Hilltop Rd 07945 — 973-543-2295
Dr. Janie Edmonds, supt. — Fax 543-2805
www.mendhamboro.org
Mountain View MS — 300/5-8
100 Dean Rd 07945 — 973-543-7075
Patricia Lambert, prin. — Fax 543-7993

West Morris Regional HSD
Supt. — See Chester
West Morris Mendham HS — 1,100/9-12
65 E Main St 07945 — 973-543-2501
Michael Matyas, prin. — Fax 543-6739

Assumption College for Sisters — Post-Sec.
350 Bernardsville Rd 07945 — 973-543-6528

Metuchen, Middlesex, Pop. 13,293
Metuchen SD — 1,800/PK-12
16 Simpson Pl 08840 — 732-321-8700
T. Pollifrone-Sinatra, supt. — Fax 321-6567
www.metuchenschools.org/metuchen
Edgar MS — 600/5-8
49 Brunswick Ave 08840 — 732-321-8770
Katherine Glutz, prin. — Fax 452-0571

Metuchen HS — 500/9-12
400 Grove Ave 08840 — 732-321-8743
John Novak, prin. — Fax 549-6415

St. Joseph HS — 800/9-12
145 Plainfield Rd 08840 — 732-549-7600
Lawrence Walsh, prin. — Fax 549-0664

Middlesex, Middlesex, Pop. 13,992
Middlesex Borough SD — 2,100/K-12
300 John F Kennedy Dr 08846 — 732-317-6000
Dr. James C. Baker, supt. — Fax 317-6006
www.middlesex.k12.nj.us
Mauger MS — 900/4-8
Fisher Ave 08846 — 732-317-6000
Robert Heidt, prin. — Fax 317-6002
Middlesex HS — 600/9-12
300 John F Kennedy Dr 08846 — 732-317-6000
Gregory Freeman, prin. — Fax 317-6008

Middletown, Monmouth, Pop. 24,000
Middletown Township SD — 10,100/K-12
59 Tindall Rd 07748 — 732-671-3850
Dr. David L. Witmer, supt. — Fax 615-9351
www.middletownk12.org/
Middletown-North HS — 1,700/9-12
63 Tindall Rd 07748 — 732-706-6061
Jeff Simon, prin. — Fax 706-6067
Middletown-South HS — 1,400/9-12
501 Nutswamp Rd 07748 — 732-706-6111
Mark Kelly, prin. — Fax 706-6058
Thompson MS — 900/6-8
1001 Middletown Lincroft Rd 07748 — 732-671-2212
Patrick Houston, prin.
Other Schools – See Leonardo, Port Monmouth

Monmouth County Vocational SD
Supt. — See Freehold
Middletown Vocational S — Vo/Tech
2 Swartzel Dr 07748 — 732-671-0650
James Johnson, prin. — Fax 671-7455

Midland Park, Bergen, Pop. 6,927
Midland Park Borough SD — 800/K-12
31 Highland Ave 07432 — 201-444-1400
August DePreker, supt. — Fax 444-3051
www.midlandparkschools.k12.nj.us
Midland Park JSHS — 500/7-12
250 Prospect St 07432 — 201-444-7400
Patricia M. Terraciano, prin. — Fax 444-0352

Milford, Hunterdon, Pop. 1,201
Holland Township SD — 700/K-8
710 Milford Warren Glen Rd 08848 — 908-995-2401
Dr. Eugene Costa, supt. — Fax 995-2011
hts.k12.nj.us
Holland Township MS — 300/5-8
710 Milford Warren Glen Rd 08848 — 908-995-2401
Nancy Yard, prin.

Millburn, Essex, Pop. 18,630
Millburn Township SD — 4,300/K-12
434 Millburn Ave 07041 — 973-376-3600
Dr. Richard L. Brodow, supt. — Fax 912-9396
www.millburn.org
Millburn HS — 1,100/9-12
462 Millburn Ave 07041 — 973-376-3600
Dr. Keith Neigel, prin. — Fax 912-8633
Millburn MS — 1,000/6-8
25 Old Short Hills Rd 07041 — 973-379-2600
Michael Cahill, prin. — Fax 912-8633

Milburn School for Hearing Handicapped — Post-Sec.
Spring & Willow Sts 07041 — 973-376-9439

Milltown, Middlesex, Pop. 7,175
Milltown SD — 700/K-8
80 Violet Ter 08850 — 732-828-0300
Dr. Linda Madison, supt. — Fax 828-0645
www.milltownps.org
Kilmer S — 400/4-8
21 W Church St 08850 — 732-828-0500
Janet Perlazzo, prin. — Fax 828-2271

Millville, Cumberland, Pop. 27,119
Millville SD — 7,700/PK-12
PO Box 5010 08332 — 856-327-7575
Dr. Shelly Schneider, supt. — Fax 825-1545
www.millville.org
Memorial Freshman HS — 1,000/8-9
500 E Broad St 08332 — 856-327-6072
Al Johnson, prin. — Fax 825-4480
Millville SHS — 1,500/10-12
200 N Wade Blvd 08332 — 856-327-6040
Dr. Christy Thompson, prin. — Fax 293-1342

Minotola, See Buena
Buena Regional SD
Supt. — See Buena
Cleary MS — 500/6-8
1501 Central Ave 08341 — 856-697-0100
Kenneth Nelson, prin. — Fax 697-9580

Monmouth Junction, Middlesex, Pop. 1,570
South Brunswick Township SD
Supt. — See North Brunswick
Crossroads North MS — 800/6-8
635 Georges Rd 08852 — 732-329-4191
Judith Black, prin. — Fax 329-1907
Crossroads South MS — 1,200/6-8
195 Major Rd 08852 — 732-329-4633
Dr. James Warfel, prin. — Fax 329-1906
South Brunswick HS — 2,400/9-12
750 Ridge Rd 08852 — 732-329-4044
Timothy Matheney, prin. — Fax 274-1237

Noor Ul-Iman S — 300/PK-12
PO Box 271 08852 — 732-329-1306

Monroe Township, Middlesex
Monroe Township SD — 4,000/K-12
423 Buckelew Ave 08831 — 732-521-2111
Ralph P. Ferrie, supt. — Fax 521-2719
monroe.k12.nj.us
Applegarth MS — 600/7-8
227 Applegarth Rd 08831 — 609-655-0604
Jeff Gorman, prin. — Fax 655-4314
Monroe Township HS — 1,200/9-12
1629 Perrineville Rd 08831 — 732-521-2882
Robert Goodall, prin. — Fax 521-2976

Montclair, Essex, Pop. 39,200
Montclair SD 6,100/K-12
22 Valley Rd 07042 973-509-4000
Dr. Frank Alvarez, supt. Fax 509-0586
www.montclair.k12.nj.us/
Glenfield MS 700/6-8
25 Maple Ave 07042 973-509-4171
Joanne Petrigliano, prin. Fax 509-4179
Montclair HS 1,800/9-12
100 Chestnut St 07042 973-509-4069
Mel Katz, prin. Fax 509-4098
Mt. Hebron MS 500/6-8
173 Bellevue Ave 07043 973-509-4220
Dr. Mark Jennings, prin. Fax 509-4218

Eastern School of Acupuncture Post-Sec.
427 Bloomfield Ave Ste 301 07042 973-746-8717
Immaculate Conception HS 300/9-12
33 Cottage Pl 07042 973-744-7445
Joann Degnan, prin. Fax 744-3926
Lacordaire Academy 200/9-12
155 Lorraine Ave 07043 973-744-1156
Sr. Suzanne McCaffrey, prin. Fax 783-9521
Montclair-Kimberley Academy 400/4-8
201 Valley Rd 07042 973-746-9800
Thomas Nammack, hdmstr. Fax 783-5777
Montclair Kimberley Academy - Upper S 400/9-12
6 Lloyd Rd 07042 973-783-8303
Thomas Nammack, hdmstr. Fax 744-4051
Montclair State University Post-Sec.
Montclair State University 07043 973-655-4000
Mountainside Hospital Post-Sec.
1 Bay Ave 07042 973-429-6850

Montvale, Bergen, Pop. 7,289
Montvale SD 1,000/PK-8
47 Spring Valley Rd 07645 201-391-1662
Susan King, supt. Fax 391-8935
www.montvale.k12.nj.us
Fieldstone MS 400/5-8
47 Spring Valley Rd 07645 201-391-9000
Paul Semendinger, prin. Fax 391-8935

Pascack Valley Regional HSD 1,600/9-12
46 Akers Ave 07645 201-358-7006
Dr. Benedict Tantillo, supt. Fax 505-4858
www.pascack.k12.nj.us
Pascack Hills HS 600/9-12
225 W Grand Ave 07645 201-358-7020
Sarah Van Gunten, prin. Fax 358-7019
Other Schools – See Hillsdale

St. Joseph Regional HS 500/9-12
40 Chestnut Ridge Rd 07645 201-391-3300
John Job, prin. Fax 391-8073

Montville, Morris, Pop. 15,600
Montville Township SD
Supt. — See Pine Brook
Lazar MS 900/6-8
123 Changebridge Rd 07045 973-331-7140
John Gallucci, prin. Fax 331-9279
Montville Township HS 1,100/9-12
100 Horseneck Rd 07045 973-331-7100
Dr. Steven Kramer, prin. Fax 334-0753

Trinity Christian S 200/PK-12
160 Changebridge Rd 07045 973-334-1785
Douglas Prol, prin. Fax 334-9282

Moorestown, Burlington, Pop. 13,242
Moorestown Township SD 4,000/K-12
803 N Stanwick Rd 08057 856-778-6600
Fax 235-0961
www.mtps.com
Allen III MS 600/7-8
801 N Stanwick Rd 08057 856-778-6620
Sharon Vitella, prin. Fax 727-9309
Moorestown HS 1,200/9-12
350 Bridgeboro Rd 08057 856-778-6610
David Yates, prin. Fax 722-8983

Moorestown Friends S 700/PK-12
110 E Main St 08057 856-235-2900
Laurence R. Van Meter, hdmstr. Fax 235-6684

Morganville, Monmouth
Marlboro Township SD
Supt. — See Marlboro
Marlboro Memorial MS 900/6-8
71 Nolan Rd 07751 732-617-5602
Joanmarie Penney, prin. Fax 972-7118

Morris Plains, Morris, Pop. 5,513
Morris Plains SD 600/PK-8
500 Speedwell Ave 07950 973-538-1650
Kenneth Knops, supt. Fax 984-2268
www.morris.k12.nj.us/mps
Borough MS 400/3-8
500 Speedwell Ave 07950 973-538-1650
Timothy Plotts, prin. Fax 540-1983

Parsippany-Troy Hills Township SD
Supt. — See Parsippany
Parsippany Hills HS 1,200/9-12
20 Rita Dr 07950 973-682-2815
Dr. Richard Konet, prin. Fax 682-2855

Morristown, Morris, Pop. 18,816
Morris SD 4,500/K-12
31 Hazel St 07960 973-292-2300
Thomas Ficarra, supt. Fax 292-2057
www.morrisschooldistrict.org
Frelinghuysen MS 900/6-8
200 W Hanover Ave 07960 973-292-2200
Ethel Minchello, prin. Fax 292-2458
Morristown HS 1,500/9-12
50 Early St 07960 973-292-2100
Linda Murphy, prin. Fax 539-5573

College of Saint Elizabeth Post-Sec.
2 Convent Rd 07960 973-290-4000
Delbarton S 500/7-12
230 Mendham Rd 07960 973-538-3231
Rev. Luke Travers, hdmstr. Fax 538-8836
Morristown-Beard S 500/6-12
70 Whippany Rd 07960 973-539-3032
Dr. Alex Curtis, hdmstr. Fax 539-1590
Morristown Memorial Hospital Post-Sec.
100 Madison Ave 07960 973-971-5177
Rabbinical College of America Post-Sec.
226 Sussex Ave 07960 973-267-9404
Shepard HS 100/9-12
10 Columba St 07960 973-984-1600
Villa Walsh Academy 200/7-12
455 Western Ave 07960 973-538-3680
Sr. Patricia Pompa, prin. Fax 538-6733

Mountain Lakes, Morris, Pop. 4,307
Mountain Lakes SD 1,500/K-12
400 Boulevard 07046 973-334-8280
Dr. John Kazmark, supt. Fax 334-2316
www.mtlakes.org
Briarcliff MS 300/6-8
93 Briarcliff Rd 07046 973-334-0342
Constance Seifert, prin. Fax 334-6857
Mountain Lakes HS 600/9-12
96 Powerville Rd 07046 973-334-8400
Lew Ludwig, prin. Fax 334-3550

Craig S 200/3-12
10 Tower Hill Rd 07046 973-334-1295
David Blanchard, hdmstr. Fax 334-1299

Mountainside, Union, Pop. 6,659
Mountainside SD 600/PK-8
1497 Woodacres Dr 07092 908-232-3232
Richard O'Malley, admin. Fax 232-1743
mountainsideschools.net/
Deerfield S 400/3-8
302 Central Ave 07092 908-232-8828
Robert Burkhardt, prin. Fax 232-7338

Mount Arlington, Morris, Pop. 5,017
Mt. Arlington SD 400/K-8
446 Howard Blvd 07856 973-398-6400
Jane Mullins Jameson, supt. Fax 398-3614
www.gti.net/mtas/
Mount Arlington MS 300/3-8
235 Howard Blvd 07856 973-398-4400
Martha Weber, prin. Fax 398-5726

Mount Ephraim, Camden, Pop. 4,497
Mt. Ephraim Borough SD 400/K-8
125 S Black Horse Pike 08059 856-931-1634
Richard Serfling, supt. Fax 931-0202
mtephraimschools.org/
Kershaw MS 200/5-8
125 S Black Horse Pike 08059 856-931-1634
Richard Serfling, prin.

Mount Holly, Burlington, Pop. 10,639
Burlington County Inst. of Technology
695 Woodlane Rd 08060 609-267-4226
Dolores Szymanski, supt. Fax 267-9788
www.bcit.cc/
Burlington Co. Institute of Technology Vo/Tech
695 Woodlane Rd 08060 609-267-4226
Daniel Money, prin. Fax 267-3752
Burlington Co. Inst of Tech Evening Vo/Tech
695 Woodlane Rd 08060 609-654-2000
John Karaska, prin.
Other Schools – See Medford

Mt. Holly Township SD 1,000/PK-8
330 Levis Dr 08060 609-267-7108
Paul Spaventa, supt. Fax 702-9082
www.mtholly.k12.nj.us
Holbein MS 400/5-8
333 Levis Dr 08060 609-267-7200
John Dileo, prin. Fax 702-9775

Rancocas Valley Regional HSD 2,200/9-12
520 Jacksonville Rd 08060 609-267-0830
Dr. Michael Moskalski, supt. Fax 265-9204
www.rancocasvalley.k12.nj.us
Rancocas Valley Regional HS 2,100/9-12
520 Jacksonville Rd 08060 609-267-0830
Dr. Michael Moskalski, prin. Fax 265-9204
Evening HS Adult
520 Jacksonville Rd 08060 609-267-0830
Camille Rosenberg, prin.

Burlington County Inst. of Technology Post-Sec.
695 Woodlane Rd 08060 609-267-4226

Mount Laurel, Burlington
Mt. Laurel Township SD 4,400/K-8
330 Mount Laurel Rd 08054 856-235-3387
Dr. Antoinette Rath, supt. Fax 235-1837
mtlaurelschools.org
Harrington MS 1,100/7-8
514 Mount Laurel Rd 08054 856-234-1610
Nancy Knight, prin. Fax 222-9754

Cittone Institute Post-Sec.
1000 Howard Blvd # 2 08054 856-722-9333

Mullica Hill, Gloucester, Pop. 1,117
Clearview Regional HSD 2,100/7-12
420 Cedar Rd 08062 856-223-2765
Patricia Carroll, supt. Fax 478-0409
www.clearviewregional.edu
Clearview Regional HS 1,300/9-12
625 Breakneck Rd 08062 856-223-2790
Kevin Kitchenman, prin. Fax 478-6705
Clearview Regional MS 800/7-8
595 Jefferson Rd 08062 856-223-2740
David Kelk, prin. Fax 223-9068

Neptune, Monmouth, Pop. 5,062
Monmouth County Vocational SD
Supt. — See Freehold
Monmouth Co. Acad of Allied Health & Sci Vo/Tech
2325 Heck Ave 07753 732-775-0058
Robert Cancro, prin. Fax 775-6646

Neptune Township SD 4,100/PK-12
3301B State Route 66 07753 732-776-2000
David Mooij, supt. Fax 776-2003
www.neptune.k12.nj.us/education/district/district.php
Neptune HS 1,300/9-12
55 Neptune Blvd 07753 732-776-2200
Edward Dever, prin. Fax 776-2253
Neptune MS 900/6-8
2100 Heck Ave 07753 732-776-2100
Peolat Smith, prin. Fax 776-2254

Jersey Shore Medical Center Post-Sec.
1945 State Route 33 07753 732-776-4603

Newark, Essex, Pop. 277,911
Essex County Vocational SD
Supt. — See Verona
Essex County Vocational HS-13th Street Vo/Tech
300 N 13th St 07107 973-483-5466
John Dolan, prin. Fax 483-6606
West Market Street Center Vocational S Vo/Tech
91 W Market St 07103 973-622-1100
Baruti Kafele, prin. Fax 623-2010

Newark SD 37,500/PK-12
2 Cedar St 07102 973-733-7333
Marion Bolden, supt. Fax 733-6834
www.nps.k12.nj.us/
Academy of Vocational Careers Vo/Tech
74 Montgomery St 07103 973-733-6911
Alan Alvarez, prin. Fax 733-6917
Arts HS 600/9-12
556 Martin Luther King Jr B 07102 973-733-7391
Dr. Norma Fair-Brown, prin. Fax 733-7395
Barringer HS 1,700/9-12
90 Parker St 07104 973-268-5125
Carmen Ruiz, prin. Fax 268-5128
Brown Academy MS 400/6-8
695 Bergen St 07108 973-733-6844
Kevin Guyton, prin. Fax 733-6887
Camden MS, 321 Bergen St 07103 600/5-8
Josephine McDowell, prin. 973-733-8351
Central HS 800/9-12
100 Summit St 07103 973-733-6897
Gregory Stewart, prin. Fax 733-8212
Chancellor Avenue MS 300/3-8
321 Chancellor Ave 07112 973-705-3870
Eugene Brown, prin. Fax 705-3003
East Side HS 1,300/9-12
238 Van Buren St 07105 973-465-4900
Mario Santos, prin. Fax 465-4936
Hillman-Jones MS 300/7-8
24 Crane St 07104 973-268-5101
Norberto Diaz, prin. Fax 268-5324
Maple Avenue S 300/4-8
33 Maple Ave 07112 973-705-3850
Daneen Washington, prin. Fax 705-3013
Marin MS 800/5-8
663 Broadway 07104 973-268-5330
Sylvia Esteves, prin. Fax 268-5972
Morton Street MS 200/6-8
75 Morton St 07103 973-733-6938
Carl Gregory, prin. Fax 733-7287
Newark Vocational S Vo/Tech
301 W Kinney St 07103 973-733-7018
Deborah DeBerry, prin. Fax 242-5431
Science HS 600/9-12
40 Rector St 07102 973-733-8689
Christine Taylor, prin. Fax 733-8236
Shabazz HS 1,200/9-12
80 Johnson Ave 07108 973-733-6760
Leila Dinkins, prin. Fax 430-9163
Technology HS Vo/Tech
223 Broadway 07104 973-481-5962
Mona Dana, prin. Fax 497-5786
University JSHS 500/7-12
55 Clinton Pl 07108 973-351-2010
Roger Leon, prin. Fax 351-2003
Vailsburg MS 600/6-8
107 Ivy St 07106 973-351-2121
Matthew Brewster, prin. Fax 374-2102
Weequahic HS 900/9-12
279 Chancellor Ave 07112 973-705-3900
Ronald Stone, prin. Fax 923-4095
West Side HS 1,300/9-12
403 S Orange Ave 07103 973-733-6977
Fernard Williams, prin. Fax 733-8941
Adult Learning Center Adult
32 Warren Pl 07102 973-733-7028
Newark Evening HS Adult
403 S Orange Ave 07103 973-374-2090
Edna Bailey, prin.

Alpha & Omega Christian S 100/PK-12
4 Fleming Ave 07105 973-465-5333
Rev. Jose Torres, dir. Fax 465-5335
Essex County College Post-Sec.
303 University Ave 07102 973-877-3000
Link Community S 100/7-8
120 Livingston St 07103 973-642-0529
Fax 642-1978
McEllis Training Institute Post-Sec.
800 Broad St 07102 973-643-6917
Mesivta of North Jersey 100/9-12
520 Broad St 07102 973-438-3211
Iris Eisenberg, admin. Fax 438-1719
Newark Boys Chorus S 100/4-8
1016 Broad St 07102 973-621-8900
Lawrence Emery, hdmstr. Fax 621-1343
New Community Workforce Development Ctr. Post-Sec.
201 Bergen St 07103 973-824-6484
New Jersey Institute of Technology Post-Sec.
University Heights 07102 973-596-3000
New Testament Church S 50/K-12
511 Orange St 07107 973-268-1310
Mollie Haynes, prin. Fax 485-4738
Our Lady of Good Counsel HS 300/9-12
243 Woodside Ave 07104 973-482-1209
Harry Hart, prin. Fax 482-4321
Rutgers-The State University of N.J. Post-Sec.
07102 973-353-5568
St. Benedict Prep S 600/7-12
520 Mrtn Lther King Jr Blvd 07102 973-643-4800
Rev. Edwin Leahy, prin. Fax 792-5721
St. Vincent Academy 300/9-12
228 W Market St 07103 973-622-1613
Sr. June Favata, dir. Fax 622-1128
Seton Hall University School of Law Post-Sec.
1 Newark Ctr 07102 973-642-8747
UMDNJ Grad. Sch. of Biomedical Sciences Post-Sec.
185 S Orange Ave 07103 973-972-4511
UMDNJ-New Jersey Dental School Post-Sec.
110 Bergen St 07103 973-972-4633
UMDNJ-New Jersey Medical School Post-Sec.
185 S Orange Ave 07103 973-972-4539
UMDNJ-Sch. of Health Related Professions Post-Sec.
65 Bergen St 07107 973-972-5453
UMDNJ-School of Nursing Post-Sec.
30 Bergen St 07107 973-972-4322

UMDNJ-University of Medicine & Dentistry | Post-Sec.
65 Bergen St 07107 | 973-982-4300

New Brunswick, Middlesex, Pop. 49,803
New Brunswick SD | 5,400/PK-12
PO Box 2683 08903 | 732-745-5300
Richard Kaplan, supt. | Fax 745-5459
www.nbps.k12.nj.us
New Brunswick HS | 1,100/9-12
1125 Livingston Ave 08901 | 732-745-5300
Leonard Sanfililppo, prin. | Fax 937-7580
New Brunswick MS | 6-8
30 Van Dyke Ave 08901 | 732-745-5300
Faye Warren, prin. | Fax 565-7621
Adult HS | Adult
268 Baldwin St 08901 | 732-846-5300
Marlene Lederman, prin. | Fax 745-5325

New Brunswick Theological Seminary | Post-Sec.
17 Seminary Pl 08901 | 732-247-5241
Rutgers-The State University of N.J. | Post-Sec.
35 College Ave 08901 | 732-932-4636
St. Peter the Apostle HS | 200/9-12
175 Somerset St 08901 | 732-846-8046
Dr. Kathleen Joyce, prin. | Fax 220-9560

New Egypt, Ocean, Pop. 2,327
Plumsted Township SD | 1,400/PK-12
117 Evergreen Rd 08533 | 609-758-6800
Jerry North, supt. | Fax 758-6808
www.newegypt.us
New Egypt HS | 500/9-12
117 Evergreen Rd 08533 | 609-758-6800
Richard Caldes, prin. | Fax 758-5683
New Egypt MS | 400/6-8
115 Evergreen Rd 08533 | 609-758-6800
Jerry Jellig, prin. | Fax 758-5538

Newfield, Gloucester, Pop. 1,628

Our Lady of Mercy Academy | 100/9-12
1001 Main Rd 08344 | 856-697-2008
Sr. Grace Marie, prin. | Fax 697-8595

New Milford, Bergen, Pop. 16,367
New Milford SD | 1,700/K-12
145 Madison Ave 07646 | 201-261-2952
Elaine Baldwin, supt. | Fax 261-8018
www.newmilfordschools.org
New Milford HS | 500/9-12
1 Snyder Cir 07646 | 201-262-0172
Dr. John Moncrief, prin. | Fax 262-4445
Owens MS | 500/6-8
470 Marion Ave 07646 | 201-265-8661
Laura Porcaro, prin. | Fax 265-5680

New Monmouth, Monmouth

Mater Dei HS | 400/9-12
538 Church St 07748 | 732-671-9100
Frank Poleski, prin. | Fax 671-9214

New Providence, Union, Pop. 11,983
New Providence SD | 2,100/K-12
356 Elkwood Ave 07974 | 908-464-9050
Ann Marie Inzano, supt. | Fax 464-9041
www.npsd.k12.nj.us
New Providence HS | 600/9-12
35 Pioneer Dr 07974 | 908-464-4700
Dr. Deborah Feinberg, prin. | Fax 464-8556
New Providence MS | 300/7-8
35 Pioneer Dr 07974 | 908-464-9161
Gina Hansen, prin. | Fax 464-5927

Newton, Sussex, Pop. 8,389
Andover Regional SD | 800/PK-8
707 Limecrest Rd 07860 | 973-383-3746
Jerry A. Clymer, supt. | Fax 579-3972
www.andoverregional.org
Long Pond S | 400/4-8
707 Limecrest Rd 07860 | 973-940-1234
T. Jon Sinclair, prin. | Fax 529-2690

Kittatinny Regional SD | 1,300/7-12
77 Halsey Rd 07860 | 973-383-1800
Robert Walker, supt. | Fax 383-6218
www.krhs.net
Kittatinny Regional JSHS | 1,300/7-12
77 Halsey Rd 07860 | 973-383-1800
Susan Kappler, prin. | Fax 383-4392

Newton SD | 1,700/PK-12
57 Trinity St 07860 | 973-383-1900
Mark Miller, supt. | Fax 383-5378
www.newtonnj.org
Halsted Street MS | 300/6-8
59 Halsted St 07860 | 973-383-7440
Kurt Walton, prin. | Fax 383-7432
Newton HS | 800/9-12
44 Ryerson Ave 07860 | 973-383-7573
Brian Doherty, prin. | Fax 383-1153

Sussex County Community College | Post-Sec.
1 College Hill Rd 07860 | 973-300-2100

North Arlington, Bergen, Pop. 15,209
North Arlington SD | 1,500/K-12
222 Ridge Rd 07031 | 201-991-6800
Dr. Oliver Stringham, supt. | Fax 991-1656
www.narlington.k12.nj.us
North Arlington HS | 500/9-12
222 Ridge Rd 07031 | 201-955-5216
Robert Kinloch, prin. | Fax 991-0188
North Arlington MS | 400/6-8
45 Beech St 07031 | 201-955-5265
Oliver Stringham, prin. | Fax 246-0703

Queen of Peace HS | 700/9-12
191 Rutherford Pl 07031 | 201-998-0792
Cathy Condon, prin. | Fax 998-3040

North Bergen, Hudson, Pop. 59,000
Hudson County Vocational SD
8511 Tonnelle Ave 07047 | 201-662-6700
Frank Gargiulo, supt.
www.hcstonline.org

Hudson Co. AVTS Adult Evening HS | Vo/Tech
2000 85th St 07047 | 201-854-3500
James Doran, prin.
Hudson County AVTS North Hudson Ctr | Vo/Tech
2000 85th St 07047 | 201-662-6801
Karol Brancato, prin. | Fax 854-4129
Other Schools – See Bayonne, Jersey City

North Bergen SD | 6,800/K-12
7317 Kennedy Blvd 07047 | 201-295-2706
Peter Fischbach, supt.
www.northbergen.k12.nj.us/
North Bergen HS | 2,100/9-12
7417 Kennedy Blvd 07047 | 201-295-2783
Paschal Tennaro, prin. | Fax 295-9521

Mesivta Ohr Naftoli | 100/9-12
8410 4th Ave 07047 | 845-357-5609
Yosef Willner, prin. | Fax 357-5601
North Hudson Academy | 50/1-12
PO Box 390 07047 | 201-865-9577

North Brunswick, Middlesex, Pop. 37,400
North Brunswick Twp. SD | 5,300/K-12
PO Box 6016 08902 | 732-289-3030
Dr. Robert Rimmer, supt. | Fax 297-8567
www.nbtschools.org
Linwood MS | 1,300/6-8
25 Linwood Pl 08902 | 732-289-3600
J. Peter Clark, prin. | Fax 247-7033
North Brunswick Twp. HS | 1,600/9-12
98 Raider Rd 08902 | 732-289-3700
Salvatore Mistretta, prin. | Fax 821-8342

South Brunswick Township SD | 8,400/K-12
231 Black Horse Ln 08902 | 732-297-7800
Gary P. McCartney Ed.D., supt. | Fax 297-8456
www.sbschools.org
Other Schools – See Monmouth Junction

Chubb Institute | Post-Sec.
651 US Highway 1 08902 | 732-448-2600
DeVry College of Technology | Post-Sec.
630 US Highway 1 08902 | 732-435-4880

North Caldwell, Essex, Pop. 7,380
West Essex Regional SD | 1,500/7-12
65 W Greenbrook Rd 07006 | 973-582-1600
Dr. Donald Merachnik, supt. | Fax 228-0559
www.westex.org
West Essex JHS | 800/7-9
65 W Greenbrook Rd 07006 | 973-228-1200
Richard Vartan, prin. | Fax 228-5852
West Essex SHS | 700/10-12
65 W Greenbrook Rd 07006 | 973-228-1200
Barbara Longo, prin. | Fax 364-1872

Northfield, Atlantic, Pop. 7,954
Northfield CSD | 1,100/K-8
2000 New Rd 08225 | 609-407-4000
Richard Stepura Ed.D., supt. | Fax 646-0608
www.ncs-nj.org/index.php?module=ContentExpress&func=d
Northfield Community MS | 500/5-8
2000 New Rd 08225 | 609-407-4008
Paul Firetto, prin. | Fax 641-2646

North Haledon, Passaic, Pop. 8,340
North Haledon SD | 600/K-8
515 High Mountain Rd 07508 | 973-427-8993
Dr. Charles Ferraro, supt. | Fax 427-4357
www.northhaledonschools.com
High Mountain MS | 300/5-8
515 High Mountain Rd 07508 | 973-427-1220
Donna Cardiello, prin. | Fax 427-7685

Eastern Christian HS | 400/9-12
50 Oakwood Ave 07508 | 973-427-0900
Jan Lucas, prin. | Fax 427-3716
Mary Help of Christians Academy | 300/9-12
659 Belmont Ave 07508 | 973-790-6200
Sr. Margaret Wilhelm, prin. | Fax 790-6125

North Plainfield, Somerset, Pop. 21,091
North Plainfield Borough SD | 3,100/K-12
33 Mountain Ave 07060 | 908-769-6060
Marilyn Birnbaum, supt. | Fax 755-5490
www.nplainfield.org
North Plainfield HS | 1,500/7-12
34 Wilson Ave 07060 | 908-769-6000
Anthony Gaita, prin. | Fax 769-6032
Adult HS | Adult
12 Harrison Ave 07060 | 908-769-6090
Rosemary McGuinness, prin. | Fax 769-6116

Reignbow Hair Fashion Institute | Post-Sec.
121 Watchung Ave 07060 | 908-754-4247

Northvale, Bergen, Pop. 4,536
Northvale SD | 600/K-8
441 Tappan Rd 07647 | 201-768-8485
Sylvan Hershey, supt. | Fax 768-4948
www.nvnet.org
Hale MS | 300/4-8
441 Tappan Rd 07647 | 201-768-0635
Michael Pinajian, dean | Fax 768-4948

Nutley, Essex, Pop. 27,400
Nutley SD | 4,000/K-12
375 Bloomfield Ave 07110 | 973-661-8798
Joseph Zarra, supt. | Fax 661-3447
www.nutleyschools.org
Franklin MS | 700/7-8
325 Franklin Ave 07110 | 973-661-8871
John Calicchio, prin. | Fax 661-3775
Nutley HS | 1,300/9-12
300 Franklin Ave 07110 | 973-661-8832
Gregory Catrambone, prin. | Fax 661-3664

Hohokus School - RETS Nutley | Post-Sec.
103 Park Ave 07110 | 973-661-0600

Oakhurst, Monmouth, Pop. 4,130
Ocean Township SD | 4,000/K-12
163 Monmouth Rd 07755 | 732-531-5600
Thomas Pagano, supt. | Fax 531-3874
www.ocean.k12.nj.us

Ocean Twp. HS | 1,300/9-12
550 W Park Ave 07755 | 732-531-5650
Julia Davidow, prin. | Fax 571-4009
Other Schools – See Ocean

Harrison Career Institute | Post-Sec.
2105 State Route 35 07755 | 732-493-1660

Oakland, Bergen, Pop. 13,616
Oakland SD | 1,600/PK-8
315 Ramapo Valley Rd 07436 | 201-337-6156
Dr. Richard Heflich, supt. | Fax 405-1237
Valley MS, 71 Oak St 07436 | 600/6-8
Dr. Christopher Lane, prin. | 201-337-8185

Ramapo Indian Hills Regional HSD | 2,100/9-12
131 Yawpo Ave 07436 | 201-416-8100
Paul Saxton, supt. | Fax 891-9672
www.rih.org
Indian Hills HS | 900/9-12
97 Yawpo Ave 07436 | 201-337-0100
Dr. Robert Onorato, prin. | Fax 337-1031
Other Schools – See Franklin Lakes

Barnstable Academy | 100/5-12
8 Wright Way 07436 | 201-651-0200
 | Fax 337-9797

Oaklyn, Camden, Pop. 4,156
Oaklyn Borough SD | 500/K-9
156 Kendall Blvd 08107 | 856-858-0335
Tommie Stringer, supt. | Fax 869-3474
www.oaklyn.k12.nj.us
Oaklyn JHS | 100/7-9
156 Kendall Blvd 08107 | 856-858-0335
James Sanders, prin. | Fax 858-1623

Oak Ridge, Passaic
Jefferson Township SD
Supt. — See Lake Hopatcong
Jefferson Twp. HS | 1,000/9-12
1010 Weldon Rd 07438 | 973-697-3535
Virginia Jones, prin. | Fax 208-8409
Jefferson Twp. MS | 900/6-8
1000 Weldon Rd 07438 | 973-697-1980
Bernard Baggs, prin. | Fax 697-1348

Ocean, Monmouth, Pop. 26,700
Ocean Township SD
Supt. — See Oakhurst
Ocean Twp. MS | 1,000/6-8
1200 W Park Ave 07712 | 732-531-5631
Larry Kostula, prin. | Fax 493-1891

Concorde School of Hair Design | Post-Sec.
Route 35 & Sunset Ave 07712 | 732-918-0505
Deal Yeshiva | 100/K-12
1515 Logan Rd 07712 | 732-663-1717
Rabbi Isaac Dwek, dean | Fax 663-1700
Hillel Yeshiva HS | 300/9-12
1027 Deal Rd 07712 | 732-493-0420
Rabbi Ralph Tawil, prin. | Fax 493-2718

Ocean City, Cape May, Pop. 15,558
Ocean City SD | 2,100/K-12
501 Atlantic Ave Ste 1 08226 | 609-399-5150
Dr. David Moyer, supt. | Fax 399-4656
www.ocean.city.k12.nj.us
Ocean City HS | 1,400/9-12
501 Atlantic Ave 08226 | 609-399-1290
Joanne Walls Ph.D., prin. | Fax 399-0265
Ocean City IS | 500/4-8
1801 Bay Ave 08226 | 609-399-5611
Dr. Pamela Vaughan, prin. | Fax 398-7089

Oceanport, Monmouth, Pop. 5,952
Oceanport Borough SD | 800/K-8
Wolf Hill Ave 07757 | 732-544-8588
James DiGiovanna, supt. | Fax 544-0386
www.oceanport.k12.nj.us
Maple Place MS, 2 Maple Pl 07757 | 400/5-8
Dr. John Amato, prin. | 732-229-0267

Ocean View, Cape May

Families United Network Academy | 50/K-12
24 Black Oak Dr 08230 | 609-390-9499
Patricia McQuarrie, prin. | Fax 390-9499

Old Bridge, Middlesex, Pop. 22,151
Old Bridge Township SD
Supt. — See Matawan
Salk MS | 1,300/6-8
155 W Greystone Rd 08857 | 732-360-4519
Kenneth Popovich, prin. | Fax 251-1690
Sandburg MS | 1,200/6-8
3439 County Road 516 08857 | 732-360-0505
Dr. Joseph Gannon, prin. | Fax 360-9676
Old Bridge Adult HS | Adult
3098 County Road 516 08857 | 732-679-0900
Dennis Kostulakos, prin. | Fax 360-1349

Old Tappan, Bergen, Pop. 5,798
Northern Valley Regional SD
Supt. — See Demarest
Northern Valley Regional HS | 1,200/9-12
150 Central Ave 07675 | 201-784-1600
Fred Hessler, prin. | Fax 768-7724

Old Tappan SD | 800/K-8
277 Old Tappan Rd 07675 | 201-664-7231
Dr. Patricia Lennon, supt. | Fax 664-4418
www.oldtappan.nvnet.org
DeWolf MS | 400/5-8
275 Old Tappan Rd 07675 | 201-664-1475
Dennis Rossi, prin. | Fax 664-8101

Oradell, Bergen, Pop. 8,025
River Dell Regional SD
Supt. — See River Edge
River Dell Regional HS | 900/9-12
55 Pyle St 07649 | 201-599-7240
Lorraine Brooks, prin. | Fax 261-3809

Bergen Catholic HS | 900/9-12
1040 Oradell Ave 07649 | 201-261-1844
Dr. Joseph Fusco, prin. | Fax 599-9507

Orange, Essex, Pop. 33,300
Orange SD | 4,400/K-12
451 Lincoln Ave 07050 | 973-677-4040
Dr. Nathan Parker, supt. | Fax 677-2518
www.orange.k12.nj.us
Orange HS | 1,000/9-12
400 Lincoln Ave 07050 | 973-677-4050
Samuel Hazell, prin. | Fax 677-3069
Orange MS | 600/7-8
400 Central Ave 07050 | 973-677-4135
Dr. Judith Kronin, prin. | Fax 677-2439

Palisades Park, Bergen, Pop. 18,007
Palisades Park SD | 1,500/K-12
270 1st St 07650 | 201-947-3560
Dr. Mark Hayes, supt. | Fax 947-4079
www.palpk.k12.nj.us
Palisades Park JSHS | 600/7-12
1 Veterans Plz 07650 | 201-941-1100
Christopher McDuffie, prin. | Fax 947-1280

Palmyra, Burlington, Pop. 7,653
Palmyra Borough SD | 1,100/K-12
301 Delaware Ave 08065 | 856-786-2963
Dr. Walter Rudder, supt. | Fax 829-9638
www.palmyra.k12.nj.us
Palmyra HS | 600/7-12
5th & Weart Blvd 08065 | 856-786-9400
Dr. Richard Perry, prin. | Fax 786-3014
Evening HS | Adult
5th & Weart Blvd 08065 | 856-786-8050
Jerome McGowen, prin. | Fax 303-1664

Paramus, Bergen, Pop. 26,503
Bergen County Vocational SD
327 E Ridgewood Ave 07652 | 201-967-2472
Robert Aloia, supt.
www.bergen.org
Bergen County Technical S - Paramus | Vo/Tech
285 Pascack Rd 07652 | 201-986-0009
Gregory Walters Ed.D., prin. | Fax 599-1288
Other Schools – See Hackensack, Teterboro

Paramus SD | 3,900/K-12
145 S Spring Valley Rd 07652 | 201-261-7800
Janice Dime Ph.D., supt. | Fax 261-5861
www.paramus.k12.nj.us
East Brook MS | 700/5-8
190 Spring Valley Rd 07652 | 201-261-7800
Willis Bott Ed.D., prin. | Fax 262-1541
Paramus HS | 1,100/9-12
99 E Century Rd 07652 | 201-261-7800
Lina Gudelis, prin. | Fax 261-3833
West Brook MS | 700/5-8
550 Roosevelt Blvd 07652 | 201-261-7800
Joan Broe, prin. | Fax 652-0376

Bergen Community College | Post-Sec.
400 Paramus Rd 07652 | 201-447-7100
Berkeley College | Post-Sec.
64 E Midland Ave 07652 | 800-446-5400
Capri Institute of Hair Design | Post-Sec.
615 Winters Ave 07652 | 201-599-0880
Cittone Institute | Post-Sec.
160 E State Rt 4 07652 | 201-828-5911
Dover Business College | Post-Sec.
East 81 Route 4 W 07652 | 201-843-8500
Frisch S | 500/9-12
243 Frisch Ct 07652 | 201-845-0555
Dr. Kalman Stein, prin. | Fax 845-4941
Paramus Catholic HS | 1,300/9-12
425 Paramus Rd 07652 | 201-445-4466
Joseph Agostino, prin. | Fax 445-3952

Park Ridge, Bergen, Pop. 8,880
Park Ridge SD | 1,300/K-12
2 Park Ave 07656 | 201-573-6000
Dr. Patricia Johnson, supt. | Fax 391-6511
www.parkridge.k12.nj.us
Park Ridge HS | 600/7-12
2 Park Ave 07656 | 201-573-6000
Richard Martinez, prin. | Fax 930-4874

Parlin, Middlesex
Sayreville SD
Supt. — See South Amboy
Sayreville MS | 1,400/6-8
800 Washington Rd 08859 | 732-525-5290
Donna Jakubik, prin. | Fax 727-5621
Sayreville War Memorial HS | 1,600/9-12
820 Washington Rd 08859 | 732-525-5252
James Brown, prin. | Fax 316-0720

Parsippany, Morris, Pop. 51,000
Parsippany-Troy Hills Township SD | 6,500/PK-12
PO Box 52 07054 | 973-263-7250
Eugene Vasile, supt. | Fax 263-7230
www.pthsd.k12.nj.us
Brooklawn MS | 800/6-8
250 Beachwood Rd 07054 | 973-428-7551
Eileen Hoehne, prin. | Fax 781-0309
Central MS | 700/6-8
1602 US Highway 46 07054 | 973-263-7125
Jeffrey Rutzky, prin. | Fax 402-1579
Parsippany HS | 1,000/9-12
309 Baldwin Rd 07054 | 973-263-7001
Anthony Sciaino, prin. | Fax 263-7347
PACE S, 140 Littleton Road 07054 | Adult
Joanne Caponegro, prin. | 973-263-7180
Other Schools – See Morris Plains

Chubb Institute | Post-Sec.
8 Sylvan Way 07054 | 973-630-4900
Parsippany Christian S | 200/PK-12
PO Box 5365 07054 | 973-539-7012
Rev. Philip Thibault, prin. | Fax 539-2527

Passaic, Passaic, Pop. 68,528
Passaic CSD | 10,800/PK-12
PO Box 388 07055 | 973-470-5201
Dr. Robert Holster, supt. | Fax 470-8984
passaic-city.k12.nj.us
Lincoln MS | 1,500/7-8
291 Lafayette Ave 07055 | 973-470-5504
John Scozzaro, prin. | Fax 470-5128
Passaic HS | 2,600/9-12
170 Paulison Ave 07055 | 973-470-5600
Carlist Creech, prin. | Fax 470-5135

Bais Yaakov of Passaic HS | 100/9-12
181 Pennington Ave 07055 | 973-365-0100
Baila Stern, prin. | Fax 365-0570
Collegiate S | 200/PK-12
22 Kent Ct 07055 | 973-777-1714
Angela Gibson, hdmstr. | Fax 777-3255
Mesivta Tiferes Rav Zvi Aryeh Zemel | 100/9-12
15 Temple Pl 07055 | 973-594-9001
Rabbi Yisroel Cohn, prin. | Fax 594-0101

Paterson, Passaic, Pop. 150,782
Paterson SD, 33 Church St 07505 | 25,300/PK-12
Dr. Michael Glascoe, supt. | 973-321-1000
www.paterson.k12.nj.us
Academy of Performing Arts | 5-8
45 Smith St 07505 | 973-321-0570
John Murez, admin. | Fax 321-0577
B.U.I.L.D. Academy | 6-8
202 Union Ave 07502 | 973-321-1000
 | Fax 321-0587
Eastside HS | 3,000/9-12
150 Park Ave 07501 | 973-321-0510
Karen Johnson, prin. | Fax 321-0516
Great Falls Academy | 9-12
259 Alabama Ave 07513 | 973-321-2380
Zatiti Moody, admin. | Fax 321-2387
HARP Academy | 9-12
175 Main St 07505 | 973-321-0561
 | Fax 321-0565
International HS | 9-12
202 Union Ave 07502 | 973-321-2281
Yolanda Burgos, prin. | Fax 321-0398
Kennedy HS | 2,600/9-12
61 Preakness Ave 07522 | 973-321-0500
Richard Roberto, prin. | Fax 321-0507
Morgan Academy | 9-12
32 Spruce St 07501 | 973-321-2540
Michael Gowdy, coord. | Fax 321-2547
MPACT Academy | 9-12
175 Main St 07505 | 973-321-0563
 | Fax 321-0376
PANTHER Academy | 9-12
201 Memorial Dr 07505 | 973-321-2290
 | Fax 321-2297
Parks Arts HS | 200/9-12
413 12th Ave 07514 | 973-321-0520
Sharon Smith, prin. | Fax 321-0527
Paterson City S 4 | 500/5-8
55 Clinton St 07522 | 973-321-0040
Mirva Rivera, prin. | Fax 321-0047
Paterson City S 7 | 200/5-8
106 Ramsey St 07501 | 973-321-0070
Courtney Glover, prin. | Fax 321-0077
Paterson Pre-Collegiate Teaching Academy | 9-12
137 Ellison St 07505 | 973-321-0550
 | Fax 321-0556
Public Safety Academy | 9-12
47 State St 07501 | 973-321-2392
John Tyson, prin. | Fax 321-2396
Sports Business Academy | 9-12
47 State St 07501 | 973-321-2392
John Tyson, prin. | Fax 321-2396
Silk City 2000 Academy/Adult S | Adult
151 Ellison St 07505 | 973-321-0760
Yolanda Burgos, prin. | Fax 321-0767

Al-Huda S | 200/K-12
154 Ellison St 07505 | 973-742-7474
HoHoKus Sch of Trade/Technical Sciences | Post-Sec.
634 Market St 07513 | 800-646-9353
Passaic Co. Community College | Post-Sec.
1 College Blvd 07505 | 973-684-6800
Paterson Catholic HS | 400/9-12
764 11th Ave 07514 | 973-278-1024
Dr. Florence Pisano, prin. | Fax 684-7244

Paulsboro, Gloucester, Pop. 6,116
Paulsboro SD | 1,300/PK-12
662 N Delaware St 08066 | 856-423-5515
Dr. Frank Scambia, supt. | Fax 423-4602
www.paulsboro.k12.nj.us
Paulsboro JSHS | 600/7-12
670 N Delaware St 08066 | 856-423-2222
Lucia Pollino, prin. | Fax 423-8915

Pemberton, Burlington, Pop. 1,248
Pemberton Township SD | 5,500/PK-12
PO Box 228 08068 | 609-893-8141
Mark Cowell, supt. | Fax 893-3295
www.pemberton.k12.nj.us
Fort MS | 900/7-8
301 Fort Dix Rd 08068 | 609-893-8141
David Roxman, prin. | Fax 894-9709
Pemberton Township HS | 1,500/9-12
148 Arneys Mount Road 08068 | 609-893-8141
Richard Nolan, prin. | Fax 894-0126
Evening HS | Adult
148 Arneys Mount Rd 08068 | 609-893-8141

Burlington County College | Post-Sec.
County Route 530 08068 | 609-894-9311

Pennington, Mercer, Pop. 2,706
Hopewell Valley Regional SD | 3,800/K-12
425 S Main St 08534 | 609-737-4000
Dr. Judith a. Ferguson, supt. | Fax 737-1418
www.hvrsd.k12.nj.us
Central HS | 1,100/9-12
259 Pennington Titusville 08534 | 609-737-4000
Joseph Mangiaracina, prin. | Fax 737-1581
Timberlane MS | 900/6-8
51 Timberlane Dr 08534 | 609-737-4000
Patricia Coats, prin. | Fax 737-2718

Mercer County Vocational SD
Supt. — See Trenton
MCVS Sypek Center Vo S | Vo/Tech
129 Bull Run Rd 08534 | 609-737-9785
Sharon Nesmith, prin. | Fax 737-3951

Pennington S | 400/6-12
112 W Delaware Ave 08534 | 609-737-1838
Penny Townsend, hdmstr. | Fax 737-2851

Pennsauken, Camden, Pop. 35,900
Camden County Technical Schools
Supt. — See Sicklerville

Pennsauken Technical HS | Vo/Tech
6008 Browning Rd 08109 | 856-663-1040
Patricia Fitzgerald, prin. | Fax 665-8011

Pennsauken Township SD | 5,400/PK-12
1695 Hylton Rd 08110 | 856-662-8505
James F. Chapman Ed.D., supt. | Fax 663-5865
www.pennsauken.net/
Pennsauken HS | 1,700/9-12
800 Hylton Rd 08110 | 856-662-8500
William Clarke, prin. | Fax 910-2612
Phifer MS | 900/7-8
8201 Park Ave 08109 | 856-662-8500
John Oliver, prin. | Fax 486-1422

Bishop Eustace Prep S | 700/9-12
5552 Route 70 08109 | 856-662-2160
Cyril Bleistine, prin. | Fax 662-0802
JDT Christian Academy | 50/K-12
3600 Earle St 08110 | 856-910-2815
Robin Chatman, prin. | Fax 910-1545
Omega Institute | Post-Sec.
7050 Kaighns Ave 08109 | 856-663-4299
Urban Promise Academy | 50/9-12
3700 Rudderow St 08110 | 856-661-1421
Lynne Rogers, admin. | Fax 661-1954

Penns Grove, Salem, Pop. 4,840
Penns Grove-Carneys Point Regional SD | 2,200/PK-12
100 Iona Ave 08069 | 856-299-4250
Joseph A. Massare Ed.D., supt. | Fax 299-5226
www.pennsgrove.k12.nj.us
Penns Grove MS | 500/6-8
351 E Maple Ave 08069 | 856-299-0576
Jean Spinelli, prin. | Fax 299-4378
Other Schools – See Carneys Point

Pennsville, Salem, Pop. 12,218
Pennsville Township SD | 2,000/K-12
30 Church St 08070 | 856-540-6210
Dr. Mark Jones, supt. | Fax 678-7565
www.psdnet.org/SchoolDistrict/framesindex.html
Pennsville Memorial HS | 600/9-12
110 S Broadway 08070 | 856-540-6220
Steven Hindman, prin. | Fax 678-2715
Pennsville MS | 500/6-8
4 William Penn Ave 08070 | 856-540-6240
Sheila Burris, prin. | Fax 678-2908

Park Bible Academy | 200/PK-12
104 Sparks Ave 08070 | 856-678-9464
Edward W. Riley, prin. | Fax 678-3696

Perth Amboy, Middlesex, Pop. 48,447
Middlesex County Vo-Tech HSD
Supt. — See East Brunswick
Perth Amboy Vocational HS | Vo/Tech
457 High St 08861 | 732-376-6300
Gerald Bohrer, prin. | Fax 376-6391
Adult HS - Perth Amboy | Adult
457 High St 08861 | 732-257-3300
Dawn Lystad, contact | Fax 376-6391

Perth Amboy SD | 8,500/PK-12
178 Barracks St 08861 | 732-376-6201
John M. Rodecker, supt. | Fax 376-6196
www.perthamboy.k12.nj.us/
McGinnis MS | 1,300/7-8
271 State St 08861 | 732-376-6040
Roland H. Jenkins, prin. | Fax 376-6047
Perth Amboy HS | 2,000/9-12
300 Eagle Ave 08861 | 732-376-6030
Rozalia Czaban, prin. | Fax 376-6275
Perth Amboy Accredited Adult HS | Adult
178 Barracks St 08861 | 732-376-6240
Ana Cruz, prin. | Fax 376-6245

Perth Amboy Catholic MS | 100/6-8
680 Catherine St 08861 | 732-442-1713
Karen Ninehan, prin. | Fax 442-6388
Raritan Bay Medical Center | Post-Sec.
530 New Brunswick Ave 08861 | 732-324-5232
Reignbow Beauty Academy | Post-Sec.
312 State St 08861 | 732-442-6007
Yeshiva Gedolah of Perth Amboy | 100/9-12
PO Box 2506 08862 | 732-826-5507
Rabbi E. Gruskin, prin. | Fax 826-0130

Petersburg, See Woodbine
Upper Township SD
Supt. — See Woodbine
Upper Township MS | 700/6-8
525 Perry Rd 08270 | 609-628-3500
Vincent Palmieri, prin. | Fax 628-3506

Phillipsburg, Warren, Pop. 15,177
Lopatcong Township SD | 900/PK-8
263 State Route 57 08865 | 908-859-0800
Dr. Michael Rossi, supt. | Fax 213-1339
www.warrennet.org/lopatcongschool
Lopatcong S | 300/6-8
321 Stonehenge Dr 08865 | 908-213-2955
Ms. Rosemary Kowalchuk, prin. | Fax 213-1339

Phillipsburg SD | 3,200/PK-12
445 Marshall St 08865 | 908-454-3400
Dr. H. Gordon Pethick, supt. | Fax 454-1746
www.pburg.k12.nj.us
Phillipsburg HS | 1,500/9-12
200 Hillcrest Blvd 08865 | 908-454-6551
Mary Jane Deutsch, prin. | Fax 213-2427
Phillipsburg MS | 600/6-8
525 Warren St 08865 | 908-454-5577
Dr. John Milone, prin. | Fax 213-2546

Pilesgrove, Salem
Salem County Vocational Technical SD
880 Route 45 08098 | 856-769-0101
William H. Adams Ed.D., supt. | Fax 769-3602
www.scvts.org
Salem Co. Arts Science & Technology HS | Vo/Tech
880 Route 45 08098 | 856-769-0101
Geoffrey W. Zoeller, prin. | Fax 769-3602
Salem County Career & Technical HS | Vo/Tech
880 Route 45 08098 | 856-769-0101
Todd Bonsall, prin. | Fax 769-4214

Pine Brook, Morris
Montville Township SD 3,900/K-12
328 Changebridge Rd 07058 973-331-7117
Dr. Mary Louise Malyska, supt. Fax 331-1307
www.montville.net
Other Schools – See Montville

Pine Hill, Camden, Pop. 11,092
Pine Hill SD 2,100/PK-12
1003 Turnerville Rd 08021 856-783-6900
Kenneth P. Koczur, supt. Fax 783-2955
www.pinehill.k12.nj.us
Overbrook Regional HS 900/9-12
1200 Turnerville Rd 08021 856-767-8000
Paul Harmelin, prin. Fax 767-3082
Pine Hill MS 500/5-8
1100 Turnerville Rd 08021 856-210-0200
Kate Klemick, prin. Fax 210-0195

Piscataway, Middlesex, Pop. 48,900
Middlesex County Vo-Tech HSD
Supt. — See East Brunswick
Piscataway Vocational HS Vo/Tech
21 Suttons Ln 08854 732-985-0717
Dr. Linda Russo, prin. Fax 985-7717

Piscataway Township SD 6,600/K-12
PO Box 1332 08855 732-572-2289
Robert L. Copeland, supt. Fax 777-1361
www.piscatawayschools.org/
Conackamack MS 500/6-8
5205 Witherspoon St 08854 732-699-1577
Dr. Suzanne Westberg, prin. Fax 699-0118
Piscataway Twp. HS 2,100/9-12
100 Behmer Rd 08854 732-981-0700
Dr. Michael A. Wanko, prin. Fax 981-1985
Quibbletown MS 600/6-8
99 Academy St 08854 732-752-0444
Mario Tursi, prin. Fax 752-5798
Schor MS 500/6-8
243 N Randolphville Rd 08854 732-752-4457
Richard Hueston, prin. Fax 424-9445

Katharine Gibbs School Post-Sec.
180 Centennial Ave 08854 732-885-1580
Timothy Christian S 600/K-12
2008 Ethel Rd 08854 732-985-0300
Dr. Ray Antocicco, admin. Fax 985-8008
UMDNJ-Robert Wood Johnson Medical School Post-Sec.
671 Hoes Ln 08854 732-235-5600
UMDNJ School of Public Health Post-Sec.
170 Frelinghuysen Rd Rm 236 08854 732-445-0199

Pitman, Gloucester, Pop. 9,274
Pitman SD 1,500/K-12
420 Hudson Ave 08071 856-589-2145
Thomas Shulte, supt. Fax 582-5465
www.pitman.k12.nj.us
Pitman HS 500/9-12
225 Linden Ave 08071 856-589-2121
Cherie Lombardo, prin. Fax 589-8855
Pitman MS, 138 E Holly Ave 08071 400/6-8
Robert Goldschmidt, prin. 856-589-0636

Pittsgrove, Salem
Pittsgrove Township SD 1,800/K-12
1076 Almond Rd 08318 856-358-3094
Loren Thomas, supt. Fax 358-6020
www.pittsgrove.org
Pittsgrove Township MS 600/5-8
1082 Almond Rd 08318 856-358-8529
Michael Clarke, prin.
Schalick HS, 718 Centerton Rd 08318 600/9-12
Matthew Jamison, prin. 856-358-2054

Pittstown, Hunterdon
Alexandria Township SD 600/K-8
557 County Road 513 08867 908-996-6811
Dr. Wendy Schadt, supt. Fax 996-3375
www.alexandria.k12.nj.us
Alexandria MS 400/4-8
557 County Road 513 08867 908-996-6811
Frances Wood, prin. Fax 996-7963

Plainfield, Union, Pop. 48,025
Plainfield SD 9,000/PK-12
504 Madison Ave 07060 908-731-4335
Dr. Paula Howard, supt. Fax 731-4336
www.plainfieldnjk12.org
Hubbard MS 400/7-8
661 W 8th St 07060 908-731-4320
Marva Fuller, prin. Fax 731-4315
Maxson MS 600/7-8
920 E 7th St 07062 908-731-4310
Phillip Williamson, prin. Fax 731-4306
Plainfield HS 1,800/9-12
950 Park Ave 07060 908-731-4390
Frank Ingargiola, prin. Fax 731-4394

Du Cret School of the Arts Post-Sec.
1030 Central Ave 07060 908-757-7171
Koinonia Academy 200/K-12
1040 Plainfield Ave 07060 908-668-9002
Muhlenberg Regional Medical Center Post-Sec.
Park Avenue And Randolph Rd 07060 908-668-2400
Union County College Post-Sec.
232 E 2nd St 07060 908-412-3559

Plainsboro, Middlesex
West Windsor-Plainsboro Regional SD
Supt. — See Princeton Junction
Community MS 1,100/6-8
55 Grovers Mill Rd 08536 609-716-5300
Dr. Arthur Downs, prin. Fax 716-5333
West Windsor-Plainsboro HS North 1,200/9-12
90 Grovers Mill Rd 08536 609-716-5100
Michael Zapicchi, prin. Fax 716-5142

Pleasantville, Atlantic, Pop. 19,016
Egg Harbor Township SD 8,400/PK-12
PO Box 31 08232 609-646-7911
Dr. Phillip Heery, supt. Fax 383-8749
www.eht.k12.nj.us
Other Schools – See Egg Harbor Township

Pleasantville SD 3,500/PK-12
PO Box 960 08232 609-383-6800
Dr. Gail Brooks, supt. Fax 677-8122
www.pleasantville.k12.nj.us
Pleasantville HS, 701 Mill Rd 08232 800/9-12
Ada Barlatt, prin. 609-383-6900
Pleasantville MS, 801 Mill Rd 08232 500/6-8
Jean Barksdale, prin. 609-383-6800

Shore Beauty School Post-Sec.
103 W Washington Ave 08232 609-645-3635

Point Pleasant, Ocean, Pop. 19,835
Point Pleasant Beach SD 900/K-12
309 Cooks Ln 08742 732-899-8840
Raymond Ellis, supt. Fax 899-1730
www.ptpleasantbch.k12.nj.us/
Point Pleasant Beach HS 400/9-12
700 Trenton Ave 08742 732-899-1817
Dr. Raymond Ellis, prin. Fax 899-1145

Point Pleasant Borough SD 3,200/K-12
2100 Panther Path 08742 732-701-1900
Robert Ciliento, supt. Fax 892-8403
www.pointpleasant.k12.nj.us/
Memorial MS 800/6-8
808 Laura Herbert Dr 08742 732-701-1900
Robert Alfonse, prin. Fax 892-0984
Point Pleasant Borough HS 1,000/9-12
808 Laura Herbert Dr 08742 732-701-1900
John Staryak, prin. Fax 892-1252

Pomona, Atlantic, Pop. 2,624

Richard Stockton College of New Jersey Post-Sec.
PO Box 195 08240 609-652-1776

Pompton Lakes, Passaic, Pop. 11,085
Pompton Lakes SD 1,800/K-12
237 Van Ave 07442 973-835-4334
Dr. Terrance R. Brennan, supt. Fax 835-1748
www.plps.org
Lakeside MS 500/6-8
316 Lakeside Ave 07442 973-835-2221
Dr. Paul Amoroso, prin. Fax 835-8088
Pompton Lakes HS 600/9-12
44 Lakeside Ave 07442 973-835-7100
Vincent Przybylinski, prin. Fax 835-1054

Institute for Therapeutic Massage Post-Sec.
125 Wanaque Ave 07442 973-839-6131
Windsor S 100/5-8
24 Wanaque Ave 07442 973-839-4050

Pompton Plains, Morris
Pequannock Township SD 2,400/K-12
538 Newark Pompton Tpke 07444 973-616-6040
Jerry Cicchelli, supt. Fax 616-6043
www.pequannock.org
Pequannock Twp. HS 800/9-12
85 Sunset Rd 07444 973-616-6000
John Lavagnino, prin. Fax 616-6029
Pequannock Valley MS 600/6-8
493 Newark Pompton Tpke 07444 973-616-6050
Dr. William Trusheim, prin. Fax 616-8370

Chancellor Academy 100/9-12
PO Box 338 07444 973-835-4989
Fax 835-0768
Netherlands Reformed Christian S 200/PK-12
164 Jacksonville Rd 07444 973-628-7400
John Vanderbrink, prin. Fax 628-0461

Port Monmouth, Monmouth, Pop. 3,558
Middletown Township SD
Supt. — See Middletown
Thorne MS, 70 Murphy Rd 07758 900/6-8
V. McKenzie, prin. 732-787-1220

Port Norris, Cumberland, Pop. 1,701
Commercial Township SD 700/PK-8
PO Box 650 08349 856-785-0840
Barry Ballard, supt. Fax 785-2354
www.commercial.k12.nj.us
Port Norris MS 200/6-8
PO Box 670 08349 856-785-1611
Peter Koza, prin. Fax 785-2556

Pottersville, Hunterdon

Purnell S 100/9-12
PO Box 500 07979 908-439-2154
Fax 439-2090

Princeton, Mercer, Pop. 13,577
Princeton Regional SD 3,300/K-12
25 Valley Rd 08540 609-806-4220
Judith A. Wilson, supt. Fax 806-4221
www.prs.k12.nj.us
Princeton HS 1,200/9-12
151 Moore St 08540 609-806-4280
Gary Snyder, prin. Fax 806-4281
Witherspoon MS 700/6-8
217 Walnut Ln 08540 609-806-4270
William Johnson, prin. Fax 806-4271

American Boychoir S 100/5-8
19 Lambert Dr 08540 609-924-5858
Fax 924-5812
Hun S of Princeton 600/6-12
176 Edgerstoune Rd 08540 609-921-7600
Dr. James Byer, hdmstr. Fax 683-4410
Princeton Day S 900/PK-12
PO Box 75 08542 609-924-6700
Dr. Judith R. Fox, hdmstr. Fax 924-8944
Princeton Theological Seminary Post-Sec.
PO Box 821 08542 609-921-8300
Princeton University 08544 Post-Sec.
609-258-3000
Raritan Valley Flying School Post-Sec.
Route 206 08540 609-921-3100
Stuart Country Day S 500/PK-12
1200 Stuart Rd 08540 609-921-2330
Sr. Frances de la Chapelle, prin. Fax 497-0784
Westminster Choir College of Rider Univ. Post-Sec.
101 Walnut Ln 08540 609-921-7100

Princeton Junction, Mercer, Pop. 2,362
West Windsor-Plainsboro Regional SD 8,200/K-12
PO Box 505 08550 609-716-5000
Robert Loretan Ph.D., supt. Fax 716-5012
www.ww-p.org
Grover MS 1,200/6-8
10 Southfield Rd 08550 609-716-5250
Steven Mayer, prin. Fax 716-5270
West Windsor-Plainsboro HS South 1,500/9-12
346 Clarksville Rd 08550 609-716-5050
Charles Rudnick, prin. Fax 716-5092
Other Schools – See Plainsboro

Rahway, Union, Pop. 26,779
Rahway SD 3,900/PK-12
1200 Kline Pl 07065 732-396-1020
Dr. William Petrino, supt. Fax 396-1391
www.rahway.net
Rahway HS 1,200/9-12
1012 Madison Ave 07065 732-396-1101
Edward Yergalonis, prin. Fax 396-2630
Rahway MS 1,000/6-8
1200 Kline Pl 07065 732-396-1025
Elaine Ross, prin. Fax 396-2633

Ramsey, Bergen, Pop. 14,490
Ramsey SD 2,800/K-12
266 E Main St 07446 201-327-2300
Dr. Roy Montesano, supt. Fax 934-6623
www.ramsey.k12.nj.us
Ramsey HS 700/9-12
266 E Main St 07446 201-785-2300
Dr. Thomas Melville, prin. Fax 818-2656
Smith MS 700/6-8
2 Monroe St 07446 201-785-2313
Dr. Richard Weiner, prin. Fax 785-2320

Don Bosco Prep HS 800/9-12
492 N Franklin Tpke 07446 201-327-8003
John Stanczak, prin. Fax 327-3397
Ho Ho Kus School Post-Sec.
10 S Franklin Tpke 07446 201-327-8877

Randolph, Morris, Pop. 19,974
Randolph Township SD 5,300/K-12
2 Emery Ave 07869 973-361-0808
Dr. Max Riley, supt. Fax 361-2405
www.rtnj.org
Randolph HS 1,500/9-12
507 Millbrook Ave 07869 973-361-2400
Carol Strowbridge, prin. Fax 361-1661
Randolph MS 1,300/6-8
507 Millbrook Ave 07869 973-366-8700
Georgiana Walsh, prin.

County College of Morris Post-Sec.
214 Center Grove Rd 07869 973-328-5000

Red Bank, Monmouth, Pop. 11,792
Red Bank Borough SD 700/PK-8
76 Branch Ave 07701 732-758-1507
Dr. John Krewer, supt. Fax 758-9539
www.rbb.k12.nj.us
Red Bank MS 300/4-8
101 Harding Rd 07701 732-758-1515
Terence Wilkins, prin. Fax 758-1518

Red Bank Catholic HS 1,100/9-12
112 Broad St 07701 732-747-1774
Robert Abatemarco, prin. Fax 747-5723

Richland, Atlantic

St. Augustine Prep S 300/9-12
PO Box 279 08350 856-697-2600
Rev. Francis Horn, prin. Fax 697-8389

Ridgefield, Bergen, Pop. 10,919
Ridgefield SD 1,700/K-12
555 Chestnut St 07657 201-945-9236
Dr. Richard Brockel, supt. Fax 945-7830
Ridgefield Memorial JSHS 700/8-12
555 Walnut St 07657 201-945-4455
Marcella Gleie, prin. Fax 945-3505

Ridgefield Park, Bergen, Pop. 12,781
Ridgefield Park SD 1,800/K-12
712 Lincoln Ave 07660 201-641-0800
Dr. John Richardson, supt. Fax 641-2203
www.rpps.net
Ridgefield Park JSHS 1,000/7-12
1 Ozzie Nelson Dr 07660 201-440-1440
Eric Koenig, prin. Fax 641-6861

Ridgewood, Bergen, Pop. 24,831
Ridgewood Village SD 5,600/K-12
49 Cottage Pl 07450 201-670-2700
Dr. John R. Porter, supt. Fax 670-2668
www.ridgewood.k12.nj.us
Franklin MS 700/6-8
335 N Van Dien Ave 07450 201-670-2780
Anthony Bencivenga, prin.
Ridgewood HS 1,600/9-12
627 E Ridgewood Ave 07450 201-670-2800
Dr. John Mucciolo, prin. Fax 444-7008
Washington MS 700/6-8
155 Washington Pl 07450 201-670-2790
George Neville, prin.

Valley Hospital Post-Sec.
223 N Van Dien Ave 07450 201-447-8002

Ringwood, Passaic, Pop. 12,704
Ringwood SD 1,400/K-8
121 Carletondale Rd 07456 973-962-7028
Dr. Patrick Martin, supt. Fax 962-9211
www.ringwoodschools.org/
Ryerson MS 500/6-8
130 Valley Rd 07456 973-962-7063
Paul Scutti, prin. Fax 962-6905

River Edge, Bergen, Pop. 10,978
River Dell Regional SD 1,400/7-12
230 Woodland Ave 07661 201-599-7206
Eugene J. Westlake Ph.D., supt. Fax 261-3809
www.riverdell.k12.nj.us

River Dell MS | 500/7-8
230 Woodland Ave 07661 | 201-599-7250
Richard Freedman, prin. | Fax 599-7257
Other Schools – See Oradell

Riverside, Burlington, Pop. 7,974
Riverside Township SD | 1,200/PK-12
112 E Washington St 08075 | 856-461-1255
Robert Goldschmidt, supt. | Fax 461-5168
www.riverside.k12.nj.us
Riverside HS | 400/9-12
112 E Washington St 08075 | 856-461-1255
Lawrence Talbot, prin. | Fax 461-7277
Riverside MS | 200/6-8
112 E Washington St 08075 | 856-461-1255
Robin Ehrich, prin. | Fax 461-7277

River Vale, Bergen, Pop. 9,410
River Vale SD | 1,300/K-12
609 Westwood Ave 07675 | 201-358-4000
David Verducci Ph.D., supt. | Fax 358-8319
www.rivervaleschools.com/
Holdrum MS | 400/6-8
393 Rivervale Rd 07675 | 201-358-4016
Jayellen Behre-Jenkins, prin. | Fax 358-8427

Robbinsville, Mercer
Washington Township SD | 1,500/K-12
1079 Washington Blvd 08691 | 609-632-0910
Dr. John Szabo, supt. | Fax 371-7964
www.wtpsmercer.k12.nj.us
Pond Road MS | 800/4-8
150 Pond Rd 08691 | 609-632-0940
Dr. Paul Gizzo, prin. | Fax 918-9011
Robbinsville HS | 9-12
155 Robbinsville Edinburg 08691 | 609-632-0950
Deborah Fadde, prin. | Fax 371-7961

Rockaway, Morris, Pop. 6,427
Morris County Vocational SD
Supt. — See Denville
Academy for Math-Science & Engineering | Vo/Tech
520 W Main St 07866 | 973-664-2301
Joseph Cacciaguida, prin.

Morris Hills Regional SD | 2,700/9-12
48 Knoll Dr 07866 | 973-664-2291
Dr. Ernest Palestis, supt. | Fax 627-6588
www.mhrd.k12.nj.us
Morris Hills HS, 520 W Main St 07866 | 1,100/9-12
Joseph Cacciaguida, prin. | 973-664-2301
Morris Knolls HS | 1,500/9-12
50 Knoll Dr 07866 | 973-664-2201
William Cleffi, prin. | Fax 586-3550
Morris Hills Adult HS | Adult
48 Knoll Dr 07866 | 973-664-2250
Robert Storm, prin.

Rockaway Borough SD | 600/K-8
103 E Main St 07866 | 973-625-8601
Emil Suarez, supt. | Fax 625-7355
Jefferson MS, 95 E Main St 07866 | 300/5-8
Terrance Fitzpatrick, prin. | 973-625-8603

Rockaway Township SD
Supt. — See Hibernia
Copeland MS | 1,000/6-8
100 Lake Shore Dr 07866 | 973-627-2465
Scott Allshouse, prin.

Roselle, Union, Pop. 21,423
Roselle Borough SD | 2,100/K-12
710 Locust St 07203 | 908-298-2040
Darlene Roberto, supt. | Fax 298-3353
www.roselleschools.org
Clark HS | 1,100/8-12
122 E 6th Ave 07203 | 908-298-2004
Nathan Fisher, prin. | Fax 259-0782

Roselle Catholic HS | 800/9-12
1 Raritan Rd 07203 | 908-245-2350
Br. Owen Ormsby, prin. | Fax 241-3869

Roselle Park, Union, Pop. 13,310
Roselle Park SD | 2,000/K-12
510 Chestnut St 07204 | 908-245-1197
Patrick Spagnoletti, supt. | Fax 245-1226
www.roselleparkschools.org
Roselle Park HS | 800/8-12
185 W Webster Ave 07204 | 908-241-4550
Frank Ferlazzo, prin. | Fax 245-6609

Rumson, Monmouth, Pop. 7,312
Rumson Borough SD | 1,000/K-8
60 Forrest Ave 07760 | 732-842-4747
Roger Caruba, supt. | Fax 842-4877
www.rumson.k12.nj.us
Forrestdale MS, 60 Forrest Ave 07760 | 600/4-8
Kathi Cronin, prin. | 732-842-0383

Rumson-Fair Haven Regional HSD | 800/9-12
74 Ridge Rd 07760 | 732-842-5456
Dr. Peter Righi, supt. | Fax 842-3139
www.rfhrhs.org
Rumson-Fair Haven HS | 800/9-12
74 Ridge Rd 07760 | 732-842-1597
Elizabeth Panella, prin. | Fax 741-1712

Runnemede, Camden, Pop. 8,541
Black Horse Pike Regional SD
Supt. — See Blackwood
Triton HS | 1,300/9-12
250 Schubert Ave 08078 | 856-939-4500
Edward Stahl, prin. | Fax 939-4724

Runnemede Borough SD | 700/K-8
505 W 3rd Ave 08078 | 856-931-5365
Joseph Sweeney, supt. | Fax 931-4446
Volz MS, 505 W 3rd Ave 08078 | 400/4-8
David Gentile, prin. | 856-931-5353

Rutherford, Bergen, Pop. 18,020
Rutherford SD | 1,700/K-12
176 Park Ave 07070 | 201-939-1717
Leslie Conlon, supt. | Fax 939-6350
www.rutherford.k12.nj.us
Pierrepont S | 400/4-8
70 E Pierrepont Ave 07070 | 201-438-7675
Margaret Vaccarino, prin. | Fax 842-0452

Rutherford HS | 800/9-12
54 Elliott Pl 07070 | 201-438-7675
John Hurley, prin. | Fax 438-7293
Union S | 400/4-8
359 Union Ave 07070 | 201-438-7675
Richard Curci, prin. | Fax 804-8248

St. Mary HS | 400/9-12
64 Chestnut St 07070 | 201-933-5220
Dr. Robert Berckes, prin. | Fax 933-0834

Saddle Brook, Bergen, Pop. 13,296
Saddle Brook Township SD | 1,600/K-12
355 Mayhill St 07663 | 201-843-2133
Dr. Harry Groveman, supt. | Fax 843-8265
www.saddlebrookschools.org/
Saddle Brook JSHS | 700/7-12
355 Mayhill St 07663 | 201-843-2880
Jim Sarto, prin. | Fax 843-4305

Helma Institute Massage Therapy | Post-Sec.
190 Midland Ave 07663 | 201-226-0056

Saddle River, Bergen, Pop. 3,689

Saddle River Day S | 300/K-12
147 Chestnut Ridge Rd 07458 | 201-327-4050
John O'Brien, hdmstr. | Fax 327-6161

Salem, Salem, Pop. 5,793
Salem CSD | 1,400/PK-12
205 Walnut St 08079 | 856-935-3800
Margaret J. Nicolosi, supt. | Fax 935-6977
www.salemnj.org
Salem HS | 600/9-12
219 Walnut St 08079 | 856-935-3900
Gregory Dunham, prin. | Fax 935-3288
Salem MS | 500/3-8
51 New Market St 08079 | 856-935-2700
John Mulhorn, prin. | Fax 935-2284

Scotch Plains, Union, Pop. 21,160
Scotch Plains-Fanwood SD | 4,800/PK-12
Evergreen Ave & Cedar St 07076 | 908-232-6161
Dr. Margaret Hayes, supt. | Fax 889-1769
www.spfk12.org
Park MS | 800/5-8
580 Park Ave 07076 | 908-322-4445
Lisa Rebimbas, prin. | Fax 561-5929
Scotch Plains-Fanwood HS | 1,400/9-12
641 Westfield Rd 07076 | 908-889-8600
David Heisey, prin. | Fax 889-8254
Terrill MS | 800/5-8
1301 Terrill Rd 07076 | 908-322-5215
Kevin Holloway, prin. | Fax 322-6813

Union County Vocational Technical SD
1776 Raritan Rd 07076 | 908-889-2900
Dr. Thomas Bistocchi, supt. | Fax 889-4336
www.ucmagnethigh.k12.nj.us
Academy for Information Technology | Vo/Tech
1776 Raritan Rd 07076 | 908-889-8288
Paul Munz, prin. | Fax 889-4399
Union County Vo-Tech HS | Vo/Tech
1776 Raritan Rd 07076 | 908-889-8288
Patrick Mauro, prin. | Fax 889-4399
Union County Adult HS | Adult
1776 Raritan Rd 07076 | 908-889-2904
Robert Glowacky, prin. | Fax 889-4940

Union Catholic Regional HS | 800/9-12
1600 Martine Ave 07076 | 908-889-1600
Sr. Percylee Hart, prin. | Fax 889-7867

Seabrook, Cumberland, Pop. 1,457
Cumberland Regional SD | 1,300/9-12
PO Box 5115 08302 | 856-451-9400
Katherine A. Kelk, supt. | Fax 455-8514
www.crhsd.org/
Cumberland Regional HS | 1,300/9-12
PO Box 5115 08302 | 856-451-9400
John J. Mitchell, prin. | Fax 455-8514

Upper Deerfield Township SD | 800/K-8
1373 Highway 77 08302 | 856-455-2267
Dr. Philip D. Exley, supt. | Fax 455-0419
Woodruff MS | 300/6-8
1373 Highway 77 08302 | 856-455-2267
James Turner, prin. | Fax 453-7077

Secaucus, Hudson, Pop. 15,735
Secaucus SD, PO Box 1496 07096 | 1,800/PK-12
Constantino Scerbo, supt. | 201-974-2004
Secaucus HS | 500/9-12
11 Millridge Rd 07094 | 201-974-2033
Patrick Impreveduto, prin. | Fax 974-0026
Secaucus MS | 300/7-8
Millridge Rd 07094 | 201-974-2025
Pascale Cocucci, prin. | Fax 974-0026

Sewell, Gloucester
Deptford Township SD
Supt. — See Deptford
Monongahela MS | 600/7-8
890 Bankbridge Rd 08080 | 856-415-9540
Carolyn Morehead, prin. | Fax 464-9284

Gloucester County Vo-Tech SD |
1360 Tanyard Rd 08080 | 856-468-1445
Frederick Keating, supt. | Fax 468-3397
www.gcit.org
Gloucester Co. Institute of Technology | Vo/Tech
1360 Tanyard Rd 08080 | 856-468-1445
Ted Frett, prin. | Fax 468-1035

Washington Township SD | 9,400/K-12
206 E Holly Ave 08080 | 856-589-6644
Dr. Cheryl Simone, supt. | Fax 582-1918
www.wtps.org
Bunker Hill MS | 800/6-8
372 Pitman Downer Rd 08080 | 856-881-7007
Mark Ebner, prin.
Chestnut Ridge MS | 800/6-8
641 Hurffville Crosskeys Rd 08080 | 856-582-3535
James Barnes, prin. | Fax 589-0683
Orchard Valley MS | 800/6-8
238 Pitman Downer Rd 08080 | 856-561-5353
Stephan Buono, prin. | Fax 589-0197

Washington Township HS | 3,100/9-12
519 Hurffville Crosskeys Rd 08080 | 856-589-8500
Rosemarie Farrow, prin. | Fax 589-4057

Gloucester County Christian S | 400/PK-12
151 Golf Club Rd 08080 | 856-589-1665
Donald Netz, prin. | Fax 582-4989
Gloucester County College | Post-Sec.
1400 Tanyard Rd 08080 | 856-468-5000

Shamong Township, Burlington, Pop. 5,765
Lenape Regional HSD | 7,500/9-12
93 Willow Grove Rd 08088 | 609-268-2000
Daniel Hicks Ph.D., supt. | Fax 268-6642
www.lr.k12.nj.us
Other Schools – See Marlton, Medford, Tabernacle

Shamong Township SD | 900/K-8
295 Indian Mills Rd 08088 | 609-268-0120
Thomas P. Christensen, supt. | Fax 268-1229
www.ims.k12.nj.us
Indian Mills Memorial MS | 400/5-8
295 Indian Mills Rd 08088 | 609-268-0440
Timothy Carroll, prin. | Fax 268-1229

Sicklerville, Camden
Camden County Technical Schools |
343 Berlin Cross Keys Rd 08081 | 856-767-7000
Gary G. Bennett Ed.D., supt. | Fax 767-3589
www.ccts.tec.nj.us
Gloucester Township Technical HS | Vo/Tech
343 Berlin Cross-Keys Rd 08081 | 856-767-7000
Charles Buchheim, prin. | Fax 767-3638
Camden County Technical Adult S | Adult
343 Berlin Cross-Keys Rd 08081 | 856-767-7002
Teri Stallone, prin.
Other Schools – See Pennsauken

Gloucester Township SD
Supt. — See Blackwood
Mullen MS, 1400 Sicklerville Rd 08081 | 1,100/6-8
Kevin Kitchenman, prin. | 856-875-8777

Camden County Technical School | Post-Sec.
343 Berlin Cross Keys Rd 08081 | 856-767-7000

Skillman, Somerset
Montgomery Township SD | 3,900/K-12
1014 Route 601 08558 | 609-466-7601
Dr. Stuart Schnur, supt. | Fax 466-0944
www.mtsd.k12.nj.us
Montgomery HS | 1,200/9-12
1016 Route 601 08558 | 609-466-7602
James Misek, prin. | Fax 874-6212
Montgomery HS Upper Campus | 800/7-8
375 Burnt Hill Rd 08558 | 609-466-7604
William Robbins, prin.

Somerdale, Camden, Pop. 5,185
Sterling HSD | 800/9-12
501 S Warwick Rd 08083 | 856-784-1287
Jack McCulley, supt. | Fax 435-1530
www.sterling.k12.nj.us
Sterling HS | 800/9-12
501 S Warwick Rd 08083 | 856-784-1333
David Tannenbaum, prin. | Fax 784-7661

Somerset, Somerset, Pop. 22,070
Franklin Township SD | 5,300/PK-12
1755 Amwell Rd 08873 | 732-873-2400
William Westfield, supt. | Fax 873-2132
www.franklinboe.org
Franklin HS, 500 Elizabeth Ave 08873 | 1,600/9-12
Orvyl Wilson, prin. | 732-302-4200
Franklin MS | 7-8
415 Francis St 08873 | 732-249-6410
Dr. Dianne Lotz, prin. | Fax 246-0770
Adult HS | Adult
415 Francis St 08873 | 732-249-6410
 | Fax 873-8393

Rutgers Prep S | 700/PK-12
1345 Easton Ave 08873 | 732-545-5600
Dr. Steven Loy, hdmstr. | Fax 214-1819

Somers Point, Atlantic, Pop. 11,618

Shore Memorial Hospital | Post-Sec.
Shore Rd 08244 | 609-653-3545

Somerville, Somerset, Pop. 12,391
Somerville Borough SD | 2,100/K-12
51 W Cliff St 08876 | 908-218-4101
Dr. Carolyn Leary, supt. | Fax 526-9668
Somerville HS | 1,000/9-12
222 Davenport St 08876 | 908-218-4108
Timothy O'Halloran, prin. | Fax 707-0971
Somerville MS, 51 W Cliff St 08876 | 300/6-8
Michael Ryan, prin. | 908-218-4107

Immaculata HS | 900/9-12
240 Mountain Ave 08876 | 908-722-0200
Sr. Mary Birster, prin. | Fax 218-7765
Raritan Valley Community College | Post-Sec.
PO Box 3300 08876 | 908-526-1200

South Amboy, Middlesex, Pop. 8,032
Sayreville SD | 4,800/PK-12
150 Lincoln St 08879 | 732-525-5224
Dr. Frank Alfano, supt. | Fax 727-5769
www.sayrevillek12.net/
Other Schools – See Parlin

South Amboy SD | 1,100/PK-12
240 John St 08879 | 732-525-2102
Robert Sheedy, supt. | Fax 727-0730
www.saboe.k12.nj.us/
South Amboy MSHS | 500/7-12
200 Gvrnr Hrold G Hffmn Plz 08879 | 732-316-7669
Dr. Patrick McCabe, prin.

Cardinal McCarrick HS | 500/9-12
310 Augusta St 08879 | 732-721-0748
Jean Kline, prin. | Fax 727-7018

Southampton, Burlington
Southampton Township SD ... 800/K-8
177 Main St 08088 ... 609-859-2256
Michael Harris, supt. ... Fax 859-1542
www.southampton.k12.nj.us
Southampton Township MS 3 ... 300/6-8
100 Warrior Way 08088 ... 609-859-2256
Lynn Kurtz, prin. ... Fax 801-0754

South Orange, Essex, Pop. 16,390
South Orange-Maplewood SD
Supt. — See Maplewood
South Orange MS ... 800/6-8
70 N Ridgewood Rd 07079 ... 973-378-2772
Kirk Smith, prin. ... Fax 378-2775

Immaculate Conception Seminary ... Post-Sec.
400 S Orange Ave 07079 ... 973-761-9575
Marylawn of the Oranges Academy ... 200/9-12
445 Scotland Rd 07079 ... 973-762-9222
Delores Thompson, prin. ... Fax 378-7975
Seton Hall University ... Post-Sec.
400 S Orange Ave 07079 ... 973-761-9000

South Plainfield, Middlesex, Pop. 22,965
South Plainfield SD ... 3,800/K-12
125 Jackson Ave 07080 ... 908-754-4620
Robert J. Rosado Ed.D., supt. ... Fax 754-3960
www.spnet.k12.nj.us
South Plainfield HS ... 1,200/9-12
200 Lake St 07080 ... 908-754-4620
Dr. Kenneth May, prin. ... Fax 756-7659
South Plainfield MS ... 600/7-8
2201 Plainfield Ave 07080 ... 908-754-4620
Steven Novak, prin. ... Fax 791-1152
Adult HS ... Adult
125 Jackson Ave 07080 ... 908-754-4620
Sophia Domogala, prin. ... Fax 561-2859

Central Career School ... Post-Sec.
126 Corporate Blvd 07080 ... 908-412-8600
Engine City Technical Institute ... Post-Sec.
901 Hadley Rd 07080 ... 800-305-3487

South River, Middlesex, Pop. 16,041
South River SD ... 1,700/K-12
15 Montgomery St 08882 ... 732-613-4000
Ronald C. Grygo, supt. ... Fax 613-4756
www.sriver.nj.org
South River HS ... 600/9-12
11 Montgomery St 08882 ... 732-613-4014
Kevin Kidney, prin. ... Fax 613-4044
South River MS ... 500/6-8
3 Montgomery St 08882 ... 732-613-4073
Dr. Richard S. Sternberg, prin. ... Fax 698-9305

Moshe Aaron Yeshiva HS ... 200/9-12
34 Charles St 08882 ... 732-613-7460
Dovid Wadler, prin. ... Fax 613-7464

Sparta, Sussex, Pop. 15,157
Sparta Township SD ... 4,000/K-12
18 Mohawk Ave 07871 ... 973-729-7886
Dr. J. Thomas Morton, supt. ... Fax 729-0576
www.sparta.org
Sparta HS ... 1,100/9-12
70 W Mountain Rd 07871 ... 973-729-6191
Richard Lio, prin. ... Fax 729-3258
Sparta MS ... 1,000/6-8
350 Main St 07871 ... 973-729-3151
Linda Nick, prin. ... Fax 729-0573

Sussex County Technical SD ...
105 N Church Rd 07871 ... 973-383-6700
Joseph Cammarata, supt. ... Fax 383-4272
www.sussex.tec.nj.us
Sussex County Technical S ... Vo/Tech
105 N Church Rd 07871 ... 973-383-6700
Joseph Cammarata, prin. ... Fax 383-4272

Pope John XXIII HS ... 800/9-12
28 Andover Rd 07871 ... 973-729-6125
Fr. Kieran McHugh, prin. ... Fax 729-3487

Spotswood, Middlesex, Pop. 8,236
Spotswood SD ... 1,600/PK-12
105 Summerhill Rd 08884 ... 732-723-2200
John Krewer Ed.D., supt. ... Fax 251-7666
www.spotswood.k12.nj.us
Spotswood HS ... 700/9-12
105 Summerhill Rd 08884 ... 732-723-2201
Thomas Calder, prin. ... Fax 251-7666
Spotswood Memorial MS ... 300/6-8
115 Summerhill Rd 08884 ... 732-723-2227
Thomas Weaver, prin. ... Fax 251-7666

Springfield, Union, Pop. 13,420
Springfield SD ... 2,000/PK-12
PO Box 210 07081 ... 973-376-1025
Michael Davino, supt. ... Fax 912-9229
www.springfieldschools.com
Dayton HS ... 500/9-12
101 Mountain Ave 07081 ... 973-376-1025
Elizabeth Cresci, prin. ... Fax 376-4570
Gaudineer MS ... 400/6-8
75 S Springfield Ave 07081 ... 973-376-1025
Timothy Kielty, prin. ... Fax 376-3259

Stanhope, Sussex, Pop. 3,688
Byram Township SD ... 1,100/K-8
12 Mansfield Dr 07874 ... 973-347-6663
Joseph Pezak, supt. ... Fax 347-9001
www.byramschools.org
Byram IS ... 500/5-8
12 Mansfield Dr 07874 ... 973-347-1019
Jack Leonard, prin. ... Fax 347-9001

Lenape Valley Regional HSD ... 700/9-12
PO Box 578 07874 ... 973-347-7600
Paul A. Palik, admin. ... Fax 347-2536
www.lvhs.org
Lenape Valley Regional HS ... 700/9-12
PO Box 578 07874 ... 973-347-7600
Dr. Marylou Coviello, prin. ... Fax 347-2536

Stewartsville, Warren
Greenwich Township SD ... 900/K-8
101 Wydham Farm Blvd 08886 ... 908-859-2022
Kevin Brennan, supt. ... Fax 859-4522
www.greenwichschool.org
Stewartsville MS ... 300/6-8
642 S Main St 08886 ... 908-859-2023
Patty Lantz, prin. ... Fax 859-1809

Stirling, Morris
Long Hill Township SD
Supt. — See Gillette
Central MS ... 300/6-8
90 Central Ave 07980 ... 908-647-2311
Richard Cimino, prin. ... Fax 647-0610

Stratford, Camden, Pop. 7,246
Stratford Borough SD ... 800/K-8
111 Warwick Rd 08084 ... 856-783-2555
Albert Brown, supt. ... Fax 309-0304
www.stratford.k12.nj.us
Yellin MS ... 500/4-8
111 Warwick Rd 08084 ... 856-783-1094
Carol Vita, prin. ... Fax 309-0304

Star Technical Institute ... Post-Sec.
43 S White Horse Pike 08084 ... 856-435-7827
UMDNJ-School of Osteopathic Medicine ... Post-Sec.
1 Medical Center Dr # 210 08084 ... 856-566-7050

Succasunna, Morris, Pop. 11,781
Roxbury Township SD ... 4,600/K-12
42 N Hillside Ave 07876 ... 973-584-6867
Dennis Mack, supt. ... Fax 252-1434
www.roxbury.org
Eisenhower MS ... 700/7-8
47 Eyland Ave 07876 ... 973-584-2973
Daniel Johnson, prin. ... Fax 584-4529
Roxbury HS ... 1,500/9-12
1 Bryant Dr 07876 ... 973-584-1200
Jeffrey Swanson, prin. ... Fax 252-1494

Capri Institute of Hair Design ... Post-Sec.
Roxbury Mall Route 10 E 07876 ... 973-584-9030

Summit, Union, Pop. 21,262
Summit CSD ... 3,400/K-12
90 Maple St 07901 ... 908-918-2100
Dr. Carolyn Deacon, supt. ... Fax 273-3656
www.summit.k12.nj.us
Summit HS ... 900/9-12
125 Kent Place Blvd 07901 ... 908-273-1494
Paul Sears, prin. ... Fax 273-2832
Summit MS ... 800/6-8
272 Morris Ave 07901 ... 908-273-1190
Dr. Theodore Stanik, prin. ... Fax 273-8320

Kent Place S ... 600/PK-12
42 Norwood Ave 07901 ... 908-273-0900
Susan C. Bosland, prin. ... Fax 273-9390
Oak Knoll S of the Holy Child ... 400/K-12
44 Blackburn Rd 07901 ... 908-522-8100
Timothy Saburn, hdmstr. ... Fax 273-4616
Oratory Prep S ... 300/7-12
1 Beverly Rd 07901 ... 908-273-1084
Timothy Lynch, hdmstr. ... Fax 273-5505

Sussex, Sussex, Pop. 2,180
High Point Regional HSD ... 1,100/9-12
299 Pidgeon Hill Rd 07461 ... 973-875-7204
Dr. John W. Hannum, supt. ... Fax 875-0904
www.hpregional.org
High Point Regional HS ... 1,100/9-12
299 Pidgeon Hill Rd 07461 ... 973-875-3101
James Platukis, prin. ... Fax 875-2756

Sussex-Wantage Regional SD ... 1,600/K-8
31 Ryan Rd 07461 ... 973-875-3175
Anthony Mistretta, supt. ... Fax 875-7175
swregional.org
Sussex MS ... 600/6-8
10 Loomis Ave 07461 ... 973-875-4138
Joseph R. Mulford, prin. ... Fax 875-6790

Swedesboro, Gloucester, Pop. 2,049
Logan Township SD ... 700/PK-8
110 School Ln 08085 ... 856-467-5133
John Herbst, supt. ... Fax 467-9012
www.logan.k12.nj.us
Logan MS ... 500/5-8
110 School Ln 08085 ... 856-467-5133
Terry Jacobs, prin. ... Fax 467-9012

Tabernacle, Burlington
Lenape Regional HSD
Supt. — See Shamong Township
Seneca HS, 110 Carranza Rd 08088 ... 1,400/9-12
John Furgione, prin. ... 609-268-4600

Tabernacle Township SD ... 900/K-8
132 New Rd 08088 ... 609-268-0153
Bernice Blum-Bart, supt. ... Fax 268-1006
www.tabernacle.k12.nj.us
Olson MS ... 500/5-8
132 New Rd 08088 ... 609-268-0153
Susan Grosser, prin. ... Fax 268-1006

Teaneck, Bergen, Pop. 39,500
Teaneck SD ... 4,300/PK-12
1 Merrison St 07666 ... 201-833-5510
John Czeterko, supt. ... Fax 837-9468
www.teaneckschools.org/
Franklin MS, 1315 Taft Rd 07666 ... 600/5-8
Barbara Pinsak, prin. ... 201-833-5451
Jefferson MS, 655 Teaneck Rd 07666 ... 700/5-8
Patricia Schwartz, prin. ... 201-833-5471
Teaneck HS ... 1,400/9-12
100 Elizabeth Ave 07666 ... 201-833-5400
Joseph White, prin. ... Fax 833-5403

Fairleigh Dickinson University ... Post-Sec.
1000 River Rd 07666 ... 201-692-2000
Holy Name Hospital School of Nursing ... Post-Sec.
690 Teaneck Rd 07666 ... 201-833-3005
Ma'ayanot Yeshiva HS for Girls ... 200/9-12
1650 Palisade Ave 07666 ... 201-833-4307
Rookie Billet, prin. ... Fax 833-0816

Schechter Regional HS ... 100/9-12
800 Broad St 07666 ... 201-837-8357
Torah Academy of Bergen County ... 200/9-12
1600 Queen Anne Rd 07666 ... 201-837-7696
Arthur Poleyeff, prin. ... Fax 837-9027

Tenafly, Bergen, Pop. 14,101
Tenafly SD ... 3,100/K-12
500 Tenafly Rd 07670 ... 201-816-4508
Dr. Darrell Lund, supt. ... Fax 569-3678
www.tenafly.k12.nj.us
Tenafly HS ... 1,000/9-12
19 Columbus Dr 07670 ... 201-816-6614
Dora Kontogiannis, prin. ... Fax 871-9184
Tenafly MS ... 700/6-8
10 Sunset Ln 07670 ... 201-816-4900
William Belluzzi, prin. ... Fax 569-0327

Teterboro, Bergen, Pop. 18
Bergen County Vocational SD
Supt. — See Paramus
Bergen County Technical S - Teterboro ... Vo/Tech
504 State Rt 46 07608 ... 201-440-0011
Andrea Sheridan, prin. ... Fax 288-6028

Teterboro School of Aeronautics ... Post-Sec.
80 Moonachie Ave 07608 ... 201-288-6300

Tinton Falls, Monmouth, Pop. 15,975
Monmouth Regional HSD ... 1,000/9-12
1 Norman J Field Way 07724 ... 732-542-1170
Patrick Collum, supt. ... Fax 542-5815
www.monmouthregional.net/
Monmouth Regional HS ... 1,000/9-12
1 Norman J Field Way 07724 ... 732-542-1170
Andrew Teeple, prin. ... Fax 542-5815
Monmouth-Ocean Ed. Serv. Comm. SD ... 9-12
100 Tornillo Way Ste 1 07712 ... 732-389-5555
Timothy Nogueira, supt. ...
www.moesc.org/
Other Schools – See Eatontown

Tinton Falls SD ... 1,700/K-8
658 Tinton Ave 07724 ... 732-460-2400
Dr. Leonard R. Kelpsh, supt. ... Fax 542-1158
www.tfs.k12.nj.us
Tinton Falls MS ... 600/6-8
674 Tinton Ave 07724 ... 732-542-0775
Dr. Marion Lamberti, prin. ... Fax 542-8723

Ranney S ... 800/PK-12
235 Hope Rd 07724 ... 732-542-4777
Lawrence Sykoff, hdmstr. ... Fax 544-1629

Toms River, Ocean, Pop. 7,524
Ocean County Vocational SD ...
137 Bey Lea Rd 08753 ... 732-240-6414
William P. Hoey, supt. ... Fax 505-8929
www.ocvts.org
Ocean County Voc-Tech S - Toms River ... Vo/Tech
1299 Old Freehold Rd 08753 ... 732-473-3100
Craig Coleman, prin. ... Fax 349-9788
Other Schools – See Brick, Jackson, Lakehurst, Waretown

Toms River Regional SD ... 16,400/K-12
1144 Hooper Ave 08753 ... 732-505-5510
Michael Ritacco, supt. ... Fax 505-9330
www.trschools.com
Toms River HS - East ... 1,800/9-12
1225 Raider Way 08753 ... 732-505-5666
Maureen Madden, prin. ... Fax 270-0909
Toms River HS - North ... 2,300/9-12
1245 Old Freehold Rd 08753 ... 732-505-5702
James Hauenstein, prin. ... Fax 341-6249
Toms River HS - South ... 1,500/9-12
55 Hyers St 08753 ... 732-505-5738
Leonard Stanziano, prin. ... Fax 341-1321
Toms River IS East ... 1,700/6-8
1519 Hooper Ave 08753 ... 732-505-5777
Jack Sohl, prin. ... Fax 286-1290
Toms River IS North ... 1,400/6-8
150 Intermediate North Way 08753 ... 732-505-5800
Irene Benn, prin. ... Fax 286-1291
Other Schools – See Beachwood

Monsignor Donovan HS ... 1,000/9-12
711 Hooper Ave 08753 ... 732-349-8801
Dr. Edward Gere, prin. ... Fax 349-8956
Ocean County College ... Post-Sec.
College Dr 08754 ... 732-255-0400
Performance Training ... Post-Sec.
1012 Cox Cro Rd 08755 ... 732-505-9119

Totowa, Passaic, Pop. 10,030
Totowa SD ... 900/K-8
10 Crews St 07512 ... 973-956-0010
Vincent Varcadipane, supt. ... Fax 956-9859
www.totowa.k12.nj.us
Memorial MS ... 400/5-8
294 Totowa Rd 07512 ... 973-942-0010
John Vanderberg, prin. ... Fax 904-1082

Trenton, Mercer, Pop. 85,314
Mercer County Vocational SD
1085 Old Trenton Rd 08690 ... 609-586-2129
Dr. Kimberly Schneider, supt. ... Fax 586-8966
www.mctec.net
MCVS Assunpink Center ... Vo/Tech
1085 Old Trenton Rd 08690 ... 609-586-5144
Lucille Jones, prin. ... Fax 586-1709
MCVS Health Careers Center ... Vo/Tech
1070 Klockner Rd 08619 ... 609-587-7640
Virginia Clevenger, prin. ... Fax 587-3304
MCVS School of Performing Arts ... Vo/Tech
1200 Old Trenton Rd 08690 ... 609-586-3550
Ryan Killeen, prin. ... Fax 586-4985
MCVS Adult Evening S ... Adult
1085 Old Trenton Rd 08690 ... 609-586-5146
Neal Orlando, prin. ... Fax 586-1709
Other Schools – See Pennington

Trenton SD 10,600/PK-12
108 N Clinton Ave 08609 609-656-4900
Dr. James Lytle, supt. Fax 989-2682
www.trenton.k12.nj.us
Dunn MS 800/6-8
401 Dayton St 08610 609-656-4700
Dr. Ruben Flores, prin. Fax 989-9693
Hedgepeth-Williams MS 500/6-8
301 Gladstone Ave 08629 609-656-4760
Christopher DeJesus, prin. Fax 989-2927
King MS 300/6-8
800 Mrtn Lther King Jr Blvd 08638 609-656-4810
Edna Margolin, prin. Fax 656-6060
Trenton Central HS 2,700/9-12
400 Chambers St 08609 609-278-7260
Maria Azzara, prin. Fax 989-2940
Daylight/Twilight HS Adult
720 Bellevue Ave 08618 609-989-2494
William Tracy, prin. Fax 656-6062

Helene Fuld Medical Center Post-Sec.
750 Brunswick Ave 08638 609-394-3174
Marie Katzenbach School for the Deaf Post-Sec.
PO Box 535 08625 609-530-3100
Meadow View Junior Academy 100/K-12
241 Bordentown Chstrfeld Rd 08620 609-298-1122
Sadrail Saint-Ulysse, prin. Fax 298-7550
Mercer County Community College Post-Sec.
N Broad & Academy Sts 08608 609-586-0505
Mercer County Community College Post-Sec.
PO Box B 08690 609-586-4800
Mercer County Vocational-Tech. School Post-Sec.
1085 Old Trenton Rd 08690 609-586-2129
Mercer Medical Center Post-Sec.
PO Box 1658 08607 609-394-4050
St. Francis Medical Center Post-Sec.
601 Hamilton Ave 08629 609-599-5000
Thomas Edison State College Post-Sec.
101 W State St 08608 609-984-1100

Union, Union, Pop. 55,000
Township of Union SD 7,800/PK-12
2369 Morris Ave 07083 908-851-6420
Dr. Theodore A. Jakubowski, supt. Fax 851-6421
www.twpunionschools.org
Burnet MS 1,200/6-8
1000 Caldwell Ave 07083 908-851-6490
Raymond Salvatore, prin. Fax 687-2645
Kawameeh MS 800/6-8
490 David Ter 07083 908-851-6570
Harold Bell, prin. Fax 687-5941
Union HS 2,500/9-12
2350 N 3rd St 07083 908-851-6500
Samuel Fortunato, prin. Fax 687-5204

European Academy of Cosmetology Post-Sec.
1126 Morris Ave 07083 908-686-4422
Healthcare Training Institute Post-Sec.
1969 Morris Ave 07083 908-851-7711
Kean University Post-Sec.
1000 Morris Ave 07083 908-527-2000
Lincoln Technical Institute Post-Sec.
2299 Vauxhall Rd 07083 908-964-7800

Union Beach, Monmouth, Pop. 6,745
Union Beach Borough SD 800/PK-8
1207 Florence Ave 07735 732-264-5405
Arthur J. Waltz Ed.D., supt. Fax 264-6109
www.ub.k12.nj.us
Adult HS Adult
1205 Florence Ave 07735 732-264-5313
Virginia Grezner, prin. Fax 264-8297

Union City, Hudson, Pop. 66,573
Union City SD, 3912 32nd St 07087 7,500/PK-12
Stanley Sanger, supt. 201-348-5852
www.union-city-nj.org/modules/AMS/
Marti MS 6-8
1800 Summit Ave 07087 201-348-5400
Geraldine Perez, prin. Fax 348-5405
Union Hill HS 1,400/9-12
3808 Hudson Ave 07087 201-348-5936
David Wilcomes, prin. Fax 348-5866
Emerson HS Adult
318 18th St 07087 201-348-5901
Robert Fazio, prin. Fax 864-2262
Evening HS, 318 18th St 07087 Adult
Dosinda Perez, prin. 201-392-3618

Mesivta Sanz Hudson County S 300/K-12
3400 New York Ave 07087 201-867-8690
Cheskel Rosenberg, admin. Fax 867-2848
Miftaahul Uloom S 100/PK-12
4607 Cottage Pl 07087 201-223-9920

Upper Saddle River, Bergen, Pop. 8,237
Upper Saddle River SD 1,300/K-8
395 W Saddle River Rd 07458 201-961-6502
Dr. Joyce Snider, supt. Fax 934-4923
www.usronline.org
Cavallini MS 400/6-8
392 W Saddle River Rd 07458 201-961-6400
Gene Solomon Ed.D., prin. Fax 236-9662

Ventnor City, Atlantic, Pop. 12,778
Ventnor CSD 1,100/K-8
400 N Lafayette Ave 08406 609-487-7918
Carmine Bonanni, supt. Fax 823-4036
www.vecc.atlnet.org
Ventnor MS 400/6-8
400 N Lafayette Ave 08406 609-487-7900
Robert Baker, prin.

Vernon, Sussex
Vernon Township SD 5,100/K-12
PO Box 99 07462 973-764-2900
Anthony J. Macerino, supt. Fax 764-0033
www.vtsd.com
Glen Meadow MS 900/7-8
PO Box 516 07462 973-764-8981
Carol Nelson Ed.D., prin. Fax 764-3295
Vernon Twp. HS 1,700/9-12
PO Box 800 07462 973-764-2960
Dennis Mudrick, prin. Fax 764-2961

Verona, Essex, Pop. 13,597
Essex County Vocational SD
900 Bloomfield Ave 07044 973-228-0377
Frank J. Cancellieri, supt. Fax 228-5910
www.essextech.org
Other Schools – See Bloomfield, Newark, West Caldwell

Verona SD 1,900/K-12
121 Fairview Ave 07044 973-239-2100
Earl Kim, supt. Fax 239-2496
www.veronaschools.org
Verona HS 600/9-12
151 Fairview Ave 07044 973-239-3300
Glenn Cesa, prin. Fax 857-7543
Whitehorne MS 600/5-8
600 Bloomfield Ave 07044 973-239-1300
Yvette McNeal, prin. Fax 857-1611

Vineland, Cumberland, Pop. 57,057
Vineland CSD 10,400/K-12
625 E Plum St 08360 856-794-6700
Dr. Clarence Hoover, supt. Fax 794-9464
www.vineland.org
D'Ippolito IS 700/5-8
1578 N Valley Ave 08360 856-794-6934
Belinda Hall, prin. Fax 507-8757
Landis IS 800/5-8
61 W Landis Ave 08360 856-794-6925
Dr. Thomas McCann, prin. Fax 507-8763
Rossi IS 600/5-8
2572 Palermo Ave 08361 856-794-6961
Lawrence Ricci, prin. Fax 507-8786
Veterans Memorial IS 900/5-8
424 S Main Rd 08360 856-794-6918
Carol Gribble, prin. Fax 507-8759
Vineland HS North 1,400/9-10
3010 E Chestnut Ave 08361 856-794-6800
Nedd Johnson, prin. Fax 507-8781
Vineland SHS - South 1,300/11-12
2880 E Chestnut Ave 08361 856-794-6800
Charles Ottinger, prin. Fax 507-8751
Vineland Adult Learning Center Adult
48 W Landis Ave 08360 856-794-6943
Gloria Kucher, prin. Fax 794-1120

Cumberland Christian S 500/K-12
1100 W Sherman Ave 08360 856-696-1600
Wayne P. Baker, hdmstr. Fax 696-0631
Cumberland County College Post-Sec.
PO Box 1500 08362 856-691-8600
Harrison Career Institute Post-Sec.
1386 S Delsea Dr 08360 856-696-0500
Sacred Heart HS 200/9-12
15 N East Ave 08360 856-691-4491
Fr. Edward Namiotka, prin. Fax 563-2453

Voorhees, Camden, Pop. 24,559
Eastern Camden County Regional HSD 2,200/9-12
PO Box 2500 08043 856-346-6740
Dr. Harold Melleby, supt. Fax 627-7894
www.eastern.k12.nj.us
Eastern Intermediate HS 1,200/9-10
PO Box 2500 08043 856-784-4441
Dr. James Talarico, prin. Fax 784-3527
Eastern SHS 1,000/11-12
PO Box 2500 08043 856-346-6720
Dr. Patricia Denholm, prin. Fax 784-1322

Voorhees Township SD 3,400/PK-8
329 Route 73 08043 856-751-8446
Raymond Brosel, supt. Fax 751-3666
www.voorhees.k12.nj.us/
Voorhees MS 1,200/6-8
1000 Holly Oak Dr 08043 856-795-2025
Charles Ronkin, prin.

Waldwick, Bergen, Pop. 9,628
Waldwick SD 1,100/PK-12
155 Summit Ave 07463 201-445-3131
John Szabo Ed.D., supt. Fax 445-0584
www.waldwick.k12.nj.us/
Waldwick HS 400/9-12
155 Wyckoff Ave 07463 201-652-9000
Vincent S. Przybylinski, prin. Fax 652-5053
Waldwick MS 6-8
155 Wyckoff Ave 07463 201-652-9000
Michael Meyers, prin. Fax 652-5053

Waldwick SDA S 100/PK-12
70 Wyckoff Ave 07463 201-652-6078
Alipia Gonzalez, prin. Fax 652-4652

Wall, Monmouth, Pop. 5,201
Monmouth County Vocational SD
Supt. — See Freehold
Communications HS of Monmouth Co. Vo/Tech
1740 New Bedford Rd 07719 732-681-1010
James Gleason, prin. Fax 681-6780
Wall Township SD 4,300/K-12
PO Box 1199 07719 732-556-2000
Dr. James F. Habel, supt. Fax 556-2101
www.wall.k12.nj.us
Wall HS 1,300/9-12
PO Box 1199 07719 732-556-2040
Steve Genco, prin. Fax 556-2104
Wall IS 1,100/6-8
PO Box 1199 07719 732-556-2500
Joseph Tonzola, prin. Fax 556-2535

Stuart School of Business Administration Post-Sec.
2400 Belmar Blvd 07719 732-681-7200

Wallington, Bergen, Pop. 11,522
Wallington SD 1,100/K-12
30 Pine St 07057 973-777-4421
Dr. Frank Cocchiola, supt. Fax 614-9391
www.wboe.org
Wallington JSHS 600/7-12
234 Main Ave 07057 973-777-0808
Joseph Pompeo, prin. Fax 777-1434

Wanaque, Passaic, Pop. 10,419
Lakeland Regional HSD 1,100/9-12
205 Conklintown Rd 07465 973-835-1900
Albert Guazzo, supt. Fax 835-2834
www.lakeland.k12.nj.us

Lakeland Regional HS 1,100/9-12
205 Conklintown Rd 07465 973-835-1900
Joseph LoCascio, prin. Fax 835-6369

Waretown, Ocean, Pop. 1,283
Ocean County Vocational SD
Supt. — See Toms River
Ocean County Voc-Tech S - Waretown Vo/Tech
423 Wells Mill Rd 08758 609-693-3434
James Rizzolo, prin. Fax 693-1514

Warren, Somerset
Warren Township SD 2,200/K-8
213 Mount Horeb Rd 07059 732-560-8700
Dr. James Crisfield, supt. Fax 560-8801
www.warrenboe.org
Warren MS 700/6-8
100 Old Stirling Rd 07059 908-753-5300
Robert Comba, prin. Fax 753-4789

Watchung Hills Regional SD 1,700/9-12
108 Stirling Rd 07059 908-647-4890
Frances Strumsland, supt. Fax 647-4852
www.whrhs.org
Watchung Hills Regional HS 1,700/9-12
108 Stirling Rd 07059 908-647-4800
Dr. Thomas DiGanci, prin. Fax 647-4852

Washington, Warren, Pop. 6,829
Warren County Vocational SD
1500 State Route 57 W 07882 908-835-2813
Dr. Alan Naimoli, supt.
www.warrennet.org/warrentech
Warren County Vo-Tech Institute Vo/Tech
1500 State Route 57 W 07882 908-835-2806
Dr. Alan Naimoli, prin.
Warren County Technical Adult HS Adult
1500 State Route 57 W 07882 908-689-0122

Warren Hills Regional HSD 2,100/7-12
89 Bowerstown Rd 07882 908-689-3143
Peter Merluzzi, supt. Fax 689-4814
www.warrenhills.org
Warren Hills Regional HS 1,300/9-12
41 Jackson Valley Rd 07882 908-689-3050
Tim O'Brien, prin. Fax 689-9640
Warren Hills Regional JHS 700/7-8
64 Carlton Ave 07882 908-689-0750
Robert Griffin, prin. Fax 689-3663

Warren County Community College Post-Sec.
475 State Route 57 W 07882 908-835-9222

Washington Township, Bergen, Pop. 9,245
Westwood Regional SD 2,500/K-12
701 Ridgewood Rd 07676 201-664-0880
Geoffrey Zoeller, supt. Fax 664-7642
www.westwood.k12.nj.us
Westwood Regional JSHS 1,100/7-12
701 Ridgewood Rd 07676 201-664-0880
Patrick Bower, prin. Fax 722-1542

Immaculate Heart Academy 800/9-12
500 Van Emburgh Ave 07676 201-445-6800
Sr. Ellen Cronan, prin. Fax 445-7416

Watchung, Somerset, Pop. 5,738
Watchung Borough SD 600/K-8
1 Dr Parenty Way 07069 908-755-8121
Dr. Patrick Parenty, supt. Fax 755-6946
www.watchungschools.com
Valley View MS 300/5-8
50 Valley View Rd 07069 908-755-4422
Pat Dye, prin. Fax 755-4035

Mt. St. Mary Academy 400/9-12
1645 US Highway 22 07069 908-757-0108
Sr. Lisa Gambacorto, dir. Fax 756-5751

Wayne, Passaic, Pop. 55,000
Passaic Co. Technical-Vocational HSD
45 Reinhardt Rd 07470 973-389-4202
Diana Lobosco, supt. Fax 790-6018
www.pcti.tec.nj.us
Passaic County Tech-Vo HS Vo/Tech
45 Reinhardt Rd 07470 973-389-4201
Diana Lobosco, prin.
Passaic County Adult HS Adult
45 Reinhardt Rd 07470 973-389-4101
Corey McKinney, prin.

Wayne Township SD 8,400/K-12
50 Nellis Dr 07470 973-633-3032
Dr. Maria Nuccetelli, supt. Fax 628-8058
www.wayneschools.com
Schuyler-Colfax JHS 1,000/6-8
1500 Hamburg Tpke 07470 973-633-3130
Dorothy Sherwood, prin. Fax 633-3195
Washington MS 1,000/6-8
68 Lenox Rd 07470 973-633-3140
MaryJane Tierney, prin. Fax 633-7590
Wayne Hills HS 1,200/9-12
272 Berdan Ave 07470 973-633-3090
Frank Markowick, prin. Fax 633-2589
Wayne MS 6-8
201 Garside Ave 07470 973-389-2128
Diane Pandolfi, prin. Fax 389-2120
Wayne Valley HS 1,400/9-12
551 Valley Rd 07470 973-633-3066
Robert Reis, prin. Fax 633-3082

Berdan Institute Post-Sec.
201 Willowbrook Blvd 07470 973-837-1818
De Paul Catholic HS 700/9-12
1512 Alps Rd 07470 973-694-3702
Thomas Smithling, prin. Fax 633-5381
William Paterson University Post-Sec.
300 Pompton Rd 07470 973-720-2000

Weehawken, Hudson, Pop. 12,385
Weehawken Township SD 1,700/PK-12
53 Liberty Pl 07086 201-867-2243
Kevin McLellan, supt.
www.weehawken.k12.nj.us
Weehawken JSHS 400/8-12
53 Liberty Pl 07086 201-867-1774
Dr. Peter Olivieri, prin. Fax 867-9370

Westampton Township, Burlington, Pop. 6,004
Westampton Township SD / 900/K-8
710 Rancocas Rd 08060 / 609-267-2053
Richard G. Ballard, supt. / Fax 267-2760
www.westampton.k12.nj.us
Westampton MS / 400/5-8
700 Rancocas Rd 08060 / 609-267-2722
Anne Lipsett, prin. / Fax 702-9017

West Berlin, Camden, Pop. 3,000
Berlin Township SD / 600/PK-8
225 Grove Ave 08091 / 856-767-9480
Brian Betze, supt. / Fax 767-8235
berlintwp.k12.nj.us
Eisenhower MS / 300/5-8
235 Grove Ave 08091 / 856-767-0203
Leslie Koller, prin. / Fax 767-7992

West Caldwell, Essex, Pop. 10,422
Caldwell-West Caldwell SD / 2,600/K-12
104 Gray St 07006 / 973-228-6979
Daniel Gerardi, supt. / Fax 228-8716
www.cwcboe.org/
Caldwell HS / 800/9-12
265 Westville Ave 07006 / 973-228-6981
Kevin M. Barnes, prin. / Fax 228-1116
Other Schools – See Caldwell

Essex County Vocational SD
Supt. — See Verona
Essex County Vocational S-West Caldwell / Vo/Tech
620 Passaic Ave 07006 / 973-575-7740
Dr. Anthony Ingenito, prin. / Fax 575-6958

Essex County College / Post-Sec.
730 Bloomfield Ave 07006 / 973-403-2560

West Deptford, Gloucester, Pop. 19,380
West Deptford Township SD / 3,000/K-12
675 Crown Rd 08066 / 856-848-4300
Edward J. Wasilewski, supt. / Fax 845-5743
www.wdeptford.k12.nj.us/
West Deptford MS / 1,000/5-8
675 Grove Rd 08066 / 856-848-1200
Charles Merkh, prin. / Fax 848-2325
Other Schools – See Westville

Westfield, Union, Pop. 29,951
Westfield SD / 5,700/K-12
302 Elm St 07090 / 908-789-4420
William Foley, supt. / Fax 789-4192
www.westfieldnjk12.org
Edison IS / 700/6-8
800 Rahway Ave 07090 / 908-789-4470
Cheryl O'Brien, prin. / Fax 789-1506
Roosevelt IS / 700/6-8
301 Clark St 07090 / 908-789-4560
Stewart Carey, prin. / Fax 789-4193
Westfield HS / 1,600/9-12
550 Dorian Rd 07090 / 908-789-4500
Dennis Fyffe, prin. / Fax 789-4230

West Long Branch, Monmouth, Pop. 8,216
Shore Regional HSD / 600/9-12
132 State Route 36 07764 / 732-222-9300
Leonard Schnappauf, supt. / Fax 222-8849
www.shoreregional.org
Shore Regional HS / 600/9-12
132 State Route 36 07764 / 732-222-9300
Leonard Schnappauf, prin. / Fax 222-8849

West Long Branch Borough SD / 800/K-8
135 Locust Ave 07764 / 732-222-5900
Dr. Joan Kelly, supt. / Fax 222-9325
www.wlbschools.com
Antonides MS / 500/4-8
135 Locust Ave 07764 / 732-222-5080
Lawrence Farley, prin. / Fax 222-8154

Deal Yeshiva / 300/K-12
PO Box 98 07764 / 732-229-1717
Dr. Judith Shoner, prin. / Fax 728-1400
Monmouth University / Post-Sec.
400 Cedar Ave 07764 / 732-571-3400

West Milford, Passaic, Pop. 26,600
West Milford Township SD / 4,600/PK-12
46 Highlander Dr 07480 / 973-697-1700
Glenn Kamp, supt. / Fax 697-8351
www.wmtps.org
Macopin MS / 800/7-8
70 Highlander Dr 07480 / 973-697-5691
Raymond Johnson, prin. / Fax 697-0301
West Milford HS / 1,400/9-12
67 Highlander Dr 07480 / 973-697-1701
Maureen Bernstock, prin. / Fax 208-0912

Westmont, Camden, Pop. 5,500
Haddon Township SD / 2,100/PK-12
500 Rhoads Ave 08108 / 856-869-7700
Mark Raivetz, supt. / Fax 854-7792
www.haddon.k12.nj.us
Haddon Twp. HS / 700/9-12
406 Memorial Ave 08108 / 856-869-7750
Victor Mignogna, prin.
Rohrer MS, 101 MacArthur Blvd 08108 / 500/6-8
Joseph Rafferty, prin. / 856-869-7770

West New York, Hudson, Pop. 46,348
West New York SD / 5,300/PK-12
6028 Broadway 07093 / 201-553-4000
Anthony Yankovich, supt. / Fax 865-2725
www.wnyschools.net
Memorial HS / 1,500/9-12
5501 Park Ave 07093 / 201-553-4110
Matthew Sinisi, prin. / Fax 864-2151
West New York MS / 7-8
201 57th St 07093 / 201-563-4160
Tony Ferrainolo, prin. / Fax 863-6698

New Horizons Beauty School / Post-Sec.
5518 Bergenline Ave 07093 / 201-866-4000
St. Joseph of the Palisades HS / 300/9-12
5400 Broadway 07093 / 201-864-9700
Michael Musante, prin. / Fax 864-0229

West Orange, Essex, Pop. 45,500
West Orange SD / 6,000/K-12
179 Eagle Rock Ave 07052 / 973-669-5400
Jerry Tarnoff, supt. / Fax 669-1432
www.westorange.k12.nj.us
Edison MS / 700/6-8
75 William St 07052 / 973-669-5360
Xavier Fitzgerald, prin. / Fax 243-9802
Roosevelt MS / 800/6-8
36 Gilbert Pl 07052 / 973-669-5373
Frank Corrado, prin. / Fax 243-9807
West Orange HS / 1,900/9-12
51 Conforti Ave 07052 / 973-669-5301
Arthur Alloggiamento, prin. / Fax 669-1260

Seton Hall Preparatory HS / 900/9-12
120 Northfield Ave 07052 / 973-325-6624
Rev. Michael Kelly, prin. / Fax 325-6652
Solomon Schecter Day S - Upper S / 400/6-12
1418 Pleasant Valley Way 07052 / 973-669-8000
Seth Linfield, hdmstr. / Fax 669-0034

West Paterson, Passaic, Pop. 11,255
West Paterson SD / 900/K-8
853 McBride Ave 07424 / 973-278-5535
Fredrick J. Lijoi, supt. / Fax 278-2568
wpschools.org
Memorial MS / 400/5-8
15 Memorial Dr 07424 / 973-256-5800
Charles Silverstein, prin. / Fax 256-5644

Berkeley College / Post-Sec.
44 Rifle Camp Rd 07424 / 973-278-5400

Westville, Gloucester, Pop. 4,473
West Deptford Township SD
Supt. — See West Deptford
West Deptford HS / 1,000/9-12
1600 Crown Point Rd 08093 / 856-848-6110
Howard Cohen, prin. / Fax 845-5774

St. John of God Community Services / Post-Sec.
1145 Delsea Dr 08093 / 856-848-4700

Westwood, Bergen, Pop. 11,010

Pascack Valley Hospital / Post-Sec.
250 Old Hook Rd 07675 / 201-358-3010

Wharton, Morris, Pop. 6,223
Wharton Borough SD / 700/K-8
137 E Central Ave 07885 / 973-361-2592
Richard Bitondo, supt. / Fax 895-2187
www.wpbs.org
MacKinnon MS / 200/6-8
137 E Central Ave 07885 / 973-361-1253
Christopher Herdman, prin. / Fax 361-4805

Whippany, Morris
Hanover Park Regional HSD
Supt. — See East Hanover
Whippany Park HS / 600/9-12
165 Whippany Rd 07981 / 973-887-3004
John Manning, prin. / Fax 887-0451

Hanover Township SD / 1,400/K-8
61 Highland Ave 07981 / 973-515-2404
Scott R. Pepper, supt. / Fax 540-1023
www.hanovertwpschools.com/
Memorial JHS / 500/6-8
61 Highland Ave 07981 / 973-515-5510
Michael J. Wasko, prin. / Fax 515-2481

White House Station, Hunterdon, Pop. 1,287
Readington Township SD / 2,400/K-8
PO Box 807 08889 / 908-534-2195
Irene G. Benfatti, supt. / Fax 534-9551
www.readington.k12.nj.us
Readington MS / 700/6-8
PO Box 700 08889 / 908-534-2113
Johanna Ruberto Ed.D., prin. / Fax 534-6802

Whiting, Ocean
Manchester Township SD / 3,200/K-12
121 Route 539 08759 / 732-350-5900
William DeFeo, supt. / Fax 350-0436
www.manchestertwp.org
Other Schools – See Manchester

Wildwood, Cape May, Pop. 5,260
Wildwood CSD / 900/PK-12
4300 Pacific Ave 08260 / 609-522-4157
Dennis Anderson, supt. / Fax 523-8161
Wildwood HS / 300/9-12
4300 Pacific Ave 08260 / 609-522-2758
Dr. Gladys Lauriello, prin. / Fax 522-7914
Wildwood MS / 200/5-8
4300 Pacific Ave 08260 / 609-522-7922
Dr. Gladys Lauriello, prin. / Fax 522-7914

Wildwood Catholic HS / 400/9-12
1500 Central Ave 08260 / 609-522-7257
Richard Turco, prin. / Fax 522-2453

Williamstown, Gloucester, Pop. 10,891
Monroe Township SD / 4,800/K-12
75 E Academy St 08094 / 856-629-6400
Robert Terrill Ed.D., supt. / Fax 262-2499
www.monroetwp.k12.nj.us
Williamstown HS / 1,600/9-12
700 N Tuckahoe Rd 08094 / 856-262-8200
Stephen F. Stumpo, prin. / Fax 262-0869
Williamstown MS / 1,400/5-8
561 Clayton Rd 08094 / 856-629-7444
Charles D. Folker, prin. / Fax 875-6757

Victory Christian S / 200/PK-12
PO Box 806 08094 / 856-629-4300
Denton McCleary, prin. / Fax 875-7703

Willingboro, Burlington, Pop. 32,400
Willingboro Township SD / 5,000/PK-12
440 Beverly Rancocas Rd 08046 / 609-835-8600
Mel Persi, supt. / Fax 835-3880
www.willingboroschools.org/
Levitt MS, 50 Salem Rd 08046 / 500/6-8
Teresa Anne Lucas, prin. / 609-835-8600
Willingboro HS / 1,300/9-12
20 S John F Kennedy Way 08046 / 609-835-8800
Robert Tull, prin. / Fax 871-0105
Willingboro Memorial JHS / 1,000/6-8
451 Van Sciver Pkwy 08046 / 609-835-8700
Adult HS, 50 Salem Rd 08046 / Adult
Jack McGee, prin. / 609-835-3810

Woodbine, Cape May, Pop. 2,677
Upper Township SD / 1,700/K-8
525 Perry Rd 08270 / 609-628-3513
Dr. Larry Hobdell, supt. / Fax 628-2002
upperschools.org/
Other Schools – See Petersburg

Woodbridge, Middlesex, Pop. 17,434
Middlesex County Vo-Tech HSD
Supt. — See East Brunswick
Woodbridge Vocational HS / Vo/Tech
1 Convery Blvd 07095 / 732-634-5858
Hector Montes, prin. / Fax 632-7073

Woodbridge Township SD / 12,700/K-12
PO Box 428 07095 / 732-602-8550
Vincent S. Smith, supt. / Fax 750-3493
www.woodbridge.k12.nj.us
Woodbridge HS / 1,600/9-12
25 Samuel Lupo Pl 07095 / 732-602-8600
Arthur Lee Warren, prin. / Fax 602-8612
Woodbridge MS / 500/6-8
525 Barron Ave 07095 / 732-602-8690
James Sullivan, prin. / Fax 855-0326
Other Schools – See Avenel, Colonia, Fords, Iselin

Berkeley College / Post-Sec.
430 Rahway Ave 07095 / 800-446-5400

Woodbury, Gloucester, Pop. 10,439
Woodbury SD / 1,500/PK-12
25 N Broad St 08096 / 856-853-0123
Joseph Jones, supt. / Fax 853-0704
www.woodburysch.com
Woodbury JSHS / 700/6-12
25 N Broad St 08096 / 856-853-0123
Daniel Mackie, prin. / Fax 853-2684

Woodbury Heights, Gloucester, Pop. 3,001
Gateway Regional SD / 1,100/7-12
775 Tanyard Rd, / 856-848-8172
Joyce Stumpo, supt. / Fax 848-2049
www.gatewayhs.com
Gateway Regional MSHS / 1,100/7-12
775 Tanyard Rd, / 856-848-8200
Dr. Ronald Davis, prin. / Fax 251-9813

Woodcliff Lake, Bergen, Pop. 5,846
Woodcliff Lake SD / 900/PK-8
100 Dorchester Rd 07677 / 201-391-6570
Dr. Edward Michaelson, supt. / Fax 930-0488
www.woodcliff-lake.com
Woodcliff MS / 300/6-8
134 Woodcliff Ave 07677 / 201-930-4840
Lauren Barbelet, prin. / Fax 391-7932

Wood Ridge, Bergen, Pop. 7,607
Wood-Ridge SD / 1,000/K-12
89 Hackensack St 07075 / 201-933-6777
Elaine Giugliano, supt. / Fax 804-9204
www.wood-ridgeschools.org
Ostrovsky MS / 200/6-8
540 Windsor Rd 07075 / 201-939-2103
Robert Recchione, prin. / Fax 939-0259
Wood-Ridge HS / 400/9-12
258 Hackensack St 07075 / 201-939-0810
Brian Purzak, prin. / Fax 939-1195

Woodstown, Salem, Pop. 3,260
Woodstown-Pilesgrove Regional SD / 1,700/PK-12
135 East Ave 08098 / 856-769-0144
Robert Bumpus, supt. / Fax 769-4549
www.woodstown.org
Woodstown HS / 700/9-12
140 East Ave 08098 / 856-769-0144
Dr. Scott Hoopes, prin. / Fax 769-4102
Woodstown MS / 400/5-8
15 Lincoln Ave 08098 / 856-769-0144
John Fargnoli, prin. / Fax 769-9425

Woolwich, Gloucester
Kingsway Regional SD / 1,700/7-12
213 Kings Hwy 08085 / 856-467-4600
Terrence Crowley, supt. / Fax 467-5382
Kingsway Regional HS / 1,300/9-12
201 Kings Hwy 08085 / 856-467-3300
Thomas Coleman, prin. / Fax 241-1932
Kingsway Regional MS / 500/7-8
213 Kings Hwy 08085 / 856-467-3300
Ave Altersitz, prin.

Wyckoff, Bergen, Pop. 15,372
Wyckoff Township SD / 2,400/K-8
241 Morse Ave 07481 / 201-848-5701
Dr. James Bender, supt. / Fax 848-5695
www.wyckoffschools.org
Eisenhower MS / 800/6-8
344 Calvin Ct 07481 / 201-848-5750
Richard Kuder, prin. / Fax 848-5682

Eastern Christian MS / 300/5-8
518 Sicomac Ave 07481 / 201-891-3663
Florence Nieuwenhuis, prin. / Fax 847-0902

Zarephath, Somerset

Somerset Christian Academy / 200/K-12
595 Weston Canal Rd, Somerset NJ 08873 / 732-356-3488
Wendell Murray, hdmstr. / Fax 868-0386
Somerset Christian College / Post-Sec.
PO Box 9035 08890 / 800-234-9305

NEW MEXICO

NEW MEXICO PUBLIC EDUCATION DEPARTMENT
300 Don Gaspar Ave, Santa Fe 87501-2786
Telephone 505-827-5800
Fax 505-827-6696
Website http://www.sde.state.nm.us

Secretary of Education   Veronica Garcia

NEW MEXICO BOARD OF EDUCATION
300 Don Gaspar Ave, Santa Fe 87501-2786

Chairperson   Eleanor Ortiz

REGIONAL EDUCATION COOPS (REC) & REGIONAL CENTER COOPS (RCC)

Central REC 5
Nina Tafoya, dir.   505-889-3412
PO Box 37440, Albuquerque 87176   Fax 889-3422
www.crecnm.org/
High Plains REC 3
Stephen Aguirre, dir.   505-445-7090
144 S 1st St, Raton 87740   Fax 445-7663
hprec.com
Northeast REC 4
Mary Schutz, dir.   505-426-2085
PO Box 927, Las Vegas 87701   Fax 454-1473
www.rec4.com

Pecos Valley REC 8
Janet Sistrunk, dir.   505-748-6100
PO Box 155, Artesia 88211   Fax 748-6160
www.pvrec8.com/
REC 2
Dr. Daniel Trujillo, dir.   505-638-5491
PO Box 230, Gallina 87017   Fax 638-0131
REC 6
Patti Harrelson, dir.   505-742-0447
3001 N Prince St, Clovis 88101   Fax 742-0455

REC 7
Belinda Morris, dir.   505-393-0755
315 E Clinton St, Hobbs 88240   Fax 393-0249
REC 9
Sandy Gladden, dir.   505-257-2368
1400 Sudderth Dr, Ruidoso 88345   Fax 257-2141
www.recixnm.org/
Southwest REC 10
Cathe North, dir., PO Box 4075   505-894-7589
Truth or Consequences 87901   Fax 894-7584

PUBLIC, PRIVATE AND CATHOLIC SECONDARY SCHOOLS

Alamogordo, Otero, Pop. 35,551
Alamogordo SD   6,800/PK-12
PO Box 650 88311   505-439-3270
Dr. Philip Knight, supt.   Fax 439-3373
aps4kids.org
Alamogordo HS   1,900/9-12
PO Box 650 88311   505-443-2000
Joe Jaramillo, prin.   Fax 443-2018
Chaparral MS   700/6-8
PO Box 650 88311   505-439-3350
Cheryl Kullman, prin.   Fax 439-3354
Mountain View MS   600/6-8
PO Box 650 88311   505-439-3330
Mike Farley, prin.   Fax 439-3355
Other Schools – See Holloman AFB

Community Christian S   200/PK-12
2907 Thunder Rd 88310   505-434-0352
Connie Higgs, admin.   Fax 437-1320
New Mexico School Visually Handicapped Post-Sec.
1900 N White Sands Blvd 88310   505-437-3505
New Mexico State University   Post-Sec.
2400 Scenic Dr 88310   505-439-3600
Olympian University of Cosmetology   Post-Sec.
1810 10th St 88310   505-437-2221

Albuquerque, Bernalillo, Pop. 471,856
Albuquerque SD   84,200/PK-12
PO Box 25704 87125   505-880-3713
Dr. Elizabeth Everitt, supt.   Fax 872-8855
www.aps.edu
Adams MS   900/6-8
5401 Glenrio Rd NW 87105   505-831-0400
Stanley Agustin, prin.   Fax 836-7760
Albuquerque HS   1,800/9-12
800 Odelia Rd NE 87102   505-843-6400
Linda Sink, prin.   Fax 848-9432
Career Enrichment Ctr   Vo/Tech
807 Mountain Rd NE 87102   505-247-3658
Katherine Sandoval, prin.   Fax 243-2447
Carter MS   1,000/6-8
8901 Bluewater Rd NW 87121   505-833-7540
Orlando Rodriguez, prin.   Fax 833-7559
Cibola HS   2,800/9-12
1510 Ellison Dr NW 87114   505-897-0110
Grace Brown, prin.   Fax 897-4251
Cleveland MS   800/6-8
6910 Natalie Ave NE 87110   505-881-9227
Susan LaBarge, prin.   Fax 881-9441
Del Norte HS   1,600/9-12
5323 Montgomery Blvd NE 87109   505-883-7222
Rebecca Almeter, prin.   Fax 880-3965
Desert Ridge MS   1,000/6-8
8400 Barstow St NE 87122   505-857-9282
Sean Joyce, prin.   Fax 857-0201
Eisenhower MS   1,000/6-8
11001 Camero Ave NE 87111   505-292-2530
Debra Hamilton, prin.   Fax 291-6884
Eldorado HS   2,200/9-12
11300 Montgomery Blvd NE 87111   505-296-4871
Yvonne Parrillo, prin.   Fax 291-6809
Garfield MS   500/6-8
3501 6th St NW 87107   505-344-1647
Rhohda Sandoval, prin.   Fax 344-6562
Grant MS   700/6-8
1111 Easterday Dr NE 87112   505-299-2113
Ed Briggs, prin.   Fax 291-6881
Harrison MS   600/6-8
3912 Isleta Blvd SW 87105   505-877-1279
Sam Obenshain, prin.   Fax 877-6797

Hayes MS   600/6-8
1100 Texas St NE 87110   505-265-7741
Jimmie Lueder, prin.   Fax 260-6108
Highland HS   2,000/9-12
4700 Coal Ave SE 87108   505-265-3711
Anthony Trujillo, prin.   Fax 348-8503
Hoover MS   800/6-8
12015 Tivoli Ave NE 87111   505-298-6896
Wayne Knight, prin.   Fax 291-6880
Jackson MS   700/6-8
10600 Indian School Rd NE 87112   505-299-7377
Ann Piper, prin.   Fax 291-6877
Jefferson MS   800/6-8
712 Girard Blvd NE 87106   505-255-8691
Ivy Langan, prin.   Fax 268-2334
Johnson MS   1,100/6-8
6811 Taylor Ranch Rd NW 87120   505-898-1492
Marcella Johnson, prin.   Fax 898-7150
Kennedy MS   500/6-8
721 Tomasita St NE 87123   505-298-6701
Ruby Ethridge, prin.   Fax 291-6879
La Cueva HS   2,200/9-12
7801 Wilshire Ave NE 87122   505-823-2327
Jo Ann Coffee, prin.   Fax 857-0177
Madison MS   900/6-8
3501 Moon St NE 87111   505-299-4735
Jim Steinhubel, prin.   Fax 323-9512
Manzano HS   2,000/9-12
12200 Lomas Blvd NE 87112   505-559-2200
Tim Whalen, prin.   Fax 291-6854
McKinley MS   700/6-8
4500 Comanche Rd NE 87110   505-881-9390
Scott Elder, prin.   Fax 880-3968
Monroe MS   1,100/6-8
6100 Paradise Blvd NW 87114   505-897-0101
Vernon Martinez, prin.   Fax 897-2371
Polk MS   400/6-8
2220 Raymac Rd SW 87105   505-877-6444
Theresa Baca, prin.   Fax 877-1618
Pyle MS   700/6-8
1820 Valdora Rd SW 87105   505-877-3770
B. Cordoba Martinez, prin.   Fax 873-8540
Rio Grande HS   1,900/9-12
2300 Arenal Rd SW 87105   505-873-0220
Al Sanchez, prin.   Fax 873-8523
Sandia HS   2,100/9-12
7801 Candelaria Rd NE 87110   505-294-1511
Michael Bachicha, prin.   Fax 291-6878
Taft MS   700/6-8
620 Schulte Rd NW 87107   505-344-4389
Stephanie Williams, prin.   Fax 761-8440
Taylor MS   600/6-8
8200 Guadalupe Trl NW 87114   505-898-3666
Nancy Romero, prin.   Fax 897-5165
Truman MS   900/6-8
9400 Benavides Rd SW 87121   505-836-3030
Judith Martin-Tafoya, prin.   Fax 836-7745
Valley HS   2,000/9-12
1505 Candelaria Rd NW 87107   505-345-9021
Anthony Griego, prin.   Fax 761-8429
Van Buren MS   600/6-8
700 Louisiana Blvd SE 87108   505-268-3833
Maria Carmen Graham, prin.   Fax 260-6104
Washington MS   600/6-8
1101 Park Ave SW 87102   505-764-2000
Cynthia Challberg-Hale, prin.   Fax 764-2022
West Mesa HS   2,600/9-12
6701 Fortuna Rd NW 87121   505-831-6993
Bianca Lopez, prin.   Fax 836-7756

Wilson MS   600/6-8
1138 Cardenas Dr SE 87108   505-268-3961
Connie Hansen, prin.   Fax 260-2000
Albuquerque Evening HS   Adult
800 Odelia Rd NE 87102   505-848-9424
Tanya Nash, prin.   Fax 848-9545
Other Schools – See Tijeras

Albuquerque Academy   1,100/6-12
6400 Wyoming Blvd NE 87109   505-828-3200
Andrew T. Watson, hdmstr.   Fax 828-3322
Albuquerque Barber College   Post-Sec.
601 San Pedro Dr Ste 100 87108   505-266-4900
Albuquerque TVI Community College   Post-Sec.
525 Buena Vista Dr SE 87106   505-224-3000
Apollo College   500/6-12
5301 Central Ave NE Ste 101 87108   800-368-7246
Bosque S   500/6-12
4000 Learning Rd NW 87120   505-898-6388
Andrew Wooden, hdmstr.   Fax 922-0392
Calvary Christian Academy   200/PK-12
1404 Lead Ave SE 87106   505-842-8681
Georgann Cowan, prin.   Fax 842-8746
DeWolff Coll of Hairstyling\Cosmetology Post-Sec.
1500 Eubank Blvd NE 87112   505-296-4100
Evangel Christian Academy   200/K-12
4501 Montgomery Blvd NE 87109   505-883-4674
Steven Barchie, prin.   Fax 883-1229
Hope Christian S   1,300/K-12
8005 Louisiana Blvd NE 87109   505-822-8868
Kelly McEachran, hdmstr.   Fax 822-8260
International Institute of the Americas Post-Sec.
4201 Central Ave NW Ste J 87105   505-880-2877
ITT Technical Institute   Post-Sec.
5100 Masthead St NE 87109   505-828-1114
Menaul S   300/6-12
301 Menaul Blvd NE 87107   505-345-7727
Gloria Griffin Mallory Ph.D., prin. Fax 345-2517
Metropolitan College   Post-Sec.
8100 Mountain Rd NE Ste 200 87110   505-888-3400
National American University   Post-Sec.
4775 Indian Sch Rd NE #200 87110   505-265-7517
New Life Baptist Academy   200/PK-12
6900 Los Volcanes Rd NW 87121   505-352-2628
Lille Allen, prin.   Fax 352-2684
New Mexico Aveda Inst de Bellas Artes   Post-Sec.
2614 Pennsylvania St NE 87110   505-294-5333
Olympian University of Cosmetology   Post-Sec.
800 Juan Tabo Blvd NE # 1-J 87123   505-765-1044
Pima Medical Institute   Post-Sec.
2201 San Pedro Dr NE 87110   505-881-1234
St. Pius X HS   1,000/9-12
5301 Saint Josephs Dr NW 87120   505-831-8400
Barbara Rothweiler, prin.   Fax 831-8413
Sandia Prep S   600/6-12
532 Osuna Rd NE 87113   505-338-3000
Dick Heath, hdmstr.   Fax 338-3099
Southwestern Indian Polytechnic Inst.
PO Box 10146 87184   505-346-2347
Temple Baptist Academy   200/PK-12
1621 Arizona St NE 87110   505-262-0969
David Baker, admin.   Fax 262-0996
The Art Center Design College   Post-Sec.
5000 Marble Ave NE 87110   505-254-7575
Universal Therapeutic Massage Institute Post-Sec.
3410 Aztec Rd NE 87107   505-888-0020
University of New Mexico   Post-Sec.
1 University Campus 87131   505-277-0111

University of Phoenix-NM Division — Post-Sec.
7471 Pan Amrcan West Fwy NE 87109 — 505-821-4800

Victory Christian S — 200/K-12
220 El Pueblo Rd NW 87114 — 505-898-3060
Glenn Frey, admin. — Fax 898-6690

Animas, Hidalgo
Animas SD — 300/PK-12
PO Box 85 88020 — 505-548-2299
Jerry Birdwell, supt. — Fax 548-2388
www.animask12.net
Animas HS — 100/9-12
PO Box 90 88020 — 505-548-2296
Ruben Aguallo, prin. — Fax 548-2649
Animas MS — 100/5-8
PO Box 68 88020 — 505-548-2296
Karla Stinehart, prin. — Fax 548-2388

Anthony, Dona Ana, Pop. 5,160
Gadsden ISD
Supt. — See Santa Teresa
Gadsden HS — 2,300/9-12
6301 Highway 28 88021 — 505-882-6300
George Foster, prin. — Fax 882-2370
Gadsden MS — 1,100/7-8
1301 Washington St 88021 — 505-882-2372
Dana Hamel, prin. — Fax 882-5227

Anton Chico, Guadalupe
Santa Rosa SD
Supt. — See Santa Rosa
Anton Chico MS — 50/6-8
PO Box 169 87711 — 505-427-6038
Lorenzo Marquez, prin. — Fax 427-4246

Artesia, Eddy, Pop. 10,518
Artesia SD — 3,600/PK-12
1106 W Quay Ave 88210 — 505-746-3585
Mike Phipps, supt. — Fax 746-6232
www.bulldogs.org
Artesia SHS — 800/10-12
1006 W Richardson Ave 88210 — 505-746-9816
Rick Stewart, prin. — Fax 746-4365
Park JHS — 600/8-9
15th & Cannon 88210 — 505-746-9892
Crit Caton, prin. — Fax 746-4462

Aztec, San Juan, Pop. 6,818
Aztec SD — 3,200/PK-12
1118 W Aztec Blvd 87410 — 505-334-9474
Dr. Linda Paul, supt. — Fax 334-9861
www.aztecschools.com
Aztec HS — 1,000/9-12
500 E Chaco St 87410 — 505-334-9414
Kirk Carpenter, prin. — Fax 599-4387
Koogler MS — 800/6-8
455 N Light Plant Rd 87410 — 505-334-6102
Richard Vogel, prin. — Fax 599-4385

Bayard, Grant, Pop. 2,419
Cobre Consolidated SD — 1,500/PK-12
PO Box 1000 88023 — 505-537-4010
Dr. Candelario Jauregui, supt. — Fax 537-5455
www.cobre.k12.nm.us
Cobre HS — 500/9-12
PO Box 749 88023 — 505-537-4020
Jess Rogers, prin. — Fax 537-5503
Snell MS — 400/6-8
PO Box 729 88023 — 505-537-4030
Jeff Gorum, prin. — Fax 537-3358

Belen, Valencia, Pop. 6,961
Belen Consolidated SD — 4,800/PK-12
520 N Main St 87002 — 505-966-1000
Kenneth Griego, supt. — Fax 966-1005
www.belen.k12.nm.us
Belen HS — 1,400/9-12
520 N Main St 87002 — 505-966-1300
Tamie Pargas, prin. — Fax 966-1350
Belen MS — 800/7-8
520 N Main St 87002 — 505-966-1600
Aubrey Tucker, prin. — Fax 966-1650

Bernalillo, Sandoval, Pop. 6,986
Bernalillo SD — 3,700/PK-12
224 N Camino Del Pueblo 87004 — 505-867-2317
Barbara Vigil-Lowder Ed.D., supt. — Fax 867-7850
www.bernalillo-schools.org
Bernalillo HS — 900/9-12
250 Isidora Sanchez Rd 87004 — 505-867-2388
Orlando Rodriguez, prin. — Fax 867-7826
Bernalillo MS — 600/6-8
485 Camino don Tomas 87004 — 505-867-3309
Allan Tapia, prin. — Fax 867-7819
Other Schools – See Santo Domingo Pueblo

Bloomfield, San Juan, Pop. 7,210
Bloomfield SD — 2,400/PK-12
325 N Bergin Ln 87413 — 505-632-3316
Harry Hayes, supt. — Fax 632-4371
www.bsin.k12.nm.us
Bloomfield HS — 700/9-12
520 N 1st St 87413 — 505-632-3373
Nancy Radford, prin. — Fax 634-3413
Mesa Alta JHS — 400/7-8
329 N Bergin Ln 87413 — 505-632-4350
Ricardo Sanchez, prin. — Fax 634-3835

Capitan, Lincoln, Pop. 1,500
Capitan SD — 600/PK-12
PO Box 278 88316 — 505-354-2239
Dr. Larry Miller, supt. — Fax 354-2240
www.capitan.k12.nm.us
Capitan HS — 200/9-12
PO Box 278 88316 — 505-354-2567
Gary Salazar, prin. — Fax 354-2240
Capitan MS — 200/6-8
PO Box 278 88316 — 505-354-2096
Bill Miller, prin. — Fax 354-2240

Carlsbad, Eddy, Pop. 25,303
Carlsbad SD — 5,900/K-12
408 N Canyon St 88220 — 505-234-3300
Charlotte Neill, supt. — Fax 234-3367
www.carlsbad.k12.nm.us
Alta Vista MS — 600/6-8
408 N Canyon St 88220 — 505-234-3316
Theodor Cordova, prin. — Fax 234-3478
Carlsbad HS — 1,800/9-12
408 N Canyon St 88220 — 505-234-3319
Tom Quintela, prin. — Fax 234-3393
Leyva MS — 800/6-8
408 N Canyon St 88220 — 505-234-3318
Janet Hunt, prin. — Fax 234-3452

Eddy County Beauty College — Post-Sec.
1115 W Mermod St 88220 — 505-885-4545
New Mexico State University — Post-Sec.
1500 University Dr 88220 — 505-234-9200

Carrizozo, Lincoln, Pop. 1,048
Carrizozo Municipal SD — 200/PK-12
PO Box 99 88301 — 505-648-2348
Sergio Castanon, supt. — Fax 648-2216
Carrizozo HS — 100/9-12
PO Box 99 88301 — 505-648-2346
Mel Holland, prin. — Fax 648-3255
Carrizozo MS — 100/6-8
PO Box 99 88301 — 505-648-2346
Mel Holland, prin. — Fax 648-3255

Casa Blanca, Cibola
Grants/Cibola County SD
Supt. — See Grants
Laguna Acoma HS — 300/9-12
PO Box 689 87007 — 505-285-2669
Jim Reed, prin. — Fax 285-5881

Chama, Rio Arriba, Pop. 1,175
Chama Valley ISD
Supt. — See Tierra Amarilla
Chama MS — 100/6-8
PO Box 337 87520 — 505-756-2161
Larkin Vigil, prin. — Fax 756-2538

Chaparral, Dona Ana, Pop. 2,962
Gadsden ISD
Supt. — See Santa Teresa
Chaparral HS — 800/8-10
290 E Lisa Dr, — 505-824-4847
James Diggs, prin. — Fax 824-4045

Cimarron, Colfax, Pop. 909
Cimarron SD — 500/PK-12
PO Box 605 87714 — 505-376-2445
Dr. Annette Johnson, supt. — Fax 376-2442
www.cimarronschools.org
Cimarron HS — 100/9-12
PO Box 605 87714 — 505-376-2241
Penny Coppedge, prin. — Fax 376-2428
Cimarron MS — 100/5-8
PO Box 605 87714 — 505-376-2512
James Gallegos, prin. — Fax 376-2217
Other Schools – See Eagle Nest

Clayton, Union, Pop. 2,225
Clayton SD — 600/PK-12
323 S 5th St 88415 — 505-374-9611
Jack Wiley, supt. — Fax 374-9881
Clayton HS — 200/9-12
323 S 5th St 88415 — 505-374-2596
John Burgess, prin. — Fax 374-9881
Clayton JHS — 100/7-8
323 S 5th St 88415 — 505-374-9543
Terrell Jones, prin. — Fax 374-9881

Cliff, Grant
Silver Consolidated SD
Supt. — See Silver City
Cliff JSHS — 200/7-12
PO Box 9 88028 — 505-535-2051
Clayton Ellwanger, prin. — Fax 535-2054

Cloudcroft, Otero, Pop. 724
Cloudcroft Municipal SD — 400/PK-12
PO Box 198 88317 — 505-682-2361
Glena Muncrief, supt. — Fax 682-2921
www.cmsbears.org
Cloudcroft HS — 200/9-12
PO Box 198 88317 — 505-682-2524
Shirley Crawford, prin. — Fax 682-1343
Cloudcroft MS — 100/6-8
PO Box 198 88317 — 505-682-3336
Fred Wright, prin. — Fax 682-2776

Clovis, Curry, Pop. 32,815
Clovis SD — 8,200/K-12
PO Box 19000 88102 — 505-769-4300
Dr. Rhonda Seidenwurm, supt. — Fax 769-4333
www.cms.k12.nm.us
Clovis SHS — 1,600/10-12
PO Box 19000 88102 — 505-769-4350
Jody Balch, prin. — Fax 769-4366
Gattis JHS — 500/7-9
PO Box 19000 88102 — 505-769-4400
Craig Terry, prin. — Fax 769-4403
Marshall JHS — 600/7-9
PO Box 19000 88102 — 505-769-4410
Diana Russell, prin. — Fax 769-4413
Yucca JHS — 800/7-9
PO Box 19000 88102 — 505-769-4420
Alan Dropps, prin. — Fax 769-4421

Clovis Christian S — 300/K-12
PO Box 608 88102 — 505-763-5311
Steve Medeiros, admin. — Fax 763-4469
Clovis Community College — Post-Sec.
417 Schepps Blvd 88101 — 505-769-2811

Corona, Lincoln, Pop. 167
Corona SD — 100/PK-12
PO Box 258 88318 — 505-849-1911
Travis Lightfoot, supt. — Fax 849-2026
Corona JSHS — 50/7-12
PO Box 258 88318 — 505-849-1911
Rick Cogdill, prin. — Fax 849-2026

Corrales, Sandoval, Pop. 7,553

Sandia View S — 100/9-12
65 Sandia View Ln 87048 — 505-898-0717
Leon M. Hill, prin. — Fax 897-7053

Crownpoint, McKinley, Pop. 2,108
Gallup-McKinley County SD
Supt. — See Gallup
Crownpoint HS — 500/9-12
PO Box 700 87313 — 505-786-5664
Bruce Helms, prin. — Fax 786-5316
Crownpoint MS — 300/6-8
PO Box 700 87313 — 505-786-5663
Rozelyn Carroll, prin. — Fax 786-5685

Cuba, Sandoval, Pop. 619
Cuba ISD — 800/PK-12
PO Box 70 87013 — 505-289-3211
Pancho Guardiola, supt. — Fax 289-3314
cuba.k12.nm.us/
Cuba HS — 500/9-12
PO Box 70 87013 — 505-289-3211
Jack Griffin, prin. — Fax 289-3314
Cuba MS — 100/6-8
PO Box 70 87013 — 505-289-3211
Raymond Lyon, prin. — Fax 289-3314

Deming, Luna, Pop. 14,381
Deming SD — 5,300/PK-12
1001 S Diamond Ave 88030 — 505-546-8841
Harvielee Moore, supt. — Fax 546-8517
www.demingps.org
Deming HS — 1,100/9-12
1100 S Nickel St 88030 — 505-546-2678
Janean Garney, prin. — Fax 544-0918
Hofacket MS — 800/8-9
1400 S Iron St 88030 — 505-546-4863
Robin Parnell, prin. — Fax 544-7217

Des Moines, Union, Pop. 157
Des Moines SD — 200/K-12
PO Box 38 88418 — 505-278-2611
Jaynee Burchard, supt. — Fax 278-2617
Des Moines JSHS — 100/7-12
PO Box 38 88418 — 505-278-2611
Jaynee Burchard, prin. — Fax 278-2617

Dexter, Chaves, Pop. 1,216
Dexter Consolidated SD — 1,100/PK-12
PO Box 159 88230 — 505-734-5420
Patricia Parsons, supt. — Fax 734-6813
www.dexterdemons.org
Dexter HS — 400/9-12
PO Box 159 88230 — 505-734-5420
Eddie Ward, prin. — Fax 734-6709
Dexter MS — 300/6-8
PO Box 159 88230 — 505-734-5420
Christy Takacs, prin. — Fax 734-6811

Dora, Roosevelt, Pop. 129
Dora SD — 200/PK-12
PO Box 327 88115 — 505-477-2216
Steve Barron, supt. — Fax 477-2464
Dora JSHS — 100/7-12
PO Box 327 88115 — 505-477-2211
Steve Barron, prin. — Fax 477-2464

Dulce, Rio Arriba, Pop. 2,438
Dulce SD — 800/K-12
PO Box 547 87528 — 505-759-3353
Loren R. Cushman, supt. — Fax 759-3533
www.dulceschools.com/
Dulce HS — 200/9-12
PO Box 547 87528 — 505-759-3282
Steve Ulmer, prin. — Fax 759-3535
Dulce MS, PO Box 547 87528 — 200/6-8
Tracie Phillips, prin. — 505-759-3646

Eagle Nest, Colfax, Pop. 297
Cimarron SD
Supt. — See Cimarron
Eagle Nest MS — 100/5-8
PO Box 287 87718 — 505-377-6991
Lee Mills, prin. — Fax 377-3646

Elida, Roosevelt, Pop. 180
Elida SD — 100/K-12
PO Box 8 88116 — 505-274-6211
Jack Burch, supt. — Fax 274-6213
www.elida.k12.nm.us/
Elida JSHS — 100/7-12
PO Box 8 88116 — 505-274-6211
Donna Tivis, prin. — Fax 274-6213

El Rito, Rio Arriba
Mesa Vista Consolidated SD — 500/PK-12
PO Box 6 87530 — 505-581-4504
Andy Torres, supt. — Fax 581-4613
Other Schools – See Ojo Caliente

Northern New Mexico Community College — Post-Sec.
87530 — 505-581-4501

Espanola, Rio Arriba, Pop. 9,762
Espanola SD — 5,100/PK-12
714 Calle Don Diego 87532 — 505-753-2254
Dr. David Cockerham, supt. — Fax 753-2321
www.k12espanola.org
Espanola MS East — 600/7-8
714 Calle Don Diego 87532 — 505-753-2293
Lewis Johnson, prin. — Fax 747-3211
Espanola Valley HS — 800/10-12
714 Calle Don Diego 87532 — 505-753-7357
Bruce Hopmeier, prin. — Fax 753-6177
Virgil MS — 800/8-9
714 Calle Don Diego 87532 — 505-753-2294
Ben Gurule, prin. — Fax 747-3211

McCurdy S — 400/PK-12
261 S Mccurdy Rd 87532 — 505-753-7221
Pamela Womack, admin. — Fax 753-7830

Miri Piri Academy 100/2-12
  01 Ram Das Guru Pl # A 87532 505-753-8604
  Nirmaljit Kaur Sandhu, prin. Fax 753-0599
Northern New Mexico College Post-Sec.
  921 N Paseo De Onate 87532 505-747-2100
Victory Christian Academy 100/K-12
  PO Box 540 87532 505-753-0039
  J.D. Miera, prin. Fax 747-0040

Estancia, Torrance, Pop. 1,559
Estancia SD 1,000/PK-12
  PO Box 68 87016 505-384-2001
  Dr. Bruce Peterson, supt. Fax 384-2015
  www.estancia.k12.nm.us
Estancia HS 300/9-12
  PO Box 68 87016 505-384-2002
  Doreen Winn, prin. Fax 384-2015
Estancia MS 200/7-8
  PO Box 68 87016 505-384-2003
  Doreen Winn, prin. Fax 384-2015

Liberty Ranch Christian S 50/PK-12
  Bluegrass Rd 87016 505-384-2530
  Edward Bragg, prin. Fax 384-2530

Eunice, Lea, Pop. 2,561
Eunice SD 600/PK-12
  PO Box 129 88231 505-394-2524
  Larry Harvey, supt. Fax 394-3006
  www.eunice.org/
Caton MS 100/6-8
  PO Box 129 88231 505-394-3338
  Dwain Haynes, prin. Fax 394-3661
Eunice HS 200/9-12
  PO Box 129 88231 505-394-2332
  Richard Hayes, prin. Fax 394-3140

Farmington, San Juan, Pop. 41,420
Farmington SD 9,700/PK-12
  PO Box 5850 87499 505-324-9840
  Janel Ryan, supt. Fax 599-8806
  www.fms.k12.nm.us/home_body.html
Farmington HS 1,700/9-12
  2200 N Sunset Ave 87401 505-324-0352
  Mark Driskell, prin. Fax 599-8832
Heights MS 700/6-8
  3700 College Blvd 87402 505-599-8611
  Dave Willden, prin. Fax 599-8673
Hermosa MS 600/6-8
  1500 E 25th St 87401 505-599-8612
  Bob Rank, prin. Fax 599-8681
Mesa View MS 600/6-8
  4451 Wildflower Dr 87401 505-599-8622
  Kim Salazar, prin. Fax 599-8646
Piedra Vista HS 1,100/9-12
  5700 College Blvd 87402 505-599-8880
  Ann Gattis, prin. Fax 599-8891
Rocinante HS Vo/Tech
  3250 E 30th St 87402 505-599-8627
  Richard Sharpe, prin. Fax 599-8731
Tibbetts MS 500/6-8
  312 E Apache St 87401 505-599-8613
  Dr. Anthony Smagacz, prin. Fax 599-8675

San Juan College Post-Sec.
  4601 College Blvd 87402 505-326-3311

Floyd, Roosevelt, Pop. 76
Floyd Municipal SD 300/PK-12
  PO Box 65 88118 505-478-2211
  Paul Benoit, supt. Fax 478-2811
  www.floydbroncos.com/
Floyd HS 100/9-12
  PO Box 65 88118 505-478-2211
  Chris Duncan, prin. Fax 478-2811
Floyd MS 100/5-8
  PO Box 65 88118 505-478-2211
  Chris Duncan, prin. Fax 478-2811

Fort Sumner, DeBaca, Pop. 1,124
Fort Sumner SD 300/PK-12
  PO Box 387 88119 505-355-7734
  Patricia Miller, supt. Fax 355-7716
  www.ftsumnerk12.com/
Fort Sumner HS 100/9-12
  PO Box 387 88119 505-355-2231
  Patti Scott, prin. Fax 355-7663
Fort Sumner MS 100/6-8
  PO Box 387 88119 505-355-2231
  Patti Scott, prin. Fax 355-7663

Gallina, Rio Arriba
Jemez Mountain SD 400/K-12
  PO Box 230 87017 505-638-5419
  Robert Archuleta, supt. Fax 638-5571
  www.jmsk12.com/
Coronado MSHS 200/6-12
  PO Box 230 87017 505-638-5549
  Felix Garcia, prin. Fax 638-5571

Gallup, McKinley, Pop. 19,868
Gallup-McKinley County SD 13,600/PK-12
  PO Box 1318 87305 505-722-7711
  Karen White, supt. Fax 721-1199
  www.gmcs.k12.nm.us/
Gallup HS 1,500/10-12
  1055 Rico St 87301 505-721-2525
  Mike Butkovich, prin. Fax 721-2556
Gallup JHS 1,600/8-9
  680 S Boardman Ave 87301 505-721-1900
  Frank Chiapetti, prin. Fax 721-1910
Other Schools – See Crownpoint, Navajo, Ramah, Thoreau, Tohatchi

Gallup Catholic HS 100/9-12
  515 Park Ave 87301 505-722-6089
  Angelo DiPalo, prin. Fax 722-6089
University of New Mexico Post-Sec.
  200 College Rd 87301 505-863-7500

Grady, Curry, Pop. 99
Grady SD 100/K-12
  PO Box 71 88120 505-357-2192
  Dr. Elizabeth Posey, supt. Fax 357-2000
Grady HS 50/9-12
  PO Box 71 88120 505-357-2192
  Darrel Bollinger, prin. Fax 357-2000
Grady MS 6-8
  PO Box 71 88120 505-357-2192
  Darrel Bollinger, prin. Fax 357-2000

Grants, Cibola, Pop. 8,972
Grants/Cibola County SD 3,800/PK-12
  PO Box 8 87020 505-285-2600
  Kilino Marquez, supt. Fax 285-2628
  www.gccs.cc/
Grants HS 1,000/9-12
  500 Mountain Rd 87020 505-285-2653
  Rick Horacek, prin. Fax 287-3126
Los Alamitos MS 500/7-8
  1100 Mount Taylor Ave 87020 505-285-2684
  Joan Gilmore, prin. Fax 285-2692
Other Schools – See Casa Blanca, New Laguna

New Mexico State University Post-Sec.
  1500 N 3rd St 87020 505-287-7981

Hagerman, Chaves, Pop. 1,153
Hagerman SD 500/PK-12
  PO Box B 88232 505-752-3254
  Steven Starkey, supt. Fax 752-3255
  bobcat.net
Hagerman HS 100/9-12
  PO Box B 88232 505-752-3283
  Guyla Maples, prin. Fax 752-3306
Hagerman MS 100/6-8
  PO Box B 88232 505-752-3283
  Guyla Maples, prin. Fax 752-0241

Hatch, Dona Ana, Pop. 1,668
Hatch Valley SD 1,500/K-12
  PO Box 790 87937 505-267-8200
  Dane Kennon, supt. Fax 267-8210
  www.hatch.k12.nm.us/
Hatch Valley HS 400/9-12
  PO Box 790 87937 505-267-8230
  Michael Gaume, prin. Fax 267-8235
Hatch Valley MS 400/6-8
  PO Box 790 87937 505-267-8250
  Claud Gobble, prin. Fax 267-8255
ACE HS Adult
  PO Box 790 87937 505-267-8225
   Fax 267-8226

Hobbs, Lea, Pop. 28,311
Hobbs Municipal SD 7,400/PK-12
  PO Box 1030 88241 505-433-0100
  Cliff Burch, supt. Fax 433-0140
  www.hobbsschools.net
Highland JHS 600/7-8
  2500 N Jefferson St 88240 505-433-1200
  John Notaro, prin. Fax 433-1203
Hobbs Freshman HS Heizer Campus 600/9-9
  100 E Stanolind Rd 88240 505-433-1100
  Pat McMurray, prin. Fax 433-1109
Hobbs HS 1,600/10-12
  800 N Jefferson St 88240 505-433-0200
  Eppie Calderon, prin. Fax 433-0203
Houston JHS 600/7-8
  300 N Houston St 88240 505-433-1300
  Jeff Cearley, prin. Fax 433-1304

College of the Southwest Post-Sec.
  6610 N Lovington Hwy 88240 505-392-6561
New Mexico Junior College Post-Sec.
  5317 N Lovington Hwy 88240 505-392-4510

Holloman AFB, Otero, Pop. 5,891
Alamogordo SD
  Supt. — See Alamogordo
Holloman MS 200/6-8
  Building 768 88330 505-479-2282
  Maria Showalter, prin. Fax 479-4041

Hondo, Lincoln
Hondo Valley SD 100/PK-12
  PO Box 55 88336 505-653-4411
  John MacCallum, supt. Fax 653-4414
Hondo HS 100/7-12
  PO Box 55 88336 505-653-4411
  John MacCallum, prin. Fax 653-4414

House, Quay, Pop. 67
House SD 300/K-12
  PO Box 673 88121 505-279-7353
  Dr. Art Brokenbek, supt. Fax 279-6201
  www.houseschools.net
House JSHS 100/7-12
  PO Box 673 88121 505-279-7353
  Dr. Art Brokenbek, prin. Fax 279-6201

Jal, Lea, Pop. 1,980
Jal SD 400/PK-12
  PO Box 1386 88252 505-395-2101
  Rick Ferguson, supt. Fax 395-2146
  www.jalnm.org
Jal JSHS 200/7-12
  PO Box 1386 88252 505-395-2277
  Elaine O'Neal, prin. Fax 395-3177

Jemez Pueblo, Sandoval, Pop. 1,301
Jemez Valley SD 400/PK-12
  8501 Highway 4 87024 505-834-7391
  Sandra Henson, supt. Fax 834-7394
  www.jvps.org
Jemez Valley HS 100/9-12
  8501 Highway 4 87024 505-834-7392
  Jay Leonard, prin. Fax 834-7676
Jemez Valley MS 100/6-8
  8501 Highway 4 87024 505-834-7393
  Claudie Thompson, prin. Fax 834-7130

Kirtland, San Juan, Pop. 3,552
Central Consolidated SD 22
  Supt. — See Shiprock
Kirtland Central HS 1,000/9-12
  550 Rd 6100 87417 505-598-5881
  Cody Diehl, prin. Fax 598-9712
Kirtland MS 500/7-8
  538 Rd 6100 87417 505-598-6114
  Charles Trujillo, prin. Fax 598-9497

Lake Arthur, Chaves, Pop. 431
Lake Arthur SD 200/PK-12
  PO Box 98 88253 505-365-2001
  Michael Grossman, supt. Fax 365-2002
Lake Arthur HS 50/9-12
  PO Box 98 88253 505-365-2001
  Dale Ballard, prin. Fax 365-2002
Lake Arthur MS 50/6-8
  PO Box 98 88253 505-365-2001
  Dale Ballard, prin. Fax 365-2002

Las Cruces, Dona Ana, Pop. 76,990
Las Cruces SD 22,900/PK-12
  505 S Main St Ste 249 88001 505-527-5807
  Louis Martinez, supt. Fax 527-5972
  www.lcps.k12.nm.us
Camino Real MS 900/6-8
  505 S Main St Ste 249 88001 505-527-6030
  Angie Dotson, prin. Fax 527-6031
Las Cruces HS 2,400/9-12
  505 S Main St Ste 249 88001 505-527-9400
  Nyeta Haines, prin. Fax 527-9767
Lynn MS 800/6-8
  505 S Main St Ste 249 88001 505-527-9445
  Gina Rivera, prin. Fax 527-9454
Mayfield HS 2,500/9-12
  505 S Main St Ste 249 88001 505-527-9415
  Chris Cook, prin. Fax 527-9420
Onate HS 1,900/9-12
  505 S Main St Ste 249 88001 505-527-9430
  Joyce Aranda, prin. Fax 527-9444
Picacho MS 700/6-8
  505 S Main St Ste 249 88001 505-527-9455
  Michael Montoya, prin. Fax 527-9459
Sierra MS 1,000/6-8
  505 S Main St Ste 249 88001 505-527-9640
  Brenda Lewis, prin. Fax 527-9768
Vista MS 900/6-8
  505 S Main St Ste 249 88001 505-527-9465
  Dan Davis, prin. Fax 527-9470
Zia MS 900/6-8
  505 S Main St Ste 249 88001 505-527-9475
  Dante Thacker, prin. Fax 527-9479
Other Schools – See White Sands

Business Skills Institute Post-Sec.
  1400 El Paseo Rd 88001 505-526-5579
Mesilla Valley Christian S 500/PK-12
  3850 Stern Dr 88001 505-525-8515
  John Foreman, admin. Fax 526-2713
New Mexico State Univ. Dona Ana Branch Post-Sec.
  PO Box 30001 88003 505-527-7500
New Mexico State University Post-Sec.
  PO Box 30001 88003 505-646-0111
Olympian University of Cosmetology Post-Sec.
  1460 Missouri Ave # 5 88001 505-523-7181

Las Vegas, San Miguel, Pop. 14,194
Las Vegas City SD 2,200/PK-12
  901 Douglas Ave 87701 505-454-5700
  Dr. Pete Campos, supt. Fax 454-6965
  cybercardinal.com/
Memorial MS 500/6-8
  901 Douglas Ave 87701 505-454-5710
  Sandra Madrid, prin. Fax 426-0303
Robertson HS 700/9-12
  901 Douglas Ave 87701 505-454-5770
  Richard Lopez, prin. Fax 425-6852

West Las Vegas SD 2,000/K-12
  179 Bridge St 87701 505-426-2300
  Joe Baca, supt. Fax 426-2332
West Las Vegas HS 500/9-12
  179 Bridge St 87701 505-426-2500
  Gene Parson, prin. Fax 426-2501
West Las Vegas MS 400/6-8
  179 Bridge St 87701 505-426-2541
  Victor Sanchez, prin. Fax 426-2542
Other Schools – See Ribera

Luna Community College Post-Sec.
  366 Luna Dr 87701 505-454-2500
New Mexico Highlands University Post-Sec.
  PO Box 9000 87701 505-454-3434

La Union, Dona Ana
Covenant Christian Academy 50/7-12
  7048 McNutt Rd 88021 505-589-3538
  Jeffrey Miller, hdmstr.

Logan, Quay, Pop. 1,046
Logan SD 200/PK-12
  PO Box 67 88426 505-487-2252
  Carolyn Franklin, supt. Fax 487-9479
Logan HS 100/9-12
  PO Box 67 88426 505-487-2252
  Gary Miller, prin. Fax 487-9479
Logan MS 6-8
  PO Box 67 88426 505-487-2252
  Gary Miller, prin. Fax 487-9479

Lordsburg, Hidalgo, Pop. 2,904
Lordsburg Municipal SD 700/PK-12
  PO Box 430 88045 505-542-9361
  Jim Barentine, supt. Fax 542-9364
  www.lmsed.org
Dugan-Tarango MS 100/7-8
  1352 Hardin St 88045 505-542-9806
  David Lackey, prin. Fax 542-9811
Lordsburg HS 200/9-12
  501 W 4th St 88045 505-542-3782
  J. Vance Lee, prin. Fax 542-3712

Los Alamos, Los Alamos, Pop. 11,455
Los Alamos SD — 3,600/PK-12
PO Box 90 87544 — 505-663-2222
Dr. James Anderson, supt. — Fax 661-6300
www.laschools.net
Los Alamos HS — 1,200/9-12
1300 Diamond Dr 87544 — 505-663-2510
Lynne Saccaro, prin. — Fax 662-6846
Los Alamos MS — 600/7-8
1 Hawk Dr 87544 — 505-663-2375
Garrett Bosarge, prin. — Fax 662-4270

University of New Mexico — Post-Sec.
4000 University Dr 87544 — 505-662-5919

Los Lunas, Valencia, Pop. 11,265
Los Lunas SD — 8,800/PK-12
PO Box 1300 87031 — 505-866-8231
Walter Gibson, supt. — Fax 865-7766
www.llschools.net/
Career Academy — Vo/Tech
PO Box 1300 87031 — 505-565-8755
Lena Mae Chavez, prin. — Fax 565-8762
Los Lunas HS — 2,400/9-12
PO Box 1300 87031 — 505-865-4646
Gina Sallie, prin. — Fax 565-2847
Los Lunas MS — 800/7-8
PO Box 1300 87031 — 505-865-7273
Russell Hague, prin. — Fax 865-9742
Manzano Vista MS — 700/7-8
PO Box 1300 87031 — 505-865-1750
Carla Cano, prin. — Fax 866-8921

Christ the King S — 50/K-12
700 Camelot Blvd SW 87031 — 505-865-9226
Rev. Alan R. Coleman, prin. — Fax 865-9226
University of New Mexico — Post-Sec.
280 La Entrada Rd 87031 — 505-925-8500

Loving, Eddy, Pop. 1,320
Loving Municipal SD — 600/PK-12
PO Box 98 88256 — 505-745-2000
David Chavez, supt. — Fax 745-2002
www.lovingschools.org
Loving HS — 200/9-12
PO Box 98 88256 — 505-745-2020
Fran McCarthy, prin. — Fax 745-2002
Loving MS — 100/6-8
PO Box 98 88256 — 505-745-2050
Jana Rodriguez, prin. — Fax 745-2052

Lovington, Lea, Pop. 9,456
Lovington Municipal SD — 2,900/PK-12
PO Box 1537 88260 — 505-739-2200
Jimmy Derrick, supt. — Fax 739-2205
lovschools.leaco.net/
Lovington JHS — 400/8-9
500 W Jefferson Ave 88260 — 505-739-2330
Darin Manes, prin. — Fax 739-2330
Lovington SHS — 500/10-12
701 W Avenue K 88260 — 505-739-2230
Robert Brown, prin. — Fax 739-2242

Magdalena, Socorro, Pop. 883
Magdalena Municipal SD — 400/PK-12
PO Box 24 87825 — 505-854-2241
Mike Chambers, supt. — Fax 854-2294
www.magdalena.k12.nm.us
Magdalena HS — 100/9-12
PO Box 629 87825 — 505-854-8034
Dwight Myers, prin. — Fax 854-2531
Magdalena MS — 100/6-8
PO Box 629 87825 — 505-854-8034
Dwight Myers, prin. — Fax 854-2531

Maxwell, Colfax, Pop. 271
Maxwell Municipal SD — 100/PK-12
PO Box 275 87728 — 505-375-2371
Dr. Kaye Peery, supt. — Fax 375-2375
www.maxwellp12.com/
Maxwell HS — 50/9-12
PO Box 275 87728 — 505-375-2371
Regina Lane, prin. — Fax 375-2375
Maxwell MS — 50/7-8
PO Box 275 87728 — 505-375-2371
Regina Lane, prin. — Fax 375-2375

Melrose, Curry, Pop. 739
Melrose SD — 300/PK-12
PO Box 275 88124 — 505-253-4269
Dr. Ronald Windom, supt. — Fax 253-4291
www.melroseschools.org
Melrose JSHS — 100/7-12
PO Box 275 88124 — 505-253-4267
Jamie Widner, prin. — Fax 253-4291

Montezuma, San Miguel

Hammer United World College — 200/11-12
PO Box 248 87731 — 505-454-4200
Dr. Philip Geier, prin. — Fax 454-4274

Mora, Mora
Mora ISD — 600/K-12
PO Box 179 87732 — 505-387-3110
Arthur S. Romero, supt. — Fax 387-3111
www.nnmt.net/~moraschools
Mora HS — 200/9-12
PO Box 180 87732 — 505-387-3122
Danny Chavez, prin. — Fax 387-3121
Mora MS — 200/6-8
PO Box 687 87732 — 505-387-3125
Loretta Chavez, prin. — Fax 387-3126

Moriarty, Torrance, Pop. 1,813
Moriarty SD — 4,200/PK-12
PO Box 2000 87035 — 505-832-4471
Karen M. Couch, supt. — Fax 832-4472
www.moriarty.k12.nm.us
Edgewood MS — 400/7-8
PO Box 2000 87035 — 505-281-7181
Barbara Gradner, prin. — Fax 832-7210

Moriarty HS — 1,300/9-12
PO Box 2000 87035 — 505-832-4254
Wayne Marshall, prin. — Fax 832-4939
Moriarty MS — 300/7-8
PO Box 2000 87035 — 505-832-6200
Dawn Tinsley, prin. — Fax 832-5919

Mosquero, Harding, Pop. 102
Mosquero Municipal SD — 100/PK-12
PO Box 258 87733 — 505-673-2271
Tim McCoy, supt. — Fax 673-2305
www.mms.k12.nm.us
Mosquero JSHS — 50/7-12
PO Box 258 87733 — 505-673-2271
Tim McCoy, prin. — Fax 673-2305

Mountainair, Torrance, Pop. 1,078
Mountainair SD — 400/PK-12
PO Box 456 87036 — 505-847-2333
Jay Mortensen, supt. — Fax 847-2843
Mountainair HS — 200/7-12
PO Box 456 87036 — 505-847-2211
Robert Chavez, prin. — Fax 847-2843

Navajo, McKinley, Pop. 1,985
Gallup-McKinley County SD
Supt. — See Gallup
Navajo MS — 200/6-8
PO Box 1286 87328 — 505-777-2390
Pauletta White, prin. — Fax 777-2375
Navajo Pine HS — 200/9-12
PO Box 1286 87328 — 505-777-2288
Fax 777-2375

Newcomb, San Juan, Pop. 388
Central Consolidated SD 22
Supt. — See Shiprock
Newcomb HS — 300/9-12
PO Box 7973 87455 — 505-696-3417
Kenneth Carmichael, prin. — Fax 696-3487
Newcomb MS — 300/6-8
PO Box 7973 87455 — 505-696-3417
Mark Madsen, prin. — Fax 696-3487

New Laguna, Cibola
Grants/Cibola County SD
Supt. — See Grants
Laguna-Acoma MS — 100/7-8
PO Box 760 87038 — 505-287-3796
Jim Reed, prin. — Fax 552-5881

Ojo Caliente, Taos
Mesa Vista Consolidated SD
Supt. — See El Rito
Mesa Vista HS — 200/9-12
PO Box 50 87549 — 505-583-2275
Polly Otero, prin. — Fax 583-9133
Mesa Vista MS — 100/7-8
PO Box 50 87549 — 505-583-2275
Polly Otero, prin. — Fax 583-9133

Pecos, San Miguel, Pop. 1,424
Pecos SD — 900/PK-12
PO Box 368 87552 — 505-757-4700
Harrell Holder Ed.D., supt. — Fax 757-8721
www.pecos.k12.nm.us
Pecos HS — 200/9-12
PO Box 368 87552 — 505-757-4720
Michael Chavez, prin. — Fax 757-2772
Pecos MS — 200/6-8
PO Box 368 87552 — 505-757-4620
Cynthia Luna, prin. — Fax 757-2561

Penasco, Taos, Pop. 648
Penasco ISD — 600/PK-12
PO Box 520 87553 — 505-587-2230
Dorothy Sanchez, supt. — Fax 587-2513
www.penasco.k12.nm.us
Penasco HS — 200/9-12
PO Box 520 87553 — 505-587-2503
Frank Fast Wolf, prin. — Fax 587-9908
Penasco MS — 200/5-8
PO Box 520 87553 — 505-587-2503
Frank Fast Wolf, prin. — Fax 587-9910

Portales, Roosevelt, Pop. 11,078
Portales Municipal SD — 2,800/PK-12
501 S Abilene Ave 88130 — 505-356-7000
Randy Fowler, supt. — Fax 356-4377
www.portalesschools.com
Portales HS — 700/9-12
201 S Knoxville St 88130 — 505-356-5831
Melvin Nusser, prin. — Fax 356-8082
Portales JHS — 400/7-8
700 E 3rd St 88130 — 505-356-7045
Steve Harris, prin. — Fax 359-0826

Eastern New Mexico University 88130 — Post-Sec.
505-562-1011

Quemado, Catron
Quemado SD — 200/PK-12
PO Box 128 87829 — 505-773-4700
Bill Green, supt. — Fax 773-4717
www.quemadoschools.org
Quemado JSHS — 100/7-12
PO Box 128 87829 — 505-773-4645
Valerie Brea, prin. — Fax 773-4717

Questa, Taos, Pop. 1,927
Questa ISD — 500/K-12
PO Box 440 87556 — 505-586-0421
Richard Romero, supt. — Fax 586-0531
www.questa.k12.nm.us
Questa HS — 200/9-12
PO Box 529 87556 — 505-586-1604
Arlene Trujillo, prin. — Fax 586-2282
Questa JHS — 100/7-8
PO Box 529 87556 — 505-586-1604
Arlene Trujillo, prin. — Fax 586-2282

Ramah, McKinley
Gallup-McKinley County SD
Supt. — See Gallup

Ramah JSHS — 300/7-12
PO Box 849 87321 — 505-783-4211
Tim Bond, prin. — Fax 783-4261

Raton, Colfax, Pop. 7,186
Raton SD — 1,400/PK-12
PO Box 940 87740 — 505-445-9111
Bill Walz, supt. — Fax 445-5641
Raton HS — 400/9-12
1535 Tiger Cir 87740 — 505-445-3541
Mary O'Neill, prin. — Fax 445-2237
Raton MS — 300/6-8
500 S 3rd St 87740 — 505-445-9881
David Castillo, prin. — Fax 445-3682

Rehoboth, McKinley

Rehoboth Christian S — 400/K-12
PO Box 41 87322 — 505-863-4412
Ron Donkersloot, supt. — Fax 863-2185

Reserve, Catron, Pop. 353
Reserve ISD — 200/PK-12
PO Box 350 87830 — 505-533-6241
Dr. Maria Fuentes-Leas, supt. — Fax 533-6647
www.reserve.k12.nm.us/
Reserve JSHS — 100/7-12
PO Box 350 87830 — 505-533-6242
Cindy Shellhorn, prin. — Fax 533-6900

Ribera, San Miguel
West Las Vegas SD
Supt. — See Las Vegas
Valley MS — 100/6-8
HC 72 Box 205 87560 — 505-426-2581
Becky Gallegos, prin. — Fax 426-2582

Rio Rancho, Sandoval, Pop. 58,981
Rio Rancho SD — 11,900/PK-12
500 Laser Dr NE 87124 — 505-896-0667
Dr. V. Sue Cleveland, supt. — Fax 896-0662
www.rrps.net
Rio Rancho HS — 2,500/10-12
301 Loma Colorado St NE 87124 — 505-896-5600
Richard Von Ancken, prin. — Fax 896-5901
Rio Rancho Mid HS — 1,900/8-9
1600 40th St NE, — 505-891-5335
Lisa Dobson, prin. — Fax 891-1180

National American University — Post-Sec.
1601 Rio Rancho Dr SE # 200 87124 — 505-891-1111

Roswell, Chaves, Pop. 44,228
Roswell ISD — 8,200/PK-12
PO Box 1437 88202 — 505-627-2500
Michael Gottlieb, supt. — Fax 627-2512
www.risd.k12.nm.us
Berrendo MS — 400/6-8
800 Marion Richards Rd 88201 — 505-627-2775
June Wilcox, prin. — Fax 625-8248
Goddard HS — 1,200/9-12
701 E Country Club Rd 88201 — 505-627-4800
Ray Burrola, prin. — Fax 627-4853
Mesa MS — 400/6-8
1601 E Bland St 88203 — 505-627-2800
Loren Bentley, prin. — Fax 625-8263
Mountain View MS — 400/6-8
312 E Mountain View Rd 88203 — 505-627-2825
Laquita Goff, prin. — Fax 625-8260
Roswell HS — 1,300/9-12
500 W Hobbs St 88203 — 505-637-3200
Brian Shea, prin. — Fax 637-3268
Sierra MS — 400/6-8
615 S Sycamore Ave 88203 — 505-627-2850
Josie Turner, prin. — Fax 625-8283

Aladdin Beauty College — Post-Sec.
108 S Union Ave 88203 — 505-623-6331
Eastern New Mexico University — Post-Sec.
PO Box 6000 88202 — 505-624-7000
Gateway Christian S — 200/PK-12
PO Box 1642 88202 — 505-622-9710
Rick Rapp, admin. — Fax 622-9739
New Mexico Military Institute — Post-Sec.
101 W College Blvd 88201 — 800-421-5376
New Mexico Military Institute — 400/9-12
101 W College Blvd 88201 — 505-624-8023
Don Beard, prin. — Fax 624-8025

Roy, Harding, Pop. 256
Roy SD — 100/PK-12
PO Box 430 87743 — 505-485-2242
Richard Hazen, supt. — Fax 485-2497
www.roy-nm-schools.net/
Roy JSHS — 100/7-12
PO Box 430 87743 — 505-485-2242
Richard Hazen, prin. — Fax 485-2497

Ruidoso, Lincoln, Pop. 8,270
Ruidoso SD — 2,400/PK-12
200 Horton Cir 88345 — 505-257-4051
Dr. J. Charles Harrison, supt. — Fax 257-4150
www.ruidoso.k12.nm.us
Ruidoso HS — 700/9-12
200 Horton Cir 88345 — 505-258-4910
Dr. Paul Wirth, prin. — Fax 258-3516
Ruidoso MS — 400/7-8
200 Horton Cir 88345 — 505-257-7324
George Heaton, prin. — Fax 257-3946

Sierra Blanca Christian Academy — 50/K-12
PO Box 2349 88355 — 505-630-0144
Shauna Dickenson, admin. — Fax 630-0144

San Jon, Quay, Pop. 288
San Jon SD — 200/PK-12
PO Box 5 88434 — 505-576-2466
Craig Stockton, supt. — Fax 576-2772
www.sanjonschools.com/
San Jon HS — 100/9-12
PO Box 5 88434 — 505-576-2466
DeLoyce Smith, prin. — Fax 576-2772

San Jon MS — 50/6-8
PO Box 5 88434 — 505-576-2466
DeLoyce Smith, prin. — Fax 576-2772

Santa Fe, Santa Fe, Pop. 66,476

Pojoaque Valley SD — 1,900/PK-12
PO Box 3468 87501 — 505-455-2282
Toni Nolan-Trujillo, supt. — Fax 455-7152
pvs.k12.nm.us/
Pojoaque Valley HS — 700/9-12
PO Box 3468 87501 — 505-455-2234
Gloria Salazar Shuttles, prin. — Fax 455-3471
Pojoaque Valley MS — 300/7-8
PO Box 3468 87501 — 505-455-2238
Eileen Chavez, prin. — Fax 455-3392

Santa Fe SD — 12,500/PK-12
610 Alta Vista St 87505 — 505-467-2000
Dr. Gloria O. Rendon, supt. — Fax 995-3300
www.sfps.info
Alameda MS — 400/7-8
450 La Madera St 87501 — 505-467-4500
Sherry Coopwood, prin. — Fax 995-3305
Capital HS — 1,200/9-12
4851 Paseo Del Sol 87507 — 505-467-1000
Darlene Ulibarri, prin. — Fax 995-3311
Capshaw MS — 400/7-8
351 W Zia Rd 87505 — 505-467-4300
Sue Lujan, prin. — Fax 989-5439
De Vargas MS — 500/7-8
1720 Llano St 87505 — 505-467-3300
Michael Hemperley, prin. — Fax 995-3307
Ortiz MS — 700/6-8
4164 S Meadows Rd 87507 — 505-467-2300
Margo Shirley, prin. — Fax 989-5597
Santa Fe HS — 1,800/9-12
2100 Yucca St 87505 — 505-467-2400
Claudia Krause-Johnson, prin. — Fax 995-3309
SER/SFPS Career Academy — Vo/Tech
2516 Cerrillos Rd 87505 — 505-467-1900
Gloria Lopez, prin. — Fax 995-3394

Christian Life Academy — 100/K-12
121 Siringo Rd 87505 — 505-984-1001
Solomon Sedillo, prin. — Fax 988-4781
College of Santa Fe — Post-Sec.
1600 Saint Michaels Dr 87505 — 505-473-6011
Desert Academy — 200/6-12
313 Camino Alire 87501 — 505-992-8284
Dr. Charles Griffin, hdmstr. — Fax 992-8270
Institute of American Indian Arts — Post-Sec.
83 A Van Nu Po 87508 — 505-424-2311
New Mexico Academy for Science & Math — 100/6-12
7300 Old Santa Fe Trl 87505 — 505-954-4000
Fernando Multedo, hdmstr. — Fax 986-9095
New Mexico School for the Deaf — Post-Sec.
1060 Cerrillos Rd 87505 — 505-827-6739
St. John's College — Post-Sec.
1160 Camino De Cruz Blanca 87505 — 505-984-6000
St. Michael HS — 700/7-12
100 Siringo Rd 87505 — 505-983-7353
Bill Armijo Ed.D., prin. — Fax 982-8722
Santa Fe Community College — Post-Sec.
6401 S Richards Ave 87508 — 505-428-1000
Santa Fe Prep S — 300/7-12
1101 Camino De Cruz Blanca 87505 — 505-982-1829
James Leonard, hdmstr. — Fax 982-2897
Sante Fe Baptist Preparatory Academy — 50/K-12
PO Box 23528 87502 — 505-471-2834
Charles Shaw, admin. — Fax 471-0545
Sante Fe Waldorf S — 200/PK-12
26 Puesta Del Sol 87508 — 505-983-9727
Faith Yoman, prin. — Fax 983-7416
Southwest Acupuncture College — Post-Sec.
1622 Galisteo St 87505 — 505-438-8884
Southwestern College — Post-Sec.
PO Box 4788 87502 — 505-471-5756

Santa Rosa, Guadalupe, Pop. 2,637

Santa Rosa SD — 700/PK-12
344 S 4th St 88435 — 505-472-3171
Dan Flores, supt. — Fax 472-5609
www.santarosa.k12.nm.us
Santa Rosa HS — 200/9-12
717 S 3rd St 88435 — 505-472-3422
George Dodge, prin. — Fax 472-3169
Santa Rosa MS — 100/6-8
244 S 4th St 88435 — 505-472-3633
Joseph M. Salas, prin. — Fax 472-3132
Other Schools – See Anton Chico

Santa Teresa, Dona Ana, Pop. 900

Gadsden ISD — 15,400/PK-12
4950 McNutt Rd 88008 — 505-882-6200
Ron Haugen, supt. — Fax 882-6229
www.gisd.k12.nm.us
Santa Teresa HS — 1,100/9-12
100 Airport Rd 88008 — 505-589-5300
Ralph Gallegos, prin. — Fax 589-5311
Santa Teresa MS — 700/7-8
PO Box 778 88008 — 505-874-7200
Millie Williams, prin. — Fax 589-2780
Other Schools – See Anthony, Chaparral

Santo Domingo Pueblo, Sandoval, Pop. 2,866

Bernalillo SD
Supt. — See Bernalillo

Santo Domingo MS — 100/6-8
PO Box 459 87052 — 505-867-4441
Richard Torralba, prin. — Fax 867-7862

Shiprock, San Juan, Pop. 7,687

Central Consolidated SD 22 — 6,900/PK-12
PO Box 1199 87420 — 505-368-4984
Dr. Linda Besett, supt. — Fax 368-5232
www.centralschools.org/
Shiprock HS — 900/9-12
PO Box 3578 87420 — 505-368-5161
Larry DeWees, prin. — Fax 368-5796
Tse' Bit'ai MS — 500/7-8
PO Box 1703 87420 — 505-368-4741
Harry Franklin, prin. — Fax 368-5105
Other Schools – See Kirtland, Newcomb

Silver City, Grant, Pop. 10,052

Silver Consolidated SD — 3,300/PK-12
2810 N Swan St 88061 — 505-956-2000
Dick Pool, supt. — Fax 956-2039
La Plata MS — 700/6-8
3500 N Silver St 88061 — 505-956-2060
John Carter, prin. — Fax 956-2098
Silver HS — 900/9-12
3200 N Silver St 88061 — 505-388-1563
James Graham, prin. — Fax 388-2927
Other Schools – See Cliff

Agape Community Christian S — 50/K-12
1301 N Santa Rita St 88061 — 505-538-3467
Douglas Bryant, prin. — Fax 538-2906
Western New Mexico University — Post-Sec.
PO Box 680 88062 — 505-538-6011

Socorro, Socorro, Pop. 8,708

Socorro SD — 2,000/PK-12
PO Box 1157 87801 — 505-835-0300
Frank Jaramillo, supt. — Fax 835-1682
www.socorro.k12.nm.us/
Sarracino MS — 400/6-8
PO Box 1157 87801 — 505-835-0283
Charles Zimmerly, prin. — Fax 835-0360
Socorro HS — 600/9-12
PO Box 1367 87801 — 505-835-0700
Daniel Padilla, prin. — Fax 835-0704

New Mexico Institute Mining & Technology — Post-Sec.
801 Leroy Pl 87801 — 505-835-5011

Springer, Colfax, Pop. 1,265

Springer SD — 200/K-12
PO Box 308 87747 — 505-483-2402
Zita Rae Lopez, supt. — Fax 483-2387
www.springerschools.org
Miranda JHS — 100/6-8
PO Box 308 87747 — 505-483-2212
Cathie Hephner, prin. — Fax 483-5012
Springer HS — 100/9-12
PO Box 308 87747 — 505-483-2406
Secundino Esquibel, prin. — Fax 483-3970

Sunland Park, Dona Ana, Pop. 13,815

International School — Post-Sec.
141 Quinella Dr 88063 — 505-589-1414

Taos, Taos, Pop. 5,008

Taos SD — 3,000/PK-12
213 Paseo Del Canon E 87571 — 505-758-5202
Dr. Marc Space, supt. — Fax 758-5298
www.taosschools.org/
Taos HS — 1,000/9-12
134 Cervantes St 87571 — 505-751-8000
Tom Trujillo, prin. — Fax 751-8001
Taos MS — 700/6-8
235 Paseo Del Canon E 87571 — 505-737-6000
Reynaldo Quintana, prin. — Fax 737-6001

National College of Midwifery — Post-Sec.
209 State Road 240 87571 — 505-758-8914
University of New Mexico — Post-Sec.
115 Civic Plaza Dr 87571 — 505-737-6200

Tatum, Lea, Pop. 685

Tatum SD — 300/PK-12
PO Box 685 88267 — 505-398-4455
T.J. Parks, supt. — Fax 398-8220
www.tatumschools.org/
Tatum JSHS — 200/7-12
PO Box 685 88267 — 505-398-4555
L. Medlin, prin. — Fax 398-8220

Texico, Curry, Pop. 1,080

Texico SD — 500/PK-12
PO Box 237 88135 — 505-482-3801
Dr. R. L. Richards, supt. — Fax 482-3650
www.texicoschools.com
Texico HS — 200/9-12
PO Box 237 88135 — 505-482-3305
Buddy Little, prin. — Fax 482-3650
Texico MS — 100/6-8
PO Box 237 88135 — 505-482-9520
Rick Stanley, prin. — Fax 482-3650

Thoreau, McKinley

Gallup-McKinley County SD
Supt. — See Gallup

Thoreau HS — 600/9-12
PO Box 96 87323 — 505-862-7488
Monique Siedschiag, prin. — Fax 862-7742
Thoreau MS — 400/6-8
PO Box 787 87323 — 505-862-7468
Alberta Noize, prin. — Fax 862-7464

Tierra Amarilla, Rio Arriba

Chama Valley SD — 500/PK-12
PO Box 10 87575 — 505-588-7285
Manuel Valdez, supt. — Fax 588-7860
www.eschs.k12.nm.us
Escalante HS — 200/9-12
PO Box 157 87575 — 505-588-7201
Fred Trujillo, prin. — Fax 588-7911
Tierra Amarilla MS — 100/6-8
PO Box 159 87575 — 505-588-7297
Fred Trujillo, prin. — Fax 588-7021
Other Schools – See Chama

Tijeras, Bernalillo, Pop. 468

Albuquerque SD
Supt. — See Albuquerque
Roosevelt MS — 600/6-8
11799 State Highway 14 S 87059 — 505-281-3316
Lee Roy Martinez, prin. — Fax 281-5120

Tohatchi, McKinley, Pop. 661

Gallup-McKinley County SD
Supt. — See Gallup
Tohatchi HS — 500/9-12
PO Box 248 87325 — 505-733-2216
— Fax 733-2216
Tohatchi MS — 300/6-8
PO Box 322 87325 — 505-733-2555
Bart Stanley, prin. — Fax 733-2556

Truth or Consequences, Sierra, Pop. 7,116

Truth or Consequences Municipal SD — 1,600/PK-12
180 N Date St 87901 — 505-894-8150
Jim Nesbitt, supt. — Fax 894-7532
www.torc.k12.nm.us
Hot Springs HS — 400/9-12
180 N Date St 87901 — 505-894-8350
Ron Williams, prin. — Fax 894-0471
Truth or Consequences MS — 400/6-8
180 N Date St 87901 — 505-894-8380
Randy Piper, prin. — Fax 894-0606

Tucumcari, Quay, Pop. 5,564

Tucumcari SD — 1,100/PK-12
PO Box 1046 88401 — 505-461-3910
Dr. William D. Reents, supt. — Fax 461-3554
www.gorattlers.org
Tucumcari HS, 1100 S 7th St 88401 — 300/9-12
Susan Montoya, prin. — 505-461-3830
Tucumcari MS, 914 S 5th St 88401 — 300/6-8
Roberta Segura, prin. — 505-461-2310

Mesalands Community College — Post-Sec.
911 S 10th St 88401 — 505-461-4413

Tularosa, Otero, Pop. 2,861

Tularosa SD — 1,000/K-12
504 1st St 88352 — 505-585-8800
Brenda Vigil, supt. — Fax 585-4439
www.tularosa.k12.nm.us
Tularosa HS — 300/9-12
504 1st St 88352 — 505-585-8866
Pam Miller, prin. — Fax 585-8112
Tularosa MS — 300/6-8
504 1st St 88352 — 505-585-8803
Diane Baker, prin. — Fax 585-4739

Vaughn, Guadalupe, Pop. 508

Vaughn SD — 100/PK-12
PO Box 489 88353 — 505-584-2283
Lorena Garcia, supt. — Fax 584-2355
Vaughn JSHS — 50/7-12
PO Box 489 88353 — 505-584-2313
Diana White, prin. — Fax 584-2355

Wagon Mound, Mora, Pop. 359

Wagon Mound SD — 200/K-12
PO Box 158 87752 — 505-666-3000
Albert Martinez, supt. — Fax 666-9001
Wagon Mound JSHS — 100/7-12
PO Box 158 87752 — 505-666-3001
Albert Martinez, prin. — Fax 666-9001

White Sands, Dona Ana, Pop. 2,616

Las Cruces SD
Supt. — See Las Cruces
White Sands MS — 100/6-8
1 Viking St 88002 — 505-678-1064
Larry Davis, prin. — Fax 678-8515

Zuni, McKinley, Pop. 5,857

Zuni SD — 1,700/K-12
PO Box A 87327 — 505-782-5511
Dr. Kaye Peery, supt. — Fax 782-5870
www.zuni.k12.nm.us
Twin Buttes HS — 100/7-12
PO Box 680 87327 — 505-782-4446
— Fax 782-4944
Zuni HS — 400/9-12
PO Box 550 87327 — 505-782-4451
Joe Westmoreland, prin. — Fax 782-5551
Zuni MS — 300/7-8
PO Box 447 87327 — 505-782-5885
Terri Sebastian, prin. — Fax 782-4370

NEW YORK

NEW YORK EDUCATION DEPARTMENT
111 Education Building, Albany 12234-0001
Telephone 518-474-5844
Fax 518-473-4909
Website http://www.nysed.gov

Commissioner of Education   Richard Mills

NEW YORK BOARD OF REGENTS
Washington Ave, Albany 12234-0001

Chancellor   Robert Bennett

BOARDS OF COOPERATIVE EDUCATIONAL SERVICES (BOCES)

Broome-Delaware-Tioga BOCES
Dr. Joseph R. Busch, supt.   607-763-3309
435 Glenwood Rd   Fax 763-3215
Binghamton 13905
www.btboces.stier.org/
Capital Region BOCES
Barbara Nagler, supt.   518-862-4900
1031 Watervliet Shaker Rd   Fax 862-4903
Albany 12205
www.capregboces.org
Cattaraugus/Allegany/Erie/Wy BOCES
Dr. Robert Olczak, supt.   585-376-8246
1825 Windfall Rd, Olean 14760   Fax 376-8452
caew-boces.wnyric.org/
Cayuga/Onondaga BOCES
Gary Gilchrist, supt.   315-253-0361
5980 S Street Rd, Auburn 13021   Fax 252-6493
cayboces.org
Champlain Valley Educational Services
Craig King, supt.   518-561-0100
PO Box 455, Plattsburgh 12901   Fax 562-1471
www.cves.org/
Delaware/Chenango/Mdsn/Otsg BOCES
Alan Pole, supt.   607-335-1233
6678 County Road 32   Fax 334-9848
Norwich 13815
www.dcmoboces.com
Dutchess BOCES
Dr. John Pennoyer, supt.   845-486-4800
5 Boces Rd, Poughkeepsie 12601   Fax 486-4981
www.dcboces.org
Eastern Suffolk BOCES
Dr. James Mapes, supt.   631-289-2200
201 Sunrise Hwy, Patchogue 11772   Fax 289-2529
www.esboces.org/
Erie 1 BOCES
Donald Ogilvie, supt.   716-821-7000
355 Harlem Rd   Fax 821-7242
West Seneca 14224
www.erie1boces.org
Erie 2-Chautauqua-Cattaraugus BOCES
Dr. Clark Godshall, supt.   716-549-4454
8685 Erie Rd, Angola 14006   Fax 549-1758
e2ccboces.wnyric.org/
Franklin-Essex-Hamilton BOCES
David DeSantis, supt.   518-483-6420
PO Box 28, Malone 12953   Fax 483-2178
www.fehb.org/
Genesee Valley BOCES
Dr. Michael Glover, supt.   585-344-7905
80 Munson St, Le Roy 14482   Fax 658-7910
www.gvboces.org
Hamilton-Fulton-Montgomery BOCES
Dr. Geoffrey Davis, supt.   518-762-4634
PO Box 665, Johnstown 12095   Fax 762-4724
www.hfmboces.org/indexmap.html

Herkimer-Fulton-Hamilton-Otsego BOCES
Sandra Simpson, supt.   315-867-2023
352 Gros Blvd, Herkimer 13350   Fax 867-2002
www.herkimer-boces.org
Jeffrsn-Lws-Hmltn-Hrkmr-Oneida BOCES
Jack Boak, supt.   315-779-7010
20104 State Route 3   Fax 785-8300
Watertown 13601
www.boces.com/
Madison-Oneida BOCES
Jacklin Pexton, supt.   315-361-5500
PO Box 168, Verona 13478   Fax 361-5595
www.moboces.org
Monroe 1 BOCES
Dr. Michael Glover, supt.   585-383-2200
41 OConnor Rd, Fairport 14450   Fax 383-6404
www.monroe.edu/
Monroe 2 - Orleans BOCES
Dr. Joseph Marinelli, supt.   585-352-2400
3599 Big Ridge Rd   Fax 352-2442
Spencerport 14559
www.monroe2boces.org
Nassau BOCES
Dr. James D. Mapes, supt.   516-396-2200
PO Box 9195, Garden City 11530   Fax 997-8742
www.nassauboces.org
Oneida-Herkimer-Madison BOCES
Howard Mettelman, supt.   315-793-8560
PO Box 70, New Hartford 13413   Fax 793-8541
www.oneida-boces.org
Onondaga-Cortland-Madison BOCES
Dr. Jessica Cohen, supt.   315-433-2600
PO Box 4754, Syracuse 13221   Fax 434-9347
www.ocmboces.org/
Orange-Ulster BOCES
Dr. Robert Hanna, supt.   845-291-0110
53 Gibson Rd, Goshen 10924   Fax 291-0118
www.ouboces.org/
Orleans-Niagara BOCES
Dr. Clark Godshall, admin.   800-836-7510
4232 Shelby Basin Rd   Fax 798-1317
Medina 14103
www.onboces.org
Oswego BOCES
Dr. Joseph Camerino, supt.   315-963-4222
179 County Route 64   Fax 963-7131
Mexico 13114
www.oswegoboces.org/
Otsego-Delaware-Schoharie-Greene BOCES
Dr. Marie Wiles, supt.   607-652-1209
159 W Main St, Stamford 12167   Fax 652-1215
www.oncboces.org

Putnam Northern Westchester BOCES
Dr. James T. Langlois, supt.   914-248-2300
200 BOCES Dr   Fax 248-2308
Yorktown Heights 10598
www.pnwboces.org
Questar III BOCES
James Baldwin, supt.   518-477-8771
10 Empire State Blvd   Fax 477-9833
Castleton on Hudson 12033
www.questar.org/
Rockland BOCES
Dr. James Ryan, supt.   845-627-4701
65 Parrott Rd, West Nyack 10994   Fax 624-1764
www.rocklandboces.org/
St. Lawrence-Lewis BOCES
Linda Gush Ph.D., supt.   315-386-4504
PO Box 231, Canton 13617   Fax 386-2099
www.sllboces.org/
Schuyler-Chemung-Tioga BOCES
Anthony Micha, supt.   607-962-3175
9579 Vocational Dr
Painted Post 14870
www.sctboces.org
Steuben-Allegany BOCES
Anthony J. Micha, supt.   607-962-3175
9579 Vocational Dr
Painted Post 14870
www.saboces.org
Sullivan County BOCES
Dr. Martin Handler, supt.   845-292-0082
6 Wierk Ave, Liberty 12754   Fax 292-8694
www.scboces.com
Tompkins-Seneca-Tioga BOCES
Dr. Ellen A. O'Donnell, supt.   607-257-1551
555 Warren Rd, Ithaca 14850   Fax 257-2825
www.tstboces.org/
Ulster BOCES
Martin Ruglis, supt.   845-255-3040
175 State Route 32 N   Fax 255-7942
New Paltz 12561
www.ulsterboces.org/
Washington-Srtg-Warren-Hmltn-Essex BOCES
Dr. John Stoothoff, supt.   518-746-3310
1153 Burgoyne Ave Ste 2   Fax 746-3309
Fort Edward 12828
wswheboces.org/
Wayne-Finger Lakes BOCES
Dr. Joseph Marinelli, supt.   315-332-7284
131 Drumlin Ct, Newark 14513   Fax 332-7425
www.wflboces.org/wflboces/index.cfm
Westchester BOCES
Ronald Smalls, supt.   914-937-3820
17 Berkley Dr, Rye Brook 10573   Fax 937-7850
www.swboces.org/
Western Suffolk BOCES
Dr. James Mapes, supt.   631-549-4900
507 Deer Park Rd, Dix Hills 11746   Fax 423-1821
www.wsboces.org/

PUBLIC, PRIVATE AND CATHOLIC SECONDARY SCHOOLS

Accord, Ulster
Rondout Valley Central SD   2,800/K-12
PO Box 9 12404   845-687-2400
Eileen Camasso, supt.   Fax 687-9577
www.rondout.k12.ny.us
Rondout Valley HS   900/9-12
PO Box 9 12404   845-687-2400
William Cafiero, prin.   Fax 687-7665
Rondout Valley MS   1,000/5-8
PO Box 9 12404   845-687-2400
Raymond Palmer, prin.   Fax 687-8980

Adams, Jefferson, Pop. 1,631
South Jefferson Central SD
Supt. — See Adams Center
Clarke MS   6-8
11060 US Route 11 13605   315-232-4531
Tom O'Brien, prin.   Fax 232-4620
South Jefferson HS   600/9-12
11060 US Route 11 13605   315-232-4531
Karen Denny, prin.   Fax 232-3728

Adams Center, Jefferson, Pop. 1,675
South Jefferson Central SD   1,400/K-12
13180 US Route 11 13606   315-583-6104
Jamie Moesel, supt.   Fax 583-6381
www.spartanpride.org
Other Schools – See Adams

Addison, Steuben, Pop. 1,778
Addison Central SD   1,300/PK-12
1 Colwell St 14801   607-359-2244
Betsy Stiker, supt.   Fax 359-2246
www.addison.wnyric.org/
Addison JSHS   600/7-12
1 Colwell St 14801   607-359-2241
Joseph Dioguardi, prin.   Fax 359-3443

Afton, Chenango, Pop. 827
Afton Central SD   700/K-12
PO Box 5 13730   607-639-8229
Elizabeth Briggs, supt.   Fax 639-1801
www.afton.stier.us

Afton JSHS   400/6-12
PO Box 5 13730   607-639-8202
David Glover, prin.   Fax 639-8257

Airmont, Rockland, Pop. 8,635

Mesifta Beth Shraga S   100/9-12
28 Saddle River Rd,   845-356-1980
S. Feivel Mendlowitz, admin.   Fax 425-2604
Rabbinical College Beth Shraga   Post-Sec.
28 Saddle River Rd,   845-356-1980

Akron, Erie, Pop. 3,048
Akron Central SD   1,700/PK-12
47 Bloomingdale Ave 14001   585-542-5010
Ronald DeCarli, supt.   Fax 542-3863
www.akronschools.org
Akron HS   500/9-12
47 Bloomingdale Ave 14001   585-542-5030
Joseph Lucenti, prin.   Fax 542-3863
Akron MS   400/6-8
47 Bloomingdale Ave 14001   585-542-5040
Virginia Williams, prin.   Fax 542-3863

Albany, Albany, Pop. 93,919
Albany CSD 9,900/PK-12
  1 Academy Park 12207 518-462-7100
  Dr. Eva C. Joseph, supt. Fax 462-7101
  www.albanyschools.org
Abrookin Voc-Tech Center Vo/Tech
  99 Kent St 12206 518-462-7278
  Don Prozik, prin. Fax 462-7174
Albany HS 2,700/9-12
  700 Washington Ave 12203 518-454-3987
  Michael Cioffi, prin. Fax 437-0476
Hackett MS 700/7-8
  45 Delaware Ave 12202 518-462-7144
   Fax 462-7161
Livingston Magnet Academy 700/6-8
  315 Northern Blvd 12210 518-462-7154
  John Pelletier, prin. Fax 465-6530
Adult Learning Center Adult
  27 Western Ave 12203 518-462-7254
  Edwin Hotaling, prin. Fax 462-7253

South Colonie Central SD 5,800/K-12
  102 Loralee Dr 12205 518-869-3576
  Michael Marcelle, supt. Fax 869-6517
  www.southcolonieschools.org
Colonie Central HS 1,900/9-12
  1 Raider Blvd 12205 518-459-1220
  David Wetzel, prin. Fax 459-8524
Lisha Kill MS 900/5-8
  68 Waterman Ave 12205 518-456-2306
  Francis Cicozza, prin. Fax 452-8165
Sand Creek MS 1,100/5-8
  329 Sand Creek Rd 12205 518-459-1333
  David Perry, prin. Fax 459-1404

Academy of the Holy Names 200/9-12
  1075 New Scotland Rd 12208 518-489-2559
  Mary Ann Vigliante, prin. Fax 438-7368
Albany Academy 400/PK-12
  135 Academy Rd 12208 518-465-1461
  Caroline Mason, hdmstr. Fax 427-7016
Albany Academy for Girls 400/PK-12
  140 Academy Rd 12208 518-463-2201
  Caroline Mason, prin. Fax 463-5096
Albany College of Pharmacy Post-Sec.
  106 New Scotland Ave 12208 518-445-7390
Albany Law School of Union University Post-Sec.
  80 New Scotland Ave 12208 518-445-2311
Austin Beauty School Post-Sec.
  527 Central Ave 12206 518-438-7879
Bishop Maginn HS 400/9-12
  99 Slingerland St 12202 518-463-2247
  Joseph Grasso, prin. Fax 463-9880
Bryant & Stratton College Post-Sec.
  1259 Central Ave 12205 518-437-1802
Center for Natural Wellness School Post-Sec.
  3 Cerone Commercial Dr 12205 518-449-2737
Christian Brothers Academy 400/6-12
  12 Airline Dr 12205 518-452-9809
  David McGuire, prin. Fax 452-9804
College of Saint Rose Post-Sec.
  432 Western Ave 12203 518-454-5150
Doane Stuart S 300/PK-12
  799 S Pearl St 12202 518-465-5222
   Fax 465-5230
Excelsior College Post-Sec.
  7 Columbia Cir 12203 518-464-8500
La Salle S 200/6-12
  391 Western Ave 12203 518-242-4731
Maimonides Hebrew Day S 100/PK-12
  PO Box 8806 12208 518-453-9363
  Marcia Rosenfield, admin. Fax 453-9362
Maria College of Albany Post-Sec.
  700 New Scotland Ave 12208 518-438-3111
Memorial Hospital School of Nursing Post-Sec.
  600 Northern Blvd 12204 518-471-3260
Orlo School of Hair Design & Cosmetology Post-Sec.
  232 N Allen St 12206 518-459-7832
Sage College of Albany Post-Sec.
  140 New Scotland Ave 12208 518-292-1717
St. Anne Institute 100/7-12
  160 N Main Ave 12206 518-437-6661
SUNY at Albany Post-Sec.
  1400 Washington Ave 12222 518-442-3300

Albertson, Nassau, Pop. 5,166
Herricks UFD
  Supt. — See New Hyde Park
Herricks MS 1,000/6-8
  7 Hilldale Dr 11507 516-625-6463
  Joseph Leccese, prin. Fax 248-3281

Albion, Orleans, Pop. 5,839
Albion Central SD 2,700/PK-12
  324 East Ave 14411 585-589-2050
  Dr. Ada Grabowski, supt.
  www.albionk12.org/
Bergerson MS, 254 East Ave 14411 900/5-8
  Kim Houserman, prin. 585-589-2020
D'Amico MS, 302 East Ave 14411 800/9-12
  Daniel Monacelli, prin. 585-589-2040

Alden, Erie, Pop. 2,674
Alden Central SD 2,000/K-12
  13190 Park St 14004 716-937-9116
  Donald Raw, supt. Fax 937-1864
  www.alden.wnyric.org
Alden HS 700/9-12
  13190 Park St 14004 716-937-9116
  Kevin Ryan, prin. Fax 937-1740
Alden MS 500/6-8
  13250 Park St 14004 716-937-9116
  Adam Stoltman, prin. Fax 937-3563

Alexander, Genesee, Pop. 506
Alexander Central SD 1,000/K-12
  3314 Buffalo St 14005 585-591-1551
  Dick Young, supt. Fax 591-2257
  www.alexander.k12.ny.us
Alexander JSHS 500/7-12
  3314 Buffalo St 14005 585-591-1551
  Kathleen Maerten, prin. Fax 591-2257

Alexandria Bay, Jefferson, Pop. 1,093
Alexandria Central SD 700/K-12
  34 Bolton Ave 13607 315-482-9971
  Peter Morgante, supt. Fax 482-9973
Alexandria Central JSHS 300/7-12
  34 Bolton Ave 13607 315-482-5113
  Ronald Hockmuth, prin. Fax 482-9973

Alfred, Allegany, Pop. 4,530

Alfred University Post-Sec.
  1 Saxon Dr 14802 607-871-2111
Alfred Univ.-NY State Coll. of Ceramics Post-Sec.
  2 Pine St 14802 607-871-2411
SUNY College of Technology 14802 Post-Sec.
   607-587-4215

Allegany, Cattaraugus, Pop. 1,839
Allegany-Limestone Central SD 1,500/PK-12
  3131 Five Mile Rd 14706 585-375-6600
  Diane Munro, supt.
  www.alli.wnyric.org/
Allegany-Limestone HS 500/9-12
  3131 Five Mile Rd 14706 585-375-6600
  Cynthia Havers, prin. Fax 375-6630
Allegany-Limestone MS 400/6-8
  3131 Five Mile Rd 14706 585-375-6600
  Timothy McMullen, prin. Fax 375-6630

Almond, Allegany, Pop. 451
Alfred-Almond Central SD 700/K-12
  6795 State Route 21 14804 607-276-2981
  Richard Nicol, supt. Fax 276-6304
  www.aacs.wnyric.org
Alfred-Almond JSHS 400/7-12
  6795 State Route 21 14804 607-276-2961
  Richard Calkins, prin. Fax 276-6304

Amenia, Dutchess, Pop. 1,057
Northeast Central SD 900/K-12
  PO Box N 12501 845-373-4100
  Dr. Richard Johns, supt. Fax 373-4102
Webutuck MSHS 400/7-12
  194 Haight Rd 12501 845-373-4114
  Ken Sauer, prin. Fax 373-8529

Kildonan S 100/2-12
  425 Morse Hill Rd 12501 845-373-8111
   Fax 373-9793

Amherst, Erie, Pop. 45,800
Amherst Central SD 3,100/K-12
  55 Kings Hwy 14226 716-362-3000
  Dennis Ford, supt. Fax 836-2537
  amherstschools.org
Amherst Central HS 1,000/9-12
  4301 Main St 14226 716-362-8100
  Jo Ann Balazs, prin. Fax 836-4972
Amherst MS 700/6-8
  55 Kings Hwy 14226 716-362-7100
  Diane Klein, prin. Fax 836-0193

Sweet Home Central SD 3,900/PK-12
  1901 Sweet Home Rd 14228 716-250-1402
  Geoffrey M. Hicks, supt. Fax 250-1374
  www.sweethomeschools.com
Sweet Home HS 1,200/9-12
  1901 Sweet Home Rd 14228 716-250-1200
  Suzanne Thomas, prin. Fax 250-1362
Sweet Home MS 900/6-8
  4150 Maple Rd 14226 716-250-1450
  Joseph Zwack, prin. Fax 250-1490

Bryant & Stratton College Post-Sec.
  40 Hazelwood Dr 14228 716-691-0012
Daemen College Post-Sec.
  4380 Main St 14226 716-839-3600
University at Buffalo SUNY Post-Sec.
  408 Capen Hall 14260 716-645-2000

Amityville, Suffolk, Pop. 9,551
Amityville UFD 3,100/PK-12
  150 Park Ave 11701 631-598-6507
  Dr. Brian Desorbe, supt. Fax 691-4108
  www.amityville.com/School/
Amityville Memorial HS 900/9-12
  250 Merrick Rd 11701 631-598-6550
  Dr. Scott Andrews, prin. Fax 264-4489
Miles MS 700/6-8
  501 Broadway 11701 631-789-6200
  George Giberti, prin. Fax 789-1655

Island Drafting & Technical Institute Post-Sec.
  128 Broadway 11701 631-691-8733

Amsterdam, Montgomery, Pop. 17,974
Broadalbin-Perth Central SD
  Supt. — See Broadalbin
Broadalbin-Perth MS 300/7-8
  1870 County Highway 107 12010 518-954-2700
  Joseph Shannon, prin. Fax 954-2709

Greater Amsterdam SD 3,400/K-12
  11 Liberty St 12010 518-843-5217
  Ronald E. Limoncelli, supt. Fax 842-0012
  www.gasd.org
Amsterdam HS 1,200/9-12
  140 Saratoga Ave 12010 518-843-4932
  Gavin Murdoch, prin. Fax 843-5432
Lynch MS 900/6-8
  55 Brandt Pl 12010 518-843-3716
  Thomas Perillo, prin. Fax 843-6287

Perth Bible Christian Academy 100/PK-12
  1863 County Highway 107 12010 518-843-0734
  Bonnie Howard, prin. Fax 843-3304

Andes, Delaware, Pop. 278
Andes Central SD 100/K-12
  PO Box 248 13731 845-676-3167
  John Bernhardt, supt. Fax 676-3181
  www.andescentralschool.org

Andes Central S 100/K-12
  PO Box 248 13731 845-676-3166
  John Bernhardt, prin. Fax 676-3181

Andover, Allegany, Pop. 1,050
Andover Central SD 400/PK-12
  31-35 Elm St 14806 607-478-8491
  William C. Berg, supt. Fax 478-8833
Andover S 400/PK-12
  31-35 Elm St 14806 607-478-8491
  Richard McInroy, prin. Fax 478-8833

Angola, Erie, Pop. 2,227
Evans-Brant Central SD (Lake Shore) 3,200/K-12
  959 Beach Rd 14006 716-926-2201
  Jeffrey Rabey, supt. Fax 549-6407
  www.lakeshore.wnyric.org
Lake Shore Central MS 800/6-8
  8855 Erie Rd 14006 716-549-2302
  Scott Smith, prin. Fax 549-4374
Lake Shore HS 1,100/9-12
  959 Beach Rd 14006 716-549-2301
  R. Terrence Redman, prin. Fax 549-4033

Annandale on Hudson, Dutchess

Bard College 12504 Post-Sec.
   845-758-6822

Ardsley, Westchester, Pop. 4,820
Ardsley UFD 2,200/K-12
  500 Farm Rd 10502 914-693-6300
  Dr. Richard Maurer, supt. Fax 693-8340
  www.ardsleyschools.org
Ardsley HS 700/9-12
  300 Farm Rd 10502 914-693-6300
  Dr. James Haubner, prin. Fax 693-6822
Ardsley MS 700/5-8
  700 Ashford Ave 10502 914-693-7564
  Jeffrey O'Donnell, prin. Fax 693-7896

Argyle, Washington, Pop. 286
Argyle Central SD 700/K-12
  5023 State Route 40 12809 518-638-8243
  Ryan Sherman, supt. Fax 638-6373
Argyle Central HS 300/9-12
  5023 State Route 40 12809 518-638-8243
   Fax 638-6373

Arkport, Steuben, Pop. 829
Arkport Central SD 600/K-12
  35 East Ave 14807 607-295-7471
  William Locke, supt. Fax 295-7473
  www.stev.net
Arkport Central S 600/K-12
  35 East Ave 14807 607-295-9823
  Melody Troy, prin. Fax 295-7473

Armonk, Westchester, Pop. 2,745
Byram Hills Central SD 2,700/K-12
  10 Tripp Ln 10504 914-273-4082
  John Chambers, supt. Fax 273-2516
  www.byramhills.org
Byram Hills HS 700/9-12
  12 Tripp Ln 10504 914-273-9200
  Dr. William Donohue, prin. Fax 273-8099
Crittenden MS 700/6-8
  10 MacDonald Ave 10504 914-273-4250
  Dr. H. Evan Powderly, prin. Fax 273-4618

Arverne, See New York
NYC Department of Education
  Supt. — See New York
JHS 198 400/5-8
  365 Beach 56th St 11692 718-945-3300
  Angela Logan, prin. Fax 945-3303

Astoria, See New York
NYC Department of Education
  Supt. — See New York
Baccalaureate S for Global Education 200/7-9
  3412 36th Ave 11106 718-361-5275
  William Stroud, prin. Fax 361-5395
Long Island City HS 3,700/9-12
  1430 Broadway 11106 718-545-7095
  William Bassell, prin. Fax 545-2980

Learning Institute for Beauty Sciences Post-Sec.
  3815 Broadway 11103 718-726-8383
St. Demetrios S 700/PK-12
  3003 30th Dr 11102 718-728-1754
  Anastasios Koularmanis, prin. Fax 726-3482
St. John's Prep HS 1,400/9-12
  2121 Crescent St 11105 718-721-7200
  William Higgins, prin. Fax 545-9385

Athol Springs, Erie

St. Francis HS 600/9-12
  S4129 Lake Shore Rd 14010 716-627-1200
  Rev. Michael Sajda, prin. Fax 627-4610

Attica, Wyoming, Pop. 2,525
Attica Central SD 1,800/K-12
  3338 E Main Street Rd 14011 585-591-0400
  Bryce Thompson, supt. Fax 591-2681
  www.atticacsd.org
Attica HS 600/9-12
  3338 E Main Street Rd 14011 585-591-0400
  Rodney Ryan, prin. Fax 591-2681
Attica JHS 600/5-8
  3338 E Main Street Rd 14011 585-591-0400
  Shawn Williams, prin. Fax 591-2681

Auburn, Cayuga, Pop. 28,121
Auburn CSD 4,900/K-12
  78 Thornton Ave 13021 315-255-8835
  John Plume, supt. Fax 253-6068
  www.auburn.cnyric.org/
Auburn HS 1,400/9-12
  250 Lake Ave 13021 315-255-8305
  David Roth, prin. Fax 255-5876

East MS 600/6-8
191 Franklin St 13021 315-255-8484
Diane Dolcemascolo, prin. Fax 255-5910
West MS 600/6-8
217 Genesee St 13021 315-255-8543
Deborah Carey, prin. Fax 255-5910

SUNY Cayuga County Community College Post-Sec.
197 Franklin St 13021 315-255-1743

Aurora, Cayuga, Pop. 719
Southern Cayuga Central SD 1,000/K-12
2384 State Route 34B 13026 315-364-7211
Peter F. Cardamone, supt. Fax 364-7863
www.southerncayuga.org
Southern Cayuga MS 300/5-8
2384 State Route 34B 13026 315-364-7098
Karen Simon, prin. Fax 364-7863
Southern Cayuga Secondary S 400/9-12
2384 State Route 34B 13026 315-364-7111
Dennis Farnsworth, prin. Fax 364-7863

Wells College Post-Sec.
PO Box 500 13026 315-364-3266

Averill Park, Rensselaer, Pop. 1,656
Averill Park Central SD 3,500/K-12
8439 Miller Hill Rd 12018 518-674-7050
Josephine Moccia Ed.D., supt. Fax 674-3802
www.averillpark.k12.ny.us/
Algonquin MS 900/6-8
333 NY Highway 351 12018 518-674-7100
Steve Beebie, prin. Fax 674-0671
Averill Park HS 1,200/9-12
146 Gettle Rd 12018 518-674-7000
Colleen Gomes, prin. Fax 674-7046

Avoca, Steuben, Pop. 991
Avoca Central SD 700/K-12
PO Box G 14809 607-566-2221
R. Christopher Roser, supt. Fax 566-8384
www.avoca.wnyric.org
Avoca Central S 700/K-12
PO Box G 14809 607-566-2221
M. Sullivan, prin. Fax 566-8384

Avon, Livingston, Pop. 2,977
Avon Central SD 1,200/K-12
191 Clinton St 14414 585-226-2455
Bruce Amey, supt. Fax 226-8202
www.avoncsd.org
Avon HS 400/9-12
245 Clinton Street Ext 14414 585-226-2455
Christopher Salinas, prin. Fax 226-8202
Avon MS 400/5-8
191 Clinton St 14414 585-226-2455
Jennifer Miller, prin. Fax 226-8202

Babylon, Suffolk, Pop. 12,759
Babylon UFD 2,000/K-12
50 Railroad Ave 11702 631-893-7925
William Bernhard, supt. Fax 893-7935
www.babylonsd.org
Babylon JSHS 1,000/7-12
50 Railroad Ave 11702 631-893-7910
Robert Visbal, prin. Fax 893-7936

Bainbridge, Chenango, Pop. 1,349
Bainbridge-Guilford Central SD 800/K-12
18 Juliand St 13733 607-967-6321
Grayson Stevens, supt. Fax 967-4231
www.bgcsd.org
Bainbridge-Guilford HS 400/9-12
18 Juliand St 13733 607-967-6323
William Zakrajsek, prin. Fax 967-4231
Bainbridge-Guilford MS 6-8
18 Juliand St 13733 607-967-6300
Victoria Gullo, prin. Fax 967-4231

Baldwin, Nassau, Pop. 22,719
Baldwin UFD 5,200/K-12
960 Hastings St 11510 516-377-9271
Dr. Robert Britto, supt. Fax 377-9421
www.baldwin.k12.ny.us/
Baldwin HS 1,600/9-12
841 Ethel T Kloberg Dr 11510 516-377-9203
Susan Knors, prin. Fax 377-9208
Baldwin JHS 1,300/6-8
3211 Schreiber Pl 11510 516-377-9321
James Brown, prin. Fax 377-9432

Baldwinsville, Onondaga, Pop. 7,190
Baldwinsville Central SD 5,900/K-12
29 E Oneida St 13027 315-638-6043
Jeanne Dangle, supt. Fax 638-6041
www.bville.org
Baker SHS 1,300/10-12
29 E Oneida St 13027 315-638-6000
Olivia Cambs, prin. Fax 638-6150
Durgee JHS 1,000/8-9
29 E Oneida St 13027 315-638-6086
William Doughty, prin. Fax 635-3970

Ballston Spa, Saratoga, Pop. 5,565
Ballston Spa Central SD 4,500/K-12
70 Malta Ave 12020 518-884-7195
Dr. John Gratto, supt. Fax 884-7101
www.bscsd.org
Ballston Spa HS 1,300/9-12
220 Ballston Ave 12020 518-884-7150
Anthony Deblois, prin. Fax 884-7199
Ballston Spa MS 1,100/6-8
210 Ballston Ave 12020 518-884-7200
Dr. Helen Stuetzel, prin. Fax 884-7234

Bardonia, Rockland, Pop. 4,487

Albertus Magnus HS 500/9-12
798 Route 304 10954 845-623-8842
Joseph Troy, prin. Fax 623-0009

Barker, Niagara, Pop. 566
Barker Central SD 1,100/PK-12
1628 Quaker Rd 14012 716-795-3832
Steven LaRock, supt. Fax 795-3283
barkercsd.net
Barker HS 400/9-12
1628 Quaker Rd 14012 716-795-3201
John Hoar, prin. Fax 795-3911
Barker MS 400/5-8
1628 Quaker Rd 14012 716-795-3203
Cheryl Cardone, prin. Fax 795-9437

Barrytown, Dutchess

Unification Theological Seminary Post-Sec.
30 Seminary Dr 12507 845-752-3100

Batavia, Genesee, Pop. 15,939
Batavia CSD 2,600/K-12
PO Box 677 14021 585-343-2480
Richard G. Stutzman, supt. Fax 344-8204
www.bataviacsd.org
Batavia HS 800/9-12
260 State St 14020 585-343-2480
Pamela Buresch, prin. Fax 344-8609
Batavia MS 600/6-8
96 Ross St 14020 585-343-2480
Sandra Griffin, prin. Fax 344-8626

Continental School of Beauty Culture Post-Sec.
215 Main St 14020 585-344-0886
Genesee Community College Post-Sec.
1 College Rd 14020 585-343-0055
New York State School for the Blind Post-Sec.
2A Richmond Ave 14020
Notre Dame HS 200/9-12
73 Union St 14020 585-343-2783
Dr. Joseph Scanlon, prin. Fax 343-7323

Bath, Steuben, Pop. 5,574
Bath Central SD 2,000/PK-12
25 Ellis Ave 14810 607-776-3301
Marion Tunney, supt. Fax 776-5021
www.bathcsd.org
Haverling HS 700/9-12
25 Ellis Ave 14810 607-776-4107
Randy Brzezinski, prin. Fax 776-5021
Haverling MS 500/6-8
25 Ellis Ave 14810 607-776-4110
Jared Fulgoni, prin. Fax 776-5625

Bayport, Suffolk, Pop. 7,702
Bayport-Blue Point UFD 2,500/K-12
189 Academy St 11705 631-472-7860
Anthony J. Annunziato, supt. Fax 472-7817
www.b-bp.k12.ny.us
Bayport-Blue Point HS 700/9-12
200 Snedecor Ave 11705 631-472-7800
Peter Sellitto, prin. Fax 472-7814
Young MS 600/6-8
602 Sylvan Ave 11705 631-472-7820
Susan Haske, prin. Fax 472-7849

Bay Shore, Suffolk, Pop. 21,279
Bay Shore UFD 5,400/K-12
75 Perkal St 11706 631-968-1115
Evelyn Holman Ph.D., supt. Fax 968-1129
www.bayshore.k12.ny.us
Bay Shore HS 1,600/9-12
155 3rd Ave 11706 631-968-1156
Edmund Frazier, prin. Fax 968-2332
Bay Shore MS 1,400/6-8
393 Brook Ave 11706 631-968-1208
LaQuita Outlaw, prin. Fax 968-2342

Brentwood UFD
Supt. — See Brentwood
West MS, 2030 Udall Rd 11706 700/6-8
Darlene Phillips, prin. 631-434-2371

Bayside, See New York
NYC Department of Education
Supt. — See New York
Bayside HS 3,000/9-12
3224 Corporal Kennedy St 11361 718-229-7600
Judith Tarlo, prin. Fax 423-9566
JHS 158 1,100/6-9
4635 Oceania St 11361 718-423-8100
Marie Nappi, prin. Fax 423-8135

Beacon, Dutchess, Pop. 16,059
Beacon CSD 3,500/PK-12
10 Education Dr 12508 845-838-6900
Vito Di Cesare, supt. Fax 838-6905
www.beaconcityschools.org/
Beacon HS 1,000/9-12
101 Matteawan Rd 12508 845-838-6900
Edward Mancari, prin. Fax 838-0796
Rombout MS 800/6-8
84 Matteawan Rd 12508 845-838-6900
Louis Valesey, prin. Fax 838-0695

Beaver Falls, Lewis
Beaver River Central SD 1,000/K-12
PO Box 179 13305 315-346-1211
Gerald Crowell, supt. Fax 346-6775
www.brcsd.org/
Beaver River MSHS 600/6-12
PO Box 179 13305 315-346-1211
Kenneth Proulx, prin. Fax 346-6775

Bedford, Westchester, Pop. 1,828
Bedford Central SD 4,100/K-12
632 S Bedford Rd 10506 914-241-6000
Dr. Debra Jackson, supt. Fax 241-6004
www.bedford.k12.ny.us
Fox Lane HS 1,200/9-12
S Bedford Rd 10506 914-241-6085
Deborah Talbot, prin. Fax 241-6064
Fox Lane MS 900/6-8
S Bedford Rd 10506 914-241-6144
Anne Marie Berardi, prin. Fax 241-6129

Rippowam Cisqua S 200/5-9
439 Cantitoe St 10506 914-244-1250
Eileen F. Lambert, hdmstr. Fax 244-1245

Bedford Hills, Westchester, Pop. 3,200

Yeshiva & Mesivta Ohel Shmuel 50/11-12
165 Haines Rd 10507 914-241-2700
Rabbi M. Waldman, prin. Fax 666-0280

Belfast, Allegany
Belfast Central SD 400/PK-12
1 King St 14711 585-365-9940
Daniel McCarthy, supt. Fax 365-2648
www.belfast.wnyric.org
Belfast S 400/PK-12
1 King St 14711 585-365-8285
Sue Picchota, prin. Fax 365-2648

Belle Harbor, Queens

Yeshiva Merkaz Hatorah of Belle Harbor 50/9-12
505 Beach 129th St, 718-474-3064
Rabbi Levi Dicker, admin. Fax 634-4510

Bellerose, Queens, Pop. 1,161
NYC Department of Education
Supt. — See New York
HS of Teaching Liberal Arts & Science 9-12
7420 Commonwealth Blvd 11426 718-736-7100
Nigel Pugh, dir. Fax 736-7125

Belleville, Jefferson
Belleville-Henderson Central SD 600/PK-12
PO Box 158 13611 315-846-5411
Robert Ike Ed.D., supt. Fax 846-5826
Belleville-Henderson Central S 600/PK-12
PO Box 158 13611 315-846-5121
Shawn Baker, prin. Fax 846-5826

Bellmore, Nassau, Pop. 16,438
Bellmore-Merrick Central HSD
Supt. — See North Merrick
Grand Avenue MS 1,100/7-8
2301 Grand Ave 11710 516-992-1100
Lewis Serra, prin. Fax 679-5068
Kennedy HS 1,200/9-12
3000 Bellmore Ave 11710 516-992-1400
Lorraine Poppe, prin. Fax 826-0526
Mepham HS 1,300/9-12
2401 Camp Ave 11710 516-992-1500
John Didden, prin. Fax 785-7590

New Jerusalem Christian Academy 50/1-12
2658 Corner Ln 11710 516-785-0276
Alan Brandenburg, prin. Fax 785-0276

Bellport, Suffolk, Pop. 2,379
South Country Central SD
Supt. — See East Patchogue
Bellport MS 1,100/6-8
35 Kreamer St 11713 631-730-1657
Gerard Cairns, prin. Fax 286-4460

Belmont, Allegany, Pop. 912
Genesee Valley Central SD 800/PK-12
1 Jaguar Dr 14813 585-268-7900
Michael Taylor, supt. Fax 268-5012
Genesee Valley HS 200/9-12
1 Jaguar Dr 14813 585-268-7900
Mary Kay Worth, prin. Fax 268-5012
Genesee Valley MS 200/5-8
1 Jaguar Dr 14813 585-268-7900
Mary Kay Worth, prin. Fax 268-5012

Bemus Point, Chautauqua, Pop. 336
Bemus Point Central SD 900/K-12
PO Box 468 14712 716-386-2375
Albert D'Attilio, supt. Fax 386-2376
www.mghs.org
Maple Grove JSHS 500/7-12
PO Box 468 14712 716-386-2855
Edward Turkasz, prin. Fax 386-2376

Bergen, Genesee, Pop. 1,215
Byron-Bergen Central SD 1,300/K-12
6917 W Bergen Rd 14416 585-494-1220
Dr. Gregory Geer, supt. Fax 494-2613
www.bbcs.k12.ny.us
Byron-Bergen HS 400/9-12
6917 W Bergen Rd 14416 585-494-1220
David Pescrillo, prin. Fax 494-2613
Byron-Bergen MS 400/5-8
6917 W Bergen Rd 14416 585-494-1220
Daniel Bedette, prin. Fax 494-2613

Berlin, Rensselaer
Berlin Central SD 1,000/K-12
PO Box 259 12022 518-658-2690
Maria A. Diamond, supt. Fax 658-3822
www.berlincentral.org/
Berlin Central JSHS 600/6-12
PO Box 259 12022 518-658-2515
Frances DelSignore, prin. Fax 658-2535

Berne, Albany
Berne-Knox-Westerlo Central SD 1,100/K-12
1738 Helderberg Trl 12023 518-872-1293
Steven Schrade, supt. Fax 872-0341
www.bkwcsd.k12.ny.us/
Berne-Knox-Westerlo JSHS 700/6-12
1738 Helderberg Trl 12023 518-872-1482
Mary Petrilli, prin. Fax 872-0341

Bethpage, Nassau, Pop. 15,761
Bethpage UFD 3,000/K-12
10 Cherry Ave 11714 516-644-4000
Dr. Richard S. Marsh, supt. Fax 931-8783
www.bethpagecommunity.com
Bethpage HS 900/9-12
10 Cherry Ave 11714 516-644-4100
John DeTommaso, prin. Fax 937-6076

Kennedy MS | 700/6-8
500 Broadway 11714 | 516-644-4200
Kerri McCarthy, prin. | Fax 937-0540

Plainedge UFD
Supt. — See North Massapequa
Plainedge MS | 800/6-8
200 Stewart Ave 11714 | 516-992-7650
Mark Nocero, prin. | Fax 992-7645

Briarcliffe College | Post-Sec.
1055 Stewart Ave 11714 | 516-918-3600

Binghamton, Broome, Pop. 46,310
Binghamton CSD | 6,100/PK-12
PO Box 2126 13902 | 607-762-8100
Peggy J. Wozniak, supt. | Fax 762-8112
www.binghamtonschools.org
Binghamton HS | 1,700/9-12
31 Main St 13905 | 607-762-8200
Albert Penna, prin. | Fax 762-6072
East MS | 700/6-8
167 E Frederick St 13904 | 607-762-8300
Michael O'Branski, prin. | Fax 762-8398
West MS | 700/6-8
W Middle Ave 13905 | 607-763-8400
Michael Holly, prin. | Fax 763-8429

Chenango Forks Central SD | 1,900/PK-12
1 Gordon Dr 13901 | 607-648-7543
Robert Bundy Ed.D., supt. | Fax 648-7560
www.cforks.org
Chenango Forks HS | 600/9-12
1 Gordon Dr 13901 | 607-648-7544
Diane Wheeler-Busch, prin. | Fax 648-7560
Chenango Forks MS | 500/6-8
1 Gordon Dr 13901 | 607-648-7576
William Burke, prin. | Fax 648-7560

Chenango Valley Central SD | 2,000/PK-12
1160 Chenango St 13901 | 607-779-4710
Carmen Ciullo, supt. | Fax 779-8610
www.cvcsd.stier.org/
Chenango Valley HS | 600/9-12
1160 Chenango St 13901 | 607-779-4743
R. Glenn Reich, prin. | Fax 779-4777
Chenango Valley MS | 300/7-8
1160 Chenango St 13901 | 607-779-4755
David Gill, prin.

Broome Community College | Post-Sec.
907 Upper Front St 13905 | 607-778-5000
Ridley-Lowell Business & Technical Inst. | Post-Sec.
116 Front St 13905 | 607-724-2941
Seton Catholic Central HS | 500/9-12
70 Seminary Ave 13905 | 607-723-5307
Kathleen Dwyer, prin. | Fax 723-4811
SUNY at Binghamton | Post-Sec.
PO Box 6001 13902 | 607-777-2000
Triple Cities School of Beauty Culture | Post-Sec.
5 Court St 13901 | 607-722-1279

Blauvelt, Rockland, Pop. 4,838
South Orangetown Central SD | 3,300/K-12
160 Van Wyck Rd 10913 | 845-680-1050
Dr. Joseph Zambito, supt. | Fax 680-1900
www.socsd.k12.ny.us
South Orangetown MS | 800/6-8
160 Van Wyck Rd 10913 | 845-680-1100
Lynn Gorey, prin. | Fax 680-1905
Other Schools – See Orangeburg

Bloomfield, Ontario, Pop. 1,258
Bloomfield Central SD | 800/K-12
Oakmount Ave 14469 | 585-657-6121
Frederick A. Wille Ed.D., supt. | Fax 657-6060
www.bloomfieldcsd.org
Bloomfield HS | 300/9-12
Oakmount Ave 14469 | 585-657-6121
Michael Reho, prin. | Fax 657-4771
Bloomfield MS | 6-8
Oakmount Ave 14469 | 585-657-6121
Janet Starwald, prin. | Fax 657-4771

Bohemia, Suffolk, Pop. 9,556
Connetquot Central SD | 6,400/K-12
780 Ocean Ave 11716 | 631-244-2215
Alan Groveman, supt. | Fax 589-0683
www.connetquot.k12.ny.us/
Connetquot HS | 1,800/9-12
190 7th St 11716 | 631-244-2226
Gregory Murtha, prin. | Fax 244-2287
Other Schools – See Oakdale, Ronkonkoma

Boiceville, Ulster
Onteora Central SD | 2,000/K-12
PO Box 300 12412 | 845-657-8851
Justine Winters, supt. | Fax 657-8742
onteora.schoolwires.com/
Onteora HS | 700/9-12
4166 State Route 28 12412 | 845-657-2373
Barbara Ruben, prin. | Fax 657-8430
Onteora MS | 400/7-8
4166 State Route 28 12412 | 845-657-1100
Gayle Kavanagh, prin. | Fax 657-7763

Bolivar, Allegany, Pop. 1,154
Bolivar-Richburg Central SD | 1,000/PK-12
100 School St 14715 | 585-928-2561
Joseph Decerbo, supt. | Fax 928-2411
www.brcs.wnyric.org
Bolivar-Richburg JSHS | 500/6-12
100 School St 14715 | 585-928-2561
Kathleen Hill, prin. | Fax 928-1368

Bolton Landing, Warren
Bolton Central SD | 300/K-12
PO Box 120 12814 | 518-644-2400
Raymond Ciccarelli, supt. | Fax 644-2124
Bolton Central S | 300/K-12
PO Box 120 12814 | 518-644-2400
James Donahue, prin. | Fax 644-2124

Boonville, Oneida, Pop. 2,102
Adirondack Central SD | 1,500/K-12
110 Ford St 13309 | 315-942-9200
Frederick Morgan, supt. | Fax 942-5522
www.adirondackcsd.org
Adirondack HS | 500/9-12
8181 State Route 294 13309 | 315-942-9250
Eric Vernold, prin. | Fax 942-9254
Adirondack MS | 400/6-12
8181 State Route 294 13309 | 315-942-9202
Patricia Thomas, prin. | Fax 942-9211

Bradford, Schuyler
Bradford Central SD | 300/K-12
2820 State Route 226 14815 | 607-583-4616
Lynn Lyndes, supt. | Fax 583-4013
www.bradfordcsd.org/bcs/site/default.asp
Bradford Central S | 300/K-12
2820 State Route 226 14815 | 607-583-4616
Geri Furterer, prin. | Fax 583-4013

Brasher Falls, Saint Lawrence, Pop. 1,271
Brasher Falls Central SD | 1,000/PK-12
PO Box 307 13613 | 315-389-5131
Stephen Putman, supt. | Fax 389-5245
St. Lawrence Central HS | 300/9-12
PO Box 307 13613 | 315-389-5131
Lynn Roy, prin. | Fax 389-5245
St. Lawrence Central MS | 300/5-8
PO Box 307 13613 | 315-389-5131
Christoper Rose, prin. | Fax 389-5245

Brentwood, Suffolk, Pop. 55,000
Brentwood UFD | 15,100/PK-12
52 3rd Ave 11717 | 631-434-2323
Leslie Black, supt. | Fax 273-6373
www.brentwood.k12.ny.us
Brentwood Freshman Center | 1,100/9-9
33 Leahy Ave 11717 | 631-434-2541
Jose Suarez, prin.
Brentwood SHS, 2 6th Ave 11717 | 2,800/10-12
Thomas O'Brien, prin. | 631-434-2204
East MS, 70 Hilltop Dr 11717 | 1,000/6-8
Kyrie Siegel, prin. | 631-434-2473
North MS, 350 Wicks Rd 11717 | 1,000/6-8
Mae Lane, prin. | 631-434-2356
South MS, 785 Candlewood Rd 11717 | 900/6-8
Kevin McNicholas, prin. | 631-434-2341
Other Schools – See Bay Shore

Academy of St. Joseph | 400/PK-12
1725 Brentwood Rd 11717 | 631-273-2406
Katharine Ventura, prin. | Fax 231-4155
Long Island University | Post-Sec.
100 2nd Ave 11717 | 631-273-5112
SUNY Suffolk County Community College | Post-Sec.
1001 Crooked Hill Rd 11717 | 631-851-6700

Brewster, Putnam, Pop. 2,178
Brewster Central SD | 3,700/K-12
30 Farm To Market Rd 10509 | 845-279-8000
Joseph Sabatella Ed.D., supt. | Fax 279-3510
www.brewsterschools.org
Brewster HS | 1,200/9-12
50 Foggintown Rd 10509 | 845-279-5051
Matthew Byrnes, prin. | Fax 279-6730
Wells MS | 900/6-8
570 Route 312 10509 | 845-279-3702
JoAnne Januzzi, prin. | Fax 279-7634

Briarcliff Manor, Westchester, Pop. 7,906
Briarcliff Manor UFD | 1,700/K-12
45 Ingham Rd 10510 | 914-941-8880
Dr. Frances Wills, supt. | Fax 941-2177
www.briarcliffschools.org
Briarcliff Manor HS | 500/9-12
444 Pleasantville Rd 10510 | 914-769-6999
James Kaishian, prin. | Fax 769-2509
Briarcliff MS | 400/6-8
444 Pleasantville Rd 10510 | 914-769-6343
Susan Howard, prin. | Fax 769-6375

Bridgehampton, Suffolk, Pop. 1,997
Bridgehampton UFD | 200/PK-12
PO Box 3021 11932 | 631-537-0271
Dr. Dianne B. Youngblood, supt. | Fax 537-9038
www.bridgehampton.k12.ny.us/
Bridgehampton S | 200/PK-12
PO Box 3021 11932 | 631-537-0271
John Pryor, prin. | Fax 537-0443

Broadalbin, Fulton, Pop. 1,401
Broadalbin-Perth Central SD | 1,900/K-12
14 School St 12025 | 518-954-2500
Robert C. Munn, supt. | Fax 954-2509
www.bpcsd.org
Broadalbin-Perth HS | 600/9-12
100 Bridge St 12025 | 518-954-2600
Robin Blowers, prin. | Fax 954-2609
Other Schools – See Amsterdam

Brockport, Monroe, Pop. 8,097
Brockport Central SD | 4,500/K-12
40 Allen St 14420 | 585-637-1810
James Fallon, supt. | Fax 637-0165
brockport.k12.ny.us
Brockport HS | 1,500/9-12
40 Allen St 14420 | 585-637-1877
Gary Levandowski, prin. | Fax 637-1867
Oliver MS | 1,200/6-8
40 Allen St 14420 | 585-637-1860
Rob Banzer, prin. | Fax 637-1869

Cornerstone Christian Academy | 100/K-12
60 Holley St 14420 | 585-637-4540
Christopher Johnson, admin. | Fax 637-4518
SUNY College at Brockport | Post-Sec.
350 New Campus Dr 14420 | 585-395-2211

Brocton, Chautauqua, Pop. 1,516
Brocton Central SD | 700/K-12
138 W Main St 14716 | 716-792-2173
John Skahill, supt. | Fax 792-9965
www.brocton.wnyric.org/

Brocton MSHS | 400/6-12
138 W Main St 14716 | 716-792-2190
Stephen Keefe, prin. | Fax 792-2246

Bronx, See New York
NYC Department of Education
Supt. — See New York
Academy for Careers in Sports | 200/9-12
701 Saint Anns Ave 10455 | 718-993-0255
Felice Lepore, prin. | Fax 993-1567
Academy of Public Relations | 6-8
778 Forest Ave 10456
Acad for Scholarship & Entrepreneurship | 6-9
1716 Southern Blvd 10460 | 718-935-3168
Zenobia White, prin.
Accion Academy | 6-8
1970 W Farms Rd 10460 | 718-378-6744
Melinda Dore, prin. | Fax 837-8674
Addams Academic Careers HS | Vo/Tech
900 Tinton Ave 10456 | 718-292-4513
Ellen O'Grady, prin. | Fax 292-1947
Astor Collegiate Academy | 9-12
925 Astor Ave 10469 | 718-944-3419
Richard Cintron, prin. | Fax 519-1565
Belmont Preparatory HS | 600/9-12
500 E Fordham Rd 10458 | 718-733-8100
Garner Bass, prin. | Fax 295-3655
Bronx Academy of Health Careers | 9-12
800 E Gun Hill Rd 10467 | 718-881-6147
Marvia Lindsay, prin. | Fax 547-1321
Bronx Academy of Letters | 200/9-12
339 Morris Ave 10451 | 718-292-1052
Joan Sullivan, prin. | Fax 292-5765
Bronx Aerospace Academy | 200/9-12
800 E Gun Hill Rd 10467 | 718-994-7823
Barbara Kirkweg, prin. | Fax 994-4974
Bronx Center for Science & Math HS | 9-12
1363 Fulton Ave 10456 | 718-992-7089
Tom Edward, prin. | Fax 590-1052
Bronx Dance Academy | 300/6-8
3617 Bainbridge Ave 10467 | 718-515-0410
Amy Jones, prin. | Fax 515-0345
Bronx Engineering & Technology Academy | 9-12
99 Terrace View Ave 10463 | 718-563-6678
Carine Davis, prin. | Fax 563-6975
Bronx Expeditionary Learning HS | 9-12
240 E 172nd St 10457 | 718-293-9569
Talana Bradley, prin. | Fax 293-9567
Bronx Guild HS | 100/9-12
1980 Lafayette Ave 10473 | 718-597-1587
Michael Soguero, prin. | Fax 597-1371
Bronx Health Sciences HS | 9-12
750 Baychester Ave 10475 | 718-548-1349
Miriam Rivas, prin.
HS for Contemporary Arts | 9-12
800 E Gun Hill Rd 10467 | 718-653-2379
Ronald Alexander, prin. | Fax 653-2866
HS for Excellence | 200/9-10
1100 Boston Rd 10456 | 718-860-1385
Wade Fuller, prin. | Fax 860-4882
Bronx HS for Law & Community Service | 700/9-12
500 E Fordham Rd 10458 | 718-410-3430
Gail Joyner-White, prin. | Fax 295-3631
Bronx HS for Performance & Stagecraft | 9-12
1619 Boston Rd 10460 | 718-541-1038
Dr. Jesus Santiago, prin.
HS for Teaching & Professions | 500/9-12
2780 Reservoir Ave 10468 | 718-364-7400
Maxine Johnson, prin. | Fax 365-7984
HS for Violin & Dance | 9-12
1100 Boston Rd 10456 | 347-542-3700
Tanya Lippold, prin.
Bronx HS for Visual Arts | 100/9-9
50 Mercy College Pl 10462 | 718-319-5160
Dr. George York, prin. | Fax 944-3409
Bronx HS for Writing & Communication | 9-12
800 E Gun Hill Rd 10467 | 718-828-5765
Steven Chernigoff, prin.
HS of American Studies | 600/9-12
2925 Goulden Ave 10468 | 718-329-2144
Myra Luftman, prin. | Fax 329-0792
Bronx HS of Business | 700/9-12
240 E 172nd St 10457 | 718-293-7200
Enrique Lizardi, prin. | Fax 992-5760
HS of Business & Technology | 700/9-12
500 E Fordham Rd 10458 | 718-733-8100
Leonard Wolff, prin. | Fax 295-3674
HS of Computers & Technology | 9-12
800 E Gun Hill Rd 10467 | 718-798-1480
Bruce Abramowitz, prin. | Fax 798-2875
Bronx HS of Science | 2,500/9-12
75 Bronx Science Blvd 10468 | 718-817-7700
Valerie Reidy, prin. | Fax 733-7951
IS 117 | 1,000/6-8
1865 Morris Ave 10453 | 718-583-7718
Delise M. Jones, prin. | Fax 583-7658
IS 129 | 800/5-8
2055 Mapes Ave 10460 | 718-933-5976
Yvette Beasley, prin. | Fax 933-8132
IS 158 | 500/6-8
800 Home St 10456 | 718-542-1155
Marsha Elliott, prin. | Fax 589-8067
IS 174 | 1,300/5-8
456 White Plains Rd 10473 | 718-617-5293
Sharon Delaney, prin. | Fax 328-3124
IS 180 | 1,000/5-8
700 Baychester Ave 10475 | 718-904-5650
Frank Uzzo, prin. | Fax 904-5655
IS 181 | 700/5-8
800 Baychester Ave 10475 | 718-904-5600
Stephen Bennett, prin. | Fax 904-5620
IS 184 | 800/6-8
778 Forest Ave 10456 | 718-292-1684
Alejandro M. Soto, prin. | Fax 292-5801
IS 190 | 300/6-8
1550 Crotona Park E 10460 | 718-620-9423
Diana J. Santiago, prin. | Fax 620-9927
IS 192 | 1,100/6-8
650 Hollywood Ave 10465 | 718-822-5317
Jeanette Vargas, prin. | Fax 239-3124

IS 206 500/5-8
2280 Aqueduct Ave 10468 718-584-1570
David Neering, prin. Fax 584-7928

IS 219 1,400/6-8
3630 3rd Ave 10456 718-681-7093
Dominic Cipollone, prin. Fax 681-7324

IS 222 800/6-8
345 Brook Ave 10454 718-292-4474
Rose Marie Mills, prin. Fax 292-4473

IS 228 6-8
4525 Manhattan College Pkwy 10471 718-884-6673
Maria Esponda, prin. Fax 884-6775

IS 229 500/5-8
275 Harlem River Park Brg 10453 718-583-6266
Dr. Ezra Matthias, prin. Fax 583-6325

IS 232 900/6-8
1700 Macombs Rd 10453 718-583-7007
Marcella Lilley, prin. Fax 583-4864

IS 254 600/6-8
2452 Washington Ave 10458 718-220-8700
Wilfred Heymans, prin. Fax 220-4881

IS 303 300/6-8
1700 Macombs Rd 10453 718-583-5466
Patricia Bentley, prin. Fax 583-2463

IS 313 500/6-8
1600 Webster Ave 10457 718-583-1736
Lauren Wilkens, prin. Fax 299-5559

IS 318 400/7-8
1919 Prospect Ave 10457 718-294-8504
Maria Lopez, prin. Fax 901-0778

IS 339 800/6-8
1600 Webster Ave 10457 718-583-6767
Jason Levy, prin. Fax 583-0281

Bronx International Academy 200/9-10
1100 Boston Rd 10456 718-620-1053
Norma Morales, prin. Fax 620-1056

JHS 22 1,400/5-8
270 E 167th St 10456 718-681-6850
Shimon Waronker, prin. Fax 681-6895

JHS 45 1,400/6-8
2502 Lorillard Pl 10458 718-584-1660
Anna Maria Giordano, prin. Fax 584-7968

JHS 80 1,200/6-8
3202 Steuben Ave 10467 718-405-6300
Lovey Mazique-Rivera, prin. Fax 405-6324

JHS 98 600/5-8
1619 Boston Rd 10460 718-589-8200
Claralee Irobunda, prin. Fax 589-8179

JHS 113 1,800/6-8
3710 Barnes Ave 10467 718-653-2130
Angela Green, prin. Fax 547-5377

JHS 118 1,200/6-8
577 E 179th St 10457 718-584-2330
Giulia Cox, prin. Fax 364-2324

JHS 123 600/6-8
1025 Morrison Ave 10472 718-328-2105
Virginia Connelly, prin. Fax 328-8561

JHS 125 800/6-8
1111 Pugsley Ave 10472 718-822-5186
Maria Guzman, prin. Fax 239-3121

JHS 127 1,100/5-8
1560 Purdy St 10462 718-892-8600
Harry Sherman, prin. Fax 892-8300

JHS 131 1,200/5-8
885 Bolton Ave 10473 718-991-7490
Rudolph Rupnarain, prin. Fax 328-6705

JHS 135 1,300/6-8
2441 Wallace Ave 10467 718-653-1237
Elizabeth White, prin. Fax 231-2957

JHS 142 1,400/6-9
3750 Baychester Ave 10466 718-231-0100
Alan Borer, prin. Fax 231-3046

JHS 143 500/8-8
120 W 231st St 10463 718-796-8170
Frank Fasolino, prin. Fax 796-7051

JHS 144 1,200/6-8
2545 Gunther Ave 10469 718-379-7400
Katina Lotakis, prin. Fax 320-0595

JHS 145 1,500/5-8
1000 Teller Ave 10456 718-681-7219
Robert Hannibal, prin. Fax 681-6913

JHS 151 400/6-8
250 Thurman Munson Way 10451 718-292-0260
John Piazza, prin. Fax 292-5704

JHS 162 1,100/6-8
600 Saint Anns Ave 10455 718-292-0880
Maryann Manzolillo, prin. Fax 292-5735

JHS 166 1,200/5-8
250 E 164th St 10456 718-681-6334
Lauren Reiss-Meredith, prin. Fax 681-6377

Bronx Lab S 9-12
800 E Gun Hill Rd 10467 718-798-4088
Marc Sternberg, prin. Fax 798-4248

Bronx Latin S, 800 Home St 10456 6-12
Leticia Pineiro, prin. 718-542-1155

Bronx Leadership Academy 600/9-12
1710 Webster Ave 10457 718-299-4274
Kenneth Gaskins, prin. Fax 299-4707

Bronx Leadership Academy II 100/9-9
1100 Boston Rd 10456 718-842-0173
Paulette Franklin, prin. Fax 893-7368

MS 101 600/5-8
2750 Lafayette Ave 10465 718-829-6372
Kim Hampton-Hewitt, prin. Fax 829-6594

MS 273 6-8
2111 Crotona Ave 10457 718-561-1617
Deborah Cimini, prin. Fax 561-2184

MS 301 400/6-8
890 Cauldwell Ave 10456 718-585-2950
Benjamin Basile, prin. Fax 401-2567

MS 302 1,100/5-8
681 Kelly St 10455 718-292-6070
Angel Rodriguez, prin. Fax 401-2958

MS 327 6-8
580 Crotona Park S 10456 718-861-0852
Manuel Ramirez, prin. Fax 861-2750

MS 331 6-8
40 W Tremont Ave 10453 718-583-4146
John Barnes, prin. Fax 583-4292

MS 390 700/5-8
1930 Andrews Ave 10453 718-583-5502
Robert Mercedes, prin. Fax 583-5556

MS 391 1,100/6-8
2225 Webster Ave 10457 718-584-0980
Donna Raskin, prin. Fax 584-1358

MS 399 800/6-8
120 E 184th St 10468 718-584-0350
Yolanda Torres, prin. Fax 584-0730

Bronx MSHS for Medical Science 3,000/7-12
240 E 172nd St 10457 718-293-7200
William Quintana, prin. Fax 992-4129

Bronx School Law Government & Justice 400/9-12
244 E 163rd St 10451 718-410-2380
Meisha Ross-Porter, prin. Fax 329-0433

Bronx S of Law & Finance 9-12
99 Terrace View Ave 10463 718-561-0113
Evan Schwartz, prin. Fax 561-0595

Bronx Studio S 6-12
928 Simpson St 10459 718-620-7311
David Vazquez, prin. Fax 620-7326

Bronx Theatre HS 100/9-12
99 Terrace View Ave 10463 718-329-2902
Deborah Effinger, prin. Fax 329-0433

Bronx Writing Academy 6-8
270 E 167th St 10456 718-293-9048
Nick Marinacci, prin. Fax 293-9748

Business S for Entrepreneurial Studies 500/6-8
977 Fox St 10459 718-991-8489
Domingo Martinez, prin. Fax 378-3352

Childs HS 2,800/9-12
800 E Gun Hill Rd 10467 718-519-7700
Monica Ortiz-Urena, prin. Fax 547-1321

Clinton HS 4,000/9-12
100 W Mosholu Pkwy S 10468 718-543-1000
Geraldine Ambrosio, prin. Fax 548-0036

Collegiate Institute of Math & Science 9-12
925 Astor Ave 10469 718-944-3321
Estelle Hans, prin. Fax 519-1565

Columbus HS 3,200/9-12
925 Astor Ave 10469 718-944-3400
Lisa Fuentes, prin. Fax 519-1565

Community S for Social Justice 600/9-12
350 Gerard Ave 10451 718-402-8481
Sue Ann Rosch, prin. Fax 402-8650

Cruz HS of Music 9-12
2780 Reservoir Ave 10468 718-733-3781
Dr. William Rodriguez, prin. Fax 733-3865

Curie MSHS 7-12
120 W 231st St 10463 718-432-6491
Rodney Fisher, prin. Fax 432-6553

Discovery HS 100/9-12
2780 Reservoir Ave 10468 718-733-3872
Scott Goldner, prin. Fax 733-3621

Dodge Career & Technology HS Vo/Tech
2474 Crotona Ave 10458 718-584-2700
Craig Shapiro, prin. Fax 584-7490

Douglass Academy 9-12
3630 3rd Ave 10456 718-538-9726
Rahesha Amon, prin. Fax 538-9796

East Bronx Academy for the Future 9-12
1716 Southern Blvd 10460 718-861-0293
Sarah Scrogin, prin. Fax 861-8634

Eximius College Preparatory Academy 6-12
1363 Fulton Ave 10456 718-992-7154
Tammy Smith, prin. Fax 590-1081

Explorations Academy 9-12
1363 Fulton Ave 10456 718-992-7252
John Nassivera, prin. Fax 590-1058

Fordham HS for the Arts 700/9-12
500 E Fordham Rd 10458 718-733-8100
Iris Blige, prin. Fax 295-3605

Foreign Langugage Academy\Global Study 300/9-12
470 Jackson Ave 10455 718-585-4024
Leba Augone, prin. Fax 585-4239

Gateway S of Environmental Research 9-12
1980 Lafayette Ave 10473 718-918-2700
Cliff Siegel, prin. Fax 792-7983

Global Enterprise Academy 200/9-12
925 Astor Ave 10469 718-944-3548
Rick Levine, prin.

Gompers HS Vo/Tech
455 Southern Blvd 10455 718-665-0950
Joyce Kittrell, prin. Fax 292-3164

Institute for Law and Public Policy 9-12
1440 Story Ave 10473 718-935-3165
Grismaldy Laboy, prin. Fax 860-5081

International S of Liberal Arts 7-12
2780 Reservoir Ave 10468 718-562-9083
Karen Maldonado, prin. Fax 562-9369

KAPPA 800/5-8
3630 3rd Ave 10456 718-590-5455
Sheri Warren, prin. Fax 681-4266

Kappa III S, 2055 Mapes Ave 10460 5-8

Kelly HS 200/9-12
965 Longwood Ave 10459 718-860-1242
Joshua Laub, prin. Fax 860-1934

Kennedy HS 4,100/9-12
99 Terrace View Ave 10463 718-562-5500
Anthony Rotunno, prin. Fax 562-5132

Kingsbridge International Academy 9-12
2780 Reservoir Ave 10468 718-562-9157
Ronald Newlon, prin. Fax 562-9413

Leadership Institute 9-12
2255 Webster Ave 10457 718-562-9485
Ronald Gonzalez, prin. Fax 562-9585

Lehman HS 3,700/9-12
3000 E Tremont Ave 10461 718-904-4286
Robert Leder, prin. Fax 904-4285

Levin HS for Media & Communications 600/9-12
240 E 172nd St 10457 718-992-3709
Nasib Hoxha, prin. Fax 922-4170

Marble Hill HS for International Studies 600/9-12
99 Terrace View Ave 10463 718-561-0973
Iris Zucker, prin. Fax 561-5612

Metropolitan HS 9-9
1181 Intervale Ave 10459 718-991-4634
Carla Theodorou, prin.

Millenium Art Academy 9-12
1980 Lafayette Ave 10473 718-824-0978
Maxine Nodel, prin. Fax 824-0963

Morris Academy for Collaborative Studies 600/9-12
1100 Boston Rd 10456 718-542-3700
Charles Osewalt, prin. Fax 991-0117

Mott Hall Bronx HS 9-12
450 Saint Pauls Pl 10456 718-588-0918
David Tinagero, prin. Fax 588-0328

Mott Haven Village Prep HS 100/9-9
701 Saint Anns Ave 10455 718-402-0571
Ana Maldonado, prin. Fax 402-0917

MSHS 141 1,000/6-12
660 W 237th St 10463 718-796-8516
Daniella Phillips, prin. Fax 796-8657

MSHS 368 6-12
2975 Tibbett Ave 10463 718-432-4300
Rose Clunie, prin. Fax 432-4310

Neruda Academy 9-12
1980 Lafayette Ave 10473 718-918-2700
Dina Heisler, prin. Fax 823-7858

New Day Academy 6-9
800 Home St 10456 718-935-3143
Paul Schwarz, prin. Fax 714-6857

New Explorers HS 200/9-12
701 Saint Anns Ave 10455 718-993-3634
Despina Zaharakis, prin. Fax 993-3614

New Millenium Business Academy 6-8
1000 Teller Ave 10456 718-588-8308
Melody Morgan, prin. Fax 681-6913

New S for Leadership and Journalism 6-8
120 W 231st St 10463 718-601-2869
Dolores Peterson, prin. Fax 601-2867

New World HS 9-10
50 Mercy College Pl 10462 718-319-5175
Fausto Salazar, prin. Fax 319-5179

Peace & Diversity Academy 9-12
3000 E Tremont Ave 10461 718-430-6395
Andrew Turay, prin. Fax 430-6335

Pelham Preparatory Academy HS 200/9-12
925 Astor Ave 10469 718-944-3401
Jane Aronoff, prin. Fax 944-3479

Public S 721X Vo/Tech
2697 Westchester Ave 10461 718-597-6404
Dr. Ilisa Sulner, prin. Fax 829-5752

Rapport S of Career Development Vo/Tech
470 Jackson Ave 10455 718-993-5581
Dolores Cooper, prin. Fax 585-4624

Renaissance HS of Musical Theater 9-12
3000 E Tremont Ave 10461 718-430-6390
Bernardo Ascona, prin. Fax 430-6313

School for Community Research & Learning 9-12
1980 Lafayette Ave 10473 347-563-4785

School for Inquiry & Social Justice 6-8
1025 Morrison Ave 10472 718-860-4181
Andrea Cyprys, prin.

School of Performing Arts 500/5-8
977 Fox St 10459 718-589-4844
Louis Corominas, prin. Fax 589-7998

Smith HS Vo/Tech
333 E 151st St 10451 718-993-5000
Rene Cassanova, prin. Fax 292-1944

South Bronx Academy for Applied Media 6-8
778 Forest Ave 10456
Roshone Ault, prin.

South Bronx HS 300/9-12
360 E 145th St 10454 718-993-4719
Brian Rosenbloom, prin. Fax 665-2363

Sports Professions HS 9-10
50 Mercy College Pl 10462 718-319-2740
Janet Gallardo, prin. Fax 319-2744

Stevenson HS 3,000/9-12
1980 Lafayette Ave 10473 718-918-2700
Gerald Martori, prin. Fax 792-7983

Taft HS 900/9-12
240 E 172nd St 10457 718-293-7200
Lisa Luft, prin. Fax 583-8742

Truman HS 2,500/9-12
750 Baychester Ave 10475 718-904-5400
Sana Nasser, prin. Fax 904-5502

Urban Assembly Math & Science MSHS 6-12
3223 Independence Ave 10463 718-432-0537
Kenneth Baum, prin. Fax 432-0467

Urban Science Academy 5-8
1000 Teller Ave 10456 718-588-8221
Patrick Kelly, prin. Fax 588-8268

Validus Preparatory Academy 9-12
1363 Fulton Ave 10456 718-992-7210
Brady Smith, prin. Fax 590-1505

Walton HS 2,900/9-12
2780 Reservoir Ave 10468 718-364-7400
John Tornifolio, prin. Fax 295-3535

West Bronx Academy for the Future 6-12
500 E Fordham Rd 10458 718-733-8100
Wilper Morales, prin.

Young Women's Leadership Academy 7-12
601 Stickball Blvd 10473 718-409-8100
Arnette Crocker, prin. Fax 409-8185

Academy of Mt. St. Ursula 500/9-12
330 Bedford Park Blvd 10458 718-364-5353
Sr. Mary Read, prin. Fax 364-2354

All Hallows S 500/9-12
111 E 164th St 10452 718-293-4545
Sean Sullivan, prin. Fax 410-8298

Aquinas HS 800/9-12
685 E 182nd St 10457 718-367-2113
Sr. Catherine Rose Quigley, prin. Fax 295-5864

Bronx Lebanon Hospital Center Post-Sec.
1650 Grand Concourse 10457 718-518-1800

Cardinal Hayes HS 1,000/9-12
650 Grand Concourse 10451 718-292-6100
Br. Christopher Keogan, prin. Fax 292-9178

Cardinal Spellman HS 1,400/9-12
1 Cardinal Spellman Pl 10466 718-881-8000
Dr. Neil McCarthy, prin. Fax 515-6615

College of Mount Saint Vincent Post-Sec.
6301 Riverdale Ave 10471 718-405-3200

College of New Rochelle Post-Sec.
332 E 149th St 10451 718-665-1310

College of New Rochelle Post-Sec.
755 Co Op City Blvd 10475 718-320-0300

CUNY Bronx Community College Post-Sec.
W 181st And University Ave 10453 718-289-5100

CUNY Lehman College Post-Sec.
250 Bedford Park Blvd W 10468 718-960-8000

Fieldston S — 800/7-12
3901 Fieldston Rd 10471 — 718-329-7300
Dr. John Love, prin. — Fax 329-7305
Fordham Preparatory HS — 900/9-12
441 E Fordham Rd 10458 — 718-367-7500
Robert Gomprecht, prin. — Fax 367-7598
Fordham University — Post-Sec.
441 E Fordham Rd 10458 — 718-817-1000
Hostos Community College - CUNY — Post-Sec.
500 Grand Concourse 10451 — 718-518-6633
Lavelle School/Blind-Visually Impaired — Post-Sec.
E 221 St & Paulding Ave 10469
Manhattan College — Post-Sec.
4513 Manhattan College Pkwy 10471 — 718-862-8000
Mercy College — Post-Sec.
1200 Waters Pl 10461 — 718-798-8952
Monroe College — Post-Sec.
2501 Jerome Ave 10468 — 718-933-6700
Monsignor Scanlan HS — 600/9-12
915 Hutchinson River Pkwy 10465 — 718-430-0100
Sr. Marie O'Donnell, prin. — Fax 892-8845
Montefiore Medical Center — Post-Sec.
111 E 210th St 10467 — 718-920-4001
Mt. St. Michael Academy — 100/6-8
4300 Murdock Ave 10466 — 718-515-6400
Lillian Dippolito, prin. — Fax 994-7729
Mt. St. Michael Academy — 100/9-12
4300 Murdock Ave 10466 — 718-515-6400
Richard Tardalo, prin. — Fax 994-7729
New York Institute for Special Education — Post-Sec.
999 Pelham Pkwy N 10469 — 718-519-7000
Our Saviour Lutheran S — 400/PK-12
1734 Williamsbridge Rd 10461 — 718-792-5665
John C. Schmidt, prin. — Fax 409-3877
Preston HS — 500/9-12
2780 Schurz Ave 10465 — 718-863-9134
Sr. Lucille Coldrick, prin. — Fax 863-6125
St. Barnabas HS — 200/9-12
425 E 240th St 10470 — 718-325-8800
Joseph Mercora, prin. — Fax 325-8820
St. Catharine Academy — 700/9-12
2250 Williamsbridge Rd 10469 — 718-882-2882
Sr. Anne Welch, prin. — Fax 231-9099
St. Pius V HS — 200/9-12
500 Courtlandt Ave 10451 — 718-292-3636
Sr. Mary Jo Lynch, prin. — Fax 402-1704
St. Raymond Academy — 300/9-12
2380 E Tremont Ave 10462 — 718-824-4220
Sr. Mary Ann D'Antonio, prin. — Fax 829-3571
St. Raymond Boys HS — 800/9-12
2151 Saint Raymonds Ave 10462 — 718-824-5050
Br. Daniel Brenner, prin. — Fax 863-8808
Salanter Akiba Riverdale HS — 100/9-12
5900 Netherland Ave 10471 — 718-548-2727
Rabbi Tully Harcsztark, prin. — Fax 548-4400
SUNY Maritime College — Post-Sec.
6 Pennyfield Ave 10465 — 718-409-7200
Veterans Affairs Medical Center — Post-Sec.
130 W Kingsbridge Rd 10468 — 718-579-1640
Yeshiva of the Telshe Alumni — Post-Sec.
4904 Independence Ave 10471 — 718-601-3523

Bronxville, Westchester, Pop. 6,515
Bronxville UFD — 1,500/K-12
177 Pondfield Rd 10708 — 914-395-0500
David Quattrone, supt. — Fax 337-7109
www.bronxville.k12.ny.us
Bronxville HS — 400/9-12
177 Pondfield Rd 10708 — 914-395-0500
Dr. Anthony Miserandino, prin. — Fax 337-1904
Bronxville MS — 400/6-8
177 Pondfield Rd 10708 — 914-395-0500
Dr. Barry Richelsoph, prin. — Fax 337-1904

Concordia College — Post-Sec.
171 White Plains Rd 10708 — 914-337-9300
Sarah Lawrence College — Post-Sec.
1 Meadway 10708 — 914-337-0700

Brookfield, Madison
Brookfield Central SD — 300/K-12
PO Box 60 13314 — 315-899-3323
Dr. Steven Szatko, supt. — Fax 899-8902
Brookfield Central S — 300/K-12
PO Box 60 13314 — 315-899-3323
Gerard M. O'Sullivan, prin. — Fax 899-8902

Brookhaven, Suffolk, Pop. 3,118
South Country Central SD
Supt. — See East Patchogue
Bellport HS — 1,300/9-12
205 Beaver Dam Rd 11719 — 631-730-1575
Lois Etzel, prin. — Fax 286-5336

Brooklyn, See New York
NYC Department of Education
Supt. — See New York
Academy for Urban Planning — 100/9-12
400 Irving Ave 11237 — 718-381-7100
Monique A. Darrisaw, prin. — Fax 418-0314
Academy of Business & Tech - Erasmus — 800/9-12
911 Flatbush Ave 11226 — 718-282-7804
Myrna Walters, prin. — Fax 462-1890
Academy of Humanities - Erasmus — 800/9-12
911 Flatbush Ave 11226 — 718-282-8223
Dr. Richard A. Forman, prin. — Fax 462-1974
All City Leadership Academy — 200/6-12
1474 Gates Ave 11237 — 718-381-9653
E. Estevez, prin. — Fax 381-9680
Automotive HS — Vo/Tech
50 Bedford Ave 11222 — 718-218-9301
Melissa Silberman, prin. — Fax 599-4351
Banneker Academy — 9-12
77 Clinton Ave 11205 — 718-797-3702
Daryl Rock, prin. — Fax 797-3862
Barton Vocational HS — Vo/Tech
901 Classon Ave 11225 — 718-636-4900
Jacqueline Foster, prin. — Fax 857-3688
B.A.S.E. — 9-12
883 Classon Ave 11225 — 718-636-5800
Veronica Peterson, prin. — Fax 789-7279

Bedford Academy HS — 9-12
1119 Bedford Ave 11216 — 718-398-3061
George Leonard, prin. — Fax 330-0944
Boys & Girls HS — 3,500/9-12
1700 Fulton St 11213 — 718-467-1700
Spencer Holder, prin. — Fax 221-0645
Brooklyn Collegiate HS — 6-12
2021 Bergen St 11233 — 718-922-1145
Amote Sias, prin. — Fax 922-2347
Brooklyn Comprehensive Night HS — 1,100/9-12
2839 Bedford Ave 11210 — 718-434-5043
Malaika Bermiss, prin. — Fax 859-0539
HS for Civil Rights — 9-12
400 Pennsylvania Ave 11207 — 718-922-6289
Laura Gibbs, prin. — Fax 922-7253
HS for Global Citizenship — 9-12
883 Classon Ave 11225 — 718-636-5800
Brad Haggerty, prin. — Fax 857-3688
HS for Public Service — 9-12
600 Kingston Ave 11203 — 718-467-7400
Benjamin Shuldiner, prin. — Fax 604-3029
HS for Service & Learning — 9-12
911 Flatbush Ave 11226 — 718-826-1683
Leonard Kassan, prin.
HS for Youth & Community Development — 9-12
911 Flatbush Ave 11226 — 718-940-8153
Marie Prendergast, prin. — Fax 462-1890
HS of Sports Management — 9-12
2865 W 19th St 11224 — 718-946-6812
Robin Pitts, prin.
HS of Telecommunications Arts & Tech — 1,100/9-12
350 67th St 11220 — 718-759-3400
Philip Weinberg, prin. — Fax 759-3490
IS 30 — 400/6-8
415 Ovington Ave 11209 — 718-491-5684
Linda Guarneri, prin. — Fax 491-0071
IS 55 — 400/6-8
2021 Bergen St 11233 — 718-495-7736
Alma Summors, prin. — Fax 270-8725
IS 68 — 1,300/6-8
956 E 82nd St 11236 — 718-241-4800
Alex Fralin, prin. — Fax 241-5582
IS 96 — 1,300/6-9
99 Avenue P 11204 — 718-236-1344
Barry M. Fein, prin. — Fax 236-2397
IS 98 — 1,200/6-8
1401 Emmons Ave 11235 — 718-891-9005
Marian Nagler, prin. — Fax 891-3865
IS 162 — 700/6-8
1390 Willoughby Ave 11237 — 718-821-4860
Barbara DeMartino, prin. — Fax 821-1728
IS 171 — 1,100/5-8
528 Ridgewood Ave 11208 — 718-647-0111
Joan Beckman, prin. — Fax 827-5834
IS 187 — 1,100/6-8
1171 65th St 11219 — 718-236-3394
Justin Berman, prin. — Fax 236-3638
IS 211 — 1,000/6-8
1001 E 100th St 11236 — 718-251-4411
Buffie Simmons-Peart, prin. — Fax 241-2053
IS 228 — 1,300/6-8
228 Avenue S 11223 — 718-375-7635
Rose Caniglia, prin. — Fax 998-4013
IS 232 — 900/6-8
905 Winthrop St 11203 — 718-773-2662
Ingrid Thomas-Clark, prin. — Fax 953-4592
IS 234 — 1,800/6-8
1875 E 17th St 11229 — 718-645-1334
Susan Schaeffer, prin. — Fax 645-7759
IS 239 — 1,300/6-8
2401 Neptune Ave 11224 — 718-266-0814
Carol Moore, prin. — Fax 266-1693
IS 246 — 1,200/6-8
72 Veronica Pl 11226 — 718-282-5230
Bently Warrington, prin. — Fax 284-6429
IS 252 — 600/6-8
1084 Lenox Rd 11212 — 718-342-1144
Mendis Brown, prin. — Fax 485-8117
IS 271 — 600/6-8
1137 Herkimer St 11233 — 718-495-7787
Rosemarie Sinclair, prin. — Fax 495-7831
IS 275 — 400/6-8
985 Rockaway Ave 11212 — 718-495-7833
Alma Summors, prin. — Fax 495-7836
IS 281 — 1,300/6-8
8787 24th Ave 11214 — 718-996-6706
Marc Spyliopulos, prin. — Fax 996-4186
IS 285 — 1,200/6-8
5909 Beverley Rd 11203 — 718-451-2200
Edward Gentile, prin. — Fax 451-0229
IS 291 — 1,000/6-8
231 Palmetto St 11221 — 718-574-0361
Dr. Nicole Ambrosia, prin. — Fax 574-1360
IS 296 — 1,000/6-8
125 Covert St 11207 — 718-574-0288
Maria De Los Barreto, prin. — Fax 574-1368
IS 303 — 1,100/6-8
501 West Ave 11224 — 718-996-0100
Gary Ingrassia, prin. — Fax 996-3785
IS 311 — 300/6-8
590 Sheffield Ave 11207 — 718-272-8371
Gail Gaines, prin. — Fax 272-8372
IS 340 — 400/6-8
227 Sterling Pl 11238 — 718-857-5516
Gloria Dupree, prin. — Fax 230-5479
IS 347 — 400/6-8
35 Starr St 11221 — 718-821-4248
John Barbella, prin. — Fax 821-1332
IS 349 — 500/6-8
35 Starr St 11221 — 718-418-6389
Roy Parris, prin. — Fax 418-6146
IS 364 — 400/6-8
1426 Freeport Loop 11239 — 718-642-3007
Dale Kelly, prin. — Fax 642-8516
IS 381 — 500/6-8
1599 E 22nd St 11210 — 718-252-0058
Mary Harrington, prin. — Fax 252-0035
IS 383 — 1,500/5-8
1300 Greene Ave 11237 — 718-574-0390
Barbara Sanders, prin. — Fax 574-1366

IS 391 — 500/6-8
790 E New York Ave 11203 — 718-493-8920
Iris Zvi, prin. — Fax 347-3549
IS 392 — 400/5-8
104 Sutter Ave 11212 — 718-498-2491
Shirley Wheeler, prin. — Fax 346-2804
JHS 14 — 1,000/6-8
2424 Batchelder St 11235 — 718-743-0220
Ilene Agranoff, prin. — Fax 769-8632
JHS 33 — 500/6-8
70 Tompkins Ave 11206 — 718-782-9500
Marissa Burson Flateau, prin. — Fax 387-3011
JHS 49 — 500/6-8
223 Graham Ave 11206 — 718-387-7697
Claytisha Walden, prin. — Fax 302-2318
JHS 50 — 800/7-9
183 S 3rd St 11211 — 718-387-4184
Denise Jamison, prin. — Fax 302-2320
JHS 62 — 1,300/6-8
700 Cortelyou Rd 11218 — 718-941-5450
Dr. Nancy Brogan, prin. — Fax 693-7433
JHS 71 — 400/6-8
215 Heyward St 11206 — 718-302-7900
Howard Finemen, prin. — Fax 302-7979
JHS 78 — 1,500/6-8
1420 E 68th St 11234 — 718-763-4701
Jennifer Canton, prin. — Fax 251-3439
JHS 88 — 900/6-8
544 7th Ave 11215 — 718-788-4482
Allen Mitchell-Altman, prin. — Fax 768-0213
JHS 117 — 600/6-8
300 Willoughby Ave 11205 — 718-230-5400
Alander Hasty, prin. — Fax 622-3570
JHS 126 — 700/7-9
424 Leonard St 11222 — 718-782-2527
Dr. Sheldon Toback, prin. — Fax 302-2319
JHS 136 — 600/6-8
4004 4th Ave 11232 — 718-965-3331
Ronnie Block - Lyons, prin. — Fax 965-9567
JHS 166 — 900/6-8
800 Van Siclen Ave 11207 — 718-649-0765
Maria Ortega, prin. — Fax 927-2172
JHS 201 — 1,500/6-8
8100 12th Ave 11228 — 718-833-9363
Madeleine Brennan, prin. — Fax 836-1786
JHS 218 — 1,200/6-8
370 Fountain Ave 11208 — 718-647-9050
Joseph Costa, prin. — Fax 827-5839
JHS 220 — 1,400/6-8
4812 9th Ave 11220 — 718-633-8200
L. M. Witek, prin. — Fax 871-7466
JHS 223 — 800/6-8
4200 16th Ave 11204 — 718-438-0155
Gertrude Adduci, prin. — Fax 871-7477
JHS 227 — 1,400/6-8
6500 16th Ave 11204 — 718-256-8218
Brenda Champion, prin. — Fax 331-7378
JHS 240 — 1,900/6-8
2500 Nostrand Ave 11210 — 718-253-3700
Elena O'Sullivan, prin. — Fax 253-0356
JHS 258 — 700/6-8
141 Macon St 11216 — 718-398-3764
Stanley Walker, prin. — Fax 857-3422
JHS 259 — 1,400/6-8
7301 Fort Hamilton Pkwy 11228 — 718-833-1000
Janice Geary, prin. — Fax 833-3419
JHS 278 — 1,100/6-8
1925 Stuart St 11229 — 718-375-3523
Debra Garofalo, prin. — Fax 998-7324
JHS 292 — 900/6-8
300 Wyona St 11207 — 718-498-6560
Everett Hughes, prin. — Fax 345-3327
JHS 302 — 1,100/6-8
350 Linwood St 11208 — 718-647-9500
Martin Weinstein, prin. — Fax 827-3294
JHS 318 — 1,000/6-8
101 Walton St 11206 — 718-782-0589
Fortunato Rubino, prin. — Fax 384-7867
MS 2 — 1,100/6-8
655 Parkside Ave 11226 — 718-462-6992
Adrienne Spencer, prin. — Fax 284-7717
MS 51 — 900/6-8
350 5th Ave 11215 — 718-369-7603
Xavier Castelli, prin. — Fax 499-4948
MS 57 — 300/6-8
125 Stuyvesant Ave 11221 — 718-574-2357
Carolyn Brunson-Williams, prin. — Fax 453-0577
MS 61 — 1,200/6-8
400 Empire Blvd 11225 — 718-774-1002
Rhonda Taylor, prin. — Fax 467-4335
MS 113 — 700/6-8
300 Adelphi St 11205 — 718-834-6734
Khalek Kirkland, prin. — Fax 596-2802
MS 143 — 400/7-8
800 Gates Ave 11221 — 718-574-2424
L. Wade, prin. — Fax 453-0383
MS 266 — 200/7-8
62 Park Pl 11217 — 718-857-2291
Michele L. Robinson, prin. — Fax 857-2347
MS 267 — 400/7-8
800 Gates Ave 11221 — 718-574-2319
Lucile Lewis, prin. — Fax 574-2320
MS 385 — 200/7-8
125 Stuyvesant Ave 11221 — 718-602-3271
Glyn Marryshow, prin. — Fax 602-3274
MS 390 — 800/6-8
1224 Park Pl 11213 — 718-493-5445
Tyona Washington, prin. — Fax 467-4522
MS 394 — 500/6-8
188 Rochester Ave 11213 — 718-756-3164
Claudette Murray, prin. — Fax 756-3177
MS 584 — 6-8
130 Rochester Ave 11213 — 718-604-1380
Verone Kennedy, prin. — Fax 604-3678
MS for Academic and Social Excellence — 6-8
1224 Park Pl 11213
MS of the Arts — 6-8
790 E New York Ave 11203 — 718-493-8920
Susan Hobson-Ransom, prin.
MS School of Integrated Learning — 6-8
1224 Park Pl 11213 — 718-493-5445
Monique Campbell, prin. — Fax 467-4522

Brooklyn Preparatory HS 9-12
300 Willoughby Ave 11205 718-789-6126
Janet Price, prin. Fax 789-6148

Brooklyn S for Music & Theater 100/9-12
883 Classon Ave 11225 718-636-5800
K. McGuire, prin. Fax 789-7279

Brooklyn Studio S 500/9-12
8310 21st Ave 11214 718-266-5032
Martin Fiasconaro, prin. Fax 266-5093

Brooklyn Tech HS Vo/Tech
29 Fort Greene Pl 11217 718-858-5150
Dr. Lee McCaskill, prin. Fax 596-7944

Bushwick HS 1,100/9-12
400 Irving Ave 11237 718-381-7100
Ana Santiago, prin. Fax 381-1905

Bushwick HS for Social Justice 100/9-12
400 Irving Ave 11237 718-381-7100
Terry C. Byam, prin. Fax 418-0192

Canarsie HS 2,400/9-12
1600 Rockaway Pkwy 11236 718-290-8600
David Harris, prin. Fax 290-8681

Carson HS for Coastal Studies 9-12
501 West Ave 11224 718-935-3288
Joanne Pierre, prin.

Dewey HS 3,100/9-12
50 Avenue X 11223 718-373-6400
Barry Fried, prin. Fax 266-4385

Douglas Academy VII HS 9-12
226 Bristol St 11212 718-485-3789
Tamika Matheson, prin. Fax 922-2761

FDNY S for Fire & Life Safety 9-12
400 Pennsylvania Ave 11207 718-922-0389
Ray Palmer, prin. Fax 922-0593

Ft. Hamilton HS 4,400/9-12
8301 Shore Rd 11209 718-748-1537
Joann Chester, prin. Fax 836-3955

Foundations Academy 9-9
265 Ralph Ave 11233 718-452-6315
Gary Biedleman, prin. Fax 452-4291

Goldstein - Sciences HS 800/9-12
1830 Shore Blvd 11235 718-368-8500
Joseph Zaza, prin. Fax 368-8555

Grady HS Vo/Tech
25 Brighton 4th Rd 11235 718-332-5000
Stephen Jackson, prin. Fax 332-2544

Harbor HS 9-12
400 Irving Ave 11237 718-381-7100
Nathan Dudley, prin. Fax 418-0128

International Arts & Business HS 100/9-12
600 Kingston Ave 11203 718-467-7400
Leonard Trerotola, prin. Fax 604-3029

International HS at Prospect Heights 9-12
883 Classon Ave 11225 718-622-6496
Alexandra Anormaliza, prin. Fax 622-6554

Jefferson HS 1,700/9-12
400 Pennsylvania Ave 11207 718-345-1801
Varleton McDonald, prin. Fax 345-2014

Lafayette HS 1,900/9-12
2630 Benson Ave 11214 718-372-3480
Jolanta Rohloff, prin. Fax 996-6684

Lane HS 3,400/9-12
999 Jamaica Ave 11208 718-647-2100
Evan Ahern, prin. Fax 235-4877

Lincoln HS 2,700/9-12
2800 Ocean Pkwy 11235 718-372-5474
Ari Hoogenboom, prin. Fax 946-5035

Madison HS 4,000/9-12
3787 Bedford Ave 11229 718-758-7200
Joseph A. Gogliormella, prin. Fax 758-7341

Maxwell Career and Technical HS Vo/Tech
145 Pennsylvania Ave 11207 718-345-9100
Zipora Steiner, prin. Fax 345-5470

McKinney S of the Arts 800/7-12
101 Park Ave 11205 718-834-6760
Paula Holmes, prin. Fax 834-6776

Middle College HS at Medgar Evers Coll 900/9-12
1186 Carroll St 11225 718-703-5400
Dr. Michael Wiltshire, prin. Fax 703-5600

Midwood HS 3,600/9-12
2839 Bedford Ave 11210 718-724-8500
Steven Zwisohn, prin. Fax 724-8515

Mott Hall IV MS 6-8
1137 Herkimer St 11233 718-485-5240
Lajuan White, prin.

Murrow HS 3,800/9-12
1600 Avenue L 11230 718-258-9283
Anthony Lodico, prin. Fax 252-2611

New Horizons S 200/6-8
317 Hoyt St 11231 718-330-9228
Mary Lou Aranyos, dir. Fax 330-9251

New Utrecht HS 2,600/9-12
1601 80th St 11214 718-232-2500
Dr. Howard Lucks, prin. Fax 259-5526

New Voices S 400/6-8
330 18th St 11215 718-330-2230
Frank Giordano, prin. Fax 330-2239

Performing Arts & Technology HS 9-12
400 Pennsylvania Ave 11207 718-922-0762
Lottie Almonte, prin. Fax 922-0953

Prospect Heights HS 1,400/9-12
883 Classon Ave 11225 718-636-5800
Laurie B. Midgette, prin. Fax 789-7279

Robeson HS of Business/Tech Vo/Tech
150 Albany Ave 11213 718-774-0300
Ira Weston, prin. Fax 467-3692

Roosevelt HS 3,300/9-12
5800 20th Ave 11204 718-256-1346
Geri Malone, prin. Fax 232-9513

Satellite East 6-8
344 Monroe St 11216 718-624-6306
Kim Mcpherson, prin. Fax 789-4823

Satellite III S 6-8
170 Gates Ave 11238 718-789-5835
Kenyatte Reid, prin. Fax 694-5333

Satellite West MS 6-8
209 York St 11201 718-834-6774
Charles Adams, prin. Fax 834-2979

School for Democracy & Leadership 6-12
600 Kingston Ave 11203 718-771-4865
Nancy Gannon, prin. Fax 771-5847

School for Human Rights 6-12
600 Kingston Ave 11203 718-467-7400
Kevin Dotson, prin.

School for International Studies 200/9-12
284 Baltic St 11201 718-330-9390
Fred Walsh, prin. Fax 875-7522

Science & Math HS - Erasmus 500/9-12
911 Flatbush Ave 11226 718-282-8079
Melanie Johnson, prin. Fax 462-1839

Science Technology & Research HS 100/9-12
911 Flatbush Ave 11226 718-282-8223
Henrietta Coursey, prin. Fax 462-1974

Secondary S for Journalism 200/9-12
237 7th Ave 11215 718-788-1514
Abbie Reif, prin. Fax 832-0273

Secondary S for Law 300/6-9
237 7th Ave 11215 718-788-1514
Larry Woodbridge, prin. Fax 499-3947

Secondary S for Research 400/6-11
237 7th Ave 11215 718-788-1514
Jill Bloomberg, prin. Fax 832-0273

Sheepshead Bay HS 3,200/9-12
3000 Avenue X 11235 718-332-2003
Reesa Levy, prin. Fax 648-9349

South Shore HS 2,000/9-12
6565 Flatlands Ave 11236 718-531-4454
Judy Henry, prin. Fax 251-0248

Stroud MS 500/6-8
750 Classon Ave 11238 718-638-4043
Claudette Essor, prin. Fax 230-5366

Sunset Park Prep MS 6-8
4004 4th Ave 11232 718-965-3331
Lola Padin, prin. Fax 965-3330

Teachers Preparatory HS 100/9-9
226 Bristol St 11212 718-498-2605
Dr. Michael Alcoff, prin. Fax 345-8069

Tilden HS 2,100/9-12
5800 Tilden Ave 11203 718-629-4523
Diane Varano, prin. Fax 629-0165

Transit Tech HS Vo/Tech
1 Wells St 11208 718-647-5204
Mark Moskowitz, prin. Fax 647-4458

Upper Bergen Academy 6-8
80 Underhill Ave 11238 718-834-6790
Linda Patterson-Weston, prin. Fax 638-0295

Upper Ten Eyck 6-8
207 Bushwick Ave 11206 718-497-0139
Brian Walsh, prin. Fax 456-8220

Urban Assembly Academy of Business 6-12
141 Macon St 11216 718-783-4842
Clyde Cole, prin. Fax 783-4869

Urban Assembly S for Law & Justice 9-12
50 Navy St 11201 718-858-1160
Elana Karopkin, prin. Fax 834-6766

Urban Assembly S for Music & Art 9-9
49 Flatbush Avenue Ext 11201 718-858-0249
Paul Thompson, prin. Fax 858-0492

Urban Assembly S for Urban Environment 6-12
70 Tompkins Ave 11206 718-359-9037
Kourtney Boyd, prin. Fax 388-0872

Van Arsdale HS 1,200/9-12
257 N 6th St 11211 718-486-2500
Fax 486-2600

WATCH HS 9-12
400 Pennsylvania Ave 11207 718-922-0650
Kim Lawrence, prin. Fax 922-0709

Westinghouse Vo & Tech HS Vo/Tech
105 Johnson St 11201 718-625-6130
John Widlund, prin. Fax 596-9434

Williamsburg HS Architecture & Design 9-12
257 N 6th St 11211 718-388-1260
Charles Pomaro, prin. Fax 486-2600

Williamsburg Prep S 9-12
257 N 6th St 11211 718-302-3549
Kathleen Elvin, prin. Fax 302-3726

Wingate HS 1,200/9-12
600 Kingston Ave 11203 718-467-7400
Herbert Hogan, prin. Fax 604-3029

Adelphi Academy 300/PK-12
8515 Ridge Blvd 11209 718-238-3308
Rosemarie B. Ferrara, dir. Fax 238-2894

Advanced Software Analysis Post-Sec.
151 Lawrence St Fl 2 11201 718-522-9073

Al-Noor S 700/PK-12
675 4th Ave 11232 718-768-7181
Nidal Abuasi, prin. Fax 768-7088

Bais Brocha Stolin Karlin 400/PK-12
4314 10th Ave 11219 718-853-1222
Rabbi Ephraim Scherman, admin. Fax 851-0112

Bais Rochel HS 900/9-12
62 Harrison Ave 11211 718-963-9287
Leah Schorr, prin. Fax 963-9571

Bais Rochel S of Boro Park 1,500/K-12
5301 14th Ave 11219 718-438-7822
Mindy Margulies, prin. Fax 438-3153

Bais Tziporah S 400/PK-12
1449 39th St 11218 718-436-8336
Moshe Melamed, dir. Fax 436-1201

Bais Yaakov Academy 700/PK-12
1213 Elm Ave 11230 718-339-4747
Lisa Wadler, prin. Fax 998-5766

Bais Yaakov Adas Yereim 300/PK-12
563 Bedford Ave 11211 718-782-2486
D. Ausch, prin. Fax 384-5885

Bais Yaakov D'Gur HS 100/9-12
1975 51st St 11204 718-338-5600
Leah Lederman, prin. Fax 338-5974

Bais Yaakov of Adas Yereim S 300/PK-12
1169 43rd St 11219 718-435-5111
Chaya Brikman, prin. Fax 435-5446

Be'er Hagolah Institute 700/K-12
671 Louisiana Ave 11239 718-642-6800
Lillian German, prin. Fax 642-4740

Beikvei Hatzoin S 200/PK-12
31 Division Ave 11211 718-486-6363
Shaindy Gross, prin. Fax 486-6639

Beis Chaya Mushka 100/PK-12
1492 Saint Johns Pl 11213 718-756-0770
Rabbi Levi Plotkin, prin. Fax 493-9336

Belz Girls S 800/PK-12
600 McDonald Ave 11218 718-871-0500
R. Grussgott, prin. Fax 435-4456

Berkeley Carroll S 500/5-12
181 Lincoln Pl 11217 718-789-6060
Robert Vitalo, hdmstr. Fax 398-3640

Berk Trade School Post-Sec.
383 Pearl St 11201 718-625-6037

Beth Chana S 300/1-12
712 Bedford Ave 11206 718-935-1845
Rabbi Mordechai Scheiner, prin. Fax 852-4364

Beth HaMedrash Shaarei Yosher Post-Sec.
4102 16th Ave # 10 11204 718-854-2290

Beth Hamedrash Shaarei Yosher 100/9-12
4102 16th Ave 11204 718-854-2290
Rabbi Aaron Steinburg, admin. Fax 436-9045

Beth HaTalmud Rabbinical College Post-Sec.
2127 82nd St 11214 718-259-2525

Beth Jacob HS 800/9-12
4421 15th Ave 11219 718-851-2255
D. Wolf, prin. Fax 435-3736

Beth Jacob S 800/PK-12
85 Parkville Ave 11230 718-633-6555
Rabbi Michoel Levi, prin. Fax 633-2930

Beth Rivkah HS 1,800/9-12
310 Crown St 11225 718-735-0400
Chaya Lane, prin. Fax 735-0422

Bet Yaakov Ateret Torah HS 100/9-12
1649 E 13th St 11229 718-382-7002
Rebecca Weiss, prin. Fax 375-7883

Bishop Ford Central Catholic HS 800/9-12
500 19th St 11215 718-360-2500
Frank Brancato, prin. Fax 360-2595

Bishop Kearney HS 1,100/9-12
2202 60th St 11204 718-236-6363
Sr. M. Thomasine Stagnitta, prin. Fax 236-7784

Bishop Loughlin Memorial HS 900/9-12
357 Clermont Ave 11238 718-857-2700
Br. Dennis Cronin, prin. Fax 398-4227

Bnos Menachem S for Girls 300/PK-10
739 E New York Ave 11203 718-493-1100
R. Katz, prin. Fax 493-4836

Bnos Yaakov Education Center 50/1-12
62 Harrison Ave 11211 718-387-7905
Gitty Lichtman, prin. Fax 387-7124

Bnos Yaakov of Boro Park 900/PK-12
1402 40th St 11218 718-851-0316
Yehudis Weiser, dean Fax 436-7280

Bnos Yaakov S for Girls 600/1-12
62 Harrison Ave 11211 718-387-7905
Rivka Levy, prin. Fax 387-7124

Bnos Yisroel Viznitz S 700/PK-12
12 Franklin Ave 11211 718-330-0222
Eva Rozman, prin. Fax 858-7387

Bnos Zion of Bobov 1,400/PK-12
5000 14th Ave 11219 718-438-3080
Rabbi Moshe Zenwirth, admin. Fax 438-3144

Bobover Yeshiva Bnei Zion S 50/6-8
1533 48th St 11219 718-435-8033
Rabbi Shlomo Kessler, prin. Fax 972-5305

Boricua College Post-Sec.
186 N 6th St 11211 718-782-2200

Brooklyn Amity S 100/K-12
2727 Coney Island Ave 11235 718-891-6100

Brooklyn Friends S 500/PK-12
375 Pearl St 11201 718-852-1029
Michael Nill, hdmstr. Fax 643-4868

Brooklyn Hospital Post-Sec.
121 Dekalb Ave 11201 718-250-8005

Brooklyn Law School Post-Sec.
250 Joralemon St 11201 718-780-7906

Career & Educational Consultants Post-Sec.
270 Flatbush Avenue Ext 11201 718-858-8500

Career Institute of Health & Technology Post-Sec.
340 Flatbush Avenue Ext 11201 718-422-1212

Central Yeshiva Tomchei Tmimim Lubavitz Post-Sec.
841 Ocean Pkwy 11230 718-434-0784

Centurion Professional Training Post-Sec.
2619 E 16th St 11235 718-646-4507

Charles Stuart School of Locksmithing Post-Sec.
1420 Kings Hwy 11229 718-339-2640

Cheder S 500/PK-12
129 Elmwood Ave 11230 718-252-6333
Rabbi Mayer Gutfreund, prin. Fax 252-4574

Christian Heritage Academy 300/PK-12
1100 E 42nd St 11210 718-377-9406
Albert Delmadge, hdmstr. Fax 338-9870

College of New Rochelle Post-Sec.
1368 Fulton St 11216 718-638-2500

CUNY Brooklyn College Post-Sec.
2900 Bedford Ave 11210 718-951-5000

CUNY Kingsborough Community College Post-Sec.
2001 Oriental Blvd 11235 718-368-5000

CUNY Medgar Evers College Post-Sec.
1650 Bedford Ave 11225 718-270-4900

Darkei Noam Rabbinical College Post-Sec.
2822 Avenue J 11210 718-338-6464

Educational Institute Oholei Torah 100/9-12
667 Eastern Pkwy 11213 718-363-0019
Rabbi Zushe Wilhelm, prin. Fax 363-1779

Followers of Jesus S 100/1-12
3065 Atlantic Ave 11208 718-235-5493
James Gochnauer, prin. Fax 477-7274

Fontbonne Hall Academy 500/9-12
9901 Shore Rd 11209 718-748-2244
Sr. Anne Clancy, prin. Fax 745-3841

Franklin Career Institute Post-Sec.
5323 5th Ave 11220 718-535-3333

Gamla College Post-Sec.
1213 Elm Ave 11230 718-339-4747

Gerer Mesivta Bais Yisroel 50/9-12
5407 16th Ave 11204 718-854-8777
Rabbi Dovid Olewski, prin. Fax 851-1265

Hair Design Institute at Fifth Avenue Post-Sec.
6711 5th Ave 11220 718-745-1000

Harma Religious Institute Yeshiva HS 200/12-12
30 Lancaster Ave 11223 718-743-3141
Rabbi Hanania Elbaz, dean Fax 743-7990

Institute of Design and Construction Post-Sec.
141 Willoughby St 11201 718-855-3661

Kehilath Yakov Rabbinical Seminary Post-Sec.
206 Wilson St 11211 718-963-1212

Learning Institute for Beauty Sciences Post-Sec.
2384 86th St 11214 718-373-2400
Long Island College Hospital Post-Sec.
397 Hicks St 11201 718-780-1953
Long Island University-Brooklyn Campus Post-Sec.
1 University Plz 11201 718-488-1000
Machon Bais Yaakov S 400/9-12
1683 42nd St 11204 718-972-7900
Rabbi Moshe Yanofsky, prin. Fax 633-4636
Machzikei Hadath Rabbinical College Post-Sec.
5407 16th Ave 11204 718-854-8777
Magen David Yeshiva HS 500/9-12
7801 Bay Pkwy 11214 718-331-4002
Norman Fisher, prin. Fax 331-2174
Masores Bais Yaakov S 500/PK-12
1395 Ocean Ave 11230 718-692-2424
Joseph Gelman, prin. Fax 692-3162
McAuley HS 300/9-12
710 E 37th St 11203 718-462-7282
Sr. Margaret Lake, prin. Fax 462-7284
Merkaz Bnos - Business School Post-Sec.
2115 Benson Ave 11214 718-234-4000
Merkaz Bnos HS 100/9-12
1400 W 6th St 11204 718-259-5600
Rabbi Chaim Waldman, dir. Fax 259-8024
Mesifta V'Yoel Moshei S 600/9-12
960 49th St 11219 718-438-7109
Rabbi Roseburg, prin.
Mesivta Eastern Parkway Rabbinical Sem. Post-Sec.
510 Dahill Rd 11218 718-438-1002
Mesivta Eitz Chaim S 300/9-12
1577 48th St 11219 718-438-2018
Rabbi Israel Licht, prin. Fax 871-9031
Mesivta Imrei Yosef Spinka 400/9-12
1460 56th St 11219 718-851-1600
Rabbi Aaron Weiss, prin. Fax 851-2915
Mesivta Lev Bonim 100/9-12
8700 Avenue K 11236 718-444-5996
Rabbi Yisroel Pearl, prin. Fax 209-0608
Mesivta Nachlas Yakov of Adas Yereim 100/9-12
185 Wilson St 11211 718-388-1751
Laslo Goldberger, prin. Fax 388-3531
Mesivta of Manhattan Beach 100/9-12
59 W End Ave 11235 718-368-1333
Rabbi Chaim Zelikovitz, prin. Fax 368-1969
Mesivta of Sea Gate 50/9-12
3803 Nautilus Ave 11224 718-449-6544
Rabbi Jonathan Tendler, prin. Fax 449-6544
Mesivta Rabbi Chaim Berlin 200/9-12
1585 Coney Island Ave 11230 718-377-8400
Rabbi Yaakov Shulman, prin. Fax 377-5883
Mesivta Tiferes Elimelech S 50/9-12
4407 12th Ave 11219 718-854-3062
Rabbi Yosef Tisser, prin. Fax 854-3062
Mesivta Torah Vodaath Seminary Post-Sec.
425 E 9th St 11218 718-941-8000
Mesivta Veretzky 100/9-12
1102 Avenue L 11230 718-252-7777
Rabbi Efraim Nussbaum, prin. Fax 252-7808
Mesivta Zichron Eliezer S 100/9-12
1543 E 9th St 11230 718-336-9629
Rabbi Zelig Friedman, prin. Fax 377-1408
Mikdash Melech Mechina HS 50/9-12
1918 E 8th St 11223 718-339-4373
Rabbi Moshe Benzecry, prin. Fax 998-9321
Mirrer Yeshiva Central Institute Post-Sec.
1795 Ocean Pkwy 11223 718-645-0536
Mirrer Yeshiva Mesivta HS 200/9-12
1795 Ocean Pkwy 11223 718-375-0771
Rabbi Dovid Rockove, prin. Fax 375-6342
Mosdos Chasidei Square 400/K-12
1373 43rd St 11219 718-436-2550
Moshe Melamid, admin. Fax 436-2658
Nazareth Regional HS 600/9-12
475 E 57th St 11203 718-763-1100
Dr. Robert Muccigrosso, prin. Fax 629-5382
Nefesh Academy 300/PK-12
2005 E 17th St 11229 718-627-4463
Sandra Newhouse, prin. Fax 645-8755
New Vistas Academy 300/PK-12
3321 Glenwood Rd 11210 718-421-1786
Helene Hamilton, prin. Fax 282-9089
New York City College of Technology CUNY Post-Sec.
300 Jay St 11201 718-260-5000
New York Methodist Hospital Post-Sec.
506 6th St 11215 718-780-3706
Northside Catholic Academy - Mt. Carmel 100/6-8
10 Withers St 11211 718-782-1110
Beverly Mulqueen, prin. Fax 782-1110
Packer Collegiate Institute 900/PK-12
170 Joralemon St 11201 718-250-0222
Fax 250-0271
Poly Prep Country Day S 800/5-12
9216 7th Ave 11228 718-836-9800
David B. Harman, prin. Fax 921-5112
Polytechnic University Post-Sec.
6 Metrotech Ctr 11201 718-260-3600
Pratt Institute Post-Sec.
200 Willoughby Ave 11205 718-636-3600
Prospect Park Bnos Leah HS 400/9-12
1601 Avenue R 11229 718-376-3337
Zlata Press, prin. Fax 376-4497
Rabbinical Academy Mesivta Rabbi Chaim Post-Sec.
1605 Coney Island Ave 11230 718-377-0777
Rabbinical Coll. Bobovr Yeshiva Bnei Zn. Post-Sec.
1577 48th St 11219 718-438-2018
Rabbinical Coll. Ch' San Sofer of NY Post-Sec.
1876 50th St 11204 718-236-1171
Rabbinical College of Ohr Shimon Yisroel Post-Sec.
215 Hewes St 11211 718-855-4092
Rabbinical Seminary Adas Yereim Post-Sec.
185 Wilson St 11211 718-388-1751
Rabbinical Seminary M'Kor Chaim Post-Sec.
1571 55th St 11219 718-851-0183
St. Ann's S 1,000/PK-12
129 Pierrepont St 11201 718-522-1660
Dr. Larry Weiss, prin. Fax 522-2599
St. Edmund Prep HS 600/9-12
2474 Ocean Ave 11229 718-743-6100
John Lorenzetti, prin. Fax 743-5243
St. Francis College Post-Sec.
180 Remsen St 11201 718-522-2300

St. Joseph HS 300/9-12
80 Willoughby St 11201 718-624-3618
Sr. Eugenia Calabrese, prin. Fax 624-2792
St. Joseph's College Post-Sec.
245 Clinton Ave 11205 718-636-6800
St. Saviour HS 300/9-12
588 6th St 11215 718-768-4406
Sr. Valeria Belanger, prin. Fax 369-2688
Shulamith Girls S 200/9-12
1277 E 14th St 11230 718-338-7154
Dr. Susan Katz, prin. Fax 258-9626
Sinai Academy 100/9-12
2025 79th St 11214 718-256-7400
Rabbi Moshe Silber, prin. Fax 256-7786
Soille Bais Yaakov HS 100/9-12
2600 Ocean Ave 11229 718-769-8160
Sora Bulka, prin. Fax 769-8640
SUNY Health Science Center Post-Sec.
450 Clarkson Ave 11203 718-270-1000
Talmudical Seminary Oholei Torah Post-Sec.
667 Eastern Pkwy 11213 718-774-5050
Talmud Torah Imrei Chaim 700/PK-12
1824 53rd St 11204 718-234-2000
Mayer Taub, admin. Fax 236-0970
Tomer Dvora HS 300/9-12
5801 16th Ave 11204 718-633-4125
Rivkah Taub, prin. Fax 633-3529
Torah Academy HS of Brooklyn 100/9-12
2066 E 9th St 11223 718-339-8844
Rabbi Avi Davidowitz, prin. Fax 339-9701
Torah Temimah Talmudical Seminary Post-Sec.
507 Ocean Pkwy 11218 718-853-8500
United Lubavitcher Yeshiva 100/9-12
PO Box 130347 11213 718-735-6607
Rabbi Menachem Minsky, prin. Fax 778-7161
United Talmudical Academy 50/4-9
82 Lee Ave 11211 718-963-9260
Rabbi Skaist, prin. Fax 963-2172
United Talmudical Academy 400/7-9
1346 53rd St 11219 718-438-7038
Rabbi Chaim Rubin, prin.
United Talmudical Seminary Post-Sec.
82 Lee Ave 11211 718-963-9770
Xaverian HS 1,300/9-12
7100 Shore Rd 11209 718-836-7100
Dr. Joseph Marino, prin. Fax 836-7114
Yeshiva Ahavas Yisroel 50/K-12
2 Lee Ave 11211 718-388-0848
Shlomo Levine, dir. Fax 628-2545
Yeshiva and Kollel Harbotzas Torah Post-Sec.
1049 E 15th St 11230 718-692-0208
Yeshiva & Mesivta Torah Temimah 1,000/K-12
555 Ocean Pkwy 11218 718-853-8500
Rabbi Yisroel Hisiger, prin. Fax 438-5779
Yeshiva & Mesivta V'Yoel Moshe D'Satmar 100/9-12
960 49th St 11219 718-854-5391
Rabbi Y.N. Berger, prin.
Yeshiva Bais Yitzchok D'Spinka 500/PK-12
575 Bedford Ave 11211 718-387-4597
Rabbi Zalman Horowitz, dean Fax 486-6645
Yeshiva Beis Meir 200/9-12
1327 38th St 11218 718-437-5844
Rabbi M. Goldberg, prin. Fax 437-4883
Yeshiva Bnai Yesucher Ber 50/9-12
467 Bedford Ave 11211 718-387-0141
Joseph Deutsch, dir. Fax 384-6691
Yeshiva Chanoch Lenaar 100/8-12
876 Eastern Pkwy 11213 718-774-8456
Rabbi Raphael Jaworowski, prin. Fax 493-2424
Yeshiva Chatzar Hakodesh 700/PK-12
1420 50th St 11219 718-436-1248
Shlomo Waldman, dir. Fax 853-8893
Yeshiva Chemdas Yisroel Kerem 50/10-12
1149 38th St 11218 718-437-7665
Rabbi Yosef Meisels, prin. Fax 437-4946
Yeshiva Congregation Toras Yufa S 100/10-10
1056 54th St 11219 718-436-5683
Yeshiva Derech Chaim Post-Sec.
1573 39th St 11218 718-438-5476
Yeshiva Gedolah Bais Yisroel Post-Sec.
2002 Avenue J 11210 718-258-7400
Yeshiva Gedolah Bais Yisroel 50/9-12
2002 Avenue J 11210 718-258-7400
Rabbi Yehuda Mintz, prin. Fax 258-2394
Yeshiva Gedolah Imrei Yosef D'Spinka Post-Sec.
1460 56th St 11219 718-972-1989
Yeshiva Gedolah of Midwood 100/11-12
201 Avenue F 11218 718-853-2400
Rabbi Chaim Pachtman, prin. Fax 853-7826
Yeshivah of Flatbush Braverman HS 800/9-12
1609 Avenue J 11230 718-377-1100
Rabbi Ronald Levy, prin. Fax 258-0933
Yeshiva Karlin Stolin Post-Sec.
1818 54th St 11204 718-232-7800
Yeshiva Ketana Toldos Yaakov 300/9-12
87 Heyward St 11206 718-852-0502
Rabbi Shimon Biston, prin. Fax 852-0512
Yeshiva Machzikei Hadas Belz 500/PK-12
1601 42nd St 11204 718-436-4445
Rabbi Aharon Friedman, dir. Fax 435-9046
Yeshiva Mesivta Arugath Habosem 400/K-12
40 Lynch St 11206 718-237-4500
Rabbi Sholom Taub, prin. Fax 237-6064
Yeshiva Mesivta Karlin Stolin 400/PK-12
1818 54th St 11204 718-232-7800
Rabbi Dovid Stein, admin. Fax 331-4833
Yeshiva Mesivta Rabbi Shlomo Kluger 500/K-12
1876 50th St 11204 718-236-1171
Rabbi Mayer Weinberger, dir. Fax 236-1119
Yeshiva Mesivta Tiferes Yisroel S 400/K-12
1271 E 35th St 11210 718-258-9006
David Schonbrun, prin. Fax 258-9055
Yeshiva Mesivta Torah Vodaath 700/K-12
425 E 9th St 11218 718-941-8000
Chaim Schilit, prin. Fax 941-8032
Yeshiva Minchas Eluzar S 50/9-12
4706 14th Ave 11219 718-972-2741
Rabbi Joshua Horowitz, prin.
Yeshiva M'Kor Chaim 50/9-12
1571 55th St 11219 718-851-0183
Rabbi Simcha Paler, prin. Fax 853-2967

Yeshiva Nesivos Chaim 100/9-12
221 Avenue F 11218 718-633-4760
Rabbi Yaakov Haltern, admin. Fax 633-2468
Yeshiva Novominsk Post-Sec.
1569 47th St 11219 718-438-2727
Yeshiva of Brooklyn-Girls 1,000/PK-12
1470 Ocean Pkwy 11230 718-376-3775
G. Bresler, prin. Fax 376-4280
Yeshiva of Nitra Rabbinical College Post-Sec.
194 Division Ave 11211 718-387-0422
Yeshiva Ohr Eliezer 100/6-12
511 Avenue R 11223 718-336-2898
Sharon Hagler, prin. Fax 336-3583
Yeshiva Ohr Hatorah 50/9-12
5822 11th Ave 11219 718-851-7956
Rabbi David Eichenstein, dir.
Yeshivas Boyan Tiferes Mordechai Shlomo 400/PK-12
1205 44th St 11219 718-435-6060
Rabbi David Endzweig, admin. Fax 435-4060
Yeshiva Shir Chodosh 50/9-10
5014 16th Ave #195 11204 718-744-4510
Rabbi Yehuda Langsam, prin. Fax 854-9436
Yeshivas Novominsk-Kol Yehuda 200/9-12
1569 47th St 11219 718-438-2727
Rabbi Shlomo Spira, prin. Fax 438-2472
Yeshivas Tiferes Academy 50/9-12
1960 Schenectady Ave 11234 718-252-0801
Rabbi Moshe Aronov, dean Fax 252-6787
Yeshivas Vyelipol HS 100/9-12
860 E 27th St 11210 718-951-1800
Zalman Friedman, prin. Fax 951-3414
Yeshivat Ateret Torah 1,000/PK-12
901 Quentin Rd 11223 718-375-7100
Rabbi Chaim Weinberg, prin. Fax 645-5097
Yeshiva Tiferes Shmiel D'Aleksander 100/9-12
PO Box 190738 11219 718-438-1818
Rabbi Boruch Singer, prin. Fax 438-7826
Yeshivat Mikdash Melech Post-Sec.
1326 Ocean Pkwy 11230 718-339-1090
Yeshiva Toldos Yitzchok Bnei Mordechai 100/PK-10
1413 45th St 11219 718-633-4802
Philip Gross, prin. Fax 972-2595
Yeshiva Toras Chesed S 200/9-12
5506 16th Ave 11204 718-972-3077
Rabbi Avrohom Pinter, prin. Fax 972-3078
Yeshiva Toras Emes Kamenitz 500/PK-12
1904 Avenue N 11230 718-375-0900
Irving Frank, prin. Fax 375-0272
Yeshivat Or Hatorah S 50/9-12
2119 Homecrest Ave 11229 718-645-4645
Rabbi Joseph Ugowitz, prin. Fax 645-4693
Yeshivat Shaare Torah Boys S 600/PK-12
1680 Coney Island Ave 11230 718-645-2142
Rabbi Nachman Cohen, coord. Fax 645-9529
Yeshivat Shaare Torah Girls HS 100/9-12
321 Avenue N 11230 718-382-4000
Leah Diskind, prin. Fax 382-7999
Yeshiva Yesode Hatorah 50/9-12
187 Hooper St 11211 718-387-6242
David Friedman, prin.
Zvi Dov Roth Academy 100/7-12
3300 Kings Hwy 11234 718-338-6921
Chana Kartaginer, prin. Fax 677-5103

Brookville, Nassau, Pop. 3,395

Long Island Lutheran HS 600/6-12
131 Brookville Rd 11545 516-626-1700
Dr. David M. Hahn, hdmstr. Fax 626-7459

Brushton, Franklin, Pop. 478
Brushton-Moira Central SD 900/K-12
758 County Route 7 12916 518-529-8948
Earle Gregory Ed.D., supt. Fax 529-6062
www.bmcsd.org
Brushton-Moira Central JSHS 400/7-12
758 County Route 7 12916 518-529-7342
Robin Jones, prin. Fax 529-6062

Buffalo, Erie, Pop. 285,018
Buffalo CSD 31,100/PK-12
713 City Hall 14202 716-851-3600
James Williams Ed.D., supt. Fax 851-3535
www.buffaloschools.org/
Austin MS, 1405 Sycamore St 14211 5-8
Kathleen Vitagliano, prin. 716-816-4460
Badillo Bilingual Academy 500/3-8
300 S Elmwood Ave 14201 716-816-3848
Donna Jackson, prin. Fax 851-3853
Bennett HS 9th Grade Magnet 9-9
120 Minnesota Ave 14214 716-838-7440
Fax 838-7444
Bennett HS 1,500/9-12
2885 Main St 14214 716-816-4250
Ramona Reynolds, prin. Fax 838-7490
Buffalo Academy Visual-Performing Arts 800/5-12
333 Clinton St 14204 716-851-3868
Kevin E. Kazmieczak, prin. Fax 851-3863
Burgard Vocational HS Vo/Tech
400 Kensington Ave 14214 716-816-4450
James Pautler, prin. Fax 838-7546
City Honors JSHS 900/5-12
186 E North St 14204 716-816-4230
Dr. Catherine F. Battaglia, prin. Fax 888-7145
Cleveland HS 1,100/9-12
110 14th St 14213 716-816-4300
Kevin Eberle, prin. Fax 888-7158
Drew Science Magnet S 7-8
1 N Meadow Dr 14214 716-816-4440
Delcene West, prin.
East HS, 820 Northampton St 14211 9-12
Geraldine Horton, prin. 716-816-4520
Grabiarz S of Excellence 800/5-8
225 Lawn Ave 14207 716-871-6000
Michael J. O'Brien, prin. Fax 871-6115
Houghton Academy 300/3-8
1515 S Park Ave 14220 716-816-4777
Elaine Vandi, prin. Fax 828-4797
Hutchinson Central Tech HS Vo/Tech
319 Suffolk St 14215 716-816-4330
David Greco, prin.

Lafayette HS | 1,000/9-12
370 Lafayette Ave 14213 | 716-816-4340
Jacquelyn Baldwin, prin. | Fax 888-7096
McKinley Vocational HS | Vo/Tech
1500 Elmwood Ave 14207 | 716-816-4480
Crystal Barton, prin. | Fax 871-6073
Middle College JHS | 9-10
290 Main St 14201 | 716-851-3763
Susan Doyle, prin. | Fax 851-3766
North Park Academy | 300/5-8
780 Parkside Ave 14216 | 716-816-3440
Angela Elmore, prin. | Fax 838-7448
Occupational Training Center | Vo/Tech
2495 Main St 14214 | 716-816-3250
Thomas Vitale, prin. | Fax 838-2226
Public MS 43 | 400/3-8
11 Benzinger St 14206 | 716-816-3260
Alvion Johnson, prin. | Fax 897-8012
Public MS 56 | 300/5-8
716 W Delavan Ave 14222 | 716-888-7100
Michael Gruber, prin. | Fax 888-7104
Public S 40 | 200/5-8
89 Clare St 14206 | 716-851-3806
| Fax 851-3807

Riverside HS | 1,100/9-12
51 Ontario St 14207 | 716-816-4360
Michael Mogavero, prin. | Fax 871-6046
Sedita Academy | 5-8
21 Lowell Pl 14213 | 716-816-3220
Debra Washington, prin. | Fax 888-2032
Seneca Vocational HS | Vo/Tech
666 E Delavan Ave 14215 | 716-897-8170
Robert Barton, prin. | Fax 897-8058
South Park HS | 1,000/9-12
150 Southside Pkwy 14220 | 716-816-4828
Paul Casseri, prin. | Fax 828-4905
West Hertel MS | 700/5-8
1369 Broadway St 14212 | 716-816-3270
Sharon Ruffin, prin. | Fax 871-6071
Adult Learning Center | Adult
389 Virginia St 14201 | 716-888-7088
Jane Ervolino, dir. | Fax 888-7097

Cheektowago-Sloan UFD | 1,500/PK-12
166 Halstead Ave 14212 | 716-891-6402
James Mazgajewski, supt. | Fax 891-6435
www.sloan.wnyric.org
Other Schools – See Cheektowaga

Kenmore-Tonawanda UFSD | 8,500/K-12
1500 Colvin Blvd 14223 | 716-874-8400
Steven A. Achramovitch, supt. | Fax 874-8624
www.kenton.k12.ny.us/
Franklin MS | 600/6-8
540 Parkhurst Blvd 14223 | 716-874-8404
Dennis Priore, prin. | Fax 874-8480
Hoover MS | 700/6-8
249 Thorncliff Rd 14223 | 716-874-8405
Margaret Hollstein, prin. | Fax 874-8470
Kenmore West HS | 1,700/9-12
33 Highland Pkwy 14223 | 716-874-8401
Douglas Smith, prin. | Fax 874-8527
Other Schools – See Kenmore, Tonawanda

Bishop Timon-St. Jude HS | 400/9-12
601 McKinley Pkwy 14220 | 716-826-3610
Thomas Sullivan, prin. | Fax 824-5833
Bryant & Stratton College | Post-Sec.
465 Main St Ste 400 14203 | 716-884-9120
Buffalo Seminary | 200/9-12
205 Bidwell Pkwy 14222 | 716-885-6780
Sandra Gilmor, hdmstr. | Fax 885-6785
Canisius College | Post-Sec.
2001 Main St 14208 | 716-883-7000
Canisius HS | 700/9-12
1180 Delaware Ave 14209 | 716-882-0466
Frank Tudini, prin. | Fax 883-1870
Central Catholic S | 300/6-8
1955 Genesee St 14211 | 716-852-6854
Patricia Duffy, prin. | Fax 852-8410
Continental School of Beauty Culture | Post-Sec.
326 Kenmore Ave 14223 | 716-833-5016
D'Youville College | Post-Sec.
320 Porter Ave 14201 | 716-881-3200
Erie Community College | Post-Sec.
121 Ellicott St 14203 | 716-842-2770
Finney HS | 100/9-12
260 Eggert Rd 14215 | 716-362-0770
Susan Thorington, prin. | Fax 895-2383
Holy Angels Academy | 200/9-12
24 Shoshone St 14214 | 716-834-7120
Jo Anne Grippi, prin. | Fax 834-7128
Medaille College | Post-Sec.
18 Agassiz Cir 14214 | 716-884-3281
Mt. Mercy Academy | 500/9-12
88 Red Jacket Pkwy 14220 | 716-825-8796
Paulette Gaske, prin. | Fax 825-0976
Nardin Academy | 400/9-12
135 Cleveland Ave 14222 | 716-881-6262
Rebecca Reeder, prin. | Fax 881-0086
National Tractor Trailer School | Post-Sec.
175 Katherine St 14210 | 716-849-6887
New York Institute of Massage | Post-Sec.
PO Box 645 14231 | 716-633-0355
Nichols S | 600/5-12
1250 Amherst St 14216 | 716-876-3500
Richard C. Bryan, hdmstr. | Fax 877-1090
Park S of Buffalo | 200/PK-12
4625 Harlem Rd 14226 | 716-839-1242
Donald Grace, prin. | Fax 839-2014
St. Mary's School for the Deaf | Post-Sec.
2253 Main St 14214
SUNY College at Buffalo | Post-Sec.
1300 Elmwood Ave 14222 | 716-878-4000
SUNY Educational Opportunity Center | Post-Sec.
465 Washington St 14203 | 716-849-6725
SUNY Empire State College | Post-Sec.
617 Main St Fl 3 14203 | 716-853-7700
Trocaire College | Post-Sec.
360 Choate Ave 14220 | 716-826-1200
University at Buffalo SUNY | Post-Sec.
Ellicott Complex Mfac # 220 14261 | 716-645-6900

Villa Maria College of Buffalo | Post-Sec.
240 Pine Ridge Rd 14225 | 716-896-0700

Burnt Hills, Saratoga
Burnt Hills-Ballston Lake CSD
Supt. — See Scotia
Burnt Hills-Ballston Lake HS | 1,100/9-12
88 Lake Hill Rd 12027 | 518-399-9141
Maryellen Symer, prin. | Fax 399-4341
O'Rourke MS | 800/6-8
173 Lake Hill Rd 12027 | 518-399-9141
Donald Germain, prin. | Fax 384-2588

Cairo, Greene, Pop. 1,273
Cairo-Durham Central SD | 1,800/K-12
PO Box 780 12413 | 518-622-8534
Sally Sharkey, supt. | Fax 622-9566
www.cairodurham.org
Cairo-Durham HS | 600/9-12
PO Box 598 12413 | 518-622-8543
William Toussaint, prin. | Fax 622-8857
Cairo-Durham MS | 500/6-8
PO Box 1139 12413 | 518-622-0490
Simon Williams, prin. | Fax 622-0493

Caledonia, Livingston, Pop. 2,256
Caledonia-Mumford Central SD | 1,100/K-12
99 North St 14423 | 585-538-3400
David Dinolfo, supt. | Fax 538-3450
www.cal-mum.org
Caledonia-Mumford HS | 400/9-12
99 North St 14423 | 585-538-3483
Thomas Woodruff, prin. | Fax 538-3470
Caledonia-Mumford MS | 300/6-8
99 North St 14423 | 585-538-3482
Robert Molisani, prin. | Fax 538-3430

Cambridge, Washington, Pop. 1,913
Cambridge Central SD | 1,100/K-12
23 W Main St 12816 | 518-677-2653
Dr. Frank Greenhall, supt. | Fax 677-3889
www.cambridgecsd.org
Cambridge HS | 500/7-12
24 S Park St 12816 | 518-677-8527
Daniel Severson, prin. | Fax 677-3246

Camden, Oneida, Pop. 2,300
Camden Central SD | 3,400/K-12
51 3rd St 13316 | 315-245-4075
Richard Keville, supt. | Fax 245-1622
www.camdenschools.org/
Camden HS | 900/9-12
55 Oswego St 13316 | 315-245-3168
Jeffrey Bryant, prin. | Fax 245-4173
Camden MS | 400/7-8
32 Union St 13316 | 315-245-0080
Mary Barker, prin. | Fax 245-0083

Camillus, Onondaga, Pop. 1,233
West Genesee Central SD | 5,100/K-12
300 Sanderson Dr 13031 | 315-487-4562
Dr. Rudolph Rubeis, supt. | Fax 487-2999
www.westgenesee.org
Camillus MS | 600/6-8
5525 Ike Dixon Rd 13031 | 315-672-3159
Robert Honcharski, prin. | Fax 672-3309
West Genesee HS | 1,700/9-12
5201 W Genesee St 13031 | 315-487-4592
Barry Copeland, prin. | Fax 487-4582
West Genesee MS | 700/6-8
500 Sanderson Dr 13031 | 315-487-4615
Earl Sanderson, prin. | Fax 487-4618

Campbell, Steuben
Campbell-Savona Central SD | 1,200/K-12
8455 County Route 125 14821 | 607-527-4548
Scott Layton, supt. | Fax 527-8363
www.campbellsavona.wnyric.org
Campbell-Savona HS | 300/9-12
8455 County Route 125 14821 | 607-527-4551
Mark Sissel, prin. | Fax 527-8363
Campbell-Savona MS | 300/6-8
8455 County Route 125 14821 | 607-527-4551
Michele Plank, prin. | Fax 527-8363

Canaan, Columbia
Berkshire UFD | 200/7-12
13640 Route 22 12029 | 518-781-3500
James Gaudette, supt. | Fax 781-4890
Berkshire JSHS | 200/7-12
13640 Route 22 12029 | 518-781-3500
Bruce Potter, prin. | Fax 781-4890

Canajoharie, Montgomery, Pop. 2,212
Canajoharie Central SD | 1,100/PK-12
136 Scholastic Way 13317 | 518-673-6302
Richard Rose, supt. | Fax 673-3177
www.canajoharieschools.org
Canajoharie HS | 400/9-12
136 Scholastic Way 13317 | 518-673-6330
Dr. Donald Bowden, prin. | Fax 673-3177
Canajoharie MS | 200/6-8
25 School District Rd 13317 | 518-673-6320
Rodney Strait, prin. | Fax 673-5557

Canandaigua, Ontario, Pop. 11,449
Canandaigua CSD | 4,100/K-12
143 N Pearl St 14424 | 585-396-3700
Dr. Stephen Uebbing, supt. | Fax 396-7306
www.canandaiguaschools.org/
Canandaigua Academy | 1,400/9-12
435 East St 14424 | 585-396-3800
Lynne Erdle, prin. | Fax 396-3806
Canandaigua MS | 1,000/6-8
215 Granger St 14424 | 585-396-3850
Ralph Undercoffler, prin. | Fax 396-3863

Finger Lakes Community College | Post-Sec.
4355 Lakeshore Dr 14424 | 585-394-3500

Canaseraga, Allegany, Pop. 582
Canaseraga Central SD | 300/K-12
PO Box 230 14822 | 607-545-6421
| Fax 545-6265
www.canaseraga.wnyric.org

Canaseraga S | 300/K-12
PO Box 230 14822 | 607-545-6421
James Anderson, prin. | Fax 545-6265

Canastota, Madison, Pop. 4,445
Canastota Central SD | 1,500/K-12
120 Roberts St 13032 | 315-697-2025
Frederick Bragan, supt. | Fax 697-6368
www.canastotacsd.org
Canastota JSHS | 700/7-12
102 Roberts St 13032 | 315-697-2003
Donna Marie Norton, prin. | Fax 697-6368

Utica School of Commerce | Post-Sec.
PO Box 462 13032 | 315-697-8200

Candor, Tioga, Pop. 839
Candor Central SD | 900/K-12
PO Box 145 13743 | 607-659-5010
Jeffrey J. Kisloski, supt. | Fax 659-7112
candor.org
Candor JSHS | 500/7-12
PO Box 145 13743 | 607-659-5020
Ryan Dougherty, prin. | Fax 659-4692

Canisteo, Steuben, Pop. 2,297
Canisteo-Greenwood SD | 1,000/PK-12
84 Greenwood St 14823 | 607-698-4225
Lorraine Patti, supt. | Fax 698-2833
www.cg.wnyric.org
Canisteo-Greenwood JSHS | 500/7-12
84 Greenwood St 14823 | 607-698-4225
Michael Wright, prin. | Fax 698-2833

Canton, Saint Lawrence, Pop. 5,961
Canton Central SD | 1,500/PK-12
99 State St 13617 | 315-386-8561
Dr. Katrina Jacobson, supt. | Fax 386-1323
www.ccsdk12.org/
McKenney MS | 600/4-8
99 State St 13617 | 315-386-8561
Arthur Quackenbush, prin. | Fax 386-1323
Williams HS | 500/9-12
99 State St 13617 | 315-386-8561
William Gregory, prin. | Fax 386-1323

St. Lawrence University | Post-Sec.
2501 Saint Lawrence Univ 13617 | 315-229-5011
SUNY Canton - College of Technology | Post-Sec.
34 Cornell Dr 13617 | 315-386-7011

Carle Place, Nassau, Pop. 5,107
Carle Place UFD | 1,500/K-12
168 Cherry Ln 11514 | 516-622-6442
Dr. Patricia Hansen, supt. | Fax 622-6447
www.cps.k12.ny.us
Carle Place MSHS | 700/7-12
168 Cherry Ln 11514 | 516-622-6400
Neil Connolly, prin. | Fax 622-6489

Carmel, Putnam, Pop. 4,800
Carmel Central SD
Supt. — See Patterson
Carmel HS | 1,600/9-12
30 Fair St 10512 | 845-225-8441
Kevin Carroll, prin. | Fax 228-2308
Fischer MS | 1,600/5-8
281 Fair St 10512 | 845-228-2300
Les Weintraub, prin. | Fax 228-2304

Carthage, Jefferson, Pop. 3,734
Carthage Central SD | 3,800/K-12
25059 County Route 197 13619 | 315-493-5000
Dr. Carl Mangee, supt. | Fax 493-6252
www.carthagecsd.org
Carthage HS | 900/9-12
36500 State Route 26 13619 | 315-493-5030
Peter Turner, prin. | Fax 493-5039
Carthage MS | 800/5-8
21986 Cole Rd 13619 | 315-493-5020
Andrea Miller, prin. | Fax 493-5029

Castleton on Hudson, Rensselaer, Pop. 1,525
Schodack Central SD | 1,200/K-12
1216 Maple Hill Rd 12033 | 518-732-2297
Douglas Hamlin, supt. | Fax 732-7710
www.schodack.k12.ny.us/
Maple Hill HS | 400/9-12
1216 Maple Hill Rd 12033 | 518-732-7701
Robert Horan, prin. | Fax 732-0494
Maple Hill MS | 500/4-8
1477 S Schodack Rd 12033 | 518-732-7736
Heather Lansing, prin. | Fax 732-0493

Cato, Cayuga, Pop. 594
Cato-Meridian Central SD | 1,300/PK-12
2851 State Route 370 13033 | 315-626-3439
Deborah D. Bobo, supt. | Fax 626-2888
www.catomeridian.org/
Cato-Meridian HS | 400/9-12
2851 State Route 370 13033 | 315-626-3317
Charles Mitchell, prin. | Fax 626-2551
Cato-Meridian MS | 400/5-8
2851 State Route 370 13033 | 315-626-3319
Sean Gleason, prin. | Fax 626-2888

Catskill, Greene, Pop. 4,360
Catskill Central SD | 1,800/K-12
343 W Main St 12414 | 518-943-4696
Kathleen P. Farrell Ph.D., supt. | Fax 943-7116
www.catskillcsd.org
Catskill HS | 500/9-12
341 W Main St 12414 | 518-943-2300
Lisa Slutzky, prin. | Fax 943-1451
Catskill MS | 300/7-8
345 W Main St 12414 | 518-943-5665
Marielena Davis, prin. | Fax 943-3001

Columbia-Greene Beauty School | Post-Sec.
342 Main St 12414 | 518-943-2224

Cattaraugus, Cattaraugus, Pop. 1,044
Cattaraugus-Little Valley Central SD
Supt. — See Little Valley

Cattaraugus-Little Valley HS | 300/10-12
25 N Franklin St 14719 | 716-257-3483
Paul Stetz, prin. | Fax 257-5108
Cattaraugus-Little Valley MS | 300/7-9
25 N Franklin St 14719 | 716-257-3483
Lawrence Studd, prin. | Fax 257-5108

Cazenovia, Madison, Pop. 2,710
Cazenovia Central SD | 1,800/K-12
31 Emory Ave 13035 | 315-655-1317
Robert Dubik, supt. | Fax 655-1375
www.caz.cnyric.org
Cazenovia JSHS | 800/8-12
31 Emory Ave 13035 | 315-655-1314
Daniel Nolan, prin. | Fax 655-1371

Cazenovia College 13035 | Post-Sec.
| 800-654-3210

Cedarhurst, Nassau, Pop. 6,121
Lawrence UFD
Supt. — See Lawrence
Lawrence HS | 1,300/9-12
2 Reilly Rd 11516 | 516-295-8000
Geoffrey Touretz, prin. | Fax 295-2754

Hebrew Academy of Five Towns HS | 500/9-12
635 Central Ave 11516 | 516-569-3807
Rabbi Zvi Bajnon, prin. | Fax 374-5761
Yeshiva Zichron Aryeh | Post-Sec.
100 Cedarhurst Ave 11516 | 516-295-5700

Centereach, Suffolk, Pop. 27,400
Middle Country Central SD | 10,700/PK-12
8 43rd St 11720 | 631-285-8005
Dr. Leonard Adler, supt. | Fax 738-2719
www.middlecountry.k12.ny.us/
Centereach HS | 1,700/9-12
14 43rd St 11720 | 631-285-8100
Alene Abrams, prin. | Fax 285-8101
Dawnwood MS, 10 43rd St 11720 | 1,400/6-8
James Donovan, prin. | 631-285-8200
Selden MS, 22 Jefferson Ave 11720 | 1,300/6-8
Barbara Phillipson, prin. | 631-285-8400
Other Schools – See Selden

Our Savior New American S | 300/PK-12
140 Mark Tree Rd 11720 | 631-588-2757
Dolores Reade, admin. | Fax 588-2617

Center Moriches, Suffolk, Pop. 5,987
Center Moriches UFD | 1,400/K-12
529 Main St 11934 | 631-878-0052
Donald A. James, supt. | Fax 878-4326
www.cmschools.org
Center Moriches HS | 500/9-12
311 Frowein Rd 11934 | 631-878-0092
Lino Bracco, prin. | Fax 878-1796
Center Moriches MS | 300/6-8
311 Frowein Rd 11934 | 631-878-2519
Patricia Cunningham, prin. | Fax 878-0362

Burket Christian S | 200/PK-12
34 Oak St 11934 | 631-878-1727
Dominick Scibetta, admin. | Fax 878-8968

Central Islip, Suffolk, Pop. 33,400
Central Islip UFD | 6,600/PK-12
PO Box 9027 11722 | 631-348-5001
Fadhilika Atiba-Weza, supt. | Fax 348-0366
www.cischools.org
Central Islip HS | 1,900/9-12
85 Wheeler Rd 11722 | 631-348-5078
Anthony Servedio, prin. | Fax 342-0161
Reed MS | 1,100/7-8
200 Half Mile Rd 11722 | 631-348-5065
Carmen Garcia-Collins, prin. | Fax 348-5159

New York Institute of Technology | Post-Sec.
211 Carleton Ave 11722 | 631-348-3000

Central Square, Oswego, Pop. 1,651
Central Square Central SD | 4,900/K-12
642 S Main St 13036 | 315-668-4220
Dr. Walter Doherty, supt. | Fax 676-4437
www.centralsquareschools.org/
Central Square MS | 1,300/6-8
248 US Route 11 13036 | 315-668-4216
Dr. Paul Darnall, prin. | Fax 668-8410
Moore HS | 1,400/9-12
44 School Dr 13036 | 315-668-4231
Thomas Douglas, prin. | Fax 668-4346

Central Valley, Orange, Pop. 1,929
Monroe-Woodbury Central SD | 7,200/K-12
278 Route 32 10917 | 845-460-6200
Joseph DiLorenzo, supt. | Fax 460-6080
www.mw.k12.ny.us
Monroe-Woodbury HS | 2,300/9-12
155 Dunderberg Rd 10917 | 845-460-7000
Aldo Filippone, prin. | Fax 460-7090
Monroe-Woodbury MS | 1,800/6-8
199 Dunderberg Rd 10917 | 845-460-6400
Elsie Rodriguez, prin. | Fax 460-6044

Champlain, Clinton, Pop. 1,163
Northeastern Clinton Central SD | 1,600/K-12
103 State Route 276 12919 | 518-298-8242
Robert J. Hebert, supt. | Fax 298-4293
www.nccscougars.org/
Northeastern Clinton HS | 600/9-12
103 State Route 276 12919 | 518-298-8638
Christine Crowley, prin. | Fax 298-4293
Northeastern Clinton MS | 500/6-8
103 State Route 276 12919 | 518-298-8681
Diane Thompson, prin. | Fax 298-4293

Chappaqua, Westchester, Pop. 6,400
Chappaqua Central SD | 4,400/K-12
PO Box 21 10514 | 914-238-7200
David A. Fleishman, supt. | Fax 238-7218
www.ccsd.ws

Bell MS | 900/5-8
50 Senter St 10514 | 914-238-6170
Martin Fitzgerald, prin. | Fax 238-2085
Greeley HS | 1,200/9-12
70 Roaring Brook Rd 10514 | 914-861-9400
Andrew Salesnick, prin. | Fax 238-4291
Seven Bridges MS | 800/5-8
PO Box 22 10514 | 914-666-7330
Donna Raskin, prin. | Fax 666-7306

Chateaugay, Franklin, Pop. 793
Chateaugay Central SD | 600/K-12
PO Box 904 12920 | 518-497-6420
Paul Harrica, supt. | Fax 497-3170
www.chateaugay.org/
Chateaugay JSHS | 300/7-12
PO Box 904 12920 | 518-497-6611
Dale Breault, prin. | Fax 497-3170

Chatham, Columbia, Pop. 1,787
Chatham Central SD | 1,500/K-12
50 Woodbridge Ave 12037 | 518-392-1501
Scott Hunter, supt. | Fax 392-2413
www.chathamcentralschools.com/
Chatham HS | 500/9-12
50 Woodbridge Ave 12037 | 518-392-1570
Ronald Davis, prin. | Fax 392-0908
Chatham MS | 500/5-8
50 Woodbridge Ave 12037 | 518-392-1560
Gordon Fitting, prin. | Fax 392-1559

Chaumont, Jefferson, Pop. 593
Lyme Central SD | 400/K-12
PO Box 219 13622 | 315-649-2417
Donnalee Dodson, supt. | Fax 649-2812
www.lymecsd.org
Lyme Central S | 400/K-12
PO Box 219 13622 | 315-649-2417
William Snyder, prin. | Fax 649-2812

Chazy, Clinton
Chazy Central Rural SD | 600/K-12
609 Miner Farm Rd 12921 | 518-846-7135
Kevin Mulligan, supt. | Fax 846-8322
www.chazy.org
Chazy Central Rural JSHS | 300/7-12
609 Miner Farm Rd 12921 | 518-846-7135
Kevin Mulligan, prin. | Fax 846-8322

Cheektowaga, Erie, Pop. 79,200
Cheektowaga Central SD | 2,400/K-12
3600 Union Rd 14225 | 716-686-3606
Delia Bonenberger, supt. | Fax 681-5232
www.cheektowagacentral.org
Cheektowaga Central HS | 800/9-12
3600 Union Rd 14225 | 716-686-3602
Steven Wright, prin. | Fax 686-3619
Cheektowaga Central MS | 600/6-8
3600 Union Rd 14225 | 716-686-3660
Cheryl Buggs, prin. | Fax 686-3669

Cheektowaga-Maryvale UFD | 2,500/K-12
1050 Maryvale Dr 14225 | 716-631-7407
Gary Brader, supt. | Fax 635-4699
www.maryvale.wnyric.org
Maryvale HS | 800/9-12
1050 Maryvale Dr 14225 | 716-631-7481
Renee Salvadore, prin. | Fax 631-7404
Maryvale MS | 700/6-8
1050 Maryvale Dr 14225 | 716-631-7425
| Fax 631-7499

Cheektowago-Sloan UFD
Supt. — See Buffalo
Kennedy HS | 400/9-12
305 Cayuga Creek Rd 14227 | 716-891-6407
Stephen Bovino, prin. | Fax 891-6430
Kennedy MS | 400/6-8
305 Cayuga Creek Rd 14227 | 716-897-7300
David Peters, prin. | Fax 891-6430

Cleveland Hill UFD | 1,600/K-12
105 Mapleview Rd 14225 | 716-836-7200
Bruce Inglis, supt. | Fax 836-0675
www.clevehill.wnyric.org/
Cleveland Hill MSHS | 800/6-12
105 Mapleview Rd 14225 | 716-836-7200
Jill Sherman, prin. | Fax 836-0675

Villa Maria Academy | 200/9-12
600 Doat St 14211 | 716-894-0398
Sr. Paul Marie Baczkowski, prin. | Fax 894-0468

Cherry Valley, Otsego, Pop. 561
Cherry Valley-Springfield Central SD | 700/PK-12
PO Box 485 13320 | 607-264-9332
Nicholas J. Savin, supt. | Fax 264-9023
www.cvscs.org
Cherry Valley-Springfield JSHS | 300/7-12
PO Box 485 13320 | 607-264-9012
Charles Strange, prin. | Fax 264-3458

Chester, Orange, Pop. 3,521
Chester UFD | 1,000/K-12
64 Hambletonian Ave 10918 | 845-469-5052
Judy L. Waligory, supt. | Fax 469-2377
chesterufsd.org
Chester Academy | 500/6-12
64 Hambletonian Ave 10918 | 845-469-2231
Neil Schweda, prin. | Fax 469-3547

Chestertown, Warren
North Warren Central SD | 600/PK-12
6110 State Route 8 12817 | 518-494-3015
Joseph R. Murphy, supt. | Fax 494-2929
www.northwarren.k12.ny.us
North Warren Central S | 600/PK-12
6110 State Route 8 12817 | 518-494-3015
Therese Andrews, prin. | Fax 494-2929

Chestnut Ridge, Rockland, Pop. 7,881
East Ramapo Central SD
Supt. — See Spring Valley

Chestnut Ridge MS | 500/7-8
892 Chestnut Ridge Rd 10977 | 845-577-6300
Maria Vergez, prin. | Fax 426-1063

Green Meadow Waldorf S | 400/PK-12
307 Hungry Hollow Rd 10977 | 845-356-2514
Kay Hoffman, prin. | Fax 356-2921

Chittenango, Madison, Pop. 4,876
Chittenango Central SD | 2,600/K-12
1732 Fyler Rd 13037 | 315-687-2669
Thomas E. Marzeski, supt. | Fax 687-9830
www.chittenangoschools.org
Chittenango HS | 800/9-12
150 Genesee St 13037 | 315-687-2621
Derek Sajnog, prin. | Fax 687-5182
Chittenango MS | 600/6-8
1732 Fyler Rd 13037 | 315-687-2648
Linda LLewellyn, prin. | Fax 687-5482

Churchville, Monroe, Pop. 1,908
Churchville-Chili Central SD | 4,500/K-12
139 Fairbanks Rd 14428 | 585-293-1800
Anne Spadafora, supt. | Fax 293-1013
www.cccsd.org
Churchville-Chili JHS | 1,200/7-9
137 Fairbanks Rd 14428 | 585-293-4541
David Hamilton, prin. | Fax 293-4501
Churchville-Chili SHS | 1,100/10-12
5786 Buffalo Rd 14428 | 585-293-4540
Bill Geraci, prin. | Fax 293-4508

Cicero, Onondaga
North Syracuse Central SD
Supt. — See North Syracuse
Cicero-North Syracuse SHS | 2,200/10-12
6002 State Route 31 13039 | 315-218-4100
James Froio, prin.

Cincinnatus, Cortland
Cincinnatus Central SD | 700/K-12
2809 Cincinnatus Rd 13040 | 607-863-4069
Steven Hubbard, supt. | Fax 863-4559
www.cincynet.cnyric.org
Cincinnatus JSHS | 300/7-12
2809 Cincinnatus Rd 13040 | 607-863-3200
Karen Heffernan, prin. | Fax 863-4559

Circleville, Orange, Pop. 1,350
Pine Bush Central SD
Supt. — See Pine Bush
Circleville MS | 600/6-8
PO Box 143 10919 | 845-361-4000
Richard Schacher, prin. | Fax 361-3811

Clarence, Erie
Clarence Central SD | 4,900/K-12
9625 Main St 14031 | 716-407-9100
Thomas Coseo Ed.D., supt. | Fax 407-9126
www.clarenceschools.org
Clarence HS, 9625 Main St 14031 | 1,500/9-12
Joseph Gentile, prin. | 716-407-9020
Clarence MS | 1,200/6-8
10150 Greiner Rd 14031 | 716-407-9200
Joel Weiss, prin.

Clayton, Jefferson, Pop. 1,830
Thousand Islands Central SD | 1,200/K-12
PO Box 1000 13624 | 315-686-5594
Dr. John Slattery, supt. | Fax 686-5511
www.1000islandsschools.org
Thousand Islands HS | 400/9-12
8481 Country Route 9 13624 | 315-686-5594
Joseph Gilfus, prin. | Fax 654-5039
Thousand Islands MS | 300/6-8
8487 County Route 9 13624 | 315-686-5594
Debra Percy, prin. | Fax 654-5038

Clifton Park, Saratoga
Shenendehowa Central SD | 8,500/K-12
5 Chelsea Pl 12065 | 518-881-0600
R. Oliver Robinson, supt. | Fax 371-9393
www.shenet.org/
Acadia MS | 700/6-8
970 Route 146 12065 | 518-881-0450
Jonathan Burns, prin. | Fax 371-3981
Gowana MS | 700/6-8
970 Route 146 12065 | 518-881-0460
Jill Bush, prin. | Fax 383-1490
Koda MS | 700/6-8
970 Route 146 12065 | 518-881-0470
Bruce Ballan, prin. | Fax 383-1532
Shenendehowa HS West | 9-9
970 Route 146 12065 | 518-881-0330
Robert Melia, prin. | Fax 383-5768
Shenendehowa SHS East | 2,000/10-12
970 Route 146 12065 | 518-881-0310
Robert Melia, prin. | Fax 383-1670

Clifton Springs, Ontario, Pop. 2,196
Phelps-Clifton Springs Central SD | 2,000/K-12
1490 State Route 488 14432 | 315-548-6420
Michael Ford, supt. | Fax 548-6429
www.midlakes.org
Midlakes HS | 700/9-12
1554 State Route 488 14432 | 315-548-6300
L. Rick Bley, prin. | Fax 548-6319
Midlakes MS | 500/6-8
1550 State Route 488 14432 | 315-548-6600
Kathy DeMay, prin. | Fax 548-6619

Climax, Greene

Grapeville Christian S | 100/K-12
2416 County Route 26 12042 | 518-966-5037
Nicole Orsino, prin. | Fax 966-4265

Clinton, Oneida, Pop. 1,922
Clinton Central SD | 1,600/K-12
75 Chenango Ave 13323 | 315-557-2253
Jeffrey Roudebush, supt. | Fax 853-8727
www.ccs.edu

Clinton HS 600/9-12
75 Chenango Ave 13323 315-557-2232
Richard Hunt, prin. Fax 853-8727
Clinton MS 400/6-8
75 Chenango Ave 13323 315-557-2260
Martin Cross, prin. Fax 853-8727

Hamilton College Post-Sec.
198 College Hill Rd 13323 315-859-4011

Clinton Corners, Dutchess

Upton Lake Christian S 100/K-12
PO Box 63 12514 845-266-3497
Dietlind Hoiem, admin. Fax 266-3828

Clintonville, Clinton
Au Sable Valley Central SD 1,300/K-12
1273 Route 9N 12924 518-834-2845
Paul Savage, supt. Fax 834-2843
www.avcs.org
Au Sable Valley HS 500/9-12
1490 Route 9N 12924 518-834-2800
Charles Chafee, prin. Fax 834-2847
Au Sable Valley MS 300/7-8
1490 Route 9N 12924 518-834-2800
Philip Mero, prin. Fax 834-2847

Clyde, Wayne, Pop. 2,222
Clyde-Savannah Central SD 1,100/K-12
215 Glasgow St 14433 315-902-3000
Richard Drahms, supt. Fax 923-2560
www.clydesavannah.org/
Clyde JSHS 500/7-12
215 Glasgow St 14433 315-902-3050
Matthew Motala, prin. Fax 923-2560

Clymer, Chautauqua
Clymer Central SD 500/K-12
8672 E Main St 14724 716-355-4444
Ralph Wilson, supt. Fax 355-4467
www.clymer.wnyric.org/
Clymer Central S 500/K-12
8672 E Main St 14724 716-355-4444
Edward Bailey, prin. Fax 355-4467

Cobleskill, Schoharie, Pop. 4,533
Cobleskill-Richmondville Central SD 2,200/K-12
155 Washington Ave 12043 518-234-4032
Samuel Shevat, supt. Fax 234-7721
www.crcs.k12.ny.us/
Golding MS 500/6-8
193 Golding Dr 12043 518-234-8368
Scott McDonald, prin. Fax 234-1018
Other Schools – See Richmondville

SUNY College of Agriculture & Technology Post-Sec.
107 Schenectady Ave 12043 518-255-5011

Cohoes, Albany, Pop. 15,303
Cohoes CSD 2,200/K-12
7 Bevan St 12047 518-237-0100
Charles Dedrick, supt. Fax 237-2912
www.cohoes.org/
Cohoes HS 700/9-12
1 Tiger Cir 12047 518-237-9100
Joseph Rajczak, prin. Fax 238-0169
Cohoes MS 500/6-8
7 Bevan St 12047 518-237-4131
Mark Perry, prin. Fax 237-2253

Cold Spring, Putnam, Pop. 1,998
Haldane Central SD 800/K-12
15 Craigside Dr 10516 845-265-9254
Dr. John DiNatale, supt. Fax 265-9213
www2.lhric.org/haldane
Haldane JSHS 400/7-12
15 Craigside Dr 10516 845-265-9254
J. Andy Irvin, prin. Fax 265-9213

Cold Spring Harbor, Suffolk, Pop. 4,789
Cold Spring Harbor Central SD 2,100/K-12
75 Goose Hill Rd 11724 631-692-8036
Whitney Vantine Ed.D., supt. Fax 367-3108
www.csh.k12.ny.us
Cold Spring Harbor JSHS 1,000/7-12
82 Turkey Ln 11724 631-692-8600
Dr. Thomas Dolan, prin. Fax 692-8016

College Point, See New York

St. Agnes Academic HS 300/9-12
1320 124th St 11356 718-353-6068
Sr. Joan Martin, prin.

Colton, Saint Lawrence
Colton-Pierrepont Central SD 400/PK-12
4921 State Highway 56 13625 315-262-2100
Martin Bregg, supt. Fax 262-2644
www.cpcs.k12.ny.us
Colton-Pierrepont JSHS 200/7-12
4921 State Highway 56 13625 315-262-2100
Randy Johnson, prin. Fax 262-2644

Commack, Suffolk, Pop. 36,400
Commack UFD
Supt. — See East Northport
Commack HS, 1 Scholar Ln 11725 2,100/9-12
Ronald Vale, prin. 631-912-2100
Commack MS 1,700/6-8
700 Vanderbilt Pkwy 11725 631-858-3500
Pamela Travis-Moore, prin.

Long Island Business Institute Post-Sec.
6500 Jericho Tpke 11725 631-499-7100

Congers, Rockland, Pop. 8,003

Rockland Country Day S 200/PK-12
34 Kings Hwy 10920 845-268-6802
James Handlin Ed.D., hdmstr. Fax 268-4644

Conklin, Broome
Susquehanna Valley Central SD 2,100/K-12
PO Box 200 13748 607-775-9100
Carol Boyce, supt. Fax 775-4575
www.svsabers.org/
Stank MS 500/6-8
1040 Conklin Rd 13748 607-775-0303
Gerardo Tagliaferri, prin. Fax 775-9142
Susquehanna Valley HS 700/9-12
1040 Conklin Rd 13748 607-775-0304
David Daniels, prin. Fax 775-4575

Cooperstown, Otsego, Pop. 1,936
Cooperstown Central SD 1,100/K-12
39 Linden Ave 13326 607-547-5364
Mary Jo McPhail, supt. Fax 547-5100
Cooperstown Central HS 400/9-12
39 Linden Ave 13326 607-547-8181
Gary Kuch, prin. Fax 547-5100
Cooperstown MS 300/6-8
39 Linden Ave 13326 607-547-5512
Michael G. Cring, prin. Fax 547-5100

Copenhagen, Lewis, Pop. 829
Copenhagen Central SD 600/K-12
PO Box 30 13626 315-688-4411
Lisa Parsons, supt. Fax 688-2001
www.ccsknights.org/
Copenhagen Central S 600/K-12
PO Box 30 13626 315-688-4411
Patricia Gibbons, prin. Fax 688-2001

Copiague, Suffolk, Pop. 20,769
Copiague UFD 4,500/K-12
2650 Great Neck Rd 11726 631-842-4015
Dr. William Bolton, supt. Fax 841-4614
www.copiague.k12.ny.us/
Copiague MS 1,100/6-8
2650 Great Neck Rd 11726 631-842-4011
Albert Voorneveld, prin. Fax 841-4630
O'Connell - Copiague HS 1,300/9-12
1100 Dixon Ave 11726 631-842-4010
Michael Hodgkiss, prin. Fax 841-4642

Corfu, Genesee, Pop. 778
Pembroke Central SD 1,400/PK-12
PO Box 38 14036 585-599-4525
Gary Mix, supt. Fax 762-9993
www.pembroke.k12.ny.us
Pembroke JSHS 700/7-12
Routes 5 & 77 14036 585-599-4525
Keith Palmer, prin. Fax 762-9993

Corinth, Saratoga, Pop. 2,483
Corinth Central SD 1,300/K-12
105 Oak St 12822 518-654-2601
Matthew Breitenbach, supt. Fax 654-6266
www.corinthcsd.com/
Corinth HS 400/9-12
105 Oak St 12822 518-654-9005
Brian Testani, prin. Fax 654-6266
Corinth MS 400/5-8
105 Oak St 12822 518-654-9005
Gregory Kreis, prin. Fax 654-6266

Corning, Steuben, Pop. 10,625
Corning CSD
Supt. — See Painted Post
Corning Free Academy MS 700/6-8
11 W 3rd St 14830 607-936-3788
Richard Kimble, prin. Fax 654-2809
Corning-Painted Post East HS 800/9-12
201 Cantigney St 14830 607-936-3746
Joseph Tobia, prin. Fax 654-2787
Northside Blodgett MS 600/6-8
143 Princeton Ave 14830 607-936-3791
Robert Rossi, prin. Fax 654-2798

Corning Christian Academy 200/PK-12
11 Aisne St 14830 607-962-4220
Dean Everhart, admin. Fax 962-4410
Corning Community College Post-Sec.
1 Academic Dr 14830 607-962-9011

Cornwall, Orange, Pop. 11,270
Cornwall Central SD
Supt. — See Cornwall on Hudson
Cornwall Central MS 1,000/5-8
122 Main St 12518 845-534-8009
Diana Musich, prin. Fax 534-7809

Cornwall on Hudson, Orange, Pop. 3,110
Cornwall Central SD 3,100/K-12
24 Idlewild Ave 12520 845-534-8009
Timothy Rehm, supt. Fax 534-4231
www.cornwallschools.com/
Other Schools – See Cornwall, New Windsor

New York Military Academy 300/7-12
78 Academy Ave 12520 845-534-3710
Fax 534-7121
Storm King S 100/7-12
314 Mountain Rd 12520 845-534-7892
Fax 534-2709

Corona, See New York
NYC Department of Education
Supt. — See New York
Arts & Business HS 800/9-12
10525 Horace Harding Expy 11368 718-271-8383
Vivian Selenikas, prin. Fax 271-7196
IS 61 1,800/6-8
9850 50th Ave 11368 718-760-3233
John O'Mahoney, prin. Fax 760-5220

Sister Clara Muhammed S 100/K-12
10501 Northern Blvd 11368 718-779-1060

Cortland, Cortland, Pop. 18,462
Cortland CSD 2,800/K-12
1 Valley View Dr 13045 607-758-4100
Laurence Spring, supt. Fax 758-4128
www.cortlandschools.org
Cortland JSHS 1,300/7-12
8 Valley View Dr 13045 607-758-4100
Steve Woodard, prin.

Cortland Christian Academy 100/K-12
15 West Rd 13045 607-756-5838
Craig Miller, admin. Fax 756-7716
SUNY College at Cortland Post-Sec.
PO Box 2000 13045 607-753-2011

Cortlandt Manor, See Peekskill
Hendrick Hudson Central SD
Supt. — See Montrose
Blue Mountain MS 700/6-8
7 Furnace Woods Rd 10567 914-736-5300
Sean Michel, prin. Fax 736-3513

Lakeland CSD
Supt. — See Shrub Oak
Panas HS 700/9-12
300 Croton Ave 10567 914-739-2823
Susan Strauss, prin. Fax 739-3545

Coxsackie, Greene, Pop. 2,876
Coxsackie-Athens Central SD 1,600/K-12
24 Sunset Blvd 12051 518-731-1710
Dr. Earle Gregory, supt. Fax 731-1729
www.coxsackie-athens.org
Coxsackie-Athens HS 500/9-12
24 Sunset Blvd 12051 518-731-1800
Dr. James Maxwell, prin. Fax 731-1809
Coxsackie-Athens MS 500/5-8
24 Sunset Blvd 12051 518-731-1850
Joseph Posillico, prin. Fax 731-1859

Craryville, Columbia
Taconic Hills Central SD 1,800/K-12
PO Box 482 12521 518-325-0310
Kraig Pritts, supt. Fax 325-3557
www.taconichills.k12.ny.us/
Taconic Hills HS 600/9-12
PO Box 536 12521 518-325-0390
John Gulisane, prin. Fax 325-9051
Taconic Hills MS 600/5-8
PO Box 536 12521 518-325-0420
Michael Hartner, prin. Fax 325-9051

Cross River, Westchester
Katonah Lewisboro UFD
Supt. — See South Salem
Jay HS 1,200/9-12
60 N Salem Rd 10518 914-763-7200
Richard Leprine, prin. Fax 763-7494
Jay MS 1,000/6-8
40 N Salem Rd 10518 914-763-7500
Douglas Both, prin. Fax 763-7665

Croton on Hudson, Westchester, Pop. 7,134
Croton-Harmon UFD 1,500/K-12
10 Gerstein St 10520 914-271-4793
Dr. Marjorie Castro, supt. Fax 271-8685
www.croton-harmonschools.org
Croton-Harmon HS 400/9-12
36 Old Post Rd S 10520 914-271-2147
Joel Adelberg, prin. Fax 271-6643
Van Cortlandt MS 400/6-8
3 Glen Pl 10520 914-271-2191
Robert Hendrickson, prin. Fax 271-6618

Crown Point, Essex
Crown Point Central SD 300/K-12
PO Box 35 12928 518-597-4200
Shari Brannock, supt. Fax 597-4121
Crown Point Central S 300/K-12
PO Box 35 12928 518-597-3285
Agatha Mace, prin. Fax 597-4121

Cuba, Allegany, Pop. 1,605
Cuba-Rushford Central SD 1,100/K-12
5476 Route 305 14727 585-968-2650
Anne Brungard, supt. Fax 968-2651
www.crcs.wnyric.org/
Cuba-Rushford HS 300/9-12
5476 Route 305 14727 585-968-2650
Judi McCarthy, prin. Fax 968-2651
Cuba-Rushford MS 300/6-8
5476 Route 305 14727 585-968-2650
Barbara Funk, prin. Fax 968-2651

Cutchogue, Suffolk, Pop. 2,627
Mattituck-Cutchogue UFD 1,500/1-12
385 Depot Ln 11935 631-298-4242
Kenny Aldrich, supt. Fax 298-8573
www.northfork.net/mhs/home.htm
Other Schools – See Mattituck

Dannemora, Clinton, Pop. 4,154
Saranac Central SD 1,600/K-12
32 Emmons St 12929 518-565-5600
Kenneth Cringle, supt. Fax 565-5617
www.saranac.org
Other Schools – See Saranac

Dansville, Livingston, Pop. 4,705
Dansville Central SD 1,700/K-12
284 Main St 14437 585-335-4000
Adele Bovard, supt. Fax 335-4002
www.dansvillecsd.org
Dansville HS 500/9-12
282 Main St 14437 585-335-4010
Joe Hochreiter, prin. Fax 335-4080
Dansville MS 400/6-8
31 Clara Barton St 14437 585-335-4020
Amy Schiavi, prin. Fax 335-4021

Davenport, Delaware
Charlotte Valley Central SD 400/K-12
15611 State Highway 23 13750 607-278-5511
Mark Dupra, supt. Fax 278-5900
Charlotte Valley S 400/K-12
15611 State Highway 23 13750 607-278-5511
Edgar Whaley, prin. Fax 278-5900

Deer Park, Suffolk, Pop. 28,300
Deer Park UFD — 4,300/PK-12
1881 Deer Park Ave 11729 — 631-274-4010
Richard E. Organisciak, supt. — Fax 242-6762
www.deerparkschools.org/
Deer Park HS — 1,100/9-12
30 Rockaway Ave 11729 — 631-274-4110
Nanine Cuttitta, prin. — Fax 243-4225
Frost MS — 1,100/6-8
450 Half Hollow Rd 11729 — 631-274-4210
Dr. Julia Bingham, prin. — Fax 242-0035

De Kalb Junction, Saint Lawrence
Hermon-DeKalb Central SD — 400/PK-12
709 E DeKalb Rd 13630 — 315-347-3442
Ann Adams, supt. — Fax 347-3817
hdcs.sllboces.org
Hermon-DeKalb Central S — 400/PK-12
709 E DeKalb Rd 13630 — 315-347-3442
Mark White, prin. — Fax 347-3817

Delanson, Schenectady, Pop. 399
Duanesburg Central SD — 1,000/K-12
133 School Rd 12053 — 518-895-2279
Dr. Mark Villanti, supt. — Fax 895-2626
dcs.neric.org
Duanesburg JSHS — 500/6-12
163 School Rd 12053 — 518-895-2355
Wilford LeForestier, prin. — Fax 895-9971

Delhi, Delaware, Pop. 2,551
Delhi Central SD — 1,000/K-12
2 Sheldon Dr 13753 — 607-746-1300
George Mack Ph.D., supt. — Fax 746-6028
delhischools.org
Delaware Academy HS — 400/9-12
2 Sheldon Dr 13753 — 607-746-2103
D. Scott Bojanich, prin. — Fax 746-1324
Delhi MS — 300/6-8
2 Sheldon Dr 13753 — 607-746-8775
Fax 746-1210

SUNY College of Technology — Post-Sec.
2 Main St 13753 — 607-746-4000

Delmar, Albany, Pop. 8,360
Bethlehem Central SD — 5,000/K-12
90 Adams Pl 12054 — 518-439-7098
Leslie Loomis, supt. — Fax 475-0352
bcsd.k12.ny.us
Bethlehem Central HS — 1,500/9-12
700 Delaware Ave 12054 — 518-439-4921
Charles Abba, prin. — Fax 439-2837
Bethlehem Central MS — 1,300/6-8
332 Kenwood Ave 12054 — 518-439-7460
Jodi Monroe, prin. — Fax 475-0092

Depew, Erie, Pop. 16,194
Depew UFD — 2,400/K-12
591 Terrace Blvd 14043 — 716-686-2253
Robert F. DeFilippo, supt. — Fax 686-2269
www.depewschools.org/
Depew HS — 800/9-12
5201 Transit Rd 14043 — 716-686-2421
Carol Townsend, prin. — Fax 686-2478
Depew MS — 800/5-8
5201 Transit Rd 14043 — 716-686-2440
Fax 686-2410

Deposit, Delaware, Pop. 1,657
Deposit Central SD — 700/K-12
171 2nd St 13754 — 607-467-5380
Oliver Blaise, supt. — Fax 467-5535
Deposit JSHS — 300/7-12
171 2nd St 13754 — 607-467-2197
John Murphy, prin. — Fax 467-5504

DeRuyter, Madison, Pop. 524
De Ruyter Central SD — 500/PK-12
711 Railroad St 13052 — 315-852-3410
Bruce R. Sharpe, supt. — Fax 852-9600
De Ruyter JSHS — 300/6-12
711 Railroad St 13052 — 315-852-3400
Edmund Ludwig, prin. — Fax 852-9600

De Witt, Onondaga, Pop. 8,244
Jamesville-DeWitt Central SD — 2,700/K-12
PO Box 606 13214 — 315-445-8304
Alice Kendrick, supt. — Fax 445-8477
www.jamesvilledewitt.org
Jamesville-DeWitt HS — 900/9-12
6845 Edinger Dr 13214 — 315-445-8340
Paul Gasparini, prin. — Fax 445-8307
Other Schools – See Jamesville

Manlius Pebble Hill S — 600/PK-12
5300 Jamesville Rd 13214 — 315-446-2452
Baxter Ball, prin. — Fax 446-2620

Dexter, Jefferson, Pop. 1,123
General Brown Central SD — 1,500/K-12
PO Box 500 13634 — 315-639-4711
Stephan Vigliotti, supt. — Fax 639-6916
www.gblions.org
Brown JSHS — 800/7-12
17643 Cemetery Rd 13634 — 315-639-6234
Mary Margaret Zehr, prin. — Fax 639-3444

Dix Hills, Suffolk, Pop. 26,100
Half Hollow Hills Central SD — 9,200/K-12
525 Half Hollow Rd 11746 — 631-592-3000
Dr. Sheldon Karnilow, supt. — Fax 592-3930
www.halfhollowhills.k12.ny.us
Candlewood MS — 1,000/6-8
1200 Carlls Straight Path 11746 — 631-592-3300
Andrew Greene, prin. — Fax 592-3921
Half Hollow Hills HS East — 1,400/9-12
50 Vanderbilt Pkwy 11746 — 631-592-3100
Al Kindelmann, prin. — Fax 592-3907
Half Hollow Hills HS West — 1,200/9-12
375 Wolf Hill Rd 11746 — 631-592-3200
Dr. James Lofrese, prin. — Fax 592-3923
Other Schools – See Melville

Five Towns College — Post-Sec.
305 N Service Rd 11746 — 631-424-7000
Upper Room Christian S — 300/PK-12
722 Deer Park Rd 11746 — 631-242-5359
Gregory Eck, prin. — Fax 242-5418

Dobbs Ferry, Westchester, Pop. 11,041
Dobbs Ferry UFD — 1,400/K-12
505 Broadway 10522 — 914-693-1506
Dr. Sidney Freund, supt. — Fax 693-1787
www2.lhric.org/dobbsferry
Dobbs Ferry HS — 400/9-12
505 Broadway 10522 — 914-693-7645
Keith Yi, prin. — Fax 693-1115
Dobbs Ferry MS — 300/6-8
505 Broadway 10522 — 914-693-7640
Marjorie Holderman, prin. — Fax 693-1115

Greenburgh 11 UFD — 300/K-12
PO Box 501 10522 — 914-693-8500
Sandra Mallah, supt. — Fax 693-4029
Greenburgh Eleven HS — 100/9-12
PO Box 501 10522 — 914-693-8500
Sandra Strang, prin. — Fax 693-4029

Long Island University — Post-Sec.
555 Broadway 10522 — 914-693-4500
Masters S — 500/5-12
49 Clinton Ave 10522 — 914-479-6400
Dr. Maureen Fonseca, hdmstr. — Fax 693-1230
Mercy College — Post-Sec.
555 Broadway 10522 — 914-674-7600
Our Lady of Victory Academy — 400/9-12
565 Broadway 10522 — 914-693-1633
Sr. Joan Agro, prin. — Fax 693-5250

Dolgeville, Herkimer, Pop. 2,105
Dolgeville Central SD — 900/PK-12
38 Slawson St 13329 — 315-429-3155
Theodore Kawryga, supt. — Fax 429-8473
dolgeville.org
Dolgeville Centeral MSHS — 400/7-12
38 Slawson St 13329 — 315-429-3155
James D. Donnelly, prin. — Fax 429-8473

Dover Plains, Dutchess, Pop. 1,847
Dover UFD — 1,700/K-12
2368 Route 22 12522 — 845-832-4500
Dr. Craig Onofry, supt. — Fax 832-4511
www.doverschools.org
Dover HS — 600/9-12
2368 Route 22 12522 — 845-832-4520
Michael Tierney, prin. — Fax 832-3924
Dover MS — 500/6-8
2368 Route 22 12522 — 845-832-4521
Michael Tierney, prin. — Fax 832-3924

Downsville, Delaware
Downsville Central SD — 400/K-12
PO Box J 13755 — 607-363-2100
Robert Mackey, supt.
www.dcseagles.org
Downsville Central S — 400/K-12
PO Box J 13755 — 607-363-2111
Philip Fusco, prin. — Fax 363-2105

Dryden, Tompkins, Pop. 1,867
Dryden Central SD — 1,700/K-12
PO Box 88 13053 — 607-844-8694
Mark J. Crawford, supt. — Fax 844-4733
www.dryden.k12.ny.us
Dryden HS — 600/9-12
PO Box 88 13053 — 607-844-8694
Richard During, prin. — Fax 844-9004
Dryden MS — 500/6-8
PO Box 88 13053 — 607-844-8694
Edmund Walsh, prin. — Fax 844-5174

Tompkins Cortland Community College — Post-Sec.
PO Box 139 13053 — 607-844-8211

Dundee, Yates, Pop. 1,689
Dundee Central SD — 900/K-12
55 Water St 14837 — 607-243-5533
Nancy Zimar, supt. — Fax 243-7912
www.dundeecs.k12.ny.us/
Dundee JSHS — 400/7-12
55 Water St 14837 — 607-243-5534
Michael Chirco, prin. — Fax 243-7912

Dunkirk, Chautauqua, Pop. 12,715
Dunkirk CSD — 2,100/K-12
620 Marauder Dr 14048 — 716-366-9300
Carl Militello, supt. — Fax 366-9399
www.dunkirk.wnyric.org
Dunkirk HS — 600/9-12
75 W 6th St 14048 — 716-366-9390
Daniel Genovese, prin. — Fax 366-0321
Dunkirk MS — 500/6-8
525 Eagle St 14048 — 716-366-9380
David Boyda, prin. — Fax 366-9357

East Amherst, Erie
Williamsville Central SD — 10,800/K-12
PO Box 5000 14051 — 716-626-8000
Dr. Howard Smith, supt. — Fax 626-8089
www.williamsvillek12.org
Casey MS — 900/5-8
105 Casey Rd 14051 — 716-626-8585
Francis McGreevy, prin. — Fax 626-8562
Transit MS — 1,100/5-8
8730 Transit Rd 14051 — 716-626-8701
Jill Pellis, prin. — Fax 626-8796
Williamsville East HS — 1,000/9-12
151 Paradise Rd 14051 — 716-626-8404
Neal Miller, prin. — Fax 626-8460
Other Schools – See Williamsville

East Aurora, Erie, Pop. 6,493
East Aurora UFD — 2,100/K-12
430 Main St 14052 — 585-687-2302
James Bodziak, supt. — Fax 652-8581
www.eaur.wnyric.org/

East Aurora HS — 700/9-12
1003 Center St 14052 — 585-687-2505
Dr. James Hoagland, prin. — Fax 687-2552
East Aurora MS — 500/6-8
430 Main St 14052 — 585-687-2453
Dennis Leach, prin. — Fax 652-8581

Christ the King Seminary — Post-Sec.
PO Box 607 14052 — 585-652-8900

Eastchester, Westchester, Pop. 18,537
Eastchester UFD — 2,500/K-12
580 White Plains Rd 10709 — 914-793-6130
Dr. Robert Siebert, supt. — Fax 793-9006
www2.lhric.org/eastchester/
Eastchester HS — 700/9-12
2 Stewart Pl 10709 — 914-793-6130
Dr. Jeffrey Capuano, prin. — Fax 793-9000
Eastchester MS — 600/6-8
550 White Plains Rd 10709 — 914-793-6130
Dr. Walter Moran, prin. — Fax 793-1699

Tuckahoe UFD
Supt. — See Tuckahoe
Tuckahoe HS — 300/9-12
65 Siwanoy Blvd 10709 — 914-337-5376
Bart Linehan, prin. — Fax 337-5168
Tuckahoe MS — 200/6-8
65 Siwanoy Blvd 10709 — 914-337-5376
Carl Albano, prin. — Fax 337-5236

East Elmhurst, See New York
NYC Department of Education
Supt. — See New York
IS 227 — 1,300/5-8
3202 Junction Blvd 11369 — 718-335-7500
Renee David, prin. — Fax 779-7186

Monsignor McClancy Memorial HS — 500/9-12
7106 31st Ave 11370 — 718-898-3800
James Carey, prin. — Fax 898-3929

East Greenbush, Rensselaer, Pop. 3,784
East Greenbush Central SD — 4,600/K-12
29 Englewood Ave 12061 — 518-477-2755
Terrance Brewer, supt. — Fax 477-4833
www.egcsd.org
Columbia HS — 1,500/9-12
962 Luther Rd 12061 — 518-207-2000
Michael Kuzdzal, prin. — Fax 207-2009
Goff MS — 1,200/6-8
35 Gilligan Rd 12061 — 518-477-2731
Deborah Marcil, prin. — Fax 477-2667

East Hampton, Suffolk, Pop. 1,354
East Hampton UFD — 2,000/PK-12
4 Long Ln 11937 — 631-329-4104
Dr. Raymond Gualtieri, supt. — Fax 329-7550
www.ehufsd.org
East Hampton HS — 1,000/9-12
2 Long Ln 11937 — 631-329-4130
Scott Farina, prin. — Fax 329-4183
East Hampton MS — 500/5-8
76 Newtown Ln 11937 — 631-329-4116
Gail Parker, prin. — Fax 329-4187

East Islip, Suffolk, Pop. 14,325

Hewlett School of East Islip — 100/PK-12
74 Suffolk Ln 11730 — 631-581-1035

East Meadow, Nassau, Pop. 37,600
East Meadow UFD
Supt. — See Westbury
East Meadow HS — 1,700/9-12
101 Carman Ave 11554 — 516-228-5331
Mark Scher, prin. — Fax 228-5339
Woodland MS — 1,300/6-8
690 Wenwood Dr 11554 — 516-564-6523
James Lethbridge, prin. — Fax 564-6519

East Moriches, Suffolk, Pop. 4,021
East Moriches UFD — 400/K-8
9 Adelaide Ave 11940 — 631-878-0162
Dr. Charles Russo, supt. — Fax 878-0186
www.eastmoriches.k12.ny.us
East Moriches MS — 400/5-8
9 Adelaide Ave 11940 — 631-878-0162
Allyn Leeds, prin. — Fax 874-0096

East Northport, Suffolk, Pop. 20,411
Commack UFD — 7,400/K-12
480 Clay Pitts Rd 11731 — 631-912-2000
Dr. James Feltman, supt. — Fax 266-2406
www.commack.k12.ny.us
Other Schools – See Commack

Northport-East Northport UFD
Supt. — See Northport
East Northport MS — 700/6-8
1075 5th Ave 11731 — 631-262-6770
Joanne Kroon, prin. — Fax 262-6773

East Norwich, Nassau, Pop. 2,698
Oyster Bay-East Norwich Central SD
Supt. — See Oyster Bay
Vernon S — 700/3-8
880 Oyster Bay Rd 11732 — 516-624-6562
Martin Malone, prin. — Fax 624-6522

East Patchogue, Suffolk, Pop. 20,195
South Country Central SD — 4,700/PK-12
189 N Dunton Ave 11772 — 631-730-1510
Dr. Susan Agruso, supt. — Fax 286-6394
www.southcountry.org
Other Schools – See Bellport, Brookhaven

Victory Christian Academy — 100/PK-12
1343 Montauk Hwy 11772 — 631-654-9284
Barbara Seaton, prin. — Fax 654-9297

East Rochester, Monroe, Pop. 6,510
East Rochester UFD — 1,300/PK-12
222 Woodbine Ave 14445 — 585-248-6302
Howard Maffucci, supt.
www.erschools.org
East Rochester JSHS — 700/5-12
200 Woodbine Ave 14445 — 585-248-6350
James Karg, prin. — Fax 248-6383

East Rockaway, Nassau, Pop. 10,341
East Rockaway UFD — 1,200/K-12
443 Ocean Ave 11518 — 516-887-8300
Arnold Dodge Ph.D., supt. — Fax 887-8308
www.eastrockawayschools.org
East Rockaway JSHS — 600/7-12
443 Ocean Ave 11518 — 516-887-8300
William Fortgang, prin. — Fax 887-8308

East Setauket, See Setauket
Three Village Central SD — 7,900/K-12
PO Box 9050 11733 — 631-730-4000
Frank Carasiti, supt.
www.3villagecsd.k12.ny.us
Melville HS — 1,800/10-12
380 Old Town Rd 11733 — 631-730-4900
Thomas Colletti, prin. — Fax 730-4901
Other Schools – See Setauket, Stony Brook

East Syracuse, Onondaga, Pop. 3,118
East Syracuse-Minoa Central SD — 3,800/PK-12
407 Fremont Rd 13057 — 315-656-7205
Dr. Donna DeSiato, supt. — Fax 656-3241
www.esmschools.org
East Syracuse-Minoa Central HS — 1,200/9-12
6400 Fremont Rd 13057 — 315-656-7242
Francis Murphy, prin. — Fax 656-4307
Pine Grove MS — 900/6-8
6318 Fremont Rd 13057 — 315-656-7265
Lee Carulli, prin. — Fax 656-2530

Bishop Grimes JSHS — 600/7-12
6653 Kirkville Rd 13057 — 315-437-0356
Sr. James Therese Downey, prin. — Fax 437-0358

Eden, Erie, Pop. 3,088
Eden Central SD — 1,800/K-12
PO Box 267 14057 — 716-992-3629
Robert Zimmerman, supt. — Fax 992-3682
www.edencentral.org/
Eden JSHS — 900/7-12
PO Box 267 14057 — 716-992-3641
Ron Buggs, prin. — Fax 992-3652

Edmeston, Otsego
Edmeston Central SD — 600/K-12
11 North St 13335 — 607-965-8931
David Rowley, supt. — Fax 965-8942
Edmeston Central S — 600/K-12
11 North St 13335 — 607-965-8931
Martha Winsor, prin. — Fax 965-8942

Eggertsville, Erie

Buffalo Academy of the Sacred Heart — 400/9-12
3860 Main St 14226 — 716-834-2101
Barbara Ochterski Ph.D., prin. — Fax 834-2944

Elba, Genesee, Pop. 679
Elba Central SD — 600/K-12
PO Box 370 14058 — 585-757-9967
Joan Cole, supt. — Fax 757-2713
www.elbacsd.org
Elba JSHS — 300/7-12
PO Box 370 14058 — 585-757-9967
Jason Smith, prin. — Fax 757-6683

Eldred, Sullivan
Eldred Central SD — 700/K-12
PO Box 249 12732 — 845-557-6141
Dr. Ivan J. Katz, supt. — Fax 557-3672
www.eldredschools.org
Eldred Central JSHS — 400/7-12
PO Box 249 12732 — 845-557-6014
Scott Krebs, prin. — Fax 557-3672

Elizabethtown, Essex
Elizabethtown-Lewis Central SD — 400/K-12
PO Box 158 12932 — 518-873-6371
Gail S. Else, supt. — Fax 873-9552
Elizabethtown-Lewis Central S — 400/K-12
PO Box 158 12932 — 518-873-6371
Amy L. Tyo, prin. — Fax 873-9552

Ellenburg Depot, Clinton
Northern Adirondack Central SD — 1,100/K-12
PO Box 164 12935 — 518-594-7060
William Scott, supt. — Fax 594-7255
Northern Adirondack JSHS — 700/6-12
PO Box 164 12935 — 518-594-3962
John Coughenour, prin. — Fax 594-7255

Ellenville, Ulster, Pop. 4,106
Ellenville Central SD — 1,800/K-12
28 Maple Ave 12428 — 845-647-0100
Lisa Wiles, supt. — Fax 647-0105
www.ecs.k12.ny.us
Ellenville HS — 600/9-12
28 Maple Ave 12428 — 845-647-0123
Tony Rigothi, prin. — Fax 647-5972
Ellenville MS — 600/5-8
28 Maple Ave 12428 — 845-647-0126
Glenn Bollin, prin. — Fax 647-0230

Ellicottville, Cattaraugus, Pop. 515
Ellicottville Central SD — 700/PK-12
5873 Route 219 S 14731 — 716-699-2368
Patricia Haynes, supt. — Fax 699-6017
Ellicottville MSHS — 400/6-12
5873 Route 219 S 14731 — 716-699-2316
Robert Miller, prin.

Elma, Erie
Iroquois Central SD — 2,900/K-12
PO Box 32 14059 — 716-652-3000
Neil Rochelle, supt. — Fax 652-9305
www.iroquois.wnyric.org
Iroquois HS — 1,000/9-12
PO Box 32 14059 — 716-652-3000
Dennis Kenney, prin. — Fax 995-2440
Iroquois MS — 800/6-8
PO Box 32 14059 — 716-652-3000
Brian Wiesinger, prin. — Fax 995-2335

Elmhurst, See New York
NYC Department of Education
Supt. — See New York
IS 5 — 1,500/6-8
5040 Jacobus St 11373 — 718-205-6788
Steven Katz, prin. — Fax 429-6518
Newtown HS — 4,100/9-12
4801 90th St 11373 — 718-595-8510
John Ficalora, prin. — Fax 699-8584
Queens Occupational Training Center — Vo/Tech
5712 94th St 11373 — 718-760-1083
Madeline Hassell, prin. — Fax 760-1920

Cathedral Prep Seminary — 200/9-12
5625 92nd St 11373 — 718-592-6800
Rev. Joseph Calise, prin. — Fax 592-5574

Elmira, Chemung, Pop. 30,336
Elmira CSD — 8,400/PK-12
951 Hoffman St 14905 — 607-735-3000
Dr. Raymond Bryant, supt. — Fax 735-3002
www.elmiracityschools.com
Broadway MS — 700/7-8
1000 Broadway St 14904 — 607-735-3300
Rose Kramarik, prin. — Fax 735-3309
Davis MS — 500/7-8
610 Lake St 14901 — 607-735-3400
Lisa Kelly, prin. — Fax 735-3409
Elmira Free Academy — 1,100/9-12
933 Hoffman St 14905 — 607-735-3100
Robert Bailey, prin. — Fax 735-3109
Southside HS — 1,200/9-12
777 S Main St 14904 — 607-735-3200
Christopher Krantz, prin. — Fax 735-3209

Arnot-Ogden Medical Center — Post-Sec.
600 Roe Ave 14905 — 607-737-4289
Arnot-Ogden Medical Center — Post-Sec.
600 Roe Ave 14905 — 607-737-4153
Elmira Business Institute — Post-Sec.
303 N Main St 14901 — 800-843-1812
Elmira Christian Academy — 100/K-12
235 E Miller St 14904 — 607-734-7195
David Cook, prin. — Fax 734-7195
Elmira College — Post-Sec.
1 Park Pl 14901 — 607-735-1800
Holy Family JHS — 100/7-8
1010 Davis St 14901 — 607-734-0336
Elizabeth Berliner, prin. — Fax 734-4977
Notre Dame HS — 300/9-12
1400 Maple Ave 14904 — 607-734-2267
Sr. Mary Walter Hickey, prin. — Fax 737-8903

Elmira Heights, Chemung, Pop. 4,072
Elmira Heights Central SD — 1,100/K-12
100 Robinwood Ave 14903 — 607-734-7114
Mary Beth Fiore, supt. — Fax 734-7134
www.heightsschools.com
Cohen MS — 300/6-8
100 Robinwood Ave 14903 — 607-734-5078
Judith Sanford, prin. — Fax 734-9382
Edison HS — 400/9-12
2083 College Ave 14903 — 607-733-5604
Al Turshman, prin. — Fax 737-7976

Elmont, Nassau, Pop. 33,600
Sewanhaka Central HSD
Supt. — See Floral Park
Elmont Memorial HS — 2,000/7-12
555 Ridge Rd 11003 — 516-488-9200
John Capozzi, prin. — Fax 488-9213

Elmsford, Westchester, Pop. 4,723
Elmsford UFD — 1,000/PK-12
98 S Goodwin Ave 10523 — 914-592-8440
Dr. Carol Franks-Randall, supt. — Fax 592-2181
www.elmsd.org
Hamilton JSHS — 400/7-12
98 S Goodwin Ave 10523 — 914-592-7311
Leonard Mecca, prin. — Fax 592-2181

Elwood, Suffolk, Pop. 10,916
Elwood UFD
Supt. — See Greenlawn
Elwood/Glenn HS — 700/9-12
478 Elwood Rd 11731 — 631-266-5410
Vincent Mulieri, prin. — Fax 368-5038
Elwood MS — 600/6-8
478 Elwood Rd 11731 — 631-266-5420
Patrick Scarola, prin. — Fax 368-2338

Endicott, Broome, Pop. 12,876
Union-Endicott Central SD — 4,700/K-12
1100 E Main St 13760 — 607-757-2811
Dr. James P. Coon, supt. — Fax 757-2809
www.uetigers.stier.org
Snapp MS — 1,000/6-8
101 S Loder Ave 13760 — 607-757-2156
Ann Marie Foley, prin. — Fax 658-7117
Union-Endicott HS — 1,400/9-12
1200 E Main St 13760 — 607-757-2181
Pamela Sellitto, prin. — Fax 757-2535

Endwell, Broome, Pop. 12,602
Maine-Endwell Central SD — 2,700/K-12
712 Farm To Market Rd 13760 — 607-754-1400
Joseph Stoner, supt. — Fax 754-1650
www.me.stier.org//main.html
Maine-Endwell HS — 900/9-12
750 Farm To Market Rd 13760 — 607-754-1400
Bonnie Hauber, prin. — Fax 754-1650

Maine-Endwell MS — 600/6-8
1119 Farm To Market Rd 13760 — 607-786-8271
Richard Otis, prin. — Fax 754-1650

Fabius, Onondaga, Pop. 350
Fabius-Pompey Central SD — 900/K-12
1211 Mill St 13063 — 315-683-5301
Martin Swenson, supt. — Fax 683-5827
www.fabiuspompey.org
Fabius-Pompey JSHS — 500/6-12
1211 Mill St 13063 — 315-683-5811
Timothy Ryan, prin. — Fax 683-5569

Fairport, Monroe, Pop. 5,690
Fairport Central SD — 7,000/K-12
38 W Church St 14450 — 585-421-2004
William Cala, supt. — Fax 421-3421
www.fairport.org
Brown MS — 1,000/6-8
665 Ayrault Rd 14450 — 585-421-2065
David Dunn, prin. — Fax 421-2136
Fairport HS — 1,600/10-12
1358 Ayrault Rd 14450 — 585-421-2100
David Paddock, prin. — Fax 421-4645
Minerva-Deland JHS — 600/9-9
140 Hulburt Rd 14450 — 585-421-2030
Pat Moriarty, prin. — Fax 421-1985
Perrin MS — 800/6-8
85 Potter Pl 14450 — 585-421-2080
Brett Provenzano, prin. — Fax 421-2097

Falconer, Chautauqua, Pop. 2,470
Falconer Central SD — 1,400/PK-12
2 East Ave N 14733 — 716-665-6624
Jane R. Fosberg, supt. — Fax 665-9265
www.falconer.wnyric.org/
Falconer HS — 500/9-12
2 East Ave N 14733 — 716-665-6624
Charles Nebral, prin. — Fax 665-9265
Falconer MS — 300/6-8
2 East Ave N 14733 — 716-665-6624
Judy Roach, prin. — Fax 665-9265

Fallsburg, Sullivan
Fallsburg Central SD — 1,400/K-12
PO Box 124 12733 — 845-434-5884
Walter Milton, supt. — Fax 434-8346
www.fallsburgcsd.net/
Fallsburg HS — 700/7-12
PO Box 124 12733 — 845-434-6800
Michael Kenniston, prin. — Fax 434-0418

Farmingdale, Nassau, Pop. 8,665
Farmingdale UFD — 8,000/K-12
50 Van Cott Ave 11735 — 631-752-6510
Dr. Roberta A. Gerold, supt.
www.farmingdale.k12.ny.us
Farmingdale HS — 1,800/9-12
150 Lincoln St 11735 — 631-752-6600
Allan Bauer, prin. — Fax 454-6196
Howitt MS — 1,000/6-8
70 Van Cott Ave 11735 — 631-752-6525
Luis Pena, prin. — Fax 752-7013

Farmingdale SUNY — Post-Sec.
2350 Broadhollow Rd 11735 — 631-420-2000

Farmingville, Suffolk, Pop. 14,842
Sachem Central SD
Supt. — See Holbrook
Sachem HS East — 9-12
177 Granny Rd 11738 — 631-716-8200
John Aleksak, prin. — Fax 716-8207

Faith Academy — 200/PK-12
1070 Portion Rd 11738 — 631-732-7088
Karen Warren, admin. — Fax 696-2799

Far Rockaway, See New York
NYC Department of Education
Supt. — See New York
Douglass Academy VI HS — 9-12
821 Bay 25th St 11691 — 718-471-2154
Linda Alfred, prin.
Far Rockaway HS — 1,200/9-12
821 Bay 25th St 11691 — 718-327-6000
Denise Hallet, prin. — Fax 327-8836
IS 53 — 1,100/6-8
1045 Nameoke St 11691 — 718-471-6900
Claude Monereau, prin. — Fax 471-6955

Beis Medrash Heichal Dovid — Post-Sec.
275 Beach 17th St 11691 — 718-868-2300
Church of God Christian Academy — 200/K-12
1336 Central Ave 11691 — 718-327-5090
Clarke JHS — 200/7-8
Beach 112th St 11694 — 718-634-4994
Geri Martinez, prin. — Fax 634-5267
Global Business Institute — Post-Sec.
1931 Mott Ave 11691 — 718-327-2220
Mesivta Chaim Shlomo S — 200/9-12
257 Beach 17th St 11691 — 718-868-2300
Rabbi Menachem Gold, prin. — Fax 868-0517
Stella Maris HS — 500/7-12
140 Beach 112th St 11694 — 718-634-4994
Geri Martinez, prin. — Fax 634-5267
Tichon Meir Moshe S — 50/9-9
716 Beach 9th St 11691 — 718-327-6645
Adina Mandel, prin. — Fax 327-8345
Torah Academy HS for Girls — 300/9-12
636 Lanett Ave 11691 — 718-327-1300
Abraham Aufrichtig, prin. — Fax 327-2315
Yeshiva of Far Rockaway S — 200/9-12
802 Hicksville Rd 11691 — 718-327-7600
Rabbi Aaron Brafman, prin. — Fax 327-1430

Fayetteville, Onondaga, Pop. 4,164
Fayetteville-Manlius Central SD
Supt. — See Manlius
Wellwood MS — 700/5-8
700 S Manlius St 13066 — 315-692-1300
John Almonte, prin. — Fax 692-1049

Fillmore, Allegany, Pop. 450
Fillmore Central SD — 500/K-12
PO Box 177 14735 — 585-567-2251
David Hanks, supt. — Fax 567-2541
www.fillmore.wnyric.org/
Fillmore Central HS — 500/5-12
PO Box 177 14735 — 585-567-2251
Kyle Faulkner, prin. — Fax 567-2541

Fishers Island, Suffolk
Fishers Island UFD — 100/PK-12
PO Box A 06390 — 631-788-7444
Jeanne Schultz, supt. — Fax 788-5562
www.fischool.com
Fishers Island Central S — 100/PK-12
PO Box A 06390 — 631-788-7444
Jeanne Schultz, prin. — Fax 788-5562

Floral Park, Nassau, Pop. 15,862
NYC Department of Education
Supt. — See New York
MS 172 — 1,200/6-9
8114 257th St 11004 — 718-831-4000
Jeffrey Slivko, prin. — Fax 831-4008

Sewanhaka Central HSD — 8,400/7-12
77 Landau Ave 11001 — 516-488-9800
Dr. John Williams, supt. — Fax 488-9899
www.sewanhaka.k12.ny.us/
Floral Park Memorial HS — 1,500/7-12
210 Locust St 11001 — 516-488-9300
Kathleen Sottile, prin. — Fax 488-9214
Sewanhaka HS — 1,600/7-12
500 Tulip Ave 11001 — 516-488-9600
Debra Lidowsky, prin. — Fax 488-9215
Other Schools – See Elmont, Franklin Square, New Hyde Park

Florida, Orange, Pop. 2,769
Florida UFD — 900/K-12
PO Box 757 10921 — 845-651-3095
Douglas Burnside, supt. — Fax 651-6801
www.floridaufsd.org
Seward Institute — 500/6-12
PO Box 757 10921 — 845-651-4038
Michael Rheaume, prin. — Fax 651-7166

Flushing, See New York
NYC Department of Education
Supt. — See New York
Bowne HS — 3,500/9-12
6325 Main St 11367 — 718-263-1919
Frank McQuail, prin. — Fax 575-4069
Flushing HS — 2,500/9-12
3501 Union St 11354 — 718-888-7500
Cornelia Gutwein, prin. — Fax 886-4255
IS 25 — 1,100/7-9
3465 192nd St 11358 — 718-961-3480
Joseph Catone, prin. — Fax 358-1563
IS 237 — 1,100/7-9
4621 Colden St 11355 — 718-353-6464
Joseph Cantara, prin. — Fax 460-6427
IS 250 — 200/5-8
7540 Parsons Blvd 11366 — 718-591-3015
Marc Rosenberg, prin. — Fax 591-3237
Flushing International HS — 9-12
14480 Barclay Ave 11355 — 718-463-2348
Joseph Luft, prin. — Fax 463-3514
JHS 168 — 700/7-9
15840 76th Rd 11366 — 718-591-9000
Judy Gewuerz, prin. — Fax 591-2340
JHS 185 — 1,000/7-9
14726 25th Dr 11354 — 718-445-3232
Valerie Sawinski, prin. — Fax 359-5352
JHS 189 — 1,000/7-9
14480 Barclay Ave 11355 — 718-359-6676
Cindy Diaz-Burgos, prin. — Fax 358-0155
JHS 216 — 1,400/6-8
6420 175th St 11365 — 718-358-2005
Reginald Landeau, prin. — Fax 358-2070
Harris HS — 1,100/9-12
14911 Melbourne Ave 11367 — 718-575-5580
Tom Cunningham, prin. — Fax 575-1366
Kennedy Community HS — 400/9-12
7540 Parsons Blvd 11366 — 718-969-5510
Ira Pernick, prin. — Fax 969-5524
Lewis HS — 3,900/9-12
5820 Utopia Pkwy 11365 — 718-357-7740
Jeffrey Scherr, prin. — Fax 357-5903

CUNY Queens College — Post-Sec.
6530 Kissena Blvd 11367 — 718-997-5000
Holy Cross HS — 900/9-12
2620 Francis Lewis Blvd 11358 — 718-886-7250
Joseph Giannuzzi, prin. — Fax 886-7257
Long Island Business Institute — Post-Sec.
3712 Prince St 11354 — 718-939-5100
Rabbinical Seminary Chofetz Chaim HS — 100/9-12
7601 147th St 11367 — 718-263-1445
Dr. William Muller, prin. — Fax 263-4918
St. Vincent Catholic Medical Center — Post-Sec.
17505 Horace Harding Expy 11365 — 718-357-0500
Shaarey B'nos Chayil - Shevach HS — 200/9-12
7509 Main St 11367 — 718-263-0525
Rachel Reifer, prin. — Fax 263-3759
Vaughn College of Aeronautics and Tech — Post-Sec.
8601 23rd Ave 11369 — 718-429-6600
Windsor S — 200/6-12
4160 Kissena Blvd 11355 — 718-359-8300

Fonda, Montgomery, Pop. 791
Fonda-Fultonville Central SD — 1,600/K-12
PO Box 1501 12068 — 518-853-4415
Glenn Goodale, supt. — Fax 853-4461
www.fondafultonvilleschools.org
Fonda-Fultonville HS — 500/9-12
PO Box 1501 12068 — 518-853-3182
Jay De Traglia, prin. — Fax 853-1239
Fonda-Fultonville MS — 500/5-8
PO Box 1501 12068 — 518-853-4747
Elizabeth Donovan, prin. — Fax 853-4461

Forest Hills, See New York
NYC Department of Education
Supt. — See New York
Forest Hills HS — 3,300/9-12
6701 110th St 11375 — 718-268-3137
Stephen Frey, prin. — Fax 793-7850
JHS 190 — 1,200/7-9
6817 Austin St 11375 — 718-830-4970
Marilyn Grant, prin. — Fax 830-4960

Bramson O R T College — Post-Sec.
6930 Austin St 11375 — 718-261-5800
Ezra Academy — 300/7-12
11945 Union Tpke 11375 — 718-263-5500
Francine Hirschman, prin. — Fax 520-9424
Kew-Forest S — 400/K-12
11917 Union Tpke 11375 — 718-268-4667
Peter Lewis, hdmstr. — Fax 268-9121
Mesivta Yesodei Yeshurun — 100/9-12
7102 113th St 11375 — 718-261-4738
Dr. Yaakov Nierman, prin. — Fax 793-1546
Midrash L'man Achai — 100/7-12
7102 113th St 11375 — 718-544-4875
Chaim Slomnicki, prin. — Fax 544-4768
Rabbinical Seminary of America — Post-Sec.
9215 69th Ave 11375 — 718-268-4700
Yeshiva Binat Chaim — 100/7-12
10616 70th Ave 11375 — 718-520-7775
Rabbi Levi Abdurakhmanov, prin. — Fax 520-0111

Forestville, Chautauqua, Pop. 747
Forestville Central SD — 600/K-12
12 Water St 14062 — 716-965-2742
John O'Connor, supt. — Fax 965-2117
www.forestville.com
Forestville Central JSHS — 400/6-12
4 Academy St 14062 — 716-965-2711
Charles Leichner, prin. — Fax 965-2102

Fort Ann, Washington, Pop. 466
Ft. Ann Central SD — 300/K-12
1 Catherine St 12827 — 518-639-5594
Maureen McNolty, supt. — Fax 639-8911
www.fortannschool.org/
Fort Ann JSHS — 300/7-12
1 Catherine St 12827 — 518-639-5594
Glenn Remington, prin. — Fax 639-8911

Fort Covington, Franklin
Salmon River Central SD — 1,600/PK-12
637 County Route 1 12937 — 518-358-6610
Glenn R. Bellinger, supt. — Fax 358-3492
Salmon River JSHS — 700/7-12
637 County Route 1 12937 — 518-358-6620
John Simons, prin. — Fax 358-9787

Fort Edward, Washington, Pop. 3,115
Fort Edward UFD — 300/K-12
220 Broadway 12828 — 518-747-4594
Stanley Maziejka, supt. — Fax 747-4289
www.fortedward.org
Fort Edward JSHS — 300/7-12
220 Broadway 12828 — 518-747-4529
John Godfrey, prin. — Fax 747-4289

Fort Montgomery, Orange, Pop. 1,450
Highland Falls-Ft. Montgomery Cntrl SD — 1,200/PK-12
21 Morgan Farm Rd 10922 — 845-446-9575
Dr. Philip Arbolino, supt. — Fax 446-3321
www.hffmcsd.org/
O'Neill HS — 600/9-12
21 Morgan Rd 10922 — 845-446-4914
Louis Trombetta, prin. — Fax 446-2123
Other Schools – See Highland Falls

Fort Plain, Montgomery, Pop. 2,243
Ft. Plain Central SD — 1,000/PK-12
25 High St 13339 — 518-993-4000
Douglas C. Burton, supt. — Fax 993-3393
www.fortplain.org
Fort Plain JSHS — 500/7-12
1 West St 13339 — 518-993-4000
Deborah Larrabee, prin. — Fax 993-2897

Frankfort, Herkimer, Pop. 2,462
Frankfort-Schuyler Central SD — 1,200/K-12
605 Palmer St 13340 — 315-894-5083
Robert Reina, supt. — Fax 895-7011
www.frankfort-schuyler.org
Frankfort-Schuyler Central JSHS — 600/6-12
605 Palmer St 13340 — 315-895-7461
Donald Stankavage, prin. — Fax 895-4032

Franklin, Delaware, Pop. 386
Franklin Central SD — 300/PK-12
PO Box 888 13775 — 607-829-3551
Michael Shea, supt. — Fax 829-2101
www.franklincsd.org
Franklin Central S — 300/PK-12
PO Box 888 13775 — 607-829-3551
Julie Lambiaso, prin. — Fax 829-2101

Franklin Square, Nassau, Pop. 29,500
Sewanhaka Central HSD
Supt. — See Floral Park
Carey HS — 1,800/7-12
230 Poppy Ave 11010 — 516-539-9400
Douglas Monaghan, prin. — Fax 565-4351

Valley Stream Central HSD
Supt. — See Valley Stream
Valley Stream North JSHS — 1,200/7-12
750 Herman Ave 11010 — 516-564-5510
Dr. Thomas Troisi, prin. — Fax 564-5539

Franklinville, Cattaraugus, Pop. 1,804
Franklinville Central SD — 1,000/PK-12
31 N Main St 14737 — 585-676-8029
Terence Dolan, supt.
Franklinville JSHS — 500/7-12
31 N Main St 14737 — 585-676-8060
Angelo Melaro, prin.

New Life Christian S — 50/K-12
Route 16 S 14737 — 585-676-2412
Dwight Coords, admin. — Fax 676-3995

Fredonia, Chautauqua, Pop. 10,569
Fredonia Central SD — 1,900/PK-12
425 E Main St 14063 — 716-679-1581
Paul J. DiFonzo, supt. — Fax 679-1555
www.fredonia.wnyric.org
Fredonia HS — 600/9-12
425 E Main St 14063 — 716-679-1581
Todd Crandall, prin. — Fax 672-8687
Fredonia MS — 500/6-8
425 E Main St 14063 — 716-679-1581
Andrew Ludwig, prin. — Fax 673-9449

SUNY College at Fredonia 14063 — Post-Sec.
716-673-3111

Freeport, Nassau, Pop. 43,726
Freeport UFD — 7,100/PK-12
235 N Ocean Ave 11520 — 516-867-5200
Dr. Eric L. Eversley, supt. — Fax 623-4759
www.freeportschools.org
Dodd MS — 1,100/7-8
25 Pine St 11520 — 516-867-5280
John O'Mard, prin. — Fax 379-6794
Freeport HS — 2,200/9-12
50 S Brookside Ave 11520 — 516-867-5300
Kimberlee Pierre, prin. — Fax 379-7592

De LaSalle S — 100/5-8
87 Pine St 11520 — 516-379-8660
Maryalice Doherty, prin. — Fax 379-8806
Freeport Christian Academy — 100/PK-10
50 N Main St 11520 — 516-546-2020
Tito Mattei, hdmstr. — Fax 546-8394

Fresh Meadows, See New York
NYC Department of Education
Supt. — See New York
Queens S of Inquiry — 6-12
15840 76th Rd 11366 — 718-935-3373
Elizabeth Ophals, prin.

St. Francis Prep S — 2,800/9-12
6100 Francis Lewis Blvd 11365 — 718-423-8810
Br. Leonard Conway, prin. — Fax 224-2108

Frewsburg, Chautauqua, Pop. 1,817
Frewsburg Central SD — 1,000/K-12
26 Institute St 14738 — 716-569-9241
Stephen J. Vanstrom, supt. — Fax 569-4681
frewsburg.wnyric.org
Frewsburg JSHS — 500/7-12
26 Institute St 14738 — 716-569-3255
Steve Vanstrom, prin. — Fax 569-4681

Friendship, Allegany, Pop. 1,423
Friendship Central SD — 400/PK-12
46 W Main St 14739 — 585-973-3534
Maureen Donahue, supt. — Fax 973-2023
Friendship Central S — 400/PK-12
46 W Main St 14739 — 585-973-3311
John Marshall, prin. — Fax 973-2023

Fulton, Oswego, Pop. 11,639
Fulton CSD — 3,900/K-12
167 S 4th St 13069 — 315-593-5510
William Lynch, supt. — Fax 598-6351
www.fulton.cnyric.org/
Bodley HS — 1,200/9-12
6 Gillard Dr 13069 — 315-593-5400
Dennis Dumas, prin. — Fax 593-5427
Fulton JHS — 700/7-8
129 Curtis St 13069 — 315-593-5440
Mark Slosek, prin. — Fax 593-5459

Gainesville, Wyoming, Pop. 296
Letchworth Central SD — 1,200/K-12
5550 School Rd 14066 — 585-493-5450
Joseph Backer, supt. — Fax 493-2762
www.letchworth.k12.ny.us/
Letchworth HS — 400/9-12
5550 School Rd 14066 — 585-493-2571
Thomas Kelleher, prin. — Fax 493-2762
Letchworth MS — 400/5-8
5550 School Rd 14066 — 585-493-2592
Jonathan Retz, prin. — Fax 493-2762

Galway, Saratoga, Pop. 214
Galway Central SD — 1,200/K-12
5317 Sacandaga Rd 12074 — 518-882-1033
Clifford Moses, supt.
www.galwaycsd.org/
Galway HS — 400/9-12
5317 Sacandaga Rd 12074 — 518-882-1221
Paul Jenkins, prin. — Fax 882-5250
Galway MS — 200/7-8
5317 Sacandaga Rd 12074 — 518-882-5047
Paul Berry, prin. — Fax 882-5850

Garden City, Nassau, Pop. 21,787
Garden City UFD — 4,200/K-12
56 Cathedral Ave 11530 — 516-478-1000
Robert Feirsen, supt. — Fax 294-1045
www.gardencity.k12.ny.us
Garden City HS — 1,100/9-12
170 Rockaway Ave 11530 — 516-478-2000
Hank Hardy, prin. — Fax 294-2639
Garden City MS — 1,100/6-8
98 Cherry Valley Ave 11530 — 516-478-3000
Peter Osroff, prin. — Fax 294-0732

Adelphi University — Post-Sec.
1 South Ave 11530 — 516-877-3000
Career Institute of Health & Technology — Post-Sec.
200 Garden City Plz Ste 100 11530 — 516-877-1225
Nassau Community College — Post-Sec.
1 Education Dr 11530 — 516-572-7501
Ultrasound Diagnostic School — Post-Sec.
711 Stewart Ave Ste 200 11530 — 516-248-6060

Waldorf S of Garden City | 400/PK-12
225 Cambridge Ave　11530 | 516-742-3434
Roxanne Murphy, admin. | Fax 742-3457

Garden City Park, Nassau, Pop. 7,437
Mineola UFD
Supt. — See Mineola
Mineola HS | 800/9-12
10 Armstrong Rd　11040 | 516-237-2600
Edward Escobar, prin. | Fax 739-4765

Garnerville, See West Haverstraw
Haverstraw-Stony Point Central SD | 6,700/PK-12
65 Chapel St　10923 | 845-942-3000
Dodge Watkins, supt. | Fax 942-3047
www.nrcsd.org
Other Schools – See Thiells

Geneseo, Livingston, Pop. 7,916
Geneseo Central SD | 900/K-12
4050 Avon Rd　14454 | 585-243-3450
Dr. Jon Hunter, supt. | Fax 243-9481
Geneseo JSHS | 500/6-12
4050 Avon Rd　14454 | 585-243-3450
Tim Hayes, prin. | Fax 243-9481

SUNY College at Geneseo | Post-Sec.
1 College Cir　14454 | 585-245-5211

Geneva, Ontario, Pop. 13,517
Geneva CSD | 2,500/K-12
649 Exchange St　14456 | 315-781-0400
Dr. Robert C. Young, supt. | Fax 781-4128
www.genevacsd.org
Geneva HS | 800/9-12
101 Carter Rd　14456 | 315-781-0402
Ann Goldfarb, prin. | Fax 781-0695
Geneva MS | 600/6-8
101 Carter Rd　14456 | 315-781-0404
Ann I. Goldfarb, prin. | Fax 781-0694

De Sales HS | 100/9-12
90 Pulteney St　14456 | 315-789-5111
Rev. Joseph Grasso, prin. | Fax 789-8230
Hobart & William Smith Colleges | Post-Sec.
Pulteney St　14456 | 315-781-3000

Germantown, Columbia
Germantown Central SD | 300/K-12
123 Main St　12526 | 518-537-6280
Donald Gooley, supt. | Fax 537-6283
www.germantown.k12.ny.us/
Germantown Central HS | 7-12
123 Main St　12526 | 518-537-6281
Karol Harlow, prin. | Fax 537-6893

Getzville, Erie, Pop. 2,300

ITT Technical Institute | Post-Sec.
PO Box 327　14068 | 716-689-2200

Ghent, Columbia

Hawthorne Valley S | 300/PK-12
330 Route 21C　12075 | 518-672-7092
Roderick Sipe, admin. | Fax 672-0181

Gilbertsville, Otsego, Pop. 350
Gilbertsville-Mt. Upton Central SD | 600/K-12
693 State Highway 51　13776 | 607-783-2207
Douglas Exley, supt. | Fax 783-2254
Gilbertsville-Mount Upton JSHS | 300/7-12
693 State Highway 51　13776 | 607-783-2207
Carl Mummenthey, prin. | Fax 783-2254

Gilboa, Schoharie
Gilboa-Conesville Central SD | 400/K-12
132 Wyckoff Rd　12076 | 607-588-7541
M. Matthew Murray, supt. | Fax 588-6820
Gilboa-Conesville Central S | 400/K-12
132 Wyckoff Rd　12076 | 607-588-7555
Virginia Keegan, prin. | Fax 588-6820

Glen Cove, Nassau, Pop. 26,781
Glen Cove CSD | 3,100/PK-12
150 Dosoris Ln　11542 | 516-759-7217
Dr. Laurence Aronstein, supt. | Fax 759-1679
www.glencove.k12.ny.us
Finley MS | 900/5-8
Forest Ave　11542 | 516-759-7241
Anael Alston, prin. | Fax 759-8774
Glen Cove HS | 1,000/9-12
150 Dosoris Ln　11542 | 516-759-7261
Joseph Hinton, prin. | Fax 759-8778

Solomon Schechter Day S of Nassau Co. | 200/6-8
27 Cedar Swamp Rd　11542 | 516-656-5500
Solomon Schechter HS of Long Island | 200/9-12
27 Cedar Swamp Rd　11542 | 516-656-5500
G. Ben Dachs, prin. | Fax 656-9822
Webb Institute | Post-Sec.
298 Crescent Beach Rd　11542 | 516-671-2213

Glendale, See New York
NYC Department of Education
Supt. — See New York
IS 119 | 1,100/6-8
7401 78th Ave　11385 | 718-326-8261
Mary Aloisio, prin. | Fax 361-2457

Glen Head, Nassau, Pop. 4,488
North Shore Central SD
Supt. — See Sea Cliff
North Shore HS | 700/9-12
450 Glen Cove Ave　11545 | 516-705-0200
Frank Banta, prin. | Fax 705-0259
North Shore MS | 700/6-8
505 Glen Cove Ave　11545 | 516-705-0300
Marc Ferris, prin. | Fax 705-0324

Glens Falls, Warren, Pop. 14,212
Glens Falls CSD | 2,500/K-12
15 Quade St　12801 | 518-792-1212
Thomas McGowan, supt. | Fax 792-1538
www.gfsd.org
Glens Falls HS | 900/9-12
10 Quade St　12801 | 518-792-6564
Jeffrey Ziegler, prin. | Fax 743-1164
Glens Falls MS | 700/6-8
20 Quade St　12801 | 518-793-3418
Christopher Reed, prin. | Fax 793-4888

Adirondack Beauty School | Post-Sec.
108 Dix Ave　12801 | 518-745-1646
Glens Falls Hospital | Post-Sec.
100 Park St　12801 | 518-792-3151

Gloversville, Fulton, Pop. 15,227
Gloversville CSD | 2,900/PK-12
PO Box 593　12078 | 518-775-5700
Daniel Connor, supt. | Fax 725-8793
www.gloversvilleschools.org
Gloversville HS | 900/9-12
199 Lincoln St　12078 | 518-725-0671
Robert Orsino, prin. | Fax 773-3674
Gloversville MS | 700/6-8
234 Lincoln St　12078 | 518-773-7351
Peter Glaser, prin. | Fax 773-9865

Goshen, Orange, Pop. 5,370
Goshen Central SD | 2,800/K-12
227 Main St　10924 | 845-294-2410
Roy Reese, supt. | Fax 294-1658
www.gcsny.org
Goshen Central HS | 900/9-12
222 Scotchtown Rd　10924 | 845-294-2434
Robert Litz, prin. | Fax 294-7696
Hooker MS | 700/6-8
41 Lincoln Ave　10924 | 845-294-2470
Michael Johndrow, prin. | Fax 294-2473

Burke Catholic HS | 600/9-12
80 Fletcher St　10924 | 845-294-5481
Fr. James Byrnes, prin. | Fax 294-0817

Gouverneur, Saint Lawrence, Pop. 4,167
Gouverneur Central SD | 1,300/K-12
133 E Barney St　13642 | 315-287-4870
Christine LaRose, supt. | Fax 287-4736
gcs.neric.org/newweb/
Gouveneur MS | 6-8
113 E Barney St　13642 | 315-287-1903
Lauren French, prin.
Gouverneur HS | 500/9-12
113 E Barney St　13642 | 315-287-1900
John Dixon, prin.

Gowanda, Cattaraugus, Pop. 2,766
Gowanda Central SD | 1,500/PK-12
10674 Prospect St　14070 | 716-532-3325
Charles J. Rinaldi, supt. | Fax 995-2156
www.gowcsd.com
Gowanda HS | 500/9-12
10674 Prospect St　14070 | 716-532-3325
Kimberly Moritz, prin. | Fax 995-2107
Gowanda MS | 500/5-8
10674 Prospect St　14070 | 716-532-3325
David Smith, prin. | Fax 995-2127

Grahamsville, Sullivan
Tri-Valley Central SD | 1,300/PK-12
34 Moore Hill Rd　12740 | 845-985-2296
Nancy George, supt. | Fax 985-0310
tvcs.k12.ny.us
Tri-Valley Secondary S | 600/7-12
34 Moore Hill Rd　12740 | 845-985-2296
Kenneth Sherman, prin. | Fax 985-7261

Grand Island, Erie
Grand Island Central SD | 3,200/K-12
1100 Ransom Rd　14072 | 716-773-8800
Dr. Thomas Ramming, supt. | Fax 773-8843
www.grandisland-cs.k12.ny.us
Connor MS | 800/6-8
1100 Ransom Rd　14072 | 716-773-8830
Bruce Benson, prin. | Fax 773-8983
Grand Island HS | 1,000/9-12
1100 Ransom Rd　14072 | 716-773-8820
Dr. James Dempsey, prin. | Fax 773-8951

Granville, Washington, Pop. 2,620
Granville Central SD | 1,500/K-12
58 Quaker St　12832 | 518-642-1051
Daniel Teplesky, supt. | Fax 642-2491
www.granvillecsd.org
Granville JSHS | 800/7-12
58 Quaker St　12832 | 518-642-1051
Daryl Hammond, prin. | Fax 642-4544

Great Neck, Nassau, Pop. 9,623
Great Neck UFD | 6,000/PK-12
345 Lakeville Rd　11020 | 516-773-1405
Dr. Ronald L. Friedman, supt. | Fax 773-6685
www.greatneck.k12.ny.us
Great Neck South HS | 1,100/9-12
341 Lakeville Rd　11020 | 516-773-1600
Randolph Ross, prin. | Fax 773-8269
Great Neck South MS | 800/6-8
349 Lakeville Rd　11020 | 516-773-1660
Dr. James R. Welsch, prin. | Fax 773-1770
Miller Great Neck North HS | 900/9-12
35 Polo Rd　11023 | 516-773-1513
Bernard Kaplan, prin. | Fax 773-8271
Sherman Great Neck North MS | 600/6-8
77 Polo Rd　11023 | 516-773-1570
Barbara Andrews, prin. | Fax 773-1760

North Shore Hebrew Academy | 50/6-8
26 Old Mill Rd　11023 | 516-487-9163
Francine Ballan, prin. | Fax 829-3933

Greene, Chenango, Pop. 1,684
Greene Central SD | 1,300/K-12
40 S Canal St　13778 | 607-656-4161
Gary Smith, supt. | Fax 656-7933
www.greenecsd.org
Greene HS | 400/9-12
40 S Canal St　13778 | 607-656-4161
D. Gordon Daniels, prin. | Fax 656-8872
Greene MS | 300/6-8
40 S Canal St　13778 | 607-656-4161
Judy Gorton, prin. | Fax 656-4520

Green Island, Albany, Pop. 2,612
Green Island UFD | 300/K-12
171 Hudson Ave　12183 | 518-273-1422
John E. McKinney, supt. | Fax 270-0818
www.greenisland.org
Heatly S | 300/K-12
171 Hudson Ave　12183 | 518-273-1422
Herb Perkins, prin. | Fax 270-0818

Greenlawn, Suffolk, Pop. 13,208
Elwood UFD | 2,500/K-12
100 Kenneth Ave　11740 | 631-266-5402
Dr. William Swart, supt. | Fax 368-2338
www.elwood.k12.ny.us
Other Schools – See Elwood

Harborfields Central SD | 3,500/K-12
2 Oldfield Rd　11740 | 631-754-5320
Dr. Janet Ceparano Wilson, supt. | Fax 261-0068
www.harborfieldscsd.net
Harborfields HS | 1,000/9-12
98 Taylor Ave　11740 | 631-754-5360
David Bennardo, prin. | Fax 754-6237
Oldfield MS | 900/6-8
2 Oldfield Rd　11740 | 631-754-5310
Joanne Giordano, prin. | Fax 754-2677

Greenport, Suffolk, Pop. 2,066
Greenport UFD | 700/K-12
720 Front St　11944 | 631-477-1950
Dr. Charles Kozora, supt. | Fax 477-2164
www.greenport.k12.ny.us/
Greenport JSHS | 300/7-12
720 Front St　11944 | 631-477-1950
Michael Comanda, prin. | Fax 477-2164

Greenvale, Nassau

Long Island University-C. W. Post Campus | Post-Sec.
720 Northern Blvd　11548 | 516-299-2000

Greenville, Greene, Pop. 9,528
Greenville Central SD | 1,300/K-12
4976 Route 81　12083 | 518-966-5070
Cheryl Dudley, supt. | Fax 966-8346
www.greenville.k12.ny.us
Greenville HS | 400/9-12
4976 Route 81　12083 | 518-966-5070
 | Fax 966-4054

Greenville MS | 400/6-8
4976 Route 81　12083 | 518-966-5070
Colleen Horton, prin. | Fax 966-5408

Greenwich, Washington, Pop. 1,880
Greenwich Central SD | 1,200/K-12
10 Gray Ave　12834 | 518-692-9542
John McGuire, supt. | Fax 692-9547
www.greenwichcsd.org/
Greenwich JSHS | 600/7-12
10 Gray Ave　12834 | 518-692-9542
Matthias Donnelly, prin. | Fax 692-8503

Greenwood Lake, Orange, Pop. 3,454
Greenwood Lake UFD | 600/1-8
PO Box 8　10925 | 845-477-7395
John Guarracino, supt. | Fax 477-7398
Other Schools – See Monroe

Groton, Tompkins, Pop. 2,497
Groton Central SD | 1,100/K-12
PO Box 99　13073 | 607-898-5301
Dr. Brenda Myers, supt. | Fax 898-4647
www.grotoncs.org
Groton HS | 300/9-12
400 Peru Rd　13073 | 607-898-5802
Eric Hartz, prin. | Fax 898-5824
Groton MS | 300/6-8
400 Peru Rd　13073 | 607-898-5803
Connie Filzen, prin. | Fax 898-5824

Guilderland, Albany
Guilderland Central SD | 5,700/K-12
6076 State Farm Rd　12084 | 518-456-6200
Gregory Aidala Ed.D., supt. | Fax 456-1152
www.guilderlandschools.org/
Farnsworth MS | 1,400/6-8
6072 State Farm Rd　12084 | 518-456-6010
Mary Summermatter, prin. | Fax 456-3747
Other Schools – See Guilderland Center

Guilderland Center, Albany
Guilderland Central SD
Supt. — See Guilderland
Guilderland Center HS | 1,900/9-12
8 School Rd　12085 | 518-861-8591
Frank Tedesco, prin. | Fax 861-5874

Hadley, Saratoga

King's S | 100/PK-12
6087 State Route 9N　12835 | 518-654-6230
Jack Salesses, dir. | Fax 654-7310

Hamburg, Erie, Pop. 9,841
Frontier Central SD | 5,600/K-12
5120 Orchard Ave　14075 | 716-926-1711
David Kurzawa, supt. | Fax 926-1776
www.frontier.wnyric.org
Frontier HS | 1,700/9-12
4432 Bay View Rd　14075 | 716-926-1720
Michael Baumann, prin. | Fax 646-2195

Frontier MS | 1,400/6-8
2751 Amsdell Rd 14075 | 716-926-1730
M. Kerry Courtney, prin. | Fax 646-2207

Hamburg Central SD | 3,900/PK-12
5305 Abbott Rd 14075 | 716-646-3220
Dr. Peter Roswell, supt. | Fax 646-3209
www.hamburg.wnyric.org/
Hamburg HS | 1,100/9-12
4111 Legion Dr 14075 | 716-646-3302
Michael Gallagher, prin. | Fax 646-3347
Hamburg MS | 900/6-8
360 Division St 14075 | 716-646-3250
Geoffrey Grace, prin. | Fax 646-3274

Hopevale UFD | 100/7-12
3780 Howard Rd 14075 | 716-648-1930
David Frahm, supt. | Fax 648-2361
www.hopevale.com
Hopevale JSHS | 100/7-12
3780 Howard Rd 14075 | 716-648-1930
Cynthia Stachowski, prin. | Fax 648-2361

Hilbert College | Post-Sec.
5200 S Park Ave 14075 | 716-649-7900
Immaculata Academy | 200/9-12
5138 S Park Ave 14075 | 716-649-6101
David Christian, prin. | Fax 646-1782

Hamilton, Madison, Pop. 3,556
Hamilton Central SD | 700/K-12
47 W Kendrick Ave 13346 | 315-824-3721
Edmund Backus, supt. | Fax 824-3745
Hamilton JSHS | 400/6-12
47 W Kendrick Ave 13346 | 315-824-2009
Dana Chapman, prin. | Fax 824-3745

Colgate University | Post-Sec.
13 Oak Dr 13346 | 315-228-1000
New Life Christian S | 100/PK-12
1528 River Rd 13346 | 315-824-2625
Patricia Richmond, prin. | Fax 824-5102

Hammond, Saint Lawrence, Pop. 297
Hammond Central SD | 300/K-12
PO Box 185 13646 | 315-324-5931
Dennis Johnson, supt. | Fax 324-6057
Hammond Central S | 300/K-12
PO Box 185 13646 | 315-324-5931
Dennis Johnson, supt. | Fax 324-6057

Hammondsport, Steuben, Pop. 712
Hammondsport Central SD | 600/K-12
PO Box 368 14840 | 607-569-5200
Christopher R. Brown, supt. | Fax 569-5212
www.hammondsportcsd.org
Hammondsport JSHS | 300/7-12
8272 Main Street Ext 14840 | 607-569-5287
Julie Sissel, prin. | Fax 569-5279

Hampton Bays, Suffolk, Pop. 7,893
Hampton Bays UFD | 1,800/K-12
86 Argonne Rd E 11946 | 631-723-2100
Joanne Loewenthal, supt. | Fax 723-2109
www.hamptonbays.k12.ny.us
Hampton Bays Secondary S | 800/7-12
88 Argonne Rd E 11946 | 631-723-2110
Dan Nolan, prin. | Fax 723-2120

Hancock, Delaware, Pop. 1,147
Hancock Central SD | 500/PK-12
67 Education Ln 13783 | 607-637-1301
Terrance Dougherty, supt. | Fax 637-2512
Hancock JSHS | 300/5-12
67 Education Ln 13783 | 607-637-1306
Michael Williams, prin. | Fax 637-2512

Hannibal, Oswego, Pop. 533
Hannibal Central SD | 1,800/K-12
PO Box 66 13074 | 315-564-7900
Michael DiFabio, supt. | Fax 564-7263
www.hannibalcsd.org/
Hannibal HS | 500/9-12
928 Cayuga St 13074 | 315-564-7910
Daniel Salisbury, prin. | Fax 564-7973
Kenney MS | 600/5-8
846 Cayuga St 13074 | 315-564-7955
Robert Wren, prin. | Fax 564-7509

Harpursville, Broome
Harpursville Central SD | 900/PK-12
PO Box 147 13787 | 607-693-8101
Kathleen M. Wood, supt. | Fax 693-1480
www.hcs.stier.org/
Harpursville HS | 400/9-12
PO Box 147 13787 | 607-693-8105
Glenn Hamilton, prin. | Fax 693-1480
Harpursville MS | 7-8
PO Box 147 13787 | 607-693-8110
Joshua Quick, prin. | Fax 693-1480

Harrison, Westchester, Pop. 25,150
Harrison Central SD | 3,300/K-12
50 Union Ave 10528 | 914-835-3300
Louis Wool, supt. | Fax 835-2950
www.harrisoncsd.org
Harrison HS | 800/9-12
255 Union Ave 10528 | 914-630-3095
Keith Schenker, prin. | Fax 835-5471
Klein MS | 800/6-8
50 Union Ave 10528 | 914-630-3033
Dr. Rosemary Brooke, prin. | Fax 777-1346

Harrisville, Lewis, Pop. 624
Harrisville Central SD | 400/K-12
PO Box 200 13648 | 315-543-2707
Rolf A. Waters, supt. | Fax 543-2360
Harrisville JSHS | 200/7-12
PO Box 200 13648 | 315-543-2920
Mary E. Curcio, prin. | Fax 543-2360

Hartford, Washington
Hartford Central SD | 300/PK-12
4704 State Route 149 12838 | 518-632-5931
Thomas Abraham, supt. | Fax 632-5231
www.hartfordcsd.org
Hartford Central HS | 300/6-12
4704 State Route 149 12838 | 518-632-5923
Patrick Sweeney, prin. | Fax 632-5231

Hartsdale, Westchester, Pop. 9,587
Greenburgh Central SD 7 | 1,700/PK-12
475 W Hartsdale Ave 10530 | 914-761-6000
Dr. Josephine Moffett, supt. | Fax 761-2354
www.greenburgh.k12.ny.us
Woodland MS | 300/7-8
475 W Hartsdale Ave 10530 | 914-761-6052
Michael Chambless, prin. | Fax 761-7670
Woodlands HS | 500/9-12
475 W Hartsdale Ave 10530 | 914-761-6052
Robert Chakar, prin. | Fax 761-7387

Cristo Rey HS | 200/9-12
112 E 106th St, | 212-996-7000
William Ford, prin. | Fax 427-7444
Maria Regina HS | 500/9-12
500 W Hartsdale Ave 10530 | 914-761-3300
Sr. Danielle Baran, prin. | Fax 761-0860
Solomon Schechter S of Westchester | 500/6-12
555 W Hartsdale Ave 10530 | 914-948-8333
Marc Medwed, prin. | Fax 948-7979
SUNY Empire State College | Post-Sec.
200 N Central Ave 10530 | 914-948-6206

Hastings on Hudson, Westchester, Pop. 8,021
Greenburgh-Graham UFD | 300/1-12
1 S Broadway 10706 | 914-478-1106
James G. Donlevy, supt. | Fax 478-0904
King HS | 200/9-12
1 S Broadway 10706 | 914-478-1161
| Fax 478-2321

Hastings on Hudson UFD | 1,700/K-12
27 Farragut Ave 10706 | 914-478-6200
Dr. John Russell, supt. | Fax 478-6209
www.hastings.k12.ny.us
Farragut MS | 600/5-8
27 Farragut Ave 10706 | 914-478-6300
Gail Kipper, prin. | Fax 478-6314
Hastings HS | 500/9-12
1 Mount Hope Blvd 10706 | 914-478-6250
Dr. Thomas Fazio, prin. | Fax 478-7842

Hauppauge, Suffolk, Pop. 19,750
Hauppauge UFD | 3,700/K-12
495 Hoffman Ln 11788 | 631-265-3630
Peter C. Scordo, supt. | Fax 265-3649
www.hauppauge.k12.ny.us
Hauppauge HS | 1,200/9-12
500 Lincoln Blvd 11788 | 631-265-3630
Dean Schlanger, prin. | Fax 979-0926
Hauppauge MS | 1,000/6-8
600 Townline Rd 11788 | 631-265-3630
Maryann Fletcher, prin. | Fax 265-9546

Learning Institute for Beauty Sciences | Post-Sec.
544 Route 111 11788 | 631-724-0440

Hawthorne, Westchester, Pop. 4,764

Polytechnic University | Post-Sec.
40 Saw Mill River Rd 10532 | 914-323-2000

Hempstead, Nassau, Pop. 53,162
Hempstead UFD | 6,100/PK-12
185 Peninsula Blvd 11550 | 516-292-7111
Dr. Nathaniel Clay, supt. | Fax 292-9471
www.hempsteadschools.org/
Hempstead HS | 1,800/9-12
201 President St 11550 | 516-292-7014
Reginald Stroughn, prin. |
Schultz MS | 1,300/6-8
70 Greenwich St 11550 | 516-292-7124
Julius Brown, prin. | Fax 292-5229

Uniondale UFD
Supt. — See Uniondale
Lawrence Road MS | 800/6-8
50 Lawrence Rd 11550 | 516-918-1500
Dr. Valerie Piedmonte, prin. | Fax 565-5023

Franklin Career Institute | Post-Sec.
91 N Franklin St 11550 | 516-481-4444
Hofstra University | Post-Sec.
100 Hofstra University 11549 | 516-463-6600
Learning Institute for Beauty Sciences | Post-Sec.
173A Fulton Ave 11550 | 516-483-6259
Sacred Heart Academy | 800/9-12
47 Cathedral Ave 11550 | 516-483-7383
Sr. Jeanne Ross, prin. | Fax 483-1016
Suburban Technical School | Post-Sec.
175 Fulton Ave 11550 | 516-481-6660

Henrietta, Monroe
Rush-Henrietta Central SD | 5,700/K-12
2034 Lehigh Station Rd 14467 | 585-359-5012
Dr. J. Kenneth Graham, supt. | Fax 359-5045
www.rhnet.org
Ninth Grade Academy | 500/9-9
2000 Lehigh Station Rd 14467 | 585-359-5550
Christopher Barker, prin. | Fax 359-5559
Roth MS | 800/6-8
4000 E Henrietta Rd 14467 | 585-359-5108
Denise Zeh, prin. | Fax 359-5164
Rush-Henrietta HS | 1,400/10-12
1799 Lehigh Station Rd 14467 | 585-359-5208
Beth Patton, prin. | Fax 359-5290
Other Schools – See West Henrietta

Herkimer, Herkimer, Pop. 7,298
Herkimer Central SD | 1,300/K-12
801 W German St 13350 | 315-866-2230
Carol Zygo, supt. |
www.herkimercsd.org/

Herkimer JSHS | 700/7-12
801 W German St 13350 | 315-866-2230
Terry Dangle, prin. | Fax 866-2234

Herkimer County Community College | Post-Sec.
100 Reservoir Rd 13350 | 315-866-0300

Heuvelton, Saint Lawrence, Pop. 787
Heuvelton Central SD | 600/K-12
PO Box 375 13654 | 315-344-2414
Susan Todd, supt. | Fax 344-2349
Heuvelton Central S | 600/K-12
PO Box 375 13654 | 315-344-2414
Michael Warden, prin. | Fax 344-2349

Hewlett, Nassau, Pop. 6,620
Hewlett-Woodmere UFD
Supt. — See Woodmere
Hewlett HS | 1,100/9-12
60 Everit Ave 11557 | 516-374-8005
Joyce Bisso, prin. | Fax 374-8173
Woodmere MS | 800/6-8
1170 Peninsula Blvd 11557 | 516-374-8068
Claudette Tableman, prin. | Fax 374-4571

Abraham HS for Girls | 300/9-12
291 Meadowview Ave 11557 | 516-374-7195
Helen Spirn, prin. | Fax 374-2532
Mesivta Ateres Yaakov HS | 200/9-12
1170 William St Ste A 11557 | 516-374-6465
Rabbi Sam Rudansky, prin. | Fax 374-1834
Reenas Bais Yakov HS | 100/9-12
1 Piermont Ave 11557 | 516-295-7453

Hicksville, Nassau, Pop. 41,400
Hicksville UFD | 5,100/PK-12
200 Division Ave 11801 | 516-733-6600
Maureen K. Bright, supt. | Fax 733-6584
www.hicksvillepublicschools.com
Hicksville HS | 1,500/9-12
180 Division Ave 11801 | 516-733-6621
Brijinder Singh, prin. | Fax 733-6626
Hicksville MS | 1,200/6-8
215 Jerusalem Ave 11801 | 516-733-6521
Stephen Aronowitz, prin. | Fax 733-6528

Holy Trinity Diocesan HS | 1,500/9-12
98 Cherry Ln 11801 | 516-433-2900
Gene Fennell, prin. | Fax 433-2827
Long Island Christian Academy | 100/K-12
80 Division Ave 11801 | 516-931-5129

Highland, Ulster, Pop. 4,492
Highland Central SD | 1,900/K-12
320 Pancake Hollow Rd 12528 | 845-691-1012
John McCarthy, supt. | Fax 691-1039
www.highland-k12.org/
Highland HS | 600/9-12
320 Pancake Hollow Rd 12528 | 845-691-3020
David Evans, prin. | Fax 691-2096
Highland MS | 500/6-8
71 Main St 12528 | 845-691-1081
Jo Burruby, prin. | Fax 691-2074

Highland Residential Center | 200/8-12
629 N Chodikee Lake Rd 12528 | 845-691-6006

Highland Falls, Orange, Pop. 3,766
Highland Falls-Ft. Montgomery Cntrl SD
Supt. — See Fort Montgomery
Highland Falls MS | 300/5-8
PO Box 287 10928 | 845-446-4761
Ellen Connors, prin. | Fax 446-0858

Hillburn, Rockland, Pop. 890
Ramapo Central SD | 4,600/K-12
45 Mountain Ave 10931 | 845-357-7783
Robert MacNaughton Ph.D., supt. | Fax 357-5707
www.ramapocentral.org
Other Schools – See Suffern

Hilton, Monroe, Pop. 5,962
Hilton Central SD | 4,400/K-12
225 West Ave 14468 | 585-392-1000
David Dimbleby, supt. | Fax 392-1038
www.hilton.k12.ny.us
Hilton HS | 1,500/9-12
400 East Ave 14468 | 585-392-1000
Brian Bartalo, prin. | Fax 392-1052
Williams MS | 700/7-8
200 School Ln 14468 | 585-392-1000
Carol Stehm, prin. | Fax 392-1054

Hinsdale, Cattaraugus
Hinsdale Central SD | 500/K-12
3701 Main St 14743 | 716-557-2227
Michael O'Brien, supt. | Fax 557-2259
www.hinsdale.wnyric.org/working.htm
Hinsdale Central S | 500/K-12
3701 Main St 14743 | 716-557-2227
Laurie Edmonston, prin. | Fax 557-2259

Holbrook, Suffolk, Pop. 27,900
Sachem Central SD | 13,600/K-12
245 Union Ave 11741 | 631-471-1336
Dr. Charles Murphy, supt. | Fax 471-1341
www.sachem.edu
Seneca MS | 1,300/6-8
850 Main St 11741 | 631-471-1850
Gemma Salvia, prin. | Fax 471-1849
Other Schools – See Farmingville, Holtsville, Lake Ronkonkoma

Holland, Erie, Pop. 1,288
Holland Central SD | 1,200/K-12
103 Canada St 14080 | 716-537-8222
Garry Stone, supt. | Fax 537-2453
Holland HS | 400/9-12
103 Canada St 14080 | 716-537-8220
James Biryla, prin. | Fax 537-2453
Holland MS | 400/5-8
11720 Partridge Rd 14080 | 716-537-8277
Eric Lawton, prin. | Fax 537-2453

Holland Patent, Oneida, Pop. 458
Holland Patent Central SD 1,800/K-12
  9601 Main St 13354 315-865-7221
  Kathleen Dans, supt. Fax 865-4057
Holland Patent Central HS 600/9-12
  9601 Main St 13354 315-865-8154
  Gordon Garrett, prin. Fax 865-4069
Holland Patent MS 500/6-8
  9601 Main St 13354 315-865-8152
  Nancy Nowicki, prin. Fax 865-7243

Holley, Orleans, Pop. 1,762
Holley Central SD 1,400/K-12
  3800 N Main Street Rd 14470 585-638-6316
  Robert D'Angelo, supt. Fax 638-7409
Holley JSHS 700/7-12
  Lynch Rd 14470 585-638-6335
  Terrance McCarthy, prin. Fax 638-7925

Hollis, See New York
NYC Department of Education
  Supt. — See New York
IS 238 1,700/6-8
  8815 182nd St 11423 718-297-9821
  Joseph Gates, prin. Fax 658-5288

Yeshiva University HS - Girls 300/9-12
  8686 Palo Alto St 11423 718-479-8550
  Rochelle Brand, prin. Fax 479-8686

Holtsville, Suffolk, Pop. 14,972
Sachem Central SD
  Supt. — See Holbrook
Sagamore MS 1,300/6-8
  57 Division St 11742 631-696-8600
  Steve Siciliano, prin. Fax 696-8620
Sequoya MS 6-8
  750 Waverly Ave 11742 631-207-7100
  Thomas Logatto, prin. Fax 207-7115

Homer, Cortland, Pop. 3,333
Homer Central SD 2,400/K-12
  PO Box 500 13077 607-749-7241
  Douglas Larison, supt. Fax 749-2312
  www.homercentral.org
Homer HS 800/9-12
  80 S West St 13077 607-749-7246
  Fred Farah, prin. Fax 749-2312
Homer JHS 400/7-8
  58 Clinton St 13077 607-749-1230
  Tom Turck, prin. Fax 749-1238

Honeoye, Ontario
Honeoye Central SD 1,100/K-12
  PO Box 170 14471 585-229-4125
  William F. Schofield, supt. Fax 229-5633
  www.honeoye.org
Honeoye JSHS 600/6-12
  PO Box 170 14471 585-229-4127
  Craig Dennison, prin. Fax 229-4879

Honeoye Falls, Monroe, Pop. 2,602
Honeoye Falls-Lima Central SD 2,600/K-12
  20 Church St 14472 585-624-7000
  Dr. Diane Reed, supt. Fax 624-7003
  www.hflcsd.org/welcome/index.php
Honeoye Falls-Lima HS 800/9-12
  83 East St 14472 585-624-7051
  Kathy Walling, prin. Fax 624-7118
Honeoye Falls-Lima MS 600/6-8
  619 Quaker Meeting House Rd 14472 585-624-7100
  Garcia Reed, prin. Fax 624-7121

Hoosick, Rensselaer

Hoosac S 100/8-12
  PO Box 9 12089 518-686-7331
    Fax 686-3370

Hoosick Falls, Rensselaer, Pop. 3,383
Hoosick Falls Central SD 1,200/K-12
  PO Box 192 12090 518-686-7012
  Roger Thompson, supt. Fax 686-9060
  www.hoosick-falls.k12.ny.us
Hoosick Falls HS 600/7-12
  PO Box 192 12090 518-686-7321
  Edward Balaban, prin. Fax 686-9060

Hopewell Junction, Dutchess, Pop. 1,786
Wappingers Central SD
  Supt. — See Wappingers Falls
Jay HS 1,900/9-12
  PO Box 38 12533 845-897-6700
  Paul Tobin, prin. Fax 897-6719

Hornell, Steuben, Pop. 8,817
Hornell CSD 1,900/K-12
  25 Pearl St 14843 607-324-1302
  George Kiley, supt. Fax 324-4060
  www.hornell.wnyric.org
Hornell HS 1,000/7-12
  134 Seneca St 14843 607-324-1303
  Sean Gaffney, prin. Fax 324-3702

St. James Mercy Hospital Post-Sec.
  411 Canisteo St 14843 607-324-3900

Horseheads, Chemung, Pop. 6,363
Horseheads Central SD 4,300/K-12
  1 Raider Ln 14845 607-739-5601
  William Congdon, supt. Fax 739-5832
  www.horseheadsdistrict.org
Horseheads HS 1,500/9-12
  401 Fletcher St 14845 607-739-5601
  James Abrams, prin. Fax 739-4299
Horseheads MS 700/7-8
  950 Sing Sing Rd 14845 607-739-6356
  William Carney, prin. Fax 739-6343

Houghton, Allegany, Pop. 1,740

Houghton Academy 200/7-12
  9790 Thayer St 14744 585-567-8115
  Philip Stockin, hdmstr. Fax 567-8048

Houghton College Post-Sec.
  PO Box 128 14744 585-567-9200

Hudson, Columbia, Pop. 7,296
Hudson CSD 2,100/K-12
  621 State Route 23B 12534 518-828-4360
  Marilyn Barry, supt. Fax 697-8777
  www.hudsoncsd.k12.ny.us
Hudson HS 600/9-12
  215 Harry Howard Ave 12534 518-828-4132
  Steven Spicer, prin. Fax 697-8418
Hudson MS 700/5-8
  102 Harry Howard Ave 12534 518-828-4650
  Thomas Gavin, prin. Fax 697-8434

Columbia-Greene Community College Post-Sec.
  4400 State Route 23 12534 518-828-4181

Hudson Falls, Washington, Pop. 6,857
Hudson Falls Central SD 2,300/K-12
  PO Box 710 12839 518-747-2121
  Mark Doody, supt. Fax 747-0951
  www.hfcsd.org
Hudson Falls HS 700/9-12
  80 E La Barge St 12839 518-747-2121
  C.J. Hebert, prin. Fax 746-9033
Hudson Falls MS 600/6-8
  131 Notre Dame St 12839 518-747-2121
  Todd Gonyeau, prin. Fax 746-2790

Huntington, Suffolk, Pop. 18,243
Huntington UFD
  Supt. — See Huntington Station
Finley JHS 700/7-8
  20 Greenlawn Rd 11743 631-673-2020
  Craig Springer, prin. Fax 425-4746
Huntington HS 1,000/9-12
  188 Oakwood Rd 11743 631-673-2003
  Dr. Carmela Leonardi, prin. Fax 425-4730

Hebrew Academy S of Academic Excellence 100/PK-9
  755 Park Ave 11743 631-425-2426
  Rabbi Moshe Labrie, dean Fax 367-0177
Seminary of the Immaculate Conception Post-Sec.
  440 W Neck Rd 11743 631-423-0483
Touro College Post-Sec.
  300 Nassau Rd 11743 631-421-2244

Huntington Station, Suffolk, Pop. 30,200
Huntington UFD 4,000/K-12
  50 Tower St 11746 631-673-2038
  John Finello, supt. Fax 423-3447
  www.hufsd.edu/
Other Schools – See Huntington

South Huntington UFD 5,500/K-12
  60 Weston St 11746 631-425-5300
  Thomas C. Shea Ed.D., supt. Fax 425-5362
  www.shufsd.org
Stimson MS 900/7-8
  401 Oakwood Rd 11746 631-425-5432
  Faye Robins, prin. Fax 425-5449
Whitman HS 1,800/9-12
  301 W Hills Rd 11746 631-425-5387
  James Polansky, prin. Fax 425-5378

St. Anthony HS 2,200/9-12
  275 Wolf Hill Rd 11747 631-271-2020
  Br. Gary Cregan, prin. Fax 547-6820

Hurley, Ulster, Pop. 4,644

Coleman HS 200/9-12
  430 Hurley Ave 12443 845-338-2750
  John P. Traverse, prin. Fax 338-0250

Hyde Park, Dutchess, Pop. 21,230
Hyde Park Central SD 4,600/K-12
  PO Box 2033 12538 845-229-4000
  Carole Pickering, supt. Fax 229-4016
  www.hydeparkschools.org
Haviland MS 1,100/6-8
  23 Haviland Rd 12538 845-229-4030
  Carol Meissner, prin. Fax 229-2475
Other Schools – See Staatsburg on Hudson

Beauty School of Middletown Post-Sec.
  RR 9 12538 845-229-6541
Culinary Institute of America Post-Sec.
  1946 Campus Dr 12538 845-451-1368

Ilion, Herkimer, Pop. 8,370
Ilion Central SD 1,800/PK-12
  PO Box 480 13357 315-894-9934
  Robert Service, supt. Fax 894-2716
  www.ilioncsd.org/
Ilion JSHS 800/7-12
  1 Golden Bomber Dr 13357 315-895-7471
  Renee Rudd, prin. Fax 894-2716

Indian Lake, Hamilton
Indian Lake Central SD 200/K-12
  28 W Main St 12842 518-648-5024
  Mark Brand, supt. Fax 648-6346
  ilcsd.org
Indian Lake Central S 200/K-12
  28 W Main St 12842 518-648-5024
  Scott Poreda, prin. Fax 648-6346

Irvington, Westchester, Pop. 6,665
Irvington UFD 2,000/K-12
  40 N Broadway 10533 914-591-8501
  Dr. Kathleen Matusiak, supt. Fax 591-3099
  irvingtonschools.org
Irvington HS 500/9-12
  40 N Broadway 10533 914-591-8648
  Dr. Scott Mosenthal, prin. Fax 591-6714
Irvington MS 500/6-8
  40 N Broadway 10533 914-591-9494
  Scott Fried, prin. Fax 591-8535

Island Park, Nassau, Pop. 4,756
Island Park UFD 800/K-8
  150 Trafalgar Blvd 11558 516-431-8100
  Dr. Edward J. Price, supt. Fax 431-7550
  www.ips.k12.ny.us
Island Park/Lincoln Orens MS 400/5-8
  150 Trafalgar Blvd 11558 516-431-7194
  Dr. Thalia Vendetti, prin. Fax 431-7550

Islip, Suffolk, Pop. 18,924
Islip UFD 3,600/K-12
  215 Main St 11751 631-859-2200
  Alan Van Cott, supt. Fax 859-2224
  www.islip.k12.ny.us
Islip HS 1,100/9-12
  2508 Union Blvd 11751 631-859-2234
  Ellen Rossman, prin. Fax 859-2227
Islip MS 900/6-8
  211 Main St 11751 631-859-2274
  Timothy Martin, prin. Fax 859-2277

Islip Terrace, Suffolk, Pop. 5,530
East Islip UFD 5,400/PK-12
  1 Craig B Gariepy Ave 11752 631-224-2000
  Dennis P. Maloney, supt. Fax 581-1617
  www.eischools.org
East Islip HS 1,600/9-12
  1 Redmen St 11752 631-224-2100
  Miriam Flynn, prin. Fax 581-4410
Islip Terrace JHS 900/7-8
  100 Redmen St 11752 631-224-2170
  Alise Becker-Santa, prin. Fax 859-3745

Ithaca, Tompkins, Pop. 30,343
Ithaca CSD 5,300/PK-12
  400 Lake St 14850 607-274-2101
  Dr. Judith Pastel, supt. Fax 274-2271
  www.icsd.k12.ny.us
Boynton MS 600/6-8
  1601 N Cayuga St 14850 607-274-2241
  Johnny Vann, prin. Fax 274-2357
De Witt MS 600/6-8
  560 Warren Rd 14850 607-257-3222
  Ronald Acerra, prin. Fax 266-3502
Ithaca HS 1,500/9-12
  1401 N Cayuga St 14850 607-274-2145
  Joe Wilson, prin. Fax 277-3061

Cornell University Post-Sec.
  410 Thurston Ave 14850 607-255-2000
Ithaca College Post-Sec.
  953 Danby Rd 14850 607-274-3011

Jackson Heights, See New York
NYC Department of Education
  Supt. — See New York
IS 145 2,000/6-8
  3334 80th St 11372 718-457-1242
  Delores Beckham, prin. Fax 335-0601
IS 230 1,000/6-8
  7310 34th Ave 11372 718-335-7648
  Sharon Terry, prin. Fax 335-7513

Garden S 400/PK-12
  3316 79th St 11372 718-335-6363
  Dr. Richard Marotta, hdmstr. Fax 565-1169
Plaza College Post-Sec.
  7409 37th Ave 11372 718-779-1430

Jamaica, See New York
NYC Department of Education
  Supt. — See New York
Business/Computer Applications S 500/9-12
  20701 116th Ave 11411 718-978-2807
  Raymond H. Warmsley, prin. Fax 978-3402
Edison Career & Tech HS Vo/Tech
  16565 84th Ave 11432 718-297-6580
  Ilona S. Posner, prin. Fax 658-0365
Hillcrest HS 3,000/9-12
  16005 Highland Ave 11432 718-658-5407
  Steven Duch, prin. Fax 739-5137
Humanities & the Arts Magnet HS 500/9-12
  20701 116th Ave 11411 718-978-2135
  Mercedes Qualls, prin. Fax 978-2309
Jamaica HS 2,300/9-12
  16701 Gothic Dr 11432 718-739-5942
  Jay Dickler, prin. Fax 739-4826
HS for Law Enforcement & Public Safety 9-12
  11625 Guy R Brewer Blvd 11434 718-977-4800
  Diahann E. Malcolm, dir. Fax 977-4802
JHS 8 800/6-8
  10835 167th St 11433 718-739-6883
  Antonia K'Tori, prin. Fax 526-2727
JHS 72 800/6-8
  13325 Guy R Brewer Blvd 11434 718-723-6200
  Chandra Williams, prin. Fax 527-1675
JHS 217 1,300/6-8
  8505 144th St 11435 718-657-1120
  Jeannette Reed, prin. Fax 291-3668
Law 500/9-12
  20701 116th Ave 11411 718-978-6432
  Carole Kelly, prin. Fax 978-6749
Martin HS 1,500/9-12
  15610 Baisley Blvd 11434 718-528-2920
  Anthony Cromer, prin. Fax 276-1846
Math Science Research & Tech Magnet HS 500/9-12
  20701 116th Ave 11411 718-978-1837
  Andrea Holt, prin. Fax 978-2063
Queens Gateway to the Health Sciences 600/7-12
  15091 87th Rd 11432 718-739-8080
  Cynthia Edwards, prin. Fax 739-8778
Queens HS for Science 600/9-12
  9450 159th St 11451 718-657-3181
  Brian Jetter, prin. Fax 657-2579
Queens S for Career Development Vo/Tech
  14210 Linden Blvd 11436 718-322-3500
  Lester Katz, prin. Fax 322-1306
Young Womens Leadership S 9-9
  10920 Union Hall St 11433 718-725-0402
  Avionne Gumbs, prin. Fax 725-0390

Al-Iman S | 300/PK-12
8989 Van Wyck Expy 11435 | 718-297-6520
Reza Naqvi, prin. | Fax 658-5530
Allen School | Post-Sec.
16318 Jamaica Ave 11432 | 718-291-2200
Archbishop Molloy HS | 1,300/9-12
8353 Manton St 11435 | 718-441-2100
Br. Roy George, prin. | Fax 849-8251
CUNY York College | Post-Sec.
9420 Guy R Brewer Blvd 11451 | 718-262-2000
Jon Louis School of Beauty | Post-Sec.
9114 Merrick Blvd 11432 | 718-658-6240
Louis Academy | 1,000/9-12
17621 Wexford Ter 11432 | 718-297-2120
Sr. Kathleen McKinney, prin. | Fax 739-0037
Machon Academy | 200/9-12
13906 86th Ave 11435 | 718-658-1862
Rabbi Yitzchok Young, prin. | Fax 658-1804
Nail Academy | Post-Sec.
16204 Jamaica Ave 11432 | 718-297-6330
New York Automotive & Diesel Institute | Post-Sec.
17818 Liberty Ave 11433 | 718-361-1300
St. John's University | Post-Sec.
8000 Utopia Pkwy 11439 | 718-990-6161

Jamestown, Chautauqua, Pop. 30,726
Jamestown CSD | 5,100/PK-12
201 E 4th St 14701 | 716-483-4420
Raymond Fashano, supt. | Fax 483-4421
www.jamestown.wnyric.org
Jamestown HS | 1,500/9-12
350 E 2nd St 14701 | 716-483-3470
Joseph Yelich, prin. | Fax 483-4399
Jefferson MS | 500/5-8
195 Martin Rd 14701 | 716-483-4411
Carm Proctor, prin. | Fax 483-4273
Persell MS | 500/5-8
375 Baker St 14701 | 716-483-4406
Philip Cammarata, prin. | Fax 483-4417
Washington MS | 600/5-8
159 Buffalo St 14701 | 716-483-4413
Daniel Bracey, prin. | Fax 483-4268

Southwestern Central SD | 1,800/K-12
600 Hunt Rd 14701 | 716-484-1136
Daniel George, supt. | Fax 488-2442
swcs.wnyric.org/
Southwestern HS | 600/9-12
600 Hunt Rd 14701 | 716-664-6273
Michael Vallely, prin. | Fax 484-1167
Southwestern MS | 500/6-8
600 Hunt Rd 14701 | 716-664-6270
Gregory Paterniti, prin. | Fax 487-0855

Bethel Baptist Christian Academy | 100/K-12
200 Hunt Rd 14701 | 716-484-7420
Clarence Lee, admin. | Fax 484-0087
Jamestown Business College | Post-Sec.
PO Box 429 14702 | 716-664-5100
Jamestown Community College | Post-Sec.
PO Box 20 14702 | 716-665-5220
Woman's Christian Assoc. Hospital | Post-Sec.
207 Foote Ave 14701 | 716-664-8110

Jamesville, Onondaga
Jamesville-DeWitt Central SD
Supt. — See De Witt
Jamesville-DeWitt MS | 900/5-8
6280 Randall Rd 13078 | 315-445-8360
Jeffrey Craig, prin. | Fax 445-8421

Jasper, Steuben
Jasper-Troupsburg Central SD | 600/PK-12
3769 State Route 417 14855 | 607-792-3675
Chad C. Groff, supt. | Fax 792-3749
Jasper-Troupsburg JSHS | 300/7-12
3769 State Route 417 14855 | 607-792-3675
Mary Vanetten, prin. | Fax 792-3749

Jefferson, Schoharie
Jefferson Central SD | 300/K-12
1332 State Route 10 12093 | 607-652-7821
Carl Mummenthey, supt. | Fax 652-7806
www.jeffersoncs.org
Jefferson Central S | 300/K-12
1332 State Route 10 12093 | 607-652-7821
John Righi, prin. | Fax 652-7806

Jeffersonville, Sullivan, Pop. 415
Sullivan West Central SD | 1,200/K-12
PO Box 308 12748 | 845-482-4610
Alan Derry, supt.
www.swcsd.org/
Other Schools – See Lake Huntington

Jericho, Nassau, Pop. 13,141
Jericho UFD | 3,200/K-12
99 Old Cedar Swamp Rd 11753 | 516-203-3600
Henry Grishman, supt. | Fax 933-2047
www.jerichoschools.org
Jericho HS | 1,000/9-12
99 Old Cedar Swamp Rd 11753 | 516-203-3610
Joe Prisinzano, prin. | Fax 681-2895
Jericho MS | 900/6-8
99 Old Cedar Swamp Rd 11753 | 516-203-3620
Cecile Wren, prin. | Fax 681-8984

Johnson City, Broome, Pop. 15,230
Johnson City Central SD | 2,600/K-12
666 Reynolds Rd 13790 | 607-763-1230
Lawrence A. Rowe, supt. | Fax 763-8761
www.jcschools.com
Johnson City HS | 900/9-12
666 Reynolds Rd 13790 | 607-763-1256
Thomas Lally, prin. | Fax 763-1211
Johnson City MS | 600/6-8
601 Columbia Dr 13790 | 607-763-1240
Margaret Kucko, prin. | Fax 763-1297

Davis College | Post-Sec.
400 Riverside Dr 13790 | 607-729-1581

St. James MS | 200/4-8
143 Main St 13790 | 607-797-5444
George Clancy, prin. | Fax 797-6794
United Health Services Hospital | Post-Sec.
33-57 Harrison St 13790 | 607-763-6000

Johnstown, Fulton, Pop. 8,516
Johnstown CSD | 2,000/PK-12
2 Wright Dr #101 12095 | 518-762-4611
John Whelan, supt.
www.johnstown.com/city/school.html
Johnstown HS | 700/9-12
2 Wright Dr 12095 | 518-762-4661
Michael Beatty, prin. | Fax 736-1489
Knox JHS | 300/7-8
400 S Perry St 12095 | 518-762-3711
David Carr, prin. | Fax 762-2775

Fulton-Montgomery Community College | Post-Sec.
2805 State Highway 67 12095 | 518-762-4651

Jordan, Onondaga, Pop. 1,367
Jordan-Elbridge Central SD | 1,700/K-12
PO Box 902 13080 | 315-689-3978
Marilyn Dominick, supt. | Fax 689-0084
www.jecsd.org
Jordan-Elbridge HS | 600/9-12
PO Box 901 13080 | 315-689-9553
Ronald Berry, prin. | Fax 689-1985
Jordan-Elbridge MS | 400/6-8
PO Box 1150 13080 | 315-689-3938
David Shafer, prin. | Fax 689-6524

Jordanville, Herkimer

Holy Trinity Orthodox Seminary | Post-Sec.
PO Box 36 13361 | 315-858-0945

Katonah, Westchester

Harvey S | 300/6-12
260 Jay St 10536 | 914-232-3161
Barry Fenstermacher, prin. | Fax 232-2986
Montfort Academy | 200/9-12
99 Valley Rd 10536 | 914-767-0325
Dave Petrillo, prin.

Keene Valley, Essex
Keene Central SD | 200/K-12
PO Box 67 12943 | 518-576-4555
Cynthia Ford-Johnston, supt. | Fax 576-4599
Keene Central S | 200/K-12
PO Box 67 12943 | 518-576-4555
Cynthia Ford-Johnston, prin. | Fax 576-4599

Kendall, Orleans
Kendall Central SD | 1,000/K-12
1932 Kendall Rd 14476 | 585-659-2741
Dr. Michael O'Laughlin, supt. | Fax 659-8903
www.monroe2boces.org/kendal
Kendall JSHS | 500/7-12
16887 Roosevelt Hwy 14476 | 585-659-2706
Carol D'Agostino, prin. | Fax 659-8988

Kenmore, Erie, Pop. 15,933
Kenmore-Tonawanda UFSD
Supt. — See Buffalo
Kenmore MS | 700/6-8
155 Delaware Rd 14217 | 716-874-8403
Elaine Thomas, prin. | Fax 874-8650

Mt. St. Mary Academy | 200/9-12
3756 Delaware Ave 14217 | 716-877-1358
Dawn Riggie, prin. | Fax 877-0548
St. Joseph Collegiate Institute | 800/9-12
845 Kenmore Ave 14223 | 716-874-4024
Robert Scott, prin. | Fax 874-4956

Keuka Park, Yates

Keuka College | Post-Sec.
PO Box 98 14478 | 315-536-4411

Kew Gardens, See New York

Yeshiva Shaar Hatorah-Grodno | 100/9-12
11706 84th Ave 11418 | 718-846-1940
Rabbi Azriel Hoschander, prin. | Fax 850-7916
Yeshiva Tifereth Moshe Dov Revel Center | 500/4-8
8306 Abingdon Rd 11415 | 718-846-7300
Rabbi Yaakov May, prin. | Fax 441-3962

Kings Park, Suffolk, Pop. 17,773
Kings Park Central SD | 3,900/K-12
101 Church St 11754 | 631-269-3210
Dr. Mary DeRose, supt. | Fax 269-0750
www.kpcsd.k12.ny.us
Kings Park HS | 1,100/9-12
200 Route 25a 11754 | 631-269-3245
Thomas Fasano, prin. | Fax 269-7472
Rogers MS | 900/6-8
97 Old Dock Rd 11754 | 631-269-3269
Ralph Cartisano, prin. | Fax 269-3282

Kings Point, Nassau, Pop. 5,175

United States Merchant Marine Academy | Post-Sec.
300 Steamboat Rd 11024 | 516-773-5000

Kingston, Ulster, Pop. 23,294
Kingston CSD | 8,200/PK-12
61 Crown St 12401 | 845-339-3000
Gerard Gretzinger, supt. | Fax 339-2249
www.kingstoncityschools.org/
Bailey MS | 1,000/6-8
Merilina Ave Ext 12401 | 845-338-6390
Alvin Goren, prin. | Fax 338-6312
Kingston HS | 2,400/9-12
403 Broadway 12401 | 845-331-1970
Marie Anderson, prin. | Fax 331-1628
Other Schools – See Lake Katrine

Gloden Hall Health Care Center | Post-Sec.
Golden Hill Dr 12401 | 845-339-4540

Lackawanna, Erie, Pop. 18,622
Lackawanna CSD | 1,900/PK-12
245 S Shore Blvd 14218 | 716-827-6767
Paul G. Hashem, supt. | Fax 827-6710
www.lackawannaschools.org
Lackawanna HS | 600/9-12
550 Martin Rd 14218 | 716-827-6727
Peter Hazzan, prin. | Fax 827-6724
Lackawanna MS | 300/7-8
550 Martin Rd 14218 | 716-827-6704
Michael Jakubowski, prin. | Fax 827-6784

Baker Hall S | 100/7-12
777 Ridge Rd 14218 | 716-828-9737
Nancy Pankow, dir. | Fax 828-9798

La Fargeville, Jefferson
La Fargeville Central SD | 300/K-12
PO Box 138 13656 | 315-658-2241
Susan Whitney, supt. | Fax 658-4223
www.gisco.net/lafargeville
La Fargeville Central HS | 300/7-12
PO Box 138 13656 | 315-658-2241
Kisun Peters, prin. | Fax 658-4223

La Fayette, Onondaga
La Fayette Central SD | 1,000/K-12
5955 US Route 20 13084 | 315-677-9728
Mark Mondanaro, supt. | Fax 677-3372
www.lafayetteschools.com
La Fayette JSHS | 500/7-12
3122 US Route 11 13084 | 315-677-5506
Paula Cowling, prin. | Fax 677-5507

Lagrangeville, Dutchess
Arlington Central SD
Supt. — See Poughkeepsie
Arlington HS | 3,100/9-12
1157 Route 55 12540 | 845-486-4860
Thomas Brooks, prin. | Fax 486-4879
Lagrange MS | 1,300/6-8
110 Stringham Rd 12540 | 845-486-4880
Eric Schetter, prin. | Fax 486-8863
Union Vale MS | 6-8
1657 E Noxon Rd 12540 | 845-223-8600
Steven Kerins, prin.

Lake George, Warren, Pop. 987
Lake George Central SD | 1,100/K-12
381 Canada St 12845 | 518-668-5456
Bruce Levin, supt. | Fax 668-2285
www.lkgeorge.org
Lake George JSHS | 600/7-12
381 Canada St 12845 | 518-668-5452
David Eagle, prin. | Fax 668-2285

Lake Grove, Suffolk, Pop. 10,602

Lake Grove School | Post-Sec.
PO Box 712 11755 | 888-585-9007

Lake Huntington, Sullivan
Sullivan West Central SD
Supt. — See Jeffersonville
Sullivan West JSHS | 800/7-12
PO Box 309 12752 | 845-932-8401
Rod McLaughlin, prin.

Lake Katrine, Ulster, Pop. 1,998
Kingston CSD
Supt. — See Kingston
Miller MS | 1,000/6-8
65 Fording Place Rd 12449 | 845-382-2960
Robert Pritchard, prin. | Fax 339-2249

Lake Luzerne, Warren, Pop. 2,042
Hadley-Luzerne Central SD | 1,100/K-12
27 Ben Rosa Park 12846 | 518-696-2112
Irwin Sussman, supt. | Fax 696-5402
www.hlcs.org
Hadley-Luzerne HS | 400/9-12
273 Lake Ave 12846 | 518-696-2112
Beecher Baker, prin. | Fax 696-2356
Townsend MS | 500/3-8
27 Hyland Dr 12846 | 518-696-2378
Patrick Cronin, prin. | Fax 696-2485

Lake Placid, Essex, Pop. 2,733
Lake Placid Central SD | 900/K-12
50 Cummins Rd 12946 | 518-523-2475
Dr. Ernest Stretton, supt. | Fax 523-3284
lakeplacidcsd.net
Lake Placid JSHS | 500/6-12
34 School St 12946 | 518-523-2474
Dr. David Messner, prin. | Fax 523-2896

Mountain Lake Children's Residence | Post-Sec.
50 Riverside Dr 12946 | 888-585-9007
National Sports Academy | 100/8-12
821 Mirror Lake Dr 12946 | 518-523-3460
Dave Wenn, hdmstr. | Fax 523-3488
North Country S | 100/4-9
PO Box 187 12946 | 518-523-9329
Fax 523-4858
Northwood S | 200/8-12
PO Box 1070 12946 | 518-523-3357
Fax 523-3405

Lake Ronkonkoma, Suffolk, Pop. 18,997
Sachem Central SD
Supt. — See Holbrook
Sachem HS North | 4,500/9-12
212 Smith Rd 11779 | 631-471-1400
James Nolan, prin. | Fax 471-1408
Samoset MS | 6-8
51 School St 11779 | 631-471-1700
Mary Cavanaugh, prin. | Fax 471-1706

Lancaster, Erie, Pop. 11,381
Lancaster Central SD — 5,800/K-12
177 Central Ave 14086 — 716-686-3201
Thomas Markle, supt. — Fax 686-3350
lancasterschools.org
Lancaster HS — 1,900/9-12
1 Forton Dr 14086 — 716-686-3250
Dan Paveljack, prin. — Fax 686-3347
Lancaster MS — 1,000/7-8
148 Aurora St 14086 — 716-686-3220
Peter Kruszynski, prin. — Fax 686-3223

St. Mary HS — 400/9-12
142 Laverack Ave 14086 — 716-683-4824
Dr. Joseph Casimino, prin. — Fax 683-4996

Lansing, Tompkins, Pop. 3,474
Lansing Central SD — 1,300/K-12
264 Ridge Rd 14882 — 607-533-4294
Dr. Mark Lewis, supt. — Fax 533-3602
www.lansingschools.org
Lansing HS — 400/9-12
300 Ridge Rd 14882 — 607-533-4652
Michelle Stone, prin. — Fax 533-4612
Lansing MS — 400/5-8
6 Ludlowville Rd 14882 — 607-533-4271
John Gizzi, prin. — Fax 533-3543

Larchmont, Westchester, Pop. 6,523
Mamaroneck UFD
Supt. — See Mamaroneck
Hommocks MS — 1,100/6-8
10 Hommocks Rd 10538 — 914-220-3300
Dr. Seth Weitzman, prin.

French-American S of NY — 700/PK-10
111 Larchmont Ave 10538 — 914-834-3002
Robert M. Leonhardt, hdmstr. — Fax 834-1284

Latham, Albany, Pop. 10,131
North Colonie Central SD — 5,600/K-12
91 Fiddlers Ln 12110 — 518-785-8591
Randy A. Ehrenberg, supt. — Fax 785-8502
www.northcolonie.org
Shaker HS — 2,000/9-12
445 Watervliet Shaker Rd 12110 — 518-785-5511
James Jackson, prin. — Fax 783-5905
Shaker JHS — 1,000/7-8
475 Watervliet Shaker Rd 12110 — 518-785-1341
Russell Moore, prin. — Fax 783-8877

Mildred Elley the College for Careers — Post-Sec.
800 New Loudon Rd Ste 5120 12110 — 518-786-0855
SUNY Empire State College — Post-Sec.
21 British American Blvd 12110 — 518-783-6203

Laurens, Otsego, Pop. 263
Laurens Central SD — 400/K-12
PO Box 301 13796 — 607-432-2050
Romona Wenck, supt. — Fax 432-4388
laurenscs.org
Laurens Central S — 400/K-12
PO Box 301 13796 — 607-432-2050
Karl Brown, prin. — Fax 432-4388

Lawrence, Nassau, Pop. 6,546
Lawrence UFD — 3,400/PK-12
PO Box 477 11559 — 516-295-7030
Dr. John Fitzsimons, supt. — Fax 239-7164
www.lawrence.org/
Lawrence MS — 900/6-8
195 Broadway 11559 — 516-295-7000
Dr. Mark Kavarsky, prin. — Fax 295-7196
Other Schools – See Cedarhurst

Hebrew Academy of Five Towns MS — 300/6-8
44 Frost Ln 11559 — 516-569-6352
Naomi Lippman, prin. — Fax 569-6457
Rambam Mesivta — 200/9-12
15 Frost Ln 11559 — 516-371-5824
Rabbi Yotav Eliach, prin. — Fax 371-4706
Shor Yoshuv Institute — Post-Sec.
1 Cedarlawn Ave 11559 — 516-239-9002

Le Roy, Genesee, Pop. 4,373
Le Roy Central SD — 1,400/K-12
2 Trigon Park 14482 — 585-768-8133
Mary Jane Brooke, supt. — Fax 768-8929
www.leroy.k12.ny.us
Le Roy JSHS — 700/7-12
9300 S Street Rd 14482 — 585-768-8131
Charles Herring, prin. — Fax 768-8929

Levittown, Nassau, Pop. 53,000
Island Trees UFD — 2,800/K-12
74 Farmedge Rd 11756 — 516-520-2100
James Parla, supt. — Fax 520-2113
www.islandtrees.org
Island Trees HS — 900/9-12
59 Straight Ln 11756 — 516-520-2135
Joseph Pisani, prin. — Fax 520-9199
Island Trees MS — 900/5-8
45 Wantagh Ave 11756 — 516-520-2157
Jon Segerdahl, prin. — Fax 520-2168

Levittown UFD — 7,700/K-12
150 Abbey Ln 11756 — 516-520-8300
Herman Sirois, supt. — Fax 520-8314
www.levittownschools.com
Division Avenue HS — 1,000/9-12
120 Division Ave 11756 — 516-520-8350
Kathleen Valentino, prin. — Fax 520-8364
MacArthur HS — 1,200/9-12
3369 N Jerusalem Rd 11756 — 516-520-8450
John Bifolco, prin. — Fax 520-8466
Salk MS — 1,000/6-8
3359 N Jerusalem Rd 11756 — 516-520-8470
Debbie Rifkin, prin. — Fax 520-8479
Wisdom Lane MS — 900/6-8
120 Center Ln 11756 — 516-520-8370
Dr. Robert Tymann, prin. — Fax 520-8380

Hunter Business School — Post-Sec.
3601 Hempstead Tpke 11756 — 516-796-1000
Learning Institute for Beauty Sciences — Post-Sec.
2981 Hempstead Tpke 11756 — 516-731-8300

Liberty, Sullivan, Pop. 3,970
Liberty Central SD — 1,900/PK-12
115 Buckley St 12754 — 845-292-6990
Lawrence A. Clarke, supt. — Fax 292-1164
www.libertyk12.org
Liberty JSHS — 700/8-12
125 Buckley St 12754 — 845-292-5400
Jack Strassman, prin. — Fax 292-7262

Lido Beach, Nassau, Pop. 2,786
Long Beach CSD — 4,500/PK-12
235 Lido Blvd 11561 — 516-897-2104
Dr. Robert Greenberg, supt. — Fax 897-2107
www.lbeach.org
Other Schools – See Long Beach

Lima, Livingston, Pop. 2,450

Lima Christian S — 200/K-12
1574 Rochester St 14485 — 585-624-3841
Ralph Dewey, prin. — Fax 624-8293

Lincolndale, Westchester
Somers Central SD
Supt. — See Somers
Somers HS — 900/9-12
PO Box 640 10540 — 914-248-8585
Linda Horisk, prin. — Fax 248-8186

Ives S — 200/7-11
PO Box 600 10540 — 914-248-7474
Dr. Frank McGowan, prin. — Fax 248-5673

Lindenhurst, Suffolk, Pop. 28,469
Lindenhurst UFD — 7,400/K-12
350 Daniel St 11757 — 631-226-6441
Neil Lederer, supt. — Fax 226-6865
www.lindenhurstschools.org
Lindenhurst HS — 2,300/9-12
300 Charles St 11757 — 631-226-6445
Daniel Giordano, prin. — Fax 226-6577
Lindenhurst MS — 1,800/6-8
350 S Wellwood Ave 11757 — 631-226-6521
Frank Naccarato, prin. — Fax 226-6554

Lisbon, Saint Lawrence
Lisbon Central SD — 600/K-12
6866 County Route 10 13658 — 315-393-4951
Ernest Witkowski, supt. — Fax 393-7666
lisboncs.schoolwires.com
Lisbon Central S — 600/K-12
6866 County Route 10 13658 — 315-393-4951
Christopher Todd, prin. — Fax 393-7666

Little Falls, Herkimer, Pop. 5,049
Little Falls CSD — 1,200/K-12
15 Petrie St 13365 — 315-823-1470
William Gokey, supt. — Fax 823-0321
lfcsd.com/
Little Falls HS — 300/9-12
1 High School Rd 13365 — 315-823-1167
Louis Patrei, prin. — Fax 823-1209
Little Falls MS — 300/6-8
1 High School Rd 13365 — 315-823-4300
Kathryn Faber, prin. — Fax 823-3920

Little Neck, See New York
NYC Department of Education
Supt. — See New York
JHS 67 — 1,200/6-9
5160 Marathon Pkwy 11362 — 718-423-8138
Zoi McGrath, prin. — Fax 423-8281

Little Valley, Cattaraugus, Pop. 1,100
Cattaraugus-Little Valley Central SD — 1,100/K-12
207 Rock City St 14755 — 716-938-9155
Louis Mcintosh Jr., supt. — Fax 938-6576
www.cattlv.wnyric.org/
Other Schools – See Cattaraugus

Liverpool, Onondaga, Pop. 2,457
Liverpool Central SD — 7,800/PK-12
195 Blackberry Rd 13090 — 315-622-7125
Janice H. Matousek, supt. — Fax 622-7124
www.liverpool.k12.ny.us
Chestnut Hill MS — 300/7-8
204 Saslon Park Dr 13088 — 315-453-0245
Scott Krell, prin. — Fax 453-0278
Liverpool HS — 2,000/10-12
4338 Wetzel Rd 13090 — 315-453-1112
— Fax 453-1246
Liverpool MS — 500/7-8
700 7th St 13088 — 315-453-0258
Robert Gaetano, prin. — Fax 453-0281
Ninth Grade Annex — 9-9
4340 Wetzel Rd 13090 — 315-453-1275
Ted Phillips, prin.
Soule Road MS — 500/7-8
8340 Soule Rd 13090 — 315-453-1283
Robert Sheitz, prin. — Fax 453-1286

Bryant & Stratton College — Post-Sec.
8687 Carling Rd 13090 — 315-472-6603
National Tractor Trailer School — Post-Sec.
PO Box 208 13088 — 315-451-2430

Livingston Manor, Sullivan, Pop. 1,482
Livingston Manor Central SD — 700/PK-12
PO Box 947 12758 — 845-439-4400
Debra Lynker, supt. — Fax 439-4717
lmcs.k12.ny.us
Livingston Manor JSHS — 300/7-12
PO Box 947 12758 — 845-439-4400
Harold Tighe, prin. — Fax 439-4717

Livonia, Livingston, Pop. 1,357
Livonia Central SD — 2,100/K-12
PO Box E 14487 — 585-346-4000
David DeLoria, supt. — Fax 346-6145
www.livoniacsd.org
Livonia HS — 700/9-12
PO Box E 14487 — 585-346-4040
Karen Bennett, prin. — Fax 346-9605
Livonia JHS — 400/7-8
PO Box E 14487 — 585-346-4050
Charles D'Imperio, prin. — Fax 346-6835

Loch Sheldrake, Sullivan

SUNY Sullivan County Community College — Post-Sec.
112 College Rd 12759 — 845-434-5750

Lockport, Robert, Niagara, Pop. 21,600
Lockport CSD, 130 Beattie Ave 14094 — 5,600/PK-12
Dr. Bruce Fraser, supt. — 716-478-4835
www.lockport.k12.ny.us
Belknap MS, 491 High St 14094 — 700/6-8
Gary Wilson, prin. — 716-478-4552
Lockport HS, 250 Lincoln Ave 14094 — 1,800/9-12
Frank Movalli, prin. — 716-478-4452
North Park MS — 600/6-8
160 Passaic Ave 14094 — 716-478-4702
James Snyder, prin.

Starpoint Central SD — 2,800/K-12
4363 Mapleton Rd 14094 — 716-210-2352
Dr. C. Douglas Whelan, supt.
www.starpointcsd.org/
Starpoint HS — 900/9-12
4363 Mapleton Rd 14094 — 716-210-2300
Gil Licata, prin.
Starpoint MS — 700/6-8
4363 Mapleton Rd 14094 — 716-210-2200
James Bryer, prin.

Christian Academy of Western New York — 100/PK-12
120 Main St 14094 — 716-433-1652
Patricia Poeller, admin. — Fax 438-0751

Locust Valley, Nassau, Pop. 3,963
Locust Valley Central SD — 2,300/K-12
99 Horse Hollow Rd 11560 — 516-674-6390
Anthony Singe, supt. — Fax 674-0138
www.lvcsd.k12.ny.us/
Locust Valley HS — 600/9-12
99 Horse Hollow Rd 11560 — 516-674-6305
Richard Shear, prin. — Fax 671-1096
Locust Valley MS — 500/6-8
99 Horse Hollow Rd 11560 — 516-674-6370
Matt Sanzone, prin. — Fax 674-3795

Friends Academy — 700/PK-12
Duck Pond Rd 11560 — 516-676-0393
William Morris, hdmstr. — Fax 393-4276
Portledge S — 400/PK-12
355 Duck Pond Rd 11560 — 516-750-3100
Stephen Hahn, hdmstr. — Fax 671-2039

Long Beach, Nassau, Pop. 35,415
Long Beach CSD
Supt. — See Lido Beach
Long Beach HS — 1,400/9-12
322 Lagoon Dr W 11561 — 516-897-2012
Nicholas Restivo, prin. — Fax 897-2052
Long Beach MS — 1,000/6-8
239 Lido Blvd 11561 — 516-897-2166
Joane Tom, prin. — Fax 897-2145

Mesivta of Long Beach — 100/9-12
205 W Beech St 11561 — 516-255-4700
Rabbi Harvey Krasnow, prin. — Fax 255-4701
Rabbinical College of Long Island — Post-Sec.
205 W Beech St 11561 — 516-255-4700

Long Island City, See New York
NYC Department of Education
Supt. — See New York
Academy of Finance & Enterprise — 9-12
3020 Thomson Ave 11101 — 718-389-3623
Gilberto Vega, prin. — Fax 389-3724
Applied Communication HS — 9-12
3020 Thomson Ave 11101 — 718-389-3163
Mary Ellen Kociszewski, prin. — Fax 389-3427
Aviation Career & Technical HS — Vo/Tech
4530 36th St 11101 — 718-361-2032
Eileen Taylor, prin. — Fax 784-8654
Bryant HS — 3,600/9-12
4810 31st Ave 11103 — 718-721-5404
C. Pellettieri, prin. — Fax 728-3478
Information Technology HS — 300/9-12
2116 44th Rd 11101 — 718-937-4270
Noralee Montemarano, dir. — Fax 281-7569
IS 10 — 1,000/6-8
4511 31st Ave 11103 — 718-726-7054
Clemente Lopes, prin. — Fax 274-1578
IS 126 — 800/6-8
3151 21st St 11106 — 718-274-8316
Dr. Candice Scott, prin. — Fax 728-6512
IS 141 — 1,100/6-8
3711 21st Ave 11105 — 718-278-6403
Anthony B. Aldorasi, prin. — Fax 278-2884
IS 204 — 1,000/6-8
3641 28th St 11106 — 718-937-1463
Thomas Semanski, prin. — Fax 937-7964
Queens Vocational HS — Vo/Tech
3702 47th Ave 11101 — 718-937-3010
Denise Vittor, prin. — Fax 392-8397
Sinatra HS — 500/9-12
2910 Thomson Ave 11101 — 718-361-9920
Donna Finn, prin. — Fax 361-9995

DeVry Institute of Technology — Post-Sec.
3020 Thomson Ave 11101 — 718-472-2728
Evangel Christian S — 400/PK-12
3921 Crescent St 11101 — 718-937-9600
Marilyn Johansson, prin. — Fax 937-1613

LaGuardia Community College / CUNY   Post-Sec.
   31-10 Thompson Ave   11101   718-482-7200
New York School for Medical Dental Asst.   Post-Sec.
   3310 Queens Blvd   11101   718-793-2330

Long Lake, Hamilton
Long Lake Central SD   100/PK-12
   PO Box 217   12847   518-624-2147
   Kevin Crampton, supt.   Fax 624-3896
Long Lake Central S   100/PK-12
   PO Box 217   12847   518-624-2147
   Lawrence Patzwald, prin.   Fax 624-3896

Loudonville, Albany, Pop. 10,822

Loudonville Christian S   300/PK-12
   374 Loudon Rd   12211   518-434-6051
   Valyn Anderson, hdmstr.   Fax 935-2258
Siena College   Post-Sec.
   515 Loudon Rd   12211   518-783-2300

Lowville, Lewis, Pop. 3,340
Lowville Central SD   1,400/K-12
   7668 N State St   13367   315-376-9000
   Kenneth J. McAuliffe, supt.   Fax 376-1933
   www.lacs-ny.org
Lowville HS   400/9-12
   7668 N State St   13367   315-376-9015
   Daniel J. Cushing, prin.   Fax 376-1933
Lowville MS   300/6-8
   7668 N State St   13367   315-376-9010
   Leueen Smithling, prin.   Fax 376-9011

Lynbrook, Nassau, Pop. 19,803
Lynbrook UFD   3,100/K-12
   111 Atlantic Ave   11563   516-887-0253
   Dr. Philip S. Cicero, supt.   Fax 887-3263
   www.lynbrook.k12.ny.us
Lynbrook HS   900/9-12
   9 Union Ave   11563   516-887-0200
   Santo Barbarino Ph.D., prin.   Fax 887-8079
Lynbrook North MS   300/6-8
   529 Merrick Rd   11563   516-887-0282
   Dean Mittleman, prin.   Fax 887-0286
Lynbrook South MS   500/6-8
   333 Union Ave   11563   516-887-0267
   Margaret Rienzi Ed.D., prin.   Fax 887-0268

Lyndonville, Orleans, Pop. 854
Lyndonville Central SD   800/K-12
   PO Box 540   14098   585-765-3101
   Barbara Deane-Williams, supt.   Fax 765-2106
Lyndonville JHS   300/5-8
   PO Box 540   14098   585-765-3142
   Mathew Penrod, prin.   Fax 765-2106
Webber HS   300/9-12
   PO Box 540   14098   585-765-3164
   Kenneth Smith, prin.   Fax 765-2106

Lyons, Wayne, Pop. 3,589
Lyons Central SD   1,000/K-12
   9 Lawrence St   14489   315-946-2200
   Richard Amundson, supt.   Fax 946-2205
   www.lyonscsd.org
Lyons HS   300/9-12
   10 Clyde Rd   14489   315-946-2220
   Harold Decook, prin.   Fax 946-2221
Lyons MS   200/7-8
   10 Clyde Rd   14489   315-946-2200
   Celine Olgin, prin.   Fax 946-2221

Mc Graw, Cortland, Pop. 1,032
Mc Graw Central SD   600/K-12
   PO Box 556   13101   607-836-3636
   Maria S. Fragnoli-Ryan, supt.   Fax 836-3635
   www.mcgrawschools.org
Mc Graw JSHS   300/7-12
   PO Box 556   13101   607-836-3600
   Patricia Plata, prin.   Fax 836-3635

Madison, Madison, Pop. 312
Madison Central SD   500/K-12
   7303 State Route 20   13402   315-893-1878
   Cynthia DeDominick, supt.   Fax 893-7111
   www.madisoncentralny.org
Madison Central S   500/K-12
   7303 State Route 20   13402   315-893-1878
   Michael Drahos, prin.   Fax 893-7111

Madrid, Saint Lawrence
Madrid-Waddington Central SD   800/K-12
   PO Box 67   13660   315-322-5746
   Kendall Straight, supt.   Fax 322-4462
   www.mwcsk12.org
Madrid-Waddington JSHS   500/6-12
   PO Box 67   13660   315-322-5746
   Joseph Ruddy, prin.   Fax 322-4462

Mahopac, Putnam, Pop. 7,755
Mahopac Central SD   5,300/K-12
   179 E Lake Blvd   10541   845-628-3415
   Robert J. Reidy Ph.D., supt.   Fax 628-5502
   www.mahopac.k12.ny.us
Mahopac HS   1,600/9-12
   421 Baldwin Place Rd   10541   845-628-3256
   Aaron Trummer, prin.   Fax 628-4380
Mahopac MS   1,300/6-8
   425 Baldwin Place Rd   10541   845-621-1330
   Ira Gurkin, prin.   Fax 628-5847

Malone, Franklin, Pop. 5,998
Malone Central SD   2,400/PK-12
   PO Box 847   12953   518-483-7800
   Stephen Shafer, supt.   Fax 483-3071
   malone.k12.ny.us/
Franklin Academy HS   800/9-12
   42 Huskie Ln   12953   518-483-7807
   Donald Merrick, prin.   Fax 483-7813
Malone MS   600/6-8
   15 Francis St   12953   518-483-7801
   John Scheide, prin.   Fax 483-9497

Malverne, Nassau, Pop. 8,879
Malverne UFD   1,800/K-12
   301 Wicks Ln   11565   516-887-6405
   Dr. Mary Ellen Freeley, supt.   Fax 596-2910
   www.malverne.k12.ny.us
Herber MS   600/5-8
   75 Ocean Ave   11565   516-887-6444
   David Zimbler, prin.   Fax 596-0525
Malverne HS   600/9-12
   80 Ocean Ave   11565   516-887-6420
   Glenda Good, prin.   Fax 887-6479

Mamaroneck, Westchester, Pop. 18,493
Mamaroneck UFD   4,700/PK-12
   1000 W Boston Post Rd   10543   914-220-3000
   Dr. Paul R. Fried, supt.
   www.mamkschools.org
Mamaroneck HS   1,400/9-12
   1000 W Boston Post Rd   10543   914-220-3100
   Dr. Mark Orfinger, prin.
Other Schools – See Larchmont

Rye Neck UFD   1,400/K-12
   310 Hornidge Rd   10543   914-777-5200
   Dr. Peter Mustich, supt.   Fax 777-5201
   www.ryeneck.k12.ny.us/
Rye Neck HS   400/9-12
   300 Hornidge Rd   10543   914-777-5200
   Dr. Barbara Ferraro, prin.   Fax 777-4801
Rye Neck MS   400/5-8
   300 Hornidge Rd   10543   914-777-5200
   Eric Lutinski, prin.   Fax 777-4701

Westchester Hebrew HS   100/9-12
   856 Orienta Ave   10543   914-698-0806
   Rabbi Majerowicz, hdmstr.   Fax 698-1330

Manhasset, Nassau, Pop. 7,718
Manhasset UFD   2,700/K-12
   200 Memorial Pl   11030   516-627-7705
   Charles Cardillo, supt.   Fax 627-1618
   www.manhasset.k12.ny.us
Manhasset HS   800/9-12
   200 Memorial Pl   11030   516-627-7600
   William Stark, prin.   Fax 627-4604
Manhasset MS   400/7-8
   200 Memorial Pl   11030   516-627-8044
   Richard McMahon, prin.   Fax 627-8157

St. Mary HS   800/9-12
   51 Clapham Ave   11030   516-627-2711
   Kevin McBride, prin.   Fax 627-3209

Manlius, Onondaga, Pop. 4,759
Fayetteville-Manlius Central SD   4,600/K-12
   8199 E Seneca Tpke   13104   315-692-1200
   Corliss Kaiser, supt.   Fax 692-1227
   www.fmschools.org
Eagle Hill MS   800/5-8
   4645 Enders Rd   13104   315-692-1400
   Mary Coughlin, prin.   Fax 692-1046
Fayetteville-Manlius HS   1,500/9-12
   8201 E Seneca Tpke   13104   315-692-1900
   James Chupaila, prin.   Fax 692-1028
Other Schools – See Fayetteville

Manorville, Suffolk, Pop. 6,198
Eastport South Manor Central SD   3,400/K-12
   149 Dayton Ave   11949   631-874-6720
   B. Allen Mannella, supt.   Fax 878-6308
   www.esmonline.org
Eastport/South Manor JSHS   1,400/7-12
   543 Moriches Middle Isle Rd   11949   631-874-6500
   Joseph A. Steimel, prin.   Fax 874-6787

Marathon, Cortland, Pop. 1,050
Marathon Central SD   1,000/K-12
   PO Box 339   13803   607-849-3251
   Timothy Turecek, supt.   Fax 849-6111
Marathon JSHS   500/7-12
   PO Box 339   13803   607-849-3251
   David Rosetti, prin.   Fax 849-3305

Marcellus, Onondaga, Pop. 1,820
Marcellus Central SD   2,100/K-12
   2 Reed Pkwy   13108   315-673-0201
   Dr. Timothy Barstow, supt.   Fax 673-1727
   mcs.rway.com
Driver MS   900/4-8
   2 Reed Pkwy   13108   315-673-0219
   Patrick Collier, prin.   Fax 673-1727
Marcellus HS   700/9-12
   1 Mustang Hl   13108   315-673-0296
   John Durkee, prin.   Fax 673-0312

Marcy, Oneida, Pop. 8,685
Whitesboro Central SD
   Supt. — See Yorkville
Whitesboro HS   1,200/9-12
   6000 State Route 291   13403   315-266-3200
   Curt Woodcock, prin.   Fax 266-3223

Margaretville, Delaware, Pop. 657
Margaretville Central SD   500/K-12
   PO Box 319   12455   845-586-2647
   John P. Riedl, supt.   Fax 586-2949
   www.margaretvillecs.org
Margaretville Central S   500/K-12
   PO Box 319   12455   845-586-2647
   Linda Taylor, prin.   Fax 586-2949

Marion, Wayne
Marion Central SD   1,100/K-12
   4034 Warner Rd   14505   315-926-2300
   Dr. J. Richard Boyes, supt.   Fax 926-5797
   www.marioncs.org/
Marion JSHS   600/7-12
   4034 Warner Rd   14505   315-926-4228
   Duane Perry, prin.   Fax 926-3114

Marlboro, Ulster, Pop. 2,200
Marlboro Central SD   2,200/K-12
   50 Cross Rd   12542   845-236-5802
   Julie Amodeo, supt.   Fax 236-5817
   www.marlboroschools.org
Marlboro Central HS   700/9-12
   50 Cross Rd   12542   845-236-5810
   Paul Hughes, prin.   Fax 236-2638
Marlboro MS   500/6-8
   1375 Route 9W   12542   845-236-5842
   Jose Sanchez, prin.   Fax 236-3634

Maspeth, See New York
NYC Department of Education
   Supt. — See New York
IS 73   1,800/6-8
   7002 54th Ave   11378   718-639-3817
   Patricia Reynolds, prin.   Fax 429-5162

Martin Luther HS   400/9-12
   6002 Maspeth Ave   11378   718-894-4000
   Elizabeth Crowe, prin.   Fax 894-1469

Massapequa, Nassau, Pop. 22,018
Massapequa UFD   8,000/K-12
   4925 Merrick Rd   11758   516-797-6160
   Dr. Lawrence Pereira, supt.   Fax 797-6072
   www.msd.k12.ny.us
Berner MS   1,400/7-8
   50 Carman Mill Rd   11758   516-797-6080
   Stephen Scarallo, prin.   Fax 797-6638
Massapequa HS   1,700/10-12
   4925 Merrick Rd   11758   516-797-6110
   James Maloney, prin.   Fax 797-6663
Massapequa HS Ames Campus   600/9-9
   198 Baltimore Ave   11758   516-797-6530
   Barbara Williams, prin.   Fax 797-6534

Plainedge UFD
   Supt. — See North Massapequa
Plainedge HS   1,100/9-12
   241 Wyngate Dr   11758   516-992-7550
   Robert Amster, prin.   Fax 992-7545

Massena, Saint Lawrence, Pop. 10,982
Massena Central SD   2,900/K-12
   84 Nightengale Ave   13662   315-764-3700
   Douglas Huntley, supt.   Fax 764-3701
   www.mcs.k12.ny.us
Leary JHS   600/7-8
   84 Nightengale Ave   13662   315-764-3720
   Roger Clough, prin.   Fax 764-3723
Massena HS   1,000/9-12
   84 Nightengale Ave   13662   315-764-3710
   Cathryn McDevitt, prin.   Fax 764-3719

Mastic Beach, Suffolk, Pop. 10,293
William Floyd UFD   10,300/K-12
   240 Mastic Beach Rd   11951   631-874-1100
   Dr. Richard Hawkins, supt.   Fax 281-3047
   www.wfsd.k12.ny.us
Floyd HS   3,200/9-12
   240 Mastic Beach Rd   11951   631-874-1120
   Robert Feeney, prin.   Fax 281-3047
Paca MS   1,400/6-8
   338 Blanco Dr   11951   631-874-1415
   Barbara Butler, prin.   Fax 281-3047
Other Schools – See Moriches

Mattituck, Suffolk, Pop. 3,902
Mattituck-Cutchogue UFD
   Supt. — See Cutchogue
Mattituck-Cutchogue JSHS   700/7-12
   15125 Main Rd   11952   631-298-8460
   James McKenna, prin.   Fax 298-8544

Mayfield, Fulton, Pop. 795
Mayfield Central SD   1,200/K-12
   27 School St   12117   518-661-8207
   Ralph Acquaro, supt.   Fax 661-7666
   www.mayfield12.com/
Mayfield JSHS   600/7-12
   27 School St   12117   518-661-8200
   Robert Husain, prin.   Fax 661-7666

Mayville, Chautauqua, Pop. 1,744
Chautauqua Lake SD   1,000/PK-12
   100 N Erie St   14757   716-753-5808
   Benjamin Spitzer, supt.   Fax 753-5813
   www.clake.org
Chautauqua Lake Central HS   300/9-12
   100 N Erie St   14757   716-753-5882
   Rosemary Andrews, prin.   Fax 753-5886
Chautauqua Lake MS   200/6-8
   100 N Erie St   14757   716-753-5872
   John Panebianco, prin.   Fax 753-5876

Mechanicville, Saratoga, Pop. 5,001
Mechanicville CSD   1,300/K-12
   25 Kniskern Ave   12118   518-664-5727
   Michael McCarthy, supt.   Fax 664-0060
Mechanicville HS   400/9-12
   25 Kniskern Ave   12118   518-664-9888
   G. Michael Apostol, prin.   Fax 664-1505
Mechanicville MS   300/6-8
   25 Kniskern Ave   12118   518-664-6303
   Kevin Duffy, prin.   Fax 664-6341

Medford, Suffolk, Pop. 21,274
Patchogue-Medford UFD
   Supt. — See Patchogue
Oregon MS   1,000/6-9
   109 Oregon Ave   11763   631-687-6800
   Lori Cannetti, prin.   Fax 758-1126
Patchogue-Medford HS   1,900/10-12
   181 Buffalo Ave   11763   631-687-6500
   J. Matuk, prin.   Fax 758-1126

Medina, Orleans, Pop. 6,308
Medina Central SD   1,900/K-12
   1 Mustang Dr   14103   585-798-2700
   Richard Galante, supt.   Fax 798-5676
   www.medinacsd.org

Medina HS 600/9-12
  2 Mustang Dr 14103 585-798-2710
  Wes Pickreign, prin. Fax 798-2787
Wise MS 500/6-8
  1016 Gwinn St 14103 585-798-2100
  Marc Graff, prin. Fax 798-1062

Orleans County Christian S 50/K-12
  PO Box 349 14103 585-798-2992
  Linda Strickland, admin. Fax 798-3766

Melville, Suffolk, Pop. 12,586
Half Hollow Hills Central SD
  Supt. — See Dix Hills
West Hollow MS 1,200/6-8
  250 Old East Neck Rd 11747 631-592-3400
  Mary Retetaliata, prin. Fax 592-3922

Katharine Gibbs School Post-Sec.
  320 S Service Rd 11747 631-370-3300
Polytechnic University Post-Sec.
  105 Maxess Rd Ste 201N 11747 631-755-4300

Merrick, Nassau, Pop. 23,042
Bellmore-Merrick Central HSD
  Supt. — See North Merrick
Calhoun HS 1,300/9-12
  1786 State St 11566 516-992-1300
  David Seinfeld, prin. Fax 867-7390
Merrick Avenue MS 1,000/7-8
  1870 Merrick Ave 11566 516-992-1200
  Caryn Frange, prin. Fax 867-6391

Mexico, Oswego, Pop. 1,567
Mexico Central SD 2,700/K-12
  40 Academy St 13114 315-963-8400
  Michael Maroun, supt. Fax 963-3325
  www.mexico.cnyric.org
Mexico HS 900/9-12
  3338 Main St 13114 315-963-8400
  Jeannie Henry, prin. Fax 963-8887
Mexico MS 900/5-8
  16 Fravor Rd 13114 315-963-8400
  William Kamalsky, prin. Fax 963-3848

Middleburgh, Schoharie, Pop. 1,469
Middleburgh Central SD 1,000/PK-12
  PO Box 606 12122 518-827-3600
  Douglas Kelley, supt. Fax 827-6632
  teacherweb.com/NY/MiddleburghCentralSchool/District/
Middleburgh HS 300/9-12
  PO Box 400 12122 518-827-3600
  Lori Petrosino, prin. Fax 827-5192
Middleburgh MS 300/6-8
  PO Box 400 12122 518-827-3600
  Douglas Kelley, prin. Fax 827-9533

Middle Island, Suffolk, Pop. 7,848
Longwood Central SD 9,200/K-12
  35 Yaphank Middle Island Rd 11953 631-345-2172
  Dr. Allan Gerstenlauer, supt. Fax 345-2166
  www.longwood.k12.ny.us
Longwood HS 2,900/9-12
  100 Longwood Rd 11953 631-345-9200
  Donald Murphy, prin. Fax 345-9279
Longwood JHS 1,500/7-8
  198 Longwood Rd 11953 631-345-2701
  Levi McIntyre, prin. Fax 345-9281

Middleport, Niagara, Pop. 1,860
Royalton-Hartland Central SD 1,200/K-12
  54 State St 14105 716-735-3031
  Paul Bona, supt. Fax 735-3660
  royhart.org/
Royalton-Hartland HS 600/9-12
  56 State St 14105 716-735-3800
  Kevin Shanley, prin. Fax 735-6128
Royalton-Hartland MS 400/5-8
  78 State St 14105 716-735-3722
  Sean Kinsley, prin. Fax 735-0047

Middletown, Orange, Pop. 25,863
Middletown CSD 7,300/K-12
  223 Wisner Ave 10940 845-341-5690
  Dr. Kenneth Eastwood, supt. Fax 343-9938
  www.middletown.k12.ny.us
Middletown HS 1,900/9-12
  20 Gardner Ave Ext 10940 845-341-5900
  George Vanderzell, prin. Fax 343-5991
Middletown Twin Towers MS 800/6-8
  112 Grand Ave 10940 845-341-5400
  Gordon Dean, prin. Fax 343-4515
Monhagen MS 800/6-8
  555 County Highway 78 10940 845-346-4800
  Eileen R. Shapiro, prin. Fax 346-4868

Beauty School of Middletown Post-Sec.
  225 Dolson Ave Ste 100 10940 845-343-2171
Harmony Christian S 300/PK-12
  1790 Route 211 E 10941 845-692-5353
  Pamela Burns, admin. Fax 692-7140
SUNY Orange County Community College Post-Sec.
  115 South St 10940 845-344-6222

Middle Village, See New York

Christ the King Regional HS 1,800/9-12
  6802 Metropolitan Ave 11379 718-366-7400
  Michael Lynch, prin. Fax 366-1165

Milford, Otsego, Pop. 487
Milford Central SD 500/K-12
  PO Box 237 13807 607-286-3341
  Peter Livshin, supt. Fax 286-7879
Milford Central S 500/K-12
  PO Box 237 13807 607-286-3349
  Lynda Bookhard, prin. Fax 286-7879

Millbrook, Dutchess, Pop. 1,544
Millbrook Central SD 1,200/K-12
  PO Box AA 12545 845-677-4200
  Michael Mahoney, supt. Fax 677-4206
  www.millbrookcsd.org/
Millbrook JSHS 600/7-12
  PO Box AA 12545 845-677-4210
  Jeffrey Matteson, prin. Fax 677-6913

Millbrook S 200/9-12
  School Rd 12545 845-677-8261
  Drew Casertano, hdmstr. Fax 677-8598

Miller Place, Suffolk, Pop. 9,315
Miller Place UFD 3,000/K-12
  275 Route 25A Unit 43 11764 631-474-2700
  Dr. Donald K. Carlisle, supt. Fax 474-0686
  www.millerplace.k12.ny.us
Miller Place HS 900/9-12
  15 Memorial Dr 11764 631-474-2723
  Seth Lipshie, prin. Fax 474-1734
North Country Road MS 800/6-8
  191 N Country Rd 11764 631-474-2710
  Susan Hodun, prin. Fax 474-5178

Mill Neck, Nassau, Pop. 839

Mill Neck Lutheran School Post-Sec.
  Frost Mill Rd B12 11765

Millwood, Westchester, Pop. 1,000

Yeshiva Kehilath Yaakov 50/11-12
  PO Box 501 10546 914-762-3010
  Rabbi Shimshon Katz, admin. Fax 762-3010

Mineola, Nassau, Pop. 19,164
Mineola UFD 2,900/PK-12
  121 Jackson Ave 11501 516-237-2001
  Dr. Lorenzo Licopoli, supt. Fax 739-4783
  www.mineola.k12.ny.us
Mineola MS 600/6-8
  200 Emory Rd 11501 516-237-2500
  Mark Barth, prin. Fax 739-4129
Other Schools – See Garden City Park

Chaminade HS 1,600/9-12
  340 Jackson Ave 11501 516-742-5555
  Br. Joseph Bellizzi, prin. Fax 742-1989
NY College Traditional Chinese Medicine Post-Sec.
  155 1st St 11501 516-739-1545
Winthrop University Hospital Post-Sec.
  259 1st St 11501 516-663-2201

Mohawk, Herkimer, Pop. 2,588
Mohawk Central SD 1,000/K-12
  28 Grove St 13407 315-867-2904
  Joyce Caputo, supt. Fax 867-2918
  www.mohawk.k12.ny.us
Mohawk JSHS 500/7-12
  28 Grove St 13407 315-866-2620
  Edward Rinaldo, prin. Fax 867-2909

Monroe, Orange, Pop. 8,052
Greenwood Lake UFD
  Supt. — See Greenwood Lake
Greenwood Lake MS 300/5-8
  1247 Lakes Rd 10950 845-986-8624
  Allan Lipsky, prin. Fax 782-2004

Kiryas Joel Village UFSD 200/PK-12
  PO Box 398, 845-782-2300
  Dr. Steven Benardo, supt. Fax 782-4176
Kiryas Joel Village S 200/PK-12
  PO Box 398, 845-782-7510
  Susan Gartenberg, prin. Fax 782-4176

Bnei Yoel S 300/PK-12
  PO Box 255, 845-783-8036
UTA Mesivta of Kiryas Joel Post-Sec.
  33 Forest Ave Ste 101 10950 845-783-9901
UTA of Kiryas Joel 5,800/K-12
  PO Box 477, 845-783-5800
  Rabbi Baruch Weinberger, prin. Fax 782-1922

Monsey, Rockland, Pop. 13,986

Ateres Bais Yaakov 200/PK-12
  236 Cherry Ln 10952 845-368-2200
  Rabbi A. Fink, dean Fax 357-2343
Bais Malka Girls S of Belz 300/PK-12
  PO Box 977 10952 845-371-0500
  C. Levine, prin. Fax 425-2629
Bais Shifra Miriam S 300/K-12
  PO Box 682 10952 845-356-0061
  Gabriel Kramarsky, admin. Fax 356-0223
Bais Usher Darkai Torah S 50/10-12
  PO Box 649 10952 845-425-1939
  Rabbi Shimon Goldbrenner, prin. Fax 352-0980
Bais Yaakov D'Rav Hirsch 100/9-12
  PO Box 671 10952 845-371-6750
  Rabbi Z. Gelley, dean Fax 371-6618
Bais Yaakov HS of Spring Valley 400/9-12
  11 Smolley Dr 10952 845-356-3113
  M. Paretzky, prin. Fax 356-3132
Bais Yaakov of Ramapo HS 100/9-12
  16 Hershel Ter 10952 845-356-0580
  Rabbi Michael Shepard, prin. Fax 356-0584
Beth Rochel School for Girls 800/K-12
  145 Saddle River Rd 10952 845-352-5000
  Rabbi Jacob Przewozman, admin. Fax 352-6571
Bnos Yisroel Girls S of Viznitz 1,000/K-12
  1 School Ter 10952 845-356-2322
  Rabbi H. Moskowitz, admin. Fax 731-3751
Kol Yaakov Torah Center Post-Sec.
  29 W Maple Ave 10952 845-425-3863
Mesivta Shaarei Arazim 100/9-12
  PO Box 523 10952 845-426-6401
  Rabbi Zev Freundlich, admin. Fax 426-6389
Mesivta Yesodei Yisroel 100/9-12
  51 Carlton Rd 10952 845-425-2520
  Dr. Yaakov Zvi Nierman, prin. Fax 425-0317

Mesivta Ziev Hatorah 100/9-12
  PO Box 814 10952 845-426-6868
  Yizchok Weinberger, dir. Fax 356-5651
Ohr Somayach Tanenbaum Educational Ctr. Post-Sec.
  PO Box 334 10952 845-425-1370
Yeshiva and Kolel Bais Medrash Elyon Post-Sec.
  73 Main St 10952 845-356-7064
Yeshiva Beth David S 500/K-12
  PO Box 136 10952 845-352-3100
  Rabbi Yehuda Lichter, prin. Fax 352-0153
Yeshiva D'Monsey Rabbinical College Post-Sec.
  2 Roman Blvd 10952 845-426-3276
Yeshiva Gedola of South Monsey 100/9-12
  10 Algonquin Cir 10952 845-356-4030
  Rabbi Eliezer Abish, prin. Fax 352-7436
Yeshiva Shaar Ephraim S 100/9-12
  PO Box 253 10952 845-426-3110
  Y. Oshry, prin. Fax 425-4721
Yeshivath Viznitz Post-Sec.
  PO Box 446 10952 845-356-1010
Yeshiva Tzoin Yosef-Pupa 400/PK-12
  PO Box 978 10952 845-371-1220
  J. Kohn, prin. Fax 371-1237
Yeshiva Viznitz 1,600/PK-12
  PO Box 446 10952 845-356-1010
  Rabbi Berl Rosenfeld, admin. Fax 356-7359

Montgomery, Orange, Pop. 3,989
Valley Central SD 5,200/K-12
  944 State Route 17K 12549 845-457-2400
  Richard M. Hooley Ed.D., supt. Fax 457-4319
  www.vcsd.k12.ny.us
Valley Central HS 1,700/9-12
  1175 State Route 17K 12549 845-457-2400
  Darryl Imperati, prin. Fax 457-4056
Valley Central MS 1,300/6-8
  1189 State Route 17K 12549 845-457-2400
  Ned Hayes, prin. Fax 457-4311

Monticello, Sullivan, Pop. 6,493
Monticello Central SD 3,500/K-12
  237 Forestburgh Rd 12701 845-794-7700
  Eileen Casey, supt. Fax 794-7710
  www.monticelloschools.net
Kaiser MS 900/6-8
  45 Breakey Ave 12701 845-796-3058
  Deborah Wood, prin. Fax 796-3099
Monticello HS 1,100/9-12
  39 Breakey Ave 12701 845-794-8840
  George Vanderzell, prin. Fax 794-8133

Montrose, Westchester
Hendrick Hudson Central SD 2,900/K-12
  61 Trolley Rd 10548 914-736-5200
  Joan Thompson, supt. Fax 736-5242
  www.henhud.k12.ny.us
Hendrick Hudson HS 900/9-12
  2166 Albany Post Rd 10548 914-736-5500
  James Mackin, prin. Fax 737-6746
Other Schools – See Cortlandt Manor

Moravia, Cayuga, Pop. 1,349
Moravia Central SD 1,000/K-12
  PO Box 1189 13118 315-497-2670
  William P. Tammaro, supt. Fax 497-2260
  www.moraviaschool.org/
Monravia JHS, PO Box 1189 13118 7-8
  Bruce MacBain, prin. 315-497-2670
Moravia HS 400/9-12
  PO Box 1189 13118 315-497-2670
  Brian Morgan, prin. Fax 497-3852

Moriches, Suffolk
William Floyd UFD
  Supt. — See Mastic Beach
Floyd MS 1,300/6-8
  630 Moriches Middle Island 11955 631-874-5500
  Carolyn Schick, prin.

Morris, Otsego, Pop. 563
Morris Central SD 500/K-12
  PO Box 40 13808 607-263-6100
  Michael Virgil, supt. Fax 263-2483
  morriscs.org
Morris Central S 500/K-12
  PO Box 40 13808 607-263-6100
  Leone Schermerhorn, prin. Fax 263-2483

Morristown, Saint Lawrence, Pop. 445
Morristown Central SD 400/K-12
  PO Box 217 13664 315-375-8814
  Beverly Ouderkirk, supt. Fax 375-8604
Morristown Central S 400/K-12
  PO Box 217 13664 315-375-8814
  Michael Willis, prin. Fax 375-8604

Morrisville, Madison, Pop. 2,102
Morrisville-Eaton Central SD 900/K-12
  PO Box 990 13408 315-684-9300
  Nelson Bauersfeld, supt. Fax 684-9399
  www.m-ecs.org
Morrisville-Eaton MSHS 500/7-12
  PO Box 990 13408 315-684-9101
  Jonathan Bryant, prin. Fax 684-9192

SUNY College of Agriculture & Technology Post-Sec.
  13408 315-684-6000

Mount Kisco, Westchester, Pop. 10,035

Yeshiva Farm Settlement S 400/9-12
  PO Box 1050 10549 914-666-9702
  Yitzchak Schwartz, admin.

Mount Morris, Livingston, Pop. 3,198
Mt. Morris Central SD 600/K-12
  30 Bonadonna Ave 14510 585-658-2568
  Kathleen Farrell, supt. Fax 658-4814
  www.mt-morris.k12.ny.us
Mount Morris JSHS 300/7-12
  30 Bonadonna Ave 14510 585-658-3331
  Mark Valentino, prin. Fax 658-4814

Mount Sinai, Suffolk, Pop. 8,023
Mt. Sinai UFD 2,400/K-12
150 N Country Rd 11766 631-870-2550
Jonathan Van Eyk, supt. Fax 473-0905
www.mtsinai.k12.ny.us
Mount Sinai HS 700/9-12
Gertrude Goodman Dr 11766 631-870-2800
Peter Ferenz, prin. Fax 928-3668
Mount Sinai MS 900/5-8
150 N Country Rd 11766 631-870-2700
Robert Grable, prin. Fax 928-3129

Mount Vernon, Westchester, Pop. 68,404
Mt. Vernon CSD 10,100/PK-12
165 N Columbus Ave 10553 914-665-5000
Brenda L. Smith, supt. Fax 665-6077
www.lhric.org/mtvernon
Davis MS 800/7-8
350 Gramatan Ave 10552 914-665-5120
Murdisia Orr, prin. Fax 665-5128
Franko MS 700/7-8
455 N High St 10552 914-665-5151
Cleveland Person, prin. Fax 665-5152
Mount Vernon HS 2,600/9-12
100 California Rd 10552 914-665-5300
Dr. Larry H. Ashley, prin. Fax 665-5281

Fortress Christian Academy 50/K-12
51 N 10th Ave 10550 914-699-9039
Rev. Dennis Karaman, admin. Fax 699-6819
Hopfer School of Nursing Post-Sec.
53 Valentine St 10550 914-664-8000
Westchester School of Beauty Culture Post-Sec.
6 Gramatan Ave 10550 914-699-2344

Munnsville, Madison, Pop. 431
Stockbridge Valley Central SD 500/K-12
PO Box 732 13409 315-495-4400
Dr. Randy Richards, supt. Fax 495-4492
www.stockbridgevalley.org
Stockbridge Valley Central S 500/K-12
PO Box 732 13409 315-495-4445
Mary Anne Iritz, prin. Fax 495-4492

Nanuet, Rockland, Pop. 14,065
Nanuet UFD 2,700/K-12
101 Church St 10954 845-627-9890
Dr. Mark McNeill, supt. Fax 624-5338
nanuet.lhric.org/
Barr MS 500/6-8
143 Church St 10954 845-627-4040
Roger Guccione, prin. Fax 624-3138
Nanuet HS 600/9-12
103 Church St 10954 845-627-9800
Dr. Vin Carella, prin. Fax 624-5520

Capri Cosmetology Learning Center Post-Sec.
251 W Route 59 10954 845-623-6339

Naples, Ontario, Pop. 1,058
Naples Central SD 1,000/K-12
136 N Main St 14512 585-374-7900
Brenda C. Keith, supt. Fax 374-5859
www.naples.k12.ny.us
Naples HS 500/7-12
136 N Main St 14512 585-374-7905
Kenneth Foster, prin. Fax 374-5859

Nedrow, Onondaga, Pop. 2,700
Onondaga Central SD 1,000/PK-12
4466 S Onondaga Rd 13120 315-492-1701
Carolyn Costello, supt. Fax 492-4650
www.ocs.cnyric.org
Onondaga JSHS 500/7-12
4479 S Onondaga Rd 13120 315-492-1705
William Rasbeck, prin. Fax 492-8567

Nesconset, Suffolk, Pop. 10,712
Smithtown Central SD
Supt. — See Smithtown
Great Hollow MS 800/6-8
150 Southern Blvd 11767 631-382-2800
Daniel Goitia, prin. Fax 382-2807

Newark, Wayne, Pop. 9,507
Newark Central SD 2,500/K-12
100 E Miller St 14513 315-332-3217
Robert Christmann, supt. Fax 332-3523
www.newark.k12.ny.us
Newark HS 800/9-12
625 Peirson Ave 14513 315-332-3242
Kevin Whitaker, prin. Fax 332-3567
Newark MS 700/6-8
701 Peirson Ave 14513 315-332-3295
Robert Palmateer, prin. Fax 332-3584

Newark Valley, Tioga, Pop. 1,046
Newark Valley Central SD 1,400/K-12
PO Box 547 13811 607-642-3221
Mary Ellen Grant, supt. Fax 642-8821
www.nvcs.stier.org/
Newark Valley JSHS 600/8-12
68 Wilson Creek Rd 13811 607-642-8351
Christopher Tennant, prin. Fax 642-5292

New Berlin, Chenango, Pop. 1,121
Unadilla Valley CSD 1,100/PK-12
PO Box F 13411 607-847-7500
Rexford A. Hurlburt, supt. Fax 847-6924
www.uvcs.k12.ny.us
Unadilla Valley HS 300/9-12
PO Box F 13411 607-847-7500
Robert E. Franklin, prin. Fax 847-8045
Unadilla Valley MS 300/6-8
PO Box F 13411 607-847-7500
Gene Chilion, prin. Fax 847-8045

Newburgh, Orange, Pop. 28,412
Newburgh Enlarged CSD 12,400/PK-12
124 Grand St 12550 845-563-3500
Dr. Annette Saturnelli, supt. Fax 563-3501
www.newburghschools.org/newburgh/newburgh.cfm

Newburgh Free Academy 2,500/10-12
201 Fullerton Ave 12550 845-563-5400
Peter Copeletti, prin. Fax 563-5405
North JHS 1,000/7-9
301 Robinson Ave 12550 845-563-8400
Ronald Jackson, prin. Fax 563-8409
South JHS 1,100/7-9
33 Monument St 12550 845-563-7000
Edward Mucci, prin. Fax 563-7019
Other Schools – See New Windsor

Mt. St. Mary College Post-Sec.
330 Powell Ave 12550 845-561-0800

New City, Rockland, Pop. 34,100
Clarkstown Central SD 9,200/K-12
62 Old Middletown Rd 10956 845-639-6419
Dr. William Heebink, supt. Fax 639-6488
www.ccsd.edu
Clarkstown North HS 1,500/9-12
151 Congers Rd 10956 845-639-6504
Harry Leonardatos, prin. Fax 638-6916
Other Schools – See West Nyack

Newcomb, Essex
Newcomb Central SD 100/PK-12
PO Box 418 12852 518-582-3341
John Mulholland, supt. Fax 582-2163
www.newcombcsd.org
Newcomb Central S 100/PK-12
PO Box 418 12852 518-582-3341
John Mulholland, prin. Fax 582-2163

Newfane, Niagara, Pop. 3,001
Newfane Central SD 2,200/PK-12
6273 Charlotteville Rd 14108 716-778-6850
Dr. James Mills, supt. Fax 778-6852
www.newfane.wnyric.org
Newfane HS, 1 Panther Dr 14108 700/9-12
Steve Burley, prin. 716-778-6551
Newfane MS, 2700 Transit Rd 14108 500/6-8
Gary Pogorzelski, prin. 716-778-6452

Newfield, Tompkins
Newfield Central SD 1,000/PK-12
247 Main St 14867 607-564-9955
William Hurley, supt. Fax 564-0055
www.newfieldschools.org
Newfield HS 300/9-12
247 Main St 14867 607-564-9955
Suzanne France, prin. Fax 564-0055
Newfield MS 200/6-8
247 Main St 14867 607-564-9955
Catherine Griggs, prin. Fax 564-0055

New Hartford, Oneida, Pop. 1,853
New Hartford Central SD 2,700/K-12
33 Oxford Rd 13413 315-624-1218
Daniel Gilligan, supt. Fax 724-8940
www.newhartfordschools.org
New Hartford SHS 700/10-12
33 Oxford Rd 13413 315-624-1214
Jennifer Spring, prin. Fax 738-9209
Perry JHS 700/7-9
9499 Weston Rd 13413 315-738-9300
Keith Levatino, prin. Fax 738-9349

New Hyde Park, Nassau, Pop. 9,526
Herricks UFD, 999 Herricks Rd 11040 3,900/K-12
Dr. John Bierwirth, supt. 516-248-3105
www.herricks.org
Herricks HS 1,300/9-12
100 Shelter Rock Rd 11040 516-248-3142
Dr. Jane Modoono, prin. Fax 248-3282
Other Schools – See Albertson

Sewanhaka Central HSD
Supt. — See Floral Park
New Hyde Park Memorial HS 1,500/7-12
500 Leonard Blvd 11040 516-488-9500
Loretta Nugent, prin. Fax 488-9506

New Lebanon, Columbia
New Lebanon Central SD 600/K-12
14665 State Route 22 12125 518-794-9016
Patrick Gabriel, supt. Fax 766-5574
www.newlebanoncsd.org
New Lebanon JSHS 300/7-12
14665 State Route 22 12125 518-794-7600
Patricia Ackley, prin. Fax 766-6265

Darrow S 100/9-12
110 Darrow Rd 12125 518-794-6000
Fax 794-7065

New Paltz, Ulster, Pop. 6,428
New Paltz Central SD 2,400/K-12
196 Main St 12561 845-256-4020
Maria Rice, supt. Fax 256-4025
www.newpaltz.k12.ny.us
New Paltz HS 800/9-12
196 Main St 12561 845-256-4100
Barbara Clinton, prin. Fax 256-4109
New Paltz MS 600/6-8
196 Main St 12561 845-256-4200
Richard Wiesenthal, prin. Fax 256-4209

SUNY College at New Paltz Post-Sec.
75 S Manheim Blvd Ste 1 12561 845-257-2121

Newport, Herkimer, Pop. 620
West Canada Valley Central SD 900/K-12
5447 State Route 28 13416 315-845-6800
Kenneth Slentz, supt.
www.westcanada.org
West Canada Valley JSHS 500/7-12
5447 State Route 28 13416 315-845-6802
Frank Sutliff, prin. Fax 845-8652

New Rochelle, Westchester, Pop. 72,582
New Rochelle CSD 10,400/PK-12
515 North Ave 10801 914-576-4300
Linda E. Kelly, supt. Fax 632-4144
www.nred.org

Leonard MS 1,200/6-8
25 Gerada Ln 10804 914-576-4339
William Evans, prin. Fax 576-4784
New Rochelle HS 3,000/9-12
265 Clove Rd 10801 914-576-4502
Don Conetta, prin. Fax 576-4284
Young MS 1,100/6-8
270 Centre Ave 10805 914-576-4360
Anthony Bongo, prin. Fax 632-2738

Blessed Sacrament-St. Gabriel HS 300/9-12
24 Shea Pl 10801 914-632-2595
Edward Sullivan, prin. Fax 632-3321
College of New Rochelle Post-Sec.
29 Castle Pl 10805 914-654-5000
Hallen S 300/K-12
97 Centre Ave 10801 914-636-6600
Carol Locascio, dir. Fax 636-2844
Iona College Post-Sec.
715 North Ave 10801 914-633-2000
Iona Preparatory S 800/9-12
255 Wilmot Rd 10804 914-632-0714
Richard Hazelton, hdmstr. Fax 632-9760
Monroe College Post-Sec.
434 Main St 10801 914-632-5400
New Testament Church S 50/K-12
138 Mayflower Ave 10801 914-966-1766
Sunil Maryil, admin. Fax 966-1766
Salesian HS 400/9-12
148 E Main St 10801 914-632-0248
John Flaherty, prin. Fax 632-1362
Thornton-Donovan S 200/K-12
100 Overlook Cir 10804 914-632-8836
Ursuline HS 800/9-12
1354 North Ave 10804 914-636-3950
Sr. Jean Nicholson, prin. Fax 636-3949

New Square, Rockland, Pop. 5,644

Avir Yaakov Girl's S 800/K-12
15 N Roosevelt Ave 10977 845-354-0874
Zlaty Hoffman, prin. Fax 354-5920

New Windsor, Orange, Pop. 8,898
Cornwall Central SD
Supt. — See Cornwall on Hudson
Cornwall Central HS 1,000/9-12
10 Dragon Dr 12553 845-534-8009
Michae Brooksl, prin. Fax 565-2754

Newburgh Enlarged CSD
Supt. — See Newburgh
Heritage JHS 800/7-9
405 Union Ave 12553 845-563-3750
Joseph Raiti, prin. Fax 563-3759

New York, New York, Pop. 8,085,742
NYC Department of Education 916,100/PK-12
52 Chambers St 10007 718-935-2000
Joel Klein, chncllr.
Academy for Environmental Science 300/9-12
410 E 100th St 10029 212-860-6025
Irene Gee, prin. Fax 860-6008
Art & Design HS 1,300/9-12
1075 2nd Ave 10022 212-752-4340
Scott Feltzin, prin. Fax 752-4945
Bard HS Early College 500/9-12
525 E Houston St 10002 212-995-8479
Raymond Peterson, prin. Fax 777-4702
Bayard Rustin HS for the Humanities 2,000/9-12
351 W 18th St 10011 212-675-5350
John Angelet, prin. Fax 255-5701
Bergtraum HS 2,700/9-12
411 Pearl St 10038 212-964-9610
Barbara Esmilla, prin. Fax 732-6622
Brandeis HS 2,400/9-12
145 W 84th St 10024 212-441-5600
Dr. Eloise Messineo, prin. Fax 877-1959
Chelsea Career & Technical Education HS Vo/Tech
131 Avenue Of The Americas 10013 212-925-1080
Timothy Timberlake, prin. Fax 941-7934
Douglas Academy 1,300/7-12
2581 Adam Clayton Powell Jr 10039 212-491-4107
Dr. Gregory Hodge, prin. Fax 491-4414
East Side Community HS 500/7-12
420 E 12th St 10009 212-460-8467
Mark Federman, prin. Fax 260-9657
Facing History S, 525 W 50th St 10019 9-12
Gillian Smith, prin. 718-935-3354
Fashion Industries HS 1,600/9-12
225 W 24th St 10011 212-255-1235
Hilda Nieto, prin. Fax 255-4756
Food & Finance HS 9-12
525 W 50th St 10019 212-586-2943
Roger E. Turgeon, prin. Fax 586-4205
Green HS of Teaching 900/8-12
421 E 88th St 10128 212-722-5240
Isabel Dimola, prin. Fax 427-8069
Greenwich Village MS 6-8
490 Hudson St 10014 212-691-7384
Isora Bailey, prin. Fax 691-9489
Health Professions & Human Services HS 1,600/9-12
345 E 15th St 10003 212-780-9175
Marta Jimenez, prin. Fax 979-7261
Henry Street S for International Studies 6-12
220 Henry St 10002 212-406-9411
Hoa Tu, prin. Fax 717-1234
Humanities Preparatory S 200/9-12
351 W 18th St 10011 212-929-4433
Vincent Brevetti, prin. Fax 929-4445
Irving HS 3,100/9-12
40 Irving Pl 10003 212-674-5000
Dr. Denise DiCarlo, prin. Fax 674-9569
Kennedy-Onassis HS 600/9-12
120 W 46th St 10036 212-391-0041
Edward Demeo, prin. Fax 391-1293
King Arts & Technology HS 700/9-12
122 Amsterdam Ave 10023 212-501-1198
Anne Geiger, prin. Fax 441-3693
King HS 600/9-12
122 Amsterdam Ave 10023 212-501-1235
Susan Kreisman, prin. Fax 501-1171

King Law Advocacy & Community Justice S 700/9-12
122 Amsterdam Ave 10023 212-501-1201
Miriam Nightengale, prin. Fax 441-3697
La Guardia HS 2,400/9-12
100 Amsterdam Ave 10023 212-496-0700
Kim Bruno, prin. Fax 724-5748
Leadership & Public Service HS 600/9-12
90 Trinity Pl 10006 212-346-0007
Ada Rosario Dolch, prin. Fax 346-0612
Lower Manhattan Arts Academy 9-12
350 Grand St 10002 718-935-3220
John Wenk, prin. Fax 982-8750
Manhattan Bridges HS 200/9-12
525 W 50th St 10019 212-262-5860
Mirza Sanchez-Medina, prin. Fax 265-1307
Manhattan HS for Science/Math 1,600/9-12
260 Pleasant Ave 10029 212-876-4639
Corinne Vinal, prin. Fax 996-5946
Manhattan Occupational Training Center Vo/Tech
250 W Houston St 10014 212-675-7926
Sheryl Watkins, prin. Fax 255-3227
Manhattan S for Career Development Vo/Tech
113 E 4th St 10003 212-477-2090
Jeffrey Rothschild, prin. Fax 228-7095
Manhattan Theatre Lab HS 9-12
6 Edgecombe Ave 10030 212-690-7367
Margaret Salvante-McCann, prin. Fax 690-8053
Marshall Academy 400/7-12
200 W 135th St 10030 212-283-8055
Dr. Sandye Johnson, prin. Fax 283-8109
Marte Valle Model HS 500/7-11
145 Stanton St 10002 212-473-8152
Jayne Godlewski, prin. Fax 475-7588
Milk HS 100/9-12
2 Astor Pl 10003 212-477-1555
Daniel Rossi, prin. Fax 674-8650
Millenium/Tribeca HS 600/9-12
75 Broad St 10004 212-825-9008
Robert Rhodes, prin. Fax 825-9095
Mott Hall HS 9-10
6 Edgecombe Ave 10030 212-690-5501
John Sullivan, prin.
Mott Hall II 6-8
234 W 109th St 10025 212-678-2960
Mary Moss, prin. Fax 504-3239
New Design HS 9-12
350 Grand St 10002 212-475-4148
Scott Conti, prin. Fax 674-2152
New Explorations Sci Tech/Math S 200/7-12
111 Columbia St 10002 212-677-5190
Celenia Chevere, prin. Fax 260-8124
Newton MS for Science Math Tech 7-8
260 Pleasant Ave 10029 212-860-6006
Majida Abdul-Karim, prin. Fax 987-4197
HS Arts 100/9-9
122 Amsterdam Ave 10023 212-799-4064
Stephen Noonan, prin. Fax 799-4171
HS for Dual Language & Asian Studies 100/9-12
350 Grand St 10002 212-475-4097
Li Yan, prin. Fax 674-1392
New York HS for Economic & Finance 700/9-12
100 Trinity Pl 10006 212-346-0708
Dr. Craig Peck, prin. Fax 346-0712
New York HS for Environmental Studies 1,500/9-12
444 W 56th St 10019 212-262-8113
Shirley Matthews, prin. Fax 262-0702
HS for History & Communication 9-12
350 Grand St 10002 347-881-6871
Alex Shub, prin.
HS for Math Science Engineering 600/9-12
138th St & Convent Ave 10031 212-281-6490
Randy J. Asher, prin. Fax 220-8204
HS of Graphic Communication Arts 1,900/9-12
439 W 49th St 10019 212-245-5925
Jerod Resnick, prin. Fax 265-1552
HS of Hospitality Management 9-12
525 W 50th St 10019 212-262-5860
Matthew Angrisani, prin. Fax 929-4445
IS 52 1,700/5-8
650 Academy St 10034 212-567-9162
Jose Rivera, prin. Fax 942-4952
IS 90 500/8-8
21 Jumel Pl 10032 212-927-8314
Sharon Weissbrot, prin. Fax 927-8334
IS 131 900/6-8
100 Hester St 10002 212-219-1204
Jane Lehrach, prin. Fax 925-6386
IS 143 1,600/6-8
511 W 182nd St 10033 212-927-7739
Ourania Pappas, prin. Fax 781-5539
IS 195 800/6-8
625 W 133rd St 10027 212-690-5848
Aura Rivera, prin. Fax 690-5999
IS 218 1,500/6-8
4600 Broadway 10040 212-567-2322
June Barnett, prin. Fax 569-7421
IS 223 400/4-8
71 Convent Ave 10027 212-927-9466
Cynthia Arndt, prin. Fax 491-3451
IS 275 200/8-8
175 W 134th St 10030 212-283-1903
Salvador Fernandez, prin. Fax 283-6319
IS 286 300/6-8
509 W 129th St 10027 212-690-5972
Sandra Small, prin. Fax 694-4124
IS 289 300/6-8
201 Warren St 10282 212-571-5659
Ellen Foote, prin. Fax 571-0739
IS 528 300/6-8
180 Wadsworth Ave 10033 212-740-4900
Norma Perez, prin. Fax 781-7302
JHS 13 500/7-8
1573 Madison Ave 10029 212-860-8935
Jacob Michelman, prin. Fax 860-5933
JHS 45 900/7-8
2351 1st Ave 10035 212-860-5838
Maria Aviles, prin. Fax 860-5837
JHS 99 600/7-8
410 E 100th St 10029 212-860-5854
Lillian Sarro, prin. Fax 876-5359
JHS 104 1,100/6-8
330 E 21st St 10010 212-674-4545
Marge Struk, prin. Fax 477-2205
JHS 164 800/7-8
401 W 164th St 10032 212-927-8380
Migdalia Carrillo, prin. Fax 923-6929
JHS 167 1,200/6-8
220 E 76th St 10021 212-535-8610
Jennifer Rehn, prin. Fax 472-9385
MS 44 600/6-8
100 W 77th St 10024 212-441-1163
David Bouie, prin. Fax 501-0912
MS 54 1,000/6-8
103 W 107th St 10025 212-678-2861
Dr. Elana Elster, prin. Fax 316-0883
MS 114 300/6-8
1458 York Ave 10021 212-439-6278
David Getz, prin. Fax 717-5606
MS 224 200/6-8
410 E 100th St 10029 212-860-6047
Liliana Sarno, prin. Fax 410-0678
MS 243 200/5-8
270 W 70th St 10023 212-678-2791
Elaine Schwartz, prin. Fax 579-9728
MS 244 200/6-8
100 W 77th St 10024 212-441-1191
Rodney Murphy, prin. Fax 501-7235
MS 245 300/6-8
100 W 77th St 10024 212-441-0873
Henry Zymeck, prin. Fax 678-5908
MS 246 200/6-8
234 W 109th St 10025 212-678-5850
Joseph Rand, prin. Fax 678-4275
MS 247 200/6-8
32 W 92nd St 10025 212-799-2653
Claudia Aguirre, prin. Fax 579-2407
MS 250 200/6-8
735 W End Ave 10025 212-866-6313
Jeanne Rotunda, dir. Fax 678-5295
MS 255 200/6-8
319 E 19th St 10003 212-614-8785
Rhonda Perry, prin. Fax 614-0095
MS 256 200/6-8
154 W 93rd St 10025 212-222-2857
Cheryl Rosen, prin. Fax 531-0586
MS 258 200/6-8
154 W 93rd St 10025 212-678-5888
John Curry, prin. Fax 961-1613
MS 260 200/6-8
320 W 21st St 10011 212-255-8860
Joseph Cassidy, prin. Fax 807-0421
MS 287 700/5-8
349 Cabrini Blvd 10040 212-927-8218
Janet Aravena, prin. Fax 795-9119
MS 322 6-8
4600 Broadway 10040 212-304-0853
Erica Zigelman, prin. Fax 567-3016
MS 332 University Neighborhood 6-8
220 Henry St 10002 212-267-5701
Cyndi Kerr, prin. Fax 267-5703
MS 860 6-9
215 W 114th St 10026 212-865-9260
Latasha Greer, prin. Fax 865-9281
MS 864, 41 W 117th St 10026 6-8
Shaniquia Singletary, prin. 646-672-0558
Pace HS 9-12
100 Hester St 10002 212-334-4663
Yvette Sy, prin. Fax 334-4919
Park West HS 1,400/9-12
525 W 50th St 10019 212-262-5860
Deonne Martin, prin. Fax 265-1307
Powell MS for Law & Social Justice 600/6-8
509 W 129th St 10027 212-690-5977
Dr. Curtis Andrews, prin. Fax 690-5980
Professional Performing Arts HS 400/6-12
328 W 48th St 10036 212-247-8652
Keith Ryan, prin. Fax 247-7514
Randolph HS 1,300/9-12
443 W 135th St 10031 212-926-0113
Maurice Collins, prin. Fax 281-2726
Roosevelt HS 700/9-12
411 E 76th St 10021 212-772-1220
Susan Elliott, prin. Fax 772-1440
School of the Future 600/6-12
127 E 22nd St 10010 212-475-8086
C. Delaura, dir. Fax 475-9273
Seward Park HS 1,100/9-12
350 Grand St 10002 212-674-7000
Doris Unger, prin. Fax 982-8730
Stuyvesant HS 3,100/9-12
345 Chambers St 10282 212-312-4800
Stanley Teitel, prin. Fax 587-3874
Talent Unlimited HS 500/9-12
317 E 67th St 10021 212-737-1530
Deena Forman, prin. Fax 737-2863
Thomas HS 2,500/9-12
111 E 33rd St 10016 212-576-0500
Steven Satin, prin. Fax 545-9648
Tompkins Square MS 7-8
600 E 6th St 10009 212-995-1430
Mark Pingitore, prin. Fax 995-9671
Urban Assembly Media HS 9-12
122 Amsterdam Ave 10023 212-501-1110
Lynette Delgado, prin. Fax 501-1111
Urban Assembly of Government & Law 9-12
350 Grand St 10002 718-935-3356
Joaquin Tamayo, prin.
Urban Assembly S Design & Construction 9-12
525 W 50th St 10019 212-586-0981
Lawrence Pendergast, prin. Fax 586-1731
Urban Assembly S of Business 9-12
420 E 12th St 10009 917-488-5415
Patricia Minaya, prin.
Wadleigh Arts HS 600/6-12
215 W 114th St 10026 212-749-5800
Karen Watts, prin. Fax 749-6463
Manhattan Comprehensive Night & Day HS Adult
240 2nd Ave 10003 212-353-2010
Howard Friedman, prin. Fax 353-1673

Other Schools – See Arverne, Astoria, Bayside, Bellerose, Bronx, Brooklyn, Corona, East Elmhurst, Elmhurst, Far Rockaway, Floral Park, Flushing, Forest Hills, Fresh Meadows, Glendale, Hollis, Jackson Heights, Jamaica, Little Neck, Long Island City, Maspeth, Oakland Gardens, Ozone Park, Queens Village, Rego Park, Richmond Hill, Ridgewood, Rockaway Park, Saint Albans, South Ozone Park, Springfield Gardens, Staten Island, Whitestone, Woodside

American Academy McAllister Institute Post-Sec.
619 W 54th St Fl 6 10019 212-757-1190
American Academy of Dramatic Arts Post-Sec.
120 Madison Ave 10016 212-686-9244
American Barber Institute Post-Sec.
252 W 29th St 10001 212-290-2289
American University in Cairo Post-Sec.
420 5th Ave Fl 3 10018 212-730-8800
Apex Technical School Post-Sec.
635 Avenue Of The Americas 10011 212-645-3300
Art Institute of New York City Post-Sec.
75 Varick St Fl 16 10013 212-226-5500
Bank Street College of Education Post-Sec.
610 W 112th St 10025 212-875-4404
Barnard College Post-Sec.
3009 Broadway 10027 212-854-5262
Bellevue Hospital Center Post-Sec.
462 1st Ave 10016 212-561-4132
Birch Wathen Lenox S 400/K-12
210 E 77th St 10021 212-861-0404
Frank Carnabuci, prin. Fax 879-5309
Boricua College Post-Sec.
3755 Broadway 10032 212-694-1000
Brearley S 700/K-12
610 E 83rd St 10028 212-744-8582
Stephanie Hull, hdmstr. Fax 472-8020
Browning S 400/K-12
52 E 62nd St 10021 212-838-6280
Stephen Clement, prin. Fax 355-5602
Calhoun S 700/PK-12
433 W End Ave 10024 212-497-6500
Steven Nelson, hdmstr. Fax 497-6530
Caliber Training Institute Post-Sec.
500 Fashion Ave Fl 2 10018 212-564-0500
Cathedral HS 1,000/9-12
350 E 56th St 10022 212-688-1545
Sr. Elizabeth Graham, prin. Fax 754-2024
Chapin S 600/K-12
100 E End Ave 10028 212-744-2335
Patricia Hayot, hdmstr. Fax 535-8138
Chubb Institute Post-Sec.
498 Fashion Ave Fl 17 10018 212-659-2116
Churchill S and Center 400/K-12
301 E 29th St 10016 212-722-0610
Kristine Baxter, hdmstr. Fax 722-1387
College of New Rochelle Post-Sec.
125 Barclay St 10007 212-815-1710
College of New Rochelle Post-Sec.
144 W 125th St 10027 212-662-7500
Collegiate S 600/K-12
260 W 78th St 10024 212-812-8500
W. Lee Pierson, prin. Fax 812-8522
Columbia Grammar & Prep S 1,000/PK-12
5 W 93rd St 10025 212-749-6200
Richard Soghoian, prin. Fax 865-4278
Columbia University Post-Sec.
168th & Broadway 10032 212-305-5756
Columbia University Post-Sec.
2960 Broadway 10027 212-854-1754
Connelly Center for Education 100/5-8
220 E 4th St 10009 212-982-2287
Kimberly Morcate, prin. Fax 984-0547
Convent of the Sacred Heart S 400/PK-12
1 E 91st St 10128 212-722-4745
Dr. Mary Blake, hdmstr. Fax 996-1784
Cooper Union Post-Sec.
30 Cooper Sq 10003 212-353-4100
Cope Institute Post-Sec.
225 Broadway Fl 2 10007 212-809-5935
County Univ. Sch. of Dental & Oral Surg. Post-Sec.
630 W 168th St 10032
Culinary Academy of New York Post-Sec.
154 W 14th St 10011 212-675-6655
CUNY Bernard M. Baruch College Post-Sec.
17 Lexington Ave 10010 212-802-2000
CUNY Borough/Manhattan Comm. College Post-Sec.
199 Chambers St 10007 212-346-8800
CUNY City College Post-Sec.
160 Convent Ave 10031 212-650-7000
CUNY Graduate Center Post-Sec.
365 5th Ave 10016 212-817-7000
CUNY Hunter College Post-Sec.
695 Park Ave 10021 212-772-4000
CUNY John Jay College Criminal Justice Post-Sec.
899 10th Ave 10019 212-237-8000
Dalton S 1,300/K-12
108 E 89th St 10128 212-423-5200
Ellen Stein, hdmstr. Fax 423-5259
De La Salle Academy 100/6-8
202 W 97th St 10025 212-316-5840
Fax 316-5998
Dominican Academy 200/9-12
44 E 68th St 10021 212-744-0195
Sr. Joan Franks, prin. Fax 744-0375
Dwight S 500/PK-12
291 Central Park W 10024 212-724-2146
Stephen Spahn, prin. Fax 724-2539
Fashion Institute of Technology Post-Sec.
227 W 27th St 10001 212-217-7999
FEGS Trades & Business School Post-Sec.
80 Vandam St 10013 212-366-8466
Folk Art Institute Post-Sec.
45 E 53rd St 10022 212-977-7170
Fordham University Post-Sec.
113 W 60th St 10023 212-636-6000
French Culinary Institute Post-Sec.
462 Broadway 10013 212-219-8890
Friends Seminary S 700/K-12
222 E 16th St 10003 212-979-5030
Robert Lauder, prin. Fax 979-5034

Gemological Institute of America Post-Sec.
580 5th Ave 10036 212-944-5900

General Theological Seminary Post-Sec.
175 9th Ave 10011 212-243-5150

Global Business Institute Post-Sec.
209 W 125th St 10027 212-663-1500

Globe Institute of Technology Post-Sec.
291 Broadway Fl 2 10007 212-349-4330

Harlem International Community S 50/PK-12
2116 Adam Clayton Powell Jr 10027 212-222-7798
Ms. Wallie Simpson, prin. Fax 222-7798

Harlem School of Technology Post-Sec.
215 W 125th St 10027 212-932-2849

Hebrew Union College Post-Sec.
1 W 4th St 10012 212-674-5300

Helene Fuld College of Nursing Post-Sec.
1879 Madison Ave 10035 212-423-2700

Heschel MS 100/6-8
314 W 91st St 10024 212-595-7817
Fax 595-6281

Heschel S 700/PK-12
270 W 89th St 10024 212-595-7087
Roanna Shorofsky, dir. Fax 595-7252

Hewitt S 500/K-12
45 E 75th St 10021 212-288-1919
Linda MacMurray Gibbs, hdmstr. Fax 472-7531

Hunter College Campus S 1,600/K-12
71 E 94th St 10128 212-860-1267
John Mucciolo, prin. Fax 289-2209

Institute of Allied Medical Professions Post-Sec.
405 Park Ave 10022 212-758-1410

Institute of Audio Research Post-Sec.
64 University Pl 10003 212-677-7590

Interboro Institute Post-Sec.
450 W 56th St 10019 212-399-0091

Jewish Theological Seminary of America Post-Sec.
3080 Broadway 10027 212-678-8000

Juilliard School Post-Sec.
60 Lincoln Center Plz 10023 212-799-5000

Katharine Gibbs School Post-Sec.
50 W 40th St 10018 212-867-9300

Keller Graduate School Post-Sec.
120 W 45th St Ste 200 10036 212-556-0002

Kings Academy 200/PK-12
2345 3rd Ave 10035 212-348-7380
Thomas Streitferdt, prin. Fax 348-0515

Laboratory Institute of Merchandising Post-Sec.
12 E 53rd St 10022 212-752-1530

LaSalle Academy 500/9-12
44 E 2nd St 10003 212-475-8940
John Quinn, prin. Fax 529-3598

La Scuola New York G. Marconi S 200/PK-12
12 E 96th St 10128 212-369-3290
B. Padolecchia Goodrich, prin. Fax 369-1164

Learning Institute for Beauty Sciences Post-Sec.
22 W 34th St 10001 212-695-4555

Lia Schorr Inst of Cosmetic Skin Care Post-Sec.
686 Lexington Ave 10022 212-486-9541

Loyola S 200/9-12
980 Park Ave 10028 212-288-3522
James Lyness, lead tchr. Fax 861-1021

LREI Little Red School House 600/PK-12
272 6th Ave 10014 212-477-5316
Philip Kassen, dir. Fax 677-9159

Lycee Francais De New York 1,300/PK-12
505 E 75th St 10021 212-369-1400
Yves Theze, prin. Fax 439-4210

Lyceum Kennedy S 200/PK-12
225 E 43rd St 10017 212-681-1877

Mandl College of Allied Health Post-Sec.
254 W 54th St 10019 212-247-3434

Manhattan HS for Girls 200/9-12
154 E 70th St 10021 212-737-6800
Ruth Assaf, prin. Fax 737-0766

Manhattan School of Computer Technology Post-Sec.
42 Broadway Fl 22 10004 212-349-9768

Manhattan School of Music Post-Sec.
120 Claremont Ave 10027 212-749-2802

Mannes College of Music Post-Sec.
150 W 85th St 10024 212-580-0210

Marymount Manhattan College Post-Sec.
221 E 71st St 10021 212-517-0400

Marymount S 500/PK-12
1026 5th Ave 10028 212-744-4486
Concepcion Alvar, hdmstr. Fax 744-0163

Memorial Sloan Kettering Cancer Center Post-Sec.
1275 York Ave 10021 212-639-6561

Mercy College - Manhattan Campus Post-Sec.
66 W 35th St 10001 212-615-3351

Mesivta Tifereth Jerusalem of America Post-Sec.
145 E Broadway 10002 212-964-2830

Mesivta Tifereth Jerusalem S 200/PK-12
145 E Broadway 10002 212-964-2830
Stanley Bronfeld, prin. Fax 349-5213

Metropolitan College of New York Post-Sec.
75 Varick St 10013 212-343-1234

Mother Cabrini HS 400/9-12
701 Fort Washington Ave 10040 212-923-3540
Brian Donahue, prin. Fax 781-2051

Mt. Sinai School of Medicine Post-Sec.
1 Gustave L Levy Pl 10029 212-241-6546

Nativity Mission MS 100/6-8
204 Forsyth St 10002 212-477-2472
Nick Romero, prin. Fax 937-3385

New School University Post-Sec.
66 W 12th St 10011 212-229-5600

New York Academy of Art Post-Sec.
111 Franklin St 10013 212-966-0300

New York Career Institute Post-Sec.
11 Park Pl Fl 4 10007 212-962-0002

New York College of Podiatric Medicine Post-Sec.
1800 Park Ave 10035 212-410-8000

New York Eye & Ear Infirmary Post-Sec.
310 E 14th St 10003 212-979-4375

New York Institute of Technology Post-Sec.
1855 Broadway 10023 212-261-1508

New York Inst. of Business Technology Post-Sec.
248 W 35th St 10001 212-725-9400

New York International Beauty School Post-Sec.
500 8th Ave Rm 803 10018 212-868-7171

New York Law School Post-Sec.
57 Worth St 10013 212-431-2888

New York Paralegal School Post-Sec.
299 Broadway Ste 200 10007 212-349-8800

New York Presbyterian Hospital Post-Sec.
525 E 68th St 10021 212-746-4000

New York School of Interior Design Post-Sec.
170 E 70th St 10021 212-472-1500

New York Theological Seminary Post-Sec.
475 Riverside Dr Ste 500 10115 212-870-1211

New York University Post-Sec.
70 Washington Sq S 10012 212-998-1212

New York University Medical Center Post-Sec.
550 1st Ave 10016 212-263-5111

Nightingale-Bamford S 600/K-12
20 E 92nd St 10128 212-289-5020
Dorothy Hutcheson, hdmstr. Fax 876-1045

Northeastern Academy 200/9-12
532 W 215th St 10034 212-569-4800
Beverly Bucknor, prin. Fax 569-6145

Notre Dame HS 200/9-12
327 W 13th St 10014 212-620-5575
John Joven, prin. Fax 620-0432

Pace University Post-Sec.
1 Pace Plz 10038 212-346-1200

Pacific College of Oriental Medicine Post-Sec.
915 Broadway Fl 3 10010 212-982-3456

Parsons School of Design Post-Sec.
66 5th Ave 10011 212-229-8953

Phillips Beth Israel School of Nursing Post-Sec.
776 Avenue of the Americas 10001 212-614-6110

Professional Business College Post-Sec.
125 Canal St 10002 212-226-7300

Professional Children's S 200/6-12
132 W 60th St 10023 212-582-3116
Dr. James Dawson, hdmstr. Fax 956-3295

Rabbi Isaac Elchanan Theological Sem. Post-Sec.
2495 Amsterdam Ave 10033 212-960-5344

Ramaz HS 500/9-12
60 E 78th St 10021 212-774-8000
Rabbi Jay Goldmintz, hdmstr. Fax 774-8099

Ramaz MS 200/5-8
114 E 85th St 10028 212-774-8040
Judith Fagin, hdmstr. Fax 774-8069

Regis HS 300/9-12
55 E 84th St 10028 212-288-1100
Rev. Vincent Biagi, prin. Fax 794-1221

Rice HS 300/9-12
74 W 124th St 10027 212-369-4100
Br. John Walderman, hdmstr. Fax 348-4631

Rockefeller University Post-Sec.
1230 York Ave 10021 212-327-8000

St. Agnes Boys HS 400/9-12
555 W End Ave 10024 212-873-9100
Br. Emil Denworth, prin. Fax 873-9292

St. George Academy HS 100/9-12
215 E 6th St 10003 212-473-3323
Peter Shyshka, prin. Fax 534-0819

St. Jean Baptiste HS 400/9-12
173 E 75th St 10021 212-288-1645
Sr. Ona Bessette, prin. Fax 288-6540

St. John's University Post-Sec.
101 Murray St 10007 212-962-4111

St. Michael Academy 400/9-12
425 W 33rd St 10001 212-563-2547
Sr. Kathleen Cusack, prin. Fax 563-9892

St. Thomas Choir S 50/4-8
202 W 58th St 10019 212-247-3311
Fax 247-3393

St. Vincent Ferrer HS 400/9-12
151 E 65th St 10021 212-535-4680
Sr. Gail Morgan, prin. Fax 988-3455

St. Vincent's Hospital & Medical Center Post-Sec.
153 W 11th St 10011 212-604-7500

School for the Deaf Post-Sec.
225 E 23rd St 10010

School of Visual Arts Post-Sec.
209 E 23rd St 10010 212-592-2000

Sessions.edu Online School of Design Post-Sec.
350 7th Ave Ste 1203 10001 212-239-3080

Solomon Schecter HS of New York 100/9-12
1 W 91st St 10024 212-877-7747

Sotheby's Institute of Art Post-Sec.
1334 York Ave 10021 212-894-1111

Spanish-American Institute Post-Sec.
215 W 43rd St 10036 212-840-7111

Spence S 600/K-12
22 E 91st St 10128 212-289-5940
Arlene Gibson, prin. Fax 860-2652

Steiner Upper S 100/7-12
15 E 78th St 10021 212-879-1101
Fax 794-1554

Studio Jewelers Post-Sec.
32 E 31st St 10016 212-686-1944

SUNY College of Optometry Post-Sec.
33 W 42nd St 10036 212-780-4900

SUNY Empire State College Post-Sec.
325 Hudson St 5th Flr 10013 212-647-7800

Swedish Institute Post-Sec.
226 W 26th St Fl 5 10001 212-924-5900

Taylor Business Institute Post-Sec.
23 W 17th St # 7 10011 800-959-9999

TCI Institute The College of Technology Post-Sec.
320 W 31st St 10001 212-594-4000

Teachers College of Columbia University Post-Sec.
525 W 120th St 10027 212-678-3000

The Institute of Culinary Education Post-Sec.
50 W 23rd St 10010 212-847-0711

Touro College Post-Sec.
27 W 23rd St # 33 10010 212-463-0400

Touro College Post-Sec.
240 E 123rd St 10035 212-722-1575

Trevor Day S 200/6-12
1 W 88th St 10024 212-426-3360
Pam Clarke, dir. Fax 873-8520

Trinity S 1,000/K-12
139 W 91st St 10024 212-873-1650
Henry Moses, hdmstr. Fax 799-3417

Tri-State College of Acupuncture Post-Sec.
80 8th Ave # 400 10011 212-242-2255

Ultrasound Diagnostic School Post-Sec.
120 E 16th St Fl 2 10003 212-645-9116

U.N. International S 1,500/K-12
2450 F D R Dr 10010 212-684-7400
Kenneth Wrye, dir. Fax 684-1382

Union Theological Seminary Post-Sec.
3041 Broadway 10027 212-662-7100

Weill Medical College of Cornell Univ Post-Sec.
1300 York Ave 10021 212-746-5454

Winston Preparatory S 100/6-12
126 W 17th St 10011 646-638-2705

Wood Tobe-Coburn School Post-Sec.
8 E 40th St 10016 212-686-9040

Xavier HS 900/9-12
30 W 16th St 10011 212-924-7900
Dr. Joseph Gerics, hdmstr. Fax 924-0303

Yeshiva Rabbi S.R. Hirsch 500/PK-12
91 Bennett Ave 10033 212-568-6200
Nathan Blaivas, prin. Fax 928-4422

Yeshiva University Post-Sec.
55 5th Ave 10003 212-790-0274

Yeshiva University Post-Sec.
500 W 185th St 10033 212-960-5400

Yeshiva University HS 300/9-12
2540 Amsterdam Ave 10033 212-960-5345
Yaacov Sklar, prin. Fax 960-0027

York Prep S 300/6-12
40 W 68th St 10023 212-362-0400
Ronald Stewart, hdmstr. Fax 362-7106

New York Mills, Oneida, Pop. 3,157

New York Mills UFD 600/K-12
1 Marauder Blvd 13417 315-768-8127
Dave Langone, supt. Fax 768-3521
www.newyorkmills.org

New York Mills JSHS 300/7-12
1 Marauder Blvd 13417 315-768-8124
Gary Hadfield, prin. Fax 768-3521

Niagara Falls, Niagara, Pop. 53,989

Niagara Falls CSD 8,800/PK-12
607 Walnut Ave 14301 716-286-4205
Carmen Granto, supt. Fax 286-4283
www.nfschools.net/

Gaskill MS 800/6-8
910 Hyde Park Blvd 14301 716-278-5820
Joseph Colburn, prin. Fax 278-5829

La Salle MS 700/6-8
7436 Buffalo Ave 14304 716-278-5880
Richard Carella, prin. Fax 283-2494

Niagara Falls HS 2,500/9-12
4455 Porter Rd 14305 716-278-5800
Mark Laurrie, prin. Fax 286-7964

Niagara MS 600/6-8
6431 Girard Ave 14304 716-278-9120
Maria Chille-Zafuto, prin. Fax 278-9122

Niagara-Wheatfield Central SD 4,100/PK-12
6700 Schultz St 14304 716-215-3003
Dr. Judith Howard, supt. Fax 215-3039
www.nwcsd.k12.ny.us
Other Schools – See Sanborn

Cheryl Fell's School of Business Post-Sec.
2541 Military Rd 14304 716-297-2750

Niagara Catholic JSHS 400/7-12
520 66th St 14304 716-283-8771
Robert DiFrancesco, prin. Fax 283-6574

St. Dominic Savio MS 500/6-8
504 66th St 14304 716-215-1461
Rose Mary Buscaglia, prin. Fax 215-1465

Niagara University, Niagara

Niagara University Post-Sec.
PO Box 9999 14109 716-285-1212

North Babylon, Suffolk, Pop. 18,081

North Babylon UFD 5,200/K-12
5 Jardine Pl 11703 631-321-3226
Randy Bos Ed.D., supt. Fax 321-3295
www.nbsd.org

Moses MS 1,300/6-8
234 Phelps Ln 11703 631-321-3251
Kathleen Hartnett, prin. Fax 587-2619

North Babylon HS 1,500/9-12
1 Phelps Ln 11703 631-321-3233
Donald Shevlin, prin. Fax 321-3327

North Collins, Erie, Pop. 1,048

North Collins Central SD 700/K-12
2045 School St 14111 716-337-0101
John McDonough, supt. Fax 337-3457
www.northcollins.com

North Collins JSHS 400/7-12
2045 School St 14111 716-337-0101
Benjamin Halsey, prin. Fax 337-3457

North Creek, Warren

Johnsburg Central SD 400/K-12
PO Box 380 12853 518-251-2814
Michael Markwica, supt. Fax 251-2562
johnsburg.k12.ny.us

Johnsburg Central S 400/K-12
PO Box 380 12853 518-251-3504
Nadine Allard, prin. Fax 251-2562

North Massapequa, Nassau, Pop. 19,365

Plainedge UFD 3,600/PK-12
241 Wyngate Dr 11758 516-992-7455
Dr. John Richman, supt. Fax 992-7446
www.plainedgeschools.org
Other Schools – See Bethpage, Massapequa

North Merrick, Nassau, Pop. 12,113

Bellmore-Merrick Central HSD 5,800/7-12
1260 Meadowbrook Rd 11566 516-992-1000
Dr. Thomas Caramore, supt. Fax 623-0151
www.bellmore-merrick.k12.ny.us
Other Schools – See Bellmore, Merrick

Northport, Suffolk, Pop. 7,671

Northport-East Northport UFD 6,400/PK-12
PO Box 210 11768 631-262-6604
Marylou McDermott, supt. Fax 262-6607
northport.k12.ny.us

Northport HS | 1,800/9-12
154 Laurel Hill Rd   11768 | 631-262-6652
Irene McLaughlin, prin. | Fax 262-6736
Northport MS | 800/6-8
11 Middleville Rd   11768 | 631-262-6750
Thomas Heinegg, prin. | Fax 262-6793
Other Schools – See East Northport

Northport VA Medical Center | Post-Sec.
79 Middleville Rd   11768 | 631-261-4400

North Salem, Westchester
North Salem Central SD | 1,400/K-12
230 June Rd   10560 | 914-669-5414
Dr. Peter R. Litchka, supt. | Fax 669-8753
northsalem.k12.ny.us
North Salem MSHS | 700/6-12
230 June Rd   10560 | 914-669-5414
Dr. Patricia Cyganovich, prin. | Fax 669-5663

North Syracuse, Onondaga, Pop. 6,863
North Syracuse Central SD | 9,800/PK-12
5355 W Taft Rd   13212 | 315-218-2151
Jerome Melvin, supt.
www.nscsd.k12.ny.us
North Syracuse JHS | 1,600/8-9
5353 W Taft Rd   13212 | 315-218-3600
Constance Turose, prin.
Other Schools – See Cicero

North Tonawanda, Niagara, Pop. 32,359
North Tonawanda CSD | 4,000/PK-12
175 Humphrey St   14120 | 716-807-3599
John H. George Ed.D., supt. | Fax 807-3522
www.ntcityschools.wnyric.org
North Tonawanda HS | 1,600/9-12
405 Meadow Dr   14120 | 716-807-3600
James Fisher, prin. | Fax 807-3639
North Tonawanda MS | 600/6-8
1500 Vanderbilt Ave   14120 | 716-807-3700
Gloria Mierzwa, prin. | Fax 807-3701

North Tonawanda Catholic S | 200/4-8
75 Keil St   14120 | 716-693-2828
Sr. Rosemarie Kutsko, prin. | Fax 693-0169

Northville, Fulton, Pop. 1,138
Northville Central SD | 500/PK-12
PO Box 608   12134 | 518-863-7000
Dr. Harry Brooks, supt. | Fax 863-7011
northvillecsd.k12.ny.us
Northville JSHS | 300/7-12
PO Box 608   12134 | 518-863-7000
Barbara Sperry, prin. | Fax 863-7011

Norwich, Chenango, Pop. 7,251
Norwich CSD | 2,200/PK-12
19 Eaton Ave   13815 | 607-334-1600
Gerard O'Sullivan, supt. | Fax 336-8652
www.ncs.stier.org
Norwich HS | 700/9-12
19 Eaton Ave   13815 | 607-334-1600
John Ross, prin. | Fax 334-6680
Norwich MS | 400/7-8
19 Eaton Ave   13815 | 607-334-1600
| Fax 334-6210

Valley Heights Christian Academy | 100/PK-12
75 Calvary Dr   13815 | 607-336-8422
Eric Schimke, prin.

Norwood, Saint Lawrence, Pop. 1,645
Norwood-Norfolk Central SD | 1,100/K-12
PO Box 194   13668 | 315-353-9951
James Short, supt. | Fax 353-2467
nncsk12.org
Norwood HS | 400/9-12
PO Box 194   13668 | 315-353-6631
Robin Fetter, prin. | Fax 353-2480
Norwood-Norfolk MS | 400/5-8
PO Box 194   13668 | 315-353-6674
Robert Stewart, prin.

Nunda, Livingston, Pop. 1,297
Keshequa Central SD | 900/K-12
PO Box 517   14517 | 585-468-2541
Lucinda Miner, supt. | Fax 468-3814
www.keshequa.org
Keshequa HS | 300/9-12
PO Box 517   14517 | 585-468-2513
Mark Mattle, prin. | Fax 468-5493
Keshequa MS | 200/6-8
PO Box 517   14517 | 585-468-2513
Doris Marsh, prin. | Fax 468-3814

Nyack, Rockland, Pop. 6,749
Nyack UFD | 2,900/K-12
13A Dickinson Ave   10960 | 845-353-7015
Dr. Valencia Douglas, supt. | Fax 353-0508
www.nyackschools.com
Nyack MS | 600/6-8
98 S Highland Ave   10960 | 845-353-7200
Jacqueline Gonzalez, prin. | Fax 353-0506
Other Schools – See Upper Nyack

Alliance Theological Seminary | Post-Sec.
350 N Highland Ave   10960 | 845-353-2020
Nyack College | Post-Sec.
1 South Boulevard   10960 | 845-358-1710

Oakdale, Suffolk, Pop. 7,875
Connetquot Central SD
Supt. — See Bohemia
Oakdale-Bohemia Road MS | 600/6-8
60 Oakdale Bohemia Rd   11769 | 631-244-2268
Dr. Terry Earley, prin. | Fax 563-6167

Dowling College | Post-Sec.
150 Idle Hour Blvd   11769 | 631-244-3000

Oakfield, Genesee, Pop. 1,759
Oakfield-Alabama Central SD | 1,100/K-12
7001 Lewiston Rd   14125 | 585-948-5211
Robert McIntosh, supt. | Fax 948-9362
www.oahornets.org
Oakfield-Alabama JSHS | 600/6-12
7001 Lewiston Rd   14125 | 585-948-5211
Lynn Muscarella, prin. | Fax 948-9362

Oakland Gardens, See New York
NYC Department of Education
Supt. — See New York
Cardozo HS | 3,900/9-12
5700 223rd St   11364 | 718-279-6500
Richard Hallman, prin. | Fax 631-7880
JHS 74 | 1,100/6-8
6115 Oceania St   11364 | 718-631-6800
Andrea Dapolito, prin. | Fax 631-6899

CUNY Queensborough Community College | Post-Sec.
22205 56th Ave   11364 | 718-631-6262

Oceanside, Nassau, Pop. 32,800
Oceanside UFD | 6,300/K-12
145 Merle Ave   11572 | 516-678-5211
Dr. Herb Brown, supt. | Fax 678-7503
www.oceanside.k12.ny.us/
Oceanside HS | 1,900/9-12
3160 Skillman Ave   11572 | 516-678-7526
Dorie Ciulla, prin. | Fax 678-6790
Oceanside MS | 1,000/7-8
186 Alice Ave   11572 | 516-678-8518
Robert Fenter, prin. | Fax 594-2365

Hochstim School of Radiography | Post-Sec.
PO Box 9007   11572 | 516-763-2030

Odessa, Schuyler, Pop. 617
Odessa-Montour Central SD | 900/K-12
PO Box 430   14869 | 607-594-3341
James Frame, supt. | Fax 594-3976
www.omschools.org
Odessa-Montour HS | 300/9-12
PO Box 430   14869 | 607-594-3341
| Fax 594-3976
Odessa-Montour MS | 200/6-8
PO Box 430   14869 | 607-594-3341
Sandra Young, prin. | Fax 594-3328

Ogdensburg, Saint Lawrence, Pop. 11,832
Ogdensburg CSD | 1,900/K-12
1100 State St   13669 | 315-393-0900
William Flynn, supt. | Fax 393-2767
www.ogdensburgk12.org/
Ogdensburg Free Academy HS | 900/7-12
1100 State St   13669 | 315-393-0900
Marsha Sawyer, prin. | Fax 393-7412

Old Forge, Herkimer
Town of Webb UFD | 400/K-12
PO Box 38   13420 | 315-369-3222
Donald Gooley, supt. | Fax 369-6216
Town of Webb S | 400/K-12
PO Box 38   13420 | 315-369-3222
Marie Schoonover, prin. | Fax 369-6216

Old Westbury, Nassau, Pop. 4,385
East Williston UFD | 1,800/K-12
11 Bacon Rd   11568 | 516-333-3758
Dr. Carolyn Harris, supt.
www.ewsdonline.org/
Wheatley HS, 11 Bacon Rd   11568 | 700/8-12
Richard Simon, prin. | 516-333-7804

Westbury UFD | 3,800/PK-12
2 Hitchcock Ln   11568 | 516-874-1829
Dr. Constance R. Clark, supt. | Fax 876-5187
www.westburyschools.org
Westbury HS | 900/9-12
1 Post Rd   11568 | 516-874-1200
Manuel Arias, prin. | Fax 876-5079
Other Schools – See Westbury

New York Institute of Technology | Post-Sec.
PO Box 8000   11568 | 516-686-7520
New York Institute of Technology | Post-Sec.
PO Box 8000   11568 | 516-686-7516
SUNY College at Old Westbury | Post-Sec.
PO Box 210   11568 | 516-876-3000
SUNY Empire State College | Post-Sec.
PO Box 130   11568 | 516-997-4700

Olean, Cattaraugus, Pop. 14,989
Olean CSD | 2,400/PK-12
410 W Sullivan St   14760 | 716-375-8018
Mark Ward, supt. | Fax 375-8047
www.oleanschools.org
Olean HS | 800/9-12
410 W Sullivan St   14760 | 716-375-8010
Barbara Lias, prin. | Fax 375-8048
Olean MS | 600/6-8
401 Wayne St   14760 | 716-375-8061
Gerald Trietley, prin. | Fax 375-8070

Archbishop Walsh HS | 100/9-12
208 N 24th St   14760 | 585-372-8122
Kathleen Baker, prin. | Fax 372-6707
Continental School of Beauty Culture | Post-Sec.
515 N Union St   14760 | 716-372-5095
Jamestown Community College   14760 | Post-Sec.
| 585-372-1661
Olean Business Institute | Post-Sec.
301 N Union St   14760 | 716-372-7978

Olmstedville, Essex
Minerva Central SD | 100/PK-12
PO Box 39   12857 | 518-251-2000
Ann Jaeger, supt. | Fax 251-2395
Minerva Central S | 100/PK-12
PO Box 39   12857 | 518-251-2000
Timothy Farrell, prin. | Fax 251-2395

Oneida, Madison, Pop. 10,956
Oneida CSD | 2,500/K-12
PO Box 327   13421 | 315-363-2550
Ronald R. Spadafora, supt. | Fax 363-6728
www.oneidany.org
Oneida HS | 700/9-12
560 Seneca St   13421 | 315-363-6901
Brian Gallagher, prin. | Fax 366-0619
Other Schools – See Wampsville

Oneonta, Otsego, Pop. 12,799
Oneonta CSD | 2,100/PK-12
189 Main St   13820 | 607-433-8200
Michael P. Shea, supt. | Fax 433-8290
oneontacsd.org
Oneonta HS | 700/9-12
130 East St   13820 | 607-433-8243
Scott Rabeler, prin. | Fax 433-8204
Oneonta MS | 400/7-8
130 East St   13820 | 607-433-8262
Kevin Johnson, prin. | Fax 433-8203

Hartwick College | Post-Sec.
West St   13820 | 607-431-4000
Lighthouse Christian Academy | 50/K-12
12 Grove St   13820 | 607-432-2031
Jacqueline Yarborough, admin. | Fax 432-3403
SUNY College at Oneonta   13820 | Post-Sec.
| 607-436-3500
Utica School of Commerce | Post-Sec.
17 Elm St   13820 | 607-432-7003

Ontario Center, Wayne
Wayne Central SD | 2,700/K-12
6076 Ontario Center Rd   14520 | 315-524-1001
Michael Havens, supt. | Fax 524-4233
www.wayne.k12.ny.us
Wayne Central MS | 700/6-8
6076 Ontario Center Rd   14520 | 315-524-2710
Robert Armocida, prin. | Fax 524-4233
Wayne HS | 900/9-12
6200 Ontario Center Rd   14520 | 315-524-1710
Joseph Siracuse, prin. | Fax 524-4233

Orangeburg, Rockland, Pop. 3,583
South Orangetown Central SD
Supt. — See Blauvelt
Tappan Zee HS | 1,000/9-12
15 Dutch Hill Rd   10962 | 845-680-1600
Lynn Trager, prin. | Fax 680-1950

Dominican College of Blauvelt | Post-Sec.
470 Western Hwy   10962 | 845-359-7800
Long Island University-Rockland Campus | Post-Sec.
70 Route 340   10962 | 845-359-7200

Orchard Park, Erie, Pop. 3,218
Orchard Park Central SD | 5,200/K-12
3330 Baker Rd   14127 | 716-209-6280
Joan Thomas, supt. | Fax 209-6353
www.opschools.org
Orchard Park HS | 1,600/9-12
4040 Baker Rd   14127 | 716-209-6440
Robert Farwell, prin.
Orchard Park MS | 1,300/6-8
60 S Lincoln Ave   14127 | 716-209-6227
James Higgins, prin.

Bryant & Stratton College | Post-Sec.
200 Red Tail   14127 | 716-677-9500
Erie Community College South | Post-Sec.
4041 Southwestern Blvd   14127 | 716-648-5400

Oriskany, Oneida, Pop. 1,438
Oriskany Central SD | 800/K-12
PO Box 539   13424 | 315-768-2058
Michael Deuel, supt. | Fax 768-1733
Oriskany JSHS | 400/7-12
PO Box 539   13424 | 315-768-2063
Andy Brown, prin. | Fax 768-4496

Ossining, Westchester, Pop. 24,229
Ossining UFD | 4,200/PK-12
190 Croton Ave   10562 | 914-941-7700
Dr. Robert Roelle, supt. | Fax 941-2794
ossiningufsd.org
Dorner MS | 900/6-8
90 Van Cortlandt Ave   10562 | 914-762-5740
Regina Cellio, prin. | Fax 762-5246
Ossining HS | 1,300/9-12
29 S Highland Ave   10562 | 914-762-5760
Joshua Mandel, prin. | Fax 762-4011

Oswego, Oswego, Pop. 18,223
Oswego CSD | 4,800/K-12
120 E 1st St   13126 | 315-341-2001
David Fischer, supt. | Fax 341-2910
www.oswego.org
Oswego HS | 1,700/9-12
2 Buccaneer Blvd   13126 | 315-341-2200
Pete Myles, prin. | Fax 341-2920
Oswego MS | 800/7-8
100 Mark Fitzgibbons Dr   13126 | 315-341-2300
Constance Evelyn, prin. | Fax 341-2390

SUNY College at Oswego   13126 | Post-Sec.
| 315-312-2500

Otego, Otsego, Pop. 998
Otego-Unadilla Central SD | 1,200/K-12
2641 State Highway 7   13825 | 607-988-5038
Dr. Rebecca Furlong, supt. | Fax 988-1039
unatego.org
Unatego JSHS | 700/6-12
2641 State Highway 7   13825 | 607-988-5000
Jeff Bennett, prin. | Fax 988-1039

Ovid, Seneca, Pop. 616
South Seneca Central SD | 1,000/PK-12
7263 Main St   14521 | 607-869-9636
Janie L. Nusser, supt. | Fax 532-8540
www.southseneca.com/

South Seneca HS
7263 Main St 14521 — 300/9-12
Robert Waller, prin. — 607-869-9636
Fax 869-9553
South Seneca MS
7263 Main St 14521 — 200/7-8
Thomas Phillips, prin. — 607-869-9636
Fax 532-8540

Owego, Tioga, Pop. 3,809
Owego-Apalachin Central SD — 2,300/K-12
36 Talcott St 13827 — 607-687-6224
Joseph Sever, supt. — Fax 687-6313
www.oacsd.org
Owego-Apalachin MS — 600/6-8
100 Elm St 13827 — 607-687-6248
Robert Devan, prin. — Fax 687-6259
Owego Free Academy — 800/9-12
1 Sheldon Guile Blvd 13827 — 607-687-6230
Ronald Pierce, prin. — Fax 687-6247

Oxford, Chenango, Pop. 1,565
Oxford Academy & Central Schools — 900/K-12
PO Box 192 13830 — 607-843-7185
Randall W. Squier, supt. — Fax 843-3241
www.oxac.org
Oxford Academy HS — 300/9-12
PO Box 192 13830 — 607-843-2025
Mark Hine, prin. — Fax 843-3231
Oxford Academy MS — 300/5-8
PO Box 192 13830 — 607-843-7185
David Hubman, prin. — Fax 843-3241

Oyster Bay, Nassau, Pop. 6,687
Oyster Bay-East Norwich Central SD — 1,800/PK-12
1 McCouns Ln 11771 — 516-624-6505
Dr. Phyllis Harrington, supt. — Fax 624-6520
oben.powertolearn.com/
Oyster Bay JSHS — 700/7-12
150 E Main St 11771 — 516-624-6524
Dennis O'Hara, prin. — Fax 624-6684
Other Schools – See East Norwich

St. Dominic HS — 500/9-12
110 Anstice St 11771 — 516-922-4888
Robert Lowenberg, prin. — Fax 922-4898

Ozone Park, See New York
NYC Department of Education
Supt. — See New York
Adams HS — 3,200/9-12
10101 Rockaway Blvd 11417 — 718-322-0500
Grace Zwillenberg, prin. — Fax 738-9077
JHS 202 — 1,300/6-8
13830 Lafayette St 11417 — 718-848-0001
William A. Moore, prin. — Fax 848-8082
JHS 210 — 2,100/6-8
9311 101st Ave 11416 — 718-845-5942
Rosalyn Allman-Manning, prin. — Fax 845-4037

Painted Post, Steuben, Pop. 1,804
Corning CSD — 5,600/PK-12
165 Charles St 14870 — 607-936-3704
Judith P. Staples Ed.D., supt. — Fax 654-2735
www.corningareaschools.com
Corning-Painted Post West HS — 900/9-12
201 Victory Hwy 14870 — 607-936-3794
John Wood, prin. — Fax 654-2771
Other Schools – See Corning

Palisades, Rockland

Lamont-Doherty Earth Observatory — Post-Sec.
10964 — 845-365-8550

Palmyra, Wayne, Pop. 3,440
Palmyra-Macedon Central SD — 2,200/K-12
151 Hyde Pkwy 14522 — 315-597-3401
Harold Ferguson Ed.D., supt. — Fax 597-3898
www.palmac.k12.ny.us
Palmyra-Macedon HS — 700/9-12
151 Hyde Pkwy 14522 — 315-597-3420
Barb Persia, prin. — Fax 597-3898
Palmyra-Macedon MS — 600/6-8
163 Hyde Pkwy 14522 — 315-597-3450
Darcy Smith, prin. — Fax 597-3460

Panama, Chautauqua, Pop. 478
Panama Central SD — 800/K-12
41 North St 14767 — 716-782-2455
Carol Hay, supt. — Fax 782-4281
www.pancent.org
Panama HS — 300/9-12
41 North St 14767 — 716-782-2455
Bert Lictus, prin. — Fax 782-4281

Parish, Oswego, Pop. 501
Altmar-Parish-Williamstown Central SD — 1,600/K-12
PO Box 97 13131 — 315-625-5251
Deborah A. Haab, supt. — Fax 625-7952
www.apw.cnyric.org
Altmar-Parish-Williamstown HS — 500/9-12
639 County Route 22 13131 — 315-625-5222
Mark Potter, prin. — Fax 625-4638
Altmar-Parish-Williamstown MS — 400/6-8
640 County Route 22 13131 — 315-625-5200
Jamie Coppola, prin. — Fax 625-4937

Parishville, Saint Lawrence
Parishville-Hopkinton Central SD — 500/K-12
PO Box 187 13672 — 315-265-4642
Thomas Burns, supt. — Fax 268-1309
phcs.neric.org
Parishville-Hopkinton JSHS — 200/7-12
PO Box 187 13672 — 315-265-4642
Darin P. Saiff, prin. — Fax 268-1309

Patchogue, Suffolk, Pop. 12,016
Patchogue-Medford UFD — 8,700/PK-12
241 S Ocean Ave 11772 — 631-687-6380
Michael Mostow, supt. — Fax 758-1126
pat-med.k12.ny.us
Saxton MS — 1,100/6-9
121 Saxton St 11772 — 631-687-6700
Linda Pickford, prin. — Fax 758-1126

South Ocean MS — 800/6-9
225 S Ocean Ave 11772 — 631-687-6600
Manuel Sanzone, prin. — Fax 758-1126
Other Schools – See Medford

Briarcliffe College — Post-Sec.
225 W Main St 11772 — 631-654-5300
St. Joseph's College — Post-Sec.
155 W Roe Blvd 11772 — 631-447-3200

Patterson, Putnam
Carmel Central SD — 5,400/K-12
PO Box 296 12563 — 845-878-2094
Dr. Marilyn Terranova, supt. — Fax 878-4337
www.ccsd.k12.ny.us
Other Schools – See Carmel

Pattersonville, Schenectady

Spencer Business & Technical Institute — Post-Sec.
795 Pattersonville Rd 12137 — 518-374-7619

Paul Smiths, Franklin

Paul Smith's College 12970 — Post-Sec.
800-421-2605

Pavilion, Genesee
Pavilion Central SD — 900/K-12
7014 Big Tree Rd 14525 — 585-584-3115
Edward Orman, supt. — Fax 584-3421
Pavilion JSHS — 600/6-12
7014 Big Tree Rd 14525 — 585-584-3070
Dr. Sheila Stellrecht, prin. — Fax 584-3421

Pawling, Dutchess, Pop. 2,259
Pawling Central SD — 1,400/K-12
7 Haight St 12564 — 845-855-4600
Frank DeLuca, supt. — Fax 855-4659
www.pawlingschools.org
Pawling HS — 400/9-12
7 Haight St 12564 — 845-855-4620
Frank Tolan, prin. — Fax 855-4617
Pawling MS — 500/5-8
7 Haight St 12564 — 845-855-4653
Cheryl Thomas, prin. — Fax 855-4134

Trinity-Pawling S — 300/7-12
700 Route 22 12564 — 845-855-3100
Archibald Smith, hdmstr. — Fax 855-3816

Pearl River, Rockland, Pop. 15,314
Pearl River UFD — 2,500/K-12
275 E Central Ave 10965 — 845-620-3900
Dr. Frank V. Auriemma, supt. — Fax 620-3927
www.pearlriver.org
Pearl River HS — 900/8-12
275 E Central Ave 10965 — 845-620-3800
William Furdon, prin. — Fax 620-3904

Iona College at Blue Hill — Post-Sec.
PO Box 1522 10965 — 845-620-1350

Peekskill, Westchester, Pop. 23,436
Peekskill CSD — 3,000/PK-12
1031 Elm St 10566 — 914-737-3300
Judith Johnson, supt. — Fax 737-3912
www.peekskillcsd.org
Peekskill HS — 800/9-12
1072 Main St 10566 — 914-737-0201
Vincent Burruano, prin. — Fax 737-2550
Peekskill MS — 500/7-8
212 Ringgold St 10566 — 914-737-4542
Walter Chadwick, prin. — Fax 737-3253

Northern Westchester Sch of Hairdressing — Post-Sec.
19 Bank St 10566 — 914-739-8400
Ohr Hameir Seminary Tifereth Israel HS — 100/9-12
PO Box 2130 10566 — 914-736-1500
Joseph Willner, prin. — Fax 736-1055
Ohr HaMeir Theological Seminary — Post-Sec.
PO Box 2130 10566 — 914-736-1500

Pelham, Westchester, Pop. 6,399
Pelham UFD — 2,500/K-12
661 Hillside Rd 10803 — 914-738-3434
Dr. Charles Wilson, supt. — Fax 738-7223
www.pelhamschools.org
Pelham Memorial HS — 700/9-12
640 Colonial Ave 10803 — 914-738-8110
Jeannine Clark, prin. — Fax 738-8122
Pelham MS — 600/6-8
28 Franklin Pl 10803 — 914-738-8190
Joseph Longobardi, prin. — Fax 738-8132

Penfield, Monroe, Pop. 30,219
Penfield Central SD — 4,900/K-12
PO Box 900 14526 — 585-249-5700
G. Susan Gray, supt. — Fax 248-8412
www.penfield.edu
Bay Trail MS — 1,200/6-8
1760 Scribner Rd 14526 — 585-249-6450
Ronald Marro, prin. — Fax 248-0735
Penfield HS — 1,600/9-12
25 Highschool Dr 14526 — 585-249-6700
Mark Van Vliet, prin. — Fax 248-2810

Penn Yan, Yates, Pop. 5,123
Penn Yan Central SD — 2,000/PK-12
1 School Dr 14527 — 315-536-3371
Ann Orman, supt. — Fax 536-0068
www.pycsd.org
Penn Yan Academy HS — 600/9-12
305 Court St 14527 — 315-536-4408
Keith Mathews, prin. — Fax 536-0341
Penn Yan MS — 500/6-8
515 Liberty St 14527 — 315-536-3366
Linda Raide, prin. — Fax 536-7769

Perry, Wyoming, Pop. 3,876
Perry Central SD — 1,100/PK-12
33 Watkins Ave 14530 — 585-237-0270
Daniel White, supt. — Fax 237-6172
www.perry.k12.ny.us
Perry HS — 400/9-12
33 Watkins Ave 14530 — 585-237-0270
Ed Stores, prin. — Fax 237-6350
Perry MS — 300/5-8
50 Olin Ave 14530 — 585-237-0270
Katherine Waite, prin. — Fax 237-3483

Peru, Clinton, Pop. 1,565
Peru Central SD — 2,200/K-12
PO Box 68 12972 — 518-643-6000
A. Paul Scott, supt. — Fax 643-2043
www.peru.com
Peru HS — 700/9-12
PO Box 68 12972 — 518-643-6400
Stephen Broadwell, prin. — Fax 643-2043
Peru MS — 600/6-8
PO Box 68 12972 — 518-643-6300
Christopher Mazzella, prin. — Fax 643-6313

Philadelphia, Jefferson, Pop. 1,533
Indian River Central SD — 3,400/K-12
32735 County Route 29 #B 13673 — 315-642-4441
Roger W. Adams, supt. — Fax 642-3738
www.ircsd.org/
Indian River HS — 800/9-12
32925 US Route 11 13673 — 315-642-3427
Troy Decker, prin. — Fax 642-5658
Indian River MS — 800/6-8
32735 County Route 29 13673 — 315-642-0125
Nancy Taylor-Schmitt, prin. — Fax 642-0802

Phoenix, Oswego, Pop. 2,211
Phoenix Central SD — 2,500/K-12
116 Volney St 13135 — 315-695-1511
Rita E. Racette, supt. — Fax 695-1201
www.phoenix.k12.ny.us
Birdlebough HS — 800/9-12
552 Main St 13135 — 315-695-1631
James McLaughlin, prin. — Fax 695-1618
Dillon MS — 600/6-8
116 Volney St 13135 — 315-695-1521
Susan Anderson, prin. — Fax 695-1523

Pine Bush, Orange, Pop. 1,445
Pine Bush Central SD — 6,000/K-12
PO Box 700 12566 — 845-744-2031
Rose Marie Stark, supt. — Fax 744-6189
www.pinebushschools.org
Crispell MS — 900/6-8
PO Box 780 12566 — 845-744-2031
John Boyle, prin. — Fax 744-2261
Pine Bush HS — 1,900/9-12
PO Box 670 12566 — 845-744-2031
Jeanette Green, prin. — Fax 744-3488
Other Schools – See Circleville

AEF Chapel Field S — 200/6-12
211 Fleury Rd 12566 — 845-778-1881
William Spanjer, prin. — Fax 778-5841

Pine Plains, Dutchess, Pop. 1,312
Pine Plains Central SD — 1,400/K-12
2829 Church St 12567 — 518-398-7181
Linda L. Kaumeyer, supt. — Fax 398-6592
www.pineplainsschools.org
Stissing Mountain HS — 400/9-12
2829 Church St 12567 — 518-398-7181
John Howe, prin. — Fax 398-6592
Stissing Mountain MS — 400/6-8
2829 Church St 12567 — 518-398-7181
Robert Hess, prin. — Fax 398-6592

Pittsford, Monroe, Pop. 1,384
Pittsford Central SD — 6,000/K-12
42 W Jefferson Rd 14534 — 585-267-1000
Mary Alice Price, supt. — Fax 267-1088
www.pittsfordschools.org
Barker Road MS — 1,500/6-8
75 Barker Rd 14534 — 585-267-1800
Michael Pero, prin. — Fax 385-5960
Calkins Road MS — 6-8
1899 Calkins Rd 14534 — 585-267-1900
Scott Reinhart, prin. — Fax 264-0053
Pittsford-Mendon HS — 1,000/9-12
472 Mendon Rd 14534 — 585-267-1600
Karl Thielking, prin. — Fax 267-1679
Pittsford-Sutherland HS — 1,000/9-12
55 Sutherland St 14534 — 585-267-1100
Elizabeth Konar, prin. — Fax 381-7687

Plainview, Nassau, Pop. 25,600
Plainview-Old Bethpage Central SD — 5,000/K-12
106 Washington Ave 11803 — 516-937-6301
Dr. Martin Brooks, supt. — Fax 937-6303
www.pob.k12.ny.us/
Mattlin MS — 800/5-8
100 Washington Ave 11803 — 516-937-6393
Dean Mittleman, prin. — Fax 937-6431
Plainview-Old Bethpage/JFK HS — 1,500/9-12
50 Kennedy Dr 11803 — 516-937-6370
James Murray, prin. — Fax 937-6433
Plainview-Old Bethpage MS — 800/5-8
121 Central Park Rd 11803 — 516-349-4750
Dr. Edward Metzendorf, prin. — Fax 349-4777

Plattsburgh, Clinton, Pop. 19,163
Beekmantown Central SD
Supt. — See West Chazy
Beekmantown HS — 600/9-12
6944 Route 22 12901 — 518-563-8787
Garth Frechette, prin. — Fax 563-8132
Beekmantown MS — 600/6-8
6944 Route 22 12901 — 518-563-8690
Sue Coonrod, prin. — Fax 563-8132

Plattsburgh CSD 1,900/PK-12
49 Broad St 12901 518-957-6002
Dr. Michelle M. Kavanaugh, supt. Fax 561-6605
www.plattscsd.org/
Plattsburgh HS 700/9-12
1 Clifford Dr 12901 518-561-7500
John Fairchild, prin. Fax 561-1895
Stafford MS 500/6-8
15 Broad St 12901 518-563-6800
Patricia Amo, prin. Fax 563-8520

Champlain Valley Physicians Hospital Post-Sec.
75 Beekman St 12901 518-561-2000
Clinton Community College Post-Sec.
136 Clinton Point Dr 12901 518-562-4200
Seton Catholic Central JSHS 400/7-12
5135 N Catherine St 12901 518-561-4031
Gwen Cote, prin. Fax 563-1193
SUNY College at Plattsburgh 12901 Post-Sec.
518-564-2000

Pleasantville, Westchester, Pop. 7,178
Pleasantville UFD 1,700/K-12
60 Romer Ave 10570 914-741-1400
Dr. Donald Antonecchia, supt. Fax 741-1499
www.pleasantvilleschools.com
Pleasantville HS 500/9-12
60 Romer Ave 10570 914-741-1420
Dr. George Cancro, prin. Fax 741-2546
Pleasantville MS 500/5-8
40 Romer Ave 10570 914-741-1450
Vivian Ossowski, prin. Fax 741-1496

Pace University Post-Sec.
861 Bedford Rd 10570 914-773-3200

Poland, Herkimer, Pop. 452
Poland Central SD 800/PK-12
74 Cold Brook St 13431 315-826-0203
John Stewart, supt. Fax 826-7516
www.polandcs.org
Poland JSHS 300/7-12
74 Cold Brook St 13431 315-826-7900
Jon Speich, prin. Fax 826-7516

Port Byron, Cayuga, Pop. 1,285
Port Byron Central SD 1,200/K-12
30 Maple Ave 13140 315-776-5728
Neil O'Brien, supt. Fax 776-4050
Lehn MS 400/5-8
30 Maple Ave 13140 315-776-8939
Sarah Feinberg, prin. Fax 776-4050
West HS 400/9-12
30 Maple Ave 13140 315-776-4598
Shawn Bissetta, prin. Fax 776-4050

Port Chester, Westchester, Pop. 27,955
Port Chester-Rye UFD
Supt. — See Rye Brook
Port Chester HS 900/9-12
1 Tamarack Rd 10573 914-934-7950
Dr. Mitchell Combs, prin. Fax 934-2998
Port Chester MS 700/6-8
113 Bowman Ave 10573 914-934-7930
Carmen Macchia, prin. Fax 934-7886

Port Henry, Essex, Pop. 1,122
Moriah Central SD 800/K-12
39 Viking Ln 12974 518-546-3301
Harold Bresett, supt. Fax 546-7895
Moriah JSHS 400/7-12
39 Viking Ln 12974 518-546-3301
Kathy Carr, prin. Fax 546-7895

Port Jefferson, Suffolk, Pop. 7,948
Port Jefferson UFD 1,300/PK-12
550 Scraggy Hill Rd 11777 631-476-4404
Dr. Robert Aloise, supt. Fax 476-4409
www.portjeff.k12.ny.us
Port Jefferson MS 300/6-8
350 Old Post Rd 11777 631-474-4440
David Klecher, prin. Fax 474-4430
Vandermeulen HS 400/9-12
350 Old Post Rd 11777 631-476-4400
Leonard Bozza, prin. Fax 476-4408

Port Jefferson Station, See Port Jefferson
Comsewogue SD 3,700/K-12
290 Norwood Ave 11776 631-474-8105
Dr. Shelley Saffer, supt. Fax 474-3568
www.comsewogue.k12.ny.us
Comsewogue HS 1,000/9-12
565 Bicycle Path 11776 631-474-8182
Jennifer Reph, prin. Fax 474-8175
Kennedy MS, 200 Jayne Blvd 11776 900/6-8
Michael Fama, prin. 631-474-8160

Port Jervis, Orange, Pop. 9,100
Port Jervis CSD 3,200/K-12
9 Thompson St 12771 845-858-3175
Joseph Dilorenzo, supt. Fax 856-1885
www.portjerviscsd.k12.ny.us/
Port Jervis HS 1,100/9-12
Route 209 12771 845-858-3100
Anthony Di Marco, prin. Fax 858-2895
Port Jervis MS 500/7-8
118 E Main St 12771 845-858-3148
Thomas Bongiovi, prin. Fax 858-2893

Portville, Cattaraugus, Pop. 1,007
Portville Central SD 1,000/K-12
500 Elm St 14770 585-933-7141
Peter Tigh Ph.D., supt. Fax 933-7161
www.portville.wnyric.org/
Portville JSHS 500/7-12
500 Elm St 14770 585-933-6704
Kevin Curran, prin. Fax 933-7161

Port Washington, Nassau, Pop. 15,387
Port Washington UFD 4,700/K-12
100 Campus Dr 11050 516-767-5000
Dr. Geoffrey N. Gordon, supt. Fax 767-5007
www.portnet.k12.ny.us

Schreiber HS 1,400/9-12
101 Campus Dr 11050 516-767-5800
John Lewis, prin. Fax 767-5807
Weber JHS 1,100/6-8
Port Washington Blvd 11050 516-767-5500
Marilyn Rodahan, prin. Fax 767-5507

Smith S 100/5-12
322 Port Washington Blvd 11050 516-365-4900

Potsdam, Saint Lawrence, Pop. 9,555
Potsdam Central SD 1,400/PK-12
29 Leroy St 13676 315-265-2000
Patrick Brady;, supt. Fax 265-2048
www.potsdam.k12.ny.us
Kingston MS 500/5-8
29 Leroy St 13676 315-265-2000
Richard Evans, prin. Fax 265-8103
Potsdam HS 500/9-12
29 Leroy St 13676 315-265-2000
J. Gregory Jadlos, prin. Fax 265-8134

Clarkson University Post-Sec.
PO Box 5500 13699 315-268-6400
SUNY College at Potsdam 13676 Post-Sec.
315-267-2000

Pottersville, Warren

Word of Life Bible Institute Post-Sec.
PO Box 129 12860 518-494-4723

Poughkeepsie, Dutchess, Pop. 30,174
Arlington Central SD 10,100/K-12
696 Dutchess Tpke 12603 845-486-4460
Frank V. Pepe, supt. Fax 486-4457
www.arlingtonschools.org
Arlington MS 1,200/6-8
601 Dutchess Tpke 12603 845-486-4480
Brendan Lyons, prin. Fax 486-4446
Other Schools – See Lagrangeville

Poughkeepsie CSD 5,000/K-12
11 College Ave 12603 845-451-4950
Robert C. Watson, supt. Fax 451-4954
www.poughkeepsieschools.org/
Poughkeepsie HS 1,200/9-12
70 Forbus St 12603 845-451-4850
Robert Murphy, prin. Fax 451-4853
Poughkeepsie MS 1,100/6-8
55 College Ave 12603 845-451-4800
Carl Pabon, prin. Fax 451-4724

Spackenkill UFD 1,800/K-12
15 Croft Rd 12603 845-463-7800
Dr. Lois Colletta, supt. Fax 463-7804
www.dcboces.org/sufsd/
Spackenkill HS 600/9-12
112 Spackenkill Rd 12603 845-463-7810
Suzanne Smith, prin. Fax 463-7826
Todd MS 500/6-8
11 Croft Rd 12603 845-463-7830
Steven Malkischer, prin. Fax 462-1109

Dutchess Community College Post-Sec.
53 Pendell Rd 12601 845-431-8000
Marist College Post-Sec.
3399 North Rd 12601 845-575-3000
Oakwood Friends S 200/6-12
22 Spackenkill Rd 12603 845-462-4200
Peter Baily, hdmstr. Fax 462-4251
Our Lady of Lourdes HS 900/9-12
131 Boardman Rd 12603 845-463-0400
Br. Michael Mullin, prin. Fax 463-0174
Poughkeepsie Day S 300/PK-12
260 Boardman Rd 12603 845-462-7600
Josie Holford, hdmstr. Fax 462-7603
Ridley-Lowell Business & Technical Inst. Post-Sec.
26 S Hamilton St 12601 845-471-0330
Tabernacle Christian Academy 200/K-12
155 Academy St 12601 845-454-2792
Timothy Hostetter, prin. Fax 483-0926
Vassar College Post-Sec.
124 Raymond Ave 12604 845-437-7000

Prattsburgh, Steuben
Prattsburg Central SD 500/PK-12
1 Academy St 14873 607-522-3795
Jeffrey Black, supt. Fax 522-6221
Prattsburg Central S 500/PK-12
1 Academy St 14873 607-522-3795
Fax 522-6221

Pulaski, Oswego, Pop. 2,358
Pulaski Central SD 1,200/K-12
2 Hinman Rd 13142 315-298-5188
Dr. Marshall Marshall, supt. Fax 298-4390
www.pacs.cnyric.org
Pulaski JSHS 600/7-12
4624 Salina St 13142 315-298-5103
Joseph McGrath, prin. Fax 298-2371

Purchase, See Harrison

Keio Academy of New York 400/9-12
3 College Rd 10577 914-694-4825
Sumio Sakomura, hdmstr. Fax 694-4830
Long Island University-Westchester Post-Sec.
735 Anderson Hill Rd 10577 800-472-3548
Manhattanville College Post-Sec.
2900 Purchase St 10577 914-694-2200
Purchase College SUNY Post-Sec.
735 Anderson Hill Rd 10577 914-251-6000

Putnam Valley, Putnam
Putnam Valley Central SD 1,900/K-12
146 Peekskill Hollow Rd 10579 845-528-8143
Gary Tutty, supt. Fax 528-0274
www.putnamvalleyschools.org
Putnam Valley HS 600/9-12
146 Peekskill Hollow Rd 10579 845-526-7847
Raymond Cooper, prin. Fax 528-4456

Putnam Valley MS 600/5-8
142 Peekskill Hollow Rd 10579 845-528-8101
Edward Hallisey, prin. Fax 528-8145

Queensbury, Warren
Queensbury UFD 3,800/K-12
429 Aviation Rd 12804 518-824-5600
Dr. Brian Howard, supt. Fax 793-4476
www.queensburyschool.org/
Queensbury HS 1,200/9-12
409 Aviation Rd 12804 518-742-6026
Michael Patton, prin. Fax 742-6043
Queensbury MS 1,000/6-8
455 Aviation Rd 12804 518-742-6035
Douglas Silvernell, prin. Fax 742-6053

SUNY Adirondack Community College Post-Sec.
640 Bay Rd 12804 518-743-2200

Queens Village, See New York
NYC Department of Education
Supt. — See New York
IS 109 1,500/6-8
21310 92nd Ave 11428 718-465-0651
Shango Blake, prin. Fax 264-1246
Van Buren HS 3,000/9-12
23017 Hillside Ave 11427 718-776-4728
Marilyn Shevell, prin. Fax 776-6807

Bethel Christian Academy 400/PK-12
21532 Jamaica Ave 11428 718-978-4357
Dr. Johnson, prin.

Randolph, Cattaraugus, Pop. 1,282
Randolph Central SD 700/PK-12
18 Main St 14772 716-358-7005
Sandra Craft, supt. Fax 358-7072
www.randolphcsd.org/
Randolph HS 300/9-12
18 Main St 14772 716-358-7007
Dave Davidson, prin. Fax 358-7072
Randolph MS 5-8
22 Main St 14772 716-358-7028
William Caldwell, prin. Fax 358-7060

Ravena, Albany, Pop. 3,356
Ravena-Coeymans-Selkirk CSD
Supt. — See Selkirk
Ravena-Coeymans-Selkirk HS 800/9-12
2025 US Route 9W 12143 518-756-5200
Hakim Jones, prin. Fax 756-3534
Ravena-Coeymans-Selkirk MS 600/6-8
2025 Route 9W 12143 518-756-5229
Ralph Lyons, prin. Fax 756-1988

Red Creek, Wayne, Pop. 508
Red Creek Central SD 1,100/K-12
PO Box 190 13143 315-754-2010
David Sholes, supt. Fax 754-8169
www.rccsd.org
Red Creek HS 400/9-12
PO Box 190 13143 315-754-2040
Noel Patterson, prin. Fax 754-2068
Red Creek MS 300/6-8
PO Box 190 13143 315-754-2070
Randall Lawrence, prin. Fax 754-2077

Red Hook, Dutchess, Pop. 1,833
Red Hook Central SD 2,300/K-12
7401 S Broadway 12571 845-758-2241
Jan Volpe Ed.D., supt. Fax 758-3366
www.redhookcentralschools.org/
Linden Avenue MS 600/6-8
65 W Market St 12571 845-758-2241
Steven Chaikin, prin. Fax 758-0688
Red Hook HS 700/9-12
103 W Market St 12571 845-758-2241
Roy Paisley, prin. Fax 758-0482

Devereux Center in New York Post-Sec.
40 Devereux Way 12571 845-758-1899
Northern Dutchess Christian S 100/K-12
59 Fisk St 12571 845-876-7300
Nancy Aierstok, prin. Fax 758-4476

Rego Park, See New York
NYC Department of Education
Supt. — See New York
JHS 157 1,400/6-9
10201 64th Ave, 718-830-4910
Vincent Suraci, prin. Fax 830-4993

Career Institute of Health & Technology Post-Sec.
9525 Queens Blvd Ste 600 11374 718-897-4868
Metropolitan Learning Institute Post-Sec.
97-45 Queens Blvd Ste 401 11374 718-897-0482

Remsen, Oneida, Pop. 523
Remsen Central SD 600/K-12
PO Box 406 13438 315-831-3797
Ann Turner, supt. Fax 831-2172
Remsen JSHS 300/7-12
PO Box 406 13438 315-831-3851
Anthony Nicotera, prin. Fax 831-2172

Rensselaer, Rensselaer, Pop. 7,743
Rensselaer CSD 1,100/PK-12
555 Broadway 12144 518-465-7509
Gordon Reynolds, supt. Fax 436-0479
www.rcsd.k12.ny.us
Rensselaer HS 300/9-12
555 Broadway 12144 518-436-8561
Dr. Michael Dawkins, prin. Fax 436-0479
Rensselaer MS 300/6-8
555 Broadway 12144 518-436-8561
Karen Urbanski, prin. Fax 436-0479

Retsof, Livingston
York Central SD, PO Box 102 14539 1,000/K-12
Thomas Manko, supt. 585-243-1730
www.riverhead.net/

York JSHS | 500/7-12
PO Box 102 14539 | 585-243-1730
David Sylvester, prin. | Fax 243-5269

Rhinebeck, Dutchess, Pop. 3,114
Rhinebeck Central SD | 1,300/K-12
PO Box 351 12572 | 845-871-5520
Joseph Phelan, supt. | Fax 876-4276
www.rhinebeckcsd.org/
Bulkeley MS | 300/6-8
PO Box 351 12572 | 845-871-5500
John Kemnitzer, prin. | Fax 871-5553
Rhinebeck HS | 400/9-12
PO Box 351 12572 | 845-871-5500
Edwin Davenport, prin. | Fax 876-8755

Richfield Springs, Otsego, Pop. 1,197
Richfield Springs Central SD | 700/K-12
PO Box 631 13439 | 315-858-0610
Robert Barraco, supt. | Fax 858-2440
www.richfieldcsd.org
Richfield Springs Central S | 700/K-12
PO Box 631 13439 | 315-858-0610
Penny Harrington, prin. | Fax 858-2440

Richmond Hill, See New York
NYC Department of Education
Supt. — See New York
Richmond Hill HS | 3,100/9-12
8930 114th St 11418 | 718-846-3335
Eileen M. May, prin. | Fax 847-0980

Bethlehem Christian Academy | 200/PK-12
9111 Lefferts Blvd 11418 | 718-850-6480
Jeremiah Grant, admin. | Fax 850-5308
Yeshiva Shaar HaTorah - Grodno | Post-Sec.
8396 117th St 11418 | 718-846-1940

Richmondville, Schoharie, Pop. 785
Cobleskill-Richmondville Central SD
Supt. — See Cobleskill
Cobleskill-Richmondville HS | 700/9-12
1353 State Route 7 12149 | 518-234-3565
David Zacher, prin. | Fax 234-1018

Ridgewood, See New York
NYC Department of Education
Supt. — See New York
Cleveland HS | 2,600/9-12
2127 Himrod St 11385 | 718-381-9600
Dominick Scarola, prin. | Fax 417-8457
IS 77 | 1,300/6-8
976 Seneca Ave 11385 | 718-366-7120
Joseph Miller, prin. | Fax 456-9512
IS 93 | 1,400/6-8
6656 Forest Ave 11385 | 718-821-4882
George Foley, prin. | Fax 456-9521

Midway Paris Beauty School | Post-Sec.
5440 Myrtle Ave 11385 | 718-418-2790

Ripley, Chautauqua, Pop. 1,189
Ripley Central SD | 200/PK-12
PO Box 688 14775 | 716-736-6201
Dr. John Hamels, supt. | Fax 736-6226
www.ripleycsd.wnyric.org
Ripley Central HS | 7-12
PO Box 688 14775 | 716-736-2631
Susan Hammond, prin. | Fax 736-6226

Riverdale, See New York

Mann HS | 900/6-12
231 W 246th St 10471 | 718-432-4000
Dr. Thomas Kelly, hdmstr. | Fax 548-2089
Riverdale Country S | 1,100/PK-12
5250 Fieldston Rd 10471 | 718-549-8810
John Johnson, hdmstr. | Fax 519-2795
Yeshiva of Telshe Alumni | 100/9-12
4904 Independence Ave 10471 | 718-601-3523
Rabbi Noson Joseph, admin. | Fax 601-2141
Yeshiva Ohavei Torah | 100/9-12
450 W 250th St 10471 | 718-432-2600
Rabbi Avrumi Portowicz, prin. | Fax 548-4106

Riverhead, Suffolk, Pop. 8,814
Riverhead Central SD | 4,900/K-12
700 Osborne Ave 11901 | 631-369-6716
Paul R. Doyle, supt. | Fax 369-6816
www.riverhead.net
Riverhead HS | 1,500/9-12
700 Harrison Ave 11901 | 631-369-6723
James McCaffrey, prin. | Fax 369-5164
Riverhead MS | 800/7-8
600 Harrison Ave 11901 | 631-369-6759
Andrea Pekar, prin. | Fax 369-6829

Central Suffolk Hospital | Post-Sec.
1300 Roanoke Ave 11901 | 631-548-6000
McGann-Mercy HS | 400/7-12
1225 Ostrander Ave 11901 | 631-727-5900
Dr. Steven Cheeseman, prin. | Fax 727-8483
SUNY Suffolk County Community College | Post-Sec.
2 Speonk Riverhead Rd 11901 | 631-548-2500

Rochester, Monroe, Pop. 215,093
Brighton Central SD | 3,600/K-12
2035 Monroe Ave 14618 | 585-242-5080
Dr. Christopher Manaseri, supt. | Fax 242-5164
www.bcsd.org
Brighton HS | 1,300/9-12
1150 Winton Rd S 14618 | 585-242-5000
Nancy Hackett, prin. | Fax 242-7364
Twelve Corners MS | 900/6-8
2643 Elmwood Ave 14618 | 585-242-5100
Terence Quinn, prin. | Fax 242-2540

East Irondequoit Central SD | 3,500/K-12
600 Pardee Rd 14609 | 585-339-1210
Susan Allen, supt. | Fax 288-0713
www.eicsd.k12.ny.us/
East Irondequoit MS | 900/6-8
155 Densmore Rd 14609 | 585-339-1400
Dr. John Boronkay, prin. | Fax 339-1409
Eastridge HS | 1,100/9-12
2350 Ridge Rd E 14622 | 585-339-1450
Matthew Laniak, prin. | Fax 339-1459

Gates Chili Central SD | 4,600/K-12
910 Wegman Rd 14624 | 585-247-5050
Richard A. Stein, supt. | Fax 340-5569
www.gateschili.org
Gates Chili HS | 1,500/9-12
910 Wegman Rd 14624 | 585-247-5050
Tim Clasgens, prin. | Fax 340-5518
Gates Chili MS | 1,100/6-8
910 Wegman Rd 14624 | 585-247-5050
Gerard Iuppa, prin. | Fax 340-5532

Greece Central SD | 12,600/PK-12
750 Maiden Ln 14615 | 585-621-1000
Dr. Josephine Kehoe, supt. | Fax 621-6967
www.greece.k12.ny.us
Apollo MS | 1,000/6-8
750 Maiden Ln 14615 | 585-966-5200
Cindy Neth, prin. | Fax 966-5239
Arcadia MS | 900/6-8
130 Island Cottage Rd 14612 | 585-966-3300
Aaron Skype, prin. | Fax 966-3339
Greece Arcadia HS | 1,400/9-12
120 Island Cottage Rd 14612 | 585-966-3000
Leslie Flick, prin. | Fax 966-3039
Greece-Athena HS | 1,400/9-12
800 Long Pond Rd 14612 | 585-966-4000
Helen Wahl, prin. | Fax 966-4039
Greece Athena MS | 1,000/6-8
800 Long Pond Rd 14612 | 585-966-4200
Richard Snyder, prin. | Fax 966-4239
Olympia HS | 1,400/9-12
1139 Maiden Ln 14615 | 585-966-5000
Christina Sloane, prin. | Fax 966-5039

Rochester CSD | 32,900/PK-12
131 W Broad St 14614 | 585-262-8100
Dr. Manuel Rivera, supt. | Fax 262-5151
www.rcsdk12.org/
BioScience & Health Careers HS | Vo/Tech
950 Norton St 14621 | 585-324-3730
Linda Kantor, prin. | Fax 336-8018
Business Finance & Entrepreneurship S | Vo/Tech
655 Colfax St 14606 | 585-324-9781
Joseph Baldino, prin. |
Charlotte HS | 600/9-12
4115 Lake Ave 14612 | 585-663-7070
Deborah Rider, prin. | Fax 621-0275
Douglass Preparatory S | 900/7-9
940 Fernwood Park 14609 | 585-482-2000
Barbara A. Hasler, prin. | Fax 654-1039
East HS | 2,100/7-12
1801 E Main St 14609 | 585-288-3130
Kathleen Lamb, prin. | Fax 654-1066
Edison Skilled Trade S | Vo/Tech
655 Colfax St 14606 | 585-647-2200
Dennis Malinowski, prin. | Fax 277-0092
Engineering & Manufacturing S @ Edison | Vo/Tech
655 Colfax St 14606 | 585-324-9782
Eldridge Moore, prin. |
Global Media Arts HS @ Franklin | Vo/Tech
950 Norton St 14621 | 585-324-3720
Dennis Francione, prin. | Fax 336-5549
Imaging & Information Tech S @ Edison | Vo/Tech
655 Colfax St 14606 | 585-324-9794
Bonnie Atkins, prin. |
Intl Finance & Economic Dev Career HS | Vo/Tech
950 Norton St 14621 | 585-324-3725
Ali Abdulmateen, prin. | Fax 336-5562
Jefferson HS | 1,200/7-12
1 Edgerton Park 14608 | 585-458-2280
Mary Andrecolich-Diaz, prin. | Fax 277-0038
Marshall HS | 1,100/7-12
180 Ridgeway Ave 14615 | 585-458-2110
Joseph Munno, prin. | Fax 277-0077
Monroe JSHS | 1,400/7-12
164 Alexander St 14607 | 585-232-1530
Linda Dianetti, prin. | Fax 262-8965
Rochester HS of the Arts | 1,000/6-12
45 Prince St 14607 | 585-242-7682
Brenda Pacheco-Rivera, prin. | Fax 256-6580
School Without Walls Foundation Academy | 7-8
110 Clinton Ave N 14604 | 585-324-3111
Daniel Drmacich, prin. |
Thomas Learning Center | 1,300/7-12
625 Scio St 14605 | 585-262-8850
Sandra Jordan, prin. | Fax 262-8872
Wilson Commencement Acad @ Wilson | 800/10-12
501 Genesee St 14611 | 585-328-3440
Marilynn Patterson Grant, prin. | Fax 464-6153
Wilson Foundation Acad @ James Madison | 900/7-9
200 Genesee St 14611 | 585-463-4100
Marilynn Patterson Grant, prin. | Fax 463-4103

West Irondequoit Central SD | 3,900/K-12
321 List Ave 14617 | 585-342-5500
Jeffrey B. Crane, supt. | Fax 266-1556
www.westirondequoit.org
Dake MS | 700/7-8
350 Cooper Rd 14617 | 585-342-2140
Timothy Terranova, prin. | Fax 336-3034
Irondequoit HS | 1,400/9-12
260 Cooper Rd 14617 | 585-336-2914
Patrick McCue, prin. | Fax 336-2929

Allendale Columbia S | 500/PK-12
519 Allens Creek Rd 14618 | 585-381-4560
Charles Hertrick, hdmstr. | Fax 383-1191
All Saints Catholic Academy | 100/7-8
170 Spencerport Rd 14606 | 585-429-6010
Monette Mahoney, prin. | Fax 429-6761

Aquinas Institute | 900/9-12
1127 Dewey Ave 14613 | 585-254-2020
Dennis Sadler, prin. | Fax 254-7401
Bexley Hall Seminary | Post-Sec.
26 Broadway 14607 | 585-546-2160
Bishop Kearney HS | 500/9-12
125 Kings Hwy S 14617 | 585-342-4000
Louis Angelo, prin. | Fax 342-4694
Bryant & Stratton College | Post-Sec.
150 Bellwood Dr 14606 | 585-720-0660
Bryant & Stratton College | Post-Sec.
1225 Jeffson Rd 14623 | 585-292-5627
Colgate Rochester Crozer Divinity School | Post-Sec.
1100 Goodman St S 14620 | 585-271-1320
Continental School | Post-Sec.
633 Jefferson Rd 14623 | 585-272-8060
David Hochstein Memorial Music School | Post-Sec.
50 Plymouth Ave N 14614 | 585-454-4596
Eastman School of Music | Post-Sec.
26 Gibbs St 14604 | 585-274-1060
Harley S | 500/PK-12
1981 Clover St 14618 | 585-442-1770
Paul Schiffman, hdmstr. | Fax 442-5758
Howard S | 200/5-12
275 Pinnacle Rd 14623 | 585-334-8010
Linda Lawrence, prin. | Fax 334-8073
McQuaid Jesuit HS | 800/7-12
1800 Clinton Ave S 14618 | 585-473-1130
William Hobbs, prin. | Fax 256-6171
Monroe Community College | Post-Sec.
1000 E Henrietta Rd 14623 | 585-292-2000
Nazareth Academy | 300/9-12
1001 Lake Ave 14613 | 585-458-8583
Louis Zona, prin. | Fax 647-8717
Nazareth College of Rochester | Post-Sec.
4245 East Ave 14618 | 585-389-2525
Nazareth Hall MS | 100/6-8
1001 Lake Ave 14613 | 585-647-8716
Sr. Elizabeth Snyder, dir. | Fax 254-5468
Northstar Christian Academy | 400/PK-12
332 Spencerport Rd 14606 | 585-429-5530
David Stein, prin. | Fax 429-7913
Ora Academy | 50/9-12
600 East Ave 14607 | 585-271-8711
Rabbi Reuven Feinberg, hdmstr. | Fax 271-8158
Our Lady of Mercy HS | 600/7-12
1437 Blossom Rd 14610 | 585-288-7120
Vilma Goetting, prin. | Fax 288-7966
Roberts Wesleyan College | Post-Sec.
2301 Westside Dr 14624 | 585-594-6000
Rochester Business Institute | Post-Sec.
1630 Portland Ave 14621 | 585-266-0430
Rochester General Hospital | Post-Sec.
1425 Portland Ave 14621 | 585-338-4430
Rochester Institute of Technology (NTID) | Post-Sec.
52 Lomb Memorial Dr 14623 | 585-475-6585
Rochester Institute of Technology | Post-Sec.
1 Lomb Memorial Dr 14623 | 585-475-2411
Rochester School for the Deaf | Post-Sec.
1545 Saint Paul St 14621 | 585-544-1240
Rochester SDA Junior Academy | 100/PK-12
309 Jefferson Ave 14611 | 585-436-5915
| Fax 436-5921
St. Bernard's Sch of Theology & Ministry | Post-Sec.
120 French Rd 14618 | 585-271-3657
St. John Fisher College | Post-Sec.
3690 East Ave 14618 | 585-385-8000
Shear Ego Intl School of Hair Design | Post-Sec.
525 Titus Ave 14617 | 585-342-0070
Siena Catholic Academy | 300/7-8
2617 East Ave 14610 | 585-381-1220
Timothy Leahy, prin. | Fax 381-1223
SUNY Empire State College | Post-Sec.
1475 Winton Rd N 14609 | 585-244-3884
Talmudical Institute of Upstate New York | Post-Sec.
769 Park Ave 14607 | 585-473-2810
Talmudical Institute of Upstate New York | 100/9-12
769 Park Ave 14607 | 585-473-2810
Rabbi M. Davidowitz, dean | Fax 442-0417
University of Rochester | Post-Sec.
Meliora Hall 14627 | 585-275-2121
University of Rochester Medical Center | Post-Sec.
14642 | 585-275-8831

Rockaway Park, See New York
NYC Department of Education
Supt. — See New York
Beach Channel HS | 2,300/9-12
10000 Beach Channel Dr 11694 | 718-945-6900
Dr. David Morris, prin. | Fax 474-7682
Channel View S for Research | 9-12
10000 Beach Channel Dr 11694 | 718-634-1970
Patricia Tubridy, prin. | Fax 634-2896
MS 180 | 900/6-8
320 Beach 104th St 11694 | 718-945-4200
Ronnie Nelson, prin. | Fax 945-8958
Scholars Academy | 6-8
320 Beach 104th St 11694 | 718-474-6818
Brian O'Connell, prin. |

Rockville Centre, Nassau, Pop. 24,397
Rockville Centre UFD | 3,600/K-12
128 Shepherd St 11570 | 516-255-8957
Dr. William Johnson, supt. | Fax 255-8810
www.rvcschools.org
South Side HS | 1,100/9-12
140 Shepherd St 11570 | 516-255-8944
Dr. Carol Burris, prin. | Fax 766-7934
South Side MS | 900/6-8
67 Hillside Ave 11570 | 516-255-8976
Shelagh McGinn, prin. | Fax 763-0914

Mercy Medical Center | Post-Sec.
PO Box 9024 11571 | 516-705-2525
Molloy College | Post-Sec.
PO Box 5002 11571 | 516-678-5000

Rocky Point, Suffolk, Pop. 8,596
Rocky Point UFD | 3,500/K-12
170 Route 25A 11778 | 631-744-1600
Dr. Carla D'ambrosio, supt. | Fax 744-0817
www.rockypointschools.org

Rocky Point HS
900/9-12
82 Rocky Point Yaphank Rd 11778
631-744-1600
William Caulfield, prin.
Fax 209-0204
Rocky Point MS
900/6-8
76 Rocky Point Yaphank Rd 11778
631-744-1600
Joseph Tanen Centamore, prin.
Fax 886-0000

Rome, Oneida, Pop. 34,512
Rome CSD
5,600/PK-12
112 E Thomas St 13440
315-338-6500
Thomas Gallagher, supt.
Fax 334-7409
www.romecsd.org/
Rome Free Academy
1,700/9-12
95 Dart Cir 13441
315-334-7200
Mark Benson, prin.
Fax 334-7236
Staley Upper ES
700/6-8
620 E Bloomfield St 13440
315-338-5300
Michael Stalteri, prin.
Fax 338-5306
Strough MS
700/6-8
801 Laurel St 13440
315-338-5200
Riccardo Ripa, prin.
Fax 338-7465

New York State School for the Deaf
Post-Sec.
401 Turin St 13440
Rome Catholic S
100/PK-12
800 Cypress St 13440
315-336-6190
Chris Moniney, prin.
Fax 336-6194

Romulus, Seneca
Romulus Central SD
600/PK-12
5705 State Route 96 14541
866-810-0345
Michael J. Midey, supt.
Fax 869-5961
www.rcs.k12.ny.us
Romulus Central HS
300/7-12
5705 State Route 96 14541
866-810-0345
Lynn Rhone, prin.
Fax 869-5961

Ronkonkoma, Suffolk, Pop. 20,391
Connetquot Central SD
Supt. — See Bohemia
Ronkonkoma MS
600/6-8
501 Peconic St 11779
631-467-6000
Charles Morea, prin.
Fax 467-6003

Roosevelt, Nassau, Pop. 15,030
Roosevelt UFD
2,400/PK-12
240 Denton Pl 11575
516-867-8616
Ronald Ross, supt.
Fax 379-0178
www.rooseveltschools.net
Roosevelt HS
700/9-12
1 Wagner Ave 11575
516-867-8667
Donald Humphrey, prin.
Fax 867-2471
Roosevelt MS
7-8
1 Wagner Ave 11575
516-867-8673
Catalina Castillo, prin.
Fax 867-2471

Roscoe, Sullivan
Roscoe Central SD
300/PK-12
6 Academy St 12776
607-498-4126
Carmine Giangreco, supt.
Fax 498-5609
www.roscoe.k12.ny.us
Roscoe Central S
300/PK-12
6 Academy St 12776
607-498-4126
Scott Haberli, prin.
Fax 498-5609

Roslyn, Nassau, Pop. 2,587
Roslyn UFD
3,200/PK-12
PO Box 367 11576
516-625-6303
David J. Helme, supt.
Fax 625-8201
www.roslynschools.org
Other Schools – See Roslyn Heights

Mesivta of Roslyn
50/9-12
2 Shelter Rock Rd 11576
516-877-2131
Howard Galin, prin.
Fax 877-2174

Roslyn Heights, Nassau, Pop. 6,405
Roslyn UFD
Supt. — See Roslyn
Roslyn HS
900/9-12
475 Round Hill Rd 11577
516-625-6337
Kevin Scanlon, prin.
Fax 625-8191
Roslyn MS
800/6-8
375 Locust Ln 11577
516-625-6410
Jack Palmadesso, prin.
Fax 625-6597

Roxbury, Delaware
Roxbury Central SD
400/K-12
53729 State Highway 30 12474
607-326-4151
Dr. Craig G. Carr, supt.
Fax 326-4154
www.roxburycs.org
Roxbury Central S
400/K-12
53729 State Highway 30 12474
607-326-4151
Thomas O'Brien, prin.
Fax 326-4154

Rush, Monroe

State Agriculture & Industrial S
100/6-12
375 Rush Scottsville Rd 14543
585-533-2663
Thomas Fitzsimmons, dir.
Fax 533-2664

Rushville, Ontario, Pop. 613
Marcus Whitman Central SD
1,600/K-12
4100 Baldwin Rd 14544
585-554-4848
Oren Cook, supt.
Fax 554-4882
www.mwcsd.org/
Whitman HS
500/9-12
4100 Baldwin Rd 14544
585-554-6441
Susan Wissick, prin.
Fax 554-5201
Whitman MS
400/6-8
4100 Baldwin Rd 14544
585-554-6442
Alan DeGroote, prin.
Fax 554-3414

Russell, Saint Lawrence
Edwards-Knox Central SD
700/K-12
PO Box 630 13684
315-562-8326
Dr. William Cartwright, supt.
Fax 562-2477
www.ekcsk12.org
Edwards-Knox JSHS
300/7-12
PO Box 630 13684
315-562-3227
Jeff Davis, prin.
Fax 562-8433

Rye, Westchester, Pop. 15,066
Rye CSD
2,700/K-12
324 Midland Ave 10580
914-967-6100
Dr. Edward Shine, supt.
Fax 967-6957
www.ryecityschools.lhric.org
Rye HS
700/9-12
1 Parsons St 10580
914-967-6100
Dr. Jim Rooney, prin.
Fax 967-4380
Rye MS
600/6-8
3 Parsons St 10580
914-967-6100
Dr. Ann Edwards, prin.
Fax 921-6189

Rye Country Day S
800/PK-12
Cedar St 10580
914-967-1417
Scott Nelson, hdmstr.
Fax 967-1418
School of the Holy Child
300/9-12
2225 Westchester Ave 10580
914-967-5622
Ann Sullivan, prin.
Fax 967-6476

Rye Brook, Westchester, Pop. 9,234
Blind Brook-Rye UFD
1,400/K-12
390 N Ridge St 10573
914-937-3600
Dr. Ronald Valenti, supt.
Fax 937-5871
blindbrook.k12.ny.us
Blind Brook HS
300/9-12
840 King St 10573
914-937-3600
Anthony Baxter, prin.
Fax 937-4509
Blind Brook MS, 840 King St 10573
300/6-8
Dr. Thomas Wolf, prin.
914-937-3600

Port Chester-Rye UFD
3,400/K-12
113 Bowman Ave 10573
914-934-7901
Charles Coletti Ph.D., supt.
Fax 934-0727
www.portchesterschools.org/
Other Schools – See Port Chester

Sackets Harbor, Jefferson, Pop. 1,394
Sackets Harbor Central SD
500/K-12
PO Box 290 13685
315-646-3575
Suzanne Tingley, supt.
Fax 646-1038
Sackets Harbor Central S
500/K-12
PO Box 290 13685
315-646-3575
Robert Wagoner, prin.
Fax 646-1038

Sag Harbor, Suffolk, Pop. 2,367
Sag Harbor HS
1,000/K-12
200 Jermain Ave 11963
631-725-5300
Kathryn Holden, supt.
Fax 725-5307
Pierson JSHS
500/6-12
200 Jermain Ave 11963
631-725-5302
Jeff Nichols, prin.
Fax 725-5314

Saint Albans, See New York
NYC Department of Education
Supt. — See New York
Pathways College Preparatory S
6-12
10989 204th St 11412
718-454-4957
Michelle Shannon, prin.
Fax 454-4892
IS 192
1,000/6-8
10989 204th St 11412
718-479-5540
Harriett Diaz, prin.
Fax 217-4645

Saint Bonaventure, Cattaraugus, Pop. 2,397

St. Bonaventure University 14778
Post-Sec.
585-375-2000

Saint James, Suffolk, Pop. 12,703
Smithtown Central SD
Supt. — See Smithtown
Nesaquake MS
6-8
478 Edgewood Ave 11780
631-382-5100
Steven Podd, prin.
Fax 382-5107
Smithtown HS East
2,800/9-12
10 School St 11780
631-382-2700
Fax 382-2707

Knox S
100/7-12
541 Long Beach Rd 11780
631-584-5500
Fax 584-6566

Saint Johnsville, Montgomery, Pop. 1,650
Oppenheim-Ephratah Central SD
500/PK-12
6486 State Highway 29 13452
518-568-2014
Dan Russom, supt.
Fax 568-2941
oecs.k12.ny.us
Oppenheim-Ephratah Central S
500/PK-12
6486 State Highway 29 13452
518-568-2014
Michele Weaver, prin.
Fax 568-2941

St. Johnsville Central SD
500/PK-12
61 Monroe St 13452
518-568-7023
Christine M. Battisti, supt.
Fax 568-5407
www.sjcsd@neric.org
Saint Johnsville MSHS
300/6-12
44 Center St 13452
518-568-2011
Greg Sova, prin.
Fax 568-2797

Saint Regis Falls, Franklin
St. Regis Falls Central SD
400/PK-12
PO Box 309 12980
518-856-9421
Patricia Dovi, supt.
Fax 856-0142
Saint Regis Falls S
400/PK-12
PO Box 309 12980
518-856-9421
Richard Hansen, prin.
Fax 856-0142

Salamanca, Cattaraugus, Pop. 5,942
Salamanca CSD
1,500/K-12
50 Iroquois Dr 14779
716-945-2403
Rick Moore, supt.
Fax 945-3964
www.salamancany.org/
Salamanca HS
400/9-12
50 Iroquois Dr 14779
716-945-2404
Donnald G. Hensel, prin.
Fax 945-5983
Salamanca MS
300/6-8
50 Iroquois Dr 14779
716-945-2405
Laurence D. Whitcomb, prin.
Fax 945-5738

Salem, Washington, Pop. 961
Salem Central SD
800/K-12
PO Box 517 12865
518-854-7855
Richard Wheeler, supt.
Fax 854-3957

Salem JSHS
400/7-12
PO Box 517 12865
518-854-7600
Daniel Jordan, prin.
Fax 854-3957

Sanborn, Niagara
Niagara-Wheatfield Central SD
Supt. — See Niagara Falls
Niagara-Wheatfield HS
1,400/9-12
2292 Saunders Settlement Rd 14132 716-215-3100
Michelle Spasiano, prin.
Fax 215-3125
Town MS
1,000/6-8
2292 Saunders Settlement Rd 14132 716-215-3150
Dr. Laura Palka, prin.
Fax 215-3160

SUNY Niagara County Community College
Post-Sec.
3111 Saunders Settlement Rd 14132 716-614-6222

Sandy Creek, Oswego, Pop. 780
Sandy Creek Central SD
1,100/K-12
PO Box 248 13145
315-387-3445
Stewart R. Amell, supt.
Fax 387-2196
www.sccs.cnyric.org/
Sandy Creek HS
400/9-12
PO Box 248 13145
315-387-3465
Maureen Shiel, prin.
Fax 387-2196
Sandy Creek MS
300/6-8
PO Box 248 13145
315-387-3465
Joanne Norton, prin.
Fax 387-2196

Saranac, Clinton
Saranac Central SD
Supt. — See Dannemora
Saranac HS
600/9-12
60 Picketts Corners Rd 12981
518-565-5800
Jonathan Parks, prin.
Fax 565-5809
Saranac JHS
400/7-8
70 Picketts Corners Rd 12981
518-565-5700
James Gratto, prin.
Fax 565-5706

Saranac Lake, Franklin, Pop. 4,974
Saranac Lake Central SD
1,600/PK-12
79 Canaras Ave 12983
518-891-5460
Scott A. Amo, supt.
Fax 891-5140
www.slcs.org
Petrova MS
400/6-8
79 Canaras Ave 12983
518-891-4221
Patricia Kenyon, prin.
Fax 891-6615
Saranac Lake HS
600/9-12
79 Canaras Ave 12983
518-891-4450
Gerald Goldman, prin.
Fax 891-6813

North Country Community College
Post-Sec.
PO Box 89 12983
518-891-2915

Saratoga Springs, Saratoga, Pop. 27,332
Saratoga Springs CSD
6,900/K-12
3 Blue Streak Blvd 12866
518-583-4709
John MacFadden, supt.
Fax 584-6624
www.saratogaschools.org
Maple Ave MS
1,700/6-8
515 Maple Ave 12866
518-587-4551
Stuart Byrne, prin.
Fax 587-5759
Saratoga Springs HS
2,100/9-12
1 Blue Streak Blvd 12866
518-587-6690
Frank Crowley, prin.
Fax 583-1671

Saratoga Central Catholic HS
200/7-12
247 S Broadway 12866
518-587-7070
Chris Signor, prin.
Fax 587-0678
Skidmore College
Post-Sec.
815 N Broadway 12866
518-580-5000
SUNY Empire State College
Post-Sec.
1 Union Ave 12866
518-587-2100
Waldorf S of Saratoga Springs
200/PK-12
122 Regent St 12866
518-587-0549
Sydney Morrell, admin.
Fax 581-1682

Saugerties, Ulster, Pop. 3,903
Saugerties Central SD
3,300/K-12
PO Box A 12477
845-247-6550
Richard R. Rhau Ed.D., supt.
Fax 246-8364
www.saugerties.k12.ny.us
Saugerties HS
1,100/9-12
PO Box A 12477
845-247-6650
Timothy Price, prin.
Fax 246-4312
Saugerties JHS
600/7-8
PO Box A 12477
845-247-6560
Donald Farris, prin.
Fax 246-4322

Sauquoit, Oneida
Sauquoit Valley Central SD
1,300/K-12
2601 Oneida St 13456
315-839-6311
Deborah Flack, supt.
Fax 839-5352
www.svcsd.org
Sauquoit Valley HS
400/9-12
2601 Oneida St 13456
315-839-6316
John Kolczynski, prin.
Fax 839-6397
Sauquoit Valley MS
300/6-8
2601 Oneida St 13456
315-839-6371
Ron Wheelock, prin.
Fax 839-6390

Sayville, Suffolk, Pop. 16,550
Sayville UFD
3,600/K-12
99 Greeley Ave 11782
631-244-6510
Dr. Rosemary Jones, supt.
Fax 244-6504
www.sayville.k12.ny.us
Sayville MS
900/6-8
291 Johnson Ave 11782
631-244-6650
Dr. Walter Schartner, prin.
Fax 244-6655
Other Schools – See West Sayville

Scarsdale, Westchester, Pop. 17,929
Edgemont UFD
1,800/K-12
300 White Oak Ln 10583
914-472-7768
Nancy Taddiken, supt.
Fax 472-6846
www.edgemont.org
Edgemont JSHS
900/7-12
200 White Oak Ln 10583
914-725-1500
William Manfredonia, prin.
Fax 725-1057

Scarsdale UFD | 4,500/K-12
2 Brewster Rd 10583 | 914-721-2412
Michael McGill, supt. | Fax 722-2822
www.scarsdaleschools.k12.ny.us
Scarsdale HS | 1,300/9-12
1057 Post Rd 10583 | 914-721-2450
John Klemme, prin. | Fax 721-2549
Scarsdale MS | 1,100/6-8
134 Mamaroneck Rd 10583 | 914-721-2600
Michael McDermott, prin. | Fax 721-2655

Schaghticoke, Rensselaer, Pop. 678
Hoosic Valley Central SD | 1,200/K-12
2 Pleasant Ave 12154 | 518-753-4450
Dr. James Seeley, supt. | Fax 753-7665
www.hoosicvalley.k12.ny.us/
Hoosic Valley HS | 400/9-12
Route 67 12154 | 518-753-4432
Patti Sawyer, prin. | Fax 753-7491
Hoosic Valley MS | 400/5-8
Route 67 12154 | 518-753-4432
Amy Goodell, prin. | Fax 753-7491

Schenectady, Schenectady, Pop. 61,016
Mohonasen Central SD | 3,300/K-12
2072 Curry Rd 12303 | 518-356-8200
Kathleen Spring, supt. | Fax 356-8247
www.mohonasen.org
Draper MS | 900/6-8
2070 Curry Rd 12303 | 518-356-8350
Patrick McGrath, prin. | Fax 356-8359
Mohonasen HS | 1,100/9-12
2072 Curry Rd 12303 | 518-356-8300
Lisa Cutting, prin. | Fax 356-8309

Niskayuna Central SD | 4,300/K-12
1239 Van Antwerp Rd 12309 | 518-377-4666
Dr. Kevin Baughman, supt. | Fax 377-4074
www.nisk.k12.ny.us
Iroquois MS | 600/6-8
2495 Rosendale Rd 12309 | 518-377-2233
David Crandall, prin. | Fax 377-2219
Niskayuna HS | 1,400/9-12
1626 Balltown Rd 12309 | 518-382-2521
John Rickert, prin. | Fax 382-2539
Van Antwerp MS | 500/6-8
2253 Story Ave 12309 | 518-370-1243
Luke Rakoczy, prin. | Fax 370-4610

Schalmont Central SD | 2,300/K-12
401 Duanesburg Rd 12306 | 518-355-9500
Dr. Valerie Kelsey, supt. | Fax 355-9203
www.schalmont.org
Schalmont HS | 800/9-12
1 Sabre Dr 12306 | 518-355-6110
Terence Nash, prin. | Fax 355-8720
Schalmont MS | 600/6-8
2 Sabre Dr 12306 | 518-355-6110
Michael Kondratowicz, prin. | Fax 355-5329

Schenectady CSD | 9,600/PK-12
108 Education Dr 12303 | 518-370-8100
John Falco, supt. | Fax 370-8173
www.schenectady.k12.ny.us
Central Park MS | 700/6-8
421 Elm St 12304 | 518-881-3660
Mary Ozarowski, prin. | Fax 881-3662
Mont Pleasant MS | 700/6-8
1121 Forest Rd 12303 | 518-370-8160
Gary Comley, prin. | Fax 370-8339
Oneida MS | 700/6-8
1629 Oneida St 12308 | 518-370-8260
Edna Baker, prin. | Fax 370-8267
Schenectady HS | 2,600/9-12
1445 The Plz 12308 | 518-370-8190
Arnold Spadafora, prin. | Fax 370-8169

Ellis Hospital School of Nursing | Post-Sec.
1101 Nott St 12308 | 518-243-4471
Mid-America Baptist Theological Seminary | Post-Sec.
2810 Curry Rd 12303 | 518-355-4000
Modern Welding School | Post-Sec.
1842 State St 12304 | 518-374-1216
Notre Dame-Bishop Gibbons HS | 400/6-12
2600 Albany St 12304 | 518-393-3131
Rick Bayhan, prin. | Fax 370-3817
SUNY Schenectady County Community Coll. | Post-Sec.
78 Washington Ave 12305 | 518-381-1200
Union College 12308 | Post-Sec.
518-388-6000

Schenevus, Otsego, Pop. 529
Schenevus Central SD | 400/K-12
159 Main St 12155 | 607-638-5530
Edmund Shultis, supt. | Fax 638-5600
Schenevus Central S | 400/K-12
159 Main St 12155 | 607-638-5881
Marie McCrea, prin. | Fax 638-5600

Schoharie, Schoharie, Pop. 1,026
Schoharie Central SD | 1,100/K-12
PO Box 430 12157 | 518-295-8132
Arthur Cotugno, supt. | Fax 295-8178
www.schoharie.k12.ny.us
Schoharie JSHS | 600/7-12
PO Box 430 12157 | 518-295-8188
Stacey Birdsall, prin. | Fax 295-8161

Schroon Lake, Essex
Schroon Lake Central SD | 300/K-12
PO Box 338 12870 | 518-532-7164
Michael Bonnewell, supt. | Fax 532-0284
www.schroonschool.org
Schroon Lake Central S | 300/K-12
PO Box 338 12870 | 518-532-7164
Michael Bonnewell, prin. | Fax 532-0284

Schuylerville, Saratoga, Pop. 1,303
Schuylerville Central SD | 1,700/K-12
14 Spring St 12871 | 518-695-3255
Dr. Leon Reed, supt. | Fax 695-6491
www.schuylervilleschools.org

Schuylerville JSHS | 700/7-12
14 Spring St 12871 | 518-695-3255
Matthew Sickles, prin. | Fax 695-3103

Scio, Allegany
Scio Central SD | 500/PK-12
3968 Washington St 14880 | 585-593-5076
Michael J. McArdle, supt. | Fax 593-3468
www.scio.wnyric.org
Scio Central S | 500/PK-12
3968 Washington St 14880 | 585-593-5510
Thomas Simon, prin. | Fax 593-0653

Scotia, Schenectady, Pop. 7,856
Burnt Hills-Ballston Lake CSD | 3,400/K-12
50 Cypress Dr 12302 | 518-399-9141
Jim Schultz, supt. | Fax 399-1882
www.bhbl.org
Other Schools – See Burnt Hills

Scotia-Glenville Central SD | 2,900/K-12
900 Preddice Pkwy 12302 | 518-382-1215
Susan Swartz, supt. | Fax 382-1222
www.sgcsd.neric.org
Scotia-Glenville HS | 900/9-12
1 Tartan Way 12302 | 518-382-1231
Lynda Castronovo, prin. | Fax 382-1251
Scotia-Glenville MS | 800/6-8
10 Prestige Pkwy 12302 | 518-382-1263
Sharyll Keller, prin. | Fax 382-1263

Schenectady Christian S | 300/K-12
36-38 Sacandaga Rd 12302 | 518-370-4272
John Bishop, hdmstr. | Fax 370-4778

Scottsville, Monroe, Pop. 2,089
Wheatland-Chili Central SD | 900/K-12
940 North Rd 14546 | 585-889-6246
Thomas Gallagher, supt. | Fax 889-6284
www.wheatland.k12.ny.us
Wheatland-Chili JSHS | 400/7-12
940 North Rd 14546 | 585-889-6245
Stephen Grimm, prin. | Fax 889-6284

Sea Cliff, Nassau, Pop. 5,034
North Shore Central SD | 2,700/K-12
112 Franklin Ave 11579 | 516-705-0350
Edward Melnick, supt. | Fax 705-0353
www.northshore.k12.ny.us/
Other Schools – See Glen Head

Seaford, Nassau, Pop. 15,597
Seaford UFD | 2,700/K-12
1600 Washington Ave 11783 | 516-592-4000
George Duffy, supt.
www.seaford.k12.ny.us/
Seaford HS | 800/9-12
1575 Seamans Neck Rd 11783 | 516-592-4300
Michael Ragon, prin.
Seaford MS, 3940 Sunset Ave 11783 | 700/6-8
Roseanne Careri, prin. | 516-592-4200

Selden, Suffolk, Pop. 20,608
Middle Country Central SD
Supt. — See Centereach
Newfield HS, 145 Marshall Dr 11784 | 1,700/9-12
Gordon Brosdal, prin. | 631-285-8300

SUNY Suffolk County Community College | Post-Sec.
533 College Rd 11784 | 631-451-4110

Selkirk, Albany
Ravena-Coeymans-Selkirk CSD | 2,400/PK-12
26 Thatcher St 12158 | 518-756-5200
Vicki Wright, supt. | Fax 767-2644
www.rcscsd.org
Other Schools – See Ravena

Seneca Falls, Seneca, Pop. 6,901
Seneca Falls Central SD | 1,500/K-12
PO Box 268 13148 | 315-568-5500
Gerald Macaluso, supt. | Fax 712-0535
www.sfcs.k12.ny.us/
Mynderse Academy | 500/9-12
105 Troy St 13148 | 315-568-5500
Anthony Ferrara, prin. | Fax 712-0523
Seneca Falls MS | 300/6-8
95 Troy St 13148 | 315-568-5500
Robert McKeveny, prin. | Fax 712-0524

Finger Lakes Christian S | 100/PK-12
2291 State Route 89 13148 | 315-568-2216
Scott VanKirk, admin. | Fax 568-6638
New York Chiropractic College | Post-Sec.
PO Box 800 13148 | 315-568-3000

Setauket, Suffolk, Pop. 13,634
Three Village Central SD
Supt. — See East Setauket
Gelinas JHS, 25 Mud Rd 11733 | 1,000/7-9
Gustave Hueber, prin. | 631-730-4700

Sharon Springs, Schoharie, Pop. 537
Sharon Springs Central SD | 400/K-12
PO Box 218 13459 | 518-284-2266
Linda H. Tharp, supt. | Fax 284-9033
www.sharonsprings.org/
Sharon Springs Central S | 400/K-12
PO Box 218 13459 | 518-284-2267
Patterson Green, prin. | Fax 284-9075

Shelter Island, Suffolk, Pop. 1,193
Shelter Island UFD | 300/K-12
PO Box 2015 11964 | 631-749-0302
Sharon Clifford, supt. | Fax 749-1262
Shelter Island Central S | 300/K-12
PO Box 2015 11964 | 631-749-0302
Sharon Clifford, prin. | Fax 749-1262

Sherburne, Chenango, Pop. 1,444
Sherburne-Earlville Central SD | 1,700/K-12
15 School St 13460 | 607-674-7300
Gayle Hellert, supt. | Fax 674-9742
secsd.org/

Sherburne-Earlville HS | 600/9-12
13 School St 13460 | 607-674-7380
Eric Schnabl, prin. | Fax 674-7368
Sherburne-Earlville MS | 400/6-8
13 School St 13460 | 607-674-7350
Jill Lee, prin. | Fax 674-7392

Sherman, Chautauqua, Pop. 692
Sherman Central SD | 500/K-12
PO Box 950 14781 | 716-761-6121
Dr. Howard Ferguson, supt. | Fax 761-6119
www.sherman.wnyric.org
Sherman S | 500/K-12
PO Box 950 14781 | 716-761-6121
David Hickey, dean | Fax 761-6119

Shoreham, Suffolk, Pop. 423
Shoreham-Wading River Central SD | 2,700/K-12
250b Route 25a 11786 | 631-821-8100
Harriet Copel Ed.D., supt. | Fax 929-3001
www.swrcsd.org
Prodell MS | 600/6-8
100 Randall Rd 11786 | 631-821-8212
Dr. Ken Wagner, prin. | Fax 821-8275
Shoreham-Wading River HS | 800/9-12
250a Route 25a 11786 | 631-821-8264
Israel Colon, prin. | Fax 821-8162

Shortsville, Ontario, Pop. 1,306
Manchester-Shortsville Central SD | 900/K-12
1506 State Route 21 14548 | 585-289-3964
Robert Leiby, supt. | Fax 289-6660
www.redjacket.org
Red Jacket HS | 300/9-12
1506 State Route 21 14548 | 585-289-3966
Timothy Benjamin, prin. | Fax 289-4755
Red Jacket MS | 200/6-8
1506 State Route 21 14548 | 585-289-3967
Charlene Harvey, prin. | Fax 289-8715

Shrub Oak, Westchester
Lakeland CSD | 6,100/K-12
1086 E Main St 10588 | 914-245-1700
Kenneth Connolly, supt. | Fax 245-7817
www.lakelandschools.org
Lakeland HS | 1,100/9-12
1349 E Main St 10588 | 914-528-0600
Richard Herlihy, prin. | Fax 528-0521
Other Schools – See Cortlandt Manor, Yorktown Heights

Sidney, Delaware, Pop. 3,936
Sidney Central SD | 1,200/K-12
95 W Main St 13838 | 607-563-2135
Dominic Nuciforo, supt. | Fax 563-2386
Sidney HS, 95 W Main St 13838 | 500/9-12
Annette Hammond, prin. | 607-563-2135
Sidney MS, 13 Pearl St E 13838 | 300/6-8
Allen Bilofsky, prin. | 607-563-2135

Silver Creek, Chautauqua, Pop. 2,857
Silver Creek Central SD | 1,200/K-12
1 Dickinson St 14136 | 716-934-2603
Gordon Salisbury, supt. | Fax 934-7597
www.silvercreek.wnyric.org/
Silver Creek HS | 400/9-12
1 Dickinson St 14136 | 716-934-2603
John Hertlein, prin. | Fax 934-2103
Silver Creek MS | 300/6-8
1 Dickinson St 14136 | 716-934-2603
Patricia Krenzer, prin. | Fax 934-2103

Sinclairville, Chautauqua, Pop. 649
Cassadaga Valley Central SD | 1,400/PK-12
PO Box 540 14782 | 716-962-5155
John C. Brown, supt. | Fax 962-5976
cvweb.wnyric.org/
Cassadaga Valley MSHS | 800/6-12
PO Box 540 14782 | 716-962-8581
Jud Foy, prin. | Fax 962-5788

Skaneateles, Onondaga, Pop. 2,596
Skaneateles Central SD | 1,800/K-12
49 E Elizabeth St 13152 | 315-291-2221
Kathryn Carlson, supt. | Fax 685-0347
www.scs.cnyric.org/
Skaneateles HS | 600/9-12
49 E Elizabeth St 13152 | 315-291-2231
Georgette Hoskins, prin. | Fax 685-0347
Skaneateles MS | 500/6-8
35 East St 13152 | 315-291-2241
Timothy Chiavara, prin. | Fax 685-0347

Slate Hill, Orange
Minisink Valley Central SD | 4,500/K-12
PO Box 217 10973 | 845-355-5110
Dr. Martha Murray, supt. | Fax 355-5119
www.minisink.com
Minisink Valley HS | 1,500/9-12
PO Box 217 10973 | 845-355-5150
John Latini, prin. | Fax 355-5198
Minisink Valley MS | 1,100/6-8
PO Box 217 10973 | 845-355-5200
Robert Peters, prin. | Fax 355-5205

Sleepy Hollow, See North Tarrytown
Tarrytown UFD | 2,500/PK-12
200 N Broadway 10591 | 914-631-9404
Dr. Howard Smith, supt. | Fax 332-6283
www.tufsd.org
Sleepy Hollow MSHS | 1,100/7-12
210 N Broadway 10591 | 914-631-8838
Carol Conklin, prin. | Fax 332-6219

Smithtown, Suffolk, Pop. 27,100
Smithtown Central SD | 11,200/K-12
26 New York Ave 11787 | 631-382-2006
Judith Elias, supt. | Fax 382-2010
www.smithtown.k12.ny.us
Accompsett MS | 6-8
660 Meadow Rd 11787 | 631-382-2300
John Nocero, prin. | Fax 382-2307
Smithtown HS West | 2,800/9-12
100 Central Rd 11787 | 631-382-2905
John Dolan, prin. | Fax 382-2910
Other Schools – See Nesconset, Saint James

Smithtown Christian S   600/PK-12
  1 Higbie Dr 11787   631-265-3334
  Rev. Salvatore Greco Ed.D., supt.   Fax 265-1079

Sodus, Wayne, Pop. 1,686
Sodus Central SD   1,100/PK-12
  PO Box 220 14551   315-483-5201
  Susan Kay Salvaggio, supt.   Fax 483-6168
  www.sodus.k12.ny.us
Sodus HS   500/9-12
  PO Box 220 14551   315-483-5203
  Eugene Hoskins, prin.   Fax 483-6168
Sodus MS   200/7-8
  PO Box 220 14551   315-483-5214
  Nelson Kise, prin.   Fax 483-6168

Solvay, Onondaga, Pop. 6,734
Solvay UFD   1,700/K-12
  103 3rd St 13209   315-468-1111
  J. Francis Manning, supt.   Fax 468-2755
  www.solvayschools.org
Solvay HS   700/9-12
  600 Gertrude Ave 13209   315-468-2551
  Joseph Rotella, prin.   Fax 484-1404
Other Schools – See Syracuse

Somers, Westchester
Somers Central SD   3,100/K-12
  334 Route 202 10589   914-277-2400
  Dr. Joanne Marien, supt.   Fax 248-7886
  www.somers.k12.ny.us/
Somers MS   700/6-8
  250 Route 202 10589   914-277-3399
  Geraldine Paige, prin.   Fax 277-2236
Other Schools – See Lincolndale

Kennedy HS   600/9-12
  54 Route 138 10589   914-232-5061
  Stephen Schmidt, prin.   Fax 232-3416

Southampton, Suffolk, Pop. 4,075
Southampton UFD   1,700/PK-12
  70 Leland Ln 11968   631-591-4510
  Dr. Linda J. Bruno, supt.   Fax 591-4528
  www.southampton.k12.ny.us
Southampton HS   600/9-12
  141 Narrow Ln 11968   631-591-4600
  Nicholas Dyno, prin.   Fax 283-6313
Southampton IS   500/5-8
  70 Leland Ln 11968   631-591-4700
  Timothy Frazier, prin.   Fax 283-6899

Long Island University-Southampton   Post-Sec.
  239 Montauk Hwy 11968   631-283-4000

South Dayton, Chautauqua, Pop. 650
Pine Valley-South Dayton Central SD   800/K-12
  7755 Route 83 14138   716-988-3293
  Vincent J. Vecchiarella, supt.   Fax 988-3139
Pine Valley Central JSHS   400/7-12
  7827 Route 83 14138   716-988-3276
  Carol Smith, prin.   Fax 988-3139

South Fallsburg, Sullivan, Pop. 2,115

Yeshiva Gedola Zichron Moshe   300/9-12
  PO Box 580 12779   845-434-5240
  Rabbi Meshulim Gorelick, prin.   Fax 434-1009
Yeshivath Zichron Moshe   Post-Sec.
  Laurel Park Rd 12779   845-434-5240

South Glens Falls, Saratoga, Pop. 3,417
South Glens Falls Central SD   3,200/PK-12
  6 Bluebird Rd 12803   518-793-9647
  Dr. James McCarthy, supt.   Fax 761-0723
  www.sgfallssd.org/
South Glens Falls HS   900/9-12
  42 Merritt Rd 12803   518-792-9987
  Jean Tedesco, prin.   Fax 792-5412
Winch MS   800/6-8
  99 Hudson St 12803   518-792-5891
  Mark Fish, prin.   Fax 793-9505

South Kortright, Delaware
South Kortright Central SD   400/K-12
  PO Box 113 13842   607-538-9111
  Benjamin Berliner, supt.   Fax 538-9205
  www.skcs.org
South Kortright Central S   400/K-12
  PO Box 113 13842   607-538-9111
  John J. Bonhotal, prin.   Fax 538-9205

Southold, Suffolk, Pop. 5,192
Southold UFD   1,000/K-12
  PO Box 40 11971   631-765-5400
  Dr. Christopher Gallagher, supt.   Fax 765-5086
  www.northfork.net/shs
Southold JSHS   500/7-12
  PO Box 40 11971   631-765-5081
  Mary Fitzpatrick, prin.   Fax 765-5086

South Otselic, Chenango
Georgetown-South Otselic Central SD   400/K-12
  PO Box 161 13155   315-653-7591
  Larry Thomas, supt.   Fax 653-7500
Otselic Valley JSHS   200/7-12
  PO Box 161 13155   315-653-7218
  Toni DeMott, prin.   Fax 653-7500

South Ozone Park, See New York
NYC Department of Education
  Supt. — See New York
JHS 226   2,100/6-8
  12110 Rockaway Blvd 11420   718-843-2260
  Sonia Nieves, prin.   Fax 835-6317

South Salem, Westchester
Katonah Lewisboro UFD   4,100/K-12
  1 Shady Ln 10590   914-763-7000
  Dr. Robert V. Lichtenfeld, supt.   Fax 763-7033
  www.k-lschools.org
Other Schools – See Cross River

South Wales, Erie

Gow S   100/7-12
  PO Box 85 14139   585-652-3450
    Fax 652-3457

Sparkill, Rockland

St. Thomas Aquinas College   Post-Sec.
  125 Route 340 10976   845-398-4000

Spencer, Tioga, Pop. 715
Spencer-Van Etten Central SD
  Supt. — See Van Etten
Spencer MS   400/5-8
  1 Center St 14883   607-589-7120
  Marcia Bishop, prin.   Fax 589-3020
Spencer-Van Etten HS   400/9-12
  PO Box 307 14883   607-589-7140
  Ann Sincock, prin.   Fax 589-3010

Spencerport, Monroe, Pop. 3,560
Spencerport Central SD   4,400/K-12
  71 Lyell Ave 14559   585-349-5000
  Mary Anne Kermis, supt.   Fax 349-5011
  www.spencerportschools.org
Cosgrove MS   1,200/6-8
  2749 Spencerport Rd 14559   585-349-5300
  Michael Canny, prin.   Fax 349-5346
Spencerport HS   1,400/9-12
  2707 Spencerport Rd 14559   585-349-5200
  Ty Zinkiewich, prin.   Fax 349-5266

Springfield Gardens, See New York
NYC Department of Education
  Supt. — See New York
Carver HS for the Sciences   9-12
  14310 Springfield Blvd 11413   718-525-6439
  Janice Sutton, prin.   Fax 525-6482
Excelsior Preparatory HS   9-12
  14310 Springfield Blvd 11413   718-525-6507
  Derek Jones, prin.   Fax 525-6276
Queens Preparatory Academy   9-12
  14310 Springfield Blvd 11413   718-935-3375
  Tashon Haywood, prin.
Springfield Gardens HS   1,500/9-12
  14310 Springfield Blvd 11413   718-341-3033
  Elizabeth McCullough, prin.   Fax 525-8495
IS 59   1,400/6-8
  13255 Ridgedale St 11413   718-527-3501
  Carleton Gordon, prin.   Fax 276-1364
IS 231   1,400/6-8
  14500 Springfield Blvd 11413   718-276-5140
  Robert Brisbane, prin.   Fax 276-2259

Christopher Robin Academy   200/1-12
  22216 Merrick Blvd 11413   718-525-1330
  Robert Donus, prin.   Fax 978-6610

Spring Valley, Rockland, Pop. 25,509
East Ramapo Central SD   8,400/PK-12
  105 S Madison Ave 10977   845-577-6000
  Jason Friedman, supt.   Fax 577-6168
  www.ercsd.k12.ny.us/
Ramapo Freshman Center   9-9
  465 Viola Rd 10977   845-577-6100
    Fax 426-1059
Ramapo HS   1,300/10-12
  400 Viola Rd 10977   845-577-6400
    Fax 426-1124
Spring Valley HS   1,300/9-12
  361 Route 59 10977   845-577-6500
  Beverly Davis, prin.   Fax 426-1127
Other Schools – See Chestnut Ridge, Suffern

Monsey Academy for Girls   100/9-12
  246 N Main St 10977   845-356-3929
  Rivka Shear, prin.   Fax 356-0328
Sunbridge College   Post-Sec.
  285 Hungry Hollow Rd 10977   845-425-0055
SUNY Rockland Community College   Post-Sec.
  766 N Main St 10977   845-352-5535
SUNY Rockland Community College   Post-Sec.
  185 N Main St 10977   845-352-5535
United Talmudical Academy   1,300/K-12
  89 S Main St 10977   845-425-0392
  Yidel Spitzer, admin.   Fax 352-7253
Yeshiva Aviir Yaakov   2,200/PK-12
  PO Box 840 10977   845-362-6600
    Fax 354-6809
Yeshiva Degel Hatorah   200/K-12
  111 Maple Ave 10977   845-356-4610
  Rabbi Moshe Schwab, prin.   Fax 356-4507
Yeshiva Toras Chaim   50/9-11
  15 Fanley Ave 10977   845-352-9126
  Mayer Schlesinger, dir.

Springville, Erie, Pop. 4,367
Springville-Griffith Inst. Central SD   2,400/K-12
  307 Newman St 14141   716-592-3230
  Dr. Brenda Peters, supt.   Fax 592-8469
  www.springvillegi.wnyric.org
Griffith Institute HS   800/9-12
  290 N Buffalo St 14141   716-592-3237
  Philip Benson, prin.   Fax 592-0674
Griffith Institute MS   600/6-8
  267 Newman St 14141   716-592-3270
  Gary Cerne, prin.   Fax 592-0746

Staatsburg on Hudson, Dutchess
Hyde Park Central SD
  Supt. — See Hyde Park
Roosevelt HS   1,400/9-12
  154 S Cross Rd 12580   845-229-4020
  Alan Gonzalez, prin.   Fax 229-4029

Stamford, Delaware, Pop. 1,223
Stamford Central SD, 1 River St 12167   500/K-12
  Gregory Sanik, supt.   607-652-7301
Stamford Central S   500/K-12
  1 River St 12167   607-652-7301
  Julie Mable, prin.   Fax 652-3446

Star Lake, Saint Lawrence, Pop. 1,092
Clifton-Fine Central SD   400/PK-12
  11 Hall Ave 13690   315-848-3335
  Dr. Paul Alioto, supt.
Clifton-Fine JSHS   200/7-12
  11 Hall Ave 13690   315-848-3333
  Susan Shene, prin.   Fax 848-3350

Staten Island, See New York
NYC Department of Education
  Supt. — See New York
CSI HS for International Studies   9-12
  2800 Victory Blvd 10314   718-982-3460
  Aimee Horowitz, prin.
Curtis HS   2,400/9-12
  105 Hamilton Ave 10301   718-273-7380
  Aurelia Curtis, prin.   Fax 273-9657
McKee Career and Technical HS   Vo/Tech
  290 Saint Marks Pl 10301   718-420-2600
  Linda Waite, prin.   Fax 981-8776
New Dorp HS   2,100/9-12
  465 New Dorp Ln 10306   718-667-8686
  Deirdre DeAngelis, prin.   Fax 987-4889
Port Richmond HS   2,600/9-12
  85 Saint Josephs Ave 10302   718-273-3600
  Tim Gannon, prin.   Fax 981-6203
Public S 721   Vo/Tech
  155 Tompkins Ave 10304   718-273-8622
  Mary McInerney, prin.   Fax 727-6994
South Richmond HS   Vo/Tech
  6581 Hylan Blvd 10309   718-984-1526
  William Bates, prin.   Fax 356-8905
IS 2   1,000/6-8
  333 Midland Ave 10306   718-987-5336
  Michelena Dibuono, prin.   Fax 987-6937
IS 7   1,300/6-8
  1270 Huguenot Ave 10312   718-356-2314
  Dr. Nora Derosa-Karby, prin.   Fax 967-0809
IS 24   1,500/6-8
  225 Cleveland Ave 10308   718-356-4200
  Rosemarie O'Neill, prin.   Fax 356-5834
IS 27   800/6-8
  11 Clove Lake Pl 10310   718-981-8800
  Dennis Bellantoni, prin.   Fax 815-4677
IS 34   1,200/6-8
  528 Academy Ave 10307   718-984-0772
  Jeffrey Preston, prin.   Fax 227-4074
IS 49   1,000/6-8
  101 Warren St 10304   718-727-6040
  Linda Hill, prin.   Fax 876-8207
IS 51   1,400/6-8
  20 Houston St 10302   718-981-0502
  Emma Della Rocca, prin.   Fax 815-3957
IS 61   1,200/6-8
  445 Castleton Ave 10301   718-727-8481
  Richard Gallo, prin.   Fax 447-2112
IS 72   1,900/6-8
  33 Ferndale Ave 10314   718-698-5757
  Peter Macellari, prin.   Fax 761-5928
IS 75   1,500/6-8
  455 Huguenot Ave 10312   718-356-0130
  Mark F. Cannizzaro, prin.   Fax 984-5302
Staten Island Tech HS   Vo/Tech
  485 Clawson St 10306   718-667-5725
  Vincent Minsicalco, prin.   Fax 987-5872
Tottenville HS   3,900/9-12
  100 Luten Ave 10312   718-356-2220
  John Tuminaro, prin.   Fax 317-0962
Wagner HS   2,600/9-12
  1200 Manor Rd 10314   718-698-4200
  Gary M. Giordano, prin.   Fax 698-5213

CUNY College of Staten Island   Post-Sec.
  2800 Victory Blvd 10314   718-982-2000
Francis HS   200/9-12
  4240 Amboy Rd 10308   718-967-0400
Monsignor Farrell HS   1,200/9-12
  2900 Amboy Rd 10306   718-987-2900
  Fr. John Paddock, prin.   Fax 987-4241
Moore Catholic HS   800/9-12
  100 Merrill Ave 10314   718-761-9200
  Douglas McManus, prin.   Fax 982-7779
Notre Dame Academy   400/9-12
  134 Howard Ave 10301   718-447-8878
  Dr. Gregory Rossicone, prin.   Fax 447-2926
St. John's University   Post-Sec.
  300 Howard Ave 10301   718-447-4343
St. John Villa Academy   600/9-12
  26 Landis Ave 10305   718-442-6240
  Sr. Antonia Zuffante, prin.   Fax 447-6729
St. Joseph by the Sea HS   1,400/9-12
  5150 Hylan Blvd 10312   718-984-6500
  Rev. Joseph Ansaldi, prin.   Fax 984-6503
St. Joseph Hill Academy   400/9-12
  850 Hylan Blvd 10305   718-447-1374
  Angela Ferrando, prin.   Fax 447-3041
St. Peter's Boys HS   700/9-12
  200 Clinton Ave 10301   718-447-1676
  John Fodera, prin.   Fax 447-4027
St. Peter's Girls HS   200/9-12
  300 Richmond Ter 10301   718-447-0304
  Florence Bricker, prin.   Fax 447-0832
St. Vincent's Medical Center   Post-Sec.
  355 Bard Ave 10310   718-876-2413
Sisters of Charity Medical Center   Post-Sec.
  75 Vanderbilt Ave 10304   718-818-6470
Staten Island Academy   400/PK-12
  715 Todt Hill Rd 10304   718-987-8100
  Diane J. Hulse, hdmstr.   Fax 979-7641
Wagner College   Post-Sec.
  1 Campus Rd 10301   718-390-3100
Yeshiva & Mesvita of Staten Island   50/9-12
  1870 Drumgoole Rd E 10309   718-356-4323
  Shloma Eidelman, dir.   Fax 356-5200
Yeshiva Tiferes Torah   200/9-12
  5 Birchard Ave 10314   718-982-0239

Stillwater, Saratoga, Pop. 1,670
Stillwater Central SD   1,300/K-12
  334 Hudson Ave 12170   518-373-6100
  Donald Flynt, supt.   Fax 664-9134

Stillwater HS 700/6-12
 334 Hudson Ave 12170 518-373-6100
 Roger Fedele, prin. Fax 664-1832

Stone Ridge, Ulster

Ulster County Community College Post-Sec.
 12484 845-687-5000

Stony Brook, Suffolk, Pop. 13,726
Three Village Central SD
 Supt. — See East Setauket
 Murphy JHS, 351 Oxhead Rd 11790 900/7-9
 Vincent Vizzo, prin. 631-730-4800

Stony Brook S 300/7-12
 1 Chapman Pkwy 11790 631-751-1800
 Robert Gustafson, hdmstr. Fax 751-4211
 SUNY at Stony Brook 11794 Post-Sec.
 631-689-6000

Suffern, Rockland, Pop. 11,014
East Ramapo Central SD
 Supt. — See Spring Valley
 Pomona MS 900/8-9
 101 Pomona Rd 10901 845-577-6200
 Brenda Shannon, prin. Fax 577-6245

Ramapo Central SD
 Supt. — See Hillburn
Suffern HS 1,400/9-12
 49 Viola Rd 10901 845-357-3800
 Patrick Faherty, prin. Fax 357-5035
Suffern JHS 1,100/6-8
 80 Hemion Rd 10901 845-357-7400
 Diana Jabis, prin. Fax 357-4563

Bat Torah - Alisa M. Flatow Yeshiva HS 100/9-12
 4 Campbell Ave 10901 845-357-0774
 Miriam S. Bak, prin. Fax 357-9482
Shaarei Torah of Rockland 100/9-12
 91 Carlton Rd W 10901 845-352-3431
 Rabbi Mordechai Wolmark, admin. Fax 352-3433
SUNY Rockland Community College Post-Sec.
 145 College Rd 10901 845-574-4000
Yeshiva Ohr Reuven 100/9-12
 259 Grandview Ave 10901 845-362-8362
 Rabbi Bezalel Rudinsky, prin. Fax 354-4830
Yeshiva Shaarei Torah of Rockland Post-Sec.
 91 Carlton Rd W 10901 845-352-3431

Syosset, Nassau, Pop. 18,967
Syosset Central SD 6,500/K-12
 99 Pell Ln 11791 516-364-5600
 Dr. Carole Hankin, supt. Fax 921-5616
 www.syosset.k12.ny.us
South Woods MS 700/6-8
 99 Pell Ln 11791 516-364-5621
 Michelle Burget, prin. Fax 921-5616
Syosset HS 2,000/9-12
 70 Southwoods Rd 11791 516-364-5675
 Jorge Schneider, prin. Fax 921-5616
Thompson MS 900/6-8
 98 Ann Dr 11791 516-364-5760
 James Kassebaum, prin. Fax 921-5616

Culinary Academy of Long Island Post-Sec.
 125 Michael Dr 11791 516-364-4344
New York College of Health Professions Post-Sec.
 6801 Jericho Tpke 11791 516-364-0808
Our Lady of Mercy Academy 500/9-12
 815 Convent Ave 11791 516-921-1047
 Sr. Adrienne Ryniewicz, prin. Fax 921-3634
Torah Academy of Long Island 50/7-12
 310A S Oyster Bay Rd # 100 11791 516-364-6262
 Myrna Wohlberg, prin. Fax 364-6299

Syracuse, Onondaga, Pop. 144,001
Solvay UFD
 Supt. — See Solvay
Solvay MS 600/4-8
 299 Bury Dr 13209 315-487-7061
 James Werbeck, prin. Fax 484-1444

Syracuse CSD 21,900/PK-12
 725 Harrison St 13210 315-435-4161
 Robert DiFlorio Ph.D., supt. Fax 435-4015
 www.syracusecityschools.com/
Central Technical-Vocational Center Vo/Tech
 258 E Adams St 13202 315-435-4300
 Donnell Hicks, prin. Fax 435-5816
Clary Magnet MS 700/6-8
 100 Amidon Dr 13205 315-435-4411
 Iverna Minor, prin. Fax 435-5832
Corcoran HS 1,400/9-12
 919 Glenwood Ave 13207 315-435-4321
 Brian Nolan, prin. Fax 435-4024
Danforth Magnet MS 500/6-8
 309 W Brighton Ave 13205 315-435-4535
 Florence Williams, prin. Fax 435-6208
Fowler HS 1,300/9-12
 227 Magnolia St 13204 315-435-4376
 Milagros Escalera, prin. Fax 435-6313
Grant MS 900/6-8
 2400 Grant Blvd 13208 315-435-4433
 Gwen McKinnon, prin. Fax 435-4856
Henninger HS 1,700/9-12
 600 Robinson St 13206 315-435-4343
 David Cecile, prin. Fax 435-6277
Johnson Vocational Center Vo/Tech
 573 E Genesee St 13202 315-435-4135
 Donnell Hicks, prin. Fax 435-6599
Levy MS 500/7-8
 111 Fellows Ave 13210 315-435-4444
 Lynne Kelly, prin. Fax 435-4443
Lincoln MS 700/6-8
 1613 James St 13203 315-435-4450
 Robert DiFlorio, prin. Fax 435-4455
Nottingham HS 1,300/9-12
 3100 E Genesee St 13224 315-435-4380
 Debra Mastropaolo, prin. Fax 435-4177

Shea MS 600/6-8
 1607 S Geddes St 13207 315-435-4480
 Margaret Morone Wilson, prin. Fax 435-6232
Westhill Central SD 2,000/K-12
 400 Walberta Rd 13219 315-426-3218
 Stephen A. Bocciolatt, supt. Fax 488-6411
 www.westhillschools.org/
Onondaga Hill MS 700/5-8
 4860 Onondaga Rd 13215 315-426-3400
 Douglas Hutson, prin. Fax 492-0156
Westhill HS 700/9-12
 4501 Onondaga Blvd 13219 315-426-3100
 Grenardo Avellino, prin. Fax 475-0319

Bishop Ludden HS 800/9-12
 815 Fay Rd 13219 315-468-2591
 Dennis Meehan, prin. Fax 468-0097
Bryant & Stratton College Post-Sec.
 953 James St 13203 315-472-6603
Christian Brothers Academy 700/7-12
 6245 Randall Rd 13214 315-446-5960
 Br. Thomas Zoppo, prin. Fax 446-3393
Crouse Hospital School of Nursing Post-Sec.
 736 Irving Ave 13210 315-470-7481
Faith Heritage S 500/PK-12
 3740 Midland Ave 13205 315-469-7777
 Lawrence Falco, hdmstr. Fax 492-7440
Le Moyne College Post-Sec.
 1419 Salt Springs Rd 13214 315-445-4100
Living Word Academy 200/PK-12
 6101 Court Street Rd 13206 315-437-6744
 Philip Mastroleo, prin. Fax 437-6766
Onondaga Community College Post-Sec.
 4941 Onondaga Rd 13215 315-498-2622
Phillips Hairstyling Institute Post-Sec.
 709 E Genesee St 13210 315-422-9656
St. Joseph's Hospital College of Nursing Post-Sec.
 206 Prospect Ave 13203 315-448-5040
Simmons Institute of Funeral Service Post-Sec.
 1828 South Ave 13207 315-475-5142
SUNY College Environ. Science - Forestry Post-Sec.
 1 Forestry Dr 13210 315-470-6500
SUNY Empire State College Post-Sec.
 219 Walton St Fl 1 13202 315-472-5799
SUNY Upstate Medical University Post-Sec.
 750 E Adams St 13210 315-464-5540
Syracuse University 13244 Post-Sec.
 315-443-1870

Tannersville, Greene, Pop. 444
Hunter-Tannersville Central SD 500/PK-12
 PO Box 1018 12485 518-589-5400
 Ralph Marino, prin. Fax 589-5403
 www.huntertannersvillecsd.org
Tannersville MSHS 300/7-12
 6094 Main St 12485 518-589-5880
 Thomas Averill, prin. Fax 589-7071

Tarrytown, Westchester, Pop. 11,411

Hackley S 800/K-12
 293 Benedict Ave 10591 914-631-0128
 Walter Johnson, hdmstr. Fax 366-2636
Marymount College Post-Sec.
 100 Marymount Ave 10591 914-631-3200

Thiells, Rockland, Pop. 5,204
Haverstraw-Stony Point Central SD
 Supt. — See Garnerville
Fieldstone Secondary S 8-9
 100 Fieldstone Dr 10984 845-942-7900
 Frank Parrino, prin. Fax 942-7910
North Rockland HS 1,900/10-12
 106 Hammond Rd 10984 845-942-3300
 Dennis Hand, prin. Fax 942-3365

Thornwood, Westchester, Pop. 7,025
Mt. Pleasant Central SD 1,800/K-12
 825 Westlake Dr 10594 914-769-5500
 Dr. Alfred Lodovico, supt. Fax 769-3733
 www.mtplcsd.org
Westlake HS 500/9-12
 825 Westlake Dr 10594 914-769-8311
 Frank Viteritti, prin. Fax 769-0596
Westlake MS 500/5-8
 825 Westlake Dr 10594 914-769-8541
 Jerry Schulman, prin. Fax 769-8550

Ticonderoga, Essex, Pop. 2,726
Ticonderoga Central SD 1,100/K-12
 9 Amherst Ave 12883 518-585-6674
 John McDonald, supt. Fax 585-2682
 www.ticonderogak12.org
Ticonderoga HS 400/9-12
 5 Calkins Pl 12883 518-585-6661
 Michael Graney, prin. Fax 585-5282
Ticonderoga MS 300/6-8
 116 Alexandria Ave 12883 518-585-7442
 Bruce Tubbs, prin. Fax 585-2716

SUNY North Country Community College Post-Sec.
 PO Box 311 12883 518-585-4454

Tioga Center, Tioga
Tioga Central SD 1,200/K-12
 3 5th Ave 13845 607-687-8000
 Patrick Dougherty, supt. Fax 687-8007
Tioga HS 400/9-12
 27 5th Ave 13845 607-687-8001
 Scot Taylor, prin. Fax 687-8010
Tioga MS 400/5-8
 27 5th Ave 13845 607-687-8004
 Cynthia Bennett, prin. Fax 687-6910

Tonawanda, Erie, Pop. 15,700
Kenmore-Tonawanda UFSD
 Supt. — See Buffalo
Kenmore East HS 1,200/9-12
 350 Fries Rd 14150 716-874-8402
 Fax 874-8443

Tonawanda CSD 2,200/K-12
 202 Broad St 14150 716-694-7784
 George W. Batterson Ed.D., supt. Fax 695-8738
 www.tona.wnyric.org
Tonawanda HS 700/9-12
 150 Hinds St 14150 716-694-7670
 Susan Frey, prin. Fax 694-7692
Tonawanda MS 600/6-8
 600 Fletcher St 14150 716-694-7660
 James Newton, prin. Fax 694-4597

Cardinal O'Hara HS 300/9-12
 39 Ohara Rd 14150 716-695-2600
 Michael Powers, prin. Fax 692-8697
MarJon School of Beauty Culture Post-Sec.
 1154 Niagara Falls Blvd 14150 716-836-6240

Troy, Rensselaer, Pop. 48,649
Brunswick Central SD 1,200/K-12
 3992 State Highway 2 12180 518-279-4600
 Dr. Teresa Snyder, supt. Fax 279-1918
 www.brittonkill.k12.ny.us
Tamarac MSHS 600/6-12
 3992 State Highway 2 12180 518-279-4600
 Christopher Rockwell, prin. Fax 279-3888

Lansingburgh Central SD 2,300/K-12
 576 5th Ave 12182 518-233-6850
 Lee Bordick, supt.
 www.lansingburgh.org
Knickerbacker MS 600/6-8
 320 7th Ave 12182 518-233-6811
 Shaun Paolino, prin. Fax 238-2518
Lansingburgh HS 700/9-12
 320 7th Ave 12182 518-233-6806
 Angelina Bergin, prin. Fax 233-6826

Troy CSD 4,300/PK-12
 1728 Tibbits Ave 12180 518-271-5210
 Lonnie Palmer, supt. Fax 271-5229
 www.troy.k12.ny.us/
Doyle MS 800/6-8
 1976 Burdett Ave 12180 518-271-5350
 James Canfield, prin. Fax 271-8160
Troy HS 1,400/9-12
 1950 Burdett Ave 12180 518-271-5300
 Dr. Brigitte Garrison, prin. Fax 274-2341

Catholic Central HS 500/7-12
 625 7th Ave 12182 518-235-7100
 Michael Piatek, prin. Fax 237-1796
La Salle Institute 600/6-12
 174 Williams Rd 12180 518-283-2500
 Robert Herzog, prin. Fax 283-6265
Oakwood Christian S 100/9-12
 260 Oakwood Ave 12182 518-271-0526
 James DuJack, hdmstr. Fax 270-1659
Redemption Christian Academy 100/PK-12
 PO Box 753 12181 518-272-6679
 John Massey, prin. Fax 270-8039
Rensselaer Polytechnic Institute Post-Sec.
 110 8th St 12180 518-276-6000
Russell Sage College Post-Sec.
 45 Ferry St 12180 518-244-2000
Russell Sage Graduate School Post-Sec.
 45 Ferry St 12180 518-244-2264
Samaritan Hospital School of Nursing Post-Sec.
 2215 Burdett Ave 12180 518-271-3285
SUNY Hudson Valley Community College Post-Sec.
 80 Vandenburgh Ave 12180 518-629-4822
Troy School of Beauty Culture Post-Sec.
 86 Congress St 12180 518-273-7741
Willard S 300/9-12
 285 Pawling Ave 12180 518-833-1300
 Trudy Hall, prin. Fax 833-1800

Trumansburg, Tompkins, Pop. 1,615
Trumansburg Central SD 1,400/K-12
 100 Whig St 14886 607-387-7551
 Cosimo Tangorra, supt. Fax 387-2807
 www.tburg.k12.ny.us
Dickerson HS 500/9-12
 100 Whig St 14886 607-387-7551
 Paula Hurley, prin. Fax 387-2807
Doig MS 500/5-8
 100 Whig St 14886 607-387-7551
 Gary Astles, prin. Fax 387-2807

Tuckahoe, Westchester, Pop. 6,243
Tuckahoe UFD 1,000/K-12
 29 Elm St 10707 914-337-6600
 Michael Yazurlo Ed.D., supt. Fax 337-3072
 www.tuckahoeschools.org/
Other Schools – See Eastchester

St. Vladimir's Orthodox Theological Sem. Post-Sec.
 575 Scarsdale Rd 10707 914-961-8313

Tully, Onondaga, Pop. 907
Tully Central SD 1,200/K-12
 PO Box 628 13159 315-696-6204
 Kraig Pritts, supt. Fax 696-6251
 www.tully.k12.ny.us/
Tully JSHS 600/7-12
 PO Box 628 13159 315-696-6235
 Curt Czarniak, prin. Fax 696-6237

Tupper Lake, Franklin, Pop. 3,900
Tupper Lake Central SD 1,100/K-12
 294 Hosley Ave 12986 518-359-3371
 Daniel Bower, supt. Fax 359-7862
 www.tupperlakecsd.net/
Tupper Lake MSHS 600/7-12
 25 Chaney Ave 12986 518-359-3322
 Pamela Martin, prin. Fax 359-7862

Turin, Lewis, Pop. 252
South Lewis Central SD 1,200/K-12
 PO Box 10 13473 315-348-2500
 Frank House, supt. Fax 348-2510
 www.southlewis.org

South Lewis HS 400/9-12
PO Box 40 13473 315-348-2520
Dr. Dan McPhail, prin. Fax 348-2510
South Lewis MS 300/6-8
PO Box 70 13473 315-348-2570
Philomena Goss, prin. Fax 348-2510

Tuxedo Park, Orange, Pop. 733
Tuxedo UFD 600/K-12
PO Box 2002 10987 845-351-4799
Joseph Zanetti, supt. Fax 351-5296
tuxedoschooldistrict.com
Baker HS 400/9-12
PO Box 2002 10987 845-351-4786
Denis Petrilak, prin. Fax 351-4823

Uniondale, Nassau, Pop. 20,328
Uniondale UFD 6,300/K-12
933 Goodrich St 11553 516-560-8824
William K. Lloyd Ph.D., supt. Fax 292-2659
www.uniondale.k12.ny.us
Turtle Hook MS 700/6-8
975 Jerusalem Ave 11553 516-918-1300
Annette O'Ferrall, prin. Fax 505-2533
Uniondale HS 1,800/9-12
933 Goodrich St 11553 516-560-8831
Florence Simmons, prin. Fax 564-8464
Other Schools – See Hempstead

Hebrew Academy of Nassau County 400/7-12
215 Oak St 11553 516-538-8161
Rabbi Joshua Schonbrun, prin. Fax 489-1142
Kellenberg Memorial HS 1,900/6-12
1400 Glenn Curtiss Blvd 11553 516-292-0200
Br. Ken Hoagland, prin. Fax 292-0877

Union Springs, Cayuga, Pop. 1,072
Union Springs Central SD 900/K-12
239 Cayuga St 13160 315-889-4101
Linda Rice, supt. Fax 889-4108
Union Springs HS 400/9-12
239 Cayuga St 13160 315-889-4110
Kimberle Ward, prin. Fax 889-4118
Union Springs MS 7-8
239 Cayuga St 13160 315-889-4112
Donald Beckers, prin. Fax 889-4108

Union Springs Academy 50/9-12
PO Box 524 13160 315-889-7314
Fax 889-7188

Upper Nyack, Rockland, Pop. 1,884
Nyack UFD
Supt. — See Nyack
Nyack HS 900/9-12
360 Christian Herald Rd 10960 845-353-7100
Phyllis Aliberto, prin. Fax 353-7119

Utica, Oneida, Pop. 59,485
Utica CSD 8,000/K-12
1115 Mohawk St 13501 315-792-2222
Marilyn Skermont, supt. Fax 792-2200
www.uticaschools.org
Donovan MS 900/7-9
1701 Noyes St 13502 315-792-2007
John Licari, prin. Fax 792-2077
Kennedy MS 800/6-8
500 Deerfield Dr E 13502 315-792-2086
Bruce Karam, prin. Fax 792-2084
Proctor HS, 1203 Hilton Ave 13501 1,600/9-12
Dolores Chainey, prin. 315-368-6100

Faxton-St. Luke's Healthcare Post-Sec.
PO Box 479 13503 315-624-6136
Mohawk Valley Community College Post-Sec.
1101 Sherman Dr 13501 315-792-5400
Munson-Williams-Proctor Institute Post-Sec.
310 Genesee St 13502 315-797-8260
Notre Dame JSHS 600/7-12
2 Notre Dame Ln 13502 315-724-5118
Bill Scott, prin. Fax 724-9460
St. Elizabeth College of Nursing Post-Sec.
2215 Genesee St 13501 315-798-8125
SUNY Institute of Technology Utica/Rome Post-Sec.
PO Box 3050 13504 315-792-7100
Tilton S at the House of Good Shepherd 100/1-11
1550 Champlin Ave 13502 315-235-7671
David Williams, dir. Fax 235-7609
Utica College Post-Sec.
1600 Burrstone Rd 13502 315-792-3111
Utica School of Commerce Post-Sec.
201 Bleecker St 13501 315-733-2307

Valatie, Columbia, Pop. 1,818
Kinderhook Central SD 2,300/K-12
2910 Route 9 12184 518-758-7575
James Dexter, supt. Fax 758-7579
www.berk.com/~ichabod/
Crane HS 700/9-12
2910 US Route 09 12184 518-758-7577
L. Collett, prin. Fax 758-2181
Crane MS 600/5-8
2910 US Route 09 12184 518-758-7676
Maureen Van Duesen, prin. Fax 758-7579

Academy of Christian Leadership 50/6-12
3429 Route 9 12184 518-784-2222
Jim Ogden, admin.

Valhalla, Westchester, Pop. 6,200
Valhalla UFD 1,400/K-12
316 Columbus Ave 10595 914-683-5040
Dr. Diane Ramos-Kelly, supt. Fax 683-5075
Valhalla HS 400/9-12
300 Columbus Ave 10595 914-683-5014
Jerry Salese, prin. Fax 683-5003
Valhalla MS 300/6-8
300 Columbus Ave 10595 914-683-5011
Fax 683-5003

New York Medical College 10595 Post-Sec.
914-594-4000

Westchester Community College Post-Sec.
75 Grasslands Rd 10595 914-785-6600
Westchester County Medical Center Post-Sec.
Grasslands Rd 10595 914-285-7276

Valley Stream, Nassau, Pop. 36,214
Valley Stream Central HSD 4,500/7-12
1 Kent Rd 11580 516-872-5601
Dr. R. Marc Bernstein, supt. Fax 872-5658
vschsd.org
Valley Stream Central SHS 1,000/10-12
135 Fletcher Ave 11580 516-561-4410
Joseph Pompilio, prin. Fax 561-4490
Valley Stream Memorial JHS 1,100/7-9
320 Fletcher Ave 11580 516-872-7710
Dr. Kathleen Walsh, prin. Fax 872-7711
Valley Stream South JSHS 1,300/7-12
150 Jedwood Pl 11581 516-791-0310
Dr. Stephen Lando, prin. Fax 791-0305
Other Schools – See Franklin Square

Business Informatics Center Post-Sec.
134 S Central Ave 11580 516-561-0050
Mesivta Or Chadash 100/9-12
322 N Corona Ave 11580 516-561-5090
Rabbi Boruch Gotteman, prin. Fax 561-5091

Van Etten, Chemung, Pop. 577
Spencer-Van Etten Central SD 1,100/PK-12
PO Box 307 14889 607-589-7100
Steven Schoonmaker, supt. Fax 589-3010
www.s-ve.org
Other Schools – See Spencer

Van Hornesville, Herkimer
Owen Young Central SD 200/K-12
PO Box 125 13475 315-858-0729
James Christmann, supt. Fax 858-2019
Young Central S 200/K-12
PO Box 125 13475 315-858-0729
James Christmann, prin. Fax 858-2019

Verona, Oneida
Vernon-Verona-Sherrill Central SD 2,400/PK-12
PO Box 128 13478 315-829-2520
Norman Reed, supt. Fax 829-4949
www.vvscentralschools.org/
Vernon-Verona-Sherrill HS 700/9-12
PO Box 128 13478 315-829-2520
Mark Wixson, prin. Fax 829-4465
Vernon-Verona-Sherrill MS 400/7-8
PO Box 128 13478 315-829-2520
James Kramer, prin. Fax 829-5966

Vestal, Broome, Pop. 5,000
Vestal Central SD 4,200/K-12
201 Main St 13850 607-757-2241
Mark A. Capobianco, supt. Fax 757-2227
www.vestal.stier.org
Vestal HS 1,300/9-12
205 Woodlawn Dr 13850 607-757-2281
Catherine Hepler, prin. Fax 757-2301
Vestal MS 1,100/6-8
600 S Benita Blvd 13850 607-757-2331
Ann Marie Loose, prin. Fax 757-2229

Ross Corners Christian Academy 300/PK-12
2101 Owego Rd 13850 607-748-3301
Toby Wyse, admin. Fax 748-3301

Victor, Ontario, Pop. 2,526
Victor Central SD 3,600/PK-12
953 High St 14564 585-924-3252
Timothy McElheran, supt. Fax 742-7090
www.victorschools.org
Victor HS 1,000/9-12
953 High St 14564 585-924-3252
Yvonne O'Shea, prin. Fax 924-9536
Victor JHS 500/7-8
953 High St 14564 585-924-3252
Miryam Matulic-Keller, prin. Fax 924-9535

Voorheesville, Albany, Pop. 2,810
Voorheesville Central SD 1,300/K-12
432 New Salem Rd 12186 518-765-3313
Linda Langevin, supt. Fax 765-2751
vcsd.neric.org/
Bouton MSHS 700/7-12
432 New Salem Rd 12186 518-765-3314
Mark Diefendorf, prin. Fax 765-5547

Wallkill, Ulster, Pop. 2,125
Wallkill Central SD 3,500/K-12
PO Box 310 12589 845-895-7100
Anthony Argulewicz, supt. Fax 895-3630
www.wallkillcsd.k12.ny.us
Wallkill HS 1,200/9-12
PO Box 310 12589 845-895-7150
David Bernsley, prin. Fax 895-8003
Wallkill MS 600/7-8
PO Box 310 12589 845-895-7175
Jason Doyle, prin. Fax 895-8036

Walton, Delaware, Pop. 2,953
Walton Central SD 1,100/K-12
47-49 Stockton Ave 13856 607-865-4116
Jonathan Buhner, supt. Fax 865-8568
www.waltoncsd.stier.org/
Walton HS 400/9-12
47-49 Stockton Ave 13856 607-865-4116
Michael Snider, prin. Fax 865-6130
Walton MS 300/6-8
47-49 Stockton Ave 13856 607-865-4116
Michael A. MacDonald, prin. Fax 865-8568

Walworth, Wayne
Gananda Central SD 1,200/K-12
1500 Dayspring Rdg 14568 315-986-3521
Patricia Roach, supt. Fax 986-2003
www.Gananda.org
Gananda / Cirillo HS 300/9-12
3195 Wiedrick Rd 14568 315-986-3521
Ken Dehn, prin. Fax 986-2003

Gananda MS 300/6-8
1500 Dayspring Rdg 14568 315-986-3521
Matthew Mahoney, prin. Fax 986-2003

Wampsville, Madison, Pop. 576
Oneida CSD
Supt. — See Oneida
Shortell MS 400/7-8
PO Box 716 13163 315-363-1050
Robin Price, prin. Fax 366-0622

Wantagh, Nassau, Pop. 18,567
Wantagh UFD 3,600/K-12
3301 Beltagh Ave 11793 516-781-8000
Carl Bonuso, supt. Fax 781-6076
www.wantaghschools.org
Wantagh HS 1,000/9-12
3297 Beltagh Ave 11793 516-679-6402
Terrance O'Connor, prin. Fax 679-6432
Wantagh MS 800/6-8
3299 Beltagh Ave 11793 516-679-6350
Dr. Jeannette Stern, prin. Fax 679-6311

Wappingers Falls, Dutchess, Pop. 4,991
Wappingers Central SD 11,800/K-12
167 Myers Corners Rd 12590 845-298-5000
Richard A. Powell, supt. Fax 298-5041
wappingersschools.org
Ketcham HS 1,700/9-12
99 Myers Corners Rd 12590 845-298-5100
Sherrill Lazarus, prin. Fax 298-5099
Van Wyck JHS 1,300/6-8
10 Hillside Lake Rd 12590 845-227-1700
Steve Shuchat, prin. Fax 221-2607
Wappingers Falls JHS 900/7-8
30 Major MacDonald Way 12590 845-298-5200
Cheryl Musante, prin. Fax 297-9620
Other Schools – See Hopewell Junction

Warrensburg, Warren, Pop. 3,204
Warrensburg Central SD 900/K-12
103 Schroon River Rd 12885 518-623-2861
Timothy Lawson, supt. Fax 623-2436
www.wcsd.org/
Warrensburg JSHS 400/7-12
103 Schroon River Rd 12885 518-623-2862
Daniel Roberts, prin. Fax 623-5089

Warsaw, Wyoming, Pop. 3,737
Warsaw Central SD 900/K-12
153 W Buffalo St 14569 585-786-8000
Philip D'Angelo, supt. Fax 786-8008
www.warsaw.k12.ny.us/
Warsaw HS 400/9-12
81 W Court St 14569 585-786-8000
Marc Czadzeck, prin. Fax 786-3193
Warsaw MS 6-8
81 W Court St 14569 585-786-8000
Gregory Feller, prin. Fax 786-3193

Warwick, Orange, Pop. 6,548
Warwick Valley Central SD 4,600/K-12
PO Box 595 10990 845-987-3000
Dr. Joseph Natale, supt. Fax 987-1147
www.warwickvalleyschools.com
Warwick Valley HS 1,600/9-12
PO Box 595 10990 845-987-3050
Randy Barbarash, prin. Fax 987-8982
Warwick Valley MS 1,100/6-8
PO Box 595 10990 845-987-3100
Virginia Lynch, prin. Fax 986-6942

Washingtonville, Orange, Pop. 6,243
Washingtonville Central SD 5,000/K-12
52 W Main St 10992 845-497-2200
Dr. Marilyn Pirkle, supt. Fax 496-2330
www.ws.k12.ny.us
Washingtonville HS 1,700/9-12
54 W Main St 10992 845-497-2200
Michael Rossi, prin. Fax 496-2212
Washingtonville MS 1,200/6-8
38 W Main St 10992 845-497-2200
Maureen Peterson, prin. Fax 496-2099

Waterford, Saratoga, Pop. 2,183
Waterford-Halfmoon UFD 900/K-12
125 Middletown Rd 12188 518-237-0800
Carl Klossner, supt. Fax 237-7335
www.whufsd.org
Waterford-Halfmoon HS 200/9-12
125 Middletown Rd 12188 518-237-0800
John Polnak, prin. Fax 237-7335
Waterford-Halfmoon MS 300/5-8
125 Middletown Rd 12188 518-237-0800
Christine Barry, prin. Fax 237-7335

Waterloo, Seneca, Pop. 5,132
Waterloo Central SD 2,000/K-12
109 Washington St 13165 315-539-1500
Randy Bos, supt. Fax 539-1504
www.flare.net/wcs/
Waterloo HS 600/9-12
65 Center St 13165 315-539-1550
John Butler, prin. Fax 539-1536
Waterloo MS 500/6-8
202 W Main St 13165 315-539-1540
Michael Ferrara, prin. Fax 539-1504

Watertown, Jefferson, Pop. 26,782
Watertown CSD 4,100/K-12
376 Butterfield Ave 13601 315-785-3700
Terry Fralick, supt. Fax 785-6855
www.watertowncsd.org
Case MS 600/7-8
1237 Washington St 13601 315-785-3870
Donald Whitney, prin. Fax 785-3731
Watertown HS 1,100/9-12
1335 Washington St 13601 315-785-3800
Stephen Williamson, prin. Fax 785-3733

Faith Fellowship Christian S 100/PK-12
131 Moore Ave 13601 315-782-9342
Donald Cronk, prin. Fax 786-0309

Immaculate Heart Central JSHS — 500/7-12
1316 Ives St 13601 — 315-788-4670
Pat Fontana, prin. — Fax 788-4672
Jefferson Community College — Post-Sec.
1220 Coffeen St 13601 — 315-786-2200
Samaritan Medical Center — Post-Sec.
830 Washington St 13601 — 315-785-4000

Waterville, Oneida, Pop. 1,690
Waterville Central SD — 1,000/K-12
381 Madison St 13480 — 315-841-3900
James Van Wormer, supt. — Fax 841-3939
Waterville JSHS — 600/6-12
381 Madison St 13480 — 315-841-3800
Sherri Walczak, prin. — Fax 841-3838

Watervliet, Albany, Pop. 10,052
Watervliet CSD — 1,400/K-12
1245 Hillside Dr 12189 — 518-629-3200
Paul Padalino, supt. — Fax 629-3265
vliet.neric.org/
Watervliet JSHS — 700/7-12
1245 Hillside Dr 12189 — 518-629-3200
Lori Caplan, prin.

Watkins Glen, Schuyler, Pop. 2,114
Watkins Glen Central SD — 1,300/K-12
301 12th St 14891 — 607-535-3219
Dr. Mary Ellen Correa, supt. — Fax 535-7238
www.sctboces.org/wgcsd
Watkins Glen Central HS — 400/9-12
301 12th St 14891 — 607-535-3210
David Warren, prin. — Fax 535-4629
Watkins Glen MS — 400/5-8
200 10th St 14891 — 607-535-3230
Kristine Somerville, prin. — Fax 535-4532

Waverly, Tioga, Pop. 4,515
Waverly Central SD — 1,800/K-12
15 Frederick St 14892 — 607-565-2841
Michael McMahon, supt. — Fax 565-4997
www.sctboces.org/waverly/
Waverly HS — 600/9-12
1 Frederick St 14892 — 607-565-8101
Kim Hollister, prin. — Fax 565-4997
Waverly MS, 1 Frederick St 14892 — 300/7-8
Diane Tymoski, prin. — 607-565-3410

Wawarsing, Ulster, Pop. 12,348

Wawarsing Christian Academy — 100/PK-12
PO Box 338 12489 — 845-647-3810
Ronald Mahany, admin. — Fax 647-1041

Wayland, Steuben, Pop. 1,851
Wayland-Cohocton Central SD — 1,800/PK-12
2350 State Route 63 14572 — 585-728-2211
Robert Cownie, supt. — Fax 728-3566
www.wccsk12.org
Wayland-Cohocton HS — 600/9-12
2350 State Route 63 14572 — 585-728-2366
William Whyte, prin. — Fax 728-2425
Wayland-Cohocton MS — 600/5-8
2350 State Route 63 14572 — 585-728-2551
Eileen Feinman, prin. — Fax 728-3556

Webster, Monroe, Pop. 5,175
Webster Central SD — 8,700/K-12
119 South Ave 14580 — 585-216-0000
Thomas Strining, supt. — Fax 265-6561
www.websterschools.org
Spry MS — 1,100/6-8
119 South Ave 14580 — 585-265-6500
Carol Clarke, prin. — Fax 265-6512
Thomas HS — 1,400/9-12
800 Five Mile Line Rd 14580 — 585-670-8000
John Walker, prin. — Fax 671-1884
Webster Schroeder HS — 1,500/9-12
875 Ridge Rd 14580 — 585-671-1880
Joseph Pustulka, prin. — Fax 671-8681
Willink MS — 1,100/6-8
900 Publishers Pkwy 14580 — 585-670-1030
Joseph Morgan, prin. — Fax 671-1978

Webster Christian S — 300/PK-12
675 Holt Rd 14580 — 585-872-5150
Keith Bell, admin. — Fax 872-5932

Weedsport, Cayuga, Pop. 1,985
Weedsport Central SD — 1,000/K-12
2821 E Brutus Street Rd 13166 — 315-834-6637
Shaun O'Connor, supt.
Weedsport JSHS — 600/6-12
2821 E Brutus Street Rd 13166 — 315-834-6652
Phillip Grome, prin. — Fax 834-8693

Wells, Hamilton
Wells Central SD — 200/PK-12
PO Box 300 12190 — 518-924-6000
Paul Williamson, supt. — Fax 924-9246
wells.neric.org
Wells S — 200/PK-12
PO Box 300 12190 — 518-924-6000
Paul Williamson, prin. — Fax 924-9246

Wellsville, Allegany, Pop. 4,833
Wellsville Central SD — 1,400/K-12
126 W State St 14895 — 585-596-2170
Byron Chandler Ed.D., supt. — Fax 596-2177
www.wellsville.wnyric.org
Wellsville HS — 500/9-12
126 W State St 14895 — 585-596-2188
Tyke Tooney, prin. — Fax 596-2180
Wellsville MS — 300/6-8
126 W State St 14895 — 585-596-2144
Mary Ellen O'Connell, prin. — Fax 596-2142

West Babylon, Suffolk, Pop. 43,700
West Babylon UFD — 4,900/K-12
10 Farmingdale Rd 11704 — 631-321-3142
Melvin Noble, supt. — Fax 661-5166
www.westbabylon.k12.ny.us

West Babylon HS — 1,500/9-12
500 Great East Neck Rd 11704 — 631-321-3003
Dr. Ellice Vassallo, prin. — Fax 321-3168
West Babylon JHS — 1,200/6-8
200 Old Farmingdale Rd 11704 — 631-321-3084
Michael Rizzo, prin. — Fax 321-3079

Commercial Driver Training School — Post-Sec.
600 Patton Ave 11704 — 631-249-1330

Westbury, Nassau, Pop. 14,283
East Meadow UFD — 8,000/K-12
718 The Plain Rd 11590 — 516-478-5776
Robert R. Dillon Ed.D., supt.
www.eastmeadow.k12.ny.us
Clarke HS — 900/9-12
740 Edgewood Dr 11590 — 516-876-7451
Dr. Vincent Cirello, prin. — Fax 876-7416
Clarke MS — 700/6-8
740 Edgewood Dr 11590 — 516-876-7401
Daniel Shewchuk, prin. — Fax 876-7407
Other Schools – See East Meadow

Westbury UFD
Supt. — See Old Westbury
Westbury MS — 900/6-8
455 Rockland St 11590 — 516-874-1208
Darnel Powell, prin. — Fax 876-5141

West Chazy, Clinton
Beekmantown Central SD — 2,100/K-12
37 Eagle Way 12992 — 518-563-8250
Mark Sposato Ed.D., supt. — Fax 563-8132
www.bcsdk12.org
Other Schools – See Plattsburgh

Westfield, Chautauqua, Pop. 3,480
Westfield Central SD — 900/K-12
203 E Main St 14787 — 716-326-2151
Laura Chabe, supt. — Fax 326-2195
www.wacs.wnyric.org/
Westfield HS — 300/9-12
203 E Main St 14787 — 716-326-2151
Jon Peterson, prin. — Fax 326-2157
Westfield MS — 200/6-8
203 E Main St 14787 — 716-326-2151
Jon Peterson, prin. — Fax 326-2157

Westhampton Beach, Suffolk, Pop. 1,949
Westhampton Beach UFD — 1,700/K-12
340 Mill Rd 11978 — 631-288-3800
Lynn Schwartz, supt. — Fax 288-8351
www.westhamptonbeach.k12.ny.us
Westhampton Beach HS — 900/9-12
49 Lilac Rd 11978 — 631-288-3800
Edward W. Casswell, prin. — Fax 288-3915
Westhampton Beach MS — 400/6-8
340 Mill Rd 11978 — 631-288-3800
Charisse Miller, prin. — Fax 288-5496

West Hempstead, Nassau, Pop. 17,689
West Hempstead UFD — 2,300/K-12
252 Chestnut St 11552 — 516-390-3107
Dr. Carol Eisenburg, supt. — Fax 489-1776
www.westhempstead.k12.ny.us
West Hempstead HS — 900/9-12
400 Nassau Blvd 11552 — 516-390-3214
Thomas Lee, prin. — Fax 489-1769
West Hempstead MS — 500/6-8
450 Nassau Blvd 11552 — 516-390-3160
Joseph Cirnigliaro, prin. — Fax 489-8946

West Henrietta, Monroe
Rush-Henrietta Central SD
Supt. — See Henrietta
Burger MS — 600/6-8
639 Erie Station Rd 14586 — 585-359-5308
Shawn Nelms, prin. — Fax 359-5333

West Islip, Suffolk, Pop. 29,000
West Islip UFD — 5,800/K-12
100 Sherman Ave 11795 — 631-893-3200
Beth Virginia Blau Ed.D., supt. — Fax 893-3212
www.westislipufsd.k12.ny.us/
Beach Street MS — 700/6-8
1765 Beach St 11795 — 631-893-3310
Anne Shierant, prin. — Fax 893-3318
Udall Road MS — 800/6-8
900 Udall Rd 11795 — 631-893-3290
Bernadette Burns, prin. — Fax 893-3301
West Islip HS — 1,700/9-12
3 Higbie Ln 11795 — 631-893-3250
Kenneth Hartill, prin. — Fax 893-3318

St. John the Baptist Diocesan HS — 900/9-12
1170 Montauk Hwy 11795 — 631-587-8000
Walter Lace, prin. — Fax 587-8996

Westmoreland, Oneida
Westmoreland Central SD — 1,200/K-12
5176 State Route 233 13490 — 315-557-2601
Antoinette Kulak, supt. — Fax 853-4602
Westmoreland HS — 400/9-12
5176 State Route 233 13490 — 315-557-2616
Rocco Migliori, prin. — Fax 853-4602
Westmoreland MS — 400/5-8
5176 State Route 233 13490 — 315-557-2618
Brian Kavanagh, prin. — Fax 853-4602

West Nyack, Rockland, Pop. 3,437
Clarkstown Central SD
Supt. — See New City
Clarkstown South HS — 1,400/9-12
31 Demarest Mill Rd 10994 — 845-624-3400
James Vitale, prin. — Fax 623-5470
Festa MS — 2,200/6-8
30 Parrott Rd 10994 — 845-639-6339
Dianne Basso, prin. — Fax 634-5874

West Point, Orange, Pop. 8,024

United States Military Academy — Post-Sec.
646 Swift Rd 10996 — 845-938-4041

Westport, Essex, Pop. 524
Westport Central SD — 300/K-12
PO Box 408 12993 — 518-962-8244
Karen Tromblee, supt. — Fax 962-4571
www.westportcs.org
Westport Central S — 300/K-12
PO Box 408 12993 — 518-962-8244
Karen Tromblee, prin. — Fax 962-4571

West Sayville, Suffolk, Pop. 4,680
Sayville UFD
Supt. — See Sayville
Sayville HS — 1,100/9-12
20 Brook St 11796 — 631-244-6600
Joseph Buderman, prin. — Fax 244-6779

West Seneca, Erie, Pop. 45,600
West Seneca Central SD — 7,200/K-12
1397 Orchard Park Rd 14224 — 716-677-3101
James Brotz, supt. — Fax 677-3104
www.wscschools.org/
East MS — 500/7-8
1445 Center Rd 14224 — 716-677-3530
Monica Witman, prin. — Fax 674-1046
West MS — 700/7-8
395 Center Rd 14224 — 716-677-3500
Brian Graham, prin. — Fax 675-6134
West Seneca East HS — 1,100/9-12
4760 Seneca St 14224 — 716-677-3300
Angela LaPaglia, prin. — Fax 677-2933
West Seneca West HS — 1,300/9-12
3330 Seneca St 14224 — 716-677-3350
Jon MacSwan, prin. — Fax 674-3551

Continental School of Beauty Culture — Post-Sec.
1050 Union Rd 14224 — 716-675-8205
Houghton College — Post-Sec.
910 Union Rd 14224 — 716-674-6363
West Seneca Christian S — 300/K-12
511 Union Rd 14224 — 716-674-1820

West Valley, Cattaraugus
West Valley Central SD — 400/PK-12
PO Box 290 14171 — 716-942-3293
Edward Ahrens, supt. — Fax 942-3440
www.wvalley.wnyric.org
West Valley Central HS — 200/9-12
PO Box 290 14171 — 716-942-3293
Edward Ahrens, prin. — Fax 942-3480

West Winfield, Herkimer, Pop. 843
Bridgewater-West Winfield Central SD — 1,400/K-12
500 Fairground Rd 13491 — 315-822-6161
Casey Barduhn, supt. — Fax 822-6162
Mount Markham HS — 500/9-12
500 Fairground Rd 13491 — 315-822-6343
Russell Kissinger, prin. — Fax 822-3486
Mount Markham MS — 500/5-8
500 Fairground Rd 13491 — 315-822-6361
Dawn Yerkie, prin. — Fax 822-6125

Whitehall, Washington, Pop. 2,644
Whitehall Central SD — 800/K-12
87 Buckley Rd 12887 — 518-499-1772
James Watson, supt. — Fax 499-1759
Whitehall JSHS — 400/7-12
87 Buckley Rd 12887 — 518-499-1770
Kelly McHugh, prin. — Fax 499-1759

White Plains, Westchester, Pop. 55,900
White Plains CSD — 6,200/K-12
5 Homeside Ln 10605 — 914-422-2019
Timothy P. Connors, supt. — Fax 422-2024
www.wpcsd.k12.ny.us
White Plains HS — 1,900/9-12
550 North St 10605 — 914-422-2182
Ivan Toper, prin. — Fax 422-2196
White Plains MS (Eastview Campus) — 6-8
350 Main St 10601 — 914-422-2223
Joseph Cloherty, prin. — Fax 422-2222
White Plains MS (Highlands Campus) — 1,400/6-8
128 Grandview Ave 10605 — 914-422-2092
Diana Knight, prin. — Fax 422-2273

Academy of Our Lady of Good Counsel HS — 400/9-12
52 N Broadway 10603 — 914-949-0178
Sr. Carol Peterson, prin. — Fax 682-3531
Archbishop Stepinac HS — 700/9-12
950 Mamaroneck Ave 10605 — 914-946-4800
Paul Carty, prin. — Fax 686-3615
Berkeley College - Westchester Campus — Post-Sec.
99 Church St 10601 — 914-694-1122
German S — 400/K-12
50 Partridge Rd 10605 — 914-948-6514
Udo Bochinger, hdmstr. — Fax 948-6529
Mercy College — Post-Sec.
277 Martine Ave 10601 — 914-948-3666
Music Conservatory of Westchester — Post-Sec.
216 Central Ave 10606 — 914-761-3715
New York School for the Deaf — Post-Sec.
555 Knollwood Rd 10603
Pace University — Post-Sec.
78 N Broadway 10603 — 914-422-4000
Pace University — Post-Sec.
1 Martine Ave 10606 — 914-442-2000
Sanford-Brown Institute — Post-Sec.
333 Westchester Ave 10604 — 914-347-6817
The College of Westchester — Post-Sec.
PO Box 710 10602 — 914-948-4442
Windward S — 300/5-12
40 W Red Oak Ln 10604 — 914-949-6968
Dr. Daniel Kahn, hdmstr. — Fax 949-8220

Whitesboro, Oneida, Pop. 3,875
Whitesboro Central SD
Supt. — See Yorkville
Whitesboro MS — 700/7-8
75 Oriskany Blvd 13492 — 315-266-3100
Mary Carbone, prin. — Fax 768-9770

Whitestone, See New York
NYC Department of Education
Supt. — See New York

JHS 194 — 900/7-9
15460 17th Ave 11357 — 718-746-0818
Anne Marie Iannizzi, prin. — Fax 746-7618

Whitesville, Allegany
Whitesville Central SD — 300/K-12
692 Main St 14897 — 607-356-3301
Douglas Wyant, supt.
Whitesville Central S — 300/K-12
692 Main St 14897 — 607-356-3301
Jennifer Fisk, prin. — Fax 356-3598

Whitney Point, Broome, Pop. 957
Whitney Point Central SD — 1,900/PK-12
PO Box 249 13862 — 607-692-8202
Dr. Carol Eaton, supt. — Fax 692-4434
www.wpcsd.org
Whitney Point HS — 600/9-12
PO Box 249 13862 — 607-692-8201
Fred Rothman, prin. — Fax 692-4434
Whitney Point MS — 500/6-8
PO Box 249 13862 — 607-692-8232
Dan Sweeney, prin. — Fax 692-4434

Williamson, Wayne
Williamson Central SD — 1,400/K-12
PO Box 900 14589 — 315-589-9661
Maria Ehresman, supt. — Fax 589-7611
www.williamsoncentral.org
Williamson HS — 400/9-12
PO Box 900 14589 — 315-589-9621
Douglas Lauf, prin. — Fax 589-8310
Williamson MS — 400/5-8
PO Box 900 14589 — 315-589-9665
John Fulmer, prin. — Fax 589-8314

Williamsville, Erie, Pop. 5,427
Williamsville Central SD
Supt. — See East Amherst
Heim MS — 900/5-8
175 Heim Rd 14221 — 716-626-8600
Charles Kramer, prin. — Fax 626-8626
Mill MS — 800/5-8
505 Mill St 14221 — 716-626-8300
Michael Calandra, prin. — Fax 626-8326
Williamsville North HS — 1,500/9-12
1595 Hopkins Rd 14221 — 716-626-8505
Robert Tubbs, prin. — Fax 626-8597
Williamsville South HS — 900/9-12
5950 Main St 14221 — 716-626-8200
Elvin Simmons, prin. — Fax 626-8207

Christian Central Academy — 400/K-12
39 Academy St 14221 — 716-634-4821
Nurline Lawrence, hdmstr. — Fax 634-5851
Erie Community College North — Post-Sec.
6205 Main St 14221 — 716-634-0800
Leon Studio One School of Hair Design — Post-Sec.
5221 Main St 14221 — 716-631-3878

Willsboro, Essex
Willsboro Central SD — 400/PK-12
PO Box 180 12996 — 518-963-4456
Stephen Broadwell, supt. — Fax 963-7577
www.willsborocsd.org/
Willsboro Central S — 400/PK-12
PO Box 180 12996 — 518-963-4456
Stephen Broadwell, prin. — Fax 963-7577

Wilson, Niagara, Pop. 1,186
Wilson Central SD — 1,100/K-12
412 Lake St 14172 — 716-751-9341
Dr. Michael Wendt, supt. — Fax 751-6556
www.wilson.wnyric.org/
Wilson HS — 500/9-12
PO Box 648 14172 — 716-751-9341
Daniel Johnson, prin. — Fax 751-9597
Wilson MS — 6-8
PO Box 648 14172 — 716-751-9341
Peter Rademacher, prin. — Fax 751-9597

Windham, Greene
Windham-Ashland-Jewett Central SD — 500/K-12
PO Box 429 12496 — 518-734-3400
John Wiktorko, supt. — Fax 734-6050
Windham-Ashland Central S — 500/K-12
PO Box 429 12496 — 518-734-3400
Mark Lybolt, prin. — Fax 734-6050

Windsor, Broome, Pop. 885
Windsor Central SD — 2,000/K-12
215 Main St 13865 — 607-655-8216
Dr. Richard H. Montgomery, supt. — Fax 655-3553
www.windsor-csd.org
Windsor Central HS — 600/9-12
1191 NY Route 79 13865 — 607-655-8250
Jason Van Fossen, prin. — Fax 655-3622

Wolcott, Wayne, Pop. 1,694
North Rose-Wolcott Central SD — 1,600/K-12
11669 Salter Colvin Rd 14590 — 315-594-3141
Daniel Starr, supt. — Fax 594-2352
www.nrwcs.org/
North Rose-Wolcott HS — 600/9-12
11631 Salter Colvin Rd 14590 — 315-594-3100
William Rotenberg, prin. — Fax 594-6235
North Rose-Wolcott MS — 400/6-8
5957 New Hartford St 14590 — 315-594-3130
John Boogaard, prin. — Fax 594-3120

Woodmere, Nassau, Pop. 15,578
Hewlett-Woodmere UFD — 3,300/PK-12
1 Johnson Pl 11598 — 516-374-8100
Les M. Omotani, supt. — Fax 374-8101
www.hewlett-woodmere.net
Other Schools – See Hewlett

Davis Renov Stahler Yeshiva HS for Boys — 300/9-12
700 Ibsen St 11598 — 516-295-7700
Harvey Feldman, prin. — Fax 295-2929
Woodmere Academy — 400/PK-12
336 Woodmere Blvd 11598 — 516-374-9000
Alan Bernstein, hdmstr. — Fax 374-4707

Woodside, See New York
NYC Department of Education
Supt. — See New York
IS 125 — 1,700/5-8
4602 47th Ave 11377 — 718-937-0320
Judy Mittler, prin. — Fax 361-2451

Greater New York Academy — 200/9-12
4132 58th St 11377 — 718-639-1752
Lillian Mitchell, prin. — Fax 639-8992
Razi S — 500/PK-12
5511 Queens Blvd 11377 — 718-779-0711
Ghassan Elcheikhali, prin. — Fax 779-0103

Woodstock, Ulster, Pop. 1,870

Woodstock Day S — 200/PK-12
PO Box 1 12498 — 845-246-3744
Steve Coleman, hdmstr. — Fax 246-0053

Worcester, Otsego
Worcester Central SD — 400/K-12
198 Main St 12197 — 607-397-8785
John T. Selover, supt. — Fax 397-9454
www.worcestercs.org
Worcester Central S — 400/K-12
198 Main St 12197 — 607-397-8785
Melissa Lane, prin. — Fax 397-9454

Wyandanch, Suffolk, Pop. 8,950
Wyandanch UFD — 2,300/PK-12
1445 Straight Path 11798 — 631-491-1012
Dr. Frank Satchel, supt. — Fax 253-0522
Olive MS, 140 Garden City Ave 11798 — 700/5-8
Gina Talbert, prin. — 631-491-1047
Wyandanch Memorial HS — 600/9-12
54 S 32nd St 11798 — 631-491-1022
Dr. Larry Spruill, prin. — Fax 491-1728

Wynantskill, Rensselaer, Pop. 3,329

Vanderheyden Hall — 100/7-12
PO Box 219 12198 — 518-283-6500

Yonkers, Westchester, Pop. 197,388
Yonkers CSD — 26,300/PK-12
1 Larkin Ctr 10701 — 914-376-8000
Bernard Pierorazio, supt. — Fax 376-8062
www.yonkerspublicschools.org
Emerson MS — 1,200/6-8
160 Bolmer Ave 10703 — 914-376-8300
Robert Riccuiti, prin. — Fax 376-8499
Gorton HS — 1,300/9-12
100 Shonnard Pl 10703 — 914-376-8350
Rocco Grassi, prin. — Fax 376-8377
Lincoln HS — 1,300/9-12
375 Kneeland Ave 10704 — 914-376-8400
Edwin Quezada, prin. — Fax 376-8414
Museum MS — 1,200/6-8
565 Warburton Ave 10701 — 914-376-8425
Christine Wagner, prin. — Fax 376-8475
Roosevelt HS — 1,500/9-12
631 Tuckahoe Rd 10710 — 914-376-8500
Jade Sharp, prin. — Fax 779-7632
Saunders Trades & Tech HS — Vo/Tech
183 Palmer Rd 10701 — 914-376-8150
Steve Mazzola, prin. — Fax 376-8154
Twain MS — 1,100/6-8
160 Woodlawn Ave 10704 — 914-376-8540
John Difiore, prin. — Fax 376-8552
Yonkers HS — 1,700/6-11
150 Rockland Ave 10705 — 914-376-8191
Ralph Vigliotti, prin. — Fax 376-4856
Yonkers MS — 1,100/6-8
150 Rockland Ave 10705 — 914-376-8200
Anthony Cioffi, prin. — Fax 376-8245

City Harvest Christian Academy — 100/PK-12
44 Hudson St 10701 — 914-964-5422
Donald Somerville, hdmstr. — Fax 476-5689
Cochran School of Nursing — Post-Sec.
967 N Broadway 10701 — 914-964-4283
Sacred Heart HS — 300/9-12
34 Convent Ave 10703 — 914-965-3114
Agnes McNamara, prin. — Fax 965-4510
St. Joseph's Seminary — Post-Sec.
201 Seminary Ave 10704 — 914-968-6200

Yorkshire, Cattaraugus, Pop. 1,340
Yorkshire-Pioneer Central SD — 2,800/K-12
PO Box 579 14173 — 585-492-9300
Jeffrey Bowen, supt. — Fax 492-9360
www.pioneer.wnyric.org/
Pioneer HS — 900/9-12
PO Box 639 14173 — 585-492-9328
Sharon Huff, prin. — Fax 492-1825
Pioneer MS — 900/5-8
PO Box 619 14173 — 585-492-9375
Ravo Root, prin. — Fax 492-9372

Yorktown Heights, Westchester, Pop. 7,690
Lakeland CSD
Supt. — See Shrub Oak
Lakeland-Copper Beech MS — 1,500/6-8
3417 Old Yorktown Rd 10598 — 914-245-1885
Jean Miccio, prin. — Fax 245-4391

Yorktown Central SD — 4,300/K-12
2725 Crompond Rd 10598 — 914-243-8000
Dr. Vincent Ziccolella, supt. — Fax 243-8003
www.yorktown.org
Strang MS — 1,000/6-8
2701 Crompond Rd 10598 — 914-243-8100
Linda Grimm, prin. — Fax 243-0016
Yorktown HS — 1,300/9-12
2727 Crompond Rd 10598 — 914-243-8050
John Sullivan, prin. — Fax 245-9256

Mercy College — Post-Sec.
2651 Strang Blvd 10598 — 914-245-6100

Yorkville, Oneida, Pop. 2,624
Whitesboro Central SD — 3,800/K-12
PO Box 304 13495 — 315-266-3303
Arnold Kaye, supt. — Fax 768-9730
www.wboro.org
Other Schools – See Marcy, Whitesboro

Youngstown, Niagara, Pop. 1,920
Lewiston-Porter Central SD — 2,200/K-12
4061 Creek Rd 14174 — 716-754-8281
Fax 754-2755
lew-port.com
Lewiston-Porter HS — 800/9-12
4061 Creek Rd 14174 — 716-286-7263
Paul Casseri, prin. — Fax 286-7852
Lewiston-Porter MS — 600/6-8
4061 Creek Rd 14174 — 716-286-7201
Vincent Dell'Oso, prin. — Fax 286-7204

NORTH CAROLINA

NORTH CAROLINA DEPT. PUBLIC INSTRUCTION
301 N Wilmington St, Raleigh 27601-1058
Telephone 919-807-3300
Fax 919-807-3445
Website http://www.dpi.state.nc.us

Superintendent of Public Instruction   June Atkinson

NORTH CAROLINA BOARD OF EDUCATION
301 N Wilmington St, Raleigh 27601-1058

Chairperson   Howard Lee

PUBLIC, PRIVATE AND CATHOLIC SECONDARY SCHOOLS

Aberdeen, Moore, Pop. 4,110
Moore County SD
  Supt. — See Carthage
Southern MS — 700/6-8
  717 Johnson St 28315 — 910-693-1550
  Debbie Warren, prin. — Fax 693-1544

Ahoskie, Hertford, Pop. 4,314
Hertford County SD
  Supt. — See Winton
Hertford County HS — 1,100/9-12
  PO Box 1326 27910 — 252-332-4096
  Larry Cooper, prin. — Fax 332-6176

Ahoskie Christian S — 100/K-12
  500 Kiwanis St 27910 — 252-332-2764
  Elaine Pool, prin.
Ridgecroft S — 300/PK-12
  PO Box 1008 27910 — 252-332-2964
  Elton Winslow, prin. — Fax 332-7586
Roanoke-Chowan Community College — Post-Sec.
  109 Community College Rd 27910 — 252-862-1200

Albemarle, Stanly, Pop. 15,408
Stanly County SD — 10,000/PK-12
  1000 N 1st St Ste 4 28001 — 704-983-5151
  Dr. Samuel DePaul, supt. — Fax 982-3618
  www.scs.k12.nc.us
Albemarle HS — 700/9-12
  311 Park Ridge Rd 28001 — 704-982-3711
  David Bright, prin. — Fax 982-9645
Albemarle MS — 600/6-8
  1811 Badin Rd 28001 — 704-982-5480
  Todd Thorpe, prin. — Fax 983-2600
Other Schools – See New London, Norwood, Oakboro

Stanly Community College — Post-Sec.
  141 College Dr 28001 — 704-982-0121

Andrews, Cherokee, Pop. 1,591
Cherokee County SD
  Supt. — See Murphy
Andrews HS — 300/9-12
  50 High School Dr 28901 — 828-321-5415
  S. Tim Coffey, prin. — Fax 321-3986
Andrews MS — 300/6-8
  2750 Business 19 28901 — 828-321-5762
  John Higdon, prin. — Fax 321-2009

Angier, Harnett, Pop. 3,880
Harnett County SD
  Supt. — See Lillington
Harnett Central HS — 1,300/9-12
  2911 Harnett Central Rd 27501 — 919-639-6161
  Ken Jernigan, prin. — Fax 639-3642
Harnett Central MS — 1,200/6-8
  2529 Harnett Central Rd 27501 — 919-639-6000
  Chris Mace, prin. — Fax 639-9617

Apex, Wake, Pop. 26,588
Wake County SD
  Supt. — See Raleigh
Apex HS — 2,000/9-12
  1501 Laura Duncan Rd 27502 — 919-387-2208
  Dr. Thomas Dixon, prin. — Fax 387-3023
Apex MS — 1,000/6-8
  400 E Moore St 27502 — 919-387-2181
  Timothy Locklair, prin. — Fax 387-2203
Lufkin Road MS — 1,000/6-8
  1002 Lufkin Rd, — 919-387-4465
  Dr. Jessie Dingle, prin. — Fax 363-1095
Middle Creek HS — 1,600/9-12
  123 Middle Creek Park Ave, — 919-773-3838
  John Williams, prin. — Fax 773-3880
Salem MS — 6-8
  6150 Old Jenks Rd, — 919-363-1870
  Matthew Wight, prin. — Fax 363-1876
West Lake MS — 1,400/6-8
  4600 W Lake Rd, — 919-662-2900
  Dr. Gregory Decker, prin. — Fax 662-2906

Archdale, Randolph, Pop. 9,241

Mount Calvary Christian S — 100/K-12
  6551 Weant Rd 27263 — 336-434-6800
  Dr. Richard Callahan, prin. — Fax 434-5267

Arden, Buncombe
Buncombe County SD
  Supt. — See Asheville
Valley Springs MS — 800/6-8
  224 Long Shoals Rd 28704 — 828-654-1785
  Thomas Keever, prin. — Fax 654-1789

Christ S — 200/8-12
  500 Christ School Rd 28704 — 828-684-6232
  Paul Krieger, hdmstr. — Fax 684-2745

Asheboro, Randolph, Pop. 22,839
Asheboro CSD — 4,400/PK-12
  PO Box 1103 27204 — 336-625-5104
  Dr. Diane Frost, supt. — Fax 625-9238
  www.asheboro.k12.nc.us
Asheboro HS — 1,200/9-12
  1221 S Park St 27203 — 336-625-6185
  Dr. Larry Riggan, prin. — Fax 625-9320
North Asheboro MS — 500/6-8
  1861 N Asheboro School Rd 27203 — 336-672-1900
  Ronald Coley, prin. — Fax 672-6267
South Asheboro MS — 600/6-8
  523 W Walker Ave 27203 — 336-629-4141
  Gwendolyn Williams, prin. — Fax 629-3761

Randolph County SD — 18,100/K-12
  2222 S Fayetteville St 27205 — 336-318-6100
  Donald Andrews, supt. — Fax 318-6155
  www.randolph.k12.nc.us
Southwestern Randolph HS — 1,300/9-12
  1641 Hopewell Friends Rd 27205 — 336-381-7747
  Chris Vecchione, prin. — Fax 381-7743
Southwestern Randolph MS — 700/6-8
  1509 Hopewell Friends Rd 27205 — 336-381-3900
  Tim Setzer, prin. — Fax 381-3905
Other Schools – See Liberty, Ramseur, Randleman, Trinity

Fayetteville Street Christian S — 200/K-12
  151 W Pritchard St 27203 — 336-629-1383
  Mike Brown, prin. — Fax 629-0067
Randolph Community College — Post-Sec.
  PO Box 1009 27204 — 336-633-0200

Asheville, Buncombe, Pop. 69,045
Asheville CSD — 3,800/PK-12
  85 Mountain St 28801 — 828-350-7000
  Robert L. Logan, supt. — Fax 255-5131
  www.asheville.k12.nc.us
Asheville HS — 1,200/9-12
  419 McDowell St 28803 — 828-255-5352
  Judd Porter, prin. — Fax 255-5316
Asheville MS — 700/6-8
  197 S French Broad Ave 28801 — 828-350-6200
  Pam Decker, prin. — Fax 255-5311

Buncombe County SD — 24,800/K-12
  175 Bingham Rd 28806 — 828-255-5921
  Cliff Dodson, supt. — Fax 255-5923
  www.buncombe.k12.nc.us/
Career Education Center — Vo/Tech
  175 Bingham Rd 28806 — 828-251-0499
  Magnolia Thomas, prin. — Fax 255-5275
Erwin HS — 1,100/9-12
  60 Lees Creek Rd 28806 — 828-232-4251
  Eddie Burchfiel, prin. — Fax 251-2893
Erwin MS — 1,100/6-8
  20 Erwin Hills Rd 28806 — 828-232-4264
  Andy Peoples, prin. — Fax 232-4247
Reynolds HS — 1,400/9-12
  1 Rocket Dr 28803 — 828-298-2500
  Regina Lambert, prin. — Fax 298-2002
Reynolds MS — 700/6-8
  2 Rocket Dr 28803 — 828-298-7484
  Robbie Adell, prin. — Fax 298-7503
Roberson HS — 1,400/9-12
  250 Overlook Rd 28803 — 828-654-1765
  Rob Weinkle, prin. — Fax 654-1768
Other Schools – See Arden, Black Mountain, Candler, Fletcher, Swannanoa, Weaverville

Asheville Buncombe Technical Comm. Coll. — Post-Sec.
  340 Victoria Rd 28801 — 828-254-1921
Asheville S — 200/9-12
  360 Asheville School Rd 28806 — 828-254-6345
  Archibald Montgomery, hdmstr. — Fax 252-8666
Atlantic University of Chinese Medicine — Post-Sec.
  64 Westgate Pkwy 28806 — 828-225-8550
Carolina Christian S — 200/PK-12
  48 Woodland Hills Rd 28804 — 828-658-8964
  Cheryl Scroggs, hdmstr. — Fax 658-8965
Carolina Day S — 700/PK-12
  1345 Hendersonville Rd 28803 — 828-274-0757
  Dr. Beverly Sgro, hdmstr. — Fax 274-0756
South College — Post-Sec.
  1567 Patton Ave 28806 — 828-252-2486

Temple Baptist S — 200/K-12
  985 1/2 Patton Ave 28806 — 828-252-3712
  William Spence, prin. — Fax 254-5119
University of North Carolina — Post-Sec.
  1 University Hts 28804 — 828-251-6600
Warren Wilson College — Post-Sec.
  PO Box 9000 28815 — 828-298-3325

Aurora, Beaufort, Pop. 580
Beaufort County SD
  Supt. — See Washington
Aurora MS — 100/6-8
  693 N 7th St 27806 — 252-322-4524
  Ted Overton, prin. — Fax 322-4474

Ayden, Pitt, Pop. 4,570
Pitt County SD
  Supt. — See Greenville
Ayden-Grifton HS — 600/9-12
  7653 NC 11 S 28513 — 252-746-4183
  Bill Frazier, prin. — Fax 746-2120
Ayden MS — 500/5-8
  1207 W 3rd St 28513 — 252-746-3672
  Keith Gould, prin. — Fax 746-9923

Bailey, Nash, Pop. 664
Nash-Rocky Mount SD
  Supt. — See Nashville
Southern Nash HS — 1,200/9-12
  6446 Southern Nash High Rd 27807 — 252-478-5450
  Rosalie Bardin, prin. — Fax 478-5953

Bakersville, Mitchell, Pop. 356
Mitchell County SD — 2,300/K-12
  72 Ledger School Rd 28705 — 828-688-4432
  Dr. William Sears, supt. — Fax 688-4095
  central.mitchell.k12.nc.us
Bowman MS — 200/5-8
  PO Box 46 28705 — 828-688-2752
  Angela Burleson, prin. — Fax 688-6002
Mitchell HS — 700/9-12
  416 Ledger School Rd 28705 — 828-688-2101
  Jack Brooks, prin. — Fax 688-4847
Other Schools – See Spruce Pine

Banner Elk, Avery, Pop. 885

Lees-McRae College — Post-Sec.
  PO Box 128 28604 — 828-898-5241

Barco, Currituck
Currituck County SD
  Supt. — See Currituck
Currituck County HS — 1,100/9-12
  4203 Caratoke Hwy 27917 — 252-453-0014
  Dr. Harper Donahoe, prin. — Fax 453-0017
Currituck County MS — 400/6-8
  4263 Caratoke Hwy 27917 — 252-453-2171
  Bill Wicks, prin. — Fax 453-0019

Battleboro, Edgecombe, Pop. 559
Edgecombe County SD
  Supt. — See Tarboro
Phillips MS — 500/4-8
  1407 Legett-Battleboro Rd 27809 — 252-446-2031
  William Etheridge, prin. — Fax 446-1629

Nash-Rocky Mount SD
  Supt. — See Nashville
Red Oak MS — 900/6-8
  3170 Red Oak Battleboro Rd 27809 — 252-451-5500
  Connie Bobbitt, prin. — Fax 451-5510

Bayboro, Pamlico, Pop. 730
Pamlico County SD — 1,800/PK-12
  507 Anderson Dr 28515 — 252-745-4171
  Rick Sherrill, supt. — Fax 745-4172
  www.pamlico.k12.nc.us
Pamlico County HS — 700/9-12
  PO Box 699 28515 — 252-745-3151
  Tom Frazier, prin. — Fax 745-3153
Pamlico County MS — 400/6-8
  15526 NC Highway 55 28515 — 252-745-4061
  Henry Rice, prin. — Fax 745-5583

Bear Creek, Chatham
Chatham County SD
  Supt. — See Pittsboro
Chatham Central HS — 500/9-12
  14950 NC Highway 902 27207 — 919-837-2251
  John Eldridge, prin. — Fax 837-2975

Beaufort, Carteret, Pop. 3,854
Carteret County SD | 8,300/PK-12
107 Safrit Dr 28516 | 252-728-4583
Dr. David Lenker, supt. | Fax 728-3028
www.carteretcountyschools.org
Beaufort MS | 300/6-8
100 Carraway St 28516 | 252-728-4520
Greg Guthrie, prin. | Fax 728-3392
East Carteret HS | 600/9-12
3263 US Highway 70 E 28516 | 252-728-3514
Ralph Holloway, prin. | Fax 728-3487
Other Schools – See Morehead City, Newport

Belhaven, Beaufort, Pop. 1,929

Pungo Christian Academy | 100/PK-12
983 W Main St 27810 | 252-943-2678
Marcy S. Morgan, prin. | Fax 943-3292

Belmont, Gaston, Pop. 8,793
Gaston County SD
Supt. — See Gastonia
Belmont MS | 700/6-8
110 N Central Ave 28012 | 704-825-9619
Audrey Devine, prin. | Fax 825-6951
South Point HS | 1,100/9-12
906 Southpoint Rd 28012 | 704-825-3351
Sheri Little, prin. | Fax 825-2820

Belmont Abbey College | Post-Sec.
100 Belmont Mount Holly Rd 28012 | 704-825-6700
Gaston Christian S | 700/PK-12
200 Mercy Dr 28012 | 704-825-9000
Daniel Patton, hdmstr. | Fax 825-9884

Benson, Johnston, Pop. 3,031
Johnston County SD
Supt. — See Smithfield
Benson MS | 500/5-8
1600 N Wall St 27504 | 919-894-3889
Sheila Singleton, prin. | Fax 894-1551
McGee's Crossroads MS | 500/6-8
13353 NC Highway 210 27504 | 919-894-6003
Barretta Haynes, prin. | Fax 894-6007
West Johnston HS | 1,300/9-12
5935 Raleigh Rd 27504 | 919-934-7333
Brookie Honeycutt, prin. | Fax 934-6906

Bessemer City, Gaston, Pop. 5,100
Gaston County SD
Supt. — See Gastonia
Bessemer City HS | 700/9-12
119 Yellow Jacket Rd 28016 | 704-629-2258
Ted Saunders, prin. | Fax 629-2775
Bessemer City MS | 600/6-8
525 Ed Wilson Rd 28016 | 704-629-3281
Lance Frady, prin. | Fax 629-4501

Bethel, Pitt, Pop. 1,682
Pitt County SD
Supt. — See Greenville
North Pitt HS | 900/9-12
5659 NC Highway 11 N 27812 | 252-825-0054
Robin Dailey, prin. | Fax 825-1310

Beulaville, Duplin, Pop. 1,080
Duplin County SD
Supt. — See Kenansville
East Duplin HS | 800/9-12
PO Box 188 28518 | 910-298-4535
Ben Thigpen, prin. | Fax 298-2021

Biscoe, Montgomery, Pop. 1,721
Montgomery County SD
Supt. — See Troy
East MS | 500/6-8
1834 US Highway 220 Alt S 27209 | 910-428-3278
Sandra Lampros, prin. | Fax 428-1279
East Montgomery HS | 600/9-12
157 Eagle Ln 27209 | 910-428-9641
Everette Johnson, prin. | Fax 428-1197

Black Mountain, Buncombe, Pop. 7,551
Buncombe County SD
Supt. — See Asheville
Owen HS | 900/9-12
99 Lake Eden Rd 28711 | 828-686-3852
Don Johnson, prin. | Fax 686-8442

Bladenboro, Bladen, Pop. 1,711
Bladen County SD
Supt. — See Elizabethtown
Bladenboro MS | 400/5-8
910 S Main St 28320 | 910-863-3232
Wilbert Stokes, prin. | Fax 863-4683
West Bladen HS | 900/9-12
1600 NC Hwy 410 S 28320 | 910-862-2130
Rick Helms, prin. | Fax 862-3328

Boiling Springs, Cleveland, Pop. 3,857

Gardner-Webb University | Post-Sec.
PO Box 817 28017 | 704-406-2361

Bolivia, Brunswick, Pop. 158
Brunswick County SD | 11,400/PK-12
35 Referendum Dr NE 28422 | 910-253-2900
Dr. Katie McGee, supt. | Fax 253-2983
www.bcswan.net
Other Schools – See Leland, Shallotte, Southport

Boone, Watauga, Pop. 13,127
Watauga County SD | 4,700/PK-12
PO Box 1790 28607 | 828-264-7190
Dr. Bobbie Short, supt. | Fax 264-7196
www.watauga.k12.nc.us
Watauga HS | 1,500/9-12
400 High School Dr 28607 | 828-264-2407
Angela Quick, prin. | Fax 264-9030

Appalachian State University | Post-Sec.
Asu Station 28608 | 828-262-2000

Boonville, Yadkin, Pop. 1,107
Yadkin County SD
Supt. — See Yadkinville
Starmount HS | 700/9-12
2516 Longtown Rd 27011 | 336-468-2891
Tony George, prin. | Fax 468-6434

Bostic, Rutherford, Pop. 328
Rutherford County SD
Supt. — See Forest City
East Rutherford MS | 800/6-8
PO Box 189 28018 | 828-245-4836
Marty Hopper, prin. | Fax 245-1491

Brevard, Transylvania, Pop. 6,693
Transylvania County SD | 3,800/K-12
400 Rosenwald Ln 28712 | 828-884-6173
Dr. Sonna Lyda, supt. | Fax 884-9524
www.transylvania.k12.nc.us
Brevard HS | 800/9-12
747 Country Club Rd 28712 | 828-884-4103
Douglas Odom, prin. | Fax 885-7355
Brevard MS | 600/6-8
198 Fisher Rd 28712 | 828-884-2091
Donna Hill, prin. | Fax 883-3150
Other Schools – See Rosman

Brevard College | Post-Sec.
400 N Broad St 28712 | 828-883-8292

Bryson City, Swain, Pop. 1,392
Swain County SD | 1,700/K-12
PO Box 2340 28713 | 828-488-3129
Robert White, supt. | Fax 488-8510
www.swaincountyschools.com
Swain County HS | 500/9-12
1415 Fontana Rd 28713 | 828-488-2152
Janet Clapsaddle, prin. | Fax 488-0523
Swain County MS | 500/6-8
135 Arlington Ave 28713 | 828-488-3480
Os Waters, prin. | Fax 488-0949

Buies Creek, Harnett, Pop. 2,085

Campbell University | Post-Sec.
PO Box 546 27506 | 910-893-1200

Bunn, Franklin, Pop. 380
Franklin County SD
Supt. — See Louisburg
Bunn HS | 800/9-12
PO Box 146 27508 | 919-496-3975
George Kelley, prin. | Fax 496-1639
Bunn MS | 800/6-8
4742 NC Highway 39 S 27508 | 919-496-7700
David Hawks, prin. | Fax 496-1404

Burgaw, Pender, Pop. 3,613
Pender County SD | 6,900/PK-12
925 Penderlea Hwy 28425 | 910-259-2187
Dr. Ted Kaniuka, supt. | Fax 259-0133
www.edline.net/pages/pender_county_schools
Burgaw MS | 300/6-8
500 S Wright St 28425 | 910-259-0149
Harold Vann Blakes, prin. | Fax 259-0150
Pender Early College HS | 9-12
100 Industrial Dr 28425 | 910-259-7178
Angela Jeffrey, prin.
Pender HS | 700/9-12
5380 NC Highway 53 W 28425 | 910-259-0162
Robbie Cauley, prin. | Fax 259-0166
West Pender MS | 300/6-8
10750 NC Highway 53 W 28425 | 910-283-5626
June Robbins, prin. | Fax 283-9537
Other Schools – See Hampstead, Rocky Point

Burlington, Alamance, Pop. 46,271
Alamance-Burlington SD | 21,700/PK-12
1712 Vaughn Rd 27217 | 336-570-6060
James Merrill Ed.D., supt. | Fax 570-6218
www.abss.k12.nc.us
Broadview MS | 700/6-8
2229 Broadview Dr 27217 | 336-570-6195
Nakia Hardy, prin. | Fax 570-6202
Cummings HS | 900/9-12
2200 N Mebane St 27217 | 336-570-6100
Charles Monroe, prin. | Fax 570-6107
Sellars-Gunn Educational Center | Vo/Tech
612 Apple St 27217 | 336-570-6130
James Pegues, prin. | Fax 570-6208
Turrentine MS | 1,100/6-8
1710 Edgewood Ave 27215 | 336-570-6150
Pat Morgan, prin. | Fax 570-6210
Williams HS | 1,300/9-12
1307 S Church St 27215 | 336-570-6161
Dr. George Griffin, prin. | Fax 570-6214
Other Schools – See Elon, Graham, Mebane

Burnsville, Yancey, Pop. 1,636
Yancy County SD | 2,500/K-12
PO Box 190 28714 | 828-682-6101
Dr. Barbara Tipton, supt. | Fax 682-7110
www.yanceync.net
Cane River MS | 300/6-8
1128 Cane River School Rd 28714 | 828-682-2202
Beverly Brown, prin. | Fax 682-3754
East Yancey MS | 300/6-8
285 Georges Fork Rd 28714 | 828-682-2281
Rick Tipton, prin. | Fax 682-3513
Mountain Heritage HS | 800/9-12
PO Box 70 28714 | 828-682-6103
Alton Robinson, prin. | Fax 682-4287

Butner, Granville, Pop. 4,679
Granville County SD
Supt. — See Oxford
Butner-Stem MS | 500/6-8
501 E D St 27509 | 919-575-9429
Donna McLamb, prin. | Fax 575-5894

Buxton, Dare
Dare County SD
Supt. — See Nags Head
Cape Hatteras JSHS | 400/6-12
PO Box 948 27920 | 252-995-5730
Lou Tonelson, prin. | Fax 995-6161

Calypso, Duplin, Pop. 436
Duplin County SD
Supt. — See Kenansville
North Duplin JSHS | 400/7-12
PO Box 306 28325 | 919-658-3051
Debra Hunter, prin. | Fax 658-9971

Camden, Camden
Camden County SD | 1,600/PK-12
174 NC Highway 343 N 27921 | 252-335-0831
John Dunn, supt. | Fax 331-2300
www.camden.k12.nc.us
Camden County HS | 500/9-12
103 US Highway 158 W 27921 | 252-338-0114
Vann Pennell, prin. | Fax 331-6792
Camden MS | 400/6-8
248 Scotland Rd 27921 | 252-338-3349
Jean Gray, prin. | Fax 331-2253

Cameron, Moore, Pop. 155
Moore County SD
Supt. — See Carthage
New Century MS | 900/6-8
1577 Union Church Rd 28326 | 910-947-1301
Cindy Holland, prin. | Fax 947-1227
Union Pines HS | 1,100/9-12
1981 Union Church Rd 28326 | 910-947-5511
Robin Lea, prin. | Fax 947-5117

Candler, Buncombe
Buncombe County SD
Supt. — See Asheville
Enka HS | 1,300/9-12
475 Enka Lake Rd 28715 | 828-670-5000
Don Icenhower, prin. | Fax 670-5007
Enka MS | 1,000/6-8
390 Asbury Rd 28715 | 828-670-5010
Pam Fourtenbary, prin. | Fax 670-5015

Mt. Pisgah Academy | 200/9-12
75 Academy Dr 28715 | 828-667-2535
Rick Anderson, prin. | Fax 667-0657

Canton, Haywood, Pop. 3,957
Haywood County SD
Supt. — See Waynesville
Canton MS | 600/6-8
60 Penland St 28716 | 828-646-3467
Greg Bailey, prin. | Fax 648-9558
Pisgah HS | 1,000/9-12
1 Black Bear Dr 28716 | 828-646-3440
Danny Miller, prin. | Fax 648-8618

Bethel Christian Academy | 200/K-12
100 Park St 28716 | 828-648-4492
Paula Rhodarmer, prin.

Carthage, Moore, Pop. 1,913
Moore County SD | 11,800/K-12
PO Box 1180 28327 | 910-947-2976
Susan Purser Ed.D., supt. | Fax 947-3011
www.mcs.k12.nc.us/
Pinckney Academy | Vo/Tech
PO Box 1423 28327 | 910-947-2342
Robin Moore, prin. | Fax 947-2404
Other Schools – See Aberdeen, Cameron, Robbins,
Southern Pines, West End

Cary, Wake, Pop. 99,824
Wake County SD
Supt. — See Raleigh
Cary HS | 2,200/9-12
638 Walnut St 27511 | 919-460-3549
Dr. David Dennis, prin. | Fax 460-3573
Davis Drive MS | 1,200/6-8
2101 Davis Dr 27519 | 919-387-3033
Linda Bird, prin. | Fax 387-3039
Green Hope HS | 2,000/9-12
2500 Carpenter Upchurch Rd 27519 | 919-380-3700
James Merrick, prin. | Fax 380-3712
Reedy Creek MS | 900/6-8
930 Reedy Creek Rd 27513 | 919-460-3504
Carla Jernigan, prin. | Fax 460-3391
West Cary MS | 1,000/6-8
1000 Evans Rd 27513 | 919-460-3528
Douglas Thilman, prin. | Fax 460-3540

Cary Academy | 700/6-12
1500 N Harrison Ave 27513 | 919-677-3873
Donald S. Berger, hdmstr. | Fax 677-4002
Cary Christian S | 700/K-12
1330 Old Apex Rd 27513 | 919-303-2560
Larry Stephenson, admin. | Fax 367-7558
Miller-Motte Technical College | Post-Sec.
2205 Walnut St 27511 | 919-532-7171

Cashiers, Jackson
Jackson County SD
Supt. — See Sylva
Blue Ridge S | 300/PK-12
95 Bobcat Dr 28717 | 828-743-2646
Carol Rector, prin. | Fax 743-5320

Catawba, Catawba, Pop. 710
Catawba County SD
Supt. — See Newton
Bandys HS | 1,000/9-12
5040 E Bandys Xrd 28609 | 828-241-3171
John Westberg, prin. | Fax 241-9402

Cerro Gordo, Columbus, Pop. 239
Columbus County SD
Supt. — See Whiteville
West Columbus HS | 700/9-12
PO Box 130 28430 | 910-654-6111
Worley Edwards, prin. | Fax 654-4082

Chadbourn, Columbus, Pop. 2,080
Columbus County SD
Supt. — See Whiteville
Chadbourn MS | 300/5-8
801 W Smith St 28431 | 910-654-4300
Georgia Spaulding, prin. | Fax 654-6809

Chapel Hill, Orange, Pop. 49,301
Chapel Hill-Carrboro CSD | 10,700/PK-12
750 S Merritt Mill Rd 27516 | 919-967-8211
Dr. Neil Pedersen, supt. | Fax 933-4560
www.chccs.k12.nc.us
Chapel Hill HS | 1,800/9-12
1709 High School Rd 27516 | 919-929-2106
Karla Eanes, prin. | Fax 929-2455
East Chapel Hill HS | 1,600/9-12
500 Weaver Dairy Rd 27514 | 919-969-2482
David Thaden, prin. | Fax 969-2492

Grey Culbreth MS 600/6-8
225 Culbreth Rd 27516 919-929-7161
Jacqueline Ellis, prin. Fax 969-2412
McDougle MS 700/6-8
900 Old Fayetteville Rd 27516 919-933-1556
Debra Scott, prin. Fax 969-2433
Phillips MS 700/6-8
606 N Estes Dr 27514 919-929-2188
Eileen Tulley, prin. Fax 969-2477
Smith MS 600/6-8
9201 Seawell School Rd 27516 919-918-2145
Valerie Reinhardt, prin. Fax 918-2079

Emerson Waldorf S 300/PK-12
6211 New Jericho Rd 27516 919-967-1858
Edward Schuldt, prin. Fax 967-2732
University of North Carolina 27599 Post-Sec.
919-962-2211
University of North Carolina Hospitals Post-Sec.
101 Manning Dr 27514 919-966-5111

Charlotte, Mecklenburg, Pop. 584,658
Charlotte/Mecklenburg Co. SD 112,500/PK-12
PO Box 30035 28230 980-343-3000
Dr. Frances Haithcock, supt. Fax 343-3647
www.cms.k12.nc.us/
Albemarle Road MS 900/6-8
6900 Democracy Dr 28212 980-343-6420
Betty Bauknight, prin. Fax 343-6501
Berry Academy of Technology Vo/Tech
1430 Alleghany St 28208 980-343-5992
Dr. David Baldaia, prin. Fax 343-5994
Bishop Spaugh MS 600/6-8
1901 Herbert Spaugh Ln 28208 980-343-6025
Jerry Brown, prin. Fax 343-6124
Carmel MS 1,100/6-8
5001 Camilla Dr 28226 980-343-6705
Nancy Hicks, prin. Fax 343-6749
Cochrane MS 600/6-8
6200 Starhaven Dr 28215 980-343-6460
Terry M. Brown, prin. Fax 343-6521
Community House MS 6-8
9500 Community House Rd 28277 980-343-0689
Gifford Lockley, prin. Fax 343-0691
Coulwood MS 1,200/6-8
500 Kentberry Dr 28214 980-343-6090
Sherry Sigmon, prin. Fax 343-6142
Davis MS 500/6-8
3343 Griffith St 28203 980-343-5832
Patricia Collins, prin. Fax 343-5860
East Mecklenburg HS 2,300/9-12
6800 Monroe Rd 28212 980-343-6430
Mark Nixon, prin. Fax 343-6437
Eastway MS 6-8
1501 Norland Dr 28205 980-343-6410
Nancy Barkemeyer, prin. Fax 343-6406
Garinger HS 1,500/9-12
1100 Eastway Dr 28205 980-343-6450
Jo Ella Ferrell, prin. Fax 343-6454
Graham MS 900/6-8
1800 Runnymede Ln 28211 980-343-5810
Dr. Kandace Williams, prin. Fax 343-5868
Harding University HS 1,400/9-12
2001 Alleghany St 28208 980-343-6007
Curtis Carroll, prin. Fax 343-6015
Independence HS 2,700/9-12
1967 Patriot Dr 28227 980-343-6900
Nancy Bartles, prin. Fax 343-6907
Kennedy MS 700/6-8
4000 Gallant Ln 28273 980-343-5540
Dr. Johnnie Gordon, prin. Fax 343-5412
King MS 900/6-8
500 Bilmark Ave 28213 980-343-0698
Dr. Mark Robinson, prin. Fax 343-0700
Martin MS 1,700/6-8
7800 IBM Dr 28262 980-343-5382
Raynard Lee, prin. Fax 343-5135
McClintock MS 900/6-8
2101 Rama Rd 28212 980-343-6425
Kris Miller, prin. Fax 343-6509
Myers Park HS 2,600/9-12
2400 Colony Rd 28209 980-343-5800
Dr. William Anderson, prin. Fax 343-5803
Northeast MS 1,000/6-8
5960 Brickstone Dr 28227 980-343-6920
Jocelyn B. Becoats, prin. Fax 343-6153
Northridge MS 1,200/6-8
7601 The Plz 28215 980-343-5015
Jamal Crawford, prin. Fax 343-5174
Northwest S of the Arts 1,200/6-12
1415 Beatties Ford Rd 28216 980-343-5500
Dr. Charles LaBorde, prin. Fax 343-5593
Northwest S of the Arts at Spirit Square 6-12
345 N College St 28202 980-343-3235
Charles LaBorde, prin. Fax 343-6938
Olympic HS 1,400/9-12
4301 Sandy Porter Rd 28273 980-343-3800
Pam Espinosa, prin. Fax 343-3803
Piedmont Open MS 900/6-8
1241 E 10th St 28204 980-343-5435
Tom Spivey, prin. Fax 343-5557
Providence HS 2,400/9-12
1800 Pineville Matthews Rd 28270 980-343-5390
Dr. Terri Cockerham, prin. Fax 343-3956
Quail Hollow MS 1,100/6-8
2901 Smithfield Church Rd 28210 980-343-3620
Mark Bosco, prin. Fax 343-3622
Randolph MS 700/6-8
4400 Water Oak Rd 28211 980-343-6700
Jackie Menser, prin. Fax 343-6741
Ranson MS 800/6-8
5850 Statesville Rd 28269 980-343-6800
Kevin Carr, prin. Fax 343-6796
Robinson MS 1,200/6-8
5925 Ballantyne Commons Pky 28277 980-343-6944
Dr. Maureen Furr, prin. Fax 343-6947
Sedgefield MS 600/6-8
2700 Dorchester Pl 28209 980-343-5840
Dr. Lawton Grier, prin. Fax 343-5862
South Charlotte MS 1,000/6-8
8040 Strawberry Ln 28277 980-343-3670
V. Christine Waggoner, prin. Fax 343-3725
South Mecklenburg HS 2,200/9-12
8900 Park Rd 28210 980-343-3600
Marian Yates, prin. Fax 343-3607
Southwest MS 800/6-8
13624 Steele Creek Rd 28273 980-343-5006
Valerie Williams, prin. Fax 343-3239
Vance HS 2,400/9-12
7600 IBM Dr 28262 980-343-5284
Katherine Rea, prin. Fax 343-5286
Waddell HS 1,100/9-12
7030 Nations Ford Rd 28217 980-343-6769
Dr. Edward Ellis, prin. Fax 343-6771
West Charlotte HS 1,500/9-12
2219 Senior Dr 28216 980-343-6060
John Modest, prin. Fax 343-6049
West Mecklenburg HS 1,500/9-12
7400 Tuckaseegee Rd 28214 980-343-6080
Dr. Craig Witherspoon, prin. Fax 343-6079
Williams MS 800/6-8
2400 Carmine St 28206 980-343-5544
Angela Bozeman, prin. Fax 343-5601
Wilson MS 600/6-8
7020 Tuckaseegee Rd 28214 980-343-6070
Shelley Hinton, prin. Fax 343-6129
Other Schools – See Davidson, Huntersville, Matthews

Adventist Christian Academy 100/PK-12
4601 Emory Ln 28211 704-366-4351
Chester Caswell, prin. Fax 367-1872
Al-Huda Islamic Academy 100/K-12
1700 Progress Ln 28205 704-537-1772
Dr. Hassan El Annani, prin.
Art Institute of Charlotte Post-Sec.
2110 Water Ridge Pkwy 28217 704-357-8020
Briar Creek Road Cottage HS 100/9-12
1451 Briar Creek Rd 28205 704-566-0409
Brookstone College of Business Post-Sec.
10125 Berkeley Place Dr 28262 704-547-8600
Carolina Beauty College Post-Sec.
5430 N Tryon St Ste O 28213 704-597-5503
Carolinas College of Health Sciences Post-Sec.
PO Box 32861 28232 704-355-5043
Central Piedmont Community College Post-Sec.
PO Box 35009 28235 704-330-2722
Charlotte Catholic HS 900/9-12
7702 Pineville Matthews Rd 28226 704-543-1127
Jerry Healy, prin. Fax 543-1217
Charlotte Christian S 1,000/PK-12
7301 Sardis Rd 28270 704-366-5657
Dr. Leo Orsino, hdmstr. Fax 366-5678
Charlotte Country Day S 1,600/PK-12
1440 Carmel Rd 28226 704-943-4500
Margaret Gragg, prin. Fax 943-4577
Charlotte Latin S 1,400/PK-12
9502 Providence Rd 28277 704-846-1100
Arch N. McIntosh, hdmstr. Fax 846-1712
DeVry University Post-Sec.
4521 Sharon Rd Ste 145 28211 704-362-2345
Dore Academy 100/K-12
1727 Providence Rd 28207 704-365-5490
David Hudspeth, hdmstr. Fax 365-5087
Dudley Beauty College Post-Sec.
1950 John McDonald Ave 28216 704-392-2564
ECPI College of Technology Post-Sec.
4800 Airport Center Pkwy 28208 704-399-1010
Fletcher S 200/K-12
8500 Sardis Rd 28270 704-365-4658
Margaret Sigmon, hdmstr. Fax 364-2978
Hairstyling Institute of Charlotte Post-Sec.
209B S Kings Dr 28204 704-334-5511
Hickory Grove Baptist Christian S 1,100/K-12
6050 Hickory Grove Rd 28215 704-531-4008
Henry Ward, admin. Fax 531-4082
Holy Trinity Catholic MS 900/6-8
3100 Park Rd 28209 704-527-7822
Carole Breerwood, prin. Fax 525-7288
Johnson & Wales University Post-Sec.
801 W Trade St 28202 980-598-1000
Johnson C. Smith University Post-Sec.
100 Beatties Ford Rd 28216 704-378-1000
King's College Post-Sec.
322 Lamar Ave 28204 704-372-0266
Lee University Charlotte Center Post-Sec.
1209 Little Rock Rd 28214 704-394-2307
Mercy School of Nursing Post-Sec.
1921 Vail Ave 28207 704-379-5841
New Life Theological Seminary Post-Sec.
PO Box 790106 28206 704-334-6882
Northside Christian Academy 800/PK-12
333 Jeremiah Blvd 28262 704-596-4074
David Kilgore, hdmstr. Fax 921-1384
Presbyterian Hospital Post-Sec.
PO Box 33549 28233 704-384-4141
Providence Day S 1,500/PK-12
5800 Sardis Rd 28270 704-887-7041
Eugene Bratek, prin. Fax 887-7042
Queens University of Charlotte Post-Sec.
1900 Selwyn Ave 28274 704-337-2212
Reformed Theological Seminary Post-Sec.
2101 Carmel Rd 28226 704-366-5066
Resurrection Christian S 100/PK-12
2940 Commonwealth Ave 28205 704-334-9898
Fax 347-0811
SonRise Christian Academy 50/K-12
4300 McKee Rd 28270 704-846-8961
S. David Johnson, hdmstr. Fax 841-4313
Southeastern School of Neuromuscular Post-Sec.
4 Woodlawn Green #200 28217 704-527-4979
United Faith Christian Academy 300/PK-12
8617 Providence Rd 28277 704-541-1742
Mark Starnes, contact Fax 540-7926
Universal College of Beauty Post-Sec.
1701 W Trade St 28216 704-333-6969
University of North Carolina Post-Sec.
9201 University City Blvd 28223 704-547-2000
Victory Christian S 300/K-12
1501 Carrier Dr 28216 704-391-7339
Michael Pratt, prin. Fax 391-0494

Cherokee, Swain

Oconaluftee Job Corps Center Post-Sec.
502 Ocnaluftee Job Corps Rd 28719 828-497-5411

Cherryville, Gaston, Pop. 5,422
Gaston County SD
Supt. — See Gastonia
Chavis MS 600/6-8
PO Box 337 28021 704-435-6045
James Montgomery, prin. Fax 435-6168
Cherryville HS 600/9-12
PO Box 779 28021 704-435-4506
Steve Huffstetler, prin. Fax 435-4989

China Grove, Rowan, Pop. 3,696
Rowan-Salisbury County SD
Supt. — See Salisbury
China Grove MS 600/6-8
1013 N Main St 28023 704-857-7038
Donald Bost, prin. Fax 857-6650
South Rowan HS 1,700/9-12
1655 Patterson St 28023 704-857-1161
Fax 855-1420

Chocowinity, Beaufort, Pop. 724
Beaufort County SD
Supt. — See Washington
Chocowinity MS 400/5-8
3831 US Highway 17 S 27817 252-946-6191
Charles Clark, prin. Fax 975-3812
Southside HS 500/9-12
5700 NC Highway 33 E 27817 252-940-1881
Todd Blumenreich, prin. Fax 940-1888

Claremont, Catawba, Pop. 1,068
Catawba County SD
Supt. — See Newton
Bunker Hill HS 900/9-12
4675 Oxford School Rd 28610 828-241-3355
Jerry Griffin, prin. Fax 241-9401
Mill Creek MS 500/7-8
1041 Shiloh Rd 28610 828-241-2711
Rob Rucker, prin. Fax 241-2743
River Bend MS 500/7-8
4670 Oxford School Rd 28610 828-241-2754
Donna Heavner, prin. Fax 241-2820

Clarkton, Bladen, Pop. 696
Bladen County SD
Supt. — See Elizabethtown
Clarkton MS of Discovery 300/6-8
PO Box 127 28433 910-647-6531
Michelle Mena, prin. Fax 647-6671

Clayton, Johnston, Pop. 11,293
Johnston County SD
Supt. — See Smithfield
Clayton HS 1,500/9-12
600 S Fayetteville St 27520 919-553-4064
Jerry Smith, prin. Fax 553-2563
Clayton MS 700/6-8
490 Guy Rd 27520 919-553-5811
Deborah Woodruff, prin. Fax 553-6978
Riverwood MS 700/6-8
204 Athletic Club Blvd, 919-359-2769
Phillip Lee, prin. Fax 359-1519

Clemmons, Forsyth, Pop. 16,118
Winston-Salem/Forsyth SD
Supt. — See Winston Salem
West Forsyth HS 2,100/9-12
1735 Lewisville Clemmons Rd 27012 336-712-4400
Kurt Telford, prin. Fax 712-4416

Clinton, Sampson, Pop. 8,636
Clinton CSD 2,800/PK-12
606 College St 28328 910-592-3132
Gene Hales, supt. Fax 592-2011
www.clinton.k12.nc.us
Clinton HS 800/9-12
1201 W Elizabeth St 28328 910-592-2067
Jeff Bell, prin. Fax 592-6185
Sampson MS 700/6-8
505 Sunset Ave 28328 910-592-3327
Terrace Miller, prin. Fax 592-2292

Sampson County SD 8,200/PK-12
PO Box 439 28329 910-592-1401
Dr. Leslie Stewart Hobbs, supt. Fax 590-2445
www.sampson.k12.nc.us/
Union HS 500/9-12
455 River Rd 28328 910-592-4026
Stuart Daugherty, prin. Fax 592-8226
Union MS 500/6-8
1190 Edmond Matthis Rd 28328 910-592-4547
Donald Boykin, prin. Fax 592-4211
Other Schools – See Dunn, Newton Grove, Roseboro, Salemburg

Sampson Community College Post-Sec.
PO Box 318 28329 910-592-8081

Clyde, Haywood, Pop. 1,336
Haywood County SD
Supt. — See Waynesville
Central Haywood JSHS 500/7-12
3215 Broad St 28721 828-627-8308
Phil Pressley, prin. Fax 627-8935

Haywood Community College Post-Sec.
185 Freedlander Dr 28721 828-627-2821

Columbia, Tyrrell, Pop. 801
Tyrrell County SD 700/PK-12
PO Box 328 27925 252-796-1121
Nelson Smith, supt. Fax 796-1492
www.tyrrell.k12.nc.us
Columbia HS 200/9-12
PO Box 419 27925 252-796-0191
Jana Rawls, prin. Fax 796-0143
Columbia MS 200/6-8
PO Box 839 27925 252-796-0369
Marcia Manning, prin. Fax 796-3639

Columbus, Polk, Pop. 994
Polk County SD 2,000/PK-12
PO Box 638 28722 828-894-3051
William Miller, supt. Fax 894-8153
www.polk.k12.nc.us
Polk County HS 700/9-12
1681 NC 108 Hwy E 28722 828-894-2525
Aaron Greene, prin. Fax 894-2093
Other Schools – See Mill Spring

Concord, Cabarrus, Pop. 58,943
Cabarrus County SD 21,800/PK-12
PO Box 388 28026 704-262-6123
Dr. Harold Winkler, supt. Fax 262-6175
www.cabarrus.k12.nc.us
Central Cabarrus HS 1,400/9-12
505 Highway 49 N 28025 704-786-0125
Brad Hinson, prin. Fax 782-1239
Concord HS 1,200/9-12
481 Burrage Rd NE 28025 704-786-4161
Carla Black, prin. Fax 782-7539

Concord MS 900/6-8
1500 Gold Rush Dr 28025 704-786-4121
James Carroll, prin. Fax 782-8632
Fries MS 800/6-8
133 Stonecrest Cir 28027 704-788-4140
Mary Beth Roth, prin. Fax 784-2086
Griffin MS 1,100/6-8
7650 Griffins Gate Dr SW 28025 704-455-4700
Dr. Jim Williams, prin. Fax 455-4780
Harris Road MS 800/6-8
1251 Patriot Plantation Blv 28027 704-782-2002
Susan Cline, prin. Fax 262-4298
Northwest Cabarrus HS 1,200/9-12
5130 NW Cabarrus Dr 28027 704-788-4111
Dan Meehan, prin. Fax 723-4114
Northwest Cabarrus MS 800/6-8
5140 NW Cabarrus Dr 28027 704-788-4135
Tim Farrar, prin. Fax 784-2649
Robinson HS 1,600/9-12
300 Pitts School Rd 28027 704-788-4500
Todd Smith, prin. Fax 262-3630
Other Schools – See Mount Pleasant

Barber-Scotia College Post-Sec.
145 Cabarrus Ave W 28025 704-789-2900
Cabarrus College of Health Sciences Post-Sec.
401 Medical Park Dr 28025 704-783-1556
Cannon S 900/PK-12
5801 Poplar Tent Rd 28027 704-786-8171
Richard Snyder, hdmstr. Fax 788-7779
Covenant Classical S 200/PK-12
3200 Patrick Henry Dr 28027 704-792-1854
Corie Crouch, hdmstr. Fax 792-2102
Empire Beauty School Post-Sec.
10075 Weddington Road Ext 28027 800-575-5983
First Assembly Christian S 800/PK-12
154 Warren C Coleman Blvd N 28027 704-793-4750
Blenda Snodderly, admin. Fax 793-4784

Connellys Springs, Burke, Pop. 1,494
Burke County SD
Supt. — See Morganton
East Burke HS 1,900/9-12
3695 E Burke Blvd 28612 828-397-5541
Rexana Lowman, prin. Fax 397-7652

Conover, Catawba, Pop. 6,772

Tri-City Christian S 300/PK-12
PO Box 1690 28613 828-465-0475
Bob Templeton, admin. Fax 466-3749

Conway, Northampton, Pop. 710
Northampton County SD
Supt. — See Jackson
Conway MS 500/6-8
400 E Main St 27820 252-585-0312
Reginald Ennett, prin. Fax 585-0335
Northampton County HS East 600/9-12
750 Northamptn County HS Rd 27820 252-585-0627
Terence Wyche, prin. Fax 585-9019

Cornelius, Mecklenburg, Pop. 16,827

New Beginnings Christian Academy 100/PK-12
18731 W Catawba Ave 28031 704-895-0214
Barbara Lambert, admin. Fax 895-9472

Cramerton, Gaston, Pop. 2,935
Gaston County SD
Supt. — See Gastonia
Cramerton MS 800/6-8
601 Cramer Mountain Rd 28032 704-824-2907
Denise McLean, prin. Fax 824-0228

Cramerton Christian Academy 400/K-12
426 Woodlawn Ave 28032 704-824-2840
Kyle Brown, prin. Fax 824-9642

Creedmoor, Granville, Pop. 2,924
Granville County SD
Supt. — See Oxford
Hawley MS 600/6-8
2173 Brassfield Rd 27522 919-528-0091
Beth Cook, prin. Fax 528-0051
South Granville HS 1,100/9-12
701 Crescent Dr 27522 919-528-1507
Harold Carver, prin. Fax 528-3389
South Granville S of Health & Life Sci 9-12
701 Crescent Dr 27522 919-693-5510
Catherine Brooks, prin.

Creswell, Washington, Pop. 270
Washington County SD
Supt. — See Plymouth
Creswell JSHS 100/7-12
PO Box 188 27928 252-797-4766
Wayne Talley, prin. Fax 797-4651

Cullowhee, Jackson, Pop. 4,029

Western Carolina University Post-Sec.
University Dr 28723 828-227-7211

Currituck, Currituck
Currituck County SD 3,700/PK-12
2958 Caratoke Hwy 27929 252-232-2223
C. Michael Warren, supt. Fax 232-3655
www.currituck.k12.nc.us
Other Schools – See Barco, Moyock

Dallas, Gaston, Pop. 3,382
Gaston County SD
Supt. — See Gastonia
Friday MS 800/6-8
1221 Ratchford Dr 28034 704-922-5297
Jessica McGee, prin. Fax 922-9841
North Gaston HS 1,100/9-12
1133 Ratchford Dr 28034 704-922-5285
Brent Boone, prin. Fax 922-7486

Gaston College Post-Sec.
201 Highway 321 S 28034 704-922-6200
Tabernacle Christian Academy 200/K-12
2128 Dallas Cherryville Hwy 28034 704-922-9143
Patricia Hedrick, prin. Fax 922-9988

Danbury, Stokes, Pop. 106
Stokes County SD 7,500/PK-12
PO Box 50 27016 336-593-8146
Dr. Larry Cartner, supt. Fax 593-2041
www.stokes.k12.nc.us
North Stokes HS 400/9-12
1350 N Stokes School Rd 27016 336-593-8134
Ronnie Mendenhall, prin. Fax 593-8882
Other Schools – See King, Lawsonville, Walnut Cove

Davidson, Mecklenburg, Pop. 8,142
Charlotte/Mecklenburg Co. SD
Supt. — See Charlotte
Davidson International Baccalaureate MS 200/6-8
PO Box 369 28036 980-343-5185
Dr. Mary Louise Jones, prin. Fax 343-5187

Davidson College Post-Sec.
PO Box 7156 28035 704-892-2000

Deep Run, Lenoir
Lenoir County SD
Supt. — See Kinston
South Lenoir HS 800/9-12
3355 NC Highway 11 S 28525 252-568-6161
Jay Thomas, prin. Fax 568-6015

Delco, Columbus
Columbus County SD
Supt. — See Whiteville
Acme-Delco MS 200/6-8
PO Box 40 28436 910-655-3200
Theresa Blanks, prin. Fax 655-6865

Denton, Davidson, Pop. 1,458
Davidson County SD
Supt. — See Lexington
South Davidson HS 500/9-12
14956 S NC Highway 109 27239 336-859-3533
Keith Overcash, prin. Fax 859-2789
South Davidson MS 400/6-8
14954 S NC Highway 109 27239 336-859-0575
Kimberly Loflin, prin. Fax 859-2789

Denver, Lincoln
Lincoln County SD
Supt. — See Lincolnton
East Lincoln HS 900/9-12
6471 Highway 73 28037 704-483-5681
Todd Black, prin. Fax 483-6751

Dobson, Surry, Pop. 1,454
Surry County SD 8,700/PK-12
PO Box 364 27017 336-386-8211
Dr. Ashley Hinson, supt. Fax 386-4279
www.surry.k12.nc.us/
Central MS 600/6-8
PO Box 768 27017 336-386-4018
Vickie Cameron, prin. Fax 386-4371
Surry Central HS 800/9-12
PO Box 8 27017 336-386-8842
Jill Reinhardt, prin. Fax 386-4424
Other Schools – See Mount Airy, Pilot Mountain

Surry Community College Post-Sec.
630 S Main St 27017 336-386-8121

Dublin, Bladen, Pop. 253

Bladen Community College Post-Sec.
PO Box 266 28332 910-862-2164

Dudley, Wayne
Wayne County SD
Supt. — See Goldsboro
Brogden MS 600/5-8
3761 US Hwy 117 South Alt 28333 919-705-6010
Earl Moore, prin. Fax 705-6000
Southern Wayne HS 1,200/9-12
124 Walter Fulcher Rd 28333 919-705-6060
Richard Sauls, prin. Fax 731-5982

Dunn, Harnett, Pop. 9,722
Harnett County SD
Supt. — See Lillington
Coats-Erwin MS 700/6-8
2833 NC Highway 55 E 28334 910-230-0300
Whit Bradham, prin. Fax 230-0306
Dunn MS 500/6-8
1301 Meadow Lark Rd 28334 910-892-1017
Stan Williams, prin. Fax 892-7923

Sampson County SD
Supt. — See Clinton
Midway HS 600/9-12
15375 Spiveys Corner Hwy 28334 910-567-6664
Gaynor Canady, prin. Fax 567-5989
Midway MS 600/6-8
1115 Roberts Grove Rd 28334 910-567-5879
Donnie Ray Naylor, prin. Fax 567-5131

Heritage Bible College Post-Sec.
PO Box 1628 28335 910-892-3178

Durham, Durham, Pop. 198,376
Durham County SD 31,000/PK-12
PO Box 30002 27702 919-560-2000
Dr. Carl Harris, supt. Fax 560-2422
www.dpsnc.net
Brogden MS 800/6-8
1001 Leon St 27704 919-560-3906
Alexis Spann, prin. Fax 560-3957
Carrington MS 1,300/6-8
227 Milton Rd 27712 919-560-3916
Julie Spencer, prin. Fax 560-3522
Chewning MS 800/6-8
5001 Red Mill Rd 27704 919-560-3914
Richard Kozak, prin. Fax 477-9189
Durham School of the Arts 1,400/6-12
400 N Duke St 27701 919-560-3926
Ron Roukema, prin. Fax 560-2217
Githens MS 1,100/6-8
4800 Old Chapel Hill Rd 27707 919-560-3966
Emmett Tilley, prin. Fax 560-3454
Hillside HS 1,500/9-12
3727 Fayetteville St 27707 919-560-3925
Eunice Sanders, prin. Fax 560-2312
Jordan HS 1,800/9-12
6806 Garrett Rd 27707 919-560-3912
Richard Webber, prin. Fax 493-2620
Lowes Grove MS 800/6-8
4418 S Alston Ave 27713 919-560-3946
Marsha Person, prin. Fax 560-2102
Middle College HS at DTCC 11-12
1637 E Lawson St 27703 919-560-2100
Dr. Charles Nolan, prin. Fax 560-3950
Neal MS 800/6-8
201 Baptist Rd 27704 919-560-3955
Myron Wilson, prin. Fax 560-3451
Northern HS 1,600/9-12
117 Tom Wilkinson Rd 27712 919-560-3956
John Colclough, prin. Fax 479-3001
Riverside HS 1,800/9-12
3218 Rose Of Sharon Rd 27712 919-560-3965
James Key, prin. Fax 560-3798
Rogers-Herr MS 600/6-8
911 W Cornwallis Rd 27707 919-560-3970
Drew Sawyer, prin. Fax 560-2439
Shepard MS 400/6-8
2401 Dakota St 27707 919-560-3938
Julia Fairley, prin. Fax 560-3945
Southern HS 1,500/9-12
800 Clayton Rd 27703 919-560-3968
Rodriguez Teal, prin. Fax 596-1951

Apex School of Theology Post-Sec.
5104 Revere Rd 27713 919-572-1625
Carolina Beauty College Post-Sec.
5106 N Roxboro St 27704 919-477-1444
Carolina Friends S 500/K-12
4809 Friends School Rd 27705 919-383-6602
Mike Hanas, prin. Fax 383-6009
Cresset Christian Academy 300/PK-12
3707 Garrett Rd 27707 919-489-2655
Gail Murphy, admin. Fax 493-8102
Duke University 27706 Post-Sec.
919-684-8111
Durham Academy 1,100/PK-12
3501 Ridge Rd 27705 919-493-9595
Edward Costello, hdmstr.
Durham Technical Community College Post-Sec.
1637 E Lawson St 27703 919-686-3300
Hill Center 200/K-12
3200 Pickett Rd 27705 919-489-7464
Sharon Maskel Ed.D., prin. Fax 489-7466
Liberty Christian S 200/K-12
3864 Guess Rd 27705 919-471-5522
Loren Kurtz, prin.
Mt. Zion Christian Academy 100/K-12
3519 Fayetteville St 27707 919-688-4245
Peggy McIlwain, prin. Fax 688-2201
North Carolina Central University Post-Sec.
PO Box 19617 27707 919-560-6100

East Bend, Yadkin, Pop. 659
Yadkin County SD
Supt. — See Yadkinville
Forbush HS 1,000/9-12
1525 Falcon Rd 27018 336-961-4644
Jeff Wallace, prin. Fax 961-2575

East Flat Rock, Henderson, Pop. 3,218
Henderson County SD
Supt. — See Hendersonville
East Henderson HS 1,000/9-12
110 Old Upward Rd 28726 828-697-4768
Ben Williams, prin. Fax 698-6123
Flat Rock MS 800/6-8
191 Preston Ln 28726 828-697-4775
Bill Reedy, prin. Fax 698-6124

Eden, Rockingham, Pop. 15,622
Rockingham County SD 14,500/PK-12
511 Harrington Hwy 27288 336-627-2600
Dr. Bill Capehart, supt. Fax 627-2660
www.rock.k12.nc.us
Holmes MS 1,000/6-8
211 N Pierce St 27288 336-623-9791
George Murphy, prin. Fax 627-0075
Morehead HS 1,200/9-12
134 N Pierce St 27288 336-627-7731
Chris Carter, prin. Fax 623-5462
Other Schools – See Madison, Mayodan, Reidsville

Edenton, Chowan, Pop. 4,981
Edenton/Chowan County SD 2,600/PK-12
PO Box 206 27932 252-482-4436
Allan Smith, supt. Fax 482-7309
www.ecps.k12.nc.us
Holmes HS 800/9-12
PO Box 409 27932 252-482-8426
William Moore, prin. Fax 482-2010
Other Schools – See Tyner

Elizabeth City, Pasquotank, Pop. 17,570
Elizabeth City/Pasquotank County SD 6,000/PK-12
PO Box 2247 27906 252-335-2981
Dr. Tony Stewart, supt. Fax 335-0974
www.ecpps.k12.nc.us
Elizabeth City MS 700/6-8
306 N Road St 27909 252-335-2974
Gerri Hill, prin. Fax 335-1751
Northeastern HS 900/9-12
963 Oak Stump Rd 27909 252-335-2932
Don Sisson, prin. Fax 335-1005
Pasquotank County HS 1,000/9-12
1064 Northside Rd 27909 252-337-6880
Patti Hamler, prin. Fax 337-6890
River Road MS 700/6-8
1701 River Rd 27909 252-333-1454
Carolyn Jennings, prin. Fax 331-1339

Albemarle Academy 200/K-12
1210 US Highway 17 S 27909 252-338-0883
Melvin Hooker, prin. Fax 338-1222
College of the Albemarle Post-Sec.
PO Box 2327 27906 252-335-0821
Elizabeth City State University Post-Sec.
1704 Weeksville Rd 27909 252-335-3400
Roanoke Bible College Post-Sec.
715 N Poindexter St 27909 252-334-2070
Victory Christian S 200/PK-12
684 Old Hertford Hwy 27909 252-264-2011
R.L. Parker, admin. Fax 264-4155

Elizabethtown, Bladen, Pop. 3,675
Bladen County SD 5,900/PK-12
PO Box 37 28337 910-862-4136
Dr. Kenneth Dinkins, supt. Fax 862-4277
www.bladen.k12.nc.us/

East Bladen HS 700/9-12
5600 NC Highway 87 E 28337 910-645-2500
Rob Spainhour, prin. Fax 645-2509
Elizabethtown MS 500/5-8
PO Box 639 28337 910-862-4071
Linda Baldwin, prin. Fax 862-7426
Other Schools – See Bladenboro, Clarkton, Tar Heel

Elkin, Surry, Pop. 4,089
Elkin CSD 1,000/PK-12
202 W Spring St 28621 336-835-3135
Dr. Barry C. Shepherd, supt. Fax 835-3756
www.elkincityschools.com
Elkin HS 300/9-12
334 Elk Spur St 28621 336-835-3858
Misty Walker, prin. Fax 835-3253
Elkin MS 7-8
300 Elk Spur St 28621 336-835-3858
Pam Helms, prin. Fax 835-3253

Elk Park, Avery, Pop. 462
Avery County SD
Supt. — See Newland
Cranberry MS 200/6-8
PO Box 38 28622 828-733-2932
Kim Davis, prin. Fax 733-6863

Ellerbe, Richmond, Pop. 1,002
Richmond County SD
Supt. — See Hamlet
Ellerbe JHS 400/6-9
128 W Ballard St 28338 910-652-3231
William Kelley, prin. Fax 652-3106

Elm City, Wilson, Pop. 1,374
Wilson County SD
Supt. — See Wilson
Elm City MS 500/6-8
215 Church St E 27822 252-236-4148
Mark L. Cockrell, prin. Fax 236-3754

Elon, Alamance, Pop. 7,053
Alamance-Burlington SD
Supt. — See Burlington
Western Alamance HS 1,100/9-12
1731 N NC Highway 87 27244 336-538-6020
Ann Davis, prin. Fax 538-6013
Western MS 800/6-8
2100 Eldon Dr 27244 336-538-6010
Dr. Lizzie Alston, prin. Fax 538-6012

Elon University Post-Sec.
2700 Campus Box 27244 336-278-2000

Enfield, Halifax, Pop. 2,332
Halifax County SD
Supt. — See Halifax
Eastman MS 300/6-8
20212 NC Highway 48 27823 252-445-3720
Fax 445-2410
Enfield MS 300/6-8
PO Box 128 27823 252-445-5502
Ruzalia Vines, prin. Fax 445-3600

Erwin, Harnett, Pop. 4,697
Harnett County SD
Supt. — See Lillington
Triton HS 1,400/9-12
215 Maynard Lake Rd 28339 910-897-8121
Brooks Matthews, prin. Fax 897-3148

Cape Fear Christian Academy 300/PK-12
138 Erwin Chapel Rd 28339 910-897-5423
Pat Sandel, admin. Fax 897-2150

Fairmont, Robeson, Pop. 2,569
Robeson County SD
Supt. — See Lumberton
Fairgrove MS 300/4-8
1953 Fairgrove School Rd 28340 910-628-8290
Craig Lowry, prin. Fax 628-6181
Fairmont HS 700/9-12
5419 Old Stage Rd 28340 910-628-6727
Lannie Edwards, prin. Fax 628-5627
Fairmont MS 600/5-8
402 Iona St 28340 910-628-9728
Joyce Canady, prin. Fax 628-0335

Farmville, Pitt, Pop. 4,557
Pitt County SD
Supt. — See Greenville
Farmville Central HS 700/9-12
3308 E Wilson St 27828 252-753-5138
Valerie Galbreth, prin. Fax 753-7873
Farmville MS 700/6-8
3914 Grimmersburg St 27828 252-753-2116
William Dorey, prin. Fax 753-7995

Fayetteville, Cumberland, Pop. 124,372
Cumberland County SD 53,000/PK-12
PO Box 2357 28302 910-678-2300
William C. Harrison Ed.D., supt. Fax 678-2339
www.ccs.k12.nc.us
Abbott MS 1,000/6-8
590 Winding Creek Rd 28305 910-323-2201
Myra Holloway, prin. Fax 485-0841
Britt HS 1,800/9-12
7403 Rockfish Rd 28306 910-429-2800
Conrad Lopes, prin. Fax 429-2810
Byrd HS 1,400/9-12
1624 Ireland Dr 28304 910-484-8121
Jackie Warner, prin. Fax 323-4127
Byrd MS 800/7-8
1616 Ireland Dr 28304 910-483-3101
Lodies Gloston, prin. Fax 483-3741
Cape Fear HS 1,500/9-12
4762 Clinton Rd, 910-483-0191
Jeffery Jernigan, prin. Fax 483-1679
Chesnutt MS 700/6-8
2121 Skibo Rd 28314 910-867-9147
Tom Hatch, prin. Fax 868-3695
Griffin MS 1,200/6-8
5551 Fisher Rd 28304 910-424-7678
Cynthia McCormic, prin. Fax 424-7602
Jeralds MS 700/6-8
2517 Ramsey St 28301 910-822-2570
Shirley Gamble, prin. Fax 822-1534
Lewis Chapel MS 800/6-8
2150 Skibo Rd 28314 910-864-1407
Kathia Ennett, prin. Fax 864-8298

Massey Hill Classical HS 300/9-12
1062 Southern Ave 28306 910-485-8761
Donna Hancock, prin. Fax 485-7950
Pine Forest HS 1,700/9-12
525 Andrews Rd 28311 910-488-2384
Mark Culbreth, prin. Fax 488-0790
Pine Forest MS 800/6-8
6901 Ramsey St 28311 910-488-2711
Dan Krumanocker, prin. Fax 630-2357
Ross Classical JSHS 900/6-12
3200 Ramsey St 28301 910-488-8415
Diane Antolak, prin. Fax 488-6209
Sanford HS 1,500/9-12
2301 Fort Bragg Rd 28303 910-484-1151
Alton Miller, prin. Fax 484-7203
Seventy-First Classical MS 600/6-8
6830 Raeford Rd 28304 910-864-0092
Joann Pearce, prin. Fax 487-8547
Seventy-First HS 1,900/9-12
6764 Raeford Rd 28304 910-867-3116
Tina Poltrock, prin. Fax 867-1445
Smith MS 1,500/6-8
1800 Seabrook Rd 28301 910-483-0153
Rene Corders, prin. Fax 483-7696
Westover HS 1,300/9-12
277 Bonanza Dr 28303 910-864-0190
Mark Smith, prin. Fax 864-5924
Westover MS 900/6-8
275 Bonanza Dr 28303 910-864-0813
Ronnie Godbolt, prin. Fax 864-7906
Williams MS 1,200/6-8
4464 Clinton Rd, 910-483-8222
Ernest Freeman, prin. Fax 483-4831
Cumberland Evening and Web Academy Adult
1624 Ireland Dr 28304 910-484-8231
Allan Jordan, prin. Fax 323-4127
Other Schools – See Hope Mills, Spring Lake

Berean Baptist Academy 300/PK-12
518 Glensford Dr 28314 910-868-2511
Donald Adams, prin. Fax 868-1550
Cornerstone Christian Academy 100/PK-12
3000 Scotty Hill Rd 28303 910-867-1166
Greg DeBruler, prin. Fax 867-2166
Fayetteville Academy 400/PK-12
3200 Cliffdale Rd 28303 910-868-5131
Richard Cameron, hdmstr. Fax 868-7351
Fayetteville Adventist Christian S 50/K-12
PO Box 64397 28306 910-484-6091
Phyllis Knight, prin.
Fayetteville Beauty College Post-Sec.
3442 Bragg Blvd 28303 910-487-0227
Fayetteville Christian S 600/PK-12
1422 Ireland Dr 28304 910-483-3905
Tammi Peters, prin. Fax 483-6966
Fayetteville State University Post-Sec.
1200 Murchison Rd 28301 910-486-1111
Fayetteville Technical Community College Post-Sec.
PO Box 35236 28303 910-678-8400
Liberty Christian Academy 300/PK-12
6548 Rockfish Rd 28306 910-424-1205
Duncan Edge, prin. Fax 424-8049
Methodist College Post-Sec.
5400 Ramsey St 28311 910-630-7000
Mitchell's Hairstyling Academy Post-Sec.
222 Tallywood Shopping Ctr 28303 910-485-6310
New Life Christian Academy 50/PK-12
1420 Hoke Loop Rd 28314 910-868-9640
Connie McLaughlin, prin. Fax 868-3300
Northwood Temple Academy 400/PK-12
4200 Ramsey St 28311 910-822-7711
Renee McLamb, hdmstr. Fax 488-7299
Trinity Christian S 200/K-12
3727 Rosehill Rd 28311 910-488-6779
Dennis Vandevender, prin.
Village Christian Academy 700/K-12
908 S Mcpherson Church Rd 28303 910-483-5500
Joan Dayton, admin. Fax 483-5335

Flat Rock, Henderson, Pop. 2,657

Blue Ridge Community College Post-Sec.
College Ave 28731 828-694-1700

Fletcher, Henderson, Pop. 4,342
Buncombe County SD
Supt. — See Asheville
Cane Creek MS 900/6-8
570 Lower Brush Creek Rd 28732 828-628-0824
Kathy Noyes, prin. Fax 628-9833

Fletcher Academy 100/9-12
PO Box 5440 28732 828-687-5100
Rob Gettys, prin. Fax 687-5102
Veritas Christian Academy 200/K-12
17 Cane Creek Rd 28732 828-681-0546
Kay Belknap, hdmstr. Fax 681-0547

Forest City, Rutherford, Pop. 7,373
Rutherford County SD 9,900/K-12
382 W Main St 28043 828-245-0252
Dr. John Kinlaw, supt. Fax 245-4151
www.rutherford.k12.nc.us
Chase HS 800/9-12
1603 Chase High Rd 28043 828-245-7668
Robert Smith, prin. Fax 248-3584
Chase MS 800/6-8
840 Chase High Rd 28043 828-247-1044
Greg Lovelace, prin. Fax 247-0551
East Rutherford HS 900/9-12
PO Box 668 28043 828-245-6424
Janet Mason, prin. Fax 247-0039
Other Schools – See Bostic, Rutherfordton

Master's Academy 100/PK-12
120 School Dr 28043 828-245-7203
Tami Schultz, admin.

Four Oaks, Johnston, Pop. 1,631
Johnston County SD
Supt. — See Smithfield
Four Oaks MS 500/6-8
1475 Boyette Rd 27524 919-963-4022
Lisa Edwards, prin. Fax 963-4123
South Johnston HS 1,000/9-12
10381 US Highway 301 S 27524 919-894-3146
Barry Honeycutt, prin. Fax 894-3229

Franklin, Macon, Pop. 3,573
Macon County SD 4,100/K-12
PO Box 1029 28744 828-524-3314
Dr. Rodney Shotwell, supt. Fax 524-5938
www.mcsk-12.org
Franklin HS 1,100/9-12
100 Panther Dr 28734 828-524-6467
Gary Sheilds, prin. Fax 524-0684
Macon MS 800/6-8
1345 Wells Grove Rd 28734 828-524-3766
Regina Cook Mathis, prin. Fax 349-3900
Other Schools – See Highlands, Topton

Trimont Christian Academy 100/PK-12
98 Promise Ln 28734 828-369-6756
Robert Ricotta, admin. Fax 524-0622

Franklinton, Franklin, Pop. 1,848
Franklin County SD
Supt. — See Louisburg
Franklinton HS 700/9-12
PO Box 520 27525 919-494-2332
Charles Fuller, prin. Fax 494-5140

Fremont, Wayne, Pop. 1,428
Wayne County SD
Supt. — See Goldsboro
Norwayne MS 1,000/6-8
1394 Norwayne School Rd 27830 919-242-3414
Barbara Wilkins, prin. Fax 242-3418

Fuquay Varina, Wake, Pop. 6,525
Wake County SD
Supt. — See Raleigh
Fuquay-Varina HS 1,500/9-12
201 Bengal Dr 27526 919-557-2511
Tony Cates, prin. Fax 557-2512
Fuquay-Varina MS 700/6-8
109 N Ennis St 27526 919-557-2727
William Blanchard, prin. Fax 557-2732

Hilltop Christian S 200/K-12
5309 Umstead Rd 27526 919-552-5612
Jeff Jones, prin.

Garner, Wake, Pop. 20,537
Johnston County SD
Supt. — See Smithfield
Cleveland MS 700/6-8
2323 Cornwallis Rd 27529 919-553-7500
Kathleen McLamb, prin. Fax 553-7798

Wake County SD
Supt. — See Raleigh
East Garner MS 800/6-8
6301 Jones Sausage Rd 27529 919-662-2339
Isaac Holton, prin. Fax 662-2357
Garner HS 1,900/9-12
2101 Spring Dr 27529 919-662-2379
Catherine Johnson, prin. Fax 662-2397
North Garner MS 900/6-8
720 Powell Dr 27529 919-662-2434
John Wall, prin. Fax 662-5637

EnVisionary I-Care Post-Sec.
133 Highway 70 W 27529 919-661-7773

Gaston, Northampton, Pop. 953
Northampton County SD
Supt. — See Jackson
Gaston MS 300/6-8
PO Box J 27832 252-537-2520
Martha Paige, prin. Fax 535-5692
Northampton County HS West 500/9-12
152 Hurricane Ln 27832 252-537-1910
Charles Chestnut, prin. Fax 537-9028

Gastonia, Gaston, Pop. 67,781
Gaston County SD 30,000/PK-12
PO Box 1397 28053 704-866-6100
Dr. Edward Sadler, supt. Fax 866-6321
www.gaston.k12.nc.us/
Ashbrook HS 1,400/9-12
2222 S New Hope Rd 28054 704-866-6600
Page Carver, prin. Fax 866-6203
Forestview HS 1,200/9-12
5545 Union Rd 28056 704-861-2625
Robert Carpenter, prin. Fax 853-3323
Grier MS 700/6-8
1622 E Garrison Blvd 28054 704-866-6086
Laura Dixon, prin. Fax 866-6116
Highland School of Technology Vo/Tech
1600 N Morris St 28052 704-810-8818
Lee Dedmon, prin. Fax 866-6105
Huss HS 1,000/9-12
1518 Edgefield Ave 28052 704-866-6610
Kelly Gwaltney, prin. Fax 866-6103
Southwest MS 900/6-8
1 Roadrunner Dr 28052 704-866-6290
Chris Germain, prin. Fax 866-6293
York-Chester MS 500/6-8
601 S Clay St 28052 704-866-6297
Cindy White, prin. Fax 866-6319
Other Schools – See Belmont, Bessemer City,
Cherryville, Cramerton, Dallas, Lowell, Mount Holly,
Stanley

Gaston Day S 400/PK-12
2001 Gaston Day School Rd 28056 704-864-7744
Dr. Richard E. Rankin, prin. Fax 865-3813
Victory Christian Academy 100/K-12
310 Carolina Ave 28052 704-865-7132
Willa McGhee, prin. Fax 867-1731

Gatesville, Gates, Pop. 284
Gates County SD 2,000/PK-12
PO Box 125 27938 252-357-1113
Dr. Robert Hahne, supt. Fax 357-0207
coserver.gates.k12.nc.us/
Central MS 500/6-8
362 US Highway 158 W 27938 252-357-0470
Shirley Vinson, prin. Fax 357-1319
Gates County HS 600/9-12
88 US Highway 158 W 27938 252-357-0720
Charles Mason, prin. Fax 357-2058

Gibsonville, Guilford, Pop. 4,447
Guilford County SD
Supt. — See Greensboro

Eastern Guilford HS 1,000/9-12
415 Peeden Dr 27249 336-274-8461
Dr. Lisa Cooke, prin. Fax 449-7392
Eastern MS 900/6-8
435 Peeden Dr 27249 336-697-3199
Michael Ferrell, prin. Fax 449-0728

Goldsboro, Wayne, Pop. 38,484
Wayne County SD 19,400/K-12
PO Box 1797 27533 919-731-5900
Dr. Steven Taylor, supt. Fax 705-6199
www.waynecountyschools.org
Dillard MS 300/6-8
1101 Devereaux St 27530 919-580-9360
Marvin McCoy, prin. Fax 736-1121
Eastern Wayne HS 1,300/9-12
1135 E New Hope Rd 27534 919-751-7120
Eugene Byrd, prin. Fax 751-7107
Eastern Wayne MS 700/6-8
3518 Central Heights Rd 27534 919-751-7110
Keith Wright, prin. Fax 751-7114
Goldsboro HS 700/9-12
PO Box 1757 27533 919-731-5930
Patricia Burden, prin. Fax 731-5914
Goldsboro MS 500/6-8
801 Lionel St 27530 919-731-5940
Sylvester Townsend, prin. Fax 731-5945
Greenwood MS 600/5-8
3209 E Ash St 27534 919-751-7100
Larry Dean, prin. Fax 751-7201
Rosewood HS 500/9-12
900 Rosewood Rd 27530 919-705-6050
David Lewis, prin. Fax 705-6055
Rosewood MS 400/6-8
541 NC Highway 581 S 27530 919-736-5050
Lisa Tart, prin. Fax 736-5055
Other Schools – See Dudley, Fremont, Mount Olive,
Pikeville, Seven Springs

Faith Christian Academy 400/K-12
1200 W Grantham St 27530 919-734-8701
Walter Sloan, prin. Fax 734-9658
Mitchell's Hairstyling Academy Post-Sec.
1021 N Spence Ave 27534 919-778-8200
Summit Christian Academy 200/PK-12
3016 Summit Rd 27534 919-759-2002
Tammy Kennedy, prin. Fax 759-0050
Wayne Christian S 500/PK-12
1201 Patetown Rd 27530 919-735-5605
Lynn Mooring, prin. Fax 735-5229
Wayne Community College Post-Sec.
PO Box 8002 27533 919-735-5151
Wayne Country Day S 300/PK-12
480 Country Day Rd 27530 919-736-1045
Todd Anderson, prin. Fax 583-9493

Graham, Alamance, Pop. 13,282
Alamance-Burlington SD
Supt. — See Burlington
Graham HS 800/9-12
903 Trollinger Rd 27253 336-570-6440
Lynn Briggs, prin. Fax 570-6446
Graham MS 700/6-8
311 E Pine St 27253 336-570-6460
Teresa Faucette, prin. Fax 570-6464
Southern Alamance HS 1,300/9-12
631 Southern High School Rd 27253 336-570-6400
Kent Byrd, prin. Fax 570-6404
Southern MS 800/6-8
771 Southern High School Rd 27253 336-570-6500
Heather Ward, prin. Fax 570-6504

Alamance Christian S 300/K-12
PO Box 838 27253 336-578-0318
Robert La Tour, prin. Fax 578-7200
Alamance Community College Post-Sec.
PO Box 8000 27253 336-578-2002

Granite Falls, Caldwell, Pop. 4,572
Caldwell County SD
Supt. — See Lenoir
Granite Falls MS 700/6-8
90 N Main St 28630 828-396-2341
Brian Suddreth, prin. Fax 396-7072

Covenant Fellowship S 100/K-12
6062 Petra Mill Rd 28630 828-396-6892
Shirley Connor, prin. Fax 396-8451

Grantsboro, Pamlico, Pop. 761

Pamlico Community College Post-Sec.
PO Box 185 28529 252-249-1851

Greensboro, Guilford, Pop. 229,110
Guilford County SD 66,700/PK-12
PO Box 880 27402 336-370-8100
Dr. Terry Grier, supt. Fax 370-8299
www.gcsnc.com/
Allen MS 900/6-8
1108 Glendale Dr 27406 336-294-7325
Jesse Pratt, prin. Fax 294-7315
Aycock MS 700/6-8
811 Cypress St 27405 336-370-8110
William Price, prin. Fax 370-8044
Brown Summit MS 6-8
4720 E NC Highway 150, 336-656-0432
Terri Spears, prin. Fax 656-0439
Dudley HS 1,300/9-12
1200 Lincoln St 27401 336-370-8130
Phyllis Martin, prin. Fax 370-8979
Grimsley HS 1,900/9-12
801 Westover Ter 27408 336-370-8180
Robert M. Gasparello, prin. Fax 370-8194
Guilford MS 900/4-8
401 College Rd 27410 336-316-5833
Cynthia Kremer, prin. Fax 316-5837
Hairston MS 800/6-8
3911 Naco Rd 27401 336-370-8050
Lewis Ferebee, prin. Fax 370-8153
Jackson MS 700/6-8
2200 Ontario St 27403 336-294-7350
Jason Johnson, prin. Fax 294-7316
Kernodle MS 900/6-8
3600 Drawbridge Pkwy 27410 336-545-3717
Charles L. Burns, prin. Fax 545-3714
Kiser MS 1,000/6-8
716 Benjamin Pkwy 27408 336-370-8240
Dr. Dorothy Harper, prin. Fax 370-8248

Lincoln Academy 4-8
1016 Lincoln St 27401 336-370-3471
Rodney Boone, prin. Fax 370-3480
Mendenhall MS 900/6-8
205 Willoughby Blvd 27408 336-545-2000
Nola Taylor, prin. Fax 545-2004
Northwest Guilford HS 1,900/9-12
5240 NW School Rd 27409 336-605-3300
Wanda Legrand, prin. Fax 605-3314
Northwest Guilford MS 1,100/6-8
5300 NW School Rd 27409 336-605-3333
Dr. William Stewart, prin. Fax 605-3325
Page HS 1,600/9-12
201 Alma Pinnix Dr 27405 336-370-8200
Dr. Terry Worrell, prin. Fax 370-8219
Smith HS 1,600/9-12
2407 S Holden Rd 27407 336-294-7300
Dr. Samuel W. Misher, prin. Fax 294-7313
Southeast Guilford HS 1,200/9-12
4530 SE School Rd 27406 336-674-4300
Keith D. Kremer, prin. Fax 674-4290
Southeast Guilford MS 1,100/6-8
4825 Woody Mill Rd 27406 336-674-4280
Sam Foust, prin. Fax 674-4276
Southern Guilford HS 900/9-12
5700 Drake Rd 27406 336-674-4250
James Gibson, prin. Fax 674-4254
Weaver Education Center Vo/Tech
300 S Spring St 27401 336-370-8282
Sarah Harrelson, prin. Fax 370-8287
Western Guilford HS 1,300/9-12
409 Friendway Rd 27410 336-316-5800
Randy Shaver, prin. Fax 316-5813
Other Schools – See Gibsonville, High Point, Jamestown,
Mc Leansville

American Hebrew Academy 100/9-12
4334 Hobbs Rd 27410 336-217-7015
Glenn Drew, prin.
Bennett College Post-Sec.
900 E Washington St 27401 336-273-4431
Brookstone College of Business Post-Sec.
7815 National Service Rd 27409 336-668-2627
Caldwell Academy 600/K-12
2900 Horse Pen Creek Rd 27410 336-665-1161
Mark Guthrie, hdmstr. Fax 665-1178
Carolina Beauty College Post-Sec.
1917 E Wendover Ave 27405 336-886-4712
Carolina Beauty College Post-Sec.
2001 E Wendover Ave 27405 336-272-2966
ECPI College of Technology Post-Sec.
7802 Airport Center Dr 27409 336-665-1400
Greensboro College Post-Sec.
815 W Market St 27401 336-272-7102
Greensboro Day S 900/PK-12
5401 Lawndale Dr 27455 336-288-8590
Ralph Davison, prin. Fax 282-2905
Guilford College Post-Sec.
5800 W Friendly Ave 27410 336-316-2000
Guilford Day S 100/1-12
3310 Horse Pen Creek Rd 27410 336-282-7044
Laura B. Mlatac, hdmstr. Fax 282-2048
Leon's Beauty School Post-Sec.
1410 W Lee St 27403 336-274-4601
Moses H. Cone Memorial Hospital Post-Sec.
1200 N Elm St 27401 336-574-7881
New Garden Friends S 300/PK-12
1128 New Garden Rd 27410 336-299-0964
Marty Goldstein, prin. Fax 292-0347
North Carolina A&T State University Post-Sec.
1601 E Market St 27411 336-334-7500
Shining Light Academy 200/K-12
4530 W Wendover Ave 27409 336-299-9688
Rev. Steve Kilby, prin.
University of North Carolina Post-Sec.
1000 Spring Garden St 27412 336-334-5000
Vandalia Christian S 700/PK-12
3919 Pleasant Garden Rd 27406 336-379-8380
Mark Weatherford, admin. Fax 379-8671

Greenville, Pitt, Pop. 67,190
Pitt County SD 21,400/PK-12
1717 W 5th St 27834 252-830-4200
Michael D. Priddy Ed.D., supt. Fax 830-4239
www.pitt.k12.nc.us/
Aycock MS 900/6-8
1325 Red Banks Rd 27858 252-756-4181
Delilah Jackson, prin. Fax 756-2408
Conley HS 1,300/9-12
2006 Worthington Rd 27858 252-756-3440
C.G. Moore, prin. Fax 756-3028
Eppes MS 500/6-8
1100 S Elm St 27858 252-757-2160
Charlie Langley, prin. Fax 757-2163
Rose HS 1,700/9-12
600 W Arlington Blvd 27834 252-321-3640
Dr. George Frazier, prin. Fax 321-3653
Wellcome MS 500/6-8
3101 N Memorial Dr 27834 252-752-5938
Dr. John Daniels, prin. Fax 752-1685
Other Schools – See Ayden, Bethel, Farmville, Winterville

East Carolina University Post-Sec.
Admissions 27858 252-328-6131
Greenville Christian Academy 400/K-12
1621 Greenville Blvd SW 27834 252-756-0939
Paul Aynes, prin.
Mitchell's Hairstyling Academy Post-Sec.
426 E Arlington Blvd 27858 252-756-3050
Pitt Community College Post-Sec.
PO Box 7007 27835 252-321-4200
Trinity Christian S 400/PK-12
3111 Golden Rd 27858 252-758-0037
Denise Mills, prin. Fax 758-0767

Grifton, Lenoir, Pop. 2,056
Lenoir County SD
Supt. — See Kinston
Savannah MS 300/6-8
2583 Cameron Langston Rd 28530 252-527-8897
Audrey Nobles, prin. Fax 527-9175

Halifax, Halifax, Pop. 326
Halifax County SD 5,700/PK-12
PO Box 468 27839 252-583-5111
Dr. Willie Gilchrist, supt. Fax 583-1474
www.halifax.k12.nc.us/
Southeast Halifax HS 700/9-12
16683 NC Highway 125 27839 252-445-2027
Fax 445-3463

Other Schools – See Enfield, Littleton, Roanoke Rapids,
Scotland Neck

Weldon CSD
Supt. — See Weldon
Weldon MS 300/6-8
PO Box 100 27839 252-536-2571
Willie Bell, prin. Fax 536-3485

Hallsboro, Columbus
Columbus County SD
Supt. — See Whiteville
Hallsboro MS 400/5-8
PO Box 248 28442 910-646-4192
Michael Mobley, prin. Fax 646-5072

Hamlet, Richmond, Pop. 5,866
Richmond County SD 8,200/PK-12
PO Box 1259 28345 910-582-5860
Dr. Larry Weatherly, supt. Fax 582-7921
www.richmond.k12.nc.us
Hamlet JHS 600/7-9
1406 Mcdonald Ave 28345 910-582-7903
Carl Ransom, prin. Fax 582-5730
Other Schools – See Ellerbe, Rockingham

Richmond Community College Post-Sec.
PO Box 1189 28345 910-582-7000

Hampstead, Pender
Pender County SD
Supt. — See Burgaw
Topsail HS 700/9-12
17445 US Highway 17 N 28443 910-270-2755
Fax 270-9290
Topsail MS 600/6-8
17385 US Highway 17 N 28443 910-270-2612
Markus Skipper, prin. Fax 270-3190

Harrells, Sampson, Pop. 206

Harrells Christian Academy 400/K-12
PO Box 88 28444 910-532-4575
Dr. Ronald Montgomery, prin. Fax 532-2958

Havelock, Craven, Pop. 22,499
Craven County SD
Supt. — See New Bern
Havelock HS 1,200/9-12
101 Webb Blvd 28532 252-444-5112
Jeffrey Murphy, prin. Fax 444-5119
Havelock MS 500/6-8
102 High School Dr 28532 252-444-5125
Wanda Simmons, prin. Fax 444-5129
Tucker Creek MS 500/6-8
200 Sermons Rd 28532 252-444-7200
Danny Tripp, prin. Fax 444-7206

Liberty Christian S 100/K-12
81 Shepard St 28532 252-447-4185
Bryan Roberts, prin. Fax 447-6736

Hayesville, Clay, Pop. 459
Clay County SD 1,300/PK-12
PO Box 178 28904 828-389-8513
Douglas Penland, supt. Fax 389-3437
www.clayschools.org/
Hayesville HS 400/9-12
205 Yellow Jacket Dr 28904 828-389-6532
Dr. Gail Criss, prin. Fax 389-6251
Hayesville MS 400/5-8
135 School Dr 28904 828-389-9924
Mark Leek, prin. Fax 389-1706

Hays, Wilkes, Pop. 1,522
Wilkes County SD
Supt. — See Wilkesboro
North Wilkes HS 700/9-12
PO Box 430 28635 336-957-8601
Annette Greene, prin. Fax 957-4787

Henderson, Vance, Pop. 16,231
Vance County SD 8,600/PK-12
PO Box 7001 27536 252-492-2127
Dr. Norman Shearin, supt. Fax 438-6119
www.vcs.k12.nc.us
Eaton-Johnson MS 1,100/6-8
500 N Beckford Dr 27536 252-438-5017
Michael Talley, prin. Fax 738-0250
Henderson MS 1,100/6-8
219 Charles St 27536 252-492-0054
Victor Fenner, prin. Fax 430-8588
Northern Vance HS 1,100/9-12
293 Warrenton Rd 27537 252-492-6041
Hugh Brady, prin. Fax 492-7878
Southern Vance HS 900/9-12
925 Garrett Rd 27537 252-430-6000
James Pickens, prin. Fax 430-0308

Crossroads Christian S 200/PK-12
583 Old County Home Rd 27537 252-431-1333
Charles Ligon, hdmstr. Fax 431-0333
Kerr-Vance Academy 400/PK-12
700 Vance Academy Rd 27537 252-492-0018
Robin Jackson, prin. Fax 438-4652
Maria Parham Hospital Post-Sec.
566 Ruin Creek Rd 27536 252-436-1130
Vance-Granville Community College Post-Sec.
PO Box 917 27536 252-492-2061
Victory Baptist S 100/K-12
PO Box 592 27536 252-492-6079
Rev. Ricky Easter, prin. Fax 492-4683

Hendersonville, Henderson, Pop. 11,123
Henderson County SD 12,300/PK-12
414 4th Ave W 28739 828-697-4733
Stephen L. Page Ed.D., supt. Fax 697-5541
www.henderson.k12.nc.us
Apple Valley MS 800/6-8
43 Fruitland Rd 28792 828-697-4545
Caroline Patterson, prin. Fax 698-6119
Hendersonville HS 600/9-12
311 8th Ave W 28791 828-697-4802
W. Robert Wilkins, prin. Fax 698-6126
Hendersonville MS 500/6-8
825 N Whitted St 28791 828-697-4800
Dr. Chuck Pressley, prin. Fax 698-6127
North Henderson HS 900/9-12
35 Fruitland Rd 28792 828-697-4500
Rebecca Friend, prin. Fax 698-6129

Rugby MS
3345 Haywood Rd 28791
Beverly Setzer, prin.
West Henderson HS
3600 Haywood Rd 28791
Dr. Jan Webster, prin.
Other Schools – See East Flat Rock

800/6-8
828-891-6566
Fax 891-6589
1,000/9-12
828-891-6571
Fax 891-6590

Hendersonville Christian S
708 Old Spartanburg Rd 28792
Kenny Young, prin.

100/K-12
828-692-0556

Hertford, Perquimans, Pop. 2,070
Perquimans County SD
PO Box 337 27944
Dr. Kenneth W. Wells, supt.
www.pcs.k12.nc.us/
Perquimans County HS
PO Box 398 27944
Melvin Harkins, prin.
Other Schools – See Winfall

1,800/PK-12
252-426-5741
Fax 426-4913

600/9-12
252-426-5778
Fax 426-1663

Hickory, Catawba, Pop. 39,476
Catawba County SD
Supt. — See Newton
Arndt MS
3350 34th Street Dr NE 28601
Jeff Taylor, prin.
Catawba Valley Early College HS
2550 Highway 70 SE 28602
Dr. Eddy Daniel, prin.
St. Stephens HS
3205 34th Street Dr NE 28601
DeAnna Taylor, prin.

700/7-8
828-256-9545
Fax 256-6748
9-12
828-485-2980
Fax 485-2981
1,200/9-12
828-256-9841
Fax 256-7159

Hickory CSD
432 4th Ave SW 28602
Dr. Duane Kirkman, supt.
www.hickory.k12.nc.us
Grandview MS
737 12th St SW 28602
Vanessa Howerton, prin.
Hickory HS
1234 3rd St NE 28601
Dr. Kim Mattox, prin.
Northview MS
302 28th Ave NE 28601
Dr. Martha Hill, prin.

4,500/PK-12
828-322-2855
Fax 322-1834

500/6-8
828-328-2289
Fax 328-2992
1,300/9-12
828-322-5860
Fax 326-7101
600/6-8
828-327-6300
Fax 327-6367

Catawba Valley Community College
2550 US Highway 70 SE 28602
Christian Family Academy
PO Box 5353 28603
David Gruver, prin.
Hickory Christian Academy
PO Box 5203 28603
Tracy Robinson, prin.
Lenoir-Rhyne College
7th Ave and 8th St 28603
Tabernacle Christian S
1225 29th Avenue Dr NE 28601
Dr. Gordon Fenlason, prin.

Post-Sec.
828-327-7000
200/K-12
828-324-4204

200/K-12
828-324-5405

Post-Sec.
828-328-1741
200/K-12
828-324-9936
Fax 324-8921

Hiddenite, Alexander
Alexander County SD
Supt. — See Taylorsville
East Alexander MS
1285 White Plains Rd 28636
Ron Hargrave, prin.

600/6-8
828-632-7565
Fax 632-4508

Highlands, Macon, Pop. 906
Macon County SD
Supt. — See Franklin
Highlands S
PO Box 940 28741
Monica Bomengen, prin.

400/K-12
828-526-2147
Fax 526-0615

High Point, Guilford, Pop. 91,543
Guilford County SD
Supt. — See Greensboro
Andrews HS
1920 McGuinn Dr 27265
Monique Brooks, prin.
Ferndale MS
701 Ferndale Blvd 27262
Carolyn Brown, prin.
High Point Central HS
801 Ferndale Blvd 27262
Revonda Johnson, prin.
Jay MS
1201 E Fairfield Rd 27263
Kevin Wheat, prin.
Penn-Griffin MS
825 E Washington Dr 27260
Bobby Ann Hayes, prin.
Southwest Guilford HS
4364 Barrow Rd 27265
George Allen Parker, prin.
Southwest Guilford MS
4368 Barrow Rd 27265
William Farkas, prin.
Welborn MS
1710 McGuinn Dr 27265
Roger Wood, prin.

1,200/9-12
336-819-2800
Fax 887-5585
700/6-8
336-819-2855
Fax 885-2854
1,400/9-12
336-819-2825
Fax 819-2991
700/6-8
336-434-8470
Fax 431-5530
700/6-8
336-819-2870
Fax 889-4841
1,300/9-12
336-819-2970
Fax 454-5175
1,100/6-8
336-819-2985
Fax 454-4015
800/6-8
336-819-2880
Fax 819-2878

Hayworth Christian S
1696 Westchester Dr 27262
Mickey Briles, admin.
High Point Christian Academy
307 N Rotary Dr 27262
Richard Hardee, admin.
High Point University
933 Montlieu Ave 27262
John Wesley College
2314 N Centennial St 27265
Tri-City Junior Academy
8000 Clinard Farms Rd 27265
Clint Sutton, prin.
Wesleyan Christian Academy
1917 N Centennial St 27262
Joel Farlow, prin.
Westchester Academy
204 Pine Tree Ln 27265
Tommy Hudgins, hdmstr.

200/PK-12
336-882-3126
Fax 882-9157
700/PK-12
336-841-8702
Fax 841-8701
Post-Sec.
336-841-9000
Post-Sec.
336-889-2262
100/K-10
336-665-9822
Fax 665-9834
1,300/PK-12
336-884-3333
Fax 884-8232
400/K-12
336-869-2128
Fax 869-9298

Hillsborough, Orange, Pop. 5,361
Orange County SD
200 E King St 27278
Dr. Shirley Carraway, supt.
www.orange.k12.nc.us

6,500/K-12
919-732-8126
Fax 732-8120

Cedar Ridge HS
1125 New Grady Brown Sch Rd 27278

Gary Thornburg, prin.
Orange HS
500 Orange High School Rd 27278
Jeffrey Dishmon, prin.
Stanback MS
3700 NC Highway 86 S 27278
Clara Daniels, prin.
Stanford MS
308 Orange High School Rd 27278
Michael Gilbert, prin.

900/9-12
919-245-4000
919-245-4000
Fax 245-4010
1,000/9-12
919-732-6133
Fax 644-7699
800/6-8
919-644-3200
Fax 644-3226
900/6-8
919-732-6121
Fax 732-6910

Abundant Life Christian Academy
512 US Highway 70 E 27278
Ken Brunson, admin.

200/PK-12
919-732-6460
Fax 732-8927

Hobgood, Halifax, Pop. 393

Hobgood Academy
201 S Beech St 27843
William Whitehurst, prin.

200/K-12
252-826-4116
Fax 826-2265

Holly Ridge, Onslow, Pop. 790
Onslow County SD
Supt. — See Jacksonville
Dixon HS
160 Dixon School Rd 28445
Lesley Eason, prin.
Dixon MS
200 Dixon School Rd 28445
Dr. Laurie Spring, prin.

600/9-12
910-347-2958
Fax 347-3932
500/6-8
910-347-2738
Fax 347-4399

Holly Springs, Wake, Pop. 12,694
Wake County SD
Supt. — See Raleigh
Holly Ridge MS
950 Holly Springs Rd 27540
Kenneth Proulx, prin.
Holly Springs HS
5329 Cass Holt Rd 27540
Luther Johnson, prin.

900/6-8
919-577-1335
Fax 577-1339
9-10
919-463-8606
Fax 463-8607

Hookerton, Greene, Pop. 485

Mount Calvary Christian Academy
PO Box 250 28538
Michael Fulcher, prin.

200/K-12
252-747-8111
Fax 747-8112

Hope Mills, Cumberland, Pop. 11,966
Cumberland County SD
Supt. — See Fayetteville
Grays Creek HS
5301 Celebration Dr 28348
Joyce Adams, prin.
Grays Creek MS
2964 School Rd 28348
Sara Whitaker, prin.
Hope Mills MS
4975 Cameron Rd 28348
Patsy Ray, prin.
South View HS
4184 Elk Mill Rd 28348
Robert Barnes, prin.
South View MS
4100 Elk Mill Rd 28348
Garda Tatum, prin.

800/9-12
910-424-8589
Fax 424-7411
500/6-8
910-483-4124
Fax 483-5296
700/6-8
910-425-5106
Fax 423-5887
1,800/9-12
910-425-8181
Fax 425-2962
900/6-8
910-424-3131
Fax 424-2402

Hudson, Caldwell, Pop. 3,064
Caldwell County SD
Supt. — See Lenoir
Caldwell County Career Center
2857 Hickory Blvd 28638
Roxy Poovey, prin.
Hudson MS
291 Pine Mountain Rd 28638
Jeff Church, prin.
South Caldwell HS
7035 Spartan Dr 28638
Michael Peake, prin.

Vo/Tech
828-726-2606
Fax 726-2463
800/6-8
828-728-4281
Fax 726-8157
1,500/9-12
828-396-2188
Fax 396-3329

Caldwell Community Coll. & Tech. Inst.
2855 Hickory Blvd 28638
Harris Chapel Christian Academy
1444 Cajah Mountain Rd 28638
Allen Norrod, prin.
Heritage Christian S
239 Mount Herman Rd 28638
Robert Setzer, prin.

Post-Sec.
828-726-2200
100/K-12
828-728-3721
Fax 728-2375
200/K-12
828-726-0055

Huntersville, Mecklenburg, Pop. 32,323
Charlotte/Mecklenburg Co. SD
Supt. — See Charlotte
Alexander MS
12201 Hambright Rd 28078
Joey Burch, prin.
Bradley MS
13345 Beatties Ford Rd 28078
Alicisa Johnson, prin.
Hopewell HS
11530 Beatties Ford Rd 28078
Kendra March, prin.
North Mecklenburg HS
11201 Old Statesville Rd 28078
Joey Burch, prin.

1,400/6-8
980-343-3830
Fax 343-3851
1,700/6-8
980-343-5750
Fax 343-5743
2,000/9-12
980-343-5988
Fax 343-5990
2,400/9-12
980-343-3840
Fax 343-3845

SouthLake Christian Academy
13901 Hagers Ferry Rd 28078
C. Wayne Parker, hdmstr.

600/K-12
704-949-2200
Fax 949-2203

Icard, Burke, Pop. 2,553
Burke County SD
Supt. — See Morganton
East Burke MS
PO Box 1150 28666
Jim Childers, prin.

900/6-8
828-397-7446
Fax 397-1086

Indian Trail, Union, Pop. 14,173
Union County SD
Supt. — See Monroe
Porter Ridge HS
2839 Ridge Rd 28079
Dr. Bryan Setser, prin.
Porter Ridge MS
2827 Ridge Rd 28079
Timothy Conner, prin.

9-12
704-292-7662
Fax 296-9733
6-8
704-225-7555
Fax 226-9844

Sun Valley MS
1409 Wesley Chapel Rd 28079
John Jones, prin.

1,300/6-8
704-296-3009
Fax 296-3045

Lake Park Christian Academy
3624 Lake Park Rd 28079
William Kamm, prin.
Metrolina Christian Academy
PO Box 1460 28079
Rick Calloway, admin.

100/K-10
704-882-6267
Fax 882-4651
900/PK-12
704-882-3375
Fax 882-4178

Iron Station, Lincoln
Lincoln County SD
Supt. — See Lincolnton
East Lincoln HS
4137 Highway 73 28080
Dr. Vista Rainey, prin.

600/6-8
704-732-0761
Fax 732-4456

Jackson, Northampton, Pop. 674
Northampton County SD
PO Box 158 27845
Dr. Kathi Gibson, supt.
www.northampton.k12.nc.us/
Other Schools – See Conway, Gaston

3,400/PK-12
252-534-1371
Fax 534-4631

Jacksonville, Onslow, Pop. 67,386
Onslow County SD
PO Box 99 28541
Ronald Singletary, supt.
www.onslow.k12.nc.us
Hunters Creek MS
85 Hunters Trl 28546
Megan Doyle, prin.
Jacksonville Commons MS
315 Commons Dr S 28546
Lynn Jackson, prin.
Jacksonville HS
1021 Henderson Dr 28540
Susie Kinder, prin.
New Bridge MS
401 New Bridge St 28540
Brent Anderson, prin.
Northside HS
365 Commons Dr S 28540
Albert James, prin.
Northwoods Park MS
904 Sioux Dr 28540
Maria Johnson, prin.
Southwest HS
1420 Burgaw Hwy 28540
Debra Bryan, prin.
Southwest MS
3000 Furia Rd 28540
Pam Baldwin, prin.
White Oak HS
1001 Piney Green Rd 28546
Paul Wiggins, prin.
Other Schools – See Holly Ridge, Richlands, Swansboro

21,700/PK-12
910-455-2211
Fax 455-1965

800/6-8
910-353-2147
Fax 353-7939
700/6-8
910-346-6888
Fax 938-1682
1,300/9-12
910-989-2048
Fax 989-2046
500/6-8
910-346-5144
Fax 346-5402
800/9-12
910-455-4868
Fax 455-4987
600/6-8
910-347-1202
Fax 347-0713
800/9-12
910-455-4888
Fax 455-3949
500/6-8
910-455-1105
Fax 455-4082
1,200/9-12
910-455-1541
Fax 938-2302

Cheveux School Hair Design and Hairport
4781 Gum Branch Rd # 1 28540
Coastal Carolina Community College
444 Western Blvd 28546
Jacksonville Christian Academy
919 Gum Branch Rd 28540
Rev. Earl Hanna, prin.
Living Water Christian S
3980 Gum Branch Rd 28540
Barbara Koebbe, prin.

Post-Sec.
910-455-5767
Post-Sec.
910-455-1221
200/K-12
910-347-2358

200/K-12
910-938-7017
Fax 938-7025

Jamestown, Guilford, Pop. 3,041
Guilford County SD
Supt. — See Greensboro
Jamestown MS
4401 Vickery Chapel Rd N 27282
Beverly Tucker, prin.
Ragsdale HS
602 High Point Rd 27282
Dr. Kathryn Rogers, prin.

1,200/6-8
336-819-2100
Fax 454-6734
1,200/9-12
336-819-2960
Fax 454-6767

Guilford Technical Community College
PO Box 309 27282

Post-Sec.
336-334-4822

Jamesville, Martin, Pop. 488
Martin County SD
Supt. — See Williamston
Jamesville JSHS
PO Box 189 27846
Helen Davis, prin.

300/7-12
252-792-4428
Fax 809-4812

Jefferson, Ashe, Pop. 1,424
Ashe County SD
PO Box 604 28640
Donnie Johnson, supt.
www.ashe.k12.nc.us/
Other Schools – See Warrensville, West Jefferson

2,700/PK-12
336-246-7175
Fax 246-7609

Kannapolis, Cabarrus, Pop. 38,178
Kannapolis CSD
100 Denver St 28083
Jo Anne A. Byerly, supt.
www.kannapolis.k12.nc.us
Brown HS
415 E 1st St 28083
Debra Morris, prin.
Kannapolis MS
1445 Oakwood Ave 28081
Daron Buckwell, prin.

3,500/K-12
704-938-1131
Fax 933-6370

1,200/9-12
704-932-6125
Fax 933-1862
7-8
704-932-4102
Fax 932-4104

Kenansville, Duplin, Pop. 875
Duplin County SD
PO Box 128 28349
Dr. Wiley Doby, supt.
www.duplinschools.net
Smith MS
PO Box 369 28349
Angela Britt, prin.
Other Schools – See Beulaville, Calypso, Rose Hill, Teachey, Warsaw

8,900/PK-12
910-296-1521
Fax 296-1396

400/6-8
910-296-0309
Fax 296-0086

James Sprunt Community College
PO Box 398 28349

Post-Sec.
910-296-2500

Kenly, Johnston, Pop. 1,652
Johnston County SD
Supt. — See Smithfield
North Johnston HS
PO Box 339 27542
Ross Renfrow, prin.

700/9-12
919-284-2031
Fax 284-6224

Kernersville, Forsyth, Pop. 20,053
Winston-Salem/Forsyth SD
Supt. — See Winston Salem
East Forsyth HS 1,800/9-12
2500 W Mountain St 27284 336-727-2265
Patricia Gainey, prin. Fax 727-8546
East Forsyth MS 6-8
4690 Old Hollow Rd 27284 336-703-6765
Dossie Poteat, prin. Fax 607-8531
Glenn HS 1,600/9-12
1600 Union Cross Rd 27284 336-771-4500
Adolphus Coplin, prin. Fax 771-4507
Kernersville MS 1,300/6-8
110 Brown Rd 27284 336-996-5566
Deborah Brooks, prin. Fax 996-1966
Southeast MS 1,200/6-8
1200 Old Salem Rd 27284 336-996-5848
Debbie Blanton-Warren, prin. Fax 996-0148

Bishop McGuiness HS 300/9-12
1725 NC Highway 66 S 27284 336-564-1010
George Repass, prin. Fax 564-1060
Dudley Cosmetology University Post-Sec.
900 E Mountain St 27284 336-996-2030
Kerwin Baptist Christian S 100/PK-12
4520 Old Hollow Rd 27284 336-993-3791
Dr. Ron Carrell, prin. Fax 996-1850

Kill Devil Hills, Dare, Pop. 6,287
Dare County SD
Supt. — See Nags Head
First Flight HS 9-12
PO Box 1758 27948 252-449-7000
Arty Tillett, prin. Fax 449-7004
First Flight MS 700/6-8
109 Run Hill Rd 27948 252-441-8888
Adrienne Palma, prin. Fax 441-7694

King, Stokes, Pop. 6,187
Stokes County SD
Supt. — See Danbury
Chestnut Grove MS 800/6-8
2185 Chestnut Grove Rd 27021 336-983-2106
Todd Martin, prin. Fax 983-2725
West Stokes HS 1,000/9-12
1400 Priddy Rd 27021 336-983-2099
Charles McAninch, prin. Fax 983-6076

Calvary Christian S 200/K-12
748 Spainhour Rd 27021 336-983-3743
Sid Main, prin. Fax 983-8426

Kings Mountain, Cleveland, Pop. 10,537
Cleveland County SD
Supt. — See Shelby
Kings Mountain HS 1,300/9-12
PO Box 1489 28086 704-734-5647
John Yarbro, prin. Fax 734-1723
Kings Mountain MS 800/7-8
1000 Phifer Rd 28086 704-734-5667
Stephen Fisher, prin. Fax 734-5615

Hope Christian Academy 100/K-12
PO Box 6 28086 704-734-0051
Raymond Sibley, prin.

Kinston, Lenoir, Pop. 22,978
Lenoir County SD 10,300/PK-12
PO Box 729 28502 252-527-1109
Dr. John Frossard, supt. Fax 527-6884
www.lenoir.k12.nc.us
Kinston HS 1,100/9-12
2601 N Queen St 28501 252-527-8067
Craig Hill, prin. Fax 527-4090
Rochelle MS 700/6-8
301 N Rochelle Blvd 28501 252-527-4290
Charity Bell, prin. Fax 527-6498
Woodington MS 800/6-8
4939 US Highway 258 S 28504 252-527-9570
Diane Heath, prin. Fax 527-3883
Other Schools – See Deep Run, Grifton, La Grange

Arendell Parrott Academy 700/PK-12
PO Box 1297 28503 252-522-4222
Dr. Ike Southerland, hdmstr. Fax 522-0672
Bethel Christian Academy 400/K-12
1936 Banks School Rd 28504 252-522-4636
Robert Struil, prin. Fax 523-7290
Lenoir Community College Post-Sec.
PO Box 188 28502 252-527-6223
Lenoir Memorial Hospital Post-Sec.
100 Airport Rd 28501 252-522-7797

Knightdale, Wake, Pop. 6,052
Wake County SD
Supt. — See Raleigh
Knightdale HS 9-12
100 Bryan Chalk Ln 27545 919-217-5350
Marvin Connelly, prin. Fax 217-5357

La Grange, Lenoir, Pop. 2,813
Lenoir County SD
Supt. — See Kinston
Frink MS 700/6-8
102 Martin Luther King Jr 28551 252-566-3326
Brent Williams, prin. Fax 566-4027
North Lenoir HS 1,000/9-12
2400 Institute Rd 28551 252-527-9184
Dexter Simms, prin. Fax 527-8672

Lake Waccamaw, Columbus, Pop. 1,420
Columbus County SD
Supt. — See Whiteville
East Columbus HS 700/9-12
PO Box 401 28450 910-646-4094
Reginald Lewis, prin. Fax 646-3779

Landis, Rowan, Pop. 2,997
Rowan-Salisbury County SD
Supt. — See Salisbury
Corriher-Lipe MS 600/6-8
214 W Rice St 28088 704-857-7946
Dr. Beverly S. Pugh, prin. Fax 855-2670

Lasker, Northampton, Pop. 99

Northeast Academy 300/PK-12
210 Church St 27845 252-539-2461
Russell Leake, hdmstr. Fax 539-3919

Laurel Hill, Scotland
Scotland County SD
Supt. — See Laurinburg
Carver MS 600/6-8
18601 Fieldcrest Rd 28351 910-462-4669
Gary Dwyer, prin. Fax 462-4674

Laurinburg, Scotland, Pop. 15,552
Scotland County SD 7,200/PK-12
322 S Main St 28352 910-276-1138
Dr. Shirley Prince, supt. Fax 277-4310
www.scsnc.org
Scotland HS 1,800/9-12
1000 W Church St 28352 910-276-7370
Roger Edwards, prin. Fax 277-4444
Spring Hill MS 500/6-8
22801 Airbase Rd 28352 910-369-0590
Harriet Jackson, prin. Fax 369-0595
Sycamore Lane MS 600/6-8
2100 Sycamore Ln 28352 910-277-4350
Rick Singletary, prin. Fax 277-4321
Other Schools – See Laurel Hill

St. Andrews Presbyterian College Post-Sec.
1700 Dogwood Mile St 28352 910-277-5000
Scotland Christian Academy 200/K-12
10300 McColl Rd 28352 910-276-7722
Rebecca Cline, prin.

Lawndale, Cleveland, Pop. 642
Cleveland County SD
Supt. — See Shelby
Burns HS 1,200/9-12
307 E Stagecoach Trl 28090 704-538-7403
Dr. Collette Deviney, prin. Fax 538-3895
Burns MS 1,000/6-8
215 Shady Grove Rd 28090 704-538-3126
Gary Blake, prin. Fax 538-3944

Lawsonville, Stokes
Stokes County SD
Supt. — See Danbury
Piney Grove MS 400/6-8
3415 Piney Grove Church Rd 27022 336-593-4000
Roger Tucker, prin. Fax 593-4003

Leland, Brunswick, Pop. 4,235
Brunswick County SD
Supt. — See Bolivia
Leland MS 700/6-8
927 Old Fayetteville Rd NE 28451 910-371-3030
Rob Knuschke, prin. Fax 371-0647
North Brunswick HS 700/9-12
PO Box 2080 28451 910-371-2261
Deanne Meadows, prin. Fax 371-0879

Lenoir, Caldwell, Pop. 17,952
Caldwell County SD 12,900/PK-12
1914 Hickory Blvd SW 28645 828-728-8407
Dr. Tom McNeel, supt. Fax 728-0012
www.caa.k12.nc.us
Gamewell MS 600/6-8
3210 Gamewell School Rd 28645 828-754-6204
Lynn Smith, prin. Fax 754-6278
Hibriten HS 1,000/9-12
550 East Blvd 28645 828-758-7376
James Sims, prin. Fax 758-9708
Lenoir MS 500/6-8
332 Greenhaven Dr NW 28645 828-758-2500
Dr. Pete Yount, prin. Fax 758-1570
West Caldwell HS 1,000/9-12
300 W Caldwell Dr 28645 828-758-5583
Chris Burton, prin. Fax 754-2783
Other Schools – See Granite Falls, Hudson

Lewisville, Forsyth, Pop. 9,332

Forsyth Country Day S 1,000/PK-12
PO Box 549 27023 336-945-3151
Henry Battle, prin. Fax 945-2907

Lexington, Davidson, Pop. 20,385
Davidson County SD 19,100/PK-12
PO Box 2057 27293 336-249-8181
Fred Mock, supt. Fax 249-1062
www.davidson.k12.nc.us
Central Davidson HS 900/9-12
2747 NC Highway 47 27292 336-357-2920
Kevin Firquin, prin. Fax 357-5175
Central Davidson MS 900/6-8
2591 NC Highway 47 27292 336-357-2310
Crystal Clodfelter, prin. Fax 357-5965
Davidson Early College S 10-12
PO Box 1287 27293 336-242-5686
Dr. Larry Allred, prin. Fax 242-5688
North Davidson HS 1,400/9-12
7227 Old US Highway 52 27295 336-731-8431
Gary Fishel, prin. Fax 731-2642
North Davidson MS 1,300/6-8
333 Critcher Dr 27295 336-731-2331
W. Bruce Johnson, prin. Fax 731-2328
Tyro MS 700/6-8
2946 Michael Rd 27295 336-853-7795
Harry Mock, prin. Fax 853-7357
West Davidson HS 800/9-12
200 Dragon Dr 27295 336-853-8082
Catherine Gentry, prin. Fax 853-7315
Other Schools – See Denton, Thomasville

Lexington CSD 2,800/PK-12
1010 Fair St 27292 336-242-1527
Rebecca Bloxam, supt. Fax 249-3206
lexcs.org
Lexington HS 800/9-12
26 Penry St 27292 336-242-1574
Greg Newlin, prin. Fax 242-1285
Lexington MS 700/6-8
100 E Hemstead St 27292 336-242-1557
Patti Kroh, prin. Fax 242-1372

Davidson County Community College Post-Sec.
PO Box 1287 27293 336-249-8186
Sheets Memorial Christian S 300/PK-12
307 Holt St 27292 336-249-4224
Dan Hightower, admin. Fax 249-6985
Union Grove Christian S 300/K-12
2295 Union Grove Rd 27295 336-764-3105
Pete Steinhaus, prin. Fax 764-8657

Liberty, Randolph, Pop. 2,663
Randolph County SD
Supt. — See Asheboro
Northeastern Randolph MS 500/6-8
3493 Ramseur Julian Rd 27298 336-622-5808
Beverly Wilson, prin. Fax 622-5868

Lillington, Harnett, Pop. 3,106
Harnett County SD 16,900/K-12
PO Box 1029 27546 910-893-8151
Dan Honeycutt, supt. Fax 893-5816
www.harnett.k12.nc.us/
Western Harnett HS 2,000/9-12
10637 NC Highway 27 W 27546 919-499-5113
Terry Hinson, prin. Fax 499-1537
Western Harnett MS 900/6-8
11135 NC Highway 27 W 27546 919-499-4497
Janice Harrington, prin. Fax 499-1788
Other Schools – See Angier, Dunn, Erwin, Spring Lake

Lincolnton, Lincoln, Pop. 10,114
Lincoln County SD 11,100/PK-12
PO Box 400 28093 704-732-2261
Dr. Jim Watson, supt. Fax 736-4321
www.lincoln.k12.nc.us
Lincoln County School of Technology Vo/Tech
1 Timpken Dr 28092 704-732-4084
David Bynum, prin. Fax 735-8292
Lincolnton HS 900/9-12
803 N Aspen St 28092 704-735-3089
Tony Worley, prin. Fax 736-4234
Lincolnton MS 700/6-8
2361 Startown Rd 28092 704-735-1120
Scott Carpenter, prin. Fax 732-6811
North Lincoln HS 800/9-12
2737 Lee Lawing Rd 28092 704-736-1969
Richard Freeman, prin. Fax 736-1966
Pumpkin Center MS 600/6-8
3980 King Wilkinson Rd 28092 704-736-0262
Rhonda Hager, prin. Fax 736-9812
West Lincoln HS 1,000/9-12
172 Shoal Rd 28092 704-276-1402
Mitchell Sherrill, prin. Fax 276-2004
West Lincoln MS 800/6-8
260 Shoal Rd 28092 704-276-1760
Glenda Walker, prin. Fax 276-2293
Other Schools – See Denver, Iron Station

Lincoln Christian Academy 100/K-12
280 Car Farm Rd 28092 704-735-5997
Clyde Smith, admin. Fax 732-3514

Littleton, Halifax, Pop. 666
Halifax County SD
Supt. — See Halifax
Northwest HS 900/9-12
8492 NC Highway 48 27850 252-586-4125
Sharon Arrington, prin. Fax 586-6240

Louisburg, Franklin, Pop. 3,103
Franklin County SD 7,800/K-12
PO Box 449 27549 919-496-4159
Dr. Bert L'Homme, supt. Fax 496-3341
www.fcschools.net
Louisburg HS 600/9-12
201 Allen Ln 27549 919-496-3725
Chris Blice, prin. Fax 496-2505
Terrell Lane MS 500/6-8
101 Terrell Ln 27549 919-496-1855
Novella Brown, prin. Fax 496-1370
Other Schools – See Bunn, Franklinton, Youngsville

Louisburg College Post-Sec.
501 N Main St 27549 919-496-2521

Lowell, Gaston, Pop. 2,644
Gaston County SD
Supt. — See Gastonia
Holbrook MS 800/6-8
418 S Church St 28098 704-824-2381
Gary Ford, prin. Fax 824-4529

Lucama, Wilson, Pop. 867
Wilson County SD
Supt. — See Wilson
Springfield MS 500/6-8
5551 Wiggins Mill Rd 27851 252-239-1347
Glenn Reaves, prin. Fax 239-1686

Lumberton, Robeson, Pop. 21,161
Robeson County SD 24,400/PK-12
PO Box 2909 28359 910-671-6000
Johnny Hunt, supt. Fax 671-6024
www.robeson.k12.nc.us
Early College HS 9-12
5160 N Fayetteville Rd 28360 910-671-6000
Wesley Revels, prin.
Littlefield MS 700/4-8
9674 NC Highway 41 N 28358 910-671-6065
David Evans, prin. Fax 618-9419
Lumberton HS 2,100/9-12
3901 Fayetteville Rd 28358 910-671-6050
Gregory Killingsworth, prin. Fax 671-6078
Lumberton JHS 600/7-8
82 Marion Rd 28358 910-738-9611
Darlene Cummings, prin. Fax 671-4350
Robeson County Career Center Vo/Tech
PO Box 2909 28359 910-671-6095
Daniel Ryberg, prin. Fax 671-6097
Other Schools – See Fairmont, Maxton, Orrum, Pembroke, Red Springs, Rowland, Saint Pauls

Robeson Community College Post-Sec.
PO Box 1420 28359 910-738-7101

Mc Leansville, Guilford, Pop. 1,154
Guilford County SD
Supt. — See Greensboro
Northeast Guilford HS 1,100/9-12
6700 Mcleansville Rd 27301 336-375-2500
Angelo Kidd, prin. Fax 375-2520
Northeast Guilford MS 900/6-8
6720 Mcleansville Rd 27301 336-375-2525
Gayland Welborn, prin. Fax 375-2534

Madison, Rockingham, Pop. 2,241
Rockingham County SD
Supt. — See Eden

Western Rockingham MS
915 Ayersville Rd 27025   900/6-8
Jonathan Craig, prin.   336-548-2168
Fax 548-1799

Maiden, Catawba, Pop. 3,191
Catawba County SD
  Supt. — See Newton
Maiden HS   600/9-12
600 W Main St 28650   828-428-8197
Dwayne Finger, prin.   Fax 428-8341
Maiden MS   7-8
518 N C Ave 28650   828-428-2326
Nan VanHoy, prin.   Fax 428-5389

Manteo, Dare, Pop. 1,208
Dare County SD
  Supt. — See Nags Head
Manteo HS   1,200/9-12
PO Box 280 27954   252-473-5841
John Luciano, prin.   Fax 473-2263
Manteo MS   300/6-8
264 N Highway 64 27954   252-473-5549
Terry McGinnis, prin.   Fax 473-2612

Marion, McDowell, Pop. 4,854
McDowell County SD   6,500/K-12
334 S Main St 28752   828-652-4535
Dr. Ira Trollinger, supt.   Fax 659-2238
www.mcdowell.k12.nc.us/
East McDowell JHS   700/7-9
676 State St 28752   828-652-7711
Nancy Guthrie, prin.   Fax 652-1469
McDowell HS   1,300/9-12
600 McDowell High Dr 28752   828-652-7920
Ben Talbert, prin.   Fax 652-1101
West McDowell JHS   900/7-9
346 W McDowell Jr High Sch 28752   828-652-3390
C. Gibson, prin.   Fax 659-1964

Marion Christian Academy   200/K-12
PO Box 1045 28752   828-652-2033
Dr. Larry Spencer, admin.   Fax 652-1853
McDowell Technical Community College   Post-Sec.
54 College Dr 28752   828-652-6021

Marshall, Madison, Pop. 832
Madison County SD   2,600/K-12
5738 US Hwy 25-70 28753   828-649-9276
Ronald Wilcox Ed.D., supt.   Fax 649-9334
www.madison.k12.nc.us
Madison HS   800/9-12
5740 US Highway 25-70 28753   828-649-2876
Daniel Metcalf, prin.   Fax 649-0104
Madison MS   600/6-8
95 Upper Brush Creek Rd 28753   828-649-2269
Carolyn Franklin, prin.   Fax 649-9015

Mars Hill, Madison, Pop. 1,720

Mars Hill College 28754   Post-Sec.
  800-543-1514

Marshville, Union, Pop. 2,601
Union County SD
  Supt. — See Monroe
East Union MS   800/6-8
6010 W Marshville Blvd 28103   704-624-2114
Dr. Beth Copenhaver, prin.   Fax 624-9302
Forest Hills HS   900/9-12
100 Forest Hills School Rd 28103   704-233-4001
Dr. Mike Zezech, prin.   Fax 233-4003

Matthews, Mecklenburg, Pop. 23,436
Charlotte/Mecklenburg Co. SD
  Supt. — See Charlotte
Butler HS   2,000/9-12
1810 Matthews Mint Hill Rd 28105   980-343-6300
Joel Ritchie, prin.   Fax 343-6315
Crestdale MS   1,200/6-8
940 Sam Newell Rd 28105   980-343-5755
Kendra March, prin.   Fax 343-5761
Mint Hill MS   900/6-8
11501 Idlewild Rd 28105   980-343-5439
Denise Watts, prin.   Fax 343-5442

Union County SD
  Supt. — See Monroe
Weddington HS   1,500/9-12
4901 Monroe Weddington Rd 28104   704-708-5530
Joe Delaney, prin.   Fax 708-6218
Weddington MS   1,200/6-8
5903 Deal Rd 28104   704-814-9772
Jan Hollis, prin.   Fax 814-9775

Bible Baptist Christian S   100/PK-12
2724 Margaret Wallace Rd 28105   704-535-1694
David King, prin.   Fax 536-1289
Covenant Day S   800/K-12
800 Fullwood Rd 28105   704-847-2385
Dr. Marni Halvorson, hdmstr.   Fax 708-6137
Empire Beauty School   Post-Sec.
11032 E Independence Blvd 28105   800-575-5983
Southern Evangelical Seminary   Post-Sec.
3000 Tilley Morris Rd 28105   704-847-5600

Maxton, Robeson, Pop. 2,520
Robeson County SD
  Supt. — See Lumberton
Townsend MS   300/5-8
105 W Carolina St 28364   910-844-5086
Walter Jackson, prin.   Fax 844-4292

Mayodan, Rockingham, Pop. 2,382
Rockingham County SD
  Supt. — See Eden
McMichael HS   1,000/9-12
6845 NC Highway 135 27027   336-427-5165
Mavis Dillon, prin.   Fax 427-5776

Mebane, Alamance, Pop. 8,464
Alamance-Burlington SD
  Supt. — See Burlington
Eastern Alamance HS   1,100/9-12
4040 Mebane Rogers Rd 27302   919-563-5991
Dave Ebert, prin.   Fax 563-6114
Hawfields MS   700/6-8
1948 S NC Highway 119 27302   919-563-5303
Todd Wirt, prin.   Fax 563-1351
Woodlawn MS   600/6-8
3970 Mebane Rogers Rd 27302   919-563-3222
Dr. John Swajkoski, prin.   Fax 563-6807

Merry Hill, Bertie

Lawrence Academy   400/PK-12
PO Box 70 27957   252-482-4748
Eric Meadows, hdmstr.   Fax 482-2215

Micro, Johnston, Pop. 482
Johnston County SD
  Supt. — See Smithfield
North Johnston MS   600/6-8
PO Box 69 27555   919-284-3374
Ray Stott, prin.   Fax 284-3399

Millers Creek, Wilkes, Pop. 1,787
Wilkes County SD
  Supt. — See Wilkesboro
West Wilkes HS   700/9-12
6598 Boone Trl 28651   336-973-4503
Stephen Moree, prin.   Fax 973-7323

Mill Spring, Polk
Polk County SD
  Supt. — See Columbus
Polk County MS   6-8
321 Wolverine Trl 28756   828-894-2215
Hank Utz, prin.   894-0191

Misenheimer, Stanly

Pfeiffer University   Post-Sec.
PO Box 960 28109   704-463-1360

Mocksville, Davie, Pop. 4,291
Davie County SD   6,000/PK-12
220 Cherry St 27028   336-751-5921
W.G. Potts, prin.   Fax 751-9013
www.davie.k12.nc.us
Davie County HS   1,600/9-12
1200 Salisbury Rd 27028   336-751-5905
Larry Bridgewater, prin.   Fax 751-4597
North Davie MS   700/6-8
497 Farmington Rd 27028   336-998-5555
Candy Poplin, prin.   Fax 998-7233
South Davie MS   800/6-8
700 Hardison St 27028   336-751-5941
Dr. Danny Cartner, prin.   Fax 751-5656

Trinity Baptist Academy   100/K-12
2722 US Highway 601 S 27028   336-284-2832
Dr. Darrell Cox, prin.

Monroe, Union, Pop. 28,222
Union County SD   26,900/PK-12
500 N Main St Ste 700 28112   704-283-3733
Dr. Ed Davis, supt.   Fax 289-1536
www.ucps.k12.nc.us
Monroe HS   900/9-12
1 High School Dr 28112   704-296-3130
Dr. Mike Webb, prin.   Fax 296-3138
Monroe MS   800/6-8
601 E Sunset Dr 28112   704-296-3120
Montrio Belton, prin.   Fax 296-3122
Parkwood HS   1,200/9-12
3220 Parkwood School Rd 28112   704-764-2900
Dr. Roger Ashford, prin.   Fax 764-2907
Parkwood MS   900/6-8
3219 Parkwood School Rd 28112   704-764-2910
Neil Hawkins, prin.   Fax 764-2914
Piedmont HS   1,400/9-12
3006 Sikes Mill Rd 28110   704-753-2810
Wanda Little, prin.   Fax 753-2815
Piedmont MS   1,200/6-8
2816 Sikes Mill Rd 28110   704-753-2840
Anne Radke, prin.   Fax 753-2846
Sun Valley HS   1,400/9-12
5211 Old Charlotte Hwy 28110   704-296-3020
Ken Roess, prin.   Fax 296-3029
Union County Career Center   Vo/Tech
600 Brewer Dr 28112   704-296-3088
Dr. Linda Presley, prin.   Fax 296-3090
Other Schools – See Indian Trail, Marshville, Matthews

Sunset Park Christian S   50/K-12
1320 S Hayne St 28112   704-283-2414
Davena Carnes, prin.   Fax 226-9595
Tabernacle Christian S   200/K-12
2900 Walkup Ave 28110   704-283-4395
Stephen Leonard, prin.

Montreat, Buncombe, Pop. 657

Montreat College   Post-Sec.
PO Box 1267 28757   828-669-8011

Mooresville, Iredell, Pop. 19,606
Iredell-Statesville SD
  Supt. — See Statesville
Brawley MS   800/6-8
664 Brawley School Rd 28117   704-664-4430
Roberta Ellis, prin.   Fax 664-9846
Lake Norman HS   1,300/9-12
186 Doolie Rd 28117   704-799-8555
David Blattner, prin.   Fax 799-1512
Lakeshore MS   500/6-8
244 Lakeshore School Dr 28117   704-799-0187
Jim Gaghan, prin.   Fax 663-6431

Mooresville CSD   4,100/PK-12
305 N Main St 28115   704-664-5553
Dr. Bruce Boyles, supt.   Fax 663-3005
www.mgsd.k12.nc.us
Mooresville HS   1,300/9-12
659 E Center Ave 28115   704-664-5545
Dr. John R. Streb, prin.   Fax 664-4381
Mooresville MS   700/7-8
160 S Magnolia St 28115   704-663-3841
Nicki Cohen, prin.   Fax 664-5101
Woods Adv Tech / Arts Center   Vo/Tech
574 W McLelland Ave 28115   704-663-3274
Dr. Randy Bolton, prin.   Fax 664-5102

Mooresville Christian Academy   100/K-12
PO Box 114 28115   704-663-4690
Betsy Harris, hdmstr.   Fax 663-2908
NASCAR Technical Institute   Post-Sec.
220 Byers Creek Rd 28117   704-658-1950

Moravian Falls, Wilkes, Pop. 1,736
Wilkes County SD
  Supt. — See Wilkesboro
Central Wilkes MS   800/6-8
3541 S NC Highway 16 28654   336-667-7453
Teresa Foster, prin.   Fax 667-5825

Morehead City, Carteret, Pop. 8,064
Carteret County SD
  Supt. — See Beaufort
Morehead City MS   500/6-8
400 Barbour Rd 28557   252-726-1126
Suzanne Kreuser, prin.   Fax 726-4980
West Carteret HS   1,200/9-12
4700 Country Club Rd 28557   252-726-1176
D. Gordon Patrick, prin.   Fax 726-6290

Carteret Community College   Post-Sec.
3505 Arendell St 28557   252-222-6000

Morganton, Burke, Pop. 17,261
Burke County SD   14,600/PK-12
PO Box 989 28680   828-439-4312
David Burleson, supt.   Fax 439-4314
www.burke.k12.nc.us
Freedom HS   2,300/9-12
511 Independence Blvd 28655   828-433-1310
Brian Oliver, prin.   Fax 439-8420
Johnson MS   500/6-8
701 Lenoir Rd 28655   828-430-7340
Jack Leonard, prin.   Fax 430-4801
Liberty MS   700/6-8
529 Enola Rd 28655   828-437-1330
Shanda McFarlin, prin.   Fax 432-2124
Table Rock MS   700/6-8
1581 NC 126 28655   828-437-5212
Sharon Colaw, prin.   Fax 439-5702
Other Schools – See Connellys Springs, Icard, Valdese

Morganton Christian Academy   100/PK-12
201 Believers Way 28655   828-437-1897
Greg Zolninger, prin.   Fax 439-8948
North Carolina School for the Deaf   Post-Sec.
517 W Fleming Dr 28655   828-433-2971
Western Piedmont Community College   Post-Sec.
1001 Burkemont Ave 28655   828-438-6000

Morrisville, Wake, Pop. 7,671
Wake County SD
  Supt. — See Raleigh
Panther Creek HS   9-10
1050 Town Hall Dr 27560   919-463-8656
Rodney Nelson, prin.   Fax 463-8666

Mount Airy, Surry, Pop. 8,394
Mt. Airy CSD   1,900/PK-12
130 Rawley Ave 27030   336-786-8355
Tim Farley, supt.   Fax 786-7553
www.mtairy.k12.nc.us
Mount Airy HS   600/9-12
1011 N South St 27030   336-789-5147
Sandy George, prin.   Fax 719-2341
Mount Airy MS   500/6-8
249 Hamburg St 27030   336-789-9021
Ross Scott, prin.   Fax 789-6074

Surry County SD
  Supt. — See Dobson
Gentry MS   500/6-8
1915 W Pine St 27030   336-786-4155
Tom Hemmings, prin.   Fax 786-6863
Meadowview MS   500/6-8
1282 Mckinney Rd 27030   336-789-0276
Angela Carson, prin.   Fax 789-0449
North Surry HS   1,000/9-12
2440 W Pine St 27030   336-789-5055
Bill Goins, prin.   Fax 786-8630

Northern Hospital of Surry County   Post-Sec.
PO Box 1101 27030   336-719-7124
White Plains Christian S   100/K-12
609 Old Highway 601 27030   336-786-9585
David Tucker, prin.

Mount Gilead, Montgomery, Pop. 1,388
Montgomery County SD
  Supt. — See Troy
West MS   600/6-8
129 NC Highway 109 S 27306   910-572-9378
Jerry Michael Penninger, prin.   Fax 572-2114
West Montgomery HS   700/9-12
147 Warrior Rd 27306   910-439-6191
Ray Massey, prin.   Fax 439-4600

Mount Holly, Gaston, Pop. 9,591
Gaston County SD
  Supt. — See Gastonia
East Gaston HS   1,400/9-12
1744 Lane Rd 28120   704-827-7251
Eddie McGinnis, prin.   Fax 827-7974
Mount Holly MS   700/6-8
124 S Hawthorne St 28120   704-827-4811
Denece Farris, prin.   Fax 822-1049

Mount Olive, Wayne, Pop. 4,488
Wayne County SD
  Supt. — See Goldsboro
Mount Olive MS   300/6-8
309 Wooten St 28365   919-658-7320
Craig Uzzell, prin.   Fax 658-7325

Mt. Olive College   Post-Sec.
634 Henderson St 28365   919-658-2502

Mount Pleasant, Cabarrus, Pop. 1,307
Cabarrus County SD
  Supt. — See Concord
Mount Pleasant HS   900/9-12
700 Walker Rd 28124   704-436-9321
Edith Sayewich, prin.   Fax 436-2909
Mount Pleasant MS   700/6-8
8325 Highway 49 S 28124   704-436-9302
Sam Treadaway, prin.   Fax 436-6112

Mount Ulla, Rowan
Rowan-Salisbury County SD
  Supt. — See Salisbury
West Rowan HS   1,300/9-12
8050 NC 801 Hwy 28125   704-278-9233
Dr. Carolyn Means, prin.   Fax 278-9733

Moyock, Currituck
Currituck County SD
Supt. — See Currituck
Moyock MS 600/5-8
216 Survey Rd 27958 252-435-2566
Virginia Arrington, prin. Fax 435-2576

Murfreesboro, Hertford, Pop. 2,347
Hertford County SD
Supt. — See Winton
Hertford County MS 600/7-8
1850 Highway 11 North 27855 252-398-4091
Sheila Porter, prin. Fax 398-5570

Chowan College Post-Sec.
PO Box 1848 27855 252-398-6500

Murphy, Cherokee, Pop. 1,562
Cherokee County SD 3,800/PK-12
911 Andrews Rd 28906 828-837-2722
Dr. Jeanette F. Hedrick, supt. Fax 837-5799
www.cherokee.k12.nc.us
Hiwassee Dam HS 200/9-12
267 Blue Eagle Cir 28906 828-644-5916
Kenny Garland, prin. Fax 644-9463
Murphy HS 600/9-12
234 High School Cir 28906 828-837-2426
Jerry Brackett, prin. Fax 837-2555
Murphy MS 400/6-8
65 Middle School Dr 28906 828-837-0160
Michael Rogers, prin. Fax 837-5814
Tri-County Early College HS 9-12
4610 E US Highway 64 28906 828-835-4298
Sue Ledford, prin.
Other Schools – See Andrews

Murphy Adventist S 50/PK-12
PO Box 620 28906 828-837-5857
Joan Bilbo, prin. Fax 835-9300
Tri-County Community College Post-Sec.
2300 E US Highway 64 28906 828-837-6810

Nags Head, Dare, Pop. 2,993
Dare County SD 4,800/PK-12
PO Box 1508 27959 252-480-8888
Dr. Sue Burgess, supt. Fax 480-8889
www.dare.k12.nc.us
Other Schools – See Buxton, Kill Devil Hills, Manteo

Nashville, Nash, Pop. 4,375
Nash-Rocky Mount SD 18,600/PK-12
930 Eastern Ave 27856 252-459-5220
Rick McMahon, supt. Fax 459-6404
www.nrms.k12.nc.us
Nash Central MS 800/6-8
1638 S 1st St 27856 252-459-5292
Lorenzo Morgan, prin. Fax 459-5297
Other Schools – See Bailey, Battleboro, Rocky Mount, Spring Hope

New Bern, Craven, Pop. 23,308
Craven County SD 14,600/PK-12
3600 Trent Rd 28562 252-514-6300
William Rivenbark, supt. Fax 514-6351
www.craven.k12.nc.us
Fields MS 600/6-8
2000 Dr M L King Jr Blvd 28560 252-514-6438
Dr. Renee Franklin, prin. Fax 514-6443
MacDonald MS 900/6-8
3127 Elizabeth Ave 28562 252-514-6450
Karen Barrow, prin. Fax 514-6456
New Bern HS 1,800/9-12
4200 Academic Dr 28562 252-514-6400
Terence Fuhrman, prin. Fax 514-6412
West Craven MS 1,000/6-8
515 NW Crvn Mddle School Rd 28562 252-514-6488
Joan Bjork, prin. Fax 514-6491
Other Schools – See Havelock, Vanceboro

Craven Community College Post-Sec.
PO Box 885 28563 252-638-4131
Ruths Chapel Christian S 200/K-12
2709 Oaks Rd 28560 252-638-1297
David Thompson, prin. Fax 638-5770

Newland, Avery, Pop. 706
Avery County SD 2,400/PK-12
PO Box 1360 28657 828-733-6006
Grace Calhoun, supt. Fax 733-8943
www.averyschools.net
Avery County HS 700/9-12
PO Box 1300 28657 828-733-0151
Mark Garrett, prin. Fax 733-1742
Avery County MS 300/6-8
PO Box 729 28657 828-733-0145
David Wright, prin. Fax 733-3506
Other Schools – See Elk Park

New London, Stanly, Pop. 322
Stanly County SD
Supt. — See Albemarle
New London Choice MS 300/6-8
PO Box 68 28127 704-463-7962
Jessie Morton, prin. Fax 463-5340
North Stanly HS 800/9-12
40206 US Highway 52 N 28127 704-463-7358
Joyce Steele, prin. Fax 463-1962

Christ the King Christian Academy 100/K-10
PO Box 279 28127 704-463-7285
John Kahl, prin. Fax 463-7285

Newport, Carteret, Pop. 3,672
Carteret County SD
Supt. — See Beaufort
Broad Creek MS 500/6-8
2382 Highway 24 28570 252-247-3135
Cathy Tomon, prin. Fax 247-5114
Croatan HS 800/9-12
1 Cougar Ln 28570 252-393-7022
Matthew Bottoms, prin. Fax 393-1223
Newport MS 500/6-8
500 E Chatham St 28570 252-223-3482
Bud Lanning, prin. Fax 223-4914

Gramercy Christian S 200/K-12
8170 Highway 70 28570 252-223-5199
Vicki Bishop, hdmstr. Fax 223-2359

Newton, Catawba, Pop. 12,682
Catawba County SD 16,700/K-12
PO Box 1010 28658 828-464-8333
Tim Markley, supt. Fax 464-0925
www.catawba.k12.nc.us
Foard HS 1,200/9-12
3407 Plateau Rd 28658 704-462-1496
Sally Bradshaw, prin. Fax 462-1988
Jacobs Fork MS 600/7-8
3431 Plateau Rd 28658 704-462-1827
Fax 462-1600
Other Schools – See Catawba, Claremont, Hickory, Maiden

Newton-Conover CSD 2,800/PK-12
605 N Ashe Ave 28658 828-464-3191
Dr. Barry Redmond, supt. Fax 466-0063
www.nccs.k12.nc.us
Newton-Conover HS 800/9-12
338 W 15th St 28658 828-465-0920
Richard Armstrong, prin. Fax 464-1412
Newton-Conover MS 700/6-8
221 W 26th St 28658 828-464-4221
Sylvia White, prin. Fax 464-5238

Newton Grove, Sampson, Pop. 610
Sampson County SD
Supt. — See Clinton
Hobbton HS 500/9-12
12201 Hobbton Hwy 28366 910-594-0242
Henry Stumpf, prin. Fax 594-1115
Hobbton MS 500/6-8
12081 Hobbton Hwy 28366 910-594-1420
Wesley Johnson, prin. Fax 594-0049

Norlina, Warren, Pop. 1,072

Norlina Christian S 100/K-12
PO Box 757 27563 252-456-3385
Abidan Shah, prin. Fax 456-3354

North Wilkesboro, Wilkes, Pop. 4,122
Wilkes County SD
Supt. — See Wilkesboro
North Wilkes MS 600/6-8
2776 Yellow Banks Rd 28659 336-696-2724
Wayne Shepherd, prin. Fax 696-4183

Wilkes Regional Medical Center Post-Sec.
PO Box 609 28659 336-651-8100

Norwood, Stanly, Pop. 2,178
Stanly County SD
Supt. — See Albemarle
South Stanly HS 500/9-12
40488 S Stanly School Rd 28128 704-474-3155
Mike Campbell, prin. Fax 474-7436
South Stanly MS 500/6-8
12492 Cottonville Rd 28128 704-474-5355
Sam Basden, prin. Fax 474-5579

Oakboro, Stanly, Pop. 1,194
Stanly County SD
Supt. — See Albemarle
West Stanly HS 1,000/9-12
16686 NC 24 27 Hwy 28129 704-485-3012
Larry Smith, prin. Fax 485-4509

Oak Ridge, Guilford, Pop. 4,056

Oak Ridge Military Academy 200/6-12
PO Box 498 27310 336-643-4131
Dr. Roy Berwick, pres. Fax 643-1797

Ocracoke, Hyde
Hyde County SD
Supt. — See Swanquarter
Ocracoke S 100/K-12
PO Box 189 27960 252-928-3251
George Ortman, prin. Fax 928-5380

Olin, Iredell
Iredell-Statesville SD
Supt. — See Statesville
North Iredell HS 1,100/9-12
156 Raider Rd 28660 704-876-4191
Mark Byrd, prin. Fax 876-1053
North Iredell MS 600/6-8
2467 Jennings Rd 28660 704-876-4802
Kelly Cooper, prin. Fax 876-6190

Orrum, Robeson, Pop. 79
Robeson County SD
Supt. — See Lumberton
Orrum MS 400/5-8
PO Box 129 28369 910-628-8408
Kent Lovett, prin. Fax 628-6285

Oxford, Granville, Pop. 8,495
Granville County SD 8,700/PK-12
101 Delacroix St 27565 919-693-4613
Thomas Williams, supt. Fax 693-7391
eclipse.gcs.k12.nc.us/
Northern Granville MS 800/7-8
3144 Webb School Rd 27565 919-693-1483
Daniel Callaghan, prin. Fax 693-1716
Webb HS 1,300/9-12
3200 Webb School Rd 27565 919-693-2521
Roy Winslow, prin. Fax 693-2589
Webb S of Health & Life Sciences 10-12
3200 Webb School Rd 27565 919-693-6411
Dr. Elizabeth Lee, prin.
Other Schools – See Butner, Creedmoor

Pantego, Beaufort, Pop. 168

Terra Ceia Christian S 200/K-12
4428 Christian School Rd 27860 252-943-2485
Ken Leys, prin. Fax 943-2139

Pembroke, Robeson, Pop. 2,702
Robeson County SD
Supt. — See Lumberton
Accelerated Learning Academy 9-12
11344 Deep Branch Rd 28372 910-671-6000
Pembroke MS 800/6-8
PO Box 1148 28372 910-521-9464
Tommy Lowry, prin. Fax 521-1562
Swett HS 1,500/9-12
PO Box 1210 28372 910-521-3253
Antonio Wilkins, prin. Fax 521-2956

University of North Carolina at Pembroke Post-Sec.
PO Box 1510 28372 910-521-6000

Pfafftown, Forsyth
Winston-Salem/Forsyth SD
Supt. — See Winston Salem
Reagan HS 9-12
3750 Transou Rd 27040 336-703-6776
Stan Elrod, prin. Fax 922-1752

Pikeville, Wayne, Pop. 701
Wayne County SD
Supt. — See Goldsboro
Aycock HS 1,200/9-12
PO Box 159 27863 919-242-3400
Randy Bledsoe, prin. Fax 242-6994

Pilot Mountain, Surry, Pop. 1,268
Surry County SD
Supt. — See Dobson
East Surry HS 600/9-12
801 W Main St 27041 336-368-2251
Tony Hall, prin. Fax 368-3035
Pilot Mountain MS 500/6-8
202 Friends St 27041 336-368-2641
Dennis Lawson, prin. Fax 368-3935

Pinehurst, Moore, Pop. 10,774

Sandhills Community College Post-Sec.
3395 Airport Rd 28374 910-692-6185

Pinetops, Edgecombe, Pop. 1,357
Edgecombe County SD
Supt. — See Tarboro
South Edgecombe MS 600/5-8
230 Pinetops Crisp Rd 27864 252-827-5083
William Wright, prin. Fax 827-2811
Southwest Edgecombe HS 1,000/9-12
5912 NC Highway 43 27864 252-827-5016
Tim Pittman, prin. Fax 827-2815

Pinetown, Beaufort
Beaufort County SD
Supt. — See Washington
Northside HS 600/9-12
7868 Free Union Church Rd 27865 252-943-6341
John Smith, prin. Fax 943-6344

Pisgah Forest, Transylvania

Schenck Civilian Conservation Center Post-Sec.
98 Schenck Dr 28768 828-862-6100

Pittsboro, Chatham, Pop. 2,379
Chatham County SD 7,300/K-12
PO Box 128 27312 919-542-3626
Dr. Ann Hart, supt. Fax 542-1380
www.chatham.k12.nc.us
Horton MS 400/5-8
PO Box 639 27312 919-542-2303
Pat Lane, prin. Fax 542-7099
Northwood HS 1,000/9-12
310 Northwood High Sch Rd 27312 919-542-4181
Joel County, prin. Fax 542-4934
Other Schools – See Bear Creek, Siler City

Plymouth, Washington, Pop. 3,994
Washington County SD 2,300/PK-12
802 Washington St 27962 252-793-5171
Julius Walker, supt. Fax 793-5062
www.washingtonco.k12.nc.us/
Plymouth HS 500/9-12
PO Box 827 27962 252-793-3031
Gloria McCray, prin. Fax 793-3986
Other Schools – See Creswell, Roper

Polkton, Anson, Pop. 1,894

South Piedmont Community College Post-Sec.
PO Box 126 28135 704-272-7635

Powellsville, Bertie, Pop. 252
Bertie County SD
Supt. — See Windsor
White MS 300/6-8
503 E Main St 27967 252-332-2491
Joanne Jones, prin. Fax 209-0994

Princeton, Johnston, Pop. 1,146
Johnston County SD
Supt. — See Smithfield
Princeton S 1,300/PK-12
PO Box 38 27569 919-936-5011
W. Kirk Denning, prin. Fax 936-2962

Raeford, Hoke, Pop. 3,484
Hoke County SD 6,600/PK-12
PO Box 370 28376 910-875-4106
Allen Strickland, supt. Fax 875-3362
www.hcs.k12.nc.us
East Hoke MS 800/6-8
4702 Fayetteville Rd 28376 910-875-5048
Sam Queen, prin. Fax 875-9307
Hoke County HS 1,500/9-12
505 S Bethel Rd 28376 910-875-2156
Mark Smith, prin. Fax 904-1644
West Hoke MS 700/6-8
200 NC Highway 211 28376 910-875-3411
Dr. James McLauchlin, prin. Fax 875-0332

Raleigh, Wake, Pop. 316,802
Wake County SD 109,600/PK-12
PO Box 28041 27611 919-850-1600
William McNeal, supt. Fax 850-1819
www.wcpss.net
Athens Drive HS 1,800/9-12
1420 Athens Dr 27606 919-233-4050
Kathryn Chontos, prin. Fax 233-4082
Broughton HS 2,200/9-12
723 Saint Marys St 27605 919-856-7810
Ray Teel, prin. Fax 856-7822
Carnage MS 1,000/6-8
1425 Carnage Dr 27610 919-856-7600
Delores Fogg, prin. Fax 856-7619

Carroll MS — 800/6-8
4520 Six Forks Rd 27609 — 919-881-1370
Mary Rich, prin. — Fax 881-5016
Centennial MS — 500/6-8
1900 Main Campus Dr 27606 — 919-233-4217
Kenneth Branch, prin. — Fax 233-4268
Daniels MS — 900/6-8
2816 Oberlin Rd 27608 — 919-881-4860
Stephen Mares, prin. — Fax 881-1418
Dillard Drive MS — 1,100/6-8
5200 Dillard Dr 27606 — 919-233-4228
Teresa Abron, prin. — Fax 854-1615
Durant Road MS — 1,600/6-8
10401 Durant Rd 27614 — 919-870-4098
Robert E. Smith, prin. — Fax 518-0021
East Millbrook MS — 1,000/6-8
3801 Spring Forest Rd 27616 — 919-850-8755
David Ansbacher, prin. — Fax 850-8770
East Wake MS — 900/6-8
2700 Old Milburnie Rd 27604 — 919-266-8500
Bradford Shackelford, prin. — Fax 266-8506
Enloe HS — 2,300/9-12
128 Clarendon Cres 27610 — 919-856-7918
A. Beth Cochran, prin. — Fax 856-7917
Leesville HS — 2,100/9-12
8409 Leesville Rd 27613 — 919-870-4250
Stephen Gainey, prin. — Fax 870-4287
Leesville Road MS — 1,100/6-8
8405 Leesville Rd 27613 — 919-870-4141
Floyd Lowman, prin. — Fax 870-4166
Ligon MS — 1,000/6-8
706 E Lenoir St 27601 — 919-856-7929
Scott Lyons, prin. — Fax 856-3745
Martin MS — 1,000/6-8
1701 Ridge Rd 27607 — 919-881-4970
Anne Deegan, prin. — Fax 881-1416
Millbrook HS — 2,000/9-12
2201 Spring Forest Rd 27615 — 919-850-8787
Dana King, prin. — Fax 850-8803
Moore Square MS — 500/6-8
301 S Person St 27601 — 919-664-5737
Elizabeth Colbert, prin. — Fax 856-8194
River Oaks MS — 6-8
4700 New Bern Ave 27610 — 919-217-3259
Susanne Warren, prin.
Sanderson HS — 1,800/9-12
5500 Dixon Dr 27609 — 919-881-4800
Cathy Moore, prin. — Fax 881-5006
Southeast Raleigh HS — 2,100/9-12
2600 Rock Quarry Rd 27610 — 919-856-2800
Beulah Wright, prin. — Fax 856-2827
Wake Early College of Health & Sciences — 9-12
2901 Holston Ln 27610 — 919-850-1793
Dr. Jim Palermo, prin.
Wakefield HS — 1,800/9-12
2200 Wakefield Pines Dr 27614 — 919-562-3600
Steve Takacs, prin. — Fax 562-3623
Wakefield MS — 1,100/6-8
2300 Wakefield Pines Dr 27614 — 919-562-3500
Mark Savage, prin. — Fax 562-3527
West Millbrook MS — 1,000/6-8
8115 Strickland Rd 27615 — 919-870-4050
Cindy Hall, prin. — Fax 870-4064
Other Schools – See Apex, Cary, Fuquay Varina, Garner, Holly Springs, Knightdale, Morrisville, Wake Forest, Wendell, Zebulon

Cardinal Gibbons HS — 900/9-12
1401 Edwards Mill Rd 27607 — 919-834-1625
Br. Michel Bettigole, prin. — Fax 834-9771
ECPI College of Technology — Post-Sec.
4101 Dole Cope Rd 27613 — 919-571-0057
Fletcher Academy — 100/1-12
400 Cedarview Ct 27609 — 919-782-5082
Junell Blaylock, prin. — Fax 782-5980
Friendship Christian S — 300/PK-12
5510 Falls of Neuse Rd 27609 — 919-872-2133
Dan Perryman, admin. — Fax 872-7451
GRACE Christian S — 300/PK-12
801 Buck Jones Rd 27606 — 866-472-2330
Kathie Thompson, prin. — Fax 783-0856
Meredith College — Post-Sec.
3800 Hillsborough St 27607 — 919-760-8600
Neuse Baptist Christian S — 400/K-12
8700 Capital Blvd 27616 — 919-876-0990
John Hughes, prin. — Fax 876-3168
North Carolina State University — Post-Sec.
PO Box 7001 27695 — 919-515-2011
North Raleigh Christian Academy — 1,200/K-12
7300 Perry Creek Rd 27616 — 919-573-7900
Dr. S.L. Sherrill, supt. — Fax 573-7901
Peace College — Post-Sec.
15 E Peace St 27604 — 919-508-2000
Raleigh Christian Academy — 500/PK-12
2110 Trawick Rd 27604 — 919-872-2215
Dwight Ausley, admin. — Fax 861-1000
Ravenscroft S — 1,100/PK-12
7409 Falls Of Neuse Rd 27615 — 919-847-0900
Doreen Kelly, hdmstr. — Fax 846-2371
St. Augustine's College — Post-Sec.
1315 Oakwood Ave 27610 — 919-516-4000
St. David's S — 500/K-12
3400 White Oak Rd 27609 — 919-782-3331
John Andrew Murray, hdmstr. — Fax 571-3330
St. Mary's College Prep S — 300/9-12
900 Hillsborough St 27603 — 919-424-4000
Theo Coonrod, hdmstr. — Fax 424-4122
School of Communication Arts — Post-Sec.
3000 Wakefield Crossing Dr 27614 — 800-288-7442
Shaw University — Post-Sec.
118 E South St 27601 — 919-546-8200
Strayer University — Post-Sec.
3200 Spring Forest Rd 27616 — 919-878-9900
Trinity Academy of Raleigh — 200/K-12
10224 Baileywick Rd 27613 — 919-786-0114
Dr. Robert Littlejohn, prin.
Wake Christian Academy — 900/K-12
5500 Wake Academy Dr 27603 — 919-772-6264
Mike Woods, admin. — Fax 779-0948
Wake Technical Community College — Post-Sec.
9101 Fayetteville Rd 27603 — 919-662-3400
Word of God Christian Academy — 200/PK-12
PO Box 14408 27620 — 919-834-8200
Anesha Pittman, prin. — Fax 899-3640

Ramseur, Randolph, Pop. 1,585
Randolph County SD
Supt. — See Asheboro

Eastern Randolph HS — 1,400/9-12
390 Eastern Randolph Rd 27316 — 336-824-2351
Parks Allen, prin. — Fax 824-6164
Southeastern Randolph MS — 700/6-8
5302 Foushee Rd 27316 — 336-824-6700
Stephanie Bridges, prin. — Fax 824-6705

Faith Christian S — 300/PK-12
5449 Brookhaven Rd 27316 — 336-824-4156
William Hohneisen, prin. — Fax 824-1012

Randleman, Randolph, Pop. 3,559
Randolph County SD
Supt. — See Asheboro
Randleman HS — 1,100/9-12
4396 Tigers Den Rd 27317 — 336-498-2682
Rick Dawes, prin. — Fax 498-2609
Randleman MS — 900/6-8
PO Box 625 27317 — 336-498-2606
Dana Albright-Johnson, prin. — Fax 498-8015

Red Springs, Robeson, Pop. 3,429
Robeson County SD
Supt. — See Lumberton
Red Springs HS — 700/9-12
509 N Vance St 28377 — 910-843-4211
Numer Locklear, prin. — Fax 843-2825
Red Springs MS — 600/5-8
302 W 2nd Ave 28377 — 910-843-3883
Richard Dixon, prin. — Fax 843-3765

Macdonald Academy — 200/PK-12
200 N College St 28377 — 910-843-4995
Jonathon Good, hdmstr. — Fax 843-8102

Reidsville, Rockingham, Pop. 14,777
Rockingham County SD
Supt. — See Eden
Reidsville HS — 1,000/9-12
1901 S Park Dr 27320 — 336-349-6361
Janet King, prin. — Fax 349-3205
Reidsville MS — 800/6-8
1903 S Park Dr 27320 — 336-342-4726
Louise Uziel, prin. — Fax 342-9434
Rockingham County HS — 1,200/9-12
180 High School Rd 27320 — 336-634-3220
Wayne Barnett, prin. — Fax 342-7794
Rockingham County MS — 900/6-8
182 High School Rd 27320 — 336-616-0073
Steve Hall, prin. — Fax 616-0870

Richlands, Onslow, Pop. 854
Onslow County SD
Supt. — See Jacksonville
Richlands HS — 700/9-12
PO Box 218 28574 — 910-324-4191
Tim Spencer, prin. — Fax 324-6688
Trexler MS — 600/6-8
PO Box 188 28574 — 910-324-4414
Susanne Long, prin. — Fax 324-3963

Roanoke Rapids, Halifax, Pop. 16,512
Halifax County SD
Supt. — See Halifax
Davie MS — 600/6-8
4391 US Highway 158 27870 — 252-519-0300
Claude Cooper, prin. — Fax 519-0222

Roanoke Rapids CSD — 3,000/PK-12
536 Hamilton St 27870 — 252-535-3111
John G. Parker, supt. — Fax 535-5919
www.rrgsd.org
Chaloner MS — 700/6-8
2100 Virginia Ave 27870 — 252-537-8540
Jimmy Kearney, prin. — Fax 537-9947
Roanoke Rapids HS — 900/9-12
800 Hamilton St 27870 — 252-537-8563
Monica Smith-Woofter, prin. — Fax 537-3606

Halifax Academy — 500/PK-12
1400 Three Bridges Rd 27870 — 252-537-8527
Glenn Wiggs, hdmstr. — Fax 308-0555

Robbins, Moore, Pop. 1,213
Moore County SD
Supt. — See Carthage
Elise MS — 200/6-8
PO Box 850 27325 — 910-948-2421
Brenda Cassady, prin. — Fax 948-4112
North Moore HS — 600/9-12
PO Box 9 27325 — 910-464-3105
Michael Tylavsky, prin. — Fax 464-5275

Robbinsville, Graham, Pop. 743
Graham County SD — 1,200/PK-12
52 Moose Branch Rd 28771 — 828-479-3413
Rick Davis, supt. — Fax 479-7950
www.graham.k12.nc.us
Robbinsville HS — 400/9-12
PO Box 625 28771 — 828-479-3330
Scott Perkins, prin. — Fax 479-1052
Robbinsville MS — 200/7-8
PO Box 940 28771 — 828-479-8484
Bruce Snyder, prin. — Fax 479-6847

Robersonville, Martin, Pop. 1,666
Martin County SD
Supt. — See Williamston
Roanoke HS — 400/9-12
21077 NC Highway 903 27871 — 252-795-4081
Vicki Dixon, prin. — Fax 795-4187
Roanoke MS — 300/6-8
21230 NC Highway 903 27871 — 252-795-3910
Clay Wagner, prin. — Fax 795-3890

Rockingham, Richmond, Pop. 9,301
Richmond County SD
Supt. — See Hamlet
Richmond SHS — 1,500/10-12
PO Box 1748 28380 — 910-997-9812
Cory Satterfield, prin. — Fax 997-9816
Rockingham JHS — 700/7-9
415 Wall St 28379 — 910-997-9827
Linwood Huffman, prin. — Fax 997-9859
Rohanen JHS — 300/7-9
252 School St 28379 — 910-997-9839
T. K. Thrower, prin. — Fax 997-8172

Temple Christian S — 200/K-12
165 Airport Rd 28379 — 910-997-3179
Rev. Joey Byrd, prin.

Rockwell, Rowan, Pop. 1,973

Rockwell Christian S — 200/K-12
PO Box 28138 — 704-279-8854
Ken Prater, prin. — Fax 279-1442

Rocky Mount, Edgecombe, Pop. 55,984
Edgecombe County SD
Supt. — See Tarboro
West Edgecombe MS — 700/4-8
6301 Nobles Mill Pond Rd 27801 — 252-446-2030
Laverne Daniels, prin. — Fax 446-1592

Nash-Rocky Mount SD
Supt. — See Nashville
Edwards MS — 1,000/6-8
720 Edwards St 27803 — 252-977-3328
Beezie Whitaker, prin. — Fax 446-5527
Nash Central HS — 900/9-12
4279 Nash Central High Rd 27804 — 252-451-2860
LeRoy Hartsfield, prin. — Fax 451-1279
Northern Nash HS — 1,500/9-12
4230 Green Hills Rd 27804 — 252-937-5600
Chip Hodges, prin. — Fax 443-5448
Parker MS — 500/6-8
1500 E Virginia St 27801 — 252-977-3486
Charles Davis, prin. — Fax 446-5756
Rocky Mount HS — 1,400/9-12
308 S Tillery St 27804 — 252-977-3085
Judy Bradshaw, prin. — Fax 985-4321

Faith Christian S — 300/K-12
PO Box 8165 27804 — 252-443-3700
Keith Griffin, hdmstr. — Fax 443-2456
Falls Road Baptist Church S — 200/K-12
113 Trevathan St 27804 — 252-977-2401
David Wredberg, prin. — Fax 977-3493
Nash Community College — Post-Sec.
PO Box 7488 27804 — 252-443-4011
North Carolina Wesleyan College — Post-Sec.
3400 N Wesleyan Blvd 27804 — 252-985-5100
Rocky Mount Academy — 400/PK-12
1313 Avondale Ave 27803 — 252-443-4126
Thomas Stevens, hdmstr. — Fax 937-7922
Showers of Blessing Christian Academy — 50/PK-12
PO Box 2916 27802 — 252-985-1848
Bernard Grant, hdmstr. — Fax 985-1360

Rocky Point, Pender
Pender County SD
Supt. — See Burgaw
Cape Fear MS — 500/6-8
1886 NC Highway 133 28457 — 910-602-3334
Leah Dove, prin. — Fax 602-3036
Trask HS — 600/9-12
14328 NC Highway 210 28457 — 910-602-6810
Randy Richardson, prin. — Fax 602-6662

Ronda, Wilkes, Pop. 469
Wilkes County SD
Supt. — See Wilkesboro
East Wilkes HS — 500/9-12
PO Box 368 28670 — 336-835-4772
Marty Hemric, prin. — Fax 835-9298
East Wilkes MS — 500/6-8
2202 Macedonia Church Rd 28670 — 336-928-9800
Jeff Peal, prin. — Fax 957-8734

Roper, Washington, Pop. 593
Washington County SD
Supt. — See Plymouth
Washington County Union MS — 600/5-8
PO Box 309 27970 — 252-793-2835
Earnell Purington, prin. — Fax 793-4411

Roseboro, Sampson, Pop. 1,276
Sampson County SD
Supt. — See Clinton
Roseboro-Salemburg MS — 400/6-8
PO Box 976 28382 — 910-525-4764
William Peterson, prin. — Fax 525-3471

Rose Hill, Duplin, Pop. 1,360
Duplin County SD
Supt. — See Kenansville
Charity MS — 600/6-8
PO Box 70 28458 — 910-289-3323
Janice Wynn, prin. — Fax 289-2064

Rosman, Transylvania, Pop. 492
Transylvania County SD
Supt. — See Brevard
Rosman HS — 400/9-12
HC 73 Box 500 28772 — 828-862-4284
Larry Clayton, prin. — Fax 862-4765
Rosman MS — 300/6-8
HC 73 Box 500 28772 — 828-862-4286
Lisa Anderson, prin. — Fax 885-8222

Rowland, Robeson, Pop. 1,128
Robeson County SD
Supt. — See Lumberton
Rowland MS — 200/6-8
408 W Chapel St 28383 — 910-422-3983
Dr. Penny Britt, prin. — Fax 422-8369
South Robeson HS — 500/9-12
3268 S Robeson Rd 28383 — 910-422-3987
Jessie McCormick, prin. — Fax 422-3221

Roxboro, Person, Pop. 8,794
Person County SD — 5,800/PK-12
304 S Morgan St Ste 25 27573 — 336-599-2191
Ronnie Bugnar, supt. — Fax 599-2194
www.person.k12.nc.us
Northern MS — 800/6-8
1935 Carver Dr. — 336-599-6344
Kelly Gentry, prin. — Fax 598-9207
Person HS — 1,700/9-12
1010 Ridge Rd 27573 — 336-599-8321
Margaret Bradsher, prin. — Fax 599-6583
Southern MS — 700/6-8
209 Southern Middle School 27573 — 336-599-6995
Bill Boston, prin. — Fax 503-0587

Piedmont Community College — Post-Sec.
PO Box 1197 27573 — 336-599-1181

Roxboro Christian Academy | 200/K-12
PO Box 1357 27573 | 336-599-0208
Lynn Bowen, prin.

Rutherfordton, Rutherford, Pop. 4,066
Rutherford County SD
  Supt. — See Forest City
R-S Central HS | 1,100/9-12
  PO Box 1119 28139 | 828-287-3304
  Tim Davis, prin. | Fax 286-2024
R-S MS | 900/6-8
  545 Charlotte Rd 28139 | 828-286-4461
  Greg Carter, prin. | Fax 286-4882

Saint Pauls, Robeson, Pop. 2,235
Robeson County SD
  Supt. — See Lumberton
Saint Pauls HS | 900/9-12
  648 N Stage Rd 28384 | 910-865-4177
  Stephen Gaskins, prin. | Fax 865-3736
Saint Pauls MS | 500/6-8
  526 W Shaw St 28384 | 910-865-4070
  Barbara Thompson, prin. | Fax 865-1599

Salemburg, Sampson, Pop. 473
Sampson County SD
  Supt. — See Clinton
Lakewood HS | 500/9-12
  245 Lakewood School Rd 28385 | 910-525-5171
  Jeff Heath, prin. | Fax 525-3344

Salisbury, Rowan, Pop. 26,548
Rowan-Salisbury County SD | 21,000/PK-12
  PO Box 2349 28145 | 704-636-7500
  Dr. Judy Grissom, supt. | Fax 630-6129
  www.rss.k12.nc.us
East Rowan HS | 1,400/9-12
  175 Saint Luke Church Rd 28146 | 704-279-5232
  G. Kelly Sparger, prin. | Fax 279-4549
Erwin MS | 900/6-8
  170 Saint Luke Church Rd 28146 | 704-279-7265
  Ray Whitaker, prin. | Fax 279-7954
Henderson Independent JSHS | 200/8-12
  1215 N Main St 28144 | 704-639-3103
  Robert Pulliam, prin. | Fax 639-3118
Knox MS | 600/6-8
  1625 W Park Rd 28144 | 704-633-2922
  Susan Heaggans, prin. | Fax 638-3538
Salisbury HS | 900/9-12
  500 Lincolnton Rd 28144 | 704-636-1221
  Dr. N. Windsor Eagle, prin. | Fax 639-3029
Southeast MS | 700/6-8
  1570 Peeler Rd 28146 | 704-638-5561
  Jamie Durant, prin. | Fax 638-5719
West Rowan MS | 800/6-8
  5925 Statesville Blvd 28147 | 704-633-4775
  Cynthia Misenheimer, prin. | Fax 633-3157
Other Schools – See China Grove, Landis, Mount Ulla, Spencer

Catawba College | Post-Sec.
  2300 W Innes St 28144 | 704-637-4111
Hood Theological Seminary | Post-Sec.
  1810 Lutheran Synod Dr 28144 | 704-636-6823
Livingstone College | Post-Sec.
  701 W Monroe St 28144 | 704-797-1000
North Hills Christian S | 200/PK-12
  2970 W Innes St 28144 | 704-636-3005
  Steve Adams, admin. | Fax 636-3597
Rowan-Cabarrus Community College | Post-Sec.
  PO Box 1595 28145 | 704-637-0760

Sanford, Lee, Pop. 23,346
Lee County SD | 9,000/K-12
  PO Box 1010 27331 | 919-774-6226
  Dr. James T. McCormick, supt. | Fax 776-0443
  www.lee.k12.nc.us
East Lee MS | 1,100/6-8
  1337 Broadway Rd 27332 | 919-776-8441
  Travis Taylor, prin. | Fax 774-7451
Lee County HS | 2,500/9-12
  1708 Nash St 27330 | 919-776-7541
  Greg Batten, prin. | Fax 718-7170
Lee Early College S | 9-12
  1105 Kelly Dr 27330 | 919-718-7259
  Robert Dietrich, prin. | Fax 718-7519
Southern Lee HS | 9-12
  2301 Tramway Rd 27332 | 919-718-2400
  Hans D. Lassiter, prin. | Fax 718-2410
West Lee MS | 1,100/6-8
  3301 Wicker St 27330 | 919-775-7351
  Stella Farrow, prin. | Fax 776-3694

Central Carolina Community College | Post-Sec.
  1105 Kelly Dr 27330 | 919-775-5401
Grace Christian S | 300/K-12
  2601 Jefferson Davis Hwy 27332 | 919-774-4415
  William Carver, prin. | Fax 774-1330
Lee Christian S | 400/PK-12
  3220 Keller Andrews Rd 27330 | 919-708-5115
  Stephen Coble, prin. | Fax 708-6933

Scotland Neck, Halifax, Pop. 2,281
Halifax County SD
  Supt. — See Halifax
Brawley MS | 300/6-8
  PO Box 449 27874 | 252-826-4513
  Allen Sledge, prin. | Fax 826-5098

Selma, Johnston, Pop. 6,333
Johnston County SD
  Supt. — See Smithfield
Selma MS | 600/5-8
  1533 US Highway 301 N 27576 | 919-965-2555
  Jennifer Moore, prin. | Fax 202-0116

Seven Springs, Wayne, Pop. 85
Wayne County SD
  Supt. — See Goldsboro
Spring Creek JSHS | 1,000/6-12
  4340 Indian Springs Rd 28578 | 919-751-7160
  Steve Clingan, prin. | Fax 751-7202

Shallotte, Brunswick, Pop. 1,490
Brunswick County SD
  Supt. — See Bolivia
Shallotte MS | 900/6-8
  225 Village Rd 28470 | 910-754-6882
  Jerry Small, prin. | Fax 754-3108

West Brunswick HS | 1,200/9-12
  550 Whiteville Rd NW 28470 | 910-754-4338
  Jim Burian, prin. | Fax 754-3110

Southeastern Christian Academy | 100/PK-12
  PO Box 1189 28459 | 910-754-4809
  Sherwood Lancaster, admin. | Fax 754-4895

Shelby, Cleveland, Pop. 21,215
Cleveland County SD | 17,900/PK-12
  130 S Post Rd Ste 2 28152 | 704-476-8000
  Steve Borders, supt. | Fax 476-8300
  www.clevelandcountyschools.org
Crest HS | 1,600/9-12
  800 Old Boiling Springs Rd 28152 | 704-482-5354
  Roger Harris, prin. | Fax 482-1187
Crest MS of Technology | 1,400/6-8
  315 Beaver Dam Church Rd 28152 | 704-482-0343
  Jeff Benfield, prin. | Fax 487-0378
Shelby HS | 900/9-12
  230 E Dixon Blvd 28152 | 704-482-3409
  Dianna Bridges, prin. | Fax 487-2869
Shelby MS | 800/6-8
  400 W Marion St 28150 | 704-482-6331
  Tim Quattlebaum, prin. | Fax 487-2889
Other Schools – See Kings Mountain, Lawndale

Cleveland Community College | Post-Sec.
  137 S Post Rd 28152 | 704-484-4000

Siler City, Chatham, Pop. 7,603
Chatham County SD
  Supt. — See Pittsboro
Chatham MS | 500/5-8
  2025 S 2nd Avenue Ext 27344 | 919-663-2414
  Brenda Griffin, prin. | Fax 663-2871
Jordan-Matthews HS | 700/9-12
  910 E Cardinal St 27344 | 919-742-2916
  David Moody, prin. | Fax 742-2201

Smithfield, Johnston, Pop. 11,462
Johnston County SD | 25,000/PK-12
  PO Box 1336 27577 | 919-934-6031
  Anthony J. Parker Ed.D., supt. | Fax 934-6035
  www.johnston.k12.nc.us
Smithfield MS | 800/6-8
  PO Box 2270 27577 | 919-934-4696
  Anne Meredith, prin. | Fax 934-7552
Smithfield-Selma HS | 1,400/9-12
  700 E Booker Dairy Rd 27577 | 919-934-5191
  Patrick Jacobs, prin. | Fax 934-3001
Other Schools – See Benson, Clayton, Four Oaks, Garner, Kenly, Micro, Princeton, Selma

Johnston Christian Academy | 200/PK-12
  PO Box 1599 27577 | 919-934-1248
  Donna Hammond, prin. | Fax 934-1289
Johnston Community College | Post-Sec.
  PO Box 2350 27577 | 919-934-3051

Snow Hill, Greene, Pop. 1,427
Greene County SD | 3,300/PK-12
  301 Kingold Blvd 28580 | 252-747-3425
  L. Stephen Mazingo, supt. | Fax 747-5942
  www.gcsedu.org/
Greene Central HS | 900/9-12
  140 School Dr 28580 | 252-747-3814
  Stephen Bryant, prin. | Fax 747-5972
Greene County MS | 800/6-8
  485 Middle School Rd 28580 | 252-747-8191
  Gregory Monroe, prin. | Fax 747-8696

Southern Pines, Moore, Pop. 11,446
Moore County SD
  Supt. — See Carthage
Pinecrest HS | 1,800/9-12
  100 Pinecrest School Rd 28387 | 910-692-6554
  Beverly McAnulty, prin. | Fax 692-0606

Calvary Christian S | 200/K-12
  400 S Bennett St 28387 | 910-692-8311
  Rev. Dan Carr, prin. | Fax 692-1992
O'Neal S | 400/PK-12
  PO Box 290 28388 | 910-692-6920
  John Neiswender, hdmstr. | Fax 692-6930

Southport, Brunswick, Pop. 2,605
Brunswick County SD
  Supt. — See Bolivia
South Brunswick HS | 1,000/9-12
  280 Cougar Rd 28461 | 910-845-2204
  Van Pennell, prin. | Fax 845-8974
South Brunswick MS | 900/6-8
  100 Cougar Rd 28461 | 910-845-2771
  Patricia Underwood, prin. | Fax 845-8972

Sparta, Alleghany, Pop. 1,818
Alleghany County SD | 1,500/PK-12
  85 Peachtree St 28675 | 336-372-4345
  Dr. Jeff Cox, supt. | Fax 372-4204
  www.alleghany.k12.nc.us
Alleghany HS | 400/9-12
  404 Trojan Ave 28675 | 336-372-4554
  Judd Starling, prin. | Fax 372-2680

Spencer, Rowan, Pop. 3,321
Rowan-Salisbury County SD
  Supt. — See Salisbury
North Rowan HS | 800/9-12
  300 N Whitehead Ave 28159 | 704-636-4420
  Rodney Bass, prin. | Fax 639-3033
North Rowan MS | 700/6-8
  512 Charles St 28159 | 704-639-3018
  Vicki Booker, prin. | Fax 639-3099

Spindale, Rutherford, Pop. 3,917
Isothermal Community College | Post-Sec.
  PO Box 804 28160 | 828-286-3636

Spring Hope, Nash, Pop. 1,255
Nash-Rocky Mount SD
  Supt. — See Nashville
Southern Nash MS | 1,100/6-8
  5301 S NC Highway 581 27882 | 252-478-4807
  Carina Bissette, prin. | Fax 478-4861

Spring Lake, Cumberland, Pop. 8,163
Cumberland County SD
  Supt. — See Fayetteville

Spring Lake MS | 700/6-8
  612 Spring Ave 28390 | 910-497-1175
  James Ellerbe, prin. | Fax 497-3467

Harnett County SD
  Supt. — See Lillington
Overhills HS | 9-12
  2495 Ray Rd 28390 | 910-436-1436
  John Castranio, prin. | Fax 436-0413
Overhills MS | 900/6-8
  2711 Ray Rd 28390 | 910-436-0009
  Rose Cooper, prin. | Fax 436-0948

Spruce Pine, Mitchell, Pop. 2,013
Mitchell County SD
  Supt. — See Bakersville
Harris MS | 300/6-8
  121 Harris St 28777 | 828-765-2321
  Chad Calhoun, prin. | Fax 765-1595

Altapass Christian S | 50/K-12
  50 Altapass Trl 28777 | 828-765-0660
  Debbie McKinney, prin.
Mayland Community College | Post-Sec.
  PO Box 547 28777 | 828-765-7351

Stanley, Gaston, Pop. 3,086
Gaston County SD
  Supt. — See Gastonia
Stanley MS | 600/6-8
  317 Hovis Rd 28164 | 704-263-2941
  Charles Ashley, prin. | Fax 263-0993

Statesville, Iredell, Pop. 24,129
Iredell-Statesville SD | 19,100/PK-12
  PO Box 911 28687 | 704-872-8931
  Dr. Terry Holliday, supt. | Fax 871-2834
  www.iss.k12.nc.us
Collaborative College for Technology | 9-12
  500 W Broad St 28677 | 704-978-5450
  Lisa Miller, prin. | Fax 978-5452
East Iredell MS | 700/6-8
  590 Chestnut Grove Rd 28625 | 704-872-4666
  Dr. Katherine Stillerman, prin. | Fax 873-6602
South Iredell HS | 800/9-12
  299 Old Mountain Rd 28677 | 704-528-4536
  David Dixon, prin. | Fax 528-0882
Statesville HS | 1,200/9-12
  474 N Center St 28677 | 704-873-3491
  Larry Rogers, prin. | Fax 878-6195
Statesville MS | 600/6-8
  321 Clegg St 28677 | 704-872-2135
  Terry Jonas, prin. | Fax 871-9279
West Iredell HS | 1,100/9-12
  213 Warrior Dr 28625 | 704-873-2181
  Todd Holden, prin. | Fax 873-0356
West Iredell MS | 900/6-8
  303 Watermelon Rd 28625 | 704-873-2887
  Pat Svanson, prin. | Fax 881-0582
Other Schools – See Mooresville, Olin, Troutman

Believers Faith Center Christian Academy | 100/PK-12
  PO Box 706 28687 | 704-873-5484
  June Gaither, prin. | Fax 871-1596
Gardner-Webb University | Post-Sec.
  PO Box 908 28687 | 704-872-3664
Hairstylist Academy | Post-Sec.
  113 Water St 28677 | 704-873-8805
Mitchell Community College | Post-Sec.
  500 W Broad St 28677 | 704-878-3200
Southview Christian S | 200/K-12
  625 Wallace Springs Rd 28677 | 704-872-9554
  Larry Duffer, prin. | Fax 872-4359
Statesville Christian S | 500/PK-12
  1210 Museum Rd 28625 | 704-873-9511
  Patrick Deveney, hdmstr. | Fax 873-0841

Stokesdale, Guilford, Pop. 3,367
Oak Level Baptist Academy | 100/K-12
  1569 Oak Level Church Rd 27357 | 336-643-9288
  Clay Walker, prin.

Stoneville, Rockingham, Pop. 989
Stone-Eden Christian S | 100/K-12
  PO Box 505 27048 | 336-573-3335
  Celeste Bailey, prin.

Sugar Grove, Watauga
Jung Tao School of Chinese Medicine | Post-Sec.
  207 Dale Adams Rd 28679 | 828-297-4181

Supply, Brunswick
Brunswick Community College | Post-Sec.
  PO Box 30 28462 | 910-755-7300

Swannanoa, Buncombe, Pop. 3,538
Buncombe County SD
  Supt. — See Asheville
Owen MS | 700/6-8
  730 Old US 70 Hwy 28778 | 828-686-7739
  Vicky Matthews, prin. | Fax 686-7938

Asheville Christian Academy | 500/PK-12
  PO Box 1089 28778 | 828-581-2200
  William George, hdmstr. | Fax 581-2218

Swanquarter, Hyde
Hyde County SD | 700/PK-12
  PO Box 217 27885 | 252-926-3281
  Dr. M. Brock Womble, supt. | Fax 926-3083
  www.hyde.k12.nc.us/
Mattamuskeet HS | 200/9-12
  20392 US Highway 264 27885 | 252-926-0221
  Linwood Smith, prin. | Fax 926-0224
Mattamuskeet MS | 200/6-8
  20400 US Highway 264 27885 | 252-926-0015
  Rosemary W. Mann, prin. | Fax 926-0016
Other Schools – See Ocracoke

Swansboro, Onslow, Pop. 1,334
Onslow County SD
  Supt. — See Jacksonville
Swansboro HS | 1,000/9-12
  161 Queens Creek Rd 28584 | 910-326-4300
  J. Beasley, prin. | Fax 326-1674

Swansboro MS
1240 W Corbett Ave   28584 — 800/6-8 — 910-326-3601
Christine Andre, prin. — Fax 326-5848

Sylva, Jackson, Pop. 2,426
Jackson County SD
398 Hospital Rd   28779 — 3,700/PK-12 — 828-586-2311
Peggy Sue Nations Ed.D., supt. — Fax 586-5450
www.jcps.k12.nc.us
Smoky Mountain HS
100 Smoky Mountain Dr   28779 — 900/9-12 — 828-586-2177
Alex Bell, prin. — Fax 586-2374
Other Schools – See Cashiers

Southwestern Community College — Post-Sec.
447 College Dr   28779 — 828-586-4091

Tabor City, Columbus, Pop. 2,602
Columbus County SD
Supt. — See Whiteville
South Columbus HS
40 Stallion Dr   28463 — 800/9-12 — 910-653-4073
Dr. Maudie Davis, prin. — Fax 653-9461
Tabor City MS
701 W 6th St   28463 — 300/6-8 — 910-653-3637
James Doll, prin. — Fax 653-2093

Tarboro, Edgecombe, Pop. 10,701
Edgecombe County SD
PO Box 7128   27886 — 7,900/PK-12 — 252-641-2600
Roland Whitted, supt. — Fax 641-5714
www.ecps.us/community/
Martin MS
400 E Johnston St   27886 — 500/7-8 — 252-641-5710
Douglas Edwards, prin. — Fax 641-5713
North Edgecombe HS
7589 NC Highway 33 NW   27886 — 400/9-12 — 252-823-3562
Derrick Jordan, prin. — Fax 823-7847
Tarboro HS
1400 W Howard Ave   27886 — 800/9-12 — 252-823-4284
Michael Lutz, prin. — Fax 823-0862
Other Schools – See Battleboro, Pinetops, Rocky Mount

Edgecombe Community College — Post-Sec.
2009 W Wilson St   27886 — 252-823-5166

Tar Heel, Bladen, Pop. 69
Bladen County SD
Supt. — See Elizabethtown
Tar Heel MS
PO Box 128   28392 — 400/5-8 — 910-862-2475
Susan Inman, prin. — Fax 872-5599

Taylorsville, Alexander, Pop. 1,846
Alexander County SD
PO Box 128   28681 — 5,600/PK-12 — 828-632-7001
Jack Hoke, supt. — Fax 632-8862
www.alexander.k12.nc.us
Alexander Central HS
223 School Dr   28681 — 1,600/9-12 — 828-632-7063
Steve Bumgarner, prin. — Fax 632-5387
West Alexander MS
85 Bulldog Ln   28681 — 700/6-8 — 828-495-4611
Susan Gantt, prin. — Fax 495-3527
Other Schools – See Hiddenite

Teachey, Duplin, Pop. 247
Duplin County SD
Supt. — See Kenansville
Wallace-Rose Hill HS
602 High School Rd   28464 — 700/9-12 — 910-285-7501
M.D. Guthrie, prin. — Fax 285-1116

Thomasville, Davidson, Pop. 25,466
Davidson County SD
Supt. — See Lexington
Brown MS
1140 Kendall Mill Rd   27360 — 800/6-8 — 336-475-8845
Randy Holmes, prin. — Fax 475-3842
East Davidson HS
1408 Lake Rd   27360 — 900/9-12 — 336-476-4814
Cathi Smith, prin. — Fax 476-2982
Ledford HS
140 Jesse Green Rd   27360 — 900/9-12 — 336-769-9671
Bill Butts, prin. — Fax 769-0650
Ledford MS
3954 N NC Highway 109   27360 — 900/6-8 — 336-476-4816
J. Evan Myers, prin. — Fax 476-1479

Thomasville CSD
400 Turner St   27360 — 2,600/K-12 — 336-474-4200
Daniel Cockman, supt. — Fax 475-0356
www.tcs.k12.nc.us
Thomasville HS
410 Unity St   27360 — 700/9-12 — 336-474-4250
Dirk Gurley, prin. — Fax 476-7430
Thomasville MS
400 Unity St   27360 — 600/6-8 — 336-474-4120
Keith Tobin, prin. — Fax 472-5081

Carolina Christian Academy — 100/K-12
367 Academy Dr   27360 — 336-472-8950
Daniel Lee, prin. — Fax 472-8920

Topton, Macon
Macon County SD
Supt. — See Franklin
Nantahala S — 100/K-12
212 Winding Stairs Rd   28781 — 828-321-4388
Chris Baldwin, prin. — Fax 321-4834

Trenton, Jones, Pop. 197
Jones County SD
320 W Jones St   28585 — 1,500/PK-12 — 252-448-2531
Ethan Lenker, supt. — Fax 448-1394
www.jonesnc.net
Jones HS
1490 NC Highway 58 S   28585 — 400/9-12 — 252-448-2451
Joletha White, prin. — Fax 448-1034
Jones MS
190 Old New Bern Rd   28585 — 300/6-8 — 252-448-3956
Steve Hill, prin. — Fax 448-1044

Trinity, Randolph, Pop. 6,818
Randolph County SD
Supt. — See Asheboro
Archdale-Trinity MS
PO Box 232   27370 — 800/7-8 — 336-431-2589
Dustin Johnson, prin. — Fax 431-1809

Trinity HS
5746 Trinity High School Dr   27370 — 1,300/9-12 — 336-861-6870
Daryl Barnes, prin. — Fax 861-8613
Uwharrie HS
1463 Pleasant Union Rd   27370 — 500/6-8 — 336-241-3900
Linda Johnson, prin. — Fax 241-3904

Troutman, Iredell, Pop. 1,651
Iredell-Statesville SD
Supt. — See Statesville
Troutman MS
PO Box 807   28166 — 400/6-8 — 704-528-5137
Judy Gaghan, prin. — Fax 528-4006

Troy, Montgomery, Pop. 3,465
Montgomery County SD
PO Box 427   27371 — 4,600/PK-12 — 910-576-6511
Dr. C. Lindsey Suggs, supt. — Fax 576-2044
www.montgomery.k12.nc.us
Other Schools – See Biscoe, Mount Gilead

Montgomery Community College — Post-Sec.
1011 Page St   27371 — 910-576-6222

Tyner, Chowan
Edenton/Chowan County SD
Supt. — See Edenton
Chowan MS
2845 Virginia Rd   27980 — 600/6-8 — 252-221-4131
Willie Koonce, prin. — Fax 221-8033

Valdese, Burke, Pop. 4,549
Burke County SD
Supt. — See Morganton
Heritage MS
1951 Enon Rd   28690 — 800/6-8 — 828-874-0731
Robert Murray, prin. — Fax 879-6330

Vanceboro, Craven, Pop. 875
Craven County SD
Supt. — See New Bern
West Craven HS
2600 Streets Ferry Rd   28586 — 1,100/9-12 — 252-244-3200
Donald Hughes, prin. — Fax 244-3207

Wadesboro, Anson, Pop. 3,463
Anson County SD
PO Box 719   28170 — 4,500/PK-12 — 704-694-4417
Dr. George Truman, supt. — Fax 694-7470
www.anson.k12.nc.us
Anson HS
PO Box 513   28170 — 1,200/9-12 — 704-694-9301
Michael McLeod, prin. — Fax 694-4570
Anson MS
PO Box 678   28170 — 700/7-8 — 704-694-3945
Howard McLean, prin. — Fax 694-5209

Anson College of Cosmetology — Post-Sec.
1217 E Caswell St   28170 — 704-694-6677

Wake Forest, Wake, Pop. 16,029
Wake County SD
Supt. — See Raleigh
Heritage MS
3500 Rogers Rd   27587 — 800/6-8 — 919-562-6204
LaVaughan Buchanan, prin. — Fax 562-6227
Wake Forest-Rolesville HS
420 Stadium Dr   27587 — 1,500/9-12 — 919-554-8611
Andre Smith, prin. — Fax 554-8617
Wake Forest-Rolesville MS
1800 S Main St   27587 — 1,200/6-8 — 919-554-8440
Elaine Hanzer, prin. — Fax 554-8435

Southeastern Baptist Theological Sem. — Post-Sec.
PO Box 1889   27588 — 919-761-2280

Walkertown, Forsyth, Pop. 4,148
Winston-Salem/Forsyth SD
Supt. — See Winston Salem
Walkertown MS
PO Box 1149   27051 — 600/6-8 — 336-595-2161
Dr. Patrick Mitze, prin. — Fax 595-3423

Walnut Cove, Stokes, Pop. 1,467
Stokes County SD
Supt. — See Danbury
Southeastern Stokes MS
1044 N Main St   27052 — 500/6-8 — 336-591-4371
Jo Beth Clark, prin. — Fax 591-8164
South Stokes HS
1100 S Stokes High Dr   27052 — 700/9-12 — 336-994-2995
Debbie Whitaker, prin. — Fax 994-2608

Warrensville, Ashe
Ashe County SD
Supt. — See Jefferson
Ashe County MS
PO Box 259   28693 — 500/7-8 — 336-384-3591
W. Bobby Ashley, prin. — Fax 384-2112

Warrenton, Warren, Pop. 774
Warren County SD
PO Box 110   27589 — 3,100/K-12 — 252-257-3184
Dr. Ray Spain, supt. — Fax 257-5357
www.wcsk12.org
Warren County HS
149 Campus Dr   27589 — 1,000/9-12 — 252-257-4413
Dr. Tony Cozart, prin. — Fax 257-1019
Warren County MS
118 Campus Dr   27589 — 800/6-8 — 252-257-3751
Danylu Hundley, prin. — Fax 257-4532

Warsaw, Duplin, Pop. 3,044
Duplin County SD
Supt. — See Kenansville
Kenan HS
1241 NC 24 & 50   28398 — 600/9-12 — 910-293-4218
— Fax 293-6744
Warsaw MS
738 W College St   28398 — 200/6-8 — 910-293-7997
Kenneth Houston, prin. — Fax 293-7397

Washington, Beaufort, Pop. 9,677
Beaufort County SD
321 Smaw Rd   27889 — 7,400/PK-12 — 252-946-6593
Dr. Jeffrey C. Moss, supt. — Fax 946-3255
www.beaufort.k12.nc.us
B.C. Education Technical Center — Vo/Tech
511 N Harvey St   27889 — 252-946-5382
Victoria Mallison, prin. — Fax 946-7964

Jones MS
230 E 8th St   27889 — 900/6-8 — 252-946-0874
Donna Moore, prin. — Fax 946-7604
Washington HS
400 Slatestone Rd   27889 — 1,100/9-12 — 252-946-0858
Steve Hagen, prin. — Fax 946-9633
Other Schools – See Aurora, Chocowinity, Pinetown

Beaufort County Community College — Post-Sec.
PO Box 1069   27889 — 252-946-6194

Waynesville, Haywood, Pop. 9,347
Haywood County SD
1230 N Main St   28786 — 8,400/PK-12 — 828-456-2400
Bill Upton, supt. — Fax 456-2438
www.haywood.k12.nc.us
Bethel MS
730 Sonoma Rd   28786 — 300/6-8 — 828-646-3442
Tom Daily, prin. — Fax 648-6259
Tuscola HS
564 Tuscola School Rd   28786 — 1,300/9-12 — 828-456-2708
Tommy Hollingsworth, prin. — Fax 456-2434
Waynesville MS
459 Brown Ave   28786 — 1,000/6-8 — 828-456-2403
Keith Roden, prin.
Other Schools – See Canton, Clyde

Weaverville, Buncombe, Pop. 2,423
Buncombe County SD
Supt. — See Asheville
North Buncombe HS
890 Clarks Chapel Rd   28787 — 1,200/9-12 — 828-645-4221
Jack Evans, prin. — Fax 645-4367
North Buncombe MS
51 N Buncombe School Rd   28787 — 600/7-8 — 828-645-7944
Vicki Biggers, prin. — Fax 645-2509

Weldon, Halifax, Pop. 1,328
Weldon CSD
301 Mulberry St   27890 — 1,100/PK-12 — 252-536-4821
J. Wendell Hall, supt. — Fax 536-3062
www.weldoncityschools.k12.nc.us
Weldon HS
415 County Rd   27890 — 300/9-12 — 252-536-4829
David Jones, prin. — Fax 536-0168
Other Schools – See Halifax

Halifax Community College — Post-Sec.
PO Box 809   27890 — 252-536-2551

Wendell, Wake, Pop. 4,322
Wake County SD
Supt. — See Raleigh
East Wake HS
5101 Rolesville Rd   27591 — 2,000/9-12 — 919-365-2625
Dr. Herman G. Horne, prin. — Fax 365-2628
East Wake S of Integrated Technology — Vo/Tech
5101 Rolesville Rd   27591 — 919-850-1600

Wentworth, Rockingham, Pop. 2,803

Rockingham Community College — Post-Sec.
PO Box 38   27375 — 336-342-4261

West End, Moore
Moore County SD
Supt. — See Carthage
West Pine MS
144 Archie Rd   27376 — 700/6-8 — 910-673-1464
Jeff Maples, prin. — Fax 673-1272

West Jefferson, Ashe, Pop. 1,076
Ashe County SD
Supt. — See Jefferson
Ashe County HS
PO Box 450   28694 — 1,000/9-12 — 336-246-2400
Phil Howell, prin. — Fax 246-2411

Whiteville, Columbus, Pop. 5,099
Columbus County SD
PO Box 729   28472 — 7,000/PK-12 — 910-642-5168
Dr. Dan Strickland, supt. — Fax 640-1010
www.columbus.k12.nc.us/
Other Schools – See Cerro Gordo, Chadbourn, Delco,
Hallsboro, Lake Waccamaw, Tabor City

Whiteville CSD
PO Box 609   28472 — 2,800/PK-12 — 910-642-4116
Dr. Danny D. McPherson, supt. — Fax 642-0564
www.whiteville.k12.nc.us
Central MS
310 S Mrtn Lthr King Jr Ave   28472 — 600/6-8 — 910-642-3546
Dr. Beverly Boone, prin. — Fax 642-7484
Whiteville HS
413 N Lee St   28472 — 800/9-12 — 910-914-4189
Kyle Ramey, prin. — Fax 914-4186

Carolina Adventist Academy — 50/K-10
3710 James B White Hwy   28472 — 910-640-0855
Evelyn Tucker, prin.
Columbus Christian Academy — 200/K-12
115 W Calhoun St   28472 — 910-642-6196
Debra N. Edwards, prin.
Southeastern Community College — Post-Sec.
PO Box 151   28472 — 910-642-7141
Waccamaw Academy — 200/K-12
PO Box 507   28472 — 910-642-7530
Denning Buchter, hdmstr. — Fax 642-6938

Wilkesboro, Wilkes, Pop. 3,206
Wilkes County SD
201 W Main St   28697 — 9,700/PK-12 — 336-667-1121
Dr. Stephen C. Laws, supt. — Fax 838-5021
www.wilkes.k12.nc.us
West Wilkes MS
1677 N NC Highway 16   28697 — 500/6-8 — 336-973-1700
Susan Blackburn, prin. — Fax 973-7423
Wilkes Central HS
1179 Moravian Falls Rd   28697 — 1,000/9-12 — 336-667-5277
Scott Kaufman, prin. — Fax 667-2091
Wilkes County Career Center — Vo/Tech
374 Lincoln Heights Rd   28697 — 336-667-3653
Al Olson, prin. — Fax 838-8947
Other Schools – See Hays, Millers Creek, Moravian Falls,
North Wilkesboro, Ronda

Wilkes Community College — Post-Sec.
PO Box 120   28697 — 336-838-6100

Williamston, Martin, Pop. 5,749
Martin County SD — 4,600/PK-12
300 N Watts St   27892 — 252-792-1575
Dr. Thomas Daly, supt. — Fax 792-1965
www.martin.k12.nc.us/
Bear Grass JSHS — 300/7-12
6344 E Bear Grass Rd   27892 — 252-792-3721
Hallet Davis, prin. — Fax 809-4814
Williamston HS — 600/9-12
200 Godwin Dr   27892 — 252-792-7881
Linda Cherry, prin. — Fax 809-4807
Williamston MS — 500/6-8
600 N Smithwick St   27892 — 252-792-1111
Lindell Wallace, prin. — Fax 792-6644
Other Schools – See Jamesville, Robersonville

Martin Community College — Post-Sec.
1161 Kehukee Park Rd   27892 — 252-792-1521

Wilmington, New Hanover, Pop. 91,137
New Hanover County SD — 22,400/PK-12
6410 Carolina Beach Rd   28412 — 910-763-5431
Dr. D. John Morris, supt. — Fax 254-4479
www.nhcs.k12.nc.us
Ashley HS — 1,500/9-12
555 Haleyburton Memorial Pk   28412 — 910-790-2360
James McAdams, prin. — Fax 790-2356
Hoggard HS — 1,700/9-12
4305 Shipyard Blvd   28403 — 910-350-2072
Dave Spencer, prin. — Fax 350-2066
Lakeside JSHS — 300/6-12
1805 S 13th St   28401 — 910-251-6161
Jerry Oates, prin. — Fax 251-6022
Laney HS — 1,800/9-12
2700 N College Rd   28405 — 910-350-2089
Robert Grimes, prin. — Fax 350-2083
Murray MS — 800/6-8
655 Haleyburton Memorial Pk   28412 — 910-790-2363
LaChawn Smith, prin. — Fax 790-2351
Myrtle Grove MS — 700/6-8
901 Piner Rd   28409 — 910-350-2100
Robin Meiers, prin. — Fax 350-2104
New Hanover HS — 1,600/9-12
1307 Market St   28401 — 910-251-6100
Chris Furr, prin. — Fax 251-6114
Noble MS — 700/6-8
6520 Market St   28405 — 910-350-2112
Al O'Briant, prin. — Fax 350-2109
Roland-Grise MS — 800/6-8
4412 Lake Ave   28403 — 910-350-2136
Will Hatch, prin. — Fax 350-2133
Trask MS — 700/6-8
2900 N College Rd   28405 — 910-350-2142
Sharon Dousharm, prin. — Fax 350-2144
Virgo MS — 400/6-8
813 Nixon St   28401 — 910-251-6150
Megan Silvey, prin. — Fax 251-6055
Williston MS — 900/6-8
401 S 10th St   28401 — 910-815-6906
Cynthia Wartel, prin. — Fax 815-6904

Cape Fear Academy — 600/PK-12
3900 S College Rd   28412 — 910-791-0287
John Meehl, hdmstr. — Fax 791-0290
Cape Fear Community College — Post-Sec.
411 N Front St   28401 — 910-251-5100
Miller-Motte Technical College — Post-Sec.
5000 Market St   28405 — 800-784-2110
Mr. David's School of Hair Design — Post-Sec.
4348 Market St # N-17   28403 — 910-763-4418
New Hanover Regional Medical Center — Post-Sec.
2131 S 17th St   28401 — 910-343-7074
University of North Carolina — Post-Sec.
601 S College Rd   28403 — 910-962-3000
Wilmington Christian Academy — 600/K-12
1401 N College St   28405 — 910-791-4248
Barren Nobles, admin. — Fax 791-4276

Wilson, Wilson, Pop. 45,921
Wilson County SD — 12,800/PK-12
PO Box 2048   27894 — 252-399-7700
Dr. Larry Price, supt. — Fax 399-2776
www.wilson.k12.nc.us/
Beddingfield HS — 1,000/9-12
4510 Old Stantonsburg Rd   27893 — 252-399-7880
Bob Pope, prin. — Fax 399-7850
Darden MS — 400/6-8
1665 Lipscomb Rd E   27893 — 252-206-4973
Alice Mills-Sadler, prin. — Fax 206-1508
Fike HS — 1,200/9-12
500 Harrison Dr N   27893 — 252-399-7905
Jim Tillman, prin. — Fax 399-7893
Forest Hills MS — 600/6-8
1210 Forest Hills Rd NW   27896 — 252-399-7913
Steve J. Ellis, prin. — Fax 399-7894
Hunt HS — 1,200/9-12
4559 Lamm Rd SW   27893 — 252-399-7930
William Williamson, prin. — Fax 399-7897
Speight MS — 400/6-8
5514 Old Stantonsburg Rd, — 252-238-3983
Jeremy Stevens, prin. — Fax 238-2104
Toisnot MS — 600/6-8
1301 Corbett Ave N   27893 — 252-399-7973
Craig Harris, prin. — Fax 399-7749
Other Schools – See Elm City, Lucama

Barton College — Post-Sec.
PO Box 5000   27893 — 252-399-6300
Community Christian S — 200/PK-12
5160 Packhouse Rd   27896 — 252-399-1376
Renita Petway, hdmstr. — Fax 243-6973
Eastern North Carolina Sch. for the Deaf — Post-Sec.
PO Box 2768   27894
Greenfield S — 200/PK-12
PO Box 3525   27895 — 252-237-8046
Janet Beaman, hdmstr. — Fax 237-1825
Mitchell's Hairstyling Academy — Post-Sec.
2620 Forest Hills Rd #A   27893 — 252-243-3158
Wilson Christian Academy — 400/K-12
PO Box 3818   27895 — 252-237-8064
Shirley Pierce, prin. — Fax 234-9164
Wilson Technical Community College — Post-Sec.
PO Box 4305   27893 — 252-291-1195

Windsor, Bertie, Pop. 2,243
Bertie County SD — 3,500/PK-12
PO Box 10   27983 — 252-794-3173
Dr. Nettie Collins-Hart, supt. — Fax 794-9727
www.bertieschools.com
Bertie HS — 1,100/9-12
715 US Highway 13 N   27983 — 252-794-3034
Wayne Mayo, prin. — Fax 794-1932
Southwestern MS — 600/6-8
819 Governors Rd   27983 — 252-794-2358
Sandra Hardy, prin. — Fax 794-3407
Other Schools – See Powellsville

Bethel Assembly Christian Academy — 200/K-12
105 Askewville Bryant St   27983 — 252-794-4034
R.O. Denton, prin.

Winfall, Perquimans, Pop. 556
Perquimans County SD
Supt. — See Hertford
Perquimans County MS — 400/6-8
PO Box 39   27985 — 252-426-7355
Jamie Liverman, prin. — Fax 426-1424

Wingate, Union, Pop. 2,665

Wingate University — Post-Sec.
201 E Wilson St   28174 — 704-233-8000

Winston Salem, Forsyth, Pop. 188,934
Winston-Salem/Forsyth SD — 49,200/PK-12
PO Box 2513   27102 — 336-727-2816
Dr. Donald L. Martin, supt. — Fax 727-2008
wsfcs.k12.nc.us
Atkins MS — 300/6-8
1215 N Cameron Ave   27101 — 336-727-2781
Sterling Garris, prin. — Fax 727-2961
Career Center — Vo/Tech
1615 Miller St   27103 — 336-727-8181
Dr. Dennis Moser, prin. — Fax 727-2115
Carter Vocational S — Vo/Tech
2700 S Main St   27127 — 336-771-4590
Dr. Jan Floyd, prin. — Fax 771-4554
Carver HS — 1,100/9-12
3545 Carver School Rd   27105 — 336-727-2987
Carol Montague, prin. — Fax 727-8211
Clemmons MS — 1,200/6-8
3785 Fraternity Church Rd   27127 — 336-774-4677
Sandra Hunter, prin. — Fax 774-4678
Hanes MS — 600/6-8
2900 Indiana Ave   27105 — 336-727-2252
Joe Childers, prin. — Fax 748-4138
Hill MS — 500/6-8
2200 Tryon St   27107 — 336-771-4515
Becky Hodges, prin. — Fax 771-4519
Jefferson MS — 1,100/6-8
3500 Sally Kirk Rd   27106 — 336-774-4630
Dr. Joyce Jones, prin. — Fax 774-4635
Meadowlark MS — 1,100/6-8
301 Meadowlark Dr   27106 — 336-922-1730
Loretta Rowland-Kitley, prin. — Fax 922-1745
Mineral Springs MS — 500/6-8
4559 Ogburn Ave   27105 — 336-661-4870
Randy Fulton, prin. — Fax 661-4857
Mt. Tabor HS — 1,800/9-12
342 Petree Rd   27106 — 336-774-4600
Martha Land, prin. — Fax 774-4606
North Forsyth HS — 1,700/9-12
5705 Shattalon Dr   27105 — 336-661-4880
Ron Jessup, prin. — Fax 661-4869
Northwest MS — 1,000/6-8
5501 Murray Rd   27106 — 336-924-5126
Brenda Peay, prin. — Fax 924-5128
Paisley MS — 800/6-10
1400 Grant Ave   27105 — 336-727-2775
Marion Couch, prin. — Fax 727-8315
Parkland HS — 1,300/9-12
1600 Brewer Rd   27127 — 336-771-4700
Dr. Tim Lee, prin. — Fax 771-4703
Philo MS — 500/6-8
410 Haverhill St   27127 — 336-771-4570
Valarie Williams, prin. — Fax 771-4578
Reynolds HS — 1,800/9-12
301 N Hawthorne Rd   27104 — 336-727-2061
Dr. Art Paschal, prin. — Fax 727-2053
School of Biotechnology — 9-12
3605 Old Greensboro Rd   27101 — 336-703-6754
Carolyn Preyar, prin. — Fax 748-3565

School of Computer Technology — 9-12
3605 Old Greensboro Rd   27101 — 336-703-6754
Brad Craddock, prin. — Fax 748-3565
School of Pre-Engineering — 9-12
3605 Old Greensboro Rd   27101 — 336-703-6754
Doug Gerringer, prin. — Fax 748-3565
Wiley MS — 900/6-8
1400 W Northwest Blvd   27104 — 336-727-2378
Ed Weiss, prin. — Fax 727-2303
Other Schools – See Clemmons, Kernersville, Pfafftown, Walkertown

Calvary Baptist Day S — 700/PK-12
5000 Country Club Rd   27104 — 336-765-5546
Martha Lennon, admin. — Fax 714-5577
Carolina Beauty College — Post-Sec.
7736 N Point Blvd Ste C   27106 — 336-759-7969
Cosmetology Inst of Beauty Arts & Sci. — Post-Sec.
807 Silas Creek Pkwy   27127 — 336-773-1472
Forsyth Technical Community College — Post-Sec.
2100 Silas Creek Pkwy   27103 — 336-723-0371
Gospel Light Christian S — 500/K-12
4940 Gospel Light Church Rd   27101 — 336-722-6100
Robert Richards, prin. — Fax 722-9640
North Carolina School of the Arts — Post-Sec.
PO Box 12189   27117 — 336-770-3291
Piedmont Baptist College — Post-Sec.
716 Franklin St   27101 — 336-725-8344
Salem Academy — 200/9-12
500 E Salem Ave   27101 — 336-721-2646
Wayne Burkette, hdmstr. — Fax 917-5340
Salem Baptist Christian S — 300/PK-12
429 S Broad St   27101 — 336-725-6113
Martha Drake, hdmstr. — Fax 725-8455
Salem College — Post-Sec.
PO Box 10548   27108 — 800-327-2536
Wake Forest University — Post-Sec.
Medical Center Blvd   27157 — 336-748-4424
Wake Forest University — Post-Sec.
PO Box 7305   27109 — 336-759-5000
Winston-Salem Barber School — Post-Sec.
1531 Silas Creek Pkwy   27127 — 336-724-1459
Winston-Salem Bible College — Post-Sec.
PO Box 777   27102 — 336-774-0900
Winston-Salem State University — Post-Sec.
601 S Mrtn Lther King Jr Dr   27110 — 336-750-2000
Woodland Baptist Christian S — 300/PK-12
3665 Patterson Ave   27105 — 336-767-6176
Steve Holley, prin. — Fax 767-9116

Winterville, Pitt, Pop. 4,660
Pitt County SD
Supt. — See Greenville
Cox MS — 1,000/6-8
2657 Church St   28590 — 252-756-3105
John Coleman, prin. — Fax 756-1081
South Central HS — 1,000/9-12
570 Forlines Rd   28590 — 252-321-3232
Will Sanderson, prin. — Fax 321-7909

Winton, Hertford, Pop. 918
Hertford County SD — 4,000/PK-12
PO Box 158   27986 — 252-358-1761
Dennis M. Deloatch, supt. — Fax 358-4745
www.hertford.k12.nc.us
Other Schools – See Ahoskie, Murfreesboro

Yadkinville, Yadkin, Pop. 2,842
Yadkin County SD — 6,000/PK-12
121 Washington St   27055 — 336-679-2051
Barbara Todd, supt. — Fax 679-4013
www.yadkin.k12.nc.us
Other Schools – See Boonville, East Bend

Yanceyville, Caswell, Pop. 2,108
Caswell County SD — 3,500/PK-12
PO Box 160   27379 — 336-694-4116
Douglas N. Barker, supt. — Fax 694-5154
www.caswellschools.org
Bartlett Yancey HS — 1,100/9-12
PO Box 27379 — 336-694-4212
Dr. Gary Cone, prin. — Fax 694-5285
Dillard MS — 900/6-8
PO Box 310   27379 — 336-694-4941
Frank Scott, prin. — Fax 694-6353

Youngsville, Franklin, Pop. 686
Franklin County SD
Supt. — See Louisburg
Cedar Creek MS — 600/6-8
2228 Cedar Creek Rd   27596 — 919-554-4463
Brooke Wheeler, prin. — Fax 570-5143

American Institute of Applied Science — Post-Sec.
100 Hunter Pl   27596 — 919-554-2500

Zebulon, Wake, Pop. 4,133
Wake County SD
Supt. — See Raleigh
Zebulon MS — 1,000/6-8
1000 Shepard School Rd   27597 — 919-404-3630
Dalphine Perry, prin. — Fax 404-3651

Heritage Christian Academy — 100/K-12
615 Mack Todd Rd   27597 — 919-269-6915
Rev. David Dupree, prin.

NORTH DAKOTA

NORTH DAKOTA DEPT. OF PUBLIC INSTRUCTION
600 E Boulevard Ave, Bismarck 58505-0660
Telephone 701-328-2260
Fax 701-328-2461
Website http://www.dpi.state.nd.us
Superintendent of Public Instruction   Wayne Sanstead

NORTH DAKOTA BOARD OF EDUCATION
600 E Boulevard Ave, Bismarck 58505-0660
Chairperson   Charles Brickner

COUNTY SUPERINTENDENTS OF SCHOOLS

Adams County Office of Education
  Patricia Carroll, supt. — 701-567-4363
  PO Box 589, Hettinger 58639 — Fax 567-2910
Barnes County Office of Education
  Edward McGough, supt. — 701-845-8500
  230 4th St NW, Valley City 58072 — Fax 845-8548
Benson County Office of Education
  Jean Olson, supt. — 701-473-5370
  PO Box 347, Minnewaukan 58351 — Fax 473-5571
  www.tradecorridor.com/minnewaukan/
Billings County Office of Education
  Virginia Bares, supt. — 701-623-4366
  PO Box 334, Medora 58645 — Fax 623-4896
Bottineau County Office of Education
  Dwane Getzlaff, supt. — 701-228-2815
  314 5th St W, Bottineau 58318 — Fax 228-3658
  www.tradecorridor.com/bottineaucounty/index.html
Bowman County Office of Education
  Lois Anderson, supt. — 701-523-3478
  PO Box 380, Bowman 58623 — Fax 523-3428
Burke County Office of Education
  Teri Baumann, supt. — 701-377-2861
  PO Box 310, Bowbells 58721 — Fax 377-2020
Burleigh County Office of Education
  Karen Kautzmann, supt. — 701-667-3315
  210 2nd Ave NW, Mandan 58554 — Fax 667-3348
  www.co.burleigh.nd.us
Cass County Office of Education
  Mike Montplaisir, supt. — 701-241-5601
  PO Box 2806, Fargo 58108 — Fax 241-5728
  www.co.cass.nd.us
Cavalier County Office of Education
  Dawn Roppel, supt. — 701-256-2229
  901 3rd St, Langdon 58249 — Fax 256-2546
Dickey County Office of Education
  Tom Strand, supt. — 701-349-3249
  PO Box 148, Ellendale 58436 — Fax 349-4639
Divide County Office of Education
  Donald Nielsen, supt. — 701-965-6313
  PO Box G, Crosby 58730 — Fax 965-6004
Dunn County Office of Education
  Reinhard Hauck, supt. — 701-573-4448
  PO Box 105, Manning 58642 — Fax 573-4444
Eddy County Office of Education
  Joan Schaefer, supt. — 701-947-5615
  524 Central Ave — Fax 947-2279
  New Rockford 58356
Emmons County Office of Education
  Del Svalen, supt. — 701-254-4486
  PO Box 338, Linton 58552 — Fax 254-4322
Foster County Office of Education
  Roger Schlotman, supt. — 701-652-2441
  PO Box 80, Carrington 58421 — Fax 652-2173
Golden Valley County Office of Education
  Virginia Bares, supt. — 701-872-4543
  PO Box 35, Beach 58621 — Fax 872-4383
  www.beachnd.com

Grand Forks County Office of Education
  David Godfread, supt. — 701-795-2777
  500 Stanford Rd — Fax 795-2770
  Grand Forks 58203
Grant County Office of Education
  Judy Zins, supt. — 701-622-3238
  PO Box 279, Carson 58529 — Fax 622-3717
Griggs County Office of Education
  Ardis Oettie, supt. — 701-797-2411
  PO Box 340, Cooperstown 58425
  www.cooperstownnd.com
Hettinger County Office of Education
  Sheila Steiner, supt. — 701-824-2500
  PO Box 668, Mott 58646 — Fax 824-2717
  ndaco.org
Kidder County Office of Education
  Kelley Binder, supt. — 701-475-2632
  PO Box 66, Steele 58482 — Fax 475-2202
  www.ndaco.org
La Moure County Office of Education
  Margaret Witt, supt. — 701-883-5301
  PO Box 128, La Moure 58458 — Fax 883-5304
Logan County Office of Education
  Gary Schumacher, supt. — 701-754-2756
  301 Broadway, Napoleon 58561 — Fax 754-2270
McHenry County Office of Education
  Maxine Rognlien, supt. — 701-537-5642
  PO Box 147, Towner 58788 — Fax 537-5969
McIntosh County Office of Education
  Coreen Schumacher, supt. — 701-288-3346
  PO Box 290, Ashley 58413 — Fax 288-3671
McKenzie County Office of Education
  Carol Kieson, supt. — 701-444-3456
  PO Box 503, Watford City 58854 — Fax 444-4113
  www.4eyes.net
McLean County Office of Education
  Lori Foss, supt. — 701-462-8541
  PO Box 1108, Washburn 58577 — Fax 462-3542
  www.tradecorridor.com/mcleancounty/
Mercer County Office of Education
  Phil Eastgate, supt. — 701-873-2298
  1021 Arthur St, Stanton 58571
Morton County Office of Education
  Karen Kautzmann, supt. — 701-667-3315
  210 2nd Ave NW, Mandan 58554 — Fax 667-3348
  www.co.morton.nd.us/
Mountrail County Office of Education
  Karen Eliason, supt. — 701-628-2145
  PO Box 69, Stanley 58784 — Fax 628-3975
Nelson County Office of Education
  Sharon Young, supt. — 701-247-2472
  210 B Ave W, Lakota 58344 — Fax 247-2943
Oliver County Office of Education
  Barbara Fleming, supt. — 701-794-8721
  PO Box 188, Center 58530 — Fax 794-3476
Pembina County Office of Education
  Dorothy L. Robinson, supt. — 701-265-4336
  301 Dakota St W, Cavalier 58220 — Fax 265-4876

Pierce County Office of Education
  Karin Fursather, supt. — 701-776-5225
  240 2nd St SE, Rugby 58368 — Fax 776-5225
Ramsey County Office of Education
  Beverly Schmidt, supt. — 701-662-7062
  524 4th Ave, Devils Lake 58301 — Fax 662-7049
Ransom County Office of Education
  Suzanne Anderson, supt. — 701-683-5823
  PO Box 112, Lisbon 58054 — Fax 683-5827
Renville County Office of Education
  LeAnn Fisher, supt. — 701-756-6301
  PO Box 68, Mohall 58761 — Fax 756-7158
  www.renvillecounty.org
Richland County Office of Education
  Harris Bailey, supt. — 701-642-7898
  418 2nd Ave N, Wahpeton 58075 — Fax 642-7701
Rolette County Office of Education
  Dwane Getzlaff, supt. — 701-477-5265
  PO Box 939, Rolla 58367 — Fax 477-6339
  www.tradecorridor.com/rolettecounty
Sargent County Office of Education
  Sherry Hosford, supt. — 701-724-6241
  PO Box 177, Forman 58032 — Fax 724-6244
Sheridan County Office of Education
  Denise Melom, supt. — 701-363-2205
  PO Box 636, Mc Clusky 58463 — Fax 363-2953
  www.ndaco.org
Sioux County Office of Education
  Barb Hettich, supt. — 701-854-3481
  PO Box L, Fort Yates 58538 — Fax 854-3854
Slope County Office of Education
  Kathy Walser, supt. — 701-879-6277
  PO Box MM, Amidon 58620 — Fax 879-6278
Stark County Office of Education
  Alice Schultz, supt. — 701-456-7630
  PO Box 130, Dickinson 58602 — Fax 456-7634
Steele County Office of Education
  Linda Leadbetter, supt. — 701-524-2110
  PO Box 275, Finley 58230 — Fax 524-1715
Stutsman County Office of Education
  Larry Olson, supt. — 701-252-9035
  511 2nd Ave SE, Jamestown 58401 — Fax 251-1603
Towner County Office of Education
  D. Allen Halley, supt. — 701-968-4346
  PO Box 603, Cando 58324 — Fax 968-4342
Traill County Office of Education
  Rebecca Braaten, supt. — 701-636-4458
  PO Box 429, Hillsboro 58045 — Fax 636-0429
Walsh County Office of Education
  Heather Narloch, supt. — 701-248-3158
  600 Cooper Ave, Grafton 58237
Ward County Office of Education
  Jodi Johnson, supt. — 701-857-6495
  PO Box 5005, Minot 58702 — Fax 857-6414
Wells County Office of Education
  Evelyn Faul, supt. — 701-547-3221
  PO Box 408, Fessenden 58438 — Fax 547-3719
Williams County Office of Education
  Grant Archer, supt. — 701-577-4580
  PO Box 2047, Williston 58802 — Fax 577-4579

PUBLIC, PRIVATE AND CATHOLIC SECONDARY SCHOOLS

Alexander, McKenzie, Pop. 212
Alexander SD 2 — 100/K-12
  PO Box 66 58831 — 701-828-3335
  Murray Kline, supt. — Fax 828-3134
  www.alexander.k12.nd.us/
Alexander HS — 50/7-12
  PO Box 66 58831 — 701-828-3335
  Murray Kline, prin. — Fax 828-3134

Anamoose, McHenry, Pop. 271
Anamoose SD 14 — 100/K-12
  706 3rd St W 58710 — 701-465-3258
  Steven Heim, supt. — Fax 465-3259
  www.anamoose.k12.nd.us
Anamoose JSHS — 100/7-12
  706 3rd St W 58710 — 701-465-3258
  Steve Heim, prin. — Fax 465-3259

Ashley, McIntosh, Pop. 822
Ashley SD 9 — 200/K-12
  703 W Main St 58413 — 701-288-3456
  Leslie B. Dale, supt. — Fax 288-3457
  www.ashley.k12.nd.us/
Ashley HS — 100/7-12
  703 W Main St 58413 — 701-288-3456
  Kendra Becker, prin. — Fax 288-3457

Beach, Golden Valley, Pop. 1,054
Beach SD 3 — 300/K-12
  PO Box 368 58621 — 701-872-4161
  Larry Helvik, supt. — Fax 872-3801
  www.beach.k12.nd.us
Beach JSHS — 200/7-12
  PO Box 368 58621 — 701-872-4161
  Brandt Gaugler, prin. — Fax 872-3801

Belcourt, Rolette, Pop. 2,458
Belcourt SD 7 — 1,700/K-12
  PO Box 440 58316 — 701-477-6471
  Viola LaFontaine, supt. — Fax 477-6470
  www.belcourt.k12.nd.us
Turtle Mountain Community HS — 600/9-12
  PO Box 440 58316 — 701-477-6471
  Rosemary Jaros, prin. — Fax 477-8821
Turtle Mountain Community MS — 400/6-8
  PO Box 440 58316 — 701-477-6471
  Louis Dauphinais, prin. — Fax 477-3973

Turtle Mountain Community College — Post-Sec.
  PO Box 340 58316 — 701-477-7862

Belfield, Stark, Pop. 833
Belfield SD 13 — 200/K-12
  PO Box 97 58622 — 701-575-4275
  Darrel Remington, supt. — Fax 575-8533
  www.belfield.k12.nd.us/
Belfield S — 200/K-12
  PO Box 97 58622 — 701-575-4275
  Jeffrey Lamprecht, prin. — Fax 575-8533

Berthold, Ward, Pop. 447
Lewis and Clark SD 161 — 300/PK-12
  PO Box 185 58718 — 701-453-3484
  Brian Nelson, supt. — Fax 453-3488
  www.lewisandclark.k12.nd.us/
Berthold HS, PO Box 185 58718 — 7-12
  Margaret Person, prin. — 701-453-3484
Other Schools – See Makoti

Beulah, Mercer, Pop. 3,073
Beulah SD 27 — 900/K-12
  204 5th St NW 58523 — 701-873-2261
  Wilfred Volesky, supt. — Fax 873-5273
  www.beulah.k12.nd.us
Beulah HS — 400/9-12
  204 5th St NW 58523 — 701-873-2261
  Kelly Rasch, prin. — Fax 873-5273
Beulah MS — 300/5-8
  1700 Central Ave N 58523 — 701-873-4325
  Gail Wold, prin. — Fax 873-2844

Binford, Griggs, Pop. 185
Midkota SD 7 — 200/K-12
  PO Box 38 58416 — 701-676-2511
  Kerwin Borgen, supt. — Fax 676-2510
  www.midkota.k12.nd.us
Other Schools – See Glenfield

Bisbee, Towner, Pop. 157
Bisbee-Egeland SD 2 — 100/K-12
  PO Box 217 58317 — 701-656-3536
  Brent Bautz, supt. — Fax 656-3205
Bisbee-Egeland JSHS — 50/7-12
  PO Box 217 58317 — 701-656-3536
  Eric Koogen, prin. — Fax 656-3205

Bismarck, Burleigh, Pop. 56,344
Bismarck SD 1 — 10,700/PK-12
  806 N Washington St 58501 — 701-355-3000
  Dr. Paul Johnson, supt. — Fax 355-3001
  www.bismarck.k12.nd.us/
Bismarck Career & Technical Center — Vo/Tech
  1500 Edwards Ave 58501 — 701-224-5402
  Dale Hoerauf, prin. — Fax 224-5552
Bismarck SHS — 1,400/10-12
  800 N 8th St 58501 — 701-221-3500
  Ken Erickson, prin. — Fax 221-3742
Century SHS — 1,100/10-12
  1000 E Century Ave 58503 — 701-250-4000
  Mike Heilman, prin. — Fax 250-4099
Horizon MS — 800/7-9
  500 Ash Coulee Dr 58503 — 701-221-3555
  Rudolph Steidl, prin. — Fax 221-3569
Simle MS — 800/7-9
  1215 N 19th St 58501 — 701-221-3570
  Russ Riehl, prin. — Fax 221-3584
Wachter MS — 800/7-9
  1107 S 7th St 58504 — 701-221-3585
  Brian Beehler, prin. — Fax 221-3592
Adult Learning Center — Adult
  806 N Washington St 58501 — 701-221-3791
  Scott Halvorson, prin. — Fax 221-3793

Bismarck State College — Post-Sec.
  PO Box 5587 58506 — 701-224-5400
Dakota Adventist Academy — 100/9-12
  15905 Sheyenne Cir 58503 — 701-258-9000
  David Chapman, admin. — Fax 258-0110
Medcenter One College of Nursing — Post-Sec.
  512 N 7th St 58501 — 701-323-6271
Medcenter One Health System — Post-Sec.
  222 N 7th St 58501 — 701-222-5413
R.D. Hairstyling College — Post-Sec.
  124 N 4th St 58501 — 701-223-8804
St. Alexius Medical Center — Post-Sec.
  PO Box 5510 58506 — 701-224-7600
St. Marys Central HS — 400/9-12
  1025 N 2nd St 58501 — 701-223-4113
  Tom Eberle, prin. — Fax 223-8629
Shiloh Christian S — 300/PK-12
  1915 Shiloh Dr 58503 — 701-221-2104
  Ross Reinhiller, admin. — Fax 224-8221
United Tribes Technical College — Post-Sec.
  3315 University Dr 58504 — 701-255-3285
University of Mary — Post-Sec.
  7500 University Dr 58504 — 701-255-7500

Bottineau, Bottineau, Pop. 2,223
Bottineau SD 1 — 800/K-12
  301 Brander St 58318 — 701-228-2266
  Jason Kersten, supt. — Fax 228-2021
  www.bottineau.k12.nd.us/
Bottineau JSHS — 400/7-12
  301 Brander St 58318 — 701-228-2266
  Ross Roemmich, prin. — Fax 228-2021

Minot State University-Bottineau Campus — Post-Sec.
  105 Simrall Blvd 58318 — 701-228-2277

Bowbells, Burke, Pop. 378
Bowbells SD 14 — 100/K-12
  PO Box 279 58721 — 701-377-2396
  Brent Johnston, supt. — Fax 377-2399
  www.bowbells.k12.nd.us/
Bowbells HS — 50/7-12
  PO Box 279 58721 — 701-377-2396
  Celeste Thingvold, prin. — Fax 377-2399

Bowman, Bowman, Pop. 1,509
Bowman SD 1 — 400/K-12
  PO Box H 58623 — 701-523-3283
  Tony Duletski, supt. — Fax 523-3849
  www.bowman.k12.nd.us
Bowman HS — 100/9-12
  PO Box H 58623 — 701-523-3283
  Wayne Olson, prin. — Fax 523-3849

Buxton, Traill, Pop. 347
Central Valley SD 3 — 300/K-12
  RR 1 Box 152B 58218 — 701-847-2220
  Marcia Hall, supt. — Fax 847-2407
  www.centralvalley.k12.nd.us/
Central Valley HS — 100/7-12
  RR 1 Box 152B 58218 — 701-847-2220
  Robert Schneck, prin. — Fax 847-2407

Cando, Towner, Pop. 1,235
Southern SD 8 — 300/K-12
  PO Box 489 58324 — 701-968-4416
  Mark Lindahl, supt. — Fax 968-4418
  www.cando.k12.nd.us/
Cando HS — 100/7-12
  PO Box 489 58324 — 701-968-4416
  Jeff Hagler, prin. — Fax 968-4418

Carrington, Foster, Pop. 2,106
Carrington SD 49 — 600/PK-12
  PO Box 48 58421 — 701-652-3136
  Charles Brickner, supt. — Fax 652-1243
  www.carrington.k12.nd.us/
Carrington JSHS — 300/8-12
  PO Box 48 58421 — 701-652-3136
  Chuck Kessler, prin. — Fax 652-1243

Casselton, Cass, Pop. 1,885
Central Cass SD 17 — 600/K-12
  802 5th St N 58012 — 701-347-5352
  Larry Gegelman, supt. — Fax 347-5354
  www.central-cass.k12.nd.us/
Central Cass HS — 300/9-12
  802 5th St N 58012 — 701-347-5352
  Steve Lorentzen, prin. — Fax 347-5354
Central Cass MS, 802 5th St 58012 — 6-8
  Mary Jelinek, prin. — 701-347-5352

Cavalier, Pembina, Pop. 1,479
Cavalier SD 6 — 500/K-12
  PO Box 410 58220 — 701-265-8417
  Francis Schill, supt. — Fax 265-8106
Cavalier HS — 200/9-12
  PO Box 410 58220 — 701-265-8417
  Daniel Stutlien, prin. — Fax 265-8106

Center, Oliver, Pop. 624
Center-Stanton SD 1 — 300/PK-12
  PO Box 248 58530 — 701-794-8778
  Royal D. Lyson, supt. — Fax 794-3659
  www.center.k12.nd.us/
Center S — 300/K-12
  PO Box 248 58530 — 701-794-8778
  Lyle Krueger, prin. — Fax 794-3659

Colfax, Richland, Pop. 93
Richland SD 44 — 300/K-12
  PO Box 49 58018 — 701-372-3713
  Wayne Ulven, supt. — Fax 372-3718
  www.richland.k12.nd.us
Richland JSHS — 200/7-12
  PO Box 49 58018 — 701-372-3713
  Neil Race, prin. — Fax 372-3718

Cooperstown, Griggs, Pop. 985
Griggs County Central SD 18 — 300/K-12
  1207 Foster Ave NE 58425 — 701-797-3114
  Wade Faul, supt. — Fax 797-3130
  www.griggs-co.k12.nd.us/
Griggs County Central JSHS — 200/7-12
  1207 Foster Ave NE 58425 — 701-797-3114
  Kirk Ham, prin. — Fax 797-3130

Crosby, Divide, Pop. 1,067
Divide County SD 1 — 300/K-12
  PO Box G 58730 — 701-965-6313
  Donald Nielsen, supt. — Fax 965-6004
  www.divide-co.k12.nd.us/
Divide County JSHS — 200/7-12
  PO Box G 58730 — 701-965-6392
  Lee Lampert, prin. — Fax 965-6942

Des Lacs, Ward, Pop. 198
United SD 7 — 600/PK-12
  PO Box 117 58733 — 701-725-4334
  Clarke S Ranum, supt. — Fax 725-4375
  www.united.k12.nd.us/
Des Lacs Burlington HS — 200/9-12
  PO Box 117 58733 — 701-725-4334
  Cory Steiner, prin. — Fax 725-4375

Devils Lake, Ramsey, Pop. 6,971
Devils Lake SD 1 — 2,000/PK-12
  1601 College Dr N 58301 — 701-662-7640
  Steven W. Swiontek, supt. — Fax 662-7646
  www.dlschools.org/
Central MS — 600/5-8
  325 7th St NE 58301 — 701-662-7664
  Robert Gibson, prin. — Fax 662-7649
Devils Lake HS — 600/9-12
  1601 College Dr N 58301 — 701-662-1200
  Ryan Hanson, prin. — Fax 662-1208
Lake Area Career & Technology Center — Vo/Tech
  205 16th St NW 58301 — 701-662-7650
  Denise Wolf, prin. — Fax 662-7658

Lake Region State College — Post-Sec.
  1801 College Dr N 58301 — 701-662-1600

Dickinson, Stark, Pop. 15,683
Dickinson SD 1 — 2,700/K-12
  PO Box 1057 58602 — 701-456-0002
  Dr. Paul Stremick, supt. — Fax 456-0035
  www.dickinson.k12.nd.us
Dickinson HS — 900/9-12
  PO Box 1057 58602 — 701-456-0030
  Ron Dockter, prin. — Fax 456-0019
Hagen JHS — 400/7-8
  PO Box 1057 58602 — 701-456-0020
  Perry Braunagel, prin. — Fax 456-0023
Southwest Community HS — Adult
  PO Box 1057 58602 — 701-456-0042
  Eileen Rowe, prin. — Fax 456-0042

Dickinson State University 58601 — Post-Sec.
   — 701-483-2507
Trinity HS — 400/7-12
  PO Box 1177 58602 — 701-483-6081
  Kelly Koppinger, admin. — Fax 483-1450

Drake, McHenry, Pop. 299
Drake SD 57 — 100/PK-12
  PO Box 256 58736 — 701-465-3732
  Dean Vorland, supt. — Fax 465-3634
Drake S — 100/PK-12
  PO Box 256 58736 — 701-465-3732
  Marvin Goplen, prin. — Fax 465-3634

Drayton, Pembina, Pop. 870
Drayton SD 19 — 200/K-12
  108 S 5th St 58225 — 701-454-3324
  Robert Klein, supt. — Fax 454-3485
Drayton JSHS — 100/7-12
  108 S 5th St 58225 — 701-454-3324
  Kerri L. Stegman, prin. — Fax 454-3485

Dunseith, Rolette, Pop. 738
Dunseith SD 1 — 500/K-12
  PO Box 789 58329 — 701-244-0480
  Lanelia DeCoteau, supt. — Fax 244-5129
  www.dunseith.k12.nd.us/
Dunseith JSHS — 200/7-12
  PO Box 789 58329 — 701-244-5249
  Jorgen Knutson, prin. — Fax 244-5129

Edgeley, LaMoure, Pop. 598
Edgeley SD 3 — 300/K-12
  PO Box 37 58433 — 701-493-2292
  Richard Diegel, supt. — Fax 493-2411
  www.edgeley.k12.nd.us/
Edgeley HS — 100/7-12
  PO Box 37 58433 — 701-493-2292
  Todd Kosel, prin. — Fax 493-2411

Edinburg, Walsh, Pop. 236
Edinburg SD 106 — 100/K-12
  PO Box 6 58227 — 701-993-8312
  David Monson, supt. — Fax 993-8313
  www.edinburg.k12.nd.us/
Edinburg HS — 100/7-12
  PO Box 6 58227 — 701-993-8312
  David Monson, prin. — Fax 993-8313

Edmore, Ramsey, Pop. 244
Edmore SD 2 — 100/7-12
  PO Box 188 58330 — 701-644-2282
  Keith Arneson, supt. — Fax 644-2222
  www.adams-edmore.k12.nd.us
Adams-Edmore JSHS — 100/7-12
  PO Box 188 58330 — 701-644-2282
  Wade Schock, prin. — Fax 644-2222

Elgin, Grant, Pop. 615
Elgin / New Leipzig SD 49 — 200/K-12
  PO Box 70 58533 — 701-584-2374
  Martin Schock, supt. — Fax 584-3018
  www.elgin.k12.nd.us
Grant County HS — 100/9-12
  PO Box 70 58533 — 701-584-2374
  Terry Bentz, prin. — Fax 584-3018

Ellendale, Dickey, Pop. 1,500
Ellendale SD 40 — 400/K-12
  PO Box 400 58436 — 701-349-3232
  Jeff Fastnacht, supt. — Fax 349-3447
  www.ellendale.k12.nd.us
Ellendale JSHS — 200/7-12
  PO Box 400 58436 — 701-349-4148
  Matthew Herman, prin. — Fax 349-3447

Trinity Bible College — Post-Sec.
  50 6th Ave S 58436 — 701-349-3621

Enderlin, Ransom, Pop. 1,070
Enderlin SD 22 — 300/K-12
  410 Bluff St 58027 — 701-437-2240
  Jon Kringen, supt. — Fax 437-2242
  www.enderlin.k12.nd.us/
Enderlin HS — 200/7-12
  410 Bluff St 58027 — 701-437-2240
  Timothy Michaelson, prin. — Fax 437-2242

Fairmount, Richland, Pop. 389
Fairmount SD 18 — 100/K-12
  PO Box 228 58030 — 701-474-5469
  Barry Loos, supt. — Fax 474-5862
  www.fairmount.k12.nd.us/
Fairmount HS — 50/7-12
  PO Box 228 58030 — 701-474-5469
  Clarke Johnson, prin. — Fax 474-5862

Fargo, Cass, Pop. 91,484
Fargo SD 1 — 9,800/PK-12
  415 4th St N 58102 — 701-446-1000
  David Flowers, supt. — Fax 446-1200
  www.fargo.k12.nd.us/
Discovery MS — 1,100/6-8
  1717 40th Ave S 58104 — 701-446-3300
  Linda Davis, prin. — Fax 446-3599

Eielson MS 6-8
1601 13th Ave 58102 701-446-1700
Brad Larson, prin. Fax 446-1799
Fargo North HS 1,200/9-12
801 17th Ave N 58102 701-446-2400
Andrew Dahlen, prin. Fax 446-2799
Fargo South SHS 1,600/10-12
1840 15th Ave S 58103 701-446-2000
Todd Bertsch, prin. Fax 446-2399
Franklin MS 700/6-8
1420 8th St N 58102 701-446-3600
John Nelson, prin. Fax 446-3899
South Campus II 300/9-9
1305 9th Ave S 58103 701-446-3200
Marcy Blikre, prin. Fax 446-3299
Evaluation & Training Center Adult
424 9th Ave S 58103 701-241-4858
Terry Paulson, prin. Fax 241-4896

Aakers College Post-Sec.
4012 19th Ave S 58103 701-277-3889
Josef's School of Hair Design Post-Sec.
627 NP Ave 58102 701-235-0011
Moler Barber College of HairStyling Post-Sec.
16 8th St S 58103 701-232-6773
North Dakota State University 58105 Post-Sec.
701-237-7211
Oak Grove Lutheran HS 200/6-12
124 N Terrace 58102 701-237-0210
Morgan Forness, pres. Fax 237-4217
Shanley HS 300/9-12
5600 25th St S 58104 701-893-3200
Don Bunce, prin. Fax 893-3277
Sr. Rosalind Gefre School Post-Sec.
3101 39th St S Ste E 58104 701-297-5993
Sullivan MS 200/6-8
5600 25th St S 58104 701-893-3200
Sean Safranski, prin. Fax 893-3277
Tri-College University 58105 Post-Sec.
701-231-8170

Fessenden, Wells, Pop. 568
Fessenden-Bowdon SD 25 200/K-12
PO Box 67 58438 701-547-3296
Terry Olschlager, supt. Fax 547-3125
www.fessenden-bowdon.k12.nd.us/
Fessenden-Bowdon HS 100/9-12
PO Box 67 58438 701-547-3296
Terry Olschlager, prin. Fax 547-3125

Finley, Steele, Pop. 470
Finley-Sharon SD 19 200/K-12
PO Box 448 58230 701-524-2420
Merlin H. Dahl, supt. Fax 524-2588
www.finley.k12.nd.us/
Finley-Sharon HS 100/7-12
PO Box 448 58230 701-524-2420
Merlin H. Dahl, prin. Fax 524-2588

Flasher, Morton, Pop. 275
Flasher SD 39 200/K-12
PO Box 267 58535 701-597-3355
Michael Severson, supt. Fax 597-3781
www.flasher.k12.nd.us/
Flasher HS 100/7-12
PO Box 267 58535 701-597-3355
Michael A. Severson, prin. Fax 597-3781

Fordville, Walsh, Pop. 248
Fordville-Lankin SD 5 100/K-12
PO Box 127 58231 701-229-3297
Jeffrey Watts, supt. Fax 229-3231
www.fordville-lankin.k12.nd.us/
Fordville Lankin HS 100/7-12
PO Box 127 58231 701-229-3297
Charles Frederickson, prin. Fax 229-3231

Forman, Sargent, Pop. 487
Sargent Central SD 6 300/K-12
575 5th St SW 58032 701-724-3205
Michael D. Campbell, supt. Fax 724-3559
www.sargent.k12.nd.us
Sargent Central HS 100/7-12
575 5th St SW 58032 701-724-3205
Brenda Grothe, prin. Fax 724-3559

Fort Totten, Benson, Pop. 867
Fort Totten SD 30 200/9-12
PO Box 239 58335 701-766-1435
Wayne Trottier, supt. Fax 766-1475
Four Winds Community HS 200/9-12
PO Box 239 58335 701-766-1412
Melvin Laducer, prin. Fax 766-1435

Cankdeska Cikana Community College Post-Sec.
PO Box 269 58335 701-766-4415

Fort Yates, Sioux, Pop. 229
Fort Yates SD 4 200/6-8
9189 Highway 24 58538 701-854-2142
Gene LaFromboise, supt. Fax 854-7488
Fort Yates MS 200/6-8
9189 Highway 24 58538 701-854-3819
John Barry, prin. Fax 854-7488

Sitting Bull College Post-Sec.
1341 92nd St 58538 701-854-3861

Gackle, Logan, Pop. 313
Gackle-Streeter SD 56 100/K-12
PO Box 375 58442 701-485-3692
Norman Fries, supt. Fax 485-3620
www.gacklestreeter.k12.nd.us/
Gackle-Streeter HS 100/7-12
PO Box 375 58442 701-485-3692
Ron Groth, prin. Fax 485-3620

Garrison, McLean, Pop. 1,272
Garrison SD 51 400/PK-12
PO Box 249 58540 701-463-2818
Steve M. Brannan, supt. Fax 463-2067
www.garrison.k12.nd.us/
Garrison JSHS 200/7-12
PO Box 249 58540 701-463-2818
Mark V. Larson, prin. Fax 463-2067

Glenburn, Renville, Pop. 349
Glenburn SD 26 300/K-12
PO Box 138 58740 701-362-7426
Robert Thom, supt. Fax 362-7349
www.glenburn.k12.nd.us/
Glenburn HS 200/7-12
PO Box 138 58740 701-362-7426
David Wisthoff, prin. Fax 362-7349

Glenfield, Foster, Pop. 127
Midkota SD 7
Supt. — See Binford
Midkota HS 100/7-12
PO Box 98 58443 701-785-2126
Gilbert Black, prin. Fax 785-2226

Glen Ullin, Morton, Pop. 839
Glen Ullin SD 48 200/K-12
PO Box 548 58631 701-348-3590
Patrick Feist, supt. Fax 348-3084
www.glen-ullin.k12.nd.us
Glen Ullin JSHS 100/7-12
PO Box 548 58631 701-348-3365
Larry Sebastian, prin. Fax 348-3084

Golden Valley, Mercer, Pop. 176
Golden Valley SD 20 50/7-12
PO Box 158 58541 701-983-4256
David Bicknese, supt. Fax 983-4257
www.goldenvalley.k12.nd.us/
Golden Valley JSHS 50/7-12
PO Box 158 58541 701-983-4256
David Bicknese, prin. Fax 983-4257

Goodrich, Sheridan, Pop. 143
Goodrich SD 16 100/K-12
PO Box 159 58444 701-884-2469
Rodney Scherbenske, supt. Fax 884-2496
Goodrich HS 50/7-12
PO Box 159 58444 701-884-2469
Daniel Klemisch, prin. Fax 884-2496

Grafton, Walsh, Pop. 4,299
Grafton SD 3 900/K-12
1548 School Rd 58237 701-352-1930
Dr. Paul R. Stremick, supt. Fax 352-1943
www.grafton.k12.nd.us/
Grafton Central MS 200/6-8
725 Griggs Ave 58237 701-352-1469
Dennis G. Hammer, prin. Fax 352-1120
Grafton HS 300/9-12
1548 School Rd 58237 701-352-1930
Darren Albrecht, prin. Fax 352-1943
North Valley Area Career & Tech Vo/Tech
1540 School Rd 58237 701-352-3705
Elizabeth Daby, prin. Fax 352-3170

Grand Forks, Grand Forks, Pop. 48,618
Grand Forks SD 1 8,200/PK-12
PO Box 6000 58206 701-746-2200
Mark Sanford, supt. Fax 772-7739
www.gfschools.org
Central HS 1,100/9-12
115 N 4th St 58203 701-746-2375
Jeffrey Schatz, prin. Fax 746-2387
Red River HS 1,300/9-12
2211 17th Ave S 58201 701-746-2400
James Stenehjem, prin. Fax 746-2406
Schroeder MS 600/6-8
800 32nd Ave S 58201 701-746-2330
Ken Schill, prin. Fax 746-2332
South MS 500/6-8
1999 47th Ave S 58201 701-746-2345
Nancy Dutot, prin. Fax 746-2355
Valley MS 500/6-8
2100 5th Ave N 58203 701-746-2360
Kevin Ohnstad, prin. Fax 746-2363
Other Schools – See Grand Forks AFB

Josef's School of Hair Design Post-Sec.
2011 S Washington St 58201 701-772-2728
North Dakota School for the Blind Post-Sec.
500 Stanford Rd 58203
University of North Dakota Post-Sec.
Box 8193 University Station 58203 701-777-2011

Grand Forks AFB, Grand Forks, Pop. 9,343
Grand Forks SD 1
Supt. — See Grand Forks
Twining S 600/4-8
1422 Louisiana St 58204 701-787-5100
Terry Brenner, prin. Fax 787-5143

Granville, McHenry, Pop. 266
TGU SD 60
Supt. — See Towner
TGU Granville HS 100/7-12
210 6th St SW 58741 701-728-6641
Tonya Hunskor, prin. Fax 728-6386

Grenora, Williams, Pop. 195
Grenora SD 99 100/K-12
PO Box 38 58845 701-694-2711
Nancy Wisness, supt. Fax 694-2717
www.grenora.k12.nd.us/
Grenora HS 50/7-12
PO Box 38 58845 701-694-2711
Nancy Wisness, prin. Fax 694-2717

Gwinner, Sargent, Pop. 715
North Sargent SD 3 200/K-12
PO Box 289 58040 701-678-2492
Sandra Willprecht, supt. Fax 678-2311
www.northsargent.k12.nd.us
North Sargent HS 100/7-12
PO Box 289 58040 701-678-2492
Randal Brockman, prin. Fax 678-2311

Halliday, Dunn, Pop. 220
Halliday SD 19 50/K-12
PO Box 188 58636 701-938-4391
Ronald Biberdorf, supt. Fax 938-4373
www.halliday.k12.nd.us/
Halliday HS 7-12
PO Box 188 58636 701-938-4391
Maureen Olson, prin. Fax 938-4373

Hankinson, Richland, Pop. 1,015
Hankinson SD 8 300/K-12
PO Box 220 58041 701-242-7516
Adam Boschee, supt. Fax 242-7434
www.hankinson.k12.nd.us/
Hankinson HS 200/7-12
PO Box 220 58041 701-242-7138
Jess Smith, prin. Fax 242-7434

Harvey, Wells, Pop. 1,826
Harvey SD 38 500/K-12
811 Burke Ave 58341 701-324-4692
Robert Marthaller, supt. Fax 324-4414
www.harvey.k12.nd.us/
Harvey HS 200/9-12
200 North St E 58341 701-324-2267
Albert Liebersbach, prin. Fax 324-2424

Hatton, Traill, Pop. 682
Hatton SD 7 300/K-12
PO Box 200 58240 701-543-3455
Jack Maus, supt. Fax 543-3459
www.hatton.k12.nd.us/
Hatton HS 100/7-12
PO Box 200 58240 701-543-3455
Kevin Rogers, prin. Fax 543-3459

Hazelton, Emmons, Pop. 219
Hazelton-Moffit-Braddock SD 6 100/K-12
PO Box 209 58544 701-782-6231
Brad Rinas, supt. Fax 782-6245
Hazelton-Moffit-Braddock HS 100/7-12
PO Box 209 58544 701-782-6231
Brad Rinas, prin. Fax 782-6245

Hazen, Mercer, Pop. 2,392
Hazen SD 3 700/PK-12
PO Box 487 58545 701-748-2345
Michael Ness, supt. Fax 748-2342
www.hazen.k12.nd.us
Hazen HS 300/9-12
PO Box 487 58545 701-748-2345
Ed Boger, prin. Fax 748-2342
Hazen MS 200/6-8
PO Box 487 58545 701-748-6649
Jerry Obenauer, prin. Fax 748-6650

Hebron, Morton, Pop. 759
Hebron SD 13 200/K-12
PO Box Q 58638 701-878-4442
George Ding, supt. Fax 878-4345
www.hebron.k12.nd.us/
Hebron HS 100/7-12
PO Box Q 58638 701-878-4442
Steven Maerschbecker, prin. Fax 878-4345

Hettinger, Adams, Pop. 1,272
Hettinger SD 13 400/K-12
PO Box 1188 58639 701-567-5315
John Campbell, supt. Fax 567-5094
www.hettinger.k12.nd.us
Hettinger HS 200/7-12
PO Box 1188 58639 701-567-4502
Brian Christopherson, prin. Fax 567-2796

Hillsboro, Traill, Pop. 1,523
Hillsboro SD 9 400/K-12
PO Box 579 58045 701-636-4360
Mike Bitz, supt. Fax 636-4362
www.hillsboro.k12.nd.us/
Hillsboro JSHS 200/7-12
PO Box 579 58045 701-636-4360
Kevin Coles, prin. Fax 636-4362

Hoople, Walsh, Pop. 274
Valley SD 12 200/PK-12
PO Box 150 58243 701-894-6226
John Oistad, supt. Fax 894-6146
www.valley.k12.nd.us/
Valley HS 100/9-12
PO Box 150 58243 701-894-6226
Douglas Bertsch, prin. Fax 894-6146

Hope, Steele, Pop. 275
Hope SD 10 100/7-12
PO Box 100 58046 701-945-2511
Arthur Mitzel, supt. Fax 945-2511
www.hope-page.k12.nd.us/
Hope-Page HS 100/7-12
PO Box 100 58046 701-945-2473
Dale Krueger, prin. Fax 945-2511

Hunter, Cass, Pop. 311
Northern Cass SD 97 500/K-12
16021 18th St SE 58048 701-874-2322
Allen Burgad, supt. Fax 874-2422
www.northerncass.k12.nd.us
Northern Cass HS 200/7-12
16021 18th St SE 58048 701-874-2322
Todd Kaylor, prin. Fax 874-2422

Inkster, Grand Forks, Pop. 99
Midway SD 128　300/K-12
3202 33rd Ave NE　58244　701-869-2432
Roger Abbe, supt.　Fax 869-2688
midway.nd.schoolwebpages.com
Midway HS　100/9-12
3202 33rd Ave NE　58244　701-869-2432
George Lee, prin.　Fax 869-2688
Midway MS　100/6-8
3202 33rd Ave NE　58244　701-869-2432
Nancy Brueckner, prin.　Fax 869-2688

Jamestown, Stutsman, Pop. 15,158
Jamestown SD 1　2,300/PK-12
PO Box 269　58402　701-252-1950
David Smette, supt.　Fax 251-2011
www.jamestown.k12.nd.us
Jamestown HS　900/9-12
PO Box 269　58402　701-252-0559
William Nold, prin.　Fax 252-8580
Jamestown MS　400/6-8
PO Box 269　58402　701-252-0317
Joseph Hegland, prin.　Fax 252-3310
James Valley Area Vo-Tech Center　Vo/Tech
PO Box 269　58402　701-252-8841
Dan Schneibel, prin.　Fax 252-3646

Carlsen Center for Children　50/K-12
301 7th Ave NW　58401　701-952-5165
Marcia Gums, prin.　Fax 952-5154
Jamestown College　Post-Sec.
6000 College Ln　58405　701-252-3467

Kenmare, Ward, Pop. 1,119
Kenmare SD 28　300/K-12
PO Box 667　58746　701-385-4996
Greg Haugland, supt.　Fax 385-4390
www.kenmare.k12.nd.us/
Kenmare JSHS　200/7-12
PO Box 667　58746　701-385-4996
Arnold Jordan, prin.　Fax 385-4390

Kensal, Stutsman, Pop. 156
Kensal SD 19　100/K-12
803 1st Ave　58455　701-435-2484
Tom Tracy, supt.　Fax 435-2486
www.kensal.k12.nd.us
Kensal HS　50/7-12
803 1st Ave　58455　701-435-2484
Allan Zerr, prin.　Fax 435-2486

Killdeer, Dunn, Pop. 700
Killdeer SD 16　400/K-12
PO Box 579　58640　701-764-5877
Gary Wilz, supt.　Fax 764-5648
www.killdeer.k12.nd.us
Killdeer HS　200/7-12
PO Box 579　58640　701-764-5877
Steve Quintus, prin.　Fax 764-5648

Kindred, Cass, Pop. 591
Kindred SD 2　700/K-12
55 1st Ave S　58051　701-428-3177
Steve Hall, supt.　Fax 428-3149
www.kindred.k12.nd.us/
Kindred HS　300/7-12
55 1st Ave S　58051　701-428-3177
Kent Packer, prin.　Fax 428-3149

Kulm, LaMoure, Pop. 404
Kulm SD 7　100/K-12
PO Box G　58456　701-647-2303
Daniel Bauer, supt.　Fax 647-2304
www.kulm.k12.nd.us/
Kulm JSHS　100/7-12
PO Box G　58456　701-647-2341
Thomas Nitschke, prin.　Fax 647-2457

Lakota, Nelson, Pop. 761
Lakota SD 66　300/K-12
PO Box 388　58344　701-247-2992
Joe Harder, supt.　Fax 247-2910
www.lakota.k12.nd.us
Lakota JSHS　100/7-12
PO Box 388　58344　701-247-2992
Joe Harder, prin.　Fax 247-2910

La Moure, LaMoure, Pop. 892
La Moure SD 8　400/K-12
PO Box 656　58458　701-883-5396
Brett Gibbs, supt.　Fax 883-5144
www.lamoure.k12.nd.us/
La Moure JSHS　200/7-12
PO Box 656　58458　701-883-5397
Mitchell Carlson, prin.　Fax 883-5144

Langdon, Cavalier, Pop. 1,934
Langdon Area SD 23　500/PK-12
715 14th Ave　58249　701-256-5291
Rich Rogers, supt.　Fax 256-2606
lhs.utma.com/
Langdon Area JSHS　300/7-12
715 14th Ave　58249　701-256-5291
Jason Schwabe, prin.　Fax 256-2606

Larimore, Grand Forks, Pop. 1,371
Larimore SD 44　600/PK-12
PO Box 769　58251　701-343-2366
Ron Stahlecker, supt.　Fax 343-2908
larimore.nd.schoolwebpages.com/
Larimore JSHS　300/7-12
PO Box 769　58251　701-343-2366
Pamela Cronin, prin.　Fax 343-2908

Leeds, Benson, Pop. 445
Leeds SD 6　200/K-12
PO Box 189　58346　701-466-2461
Joel Braaten, supt.　Fax 466-2422
Leeds JSHS　100/7-12
PO Box 189　58346　701-466-2461
Jason Gullickson, prin.　Fax 466-2422

Lidgerwood, Richland, Pop. 754
Lidgerwood SD 28　200/K-12
PO Box 468　58053　701-538-7341
Tony Grubb, supt.　Fax 538-4483
www.lidgerwood.k12.nd.us/
Lidgerwood HS　100/7-12
PO Box 468　58053　701-538-7341
Tony Grubb, prin.　Fax 538-4483

Lignite, Burke, Pop. 166
Burke Central SD 36　100/K-12
PO Box 91　58752　701-933-2821
Mike Klabo, supt.　Fax 933-2823
Burke Central HS　100/7-12
PO Box 91　58752　701-933-2821
Mike Klabo, prin.　Fax 933-2823

Linton, Emmons, Pop. 1,209
Linton SD 36　300/K-12
PO Box 970　58552　701-254-4138
Steven Nelson, supt.　Fax 254-4313
www.linton.k12.nd.us
Linton HS　100/9-12
PO Box 970　58552　701-254-4717
Steven Nelson, prin.　Fax 254-4313
Linton MS　6-8
PO Box 970　58552　701-254-4173
Brian Flyberg, prin.　Fax 254-0159

Lisbon, Ransom, Pop. 2,259
Lisbon SD 19　600/K-12
PO Box 593　58054　701-683-4106
Steven Johnson, supt.　Fax 683-4414
www.lisbon.k12.nd.us
Lisbon HS　200/9-12
PO Box 593　58054　701-683-4106
Philip Martin, prin.　Fax 683-4414
Lisbon MS　200/5-8
PO Box 593　58054　701-683-4108
Elinor Meckle, prin.　Fax 683-4111

Mc Clusky, Sheridan, Pop. 428
Mc Clusky SD 19　100/K-12
PO Box 499　58463　701-363-2470
Rodney Scherbenske, supt.　Fax 363-2239
mcclusky.nd.schoolwebpages.com/
Mc Clusky JSHS　100/7-12
PO Box 499　58463　701-363-2470
Daniel Klemisch, prin.　Fax 363-2239

Mc Ville, Nelson, Pop. 501
Dakota Prairie SD 1　300/K-12
PO Box 337,　701-322-4771
Loren D. Scheer, supt.　Fax 322-5128
www.dakotaprairie.k12.nd.us/
Other Schools – See Petersburg

Maddock, Benson, Pop. 480
Maddock SD 9　200/K-12
PO Box 398　58348　701-438-2531
Brian Bubach, supt.　Fax 438-2620
www.maddock.k12.nd.us
Maddock HS　100/7-12
PO Box 398　58348　701-438-2531
Kimberly Anderson, prin.　Fax 438-2620

Makoti, Ward, Pop. 141
Lewis and Clark SD 161
Supt. — See Berthold
North Shore HS　100/7-12
PO Box 127　58756　701-726-5591
Janene M. Lee, prin.　Fax 726-5701

Mandan, Morton, Pop. 16,781
Mandan SD 1　3,300/PK-12
309 Collins Ave　58554　701-663-9531
Wilfred Volesky, supt.　Fax 663-0328
www.mandan.k12.nd.us
Mandan HS　1,100/9-12
905 8th Ave NW　58554　701-663-9532
Mark Andresen, prin.　Fax 663-5398
Mandan JHS　500/7-8
406 4th St NW　58554　701-663-7491
Harlan Haak, prin.　Fax 667-0984

Mandaree, McKenzie, Pop. 367
Mandaree SD 36　200/K-12
PO Box 488　58757　701-759-3311
Anna Rubia, supt.　Fax 759-3493
www.mandaree.k12.nd.us/
Mandaree HS　100/9-12
PO Box 488　58757　701-759-3311
Carolyn Bluestone, prin.　Fax 759-3493
Mandaree MS　50/7-8
PO Box 488　58757　701-759-3188
Carolyn Bluestone, prin.　Fax 759-3493

Marion, LaMoure, Pop. 135
Litchville-Marion SD 46　200/K-12
PO Box 159　58466　701-669-2262
James Gross, supt.　Fax 669-2316
www.litchville-marion.k12.nd.us/
Litchville-Marion JSHS　100/7-12
PO Box 159　58466　701-669-2262
Steven Larson, prin.　Fax 669-2316

Max, McLean, Pop. 270
Max SD 50　200/K-12
PO Box 297　58759　701-679-2685
Elroy Burkle, supt.　Fax 679-2245
www.max.k12.nd.us/
Max HS　100/7-12
PO Box 297　58759　701-679-2685
Elroy Burkle, prin.　Fax 679-2245

Mayville, Traill, Pop. 1,914
Mayville-Portland CG SD 14　600/K-12
900 Main St W　58257　701-788-2281
Michael Bradner, supt.　Fax 788-2959
www.mayportcg.com/

Mayville-Portland CG HS　200/9-12
900 Main St W　58257　701-788-2281
Scott Ulland, prin.　Fax 788-2959
Mayville-Portland CG MS　100/6-8
900 Main St W　58257　701-788-2281
Jeffrey Houdek, prin.　Fax 788-2959

Mayville State University　Post-Sec.
330 3rd St NE　58257　701-786-2301

Medina, Stutsman, Pop. 317
Medina SD 3　200/PK-12
PO Box 547　58467　701-486-3121
James Dunnigan, supt.　Fax 486-3138
www.medina.k12.nd.us
Medina HS　100/9-12
PO Box 547　58467　701-486-3121
James Dunnigan, prin.　Fax 486-3138

Milnor, Sargent, Pop. 695
Milnor SD 2　200/K-12
PO Box 369　58060　701-427-5237
Diann Aberle, supt.　Fax 427-5304
www.milnor.k12.nd.us
Milnor HS　7-12
PO Box 369　58060　701-427-5237
Patrick Adair, prin.　Fax 427-5304

Minnewaukan, Benson, Pop. 308
Minnewaukan SD 5　100/K-12
PO Box 348　58351　701-473-5306
Myron Jury, supt.　Fax 473-5420
www.minnewaukan.k12.nd.us/
Minnewaukan HS　100/7-12
PO Box 348　58351　701-473-5306
Ronald Carlson, prin.　Fax 473-5420

Minot, Ward, Pop. 35,424
Minot SD 1　6,800/PK-12
215 2nd St SE　58701　701-857-4422
Dr. David Looysen, supt.　Fax 857-4432
www.minot.k12.nd.us/
Central Campus HS　1,000/9-10
215 1st St SE　58701　701-857-4660
Keith Altendorf, prin.　Fax 857-4636
Hill MS　600/6-8
1000 6th St SW　58701　701-857-4477
Leslie Anderson, prin.　Fax 857-4479
Magic City Campus HS　1,000/11-12
1100 11th Ave SW　58701　701-857-4500
Mark Vollmer, prin.　Fax 857-4521
Memorial MS　200/7-8
1 Rocket Rd　58704　701-727-3300
Tom Holtz, prin.　Fax 727-3303
Ramstad MS　500/6-8
501 Lincoln Ave　58703　701-857-4465
Jim Tschetter, prin.　Fax 857-4464

Bishop Ryan S　400/K-12
316 11th Ave NW　58703　701-838-3355
Terry Voiles, prin.　Fax 837-8914
Headquarters Academy of Hair Design　Post-Sec.
108 Main St S　58701　701-852-8329
Minot State University　Post-Sec.
500 University Ave W　58707　701-858-3350
Our Redeemer's Christian S　300/K-12
700 16th Ave SE　58701　701-839-0772
Julie Smesrud, prin.　Fax 858-0994
Trinity Medical Center　Post-Sec.
3 Burdick Expy　58701　701-857-5000

Minto, Walsh, Pop. 627
Minto SD 20　200/K-12
PO Box 377　58261　701-248-3479
Harold Mach, supt.　Fax 248-3001
www.minto.k12.nd.us/
Minto HS　100/7-12
PO Box 377　58261　701-248-3400
Frank Mitzel, prin.　Fax 248-3001

Mohall, Renville, Pop. 771
Mohall-Lansford-Sherwood SD 1　300/PK-12
PO Box 187　58761　701-756-6896
Kelly Taylor, supt.　Fax 756-6549
www.mohall.k12.nd.us/
Mohall HS　100/7-12
PO Box 187　58761　701-756-6660
Lenora Stevenson, prin.　Fax 756-6549
Other Schools – See Sherwood

Montpelier, Stutsman, Pop. 98
Montpelier SD 14　100/K-12
PO Box 10　58472　701-489-3348
Lynn Krueger, supt.　Fax 489-3349
www.montpelier.k12.nd.us
Montpelier HS　100/7-12
PO Box 10　58472　701-489-3348
Lynn Krueger, prin.　Fax 489-3349

Mott, Hettinger, Pop. 757
Mott/Regent SD 1　300/K-12
205 Dakota Ave　58646　701-824-2249
Myron Schweitzer, supt.　Fax 824-2249
mott.nd.schoolwebpages.com/
Mott / Regent HS　100/9-12
205 Dakota Ave　58646　701-824-2795
Myron Schweitzer, prin.　Fax 824-2249
Other Schools – See Regent

Munich, Cavalier, Pop. 246
Munich SD 19　100/K-12
PO Box 39　58352　701-682-5321
Elroy Burkle, supt.　Fax 682-5323
www.munich.k12.nd.us
Munich HS　100/7-12
PO Box 39　58352　701-682-5321
Kurt Hayes, prin.　Fax 682-5323

Napoleon, Logan, Pop. 794
Napoleon SD 2 — 200/K-12
PO Box 69 58561 — 701-754-2244
Jon C. Starkey, supt. — Fax 754-2233
www.napoleon.k12.nd.us/
Napoleon HS — 100/7-12
PO Box 69 58561 — 701-754-2244
Kip R. Schmidt, prin. — Fax 754-2233

Newburg, Bottineau, Pop. 85
Newburg United SD 54 — 100/K-12
PO Box 427 58762 — 701-272-6151
Jason A. Kertsen, supt. — Fax 272-6117
www.newburg.k12.nd.us/
Newburg United HS — 50/7-12
PO Box 427 58762 — 701-272-6151
Carl Selvig, prin. — Fax 272-6117

New England, Hettinger, Pop. 513
New England SD 9 — 200/K-12
PO Box 307 58647 — 701-579-4160
Noel Lunde, supt. — Fax 579-4462
www.new-england.k12.nd.us
New England HS — 100/7-12
PO Box 307 58647 — 701-579-4160
Lawrence Lechler, prin. — Fax 579-4462

New Rockford, Eddy, Pop. 1,370
New Rockford SD 1 — 400/K-12
437 1st Ave N 58356 — 701-947-5036
Kurt Eddy, supt. — Fax 947-2195
www.newrockford.k12.nd.us/
New Rockford HS — 200/7-12
437 1st Ave N 58356 — 701-947-5036
David Libis, prin. — Fax 947-2195

New Salem, Morton, Pop. 897
New Salem SD 7 — 400/PK-12
PO Box 378 58563 — 701-843-7846
Gordon Davis, supt. — Fax 843-7011
www.newsalem.k12.nd.us/
New Salem JSHS — 200/7-12
PO Box 378 58563 — 701-843-7610
Keith Jacobson, prin. — Fax 843-7011

New Town, Mountrail, Pop. 1,339
New Town SD 1 — 800/PK-12
PO Box 700 58763 — 701-627-3650
Edward Slocum, supt. — Fax 627-3689
www.new-town.k12.nd.us/
New Town HS — 200/9-12
PO Box 700 58763 — 701-627-3658
Spencer Wilkinson, prin. — Fax 627-3689
New Town MS — 200/6-8
PO Box 700 58763 — 701-627-3660
Fax 627-3689

Fort Berthold Community College — Post-Sec.
PO Box 490 58763 — 701-627-4738

Northwood, Grand Forks, Pop. 915
Northwood SD 129 — 300/K-12
PO Box 250 58267 — 701-587-5221
Jack Maus, supt. — Fax 587-5423
www.northwood.k12.nd.us
Northwood HS — 200/7-12
PO Box 250 58267 — 701-587-5221
Matthew Strinden, prin. — Fax 587-5423

Oakes, Dickey, Pop. 1,864
Oakes SD 41 — 600/PK-12
804 Main Ave 58474 — 701-742-3234
Arthur Conklin, supt. — Fax 742-2812
www.oakes.k12.nd.us
Oakes JSHS — 200/7-12
804 Main Ave 58474 — 701-742-3234
Donald Warren, prin. — Fax 742-2812
Southeast Vocational Technical Center — Vo/Tech
PO Box 372 58474 — 701-742-3248
Marlin Aagenus, prin. — Fax 742-3152

Park River, Walsh, Pop. 1,457
Park River SD 78 — 400/K-12
PO Box 240 58270 — 701-284-7164
Harold F. Knoll, supt. — Fax 284-7936
www.parkriver.k12.nd.us/
Park River HS — 200/7-12
PO Box 240 58270 — 701-284-7164
David Beckman, prin. — Fax 284-7936

Parshall, Mountrail, Pop. 1,009
Parshall SD 3 — 300/PK-12
PO Box 158 58770 — 701-862-3129
Stephen R. Cascaden, supt. — Fax 862-3801
Parshall JSHS — 200/7-12
PO Box 158 58770 — 701-862-3129
Mark Grueneich, prin. — Fax 862-3801

Pembina, Pembina, Pop. 610
North Border SD 100 — 400/K-12
155 S 3rd St 58271 — 701-825-6261
Wade Defoe, supt. — Fax 825-6645
Pembina HS — 100/9-12
PO Box 409 58271 — 701-825-6261
Jeff Carpenter, prin. — Fax 825-6645
Pembina MS — 50/7-8
PO Box 409 58271 — 701-825-6261
Jeff Carpenter, prin. — Fax 825-6645
Other Schools – See Walhalla

Petersburg, Nelson, Pop. 177
Dakota Prairie SD 1
Supt. — See Mc Ville
Dakota Prairie HS — 200/7-12
PO Box 37 58272 — 701-345-8233
Janet Edlund, prin. — Fax 345-8251

Pingree, Stutsman, Pop. 62
Pingree Buchanan SD 10 — 200/K-12
111 Lincoln Ave 58476 — 701-252-5563
Dennis Adair, supt. — Fax 252-2245
www.pingree.k12.nd.us/
Pingree Buchanan JSHS — 100/8-12
111 Lincoln Ave 58476 — 701-252-5563
Shannon Faller, prin. — Fax 252-2245

Powers Lake, Burke, Pop. 284
Powers Lake SD 27 — 100/K-12
PO Box 346 58773 — 701-464-5432
Delbert Fry, supt. — Fax 464-5435
Powers Lake JSHS — 100/7-12
PO Box 346 58773 — 701-464-5432
Ruth Ann Larshus, prin. — Fax 464-5435

Ray, Williams, Pop. 522
Nesson SD 2 — 200/K-12
PO Box 564 58849 — 701-568-3301
Daniel Anderson, supt. — Fax 568-3302
Ray HS — 100/7-12
PO Box 564 58849 — 701-568-3301
Arley Larson, prin. — Fax 568-3302

Regent, Hettinger, Pop. 195
Mott/Regent SD 1
Supt. — See Mott
Mott/Regent MS at Regent — 100/5-8
PO Box 219 58650 — 701-563-4315
Deb Vining, prin. — Fax 563-4315

Rhame, Bowman, Pop. 177
Rhame SD 17 — 100/K-12
PO Box 250 58651 — 701-279-5523
Anthony T. Duletski, supt. — Fax 279-5750
www.rhame.k12.nd.us/
Rhame HS — 50/9-12
PO Box 250 58651 — 701-279-5523
Niel R. Hinek, prin. — Fax 279-5750

Richardton, Stark, Pop. 589
Richardton-Taylor SD 34 — 300/K-12
PO Box 289 58652 — 701-974-2111
Gerald Quintus, supt. — Fax 974-2161
Richardton-Taylor HS — 200/7-12
PO Box 289 58652 — 701-974-2111
Ron Dazell, prin. — Fax 974-2161

Rocklake, Towner, Pop. 178
North Central SD 28 — 100/K-12
PO Box 188 58365 — 701-266-5539
Wayne Lingen, supt. — Fax 266-5533
www.rocklake.k12.nd.us/
North Central HS — 50/7-12
PO Box 188 58365 — 701-266-5539
Dean Ralston, prin. — Fax 266-5533

Rogers, Barnes, Pop. 59
North Central SD 65 — 200/K-12
10860 20 1/2 St SE 58479 — 701-646-6202
Doug Jacobson, supt. — Fax 646-6566
www.rogers.k12.nd.us/
North Central HS — 100/7-12
10860 20 1/2 St SE 58479 — 701-646-6202
Daren Christianson, prin. — Fax 646-6566

Rolette, Rolette, Pop. 535
Rolette SD 29 — 200/K-12
PO Box 97 58366 — 701-246-3595
Bradley N. Webster, supt. — Fax 246-3452
www.rolettepublicschools.com
Rolette JSHS — 100/7-12
PO Box 97 58366 — 701-246-3595
Bradley Webster, prin. — Fax 246-3452

Rolla, Rolette, Pop. 1,423
Mt. Pleasant SD 4 — 300/PK-12
201 5th St NE 58367 — 701-477-3151
Robert Lech, supt. — Fax 477-5001
www.rolla.k12.nd.us
Mt. Pleasant HS — 200/7-12
201 5th St NE 58367 — 701-477-3151
Randy Loing, prin. — Fax 477-5001

Roseglen, McLean
White Shield SD 85 — 100/K-12
2 2nd Ave W 58775 — 701-743-4350
Ioane Schmidt, supt. — Fax 743-4501
www.white-shield.k12.nd.us/
White Shield HS — 50/9-12
2 2nd Ave W 58775 — 701-743-4350
Fax 743-4501

Rugby, Pierce, Pop. 2,808
Rugby SD 5 — 600/PK-12
1123 S Main Ave 58368 — 701-776-5201
Jeffery Lind, supt. — Fax 776-5091
www.rugby.k12.nd.us/
Rugby JSHS — 300/7-12
1123 S Main Ave 58368 — 701-776-5201
David Zwingel, prin. — Fax 776-5091

Saint John, Rolette, Pop. 357
St. John SD 3 — 300/K-12
PO Box 200 58369 — 701-477-5651
Donald Davis, supt. — Fax 477-8195
www.stjohn.k12.nd.us
Saint John HS — 100/7-12
PO Box 200 58369 — 701-477-5651
Randall Cale, prin. — Fax 477-8195

Saint Thomas, Pembina, Pop. 424
Saint Thomas SD 43 — 100/K-12
PO Box 150 58276 — 701-257-6424
Larry Durand, supt. — Fax 257-6461
Saint Thomas HS — 100/7-12
PO Box 150 58276 — 701-257-6424
David Hanson, prin. — Fax 257-6461

Sawyer, Ward, Pop. 357
Sawyer SD 16 — 100/K-12
PO Box 167 58781 — 701-624-5167
Daniel Larson, supt. — Fax 624-5482
Sawyer HS — 100/7-12
PO Box 167 58781 — 701-624-5167
Daniel D. Larson, prin. — Fax 624-5482

Scranton, Bowman, Pop. 284
Scranton SD 33 — 200/K-12
PO Box 126 58653 — 701-275-8897
John L. Pretzer, supt. — Fax 275-6221
www.scrantonpublicschool.homestead.com/
Scranton HS — 100/7-12
PO Box 126 58653 — 701-275-8266
Dennis Schaff, prin. — Fax 275-6221

Selfridge, Sioux, Pop. 219
Selfridge SD 8 — 100/K-12
PO Box 45 58568 — 701-422-3353
William Dietz, supt. — Fax 422-3348
Selfridge HS — 50/7-12
PO Box 45 58568 — 701-422-3353
William Dietz, prin. — Fax 422-3348

Sherwood, Renville, Pop. 238
Mohall-Lansford-Sherwood SD 1
Supt. — See Mohall
Sherwood HS — 100/7-12
PO Box 9 58782 — 701-459-2214
Robby Voight, prin. — Fax 459-2749

Sheyenne, Eddy, Pop. 301
Sheyenne SD 12 — 100/K-12
320 Sunnyside Ave 58374 — 701-996-3461
Charles Guthrie, supt. — Fax 996-2491
Sheyenne HS — 50/9-12
320 Sunnyside Ave 58374 — 701-996-3461
Charles Guthrie, prin. — Fax 996-2491

Solen, Sioux, Pop. 86
Solen SD 3 — 200/PK-12
PO Box 128 58570 — 701-445-3331
Alan Bjornson, supt. — Fax 445-3323
Solen HS — 100/7-12
PO Box 128 58570 — 701-445-3331
Alan C. Bjornson, prin. — Fax 445-3323

South Heart, Stark, Pop. 294
South Heart SD 9 — 300/K-12
PO Box 159 58655 — 701-677-5671
Loren Mathson, supt. — Fax 677-5616
www.southheart.k12.nd.us/
South Heart HS — 100/9-12
PO Box 159 58655 — 701-677-5671
Curt M. Pierce, prin. — Fax 677-5616

Stanley, Mountrail, Pop. 1,236
Stanley SD 2 — 400/K-12
PO Box 10 58784 — 701-628-3811
Wayne Stanley, supt. — Fax 628-3358
Stanley JSHS — 200/7-12
PO Box 10 58784 — 701-628-2342
Kevin Hoherz, prin. — Fax 628-3358

Starkweather, Ramsey, Pop. 148
Starkweather SD 44 — 100/K-12
PO Box 45 58377 — 701-292-4381
Elroy Burkle, supt. — Fax 292-5714
www.starkweather.k12.nd.us/
Starkweather HS — 50/7-12
PO Box 45 58377 — 701-292-4381
Dennis Dockter, prin. — Fax 292-5714

Steele, Kidder, Pop. 720
Steele-Dawson SD 26 — 300/K-12
PO Box 380 58482 — 701-475-2243
Ken Miller, supt. — Fax 475-2737
Steele-Dawson HS — 100/7-12
PO Box 380 58482 — 701-475-2243
Darnell Schmidt, prin. — Fax 475-2737

Strasburg, Emmons, Pop. 509
Strasburg SD 15 — 200/K-12
PO Box 308 58573 — 701-336-2667
James Eiseman, supt. — Fax 336-7490
www.strasburg.k12.nd.us/
Strasburg JSHS — 100/7-12
PO Box 308 58573 — 701-336-2667
Joel Hedtke, prin. — Fax 336-7490

Surrey, Ward, Pop. 889
Surrey SD 41 — 400/PK-12
PO Box 40 58785 — 701-839-8867
Robert Briggs, supt. — Fax 838-8822
www.surrey.k12.nd.us
Surrey HS — 200/7-12
PO Box 40 58785 — 701-838-3282
David Gerding, prin. — Fax 838-1262

Tappen, Kidder, Pop. 198
Tappen SD 28 — 100/K-12
PO Box 127 58487 — 701-327-4256
Gerald Christianson, admin. — Fax 327-4255
www.tappen.k12.nd.us
Tappen HS — 100/7-12
PO Box 127 58487 — 701-327-4256
Tom Six, prin. — Fax 327-4255

Thompson, Grand Forks, Pop. 985
Thompson SD 61 — 400/K-12
PO Box 269 58278 — 701-599-2765
Ron Stahlecker, supt. — Fax 599-2819
www.thompson.k12.nd.us
Thompson HS — 200/7-12
PO Box 269 58278 — 701-599-2765
Jim Larson, prin. — Fax 599-2819

Tioga, Williams, Pop. 1,100
Tioga SD 15 — 300/K-12
 PO Box 69 58852 — 701-664-2333
 David S. Rust, supt. — Fax 664-4441
 www.tioga.k12.nd.us
Tioga HS — 100/7-12
 PO Box 279 58852 — 701-664-3606
 Todd Lee, prin. — Fax 664-3356

Tower City, Cass, Pop. 244
Maple Valley SD 4 — 300/K-12
 PO Box 168 58071 — 701-749-2570
 Roger Mulvaney, supt. — Fax 749-2313
 www.maple-valley.k12.nd.us/
Maple Valley HS — 100/7-12
 PO Box 168 58071 — 701-749-2570
 Gary Milbrandt, prin. — Fax 749-2313

Towner, McHenry, Pop. 541
TGU SD 60 — 400/K-12
 PO Box 270 58788 — 701-537-5414
 Debby Marshall, supt. — Fax 537-5413
TGU Towner HS — 100/9-12
 PO Box 270 58788 — 701-537-5414
 Greg Foster, prin. — Fax 537-5413
Other Schools – See Granville

Turtle Lake, McLean, Pop. 550
Turtle Lake Mercer SD 72 — 200/K-12
 PO Box 160 58575 — 701-448-2365
 Timothy Ketterling, supt. — Fax 448-2368
 www.tlm.k12.nd.us/
Turtle Lake Mercer HS — 100/7-12
 PO Box 160 58575 — 701-448-2365
 Robert Martin, prin. — Fax 448-2368

Tuttle, Kidder, Pop. 98
Tuttle-Pettibone SD 20 — 50/7-12
 PO Box 8 58488 — 701-867-2564
 Robert Stringer, supt. — Fax 867-2565
 www.tuttle-pettibone.k12.nd.us/
Tuttle-Pettibone JSHS — 50/7-12
 PO Box 8 58488 — 701-867-2564
 Larry Grooters, prin. — Fax 867-2565

Underwood, McLean, Pop. 773
Underwood SD 8 — 200/K-12
 PO Box 100 58576 — 701-442-3201
 Dale Ekstrom, supt. — Fax 442-3704
 www.underwood.k12.nd.us/
Underwood HS — 100/7-12
 PO Box 100 58576 — 701-442-3201
 Gene Utecht, prin. — Fax 442-3704

Valley City, Barnes, Pop. 6,420
Valley City SD 2 — 900/PK-12
 460 Central Ave N 58072 — 701-845-0483
 Dean Koppelman, supt. — Fax 845-4109
 www.valley-city.k12.nd.us
Sheyenne Valley Area Career & Tech Ctr. — Vo/Tech
 PO Box 30 58072 — 701-845-0256
 Jeffrey Bopp, prin. — Fax 845-0003
Valley City HS — 400/9-12
 493 Central Ave N 58072 — 701-845-0483
 Kim Knodle, prin. — Fax 845-2762
Valley City JHS — 200/7-8
 493 Central Ave N 58072 — 701-845-0483
 Al Cruchet, prin. — Fax 845-2762

Valley City State University — Post-Sec.
 101 College St SW 58072 — 701-845-7990

Velva, McHenry, Pop. 1,005
Velva SD 1 — 400/K-12
 PO Box 179 58790 — 701-338-2022
 Steven Dick, supt. — Fax 338-2023
 velva.nd.schoolwebpages.com/
Velva HS — 200/7-12
 PO Box 179 58790 — 701-338-2022
 Kelly D. Peters, prin. — Fax 338-2023

Wahpeton, Richland, Pop. 8,443
Wahpeton SD 37 — 1,600/PK-12
 1505 11th St N 58075 — 701-642-6741
 Michael Connell, supt. — Fax 642-4908
Southeast Region Career & Technology Ctr — Vo/Tech
 2101 9th St N 58075 — 701-642-8701
 Dan Rood, dir. — Fax 642-3811
Wahpeton HS — 500/9-12
 1021 11th St N 58075 — 701-642-2604
 Clark Gripentrog, prin. — Fax 642-1330
Wahpeton MS — 400/6-8
 1209 Loy Ave 58075 — 701-642-6687
 Beverly Jacobson, prin. — Fax 642-5622

North Dakota State College of Science — Post-Sec.
 800 6th Ave N 58075 — 701-671-1130

Walhalla, Pembina, Pop. 1,008
North Border SD 100
 Supt. — See Pembina
Walhalla HS — 100/9-12
 PO Box 558 58282 — 701-549-3751
 Cynthia Gendreau, prin. — Fax 549-3753

Warwick, Benson, Pop. 75
Warwick SD 29 — 200/K-12
 PO Box 7 58381 — 701-294-2561
 Maynard Loibl, supt. — Fax 294-2626
Warwick HS — 100/7-12
 PO Box 7 58381 — 701-294-2561
 Gene Riedinger, prin. — Fax 294-2626

Washburn, McLean, Pop. 1,328
Washburn SD 4 — 300/K-12
 PO Box 280 58577 — 701-462-3228
 Robert Tollefson, supt. — Fax 462-3561
 www.washburn.k12.nd.us
Washburn HS — 200/7-12
 PO Box 280 58577 — 701-462-3221
 Glen Weinmann, prin. — Fax 462-3561

Watford City, McKenzie, Pop. 1,376
McKenzie County SD 1 — 600/K-12
 PO Box 589 58854 — 701-444-3626
 Steven Holen, supt. — Fax 444-6345
Watford City JSHS — 300/7-12
 PO Box 589 58854 — 701-444-3624
 Jay Diede, prin. — Fax 444-3612

West Fargo, Cass, Pop. 16,431
West Fargo SD 6 — 5,300/PK-12
 207 Main Ave W 58078 — 701-356-2000
 Charles Cheney, supt. — Fax 356-2009
 www.west-fargo.k12.nd.us
Cheney MS — 900/6-8
 825 17th Ave E 58078 — 701-356-2090
 Rob Kaspari, prin. — Fax 356-2099
West Fargo HS — 1,600/9-12
 801 9th St E 58078 — 701-356-2050
 Gary Clark, prin. — Fax 356-2060

Westhope, Bottineau, Pop. 503
Westhope SD 17, 395 Main St 58793 — 100/K-12
 William Thibault, supt. — 701-245-6444
 www.westhope.k12.nd.us
Westhope HS, 395 Main St 58793 — 100/7-12
 William Thibault, prin. — 701-245-6444

Wildrose, Williams, Pop. 125
Wildrose-Alamo SD 91 — 50/K-12
 PO Box 697 58795 — 701-539-2261
 Marlyn Vatne, supt. — Fax 539-2270
 www.wildrose.k12.nd.us/
Wildrose-Alamo HS — 50/7-12
 PO Box 697 58795 — 701-539-2261
 Kyle Christensen, prin. — Fax 539-2270

Williston, Williams, Pop. 12,224
Williston SD 1 — 2,200/K-12
 PO Box 1407 58802 — 701-572-1580
 Warren Larson, supt. — Fax 572-3547
 www.williston.k12.nd.us
Williston HS — 800/9-12
 PO Box 1407 58802 — 701-572-0967
 Chris Kittleson, prin. — Fax 572-5449
Williston JHS — 300/7-12
 PO Box 1407 58802 — 701-572-5618
 Marcia Armogost, prin. — Fax 774-3109

Trinity Christian S — 200/PK-12
 2419 9th Ave W 58801 — 701-774-9056
 Doug Black, admin. — Fax 774-3158
Williston State College — Post-Sec.
 PO Box 1326 58802 — 701-774-4200

Wilton, McLean, Pop. 769
Montefiore SD 1 — 200/K-12
 PO Box 249 58579 — 701-734-6559
 Robert Tollefson, supt. — Fax 734-6944
 www.wilton.k12.nd.us
Wilton HS — 100/7-12
 PO Box 249 58579 — 701-734-6331
 Roger Norris, prin. — Fax 734-6944

Wimbledon, Barnes, Pop. 220
Wimbledon Courtenay SD 82 — 200/K-12
 PO Box 255 58492 — 701-435-2493
 Douglas Jacobson, supt. — Fax 435-2365
 www.wimbledoncourtenay.k12.nd.us/
Wimbledon Courtenay HS — 100/7-12
 PO Box 255 58492 — 701-435-2494
 Darrin Roach, prin. — Fax 435-2365

Wing, Burleigh, Pop. 119
Wing SD 28 — 100/K-12
 PO Box 130 58494 — 701-943-2310
 Gene Kotaska, supt. — Fax 943-2318
 www.wing.k12.nd.us/
Wing HS — 50/7-12
 PO Box 130 58494 — 701-943-2319
 Gary Simmons, prin. — Fax 943-2318

Wishek, McIntosh, Pop. 1,063
Wishek SD 19 — 300/K-12
 PO Box 247 58495 — 701-452-2892
 Brian Duchscherer, supt. — Fax 452-4273
 www.wishek.k12.nd.us
Wishek JSHS — 100/7-12
 PO Box 247 58495 — 701-452-2995
 Perry Turner, prin. — Fax 452-4273

Wolford, Pierce, Pop. 48
Wolford SD 1 — 100/K-12
 PO Box 478 58385 — 701-583-2387
 Larry Zavada, supt. — Fax 583-2519
 www.wolford.k12.nd.us/
Wolford HS — 50/7-12
 PO Box 478 58385 — 701-583-2387
 Diane Fritel, prin. — Fax 583-2519

Wyndmere, Richland, Pop. 513
Wyndmere SD 42 — 300/K-12
 PO Box 190 58081 — 701-439-2287
 Rick Jacobson, supt. — Fax 439-2804
 www.wyndmere.k12.nd.us/
Wyndmere HS — 200/7-12
 PO Box 190 58081 — 701-439-2287
 Chris Swenson, prin. — Fax 439-2804

Zeeland, McIntosh, Pop. 132
Zeeland SD 4 — 100/K-12
 PO Box 2 58581 — 701-423-5429
 Corbley Ogren, supt. — Fax 423-5465
 www.zeeland.k12.nd.us/
Zeeland HS — 50/7-12
 PO Box 2 58581 — 701-423-5429
 Corbley Ogren, prin. — Fax 423-5465

OHIO

OHIO DEPARTMENT OF EDUCATION
25 S Front St, Columbus 43215-4183
Telephone 877-644-6338
Website http://www.ode.state.oh.us

Superintendent of Public Instruction   Susan Tave Zelman

OHIO BOARD OF EDUCATION
25 S Front St, Columbus 43215-4104

President   Sue Westendorf

EDUCATIONAL SERVICE CENTERS (ESC)

Allen County ESC
Brian Rockhold, supt.   419-222-1836
1920 Slabtown Rd, Lima 45801   Fax 224-0718
www.noacsc.org/allen/ac/
Ashtabula County ESC
Richard Crepage, supt.   440-576-9023
PO Box 186, Jefferson 44047   Fax 576-3065
www.ashtabulaesc.org/
Athens-Meigs Counties ESC
John Costanzo, supt.   740-593-8001
507 Richland Ave Ste 108   Fax 593-5968
Athens 45701
Auglaize County ESC
Patrick Niekamp, supt.   419-738-3422
1045 Dearbaugh Ave Ste 2   Fax 738-1267
Wapakoneta 45895
www.auglaizeesc.k12.oh.us/
Belmont County ESC
Michael Crawford, supt.   740-695-9773
101 N Market St   Fax 695-2177
Saint Clairsville 43950
www.belmontcountyesc.k12.oh.us/
Brown County ESC
James Frazier, supt.   937-378-6118
325 W State St, Georgetown 45121   Fax 378-4286
www.browncountyesc.org/
Butler County ESC
Daniel Hare, supt.   513-887-3710
1910 Fairgrove Ave Ste B   Fax 887-3709
Hamilton 45011
www.bcesc.org/
Clark County ESC
Bruce E. Stewart, supt.   937-325-7671
30 Warder St Ste 120   Fax 325-9915
Springfield 45504
www.clarkesc.k12.oh.us/
Clermont County ESC
Glenn Alexander, supt.   513-735-8300
2400 Clermont Center Dr   Fax 735-8371
Batavia 45103
www.clermontcountyschools.org
Columbiana County ESC
Anna Vaughn, supt.   330-424-9591
38720 Saltwell Rd, Lisbon 44432   Fax 424-9481
www.ccesc.k12.oh.us/
Cuyahoga County ESC
Harry Eastridge, supt.   216-524-3000
5811 W Canal Rd   Fax 524-3683
Valley View 44125
www.cuyahoga.k12.oh.us/
Darke County ESC
Michael Gray, supt.   937-548-4915
5279 Education Dr   Fax 548-8920
Greenville 45331
www.darke.k12.oh.us
Delaware-Union Counties ESC
Dr. James Crawford, supt.   740-548-7880
4565 Columbus Pike   Fax 548-4465
Delaware 43015
www.duesc.org
Erie-Huron-Ottawa Counties ESC
William B. Lally, supt.   419-625-6274
2900 Columbus Ave   Fax 627-1104
Sandusky 44870
www.ehoesc.org/
Fairfield County ESC
J. Larry Miller, supt.   740-653-3193
995 Liberty Dr, Lancaster 43130   Fax 653-4053
Franklin County ESC
Bart Anderson, supt.   614-445-3750
1717 Alum Creek Dr   Fax 445-3767
Columbus 43207
www.fcesc.org/
Gallia-Vinton Counties ESC
Denise Shockley, supt.   740-245-0593
PO Box 178, Rio Grande 45674   Fax 245-0596
Geauga County ESC
Matthew Galemmo, supt.   440-285-2222
470 Center St Bldg 2   Fax 286-7106
Chardon 44024
www.gcesc.k12.oh.us/
Greene County ESC
Terry Thomas, supt., 360 E Enon Rd   937-767-1303
Yellow Springs 45387   Fax 767-1025
www.greene.k12.oh.us/

Guernsey Monroe Noble ESC
Carol Austin, supt.   740-439-3558
749 Wheeling Ave   Fax 439-0012
Cambridge 43725
www.gmnesc.k12.oh.us/
Hamilton County ESC
David Distel, supt.   513-674-4200
11083 Hamilton Ave   Fax 742-8339
Cincinnati 45231
www.hcesc.org/
Hancock County ESC
Larry Busdeker, supt.   419-422-7525
7746 County Road 140   Fax 422-8766
Findlay 45840
www.hancockcountyesc.org/
Hardin County ESC
Ron Morrison, supt.   419-674-2288
1211 W Lima St #A, Kenton 43326   Fax 675-3309
www.hardinesc.k12.oh.us/
Jefferson County ESC
Craig Closser, supt.   740-283-3347
2023 Sunset Blvd   Fax 283-2709
Steubenville 43952
www.jcesc.k12.oh.us/
Knox County ESC
David Southward, supt.   740-393-6767
308 Martinsburg Rd   Fax 393-6812
Mount Vernon 43050
www.treca.org/schools/knoxesc/ppp.html
Lake County ESC
Linda Williams, supt.   440-350-2563
30 S Park Pl Ste 320   Fax 350-2566
Painesville 44077
www.lcesc.k12.oh.us/
Lawrence County ESC
Harold Shafer, supt.   740-532-4223
111 S 4th St, Ironton 45638   Fax 532-7226
Licking County ESC
Nelson McCray, supt.   740-349-6084
675 Price Rd NE, Newark 43055   Fax 349-6107
www.lcesc.org/
Logan County ESC
Joyce Roberts, supt.   937-599-5195
121 S Opera St   Fax 599-1959
Bellefontaine 43311
www.loganesc.k12.oh.us/
Lorain County ESC
Thomas Rockwell, supt.   440-324-5777
1885 Lake Ave, Elyria 44035   Fax 324-7355
www.leeca.esu.k12.oh.us/ESC/
Lucas County ESC
Sandra Frisch, supt.   419-245-4150
2275 Collingwood Blvd   Fax 245-4186
Toledo 43620
www.lucas.k12.oh.us/
Madison-Champaign Counties ESC
Judy Saylor, supt.   937-484-1557
1512 S US Highway 68   Fax 484-1571
Urbana 43078
www.mccesc.k12.oh.us/
Mahoning County ESC
Richard Denaman, supt.   330-965-7828
100 DeBartolo Pl Ste 105   Fax 965-7902
Youngstown 44512
www.mcesc.k12.oh.us
Medina County ESC
William J. Koran, supt.   330-723-6393
124 W Washington St   Fax 723-0573
Medina 44256
www.medina-esc.k12.oh.us
Mercer County ESC
Eugene Linton, supt.   419-586-6628
441 E Market St, Celina 45822   Fax 586-3377
www.noacsc.org/mercer/mc/
Miami County ESC
John Decker, supt.   937-440-8050
510 W Water St Ste 210   Fax 440-5485
Troy 45373
www.miami.k12.oh.us/
Mid-Ohio ESC
Gregg Reink, supt.   419-774-5520
890 W 4th St, Mansfield 44906   Fax 774-5523
www.moesc.k12.oh.us/

Montgomery County ESC
Donald R. Thompson, supt.   937-225-4598
200 S Keowee St, Dayton 45402   Fax 496-7426
www.montgomery.k12.oh.us
Muskingum Valley ESC
Richard Murry, supt.   740-452-4518
205 N 7th St, Zanesville 43701   Fax 455-6702
www.mvesc.k12.oh.us/
North Central Ohio ESC
David J. Getter, supt.   419-447-2927
244 S Washington St, Tiffin 44883   Fax 447-2825
www.ncoesc.esu.k12.oh.us/
Northwest Ohio ESC
John Wilhelm, supt.   419-335-1070
PO Box 552, Wauseon 43567   Fax 335-5464
www.nwoesc.k12.oh.us/
Perry-Hocking Counties ESC
Dale Dickson, supt., 1605 Airport Rd   740-342-3502
New Lexington 43764   Fax 342-1961
www.gmntrico4u.org/counties/perry/phesc.html
Pickaway County ESC
David Beavers, supt.   740-474-7529
2050 Stoneridge Dr   Fax 474-7251
Circleville 43113
pickawayesc.org/
Portage County ESC
Dewey Chapman, supt.   330-297-1436
224 W Riddle Ave, Ravenna 44266   Fax 297-1113
www.portagenet.sparcc.org/
Preble County ESC
Paul L. Erslan, supt.   937-456-1187
597 Hillcrest Dr, Eaton 45320   Fax 456-3253
www.preblecountyesc.org
Putnam County ESC
Jan Osborn, supt.   419-523-5951
PO Box 190, Ottawa 45875   Fax 523-6126
putnam.noacsc.org/
Ross-Pike Counties ESC
Philip Satterfield, supt.   740-702-3120
475 Western Ave Ste E   Fax 702-3123
Chillicothe 45601
gsn.k12.oh.us/RossCO/
Sandusky County ESC
Barbara Marshall, supt.   419-332-8214
500 W State St, Fremont 43420   Fax 332-6707
www.sandusky.k12.oh.us/
Shelby County ESC
Mary Lou Holly, supt.   937-498-1354
129 E Court St, Sidney 45365   Fax 498-4850
scesc.woco-k12.org
South Central Ohio ESC
Darren C. Jenkins, supt.   740-354-7761
411 Court St Rm 105   Fax 353-1882
Portsmouth 45662
www.scoesc.k12.oh.us/
Southern Ohio ESC
Robert Dalton, supt.   937-382-6921
62 Laurel Dr, Wilmington 45177   Fax 383-3171
www.cfhesd.k12.oh.us/
Stark County ESC
Larry Morgan, supt.   330-492-8136
2100 38th St NW, Canton 44709   Fax 492-6381
www.stark.k12.oh.us/
Summit County ESC
Patrick Corbett, supt.   330-945-5600
420 Washington Ave #200   Fax 945-6222
Cuyahoga Falls 44221
www.cybersummit.org/
Tri-County ESC
Edward Swartz, supt.   330-345-6771
741 Winkler Dr, Wooster 44691   Fax 345-7622
www.youresc.k12.oh.us/
Trumbull County ESC
Anthony D'Ambrosio Ed.D., supt.   330-675-2800
347 N Park Ave, Warren 44481   Fax 675-2814
www.trumbull.k12.oh.us/
Tuscarawas-Carroll-Harrison Counties ESC
Robert Fogler, supt., 834 E High Ave   330-308-9939
New Philadelphia 44663   Fax 308-0964
www.tchesc.k12.oh.us/
Warren County ESC
John Lazares, supt.   513-695-2900
320 E Silver St, Lebanon 45036   Fax 695-2961
www.warren.k12.oh.us/

Washington County ESC
Roger L. Bartunek, supt. 740-373-6669
PO Box 1A, Marietta 45750 Fax 376-5809
www.gmntrico4u.org/counties/washington/wcesc.html

Western Buckeye ESC
Kevin L. Dangler, supt. 419-238-4746
10730 Lincoln Hwy Fax 238-6259
Van Wert 45891
www.noacsc.org/vanwert/wb/
Wood County ESC
Douglas Garman, supt. 419-354-9010
1867 N Research Dr Fax 354-1146
Bowling Green 43402
www.wood.k12.oh.us/

PUBLIC, PRIVATE AND CATHOLIC SECONDARY SCHOOLS

Aberdeen, Brown, Pop. 1,673
Ripley-Union-Lewis-Huntington Local SD
Supt. — See Ripley
Ripley-Union-Lewis-Huntington MS 5-8
2300 Rains Eitel Rd 45101 937-795-8001
Machael Kennedy, prin.

Ada, Hardin, Pop. 5,583
Ada EVD 900/K-12
435 Grand Ave 45810 419-634-6421
Raymond Getz, supt. Fax 634-0311
www.ada.k12.oh.us
Ada JSHS 400/7-12
435 Grand Ave 45810 419-634-2746
Dennis Bahmer, prin. Fax 634-4153

Ohio Northern University Post-Sec.
525 S Main St 45810 419-772-2000

Akron, Summit, Pop. 212,215
Akron CSD 28,400/K-12
70 N Broadway St 44308 330-761-1661
Dr. Sylvester Small, supt. Fax 761-3225
www.akronschools.com
Adult Vocational Services Vo/Tech
147 Park St 44308 330-761-1385
Arden Scholles, dir. Fax 761-1388
Buchtel HS 700/9-12
1040 Copley Rd 44320 330-873-3300
Deborah Houchins, prin. Fax 873-3307
Central-Hower HS 900/9-12
123 S Forge St 44308 330-761-1605
Addie Veasley, prin. Fax 761-1614
East HS 800/9-12
80 Brittain Rd 44305 330-794-4100
Anthony Lane, prin. Fax 794-4107
Ellet HS 1,100/9-12
309 Woolf Ave 44312 330-794-4120
M. Constance Hardy, prin. Fax 794-4130
Firestone HS 1,200/9-12
333 Rampart Ave 44313 330-873-3315
LaVonne Humphrey, prin. Fax 873-3318
Garfield HS 1,300/9-12
435 N Firestone Blvd 44301 330-773-6831
Rebecca DeCapua, prin. Fax 773-3403
Goodrich MS 700/6-8
700 Lafollette St 44306 330-773-6689
Jo Anne Orlando, prin. Fax 773-7807
Goodyear MS 700/6-8
49 N Martha Ave 44305 330-794-4135
Joyce Gerber, prin. Fax 794-4142
Hyre MS 900/6-8
2443 Wedgewood Dr 44312 330-794-4144
Julia Mann, prin. Fax 794-4143
Innes MS 900/6-8
1999 East Ave 44314 330-848-5210
Norris Kelly, prin. Fax 848-5217
Jennings MS 700/6-8
225 E Tallmadge Ave 44310 330-761-1715
Nicki Embly, prin. Fax 761-1713
Kenmore HS 900/9-12
2140 13th St SW 44314 330-848-4141
Elizabeth Neidert, prin. Fax 848-5270
Kent MS 800/6-8
1445 Hammel St 44306 330-773-7631
Larry Petry, prin. Fax 773-6442
Litchfield MS 700/6-8
1540 Fairfax Rd 44313 330-873-3330
James McCoy, prin. Fax 873-3337
Miller-South Education Center MS 500/4-8
1055 East Ave 44307 330-761-1765
Kathleen Ashcroft, prin. Fax 761-1764
North HS 700/9-12
985 Gorge Blvd 44310 330-761-2665
Lawrence Weigle, prin. Fax 761-2661
Perkins MS 700/6-8
630 Mull Ave 44313 330-873-3340
Felisha Cheatem, prin. Fax 873-3347
Riedinger MS 600/6-8
77 W Thornton St 44311 330-761-1345
Traci Buckner, prin. Fax 761-1349
Evening HS Adult
985 Gorge Blvd 44310 330-761-2680
Frank Kalain, coord. Fax 761-2661

Coventry Local SD 2,200/K-12
3257 Cormany Rd 44319 330-644-8489
Gary Zoldesy, supt. Fax 644-0159
www.coventrylocalschools.com
Coventry JHS 400/8-9
3257 Cormany Rd 44319 330-644-2232
Cynthia McDonald, prin. Fax 644-0331
Coventry SHS 600/10-12
3089 Manchester Rd 44319 330-644-3004
Jon Hibian, prin. Fax 644-4222

Manchester Local SD 1,500/K-12
6075 Manchester Rd 44319 330-882-6926
Sam Reynolds, supt. Fax 882-0013
www.panthercountry.org/
Manchester HS 500/9-12
437 W Nimisila Rd 44319 330-882-3291
James France, prin. Fax 882-5696
Manchester MS 500/5-8
760 W Nimisila Rd 44319 330-882-3812
James Miller, prin. Fax 882-2013

Springfield Local SD 3,000/K-12
2960 Sanitarium Rd 44312 330-798-1111
Jerome Pecko, supt. Fax 798-1161
www.springfield-lucas.k12.oh.us/
Springfield HS 1,000/9-12
2966 Sanitarium Rd 44312 330-798-1002
Cynthia Frola, prin. Fax 798-1162
Spring Hill JHS 500/7-8
660 Lessig Ave 44312 330-798-1003
Robert Bauer, prin. Fax 798-1163

Akron General Medical Center Post-Sec.
400 Wabash Ave 44307 330-846-6548
Akron Institute Post-Sec.
1600 S Arlington St Ste 100 44306 330-724-1600
Archbishop Hoban HS 800/9-12
1 Holy Cross Blvd 44306 330-773-6658
Mary Anne Beiting, prin. Fax 773-9100
Brown Mackie College Post-Sec.
2791 Mogadore Rd 44312 330-733-8766
Children's Hospital & Medical Center Post-Sec.
1 Perkins Sq 44308 330-379-8293
Cooperative Medical Technology Program Post-Sec.
1 Perkins Sq 44308 330-543-8720
Mogadore Christian Academy 100/K-12
3603 Carper Ave 44312 330-628-8482
Dennis Calaway, prin. Fax 628-2677
Our Lady of the Elms HS 300/9-12
1375 W Exchange St 44313 330-867-0880
Lisa K. Massello, prin. Fax 864-6488
Our Lady of the Elms JHS 100/7-8
1375 W Exchange St 44313 330-867-0880
Lisa K. Massello, prin. Fax 864-6488
St. Vincent-St. Mary HS 500/9-12
15 N Maple St 44303 330-253-9113
David Rathz, prin. Fax 996-0020
University of Akron Post-Sec.
381 Buchtel Mall 44304 330-972-7111

Albany, Athens, Pop. 839
Alexander Local SD 1,700/PK-12
6091 Ayers Rd 45710 740-698-8831
Robert Bray, supt. Fax 698-2038
www.alexanderschools.org/
Alexander HS 600/9-12
6125 School Rd 45710 740-698-8831
Frank Doudna, prin. Fax 698-3614
Alexander MS 400/6-8
6115 School Rd 45710 740-698-8831
Frank Doudna, prin. Fax 698-8833

Alliance, Stark, Pop. 22,892
Alliance CSD 3,200/K-12
200 Glamorgan St 44601 330-821-2100
Stephen Stohla, supt. Fax 821-0202
www.aviators.stark.k12.oh.us/
Alliance HS 1,000/9-12
400 Glamorgan St 44601 330-829-2245
Robert Gress, prin. Fax 823-4920
Alliance MS 800/6-8
3205 S Union Ave 44601 330-829-2254
Rae Ellen Dale, prin. Fax 823-0872

Marlington Local SD 2,700/K-12
10320 Moulin Ave NE 44601 330-823-7458
Tony D. Scott, supt. Fax 823-7759
www.dukes.stark.k12.oh.us/
Marlington HS 1,000/9-12
10450 Moulin Ave NE 44601 330-823-1300
Jim Nicodemo, prin. Fax 829-1986
Marlington MS 700/6-8
10325 Moulin Ave NE 44601 330-823-7566
Steve Viscounte, prin.

Good Shepherd S 50/K-12
7775 Pontius St NE 44601 330-935-0623
Rev. Gary Spencer, admin. Fax 935-0433
Mt. Union College Post-Sec.
1972 Clark Ave 44601 330-821-5320

Amanda, Fairfield, Pop. 717
Amanda-Clearcreek Local SD 1,600/K-12
328 E Main St 43102 740-969-7250
James Dick, supt. Fax 969-7620
www.amanda.k12.oh.us
Amanda-Clearcreek HS 500/9-12
328 E Main St 43102 740-969-7251
Jon Saxton, prin.
Other Schools – See Stoutsville

Amherst, Lorain, Pop. 11,738
Amherst EVD 4,100/K-12
185 Forest St 44001 440-988-4406
Robert Boynton, supt. Fax 988-4413
www.amherst.k12.oh.us
Amherst JHS 700/7-8
548 Milan Ave 44001 440-988-0324
Michael Diamond, prin. Fax 988-0328
Steele HS 1,300/9-12
450 Washington St 44001 440-988-4433
Michael Gillam, prin. Fax 988-5087

Andover, Ashtabula, Pop. 1,249
Pymatuning Valley Local SD 1,400/K-12
PO Box 1180 44003 440-293-6488
John Rose, supt. Fax 293-7654
www.pvschools.k12.oh.us/
Pymatuning Valley HS 500/9-12
PO Box 1180 44003 440-293-6263
Andrew Kuthy, prin. Fax 293-7214
Pymatuning Valley MS 600/4-8
PO Box 1180 44003 440-293-6981
Michael Chokshi, prin. Fax 293-7237

Anna, Shelby, Pop. 1,392
Anna Local SD 1,200/K-12
PO Box 169 45302 937-394-2011
Dr. John Granger, supt. Fax 394-7658
www.anna.k12.oh.us
Anna MSHS 700/6-12
PO Box 169 45302 937-394-2011
Andrew Bixler, prin. Fax 394-7658

Ansonia, Darke, Pop. 1,123
Ansonia Local SD 700/K-12
PO Box 279 45303 937-337-4000
James Atchley, supt. Fax 337-9520
www.ansonia.k12.oh.us/
Ansonia HS 200/9-12
PO Box 279 45303 937-337-5591
Steve Garman, prin. Fax 337-9520
Ansonia MS 200/5-8
PO Box 279 45303 937-337-5591
Stephen Garman, prin. Fax 337-9520

Antwerp, Paulding, Pop. 1,659
Antwerp Local SD 700/K-12
303 S Harrmann Rd 45813 419-258-5421
Mark Hartman, supt. Fax 258-4041
www.noacsc.org/paulding/aw/
Antwerp Local HS 200/9-12
303 S Harrmann Rd 45813 419-258-5421
Stephen Arnold, prin. Fax 258-4041
Antwerp Local MS 200/6-8
303 S Harrmann Rd 45813 419-258-5420
Stephen Arnold, prin. Fax 258-4041

Apple Creek, Wayne, Pop. 988
Southeast Local SD 1,700/K-12
9048 Dover Rd 44606 330-698-3001
Steven A. Sayers, supt. Fax 698-5000
www.southeast.k12.oh.us
Lea MS 200/7-8
9130 Dover Rd 44606 330-698-3151
Holly Lawver, prin. Fax 698-1922
Waynedale HS 500/9-12
9050 Dover Rd 44606 330-698-3071
William Seder, prin. Fax 698-1432

Arcadia, Hancock, Pop. 580
Arcadia Local SD 600/K-12
19033 State Route 12 44804 419-894-6431
Laurie Walles, supt. Fax 894-6970
www.noacsc.org/hancock/ad/
Arcadia JSHS 300/7-12
19033 State Route 12 44804 419-894-6431
Thom Loomis, prin. Fax 894-6970

Arcanum, Darke, Pop. 2,043
Arcanum Butler Local SD 1,100/K-12
2 Weisenbarger Ct 45304 937-692-5174
Wayne Combs, supt. Fax 692-5959
www.arcanum-butler.k12.oh.us
Arcanum HS 400/9-12
310 N Main St 45304 937-692-5175
Pat McBride, prin. Fax 692-5959
Butler MS 300/6-8
1481 State Route 127 45304 937-678-6571
Kirby Tippla, prin. Fax 678-6581

Archbold, Fulton, Pop. 4,443
Archbold Area Local SD 1,400/K-12
600 Lafayette St 43502 419-445-5579
Kenneth Cline, supt. Fax 445-8536
www.archbold.k12.oh.us
Archbold HS 500/9-12
600 Lafayette St 43502 419-445-5579
Marcia Rozevink, prin. Fax 445-8536
Archbold MS 500/5-8
306 Stryker St 43502 419-446-2726
Mike Pressler, prin. Fax 445-8402

Four County Career Center SD
22900 State Route 34 43502 419-267-3331
Dr. David A. Nicholls, supt. Fax 267-5234
www.fourcounty.net
Four County Career Center Vo/Tech
22900 State Route 34 43502 419-267-3331
Fax 267-5234

Northwest State Community College Post-Sec.
22600 State Route 34 43502 419-267-5511

Arlington, Hancock, Pop. 1,344
Arlington Local SD 600/K-12
PO Box 260 45814 419-365-5121
David A. Rossman, supt. Fax 365-1282
www.noacsc.org/hancock/ag
Arlington JSHS 300/7-12
PO Box 260 45814 419-365-5121
Teri Kubbs, prin. Fax 365-1282

Ashland, Ashland, Pop. 21,449
Ashland CSD 3,800/K-12
PO Box 160 44805 419-289-1117
James Jones, supt. Fax 289-9534
www.ashland-city.k12.oh.us

Ashland HS — 1,200/9-12
1440 King Rd 44805 — 419-289-7968
Robert Lake, prin. — Fax 281-8796
Ashland MS — 600/7-8
345 Cottage St 44805 — 419-289-7966
Mike Heimann, prin. — Fax 289-2303

Ashland County-West Holmes JVSD
1783 State Route 60 44805 — 419-289-3313
Michael McDaniel, supt. — Fax 289-3729
www.acwhcc-jvs.k12.oh.us
Ashland Co. - West Holmes JVS Career Ctr — Vo/Tech
1783 State Route 60 44805 — 419-289-3313
Stanley Valentine, prin. — Fax 289-3729

Crestview Local SD — 1,300/PK-12
1575 State Route 96 44805 — 419-895-1700
Steven Willeke, supt. — Fax 895-1733
www.crestview-richland.k12.oh.us
Crestview HS — 400/9-12
1575 State Route 96 44805 — 419-895-1700
Debbie Reidy, prin. — Fax 895-3103
Crestview MS — 500/4-8
1575 State Route 96 44805 — 419-895-1700
John McNeely, prin. — Fax 895-1733

Mapleton Local SD — 1,000/K-12
2 Mountie Dr 44805 — 419-945-2188
Lori Lytle, supt. — Fax 945-8114
www.mapleton.k12.oh.us/
Mapleton HS — 400/9-12
1 Mountie Dr 44805 — 419-945-2188
Jeff Hill, prin. — Fax 945-2123
Mapleton MS — 200/6-8
635 County Road 801 44805 — 419-945-2188
Scott Smith, prin. — Fax 652-3541

Ashland County-West Holmes Career Center — Post-Sec.
1783 State Route 60 44805 — 419-289-3313
Ashland Theological Seminary — Post-Sec.
910 Center St 44805 — 419-289-5161
Ashland University — Post-Sec.
401 College Ave 44805 — 419-289-4142

Ashtabula, Ashtabula, Pop. 20,355
Ashtabula Area CSD — 4,600/K-12
PO Box 290 44005 — 440-993-2500
William Licate, supt. — Fax 993-2626
www.aacs.net
Columbus JHS — 300/7-8
1326 Columbus Ave 44004 — 440-993-2618
Sylvia Atkinson, prin. — Fax 992-0331
Lakeside 9 — 400/9-9
221 Lake Ave 44004 — 440-993-2553
John Rose, prin. — Fax 993-2558
Lakeside HS — 900/10-12
401 W 44th St 44004 — 440-993-2522
James Candela, prin. — Fax 993-2647
West JHS — 400/7-8
1231 W 47th St 44004 — 440-993-2577
Patricia Craft, prin. — Fax 993-2585

Buckeye Local SD — 2,300/K-12
3436 Edgewood Dr 44004 — 440-998-4411
Nancy L. Williams, supt. — Fax 992-8369
www.buckeyeschools.net/
Braden JHS — 400/7-8
3436 Edgewood Dr 44004 — 440-998-0550
Charles Schlick, prin.
Edgewood HS — 800/9-12
2428 Blake Rd 44004 — 440-997-5301
Timothy Essig, prin. — Fax 998-6143

Kent State University-Ashtabula Campus — Post-Sec.
3325 W 13th St 44004 — 440-964-3322
SS. John & Paul HS — 200/7-12
541 W 34th St 44004 — 440-997-5531
Albina Larson, prin. — Fax 998-1661

Ashville, Pickaway, Pop. 3,201
Teays Valley Local SD — 3,200/K-12
385 Circleville Ave 43103 — 740-983-4111
Ronald Thornton, supt. — Fax 983-4158
www.teays-valley.k12.oh.us
Teays Valley HS — 900/9-12
3887 State Route 752 43103 — 740-983-3131
Jeffrey Sheets, prin. — Fax 983-4158
Teays Valley MS — 800/6-8
383 Circleville Ave 43103 — 740-983-4074
Kyle Wolfe, prin. — Fax 983-4158

Athens, Athens, Pop. 22,220
Athens CSD
Supt. — See The Plains
Athens MS, 51 W State St 45701 — 400/7-8
Paul Grippa, prin. — 740-593-7107

Ohio University — Post-Sec.
120 Chubb Hall 45701 — 740-593-1000

Attica, Seneca, Pop. 926
Seneca East Local SD — 1,100/K-12
PO Box 462 44807 — 419-426-7041
Michael Wank, supt. — Fax 426-5514
www.seneca-east.k12.oh.us/home/main.htm
Seneca East HS — 400/9-12
PO Box 462 44807 — 419-426-3312
Judy Watson, prin. — Fax 426-5400
Other Schools – See Republic

Atwater, Portage
Waterloo Local SD — 1,400/K-12
1464 Industry Rd 44201 — 330-947-2664
Robert Wolf, supt. — Fax 947-2847
www.viking.portage.k12.oh.us
Waterloo HS — 400/9-12
1464 Industry Rd 44201 — 330-947-2124
Nick Hulea, prin. — Fax 947-1911
Waterloo MS — 300/6-8
1464 Industry Rd 44201 — 330-947-0033
Paul Woodard, prin. — Fax 947-4073

Aurora, Portage, Pop. 14,270
Aurora CSD — 2,600/PK-12
102 E Garfield Rd 44202 — 330-995-7702
Russell Bennett, supt. — Fax 562-4892
www.aurora-schools.org
Aurora HS — 900/9-12
109 W Pioneer Trl 44202 — 330-562-3501
Dr. Russell Jones, prin. — Fax 562-3588
Harmon MS — 700/6-8
130 Aurora Hudson Rd 44202 — 330-562-3375
Will Laine, prin. — Fax 562-4796

Austinburg, Ashtabula
Grand River Academy — 100/9-12
PO Box 222 44010 — 440-275-2811
Randy Blum, hdmstr. — Fax 275-1825

Austintown, Mahoning, Pop. 31,500
Hair Academy — Post-Sec.
6000 Mahoning Ave 44515 — 330-792-6504

Avon, Lorain, Pop. 13,877
Avon Local SD — 1,800/K-12
35573 Detroit Rd 44011 — 440-937-4680
Jim Reitenbach, supt. — Fax 937-4688
www.avon.k12.oh.us
Avon HS, 37545 Detroit Rd 44011 — 600/9-12
Chad Coffman, prin. — 440-934-6171
Avon MS — 400/7-8
3075 Stoney Ridge Rd 44011 — 440-934-3800
Craig Koehler, prin.

Avon Lake, Lorain, Pop. 19,782
Avon Lake CSD — 3,300/K-12
175 Avon Belden Rd 44012 — 440-933-6210
Robert D. Scott, supt. — Fax 933-6711
www.avonlakecityschools.org
Avon Lake HS — 1,100/9-12
175 Avon Belden Rd 44012 — 440-933-6290
Timothy Freeman, prin. — Fax 930-2798
Learwood MS — 500/7-8
340 Lear Rd 44012 — 440-933-8142
Jane Ramsay, prin. — Fax 933-8406

Bainbridge, Ross, Pop. 1,022
Paint Valley Local SD — 1,200/K-12
7454 US Highway 50 W 45612 — 740-634-2826
Gary E. Uhrig, supt. — Fax 634-2890
gsn.k12.oh.us/PaintValley/index.htm
Paint Valley HS — 400/9-12
7454 US Highway 50 W 45612 — 740-634-3582
H. Dwight Goins, prin. — Fax 634-3518
Paint Valley MS — 300/6-8
7454 US Highway 50 W 45612 — 740-634-3454
Brent Taylor, prin. — Fax 634-3459

Baltimore, Fairfield, Pop. 2,901
Liberty Union-Thurston Local SD — 1,400/K-12
621 W Washington St 43105 — 740-862-4171
Paul E. Mathews, supt. — Fax 862-2015
www.libertyunion.org
Liberty Union HS — 400/9-12
500 W Washington St 43105 — 740-862-4107
Mark Fullen, prin. — Fax 862-4100
Liberty Union MS — 400/5-8
600 W Washington St 43105 — 740-862-4126
Henry Gavarkavich, prin. — Fax 862-2015

Barberton, Summit, Pop. 27,462
Barberton CSD — 4,000/K-12
479 Norton Ave 44203 — 330-753-1025
Dr. Elizabeth J. Lolli, supt. — Fax 848-0884
www.barbertonschools.org
Barberton HS — 1,300/9-12
555 Barber Rd 44203 — 330-753-1084
Kirk Koennecke, prin. — Fax 848-5517
Highland MS — 500/6-8
1152 Belleview Ave 44203 — 330-848-4243
— Fax 848-4221
Light MS — 500/6-8
292 Robinson Ave 44203 — 330-848-4236
Jason Ondrus, prin. — Fax 848-1272

Barnesville, Belmont, Pop. 4,196
Barnesville EVD — 1,300/K-12
210 W Church St 43713 — 740-425-3615
Randy Lucas, supt. — Fax 425-5000
www.barnesville.k12.oh.us/
Barnesville HS — 400/9-12
910 Shamrock Dr 43713 — 740-425-3617
Jeff Crosier, prin. — Fax 425-9254
Barnesville MS — 400/5-8
970 Shamrock Dr 43713 — 740-425-3116
Erin Olexo, prin. — Fax 425-9204

Olney Friends S — 100/9-12
61830 Sandy Ridge Rd 43713 — 740-425-3655
Richard F. Sidwell, hdmstr. — Fax 425-3202

Bascom, Seneca
Hopewell-Loudon Local SD — 900/K-12
PO Box 400 44809 — 419-937-2216
Geoffrey Palmer, supt. — Fax 937-2516
www.hlschool.org/
Hopewell-Loudon Local JSHS — 400/7-12
PO Box 400 44809 — 419-937-2216
Bill Dobbins, prin. — Fax 937-2516

Batavia, Clermont, Pop. 1,649
Batavia Local SD — 1,900/K-12
800 Bauer Ave 45103 — 513-732-2343
Barbara Bradley Ed.D., supt. — Fax 732-3221
www.bataviaschools.org
Batavia HS — 500/9-12
1 Bull Dog Pl 45103 — 513-732-2341
Jamie Corrill, prin. — Fax 732-3221
Batavia MS, 800 Bauer Ave 45103 — 600/5-8
Karyn Strong, prin. — 513-732-9534

Clermont-Northeastern Local SD — 2,000/PK-12
2792 US Highway 50 45103 — 513-625-5478
Ralph Shell, supt. — Fax 625-6080
www.cneschools.org
Clermont-Northeastern HS — 700/9-12
5327 Hutchinson Rd 45103 — 513-625-1211
Robert Humble, prin. — Fax 625-3328
Clermont-Northeastern MS — 600/5-8
5347 Hutchinson Rd 45103 — 513-625-7075
Kathy Sabo, prin. — Fax 625-3325

West Clermont Local SD
Supt. — See Cincinnati
Amelia HS — 1,300/9-12
1351 Clough Pike 45103 — 513-947-7400
Keith Hickman, prin. — Fax 753-2419
Amelia MS — 1,100/6-8
1341 Clough Pike 45103 — 513-947-7500
David Mack, prin. — Fax 753-7851

University of Cincinnati — Post-Sec.
4200 Clermont College Dr 45103 — 513-732-5200

Bath, Summit
Revere Local SD
Supt. — See Richfield
Revere MS — 700/6-8
PO Box 339 44210 — 330-666-4155
Frank Surace, prin. — Fax 659-3795

Bay Village, Cuyahoga, Pop. 15,731
Bay Village CSD — 2,400/K-12
377 Dover Center Rd 44140 — 440-617-7300
Clinton Keener, supt. — Fax 617-7301
www.bayvillageschools.com
Bay HS — 800/9-12
29230 Wolf Rd 44140 — 440-617-7400
James Cahoon, prin. — Fax 617-7401
Bay MS — 700/5-8
27725 Wolf Rd 44140 — 440-617-7600
Sean McAndrews, prin. — Fax 617-7601

Beachwood, Cuyahoga, Pop. 11,906
Beachwood CSD — 1,600/PK-12
24601 Fairmount Blvd 44122 — 216-464-2600
Dr. Richard A. Markwardt, supt. — Fax 292-2340
www.beachwood.k12.oh.us
Beachwood HS — 700/9-12
25100 Fairmount Blvd 44122 — 216-831-2080
Roy Warren, prin. — Fax 292-4169
Beachwood MS — 200/7-8
2860 Richmond Rd 44122 — 216-831-0355
Edward Bernetich, prin. — Fax 831-1891

Stone Yavne HS — 200/7-12
2475 S Green Rd 44122 — 216-691-5838
Lois Mager, prin.

Beallsville, Monroe, Pop. 425
Switzerland of Ohio Local SD
Supt. — See Woodsfield
Beallsville JSHS — 200/7-12
PO Box 262 43716 — 740-926-1302
Todd Christman, prin. — Fax 926-1394

Beaver, Pike, Pop. 468
Eastern Local SD — 800/K-12
1170 Tile Mill Rd 45613 — 740-226-4851
Dr. Charles Shreve, supt. — Fax 226-1331
Eastern HS — 300/9-12
1170 Tile Mill Rd 45613 — 740-226-1544
Steve Kempf, prin. — Fax 226-6322
Eastern MS — 200/6-8
1170 Tile Mill Rd 45613 — 740-226-1544
Steve Kempf, prin. — Fax 226-6322

Beavercreek, Greene, Pop. 39,196
Beavercreek CSD — 7,100/PK-12
3040 Kemp Rd 45431 — 937-426-1522
Dennis A. Morrison, supt. — Fax 429-7517
www.beavercreek.k12.oh.us/
Ankeney MS — 900/6-8
4085 Shakertown Rd 45430 — 937-429-7567
Pam Taiclet, prin. — Fax 429-7685
Beavercreek HS — 2,400/9-12
2660 Dayton Xenia Rd 45434 — 937-429-7547
Marian West, prin. — Fax 429-7546
Ferguson MS — 900/6-8
2680 Dayton Xenia Rd 45434 — 937-429-7577
Gary Creviston, prin. — Fax 429-7686

Bedford, Cuyahoga, Pop. 13,790
Bedford CSD — 3,800/K-12
475 Northfield Rd 44146 — 440-439-1500
Martha A. Motsco, supt. — Fax 439-4850
www.bedford.k12.oh.us
Bedford HS — 1,200/9-12
481 Northfield Rd 44146 — 440-786-3521
Joanie A. Hines Ed.D., prin. — Fax 439-4627
Other Schools – See Bedford Heights

St. Peter Chanel HS — 400/9-12
480 Northfield Rd 44146 — 440-232-5900
Roger Abood, prin. — Fax 232-9283

Bedford Heights, Cuyahoga, Pop. 11,189
Bedford CSD
Supt. — See Bedford
Heskett MS — 700/7-8
5771 Perkins Rd 44146 — 440-439-4450
Kathryn Powers, prin. — Fax 786-3572

Bellaire, Belmont, Pop. 4,766
Bellaire SD — 1,500/K-12
340 34th St 43906 — 740-671-1826
John Stinoski, supt. — Fax 671-6002
www.bellaire.k12.oh.us
Bellaire HS — 500/9-12
349 35th St 43906 — 740-676-3652
Frank Danadic, prin. — Fax 671-6024
Bellaire MS — 500/5-8
54555 Bellaire-Neffs Rd 43906 — 740-676-1635
— Fax 676-3014

St. John Central HS | 200/9-12
3625 Guernsey St 43906 | 740-676-4932
C. Gary Hill, prin. | Fax 676-4934

Bellbrook, Greene, Pop. 6,966
Sugarcreek Local SD | 2,800/PK-12
60 E South St 45305 | 937-848-6251
Keith St Pierre, supt. | Fax 848-5018
www.sugarcreek.k12.oh.us
Bellbrook HS | 900/9-12
3737 Upper Bellbrook Rd 45305 | 937-848-3737
Christopher Baker, prin. | Fax 848-5016
Bellbrook JHS | 700/6-8
3777 Upper Bellbrook Rd 45305 | 937-848-3777
Jenness Sigman, prin. | Fax 848-5066

Bellefontaine, Logan, Pop. 12,980
Bellefontaine CSD | 2,800/K-12
820 Ludlow Rd 43311 | 937-593-9060
Larry Anderson, supt. | Fax 599-1346
www.bellefontaine.k12.oh.us/
Bellefontaine HS | 900/9-12
555 E Lake Ave 43311 | 937-593-0545
Maureen Yoder, prin. | Fax 593-0575
Bellefontaine MS | 700/6-8
509 N Park St 43311 | 937-593-9010
Michael Hassel, prin. | Fax 593-9030

Benjamin Logan Local SD | 2,000/K-12
4740 County Road 26 43311 | 937-593-9211
Stanley P. Mounts, supt. | Fax 599-4059
www.benlogan.k12.oh.us
Logan HS | 600/9-12
6609 State Route 47 E 43311 | 937-592-1666
Scott Albert, prin. | Fax 599-4061
Logan MS | 700/5-8
4626 County Road 26 43311 | 937-599-2386
James Cox, prin. | Fax 599-4062

Ohio Hi-Point JVSD | 2,000/9-12
2280 State Route 540 43311 | 937-599-3010
Kimberly S. Wilson, supt. | Fax 599-2318
www.ohp.k12.oh.us
Ohio Hi-Point Joint Vocational S | Vo/Tech
2280 State Route 540 43311 | 937-599-3010
| Fax 599-2318

Bellevue, Huron, Pop. 8,111
Bellevue CSD | 2,300/K-12
125 North St 44811 | 419-484-5000
Stephen Schumm, supt. | Fax 483-0723
www.bellevueschools.org
Bellevue HS | 800/9-12
200 Oakland Ave 44811 | 419-484-5070
Francis Scruci, prin. | Fax 483-7157
Bellevue JHS, 215 North St 44811 | 400/7-8
John Redd, prin. | 419-484-5060

Bellville, Richland, Pop. 1,743
Clear Fork Valley Local SD | 2,000/K-12
92 Hines Ave 44813 | 419-886-3855
Daniel Freund, supt. | Fax 886-2237
www.clearfork.k12.oh.us
Clear Fork HS | 600/9-12
987 State Route 97 E 44813 | 419-886-2601
Ralph Moore, prin. | Fax 886-4749
Clear Fork MS | 500/6-8
987 State Route 97 E 44813 | 419-886-3111
Brian Brown, prin. | Fax 886-4749

Belmont, Belmont, Pop. 524
Union Local SD
Supt. — See Morristown
Union Local HS | 500/9-12
66779 Belmont Morristown Rd 43718 | 740-782-1181
Rick Jones, prin. | Fax 782-1346
Union Local MS | 400/6-8
66859 Belmont Morristown Rd 43718 | 740-782-1388
Joel Davia, prin. | Fax 782-1474

Beloit, Mahoning, Pop. 1,007
West Branch Local SD | 2,100/K-12
14277 S Main St 44609 | 330-938-9324
Dr. Scott Weingart, supt. | Fax 938-6815
www.westbranch.k12.oh.us/
West Branch HS | 800/9-12
14277 S Main St 44609 | 330-938-2183
Joseph Knoll, prin. | Fax 938-6815
West Branch MS | 600/6-8
14409 Beloit Snodes Rd 44609 | 330-938-4300
Matthew Manley, prin. | Fax 938-6815

Belpre, Washington, Pop. 6,570
Belpre CSD | 1,300/K-12
2014 Washington Blvd 45714 | 740-423-9511
Harry Fleming, supt. | Fax 423-3050
www.belpre.k12.oh.us
Belpre HS | 400/9-12
612 3rd St 45714 | 740-423-3000
Bob Hattman, prin. | Fax 423-3003
Belpre MS | 500/4-8
2000 Rockland Ave 45714 | 740-423-3010
Kathy Garrison, prin. | Fax 423-3012

Berea, Cuyahoga, Pop. 18,505
Berea CSD | 7,500/K-12
390 Fair St 44017 | 440-243-6000
Derran Wimer, supt. | Fax 234-2309
www.berea.k12.oh.us
Berea HS | 1,200/9-12
165 E Bagley Rd 44017 | 440-234-5418
Jeff Grosse, prin. | Fax 891-0317
Roehm MS | 700/6-8
7220 Pleasant Ave 44017 | 440-234-1326
Harold Booker, prin. | Fax 891-3764
Other Schools – See Brook Park, Middleburg Heights

Baldwin-Wallace College | Post-Sec.
275 Eastland Rd 44017 | 440-826-2900

Bergholz, Jefferson, Pop. 753
Edison Local SD
Supt. — See Hammondsville

Springfield MS | 400/5-8
4569 County Road 75 43908 | 740-768-2420
Robert Gill, prin. | Fax 768-2403

Berlin, Holmes
East Holmes Local SD | 1,700/PK-12
PO Box 182 44610 | 330-893-2610
Joe Wengerd, supt. | Fax 893-2838
www.eastholmes.k12.oh.us
Hiland JSHS | 400/7-12
PO Box 275 44610 | 330-893-2626
Matthew Johnson, prin. | Fax 893-3570
Other Schools – See Charm

Berlin Center, Mahoning
Western Reserve Local SD | 800/K-12
13850 W Akron Canfield Rd 44401 | 330-547-4100
Charles Swindler, supt. | Fax 547-9302
www.westernreserve.k12.oh.us
Western Reserve HS | 300/9-12
13850 W Akron Canfield Rd 44401 | 330-547-3911
Jeffrey Zatchok, prin. | Fax 547-9302
Western Reserve MS | 300/5-8
15904 W Akron Canfield Rd 44401 | 330-547-3941
Dennis Zinz, prin. | Fax 547-9302

Berlin Heights, Erie, Pop. 664
Berlin-Milan Local SD
Supt. — See Milan
Berlin-Milan MS | 400/6-8
20 Center St 44814 | 419-588-2078
Douglas Crooks, prin. | Fax 588-3212

Bethel, Clermont, Pop. 2,570
Bethel-Tate Local SD | 2,000/K-12
112 N Union St 45106 | 513-734-2238
James Smith, supt. | Fax 734-4792
www.betheltate.org
Bethel-Tate HS | 600/9-12
3420 State Route 125 45106 | 513-734-2271
Mimi Webb, prin. | Fax 734-1355
Bethel-Tate MS | 500/6-8
649 W Plane St 45106 | 513-734-2261
Steve Gill, prin. | Fax 734-0888

U.S. Grant JVSD | 2,000/9-12
718 W Plane St 45106 | 513-734-6222
Ken Morrison, supt. | Fax 734-4758
www.grantcareer.com
Grant Career Center | Vo/Tech
718 W Plane St 45106 | 513-734-6222
Kenneth Kappel, prin. | Fax 734-4758

Bethesda, Belmont, Pop. 1,399

Faith Community Christian HS | 50/9-12
321 3rd St, | 740-484-1437
April Woods, admin. | Fax 484-1435

Bettsville, Seneca, Pop. 765
Bettsville Local SD | 300/K-12
PO Box 6 44815 | 419-986-5166
Randy Pawlowski, supt. | Fax 986-6039
www.bettsville.k12.oh.us/
Bettsville HS | 100/9-12
PO Box 6 44815 | 419-986-5166
David Madaras, prin. | Fax 986-6039
Bettsville MS | 100/5-8
PO Box 6 44815 | 419-986-5166
David Madaras, prin. | Fax 986-6039

Beverly, Washington, Pop. 1,257
Fort Frye Local SD | 1,200/K-12
PO Box 1149 45715 | 740-984-2497
Robert Heinlein, supt. | Fax 984-8784
www.fortfrye.k12.oh.us
Ft. Frye JSHS | 600/7-12
PO Box 1089 45715 | 740-984-2376
Susan Rauch, prin. | Fax 984-4361

Bexley, Franklin, Pop. 12,632
Bexley CSD | 2,200/K-12
348 S Cassingham Rd 43209 | 614-231-7611
Michael Johnson, supt. | Fax 231-8448
www.bexley.k12.oh.us/
Bexley HS | 700/9-12
326 S Cassingham Rd 43209 | 614-231-4591
John Kellogg, prin. | Fax 338-2087
Bexley MS | 400/7-8
300 S Cassingham Rd 43209 | 614-237-4277
Harley Williams, prin. | Fax 338-2090

Blanchester, Clinton, Pop. 4,308
Blanchester Local SD | 1,500/K-12
3580 State Route 28 45107 | 937-783-3523
Rick Burton, supt. | Fax 783-2990
www.blanchester.k12.oh.us/
Blanchester HS | 500/9-12
4000 State Route 28 45107 | 937-783-2461
John Skaggs, prin. | Fax 783-5666
Blanchester MS | 400/6-8
4004 State Route 28 45107 | 937-783-3642
Brian Ruckel, prin. |

Bloomdale, Wood, Pop. 711
Elmwood Local SD | 800/K-12
7650 Jerry City Rd 44817 | 419-655-2583
Steven Pritts, supt. | Fax 655-3995
www.elmwood.k12.oh.us
Elmwood HS | 400/9-12
7650 Jerry City Rd 44817 | 419-655-2583
Tom Bentley, prin. |
Elmwood MS | 300/5-8
7650 Jerry City Rd 44817 | 419-655-2583
Jesse Steiner, prin. |

Bloomingburg, Fayette, Pop. 862
Miami Trace Local SD
Supt. — See Washington Court House
Miami Trace JHS | 400/7-8
103 Main St 43106 | 740-437-7344
Eric Wayne, prin. | Fax 437-6061

Bloomingdale, Jefferson, Pop. 219
Jefferson County JVSD | 740-264-5545
1509 County Road 22A 43910 | Fax 264-3144
T. Dale Edwards, supt. |
www.jcjvs.k12.oh.us
Jefferson County Joint Vocational HS | Vo/Tech
1509 County Road 22A 43910 | 740-264-5545
Todd Phillipson, prin. | Fax 264-3144

Bluffton, Allen, Pop. 3,963
Bluffton EVD | 1,200/K-12
102 S Jackson St 45817 | 419-358-5901
Rodney Russell, supt. | Fax 358-4871
www.bluffton.noacsc.org/
Bluffton HS | 400/9-12
106 W College Ave 45817 | 419-358-7941
Gregory Denecker, prin. | Fax 358-6586
Bluffton MS | 300/6-8
116 S Jackson St 45817 | 419-358-7961
Dean Giesige, prin. | Fax 358-4871

Bluffton University | Post-Sec.
1 University Dr 45817 | 419-358-3000

Boardman, Mahoning, Pop. 37,100

Hondros College | Post-Sec.
7410 South Ave 44512 | 330-896-9666

Botkins, Shelby, Pop. 1,192
Botkins Local SD | 600/K-12
PO Box 550 45306 | 937-693-4241
Connie Schneider, supt. | Fax 693-2557
www.botkins.k12.oh.us
Botkins JSHS | 300/7-12
PO Box 550 45306 | 937-693-4241
Cheryl Fark, prin. | Fax 693-2557

Bowerston, Harrison, Pop. 421
Conotton Valley Union Local SD
Supt. — See Sherrodsville
Conotton Valley JSHS | 200/7-12
7205 Cumberland Rd SW 44695 | 740-269-2711
Al Kennedy, prin. | Fax 269-4405

Bowling Green, Wood, Pop. 29,382
Bowling Green CSD | 3,000/K-12
140 S Grove St 43402 | 419-352-3576
Hugh Caumartin, supt. | Fax 352-1701
www.bgcs.k12.oh.us
Bowling Green HS | 1,100/9-12
530 W Poe Rd 43402 | 419-354-0100
Jeff Dever, prin. | Fax 354-1839
Bowling Green JHS | 500/7-8
215 W Wooster St 43402 | 419-354-0200
Lee Vincent, prin. | Fax 353-1958

Bowling Green State University | Post-Sec.
110 McFall Ctr 43403 | 419-372-2478

Bradford, Miami, Pop. 1,832
Bradford EVD | 700/K-12
760 Railroad Ave 45308 | 937-448-2770
Barbara Townsend, supt. | Fax 448-2493
www.bradford.k12.oh.us/
Bradford JSHS | 400/6-12
750 Railroad Ave 45308 | 937-448-2719
Anthony Meinerding, prin. | Fax 448-2742

Brecksville, Cuyahoga, Pop. 13,474
Brecksville-Broadview Heights CSD | 4,600/K-12
6638 Mill Rd 44141 | 440-740-4010
Steven Farnsworth, supt. | Fax 740-4014
www.bbhcsd.org
Other Schools – See Broadview Heights

Cuyahoga Valley Career Center SD
8001 Brecksville Rd 44141 | 440-526-5200
Roscoe E. Schlachter, supt. | Fax 746-8298
www.cvcc.k12.oh.us
Cuyahoga Valley Career Center | Vo/Tech
8001 Brecksville Rd 44141 | 440-526-5200
Richard Rybak, prin. | Fax 838-8929

Bridgeport, Belmont, Pop. 2,125
Bridgeport EVD | 800/K-12
501 Bennett St 43912 | 740-635-1713
Mark Matz, supt. | Fax 635-6003
www.bevs.k12.oh.us/
Bridgeport HS | 300/9-12
501 Bennett St 43912 | 740-635-0853
Rob Zitzelsberger, prin. | Fax 635-6003
Kirkwood MS, 501 Bennett St 43912 | 200/6-8
Rob Zitzelsberger, prin. | 740-635-0853

Brilliant, Jefferson, Pop. 1,604
Buckeye Local SD
Supt. — See Dillonvale
Buckeye North MS | 200/6-8
1004 3rd St 43913 | 740-598-4540
Joyce Palmer, prin. | Fax 598-4145

Bristolville, Trumbull
Bristol Local SD | 800/K-12
PO Box 260 44402 | 330-889-3053
Dr. Marty Santillo, supt. | Fax 889-2529
www.bristol.k12.oh.us
Bristol HS | 400/7-12
PO Box 260 44402 | 330-889-2621
Gene Jones, prin. | Fax 889-2529

Broadview Heights, Cuyahoga, Pop. 16,721
Brecksville-Broadview Heights CSD
Supt. — See Brecksville
Brecksville-Broadview Heights HS | 1,500/9-12
6380 Mill Rd 44147 | 440-740-4700
Brian Wilch, prin. | Fax 740-4704
Brecksville-Broadview Heights MS | 1,100/6-8
6376 Mill Rd 44147 | 440-740-4400
Wendy Baker, prin. | Fax 740-4404

Lawrence S | 200/1-12
1551 E Wallings Rd 44147 | 440-526-0003
Mimi Mayer, prin. | Fax 526-0595

Vatterott College - Cleveland | Post-Sec.
5025 E Royalton Rd 44147 | 440-526-1660

Brookfield, Trumbull
Brookfield Local SD | 1,400/K-12
PO Box 209 44403 | 330-448-4930
Michael Notar, supt. | Fax 448-5026
www.brookfield.k12.oh.us/
Brookfield HS, PO Box 209 44403 | 500/9-12
John Yensick, prin. | 330-448-3001
Brookfield MS | 500/5-8
PO Box 209 44403 | 330-448-3003
Tim Filipovich, prin. | Fax 448-5028

Brooklyn, Cuyahoga, Pop. 11,276
Brooklyn CSD | 1,300/K-12
9200 Biddulph Rd 44144 | 216-485-8110
Jefferey Lampert, supt. | Fax 485-8118
www.brooklyn.k12.oh.us/
Brooklyn HS | 400/9-12
9200 Biddulph Rd 44144 | 216-485-8162
Gretchen Derethik, prin. | Fax 485-8124
Brooklyn MS | 300/6-8
9200 Biddulph Rd 44144 | 216-485-8127
Tom Russo, prin. | Fax 485-8118

Brook Park, Cuyahoga, Pop. 20,679
Berea CSD
Supt. — See Berea
Ford MS | 1,100/6-8
17001 Holland Rd 44142 | 216-433-1133
Michael Pelegrino, prin. | Fax 676-2072

Brookville, Montgomery, Pop. 5,279
Brookville Local SD | 1,600/K-12
325 Simmons Ave 45309 | 937-833-2181
Timothy Hopkins, supt. | Fax 833-2787
www.brookville.k12.oh.us/
Brookville HS | 500/9-12
1 Blue Pride Dr 45309 | 937-833-6761
Chris Bronner, prin. | Fax 833-6302
Brookville IS | 600/4-8
2 Blue Pride Dr 45309 | 937-833-6731
Brian Boyd, prin. | Fax 833-6756

Brunswick, Medina, Pop. 34,788
Brunswick CSD | 7,200/K-12
3643 Center Rd 44212 | 330-225-7731
James Hayas, supt. | Fax 273-0507
www.brunswickschools.org
Brunswick HS | 2,200/9-12
3581 Center Rd 44212 | 330-225-7731
Michael Mayell, prin. | Fax 225-5393
Edwards MS | 500/6-8
1497 Pearl Rd 44212 | 330-225-7731
Kent Morgan, prin. | Fax 273-0519
Visintainer MS | 500/6-8
1459 Pearl Rd 44212 | 330-225-7731
Carol Yost, prin. | Fax 273-0400
Willetts MS | 700/6-8
1045 Hadcock Rd 44212 | 330-225-7731
Mike Hodson, prin. | Fax 273-0222

Bryan, Williams, Pop. 8,241
Bryan CSD | 2,300/PK-12
1350 Fountain Grove Dr 43506 | 419-636-6973
James Gunner, supt. | Fax 636-0313
www.bryan.k12.oh.us
Bryan HS | 800/9-12
150 S Portland St 43506 | 419-636-4536
Norm Glismann, prin. | Fax 636-0313
Bryan MS | 900/4-8
1301 Center St 43506 | 419-636-6766
Beth Hollabaugh, prin. | Fax 636-6903

Bucyrus, Crawford, Pop. 12,945
Bucyrus CSD | 2,000/PK-12
630 Jump St 44820 | 419-562-4045
Paul Johnson Ph.D., supt. | Fax 562-3990
www.bucyrus.k12.oh.us
Bucyrus HS | 600/9-12
900 W Perry St 44820 | 419-562-7721
James C. Oyster, prin. | Fax 562-7819
Bucyrus MS | 600/5-8
245 Woodlawn Ave 44820 | 419-562-0003
Wm. Todd Roll, prin. | Fax 562-1773

Wynford Local SD | 1,100/K-12
3288 Holmes Center Rd 44820 | 419-562-7828
Samuel L. Preston, supt. | Fax 562-7825
www.wynford.k12.oh.us
Wynford JSHS | 500/7-12
3288 Holmes Center Rd 44820 | 419-562-7828
Scott Langenderfer, prin. | Fax 562-7825

Burton, Geauga, Pop. 1,444
Berkshire Local SD | 1,200/K-12
PO Box 364 44021 | 440-834-4123
James Knapp, supt. | Fax 834-2058
www.berkshire.k12.oh.us
Berkshire JSHS | 700/7-12
PO Box 365 44021 | 440-834-4110
Steve Reedy, prin. | Fax 834-0440

Kent State University-Geauga Campus | Post-Sec.
14111 Claridon Troy Rd 44021 | 440-834-4187

Byesville, Guernsey, Pop. 2,611
Rolling Hills Local SD
Supt. — See Cambridge
Meadowbrook HS | 700/9-12
58615 Marietta Rd 43723 | 740-685-2566
Charles Chippi, prin. | Fax 685-2797
Meadowbrook MS | 500/6-8
58607 Marietta Rd 43723 | 740-685-2561
Larry Touvell, prin. | Fax 685-2628

Cadiz, Harrison, Pop. 3,373
Belmont-Harrison Area JVSD
Supt. — See Saint Clairsville
Harrison Career Center | Vo/Tech
82500 Cadiz Jewett Rd 43907 | 740-942-2148
Kenneth Woodford, prin. | Fax 695-4866

Harrison Hills CSD
Supt. — See Hopedale
Harrison Central HS | 600/9-12
440 E Market St 43907 | 740-912-7700
James Rocchi, prin.

Caldwell, Noble, Pop. 1,760
Caldwell EVD | 1,000/K-12
516 Fairground St 43724 | 740-732-5637
William Brelsford, supt. | Fax 732-7303
www.caldwell.k12.oh.us
Caldwell HS, 516 Fairground St 43724 | 300/9-12
J. Scott Cleland, prin. | 740-732-5634

Caledonia, Marion, Pop. 565
River Valley Local SD | 1,800/K-12
197 Brocklesby Rd 43314 | 740-725-5400
Thomas G. Shade, supt. | Fax 725-5499
www.rivervalley.k12.oh.us
River Valley HS | 600/9-12
4280 Marion Mount Gilead Rd 43314 | 740-725-5800
David R. Gorenflo, prin. | Fax 725-5899
River Valley MS | 500/6-8
4334 Marion Mount Gilead Rd 43314 | 740-725-5700
Glenn E. Crawford, prin. | Fax 725-5799

Cambridge, Guernsey, Pop. 11,596
Cambridge CSD | 2,700/K-12
6111 Fairdale Dr 43725 | 740-439-5021
Susan Purdue, supt. | Fax 439-9284
www.cambridge.k12.oh.us/
Cambridge HS | 800/9-12
65328 Creek Rd 43725 | 740-435-1100
Frank Blake, prin. | Fax 435-1101
Cambridge MS | 600/6-8
65370 Creek Rd 43725 | 740-435-1140
Doug Thoburn, prin. | Fax 435-1141

Rolling Hills Local SD | 2,200/K-12
60851 Southgate Rd 43725 | 740-432-5370
Gary Norris, supt. | Fax 435-8312
www.omeresa.net/Schools/Meadowbrook/
Other Schools – See Byesville

Camden, Preble, Pop. 2,291
Preble-Shawnee Local SD | 1,300/K-12
124 Barbee St 45311 | 937-452-3323
Kleetis McGhee, supt. | Fax 452-3926
www.preble-shawnee.k12.oh.us
Preble-Shawnee HS | 500/9-12
5495 Somers Gratis Rd 45311 | 937-787-3541
Richard McKee, prin. | Fax 787-3664
Preble-Shawnee JHS | 300/7-8
5495 Somers Gratis Rd 45311 | 937-787-3519
Dianna Whitis, prin. | Fax 787-3664

Campbell, Mahoning, Pop. 9,020
Campbell CSD | 1,600/K-12
280 6th St 44405 | 330-799-8777
Thomas Robey, supt. | Fax 799-0875
www.campbell.k12.oh.us
Campbell MS | 500/5-8
2002 Community Cir 44405 | 330-799-0054
Marcia Norris, prin. | Fax 799-8259
Memorial HS | 500/9-12
280 6th St 44405 | 330-799-1515
Richard Gozur, prin. | Fax 799-6390

Canal Fulton, Stark, Pop. 5,017
Northwest Local SD | 1,900/K-12
104 Market St W 44614 | 330-854-2291
Dennis Lambes, supt.
www.northwest.sparcc.org/
Northwest HS | 800/9-12
8590 Erie Ave N 44614 | 330-854-2205
Stephen Jones, prin. | Fax 854-2030
Northwest MS | 400/7-8
8540 Erie Ave N 44614 | 330-854-3303
Robert Venables, prin. | Fax 854-5883

Canal Winchester, Franklin, Pop. 5,193
Canal Winchester Local SD | 2,600/K-12
290 Washington St 43110 | 614-837-4533
Jeff Childers, supt. | Fax 833-2165
www.canalwin.k12.oh.us
Canal Winchester HS | 700/9-12
300 Washington St 43110 | 614-833-2157
Lynn Landis, prin. | Fax 833-2163
Canal Winchester MS | 400/7-8
100 Washington St 43110 | 614-833-2151
Cassandra Miller, prin. | Fax 833-2173

Harvest Preparatory S | 600/PK-12
4595 Gender Rd 43110 | 614-837-1990
Jack Johnson, hdmstr. | Fax 837-9591

Canfield, Mahoning, Pop. 7,188
Canfield Local SD | 3,100/K-12
100 Wadsworth St 44406 | 330-533-3303
Dante J. Zambrini, supt. | Fax 533-6827
canfield.access-k12.org
Canfield HS | 1,100/9-12
100 Cardinal Dr 44406 | 330-533-5507
Abby Barone, prin. | Fax 533-1919
Canfield Village MS | 1,000/5-8
42 Wadsworth St 44406 | 330-533-5544
Ronald Infante, prin. | Fax 702-7064

Mahoning County JVSD |
7300 N Palmyra Rd 44406 | 330-729-4000
Roan M. Craig, supt. | Fax 729-4050
Mahoning County Career & Technical Ctr | Vo/Tech
7300 N Palmyra Rd 44406 | 330-729-4000
Edward Kapusinski, dir. | Fax 729-4015

Canton, Stark, Pop. 79,255
Canton CSD | 12,500/PK-12
617 Mckinley Ave SW 44707 | 330-438-2500
Dianne Talarico, supt. | Fax 455-0682
www.ccsdistrict.org
Crenshaw MS | 900/6-8
2525 19th St NE 44705 | 330-454-7717
Edward A Rehfus, prin. | Fax 588-2120
Early College HS | 9-12
231 Mckinley Ave NW 44702 | 330-458-3950
Tom Forbes, prin.

Freshman Academy | 300/9-9
1510 Clarendon Ave NW 44708 | 330-451-3334
Marilyn Van Almen, prin.
Hartford MS | 400/6-8
1824 3rd St SE 44707 | 330-453-6012
Stephanie L. Patrick, prin. | Fax 453-5096
Lehman MS | 600/6-8
1400 Broad Ave NW 44708 | 330-456-1963
David I. McDermott, prin. | Fax 456-6431
McKinley HS | 2,000/9-12
2323 17th St NW 44708 | 330-438-2712
Jeffrey Talbert, prin. | Fax 580-2712
Souers MS | 700/6-8
2800 13th St SW 44710 | 330-456-8779
Barbara Maceyak, prin. | Fax 438-2788
Timken HS | 900/9-12
521 Tuscarawas St W 44702 | 330-438-2602
Kim Redmond, prin. | Fax 580-3508
Community Educational Services | Adult
617 Mckinley Ave SW 44707 | 330-438-2559
John Pieper, prin.

Canton Local SD | 2,500/K-12
4526 Ridge Ave SE 44707 | 330-484-8010
Teresa Purses, supt. | Fax 484-8032
www.cantonlocal.org
Canton South HS | 900/9-12
600 Faircrest St SE 44707 | 330-484-8000
G. Ira Wentworth, prin. | Fax 484-8013
Faircrest Memorial MS | 600/6-8
616 Faircrest St SW 44706 | 330-484-8015
Timothy Welker, prin. | Fax 484-8033

Plain Local SD | 6,100/K-12
901 44th St NW 44709 | 330-492-3500
Jacqueline DeGarmo, supt. | Fax 493-5542
www.plainlocal.org/
Glenoak HS | 2,100/9-12
1015 44th St NW 44709 | 330-492-7768
Mark Hartman, prin. | Fax 493-5541
Pleasant View S for Arts | 400/4-8
3000 Columbus Rd NE 44705 | 330-452-7453
C. Digman, prin. | Fax 452-6657
Taft MS | 600/6-8
3829 Guilford Ave NW 44718 | 330-493-5505
Cynthia Donnelly, prin. | Fax 493-5508
Other Schools – See North Canton

Aultman Hospital | Post-Sec.
2600 6th St SW 44710 | 330-438-6241
Central Catholic HS | 700/9-12
4824 Tuscarawas St W 44708 | 330-478-2131
Fr. Robert Kaylor, prin. | Fax 478-6086
Heritage Christian S | 400/PK-12
2107 6th St SW 44706 | 330-452-8271
Howard Pizor, prin. | Fax 452-0672
Malone College | Post-Sec.
515 25th St NW 44709 | 330-471-8100
National Beauty College | Post-Sec.
4642 Cleveland Ave NW 44709 | 330-499-9444
Timken Mercy Medical Center | Post-Sec.
1320 Mercy Dr NW 44708 | 330-489-1001

Cardington, Morrow, Pop. 1,979
Cardington-Lincoln Local SD | 1,200/K-12
121 Nichols St 43315 | 419-864-3691
Mark Wilcheck, supt. | Fax 864-0946
Cardington-Lincoln HS | 400/9-12
349 Chesterville Ave 43315 | 419-864-2691
William Clauss, prin. | Fax 864-9515
Cardington-Lincoln MS | 300/6-8
349 Chesterville Ave 43315 | 419-864-0609
Roger Jury, prin. | Fax 864-9515

Carey, Wyandot, Pop. 3,864
Carey EVD | 900/K-12
357 E South St 43316 | 419-396-7922
Raymond Funk, supt. | Fax 396-3158
carey.k12.oh.us/
Carey JSHS | 500/7-12
357 E South St 43316 | 419-396-7638
Karl Vehre, prin. | Fax 396-3158

Carlisle, Warren, Pop. 5,522
Carlisle Local SD | 1,800/K-12
724 Fairview Dr 45005 | 937-746-0710
Timothy J. McLinden, supt. | Fax 746-0438
www.carlisle-local.k12.oh.us
Carlisle HS | 600/9-12
250 Jamaica Rd 45005 | 937-746-4481
Matt Bishop, prin. | Fax 937-6578
Chamberlain MS | 400/6-8
720 Fairview Dr 45005 | 937-746-3227
Mike Milner, prin. | Fax 746-0519

Carroll, Fairfield, Pop. 479
Bloom-Carroll Local SD | 1,500/K-12
PO Box 338 43112 | 614-837-6560
James Herd, supt. | Fax 756-7466
www.bloom-carroll.k12.oh.us
Bloom-Carroll HS | 500/9-12
5240 Plum Rd 43112 | 740-756-4318
Roger Mace, prin. | Fax 756-9525
Bloom-Carroll MS | 300/6-8
PO Box 338 43112 | 740-756-9231
Timothy Winland, prin. | Fax 756-7466

Eastland-Fairfield Career & Technical SD
Supt. — See Groveport
Fairfield Career Center | Vo/Tech
4000 Columbus Lncster Rd NW 43112
| 614-837-9443
Bonnie Hopkins, prin. | Fax 837-9447

Carrollton, Carroll, Pop. 3,306
Carrollton EVD | 2,700/PK-12
252 3rd St NE 44615 | 330-627-2181
Kevin J. Spears, supt. | Fax 627-2182
www.carrollton.k12.oh.us
Bell-Herron MS, 252 3rd St NE 44615 | 600/6-8
Robert Mehno, prin. | 330-627-7188
Carrollton HS, 252 3rd St NE 44615 | 1,000/9-12
David Davis, prin. | 330-627-2134

Casstown, Miami, Pop. 315
Miami East Local SD 1,100/K-12
3825 N State Route 589 45312 937-335-7505
Todd Rappold, supt. Fax 335-6309
www.miamieast.k12.oh.us
Miami East HS 500/9-12
3825 N State Route 589 45312 937-335-7070
Tim Williams, prin. Fax 335-7505
Miami East JHS 300/6-8
4025 N State Route 589 45312 937-335-5439
Allen Mack, prin. Fax 332-7927

Castalia, Erie, Pop. 925
Margaretta Local SD 1,500/K-12
305 S Washington St 44824 419-684-5322
Edward Kurt, supt. Fax 684-9003
www.margaretta.k12.oh.us/
Margaretta JSHS, 209 Lowell St 44824 700/7-12
Keith Bonnigson, prin. 419-684-5351

Cedarville, Greene, Pop. 4,085
Cedar Cliff Local SD 700/K-12
PO Box 45 45314 937-766-6000
David Baits, supt. Fax 766-4717
www.cedarcliff.k12.oh.us
Cedarville JSHS 300/7-12
PO Box 45 45314 937-766-1871
Virginia Potter, prin. Fax 766-5211

Cedarville University Post-Sec.
251 N Main St 45314 937-766-2211

Celina, Mercer, Pop. 10,275
Celina CSD 3,100/K-12
585 E Livingston St 45822 419-586-8300
Matt Miller, supt. Fax 586-7046
www.celinaschools.org
Celina HS 1,200/9-12
715 E Wayne St 45822 419-586-8300
Curt Shellabarger, prin. Fax 584-0307
Celina MS 500/7-8
615 Holly St 45822 419-586-8300
Ann Esselstein, prin. Fax 586-9166

Wright State University Post-Sec.
7600 State Route 703 45822 419-586-0300

Centerburg, Knox, Pop. 1,469
Centerburg Local SD 1,100/K-12
175 Union St 43011 740-625-6346
Dorothy B. Holden, supt. Fax 625-9939
Centerburg HS 300/9-12
3782 Columbus Rd 43011 740-625-6055
John Morgan, prin. Fax 625-5799
Centerburg MS 300/6-8
3782 Columbus Rd 43011 740-625-6055
Mike Hebenthal, prin. Fax 625-5799

Centerville, Montgomery, Pop. 23,273
Centerville CSD 8,000/K-12
111 Virginia Ave 45458 937-433-8841
Gary P. Smiga, supt. Fax 438-6057
www.centerville.k12.oh.us
Centerville HS 2,700/9-12
500 E Franklin St 45459 937-439-3500
Eileen Booher, prin. Fax 439-3574
Magsig MS 600/6-8
192 W Franklin St 45459 937-433-0965
S. Westendorf-Wozniak, prin. Fax 433-5256
Tower Heights MS 600/6-8
195 N Johanna Dr 45459 937-434-0383
Clint Freese, prin. Fax 434-3033
Other Schools – See Dayton

RETS Technical Center Post-Sec.
555 E Alex Bell Rd 45459 937-433-3410
Spring Valley Academy 400/K-12
1461 E Spring Valley Pike 45458 937-433-0790
Bradley Durby, prin. Fax 433-0914

Chagrin Falls, Cuyahoga, Pop. 3,912
Chagrin Falls EVD 2,000/PK-12
400 E Washington St 44022 440-247-4363
Dr. David Axner, supt. Fax 247-5883
www.chagrin-falls.k12.oh.us
Chagrin Falls HS 700/9-12
400 E Washington St 44022 440-247-2072
Robert Hunt, prin. Fax 247-2071
Chagrin Falls MS 300/7-8
342 E Washington St 44022 440-247-4746
Eileen Parmelee, prin. Fax 247-4855

Kenston Local SD 3,100/K-12
17419 Snyder Rd 44023 440-543-9677
Robert Lee, supt. Fax 543-8634
www.kenstonlocal.com
Kenston HS 1,000/9-12
17425 Snyder Rd 44023 440-543-9821
Christopher Lewis, prin. Fax 543-9021
Kenston MS 800/6-8
17419 Snyder Rd 44023 440-543-8241
Patricia Brockway, prin. Fax 543-4851

English Nanny and Governess School Post-Sec.
37 S Franklin St 44022 440-247-0600

Chardon, Geauga, Pop. 5,270
Chardon Local SD 3,200/K-12
428 North St 44024 440-285-4052
Joseph Bergant, supt. Fax 285-7229
www.chardon.k12.oh.us
Chardon HS 1,100/9-12
151 Chardon Ave 44024 440-285-4057
Doug Delong, prin. Fax 285-9463
Chardon MS 800/6-8
424 North St 44024 440-285-4062
Tom Solet, prin. Fax 286-0461

Notre Dame-Cathedral Latin HS 800/9-12
13000 Auburn Rd 44024 440-286-6226
Sr. Margaret Gorman, prin. Fax 286-7199

Charm, Holmes
East Holmes Local SD
Supt. — See Berlin
Wise MS, PO Box 159 44617 100/5-8
Jon Wilson, prin. 330-893-2505

Chesapeake, Lawrence, Pop. 856
Chesapeake Union EVD 1,300/K-12
10183 County Road 1 45619 740-867-3135
Samuel Hall, supt. Fax 867-3136
www.peake.k12.oh.us
Chesapeake HS 400/9-12
10181 County Road 1 45619 740-867-5958
Joseph Rase, prin. Fax 867-1130
Chesapeake MS 400/5-8
10335 County Road 1 45619 740-867-3972
Kim Wells, prin. Fax 867-1120

Lawrence County JVSD
11627 State Route 243 45619 740-867-6641
Stephen Dodgion, supt. Fax 867-2009
www.collins-cc.k12.oh.us
Lawrence County Joint Vocational SHS Vo/Tech
11627 State Route 243 45619 740-867-6641
Fax 867-2009

Collins Career Center Post-Sec.
11627 State Route 243 45619 740-867-6641

Cheshire, Gallia, Pop. 85
Gallia County Local SD
Supt. — See Gallipolis
Kyger Creek MS 200/5-8
350 Watson Grove Rd 45620 740-367-7721
Silos Johnson, prin. Fax 367-5005
River Valley HS 600/9-12
1428 Little Kyger Rd 45620 740-367-7377
J. Michael Jacobs, prin. Fax 367-7249

Chesterland, Geauga, Pop. 2,078
West Geauga Local SD 2,500/K-12
8615 Cedar Rd 44026 440-729-5900
Anthony Podojil, supt. Fax 729-5939
www.westgeauga.k12.oh.us
West Geauga HS 900/9-12
13401 Chillicothe Rd 44026 440-729-5950
Joseph Mueller, prin. Fax 729-5959
West Geauga MS 600/6-8
8611 Cedar Rd 44026 440-729-5940
James Kish, prin. Fax 729-5909

Chillicothe, Ross, Pop. 22,170
Chillicothe CSD 3,400/K-12
235 Cherry St 45601 740-775-4250
Roger Crago, supt. Fax 775-4270
www.chillicothe.k12.oh.us
Chillicothe HS 1,100/9-12
381 Yoctangee Pkwy 45601 740-702-2287
John Payne, prin. Fax 773-1097
Smith MS 600/6-8
345 Arch St 45601 740-773-2241
Robert Crabtree, prin. Fax 774-9482

Huntington Local SD 1,400/K-12
188 Huntsman Rd 45601 740-663-5892
John Barr, supt. Fax 663-6078
www.hunt.k12.oh.us/
Huntington HS 400/9-12
188 Huntsman Rd 45601 740-663-2230
Tim Butler, prin. Fax 663-5042
Huntington MS 300/6-8
188 Huntsman Rd 45601 740-663-6079
Alice Kellough, prin. Fax 663-6080

Pickaway-Ross County JVSD
895 Crouse Chapel Rd 45601 740-642-1200
Brett Smith, supt. Fax 642-1399
www.pickawayross.com
Pickaway-Ross Career & Technology Center Vo/Tech
895 Crouse Chapel Rd 45601 740-642-1200
Judy Wells, prin. Fax 642-1399

Southeastern Local SD 900/K-12
2003 Lancaster Rd 45601 740-774-2003
Brian Justice, supt. Fax 774-1687
www.sepanthers.k12.oh.us/
Southeastern HS 300/9-12
2003 Lancaster Rd 45601 740-774-2003
Leonard Steyer, prin. Fax 774-1684
Southeastern MS 200/5-8
2003 Lancaster Rd 45601 740-774-2003
David Shea, prin. Fax 774-1684

Union-Scioto Local SD 1,800/K-12
1565 Egypt Pike 45601 740-773-4102
Dwight Garrett, supt. Fax 775-2852
gsn.k12.oh.us/unioto/index.htm
Unioto HS 600/9-12
14193 Pleasant Valley Rd 45601 740-773-4105
James Osborne, prin. Fax 774-9158
Unioto JHS 300/7-8
160 Moundsville Rd 45601 740-773-5211
Ron Lovely, prin. Fax 772-2974

Zane Trace Local SD 1,800/K-12
946 State Route 180 45601 740-775-1355
Ernest Hamilton, supt. Fax 773-0249
gsn.k12.oh.us:16080/zanetrace/
Zane Trace HS 700/7-12
946 State Route 180 45601 740-775-1809
Todd Holdren, prin. Fax 775-1301
Zane Trace MS 500/5-8
946 State Route 180 45601 740-773-9854
Bret Mavis, prin.

Ohio University Post-Sec.
PO Box 629 45601 740-774-7200
Recording Workshop Post-Sec.
455 Massieville Rd 45601 740-663-1000
Southeastern Business College Post-Sec.
1855 Western Ave 45601 740-774-6300

Cincinnati, Hamilton, Pop. 317,361
Cincinnati CSD, PO Box 5381 45201 34,800/PK-12
Rosa Blackwell, supt. 513-363-0000
www.cps-k12.org
Aiken Traditional HS 400/9-12
5641 Belmont Ave 45224 513-363-6600
Susan Raudabaugh, prin. Fax 363-6620
Bloom Accelerated MS 300/6-8
1941 Baymiller St 45214 513-363-6500
Joseph Porter, prin. Fax 363-6520
Clark Montessori S 600/7-12
3030 Erie Ave 45208 513-363-7100
Thomas Rothwell, prin. Fax 363-7120
Creative & Performing Arts S 1,000/4-12
1310 Sycamore St 45202 513-363-8000
Clarence Crum, prin. Fax 363-8020
Dater HS 700/7-12
2146 Ferguson Rd 45238 513-363-7200
Beverly Eby, prin. Fax 363-7220
Hughes Center HS 1,500/9-12
2515 Clifton Ave 45219 513-363-7500
Michael Holbrook, prin. Fax 363-7545
Jacobs HS 500/7-12
5641 Belmont Ave 45224 513-363-7400
Susan Raudabaugh, prin. Fax 363-7420
Shroder Paideia Academy 600/7-12
3500 Lumford Pl 45213 513-363-6900
Yenetta Harper, prin. Fax 363-6920
Taft HS 600/9-12
420 Ezzard Charles Dr 45214 513-363-8200
Anthony Smith, prin. Fax 363-8220
Walnut Hills JSHS 1,900/7-12
3250 Victory Pkwy 45207 513-363-8400
Marvin Koenig, prin. Fax 363-8420
Western Hills HS 1,100/9-12
2144 Ferguson Rd 45238 513-363-8900
Stephanie Morton, prin. Fax 363-8920
Withrow HS 400/10-12
2488 Madison Rd 45208 513-363-9000
Charlene Cleveland, prin. Fax 363-9020
Woodward Career Technical S Vo/Tech
7001 Reading Rd 45237 513-363-9300
J. Larry Ballew, prin. Fax 363-9320
Woodward SHS 200/11-12
7001 Reading Rd 45237 513-363-9500
Sammy Yates, prin. Fax 363-9520

Deer Park Community CSD 1,400/K-12
8688 Donna Ln 45236 513-891-0222
Kimberlee Gray, supt. Fax 891-2930
www.deerparkcityschools.org
Deer Park JSHS 700/7-12
8351 Plainfield Rd 45236 513-891-0010
Michelle Walker-Glenn, prin. Fax 891-3845

Finneytown Local SD 1,800/K-12
8916 Fontainebleau Ter 45231 513-728-3700
Randall Parsons, supt. Fax 931-0986
www.finneytown.org
Finneytown HS 900/7-12
8916 Fontainebleau Ter 45231 513-931-0712
Gregg Tracy, prin. Fax 728-7230

Forest Hills Local SD 7,500/K-12
7550 Forest Rd 45255 513-231-3600
John B. Patzwald Ph.D., supt. Fax 231-3830
www.foresthills.edu
Anderson HS 1,500/9-12
7560 Forest Rd 45255 513-232-2772
Diana Carter, prin. Fax 232-3146
Nagel MS 1,200/7-8
1500 Nagel Rd 45255 513-474-5407
Natasha Adams, prin. Fax 474-5584
Turpin HS 1,100/9-12
2650 Bartels Rd 45244 513-232-7770
Peggy Johnson, prin. Fax 232-9047

Great Oaks Institute of Technology
3254 E Kemper Rd 45241 513-771-8840
Roberta White, supt. Fax 771-6575
www.greatoaks.com
Diamond Oaks CDC Vo/Tech
6375 Harrison Ave 45247 513-574-1300
Dave Buchwalter, prin. Fax 574-3953
Scarlet Oaks CDC Vo/Tech
3254 E Kemper Rd 45241 513-771-8810
Nancy Mulvey, prin. Fax 771-4928
Other Schools – See Milford, Wilmington

Indian Hill EVD 2,200/K-12
6855 Drake Rd 45243 513-272-4500
Jane Knudson Ed.D., supt. Fax 272-4512
www.ih.k12.oh.us
Indian Hill HS 700/9-12
6865 Drake Rd 45243 513-272-4550
Terence Barton, prin. Fax 272-4557
Indian Hill MS 500/6-8
6845 Drake Rd 45243 513-272-4642
Brian Frank, prin. Fax 272-4690

Lockland CSD 700/K-12
210 N Cooper Ave 45215 513-563-5000
Donna Hubbard, supt. Fax 563-9611
www.locklandschools.org
Other Schools – See Lockland

Madeira CSD 1,500/K-12
7465 Loannes Dr 45243 513-985-6070
Stephen M. Kramer, supt. Fax 985-6072
www.madeiracityschools.org
Madeira HS 500/9-12
7465 Loannes Dr 45243 513-891-8222
Chris Mate, prin. Fax 985-6089
Other Schools – See Milford

Mariemont CSD 1,700/K-12
6743 Chestnut St 45227 513-272-7500
Gerald Harris, supt. Fax 527-3436
www.mariemontschools.org
Mariemont HS 500/9-12
3812 Pocahontas Ave 45227 513-272-7600
Jim Renner, prin. Fax 527-5991

Mariemont JHS 300/7-8
6743 Chestnut St 45227 513-272-7300
Keith Koehne, prin. Fax 527-3432

Mt. Healthy CSD 4,000/PK-12
7615 Harrison Ave 45231 513-729-0077
David Horine, supt. Fax 728-4692
www.mthcs.org/
Mt. Healthy HS 1,100/9-12
2046 Adams Rd 45231 513-728-7644
Jack Fisher, prin. Fax 728-4695
North MS 300/7-8
2170 Struble Rd 45231 513-742-6016
Eugene Blalock, prin. Fax 728-4691
South MS 300/7-8
1917 Miles Rd 45231 513-742-0666
Kevin Mays, prin. Fax 742-2797

North College Hill CSD 1,500/K-12
1498 W Galbraith Rd 45231 513-728-4770
Gary Gellert, supt. Fax 728-4774
www.nchcityschools.org
North College Hill JSHS 700/7-12
1620 W Galbraith Rd 45239 513-728-4783
Kelly Hughes, prin. Fax 728-4791

Northwest Local SD 10,700/PK-12
3240 Banning Rd 45239 513-923-1000
Richard Glatfelter, supt. Fax 923-3644
www.nwlsd.org
Colerain MS 2,100/9-12
8801 Cheviot Rd 45251 513-385-6424
Maureen Heintz, prin. Fax 741-5032
Colerain MS 700/6-8
4700 Poole Rd 45251 513-385-8490
Mark Farmer, prin. Fax 385-6685
Northwest HS 1,300/9-12
10761 Pippin Rd 45231 513-851-7300
Bob Reynolds, prin. Fax 742-6376
Pleasant Run MS 1,000/6-8
11770 Pippin Rd 45231 513-851-2400
David Maine, prin. Fax 851-7071
White Oak MS 800/6-8
3130 Jessup Rd 45239 513-741-4300
Traci Rea, prin. Fax 741-0717

Oak Hills Local SD 8,100/K-12
6325 Rapid Run Rd 45233 513-574-3200
Patricia Brenneman, supt. Fax 598-2947
www.oakhills.k12.oh.us
Bridgetown MS 700/6-8
3900 Race Rd 45211 513-574-3511
Tim Cybulski, prin. Fax 574-6689
Delhi MS 600/6-8
5280 Foley Rd 45238 513-922-8400
Marni Durham, prin. Fax 922-8472
Oak Hills HS 3,000/9-12
3200 Ebenezer Rd 45248 513-922-2300
Jeff Brandt, prin. Fax 451-3795
Rapid Run MS 600/6-8
6345 Rapid Run Rd 45233 513-574-3200
Robert Sehlhorst, prin.

Princeton CSD 6,000/PK-12
25 W Sharon Rd 45246 513-771-8560
Aaron Mackey, supt. Fax 771-3454
www.princeton.k12.oh.us
Community MS 1,000/6-8
11157 Chester Rd 45246 513-552-8500
Mario Basora, prin. Fax 552-8511
Princeton HS 1,900/9-12
11080 Chester Rd 45246 513-552-8200
Raymond Spicher, prin. Fax 552-8224

Sycamore CSD 5,700/K-12
4881 Cooper Rd 45242 513-686-1700
Dr. Adrienne James, supt. Fax 791-4873
www.sycamoreschools.org
Sycamore HS 2,000/9-12
7400 Cornell Rd 45242 513-686-1770
Kenji Matsudo, prin. Fax 489-7425
Sycamore JHS 1,000/7-8
5757 Cooper Rd 45242 513-686-1760
Karen Naber, prin. Fax 891-3162

West Clermont Local SD 9,000/K-12
4350 Aicholtz Rd 45245 513-943-5000
Gary Brooks, supt. Fax 752-6158
www.westcler.k12.oh.us
Glen Este HS 1,400/9-12
4342 Glen Este Wthmsvlle Rd 45245 513-947-7600
Dennis Ashworth, prin. Fax 943-7090
Glen Este MS 1,100/6-8
4342 Glen Este Wthmsvlle Rd 45245 513-947-7700
Kevin Thacker, prin. Fax 753-3462
Other Schools – See Batavia

Winton Woods CSD 4,100/K-12
1215 W Kemper Rd 45240 513-619-2300
Camille Nasbe, supt. Fax 619-2309
www.wintonwoods.org
Winton Woods HS 1,300/9-12
1231 W Kemper Rd 45240 513-619-2420
Anita Williams, prin.
Winton Woods MS 700/7-8
147 Farragut Rd 45218 513-619-2240
Beverly Hood, prin.

Aldersgate Christian Academy 200/K-12
1810 Young St 45202 513-721-7944
David Crosley, prin. Fax 721-1357
Antonelli College Post-Sec.
124 E 7th St 45202 800-505-4338
Art Academy of Cincinnati Post-Sec.
1212 Jackson St 45202 513-562-6262
Art Institute of Cincinnati Post-Sec.
1171 E Kemper Rd 45246 513-751-1206
Art Institute of Ohio - Cincinnati Post-Sec.
1011 Glendale-Milford Rd 45215 513-771-2829
Athenaeum of Ohio Post-Sec.
6616 Beechmont Ave 45230 513-231-2223
Bacon HS 700/9-12
4320 Vine St 45217 513-641-1300
Thomas Devolve, prin. Fax 641-0498

Brown Mackie College Post-Sec.
1011 Glendale Milford Rd 45215 513-771-2424
Central Baptist Academy 200/K-12
7645 Winton Rd 45224 513-521-5481
Richard Voiles, admin. Fax 521-5481
Christ Hospital Post-Sec.
2139 Auburn Ave 45219 513-369-2201
Christian Center Academy 200/PK-12
717 Barg Salt Run Rd 45244 513-528-7123
Pamela Walling, prin. Fax 528-7130
Cincinnati Christian University Post-Sec.
PO Box 4320 45204 513-244-8100
Cincinnati College of Mortuary Science Post-Sec.
645 W North Bend Rd 45224 513-761-2020
Cincinnati Country Day S 900/K-12
6905 Given Rd 45243 513-561-7298
Dr. Robert Macrae, hdmstr. Fax 527-7600
Cincinnati Hills Christian Academy 400/5-8
11300 Snider Rd 45249 513-247-0900
Rob Hall, prin. Fax 247-9362
Cincinnati Hills Christian Academy 400/9-12
11525 Snider Rd 45249 513-247-0900
Dave Walker, prin. Fax 247-0982
Cincinnati State Technical & Comm Coll Post-Sec.
3520 Central Pkwy 45223 513-569-1500
College of Art Advertising Post-Sec.
4343 Bridgetown Rd 45211 513-574-1010
College of Mount Saint Joseph Post-Sec.
5701 Delhi Rd 45233 513-244-4200
Elder HS 1,100/9-12
3900 Vincent Ave 45205 513-921-3744
Thomas Otten, prin. Fax 921-8123
God's Bible School and College Post-Sec.
1810 Young St 45202 513-721-7944
Good Samaritan Hospital Post-Sec.
375 Dixmyth Ave 45220 513-872-1983
Hebrew Union College Post-Sec.
3101 Clifton Ave 45220 513-221-1875
Hillside Christian Academy 50/K-12
5554 Muddy Creek Rd 45238 513-451-3777
Terrance Bledsoe, admin.
Hondros College Post-Sec.
4675 Cornell Rd Ste 175 45241 513-247-9711
Institute of Medical & Dental Technology Post-Sec.
375 Glensprings Dr Ste 201 45246 513-851-8500
International Academy of Hair Design Post-Sec.
8419 Colerain Ave 45239 513-741-4777
ITT Technical Institute Post-Sec.
4750 Wesley Ave 45212 513-531-8300
La Salle HS 900/9-12
3091 N Bend Rd 45239 513-741-3000
Thomas Luebbe, prin. Fax 741-2666
Marinello-Eastern Hills Academy Post-Sec.
7681 Beechmont Ave 45255 513-231-8621
McAuley HS 800/9-12
6000 Oakwood Ave 45224 513-681-1800
Cheryl Sucher, prin. Fax 681-1802
McNicholas HS 800/9-12
6536 Beechmont Ave 45230 513-231-3500
Thomas Bill, prin. Fax 231-1351
Miami Valley Christian Academy 300/K-12
6830 School St 45244 513-272-6822
Lynda Lunn, prin. Fax 272-3711
Moeller HS 1,000/9-12
9001 Montgomery Rd 45242 513-791-1680
Blane M. Collison, prin. Fax 792-3443
Moler-Hollywood Beauty College Post-Sec.
130 E 6th St Fl 2 45202 513-621-5262
Mother of Mercy HS 600/9-12
3036 Werk Rd 45211 513-661-2740
Sr. Nancy Merkle, prin. Fax 661-1842
Norwood Christian Academy 100/K-12
2041 Courtland Ave 45212 513-458-2140
Gary Arthur, prin. Fax 458-2142
Ohio Center for Broadcasting Post-Sec.
6703 Madison Rd 45227 513-271-6060
Purcell-Marian HS 400/9-12
2935 Hackberry St 45206 513-751-1230
Albert Early, prin. Fax 751-1395
Reg. Inst. for Torah & Secular Studies 50/9-12
PO Box 37383 45222 513-631-0083
Fax 631-0947
St. Rita School for the Deaf Post-Sec.
1720 Glendale Milford Rd 45215 513-771-7600
St. Ursula Academy 700/9-12
1339 E Mcmillan St 45206 513-961-3410
Frances Romweber, prin. Fax 961-3856
St. Xavier HS 1,500/9-12
600 W North Bend Rd 45224 513-761-7600
David Mueller, prin. Fax 842-1610
Seton HS 600/9-12
3901 Glenway Ave 45205 513-471-2600
Susan Gibbons, prin. Fax 471-0529
Seven Hills S 1,100/PK-12
5400 Red Bank Rd 45227 513-271-9027
Sandra J. Theunick, hdmstr. Fax 271-2471
Southwestern College of Business Post-Sec.
630 Vine St Ste 200 45202 513-421-3212
Southwestern College of Business Post-Sec.
149 Northland Blvd 45246 513-874-0432
Summit Country Day S 1,100/PK-12
2161 Grandin Rd 45208 513-871-4700
Tom Monaco, prin. Fax 533-5373
Temple Baptist College Post-Sec.
11965 Kenn Rd 45240 513-851-3800
Tri County Bible College Post-Sec.
111 Kemper Rd 45246 513-671-8340
Union Institute & University Post-Sec.
440 E McMillan St 45206 513-861-6400
University of Cincinnati Post-Sec.
2700 Clifton Ave 45220 513-556-6000
University of Cincinnati Post-Sec.
9555 Plainfield Rd 45236 513-745-5600
University of Cincinnati/OMI College Post-Sec.
2220 Victory Pkwy 45206 513-556-6567
Univ. of Cincinnati Coll. Allied Health Post-Sec.
PO Box 670394 45267 513-558-7495
Ursuline Academy 600/9-12
5535 Pfeiffer Rd 45242 513-791-5791
Adele Iwanusa, prin. Fax 791-5802
Western Hills Sch of Beauty & Hair Dsgn. Post-Sec.
6490 Glenway Ave 45211 513-574-3818
Xavier University Post-Sec.
3800 Victory Pkwy 45207 513-745-3000

Circleville, Pickaway, Pop. 13,400
Circleville CSD 2,500/K-12
388 Clark Dr 43113 740-474-4340
Tyrus Ankrom, supt. Fax 474-6600
www.circlevillecityschools.org/
Circleville HS 700/9-12
380 Clark Dr 43113 740-474-4846
Paul Vitartas, prin. Fax 474-3987
Everts MS 600/6-8
520 S Court St 43113 740-474-2345
Kirk McMahon, prin. Fax 477-6384

Logan Elm Local SD 2,300/K-12
9579 Tarlton Rd 43113 740-474-7501
C. Asa Bradbury, supt. Fax 477-6525
www.loganelmschools.com/
Logan Elm HS 700/9-12
9575 Tarlton Rd 43113 740-474-7503
Sally Kleon, prin. Fax 477-6525
McDowell-Exchange JHS 400/7-8
9579 Tarlton Rd 43113 740-474-7538
Rodney Brobst, prin. Fax 477-6525

Circleville Bible College Post-Sec.
PO Box 458 43113 740-474-8896

Clarksville, Clinton, Pop. 499
Clinton-Massie Local SD 1,800/K-12
2556 Lebanon Rd 45113 937-289-2471
Ronald Rudduck, supt. Fax 289-3313
www.clinton-massie.k12.oh.us
Clinton-Massie HS 500/9-12
2556 Lebanon Rd 45113 937-289-2109
Randy Dunlap, prin. Fax 289-3313
Clinton-Massie MS 400/6-8
2556 Lebanon Rd 45113 937-289-2932
Mark McCormick, prin. Fax 289-3313

Clayton, Montgomery, Pop. 13,268
Miami Valley Career Tech SD
6800 Hoke Rd 45315 937-837-7781
John Boggess, supt. Fax 837-5318
www.mvctc.com
Miami Valley Career Tech Center Vo/Tech
6800 Hoke Rd 45315 937-837-7781
Jack Poore, prin. Fax 837-5318

Northmont CSD
Supt. — See Englewood
Northmont HS 2,000/9-12
4916 National Rd 45315 937-832-6000
P. Eugene Klaus, prin. Fax 832-6001
Northmont MS 1,000/7-8
4810 National Rd 45315 937-832-6500
David Weekley, prin. Fax 832-6501

Cleveland, Cuyahoga, Pop. 461,324
Cleveland CSD 83,600/PK-12
1380 E 6th St 44114 216-574-8000
Fax 574-8193
www.cmsdnet.net
Academy of Creative Expression 9-12
1349 E 79th St 44103 216-431-5361
Denetris Anderson, prin. Fax 432-4543
Academy of Human Services 9-12
1349 E 79th St 44103 216-431-5361
Michelle Madison, prin. Fax 432-4543
Addams Business Career Center 600/9-12
2373 E 30th St 44115 216-621-2131
Deborah Franklin, prin. Fax 696-8843
Business Entrepreneurship & Tech Academy 9-12
17100 Harvard Ave 44128 216-921-1450
Perry Myles, prin. Fax 295-2455
Cleveland School of Arts HS 700/6-12
2064 Stearns Rd 44106 216-791-2496
Barbara Walton, prin. Fax 421-7689
Collinwood HS 1,900/9-12
15210 Saint Clair Ave 44110 216-451-8782
Deborah Moore, prin. Fax 268-6057
Dreams Academy 9-12
17100 Harvard Ave 44128 216-921-1450
Christy Nickerson, prin. Fax 295-2455
Eagle Academy 9-12
17100 Harvard Ave 44128 216-921-1450
Steven Mietus, prin. Fax 295-2455
East HS 1,200/9-12
1349 E 79th St 44103 216-431-5361
Brenda Washington, admin. Fax 432-4543
East Tech Annex Vo/Tech
1935 Euclid Ave 44115 216-621-5202
Gene Zuckerman, prin. Fax 795-8880
East Tech HS Vo/Tech
2439 E 55th St 44104 216-431-2626
Robert McKinnie, admin. Fax 431-4631
Glenville HS 1,700/9-12
650 E 113th St 44108 216-268-6000
Jacqueline Bell, admin. Fax 541-7666
Hayes HS Vo/Tech
4600 Detroit Ave 44102 216-631-1528
David Volosin, prin. Fax 634-2175
Health Career Center HS Vo/Tech
1740 E 32nd St 44114 216-579-9984
Sheree Ray, prin. Fax 621-8982
High Tech Academy 10-12
2900 Community College Ave 44115
Kenneth Hale, prin. 216-987-4675
Institute of Business & Law 9-12
1349 E 79th St 44103 216-431-5361
Gerard Leslie, prin. Fax 432-4543
Kennedy HS 2,000/9-12
17100 Harvard Ave 44128 216-921-1450
Charita Crockrom, admin. Fax 295-2455
King S for Law 900/6-12
1651 E 71st St 44103 216-431-6858
Donald Jolly, prin. Fax 431-5180
Leadership & Human Services Institute Vo/Tech
2439 E 55th St 44104 216-431-2626
Dale Laux, prin. Fax 431-4631
Leadership & Urban Awareness Academy 9-12
17100 Harvard Ave 44128 216-921-1450
Erin Frew, prin. Fax 295-2455
Lighthouse Academy Vo/Tech
2439 E 55th St 44104 216-431-2626
Cheryl Taylor, prin. Fax 431-4631

Lincoln-West HS 1,600/9-12
3202 W 30th St 44109 216-631-1505
Valentina Mickey, prin. Fax 634-2403
Marshall HS 2,000/9-12
3952 W 140th St 44111 216-251-5740
Rhonda Saegert, prin. Fax 476-4482
Morgan S of Science 700/6-9
4016 Woodbine Ave 44113 216-281-6188
Laverne Hooks, prin. Fax 634-2113
Prodigy Academy 9-12
17100 Harvard Ave 44128 216-921-1450
Joyce Hunter, prin. Fax 295-2455
Renaissance S of Fine Arts 9-12
650 E 113th St 44108 216-268-6000
Hubert Watson, prin. Fax 541-7666
Rhodes HS 1,800/9-12
5100 Biddulph Ave 44144 216-351-6285
Wayne Marok, admin. Fax 749-8130
Roosevelt MS 800/6-8
800 Linn Dr 44108 216-541-0587
Marsha Brooks, prin. Fax 541-7667
School of Applied Design & Technology 9-12
1349 E 79th St 44103 216-431-5361
Patrick McNichols, prin. Fax 432-4543
School of Business & Internatnl Affairs 9-12
650 E 113th St 44108 216-268-6000
Anthony Riccio, prin. Fax 541-7666
School of Health Leadership & Wellness 9-12
650 E 113th St 44108 216-268-6000
Sophronia Hairston, prin. Fax 541-7666
School of Inquiry/Innovation & Tech 9-12
5100 Biddulph Ave 44144 216-351-6285
Donald Strinka, prin. Fax 749-8130
School of Leadership 9-12
5100 Biddulph Ave 44144 216-351-6285
Craig Strom, prin. Fax 749-8130
School of Science & Technology 9-12
650 E 113th St 44108 216-268-6000
Marion Wallace, prin. Fax 541-7666
Shuler MS 1,200/6-10
13501 Terminal Ave 44135 216-671-0272
Marilyn Cargile, prin. Fax 476-4212
South HS 1,700/9-12
7415 Broadway Ave 44105 216-641-0410
Timothy Bigenho, prin. Fax 441-8242
Technology Institute Vo/Tech
2439 E 55th St 44104 216-431-2626
Brian Register, prin. Fax 431-4631
Young S 700/6-11
17900 Harvard Ave 44128 216-283-5220
Alisa McKinnie, prin. Fax 295-3547
Cleveland Extension HS @ Hayes Annex Adult
4600 Detroit Ave 44102 216-651-3840
David Volosin, prin. Fax 634-7143
Cleveland Skills & Career Center Adult
3122 Euclid Ave 44115 216-361-4770
Debbie Sutula, coord. Fax 361-1664

Orange CSD 2,300/PK-12
32000 Chagrin Blvd 44124 216-831-8600
Daniel Lukich, supt. Fax 831-5049
www.orangeschools.org
Brady MS 500/6-8
32000 Chagrin Blvd 44124 216-831-8600
Stephen Hegner, prin. Fax 839-1335
Orange HS 800/9-12
32000 Chagrin Blvd 44124 216-831-8581
Daniel Hanstein, prin. Fax 831-4846

Academy of Court Reporting Post-Sec.
2044 Euclid Ave 44115 216-861-3222
ATS Institute of Technology Post-Sec.
230 Alpha Park 44143 440-449-1700
Beatrice Academy of Beauty Post-Sec.
10500 Cedar Ave 44106 216-421-2313
Benedictine HS 400/9-12
2900 Martin Luther King Jr 44104 216-421-2080
Sal Miroglotta, prin. Fax 421-1100
Bryant & Stratton College Post-Sec.
12955 Snow Rd 44130 216-265-3151
Bryant & Stratton College Post-Sec.
1700 E 13th St 44114 216-771-1700
Case Western Reserve University Post-Sec.
10900 Euclid Ave 44106 216-368-2000
Cleveland Central Catholic HS 600/9-12
6550 Baxter Ave 44105 216-441-4700
Karl Ertle, prin. Fax 441-8353
Cleveland Clinic Foundation Post-Sec.
9500 Euclid Ave 44195 216-445-5719
Cleveland Institute Dental Medical Asst. Post-Sec.
2450 Prospect Ave E 44115 216-241-2930
Cleveland Institute of Art Post-Sec.
11141 East Blvd 44106 216-421-7000
Cleveland Institute of Electronics Post-Sec.
1776 E 17th St 44114 216-781-9400
Cleveland Institute of Music Post-Sec.
11021 East Blvd 44106 216-795-3107
Cleveland State University Post-Sec.
2121 Euclid Ave 44115 216-687-2000
Cleveland Veterans Affairs Medical Ctr Post-Sec.
10701 East Blvd 44106 216-421-3028
Cuyahoga Community College Post-Sec.
2900 Community College Ave 44115 216-987-4000
Fairview General Hospital Post-Sec.
18101 Lorain Ave 44111 216-476-7000
John Carroll University Post-Sec.
20700 N Park Blvd 44118 216-397-1886
Keller Graduate School Post-Sec.
200 Public Sq Ste 150 44114 216-781-8000
Laura/Alvin Siegal Coll Judaic Studies Post-Sec.
26500 Shaker Blvd 44122 216-464-4050
Meridia Health System Post-Sec.
17325 Euclid Ave 44112 440-446-8260
MetroHealth Medical Center Post-Sec.
2500 Metrohealth Dr 44109 216-459-5700
Myers University Post-Sec.
3921 Chester Ave 44114 216-361-2769
Notre Dame College Post-Sec.
4545 College Rd 44121 216-381-1680
Ohio College of Podiatric Medicine Post-Sec.
10515 Carnegie Ave 44106 216-231-3300
Ohio Technical College Post-Sec.
1374 E 51st St 44103 216-881-1700
Remington College Post-Sec.
14445 Broadway Ave 44125 216-475-7520
St. Ignatius HS 1,300/9-12
1911 W 30th St 44113 216-651-0222
Peter H. Corrigan, prin. Fax 651-6313
St. Joseph Academy 600/9-12
3430 Rocky River Dr 44111 216-251-6788
Jacqualine Kasprowski, prin. Fax 251-5809
St. Luke's Medical Center Post-Sec.
2351 E 22nd St 44115 216-368-7000
St. Martin de Porres HS 200/9-12
6111 Lausche Ave 44103 216-881-1689
Mary Ann Vogel, prin. Fax 881-8303
Sanford-Brown College Post-Sec.
17535 Rosbough Blvd Ste 100 44130 440-239-9640
Southwest General Hospital Post-Sec.
18697 Bagley Rd 44130 440-816-6801
Total Technical Institute Post-Sec.
8720 Brookpark Rd 44129 216-485-0900
University Hospital of Cleveland Post-Sec.
11100 Euclid Ave 44106 216-844-7565
Ursuline College Post-Sec.
2550 Lander Rd 44124 440-449-4200
Villa Angela/St. Joseph HS 500/9-12
18491 Lake Shore Blvd 44119 216-481-8414
Janice Roccosalva, prin. Fax 486-1035

Cleveland Heights, Cuyahoga, Pop. 49,016
Cleveland Hts - University Hts CSD
Supt. — See University Heights
Cleveland Heights HS 2,100/9-12
13263 Cedar Rd 44118 216-371-7101
Darcel Williams, prin. Fax 371-6506
Monticello MS 600/6-8
3665 Monticello Blvd 44121 216-371-6520
Renee Cavor, prin. Fax 397-5967
Roxboro MS 600/6-8
2400 Roxboro Rd 44106 216-371-7440
Brian Sharosky, prin. Fax 397-3857

Beaumont HS 400/9-12
3301 N Park Blvd 44118 216-321-2954
Margaret Connell, prin. Fax 321-3947
Hebrew Academy of Cleveland 700/PK-12
1860 S Taylor Rd 44118 216-321-5838
Rabbi Simcha Dessler, dir. Fax 932-4597
Lutheran East HS 100/9-12
3565 Mayfield Rd 44118 216-382-6100
Clarence Griffin, prin. Fax 382-6119
Mosdos Ohr HaTorah S - Girls 300/PK-12
1700 S Taylor Rd 44118 216-321-1547
Brina Fried, prin. Fax 321-7505
Saperstein HS for Boys 100/7-12
1975 Lyndway Rd 44121 216-382-6495
Rabbi N.W. Dessler, dean Fax 291-5127

Cleves, Hamilton, Pop. 2,641
Three Rivers Local SD 2,100/K-12
92 Cleves Ave 45002 513-941-6400
Rhonda Bohannon, supt. Fax 467-3207
www.threeriversschools.org
Three Rivers MS 600/6-8
8575 Bridgetown Rd 45002 513-467-3500
Thomas Huber, prin. Fax 467-3504
Other Schools – See North Bend

Clyde, Sandusky, Pop. 6,047
Clyde-Green Springs EVD 2,300/K-12
106 S Main St 43410 419-547-0588
Todd Helms, supt. Fax 547-8644
www.clyde.k12.oh.us
Clyde HS 800/9-12
1015 Race St 43410 419-547-9511
Joe Webb, prin. Fax 639-3788
McPherson MS 400/7-8
201 Spring St 43410 419-547-9150
Gregg Elchert, prin. Fax 547-8644

Coal Grove, Lawrence, Pop. 2,056
Dawson-Bryant Local SD 1,300/K-12
222 Lane St 45638 740-532-6451
James Payne, supt. Fax 533-6006
Dawson-Bryant HS 400/9-12
1 Hornet Ln 45638 740-532-6345
Steven Easterling, prin. Fax 533-6014
Dawson-Bryant MS 300/6-8
1 Hornet Ln 45638 740-532-1664
Gary Dutey, prin. Fax 533-6006

Coldwater, Mercer, Pop. 4,457
Coldwater EVD 1,600/K-12
310 N 2nd St 45828 419-678-2611
Richard Seas, supt. Fax 678-3100
cw.noacsc.org
Coldwater HS 500/9-12
310 N 2nd St 45828 419-678-4821
Steve Keller, prin. Fax 678-3100
Coldwater JHS 500/5-8
310 N 2nd St 45828 419-678-3331
Jerry Kanney, prin. Fax 678-3100

Collins, Huron
Western Reserve Local SD 1,400/K-12
3765 State Route 20 44826 419-660-8508
Jerry Wolf, supt. Fax 660-8429
www.western-reserve.org
Western Reserve HS 400/9-12
3841 State Route 20 44826 419-668-8470
Thomas Lehman, prin. Fax 663-5916
Western Reserve MS 200/7-8
3841 State Route 20 44826 419-668-1924
Thomas Lehman, prin.

Columbiana, Columbiana, Pop. 5,703
Columbiana EVD 1,000/K-12
700 Columbiana Waterford Rd 44408 330-482-5352
Ronald Iarussi, supt. Fax 482-5361
www.columbiana.k12.oh.us
Columbiana HS 300/9-12
700 Columbiana Waterford Rd 44408 330-482-3818
Timothy Saxton, prin. Fax 482-5360
South Side MS 300/5-8
720 Columbiana Waterford Rd 44408 330-482-5354
Ray Wagner, prin. Fax 482-6332
Crestview Local SD 1,100/K-12
44100 Crestview Rd Ste A 44408 330-482-5526
John Dilling, supt. Fax 482-5367
www.crestviewlocal.k12.oh.us/
Crestview HS 400/9-12
44100 Crestview Rd Ste B 44408 330-482-4744
John Gecina, prin. Fax 482-5369
Crestview MS 400/5-8
44100 Crestview Rd Ste C 44408 330-482-4648
David Mackay, prin. Fax 482-5374

Heartland Christian S 300/PK-12
28 Pittsburgh St 44408 330-482-2331
Dallas Lehman, admin. Fax 482-2413

Columbia Station, Lorain
Columbia Local SD 1,100/K-12
25796 Royalton Rd 44028 440-236-5008
John Kuhn, supt. Fax 236-8817
www.columbia.k12.oh.us/
Columbia HS 400/9-12
14168 W River Rd 44028 440-236-5001
Graig Bansek, prin. Fax 236-3081
Columbia MS 400/5-8
13646 W River Rd 44028 440-236-5741
James Cottom, prin. Fax 236-9274

Columbus, Franklin, Pop. 728,432
Columbus CSD 59,000/K-12
270 E State St 43215 614-365-5000
Gene T. Harris, supt. Fax 365-5689
www.columbus.k12.oh.us/
Barrett Urban Academy 500/6-8
345 E Deshler Ave 43206 614-365-5514
Cary Cordell, prin. Fax 365-5512
Beechcroft HS 900/9-12
6100 Beechcroft Rd 43229 614-365-5364
Thomas Reed, prin. Fax 365-6963
Beery MS 500/6-8
2740 Lockbourne Rd 43207 614-365-5414
Henderson O. Days, prin. Fax 365-5412
Briggs HS 900/9-12
2555 Briggs Rd 43223 614-365-5915
Kurt Yancey, prin. Fax 365-6964
Brookhaven HS 1,000/9-12
4077 Karl Rd 43224 614-365-5985
Talisha Dixon, prin. Fax 365-6965
Buckeye MS 700/6-8
2950 Parsons Ave 43207 614-365-5417
Fax 365-5895
Centennial HS 800/9-12
1441 Bethel Rd 43220 614-365-5491
Frances L. Hershey, prin. Fax 365-6967
Champion MS 400/6-8
1270 Hawthorne Ave 43203 614-365-6082
Joseph Santa-Emma, prin. Fax 365-6080
Clinton MS 700/6-8
3940 Karl Rd 43224 614-365-5996
Thomas Sweeney, prin. Fax 365-5999
Crestview MS 500/6-8
251 E Weber Rd 43202 614-365-6014
Debra Tracy, prin. Fax 365-8135
Dominion MS 500/6-8
330 E Dominion Blvd 43214 614-365-6020
Carole Pressman, prin. Fax 365-6018
East HS 900/9-12
1500 E Broad St 43205 614-365-6096
Edward P. Johnson, prin. Fax 365-6966
Eastmoor Academy HS 800/9-12
417 S Weyant Ave 43213 614-365-6158
Darryl Sanders, prin. Fax 365-6960
Eastmoor MS 600/6-8
3450 Medway Ave 43213 614-365-6166
Debra Odom, prin. Fax 365-6164
Fort Hayes Career Center Vo/Tech
546 Jack Gibbs Blvd 43215 614-365-6681
Milton Ruffin, dir. Fax 365-6988
Hilltonia MS 700/6-8
2345 W Mound St 43204 614-365-5937
Jerrilyn Eddington, prin. Fax 365-8015
Independence HS 900/9-12
5175 Refugee Rd 43232 614-365-5372
Michael Dodds, prin. Fax 365-8286
Indianola MS 400/6-8
420 E 19th Ave 43201 614-365-5575
Donna H. LeBeau, prin. Fax 365-5577
Johnson Park MS 700/6-8
1130 S Waverly St 43227 614-365-6501
Charmaine W. Tinker, prin. Fax 365-8698
Linden-McKinley HS 700/9-12
1320 Duxberry Ave 43211 614-365-5583
Carlton Jenkins, prin. Fax 365-6968
Linmoor MS 400/6-8
2001 Hamilton Ave 43211 614-365-5595
Michelle Myles, prin. Fax 365-5594
Marion-Franklin HS 900/9-12
1265 Koebel Rd 43207 614-365-5432
Brian J. Terrell, prin. Fax 365-6625
Medina MS 700/6-8
1425 Huy Rd 43224 614-365-6050
Sherri C. Edwards, prin. Fax 365-8136
Mifflin HS 900/9-12
3245 Oak Spring St 43219 614-365-5466
Laura Commodore-Young, prin. Fax 365-6628
Northeast Career Ctr Vo/Tech
3871 Stelzer Rd 43219 614-365-5478
Shirley Moore, dir. Fax 365-5484
Northland HS 1,300/9-12
1919 Northcliff Dr 43229 614-365-5342
Duane R. Bland, prin. Fax 365-6479
Ridgeview MS 500/6-8
4241 Rudy Rd 43214 614-365-5506
Keith M. Harris, prin. Fax 365-5505
Sherwood MS 600/6-8
1400 Shady Lane Rd 43227 614-365-5393
Anthony J. Wade, prin. Fax 365-8351
Southeast Career Center Vo/Tech
3500 Alum Creek Dr 43207 614-365-5442
Michael Ochab, dir. Fax 365-6985
Southmoor MS 500/6-8
1201 Moler Rd 43207 614-365-5550
Murphy Moultry, prin. Fax 365-6637

South Urban Academy HS · 800/9-12
1160 Ann St 43206 · 614-365-5541
Johnetta D. Wiley, prin. · Fax 365-5538
Starling MS · 600/6-8
120 S Central Ave 43222 · 614-365-5945
· Fax 365-5942
Walnut Ridge HS · 1,100/9-12
4841 E Livingston Ave 43227 · 614-365-5400
Timothy Carpenter, prin. · Fax 365-5662
Wedgewood MS · 600/6-8
3771 Eakin Rd 43228 · 614-365-5947
Loy M. Koeller, prin. · Fax 365-5950
West HS · 1,100/9-12
179 S Powell Ave 43204 · 614-365-5956
Arnold Holmes, prin. · Fax 365-6970
Westmoor MS · 700/6-8
3001 Valleyview Dr 43204 · 614-365-5974
Kathleen E. Squires, prin. · Fax 365-6705
Whetstone HS · 1,000/9-12
4405 Scenic Dr 43214 · 614-365-6060
Cheryl A. Norman, prin. · Fax 365-6971
Woodward Park MS · 1,000/6-8
5151 Karl Rd 43229 · 614-365-5354
Jill Spanheimer, prin. · Fax 365-5357
Yorktown MS · 700/6-8
5600 E Livingston Ave 43232 · 614-365-5408
Pamela Smith, prin. · Fax 365-5411
Other Schools – See Dublin

Hamilton Local SD · 3,000/K-12
1055 Rathmell Rd 43207 · 614-491-8044
Christopher Lester, supt. · Fax 491-8323
www.hamilton-local.k12.oh.us
Hamilton MS · 500/7-8
775 Rathmell Rd 43207 · 614-491-3468
Terry McCray, prin. · Fax 491-0260
Hamilton Township HS · 800/9-12
4999 Lockbourne Rd 43207 · 614-491-3330
Jeffrey Endres, prin. · Fax 492-1495

South-Western CSD
Supt. — See Grove City
Finland MS · 700/7-8
1825 Finland Ave 43223 · 614-801-3600
Jim Voyles, prin. · Fax 278-6334
Franklin Heights HS · 1,200/9-12
1001 Demorest Rd 43204 · 614-801-3200
Gary Barber, prin. · Fax 278-6303
Norton MS · 600/7-8
215 Norton Rd 43228 · 614-801-3700
Bill Mullins, prin. · Fax 870-5528

Worthington CSD
Supt. — See Worthington
McCord MS · 400/7-8
1500 Hard Rd 43235 · 614-883-3550
Michael Kuri, prin. · Fax 883-3560
Worthington Kilbourne HS · 1,600/9-12
1499 Hard Rd 43235 · 614-883-2550
Ed Dunaway, prin. · Fax 883-2560

Academy of Court Reporting · Post-Sec.
630 E Broad St 43215 · 614-221-7770
American Inst. of Alternative Medicine · Post-Sec.
6685 Doubletree Ave 43229 · 614-825-6278
American School of Technology · Post-Sec.
2100 Morse Rd # 4599 43229 · 614-436-4820
Arthur James Cancer Hospital · Post-Sec.
300 W 10th Ave 43210 · 614-293-5485
Bexley Hall University · Post-Sec.
583 Sheridan Ave 43209 · 614-231-3095
Bishop Hartley HS · 600/9-12
1285 Zettler Rd 43227 · 614-237-5421
Mike Winters, prin. · Fax 237-3809
Bishop Ready HS · 500/9-12
707 Salisbury Rd 43204 · 614-276-5263
Celene Seamen, prin. · Fax 276-5116
Bishop Waterson HS · 1,100/9-12
99 E Cooke Rd 43214 · 614-268-8671
Marian Hutson, prin. · Fax 268-0551
Bradford School · Post-Sec.
2469 Stelzer Rd 43219 · 614-416-6200
Capital University · Post-Sec.
2199 E Main St 43209 · 614-236-6011
Capital University Law School · Post-Sec.
303 E Broad St 43215 · 614-236-6500
Columbus College of Art & Design · Post-Sec.
107 N 9th St 43215 · 614-224-9101
Columbus School for Girls · 700/PK-12
56 S Columbia Ave 43209 · 614-252-0781
Diane B. Cooper, hdmstr. · Fax 252-0571
Columbus State Community College · Post-Sec.
550 E Spring St 43215 · 614-287-2400
Columbus Torah Academy · 300/K-12
181 Noe Bixby Rd 43213 · 614-864-0299
Marcia Hershfield, prin. · Fax 864-2218
DeVry University · Post-Sec.
1350 Alum Creek Dr 43209 · 614-253-7291
Franklin University · Post-Sec.
201 S Grant Ave 43215 · 614-341-6300
HARDI Home Study Institute · Post-Sec.
1389 Dublin Rd 43215 · 614-488-1835
Keller Graduate School · Post-Sec.
8800 Lyra Dr Ste 120 43240 · 614-252-8850
Liberty Christian Academy · 600/PK-12
4938 Beatrice Dr 43227 · 614-864-5332
LaVonne McIlrath, admin. · Fax 864-5381
Marburn Academy · 100/K-12
1860 Walden Dr 43229 · 614-433-0822
Earl Oremus, prin.
Mt. Carmel College of Nursing · Post-Sec.
127 S Davis Ave 43222 · 614-234-5800
Nationwide Beauty Academy · Post-Sec.
5300 WestPointe Plaza Dr 43228 · 614-921-9109
Ohio Dominican University · Post-Sec.
1216 Sunbury Rd 43219 · 614-253-2741
Ohio Institute of Health Careers · Post-Sec.
1880 E Dublin Granville Rd 43229 · 614-891-5030
Ohio School for the Deaf · Post-Sec.
500 Morse Rd 43214
Ohio State College of Barber Styling · Post-Sec.
4614 E Broad St 43213 · 614-868-1015
Ohio State Sch of Cosmetology Northland · Post-Sec.
4390 Karl Rd 43224 · 614-263-1861

Ohio State School for the Blind · Post-Sec.
5220 N High St 43214
Ohio State School of Cosmetology · Post-Sec.
3717 S High St 43207 · 614-491-0492
Ohio State University · Post-Sec.
154 W 12th Ave 43210 · 614-292-6446
Ohio State University Hospitals · Post-Sec.
450 W 10th Ave 43210 · 614-293-5555
Pontifical College Josephinum · Post-Sec.
7625 N High St 43235 · 614-885-5585
St. Charles Prep S · 500/9-12
2010 E Broad St 43209 · 614-252-6714
Dominic Cavello, prin. · Fax 251-6800
St. Francis De Sales HS · 1,000/9-12
4212 Karl Rd 43224 · 614-267-7808
Dan Garrick, prin. · Fax 265-3375
Spa School · Post-Sec.
5050 N High St 43214 · 614-888-1092
Technology Education College · Post-Sec.
2745 Winchester Pike 43232 · 614-759-7700
Tree of Life Christian HS · 300/6-12
935 Northridge Rd 43224 · 614-263-2688
Todd Marrah, prin. · Fax 263-6450
Trinity Lutheran Seminary · Post-Sec.
2199 E Main St 43209 · 614-235-4136
Wellington S · 600/K-12
3650 Reed Rd 43220 · 614-457-7883
Richard O'Hara, hdmstr. · Fax 442-3286

Columbus Grove, Putnam, Pop. 2,169
Columbus Grove Local SD · 800/K-12
201 W Cross St 45830 · 419-659-2639
Robert Jennell, supt. · Fax 659-5134
Columbus Grove HS · 300/9-12
201 W Cross St 45830 · 419-659-2156
Chris Pfahler, prin. · Fax 659-5134
Columbus Grove MS · 200/5-8
201 W Cross St 45830 · 419-659-2631
James Kincaid, prin. · Fax 659-5134

Concord, Lake
Auburn Vocational SD
8140 Auburn Rd 44077 · 440-357-7542
G. Thomas Schultz, supt. · Fax 357-0310
www.auburncc.org
Auburn Career Center · Vo/Tech
8140 Auburn Rd 44077 · 440-357-7542
Mary Ann Bittner, prin. · Fax 357-0227

Conneaut, Ashtabula, Pop. 12,666
Conneaut Area CSD · 1,600/K-12
263 Liberty St 44030 · 440-593-7200
Mary Zappitelli, supt. · Fax 593-6253
www.conneautschools.org
Conneaut HS · 700/9-12
381 Mill St 44030 · 440-593-7210
Kent Houston, prin. · Fax 593-6899
Conneaut MS · 600/6-8
230 Gateway Ave 44030 · 440-593-7240
Linda Bernay, prin. · Fax 593-6253

Continental, Putnam, Pop. 1,170
Continental Local SD · 700/K-12
5211 State Route 634 45831 · 419-596-3671
Sandra Muir, supt. · Fax 596-3861
cn2.noacsc.org
Continental HS · 200/9-12
5211 State Route 634 45831 · 419-596-3871
Larry Claypool, prin. · Fax 596-2651
Continental MS · 200/6-8
5211 State Route 634 45831 · 419-596-4571
Larry Claypool, prin. · Fax 596-2651

Convoy, Van Wert, Pop. 1,083
Crestview Local SD · 1,000/K-12
531 E Tully St 45832 · 419-749-9100
John Basinger, supt. · Fax 749-4235
www.crestviewknights.com/
Crestview JSHS · 500/7-12
531 E Tully St 45832 · 419-749-9100
Mike Biro, prin. · Fax 749-2484

Copley, Summit, Pop. 11,130
Copley-Fairlawn CSD · 3,200/K-12
3797 Ridgewood Rd 44321 · 330-664-4800
Edward Myracle, supt. · Fax 664-4811
www.copley-fairlawn.org
Copley-Fairlawn MS · 1,000/5-8
1531 S Clvland Massillon Rd 44321 · 330-664-4875
Robert Whitaker, prin. · Fax 664-4912
Copley HS · 1,000/9-12
3807 Ridgewood Rd 44321 · 330-664-4822
William Steffen, prin. · Fax 664-4951

Ohio College of Massotherapy · Post-Sec.
225 Heritage Woods Dr 44321 · 330-665-1084

Corning, Perry, Pop. 611
Southern Local SD · 1,000/K-12
10397 State Route 155 SE #1 43730 · 740-394-2402
Cindy Hartman, supt. · Fax 394-2083
www.spsd.k12.oh.us/
Miller HS · 300/9-12
10397 State Route 155 SE 43730 · 740-394-2426
Ralph Holbert, prin. · Fax 394-2083
Miller MS · 300/5-8
10397 State Route 155 SE 43730 · 740-394-1173
Larry Hoover, prin. · Fax 394-2083

Cortland, Trumbull, Pop. 6,703
Lakeview Local SD · 2,200/K-12
300 Hillman Dr 44410 · 330-637-8741
Robert Wilson, supt. · Fax 638-1060
Lakeview HS · 700/9-12
300 Hillman Dr 44410 · 330-637-4921
Fred Kunar, prin. · Fax 638-1060
Lakeview MS · 600/6-8
640 Wakefield Dr 44410 · 330-637-4360
Nancy Krygowski, prin. · Fax 638-1060

Maplewood Local SD · 1,300/K-12
2414 Greenville Rd 44410 · 330-637-7506
Beverly R. Hoagland, supt. · Fax 637-6616
www.maplewood.k12.oh.us/
Maplewood HS · 600/7-12
2414 Greenville Rd 44410 · 330-637-8466
Ruth Zitnik, prin. · Fax 637-0496
Maplewood MS · 400/5-8
4174 Greenville Rd 44410 · 330-924-2401
Kevin Spicher, prin. · Fax 924-5151

Coshocton, Coshocton, Pop. 11,630
Coshocton CSD · 1,900/K-12
1207 Cambridge Rd 43812 · 740-622-1901
Wade Lucas, supt. · Fax 623-5803
www.coshoctonredskins.com/
Coshocton JSHS · 900/7-12
1205 Cambridge Rd 43812 · 740-622-9433
Bill Hartmeyer, prin. · Fax 623-0774

Coshocton County JVSD
23640 Airport Rd 43812 · 740-622-0211
Donna Johnson, supt. · Fax 623-4651
www.coshocton-jvs.k12.oh.us/
Coshocton County Career Center · Vo/Tech
23640 Airport Rd 43812 · 740-622-0211
Eddie Dovenbarger, prin. · Fax 623-4651

Coshocton Christian S · 100/PK-12
23891 Airport Rd 43812 · 740-622-5052
Aimee Horton, prin. · Fax 622-9244

Covington, Miami, Pop. 2,555
Covington EVD · 900/K-12
25 N Grant St 45318 · 937-473-2249
Randy G. Earl, supt. · Fax 473-3730
www.covington.k12.oh.us
Covington HS · 300/9-12
807 Chestnut St 45318 · 937-473-3746
Chad Mason, prin. · Fax 473-3889
Covington MS · 200/6-8
25 N Grant St 45318 · 937-473-2833
Paula Jurgens, prin. · Fax 473-8189

Crestline, Crawford, Pop. 4,974
Crestline EVD · 800/K-12
PO Box 350 44827 · 419-683-3647
Mark Stock, supt. · Fax 683-2330
www.crestline.k12.oh.us
Crestline HS · 300/8-12
7854 Oldfield Rd 44827 · 419-683-3647
Douglas Potts, prin. · Fax 683-9063

Creston, Wayne, Pop. 2,149
North Central Local SD · 1,400/K-12
350 S Main St 44217 · 330-435-6382
Larry Acker, supt. · Fax 435-4633
www.northcentral.k12.oh.us/
Creston MS · 400/5-8
PO Box 4443 44217 · 330-435-4255
Karen O'Hare, prin. · Fax 435-4633
Norwayne HS · 500/9-12
350 S Main St 44217 · 330-435-4276
Douglas Zimmerly, prin. · Fax 435-4633

Crooksville, Perry, Pop. 2,530
Crooksville EVD · 1,200/K-12
4065 School Dr 43731 · 740-982-7040
Steven Pompey, supt. · Fax 982-3551
www.crooksville.k12.oh.us/
Crooksville HS · 300/9-12
4075 Ceramic Way 43731 · 740-982-7015
Jacqueline Bolyard, prin. · Fax 982-3086
Crooksville MS · 300/6-8
12400 Tunnel Hill Rd 43731 · 740-982-7010
Gary Stall, prin. · Fax 982-5087

Crown City, Gallia, Pop. 425
Gallia County Local SD
Supt. — See Gallipolis
South Gallia HS · 200/9-12
266 Mercerville Rd 45623 · 740-256-6379
Scot West, prin. · Fax 256-6007

Cutler, Washington
Warren Local SD
Supt. — See Vincent
Bartlett S · 100/4-8
2035 State Route 550 45724 · 740-551-2461
Tom Perkins, prin. · Fax 551-2237

Cuyahoga Falls, Summit, Pop. 50,375
Cuyahoga Falls CSD · 4,700/K-12
PO Box 396 44222 · 330-926-3800
Dr. Edwin S. Holland, supt. · Fax 920-1074
www.cfalls.summit.k12.oh.us
Bolich MS · 600/6-8
2630 13th St 44223 · 330-926-3801
Chris McBurney, prin. · Fax 920-3737
Cuyahoga Falls HS · 1,700/9-12
2300 4th St 44221 · 330-926-3808
Nicholas Valentine, prin. · Fax 916-6013
Roberts MS · 400/6-8
3333 Charles St 44221 · 330-926-3809
Thomas Ratcliff, prin. · Fax 920-3748

Cuyahoga Valley Christian Academy · 900/7-12
4687 Wyoga Lake Rd 44224 · 330-929-0575
Jon Holley, prin. · Fax 929-0156
National Institute of Technology · Post-Sec.
2545 Bailey Rd 44221 · 330-923-9959
Riggs Le Mar Beauty College · Post-Sec.
3464 Hudson Dr 44221 · 330-945-4045

Cuyahoga Heights, Cuyahoga, Pop. 578
Cuyahoga Heights Local SD · 900/PK-12
4820 E 71st St 44125 · 216-429-5700
Peter Guerrera, supt. · Fax 341-3737
www.cuyhts.k12.oh.us
Cuyahoga Heights HS · 300/9-12
4820 E 71st St 44125 · 216-429-5707
Lora Garrett, prin. · Fax 429-5706
Cuyahoga Heights MS · 200/6-8
4840 E 71st St 44125 · 216-429-5757
Tom Burton, prin. · Fax 429-5735

Dalton, Wayne, Pop. 1,588
Dalton Local SD 1,000/K-12
PO Box 514 44618 330-828-2267
Fred Blosser, supt. Fax 828-2800
www.dalton.k12.oh.us
Dalton IS 200/6-8
PO Box 514 44618 330-828-2405
Broc Bidlack, prin. Fax 828-2801
Dalton Local HS 300/9-12
PO Box 514 44618 330-828-2261
Scott Beatty, prin. Fax 828-2904

Danville, Knox, Pop. 1,100
Danville Local SD 600/K-12
PO Box 30 43014 740-599-6116
Damien O. Bawn, supt. Fax 599-5417
www.danville.k12.oh.us/
Danville HS 200/9-12
PO Box 30 43014 740-599-6116
Roxanna Reiheld, prin. Fax 599-5418
Danville MS, PO Box 30 43014 100/7-8
Roxanna Reihold, prin. 740-599-6116

Dayton, Montgomery, Pop. 161,696
Centerville CSD
Supt. — See Centerville
Watts MS 600/6-8
7056 McEwen Rd 45459 937-434-0370
Brian Miller, prin. Fax 434-2907

Dayton CSD 20,100/PK-12
115 S Ludlow St 45402 937-542-3000
Percy A. Mack Ph.D., supt. Fax 542-3188
www.dps.k12.oh.us
Belmont HS 1,100/9-12
2323 Mapleview Ave 45420 937-542-6460
Joye Stier, prin. Fax 542-6461
Dunbar HS 900/9-12
2222 Richley Dr 45408 937-542-6760
Phyllis Combs, prin. Fax 542-6761
Fairview MS 700/7-8
2408 Philadelphia Dr 45406 937-542-6050
Vondia Jackson, prin. Fax 542-6051
Kiser MS 200/8-8
1401 Leo St 45404 937-542-6130
Jacqueline Ringer, prin. Fax 542-6131
Meadowdale HS 1,200/9-12
4417 Williamson Dr 45416 937-542-7030
Dora A. Carson, prin. Fax 542-7031
Miami Chapel MS 700/4-8
1630 Miami Chapel Rd 45408 937-542-5440
Maurice Sadler, prin. Fax 542-5441
Patterson Career Academy Vo/Tech
441 River Corridor Dr 45402 937-542-7180
Sheryl Lenehan, prin. Fax 542-7181
Stivers School for the Arts 800/7-12
325 Homewood Ave 45405 937-542-7380
Erin Dooley, prin. Fax 542-7381
White HS 1,100/9-12
501 Niagara Ave 45405 937-542-6610
Gerry Griffith, prin. Fax 542-6611
Wright MS 700/7-8
1361 Huffman Ave 45403 937-542-6380
Shirley Frederick, prin. Fax 542-6381

Jefferson Township Local SD 700/K-12
2625 S Union Rd 45418 937-835-5682
Dr. Norris Brown, supt. Fax 835-5955
www.jeffersontwp.k12.oh.us/
Jefferson HS 400/7-12
2701 S Union Rd 45418 937-295-5691
Bert Seard, prin. Fax 835-5693

Mad River Local SD 3,400/K-12
801 Old Harshman Rd 45431 937-259-6606
Alex DiNino, supt. Fax 259-6607
www.madriver.k12.oh.us
Mad River MS 600/7-8
1801 Harshman Rd 45424 937-237-4265
Mark Henderson, prin. Fax 237-4273
Stebbins HS 1,100/9-12
1900 Harshman Rd 45424 937-237-4250
Dr. Todd Nichols, prin. Fax 237-4262

Northridge Local SD 1,500/K-12
2011 Timber Ln 45414 937-278-5885
Tod Perez, supt. Fax 276-8351
www.northridge-montgomery.k12.oh.us
Dennis MS 500/6-8
5120 N Dixie Dr 45414 937-274-2136
Timothy Whitestone, prin. Fax 276-8354
Northridge HS 500/9-12
2251 Timber Ln 45414 937-275-7469
David Jackson, prin. Fax 275-8434

Oakwood CSD 2,000/K-12
20 Rubicon Rd 45409 937-297-5332
Mary Jo Scalzo Ph.D., supt. Fax 297-5345
www.oakwoodschools.org
Oakwood HS 600/9-12
1200 Far Hills Ave 45419 937-297-5325
Joseph Boyle, prin. Fax 297-5348
Oakwood JHS 300/7-8
1200 Far Hills Ave 45419 937-297-5328
John Kronour, prin. Fax 297-7807

Trotwood-Madison CSD
Supt. — See Trotwood
Trotwood-Madison MS 900/6-9
3594 N Snyder Rd 45426 937-854-0017
Kevin Bell, prin. Fax 854-8433

Vandalia-Butler CSD
Supt. — See Vandalia
Smith MS 500/5-8
3625 Little York Rd 45414 937-415-7000
Laura Bemus, prin. Fax 415-7051

Carousel Beauty College Post-Sec.
125 E 2nd St 45402 937-223-3572
Carroll HS 1,000/9-12
4524 Linden Ave 45432 937-253-8188
Joseph Sens, prin. Fax 258-7001
Chaminade-Julienne HS 1,000/9-12
505 S Ludlow St 45402 937-461-3740
John Marshall, prin. Fax 461-6256
Dayton Barber College Post-Sec.
28 W 5th St 45402 937-222-9101
Dominion Academy of Dayton 100/4-12
925 N Main St 45405 937-224-8555
Fax 224-4485
International College of Broadcasting Post-Sec.
6 S Smithville Rd 45431 937-258-8251
ITT Technical Institute Post-Sec.
3325 Stop 8 Rd 45414 937-454-2267
Miami-Jacobs College Post-Sec.
110 N Patterson Blvd 45402 937-222-7337
Miami Valley Hospital Post-Sec.
1 Wyoming St 45409 937-223-6192
Miami Valley S 500/PK-12
5151 Denise Dr 45429 937-434-4444
Thomas Brereton, hdmstr. Fax 434-1033
Ohio Institute of Photography & Tech Post-Sec.
2029 Edgefield Rd 45439 937-294-6155
Sinclair Community College Post-Sec.
444 W 3rd St 45402 937-512-2500
Southwestern College of Business Post-Sec.
111 W 1st St Ste 1140 45402 937-224-0061
University of Dayton Post-Sec.
300 College Park Ave 45469 937-229-1000
Wright State University Post-Sec.
3640 Colonel Glenn Hwy 45435 937-775-3333

Defiance, Defiance, Pop. 16,163
Ayersville Local SD 900/K-12
28046 Watson Rd 43512 419-395-1111
Tod A. Hug, supt. Fax 395-9990
www.ayersville.k12.oh.us
Ayersville HS 300/9-12
28046 Watson Rd 43512 419-395-1111
Cameron VanArsdalen, prin. Fax 395-2566
Ayersville MS 300/5-8
28046 Watson Rd 43512 419-395-1111
Bruce Brown, prin. Fax 395-9990

Defiance CSD 2,500/K-12
629 Arabella St 43512 419-782-0070
Richard Motuelle Ed.D., supt. Fax 782-4395
www.defiancecityschools.org
Defiance HS 900/9-12
1755 Palmer Dr 43512 419-784-2777
Fred Boring, prin. Fax 784-0102
Defiance JHS 400/7-8
629 Arabella St 43512 419-782-0050
Kelly Davis, prin. Fax 782-0060

Northeastern Local SD 1,200/K-12
5921 Domersville Rd 43512 419-497-3461
James Roach, supt. Fax 497-3401
www.tinora.k12.oh.us
Tinora HS 400/9-12
5921 Domersville Rd 43512 419-497-2621
Philip Nofziger, prin. Fax 497-3401
Tinora JHS 200/7-8
5921 Domersville Rd 43512 419-497-2361
G. Kent Adams, prin. Fax 497-3401

Defiance College Post-Sec.
701 N Clinton St 43512 419-784-4010

De Graff, Logan, Pop. 1,189
Riverside Local SD 500/K-12
2096 County Road 24 S 43318 937-585-5981
Bernie Pachmayer, supt. Fax 585-4599
www.riverside.k12.oh.us
Riverside HS 300/9-12
2096 County Road 24 S 43318 937-585-5981
Mike Edwards, prin. Fax 585-4599
Riverside MS 5-8
2096 County Road 24 S 43318 937-585-5981
Tim Walls, prin. Fax 585-4599

Delaware, Delaware, Pop. 28,358
Buckeye Valley Local SD 2,200/K-12
679 Coover Rd 43015 740-369-8735
John Schiller, supt. Fax 363-7654
www.buckeyevalley.k12.oh.us
Buckeye Valley HS 700/9-12
901 Coover Rd 43015 740-363-1349
Davis Baker, prin. Fax 363-9380
Buckeye Valley MS 500/6-8
683 Coover Rd 43015 740-363-6626
Andrew Miller, prin. Fax 363-4483

Delaware Area Career Center
4565 Columbus Pike 43015 740-548-0708
Patricia Foor, supt. Fax 549-1397
www.delawareareacc.org
Delaware Area Career Center North Campus Vo/Tech
1610 State Route 521 43015 740-363-1993
Mary Paulins, prin. Fax 362-6461
Delaware Area Career Center South Campus Vo/Tech
4565 Columbus Pike 43015 740-548-0708
Dale Hayes, prin. Fax 548-0710
Delaware Area Career Ctr Adult Education Adult
4565 Columbus Pike 43015 740-548-0708
Sue Rowland, prin. Fax 549-1397

Delaware CSD 4,400/K-12
248 N Washington St 43015 740-833-1100
Dr. Mary Anne Ashworth, supt. Fax 833-1149
www.dcs.k12.oh.us
Dempsey MS 700/7-8
599 Pennsylvania Ave 43015 740-833-1800
Paul King, prin. Fax 833-1899
Hayes HS 1,300/9-12
289 Euclid Ave 43015 740-833-1010
James Peterson, prin. Fax 833-1099

Bethany Academy 100/K-10
500 N Liberty St 43015 740-362-5540
Jerry Smith, admin.
Delaware Christian S 300/K-12
45 Belle Ave 43015 740-363-8425
Gordon McDonald, admin. Fax 369-8378
Methodist Theological School in Ohio Post-Sec.
3081 Columbus Pike 43015 740-363-1146
Ohio Wesleyan University Post-Sec.
61 S Sandusky St 43015 740-368-2000

Delphos, Allen, Pop. 6,872
Delphos CSD 1,100/K-12
234 N Jefferson St 45833 419-692-2509
Bruce Sommers, supt. Fax 692-2653
www.noacsc.org/allen/dl/
Jefferson HS 300/9-12
901 Wildcat Ln 45833 419-695-1786
Robert Kiracofe, prin. Fax 692-2287
Jefferson MS 200/6-8
227 N Jefferson St 45833 419-695-2523
Terry Moreo, prin. Fax 692-2302

St. John HS 400/9-12
515 E 2nd St 45833 419-692-5371
Donald Huysman, prin. Fax 879-6874

Delta, Fulton, Pop. 2,921
Pike-Delta-York Local SD 1,500/K-12
504 Fernwood St 43515 419-822-3391
Robin Rayfield, supt. Fax 822-4478
www.pdy.k12.oh.us
Pike-Delta-York HS 500/9-12
605 Taylor St 43515 419-822-8247
Randall Lintermoot, prin. Fax 822-5921
Pike-Delta-York MS 400/6-8
1101 Panther Pride Dr 43515 419-822-9118
Dennis Ford, prin. Fax 822-8490

Dennison, Tuscarawas, Pop. 2,941
Claymont CSD 2,300/K-12
201 N 3rd St 44621 740-922-5478
Gary Hunter, supt. Fax 922-7325
www.claymont.k12.oh.us
Other Schools – See Uhrichsville

Diamond, Mahoning

TDDS Technical Institute Post-Sec.
1688 N Pricetown Rd 44412 330-538-2216

Dillonvale, Jefferson, Pop. 767
Buckeye Local SD 2,300/K-12
6898 State Route 150 43917 740-769-7395
Joseph Pielech, supt. Fax 769-2361
omeresa.net/schools/buckeye
Other Schools – See Brilliant, Rayland, Tiltonsville

Dola, Hardin
Hardin Northern Local SD 500/K-12
11589 State Route 81 45835 419-759-2331
Jeff Price, supt. Fax 759-2581
Hardin Northern JSHS 200/7-12
11589 State Route 81 45835 419-759-3515
Bradd Molk, prin. Fax 759-2581

Dover, Tuscarawas, Pop. 12,345
Dover CSD 2,600/K-12
219 W 6th St 44622 330-364-1906
Robert Hamm, supt. Fax 343-7070
www.dover.k12.oh.us/
Dover HS 900/9-12
520 N Walnut St 44622 330-364-7148
Karie McCrate, prin. Fax 364-7142
Dover MS 600/6-8
2131 N Wooster Ave 44622 330-364-7121
Thomas Jones, prin. Fax 364-7127

Doylestown, Wayne, Pop. 2,819
Chippewa Local SD 1,400/K-12
56 N Portage St 44230 330-658-6368
Steve Caples, supt. Fax 658-5842
www.chippewa.k12.oh.us
Chippewa HS 500/9-12
100 Valley View Rd 44230 330-658-2011
Jeff Schleich, prin. Fax 658-3339
Chippewa MS 400/5-8
257 High St 44230 330-658-2214
Sandy Stebly, prin. Fax 658-5842

Dresden, Muskingum, Pop. 1,423
Tri-Valley Local SD 3,100/K-12
36 E Muskingum Ave 43821 740-754-1572
C. Douglas Spade, supt. Fax 754-6400
www.tri-valley.k12.oh.us
Tri-Valley HS 900/9-12
46 E Muskingum Ave 43821 740-754-2921
James Pottmeyer, prin. Fax 754-6409
Tri-Valley MS 500/7-8
1358 Main St 43821 740-754-3531
Margaret Wilcox, prin. Fax 754-1879

Dublin, Franklin, Pop. 33,606
Columbus CSD
Supt. — See Columbus
Northwest Career Ctr Vo/Tech
2960 Cranston Dr 43017 614-365-5325
Charles Richardson, dir. Fax 365-5621

Dublin CSD 14,100/K-12
7030 Coffman Rd 43017 614-764-5913
Dr. Linda Fenner, supt. Fax 761-5899
www.dublinschools.net
Davis MS 700/6-8
2400 Sutter Pkwy 43016 614-761-5820
David Nosker, prin. Fax 761-5893
Dublin Coffman HS 2,000/9-12
6780 Coffman Rd 43017 614-764-5900
Tracey Miller, prin. Fax 764-5925
Dublin Jerome HS 1,800/9-12
8300 Hyland Croy Rd 43016 614-764-5913
Steven Best, prin. Fax 873-1937
Dublin Scioto HS 1,600/9-12
4000 Hard Rd 43016 614-717-2464
Marina Davis, prin. Fax 717-2484
Grizzell MS 800/6-8
8705 Avery Rd 43017 614-798-3569
Timothy Barton, prin. Fax 761-6514
Karrer MS 800/6-8
7245 Tullymore Dr 43016 614-873-0459
Rick Weininger, prin. Fax 718-8505

Sells MS | 600/6-8
150 W Bridge St 43017 | 614-764-5919
Carol King, prin. | Fax 764-5923

Duncan Falls, Muskingum
Franklin Local SD | 2,400/K-12
PO Box 428 43734 | 740-674-5203
David N. Branch, supt. | Fax 674-5214
www.franklin-local.k12.oh.us
Other Schools – See Philo, Roseville

East Canton, Stark, Pop. 1,611
Osnaburg Local SD | 900/K-12
310 Browning Ct N 44730 | 330-488-1609
Tom Davis, supt. | Fax 488-4001
ecweb.sparcc.org
East Canton HS | 300/9-12
310 Browning Ct N 44730 | 330-488-0316
Chris Corbi, prin. | Fax 488-4001
East Canton MS | 400/4-8
310 Browning Ct N 44730 | 330-488-0229
Dave Fischer, prin. | Fax 488-4001

East Cleveland, Cuyahoga, Pop. 26,255
East Cleveland CSD | 4,800/K-12
15305 Terrace Rd 44112 | 216-268-6550
Myrna Loy Corley, supt. | Fax 268-6676
www.east-cleveland.k12.oh.us
Heritage MS, 14410 Terrace Rd 44112 | 400/8-8
Beverly Bright-Lloyd, prin. | 216-268-6610
Shaw HS | 1,300/9-12
15320 Euclid Ave 44112 | 216-268-6500
Sandra Brown, prin. | Fax 268-6676

Huron School of Nursing | Post-Sec.
13951 Terrace Rd 44112 | 216-761-7996

Eastlake, Lake, Pop. 19,990
Willoughby-Eastlake CSD
Supt. — See Willoughby
Eastlake MS | 600/6-8
35972 Lake Shore Blvd 44095 | 440-942-5696
Ralph Young, prin. | Fax 918-8973
North HS | 1,500/9-12
34041 Stevens Blvd 44095 | 440-975-3666
Jeffrey Meddock, prin. | Fax 975-3671

East Liverpool, Columbiana, Pop. 12,611
East Liverpool CSD | 2,600/K-12
500 Maryland St 43920 | 330-386-7132
Douglas Hiscox, supt. | Fax 386-8763
eastliverpool.k12.oh.us
East Liverpool HS | 1,000/9-12
100 Maine Blvd 43920 | 330-386-8750
Linda Henderson, prin. | Fax 386-8753
East Liverpool MS | 700/6-8
810 W 8th St 43920 | 330-386-8765
Patrick Poling, prin. | Fax 382-7670

East Liverpool Christian S | 200/PK-12
46682 Florence St 43920 | 330-385-5588
Janice Moegerle, prin. | Fax 385-1267
Kent State University-East Liverpool | Post-Sec.
400 E 4th St 43920 | 330-385-3805
Ohio Valley College of Technology | Post-Sec.
PO Box 7000 43920 | 330-385-1070

East Palestine, Columbiana, Pop. 4,835
East Palestine CSD | 1,400/K-12
200 N North Ave 44413 | 330-426-4191
Jeffrey Richardson, supt. | Fax 426-9592
www.epschools.k12.oh.us/
East Palestine HS | 500/9-12
360 W Grant St 44413 | 330-426-9401
Gary Contini, prin. | Fax 426-5105
East Palestine MS | 400/6-8
320 W Grant St 44413 | 330-426-9451
Lynn Campbell, prin.

Eaton, Preble, Pop. 8,170
Eaton Community SD | 2,300/K-12
307 N Cherry St 45320 | 937-456-1107
Dr. Joe DeLuca, supt. | Fax 472-1057
eaton-city.k12.oh.us
Eaton HS | 700/9-12
600 Hillcrest Dr 45320 | 937-456-1141
Brad Neavin, prin. | Fax 456-1143
Eaton MS | 500/6-8
311 N Cherry St 45320 | 937-456-2286
Kern Carpenter, prin. | Fax 456-2022

Edgerton, Williams, Pop. 2,050
Edgerton Local SD | 700/K-12
111 E River St 43517 | 419-298-2112
Charles A. Koch, supt. | Fax 298-2281
www.edgerton.k12.oh.us/
Edgerton HS | 300/9-12
111 E River St 43517 | 419-298-2331
Jeffrey Snyder, prin. | Fax 298-2281
Edgerton MS | 100/7-8
217 E River St 43517 | 419-298-2166
Jeffrey Snyder, prin. | Fax 298-2281

Edon, Williams, Pop. 872
Edon-Northwest Local SD | 700/K-12
802 W Indiana St 43518 | 419-272-3213
Michael Struble, supt. | Fax 272-2240
www.edon.k12.oh.us/
Edon HS | 300/9-12
802 W Indiana St 43518 | 419-272-3113
Robert Morton, prin. | Fax 272-2240
Edon MS | 200/5-8
802 W Indiana St 43518 | 419-272-3213
Robert Morton, prin. | Fax 272-2240

Elida, Allen, Pop. 1,901
Elida Local SD | 2,400/K-12
4380 Sunnydale St 45807 | 419-331-4155
Don Diglia, supt. | Fax 331-1656
home.elida.k12.oh.us/
Elida HS | 900/9-12
101 E North St 45807 | 419-331-4115
Sarah Burden, prin. | Fax 339-3523
Elida MS | 600/6-8
4500 Sunnydale St 45807 | 419-331-2505
Herbert Purton, prin. | Fax 331-6822

Elmore, Ottawa, Pop. 1,401
Woodmore Local SD
Supt. — See Woodville
Woodmore JSHS | 600/7-12
633 Fremont St 43416 | 419-862-2721
Hobart Johnson, prin. | Fax 862-3835

Elyria, Lorain, Pop. 56,096
Elyria CSD | 8,000/K-12
42101 Griswold Rd 44035 | 440-284-8000
Paul Rigda, supt. | Fax 284-0678
www.elyriaschools.org
Eastern Heights JHS | 400/7-8
528 Garford Ave 44035 | 440-284-8015
Kimberly Blevins, prin.
Elyria HS | 2,000/9-12
311 6th St 44035 | 440-284-8300
Dianne Quinn, prin. | Fax 323-2543
Northwood JHS | 500/7-8
700 Gulf Rd 44035 | 440-284-8016
Thomas Jama, prin. | Fax 284-1546
Westwood JHS | 400/7-8
42350 Adelbert St 44035 | 440-284-8017
Gregory Horace, prin. | Fax 284-1055

Elyria Catholic HS | 600/9-12
725 Gulf Rd 44035 | 440-365-1821
Andrew Krakowiak, prin. | Fax 365-7536
First Baptist Christian S | 200/PK-12
11400 Lagrange Rd 44035 | 440-458-5185
Brenda Milam, admin. | Fax 458-8717
Lorain County Community College | Post-Sec.
1005 Abbe Rd N 44035 | 440-365-5222
Ohio Institute of Health Careers | Post-Sec.
631 Griswold Rd 44035 | 800-725-0882
Open Door Christian HS | 300/7-12
8287 W Ridge Rd 44035 | 440-322-6386
Darrell Dunckel, prin. | Fax 284-6033

Englewood, Montgomery, Pop. 12,460
Northmont CSD | 5,800/K-12
4001 Old Salem Rd 45322 | 937-832-5000
Dr. Gale Mabry, supt. | Fax 832-5001
www.northmontschools.com/
Other Schools – See Clayton

Enon, Clark, Pop. 2,573
Greenon Local SD | 2,000/K-12
500 Enon-Xenia Rd 45323 | 937-864-1202
Denny Howell, supt. | Fax 864-2470
www.greenon.k12.oh.us
Indian Valley MS | 600/5-8
510 Enon-Xenia Rd 45323 | 937-864-7348
Cathie Scott, prin. | Fax 864-6009
Other Schools – See Springfield

Etna, Licking
Southwest Licking Local SD | 3,500/K-12
PO Box 180 43018 | 740-927-3941
Forest Yocum, supt. | Fax 927-4648
www.swl.k12.oh.us
Other Schools – See Pataskala

Euclid, Cuyahoga, Pop. 51,260
Euclid CSD | 7,500/K-12
651 E 222nd St 44123 | 216-261-2900
Dr. Joffrey Jones, supt. | Fax 261-3120
www.euclid.k12.oh.us
AIID | 9-12
711 E 222nd St 44123 | 216-797-7825
William Baylis, prin. | Fax 797-7900
Business & Communications S | 9-12
711 E 222nd St 44123 | 216-797-7821
Ed Klein, prin. | Fax 797-7900
Euclid Academy of the Arts | 9-12
711 E 222nd St 44123 | 216-797-7813
Tina Elliott, prin. | Fax 797-7900
Euclid Central MS | 1,100/6-8
20701 Euclid Ave 44117 | 216-797-5300
Hans Pesch, prin. | Fax 797-5333
Forest Park MS | 500/6-8
27000 Elinore Ave 44132 | 216-797-4700
Charlie Smialek, prin. | Fax 797-4710
International Academy | 9-12
711 E 222nd St 44123 | 216-797-7831
Claudia Spencer, prin. | Fax 797-7900
Professional Path S | 9-12
711 E 222nd St 44123 | 216-797-7809
Elie Thomas, prin. | Fax 797-7900
Science Technology Engineering & Math S | 2,100/9-12
711 E 222nd St 44123 | 216-797-7801
Ron Seymour, prin. | Fax 797-7900

Fairborn, Greene, Pop. 32,474
Fairborn CSD | 3,500/PK-12
306 E Whittier Ave 45324 | 937-878-3961
Dave Scarberry, supt. | Fax 879-8180
www.fairborn.k12.oh.us
Baker MS | 900/6-8
200 Lincoln Dr 45324 | 937-878-4681
William Howard, prin. | Fax 879-8193
Fairborn HS | 1,600/9-12
900 E Dayton Yellow Springs 45324 | 937-879-3611
Robert Cotter, prin. | Fax 879-8190

Creative Images-Matrix Design Academy | Post-Sec.
1076 Kauffman Ave 45324 | 937-878-9555
Hondros College | Post-Sec.
1810 Successful Dr 45324 | 937-431-1808

Fairfield, Butler, Pop. 42,544
Butler Technology & Career Development S
3603 Hamilton Middletown Rd 45011 | 513-868-1911
Robert D. Sommers, supt. | Fax 868-9348
www.butlertech.org
Lee Career-Technology Center | Vo/Tech
3603 Hamilton Middletown Rd 45011 | 513-868-6300
Bob Thompson, prin. | Fax 868-1701
Options Arts Academy | Vo/Tech
101 S Monument Ave 45011 | 513-863-8873
Jackie Quay, prin.
Other Schools – See Hamilton, Monroe

Fairfield CSD | 9,500/K-12
211 Donald Dr 45014 | 513-829-6300
Robert Farrell, supt. | Fax 829-0148
www.fairfieldcityschools.com
Fairfield Freshman HS | 700/9-9
5050 Dixie Hwy 45014 | 513-829-8300
Dan Beckenhaupt, prin. | Fax 829-4733
Fairfield MS | 1,600/7-8
1111 Nilles Rd 45014 | 513-829-4433
Megan Graham, prin. | Fax 829-6480
Fairfield SHS | 2,200/10-12
8800 Holden Blvd 45014 | 513-942-2999
Paul Waller, prin. | Fax 942-3288

Moler-Pickens Beauty College | Post-Sec.
5951 Boymel Dr Ste S 45014 | 513-874-5116

Fairlawn, Summit, Pop. 7,287

Academy of Court Reporting | Post-Sec.
2930 W Market St 44333 | 330-867-4030
Gerber Akron Beauty School | Post-Sec.
33 Shiawassee Ave 44333 | 330-867-6200

Fairport Harbor, Lake, Pop. 3,192
Fairport Harbor EVD | 600/K-12
329 Vine St 44077 | 440-354-5400
William Clark, supt. | Fax 354-1724
www.fairport.k12.oh.us/home.htm
Fairport Harding JSHS | 300/7-12
329 Vine St 44077 | 440-354-3592
Marilyn Foote, prin. | Fax 354-5426

Fairview Park, Cuyahoga, Pop. 17,087
Fairview Park CSD | 1,800/K-12
20770 Lorain Rd 44126 | 440-331-5500
Brion Deitsch, supt. | Fax 356-3545
www.leeca.org/fairview
Fairview HS | 700/9-12
4507 W 213th St 44126 | 440-356-3500
Cary Willgren, prin. | Fax 356-3529
Mayer MS | 300/7-8
21200 Campus Dr 44126 | 440-356-3510
Molly Jewitt, prin. | Fax 895-2191

Fairview Academy | Post-Sec.
22610 Lorain Rd 44126 | 440-734-5555

Fayette, Fulton, Pop. 1,323
Gorham Fayette Local SD | 500/K-12
PO Box 309 43521 | 419-237-2573
David Hankins, supt. | Fax 237-3125
www.gorham-fayette.k12.oh.us
Gorham Fayette JSHS | 200/7-12
PO Box 309 43521 | 419-237-2114
James Marquette, prin. | Fax 237-3125

Fayetteville, Brown, Pop. 380
Fayetteville-Perry Local SD | 1,000/K-12
501 S Apple St 45118 | 513-875-2423
Roy Hill, supt. | Fax 875-2703
www.fp.k12.oh.us
Fayetteville-Perry HS | 300/9-12
501 S Apple St 45118 | 513-875-3520
Raegan White, prin. | Fax 875-4512
Fayetteville-Perry MS | 300/5-8
601 S Apple St 45118 | 513-875-2829
David Tatman, prin. | Fax 875-4523

Chatfield College | Post-Sec.
20918 State Route 251 45118 | 513-875-3344

Felicity, Clermont, Pop. 912
Felicity-Franklin Local SD | 1,200/PK-12
PO Box 839 45120 | 513-876-2113
Jeffery T. Weir, supt. | Fax 876-2519
www.felicityfranklinschools.org/
Felicity-Franklin Local HS | 400/9-12
PO Box 839 45120 | 513-876-2113
Chris Allen, prin. | Fax 876-2560
Felicity-Franklin Local MS | 400/5-8
PO Box 839 45120 | 513-876-2113
Marty Paeltz, prin. | Fax 876-2519

Findlay, Hancock, Pop. 39,797
Findlay CSD | 6,800/K-12
227 S West St 45840 | 419-425-8212
Dr. Dean Wittwer, supt. | Fax 425-8203
www.findlaycityschools.org
Central MS | 500/6-8
200 W Main Cross St 45840 | 419-425-8257
Christopher Renn, prin. | Fax 427-5453
Donnell MS | 500/6-8
301 Baldwin Ave 45840 | 419-425-8370
Stephanie Roth, prin. | Fax 425-5454
Findlay HS | 2,100/9-12
1200 Broad Ave 45840 | 419-425-8289
Craig Kupferberg, prin. | Fax 427-5448
Glenwood MS | 400/6-8
1715 N Main St 45840 | 419-425-8373
Bruce Otley, prin. | Fax 427-5455
Millstream East Vocational S | Vo/Tech
620 Lynn St 45840 | 419-425-8214
Edith Wannemacher, prin. | Fax 427-5461
Millstream South Vocational S | Vo/Tech
1100 Broad Ave 45840 | 419-425-8277
Kathy Siebenaler-Wilson, prin. | Fax 427-5469

Liberty-Benton Local SD | 1,300/K-12
9190 County Road 9 45840 | 419-422-8526
Dennis Recker, supt. | Fax 422-5108
www.noacsc.org/hancock/lb/
Liberty-Benton HS | 400/9-12
9190 County Road 9 45840 | 419-424-5351
Brenda Frankart, prin. | Fax 422-5108
Liberty Benton MS | 300/6-8
9050 W State Route 12 45840 | 419-422-9166
Steven Gfell, prin. | Fax 422-5108

Brown Mackie College | Post-Sec.
1700 Fostoria Ave Ste 100 45840 | 888-296-5059
Owens Community College | Post-Sec.
300 Davis St 45840 | 567-429-3500

University of Findlay | Post-Sec.
1000 N Main St 45840 | 419-422-8313
Winebrenner Theological Seminary | Post-Sec.
950 N Main St 45840 | 419-434-4200

Fort Jennings, Putnam, Pop. 429
Jennings Local SD | 500/K-12
PO Box 98 45844 | 419-286-2238
Frank Sukup, supt. | Fax 286-2240
Fort Jennings JSHS | 200/7-12
PO Box 98 45844 | 419-286-2238
Nicholas Langhals, prin. | Fax 286-2240

Fort Loramie, Shelby, Pop. 1,432
Fort Loramie Local SD | 800/K-12
PO Box 26 45845 | 937-295-3931
Larry Ludlow, supt. | Fax 295-2758
www.loramie.k12.oh.us/
Fort Loramie JSHS | 400/7-12
PO Box 290 45845 | 937-295-3342
Michael Roche, prin. | Fax 295-2758

Fort Recovery, Mercer, Pop. 1,305
Fort Recovery Local SD | 1,100/PK-12
PO Box 604 45846 | 419-375-4139
David R. Riel, supt. | Fax 375-1058
www.noacsc.org/mercer/fr/
Fort Recovery HS | 300/9-12
400 E Butler St 45846 | 419-375-4111
Edward Snyder, prin. | Fax 375-2039
Fort Recovery MS | 200/6-8
865 Sharpsburg Rd 45846 | 419-375-2815
Ted Shuttleworth, prin. | Fax 375-1126

Fostoria, Seneca, Pop. 13,720
Fostoria CSD | 2,200/PK-12
500 Parkway Dr 44830 | 419-435-8163
Dr. Cynthia A. Lemmerman, supt. | Fax 436-4109
www.fostoria.k12.oh.us/
Fostoria HS | 700/9-12
1001 Park Ave 44830 | 419-436-4110
Jude Meyers, prin. | Fax 436-4118
Fostoria MS | 500/6-8
1202 H L Ford Dr 44830 | 419-436-4120
Kathleen Leitzy, prin. | Fax 436-4169

Lakota Local SD
Supt. — See Risingsun
Lakota JHS | 200/7-8
8351 W County Road 28 44830 | 419-435-2497
James Balsizer, prin. | Fax 435-9401

St. Wendelin HS | 300/9-12
533 N Countyline St 44830 | 419-435-8144
David Alt, prin. | Fax 436-4042

Fowler, Trumbull
Mathews Local SD
Supt. — See Vienna
Neal MS, PO Box 179 44418 | 200/6-8
Pat Vidis, prin. | 330-637-3066

Frankfort, Ross, Pop. 1,012
Adena Local SD | 1,200/K-12
3367 County Road 550 45628 | 740-998-4633
Michael Kinnamon, supt. | Fax 998-4632
adena.k12.oh.us/
Adena HS | 400/9-12
3367 County Road 550 45628 | 740-998-2313
Michael Francis, prin. | Fax 998-2314
Adena MS | 300/6-8
3367 County Road 550 45628 | 740-998-2313
Richard D. Clark, prin. | Fax 998-2314

Franklin, Warren, Pop. 12,065
Franklin CSD | 2,700/K-12
150 E 6th St 45005 | 937-746-1699
Steven Buerschen, supt. | Fax 743-4135
www.franklin-city.k12.oh.us
Franklin HS | 900/9-12
750 E 4th St 45005 | 937-743-8610
Dave Gregory, prin. | Fax 743-8623
Franklin MS | 500/6-8
136 E 6th St 45005 | 937-743-8630
James Martin, prin. | Fax 743-8637

Fenwick HS | 500/9-12
4485 State Route 122 45005 | 513-423-0723
Catherine Mulligan, prin. | Fax 420-8690
Middletown Christian S | 500/PK-12
3011 Union Rd 45005 | 513-423-4542
Mark Spradling, prin. | Fax 261-6841
Southwestern College | Post-Sec.
201 E 2nd St 45005 | 937-746-6633

Franklin Furnace, Scioto, Pop. 1,212
Green Local SD | 700/K-12
4070 Gallia Pike 45629 | 740-354-9221
Frank Barnett, supt. | Fax 355-8975
www.green.k12.oh.us
Green JSHS | 400/7-12
4057 Gallia Pike 45629 | 740-354-9150
David Hopper, prin. | Fax 355-9094

Fredericktown, Knox, Pop. 2,552
Fredericktown Local SD | 1,200/K-12
134 W 2nd St 43019 | 740-694-2956
Dan Humphrey, supt. | Fax 694-0956
www.fredericktown.net/schools.htm
Fredericktown HS | 400/9-12
117 Columbus Rd 43019 | 740-694-2726
Gary Chapman, prin. | Fax 694-0956
Fredericktown IS | 500/4-8
31 Taylor St 43019 | 740-694-2966
Emily Funston, prin. | Fax 694-0956

Fremont, Sandusky, Pop. 17,236
Fremont CSD | 4,500/K-12
1220 Cedar St Ste A 43420 | 419-332-6454
Donald G. King, supt. | Fax 334-5454
www.fremont.k12.oh.us
Fremont MS | 1,000/7-9
501 Croghan St 43420 | 419-332-5569
Jon Detwiler, prin. | Fax 334-5494

Fremont Ross SHS | 1,000/10-12
1100 North St 43420 | 419-332-8221
Sandra Werling, prin. | Fax 334-5450

Vanguard-Sentinel Career Centers
1306 Cedar St 43420 | 419-332-2626
David Danhoff, supt. | Fax 334-4308
www.vscc.k12.oh.us/
Technology Center | Vo/Tech
1220 Cedar St Ste C 43420 | 419-334-5698
Thomas Gerschutz, prin. | Fax 334-2609
Vanguard Career Center | Vo/Tech
1306 Cedar St 43420 | 419-332-2626
Terri Clark, dir. | Fax 334-5692
Vanguard-Sentinel Adult Career Center | Vo/Tech
1220 Career St Ste B 43420 | 419-334-6901
Tom Gerschutz, dir. | Fax 334-5696
Other Schools – See Tiffin

St. Joseph Central HS | 300/9-12
702 Croghan St 43420 | 419-332-9947
Mike Gabel, prin. | Fax 332-4945
Terra State Community College | Post-Sec.
2830 Napoleon Rd 43420 | 419-334-8400

Gahanna, Franklin, Pop. 33,224
Gahanna-Jefferson CSD | 6,800/K-12
160 S Hamilton Rd 43230 | 614-471-7065
Gregg Morris, supt. | Fax 478-5568
www.gahannaschools.org
Gahanna MS East | 600/6-8
730 Clotts Rd 43230 | 614-478-5550
Dwight Carter, prin. | Fax 478-5544
Gahanna MS South | 600/6-8
349 Shady Spring Dr 43230 | 614-337-3730
Angie Adrean, prin. | Fax 337-3734
Gahanna MS West | 600/6-8
350 N Stygler Rd 43230 | 614-478-5570
John Rathburn, prin. | Fax 337-3771
Lincoln HS | 2,200/9-12
140 S Hamilton Rd 43230 | 614-478-5500
Mark White, prin. | Fax 337-3769

Columbus Academy | 1,000/PK-12
PO Box 30745 43230 | 614-475-2311
John MacKenzie, prin. | Fax 475-0396
Gahanna Christian Academy | 500/PK-12
817 N Hamilton Rd 43230 | 614-471-9270
Rev. Lawrence Bates, supt. | Fax 471-9201

Galena, Delaware, Pop. 387
Big Walnut Local SD | 2,600/K-12
PO Box 218 43021 | 740-965-2706
Melissa Conrath, supt.
www.bigwalnut.k12.oh.us/
Other Schools – See Sunbury

Galion, Crawford, Pop. 11,491
Galion CSD | 1,500/PK-12
200 W Church St 44833 | 419-468-3432
Dennis Rose, supt. | Fax 468-4333
www.ncocc-k12.org/galion
Galion HS | 700/9-12
200 N Union St 44833 | 419-468-6500
Joe Gotchall, prin. | Fax 468-4333
Galion MS | 400/6-8
200 W Walnut St 44833 | 419-468-3134
Andrew Johnson, prin. | Fax 468-4333

Northmor Local SD | 1,200/K-12
5247 County Road 29 44833 | 419-946-8861
Brent Winand, supt. | Fax 947-6255
www.ncocc-k12.org/northmor
Northmor HS | 600/7-12
5353 County Road 29 44833 | 419-946-3946
Dennis Ervin, prin. | Fax 947-7545

Gallipolis, Gallia, Pop. 4,176
Gallia County Local SD | 2,500/K-12
230 Shawnee Ln 45631 | 740-446-7917
Charla C. Evans, supt. | Fax 446-3187
gallialocal.org
Other Schools – See Cheshire, Crown City

Gallipolis CSD | 2,300/K-12
61 State St 45631 | 740-446-3211
Jack Payton, supt. | Fax 446-6433
gallipoliscityschools.k12.oh.us
Gallia Academy JSHS | 1,100/7-12
340 4th Ave 45631 | 740-446-3212
Bruce Wilson, prin. | Fax 446-3436

Gallipolis Career College | Post-Sec.
1176 Jackson Pike # 312 45631 | 740-446-4367
Gallipolis State Institute | Post-Sec.
Ohio Valley Christian S | 200/K-12
455 3rd Ave 45631 | 740-446-0374
Dr. Frederick Williams, admin. | Fax 446-8593

Galloway, Franklin
South-Western CSD
Supt. — See Grove City
Westland HS | 1,600/9-12
146 Galloway Rd 43119 | 614-851-7000
James Grube, prin. | Fax 870-5531

Gambier, Knox, Pop. 1,986

Kenyon College | Post-Sec.
1 Kenyon College 43022 | 740-427-5000

Garfield Heights, Cuyahoga, Pop. 29,881
Garfield Heights CSD | 3,800/K-12
5640 Briarcliff Dr 44125 | 216-475-8100
Jeanne Sternad, supt. | Fax 475-1824
www.garfieldheightscityschools.com/
Garfield Heights HS | 1,200/9-12
4900 Turney Rd 44125 | 216-662-2800
Terrance Olszewski, prin. | Fax 271-6183
Garfield Heights MS | 900/6-8
12000 Mapleleaf Dr 44125 | 216-475-8105
Marlene Remiesch, prin. | Fax 475-8146

Archbishop Lyke-St Timothy S | 300/5-8
4351 E 131st St 44105 | 216-581-3517
Margarete Smith, prin. | Fax 581-6204
Trinity HS | 700/9-12
12425 Granger Rd 44125 | 216-581-1644
Joseph A. Waler, prin. | Fax 581-9348

Garrettsville, Portage, Pop. 2,223
James A. Garfield Local SD | 1,600/K-12
10235 State Route 88 44231 | 330-527-4336
Charles Klamer, supt. | Fax 527-5941
garfield.sparcc.org/
Garfield HS | 500/9-12
10233 State Route 88 44231 | 330-527-4341
Neil Wallace, prin. | Fax 527-5636
Garfield MS | 300/7-8
10231 State Route 88 44231 | 330-527-2151
Rosalice Manlove, prin. | Fax 527-2601

Gates Mills, Cuyahoga, Pop. 2,432

Gilmour Academy MS | 100/7-8
34001 Cedar Rd 44040 | 440-473-8111
Yvonne Saunders, prin. | Fax 473-8112
Gilmour Academy Upper S | 300/9-12
34001 Cedar Rd 44040 | 440-473-8090
Br. Robert Lavelle, prin. | Fax 473-8093
Hawken S | 400/9-12
PO Box 8002 44040 | 440-423-4446
James Berkman, hdmstr. | Fax 423-2975

Geneva, Ashtabula, Pop. 6,511
Geneva CSD | 3,000/K-12
135 S Eagle St 44041 | 440-466-4831
Ronald Donatone, supt. | Fax 466-0908
www.genevaschools.org/
Geneva HS | 1,000/9-12
839 Sherman St 44041 | 440-466-4831
Joanna Daniels, prin. | Fax 466-6036
Geneva JHS | 500/7-8
839 Sherman St 44041 | 440-466-4831
Richard Belconis, prin. | Fax 466-6036

Genoa, Ottawa, Pop. 2,346
Genoa Area Local SD | 1,700/K-12
2810 N Genoa Clay Center Rd 43430 | 419-855-7741
Dennis Mock, supt. | Fax 855-4030
www.genoaschools.com
Genoa Area HS | 600/9-12
2980 N Genoa Clay Center Rd 43430 | 419-855-7735
James Henline, prin. | Fax 855-7739
Genoa Area MS | 400/6-8
2950 N Genoa Clay Center Rd 43430 | 419-855-7781
Kevin Katafias, prin. | Fax 855-7784

Georgetown, Brown, Pop. 3,786
Georgetown EVD | 1,100/K-12
1043 Mount Orab Pike 45121 | 937-378-3730
Michael Smith, supt. | Fax 378-2219
www.gtownschools.org/
Georgetown JSHS | 500/7-12
987 Mount Orab Pike 45121 | 937-378-6730
Perianne Germann, prin. | Fax 378-2442

Southern Hills JVSD | 937-378-6131
9193 Hamer Rd 45121 | Fax 378-4577
Charles Guarino, supt.
www.shcc.k12.oh.us
Southern Hills Career Center | Vo/Tech
9193 Hamer Rd 45121 | 937-378-6131
Tim Chadwell, prin. | Fax 378-4577

Germantown, Montgomery, Pop. 5,043
Valley View Local SD | 2,000/K-12
64 Comstock St 45327 | 937-855-6581
Sherry Parr, supt. | Fax 855-7156
www.valleyview.k12.oh.us
Valley View HS | 700/9-12
6027 Frmrsvll Germantn Pike 45327 | 937-855-4116
Steve Anderson, prin. | Fax 855-4739
Valley View MS | 500/6-8
64 Comstock St 45327 | 937-855-4203
Harold Bowman, prin. | Fax 855-7156

Germantown Christian S | 100/K-12
9440 Eby Rd 45327 | 937-855-7334
Patricia Irwin, prin. | Fax 855-7746

Gibsonburg, Sandusky, Pop. 2,454
Gibsonburg EVD | 1,200/PK-12
301 S Sunset Ave 43431 | 419-637-2479
Richard Freeborn, supt. | Fax 637-3029
www.gibsonburg.k12.oh.us/
Gibsonburg HS | 400/9-12
740 S Main St 43431 | 419-637-2873
Thom Loomis, prin. | Fax 637-2046
Gibsonburg MS | 300/6-8
740 S Main St 43431 | 419-637-7954
Danny Kissell, prin. | Fax 637-2046

Girard, Trumbull, Pop. 10,654
Girard CSD | 1,800/K-12
704 E Prospect St 44420 | 330-545-2596
Joseph Jeswald, supt. | Fax 545-2597
Girard HS | 600/9-12
31 N Ward Ave 44420 | 330-545-5431
Ronald Ragozine, prin. | Fax 545-5440
Girard JHS | 300/7-8
31 N Ward Ave 44420 | 330-545-5431
William Ryser, prin. | Fax 545-5440

Glouster, Athens, Pop. 2,041
Trimble Local SD | 1,000/K-12
1 Tomcat Dr 45732 | 740-767-4444
Cindy Johnston, supt. | Fax 767-4901
trimble.k12.oh.us/
Trimble HS | 300/9-12
1 Tomcat Dr 45732 | 740-767-3434
John Abdella, prin. | Fax 767-4901
Trimble MS | 300/5-8
18500 Jacksonville Rd 45732 | 740-767-2810
Darrell Dugan, prin. | Fax 767-9523

Gnadenhutten, Tuscarawas, Pop. 1,287
Indian Valley Local SD | 2,000/K-12
PO Box 171 44629 | 740-254-4334
Randall Cadle, supt. | Fax 254-9271
www.ivschools.org/
Indian Valley HS | 900/7-12
PO Box 130 44629 | 740-254-4262
Martha Roudebush, prin. | Fax 254-4911

Goshen, Clermont
Goshen Local SD | 2,500/K-12
6694 Goshen Rd 45122 | 513-722-2222
Charlene Thomas, supt. | Fax 722-3767
www.goshenlocalschools.org
Goshen HS | 800/9-12
6707 Goshen Rd 45122 | 513-722-2227
John Strathern, prin. | Fax 722-2247
Goshen MS | 600/6-8
6692 Goshen Rd 45122 | 513-722-2226
Troy Smith, prin. | Fax 722-2246

Cozaddale Baptist Academy | 100/K-12
10632 Eltzroth Rd 45122 | 513-722-2064
C. Lee Carr, admin. | Fax 722-0096

Grafton, Lorain, Pop. 6,105
Midview Local SD | 1,700/K-12
1010 Vivian Dr 44044 | 440-926-3737
Howard Dulmage, supt. | Fax 926-2675
www.midviewk12.org
Midview HS | 1,100/9-12
38199 Capel Rd 44044 | 440-748-2124
Susan Bobola, prin. | Fax 748-5277
Midview MS | 600/7-8
37999 Capel Rd 44044 | 440-748-2122
Scott Goggin, prin. | Fax 748-0131

Grand Rapids, Wood, Pop. 990
Otsego Local SD
Supt. — See Tontogany
Otsego MS | 300/7-8
23939 2nd St 43522 | 419-832-2261
Ray Graves, prin. | Fax 832-0487

Grandview Heights, Franklin, Pop. 6,452
Grandview Heights CSD | 1,000/K-12
1587 W 3rd Ave 43212 | 614-481-3600
D. Steven Allen, supt. | Fax 481-3648
www.grandviewschools.org/
Grandview Heights HS | 400/9-12
1587 W 3rd Ave 43212 | 614-481-3620
Steven Andersson, prin. | Fax 481-3648
Grandview Heights MS | 200/7-8
1240 Oakland Ave 43212 | 614-481-3632
Robert Baeslack, prin. | Fax 481-3648

Granville, Licking, Pop. 5,125
Granville EVD | 2,100/K-12
PO Box 417 43023 | 740-587-8101
Kathleen Lowery, supt. | Fax 587-8191
www.granville.k12.oh.us/
Granville HS | 700/9-12
248 New Burg St 43023 | 740-587-8105
Charles Dilbone, prin. | Fax 587-8195
Granville MS | 300/7-8
210 New Burg St 43023 | 740-587-8104
Lisa Sealover-Ormond, prin. | Fax 587-8194

Denison University | Post-Sec.
PO Box B 43023 | 740-587-0810
Granville Christian Academy | 300/K-12
1820 Newark Granville Rd 43023 | 740-587-4423
Nancy Warner, prin. | Fax 587-1266

Green, Summit, Pop. 23,378
Green Local SD | 4,100/K-12
PO Box 218 44232 | 330-896-7500
David Macali, supt. | Fax 896-7580
www.green.summit.k12.oh.us
Other Schools – See Uniontown

Portage Lakes JVSD | 330-896-8200
PO Box 248 44232 | Fax 896-8297
Mark Lukens, supt.
Portage Lakes Career Center | Vo/Tech
PO Box 248 44232 | 330-896-8200
Paulette Prince, prin. | Fax 896-8297

Green Camp, Marion, Pop. 330
Elgin Local SD
Supt. — See Marion
Elgin JHS | 300/7-8
PO Box 214 43322 | 740-528-2320
Brian Napper, prin. | Fax 528-2618

Greenfield, Highland, Pop. 4,939
Greenfield EVD | 2,200/PK-12
200 N 5th St 45123 | 937-981-2152
Terrence Fouch, supt. | Fax 981-4395
greenfield.k12.oh.us
Greenfield MS | 600/5-8
200 N 5th St 45123 | 937-981-2197
Howard Zody, prin. | Fax 981-0417
McClain HS | 700/9-12
200 N 5th St 45123 | 937-981-7731
Dan Strain, prin. | Fax 981-4792

Greenville, Darke, Pop. 13,234
Greenville CSD | 3,400/K-12
215 W 4th St 45331 | 937-548-3185
Greg Taylor, supt. | Fax 548-6943
www.greenville.k12.oh.us
Greenville HS | 1,100/9-12
100 Greenwave Way 45331 | 937-548-4188
Jeff Hobbs, prin. | Fax 548-3082
Greenville JHS | 500/7-8
131 Central Ave 45331 | 937-548-3202
Jack Schulte, prin. | Fax 548-3315

Greenwich, Huron, Pop. 1,547
South Central Local SD | 900/K-12
3305 Greenwich Angling Rd 44837 | 419-752-3815
Lowell Etzler, supt. | Fax 752-0182
buford.willard-oh.com/southcentral/

South Central HS | 300/9-12
3305 Greenwich Angling Rd 44837 | 419-752-3354
Benjamin Chaffee, prin. | Fax 752-6927

Grove City, Franklin, Pop. 29,165
South-Western CSD | 20,800/PK-12
3805 Marlane Dr 43123 | 614-801-3000
Dr. R. Kirk Hamilton, supt. | Fax 871-2781
www.swcs.k12.oh.us
Brookpark MS | 600/7-8
2803 Southwest Blvd 43123 | 614-801-3500
Bob Rains, prin. | Fax 871-6512
Central Crossing HS | 1,400/9-12
4500 Big Run South Rd 43123 | 614-801-6500
Ed Palmer, prin. | Fax 801-6690
Grove City HS | 1,600/9-12
4665 Hoover Rd 43123 | 614-801-3300
Kathryn Buckerfield, prin. | Fax 871-6563
Jackson MS | 600/7-8
2271 Holton Rd 43123 | 614-801-3800
Elizabeth Watkins, prin. | Fax 801-3818
Pleasant View MS | 800/7-8
7255 Kropp Rd 43123 | 614-801-3900
Thom Gamertsfelder, prin. | Fax 870-5530
South-Western Career Academy | Vo/Tech
4750 Big Run South Rd 43123 | 614-801-3400
Shirley Moore, prin. | Fax 801-6138
Other Schools – See Columbus, Galloway

Grove City Christian S | 600/K-12
PO Box 728 43123 | 614-875-3000
Cindy Bigelow, prin. | Fax 875-8933

Groveport, Franklin, Pop. 4,367
Eastland-Fairfield Career & Technical SD | 614-836-4530
4300 Amalgamated Pl 43125 | Fax 836-0203

www.eastland-fairfield.com
Eastland Career Center | Vo/Tech
4465 S Hamilton Rd 43125 | 614-836-5725
Deb Stephenson, prin. | Fax 836-4525
Other Schools – See Carroll

Groveport Madison Local SD | 5,800/K-12
5940 Clyde Moore Dr 43125 | 614-492-2520
Scott McKenzie, supt. | Fax 492-2533
www.gocruisers.org
Groveport Madison HS | 1,600/9-12
4475 S Hamilton Rd 43125 | 614-836-4964
Donis Toler, prin. | Fax 836-4690
Groveport Madison JHS | 200/8-8
751 Main St 43125 | 614-836-4957
Zoraba Ross, prin. | Fax 836-4999

Fairfield Career Center | Post-Sec.
4465 S Hamilton Rd 43125 | 614-836-5725
Madison Christian S | 500/PK-12
3565 Bixby Rd 43125 | 614-497-3456
Gary Ramin, prin. | Fax 497-3057

Hamilton, Butler, Pop. 60,763
Butler Technology & Career Development S
Supt. — See Fairfield
Options Business Academy | Vo/Tech
105 N 2nd St 45011 | 513-887-0001
Harold Niehaus, prin.

Edgewood CSD
Supt. — See Trenton
Edgewood MS | 800/6-8
3440 Busenbark Rd 45011 | 513-867-7430
Judith Scherrer, prin. | Fax 867-7571

Hamilton CSD | 9,000/K-12
PO Box 627 45012 | 513-887-5000
Janet Baker, supt. | Fax 887-5014
hamiltoncityschools.com/
Garfield MS | 600/7-8
250 N Fair Ave 45011 | 513-887-5035
Patricia Blake, prin. | Fax 887-4700
Hamilton Freshman HS | 200/9-9
2260 NW Washington Blvd 45013 | 513-896-3400
Gregory Rulon, prin.
Hamilton SHS | 2,100/10-12
1165 Eaton Ave 45013 | 513-868-7700
Dennis Malone, prin. | Fax 887-4810
Wilson MS | 500/7-8
714 Eaton Ave 45013 | 513-887-5170
Sheryl Burk, prin. | Fax 887-5186

Lakota Local SD
Supt. — See Liberty
Lakota Plains JHS | 700/6-8
5500 Princeton Rd 45011 | 513-644-1130
Michael Holbrook, prin. | Fax 644-1135

New Miami Local SD | 900/K-12
600 Seven Mile Ave 45011 | 513-863-0833
Robert Bierly, supt. | Fax 863-0497
New Miami JSHS | 400/7-12
600 Seven Mile Ave 45011 | 513-863-4917
Tom Alf, prin. | Fax 896-3956

Ross Local SD | 2,600/K-12
3371 Hamilton Cleves Rd 45013 | 513-863-1253
M. Todd Yohey, supt. | Fax 863-6250
www.rosd.k12.oh.us
Ross HS | 800/9-12
3601 Hamilton Cleves Rd 45013 | 513-863-1252
Keith Klinefelter, prin. | Fax 863-8340
Ross MS | 800/5-8
3425 Hamilton Cleves Rd 45013 | 513-863-1251
Christopher Saylor, prin. | Fax 863-0066

Badin HS | 600/9-12
571 Hamilton New London Rd 45013 | 513-863-3993
Frank M. Margello, prin. | Fax 785-2844
Cincinnati Christian HS | 400/6-12
7474 Morris Rd 45011 | 513-892-8500
Brian Hitchcock Ph.D., hdmstr. | Fax 892-0516
Miami University-Hamilton Campus | Post-Sec.
1601 University Blvd 45011 | 513-785-3000

Hamler, Henry, Pop. 693
Patrick Henry Local SD | 800/K-12
6900 State Route 18 43524 | 419-274-5451
Susan Miko, supt. | Fax 274-1641
www.patrickhenry.k12.oh.us/
Henry HS, 6900 State Route 18 43524 | 400/9-12
Gregg Pettit, prin. | 419-274-3015
Henry MS, E050 County Road 7 43524 | 300/5-8
Keith Ruhe, prin. | 419-274-3431

Hammondsville, Jefferson
Edison Local SD | 2,700/PK-12
14890 State Route 213 43930 | 330-532-3199
Lisa Carmichael, supt. | Fax 532-2860
www.edisonlocal.k12.oh.us/
Stanton MS | 400/5-8
14890 State Route 213 43930 | 330-532-1594
Douglas Eckley, prin. | Fax 532-1594
Other Schools – See Bergholz, Richmond

Hannibal, Monroe
Switzerland of Ohio Local SD
Supt. — See Woodsfield
River HS | 300/9-12
PO Box 37 43931 | 740-483-1358
Vincent Monseau, prin. | Fax 483-2321

Hanoverton, Columbiana, Pop. 391
United Local SD | 1,500/K-12
8143 State Route 9 44423 | 330-223-1521
Thomas Davis, supt. | Fax 223-2363
www.united.k12.oh.us/
United JSHS | 800/7-12
8143 State Route 9 44423 | 330-223-7102
William Young, prin. | Fax 223-2363

Harrison, Hamilton, Pop. 7,478
Southwest Local SD | 3,900/K-12
230 S Elm St 45030 | 513-367-4139
Daniel Lawler, supt. | Fax 367-2287
www.southwestschools.org
Harrison HS | 1,300/9-12
9860 West Rd 45030 | 513-367-4169
Susan Thomas, supt. | Fax 367-7251
Harrison MS | 700/7-8
9830 West Rd 45030 | 513-367-4831
Don Jostworth, prin. | Fax 367-0370

Christ Centered S | 100/PK-12
220 Sunset Ave 45030 | 513-367-4564
Jerry Goodbar, admin. | Fax 367-7981

Harrod, Allen, Pop. 482
Allen East Local SD | 1,100/K-12
9520 Harrod Rd 45850 | 419-648-3333
Michael Richards, supt. | Fax 648-5282
www.noacsc.org/allen/ae
Allen East MS | 400/4-8
9520 Harrod Rd 45850 | 419-648-3571
Larry Altenburger, prin. | Fax 648-5282
Other Schools – See Lafayette

Hartville, Stark, Pop. 2,236
Lake Local SD
Supt. — See Uniontown
Lake MS | 800/6-8
12001 Market Ave N 44632 | 330-877-4290
Jeffrey Durbin, prin. | Fax 877-1384

Lake Center Christian S | 600/K-11
12893 Kaufman Ave NW 44632 | 330-877-2049
Matthew McMullen, supt. | Fax 877-2040

Haviland, Paulding, Pop. 170
Wayne Trace Local SD | 1,200/PK-12
4915 US Route 127 45851 | 419-399-4113
Kenneth Doseck, supt. | Fax 263-2377
www.noacsc.org/paulding/wt/
Wayne Trace JSHS | 600/7-12
4915 US Route 127 45851 | 419-399-4100
Kevin Wilson, prin. | Fax 622-3037

Heath, Licking, Pop. 8,704
Heath CSD | 1,700/K-12
107 Lancaster Dr 43056 | 740-522-2816
Tom Forman, supt. | Fax 522-4697
www.heath.k12.oh.us/
Heath HS | 500/9-12
300 Licking View Dr 43056 | 740-788-3300
Terry Kopchak, prin. | Fax 788-3322
Heath MS | 400/6-8
310 Licking View Dr 43056 | 740-788-3200
Jim Forgrave, prin. | Fax 788-3209

Hebron, Licking, Pop. 2,067
Lakewood Local SD | 2,300/K-12
PO Box 70 43025 | 740-928-5878
Jay Gault, supt. | Fax 928-3152
www.lakewoodlocal.k12.oh.us/
Lakewood HS | 700/9-12
PO Box 70 43025 | 740-928-4526
Larry Bevard, prin. | Fax 928-3731
Lakewood MS | 500/6-8
PO Box 70 43025 | 740-928-8330
Arnold Ettenhofer, prin. | Fax 928-5627

Hicksville, Defiance, Pop. 3,565
Hicksville EVD | 1,000/K-12
105 W Smith St 43526 | 419-542-7665
Kevin Miller, supt. | Fax 542-8534
www.hicksvilleschools.org/
Hicksville JSHS | 500/7-12
105 W Smith St 43526 | 419-542-7636
Sue Dangler, prin. | Fax 542-8534

Highland Heights, Cuyahoga, Pop. 8,512
Mayfield CSD
Supt. — See Mayfield Heights
CEVEC | Vo/Tech
211 Alpha Park 44143 | 440-995-7451
Robert Ross, prin. | Fax 995-7455

Highland Hills, Cuyahoga, Pop. 1,605

Cuyahoga Community College — Post-Sec.
25444 Harvard Rd 44122 — 216-987-2019

Hilliard, Franklin, Pop. 25,808
Hilliard CSD — 14,100/PK-12
5323 Cemetery Rd 43026 — 614-771-4273
Dale A. McVey, supt. — Fax 777-2424
www.hilliard.k12.oh.us
Hilliard Darby HS — 2,100/9-12
4200 Leppert Rd 43026 — 614-527-4200
David Stewart, prin. — Fax 527-4206
Hilliard Davidson HS — 1,900/9-12
5100 Davidson Rd 43026 — 614-771-2299
John Bandow, prin. — Fax 529-7406
Hilliard Heritage MS — 800/7-8
5670 Scioto Darby Rd 43026 — 614-771-2800
Suzanne McCoy, prin. — Fax 771-2808
Hilliard Memorial MS — 700/7-8
5600 Scioto Darby Rd 43026 — 614-334-3057
Douglas Lowery, prin. — Fax 334-3058
Weaver MS — 700/7-8
4600 Avery Rd 43026 — 614-529-7424
Edward O'Reilly, prin. — Fax 529-7425

Hillsboro, Highland, Pop. 6,632
Hillsboro CSD — 2,800/K-12
338 W Main St 45133 — 937-393-3475
Art Reiber, supt. — Fax 393-5841
www.hillsboro.k12.oh.us
Hillsboro HS — 800/9-12
358 W Main St 45133 — 937-393-3485
Larry Stall, prin. — Fax 393-5842
Hillsboro MS — 500/6-8
358 W Main St 45133 — 937-393-9877
Rick Earley, prin. — Fax 393-5843

Southern State Community College — Post-Sec.
100 Hobart Dr 45133 — 937-393-3431

Hiram, Portage, Pop. 1,231

Hiram College — Post-Sec.
PO Box 96 44234 — 330-569-3211

Holgate, Henry, Pop. 1,181
Holgate Local SD — 500/K-12
103 Frazier Ave 43527 — 419-264-5141
James Reiter, supt. — Fax 264-1965
www.holgate.k12.oh.us/
Holgate JSHS — 300/6-12
103 Frazier Ave 43527 — 419-264-2521
Bruce Kidder, prin. — Fax 264-1965

Holland, Lucas, Pop. 1,319
Springfield Local SD — 3,700/K-12
6900 Hall St 43528 — 419-867-5600
Dr. Cynthia Beekley, supt. — Fax 867-5700
www.springfield-lucas.k12.oh.us
Springfield HS — 1,200/9-12
1470 S Mccord Rd 43528 — 419-867-5633
Michael O'Shea, prin. — Fax 867-5618
Springfield MS — 900/6-8
7001 Madison Ave 43528 — 419-867-5644
Matt Geha, prin. — Fax 867-5732

Hondros College — Post-Sec.
6135 Trust Dr Ste 110 43528 — 419-865-0070

Hopedale, Harrison, Pop. 986
Harrison Hills CSD — 2,100/K-12
PO Box 356 43976 — 740-942-7800
Jim Drexler, supt. — Fax 942-7808
www.harrisonhills.k12.oh.us/
Other Schools – See Cadiz, Scio

Houston, Shelby
Hardin-Houston Local SD — 900/K-12
5300 Houston Rd 45333 — 937-295-3010
John Schey, supt. — Fax 295-3737
www.houston.k12.oh.us
Houston JSHS — 400/7-12
5300 Houston Rd 45333 — 937-295-3010
Rick Russell, prin. — Fax 295-3737

Howard, Knox
East Knox Local SD — 1,100/K-12
PO Box 68 43028 — 740-599-7493
John Marschhausen, supt. — Fax 599-5863
www.eastknox.k12.oh.us/index2.html
East Knox HS — 600/7-12
PO Box 128 43028 — 740-599-7007
Gary Comstock, prin. — Fax 599-2922

Hoytville, Wood, Pop. 299
Mc Comb Local SD
Supt. — See Mc Comb
Mc Comb Local MS — 200/6-8
PO Box 157 43529 — 419-278-8194
Jerry Wolford, prin. — Fax 278-7166

Hubbard, Trumbull, Pop. 8,105
Hubbard EVD — 2,300/K-12
150 Hall Ave 44425 — 330-534-1921
Richard J. Buchenic, supt. — Fax 534-0522
www.hubbard.k12.oh.us/
Hubbard HS — 900/9-12
350 Hall Ave 44425 — 330-534-1113
Larry Lushinsky, prin. — Fax 534-2865
Reed MS — 700/5-8
150 Hall Ave 44425 — 330-534-1129
Jon Young, prin. — Fax 534-0522

Huber Heights, Montgomery, Pop. 38,240
Huber Heights CSD — 6,700/K-12
5954 Longford Rd 45424 — 937-237-6300
William Kirby, supt. — Fax 237-6307
www.huberheights.k12.oh.us/
Studebaker MS — 800/6-8
5950 Longford Rd 45424 — 937-237-6345
Tom Heid, prin.
Wayne HS — 2,200/9-12
5400 Chambersburg Rd 45424 — 937-233-6431
John Allen, prin. — Fax 237-6321
Weisenborn MS — 800/6-8
6061 Troy Pike 45424 — 937-237-6350
Kathy Leary, prin.

Carousel of Miami Valley Beauty College — Post-Sec.
7809 Waynetowne Blvd 45424 — 937-233-8818

Hudson, Summit, Pop. 23,053
Hudson CSD — 5,500/K-12
2400 Hudson Aurora Rd 44236 — 330-653-1200
Maryann Wolowiec, supt. — Fax 653-1474
www.hudson.edu
Hudson HS — 1,800/9-12
2500 Hudson Aurora Rd 44236 — 330-653-1416
Jay Tyree, prin. — Fax 653-1481
Hudson MS — 1,400/6-8
77 N Oviatt St 44236 — 330-653-1316
Charles DiLauro, prin. — Fax 653-1368

Brighton College — Post-Sec.
85 S Main St Ste B 44236 — 800-231-3803
Western Reserve Academy — 400/9-12
115 College St 44236 — 330-650-4400
Henry Flanagan, hdmstr. — Fax 650-9754

Hunting Valley, Cuyahoga, Pop. 717

University S — 400/9-12
2785 Som Center Rd 44022 — 216-831-2200
Stephen Murray, prin. — Fax 831-0402

Huron, Erie, Pop. 7,718
Huron CSD — 1,700/PK-12
712 Cleveland Rd E 44839 — 419-433-3911
Fred Fox, supt. — Fax 433-7095
www.huron-city.k12.oh.us/
Huron HS — 500/9-12
710 Cleveland Rd W 44839 — 419-433-3171
John Ruf, prin. — Fax 433-2339
McCormick MS — 500/5-8
325 Ohio St 44839 — 419-433-5658
Mark Doughty Ph.D., prin. — Fax 433-8427

Bowling Green State University — Post-Sec.
1 University Dr 44839 — 419-433-5560

Independence, Cuyahoga, Pop. 7,096
Independence Local SD — 1,100/PK-12
7733 Stone Rd 44131 — 216-642-5850
David Laurenzi, supt. — Fax 642-3482
www.independence.k12.oh.us
Independence HS — 400/9-12
6001 Archwood Rd 44131 — 216-642-5860
Richard Forney, prin. — Fax 642-5886
Independence MS — 400/5-8
6111 Archwood Rd 44131 — 216-642-5865
Edward Vittardi, prin. — Fax 520-7002

Ironton, Lawrence, Pop. 11,230
Ironton CSD — 1,600/K-12
105 S 5th St 45638 — 740-532-4133
Dean Nance, supt. — Fax 532-2314
www.tigertown.com
Ironton HS — 500/9-12
1701 S 7th St 45638 — 740-532-3911
Joseph Rowe, prin. — Fax 533-6027
Ironton JHS — 200/7-8
1701 S 7th St 45638 — 740-532-9458
Toben Schreck, prin. — Fax 533-6039

Rock Hill Local SD — 1,900/K-12
2325 County Road 26 Unit A 45638 — 740-532-7030
Steve Lambert, supt. — Fax 532-7043
rockhill.org/
Rock Hill HS — 600/9-12
2415 County Road 26 45638 — 740-533-7012
Dennis Hankins, prin.
Rock Hill MS — 500/6-8
2171 County Road 26 45638 — 740-532-7026
Wes Hairston, prin.

Ohio University Southern Campus — Post-Sec.
1804 Liberty Ave 45638 — 740-533-4600
St. Joseph Central HS — 100/7-12
912 S 6th St 45638 — 740-532-0485
James Mains, prin. — Fax 532-3699

Irwin, Union

Rosedale Bible College — Post-Sec.
2270 Rosedale Rd 43029 — 740-857-1311

Jackson, Jackson, Pop. 6,159
Jackson CSD — 2,500/K-12
450 Vaughn St 45640 — 740-286-6442
Stephen P. Anderson, supt. — Fax 286-6445
www.jcs.k12.oh.us
Jackson HS, 500 Vaughn St 45640 — 900/9-12
Kevin Rice, prin. — 740-286-7575
Jackson MS — 700/6-8
11507 Chillicothe Pike 45640 — 740-286-7586
Paul Blankenship, prin.

Southeastern Business College — Post-Sec.
504 McCarty Ln 45640 — 740-286-1554

Jackson Center, Shelby, Pop. 1,461
Jackson Center Local SD — 600/K-12
PO Box 849 45334 — 937-596-6053
Dr. John C. Cline, supt. — Fax 596-6490
Jackson Center JSHS — 300/7-12
PO Box 849 45334 — 937-596-6149
Ross Klima, prin. — Fax 596-6490

Jacksontown, Licking

Excel Academy, PO Box 109 43030 — 100/K-12
Marlene Jacob, prin. — 740-323-1102

Jamestown, Greene, Pop. 1,881
Greeneview Local SD — 1,300/K-12
4 S Charleston Rd 45335 — 937-675-2728
Valerie Browning Ph.D., supt. — Fax 675-6807
www.greeneview.k12.oh.us
Greenview HS — 700/8-12
4710 Cottonville Rd 45335 — 937-675-9711
Wallace Campbell, prin. — Fax 675-6805

Jefferson, Ashtabula, Pop. 3,534
Ashtabula County JVSD
1565 State Route 167 44047 — 440-576-6015
Jerome Brockway, supt. — Fax 576-6502
www.acjvs.org
Ashtabula County Joint Vocational S — Vo/Tech
1565 State Route 167 44047 — 440-576-6015
Jon Whipple, prin. — Fax 576-6502

Jefferson Area Local SD — 2,300/K-12
45 E Satin St 44047 — 440-576-9180
Kevin S. Turner, supt. — Fax 576-9876
jefferson.k12.oh.us/
Jefferson Area JSHS — 1,100/7-12
125 S Poplar St 44047 — 440-576-4731
Thomas Harrison, prin. — Fax 576-9876

Jeromesville, Ashland, Pop. 483
Hillsdale Local SD — 1,200/K-12
485 Township Rd 1902 44840 — 419-368-8231
Joel Roscoe, supt. — Fax 368-7504
www.hillsdale.k12.oh.us/
Hillsdale HS — 400/9-12
485 Township Rd 1902 44840 — 419-368-6841
Kevin Reidy, prin. — Fax 368-7504
Hillsdale MS — 400/5-8
PO Box 57 44840 — 419-368-4911
Tom Gaus, prin. — Fax 368-3613

Johnstown, Licking, Pop. 3,650
Johnstown-Monroe Local SD — 1,500/K-12
441 S Main St 43031 — 740-967-6846
Tom Suriano, supt. — Fax 967-1106
johnstown.k12oh.us
Adams MS — 400/6-8
80 W Maple St 43031 — 740-967-8766
Angela Pollock, prin. — Fax 967-0051
Johnstown-Monroe HS — 500/9-12
401 S Oregon St 43031 — 740-967-2721
Kim Jakeway, prin. — Fax 967-1140

Northridge Local SD — 1,400/K-12
6097 Johnstown Utica Rd 43031 — 740-967-6631
Jacqueline Henderson, supt. — Fax 967-5022
northridge.k12.oh.us
Northridge HS — 400/9-12
6066 Johnstown Utica Rd 43031 — 740-967-6651
Chris Vail, prin. — Fax 967-6958
Northridge MS — 300/6-8
6066 Johnstown Utica Rd 43031 — 740-967-6671
Amy Anderson, prin. — Fax 967-7083

Kalida, Putnam, Pop. 1,093
Kalida Local SD — 700/K-12
PO Box 269 45853 — 419-532-3534
Mark Neal, supt. — Fax 532-2277
www.kalida.k12.oh.us
Kalida JSHS — 300/7-12
PO Box 269 45853 — 419-532-3529
Donald Horstman, prin. — Fax 532-2277

Kansas, Sandusky
Lakota Local SD
Supt. — See Risingsun
Lakota HS — 400/9-12
5186 County Road 13 44841 — 419-986-5161
Tony Anastasio, prin. — Fax 986-5436

Kelleys Island, Erie, Pop. 369
Kelleys Island Local SD — 50/K-12
PO Box 349 43438 — 419-746-2730
Phil Thiede, supt. — Fax 746-2271
www.kelleys.k12.oh.us/
Kelleys Island S — 50/K-12
PO Box 349 43438 — 419-746-2730
Phil Thiede, prin. — Fax 746-2271

Kent, Portage, Pop. 28,082
Kent CSD — 3,800/PK-12
321 N Depeyster St 44240 — 330-673-6515
Marc Crail, supt. — Fax 677-6166
kent.k12.oh.us
Central HS — 9-12
200 N Mantua St 44240 — 330-676-4181
Fax 676-4303
Roosevelt HS — 1,300/9-12
1400 N Mantua St 44240 — 330-673-9595
Roger Sidoti, prin. — Fax 673-9217
Stanton MS — 800/6-8
1175 Hudson Rd 44240 — 330-673-6693
Dr. Timothy Dortch, prin. — Fax 673-1561

Kent State University — Post-Sec.
PO Box 5190 44242 — 330-672-2444

Kenton, Hardin, Pop. 8,181
Kenton CSD — 2,000/K-12
222 W Carrol St 43326 — 419-673-0775
Doug Roberts, supt. — Fax 673-3180
www.kentoncityschools.org/
Kenton HS — 700/9-12
200 Harding Ave 43326 — 419-673-1286
Archibald Rodgers, prin. — Fax 675-5200
Kenton MS — 500/6-8
300 Oriental St 43326 — 419-673-1237
Steven Ickes, prin. — Fax 673-1626

Kettering, Montgomery, Pop. 56,494
Kettering CSD — 7,600/K-12
3750 Far Hills Ave 45429 — 937-499-1400
Robert Mengerink, supt. — Fax 499-1519
www.kettering.k12.oh.us
Kettering-Fairmont HS — 2,500/9-12
3301 Shroyer Rd 45429 — 937-499-1600
James Schoenlein, prin. — Fax 499-1661

Kettering MS | 1,100/6-8
3000 Glengarry Dr 45420 | 937-499-1550
Kyle Ramey, prin. | Fax 499-1598
Van Buren JHS | 700/6-8
3775 Shroyer Rd 45429 | 937-499-1800
Matthew Rugh, prin. | Fax 499-1820

Archbishop Alter HS | 700/9-12
940 E David Rd 45429 | 937-434-4434
Sr. Katie Hoelscher, prin. | Fax 434-0507
Carousel Beauty College | Post-Sec.
3120 Woodman Dr 45420 | 937-298-5752
Kettering College of Medical Arts | Post-Sec.
3737 Southern Blvd 45429 | 800-433-5262
School of Advertising Art | Post-Sec.
1725 E David Rd 45440 | 937-294-0592

Kidron, Wayne

Central Christian S, PO Box 9 44636 | 300/5-12
Joyce Taylor, prin. | 330-857-7311

Kings Mills, Warren
Kings Local SD | 3,800/K-12
PO Box 910 45034 | 513-398-8050
Charles Mason, supt. | Fax 229-7590
www.kingslocal.k12.oh.us
Kings HS | 1,100/9-12
5500 Columbia Rd 45034 | 513-398-8050
Tom Higgins, prin. | Fax 459-2941
Kings JHS | 600/7-8
5620 Columbia Rd 45034 | 513-398-8050
James Acton, prin. | Fax 459-2951

Kinsman, Trumbull
Joseph Badger Local SD | 1,100/K-12
8317 Main St 44428 | 330-876-1051
David D. Bair, supt. | Fax 876-1053
www.joseph-badger.k12.oh.us/
Badger HS | 400/9-12
8319 Main St 44428 | 330-876-8011
Alan Harris, prin. | Fax 876-8014
Badger MS | 300/6-8
6144 Youngstown Conneaut Rd 44428 | 330-772-4731
Robert Moon, prin. | Fax 876-1053

Kirtland, Lake, Pop. 6,970
Kirtland Local SD | 1,100/K-12
9252 Chillicothe Rd 44094 | 440-256-3311
Stan Lipinski, supt. | Fax 256-3831
www.kirtland.k12.oh.us
Kirtland HS | 300/9-12
9150 Chillicothe Rd 44094 | 440-256-3366
Jack Thompson, prin. | Fax 256-1042
Kirtland MS | 200/6-8
9152 Chillicothe Rd 44094 | 440-256-3358
Harry Siskind, prin. | Fax 256-3928

Lakeland Community College | Post-Sec.
7700 Clocktower Dr 44094 | 440-953-7000

Lafayette, Allen, Pop. 296
Allen East Local SD
Supt. — See Harrod
Allen East HS | 400/9-12
PO Box 7186 45854 | 419-649-6311
Gary DeLuca, prin. | Fax 649-8900

La Grange, Lorain, Pop. 1,551
Keystone Local SD | 1,800/K-12
PO Box 65 | 440-355-5131
Dr. Gary Friedt, supt. | Fax 355-6052
www.keystone.k12.oh.us
Keystone HS | 600/9-12
PO Box 65 | 440-355-5132
Thomas Clary, prin. | Fax 355-6052
Keystone MS | 600/5-8
PO Box 65 | 440-355-5133
Timothy Jenkins, prin. | Fax 355-6052

Lakeside, Ottawa
Danbury Local SD | 600/K-12
9451 E Harbor Rd 43440 | 419-798-5185
Martin Fanning, supt. | Fax 798-2260
www.danbury.k12.oh.us
Danbury JSHS | 300/7-12
9451 E Harbor Rd 43440 | 419-798-4037
Karen Abbott, prin. | Fax 798-2262

Lakewood, Cuyahoga, Pop. 54,378
Lakewood CSD | 6,300/K-12
1470 Warren Rd 44107 | 216-529-4092
David Estrop, supt. | Fax 228-5812
www.lakewoodcityschools.org/
Emerson MS | 700/6-8
13439 Clifton Blvd 44107 | 216-529-4241
Vincent Barra, prin. | Fax 529-4463
Harding MS | 500/6-8
16600 Hilliard Rd 44107 | 216-529-4261
Gene Hancock, prin. | Fax 529-4708
Lakewood HS | 2,500/9-12
14100 Franklin Blvd 44107 | 216-529-4021
William Wagner, prin. | Fax 529-4459
Mann MS | 400/6-8
1215 W Clifton Blvd 44107 | 216-529-4287
Michael Pellegrino, prin. | Fax 529-4249

St. Edward HS | 900/9-12
13500 Detroit Ave 44107 | 216-221-3776
Eugene Boyer, prin. | Fax 221-4609
Virginia Marti College of Art & Design | Post-Sec.
11724 Detroit Ave 44107 | 216-221-8564

Lancaster, Fairfield, Pop. 35,914
Fairfield Union Local SD
Supt. — See Rushville
Fairfield Union HS | 600/9-12
6401 Cincinnati Zanesville 43130 | 740-536-7306
Dale Ferbrache, prin. | Fax 536-7911
Fairfield Union JHS | 300/7-8
6401 Cincinnati Zanesville 43130 | 740-536-7846
Dale Ferbrache, prin. | Fax 536-7911

Lancaster CSD | 5,300/K-12
345 E Mulberry St 43130 | 740-687-7300
Denise Callihan, supt. | Fax 687-7303
www.lancaster.k12.oh.us
Ewing JHS | 600/6-8
825 E Fair Ave 43130 | 740-687-7347
John Zishka, prin. | Fax 687-3446
Lancaster HS | 1,800/9-12
1312 Granville Pike 43130 | 740-681-7500
Steve Wigton, prin. | Fax 681-7505
Sherman JHS | 500/6-8
701 Union St 43130 | 740-687-7344
Greg Stickel, prin. | Fax 687-3443

Fairfield Christian Academy | 700/PK-12
1965 N Columbus St 43130 | 740-654-2889
Megan Peters, supt. | Fax 654-7689
Fisher Catholic HS | 300/9-12
1803 Granville Pike 43130 | 740-654-1231
James Condron, prin. | Fax 654-1233
Ohio University | Post-Sec.
1570 Granville Pike 43130 | 740-654-6711
Southeastern Business College | Post-Sec.
1522 Sheridan Dr 43130 | 740-687-6126

Latham, Pike
Western Local SD | 900/K-12
PO Box 130 45646 | 740-493-3113
Joseph Morrison, supt. | Fax 493-2065
Western HS | 400/7-12
PO Box 130 45646 | 740-493-2514
Phillip Howard, prin. | Fax 493-8513

Leavittsburg, Trumbull
LaBrae Local SD | 800/K-12
1001 N Leavitt Rd 44430 | 330-898-0800
Ronald Joseph, supt. | Fax 898-6112
LaBrae HS | 400/9-12
1001 N Leavitt Rd 44430 | 330-898-0800
Douglas Hitchcock, prin. | Fax 898-6112
LaBrae MS, 1001 N Leavitt Rd 44430 | 6-8
Milajean Harkabus, prin. | 330-898-0800

Lebanon, Warren, Pop. 18,766
Lebanon CSD | 2,900/K-12
700 Holbrook Ave 45036 | 513-934-5770
Mark North, supt. | Fax 932-5906
www.lebanon.k12.oh.us
Lebanon HS | 1,400/9-12
1916 Drake Rd 45036 | 513-934-5100
Dr. Samuel Ison, prin. | Fax 933-2150
Lebanon JHS | 7-8
160 Miller Rd 45036 | 513-934-5300
Tom Olson, prin. | Fax 932-9436

Warren County Vocational SD
3525 N State Route 48 45036 | 513-932-5677
Margaret Hess, supt. | Fax 932-3810
wccareercenter.com
Warren County Career Center | Vo/Tech
3525 N State Route 48 45036 | 513-932-5677
Gary Patton, dir. | Fax 932-3810

New England School of Hair Design | Post-Sec.
12 Interchange Dr 03784 | 603-298-5199

Leesburg, Highland, Pop. 1,304
Fairfield Local SD | 900/K-12
11611 State Route 771 45135 | 937-780-2221
Scott Wilson, supt. | Fax 780-6900
www.fairfield-highland.k12.oh.us
Fairfield HS | 300/9-12
11611 State Route 771 45135 | 937-780-2966
Daniel Staggs, prin. | Fax 780-2841
Fairfield MS | 300/5-8
11611 State Route 771 45135 | 937-780-2977
Michael G. Daye, prin. | Fax 780-2841

Lees Creek, Clinton
East Clinton Local SD | 1,600/K-12
97 College St 45138 | 937-584-2461
Gary R. West, supt. | Fax 584-2817
www.east-clinton.k12.oh.us
East Clinton HS | 500/9-12
PO Box 19 45138 | 937-584-2474
Kevin Snarr, prin. | Fax 584-4842
East Clinton MS | 400/6-8
PO Box 19 45138 | 937-584-9267
Terry Enochs, prin. | Fax 584-9558

Leetonia, Columbiana, Pop. 2,009
Leetonia EVD | 900/K-12
450 Walnut St 44431 | 330-427-6594
Thomas S. Inchak, supt. | Fax 427-1136
www.leetonia.k12.oh.us
Leetonia HS | 300/9-12
450 Walnut St 44431 | 330-427-2115
Michael Ferguson, prin. | Fax 427-6904
Leetonia MS | 300/5-8
450 Walnut St 44431 | 330-427-2444
Elizabeth Goerig, prin. | Fax 427-2549

Leipsic, Putnam, Pop. 2,231
Leipsic Local SD | 700/K-12
232 Oak St 45856 | 419-943-2165
Alice L. Dewar, supt. | Fax 943-4331
www.noacsc.org/putnam/1p/
Leipsic JSHS | 400/7-12
232 Oak St 45856 | 419-943-2164
Nancey Schortgen, prin. | Fax 943-2185

Lewisburg, Preble, Pop. 1,788
Tri-County North Local SD | 1,200/K-12
PO Box 40 45338 | 937-962-2671
Stephen Grant, supt. | Fax 962-4731
Tri-County North HS | 400/9-12
PO Box 610 45338 | 937-962-2675
William Derringer, prin. | Fax 962-4731
Tri-County North MS | 400/5-8
PO Box 699 45338 | 937-962-2631
Joseph Finkbine, prin. | Fax 962-4731

Lewis Center, Delaware, Pop. 300
Olentangy Local SD | 9,400/K-12
814 Shanahan Rd Ste 100 43035 | 740-657-4050
Dr. William Reimer, supt. | Fax 657-4099
www.olentangy.k12.oh.us
Olentangy HS | 1,200/9-12
675 Lewis Center Rd 43035 | 740-657-4100
Melinda Farry, prin. | Fax 657-4199
Olentangy Orange MS | 900/6-8
2680 E Orange Rd 43035 | 740-657-5300
James Wightman, prin. | Fax 657-5399
Olentangy Shanahan MS | 1,000/6-8
814 Shanahan Rd 43035 | 740-657-4300
Dennis Harden, prin. | Fax 657-4398
Other Schools – See Powell

Lewistown, Logan
Indian Lake Local SD | 2,000/K-12
6210 State Route 235 N 43333 | 937-686-8601
Dr. William McGlothlin, supt. | Fax 686-8421
www.indianlake.k12.oh.us
Indian Lake HS | 600/9-12
6210 State Route 235 N 43333 | 937-686-8851
Denny Shaner, prin. | Fax 686-0024
Indian Lake MS | 700/5-8
8920 County Road 91 43333 | 937-686-8833
Charles Blair, prin. | Fax 686-8993

Lexington, Richland, Pop. 4,117
Lexington Local SD | 2,800/K-12
103 Clever Ln 44904 | 419-884-2132
James Ziegelhofer, supt. | Fax 884-3129
www.lexington.k12.oh.us
Lexington HS | 900/9-12
103 Clever Ln 44904 | 419-884-1111
James Goode, prin. | Fax 884-2340
Lexington JHS | 500/7-8
90 Frederick St 44904 | 419-884-2112
William Ferguson, prin. | Fax 884-0134

Liberty, Butler
Lakota Local SD | 16,100/K-12
5572 Princeton Rd 45011 | 513-874-5505
Dr. Philip Ehrhardt, supt. | Fax 644-1167
www.lakotaonline.com
Other Schools – See Hamilton, Middletown, West Chester

Liberty Center, Henry, Pop. 1,118
Liberty Center Local SD | 1,200/K-12
PO Box 434 43532 | 419-533-5011
Jack Loudin, supt. | Fax 533-5036
www.libertycenter.k12.oh.us/
Liberty Center HS | 300/9-12
PO Box 434 43532 | 419-533-6641
| Fax 533-5036
Liberty Center MS | 400/5-8
PO Box 434 43532 | 419-533-0020
Beverly Jump, prin. | Fax 533-5036

Lima, Allen, Pop. 40,549
Apollo JVSD | 3325 Shawnee Rd 45806 | 419-998-2908
J. Chris Pfister, supt. | Fax 998-2929
www.apollocareercenter.com
Apollo Career Ctr Joint Vocational JSHS | Vo/Tech
3325 Shawnee Rd 45806 | 419-998-2908
Doug Bodey, dir. | Fax 998-2929

Bath Local SD | 2,100/K-12
2650 Bible Rd 45801 | 419-221-0807
William Lodermeier, supt. | Fax 221-0983
www.noacsc.org/allen/ba
Bath HS | 700/9-12
2850 Bible Rd 45801 | 419-221-0366
Richard Gross, prin. | Fax 221-0766
Bath MS | 700/5-8
2700 Bible Rd 45801 | 419-221-1839
Bradley Clark, prin. | Fax 221-2431

Lima CSD | 4,600/K-12
515 Calumet Ave 45804 | 419-996-3400
Karel Oxley, supt. | Fax 996-3401
www.limacityschools.org
Lima HS | 1,300/9-12
1 Spartan Way 45801 | 419-996-3000
Douglas Kent, prin. | Fax 996-3001
North MS | 600/5-8
1135 N West St 45801 | 419-996-3100
Mark Vaughn, prin. | Fax 996-3101
South MS | 500/5-8
755 Saint Johns Ave 45804 | 419-996-3190
Mitchell Black, prin. | Fax 996-3191
West MS | 500/5-8
503 N Cable Rd 45805 | 419-996-3150
Rise Light, prin. | Fax 996-3151

Perry Local SD | 800/K-12
2770 E Breese Rd 45806 | 419-221-2770
Michael Lamb, supt. | Fax 221-2773
www.noacsc.org/allen/pe/index.htm
Perry HS | 400/7-12
2770 E Breese Rd 45806 | 419-221-2774

Shawnee Local SD | 2,600/K-12
3255 Zurmehly Rd 45806 | 419-998-8031
Paul Nardini, supt. | Fax 998-8050
shawnee.noacsc.org/
Shawnee HS | 900/9-12
3333 Zurmehly Rd 45806 | 419-998-8000
Don Wade, prin. | Fax 998-8026
Shawnee MS | 900/5-8
3235 Zurmehly Rd 45806 | 419-998-8057
Tony Cox, prin. | Fax 998-8050

James A. Rhodes State Coll | Post-Sec.
4240 Campus Dr 45804 | 419-995-8000
Liberty Christian S | 50/PK-12
801 Bellefontaine Ave 45801 | 419-229-6266
Nadine Schwartz, admin. | Fax 229-6266
Lima Central Catholic HS | 400/9-12
720 S Cable Rd 45805 | 419-222-4276
Rev. Todd M. Dominique, pres. | Fax 222-6933
Ohio State Beauty Academy | Post-Sec.
57 Town Sq 45801 | 419-229-7896

Ohio State University-Lima Campus — Post-Sec.
4240 Campus Dr 45804 — 419-221-1641
Temple Christian S — 300/PK-12
982 Brower Rd 45801 — 419-227-1644
Bruce Bowman, supt. — Fax 227-6635
University of Northwestern Ohio — Post-Sec.
1441 N Cable Rd 45805 — 419-227-3141

Lisbon, Columbiana, Pop. 2,872
Beaver Local SD — 2,400/K-12
13093 State Route 7 44432 — 330-385-6831
Willard C. Adkins, supt. — Fax 386-8711
www.beaver.k12.oh.us/
Beaver Local HS — 800/9-12
13187 State Route 7 44432 — 330-386-8700
Janet Christen, prin. — Fax 386-8720
Beaver Local MS — 800/5-8
13052 State Route 7 44432 — 330-386-8707
Thomas Sapp, prin. — Fax 382-0317

Columbiana County JVSD —
9364 State Route 45 44432 — 330-424-9561
Edna Anderson, supt. — Fax 424-9719
Columbiana County Joint Vocational SHS — Vo/Tech
9364 State Route 45 44432 — 330-424-9561
Rick Istnick, prin. — Fax 424-9719

Lisbon EVD — 1,100/K-12
317 N Market St 44432 — 330-424-7714
Donald Thompson, supt. — Fax 424-0135
www.lisbon.k12.oh.us/
Anderson JSHS — 600/7-12
260 W Pine St 44432 — 330-424-3215
Donald Mook, prin. — Fax 424-1004

Lockland, Hamilton, Pop. 3,505
Lockland CSD
Supt. — See Cincinnati
Lockland JSHS — 300/7-12
249 W Forrer St 45215 — 513-563-5000
Ben Hubbard, prin. — Fax 563-9611

Lodi, Medina, Pop. 3,239
Cloverleaf Local SD — 2,200/K-12
8525 Friendsville Rd 44254 — 330-948-2500
Dr. Bruce Hulme, supt. — Fax 948-1034
www.cls.k12.oh.us
Cloverleaf HS — 1,200/9-12
8525 Friendsville Rd 44254 — 330-948-2500
Robert Hevener, prin. — Fax 948-4068
Other Schools – See Seville

Logan, Hocking, Pop. 6,870
Logan-Hocking Local SD — 3,400/PK-12
121 S Spring St 43138 — 740-385-8517
Stephen Stirn, supt. — Fax 385-3683
www.loganhocking.k12.oh.us
Logan-Hocking HS — 1,300/9-12
50 North St 43138 — 740-385-2069
Jeff Daubenmire, prin. — Fax 385-9564
Logan-Hocking MS — 1,000/6-8
1 Middleschool Dr 43138 — 740-385-8764
Myles Kiphen, prin. — Fax 385-9547

London, Madison, Pop. 9,087
London CSD — 1,800/PK-12
60 S Walnut St 43140 — 740-852-5700
Thomas Coyne, supt. — Fax 852-7360
www.london.k12.oh.us/
London HS — 600/9-12
336 Elm St 43140 — 740-852-5705
Jeff Thompson, prin. — Fax 852-3078
London JHS — 300/7-8
60 S Walnut St 43140 — 740-852-5700
Mark Elliott, prin. — Fax 845-2869

Madison-Plains Local SD — 1,500/K-12
55 Linson Rd 43140 — 740-852-3712
Daniel L. Shull, supt. — Fax 852-5895
Madison-Plains HS — 500/9-12
800 Linson Rd 43140 — 740-852-0364
Chris Clark, prin. — Fax 852-3046
Madison-Plains MS — 400/6-8
9940 State Route 38 SW 43140 — 740-852-1707
John Woodason, prin. — Fax 852-6351

Madison Clark Christian Academy — 100/K-12
2600 US Hwy 40 NE 43140 — 740-845-1175
Karen Keigley, prin.

Lorain, Lorain, Pop. 67,955
Clearview Local SD — 1,500/K-12
4700 Broadway 44052 — 440-233-5412
Rick Buckosh, supt. — Fax 233-6034
www.clearview.k12.oh.us/
Clearview HS — 500/9-12
4700 Broadway 44052 — 440-233-6313
Daniel Parent, prin. — Fax 233-6311
Durling MS — 500/5-8
100 N Ridge Rd W 44053 — 440-233-6869
Jerome Davis, prin. — Fax 233-6204

Lorain CSD — 10,000/K-12
2350 Pole Ave 44052 — 440-233-2271
Dr. Dee Morgan, supt. — Fax 282-9151
www.lorainschools.org
King HS — 1,400/9-12
2600 Ashland Ave 44052 — 440-282-9191
Duane Davis, prin. — Fax 282-1831
Southview HS — 1,300/9-12
2270 E 42nd St 44055 — 440-277-7271
David Hall, prin. — Fax 277-9566
Whittier MS — 600/7-8
3201 Seneca Ave 44055 — 440-277-7261
Roberto Davila, prin. — Fax 277-1560
Wilson MS — 1,000/7-8
602 Washington Ave 44052 — 440-244-0200
Christine Pankey, prin. — Fax 245-1387

Sheffield-Sheffield Lake CSD
Supt. — See Sheffield Lake
Brookside HS — 600/9-12
1812 Harris Rd 44054 — 440-949-4220
Burton Daugherty, prin. — Fax 949-4204

Sheffield MS — 500/6-8
1919 Harris Rd 44054 — 440-949-4228
David Riley, prin. — Fax 949-4204

Northern Institute of Cosmetology — Post-Sec.
667 Broadway 44052 — 440-244-4282
Ohio Business College — Post-Sec.
1907 N Ridge Rd E 44055 — 440-277-0021

Lore City, Guernsey, Pop. 304
East Guernsey Local SD
Supt. — See Old Washington
Buckeye Trail HS — 400/9-12
65555 Wintergreen Rd 43755 — 740-489-5005
Timothy VanCamp, prin. — Fax 489-9839
Buckeye Trail MS — 6-8
65553 Wintergreen Rd 43755 — 740-489-5100
Lonnie Caudill, prin. — Fax 489-9049

Loudonville, Ashland, Pop. 2,997
Loudonville-Perrysville EVD — 1,300/K-12
210 E Main St 44842 — 419-994-3912
John Miller, supt. — Fax 994-3912
www.lpschools.k12.oh.us
Loudonville HS — 400/9-12
421 Campus Ave 44842 — 419-994-4101
Ben Blubaugh, prin. — Fax 994-3485
Other Schools – See Perrysville

Louisville, Stark, Pop. 9,138
Louisville CSD — 3,200/K-12
418 E Main St 44641 — 330-875-1666
Clyde Lepley, supt. — Fax 875-7603
www.leopard.stark.k12.oh.us/
Louisville HS — 1,000/9-12
1201 S Nickelplate St 44641 — 330-875-1438
Polly Doyle, prin. — Fax 875-7606
Louisville MS — 800/6-8
1307 S Nickelplate St 44641 — 330-875-5597
David Varner, prin. — Fax 875-7620

St. Thomas Aquinas HS — 500/9-12
2121 Reno Dr 44641 — 330-875-1631
Joseph Vagedes, prin. — Fax 875-8469

Loveland, Hamilton, Pop. 11,302
Loveland CSD — 4,300/PK-12
757 S Lebanon Rd 45140 — 513-683-5600
Kevin S. Boys Ed.D., supt. — Fax 683-5697
www.lovelandschools.org/
Loveland HS — 1,200/9-12
1 Tiger Trl 45140 — 513-683-1920
Molly Moorhead, prin. — Fax 677-7952
Loveland MS — 700/7-8
801 S Lebanon Rd 45140 — 513-683-3100
Erica Kramer, prin. — Fax 677-7986

Lowellville, Mahoning, Pop. 1,202
Lowellville Local SD — 600/K-12
52 Rocket Pl 44436 — 330-536-6318
Rocco Nero, supt. — Fax 536-8468
www.lowellville.k12.oh.us/
Lowellville JSHS — 300/7-12
52 Rocket Pl 44436 — 330-536-8426
Samuel Ramunno, prin. — Fax 536-8468

Lucas, Richland, Pop. 609
Lucas Local SD — 600/PK-12
84 Lucas North Rd 44843 — 419-892-2338
William A. Huber, supt. — Fax 892-1138
www.lucascubs.org
Lucas HS — 200/9-12
5 1st Ave 44843 — 419-892-2338
Rodney Hopton, prin. — Fax 892-1138

Lucasville, Scioto, Pop. 1,575
Scioto County JVSD —
951 Vern Riffe Dr 45648 — 740-259-5522
Stan Jennings, supt. — Fax 259-2632
www.scjvs.com
Scioto County Joint Vocational HS — Vo/Tech
951 Vern Riffe Dr 45648 — 740-259-5522
Don Gibson, dir. — Fax 259-2632

Valley Local SD — 1,200/K-12
PO Box 888 45648 — 740-259-3115
Paul Miller, supt. — Fax 259-2314
www.valley.k12.oh.us/
Valley HS — 400/9-12
1821 State Route 728 45648 — 740-259-5551
Michael Yeagle, prin.
Valley MS, 393 Indian Dr 45648 — 400/5-8
Don Miller, prin. — 740-259-2651

Lynchburg, Highland, Pop. 1,402
Lynchburg-Clay Local SD — 1,300/K-12
PO Box 515 45142 — 937-364-2338
Gregory Hawk, supt. — Fax 364-2339
www.lynchclay.k12.oh.us
Lynchburg-Clay HS — 400/9-12
6762 State Route 134 45142 — 937-364-2250
Michelle Williamson, prin. — Fax 364-6133
Lynchburg-Clay MS — 300/6-8
8250 State Route 134 45142 — 937-364-2811
Eric Magee, prin. — Fax 364-2159

Lyndhurst, Cuyahoga, Pop. 14,875
South Euclid-Lyndhurst CSD — 4,500/K-12
5044 Mayfield Rd 44124 — 216-691-2000
William Zelei, supt. — Fax 691-2033
www.sel.k12.oh.us
Brush HS — 1,600/9-12
4875 Glenlyn Rd 44124 — 216-691-2065
Elaine Vrabel, prin. — Fax 691-2064
Memorial JHS — 700/7-8
1250 Professor Rd 44124 — 216-691-2140
Tim Jarvie, prin. — Fax 691-2159

Cleveland Institute Dental Medical Asst. — Post-Sec.
5564 Mayfield Rd 44124 — 440-473-6273
Inner State Beauty School — Post-Sec.
5150 Mayfield Rd 44124 — 440-442-4500

Mc Arthur, Vinton, Pop. 1,645
Vinton County Local SD — 2,600/PK-12
307 W High St 45651 — 740-596-5218
John Simmons, supt. — Fax 596-3142
vinton.k12.oh.us
Vinton County HS — 700/9-12
63910 US Highway 50 45651 — 740-596-5258
Kevin Waddell, prin. — Fax 596-3003
Vinton County JHS — 400/7-8
57710 US Highway 50 45651 — 740-596-5243
Dee Caudill, prin. — Fax 596-3815

Mc Comb, Hancock, Pop. 1,632
Mc Comb Local SD — 800/K-12
PO Box 877 45858 — 419-293-3979
Timothy Scherer, supt. — Fax 293-2412
www.noacsc.org/hancock/mb
Mc Comb Local HS — 300/9-12
PO Box 877 45858 — 419-293-3853
Greg Williamson, prin. — Fax 293-3107
Other Schools – See Hoytville

Mc Connelsville, Morgan, Pop. 1,829
Morgan Local SD — 2,200/K-12
PO Box 509 43756 — 740-962-2782
Scott M. Davis, supt. — Fax 962-4931
www.mlsd.k12.oh.us/
Morgan HS — 700/9-12
800 Raider Dr 43756 — 740-962-2944
Anita Eldridge, prin. — Fax 962-6005
Morgan JHS — 400/7-8
820 Junior Raider Dr 43756 — 740-962-2833
Timothy Hopkins, prin. — Fax 962-3389

Mc Dermott, Scioto
Northwest Local SD — 1,800/K-12
800 Mohawk Dr 45652 — 740-259-5558
Ruth Teeters, supt. — Fax 259-3476
www.northwest.k12.oh.us
Northwest HS — 600/9-12
914 Mohawk Dr 45652 — 740-259-2366
Edward Crabtree, prin. — Fax 259-5655
Northwest MS — 400/6-8
692 Mohawk Dr 45652 — 740-259-2528
Todd Jenkins, prin. — Fax 259-5731

Mc Donald, Trumbull, Pop. 3,501
McDonald Local SD — 900/K-12
600 Iowa Ave 44437 — 330-530-8051
Michael Wasser, supt. — Fax 530-7041
www.mcdonald.k12.oh.us
McDonald JSHS — 400/7-12
600 Iowa Ave 44437 — 330-530-8051
John Larocca, prin. — Fax 530-7041

Macedonia, Summit, Pop. 10,087
Nordonia Hills CSD
Supt. — See Northfield
Nordonia HS — 1,300/9-12
8006 S Bedford Rd 44056 — 330-468-4601
Charles Vrabel, prin. — Fax 468-0045

Mc Guffey, Hardin, Pop. 572
Upper Scioto Valley Local SD — 800/K-12
PO Box 305 45859 — 419-757-4451
Nancy Wood Allison, supt. — Fax 757-0590
www.usv.woco-k12.org/
Upper Scioto Valley HS — 200/9-12
PO Box 305 45859 — 419-757-3231
Craig Hurley, prin. — Fax 757-2590
Upper Scioto Valley MS — 200/6-8
PO Box 305 45859 — 419-757-2551
Craig Hurley, prin. — Fax 757-3112

Madison, Lake, Pop. 2,990
Madison Local SD — 3,500/K-12
6741 N Ridge Rd 44057 — 440-428-2166
James Herrholtz, supt. — Fax 946-6472
www.madison-richland.k12.oh.us/
Madison HS — 1,100/9-12
3100 Burns Rd 44057 — 440-428-2161
William Fisher, prin. — Fax 428-2165
Madison MS — 800/6-8
1941 Red Bird Rd 44057 — 440-428-1196
Heidi Stark, prin. — Fax 428-9389

Magnolia, Stark, Pop. 926
Sandy Valley Local SD — 1,600/K-12
5362 State Route 183 NE 44643 — 330-866-3339
Rock Vanfossen, supt. — Fax 866-5238
cardweb.stark.k12.oh.us/
Sandy Valley JSHS — 800/7-12
5362 State Route 183 NE 44643 — 330-866-9371
Nicki Howard, prin. — Fax 866-2490

Malvern, Carroll, Pop. 1,233
Brown Local SD — 900/K-12
401 W Main St 44644 — 330-863-1170
Connie Griffin, supt. — Fax 863-1172
www.hornet.sparcc.org
Malvern MSHS — 500/6-12
401 W Main St 44644 — 330-863-1355
Douglas Schmidt, prin. — Fax 863-1915

Mansfield, Richland, Pop. 50,688
Madison Local SD — 3,500/K-12
1379 Grace St 44905 — 419-589-2600
Dr. David Williamson, supt. — Fax 589-3653
www.madison-richland.k12.oh.us
Madison Comprehensive HS — 800/10-12
600 Esley Ln 44905 — 419-589-2112
Allen Pease, prin. — Fax 589-2533
Madison JHS — 900/7-9
690 Ashland Rd 44905 — 419-522-0471
Timothy Rupert, prin. — Fax 522-1463

Mansfield CSD — 5,200/K-12
PO Box 1448 44901 — 419-525-6400
Dr. P. Joseph Madak, supt. — Fax 525-6415
www.tygerpride.com
Malabar MS — 800/6-8
205 W Cook Rd 44907 — 419-525-6374
Joann Hipsher, prin. — Fax 525-6376
Mansfield HS — 1,100/9-12
124 N Linden Rd 44906 — 419-525-6369
Virginia Dias, prin. — Fax 524-2210

Simpson MS 500/6-8
218 W 4th St 44903 419-525-6348
Shawn Perry, prin. Fax 525-6350

Ontario Local SD 1,800/PK-12
457 Shelby Ontario Rd 44906 419-747-4311
Daryl Hall, supt. Fax 747-6859
www.ncocc-k12.org/ontario
Ontario HS 600/9-12
467 Shelby Ontario Rd 44906 419-529-3969
Jim Klenk, prin. Fax 529-5649
Ontario MS 400/6-8
447 Shelby Ontario Rd 44906 419-529-5507
Monty Perry, prin. Fax 529-7058

Mansfield Christian HS 300/7-12
500 Logan Rd 44907 419-756-5651
Dr. Cy Smith, prin. Fax 756-7470
MedCentral College of Nursing Post-Sec.
335 Glessner Ave 44903 419-520-2600
North Central State College Post-Sec.
PO Box 698 44901 419-755-4800
Ohio State University-Mansfield Campus Post-Sec.
1680 University Dr 44906 419-755-4011
St. Peter HS 200/9-12
104 W 1st St 44902 419-524-0979
Tressa Reith, prin. Fax 524-3336
Temple Christian S 300/K-12
752 Stewart Rd N 44905 419-589-9707
Robert Kurtz, prin. Fax 589-7213

Mantua, Portage, Pop. 1,025
Crestwood Local SD 1,800/K-12
4565 W Prospect St 44255 330-274-8511
Joseph Iacano, supt. Fax 274-3710
www.crestwood.sparcc.org/
Crestwood HS 900/9-12
10919 Main St 44255 330-274-2214
Pearl Austin, prin. Fax 274-3150
Crestwood MS 700/6-8
10880 John Edward Dr 44255 330-274-2249
Ann Salva, prin. Fax 274-3705

Maple Heights, Cuyahoga, Pop. 25,490
Maple Heights CSD 3,600/K-12
14605 Granger Rd 44137 216-587-6100
Dr. Charles Keenan, supt. Fax 518-2674
www.mapleheightsk12.com
Maple Heights HS 1,100/9-12
5500 Clement Ave 44137 216-587-3200
Nancy Santilli, prin. Fax 587-3259
Milkovich MS 700/7-8
5460 West Blvd 44137 216-587-3200
Tracy Williams, prin. Fax 587-6166

Marengo, Morrow, Pop. 315
Highland Local SD 1,800/K-12
6506 State Route 229 43334 419-768-2206
Timothy Hilborn, supt. Fax 768-3115
www.highland.k12.oh.us/
Other Schools – See Sparta

Maria Stein, Mercer
Marion Local SD 1,000/K-12
7956 State Route 119 45860 419-925-4294
Dr. Andrew Smith, supt. Fax 925-0212
marionlocal.k12.oh.us/
Marion HS 300/9-12
1901 State Route 716 45860 419-925-4597
Dr. Ronald Hertel, prin. Fax 925-5111

Marietta, Washington, Pop. 14,035
Marietta CSD 3,200/K-12
701 3rd St 45750 740-374-6500
Dr. Doug Baker, supt. Fax 374-6506
mariettacityschools.k12.oh.us
Marietta HS 1,100/9-12
208 Davis Ave 45750 740-374-6540
Michael Elliott, prin. Fax 376-2462
Marietta MS 700/6-8
242 N 7th St 45750 740-374-6530
Mark Doebrich, prin. Fax 374-6531

Washington County JVSD
21740 State Route 676 45750 740-373-2766
Roger Bartunek, supt. Fax 373-9026
www.thecareercenter.net
Washington County Career Center Vo/Tech
21740 State Route 676 45750 740-373-2766
Dennis Blatt, prin. Fax 373-9026

Marietta College Post-Sec.
215 5th St 45750 740-376-4600
Memorial Hospital Post-Sec.
401 Matthew St 45750 740-374-1412
Valley Beauty School Post-Sec.
1315 Cisler Dr 45750 740-373-3617
Washington State Community College Post-Sec.
710 Colegate Dr 45750 740-374-8716

Marion, Marion, Pop. 37,300
Elgin Local SD 1,600/K-12
4616 Larue Prospect Rd W 43302 740-382-1101
Doug Ute, supt. Fax 382-1672
www.treca.org/schools/elgin/
Elgin HS 500/9-12
1239 Keener Rd S 43302 740-383-5118
Robert Britton, prin. Fax 383-4225
Other Schools – See Green Camp

Marion CSD 3,400/K-12
910 E Church St 43302 740-387-3300
Dr. William Zwick, supt. Fax 223-4400
www.marioncityschools.org/
Grant MS, 420 Presidential Dr 43302 400/6-8
Kathy McKinniss, prin. 740-223-4900
Harding HS 1,600/9-12
1500 Harding Hwy E 43302 740-223-4700
Mike McCreary, prin.

Pleasant Local SD 1,400/K-12
1107 Owens Rd W 43302 740-389-4476
John Bruno, supt. Fax 389-6985
www.pleasant.treca.org/index.html
Pleasant HS 500/9-12
1101 Owens Rd W 43302 740-389-2389
Brian Sparling, prin. Fax 389-3904
Pleasant MS 400/6-8
3507 Smeltzer Rd 43302 740-389-5167
Joe Kume, prin. Fax 389-5111

Tri-Rivers JVSD
2222 Marion Mount Gilead Rd 43302 740-389-4681
Charles R. Barr, supt. Fax 389-2963
www.tririvers.com
Tri-Rivers Career Center Vo/Tech
2222 Marion Mount Gilead Rd 43302 740-389-4681
Larry Hickman, dir. Fax 389-2963

Marion Catholic Preparatory JSHS 100/7-12
1001 Mount Vernon Ave 43302 740-389-2381
Fran Voll, prin. Fax 389-5243
Marion General Hospital Post-Sec.
1000 McKinley Park Dr 43302 740-383-8700
Marion Technical College Post-Sec.
1467 Mount Vernon Ave 43302 740-389-4636
Ohio State University-Marion Post-Sec.
1465 Mount Vernon Ave 43302 740-389-6786

Martins Ferry, Belmont, Pop. 7,021
Martins Ferry CSD 1,500/K-12
633 Hanover St 43935 740-633-1732
Nick Stankovich, supt. Fax 633-5666
www.mfcsd.k12.oh.us/
Martins Ferry HS 600/8-12
810 Hanover St 43935 740-633-0684
Jeff Oberdick, prin. Fax 635-6103

Marysville, Union, Pop. 16,245
Marysville EVD 4,700/K-12
1000 Edgewood Dr 43040 937-644-8105
Larry Zimmerman, supt. Fax 644-1849
www.marysville.k12.oh.us
Marysville HS 1,400/9-12
800 Amrine Mill Rd 43040 937-642-0010
Gregory Hanson, prin. Fax 642-2033
Marysville MS 700/7-8
833 N Maple St 43040 937-642-1721
M. Sweeney, prin. Fax 642-2170

Christian Academy 50/PK-12
PO Box 435 43040 937-644-0911
Donna Moceri, prin. Fax 644-0911

Mason, Warren, Pop. 27,308
Mason CSD 8,500/K-12
211 N East St 45040 513-398-0474
Kevin Bright, supt. Fax 398-4554
www.masonohioschools.com
Mason HS 2,100/9-12
6100 S Mason Montgomery Rd 45040 513-398-5025
Dr. Dave Allen, prin. Fax 459-7348
Mason MS 1,400/7-8
6370 Mason Montgomery Rd 45040 513-398-9035
Tonya McCall, prin. Fax 459-0904

Mars Hill Academy 200/K-12
6170 Irwin Simpson Rd 45040 513-770-3223
Tom McCoy, hdmstr. Fax 770-3443
Montessori Academy of Cincinnati 200/PK-10
8293 Duke Blvd 45040 513-398-7773
Patricia Elder, prin. Fax 398-1031

Massillon, Stark, Pop. 31,542
Jackson Local SD 5,500/K-12
7984 Fulton Dr NW 44646 330-830-8000
Cheryl Haschak, supt. Fax 830-8008
jackson.stark.k12.oh.us
Jackson HS 1,800/9-12
7600 Fulton Dr NW 44646 330-837-3501
Rick Campbell, prin. Fax 830-8069
Jackson Memorial MS 1,400/6-8
7355 Mudbrook Rd NW 44646 330-830-8034
Gary Wenning, prin. Fax 830-8068

Massillon CSD 3,000/K-12
207 Oak Ave SE 44646 330-830-1810
Alfred Hennon, supt. Fax 830-0953
www.massillon.sparcc.org
Massillon MS, 250 29th St NW 44647 5-8
Diane Lukac, prin. 330-830-3902
Washington HS 1,400/9-12
1 Paul E Brown Dr SE 44646 330-830-1800
Mark Fortner, prin. Fax 832-1954

Perry Local SD 4,900/PK-12
4201 13th St SW 44646 330-477-8121
John Richard, supt. Fax 478-6184
perrynet.stark.k12.oh.us
Edison JHS 800/8-9
4201 13th St SW 44646 330-478-6167
Richard Chaddock, prin. Fax 477-4612
Perry SHS 1,200/10-12
3737 13th St SW 44646 330-477-3486
Mark Dean, prin. Fax 478-6180

Stark County Area Vocational SD
6805 Richville Dr SW 44646 330-832-1591
Larry Morgan, supt. Fax 832-9850
Drage Career-Technical Center Vo/Tech
6805 Richville Dr SW 44646 330-832-9856
Richard Faiello, prin. Fax 832-9850

Tuslaw Local SD 500/K-12
1835 Manchester Ave NW 44647 330-837-7813
Alan Osler, supt. Fax 837-7804
Tuslaw HS 500/9-12
1847 Manchester Ave NW 44647 330-837-7800
Robert Sattler, prin. Fax 837-6016
Tuslaw MS 3-8
1723 Manchester Ave NW 44647 330-837-7807
David Ryder, prin. Fax 837-6015

Massillon Christian S 100/K-12
965 Overlook Ave SW 44647 330-833-1039
Robert Sampsel, prin. Fax 830-5981

Maumee, Lucas, Pop. 14,705
Maumee CSD 2,800/K-12
2345 Detroit Ave 43537 419-893-3200
Gregory Smith, supt. Fax 891-5387
www.maumee.k12.oh.us
Gateway MS 700/6-8
900 Gibbs St 43537 419-893-3386
Christopher Conroy, prin. Fax 893-2263
Maumee HS 1,000/9-12
1147 Saco St 43537 419-893-8778
Larry Caffro, prin. Fax 893-5621

Mayfield, Cuyahoga, Pop. 3,351
Mayfield CSD
Supt. — See Mayfield Heights
Mayfield HS 2,000/8-12
6116 Wilson Mills Rd 44143 440-995-6900
Tony Loewer, prin. Fax 995-6805

Mayfield Heights, Cuyahoga, Pop. 18,922
Mayfield CSD 4,600/K-12
1101 SOM Center RD 44124 440-995-6800
Phillip Price Ph.D., supt. Fax 995-7205
www.mayfield.k12.oh.us
Other Schools – See Highland Heights, Mayfield

Mechanicsburg, Champaign, Pop. 1,731
Mechanicsburg EVD 800/K-12
60 High St 43044 937-834-2453
Herbert Swiger, supt. Fax 834-3954
www.mechanicsburg.k12.oh.us
Mechanicsburg HS 400/7-12
60 High St 43044 937-834-2453
David Perin, prin. Fax 834-7103

Medina, Medina, Pop. 26,487
Buckeye Local SD 2,400/K-12
3044 Columbia Rd 44256 330-722-8257
Craig Bailey, supt. Fax 722-5793
www.buckeye.k12.oh.us
Buckeye HS 800/9-12
3084 Columbia Rd 44256 330-722-3604
N. Marty Brand, prin. Fax 722-8257
Buckeye JHS 400/7-8
3024 Columbia Rd 44256 330-725-0118
Roger Cramer, prin. Fax 722-8257

Highland Local SD 3,300/PK-12
3880 Ridge Rd 44256 330-239-1901
Bruce Armstrong, supt. Fax 239-2456
www.highlandschools.org
Highland HS 900/9-12
4150 Ridge Rd 44256 330-239-1901
Chuck Grimes, prin. Fax 239-7385
Highland MS 700/6-8
3880 Ridge Rd 44256 330-239-1901
John Deuber, prin. Fax 239-7388

Medina CSD 7,200/PK-12
140 W Washington St 44256 330-725-8831
Jeffrey W. Weaver Ph.D., supt. Fax 764-3501
www.mcsoh.org
Claggett MS 800/6-8
420 E Union St 44256 330-636-3600
Jo Maurer, prin. Fax 725-9349
Medina HS 2,300/9-12
777 E Union St 44256 330-636-3200
Randy Stepp, prin. Fax 725-3521
Root MS 900/6-8
333 W Sturbridge Dr 44256 330-636-3500
Thomas McKenna, prin. Fax 764-1471

Medina County JVSD
1101 W Liberty St 44256 330-725-8461
Thomas Horwedel, supt. Fax 725-5870
www.mccc-jvsd.org
Medina County Career Center Vo/Tech
1101 W Liberty St 44256 330-725-8461
Linda Bowers, prin. Fax 725-5870

Hamrick Truck Driving School Post-Sec.
1156 Medina Rd 44256 330-239-2229
Medina County Career Center Post-Sec.
1101 W Liberty St 44256 330-725-8461

Mentor, Lake, Pop. 50,004
Mentor EVD 9,100/K-12
6451 Center St 44060 440-255-4444
Dr. Jacqueline A. Hoynes, supt. Fax 255-4622
www.mentorschools.com
Memorial JHS 800/7-9
8979 Mentor Ave 44060 440-974-2250
Larry Luciano, prin. Fax 974-2259
Mentor SHS 2,400/10-12
6477 Center St 44060 440-974-5300
Joseph Spiccia, prin. Fax 974-5216
Ridge JHS 700/7-9
7860 Johnnycake Ridge Rd 44060 440-974-5400
Megan Kinsey, prin. Fax 974-5285
Shore JHS 900/7-9
5670 Hopkins Rd 44060 440-257-8750
Douglas Baker, prin. Fax 257-8761

Brown Aveda Institute Post-Sec.
8816 Mentor Ave 44060 440-255-9494
Cleveland Institute Dental Medical Asst. Post-Sec.
5733 Hopkins Rd 44060 440-946-9530
Hondros College Post-Sec.
7350 Industrial Park Blvd 44060 440-918-0080
Lake Catholic HS 900/9-12
6733 Reynolds Rd 44060 440-951-0077
Sr. Ann Waldron, prin. Fax 974-9087

Metamora, Fulton, Pop. 582
Evergreen Local SD 800/K-12
14544 County Road 6 43540 419-644-3521
Kenneth L. Jones, supt. Fax 644-6070
www.evergreen.k12.oh.us

Evergreen HS 500/9-12
14544 County Road 6 43540 419-644-2951
Mark Basilius, prin. Fax 644-6070
Evergreen MS 300/6-8
14544 County Road 6 43540 419-644-2331
Thomas Shafer, prin. Fax 644-9203

Miamisburg, Montgomery, Pop. 19,857
Miamisburg CSD 5,300/K-12
540 Park Ave 45342 937-866-3381
Dr. Gary Schomburg, supt. Fax 865-5250
www.miamisburgcityschools.org
Miamisburg HS 1,500/9-12
1860 Belvo Rd 45342 937-866-0771
Jim Ingham, prin. Fax 865-5267
Wantz MS 900/7-8
117 S 7th St 45342 937-866-3431
Susan Jandes, prin. Fax 866-6891

Dayton Christian HS 500/9-12
9391 Washington Church Rd 45342 937-291-7201
David Rough, prin. Fax 291-7202
Dayton Christian MS 300/5-8
9391 Washington Church Rd 45342 937-291-7201
Rich Garrett, prin. Fax 291-7202
Miamisburg Christian Academy 50/K-12
8500 S Union Rd 45342 937-866-6226
Charles Maqsud, prin. Fax 866-0112

Middleburg Heights, Cuyahoga, Pop. 15,680
Berea CSD
Supt. — See Berea
Midpark HS 1,300/9-12
7000 Paula Dr 44130 216-676-8400
Bela Molnar, prin. Fax 676-2070

Polaris JVSD
7285 Old Oak Blvd 44130 440-891-7600
Linda Schwarzbach, supt. Fax 826-4330
www.polaris.edu
Polaris Career Ctr Career Technical SHS Vo/Tech
7285 Old Oak Blvd 44130 440-891-7600
Bob Timmons, prin. Fax 243-3952

Middlefield, Geauga, Pop. 2,396
Cardinal Local SD 1,500/K-12
PO Box 188 44062 440-632-0261
James Campbell, supt. Fax 632-5886
www.cardinal.k12.oh.us
Cardinal HS 400/9-12
PO Box 7 44062 440-632-0264
Dave Ritter, prin. Fax 632-1734
Cardinal MS 300/6-8
PO Box 879 44062 440-632-0263
James Millet, prin. Fax 632-0294

Middletown, Butler, Pop. 51,941
Lakota Local SD
Supt. — See Liberty
Lakota East SHS 1,600/10-12
6840 Lakota Ln 45044 513-755-7211
Ruth Barber, prin. Fax 759-8633
Liberty JHS 900/6-8
7055 Dutchland Blvd 45044 513-777-4420
Ronald Spurlock, prin. Fax 777-7950

Madison Local SD 1,600/K-12
1324 Middletown Eaton Rd 45042 513-420-4750
Jan Kesselring, supt. Fax 420-4781
www.madison-local.k12.oh.us/
Madison JSHS 800/7-12
5797 W Alexandria Rd 45042 513-420-4760
Curtis Philpot, prin. Fax 420-4914

Middletown CSD 6,900/K-12
1515 Girard Ave 45044 513-423-0781
Dr. Steve Price, supt. Fax 420-4579
www.middletowncityschools.com
Middletown HS 1,800/9-12
601 N Breiel Blvd 45042 513-420-4500
Dennis Newell, prin. Fax 420-4648
Vail MS 800/7-8
1415 Girard Ave 45044 513-420-4528
Michael Valenti, prin. Fax 420-4527
Other Schools – See Monroe

Carousel Beauty College Post-Sec.
633 S Breiel Blvd 45044 513-422-2962
Miami University-Middletown Campus Post-Sec.
4200 N University Blvd 45042 513-727-3200
Middletown Regional Hospital Post-Sec.
105 McKnight Dr 45044 513-420-5100

Milan, Erie, Pop. 1,407
Berlin-Milan Local SD 1,900/PK-12
140 S Main St 44846 419-499-4272
David Snook, supt. Fax 499-4859
www.berlin-milan.org
Edison HS 600/9-12
2603 State Route 113 E 44846 419-499-4652
Jeffrey Goodwin, prin. Fax 499-2035
Other Schools – See Berlin Heights

EHOVE JVSD
316 Mason Rd W 44846 419-499-4663
Joseph DeRose, supt. Fax 499-4076
www.ehove.net
EHOVE Career Center Vo/Tech
316 Mason Rd W 44846 419-499-4663
Judith Driscoll, dir. Fax 499-5390

Milford, Clermont, Pop. 6,404
Great Oaks Institute of Technology
Supt. — See Cincinnati
Live Oaks CDC Vo/Tech
5956 Buckwheat Rd 45150 513-575-1900
Dan Cox, prin. Fax 575-0805

Madeira CSD
Supt. — See Cincinnati
Madeira MS 500/5-8
527 Lila Ave 45150 513-561-5555
Robert Kramer, prin. Fax 272-4145

Milford EVD 6,200/K-12
777 Garfield Ave 45150 513-831-1314
John Frye, supt. Fax 831-3208
www.milfordschools.org
Milford HS 2,000/9-12
1 Eagles Way 45150 513-831-2990
Dr. Ray Bauer, prin. Fax 831-9714
Milford JHS 1,000/7-8
5735 Pleasant Hill Rd 45150 513-831-1900
Chris Davis, prin. Fax 248-3451

St. Andrew /St. Elizabeth Ann Seton S 300/5-8
555 Main St 45150 513-831-5277
Donna Beebe, prin. Fax 831-8436

Milford Center, Union, Pop. 669
Fairbanks Local SD 900/K-12
11158 State Route 38 43045 937-349-3731
Jim Craycraft, supt. Fax 349-8885
www.fairbanks.k12.oh.us/
Fairbanks HS 300/9-12
11158 State Route 38 43045 937-349-3721
Jeff Parker, prin. Fax 349-2011
Fairbanks MS 300/5-8
11158 State Route 38 43045 937-349-6841
Patricia Lucas, prin. Fax 349-2013

Millbury, Wood, Pop. 1,148
Lake Local SD 1,700/K-12
PO Box 151 43447 419-836-2552
Paul Orshoski, supt. Fax 836-1755
www.lakelocal.k12.oh.us
Lake HS 600/9-12
28080 Lemoyne Rd 43447 419-661-6640
Marty Schloegl, prin. Fax 661-6650
Lake JHS 400/6-8
28100 Lemoyne Rd 43447 419-661-6660
Tim Jackson, prin. Fax 661-6664

Miller City, Putnam, Pop. 132
Miller City-New Cleveland Local SD 500/K-12
PO Box 38 45864 419-876-3172
William Kreinbrink, supt. Fax 876-3849
ml.noacsc.org
Miller City-New Cleveland HS 100/9-12
PO Box 38 45864 419-876-3173
Kevin McGlaughlin, prin. Fax 876-2020
Miller City-New Cleveland MS 100/6-8
PO Box 38 45864 419-876-3174
Kevin McGlaughlin, prin. Fax 876-2020

Millersburg, Holmes, Pop. 3,500
West Holmes Local SD 2,800/K-12
28 W Jackson St 44654 330-674-3546
Joseph Parish, supt. Fax 674-1177
www.westholmes.k12.oh.us
West Holmes HS 900/9-12
10909 State Route 39 44654 330-674-6085
Jay Arbaugh, prin. Fax 674-0818
West Holmes MS 700/6-8
10901 State Route 39 44654 330-674-4761
Maureen Businger, prin. Fax 674-2311

Millersport, Fairfield, Pop. 961
Walnut Township Local SD 700/K-12
PO Box 278 43046 740-467-2802
S. Edward Abram, supt. Fax 467-3494
Millersport JSHS 400/7-12
PO Box 278 43046 740-467-2929
Roger Montgomery, prin. Fax 467-3494

Mineral Ridge, Trumbull, Pop. 3,928
Weathersfield Local SD 1,100/K-12
3750 Main St 44440 330-652-0287
Michael Hanshaw, supt. Fax 544-7476
www.weathersfield.k12.oh.us/
Mineral Ridge HS 300/9-12
1334 Seaborn St 44440 330-652-1451
Lew Lowery, prin. Fax 505-9374
Mineral Ridge MS 300/5-8
3750 Main St 44440 330-652-2120
Bill Koppel, prin. Fax 544-7476

Minerva, Stark, Pop. 3,966
Minerva Local SD 2,200/K-12
303 Latzer Ave 44657 330-868-4332
Douglas Marrah, supt. Fax 868-4731
lion.stark.k12.oh.us/
Minerva HS 600/9-12
501 Almeda Ave 44657 330-868-4134
Carl Michael, prin. Fax 868-6555
Minerva MS 500/6-8
600 E Line St 44657 330-868-4497
Richard Mikes, prin. Fax 868-6122

Minford, Scioto
Minford Local SD 1,600/K-12
PO Box 204 45653 740-820-3896
Dennis Meade, supt. Fax 820-3334
www.minford.k12.oh.us/
Minford HS 500/9-12
PO Box 204 45653 740-820-3445
Robert Shaffer, prin. Fax 820-4484
Minford MS 600/4-8
PO Box 204 45653 740-820-2181
Kevin Lloyd, prin. Fax 820-2191

Mingo Junction, Jefferson, Pop. 3,472
Indian Creek Local SD
Supt. — See Wintersville
Indian Creek JHS 300/7-8
110 Steuben St 43938 740-266-2916
Mark Furda, prin. Fax 535-9100

Jefferson County Christian S 200/PK-12
2501 Commercial Ave 43938 740-535-1337
Diane Hutchison, prin.

Minster, Auglaize, Pop. 2,787
Minster Local SD 900/K-12
100 E 7th St 45865 419-628-3397
Gayl Ray, supt. Fax 628-2495
www.minster.k12.oh.us
Minster HS 300/9-12
100 E 7th St 45865 419-628-2324
Carl Brown, prin. Fax 628-2495
Minster MS 400/4-8
50 E 7thSt 45865 419-628-4174
Michael Lee, prin. Fax 628-2482

Mogadore, Summit, Pop. 3,954
Field Local SD 2,300/K-12
1473 Saxe Rd 44260 330-673-2659
David A. Redd, supt. Fax 677-2513
www.fieldschools.com
Field MS 600/7-9
1379 Saxe Rd 44260 330-673-4176
Beth Coleman, prin. Fax 673-0942
Field SHS 500/10-12
2900 State Route 43 44260 330-673-9591
Michael Harris, prin. Fax 677-2510

Mogadore Local SD 900/K-12
1 S Cleveland Ave 44260 330-628-9946
Terry Byers, supt. Fax 628-6661
www.mogadore.summit.k12.oh.us
Mogadore JSHS 400/7-12
130 S Cleveland Ave 44260 330-628-9943
Michael Herchik, prin. Fax 628-6657

Monclova, Lucas

Monclova Christian Academy 200/K-12
7819 Monclova Rd 43542 419-866-7630
Marvin Osborn, admin. Fax 868-1062

Monroe, Butler, Pop. 8,821
Butler Technology & Career Development S
Supt. — See Fairfield
Greentree Health Science Academy Vo/Tech
225 Macready Ave 45050 513-539-0818
Tod Baldwin, prin. Fax 539-1129

Middletown CSD
Supt. — See Middletown
Verity MS 500/6-8
101 W Elm St 45050 513-539-0318
Greg Williams, prin. Fax 539-0321

Monroe Local SD 1,500/K-12
30 Overbrook Dr Ste D 45050 513-539-2536
Arnol Elam, supt. Fax 539-2648
www.monroelocalschools.com/
Monroe HS, 220 Yankee Rd 45050 500/9-12
Robert Leahy, prin. 513-539-8471
Monroe JHS, 210 Yankee Rd 45050 300/7-8
Steven Jackson, prin. 513-539-8471

Monroeville, Huron, Pop. 1,412
Monroeville Local SD 700/K-12
101 West St 44847 419-465-2610
Carol Girton, supt. Fax 465-4263
www.monroeville.k12.oh.us
Monroeville JSHS 400/7-12
101 West St 44847 419-465-2531
David Stubblebine, prin. Fax 465-4580

Montpelier, Williams, Pop. 4,182
Montpelier EVD 1,200/K-12
PO Box 193 43543 419-485-3676
Pam Campbell, supt. Fax 485-4318
www.montpelier.k12.oh.us/
Montpelier HS 300/9-12
309 E Main St 43543 419-485-3186
Ed Ewers, prin. Fax 485-3487
Superior MS 400/4-8
10079 State Route 576 43543 419-485-5546
Randy Stuckey, prin. Fax 485-0816

Morral, Marion, Pop. 393
Ridgedale Local SD 900/PK-12
3103 Hillman Ford Rd 43337 740-382-6065
Eric Hoffman, supt. Fax 383-6538
www.treca.org/schools/ridge/
Ridgedale JSHS 600/6-12
3165 Hillman Ford Rd 43337 740-382-6065
Clayton Born, prin. Fax 387-8525

Morristown, Belmont, Pop. 300
Union Local SD 1,500/K-12
PO Box 300 43759 740-782-1978
H. Kirk Glasgow, supt. Fax 695-5066
www.union-local.k12.oh.us
Other Schools – See Belmont

Morrow, Warren, Pop. 1,422
Little Miami Local SD 3,200/K-12
5819 Morrow Rossburg Rd 45152 513-899-2264
Daniel Bennett, supt. Fax 899-3244
www.littlemiamischools.com
Little Miami HS 900/9-12
3001 E US Highway 22 And 3 45152 513-899-3781
John Spieser, prin. Fax 899-4912
Little Miami JHS 500/7-8
605 Welch Rd 45152 513-899-3408
Brian Bailey, prin. Fax 899-3196

Mount Blanchard, Hancock, Pop. 475
Riverdale Local SD 800/K-12
20613 State Route 37 45867 419-694-4994
Dr. Joyce Plummer, supt. Fax 694-6465
www.riverdale.k12.oh.us
Riverdale HS 300/9-12
20613 State Route 37 45867 419-694-2211
Deb Frey, prin. Fax 694-5008
Riverdale MS 200/6-8
20613 State Route 37 45867 419-694-2211
Deb Frey, prin. Fax 694-5008

Mount Gilead, Morrow, Pop. 3,470
Mt. Gilead EVD 1,400/K-12
145 1/2 N Cherry St 43338 419-946-1646
Robert P. Alexander, supt. Fax 946-3651
www.treca.org/schools/mtg/
Mount Gilead HS 500/9-12
338 W Park Ave 43338 419-947-6065
Debra Clauss, prin. Fax 946-3263

Mount Gilead MS | 300/6-8
145 N Cherry St 43338 | 419-947-9517
Sean Smith, prin. | Fax 947-9518

Gilead Christian S South Campus | 100/7-12
3613 Township Road 115 43338 | 419-946-5990
Jim McMillan, admin.

Mount Orab, Brown, Pop. 2,701
Western Brown Local SD | 3,400/K-12
524 W Main St 45154 | 937-444-2044
Jeffrey A. Royalty, supt. | Fax 444-4303
www.wb.k12.oh.us/
Mount Orab MS | 800/5-8
472 W Main St 45154 | 937-444-2529
Kevin Kratzer, prin. | Fax 444-4268
Western Brown HS | 1,000/9-12
476 W Main St 45154 | 937-444-2544
Ray Wisby, prin. | Fax 444-4355

Mount Vernon, Knox, Pop. 15,826
Knox County JVSD | 740-397-5820
306 Martinsburg Rd 43050
Ray Richardson, supt. | Fax 397-7040
Knox County Career Center | Vo/Tech
306 Martinsburg Rd 43050 | 740-397-5820
Rick Hornick, dir. | Fax 397-7040

Mt. Vernon CSD | 4,100/K-12
300 Newark Rd 43050 | 740-397-7422
R. Jeff Maley, supt. | Fax 393-5949
www.mt-vernon.k12.oh.us
Mount Vernon HS | 1,400/9-12
300 Martinsburg Rd 43050 | 740-393-5900
Kathy Kasler, prin. | Fax 397-6018
Mount Vernon MS | 1,000/6-8
298 Martinsburg Rd 43050 | 740-392-6867
Deborah McDaniel, prin. | Fax 392-3369

Christian Star Academy | 50/PK-12
7 E Sugar St 43050 | 740-393-0251
Suzanne Feasel, admin. | Fax 393-0067
Knox County Career Center | Post-Sec.
306 Martinsburg Rd 43050 | 740-397-5820
Mt. Vernon Academy | 200/9-12
PO Box 311 43050 | 740-397-5411
David Daniels, prin. | Fax 397-3901
Mt. Vernon Nazarene University | Post-Sec.
800 Martinsburg Rd 43050 | 740-397-9000

Mount Victory, Hardin, Pop. 595
Ridgemont Local SD | 600/PK-12
330 Taylor St W 43340 | 937-354-2441
Bruce Gast, supt. | Fax 354-2194
www.ridgemont.k12.oh.us
Other Schools – See Ridgeway

Mowrystown, Highland, Pop. 384
Bright Local SD | 800/PK-12
PO Box 9 45155 | 937-442-3114
Dee Wright, supt. | Fax 442-6655
www.bright.k12.oh.us/
Whiteoak JSHS | 400/7-12
PO Box 297 45155 | 937-442-2241
J. R. Roush, prin. | Fax 442-6655

Munroe Falls, Summit, Pop. 5,320
Stow-Munroe Falls CSD
Supt. — See Stow
Kimpton MS | 1,000/7-8
380 N River Rd 44262 | 330-689-5288
Maria DiTommaso, prin. | Fax 686-4718

Napoleon, Henry, Pop. 9,279
Napoleon Area CSD | 2,400/K-12
701 Briarheath Ave Ste 108 43545 | 419-599-7015
David Watson, supt. | Fax 599-7035
www.napoleon.k12.oh.us/default.htm
Napoleon HS | 900/9-12
701 Briarheath Ave # 123 43545 | 419-599-1050
Jeffrey Schlade, prin. | Fax 599-8537
Napoleon MS | 500/6-8
303 W Main St 43545 | 419-592-6991
Tony Borton, prin. | Fax 599-7638

Navarre, Stark, Pop. 1,440
Fairless Local SD | 1,900/K-12
11885 Navarre Rd SW 44662 | 330-767-3577
Mona Fair, supt. | Fax 767-3298
falcon.stark.k12.oh.us
Fairless HS | 600/9-12
11885 Navarre Rd SW 44662 | 330-767-3444
Larry Chambliss, prin. | Fax 767-3298
Fairless JHS | 300/7-8
11885 Navarre Rd SW 44662 | 330-767-3444

Nelsonville, Athens, Pop. 5,483
Nelsonville-York CSD | 1,300/PK-12
2 Buckeye Dr 45764 | 740-753-4441
Ted Bayat, supt. | Fax 753-1968
www.nelsonvilleyork.k12.oh.us/
Nelsonville-York HS | 400/9-12
1 Buckeye Dr 45764 | 740-753-4441
Charles McClelland, prin. | Fax 753-1420
Nelsonville-York JHS | 200/7-8
14455 Kimberley Rd 45764 | 740-753-4441
Joseph Malesick, prin. | Fax 753-1087

Tri County JVSD
15676 State Route 691 45764 | 740-753-3511
William Wittman, supt. | Fax 753-5376
www.tricountyhightech.com
Tri County Career Center | Vo/Tech
15676 State Route 691 45764 | 740-753-3511
Linda Fife, prin. | Fax 753-5376

Hocking College | Post-Sec.
3301 Hocking Pkwy 45764 | 800-282-4163
Nelsonville Christian Academy | 100/PK-12
803 Burr Oak Blvd 45764 | 740-753-4002
Wendy Sayers, admin. | Fax 753-3943

New Albany, Franklin, Pop. 5,212
New Albany - Plain Local SD | 2,900/K-12
99 W Main St Fl 2 43054 | 614-855-2040
Dr. Steve Castle, supt. | Fax 855-2043
www.new-albany.k12.oh.us
New Albany HS | 600/9-12
7600 Fodor Rd 43054 | 614-413-8300
Scott Stewart, prin. | Fax 413-8301
New Albany MS | 700/6-8
6600 E Dublin Granville Rd 43054 | 614-413-8500
Madeline Partlow, prin. | Fax 413-8501

Newark, Licking, Pop. 46,601
Career & Technology Educ Ctr Licking Co.
150 Price Rd 43055 | 740-366-3351
Ronald A. Cassidy, supt. | Fax 366-6215
Career & Technology Educ Ctr Licking Co. | Vo/Tech
150 Price Rd 43055 | 740-366-3351
Mary K. Andrews, dir. | Fax 366-6215

Licking Valley Local SD | 2,200/K-12
1379 Licking Valley Rd 43055 | 740-763-3525
Susan Hatcher, supt. | Fax 763-0471
www.lickingvalley.k12.oh.us/
Licking Valley HS | 700/9-12
100 Hainsview Dr 43055 | 740-763-3721
David Hile, prin. | Fax 763-0847
Licking Valley MS | 500/6-8
1379 Licking Valley Rd 43055 | 740-763-3396
Rick Nabors, prin. | Fax 763-2612

Newark CSD | 7,000/K-12
85 E Main St 43055 | 740-345-9891
Keith Richards, supt. | Fax 345-7495
www.newarkcityschools.org
Lincoln MS | 400/6-8
471 E Main St 43055 | 740-345-4440
Les Richards, prin. | Fax 328-2042
Newark HS | 1,900/9-12
314 Granville St 43055 | 740-345-9831
Jesse Truett, prin. | Fax 328-2232
Roosevelt MS | 300/7-8
621 Mount Vernon Rd 43055 | 740-349-2320
Elizabeth Phelps, prin. | Fax 328-2043
Wilson MS | 400/7-8
805 W Church St 43055 | 740-349-2315
John Davis, prin. | Fax 328-2045

Central Ohio Technical College | Post-Sec.
1179 University Dr 43055 | 740-366-1351
Newark Catholic HS | 300/9-12
1 Green Wave Dr 43055 | 740-344-3594
Beth Hill, prin. | Fax 344-0421
Ohio State University-Newark | Post-Sec.
1179 University Dr 43055 | 740-366-3321

New Boston, Scioto, Pop. 2,230
New Boston Local SD | 400/K-12
522 Glenwood Ave 45662 | 740-456-4626
Jerry Skiver, supt. | Fax 456-5252
Glenwood HS | 200/7-12
522 Glenwood Ave 45662 | 740-456-4559
Melinda Burnside, prin. | Fax 456-5252

Southeastern Business College | Post-Sec.
3879 Rhodes Ave Ste A 45662 | 740-456-4124

New Bremen, Auglaize, Pop. 2,965
New Bremen Local SD | 1,000/K-12
901 E Monroe St 45869 | 419-629-8606
Dr. Larry Smith, supt. | Fax 629-0115
www.bremen.k12.oh.us
New Bremen HS | 300/9-12
901 E Monroe St 45869 | 419-629-8606
Frank Borchers, prin. | Fax 629-2973

Grand Lake Christian S | 50/PK-12
212 S Walnut St 45869 | 419-629-4527
Teresa Howell, prin. | Fax 629-4527

Newbury, Geauga, Pop. 3,973
Newbury Local SD | 800/K-12
14775 Auburn Rd 44065 | 440-564-5501
Richard Wagner, supt. | Fax 564-9460
newbury.k12.oh.us
Newbury JSHS | 400/7-12
14775 Auburn Rd 44065 | 440-564-2281
Judith Miller, prin. | Fax 564-9788

New Carlisle, Clark, Pop. 5,655
Tecumseh Local SD | 3,300/PK-12
9760 W National Rd 45344 | 937-845-3576
Jim Gay, supt. | Fax 845-4453
www.tecumseh.k12.oh.us
New Carlisle MS | 400/6-8
1203 Kennison Ave 45344 | 937-845-4460
Cecil Foley, prin. | Fax 845-4462
Olive Branch MS | 500/6-8
9712 W National Rd 45344 | 937-845-4465
Bradley Martin, prin. | Fax 845-4467
Tecumseh HS | 1,100/9-12
9830 W National Rd 45344 | 937-845-4500
Michael Ostendorf, prin. | Fax 845-4547

Newcomerstown, Tuscarawas, Pop. 3,973
Newcomerstown EVD | 1,200/K-12
702 S River St 43832 | 740-498-8373
Jeffrey Staggs, supt. | Fax 498-8375
www.nct.k12.oh.us
Newcomerstown HS | 400/9-12
659 Beaver St 43832 | 740-498-5111
Randy Addy, prin. | Fax 498-4994
Newcomerstown MS | 300/6-8
325 W Main St 43832 | 740-498-8151
Timothy Sherman, prin. | Fax 498-4991

New Concord, Muskingum, Pop. 2,744
East Muskingum Local SD | 2,000/K-12
13505 John Glenn School Rd 43762 | 740-826-7655
Jim Heagen, supt. | Fax 826-7194
www.east-muskingum.k12.oh.us
East Muskingum MS | 500/6-8
13120 John Glenn School Rd 43762 | 740-826-7631
David Scholl, supt. | Fax 826-4392

Glenn HS | 700/9-12
13115 John Glenn School Rd 43762 | 740-826-7641
Frank Gregory, prin. | Fax 826-3039

Muskingum College | Post-Sec.
147 Center St 43762 | 740-826-8211

New Knoxville, Auglaize, Pop. 901
New Knoxville Local SD | 500/K-12
PO Box 476 45871 | 419-753-2431
Charles Rowen, supt. | Fax 753-2333
www.nk.k12.oh.us
New Knoxville HS | 200/7-12
PO Box 476 45871 | 419-753-2431
Michael Pohlman, prin. | Fax 753-2333

New Lebanon, Montgomery, Pop. 4,242
New Lebanon Local SD | 1,300/K-12
278 E Main St 45345 | 937-687-1301
Michael C. Eckert, supt. | Fax 687-7321
www.newlebanon.k12.oh.us/
Dixie HS | 400/9-12
300 S Fuls Rd 45345 | 937-687-1366
Chad Hill, prin. | Fax 687-7074
Dixie MS | 400/5-8
200 S Fuls Rd 45345 | 937-687-3508
Martin Tucker, prin. | Fax 687-7705

New Lexington, Perry, Pop. 4,712
New Lexington CSD | 2,000/K-12
101 3rd Ave 43764 | 740-342-4133
Larry Rentschler, supt. | Fax 342-6051
www.nlcs.k12.oh.us
New Lexington HS | 600/9-12
2547 Panther Dr NE 43764 | 740-342-3528
Tonya Sherburne, prin. | Fax 342-4765
New Lexington MS | 500/6-8
2549 Panther Dr NE 43764 | 740-342-4128
Tonya Cline, prin. | Fax 342-6071

New London, Huron, Pop. 2,693
New London Local SD | 1,200/K-12
2 Wildcat Dr 44851 | 419-929-8433
Gary Graham, supt. | Fax 929-4108
www.newlondon.k12.oh.us/
New London HS | 300/9-12
1 Wildcat Dr 44851 | 419-929-1586
Mary Lou Harris, prin. | Fax 929-9513
New London MS | 300/6-8
1 Wildcat Dr 44851 | 419-929-5409
Mary Lou Harris, prin. | Fax 929-9513

New Madison, Darke, Pop. 788
Tri-Village Local SD | 800/K-12
PO Box 31 45346 | 937-996-6261
Anthony Thomas, supt. | Fax 996-5537
www.tri-village.k12.oh.us
Tri-Village JSHS | 400/7-12
PO Box 31 45346 | 937-996-1511
William Moore, prin. | Fax 996-0307

New Matamoras, Washington, Pop. 1,019
Frontier Local SD | 1,000/K-12
44870 State Route 7 45767 | 740-865-3473
| Fax 865-2010
flsd.k12.oh.us/
Frontier HS | 300/9-12
44870 State Route 7 45767 | 740-865-3441
Troy Thacker, prin. | Fax 865-2011

New Middletown, Mahoning, Pop. 1,644
Springfield Local SD | 1,200/K-12
PO Box 549 44442 | 330-542-2929
Debra Mettee, supt. | Fax 542-9453
www.springfield.k12.oh.us
Springfield HS | 400/9-12
11335 Yngstwn Pittsburgh Rd 44442 | 330-542-3626
Anthony De Felice, prin. | Fax 542-9453
Springfield IS | 400/5-8
11333 Yngstwn Pittsburgh Rd 44442 | 330-542-3624
Jerome Hiznay, prin. | Fax 542-2159

New Paris, Preble, Pop. 1,562
National Trail Local SD | 1,100/K-12
6940 Oxford Gettysburg Rd 45347 | 937-437-3333
Clinton Moore, supt. | Fax 437-7865
National Trail HS | 400/9-12
6940 Oxford Gettysburg Rd 45347 | 937-437-3333
Mark Wiseman, prin. | Fax 437-8270
National Trail MS | 300/5-8
6940 Oxford Gettysburg Rd 45347 | 937-437-3333
Mark Wiseman, prin. | Fax 437-7306

New Philadelphia, Tuscarawas, Pop. 17,363
Buckeye JVSD
545 University Dr NE 44663 | 330-339-2288
Paul Hickman, supt. | Fax 339-5159
www.bjvs.k12.oh.us/
Buckeye Career Center | Vo/Tech
545 University Dr NE 44663 | 330-339-2288
| Fax 339-5159

New Philadelphia CSD | 3,000/K-12
248 Front Ave SW 44663 | 330-364-0600
Richard J. Varrati, supt. | Fax 364-9310
www.npschools.org
New Philadelphia HS | 1,000/9-12
343 Ray Ave NW 44663 | 330-364-0644
Rick Sattler, prin. | Fax 364-0633
Welty MS | 700/6-8
315 4th St NW 44663 | 330-364-0645
Scott Jenkins, prin. | Fax 364-0633

Central Catholic HS | 100/9-12
777 3rd St NE 44663 | 330-343-3302
David DiDonato, prin. | Fax 343-6388
Kent State University | Post-Sec.
330 University Dr NE 44663 | 330-339-3391

New Richmond, Clermont, Pop. 2,356
New Richmond EVD | 2,400/K-12
212 Market St 45157 | 513-553-2616
Thomas Durbin, supt. | Fax 553-6431
www.nrschools.org

New Richmond HS | 800/9-12
1131 Bethel New Richmond Rd 45157 513-553-3191
Diana Spinnati, prin. | Fax 553-2531
New Richmond MS | 400/7-8
1135 Bethel New Richmond Rd 45157 513-553-3161
Adam Bird, prin. | Fax 553-2604

New Riegel, Seneca, Pop. 219
New Riegel Local SD | 400/K-12
44 N Perry St 44853 | 419-595-2265
John P. Nolan, supt. | Fax 595-2901
www.new-riegel.k12.oh.us
New Riegel JSHS | 200/7-12
44 N Perry St 44853 | 419-595-2256
Rick Gagnon, prin. | Fax 595-2901

Newton Falls, Trumbull, Pop. 4,892
Newton Falls EVD | 1,500/K-12
909 1/2 Milton Blvd 44444 | 330-872-5445
David Wilson, supt. | Fax 872-3351
www.newton-falls.k12.oh.us/
Newton Falls JSHS | 700/7-12
907 Milton Blvd 44444 | 330-872-5121
John Crowder, prin. | Fax 872-3351

New Washington, Crawford, Pop. 965
Buckeye Central Local SD | 700/K-12
306 S Kibler St 44854 | 419-492-2864
Ronald Cirata, supt. | Fax 492-2039
www.buckeye-central.k12.oh.us
Buckeye Central JSHS | 300/7-12
306 S Kibler St 44854 | 419-492-2266
Jay Zeiter, prin. | Fax 492-2039

Niles, Trumbull, Pop. 20,337
Niles CSD | 2,900/K-12
100 West St 44446 | 330-652-2509
Rocco Adduci, supt. | Fax 652-3522
www.niles.k12.oh.us/
McKinley HS | 900/9-12
616 Dragon Dr 44446 | 330-652-9968
Mark Pallante, prin. | Fax 505-0755
Niles MS | 700/6-8
411 Brown St 44446 | 330-652-5656
Robert Marino, prin. | Fax 652-9158

ETI Technical College | Post-Sec.
2076 Youngstown Warren Rd 44446 330-652-9919
Raphael's School of Beauty Culture | Post-Sec.
1324 Youngstown Warren Rd 44446 330-652-1559
Victory Christian S | 100/K-12
2053 Pleasant Valley Rd 44446 | 330-539-9827
Jeanne Hanselman, prin. | Fax 539-9828

North Baltimore, Wood, Pop. 3,330
North Baltimore Local SD | 800/K-12
201 S Main St 45872 | 419-257-3531
Kyle Clark, supt. | Fax 257-2008
www.northbaltimoreschools.org/
North Baltimore HS | 200/9-12
124 S 2nd St 45872 | 419-257-3464
Greg Clark, prin. | Fax 257-3601
North Baltimore MS | 100/7-8
124 S 2nd St 45872 | 419-257-3464
Gregory Clark, prin. | Fax 257-3044

North Bend, Hamilton, Pop. 606
Three Rivers Local SD
Supt. — See Cleves
Taylor HS | 600/9-12
36 E Harrison Ave 45052 | 513-467-3200
Randal Mechlenborg, prin. | Fax 467-3204

North Bloomfield, Trumbull
Bloomfield-Mespo Local SD | 400/K-12
2077 Park West Rd 44450 | 440-685-4710
Frank DiPiero, supt. | Fax 685-4751
www.bloomfield.k12.oh.us
Bloomfield MSHS | 200/6-12
2077 Park West Rd 44450 | 440-685-4711
Steve Kobus, prin.

North Canton, Stark, Pop. 16,722
North Canton CSD | 4,900/PK-12
525 7th St NE 44720 | 330-497-5600
Michael Gallina, supt. | Fax 497-5618
www.northcanton.sparcc.org/~nccs/
Hoover HS | 1,700/9-12
525 7th St NE 44720 | 330-497-5620
Anthony Pallija, prin. | Fax 497-5606
North Canton MS | 1,100/6-8
605 Fair Oaks Ave SW 44720 | 330-497-5635
John Stanley, prin. | Fax 497-5659

Plain Local SD
Supt. — See Canton
Middlebranch MS | 700/6-8
7500 Middlebranch Ave NE, Canton OH 44721
| 330-493-5525
Mark Filicky, prin. | Fax 493-5528

Brown Mackie College | Post-Sec.
1320 W Maple St 44720 | 330-494-1214
Kent State University-Stark Campus | Post-Sec.
6000 Frank Ave NW 44720 | 330-499-9600
Stark State College of Technology | Post-Sec.
6200 Frank Ave NW 44720 | 330-494-6170
Walsh University | Post-Sec.
2020 E Maple St 44720 | 800-362-9846

North Eaton, Lorain

Christian Community S | 200/K-12
35716 Royalton Rd 44044 | 440-748-6224
Richard Willis, hdmstr. | Fax 748-1007

Northfield, Summit, Pop. 3,771
Nordonia Hills CSD | 3,800/K-12
9370 Olde 8 Rd 44067 | 330-467-0580
J. Wayne Blankenship, supt. | Fax 468-0152
www.nordonia.summit.k12.oh.us
Nordonia MS | 600/7-8
73 Leonard Ave 44067 | 330-467-0584
Dave Wilson, prin. | Fax 468-6719
Other Schools – See Macedonia

North Jackson, Mahoning
Jackson-Milton Local SD | 900/K-12
14110 Mahoning Ave 44451 | 330-538-3232
Warne Palmer, supt. | Fax 538-2259
www.jacksonmilton.k12.oh.us/
Jackson-Milton HS | 300/9-12
10748 Mahoning Ave 44451 | 330-538-3308
Joseph Malmisur, prin. | Fax 538-0821
Jackson-Milton MS | 200/6-8
10748 Mahoning Ave 44451 | 330-538-4054
Lisa Whitacre, prin.

North Lewisburg, Union, Pop. 1,605
Triad Local SD | 1,100/K-12
7920 Brush Lake Rd 43060 | 937-826-4961
Dan Kaffenbarger, supt. | Fax 826-3281
www.triad.k12.oh.us
Triad HS | 300/9-12
8099 Brush Lake Rd 43060 | 937-826-3771
Kyle Huffman, prin. | Fax 826-2002
Triad MS | 400/5-8
7941 Brush Lake Rd 43060 | 937-826-3071
Scott Blackburn, prin. | Fax 826-1000

North Lima, Mahoning
South Range Local SD | 1,300/K-12
11836 South Ave 44452 | 330-549-5226
James Hall, supt. | Fax 549-4740
www.southrange.k12.oh.us/
South Range HS | 400/9-12
11836 South Ave 44452 | 330-549-2163
Dennis Dunham, prin. | Fax 549-0214
Other Schools – See Salem

Tri-State College of Massotherapy | Post-Sec.
9159 Market St # 26 44452 | 330-629-9998

North Olmsted, Cuyahoga, Pop. 33,481
North Olmsted CSD | 4,600/PK-12
27425 Butternut Ridge Rd 44070 | 440-779-3549
Dr. Kurt Stanic, supt. | Fax 779-3505
www.northolmstedschools.org/
North Olmsted HS | 1,600/9-12
5755 Burns Rd 44070 | 440-779-8825
Paul Sink, prin. | Fax 777-2216
North Olmsted MS | 800/7-8
27351 Butternut Ridge Rd 44070 | 440-779-8501
Steve Barrett, prin. | Fax 779-8510

Hearts for Jesus Christ Christian S | 200/K-12
27113 Brookpark Rd Ext #179 44070
Kitt Chmura, admin. | 216-226-2750
Remington College-Cleveland West Campus Post-Sec.
26350 Brookpark Rd 44070 | 440-777-2560

North Ridgeville, Lorain, Pop. 24,294
North Ridgeville CSD | 3,100/K-12
5490 Mills Creek Ln 44039 | 440-327-4444
Larry Bowersox, supt. | Fax 327-9774
www.nrcs.k12.oh.us
North Ridgeville HS | 1,100/9-12
34600 Bainbridge Rd 44039 | 440-327-1992
Patricia Bahr, prin. | Fax 327-4056
North Ridgeville MS | 800/6-8
35895 Center Ridge Rd 44039 | 440-353-1180
John Komperda, prin. | Fax 353-1144

Lake Ridge Academy | 400/K-12
37501 Center Ridge Rd 44039 | 440-327-1175
Deborah M. Cook, hdmstr. | Fax 353-0324

North Robinson, Crawford, Pop. 205
Colonel Crawford Local SD | 1,000/K-12
PO Box 7 44856 | 419-562-4666
Ted Bruner, supt. | Fax 562-3304
www.colonel-crawford.k12.oh.us/
Crawford HS | 400/9-12
PO Box 7 44856 | 419-562-4666
James Trainer, prin. | Fax 562-3304
Crawford IS | 300/6-8
PO Box 7 44856 | 419-562-3503
Steve Mohr, prin. | Fax 562-3304

North Royalton, Cuyahoga, Pop. 29,598
North Royalton CSD | 4,300/PK-12
6579 Royalton Rd 44133 | 440-237-8800
Randy S. Boroff, supt. | Fax 582-7336
www.northroyaltonsd.org
North Royalton HS | 1,500/9-12
14713 Ridge Rd 44133 | 440-582-7801
Carol Moehring, prin. | Fax 582-7337
North Royalton MS | 1,500/5-8
14709 Ridge Rd 44133 | 440-582-9120
Donald DiLillo, prin. | Fax 582-7366

Northwood, Wood, Pop. 5,484
Northwood Local SD | 1,000/K-12
600 Lemoyne Rd 43619 | 419-691-3888
| Fax 697-2470
www.northwood.k12.oh.us
Northwood HS | 300/9-12
700 Lemoyne Rd 43619 | 419-691-4651
Joe Gagel, prin. | Fax 691-2846
Northwood MS | 200/6-8
500 Lemoyne Rd 43619 | 419-691-4621
Amy Klinger, prin. | Fax 697-2479

Toledo Academy of Beauty Culture - East | Post-Sec.
2592 Woodville Rd 43619 | 419-693-7257

Norton, Summit, Pop. 11,648
Norton CSD | 2,600/PK-12
4128 Cleveland Massillon Rd 44203 | 330-825-0863
Karen Wilson, supt. | Fax 825-0929
www.nortonschools.org
Norton HS | 800/9-12
4108 Cleveland Massillon Rd 44203 | 330-825-7300
Rolland Gerstenmaier, prin. | Fax 825-4275
Norton MS | 800/5-8
3390 Cleveland Massillon Rd 44203 | 330-825-5607
Suzanne Miller, prin. | Fax 825-1461

Akron Machining Institute | Post-Sec.
2959 Barber Rd 44203 | 330-745-1111

Norwalk, Huron, Pop. 16,353
Norwalk CSD | 2,800/K-12
134 Benedict Ave 44857 | 419-668-2779
Dr. Wayne Babcanec, supt. | Fax 663-3302
www.norwalk-city.k12.oh.us
Norwalk HS | 800/9-12
350 Shady Lane Dr 44857 | 419-668-2079
Robert Duncan, prin.
Norwalk MS, 64 Christie Ave 44857 | 500/7-8
James Hagemeyer, prin. | 419-668-8370

St. Paul HS | 300/9-12
93 E Main St 44857 | 419-668-3005
Valerie French, prin. | Fax 668-6417

Norwood, Hamilton, Pop. 20,781
Norwood CSD | 2,600/K-12
2132 Williams Ave 45212 | 513-924-2500
Steve L. Collier, supt. | Fax 396-6420
www.norwoodschools.org
Norwood HS | 800/9-12
2020 Sherman Ave 45212 | 513-924-2800
Terri Holden, prin. | Fax 396-5559
Norwood MS | 400/7-8
2060 Sherman Ave 45212 | 513-924-2700
Sharon Freyhof, prin. | Fax 396-5537

Oak Harbor, Ottawa, Pop. 2,819
Benton Carroll Salem Local SD | 2,000/K-12
11685 W State Route 163 43449 | 419-898-6210
Diane Kershaw, supt. | Fax 898-4303
www.bcs.k12.oh.us/
Oak Harbor HS | 700/9-12
11661 W State Route 163 43449 | 419-898-6216
Keith Thorbahn, prin. | Fax 898-0116
Oak Harbor MS | 500/6-8
315 N Church St 43449 | 419-898-6217
Marie Wittman, prin. | Fax 898-1613

Oak Hill, Jackson, Pop. 1,662
Oak Hill Union Local SD | 1,200/K-12
265 W Cross St 45656 | 740-682-7595
William Ramsey, supt. | Fax 682-6998
www.oakhill.k12.oh.us
Oak Hill MSHS | 700/6-12
5063 State Road 93 N 45656 | 740-682-7055
Regina Boggs, prin. | Fax 682-6075

Oberlin, Lorain, Pop. 8,139
Firelands Local SD | 2,200/K-12
11970 Vermilion Rd 44074 | 440-965-5821
Dr. Thomas Diringer, supt. | Fax 965-5990
www.firelandsschools.org/
Firelands HS | 700/9-12
10643 Vermilion Rd 44074 | 440-965-5351
Paul Haeuptle, prin. | Fax 965-5296
Other Schools – See South Amherst

Lorain County JVSD | 440-774-1051
15181 State Route 58 44074
William Randall, supt. | Fax 774-2144
www.lcjvs.com/
Burton Vocational Center HS | Vo/Tech
15181 State Route 58 44074 | 440-774-1051
Jo Ann Kuebbeler, prin. | Fax 774-2144
Oberlin CSD | 1,100/K-12
153 N Main St 44074 | 440-774-1458
| Fax 774-4492
www.oberlin.k12.oh.us
Langston MS | 300/6-8
150 N Pleasant St 44074 | 440-775-7961
Ronald Thomas, prin. | Fax 776-4520
Oberlin HS | 300/9-12
281 N Pleasant St 44074 | 440-774-1295
Larry Thomas, prin. | Fax 774-5099

Oberlin College | Post-Sec.
101 N Professor St 44074 | 440-775-8121

Old Fort, Seneca
Old Fort Local SD | 600/K-12
PO Box 64 44861 | 419-992-4291
Richard Selvey, supt. | Fax 992-4293
www.old-fort.k12.oh.us/
Old Fort JSHS | 300/7-12
PO Box 64 44861 | 419-992-4291
Laura Keller, prin. | Fax 992-4293

Old Washington, Guernsey, Pop. 270
East Guernsey Local SD | 700/K-12
PO Box 128 43768 | 740-489-5190
Robert Greenwood, supt. | Fax 489-9813
www.eguernsey.k12.oh.us
Other Schools – See Lore City

Olmsted Falls, Cuyahoga, Pop. 8,445
Olmsted Falls CSD | 3,300/K-12
PO Box 38010 44138 | 440-427-6000
Todd Hoadley, supt. | Fax 427-6010
www.ofcs.k12.oh.us/
Olmsted Falls HS | 1,100/9-12
26939 Bagley Rd 44138 | 440-427-6100
Robert Trapp, prin. | Fax 427-6110
Olmsted Falls MS | 800/6-8
27045 Bagley Rd 44138 | 440-427-6200
Mark Kurz, prin. | Fax 427-6210

Oregon, Lucas, Pop. 19,419
Oregon CSD | 3,800/K-12
5721 Seaman St 43616 | 419-693-0661
John C. Hall, supt. | Fax 698-6016
www.oregon.k12.oh.us
Clay HS | 1,200/9-12
5665 Seaman St 43616 | 419-693-0665
Michael Zalar, prin. | Fax 698-6047
Eisenhower MS | 500/6-8
331 N North Curtice Rd 43618 | 419-836-8498
Mark Verroco, prin. | Fax 836-2005
Fassett MS | 500/6-8
3025 Starr Ave 43616 | 419-693-0455
Dean Ensey, prin. | Fax 698-6048

Cardinal Stritch HS | 400/9-12
3225 Pickle Rd   43616 | 419-693-0465
Tim Mahoney, prin. | Fax 693-0465
St. Charles Hospital | Post-Sec.
2600 Navarre Ave   43616 | 419-698-7341

Orrville, Wayne, Pop. 8,506
Orrville CSD | 1,200/K-12
815 N Ella St   44667 | 330-682-4651
Jeffrey Patterson, supt. | Fax 682-0073
www.orrville.k12.oh.us
Orrville HS | 600/9-12
841 N Ella St   44667 | 330-682-4661
Richard Gardner, prin. | Fax 682-0073
Orrville JHS | 300/7-8
217 E Church St   44667 | 330-682-1791
James Curtis, prin. | Fax 682-2743

Kingsway Christian S | 200/K-12
11138 Old Lincoln Way E   44667 | 330-683-0012
James Williams, admin. | Fax 683-0017
University of Akron-Wayne College | Post-Sec.
1901 Smucker Rd   44667 | 330-683-2010

Orwell, Ashtabula, Pop. 1,532
Grand Valley Local SD | 500/K-12
11 Grand Valley Ave Ste A   44076 | 440-437-6260
John Sheets, supt. | Fax 437-1025
www.grand-valley.k12.oh.us
Grand Valley HS | 400/9-12
11 Grand Valley Ave Ste C   44076 | 440-437-6260
Stephen Sisko, prin. | Fax 437-6254
Grand Valley MS | 5-8
11 Grand Valley Ave Ste D   44076 | 440-437-6260
Lowell Moodt, prin. | Fax 437-6156

Ottawa, Putnam, Pop. 4,491
Ottawa-Glandorf Local SD | 1,600/K-12
630 Glendale Ave   45875 | 419-523-5261
Kevin Brinkman, supt. | Fax 523-5978
og.noacsc.org/
Ottawa-Glandorf HS | 700/9-12
630 Glendale Ave   45875 | 419-523-5702
William Hanna, prin. | Fax 523-6346

Ottoville, Putnam, Pop. 855
Ottoville Local SD | 600/K-12
PO Box 248   45876 | 419-453-3356
Kenneth Amstutz, supt. | Fax 453-3367
www.noacsc.org/putnam/ov/
Ottoville JSHS | 300/7-12
PO Box 248   45876 | 419-453-3358
Wilbur Altenburger, prin. | Fax 453-3367

Oxford, Butler, Pop. 22,283
Talawanda CSD | 3,100/K-12
131 W Chestnut St   45056 | 513-523-4716
Dr. Philip F. Cagwin, supt. | Fax 523-1145
www.talawanda.org
Talawanda HS | 1,100/9-12
101 W Chestnut St   45056 | 513-523-4137
Dr. David Isaacs, prin. | Fax 523-0504
Talawanda MS | 800/6-8
4030 Oxford Reily Rd   45056 | 513-523-1989
Sharon Lytle, prin. | Fax 523-5144

Miami University | Post-Sec.
E High St   45056 | 513-529-1809

Painesville, Lake, Pop. 17,428
Painesville City Local SD | 2,700/K-12
58 Jefferson St   44077 | 440-392-5060
Michael Hanlon Ph.D., supt. | Fax 392-5089
www.painesville-city.k12.oh.us
Harvey HS | 600/9-12
167 W Washington St   44077 | 440-392-5110
Kimberly Martin, prin. | Fax 392-5119
Hobart MS | 600/6-8
200 W Walnut Ave   44077 | 440-392-5250
Denise Ward, prin. | Fax 392-5259

Painesville Township Local SD | 4,400/K-12
585 Riverside Dr   44077 | 440-352-0668
Dr. Michael Shoaf, supt. | Fax 639-1959
www.townshipschools.com
Riverside JSHS | 1,800/8-12
585 Riverside Dr   44077 | 440-352-3341
David Toth, prin. | Fax 352-0695

Lake Erie College | Post-Sec.
391 W Washington St   44077 | 440-352-3361

Pandora, Putnam, Pop. 1,214
Pandora-Gilboa Local SD | 600/K-12
410 Rocket Rdg   45877 | 419-384-3227
Dale Lewellen, supt. | Fax 384-3230
www.pg.noacsc.org
Pandora-Gilboa HS | 200/9-12
410 Rocket Rdg   45877 | 419-384-3225
Mel Heitmeyer, prin. | Fax 384-3230
Pandora-Gilboa MS | 200/5-8
410 Rocket Rdg   45877 | 419-384-3225
John Stoner, prin. | Fax 384-3230

Parma, Cuyahoga, Pop. 83,861
Parma CSD | 13,200/K-12
6726 Ridge Rd   44129 | 440-842-5300
Dr. Sarah Zatik, supt. | Fax 885-2452
www.parmacityschools.org/
Greenbriar MS | 800/7-8
11810 Huffman Rd   44130 | 440-885-2368
Frank Spisak, prin. | Fax 885-8353
Normandy HS | 1,200/9-12
2500 W Pleasant Valley Rd   44134 | 440-885-2400
Chris Jayjack, prin. | Fax 885-2402
Parma HS | 1,600/9-12
6285 W 54th St   44129 | 440-885-2300
Cassandra Johnson, prin. | Fax 885-8684
Shiloh MS | 800/7-8
2303 Grantwood Dr   44134 | 440-885-8485
Phyllis Spears, prin. | Fax 885-8486
Other Schools – See Parma Heights, Seven Hills

Padua Franciscan HS | 1,100/9-12
6740 State Rd   44134 | 440-845-2444
Christopher Keavy, prin. | Fax 845-5710
Parma Community General Hospital | Post-Sec.
7007 Powers Blvd   44129 | 440-743-3000

Parma Heights, Cuyahoga, Pop. 21,209
Parma CSD
Supt. — See Parma
Valley Forge HS | 1,700/9-12
9999 Independence Blvd   44130 | 440-885-2330
Steele Nowlin, prin. | Fax 885-8412

Cuyahoga Community College | Post-Sec.
11000 W Pleasant Valley Rd   44130 | 440-842-7773
Holy Name HS | 1,100/9-12
6000 Queens Hwy   44130 | 440-886-0300
Benjamin Farmer, prin. | Fax 886-1267

Pataskala, Licking, Pop. 11,850
Licking Heights Local SD
Supt. — See Summit Station
Licking Heights HS | 800/7-12
4000 Mink St SW   43062 | 740-927-9046
Stephen Hackett, prin. | Fax 927-9043

Southwest Licking Local SD
Supt. — See Etna
Watkins Memorial HS | 1,000/9-12
8868 Watkins Rd SW   43062 | 740-927-3846
Steve Donahue, prin. | Fax 964-0088
Watkins MS | 900/6-8
8808 Watkins Rd SW   43062 | 740-927-5767
Lynn Lanning, prin. | Fax 927-2337

Paulding, Paulding, Pop. 3,442
Paulding EVD | 1,800/PK-12
405 N Water St   45879 | 419-399-4656
William Shugars, supt. | Fax 399-2404
pv.noacsc.org
Paulding HS | 500/9-12
405 N Water St   45879 | 419-399-4656
Carl Metzger, prin. | Fax 399-2404
Paulding MS | 400/6-8
405 N Water St   45879 | 419-399-4656
David Stallkamp, prin. | Fax 399-2404

Peebles, Adams, Pop. 1,793
Adams County/Ohio Valley SD
Supt. — See West Union
Peebles HS | 500/7-12
25719 State Route 41   45660 | 937-587-2681
Eric Meredith, prin. | Fax 587-5236

Pemberville, Wood, Pop. 1,339
Eastwood Local SD | 1,900/K-12
4800 Sugar Ridge Rd   43450 | 419-833-6411
Brent Welker, supt. | Fax 833-4915
www.eastwood.k12.oh.us/
Eastwood HS | 700/9-12
4900 Sugar Ridge Rd   43450 | 419-833-3611
Jeff Hill, prin. | Fax 833-6014
Eastwood MS | 500/6-8
4800 Sugar Ridge Rd   43450 | 419-833-6011
John Obrock, prin. | Fax 833-7454

Peninsula, Summit, Pop. 669
Woodridge Local SD | 1,800/K-12
4411 Quick Rd   44264 | 330-928-9074
Dr. Jeffrey Graham, supt. | Fax 928-1542
www.woodridge.k12.oh.us/
Woodridge HS | 500/9-12
4440 Quick Rd   44264 | 330-929-3191
Phil Hatton, prin. | Fax 928-5036
Woodridge MS | 400/6-8
4451 Quick Rd   44264 | 330-928-7420
Jim Nicodemo, prin. | Fax 928-5645

Perry, Lake, Pop. 1,225
Perry Local SD | 1,900/K-12
4325 Manchester Rd   44081 | 440-259-3881
Michael Sawyers, supt. | Fax 259-3607
www.perry-lake.k12.oh.us
Perry HS | 600/9-12
1 Success Blvd   44081 | 440-259-3511
Doug Jenkins, prin. | Fax 259-9290
Perry MS | 600/5-8
2 Learning Ln   44081 | 440-259-3026
Ann Spurrier, prin. | Fax 259-5149

Perrysburg, Wood, Pop. 16,840
Penta County JVSD | 419-666-1120
30095 Oregon Rd   43551 | Fax 666-6049
Frederick Susor, supt.
www.pentacareercenter.org
Penta Career Center | Vo/Tech
30095 Oregon Rd   43551 | 419-666-1120
Ronald Simon, prin. | Fax 666-6049

Perrysburg EVD | 4,300/K-12
140 E Indiana Ave   43551 | 419-874-9131
Michael L. Cline, supt. | Fax 872-8820
www.perrysburg.k12.oh.us
Perrysburg HS | 1,400/9-12
13385 Roachton Rd   43551 | 419-874-3181
Michael Short, prin. | Fax 872-8813
Perrysburg JHS | 1,100/6-8
550 E South Boundary St   43551 | 419-874-9193
Patrick Calvin, prin. | Fax 872-8812

Perrysville, Ashland, Pop. 830
Loudonville-Perrysville EVD
Supt. — See Loudonville
Perrysville JHS | 200/7-8
PO Box 426   44864 | 419-938-7193
John Lance, prin. | Fax 938-3304

Pettisville, Fulton
Pettisville Local SD | 600/K-12
PO Box 53001   43553 | 419-446-2705
Stephen Switzer, supt. | Fax 445-2992
blackbirds.pettisville.k12.oh.us/
Pettisville HS | 300/7-12
PO Box 53001   43553 | 419-446-2705
Michael Lane, prin. | Fax 445-2992

Philo, Muskingum, Pop. 765
Franklin Local SD
Supt. — See Duncan Falls
Philo HS | 700/9-12
200 Broad St   43771 | 740-674-4355
Michael Dorman, prin. | Fax 674-5202
Philo JHS | 400/6-8
225 Market St   43771 | 740-674-5210
Tony Sines, prin. | Fax 674-5217

Pickerington, Fairfield, Pop. 12,627
Pickerington Local SD | 8,800/K-12
777 Long Rd   43147 | 614-833-2110
Dr. Robert H. Thiede, supt. | Fax 833-2143
www.pickerington.k12.oh.us
Pickerington HS Central | 1,200/9-12
300 Opportunity Way   43147 | 614-833-3025
Charles Kemper, prin. | Fax 833-3062
Pickerington HS North | 1,400/9-12
7800 Refugee Rd   43147 | 614-830-2700
Mike Smith, prin. | Fax 833-3660
Pickerington Lakeview JHS | 800/7-8
12445 Ault Rd   43147 | 614-830-2200
Jim Sotlar, prin. | Fax 834-3267
Pickerington Ridgeview JHS | 600/7-8
130 Hill Rd S   43147 | 614-833-2100
Charles Byers, prin. | Fax 833-2127

Piketon, Pike, Pop. 1,962
Pike County Area JVSD | 740-289-2721
PO Box 577   45661 | Fax 289-8891
Stephen E. Martin, supt.
www.pikectc.org
Riffe Career Technology Center | Vo/Tech
PO Box 577   45661 | 740-289-2721
Keith Smith Ph.D., dir. | Fax 289-2527

Scioto Valley Local SD | 1,600/K-12
PO Box 600   45661 | 740-289-4456
Dennis Thompson, supt. | Fax 289-3065
www.svross.k12.oh.us
Piketon JSHS | 800/7-12
PO Box 488   45661 | 740-289-2254
Steve McCann, prin. | Fax 289-1514

Miracle City Academy | 100/9-12
204 Commercial Blvd   45661 | 740-289-2787
Malcolm Cisco, prin. | Fax 289-2013

Pioneer, Williams, Pop. 1,431
North Central Local SD | 700/K-12
400 E Baubice St   43554 | 419-737-2392
Stephen Lewis, supt. | Fax 737-3361
North Central JSHS | 300/7-12
400 E Baubice St   43554 | 419-737-2366
Paul Allison, prin. | Fax 737-3361

Piqua, Miami, Pop. 20,728
Piqua CSD | 3,900/K-12
719 E Ash St   45356 | 937-773-4321
Dr. Karen Mantia, supt. | Fax 778-4518
portal2.piqua.org/
Piqua HS | 1,300/9-12
1 Indian Trl   45356 | 937-773-6314
Katherine Davisson, prin. | Fax 774-6414
Piqua JHS | 700/7-8
1 Tomahawk Trl   45356 | 937-778-2997
Edward McCord, prin. | Fax 773-3574

Upper Valley JVSD | 937-778-1980
8811 Career Dr   45356 | Fax 778-0103
Karl Wilson, supt.
www.uvjvs.org
Upper Valley Joint Vocational S | Vo/Tech
8811 Career Dr   45356 | 937-778-1980
Michael Shellabarger, dir. | Fax 778-4677

Edison State Community College | Post-Sec.
1973 Edison Dr   45356 | 937-778-8600
Piqua Catholic S - North | 200/4-8
503 W North St   45356 | 937-773-1564
Anthony Frierott, prin. | Fax 773-0380

Pitsburg, Darke, Pop. 389
Franklin-Monroe Local SD | 700/K-12
PO Box 78   45358 | 937-692-8637
David Gray, supt. | Fax 692-6547
www.franklin-monroe.k12.oh.us/
Franklin-Monroe JSHS | 400/7-12
PO Box 78   45358 | 937-692-8761
David Deskins, prin. | Fax 692-8740

Plain City, Madison, Pop. 3,167
Central Ohio JVSD | 614-873-4666
7877 US Highway 42 S   43064 | Fax 873-8761
Carl J. Berg, supt.
www.tollestech.com
Tolles Career & Technical Center | Vo/Tech
7877 US Highway 42 S   43064 | 614-873-4666
Steve Hull, supt. | Fax 873-6909

Jonathan Alder Local SD | 1,500/PK-12
9200 US Highway 42 S   43064 | 614-873-5621
Douglas Carpenter Ph.D., supt. | Fax 873-8462
www.alder.k12.oh.us
Alder HS | 600/9-12
9200 US Highway 42 S   43064 | 614-873-4642
Phil Harris, prin.
Alder JHS | 7-8
6440 Kilbury Huber Rd   43064 | 614-873-4635
Jud Ross, prin. | Fax 873-0845

Pleasant Hill, Miami, Pop. 1,131
Newton Local SD | 600/K-12
PO Box 803   45359 | 937-676-3271
Kent A. Shafer, supt. | Fax 676-2054
Newton JSHS | 300/7-12
PO Box 803   45359 | 937-676-3081
Andrew White, prin. | Fax 676-3258

Pleasant Plain, Warren, Pop. 159

Village Christian S | 200/PK-12
PO Box 48   45162 | 513-877-2143
Dwight Hesson, supt. | Fax 877-2102

Plymouth, Huron, Pop. 1,866
Plymouth-Shiloh Local SD — 1,000/K-12
365 Sandusky St 44865 — 419-687-4733
James Metcalf, supt. — Fax 687-1541
www.plymouth.k12.oh.us/
Plymouth HS — 300/9-12
400 Trux St 44865 — 419-687-8200
John Hart, prin. — Fax 687-8175
Shiloh MS — 200/6-8
400 Trux St 44865 — 419-687-4061
Bradley Turson, prin. — Fax 887-8175

Poland, Mahoning, Pop. 2,780
Poland Local SD — 2,500/K-12
30 Riverside Dr 44514 — 330-757-7000
Robert Zorn, supt. — Fax 757-2390
www.polandbulldogs.com/
Poland MS — 400/7-8
47 College St 44514 — 330-757-7003
Susan Sause, prin. — Fax 757-2390
Poland Seminary HS — 900/9-12
3199 Dobbins Rd 44514 — 330-757-7018
Robert Rostan, prin. — Fax 757-2390

Pomeroy, Meigs, Pop. 1,997
Meigs Local SD — 1,900/K-12
PO Box 272 45769 — 740-992-2153
William Buckley, supt. — Fax 992-7814
www.ml.k12.oh.us/
Meigs HS — 700/9-12
42091 Pomeroy Pike 45769 — 740-992-2158
Dennis Eichinger, prin. — Fax 992-5839
Meigs MS — 500/6-8
42353 Charles Chancey Dr 45769 — 740-992-3058
Mary Hawk, prin. — Fax 992-6952

Port Clinton, Ottawa, Pop. 6,316
Port Clinton CSD — 1,900/K-12
431 Portage Dr 43452 — 419-732-2102
Patrick Adkins, supt. — Fax 734-4527
www.port-clinton.k12.oh.us
Port Clinton HS — 700/9-12
821 Jefferson St 43452 — 419-734-2147
Gaylord Moore, prin. — Fax 734-4276
Port Clinton MS — 300/7-8
110 E 4th St 43452 — 419-734-4448
Robert Nobles, prin. — Fax 734-4440

Portsmouth, Scioto, Pop. 19,913
Clay Local SD — 600/K-12
44 Clay High St 45662 — 740-354-6645
Anthony Mantell, supt. — Fax 354-5746
clay.k12.oh.us/
Clay HS — 300/7-12
44 Clay High St 45662 — 740-354-6644
Todd Warnock, prin. — Fax 354-5746
Portsmouth CSD — 2,100/K-12
923 Findlay St 45662 — 740-354-5663
Wyvonna Broughton, supt. — Fax 354-8872
www.portsmouth.k12.oh.us
Portsmouth HS — 500/9-12
1149 Gallia St 45662 — 740-353-2398
Ann Charles, prin. — Fax 354-3494
Portsmouth JHS — 300/7-8
1149 Gallia St 45662 — 740-353-6129
Tom Smith, prin. — Fax 353-6340

Washington-Nile Local SD
Supt. — See West Portsmouth
Portsmouth West HS — 500/9-12
15332 US Highway 52 45663 — 740-858-1103
Anthony Bazler, prin. — Fax 858-1110

Notre Dame JSHS — 200/7-12
2220 Sunrise Ave 45662 — 740-353-0719
Kathy Milligan, prin. — Fax 353-2526
Paramount Beauty Academy — Post-Sec.
1745 11th St 45662 — 740-353-2436
Shawnee State University — Post-Sec.
940 2nd St 45662 — 740-354-3205

Powell, Delaware, Pop. 8,179
Olentangy Local SD
Supt. — See Lewis Center
Olentangy Liberty HS — 800/9-12
3584 Home Rd 43065 — 740-657-4200
Eric Gordon, prin. — Fax 657-4299
Olentangy Liberty MS — 900/6-8
7940 Liberty Rd N 43065 — 740-657-4400
Gena Williams, prin. — Fax 657-4499

Learning Unlimited-Village Academy — 400/K-12
284 S Liberty St 43065 — 614-841-0050
Susan Lasley, prin. — Fax 841-0501

Proctorville, Lawrence, Pop. 615
Fairland Local SD — 1,800/K-12
228 Private Dr 10010 45669 — 740-886-3100
Jerry McConnell, supt. — Fax 886-7253
fairland.k12.oh.us/
Fairland HS — 600/9-12
21360 State Route 243 45669 — 740-886-3250
David Judd, prin. — Fax 886-6738
Fairland MS — 400/6-8
7875 State Route 7 45669 — 740-886-3200
Michael Whitley, prin. — Fax 886-5125

Put in Bay, Ottawa, Pop. 135
Put-in-Bay Local SD — 100/K-12
PO Box 659 43456 — 419-285-3614
James Stauffer, supt. — Fax 285-2137
www.put-in-bay.k12.oh.us
Put-in-Bay JSHS — 50/7-12
PO Box 659 43456 — 419-285-3614
James Stauffer, supt. — Fax 285-2137

Racine, Meigs, Pop. 769
Southern Local SD — 700/K-12
920 Elm St 45771 — 740-949-2669
Robert Grueser, supt. — Fax 949-3309
www.seovec.org/southern/
Southern HS — 200/9-12
920 Elm St 45771 — 740-949-2611
Mark Miller, prin. — Fax 949-3309

Ravenna, Portage, Pop. 11,506
Maplewood Career Center SD
7075 State Route 88 44266 — 330-296-2892
Randall Griffith, supt. — Fax 296-5680
www.maplenet.sparcc.org
Maplewood Career Center — Vo/Tech
7075 State Route 88 44266 — 330-296-2892
— Fax 296-5680

Ravenna CSD — 3,200/PK-12
507 E Main St 44266 — 330-296-9679
Dr. Tim Calfee, supt. — Fax 297-4158
www.ravenna.portage.k12.oh.us
Brown MS, 228 S Scranton St 44266 — 500/7-8
Judy Paydock, prin. — 330-296-3849
— Fax 296-3849
Ravenna HS — 900/9-12
345 E Main St 44266 — 330-296-3844
Michael Bradley, prin. — Fax 296-1855

Southeast Local SD — 2,500/K-12
8245 Tallmadge Rd 44266 — 330-654-5841
Linda Fuline, supt. — Fax 654-9110
se-web.portage.k12.oh.us/
Southeast HS — 700/9-12
8423 Tallmadge Rd 44266 — 330-654-5841
Gregory Newell, prin. — Fax 654-9110
Southeast MS — 500/6-8
8540 Tallmadge Rd 44266 — 330-654-5842
David Cappuzzello, prin. — Fax 654-9110

Bohecker's Business College — Post-Sec.
653 Enterprise Pkwy 44266 — 800-794-2856

Rawson, Hancock, Pop. 472
Cory-Rawson Local SD — 700/K-12
3930 County Road 26 45881 — 419-963-3415
Richard Steiner, supt. — Fax 963-4400
cory-rawson.k12.oh.us
Cory-Rawson HS — 300/9-12
3930 County Road 26 45881 — 419-963-2611
Mark Willeke, prin. — Fax 963-4400
Cory-Rawson MS — 200/5-8
3930 County Road 26 45881 — 419-963-3161
Daniel Grime, prin. — Fax 963-4400

Rayland, Jefferson, Pop. 413
Buckeye Local SD
Supt. — See Dillonvale
Buckeye HS — 800/9-12
10692 State Route 150 43943 — 740-859-2196
Scott Celestin, prin. — Fax 859-2857

Reading, Hamilton, Pop. 10,747
Reading Community CSD — 1,400/K-12
1301 Bonnell St 45215 — 513-554-1800
L. Scott Inskeep, supt. — Fax 483-6754
www.readingschools.org
Reading Community JSHS — 700/7-12
810 E Columbia Ave 45215 — 513-733-4422
Charles LaFata, prin. — Fax 483-6766

Mt. Notre Dame HS — 800/9-12
711 E Columbia Ave 45215 — 513-821-3044
Maureen Baldock, prin. — Fax 821-6068

Reedsville, Meigs
Eastern Local SD — 800/K-12
50008 State Route 681 45772 — 740-667-6079
Ricky D. Edwards, supt. — Fax 667-3978
www.el.k12.oh.us/2004/index.shtml
Eastern HS — 200/9-12
38900 State Route 7 45772 — 740-985-3329
John Linder, prin. — Fax 667-3978

Republic, Seneca, Pop. 597
Seneca East Local SD
Supt. — See Attica
Seneca East JHS — 200/7-8
PO Box 39 44867 — 419-585-4291
— Fax 585-5010

Reynoldsburg, Franklin, Pop. 32,878
Reynoldsburg CSD — 6,500/K-12
7244 E Main St 43068 — 614-501-1020
Dr. Richard Ross, supt. — Fax 501-1050
reynoldsburg.schoolnet.com
Reynoldsburg HS — 2,000/9-12
6699 E Livingston Ave 43068 — 614-501-4000
Diane Mankins, prin. — Fax 575-3098
Reynoldsburg JHS — 1,100/7-8
2300 Baldwin Pl 43068 — 614-367-1600
Robert Stamps, prin. — Fax 367-1625

Ohio State School of Cosmetology East — Post-Sec.
6320 E Livingston Ave 43068 — 614-868-1601

Richfield, Summit, Pop. 3,517
Revere Local SD — 2,800/K-12
3496 Everett Rd 44286 — 330-666-4155
James J. Ritchie, supt. — Fax 659-3127
www.revere.k12.oh.us
Revere HS — 900/9-12
3420 Everett Rd 44286 — 330-659-6111
Bill Adams, prin. — Fax 659-6407
Other Schools – See Bath

Richmond, Jefferson, Pop. 470
Edison Local SD
Supt. — See Hammondsville
Edison HS — 800/9-12
9890 State Route 152 43944 — 740-765-4313
Richard Wilinski, prin. — Fax 765-4961

Richmond Heights, Cuyahoga, Pop. 10,855
Richmond Heights Local SD — 1,100/K-12
447 Richmond Rd 44143 — 216-692-8485
Walter Calinger, supt. — Fax 692-2820
www.richmond-heights.k12.oh.us
Richmond Heights HS — 300/9-12
447 Richmond Rd 44143 — 216-692-0094
Terry Wallace, prin. — Fax 692-2820
Richmond Heights MS — 300/6-8
447 Richmond Rd 44143 — 216-692-7395
Betty Mateen, prin. — Fax 692-2820

Richwood, Union, Pop. 2,177
North Union Local SD — 1,400/K-12
12920 State Route 739 43344 — 740-943-2509
Carol Young, supt. — Fax 943-2534
www.n-union.k12.oh.us
North Union HS — 400/9-12
401 N Franklin St 43344 — 740-943-3012
Eric Holman, prin. — Fax 943-2534
North Union MS — 400/6-8
16 Norris St 43344 — 740-943-2369
Diana Martin, prin. — Fax 943-9279

Ridgeway, Hardin, Pop. 349
Ridgemont Local SD
Supt. — See Mount Victory
Ridgemont JSHS — 300/7-12
162 E Hale St 43345 — 937-363-2701
Chad Cunningham, prin. — Fax 363-2066

Rio Grande, Gallia, Pop. 916
Gallia-Jackson-Vinton JVSD
PO Box 157 45674 — 740-245-5334
Daniel Lewis, supt. — Fax 245-9465
Buckeye Hills Career Center — Vo/Tech
PO Box 157 45674 — 740-245-5334
Truman Noe, dir. — Fax 245-9465

University of Rio Grande — Post-Sec.
General Delivery 45674 — 740-245-5353

Ripley, Brown, Pop. 1,791
Ripley-Union-Lewis-Huntington Local SD — 1,000/K-12
120 Main St 45167 — 937-392-4396
Dr. C. Stephen Oborn, supt. — Fax 392-7003
www.ripley.k12.oh.us
Ripley-Union-Lewis-Huntington HS — 500/9-12
1317 S 2nd St 45167 — 937-392-4384
Gary Scarth, prin. — Fax 392-7017
Other Schools – See Aberdeen

Risingsun, Wood, Pop. 602
Lakota Local SD — 1,100/PK-12
PO Box 5 43457 — 419-457-2911
Christopher J. Boyd, supt. — Fax 457-0535
www.lakota-sandusky.k12.oh.us
Other Schools – See Fostoria, Kansas

Rittman, Wayne, Pop. 6,272
Rittman EVD — 1,200/K-12
220 N 1st St 44270 — 330-927-7400
Orville Ullman, supt. — Fax 927-7405
www.rittman.k12.oh.us
Rittman HS — 400/8-12
100 Saurer St 44270 — 330-927-7140
Joseph Magnacca, prin. — Fax 927-7145

Rockford, Mercer, Pop. 1,111
Parkway Local SD — 1,100/K-12
401 S Franklin St 45882 — 419-363-3045
Douglas Karst, supt. — Fax 363-3045
phstech.noacsc.org/parkway/
Parkway HS — 400/9-12
401 S Franklin St 45882 — 419-363-2894
Gregory Puthoff, prin. — Fax 363-3045
Other Schools – See Willshire

Rocky River, Cuyahoga, Pop. 20,188
Rocky River CSD — 2,600/K-12
21600 Center Ridge Rd 44116 — 440-333-6000
Dennis Allen, supt. — Fax 356-6014
www.lnoca.org/~rrcs/
Rocky River HS — 800/9-12
20951 Detroit Rd 44116 — 440-356-6800
Debra Bernard, prin. — Fax 331-2189
Rocky River MS — 600/6-8
1631 Lakeview Ave 44116 — 440-356-6870
David Root, prin. — Fax 356-6881

Lutheran West HS — 400/9-12
3850 Linden Rd 44116 — 440-333-1660
John Buetow, prin. — Fax 333-1729
Magnificat HS — 800/9-12
20770 Hilliard Blvd 44116 — 440-331-1572
Sr. Mary Pat Cook, prin. — Fax 331-7257

Rootstown, Portage
Rootstown Local SD — 1,300/K-12
4140 State Route 44 44272 — 330-325-9911
William M. Stauffer, supt. — Fax 325-4105
rootstown.sparcc.org
Rootstown HS — 400/9-12
4140 State Route 44 44272 — 330-325-7911
Andrew Hawkins, prin. — Fax 325-8506
Rootstown MS — 300/6-8
4140 State Route 44 44272 — 330-325-9956
Neal Beans, prin. — Fax 325-8505

Northeastern Ohio Univ Coll of Medicine — Post-Sec.
PO Box 95 44272 — 330-325-2511

Roseville, Perry, Pop. 1,933
Franklin Local SD
Supt. — See Duncan Falls
Roseville MS — 200/5-8
76 W Athens Rd 43777 — 740-697-7317
Bruce King, prin. — Fax 697-7186

Rossford, Wood, Pop. 6,357
Rossford EVD — 2,000/K-12
601 Superior St 43460 — 419-666-2010
Luci Gernot, supt. — Fax 661-2856
www.rossford.k12.oh.us
Rossford HS — 600/9-12
701 Superior St 43460 — 419-666-5262
Ronald Grimm, prin. — Fax 661-2843
Rossford JHS — 300/7-8
651 Superior St 43460 — 419-666-5254
Lester Pierson, prin. — Fax 661-2890

Rushville, Fairfield, Pop. 270
Fairfield Union Local SD — 2,000/K-12
7698 Main St 43150 — 740-536-7384
Clark Davis, supt. — Fax 536-9132
www.fairfield-union.k12.oh.us/
Other Schools – See Lancaster

Russia, Shelby, Pop. 584
Russia Local SD — 400/K-12
  PO Box 8 45363 — 937-295-3454
  Michael Moore, supt. — Fax 526-9519
Russia JSHS — 200/7-12
  PO Box 8 45363 — 937-295-3454
  Vernon Rosenbeck, prin. — Fax 526-9519

Saint Bernard, Hamilton, Pop. 4,640
St. Bernard-Elmwood Place CSD — 1,200/PK-12
  105 Washington Ave 45217 — 513-482-7121
  Dr. Carroll Roberts, supt. — Fax 641-0066
  stbernard.hccanet.org/
Saint Bernard-Elmwood Place JSHS — 500/7-12
  4615 Tower Ave 45217 — 513-482-7100
  Janie Acra, prin. — Fax 641-4878

Saint Clairsville, Belmont, Pop. 5,025
Belmont-Harrison Area JVSD — 740-695-9130
  110 Fox Shannon Pl 43950 — Fax 695-5340
  Charles V. Bizzari, supt.
  www.bhcareercenter.com/
Belmont Career Center — Vo/Tech
  110 Fox Shannon Pl 43950 — 740-695-9130
  Charles L. Strahl, prin. — Fax 695-5340
Other Schools – See Cadiz

St. Clairsville-Richland CSD — 1,600/K-12
  108 Woodrow Ave 43950 — 740-695-1624
  F. William Zanders, supt. — Fax 695-1627
  www.stcs.k12.oh.us/
St. Clairsville HS — 600/9-12
  102 Woodrow Ave 43950 — 740-695-1584
  Walt Skaggs, prin. — Fax 695-2513
St. Clairsville MS — 400/6-8
  104 Woodrow Ave 43950 — 740-695-1591
  Diane Thompson, prin. — Fax 695-2317

Belmont Technical College — Post-Sec.
  120 Fox Shannon Pl 43950 — 740-695-9500
Ohio University — Post-Sec.
  45425 National Rd W 43950 — 740-695-1720

Saint Henry, Mercer, Pop. 2,301
St. Henry Consolidated Local SD — 1,100/K-12
  391 E Columbus St 45883 — 419-678-4834
  Rodney Moorman, supt. — Fax 678-1724
  noacsc.org/mercer/sh
Saint Henry HS — 400/9-12
  391 E Columbus St 45883 — 419-678-4834
  Frank Griesdorn, prin. — Fax 678-1724
Saint Henry MS — 400/5-8
  381 E Columbus St 45883 — 419-678-4834
  Julie Laipply, prin. — Fax 678-1724

Saint Marys, Auglaize, Pop. 8,276
St. Mary's CSD — 2,300/K-12
  101 W South St 45885 — 419-394-4312
  Kenneth Baker, supt. — Fax 394-5638
  www.ridertown.com/news/pages/mainsch.html
McBroom MS — 400/7-8
  210 S Front St 45885 — 419-394-2112
  Newton Triplett, prin. — Fax 394-3022
Memorial HS — 900/9-12
  101 W South St 45885 — 419-394-4011
  Michael Makley, prin. — Fax 394-1932

Saint Paris, Champaign, Pop. 1,984
Graham Local SD — 2,200/K-12
  370 E Main St 43072 — 937-663-4123
  James Zerkle, supt. — Fax 663-4670
  www.graham.k12.oh.us
Graham HS — 700/9-12
  7800 US Highway 36 43072 — 937-663-4127
  Larry Moore, prin. — Fax 663-0396
Graham MS — 500/6-8
  9644 US Highway 36 43072 — 937-663-5339
  Jacob Conley, prin. — Fax 663-4674

Operation Rebirth Christian Academy — 50/K-12
  1638 Apple Rd 43072 — 937-663-5765
  James Brian, dir. — Fax 663-4949

Salem, Columbiana, Pop. 12,101
Salem CSD — 1,900/K-12
  1226 E State St 44460 — 330-332-0316
  Stephen Larcomb, supt. — Fax 332-8936
  www.salem.k12.oh.us
Salem HS — 800/9-12
  1200 E 6th St 44460 — 330-332-8905
  Joseph Shivers, prin. — Fax 332-8943
Salem JHS — 400/7-8
  1200 E 6th St 44460 — 330-332-8914
  Sean Kirkland, prin. — Fax 332-8923

South Range Local SD
  Supt. — See North Lima
South Range MS — 500/4-8
  7600 W South Range Rd 44460 — 330-533-3335
  Al Toth, prin. — Fax 533-7593

Allegheny Wesleyan College — Post-Sec.
  2161 Woodsdale Rd 44460 — 800-292-3153
Kent State University-Salem Campus — Post-Sec.
  2491 State Route 45 S 44460 — 330-332-0361
Salem Wesleyan Academy — 100/K-12
  1095 Newgarden Ave 44460 — 330-332-4819
  Dan Forrider, prin. — Fax 332-4819

Salineville, Columbiana, Pop. 1,357
Southern Local SD — 900/K-12
  38095E State Route 39 43945 — 330-679-2343
  Fred Burns, supt. — Fax 679-0193
  www.southern.k12.oh.us
Southern Local JSHS — 400/7-12
  38095E State Route 39 43945 — 330-679-2305
  Dennis Spisak, prin. — Fax 679-3005

Sandusky, Erie, Pop. 27,030
Perkins Local SD — 2,200/K-12
  1210 E Bogart Rd 44870 — 419-625-0484
  Sharon Buccieri, supt. — Fax 621-2052
  www.perkins.k12.oh.us

Perkins HS — 800/9-12
  3714 Campbell St 44870 — 419-625-1252
  Chris Gastier, prin. — Fax 625-1253
Perkins MS — 600/6-8
  3700 South Ave 44870 — 419-625-0132
  Dean Janitzki, prin. — Fax 625-0523

Sandusky CSD — 3,700/K-12
  407 Decatur St 44870 — 419-626-6940
  William F. Pahl, supt. — Fax 621-2784
  www.scs-k12.net
Jackson JHS — 300/8-8
  314 W Madison St 44870 — 419-621-2818
  Scott Matheny, prin. — Fax 621-2824
Sandusky Career Center — Vo/Tech
  2130 Hayes Ave 44870 — 419-625-9294
  Viki Kaszonyi, dir. — Fax 621-2893
Sandusky HS — 1,200/9-12
  2130 Hayes Ave 44870 — 419-621-2743
  Dan Poggiali, prin. — Fax 621-2751

Firelands Regional Medical Center — Post-Sec.
  1912 Hayes Ave 44870 — 419-557-7111
Ohio Business College — Post-Sec.
  4020 Milan Rd 44870 — 419-627-8345
St. Mary Central Catholic HS — 200/9-12
  410 W Jefferson St 44870 — 419-626-1892
  Michael Cole, prin. — Fax 621-2252
St. Mary S — 400/4-8
  530 Decatur St 44870 — 419-626-1648
  Douglas Solet, prin. — Fax 621-0404

Sarahsville, Noble, Pop. 198
Noble Local SD — 1,200/K-12
  20977 Zep Rd E 43779 — 740-732-2084
  Daniel Doyle, supt. — Fax 732-7669
  www.gozeps.org/
Shenandoah HS — 400/9-12
  49346 Seneca Lake Rd 43779 — 740-732-2361
  Sharon Miller, prin. — Fax 732-6474

Sardinia, Brown, Pop. 890
Eastern Local SD — 1,500/K-12
  PO Box 500 45171 — 937-378-3981
  Alan Simmons, supt. — Fax 695-9046
  www.eb.k12.oh.us
Eastern HS — 500/9-12
  PO Box 49 45171 — 937-378-6016
  Ted Downing, prin. — Fax 695-0303
Eastern JHS — 200/7-8
  PO Box 25 45171 — 937-378-6720
  Rob Beucler, prin. — Fax 695-1299

Southern State Community College — Post-Sec.
  12681 US Route 62 45171 — 937-695-0307

Scio, Harrison, Pop. 786
Harrison Hills CSD
  Supt. — See Hopedale
Harrison JHS, 322 W Main St 43988 — 300/7-8
  Mark Kowalski, prin. — 740-942-7600

Seaman, Adams, Pop. 1,060
Adams County/Ohio Valley SD
  Supt. — See West Union
North Adams HS — 500/7-12
  96 Green Devil Dr 45679 — 937-386-2528
  Rodney Wallace, prin. — Fax 386-2888

Sebring, Mahoning, Pop. 4,744
Sebring Local SD — 800/K-12
  510 N 14th St 44672 — 330-938-6165
  Howard Friend, supt. — Fax 938-4701
McKinley JSHS — 300/7-12
  225 E Indiana Ave 44672 — 330-938-2963
  Brian Coffee, prin. — Fax 938-9455

Senecaville, Guernsey, Pop. 453
Mid-East Career & Technology Center JVSD
  Supt. — See Zanesville
Mid-East Career & Tech Ctr - Buffalo — Vo/Tech
  57090 Vocational Rd 43780 — 740-685-2516
  Joseph Smith, dir. — Fax 685-2518

Seven Hills, Cuyahoga, Pop. 12,098
Parma CSD
  Supt. — See Parma
Hillside MS — 600/7-8
  1 Educational Park Dr 44131 — 440-885-2373
  Larry Minamyer, prin. — Fax 885-8448

DeVry University — Post-Sec.
  6000 Lombardo Ctr 44131 — 216-328-8754
Hondros College — Post-Sec.
  4100 Rockside Rd 44131 — 216-524-1143

Seville, Medina, Pop. 2,259
Cloverleaf Local SD
  Supt. — See Lodi
Cloverleaf MS — 600/7-8
  7500 Buffham Rd 44273 — 330-948-2500
  Ronald Tisher, prin. — Fax 721-3619

Shadyside, Belmont, Pop. 3,608
Shadyside Local SD — 900/K-12
  3890 Lincoln Ave 43947 — 740-676-3121
  Gerald Narcisi, supt. — Fax 676-6616
  www.shadyside.k12.oh.us
Shadyside JSHS — 400/7-12
  3890 Lincoln Ave 43947 — 740-676-3235
  Lawrence Falbo, prin. — Fax 676-6616

Shaker Heights, Cuyahoga, Pop. 28,459
Shaker Heights CSD — 5,600/K-12
  15600 Parkland Dr 44120 — 216-295-4000
  Mark Freeman, supt. — Fax 295-4340
  www.shaker.org
Shaker Heights HS — 1,800/9-12
  15911 Aldersyde Dr 44120 — 216-295-4200
  Michael Griffith, prin. — Fax 295-4277
Shaker Heights MS — 1,000/7-8
  20600 Shaker Blvd 44122 — 216-295-4100
  Randall Yates, prin. — Fax 295-4129

Hathaway Brown S — 800/PK-12
  19600 N Park Blvd 44122 — 216-932-4214
  William Christ, hdmstr. — Fax 371-1501
Laurel S — 700/K-12
  1 Lyman Cir 44122 — 216-464-1441
  Ann Klotz, prin. — Fax 464-8483

Sheffield Lake, Lorain, Pop. 9,222
Sheffield-Sheffield Lake CSD — 2,000/K-12
  1824 Harris Rd 44054 — 440-949-6181
  Will Folger, supt. — Fax 949-4204
  www.sheffield.k12.oh.us
Other Schools – See Lorain

Shelby, Richland, Pop. 9,579
Pioneer Career & Technology JVSD — 419-347-7926
  27 Ryan Rd 44875 — Fax 347-4709
  Donald Plotts, supt.
Pioneer Career & Technology S — Vo/Tech
  27 Ryan Rd 44875 — 419-347-7744
  — Fax 347-4977

Shelby CSD — 1,600/K-12
  25 High School Ave 44875 — 419-342-3520
  Charles A. Speelman, supt. — Fax 347-3586
  www.shelby-city.k12.oh.us
Shelby HS — 800/9-12
  109 W Smiley Ave 44875 — 419-342-5065
  David Jones, prin. — Fax 342-5095
Shelby MS — 400/7-8
  16 Park Ave 44875 — 419-347-5451
  Tim Tarvin, prin. — Fax 347-2095

Sherrodsville, Carroll, Pop. 320
Conotton Valley Union Local SD — 500/K-12
  PO Box 187 44675 — 740-269-2000
  Jeff Bleininger, supt. — Fax 269-7901
  www.conottonvalley.k12.oh.us
Other Schools – See Bowerston

Sherwood, Defiance, Pop. 792
Central Local SD — 1,200/K-12
  6289 US Highway 127 43556 — 419-658-2808
  David E. Bagley, supt. — Fax 658-4010
  www.centrallocal.k12.oh.us/default.htm
Fairview HS — 400/9-12
  6289 US Highway 127 43556 — 419-658-2378
  Troy Merillat, prin. — Fax 658-4011
Fairview MS — 300/6-8
  6289 US Highway 127 43556 — 419-658-2331
  Robert Lloyd, prin. — Fax 658-4010

Sidney, Shelby, Pop. 20,254
Fairlawn Local SD — 500/K-12
  18800 Johnston Rd 45365 — 937-492-1974
  Steve Mascho, supt. — Fax 492-8613
  www.fairlawn.k12.oh.us
Fairlawn MSHS — 300/6-12
  18800 Johnston Rd 45365 — 937-492-5930
  Jo DeMotte, prin. — Fax 492-8613

Sidney CSD — 3,500/K-12
  750 S 4th Ave 45365 — 937-497-2200
  Dr. Michael Trego, supt. — Fax 497-2211
  www.sidney.k12.oh.us
Sidney HS — 1,100/9-12
  1215 Campbell Rd 45365 — 937-497-2238
  Jeff Hobbs, prin. — Fax 497-2216
Sidney MS — 900/6-8
  980 Fair Rd 45365 — 937-497-2225
  Gene Gooding, prin. — Fax 497-2204

Christian Academy S — 200/K-12
  2151 W Russell Rd 45365 — 937-492-7556
  Mary Smith, supt. — Fax 492-5399
Lehman HS — 300/9-12
  2400 St Marys Rd 45365 — 937-498-1161
  David M. Barhorst, prin. — Fax 492-9877

Smithville, Wayne, Pop. 1,319
Green Local SD — 1,400/K-12
  PO Box 438 44677 — 330-669-3921
  Ken Boyer, supt. — Fax 669-2121
  www.green-local.k12.oh.us/
Greene MS — 400/5-8
  PO Box 367 44677 — 330-669-2751
  Howard Morris, prin. — Fax 669-2121
Smithville HS — 400/9-12
  PO Box 156 44677 — 330-669-3165
  Rich Bellanco, prin. — Fax 669-2999

Wayne County JVSD — 330-669-2134
  518 W Prospect St 44677 — Fax 669-2095
  Kip Crain, supt.
  www.wcscc.org
Wayne County Schools Career Center — Vo/Tech
  518 W Prospect St 44677 — 330-669-2134
  Michael Hall, prin. — Fax 669-2095

Solon, Cuyahoga, Pop. 22,248
Solon CSD — 5,200/PK-12
  33800 Inwood Dr 44139 — 440-248-1600
  Joseph Regano, supt. — Fax 248-7665
  www.solonschools.org
Solon HS — 1,700/9-12
  33600 Inwood Dr 44139 — 440-349-6230
  George Steyer, prin. — Fax 349-8041
Solon MS — 900/7-8
  6835 Som Center Rd 44139 — 440-349-3848
  Eugenia Robinson-Green, prin. — Fax 349-8034

South Amherst, Lorain, Pop. 1,817
Firelands Local SD
  Supt. — See Oberlin
South Amherst MS — 700/5-8
  152 W Main St 44001 — 440-986-7021
  Tony Reaser, prin. — Fax 986-7022

South Charleston, Clark, Pop. 1,813
Southeastern Local SD — 900/K-12
  PO Box Z 45368 — 937-462-8388
  John Weaver, supt. — Fax 462-7915
  www.southeastern.k12.oh.us/

Miami View MS 300/5-8
230 Clifton Rd 45368 937-462-8364
Karen Jines, prin. Fax 462-7914
Southeastern HS 300/9-12
PO Box Z 45368 937-462-8308
Susan Cline, prin. Fax 462-8394

South Euclid, Cuyahoga, Pop. 22,860

Regina HS 300/9-12
1857 S Green Rd 44121 216-382-2110
Sr. Maureen Burke, prin. Fax 382-3555

Southington, Trumbull
Southington Local SD 700/K-12
4432 State Route 305 44470 330-898-7480
Frank Danso, supt. Fax 898-4828
www.southington.k12.oh.us/
Chalker HS 200/9-12
4432 State Route 305 44470 330-898-1781
Nicholas Roberts, prin. Fax 898-4828
Southington MS 200/5-8
4432 State Route 305 44470 330-898-1781
Fax 898-4828

South Point, Lawrence, Pop. 3,831
South Point Local SD 1,900/K-12
203 Park Ave 45680 740-377-4315
Ken Cook, supt. Fax 377-9735
www.southpoint.k12.oh.us
South Point HS 600/9-12
302 High St 45680 740-377-4323
George York, prin. Fax 377-4325
South Point MS, 201 Park Ave 45680 400/6-8
Les York, prin. 740-377-4343

South Vienna, Clark, Pop. 502
Northeastern Local SD
Supt. — See Springfield
South Vienna MS 400/6-8
140 W Main St 45369 937-568-4765
Ted Williams, prin. Fax 568-4988

South Webster, Scioto, Pop. 744
Bloom-Vernon Local SD 1,000/K-12
PO Box 237 45682 740-778-2281
Rick Carrington, supt. Fax 778-2526
www.bv.k12.oh.us
South Webster JSHS 400/7-12
PO Box 100 45682 740-778-2320
Robert Johnson, prin. Fax 778-3227

Sparta, Morrow, Pop. 203
Highland Local SD
Supt. — See Marengo
Highland HS 500/9-12
PO Box 98 43350 419-768-3101
Debra Ruhl, prin. Fax 768-3560
Highland MS 400/6-8
PO Box 68 43350 419-768-2781
Rob Terrill, prin. Fax 768-2742

Spencerville, Allen, Pop. 2,230
Spencerville Local SD 1,000/K-12
600 School St 45887 419-647-4111
Joel Hatfield, supt. Fax 647-6498
www.spencervillebearcats.com
Spencerville HS 300/9-12
600 School St 45887 419-647-4111
Shawn Brown, prin. Fax 647-6498
Spencerville MS 200/6-8
436 E 4th St 45887 419-647-4112
Dennis Fuge, prin. Fax 647-6498

Springboro, Warren, Pop. 15,051
Springboro Community SD 4,300/K-12
1685 S Main St 45066 937-748-3960
David Baker Ph.D., supt. Fax 748-3956
www.springboro.org
Springboro HS 1,200/9-12
1675 S Main St 45066 937-748-3950
Dr. Ron Malone, prin. Fax 748-3983
Springboro JHS 1,000/6-8
1605 S Main St 45066 937-748-3953
Phil Rench, prin. Fax 748-3964

Ridgeville Christian S 400/PK-12
946 E Lower Springboro Rd 45066 513-932-6407
Marvin Retzer, admin. Fax 932-8453

Springfield, Clark, Pop. 64,483
Clark-Shawnee Local SD 2,500/K-12
3680 Selma Rd 45502 937-328-5378
Debbie Finkes, supt. Fax 328-5379
www.clark-shawnee.k12.oh.us/
Shawnee HS 900/9-12
1675 E Possum Rd 45502 937-325-9296
Nathan Dockter, prin. Fax 328-5389

Greenon Local SD
Supt. — See Enon
Greenon HS 700/9-12
3950 S Tecumseh Rd 45502 937-325-7343
Robert McClure, prin. Fax 328-7527

Northeastern Local SD 3,600/K-12
1414 Bowman Rd 45502 937-325-7615
Richard Broderick, supt. Fax 328-6592
www.northeastern.k12.oh.us
Kenton Ridge HS 700/9-12
4444 Middle Urbana Rd 45503 937-390-1274
Charles Foss, prin. Fax 390-0013
Northeastern HS 500/9-12
1480 Bowman Rd 45502 937-328-6575
Mark Klopfenstein, prin. Fax 328-6581
Northridge MS 500/6-8
4445 Ridgewood Rd E 45503 937-399-2852
Sharon Beck, prin. Fax 342-4631
Other Schools – See South Vienna

Northwestern Local SD 1,900/K-12
5610 Troy Rd 45502 937-964-1318
Kevin Lacey, supt. Fax 964-6019
www.northwestern.k12.oh.us
Northwestern HS 700/9-12
5650 Troy Rd 45502 937-964-1324
Lori Swafford, prin. Fax 964-6006
Northwestern MS 600/5-8
5610 Troy Rd 45502 937-964-1391
Rick Yontz, prin. Fax 964-6000

Springfield CSD 8,900/K-12
700 S Limestone St 45505 937-505-2800
Dr. Edna Jean Harper, supt. Fax 328-6855
www.spr.k12.oh.us/
Clark MS 400/6-8
1500 W Jefferson St 45506 937-505-4170
Michael Renkiewicz, prin. Fax 325-9358
Hayward MS 400/6-8
1700 Clifton Ave 45505 937-505-4190
Susie Samuels, prin. Fax 323-9812
Roosevelt MS 500/6-8
721 E Home Rd 45503 937-505-4370
Monte Brigham, prin. Fax 342-0280
Schaefer MS 500/6-8
147 S Fostoria Ave 45505 937-505-4390
Kathy Klosterman, prin. Fax 325-9974
Springfield North HS 1,400/9-12
701 E Home Rd 45503 937-342-4100
JoEtta Cooper, prin. Fax 342-4121
Springfield South HS 1,100/9-12
700 S Limestone St 45505 937-328-2027
Pauline Swan, prin. Fax 328-6866

Springfield-Clark County JVSD 300/7-12
1901 Selma Rd 45505 937-325-7368
Randall Richardson, supt. Fax 325-7452
Springfield-Clark County Joint Vo SHS Vo/Tech
1901 Selma Rd 45505 937-325-7368
Susan Backus, dir. Fax 325-7452

Carousel Beauty College Post-Sec.
1475 Upper Valley Pike #956 45504 937-323-0277
Catholic Central JSHS 300/7-12
1200 E High St 45505 937-325-9204
Jeanne Kunay, prin. Fax 328-7426
Clark State Community College Post-Sec.
570 E Leffel Ln 45505 937-325-0691
Community Hospital School of Nursing Post-Sec.
2615 E High St 45505 937-328-8905
Emmanuel Christian Academy 400/K-12
2177 Emmanuel Way 45502 937-390-3777
George B. Simon Ph.D., admin. Fax 390-0966
Nightingale Montessori S 100/K-12
1106 E High St 45505 937-324-0336
Nancy Schwab, prin. Fax 398-0086
Wittenberg University Post-Sec.
PO Box 720 45501 937-327-6231

Steubenville, Jefferson, Pop. 19,568
Steubenville CSD 2,200/PK-12
PO Box 189 43952 740-283-3767
Richard Ranallo, supt. Fax 283-8930
www.steubenville.k12.oh.us/
Harding MS 500/6-8
2002 Sunset Blvd 43952 740-282-3481
Rob Rembold, prin. Fax 283-8949
Steubenville HS 700/9-12
420 N 4th St 43952 740-282-9741
Shawn Crosier, prin. Fax 283-8943

Catholic Central HS 400/9-12
320 West View Ave 43952 740-264-5538
Denise McKeown, prin. Fax 264-5443
Century School of Cosmetology Post-Sec.
434 Market St 43952 740-282-3312
Franciscan University of Steubenville Post-Sec.
100 Franciscan Way 43952 800-783-6220
Jefferson Community College Post-Sec.
4000 Sunset Blvd 43952 740-264-5591
Ohio Valley Hospital Post-Sec.
1 Ross Park Blvd 43952 740-283-7273
Trinity Medical Center East Post-Sec.
380 Summit Ave 43952 740-283-7213

Stewart, Athens
Federal Hocking Local SD 1,400/PK-12
PO Box 117 45778 740-662-6691
James R. Patsey, supt. Fax 662-5065
www.federalhocking.k12.oh.us
Federal Hocking HS 500/9-12
8461 State Route 144 45778 740-662-6691
Dr. George Wood, prin. Fax 662-3805
Federal Hocking MS 300/6-8
8461 State Route 144 45778 740-662-6691
Sonya White, prin. Fax 662-5065

Stoutsville, Fairfield, Pop. 586
Amanda-Clearcreek Local SD
Supt. — See Amanda
Amanda-Clearcreek MS 400/6-8
9096 Walnut St 43154 740-969-7252
Kenneth Dille, prin.

Stow, Summit, Pop. 34,290
Stow-Munroe Falls CSD 6,100/PK-12
4350 Allen Rd 44224 330-689-5445
Edward VandenBulke, supt. Fax 688-1629
www.stow.summit.k12.oh.us
Stow-Munroe Falls HS 2,000/9-12
3227 Graham Rd 44224 330-689-5300
Cynthia Finley, prin. Fax 678-3899
Other Schools – See Munroe Falls

Walsh Jesuit HS 800/9-12
4550 Wyoga Lake Rd 44224 330-929-4205
Fr. James Prehn, prin. Fax 929-9749

Strasburg, Tuscarawas, Pop. 2,453
Strasburg-Franklin Local SD 700/K-12
140 N Bodmer Ave 44680 330-878-5571
Palmer Fogler, supt. Fax 878-7900

Strasburg-Franklin HS 300/7-12
140 N Bodmer Ave 44680 330-878-5571
Jeff Gyurko, prin. Fax 878-7900

Streetsboro, Portage, Pop. 13,822
Streetsboro CSD 2,100/K-12
9000 Kirby Ln 44241 330-626-4900
Thomas M. Giovangnoli, supt. Fax 626-8102
www.rockets.sparcc.org
Streetsboro HS 600/9-12
1900 Annalane Dr 44241 330-626-4902
James Montaquila, prin. Fax 626-8103
Streetsboro MS 300/7-8
1951 Annalane Dr 44241 330-626-4905
George Hammond, prin. Fax 626-8104

Strongsville, Cuyahoga, Pop. 44,560
Strongsville CSD 7,300/K-12
13200 Pearl Rd 44136 440-572-7010
James Gray, supt. Fax 572-7041
strongnet.org
Albion MS 600/7-8
11109 Webster Rd 44136 440-572-7070
Jeff Stanton, prin. Fax 572-7079
Center MS 600/7-8
13200 Pearl Rd 44136 440-572-7090
Jeff Martin, prin. Fax 572-7094
Strongsville HS 2,400/9-12
20025 Lunn Rd 44149 440-572-7100
Karen Hollo, prin. Fax 572-7107

ITT Technical Institute Post-Sec.
14955 W Sprague Rd 44136 440-234-9091

Struthers, Mahoning, Pop. 11,334
Struthers CSD 2,000/K-12
99 Euclid Ave 44471 330-750-1061
Dr. Sandra DiBacco, supt. Fax 750-5516
www.struthers.k12.oh.us/
Struthers HS 600/9-12
111 Euclid Ave 44471 330-750-1062
Mary Ann Meadows, prin. Fax 750-5516
Struthers MS 600/5-8
800 5th St 44471 330-750-1064
Jacqueline Kuffel, prin. Fax 750-5516

Youngstown College of Massotherapy Post-Sec.
14 Highland Ave 44471 330-755-1406

Stryker, Williams, Pop. 1,398
Stryker Local SD 500/K-12
400 S Defiance St 43557 419-682-6961
Russ Griggs, supt. Fax 682-2646
www.nwoca.org/~stryker_www/
Stryker JSHS 300/7-12
400 S Defiance St 43557 419-682-4591
Denise Meyer, prin. Fax 682-3508

Living Word Christian S 100/K-12
22754 County Road B50 43557 419-682-1750
James Garrett, admin. Fax 682-1440

Sugarcreek, Tuscarawas, Pop. 2,159
Garaway Local SD 1,200/K-12
146 Dover Rd NW 44681 330-852-2421
Ted Gerber, supt. Fax 852-2991
www.garaway.k12.oh.us/
Garaway JSHS 600/7-12
146 Dover Rd NW 44681 330-852-2422
Teresa Alberts, prin. Fax 852-4382

Sugar Grove, Fairfield, Pop. 441
Berne Union Local SD 1,000/K-12
506 N Main St 43155 740-746-8341
Thomas Wolfe, supt. Fax 746-9824
berne-union.k12.oh.us
Berne Union HS 300/9-12
506 N Main St 43155 740-746-9956
Robert Starr, prin. Fax 746-9824
Berne Union MS 300/5-8
506 N Main St 43155 740-746-9738
Terry McCray, prin. Fax 746-9824

Sullivan, Ashland
Black River Local SD 1,700/PK-12
257A County Road 40 44880 419-736-3300
Janice Wyckoff, supt. Fax 736-3308
www.blackriver.k12.oh.us/
Black River HS 500/9-12
233 County Road 40 44880 419-736-3303
Bruce Lorincz, prin. Fax 736-3302
Black River MS 400/6-8
257 County Road 40 44880 419-736-3304
Cathy Aviles, prin. Fax 736-3309

Summit Station, Licking, Pop. 1,380
Licking Heights Local SD 2,000/K-12
6539 Summit Rd SW 43073 740-927-6926
Janice Streit, supt. Fax 927-9043
www.licking-heights.k12.oh.us/
Other Schools – See Pataskala

Sunbury, Delaware, Pop. 3,051
Big Walnut Local SD
Supt. — See Galena
Big Walnut HS, PO Box 5001 43074 900/9-12
Charles Workman, prin. 740-965-3766
Big Walnut MS, PO Box 5002 43074 600/6-8
Steve House, prin. 740-965-3006

Swanton, Fulton, Pop. 3,331
Swanton Local SD 1,500/K-12
108 N Main St 43558 419-826-7085
Neil Weber, supt. Fax 825-1197
www.swanton.k12.oh.us
Swanton HS 500/9-12
601 N Main St 43558 419-826-3045
James Tokarsky, prin. Fax 826-1611
Swanton MS 400/6-8
206 Cherry St 43558 419-826-4016
Paulette Raczkowski, prin. Fax 826-5176

Sycamore, Wyandot, Pop. 896
Mohawk Local SD — 1,100/K-12
295 State Highway 231 44882 — 419-927-2414
Sam Martin, supt. — Fax 927-2393
www.mohawk.k12.oh.us/
Mohawk HS — 400/9-12
295 State Highway 231 44882 — 419-927-6292
Jodi Gaietto, prin.

Sylvania, Lucas, Pop. 19,027
Sylvania CSD — 7,700/K-12
PO Box 608 43560 — 419-824-8500
Bradley Rieger, supt. — Fax 824-8503
www.sylvania.k12.oh.us
Arbor Hills JHS — 700/6-8
5334 Whiteford Rd 43560 — 419-824-8640
Scott Nelson, prin. — Fax 824-8659
McCord JHS — 700/6-8
4304 N Mccord Rd 43560 — 419-824-8650
Jeff Robbins, prin. — Fax 824-8619
Northview HS — 1,400/9-12
5403 Silica Dr 43560 — 419-824-8570
Stewart Jesse, prin. — Fax 824-8698
Southview HS — 1,300/9-12
7225 Sylvania Ave 43560 — 419-824-8580
Dave McMurray, prin. — Fax 824-8678
Timberstone JHS — 700/6-8
9000 Sylvania Ave 43560 — 419-824-8680
Jack Smith, prin. — Fax 824-8690

Lourdes College — Post-Sec.
6832 Convent Blvd 43560 — 419-885-3211

Tallmadge, Summit, Pop. 17,165
Tallmadge CSD — 2,700/K-12
486 East Ave 44278 — 330-633-3291
Dr. Vincent Frammartino, supt. — Fax 633-5331
www.tallmadge.k12.oh.us/index.htm
Tallmadge HS — 900/9-12
484 East Ave 44278 — 330-633-5505
Jeff Ferguson, prin. — Fax 630-5986
Tallmadge MS — 700/6-8
76 North Ave 44278 — 330-633-4994
Gregory Misch, prin. — Fax 630-5984

Tallmadge Christian Academy — 100/K-12
508 Newton St 44278 — 330-784-1284
— Fax 784-1364

The Plains, Athens, Pop. 2,644
Athens CSD — 2,900/K-12
25 S Plains Rd 45780 — 740-797-4544
Carl Martin, supt. — Fax 797-2486
athenscity.k12.oh.us/
Athens HS — 900/9-12
1 High School Rd 45780 — 740-797-4521
Mike Meek, prin. — Fax 797-4072
Other Schools – See Athens

Thompson, Geauga
Ledgemont Local SD — 600/K-12
16200 Burrows Rd 44086 — 440-298-3341
John Marshall, supt. — Fax 298-3342
www.ledgemont.k12.oh.us
Ledgemont HS — 200/9-12
16700 Thompson Rd 44086 — 440-298-3343
Beto Gage, prin. — Fax 298-1481

Thornville, Perry, Pop. 794
Northern Local SD — 2,300/K-12
8700 Sheridan Dr 43076 — 740-743-1303
Jack Porter, supt. — Fax 743-3301
www.nlsd.k12.oh.us
Sheridan HS — 800/9-12
8725 Sheridan Dr 43076 — 740-743-1335
Rick Caldwell, prin. — Fax 743-3311
Sheridan MS — 500/6-8
8660 Sheridan Dr 43076 — 740-743-1315
Thomas Dorman, prin. — Fax 743-3301

Tiffin, Seneca, Pop. 17,497
Tiffin CSD — 3,000/K-12
244 S Monroe St 44883 — 419-447-2515
Donald Coletta, supt. — Fax 448-5202
www.tiffin.k12.oh.us
Columbian HS — 1,000/9-12
300 S Monroe St 44883 — 419-447-6331
Larry Kisabeth, prin. — Fax 448-5252
Tiffin MS — 700/6-8
103 Shepherd Dr 44883 — 419-447-3358
J. Kevin Campbell, prin. — Fax 448-5250

Vanguard-Sentinel Career Centers
Supt. — See Fremont
Sentinel Career Center — Vo/Tech
793 E Township Rd 201 44883 — 419-448-1212
Henry Elchert, prin. — Fax 447-2544

Calvert HS — 300/9-12
152 Madison St 44883 — 419-447-3844
Anthony Mass, prin. — Fax 447-2922
Heidelberg College — Post-Sec.
310 E Market St 44883 — 419-448-2000
Tiffin Academy of Hair Design — Post-Sec.
104 E Market St 44883 — 419-447-3111
Tiffin University — Post-Sec.
155 Miami St 44883 — 800-968-6446

Tiltonsville, Jefferson, Pop. 1,267
Buckeye Local SD
Supt. — See Dillonvale
Buckeye Southwest MS — 300/6-8
100 Walden Ave 43963 — 740-859-2357
George Bell, prin. — Fax 859-2660

Tipp City, Miami, Pop. 9,285
Bethel Local SD — 900/K-12
7490 State Route 201 45371 — 937-845-9414
David Henagen, supt. — Fax 845-5007
www.bethel.k12.oh.us
Bethel HS — 400/9-12
7490 State Route 201 45371 — 937-845-9487
David Vail, prin. — Fax 845-5007

Bethel JHS — 200/7-8
7490 State Route 201 45371 — 937-845-9430
Mike Johnston, prin. — Fax 845-5007
Tipp City EVD — 2,300/K-12
90 S Tippecanoe Dr 45371 — 937-667-8444
John Zigler, supt. — Fax 667-6886
www.tippcityschools.com/
Tippecanoe HS — 800/9-12
615 E Kessler Cowlesville 45371 — 937-667-8448
Charles Wray, prin. — Fax 667-0912
Tippecanoe MS — 400/6-8
555 N Hyatt St 45371 — 937-667-8454
Greg Southers, prin. — Fax 667-0874

Toledo, Lucas, Pop. 308,973
Ottawa Hills Local SD — 1,000/K-12
3600 Indian Rd 43606 — 419-536-6371
Gail Mirrow, supt. — Fax 534-5380
www.ohschools.k12.oh.us
Ottawa Hills JSHS — 500/7-12
2532 Evergreen Rd 43606 — 419-534-5376
Katherine Hurst, prin. — Fax 534-5384
Toledo CSD — 33,300/PK-12
420 E Manhattan Blvd 43608 — 419-729-8200
Dr. Eugene T.W. Sanders, supt. — Fax 729-8425
www.tps.org
Bowsher HS — 1,300/9-12
3548 S Detroit Ave 43614 — 419-671-2000
Larry Black, prin. — Fax 389-5055
Byrnedale JHS — 800/7-8
3645 Glendale Ave 43614 — 419-382-3427
Karen Schultz-Gray, prin. — Fax 385-3911
DeVeaux JHS — 1,000/7-8
2626 W Sylvania Ave 43613 — 419-475-4213
John Mann, prin. — Fax 473-2123
East Toledo JHS — 800/7-8
355 Dearborn Ave 43605 — 419-691-5781
R. C. Morrison, prin. — Fax 697-2541
Jones JHS — 700/7-8
550 Walbridge Ave 43609 — 419-244-8391
Pamela King, prin. — Fax 249-8261
Leverette JHS — 700/7-8
1111 E Manhattan Blvd 43608 — 419-726-3449
— Fax 729-8826
Libbey HS — 1,000/9-12
1250 Western Ave 43609 — 419-671-5110
— Fax 385-8246
McTigue JHS — 700/7-8
5700 Hill Ave 43615 — 419-531-4264
Cheryl King, prin. — Fax 534-5829
Robinson JHS — 600/7-8
1007 Grand Ave 43606 — 419-244-3753
Deborah Rivers, prin. — Fax 255-6002
Rogers HS — 1,200/9-12
5539 Nebraska Ave 43615 — 419-671-1000
Tony Brashear, prin. — Fax 534-5824
Scott HS — 1,400/9-12
2400 Collingwood Blvd 43620 — 419-671-4112
— Fax 249-8248
Start HS — 1,800/9-12
2100 Tremainsville Rd 43613 — 419-671-3000
Raymond Russell, prin. — Fax 479-3151
Toledo Technology Academy — Vo/Tech
3301 Upton Ave 43613 — 419-479-3161
— Fax 479-3192
Waite HS — 1,400/9-12
301 Morrison Dr 43605 — 419-671-7000
David Yenrick, prin. — Fax 697-2511
Woodward HS — 1,200/9-12
600 E Streicher St 43608 — 419-671-6000
Ron Spitulski, prin. — Fax 729-7055

Washington Local SD — 6,800/K-12
3505 W Lincolnshire Blvd 43606 — 419-473-8220
Michael Carmean, supt. — Fax 473-8247
www.washloc.k12.oh.us
Washington JHS — 600/8-10
5700 Whitmer Dr 43613 — 419-473-8449
Lynita Bigelow, prin. — Fax 473-8340
Whitmer HS — 2,100/9-12
5601 Clegg Dr 43613 — 419-473-8490
Brad Faust, prin. — Fax 473-8461

Central Catholic HS — 1,200/9-12
2550 Cherry St 43608 — 419-255-2280
Michael Kaucher, prin. — Fax 259-2848
Davis College — Post-Sec.
4747 Monroe St 43623 — 419-473-2700
Emmanuel Baptist Christian S — 500/PK-12
4607 W Laskey Rd 43623 — 419-885-3558
Robert Flamm, prin. — Fax 885-0139
Maumee Valley Country Day S — 500/PK-12
1715 S Reynolds Rd 43614 — 419-381-1313
Hiram Goza, hdmstr. — Fax 381-9941
Medical University of Ohio — Post-Sec.
3000 Arlington Ave 43614 — 419-383-4000
Mercy College of Northwest Ohio — Post-Sec.
2221 Madison Ave 43624 — 419-251-1279
Notre Dame Academy — 600/9-12
3535 W Sylvania Ave 43623 — 419-475-9359
Kim Grilliot, prin. — Fax 724-2640
Owens Community College — Post-Sec.
PO Box 10000 43699 — 567-661-7000
Professional Skills Institute — Post-Sec.
20 Arco Dr 43607 — 419-531-9610
Riverside Hospital — Post-Sec.
3404 W Sylvania Ave 43623 — 419-729-6059
St. Francis De Sales HS — 700/9-12
2323 W Bancroft St 43607 — 419-531-1618
Andy Hill, prin. — Fax 531-9740
St. Johns Jesuit Academy — 200/7-8
5901 Airport Hwy 43615 — 419-865-5743
Christopher Knight, prin. — Fax 861-5002
St. John's Jesuit HS — 800/9-12
5901 Airport Hwy 43615 — 419-865-5743
Tim Malone, prin. — Fax 861-5002
St. Ursula Academy — 600/9-12
4025 Indian Rd 43606 — 419-531-1693
Jane McGee, prin. — Fax 534-5777
Stautzenberger College — Post-Sec.
5355 Southwyck Blvd 43614 — 419-866-0261

Toledo Academy of Beauty Culture - North — Post-Sec.
5020 Lewis Ave 43612 — 419-478-5325
Toledo Academy of Beauty Culture - South — Post-Sec.
1554 S Byrne Rd 43614 — 419-381-7218
Toledo Christian S — 900/K-12
2303 Brookford Dr 43614 — 419-389-8700
Dan Bragg, supt. — Fax 724-2117
Toledo Islamic Academy — 200/K-12
4404 Secor Rd 43623 — 419-292-1491
Carolyn al-Qadi, prin. — Fax 292-0444
University of Toledo — Post-Sec.
2801 W Bancroft St 43606 — 419-530-4636

Tontogany, Wood, Pop. 366
Otsego Local SD — 1,600/K-12
PO Box 290 43565 — 419-823-4381
Joseph Long, supt. — Fax 823-3035
www.otsegoknights.org
Otsego HS — 500/9-12
PO Box 290 43565 — 419-823-4911
David Drewyor, prin. — Fax 823-6421
Other Schools – See Grand Rapids

Toronto, Jefferson, Pop. 5,537
Toronto CSD — 1,000/PK-12
300 Myers St 43964 — 740-537-2456
Frank Vostatek, supt. — Fax 537-1102
www.torontocityschools.k12.oh.us
Karaffa MS, 1307 Dennis Way 43964 — 200/6-8
Linda Davis-Rex, prin. — 740-537-2471
Toronto HS, 300 Myers St 43964 — 300/9-12
Robert Reeves, prin. — 740-537-2442

Trenton, Butler, Pop. 9,953
Edgewood CSD — 3,600/PK-12
3500 Busenbark Rd 45067 — 513-863-4692
Tom York, supt. — Fax 867-7421
www.edgewoodschools.com/index.cfm
Edgewood HS — 1,000/9-12
5005 Oxford State Rd 45067 — 513-867-7425
Bob Buchheim, prin. — Fax 867-7428
Other Schools – See Hamilton

Trotwood, Montgomery, Pop. 27,070
Trotwood-Madison CSD — 3,700/K-12
444 S Broadway St 45426 — 937-854-3050
Lowell Draffen, supt. — Fax 854-3057
www.trotwood.k12.oh.us/
Trotwood-Madison HS — 1,100/9-12
4440 N Union Rd 45426 — 937-854-0878
Gerald Cox, prin. — Fax 854-0594
Other Schools – See Dayton

United Theological Seminary — Post-Sec.
4501 Denlinger Rd 45426 — 800-322-5817

Troy, Miami, Pop. 22,169
Troy CSD — 4,500/K-12
500 N Market St 45373 — 937-332-6700
Tom Dunn, supt. — Fax 332-6771
www.troy.k12.oh.us
Troy HS — 1,500/9-12
151 Staunton Rd 45373 — 937-332-6710
Steve Moeckel, prin. — Fax 332-6738
Troy JHS — 700/7-8
556 Adams St 45373 — 937-332-6720
Tom Mercer, prin. — Fax 332-6739

Hobart Institute of Welding Technology — Post-Sec.
400 Trade Sq E 45373 — 800-332-9448
Troy Christian HS — 400/7-12
700 S Dorset Rd 45373 — 937-339-5692
Steve Peterson, prin. — Fax 335-6258

Twinsburg, Summit, Pop. 17,236
Twinsburg CSD — 4,000/PK-12
11136 Ravenna Rd 44087 — 330-486-2000
Steve Marlow, supt. — Fax 425-7216
twinsburg.k12.oh.us
Chamberlin MS — 600/7-8
10270 Ravenna Rd 44087 — 330-486-2281
Belinda Scott, prin. — Fax 963-8313
Twinsburg HS — 1,100/9-12
10084 Ravenna Rd 44087 — 330-486-2400
Michael Swank, prin. — Fax 405-7406

Uhrichsville, Tuscarawas, Pop. 5,696
Claymont CSD
Supt. — See Dennison
Claymont HS — 800/9-12
4205 Indian Hill Rd SE 44683 — 740-922-3471
Larry Amicone, prin. — Fax 922-1031
Claymont JHS — 300/7-8
215 E 6th St 44683 — 740-922-5241
Michael Wright, prin. — Fax 922-7330

Union City, Darke, Pop. 1,711
Mississinawa Valley Local SD — 700/K-12
1469 State Road 47 E 45390 — 937-968-5656
W. Joe Scholler, supt. — Fax 968-6731
www.mississinawa.k12.oh.us
Mississinawa Valley JSHS — 300/7-12
10480 Staudt Rd 45390 — 937-968-4464
Clarence Perry, prin. — Fax 968-3434

Uniontown, Stark, Pop. 3,074
Green Local SD
Supt. — See Green
Green HS — 1,300/9-12
1474 Boettler Rd 44685 — 330-896-7575
Gary Geis, prin. — Fax 896-7549
Green MS — 1,000/6-8
1711 Steese Rd 44685 — 330-896-7710
Brian Reed, prin. — Fax 896-7760

Lake Local SD — 3,300/K-12
11936 King Church Ave NW 44685 — 330-877-9383
William Stetler, supt. — Fax 877-4754
www.lakelocal.org
Lake HS — 1,100/9-12
1025 Lake Center St NW 44685 — 330-877-4282
Jeffrey Wendorf, prin. — Fax 877-0853
Other Schools – See Hartville

Hondros College
1505 Crprt Woods Pky #100 44685 — Post-Sec. — 330-896-9666

University Heights, Cuyahoga, Pop. 13,723
Cleveland Hts - University Hts CSD — 6,700/K-12
2155 Miramar Blvd 44118 — 216-371-7171
Deborah Delisle, supt. — Fax 397-3880
www.chuh.org
Wiley MS — 500/6-8
2181 Miramar Blvd 44118 — 216-371-7270
Denine Goolsby, prin. — Fax 397-5968
Other Schools – See Cleveland Heights

Fuchs Mizrachi S — 400/PK-12
2301 Fenwick Rd 44118 — 216-932-0220
Rabbi Pinchos Hecht, hdmstr. — Fax 932-0345

Upper Arlington, Franklin, Pop. 32,406
Upper Arlington CSD — 5,600/K-12
1950 N Mallway Dr 43221 — 614-487-5000
Jeffrey Weaver Ph.D., supt. — Fax 487-5012
www.uaschools.org
Hastings MS — 700/6-8
1850 Hastings Ln 43220 — 614-487-5100
Beverly Von Zielonka, prin. — Fax 487-5116
Jones MS — 600/6-8
2100 Arlington Ave 43221 — 614-487-5080
Karen Pettus, prin. — Fax 487-5307
Upper Arlington HS — 1,900/9-12
1650 Ridgeview Rd 43221 — 614-487-5200
Kip Greenhill, prin. — Fax 487-5238

Upper Sandusky, Wyandot, Pop. 6,458
Upper Sandusky EVD — 1,500/K-12
800 N Sandusky Ave Ste A 43351 — 419-294-2307
Steven Puchta, supt. — Fax 294-6891
www.uppersandusky.k12.oh.us
Union MS — 600/4-8
390 W Walker St 43351 — 419-294-5721
James Wheeler, prin. — Fax 294-2586
Upper Sandusky HS — 600/9-12
800 N Sandusky Ave 43351 — 419-294-2308
James Clifford, prin. — Fax 294-6889

Urbana, Champaign, Pop. 11,597
Urbana CSD — 2,300/K-12
711 Wood St 43078 — 937-653-1402
Dr. Susan McCarty, supt. — Fax 652-3845
www.urbana.k12.oh.us
Urbana HS — 600/9-12
500 Washington Ave 43078 — 937-653-1412
Charles Thiel, prin. — Fax 653-1487
Urbana JHS — 300/7-8
500 Washington Ave 43078 — 937-653-1439
Kristin Mays, prin.

Urbana University — Post-Sec.
579 College Way 43078 — 937-484-1301

Utica, Licking, Pop. 2,074
North Fork Local SD — 1,900/K-12
PO Box 497 43080 — 740-892-3666
Thomas Slater, supt. — Fax 892-2937
www.northfork.k12.oh.us
Utica HS — 600/9-12
PO Box 677 43080 — 740-892-2855
C. Mark McDaniel, prin. — Fax 892-2090
Utica JHS — 300/7-8
PO Box 647 43080 — 740-892-2691
Paul Galloway, prin. — Fax 892-2203

Valley View, Cuyahoga, Pop. 2,157

Ohio Center for Broadcasting — Post-Sec.
9000 Sweet Valley Dr 44125 — 216-447-9117

Van Buren, Hancock, Pop. 316
Van Buren Local SD — 900/K-12
217 S Main St 45889 — 419-299-3578
Timothy Myers, supt. — Fax 299-3668
www.noacsc.org/hancock/vb/
Van Buren HS — 300/9-12
217 S Main St 45889 — 419-299-3384
Michael Brand, prin. — Fax 299-3668
Van Buren MS — 200/6-8
217 S Main St 45889 — 419-299-3385
Jason Clark, prin. — Fax 299-3668

Vandalia, Montgomery, Pop. 14,495
Vandalia-Butler CSD — 3,500/K-12
306 S Dixie Dr 45377 — 937-415-6400
Dr. Christy Donnelly, supt. — Fax 415-6429
www.vandaliabutlerschools.org
Butler HS — 1,200/9-12
600 S Dixie Dr 45377 — 937-415-6300
Jeff Cassell, prin. — Fax 415-6457
Morton MS — 500/5-8
231 W National Rd 45377 — 937-415-6600
Gary Miller, prin. — Fax 415-6648
Other Schools – See Dayton

Vanlue, Hancock, Pop. 369
Vanlue Local SD — 300/K-12
PO Box 250 45890 — 419-387-7724
Timothy Kruse, supt. — Fax 387-7722
www.noacsc.org/hancock/vl/
Vanlue JSHS — 200/7-12
PO Box 250 45890 — 419-387-7724
Scott Hall, prin. — Fax 387-7722

Van Wert, Van Wert, Pop. 10,599
Lincolnview Local SD — 800/K-12
15945 Middle Point Rd 45891 — 419-238-6493
Doug Fries, supt. — Fax 968-2227
www.noacsc.org/vanwert/lv/main.html
Lincolnview HS — 400/7-12
15945 Middle Point Rd 45891 — 419-238-1289
Kelly Dye, prin. — Fax 968-2227

Van Wert CSD — 2,300/K-12
205 W Crawford St 45891 — 419-238-0648
Cathy Hoffman, supt. — Fax 238-3974
www.vanwertcougars.net
Van Wert HS — 700/9-12
205 W Crawford St 45891 — 419-238-3350
William Clifton, prin. — Fax 238-0526
Van Wert MS — 400/7-8
305 W Crawford St 45891 — 419-238-0727
Mary Riepenhoff, prin. — Fax 238-7166

Vantage Career Center — Vo/Tech
818 N Franklin St 45891 — 419-238-5411
Dr. Stephen D. Mercer, supt. — Fax 238-4058
vantagecareercenter.com
Vantage Career Center — Vo/Tech
818 N Franklin St 45891 — 419-238-5411
Bob Vennekotter, dir. — Fax 238-4058

Vermilion, Erie, Pop. 10,940
Vermilion Local SD — 2,500/K-12
1230 Beechway Dr 44089 — 440-967-5210
Bruce Keller, supt. — Fax 967-0740
vermilionschools.org
Sailorway MS — 600/6-8
5355 Sailorway Dr 44089 — 440-967-6196
Heidi Riddle, prin. — Fax 967-5720
Vermilion HS — 800/9-12
1250 Sanford St 44089 — 440-967-3183
Michael Colatruglio, prin. — Fax 967-8317

Versailles, Darke, Pop. 2,546
Versailles EVD — 1,400/K-12
PO Box 313 45380 — 937-526-4773
Tom Doseck, supt. — Fax 526-5745
www.versailles.k12.oh.us
Versailles JSHS — 700/7-12
PO Box 313 45380 — 937-526-4427
Roger McEldowney, prin. — Fax 526-4356

Vienna, Trumbull, Pop. 1,067
Mathews Local SD — 1,000/K-12
4434 Warren Sharon Rd Ste B 44473 — 330-394-1800
Lee Seiple, supt. — Fax 394-1930
www.mathews.k12.oh.us
Mathews HS — 300/9-12
4429 Warren Sharon Rd 44473 — 330-394-1138
Louis Demarco, prin.
Other Schools – See Fowler

Vincent, Washington
Warren Local SD — 2,700/K-12
220 Sweetapple Rd 45784 — 740-678-2366
Thomas Gibbs, supt. — Fax 678-8275
www.warrenlocal.k12.oh.us/
Warren HS — 800/9-12
130 Warrior Dr 45784 — 740-678-2393
Dan Leffingwell, prin. — Fax 678-2783
Other Schools – See Cutler

Wadsworth, Medina, Pop. 19,462
Wadsworth CSD — 4,700/PK-12
360 College St 44281 — 330-336-3571
Dale Fortner, supt. — Fax 334-5242
www.wadsworth.k12.oh.us/
Wadsworth HS — 1,600/9-12
625 Broad St 44281 — 330-335-1400
Brian Williams, prin. — Fax 335-1376
Wadsworth MS — 700/7-8
150 Silvercreek Rd 44281 — 330-335-1410
Roger Wright, prin. — Fax 336-3820

Reimer Road Baptist Christian S — 200/PK-12
PO Box 128 44282 — 330-334-1480
Rev. Jim Newton, prin. — Fax 336-3064

Wapakoneta, Auglaize, Pop. 9,518
Auglaize County ESC
1045 Dearbaugh Ave Ste 2 45895 — 419-738-3422
Patrick Niekamp, supt. — Fax 738-1267
www.auglaizeesc.k12.oh.us/
Auglaize County HS — 7-12
1045 Dearbaugh Ave 45895 — 419-739-7489

Wapakoneta CSD — 3,100/K-12
1102 Gardenia Dr 45895 — 419-739-2900
Dean Wittwer, supt. — Fax 739-2918
www.noacsc.org/auglaize/wk/
Wapakoneta HS, 1 Redskin Trl 45895 — 1,300/8-12 — 419-739-5200
Robert Askins, prin.

Warren, Trumbull, Pop. 46,608
Champion Local SD — 1,700/K-12
5759 Mahoning Ave NW 44483 — 330-847-2330
Pamela Hood, supt. — Fax 847-2336
www.champion.k12.oh.us
Champion HS — 600/9-12
5976 Mahoning Ave NW 44483 — 330-847-2305
Michele Bonno, prin. — Fax 847-2353
Champion MS — 600/5-8
5435 Kuszmaul Ave NW 44483 — 330-847-2340
Mary Rose Walker, prin. — Fax 847-3624

Howland Local SD — 3,200/K-12
8200 South St SE 44484 — 330-856-8200
John Rubesich, supt. — Fax 856-8214
www.howlandschools.com
Howland HS — 1,000/9-12
200 Shaffer Dr NE 44484 — 330-856-8220
Frank Thomas, prin. — Fax 856-7827
Howland MS — 800/6-8
8100 South St SE 44484 — 330-856-8250
Barbara Sullivan, prin. — Fax 856-2157

Lordstown Local SD — 500/K-12
1824 Salt Springs Rd W 44481 — 330-824-2534
Douglas E. Shamp, supt. — Fax 824-2847
www.lordstown.k12.oh.us/
Lordstown JSHS — 200/7-12
1824 Salt Springs Rd W 44481 — 330-824-2581
Anthony J. Calderone, prin. — Fax 824-2586

Trumbull Career & Technical Center — 528 Educational Hwy NW 44483
Wayne McClain, supt. — 330-847-0503 — Fax 847-0339
www.tctc.k12.oh.us
Trumbull Career & Technical Center — Vo/Tech
528 Educational Hwy NW 44483 — 330-847-0503
Gary Hoffman, dir. — Fax 847-0339

Warren CSD — 6,200/K-12
261 Monroe St NW 44483 — 330-841-2321
Dr. Kathryn Hellweg, supt. — Fax 395-4728
www.warrenschools.k12.oh.us
East MS — 600/5-8
1470 South St SE 44483 — 330-841-2255
James Mitolo, prin. — Fax 841-2257
Harding HS — 1,900/9-12
860 Elm Rd NE 44483 — 330-841-2316
— Fax 841-2289
Turner MS — 500/5-8
1443 Mahoning Ave NW 44483 — 330-841-2379
— Fax 841-2378
Warren Western Reserve MS — 1,000/5-8
200 Loveless Ave SW 44485 — 330-841-2345
Linda Reigelman, prin. — Fax 373-6065

John F. Kennedy HS — 400/9-12
2550 Central Parkway Ave SE 44484 — 330-369-1804
June Drennen, prin. — Fax 369-1125
Kent State University-Trumbull Campus — Post-Sec.
4314 Mahoning Ave NW 44483 — 330-678-4281
NDS/Queen of Apostles S — 100/4-8
1461 Moncrest Dr NW 44485 — 330-399-5411
Mary Jo Dugan, prin. — Fax 399-7364
Trumbull Business College — Post-Sec.
3200 Ridge Ave SE 44484 — 330-369-3200
Warren Christian S — 200/K-12
2640 Parkman Rd NW 44485 — 330-898-3840
Dwight Long, prin. — Fax 898-1757

Warrensville Heights, Cuyahoga, Pop. 14,719
Warrensville Heights CSD — 2,800/K-12
4500 Warrensville Center Rd 44128 — 216-295-7710
Dr. Marc Gray, supt. — Fax 921-5902
www.warrensville.k12.oh.us
Warrensville Heights HS — 800/9-12
4270 Northfield Rd 44128 — 216-752-8585
Henry Pettiegrew, prin. — Fax 752-8116
Warrensville Heights MS — 500/7-8
4285 Warrensville Center Rd 44128 — 216-752-4050
Phyllis Wren, prin. — Fax 752-5813

ITT Technical Institute — Post-Sec.
4700 Richmond Rd 44128 — 216-896-6500

Warsaw, Coshocton, Pop. 782
River View Local SD — 2,500/K-12
26496 State Route 60 43844 — 740-824-3521
Kyle Kanuckel, supt. — Fax 824-3760
www.river-view.k12.oh.us
River View HS — 800/9-12
26496 State Route 60 43844 — 740-824-3521
David Hire, prin. — Fax 824-4746
River View JHS — 400/7-8
26546 State Route 60 43844 — 740-824-3521
Alan English, prin. — Fax 824-5241

Washington Court House, Fayette, Pop. 13,471
Miami Trace Local SD — 2,700/K-12
1400 US Highway 22 NW 43160 — 740-335-3010
Daniel W. Roberts, supt. — Fax 335-5675
www.miamitrace.k12.oh.us
Miami Trace HS — 900/9-12
3722 State Route 41 NW 43160 — 740-335-5891
Jeff Spears, prin. — Fax 636-2010
Other Schools – See Bloomingburg

Washington Courthouse CSD — 2,300/K-12
306 Highland Ave 43160 — 740-335-6620
Keith Brown, supt. — Fax 335-1245
www.washingtonch.k12.oh.us
Washington HS — 600/9-12
1200 Willard St 43160 — 740-335-0820
Jeff Hodson, prin. — Fax 335-0842
Washington MS — 600/6-8
318 N North St 43160 — 740-335-0291
Steve Ross, prin. — Fax 333-3606

Waterford, Washington
Wolf Creek Local SD — 700/K-12
PO Box 67 45786 — 740-984-2373
Robert Caldwell, supt. — Fax 984-4420
www.wolfcreek.k12.oh.us
Waterford HS — 200/9-12
PO Box 67 45786 — 740-984-2373
Randy Shrider, prin. — Fax 984-4420

Wauseon, Fulton, Pop. 7,183
Wauseon EVD — 2,100/K-12
126 S Fulton St 43567 — 419-335-6616
Marc Robinson, supt. — Fax 335-3978
www.wauseon.k12.oh.us
Burr Road MS — 500/6-8
717 Burr Rd 43567 — 419-335-2701
William Friess, prin. — Fax 335-0089
Wauseon HS — 700/9-12
840 Parkview St 43567 — 419-335-5756
Joseph Sevenich, prin. — Fax 335-4228

Waverly, Pike, Pop. 5,086
Waverly CSD — 2,100/K-12
1 Tiger Dr 45690 — 740-947-4770
Cheryl Francis, supt. — Fax 947-4483
www.waverly.k12.oh.us
Waverly HS — 700/9-12
1 Tiger Dr 45690 — 740-947-7701
David Surrey, prin. — Fax 947-8877
Waverly JHS — 500/6-8
3 Tiger Dr 45690 — 740-947-4527
Ruth Teeters, prin. — Fax 947-8047

Waynesfield, Auglaize, Pop. 808
Waynesfield-Goshen Local SD — 600/K-12
500 N Westminster St 45896 — 419-568-2391
Earnie Jones, supt. — Fax 568-8024
www.waynesfield.k12.oh.us/

Waynesfield-Goshen Local HS 300/6-12
500 N Westminster St 45896 419-568-5261
Thomas Winkler, prin. Fax 568-8024

Waynesville, Warren, Pop. 2,833
Wayne Local SD 1,400/K-12
659 Dayton Rd 45068 513-897-6971
Thomas Isaacs, supt. Fax 897-9605
www.wayne-local.k12.oh.us
Waynesville HS 500/9-12
735 Dayton Rd 45068 513-897-2776
Randy Gebhardt, prin. Fax 897-2713
Waynesville MS 300/6-8
723 Dayton Rd 45068 513-897-4706
Michael Doyle, prin. Fax 897-9605

Wellington, Lorain, Pop. 4,560
Wellington EVD 1,600/K-12
201 S Main St 44090 440-647-4286
Victor Cardenzana, supt. Fax 647-4806
www.wellington.k12.oh.us
McCormick MS 700/4-8
201 S Main St 44090 440-647-2342
Tom Durham, prin. Fax 647-7310
Wellington HS 500/9-12
629 N Main St 44090 440-647-3734
Darren Conley, prin. Fax 647-7318

Wellston, Jackson, Pop. 5,994
Wellston CSD 1,900/PK-12
1 E Broadway St 45692 740-384-2152
Dan Brisker, supt. Fax 384-3948
www.wcs.k12.oh.us
Wellston HS 500/9-12
200 Golden Rocket Dr 45692 740-384-2162
Lisa Harley, prin. Fax 384-9581
Wellston MS 400/6-8
227 Golden Rocket Dr 45692 740-384-2251
Barbara White, prin. Fax 384-9801

Wellsville, Columbiana, Pop. 4,089
Wellsville Local SD 800/K-12
929 Center St 43968 330-532-2643
Ken Halbert, supt. Fax 532-6204
www.wellsvlle.k12.oh.us
Daw MS, 929 Center St 43968 300/4-8
David Buzzard, prin. 330-532-1372
Wellsville HS 300/9-12
1 Bengal Blvd 43968 330-532-1188
Richard Bereschik, prin. Fax 532-9004

West Alexandria, Preble, Pop. 1,359
Twin Valley Community Local SD 1,100/K-12
100 Education Dr 45381 937-839-4688
Larry Russell, supt. Fax 839-4898
www.tvs.k12.oh.us
Twin Valley South HS 400/9-12
100 Education Dr 45381 937-839-4693
Scott Cottingim, prin. Fax 839-4898
Twin Valley South MS 200/6-8
100 Education Dr 45381 937-839-4165
Richard Brownlee, prin. Fax 839-4858

West Carrollton, Montgomery, Pop. 14,072
West Carrollton CSD 3,900/PK-12
430 E Pease Ave 45449 937-859-5121
Rusty Clifford, supt. Fax 859-5250
www.westcarrolltonschools.com
West Carrollton HS 1,100/9-12
5833 Student St 45449 937-859-5121
Dr. Mildred Chamberlin, prin. Fax 435-2315
West Carrollton MS 900/6-8
424 E Main St 45449 937-859-5121
John Runzo, prin. Fax 859-2780

West Chester, Butler
Lakota Local SD
Supt. — See Liberty
Hopewell JHS 500/7-8
8200 Cox Rd 45069 513-777-2258
David Pike, prin. Fax 777-1908
Lakota Freshman HS 1,200/9-9
5050 Tylersville Rd 45069 513-874-8390
Keith Kline, prin. Fax 874-8236
Lakota Ridge JHS 700/7-8
6199 Beckett Ridge Blvd 45069 513-777-0552
Ed Rudder, prin. Fax 777-0919
Lakota West SHS 1,800/10-12
8940 Union Centre Blvd 45069 513-874-5699
Richard Hamilton, prin. Fax 682-4134

Westerville, Franklin, Pop. 34,922
Westerville CSD 15,000/K-12
336 S Otterbein Ave 43081 614-797-5700
George Tombaugh, supt. Fax 797-5701
www.westerville.k12.oh.us
Blendon MS 600/6-8
223 S Otterbein Ave 43081 614-797-6400
David Baker, prin. Fax 797-6401
Genoa MS 900/6-8
5948 S Old 3C Hwy 43082 614-797-6500
Suzanne Kile, prin. Fax 797-6501
Heritage MS 900/6-8
390 N Spring Rd 43082 614-797-6600
Felicia Harper, prin. Fax 797-6601
Walnut Springs MS 900/6-8
888 E Walnut St 43081 614-797-6700
Matt Lutz, prin. Fax 797-6701
Westerville Central HS 1,700/9-12
7118 Mount Royal Ave 43082 614-797-6800
Todd Meyer, prin. Fax 797-6801
Westerville-North HS 1,900/9-12
950 County Line Rd 43081 614-797-6200
Curtis Jackowski, prin. Fax 797-6201
Westerville-South HS 1,700/9-12
303 S Otterbein Ave 43081 614-797-6000
Keith Bell, prin. Fax 797-6001

Hondros College Post-Sec.
4140 Executive Pkwy 43081 614-508-7277
Ohio State Cosmetology School Post-Sec.
5970 Westerville Rd 43081 614-890-3535
Otterbein College Post-Sec.
78 W Home St 43081 614-890-3000

Worthington Christian MS 200/6-8
8225 Worthington Galena Rd 43081 614-431-8230
Richard Dray, prin. Fax 431-8216

West Jefferson, Madison, Pop. 4,266
Jefferson Local SD 1,300/PK-12
906 W Main St 43162 614-879-7654
William Mullett, supt. Fax 879-5376
www.west-jefferson.k12.oh.us
Memorial MS 300/6-8
177 S Frey Ave 43162 614-879-8345
Debbie Omen, prin. Fax 879-5399
West Jefferson HS 400/9-12
1 Roughrider Dr 43162 614-879-7681
Dave Metz, prin. Fax 879-5381

West Lafayette, Coshocton, Pop. 2,330
Ridgewood Local SD 1,500/K-12
301 S Oak St 43845 740-545-6354
William Caudill, supt. Fax 545-6336
www.ridgewood.k12.oh.us
Ridgewood HS 500/9-12
602 Johnson St 43845 740-545-6345
Rick Raach, prin. Fax 545-5311
Ridgewood MS 400/6-8
517 S Oak St 43845 740-545-6335
Mike Masloski, prin. Fax 545-5300

Westlake, Cuyahoga, Pop. 32,024
Westlake CSD 3,900/K-12
27200 Hilliard Blvd 44145 440-871-7300
James Costanza, supt. Fax 871-6034
www.westlake.k12.oh.us
Burneson MS 700/7-8
2240 Dover Center Rd 44145 440-835-6340
G. Newman, prin. Fax 835-5987
Westlake HS 1,200/9-12
27830 Hilliard Blvd 44145 440-250-1002
Tim Freeman, prin. Fax 835-5572

West Liberty, Champaign, Pop. 1,790
West Liberty-Salem Local SD 1,200/K-12
7208 US Highway 68 N 43357 937-465-1075
Steve Thompson, supt. Fax 465-1095
www.wls.k12.oh.us
West Liberty-Salem MSHS 700/6-12
7208 US Highway 68 N 43357 937-465-1060
Greg Johnson, prin. Fax 465-1095

West Milton, Miami, Pop. 4,663
Milton-Union EVD 1,800/K-12
112 S Spring St 45383 937-884-7910
Dr. James Barney, supt. Fax 884-7911
www.milton-union.k12.oh.us
Milton-Union HS 600/9-12
221 Jefferson St 45383 937-884-7940
Brian Powderly, prin.
Milton-Union MS 400/6-8
146 S Spring St 45383 937-884-7930
Dr. Ginny Rammel, prin.

West Portsmouth, Scioto, Pop. 3,551
Washington-Nile Local SD 1,700/K-12
15332 US Highway 52 45663 740-858-1111
Patricia Ciraso, supt. Fax 858-1110
www.west.k12.oh.us
Portsmouth West MS 400/6-8
1420 13th St 45663 740-858-6668
Christopher Jordan, prin. Fax 858-1110
Other Schools – See Portsmouth

West Salem, Wayne, Pop. 1,503
Northwestern Local SD 1,100/K-12
7571 N Elyria Rd 44287 419-846-3151
Jeffrey Layton, supt. Fax 846-3361
www.northwestern-wayne.k12.oh.us
Northwestern HS 500/9-12
7473 N Elyria Rd 44287 419-846-3833
Michael Burkholder, prin. Fax 846-3163
Northwestern MS 300/6-8
7569 N Elyria Rd 44287 419-846-3974
Robert Dorety, prin. Fax 846-3750

West Union, Adams, Pop. 3,033
Adams County/Ohio Valley SD 3,900/K-12
141 Lloyd Rd 45693 937-544-5586
Charles Kimble, supt. Fax 544-3720
www.ohiovalley.k12.oh.us
Ohio Valley Career & Technical Center Vo/Tech
175 Lloyd Rd 45693 937-544-2336
Tad Mitchell, prin. Fax 544-5176
West Union HS 600/7-12
97 Dragon Lair Dr 45693 937-544-5553
Dennis Sizemore, prin. Fax 544-5361
Other Schools – See Peebles, Seaman

Adams County Christian S 200/K-12
187 Willow Dr 45693 937-544-5502
Shirley Lewis, admin. Fax 544-5503

West Unity, Williams, Pop. 1,738
Millcreek-West Unity Local SD 800/K-12
113 S Defiance St 43570 419-924-2365
Deb Piotrowski, supt. Fax 924-2367
www.hilltop.k12.oh.us
Hilltop HS 400/7-12
113 S Defiance St 43570 419-924-2365
Mick Belcher, prin. Fax 924-2367

Wheelersburg, Scioto, Pop. 5,113
Wheelersburg Local SD 1,500/K-12
PO Box 340 45694 740-574-8484
Mark Knapp, supt. Fax 574-6134
www.burg.k12.oh.us
Wheelersburg HS 400/9-12
701 Pirate Dr 45694 740-574-2527
Matthew McCorkle, prin. Fax 574-6178
Wheelersburg MS 500/5-8
1731 Dogwood Ridge Rd 45694 740-574-2515
Amber Fannin, prin. Fax 574-9201

Whitehall, Franklin, Pop. 18,611
Whitehall CSD 3,000/K-12
625 S Yearling Rd 43213 614-417-5000
Judyth Dobbert-Meloy, supt. Fax 417-5023
www.whitehall.k12.oh.us

Rosemore MS 700/6-8
4735 Kae Ave 43213 614-417-5200
Mark Trace, prin. Fax 417-5212
Whitehall-Yearling HS 900/9-12
675 S Yearling Rd 43213 614-417-5100
Dondra Maney, prin. Fax 417-5133

Whitehouse, Lucas, Pop. 2,961
Anthony Wayne Local SD 3,900/K-12
PO Box 2487 43571 419-877-5377
Randy Hardy, supt. Fax 877-9352
www.anthonywayneschools.org
Wayne HS 1,200/9-12
5967 Finzel Rd 43571 419-877-0466
James Conner, prin. Fax 877-5028
Wayne JHS 600/7-8
6035 Finzel Rd 43571 419-877-5342
Jeffrey Schwerer, prin. Fax 877-4908

Wickliffe, Lake, Pop. 13,299
Wickliffe CSD 1,500/K-12
2221 Rockefeller Rd 44092 440-943-6900
Robert Smith, supt. Fax 943-7738
www.wickliffe-city.k12.oh.us
Wickliffe HS 500/9-12
2255 Rockefeller Rd 44092 440-944-0800
Vicki Wheatley, prin. Fax 943-7738
Wickliffe MS 500/5-8
29240 Euclid Ave 44092 440-943-3220
Bill Porter, prin. Fax 943-7755

Bryant & Stratton College Post-Sec.
27557 Chardon Rd 44092 440-944-6800
Rabbinical College of Telshe Post-Sec.
28400 Euclid Ave 44092 440-943-5300
St. Mary Seminary/Graduate Sch. Theology Post-Sec.
28700 Euclid Ave 44092 440-943-7600
Telshe HS 100/9-12
28400 Euclid Ave 44092 440-943-5300
Rabbi Zev Poss, prin. Fax 943-5303

Wilberforce, Greene, Pop. 2,639

Central State University Post-Sec.
PO Box 1004 45384 937-376-6011
Payne Theological Seminary Post-Sec.
PO Box 474 45384 937-376-2946
Wilberforce University Post-Sec.
PO Box 1001 45384 937-376-2911

Willard, Huron, Pop. 6,869
Willard CSD 2,400/PK-12
PO Box 150 44890 419-935-1541
Dennis Doughty, supt. Fax 935-8491
www.willard.k12.oh.us
Willard HS 700/9-12
PO Box 410 44890 419-935-0181
Jeff Ritz, prin. Fax 933-6701
Willard MS, 949 S Main St 44890 600/5-8
Dan Major, prin. 419-933-8312

Williamsburg, Clermont, Pop. 2,316
Williamsburg Local SD 1,000/K-12
549 W Main St Ste A 45176 513-724-3077
Jeffery Weir, supt. Fax 724-1504
www.williamsburg.k12.oh.us/
Williamsburg MSHS 500/6-12
500 S 5th St 45176 513-724-2211
Matthew Earley, prin. Fax 724-6577

Williamsport, Pickaway, Pop. 994
Westfall Local SD 1,600/K-12
19463 Pherson Pike 43164 740-986-3671
Randall Cotner, supt. Fax 986-8375
gsn.k12.oh.us/westfall/default.htm
Westfall HS 500/9-12
19463 Pherson Pike 43164 740-986-2911
Dennis Karshner, prin. Fax 986-8375
Westfall MS 400/6-8
19545 Pherson Pike 43164 740-986-2941
Kent Wolfe, prin. Fax 986-6751

Willoughby, Lake, Pop. 22,488
Willoughby-Eastlake CSD 8,600/K-12
37047 Ridge Rd 44094 440-946-5000
Dr. Keith Miller, supt. Fax 946-4671
www.willoughby-eastlake.k12.oh.us
South HS 1,200/9-12
5000 Shankland Rd 44094 440-975-3647
Paul Lombardo, prin. Fax 975-3645
Willoughby-Eastlake Tech Ctr Vo/Tech
25 Public Sq 44094 440-946-7085
Richard Hart, prin. Fax 975-3741
Willoughby MS 900/4-8
36901 Ridge Rd 44094 440-975-3600
Gary Barta, prin. Fax 975-3618
Other Schools – See Eastlake, Willowick

Andrews S 200/6-12
38588 Mentor Ave 44094 440-942-3600
David Rath, hdmstr. Fax 942-3660
Cornerstone Christian Academy 200/K-12
2846 SOM Center Rd 44094 440-943-9260
Daniel Buell Ph.D., admin. Fax 943-9262

Willowick, Lake, Pop. 14,072
Willoughby-Eastlake CSD
Supt. — See Willoughby
Willowick MS 700/6-8
31500 Royalview Dr 44095 440-943-2950
Loretta Rodman, prin. Fax 943-9964

Willow Wood, Lawrence
Symmes Valley Local SD 900/K-12
14778 State Route 141 45696 740-643-2451
Thomas Ben, supt. Fax 643-1219
www.symmesvalley.k12.oh.us
Symmes Valley HS 300/9-12
14778 State Route 141 45696 740-643-2371
Jeff Saunders, prin. Fax 643-1219

Willshire, Van Wert, Pop. 459
Parkway Local SD
Supt. — See Rockford

Parkway MS | 300/6-8
PO Box C 45898 | 419-495-2000
Steve Baumgartner, prin. | Fax 495-2202

Wilmington, Clinton, Pop. 12,187
Great Oaks Institute of Technology
Supt. — See Cincinnati
Laurel Oaks CDC | Vo/Tech
300 Oak Dr 45177 | 937-382-1411
Ron Webber, prin. | Fax 383-2095

Wilmington CSD | 3,200/K-12
341 S Nelson Ave 45177 | 937-382-1641
Philip Warner, supt. | Fax 382-1645
www.wilmingtoncityschool.com
O'Borror MS | 700/6-8
275 Thorne Ave 45177 | 937-382-7556
Nicole Wilson, prin. | Fax 382-3295
Wilmington HS | 1,000/9-12
300 Richardson Pl 45177 | 937-382-7716
Ronald Sexton, prin. | Fax 382-1139

Southern State Community College | Post-Sec.
1850 Davids Dr 45177 | 937-382-6645
Wilmington College | Post-Sec.
251 Ludovic St 45177 | 937-382-6661

Windham, Portage, Pop. 2,766
Windham EVD | 1,100/PK-12
9530 Bauer Ave 44288 | 330-326-2711
Ronald Niemiec, supt. | Fax 326-2134
Windham HS | 300/9-12
9530 Bauer Ave 44288 | 330-326-3916
Carol Kropinak, prin. | Fax 326-2052
Windham JHS | 200/6-8
9530 Bauer Ave 44288 | 330-326-3490
Carol Kropinak, prin. | Fax 326-3713

Wintersville, Jefferson, Pop. 3,824
Indian Creek Local SD | 2,300/PK-12
587 Bantam Ridge Rd 43953 | 740-264-3502
Jene Watkins, supt. | Fax 266-2915
www.indian-creek.k12.oh.us
Indian Creek HS | 700/9-12
200 Park Dr 43953 | 740-264-1163
John Craig, prin. | Fax 266-2929
Other Schools – See Mingo Junction

Woodsfield, Monroe, Pop. 2,535
Switzerland of Ohio Local SD | 2,800/K-12
304 Mill St 43793 | 740-472-5801
Mike Staggs, supt. | Fax 472-5806
www.swissohio.k12.oh.us/switzerland_of_ohio.htm
Monroe Central HS | 300/9-12
46605 State Route 78 43793 | 740-458-1246
Marc Ring, prin.
Swiss Hills Career Center | Vo/Tech
46601 State Route 78 43793 | 740-472-0722
Marc Ring, prin. | Fax 472-0367
Other Schools – See Beallsville, Hannibal

Woodville, Sandusky, Pop. 1,990
Woodmore Local SD | 1,200/K-12
708 W Main St 43469 | 419-849-2381
Michael Eaglowski, supt. | Fax 849-2132
www.woodmore.k12.oh.us/
Other Schools – See Elmore

Wooster, Wayne, Pop. 25,322
Triway Local SD | 2,100/K-12
3205 Shreve Rd 44691 | 330-264-9491
David Rice, supt. | Fax 262-3955
www.tccsa.net/dp/trwy
Triway HS | 700/9-12
3205 Shreve Rd 44691 | 330-264-8685
Scott Wharton, prin. | Fax 262-3955
Triway JHS | 300/7-8
3145 Shreve Rd 44691 | 330-264-2114
Mitchell Caraway, prin. | Fax 264-6025

Wooster CSD | 3,900/K-12
144 N Market St 44691 | 330-264-0869
Dr. Dan Good, supt. | Fax 262-3407
www.wooster.k12.oh.us
Edgewood MS | 600/7-8
2695 Graustark Path 44691 | 330-345-6475
Anita Jorney-Gifford, prin. | Fax 345-8237
Wooster HS | 1,300/9-12
515 Oldman Rd 44691 | 330-345-4000
Jerry Parsons, prin. | Fax 345-3501

College of Wooster | Post-Sec.
1189 Beall Ave 44691 | 330-263-2000
Ohio State University-A & T Institute | Post-Sec.
1328 Dover Rd 44691 | 330-264-3911

Worthington, Franklin, Pop. 13,602
Worthington CSD | 9,400/K-12
200 E Wilson Bridge Rd 43085 | 614-883-3000
Rick Fenton, supt. | Fax 883-3010
www.worthington.k12.oh.us
Kilbourne MS | 400/7-8
50 E Dublin Granville Rd 43085 | 614-883-3500
Pamela VanHorn, prin. | Fax 883-3510
Perry MS | 400/7-8
2341 Snouffer Rd 43085 | 614-883-3600
Jeff Maddox, prin. | Fax 883-3610
Worthington HS | 1,700/9-12
300 W Dublin Granville Rd 43085 | 614-883-2250
Richard Littell, prin. | Fax 883-2260
Worthingway MS | 400/7-8
6625 Guyer St 43085 | 614-883-3650
Santha Stall, prin. | Fax 883-3660

Other Schools – See Columbus

Worthington Christian HS | 400/9-12
6670 Worthington Galena Rd 43085 | 614-431-8210
Thomas Anglea, prin. | Fax 431-8213

Wyoming, Hamilton, Pop. 7,987
Wyoming CSD | 2,000/K-12
420 Springfield Pike 45215 | 513-772-2343
Dr. Gail Kist-Kline, supt. | Fax 672-3355
www.wyomingcityschools.org
Wyoming HS | 700/9-12
106 Pendery Ave 45215 | 513-761-1722
Annie Wade, prin. | Fax 679-3611
Wyoming MS | 600/5-8
17 Wyoming Ave 45215 | 513-761-7248
Kathy Ryan, prin. | Fax 761-7319

Xenia, Greene, Pop. 23,822
Greene County JVSD | Vo/Tech
2960 W Enon Rd 45385 | 937-372-6941
Marsha Leonard, supt. | Fax 372-8283
www.greeneccc.com
Greene County Career Center | Vo/Tech
2960 W Enon Rd 45385 | 937-372-6941
Manfred Stamguts, prin. | Fax 372-8283

Xenia Community SD | 5,100/K-12
578 E Market St 45385 | 937-376-2961
Jeffrey K. Lewis Ed.D., supt. | Fax 372-4701
www.xenia.k12.oh.us
Central MS | 600/6-8
425 Edison Blvd 45385 | 937-372-7635
Mike Earley, prin. | Fax 374-4410
Warner MS | 600/6-8
600 Buckskin Trl 45385 | 937-376-9488
Dr. Peg McAtee, prin. | Fax 374-4228
Xenia HS | 1,500/9-12
303 Kinsey Rd 45385 | 937-372-6983
Reinhold Finkes, prin. | Fax 374-4390

Dayton Christian S - Xenia Christian HS | 300/7-12
1101 Wesley Ave 45385 | 937-372-9754
Alan Stock, prin. | Fax 372-0098
Freedom Christian Academy | 50/K-12
1067 US Route 68 S 45385 | 937-372-9399
Charles Savage, prin.
Xenia Nazarene Christian S | 200/K-12
1204 W 2nd St 45385 | 937-372-4362
Charlene Crisp, prin. | Fax 372-1074

Yellow Springs, Greene, Pop. 3,702
Yellow Springs EVD | 700/K-12
201 S Walnut St 45387 | 937-767-7381
Anthony Armocida Ph.D., supt. | Fax 767-6604
www.yellow-springs.k12.oh.us/
Yellow Springs HS / McKinney MS | 400/7-12
420 E Enon Rd 45387 | 937-767-7224
John Gudgel, prin. | Fax 767-6154

Antioch College | Post-Sec.
795 Livermore St 45387 | 937-754-5000
Antioch University McGregor | Post-Sec.
800 Livermore St 45387 | 937-767-6321

Youngstown, Mahoning, Pop. 79,271
Austintown Local SD | 5,000/K-12
225 Idaho Rd 44515 | 330-797-3900
Douglas Heuer, supt. | Fax 797-3943
www.austintown.k12.oh.us
Austintown MS | 900/5-8
5800 Mahoning Ave 44515 | 330-797-3900
Daniel Bokesch, prin. | Fax 797-3965
Fitch HS | 1,700/9-12
4560 Falcon Dr 44515 | 330-797-3900
Douglas McGlynn, prin. | Fax 797-3944
Ohl MS | 700/5-8
255 Idaho Rd 44515 | 330-797-3900
Dennis Rice, prin. | Fax 797-3964

Boardman Local SD | 4,900/K-12
7410 Market St 44512 | 330-726-3404
Frank Lazzeri, supt. | Fax 726-3432
www.boardman.k12.oh.us
Boardman HS | 1,600/9-12
7777 Glenwood Ave 44512 | 330-758-7511
Tim Saxton, prin. | Fax 758-7515
Center MS, 7410 Market St 44512 | 800/5-8
Randall Ebie, prin. | 330-726-3400
Glenwood MS | 700/5-8
7635 Glenwood Ave 44512 | 330-726-3414
Anthony Alvino, prin.

Liberty Local SD | 1,800/K-12
4115 Shady Rd 44505 | 330-759-0807
Lawrence Prince, supt. | Fax 759-1209
www.liberty.k12.oh.us
Guy MS | 600/5-8
4115 Shady Rd 44505 | 330-759-1733
Mark Lucas, prin. | Fax 759-4507
Liberty HS | 700/9-12
1 Leopard Way 44505 | 330-759-2301
John Young, prin. | Fax 759-4506

Youngstown CSD | 8,300/K-12
PO Box 550 44501 | 330-744-6900
Wendy Webb Ed.D., supt. | Fax 743-1557
www.youngstown.k12.oh.us/
Alpha: S of Excellence for Boys | 7-8
2546 Hillman St 44507
Bruce Palmer, prin.

Athena: S of Excellence for Girls | 300/7-8
1061 Lyden Ave 44505
Sandra Smith, prin.
Chaney HS | 900/9-12
731 S Hazelwood Ave 44509 | 330-744-8822
Robert Spencer, prin. | Fax 480-1909
East MS | 600/5-8
1544 E High Ave 44505 | 330-744-8845
Sandra Mislevy, prin. | Fax 480-1910
Hayes MS | 500/5-8
1616 Ford Ave 44504 | 330-744-7602
Carol Staten, prin. | Fax 480-1905
Rayen HS | 900/9-12
250 Benita Ave 44504 | 330-744-8550
Henrietta Williams, prin. | Fax 480-1912
Volney Rogers JHS | 400/7-8
2400 S Schenley Ave 44511 | 330-744-7996
Marilyn Mastronardi, prin. | Fax 480-1908
Wilson HS | 900/9-12
2725 Gibson St 44502 | 330-744-8525
Melvin Lars, prin. | Fax 480-1911
Choffin Career & Technical Center | Adult
200 E Wood St 44503 | 330-744-8700
Joseph Meranto, prin.

Cardinal Mooney HS | 600/9-12
2545 Erie St 44507 | 330-788-5007
Sr. Jane Kudlacz, prin. | Fax 788-4511
ITT Technical Institute | Post-Sec.
1030 N Meridian Rd 44509 | 330-270-1600
St. Elizabeth Hospital | Post-Sec.
PO Box 1790 44501 | 330-746-7211
Ursuline HS | 600/9-12
750 Wick Ave 44505 | 330-744-4563
Patricia Fleming, prin. | Fax 744-3358
Watkins Christian Academy | 200/K-12
2122 E High Ave 44505 | 330-746-5626
Raymond McElroy, prin.
Western Reserve Care System | Post-Sec.
345 Oak Hill Ave 44502 | 330-747-0777
Youngstown Christian S | 400/PK-12
4401 Southern Blvd 44512 | 330-788-8088
Anthony Agresta, prin. | Fax 788-2875
Youngstown State University | Post-Sec.
1 University Plz 44555 | 330-742-3000

Zanesville, Muskingum, Pop. 25,277
Maysville Local SD | 2,200/K-12
PO Box 1818 43702 | 740-453-0754
Gary Reed, supt. | Fax 455-4081
www.maysville.k12.oh.us/
Maysville HS, 3725 Panther Dr 43701 | 700/9-12
Mark Ulbrich, prin. | 740-454-7999
Maysville MS | 500/6-8
3725 Panther Dr 43701 | 740-454-7982

Mid-East Career & Technology Center JVSD | 740-454-0105
400 Richards Rd 43701 | Fax 454-0731
William A. Bussey, supt.
www.mid-east.k12.oh.us/
Mid-East Career & Tech Ctr - Zanesville | Vo/Tech
400 Richards Rd 43701 | 740-454-0101
Alice K. Hite, dir. | Fax 454-0723
Other Schools – See Senecaville

West Muskingum Local SD | 1,800/K-12
4880 West Pike 43701 | 740-455-4052
Marvin Wourms, supt. | Fax 455-4063
www.westm.k12.oh.us
West Muskingum HS | 600/9-12
150 Kimes Rd 43701 | 740-455-4052
Ed Miller, prin.
West Muskingum MS | 500/6-8
100 Kimes Rd 43701 | 740-455-4055
Jim Spisak, prin. | Fax 455-9717

Zanesville CSD | 3,200/PK-12
160 N 4th St 43701 | 740-454-9751
| Fax 455-4325
www.zanesville.k12.oh.us
Cleveland MS, 968 Pine St 43701 | 400/6-8
Flora Martin, prin. | 740-453-0636
Roosevelt MS, 1429 Blue Ave 43701 | 400/6-8
Charlene Lewis, prin. | 740-453-0711
Zanesville HS | 1,100/9-12
1701 Blue Ave 43701 | 740-453-0335
Richard Sykes, prin. | Fax 455-4329

Bishop Rosecrans HS | 200/9-12
1040 E Main St 43701 | 740-452-7504
Richard Smith, prin. | Fax 455-5080
Muskingum Christian Academy | 100/K-12
1018 Marietta St 43701 | 740-454-7116
Ralph Weaver, prin. | Fax 454-7174
Ohio University | Post-Sec.
1425 Newark Rd 43701 | 740-453-0762
Valley Beauty School | Post-Sec.
627 Main St 43701 | 740-452-6821
Zane State College | Post-Sec.
1555 Newark Rd 43701 | 740-454-2501

Zoarville, Tuscarawas
Tuscarawas Valley Local SD | 1,700/PK-12
2637 Tuscarawas Valley NE 44656 | 330-859-2213
Mark A. Murphy, supt. | Fax 859-2706
www.tuskyvalley.k12.oh.us
Tuscarawas Valley HS | 500/9-12
2637 Tuscarawas Valley NE 44656 | 330-859-2421
Jeff Raynor, prin. | Fax 859-8805
Tuscarawas Valley MS | 600/6-8
2633 Tuscarawas Valley NE 44656 | 330-859-2427
Richard Price, prin. | Fax 859-8845

OKLAHOMA

OKLAHOMA DEPARTMENT OF EDUCATION
2500 N Lincoln Blvd, Oklahoma City 73105-4504
Telephone 405-521-3301
Fax 405-521-6205
Website http://www.sde.state.ok.us
Superintendent of Public Instruction   Sandy Garrett

OKLAHOMA BOARD OF EDUCATION
2500 N Lincoln Blvd, Oklahoma City 73105-4504
Chairperson   Sandy Garrett

INTERLOCAL COOPERATIVES (IC)

Atoka-Coal Counties IC
  Chris Edgar, dir. — 580-889-2664
  PO Box 1231, Atoka 74525 — Fax 889-6302
Cherokee County IC
  Sheryl Lynn Rountree, dir. — 918-456-1064
  15481 N Jarvis Rd — Fax 456-1041
  Tahlequah 74464
Choctaw Nation IC
  Terry Ragan, dir. — 580-931-0691
  PO Box 602, Durant 74702 — Fax 931-0683
Five Star IC
  Nancy Anderson, dir. — 918-225-5600
  1405 E Moses St, Cushing 74023 — Fax 225-3026
  www.fsilc.k12.ok.us

Garfield County IC
  Gerald Hoeltzel, dir. — 580-233-3071
  PO Box 10036, Enid 73706 — Fax 233-3072
McCurtain County IC
  Cindy Duncan, dir. — 580-286-3344
  103 NE A Ave, Idabel 74745 — Fax 286-5598
  www.mccareok.com/
NewNet 66 IC
  Mike Pennell, dir. — 918-633-6896
  310 N Weenonah Ave
  Claremore 74017

Osage County IC
  Gerald Harris, dir. — 918-885-2667
  207 E Main St, Hominy 74035 — Fax 885-6742
  www.ocic.k12.ok.us/
Pooled Investment IC
  Jack Harrell, pres. — 405-375-3696
  2901 N Lincoln Blvd — Fax 375-3696
  Oklahoma City 73105
Seminole County IC
  Dr. Audie Woodard, dir. — 405-382-6121
  630 Golf Rd, Seminole 74868 — Fax 382-5254
Tri-County IC
  Ty Harman, dir. — 580-673-2310
  PO Box 217, Fox 73435 — Fax 673-2309

PUBLIC, PRIVATE AND CATHOLIC SECONDARY SCHOOLS

Achille, Bryan, Pop. 516
Achille ISD — 400/PK-12
  PO Box 280 74720 — 580-283-3775
  Dr. Charles Caughern, supt. — Fax 283-3787
Achille HS, PO Box 280 74720 — 100/9-12
  Vernon Johnson, prin. — 580-283-3775

Ada, Pontotoc, Pop. 16,008
Ada ISD — 2,600/PK-12
  PO Box 1359 74821 — 580-310-7200
  Pat Harrison, supt. — Fax 310-7206
  www.adapss.com/
Ada JHS, 223 W 18th St 74820 — 600/7-9
  David Smith, prin. — 580-310-7260
Ada SHS, 1400 Stadium Dr 74820 — 500/10-12
  Bill Nelson, prin. — 580-310-7220

Byng ISD — 1,700/PK-12
  500 S New Bethel Blvd 74820 — 580-436-3020
  Steven Crawford, supt. — Fax 436-3052
  www.byngschools.com
Byng JHS — 300/7-9
  500 S New Bethel Blvd 74820 — 580-310-6743
  Jim Wright, prin. — Fax 310-6741
Byng SHS — 300/10-12
  500 S New Bethel Blvd 74820 — 580-310-6732
  Alex Souza, prin. — Fax 310-6730

Latta ISD — 700/PK-12
  13925 County Road 1560 74820 — 580-332-2092
  Cliff Johnson, supt. — Fax 332-3116
  www.latta.k12.ok.us/
Latta JHS — 200/7-9
  13925 County Road 1560 74820 — 580-332-8180
  Stan Cochran, prin.
Latta SHS — 200/10-12
  13925 County Road 1560 74820 — 580-332-3300
  Stan Cochran, prin.

OK Dept. of Voc. & Tech. Education
  Supt. — None
Pontotoc Technology Center — Vo/Tech
  601 W 33rd St 74820 — 580-310-2200
  Greg Pierce, supt. — Fax 436-0236

Vanoss ISD — 500/PK-12
  4665 County Road 1555 74820 — 580-759-2251
  Cheryl Melton, supt. — Fax 759-3080
  www.vanoss.k12.ok.us
Vanoss HS — 200/9-12
  4665 County Road 1555 74820 — 580-759-2503
  Gary Self, prin. — Fax 759-3080

East Central University — Post-Sec.
  1100 E 14th St 74820 — 580-332-8000
Valley View Regional Hospital — Post-Sec.
  430 N Monte Vista St 74820 — 580-332-2323

Adair, Mayes, Pop. 699
Adair ISD — 900/PK-12
  PO Box 197 74330 — 918-785-2424
  Tom Linihan, supt. — Fax 785-2491
  adairschools.org
Adair HS — 300/9-12
  PO Box 197 74330 — 918-785-2424
  Clifton Collins, prin. — Fax 785-2491

Adair MS — 200/6-8
  PO Box 197 74330 — 918-785-2425
  Richard Flanary, prin. — Fax 785-2491

Afton, Ottawa, Pop. 1,100
Afton ISD — 400/K-12
  PO Box 100 74331 — 918-257-8303
  Randy Gardner, supt. — Fax 257-4846
  www.aftonschools.net/
Afton HS — 100/9-12
  PO Box 100 74331 — 918-257-8305
  Alan Lauchner, prin. — Fax 257-4846

OK Dept. of Voc. & Tech. Education
  Supt. — None
Northeast Oklahoma Tech Center N Campus — Vo/Tech
  PO Box 219 74331 — 918-257-8324
  Charles Addington, prin. — Fax 257-4342

Agra, Lincoln, Pop. 357
Agra ISD — 400/PK-12
  PO Box 279 74824 — 918-375-2262
  Wesley McFarland, supt. — Fax 375-2263
  www.agra.k12.ok.us/
Agra HS — 100/9-12
  PO Box 279 74824 — 918-375-2261
  John Lazenby, prin. — Fax 375-2263

Alex, Grady, Pop. 642
Alex ISD — 400/K-12
  PO Box 188 73002 — 405-785-2605
  Norvel Heston, supt. — Fax 785-2914
  www.alex.k12.ok.us/
Alex JSHS — 200/7-12
  PO Box 188 73002 — 405-785-2264
  Tim Persinger, prin. — Fax 785-9976

Aline, Alfalfa, Pop. 205
Aline-Cleo ISD — 100/PK-12
  PO Box 49 73716 — 580-463-2255
  Dwayne Noble, supt. — Fax 463-2256
  www.alinecleo.k12.ok.us
Aline-Cleo Springs JSHS — 100/9-12
  PO Box 49 73716 — 580-463-2256
  Jim Patton, prin. — Fax 463-2256

Allen, Pontotoc, Pop. 948
Allen ISD — 400/PK-12
  PO Box 430 74825 — 580-857-2417
  David Lassiter, supt. — Fax 857-2636
  www.allen.k12.ok.us/
Allen HS — 100/9-12
  PO Box 430 74825 — 580-857-2416
  Rip Garcia, prin. — Fax 857-2636

Altus, Jackson, Pop. 20,559
Altus ISD — 4,300/PK-12
  PO Box 558 73522 — 580-481-2100
  Bob Drury, supt. — Fax 481-2129
  www.altusschools.k12.ok.us
Altus JHS — 600/8-9
  PO Box 558 73522 — 580-481-2173
  Roe Worbes, prin. — Fax 481-2547
Altus SHS — 900/10-12
  PO Box 558 73522 — 580-481-2167
  Mark Haught, prin. — Fax 481-2545

CareerTech Skills Centers
  Supt. — None
  Dom Garrison, supt.
Altus Skills Center — Vo/Tech
  PO Box 668 73522 — 580-477-1617

Navajo ISD — 500/K-12
  15695 S County Road 210 73521 — 580-482-7742
  Gary Montgomery, supt. — Fax 482-7749
  www.western.cc.ok.us/~navajo/
Navajo JSHS — 200/7-12
  15695 S County Road 210 73521 — 580-482-7742
  Floyd Roach, prin. — Fax 482-7749

OK Dept. of Voc. & Tech. Education
  Supt. — None
Southwest Technology Center — Vo/Tech
  711 W Tamarack Rd 73521 — 580-477-2250
  Dr. June Knight, supt. — Fax 477-0138

Western Oklahoma State College — Post-Sec.
  2801 N Main St 73521 — 580-477-2000

Alva, Woods, Pop. 5,034
Alva ISD — 1,000/PK-12
  418 Flynn St 73717 — 580-327-4823
  Don L. Rader, supt. — Fax 327-2965
  www.alvaschools.com
Alva HS — 300/9-12
  501 14th St 73717 — 580-327-3682
  Steve Parkhurst, prin. — Fax 327-4240
Alva MS — 200/6-8
  800 Flynn St 73717 — 580-327-0608
  Terry Conder, prin. — Fax 327-4255

CareerTech Skills Centers
  Supt. — None
  Dom Garrison, supt.
Alva Skills Center — Vo/Tech
  RR 1 Box 48 73717 — 580-327-0783

OK Dept. of Voc. & Tech. Education
  Supt. — None
Northwest Technology Center — Vo/Tech
  1801 11th St 73717 — 580-327-0344
  Freelin Roberts, supt. — Fax 327-5467

Northwestern Oklahoma State University — Post-Sec.
  709 Oklahoma Blvd 73717 — 580-327-1700

Amber, Grady, Pop. 510
Amber-Pocasset ISD — 400/PK-12
  PO Box 38 73004 — 405-224-5768
  Jack Jerman, supt. — Fax 224-5115
Amber-Pocasset JSHS — 200/7-12
  PO Box 38 73004 — 405-224-4017
  Jerry Gravlee, prin. — Fax 224-5115

Anadarko, Caddo, Pop. 6,539
Anadarko ISD — 2,700/PK-12
  1400 S Mission St 73005 — 405-247-6605
  Tom Cantrell, supt. — Fax 247-6819
Anadarko HS — 600/9-12
  1400 Warrior Dr 73005 — 405-247-2486
  Mary Swanson, prin. — Fax 247-7066
Anadarko MS — 500/6-8
  900 W College St 73005 — 405-247-6671
  Doug Hall, prin. — Fax 247-3666

Antlers, Pushmataha, Pop. 2,534
Antlers ISD 1,000/K-12
PO Box 627 74523 580-298-5504
Mark Virden, supt. Fax 298-4006
www.antlers.k12.ok.us
Antlers HS 300/9-12
PO Box 627 74523 580-298-2141
Bryan McNutt, prin. Fax 298-4019
Obuch MS 300/6-8
PO Box 627 74523 580-298-3308
Jerry Brown, prin. Fax 298-4012

Apache, Caddo, Pop. 1,598
Boone-Apache ISD 600/PK-12
PO Box 354 73006 580-588-3369
James Hooper, supt. Fax 588-3400
Apache HS 200/9-12
PO Box 354 73006 580-588-3358
Karen Rodenberg, prin. Fax 588-2079
Apache MS, PO Box 354 73006 100/7-8
Jayne Ivy, prin. 580-588-2122

Arapaho, Custer, Pop. 713
Arapaho ISD 300/PK-12
PO Box 160 73620 580-323-3261
Bob Haggard, supt. Fax 323-5886
www.arapaho.k12.ok.us/
Arapaho HS 100/9-12
PO Box 160 73620 580-323-3261
Ken Downs, prin. Fax 323-3469

Ardmore, Carter, Pop. 23,928
Ardmore ISD 3,000/PK-12
PO Box 1709 73402 580-226-7650
Dr. Ruth Ann Carr, supt. Fax 226-7652
www.ardmore.k12.ok.us
Ardmore HS 800/9-12
PO Box 1709 73402 580-226-7680
Shirley Morgan, prin. Fax 221-3012
Ardmore MS 600/6-8
PO Box 1709 73402 580-223-2475
Ron Beach, prin. Fax 221-3060

CareerTech Skills Centers
Supt. — None
Dom Garrison, supt.
Ardmore Skills Center Vo/Tech
204 Scenic State Highway 77 73401 580-223-4049

Dickson ISD 1,200/K-12
4762 State Highway 199 73401 580-223-9557
Sherry Howe, supt. Fax 223-7947
www.dickson.k12.ok.us/
Dickson HS 400/9-12
4762 State Highway 199 73401 580-226-0633
Mike Martin, prin. Fax 223-7011
Dickson JHS 200/7-8
4762 State Highway 199 73401 580-223-2700
Brad Jones, prin. Fax 223-7947

OK Dept. of Voc. & Tech. Education
Supt. — None
Southern Oklahoma Technology Center Vo/Tech
2610 Sam Noble Pkwy 73401 580-223-2070
Dr. Bob Gragg, supt. Fax 223-2120

Plainview ISD 1,300/PK-12
1140 S Plainview Rd 73401 580-223-6319
Steve Merlyn, supt. Fax 490-3190
www.plainview.k12.ok.us/
Plainview HS 300/9-12
1140 S Plainview Rd 73401 580-223-5877
Tim Parham, prin. Fax 490-3191
Plainview MS 300/6-8
1140 S Plainview Rd 73401 580-223-6502
Lisa Hartman, prin.

Ardmore Adventist Academy 50/1-12
154 Beaver Academy Rd 73401 580-223-4948
Oklahoma State Horseshoeing School Post-Sec.
4802 Dogwood Rd 73401 580-223-0064

Arkoma, LeFlore, Pop. 2,185
Arkoma ISD 400/K-12
PO Box 349 74901 918-875-3351
Katie Blagg, supt. Fax 875-3780
www.arkoma.k12.ok.us/
Arkoma HS 100/9-12
PO Box 349 74901 918-875-3353
Rita Pope, prin. Fax 875-3780

Arnett, Ellis, Pop. 505
Arnett ISD 200/PK-12
PO Box 317 73832 580-885-7811
Rusty Puffinbarger, supt. Fax 885-7922
www.arnett.k12.ok.us/
Arnett HS 50/9-12
PO Box 317 73832 580-885-7285
Bob Dobrinski, prin. Fax 885-7922

Asher, Pottawatomie, Pop. 430
Asher ISD, PO Box 168 74826 200/PK-12
Terry Grissom, supt. 405-784-2332
www.asher.k12.ok.us
Asher HS, PO Box 168 74826 100/9-12
Jamie Chambers, prin. 405-784-2331

Atoka, Atoka, Pop. 2,983
Atoka ISD 900/PK-12
PO Box 720 74525 580-889-6611
Mark McPherson, supt. Fax 889-2513
atoka.org
Atoka HS 400/9-12
PO Box 720 74525 580-889-3361
Brian Armstrong, prin. Fax 889-6453
McCall MS 200/6-8
PO Box 720 74525 580-889-5640
Chad Graham, prin. Fax 889-4064

OK Dept. of Voc. & Tech. Education
Supt. — None
Kiamichi Technology Center Vo/Tech
PO Box 240 74525 580-889-7321
Elaine Gee, dir. Fax 889-5642

Tushka ISD 400/PK-12
204 S Pecan St 74525 580-889-7355
Bill Pingleton, supt. Fax 889-6144
Tushka HS 100/9-12
204 S Pecan St 74525 580-889-7355
Matt Simpson, prin. Fax 889-6144

Balko, Beaver
Balko ISD 100/PK-12
RR 1 Box 37 73931 580-646-3385
Ricky McCullough, supt. Fax 646-3499
Balko HS 50/9-12
RR 1 Box 37 73931 580-646-3385
Ricky McCullough, prin. Fax 646-3499

Barnsdall, Osage, Pop. 1,289
Barnsdall ISD 400/K-12
PO Box 629 74002 918-847-2271
Rick Loggins, supt. Fax 847-3029
www.barnsdall.k12.ok.us/
Barnsdall HS, PO Box 629 74002 100/10-12
Sam Wofford, prin. 918-847-2721
Barnsdall JHS, PO Box 629 74002 100/7-9
Sam Wofford, prin. 918-847-2721

Bartlesville, Washington, Pop. 34,708
Bartlesville ISD 6,000/PK-12
PO Box 1357 74005 918-336-8600
Dr. Gary Quinn, supt. Fax 337-3643
www.bps-ok.org
Bartlesville Mid HS 1,000/9-10
PO Box 1357 74005 918-333-4444
Jason Langham, prin. Fax 335-6311
Bartlesville SHS 900/11-12
PO Box 1357 74005 918-336-3311
Chuck McCauley, prin. Fax 337-6226
Central MS 800/6-8
PO Box 1357 74005 918-336-9302
Greg Tackett, prin. Fax 337-6270
Madison MS 700/6-8
PO Box 1357 74005 918-333-3176
Lexie Radebaugh, prin. Fax 335-6377

OK Dept. of Voc. & Tech. Education
Supt. — None
Tri-County Technology Center Vo/Tech
6101 Nowata Rd 74006 918-333-2422
Anita Risner, supt. Fax 331-3274

Oklahoma Wesleyan University Post-Sec.
2201 Silver Lake Rd 74006 918-333-6151
Wesleyan Christian S 200/K-12
1780 Silver Lake Rd 74006 918-333-8631
Kevin Brown, prin. Fax 333-8632

Battiest, McCurtain
Battiest ISD 300/PK-12
PO Box 199 74722 580-241-7810
Stephen Lowrie, supt. Fax 241-7847
www.battiest.k12.ok.us/
Battiest HS 100/9-12
PO Box 199 74722 580-241-5550
Jon Holmes, prin. Fax 241-7847

Beaver, Beaver, Pop. 1,478
Beaver ISD 400/K-12
PO Box 580 73932 580-625-3444
Scott Kinsey, supt. Fax 625-3690
Beaver HS 100/9-12
PO Box 580 73932 580-625-3444
Michael McVay, prin. Fax 625-3690

Beggs, Okmulgee, Pop. 1,378
Beggs ISD 1,100/PK-12
1201 W 9th St 74421 918-267-3628
Marsha Norman, supt. Fax 267-3635
www.beggs.k12.ok.us
Beggs HS 300/9-12
1201 W 9th St 74421 918-267-3625
Merrill Masters, prin. Fax 267-3624
Beggs MS 300/5-8
1201 W 9th St 74421 918-267-4916
Cindy Swearingen, prin. Fax 267-4779

Bennington, Bryan, Pop. 293
Bennington ISD 200/K-12
PO Box 10 74723 580-847-2737
James Parrish, supt. Fax 847-2787
www.benningtonisd.org/
Bennington HS 100/9-12
PO Box 10 74723 580-847-2310
David Dewalt, prin. Fax 847-2787

Bethany, Oklahoma, Pop. 20,009
Bethany ISD 1,300/PK-12
6721 NW 42nd St 73008 405-789-3801
Dr. Kent Shellenberger, supt. Fax 499-4606
www.bps.k12.ok.us
Bethany HS 400/9-12
6721 NW 42nd St 73008 405-789-6370
Rocky George, prin. Fax 499-4634
Bethany MS, 6721 NW 42nd St 73008 300/6-8
Sherry Adkison, prin. 405-787-3240

Putnam City ISD
Supt. — See Oklahoma City
Western Oaks MS 600/6-8
7210 NW 23rd St 73008 405-789-4434
Lynette Thompson, prin. Fax 491-7616

Southern Nazarene University Post-Sec.
6729 NW 39th Expy 73008 405-789-6400
Southwestern Christian University Post-Sec.
PO Box 340 73008 405-789-7661

Billings, Noble, Pop. 560
Billings ISD 100/PK-12
PO Box 39 74630 580-725-3271
Les Justus, supt. Fax 725-3278
www.billings.k12.ok.us
Billings HS 50/9-12
PO Box 39 74630 580-725-3271
Les Justus, prin. Fax 725-3278

Binger, Caddo, Pop. 709
Binger-Oney ISD 300/K-12
PO Box 280 73009 405-656-2304
Sharon Kniffin, supt. Fax 656-2267
www.binger-oney.k12.ok.us/
Binger-Oney HS 100/9-12
PO Box 280 73009 405-656-2304
Kent Sexton, prin. Fax 656-2267

Bixby, Tulsa, Pop. 16,611
Bixby ISD 3,800/PK-12
109 N Armstrong St 74008 918-366-2200
Dr. Mary Jane Bias, supt. Fax 366-4241
www.bixbyps.org
Bixby HS 1,200/9-12
109 N Armstrong St 74008 918-366-2218
David Rickner, prin. Fax 366-2350
Bixby MS 600/7-8
109 N Armstrong St 74008 918-366-2203
Sean Spellecy, prin. Fax 366-2337

Blackwell, Kay, Pop. 7,423
Blackwell ISD 1,400/PK-12
201 E Blackwell Ave 74631 580-363-2570
Lesa Ward, supt. Fax 363-5513
www.blackwell.k12.ok.us/
Blackwell HS 400/9-12
303 E Coolidge Ave 74631 580-363-3542
Dan Bringham, prin. Fax 363-2133
Blackwell MS 300/6-8
1041 S 1st St 74631 580-363-2100
Eric Webb, prin. Fax 363-7010

Blair, Jackson, Pop. 850
Blair ISD 300/K-12
PO Box 428 73526 580-563-2632
Gary McLaughlin, supt. Fax 563-9166
www.blairschool.org
Blair HS 100/9-12
PO Box 428 73526 580-563-2486
Mike Rutherford, prin. Fax 563-9166

Blanchard, McClain, Pop. 3,178
Blanchard ISD 1,000/K-12
211 N Tyler Ave 73010 405-485-3391
Sandra Park, supt. Fax 485-2985
www.blanchard.k12.ok.us/
Blanchard IS 4-9
400 N Harrison Ave 73010 405-485-3396
Alan Schinnerer, prin.
Blanchard MS 300/6-8
400 N Harrison Ave 73010 405-485-3553
Jeff Funk, prin. Fax 485-9103
Blanchard SHS 300/10-12
400 N Harrison Ave 73010 405-485-3392
Glen Castle, prin. Fax 485-9549

Bridge Creek ISD 1,100/K-12
2209 E Sooner Rd 73010 405-387-4880
Terry Brown, supt. Fax 387-4882
www.bridgecreek.k12.ok.us/
Bridge Creek HS 300/9-12
2209 E Sooner Rd 73010 405-387-3981
K.B. Wedel, prin.
Bridge Creek MS 300/6-8
2209 E Sooner Rd 73010 405-387-9681
Dan Beck, prin.

Bluejacket, Craig, Pop. 273
Bluejacket ISD 200/PK-12
PO Box 29 74333 918-784-2365
Almeda Carroll, supt. Fax 784-2130
www.bluejacket.k12.ok.us
Bluejacket JSHS 100/6-12
PO Box 29 74333 918-784-2133
Marion Neighbors, prin. Fax 784-2130

Boise City, Cimarron, Pop. 1,384
Boise City ISD 300/K-12
PO Box 1116 73933 580-544-3110
Dan Faulkner, supt. Fax 544-2972
www.boisecity.k12.ok.us/
Boise City HS, PO Box 1115 73933 100/9-12
Kim Jenkins, prin. 580-544-3111

Bokchito, Bryan, Pop. 567
Rock Creek SD 500/PK-12
200 E Steakley St 74726 580-295-3137
Preston Burns, supt. Fax 295-3762
www.rockcreekisd.net
Rock Creek HS 100/9-12
200 E Steakley St 74726 580-295-3761
John Cartwright, prin. Fax 295-3854

Bokoshe, LeFlore, Pop. 457
Bokoshe ISD 300/PK-12
PO Box 158 74930 918-969-2491
Greg Fouse, supt. Fax 969-2493
www.bokoshe.k12.ok.us
Bokoshe HS, PO Box 158 74930 100/10-12
Dearl Tobey, prin. 918-969-2341
Bokoshe MS, PO Box 158 74930 100/7-9
Dearl Tobey, prin. 918-969-2341

Boley, Okfuskee, Pop. 1,110
Boley ISD 100/PK-12
PO Box 248 74829 918-667-3324
Gretana Gonzales, supt. Fax 667-3476
Boley HS 50/9-12
PO Box 248 74829 918-667-3324
Gretana Gonzales, prin. Fax 667-3476

CareerTech Skills Centers
Supt. — None
Dom Garrison, supt.
Boley Skills Center Vo/Tech
PO Box 1908 74829 918-667-3768

Boswell, Choctaw, Pop. 709
Boswell ISD 400/PK-12
PO Box 839 74727 580-566-2558
William Stokes, supt. Fax 566-2265
www.boswell.k12.ok.us/
Boswell HS 100/9-12
PO Box 839 74727 580-566-2735
Gerald Stegall, prin. Fax 566-2265

Boswell MS
  PO Box 839 74727   100/7-8
  John Jennings, prin.   580-566-2785
                                     Fax 566-2265

Bowlegs, Seminole, Pop. 369
  Bowlegs ISD, PO Box 88 74830   300/PK-12
  Bobbette Hamilton, supt.   405-398-4172
  www.bowlegs.k12.ok.us
  Bowlegs HS   100/9-12
  PO Box 88 74830   405-398-4321
  David Morris, prin.   Fax 398-4327

Boynton, Muskogee, Pop. 277
  Boynton-Moton ISD   200/PK-12
  PO Box 97 74422   918-472-7330
  Steve Henson, supt.   Fax 472-7410
  Boynton-Moton HS   100/9-12
  PO Box 97 74422   918-472-7310
  Gary Calip, prin.   Fax 472-7410

Braggs, Muskogee, Pop. 310
  Braggs ISD   200/PK-12
  PO Box 59 74423   918-487-5265
  Harry Atkins, supt.   Fax 487-7171
  www.braggs.k12.ok.us
  Braggs HS   100/9-12
  PO Box 59 74423   918-487-5265
  Chad Hance, prin.   Fax 487-7171

Braman, Kay, Pop. 237
  Braman ISD   100/K-12
  PO Box 130 74632   580-385-2191
  Mat Luse, supt.   Fax 385-2193
  Braman HS   50/9-12
  PO Box 130 74632   580-385-2191
  Mat Luse, prin.   Fax 385-2193

Bristow, Creek, Pop. 4,307
  Bristow ISD   1,700/PK-12
  134 W 9th Ave 74010   918-367-5555
  Dr. Jeanene Barnett, supt.   Fax 367-5848
  www.bristow.k12.ok.us
  Bristow HS   500/9-12
  134 W 9th Ave 74010   918-367-2241
  Curtis Shelton, prin.   Fax 367-5849
  Bristow MS   400/6-8
  134 W 9th Ave 74010   918-367-3551
  Brian Lomenick, prin.   Fax 367-1362

Broken Arrow, Tulsa, Pop. 83,607
  Broken Arrow ISD   15,100/PK-12
  601 S Main St 74012   918-259-4300
  Dr. Jim Sisney, supt.   Fax 258-0399
  www.ba.k12.ok.us
  Broken Arrow North Intermediate HS 1,100/9-10
  808 E College St 74012   918-259-4320
  Steven Nida, prin.   Fax 258-0796
  Broken Arrow SHS   2,100/11-12
  1901 E Albany St 74012   918-259-4310
  Rob Armstrong, prin.   Fax 355-3676
  Broken Arrow South Intermediate HS 1,100/9-10
  301 W New Orleans St 74011   918-259-4330
  Richard Dale, prin.   Fax 451-1964
  Centennial MS   700/6-8
  225 E Omaha St 74012   918-259-4340
  Amy Fichtner, prin.   Fax 251-8347
  Childers MS   700/6-8
  301 E Tucson St 74011   918-259-4350
  Elizabeth Burns, prin.   Fax 451-5465
  Haskell MS   800/6-8
  412 S 9th St 74012   918-259-4360
  Phil Tucker, prin.   Fax 251-8685
  Oliver MS   800/6-8
  3100 W New Orleans St 74011   918-259-4590
  Tom Sorrells, prin.   Fax 250-8185
  Sequoyah MS   600/6-8
  2701 S Elm Pl 74012   918-259-4370
  Dr. Lisa Lawrence, prin.   Fax 451-2167

  OK Dept. of Voc. & Tech. Education
  Supt. — None
  Tulsa Tech Center Broken Arrow Campus   Vo/Tech
  4600 S Olive Ave 74011   918-828-3000
  Brad Wayman, dir.   Fax 828-3009

  Union ISD
  Supt. — See Tulsa
  Union Eighth Grade Center   1,100/8-8
  6501 S Garnett Rd 74012   918-250-9541
  Tim Neller, prin.   Fax 461-3899
  Union Intermediate HS   2,100/9-10
  7616 S Garnett Rd 74012   918-254-8644
  John Chargois, prin.   Fax 252-4779
  ─────────────────────────
  Broken Arrow Beauty College   Post-Sec.
  400 S Elm Pl 74012   918-251-9660
  Grace Christian S   500/PK-12
  9610 S Garnett Rd 74012   918-249-9100
  Dr. Ken Stewart, supt.   Fax 317-5156
  Summit Christian Academy   400/K-12
  200 E Broadway St 74012   918-251-1997
  Jolinda Moss, prin.   Fax 251-5688

Broken Bow, McCurtain, Pop. 4,132
  Broken Bow ISD   1,800/PK-12
  108 W 5th St 74728   580-584-3306
  Carolyn Davis, supt.   Fax 584-9482
  www.bbisd.org
  Broken Bow HS   600/9-12
  108 W 5th St 74728   580-584-3365
  Daryl Williams, prin.   Fax 584-2064
  Rector Johnson MS   400/6-8
  108 W 5th St 74728   580-584-9603
  David Williams, prin.   Fax 584-2549

Buffalo, Harper, Pop. 1,139
  Buffalo ISD   200/K-12
  PO Box 130 73834   580-735-2419
  Terry Chapman, supt.   Fax 735-2619
  www.buffalo.k12.ok.us
  Buffalo S   200/K-12
  PO Box 130 73834   580-735-2448
  Sarah Yauk, prin.   Fax 735-2619

Burlington, Alfalfa, Pop. 152
  Burlington ISD   200/PK-12
  PO Box 17 73722   580-431-2501
  Glen Elliott, supt.   Fax 431-2237
  Burlington HS, PO Box 17 73722   100/9-12
  Darrel Humphries, prin.   580-431-2222

Burneyville, Love
  Turner ISD   300/PK-12
  PO Box 159 73430   580-276-2200
  James Gilmartin, supt.   Fax 276-2006
  www.turnerisd.org
  Turner HS, PO Box 159 73430   100/9-12
  Michael Palmer, prin.   580-276-3873

Burns Flat, Washita, Pop. 1,725
  Burns Flat-Dill City ISD   600/K-12
  PO Box 129 73624   580-562-4844
  Rick E. Garrison, supt.   Fax 562-4847
  Burns Flat-Dill City JSHS   300/7-12
  PO Box 129 73624   580-562-4846
  Joe Oliver, prin.

  OK Dept. of Voc. & Tech. Education
  Supt. — None
  Western Technology Center   Vo/Tech
  PO Box 1469 73624   580-562-3181
  Gene Orsack, supt.   Fax 562-4476

Butler, Custer, Pop. 329
  Butler ISD   100/PK-12
  PO Box 127 73625   580-664-3295
  Rod McDonald, supt.   Fax 664-5286
  www.butler.k12.ok.us/
  Butler HS   50/9-12
  PO Box 127 73625   580-664-3295
  Leon Beall, prin.   Fax 664-5286

Cache, Comanche, Pop. 2,397
  Cache ISD   1,300/PK-12
  201 W H Ave 73527   580-429-3266
  Randy Batt, supt.   Fax 429-3271
  www.cache.k12.ok.us
  Cache HS, 201 W H Ave 73527   400/9-12
  Gary Michael, prin.   580-429-3214
  Cache MS, 201 W H Ave 73527   300/6-8
  Debbie Hoffman, prin.   580-429-8489

Caddo, Bryan, Pop. 950
  Caddo ISD   400/PK-12
  PO Box 128 74729   580-367-2208
  Richard Thomas, supt.   Fax 367-2837
  www.caddoisd.org
  Caddo HS   100/9-12
  PO Box 128 74729   580-367-2208
  Patrick Mitchell, prin.   Fax 367-2837

Calera, Bryan, Pop. 1,767
  Calera ISD   600/PK-12
  PO Box 386 74730   580-434-5700
  Aaron Newcomb, supt.   Fax 434-5800
  www.caleraisd.k12.ok.us
  Calera HS, PO Box 386 74730   200/9-12
  Karen Hughes, prin.   580-434-5158

Calumet, Canadian, Pop. 520
  Calumet ISD   200/K-12
  PO Box 10 73014   405-893-2222
  Keith Weldon, supt.   Fax 893-8019
  Calumet HS   100/9-12
  PO Box 10 73014   405-893-2222
  Jimmie Smith, prin.   Fax 893-8019
  Calumet JHS   50/7-8
  PO Box 10 73014   405-893-2222
  Jimmie Smith, prin.   Fax 893-8019

Calvin, Hughes, Pop. 271
  Calvin ISD   200/PK-12
  PO Box 127 74531   405-645-2411
  Jon Tuck, supt.   Fax 645-2384
  www.calvin.k12.ok.us
  Calvin HS   100/9-12
  PO Box 127 74531   405-645-2411
  Curtis Fitzgerald, prin.   Fax 645-2384

Cameron, LeFlore, Pop. 317
  Cameron ISD   500/PK-12
  PO Box 190 74932   918-654-3225
  Dennis Shoup, supt.   Fax 654-7387
  www.cameron.k12.ok.us/
  Cameron HS   200/9-12
  PO Box 190 74932   918-654-3412
  Carolyn White, prin.   Fax 654-3826

Canadian, Pittsburg, Pop. 240
  Canadian ISD   400/PK-12
  PO Box 168 74425   918-339-7251
  Rodney Karch, supt.   Fax 339-2393
  Canadian HS, PO Box 168 74425   100/9-12
  Bud Rattan, prin.   918-339-2705

Caney, Atoka, Pop. 203
  Caney ISD   200/PK-12
  PO Box 60 74533   580-889-1996
  Tommy Johnson, supt.   Fax 889-5033
  www.caneyisd.org/
  Caney HS   100/9-12
  PO Box 60 74533   580-889-6607
  Phil Daniel, prin.   Fax 889-7922

Canton, Blaine, Pop. 597
  Canton ISD   400/PK-12
  PO Box 639 73724   580-886-3516
  Gayle Hajny, supt.   Fax 886-3501
  www.canton.k12.ok.us
  Canton HS, PO Box 639 73724   100/9-12
  DeWayne Sinclair, prin.   580-886-2256

Canute, Washita, Pop. 514
  Canute ISD   200/K-12
  PO Box 490 73626   580-472-3295
  Mike Maddox, supt.   Fax 472-3187
  Canute HS   100/9-12
  PO Box 490 73626   580-472-3782
  Kevin Merz, prin.   Fax 472-3187

Carnegie, Caddo, Pop. 1,593
  Carnegie ISD   600/K-12
  RR 2 Box 67 73015   580-654-1470
  Donny Darrow, supt.   Fax 654-1644
  www.carnegieschools.com
  Carnegie JHS, RR 2 Box 67 73015   100/7-9
  Donny Darrow, dean   580-654-1766
  Carnegie SHS   200/10-12
  RR 2 Box 67 73015   580-654-1266
  Lonnie Bliss, prin.   Fax 654-2772

Carney, Lincoln, Pop. 647
  Carney ISD   200/PK-12
  PO Box 240 74832   405-865-2344
  Dewayne Osborn, supt.   Fax 865-2345
  Carney HS, PO Box 240 74832   100/9-12
  Kimberly Powell, prin.   405-865-2344

Cashion, Kingfisher, Pop. 652
  Cashion ISD   400/K-12
  PO Box 100 73016   405-433-2741
  Greg Holleyman, supt.   Fax 433-2646
  Cashion HS   100/9-12
  PO Box 100 73016   405-433-2575
  Bill Hoots, prin.   Fax 433-2646

Catoosa, Rogers, Pop. 5,838
  Catoosa SD   2,300/PK-12
  2000 S Cherokee St 74015   918-266-8603
  Larry Cale, supt.   Fax 266-1525
  www.catoosa.k12.ok.us
  Catoosa HS   700/9-12
  2000 S Cherokee St 74015   918-266-8619
  Connie Cypert, prin.   Fax 266-1486
  Wells MS   500/6-8
  2000 S Cherokee St 74015   918-266-8623
  George Linihan, prin.   Fax 266-1282

Cement, Caddo, Pop. 522
  Cement ISD   200/PK-12
  PO Box 60 73017   405-489-3216
  Connie Claborn, supt.   Fax 489-3219
  Cement HS   100/9-12
  PO Box 60 73017   405-489-3218
  Marion Claborn, prin.   Fax 489-3219

Chandler, Lincoln, Pop. 2,824
  Chandler ISD   1,200/PK-12
  901 S CHS 74834   405-258-1450
  Don Gray, supt.   Fax 258-2657
  www.chandler.k12.ok.us/
  Chandler HS   300/9-12
  901 S CHS 74834   405-258-1269
  Joe Telford, prin.   Fax 240-5715
  Chandler JHS   200/7-8
  901 S CHS 74834   405-258-0183
  Mark Howard, prin.   Fax 258-1850

Chattanooga, Comanche, Pop. 434
  Chattanooga ISD   300/PK-12
  PO Box 129 73528   580-597-3347
  Chuck Hood, supt.   Fax 597-3344
  www.chatty.k12.ok.us/
  Chattanooga HS, PO Box 129 73528   100/9-12
  Jerry Brown, prin.   580-597-3347

Checotah, McIntosh, Pop. 3,484
  Checotah ISD   1,500/PK-12
  PO Box 289 74426   918-473-5610
  Robert Bible, supt.   Fax 473-1020
  Checotah HS   400/9-12
  PO Box 289 74426   918-473-2239
  Pam Keeter, prin.   Fax 473-2532
  Checotah MS   300/7-8
  PO Box 289 74426   918-473-5912
  Brian Terry, prin.   Fax 473-1020

Chelsea, Rogers, Pop. 2,213
  Chelsea ISD   1,100/PK-12
  206 E 4th St 74016   918-789-2528
  Mike Martin, supt.   Fax 789-3271
  www.chelseadragons.net
  Chelsea HS, 206 E 4th St 74016   300/9-12
  Paul Gruenberg, prin.   918-789-2533
  Chelsea JHS, 206 E 4th St 74016   200/7-8
  Meg Moss, prin.   918-789-2521

Cherokee, Alfalfa, Pop. 1,559
  Cherokee ISD   400/PK-12
  PO Box 325 73728   580-596-3391
  Lance Miller, supt.   Fax 596-2217
  Cherokee HS, PO Box 325 73728   100/9-12
  Darral Barnett, prin.   580-596-3391

Cheyenne, Roger Mills, Pop. 714
  Cheyenne ISD   200/K-12
  PO Box 650 73628   580-497-2666
  Alton Rawlins, supt.   Fax 497-3373
  www.cheyenne.k12.ok.us
  Cheyenne HS, PO Box 650 73628   100/9-12
  Phillip Butler, prin.   580-497-3371

Chickasha, Grady, Pop. 16,345
  Chickasha ISD   2,800/PK-12
  900 W Choctaw Ave 73018   405-222-6500
  Jim Glaze, supt.   Fax 222-6590
  chickasha.ok.schoolwebpages.com
  Chickasha HS   900/9-12
  900 W Choctaw Ave 73018   405-222-6550
  Beth Reigh-Edwards, prin.   Fax 222-6558
  Chickasha MS   600/6-8
  900 W Choctaw Ave 73018   405-222-6530
  Debra Reynolds, prin.   Fax 222-6594

  OK Dept. of Voc. & Tech. Education
  Supt. — None
  Canadian Valley Technology Center   Vo/Tech
  1401 W Michigan Ave 73018   405-224-7220
  Dr. Earl Cowan, supt.   Fax 222-3839
  ─────────────────────────
  Academy of Cosmetology   Post-Sec.
  607 W Grand Ave 73018   405-222-2323
  University of Sciences & Arts of OK Post-Sec.
  PO Box 82345 73018   405-224-3140

Choctaw, Oklahoma, Pop. 10,156
Choctaw/Nicoma Park ISD 4,500/PK-12
12880 NE 10th St 73020 405-769-4859
Dr. Jim McCharen, supt. Fax 769-9821
www.cnpschools.org
Choctaw HS 1,100/10-12
14300 NE 10th St 73020 405-390-8899
Donny Black, prin. Fax 390-2275
Choctaw JHS 600/7-9
14667 NE 3rd St 73020 405-390-2207
JeanAnn Gaona, prin. Fax 390-4439
Nicoma Park JHS 500/7-9
1321 Hickman Ave 73020 405-769-3106
David Reid, prin. Fax 769-9355

OK Dept. of Voc. & Tech. Education
Supt. — None
Eastern Oklahoma County Technology Ctr Vo/Tech
4601 N Choctaw Rd 73020 405-390-9591
Dr. Terry Underwood, supt. Fax 390-9598

Chouteau, Mayes, Pop. 1,958
Chouteau-Mazie ISD 1,100/PK-12
PO Box 969 74337 918-476-8336
Tom Turner, supt. Fax 476-8538
Chouteau-Mazie HS 300/9-12
PO Box 969 74337 918-476-8336
Donny Trammell, prin. Fax 476-8372
Chouteau-Mazie MS 200/6-8
PO Box 969 74337 918-476-8336
Charles Arnall, prin. Fax 476-8306

Claremore, Rogers, Pop. 16,773
Claremore ISD 4,100/PK-12
310 N Weenonah Ave 74017 918-699-7300
J. Michael McClaren, supt. Fax 341-8447
www.claremore.k12.ok.us
Claremore HS 1,200/9-12
1910 N Florence Ave 74017 918-341-0724
Fax 343-6331
Rogers JHS 600/7-8
1915 N Florence Ave 74017 918-341-7411
Terry Adams, prin. Fax 343-6332

Sequoyah ISD 1,400/PK-12
16441 S 4180 Rd 74017 918-341-5472
Terry Saul, supt. Fax 341-5764
www.sequoyaheagles.net
Sequoyah MS 300/7-9
16405 S 4180 Rd 74017 918-341-5537
Troy Steidley, prin. Fax 343-8102
Sequoyah SHS 300/10-12
16401 S 4180 Rd 74017 918-341-0642
Steve Johnson, prin. Fax 343-8105

Verdigris ISD 1,100/PK-12
8104 E 540 Rd, 918-266-7227
Michael Payne, supt. Fax 266-3910
vps.k12.ok.us
Verdigris HS 300/9-12
8104 E 540 Rd, 918-266-2336
Randall Risenhoover, prin. Fax 266-3910
Verdigris MS 300/5-8
8104 E 540 Rd, 918-266-6343
Steve Perdue, prin. Fax 266-1554

Claremore Beauty College Post-Sec.
200 N Cherokee Ave 74017 918-341-4370
Claremore Christian S 100/PK-12
1055 W Blue Starr Dr 74017 918-341-1805
Ryan Mullins, prin. Fax 341-1011
Rogers State University Post-Sec.
1701 W Will Rogers Blvd 74017 918-343-7777

Clarita, Coal
Olney ISD 100/PK-12
PO Box 129 74535 580-428-3293
Jerry Romines, supt. Fax 428-3310
www.olney.k12.ok.us/
Olney HS 50/9-12
PO Box 129 74535 580-428-3293
Jerry Romines, prin. Fax 428-3310

Clayton, Pushmataha, Pop. 728
Clayton ISD 400/PK-12
PO Box 190 74536 918-569-4492
Frank Kirchoffner, supt. Fax 569-7757
www.clayton.k12.ok.us
Clayton HS 200/9-12
PO Box 190 74536 918-569-4156
Jim Dominick, prin. Fax 569-4680

Cleveland, Pawnee, Pop. 3,241
Cleveland ISD 1,700/PK-12
600 N Gilbert Ave 74020 918-358-2210
Dennis Smith, supt. Fax 358-3071
www.clevelandtigers.com/
Cleveland HS 500/9-12
323 N Gilbert Ave 74020 918-358-2210
Alan Baker, prin. Fax 358-2141
Cleveland MS 400/6-8
322 N Gilbert Ave 74020 918-358-2210
Noel Nation, prin. Fax 358-2534

Clinton, Custer, Pop. 8,364
Clinton ISD 1,800/PK-12
PO Box 729 73601 580-323-1800
Perry Adams, supt. Fax 323-1804
www.clinton.k12.ok.us/
Clinton HS 500/9-12
PO Box 729 73601 580-323-1230
Steve Hill, prin. Fax 323-1236
Clinton MS 300/7-8
PO Box 729 73601 580-323-4228
Peggy Constien, prin. Fax 323-3896

Coalgate, Coal, Pop. 1,956
Coalgate ISD 700/PK-12
PO Box 368 74538 580-927-2351
Joe A. McCulley, supt. Fax 927-2694
www.coalgateschools.org
Byrd MS 100/7-8
PO Box 368 74538 580-927-3560
Adam Beauchamp, prin. Fax 927-4031
Coalgate HS 200/9-12
PO Box 368 74538 580-927-2592
Jim Girten, prin. Fax 927-4020

Colbert, Bryan, Pop. 1,085
Colbert ISD 800/PK-12
PO Box 310 74733 580-296-2624
Jarvis Dobbs, supt. Fax 296-2088
www.colbert.k12.ok.us/
Colbert HS, PO Box 310 74733 200/9-12
William Goodson, prin. 580-296-2590
Colbert MS, PO Box 310 74733 100/7-8
Andy Goodson, prin. 580-296-2590

Colcord, Delaware, Pop. 857
Colcord ISD 600/PK-12
PO Box 188 74338 918-326-4116
Kelly Hampton, supt. Fax 326-4471
Colcord HS 300/9-12
PO Box 188 74338 918-326-4107
Jerry Swank, prin. Fax 326-4493
Colcord MS 6-8
PO Box 188 74338 918-326-4852
Robert Hampton, prin. Fax 326-4468

Coleman, Johnston
Coleman ISD 200/PK-12
PO Box 188 73432 580-937-4418
Rick Webb, supt. Fax 937-4866
Coleman HS 100/9-12
PO Box 188 73432 580-937-4418
Rick Webb, prin. Fax 937-4866

Collinsville, Tulsa, Pop. 4,263
Collinsville ISD 2,200/PK-12
1119 W Broadway St 74021 918-371-2386
Pat Herald, supt. Fax 371-4285
www.collinsville.k12.ok.us/
Collinsville HS 600/9-12
2400 W Broadway St 74021 918-371-3382
Cory Slagle, prin. Fax 371-6904
Collinsville MS 500/6-8
1424 W Spring St 74021 918-371-2541
Kelly Hamlin, prin. Fax 371-1302

Comanche, Stephens, Pop. 1,502
Comanche ISD 1,000/K-12
1030 Ash Ave 73529 580-439-2900
Terry Davidson, supt. Fax 439-2907
Comanche HS 300/9-12
1030 Ash Ave 73529 580-439-2933
Steven Dunham, prin. Fax 439-2950
Comanche MS 200/6-8
1030 Ash Ave 73529 580-439-2922
Steven Dunham, prin. Fax 439-2979

Commerce, Ottawa, Pop. 2,581
Commerce ISD 800/PK-12
420 D St 74339 918-675-4316
Jim Haynes, supt. Fax 675-4464
www.commercetigers.net
Commerce HS 200/9-12
420 D St 74339 918-675-4343
Jim Buttram, prin. Fax 675-4682
Commerce MS 200/6-8
500 Commerce St 74339 918-675-4101
Herb Logan, prin. Fax 675-5353

Copan, Washington, Pop. 805
Copan ISD 400/PK-12
PO Box 429 74022 918-532-4490
Steve Stanley, supt. Fax 532-4568
www.copan.k12.ok.us/
Copan HS, PO Box 429 74022 200/9-12
Jay Vernon, prin. 918-532-4344

Cordell, Washita, Pop. 2,809
Cordell ISD 600/PK-12
PO Box 290 73632 580-832-3420
Tim Puett, supt. Fax 832-4108
www.cordell.k12.ok.us
Cordell JHS, PO Box 290 73632 100/7-9
Larry R. Johnson, prin. 580-832-2233
Cordell SHS, PO Box 290 73632 100/10-12
Larry R. Johnson, prin. 580-832-3432

Corn, Washita, Pop. 571
Washita Heights ISD 200/PK-12
PO Box 8 73024 580-343-2228
Tim Merchant, supt. Fax 343-2259
whchiefs.k12.ok.us
Washita Heights HS 100/9-12
PO Box 8 73024 580-343-2298
Jim Shelton, prin. Fax 343-2259

Corn Bible Academy 100/7-12
PO Box 38 73024 580-343-2262
Mark Thiessen, prin. Fax 343-2261

Council Hill, Muskogee, Pop. 129
Midway ISD 200/PK-12
PO Box 127 74428 918-474-3434
Don Ford, supt. Fax 474-3636
Midway HS 100/9-12
PO Box 127 74428 918-474-3434
Curt Been, prin. Fax 474-3636

Covington, Garfield, Pop. 545
Covington-Douglas ISD 300/PK-12
PO Box 9 73730 580-864-7481
Sam McElvany, supt. Fax 864-7644
www.c-d.k12.ok.us
Covington-Douglas HS 100/9-12
PO Box 9 73730 580-864-7482
Dena Stewart, prin. Fax 864-7644

Coweta, Wagoner, Pop. 7,781
Coweta ISD 2,700/PK-12
PO Box 550 74429 918-486-6506
Sean McDaniel, supt. Fax 486-4167
www.cowetaps.com/
Coweta JHS 600/7-9
PO Box 550 74429 918-486-2127
Mike Lingo, prin. Fax 486-7307
Coweta SHS 500/10-12
PO Box 550 74429 918-486-4474
Randy Craven, prin. Fax 486-1062

Coyle, Logan, Pop. 346
Coyle ISD 400/PK-12
PO Box 287 73027 405-466-2242
Rick Kibbe, supt. Fax 466-2448
www.coyle.k12.ok.us
Coyle HS 100/9-12
PO Box 287 73027 405-466-2242
Trina Liles, prin. Fax 466-2448

Crescent, Logan, Pop. 1,293
Crescent ISD 600/PK-12
PO Box 719 73028 405-969-3738
Steve Shiever, supt. Fax 969-2003
www.crescentok.com/
Crescent HS 200/9-12
PO Box 719 73028 405-969-2545
Rick McCombs, prin. Fax 969-2003
Crescent JHS 100/6-8
PO Box 719 73028 405-969-2545
Wayne Owens, prin. Fax 969-2003

Cromwell, Seminole, Pop. 261
Butner ISD 300/PK-12
PO Box 157 74837 405-944-5530
Gary D. Pollard, supt. Fax 944-5746
Butner HS 100/9-12
PO Box 157 74837 405-944-5526
Randy Wassam, prin. Fax 944-5746

Crowder, Pittsburg, Pop. 437
Crowder ISD 400/PK-12
PO Box B 74430 918-334-3203
David Jones, supt. Fax 334-3295
Crowder HS, PO Box B 74430 100/9-12
Jennifer Smith, prin. 918-334-3204

Cushing, Payne, Pop. 8,510
Cushing ISD 1,800/PK-12
PO Box 1609 74023 918-225-3425
Eddie L. Williams, supt. Fax 225-5256
Cushing HS, 1700 E Walnut St 74023 500/9-12
James Lauerman, prin. 918-225-6622
Cushing MS, 316 N Steele Ave 74023 400/6-8
Terry Morgan, prin. 918-225-1311

Cyril, Caddo, Pop. 1,165
Cyril ISD 400/K-12
PO Box 449 73029 580-464-2419
Jim Conger, supt. Fax 464-2445
Cyril HS 100/9-12
PO Box 449 73029 580-464-2272
R. Joe Kelsey, prin. Fax 464-2445

Dale, Pottawatomie, Pop. 100
Dale ISD 700/PK-12
300 Smith Ave 74851 405-964-5558
Charles Dickinson, supt. Fax 964-5559
www.dale.k12.ok.us
Dale JSHS 300/7-12
300 Smith Ave 74851 405-964-5555
Harold Jones, prin. Fax 964-5539

Davenport, Lincoln, Pop. 878
Davenport ISD 400/PK-12
PO Box 849 74026 918-377-2277
John Greenfield, supt. Fax 377-2553
www.davenport.k12.ok.us/
Davenport HS 100/9-12
PO Box 849 74026 918-377-2278
Daniel Accord, prin. Fax 377-2553

Davidson, Tillman, Pop. 361
Davidson ISD 100/PK-12
PO Box 338 73530 580-568-2423
Phillip Ratcliff, supt. Fax 568-2423
Davidson HS 50/9-12
PO Box 338 73530 580-568-2261
Phillip Ratcliff, prin. Fax 568-2423

Davis, Murray, Pop. 2,609
Davis ISD 900/K-12
400 E Atlanta Ave 73030 580-369-2386
Monte Thompson, supt. Fax 369-3507
www.davis.k12.ok.us/
Davis HS 300/9-12
400 E Atlanta Ave 73030 580-369-5541
Jack Kapella, prin. Fax 369-3071
Davis MS 300/5-8
400 E Atlanta Ave 73030 580-369-5565
Sheri Knight, prin. Fax 369-3289

Del City, Oklahoma, Pop. 22,171
Midwest City-Del City ISD
Supt. — See Midwest City
Del City SHS 1,100/10-12
1900 S Sunnylane Rd 73115 405-677-5777
Annette Nantois, prin. Fax 671-8675
Del Crest JHS 500/7-9
4731 Judy Dr 73115 405-671-8615
Jason Brown, prin. Fax 671-8618
Kerr JHS 700/7-9
2300 Linda Ln 73115 405-671-8625
Brian Eccellente, prin. Fax 671-8626

Christian Heritage Academy 600/PK-12
4400 SE 27th St 73115 405-672-1787
Ralph Bullard, hdmstr. Fax 672-1839
Mid-Del Christian S 400/PK-12
PO Box 15300, Oklahoma City OK 73155
405-677-6000
Jim Howard, admin. Fax 677-6066

Depew, Creek, Pop. 568
Depew ISD 300/PK-12
PO Box 257 74028 918-324-5466
Bruce Terronez, supt. Fax 324-5336
Depew HS 200/9-12
PO Box 257 74028 918-324-5543
Bruce McKinzie, prin. Fax 324-5336

Dewar, Okmulgee, Pop. 913
Dewar ISD ... 400/PK-12
  PO Box 790 74431 ... 918-652-9625
  Billy Green, supt. ... Fax 652-3096
  www.dewar.k12.ok.us/
Dewar HS ... 100/9-12
  PO Box 790 74431 ... 918-652-9625
  Todd Been, prin. ... Fax 652-3096
Dewar MS ... 6-8
  PO Box 790 74431 ... 918-652-9625
  Kate McDonald, prin. ... Fax 652-3096

Dewey, Washington, Pop. 3,296
Dewey ISD ... 1,100/K-12
  1 Bulldogger Rd 74029 ... 918-534-2241
  Paul Smith, supt. ... Fax 534-0149
  www.dewey.k12.ok.us
Dewey HS, 1 Bulldogger Rd 74029 ... 400/9-12
  Jack Golden, prin. ... 918-534-0933
Dewey MS, 1 Bulldogger Rd 74029 ... 300/6-8
  Leta Moreland, prin. ... 918-534-0111

Dibble, McClain, Pop. 288
Dibble ISD ... 600/PK-12
  PO Box 9 73031 ... 405-344-6375
  Bill Bentley, supt. ... Fax 344-6977
  www.dibble.k12.ok.us
Dibble HS, PO Box 9 73031 ... 200/9-12
  Chad Clanton, prin. ... 405-344-6380

Dover, Kingfisher, Pop. 363
Dover ISD ... 200/PK-12
  PO Box 195 73734 ... 405-828-4206
  Floyd Kirk, supt. ... Fax 828-7150
  www.dover.k12.ok.us
Dover S ... 200/PK-12
  PO Box 195 73734 ... 405-828-4205
  Wade Detrick, prin. ... Fax 828-8019

Drummond, Garfield, Pop. 393
Drummond ISD ... 300/PK-12
  PO Box 240 73735 ... 580-493-2216
  Denver Rowley, supt. ... Fax 493-2273
  www.drummond.k12.ok.us/
Drummond HS, PO Box 240 73735 ... 100/9-12
  Denver Rowley, prin. ... 580-493-2271

Drumright, Creek, Pop. 2,886
Drumright SD ... 700/PK-12
  301 S Pennsylvania Ave 74030 ... 918-352-2492
  H T Gee, supt. ... Fax 352-4430
  www.drumright.k12.ok.us/
Drumright HS ... 200/9-12
  301 S Pennsylvania Ave 74030 ... 918-352-2152
  Jim Frazier, prin. ... Fax 352-9845
Edison MS, 300 E Pine St 74030 ... 200/6-8
  Beverly Carlile, prin. ... 918-352-2318

OK Dept. of Voc. & Tech. Education
  Supt. — None
Central Tech ... Vo/Tech
  3 Central Tech Cir 74030 ... 918-352-2551
  Phil Waul, supt. ... Fax 352-2441

Olive ISD ... 400/PK-12
  9352 S 436th West Ave 74030 ... 918-352-9567
  Charles Lewis, supt. ... Fax 352-4379
  www.olive.k12.ok.us/
Olive HS ... 100/9-12
  9352 S 436th West Ave 74030 ... 918-352-9568
  Sam Ahtone, prin.

Duke, Jackson, Pop. 392
Duke ISD ... 200/PK-12
  PO Box 160 73532 ... 580-679-3014
  Steven Peretto, supt. ... Fax 679-3017
  www.dukeschools.com/
Duke HS, PO Box 160 73532 ... 100/9-12
  Kevin Cansler, prin. ... 580-679-3311

Duncan, Stephens, Pop. 22,031
Duncan ISD ... 3,400/PK-12
  PO Box 1548 73534 ... 580-255-0686
  Dr. Sherry Labyer, supt. ... Fax 252-2453
  www.duncanpublicschools.org
Duncan HS ... 1,100/9-12
  PO Box 1548 73534 ... 580-255-0700
  Gary Reed, prin. ... Fax 252-2445
Duncan MS ... 800/6-8
  PO Box 1548 73534 ... 580-470-8106
  Mike Toone, prin. ... Fax 470-8743

Empire ISD ... 600/PK-12
  9450 W Cherokee Rd 73533 ... 580-252-5392
  Jim Motes, supt. ... Fax 252-4231
  www.empireschools.org
Empire HS ... 200/9-12
  9450 W Cherokee Rd 73533 ... 580-255-7515
  Robert Grider, prin.

OK Dept. of Voc. & Tech. Education
  Supt. — None
Red River Technology Center ... Vo/Tech
  PO Box 1807 73534 ... 580-255-2903
  Jerry Morris, supt. ... Fax 255-0491

Durant, Bryan, Pop. 14,565
Durant ISD ... 3,000/PK-12
  PO Box 1160 74702 ... 580-924-1276
  Terry James Ph.D., supt. ... Fax 924-6019
  www.durantisd.org
Durant HS ... 900/9-12
  802 W Walnut St 74701 ... 580-924-4424
  Steve Wlodarczyk, supt. ... Fax 924-3642
Durant MS ... 500/7-8
  410 N 6th Ave 74701 ... 580-924-1321
  Jim Corley, prin. ... Fax 924-8278

OK Dept. of Voc. & Tech. Education
  Supt. — None
Kiamichi Technology Center ... Vo/Tech
  810 Waldron Dr 74701 ... 580-924-7081
  Michael Goodwin, dir. ... Fax 924-2790

Silo ISD ... 600/PK-12
  122 W Bourne St 74701 ... 580-924-7003
  Tim Smith, supt. ... Fax 920-7988
  www.siloisd.org
Silo JSHS ... 200/7-12
  122 W Bourne St 74701 ... 580-924-7000
  Ron Slawson, prin. ... Fax 924-7045

Southeastern Oklahoma State University ... Post-Sec.
  Station A 74701 ... 580-924-0121
Southern School of Beauty ... Post-Sec.
  140 W Main St 74701 ... 580-924-1049
Victory Life Academy ... 300/K-12
  3412 W University Blvd 74701 ... 580-920-0850
  Ron Craig, prin. ... Fax 920-1794

Dustin, Hughes, Pop. 448
Dustin ISD ... 100/PK-12
  PO Box 390660 74839 ... 918-656-3230
  Kelly Berry, supt. ... Fax 656-3242
  www.dustin.k12.ok.us/
Dustin HS, PO Box 390660 74839 ... 50/9-12
  Kevin Weiher, prin. ... 918-656-3230

Eagletown, McCurtain
Eagletown ISD ... 300/PK-12
  PO Box 38 74734 ... 580-835-2242
  Kent Hendon, supt. ... Fax 835-7420
Eagletown HS ... 100/9-12
  PO Box 38 74734 ... 580-835-2242
  Mike Bryan, prin. ... Fax 835-7420

Earlsboro, Pottawatomie, Pop. 653
Earlsboro ISD ... 200/K-12
  PO Box 10 74840 ... 405-997-5616
  Wade Stafford, supt. ... Fax 997-3181
Earlsboro HS ... 100/9-12
  PO Box 10 74840 ... 405-997-5252
  Mark Maloy, prin. ... Fax 997-3181

Edmond, Oklahoma, Pop. 71,643
Deer Creek ISD ... 2,000/K-12
  20825 N MacArthur Blvd 73003 ... 405-348-6100
  Kaye Jones, supt. ... Fax 348-3049
  www.deercreek.k12.ok.us
Deer Creek HS ... 600/9-12
  6101 NW 206th St 73003 ... 405-348-5720
  Richard Vrooman, prin. ... Fax 359-3155
Deer Creek MS ... 500/6-8
  21175 N Macarthur Blvd 73003 ... 405-348-4830
  Toni Jones, prin. ... Fax 359-3163

Edmond ISD ... 17,700/PK-12
  1001 W Danforth Rd 73003 ... 405-340-2800
  Dr. David Goin, supt. ... Fax 340-2835
  www.edmondschools.net/
Central MS ... 900/6-8
  500 E 9th St 73034 ... 405-340-2890
  Tara Fair, prin. ... Fax 340-3961
Cheyenne MS ... 800/6-8
  1271 W Covell Rd 73003 ... 405-330-7380
  Dr. Debbie Bendick, prin. ... Fax 330-7397
Cimarron MS ... 700/6-8
  3701 S Bryant Ave 73013 ... 405-340-2935
  Joe Fine, prin. ... Fax 330-3398
Edmond Memorial HS ... 2,000/9-12
  1000 E 15th St 73013 ... 405-340-2850
  Kyle Heath, prin. ... Fax 340-2856
Edmond North HS ... 2,000/9-12
  215 W Danforth Rd 73003 ... 405-340-2875
  Dr. Ed Story, prin. ... Fax 330-7349
Edmond Santa Fe HS ... 1,800/9-12
  1901 W 15th St 73013 ... 405-340-2230
  Vickie Simpson, prin. ... Fax 340-2240
Sequoyah MS ... 900/6-8
  1125 E Danforth Rd 73034 ... 405-340-2900
  Jeff Edwards, prin. ... Fax 340-2909
Summit MS ... 700/6-8
  1703 NW 150th St 73013 ... 405-340-2920
  Desarae Witmer, prin. ... Fax 340-2933

Oklahoma Christian S ... 800/PK-12
  PO Box 509 73083 ... 405-341-2265
  Dallas Caldwell, hdmstr. ... Fax 341-4710
University of Central Oklahoma ... Post-Sec.
  100 N University Dr 73034 ... 405-974-2000

Eldorado, Jackson, Pop. 504
Eldorado ISD ... 100/PK-12
  PO Box J 73537 ... 580-633-2219
  Mark Baumann, supt. ... Fax 633-2316
Eldorado HS ... 50/9-12
  PO Box J 73537 ... 580-633-2219
  Jackie Kenmore, prin. ... Fax 633-2316

Elgin, Comanche, Pop. 1,217
Elgin ISD ... 1,300/PK-12
  PO Box 369 73538 ... 580-492-3663
  Tom Crimmins, supt. ... Fax 492-4084
  www.elgin.k12.ok.us/
Elgin HS ... 400/9-12
  PO Box 369 73538 ... 580-492-3670
  Shari Pillow, prin. ... Fax 492-3697
Elgin MS ... 400/5-8
  PO Box 369 73538 ... 580-492-3655
  Sammy Jackson, prin. ... Fax 492-3658

Elk City, Beckham, Pop. 10,511
CareerTech Skills Centers
  Supt. — None
  Dom Garrison, supt.
Elk City Skills Center ... Vo/Tech
  PO Box 1071 73648 ... 580-243-5517

Elk City ISD ... 2,000/PK-PK, 1-
  222 W Broadway Ave 73644 ... 580-225-0175
  Galeard Roper, supt. ... Fax 225-8644
  www.elkcityschools.com/
Elk City HS ... 500/10-12
  222 W Broadway Ave 73644 ... 580-225-0105
  Rick McNeil, prin. ... Fax 225-1359
Elk City JHS ... 300/8-9
  222 W Broadway Ave 73644 ... 580-225-0476
  Jamey Cook, prin. ... Fax 225-0208

Merritt ISD ... 500/PK-12
  RR 4 Box 7195 73644 ... 580-225-5460
  Gary Higgins, supt. ... Fax 225-5469
Merritt HS ... 100/9-12
  RR 4 Box 7195 73644 ... 580-225-5460
  Jeff Daugherty, prin. ... Fax 225-5469

Elmore City, Garvin, Pop. 762
Elmore City-Pernell ISD ... 500/PK-12
  100 N Muse Ave 73433 ... 580-788-2566
  Jim Smith, supt. ... Fax 788-4665
  www.ecphs.k12.ok.us
Elmore City-Pernell JSHS ... 200/7-12
  100 N Muse Ave 73433 ... 580-788-2565
  Burl Solie, prin. ... Fax 788-4665

El Reno, Canadian, Pop. 15,938
El Reno ISD ... 2,600/PK-12
  PO Box 580 73036 ... 405-262-1703
  Dr. Jeff Mills, supt. ... Fax 262-8620
  www.elreno.k12.ok.us
El Reno HS ... 1,100/8-12
  PO Box 580 73036 ... 405-262-3254
  Matt Goucher, prin. ... Fax 262-8629

OK Dept. of Voc. & Tech. Education
  Supt. — None
Canadian Valley Technology Center ... Vo/Tech
  6505 E US Highway 66 73036 ... 405-422-2200
  Dr. Earl Cowan, supt. ... Fax 422-2354

Canadian Valley Area Voc-Tech School ... Post-Sec.
  6505 E US Highway 66 73036 ... 405-262-2629
Redlands Community College ... Post-Sec.
  1300 S Country Club Rd 73036 ... 405-262-2552

Enid, Garfield, Pop. 46,436
Chisholm HS ... 900/PK-12
  300 Colorado Ave 73701 ... 580-237-5512
  Roydon Tilley, supt. ... Fax 234-5334
  www.chisholm.k12.ok.us
Chisholm HS ... 300/9-12
  4018 W Carrier Rd 73703 ... 580-233-2852
  Scot Trower, prin. ... Fax 233-9325
Chisholm MS ... 200/6-8
  4202 W Carrier Rd 73703 ... 580-234-0234
  Jaymie Morley, prin. ... Fax 234-0343

Enid ISD ... 6,400/PK-12
  500 S Independence St 73701 ... 580-234-5270
  Dr. Garland Keithly, supt. ... Fax 249-3565
  enidpublicschools.org/
Emerson JHS ... 500/7-9
  700 W Elm Ave 73701 ... 580-237-3017
  Kimberly Jones, prin. ... Fax 249-3587
Enid HS ... 1,300/10-12
  611 W Wabash Ave 73701 ... 580-234-2404
  Jim Beierschmitt, prin. ... Fax 249-3576
Longfellow JHS ... 500/7-9
  900 E Broadway Ave 73701 ... 580-234-7022
  Ron Few, prin. ... Fax 249-3586
Waller JHS ... 500/7-9
  2604 W Randolph Ave 73703 ... 580-234-5931
  John Garvie, prin. ... Fax 249-3585

OK Dept. of Voc. & Tech. Education
  Supt. — None
Autry Technology Center ... Vo/Tech
  1201 W Willow Rd 73703 ... 580-242-2750
  Dr. Jim Strate, supt. ... Fax 233-8262

Enid Beauty College ... Post-Sec.
  1601 E Broadway Ave 73701 ... 580-237-6677
Oklahoma Bible Academy ... 300/7-12
  5913 W Chestnut Ave 73703 ... 580-242-4104
  Tim Kuhns, hdmstr. ... Fax 242-4106
O T Autry Area Vocational Tech Center ... Post-Sec.
  1201 W Willow Rd 73703 ... 580-242-2750
St. Mary's Hospital ... Post-Sec.
  305 S 5th St 73701 ... 580-233-6100

Erick, Beckham, Pop. 1,010
Erick ISD ... 200/K-12
  PO Box 9 73645 ... 580-526-3476
  Phil Compton, supt. ... Fax 526-3308
Erick HS, PO Box 9 73645 ... 100/9-12
  Darren Sharp, prin. ... 580-526-3351

Eufaula, McIntosh, Pop. 2,723
Eufaula ISD ... 1,100/K-12
  PO Box 609 74432 ... 918-689-2152
  Bill Wilson, supt. ... Fax 689-1080
  www.eufaula.k12.ok.us/
Eufaula HS ... 400/9-12
  PO Box 609 74432 ... 918-689-2556
  Steve Butcher, prin. ... Fax 689-1099
Eufaula MS ... 300/6-8
  PO Box 609 74432 ... 918-689-2711
  Chris Whelan, prin. ... Fax 689-2874

Fairfax, Osage, Pop. 1,518
Woodland SD ... 500/PK-12
  PO Box 487 74637 ... 918-642-3295
  David Payne, supt. ... Fax 642-5754
  www.woodland.k12.ok.us
Woodland HS ... 100/9-12
  PO Box 487 74637 ... 918-642-3295
  Tom Scully, prin. ... Fax 642-5754
Woodland MS ... 200/5-8
  PO Box 487 74637 ... 918-738-4286
  Bobby Rose, prin. ... Fax 738-4287

Fairland, Ottawa, Pop. 1,010
Fairland ISD ... 500/PK-12
  PO Box 689 74343 ... 918-676-3811
  Charles Thomas, supt. ... Fax 676-3594
  www.fairlandowls.com
Fairland HS, PO Box 689 74343 ... 100/9-12
  Mark Malcom, prin. ... 918-676-3246

Fairview, Major, Pop. 2,662
Fairview ISD 700/PK-12
408 E Broadway 73737 580-227-2531
Rocky Burchfield, supt. Fax 227-2642
www.fairviewhigh.com
Chamberlain MS 200/6-8
1000 E Elm St 73737 580-227-2555
Billy Sacket, prin. Fax 227-2642
Fairview HS 200/9-12
316 N 8th Ave 73737 580-227-4446
Mark Van Meter, prin. Fax 227-1004

OK Dept. of Voc. & Tech. Education
Supt. — None
Northwest Technology Center Vo/Tech
PO Box 250 73737 580-227-3708
Fax 227-2651

Fargo, Ellis, Pop. 322
Fargo ISD 200/PK-12
PO Box 200 73840 580-698-2298
Mike Woods, supt. Fax 698-8019
www.fargo.k12.ok.us
Fargo HS 100/9-12
PO Box 200 73840 580-698-2298
Sherri Long, prin. Fax 698-8019

Felt, Cimarron
Felt ISD 100/PK-12
PO Box 47 73937 580-426-2220
Barbalee Blair, supt. Fax 426-2799
www.felt.k12.ok.us
Felt HS 50/9-12
PO Box 47 73937 580-426-2220
Lewetta Hefley, prin. Fax 426-2799

Fittstown, Pontotoc
Stonewall ISD
Supt. — See Stonewall
McLish MS 50/PK-PK, 5-
PO Box 29 74842 580-777-2221
Jack Wofford, prin. Fax 777-2222

Fletcher, Comanche, Pop. 1,027
Fletcher ISD 500/PK-12
PO Box 489 73541 580-549-6015
Kathryn Turner, supt. Fax 549-6016
www.fletcherschools.org/
Fletcher JHS 100/7-9
PO Box 489 73541 580-549-6015
Julia Poteete, prin. Fax 549-6016
Fletcher SHS, PO Box 489 73541 100/10-12
Julia Poteete, prin. 580-549-6015

Forgan, Beaver, Pop. 511
Forgan ISD 200/PK-12
PO Box 406 73938 580-487-3366
Kenny Roe, supt. Fax 487-3368
www.forgan.k12.ok.us
Forgan HS 100/9-12
PO Box 406 73938 580-487-3366
Travis Smalts, prin. Fax 487-3368

Fort Cobb, Caddo, Pop. 655
Fort Cobb-Broxton ISD 400/PK-12
PO Box 130 73038 405-643-2336
Dennis Klugh, supt. Fax 643-2547
Fort Cobb-Broxton HS 100/9-12
PO Box 130 73038 405-643-2820
Kyle Lierle, prin. Fax 643-3115
Fort Cobb-Broxton MS 100/6-8
PO Box 130 73038 405-643-2820
James Biddy, prin.

OK Dept. of Voc. & Tech. Education
Supt. — None
Caddo-Kiowa Technology Center Vo/Tech
PO Box 190 73038 405-643-5511
Jerry Martin, supt. Fax 643-2144

Fort Gibson, Muskogee, Pop. 4,170
Fort Gibson ISD 1,800/PK-12
500 Ross Ave 74434 918-478-2474
Derald Glover, supt. Fax 478-8533
www.ftgibson.k12.ok.us
Fort Gibson HS 500/9-12
500 Ross Ave 74434 918-478-2452
Gary Sparks, prin. Fax 478-6244
Fort Gibson MS 400/6-8
500 Ross Ave 74434 918-478-2471
Gregory Phares, prin. Fax 478-6412

Fort Supply, Woodward, Pop. 325
CareerTech Skills Centers
Supt. — None
Dom Garrison, supt.
Fort Supply Skills Center Vo/Tech
PO Box 130 73841 580-766-2089

Fort Supply ISD 100/PK-12
PO Box 160 73841 580-766-2611
Pat Howell, supt. Fax 766-8019
Fort Supply HS, PO Box 160 73841 50/9-12
Pat Howell, prin. 580-766-2611

Fort Towson, Choctaw, Pop. 613
Fort Towson ISD 400/PK-12
PO Box 39 74735 580-873-2712
Jo Miller, supt. Fax 873-1053
www.forttowson.k12.ok.us/
Fort Towson HS 100/9-12
PO Box 39 74735 580-873-2325
Phillip Ware, prin. Fax 873-2712

Fox, Carter
Fox ISD 300/PK-12
PO Box 248 73435 580-673-2081
Brent Phelps, supt. Fax 673-2389
www.foxps.k12.ok.us
Fox HS 100/9-12
PO Box 248 73435 580-673-2082
Randy Harris, prin. Fax 673-2389

Foyil, Rogers, Pop. 263
Foyil ISD 700/PK-12
PO Box 49 74031 918-341-1113
Michael Mcgregor, supt. Fax 341-1223
www.foyil.k12.ok.us
Foyil JSHS 300/7-12
PO Box 49 74031 918-342-1782
Rick Antle, prin. Fax 341-1223

Frederick, Tillman, Pop. 4,378
Frederick ISD 1,000/PK-12
PO Box 370 73542 580-335-5516
Tony O'Brien, supt. Fax 335-2324
www.frederickbombers.net
Frederick HS, PO Box 610 73542 300/9-12
James Redeker, prin. 580-335-5521
Frederick MS, PO Box 490 73542 200/6-8
Ruth Ann Hoover, prin. 580-335-2014

OK Dept. of Voc. & Tech. Education
Supt. — None
Great Plains Technology Center Vo/Tech
2001 E Gladstone Ave 73542 580-335-5525
Gary Tyler, dir. Fax 335-2209

Freedom, Woods, Pop. 263
Freedom ISD 100/PK-12
PO Box 5 73842 580-621-3271
Christie Riley, supt. Fax 621-3699
www.freedomschools.k12.ok.us
Freedom HS 50/9-12
PO Box 5 73842 580-621-3272
Christie Riley, prin. Fax 621-3699

Gage, Ellis, Pop. 411
Gage ISD 100/K-12
PO Box 60 73843 580-923-7666
Doug Taylor, supt. Fax 923-7907
www.gage.k12.ok.us/
Gage JSHS 100/7-12
PO Box 60 73843 580-923-7909
Doug Taylor, prin. Fax 923-7907

Gans, Sequoyah, Pop. 211
Gans ISD 400/PK-12
PO Box 70 74936 918-775-2236
Brenda Taylor, supt. Fax 775-5145
www.gans.k12.ok.us
Gans HS 100/9-12
PO Box 70 74936 918-775-2236
Larry Calloway, prin. Fax 775-5145

Garber, Garfield, Pop. 818
Garber ISD 300/PK-12
PO Box 539 73738 580-863-2220
Jim Lamer, supt. Fax 863-2259
www.garber.k12.ok.us/
Garber HS, PO Box 539 73738 100/9-12
Marc Hatton, prin. 580-863-2231

Geary, Blaine, Pop. 1,223
Geary ISD 500/PK-12
PO Box 188 73040 405-884-2989
Bill Caruthers, supt. Fax 884-2099
www.geary.k12.ok.us
Geary JHS, PO Box 188 73040 100/7-9
Tom Deighan, prin. 405-884-2362
Geary SHS, PO Box 188 73040 100/10-12
Tom Deighan, prin. 405-884-2362

Geronimo, Comanche, Pop. 962
Geronimo ISD 200/PK-12
PO Box 99 73543 580-355-3801
Danny McCuiston, supt. Fax 357-8307
www.geronimo.k12.ok.us
Geronimo HS 100/9-12
PO Box 99 73543 580-355-3160
Brent Crow, prin. Fax 355-9670

Glencoe, Payne, Pop. 592
Glencoe ISD 400/PK-12
PO Box 218 74032 580-669-2261
Pat Gougler, supt. Fax 669-2961
www.glencoe.k12.ok.us
Glencoe HS 100/9-12
PO Box 218 74032 580-669-2261
Pat Gougler, prin. Fax 669-2961

Glenpool, Tulsa, Pop. 8,407
Glenpool ISD 2,100/PK-12
PO Box 1149 74033 918-322-9500
Kathy Coley, supt. Fax 322-1529
www.glenpool.k12.ok.us
Glenpool HS 600/9-12
PO Box 1149 74033 918-322-9500
Bruce Snider, prin. Fax 322-1012
Glenpool MS 500/6-8
PO Box 1149 74033 918-322-9500
Danna Garland, prin. Fax 322-9333

Goodwell, Texas, Pop. 1,175
Goodwell ISD 200/PK-12
PO Box 580 73939 580-349-2271
Robert Miller, supt. Fax 349-2531
www.gpseagles.org
Goodwell HS 50/9-12
PO Box 580 73939 580-349-2271
Steve Carroll, prin. Fax 349-2531

Yarbrough ISD 100/PK-12
RR 1 Box 31 73939 580-545-3327
Jim Wiggin, supt. Fax 545-3392
Yarbrough HS 50/9-12
RR 1 Box 31 73939 580-545-3328
Terry Mulbery, prin. Fax 545-3392

Oklahoma Panhandle State University Post-Sec.
PO Box 430 73939 580-349-2611

Gore, Sequoyah, Pop. 887
Gore ISD 600/K-12
PO Box 580 74435 918-489-5587
Patricia Cox, supt. Fax 489-5664
www.gore.k12.ok.us/
Gore HS 200/9-12
PO Box 580 74435 918-489-5587
Steven Barrick, prin. Fax 489-5664
Gore MS 200/6-8
PO Box 580 74435 918-487-5191
Richard Moseley, prin. Fax 489-5664

Gracemont, Caddo, Pop. 331
Gracemont ISD 200/PK-12
PO Box 5 73042 405-966-2236
Larry Mills, supt. Fax 966-2395
Gracemont HS 100/9-12
PO Box 5 73042 405-966-2234
Wayne Taggart, prin. Fax 966-2395

Grandfield, Tillman, Pop. 1,047
Grandfield ISD 300/PK-12
PO Box 639 73546 580-479-5237
Ed Turlington, supt. Fax 479-3381
www.grandfield.k12.ok.us/
Grandfield HS 100/9-12
PO Box 639 73546 580-479-3140
Judd Matthes, prin. Fax 479-5563

Granite, Greer, Pop. 1,897
CareerTech Skills Centers
Supt. — None
Dom Garrison, supt.
Granite Skills Center Vo/Tech
PO Box 86 73547 580-535-2186

Granite ISD 300/PK-12
PO Box 98 73547 580-535-2104
Loren Tackett, supt. Fax 535-2106
Granite HS 100/9-12
PO Box 98 73547 580-535-2104
Janice Crume, prin. Fax 535-2106

Grove, Delaware, Pop. 5,574
Grove ISD 2,300/PK-12
PO Box 450789 74345 918-786-3003
Tom Steen, supt. Fax 786-9365
www.ridgerunners.net
Grove HS, PO Box 450789 74345 700/9-12
Mike Teel, prin. 918-786-2208
Grove MS, PO Box 450789 74345 500/6-8
Don Barr, prin. 918-786-2209

Guthrie, Logan, Pop. 10,110
Guthrie ISD 3,200/PK-12
802 E Vilas Ave 73044 405-282-8900
Terry Simpson, supt. Fax 282-5904
www.guthrie.k12.ok.us
Guthrie HS 900/9-12
200 N Crooks Dr 73044 405-282-5906
Carl Clark, prin. Fax 282-8823
Guthrie JHS 500/7-8
705 E Oklahoma Ave 73044 405-282-5936
Tim Rawls, prin. Fax 282-5985

Guymon, Texas, Pop. 10,565
Guymon ISD 2,400/PK-12
PO Box 1307 73942 580-338-4340
Bob Neel, supt. Fax 338-3812
156.110.79.11/
Central JHS, PO Box 1307 73942 400/7-8
Andrew Wright, prin. 580-338-4360
Guymon HS 600/9-12
PO Box 1307 73942 580-338-4350
Lowell Doss, prin. Fax 338-0994

Haileyville, Pittsburg, Pop. 890
Haileyville ISD 400/PK-12
PO Box 29 74546 918-297-2626
David Cravens, supt. Fax 297-7136
haileyville.ok.schoolwebpages.com
Haileyville HS, PO Box 29 74546 100/9-12
Roger Hemphill, prin. 918-297-2627

Hammon, Roger Mills, Pop. 439
Hammon ISD 200/PK-12
PO Box 279 73650 580-473-2221
Randy Ann Stickney, supt. Fax 473-2464
Hammon HS 100/9-12
PO Box 279 73650 580-473-2737
Richard Megli, prin. Fax 473-2464

Hanna, McIntosh, Pop. 133
Hanna ISD 100/PK-12
PO Box 10 74845 918-657-2523
Patricia Berry, supt. Fax 657-2424
Hanna HS, PO Box 10 74845 50/9-12
Michael Parsons, prin. 918-657-2527

Hardesty, Texas, Pop. 271
Hardesty ISD 100/PK-12
PO Box 129 73944 580-888-4258
David Brewer, supt. Fax 888-4560
www.hardesty.k12.ok.us
Hardesty HS 50/9-12
PO Box 129 73944 580-888-4258
David Brewer, prin. Fax 888-4560

Harrah, Oklahoma, Pop. 4,912
Harrah ISD 2,200/PK-12
20670 Walker St 73045 405-454-6244
Dr. Dean Hughes, supt. Fax 454-0022
www.harrahschools.com
Harrah HS 500/10-12
20370 Elm St 73045 405-454-2416
Dale Munyon, prin. Fax 454-6842
Harrah JHS 400/8-9
1480 N Dobbs Rd 73045 405-454-6331
John Hunt, prin. Fax 454-6361

Hartshorne, Pittsburg, Pop. 2,069
Hartshorne ISD 800/PK-12
520 S 5th St 74547 918-297-2534
James Barnes, supt. Fax 297-2698
www.hartshorne.k12.ok.us
Hartshorne JHS 200/7-9
520 S 5th St 74547 918-297-2433
John Bernardi, prin. Fax 297-2698
Hartshorne SHS 200/10-12
520 S 5th St 74547 918-297-2536
Mark Ichord, prin. Fax 297-2025

Haskell, Muskogee, Pop. 1,791
Haskell ISD — 1,000/PK-12
PO Box 278 74436 — 918-482-5221
Dr. Landon Berry, supt. — Fax 482-3346
www.haskell.k12.ok.us
Beavers MS — 200/6-8
PO Box 278 74436 — 918-482-5221
Michael Broyles, prin. — Fax 482-3346
Haskell HS — 300/9-12
PO Box 278 74436 — 918-482-5223
John Munger, prin. — Fax 482-3346

Haworth, McCurtain, Pop. 352
Haworth ISD — 600/PK-12
HC 73 Box 1 74740 — 580-245-1406
Donald Ray, supt. — Fax 245-2265
www.haworth.k12.ok.us
Haworth JHS, HC 73 Box 1 74740 — 200/7-9
John Crabtree, prin. — 580-245-1461
Haworth SHS, HC 73 Box 1 74740 — 100/10-12
Craig Wall, prin. — 580-245-1440

Healdton, Carter, Pop. 2,775
Healdton ISD — 600/PK-12
PO Box 490 73438 — 580-229-0566
Don Lewis, supt. — Fax 229-1522
Healdton HS, PO Box 490 73438 — 200/9-12
Greg Raper, prin. — 580-229-0540
Healdton MS — 100/6-8
PO Box 490 73438 — 580-229-0303
Greg Raper, prin. — Fax 229-1475

Heavener, LeFlore, Pop. 3,199
Heavener ISD — 900/PK-12
PO Box 698 74937 — 918-653-7223
Edward Wilson, supt. — Fax 653-7843
www.heavener.k12.ok.us
Heavener HS, PO Box 698 74937 — 300/9-12
Jerry Williams, prin. — 918-653-4436

Helena, Alfalfa, Pop. 1,412
CareerTech Skills Centers
Supt. — None
Dom Garrison, supt.
Helena Skills Center — Vo/Tech
PO Box 286 73741 — 580-852-3221

Timberlake ISD — 300/PK-12
PO Box 287 73741 — 580-852-3307
R.O. Lingengelter, supt. — Fax 852-3280
www.tlake.k12.ok.us
Timberlake HS — 100/9-12
PO Box 287 73741 — 580-852-3281
Cliff Benson, prin. — Fax 852-3280

Hennessey, Kingfisher, Pop. 2,024
Hennessey ISD — 800/PK-12
604 E Oklahoma St 73742 — 405-853-4321
Uwe Gordon, supt. — Fax 853-4439
www.hps.k12.ok.us
Hennessey HS — 200/9-12
707 E Oklahoma St 73742 — 405-853-4394
David Parker, prin. — Fax 853-4644
Hennessey MS — 200/5-8
120 N Mitchell Rd 73742 — 405-853-4303
Doug Stafford, prin. — Fax 853-4848

Henryetta, Okmulgee, Pop. 6,042
Henryetta ISD — 1,200/PK-12
1801 W Troy Aikman Dr 74437 — 918-652-6523
Dan Edwards, supt. — Fax 652-6510
www.henryetta.k12.ok.us
Henryetta HS — 400/9-12
1800 W Troy Aikman Dr 74437 — 918-652-6571
Brad Wion, prin. — Fax 652-6572
Henryetta MS — 300/6-8
1700 W Troy Aikman Dr 74437 — 918-652-6578
Keith Flanary, prin. — Fax 652-6506

Wilson ISD — 300/PK-12
8867 Chestnut Rd 74437 — 918-652-3374
Rick Hatfield, supt. — Fax 652-8140
www.wpstigers.k12.ok.us
Wilson HS — 100/9-12
8867 Chestnut Rd 74437 — 918-652-3384
Andrea James, prin. — Fax 650-9725

Hinton, Caddo, Pop. 2,172
Hinton ISD — 600/PK-12
PO Box 1036 73047 — 405-542-3257
Harvey Mead, supt. — Fax 542-3286
www.hinton.k12.ok.us
Hinton HS — 200/9-12
PO Box 1036 73047 — 405-542-3235
Jeff Thompson, prin. — Fax 542-3286
Hinton MS — 100/6-8
PO Box 1036 73047 — 405-542-3235
Jason Reece, prin. — Fax 542-3286

Hobart, Kiowa, Pop. 3,878
Hobart ISD — 900/PK-12
PO Box 899 73651 — 580-726-5691
Roger Hill, supt. — Fax 726-2855
www.hobart.k12.ok.us
Hobart HS, PO Box 899 73651 — 300/9-12
Rod Maynard, prin. — 580-726-5611
Hobart MS, PO Box 899 73651 — 200/6-8
Benny Barnett, prin. — 580-726-5615

Hodgen, LeFlore
CareerTech Skills Centers
Supt. — None
Dom Garrison, supt.
Hamilton Skills Center — Vo/Tech
PO Box 250 74939 — 918-653-7831

Holdenville, Hughes, Pop. 5,575
Holdenville ISD — 1,200/PK-12
210 Grimes Ave 74848 — 405-379-5483
Shellie Gammill, supt. — Fax 379-5874
www.holdenville.k12.ok.us
Holdenville HS — 300/9-12
210 Grimes Ave 74848 — 405-379-6893
Daniel Pittman, prin. — Fax 379-2012
Holdenville JHS — 200/7-8
210 Grimes Ave 74848 — 405-379-3387
Les White, prin. — Fax 379-2012

Moss ISD — 300/PK-12
8087 E 134 Rd 74848 — 405-379-7251
Louis Maggia, supt. — Fax 379-2333
www.mossps.k12.ok.us/
Moss HS — 100/9-12
8087 E 134 Rd 74848 — 405-379-7251
Bob Sifers, prin. — Fax 379-2333

Hollis, Harmon, Pop. 2,108
Hollis ISD — 600/PK-12
PO Box 193 73550 — 580-688-3450
Wilmer Cooper, supt. — Fax 688-2532
www.hollis.k12.ok.us
Hollis HS, PO Box 193 73550 — 200/9-12
Ron Smith, prin. — 580-688-2707
Hollis MS, PO Box 193 73550 — 100/6-8
Ron Smith, prin. — 580-688-2707

Hominy, Osage, Pop. 3,766
Hominy ISD — 700/PK-12
200 S Pettit Ave 74035 — 918-885-6511
Russell Hall, supt. — Fax 885-2538
www.hominy.k12.ok.us/
Hominy HS, 200 S Pettit Ave 74035 — 200/9-12
Doyle Edwards, prin. — 918-885-2141
Hominy MS, 200 S Pettit Ave 74035 — 100/7-8
Doyle Edwards, prin. — 918-885-6253

Hooker, Texas, Pop. 1,704
Hooker ISD — 500/K-12
PO Box 247 73945 — 580-652-2162
Freida Burgess, supt. — Fax 652-3118
Hooker HS, PO Box 247 73945 — 200/9-12
Chuck Karpe, prin. — 580-652-2516

Howe, LeFlore, Pop. 708
Howe ISD — 400/PK-12
PO Box 259 74940 — 918-658-3666
Scott Parks, supt. — Fax 658-2233
www.howeschools.org
Howe HS — 100/9-12
PO Box 259 74940 — 918-658-3368
Jo Wright, prin. — Fax 658-2233

Hugo, Choctaw, Pop. 5,569
Hugo ISD — 1,300/K-12
208 N 2nd St 74743 — 580-326-6483
Jim Washburn, supt. — Fax 326-2480
Hugo HS — 400/9-12
201 E Brown St 74743 — 580-326-9648
Doyle Patterson, prin. — Fax 326-4811
Hugo MS — 200/7-8
208 N 2nd St 74743 — 580-326-3365
Darnell Shanklin, prin. — Fax 326-7352

OK Dept. of Voc. & Tech. Education
Supt. — None
Kiamichi Technology Center — Vo/Tech
PO Box 699 74743 — 580-326-6491
Dr. Charles Wibben, dir. — Fax 326-5696

School of Hair Design — Post-Sec.
116 W Jackson St 74743 — 580-326-7338

Hulbert, Cherokee, Pop. 534
Hulbert ISD — 600/PK-12
PO Box 188 74441 — 918-772-2501
Todd Kimrey, supt. — Fax 772-2766
www.hulbertriders.com
Hulbert JSHS — 300/7-12
PO Box 188 74441 — 918-772-2565
Erik Puckett, prin. — Fax 772-1275

Hydro, Caddo, Pop. 1,037
Hydro-Eakly SD — 500/PK-12
529 E 6th St 73048 — 405-663-2774
Delbo Leach, supt. — Fax 663-2139
www.hydroeakly.k12.ok.us/
Hydro MSHS — 200/6-12
529 E 6th St 73048 — 405-663-2246
Kim Hale, prin. — Fax 663-2139

Idabel, McCurtain, Pop. 6,946
Idabel ISD — 1,600/PK-12
200 NE C Ave 74745 — 580-286-7639
Jane Wooten, supt. — Fax 286-5585
www.idabelps.org
Idabel HS — 500/9-12
901 Lincoln Rd 74745 — 580-286-7693
Ted Brewer, prin. — Fax 286-6755
Idabel MS — 300/6-8
100 NE D Ave 74745 — 580-286-6558
Curtis Fuller, prin. — Fax 286-8272

OK Dept. of Voc. & Tech. Education
Supt. — None
Kiamichi Technology Center — Vo/Tech
RR 3 Box 177 74745 — 580-286-7555
Johnnie Meredith, dir. — Fax 286-3753

School of Hair Design — Post-Sec.
1437 SE Washington St 74745 — 580-286-7840

Indiahoma, Comanche, Pop. 367
Indiahoma ISD — 200/PK-12
PO Box 8 73552 — 580-246-3448
Deanna Voegeli, supt. — Fax 246-3372
www.indiahoma.k12.ok.us
Indiahoma HS — 100/9-12
PO Box 8 73552 — 580-246-3202
Doran Smith, prin. — Fax 246-3372

Indianola, Pittsburg, Pop. 191
Indianola ISD — 300/PK-12
PO Box 119 74442 — 918-823-4231
William Martin, supt. — Fax 823-4234
Indianola HS, PO Box 119 74442 — 100/9-12
Gina Barlow, prin. — 918-823-4231

Inola, Rogers, Pop. 1,677
Inola ISD — 1,300/PK-12
PO Box 1149 74036 — 918-543-2255
Jake Crutchfield, supt. — Fax 543-8754
www.inola.k12.ok.us
Inola HS — 400/9-12
PO Box 789 74036 — 918-543-2404
Robert Kinnick, prin. — Fax 543-2345
Inola MS — 400/5-8
PO Box 819 74036 — 918-543-2434
Vickie Johnson, prin. — Fax 543-6268

Jay, Delaware, Pop. 2,713
Jay ISD — 1,700/K-12
PO Box 630 74346 — 918-253-4293
David Schachle, supt. — Fax 253-8970
www.jay.k12.ok.us
Jay HS — 500/9-12
PO Box 630 74346 — 918-253-4466
Dennis Snell, prin. — Fax 253-6249
Jay MS — 400/6-8
PO Box 630 74346 — 918-253-8510
Judy Larmon, prin. — Fax 253-3342

Jenks, Tulsa, Pop. 11,560
Jenks ISD — 8,900/PK-12
205 E B St 74037 — 918-299-4411
Dr. Kirby Lehman, supt. — Fax 299-9197
jenksps.org
Jenks Freshman Academy — 800/9-9
205 E B St 74037 — 918-299-4411
Stephen Mathews, prin. — Fax 298-0807
Jenks HS — 2,100/10-12
205 E B St 74037 — 918-299-4411
Mike Means, prin. — Fax 298-0336
Other Schools – See Tulsa

Jenks Beauty College — Post-Sec.
535 W Main St 74037 — 918-299-0901
Jenks Christian Academy — 200/PK-12
2525 W Main St 74037 — 918-299-8181
David Haynes, prin. — Fax 299-3643

Jones, Oklahoma, Pop. 2,607
Jones ISD — 1,000/PK-12
412 SW 3rd St 73049 — 405-399-9215
Mike Steele, supt. — Fax 399-9212
www.joneshs.k12.ok.us
Jones HS — 300/9-12
304 Hawaii St 73049 — 405-399-9122
Carl Johnson, prin. — Fax 399-9212
Jones MS — 200/7-8
16011 E Wilshire Blvd 73049 — 405-399-9114
Pam Lucas, prin. — Fax 399-6101

Kansas, Delaware, Pop. 715
Kansas ISD — 800/K-12
PO Box 196 74347 — 918-868-2562
Jim Burgess, supt. — Fax 868-3103
www.kansasokschools.com/
Kansas HS — 300/9-12
PO Box 196 74347 — 918-868-3308
Ned Phillips, prin. — Fax 868-3103
Kansas JHS — 200/6-8
PO Box 196 74347 — 918-868-5308
Bryon Arnold, prin. — Fax 868-5582

OK Dept. of Voc. & Tech. Education
Supt. — None
Northeast Oklahoma Tech Center E Campus — Vo/Tech
PO Box 30 74347 — 918-868-3535
Rick Craig, prin. — Fax 868-3530

Kellyville, Creek, Pop. 919
Kellyville ISD — 1,200/PK-12
PO Box 99 74039 — 918-247-6133
Ronald Jackson, supt. — Fax 247-6120
www.kellyvilleschools.org/
Kellyville HS, PO Box 99 74039 — 400/9-12
Charles Nance, prin. — 918-247-6333
Kellyville MS, PO Box 99 74039 — 200/7-8
John Castillo, prin. — 918-247-6333

Keota, Haskell, Pop. 526
Keota ISD — 400/PK-12
PO Box 160 74941 — 918-966-3950
Charles Brown, supt. — Fax 966-3247
www.keota.k12.ok.us
Keota HS — 100/9-12
PO Box 160 74941 — 918-966-3950
Terry Shaw, prin. — Fax 966-3247

Ketchum, Mayes, Pop. 289
Ketchum ISD — 500/PK-12
PO Box 720 74349 — 918-782-3241
Mark Alexander, supt. — Fax 782-9018
Ketchum HS — 200/9-12
PO Box 720 74349 — 918-782-4481
Louise Brackett, prin. — Fax 782-4848
Ketchum MS, PO Box 720 74349 — 6-8
Rick Pool, prin. — 918-782-3242

Keyes, Cimarron, Pop. 386
Keyes ISD — 100/PK-12
PO Box 47 73947 — 580-546-7231
Richard Gleave, supt. — Fax 546-7338
www.keyes.k12.ok.us
Keyes HS — 50/9-12
PO Box 47 73947 — 580-546-7231
Richard Gleave, prin. — Fax 546-7338

Kiefer, Creek, Pop. 1,090
Kiefer ISD — 400/PK-12
PO Box 850 74041 — 918-321-3421
Charles Montalbano, supt. — Fax 321-5216
www.kiefer.k12.ok.us/
Kiefer HS, PO Box 850 74041 — 100/9-12
Gayla Johnson, prin. — 918-321-3533
Rongey MS, PO Box 850 74041 — 100/7-8
Gayla Johnson, prin. — 918-321-3421

Kingfisher, Kingfisher, Pop. 4,452
Kingfisher ISD 1,200/PK-12
PO Box 29 73750 405-375-4194
Max Thomas, supt. Fax 375-5565
www.kingfisher.k12.ok.us
Kingfisher HS 400/9-12
PO Box 29 73750 405-375-4191
Charles Willis, prin. Fax 375-4456
Kingfisher MS, PO Box 29 73750 300/5-8
Andy Evans, prin. 405-375-6607

Kingston, Marshall, Pop. 1,444
Kingston ISD 1,100/PK-12
PO Box 370 73439 580-564-9033
Jay McAdams, supt. Fax 564-9516
www.kingston.k12.ok.us
Kingston HS 300/9-12
PO Box 370 73439 580-564-2384
Donna Anderson, prin. Fax 564-0901
Kingston MS 300/6-8
PO Box 370 73439 580-564-2996
Steve Dean, prin. Fax 564-0902

Kinta, Haskell, Pop. 247
Kinta ISD 200/PK-12
PO Box 219 74552 918-768-3338
Patricia Deville, supt. Fax 768-3221
Kinta HS, PO Box 219 74552 100/9-12
Gerald Fishinghawk, prin. 918-768-3339

Kiowa, Pittsburg, Pop. 694
Kiowa ISD 300/PK-12
PO Box 6 74553 918-432-5631
Michael W. Kellogg, supt. Fax 432-5683
www.kiowa.k12.ok.us
Kiowa HS, PO Box 6 74553 100/9-12
Garry Walden, prin. 918-432-5641

Konawa, Seminole, Pop. 1,429
Konawa ISD 800/PK-12
RR 1 Box 3 74849 580-925-3244
Dr. Jim Beckham, supt. Fax 925-2146
www.konawa.k12.ok.us
Konawa JHS 200/6-9
RR 1 Box 3 74849 580-925-3222
Larry Marlow, prin. Fax 925-2146
Konawa SHS 200/10-12
RR 1 Box 3 74849 580-925-3221
Gary Stidham, prin. Fax 925-2146

Kremlin, Garfield, Pop. 236
Kremlin-Hillsdale ISD 200/PK-12
PO Box 198 73753 580-874-2284
Tom Pearson, supt. Fax 874-4488
Kremlin-Hillsdale HS 100/9-12
PO Box 198 73753 580-874-2281
Jon Buller, prin.

Lahoma, Garfield, Pop. 572
Cimarron ISD 300/PK-12
PO Box 8 73754 580-796-2204
Steve Walker, supt. Fax 796-2350
www.cimarron.k12.ok.us
Cimarron HS 100/9-12
PO Box 8 73754 580-796-2204
Gene Novosad, prin. Fax 796-2350

Lamont, Grant, Pop. 450
Deer Creek-Lamont ISD 200/PK-12
PO Box 10 74643 580-388-4335
Mark Taylor, supt. Fax 388-4341
www.dcla.k12.ok.us/
Deer Creek-Lamont HS 100/9-12
PO Box 10 74643 580-388-4333
David Zachary, prin.

Lane, Atoka
CareerTech Skills Centers
Supt. — None
Dom Garrison, supt.
McLeod Skills Center Vo/Tech
PO Box 156 74555 580-889-7275

Langston, Logan, Pop. 1,678

Langston University Post-Sec.
PO Box 907 73050 405-466-2231

Laverne, Harper, Pop. 1,046
Laverne ISD 400/PK-12
PO Box 40 73848 580-921-3362
Ed Thomas, supt. Fax 921-3636
www.laverne.k12.ok.us
Laverne HS 200/6-12
PO Box 40 73848 580-921-3361
Todd Overstreet, prin. Fax 921-3936

Lawton, Comanche, Pop. 91,730
CareerTech Skills Centers
Supt. — None
Dom Garrison, supt.
Lawton Skills Center Vo/Tech
605 SW Coombs Rd 73501 580-355-4921

Lawton ISD 14,900/PK-12
PO Box 1009 73502 580-357-6900
Barry Beauchamp, supt. Fax 585-6319
www.lawtonps.org
Central MS 700/6-8
1201 NW Fort Sill Blvd 73507 580-355-8544
Gene Shelkett, prin. Fax 585-6452
Eisenhower JHS 1,200/7-9
5702 W Gore Blvd 73505 580-353-1040
Rick Owens, prin. Fax 585-6436
Eisenhower SHS 1,400/10-12
5202 W Gore Blvd 73505 580-355-9144
Maria Anderson, prin. Fax 585-6329
Lawton HS 1,500/9-12
601 NW Fort Sill Blvd 73507 580-355-5170
Rick Kitzrow, prin. Fax 585-6433
MacArthur HS 800/9-12
4402 E Gore Blvd 73501 580-355-5230
Robert Roshell, prin. Fax 585-6434
MacArthur MS 600/6-8
510 NE 45th St 73507 580-353-5111
Mark Mattingly, prin. Fax 585-6435
Tomlinson MS 600/6-8
702 NW Homestead Dr 73505 580-585-6416
Dick Adams, prin. Fax 585-6451

OK Dept. of Voc. & Tech. Education
Supt. — None
Great Plains Technology Center Vo/Tech
4500 SW Lee Blvd 73505 580-355-6371
James Nesbitt, supt. Fax 250-5677

Cameron University Post-Sec.
2800 W Gore Blvd 73505 580-581-2200
Comanche Co. Memorial Hospital Post-Sec.
PO Box 129 73502 580-355-8620
Eve's College of Hairstyling Post-Sec.
912 SW C Ave 73501 580-355-6620
Great Plains Area Voc. Tech. School Post-Sec.
4500 SW Lee Blvd 73505 580-355-6371
Lawton Christian HS 200/7-12
1 NW Crusader Dr 73505 580-536-6885
Tom Lewis, admin. Fax 536-5242
Platt College Post-Sec.
112 SW 11th St 73501 580-355-4416

Leedey, Dewey, Pop. 333
Leedey ISD 200/PK-12
PO Box 67 73654 580-488-3424
Marc Montrose, supt. Fax 488-3428
Leedey HS, PO Box 67 73654 50/9-12
Ronnie Dupree, prin. 580-488-3377

Le Flore, LeFlore, Pop. 169
Leflore SD 200/PK-12
PO Box 147, 918-753-2345
James Caughern, supt. Fax 753-2604
www.leflorepss.k12.ok.us/
Leflore HS, PO Box 147, 100/9-12
L.D. Boatright, prin. 918-753-2253

Lexington, Cleveland, Pop. 2,120
CareerTech Skills Centers
Supt. — None
Dom Garrison, supt.
Harp Skills Center Vo/Tech
PO Box 550 73051 405-527-4848
Lexington Skills Center Vo/Tech
PO Box 550 73051 405-527-2191

Lexington ISD 1,000/PK-12
420 NE 4th St 73051 405-527-7236
Denny Prince, supt. Fax 527-9517
www.lexington.k12.ok.us/
Lexington HS 300/9-12
420 NE 4th St 73051 405-527-7236
Randall Fuller, prin. Fax 527-9517
Lexington MS 300/5-8
420 NE 4th St 73051 405-527-7236
Gary Jones, prin. Fax 527-9517

Lindsay, Garvin, Pop. 2,886
Lindsay ISD 1,100/PK-12
800 W Creek St 73052 405-756-3131
Doyle Greteman, supt. Fax 756-8819
www.lindsay.k12.ok.us
Lindsay HS, 800 W Creek St 73052 300/9-12
Tom Inman, prin. 405-756-3132
Lindsay MS, 800 W Creek St 73052 200/6-8
Bob Ashley, prin. 405-756-3133

Locust Grove, Mayes, Pop. 1,405
Locust Grove ISD 1,500/PK-12
PO Box 399 74352 918-479-5243
David Cash, supt. Fax 479-6468
www.lg.k12.ok.us
Locust Grove HS 400/9-12
PO Box 399 74352 918-479-5247
Howard Hill, prin. Fax 479-2743
Locust Grove MS 300/6-8
PO Box 399 74352 918-479-5244
Charles Coleman, prin. Fax 479-2930

Lone Grove, Carter, Pop. 4,868
Lone Grove ISD 1,500/PK-12
PO Box 1330 73443 580-657-3131
Gary Scott, supt. Fax 657-4355
www.lonegrove.k12.ok.us/
Lone Grove JHS 200/8-9
PO Box 1330 73443 580-657-2419
Derek Hallum, prin. Fax 657-6624
Lone Grove SHS 300/10-12
PO Box 1330 73443 580-657-3133
Russell Noland, prin. Fax 657-6624

Lone Wolf, Kiowa, Pop. 481
Lone Wolf ISD 100/PK-12
PO Box 158 73655 580-846-9091
James Sutherland, supt. Fax 846-5266
Lone Wolf HS 50/9-12
PO Box 158 73655 580-846-9091
James Sutherland, prin. Fax 846-5266

Lookeba, Caddo, Pop. 130
Lookeba-Sickles ISD 200/PK-12
RR 1 Box 34 73053 405-457-6623
Dennis Byrd, supt. Fax 457-6619
Lookeba-Sickles HS 100/9-12
RR 1 Box 34 73053 405-457-6621
Kirk Wilson, prin.

Luther, Oklahoma, Pop. 496
Luther ISD 800/K-12
PO Box 430 73054 405-277-3233
W.B. Wilson, supt. Fax 277-3498
lutherlions.org
Luther HS 200/9-12
PO Box 430 73054 405-277-3263
Jan Scheffler, prin. Fax 277-3630
Luther MS 200/6-8
PO Box 430 73054 405-277-3264
Barry Gunn, prin. Fax 277-3877

Mc Alester, Pittsburg, Pop. 17,566
CareerTech Skills Centers
Supt. — None
Dom Garrison, supt.
Brannon Skills Center Vo/Tech
PO Box 1999, 918-426-4470

McAlester ISD 2,400/PK-12
PO Box 1027, 918-423-4771
Lucy Smith, supt. Fax 423-8166
www.mcalester.k12.ok.us/
McAlester HS 900/9-12
PO Box 1027, 918-423-4776
Allen Wadsworth, prin. Fax 423-8689
Puterbaugh MS 400/7-8
PO Box 1027, 918-423-5445
Randy Hughes, prin. Fax 423-7021

OK Dept. of Voc. & Tech. Education
Supt. — None
Kiamichi Technology Center Vo/Tech
301 Kiamichi Dr, 918-426-0940
Joe Ann Vermillion, dir. Fax 426-1626

Mc Curtain, Haskell, Pop. 474
McCurtain ISD 300/PK-12
PO Box 189, 918-945-7237
Darrell Adcock, supt. Fax 945-7064
www.mccurtain.k12.ok.us/
McCurtain HS, PO Box 189, 100/9-12
Perry Arnwine, prin. 918-945-7236

Mc Loud, Pottawatomie, Pop. 2,821
CareerTech Skills Centers
Supt. — None
Dom Garrison, supt.
Bassett Skills Center Vo/Tech
29501 Kickapoo Rd, 405-964-5540

Mc Loud ISD 1,300/K-12
PO Box 240, 405-964-3314
Ronnie Renfrow, supt. Fax 964-2801
mcloud.k12.ok.us
Mc Loud HS 500/9-12
PO Box 60, 405-964-3311
Leigh Todd, prin. Fax 964-3498
Mc Loud JHS 300/7-8
PO Box 730, 405-964-3312
Doug Van Scoyoc, prin. Fax 964-7530

Macomb, Pottawatomie, Pop. 63
Macomb ISD 400/PK-12
36591 State Highway 59B 74852 405-598-3892
Randy Cottrell Ed.D., supt. Fax 598-8041
Macomb HS 100/9-12
36591 State Highway 59B 74852 405-598-5420
Greg Hinkle, prin. Fax 598-3295

Madill, Marshall, Pop. 3,519
Madill ISD 1,400/K-12
601 W McArthur St 73446 580-795-3303
John Carter, supt. Fax 795-3210
www.madillok.com
Madill HS 400/9-12
700 S 5th Ave 73446 580-795-3339
Monte Womack, prin. Fax 795-2657
Madill MS 500/5-8
601 W McArthur St 73446 580-795-7373
Steve Wilburn, prin. Fax 795-6930

Mangum, Greer, Pop. 2,753
Mangum ISD 700/PK-12
400 N Pennsylvania Ave 73554 580-782-3371
Mike Southall, supt. Fax 782-2313
www.mangum.k12.ok.us/
Mangum HS 100/10-12
301 N Oklahoma Ave 73554 580-782-3343
Micky Lively, prin. Fax 782-3265
Mangum JHS 200/7-9
400 N Oklahoma Ave 73554 580-782-2702
Mary Jane Scott, prin. Fax 782-5911

Mannford, Creek, Pop. 2,217
Mannford ISD 1,600/K-12
PO Box 100 74044 918-865-4062
Dr. Emet Callaway, supt. Fax 865-3405
www.mannford.k12.ok.us
Mannford HS 500/9-12
PO Box 100 74044 918-865-3841
Roger Moore, prin. Fax 865-2813
Mannford MS 400/6-8
PO Box 100 74044 918-865-4680
Molly Gregory, prin. Fax 865-2862

Marietta, Love, Pop. 2,431
Marietta ISD 900/PK-12
PO Box 289 73448 580-276-9444
James Howard, supt. Fax 276-4037
www.marietta.k12.ok.us
Marietta HS 300/9-12
PO Box 289 73448 580-276-3204
Larry Case, prin. Fax 276-1208
Marietta MS 200/6-8
PO Box 289 73448 580-276-3886
Jeff Dooley, prin. Fax 276-1203

Marlow, Stephens, Pop. 4,486
Bray-Doyle ISD 400/K-12
1205 S Brooks Rd 73055 580-658-5076
R. Kevin McKinley, supt. Fax 658-5888
Bray-Doyle HS 100/9-12
1205 S Brooks Rd 73055 580-658-5071
Jack Williams, prin.

Central High ISD 400/PK-12
RR 3 Box 249 73055 580-658-6858
Bennie Newton, supt. Fax 658-8010
www.central.k12.ok.us
Central HS 100/9-12
RR 3 Box 249 73055 580-658-2929
Mark Perry, prin. Fax 658-8010

Marlow ISD | 1,400/PK-12
PO Box 73 73055 | 580-658-2719
George E. Coffman, supt. | Fax 658-6455
www.marlow.k12.ok.us
Marlow HS | 400/9-12
PO Box 73 73055 | 580-658-1516
Tom Cosgrove, prin. | Fax 658-1520
Marlow MS | 300/6-8
PO Box 73 73055 | 580-658-2619
Tommy Williams, prin. | Fax 658-1169

Mason, Okfuskee
Mason ISD | 300/PK-12
RR 1 Box 143B 74859 | 918-623-0231
Don Davenport, supt. | Fax 623-0884
www.mason.k12.ok.us/
Mason HS | 100/9-12
RR 1 Box 143B 74859 | 918-623-0107
Eddie Weaver, prin. | Fax 623-0147

Maud, Pottawatomie, Pop. 1,148
Maud ISD | 400/PK-12
PO Box 130 74854 | 405-374-2416
J.E. Pryor, supt. | Fax 374-2628
www.maud.k12.ok.us/
Maud HS | 100/9-12
PO Box 130 74854 | 405-374-2425
Garrett Davis, prin. | Fax 374-2895

Maysville, Garvin, Pop. 1,294
Maysville ISD | 400/PK-12
600 1st St 73057 | 405-867-5595
Robert Moody, supt. | Fax 867-4864
www.maysville.k12.ok.us
Maysville JSHS | 200/7-12
600 1st St 73057 | 405-867-4410
Lee Hughes, prin. | Fax 867-4864

Medford, Grant, Pop. 1,133
Medford ISD | 300/PK-12
301 N Main St 73759 | 580-395-2392
Jason Sternberger, supt. | Fax 395-2391
www.medford.k12.ok.us/
Medford JSHS | 100/7-12
301 N Main St 73759 | 580-395-2392
Mickey Geurkink, prin. | Fax 395-2391

Meeker, Lincoln, Pop. 976
Meeker SD | 900/PK-12
PO Box 68 74855 | 405-279-3511
Robert Hightower, supt. | Fax 279-2765
www.meeker.k12.ok.us
Meeker HS, PO Box 68 74855 | 300/9-12
Rita Palmer, prin. | 405-279-2113
Meeker MS, PO Box 68 74855 | 200/6-8
Mike Hill, prin. | 405-279-2414

Miami, Ottawa, Pop. 13,485
Miami ISD | 2,300/K-12
418 G St SE 74354 | 918-542-8455
William Stephens, supt. | Fax 542-1236
www.miami.k12.ok.us
Miami HS | 600/9-12
2000 E Central Ave 74354 | 918-542-4421
Mike Reece, prin. | Fax 542-7421
Rogers MS | 600/6-8
504 Goodrich Blvd 74354 | 918-542-5588
Mark Stanton, prin. | Fax 542-4400

Northeastern Oklahoma A&M College | Post-Sec.
200 I St NE 74354 | 918-542-8441

Midwest City, Oklahoma, Pop. 54,662
Midwest City-Del City ISD | 14,300/PK-12
7217 SE 15th St 73110 | 405-737-4461
William Scoggan M.Ed., supt. | Fax 739-1615
www.mid-del.net
Albert JHS | 900/7-9
2515 S Post Rd 73130 | 405-739-1761
Joyce Honey, prin. | Fax 739-1780
Albert SHS | 800/10-12
2009 S Post Rd 73130 | 405-739-1726
Silvya Kirk Ph.D., prin. | Fax 739-1685
Eubanks Mid-Del Technology Center | Vo/Tech
1621 Maple Dr 73110 | 405-739-1707
Debbie Neugent, prin. | Fax 739-1716
Jarman JHS | 600/7-9
5 W MacArthur Dr 73110 | 405-739-1771
Rick Croslin, prin. | Fax 739-1773
Midwest City SHS | 1,200/10-12
213 Elm St 73110 | 405-739-1741
Ron Stearns, prin. | Fax 739-1675
Monroney JHS | 700/7-9
7400 E Reno Ave 73110 | 405-739-1786
Chris Reynolds, prin. | Fax 739-1789
Other Schools – See Del City

OK Dept. of Voc. & Tech. Education
Supt. — None
Mid-Del Technology Center | Vo/Tech
1621 Maple Dr 73110 | 405-739-1707
| Fax 739-1716

Rose State College | Post-Sec.
6420 SE 15th St 73110 | 405-733-7300

Milburn, Johnston, Pop. 310
Milburn ISD | 200/PK-12
PO Box 429 73450 | 580-443-5522
Kenneth Keeling, supt. | Fax 443-5303
www.milburn.k12.ok.us
Milburn HS | 100/9-12
PO Box 429 73450 | 580-443-5522
Debbie Speers, prin. | Fax 443-5303

Mill Creek, Johnston, Pop. 338
Mill Creek ISD | 200/PK-12
PO Box 118 74856 | 580-384-5514
Richard Bowen, supt. | Fax 384-3920
www.millcreek.k12.ok.us
Mill Creek HS | 100/9-12
PO Box 118 74856 | 580-384-5447
Kathy Bowen, prin. | Fax 384-3920

Minco, Grady, Pop. 1,713
Minco ISD | 500/PK-12
PO Box 428 73059 | 405-352-4867
Richard Brownen, supt. | Fax 352-4006
www.minco.k12.ok.us
Minco HS | 200/9-12
PO Box 428 73059 | 405-352-4377
Robert Odam, prin. | Fax 352-4006
Minco MS | 100/6-8
PO Box 428 73059 | 405-352-4377
Troy Wittrock, prin. | Fax 352-4006

Moore, Cleveland, Pop. 44,987
Moore ISD | 19,000/PK-12
1500 SE 4th St 73160 | 405-793-3188
Deborah Arato, supt. | Fax 793-3050
www.moore.k12.ok.us
Central JHS | 900/7-9
400 N Broadway St 73160 | 405-793-3265
David Peak, prin. | Fax 895-7398
Highland East JHS | 900/7-9
1200 SE 4th St 73160 | 405-793-3200
John Marren, prin. | Fax 793-3198
Highland West JHS | 700/7-9
901 N Santa Fe Ave 73160 | 405-793-3210
Peggy Pate, prin. | Fax 793-3218
Moore HS | 1,900/10-12
300 N Eastern Ave 73160 | 405-793-3100
Mike Coyle, prin. | Fax 793-3140
Other Schools – See Oklahoma City

Hillsdale Free Will Baptist College | Post-Sec.
PO Box 7208 73153 | 405-912-9000
Oklahoma City Christian Academy | 100/PK-12
1005 SW 4th St 73160 | 405-794-9000
Oklahoma Health Academy | Post-Sec.
1939 N Moore Ave 73160 | 405-912-2777

Mooreland, Woodward, Pop. 1,206
Mooreland ISD | 500/K-12
PO Box 75 73852 | 580-994-5388
Terry Kellner, supt. | Fax 994-5900
www.mooreland.k12.ok.us
Mooreland HS | 100/9-12
PO Box 75 73852 | 580-994-5426
Ron Wilson, prin. | Fax 994-2344

Morris, Okmulgee, Pop. 1,327
Morris ISD | 1,100/PK-12
PO Box 80 74445 | 918-733-9072
James Lyons, supt. | Fax 733-4205
Morris HS | 400/9-12
PO Box 80 74445 | 918-733-4198
Andrew Ewton, prin. | Fax 733-2857
Morris MS | 200/6-8
PO Box 80 74445 | 918-733-4551
Greg Large, prin. | Fax 733-4618

Morrison, Noble, Pop. 629
Morrison ISD | 500/PK-12
PO Box 176 73061 | 580-724-3341
Dennis Casey, supt. | Fax 724-3004
www.morrison.k12.ok.us
Morrison HS, PO Box 176 73061 | 100/9-12
David Cartmell, prin. | 580-724-3307

Mounds, Creek, Pop. 1,158
Liberty ISD | 600/PK-12
2727 E 201st St S 74047 | 918-366-8496
Dr. Kent Holbrook, supt. | Fax 366-8497
www.liberty.k12.ok.us
Liberty HS, 2727 E 201st St S 74047 | 200/9-12
Randy Hess, prin. | 918-366-8784
Liberty MS, 2727 E 201st St S 74047 | 100/6-8
Patty Medill, prin. | 918-366-8494

Mounds ISD | 800/PK-12
PO Box 189 74047 | 918-827-6100
Dennis Campbell, supt. | Fax 827-3704
www.mounds.k12.ok.us/
Mounds HS, PO Box 189 74047 | 200/9-12
Kevin Collins, prin. | 918-827-6200

Mountain View, Kiowa, Pop. 849
Mountain View-Gotebo ISD | 300/K-12
RR 2 Box 88 73062 | 580-347-2211
Paula Squires, supt. | Fax 347-2869
Mountain View-Gotebo HS | 100/9-12
RR 2 Box 88 73062 | 580-347-2211
Jason James, prin.

Moyers, Pushmataha
Moyers SD | 200/K-12
PO Box 88 74557 | 580-298-5549
Donna Dudley, supt. | Fax 298-2022
www.moyers.k12.ok.us/
Moyers HS | 100/9-12
PO Box 88 74557 | 580-298-6951
LaWanda Vaughn, prin. | Fax 298-2022

Muldrow, Sequoyah, Pop. 3,136
Muldrow ISD | 1,600/PK-12
PO Box 660 74948 | 918-427-7406
Roger Sharp, supt. | Fax 427-6088
www.muldrow.k12.ok.us
Muldrow HS | 500/9-12
PO Box 660 74948 | 918-427-3274
David Rhodes, prin. | Fax 427-1035
Muldrow MS | 400/5-8
PO Box 660 74948 | 918-427-5421
Montea Wight, prin. | Fax 427-1034

Muskogee, Muskogee, Pop. 38,635
Hilldale ISD | 1,800/PK-12
500 E Smith Ferry Rd 74403 | 918-683-0273
D. B. Merrill, supt. | Fax 683-8725
www.hilldale.k12.ok.us
Hilldale HS | 500/9-12
300 E Smith Ferry Rd 74403 | 918-683-3253
Dwayne Pemberton, prin. | Fax 683-0622
Hilldale MS | 400/6-8
400 E Smith Ferry Rd 74403 | 918-683-0763
John Engelbrecht, prin. | Fax 683-0766

Muskogee ISD | 8,000/PK-12
202 W Broadway St 74401 | 918-684-3700
Michael Garde, supt. | Fax 684-3827
www.mpsi20.org
Muskogee 7th & 8th Grade Center | 900/7-8
Callahan & North S St 74403 | 918-684-3775
Pam Bradley, prin. | Fax 684-3776
Muskogee HS | 1,700/9-12
3200 E Shawnee Rd 74403 | 918-684-3750
Gary Bivin, prin. | Fax 684-3751

OK Dept. of Voc. & Tech. Education
Supt. — None
Indian Capital Technology Center | Vo/Tech
2403 N 41st St E 74403 | 918-686-7565
Tom Stiles, supt. | Fax 686-7564
Indian Capital Technology Center | Vo/Tech
2403 N 41st St E 74403 | 918-687-6383
Jerry Belton, dir. | Fax 687-6624

Bacone College | Post-Sec.
2299 Old Bacone Rd 74403 | 918-781-7340
Muskogee General Hospital | Post-Sec.
300 Rockefeller Dr 74401 | 918-682-5501
Parkview School OK School for the Blind | Post-Sec.
3300 Gibson St 74403 | 918-682-6641
Virgil's Beauty College | Post-Sec.
111 S 9th St 74401 | 918-682-9429

Mustang, Canadian, Pop. 14,551
Mustang ISD | 6,900/PK-12
906 S Heights Dr 73064 | 405-376-2461
Karl Springer, supt. | Fax 376-7333
www.mustangps.org
Mustang HS | 1,600/10-12
906 S Heights Dr 73064 | 405-376-2404
Terry Tipton, prin. | Fax 376-7347
Mustang MS | 900/6-8
906 S Heights Dr 73064 | 405-376-2448
Linda Wilkes, prin. | Fax 376-7373
Mustang Mid HS | 600/9-9
906 S Heights Dr 73064 | 405-376-7855
Kenny Nelson, prin. | Fax 376-7852
Mustang North MS | 800/6-8
906 S Heights Dr 73064 | 405-324-2236
Ralph Smith, prin. | Fax 324-2258

Mutual, Woodward, Pop. 74
Sharon-Mutual ISD | 300/PK-12
RR 1 Box 290 73853 | 580-989-3210
Doug Evans, supt. | Fax 989-3241
www.smps.k12.ok.us
Sharon-Mutual HS | 100/9-12
RR 1 Box 290 73853 | 580-989-3231
Clint Ford, prin.

Newcastle, McClain, Pop. 5,814
Newcastle ISD | 1,100/K-12
101 N Main St 73065 | 405-387-2890
Robert Everett, supt. | Fax 387-3482
www.newcastle.k12.ok.us
Newcastle HS | 400/9-12
101 N Main St 73065 | 405-387-4304
Joe Cox, prin. | Fax 387-3461
Newcastle MS | 300/6-8
418 NW 10th St 73065 | 405-387-3139
Randy Scott, prin. | Fax 387-5563

Newkirk, Kay, Pop. 2,188
Newkirk ISD | 700/PK-12
PO Box 91 74647 | 580-362-2388
Carl Barnes, supt. | Fax 362-3413
www.newkirk.k12.ok.us
Newkirk HS | 200/9-12
PO Box 91 74647 | 580-362-6241
Dwight Winburn, prin. | Fax 362-6242
Newkirk MS | 200/6-8
PO Box 485 74647 | 580-362-2516
Jim Wiersig, prin. | Fax 362-1150

Ninnekah, Grady, Pop. 1,036
Ninnekah ISD | 400/PK-12
PO Box 275 73067 | 405-224-4092
Todd Bunch, supt. | Fax 224-4096
www.ninnekah.k12.ok.us/
Ninnekah HS | 100/9-12
PO Box 275 73067 | 405-224-4299
David Pitts, prin. | Fax 224-4665
Ninnekah JHS | 100/7-8
PO Box 275 73067 | 405-224-4299
David Pitts, prin. | Fax 224-4665

Noble, Cleveland, Pop. 5,402
Noble ISD | 2,800/PK-12
PO Box 499 73068 | 405-872-3452
Curtis Inge, supt. | Fax 872-3271
www.nobleps.com
Noble HS | 800/9-12
4601 E Etowah Rd 73068 | 405-872-3441
Frank Soloman, prin. | Fax 872-9824
Noble MS | 700/6-8
1201 N 8th St 73068 | 405-872-3495
Gary Lundy, prin. | Fax 872-8670

Norman, Cleveland, Pop. 99,197
Little Axe ISD | 1,200/PK-12
2000 168th Ave NE 73026 | 405-329-7691
Barry Damrill, supt. | Fax 579-2929
littleaxe.k12.ok.us
Little Axe HS | 400/9-12
2000 168th Ave NE 73026 | 405-329-1612
Bob Hicks, prin. | Fax 329-2914
Little Axe MS | 300/6-8
2000 168th Ave NE 73026 | 405-329-2156
Dalton Griffin, prin. | Fax 579-2937

Norman ISD | 12,600/PK-12
131 S Flood Ave 73069 | 405-364-1339
Dr. Joseph Siano, supt. | Fax 366-5851
www.norman.k12.ok.us
Alcott MS | 600/6-8
1919 W Boyd St 73069 | 405-366-5845
Dana Morris, prin. | Fax 447-6572

Irving MS 600/6-8
125 Vicksburg Ave 73071 405-366-5941
Jerry Privett, prin. Fax 366-5944
Longfellow MS 600/6-8
215 N Ponca Ave 73071 405-366-5948
Darien Moore, prin. Fax 366-5952
Norman HS 1,800/9-12
911 W Main St 73069 405-366-5812
Dr. Lynne Chesley, prin. Fax 366-5945
Norman North HS 2,100/9-12
1809 Stubbeman Ave 73069 405-366-5954
Jerry Winkle, prin. Fax 573-3590
Whittier MS 900/6-8
2000 W Brooks St 73069 405-366-5956
Sharon Dean, prin. Fax 447-6562

OK Dept. of Voc. & Tech. Education
Supt. — None
Moore Norman Technology Center Vo/Tech
4701 12th Ave NW 73069 405-364-5763
Dr. John Hunter, supt. Fax 217-8277

Blue Eagle Christian Academy 50/PK-12
2404 Classen Blvd 73071 405-364-7200
Bertha Symes, admin.
Community Christian S 700/PK-12
3002 Broce Dr 73072 405-329-2500
Barbara Ohsfeldt, admin. Fax 329-3510
University of Oklahoma at Norman Post-Sec.
660 Parrington Oval 73019 405-325-0311

Nowata, Nowata, Pop. 4,035
Nowata ISD 1,100/PK-12
707 W Osage Ave 74048 918-273-3425
Fred Bailey, supt. Fax 273-2105
www.nowataps.k12.ok.us/
Nowata HS, 707 W Osage Ave 74048 300/9-12
Michelle Childs, prin. 918-273-2221
Nowata MS, 707 W Osage Ave 74048 300/6-8
Kathy Berry, prin. 918-273-1346

Oaks, Delaware, Pop. 422
Oaks-Mission ISD 300/PK-12
PO Box 160 74359 918-868-2183
Wyman Thompson, supt. Fax 868-2707
Oaks-Mission HS, PO Box 160 74359 100/9-12
David Hampton, prin. 918-868-2499

Oilton, Creek, Pop. 1,109
Oilton ISD 300/PK-12
PO Box 130 74052 918-862-3954
Matt Posey, supt. Fax 862-3955
Oilton HS 100/9-12
PO Box 130 74052 918-862-3272
Tony McCool, prin. Fax 862-3763

Okarche, Kingfisher, Pop. 1,143
Okarche ISD 300/PK-12
PO Box 276 73762 405-263-7300
Robert Barnett, supt. Fax 263-7515
www.okarche.k12.ok.us/
Okarche HS 100/10-12
PO Box 276 73762 405-263-7212
Wynona Knopp, prin. Fax 263-7515
Okarche JHS, PO Box 276 73762 100/7-9
Wynona Knopp, prin. 405-263-7212

Okay, Wagoner, Pop. 603
Okay ISD 500/PK-12
PO Box 830 74446 918-682-2548
Mickey Igert, supt. Fax 683-8331
www.okayschool.k12.ok.us/
Okay HS 200/9-12
PO Box 830 74446 918-682-0371
Donald Branscum, prin. Fax 682-7653

Okeene, Blaine, Pop. 1,213
Okeene ISD 300/K-12
PO Box 409 73763 580-822-3268
Ron Pittman, supt. Fax 822-4123
Okeene JSHS 200/7-12
PO Box 409 73763 580-822-3219
Jeremy Osmus, prin. Fax 822-4123

Okemah, Okfuskee, Pop. 3,003
Okemah ISD 900/PK-12
107 W Date St 74859 918-623-1874
Tom Condict, supt. Fax 623-1203
www.okemah.k12.ok.us
Okemah HS 300/9-12
704 E Date St 74859 918-623-1274
Tom Howell, prin. Fax 623-1884
Okemah MS 300/4-8
107 W Date St 74859 918-623-0212
Tony Dean, prin. Fax 623-9151

Oklahoma City, Oklahoma, Pop. 523,303
CareerTech Skills Centers
Supt. — None
Dom Garrison, supt.
Hillside Skills Center Vo/Tech
3300 N Martin Luther King 73111 405-425-2942
Mansion Apprenticeship Skills Ctr Vo/Tech
PO Box 36248 73136 405-528-4561

Crooked Oak ISD 1,200/PK-12
1901 SE 15th St 73129 405-677-5252
Shannon Goodsell, supt. Fax 670-8070
www.crookedoak.k12.ok.us
Crooked Oak HS 300/9-12
1901 SE 15th St 73129 405-677-4063
Verna Shelton, prin. Fax 677-8072
Crooked Oak MS 300/6-8
1901 SE 15th St 73129 405-672-0231
Ken Attebery, prin. Fax 670-2256

Millwood ISD 1,100/PK-12
6724 N Martin Luther King 73111 405-478-1336
Dr. Gloria Griffin, supt. Fax 478-4698
www.millwood.k12.ok.us
Millwood HS 300/9-12
6718 N Martin Luther King 73111 405-478-0504
Nanette Thomas, prin.

Moore ISD
Supt. — See Moore
Brink JHS 1,100/7-9
11420 S Western Ave 73170 405-692-5620
Janet Southard, prin. Fax 692-5634
West JHS 1,000/7-9
9400 S Pennsylvania Ave 73159 405-692-5600
Dr. Michaele Benn, prin. Fax 692-5660
Westmoore SHS 2,100/10-12
12613 S Western Ave 73170 405-691-8000
Mark Hunt, prin. Fax 692-5711

OK Dept. of Voc. & Tech. Education
Supt. — None
Metro Tech Vo/Tech
1900 Springlake Dr 73111 405-424-8324
Dr. James Branscum, supt. Fax 424-5419
Metro Tech-Aviation Career Center Vo/Tech
5600 S MacArthur Blvd 73179 405-685-0008
Peter Lee, dir. Fax 681-5644
Metro Tech South Bryant Campus Vo/Tech
4901 S Bryant Ave 73129 405-424-8324
John Robinson, dir. Fax 670-6895
Metro Tech-Springlake Campus Vo/Tech
1900 Springlake Dr 73111 405-424-8324
Fax 528-1512
Tuttle-Portland Campus Vo/Tech
12777 N Rockwell Ave 73142 405-717-7799
Dr. Kay Martin, supt. Fax 755-0028
Tuttle-Rockwell Campus Vo/Tech
12777 N Rockwell Ave 73142 405-717-7799
Dr. Kay Martin, supt. Fax 717-4112

Oklahoma City ISD 38,400/PK-12
900 N Klein Ave 73106 405-587-0000
Fax 587-0443
www.okcps.org/
Capitol Hill HS 1,100/9-12
500 SW Grand Blvd 73109 405-616-1210
Jimmy Dew, prin. Fax 636-5007
Classen S of Advanced Studies 1,100/6-12
1901 N Ellison Ave 73106 405-556-5070
Dr. Ronald Maxfield, prin. Fax 556-5080
Douglass HS 900/7-12
900 N Martin Luther King Av 73117 405-424-4391
Vallene Cooks, prin. Fax 425-4656
Grant HS 1,400/9-12
5016 S Pennsylvania Ave 73119 405-685-6621
Phillip Wallace, prin. Fax 686-4006
Hoover MS 800/6-8
2401 NW 115th Ter 73120 405-751-1210
Carole Thompson, prin. Fax 752-6803
Jackson MS 700/6-8
2601 S Villa Ave 73108 405-634-6357
Steve Johnson, prin. Fax 636-5078
Jefferson MS 1,000/6-8
6800 S Blackwelder Ave 73159 405-632-2341
Gloria Torres, prin. Fax 636-5084
Marshall HS 800/9-12
9017 N University Ave 73114 405-848-6871
Cleo McGlory, prin. Fax 841-3109
Northeast Academy for Health Sci./Eng. 900/6-12
3100 N Kelley Ave 73111 405-424-1491
Dr. Brian Staples, prin. Fax 425-4609
Northwest Classen HS 1,400/9-12
2801 NW 27th St 73107 405-942-5551
Richard Lafavers, prin. Fax 942-3900
Roosevelt MS 900/6-8
3233 SW 44th St 73119 405-685-7795
Marilyn Vrooman, prin. Fax 686-4059
Southeast HS 800/9-12
5401 S Shields Blvd 73129 405-636-5008
Dr. Michael Maples, prin. Fax 636-5024
Taft MS 1,000/6-8
2901 NW 23rd St 73107 405-946-1431
Lisa Johnson, prin. Fax 945-1126
Webster MS 700/6-8
6708 S Santa Fe Ave 73139 405-632-6653
Richard Brown, prin. Fax 636-5094
Other Schools – See Spencer

Putnam City ISD 19,100/PK-12
5401 NW 40th St 73122 405-495-5200
Dr. Jim Capps, supt. Fax 495-8648
www.putnamcityschools.org
Central MS 900/6-8
4020 N Grove Ave 73122 405-787-3660
Christie Baker, prin. Fax 491-7536
Cooper MS 900/6-8
8001 River Bend Blvd 73132 405-720-9887
Jennifer DeSouza, prin. Fax 728-5632
Hefner MS 1,200/6-8
8400 N Macarthur Blvd 73132 405-721-2411
Lise Finley, prin. Fax 728-5645
Mayfield MS 700/6-8
1600 N Purdue Ave 73127 405-947-8693
Dr. Dick Balenseifen, prin. Fax 948-9000
Putnam City HS 2,000/9-12
5300 NW 50th St 73122 405-789-4350
Dr. Don Wentroth, prin. Fax 789-1662
Putnam City North HS 2,200/9-12
11800 N Rockwell Ave 73162 405-722-4220
Dr. Brian Chastain, prin. Fax 721-4946
Putnam City West HS 1,800/9-12
8500 NW 23rd St 73127 405-787-1140
Buster Meeks, prin. Fax 491-7602
Other Schools – See Bethany

Western Heights ISD 3,100/PK-12
8401 SW 44th St 73179 405-350-3410
Joe Kitchens, supt. Fax 745-6322
www.westernheights.k12.ok.us
Western Heights HS 800/9-12
8201 SW 44th St 73179 405-350-3435
Jean Adams, prin. Fax 745-6315
Western Heights MS 700/6-8
8435 SW 44th St 73179 405-350-3455
Dewayne White, prin. Fax 745-6341

Bishop McGuinness HS 700/9-12
801 NW 50th St 73118 405-842-6638
David Morton, prin. Fax 858-9550
Casady S 900/PK-12
PO Box 20390 73156 405-749-3100
Charles Britton, hdmstr. Fax 749-3223
CC's Cosmetology College Post-Sec.
4439 NW 50th St 73112 405-943-2300
Central State Beauty Academy Post-Sec.
8494 NW Expressway St 73162 405-722-4499
Heritage College Post-Sec.
7100 S I 35 Srvce Rd #7118 73149 405-631-3399
Heritage Hall S 800/PK-12
1800 NW 122nd St 73120 405-749-3001
Guy Bramble, hdmstr. Fax 751-7372
Hollywood Cosmetology Center Post-Sec.
PO Box 890488 73189 405-364-3375
ITT Technical Institute Post-Sec.
1900 NW Expressway St #305R 73118
405-810-4100
Metro Area Vocational Technical School Post-Sec.
1900 Springlake Dr 73111 405-424-8324
Metropolitan College Post-Sec.
1900 NW Expressway R302 73118 405-843-1000
Mid-America Christian University Post-Sec.
3500 SW 119th St 73170 405-691-3800
Mt. St. Mary's HS 200/9-12
2801 S Shartel Ave 73109 405-631-8865
Talita DeNegrl, prin. Fax 631-9209
Oklahoma Christian University Post-Sec.
PO Box 11000 73136 405-425-5000
Oklahoma City Community College Post-Sec.
7777 S May Ave 73159 405-682-1611
Oklahoma City University Post-Sec.
2501 N Blackwelder Ave 73106 405-521-5000
Oklahoma State University-Oklahoma City Post-Sec.
900 N Portland Ave 73107 405-947-4421
Parkview Adventist Academy 50/K-10
4201 N Martin Luther King 73111 405-427-6525
Fax 427-1154
Platt College Post-Sec.
309 S Ann Arbor Ave 73128 405-946-7799
Platt College Post-Sec.
2727 W Memorial Rd 73134 405-749-2433
State Barber and Hair Design College Post-Sec.
2514 S Agnew Ave 73108 405-631-8621
Tuttle Vocational Technical Center Post-Sec.
12777 N Rockwell Ave 73142 405-722-7799
University Hospital of Oklahoma City Post-Sec.
PO Box 26307 73126 405-271-4000
University of Oklahoma Health Sciences Post-Sec.
1000 Stanton L Young Blvd 73190 405-271-4000
Vatterott College Post-Sec.
4621 NW 23rd St 73127 405-945-0088
Wright Business School Post-Sec.
2219 SW 74th St Ste 122 73159 405-681-2300

Okmulgee, Okmulgee, Pop. 12,727
OK Dept. of Voc. & Tech. Education
Supt. — None
Green Country Technology Center Vo/Tech
PO Box 1217 74447 918-758-0840
Danne Spurlock, supt. Fax 758-0422

Okmulgee ISD 2,000/PK-12
PO Box 1346 74447 918-758-2000
Paul McGee, supt. Fax 758-2088
www.okmulgee.k12.ok.us
Okmulgee HS 600/9-12
415 W 3rd St 74447 918-758-2075
David Parker, prin. Fax 758-2096
Okmulgee MS 500/6-8
1421 Martin Luther King Dr 74447 918-758-2050
John Whitfield, prin. Fax 758-2095

Oklahoma State University-Okmulgee Post-Sec.
1801 E 4th St 74447 800-722-4471

Oktaha, Muskogee, Pop. 334
Oktaha ISD 600/PK-12
PO Box 9 74450 918-687-7556
Jerry Needham, supt. Fax 687-0074
Oktaha HS, PO Box 9 74450 200/9-12
Neoma Buckley, prin. 918-687-3672

Olustee, Jackson, Pop. 657
Olustee ISD 200/PK-12
PO Box 70 73560 580-648-2243
Roger Allen, supt. Fax 648-2501
Olustee HS 100/9-12
PO Box 70 73560 580-648-2243
Darinda Welch, prin. Fax 648-2501

Omega, Kingfisher
Lomega ISD 200/PK-12
RR 1 Box 46 73764 405-729-4215
Steve Mendell, supt. Fax 729-4666
www.lomega.k12.ok.us
Lomega HS 100/9-12
RR 1 Box 46 73764 405-729-4281
Karen Castonguay, prin. Fax 729-4666

OK Dept. of Voc. & Tech. Education
Supt. — None
Chisholm Trail Technology Center Vo/Tech
RR 1 Box 60 73764 405-729-8324
Tim Geis, supt. Fax 729-8335

Oologah, Rogers, Pop. 1,026
Oologah-Talala ISD 1,700/K-12
PO Box 189 74053 918-443-6000
Rick Thomas, supt. Fax 443-9088
www.oologah.k12.ok.us
Oologah HS 500/9-12
PO Box 189 74053 918-443-6211
Jack Chambers, prin. Fax 443-2418
Oologah MS 400/6-8
PO Box 189 74053 918-443-6151
Melissa Overcash, prin. Fax 443-2875

Orlando, Logan, Pop. 209
Mulhall-Orlando ISD 200/PK-12
PO Box 8 73073 580-455-2211
Dr. Don Sjoberg, supt. Fax 455-8019
www.mulhall-orlando.k12.ok.us

Mulhall-Orlando HS | 100/9-12
PO Box 8 73073 | 580-455-2212
Walter Howell, prin. | Fax 455-8019

Owasso, Tulsa, Pop. 21,634
Owasso ISD | 7,300/K-12
1501 N Ash St 74055 | 918-272-5367
Dr. Clark Ogilvie, supt. | Fax 272-8111
www.owasso.k12.ok.us
Owasso Eighth Grade Center | 600/8-8
1501 N Ash St 74055 | 918-272-6274
Deirdre Hodge, prin.
Owasso HS, 1501 N Ash St 74055 | 1,000/11-12
Stan Trout, prin. | 918-272-5334
Owasso Mid HS, 1501 N Ash St 74055 | 1,200/9-10
Sam Herriman, prin. | 918-274-3000

Paden, Okfuskee, Pop. 444
Paden ISD | 300/PK-12
PO Box 370 74860 | 405-932-5053
Keith Kincade, supt. | Fax 932-4132
www.paden.k12.ok.us/
Paden HS, PO Box 370 74860 | 100/9-12
Keith Kincade, prin. | 405-932-4465

Panama, LeFlore, Pop. 1,383
Panama ISD | 700/PK-12
PO Box 1680 74951 | 918-963-2217
Darthur Drummonds, supt. | Fax 963-4860
www.panama.k12.ok.us/
Panama HS | 200/9-12
PO Box 1680 74951 | 918-963-2215
Larry Brooks, prin. | Fax 963-2638
Panama MS | 200/6-8
PO Box 1680 74951 | 918-963-2213
Grant Ralls, prin. | Fax 963-2463

Panola, Latimer
Panola ISD | 300/PK-12
PO Box 6 74559 | 918-465-3298
Alan Lumpkins, supt. | Fax 465-3656
www.panola.k12.ok.us/
Panola HS | 100/9-12
PO Box 6 74559 | 918-465-3813
Linda Albright, prin. | Fax 465-2996

Paoli, Garvin, Pop. 653
Paoli ISD | 300/PK-12
PO Box 278 73074 | 405-484-7336
Rick Worden, supt. | Fax 484-7268
www.paoli.k12.ok.us/
Paoli HS, PO Box 278 73074 | 100/9-12
Greg Benson, prin. | 405-484-7336

Park Hill, Cherokee
Keys SD | 700/PK-12
26622 S 520 Rd 74451 | 918-458-1835
Jerry Hood, supt. | Fax 456-7502
www.keys.k12.ok.us
Keys HS | 200/9-12
26622 S 520 Rd 74451 | 918-458-1835
Jerry Hood, prin. | Fax 456-7502

Pauls Valley, Garvin, Pop. 6,179
Pauls Valley ISD | 1,300/PK-12
PO Box 780 73075 | 405-238-6453
Bobby D. Russell, supt. | Fax 238-9178
www.paulsvalley.k12.ok.us
Pauls Valley JHS | 300/7-9
PO Box 780 73075 | 405-238-1239
Martha Graham, prin. | Fax 238-1410
Pauls Valley SHS | 300/10-12
PO Box 780 73075 | 405-238-6497
Pete Campbell, prin. | Fax 238-1236

Pawhuska, Osage, Pop. 3,571
Pawhuska ISD | 1,000/PK-12
1801 McKenzie St 74056 | 918-287-1281
Jack Miles, supt. | Fax 287-4461
www.pawhuska.k12.ok.us
Pawhuska HS | 300/9-12
621 E 15th St 74056 | 918-287-1262
Robert Schornick, prin. | Fax 287-1236
Pawhuska JHS | 100/7-8
615 E 15th St 74056 | 918-287-1264
Jon Culver, prin. | Fax 287-2062

Pawnee, Pawnee, Pop. 2,200
Pawnee ISD | 800/PK-12
615 Denver St 74058 | 918-762-3676
Ned Williams, supt. | Fax 762-2704
Pawnee HS, 615 Denver St 74058 | 200/9-12
Chris Jenkins, prin. | 918-762-3676
Pawnee MS, 605 Denver St 74058 | 200/6-8
David Tanner, prin. | 918-762-3055

Perkins, Payne, Pop. 2,316
Perkins-Tryon ISD | 1,300/PK-12
PO Box 549 74059 | 405-547-5703
James Ramsey, supt. | Fax 547-2020
www.p-t.k12.ok.us
Perkins-Tryon HS | 300/10-12
PO Box 549 74059 | 405-547-5724
Margaret Hrencher, prin. | Fax 547-5760
Perkins-Tryon JHS | 300/7-9
PO Box 549 74059 | 405-547-5715
Mark Shelton, prin. | Fax 547-5761

Perry, Noble, Pop. 5,138
Perry ISD | 1,200/PK-12
900 Fir St 73077 | 580-336-4511
Brent Koontz, supt. | Fax 336-5185
www.perry.k12.ok.us
Perry HS | 400/9-12
900 Fir St 73077 | 580-336-4415
Dr. Linda Powers, prin. | Fax 336-5185
Perry MS, 1303 N 15th St 73077 | 200/6-8
Ranay Roth, prin. | 580-336-2577

Picher, Ottawa, Pop. 1,617
Picher-Cardin ISD | 400/PK-12
PO Box 74360 | 918-673-1714
Robert Walker, supt. | Fax 673-1718
Picher-Cardin JSHS | 200/7-12
PO Box 280 74360 | 918-673-1713
Bruce Chrz, prin.

Piedmont, Canadian, Pop. 4,088
Piedmont ISD | 1,600/K-12
713 Piedmont Rd N 73078 | 405-373-2311
Mike Hyatt, supt. | Fax 373-0912
piedmont.k12.ok.us
Piedmont HS | 500/9-12
823 2nd St NW 73078 | 405-373-5011
Todd Garrison, prin. | Fax 373-3055
Piedmont MS | 400/6-8
808 2nd St NW 73078 | 405-373-1315
Jacky Parish, prin. | Fax 373-5006

Pittsburg, Pittsburg, Pop. 282
Pittsburg ISD | 200/PK-12
PO Box 200 74560 | 918-432-5062
Tony Potts, supt. | Fax 432-5312
Pittsburg HS, PO Box 200 74560 | 100/9-12
Tony Potts, prin. | 918-432-5513

Pocola, LeFlore, Pop. 4,255
Pocola ISD | 900/PK-12
PO Box 640 74902 | 918-436-2424
James Warden, supt. | Fax 436-2437
www.pocola.k12.ok.us
Pocola HS | 200/9-12
PO Box 640 74902 | 918-436-2042
Randy Ragland, prin. | Fax 436-2920
Pocola MS, PO Box 640 74902 | 200/6-8
Betty Freeman, prin. | 918-436-2091

Ponca City, Kay, Pop. 25,596
OK Dept. of Voc. & Tech. Education
Supt. — None
Pioneer Technology Center | Vo/Tech
2101 N Ash St 74601 | 580-762-8336
Dr. Doug Major, supt. | Fax 762-1175

Ponca City ISD | 5,700/PK-12
111 W Grand Ave 74601 | 580-767-8000
David Pennington, supt. | Fax 767-8007
www.poncacity.k12.ok.us
East MS | 400/8-8
612 E Grand Ave 74601 | 580-767-8010
Barbara Davis, prin. | Fax 762-5301
Ponca City HS | 1,800/9-12
927 N 5th St 74601 | 580-767-9500
John Woody, prin. | Fax 767-9515

Ponca City Beauty College | Post-Sec.
122 N 1st St 74601 | 888-557-6709

Pond Creek, Grant, Pop. 862
Pond Creek-Hunter ISD | 300/PK-12
PO Box 56 73766 | 580-532-4242
Joel Quinn, supt. | Fax 532-4965
www.pondcreek-hunter.k12.ok.us
Pond Creek-Hunter HS | 200/7-12
PO Box 56 73766 | 580-532-4241
Kurt Neal, prin. | Fax 532-4965

Porter, Wagoner, Pop. 576
Porter Consolidated SD | 500/PK-12
PO Box 120 74454 | 918-483-2401
Mark Fenton, supt. | Fax 483-2310
Porter Consolidated HS | 100/9-12
PO Box 120 74454 | 918-483-7011
Larry Shackelford, prin. | Fax 483-2310

Porum, Muskogee, Pop. 732
Porum ISD | 500/PK-12
PO Box 189 74455 | 918-484-5121
Mark Calavan, supt. | Fax 484-2310
www.porum.k12.ok.us/
Porum HS | 200/9-12
PO Box 189 74455 | 918-484-5122
Don Cox, prin. | Fax 484-5121

Poteau, LeFlore, Pop. 7,990
OK Dept. of Voc. & Tech. Education
Supt. — None
Kiamichi Technology Center | Vo/Tech
PO Box 825 74953 | 918-647-4525
Joe Carrick, dir. | Fax 647-4527

Poteau ISD | 2,000/PK-12
100 Mockingbird Ln 74953 | 918-647-7700
Dr. Dan Foreman, supt. | Fax 647-9357
www.poteau.k12.ok.us
Kidd MS | 500/6-8
100 Mockingbird Ln 74953 | 918-647-7741
Lorraine Caldwell, prin. | Fax 647-4286
Poteau HS | 600/9-12
100 Mockingbird Ln 74953 | 918-647-7716
John Spencer, prin. | Fax 647-4383

Carl Albert State College | Post-Sec.
1507 S McKenna St 74953 | 918-647-1200
Poteau Beauty College | Post-Sec.
301 Turman St 74953 | 918-647-4119

Prague, Lincoln, Pop. 2,110
Prague ISD | 1,000/PK-12
3504 NBU 74864 | 405-567-4455
Rick Martin, supt. | Fax 567-3095
Prague HS | 300/9-12
3504 NBU 74864 | 405-567-2281
David Smith, supt. | Fax 567-4982
Prague MS | 200/6-8
3504 NBU 74864 | 405-567-2281
Andrea Sealock, prin. | Fax 567-3095

Preston, Okmulgee
Preston ISD | 500/PK-12
PO Box 40 74456 | 918-756-3388
Mark Hudson, supt. | Fax 756-2122
www.preston.k12.ok.us/
Preston HS | 200/9-12
PO Box 40 74456 | 918-756-8636
Pam Snowden, prin. | Fax 756-2122

Prue, Osage, Pop. 443
Prue ISD | 400/PK-12
PO Box 130 74060 | 918-242-3351
Joe Hulsey, supt. | Fax 242-3392
www.prue.k12.ok.us/

Prue HS | 100/9-12
PO Box 130 74060 | 918-242-3384
Deborah Tennison, prin. | Fax 242-3888

Pryor, Mayes, Pop. 8,921
OK Dept. of Voc. & Tech. Education
Supt. — None
Northeast Oklahoma Tech Center S Campus | Vo/Tech
PO Box 825 74362 | 918-825-5555
 | Fax 825-6281
Northeast Oklahoma Technology Center | Vo/Tech
PO Box 487 74362 | 918-825-7040
Dell Heavener, supt. | Fax 825-3176

Pryor ISD | 2,400/PK-12
PO Box 548 74362 | 918-825-1255
Dr. Larry Burdick, supt. | Fax 825-3938
www.pryor.k12.ok.us
Pryor JHS | 500/7-9
PO Box 548 74362 | 918-825-2371
Terry Gwartney, prin. | Fax 825-3950
Pryor SHS | 500/10-12
PO Box 548 74362 | 918-825-2340
Bill Gage, prin. | Fax 825-3914

Bradford Christian S | 100/K-12
2320 NE 1st St 74361 | 918-825-7038
Patrick Mayer, prin. | Fax 825-7037
Pryor Beauty College | Post-Sec.
330 W Graham Ave 74361 | 918-825-2795

Purcell, McClain, Pop. 5,627
Purcell ISD | 1,400/PK-12
919 N 9th Ave 73080 | 405-527-2146
Dr. Tony Christian, supt. | Fax 527-6366
purcellps.k12.ok.us
Purcell JHS | 300/7-9
919 N 9th Ave 73080 | 405-527-2146
Steve Musgrove, prin. | Fax 527-4454
Purcell SHS | 200/10-12
201 Lester Ln 73080 | 405-527-6591
Tony Christian, prin. | Fax 527-6593

Christian Crusaders Academy | 50/PK-12
PO Box 244 73080 | 405-527-9834
Coralee Cox, admin. | Fax 527-8318

Quapaw, Ottawa, Pop. 975
Quapaw ISD | 700/PK-12
305 W 1st St 74363 | 918-674-2501
Dennis Earp, supt. | Fax 674-2721
Quapaw HS | 200/9-12
305 W 1st St 74363 | 918-674-2474
Terry Tyree, prin. | Fax 674-2721
Quapaw MS | 200/6-8
305 W 1st St 74363 | 918-674-2496
Larry Radford, prin. | Fax 674-2721

Quinton, Pittsburg, Pop. 1,075
Quinton ISD | 500/PK-12
PO Box 670 74561 | 918-469-3100
Sherri A. Prentice, supt. | Fax 469-3308
www.quinton.k12.ok.us/
Quinton HS | 100/9-12
PO Box 670 74561 | 918-469-3309
J. David Smith, prin. | Fax 469-2310

Ramona, Washington, Pop. 568
Caney Valley ISD | 800/K-12
PO Box 410 74061 | 918-536-2500
James Knox, supt. | Fax 536-2600
www.cvalley.k12.ok.us/
Caney Valley HS | 200/9-12
PO Box 410 74061 | 918-536-3425
Debra Keil, prin. | Fax 536-7105
Caney Valley MS, PO Box 410 74061 | 200/6-8
Tom Maddox, prin. | 918-536-2705

Randlett, Cotton, Pop. 521
Big Pasture ISD | 200/PK-12
PO Box 167 73562 | 580-281-3831
Ernest Copus, supt. | Fax 281-3299
Big Pasture HS | 100/9-12
PO Box 167 73562 | 580-281-3276
Jimmy Smith, prin. | Fax 281-3299

Rattan, Pushmataha, Pop. 244
Rattan ISD | 500/PK-12
PO Box 44 74562 | 580-587-2546
Bruce Lawless, supt. | Fax 587-4000
www.rattan.k12.ok.us
Rattan JHS | 100/7-9
PO Box 44 74562 | 580-587-2715
Neil Birchfield, prin. | Fax 587-2476
Rattan SHS | 100/10-12
PO Box 44 74562 | 580-587-2715
Neil Birchfield, prin. | Fax 587-2476

Red Oak, Latimer, Pop. 572
Red Oak ISD | 200/PK-12
PO Box 310 74563 | 918-754-2426
Dr. W. Ross Nixon, supt. | Fax 754-2898
Red Oak HS | 100/9-12
PO Box 310 74563 | 918-754-2283
Bryan Deatherage, prin. | Fax 754-2898

Red Rock, Noble, Pop. 290
Frontier SD | 400/PK-12
PO Box 130 74651 | 580-723-4361
Terri Taflinger, supt. | Fax 723-4516
www.frontierok.com
Frontier HS | 100/9-12
PO Box 130 74651 | 580-723-4360
Randy Robinson, prin. | Fax 723-4516

Reydon, Roger Mills, Pop. 166
Reydon ISD | 100/PK-12
PO Box 10 73660 | 580-655-4375
Phil Drouhard, supt. | Fax 655-4622
Reydon HS, PO Box 10 73660 | 50/9-12
Phil Drouhard, prin. | 580-655-4375

Ringling, Jefferson, Pop. 1,093
Ringling ISD — 500/PK-12
  PO Box 1010 73456 — 580-662-2385
  Grey Shivers, supt. — Fax 662-2683
  www.ringling.k12.ok.us/
Ringling HS, PO Box 1010 73456 — 100/10-12
  Bill Fincher, prin. — 580-662-2386
Ringling JHS, PO Box 1010 73456 — 100/7-9
  Bill Fincher, prin. — 580-662-2386

Ringwood, Major, Pop. 421
Ringwood ISD — 400/PK-12
  PO Box 239 73768 — 580-883-2202
  Ray Johnson, supt. — Fax 883-2220
  www.ringwood.k12.ok.us/
Ringwood HS — 100/9-12
  PO Box 239 73768 — 580-883-2201
  C.W. White, prin. — Fax 883-2220

Ripley, Payne, Pop. 452
Ripley ISD — 400/PK-12
  PO Box 97 74062 — 918-372-4567
  Dr. Kenny Beams, supt. — Fax 372-4608
  www.ripley.k12.ok.us/
Ripley HS — 100/9-12
  PO Box 97 74062 — 918-372-4245
  Les Tilley, prin. — Fax 372-4608

Roff, Pontotoc, Pop. 722
Roff ISD — 300/PK-12
  PO Box 157 74865 — 580-456-7663
  Ron Brown, supt. — Fax 456-7245
  www.geocities.com/roffschool
Roff HS — 100/9-12
  PO Box 157 74865 — 580-456-7252
  George Tidwell, prin. — Fax 456-7499

Roland, Sequoyah, Pop. 2,977
Roland ISD — 1,300/PK-12
  RR 1 Box 1 74954 — 918-427-4601
  Paul R. Wood, supt. — Fax 427-1785
  www.rolandschools.org
Roland JHS — 300/7-9
  RR 1 Box 1 74954 — 918-427-4631
  Charles Morton, prin. — Fax 427-0093
Roland SHS — 300/10-12
  RR 1 Box 1 74954 — 918-427-7419
  Gary Lattimore, prin. — Fax 427-6993

Rush Springs, Grady, Pop. 1,283
Rush Springs ISD — 600/PK-12
  PO Box 308 73082 — 580-476-3929
  David Divine, supt. — Fax 476-2018
  www.rushsprings.k12.ok.us
Rush Springs HS — 200/9-12
  PO Box 308 73082 — 580-476-3596
  Mike Zurline, prin. — Fax 476-2018
Rush Springs MS — 100/6-8
  PO Box 308 73082 — 580-476-3447
  Shawn Haskins, prin. — Fax 476-2148

Ryan, Jefferson, Pop. 858
Ryan ISD — 200/PK-12
  PO Box 369 73565 — 580-757-2308
  Larry Ninman, supt. — Fax 757-2609
Ryan HS, PO Box 369 73565 — 100/9-12
  Pete Maples, prin. — 580-757-2296

Salina, Mayes, Pop. 1,434
Salina ISD — 800/PK-12
  PO Box 98 74365 — 918-434-5091
  Vol Woods, supt. — Fax 434-5346
  www.salina.k12.ok.us
Salina HS — 200/9-12
  PO Box 98 74365 — 918-434-5347
  Tony Thomas, prin. — Fax 434-5537
Salina MS — 200/6-8
  PO Box 98 74365 — 918-434-5311
  Sally Cox, prin. — Fax 434-5173

Sallisaw, Sequoyah, Pop. 8,383
Central ISD — 500/PK-12
  RR 1 Box 36 74955 — 918-775-5525
  Max Tanner, supt. — Fax 775-8557
  centralps.k12.ok.us
Central HS — 200/9-12
  RR 1 Box 36 74955 — 918-775-5525
  Ron Winans, prin. — Fax 775-8557

OK Dept. of Voc. & Tech. Education
  Supt. — None
Indian Capital Technology Center — Vo/Tech
  HC 61 Box 12 74955 — 918-775-9119
  Randy Martin, dir. — Fax 775-7305

Sallisaw ISD — 2,000/PK-12
  701 J T Stites Blvd 74955 — 918-775-5544
  Ronald Wyrick, supt. — Fax 775-1257
Sallisaw HS — 600/9-12
  2301 W Ruth Ave 74955 — 918-775-7761
  Ernie Martens, prin. — Fax 775-1275
Spear MS, 211 S Main St 74955 — 400/6-8
  Greg Cast, prin. — 918-775-3015

Sand Springs, Tulsa, Pop. 17,695
Sand Springs ISD — 5,800/PK-12
  PO Box 970 74063 — 918-246-1400
  Lloyd Snow, supt. — Fax 246-1401
  www.sandsprings.k12.ok.us/
Boyd JHS — 1,000/6-8
  PO Box 970 74063 — 918-246-1535
  Dr. Richard Rosenberger, prin. — Fax 246-1544
Central 9th Grade Center — 200/9-9
  PO Box 970 74063 — 918-246-1440
  Randy Dean, prin. — Fax 246-1446
Page HS — 1,200/9-12
  PO Box 970 74063 — 918-246-1470
  Robert Franklin, prin. — Fax 246-1480

Moriah Christian Academy — 100/K-10
  680 E 41st St 74063 — 918-241-8410
  Kim Ervin, admin.
Sand Springs Beauty College — Post-Sec.
  28 E 2nd St 74063 — 918-245-6627

Sapulpa, Creek, Pop. 19,759
OK Dept. of Voc. & Tech. Education
  Supt. — None
Central Tech — Vo/Tech
  1720 S Main St 74066 — 918-224-9300
  David Main, dir. — Fax 224-3190

Sapulpa ISD — 4,400/PK-12
  1 S Mission St 74066 — 918-224-3400
  Dr. Joe W. Crowder, supt. — Fax 227-3287
  www.sapulpa.k12.ok.us
Sapulpa JHS — 700/8-9
  7 S Mission St 74066 — 918-224-6710
  Derald Buckley, prin. — Fax 227-0473
Sapulpa SHS — 1,100/10-12
  3 S Mission St 74066 — 918-224-6560
  Jenyfer Glisson, prin. — Fax 224-0174

Sasakwa, Seminole, Pop. 147
Sasakwa ISD — 200/PK-12
  PO Box 323 74867 — 405-941-3213
  Jim Mathews, supt. — Fax 941-3561
Sasakwa HS — 100/9-12
  PO Box 323 74867 — 405-941-3250
  Buddy Canning, prin. — Fax 941-3561

Savanna, Pittsburg, Pop. 743
Savanna ISD — 500/PK-12
  PO Box 266 74565 — 918-548-3777
  Mitch Tidwell, supt. — Fax 548-3836
  www.savanna.k12.ok.us/
Savanna HS — 300/9-12
  PO Box 266 74565 — 918-548-3887
  Gary Reeder, prin. — Fax 548-3836

Sayre, Beckham, Pop. 4,221
OK Dept. of Voc. & Tech. Education
  Supt. — None
Western Technology Center — Vo/Tech
  RR 4 Box 132 73662 — 580-928-2097
  Andy Humble, dir. — Fax 928-9827

Sayre ISD — 700/PK-12
  716 NE Highway 66 73662 — 580-928-5531
  Todd Winn, supt. — Fax 928-5538
  www.sayre.k12.ok.us
Sayre HS — 200/9-12
  716 NE Highway 66 73662 — 580-928-5576
  Shane Dent, prin. — Fax 928-3045
Sayre MS — 200/6-8
  716 NE Highway 66 73662 — 580-928-5578
  Monica Brower, prin. — Fax 928-3045

Southwestern Oklahoma State University — Post-Sec.
  409 E Mississippi Ave 73662 — 580-928-5533

Schulter, Okmulgee, Pop. 614
Schulter ISD — 200/PK-12
  PO Box 203 74460 — 918-652-8219
  Alfred Gaches, supt. — Fax 652-8474
Schulter HS — 100/9-12
  PO Box 203 74460 — 918-652-8200
  Allen Callahan, prin. — Fax 652-8474

Seiling, Dewey, Pop. 826
Seiling ISD — 400/PK-12
  PO Box 780 73663 — 580-922-7383
  Bob Bush, supt. — Fax 922-8019
  www.seiling.k12.ok.us
Seiling JSHS — 200/7-12
  PO Box 780 73663 — 580-922-7382
  C. Oakes, prin. — Fax 922-8019

Seminole, Seminole, Pop. 6,756
Seminole ISD — 1,300/PK-12
  PO Box 1031 74818 — 405-382-5085
  Jeff Pritchard, supt. — Fax 382-8281
  www.sps.k12.ok.us
Seminole HS — 400/9-12
  PO Box 1031 74818 — 405-382-1415
  John Walker, prin. — Fax 382-1062
Seminole MS — 200/7-8
  PO Box 1031 74818 — 405-382-5065
  Michelle Sneed, prin. — Fax 382-8653

Strother ISD — 300/PK-12
  RR 3 Box 265 74868 — 405-382-4014
  Lowell B. Wallace, supt. — Fax 382-3339
Strother HS — 100/9-12
  RR 3 Box 265 74868 — 405-382-0982
  John Plunkett, prin. — Fax 382-9430

Varnum ISD — 300/PK-12
  11929 NS 355 74868 — 405-382-1448
  John Cope, supt. — Fax 382-8618
Varnum HS — 100/9-12
  11929 NS 355 74868 — 405-382-1408
  Mark Wynn, prin. — Fax 382-8618

Seminole State College — Post-Sec.
  PO Box 351 74818 — 405-382-9950

Sentinel, Washita, Pop. 834
Sentinel ISD — 300/K-12
  PO Box 640 73664 — 580-393-2101
  Hal Holt, supt. — Fax 393-2101
  www.sentinel.k12.ok.us/
Thomas HS — 100/9-12
  PO Box 640 73664 — 580-393-2112
  Paula Combs, prin. — Fax 393-4334

Shattuck, Ellis, Pop. 1,254
Shattuck ISD — 200/PK-12
  PO Box 159 73858 — 580-938-2586
  Mack Morse, supt. — Fax 938-8019
  www.shattuck.k12.ok.us/
Shattuck HS — 100/9-12
  PO Box 159 73858 — 580-938-2586
  Randy Holley, prin. — Fax 938-8019

Shawnee, Pottawatomie, Pop. 29,446
Bethel HS — 1,200/K-12
  36000 Clearpond Rd 74801 — 405-273-0385
  David Glover, supt. — Fax 273-5056
  www.bethel.k12.ok.us

Bethel HS — 400/9-12
  36000 Clearpond Rd 74801 — 405-273-3633
  Steve Carpenter, prin. — Fax 273-5056
Bethel MS — 300/6-8
  36000 Clearpond Rd 74801 — 405-273-5944
  Gary Cartwright, prin. — Fax 273-5056

OK Dept. of Voc. & Tech. Education
  Supt. — None
Cooper Technology Center — Vo/Tech
  1 John C Bruton Blvd 74804 — 405-273-7493
  Marty Lewis, supt. — Fax 273-4704

Shawnee ISD — 3,700/PK-12
  326 N Union Ave 74801 — 405-273-0653
  Marilyn Bradford, supt. — Fax 273-6818
  www.shawnee.k12.ok.us
Shawnee HS — 1,200/9-12
  1001 N Kennedy Ave 74801 — 405-275-3084
  Lee Hamilton, prin.
Shawnee MS — 800/6-8
  4300 N Union Ave 74804 — 405-273-0403
  James Taffee, prin.

Family of Faith Christian S — 100/K-12
  PO Box 1442 74802 — 405-273-5331
  Christopher Belyeu, admin. — Fax 273-5331
Family of Faith College — Post-Sec.
  PO Box 1805 74802 — 405-273-5331
Liberty Academy — 300/PK-12
  PO Box 1176 74802 — 405-273-3022
  Lenore Matthews, admin. — Fax 273-3029
Oklahoma Baptist University — Post-Sec.
  500 W University St 74804 — 405-275-2850
St. Gregory's University — Post-Sec.
  1900 W Macarthur St 74804 — 405-878-5100
Shawnee Beauty College — Post-Sec.
  410 E Main St 74801 — 405-275-3182

Shidler, Osage, Pop. 523
Shidler ISD — 200/K-12
  PO Box 85 74652 — 918-793-2021
  Stephen Cargill, supt. — Fax 793-2061
  www.shidler.k12.ok.us
Shidler HS — 100/7-12
  PO Box 85 74652 — 918-793-2461
  Bob Campo, prin. — Fax 793-2062

Skiatook, Tulsa, Pop. 5,879
Skiatook ISD — 2,300/PK-12
  355 S Osage St 74070 — 918-396-1792
  Gary Johnson, supt. — Fax 396-1799
  www.skiatook.k12.ok.us/
Newman MS — 500/6-8
  355 S Osage St 74070 — 918-396-3922
  Steve Cantrell, prin. — Fax 396-1799
Skiatook HS — 700/9-12
  355 S Osage St 74070 — 918-396-1790
  Donna Brogan, prin. — Fax 396-1799

Smithville, McCurtain, Pop. 111
Smithville ISD — 300/PK-12
  PO Box 8 74957 — 580-244-3333
  Delbert McBroom, supt. — Fax 244-7214
  www.smithville.k12.ok.us
Smithville HS — 100/9-12
  PO Box 8 74957 — 580-244-3281
  Curtis McDaniel, prin. — Fax 244-7277
Smithville MS, PO Box 8 74957 — 50/6-8
  Stacy Nichols, prin. — 580-244-7212

Snyder, Kiowa, Pop. 1,475
Snyder ISD — 500/PK-12
  PO Box 368 73566 — 580-569-2773
  Dr. DeDe Graham, supt. — Fax 569-4205
  www.snyder.k12.ok.us
Snyder HS, PO Box 368 73566 — 200/9-12
  Robert Trammell, prin. — 580-569-2730
Snyder MS, PO Box 368 73566 — 200/4-8
  Carol McPhail, prin. — 580-569-2691

Soper, Choctaw, Pop. 303
Soper ISD — 300/K-12
  PO Box 149 74759 — 580-345-2757
  Olen Jestis, supt. — Fax 345-2896
  www.soperisd.org
Soper HS — 100/9-12
  PO Box 149 74759 — 580-345-2212
  Monte Sill, prin. — Fax 345-2896

South Coffeyville, Nowata, Pop. 804
Oklahoma Union SD — 600/PK-12
  RR 1 Box 377-7 74072 — 918-255-6550
  Dr. Robert Jobe, supt. — Fax 255-6817
  www.okunion.k12.ok.us/
Oklahoma Union HS — 200/9-12
  RR 1 Box 377-7 74072 — 918-255-6550
  Steve Barth, prin. — Fax 255-6817
Oklahoma Union MS — 100/6-8
  RR 1 Box 377-7 74072 — 918-255-6550
  Teresa Kelley, prin. — Fax 255-6817

South Coffeyville ISD — 300/PK-12
  PO Box 190 74072 — 918-255-6202
  Colt Shaw, supt. — Fax 255-6230
South Coffeyville HS — 100/9-12
  PO Box 190 74072 — 918-255-6087
  Clem Haddox, prin. — Fax 255-6230

Spencer, Oklahoma, Pop. 3,770
Oklahoma City ISD
  Supt. — See Oklahoma City
Rogers MS — 300/7-8
  4000 Spencer Rd 73084 — 405-771-3205
  Michael Brown, prin. — Fax 771-2114
Star Academy — 600/9-12
  8917 NE 23rd 73084 — 405-769-4627
  Deborah Ealy, prin. — Fax 769-9125
Star Spencer HS — 600/9-12
  3001 Spencer Rd 73084 — 405-587-8800
  Dr. Sally Cole, prin. — Fax 771-2105

Sperry, Tulsa, Pop. 1,038
Sperry ISD　800/PK-12
　PO Box 610　74073　918-288-6258
　Jerry Burd, supt.　Fax 288-7067
　www.sperry.k12.ok.us
Sperry HS　300/9-12
　PO Box 610　74073　918-288-7213
　James White, prin.　Fax 288-7230
Sperry MS　300/6-8
　PO Box 610　74073　918-288-7213
　Dennis Holland, prin.　Fax 288-7231

Oklahoma Farriers College　Post-Sec.
　PO Box 788　74073　918-288-7221

Spiro, LeFlore, Pop. 2,253
OK Dept. of Voc. & Tech. Education
　Supt. — None
Kiamichi Technology Center　Vo/Tech
　610 SW 3rd St　74959　918-962-3722
　Joe Carrick, dir.　Fax 962-4627

Spiro ISD　900/K-12
　600 W Broadway St　74959　918-962-2463
　J. L. Williams, supt.　Fax 962-2757
　www.spiro.k12.ok.us/
Spiro HS, 600 W Broadway St　74959　300/9-12
　Tracy Saling, prin.　918-962-2493
Spiro MS, 600 W Broadway St　74959　300/6-8
　Russell Thornton, prin.　918-962-2488

Springer, Carter, Pop. 587
Springer ISD　200/PK-12
　PO Box 249　73458　580-653-2656
　Paula Oliver, supt.　Fax 653-2666
　www.springer.k12.ok.us/
Springer HS, PO Box 249　73458　50/9-12
　Brenda Foster, prin.　580-653-2471

Sterling, Comanche, Pop. 761
Sterling ISD　400/PK-12
　PO Box 158　73567　580-365-4307
　Jay Zehr, supt.　Fax 365-4705
　www.sterling.k12.ok.us/
Sterling HS, PO Box 158　73567　100/9-12
　Craig Shaw, prin.　580-365-4303

Stigler, Haskell, Pop. 2,777
OK Dept. of Voc. & Tech. Education
　Supt. — None
Kiamichi Technology Center　Vo/Tech
　1410 Old Military Rd　74462　918-967-2801
　Jim Eakle, dir.　Fax 967-2803

Stigler ISD　1,300/PK-12
　302 NW E St　74462　918-967-2805
　Greg Kasbaum, supt.　Fax 967-4550
　www.stigler.k12.ok.us
Stigler HS　400/9-12
　302 NW E St　74462　918-967-8834
　David Morgan, prin.　Fax 967-8974
Stigler MS　400/5-8
　302 NW E St　74462　918-967-2521
　Rick Prentice, prin.　Fax 967-5125

Stillwater, Payne, Pop. 41,320
OK Dept. of Voc. & Tech. Education
　Supt. — None
Meridian Technology Center　Vo/Tech
　1312 S Sangre Rd　74074　405-377-3333
　Dr. Andrea Kelly, supt.　Fax 372-3466
Other Schools – See Ada OK, Afton OK, Altus OK, Alva OK, Ardmore OK, Atoka OK, Bartlesville OK, Broken Arrow OK, Burns Flat OK, Chickasha OK, Choctaw OK, Drumright OK, Duncan OK, Durant OK, El Reno OK, Enid OK, Fairview OK, Fort Cobb OK, Frederick OK, Hugo OK, Idabel OK, Kansas OK, Lawton OK, Mc Alester OK, Midwest City OK, Muskogee OK, Norman OK, Oklahoma City OK, Okmulgee OK, Omega OK, Ponca City OK, Poteau OK, Pryor OK, Sallisaw OK, Sapulpa OK, Sayre OK, Shawnee OK, Spiro OK, Stigler OK, Stilwell OK, Tahlequah OK, Talihina OK, Tinker AFB OK, Tulsa OK, Wayne OK, Wetumka OK, Wilburton OK, Woodward OK

Stillwater ISD　5,400/PK-12
　PO Box 879　74076　405-533-6300
　Dr. Walter Swanson, supt.　Fax 743-6311
　www.stillwater.k12.ok.us
Stillwater JHS　700/8-9
　PO Box 879　74076　405-533-6420
　Trent Swanson, prin.　Fax 743-6444
Stillwater SHS　1,200/10-12
　PO Box 879　74076　405-533-6450
　Mike Turk, prin.　Fax 743-6488

Indian Meridian Vocational Tech School　Post-Sec.
　1312 S Sangre Rd　74074　405-377-3333
Oklahoma State University　74078　Post-Sec.
　405-744-5000
Stillwater Beauty Academy　Post-Sec.
　1684 Cimarron Plz　74075　405-377-4100
Sunnybrook Christian S　100/PK-12
　421 E Richmond Rd　74075　405-377-3748
　Genevieve Hurst, admin.　Fax 372-2505

Stilwell, Adair, Pop. 3,419
OK Dept. of Voc. & Tech. Education
　Supt. — None
Indian Capital Technology Center　Vo/Tech
　RR 4 Box 3320　74960　918-696-3111
　Tony Pivec, dir.　Fax 696-3111

Stilwell ISD　1,400/PK-12
　1801 W Locust St　74960　918-696-7001
　Marion Bayles, supt.　Fax 696-2193
　www.stilwell.k12.ok.us
Stilwell HS　600/9-12
　1801 W Locust St　74960　918-696-7276
　Alicia Ketcher, prin.　Fax 696-4695
Stilwell MS　300/5-8
　12 N 7th St　74960　918-696-2685
　Larry Callison, prin.　Fax 696-7761

Stonewall, Pontotoc, Pop. 465
Stonewall ISD　200/PK-12
　600 Highschool　74871　580-265-4241
　Kevin Flowers, supt.　Fax 265-4536
Stonewall HS　100/9-12
　600 Highschool　74871　580-265-4242
　Tamara Newberry, prin.　Fax 265-4231
Other Schools – See Fittstown

Stratford, Garvin, Pop. 1,482
Stratford ISD　600/PK-12
　PO Box 589　74872　580-759-3615
　Brent Walden, supt.　Fax 759-2669
　www.stratfordisd.org
Stratford JSHS　200/7-12
　PO Box 589　74872　580-759-2381
　Patrick Mitchell, prin.　Fax 759-2669

Stringtown, Atoka, Pop. 401
CareerTech Skills Centers
　Supt. — None
　Dom Garrison, supt.
Stringtown Skills Center　Vo/Tech
　PO Box 159　74569　580-346-7411

Stringtown ISD　200/PK-12
　PO Box 130　74569　580-346-7423
　Richard Quaid, supt.　Fax 346-7726
　www.stringtown.k12.ok.us
Stringtown HS　100/9-12
　PO Box 130　74569　580-346-7741
　Dirk Walden, dean　Fax 346-7949

Stroud, Lincoln, Pop. 2,747
Stroud ISD　800/PK-12
　212 W 7th St　74079　918-968-2541
　Rick McDaniel, supt.　Fax 968-2582
　www.stroud.k12.ok.us
Stroud HS　200/9-12
　212 W 7th St　74079　918-968-2542
　Joe VanTuyl, prin.　Fax 968-3656
Stroud MS　200/6-8
　212 W 7th St　74079　918-968-2200
　Marsha Thompson, prin.　Fax 968-2391

Stuart, Hughes, Pop. 218
Stuart ISD　300/PK-12
　8837 4th St　74570　918-546-2476
　Bill San Millan, supt.　Fax 546-2329
　www.stuart.k12.ok.us/
Stuart HS　100/9-12
　8837 4th St　74570　918-546-2474
　Tracy Blasengame, prin.　Fax 546-2329

Sulphur, Murray, Pop. 4,810
Sulphur ISD　1,300/PK-12
　1021 W 9th St　73086　580-622-2061
　Keith Foreman, supt.　Fax 622-6789
　www.sulphur.k12.ok.us
Sulphur HS　400/9-12
　1021 W 9th St　73086　580-622-3174
　Jim Dixon, prin.　Fax 622-5735
Sulphur JHS　200/7-8
　1021 W 9th St　73086　580-622-4010
　Billie Pyle, prin.　Fax 622-3900

Oklahoma School for the Deaf　Post-Sec.
　1100 E Oklahoma Ave　73086　580-622-4900

Sweetwater, Roger Mills, Pop. 68
Sweetwater ISD　100/PK-12
　RR 1 Box 6　73666　580-534-2272
　Don Riley, supt.　Fax 534-2273
Sweetwater HS　50/9-12
　RR 1 Box 6　73666　580-534-2272
　Don Riley, prin.　Fax 534-2273

Taft, Muskogee, Pop. 417
CareerTech Skills Centers
　Supt. — None
　Dom Garrison, supt.
Taft Skills Center Dunn Campus　Vo/Tech
　PO Box 245　74463　918-683-8669
Taft Skills Center Warrior Campus　Vo/Tech
　PO Box 245　74463　918-683-8365

Tahlequah, Cherokee, Pop. 15,405
OK Dept. of Voc. & Tech. Education
　Supt. — None
Indian Capital Technology Center　Vo/Tech
　PO Box 497　74465　918-456-2594
　Wilson Fargo, dir.　Fax 456-0140

Tahlequah ISD　3,300/PK-12
　PO Box 517　74465　918-458-4100
　Paul Hurst, supt.　Fax 458-4103
　www.tahlequah.k12.ok.us
Tahlequah HS　1,000/9-12
　591 Pendleton St　74464　918-458-4150
　Dr. Nick Migliorino, prin.　Fax 458-4135
Tahlequah MS　900/5-8
　871 Pendleton St　74464　918-458-4140
　　Fax 458-4108

Beauty Technical College　Post-Sec.
　PO Box 1506　74465　918-456-6360
Northeastern State University　Post-Sec.
　600 N Grand Ave　74464　918-456-5511

Talihina, Latimer, Pop. 1,216
Buffalo Valley ISD　200/K-12
　RR 2 Box 3505　74571　918-522-4426
　Ira Harris, supt.　Fax 522-4287
　www.buffalovalley.k12.ok.us
Buffalo Valley HS　100/9-12
　RR 2 Box 3505　74571　918-522-4803
　Betty Smallwood, prin.　Fax 522-4287

OK Dept. of Voc. & Tech. Education
　Supt. — None
Kiamichi Technology Center　Vo/Tech
　RR 2 Box 1800　74571　918-567-7264
　Shelley Free, dir.　Fax 567-3359

Talihina ISD　600/PK-12
　PO Box 38　74571　918-567-2259
　Ray Henson, supt.　Fax 567-3507
　www.talihina.k12.ok.us/
Talihina JHS　74571　100/7-9
　Robert Perryman, prin.　918-567-2138
Talihina SHS, PO Box 38　74571　100/10-12
　Robert Perryman, prin.　918-567-2266

Taloga, Dewey, Pop. 360
Taloga ISD　100/PK-12
　PO Box 158　73667　580-328-5577
　Rick Ruckman, supt.　Fax 328-5237
　www.taloga.k12.ok.us
Taloga HS　50/9-12
　PO Box 158　73667　580-328-5586
　Rick Ruckman, prin.　Fax 328-5237

Tecumseh, Pottawatomie, Pop. 6,264
Tecumseh ISD　2,000/K-12
　1301 E Highland St　74873　405-598-3739
　Tom Wilsie, supt.　Fax 598-2861
　www.tecumseh.k12.ok.us
Tecumseh HS　700/9-12
　901 N 13th St　74873　405-598-2113
　James Blue, prin.　Fax 598-2432
Tecumseh MS　500/6-8
　315 W Park St　74873　405-598-3744
　Karen Kinsey, prin.　Fax 598-1948

Temple, Cotton, Pop. 1,146
Temple ISD　200/PK-12
　PO Box 400　73568　580-342-6230
　Randy Davenport, supt.　Fax 342-6463
　www.temple.k12.ok.us/
Temple HS　100/9-12
　PO Box 400　73568　580-342-6221
　Darrell Lamar, prin.　Fax 342-6463

Texhoma, Texas, Pop. 906
Texhoma ISD　300/PK-12
　PO Box 648　73949　580-423-7433
　Eric Smith, supt.　Fax 423-7096
　www.texhoma61.net/
Texhoma HS　100/9-12
　PO Box 648　73949　580-423-7371
　Steve Neptune, prin.　Fax 423-7096

Thackerville, Love, Pop. 409
Thackerville ISD　300/PK-12
　PO Box 377　73459　580-276-2630
　David Herron, supt.　Fax 276-2638
　www.thackervilleschools.org
Thackerville HS　100/9-12
　PO Box 377　73459　580-276-3610
　Jamie Mitchell, prin.　Fax 276-2638

Thomas, Custer, Pop. 1,160
Thomas-Fay-Custer USD　500/PK-12
　PO Box 190　73669　580-661-3527
　Rob Royalty, supt.　Fax 661-3589
Thomas JSHS　200/7-12
　PO Box 190　73669　580-661-3522
　Craig McVay, prin.　Fax 661-3589

Tinker AFB, See Oklahoma City
OK Dept. of Voc. & Tech. Education
　Supt. — None
Mid-Del-Tinker Career Tech　Vo/Tech
　Building 1 D Ave　73145　405-734-7266
　Dave Williams, dir.　Fax 737-2330

Tipton, Tillman, Pop. 866
Tipton ISD　300/K-12
　PO Box 340　73570　580-667-5268
　Brad Overton, supt.　Fax 667-5267
　www.tiptonps.k12.ok.us
Tipton HS　100/9-12
　PO Box 340　73570　580-667-5268
　Cliff McCown, prin.　Fax 667-5478
Tipton MS　7-8
　PO Box 340　73570　580-667-5268
　Cliff McCown, prin.　Fax 667-5325
Tipton SOJC Manitou Site　100/8-12
　PO Box 340　73570　580-397-3511
　Jim Linker, prin.　Fax 667-5267

Tishomingo, Johnston, Pop. 3,186
Tishomingo ISD　900/PK-12
　1300 E Main St　73460　580-371-9190
　Ronald Hutchings, supt.　Fax 371-3765
　www.tishomingo.k12.ok.us/
Tishomingo HS, 1300 E Main St　73460　300/9-12
　Leo McCallay, prin.　580-371-2322
Tishomingo MS, 1300 E Main St　73460　200/6-8
　Larry Davis, prin.　580-371-3602

Murray State College　Post-Sec.
　1 Murray Campus St　73460　580-371-2371

Tonkawa, Kay, Pop. 3,160
Tonkawa ISD　800/PK-12
　500 E North Ave　74653　580-628-3597
　Rod Reese, supt.　Fax 628-5132
　www.tonkawa.k12.ok.us/
Tonkawa JSHS　400/6-12
　500 E North Ave　74653　580-628-2566
　Kyle Simpson, prin.　Fax 628-3646

Northern Oklahoma College　Post-Sec.
　PO Box 310　74653　580-628-6200

Tulsa, Tulsa, Pop. 387,807
Berryhill ISD　800/PK-12
　3128 S 63rd West Ave　74107　918-446-1966
　Mike Campbell, supt.　Fax 446-6370
　www.berryhill.k12.ok.us
Berryhill JHS　300/7-9
　3128 S 63rd West Ave　74107　918-446-8765
　Jo Etta Terrell, prin.　Fax 445-6018
Berryhill SHS　300/10-12
　3128 S 63rd West Ave　74107　918-446-1636
　Charles Prater, prin.　Fax 445-6015

Jenks ISD
Supt. — See Jenks
Jenks MS, 3019 E 101st St 74137 1,500/7-8
Rob Miller, prin. 918-299-4411

OK Dept. of Voc. & Tech. Education
Supt. — None
Tulsa County Technology Center Vo/Tech
PO Box 477200 74147 918-828-5000
Dr. Gene Callahan, supt. Fax 828-5009
Tulsa Tech Center Peoria Vo/Tech
PO Box 477200 74147 918-828-2000
Sharon Schaub, dir. Fax 828-2009
Tulsa Techn Center Riverside Campus Vo/Tech
PO Box 477200 74147 918-828-4000
Fax 828-4009
Tulsa Technology Center-Lemley Vo/Tech
PO Box 477200 74147 918-828-1000
Sandee Tackett, dir. Fax 828-1009

Tulsa ISD 41,200/PK-12
PO Box 470208 74147 918-746-6800
David E. Sawyer Ed.D., supt. Fax 746-6850
www.tulsaschools.org
Byrd MS 800/6-8
7502 E 57th St 74145 918-833-9520
Garry Nichols, prin. Fax 833-9551
Carver MS 600/6-8
624 E Oklahoma Pl 74106 918-925-1420
Cleta Driver, prin. Fax 925-1450
Central HS 1,000/9-12
3101 W Edison St 74127 918-833-8400
Jean Keeton, prin. Fax 833-8417
Cleveland MS 600/6-8
724 N Birmingham Ave 74110 918-746-9400
Kris Serna, prin. Fax 746-9426
Clinton MS, 2224 W 41st St 74107 600/6-8
Laura Undernehr, prin. 918-746-8640
East Central HS 1,200/9-12
12150 E 11th St 74128 918-746-9700
Tom O'Malley, prin. Fax 746-9760
Edison Preparatory HS 1,000/9-12
2906 E 41st St 74105 918-746-8500
Steve Mayfield, prin.
Edison Preparatory MS 900/6-8
2800 E 41st St 74105 918-746-8500
Steve Mayfield, prin.
Foster MS, 12121 E 21st St 74129 700/6-8
Darin Schmidt, prin. 918-746-9500
Hale HS 1,000/9-12
6960 E 21st St 74129 918-925-1200
Chris Johnson, prin. Fax 925-1262
Hamilton MS 600/6-8
2316 N Norwood Pl 74115 918-746-9440
Carla Westbrook, prin. Fax 746-9447
Lewis & Clark MS 700/6-8
737 S Garnett Rd 74128 918-746-9540
Ginger Bunnell, prin.
Madison MS 400/6-8
4132 W Cameron St 74127 918-833-8860
Dr. Raushan Alexander, prin.
Memorial HS 1,400/9-12
5840 S Hudson Ave 74135 918-833-9600
John McGinnis, prin.
Monroe MS, 2010 E 48th St N 74130 500/7-8
Emmitt Millhouse, prin. 918-833-8900
Nimitz MS 400/6-8
3111 E 56th St 74105 918-746-8800
Earlene Gathright, prin. Fax 746-8826
Rogers HS, 3909 E 5th Pl 74112 1,100/9-12
Tenna Whitsel, prin. 918-833-9000
Thoreau Demonstration Academy 500/6-8
7370 E 71st St 74133 918-833-9700
Thomas Padalino, prin.
Tulsa School for Science & Technology Vo/Tech
4929 N Peoria Ave 74126 918-833-8500
Jerome Williams, prin. Fax 833-8559
Washington HS 1,300/9-12
1514 E Zion St 74106 918-925-1000
Debi Boyles, prin. Fax 928-1001
Webster HS 600/9-12
1919 W 40th St 74107 918-746-8000
Phillip Garland, prin. Fax 746-8056
Whitney MS 800/6-8
2177 S 67th East Ave 74129 918-746-9260
Derrick Schmidt, prin.
Wilson MS 700/6-8
1127 S Columbia Ave 74104 918-833-9340
Bobbie Booker, prin.

Union ISD 13,900/PK-12
5656 S 129th East Ave 74134 918-459-5432
Cathy Burden, supt. Fax 459-3399
www.unionps.org
Union HS 1,900/11-12
6636 S Mingo Rd 74133 918-459-2638
Dave Stauffer, prin. Fax 459-5510
Other Schools – See Broken Arrow

Bishop Kelley HS 1,000/9-12
3905 S Hudson Ave 74135 918-627-3390
Alan Weyland, pres. Fax 664-2134
Career Point Institute Post-Sec.
3138 S Garnett Rd 74146 918-622-4100
Cascia Hall Prep S 700/6-12
2520 S Yorktown Ave 74114 918-746-2600
Rev. Bernard C. Scianna, hdmstr. Fax 746-2636
CC's Cosmetology College Post-Sec.
11630 E 21st St 74129 918-234-9444
Evangelistic Temple S 300/PK-12
1339 E 55th St 74105 918-743-5597
Randy Fulmer, prin. Fax 747-3457
Holland Hall 1,000/PK-12
5666 E 81st St 74137 918-481-1111
Mark Desjardins Ph.D., hdmstr. Fax 481-1145
Lincoln Christian S 600/K-12
1003 N 129th East Ave 74116 918-234-8863
Br. Jim Wideman, admin. Fax 270-8527
Metro Christian Academy 1,000/K-12
6363 S Trenton Ave 74136 918-745-9868
Tim Cameron, hdmstr. Fax 747-8724
Metropolitan College Post-Sec.
10820 E 45th St Ste 101 74146 918-627-9300
Mingo Valley Christian S 300/PK-12
8720 E 61st St 74133 918-294-0404
Dennis Queen, prin. Fax 294-0555
Oklahoma Health Academy Post-Sec.
2865 E Skelly Dr Ste 224 74105 918-748-9900
Oral Roberts University Post-Sec.
7777 S Lewis Ave 74171 918-495-6161
OSU College of Osteopathic Medicine Post-Sec.
1111 W 17th St 74107 918-582-1972
Phillips Theological Seminary Post-Sec.
901 N Mingo Rd 74116 918-610-8303
Platt College Post-Sec.
3801 S Sheridan Rd 74145 918-663-9000
St. Francis Hospital Post-Sec.
6161 S Yale Ave 74136 918-494-1370
Spartan Coll of Aeronautics & Technology Post-Sec.
8820 E Pine St 74115 800-331-1204
Technical Institute of Cosmetology Arts Post-Sec.
822 E 6th St 74120 918-660-8828
Tulsa Adventist Jr Academy 50/K-10
900 S New Haven Ave 74112 918-834-1107
Fax 834-2151
Tulsa Community College Post-Sec.
6111 E Skelly Dr Ste 200 74135 918-595-7000
Tulsa Community College Post-Sec.
3727 E Apache St 74115 918-595-7000
Tulsa County Area Voc Tech District 18 Post-Sec.
3420 S Memorial Dr 74145 918-627-7200
Tulsa Welding School Post-Sec.
2545 E 11th St 74104 918-587-6789
University of Tulsa Post-Sec.
600 S College Ave 74104 918-631-2000
Vatterott College - Tulsa Post-Sec.
555 S Memorial Dr 74112 918-835-8288
Victory Christian S 1,300/K-12
7700 S Lewis Ave 74136 918-491-7720
Dr. Dennis Demuth, supt. Fax 491-7727
Wright Christian Academy 300/PK-12
11391 E Admiral Pl 74116 918-438-0922
Jeff Brown, admin. Fax 438-0700

Tupelo, Coal, Pop. 370
Tupelo ISD 200/PK-12
PO Box 239 74572 580-845-2460
Tony Stevens, supt. Fax 845-2565
www.tupelo.k12.ok.us
Tupelo HS 100/9-12
PO Box 239 74572 580-845-2381
Kevin Mann, prin. Fax 845-2565

Turpin, Beaver
Turpin SD 500/PK-12
PO Box 187 73950 580-778-3333
Glyndel Holland, supt. Fax 778-3179
www.turpin.k12.ok.us
Turpin HS 100/9-12
PO Box 187 73950 580-778-3333
Bret Rider, prin. Fax 778-3733

Tuttle, Grady, Pop. 4,852
Tuttle ISD 1,300/K-12
PO Box 780 73089 405-381-2605
Lee M. Coker, supt. Fax 381-4008
Tuttle HS 400/9-12
PO Box 780 73089 405-381-2396
Pat Ragsdale, prin. Fax 381-4637
Tuttle MS 300/6-8
PO Box 780 73089 405-381-2062
Jim Stewart, prin. Fax 381-4630

Tyrone, Texas, Pop. 853
Tyrone ISD 300/PK-12
PO Box 168 73951 580-854-6298
Dave Easterday, supt. Fax 854-6474
Tyrone HS 100/9-12
PO Box 168 73951 580-854-6298
Melea Welch, prin. Fax 854-6474

Union City, Canadian, Pop. 1,425
Union City ISD 200/PK-12
PO Box 279 73090 405-483-3531
Todd Carel, supt. Fax 483-5599
Union City HS 100/9-12
PO Box 279 73090 405-483-5326
Todd Carel, prin. Fax 483-5199

Valliant, McCurtain, Pop. 760
Valliant ISD 1,000/PK-12
604 E Lucas St 74764 580-933-7232
Debbie Golden, supt. Fax 933-7289
www.vpsd.org
Valliant HS 300/9-12
604 E Lucas St 74764 580-933-7292
Don Mullenix, prin. Fax 933-7278
Valliant MS 300/6-8
604 E Lucas St 74764 580-933-4253
Wren Baker, prin. Fax 933-4254

Velma, Stephens, Pop. 660
Velma-Alma ISD 400/K-12
PO Box 8 73491 580-444-3355
Jerry Garrett, supt. Fax 444-2554
Velma-Alma HS 200/9-12
PO Box 8 73491 580-444-3356
Mike Thompson, prin. Fax 444-2554

Verden, Grady, Pop. 664
Verden ISD 300/PK-12
PO Box 99 73092 405-453-7247
David Davidson, supt. Fax 453-7246
www.verden.k12.ok.us/
Verden HS 100/8-12
PO Box 99 73092 405-453-7836
Clint Shirley, prin. Fax 453-7246

Vian, Sequoyah, Pop. 1,375
Vian ISD 900/PK-12
PO Box 434 74962 918-773-5798
Lawrence Barnes, supt. Fax 773-3051
www.vian.k12.ok.us/
Vian HS 200/9-12
PO Box 434 74962 918-773-5475
Bob Thomas, prin. Fax 773-3051
Vian MS 200/6-8
PO Box 434 74962 918-773-8631
Dr. Carla Wortman, prin. Fax 773-3051

Vici, Dewey, Pop. 645
Vici ISD 300/PK-12
PO Box 60 73859 580-995-4744
Kim Stephens, supt. Fax 995-3101
www.vicischools.k12.ok.us
Vici HS 100/9-12
PO Box 60 73859 580-995-4251
Greg Gregory, prin. Fax 995-3101

Vinita, Craig, Pop. 5,969
Vinita ISD 1,700/PK-12
PO Box 408 74301 918-256-6778
Michael Garde, supt. Fax 256-5617
www.vinitahornets.com
Vinita HS, PO Box 408 74301 500/9-12
Rusty Rankin, prin. 918-256-6777
Vinita MS, PO Box 408 74301 400/6-8
Jeff Williams, prin. 918-256-2402

White Oak ISD 200/PK-12
27355 S 4340 Rd 74301 918-256-4484
J.D. Parkerson, supt. Fax 256-4486
White Oak HS 100/9-12
27355 S 4340 Rd 74301 918-256-4484
J.D. Parkerson, prin.

Ketchum Adventist Junior Academy 50/1-10
35369 S Highway 82 74301 918-782-2986
Fax 782-1567

Wagoner, Wagoner, Pop. 7,818
Wagoner ISD 2,400/PK-12
PO Box 508 74477 918-485-4046
Janice Aldridge, supt. Fax 485-8710
www.wagonerps.org
Wagoner HS 600/9-12
300 Bulldog Cir 74467 918-485-5553
Jerry Adams, prin. Fax 485-8886
Wagoner MS 600/6-8
500 Bulldog Cir 74467 918-485-9541
Darrell Morgan, prin. Fax 485-4149

Wakita, Grant, Pop. 411
Wakita ISD 100/PK-12
PO Box 45 73771 580-594-2261
Gerald Miller, supt. Fax 594-2263
www.wakita.k12.ok.us
Wakita HS 100/7-12
PO Box 45 73771 580-594-2262
Kelly Childress, prin. Fax 594-2263

Walters, Cotton, Pop. 2,614
Walters ISD 700/PK-12
418 S Broadway St 73572 580-875-2568
Larry M. Stogner, supt. Fax 875-2831
blued.org
Walters HS 200/9-12
418 S Broadway St 73572 580-875-3257
Mike Darnell, prin. Fax 875-6097
Walters MS, 418 S Broadway St 73572 200/6-8
Jimmie Dedmon, prin. 580-875-3214

Wanette, Pottawatomie, Pop. 416
Wanette ISD 300/PK-12
PO Box 161 74878 405-383-2656
Glenn Haswell, supt. Fax 383-2449
www.wanette.k12.ok.us/
Wanette HS, PO Box 161 74878 100/9-12
Glenne Whisenhunt, prin. 405-383-2254

Wapanucka, Johnston, Pop. 443
Wapanucka ISD 200/PK-12
PO Box 188 73461 580-937-4466
Stanley Williams, supt. Fax 937-4804
Wapanucka HS, PO Box 188 73461 100/9-12
Max Rowland, prin. 580-937-4288

Warner, Muskogee, Pop. 1,446
Warner ISD 700/PK-12
RR 1 Box 1240 74469 918-463-5171
Monte Madewell, supt. Fax 463-2542
Warner HS 200/9-12
RR 1 Box 1240 74469 918-463-5172
Steve McGinnis, prin. Fax 463-2378
Warner MS, RR 1 Box 1240 74469 200/6-8
Steve McGinnis, prin. 918-463-2197

Connors State College Post-Sec.
RR 1 Box 1000 74469 918-463-2931

Washington, McClain, Pop. 518
Washington ISD 800/PK-12
PO Box 98 73093 405-288-6190
A.J. Brewer, supt. Fax 288-6214
www.washington.k12.ok.us/
Washington HS 200/9-12
PO Box 98 73093 405-288-2354
David Crabbe, prin. Fax 288-6214
Washington MS 200/6-8
PO Box 98 73093 405-288-2428
Stuart McPherson, prin. Fax 288-6214

Watonga, Blaine, Pop. 4,457
Watonga ISD 1,400/PK-12
PO Box 310 73772 580-623-7364
Dr. Craig Cummins, supt. Fax 623-7370
www.watonga.k12.ok.us
Watonga HS 300/9-12
PO Box 310 73772 580-623-4961
Curtis Janko, prin. Fax 623-8019
Watonga MS 200/6-8
PO Box 310 73772 580-623-7361
Robin Roof, prin. Fax 623-7371

Watts, Adair, Pop. 323
Watts ISD 300/PK-12
RR 2 Box 1 74964 918-422-5311
Rita Bunch, supt. Fax 422-5556
wattsschool.com

Watts HS 100/9-12
RR 2 Box 1 74964 918-422-5132
Martin Bradford, prin. Fax 422-5556

Waukomis, Garfield, Pop. 1,228
Pioneer-Pleasant Vale ISD 600/PK-12
6520 E Wood Rd 73773 580-758-3282
Bill Noak, supt. Fax 758-1541
www.ppv.k12.ok.us/
Pioneer-Pleasant Vale HS 200/9-12
6520 E Wood Rd 73773 580-758-3282
Randy Schneider, prin.
Pioneer-Pleasant Vale JHS 100/7-8
6520 E Wood Rd 73773 580-758-3282
Randy Schneider, prin.

Waukomis ISD 300/K-12
PO Box 729 73773 580-758-3247
Dwain Jindra, supt. Fax 758-3834
www.waukomis.k12.ok.us
Waukomis HS 100/9-12
PO Box 729 73773 580-758-3245
Janet Blocke, prin. Fax 758-3834

Waurika, Jefferson, Pop. 1,891
Waurika ISD 500/PK-12
PO Box 330 73573 580-228-3373
Roxie Terry, supt. Fax 228-3428
Waurika MSHS 200/6-12
PO Box 330 73573 580-228-3373
Dale Spradlin, prin. Fax 228-3428

Wayne, McClain, Pop. 712
OK Dept. of Voc. & Tech. Education
Supt. — None
Mid-America Technology Center Vo/Tech
PO Box H 73095 405-449-3391
Dale Nye, supt. Fax 449-7321

Wayne ISD 400/PK-12
PO Box 40 73095 405-449-3646
David Powell, supt. Fax 449-7095
www.wayne.k12.ok.us
Wayne HS 100/9-12
PO Box 40 73095 405-449-3317
James Lewis, prin. Fax 449-7095
Wayne MS 100/6-8
PO Box 40 73095 405-449-7047
Billy Lucas, prin. Fax 449-7095

Waynoka, Woods, Pop. 930
Waynoka ISD 300/PK-12
RR 1 Box 1 73860 580-824-6561
Dale Ross, supt. Fax 824-0656
www.waynoka.k12.ok.us/
Waynoka HS, RR 1 Box 1 73860 100/9-12
Michael Meriwether, prin. 580-824-4341

Weatherford, Custer, Pop. 9,510
Weatherford ISD 1,700/PK-12
516 N Broadway St 73096 580-772-3327
Bill Seitter, supt. Fax 774-0821
www.wpsok.org
Weatherford HS 500/9-12
1500 N Washington St 73096 580-772-3385
James Ritz, prin. Fax 774-1939
Weatherford MS 400/6-8
509 N Custer St 73096 580-772-2270
Mark Shadid, prin. Fax 774-1981

Southwestern Oklahoma State University Post-Sec.
100 Campus Dr 73096 580-772-6611

Webbers Falls, Muskogee, Pop. 733
Webbers Falls ISD 300/PK-12
PO Box 300 74470 918-464-2580
Dudley Hume, supt. Fax 464-2313
www.webbersfalls.k12.ok.us/
Webbers Falls HS 100/9-12
PO Box 300 74470 918-464-2334
Ed Cannaday, prin. Fax 464-2313

Welch, Craig, Pop. 597
Welch ISD 400/PK-12
PO Box 189 74369 918-788-3319
Dr. Clark McKeon, supt. Fax 788-3734
welchwildcats.net
Welch JSHS 200/7-12
PO Box 189 74369 918-788-3222
Noah Francis, prin. Fax 788-3734

Weleetka, Okfuskee, Pop. 983
Graham ISD 100/PK-12
RR 1 Box 91 74880 918-652-8935
Dusty Chancey, supt. Fax 652-2422
www.graham.k12.ok.us
Graham HS 100/9-12
RR 1 Box 91 74880 918-652-8935
Dusty Chancey, prin. Fax 652-2422

Weleetka ISD 500/PK-12
PO Box 278 74880 405-786-2442
Dan Parrish, supt. Fax 786-2625
www.weleetka.k12.ok.us
Weleetka HS 100/10-12
PO Box 278 74880 405-786-2203
Ron Hunter, prin. Fax 786-2625
Weleetka JHS, PO Box 278 74880 100/7-9
Ron Hunter, prin. 405-786-2204

Wellston, Lincoln, Pop. 824
Wellston ISD 800/PK-12
PO Box 60 74881 405-356-2534
Dwayne Danker, supt. Fax 356-2838
Wellston HS 200/9-12
PO Box 60 74881 405-356-2533
Ethel Grubbs, prin. Fax 356-2838
Wellston MS 200/6-8
PO Box 60 74881 405-356-2533
Mark Grubbs, prin. Fax 356-2838

Westville, Adair, Pop. 1,612
Westville ISD 700/PK-12
PO Box 410 74965 918-723-3181
Dan Collins, supt. Fax 723-3042
www.westville.k12.ok.us
Westville JHS 200/7-9
PO Box 410 74965 918-723-3432
Jackie Smith, prin. Fax 723-3042
Westville SHS 200/10-12
PO Box 410 74965 918-723-5644
Jeff Collyge, prin. Fax 723-5644

Wetumka, Hughes, Pop. 1,421
OK Dept. of Voc. & Tech. Education
Supt. — None
West Watkins Technology Center Vo/Tech
7892 Highway 9 74883 405-452-5500
Jim Moore, supt. Fax 452-5706

Wetumka ISD 400/PK-12
410 E Benson St 74883 405-452-5150
Michael Jaggars, supt. Fax 452-3052
www.wetumka.k12.ok.us/
Wetumka HS 100/9-12
410 E Benson St 74883 405-452-3291
Ed Jones, prin. Fax 452-5836

Wewoka, Seminole, Pop. 3,417
New Lima ISD 300/PK-12
116 Gross St 74884 405-257-5771
Carroll Brooksher, supt. Fax 257-2587
www.newlima.k12.ok.us
New Lima HS 100/7-12
116 Gross St 74884 405-257-5771
Gil Turpin, prin. Fax 257-2587

Wewoka ISD 700/PK-12
PO Box 870 74884 405-257-5475
Carl Moore, supt. Fax 257-2303
www.wps.k12.ok.us/
Wewoka HS 200/9-12
PO Box 870 74884 405-257-5473
Kenneth Pattison, prin. Fax 257-2303
Wewoka MS 100/6-8
PO Box 870 74884 405-257-2340
Darrell Brown, prin. Fax 257-2303

Whitesboro, LeFlore
Whitesboro ISD 200/PK-12
PO Box 150 74577 918-567-2556
Dr. John Turner, supt. Fax 567-2842
Whitesboro HS, PO Box 150 74577 100/9-12
John Elrod, prin. 918-567-2624

Wilburton, Latimer, Pop. 2,932
OK Dept. of Voc. & Tech. Education
Supt. — None
Kiamichi Technology Center Vo/Tech
PO Box 548 74578 918-465-2324
Dr. Greg Winters, supt. Fax 465-3666

Wilburton ISD 800/PK-12
1201 W Blair Ave 74578 918-465-2100
Charles Enis, supt. Fax 465-3086
Wilburton JHS 300/7-9
1201 W Blair Ave 74578 918-465-2281
Tressa Taylor Moore, prin.
Wilburton SHS 200/10-12
1201 W Blair Ave 74578 918-465-3125
Nancy Taylor, prin.

Eastern Oklahoma State College Post-Sec.
1301 W Main St 74578 918-465-2361

Wilson, Carter, Pop. 1,605
Wilson ISD 500/PK-12
1860 Hewitt Rd 73463 580-668-2306
Lynn Henderson, supt. Fax 668-2170
www.wilson.k12.ok.us/
Wilson HS 100/9-12
1860 Hewitt Rd 73463 580-668-2317
Gary Labeth, prin. Fax 668-2170

Wister, LeFlore, Pop. 1,014
Wister ISD 500/PK-12
201 Logan St 74966 918-655-3132
Jerry Carpenter, supt. Fax 655-7402
www.wisterschools.org/
Wister HS 100/9-12
201 Logan St 74966 918-655-7276
Doug Hall, prin. Fax 655-7402

Woodward, Woodward, Pop. 11,789
OK Dept. of Voc. & Tech. Education
Supt. — None
High Plains Technology Center Vo/Tech
3921 34th St 73801 580-256-6618
Dr. Don Dale, supt. Fax 571-6190

Woodward ISD 2,500/PK-12
PO Box 668 73802 580-256-6063
Bill Denton, supt. Fax 256-4391
www.woodwardps.net
Woodward HS 700/9-12
PO Box 668 73802 580-256-5329
Kirk Warnick, prin. Fax 256-8716
Woodward MS South 300/7-8
PO Box 668 73802 580-256-7901
Frank Harrington, prin. Fax 256-8014

Woodward Beauty College Post-Sec.
502 Texas St 73801 580-256-7520

Wright City, McCurtain, Pop. 816
Wright City ISD 500/PK-12
PO Box 329 74766 580-981-2824
David Hawkins, supt. Fax 981-2115
Wright City HS, PO Box 329 74766 100/9-12
Bob Finley, prin. 580-981-2558
Wright City JHS, PO Box 329 74766 100/7-8
Bob Finley, prin. 580-981-2558

Wyandotte, Ottawa, Pop. 359
Wyandotte ISD 800/K-12
PO Box 360 74370 918-678-2255
Duane Thomas, supt. Fax 678-2304
www.wyandotteschools.net
Wyandotte HS 200/9-12
PO Box 360 74370 918-678-2222
Marcia Kruse, prin. Fax 678-3906
Wyandotte MS 200/6-8
PO Box 360 74370 918-678-2222
Chris Gwartney, prin. Fax 678-3906

Wynnewood, Garvin, Pop. 2,322
Wynnewood ISD 700/PK-12
702 E Kerr Blvd 73098 405-665-2004
Bill Weldon, supt. Fax 665-5425
www.wynnewood.k12.ok.us/
Wynnewood HS 200/9-12
702 E Kerr Blvd 73098 405-665-2045
John Turner, prin.
Wynnewood MS 200/5-8
702 E Kerr Blvd 73098 405-665-4105
Mitzi Winters, prin.

Wynona, Osage, Pop. 540
Wynona ISD 200/PK-12
PO Box 700 74084 918-846-2467
Dixie Heard, supt. Fax 846-2883
Wynona HS, PO Box 700 74084 100/9-12
Mark Allgood, prin. 918-846-2467

Yale, Payne, Pop. 1,328
Yale ISD 500/PK-12
315 E Chicago Ave 74085 918-387-2434
Mike Wilson, supt. Fax 387-2503
www.yale.k12.ok.us/
Yale HS 200/9-12
315 E Chicago Ave 74085 918-387-2282
Dodds Terrell, prin. Fax 387-2503
Yale JHS 100/7-8
315 E Chicago Ave 74085 918-387-2118
Dodds Terrell, prin. Fax 387-2503

Yukon, Canadian, Pop. 21,152
Yukon ISD 4,900/K-12
600 Maple St 73099 405-354-2587
Dr. Larry Birden, supt. Fax 354-4208
www.yukonps.com
Independence MS 700/6-8
500 E Vandamet Ave 73099 405-354-5274
Tresa Smith, prin. Fax 354-0921
Lakeview MS 700/6-8
2700 N Mustang Rd 73099 405-350-2630
Rodney Weidenmaier, prin. Fax 350-2632
Yukon HS 9-10
1029 Garth Brooks Blvd 73099 405-354-6692
Shirley Tucker, prin. Fax 354-6640
Yukon HS 900/11-12
1000 Yukon Ave 73099 405-354-6661
Dyton Coleman, prin. Fax 354-8411

Southwest Covenant S 300/PK-12
2250 N Mustang Rd 73099 405-354-0772
G. Max DeWeese, hdmstr. Fax 350-2670
Yukon Beauty College Post-Sec.
1231 Garth Brooks Blvd 73099 405-354-3172

OREGON

OREGON DEPARTMENT OF EDUCATION
255 Capitol St NE, Salem 97310-0406
Telephone 503-947-5600
Fax 503-378-5156
Website http://www.ode.state.or.us

Superintendent of Public Instruction   Susan Castillo

OREGON BOARD OF EDUCATION
255 Capitol St NE, Salem 97310-0406

Steve Bogart   Chairperson

EDUCATION SERVICE DISTRICTS (ESD)

Clackamas ESD
Milt Dennison, supt.
4011 SE Lake Rd, Milwaukie 97222 — 503-675-4000 Fax 675-4200
www.clackesd.k12.or.us
Douglas ESD
Jonathan Hill, supt.
1871 NE Stephens St — 541-440-4777 Fax 440-4771
Roseburg 97470
www.douglasesd.k12.or.us
Grant ESD
Anthony Lanni, supt.
835 S Canyon Blvd — 541-575-1349 Fax 575-3601
John Day 97845
www.grantesd.k12.or.us
Harney ESD
Dennis Mills, supt.
450 N Buena Vista Ave — 541-573-2426 Fax 573-1822
Burns 97720
www.harneyesd.k12.or.us
High Desert ESD
Dennis Dempsey, supt.
145 SE Salmon Ave Ste A — 541-693-5600 Fax 693-5601
Redmond 97756
www.hdesd.k12.or.us
Jefferson ESD
Guy Fisher, supt.
295 SE Buff St, Madras 97741 — 541-475-2804 Fax 475-2827
Lake ESD
Judith May, supt.
357 N L St, Lakeview 97630 — 541-947-3371 Fax 947-3373
www.lakeesd.k12.or.us/

Lane ESD
Mike Vermillion, supt.
1200 Highway 99 N, Eugene 97402 — 541-461-8200 Fax 461-8298
www.lane.k12.or.us
Linn-Benton-Lincoln ESD
Robert Nelson, supt.
905 4th Ave SE, Albany 97321 — 541-812-2600 Fax 926-6047
www.lblesd.k12.or.us
Malheur ESD
Tim Labrousse, supt.
363 A St W, Vale 97918 — 541-473-3138 Fax 473-3915
www.malesd.k12.or.us
Multnomah ESD
Edward Schmitt, supt.
PO Box 301039, Portland 97294 — 503-255-1841 Fax 257-1525
www.mesd.k12.or.us
North Central ESD
Anthony Lanni, supt.
PO Box 637, Condon 97823 — 541-384-2732 Fax 384-2752
www.ncesd.k12.or.us
Northwest Regional ESD
Jim Mabbott, supt.
5825 NE Ray Cir, Hillsboro 97124 — 503-614-1428 Fax 614-1440
www.nwresd.k12.or.us
Region 9 ESD
James Carnes Ed.D., supt.
400 E Scenic Dr Ste 207 — 541-298-5155 Fax 296-2965
The Dalles 97058
www.r9esd.k12.or.us

Region 18 ESD
Edward Jensen, supt.
107 SW 1st St Ste 105 — 541-426-4997 Fax 426-3732
Enterprise 97828
www.wallowaesd.k12.or.us/
South Coast ESD
Rick Howell, supt.
1350 Teakwood Ave — 541-269-1611 Fax 266-4040
Coos Bay 97420
www.scesd.k12.or.us
Southern Oregon ESD
Steve Boyarsky, supt.
101 N Grape St, Medford 97501 — 541-776-8590 Fax 779-2018
www.soesd.k12.or.us
Umatilla-Morrow ESD
George Murdock, supt.
2001 SW Nye Ave — 541-276-6616 Fax 276-4252
Pendleton 97801
www.umesd.k12.or.us
Union/Baker ESD
Jack Adams, supt.
10100 N McAlister Rd — 541-963-4106 Fax 963-7256
La Grande 97850
www.ubesd.k12.or.us
Willamette ESD
Maureen Casey, supt.
2611 Pringle Rd SE, Salem 97302 — 503-588-5330 Fax 363-5787
www.wesd.org

PUBLIC, PRIVATE AND CATHOLIC SECONDARY SCHOOLS

Adel, Lake
Adel SD 21
Supt. — See Lakeview
Adel S — 50/4-8
PO Box 117 97620 — 541-947-3818
John Griffin, prin. — Fax 947-5419

Adrian, Malheur, Pop. 145
Adrian SD 61 — 200/K-12
PO Box 108 97901 — 541-372-3744
Gene Mills, supt. — Fax 372-5380
www.adriansd.com
Adrian HS — 100/9-12
PO Box 108 97901 — 541-372-2335
Gene Mills, prin. — Fax 372-5380

Albany, Linn, Pop. 43,091
Greater Albany SD 8J — 8,400/K-12
718 7th Ave SW 97321 — 541-967-4501
Pat Bedore, supt. — Fax 967-4587
www.8j.net
Calapooia MS — 800/6-8
830 24th Ave SE, — 541-967-4555
Pat Wiedmann, prin. — Fax 924-3702
Memorial MS — 600/6-8
1050 Queen Ave SW 97321 — 541-967-4537
Chris Phillips, prin. — Fax 924-3703
North Albany MS — 600/6-8
1205 NW North Albany Rd 97321 — 541-967-4541
Randy Lary, prin. — Fax 924-3704
South Albany HS — 1,200/9-12
3705 Columbus St SE, — 541-967-4522
Chris Equinoa, prin. — Fax 924-3700
West Albany HS — 1,300/9-12
1130 Queen Ave SW 97321 — 541-967-4545
Susie Orsborn, prin. — Fax 924-3701

Fairview Christian S — 100/K-12
35100 Goltra Rd SE, — 541-928-4219
Ray Allen, prin. — Fax 928-2140
Linn-Benton Community College — Post-Sec.
6500 Pacific Blvd SW 97321 — 541-917-4999

Aloha, Washington, Pop. 43,600

Life Christian S — 200/PK-12
5585 SW 209th Ave 97007 — 503-259-1329
Adam Kronberger, prin. — Fax 649-5484

Magee Brothers Beaverton Sch of Beauty — Post-Sec.
18295A SW Tualatin Valley 97007 — 503-649-1388

Alsea, Benton
Alsea SD 7J — 200/K-12
PO Box B 97324 — 541-487-4305
Jason Larson, supt. — Fax 487-4089
www.alsea.k12.or.us/
Alsea HS, PO Box B 97324 — 100/9-12
Jason Larson, prin. — 541-487-4305

Amity, Yamhill, Pop. 1,469
Amity SD 4J — 900/K-12
PO Box 138 97101 — 503-835-2171
Reg McShane, supt. — Fax 835-5050
www.amity.k12.or.us
Amity HS — 300/9-12
PO Box 138 97101 — 503-835-2181
Mike Solem, prin. — Fax 835-6113
Amity MS — 200/6-8
PO Box 138 97101 — 503-835-0518
Dave Lund, prin. — Fax 835-0418

Perrydale SD 21 — 200/K-12
7445 Perrydale Rd 97101 — 503-835-3184
Robin Stoutt, supt. — Fax 835-0631
www.perrydale.k12.or.us
Perrydale JSHS — 200/6-12
7445 Perrydale Rd 97101 — 503-835-3184
Justin Huntley, prin. — Fax 835-0631

Arlington, Gilliam, Pop. 492
Arlington SD 3 — 200/K-12
PO Box 10 97812 — 541-454-2632
Mike Keown, supt. — Fax 454-2137
www.honkernet.net
Arlington HS — 100/9-12
PO Box 10 97812 — 541-454-2632
Mike Keown, prin. — Fax 454-2137

Ashland, Jackson, Pop. 20,406
Ashland SD 5 — 2,800/K-12
885 Siskiyou Blvd 97520 — 541-482-2811
Juli DiChiro, supt. — Fax 482-2185
www.ashland.k12.or.us/splash/
Ashland HS — 1,200/9-12
201 S Mountain Ave 97520 — 541-482-8771
Jeff Schlecht, prin. — Fax 482-2172
Ashland MS — 700/6-8
100 Walker Ave 97520 — 541-482-1611
Dale Rooklyn, prin. — Fax 482-8112

Southern Oregon University — Post-Sec.
1250 Siskiyou Blvd 97520 — 541-552-7672

Astoria, Clatsop, Pop. 9,660
Astoria SD 1 — 1,500/K-12
785 Alameda Ave 97103 — 503-325-6441
Michael Sowder, supt. — Fax 325-6524
www.astoria.k12.or.us/
Astoria HS — 800/9-12
1001 W Marine Dr 97103 — 503-325-3911
Larry Lockett, prin. — Fax 325-2891
Astoria MS — 300/7-8
1100 Klaskanine Ave 97103 — 503-325-4331
Keith Neal, prin. — Fax 325-3040

Knappa SD 4 — 600/K-12
41535 Old Highway 30 97103 — 503-458-6166
Rick Pass, supt. — Fax 458-5466
Knappa HS — 200/9-12
41535 Old Highway 30 97103 — 503-458-6166
Nanette Hagen, prin. — Fax 458-5466

Astoria Beauty College — Post-Sec.
1180 Commercial St 97103 — 503-325-3163
Clatsop Community College — Post-Sec.
1653 Jerome Ave 97103 — 503-325-0910

Athena, Umatilla, Pop. 1,215
Athena-Weston SD 29RJ — 600/K-12
375 S 5th St 97813 — 541-566-3551
Richard Hensel, supt. — Fax 566-9454
www.athwest.k12.or.us/
Weston-McEwen HS — 200/9-12
540 E Main St 97813 — 541-566-3555
Brian Schimel, prin. — Fax 566-2751
Other Schools — See Weston

Aurora, Marion, Pop. 657
North Marion SD 15 — 1,800/PK-12
20256 Grim Rd NE 97002 — 503-678-7100
Linda Reeves, supt. — Fax 678-1473
www.nmarion.k12.or.us
North Marion HS — 600/9-12
20167 Grim Rd NE 97002 — 503-678-7123
Glenn Elliott, prin. — Fax 678-7186
North Marion MS — 400/6-8
20246 Grim Rd NE 97002 — 503-678-7118
Sharon Baum, prin. — Fax 678-7185

Baker City, Baker, Pop. 9,671
Baker SD 5J   2,100/PK-12
2090 4th St   97814   541-524-2260
Don Ulrey, supt.   Fax 524-2564
www.baker.k12.or.us
Baker HS   700/9-12
2500 E St   97814   541-524-2600
Jerry Peacock, prin.   Fax 524-2699
Baker MS   300/7-8
2320 Washington Ave   97814   541-524-2500
Minda Vaughan, prin.   Fax 524-2563

Bandon, Coos, Pop. 2,827
Bandon SD 54   800/K-12
455 9th St SW   97411   541-347-4411
Kenny Kent, supt.   Fax 347-3974
Bandon HS   300/9-12
550 9th St SW   97411   541-347-4413
Gaye Knapp, prin.   Fax 347-3714
Harbor Lights MS   300/5-8
390 9th St SW   97411   541-347-4415
Gerald Prickett, prin.   Fax 347-1280

Bandon Pacific Christian S   50/PK-12
PO Box 949   97411   541-347-4157
Robbyn Sands, prin.   Fax 347-4157

Banks, Washington, Pop. 1,521
Banks SD 13   1,200/K-12
450 S Main St   97106   503-324-8591
Marvin Ott, supt.   Fax 324-6969
www.banks.k12.or.us
Banks HS   400/9-12
450 S Main St   97106   503-324-2281
Jim Foster, prin.   Fax 324-8221
Banks JHS   200/7-8
450 S Main St   97106   503-324-3111
Mark Everett, prin.   Fax 324-7441

Beaver, Tillamook
Nestucca Valley SD 101
Supt. — See Cloverdale
Nestucca Valley MS   200/6-8
PO Box 77   97108   503-398-5545
Jim Goodberry, prin.   Fax 398-5831

Beaverton, Washington, Pop. 80,520
Beaverton SD 48J   35,000/K-12
16550 SW Merlo Rd   97006   503-591-8000
Jerome Colonna, supt.   Fax 591-4415
www.beavton.k12.or.us
Aloha HS   1,900/9-12
18550 SW Kinnaman Rd   97007   503-259-4700
Vicki Lukich, prin.   Fax 259-4713
Beaverton HS   2,000/9-12
13000 SW 2nd St   97005   503-259-5000
Janice Adams, prin.   Fax 259-4990
Conestoga MS   1,100/6-8
12250 SW Conestoga Dr   97008   503-524-1345
Dan Zenor, prin.   Fax 524-1349
Five Oaks MS   1,100/6-8
1600 NW 173rd Ave   97006   503-533-1900
Mike Chamberlain, prin.   Fax 533-1898
Highland Park MS   1,100/6-8
7000 SW Wilson Ave   97008   503-672-3640
Allan Deckard, prin.   Fax 672-3644
Meadow Park MS   800/6-8
14100 SW Downing St   97006   503-672-3660
Jill O'Neill, prin.   Fax 672-3664
Mountain View MS   1,100/6-8
17500 SW Farmington Rd   97007   503-259-3890
Joann Hulquist, prin.   Fax 259-3894
School of Science & Technology   Vo/Tech
1841 SW Merlo Dr   97006   503-259-5575
Gregory Parcher, prin.   Fax 259-5588
Southridge HS   2,000/9-12
9625 SW 125th Ave   97008   503-259-5400
Amy Gordon, prin.   Fax 259-5425
Whitford MS   900/6-8
7935 SW Scholls Ferry Rd   97008   503-672-3680
Matthew Casteel, prin.   Fax 672-3684
Other Schools – See Portland

Oregon Graduate Institute/Science & Tech   Post-Sec.
20000 NW Walker Rd   97006   503-748-1121
Valley Catholic HS   500/7-12
4275 SW 148th Ave   97007   503-644-3745
Ross Thomas, prin.   Fax 646-4054

Bend, Deschutes, Pop. 59,779
Bend-LaPine Administrative SD 1   13,700/K-12
520 NW Wall St   97701   541-383-6000
Douglas Nelson, supt.   Fax 383-6003
www.bend.k12.or.us
Bend HS   1,300/9-12
230 NE 6th St   97701   541-383-6290
Mark Neffendorf, prin.   Fax 383-6465
Cascade MS   700/6-8
19619 SW Mountaineer Way   97702   541-383-6230
David Haack, prin.   Fax 383-6255
High Desert MS   700/6-8
61111 27th St   97702   541-383-6480
Gary DeFrang, prin.   Fax 383-6499
Mountain View HS   1,400/9-12
2755 NE 27th St   97701   541-383-6360
Robert Jones, prin.   Fax 383-6469
Pilot Butte MS   600/6-8
1501 NE Neff Rd   97701   541-383-6260
Kathryn Legace, prin.   Fax 383-6286
Sky View MS   600/6-8
63555 18th St   97701   541-383-6479
Melissa Goff, prin.   Fax 322-5217
Summit HS   1,200/9-12
2855 NW Clearwater Dr   97701   541-322-3300
Lynn Baker, prin.   Fax 322-3310
Other Schools – See La Pine

Central Oregon Community College   Post-Sec.
2600 NW College Way   97701   541-383-7500
Morning Star Christian S   200/PK-12
19741 Baker Rd   97702   541-382-5091
Rev. Ken Marks, admin.   Fax 382-0268

Phagans' Central Oregon Beauty College   Post-Sec.
355 NE 2nd St   97701   541-382-6171
Three Sisters SDA S   50/K-10
21155 Tumalo Rd   97701   541-389-2091
Randy Thornton, prin.   Fax 389-2091

Blachly, Lane
Blachly SD 90   100/K-12
20264 Blachly Grange Rd   97412   541-925-3262
Bob De La Vergne, supt.   Fax 925-3062
www.blachly.k12.or.us/
Triangle Lake S   100/K-12
20264 Blachly Grange Rd   97412   541-925-3262
Bob De La Vergne, prin.   Fax 925-3062

Boardman, Morrow, Pop. 3,028
Morrow SD 1
Supt. — See Lexington
Riverside JSHS   600/7-12
210 NE Boardman Ave   97818   541-481-2525
Dirk Dirksen, prin.   Fax 481-2047

Bonanza, Klamath, Pop. 414
Klamath County SD
Supt. — See Klamath Falls
Bonanza S   500/K-12
PO Box 128   97623   541-545-6581
Charlene Soule, prin.   Fax 545-1719

Klamath-Lake Co. Youth Ranch   50/9-12
5800 Happy Hollow Ln   97623   541-545-6742

Boring, Clackamas
Oregon Trail SD 46
Supt. — See Sandy
Boring MS   400/6-8
27801 SE Dee St   97009   503-668-9393
Scott Maltman, prin.   Fax 668-5291

Brookings, Curry, Pop. 5,878
Brookings-Harbor SD 17-C   1,800/K-12
629 Easy St   97415   541-469-7443
Chris Nichols, supt.   Fax 469-6599
www.brookings.k12.or.us
Azalea MS   500/6-8
629 Easy St   97415   541-469-7427
Michael Dillenburg, prin.   Fax 469-7080
Brookings-Harbor HS   600/9-12
629 Easy St   97415   541-469-2108
George Park, prin.   Fax 469-6570

Brookings Harbor Christian S   100/PK-10
PO Box 5809   97415   541-469-6478
Christine Hudson, admin.   Fax 412-7242

Brooks, Marion

Willamette Valley Christian S   200/K-12
PO Box 9088   97305   503-393-5236
Gary Glassco, admin.   Fax 485-8203

Brownsville, Linn, Pop. 1,480
Central Linn SD 552   600/K-12
331 E Blakely Ave   97327   541-466-3105
Max Harrell, supt.   Fax 466-3180
www.centrallinn.k12.or.us
Other Schools – See Halsey

Burns, Harney, Pop. 2,880
Harney County SD 3   1,100/K-12
550 N Court Ave   97720   541-573-6811
David L. Courtney, supt.   Fax 573-7557
www.burnsschools.k12.or.us
Burns HS   300/9-12
1100 Oregon Ave   97720   541-573-2044
Ron Wassom, prin.   Fax 573-5456
Other Schools – See Hines

Butte Falls, Jackson, Pop. 437
Butte Falls SD 91   200/K-12
PO Box 228   97522   541-865-3563
Steve Pine, supt.   Fax 865-3217
www.buttefallsschools.org/
Butte Falls MSHS   100/7-12
PO Box 167   97522   541-865-3563
Steve Pine, prin.   Fax 865-7810

Camas Valley, Douglas
Camas Valley SD 21J   100/K-12
PO Box 97   97416   541-445-2131
Vince Swagerty, supt.   Fax 445-2041
Camas Valley S   100/K-12
PO Box 97   97416   541-445-2131
Vince Swagerty, prin.   Fax 445-2041

Canby, Clackamas, Pop. 14,238
Canby SD 86   5,200/K-12
1110 S Ivy   97013   503-266-7861
Deborah Sommer, supt.   Fax 266-0022
www.canby.k12.or.us
Ackerman MS   1,000/6-8
350 SE 13th Ave   97013   503-263-7140
Joel Sebastian, prin.   Fax 266-7489
Baker Prairie MS   6-8
1859 S Township Rd   97013   503-263-7170
Lou Bailey, prin.   Fax 263-7189
Canby HS   1,700/9-12
721 SW 4th Ave   97013   503-263-7200
Pat Johnson, prin.   Fax 263-7211

Canyon City, Grant, Pop. 611
Grant SD 3   800/K-12
401 N Canyon City Blvd   97820   541-575-1280
Newell Cleaver, supt.   Fax 575-0928
www.grantesd.k12.or.us
Other Schools – See John Day, Mount Vernon

Canyonville, Douglas, Pop. 1,382

Canyonville Christian Academy   200/6-12
PO Box 1100   97417   541-839-4401
Cathy Lovato, admin.   Fax 839-6228

Cascade Locks, Hood River, Pop. 1,112
Hood River County SD
Supt. — See Hood River
Cascade Locks S   200/K-12
PO Box 279   97014   541-374-8467
Chris Daniels, prin.   Fax 374-8446

Cave Junction, Josephine, Pop. 1,395
Three Rivers County SD
Supt. — See Grants Pass
Byrne MS   400/6-8
101 S Junction Ave   97523   541-592-2163
Tom Hewkin, prin.   Fax 592-4851
Illinois Valley HS   500/9-12
River St & Laurel Rd   97523   541-592-2116
JoAnn Bethany, prin.   Fax 592-4853

Central Point, Jackson, Pop. 14,630
Central Point SD 6   4,700/K-12
300 Ash St   97502   541-494-6200
Randal Gravon, supt.   Fax 664-1637
www.district6.org
Crater HS   1,600/9-12
655 N 3rd St   97502   541-494-6300
Kirk Gibson, prin.   Fax 664-7589
Scenic MS   900/6-8
1955 Scenic Ave   97502   541-494-6400
Sheila Henson, prin.   Fax 664-8534
Other Schools – See Gold Hill

Chiloquin, Klamath, Pop. 719
Klamath County SD
Supt. — See Klamath Falls
Chiloquin JSHS   300/7-12
PO Box 397   97624   541-783-2321
Doug Wilson, prin.   Fax 783-2792

Christmas Valley, Lake

Solid Rock Christian S   50/K-12
PO Box 745   97641   541-576-2895
Dell Renee Wilson, prin.

Clackamas, Clackamas, Pop. 2,578
North Clackamas SD 12
Supt. — See Milwaukie
Clackamas HS   1,900/9-12
14486 SE 122nd Ave   97015   503-353-5800
Jan Miner, prin.   Fax 353-5815
Sunrise MS   1,000/7-8
14331 SE 132nd Ave   97015   503-353-5750
Terrence Smyth, prin.   Fax 353-5765

Pioneer Pacific College   Post-Sec.
8800 SE Sunnyside Rd   97015   503-654-8000

Clatskanie, Columbia, Pop. 1,608
Clatskanie SD 6J   900/K-12
PO Box 678   97016   503-728-0587
Mike Corley, supt.   Fax 728-0608
www.clat6j.k12.or.us/
Clatskanie MSHS   500/7-12
PO Box 68   97016   503-728-2146
Gary Mounce, prin.   Fax 728-4632

Cloverdale, Tillamook
Nestucca Valley SD 101   600/K-12
36925 Highway 101 S   97112   503-392-4892
Bob Simonson, supt.   Fax 392-9061
www.nestucca.k12.or.us
Nestucca HS   200/9-12
PO Box 38   97112   503-392-3194
Randy Wharton, prin.   Fax 392-3724
Other Schools – See Beaver

Colton, Clackamas
Colton SD 53   700/K-12
30429 S Grays Hill Rd   97017   503-824-3535
Steve Dickenson, supt.   Fax 824-3530
www.colton.k12.or.us
Colton HS   300/9-12
30205 S Wall St   97017   503-824-2311
Jeff Davis, prin.   Fax 824-2312
Colton MS   200/6-8
21580 S Schieffer Rd   97017   503-824-2319
Clarice Schorzman, prin.   Fax 824-2309

Condon, Gilliam, Pop. 703
Condon SD 25J   200/K-12
PO Box 615   97823   541-384-2581
Gene Carlson, supt.   Fax 384-2585
www.condon.k12.or.us
Condon HS   100/9-12
PO Box 575   97823   541-384-2441
Gene Carlson, prin.   Fax 384-2504

Coos Bay, Coos, Pop. 15,345
Coos Bay SD 9   3,600/K-12
PO Box 509   97420   541-267-3104
Karen Gray, supt.   Fax 269-5366
www.coos.k12.or.us
Marshfield HS   1,200/9-12
PO Box 509   97420   541-267-1405
Robert Line, prin.   Fax 269-0161
Sunset MS   600/7-8
PO Box 509   97420   541-888-1242
Travis Howard, prin.   Fax 888-9814

Southwestern Oregon Community College   Post-Sec.
1988 Newmark Ave   97420   541-888-2525

Coquille, Coos, Pop. 4,144
Coquille SD 8   1,000/K-12
790 W 17th St   97423   541-396-2181
John Kinnee, supt.   Fax 396-5015
www.coquille.k12.or.us/
Coquille HS   400/9-12
499 W Central St   97423   541-396-2163
Patrick Royal, prin.   Fax 396-4635
Coquille Valley S   400/4-8
1115 N Baxter St   97423   541-396-2914
Mark Nortness, prin.   Fax 396-4543

Corbett, Multnomah
Corbett SD 39 600/K-12
35800 Historic Columbia Riv 97019 503-695-3612
Robert Dunton, supt. Fax 695-3641
www.corbett.k12.or.us
Corbett HS 200/10-12
35800 Historic Columbia Riv 97019 503-695-3600
Randy Trani, prin. Fax 695-3641
Corbett MS 100/7-9
35800 Historic Columbia Riv 97019 503-695-3636
Randy Trani, prin. Fax 695-3641

Corvallis, Benton, Pop. 50,126
Corvallis SD 509J 7,100/K-12
PO Box 3509J 97339 541-757-5811
Dawn Tarzian, supt. Fax 757-5703
www.csd509j.net/
Cheldelin MS 800/6-8
987 NE Conifer Blvd 97330 541-757-5971
Dawn Corliss, prin. Fax 757-4596
Corvallis HS 1,400/9-12
1400 NW Buchanan Ave 97330 541-757-5871
Jay Conroy, prin. Fax 757-5875
Crescent Valley HS 1,100/9-12
4444 NW Highland Dr 97330 541-757-5801
Cherie Stroud, prin. Fax 757-4522
Pauling MS 600/6-8
1111 NW Cleveland Ave 97330 541-757-5961
James Wickman, prin. Fax 757-4598

Oregon State University 97333 Post-Sec.
541-737-0123
Phagans' Beauty College Post-Sec.
142 SW 2nd St 97333 541-753-6466
Santiam Christian S 900/PK-12
7220 NE Arnold Ave 97330 541-745-5524
Stanton Baker, supt. Fax 745-6338

Cottage Grove, Lane, Pop. 8,514
South Lane SD 45J3 2,900/K-12
PO Box 218 97424 541-942-3381
Krista Parent, supt. Fax 942-8098
www.slane.k12.or.us/dsc
Cottage Grove HS 900/9-12
PO Box 160 97424 541-942-3391
Donn Pollard, prin. Fax 942-7492
Lincoln MS 700/6-8
1565 S 4th St 97424 541-942-3316
Brian McCasline, prin. Fax 942-9801

Cove, Union, Pop. 605
Cove SD 15 200/K-12
PO Box 68 97824 541-568-4424
Jeff Clark, supt. Fax 568-4251
Cove S 200/K-12
PO Box 68 97824 541-568-4424
Toby Koehn, prin. Fax 568-4251

Crane, Harney
Harney County UNHSD 1J 100/9-12
PO Box 828 97732 541-493-2641
Tim Adsit, supt. Fax 493-2051
Crane Union HS 100/9-12
PO Box 828 97732 541-493-2641
Tim Adsit, prin. Fax 493-2051

Creswell, Lane, Pop. 4,024
Creswell SD 40 1,200/K-12
998 A St 97426 541-895-6000
Rick Stuber, supt. Fax 895-6019
www.creswell.k12.or.us
Creswell HS 400/9-12
33390 Nieblock Ln 97426 541-895-6020
Jan Ophus, prin. Fax 895-6089
Creswell MS 300/6-8
655 W Oregon Ave 97426 541-895-6090
Shirley Burrus, prin. Fax 895-6139

Creswell Christian S 100/K-10
PO Box 217 97426 541-895-4622
Rebecca Lake, admin.

Culver, Jefferson, Pop. 805
Culver SD 4 600/K-12
PO Box 228 97734 541-546-2541
Linda Florence, supt. Fax 546-7517
www.culver.k12.or.us/
Culver HS 200/9-12
PO Box 228 97734 541-546-2251
Brian Wolf, prin. Fax 546-2201
Culver MS 200/6-8
PO Box 228 97734 541-546-3090
Alice Smith, prin. Fax 546-2137

Dallas, Polk, Pop. 13,221
Dallas SD 2 3,100/K-12
111 SW Ash St 97338 503-623-5594
Christy Perry, supt. Fax 623-5597
www.dallas.k12.or.us
Dallas HS 1,000/9-12
1250 SE Holman Ave 97338 503-623-8336
Keith Ussery, prin. Fax 623-4669
LaCreole MS 800/6-8
701 SE Lacreole Dr 97338 503-623-6662
Diane Baumgartner, prin. Fax 623-8477

Damascus, Clackamas
Gresham-Barlow SD 10J
Supt. — See Gresham
Damascus MS 400/5-8
14151 SE 242nd Ave, 503-658-3171
Lori Walter, prin. Fax 658-6275

Damascus Christian S 300/K-12
14251 SE Rust Way, 503-658-4100
Timothy Oakley, admin. Fax 658-5827

Days Creek, Douglas

Milo Adventist Academy 100/9-12
PO Box 278 97429 541-825-3200
Fax 825-3723

Dayton, Yamhill, Pop. 2,175
Dayton SD 8 1,100/K-12
526 Ferry St 97114 503-864-2215
Janelle Beers, supt. Fax 864-3927
www.dayton.k12.or.us
Dayton HS 300/9-12
801 Ferry St 97114 503-864-2273
Roger Lorenzen, prin. Fax 864-2932
Dayton JHS 200/6-8
801 Ferry St 97114 503-864-2246
Jami Fluke, prin. Fax 864-3697

Dayville, Grant, Pop. 125
Dayville SD 16J 100/K-12
PO Box C 97825 541-987-2412
Maurice Thorne, supt. Fax 987-2155
Dayville S 100/K-12
PO Box C 97825 541-987-2412
Maurice Thorne, prin. Fax 987-2155

Drain, Douglas, Pop. 1,028
North Douglas SD 22 400/K-12
PO Box 428 97435 541-836-2223
Dan Forbess, supt. Fax 836-7558
North Douglas HS 100/9-12
PO Box 488 97435 541-836-2222
Lesa Haley, prin. Fax 836-2387

Dufur, Wasco, Pop. 584
Dufur SD 29 300/K-12
802 NE 5th St 97021 541-467-2509
Jack Henderson, supt. Fax 467-2589
www.dufur.k12.or.us
Dufur S 300/K-12
802 NE 5th St 97021 541-467-2509
Bert Wyatt, prin. Fax 467-2589

Eagle Point, Jackson, Pop. 6,306
Jackson County SD 9 4,200/K-12
PO Box 548 97524 541-830-1200
Dr. William Feusahrens, supt. Fax 830-6550
www.eaglepnt.k12.or.us
Eagle Point HS 1,100/9-12
PO Box 198 97524 541-830-1300
Mari Brabbin, prin. Fax 830-6682
Eagle Point MS 500/6-8
PO Box 218 97524 541-830-1250
Wayne Gallagher, prin. Fax 830-6086
Other Schools – See Shady Cove, White City

Echo, Umatilla, Pop. 682
Echo SD 5 200/K-12
600 E Gerone St 97826 541-376-8436
Rob Waite, supt. Fax 376-8473
www.echo.k12.or.us/
Echo S 200/K-12
600 E Gerone St 97826 541-376-8436
Norm Stewart, prin. Fax 376-8473

Elgin, Union, Pop. 1,647
Elgin SD 23 500/K-12
PO Box 68 97827 541-437-1211
Kerma Berry, supt. Fax 437-1231
www.elgin.k12.or.us
Elgin HS 100/9-12
PO Box 68 97827 541-437-2021
Kerma Berry, prin. Fax 437-1705

Elkton, Douglas, Pop. 148
Elkton SD 34 200/K-12
PO Box 390 97436 541-584-2228
Rhonda Zosel, supt. Fax 584-2227
www.elkton.k12.or.us/
Elkton HS 100/9-12
PO Box 390 97436 541-584-2228
Rhonda Zosel, prin. Fax 584-2227

Elmira, Lane
Fern Ridge SD 28J 1,500/K-12
88834 Territorial Rd 97437 541-935-2253
Ivan Hernandez, supt. Fax 935-8222
www.fernridge.k12.or.us
Elmira HS 500/9-12
24936 Fir Grove Ln 97437 541-935-8200
Karen McKenzie, prin. Fax 935-8205
Fern Ridge MS 400/6-8
88831 Territorial Rd 97437 541-935-8230
Doug Kartub, prin. Fax 935-8234

Enterprise, Wallowa, Pop. 1,835
Enterprise SD 21 400/K-12
201 SE 4th St 97828 541-426-3193
Brad Royse, supt. Fax 426-3504
www.enterprise.k12.or.us/
Enterprise HS 200/7-12
201 SE 4th St 97828 541-426-3193
Blake Carlsen, prin. Fax 426-3504

Enterprise SDA S 50/K-10
PO Box N 97828 541-426-8339
Dan Webster, prin. Fax 426-8339

Estacada, Clackamas, Pop. 2,395
Estacada SD 108 2,300/K-12
255 NE 6th Ave 97023 503-630-6871
Michael Call, supt. Fax 630-8513
www.estacada.k12.or.us
Estacada HS 800/9-12
355 NE 6th Ave 97023 503-630-6871
Rick Slater, prin. Fax 630-8699
Estacada JHS 400/7-8
500 NE Main St 97023 503-630-6871
Kevin Olds, prin. Fax 630-8693

Eugene, Lane, Pop. 142,185
Bethel SD 52 5,900/K-12
4640 Barger Dr 97402 541-689-3280
Steve Hull, supt. Fax 689-0719
www.bethel.k12.or.us
Cascade MS 500/6-8
1525 Echo Hollow Rd 97402 541-689-0641
Glen Martz, prin. Fax 689-9622
Kalapuya HS 100/9-12
1200 N Terry St 97402 541-607-9853
Fred Crisman, prin. Fax 607-9857
Shasta MS 500/6-8
4656 Barger Dr 97402 541-688-9611
Bert Eliason, prin. Fax 689-9382
Willamette HS 1,500/9-12
1801 Echo Hollow Rd 97402 541-689-0731
Jim Jamieson, prin. Fax 689-7119

Crow-Applegate-Lorane SD 66 300/K-12
85955 Territorial Hwy 97402 541-935-2100
Eileen Palmer, supt. Fax 935-6107
www.cal.k12.or.us
Crow MSHS 100/7-12
25863 Crow Rd 97402 541-935-2227
Ron Osibov, prin. Fax 935-6829

Eugene SD 4J 18,800/K-12
200 N Monroe St 97402 541-687-3123
George Russell, supt. Fax 687-3691
www.4j.lane.edu
Churchill HS 1,400/9-12
1850 Bailey Hill Rd 97405 541-687-3421
Dennis Biggerstaff, prin. Fax 687-3682
Jefferson MS 400/6-8
1650 W 22nd Ave 97405 541-687-3221
Arbrella Luvert, prin. Fax 687-3675
Kelly MS 600/6-8
850 Howard Ave 97404 541-687-3224
Tim Rochholz, prin. Fax 687-3676
Kennedy MS 600/6-8
2200 Bailey Hill Rd 97405 541-687-3241
Laurie Henry, prin. Fax 687-3677
Madison MS 500/6-8
875 Wilkes Dr 97404 541-687-3278
Nancy Pollard, prin. Fax 687-3678
Monroe MS 600/6-8
2800 Bailey Ln 97401 541-687-3254
Rick Gaultney, prin. Fax 687-3679
North Eugene HS 1,200/9-12
200 Silver Ln 97404 541-687-3261
Peter Tromba, prin. Fax 687-3683
Roosevelt MS 700/6-8
680 E 24th Ave 97405 541-687-3227
Morley Hegstrom, prin. Fax 687-3680
Sheldon HS 1,600/9-12
2455 Willakenzie Rd 97401 541-687-3381
Bob Bolden, prin. Fax 687-3684
South Eugene HS 1,700/9-12
400 E 19th Ave 97401 541-687-3201
Randy Bernstein, prin. Fax 687-3685
Spencer Butte MS 400/6-8
500 E 43rd Ave 97405 541-687-3237
Cydney Vandercar, prin. Fax 687-3681
Young MS 600/6-8
2555 Gilham Rd 97408 541-687-3234
Sara Cramer, prin. Fax 687-3674

Eugene Bible College Post-Sec.
2155 Bailey Hill Rd 97405 541-485-1780
Gutenberg College Post-Sec.
1883 University St 97403 541-683-5141
Lane Community College Post-Sec.
4000 E 30th Ave 97405 541-747-4501
Lifegate Christian S 100/K-12
1052 Fairfield Ave 97402 541-689-5847
Tom Gregersen, admin. Fax 689-6028
Marist HS 500/9-12
1900 Kingsley Rd 97401 541-686-2234
Perry Martin, prin. Fax 485-3959
Northwest Christian College Post-Sec.
828 E 11th Ave 97401 541-343-1641
Oak Hill S 100/K-12
86397 Eastway Dr 97405 541-744-0954
Elliott Grey, hdmstr. Fax 741-6968
University of Oregon Post-Sec.
1217 University Of Oregon 97403 541-346-1000
Wellsprings Friends S 100/9-12
3590 W 18th Ave 97402 541-686-1223
Dennis Hoerner, hdmstr. Fax 687-1493

Fairview, Multnomah, Pop. 8,749
Reynolds SD 7 10,100/K-12
1204 NE 201st Ave 97024 503-661-7200
Terry Kneisler, supt. Fax 667-6932
www.reynolds.k12.or.us
Reynolds MS 1,000/6-8
1200 NE 201st Ave 97024 503-665-8166
Yuki Monteith, prin. Fax 667-6751
Other Schools – See Portland, Troutdale

Falls City, Polk, Pop. 995
Falls City SD 57 200/K-12
111 N Main St 97344 503-787-3521
Peter Tarzian, supt. Fax 787-1507
www.fallscity.k12.or.us
Falls City HS 100/9-12
111 N Main St 97344 503-787-3521
Peter Tarzian, prin. Fax 787-1507

Finn Rock, Lane
McKenzie SD 68 300/K-12
51187 Blue River Dr, Vida OR 97488 541-822-3338
Susan Taylor Greene, supt. Fax 822-8014
www.mckenzie.k12.or.us
McKenzie JSHS 200/6-12
51187 Blue River Dr, Vida OR 97488 541-822-3313
Jim Seversen, prin. Fax 822-8014

Florence, Lane, Pop. 7,583
Siuslaw SD 97J 1,600/K-12
2111 Oak St 97439 541-997-2651
Gerald Hamilton, supt. Fax 997-6748
www.siuslaw.k12.or.us
Siuslaw HS 600/9-12
2975 Oak St 97439 541-997-3448
Larry Martindale, prin. Fax 997-4160
Siuslaw MS 400/6-8
2525 Oak St 97439 541-997-8241
Nancy May, prin. Fax 997-4161

Forest Grove, Washington, Pop. 18,880
Forest Grove SD 15 — 5,700/K-12
1728 Main St 97116 — 503-357-6171
Jack Musser, supt. — Fax 359-2520
www.fgsd.k12.or.us
Armstrong MS — 900/7-8
1777 Mountain View Ln 97116 — 503-359-2465
Sherry Adams, prin. — Fax 359-2560
Forest Grove HS — 1,600/9-12
1401 Nichols Ln 97116 — 503-359-2432
John O'Neill, prin. — Fax 359-2521

Pacific University — Post-Sec.
2043 College Way 97116 — 800-635-0561

Fossil, Wheeler, Pop. 453
Fossil SD 21J — 100/K-12
PO Box 206 97830 — 541-763-4384
Mike Hughes, supt. — Fax 763-2099
Wheeler HS — 50/9-12
PO Box 266 97830 — 541-763-4146
Mike Hughes, prin. — Fax 763-4010

Gaston, Washington, Pop. 744
Gaston SD 511J — 500/K-12
PO Box 68 97119 — 503-985-0210
Terry Mahler, supt. — Fax 985-3366
www.gaston.k12.or.us
Gaston JSHS — 300/7-12
PO Box 68 97119 — 503-985-7516
Mike Durbin, prin. — Fax 985-3279

Gervais, Marion, Pop. 2,161
Gervais SD 1 — 1,100/K-12
PO Box 100 97026 — 503-792-3801
Larry Glaze, supt. — Fax 792-3809
www.gervais.k12.or.us
Gervais HS — 300/9-12
PO Box 195 97026 — 503-792-3656
Chuck Borberg, prin. — Fax 792-3770
Gervais MS — 400/5-8
PO Box 176 97026 — 503-792-3624
Ken Stott, prin. — Fax 792-3626

Gilchrist, Klamath
Klamath County SD
Supt. — See Klamath Falls
Gilchrist S — 300/K-12
PO Box 668 97737 — 541-433-2295
Christie Gestvang, prin. — Fax 433-2688

Gladstone, Clackamas, Pop. 11,978
Gladstone SD 115 — 2,200/K-12
17789 Webster Rd 97027 — 503-655-2777
Bob Stewart, supt. — Fax 655-5201
www.gladstone.k12.or.us
Gladstone HS — 800/9-12
18800 Portland Ave 97027 — 503-655-2544
Stu Evans, prin. — Fax 655-0320
Kraxberger MS — 700/5-8
17777 Webster Rd 97027 — 503-655-3636
Joni Cesario, prin. — Fax 650-2596

Grace Christian S — 300/PK-12
6460 Glen Echo Ave 97027 — 503-655-1702
Mardel Watterud, prin. — Fax 655-1702

Glendale, Douglas, Pop. 886
Glendale SD 77 — 500/K-12
PO Box E 97442 — 541-832-2133
Lloyd Hartley, supt. — Fax 832-3183
www.glendale.k12.or.us
Glendale JSHS — 200/7-12
PO Box E 97442 — 541-832-2171
Tom McCormick, prin. — Fax 832-2486

Glide, Douglas
Glide SD 12 — 800/PK-12
301 Glide Loop Dr 97443 — 541-496-3521
Don Schrader, supt. — Fax 496-4300
www.glide.k12.or.us
Glide HS — 300/9-12
18990 N Umpqua Hwy 97443 — 541-496-3554
Pam Maurice, prin. — Fax 496-4304
Glide MS — 100/7-8
301 Glide Loop Dr 97443 — 541-496-3516
Ira Weir, prin. — Fax 496-4302

Gold Beach, Curry, Pop. 1,911
Central Curry SD 1 — 1,000/K-12
29516 Ellensburg Ave 97444 — 541-247-2003
Tom Denning, supt. — Fax 247-9717
www.ccsd.k12.or.us
Gold Beach HS — 300/9-12
29516 Ellensburg Ave 97444 — 541-247-6647
Jennifer Dukek, prin. — Fax 247-4557

Gold Hill, Jackson, Pop. 1,072
Central Point SD 6
Supt. — See Central Point
Hanby MS — 300/6-8
806 6th Ave 97525 — 541-494-6800
Dennis Allen, prin. — Fax 855-1120

Grand Ronde, Polk
Willamina SD 30J
Supt. — See Willamina
Willamina MS at Grand Ronde — 300/6-8
PO Box 7 97347 — 503-879-5210
Kathy Long, prin. — Fax 879-5249

Grants Pass, Josephine, Pop. 25,700
Grants Pass SD 7 — 5,800/K-12
725 NE Dean Dr 97526 — 541-474-5700
Steve Iverson, supt. — Fax 474-5705
www.grantspass.k12.or.us
Grants Pass HS — 1,800/9-12
830 NE 9th St 97526 — 541-474-5710
Aaron Anderson, prin. — Fax 474-5717
North MS — 800/6-8
1725 NW Highland Ave 97526 — 541-474-5740
Dan Smith, prin. — Fax 474-5739

South MS — 700/6-8
350 W Harbeck Rd 97527 — 541-474-5750
Renee Cardiff, prin. — Fax 474-9742

Three Rivers County SD — 5,900/K-12
8550 New Hope Rd 97527 — 541-862-3111
Jerry C. Fritts, supt. — Fax 862-3119
www.threerivers.k12.or.us
Fleming MS — 500/6-8
6001 Monument Dr 97526 — 541-476-8284
John George, prin. — Fax 471-2458
Hidden Valley HS — 900/9-12
651 Murphy Creek Rd 97527 — 541-862-2124
Dennis Misner, prin. — Fax 862-2872
Lincoln Savage MS — 500/6-8
8551 New Hope Rd 97527 — 541-862-2171
Tom Wiik, prin. — Fax 862-2713
North Valley HS — 800/9-12
6741 Monument Dr 97526 — 541-479-3388
Linda Hugle, prin. — Fax 471-2462
Other Schools — See Cave Junction

Grants Pass SDA Junior Academy — 100/K-10
2250 NW Heidi Ln 97526 — 541-479-2293
Roger Knauff, prin. — Fax 479-8412
New Hope Christian S — 300/PK-12
5961 New Hope Rd 97527 — 541-476-4588
Terell Bowdoin, admin. — Fax 474-7626
Phagans' Grants Pass College of Beauty — Post-Sec.
304 NE Agness Ave Ste F 97526 — 541-479-6678
Rogue Community College — Post-Sec.
3345 Redwood Hwy 97527 — 541-956-7500

Gresham, Multnomah, Pop. 95,816
Centennial SD 28J
Supt. — See Portland
Centennial HS — 1,800/9-12
3505 SE 182nd Ave 97030 — 503-661-7612
Mark Baier, prin. — Fax 661-5296

Gresham-Barlow SD 10J — 11,700/K-12
1331 NW Eastman Pkwy 97030 — 503-618-2450
Ken Noah, supt. — Fax 661-1589
www.gresham.k12.or.us
Barlow HS — 1,800/9-12
5105 SE 302nd Ave 97080 — 503-674-5600
James Hiu, prin. — Fax 674-5645
Clear Creek MS — 700/6-8
219 NE 219th Ave 97030 — 503-492-6700
John Koch, prin. — Fax 492-6707
Gresham HS — 1,800/9-12
1200 N Main Ave 97030 — 503-674-5500
Carol Daiberl, prin. — Fax 674-5549
McCarty MS — 600/6-8
1400 SE 5th St 97080 — 503-665-0148
Tim Tutty, prin. — Fax 669-1892
Russell MS — 800/6-8
3625 SE Powell Valley Rd 97080 — 503-667-6900
Randy Bryant, prin. — Fax 492-6708
Springwater Trail HS — 100/9-12
1440 SE Fleming Ave 97080 — 503-667-4669
Larry Bentz, prin. — Fax 667-3697
West Orient MS — 400/6-8
29805 SE Orient Dr 97080 — 503-663-3323
Teresa Ketelson, prin. — Fax 663-2504
Other Schools — See Damascus

Mt. Hood Community College — Post-Sec.
26000 SE Stark St 97030 — 503-491-6422
Phonics Factory — 300/PK-10
PO Box 2128 97030 — 503-661-5632
Brian Mayer, admin. — Fax 907-5827

Halfway, Baker, Pop. 327
Pine Eagle SD 61 — 300/K-12
377 N Main St 97834 — 541-742-2811
Thomas Crane, supt. — Fax 742-2810
www.pineeagle.k12.or.us/
Pine Eagle HS — 100/9-12
400 Cornucopia Hwy 97834 — 541-742-2421
Thomas Crane, prin. — Fax 742-2422

Halsey, Linn, Pop. 728
Central Linn SD 552
Supt. — See Brownsville
Central Linn HS — 300/7-12
32433 Highway 228 97348 — 541-369-2811
Michael Bremont, prin. — Fax 369-3455

Harper, Malheur
Harper SD 66 — 100/K-12
PO Box 800 97906 — 541-358-2473
Dennis Savage, supt. — Fax 358-2488
Harper S — 100/K-12
PO Box 800 97906 — 541-358-2473
Dennis Savage, prin. — Fax 358-2488

Harrisburg, Linn, Pop. 2,908
Harrisburg SD 7J — 800/K-12
PO Box 208 97446 — 541-995-6626
Ron Worrell, supt. — Fax 995-3453
www.harrisburg.k12.or.us
Harrisburg HS — 200/9-12
PO Box 209 97446 — 541-995-6626
Larry Cote, prin. — Fax 995-6697
Harrisburg MS — 200/6-8
PO Box 317 97446 — 541-995-6551
Jon St. Germaine, prin. — Fax 995-5120

Helix, Umatilla, Pop. 184
Helix SD 1 — 200/K-12
PO Box 398 97835 — 541-457-2175
Barbara Ceniga, supt. — Fax 457-2481
www.helix.k12.or.us/
Helix S — 200/K-12
PO Box 398 97835 — 541-457-2175
Barbara Ceniga, prin. — Fax 457-2481

Heppner, Morrow, Pop. 1,435
Morrow SD 1
Supt. — See Lexington

Heppner JSHS — 200/7-12
PO Box 67 97836 — 541-676-9138
Daye Stone, prin. — Fax 676-5836

Hermiston, Umatilla, Pop. 14,086
Hermiston SD 8 — 4,400/K-12
341 NE 3rd St 97838 — 541-667-6000
Darce Driskel, supt. — Fax 667-6050
www.hermiston.k12.or.us
Hermiston HS — 1,300/9-12
600 S 1st St 97838 — 541-667-6100
Sean Gallagher, prin. — Fax 667-6150
Larive MS — 400/6-8
199 E Ridgeway Ave 97838 — 541-667-6200
Phil Starkey, prin. — Fax 667-6250
Sandstone MS — 600/6-8
400 NE 10th St 97838 — 541-667-6300
Pat Consoliver, prin. — Fax 667-6350

Hillsboro, Washington, Pop. 77,709
Hillsboro SD 1J — 19,300/K-12
3083 NE 49th Pl 97124 — 503-844-1500
Jeremy Lyon, supt. — Fax 844-1540
www.hsd.k12.or.us
Brown MS — 900/7-8
1505 SW Cornelius Pass Rd 97123 — 503-844-1070
Lu Fontaine Biado, prin. — Fax 693-1171
Century HS — 1,600/9-12
2000 SE Century Blvd 97123 — 503-848-6500
Ted Zehr, prin. — Fax 848-1825
Evergreen MS — 800/7-8
29850 NW Evergreen Rd 97124 — 503-844-1400
Dave Parker, prin. — Fax 693-1706
Glencoe HS — 1,500/9-12
2700 NW Glencoe Rd 97124 — 503-844-1900
Carol Loughner, prin. — Fax 640-5604
Hillsboro HS — 1,400/9-12
3285 SE Rood Bridge Rd 97123 — 503-844-1980
Dottie Bertelli, prin. — Fax 693-0645
Liberty HS — 1,200/9-12
21945 NW Wagon Way 97124 — 503-844-1250
Gregg O'Mara, prin. — Fax 844-5851
Poynter MS — 800/7-8
1535 NE Grant St 97124 — 503-844-1580
Greg Timmons, prin. — Fax 640-8965
Thomas MS — 500/7-8
645 NE Lincoln St 97124 — 503-844-1050
Mario Alba, prin. — Fax 640-6347

Airman Proficiency Center — Post-Sec.
3565 NE Cornell Rd 97124 — 503-648-2831
Faith Bible Christian HS — 100/9-12
4435 SE Tualatin Valley Hwy 97123 — 503-681-8254
Jim Cochran, prin. — Fax 681-9274
Heritage Christian S — 100/6-12
1679 SE Enterprise Cir 97123 — 503-640-1027
Linda Sloane, hdmstr. — Fax 846-0609
Northwest College of Hair Design — Post-Sec.
210 SE 4th Ave 97123 — 503-844-7320
Tualatin Valley Junior Academy — 300/K-10
21975 SW Baseline Rd 97123 — 503-649-5518
Jesse Cone, prin. — Fax 642-7654

Hines, Harney, Pop. 1,560
Harney County SD 3
Supt. — See Burns
Hines MS — 300/6-8
PO Box 38 97738 — 541-573-6436
Katie Baltzor, prin. — Fax 573-7255

Hood River, Hood River, Pop. 6,139
Hood River County SD — 3,900/K-12
PO Box 920 97031 — 541-386-2511
Dr. Pat Evenson-Brady, supt. — Fax 387-5007
www.hoodriver.k12.or.us/
Hood River MS — 400/6-8
1602 May St 97031 — 541-386-2114
Robert Dias, prin. — Fax 386-5070
Hood River Valley HS — 1,200/9-12
1220 Indian Creek Rd 97031 — 541-386-4500
Martha Capovilla, prin. — Fax 386-2400
Wy'East MS — 500/6-8
3000 Wyeast Rd 97031 — 541-354-1548
Ed Drew, prin. — Fax 354-5120
Other Schools — See Cascade Locks

Horizon Christian S — 200/K-12
1889 Belmont Dr 97031 — 541-387-3200
Christopher Herring, admin. — Fax 386-3651
Mid-Columbia Adventist Academy — 50/6-12
1100 22nd St 97031 — 541-386-3187
Peter Hardy, prin. — Fax 386-5702

Huntington, Baker, Pop. 494
Huntington SD 16J — 100/K-12
520 3rd St E 97907 — 541-869-2204
Gerald Hopkins, supt. — Fax 869-2444
Huntington S — 100/K-12
520 3rd St E 97907 — 541-869-2204
Gerald Hopkins, prin. — Fax 869-2444

Imbler, Union, Pop. 282
Imbler SD 11 — 300/K-12
PO Box 164 97841 — 541-534-5331
Doug Hislop, supt. — Fax 534-9560
www.imbler.k12.or.us
Imbler JSHS — 100/7-12
PO Box 164 97841 — 541-534-5331
Mike Mills, prin. — Fax 534-9560

Independence, Polk, Pop. 6,974
Central SD 13J — 2,600/K-12
1610 Monmouth St 97351 — 503-838-0030
Joseph Hunter, supt. — Fax 838-0033
www.central.k12.or.us
Central HS, 1530 Monmouth St 97351 — 800/9-12
Sylvia Warren, prin. — 503-838-0480
Talmadge MS — 400/7-8
510 S 16th St 97351 — 503-838-1424
Beau Horn, prin. — Fax 606-2436

Ione, Morrow, Pop. 332
Ione SD R2 200/K-12
PO Box 167 97843 541-422-7131
Bryn Browning, supt. Fax 422-7555
www.ione.k12.or.us
Ione S 200/K-12
PO Box 167 97843 541-422-7131
Bryn Browning, prin. Fax 422-7555

Irrigon, Morrow, Pop. 1,799
Morrow SD 1
Supt. — See Lexington
Irrigon JSHS 7-12
315 E Wyoming Ave 97844 541-922-5551
Tom Crane, prin. Fax 922-5558

Island City, Union, Pop. 917
Union/Baker ESD
Supt. — See La Grande
Union County Education Ctr Adult
10214 Wallowa Lake Hwy 97850 541-963-0920
Mary Apple, prin. Fax 963-2689

Jacksonville, Jackson, Pop. 2,238

Adventure Academy USA 50/9-12
9730 Highway 238 97530 206-427-0931
D.B. Palmer, dir.
Cascade Christian HS 300/9-12
525 E St 97530 541-899-2060
Melvin Ray Johnson, admin. Fax 899-2230

Jefferson, Marion, Pop. 2,594
Jefferson SD 14J 900/K-12
1328 N 2nd St 97352 541-327-3337
Bob Wadlow, supt. Fax 327-2960
www.jefferson.k12.or.us
Jefferson HS 300/9-12
336 Talbot Rd SE 97352 541-327-3337
Cathy Emmert, prin. Fax 327-1867
Jefferson MS 200/6-8
1334 N 2nd St 97352 541-327-3337
Monica Lawson, prin. Fax 327-2960

John Day, Grant, Pop. 1,657
Grant SD 3
Supt. — See Canyon City
Grant Union HS 300/9-12
911 S Canyon Blvd 97845 541-575-1799
Mark Witty, prin. Fax 575-2754

Jordan Valley, Malheur, Pop. 233
Jordan Valley SD 3 100/K-12
PO Box 99 97910 541-586-2213
Michael Sessions, supt. Fax 586-2568
Jordan Valley HS 100/7-12
PO Box 99 97910 541-586-2213
Michael Sessions, prin. Fax 586-2569

Joseph, Wallowa, Pop. 1,021
Joseph SD 6 400/K-12
PO Box W 97846 541-432-7311
Rhonda Shirley, supt. Fax 432-1100
Joseph HS 100/9-12
PO Box W 97846 541-432-7311
Sherri Kilgore, prin. Fax 432-1100
Joseph MS 100/5-8
PO Box W 97846 541-432-7311
Sherri Kilgore, prin. Fax 432-1100

Junction City, Lane, Pop. 5,237
Junction City SD 69 1,900/K-12
325 Maple St 97448 541-998-6311
Kathleen Rodden-Nord, supt. Fax 998-3926
www.junctioncity.k12.or.us
Junction City HS 600/9-12
1135 W 6th Ave 97448 541-998-2343
Kathryn Hedrick, prin. Fax 998-6303
Oaklea MS 600/5-8
1515 Rose St 97448 541-998-3381
Tom Endersby, prin. Fax 998-3383

Keizer, Marion, Pop. 34,154
Salem-Keizer SD 24J
Supt. — See Salem
Claggett Creek MS 1,000/6-8
1810 Alder Dr NE 97303 503-399-3701
Melissa Cole, prin. Fax 399-3708
McNary HS 1,900/9-12
595 Chemawa Rd N 97303 503-399-3233
Ken Parshall, prin. Fax 391-4025
Whiteaker MS 800/6-8
1605 Lockhaven Dr NE 97303 503-399-3224
Larry Goss, prin. Fax 375-7872

Klamath Falls, Klamath, Pop. 19,286
Klamath County SD 6,500/K-12
10501 Washburn Way 97603 541-883-5000
Greg Thede, supt. Fax 883-6677
www.kcsd.k12.or.us
Brixner JHS 500/7-8
4727 Homedale Rd 97603 541-883-5025
Larry Headden, prin. Fax 883-5019
Henley HS 700/9-12
8245 Highway 39 97603 541-883-5040
Mark Greif, prin. Fax 883-6663
Henley MS 400/7-8
7925 Highway 39 97603 541-883-5050
Polly Beam, prin. Fax 883-5012
Other Schools – See Bonanza, Chiloquin, Gilchrist, Merrill

Klamath Falls CSD 4,000/K-12
1336 Avalon St 97603 541-883-4700
Cecilia Amuchastegui, supt. Fax 850-2766
www.kfalls.k12.or.us
Klamath Union HS 1,000/9-12
1300 Monclaire St 97601 541-883-4710
Jeff Bullock, prin. Fax 885-4276
Mazama HS 900/9-12
3009 Summers Ln 97603 541-883-4730
Terry Bennett, prin. Fax 885-6760

Ponderosa JHS 500/7-8
2554 Main St 97601 541-883-4740
Bob Vian, prin. Fax 885-4286
Klamath Adult Learning Ctr. Adult
2856 Eberlein Ave 97603 541-883-4719
Fax 885-4281

College of Cosmetology Post-Sec.
357 E Main St 97601 541-882-6644
Hosanna Christian S 300/PK-12
5000 Hosanna Way 97603 541-882-7732
Dan Dickey, admin. Fax 882-6940
Klamath Community College Post-Sec.
7390 S 6th St 97603 541-882-3521
Oregon Institute of Technology Post-Sec.
3201 Campus Dr 97601 541-885-1000
Triad S 200/PK-12
4849 S 6th St 97603 541-885-7940
David Wehr, prin. Fax 884-8725

La Grande, Union, Pop. 12,282
La Grande SD 1 2,300/K-12
708 K Ave Ste 100 97850 541-663-3202
Jay Rowell, supt. Fax 663-3211
www.lagrande.k12.or.us
La Grande HS 800/9-12
708 K Ave 97850 541-663-3301
Doug Potter, prin. Fax 663-3313
La Grande MS 400/7-8
1108 4th St 97850 541-663-3421
Jim Boen, prin. Fax 663-3422

Union/Baker ESD
10100 N McAlister Rd 97850 541-963-4106
Jack Adams, supt. Fax 963-7256
www.ubesd.k12.or.us
Other Schools – See Island City

Eastern Oregon University Post-Sec.
1 University Blvd 97850 541-962-3393

Lake Oswego, Clackamas, Pop. 36,085
Lake Oswego SD 7J 6,900/K-12
PO Box 70 97034 503-534-2000
William Korach, supt. Fax 534-2030
www.loswego.k12.or.us
Lake Oswego HS 1,200/9-12
PO Box 310 97034 503-534-2313
Bruce Plato, prin. Fax 534-2327
Lake Oswego JHS 600/7-8
2500 Country Club Rd 97034 503-534-2335
Ann Gerson, prin. Fax 534-2341
Lakeridge HS 1,100/9-12
PO Box 739 97034 503-534-2319
Mike Lehman, prin. Fax 534-2392
Waluga JHS 600/7-8
4700 Jean Rd 97035 503-534-2343
Steve Sherrell, prin. Fax 534-2276

Westside Christian HS 300/9-12
4565 Carman Dr 97035 503-697-4711
Andy Sears, prin. Fax 697-4605

Lakeview, Lake, Pop. 2,446
Adel SD 21 50/4-8
357 N L St 97630 541-947-5418
Fax 947-3373
Other Schools – See Adel

Lakeview SD 7 900/K-12
1341 S 1st St 97630 541-947-3347
Judy Graham, supt. Fax 947-3386
Daly MS 100/7-8
220 S H St 97630 541-947-2257
Lane Stratton, prin. Fax 947-3506
Lakeview HS 300/9-12
906 S 3rd St 97630 541-947-2287
Robert Nash, prin. Fax 947-3601

La Pine, Deschutes
Bend-LaPine Administrative SD 1
Supt. — See Bend
La Pine HS 500/9-12
PO Box 306 97739 541-322-5360
Charles Beck, prin. Fax 322-5352
La Pine MS 500/5-8
PO Box 305 97739 541-536-5967
Patricia Yaeger, prin. Fax 536-5787

Lebanon, Linn, Pop. 13,271
Lebanon Community SD 9 4,400/K-12
485 S 5th St 97355 541-451-8511
James Robinson, supt. Fax 451-8519
www.lebanon.k12.or.us
Lebanon HS 1,300/9-12
1700 S 5th St 97355 541-451-8555
Ken Ray, prin. Fax 451-8550
Seven Oak MS 600/6-8
550 Cascade Dr 97355 541-451-8416
Ed Sansom, prin. Fax 451-8431

East Linn Christian Academy 100/7-12
31498 SW 5th St 97355 541-259-2324
Jim Hill, prin. Fax 451-3800

Lexington, Morrow, Pop. 273
Morrow SD 1 2,000/K-12
PO Box 368 97839 541-989-8202
Mark Burrows, supt. Fax 989-8470
www.morrow.k12.or.us
Other Schools – See Boardman, Heppner, Irrigon

Lincoln City, Lincoln, Pop. 7,399
Lincoln County SD
Supt. — See Newport
Taft HS 700/7-12
3780 SE Spy Glass Ridge Dr 97367 541-996-2115
Steve Kilduff, prin. Fax 996-4335

Lincoln City SDA Junior Academy 100/1-12
2126 NE Surf Ave 97367 541-994-5181
Fax 994-9034

Logsden, Lincoln

Logsden Christian S 50/K-12
6631 Logsden Rd 97357 541-444-2820
Martha Eisele, prin. Fax 444-2820

Long Creek, Grant, Pop. 208
Long Creek SD 17 100/PK-12
PO Box 429 97856 541-421-3896
Tim Sprenger, supt. Fax 421-3012
Long Creek S 100/PK-12
PO Box 429 97856 541-421-3896
Tim Sprenger, prin. Fax 421-3012

Lowell, Lane, Pop. 905
Lowell SD 71 300/K-12
65 S Pioneer 97452 541-937-8405
Debbie Egan, supt. Fax 937-2112
www.lowell.k12.or.us
Lowell JSHS 100/8-12
65 S Pioneer 97452 541-937-2124
Karl Miller, prin. Fax 937-2112

Mc Minnville, Yamhill, Pop. 23,136
McMinnville SD 40 5,700/K-12
1500 NE Baker St, 503-565-4000
Maryalice Russell, supt. Fax 565-4030
www.msd.k12.or.us
Duniway MS 600/6-8
575 NW Michelbook Ln, 503-565-4400
Cathy Carnahan, prin. Fax 565-4414
McMinnville HS 1,700/9-12
615 NE 15th St, 503-565-4200
Kris Olsen, prin. Fax 565-4244
Patton MS 700/6-8
1175 NE 19th St, 503-565-4500
Jim Torgerson, prin. Fax 565-4515

Linfield College Post-Sec.
900 SE Baker St, 503-434-2200

Madras, Jefferson, Pop. 5,128
Jefferson County SD 509J 3,100/K-12
445 SE Buff St 97741 541-475-6192
Keith Johnson, supt. Fax 475-6856
www.whitebuffalos.net/
Jefferson County MS 800/6-8
1180 SE City View St 97741 541-475-7253
Steve Johnson, prin. Fax 475-4825
Madras HS 900/9-12
390 SE 10th St 97741 541-475-7265
Gary Carlton, prin. Fax 475-7744

Mapleton, Lane
Mapleton SD 32 200/K-12
10868 E Mapleton Rd 97453 541-268-4312
Kyle Tucker, supt. Fax 268-4632
www.mapleton.k12.or.us
Mapleton MSHS 100/7-12
10868 E Mapleton Rd 97453 541-268-4322
Kyle Tucker, prin. Fax 268-4632

Marcola, Lane
Marcola SD 79J 300/K-12
38300 Wendling Rd 97454 541-933-2817
Rolla Weber, supt. Fax 933-2338
www.marcola.k12.or.us
Mohawk HS 100/9-12
38300 Wendling Rd 97454 541-933-2512
W. Rolla Weber, prin. Fax 933-2338

Marylhurst, Clackamas

Marylhurst University Post-Sec.
PO Box 261 97036 800-634-9982

Maupin, Wasco, Pop. 406
South Wasco County SD 1 300/K-12
PO Box 346 97037 541-395-2645
Dennis Hickey, supt. Fax 395-2679
www.swasco.net
South Wasco County HS 100/7-12
PO Box 347 97037 541-395-2225
Roger Richmond, prin. Fax 395-2223

Medford, Jackson, Pop. 66,638
Medford SD 549C 13,300/K-12
500 Monroe St 97501 541-842-3621
Dr. Philip Long, supt. Fax 842-1087
www.medford.k12.or.us
Hedrick MS 1,000/7-8
1501 E Jackson St 97504 541-842-3700
Paul Cataldo, prin. Fax 842-1548
McLoughlin MS 1,100/7-8
320 W 2nd St 97501 541-842-3720
Amy Tiger, prin. Fax 842-1652
North Medford HS 2,000/9-12
1900 N Keene Way Dr 97504 541-842-3670
Ron Williams, prin. Fax 842-5206
South Medford HS 1,800/9-12
815 S Oakdale Ave 97501 541-842-3680
Kevin Campbell, prin. Fax 842-1513

Abdill Career College Post-Sec.
843 E Main St Ste 203 97504 541-779-8384
Phagans' Medford Beauty School Post-Sec.
2320 Poplar Dr 97504 541-772-6155
Rogue Valley Adventist Academy 200/K-12
3675 S Stage Rd 97501 541-773-2988
Fax 779-7575
St. Mary's S 300/6-12
816 Black Oak Dr 97504 541-773-7877
Frank Phillips, prin. Fax 772-8973

Merrill, Klamath, Pop. 894
Klamath County SD
Supt. — See Klamath Falls
Lost River JSHS 300/7-12
23330 Highway 50 97633 541-798-5666
Dan Duncan, prin. Fax 798-5072

Mill City, Linn, Pop. 1,563
Santiam Canyon SD 129J — 700/K-12
PO Box 197 97360 — 503-897-2321
Brad Yates, supt. — Fax 897-4004
www.santiam.k12.or.us
Mill City MS — 200/5-8
PO Box 198 97360 — 503-897-2368
James Beck, prin. — Fax 897-4034
Santiam HS — 200/9-12
PO Box 199 97360 — 503-897-2311
David Plotts, prin. — Fax 897-3154

Milton Freewater, Umatilla, Pop. 5,886
Milton-Freewater USD 7 — 1,900/K-12
138 S Main St 97862 — 541-938-3551
Marilyn McBride, supt. — Fax 938-6704
www.miltfree.k12.or.us
Central MS — 400/6-8
306 SW 2nd Ave 97862 — 541-938-5504
Steve Carnes, prin. — Fax 938-6615
McLoughlin HS — 500/9-12
120 S Main St 97862 — 541-938-5591
Ralph Brown, prin. — Fax 938-5593

Milwaukie, Clackamas, Pop. 20,638
North Clackamas SD 12 — 15,500/K-12
4444 SE Lake Rd 97222 — 503-653-3600
Ron Naso, supt. — Fax 653-3625
www.nclack.k12.or.us
Alder Creek MS — 800/7-8
13801 SE Webster Rd 97267 — 503-353-5700
Charles Foote, prin. — Fax 353-5715
Milwaukie HS — 1,400/9-12
11300 SE 23rd Ave 97222 — 503-353-5830
Kelly Carlisle, prin. — Fax 353-5845
Putnam HS — 1,400/9-12
4950 SE Roethe Rd 97267 — 503-353-5860
Cindy Quintanilla, prin. — Fax 353-5875
Rowe HS — 700/7-8
3606 SE Lake Rd 97222 — 503-353-5725
Larry Becker, prin. — Fax 353-5740
Sabin Skills Center — Vo/Tech
14211 SE Johnson Rd 97267 — 503-653-3812
Ron Munkres, prin. — Fax 653-3718
Other Schools – See Clackamas

LaSalle HS — 600/9-12
11999 SE Fuller Rd 97222 — 503-659-4155
William George, prin. — Fax 659-2535
Northwest College of Hair Design — Post-Sec.
6128 SE King Rd 97222 — 503-659-2834
Phagans' School of Hair Design — Post-Sec.
16550 SE McLoughlin Blvd 97267 — 503-652-2668
Portland Waldorf S — 100/PK-12
2300 SE Harrison St 97222 — 503-654-2200
Fax 652-5162

Mitchell, Wheeler, Pop. 165
Mitchell SD 55 — 100/K-12
PO Box 247 97750 — 541-462-3311
Michael Carroll, supt. — Fax 462-3849
www.mitchell.k12.or.us
Mitchell S — 100/K-12
PO Box 247 97750 — 541-462-3311
Michael Carroll, prin. — Fax 462-3849

Molalla, Clackamas, Pop. 6,075
Molalla River SD 35 — 2,800/K-12
PO Box 188 97038 — 503-829-2359
Wayne Kostur, supt. — Fax 829-5540
www.molallariv.k12.or.us
Molalla HS — 800/9-12
PO Box 309 97038 — 503-829-2355
Kevin Ricker, prin. — Fax 829-6382
Molalla River MS — 700/6-8
PO Box 225 97038 — 503-829-6133
Robert Espenel, prin. — Fax 829-5680

Monmouth, Polk, Pop. 8,109

Mid Valley Christian Academy — 100/PK-12
1483 N 16th St 97361 — 503-838-2818
Candice Thomas, admin.
Western Oregon University — Post-Sec.
345 Monmouth Ave N 97361 — 877-877-1593

Monroe, Benton, Pop. 594
Monroe SD 1J — 400/K-12
365 N 5th St 97456 — 541-847-6292
Randall Crowson, supt. — Fax 847-6290
www.monroe.k12.or.us/sd1j.htm
Monroe HS — 100/9-12
365 N 5th St 97456 — 541-847-5161
Bill Crowson, prin. — Fax 847-6161

Bellfountain Cornerstone Christian S — 50/PK-12
25398 Dawson Rd 97456 — 541-424-2161
Gregory McGowan, prin. — Fax 424-2162

Monument, Grant, Pop. 137
Monument SD 8 — 100/K-12
PO Box 127 97864 — 541-934-2646
Scott Langkamp, supt. — Fax 934-2005
Monument S — 100/K-12
PO Box 127 97864 — 541-934-2646
Scott Langkamp, prin. — Fax 934-2005

Moro, Wasco, Pop. 304
Sherman County SD
Supt. — See Wasco
Sherman JSHS — 200/7-12
65912 High School Loop 97039 — 541-565-3500
Bob Vian, prin. — Fax 565-3319

Mount Angel, Marion, Pop. 3,319
Mt. Angel SD 91 — 800/K-12
PO Box 458 97362 — 503-845-2345
Robert Young, supt. — Fax 845-2789
www.masd.mtangel.k12.or.us
Kennedy HS — 200/9-12
890 E Marquam St 97362 — 503-845-6128
Bryan Starr, prin. — Fax 845-2789

Mount Angel MS — 200/6-8
460 E Marquam St 97362 — 503-845-6137
Dave Carlson, prin. — Fax 845-2856

Mount Vernon, Grant, Pop. 550
Grant SD 3
Supt. — See Canyon City
Mount Vernon MS — 200/6-8
PO Box 648 97865 — 541-932-4733
Monty Nash, prin. — Fax 932-4980

Myrtle Creek, Douglas, Pop. 3,479
South Umpqua SD 19 — 1,900/K-12
558 Chadwick Ln 97457 — 541-863-3115
Bill Burnett, supt. — Fax 863-5212
www.susd.k12.or.us
Coffenberry MS — 400/6-8
591 Rice St 97457 — 541-863-3104
Doug Park, prin. — Fax 863-5187
South Umpqua HS — 600/9-12
501 Chadwick Ln 97457 — 541-863-3118
Brody Guthrie, prin. — Fax 863-5486

Myrtle Point, Coos, Pop. 2,453
Myrtle Point SD 41 — 800/K-12
212 Spruce St 97458 — 541-572-2811
Robert Smith, supt. — Fax 572-5401
www.mpsd.k12.or.us/
Myrtle Point JSHS — 400/7-12
717 4th St 97458 — 541-572-2811
Greg Tippett, prin. — Fax 572-5221

Newberg, Yamhill, Pop. 19,732
Newberg SD 29J — 5,000/K-12
714 E 6th St 97132 — 503-554-5000
Dr. Paula Radich, supt. — Fax 537-9474
www.newberg.k12.or.us
Chehalem Valley MS — 700/6-8
403 W Foothills Dr 97132 — 503-554-4600
Kevin Engelen, prin. — Fax 537-3239
Mountain View MS — 600/6-8
2015 N Emery Dr 97132 — 503-554-4500
Wayne Strong, prin. — Fax 537-3337
Newberg HS — 1,600/9-12
2400 Douglas Ave 97132 — 503-554-4400
Bill Smethurst, prin. — Fax 538-6560

George Fox University — Post-Sec.
414 N Meridian St 97132 — 503-538-8383
Lewis Academy — 200/PK-12
PO Box 938 97132 — 503-538-0114
Wade Witherspoon, admin. — Fax 538-4113
Open Bible Christian S — 200/K-12
1605 N College St 97132 — 503-538-9833
Frank Canepa, prin. — Fax 538-4649

Newport, Lincoln, Pop. 9,548
Lincoln County SD — 5,200/K-12
PO Box 1110 97365 — 541-265-9211
Tom Rinearson, supt. — Fax 265-3231
www.lincoln.k12.or.us
Newport HS — 700/9-12
322 NE Eads St 97365 — 541-265-9281
Suzanne Dalton, prin. — Fax 574-2228
Newport MS — 400/6-8
825 NE 7th St 97365 — 541-265-6601
Marsha Eckelman, prin. — Fax 265-6493
Newton Magnet S — 100/6-8
825 NE 7th St 97365 — 541-574-2238
Marsha Eckelman, prin.
Other Schools – See Lincoln City, Toledo, Waldport

Phagans' Newport Academy of Cosmetology — Post-Sec.
333 SW 7th St 97365 — 541-265-3083

North Bend, Coos, Pop. 9,565
North Bend SD 13 — 2,300/K-12
1913 Meade St 97459 — 541-756-2521
Charles Bugge, supt. — Fax 756-1313
www.nbend.k12.or.us
North Bend HS — 700/9-12
2323 Pacific St 97459 — 541-756-8328
Bill Lucero, prin. — Fax 756-6945
North Bend MS — 600/5-8
1500 16th St 97459 — 541-756-8341
Scott Edmondson, prin. — Fax 756-6460
Oregon Coast Technology S — Vo/Tech
1913 Meade St 97459 — 541-756-8307
James Moyer, dir. — Fax 756-1313

Kingsview Christian S — 200/PK-12
1850 Clark St 97459 — 541-756-1411
Rick Wetherell, admin. — Fax 756-0105

North Powder, Union, Pop. 488
North Powder SD 8J — 200/K-12
PO Box 10 97867 — 541-898-2244
Lance Dixon, supt. — Fax 898-2046
www.npowder.k12.or.us
Powder Valley S — 200/K-12
PO Box 10 97867 — 541-898-2244
Lance Dixon, prin. — Fax 898-2046

Nyssa, Malheur, Pop. 3,080
Nyssa SD 26 — 1,100/K-12
804 Adrian Blvd 97913 — 541-372-2275
Donald Grotting, supt. — Fax 372-2204
www.nyssa.k12.or.us
Nyssa HS — 300/9-12
824 Adrian Blvd 97913 — 541-372-2287
Ken Ball, prin. — Fax 372-5634
Nyssa MS — 300/6-8
101 S 11th St 97913 — 541-372-3891
Jana Iverson, prin. — Fax 372-3260

Oakland, Douglas, Pop. 960
Oakland SD 1 — 600/K-12
PO Box 390 97462 — 541-459-4341
Dan Forbess, supt. — Fax 459-4120
www.oakland.k12.or.us
Lincoln MS — 200/5-8
PO Box 420 97462 — 541-459-3407
Rod Kalmbach, prin. — Fax 459-9167

Oakland HS — 200/9-12
PO Box 479 97462 — 541-459-2597
Greg Knee, prin. — Fax 459-4765

Oakridge, Lane, Pop. 3,167
Oakridge SD 76 — 700/K-12
76499 Rose St 97463 — 541-782-2813
John Lehmann, supt. — Fax 782-2982
www.oakridge.k12.or.us/
Oakridge HS — 200/9-12
47997 W 1st St 97463 — 541-782-2231
Donald Kordosky, prin. — Fax 782-4692
Other Schools – See Westfir

Ontario, Malheur, Pop. 10,964
Ontario SD 8C — 2,800/K-12
195 SW 3rd Ave 97914 — 541-889-5374
Dr. Dennis Carter, supt. — Fax 889-8553
www.ontario.k12.or.us
Ontario HS — 700/9-12
1115 W Idaho Ave 97914 — 541-889-5309
Bret Uptmor, prin. — Fax 889-8117
Ontario MS — 700/6-8
573 SW 2nd Ave 97914 — 541-889-5377
LaVelle Cornwell, prin. — Fax 881-0060

Treasure Valley Community College — Post-Sec.
650 College Blvd 97914 — 541-881-8822

Oregon City, Clackamas, Pop. 28,407
Oregon City SD 62 — 8,100/K-12
PO Box 2110 97045 — 503-785-8000
Roger Rada, supt. — Fax 657-2492
www.orecity.k12.or.us
Gardiner MS — 600/7-8
180 Ethel St 97045 — 503-785-8200
Chris Mills, prin. — Fax 650-5482
Ogden MS — 700/7-8
14133 Donovan Rd 97045 — 503-785-8300
John Olson, prin. — Fax 657-2508
Oregon City HS — 2,200/9-12
19761 Beavercreek Rd 97045 — 503-785-8900
Nancy Bush-Lange, prin. — Fax 785-8578

Clackamas Community College — Post-Sec.
19600 Molalla Ave 97045 — 503-657-6958
North Clackamas Christian S — 300/PK-12
19575 Sebastian Way 97045 — 503-655-5961
Joseph Morgan, admin. — Fax 655-4875

Paisley, Lake, Pop. 247
Paisley SD 11 — 100/K-12
PO Box 97 97636 — 541-943-3111
Mark Jeffrey, supt. — Fax 943-3129
Paisley S — 100/K-12
PO Box 97 97636 — 541-943-3111
Mark Jeffery, prin. — Fax 943-3129

Pendleton, Umatilla, Pop. 16,458
Pendleton SD 16 — 3,400/K-12
1207 SW Frazer Ave 97801 — 541-276-6711
Jim Keene, supt. — Fax 278-3208
www.pendleton.k12.or.us
Pendleton HS — 1,000/9-12
1800 NW Carden Ave 97801 — 541-276-3621
Tom Lovell, prin. — Fax 966-9268
Sunridge MS — 800/6-8
700 SW Runnion Ave 97801 — 541-276-4560
Susan DeMarsh, prin. — Fax 276-4724

Blue Mountain Community College — Post-Sec.
PO Box 100 97801 — 541-276-1260
Harris Junior Academy — 50/K-10
3121 SW Hailey Ave 97801 — 541-276-0615
Fax 276-3465

Philomath, Benton, Pop. 4,198
Philomath SD 17J — 1,800/K-12
1620 Applegate St 97370 — 541-929-3169
Pete Tuana, supt. — Fax 929-3991
www.philomath.k12.or.us
Philomath HS — 600/9-12
2054 Applegate St 97370 — 541-929-3211
Kent Sherwood, prin. — Fax 929-3244
Philomath MS — 500/6-8
2021 Chapel Dr 97370 — 541-929-3167
Larry Sleeman, prin. — Fax 929-3180

Phoenix, Jackson, Pop. 4,385
Phoenix-Talent SD 4 — 2,700/K-12
PO Box 698 97535 — 541-535-1517
Ben Bergreen, supt. — Fax 535-3928
www.phoenix.k12.or.us
Phoenix HS — 800/9-12
PO Box 697 97535 — 541-535-1526
Jani Hale, prin. — Fax 535-7511
Other Schools – See Talent

Pilot Rock, Umatilla, Pop. 1,530
Pilot Rock SD 2 — 400/K-12
PO Box BB 97868 — 541-443-8291
Gordon Munck, supt. — Fax 443-8000
www.pilotrock.k12.or.us
Pilot Rock JSHS — 200/7-12
PO Box BB 97868 — 541-443-2671
Ed Sherman, prin. — Fax 443-2120

Pleasant Hill, Lane
Pleasant Hill SD 1 — 1,100/K-12
36386 Highway 58 97455 — 541-746-9646
Steve Waddell, supt. — Fax 746-2537
www.pleasanthill.k12.or.us/
Pleasant Hill HS — 400/9-12
36386 Highway 58 97455 — 541-747-4541
Tony Scurto, prin. — Fax 744-3351
Pleasant Hill MS — 400/5-8
36386 Highway 58 97455 — 541-746-8311
Mary Ritter, prin. — Fax 744-3352

Emerald Christian Academy — 100/K-10
35582 Zephyr Way 97455 — 541-746-1708
Fax 746-8353

Portland, Multnomah, Pop. 538,544

Beaverton SD 48J
Supt. — See Beaverton

Cedar Park MS — 1,000/6-8
11100 SW Park Way 97225 — 503-672-3620
Linda Hall, prin. — Fax 672-3626

Stoller MS — 1,100/6-8
14141 NW Laidlaw Rd 97229 — 503-533-1910
Florence Richey, prin. — Fax 533-1914

Sunset HS — 1,900/9-12
13840 NW Cornell Rd 97229 — 503-259-5050
Carl Mead, prin. — Fax 259-5066

Westview HS — 2,300/9-12
4200 NW 185th Ave 97229 — 503-259-5218
Matt Coleman, prin. — Fax 259-5230

Centennial SD 28J — 6,300/K-12
18135 SE Brooklyn St 97236 — 503-760-7990
Robert McKean, supt. — Fax 762-3689
www.centennial.k12.or.us

Centennial HS — 1,000/7-8
17650 SE Brooklyn St 97236 — 503-762-3206
Doug Cook, prin. — Fax 762-3236

Other Schools – See Gresham

David Douglas SD 40 — 8,400/K-12
1500 SE 130th Ave 97233 — 503-252-2900
Barbara Rommel, supt. — Fax 261-8208
www.ddouglas.k12.or.us

Douglas HS — 2,600/9-12
1001 SE 135th Ave 97233 — 503-261-8300
Randy Hutchinson, prin. — Fax 261-8399

Light MS — 900/6-8
10800 SE Washington St 97216 — 503-256-6511
Mark Gaulke, prin. — Fax 261-8423

Ott MS — 700/6-8
12500 SE Ramona St 97236 — 503-256-6510
Natalie Osburn, prin. — Fax 261-8403

Russell MS — 6-8
3955 SE 112th Ave 97266 — 503-256-6519
Charlene Bassine, prin. — Fax 761-7246

Parkrose SD 3 — 3,700/K-12
10636 NE Prescott St 97220 — 503-408-2100
Michael Taylor, supt. — Fax 408-2140
www.parkrose.k12.or.us

Parkrose HS — 1,200/9-12
12003 NE Shaver St 97220 — 503-408-2600
Roy Reynolds, prin. — Fax 408-2739

Parkrose MS — 900/6-8
11800 NE Shaver St 97220 — 503-408-2700
Penny Alby, prin. — Fax 408-2998

Portland SD 1J — 38,900/PK-12
PO Box 3107 97208 — 503-916-3200
Vicki Phillips, supt. — Fax 916-3110
www.pps.k12.or.us/

Beaumont MS — 500/6-8
4043 NE Fremont St 97212 — 503-916-5610
Sherie Knutsen, prin. — Fax 916-2609

Benson Polytechnic HS — Vo/Tech
546 NE 12th Ave 97232 — 503-916-5100
Christie Plinski, prin. — Fax 916-2690

Binnsmead MS — 700/6-8
2225 SE 87th Ave 97216 — 503-916-5700
John Hinds, prin. — Fax 916-2610

Cleveland HS — 1,400/9-12
3400 SE 26th Ave 97202 — 503-916-5120
Paul Cook, prin. — Fax 916-2692

Fernwood MS — 600/6-8
1915 NE 33rd Ave 97212 — 503-916-6480
Linda Kapranos, prin. — Fax 916-2626

Franklin HS — 1,400/9-12
5405 SE Woodward St 97206 — 503-916-5140
Opal Chancler-Moore, prin. — Fax 916-2694

George MS — 400/6-8
10000 N Burr Ave 97203 — 503-916-6262
Beth Madison, prin. — Fax 916-2627

Grant HS — 1,800/9-12
2245 NE 36th Ave 97212 — 503-916-5160
Toni Hunter, prin. — Fax 916-2695

Gray MS — 500/6-8
5505 SW 23rd Ave, — 503-916-5676
Willie Poinsette, prin. — Fax 916-2629

Gregory Heights MS — 700/6-8
7334 NE Siskiyou St 97213 — 503-916-5600
Bonnie Hobson, prin. — Fax 916-2599

Hosford International MS — 400/6-8
2303 SE 28th Pl 97214 — 503-916-5640
Melissa Sandven, prin. — Fax 916-2637

Jackson MS — 700/6-8
10625 SW 35th Ave 97219 — 503-916-5680
John Danielson, prin. — Fax 916-2640

Jefferson HS — 9-12
5210 N Kerby Ave 97217 — 503-916-5180
Larry Dashiell, prin. — Fax 916-2698

Kellogg MS — 600/6-8
3330 SE 69th Ave 97206 — 503-916-5707
Margaret Lewis, prin. — Fax 916-2643

Lane MS — 600/6-8
7200 SE 60th Ave 97206 — 503-916-6355
Karl Logan, prin. — Fax 916-2648

Lincoln HS — 1,500/9-12
1600 SW Salmon St 97205 — 503-916-5200
Peter Hamilton, prin. — Fax 916-2700

Madison HS — 1,100/9-12
2735 NE 82nd Ave 97220 — 503-916-5220
Patricia Thompson, prin. — Fax 916-2702

Marshall HS — 9-12
3905 SE 91st Ave 97266 — 503-916-5240
John Wilhelmi, prin. — Fax 916-2703

Mt. Tabor MS — 700/6-8
5800 SE Ash St 97215 — 503-916-5646
Cynthia Gilliam, prin. — Fax 916-2659

Ockley Green MS — 400/6-8
6031 N Montana Ave 97217 — 503-916-5660
Joseph Malone, prin. — Fax 916-2661

Portsmouth MS — 400/6-8
5103 N Willis Blvd 97203 — 503-916-5666
Paul Steger, prin. — Fax 916-2663

Roosevelt HS — 9-12
6941 N Central St 97203 — 503-916-5260
Andrew Kelly, prin. — Fax 916-2704

Sellwood MS — 600/6-8
8300 SE 15th Ave 97202 — 503-916-5656
Frank Scotto, prin. — Fax 916-2672

Tubman MS — 300/7-8
2231 N Flint Ave 97227 — 503-916-5630
Marcia Johnson, prin. — Fax 916-2677

Vocational Village HS — Vo/Tech
4039 NE Alberta Ct 97211 — 503-916-5747
A.J. Morrison, admin. — Fax 916-2680

West Sylvan MS — 600/7-8
8111 SW West Slope Dr 97225 — 503-916-5690
Allison Couch, prin. — Fax 916-2681

Wilson HS — 1,500/9-12
1151 SW Vermont St 97219 — 503-916-5280
Carla Randall, prin. — Fax 916-2705

Portland Evening HS — Adult
546 NE 12th Ave 97232 — 503-916-5720
Macaree Traynham, admin. — Fax 916-2691

Portland Night S — Adult
2245 NE 36th Ave 97212 — 503-916-6486
Charlene Turenne, prin. — Fax 916-2696

Reynolds SD 7
Supt. — See Fairview

Lee MS — 800/6-8
1121 NE 172nd Ave 97230 — 503-255-5686
Carla Sosanya, prin. — Fax 252-0522

Riverdale SD 51J — 600/K-12
11733 SW Breyman Ave 97219 — 503-636-8611
Dr. Thomas Hagerman, supt. — Fax 635-6342
www.riverdale.k12.or.us

Riverdale HS — 200/9-12
9727 SW Terwilliger Blvd 97219 — 503-892-0722
Anne Cass, prin. — Fax 892-0723

Apollo College — Post-Sec.
2004 Lloyd Ctr Fl 3 97232 — 503-761-6100

Art Institute of Portland — Post-Sec.
1122 NW Davis St 97209 — 503-228-6528

Australasian College of Health Sciences — Post-Sec.
5940 SW Hood Ave, — 503-244-0726

Beau Monde College Acad of Cosmetology — Post-Sec.
11131 NE Halsey St 97220 — 503-252-7444

Beau Monde College of Hair Design — Post-Sec.
1221 SW 12th Ave 97205 — 503-226-7355

Birthingway College of Midwifery — Post-Sec.
12113 SE Foster Rd 97266 — 503-760-3131

Cascade College — Post-Sec.
9101 E Burnside St 97216 — 800-550-7678

Catlin Gabel S — 700/PK-12
8825 SW Barnes Rd 97225 — 503-297-1894
Dr. Lark Palma, prin. — Fax 297-0139

Central Catholic HS — 800/9-12
2401 SE Stark St 97214 — 503-235-3138
Ronald Edwards, prin. — Fax 233-0073

City Christian S — 300/PK-12
9200 NE Fremont St 97220 — 503-252-5207
Ed Mason, prin. — Fax 257-2221

College of Legal Arts — Post-Sec.
8909 SW Barbur Blvd 97219 — 503-223-5100

Columbia Christian S — 300/PK-12
413 NE 91st Ave 97220 — 503-252-8577
Morgan Outlaw, prin. — Fax 252-2108

Concorde Career Institute — Post-Sec.
1827 NE 44th Ave 97213 — 503-281-4181

Concordia University — Post-Sec.
2811 NE Holman St 97211 — 503-288-9371

De La Salle North HS — 200/9-12
7654 N Delaware Ave 97217 — 503-285-9385
John Huelskamp, prin. — Fax 285-9546

DeVry University — Post-Sec.
9755 SW Barnes Rd Ste 150 97225 — 503-296-7468

Edison HS — 100/9-12
9020 SW Bvrtn Hillsdale Hwy 97225 — 503-297-2336

George Fox University — Post-Sec.
12753 SW 68th Ave 97223 — 503-639-0559

Heald College - Portland — Post-Sec.
625 SW Broadway Ste 400 97205 — 503-229-0492

ITT Technical Institute — Post-Sec.
6035 NE 78th Ct 97218 — 503-255-6500

Jesuit HS — 1,000/9-12
9000 SW Beaverton Hillsdale 97225 — 503-292-2663
Sandy Satterberg, prin. — Fax 291-5464

Lewis & Clark College — Post-Sec.
0615 SW Palatine Hill Rd 97219 — 503-768-7000

Linfield College — Post-Sec.
2215 NW Northrup St 97210 — 503-229-7161

Multnomah Bible Coll. & Biblical Sem. — Post-Sec.
8435 NE Glisan St 97220 — 503-255-0332

National Coll. of Naturopathic Medicine — Post-Sec.
049 SW Porter St 97201 — 503-499-4343

Open Meadow Alternative S — 100/9-12
7654 N Crawford St 97203 — 503-285-0508
Rosemary Donnelly, prin. — Fax 285-0798

Oregon College of Art & Craft — Post-Sec.
8245 SW Barnes Rd 97225 — 503-297-5544

Oregon College of Oriental Medicine — Post-Sec.
10525 SE Cherry Blossom Dr 97216 — 503-253-3443

Oregon Episcopal S — 800/PK-12
6300 SW Nicol Rd 97223 — 503-246-7771
Dulaney Bennett, hdmstr. — Fax 293-1105

Oregon Health & Science University — Post-Sec.
3181 SW Sam Jackson Park Rd, — 503-494-7800

Pacific Northwest College of Art — Post-Sec.
1241 NW Johnson St 97209 — 503-821-8972

Phagans' School of Hair Design — Post-Sec.
1542 NE Weidler St 97232 — 503-239-0838

Portland Adventist Academy — 300/9-12
1500 SE 96th Ave 97216 — 503-255-8372
— Fax 255-5132

Portland Christian JSHS — 400/7-12
12425 NE San Rafael St 97230 — 503-256-3960
Kevin Barrows, prin. — Fax 256-2773

Portland Community College — Post-Sec.
PO Box 19000 97280 — 503-244-6111

Portland Lutheran S — 300/PK-12
740 SE 182nd Ave 97233 — 503-667-3199
Donn Maier, prin. — Fax 667-4520

Portland State University — Post-Sec.
PO Box 751 97207 — 503-725-3000

Reed College — Post-Sec.
3202 SE Woodstock Blvd 97202 — 503-771-1112

St. Andrew Nativity S — 50/6-8
806 NE Alberta St 97211 — 503-335-9600
Fr. Jeff McDougall, prin. — Fax 335-9494

St. Mary Academy — 600/9-12
1615 SW 5th Ave 97201 — 503-228-8306
Pat Barr, prin. — Fax 223-0995

St. Vincent Hospital & Medical Center — Post-Sec.
9205 SW Barnes Rd 97225 — 503-216-3031

Serendipity Center — 100/K-12
PO Box 33350 97292 — 503-761-7139
Patrick Sliger, prin. — Fax 761-7917

University of Portland — Post-Sec.
5000 N Willamette Blvd 97203 — 503-943-7911

Veterans Administration Medical Center — Post-Sec.
PO Box 1034 97207 — 503-220-8262

Walla Walla College School of Nursing — Post-Sec.
10345 SE Market St 97216 — 503-251-6115

Warner Pacific College — Post-Sec.
2219 SE 68th Ave 97215 — 503-517-1000

Western Business College — Post-Sec.
425 SW Washington St 97204 — 503-222-3225

Western Culinary Institute — Post-Sec.
921 SW Morrison St Ste 400 97205 — 503-223-2245

Western Seminary — Post-Sec.
5511 SE Hawthorne Blvd 97215 — 503-517-1800

Western States Chiropractic College — Post-Sec.
2900 NE 132nd Ave 97230 — 503-256-3180

Port Orford, Curry, Pop. 1,153

Port Orford-Langlois SD 2J — 400/K-12
PO Box 8 97465 — 541-348-2337
Daniel Morin, supt. — Fax 348-2228
www.2cj.com

Pacific HS — 100/9-12
PO Box 8 97465 — 541-348-2293
Daniel Morin, prin. — Fax 348-2389

Powers, Coos, Pop. 736

Powers SD 31 — 100/K-12
PO Box 479 97466 — 541-439-2291
Matt Shorb, supt. — Fax 439-2875
www.powers.k12.or.us

Powers HS — 100/7-12
PO Box 479 97466 — 541-439-3093
Jody Cyr, prin. — Fax 439-2875

Prairie City, Grant, Pop. 990

Prairie City SD 4 — 200/K-12
PO Box 345 97869 — 541-820-3314
Kevin Purnell, supt. — Fax 820-4352
www.grantesd.k12.or.us

Prairie City S — 200/K-12
PO Box 345 97869 — 541-820-3314
Kevin Purnell, prin. — Fax 820-4352

Prineville, Crook, Pop. 8,115

Crook County Unit SD — 3,200/K-12
471 NE Ochoco Plaza Dr 97754 — 541-447-5664
Steve Swisher, supt. — Fax 447-3645
www.crookcounty.k12.or.us

Crook County HS — 1,000/9-12
1100 SE Lynn Blvd 97754 — 541-416-6900
Rick Knode, prin. — Fax 416-6907

Crook County MS — 700/6-8
100 NE Knowledge St 97754 — 541-447-6283
Rocky Miner, prin. — Fax 447-3293

Crook County Christian S — 200/PK-12
839 S Main St 97754 — 541-416-0114
Sue Uptain, prin. — Fax 447-2873

Prospect, Jackson

Prospect SD 59 — 200/K-12
PO Box 40 97536 — 541-560-3653
Don Alexander, supt. — Fax 560-3644

Prospect S — 200/K-12
PO Box 40 97536 — 541-560-3653
Diane McMahan, prin. — Fax 560-3644

Rainier, Columbia, Pop. 1,787

Rainier SD 13 — 1,300/K-12
PO Box 160 97048 — 503-556-3777
R. Michael Carter, supt. — Fax 556-3778
www.rainier.k12.or.us

Rainier JSHS — 600/7-12
PO Box 280 97048 — 503-556-4215
Jeff Gilbert, prin. — Fax 556-1120

Redmond, Deschutes, Pop. 16,822

Redmond SD 2J — 5,700/K-12
145 SE Salmon Ave 97756 — 541-923-5437
Vickie Fleming, supt. — Fax 923-5142
www.redmond.k12.or.us

Gregory MS — 6-8
1220 NW Upas Ave 97756 — 541-526-6440
Mike McIntosh, prin. — Fax 526-6441

Obsidian MS — 800/6-8
1335 SW Obsidian Ave 97756 — 541-923-4900
Joe Beck, prin. — Fax 923-6509

Redmond HS — 1,700/9-12
675 SW Rimrock Way 97756 — 541-923-4800
Jon Bullock, prin. — Fax 548-0809

Central Christian S — 200/PK-12
PO Box 639 97756 — 541-548-7803
Bill Mahnke, prin. — Fax 548-2801

Reedsport, Douglas, Pop. 4,348

Reedsport SD 105 — 900/K-12
100 Ranch Rd 97467 — 541-271-3656
Forrest Bell, supt. — Fax 271-3658

Reedsport JSHS — 400/7-12
2260 Longwood Dr 97467 — 541-271-2141
Patrick Gross, prin. — Fax 271-2143

Riddle, Douglas, Pop. 1,011
Riddle SD 70 500/K-12
PO Box 45 97469 541-874-3131
Dave Gianotti, supt. Fax 874-2345
Riddle JSHS, PO Box 45 97469 200/7-12
Terry Prestianni, prin. 541-874-2251

Rockaway, Tillamook, Pop. 1,074
Neah-Kah-Nie SD 56 800/K-12
PO Box 28 97136 503-355-2222
Jay Kosik, supt. Fax 355-3434
www.neahkahnie.k12.or.us
Neah-Kah-Nie JSHS 400/7-12
24705 Highway 101 N 97136 503-355-2272
Kristi Woika, prin. Fax 355-8200

Rogue River, Jackson, Pop. 1,890
Rogue River SD 35 1,200/K-12
PO Box 1045 97537 541-582-3235
Charles Hellman, supt. Fax 582-1600
www.rogueriver.k12.or.us
Rogue River HS 400/9-12
PO Box 1045 97537 541-582-3297
Dave Orr, prin. Fax 582-6005
Rogue River MS 300/6-8
PO Box 1045 97537 541-582-3233
Kathi Sue Summers, prin. Fax 582-6004

Roseburg, Douglas, Pop. 20,162
Douglas County SD 4 6,300/K-12
1419 NW Valley View Dr 97470 541-440-4015
Lee Paterson, supt. Fax 440-4003
www.roseburg.k12.or.us
Fremont MS 600/6-8
850 W Keady Ct 97470 541-440-4055
Tim Wilson, prin. Fax 440-4060
Lane MS 600/6-8
2153 NE Vine St 97470 541-440-4104
Doug Freeman, prin. Fax 440-4100
Roseburg HS 1,800/9-12
400 W Harvard Ave 97470 541-440-4142
Karen Goirigolzarri, prin. Fax 440-8296

Phoenix S of Roseburg 100/7-12
3131 NE Diamond Lake Blvd 97470 541-673-3036
Ron Breyne, prin. Fax 957-5906
Roseburg Beauty College Post-Sec.
700 SE Stephens St 97470 541-673-5533
Roseburg Junior Academy 100/K-10
1653 NW Troost St 97470 541-673-5278
Fax 672-9785
Umpqua Community College Post-Sec.
PO Box 967 97470 541-440-4600
Umpqua Valley Christian S 200/K-12
359 Roberts Creek Rd 97470 541-679-4964
David York, prin. Fax 679-1881

Saint Benedict, Marion, Pop. 55

Mt. Angel Seminary Post-Sec.
1 Abbey Dr 97373 503-845-3951

Saint Helens, Columbia, Pop. 11,209
Saint Helens SD 502 3,500/K-12
474 N 16th St 97051 503-366-7240
Patricia Adams, supt. Fax 397-1907
www.sthelens.k12.or.us
Saint Helens HS 1,000/9-12
2375 Gable Rd 97051 503-397-1900
Brian Heinze, prin. Fax 397-1828
Saint Helens MS 600/7-8
354 N 15th St 97051 503-366-7300
Paul Berg, prin. Fax 366-7306

Saint Paul, Marion, Pop. 395
St. Paul SD 45 200/PK-12
20449 Main St NE 97137 503-633-2541
Bruce Shull, supt. Fax 633-2540
www.stpaul.k12.or.us
Saint Paul HS 100/7-12
20449 Main St NE 97137 503-633-2541
Debbie Eder, prin. Fax 633-2540

Salem, Marion, Pop. 142,914
Salem-Keizer SD 24J 37,700/K-12
PO Box 12024 97309 503-399-3000
Dr. Kay Baker, supt. Fax 399-5579
www.salkeiz.k12.or.us
Crossler MS 700/6-8
1155 Davis Rd S 97306 503-399-3444
Jim Adams, prin. Fax 391-4005
Houck MS 1,100/6-8
1155 Connecticut Ave SE, 503-399-3446
Elizabeth Ryan, prin. Fax 391-4167
Judson MS 900/6-8
4512 Jones Rd SE 97302 503-399-3201
Debra Faber, prin. Fax 391-4041
Leslie MS 900/6-8
3850 Pringle Rd SE 97302 503-399-3206
Steve Nelson, prin. Fax 399-3479
McKay HS 1,900/9-12
2440 Lancaster Dr NE 97305 503-399-3080
Cynthia Richardson, prin. Fax 375-7807
North Salem HS 1,800/9-12
765 14th St NE 97301 503-399-3241
John Honey, prin. Fax 375-7808
Parrish MS 700/6-8
802 Capitol St NE 97301 503-399-3210
Harold Kaiser, prin. Fax 391-4004
South Salem HS 1,800/9-12
1910 Church St SE 97302 503-399-3252
Willese Everson, prin. Fax 375-7805
Sprague HS 1,800/9-12
2373 Kuebler Rd S 97302 503-399-3261
Cheryl Bower, prin. Fax 391-4046
Stephens MS 1,000/6-8
4962 Hayesville Dr NE 97305 503-399-3442
Neil Anderson, prin. Fax 391-4079
Waldo MS 800/6-8
2805 Lansing Ave NE 97301 503-399-3215
Joe LaFountaine, prin. Fax 391-4070
Walker MS 900/6-8
1075 8th St NW 97304 503-399-3220
Tricia Nelson, prin. Fax 399-5540
West Salem HS 1,400/9-12
1776 Titan Dr NW 97304 503-399-5533
Ed John, prin. Fax 584-5004
Other Schools – See Keizer

Academy of Hair Design Post-Sec.
305 Court St NE 97301 503-585-8122
Blanchet S 300/7-12
4373 Market St NE 97301 503-391-2639
Robert Weber, prin. Fax 399-1259
Chemeketa Community College Post-Sec.
PO Box 14007 97309 503-399-5000
College of Hair Design Careers Post-Sec.
1684 Clay St NE 97301 503-588-5888
Corban College Post-Sec.
5000 Deer Park Dr SE, 97317 503-581-8600
Livingstone Adventist Academy 300/K-12
5771 Fruitland Rd NE, 503-363-9408
Barbara Livesay, prin. Fax 363-5721
Oregon State School for the Blind Post-Sec.
700 Church St SE 97301
Oregon State School for the Deaf Post-Sec.
999 Locust St NE 97301
Phagans' School of Beauty Post-Sec.
622 Lancaster Dr NE 97301 503-363-6800
Salem Academy 600/PK-12
942 Lancaster Dr NE 97301 503-378-1219
Dr. Benjamin Potloff, supt. Fax 375-3522
Western Mennonite S 200/6-12
9045 Wallace Rd NW 97304 503-363-2000
Darrel Camp, prin. Fax 370-9455
Willamette University Post-Sec.
900 State St 97301 503-370-6300

Sandy, Clackamas, Pop. 7,186
Oregon Trail SD 46 4,300/K-12
PO Box 547 97055 503-668-5541
Clementina Salinas, supt. Fax 668-7906
www.ortrail.k12.or.us
Cedar Ridge MS 400/6-8
17225 Smith Ave 97055 503-668-8067
Molly Knudsen, prin. Fax 668-3977
Sandy HS 1,400/9-12
17100 SE Bluff Rd 97055 503-668-8011
Jim Saxton, prin. Fax 668-7646
Other Schools – See Boring, Welches

Scappoose, Columbia, Pop. 5,506
Scappoose SD 1J 2,200/K-12
33589 High School Way 97056 503-543-6374
Paul Peterson, supt. Fax 543-7011
www.scappoose.k12.or.us
Scappoose HS 700/9-12
33700 High School Way 97056 503-543-6376
Sue Hays, prin. Fax 543-3796
Scappoose MS 400/7-8
52265 Columbia River Hwy 97056 503-543-7163
Neal Lordos, prin. Fax 543-7917

Scio, Linn, Pop. 698
Scio SD 95 600/K-12
38875 NW 1st Ave 97374 503-394-3261
Gary Tempel, supt. Fax 394-3920
www.scio.k12.or.us/
Scio HS 300/9-12
38875 NW 1st Ave 97374 503-394-3276
Scott Linenberger, prin. Fax 394-3236
Scio MS 100/6-8
38875 NW 1st Ave 97374 503-394-3271
Kerry Lau, prin. Fax 394-4042

Seaside, Clatsop, Pop. 5,916
Jewell SD 8 200/K-12
83874 Highway 103 97138 503-755-2451
John Seeley, supt. Fax 755-0616
www.jewell.k12.or.us/
Jewell S 200/K-12
83874 Highway 103 97138 503-755-2451
John Seeley, prin. Fax 755-0616

Seaside SD 10 1,700/K-12
1801 S Franklin St 97138 503-738-5591
Doug Dougherty, supt. Fax 738-3471
www.seaside.k12.or.us/
Broadway MS 400/6-8
1120 Broadway St 97138 503-738-6892
Sheila Roley, prin. Fax 738-3900
Seaside HS 600/9-12
1901 N Holladay Dr 97138 503-738-5586
Don Wickersham, prin. Fax 738-5589

Shady Cove, Jackson, Pop. 2,336
Jackson County SD 9
Supt. — See Eagle Point
Shady Cove S 300/3-8
PO Box 138 97539 541-878-1400
Dan Johnson, prin. Fax 830-6226

Sheridan, Yamhill, Pop. 5,515
Sheridan SD 48J 900/K-12
435 S Bridge St 97378 503-843-2433
Roy Williams, supt. Fax 843-3505
www.sheridan.k12.or.us
Sheridan HS 300/9-12
433 S Bridge St 97378 503-843-2162
A.J. Grauer, prin. Fax 843-3466

Delphian S 200/PK-12
20950 SW Rock Creek Rd 97378 800-626-6610
West Valley Academy 50/K-12
PO Box 127 97378 503-843-4123

Sherwood, Washington, Pop. 13,901
Sherwood SD 88J 3,400/K-12
23295 SW Main St 97140 503-625-8100
Dan Jamison, supt. Fax 625-8101
www.sherwood.k12.or.us
Sherwood HS 800/9-12
16956 SW Meinecke Rd 97140 503-625-8200
Michelle DeBoard, prin. Fax 625-8201
Sherwood MS 800/6-8
21970 SW Sherwood Blvd 97140 503-925-2600
Anna Pittioni, prin. Fax 925-2601

Silver Lake, Lake
North Lake SD 14 200/K-12
56566 Fort Rock Rd 97638 541-576-2121
Ryan Mattingly, supt. Fax 576-2705
North Lake S 200/K-12
56566 Fort Rock Rd 97638 541-576-2121
Ryan Mattingly, prin. Fax 576-2705

Silverton, Marion, Pop. 7,781
Silver Falls SD 4J 3,200/K-12
1456 Pine St 97381 503-873-5303
Craig Roessler, supt. Fax 873-2936
ww3.silverfalls.k12.or.us/
Silverton HS Pine Street Campus 9-9
1456 Pine St 97381 503-873-1970
Jodi Drescher, prin. Fax 873-1441
Silverton HS Schlador Street Campus 800/10-12
802 Schlador St 97381 503-873-6331
Jodi Drescher, prin. Fax 873-8606
Twain MS 300/7-8
425 N Church St 97381 503-873-5317
Andy Bellando, prin. Fax 873-7108

Sisters, Deschutes, Pop. 1,156
Sisters SD 6 1,200/K-12
PO Box 5099 97759 541-549-8521
Ted Thonstad, supt. Fax 549-8951
www.outlawnet.com/outlaw/ssd
Sisters HS 500/9-12
1700 W McKinney Butte Rd 97759 541-549-4045
Bob Macauley, prin. Fax 549-4051
Sisters MS 300/6-8
15200 McKenzie Rd 97759 541-549-2099
Lora Nordquist, prin. Fax 549-2098

Spray, Wheeler, Pop. 136
Spray SD 1 100/K-12
PO Box 230 97874 541-468-2226
Paul Young, supt. Fax 468-2630
www.spray.k12.or.us
Spray S 100/K-12
PO Box 230 97874 541-468-2226
Paul Young, prin. Fax 468-2630

Springfield, Lane, Pop. 54,773
Springfield SD 19 10,900/K-12
525 Mill St 97477 541-747-3331
Nancy Golden, supt. Fax 726-3312
www.sps.lane.edu
Briggs MS 500/6-8
2355 Yolanda Ave 97477 541-744-6350
Mike Riplinger, prin. Fax 744-6354
Hamlin MS 500/6-8
326 Centennial Blvd 97477 541-744-6356
Mindy Stinson, prin. Fax 744-6360
Springfield HS 1,500/9-12
875 7th St 97477 541-744-4700
Chris Reiersgaard, prin. Fax 744-4144
Springfield MS 300/6-8
1084 G St 97477 541-744-6362
Jeff Mather, prin. Fax 744-6366
Stewart MS 700/6-8
900 S 32nd St 97478 541-988-2520
Dawn Strong, prin. Fax 988-2530
Thurston HS 1,500/9-12
333 58th St 97478 541-744-5000
Ed Mendelssohn, prin. Fax 744-5029
Thurston MS 600/6-8
6300 Thurston Rd 97478 541-744-6368
Carl Swan, prin. Fax 744-6372

Pioneer Pacific College Post-Sec.
3800 Sports Way 97477 541-684-4644
Springfield College of Beauty Post-Sec.
307 Q St 97477 541-746-4473

Stanfield, Umatilla, Pop. 1,980
Stanfield SD 61 600/K-12
1120 N Main St 97875 541-449-8766
Dale Nees, supt. Fax 449-8768
www.stanfield.k12.or.us
Stanfield Secondary S 200/7-12
1120 N Main St 97875 541-449-3851
Steve Staniak, prin. Fax 449-8751

Stayton, Marion, Pop. 7,060
North Santiam SD 29J 2,500/K-12
1155 N 3rd Ave 97383 503-769-6924
B.J. Hollensteiner, supt. Fax 769-3578
www.northsantiamsd.com
Stayton HS 800/9-12
757 W Locust St 97383 503-769-2171
Charlotte Klampe, prin. Fax 769-6050
Stayton MS 500/5-8
1021 Shaff Rd 97383 503-769-2198
Randy LaFollett, prin. Fax 769-9524

Regis HS 200/9-12
550 W Regis St 97383 503-769-2159
Tony Guevara, prin. Fax 769-1706

Sutherlin, Douglas, Pop. 7,178
Sutherlin SD 130 1,600/K-12
531 E Central Ave 97479 541-459-2228
John Lahley, supt. Fax 459-2484
www.sutherlin.k12.or.us
Sutherlin HS 500/9-12
500 E Fourth Ave 97479 541-459-9551
Marty Gary, prin. Fax 459-4887
Sutherlin MS 300/7-8
649 E Fourth Ave 97479 541-459-2668
Steve Perkins, prin. Fax 459-2047

Sweet Home, Linn, Pop. 8,238
Sweet Home SD 55 2,400/K-12
1920 Long St 97386 541-367-7126
Larry Horton, supt. Fax 367-7105
www.sweethome.k12.or.us

Sweet Home HS 800/9-12
1641 Long St 97386 541-367-7145
Patricia Stineff, prin. Fax 367-7196
Sweet Home JHS 400/7-8
880 22nd Ave 97386 541-367-7187
Hal Huschka, prin. Fax 367-7107

Talent, Jackson, Pop. 5,623
Phoenix-Talent SD 4
Supt. — See Phoenix
Talent MS 700/6-8
PO Box 359 97540 541-535-1552
Patti Kinney, prin. Fax 535-7532

Tangent, Linn, Pop. 954

Central Valley Junior Academy 50/1-10
31630 Highway 34 97389 541-928-7820
Fax 967-4410

The Dalles, Wasco, Pop. 11,317
North Wasco County SD 21 2,300/K-12
3632 W 10th St 97058 541-296-6149
Candy Armstrong, supt. Fax 298-6018
www.nwasco.k12.or.us
The Dalles MS 500/6-8
1100 E 12th St 97058 541-296-4616
Jan Anderson, prin. Fax 298-6196
The Dalles - Wahtonka HS 500/10-12
220 E 10th St 97058 541-296-4601
Stephen Jupe, prin. Fax 298-4964
Wahtonka 9th Grade S 100/9-9
3601 W 10th St 97058 541-296-4633
Tim McGlothlin, prin. Fax 296-2358

Tigard, Washington, Pop. 45,538
Tigard-Tualatin SD 23J 11,800/K-12
6960 SW Sandburg St 97223 503-431-4000
Rob Saxton, supt. Fax 431-4047
www.ttsd.k12.or.us
Fowler MS 900/6-8
10865 SW Walnut St 97223 503-431-5000
Ted Feller, prin. Fax 431-5010
Tigard HS 1,900/9-12
9000 SW Durham Rd 97224 503-431-5400
Pam Henslee, prin. Fax 431-5410
Twality MS 1,100/6-8
14650 SW 97th Ave 97224 503-431-5200
Pat Sharp, prin. Fax 431-5210
Other Schools – See Tualatin

Phagans' Tigard Beauty School Post-Sec.
8820 SW Center St 97223 503-639-6107

Tillamook, Tillamook, Pop. 4,487
Tillamook SD 9 2,100/K-12
6825 Officer Row 97141 503-842-4414
Randy Schild, supt. Fax 842-6854
www.tillamook.k12.or.us
Tillamook HS 700/9-12
2605 12th St 97141 503-842-2566
Bruce Rhodes, prin. Fax 842-1340
Tillamook JHS 300/7-8
3906 Alder Ln 97141 503-842-7531
Elroy Thompson, prin. Fax 842-1349

Tillamook Adventist S 100/K-12
4300 12th St 97141 503-842-6533
Steven McKeone, prin. Fax 842-6236

Toledo, Lincoln, Pop. 3,409
Lincoln County SD
Supt. — See Newport
Toledo HS 600/7-12
1800 NE Sturdevant Rd 97391 541-336-5104
Paula Priest, prin. Fax 336-2970

Troutdale, Multnomah, Pop. 14,851
Reynolds SD 7
Supt. — See Fairview
Morey MS 700/6-8
2801 SW Lucas Ave 97060 503-491-1935
Tony Mann, prin. Fax 491-0245
Reynolds HS 2,500/9-12
1698 SW Cherry Park Rd 97060 503-667-3186
Kevin Kannier, prin. Fax 669-0776

Tualatin, Washington, Pop. 24,790
Tigard-Tualatin SD 23J
Supt. — See Tigard
Hazelbrook MS 900/6-8
11300 SW Hazelbrook Rd 97062 503-431-5100
Ernie Brown, prin. Fax 431-5110
Tualatin HS 1,800/9-12
22300 SW Boones Ferry Rd 97062 503-431-5600
Jeff Smith, prin. Fax 431-5610

West Linn-Wilsonville SD 3J 7,900/K-12
22210 SW Stafford Rd 97062 503-673-7000
Roger Woehl, supt. Fax 673-7001
www.wlwv.k12.or.us
Other Schools – See West Linn, Wilsonville

Turner, Marion, Pop. 1,508
Cascade SD 5 2,300/K-12
10226 Marion Rd SE 97392 503-749-8488
F. James McBride, supt. Fax 749-8321
www.cascade.k12.or.us
Cascade HS 700/9-12
10226 Marion Rd SE 97392 503-749-8490
Darin Drill, prin. Fax 749-8324

Cascade JHS 500/6-8
10226 Marion Rd SE 97392 503-749-8489
Leanne Deffenbaugh, prin. Fax 749-8323

Ukiah, Umatilla, Pop. 255
Ukiah SD 80 100/K-12
PO Box 218 97880 541-427-3731
Dan Korber, supt. Fax 427-3730
www.ukiah.k12.or.us
Ukiah S 100/K-12
PO Box 218 97880 541-427-3731
Dan Korber, prin. Fax 427-3730

Umatilla, Umatilla, Pop. 5,154
Umatilla SD 6R 1,300/K-12
1001 6th St 97882 541-922-6500
Brian Say, supt. Fax 922-6507
www.umatilla.k12.or.us/
Brownell MS 300/6-8
1460 7th St 97882 541-922-6625
Bill Varady, prin. Fax 922-6507
Umatilla HS 300/9-12
1460 7th St 97882 541-922-6525
John Thomas, prin. Fax 922-6599

Union, Union, Pop. 1,949
Union SD 5 500/K-12
PO Box K 97883 541-562-6115
Mike Wood, supt. Fax 562-8116
union.k12.or.us
Union JSHS 200/7-12
PO Box 908 97883 541-562-5166
James Taylor, prin. Fax 562-8116

Unity, Baker, Pop. 128
Burnt River SD 30J 100/K-12
PO Box 8 97884 541-446-3466
Robert Otheim, supt. Fax 446-3581
Burnt River S 100/K-12
PO Box 8 97884 541-446-3336
Robert Otheim, prin. Fax 446-3581

Vale, Malheur, Pop. 1,940
Vale SD 84 900/K-12
403 E St W 97918 541-473-0201
Matthew Hawley, supt. Fax 473-3294
www.vale.k12.or.us
Vale HS 300/9-12
505 Viking Dr 97918 541-473-3181
Dave Enright, prin. Fax 473-2364
Vale MS 100/7-8
403 E St W 97918 541-473-0241
Mary Jo Sharp, prin. Fax 473-3293

Vernonia, Columbia, Pop. 2,244
Vernonia SD 47J 400/K-12
475 Bridge St 97064 503-429-5891
Michael Funderburg, supt. Fax 429-7742
www.vernonia.k12.or.us/
Vernonia HS 200/9-12
299 Bridge St 97064 503-429-3521
Curt Scholl, prin. Fax 429-7049
Vernonia MS 6-8
249 Bridge St 97064 503-429-0487
Nate Underwood, prin. Fax 429-4731

Vida, Lane

McKenzie River Christian S 100/K-12
PO Box I 97488 541-896-0554
Russ Conklin, prin. Fax 896-0554

Waldport, Lincoln, Pop. 2,043
Lincoln County SD
Supt. — See Newport
Waldport HS 300/9-12
PO Box 370 97394 541-563-3243
Von Taylor, prin. Fax 563-4145

Wallowa, Wallowa, Pop. 841
Wallowa SD 12 300/K-12
PO Box 425 97885 541-886-2061
John Nesemann, supt. Fax 886-7355
www.wallowa.k12.or.us/
Wallowa JSHS 100/7-12
PO Box 425 97885 541-886-2951
John Nesemann, prin. Fax 886-7355

Warrenton, Clatsop, Pop. 4,205
Warrenton-Hammond SD 30 900/K-12
820 SW Cedar Ave 97146 503-861-2281
Craig Brewington, supt. Fax 861-2911
www.whsd.k12.or.us/
Warrenton HS 300/9-12
1700 S Main Ave 97146 503-861-3317
Rod Heyen, prin. Fax 861-2997

Wasco, Sherman, Pop. 343
Sherman County SD 300/K-12
PO Box 66 97065 541-442-5777
Angela Thompson, supt. Fax 442-5778
www.sherman.k12.or.us/District/
Other Schools – See Moro

Welches, Clackamas
Oregon Trail SD 46
Supt. — See Sandy
Welches MS 200/6-8
24903 E Salmon River Rd 97067 503-622-3166
Mike Sutton, prin. Fax 622-3398

Westfir, Lane, Pop. 279
Oakridge SD 76
Supt. — See Oakridge
Westridge MS 300/5-8
46433 Westfir Rd 97492 541-782-2731
Bill Krei, prin. Fax 782-4647

West Linn, Clackamas, Pop. 24,696
West Linn-Wilsonville SD 3J
Supt. — See Tualatin
Athey Creek MS 600/6-8
2900 SW Borland Rd 97068 503-673-7400
Michael Shay, prin. Fax 638-8302
Rosemont Ridge MS 700/6-8
20001 S Salamo Rd 97068 503-673-7550
Debi Briggs Crispin, prin. Fax 657-8720
West Linn HS 1,600/9-12
5464 W A St 97068 503-673-7800
Kim Noah, prin. Fax 657-8710

Weston, Umatilla, Pop. 713
Athena-Weston SD 29RJ
Supt. — See Athena
Athena-Weston MS 200/6-8
PO Box 158 97886 541-566-3548
Mary Pilgreen, prin. Fax 566-2326

White City, Jackson, Pop. 5,891
Jackson County SD 9
Supt. — See Eagle Point
White Mountain MS 400/6-8
550 Wilson Way 97503 541-830-6315
Lynn Eccleston, prin. Fax 830-6751

Willamina, Yamhill, Pop. 1,849
Willamina SD 30J 1,000/K-12
324 SE Adams St 97396 503-876-4525
Gus Forster, supt. Fax 876-3610
www.willamina.k12.or.us
Willamina HS 300/9-12
1100 NE Oaken Hills Dr 97396 503-876-2545
Tim France, prin. Fax 876-2511
Other Schools – See Grand Ronde

Wilsonville, Clackamas, Pop. 15,211
West Linn-Wilsonville SD 3J
Supt. — See Tualatin
Wilsonville HS 900/9-12
PO Box 3770 97070 503-673-7600
Andy Sommer, prin. Fax 682-0917
Wood MS 600/6-8
PO Box 705 97070 503-673-7500
Barbara Soisson, prin. Fax 682-9109

Pioneer Pacific College Post-Sec.
27501 SW Parkway Ave 97070 503-682-3903
Pioneer Pacific College Post-Sec.
27375 SW Parkway Ave 97070 503-682-1862

Winston, Douglas, Pop. 4,732
Winston-Dillard SD 116 1,600/K-12
620 Elwood St 97496 541-679-3000
Duane Yecha, supt. Fax 679-4819
www.wdsd.org
Douglas HS 500/9-12
1381 NW Douglas Blvd 97496 541-679-3001
Kevin McDaniel, prin. Fax 679-7284
Winston MS 300/7-8
330 Thompson Ave 97496 541-679-3002
Charan Cline, prin. Fax 679-3026

Woodburn, Marion, Pop. 21,747
Woodburn SD 103 3,400/K-12
965 N Boones Ferry Rd 97071 503-981-9555
Walt Blomberg, supt. Fax 981-8018
www.woodburn.k12.or.us
Academy of International Studies 9-12
1785 N Front St 97071 503-981-2600
Chuck Ransom, prin. Fax 981-2675
French Prairie MS 500/6-8
1025 N Boones Ferry Rd 97071 503-981-2650
Eric Swenson, prin. Fax 981-2724
Valor MS 500/6-8
450 Parr Rd 97071 503-981-2750
Bill Rhoades, prin. Fax 981-2790
Wellness Business and Sports S 9-12
1785 N Front St 97071 503-981-2600
Leo Colegio, prin. Fax 981-2675
Woodburn Academy of Art/Science & Tech 9-12
1785 N Front St 97071 503-981-2600
Geri Federico, prin. Fax 981-2675
Woodburn Arts and Communication Academy 9-12
1785 N Front St 97071 503-981-2600
Jennifer Dixon, prin. Fax 981-2675

Yamhill, Yamhill, Pop. 794
Yamhill-Carlton SD 1 1,200/K-12
PO Box 68 97148 503-662-4911
Steve Chiovaro, supt. Fax 662-4931
www.ycsd.k12.or.us
Yamhill-Carlton HS 500/9-12
275 N Maple St 97148 503-662-3228
James Orth, prin. Fax 662-3220

Yoncalla, Douglas, Pop. 1,048
Yoncalla SD 32 400/K-12
PO Box 568 97499 541-849-2782
Art Johns, supt. Fax 849-2190
www.yoncalla.k12.or.us
Yoncalla HS, PO Box 568 97499 100/9-12
Brian Berry, prin. 541-849-2175

PENNSYLVANIA

PENNSYLVANIA DEPARTMENT OF EDUCATION
333 Market St, Harrisburg 17101-2210
Telephone 717-783-6788
Fax 717-787-7222
Website http://www.pde.psu.edu
Secretary of Education   Gerald Zahorchak

PENNSYLVANIA BOARD OF EDUCATION
333 Market St, Harrisburg 17101-2210
Chairperson   Karl Girton

INTERMEDIATE UNITS (IU)

Allegheny IU 3
Dr. Donna Durno, dir. — 412-394-5700
475 Waterfront Dr E — Fax 394-5706
Homestead 15120
www.aiu3.net/

Appalachia IU 8
Dr. Michael Dillon, dir. — 814-940-0223
4500 6th Ave, Altoona 16602 — Fax 472-5033
www.iu08.org/

ARIN IU 28
Dr. Robert Coad, dir. — 724-463-5300
2895 W Pike Rd, Indiana 15701 — Fax 463-5315
www.arin.k12.pa.us

Beaver Valley IU 27
Thomas Zelesnik, dir. — 724-774-7800
225 Center Grange Rd — Fax 774-4751
Aliquippa 15001
www.bviu.org/bviu/site/default.asp

Berks County IU 14
Dr. Nancy G. Almon, dir. — 610-987-2248
PO Box 16050, Reading 19612 — Fax 987-8400
www.berksiu.org

Blast IU 17
Thomas Shivetts, dir. — 570-323-8561
PO Box 3609, Williamsport 17701
www.iu17.org

Bucks County IU 22
Richard Coe Ed.D., dir. — 215-348-2940
705 N Shady Retreat Rd — Fax 489-7874
Doylestown 18901
www.bciu.k12.pa.us

Capital Area IU 15
Dr. Glenn Zehner, dir. — 717-732-8400
PO Box 489, Summerdale 17093 — Fax 732-8421
www.caiu.k12.pa.us

Carbon-Lehigh IU 21
Dr. Frank Ferrari, dir. — 610-769-4111
4750 Orchard Rd — Fax 769-1290
Schnecksville 18078
www.cliu.org

Central IU 10
Dr. Nancy Robbins, dir. — 814-342-0884
345 Link Rd, West Decatur 16878 — Fax 342-5137
www.ciu10.com

Central Susquehanna IU 16
Dr. Robert Witten, dir. — 570-523-1155
PO Box 213, Lewisburg 17837 — Fax 524-7104
www.csiu.org/

Chester County IU 24
Dr. John Baillie, dir. — 484-237-5000
455 Boot Rd, Downingtown 19335 — Fax 237-5154
www.cciu.org/

IU 1
Dr. Lawrence J. O'Shea, dir. — 724-938-3241
1 Intermediate Unit Dr — Fax 938-8722
Coal Center 15423
www.iu1.k12.pa.us/

Colonial IU 20
Dr. Charlene Brennan, dir. — 610-252-5550
6 Danforth Rd, Easton 18045 — Fax 252-5740
www.ciu20.org

Delaware County IU 25
Harry Jamison Ph.D., dir. — 610-938-9000
200 Yale Ave, Morton 19070 — Fax 565-1315
www.dciu.org/

Lancaster-Lebanon IU 13
Dr. James Scott, dir. — 717-569-7331
1110 Enterprise Rd — Fax 560-6110
East Petersburg 17520
www.iu13.k12.pa.us

Lincoln IU 12
Dr. Michael Clemens, dir. — 717-624-4616
PO Box 70, New Oxford 17350 — Fax 624-6519
www.iu12.org

Luzerne IU 18
Michael Ostrowski, dir. — 570-287-9681
PO Box 1649, Kingston 18704 — Fax 287-5721
www.liu18.org/

Midwestern IU 4
Angelo Pezzuolo, dir. — 724-458-6700
453 Maple St, Grove City 16127 — Fax 458-5083
www.miu4.k12.pa.us/

Montgomery County IU 23
Dr. Jerry Shiveley, dir. — 610-539-8550
1605 W Main St, Norristown 19403 — Fax 539-5973
www.mciu.k12.pa.us

Northeastern Educational IU 19
Dr. Fred Rosetti, dir. — 570-876-9200
1200 Line St, Archbald 18403 — Fax 876-8660
www.neiu.org

Northwest Tri-County IU 5
David Minnis, dir. — 814-734-5610
252 Waterford St #5 — Fax 734-5806
Edinboro 16412
www.iu5.org/

Philadelphia IU 26
Paul G. Vallas, dir. — 215-299-7000
440 N Broad St, Philadelphia 19130 — Fax 299-4687

Pittsburgh/Mt. Oliver IU 2
Mark Roosevelt, dir. — 412-363-0851
515 N Highland Ave — Fax 488-7271
Pittsburgh 15206

Riverview IU 6
Dr. William Kaufman, dir. — 814-226-7103
270 Mayfield Rd, Clarion 16214 — Fax 226-4850
www.riu6.org/

Schuylkill IU 29
Dr. Gerald Achenbach, dir. — 570-544-9131
PO Box 130, Mar Lin 17951 — Fax 544-6412
www.iu29.org/

Seneca Highlands IU 9
M. Wetzel, dir. — 814-887-5512
PO Box 1566, Smethport 16749 — Fax 887-2157
www.iu9.org

Tuscarora IU 11
Richard Daubert, dir. — 717-899-7143
2527 US Highway 522 S
Mc Veytown 17051
www.tiu.k12.pa.us/

Westmoreland IU 7
Bruce Paul, dir. — 724-836-2460
RR 12 Box 205, Greensburg 15601 — Fax 836-1747
wiu.k12.pa.us/

PUBLIC, PRIVATE AND CATHOLIC SECONDARY SCHOOLS

Abington, Montgomery, Pop. 56,600
Abington SD — 7,000/K-12
970 Highland Ave 19001 — 215-884-4700
Amy Sichel Ph.D., supt. — Fax 881-2545
www.abington.k12.pa.us
Abington JHS — 1,900/7-9
2056 Susquehanna Rd 19001 — 215-884-4700
Cornelius McCarthy, prin. — Fax 517-2894
Abington SHS — 1,900/10-12
900 Highland Ave 19001 — 215-884-4700
Robert Burt, prin. — Fax 886-1871

Abington Memorial Hospital — Post-Sec.
1200 Old York Rd 19001 — 215-576-2000
Pennsylvania State University — Post-Sec.
1600 Woodland Rd 19001 — 215-881-7300

Albion, Erie, Pop. 1,573
Northwestern SD — 1,900/K-12
100 Harthan Way 16401 — 814-756-9400
Dr. Lynn Corder, supt. — Fax 756-9414
www.nwsd.org
Northwestern HS — 600/9-12
200 Harthan Way 16401 — 814-756-9400
Daniel Shreve, prin. — Fax 756-0472
Northwestern MS — 500/6-8
150 Harthan Way 16401 — 814-756-9400
Sandi Shaner, prin.

Alexandria, Huntingdon, Pop. 390
Juniata Valley SD — 900/K-12
PO Box 318 16611 — 814-669-9150
James Foster, supt. — Fax 669-4492
www.iu11.org/~jvweb/
Juniata Valley JSHS — 400/7-12
PO Box 318 16611 — 814-669-4401
Mark Loucks, prin. — Fax 669-4421

Wrightco Technologies Tech Training Inst — Post-Sec.
HCR 1 Box 22 16611 — 814-669-4241

Aliquippa, Beaver, Pop. 11,324
Aliquippa SD — 1,500/K-12
100 Harding Ave 15001 — 724-857-7500
John Thomas, supt. — Fax 857-3404
www.aliquippa.k12.pa.us
Aliquippa HS — 500/9-12
100 Harding Ave 15001 — 724-857-7500
Gary Monahan, prin. — Fax 375-0593
Aliquippa MS — 500/5-8
100 Harding Ave 15001 — 724-857-7500
Peter Carbone, prin. — Fax 857-3404

Hopewell Area SD — 2,900/K-12
2354 Brodhead Rd 15001 — 724-375-6691
Dr. Terry Mack, supt. — Fax 375-0942
www.hopewell.k12.pa.us
Hopewell HS — 1,000/9-12
1215 Longvue Ave 15001 — 724-378-8565
Michael Allison, prin. — Fax 378-4952
Hopewell JHS — 900/5-8
2354 Brodhead Rd 15001 — 724-375-7765
Dr. James Walsh, prin. — Fax 378-2594

Allentown, Lehigh, Pop. 105,958
Allentown CSD — 16,800/PK-12
PO Box 328 18105 — 484-765-4000
Karen Angello Ph.D., supt. — Fax 765-4225
www.allentownsd.org/
Allen HS — 3,300/9-12
126 N 17th St 18104 — 484-765-5000
Keith Falko, prin. — Fax 765-5010
Dieruff HS — 1,800/9-12
815 N Irving St 18109 — 484-765-5500
James Moniz, prin. — Fax 765-5512

Harrison-Morton MS — 900/6-8
137 N 2nd St 18101 — 484-765-5700
Burdette Chapel, prin. — Fax 765-5715
Raub MS — 900/6-8
102 S Saint Cloud St 18104 — 484-765-5300
Regina Finlayson, prin. — Fax 765-5310
South Mountain MS — 1,300/6-8
709 W Emmaus Ave 18103 — 484-765-4300
Ralph Lovelidge, prin. — Fax 765-4310
Trexler MS — 1,000/6-8
851 N 15th St 18102 — 484-765-4600
Karl Foerster, prin. — Fax 765-4610

Parkland SD — 8,700/K-12
1210 Springhouse Rd 18104 — 610-351-5503
Dr. Louise Donohue, supt. — Fax 351-5509
www.parklandsd.org
Parkland HS — 2,900/9-12
2700 N Cedar Crest Blvd 18104 — 610-351-5600
Richard Sniscak, prin. — Fax 351-5656
Springhouse MS — 900/6-8
1200 Springhouse Rd 18104 — 610-351-5700
Michelle Minotti, prin. — Fax 351-5748
Other Schools – See Orefield

Salisbury Twp. SD — 1,800/K-12
1140 Salisbury Rd 18103 — 610-797-2062
Mary Anne Wright, supt. — Fax 791-9983
www.salisbury.k12.pa.us/
Salisbury HS — 500/10-12
500 E Montgomery St 18103 — 610-797-4107
J. William Hume, prin. — Fax 797-1972
Salisbury MS — 600/6-9
3301 Devonshire Rd 18103 — 610-791-0830
Robert Cassidy, prin. — Fax 797-9648

Allentown Central Catholic HS | 900/9-12
301 N 4th St 18102 | 610-437-4601
Ronald Taylor, prin. | Fax 437-6760
Allentown School of Cosmetology | Post-Sec.
1921 Union Blvd 18109 | 610-437-4626
Cedar Crest College | Post-Sec.
100 College Dr 18104 | 610-437-4471
Harrison Career Institute | Post-Sec.
2102 Union Blvd 18109 | 610-434-9963
Lehigh Valley Christian HS | 200/9-12
1414 E Cedar St 18109 | 610-821-9443
Charles Bloomfield, prin. | Fax 821-5527
Lehigh Valley Hospital & Health Network | Post-Sec.
PO Box 7017 18105 | 610-402-2556
Lincoln Technical Institute | Post-Sec.
5151 W Tilghman St 18104 | 610-398-5300
Muhlenberg College | Post-Sec.
2400 W Chew St 18104 | 610-821-3100
Pennsylvania School of Business | Post-Sec.
406 W Hamilton St 18101 | 610-264-8029
Sacred Heart Hospital | Post-Sec.
421 W Chew St 18102 | 610-776-4745
Welder Training & Testing Institute | Post-Sec.
729 E Highland St 18109 | 610-437-9720

Allison Park, Allegheny, Pop. 6,000
Area Vocational Technical School
Supt. — None
Beattie Career Center | Vo/Tech
9600 Babcock Blvd 15101 | 412-366-2800
Kathryn Bamberger, prin. | Fax 366-9600

Hampton Township SD | 3,200/K-12
4591 School Dr 15101 | 412-492-6302
Dr. Lawrence Korchnak, supt. | Fax 487-6898
www.htsd.k12.pa.us
Hampton HS | 1,100/9-12
2929 McCully Rd 15101 | 412-492-6378
Jeffrey Finch, prin. | Fax 486-7050
Hampton MS | 800/6-8
4589 School Dr 15101 | 412-492-6358
Kenneth DiDonato, prin. | Fax 487-7544

Altoona, Blair, Pop. 47,980
Altoona Area SD | 8,200/PK-12
1415 6th Ave 16602 | 814-946-8211
Dr. Dennis Murray, supt. | Fax 946-8375
www.aasdcat.com/aasd/
Altoona Area SHS | 1,900/10-12
1415 6th Ave 16602 | 814-946-8273
Sharon Fasenmyer, prin.
Keith JHS | 1,000/7-9
1318 19th Ave 16601 | 814-946-8355
John Wilson, prin. | Fax 946-8557
Roosevelt JHS | 1,000/7-9
1501 7th Ave 16602 | 814-946-8340
Lori Mangan, prin. | Fax 946-8429

Area Vocational Technical School
Supt. — None
Greater Altoona CTC | Vo/Tech
1500 4th Ave 16602 | 814-946-8450
Dr. Lanny Ross, prin. | Fax 946-8351

Altoona Beauty School | Post-Sec.
1528 Valley View Blvd 16602 | 814-942-3141
Altoona Hospital | Post-Sec.
620 Howard Ave 16601 | 814-946-2223
Bishop Guilfoyle HS | 400/9-12
2400 Pleasant Valley Blvd 16602 | 814-944-4014
Robert Gervinski, prin. | Fax 944-8695
Computer Learning Network | Post-Sec.
2900 Fairway Dr 16602 | 814-944-5643
Great Commission S | 100/K-12
1100 6th Ave 16602 | 814-942-9710
Van Wiedemann, admin. | Fax 942-7147
Pennsylvania State University | Post-Sec.
3000 Ivyside Park 16601 | 814-949-5000
Pruonto's Hair Design Institute | Post-Sec.
705 12th St 16602 | 814-944-4494
South Hills School of Business & Tech. | Post-Sec.
508 58th St 16602 | 814-944-6134

Alverton, Westmoreland
Southmoreland SD
Supt. — See Scottdale
Southmoreland HS | 700/9-12
PO Box A 15612 | 724-887-2019
Carolyn Adams, prin. | Fax 887-2980
Southmoreland JHS | 400/7-8
PO Box B 15612 | 724-887-2034
Timothy Scott, prin. | Fax 887-2032

Ambler, Montgomery, Pop. 6,426
Wissahickon SD | 4,500/K-12
601 Knight Rd 19002 | 215-619-8000
Dr. Stanley Durtan, supt. | Fax 619-8002
wsdweb.org
Wissahickon HS | 1,400/9-12
521 Houston Rd 19002 | 215-619-8112
William Hayes, prin. | Fax 619-8113
Wissahickon MS | 1,100/6-8
500 Houston Rd 19002 | 215-619-8110
Lynda Fields, prin. | Fax 619-8111

Ambler Beauty Academy | Post-Sec.
50 E Butler Ave 19002 | 215-643-5994
Temple University 19002 | Post-Sec.
| 215-283-1252

Ambridge, Beaver, Pop. 7,460
Ambridge Area SD | 3,000/K-12
740 Park Rd 15003 | 724-266-2833
Dr. Kenneth E. Voss, supt. | Fax 266-3981
www.ambridge.k12.pa.us
Ambridge Area HS | 1,000/9-12
909 Duss Ave 15003 | 724-266-2833
Alan Fritz, prin. | Fax 266-5056
Other Schools – See Freedom

Trinity Episcopal School for Ministry | Post-Sec.
311 11th St 15003 | 724-266-3838

Annville, Lebanon, Pop. 4,294
Annville-Cleona SD | 1,700/K-12
520 S White Oak St 17003 | 717-867-7600
Marsha Zehner, supt. | Fax 867-7610
www.acschools.org
Annville-Cleona JSHS | 800/7-12
500 S White Oak St 17003 | 717-867-7700
Bernard Kepler, prin. | Fax 867-7720

Lebanon Valley College | Post-Sec.
101 N College Ave 17003 | 717-867-6100

Apollo, Armstrong, Pop. 1,712
Apollo-Ridge SD | 1,200/K-12
Star Route 15613 | 724-478-6000
Michael Vranesevic Ed.D., supt. | Fax 478-1149
www.apolloridge.com/
Other Schools – See Spring Church

Orchard Hills Christian Academy | 50/1-12
385 Kings Rd 15613 | 724-478-3455
Sandra Cornell, prin. | Fax 478-1174

Archbald, Lackawanna, Pop. 6,213
Valley View SD | 2,600/K-12
1 Columbus Dr 18403 | 570-876-5080
Joseph M. Daley, prin. | Fax 876-6365
www.valleyviewsd.org/
Valley View HS | 800/9-12
1 Columbus Dr 18403 | 570-876-4110
Donald Kanavy, prin. | Fax 803-0217
Valley View MS | 600/6-8
1 Columbus Dr 18403 | 570-876-6461
Gary Violanti, prin. | Fax 803-0276

Ardmore, Montgomery, Pop. 12,646
Lower Merion SD | 6,700/K-12
301 E Montgomery Ave 19003 | 610-645-1800
Dr. Jamie P. Savedoff, supt. | Fax 645-9772
www.lmsd.org
Lower Merion HS | 1,500/9-12
245 E Montgomery Ave 19003 | 610-645-1810
David Piperato, prin.
Other Schools – See Bala Cynwyd, Narberth, Rosemont

Torah Academy of Greater Philadelphia | 400/K-12
PO Box 310 19003 | 610-642-7870
Rabbi Joshua Levy, prin. | Fax 642-2265

Armagh, Indiana, Pop. 127
United SD | 1,300/K-12
10780 Route 56 Hwy E 15920 | 814-446-5618
Rick Huffman, supt. | Fax 446-6615
www.unitedsd.net/
United JSHS | 600/7-12
10780 Route 56 Hwy E 15920 | 814-446-5615
Lewis Kindja, prin. | Fax 446-6615

Arnold, Westmoreland, Pop. 5,485
New Kensington-Arnold SD
Supt. — See New Kensington
Valley MS, 1701 Alcoa Dr 15068 | 600/6-8
Brian Magill, prin. | 724-335-2511

Ashland, Schuylkill, Pop. 3,184
North Schuylkill SD | 2,000/K-12
15 Academy Ln 17921 | 570-874-0466
Robert Franklin, supt. | Fax 874-3334
www.northschuylkill.net
North Schuylkill JSHS | 1,000/7-12
15 Academy Ln 17921 | 570-874-0495
Sharon J. Snyder, prin. | Fax 874-1531

Cardinal Brennan JHSH | 200/7-12
130 Academy Ln 17921 | 570-874-3921
Dr. Jaclyn M. Fowler, prin. | Fax 874-2239

Aston, Delaware
Area Vocational Technical School
Supt. — None
Delaware County Technical HS Aston | Vo/Tech
700 Crozerville Rd 19014 | 610-459-3050
Mary Kelly, prin.

Chichester SD | 3,600/K-12
401 Cherry Tree Rd 19014 | 610-485-6881
Michael T. Golde, supt. | Fax 485-3086
www.chichesterschools.net
Other Schools – See Boothwyn

Penn-Delco SD | 3,300/K-12
2821 Concord Rd 19014 | 610-497-6300
Dr. Leslye Abrutyn, supt. | Fax 497-1798
www.pdsd.org
Northley MS | 900/6-8
2801 Concord Rd 19014 | 610-497-6300
Pete Donaghy, prin. | Fax 497-5737
Sun Valley HS | 1,100/9-12
2881 Pancoast Ave 19014 | 610-497-6300
Tom Jakubczwk, prin. | Fax 497-2863

American Christian S | 200/K-12
4150 Market St 19014 | 610-497-0700
Vicki Conteh, admin. | Fax 497-0785
Neumann College | Post-Sec.
1 Neumann Dr 19014 | 610-459-0905

Atglen, Chester, Pop. 1,302
Octorara Area SD | 2,700/K-12
228 Highland Rd # 1 19310 | 610-593-8238
Dr. Thomas Newcome, supt. | Fax 593-6425
www.octorara.k12.pa.us
Octorara Area HS | 800/9-12
226 Highland Rd 19310 | 610-593-8253
Dr. Robert Lewis, prin. | Fax 593-8256
Octorara Area MS | 700/6-8
228 Highland Rd 19310 | 610-593-8223
Douglas Groover, prin. | Fax 593-5185

Athens, Bradford, Pop. 3,328
Athens Area SD | 2,000/K-12
204 Willow St 18810 | 570-888-7766
Douglas A. Ulkins, supt. | Fax 888-3186
www.athensasd.k12.pa.us

Athens Area HS | 600/10-12
401 W Frederick St 18810 | 570-888-7766
Beth Schulze, prin. | Fax 888-4038
Rowe JHS | 400/8-9
116 W Pine St Ste 1 18810 | 570-888-7766
Scott Webster, prin. | Fax 888-9536

Valley Christian Academy | 50/K-12
207 Pennsylvania Ave 18810 | 570-888-4000
Rev. Thelma Wright, admin. | Fax 823-6011

Austin, Potter, Pop. 621
Austin Area SD | 300/PK-12
138 Costello Ave 16720 | 814-647-8603
Matthew Hutcheson, supt. | Fax 647-8869
www.austinsd.org
Austin Area JSHS | 100/7-12
138 Costello Ave 16720 | 814-647-8603
Matthew Hutcheson, prin. | Fax 647-8869

Avella, Washington
Avella Area SD | 700/K-12
1000 Avella Rd 15312 | 724-356-2218
Robert Loughry, supt. | Fax 356-2207
www.avella.hky.com/
Avella Area HS | 400/7-12
1000 Avella Rd 15312 | 724-356-2216
Wayde Killmeyer, prin. | Fax 356-7905

Avis, Clinton, Pop. 1,469
Walnut Street Christian S | 100/PK-12
PO Box 616 17721 | 570-398-1080
George Grossman, prin. | Fax 753-5728

Baden, Beaver, Pop. 4,240
Quigley HS | 200/9-12
200 Quigley Dr 15005 | 724-869-2188
Dr. Madonna Helbing, prin. | Fax 869-3091

Bala Cynwyd, Montgomery, Pop. 8,000
Lower Merion SD
Supt. — See Ardmore
Bala-Cynwyd MS | 900/6-8
510 Bryn Mawr Ave 19004 | 610-645-1480
Dr. Patricia Haupt, prin.

Bangor, Northampton, Pop. 5,275
Bangor Area SD | 3,700/K-12
123 Five Points Richmond Rd 18013 | 610-588-2163
John Reinhart, supt. | Fax 599-7040
www.bangor.k12.pa.us
Bangor Area HS | 1,200/9-12
187 Five Points Richmond Rd 18013 | 610-599-7011
Frank DeFelice, prin. | Fax 599-7043
Bangor Area MS | 600/7-8
401 Five Points Richmond Rd 18013 | 610-599-7012
Edward Brandt, prin. | Fax 599-7045

Bartonsville, Monroe
Area Vocational Technical School
Supt. — None
Monroe Career & Tech Institute | Vo/Tech
PO Box 66 18321 | 570-629-2001
Patricia Moyer, dir. | Fax 629-9698

Beaver, Beaver, Pop. 4,603
Beaver Area SD | 2,100/K-12
855 2nd St 15009 | 724-774-4010
Dr. John Hansen, supt. | Fax 774-8770
www.basd.k12.pa.us/index2.php
Beaver Area HS | 700/9-12
Gypsy Glen Rd 15009 | 724-774-0251
Brian White, prin. | Fax 774-3926
Beaver Area MS | 300/7-8
Gypsy Glen Rd 15009 | 724-774-0253
Brian White, prin. | Fax 774-3926

Medical Center of Beaver County | Post-Sec.
1000 Dutch Ridge Rd 15009 | 724-728-7000

Beaver Falls, Beaver, Pop. 9,632
Big Beaver Falls Area SD | 1,500/K-12
1503 8th Ave 15010 | 724-843-3470
Donna Nugent, supt. | Fax 843-2360
www.tigerweb.org
Beaver Falls Area HS | 600/9-12
1701 8th Ave 15010 | 724-843-7470
Thomas Karczewski, prin. | Fax 843-0892
Beaver Falls MS | 500/6-8
1601 8th Ave 15010 | 724-846-5470
Thomas House, prin. | Fax 846-2579

Blackhawk SD | 2,800/K-12
500 Blackhawk Rd 15010 | 724-846-6600
Dr. Alan Guandolo, supt. | Fax 846-2021
www.bsd.k12.pa.us
Blackhawk JSHS | 1,200/8-12
500 Blackhawk Rd 15010 | 724-846-9600
Scott Nelson, prin. | Fax 891-7113

Beaver County Christian HS | 100/9-12
510 37th St 15010 | 724-843-3002
Doug Carson, prin. | Fax 843-5224
Beaver Falls Beauty Academy | Post-Sec.
720 13th St 15010 | 724-843-7700
Geneva College | Post-Sec.
3200 College Ave 15010 | 724-846-5100

Beaver Springs, Snyder
Midd-West SD
Supt. — See Middleburg
West Snyder MS | 300/5-8
645 Snyder Ave 17812 | 570-658-8144
David Harrison, prin. | Fax 658-7287

Bedford, Bedford, Pop. 3,057
Bedford Area SD | 2,400/K-12
330 E John St 15522 | 814-623-4290
Dr. Patrick Crawford, supt. | Fax 623-4299
www.bedford.k12.pa.us
Bedford HS | 600/9-12
330 E John St 15522 | 814-623-4250
Kerry Barefoot, prin. | Fax 623-4265

Bedford MS 500/6-8
440 E Watson St 15522 814-623-4200
Max A. Shoemaker, prin. Fax 623-4214
Other Schools – See Hyndman

Bellefonte, Centre, Pop. 6,352
Bellefonte Area SD 3,000/K-12
318 N Allegheny St 16823 814-355-4814
James T. Masullo, supt. Fax 353-5342
www.basd.net
Bellefonte Area HS 1,000/9-12
830 E Bishop St 16823 814-355-4833
Anne Hutcheson, prin. Fax 353-5320
Bellefonte Area MS 800/6-8
100 N School St 16823 814-355-5466
Karen Krisch, prin. Fax 353-5350

Belle Vernon, Fayette, Pop. 1,176
Belle Vernon Area SD 3,000/K-12
270 Crest Ave 15012 724-929-5262
Robert J. Nagy, supt. Fax 930-9460
www.bvasd.net/
Belle Vernon Area HS 900/9-12
425 Crest Ave 15012 724-929-9800
Gregory J. Zborovancik, prin.
Bellmar MS, 500 Perry Ave 15012 400/6-8
Stephen Russell, prin. 724-929-9030
Rostraver MS, 250 Crest Ave 15012 400/6-8
Dr. John K Fohmar, prin. 724-929-2993

Belleville, Mifflin, Pop. 1,589

Belleville Mennonite S 200/PK-12
PO Box 847 17004 717-935-2184
R. Ann Kanagy, supt. Fax 935-5641

Bellwood, Blair, Pop. 1,942
Bellwood-Antis SD 1,400/K-12
400 Martin St 16617 814-742-2271
G. Brian Toth, supt. Fax 742-9049
tuckahoe.blwd.k12.pa.us
Bellwood-Antis HS 400/9-12
400 Martin St 16617 814-742-2274
Diane Williams, prin. Fax 742-9817
Bellwood-Antis MS 400/5-8
400 Martin St 16617 814-742-2273
Robert Fisher, prin. Fax 742-9817

Bensalem, Bucks, Pop. 59,700
Bensalem Township SD 6,500/K-12
3000 Donallen Dr 19020 215-750-2800
Dr. Victoria C. Gehrt, supt. Fax 359-0181
www.bensalemschools.org
Bensalem HS 2,100/9-12
4319 Hulmeville Rd 19020 215-750-2800
Francis Perry, prin. Fax 245-4875
Shafer MS 400/7-8
3333 Hulmeville Rd 19020 215-750-2800
William Incollingo, prin. Fax 244-2964
Snyder MS 300/7-8
3330 Hulmeville Rd 19020 215-750-2800
Dr. James Lynch, prin. Fax 244-2851

Bensalem Baptist S 100/K-12
3351 Richlieu Rd 19020 215-639-5433
B.W. Love, prin. Fax 639-5469
De La Salle Vocational HS Vo/Tech
PO Box 344 19020 215-464-0344
Ann Walker, prin. Fax 638-3767
Holy Family University Post-Sec.
1311 Bristol Pike 19020 215-637-7700
Holy Ghost Prep S 500/9-12
2429 Bristol Pike 19020 215-639-2102
Paul Pomeroy, prin. Fax 639-4225
ITT Technical Institute Post-Sec.
3330 Tillman Dr 19020 215-244-8871

Bentleyville, Washington, Pop. 2,459
Bentworth SD 1,200/K-12
150 Bearcat Dr 15314 724-239-2861
Paul J. Rach Ph.D., supt. Fax 239-2865
bentworth.org
Bentworth HS 400/9-12
75 Bearcat Dr 15314 724-239-5911
Kevin Fortuna, prin. Fax 239-4010
Other Schools – See Ellsworth

Benton, Columbia, Pop. 935
Benton Area SD 800/K-12
600 Green Acres Rd 17814 570-925-6651
Gary Powlus, supt. Fax 925-6973
www.bentonsd.k12.pa.us/
Benton Area MSHS 400/7-12
600 Green Acres Rd 17814 570-925-2651
Joseph Goode, prin. Fax 925-0956

Berlin, Somerset, Pop. 2,153
Berlin-Brothersvalley SD 900/K-12
1025 Main St 15530 814-267-4621
Wayne C. Henderson, supt. Fax 267-6060
bbsd.com
Berlin-Brothersvalley HS 300/9-12
1025 Main St 15530 814-267-4622
Thomas Vent, prin. Fax 267-6060
Berlin Brothersvalley MS 300/5-8
1025 Main St 15530 814-267-6931
Pamela Webreck, prin. Fax 267-6060

Bernville, Berks, Pop. 865
Tulpehocken Area SD 1,700/K-12
428 New Schaefferstown Rd 19506 610-488-9555
Elizabeth Massar, supt. Fax 488-7914
www.tulpehocken.org
Tulpehocken Area JSHS 800/7-12
430 New Schaefferstown Rd 19506 610-488-6286
Greg Protzman, prin. Fax 488-7976

Berwick, Columbia, Pop. 10,500
Berwick Area SD 3,400/K-12
500 Line St 18603 570-759-6400
James Kraky, supt. Fax 759-6439
www.berwicksd.org
Berwick Area HS 900/9-12
1100 Fowler Ave 18603 570-759-6400
Richard Walton, prin. Fax 759-6466

Berwick Area MS 900/6-8
1100 Evergreen Dr 18603 570-759-6400
Ralph Norce, prin. Fax 759-7978

Berwyn, See Devon
Tredyffrin-Easttown SD 5,700/K-12
738 1st Ave 19312 610-240-1900
Dr. Daniel Waters, supt. Fax 240-1965
www.tesd.net/
Conestoga HS 1,800/9-12
200 Irish Rd 19312 610-240-1000
Timothy Donovan, prin. Fax 240-1055
Tredyffrin-Easttown MS 900/5-8
801 Conestoga Rd 19312 610-240-1200
Mark Cataldi, prin. Fax 240-1225
Other Schools – See Wayne

Bessemer, Lawrence, Pop. 1,138
Mohawk Area SD 2,000/K-12
PO Box 25 16112 724-667-7723
Dr. Timothy F. McNamee, supt. Fax 667-0602
www.mohawk.k12.pa.us
Mohawk JSHS 1,000/7-12
PO Box 25 16112 724-667-7782
Frank Robinson, prin. Fax 667-0602

Bethel Park, Allegheny, Pop. 32,915
Bethel Park SD 5,200/K-12
301 Church Rd 15102 412-854-8402
Dr. Thomas Knight, supt. Fax 854-8430
www.bpsd.org
Bethel Park HS 1,900/9-12
309 Church Rd 15102 412-854-8581
David Helsinki, prin. Fax 854-8559
Independence MS 800/7-8
2807 Bethel Church Rd 15102 412-854-8677
David Muench, prin. Fax 854-8732

Bethlehem, Northampton, Pop. 72,570
Area Vocational Technical School
Supt. — None
Bethlehem AVTS Vo/Tech
3300 Chester Ave 18020 610-866-8013
Brian Williams, prin. Fax 866-6124

Bethlehem Area SD 14,800/K-12
1516 Sycamore St 18017 610-861-0500
Dr. Joseph A. Lewis, supt. Fax 807-5599
www.beth.k12.pa.us/
Broughal MS 600/6-8
125 W Packer Ave 18015 610-866-5041
Joseph Santoro, prin. Fax 807-5909
East Hills MS 1,400/6-8
2005 Chester Rd 18017 610-867-0541
Edward J. Crawford, prin. Fax 807-5941
Freedom HS 1,900/9-12
3149 Chester Ave 18020 610-867-5843
Roger Washburn, prin. Fax 867-7360
Liberty HS 2,800/9-12
1115 Linden St 18018 610-691-7200
Dean Donaher, prin. Fax 691-0741
Nitschmann MS 1,000/6-8
909 W Union Blvd 18018 610-866-5781
John Acerra, prin. Fax 866-1435
Northeast MS 800/6-8
1110 Fernwood St 18018 610-868-8581
Roberta Whitcomb, prin. Fax 807-5997

Bethlehem Catholic HS 800/9-12
2133 Madison Ave 18017 610-866-0791
Richard Culver, prin. Fax 866-9892
Lehigh University Post-Sec.
27 Memorial Dr W 18015 610-758-3000
Moravian Academy MS 200/6-8
11 W Market St 18018 610-866-6677
Barnaby J. Roberts, hdmstr. Fax 866-6337
Moravian Academy - Upper S Campus 200/9-12
4313 Green Pond Rd 18020 610-691-1600
Barnaby J. Roberts, hdmstr. Fax 691-3354
Moravian College Post-Sec.
1200 Main St 18018 610-861-1300
Moravian Theological Seminary Post-Sec.
1200 Main St 18018 610-861-1516
Northampton Co. Area Community College Post-Sec.
3835 Green Pond Rd 18020 610-861-5300
St. Luke's Hospital Post-Sec.
801 Ostrum St 18015 610-954-3400

Biglerville, Adams, Pop. 1,129
Upper Adams SD 1,800/K-12
PO Box 847 17307 717-677-7191
Eric Eshbach, supt. Fax 677-9807
www.uasd.k12.pa.us
Biglerville HS 500/9-12
161 N Main St 17307 717-677-7191
Richard Sterner, prin. Fax 677-0142
Upper Adams MS 300/7-8
161 N Main St 17307 717-677-7191
David Zinn, prin. Fax 677-0219

Birdsboro, Berks, Pop. 5,161
Daniel Boone Area SD 3,500/K-12
PO Box 490 19508 610-582-6140
David Robbins, supt. Fax 582-0059
www.dboone.k12.pa.us/
Boone Area HS 1,000/9-12
PO Box 450 19508 610-582-6100
William McIlmoyle, prin. Fax 582-5400
Other Schools – See Douglassville

Berks Christian S 200/K-12
926 Philadelphia Ter 19508 610-582-1000
Robert Becker, admin. Fax 404-0126

Blairsville, Indiana, Pop. 3,489
Blairsville-Saltsburg SD 2,200/K-12
102 School Ln 15717 724-459-5500
H. Robert Mencer Ed.D., supt. Fax 459-9209
www.b-ssd.org
Blairsville HS 400/9-12
100 School Ln 15717 724-459-8882
Timothy Haselhoff, prin. Fax 459-3392
Blairsville MS 300/6-8
104 School Ln 15717 724-459-8880
Joyce Henderson, prin. Fax 459-0213
Other Schools – See Saltsburg

WyoTech Blairsville Post-Sec.
500 Innovation Dr 15717 724-459-9500

Bloomsburg, Columbia, Pop. 12,652
Area Vocational Technical School
Supt. — None
Columbia-Montour AVTS Vo/Tech
5050 Sweppenheiser Dr 17815 570-784-8040
Steven Walk, prin. Fax 784-3565

Bloomsburg Area SD 1,800/K-12
728 E 5th St 17815 570-784-5000
Joseph Kelly, supt. Fax 387-8832
bloomsburgasd.schoolwires.com
Bloomsburg Area HS 500/9-12
1200 Railroad St 17815 570-784-6100
Daniel Bonomo, prin. Fax 387-3492
Bloomsburg Area MS 500/6-8
1100 Railroad St 17815 570-784-9100
Lee Gump, prin. Fax 387-3491

Central Columbia SD 2,200/K-12
4777 Old Berwick Rd 17815 570-784-2850
Harry Mathias, supt. Fax 387-0192
www.centralcolumbia.k12.pa.us/
Central Columbia HS 700/9-12
4777 Old Berwick Rd 17815 570-784-2833
Robert Lombardo, prin. Fax 784-0863
Central Columbia MS 800/5-8
4777 Old Berwick Rd 17815 570-784-6103
John Kurelia, prin. Fax 784-4935

Bloomsburg University of Pennsylvania Post-Sec.
400 E 2nd St 17815 570-389-4000
Columbia County Christian S 200/PK-12
123 Schoolhouse Rd 17815 570-784-2977
Scott Shaw, admin. Fax 784-1755
Keystone National High School Post-Sec.
420 W 5th St 17815 570-784-5220

Blossburg, Tioga, Pop. 1,470
Southern Tioga SD 2,200/K-12
241 Main St 16912 570-638-2183
Joseph M. Kalata, supt. Fax 638-3512
www.southerntioga.org
North Penn JSHS 300/7-12
300 Morris St 16912 570-638-2158
Albert Lindner, prin. Fax 638-2150
Other Schools – See Liberty, Mansfield

Blue Bell, Montgomery, Pop. 6,091

Montgomery County Community College Post-Sec.
340 Dekalb Pike 19422 215-641-6300
Reformed Episcopal Seminary Post-Sec.
826 2nd Ave 19422 610-292-9852

Boiling Springs, Cumberland, Pop. 1,978
South Middleton SD 2,100/K-12
4 Forge Rd 17007 717-240-2618
Patricia B. Sanker Ed.D., supt. Fax 258-1214
www.bubblers.k12.pa.us
Boiling Springs HS 700/9-12
4 Forge Rd 17007 717-258-6484
Joseph Mancuso, prin. Fax 258-5014
Yellow Breeches MS 500/6-8
4 Forge Rd 17007 717-258-6484
Frederick Withum, prin. Fax 258-0301

Boothwyn, Delaware, Pop. 5,069
Chichester SD
Supt. — See Aston
Chichester HS 1,200/9-12
3333 Chichester Ave 19061 610-485-6881
James Donnelly, prin. Fax 485-6510
Chichester MS 1,200/5-8
925 Meetinghouse Rd 19061 610-485-6881
Salvatore Salamone, prin. Fax 494-3064

Boswell, Somerset, Pop. 1,316
North Star SD 1,400/K-12
1200 Morris Ave 15531 814-629-5631
Dennis P. Leyman, supt. Fax 629-6181
www.northstar.k12.pa.us
North Star HS 400/9-12
400 Ohio St 15531 814-629-6651
Joseph Bradley, prin. Fax 629-9346

Boyertown, Berks, Pop. 3,912
Boyertown Area SD 6,900/K-12
911 Montgomery Ave 19512 610-367-6031
Dr. Harry Morgan, supt. Fax 369-7620
basd.netjunction.com
Boyertown Area JHS West 900/7-9
380 S Madison St 19512 610-369-7471
Gregory Galtere, prin.
Boyertown Area SHS 1,600/10-12
120 N Monroe St 19512 610-369-7435
Daniel Goffredo, prin. Fax 369-7533
Other Schools – See Gilbertsville

Bradford, McKean, Pop. 8,826
Bradford Area SD 2,400/PK-12
PO Box 375 16701 814-362-3841
Sandra Romanowski, supt. Fax 362-2552
www.bradfordareaschools.org
Bradford Area HS 1,000/9-12
81 Interstate Pkwy 16701 814-362-3845
Kenneth Coffman, prin. Fax 362-1765
Fretz MS 800/6-8
140 Lorana Ave 16701 814-362-3500
Tina Slaven, prin. Fax 362-1812

Bradford Regional Medical Center Post-Sec.
116 Interstate Pkwy 16701 814-362-8292
University of Pittsburgh at Bradford Post-Sec.
300 Campus Dr 16701 814-362-7500

Bridgeville, Allegheny, Pop. 5,160
Chartiers Valley SD
Supt. — See Pittsburgh
Chartiers Valley HS 1,100/9-12
50 Thoms Run Rd 15017 412-429-2273
Dr. Terri Flynn, prin. Fax 276-5808

Chartiers Valley MS | 800/6-8
50 Thoms Run Rd   15017 | 412-429-2220
Betsy Sapienza, prin. | Fax 429-2226

Bristol, Bucks, Pop. 9,947
Bristol Borough SD | 1,100/PK-12
420 Buckley St   19007 | 215-781-1015
Dr. Broadus W. Davis, supt. | Fax 781-1012
www.bbsd.org/
Bristol HS, 1801 Wilson Ave   19007 | 400/9-12
Thomas Shaffer, prin. | 215-781-1030
Bristol MS, 1801 Wilson Ave   19007 | 7-8
Thomas Shaffer, prin. | 215-781-1034

Bristol Township SD
Supt. — See Levittown
Roosevelt MS | 1,000/7-9
1001 New Rodgers Rd   19007 | 215-788-0436
Ruth Geisel, prin. | Fax 788-2629

Pennco Tech | Post-Sec.
3815 Otter St   19007 | 215-824-3200

Brockway, Jefferson, Pop. 2,137
Brockway Area SD | 1,200/K-12
40 North St   15824 | 814-265-8411
Stephen Zarlinski, supt. | Fax 265-8498
www.brockway.k12.pa.us/
Brockway Area JSHS | 600/7-12
100 Alexander St   15824 | 814-265-8414
Denise Carlini, prin. | Fax 265-8413

Brodheadsville, Monroe, Pop. 1,389
Pleasant Valley SD | 9,600/K-12
1 School Ln   18322 | 570-402-1000
Dr. Frank Pullo, supt. | Fax 992-7275
www.pvbears.org/
Pleasant Valley MS | 1,200/8-9
Route 115   18322 | 570-402-1000
Howard Drake, prin. | Fax 992-6968
Pleasant Valley SHS | 1,600/10-12
Route 209   18322 | 570-402-1000
John Gress, prin. | Fax 992-7733

Brookhaven, Delaware, Pop. 7,893

Christian Academy | 400/K-12
4301 Chandler Dr   19015 | 610-872-7600
Anita Gray, prin. | Fax 876-2173

Brookville, Jefferson, Pop. 4,151
Brookville Area SD | 1,900/K-12
PO Box 479   15825 | 814-849-8372
James Estep, supt. | Fax 849-6842
www.brookville.k12.pa.us
Brookville Area JSHS | 900/7-12
PO Box 479   15825 | 814-849-1106
Keith Wolfe, prin. | Fax 849-1117

Broomall, Delaware, Pop. 10,930
Marple-Newtown SD
Supt. — See Newtown Square
Paxon Hollow MS | 800/6-8
815 Paxon Hollow Rd   19008 | 610-359-4320
Stephen Subers Ed.D., prin.

CHI Institute/RETS Campus | Post-Sec.
1991 Sproul Rd Ste 42   19008 | 610-353-7630

Brownstown, Lancaster, Pop. 851
Area Vocational Technical School
Supt. — None
Lancaster County CTC-Brownstown | Vo/Tech
PO Box 519   17508 | 717-859-5100
James Benedict, prin. | Fax 859-4529

Brownsville, Fayette, Pop. 2,715
Brownsville Area SD | 1,900/K-12
1025 Lewis St   15417 | 724-785-2021
Lawrence Golembiewski, supt. | Fax 785-6988
www.basd.org
Brownsville Area HS | 600/9-12
1 Falcon Dr   15417 | 724-785-8200
Richard Gates, prin. | Fax 785-8930
Brownsville MS | 300/7-8
2 Falcon Dr   15417 | 724-785-2155
Vincent Nosser, prin. | Fax 785-2502

Bryn Athyn, Montgomery, Pop. 1,367

Academy of the New Church-Boys | 100/9-12
PO Box 707   19009 | 215-947-4200
| Fax 938-2617
Academy of the New Church-Girls | 100/9-12
PO Box 707   19009 | 215-938-2595
| Fax 938-2617
Bryn Athyn College of the New Church
PO Box 717   19009 | 215-938-2543

Bryn Mawr, Montgomery, Pop. 3,271

American College | Post-Sec.
270 S Bryn Mawr Ave   19010 | 610-526-1000
Baldwin S | 600/PK-12
701 Montgomery Ave   19010 | 610-525-2700
Sally Powell, hdmstr. | Fax 525-7534
Bryn Mawr College | Post-Sec.
101 N Merion Ave   19010 | 610-526-5000
Country Day S of the Sacred Heart | 400/PK-12
480 S Bryn Mawr Ave   19010 | 610-527-3915
Sr. Matthew MacDonald, hdmstr. | Fax 527-0942
Harcum Junior College | Post-Sec.
750 Montgomery Ave   19010 | 610-525-4100
Hill Top Preparatory S | 100/6-12
737 S Ithan Ave   19010 | 610-527-3230
Leslie McLean, hdmstr. | Fax 527-7683
Rosemont College | Post-Sec.
1400 Montgomery Ave   19010 | 610-527-0200
Shipley S | 900/PK-12
814 Yarrow St   19010 | 610-525-4300
Steven Piltch, prin. | Fax 525-5082

Burgettstown, Washington, Pop. 1,536
Burgettstown Area SD | 1,500/K-12
100 Bavington Rd   15021 | 724-947-3324
Deborah Jackson, supt. | Fax 947-8143
www.burgettstown.k12.pa.us
Burgettstown MSHS | 700/7-12
104 Bavington Rd   15021 | 724-947-8100
Tracy Schooley, prin. | Fax 947-3325

Tri State Christian Academy | 100/K-12
750 Steubenville Pike   15021 | 724-947-8722
M. R. Hawley, admin. | Fax 947-0821

Butler, Butler, Pop. 14,766
Area Vocational Technical School
Supt. — None
Butler County AVTS | Vo/Tech
210 Campus Ln   16001 | 724-282-0735
Dr. Joseph Cunningham, prin. | Fax 282-7448

Butler Area SD | 8,300/K-12
110 Campus Ln   16001 | 724-287-8721
Dr. Edward Fink, supt.
www.butler.k12.pa.us
Butler Area Intermediate HS | 1,400/9-10
551 Fairground Hill Rd   16001 | 724-287-8721
John Wyllie, prin.
Butler Area JHS | 1,300/7-8
225 E North St   16001 | 724-287-8721
James Allen, prin. | Fax 287-4996
Butler Area SHS | 1,300/11-12
120 Campus Ln   16001 | 724-287-8721
Dale Lumley, prin. | Fax 287-1596

Butler Beauty School | Post-Sec.
233 S Main St   16001 | 724-287-0708
Butler County Community College | Post-Sec.
PO Box 1203   16003 | 724-287-8711

Cairnbrook, Somerset
Shade-Central CSD | 600/K-12
203 McGregor Ave   15924 | 814-754-4648
Hubert Donahue Ph.D., supt. | Fax 754-5848
www.shade.k12.pa.us
Shade JSHS | 300/7-12
203 McGregor Ave   15924 | 814-754-4648
Joseph Kimmel, prin.

California, Washington, Pop. 5,472
California Area SD | 800/K-12
750 Orchard St   15419 | 724-938-2511
Dr. Robert T. Marks, supt. | Fax 938-2587
www.calsd.k12.pa.us/
Other Schools – See Coal Center

California University of Pennsylvania | Post-Sec.
250 University Ave   15419 | 724-938-4000

Cambridge Springs, Crawford, Pop. 2,309
Penncrest SD
Supt. — See Saegertown
Cambridge Springs JSHS | 600/7-12
698 Venango Ave   16403 | 814-398-4631
David Nuhfer, prin. | Fax 398-8343

Camp Hill, Cumberland, Pop. 7,533
Camp Hill SD | 1,100/K-12
2627 Chestnut St   17011 | 717-901-2400
Connie R. Kindler, supt. | Fax 901-2416
www.camphillsd.k12.pa.us
Camp Hill HS | 400/9-12
100 S 24th St   17011 | 717-901-2500
James Robertson, prin. | Fax 901-2614
Camp Hill MS | 300/6-8
2401 Chestnut St   17011 | 717-901-2450
Mark Dolan, prin. | Fax 901-2573

West Shore SD
Supt. — See Lewisberry
Allen MS, 4225 Gettysburg Rd   17011 | 500/6-8
Tammi Jones, prin. | 717-901-9552
Cedar Cliff HS | 1,400/9-12
1301 Carlisle Rd   17011 | 717-737-8654
Mark Maldet, prin. | Fax 737-0874

Holy Spirit Hospital | Post-Sec.
505 N 21st St   17011 | 717-763-2106
Trinity HS | 600/9-12
3601 Simpson Ferry Rd   17011 | 717-761-1116
Dr. Nancy Burke, admin. | Fax 761-7309

Canonsburg, Washington, Pop. 8,716
Area Vocational Technical School
Supt. — None
Western Area CTC | Vo/Tech
688 Western Ave   15317 | 724-746-2890
Dr. Joseph Iannetti, prin. | Fax 746-0817

Canon-McMillan SD | 4,300/K-12
1 N Jefferson Ave   15317 | 724-746-2940
Nick Bayat Ed.D., supt. | Fax 746-9184
www.cmsd.k12.pa.us
Canon-McMillan HS | 1,300/9-12
314 Elm Street Ext   15317 | 724-745-1400
Linda Nichols, prin. | Fax 745-2258
Canonsburg MS | 700/7-8
25 E College St   15317 | 724-745-9030
Greg Taranto, prin. | Fax 873-5230

Canton, Bradford, Pop. 1,755
Canton Area SD | 1,200/K-12
139 E Main St   17724 | 570-673-3191
W. Jeffrey Johnston, supt. | Fax 673-3680
www.canton.k12.pa.us
Canton JSHS | 600/7-12
139 E Main St   17724 | 570-673-5134
Chris Bigger, prin. | Fax 673-3680

Carbondale, Lackawanna, Pop. 9,487
Carbondale Area SD | 1,500/K-12
101 Brooklyn St   18407 | 570-282-4660
Dominick Famularo, supt. | Fax 282-6988
gateway.ca.k12.pa.us
Carbondale Area JSHS | 800/7-12
101 Brooklyn St   18407 | 570-282-4600
Joseph Farrell, prin. | Fax 282-7341

Carlisle, Cumberland, Pop. 18,110
Carlisle Area SD | 4,800/K-12
623 W Penn St   17013 | 717-240-6800
Mary Kay Durham, supt. | Fax 240-6898
www.carlisleschools.org
Carlisle HS | 1,700/9-12
623 W Penn St   17013 | 717-240-6800
Gary Worley, prin. | Fax 240-7145
Lamberton MS | 600/6-8
623 W Penn St   17013 | 717-240-6800
| Fax 240-2066
Wilson MS | 600/6-8
623 W Penn St   17013 | 717-240-6800
| Fax 240-2050

Bethel Christian Academy | 200/PK-12
1412 Holly Pike, | 717-249-3692
Robert Jay, prin. | Fax 240-0644
Dickinson College | Post-Sec.
PO Box 1773   17013 | 717-243-5121
Penn State Dickinson School of Law | Post-Sec.
150 S College St   17013 | 717-240-5000

Carmichaels, Greene, Pop. 538
Carmichaels Area SD | 1,100/K-12
225 N Vine St   15320 | 724-966-5045
Jim Zalar, supt. | Fax 966-8793
www.carmarea.org/Carm_Web/MainIndex.htm
Carmichaels Area JSHS | 500/7-12
300 W Greene St   15320 | 724-966-5045
Lyn Shlosky, prin. | Fax 966-5556

Carnegie, Allegheny, Pop. 8,265
Carlynton SD | 1,600/K-12
435 Kings Hwy   15106 | 412-429-8400
Michael Panza, supt. | Fax 429-2502
www.carlynton.k12.pa.us
Carlynton JSHS | 800/7-12
435 Kings Hwy   15106 | 412-429-2500
James Muraco, prin. | Fax 429-2508

Catasauqua, Lehigh, Pop. 6,506
Catasauqua Area SD | 1,700/K-12
201 N 14th St   18032 | 610-264-5571
Robert J. Spengler, supt. | Fax 264-5618
www.cattysd.org
Lincoln MS | 600/5-8
330 Howertown Rd   18032 | 610-264-4341
Melissa Inselmann, prin. | Fax 264-5458
Other Schools – See Northampton

Catawissa, Columbia, Pop. 1,555
Southern Columbia Area SD | 1,400/K-12
800 Southern Dr   17820 | 570-356-2931
Dr. Alan J. Lonoconus, supt. | Fax 356-2892
www.scolumbiasd.k12.pa.us/
Southern Columbia HS | 500/9-12
812 Southern Dr   17820 | 570-356-3450
Paul Caputo, prin. | Fax 356-2835
Southern Columbia MS | 500/5-8
810 Southern Dr   17820 | 570-356-3400
James Becker, prin. | Fax 356-2835

Center Valley, Lehigh
Southern Lehigh SD | 3,000/K-12
5775 Main St   18034 | 610-282-3121
Joseph P. Liberati, supt. | Fax 282-0193
www.slsd.org
Southern Lehigh HS | 1,000/9-12
5800 Main St   18034 | 610-282-1421
Christine Siegfried, prin. | Fax 282-2965
Southern Lehigh MS | 700/6-8
3715 Preston Ln   18034 | 610-282-3700
R. Ann Pope, prin. | Fax 282-2963

DeSales University | Post-Sec.
2755 Station Ave   18034 | 610-282-1100
Lehigh Valley College | Post-Sec.
2809 Saucon Valley Rd   18034 | 800-227-9109

Chalfont, Bucks, Pop. 4,061
Central Bucks SD
Supt. — See Doylestown
Unami MS | 900/7-9
160 Moyer Rd   18914 | 267-893-3400
Gary Fuller, prin. | Fax 893-5820

Chambersburg, Franklin, Pop. 17,864
Area Vocational Technical School
Supt. — None
Franklin County CTC | Vo/Tech
2463 Loop Rd   17201 | 717-263-9033
Jim Duffy, prin. | Fax 263-6568

Chambersburg Area SD | 7,900/PK-12
435 Stanley Ave   17201 | 717-263-9281
Dr. Edwin Sponseller, supt.
www.chambersburg.k12.pa.us
Chambersburg Area SHS | 1,800/10-12
511 S 6th St   17201 | 717-261-3328
Dr. Barry Purvis, prin. | Fax 261-3490
Faust JHS | 1,300/8-9
1957 Scotland Ave   17201 | 717-261-3369
Dr. Rick Keller, prin. | Fax 261-3379

Cumberland Valley Christian S | 400/PK-12
600 Miller St   17201 | 717-264-3266
Carl McKee, prin. | Fax 264-0416
Shalom Christian Academy | 500/PK-12
126 Social Island Rd   17201 | 717-375-2223
Conrad Swartzentruber, admin. | Fax 375-2224
Wilson College | Post-Sec.
1015 Philadelphia Ave   17201 | 717-264-4141
Wrightco Technologies Tech Training Inst | Post-Sec.
225 Sollenberger Rd   17201 | 717-263-8142

Champion, Fayette

Champion Christian S | 100/PK-12
2166 Indian Head Rd   15622 | 724-455-2122
Merle Skinner, pres. | Fax 455-6651

Charleroi, Washington, Pop. 4,738
Area Vocational Technical School
Supt. — None

Mon Valley CTC   Vo/Tech
1 Guttman Blvd 15022   724-489-9581
Bradley Deicas, prin.

Charleroi SD   1,700/K-12
125 Fecsen Dr 15022   724-483-3509
Dr. Brad Ferko, supt.   Fax 483-3776
www.charleroisd.org
Charleroi Area HS   500/9-12
100 Fecsen Dr 15022   724-483-3575
Jeff Taylor, prin.   Fax 483-2294
Charleroi Area MS   400/6-8
100 Fecsen Dr 15022   724-483-3600
Mary Tickner, prin.   Fax 489-9128

Chester, Delaware, Pop. 37,017
Chester-Upland SD   4,900/K-12
1720 Melrose Ave 19013   610-447-3600
Dr. Charles A. Scott, supt.   Fax 447-3616
www.chesteruplandsd.org/
Chester HS   1,500/9-12
200 W 9th St 19013   610-447-3772
John Echler, prin.   Fax 447-3682
Parry MS   400/5-8
501 W 9th St 19013   610-447-3777
Denise Johnson, prin.   Fax 447-3778
Showalter MS   600/5-8
1100 W 10th St 19013   610-447-3650
H. Stephen Brady, prin.   Fax 447-3653
Smedley MS   400/6-8
1701 Upland St 19013   610-447-3660
Howard Johnson, prin.   Fax 447-3661

Widener University   Post-Sec.
1 University Pl 19013   610-499-4000

Chesterbrook, Chester, Pop. 4,561

DeVry University   Post-Sec.
701 Lee Rd Ste 103 19087   610-889-9980

Cheswick, Allegheny, Pop. 1,846
Allegheny Valley SD   1,200/K-12
300 Pearl Ave 15024   724-274-5300
Charles J. Territo Ph.D., supt.   Fax 274-8040
www.avsd.k12.pa.us
Other Schools – See Springdale

Cheswick Christian Academy   200/K-12
1407 Pittsburgh St 15024   724-274-4566
Todd Rosio, prin.   Fax 274-8300

Cheyney, Delaware

Cheyney University of Pennsylvania   Post-Sec.
PO Box 200 19319   610-399-2000

Clairton, Allegheny, Pop. 8,204
Area Vocational Technical School
Supt. — None
Steel Center AVTS   Vo/Tech
565 N Lewis Run Rd 15025   412-469-3200
John Sandrene, prin.

Clairton CSD   900/K-12
501 Waddell Ave 15025   412-233-7090
Dr. Robert J. David, supt.   Fax 233-4982
www.clairton.k12.pa.us/
Clairton HS   300/9-12
501 Waddell Ave 15025   412-233-9200
Donald MacFann, prin.   Fax 233-3243
Clairton MS   300/5-8
501 Waddell Ave 15025   412-233-9200
Susan Hicks, prin.   Fax 233-3243

Claridge, Westmoreland
Penn-Trafford SD
Supt. — See Harrison City
Penn MS   700/6-8
PO Box 399 15623   724-744-4431
Ronald Darragh, prin.   Fax 744-1215

Clarion, Clarion, Pop. 5,953
Clarion Area SD   900/K-12
221 Liberty St 16214   814-226-6110
George White, supt.   Fax 226-9292
www.clarion-schools.com
Clarion Area JSHS   500/7-12
219 Liberty St 16214   814-226-8112
Todd MacBeth, prin.   Fax 226-9004

Clarion University of Pennsylvania   Post-Sec.
840 Wood St 16214   814-393-2000

Clarks Summit, Lackawanna, Pop. 5,044
Abington Heights SD   3,700/K-12
200 E Grove St 18411   570-586-2511
Michael Mahon, supt.   Fax 586-1756
www.ahsd.org
Abington Heights HS   1,300/9-12
222 Noble Rd 18411   570-585-5300
Susan Sallavanti, prin.   Fax 586-9093
Abington Heights MS   1,200/5-8
1555 Newton Ransom Blvd 18411   570-586-1281
Edward Kairis, prin.   Fax 586-6361

Baptist Bible College and Seminary   Post-Sec.
PO Box 800 18411   570-586-2400
Lourdesmont HS   100/7-12
537 Venard Rd 18411   570-587-4741
Barry Rogers, dir.   Fax 586-0030
Summit Christian Academy   100/7-12
660 Griffin Pond Rd 18411   570-587-1545
Tim Connor, admin.   Fax 586-5849

Claysburg, Blair, Pop. 1,399
Claysburg-Kimmel SD   900/K-12
RR 1 Box 522 16625   814-239-5141
James O'Harrow, supt.   Fax 239-5896
www.cksd.k12.pa.us
Claysburg-Kimmel JSHS   400/7-12
RR 1 Box 522 16625   814-239-5141
Dr. Gunter Moritz, prin.   Fax 239-8949

Claysville, Washington, Pop. 703
McGuffey SD   2,400/K-12
PO Box 431 15323   724-663-7745
Joseph Stefka, supt.   Fax 663-5465
mcguffey.k12.pa.us
McGuffey HS   800/9-12
86 McGuffey Dr 15323   724-948-3328
Keith Kucherawy, prin.   Fax 948-3344
McGuffey MS   500/6-8
86 McGuffey Dr 15323   724-948-3323
Beverly Arbore, prin.   Fax 948-2413

Clearfield, Clearfield, Pop. 6,413
Area Vocational Technical School
Supt. — None
Clearfield County CTC   Vo/Tech
1620 River Rd 16830   814-765-5308
Lois Richards, prin.   Fax 765-5474

Clearfield Area SD   2,800/K-12
PO Box 710 16830   814-765-5511
Dr. Denise Keltz, supt.   Fax 765-5515
www.clearfield.org
Clearfield Area HS   1,000/9-12
PO Box 910 16830   814-765-2401
John Law, prin.   Fax 765-2405
Clearfield Area MS   800/5-8
PO Box 710 16830   814-765-5302
Timothy Meckey, prin.   Fax 765-4604

Clearfield Alliance Christian S   100/K-12
56 Alliance Rd 16830   814-765-0216
Dr. Duane White, prin.   Fax 765-8846
Clearfield Beauty Academy   Post-Sec.
22 N 3rd St 16830   814-765-2022
Clearfield Hospital   Post-Sec.
PO Box 992 16830   814-768-2496
Lock Haven University-Clearfield Campus   Post-Sec.
PO Box 1410 16830   814-765-0559

Clymer, Indiana, Pop. 1,489
Penns Manor Area SD   1,000/K-12
6003 Route 553 Hwy 15728   724-254-2666
Dr. Thomas Sgriccia, supt.   Fax 254-3418
www.pennsmanor.org/
Penns Manor Area JSHS   500/7-12
6003 Route 553 Hwy 15728   724-254-2666
Daren Johnston, prin.   Fax 254-3418

Coal Center, Washington, Pop. 133
California Area SD
Supt. — See California
California Area HS   400/9-12
293 Malden Rd 15423   724-785-5800
Brian Jackson, prin.   Fax 785-8860
California Area MS   6-8
293 Malden Rd 15423   724-785-5800
Raymond Huffman, prin.   Fax 785-5458

Coal Township, Northumberland, Pop. 9,922
Area Vocational Technical School
Supt. — None
Northumberland County AVTS   Vo/Tech
1700 W Montgomery St 17866   570-644-0304
James Lewis, prin.

Shamokin Area SD   2,600/PK-12
2000 W State St 17866   570-648-5752
Stephen Curran, supt.   Fax 648-2592
www.indians.k12.pa.us/
Shamokin Area JSHS   1,300/7-12
2000 W State St 17866   570-648-5731
Chris Venna, prin.

Our Lady of Lourdes Regional HS   200/9-12
2001 Clinton Ave 17866   570-644-0375
John McKay, admin.   Fax 644-7655
Queen of Peace MS   200/5-8
821 W Chestnut St 17866   570-644-0502
Sr. Margaret McCullough, prin.   Fax 644-0502

Coatesville, Chester, Pop. 11,221
Area Vocational Technical School
Supt. — None
Center for Arts & Tech - Brandywine   Vo/Tech
1635 E Lincoln Hwy 19320   610-384-1585
Richard Saylor, prin.

Coatesville Area SD   7,300/K-12
545 E Lincoln Hwy 19320   610-466-2400
    Fax 383-1426
www.coatesville.k12.pa.us/
Coatesville Area 9-10 Center   1,300/9-10
1425 E Lincoln Hwy 19320   610-383-3735
Richard Como, prin.   Fax 383-3723
Coatesville Area SHS 11 - 12 Center   1,000/11-12
1445 E Lincoln Hwy 19320   610-383-3730
Richard Como, prin.   Fax 383-3725
North Brandywine MS   600/6-8
256 Reeceville Rd 19320   610-383-3745
Dr. Anthony Irvin, prin.   Fax 383-3749
Scott MS   700/6-8
800 Olive St 19320   610-383-6946
    Fax 383-7110
South Brandywine MS   600/6-8
600 Doe Run Rd 19320   610-383-3750
Orysia Stanko, prin.   Fax 383-3754

Brandywine Hospital   Post-Sec.
201 Reeceville Rd 19320   610-383-9000
Lan-Chester Christian S   100/PK-12
200 Airport Rd 19320   610-383-5784
Dr. Paul Foster, admin.   Fax 383-5894

Cochranton, Crawford, Pop. 1,114
Crawford Central SD
Supt. — See Meadville
Cochranton JSHS   500/7-12
PO Box 127 16314   814-425-7421
Donald K. Wigton, prin.   Fax 425-2071

Collegeville, Montgomery, Pop. 4,564
Perkiomen Valley SD   6,100/K-12
3 Iron Bridge Dr 19426   610-489-8506
Dr. Priscilla Feir, supt.   Fax 489-8574
www.pvsd.org

Perkiomen Valley HS   1,300/9-12
509 Gravel Pike 19426   610-489-1230
John Romanoski, prin.   Fax 489-1921
Other Schools – See Zieglerville

Spring-Ford Area SD   6,000/K-12
199 Bechtel Rd 19426   610-705-6000
Dr. Genevieve Coale, supt.   Fax 705-6245
www.spring-ford.net
Other Schools – See Royersford

Ursinus College   Post-Sec.
PO Box 1000 19426   610-409-3000
Valley Forge Baptist Academy   200/K-12
616 S Trappe Rd 19426   610-792-1884
Lois Rall, prin.

Columbia, Lancaster, Pop. 10,201
Columbia Borough SD   1,500/K-12
98 S 6th St 17512   717-684-2283
Kenneth Klawitter, supt.   Fax 681-2617
www.columbia.k12.pa.us
Columbia JSHS   700/7-12
901 Ironville Pike 17512   717-684-7500
Virginia Babic, prin.   Fax 681-2219

NAWCC School of Horology   Post-Sec.
514 Poplar St 17512   717-684-8261

Commodore, Indiana
Purchase Line SD, PO Box 374 15729   1,200/K-12
Dr. Richard Makin, supt.   724-254-4312
www.plsd.k12.pa.us/
Purchase Line JSHS   600/7-12
PO Box 374 15729   724-254-4312
James Price, prin.

Confluence, Somerset, Pop. 810
Turkeyfoot Valley Area SD   400/K-12
172 Turkeyfoot Rd 15424   814-395-3621
Ron Keefer, supt.   Fax 395-3366
Turkeyfoot Valley Area JSHS   200/7-12
172 Turkeyfoot Rd 15424   814-395-3622
Darlene Sherrard, prin.   Fax 395-3366

Conneaut Lake, Crawford, Pop. 687
Conneaut SD
Supt. — See Linesville
Conneaut Lake JSHS   500/7-12
10331 US Highway 6 16316   814-382-5315
Richard Rossi, prin.   Fax 382-0165

Conneautville, Crawford, Pop. 820
Conneaut SD
Supt. — See Linesville
Conneaut Valley JSHS   400/7-12
22154 State Highway 18 16406   814-587-2091
Kevin Burns, prin.   Fax 587-2094

Connellsville, Fayette, Pop. 8,765
Area Vocational Technical School
Supt. — None
North Fayette County AVTS   Vo/Tech
720 Locust St 15425   724-626-0236
Albert Canaan, prin.

Connellsville Area SD   5,100/K-12
125 N 7th St 15425   724-628-3300
James Duncan, supt.   Fax 628-9002
www.casdfalcons.org
Connellsville Area SHS   1,100/10-12
201 Falcon Dr 15425   724-628-1350
Tammy Duncan, prin.   Fax 628-0280
Connellsville JHS East   700/7-9
710 Locust St 15425   724-628-8910
Charles Geyer, prin.
Connellsville JHS West   500/7-9
215 Falls Ave 15425   724-628-4497
John Schroyer, prin.

Geibel Catholic HS   300/9-12
611 E Crawford Ave 15425   724-628-5600
Vincent Mascia, prin.   Fax 626-5700

Coraopolis, Allegheny, Pop. 5,914
Cornell SD   700/K-12
1099 Maple Street Ext 15108   412-264-5010
Dennis Johnson, supt.   Fax 264-1445
www.cornell.k12.pa.us
Cornell JSHS   300/7-12
1099 Maple Street Ext 15108   412-264-5010
Dr. Erv Weischedel, prin.   Fax 264-1445

Montour SD
Supt. — See Mc Kees Rocks
Williams MS   800/6-8
0 Porters Hollow Rd 15108   412-771-8802
Melissa Santia, prin.   Fax 771-3772

Moon Area SD   3,800/K-12
8353 University Blvd 15108   412-264-9440
Dr. Alexander Meta, supt.   Fax 264-3268
www.masd.k12.pa.us
Other Schools – See Moon Township

Our Lady of Sacred Heart HS   300/9-12
1504 Woodcrest Ave 15108   412-264-5140
Sr. Francine Horos, prin.   Fax 264-4143
Robert Morris University   Post-Sec.
881 Narrows Run Rd 15108   412-262-8200

Corry, Erie, Pop. 6,685
Corry Area SD   2,500/K-12
800 E South St 16407   814-664-4677
Dr. Brian M. Dougherty, supt.   Fax 664-9645
www.corrysd.net
Corry Area HS   800/9-12
534 E Pleasant St 16407   814-665-8297
Kelly Cragg, prin.   Fax 664-3650
Corry MS   400/7-8
534 E Pleasant St 16407   814-665-8297
Gail Swank, prin.   Fax 664-3650

Coudersport, Potter, Pop. 2,641
Coudersport Area SD — 1,000/K-12
  698 Dwight St 16915 — 814-274-9480
  George A. Nuffer, supt. — Fax 274-7551
  www.coudersportschools.com
Coudersport Area JSHS — 500/7-12
  698 Dwight St 16915 — 814-274-8500
  Ernie Kuratomi, prin. — Fax 274-8053

Cranberry Township, Butler

Pittsburgh Technical Institute — Post-Sec.
  850 Cranberry Woods 16066 — 866-233-5556

Cresson, Cambria, Pop. 1,567
Penn-Cambria SD — 1,900/K-12
  201 6th St 16630 — 814-886-8121
  John Augustine, supt. — Fax 886-4809
  www.pcam.org
Penn Cambria HS — 700/9-12
  401 Linden Ave 16630 — 814-886-8188
  Guy A. Monica, prin. — Fax 884-3977
Other Schools – See Gallitzin

Mount Aloysius College — Post-Sec.
  7373 Admiral Peary Hwy 16630 — 814-886-4131

Curwensville, Clearfield, Pop. 2,578
Curwensville Area SD — 1,300/K-12
  650 Beech St 16833 — 814-236-1101
  Norman Hatten, supt. — Fax 236-1103
  www.curwensville.org/
Curwensville Area JSHS — 600/7-12
  650 Beech St 16833 — 814-236-1100
  Alan Nichol, prin. — Fax 236-2392

Dallas, Luzerne, Pop. 2,504
Dallas SD — 2,600/K-12
  PO Box 2000 18612 — 570-674-7221
  Frank P. Galicki, supt. — Fax 674-7295
  www.dallassd.com/
Dallas HS — 800/9-12
  PO Box 2000 18612 — 570-674-7230
  James McGovern, prin. — Fax 674-6843
Dallas MS — 600/6-8
  PO Box 2000 18612 — 570-674-7245
  Anthony Martinelli, prin. — Fax 674-7219

College Misericordia — Post-Sec.
  301 Lake St 18612 — 570-674-6400

Dallastown, York, Pop. 4,067
Dallastown Area SD — 5,300/K-12
  700 New School Ln 17313 — 717-244-4021
  Dr. Stewart Weinberg, supt. — Fax 246-0597
  www.dallastown.net/
Dallastown Area HS — 1,600/9-12
  700 New School Ln 17313 — 717-244-4021
  Dr. Alan Fauth, prin. — Fax 244-8813
Dallastown Area MS — 1,400/6-8
  700 New School Ln 17313 — 717-244-4021
  Dr. Robert Krantz, prin. — Fax 244-0350

Danville, Montour, Pop. 4,711
Danville Area SD — 2,600/K-12
  600 Walnut St 17821 — 570-271-3268
  Steven P. Keifer, supt. — Fax 275-7712
  www.danville.k12.pa.us
Danville Area HS — 800/9-12
  600 Walnut St 17821 — 570-271-3268
  Margaret Auten, prin. — Fax 275-5463
Danville Area MS — 700/6-8
  120 Northumberland St 17821 — 570-271-3268
  Kevin Duckworth, prin. — Fax 275-1281

Geisinger Medical Center — Post-Sec.
  100 N Academy Ave 17822 — 570-271-5200

Darby, Delaware, Pop. 10,136
William Penn SD
  Supt. — See Lansdowne
Penn Wood West JHS — 700/7-9
  121 Summit St 19023 — 610-586-1804
  Dr. Pamela Welmon, prin. — Fax 586-7372

Davidsville, Somerset, Pop. 1,167
Conemaugh Township Area SD — 1,100/K-12
  PO Box 407 15928 — 814-479-7575
  Dr. Joseph DiBartola, supt. — Fax 479-2620
  www.ctasd.org
Conemaugh Township Area JSHS — 600/7-12
  PO Box 407 15928 — 814-479-4014
  David Koba, prin. — Fax 479-2038

Denver, Lancaster, Pop. 3,461
Cocalico SD — 3,500/K-12
  PO Box 800 17517 — 717-336-1413
  Bruce Sensenig, supt. — Fax 336-1415
  www.cocalico.k12.pa.us/
Cocalico HS — 1,100/9-12
  PO Box 800 17517 — 717-336-1421
  Andrew Terry, prin. — Fax 336-1486
Cocalico MS — 900/6-8
  PO Box 800 17517 — 717-336-1471
  Donald Jones, prin. — Fax 336-1482

Derry, Westmoreland, Pop. 2,905
Derry Area SD — 2,700/K-12
  982 N Chestnut Street Ext 15627 — 724-694-1401
  Joseph a. Bellissimo, supt. — Fax 694-1429
  wiu.k12.pa.us/derry
Derry Area HS — 900/9-12
  988 N Chestnut Street Ext 15627 — 724-694-2780
  Kathy Perry, prin. — Fax 694-1489
Derry Area MS — 700/6-8
  994 N Chestnut Street Ext 15627 — 724-694-8231
  David Sroka, prin. — Fax 694-1459

Devon, Chester, Pop. 5,019

Devon Preparatory S — 200/6-12
  363 N Valley Forge Rd 19333 — 610-688-7337
  Rev. James Shea, hdmstr. — Fax 688-2409

Dillsburg, York, Pop. 2,187
Northern York County SD — 3,200/K-12
  149 S Baltimore St 17019 — 717-432-8691
  Brian Small, supt. — Fax 432-1421
  www.northernpolarbears.com
Northern HS — 1,100/9-12
  653 S Baltimore St 17019 — 717-432-8691
  Steve Bowman, prin. — Fax 432-0375
Northern MS — 800/6-8
  655 S Baltimore St 17019 — 717-432-8691
  Sylvia Murray, prin. — Fax 432-5889

Dimock, Susquehanna
Area Vocational Technical School
  Supt. — None
Susquehanna County Career & Tech. Center — Vo/Tech
  PO Box 100 18816 — 570-278-9229
  Alice Davis, dir. — Fax 278-3913

Elk Lake SD — 1,500/K-12
  PO Box 100 18816 — 570-278-1106
  William Bush, supt. — Fax 278-4838
  www.elklakeschool.org
Elk Lake JSHS — 800/7-12
  PO Box 100 18816 — 570-278-1106
  Kenneth Cuomo, prin. — Fax 278-4838

Dingmans Ferry, Pike
Delaware Valley SD
  Supt. — See Milford
Dingman-Delaware MS — 700/6-8
  1365 Route 739 18328 — 570-296-3140
  Joseph Caramanica, prin. — Fax 296-3170

East Stroudsburg Area SD
  Supt. — See East Stroudsburg
East Stroudsburg HS North — 1,100/9-12
  HC 12 Box 690 18328 — 570-588-4420
  Patricia Mulroy, prin. — Fax 588-4421
Lehman IS — 900/6-8
  HC 12 Box 695 18328 — 570-588-4411
  Stephen Zall, prin. — Fax 588-4411

Douglassville, Berks
Daniel Boone Area SD
  Supt. — See Birdsboro
Boone Area MS — 900/6-8
  1845 Weavertown Rd 19518 — 610-689-6300
  Thomas Hankel, prin. — Fax 689-6306

Dover, York, Pop. 1,915
Dover Area SD — 3,500/K-12
  2 School Ln 17315 — 717-292-3671
  Dr. Richard D. Nilsen, supt. — Fax 292-9659
  www.dover.k12.pa.us
Dover Area HS — 1,100/9-12
  46 W Canal St 17315 — 717-292-3671
  Joel Riedel, prin. — Fax 292-7303
Dover Area IS — 600/7-8
  4500 Intermediate Ave 17315 — 717-292-3671
  Kenneth Walter, prin. — Fax 292-9849

Downingtown, Chester, Pop. 7,849
Downingtown Area SD — 10,700/K-12
  126 Wallace Ave 19335 — 610-269-8460
  Dr. Sandra Griffin, supt. — Fax 873-1404
  www.dasd.org
Downingtown HS - West Campus — 1,600/9-12
  445 Manor Ave 19335 — 610-269-4400
  Dr. Tony Watson, prin. — Fax 269-1801
Downingtown MS — 1,300/6-8
  115 Rock Raymond Rd 19335 — 610-518-0685
  Thomas Mulvey, prin. — Fax 518-0685
Other Schools – See Exton

Bishop Shanahan HS — 800/9-12
  220 Woodbine Rd 19335 — 610-518-1300
  Sr. Maureen McDermott, prin. — Fax 343-6228

Doylestown, Bucks, Pop. 8,185
Central Bucks SD — 21,600/K-12
  16 Weldon Dr 18901 — 267-893-2000
  Dr. N. Robert Laws, supt. — Fax 893-5800
  www.cbsd.org
Central Bucks SHS - East — 2,100/10-12
  2804 Holicong Rd, — 267-893-2300
  Dr. A. Joseph Jennelle, prin. — Fax 794-5446
Central Bucks SHS - West — 2,000/10-12
  375 W Court St 18901 — 267-893-2500
  J. Kevin Munnelly, prin. — Fax 348-9832
Holicong MS — 1,100/7-9
  2900 Holicong Rd, — 267-893-2700
  Jason Bucher, prin.
Lenape MS — 800/7-9
  313 W State St 18901 — 267-893-2800
  H. Nicholas Chubb Ed.D., prin. — Fax 345-4699
Tohickon MS — 1,100/7-9
  5051 Old Easton Rd 18901 — 267-893-3300
  John L. Skari, prin. — Fax 893-5819
Other Schools – See Chalfont, Warrington

Delaware Valley College — Post-Sec.
  700 E Butler Ave 18901 — 215-345-1500

Dresher, Montgomery
Upper Dublin SD
  Supt. — See Maple Glen
Sandy Run MS — 1,100/6-8
  520 Twining Rd 19025 — 215-576-3251
  Neil Evans, prin. — Fax 572-3886

Bethel Seminary of the East — Post-Sec.
  1605 Limekiln Pike 19025 — 215-641-4801

Drexel Hill, Delaware, Pop. 29,300
Upper Darby SD — 12,200/K-12
  4611 Bond Ave 19026 — 610-789-7200
  Joseph A. Galli, supt. — Fax 789-8671
  www.udsd.k12.pa.us
Drexel Hill MS, 3001 State Rd 19026 — 1,400/6-8
  Jonathan Ross, prin. — 610-853-4580
Upper Darby HS — 3,900/9-12
  601 N Lansdowne Ave 19026 — 610-622-7000
  Geoffrey Kramer, prin. — Fax 622-7844
Other Schools – See Upper Darby

Archbishop Prendergast HS — 1,000/9-12
  401 N Lansdowne Ave 19026 — 610-259-0265
  Sr. Catherine Robinson, prin. — Fax 259-3676
Monsignor Bonner HS — 1,000/9-12
  403 N Lansdowne Ave 19026 — 610-259-0280
  Dr. Thomas Rooney, prin. — Fax 259-1630

Du Bois, Clearfield, Pop. 8,117
Du Bois Area SD — 4,500/K-12
  500 Liberty Blvd 15801 — 814-371-2700
  Sharon Kirk, supt. — Fax 371-2544
  www.dasd.k12.pa.us
Du Bois Area HS — 1,400/9-12
  425 Orient Ave 15801 — 814-371-8111
  Timothy Glunt, prin. — Fax 371-3928
Du Bois Area MS — 1,100/6-8
  404 Liberty Blvd 15801 — 814-375-8770
  Daniel Hawkins, prin. — Fax 375-8780

DuBois Business College — Post-Sec.
  1 Beaver Dr 15801 — 814-371-6920
Du Bois Central Catholic HS — 200/9-12
  PO Box 567 15801 — 814-371-3060
  Fr. Mark Swoger, hdmstr. — Fax 371-3215
Du Bois Central Catholic MS — 100/6-8
  PO Box 567 15801 — 814-371-3060
  Fr. Mark Swoger, prin. — Fax 371-3215
First Baptist Academy — 100/PK-12
  199 Eastern Ave 15801 — 814-371-7395
  Greg Reese, prin. — Fax 371-7399
PA Academy of Cosmetic Arts & Sciences — Post-Sec.
  19 N Brady St 15801 — 814-371-4151
Pennsylvania State University — Post-Sec.
  College Place 15801 — 814-375-4700
Triangle Tech — Post-Sec.
  PO Box 551 15801 — 814-371-2090

Duke Center, McKean
Otto-Eldred SD — 800/K-12
  143 Sweitzer Dr 16729 — 814-966-3214
  Robert Falk, supt. — Fax 966-3911
  www.ottoeldred.org
Otto-Eldred JSHS — 400/7-12
  143 Sweitzer Dr 16729 — 814-966-3212
  Matthew Splain, prin. — Fax 966-3911

Duncannon, Perry, Pop. 1,476
Susquenita SD — 2,300/K-12
  1725 Schoolhouse Rd 17020 — 717-957-6000
  Kenneth A. Viani, supt. — Fax 834-5523
  www.susq.k12.pa.us/
Susquenita HS — 700/9-12
  1725 Schoolhouse Rd 17020 — 717-957-6000
  Nancy Valdez, prin. — Fax 834-6653
Susquenita MS — 800/5-8
  1725 Schoolhouse Rd 17020 — 717-957-6000
  Steve Blasco, prin. — Fax 957-9334

Duncansville, Blair, Pop. 1,214

Blair County Christian S — 100/PK-12
  PO Box 840 16635 — 814-696-3702
  Jeff Adams, prin. — Fax 696-2783

Dunmore, Lackawanna, Pop. 13,715
Dunmore SD — 1,700/K-12
  300 W Warren St 18512 — 570-343-2110
  Richard McDonald, supt. — Fax 343-1458
  www.dunmoreschooldistrict.net/
Dunmore HS — 500/9-12
  300 W Warren St 18512 — 570-346-2043
  James Forgione, prin. — Fax 343-1458
Dunmore MS — 300/7-8
  300 W Warren St 18512 — 570-346-2043
  John Barrett, prin. — Fax 343-1458

Bishop O'Hara HS — 400/9-12
  501 E Drinker St 18512 — 570-346-7541
  Anita Sirak, prin. — Fax 348-1070
Pennsylvania State University — Post-Sec.
  120 Ridgeview Dr 18512 — 570-963-4757

Duquesne, Allegheny, Pop. 7,116
Duquesne CSD — 900/PK-12
  300 Kennedy Ave 15110 — 412-466-5300
  Jacquelyn D. Webb Ph.D., supt. — Fax 466-7599
Duquesne HS — 200/9-12
  300 Kennedy Ave 15110 — 412-466-0714
  Daniel Stephens, prin. — Fax 466-2197

Cornerstone Leadership Academy — 50/7-12
  PO Box 567 15110 — 412-466-0480
  Audra Moore, prin. — Fax 466-0484

Dushore, Sullivan, Pop. 632
Sullivan County SD — 800/K-12
  PO Box 346 18614 — 570-928-8194
  Dr. Kathryn Gruber, supt. — Fax 928-8196
  www.sulcosd.k12.pa.us
Other Schools – See Laporte

East Greenville, Montgomery, Pop. 3,104
Upper Perkiomen SD — 3,400/K-12
  201 W 5th St 18041 — 215-679-7961
  Dr. Timothy Kirby, supt. — Fax 679-0885
  mciu.org/~upsd/
Upper Perkiomen MS — 1,000/5-8
  510 Jefferson St 18041 — 215-679-6288
  Duane Wickard, prin. — Fax 679-3091
Other Schools – See Pennsburg

Easton, Northampton, Pop. 26,189
Area Vocational Technical School
  Supt. — None
Career Inst of Technology — Vo/Tech
  5335 Kesslersville Rd 18040 — 610-258-2857
  Ronald Rehrig, prin.

Easton Area SD — 8,400/K-12
  811 Northampton St 18042 — 610-250-2400
  Dr. Dennis L. Riker, supt. — Fax 923-8954
  www.eastonsd.org
Easton Area HS — 2,600/9-12
  2601 William Penn Hwy 18045 — 610-250-2481
  William Rider, prin. — Fax 250-2483

Shawnee MS 1,400/7-8
1010 Echo Trl 18040 610-250-2460
Stephen Furst, prin. Fax 250-2613

Wilson Area SD 2,300/K-12
2040 Washington Blvd 18042 484-373-6000
Douglas Wagner, supt. Fax 258-6421
www.wilsonareasd.org
Lauer MS 600/6-8
2400 Firmstone St 18042 484-373-6110
Dennis Harper, prin. Fax 258-4014
Wilson Area HS 700/9-12
424 Warrior Ln 18042 484-373-6030
John Martuscelli, prin. Fax 258-8831

Lafayette College Post-Sec.
High St 18042 610-330-5000
Notre Dame HS 500/9-12
3417 Church Rd 18045 610-868-1431
Joseph Kramer, prin. Fax 868-6710
Rock Christian Academy 50/PK-12
PO Box 636 18044 610-253-8161
Arlene Santos, admin. Fax 250-8794

East Stroudsburg, Monroe, Pop. 10,385
East Stroudsburg Area SD 7,600/K-12
PO Box 298 18301 570-424-8500
Dr. Rachael Heath, supt. Fax 424-5646
www.esasd.net
East Stroudsburg HS South 1,400/9-12
279 N Courtland St 18301 570-424-8471
Irene Duggins, prin. Fax 420-8353
Lambert IS 1,100/6-8
2000 Milford Rd 18301 570-424-8430
Michael Catrillo, prin. Fax 476-0464
Other Schools – See Dingmans Ferry

East Stroudsburg University of PA Post-Sec.
200 Prospect St 18301 570-424-3211
Notre Dame JSHS 300/5-12
60 Spangenburg Ave 18301 570-421-0466
Jeffrey Lyons, prin. Fax 476-0629

Ebensburg, Cambria, Pop. 2,989
Area Vocational Technical School
Supt. — None
Admiral Peary AVTS Vo/Tech
948 Ben Franklin Hwy 15931 814-472-6490
Mark Kudlawiec, prin. Fax 472-6494

Central Cambria SD 1,900/K-12
208 Schoolhouse Rd 15931 814-472-8870
Dr. Susan W. Makosy, supt. Fax 472-9695
www.cchs.k12.pa.us/
Central Cambria HS 700/9-12
204 Schoolhouse Rd 15931 814-472-8860
Kenneth Bussard, prin. Fax 472-8886
Central Cambria MS 400/6-8
205 W Highland Ave 15931 814-472-6505
Kimberly McDermott, prin. Fax 472-4187

Bishop Carroll HS 300/9-12
728 Ben Franklin Hwy 15931 814-472-7500
Deborah Meckey, prin. Fax 472-8020
Pennsylvania Institute of Taxidermy Post-Sec.
118 Industrial Park Rd 15931 814-472-4510
Wrightco Technologies Tech Training Inst Post-Sec.
728 Ben Franklin Hwy 15931 814-472-5211

Edinboro, Erie, Pop. 7,073
General McLane SD 2,500/K-12
11771 Edinboro Rd 16412 814-734-1033
Alan J. Karns, supt. Fax 734-4635
www.generalmclane.org
McLane HS 900/9-12
11761 Edinboro Rd 16412 814-734-1602
Richard Scaletta, prin. Fax 734-5250
Parker MS 800/5-8
11781 Edinboro Rd 16412 814-734-1151
Annette Rilling, prin. Fax 734-7485

Edinboro University of Pennsylvania Post-Sec.
16444 814-732-2000

Elderton, Armstrong, Pop. 352
Armstrong SD
Supt. — See Ford City
Elderton JSHS 400/7-12
Lytle St 15736 724-354-2153
David Kristofic, prin. Fax 354-4303

Elizabeth, Allegheny, Pop. 1,559
Elizabeth Forward SD 2,900/K-12
401 Rock Run Rd 15037 412-896-2300
Paul Mueller, supt. Fax 751-9483
www.efsd.net
Elizabeth Forward HS 1,000/9-12
1000 Weigles Hill Rd 15037 412-896-2349
Dr. David Bowlin, prin. Fax 384-2030
Elizabeth Forward MS 800/6-8
401 Rock Run Rd 15037 412-896-2335
Jennifer Melliton, prin. Fax 751-6669

Elizabethtown, Lancaster, Pop. 11,898
Elizabethtown Area SD 4,000/K-12
600 E High St 17022 717-367-1521
Dr. Allan Thrush, supt. Fax 367-1920
www.etown.k12.pa.us
Elizabethtown Area HS 1,300/9-12
600 E High St 17022 717-367-1533
Richard Schwarzman, prin. Fax 367-4149
Elizabethtown Area MS 900/6-8
600 E High St 17022 717-361-7525
Richard Schwarzman, prin. Fax 361-2597

Elizabethtown College Post-Sec.
1 Alpha Dr 17022 717-361-1000
Mt. Calvary Christian S 400/PK-12
629 Holly St 17022 717-367-1649
Kenneth Howard, admin. Fax 367-5672

Elizabethville, Dauphin, Pop. 1,313
Upper Dauphin Area SD
Supt. — See Lykens
Upper Dauphin Area HS 400/9-12
220 N Church St 17023 717-362-8181
Timothy Foley, prin. Fax 362-8088

Elkins Park, Montgomery, Pop. 4,700
Cheltenham Township SD 4,700/K-12
1000 Ashbourne Rd 19027 215-886-9500
Christopher McGinley, supt. Fax 884-3029
www.cheltenham.org
Other Schools – See Wyncote

Medical College Hospitals Post-Sec.
60 Township Line Rd 19027 215-663-6150
Pennsylvania College of Optometry Post-Sec.
8360 Old York Rd 19027 215-780-1400
Temple University Tyler School of Art Post-Sec.
7725 Penrose Ave 19027 215-782-2875

Elkland, Tioga, Pop. 1,739
Northern Tioga SD 2,600/K-12
117 Coates Ave 16920 814-258-5642
Timothy Bowers, supt. Fax 258-7083
www.ntiogasd.org
Elkland Area JSHS 300/7-12
110 Ellison Rd 16920 814-258-5115
Thomas Butler, prin. Fax 258-7700
Other Schools – See Tioga, Westfield

Elliottsburg, Perry
West Perry SD 2,900/K-12
2606 Shermans Valley Rd 17024 717-789-3934
Dr. David R. Hoover, supt. Fax 789-4997
www2.pa.net/wpsd
West Perry HS 900/9-12
2608 Shermans Valley Rd 17024 717-789-3931
Fax 789-2110
West Perry MS 700/6-8
2620 Shermans Valley Rd 17024 717-789-3012
Bernard Danko, prin. Fax 789-3393

Ellsworth, Washington, Pop. 1,052
Bentworth SD
Supt. — See Bentleyville
Bentworth MS 200/7-8
89 Pine St 15331 724-239-4431
Kevin Fortuna, prin. Fax 239-5889

Ellwood City, Lawrence, Pop. 8,386
Ellwood City Area SD 2,200/K-12
501 Crescent Ave 16117 724-752-1591
Frank P. Aloi, supt. Fax 752-0743
www.ellwood.k12.pa.us
Lincoln JSHS 1,100/7-12
501 Crescent Ave 16117 724-752-1591
Joseph Mancini, prin. Fax 752-0743

Riverside Beaver County SD 1,400/K-12
318 Country Club Dr 16117 724-758-7512
Dr. David J. Parry, supt. Fax 758-2070
www.riverside.k12.pa.us
Riverside HS 700/9-12
300 Country Club Dr 16117 724-758-7512
Dr. Janice Dunmire, prin. Fax 758-7519
Riverside MS 300/7-8
302 Country Club Dr 16117 724-758-7512
Raymond Santillo, prin. Fax 758-0919

Elverson, Chester, Pop. 1,107
Twin Valley SD 3,200/K-12
4851 N Twin Valley Rd 19520 610-286-8611
Judith Funk, supt. Fax 286-8608
www.tvsd.org
Twin Valley HS 1,000/9-12
4897 N Twin Valley Rd 19520 610-286-8600
Steven Gerhard, prin. Fax 286-8604
Twin Valley MS 800/6-8
970 Clymer Hill Rd 19520 610-286-8660
Kim Donahue, prin. Fax 286-8662

Emmaus, Lehigh, Pop. 11,243
East Penn SD 6,900/K-12
800 Pine St 18049 610-966-8300
Dr. George Ziolkowski, supt. Fax 966-8339
www.eastpenn.k12.pa.us/
Emmaus HS 2,400/9-12
500 N Macungie St 18049 610-966-1651
Elizabeth Drake, prin.
Other Schools – See Macungie

Emporium, Cameron, Pop. 2,419
Cameron County SD 1,000/K-12
601 Woodland Ave 15834 814-486-4000
Dr. Stephen Bugaj, supt. Fax 486-1721
www.cameroncountyschools.org/
Cameron County JSHS 500/7-12
601 Woodland Ave 15834 814-486-4000
Myron Crumrine, prin. Fax 486-3643

Enola, Cumberland, Pop. 5,961
East Pennsboro Area SD 2,800/K-12
890 Valley St 17025 717-732-3601
Dr. Linda Bigos, supt. Fax 732-8927
www.epasd.k12.pa.us
East Pennsboro Area HS 900/9-12
425 W Shady Ln 17025 717-732-0723
Craig Robbins, prin. Fax 732-8932
East Pennsboro Area MS 900/5-8
529 N Enola Dr 17025 717-732-0771
Stephen Andrejack, prin.

Ephrata, Lancaster, Pop. 13,158
Ephrata Area SD 4,200/K-12
803 Oak Blvd 17522 717-721-1400
Dr. Gerald B. Rosati, supt. Fax 733-1841
easdpa.org
Ephrata HS, 803 Oak Blvd 17522 1,400/9-12
Charles Doll, prin. 717-721-1478
Ephrata MS 1,000/6-8
957 Hammon Ave 17522 717-721-1468
Kevin Fillgrove, prin. Fax 738-1930
Washington Educational Center Adult
26 Marshall St 17522 717-721-1150
Paul Murr, dir. Fax 721-1152

Farmersville Mennonite S 100/1-10
65 E Farmersville Rd 17522 717-354-5070
James Nolt, prin.
Grandview Heights Christian Academy 100/K-12
110 Durlach Rd 17522 717-738-0895
Jeanne Weber, prin. Fax 738-1002
Pleasant Valley Mennonite S 200/1-12
144 Pleasant Valley Rd 17522 717-738-1833
Larry Weaver, prin. Fax 738-3941

Erdenheim, Montgomery
Springfield Township SD
Supt. — See Oreland
Springfield Township HS 900/8-12
1801 Paper Mill Rd 19038 215-233-6000
Joseph Roy, prin. Fax 233-0691

Antonelli Institute - Art & Photography Post-Sec.
300 Montgomery Ave 19038 215-836-2222
Philadelphia-Montgomery Christian Acad. 300/6-12
35 Hillcrest Rd 19038 215-233-0782
Tom Sorkness, prin. Fax 233-0829

Erie, Erie, Pop. 101,373
Area Vocational Technical School
Supt. — None
City of Erie Regional Career & Tech S Vo/Tech
3325 Cherry St 16508 814-874-6225
David Kranking, dir.
Erie County Technical S Vo/Tech
8500 Oliver Rd 16509 814-864-0641
Aldo Jackson Ph.D., dir. Fax 864-9400

Erie CSD 13,600/K-12
148 W 21st St 16502 814-874-6000
Dr. James Barker, supt. Fax 874-6010
esd.iu5.org/
Central HS 1,300/9-12
3325 Cherry St 16508 814-874-6200
Gerald Mifsud, prin. Fax 874-6207
East HS 1,000/9-12
1001 Atkins St 16503 814-874-6400
Thomas James, prin. Fax 874-6407
Northwest Pennsylvania Collegiate Acad 9-12
2825 State St 16508 814-874-6300
Lori Gornall, dean Fax 874-6305
Roosevelt MS 700/6-8
2300 Cranberry St 16502 814-874-6800
Ina Fisher, prin. Fax 874-6807
Vincent HS 700/9-12
1330 W 8th St 16502 814-874-6500
Kenneth Brasington, prin. Fax 874-6507
Wilson MS 800/6-8
718 E 28th St 16504 814-874-6600
Pat Dean, prin. Fax 874-6607
Adult Learning Center Adult
444 W 18th St 16502 814-874-6175
David Kranking, prin. Fax 874-6117

Iroquois SD 1,200/K-12
4231 Morse St 16511 814-899-7643
Joseph Buzanowski Ed.D., supt. Fax 898-2099
Iroquois JSHS 600/7-12
4301 Main St 16511 814-899-7643
Brian Uplinger, prin. Fax 898-4105

Millcreek Township SD 7,100/K-12
3740 W 26th St 16506 814-835-5300
Dr. Dean Maynard, supt. Fax 835-5371
www.mtsd.org
McDowell Intermediate HS 1,200/9-10
3320 Caughey Rd 16506 814-835-5487
Thomas Maciulewicz, prin. Fax 835-5417
McDowell SHS 1,100/11-12
3580 W 38th St 16506 814-835-5403
Timothy Rankin, prin. Fax 835-5521
Westlake MS 500/6-8
4330 W Lake Rd 16505 814-835-5756
Marty Kaverman, prin. Fax 835-5770
Wilson MS 600/6-8
900 W 54th St 16509 814-835-5569
David Koma, prin. Fax 835-5582
Other Schools – See Fairview

Wattsburg Area SD 1,700/K-12
10782 Wattsburg Rd 16509 814-824-3400
Frank Bova, supt. Fax 824-5200
www.wattsburg.org/
Seneca HS 600/9-12
10770 Wattsburg Rd 16509 814-824-3400
Tom Rinke, prin. Fax 825-2262
Wattsburg Area MS 500/5-8
10774 Wattsburg Rd 16509 814-824-3400
Kenneth Berlin, prin. Fax 825-6337

Bethel Christian S of Erie 100/K-12
1781 W 38th St 16508 814-868-2365
Dennis Gillenwater, prin. Fax 864-7674
Cathedral Prep HS 600/9-12
225 W 9th St 16501 814-453-7737
Rev. Scott Jabo, hdmstr. Fax 455-5462
Erie Business Center Post-Sec.
246 W 9th St 16501 814-456-7504
Erie Institute of Technology Post-Sec.
5539 Peach St 16509 814-868-9900
First Assembly Christian Academy 400/PK-12
8150 Oliver Rd 16509 814-866-6979
John D. Richardson, admin. Fax 866-5829
Gannon University Post-Sec.
109 University Sq 16541 814-871-7000
GECAC Training Institute Post-Sec.
1006 W 10th St 16502 814-451-5610
Great Lakes Institute of Technology Post-Sec.
5100 Peach St 16509 814-864-6666
Lake Erie College\Osteopathic Medicine Post-Sec.
1858 W Grandview Blvd 16509 814-866-6641
Mercyhurst College Post-Sec.
501 E 38th St 16546 814-824-2000
Mercyhurst Prep S 800/9-12
538 E Grandview Blvd 16504 814-824-2210
Margaret Aste, prin. Fax 824-3638
Pennsylvania State University Post-Sec.
5091 Station Rd 16563 814-898-6000
Toni & Guy Hairdressing Academy Post-Sec.
930 Peach St 16501 800-775-4187
Triangle Tech Post-Sec.
2000 Liberty St 16502 814-453-6016
Tri-State Business Institute Post-Sec.
5757 W Ridge Rd 16506 814-838-7673

Villa Maria Academy
2403 W 8th St 16505
Cynthia Martone, prin.
600/9-12
814-838-2061
Fax 836-0881

Everett, Bedford, Pop. 1,912
Area Vocational Technical School
Supt. — None
Bedford Co. Technical Center
195 Pennknoll Rd 15537
Allen Sell, prin.
Vo/Tech
814-623-2760
Fax 623-7234

Everett Area SD
427 E South St 15537
Rodney L. Green, supt.
everett.k12.pa.us
Everett Area JSHS
1 Renaissance Cir 15537
Jonathan Donelson, prin.
1,500/K-12
814-652-9114
Fax 652-6191

800/7-12
814-652-9114
Fax 652-0107

Exeter, Luzerne, Pop. 6,023
Wyoming Area SD
20 Memorial St 18643
Raymond J. Bernardi, supt.
www.wyomingarea.org
Wyoming Area JSHS
20 Memorial St 18643
Vito Quaglia, prin.
2,600/K-12
570-655-3733
Fax 883-1280

1,300/7-12
570-655-2836
Fax 883-1280

Exton, Chester, Pop. 2,550
Downingtown Area SD
Supt. — See Downingtown
Downingtown HS - East Campus
50 Devon Dr 19341
Linwood Smith, prin.
Lionville MS
550 W Uwchlan Ave 19341
Judy Groh, prin.
1,500/9-12
610-363-6400
Fax 903-1047
1,400/6-8
610-524-6300
Fax 524-0152

Automotive Training Center
114 Pickering Way 19341
CFS the School at Church Farm
1001 Lancaster Ave 19341
Post-Sec.
610-363-6716
200/7-12
610-363-7500
Fax 363-5367
Universal Technical Institute
750 Pennsylvania Dr 19341
Post-Sec.
877-884-3986

Factoryville, Wyoming, Pop. 1,160
Lackawanna Trail SD
PO Box 85 18419
Robert Jurbala, supt.
Lackawanna Trail JSHS
PO Box 85 18419
Matthew Rakauskas, prin.
1,400/K-12
570-945-5184
Fax 945-3154
700/7-12
570-945-5181
Fax 945-3832

New Hope Academy
PO Box 295 18419
Nick Gatoura, prin.
50/8-12
570-945-0161
Fax 945-0163

Fairfield, Adams, Pop. 499
Fairfield Area SD
4840 Fairfield Rd 17320
Dr. Gary A. Miller, supt.
www.fairfieldpaschools.org/
Fairfield Area HS
4840 Fairfield Rd 17320
Wayne Sherrard, prin.
Fairfield Area MS
4840 Fairfield Rd 17320
Beth Bender, prin.
1,300/K-12
717-642-8228
Fax 642-2036

400/9-12
717-642-8228
Fax 642-2004
400/5-8
717-642-8228
Fax 642-2005

Fairless Hills, Bucks, Pop. 9,026
Area Vocational Technical School
Supt. — None
Bucks County Technical HS
610 Wistar Rd 19030
Scott Parks, prin.
Vo/Tech
215-949-1700

Bristol Township SD
Supt. — See Levittown
Armstrong MS
475 Wistar Rd 19030
Larry Funk, prin.
1,000/7-9
215-945-4940
Fax 945-1664

Pennsbury SD
Supt. — See Levittown
Pennsbury HS East
705 Hood Blvd 19030
William Katz, prin.
Pennsbury HS West
608 S Olds Blvd 19030
Lisa Becker, prin.
1,700/11-12
215-949-6700
Fax 949-3896
1,700/9-10
215-949-6780
Fax 949-6857

Conwell-Egan HS
611 Wistar Rd 19030
Maryjane McHugh, prin.
Faith Baptist Christian Academy
1515 Wistar Rd 19030
Dr. Mae Dunkley, prin.
1,400/9-12
215-945-6200
Fax 945-6206
100/PK-12
215-946-2100

Fairview, Erie, Pop. 216
Fairview SD
7460 McCray Rd 16415
Larry D. Kessler, supt.
www.fairviewschools.org/
Fairview HS
7460 McCray Rd 16415
Sam Signorio, prin.
Fairview MS
4967 Avonia Rd 16415
James Logue, prin.
1,600/K-12
814-474-2600
Fax 474-5497

500/9-12
814-474-2600
Fax 474-1367
500/5-8
814-474-2600
Fax 474-1640

Millcreek Township SD
Supt. — See Erie
Walnut Creek MS
5901 Sterrettania Rd 16415
Timothy Stoops, prin.
600/6-8
814-835-5700
Fax 835-5710

Farrell, Mercer, Pop. 5,959
Farrell Area SD
1600 Roemer Blvd 16121
Richard R. Rubano, supt.
www.farrellareaschools.com
Farrell Area MSHS
1700 Roemer Blvd 16121
Lee Vincent McFerren, prin.
1,000/PK-12
724-346-6585
Fax 346-0223

500/7-12
724-346-6585
Fax 346-2381

Fawn Grove, York, Pop. 457
South Eastern SD
104 E Main St 17321
Thomas C. McShane, supt.
www.sesdweb.net/
Kennard-Dale HS
393 Main St 17321
John Sengia, prin.
South Eastern MS - East
375 Main St 17321
Kathleen Harvey, prin.
3,300/K-12
717-382-4843
Fax 382-4769

900/9-12
717-382-4871
Fax 382-4869
600/7-8
717-382-4851
Fax 382-9033

Feasterville, Bucks, Pop. 6,696
Neshaminy SD
Supt. — See Langhorne
Poquessing MS
300 Heights Ln 19053
Ron Sayre, prin.
700/6-9
215-322-0350

Bucks County School of Beauty Culture
1761 Bustleton Pike 19053
Post-Sec.
215-322-0666

Finleyville, Washington, Pop. 448
Ringgold SD
Supt. — See New Eagle
Finley MS
6023 State Route 88 15332
Wendy Burke, prin.
600/6-8
724-348-7154
Fax 348-8839

Fishertown, Bedford
Chestnut Ridge SD
3281 Valley Rd 15539
Dr. Thomas Otis, supt.
lion.crsd.k12.pa.us
Chestnut Ridge MS
3281 Valley Rd 15539
David R. Goodin, prin.
Other Schools – See New Paris
1,800/K-12
814-839-4195
Fax 839-2088

600/5-8
814-839-4195
Fax 839-2088

Fleetwood, Berks, Pop. 3,971
Fleetwood Area SD
801 N Richmond St 19522
Dr. Paul B. Eaken, supt.
www.fleetwoodasd.k12.pa.us
Fleetwood Area HS
803 N Richmond St 19522
Robert Dziedzic, prin.
Fleetwood Area MS
407 N Richmond St 19522
Christopher Redding, prin.
2,600/K-12
610-944-9598
Fax 944-9408

800/9-12
610-944-7656
Fax 944-6952
900/5-8
610-944-7634
Fax 944-5307

Flinton, Cambria
Glendale SD
1466 Beaver Valley Rd 16640
Dr. Dennis Bruno, supt.
www.gsd1.org
Glendale JSHS
1466 Beaver Valley Rd 16640
Gary Walstrom, prin.
900/K-12
814-687-3402
Fax 687-3341

500/7-12
814-687-4261
Fax 687-4718

Flourtown, Montgomery, Pop. 4,754

Mt. St. Joseph Academy
120 W Wissahickon Ave 19031
Sr. Karen Dietrich, prin.
500/9-12
215-233-3177
Fax 233-4734

Fogelsville, Lehigh

Pennsylvania State University
8380 Mohr Ln 18051
Post-Sec.
610-285-5000

Folcroft, Delaware, Pop. 6,933
Area Vocational Technical School
Supt. — None
Delaware County Technical HS - Folcroft
701 Henderson Blvd 19032
Dr. Darla Glantz, prin.
Vo/Tech
610-583-7620
Fax 583-6537

Southeast Delco SD
1560 Delmar Dr 19032
Dr. Trudie Bennett, supt.
www.sedelco.k12.pa.us
Other Schools – See Sharon Hill
4,500/K-12
610-522-4300
Fax 461-4874

Folsom, Delaware, Pop. 8,173
Ridley SD
901 Morton Ave Ste 100 19033
Dr. Nicholas Ignatuk, supt.
www.ridleysd.k12.pa.us
Ridley HS
901 Morton Ave 19033
William E. Mills, prin.
Other Schools – See Ridley Park
5,600/K-12
610-534-1900
Fax 534-2335

2,000/9-12
610-237-8034
Fax 534-2335

Ford City, Armstrong, Pop. 3,340
Area Vocational Technical School
Supt. — None
Lenape Tech S
2215 Chaplin Ave 16226
Dawn Kocher-Taylor, prin.
Vo/Tech
724-763-7116

Armstrong SD
410 Main St 16226
Dr. William Kerr, supt.
www.asd.k12.pa.us
Ford City JSHS
1100 4th Ave 16226
Timothy Sedgwick, prin.
Other Schools – See Elderton, Kittanning, Rural Valley
6,500/K-12
724-763-7151
Fax 763-7295

800/7-12
724-763-5289
Fax 763-7813

Forest City, Susquehanna, Pop. 1,795
Forest City Regional SD
100 Susquehanna St 18421
Dr. Robert Vadella, supt.
www.forestcityschool.org/
Forest City Regional JSHS
100 Susquehanna St 18421
Anthony Rusnak, prin.
900/PK-12
570-785-2400
Fax 785-9557

400/7-12
570-785-2402
Fax 785-9557

Fort Washington, Montgomery, Pop. 3,699
Upper Dublin SD
Supt. — See Maple Glen
Upper Dublin HS
800 Loch Alsh Ave 19034
Charles Rittenhouse, prin.
1,500/9-12
215-643-8900
Fax 643-0229

DeVry University
1140 Virginia Dr 19034
Germantown Academy
PO Box 287 19034
James Connor, prin.
Post-Sec.
215-591-5700
1,100/PK-12
215-646-3300
Fax 646-1216

Forty Fort, Luzerne, Pop. 4,399

Allied Medical & Technical Institute
166 Slocum St 18704
Post-Sec.
570-288-8400

Foxburg, Clarion, Pop. 269
Allegheny-Clarion Valley SD
PO Box 100 16036
Dr. Patrick Lukasavich, supt.
www.acvsd.org/
Allegheny-Clarion Valley JSHS
PO Box 345 16036
Robert Collett, prin.
1,000/K-12
724-659-5820
Fax 659-2963

500/7-12
724-659-4661
Fax 659-4774

Frackville, Schuylkill, Pop. 4,235
Area Vocational Technical School
Supt. — None
Schuylkill Technology Center - North
101 Technology Dr 17931
Vo/Tech
570-874-1034
Fax 874-4028

Franklin, Venango, Pop. 7,397
Franklin Area SD
417 13th St 16323
Ronald Paranick, supt.
www.fasd.k12.pa.us/
Franklin Area HS
246 Pone Ln 16323
William Vonada, prin.
Franklin Area MS
246 Pone Ln 16323
Dale Ishman, prin.
2,300/K-12
814-432-8917
Fax 437-5754

800/9-12
814-432-2121
Fax 432-5031
400/7-8
814-432-2224
Fax 437-1491

Valley Grove SD
429 Wiley Ave 16323
Jeffrey A. Clark, supt.
Rocky Grove JSHS
403 Rocky Grove Ave 16323
1,000/K-12
814-432-4919
Fax 437-1243
500/7-12
814-437-3759
Fax 437-1062

Fredericksburg, Lebanon, Pop. 3,607
Northern Lebanon SD
PO Box 100 17026
Dr. Don Bell, supt.
www.norleb.k12.pa.us
Northern Lebanon HS
PO Box 100 17026
David Woods, prin.
Northern Lebanon MS
PO Box 100 17026
David Yavoich, prin.
2,000/K-12
717-865-2117
Fax 865-0606

800/9-12
717-865-2117
Fax 865-7818
7-8
717-865-2117
Fax 865-5835

Fredericktown, Washington, Pop. 1,237
Bethlehem-Center SD
194 Crawford Rd 15333
Vicki L. Monas, supt.
www.bc.k12.pa.us
Bethlehem-Center HS
179 Crawford Rd 15333
Dr. Richard Martin, prin.
Bethlehem-Center MS
136 Crawford Rd 15333
Rick Showalter, prin.
1,400/K-12
724-267-4910
Fax 267-4904

400/9-12
724-267-4944
Fax 267-4907
300/6-8
724-267-4935
Fax 267-4937

Freedom, Beaver, Pop. 1,695
Ambridge Area SD
Supt. — See Ambridge
Ambridge Area JHS
401 1st St 15042
Megan Mealie, prin.
500/7-8
724-266-2833
Fax 869-5321

Freedom Area SD
1701 8th Ave 15042
Dr. Ronald Sofo, supt.
www.freedom.k12.pa.us
Freedom Area HS
1190 Bulldog Dr 15042
Dr. Robert Staub, prin.
Freedom Area MS
1701 8th Ave 15042
Dr. William Renko, prin.
1,800/K-12
724-775-7644
Fax 775-7434

600/9-12
724-775-7400
Fax 775-7753
600/5-8
724-775-7641
Fax 775-7748

Freeland, Luzerne, Pop. 3,507

MMI Prep S
154 Centre St 18224
William Shergalis Ph.D., pres.
200/6-12
570-636-1108
Fax 636-0742

Freeport, Armstrong, Pop. 1,899
Freeport Area SD
Supt. — See Sarver
Freeport Area JHS
325 4th St 16229
Robert Isenberg, prin.
300/7-8
724-295-9020
Fax 295-4630

Galeton, Potter, Pop. 1,345
Galeton Area SD
25 Bridge St 16922
Terry J. Erway, supt.
www.gasd.net
Galeton Area S
25 Bridge St 16922
Kay Stuart, prin.
500/PK-12
814-435-6571
Fax 435-6981

500/PK-12
814-435-6571
Fax 435-6981

Gallitzin, Cambria, Pop. 1,697
Penn-Cambria SD
Supt. — See Cresson
Penn Cambria MS
401 Division St 16641
Cathy Adams, prin.
500/6-8
814-886-4181
Fax 886-9308

Gap, Lancaster, Pop. 1,226

Fairhaven Christian S
1031 Simmontown Rd 17527
Curtis Stoltzfus, prin.
100/1-12
717-442-9840

Geigertown, Berks

High Point Baptist Academy 300/PK-12
200 Chapel Rd 19523 610-286-5942
Ken Lang, prin. Fax 286-7525

Gettysburg, Adams, Pop. 7,825
Gettysburg Area SD 3,400/K-12
900 Biglerville Rd 17325 717-334-6254
Dr. David Mowery, supt. Fax 334-5220
www.gettysburg.k12.pa.us
Gettysburg Area HS 1,200/9-12
1130 Old Harrisburg Rd 17325 717-334-6254
Richard Gulas, prin. Fax 334-9190
Gettysburg Area MS 800/6-8
37 Lefever St 17325 717-334-6254
Steven Litten, prin. Fax 334-6999

Adams County Christian Academy 100/PK-12
1865 Biglerville Rd 17325 717-334-9177
Kimberly Mentzer, admin. Fax 334-7691
Freedom Christian S 100/K-12
3185 York Rd 17325 717-624-3884
Karen Trout, admin. Fax 624-1562
Gettysburg College Post-Sec.
300 N Washington St 17325 717-337-6000
Lutheran Theological Seminary Post-Sec.
61 Seminary Rdg 17325 717-334-6286

Gibsonia, Allegheny, Pop. 3,500
Pine-Richland SD 3,700/K-12
702 Warrendale Rd 15044 724-625-7773
Dr. James Manley, supt. Fax 625-1490
www.pinerichland.org
Pine-Richland HS 1,100/9-12
700 Warrendale Rd 15044 724-625-4444
Dr. Laura Davis, prin. Fax 625-4640
Pine-Richland MS 900/6-8
100 Logan Rd 15044 724-625-3111
Dr. Kathleen Harrington, prin. Fax 625-3144

Aquinas Academy 200/K-12
2308 W Hardies Rd 15044 724-444-0722
Leslie Mitros, hdmstr. Fax 444-0750

Gilbertsville, Montgomery, Pop. 3,994
Boyertown Area SD
Supt. — See Boyertown
Boyertown Area JHS East 800/7-9
2020 Big Rd 19525 610-754-9550
Andrew Ruppert, prin.

Girard, Erie, Pop. 3,082
Girard SD 2,000/K-12
1135 Lake St 16417 814-774-5666
Dr. James Tracy, supt. Fax 774-4220
www.gsd.k12.pa.us
Girard HS 600/9-12
1135 Lake St 16417 814-774-5607
Gregg McClelland, prin. Fax 774-2239
Rice Avenue MS 700/5-8
1100 Rice Ave 16417 814-774-5604
Dave Koma, prin. Fax 774-5259

Girard Alliance Christian Academy 100/K-12
229 Rice Ave 16417 814-774-9537
Karen Brumagin, admin. Fax 774-2552

Glen Mills, Delaware
Garnet Valley SD, 80 Station Rd 19342 4,000/K-12
Dr. Anthony Costello, supt. 610-579-7300
www.garnetvalleyschools.com/
Garnet Valley HS 1,100/9-12
552 Smithbridge Rd 19342 610-579-7745
Dr. Joseph Hook, prin.
Garnet Valley MS 1,000/6-8
601 Smithbridge Rd 19342 610-579-5100
Michael Christian, prin.

Glen Rock, York, Pop. 1,809
Southern York County SD 3,300/K-12
PO Box 128 17327 717-235-4811
Thomas Hensley, supt. Fax 235-0863
www.syc.k12.pa.us
Southern MS 600/7-8
PO Box 128 17327 717-235-4811
Kevin L. Helmeczi, prin. Fax 227-9681
Susquehannock HS 1,100/9-12
PO Box 128 17327 717-235-4811
Brian Cashman, prin. Fax 227-1951

Glenshaw, Allegheny
Shaler Area SD 5,600/K-12
1800 Mount Royal Blvd 15116 412-492-1200
Donald Lee, supt. Fax 492-1293
www.sasd.k12.pa.us
Shaler Area IS 1,000/8-9
1810 Mount Royal Blvd 15116 412-492-1200
David McQuade, prin. Fax 492-1237
Other Schools – See Pittsburgh

Glenside, Montgomery, Pop. 8,704

Arcadia University Post-Sec.
450 S Easton Rd 19038 215-572-2900
LaSalle College HS 900/9-12
8605 Cheltenham Ave 19038 215-233-2911
Joseph Marchese, prin. Fax 233-1418
Princeton Information Technology Center Post-Sec.
137 S Easton Rd 19038 215-576-7377
Won Institute of Graduate Studies Post-Sec.
137 S Easton Rd 19038 215-884-8942

Grantham, Cumberland

Messiah College Post-Sec.
1 S College Ave 17027 717-766-2511

Greencastle, Franklin, Pop. 3,736
Greencastle-Antrim SD 2,700/K-12
500 Leitersburg St 17225 717-597-2187
Dr. Preston D. Rearick, supt. Fax 597-2180
www.greencastle.k12.pa.us

Greencastle-Antrim HS 900/9-12
300 S Ridge Ave 17225 717-597-2186
Edward Rife, prin. Fax 597-2912
Greencastle-Antrim MS 700/6-8
370 S Ridge Ave 17225 717-597-2185
Linda Lewis, prin. Fax 597-6468

Green Lane, Montgomery, Pop. 593

Intl Academy of Advanced Reflexology Post-Sec.
1701 Snyder Rd 18054 215-234-0307

Greensboro, Greene, Pop. 285
Southeastern Green SD 700/K-12
1000 Mapletown Rd 15338 724-943-3630
Dr. Philip J. Savini, supt. Fax 943-3052
Mapletown JSHS 300/7-12
1000 Mapletown Rd 15338 724-943-3401
Richard Hauger, prin. Fax 943-4769

Greensburg, Westmoreland, Pop. 15,525
Greensburg-Salem SD 3,500/K-12
1 Academy Hill Pl 15601 724-832-2901
Thomas Kameral, supt. Fax 832-2968
www.greensburgsalem.org
Greensburg-Salem HS 1,200/9-12
65 Mennel Dr 15601 724-832-2960
Dr. Lisa Mason, prin. Fax 832-2971
Greensburg-Salem MS 900/6-8
301 N Main St 15601 724-832-2930
Tammy Wolicki, prin. Fax 832-2939

Hempfield Area SD 6,700/K-12
4347 State Route 136 15601 724-834-2590
Dr. Wayne Doyle, supt. Fax 837-8681
www.hempfieldarea.k12.pa.us
Harrold MS 600/6-8
1368 Middletown Rd 15601 724-850-2301
Rebecca Gardner, prin. Fax 850-2302
Hempfield Area HS 2,100/9-12
4345 State Route 136 15601 724-834-9000
Kathy Charlton, prin. Fax 850-2090
Wendover MS 500/6-8
425 Wendover Jr High Rd 15601 724-838-4070
Deanna Mikesic, prin. Fax 838-4071
Other Schools – See Irwin

Dominion Christian Academy 50/K-12
PO Box 1611 15601 724-830-8100
Roy Smith, admin. Fax 830-8105
Greensburg Central Catholic HS 600/9-12
901 Armory Dr 15601 724-834-0310
Terry Meehan, prin. Fax 834-2472
Seton Hill University Post-Sec.
Seton Hill Dr 15601 724-834-2200
Triangle Tech Post-Sec.
222 E Pittsburgh St # A 15601 724-832-1050
University of Pittsburgh Post-Sec.
1150 Mount Pleasant Rd 15601 724-837-7040
Westmoreland Christian Academy 100/PK-12
122 Elgin Dr 15601 724-853-8308
Dr. David Erdman, admin. Fax 853-8308

Greenville, Mercer, Pop. 6,434
Greenville Area SD 1,600/K-12
9 Donation Rd 16125 724-588-2502
Dr. Patricia M. Homer, supt. Fax 588-5024
www.greenville.k12.pa.us
Greenville JSHS 800/7-12
9 Donation Rd 16125 724-588-2500
Stephen K. Ross, prin. Fax 588-4397

Reynolds SD 1,500/K-12
531 Reynolds Rd 16125 724-646-3240
Maddox B. Stokes Ph.D., supt. Fax 646-3243
www.reynolds.k12.pa.us
Reynolds JSHS 800/7-12
531 Reynolds Rd 16125 724-646-3221
Joseph A. Torck, prin. Fax 646-3266

Thiel College Post-Sec.
75 College Ave 16125 724-589-2000

Grove City, Mercer, Pop. 7,801
Grove City Area SD 3,100/K-12
511 Highland Ave 16127 724-458-6733
Dr. Robert Post, supt. Fax 458-5868
www.grovecity.k12.pa.us
Grove City Area HS 800/9-12
511 Highland Ave 16127 724-458-5456
Joseph Skibinski, prin. Fax 450-0678
Grove City Area MS 400/7-8
130 E Main St 16127 724-458-8040
James Anderson, prin. Fax 450-0780
Republic JSHS 800/5-12
200 George Junior Rd 16127 724-450-9330
Tammi Martin, prin. Fax 458-7455

Grove City Christian Academy 100/PK-10
107 Breckenridge St 16127 724-458-5253
Grove City College Post-Sec.
100 Campus Dr 16127 724-458-2000

Guys Mills, Crawford
Penncrest SD
Supt. — See Saegertown
Maplewood JSHS 800/7-12
30383 Guys Mills Rd 16327 814-789-3666
Michael Henegan, prin. Fax 789-2409

Faith Builders Christian S 100/K-12
PO Box 127 16327 814-789-2303
Gerald E. Miller, prin. Fax 789-3396

Gwynedd Valley, Montgomery

Gwynedd-Mercy Academy 400/9-12
PO Box 902 19437 215-646-8815
Sr. Kathleen Boyce, prin. Fax 646-4361
Gwynedd-Mercy College Post-Sec.
PO Box 901 19437 215-646-7300

Hadley, Mercer
Commodore Perry SD 700/K-12
3002 Perry Hwy 16130 724-253-3255
Michael Stahlman, supt. Fax 253-3467
Perry JSHS 400/7-12
3002 Perry Hwy 16130 724-253-2232
Leslie Cattron, prin. Fax 253-3467

Halifax, Dauphin, Pop. 857
Halifax Area SD 1,200/K-12
3940 Peters Mountain Rd 17032 717-896-3416
James Dull, supt. Fax 896-3976
www.hasd.us
Halifax Area HS 400/9-12
3940 Peters Mountain Rd 17032 717-896-3416
Eric Lacianca, prin. Fax 896-3976
Halifax Area MS 300/6-8
3940 Peters Mountain Rd 17032 717-896-3416
Robert Hassinger, prin. Fax 896-3976

Hamburg, Berks, Pop. 4,112
Hamburg Area SD 2,400/K-12
Windsor St 19526 610-562-2241
Dr. William N. Kiefer, supt. Fax 562-2634
www.hasdhawks.org
Hamburg Area HS, Windsor St 19526 900/9-12
Christopher Spohn, prin. 610-562-3861
Hamburg Area MS, Windsor St 19526 700/6-8
Stephen Seier, prin. 610-562-3990

Blue Mountain Academy 200/9-12
2363 Mountain Rd 19526 610-562-2291
Spencer Hannah, prin. Fax 562-8050

Hanover, York, Pop. 14,835
Hanover Public SD 1,700/K-12
403 Moul Ave 17331 717-637-9000
Dr. Jill M. Dillon, supt. Fax 630-4617
www.hpsd.k12.pa.us
Hanover HS 500/9-12
401 Moul Ave 17331 717-637-9000
Karen Schoonover, prin. Fax 630-4634
Hanover MS 500/5-8
300 Keagy Ave 17331 717-637-9000
Pamela Smith, prin. Fax 630-4632

South Western SD 5,000/K-12
225 Bowman Rd 17331 717-632-2500
Barbara Rupp, supt. Fax 632-7993
www.swsd.k12.pa.us/
Markle IS 1,100/6-8
225 Bowman Rd 17331 717-632-2500
Alan Moyer, prin. Fax 633-7073
South Western HS 1,200/9-12
200 Bowman Rd 17331 717-632-2500
Walt Graves, prin. Fax 633-4819

Empire Beauty School Post-Sec.
1000 Carlisle St 17331 717-633-6201
St. Joseph MS 100/6-8
5125 Grandview Rd 17331 717-632-0118
Susan Mummert, prin. Fax 632-0030

Hanover Twp, Lehigh
Hanover Area SD 2,100/K-12
1600 Sans Souci Pkwy 18706 570-831-2313
James Sabatini, supt. Fax 822-6776
www.hanoverarea.org
Hanover Area JSHS 1,000/7-12
1600 Sans Souci Pkwy 18706 570-831-2300
David Fisher, prin. Fax 831-2316

Harborcreek, Erie
Harbor Creek SD 2,100/K-12
6375 Buffalo Rd 16421 814-897-2100
Dr. David Smith, supt. Fax 897-2142
www.hcsd.iu5.org
Harbor Creek JSHS 1,100/7-12
6375 Buffalo Rd 16421 814-897-2100
Ed Zenewicz, prin. Fax 898-4245

Harmony, Butler, Pop. 916
Seneca Valley SD 7,600/K-12
124 Seneca School Rd 16037 724-452-6040
Dr. Donald Tylinski, supt. Fax 452-6105
www.svsd.net/
Seneca Valley Intermediate HS 1,200/9-10
126 Seneca School Rd 16037 724-452-6040
Alan Cumo, prin. Fax 452-3718
Seneca Valley MS 1,200/7-8
122 Seneca School Rd 16037 724-452-6040
Tracy Vitale, prin. Fax 452-0331
Seneca Valley SHS 1,100/11-12
128 Seneca School Rd 16037 724-452-6040
Mark Korcinsky, prin. Fax 452-8357

Harrisburg, Dauphin, Pop. 48,322
Area Vocational Technical School
Supt. — None
Dauphin County AVTS Vo/Tech
6001 Locust Ln 17109 717-652-3170
Dr. Robert Clark, prin. Fax 652-9326

Central Dauphin SD 10,400/K-12
600 Rutherford Rd 17109 717-545-4703
John Scola, supt. Fax 545-5624
www.cdschools.org
Central Dauphin East HS 1,500/9-12
626 Rutherford Rd 17109 717-541-1662
Todd Neuhard, prin. Fax 545-7139
Central Dauphin East MS 900/6-8
628 Rutherford Rd 17109 717-545-4703
Robert Holbrook, prin. Fax 657-4987
Central Dauphin HS 1,800/9-12
437 Piketown Rd 17112 717-703-5360
Richard Mazzatesta, prin. Fax 703-5730
Central Dauphin MS 6-8
4600 Locust Ln 17109 717-540-4606
Dr. Pamela Boyd, prin. Fax 545-6931
Linglestown MS 700/6-8
1200 N Mountain Rd 17112 717-657-3060
Carol Johnson, prin. Fax 657-0537
Other Schools – See Steelton

Harrisburg SD — 8,300/K-12
2101 N Front St Bldg 2 17110 — 717-703-4000
Dr. Gerald W. Kohn, supt. — Fax 703-4115
www.hbgsd.k12.pa.us
Harrisburg Career & Technology Academy — Vo/Tech
2915 N 3rd St 17110 — 717-703-4349
Gregory Williams, prin. — Fax 703-4355
Harrisburg HS — 1,700/9-12
2451 Market St 17103 — 717-703-4300
Evangeline Kimber, prin. — Fax 703-4333
Harrisburg University Science & Tech HS — Vo/Tech
215 Market St 17101 — 717-703-1901
Lisa Waller, dir.

Susquehanna Township SD — 3,100/K-12
3550 Elmerton Ave 17109 — 717-657-5100
David W. Volkman, supt. — Fax 657-2919
www.hannasd.org
Susquehanna Twp. HS — 1,000/9-12
3500 Elmerton Ave 17109 — 717-657-5117
Kermit R. Leitner, prin. — Fax 657-2919
Susquehanna Twp. MS — 800/6-8
801 Wood St 17109 — 717-657-5125
Michael Jones, prin. — Fax 657-2919

Academy of Medical Arts and Business — Post-Sec.
2301 Academy Dr 17112 — 717-545-4747
Bishop McDevitt HS — 700/9-12
2200 Market St 17103 — 717-236-7973
Sr. Mary Anne Bednar, prin. — Fax 234-1270
Covenant Christian Academy — 200/K-11
6098 Locust Ln 17109 — 717-540-9885
Dr. Christopher Perrin, prin.
Empire Beauty School — Post-Sec.
3941 Jonestown Rd 17109 — 717-652-8500
Harrisburg Area Community College — Post-Sec.
1 Hacc Dr 17110 — 717-780-2300
Harrisburg Christian S — 300/K-12
PO Box 6464 17112 — 717-545-3728
Tom Wieland, prin. — Fax 545-9370
Thompson Institute — Post-Sec.
5650 Derry St 17111 — 717-564-4112
Widener University School of Law — Post-Sec.
PO Box 69380 17106 — 717-541-3900

Harrison City, Westmoreland
Penn-Trafford SD — 4,800/K-12
PO Box 530 15636 — 724-744-4496
Dr. Deborah Kolonay, supt. — Fax 744-4016
www.penntrafford.org
Penn-Trafford HS — 1,600/9-12
PO Box 530 15636 — 724-744-4471
Scott Inglese, prin. — Fax 744-1214
Other Schools – See Claridge, Trafford

Hatboro, Montgomery, Pop. 7,381
Upper Moreland Township SD
Supt. — See Willow Grove
Upper Moreland MS — 800/6-8
4000 Orangemans Rd 19040 — 215-674-4185
Thomas Mulvey, prin. — Fax 956-1906

Hatfield, Montgomery, Pop. 2,880
North Penn SD
Supt. — See Lansdale
Pennfield MS — 900/7-9
726 Forty Foot Rd 19440 — 215-368-9600
Dr. Barbara Galloway, prin. — Fax 368-9791

Biblical Theological Seminary — Post-Sec.
200 N Main St 19440 — 800-235-4021

Haverford, Montgomery, Pop. 6,000

Haverford College — Post-Sec.
370 Lancaster Ave 19041 — 610-896-1000
Haverford S — 1,000/PK-12
450 Lancaster Ave 19041 — 610-642-3020
Joseph Cox, prin. — Fax 649-4898

Havertown, Delaware, Pop. 30,000
Haverford Township SD — 5,500/K-12
1801 Darby Rd 19083 — 610-853-5900
David B. VanWinkle Ph.D., supt. — Fax 789-5379
www.haverford.k12.pa.us
Haverford HS — 1,800/9-12
200 Mill Rd 19083 — 610-853-5900
Nicholas Rotoli, prin. — Fax 853-5952
Haverford MS — 1,300/6-8
1701 Darby Rd 19083 — 610-853-5900
Carol Restifo, prin. — Fax 853-5937

Talent Academy — Post-Sec.
1345 W Chester Pike 19083 — 610-352-1401

Hawley, Pike, Pop. 1,304
Wallenpaupack Area SD — 4,000/K-12
HC 6 Box 6075 18428 — 570-226-4557
Michael Silsby, supt. — Fax 226-0638
www.paupack.ptd.net
Wallenpaupack Area HS — 1,300/9-12
HC 6 Box 6075 18428 — 570-226-4557
Jay Starnes, prin. — Fax 251-3153
Wallenpaupack Area MS — 1,000/6-8
HC 6 Box 6071 18428 — 570-226-4557
Diane Szader, prin. — Fax 251-3165

Hazleton, Luzerne, Pop. 22,492
Area Vocational Technical School
Supt. — None
Hazleton Area Career Center — Vo/Tech
1451 W 23rd St 18202 — 570-459-3172
Tom Allen, prin.

Hazleton Area SD — 9,500/K-12
1515 W 23rd St 18202 — 570-459-3111
Frank Victor Ph.D., supt. — Fax 459-3118
www.hasd.k12.pa.us
Hazleton Area Career Center — Vo/Tech
1451 W 23rd St 18202 — 570-459-3172
Clarence John, prin. — Fax 459-3181
Hazleton Area HS — 3,100/9-12
1601 W 23rd St 18202 — 570-459-3221
Robert Stefanovich, prin. — Fax 459-3242

Academy of Hair Design — Post-Sec.
1057 N Church St # A 18202 — 570-784-1020
Bishop Hafey JSHS — 600/7-12
1700 W 22nd St 18202 — 570-455-9431
P.J. Melvin, prin. — Fax 455-2847
Immanuel Christian S — 100/K-12
725 N Locust St 18201 — 570-459-1111
Kelly Knowlden, prin. — Fax 459-6920
Pennsylvania State University — Post-Sec.
Hazelton Campus 18201 — 570-450-3000

Hegins, Schuylkill
Tri-Valley SD
Supt. — See Valley View
Tri-Valley JSHS — 500/7-12
155 E Main St 17938 — 570-682-3125
Mark Snyder, prin. — Fax 682-9873

Hellertown, Northampton, Pop. 5,580
Saucon Valley SD — 2,300/K-12
2097 Polk Valley Rd 18055 — 610-838-7026
Dr. Richard Grove, supt. — Fax 838-6419
www.svpanthers.org
Saucon Valley HS — 700/9-12
2100 Polk Valley Rd 18055 — 610-838-7001
Dr. Curtis Dietrich, prin. — Fax 838-2365
Saucon Valley MS — 600/6-8
2095 Polk Valley Rd 18055 — 610-838-7071
Pamela Bernardo, prin. — Fax 838-7473

Herminie, Westmoreland
Yough SD — 2,600/K-12
915 Lowber Rd 15637 — 724-446-7272
Lawrence J. Nemec, supt. — Fax 446-5017
www.yough.net
Yough HS — 800/9-12
919 Lowber Rd 15637 — 724-446-5520
Earl Thompson, prin. — Fax 446-6008
Other Schools – See Ruffs Dale

Hermitage, Mercer, Pop. 16,521
Hermitage SD — 2,300/K-12
411 N Hermitage Rd 16148 — 724-981-8750
Karen Ionta, supt. — Fax 981-5080
www.hermitage.k12.pa.us
Hermitage MS — 400/7-8
123 N Hermitage Rd 16148 — 724-981-8750
Bob Kwiat, prin. — Fax 347-4514
Hickory HS — 800/9-12
640 N Hermitage Rd 16148 — 724-981-8750
Eric Trosch, prin. — Fax 347-4558

Kennedy Catholic HS — 400/9-12
2120 Shenango Valley Fwy 16148 — 724-346-5531
Dr. Peter P. Iacino, prin. — Fax 346-3011
Penn State Cosmetology Academy — Post-Sec.
2200 E State St 16148 — 724-347-4503

Herndon, Northumberland, Pop. 370
Line Mountain SD
Supt. — See Trevorton
Line Mountain JSHS — 600/7-12
RR 1 Box 1660 17830 — 570-758-2011
Karen Wiest, prin. — Fax 758-1514

Hershey, Dauphin, Pop. 11,860
Derry Township SD — 3,400/K-12
PO Box 898 17033 — 717-534-2501
Dr. Linda Brewer, supt. — Fax 533-4357
www.hershey.k12.pa.us
Hershey HS — 1,100/9-12
PO Box 898 17033 — 717-531-2244
Mike Murphy, prin. — Fax 534-2684
Hershey MS — 900/6-8
PO Box 898 17033 — 717-531-2222
Sue King, prin. — Fax 531-2245

Hershey S — 1,200/PK-12
PO Box 830 17033 — 717-520-2000
John O'Brien, pres. — Fax 520-2002
Milton S. Hershey Medical Center Hosp. — Post-Sec.
PO Box 850 17033 — 717-531-8803
Penn State Hershey College of Medicine — Post-Sec.
500 University Dr 17033 — 717-534-8521

Hilltown, Bucks

St. Agnes-Sacred Heart S — 300/5-8
Route 152 & Broad St 18927 — 215-822-9174
Margaret Graham, prin. — Fax 822-7942

Holland, Bucks, Pop. 5,300
Council Rock SD
Supt. — See Newtown
Council Rock HS South — 2,000/9-12
2002 Rock Way 18966 — 215-944-1100
Michael Holland, prin. — Fax 944-1145
Holland MS — 700/7-8
400 E Holland Rd 18966 — 215-968-0854
Michael Lecker, prin. — Fax 968-1475

Villa Joseph Marie HS — 300/9-12
1180 Holland Rd 18966 — 215-357-8810
Mary Elaine, prin. — Fax 357-2477

Hollidaysburg, Blair, Pop. 5,312
Hollidaysburg Area SD — 3,800/K-12
201 Jackson St 16648 — 814-695-8702
Dr. Paul Gallagher, supt. — Fax 695-2315
www.tigerwires.com
Hollidaysburg Area JHS — 1,000/7-9
1000 Hewit St 16648 — 814-695-4426
Edward Barton, prin. — Fax 696-2959
Hollidaysburg Area SHS — 1,100/10-12
1500 N Montgomery St 16648 — 814-695-4416
Linda McCall, prin. — Fax 696-2958

Hollsopple, Somerset

Johnstown Christian S — 300/PK-12
125 Christian School Rd 15935 — 814-288-2588
Linda Gundlach, admin. — Fax 288-1447

Homer City, Indiana, Pop. 1,787
Homer-Center SD — 1,000/K-12
65 Wildcat Ln 15748 — 724-479-8080
Dr. Joseph Marcoline, supt.
homercenter.org/
Homer-Center JSHS — 500/7-12
70 Wildcat Ln 15748 — 724-479-8026
Rick Foust, prin. — Fax 479-2208

Honesdale, Wayne, Pop. 4,900
Wayne Highlands SD — 3,100/K-12
474 Grove St 18431 — 570-253-4661
Paul Edwards, supt. — Fax 253-9409
www.neiu.org/WWW/WH/
Honesdale HS — 1,000/9-12
459 Terrace St 18431 — 570-253-2046
James Rodda, prin. — Fax 253-1502
Wayne Highlands MS — 600/6-8
482 Grove St 18431 — 570-253-5900
Kurt Eisele, prin. — Fax 253-5259

Hookstown, Beaver, Pop. 147
South Side Area SD — 1,400/K-12
4949 State Route 151 15050 — 724-573-9581
Dr. Robert Del Greco, supt. — Fax 573-0414
www.sssd.k12.pa.us/
South Side HS — 400/9-12
4949 State Route 151 15050 — 724-573-9581
Vincent Trombetta, prin. — Fax 573-0449
South Side MS — 400/6-8
4949 State Route 151 15050 — 724-573-9581
Thomas Ralston, prin. — Fax 573-0449

Horsham, Montgomery, Pop. 15,051
Hatboro-Horsham SD — 5,500/K-12
229 Meetinghouse Rd 19044 — 215-672-5660
Dr. William A. Lessa, supt. — Fax 675-2201
www.hatboro-horsham.org
Hatboro-Horsham HS — 1,800/9-12
899 Horsham Rd 19044 — 215-441-7900
Dennis Williams, prin. — Fax 441-7940
Keith Valley MS — 1,400/6-8
227 Meetinghouse Rd 19044 — 215-956-2910
Jonathan Kircher, prin. — Fax 674-0762

Houston, Washington, Pop. 1,284
Chartiers-Houston SD — 1,200/K-12
2020 W Pike St 15342 — 724-746-1400
Charles Mahoney, supt. — Fax 746-3971
www.chbucs.k12.pa.us/
Chartiers-Houston JSHS — 600/7-12
2050 W Pike St 15342 — 724-745-3350
Thomas Dirda, prin. — Fax 745-3495

Houtzdale, Clearfield, Pop. 914
Moshannon Valley SD — 1,200/K-12
4934 Green Acre Rd 16651 — 814-378-7609
Michael Slavinski Ed.D., supt. — Fax 378-7100
www.movalley.org
Moshannon Valley JSHS — 600/7-12
4934 Green Acre Rd 16651 — 814-378-7616
Dr. Jack Cunning, prin. — Fax 378-5205

Hughesville, Lycoming, Pop. 2,133
Area Vocational Technical School
Supt. — None
Lycoming CTC — Vo/Tech
293 Cemetery St 17737 — 570-584-2300
John Pulver, prin.

East Lycoming SD — 1,800/K-12
349 Cemetery St 17737 — 570-584-2131
David L. Price, supt. — Fax 584-5701
www.eastlycoming.net
Hughesville JSHS — 900/7-12
349 Cemetery St 17737 — 570-584-5111
Ron Lorson, prin. — Fax 584-5378

Hummelstown, Dauphin, Pop. 4,365
Lower Dauphin SD — 3,900/K-12
291 E Main St 17036 — 717-566-5300
Sherri Smith, supt. — Fax 566-3670
www.ldsd.org
Lower Dauphin HS — 1,200/9-12
201 S Hanover St 17036 — 717-566-5330
Jeffrey Hughes, prin. — Fax 566-3970
Lower Dauphin MS — 1,000/6-8
251 Quarry Rd 17036 — 717-566-5310
Robert K. Schultz, prin. — Fax 566-5383

Hershey Christian S — 200/K-12
330 Hilltop Rd 17036 — 717-533-4900
Timothy D. Rockafellow, admin. — Fax 533-0908

Huntingdon, Huntingdon, Pop. 6,864
Huntingdon Area SD — 2,400/K-12
2400 Cassady Ave Ste 2 16652 — 814-643-4140
Jill Adams, supt. — Fax 643-6244
www.hasd.tiu.k12.pa.us/
Huntingdon Area HS — 800/9-12
2400 Cassady Ave 16652 — 814-643-1080
Arthur Waleski, prin. — Fax 643-3800
Huntingdon Area MS — 600/6-8
2500 Cassady Ave 16652 — 814-643-2900
Patricia Wargo, prin. — Fax 643-6513

Calvary Christian Academy — 100/K-12
300 Standing Stone Ave 16652 — 814-643-4075
Donald Kidd, prin. — Fax 643-4094
DuBois Business College — Post-Sec.
1001 Moore St 16652 — 814-641-0440
Juniata College — Post-Sec.
1700 Moore St 16652 — 814-641-3000

Huntingdon Valley, Montgomery, Pop. 10,000
Lower Moreland Township SD — 1,800/K-12
2551 Murray Ave 19006 — 215-938-0270
Dr. David Archibald, supt. — Fax 947-6933
www.lmtsd.org
Lower Moreland HS — 600/9-12
555 Red Lion Rd 19006 — 215-938-0220
Gregory Doviak, prin. — Fax 947-0333
Murray Avenue MS — 700/4-8
2551 Murray Ave 19006 — 215-938-0230
Frank McKee, prin. — Fax 947-3697

Huntingdon Valley Christian Academy 100/PK-10
1845 Byberry Rd 19006 215-947-6595
Gary Davis, prin. Fax 947-4277

Hyndman, Bedford, Pop. 981
Bedford Area SD
Supt. — See Bedford
Hyndman MSHS 200/7-12
PO Box 695 15545 814-842-3918
Brian Keagy, prin. Fax 842-6246

Immaculata, Chester

Immaculata University 19345 Post-Sec.
  610-647-4400

Imperial, Allegheny, Pop. 3,449
West Allegheny SD 3,200/K-12
PO Box 55 15126 724-695-3422
John S. DiSanti Ph.D., supt. Fax 695-3788
www.westallegheny.k12.pa.us/
West Allegheny HS 1,000/9-12
205 W Allegheny Rd 15126 724-695-5245
Daniel Smith, prin.
West Allegheny MS 800/6-8
207 W Allegheny Rd 15126 724-695-8979
Dr. Janet Walsh, prin. Fax 695-8211

Indiana, Indiana, Pop. 14,636
Area Vocational Technical School
Supt. — None
Indiana County Technology Center Vo/Tech
441 Hamill Rd 15701 724-349-6700
John Jahoda, prin.

Indiana Area SD 3,200/K-12
501 E Pike Rd 15701 724-463-8713
Dr. Kathleen Kelley, supt. Fax 463-0868
www.iasd.cc
Indiana Area JHS 900/7-9
245 N 5th St 15701 724-463-8568
Dr. Luanne Kokolis, prin. Fax 463-2133
Indiana Area SHS 800/10-12
450 N 5th St 15701 724-463-8562
Paula Daskivich, prin. Fax 463-9709

Cambria-Rowe Business College Post-Sec.
422 S 13th St 15701 724-463-0222
Indiana University of Pennsylvania Post-Sec.
15705 724-357-2100

Industry, Beaver, Pop. 1,877
Western Beaver County SD
Supt. — See Midland
Western Beaver County JSHS 500/7-12
216 Engle Rd 15052 724-643-8500
Barry Borza, prin. Fax 643-8504

Irwin, Westmoreland, Pop. 4,237
Hempfield Area SD
Supt. — See Greensburg
West Hempfield MS 400/6-8
156 Northumberland Dr 15642 724-850-2140
David Waryanka, prin. Fax 850-2141

Norwin SD
Supt. — See North Huntingdon
Norwin MS 800/7-8
10870 Mockingbird Dr 15642 724-863-5707
Robert Randolph, prin. Fax 863-5408

Jamestown, Mercer, Pop. 615
Jamestown Area SD 700/K-12
PO Box 217 16134 724-932-5557
Dr. Douglas Allen, supt. Fax 932-5632
Jamestown Area JSHS 400/7-12
PO Box 217 16134 724-932-3186
Brian Keyser, prin.

Jamison, Bucks
Area Vocational Technical School
Supt. — None
Middle Bucks Institute of Tech Vo/Tech
2740 York Rd 18929 215-343-2480
Dr. Michael Erwin, dir.

Jeannette, Westmoreland, Pop. 10,369
Jeannette CSD 800/K-12
Park St 15644 724-523-5497
Vincent Aiello, supt. Fax 523-3289
wiu.k12.pa.us/jeannette/
Jeannette HS 400/9-12
200 Florida Ave 15644 724-523-5591
Sharon Marks, prin. Fax 523-5534
Jeannette McKee MS 400/6-8
1000 Lowry Ave 15644 724-527-1591
Christopher Brasco, prin. Fax 523-6792

Christian Fellowship Academy 200/PK-12
2005 Ridge Rd 15644 724-523-2358
Sharon Herbster, prin. Fax 523-5439
Monsour Medical Center Post-Sec.
70 Lincoln Hwy E 15644 724-527-0600

Jefferson, Allegheny, Pop. 979
Jefferson-Morgan SD 800/K-12
1351 Jefferson Rd 15344 724-883-2310
Charles P. Rembold Ph.D., supt. Fax 883-4942
www.jmsd.org/
Jefferson-Morgan HS 300/9-12
PO Box 158 15344 724-883-2310
Thomas Katruska, prin. Fax 883-3786
Jefferson-Morgan MS 7-8
PO Box 158 15344 724-883-2310
Carol Korber, prin. Fax 883-3786

Jefferson Hills, Allegheny, Pop. 9,685
West Jefferson Hills SD 2,900/K-12
835 Old Clairton Rd 15025 412-655-8450
Dr. John P. Lozosky, supt. Fax 655-9544
www.wjhsd.net
Jefferson HS 1,000/9-12
310 Old Clairton Rd 15025 412-655-8610
Dr. Bart Rocco, prin. Fax 655-8618
Other Schools – See Pittsburgh

Jenkintown, Montgomery, Pop. 4,459
Jenkintown SD 600/K-12
325 Highland Ave 19046 215-885-3722
Dr. Raymond J. Boccuti, supt. Fax 885-2090
www.jenkintown.org/
Jenkintown JSHS 300/7-12
325 Highland Ave 19046 215-884-1801
Dr. Lorraine Trollinger, prin. Fax 885-2090

Abington Friends S 800/PK-12
575 Washington Ln 19046 215-886-4350
Richard Nourie, hdmstr. Fax 886-9143
Manor College Post-Sec.
700 Fox Chase Rd 19046 215-885-2360
St. Basil Academy 400/9-12
711 Fox Chase Rd 19046 215-885-3771
Sr. Carla Hernandez, prin. Fax 885-4025

Jermyn, Lackawanna, Pop. 2,265
Lakeland SD 1,600/K-12
1593 Lakeland Dr 18433 570-254-9485
Dr. Margaret Billings-Jones, supt. Fax 254-9224
www.lakelandsd.org
Lakeland JSHS 800/7-12
1593 Lakeland Dr 18433 570-254-9485
Joseph Hanni, prin. Fax 254-6730

Jersey Shore, Lycoming, Pop. 4,479
Jersey Shore Area SD 3,000/K-12
175 A and P Dr 17740 570-398-1561
Richard J. Emery, supt. Fax 398-5089
www.jsasd.k12.pa.us
Jersey Shore Area MS 800/6-8
601 Thompson St 17740 570-398-7400
Reed Mellinger, prin. Fax 398-5618
Jersey Shore Area SHS 1,000/9-12
701 Cemetery St 17740 570-398-7170
Mary Thomas, prin. Fax 398-5612

Jim Thorpe, Carbon, Pop. 4,827
Area Vocational Technical School
Supt. — None
Carbon Career & Technical Institute Vo/Tech
150 W 13th St 18229 570-325-3682
Dr. Robert Mauro, prin.

Jim Thorpe Area SD 1,800/K-12
410 Center Ave 18229 570-325-3691
Keith M. Boyer, supt. Fax 325-3699
www.jtasd.k12.pa.us/index.html
Jim Thorpe Area HS 900/7-12
1 Olympian Way 18229 570-325-3663
Thomas Lesisko, prin. Fax 325-8973

Johnsonburg, Elk, Pop. 2,891
Johnsonburg Area SD 800/K-12
315 High School Rd 15845 814-965-2536
Walter Fitch, supt. Fax 965-5809
Johnsonburg Area JSHS 400/7-12
315 High School Rd 15845 814-965-2556
Donald Wismar, prin. Fax 965-5809

Johnstown, Cambria, Pop. 22,957
Area Vocational Technical School
Supt. — None
Greater Johnstown AVTS Vo/Tech
445 Schoolhouse Rd 15904 814-269-4545
William Heim, prin.

Conemaugh Valley SD 1,000/K-12
1451 Frankstown Rd 15902 814-535-3957
William Rushin, supt. Fax 536-8902
Conemaugh Valley JSHS 400/7-12
1342 William Penn Ave 15906 814-535-5523
James Cekada, prin. Fax 536-4025

Ferndale Area SD 800/K-12
100 Dartmouth Ave 15905 814-535-1507
Dr. Christine Oldham, supt. Fax 535-8527
www.fasdk12.org/index800600.html
Ferndale Area JSHS 400/7-12
600 Harlan Ave 15905 814-288-5757
Kathy Nagle, prin. Fax 288-5224

Greater Johnstown SD 3,500/PK-12
1091 Broad St 15906 814-533-5651
Barbara Parkins, supt. Fax 533-5655
www.gjsd.net
Greater Johnstown HS 1,200/9-12
222 Central Ave 15902 814-533-5603
Dan Resenic, prin. Fax 533-5698
Greater Johnstown MS 800/6-8
280 Decker Ave 15906 814-533-5570
Darren Buchko, prin. Fax 533-5564

Richland SD 1,600/K-12
220 Highfield St Ste 102 15904 814-266-6063
Gerald Davitch, supt. Fax 266-7349
www.richlandsd.com/
Richland HS 700/8-12
220 Highfield St 15904 814-266-6081
Thomas Fleming, prin. Fax 269-9506

Westmont Hilltop SD 1,700/K-12
827 Diamond Blvd 15905 814-255-6751
Dr. Susan J. Anderson, supt. Fax 255-7735
Westmont Hilltop HS 600/9-12
200 Fair Oaks Dr 15905 814-255-8726
William W. Marshall, prin. Fax 255-2704
Westmont Hilltop MS 500/5-8
827 Diamond Blvd 15905 814-255-8704
Carole M. Kakabar, prin. Fax 255-8783

Bishop McCort HS 500/9-12
25 Osborne St 15905 814-536-8991
Kenneth Salem, prin. Fax 535-4118
Cambria County Christian S 100/K-12
561 Pike Rd 15909 814-749-7406
Charlie Fenchak, admin. Fax 749-7028
Cambria-Rowe Business College Post-Sec.
221 Central Ave 15902 814-536-5168
Commonwealth Technical Institute Post-Sec.
727 Goucher St 15905 814-255-8200
Conemaugh Valley Memorial Hospital Post-Sec.
1086 Franklin St 15905 814-534-9118

Greater Johnstown Area Voc Tech School Post-Sec.
445 Schoolhouse Rd 15904 814-266-6073
PA Academy of Cosmetic Arts & Sciences Post-Sec.
2445 Bedford St 15904 814-269-3444
Pennsylvania Highlands Community College Post-Sec.
PO Box 68 15907 814-532-5300
University of Pittsburgh at Johnstown Post-Sec.
450 Schoolhouse Rd 15904 814-269-7000

Jonestown, Lebanon, Pop. 1,009

Blue Mountain Christian S 100/K-12
14 Silvertown Rd 17038 717-865-9650
Elwood Heisey, admin. Fax 865-4732

Kane, McKean, Pop. 3,972
Kane Area SD 1,400/K-12
400 W Hemlock Ave 16735 814-837-9570
Sandra Chlopecki, supt. Fax 837-7450
www.kasd.net
Kane Area HS 400/9-12
300 Hemlock Ave 16735 814-837-6821
Jeff Kepler, prin. Fax 837-6158
Kane Area MS 400/6-8
400 W Hemlock Ave 16735 814-837-6030
James Wortman, prin. Fax 837-9133

Karns City, Butler, Pop. 239
Karns City Area SD 1,800/K-12
1446 Kittanning Pike 16041 724-756-2030
Larry Henry, supt. Fax 756-2121
www.karnscity.k12.pa.us
Karns City JSHS 900/7-12
1446 Kittanning Pike 16041 724-756-2030
Dave Beck, prin. Fax 756-2121

Kennett Square, Chester, Pop. 5,271
Kennett Consolidated SD 4,700/K-12
300 E South St 19348 610-444-6600
Dr. Rudolph Karkosak, supt. Fax 444-6614
kcsd.org
Kennett HS 1,100/9-12
100 E South St 19348 610-444-6623
Wesley McDowell, prin. Fax 444-6237
Other Schools – See Landenberg

Unionville-Chadds Ford SD 3,900/K-12
740 Unionville Rd 19348 610-347-0970
Dr. John F. Kenney, supt. Fax 347-0976
www.ucfsd.org
Patton MS 1,000/6-8
760 Unionville Rd 19348 610-347-2000
Bruce Vosburgh, prin. Fax 347-0421
Unionville HS 1,200/9-12
750 Unionville Rd 19348 610-347-1600
Jim Fulginiti, prin. Fax 347-1890

Kimberton, Chester

Kimberton Waldorf S 300/PK-12
PO Box 350 19442 610-933-3635
Paula Moraine, chrpsn. Fax 935-6985

King of Prussia, Montgomery, Pop. 18,406
Upper Merion Area SD 3,400/K-12
435 Crossfield Rd 19406 610-337-6000
  Fax 337-9468

www.umasd.org
Upper Merion HS 1,200/9-12
440 Crossfield Rd 19406 610-337-6032
  Fax 337-6051
Upper Merion MS 1,100/5-8
450 Crossfield Rd 19406 610-337-6053
John Adiletto, prin. Fax 768-1750

ITT Technical Institute Post-Sec.
760 Moore Rd 19406 610-491-8004

Kingsley, Susquehanna
Mountain View SD 1,400/K-12
RR 1 Box 339A 18826 570-434-2180
Arthur Chambers, supt. Fax 434-2404
Mountain View JSHS 800/7-12
RR 1 Box 339 18826 570-434-2501
Mary Jo Walsh, prin. Fax 434-9582

Kingston, Luzerne, Pop. 13,368
Area Vocational Technical School
Supt. — None
West Side AVTS, 75 Evans St 18704 Vo/Tech
Peter Halesey, prin. 570-288-8493

Wyoming Valley West SD 5,100/K-12
450 N Maple Ave 18704 570-288-6551
August J. Piazza, supt. Fax 288-1564
www.wvwspartans.org
Wyoming Valley West MS 1,400/6-8
201 Chester St 18704 570-287-2131
David Tosh, prin. Fax 287-6343
Other Schools – See Plymouth

Academy of Creative Hair Design Post-Sec.
252 W Side Mall # 1 18704 570-288-4574
Bishop O'Reilly HS 300/9-12
316 N Maple Ave 18704 570-288-1404
Susan Dennen, prin. Fax 288-6634
Wyoming Seminary 400/9-12
201 N Sprague Ave 18704 570-270-2100
Jeremy Packard, hdmstr. Fax 270-2199

Kintnersville, Bucks
Palisades SD 2,100/K-12
39 Thomas Free Dr 18930 610-847-5131
Francis V. Barnes Ph.D., supt. Fax 847-8116
www.palisadessd.org
Palisades HS 700/9-12
35 Church Hill Rd 18930 610-847-5131
Richard Heffernan, prin. Fax 847-2562
Palisades MS 500/6-8
4710 Durham Rd 18930 610-847-5131
Edward Baumgartner, prin. Fax 847-2691

Kinzers, Lancaster
Pequea Valley SD 2,000/K-12
PO Box 130 17535 717-768-5530
Ann Keim, supt. Fax 768-7176
www.pvsd.k12.pa.us
Pequea Valley HS 600/9-12
PO Box 287 17535 717-768-5500
Patrick Hallock, prin. Fax 768-5523
Pequea Valley IS 500/6-8
PO Box 257 17535 717-768-5535
Brian Bliss, prin. Fax 768-5656

Kittanning, Armstrong, Pop. 4,556
Armstrong SD
Supt. — See Ford City
Kittanning Area MS 700/6-8
210 N Mckean St 16201 724-543-1295
Michael S. Cominos, prin. Fax 543-1155
Kittanning HS 700/9-12
1200 Orr Ave 16201 724-543-1591
James Rummel, prin. Fax 543-1712

Armstrong County Memorial Hospital Post-Sec.
1 Nolte Dr 16201 724-543-8404
Kittanning Beauty School Post-Sec.
120 Market St 16201 800-833-4247

Knox, Clarion, Pop. 1,137
Keystone SD 1,200/K-12
451 Huston Ave 16232 814-797-5921
H.D. Sinopoli, supt. Fax 797-2382
www.keyknox.com
Keystone JSHS 600/7-12
700 Beatty Ave 16232 814-797-1261
Doug Mays, prin. Fax 797-2868

Kutztown, Berks, Pop. 5,067
Kutztown Area SD 1,800/K-12
50 Trexler Ave 19530 610-683-7361
Dr. Brenda Winkler, supt. Fax 683-7230
www.kasd.org
Kutztown Area HS 600/9-12
50 Trexler Ave 19530 610-683-7346
Eric Erb, prin. Fax 894-4801
Kutztown Area MS 500/6-8
10 Deisher Ln 19530 610-683-3575
Matthew Smith, prin. Fax 683-5460

Kutztown University of Pennsylvania Post-Sec.
19530 610-683-4000

Lake Ariel, Wayne
Western Wayne SD
Supt. — See South Canaan
Western Wayne HS 700/9-12
RR 8 Box 8175 18436 570-937-4113
R. Jay Starnes, prin. Fax 937-4707
Western Wayne MS 600/6-8
RR 8 Box 8170 18436 570-937-3010
Peter Chapla, prin. Fax 937-3440

Canaan Christian Academy 200/PK-12
30 Hemlock Rd 18436 570-937-4848
David Marquette, prin. Fax 937-4800

Lampeter, Lancaster
Lampeter-Strasburg SD 2,700/K-12
PO Box 428 17537 717-464-3311
Dr. Robert A. Frick, supt. Fax 464-4699
www.l-spioneers.org
Lampeter-Strasburg HS 1,000/9-12
PO Box 428 17537 717-464-3311
Carroll Staub, prin. Fax 464-2367
Meylin MS 800/6-8
PO Box 428 17537 717-464-3311
Michael Burcin, prin. Fax 509-0289

Lancaster, Lancaster, Pop. 55,351
Conestoga Valley SD 3,900/K-12
2110 Horseshoe Rd 17601 717-397-2421
Dr. Gerald Huesken, supt. Fax 397-0442
www.cvsd.k12.pa.us
Conestoga Valley HS 1,200/9-12
2110 Horseshoe Rd 17601 717-397-5231
Brian Ginter, prin. Fax 397-8841
Conestoga Valley MS 700/7-8
500 Mount Sidney Rd 17602 717-397-1294
Robert Houghton, prin. Fax 397-4404

Hempfield SD
Supt. — See Landisville
Centerville MS 700/7-8
865 Centerville Rd 17601 717-898-5580
William Cackovic, prin. Fax 898-5513

Manheim Township SD
Supt. — See Lititz
Manheim Twp. HS 1,700/9-12
PO Box 5134 17606 717-560-3097
David Hanna, prin. Fax 569-2806
Manheim Twp. MS 1,300/6-8
PO Box 5134 17606 717-560-3111
Christopher Adams, prin. Fax 569-1670

Penn Manor SD 5,300/K-12
2950 Charlestown Rd 17603 717-872-9500
Donald F. Stewart, supt. Fax 872-9505
www.pennmanor.net
Manor MS 600/7-8
2950 Charlestown Rd 17603 717-872-9510
Dana Edwards, prin. Fax 872-9505
Other Schools – See Millersville, Pequea

SD of Lancaster 12,300/K-12
1020 Lehigh Ave 17602 717-291-6121
Dr. Rita Bishop, supt. Fax 396-6844
www.lancaster.k12.pa.us
Hand MS 600/6-8
431 S Ann St 17602 717-291-6161
Larry Mays, prin. Fax 399-6407
Lincoln MS 700/6-8
1001 Lehigh Ave 17602 717-291-6187
Josh Keene, prin. Fax 399-6408
McCaskey East HS 1,500/9-12
1051 Lehigh Ave 17602 717-291-6172
Damaso Albino, prin. Fax 391-8601
McCaskey HS 2,900/9-12
445 N Reservoir St 17602 717-291-6211
Dwight Nolt, prin. Fax 390-2567
Reynolds MS 600/6-8
605 W Walnut St 17603 717-291-6257
Arnold Raffone, prin. Fax 399-6409
Wheatland MS 700/6-8
919 Hamilton Park Dr 17603 717-291-6285
Marty Slaugh, prin. Fax 399-6411

Blue Rock Mennonite S 100/9-12
3453 Blue Rock Rd 17603 717-872-9493
Consolidated School of Business Post-Sec.
2124 Ambassador Cir 17603 717-394-6211
Dayspring Christian Academy 300/PK-12
1008 New Holland Ave 17601 717-295-6400
Michael Myers, hdmstr. Fax 295-6410
Empire Beauty School Post-Sec.
1801 Columbia Ave 17603 717-394-8561
Franklin & Marshall College Post-Sec.
PO Box 3003 17604 717-291-3911
Lancaster Bible College Post-Sec.
901 Eden Rd 17601 717-569-7071
Lancaster Christian S 300/K-12
651 Lampeter Rd 17602 717-392-8092
Paula Frey, prin. Fax 509-3094
Lancaster Country Day S 500/PK-12
725 Hamilton Rd 17603 717-392-2916
Michael Mersky, prin. Fax 392-0425
Lancaster General College of Nursing Post-Sec.
410 N Lime St 17602 717-544-6912
Lancaster HS 700/9-12
650 Juliette Ave 17601 717-509-0315
Dermot Garrett, prin. Fax 509-0312
Lancaster Mennonite S 1,300/K-12
2176 Lincoln Hwy E 17602 717-299-0436
J. Richard Thomas, supt. Fax 299-0823
Lancaster School of Cosmetology Post-Sec.
50 Ranck Ave 17602 717-299-0200
Lancaster Theological Seminary Post-Sec.
555 W James St 17603 717-393-0654
Living Word Academy 400/PK-12
2384 New Holland Pike 17601 717-556-0711
Ray Casey, admin. Fax 656-4868
Pennsylvania College of Art and Design Post-Sec.
PO Box 59 17608 717-396-7833
Resurrection MS 200/4-8
521 E Orange St 17603 717-392-3083
Brenda Weaver, prin. Fax 735-7793
Thaddeus Stevens College of Technology Post-Sec.
750 E King St 17602 717-299-7730
York Technical Institute Post-Sec.
3050 Hempland Rd 17601 800-227-9675

Landenberg, Chester
Kennett Consolidated SD
Supt. — See Kennett Square
Kennett MS, 195 Sunny Dell Rd 19350 700/7-8
John Carr, prin. 610-268-5800

Landisville, Lancaster, Pop. 4,239
Hempfield SD 7,200/K-12
200 Church St 17538 717-898-5564
Dr. David E. Poore, supt. Fax 898-5628
www.hempfieldsd.org
Hempfield HS 2,400/9-12
200 Stanley Ave 17538 717-898-5510
John Sparmblack, prin. Fax 898-5518
Landisville MS 600/7-8
340 Mumma Dr 17538 717-898-5607
Dr. Nancy Herr, prin. Fax 898-1603
Other Schools – See Lancaster

Langhorne, Bucks, Pop. 1,987
Neshaminy SD 9,400/K-12
2001 Old Lincoln Hwy 19047 215-752-6300
P. Howard Wilson, supt. Fax 752-6374
www.neshaminy.k12.pa.us
Maple Point MS 1,100/6-9
2250 Langhorne Yardley Rd 19047 215-752-6900
Mark Collins, prin.
Neshaminy MS 700/6-9
1200 Langhorne Newtown Rd 19047 215-752-3600
Karen Wychock, prin. Fax 702-0363
Neshaminy SHS 2,400/10-12
2001 Old Lincoln Hwy 19047 215-752-6451
Alex Menio, prin. Fax 752-6320
Other Schools – See Feasterville, Levittown

Philadelphia Biblical University Post-Sec.
200 Manor Ave 19047 215-752-5800
Woods Services Post-Sec.
PO Box 36 19047 800-782-3646

Lansdale, Montgomery, Pop. 16,115
Area Vocational Technical School
Supt. — None
North Montco Tech Career Center Vo/Tech
1265 Sumneytown Pike 19446 215-368-1177
Michael Lucas, prin.

North Penn SD 13,600/K-12
401 E Hancock St 19446 215-368-0400
Dr. Robert Hassler, supt. Fax 368-3161
www.npenn.org
North Penn SHS 3,300/10-12
1340 S Valley Forge Rd 19446 215-368-9800
Burton Hynes, prin. Fax 855-0632
Penndale MS 1,500/7-9
400 Penn St 19446 215-368-2700
Debra Harper, prin. Fax 368-6817
Other Schools – See Hatfield, North Wales

Calvary Baptist Christian S 300/K-12
1380 S Valley Forge Rd 19446 215-368-1100
Randy Thaxton, prin. Fax 368-1003
Calvary Baptist Theological Seminary Post-Sec.
1380 S Valley Forge Rd 19446 215-368-7538
Dock Mennonite HS 400/9-12
1000 Forty Foot Rd 19446 215-362-2675
Elaine Moyer, prin. Fax 362-2943
Lansdale Catholic HS 900/9-12
700 Lansdale Ave 19446 215-362-6160
Linda Robinson, prin. Fax 362-5746
Lansdale School of Cosmetology Post-Sec.
215 W Main St 19446 215-362-2322

Lansdowne, Delaware, Pop. 10,861
William Penn SD 5,600/K-12
100 Green Ave 19050 610-284-8000
Dana T. Bedden, supt. Fax 284-8054
www.wpsd.k12.pa.us
Penn Wood SHS 1,200/10-12
100 Green Ave 19050 610-284-8080
John Leary, prin. Fax 284-2141
Other Schools – See Darby, Yeadon

Lansford, Carbon, Pop. 4,198
Panther Valley SD 1,500/K-12
PO Box 40 18232 570-645-4248
J. Christopher West, supt. Fax 645-6232
www.panthervalley.org/
Panther Valley HS 400/9-12
PO Box 40 18232 570-645-2171
Martin Mersky, prin. Fax 645-2507
Panther Valley MS 400/6-8
PO Box 40 18232 570-645-2175
Amanda Zaremba, prin. Fax 645-9723

La Plume, Lackawanna

Keystone College Post-Sec.
PO Box 50 18440 570-945-5141

Laporte, Sullivan, Pop. 280
Sullivan County SD
Supt. — See Dushore
Sullivan County JSHS 400/7-12
PO Box 98 18626 570-946-7001
Linda Rogers, prin. Fax 946-5070

Latrobe, Westmoreland, Pop. 8,747
Area Vocational Technical School
Supt. — None
Eastern Westmoreland CTC Vo/Tech
4904 State Route 982 15650 724-539-9788
Marie Bowers, prin. Fax 539-1907

Greater Latrobe SD 4,300/K-12
410 Main St 15650 724-539-4200
Dr. William Stavisky, supt. Fax 539-4202
greaterlatrobe.schoolwires.com/
Greater Latrobe JHS 1,100/7-9
130 High School Rd 15650 724-539-4265
John Kozusko, prin. Fax 539-4223
Greater Latrobe SHS 1,000/10-12
131 High School Rd 15650 724-539-4225
Georgia Teppert, prin. Fax 539-4295

Latrobe Area Hospital Post-Sec.
101 W 2nd Ave 15650 724-537-1001
St. Vincent College Post-Sec.
300 Fraser Purchase Rd 15650 724-539-9761
St. Vincent Seminary Post-Sec.
300 Fraser Purchase Rd 15650 724-537-4592

Laureldale, Berks, Pop. 3,729
Muhlenberg SD 3,000/K-12
801 E Bellevue Ave 19605 610-921-8000
Dr. Joseph Yarworth, supt. Fax 921-8076
www.muhlsd.berksiu.k12.pa.us/
Muhlenberg HS 1,000/9-12
Sharp Ave & Frances St 19605 610-921-8078
Scott Schwenk, prin. Fax 921-7925
Muhlenberg MS 800/6-8
801 E Bellevue Ave 19605 610-921-8034
Donna Albright, prin. Fax 921-8038

Lebanon, Lebanon, Pop. 23,894
Area Vocational Technical School
Supt. — None
Lebanon Co. Career & Technology Center Vo/Tech
833 Metro Dr 17042 717-273-8551
Stephen Kachniasz, dir. Fax 273-0534

Cornwall-Lebanon SD 4,700/K-12
105 E Evergreen Rd 17042 717-272-2031
Thomas Sherk, supt. Fax 274-2786
www.clsd.k12.pa.us
Cedar Crest HS 1,500/9-12
115 E Evergreen Rd 17042 717-272-2033
David Helsel, prin. Fax 273-3250
Cedar Crest MS 1,200/6-8
101 E Evergreen Rd 17042 717-272-2032
Philip Domencic, prin. Fax 228-1437

Lebanon SD 4,200/PK-12
1000 S 8th St 17042 717-273-9391
Dr. Marianne T. Bartley, supt. Fax 270-6778
www.lebanon.k12.pa.us
Lebanon HS 1,100/9-12
1000 S 8th St 17042 717-273-9391
Thomas Jordan, prin. Fax 270-6778
Lebanon MS 900/6-8
350 N 8th St 17046 717-273-9391
Mary Garrett, prin. Fax 270-6859

Empire Beauty School Post-Sec.
1776 Quentin Rd 17042 717-272-3323
Lebanon Catholic S 500/K-12
1400 Chestnut St 17042 717-273-3731
David Chauvette, admin. Fax 274-5167
Lebanon Christian Academy 100/K-12
875 Academy Dr 17046 717-273-8114
Jeff Griffith, prin. Fax 272-1886
Lebanon County Career School Post-Sec.
18 E Weidman St 17046 800-694-8804
New Covenant Christian S 200/PK-12
452 Ebenezer Rd 17046 717-274-2423
Dr. Timothy Deibler, admin. Fax 274-9830

Leechburg, Armstrong, Pop. 2,324
Kiski Area SD 4,500/K-12
250 Hyde Park Rd 15656 724-845-2022
Dr. John Meighan, supt. Fax 842-0444
www.kiskiarea.com
Kiski Area HS 1,500/9-12
250 Hyde Park Rd 15656 724-845-8181
William McClarnon, prin. Fax 842-0403

Kiski Area IS 800/7-8
260 Hyde Park Rd 15656 724-845-2219
Patrick Hefflin, prin. Fax 845-3208

Leechburg Area SD 900/K-12
210 Penn Ave 15656 724-842-9681
James A. Budzilek Ed.D., supt. Fax 845-2241
www.leechburg.k12.pa.us
Leechburg Area HS 300/9-12
215 1st St 15656 724-842-0571
Karen Hulse, prin. Fax 845-4761
Leechburg Area MS 200/6-8
215 1st St 15656 724-842-0571
Karen Hulse, prin. Fax 845-4761

Leesport, Berks, Pop. 1,845
Area Vocational Technical School
Supt. — None
Berks CTC - West Vo/Tech
1057 County Road 19533 610-374-4073
James Casper, prin. Fax 987-6106

Schuylkill Valley SD 1,900/K-12
929 Lakeshore Dr 19533 610-916-0957
Dr. Solomon Lausch, supt. Fax 926-3960
www.schuylkillvalley.org/
Schuylkill Valley HS 600/9-12
929 Lakeshore Dr 19533 610-926-1706
David Haughney, prin. Fax 926-8341
Schuylkill Valley MS 500/6-8
114 Ontelaunee Dr 19533 610-926-7111
Judith Sargent, prin. Fax 926-3321

Leetsdale, Allegheny, Pop. 1,188
Quaker Valley SD
Supt. — See Sewickley
Quaker Valley SHS 500/10-12
625 Beaver St 15056 412-749-6000
Dr. Heidi Ondek, prin. Fax 749-6011

Lehighton, Carbon, Pop. 5,513
Lehighton Area SD 2,400/K-12
1000 Union St 18235 610-377-4490
Trent Bocan, supt. Fax 377-2423
www.uslawcenter.com/lasd/
Lehighton Area HS, 1 Indian Ln 18235 800/9-12
Dr. Gary Von Norman, prin. 610-377-6180
Lehighton Area MS 800/5-8
301 Beaver Run Rd 18235 610-377-6535
Timothy Kach, prin.

Lehman, Luzerne
Lake-Lehman SD 2,200/K-12
PO Box 38 18627 570-675-2165
Michael J. Healey, supt. Fax 675-7657
www.lake-lehman.k12.pa.us/
Lake-Lehman JSHS 1,000/7-12
PO Box 38 18627 570-675-7458
Tracey Wagner, prin. Fax 675-2951

Pennsylvania State University Post-Sec.
PO Box PSU 18627 570-675-2171

Lemoyne, Cumberland, Pop. 3,969
West Shore SD
Supt. — See Lewisberry
Lemoyne MS, 701 Market St 17043 500/6-8
Robert Savidge, prin. 717-761-6345

Leola, Lancaster, Pop. 5,685

Veritas Academy 100/K-12
26 Hillcrest Ave 17540 717-556-0690
G. Tyler Fischer, hdmstr. Fax 556-0736

Lester, Delaware

All-State Career School Post-Sec.
501 Seminole St 19029 610-521-1818

Levittown, Bucks, Pop. 53,700
Bristol Township SD 9,100/K-12
6401 Mill Creek Rd 19057 215-943-3200
Ellen Budman, supt. Fax 949-2210
www.bucksiu.org/btsd/
Franklin MS 900/7-9
6403 Mill Creek Rd 19057 215-949-8903
Stanley Vitale, prin. Fax 547-8415
Truman HS 1,500/10-12
3001 Green Ln 19057 215-547-3000
William Haws, prin. Fax 547-4802
Other Schools – See Bristol, Fairless Hills

Neshaminy SD
Supt. — See Langhorne
Sandburg MS, 30 Harmony Rd 19056 700/6-9
Dawn Kelly, prin. 215-943-0360

Pennsbury SD 11,200/K-12
134 Yardley Ave 19054 215-428-4100
Ralph Nuzzolo, supt. Fax 295-8912
www.pennsbury.k12.pa.us
Other Schools – See Fairless Hills, Yardley

Levittown Beauty Academy Post-Sec.
8919 New Falls Rd 19054 215-943-0298

Lewisberry, York, Pop. 387
West Shore SD 8,300/K-12
507 Fishing Creek Rd 17339 717-938-9577
Dr. Richard Domencic, supt. Fax 938-2779
www.wssd.k12.pa.us
Crossroads MS 800/6-8
535 Fishing Creek Rd 17339 717-932-1295
David Zuilkoski, prin.
Red Land HS 1,300/9-12
560 Fishing Creek Rd 17339 717-938-6561
Edward Novosel, prin. Fax 938-0886
Other Schools – See Camp Hill, Lemoyne, New Cumberland

Lewisburg, Union, Pop. 5,499
Lewisburg Area SD 1,800/K-12
PO Box 351 17837 570-523-3220
Dr. Mark DiRocco, supt. Fax 522-3278
www.dragon.k12.pa.us
Eichhorn MS 400/6-8
2057 Washington Ave 17837 570-523-3220
Tracy Krum, prin. Fax 522-3331
Lewisburg Area HS 600/9-12
815 Market St 17837 570-523-3220
James Zack, prin. Fax 524-9484

Bucknell University 17837 Post-Sec.
570-577-2000

Lewistown, Mifflin, Pop. 8,752
Area Vocational Technical School
Supt. — None
Mifflin-Juniata CTC, 700 Pitt St 17044 Vo/Tech
Kevin O'Donnell, prin. 717-248-3933

Mifflin County SD 5,600/K-12
201 8th St 17044 717-248-0148
David Runk, supt. Fax 248-5345
www.mcsdk12.org
Indian Valley HS 1,000/9-12
700 Cedar St 17044 717-248-5441
Ronald Varner, prin. Fax 242-5806
Lewistown Area HS 900/9-12
2 Manor Dr 17044 717-242-1401
Vance S. Varner, prin. Fax 242-5810
Lewistown MS 500/6-8
212 Green Ave 17044 717-242-5801
Mark K. Hidlay, prin. Fax 242-5804
Other Schools – See Mc Veytown, Reedsville

Mifflin-Juniata Career & Technology Ctr Post-Sec.
700 Pitt St 17044 717-248-3933
South Hills School of Business & Tech. Post-Sec.
124 E Market St 17044 717-248-8140

Liberty, Tioga, Pop. 2,810
Southern Tioga SD
Supt. — See Blossburg
Liberty JSHS 300/7-12
PO Box 135 16930 570-324-2071
Francis Jaquish, prin. Fax 324-2313

Ligonier, Westmoreland, Pop. 1,646
Ligonier Valley SD 2,100/K-12
339 W Main St 15658 724-238-5696
Stephen Whisdosh Ed.D., supt. Fax 238-7877
wiu.k12.pa.us/ligonier/
Ligonier Valley HS 500/9-12
40 Springer Rd 15658 724-238-9531
Ronald Baldonieri, prin. Fax 238-2675
Ligonier Valley MS 400/5-8
536 Bell St 15658 724-238-6412
David Steimer, prin. Fax 238-2358
Other Schools – See New Florence

Limerick, Montgomery
Area Vocational Technical School
Supt. — None
Western Center for Technical Study Vo/Tech
77 Gratersford Rd 19468 610-489-7272
Maryann Jukubczyk, prin.

Chapel Christian Academy 200/K-12
378 W Ridge Pike 19468 610-489-6215
Rev. Richard Corbin, prin.

Lincoln University, Chester

Lincoln University Post-Sec.
PO Box 179 19352 610-932-8300

Linesville, Crawford, Pop. 1,139
Conneaut SD 2,800/K-12
219 W School Dr 16424 814-683-5900
Dick Astor, supt. Fax 683-4127
connwww.iu5.org
Linesville HS 500/7-12
302 W School Dr 16424 814-683-5551
Steven Chizewick, prin. Fax 683-5221
Other Schools – See Conneaut Lake, Conneautville

Lititz, Lancaster, Pop. 8,957
Manheim Township SD 5,800/K-12
2933 Lititz Pike 17543 717-569-8231
Dr. Kevin Singer, supt. Fax 569-3729
www.mtwp.k12.pa.us
Other Schools – See Lancaster

Warwick SD 4,600/K-12
301 W Orange St 17543 717-626-3734
Dr. Stephen Iovino, supt. Fax 626-3850
www.warwick.k12.pa.us/
Warwick HS 1,500/9-12
301 W Orange St 17543 717-626-3700
Penny Mason, prin. Fax 626-6199
Warwick MS 800/7-8
401 Maple St 17543 717-626-3701
Michael O'Hara, prin. Fax 627-6089

Linden Hall S for Girls 100/6-12
212 E Main St 17543 717-626-8512
Dr. Vincent Stumpo, hdmstr. Fax 627-1384
Lititz Christian S 300/1-12
501 W Lincoln Ave 17543 717-626-9518
Michael Rohrer, prin. Fax 626-5683

Littlestown, Adams, Pop. 4,036
Littlestown Area SD 2,400/K-12
162 Newark St 17340 717-359-4146
Dr. Robert McConaghy, supt. Fax 359-9617
www.lasd.k12.pa.us
Littlestown HS 800/9-12
200 E Myrtle St 17340 717-359-4146
Bryant Meckley, prin. Fax 359-9461
Maple Avenue MS 600/6-8
75 Maple Ave 17340 717-359-4146
Jeffrey Bair, prin. Fax 359-9617

Lock Haven, Clinton, Pop. 8,957
Keystone Central SD 4,900/K-12
95 W 4th St 17745 570-893-4900
Dr. Donald Wills, supt. Fax 893-4923
www.kcsd.k12.pa.us
Other Schools – See Mill Hall, Renovo

Lock Haven University Post-Sec.
401 N Fairview St 17745 570-893-2011

Loretto, Cambria, Pop. 1,143

St. Francis University Post-Sec.
PO Box 600 15940 814-472-3000

Lower Burrell, Westmoreland, Pop. 12,531
Burrell SD 2,200/K-12
1021 Puckety Church Rd 15068 724-334-1406
Anna Mary Palermo Ph.D., supt. Fax 334-1429
www.burrell.k12.pa.us
Burrell HS 700/9-12
1021 Puckety Church Rd 15068 724-334-1403
Michael Stofa, prin. Fax 334-1420
Huston MS 600/6-8
1020 Puckety Church Rd 15068 724-334-1443
Shannon Wagner, prin. Fax 334-1434

Newport Business Institute Post-Sec.
945 Greensburg Rd 15068 724-339-7542
Oakbridge Academy of Arts Post-Sec.
1250 Greensburg Rd 15068 724-335-5336

Loysburg, Bedford
Northern Bedford County SD 1,200/PK-12
152 NBC Dr 16659 814-766-2221
William Wade, supt. Fax 766-3772
nbcsd.k12.pa.us
Northern Bedford County MSHS 600/6-12
152 NBC Dr 16659 814-766-2221
Wayne Sherlock, prin. Fax 766-3772

Lykens, Dauphin, Pop. 1,888
Upper Dauphin Area SD 1,400/K-12
5668 State Route 209 17048 717-362-8134
Barry Clippinger, supt. Fax 362-3050
www.udasd.org/
Upper Dauphin Area MS 500/5-8
5668 State Route 209 17048 717-362-8177
Daniel Bulinski, prin. Fax 362-6567
Other Schools – See Elizabethville

Mc Alisterville, Juniata
Juniata County SD
Supt. — See Mifflintown
East Juniata JSHS 600/7-12
RR 2 Box 2411 17049 717-463-2111
Dr. Delmar Hart, prin. Fax 463-3268

Juniata Mennonite S 200/K-12
PO Box 278 17049 717-463-2898
Andrew Meiser, prin. Fax 463-0134

Mc Clellandtown, Fayette
Albert Gallatin Area SD
Supt. — See Uniontown
Gallatin North MS 400/6-8
113 College Ave 15458 724-737-5423
James Patitucci, prin. Fax 737-5312

Mc Clure, Snyder, Pop. 1,056

Mifflin Co. Christian Academy 100/PK-12
5113 Back Maitland Rd 17841 717-543-2200
Craig Todd, admin. Fax 242-1700

Mc Connellsburg, Fulton, Pop. 1,079
Area Vocational Technical School
Supt. — None
Fulton County AVTS Vo/Tech
151 E Cherry St 17233 717-485-3195
Elizabeth Cheatle, prin.

Central Fulton SD 1,000/PK-12
151 E Cherry St 17233 717-485-3183
Dr. Julia Cigola, supt. Fax 485-5984
www.cfsd.info
Mc Connellsburg HS 300/9-12
151 E Cherry St 17233 717-485-3195
John Heuston, prin. Fax 485-0175
Mc Connellsburg MS 300/6-8
151 E Cherry St 17233 717-485-4209
Todd Beatty, prin. Fax 485-0175

Mc Donald, Washington, Pop. 2,246
Fort Cherry SD 1,300/K-12
110 Fort Cherry Rd 15057 724-796-1551
Robert Dinnen Ph.D., supt. Fax 796-0065
www.fortcherry.org
Fort Cherry JSHS 700/7-12
110 Fort Cherry Rd 15057 724-796-1551
Alfred H. McGivern, prin. Fax 356-2769

South Fayette Township SD 1,900/K-12
2250 Old Oakdale Rd 15057 412-221-4542
Dr. Linda Hippert, supt. Fax 693-0490
www.southfayette.org
South Fayette Township HS 500/9-12
2246 Old Oakdale Rd 15057 412-221-4542
Ann Bisignani, prin. Fax 693-9843
South Fayette Township MS 600/5-8
2254 Old Oakdale Rd 15057 412-221-4542
Karen Labutta, prin. Fax 693-0860

Mc Keesport, Allegheny, Pop. 23,343
Area Vocational Technical School
Supt. — None
McKeesport Area Tech Center Vo/Tech
1960 Eden Park Blvd 15132 412-664-3690
Dr. Julia Stewart, prin.

McKeesport Area SD 4,500/K-12
3590 Oneil Blvd 15132 412-664-3610
Patrick A. Risha, supt. Fax 664-3638
www.mckasd.com
Founders Hall MS 500/7-8
3600 Oneil Blvd 15132 412-664-3690
Dr. Timothy Gabauer, prin.
McKeesport Area HS 1,500/9-12
1960 Eden Park Blvd 15132 412-664-3650
Harry Bauman, prin.

South Allegheny SD 1,500/K-12
2743 Washington Blvd 15133 412-675-3070
Elaine M. Brown, supt. Fax 672-2836
www.southallegheny.org
South Allegheny HS 600/9-12
2743 Washington Blvd 15133 412-675-3070
Keith Gephart, prin. Fax 673-4903
South Allegheny MS 7-8
2743 Washington Blvd 15133 412-675-3070
Christopher Gretz, prin. Fax 673-4905

Pennsylvania State University Post-Sec.
0 University Dr 15132 412-675-9000
Serra Catholic HS 300/9-12
200 Hershey Dr 15132 412-751-2020
Michael Luft, prin. Fax 751-3488

Mc Kees Rocks, Allegheny, Pop. 7,235
Montour SD 3,300/K-12
223 Clever Rd 15136 412-490-6500
Dr. Joseph Findley, supt. Fax 490-0828
www.montourschools.com
Montour HS 1,100/9-12
223 Clever Rd 15136 412-490-6500
Patrick Dworakowski, prin. Fax 494-9747
Other Schools – See Coraopolis

Sto-Rox SD 1,500/K-12
600 Russellwood Ave 15136 412-778-8871
Fran Serenka, supt. Fax 771-5205
www.srsd.k12.pa.us
Sto-Rox HS 500/9-12
1105 Valley St 15136 412-771-3213
Kim Crummie, prin. Fax 771-8395
Sto-Rox MS 400/6-8
298 Ewing Rd 15136 412-771-3213
Janell Logue-Belden, prin. Fax 771-3848

Ohio Valley General Hospital Post-Sec.
25 Heckel Rd 15136 412-777-6207
Robinson Township Christian S 100/PK-12
77 Phillips Ln 15136 412-787-5919
Patty Rotellini, prin. Fax 787-1558

Mc Murray, Washington, Pop. 4,082
Peters Township SD 3,900/K-12
631 E McMurray Rd 15317 724-941-6251
Dr. Diane Kirk, supt. Fax 941-6565
www.ptsd.k12.pa.us
Peters Twp. HS 1,300/9-12
264 E McMurray Rd 15317 724-941-6250
Dr. William Englert, prin. Fax 942-0915
Peters Twp. MS 600/7-8
625 E McMurray Rd 15317 724-941-2688
Dr. Anthony Merante, prin. Fax 941-1426

Mc Sherrystown, Adams, Pop. 3,702

Delone Catholic HS 500/9-12
140 S Oxford Ave 17344 717-637-5969
Dr. Maureen Thiec, prin. Fax 637-0442

Macungie, Lehigh, Pop. 3,078
East Penn SD
Supt. — See Emmaus
Eyer MS, 5616 Buckeye Rd 18062 700/6-8
Dr. Douglas Wells, prin. 610-965-1600
Lower Macungie MS 1,100/6-8
6299 Lower Macungie Rd 18062 610-395-8593
Robert Misko, prin.

Salem Christian S 200/K-12
8031 Salem Bible Church Rd 18062 610-966-5823
Warren Skuret, admin. Fax 965-8368

Mc Veytown, Mifflin, Pop. 389
Mifflin County SD
Supt. — See Lewistown
Strodes Mills MS 200/6-8
205 Chestnut Ridge Rd 17051 717-248-5488
E. Terry Styers, prin. Fax 242-5839

Mahanoy City, Schuylkill, Pop. 4,499
Mahanoy Area SD 1,100/K-12
1 Golden Bear Dr 17948 570-773-3443
Anthony J. Crimaldi, supt. Fax 773-2913
Mahanoy Area HS 400/9-12
1 Golden Bear Dr 17948 570-773-3443
William Hume, prin. Fax 773-2913
Mahanoy Area MS 400/5-8
1 Golden Bear Dr 17948 570-773-3443
Joie Green, prin. Fax 773-4034

McCann School of Business & Technology Post-Sec.
47 S Main St 17948 570-773-1820

Malvern, Chester, Pop. 3,083
Great Valley SD 3,800/K-12
47 Church Rd 19355 610-889-2100
Rita Jones Ed.D., supt. Fax 889-2120
www.gvsd.org
Great Valley HS 1,100/9-12
225 Phoenixville Pike 19355 610-889-1900
John Fidler, prin. Fax 695-8901
Great Valley MS 1,000/6-8
255 Phoenixville Pike 19355 610-644-6440
Stephen Swymer Ed.D., prin. Fax 889-1166

Devereux Beneto Center Post-Sec.
655 Sugartown Rd # 297 19355 800-935-6789
Malvern Prep S 600/6-12
418 S Warren Ave 19355 484-595-1100
James Stewart, hdmstr. Fax 595-1124
Penn State Great Valley School Post-Sec.
30 E Swedesford Rd 19355 610-648-3200
Phelps S 200/7-12
583 Sugartown Rd 19355 610-644-1754
Norman Phelps, admin. Fax 644-6679
Villa Maria Academy 400/9-12
370 Old Lincoln Hwy 19355 610-644-2551
Sr. Marita Carmel, prin. Fax 644-2866

Manchester, York, Pop. 2,417
Northeastern York SD 2,800/PK-12
41 Harding St 17345 717-266-3667
Dr. Dennis Baughman, supt. Fax 266-5792
www.nesd.k12.pa.us
Northeastern HS 800/9-12
300 High St 17345 717-266-3644
Dennis Ashton, prin. Fax 266-0616
Northeastern MS 600/7-8
198 N Hartman St 17345 717-266-3676
Michael Alessandroni, prin. Fax 266-9735

Manheim, Lancaster, Pop. 4,721
Manheim Central SD 3,100/K-12
71 N Hazel St 17545 717-665-3422
Carol Saylor, supt. Fax 665-7631
www.manheimcentral.org
Manheim Central HS 1,100/9-12
400 Adele Ave 17545 717-665-2451
Arlen Mummau, prin. Fax 665-9174
Manheim Central MS 500/7-8
123 E Gramby St 17545 717-665-2246
Lou Martarano, prin. Fax 665-9108

Mansfield, Tioga, Pop. 3,412
Southern Tioga SD
Supt. — See Blossburg
Mansfield JSHS 500/7-12
73 W Wellsboro St 16933 570-662-2674
Denise Drabick, prin. Fax 662-2808

Mansfield University of Pennsylvania Post-Sec.
Academy St 16933 570-662-4000
New Covenant Academy 200/PK-12
310 Extension St 16933 570-662-2996
Terry L. Mickey, hdmstr. Fax 662-0272

Maple Glen, Montgomery, Pop. 5,881
Upper Dublin SD 4,400/K-12
1580 Fort Washington Ave 19002 215-643-8800
Michael Pladus Ed.D., supt. Fax 643-8803
www.udsd.org
Other Schools – See Dresher, Fort Washington

Marienville, Forest
Forest Area SD
Supt. — See Tionesta
East Forest JSHS 100/7-12
120 W Birch St 16239 814-927-6688
Michael Hardy, prin. Fax 927-8452

Marietta, Lancaster, Pop. 2,639
Donegal SD
Supt. — See Mount Joy
Donegal MS 600/6-8
1175 River Rd 17547 717-426-4915
Judy Sammet, prin. Fax 426-2417

Marion Center, Indiana, Pop. 436
Marion Center Area SD 1,700/PK-12
PO Box 156 15759 724-397-5551
Francis Fregly, supt. Fax 397-9144
www.mcasd.net/
Marion Center Area HS 800/7-12
PO Box 209 15759 724-397-5551
Thomas Trunzo, prin.

Marklesburg, Fayette, Pop. 277
Uniontown Area SD
Supt. — See Uniontown
McMullen MS 200/6-8
4773 National Pike 15459 724-329-8811
Edward Fearer, prin.

Mar Lin, Schuylkill
Area Vocational Technical School
Supt. — None
Schuylkill Technology Center - South Vo/Tech
PO Box 110 17951 570-544-4748
Kurt Lynch, prin. Fax 544-3895

Mars, Butler, Pop. 1,721
Mars Area SD 2,600/K-12
545 Route 228 16046 724-625-1518
Dr. William Pettigrew, supt. Fax 625-1060
www.marsk12.org
Mars Area HS 900/9-12
520 Route 228 16046 724-625-1581
Anna Saker, prin. Fax 625-4477
Mars Area MS 700/6-8
1775 Three Degree Rd 16046 724-625-3145
Richard Cornell, prin. Fax 625-4470

Martinsburg, Blair, Pop. 2,193
Spring Cove SD
Supt. — See Roaring Spring
Central HS, RR 1 Box 420 16662 700/9-12
David Crumrine, prin. 814-793-2111

Meadville, Crawford, Pop. 13,410
Area Vocational Technical School
Supt. — None
Crawford County AVTS Vo/Tech
860 Thurston Rd 16335 814-724-6024
Neil Donovan, prin. Fax 337-0602

Crawford Central SD 4,200/K-12
11280 Mercer Pike 16335 814-724-3960
Michael E. Dolecki, supt. Fax 333-8731
www.craw.org
Meadville Area HS 1,000/9-12
930 North St 16335 814-336-1121
James T. Morgan, prin. Fax 337-1486
Meadville Area MS 500/7-8
974 North St 16335 814-333-1188
Rebecca James, prin. Fax 333-2799
Other Schools – See Cochranton

Allegheny College Post-Sec.
520 N Main St 16335 814-332-3100
Business Institute of Pennsylvania Post-Sec.
632 Arch St 16335 814-724-0700
Calvary Baptist Christian Academy 200/PK-12
543 Randolph St 16335 814-724-6606
Durwood Abbey, prin.

Mechanicsburg, Cumberland, Pop. 8,901
Area Vocational Technical School
Supt. — None
Cumberland-Perry AVTS Vo/Tech
110 Old Willow Mill Rd 17050 717-697-0354
Mary Rodman, prin. Fax 697-0592

Cumberland Valley SD 7,700/K-12
6746 Carlisle Pike 17050 717-697-8261
B. Jean Walker, supt. Fax 795-7084
www.cvschools.org
Cumberland Valley HS 2,500/9-12
6746 Carlisle Pike 17050 717-766-0217
Steven Kirkpatrick, prin. Fax 795-8940
Eagle View MS 1,100/6-8
6746 Carlisle Pike 17050 717-766-0217
Kaye Wishard, prin. Fax 697-3738
Good Hope MS 900/6-8
451 Skyport Rd 17050 717-761-1865
Matthew LaBuda, prin. Fax 761-5910
Mechanicsburg Area SD 3,400/K-12
100 E Elmwood Ave 17055 717-691-4500
Joseph Hood, supt. Fax 691-3438
www.mbgsd.org
Mechanicsburg Area HS 1,100/9-12
500 S Broad St 17055 717-691-4530
David Harris, prin. Fax 691-7632
Mechanicsburg Area MS 900/6-8
1750 S Market St 17055 717-691-4560
Leonard Ference, prin. Fax 791-7977

Computer Learning Network Post-Sec.
401 E Winding Hill Rd # 101 17055 717-761-1481
Emmanuel Baptist Christian Academy 200/PK-12
4681 E Trindle Rd 17050 717-761-7000
F. Ross Ritchey, prin. Fax 761-3207
Faith Tabernacle S 100/1-12
1410 Good Hope Rd 17050 717-975-0641
Fax 975-9920
ITT Technical Institute Post-Sec.
5020 Louise Dr 17055 717-691-9263

Media, Delaware, Pop. 5,472
Rose Tree Media SD 4,000/K-12
308 N Olive St 19063 610-627-6000
Dr. Denise Kerr, supt. Fax 565-5317
www.rtmsd.org
Penncrest HS 1,300/9-12
134 Barren Rd 19063 610-627-6200
Kenneth Batchelor, prin. Fax 891-0898
Springton Lake MS 1,000/6-8
1900 N Providence Rd 19063 610-627-6500
Joyce Jeuell, prin. Fax 566-8665

Delaware County Community College Post-Sec.
901 Media Line Rd 19063 610-359-5000
Pennsylvania Institute of Technology Post-Sec.
800 Manchester Ave 19063 610-892-1500
Pennsylvania State University Post-Sec.
25 Yearsley Mill Rd 19063 610-892-1350
Williamson Free School of Mech. Trades Post-Sec.
106 S New Middletown Rd 19063 610-566-1776

Melrose Park, Montgomery, Pop. 6,500

Gratz College Post-Sec.
7605 Old York Rd 19027 215-635-7300
Saligman MS 100/6-8
7613 Old York Rd 19027 215-635-3303
Susan B. Friedman, prin. Fax 635-3325

Mercer, Mercer, Pop. 2,313
Area Vocational Technical School
Supt. — None
Mercer County Career Center Vo/Tech
PO Box 152 16137 724-662-3000
Rachel Martin, prin. Fax 662-1025

Mercer Area SD 1,500/K-12
545 W Butler St 16137 724-662-5100
Dr. William Gathers, supt. Fax 662-5109
www.mercer.k12.pa.us
Mercer Area HS 500/9-12
545 W Butler St 16137 724-662-5104
Dr. Hendley Hoge, prin. Fax 662-2993
Mercer Area MS 200/7-8
545 W Butler St 16137 724-662-5105
Ronald Rowe, prin. Fax 662-2993

Mercersburg, Franklin, Pop. 1,542
Tuscarora SD 2,600/K-12
118 E Seminary St 17236 717-328-3127
Dr. Thomas A. Stapleford, supt. Fax 328-9316
www.tus.k12.pa.us/
Buchanan HS 800/9-12
4773 Fort Loudon Rd 17236 717-328-2146
Rodney Benedick, prin. Fax 328-5428
Buchanan MS 600/6-8
5191 Fort Loudon Rd 17236 717-328-5221
Charles Rahauser, prin. Fax 328-9081

Mercersburg Academy 400/9-12
300 E Seminary St 17236 717-328-6113
Douglas Hale, hdmstr. Fax 328-9072

Merion Station, Montgomery, Pop. 700

Akiba Hebrew Academy 300/6-12
223 N Highland Ave 19066 610-667-4070
Rabbi Philip Field, prin. Fax 667-1046
Episcopal Academy 1,100/PK-12
376 N Latches Ln 19066 610-667-9612
Hamilton Clark, hdmstr. Fax 667-8629
Merion Mercy Academy 400/9-12
511 Montgomery Ave 19066 610-664-6655
Sr. Regina Ward, prin. Fax 664-6322

Mertztown, Berks
Brandywine Heights Area SD 2,000/K-12
103 Old Topton Rd 19539 610-682-5100
Dr. John Curtin, supt. Fax 682-5136
www.bhasd.k12.pa.us/

Brandywine Heights Area HS 700/9-12
103 Old Topton Rd 19539 610-682-5102
Demetrios Thermenos, prin. Fax 682-5139
Other Schools – See Topton

Gateway Christian S 100/K-12
245 Fredericksville Rd 19539 610-682-2748
Arthur Dexter, prin. Fax 682-9670

Meyersdale, Somerset, Pop. 2,387
Meyersdale Area SD 1,100/K-12
309 Industrial Park Rd 15552 814-634-5123
Curtis Kerns, supt. Fax 634-0832
www.masd.net
Meyersdale Area HS 400/9-12
1349 Shaw Mines Rd 15552 814-634-8311
John Wiltrout, prin. Fax 634-5100
Meyersdale Area MS 200/6-8
1353 Shaw Mines Rd 15552 814-634-1437

Middleburg, Snyder, Pop. 1,369
Midd-West SD 1,500/K-12
568 E Main St 17842 570-837-0046
William L. Houser, supt. Fax 837-3018
www.mwsd.cc
Middleburg MS 6-8
10 Dock Hill Rd 17842 570-837-0551
Donna Samuelson, prin. Fax 837-5061
Midd-West HS 500/9-12
540 E Main St 17842 570-837-0046
Ronald Renshaw, prin. Fax 837-5267
Other Schools – See Beaver Springs

Middlebury Center, Tioga, Pop. 200

Tioga Co. Christian Academy 100/K-12
PO Box 103 16935 570-376-2202
Fax 376-2587

Middletown, Dauphin, Pop. 9,105
Middletown Area SD 2,500/K-12
55 W Water St 17057 717-948-3304
Audrey Utley Ed.D., supt. Fax 948-3329
www.raiderweb.org
Feaser MS 600/6-8
214 N Race St 17057 717-948-3390
Russ Eppinger, prin. Fax 948-3392
Middletown Area HS 700/9-12
1155 N Union St 17057 717-948-3333
Scott Rohrer, prin. Fax 948-3359

Harrisburg Institute of Trade & Tech. Post-Sec.
3000 Pineford Dr 17057 717-944-2731
Pennsylvania State University Post-Sec.
777 W Harrisburg Pike 17057 717-948-6000

Midland, Beaver, Pop. 3,018
Western Beaver County SD 900/K-12
343 Ridgemont Dr 15059 724-643-9310
Dr. Maureen Ungarean, supt. Fax 643-8048
www.westernbeaver.org/
Other Schools – See Industry

Mifflinburg, Union, Pop. 3,567
Mifflinburg Area SD 2,200/K-12
PO Box 285 17844 570-966-8200
Barry Tomasetti, supt. Fax 966-8210
www.mifflinburg.org
Mifflinburg Area HS 800/9-12
75 Market St 17844 570-966-8230
Glenn Fogel, prin. Fax 966-8260
Mifflinburg Area MS 600/6-8
100 Mabel St 17844 570-966-8290
Marion Lynn, prin. Fax 966-8304

Shady Grove Christian S 100/1-12
124 Turkey Run Rd 17844 570-966-9333
Randall Yoder, prin. Fax 966-9333

Mifflintown, Juniata, Pop. 844
Juniata County SD 3,200/K-12
HC 63 Box 7D 17059 717-436-2111
Fax 436-2777
www.jcsd.k12.pa.us
Juniata HS 700/9-12
RR 4 Box 259 17059 717-436-2193
Edward Apple, prin. Fax 436-2858
Tuscarora MS 500/6-8
RR 4 Box 118 17059 717-436-2165
Ralph Baker, prin. Fax 436-5999
Other Schools – See Mc Alisterville

Milford, Pike, Pop. 1,176
Delaware Valley SD 4,700/K-12
236 Route 6 And 209 18337 570-296-1800
Dr. Candis Finan, supt. Fax 296-3172
www.dvsd.org
Delaware Valley HS 9-10 9-10
256 Route 6 and 209 18337 570-409-2001
Michael Lacika, prin. Fax 409-2002
Delaware Valley HS 11-12 800/11-12
252 Route 6 And 209 18337 570-296-1850
Joseph Casmus, prin. Fax 296-3160
Delaware Valley MS 400/7-8
258 Route 6 And 209 18337 570-296-1830
Peter Ioppolo, prin. Fax 296-3162
Other Schools – See Dingmans Ferry

Mill Creek, Huntingdon, Pop. 341
Area Vocational Technical School
Supt. — None
Huntingdon County CTC Vo/Tech
PO Box E 17060 814-643-0951
Kenneth Parker, prin.

Millersburg, Dauphin, Pop. 2,510
Millersburg Area SD 900/K-12
799 Center St 17061 717-692-2108
John Fronk, supt. Fax 692-2895
www.mlbgsd.k12.pa.us/
Millersburg Area HS 300/9-12
799 Center St 17061 717-692-2108
S. Kirk Miller, prin.
Millersburg Area MS 200/6-8
799 Center St 17061 717-692-2108
Jeffrey Prouse, prin.

Millerstown, Perry, Pop. 679
Greenwood SD 700/K-12
405 E Sunbury St 17062 717-589-3117
Ed Burns, supt. Fax 589-3013
www.greenwoodsd.org
Greenwood HS 300/9-12
405 E Sunbury St 17062 717-589-3116
Nicholas Guarente, prin. Fax 589-7096
Greenwood MS 7-8
405 E Sunbury St 17062 717-589-3116
Nicholas Guarente, prin. Fax 589-7096

Millersville, Lancaster, Pop. 7,573
Penn Manor SD
Supt. — See Lancaster
Penn Manor HS 1,800/9-12
PO Box 1001 17551 717-872-9520
Janice Mindish, prin. Fax 872-0934

Millersville University of Pennsylvania Post-Sec.
PO Box 1002 17551 717-872-3024

Mill Hall, Clinton, Pop. 1,503
Area Vocational Technical School
Supt. — None
Keystone Central CTC Vo/Tech
64 Keystone Central Dr 17751 570-748-6584
Samuel Marolo, prin. Fax 748-5467

Keystone Central SD
Supt. — See Lock Haven
Central Mountain HS 1,300/9-12
64 Keystone Central Dr 17751 570-893-4646
Karen Probst, prin. Fax 893-4946
Central Mountain MS 1,000/6-8
200 Ben Ave 17751 570-726-3141
Norman Palovecsik, prin. Fax 726-7227

Millville, Columbia, Pop. 969
Millville Area SD 800/K-12
PO Box 260 17846 570-458-5538
Kathleen Stark Ed.D., supt. Fax 458-5584
www.millville.k12.pa.us
Millville Area JSHS 400/7-12
PO Box 260 17846 570-458-5538
Brian Seely, prin. Fax 458-5583

Milton, Northumberland, Pop. 6,539
Milton Area SD 2,500/K-12
700 Mahoning St 17847 570-742-7614
Dr. William Clark, supt. Fax 742-4523
www.milton.k12.pa.us
Milton Area HS 800/K-12
700 Mahoning St 17847 570-742-7611
Bryan Noaker, prin. Fax 742-4928
Milton Area MS 600/6-8
700 Mahoning St 17847 570-742-7685
V. David Brown, prin. Fax 742-4857

Meadowbrook Christian S 300/PK-12
363 Stamm Rd 17847 570-742-2638
W. Randall Reddinger, admin. Fax 742-4710

Minersville, Schuylkill, Pop. 4,416
Minersville Area SD 1,200/PK-12
PO Box 787 17954 570-544-4764
M. Joseph Brady, supt. Fax 544-6162
www.battlinminers.com
Minersville Area JSHS 600/7-12
PO Box 787 17954 570-544-4761
Andrew M. Terry, prin. Fax 544-5866

Mohrsville, Berks

King's Academy 200/K-12
1562 Main St 19541 610-926-9639
Barbara Ann Wilcox, admin. Fax 926-8089

Monaca, Beaver, Pop. 6,077
Area Vocational Technical School
Supt. — None
Beaver County AVTS Vo/Tech
145 Poplar Dr 15061 724-728-5800
Robert George, prin. Fax 725-2299

Center Area SD 2,000/K-12
160 Baker Rd Ext 15061 724-775-5600
Dr. Daniel Matsook, supt. Fax 775-4302
www.casd.k12.pa.us
Center Area HS 700/9-12
160 Baker Rd Ext 15061 724-775-4300
Anthony Mendicino, prin. Fax 775-4302
Center Area MS 500/6-8
160 Baker Rd Ext 15061 724-775-8200
Michael McCullough, prin. Fax 775-4302

Monaca SD 800/K-12
1500 Allen Ave 15061 724-775-3252
Dr. Michael Thomas, supt. Fax 775-3633
Monaca JSHS 400/7-12
1500 Allen Ave 15061 724-775-4320
Robert Postupac, prin. Fax 770-9074

Community College of Beaver County Post-Sec.
1 Campus Dr 15061 724-775-8561
Pennsylvania State University Post-Sec.
Broadhead Rd 15061 724-773-3500

Monessen, Westmoreland, Pop. 8,467
Monessen CSD 1,100/K-12
1275 Rostraver St 15062 724-684-3600
Cynthia L. Chelen, supt. Fax 684-6782
www.monessen.k12.pa.us/index.html
Monessen HS 300/9-12
1245 State Rd 15062 724-684-7100
Randall Marino, prin. Fax 684-7925
Monessen MS 300/6-8
1245 State Rd 15062 724-684-6202
Randall Marino, prin. Fax 684-7925

Douglas Education Center Post-Sec.
130 7th St 15062 724-684-3684

Monongahela, Washington, Pop. 4,613
Ringgold SD
Supt. — See New Eagle

Carroll MS 300/6-8
120 Alexander Ave 15063 724-258-8454
Deborah DiMaglio, prin. Fax 258-4109
Ringgold HS 1,200/9-12
1 Ram Dr 15063 724-258-2200
Dwane Homa, prin. Fax 258-7360

Monroeville, Allegheny, Pop. 28,591
Area Vocational Technical School
Supt. — None
Forbes Road CTC Vo/Tech
607 Beatty Rd 15146 412-373-8100
Quentin Martin, prin. Fax 373-8106

Gateway SD 4,400/K-12
9000 Gateway Campus Blvd 15146 412-372-5300
Dr. Cleveland Steward, supt. Fax 373-5731
www.gatewayk12.org
Gateway HS 1,600/9-12
3000 Gateway Campus Blvd 15146 412-373-5744
William Short, prin. Fax 373-5872
Gateway MS 1,300/6-8
4450 Old William Penn Hwy 15146 412-373-5780
Andrew Leopold, prin. Fax 373-5794

Career Training Academy Post-Sec.
4314 Old William Penn # 103 15146 412-373-3900
Community College of Allegheny County Post-Sec.
595 Beatty Rd 15146 724-325-1327
Empire Beauty School Post-Sec.
320 Mall Blvd 15146 412-373-7727
Greater Works Christian S 300/PK-12
301 College Park Dr 15146 724-327-6500
J. R. Gardner, hdmstr. Fax 325-4602
ITT Technical Institute Post-Sec.
105 Mall Blvd # 200 15146 412-856-5920
Western School of Health & Bus. Careers Post-Sec.
1 Monroeville Ctr 15146 412-373-6400

Mont Alto, Franklin, Pop. 1,369

Pennsylvania State University Post-Sec.
Mont Alto Campus 17237 717-749-6000

Montgomery, Lycoming, Pop. 1,635
Montgomery Area SD 1,000/K-12
120 Penn St 17752 570-547-1608
Daphne Ross, supt. Fax 547-6271
www.montasd.org
Montgomery HS 300/9-12
120 Penn St 17752 570-547-1608
Wayne Brookhart, prin. Fax 547-6755
Montgomery MS 200/6-8
120 Penn St 17752 570-547-1608
Wayne Brookhart, prin. Fax 547-6755

Montoursville, Lycoming, Pop. 4,617
Loyalsock Township SD 1,200/K-12
1720 Sycamore Rd 17754 570-326-6508
Richard J. Mextorf Ed.D., supt. Fax 326-0770
www.ltsd.k12.pa.us
Other Schools – See Williamsport

Montoursville Area SD 2,100/K-12
50 N Arch St 17754 570-368-2491
Dr. Albert J. Cunningham, supt.
www.montoursville.k12.pa.us/
McCall MS, 600 Willow St 17754 700/5-8
Jeffrey Moore, prin. 570-368-2441
Montoursville Area HS 700/9-12
100 N Arch St 17754 570-368-2611
C. Raymond Huff, prin.

Montrose, Susquehanna, Pop. 1,617
Montrose Area SD 1,900/K-12
80 High School Rd 18801 570-278-6221
Michael F. Ognosky, supt. Fax 278-4798
www.masd.info/
Montrose JSHS 1,000/7-12
50 High School Rd 18801 570-278-6223
Fax 278-9143

Moon Township, Allegheny, Pop. 10,187
Moon Area SD
Supt. — See Coraopolis
Moon Area MS 900/6-8
8353 University Blvd 15108 412-262-4140
Julie Moore, prin. Fax 264-3013
Moon HS 1,100/9-12
904 Beaver Grade Rd 15108 412-262-9040
Michael Hauser, prin. Fax 264-1271

Moosic, Lackawanna, Pop. 5,679

Empire Beauty School Post-Sec.
3370 Birney Ave 18507 570-823-5987

Morgantown, Lancaster

Conestoga Christian S 300/K-12
2760 Main St 19543 610-286-0353
Susan Yoder, admin. Fax 286-0350

Morrisdale, Clearfield
West Branch Area SD 1,300/K-12
356 Allport Cutoff 16858 814-345-6832
Arleen Multhauf, supt. Fax 345-5220
www.westbranch.org
West Branch Area JSHS 800/6-12
356 Allport Cutoff 16858 814-345-5615
Ronald A. Matchock, prin. Fax 345-6116

Morrisville, Bucks, Pop. 9,955
Morrisville Boro SD 1,000/K-12
550 W Palmer St 19067 215-736-2681
Elizabeth Hammond Yonson Ed.D., supt. Fax 736-2413
mv.org
Morrisville Borough JSHS 500/6-12
550 W Palmer St 19067 215-736-5260
Fax 736-3958

Morton, Delaware, Pop. 2,688
Area Vocational Technical School
Supt. — None

Delaware County AVTS — Vo/Tech
200 Yale Ave 19070 — 610-938-9000
Dr. Philip Lachimia, prin.

Moscow, Lackawanna, Pop. 1,890
North Pocono SD — 3,200/K-12
701 Church St 18444 — 570-842-7659
Dr. Louis DeFazio, supt. — Fax 842-0886
www.npsd.net
North Pocono HS — 1,100/9-12
701 Church St 18444 — 570-842-7606
Colin Fureaux, prin. — Fax 842-2163
North Pocono MS — 800/6-8
701 Church St 18444 — 570-842-4588
Edward Bugno, prin. — Fax 842-1783

St. Gregory's Academy — 100/9-12
RR 8 Box 8214 18444 — 570-842-8212
E. Howard Clark, hdmstr. — Fax 842-4513

Mount Braddock, Fayette

West Virginia Career Institute — Post-Sec.
PO Box 278 15465 — 724-437-4600

Mount Carmel, Northumberland, Pop. 6,161
Mt. Carmel Area SD — 1,800/PK-12
600 W 5th St 17851 — 570-339-1500
Cheryl Latorre, supt.
www.mca.k12.pa.us
Mt. Carmel Area JSHS — 900/7-12
600 W 5th St 17851 — 570-339-1500
— Fax 339-0487

Mount Joy, Lancaster, Pop. 6,865
Area Vocational Technical School
Supt. — None
Lancaster County CTC-Mt. Joy — Vo/Tech
PO Box 537 17552 — 717-653-3000
Joseph Trynosky, prin. — Fax 653-0901

Donegal SD — 2,200/K-12
1051 Koser Rd 17552 — 717-653-1447
Linda M. Abele, supt. — Fax 492-1350
www.donegal.k12.pa.us
Donegal HS — 800/9-12
915 Anderson Ferry Rd 17552 — 717-653-1871
John L. Felix, prin. — Fax 492-1241
Other Schools – See Marietta

Janus S — 100/1-12
205 Lefever Rd 17552 — 717-653-0025
— Fax 653-0696
Sonlight River Brethren S — 50/K-12
4075 Siegrist Rd 17552 — 717-684-7887
Jonas Sauder, prin.

Mount Pleasant, Westmoreland, Pop. 4,584
Mount Pleasant Area SD — 2,500/K-12
RR 4 Box 2222 15666 — 724-547-4100
Frank Watson, supt. — Fax 547-0629
www.mpasd.net
Mount Pleasant Area JSHS — 1,300/7-12
RR 4 Box 2222 15666 — 724-547-4100
Terry Struble, prin. — Fax 547-0526

Mount Carmel Christian S — 100/K-12
1231 Mount Pleasant Rd 15666 — 724-887-7169
Sherwood Edward, prin.

Mount Union, Huntingdon, Pop. 2,432
Mt. Union Area SD — 1,500/K-12
28 W Market St 17066 — 814-542-8631
Dr. Jerry Dunkle, supt. — Fax 542-8633
www.muasd.org/
Mt. Union Area JSHS — 700/7-12
706 N Shaver St 17066 — 814-542-2518
Curt Whitsel, prin. — Fax 542-5451

Muncy, Lycoming, Pop. 2,564
Muncy SD — 1,100/K-12
46 S Main St 17756 — 570-546-3125
Lawrence Potash, supt. — Fax 546-6676
www.muncysd.org
Muncy JSHS — 500/7-12
200 W Penn St 17756 — 570-546-3127
Calvin Barto, prin. — Fax 546-7688

Munhall, Allegheny, Pop. 11,854
Steel Valley SD — 2,000/K-12
220 E Oliver Rd 15120 — 412-464-3650
Dr. Alex Warren, supt. — Fax 464-3626
www.svsd.k12.pa.us
Steel Valley HS — 700/9-12
3113 Main St 15120 — 412-464-3690
Nancy Hines, prin. — Fax 464-3609
Steel Valley MS — 500/6-8
3114 Main St 15120 — 412-464-3645
John Ackermann, prin. — Fax 464-3642

Murrysville, Westmoreland, Pop. 19,098
Franklin Regional SD — 3,800/K-12
3210 School St 15668 — 724-327-5456
Dr. Peter D'Arcangelo, supt. — Fax 327-6149
www.franklinregional.k12.pa.us
Franklin Regional HS — 1,300/9-12
3200 School Rd 15668 — 724-327-5456
Joan Mellon, prin. — Fax 327-9256
Franklin Regional MS — 900/6-8
4660 Old William Penn Hwy 15668 — 724-327-5456
Shelley Shaneyfelt, prin. — Fax 733-0949

Myerstown, Lebanon, Pop. 3,111
Eastern Lebanon County SD — 2,400/K-12
180 Elco Dr 17067 — 717-866-7117
Dr. Ronald Hetrick, supt. — Fax 866-7084
www.elco.k12.pa.us
Eastern Lebanon County HS — 800/9-12
180 Elco Dr 17067 — 717-866-7447
Randall Grove, prin. — Fax 866-7287
Eastern Lebanon County MS — 600/6-8
60 Evergreen Dr 17067 — 717-866-6591
Keith DuBois, prin. — Fax 866-5837

Evangelical School of Theology — Post-Sec.
121 S College St 17067 — 717-866-5775
Lebanon Valley Christian S — 100/1-12
7821 Lancaster Ave 17067 — 717-933-5171
Myerstown Mennonite S — 100/1-12
739 E Lincoln Ave 17067 — 717-866-5667
Anthony Hurst, prin. — Fax 866-8652

Nanticoke, Luzerne, Pop. 10,533
Greater Nanticoke Area SD — 1,700/K-12
427 Kosciuszko St 18634 — 570-735-1270
Anthony Perrone, supt. — Fax 735-1350
www.gnasd.com
Greater Nanticoke Area HS — 900/8-12
425 Kosciuszko St 18634 — 570-735-7781
Mary Ann Jarolen, prin. — Fax 733-1002

Luzerne County Community College — Post-Sec.
1333 S Prospect St 18634 — 570-740-0200

Nanty Glo, Cambria, Pop. 3,024
Blacklick Valley SD — 700/K-12
555 Birch St 15943 — 814-749-9211
Donald Thomas, supt. — Fax 749-8627
bvsd.k12.pa.us
Blacklick Valley JSHS — 300/7-12
555 Birch St 15943 — 814-749-9213
Michael McDermott, prin.

Narberth, Montgomery, Pop. 4,213
Lower Merion SD
Supt. — See Ardmore
Welsh Valley MS, 325 Tower Ln 19072 — 800/6-8
Dr. Alan Rosenau, prin. — 610-645-1420

Narvon, Lancaster

Twin Valley Bible Academy — 100/K-12
105 Shirktown Rd 17555 — 610-286-6646
Thomas Taylor, prin.

Natrona Heights, Allegheny, Pop. 11,400
Highlands SD — 2,700/PK-12
PO Box 288 15065 — 724-226-2400
Randall Kahler, supt. — Fax 226-8437
www.goldenrams.com
Highlands HS — 900/9-12
1500 Pacific Ave 15065 — 724-226-1000
Thomas Shirey, prin. — Fax 226-9611
Highlands MS — 600/6-8
1350 Broadview Blvd 15065 — 724-226-0600
Frank Moxie, prin. — Fax 226-3287

Allegheny Valley Hospital — Post-Sec.
1301 Carlisle St 15065 — 724-226-7000
St. Joseph HS — 200/9-12
800 Montana Ave 15065 — 724-224-5552
Beverly Kaniecki, prin. — Fax 224-3205

Nazareth, Northampton, Pop. 6,009
Nazareth Area SD — 4,400/K-12
1 Education Dr 18064 — 610-759-1170
Dr. Victor Lesky, supt. — Fax 759-9637
www.nazarethasd.k12.pa.us
Nazareth Area HS — 1,500/9-12
501 E Center St 18064 — 610-759-1730
Judith Swigart, prin. — Fax 746-2599
Nazareth Area MS — 1,100/6-8
355 Tatamy Rd 18064 — 610-759-3350
Jane Callaghan, prin. — Fax 759-3725

Needmore, Fulton

Fulton County Community Christian S — 100/PK-12
PO Box 235 17238 — 717-573-4400
Russell Cheek, prin. — Fax 573-2731

New Berlin, Union, Pop. 829
Area Vocational Technical School
Supt. — None
SUN Area Career & Technology Center — Vo/Tech
PO Box 527 17855 — 570-966-1034
John Bohn, dir. — Fax 966-9492

New Bethlehem, Clarion, Pop. 1,017
Redbank Valley SD — 1,400/K-12
920 Broad St 16242 — 814-275-2426
John M. Cornish Ed.D., supt. — Fax 275-2428
www.redbankvalley.net/
Redbank Valley JSHS — 700/7-12
910 Broad St 16242 — 814-275-2424
Stephen Dobransky, prin. — Fax 275-2428

New Bloomfield, Perry, Pop. 1,084

Carson Long Military Institute — 200/6-12
PO Box 98 17068 — 717-582-2121
Carson Holman, prin. — Fax 582-8763

New Brighton, Beaver, Pop. 6,384
New Brighton Area SD — 2,000/K-12
3225 43rd St 15066 — 724-843-1795
John Osheka Ed.D., supt. — Fax 843-6144
www.nbsd.k12.pa.us
New Brighton Area HS — 600/9-12
3200 43rd St 15066 — 724-846-1050
Edward Kasparek, prin.
New Brighton Area MS — 500/6-8
901 Penn Ave 15066 — 724-846-8100
Dr. David Pietro, prin.

New Castle, Lawrence, Pop. 25,338
Area Vocational Technical School
Supt. — None

Lawrence County AVTS — Vo/Tech
750 Phelps Way 16101 — 724-658-3583
Andrew Tommelleo, prin. — Fax 658-8530

Laurel SD — 1,400/K-12
2497 Harlansburg Rd 16101 — 724-658-8940
Dr. Sandra L. Hennon, supt. — Fax 658-2992
www.laurel.k12.pa.us
Laurel JSHS — 600/7-12
2497 Harlansburg Rd 16101 — 724-658-9056
Harold Dunn, prin. — Fax 658-2992

Neshannock Township SD — 1,300/K-12
3834 Mitchell Rd 16105 — 724-658-4793
Dr. Michael Hink, supt. — Fax 658-1828
www.neshannock.k12.pa.us
Neshannock JSHS — 600/7-12
3834 Mitchell Rd 16105 — 724-658-5513
Scott Seltzer, prin. — Fax 657-8169

New Castle Area SD — 3,700/PK-12
420 Fern St 16101 — 724-656-4756
George J. Gabriel, supt. — Fax 656-4767
www.ncasd.com
New Castle HS — 1,000/9-12
300 E Lincoln Ave 16101 — 724-656-4700
John Sarandrea, prin. — Fax 658-3916
New Castle JHS — 600/7-8
310 E Lincoln Ave 16101 — 724-656-4700
Jacqueline Respress, prin. — Fax 658-6276

Shenango Area SD — 1,400/K-12
2501 Old Pittsburgh Rd 16101 — 724-658-7287
Lawrence R. Connelly, supt. — Fax 658-5370
Shenango HS — 700/7-12
2550 Ellwood Rd 16101 — 724-658-5537
Michael Schreck, prin. — Fax 658-7584

Union Area SD — 800/K-12
500 S Scotland Ln 16101 — 724-658-4775
Dr. Dean A. Casello, supt. — Fax 658-5151
www.union.k12.pa.us
Union Area MSHS — 500/5-12
2106 Camden Ave 16101 — 724-658-4501
Robert Hooven, prin. — Fax 658-8617

Erie Business Center South — Post-Sec.
170 Cascade Galleria 16101 — 724-658-9066
Jameson Memorial Hosp School of Nursing — Post-Sec.
1211 Wilmington Ave 16105 — 724-656-4240
New Castle School of Beauty Culture — Post-Sec.
314 E Washington St 16101 — 724-654-6611

New Cumberland, Cumberland, Pop. 7,230
West Shore SD
Supt. — See Lewisberry
New Cumberland MS — 400/6-8
331 8th St 17070 — 717-774-0162
Karen Hertzler, prin.

New Eagle, Washington, Pop. 2,315
Ringgold SD — 3,800/K-12
400 Main St 15067 — 724-258-9329
Edward Repka, supt. — Fax 258-5363
www.ringgold.org
Other Schools – See Finleyville, Monongahela

New Florence, Westmoreland, Pop. 764
Ligonier Valley SD
Supt. — See Ligonier
Laurel Valley MSHS — 400/7-12
114 Education Ln 15944 — 724-238-4034
Matthew McNickle, prin. — Fax 235-9415

New Holland, Lancaster, Pop. 5,197
Eastern Lancaster County SD — 3,500/K-12
PO Box 609 17557 — 717-354-1500
Dr. Saundra Hoover, supt. — Fax 354-1512
www.elanco.k12.pa.us
Garden Spot HS — 1,200/9-12
PO Box 609 17557 — 717-354-1555
Donald Reed, prin. — Fax 354-1534
Garden Spot MS, PO Box 609 17557 — 600/7-8
Joyce Wilkinson, prin. — 717-354-1561

New Hope, Bucks, Pop. 2,263
New Hope-Solebury SD — 1,000/K-12
180 W Bridge St 18938 — 215-862-2552
Barbara Burke-Stevenson, supt. — Fax 744-6012
www.nhsd.org/
New Hope-Solebury HS — 400/9-12
180 W Bridge St 18938 — 215-862-2028
Stephen Young, prin. — Fax 862-3198
New Hope-Solebury MS — 400/6-8
180 W Bridge St 18938 — 215-862-0608
Khalid Mumin, prin. — Fax 862-2862

Solebury S — 200/7-12
6832 Phillips Mill Rd 18938 — 215-862-5261
John Brown, hdmstr. — Fax 862-3366

New Kensington, Westmoreland, Pop. 14,279
Area Vocational Technical School
Supt. — None
Northern Westmoreland County AVTS — Vo/Tech
705 Stevenson Blvd 15068 — 724-335-9389
Marsha Welsh, prin. — Fax 337-9010

New Kensington-Arnold SD — 2,600/PK-12
701 Stevenson Blvd 15068 — 724-335-8581
Thomas Wilczek, supt. — Fax 337-6519
nkasd.com
Valley HS, 703 Stevenson Blvd 15068 — 800/9-12
Kellie Abbott, prin. — 724-337-4536
Other Schools – See Arnold

Career Training Academy — Post-Sec.
950 5th Ave 15068 — 724-337-1000
Citizens General Hospital — Post-Sec.
651 4th Ave 15068 — 724-337-5090
Pennsylvania State University — Post-Sec.
3550 7th Street Rd 15068 — 724-334-5466

Newmanstown, Lebanon, Pop. 1,410

Millbach Mennonite S | 100/K-12
601 State Route 419 17073 | 717-949-2111
Bruce Good, prin.

New Milford, Susquehanna, Pop. 848

Blue Ridge SD | 1,200/K-12
RR 3 Box 220 18834 | 570-465-3141
Robert McNamara, supt. | Fax 465-3148
brsd.org
Blue Ridge HS | 400/K-12
RR 3 Box 220 18834 | 570-465-3144
John Manchester, prin. | Fax 465-3148
Blue Ridge MS | 300/6-8
RR 3 Box 220 18834 | 570-465-3177
Matthew Nebzydoski, prin. | Fax 465-3148

New Oxford, Adams, Pop. 1,736

Conewago Valley SD | 2,800/K-12
130 Berlin Rd 17350 | 717-624-2157
Dr. Daniel Trimmer, supt. | Fax 624-5020
www.conewago.k12.pa.us
New Oxford HS | 1,200/9-12
130 Berlin Rd 17350 | 717-624-2157
Michael O'Brien, prin. | Fax 624-5021
New Oxford MS | 600/7-8
130 Berlin Rd 17350 | 717-624-2157
Gretchen Gates, prin. | Fax 624-6560

New Paris, Bedford, Pop. 208

Chestnut Ridge SD
Supt. — See Fishertown
Chestnut Ridge HS | 600/9-12
2588 Quaker Valley Rd 15554 | 814-839-4195
George A. Knisely, prin. | Fax 839-0018

Newport, Perry, Pop. 1,465

Newport SD | 1,300/K-12
PO Box 9 17074 | 717-567-3806
Dr. Steven P. Messner, supt. | Fax 567-6468
www.newportsd.org
Newport JSHS | 600/7-12
PO Box 9 17074 | 717-567-3806
Kerry Helm, prin. | Fax 567-7402

New Stanton, Westmoreland, Pop. 2,003

Area Vocational Technical School
Supt. — None
Central Westmoreland CTC | Vo/Tech
240 Arona Rd 15672 | 724-925-3532
Clentin Martin, prin. | Fax 925-1423

Newtown, Bucks, Pop. 2,285

Council Rock SD | 12,500/K-12
30 N Chancellor St 18940 | 215-944-1000
Mark Klein, supt. | Fax 944-1031
www.crsd.org
Council Rock HS North | 2,200/9-12
62 Swamp Rd 18940 | 215-944-1300
Susan McCarthy, prin. | Fax 944-1387
Newtown MS | 900/7-8
116 Richboro Rd 18940 | 215-968-7200
Barry Desko, prin. | Fax 968-1476
Other Schools – See Holland, Richboro

Bucks County Community College | Post-Sec.
Swamp Rd 18940 | 215-968-8000
George S | 500/9-12
PO Box 4000 18940 | 215-579-6500
Nancy Starmer, hdmstr. | Fax 579-6507
Holy Family University 18940 | Post-Sec.
 | 215-504-2000
La Salle University | Post-Sec.
33 University Dr 18940 | 215-579-7335

Newtown Square, Delaware, Pop. 11,300

Marple-Newtown SD | 3,400/K-12
40 Media Line Rd #206 19073 | 610-359-4200
Merle Horowitz, supt. | Fax 723-3340
www.mnsd.net
Marple-Newtown HS | 1,200/9-12
120 Media Line Rd 19073 | 610-359-4218
John Sanville, prin. | Fax 356-2194
Other Schools – See Broomall

Delaware County Christian S | 900/PK-12
462 Malin Rd 19073 | 610-353-6522
Dr. Stephen Dill, hdmstr. | Fax 356-9684

New Tripoli, Lehigh

Northwestern Lehigh SD | 2,400/K-12
6493 Route 309 18066 | 610-298-8661
John M. Gould Ph.D., supt. | Fax 298-8002
www.nwlehighsd.org
Northwestern Lehigh HS | 800/9-12
6493 Route 309 18066 | 610-298-8661
Dennis Nemes, prin. | Fax 298-4645
Northwestern Lehigh MS | 700/5-8
6636 Northwest Rd 18066 | 610-298-8661
Kathleen Kelley, prin. | Fax 298-8118

Newville, Cumberland, Pop. 1,339

Big Spring SD | 3,200/K-12
45 Mount Rock Rd 17241 | 717-776-2000
Richard Fry, supt. | Fax 776-4428
www.bigspring.k12.pa.us
Big Spring HS | 1,000/9-12
100 Mount Rock Rd 17241 | 717-776-2000
John Scudder, prin. | Fax 776-2433
Big Spring MS | 800/6-8
47 Mount Rock Rd 17241 | 717-776-2000
Linda Wilson, prin. | Fax 776-2468

New Wilmington, Lawrence, Pop. 2,515

Wilmington Area SD | 1,600/K-12
300 Wood St 16142 | 724-656-8866
C. Joyce Nicksick, supt. | Fax 946-8982
www.wilmington.k12.pa.us/
Wilmington Area HS | 500/9-12
350 Wood St 16142 | 724-656-8866
William Lyon, prin.
Wilmington Area MS | 500/5-8
400 Wood St 16142 | 724-656-8866
Benjamin Fennick, prin.

Westminster College 16172 | Post-Sec.
 | 724-946-7100

Norristown, Montgomery, Pop. 31,069

Methacton SD | 5,200/K-12
1001 Kriebel Mill Rd 19403 | 610-489-5000
Dr. Jeffrey A. Miller, supt. | Fax 489-5019
www.methacton.org
Arcola IS | 1,300/6-8
4000 Eagleville Rd 19403 | 610-489-5000
Mary Anne DelCollo, prin. | Fax 831-5317
Methacton HS | 1,600/9-12
1001 Kriebel Mill Rd 19403 | 610-489-5000
Frederick Cummins, prin. | Fax 489-8165
Norristown Area SD | 6,300/K-12
401 N Whitehall Rd 19403 | 610-630-5000
Dr. Lisa J. Andrejko, supt. | Fax 630-5013
www.nasd.k12.pa.us
East Norriton MS | 500/5-8
330 Roland Dr 19401 | 610-275-6520
Gary Engler, prin. | Fax 272-0531
Eisenhower MS | 700/5-8
1601 Markley St 19401 | 610-277-8720
Nicole Poncheri, prin. | Fax 270-2901
Norristown Area HS | 1,900/9-12
1900 Eagle Dr 19403 | 610-630-5000
Joseph Howell, prin. | Fax 630-5115
Stewart MS | 800/5-8
1315 W Marshall St 19401 | 610-275-6870
Rachel Holler, prin. | Fax 272-0560

Kennedy-Kenrick HS | 600/9-12
250 E Johnson Hwy 19401 | 610-275-2846
Rosemary Naab, prin. | Fax 277-6699
MBF Center | Post-Sec.
25 E Marshall St 19401 | 610-292-0710
Pathway School | Post-Sec.
162 Egypt Rd 19403 | 610-277-0660

Northampton, Northampton, Pop. 9,599

Catasauqua Area SD
Supt. — See Catasauqua
Catasauqua HS | 500/9-12
2500 N Bullshead Rd 18067 | 610-264-0506
Bruce Krasley, prin. | Fax 264-9768

Northampton Area SD | 5,600/K-12
2014 Laubach Ave 18067 | 610-262-7811
Dr. Linda J. Firestone, supt. | Fax 262-1150
www.northampton.k12.pa.us
Northampton Area HS | 1,900/9-12
1619 Laubach Ave 18067 | 610-262-7812
Dr. Kathleen Ott, prin. | Fax 262-3024
Northampton Area MS | 1,000/7-8
1617 Laubach Ave 18067 | 610-262-7812
Karen Fleming, prin. | Fax 262-6583

North East, Erie, Pop. 4,469

North East SD | 1,900/K-12
50 E Division St 16428 | 814-725-8671
Dr. Judith A. Miller, supt. | Fax 725-9380
www.nesd1.k12.pa.us/
North East HS | 700/9-12
1901 Freeport Rd 16428 | 814-725-8672
Regan Tanner, prin. | Fax 725-3357
North East MS | 500/6-8
1903 Freeport Rd 16428 | 814-725-8672
Gregory Beardsley, prin. | Fax 725-1086

Northern Cambria, Cambria, Pop. 4,080

Northern Cambria SD | 1,300/K-12
601 Joseph St 15714 | 814-948-5481
Dr. Thomas A Estep, supt. | Fax 948-6058
www.ncsd.k12.pa.us/
Northern Cambria HS | 400/9-12
813 35th St 15714 | 814-948-6800
Dennis Colbert, prin. | Fax 948-9810
Northern Cambria MS | 300/6-8
601 Joseph St 15714 | 814-948-5880
Thomas Rocco, prin.

North Huntingdon, Westmoreland, Pop. 28,158

Norwin SD | 5,200/K-12
281 McMahon Dr 15642 | 724-861-3000
Dr. John C. Boylan, supt. | Fax 863-9467
www.norwinsd.org
Norwin HS | 1,700/9-12
251 Mcmahon Dr 15642 | 724-861-3005
Dr. Edward Federinko, prin. | Fax 861-0581
Other Schools – See Irwin

Northumberland, Northumberland, Pop. 3,638

Northumberland Christian S | 200/K-12
205 Queen St 17857 | 570-473-9786
Sunbury Christian Academy | 200/K-12
135 Spruce Hollow Rd 17857 | 570-473-7592
Nancy Gross, admin. | Fax 473-7531

North Versailles, Allegheny, Pop. 12,302

East Allegheny SD | 2,000/K-12
1150 Jacks Run Rd 15137 | 412-824-8012
Dr. Thomas Knight, supt. | Fax 824-1062
www.eawildcats.net
East Allegheny JSHS | 1,000/7-12
1150 Jacks Run Rd 15137 | 412-824-9700
Garrette Edmonds, prin. | Fax 825-4570

All-State Career School | Post-Sec.
97 2nd St 15137 | 412-823-1818

North Wales, Montgomery, Pop. 3,341

North Penn SD
Supt. — See Lansdale
Pennbrook MS | 1,000/7-9
1201 E Walnut St 19454 | 215-699-9287
Allyn Roche, prin. | Fax 699-0151

Lansdale School of Business | Post-Sec.
201 Church Rd 19454 | 215-699-5700

North Warren, Warren

Warren County SD | 4,900/K-12
185 Hospital Dr 16365 | 814-723-6900
John H. Grant, supt. | Fax 723-4244
www.wcsdpa.org
Other Schools – See Russell, Sheffield, Warren,
Youngsville

Oakdale, Allegheny, Pop. 1,502

Area Vocational Technical School
Supt. — None
Parkway West AVTS | Vo/Tech
7101 Steubenville Pike 15071 | 412-923-1772
Jack Highfield, prin. | Fax 787-7257

Pittsburgh Technical Institute | Post-Sec.
1111 McKee Rd 15071 | 800-784-9675

Oakmont, Allegheny, Pop. 6,727

Riverview SD | 1,300/K-12
701 10th St 15139 | 412-828-1800
C. Erdeljac, supt. | Fax 828-9346
www.rsd.k12.pa.us
Riverview HS | 700/7-12
100 Hulton Rd 15139 | 412-828-1800
Thomas Graham, prin. | Fax 828-6296

Oil City, Venango, Pop. 11,132

Area Vocational Technical School
Supt. — None
Venango Technology Center | Vo/Tech
1 Vo Tech Dr 16301 | 814-677-3097
Rod Tarr, dir. | Fax 676-0075

Oil City Area SD | 2,500/K-12
PO Box 929 16301 | 814-676-1867
Joseph Carrico, supt. | Fax 676-2211
www.ocasd.org
Oil City Area MS | 600/6-8
8 Lynch Blvd 16301 | 814-676-5702
Scott Stahl, prin. | Fax 676-2306
Oil City HS | 900/9-12
10 Lynch Blvd 16301 | 814-676-2771
Richard Breene, prin. | Fax 677-7256

Clarion University - Venango Campus | Post-Sec.
1801 W 1st St 16301 | 814-676-6591
DuBois Business College | Post-Sec.
701 E 3rd St 16301 | 814-677-1322
Venango Catholic HS | 100/9-12
1505 W 1st St 16301 | 814-677-3098
Rev. John Malthaner, prin. | Fax 676-4453

Old Forge, Lackawanna, Pop. 8,603

Old Forge SD | 1,000/K-12
300 Marion St 18518 | 570-457-6721
Dr. Gene Camoni, supt. | Fax 457-8389
www.ofsd.cc/
Old Forge JSHS | 500/7-12
300 Marion St 18518 | 570-457-6721
Jeffery Hatala, prin. | Fax 414-0997

Triboro Christian Academy | 100/PK-12
100 S Main St 18518 | 570-457-5392
Erika Weber, prin. | Fax 451-0807

Oley, Berks

Area Vocational Technical School
Supt. — None
Berks CTC - East | Vo/Tech
3307 Friedensburg Rd 19547 | 610-987-6201
Lisa Greenawalt, prin. | Fax 987-6106

Oley Valley SD | 2,100/K-12
17 Jefferson St 19547 | 610-987-4100
Jeffrey Zackon Ed.D., supt. | Fax 987-4138
www.oleyvalleysd.org
Oley Valley HS | 700/9-12
17 Jefferson St 19547 | 610-987-4100
Darrell Markley, prin. | Fax 987-4138
Oley Valley MS | 600/6-8
3247 Friedensburg Rd 19547 | 610-987-4100
Eileen Lightcap, prin. | Fax 987-4240

Orefield, Lehigh

Parkland SD
Supt. — See Allentown
Orefield MS | 1,300/6-8
2675 PA Route 309 18069 | 610-351-5750
Rodney Troutman, prin. | Fax 351-5799

Oreland, Montgomery, Pop. 5,695

Springfield Township SD | 2,100/K-12
1901 Paper Mill Rd 19075 | 215-233-6000
Roseann B. Nyiri Ed.D., supt. | Fax 233-5815
www.sdst.org
Other Schools – See Erdenheim

Orwigsburg, Schuylkill, Pop. 3,020

Blue Mountain SD | 2,900/K-12
PO Box 188 17961 | 570-366-0515
Dr. William H. Hall, supt. | Fax 366-0838
www.bmsd.org
Blue Mountain MS | 700/6-8
PO Box 279 17961 | 570-366-0546
James S. McGonigle, prin. | Fax 366-2513
Other Schools – See Schuylkill Haven

Oxford, Chester, Pop. 4,636

Oxford Area SD | 3,300/K-12
125 Bell Tower Ln 19363 | 610-932-6600
Dr. Mary Jane Gales, supt. | Fax 932-6648
www.oxford.k12.pa.us
Oxford Area HS | 1,000/9-12
705 Waterway Rd 19363 | 610-932-6640
David Madden, prin. | Fax 932-6649
Penn's Grove S | 600/7-8
602 Garfield St 19363 | 610-932-6615
Henry Longenberger, prin. | Fax 932-6619

Palmerton, Carbon, Pop. 5,248

Palmerton Area SD | 2,000/K-12
PO Box 350 18071 | 610-826-2364
Michael W. Michaels, supt. | Fax 826-4958
www.palmerton.org/

Palmerton Area HS 600/9-12
3525 Fireline Rd 18071 610-826-3155
Kathleen Egan, prin. Fax 826-4929
Palmerton Area JHS 300/7-8
3529 Fireline Rd 18071 610-826-2492
Thaddeus Kosciolek, prin. Fax 826-2366

Palmyra, Lebanon, Pop. 6,977
Palmyra Area SD 2,900/K-12
1125 Park Dr 17078 717-838-3144
Dr. Larry Schmidt, supt. Fax 838-5105
www.palmyra.k12.pa.us/
Palmyra Area HS 900/9-12
1125 Park Dr 17078 717-838-1331
Kelly Harbaugh, prin. Fax 838-7915
Palmyra Area MS 700/6-8
50 W Cherry St 17078 717-838-2119
Chris Demers, prin. Fax 838-4402

Paoli, Chester, Pop. 5,603

Delaware Valley Friends S 200/7-12
19 E Central Ave 19301 610-640-4150
Katherine Schantz, hdmstr. Fax 296-9970
Royer-Greaves School for Blind Post-Sec.
118 S Valley Rd 19301

Patton, Cambria, Pop. 1,948
Cambria Heights SD 1,500/K-12
PO Box 66 16668 814-674-3626
Dr. Lawrence Wess, supt. Fax 674-5411
chsd.k12.pa.us
Cambria Heights HS 600/9-12
PO Box 6 16668 814-674-3601
Timothy Laurito, prin. Fax 674-5605
Cambria Heights MS 400/6-8
PO Box 216 16668 814-674-6290
David Caldwell, prin. Fax 674-5054

Pen Argyl, Northampton, Pop. 3,620
Pen Argyl Area SD 2,000/K-12
1620 Teels Rd 18072 610-863-3191
William Haberl Ed.D., supt. Fax 863-7040
www.penargyl.k12.pa.us
Pen Argyl Area HS 600/9-12
501 W Laurel Ave 18072 610-863-1293
John Smith, prin. Fax 863-7660
Wind Gap MS 800/4-8
1620 Teels Rd 18072 610-863-9093
Terry Barry, prin. Fax 863-3817

Pennsburg, Montgomery, Pop. 3,208
Upper Perkiomen SD
Supt. — See East Greenville
Upper Perkiomen HS 1,100/9-12
2 Walt Rd 18073 215-679-5935
John Semet, prin. Fax 679-0911

Perkiomen S 300/5-12
PO Box 130 18073 215-679-9511
George Allison, hdmstr. Fax 679-9101

Penns Creek, Snyder

Penn View Christian Academy 100/PK-12
125 Penn View Dr 17862 570-837-1855
Fax 837-1865

Pequea, Lancaster
Penn Manor SD
Supt. — See Lancaster
Marticville MS 400/7-8
356 Frogtown Rd 17565 717-291-9854
Anne Carroll, prin. Fax 284-5954

Perkasie, Bucks, Pop. 8,806
Area Vocational Technical School
Supt. — None
Upper Bucks County AVTS Vo/Tech
3115 Ridge Rd 18944 215-795-2911
David Warren, prin. Fax 795-0530

Pennridge SD 7,100/K-12
1506 N 5th St 18944 215-257-5011
Dr. Robert Kish, supt. Fax 453-8699
www.bucksiu.org/pennridge/psd/psd.htm
Pennridge Central MS 700/7-8
144 N Walnut St 18944 215-258-0939
Dr. Thomas Rutter, prin. Fax 258-0938
Pennridge HS 2,300/9-12
1400 N 5th St 18944 215-453-2744
Thomas Creeden, prin. Fax 257-4986
Pennridge South MS 500/7-8
610 S 5th St 18944 215-257-0467
Dr. Margaret Kantes, prin. Fax 257-3094

Perryopolis, Fayette, Pop. 1,737
Frazier SD 1,100/K-12
142 Constitution St 15473 724-736-4432
Fax 736-0688
www.frazierschooldistrict.org
Frazier HS 400/9-12
142 Constitution St 15473 724-736-4426
Kathleen Janci, prin. Fax 736-0688
Frazier MS 300/6-8
142 Constitution St 15473 724-736-4428
Fax 736-0688

Philadelphia, Philadelphia, Pop. 1,479,339
Area Vocational Technical School
Supt. — None
Bok Technical HS Vo/Tech
1901 S 9th St 19148 215-952-6200
Larry Melton, prin. Fax 952-6410
Dobbins AVTS Vo/Tech
2150 W Lehigh Ave 19132 215-227-4421
Charles Whiting, prin. Fax 227-5087
Edison/Fareira Skills HS Vo/Tech
151 W Luzerne St 19140 215-324-9599
Dr. Jose Lebron, prin. Fax 329-4628
Mastbaum AVTS Vo/Tech
3116 Frankford Ave 19134 215-291-4703
M. Sandra Dean, prin. Fax 291-4807
Philadelphia AVTS Vo/Tech
440 N Broad St 19130 215-875-3801
Albert Bichner, prin.
Randolph AVTS Vo/Tech
3101 Henry Ave 19129 215-227-4407
Peggy Johnson, prin. Fax 227-5087
Saul Agriculture S Vo/Tech
7100 Henry Ave 19128 215-487-4467
Thomas Scott, prin.
School for Exceptional Adults AVTS Vo/Tech
1400 W Olney Ave 19141 215-299-3699
Swenson Arts & Technology HS Vo/Tech
2750 Red Lion Rd 19114 215-961-2009
David Kipphut, prin. Fax 961-2081

Philadelphia CSD 182,400/PK-12
440 N Broad St 19130 215-400-4000
Paul G. Vallas, supt.
www.phila.k12.pa.us
Audenried HS 600/9-12
S 11th St at Catherine St 19147 215-351-7614
Dr. Bessie L. Young, prin.
Baldi MS 1,200/6-8
8801 Verree Rd 19115 215-961-2003
Frances Heinze, prin. Fax 961-2116
Barratt MS 600/5-8
1599 Wharton St 19146 215-952-6217
Roy McKinney, prin. Fax 952-8583
Bartram HS 2,100/9-12
2401 S 67th St 19142 215-492-6450
Constance McAlister, prin. Fax 492-6117
Beeber MS 900/6-8
5925 Malvern Ave 19131 215-581-5513
Deborah Jumpp, prin. Fax 581-5694
Bodine HS for International Affairs 500/9-12
1101 N 4th St 19123 215-351-7331
Dr. Ann Gardner, prin. Fax 351-7370
Carver HS for Engineering & Science 600/9-12
1600 W Norris St 19121 215-684-5079
Linda Ahmed, prin. Fax 684-5151
Central East MS 1,100/5-8
238 E Wyoming Ave 19120 215-456-3012
Ralph Burnley, prin. Fax 456-0122
Central HS 2,400/9-12
1700 W Olney Ave 19141 215-276-5262
Dr. Sheldon Pavel, prin. Fax 276-4721
Clemente MS 1,300/5-8
122 W Erie Ave 19140 215-291-5400
Patricia Mazzuca, prin. Fax 291-5036
Conwell MS 900/5-8
1849 E Clearfield St 19134 215-291-4722
Ed Hoffman, prin. Fax 291-5019
Cooke MS 800/5-8
1300 W Louden St 19141 215-456-3002
Gerald Branch, prin. Fax 456-3185
Creative & Performing Arts HS 700/9-12
901 S Broad St 19147 215-952-2462
Johnny Whaley, prin. Fax 952-6472
Elverson MS 100/8-8
2118 N 13th St 19122 215-684-5091
Bruce Ryan, prin. Fax 684-5507
Fels HS 1,500/9-12
901 Devereaux Ave 19111 215-537-2516
Chris Sadjian-Peacock, prin. Fax 537-2556
Fitzsimons HS 800/7-10
2601 W Cumberland St 19132 215-227-4431
Richard Jenkins, prin. Fax 227-8662
Frankford HS 2,000/9-12
5000 Oxford Ave 19124 215-537-2519
Richard Mantell, prin. Fax 537-2598
Franklin HS 1,200/9-12
550 N Broad St 19130 215-299-4662
Chris Johnson, prin. Fax 299-7285
Furness HS 1,200/9-12
1900 S 3rd St 19148 215-952-6226
Hiromi Hernandez, prin. Fax 952-8635
Germantown HS 1,900/9-12
40 E High St 19144 215-951-4004
Catherine Murphy, prin. Fax 843-8946
Gillespie MS 700/6-8
1801 W Pike St 19140 215-227-4409
Sandra Hall, prin. Fax 227-4676
Gratz HS 2,000/9-12
1798 W Hunting Park Ave 19140 215-227-4408
Dr. Delores Williams, prin. Fax 227-7194
Harding MS 1,200/6-8
2000 Wakeling St 19124 215-537-2528
Terri Hargett, prin. Fax 537-2850
Jones MS 1,000/5-8
2099 E Willard St 19134 215-291-4709
Mary Rita Shelton, prin. Fax 291-4754
Kensington Business Finance HS 1,500/9-12
2051 E Cumberland St 19125 215-291-4700
Eileen Maicon, prin. Fax 291-5833
Kensington CAPA 1,500/9-12
2051 E Cumberland St 19125 215-291-4700
Adele Pride, prin. Fax 291-5833
Kensington Culinary Arts HS 9-12
2463 Emerald St 19125 215-291-5185
Reuben Yarmus, prin. Fax 291-6320
King HS 1,900/9-12
6100 Stenton Ave 19138 215-276-5253
Jane Adams, prin. Fax 276-5844
LaBrum MS 400/6-8
10800 Hawley Rd 19154 215-281-2607
Lois Forrester Frye, prin. Fax 281-5800
Lamberton HS 9-12
7501 Woodbine Ave 19151 215-581-5647
Florence Johnson, prin. Fax 581-5648
Leeds MS 700/6-8
1100 E Mount Pleasant Ave 19150 215-248-6602
Stephanie Mitchell, prin. Fax 248-6623
Lewis MS 700/6-8
5900 Ardleigh St 19138 215-276-5830
Woolworth Davis, prin. Fax 549-5213
Lincoln HS 2,500/9-12
3201 Ryan Ave 19136 215-335-5653
Dr. Donald Donley, prin. Fax 335-5997
Masterman MSHS 1,200/5-12
1699 Spring Garden St 19130 215-299-4661
John Frangipani, prin. Fax 299-3425
Meehan MS 1,000/6-8
3001 Ryan Ave 19152 215-335-5654
Mary Jackson, prin. Fax 335-5992
Northeast HS 3,500/9-12
1601 Cottman Ave 19111 215-728-5018
Kelly Barton, prin. Fax 728-5004
Olney HS East 2,300/9-12
100 W Duncannon Ave 19120 215-456-3014
Newton Brown, prin. Fax 456-3064
Olney HS West 9-12
100 W Duncannon Ave 19120 215-456-0109
Rita Hardy, prin. Fax 456-0442
Overbrook HS 2,000/9-12
5898 Lancaster Ave 19131 215-581-5507
Ethelyn Young, prin. Fax 581-3406
Peirce MS 500/6-8
2400 Christian St 19146 215-875-5743
Joseph Ritvalski, prin. Fax 875-5757
Penn HS 1,400/9-12
1333 N Broad St 19122 215-684-5900
Leonard Heard, prin. Fax 684-8976
Penn Treaty MS 700/5-8
600 E Thompson St 19125 215-291-4715
Dr. Donald Anticoli, prin. Fax 291-5172
Pepper MS 1,200/5-8
2901 S 84th St 19153 215-492-6457
Yolanda Armstrong, prin. Fax 492-1844
Philadelphia HS for Girls 1,200/9-12
1400 W Olney Ave 19141 215-276-5258
Dr. Geraldine Myles, prin. Fax 276-5738
Philadelphia Regional HS 200/9-12
1118 Market St 19107 215-299-3510
Ernestine Caldwell, prin. Fax 299-3513
Pickett MS 600/5-8
5700 Wayne Ave 19144 215-951-4002
Judy Seibert Burns, prin. Fax 951-4177
Rhodes Academy 6-12
2900 W Clearfield St 19132 215-227-4402
Linda Wayman, prin. Fax 227-4926
Roosevelt MS 700/6-8
430 E Washington Ln 19144 215-951-4170
Rose Ford, prin. Fax 951-7762
Roxborough HS 1,200/9-12
6498 Ridge Ave 19128 215-487-4464
Dr. Rebecca Mitchell, prin. Fax 487-4843
Rush MS 1,000/6-8
11081 Knights Rd 19154 215-281-2603
Gene McLaughlin, prin. Fax 281-3334
Sayre HS 9-12
5800 Walnut St 19139 215-471-2904
Joseph Starinieri, prin. Fax 471-3486
Shaw MS 600/5-8
5400 Warrington Ave 19143 215-727-2161
Sharif El-Mekki, prin. Fax 727-2248
Shoemaker MS 400/7-8
5301 Media St 19131 215-581-5501
Margaret Holloman, prin. Fax 581-5929
South Philadelphia HS 1,300/9-12
2101 S Broad St 19148 215-952-6220
Dr. Kevin King, prin. Fax 551-2275
Stetson MS 900/5-8
3200 B St 19134 215-291-4720
Kathleen Fitzpatrick, prin. Fax 291-4168
Stoddart-Fleisher MS 200/7-8
540 N 13th St 19123 215-351-7375
Thomas Davidson, prin. Fax 351-7377
Strawberry Mansion HS 1,100/9-12
3133 Ridge Ave 19121 215-684-5089
Lois Powell-Mondesire, prin. Fax 684-5380
Sulzberger MS 800/6-8
4725 Fairmount Ave 19139 215-581-5510
Adrienne Wooden, prin. Fax 878-8006
Thomas MS 400/5-8
927 Johnston St 19148 215-952-6225
Roslynn Sample Green, prin. Fax 952-8514
Tilden MS 1,200/5-8
6601 Elmwood Ave 19142 215-492-6454
Michelle Burns, prin. Fax 492-6128
Turner MS 800/6-8
5900 Baltimore Ave 19143 215-471-2906
Veronica Alston, prin. Fax 471-8745
University City HS 1,900/9-12
3601 Filbert St 19104 215-387-5100
John Chapman, prin. Fax 387-6362
Vare MS 700/5-8
2100 S 24th St 19145 215-952-8611
Patricia Cox, prin. Fax 952-8520
Vaux MSHS 1,100/8-12
2300 W Master St 19121 215-684-5068
Sandra Pearson, prin. Fax 684-5430
Wagner MS 800/6-8
1701 W Chelten Ave 19126 215-276-5252
Penny Nixon, prin. Fax 276-5849
Wanamaker MS 100/8-8
1111 Cecil B Moore Ave 19122 215-684-5210
Dr. Bea Mickey, prin.
Washington HS 2,700/9-12
10175 Bustleton Ave 19116 215-961-2001
Alan E. Liebowitz, prin. Fax 961-2545
Washington Jr. MS 1,200/5-8
201 E Olney Ave 19120 215-456-0422
Michael Rosenberg, prin. Fax 456-2181
West Philadelphia HS 1,500/9-12
4700 Walnut St 19139 215-471-2902
Clifton James, prin. Fax 471-6402
Wilson MS 1,200/6-8
1800 Cottman Ave 19111 215-728-5015
James McWilliams, prin. Fax 728-5051

Albert Einstein Medical Center Post-Sec.
5501 Old York Rd 19141 215-456-7010
American Beauty Academy Post-Sec.
6912 Frankford Ave 19135 215-331-1515
ARAMARK Healthcare Support Services Post-Sec.
1101 Market St Fl 12 19107 610-687-8600
Archbishop Ryan HS 2,400/9-12
11201 Academy Rd 19154 215-637-1800
Helen Chaykowsky, prin. Fax 637-8833
Art Institute of Philadelphia Post-Sec.
1622 Chestnut St 19103 215-567-7080
Aviation Institute of Maintenance Post-Sec.
3001 Grant Ave 19114 215-676-7700
Berean Institute Post-Sec.
1901 W Girard Ave 19130 215-763-4833
Bethel Baptist Academy 100/K-12
2210 E Susquehanna Ave 19125 215-426-1909
Joseph White, prin. Fax 426-6758
Better Way Academy 50/K-12
PO Box 29508 19144 215-844-5000
Patrice Johnson, dir.

Blair Christian Academy 200/PK-12
220 W Upsal St 19119 215-438-6557
Karen R. Jenkins, admin. Fax 438-0661
Calvary Christian Academy 1,000/PK-12
13500 Philmont Ave 19116 215-969-1579
Dr. Samuel Pennington, hdmstr. Fax 969-9732
Cardinal Dougherty HS 1,100/9-12
6301 N 2nd St 19120 215-276-2300
Dr. Thomas Rooney, prin. Fax 276-2306
Center for Innovative Training & Educ. Post-Sec.
714 Market St Ste 433 19106 215-922-6555
Chestnut Hill Academy 500/PK-12
500 W Willow Grove Ave 19118 215-247-4700
Francis P. Steel, hdmstr. Fax 242-4055
Chestnut Hill College Post-Sec.
9601 Germantown Ave 19118 215-248-7000
Cittone Institute Post-Sec.
3600 Market St 19104 215-382-1553
City Center Academy 100/9-12
315 S 17th St 19103 215-731-1930
Raymond Withers, prin. Fax 735-3960
Community College of Philadelphia Post-Sec.
1700 Spring Garden St 19130 215-751-8000
Crefeld S, 8836 Crefeld St 19118 100/7-12
Mark Piechota, dir. 215-242-5545
Crooked Places Made Straight Chr Academy 100/K-12
711 S 50th St 19143 215-726-4151
Dr. Winona Stewart, prin.
Curtis Institute of Music Post-Sec.
1726 Locust St 19103 215-893-5252
Delaware Valley Academy-Medical & Dental Post-Sec.
3330 Grant Ave 19114 215-676-1200
DeVry University Post-Sec.
1800 JFK Blvd Ste 104 19103 866-863-3879
Drexel University Post-Sec.
3141 Chestnut St 19104 215-895-2000
Empire Beauty School Post-Sec.
2632 S Broad St 19145 215-465-8803
Empire Beauty School Post-Sec.
4026 Woodhaven Rd 19154 215-637-3700
Empire Beauty School Post-Sec.
1522 Chestnut St 19102 215-568-3980
Episcopal Hospital Post-Sec.
100 E Lehigh Ave 19125 215-427-7168
Faith Tabernacle S 200/1-12
3620 N Randolph St 19140 215-221-0909
Craig Bickings, prin. Fax 229-3204
Father Judge HS 1,400/9-12
3301 Solly Ave 19136 215-338-9494
Dr. Joseph DeAngelis, prin. Fax 338-0250
First Century Gospel S 100/K-10
6807 Rising Sun Ave 19111 215-742-6615
Dick Wakefield, prin.
Frankford Hospital Post-Sec.
4918 Penn St 19124 215-831-2362
Friends Select S 500/PK-12
17th St & Benjamin Franklin 19103 215-561-5900
Rose Hagan, hdmstr. Fax 864-2979
Germantown Friends S 900/K-12
31 W Coulter St 19144 215-951-2300
Richard Wade, hdmstr. Fax 951-2312
Girard College S 700/1-12
2101 S College Ave 19121 215-787-2600
Dominic M. Cermele, pres. Fax 787-2725
Graves Christian Academy 100/K-12
5447 Chester Ave 19143 215-727-7795
Hallahan HS 800/9-12
311 N 19th St 19103 215-563-8930
Margaret Gallagher, prin. Fax 563-3809
Harrison Career Institute Post-Sec.
1619 Walnut St Fl 3 19103 215-640-0177
Holy Family University Post-Sec.
9801 Frankford Ave 19114 215-637-7700
Hope Church S 200/K-12
6707 Old York Rd 19126 215-927-7770
Dr. Suzette Ajedho, prin. Fax 927-8070
Hussian School of Art Post-Sec.
1118 Market St 19107 215-981-0900
International Christian HS 200/9-12
413 E Tabor Rd 19120 215-455-9334
Robert DiStefano, prin. Fax 455-7198
Ivy Leaf S, 6929 N Broad St 19126 200/4-8
Mattie Wilkinson, prin. 215-549-2670
Jean Madeline Educ. Ctr. for Cosmetology Post-Sec.
315A Bainbridge St 19147 215-238-9998
JNA Institute of Culinary Arts Post-Sec.
1212 S Broad St 19146 215-468-8800
La Salle University Post-Sec.
1900 W Olney Ave 19141 215-951-1000
Lincoln Technical Institute Post-Sec.
9191 Torresdale Ave 19136 215-335-0800
Little Flower HS 800/9-12
1000 W Lycoming St 19140 215-455-6900
Sr. Kathleen Klarich, prin. Fax 329-0478
L.T. International Beauty School Post-Sec.
1238 Spring Garden St 19123 215-922-4478
Lutheran Theological Seminary Post-Sec.
7301 Germantown Ave 19119 215-248-4616
Mercy Vocational HS Vo/Tech
2900 W Hunting Park Ave 19129 215-226-1225
Sr. Rosemary Herron, prin. Fax 228-6337
Messiah College Post-Sec.
2026 N Broad St 19121 215-769-2526
Methodist Hospital Post-Sec.
2301 S Broad St 19148 215-952-9402
Metropolitan Career Center Post-Sec.
162 W Chelten Ave 19144 215-843-6615
Metropolitan Career Center Post-Sec.
100 S Broad St Ste 830 19110 215-568-9215
Moore College of Art and Design Post-Sec.
20th & Race St 19103 215-568-4000
Nazareth Academy 500/9-12
4001 Grant Ave 19114 215-637-7676
Sr. Mary Joan Jacobs, prin. Fax 637-8523
Nazareth Hospital Post-Sec.
2601 Holme Ave 19152 215-335-6000
Northeast Catholic HS 1,000/9-12
1842 Torresdale Ave 19124 215-831-1234
Rev. Nicholas Waseline, prin. Fax 743-0926
Northeastern Hospital School of Nursing Post-Sec.
2301 E Allegheny Ave 19134 215-291-3145
Northeast Prep S 100/7-12
1309 Cottman Ave 19111 215-342-5500
Howard Schwartz, dir. Fax 342-8866
Orleans Technical Institute Post-Sec.
1330 Rhawn St 19111 215-728-4700

Orleans Technical Institute Center City Post-Sec.
1845 Walnut St Ste 700 19103 215-854-1853
Overbrook School for the Blind Post-Sec.
6333 Malvern Ave 19151 215-877-0313
Peirce College Post-Sec.
1420 Pine St 19102 215-545-6400
Pennsylvania Academy of the Fine Arts Post-Sec.
118 N Broad St 19102 215-972-7600
Pennsylvania Hospital Post-Sec.
800 Spruce St 19107 215-829-3312
Pennsylvania School for the Deaf Post-Sec.
100 W School House Ln 19144
Philadelphia Coll. Osteopathic Medicine Post-Sec.
4170 City Ave 19131 215-871-6700
Philadelphia Mennonite HS 100/9-12
860 N 24th St 19130 215-769-5363
Dr. Barbara Moses, prin. Fax 769-4063
Philadelphia University Post-Sec.
4201 Henry Ave 19144 215-951-2700
Restaurant School at Walnut Hill College Post-Sec.
4207 Walnut St 19104 215-222-4200
Rittenhouse Academy 100/9-12
1516 Spruce St 19102 215-684-3434
Harvey Levitan, dir.
Roman Catholic HS 800/9-12
301 N Broad St 19107 215-627-1270
Robert O'Neill, prin. Fax 627-4979
Roxborough Memorial Hospital Post-Sec.
5800 Ridge Ave 19128 215-487-4459
St. Hubert HS 1,500/9-12
7320 Torresdale Ave 19136 215-624-6840
Sr. Marie Hart, prin. Fax 624-5940
St. John Neumann/St. Maria Goretti HS 800/9-12
1736 S 10th St 19148 215-465-8437
Patricia Sticco, prin. Fax 462-2410
St. Joseph's Prep S 1,000/9-12
1733 W Girard Ave 19130 215-978-1950
Dr. Michael J. Coury, pres. Fax 765-1710
St. Joseph's University Post-Sec.
5600 City Ave 19131 610-660-1000
St. Monica MS 400/5-8
16th & Porter Sts 19145 215-467-5338
Sr. Rita Murphy, prin. Fax 467-4599
Settlement Music School Post-Sec.
416 Queen St 19147 215-336-0400
Sister Clara Muhammad S 200/PK-12
PO Box 8026 19101 215-844-6616
Malik Mubashshi, prin. Fax 877-2020
Springside S 600/PK-12
8000 Cherokee St 19118 215-247-7200
Priscilla G. Sands, hdmstr. Fax 248-6377
Star Technical Institute Post-Sec.
9121 Roosevelt Blvd 19114 215-969-5877
Talmudical Yeshiva of Philadelphia Post-Sec.
6063 Drexel Rd 19131 215-477-1000
Talmudical Yeshiva of Philadelphia 100/9-12
6063 Drexel Rd 19131 215-477-1000
Rabbi Uri Mandelbaum, prin. Fax 477-5065
Temple University Post-Sec.
Broad St & Montgomery Ave 19122 215-204-7000
Temple University Post-Sec.
3307 N Broad St 19140 215-787-7000
Temple University Center City Post-Sec.
1515 Market St 19102 215-204-8822
Temple Univ School of Podiatric Medicine Post-Sec.
8th & Race St 19107 215-629-0300
Thomas Jefferson University Post-Sec.
111 S 11th St 19107 215-955-6000
Thompson Institute Post-Sec.
3010 Market St 19104 215-387-1530
University of Pennsylvania Post-Sec.
3400 Spruce St 19104 215-898-5000
University of the Arts Post-Sec.
320 S Broad St 19102 215-717-6000
University of the Sciences Philadelphia Post-Sec.
600 S 43rd St 19104 215-596-8800
Westminster Theological Seminary Post-Sec.
PO Box 27009 19118 215-887-5511
West Philadphia Catholic HS 800/9-12
4501 Chestnut St 19139 215-386-2244
Sr. Mary Bur, prin. Fax 222-1651

Philipsburg, Centre, Pop. 3,049
Philipsburg-Osceola Area SD 2,100/K-12
200 Short St 16866 814-342-1050
Dr. Sonja Brobeck, supt. Fax 342-7208
www.pomounties.org/
Philipsburg-Osceola Area HS 600/9-12
502 Phillips St 16866 814-342-1521
Charles Young, prin.
Philipsburg-Osceola JHS 300/7-8
100 N 6th St 16866 814-342-4860
Robert Rocco, prin.

South Hills School of Business & Tech. Post-Sec.
200 Shadylane Dr 16866 814-342-7427

Phoenixville, Chester, Pop. 14,739
Area Vocational Technical School
Supt. — None
Center for Arts & Tech - Pickering Vo/Tech
1580 Charlestown Rd 19460 610-933-8877
Dr. Ronald Husband, prin.

Phoenixville Area SD 3,200/K-12
PO Box 809 19460 484-927-5000
David R. Noyes Ed.D., supt. Fax 983-9537
www.pasd.com
Phoenixville Area HS 900/9-12
1200 Gay St 19460 484-927-5100
Richard Kaskey, prin. Fax 933-6009
Phoenixville Area MS 800/6-8
1330 Main St 19460 484-927-5200
Dr. Troy Czukoski, prin. Fax 933-6121

Valley Forge Christian College Post-Sec.
1401 Charlestown Rd 19460 610-935-0450

Pine Forge, Berks

Pine Forge Academy 200/9-12
PO Box 338 19548 610-326-5800
Cynthia Pool-Gibson, prin. Fax 326-4260

Pine Grove, Schuylkill, Pop. 2,098
Pine Grove Area SD 1,800/K-12
103 School St 17963 570-345-2731
Dr. Terence R. Maher, supt. Fax 345-6473
www.pgasd.com
Pine Grove Area HS 600/9-12
101 School St 17963 570-345-2731
Fax 345-8326
Pine Grove Area MS 600/5-8
105 School St 17963 570-345-2731
Steve Brill, prin. Fax 345-6075

Pittsburgh, Allegheny, Pop. 325,337
Area Vocational Technical School
Supt. — None
Connelley Skill Center Vo/Tech
1501 Bedford Ave 15219 412-338-3700
Fax 338-3708
Pittsburgh AVTS Vo/Tech
850 Boggs Ave 15211 412-488-2500
Darla DelDuca, prin.

Avonworth SD 1,300/K-12
258 Josephs Ln 15237 412-369-8738
Dr. Valerie McDonald, supt. Fax 369-8746
www.avonworth.k12.pa.us
Avonworth HS 400/9-12
304 Josephs Ln 15237 412-366-6360
Dr. Margaret Boden, prin. Fax 366-7603
Avonworth MS 300/6-8
256 Josephs Ln 15237 412-366-9650
Dr. Robert Susini, prin. Fax 358-9621

Baldwin-Whitehall SD 5,000/K-12
4900 Curry Rd 15236 412-885-7810
Dr. Donna Milanovich, supt. Fax 885-7802
www.baldwin.k12.pa.us
Baldwin HS 1,800/9-12
4653 Clairton Blvd 15236 412-885-7500
Dr. Todd Keruskin, prin. Fax 885-6652
Harrison MS 700/7-8
129 Windvale Dr 15236 412-885-7530
Andrea Dorfzaun, prin. Fax 885-6766

Brentwood Borough SD 1,300/K-12
3601 Brownsville Rd 15227 412-881-2227
Dr. Anne E. Stephens, supt. Fax 881-1640
Brentwood HS 500/9-12
3601 Brownsville Rd 15227 412-881-4940
Ronald Dufalla Ph.D., prin. Fax 881-4170
Brentwood MS 300/6-8
3601 Brownsville Rd 15227 412-881-4940
Lawrence Kushner Ph.D., prin. Fax 881-4170

Chartiers Valley SD 3,500/K-12
2030 Swallow Hill Rd 15220 412-429-2201
Anthony Skender, supt. Fax 429-2237
www.cvsd.net
Other Schools – See Bridgeville

Fox Chapel Area SD 4,600/K-12
611 Field Club Rd 15238 412-963-9600
Dr. Anne Stephens, supt. Fax 967-0697
www.fcasd.edu
Dorseyville MS 1,100/6-8
550 Saxonburg Rd 15238 412-967-2520
Rox Serrao, prin. Fax 967-2531
Fox Chapel Area HS 1,600/9-12
611 Field Club Rd 15238 412-967-2433
Kenneth Williams, prin. Fax 967-0697

Keystone Oaks SD 2,500/K-12
1000 Kelton Ave 15216 412-571-6000
Dr. William Urbanek, supt. Fax 571-6006
www.kosd.org
Keystone Oaks HS 900/9-12
1000 Kelton Ave 15216 412-571-6040
Scott Hagy, prin. Fax 571-6043
Keystone Oaks MS 600/6-8
1002 Kelton Ave 15216 412-571-6146
Annette Todd, prin. Fax 571-6092

Mt. Lebanon SD 5,600/K-12
7 Horsman Dr 15228 412-344-2077
Dr. George Wilson, supt. Fax 344-2047
www.mtlsd.org
Jefferson MS 700/6-8
21 Moffett St 15243 412-344-2123
Joan Zacharias, prin. Fax 344-1252
Mellon MS 700/6-8
11 Castle Shannon Blvd 15228 412-344-2122
Vincent Barone, prin. Fax 344-0590
Mt. Lebanon HS 1,900/9-12
155 Cochran Rd 15228 412-344-2003
Dr. Zeb Jansante, prin. Fax 344-2021

North Allegheny SD 8,200/K-12
200 Hillvue Ln 15237 412-366-2100
Dr. Patricia Green, supt. Fax 369-5513
www.northallegheny.org
Carson MS 700/6-8
200 Hillvue Ln 15237 412-369-5520
Brian Miller, prin. Fax 630-5819
Ingomar MS 500/6-8
1521 Ingomar Heights Rd 15237 412-369-5470
Tammy Andreyko, prin. Fax 366-4487
North Allegheny Intermediate HS 1,400/9-10
350 Cumberland Rd 15237 412-369-5530
Dr. Jo Welter, prin. Fax 369-4825
Other Schools – See Wexford

North Hills SD 4,900/K-12
135 6th Ave 15229 412-318-6000
Dr. Joseph Clapper, supt. Fax 318-1084
www.nhsd.k12.pa.us
North Hills JHS 1,300/7-9
55 Rochester Rd 15229 412-318-1450
John Kreider, prin. Fax 318-1453
North Hills SHS 1,400/10-12
53 Rochester Rd 15229 412-318-1400
Patrick Mannarino, prin. Fax 318-1403

Northgate SD 1,500/K-12
591 Union Ave 15202 412-734-8001
Dr. Reggie Bonfield, supt. Fax 734-8008
www.northgate.k12.pa.us
Northgate MSHS 800/7-12
589 Union Ave 15202 412-734-8002
John Wilkinson, prin. Fax 734-8086

Penn Hills SD 5,900/K-12
309 Collins Dr 15235 412-793-7000
Dr. Patricia Gennari, supt. Fax 793-6402
www.phsd.k12.pa.us
Linton MS 2,100/6-9
250 Aster St 15235 412-795-3000
Sherryl Duff-Conrad, prin. Fax 795-6087
Penn Hills SHS 1,500/10-12
12200 Garland Dr 15235 412-793-7000
Richard Kruglak, prin. Fax 793-9401

Pittsburgh CSD 33,400/PK-12
341 S Bellefield Ave 15213 412-622-3600
Mark Roosevelt, supt. Fax 622-3604
www.pghboe.net
Allderdice HS 1,500/9-12
2409 Shady Ave 15217 412-422-4800
Dr. Cassandra Kemp, prin. Fax 571-7305
Allegheny Traditional Academy 300/6-8
810 Arch St 15212 412-323-4115
Dr. Jerri Lynn Lippert, prin. Fax 323-4114
Arsenal MS 500/6-8
3900 Butler St 15201 412-622-5740
Debra Rucki, prin. Fax 622-5743
Brashear HS 1,300/9-12
590 Crane Ave 15216 412-571-7300
Dr. Ruthanne Reginella, prin. Fax 571-7372
Carrick HS 1,400/9-12
125 Parkfield St 15210 412-885-7700
Anita Burley, prin. Fax 885-7752
Columbus MS 500/6-8
1805 Buena Vista St 15212 412-323-4170
Kevin McGuire, prin. Fax 323-3164
Frick International Studies Academy 700/6-8
107 Thackeray St 15213 412-622-5980
Wayne Walters, prin. Fax 622-5983
Greenway MS 400/6-8
1400 Crucible St 15205 412-928-2800
Scott Grosh, prin. Fax 928-2832
Knoxville MS 400/6-8
324 Charles St 15210 412-488-2910
Toni Kendrick, prin. Fax 488-4292
Langley HS 700/9-12
2940 Sheraden Blvd 15204 412-778-2100
Linda Baehr, prin. Fax 778-2106
Milliones MS 600/6-8
3117 Centre Ave 15219 412-622-5900
Meredith Murray, prin. Fax 622-5925
Oliver HS 1,000/9-12
2323 Brighton Rd 15212 412-323-3250
Tawayne Weems, prin. Fax 323-3294
Peabody HS 700/9-12
515 N Highland Ave 15206 412-665-2050
Sophia Facaros, prin. Fax 665-2077
Perry Traditional Academy 1,000/9-12
3875 Perrysville Ave 15214 412-323-3400
Jacqueline Blakey-Tate, prin. Fax 323-3404
Pittsburgh Classical Academy 300/6-8
1463 Chartiers Ave 15220 412-928-3110
Carolyn Heinzl, prin. Fax 928-3106
Pittsburgh HS / Creative & Perform. Arts 400/9-12
111 9th St 15222 412-338-6100
Michael Thorsen, prin. Fax 338-6143
Prospect MS 300/6-8
161 Prospect St 15211 412-488-3391
Henrietta Abraham, prin. Fax 488-6838
Reizenstein MS 900/6-8
129 Denniston Ave 15206 412-665-2260
Dr. Craig Jackson, prin. Fax 665-4988
Rogers Creative & Performing Arts S 300/6-8
5525 Columbo St 15206 412-665-2000
Dr. Lynda Lewis, prin. Fax 665-2006
Rooney MS 400/6-8
3530 Fleming Ave 15212 412-732-6700
Dr. Valerie Harris, prin. Fax 732-6706
Schenley HS 1,400/9-12
4101 Bigelow Blvd 15213 412-622-8200
Howard Bullard, prin. Fax 622-8238
Schiller Classical Academy 300/6-8
1018 Peralta St 15212 412-323-4190
Dr. Richard Gutkind, prin. Fax 323-4192
South Brook MS 400/6-8
779 Dunster St 15226 412-572-8170
Gina Reichert, prin. Fax 572-8177
South Hills MS 400/6-8
595 Crane Ave 15216 412-572-8130
Dr. Deborah Ann Cox, prin. Fax 572-8148
Sterrett Classical Academy 400/6-8
7100 Reynolds St 15208 412-247-7870
Sarah Sumpter, prin. Fax 247-7877
Washington Polytechnic Academy Vo/Tech
169 40th St 15201 412-622-3480
Dalhart Dobbs, prin. Fax 622-3482
Westinghouse HS 600/9-12
1101 N Murtland St 15208 412-665-3940
Dr. Shemeca Crenshaw, prin. Fax 665-4977

Plum Borough SD 4,400/K-12
200 School Rd 15239 412-795-0100
George I. Cooke Ed.D., supt. Fax 795-9115
www.pbsd.k12.pa.us
O'Block JHS 700/7-8
440 Presque Isle Dr 15239 724-733-2400
Margaret Evans, prin. Fax 327-6880
Plum HS 1,500/9-12
900 Elicker Rd 15239 412-795-4880
Pamela Kinzler, prin. Fax 795-6823

Shaler Area SD
Supt. — See Glenshaw
Shaler Area HS 1,500/10-12
381 Wible Run Rd 15209 412-492-1200
William Suit, prin. Fax 684-1076

Upper St. Clair SD
Supt. — See Upper Saint Clair
Ft. Couch MS 600/7-8
515 Fort Couch Rd 15241 412-833-1600
Joseph DeMar, prin. Fax 854-3095
Upper Saint Clair HS 1,400/9-12
1825 Mclaughlin Run Rd 15241 412-833-1600
Timothy Steinhauer, prin. Fax 833-4889

West Jefferson Hills SD
Supt. — See Jefferson Hills
Pleasant Hills MS 700/6-8
404 National Dr 15236 412-655-8680
Suzan Petersen, prin. Fax 655-5691

Woodland Hills SD 5,800/K-12
2430 Greensburg Pike 15221 412-731-1300
Roslynne H. Wilson Ed.D., supt. Fax 731-1562
www.whsd.k12.pa.us
Woodland Hills HS 1,900/9-12
2550 Greensburg Pike 15221 412-244-1100
Howard Weber, prin. Fax 242-2344
Woodland Hills JHS - West 600/7-8
7600 Evans St 15218 412-351-0698
Linda Marcolini, prin. Fax 351-5841
Other Schools – See Turtle Creek

Art Institute of Pittsburgh Post-Sec.
420 Blvd Of The Allies 15219 412-263-6600
Bidwell Training Center Post-Sec.
1815 Metropolitan St 15233 412-323-4000
Bishop Canevin Catholic HS 400/9-12
2700 Morange Rd 15205 412-922-7400
Kenneth Sinagra, prin. Fax 922-7403
Bradford School Post-Sec.
125 W Station Square Dr 15219 412-391-6710
Career Training Academy Post-Sec.
1500 Northway Mall 15237 412-367-4000
Carlow University Post-Sec.
3333 5th Ave 15213 412-578-6000
Carnegie Mellon University Post-Sec.
5000 Forbes Ave 15213 412-268-2000
Center for Emergency Medicine/Western PA Post-Sec.
230 McKee Pl # 500 15213 412-647-4665
Central District Catholic HS 800/9-12
4720 5th Ave 15213 412-621-8189
Br. Richard Grzeskiewicz, prin. Fax 208-0555
Chatham College Post-Sec.
Woodland Rd 15232 412-365-1100
Community College of Allegheny County Post-Sec.
808 Ridge Ave 15212 412-237-2525
Community College of Allegheny County Post-Sec.
8701 Perry Hwy 15237 412-366-7000
Cornell-Abraxas Pittsburgh S 100/7-12
437 Turrett St 15206 412-954-0018
Olivia Doswell, dir.
Craig Academy 100/2-12
751 N Negley Ave 15206 412-361-2801
Denise Sedlacek, dir.
Dean Institute of Technology Post-Sec.
1501 W Liberty Ave 15226 412-531-4433
DeVry University Post-Sec.
210 6th Ave Ste 200 15222 412-642-9072
Duffs Business Institute Post-Sec.
100 Forbes Ave # 1200 15222 412-261-4520
Duquesne University Post-Sec.
600 Forbes Ave 15282 412-396-6000
Ellis S 500/K-12
6425 5th Ave 15206 412-661-5992
Mary H. Grant, hdmstr. Fax 661-3979
Empire Beauty School Post-Sec.
1000 McKnight Park Dr #1006 15237 800-575-5983
Grace Non-Traditional Academy 50/7-12
8610 Bricelyn St 15221 412-244-8233
Ronald Malamisuro, hdmstr. Fax 243-1465
Hillel Academy of Pittsburgh 300/K-12
5685 Beacon St 15217 412-521-8131
Dr. Nina Butler, prin. Fax 521-5150
Home for Crippled Children Post-Sec.
1426 Denniston St 15217
ICM School of Business & Medical Careers Post-Sec.
10 Wood St 15222 412-261-2647
Imani Christian Academy 200/K-12
235 Eastgate Dr 15235 412-731-7982
Edward Matthews, prin. Fax 436-1020
International Academy of Design & Tech Post-Sec.
555 Grant St 15219 412-391-4197
ITT Technical Institute Post-Sec.
10 Parkway Ctr 15220 412-937-9150
La Roche College Post-Sec.
9000 Babcock Blvd 15237 412-536-1272
Mercy Hospital School of Nursing Post-Sec.
1401 Blvd Of The Allies 15219 412-232-7940
Mt. Alvernia HS 100/9-12
146 Hawthorne Rd 15209 412-821-3858
Kimberly Minick, prin. Fax 821-2910
North Catholic HS 400/9-12
1400 Troy Hill Rd 15212 412-321-4823
Dr. Edward Scheid, prin. Fax 321-0599
North Hills Beauty Academy Post-Sec.
434 Perry Hwy 15229 412-931-8563
Oakland Catholic HS 500/9-12
144 N Craig St 15213 412-682-6633
Dr. Maureen Marsteller, prin. Fax 682-2496
Pennsylvania Culinary Institute Post-Sec.
717 Liberty Ave 15222 412-566-2433
Pennsylvania Gunsmith School Post-Sec.
812 Ohio River Blvd 15202 412-766-1812
PIA School of Specialized Technology Post-Sec.
PO Box 10897 15236 412-462-9011
Pittsburgh Institute of Mortuary Science Post-Sec.
5808 Baum Blvd 15206 412-362-8500
Pittsburgh Technical Institute Post-Sec.
635 Smithfield St 15222 412-809-5100
Pittsburgh Theological Seminary Post-Sec.
616 N Highland Ave 15206 412-362-5610
Point Park University Post-Sec.
201 Wood St 15222 412-391-4100
Point Park Univ.-St. Francis Med. Ctr. Post-Sec.
201 Wood St 15222 412-392-3879
Pressley Ridge School Post-Sec.
530 Marshall Ave 15214 412-442-4468
Reformed Presbyterian Theological Sem. Post-Sec.
7418 Penn Ave 15208 412-731-8690

Robert Morris College Post-Sec.
600 5th Ave 15219 412-227-6800
Rosedale Technical Institute Post-Sec.
215 Beecham Dr Ste 2 15205 412-521-6200
St. Margaret Hospital School of Nursing Post-Sec.
221 7th St Ste 100 15238 412-784-4980
Seton-LaSalle HS 500/9-12
1000 McNeilly Rd 15226 412-561-3583
Sr. Patricia Laffey, prin. Fax 441-2798
Shady Side Academy 400/9-12
423 Fox Chapel Rd 15238 412-968-3000
Thomas Southard, pres. Fax 968-3006
Shady Side Academy MS 100/6-8
500 Squaw Run Rd E 15238 412-968-3100
Fax 968-3008
Shadyside Hospital Post-Sec.
5230 Centre Ave 15232 412-622-2010
South Hills Beauty Academy Post-Sec.
3269 W Liberty Ave 15216 412-561-3381
Triangle Tech Post-Sec.
1940 Perrysville Ave 15214 412-359-1000
Trinity Christian S 400/K-12
299 Ridge Ave 15221 412-242-8886
Dale McLane, supt. Fax 242-8859
University Health Center Post-Sec.
300 Halket St 15213 412-641-4664
University of Pittsburgh Post-Sec.
4200 5th Ave 15260 412-624-4141
UPMC School of Medical Imaging Post-Sec.
3434 Forbes Ave 15213 412-647-3528
Vet Tech Institute Post-Sec.
125 7th St 15222 412-391-7021
Vincentian Academy 200/9-12
8200 McKnight Rd 15237 412-364-1616
Sr. Camille Panich, prin. Fax 367-5722
Western Pennsylvania Hospital Post-Sec.
4900 Friendship Ave 15224 412-578-5538
Western Pennsylvania School for Blind Post-Sec.
Bayard at Bellefield 15213
Western Pennsylvania School for the Deaf Post-Sec.
300 E Swissvale Ave 15218 412-371-7000
Western School of Health & Bus. Careers Post-Sec.
421 7th Ave 15219 412-281-2600
Winchester Thurston S 600/PK-12
555 Morewood Ave 15213 412-578-7500
Gary J. Niels, hdmstr. Fax 578-7504
Yeshiva Achei Tmimim S 400/PK-12
PO Box 81868 15217 412-422-7300
Mindy Schiffrin, admin. Fax 422-5930

Pittston, Luzerne, Pop. 7,807
Pittston Area SD 3,200/K-12
5 Stout St 18640 570-654-2271
Dr. Ross Scarantino, supt. Fax 654-5548
www.pittstonarea.com
Pittston Area HS 1,100/9-12
5 Stout St 18640 570-654-3541
Dr. John Lussi, prin. Fax 602-0823
Pittston Area MS 700/6-8
120 New St 18640 570-655-2927
George Cosgrove, prin. Fax 654-0862

Seton Catholic HS 300/9-12
37 William St 18640 570-654-4831
James Redington, prin. Fax 654-2599

Plains, Luzerne, Pop. 4,694
Wilkes-Barre Area SD
Supt. — See Wilkes Barre
Solomon/Plains JHS 500/7-8
43 Abbott St 18705 570-826-7224
James Lasiewicki, prin. Fax 820-3715

Pleasant Gap, Centre, Pop. 1,699
Area Vocational Technical School
Supt. — None
Central PA Institute of Science & Tech. Vo/Tech
540 N Harrison Rd 16823 814-359-2793
Dr. Gregory Michelone, dir. Fax 359-2599

Plumsteadville, Bucks

Plumstead Christian HS 300/6-12
PO Box 216 18949 215-766-8073
Timothy Reber, prin. Fax 766-2033

Plymouth, Luzerne, Pop. 6,250
Wyoming Valley West SD
Supt. — See Kingston
Wyoming Valley West HS 1,500/9-12
150 Wadham St 18651 570-779-5361
Irvin DeRemer, prin. Fax 779-9510

Plymouth Meeting, Montgomery, Pop. 6,241
Area Vocational Technical School
Supt. — None
Center for Tech Studies-Montgomery Co Vo/Tech
821 Plymouth Rd 19462 610-277-2301
Walter Slouch, prin.

Colonial SD 4,600/K-12
230 Flourtown Rd 19462 610-834-1670
Vincent F. Cotter, supt. Fax 834-7535
www.colonialsd.org
Colonial MS 1,100/6-8
716 Belvoir Rd 19462 610-275-5100
Robert Fahler, prin. Fax 278-2447
Plymouth-Whitemarsh HS 1,500/9-12
201 E Germantown Pike 19462 610-825-1500
Monica Sullivan, prin. Fax 832-0766

Pocono Summit, Monroe
Pocono Mountain SD
Supt. — See Swiftwater
Pocono Mountain West HS 1,500/10-12
HC 89 Box 2002 18346 570-839-7121
Jawn Herman, prin. Fax 839-5968
Pocono Mountain West JHS 8-9
HC 89 Box 2002 18346 570-839-7121
Dr. Eric Vogt, prin.

Point Marion, Fayette, Pop. 1,289
Albert Gallatin Area SD
Supt. — See Uniontown
Gallatin South MS 400/6-8
224 New Genevia Rd 15474 724-725-5241
Ralph Garcia, prin. Fax 725-5424

Portage, Cambria, Pop. 2,738
Portage Area SD — 700/PK-12
84 Mountain Ave 15946 — 814-736-9636
Dr. Andrew J. Kittell, supt. — Fax 736-9634
www.portageareasd.org
Portage Area JSHS — 400/8-12
85 Mountain Ave 15946 — 814-736-9636
Thomas Kakabar, prin. — Fax 736-9597

Port Allegany, McKean, Pop. 2,309
Area Vocational Technical School
Supt. — None
Seneca Highlands AVTS — Vo/Tech
219 Edison Bates Dr 16743 — 814-642-2573
Donald Raydo, prin.

Port Allegany SD — 1,100/K-12
20 Oak St 16743 — 814-642-2596
Martin Flint, supt. — Fax 642-9574
www.pahs.net
Port Allegany JSHS — 600/7-12
20 Oak St 16743 — 814-642-2544
Mare Budd, prin. — Fax 642-9574

Portersville, Butler, Pop. 266

Portersville Christian S — 300/K-12
343 E Portersville Rd 16051 — 724-368-8787
Patricia Watters, admin. — Fax 368-3100

Pottstown, Montgomery, Pop. 21,793
Owen J. Roberts SD — 4,200/K-12
901 Ridge Rd 19465 — 610-469-5100
Dr. Myra Forrest, supt. — Fax 469-0748
www.ojrsd.com
Roberts HS — 1,300/9-12
981 Ridge Rd 19465 — 610-469-5101
George Carlino, prin. — Fax 469-5898
Roberts MS, 881 Ridge Rd 19465 — 1,000/6-8
Dr. David Blozowich, prin. — 610-469-5102

Pottsgrove SD — 3,200/K-12
1301 Kauffman Rd 19464 — 610-327-2277
Sharon Richardson, supt. — Fax 327-2530
www.pgsd.org
Pottsgrove HS — 1,100/9-12
1345 Kauffman Rd 19464 — 610-326-5105
Joyce Wishart, prin. — Fax 970-6191
Pottsgrove MS — 800/6-8
1351 N Hanover St 19464 — 610-326-8243
Dr. Regina Hove, prin. — Fax 718-0581

Pottstown SD — 3,300/PK-12
PO Box 779 19464 — 610-323-8200
Dr. Anthony A. Goreno, supt. — Fax 326-6540
pottstownschools.com
Pottstown HS — 900/9-12
750 N Washington St 19464 — 610-970-6700
Stephen Rodriguez, prin. — Fax 970-1363
Pottstown MS — 700/6-8
600 N Franklin St 19464 — 610-970-6665
Wayne Thomas, prin. — Fax 970-8738

Antonelli Medical & Professional Inst — Post-Sec.
1700 Industrial Hwy 19464 — 610-323-7270
Coventry Christian S — 400/PK-12
962 E Schuylkill Rd 19465 — 610-326-3366
Mark E. Niehls, supt. — Fax 326-9370
Empire Beauty School — Post-Sec.
141 High St 19464 — 610-327-1313
Hill S — 500/9-12
717 E High St 19464 — 610-326-1000
David Dougherty, hdmstr. — Fax 705-1753
St. Pius X HS — 500/9-12
844 N Keim St 19464 — 610-326-8990
Rev. Joseph Bongard, prin. — Fax 323-8594
West-Mont Christian Academy — 300/PK-12
873 S Hanover St 19465 — 610-326-7690
Dr. James Smock, admin. — Fax 326-7126

Pottsville, Schuylkill, Pop. 14,990
Area Vocational Technical School
Supt. — None
Schuylkill Technology Center - Airport — Vo/Tech
240 Airport Rd 17901 — 570-544-4904
Albert Gurka, prin.

Pottsville Area SD — 3,100/K-12
1501 Laurel Blvd 17901 — 570-621-2900
Dr. James Gallagher, supt. — Fax 621-2025
www.pottsville.k12.pa.us/
Lengel MS — 900/5-8
1541 Laurel Blvd 17901 — 570-621-2923
Edward Hauck, prin. — Fax 621-2999
Pottsville Area HS — 1,200/9-12
16th and Elk Ave 17901 — 570-621-2960
Joseph Opalenick, prin. — Fax 621-2037

Empire Beauty School — Post-Sec.
324 N Centre St 17901 — 570-622-6060
McCann School of Business & Technology — Post-Sec.
2650 Woodglen Rd 17901 — 570-622-7622
Nativity BVM HS — 300/9-12
1 Lawtons Hl 17901 — 570-622-8110
Rev. Ronald Jankaitis, prin. — Fax 622-0454
Pottsville Hospital School of Nursing — Post-Sec.
420 S Jackson St 17901 — 570-621-5028
Schuylkill Institute of Business & Tech. — Post-Sec.
118 S Centre St Ste 2 17901 — 570-622-4835

Prospect Park, Delaware, Pop. 6,494
Interboro SD — 4,000/K-12
900 Washington Ave 19076 — 610-461-6700
Dr. Lois Snyder, supt. — Fax 583-1678
www.interboro.k12.pa.us
Interboro HS — 1,400/9-12
500 16th Ave 19076 — 610-237-6410
Paul S. Gibson Ed.D., prin. — Fax 237-8103

Pulaski, Lawrence

New Castle School of Trades — Post-Sec.
New Castle Youngstown Rd 16143 — 724-964-8811

Punxsutawney, Jefferson, Pop. 6,150
Punxsutawney Area SD — 4,200/K-12
475 Beyer Ave 15767 — 814-938-5151
Dr. J. Frantz, supt. — Fax 938-6677
www.punxsy.k12.pa.us/
Punxsutawney Area HS — 900/9-12
450 N Findley St 15767 — 814-938-5151
David E. London, prin. — Fax 938-5101
Punxsutawney Area MS — 500/7-8
465 Beyer Ave 15767 — 814-938-5151
Richard Galluzzi, prin.

Punxsutawney Christian S — 200/PK-12
105 W Mahoning St 15767 — 814-939-7010
Pat Woods, admin. — Fax 939-7011
Punxy Beauty School of Cosmetology Arts — Post-Sec.
222 N Findley St 15767 — 814-938-8811

Quakertown, Bucks, Pop. 8,816
Quakertown Community SD — 4,800/K-12
600 Park Ave 18951 — 215-529-2000
James Scanlon Ed.D., supt. — Fax 529-2042
www.qcsd.org/
Freshman Center — 9-9
349 S 9th St 18951 — 267-371-1200
Suzanne Vincent, prin. — Fax 371-1201
Milford MS — 600/6-8
2255 Allentown Rd 18951 — 215-529-2210
Derek Peiffer, prin. — Fax 529-2211
Quakertown Community HS — 1,200/10-12
600 Park Ave 18951 — 215-529-2060
Mario Galante, prin. — Fax 529-2061
Strayer MS — 600/6-8
1200 Ronald Reagan Dr 18951 — 215-529-2290
Richard Zinck Ed.D., prin. — Fax 529-2291

Quarryville, Lancaster, Pop. 2,079
Solanco SD — 3,900/K-12
121 S Hess St 17566 — 717-786-8401
Jon Rednak Ed.D., supt. — Fax 786-8245
www.solanco.k12.pa.us
Smith MS — 500/6-8
645 Kirkwood Pike 17566 — 717-786-2244
James Close, prin. — Fax 786-8796
Solanco HS — 1,300/9-12
585 Solanco Rd 17566 — 717-786-2151
Gerard Rosolie, prin. — Fax 786-1808
Swift MS — 500/6-8
1866 Robert Fulton Hwy 17566 — 717-548-2187
Suzanne Herr, prin. — Fax 548-3350

Radnor, Delaware, Pop. 31,300
Radnor Township SD
Supt. — See Wayne
Radnor HS — 1,100/9-12
130 King Of Prussia Rd 19087 — 610-293-0855
Joane Eby, prin. — Fax 989-9146

Archbishop Carroll HS — 1,000/9-12
211 Matsonford Rd 19087 — 610-688-7610
Carol Ann Blair, prin. — Fax 688-8326
Cabrini College — Post-Sec.
610 King Of Prussia Rd 19087 — 610-902-8100

Reading, Berks, Pop. 80,305
Antietam SD — 900/K-12
100 Antietam Rd 19606 — 610-779-0554
Dr. Lawrence Mayes, supt. — Fax 779-4424
www.antietamsd.org
Antietam MSHS — 500/7-12
100 Antietam Rd 19606 — 610-779-3545
Melissa G. Herb, prin. — Fax 779-0378

Area Vocational Technical School
Supt. — None
Reading-Muhlenberg AVTS — Vo/Tech
PO Box 13068 19612 — 610-921-7306
Gerard Cunningham, admin. — Fax 921-7367

Exeter Township SD — 4,100/K-12
3650 Perkiomen Ave 19606 — 610-779-0700
Nicholas Corbo, supt. — Fax 779-7104
www.exeter.k12.pa.us/
Exeter Twp. HS — 1,300/9-12
201 E 37th St 19606 — 610-779-3060
James Smith, prin. — Fax 370-0518
Exeter Twp. JHS — 700/7-8
151 E 39th St 19606 — 610-779-3320
Eric Flamm, prin. — Fax 370-0678

Reading SD — 16,500/PK-12
800 Washington St 19601 — 610-371-5611
Dr. Thomas Chapman, supt. — Fax 371-5971
www.readingsd.org
Northeast MS — 1,200/6-8
1216 N 13th St 19604 — 610-371-5774
Eric Turman, prin. — Fax 371-5784
Northwest MS — 1,100/6-8
1000 N Front St 19601 — 610-371-5882
Dennis Campbell, prin. — Fax 371-5881
Reading HS — 4,000/9-12
801 N 13th St 19604 — 610-371-5710
Wynton Butler, prin. — Fax 371-5723
Southern MS — 900/6-8
931 Chestnut St 19602 — 610-371-5802
Alan Futrick, prin. — Fax 371-5814
Southwest MS — 700/6-8
300 Chestnut St 19602 — 610-371-5934
Yolanda Williams, prin. — Fax 371-5950

Albright College — Post-Sec.
PO Box 15234 19612 — 610-921-2381
Alvernia College — Post-Sec.
400 Saint Bernardine St 19607 — 610-796-8200
Central Catholic HS — 400/9-12
1400 Hill Rd 19602 — 610-373-4178
Thomas Mirabella, prin. — Fax 375-4898
Empire Beauty School — Post-Sec.
2302 N 5th Street Hwy 19605 — 610-372-2777
Fairview Christian S — 100/K-12
410 S 14th St 19602 — 610-372-8826
Jay Fox, prin. — Fax 478-0896
Harrison Career Institute — Post-Sec.
645 Penn St 19601 — 610-374-2469

Holy Name HS — 300/9-12
955 E Wyomissing Blvd 19611 — 610-374-8361
Keith Laser, prin. — Fax 374-4309
Pace Institute — Post-Sec.
606 Court St 19601 — 610-375-7223
Pennsylvania State University — Post-Sec.
PO Box 7009 19610 — 610-320-4800
Reading Adventist Junior Academy — 100/1-10
309 N Kenhorst Blvd 19607 — 610-777-8424
Fax 603-0129
Reading Area Community College — Post-Sec.
PO Box 1706 19603 — 610-372-4721
Reading Hospital & Medical Center — Post-Sec.
PO Box 16052 19612 — 610-378-6664
St. Joseph's Hospital — Post-Sec.
PO Box 316 19603 — 610-378-2000

Red Lion, York, Pop. 6,093
Red Lion Area SD — 5,500/K-12
696 Delta Rd 17356 — 717-244-4518
Larry Macaluso, supt. — Fax 244-2196
www.rlasd.k12.pa.us
Red Lion Area JHS — 1,000/7-8
200 Country Club Rd 17356 — 717-244-1448
Kurt Fassnacht, prin. — Fax 244-6160
Red Lion Area SHS — 1,600/9-12
200 Horace Mann Ave 17356 — 717-246-1611
Charles Humberd, prin. — Fax 246-9181

Red Lion Christian S — 300/K-12
105 Springvale Rd 17356 — 717-244-3905
Steve Schmuck, prin. — Fax 246-3738

Reedsville, Mifflin, Pop. 1,030
Mifflin County SD
Supt. — See Lewistown
Indian Valley MS — 800/6-8
125 Kish Rd 17084 — 717-667-2123
Mark A. Crosson, prin. — Fax 667-6608

Renovo, Clinton, Pop. 1,255
Keystone Central SD
Supt. — See Lock Haven
Bucktail Area JSHS — 300/7-12
1300 Bucktail Ave 17764 — 570-923-1166
Kurt Smith, prin. — Fax 923-2233

Reynoldsville, Jefferson, Pop. 2,658
Area Vocational Technical School
Supt. — None
Jefferson County-Dubois AVTS — Vo/Tech
576 Vo Tech Rd 15851 — 814-653-8265
W. Barnett Knorr, prin. — Fax 653-8425

Richboro, Bucks, Pop. 5,332
Council Rock SD
Supt. — See Newtown
Richboro MS — 500/7-8
98 Upper Holland Rd 18954 — 215-355-0500
William Bell, prin. — Fax 355-3230

Ridgway, Elk, Pop. 4,419
Ridgway Area SD — 1,100/K-12
PO Box 447 15853 — 814-773-3146
Gary K. Elder, supt. — Fax 776-4299
www.ridgwayareaschooldistrict.com/
Ridgway Area HS — 400/9-12
PO Box 447 15853 — 814-773-3164
Heather Vargas, prin. — Fax 776-4247
Ridgway Area MS — 200/6-8
PO Box 447 15853 — 814-773-3156
William Connelly, prin. — Fax 776-4239

North Central Industrial Tech. Ed. Ctr. — Post-Sec.
651 Montmorenci Rd 15853 — 814-772-1012

Ridley Park, Delaware, Pop. 7,103
Ridley SD
Supt. — See Folsom
Ridley MS, 400 Free St 19078 — 1,400/6-8
Gail Heinemeyer, prin. — 610-237-8034

Rimersburg, Clarion, Pop. 1,014
Union SD — 800/K-12
354 Baker St #2 16248 — 814-473-6311
Lawrence Bornak, supt. — Fax 473-8201
www.unionsd.net/
Union JSHS, 354 Baker St #1 16248 — 400/7-12
Carl Salser, prin. — 814-473-3121

Roaring Spring, Blair, Pop. 2,335
Spring Cove SD — 1,900/K-12
1100 E Main St 16673 — 814-224-5124
Dr. Kathy Wunder, supt. — Fax 224-5516
springcove.schoolnet.com
Spring Cove MS — 500/6-8
1150 E Main St 16673 — 814-224-2106
Charles Kensinger, prin.
Other Schools – See Martinsburg

Robesonia, Berks, Pop. 2,027
Conrad Weiser Area SD — 2,800/K-12
44 Big Spring Rd 19551 — 610-693-8545
Robert L. Urzillo, supt. — Fax 693-8586
www.conradweiser.org
Weiser HS — 900/9-12
44 Big Spring Rd 19551 — 610-693-8528
Betsy Adams, prin. — Fax 693-8511
Weiser MS — 1,000/5-8
347 E Penn Ave 19551 — 610-693-8514
Joseph Torchia, prin. — Fax 693-8543

Rochester, Beaver, Pop. 3,868
Rochester Area SD — 1,200/K-12
540 Reno St 15074 — 724-775-7500
Dr. C. Dean Galitsis, supt. — Fax 775-6942
www.rasd.org/
Rochester Area HS — 400/9-12
540 Reno St 15074 — 724-775-7500
Walter Gaida, prin. — Fax 775-9268
Rochester Area MS — 300/6-8
540 Reno St 15074 — 724-775-7500
Marianne LeDonne, prin. — Fax 775-9267

Rockwood, Somerset, Pop. 947
 Rockwood Area SD 900/K-12
  439 Somerset Ave 15557 814-926-4913
  Vincent Capricci, supt. Fax 926-2880
  www.rockwoodschools.org
 Rockwood Area JSHS 400/7-12
  437 Somerset Ave 15557 814-926-4631
  Mark Bower, prin. Fax 926-2631

Rome, Bradford, Pop. 383
 Northeast Bradford SD 900/K-12
  RR 1 Box 211B 18837 570-744-2521
  G. Mathew Gordon, supt. Fax 744-2933
  www.neb.k12.pa.us
 Northeast Bradford JSHS 500/7-12
  RR 1 Box 211B 18837 570-744-2521
  Heather McPherson, prin. Fax 744-2933

Rosemont, Montgomery
 Lower Merion SD
  Supt. — See Ardmore
 Harriton HS, 600 N Ithan Ave 19010 800/9-12
  Steven Kline, prin. 610-658-3950

 Irwin S 600/K-12
  S Ithan Ave & Conestoga Rd 19010 610-525-8400
  Fax 525-8908

Roseto, Northampton, Pop. 1,660

 Faith Christian S 200/K-12
  122 Dante St 18013 610-588-3414
  Robert Tomlinson, admin. Fax 588-8103
 Pius X HS 300/7-12
  580 3rd Ave 18013 610-588-3291
  Thomas Klepeisz, prin. Fax 599-3048

Royersford, Montgomery, Pop. 4,321
 Spring-Ford Area SD
  Supt. — See Collegeville
 Spring-Ford HS 1,700/9-12
  350 S Lewis Rd 19468 610-705-6001
  Patrick Nugent, prin. Fax 705-6258
 Spring-Ford MS 8th Grade Center 500/8-8
  700 Washington St 19468 610-705-6002
  Michael Siggins, prin. Fax 705-6255

Ruffs Dale, Westmoreland
 Yough SD
  Supt. — See Herminie
 Yough MS 700/6-8
  171 State Route 31 15679 724-872-5164
  Thomas Paterline, prin. Fax 872-5319

Rural Valley, Armstrong, Pop. 896
 Armstrong SD
  Supt. — See Ford City
 West Shamokin JSHS 700/7-12
  RR 2 Box 154A 16249 724-783-7040
  Rick Burns, prin. Fax 783-6747

Russell, Warren
 Warren County SD
  Supt. — See North Warren
 Eisenhower MSHS 600/7-12
  RR 2 Box 2276 16345 814-757-8878
  Pat Cronmiller, prin. Fax 757-8516

 Calvary Chapel Christian S 100/PK-12
  PO Box 579 16345 814-757-8744
  James Hunt, prin. Fax 757-8745

Russellton, Allegheny, Pop. 1,691
 Deer Lakes SD 2,100/K-12
  PO Box 10 15076 724-265-5300
  Mark King, supt. Fax 265-5025
  www.deerlakes.net
 Deer Lakes HS 700/9-12
  PO Box 40 15076 724-265-5320
  William McClarnon, prin. Fax 265-3970
 Deer Lakes MS 500/6-8
  PO Box 20 15076 724-265-5310
  Dr. Thomas Lesniewski, prin. Fax 265-3711

Saegertown, Crawford, Pop. 1,070
 Penncrest SD 3,900/K-12
  PO Box 808 16433 814-763-2323
  Richard Borchilo, supt. Fax 763-5129
  www.penncrest.iu5.org
 Saegertown JSHS 600/7-12
  18079 Mook Rd 16433 814-763-2615
  Randall Deemer, prin. Fax 763-6702
 Other Schools – See Cambridge Springs, Guys Mills

 French Creek Valley Christian S 100/PK-12
  420 North St 16433 814-763-3282
  Robert Holleman, prin.

Saint Davids, Delaware

 Eastern University Post-Sec.
  1300 Eagle Rd 19087 610-341-5800

Saint Marys, Elk, Pop. 14,182
 Saint Marys Area SD 2,600/K-12
  977 S Saint Marys St 15857 814-834-7831
  J. Paul Robertson, supt. Fax 781-2190
  smasd.org
 Saint Marys Area HS 900/9-12
  977 S Saint Marys St 15857 814-834-7831
  Joshua Williams, prin. Fax 781-2190
 Saint Marys Area MS 600/6-8
  979 S Saint Marys St 15857 814-834-7831
  Murray Meeper, prin. Fax 781-2191

 Elk County Catholic HS 400/9-12
  600 Maurus St 15857 814-834-7800
  John Kowach, hdmstr. Fax 781-3441
 St. Marys Catholic S 200/6-8
  325 Church St 15857 814-834-2665
  Mary Agnes Marshall, prin. Fax 834-5339

Salisbury, Somerset, Pop. 847
 Salisbury-Elk Lick SD 400/K-12
  PO Box 68 15558 814-662-2733
  Dr. David Welling, supt. Fax 662-2544
  www.selsd.com
 Salisbury-Elk Lick JSHS 200/7-12
  PO Box 68 15558 814-662-2741
  Eugene Wengerd, prin. Fax 662-2091

Saltsburg, Indiana, Pop. 923
 Blairsville-Saltsburg SD
  Supt. — See Blairsville
 Saltsburg MSHS 500/7-12
  84 Trojan Ln 15681 724-639-3547
  Eric Kostic, prin. Fax 639-0071

 Kiski S 200/9-12
  1888 Brett Ln 15681 724-639-3586
  Christopher Brueningsen, hdmstr. Fax 639-8467

Sarver, Butler
 Freeport Area SD 2,000/K-12
  621 S Pike Rd 16055 724-295-5141
  Joseph P. Malak Ed.D., supt. Fax 295-3001
  www.freeport.k12.pa.us
 Freeport Area HS 600/9-12
  625 S Pike Rd 16055 724-295-5143
  Robert Schleiden, prin. Fax 295-2390
 Other Schools – See Freeport

 Evangel Heights Christian Academy 200/PK-12
  120 Beale Rd 16055 724-295-9199
  Gary Bracewell, dir. Fax 295-9009

Saxonburg, Butler, Pop. 1,640
 South Butler County SD 2,900/K-12
  328 Knoch Rd 16056 724-352-1700
  Dr. Patrick T. O'Toole, supt. Fax 352-3622
  www.southbutler.k12.pa.us
 Knoch HS 1,000/9-12
  345 Knoch Rd 16056 724-352-1700
  Joanne Galardy, prin. Fax 352-0160
 Knoch MS 700/6-8
  754 Dinnerbell Rd 16056 724-352-1700
  James George, prin. Fax 352-0170

Saxton, Bedford, Pop. 781
 Tussey Mountain SD 1,200/K-12
  199 Front St 16678 814-635-3670
  Dr. Ronald D. McCahan, supt. Fax 635-3928
  www.tmsd.net/
 Tussey Mountain JSHS 600/7-12
  199 Front St 16678 814-635-2975
  Mike Panek, prin.

Sayre, Bradford, Pop. 5,659
 Sayre Area SD 1,200/PK-12
  333 W Lockhart St 18840 570-888-7615
  Dr. Donald Houck, supt. Fax 888-8248
  www.sayresd.org
 Sayre Area JSHS 600/7-12
  331 W Lockhart St 18840 570-888-6622
  Samuel Cessna, prin. Fax 882-9385

 Robert Packer Hospital Post-Sec.
  1 Guthrie Sq 18840 570-888-6666

Schnecksville, Lehigh, Pop. 1,780
 Area Vocational Technical School
  Supt. — None
 Lehigh Career & Technical Institute Vo/Tech
  4500 Education Park Dr 18078 610-799-1323
  Dr. Clyde Hornberger, prin.

 Lehigh Carbon Community College Post-Sec.
  4525 Education Park Dr 18078 610-799-2121

Schuylkill Haven, Schuylkill, Pop. 5,377
 Blue Mountain SD
  Supt. — See Orwigsburg
 Blue Mountain HS 1,000/9-12
  1076 W Market St 17972 570-366-0511
  Cynthia A. Knauer, prin. Fax 366-1965

 Schuylkill Haven Area SD 1,400/K-12
  120 Haven St 17972 570-385-6705
  Richard Rada, supt. Fax 385-6736
  www.haven.k12.pa.us/
 Schuylkill Haven Area HS 500/8-12
  120 Haven St 17972 570-385-6717
  Charles Grabusky, prin. Fax 385-6736

 Pennsylvania State University Post-Sec.
  200 University Dr 17972 570-385-6000

Scottdale, Westmoreland, Pop. 4,631
 Southmoreland SD 2,300/K-12
  609 Parker Ave 15683 724-887-2000
  Dr. John K. Halfhill, supt. Fax 887-2055
  www.southmoreland.net
 Other Schools – See Alverton

Scranton, Lackawanna, Pop. 74,320
 Area Vocational Technical School
  Supt. — None
 CTC of Lackawanna County Vo/Tech
  3201 Rockwell Ave 18508 570-346-8471
  Vincent Nallo, prin. Fax 342-4251

 Scranton SD 8,900/PK-12
  425 N Washington Ave 18503 570-348-3400
  Michael Sheridan, supt. Fax 348-3563
  www.scrsd.org/
 Northeast IS, 721 Adams Ave 18510 900/6-8
  Barbara Dixon, prin. 570-348-3651
 Scranton HS 1,800/9-12
  63 Munchak Way 18508 570-348-3481
  Robert McTiernan, prin. Fax 348-3561
 South Scranton IS 500/6-8
  355 Maple St 18505 570-348-3631
  Charles Gawhiler, prin.
 West Scranton HS 900/9-12
  1201 Luzerne St 18504 570-348-3616
  Kevin Rogan, prin. Fax 348-3594

 West Scranton IS 700/6-8
  Fellows St & Parrott Ave 18504 570-348-3475
  Dr. Charlotte Slocum, prin.

 Allied Medical & Technical Careers Post-Sec.
  517 Ash St 18509 570-558-1818
 Bais Yaakov of Scranton 100/9-12
  537 Monroe Ave 18510 570-347-5003
  Esther Elefant, prin. Fax 347-5003
 Bishop Hannan HS 400/9-12
  330 Wyoming Ave 18503 570-346-4643
  James Marcks, prin. Fax 346-0048
 Center for Innovative Training & Educ. Post-Sec.
  135 Franklin Ave 18503 570-922-6555
 Education Direct Post-Sec.
  925 Oak St 18515 570-342-7701
 Eisner Yeshiva HS 100/9-12
  930 Hickory St 18505 570-346-1747
  Charles Gahwiler, prin.
 Johnson College Post-Sec.
  3427 N Main Ave 18508 570-342-6404
 Lackawanna College Post-Sec.
  501 Vine St 18509 570-961-7810
 Marywood University Post-Sec.
  2300 Adams Ave 18509 570-348-6211
 St. Paul S 200/4-8
  1527 Penn Ave 18509 570-343-7880
  Elizabeth Murray, prin. Fax 343-0069
 Scranton Prep S 800/9-12
  1000 Wyoming Ave 18509 570-941-7737
  Patrick Marx, prin. Fax 941-6118
 Scranton State School for the Deaf Post-Sec.
  1800 N Washington Ave 18509
 University of Scranton Post-Sec.
  800 Linden St 18510 570-941-7400
 Yeshiva Beth Moshe Post-Sec.
  930 Hickory St 18505 570-346-1747
 Yeshiva Beth Moshe 100/9-12
  PO Box 1141 18501 570-346-1747
  Rabbi Chaim Bressler, prin. Fax 346-2251

Selinsgrove, Snyder, Pop. 5,436
 Selinsgrove Area SD 2,900/K-12
  401 18th St 17870 570-374-1144
  Dr. Frederick C. Johnson, supt. Fax 372-2241
  www.seal-pa.org/
 Selinsgrove Area HS 1,000/9-12
  500 Broad St 17870 570-374-1144
  Reed Messmore, prin. Fax 372-2240
 Selinsgrove Area MS 700/6-8
  401 18th St 17870 570-374-1144
  George Pyle, prin. Fax 372-2288

 Gospel Christian Academy 50/PK-12
  RR 2 Box 190 17870 570-743-7754
  Kii Fisher, admin. Fax 743-7746
 Susquehanna University Post-Sec.
  514 University Ave 17870 570-374-0101

Sellersville, Bucks, Pop. 4,516

 Faith Christian Academy 300/K-12
  700 N Main St 18960 215-257-5031
  Robert Clymer, prin. Fax 257-3327
 Upper Bucks Christian S 300/K-12
  754 E Rockhill Rd 18960 215-536-9200
  Steve Cruice, prin. Fax 536-2229

Seneca, Venango, Pop. 1,029
 Cranberry Area SD 1,300/K-12
  3 Education Dr 16346 814-676-5628
  Dr. Nicholas A. Bodnar, supt. Fax 677-5728
  www.cranberrysd.org/
 Cranberry Area JSHS 800/7-12
  1 Education Dr 16346 814-676-8504
  George S. Suolos, prin. Fax 676-5156

 Christian Life Academy 100/K-12
  PO Box 207 16346 814-676-9360
  Michael Lloyd, admin. Fax 676-2908
 Northwest Medical Center Post-Sec.
  100 Fairfield Dr 16346 814-677-1711

Sewickley, Allegheny, Pop. 3,769
 Quaker Valley SD 2,100/K-12
  203 Graham St 15143 412-749-3600
  Dr. R. Longo, supt. Fax 749-3601
  www.qvsd.org/qvsd/site/default.asp
 Quaker Valley MS 500/7-9
  201 Graham St 15143 412-749-5079
  Dr. Kenneth Powell, prin.
 Other Schools – See Leetsdale

 Eden Christian Academy 100/7-12
  318 Nicholson Rd 15143 412-741-2825
  Thomas Aiken, hdmstr. Fax 324-1101
 Sewickley Academy 800/PK-12
  315 Academy Ave 15143 412-741-2230
  Kolia J. O'Connor, hdmstr. Fax 741-1411
 Sewickley Valley Hospital Post-Sec.
  700 Blackburn Rd 15143 412-741-6600
 The Education Center at Watson Inst. Post-Sec.
  301 Campmeeting Rd 15143 412-741-1800

Shamokin Dam, Snyder, Pop. 1,479

 Empire Beauty School Post-Sec.
  PO Box 397 17876 570-743-1410

Shanksville, Somerset, Pop. 236
 Shanksville-Stonycreek SD 500/K-12
  PO Box 128 15560 814-267-4649
  Dr. Rosemarie Tipton, supt. Fax 267-4372
  www.sssd.com
 Shanksville-Stonycreek JSHS 300/6-12
  PO Box 128 15560 814-267-4649
  Constance Hummel, prin. Fax 267-4372

Sharon, Mercer, Pop. 15,735
 Sharon CSD 2,400/K-12
  215 Forker Blvd 16146 724-981-6390
  Dr. Donna M. DeBonis, supt. Fax 981-0844
  www.sharon.k12.pa.us/

Sharon JSHS
1129 E State St 16146
Robert Alcaro, prin.

1,100/7-12
724-983-4030
Fax 981-0840

Business Institute of Pennsylvania
335 Boyd Dr 16146
Pennsylvania State University
147 Shenango Ave 16146
Sharon Regional Health System
740 E State St 16146

Post-Sec.
724-983-0700
Post-Sec.
724-983-5800
Post-Sec.
724-983-3865

Sharon Hill, Delaware, Pop. 5,386
Southeast Delco SD
Supt. — See Folcroft
Academy Park HS
300 Calcon Hook Rd 19079
Dale Weaver, prin.

1,200/9-12
610-522-4330
Fax 522-4335

Venus Beauty Academy
1033 Chester Pike 19079

Post-Sec.
610-586-2500

Sharpsville, Mercer, Pop. 4,338
Sharpsville Area SD
701 S 7th St 16150
Dr. Mark Ferrara, supt.
www.sharpsville.k12.pa.us/
Sharpsville Area HS
301 Blue Devil Way 16150
Kirk Scurpa, prin.
Sharpsville Area MS
303 Blue Devil Way 16150
John Vannoy, prin.

1,300/K-12
724-962-7874
Fax 962-7873

400/9-12
724-962-7861
Fax 962-7730
300/6-8
724-962-7863

Sheffield, Warren, Pop. 1,294
Warren County SD
Supt. — See North Warren
Sheffield Area MSHS
HC 1 Box 600 16347
James Evers, prin.

500/6-12
814-968-3720
Fax 968-4233

Shelocta, Armstrong, Pop. 123

Wrightco Technologies Tech Training Inst
Route 422 W 15774

Post-Sec.
724-354-5162

Shenandoah, Schuylkill, Pop. 5,387
Shenandoah Valley SD
805 W Centre St 17976
Dr. Stanley Rakowsky, supt.
www.shenandoah.k12.pa.us
Shenandoah Valley JSHS
805 W Centre St 17976
Phillip Andras, prin.

1,000/PK-12
570-462-1936
Fax 462-4611

500/7-12
570-462-1957
Fax 462-2982

Shickshinny, Luzerne, Pop. 921
Northwest Area SD
243 Thorne Hill Rd 18655
Nancy Tkatch, supt.
www.northwest.k12.pa.us/
Northwest Area JSHS
243 Thorne Hill Rd 18655
Ronald Powlus, prin.

1,400/K-12
570-542-4126

600/7-12
570-542-4126

Shillington, Berks, Pop. 5,009
Governor Mifflin SD
10 S Waverly St 19607
Dr. Mary T. Weiss, supt.
www.governormifflinsd.org
Mifflin HS
101 S Waverly St 19607
John Sengia, prin.
Mifflin MS
130 East Lancaster Ave 19607
James Howland, prin.

4,200/K-12
610-775-1461
Fax 775-6586

1,400/9-12
610-775-5089
Fax 796-7471
700/7-8
610-775-1465
Fax 685-3760

Shinglehouse, Potter, Pop. 1,228
Oswayo Valley SD
PO Box 610 16748
Charles R. Wicker, supt.
www.oswayo.com/
Oswayo Valley MSHS
PO Box 610 16748
Erik Kincade, prin.

600/PK-12
814-697-7175
Fax 697-7439

300/6-12
814-697-6132
Fax 697-6375

Shippensburg, Cumberland, Pop. 5,620
Shippensburg Area SD
317 N Morris St 17257
Dr. Jacqueline Lesney, supt.
www.ship.k12.pa.us
Shippensburg Area HS
201 Eberly Dr 17257
Dr. H. Frederick Shilling, prin.
Shippensburg Area MS
101 Park Pl 17257
Teri Mowery, prin.

3,300/K-12
717-530-2700
Fax 530-2724

1,000/9-12
717-530-2730
Fax 530-2835
800/6-8
717-530-2750
Fax 530-2757

Shippensburg University
1871 Old Main Dr 17257

Post-Sec.
717-477-7447

Shippenville, Clarion, Pop. 490
Area Vocational Technical School
Supt. — None
Clarion County Career Center
447 Career Way 16254
William Powell, dir.

Vo/Tech
814-226-4391
Fax 226-7350

Shiremanstown, Cumberland, Pop. 1,499

Bible Baptist S
201 W Main St 17011
George Wiedman, admin.

500/PK-12
717-737-3550
Fax 761-3977

Sidman, Cambria, Pop. 1,189
Forest Hills SD
PO Box 158 15955
Donald Bailey, supt.
www.fhsd.k12.pa.us/
Forest Hills HS
PO Box 325 15955
R. Bernazzoli, prin.
Forest Hills MS
1427 Frankstown Rd 15955
Raymond Wotkowski, prin.

2,300/K-12
814-487-7613
Fax 487-7775

500/10-12
814-487-7613
Fax 487-2371
600/7-9
814-495-4611
Fax 495-7367

Sinking Spring, Berks, Pop. 3,153
Wilson SD
Supt. — See West Lawn
Wilson Southern JHS
3100 Iroquois Ave 19608
Luke Hadfield, prin.

700/7-9
610-670-0180
Fax 670-4815

Slatington, Lehigh, Pop. 4,373
Northern Lehigh SD
1201 Shadow Oaks Ln 18080
Dr. Nicholas P. Sham, supt.
www.nlsd.org
Northern Lehigh HS
1 Bulldog Ln 18080
Philip Bertolino, prin.
Northern Lehigh MS
600 Diamond St 18080
David Papay, prin.

1,600/K-12
610-767-9800
Fax 767-9809

700/9-12
610-767-9833
Fax 767-9853
300/7-8
610-767-9812
Fax 767-9850

Slippery Rock, Butler, Pop. 3,028
Slippery Rock Area SD
201 Kiester Rd 16057
Dr. Marianne Lee Beaton, supt.
www.slipperyrock.k12.pa.us
Slippery Rock Area HS
201 Kiester Rd 16057
Harry Beil, prin.
Slippery Rock Area MS
201 Kiester Rd 16057
Joseph Raykle, prin.

2,800/K-12
724-794-2960
Fax 794-2001

800/9-12
724-794-2960
Fax 794-1952
600/6-8
724-794-2960

Slippery Rock University
14 Maltby Ave 16057

Post-Sec.
724-738-9000

Smethport, McKean, Pop. 1,654
Smethport Area SD
414 S Mechanic St 16749
George J. Romanowski, supt.
www.smethporthubbers.net
Smethport Area JSHS
412 S Mechanic St 16749
Robert Miller, prin.

1,000/K-12
814-887-5543
Fax 887-5544

500/7-12
814-887-5545
Fax 887-5546

Somerset, Somerset, Pop. 6,617
Area Vocational Technical School
Supt. — None
Somerset County Technology Center
281 Technology Dr 15501
Robert Friedline, prin.

Vo/Tech
814-443-3651
Fax 445-6716

Somerset Area SD
645 S Columbia Ave Ste 110 15501
Dr. David Pastrick, supt.
sasdpa.net
Somerset Area JHS
645 S Columbia Ave Ste 120 15501
Jeff Boyer, prin.
Somerset Area SHS
645 S Columbia Ave Ste 130 15501
Mark Gross, prin.

2,800/K-12
814-443-2831
Fax 443-1964

700/7-9
814-443-2831
Fax 444-3301
700/10-12
814-443-2831
Fax 444-3202

Somerset Community Hospital
225 S Center Ave 15501

Post-Sec.
814-443-5221

Souderton, Montgomery, Pop. 6,768
Souderton Area SD
760 Lower Rd 18964
Charles D. Amuso Ed.D., supt.
www.soudertonsd.org
Indian Crest JHS
139 Harleysville Pike 18964
Jeff Palmer, prin.
Souderton Area HS
41 N School Ln 18964
Sam Varano, prin.

6,600/K-12
215-723-6061
Fax 723-8897

1,100/8-9
215-723-9193
Fax 723-8897
1,500/10-12
215-723-2808
Fax 723-6352

Southampton, Bucks, Pop. 11,500
Centennial SD
Supt. — See Warminster
Klinger MS
1415 2nd Street Pike 18966
Joseph Nawn, prin.

800/6-8
215-364-5950

CHI Institute
520 Street Rd 18966

Post-Sec.
215-357-5100

South Canaan, Wayne
Western Wayne SD
PO Box 500 18459
Andrew Falonk, supt.
www.westernwayne.org
Other Schools – See Lake Ariel

2,500/PK-12
570-937-4270
Fax 937-4105

St. Tikhon's Orthodox Theological Sem.
PO Box 130 18459

Post-Sec.
570-937-4411

South Park, Allegheny
South Park SD
2005 Eagle Ridge Rd 15129
Richard Bucchianeri, supt.
www.sparksd.org
South Park HS
2005 Eagle Ridge Dr 15129
Dr. Patricia Smith, prin.
South Park MS
2500 Stewart Rd 15129
Douglas Broglie, prin.

2,200/K-12
412-655-3111
Fax 655-2952

800/9-12
412-655-4900
Fax 655-1463
700/5-8
412-831-7200
Fax 831-7204

South Williamsport, Lycoming, Pop. 6,240
South Williamsport Area SD
515 W Central Ave 17702
Thomas C. Farr, supt.
www.mounties.k12.pa.us
South Williamsport Area JSHS
700 Percy St 17702
Paul Anderson, prin.

1,500/K-12
570-327-1581
Fax 326-0641

800/7-12
570-326-2684
Fax 326-2687

Spring Church, Armstrong
Apollo-Ridge SD
Supt. — See Apollo
Apollo-Ridge HS
HC 62 Box 46A 15686
James Thimons, prin.
Apollo-Ridge MS
HC 62 Box 46B 15686
Donna Sybert, prin.

500/9-12
724-478-6000
Fax 478-9775
400/6-8
724-478-6000
Fax 478-3730

Springdale, Allegheny, Pop. 3,718
Allegheny Valley SD
Supt. — See Cheswick
Springdale JSHS
501 Butler Rd 15144
Janice Nuzzo Ph.D., prin.

600/7-12
724-274-2100
Fax 274-2106

Springfield, Delaware, Pop. 24,160
Springfield SD
111 W Leamy Ave 19064
Dr. Joseph O'Brien, supt.
www.springfieldsd-delco.org
Richardson MS
20 W Woodland Ave 19064
Frank McKnight, prin.
Springfield HS
49 W Leamy Ave 19064
Dr. Bridget Kelly, prin.

3,400/K-12
610-938-6000
Fax 938-6005

1,100/5-8
610-938-6300
Fax 938-6305
1,200/9-12
610-938-6100
Fax 938-6105

Cardinal O'Hara HS
1701 S Sproul Rd 19064
William Miles Ed.D., prin.
Chubb Institute-Keystone School
400 S State Rd 19064

1,600/9-12
610-544-3800
Fax 544-1189
Post-Sec.
610-543-1747

Spring Grove, York, Pop. 2,168
Spring Grove Area SD
100 E College Ave 17362
Dr. David Stricker, supt.
www.sgasd.org
Spring Grove Area MS
1472 Roth Church Rd 17362
Rosemary Aldinger, prin.
Spring Grove HS
Hanover & Jackson Sts 17362
Steven Brown, prin.

3,900/K-12
717-225-4731
Fax 225-6028

700/7-8
717-225-4731
Fax 225-0146
1,300/9-12
717-225-4731
Fax 225-0736

Spring Mills, Centre
Penns Valley Area SD
4528 Penns Valley Rd 16875
Dr. Robert Lees, supt.
www.pennsvalley.org
Penns Valley Area JSHS
4545 Penns Valley Rd 16875
Albert D'Ambrosia, prin.

1,400/K-12
814-422-8814
Fax 422-8020

800/7-12
814-422-8854
Fax 422-8280

State College, Centre, Pop. 39,728
State College Area SD
131 W Nittany Ave 16801
Dr. Patricia Best, supt.
www.scasd.org
Mount Nittany MS
656 Brandywine Dr 16801
Jason Perrin, prin.
Park Forest MS
2180 School Dr 16803
David Dolbin, prin.
State College Area HS
653 Westerly Pkwy 16801
Craig Butler, prin.

7,300/K-12
814-231-1011
Fax 231-4130

900/6-8
814-466-5133
Fax 466-5140
900/6-8
814-237-5301
Fax 272-0196
2,600/9-12
814-231-1111
Fax 231-5024

Empire Beauty School
206 W Hamilton Ave 16801
Grace Prep S
1117 William St 16801
Robert Gresh, admin.
South Hills School of Business & Tech.
480 Waupelani Dr 16801

Post-Sec.
814-238-1961
50/9-12
814-867-1177
Fax 867-3555
Post-Sec.
888-282-7427

Steelton, Dauphin, Pop. 5,781
Central Dauphin SD
Supt. — See Harrisburg
Swatara MS
1101 Highland St 17113
Michael Jordan, prin.

600/6-8
717-939-9363
Fax 939-2156

Steelton-Highspire SD
PO Box 7645 17113
Dr. Norma Mateer, supt.
www.shsd.k12.pa.us
Steelton-Highspire JSHS
250 Reynders St 17113
Paul Cronin, prin.

1,300/K-12
717-939-9823
Fax 939-8241

600/7-12
717-939-9895
Fax 939-8241

Stoneboro, Mercer, Pop. 1,076
Lakeview SD
2482 Mercer St 16153
Dr. Paulette Savolskis, supt.
www.lakeview.k12.pa.us/
Lakeview HS
2482 Mercer St 16153
David Sapala, prin.
Lakeview MS
2482 Mercer St 16153
Fred McConnell, prin.

1,300/K-12
724-376-7911
Fax 376-7910

400/9-12
724-376-7911
Fax 376-7910
400/5-8
724-376-7911
Fax 376-7910

Stoneboro Wesleyan Methodist S
947 Fredonia Rd 16153
Roger Patterson, prin.

100/K-12
724-376-3319
Fax 376-3319

Strafford, Chester, Pop. 4,500

Woodlynde S
445 Upper Gulph Rd 19087
John Murray, hdmstr.

300/1-12
610-687-9660
Fax 687-4752

Strattanville, Clarion, Pop. 527
Clarion-Limestone Area SD
4091 C L School Rd 16258
J. Richard Slack, supt.
www.clarion-limestoneschool.com
Clarion-Limestone JSHS
4091 C L School Rd 16258
Michael Drzewiecki, prin.

1,100/K-12
814-764-5111
Fax 764-5729

500/7-12
814-764-5111
Fax 764-5274

Stroudsburg, Monroe, Pop. 6,127
Stroudsburg Area SD
123 Linden St 18360
Frederick Hackett, supt.
www.sburg.org
Stroudsburg HS
1100 W Main St 18360
Jeff Sodi, prin.
Stroudsburg JHS
1198 Chipperfield Dr 18360
Dr. Maryellen Mross, prin.

3,900/K-12
570-421-1990
Fax 424-5986

1,300/10-12
570-421-1991
Fax 424-1383
900/8-9
570-424-4848
Fax 424-4839

Stroudsburg School of Cosmetology — Post-Sec.
100 N 8th St 18360 — 570-421-3387

Summerdale, Cumberland

Central Pennsylvania College — Post-Sec.
College Hill & Valley Rds 17093 — 717-732-0702

Sunbury, Northumberland, Pop. 10,277
Shikellamy SD — 3,200/K-12
200 Island Blvd 17801 — 570-286-3720
Dr. James Hartman, supt. — Fax 286-3776
www.shikbraves.org
Rice MS — 400/6-8
4th & Hanover Sts, — 570-473-3547
Frank Boyer, prin. — Fax 473-4483
Shikellamy HS — 1,100/9-12
600 Walnut St 17801 — 570-286-3713
Terry Roden, prin. — Fax 286-3775
Sunbury MS — 400/6-8
115 Fairmount Ave 17801 — 570-286-3736
Michael Hubicki, prin. — Fax 286-3780

ICT School of Welding — Post-Sec.
358 Market St 17801 — 570-988-3960
McCann School of Business & Technology — Post-Sec.
1147 N 4th St 17801 — 570-286-3058
Triangle Tech — Post-Sec.
RR 1 Box 51 17801 — 570-988-0700

Susquehanna, Susquehanna, Pop. 1,702
Susquehanna Community SD — 1,000/K-12
RR 3 Box 5A 18847 — 570-853-4921
Bronson Stone, supt. — Fax 853-3768
www.scschools.org/
Susquehanna Community JSHS — 500/7-12
RR 3 Box 5A 18847 — 570-853-4921
Michael Lisowski, prin. — Fax 853-3918

Swarthmore, Delaware, Pop. 6,154

Swarthmore College — Post-Sec.
500 College Ave 19081 — 610-328-8000

Swiftwater, Monroe
Pocono Mountain SD — 9,600/K-12
PO Box 200 18370 — 570-839-7121
Dr. Dwight Pfennig, supt. — Fax 895-4768
www.pmsd.org
Pocono Mountain East HS — 1,900/9-12
PO Box 200 18370 — 570-839-7121
Todd Burns, prin. — Fax 839-5934
Swiftwater IS — 900/7-8
PO Box 200 18370 — 570-839-7121
Tom Barbush, prin. — Fax 839-5935
Other Schools – See Pocono Summit

Tamaqua, Schuylkill, Pop. 6,878
Tamaqua Area SD — 2,200/K-12
PO Box 112 18252 — 570-668-2570
Frederick T. Bausch, supt. — Fax 668-6850
www.tamaqua.k12.pa.us/
Tamaqua Area HS — 700/9-12
PO Box 90 18252 — 570-668-1901
Raymond Kinder, prin. — Fax 668-2970
Tamaqua Area MS — 600/6-8
PO Box 90 18252 — 570-668-1210
Ruth Ann Gardiner, prin. — Fax 668-5027

Marian HS — 400/9-12
166 Marian Ave 18252 — 570-467-3335
Sr. Bernard Agnes Smith, prin. — Fax 467-0186

Taylor, Lackawanna, Pop. 6,325
Riverside SD — 1,400/K-12
300 Davis St 18517 — 570-562-2121
Salvatore F. Luzio, supt. — Fax 562-3205
ns.neiu.k12.pa.us/WWW/RS/index.html
Riverside JSHS — 700/7-12
310 Davis St 18517 — 570-562-2121
Joseph Moceyunas, prin. — Fax 562-7551

Thompson, Susquehanna, Pop. 287

Faith Mountain Christian Academy — 50/PK-12
RR 2 Box 99 18465 — 570-465-2220
Lois Frantz, prin. — Fax 465-2220

Three Springs, Huntingdon, Pop. 433
Southern Huntingdon County SD — 1,300/K-12
RR 2 Box 1124 17264 — 814-447-5529
Charles McCabe, supt. — Fax 447-3967
www.shcsd.k12.pa.us
Southern Huntingdon County MSHS — 700/6-12
RR 2 Box 1124 17264 — 814-447-5529
M. Brouse, prin. — Fax 447-3750

Throop, Lackawanna, Pop. 3,945
Mid Valley SD — 1,500/K-12
52 Underwood Rd 18512 — 570-307-1119
Dr. Joseph Crotti, supt. — Fax 307-1107
www.mvsd.us
Mid Valley JSHS — 800/7-12
52 Underwood Rd 18512 — 570-307-2180
Randy Parry, prin.

Tioga, Tioga, Pop. 617
Northern Tioga SD
Supt. — See Elkland
Williamson JSHS — 600/7-12
RR 2 Box 205 16946 — 570-827-2191
Diana Barnes, prin. — Fax 827-3557

Tionesta, Forest, Pop. 597
Forest Area SD — 700/K-12
210 Vine St 16353 — 814-755-4491
Duane Vicini, supt. — Fax 755-2426
West Forest JSHS — 200/7-12
HC 2 Box 15 16353 — 814-755-3611
Joseph Carrico, prin. — Fax 755-2427
Other Schools – See Marienville

North Clarion County SD — 700/K-12
10439 Route 36 16353 — 814-744-8536
Rodney Hartle, supt. — Fax 744-9378
www.northclarion.org/
North Clarion County JSHS — 400/7-12
10439 Route 36 16353 — 814-744-8544
Theodore Pappas, prin. — Fax 744-8762

Titusville, Crawford, Pop. 5,890
Titusville Area SD — 2,500/PK-12
221 N Washington St 16354 — 814-827-2715
Dr. John Reagle, supt. — Fax 827-7761
www.gorockets.org/
Titusville Area HS — 800/9-12
302 E Walnut St 16354 — 814-827-9687
Amanda Hetrick, prin. — Fax 827-7761
Titusville MS, 415 Water St 16354 — 600/6-8
Michael McGaughey, prin. — 814-827-2717

University of Pittsburgh at Titusville — Post-Sec.
504 E Main St # 287 16354 — 814-827-4400

Topton, Berks, Pop. 1,943
Brandywine Heights Area SD
Supt. — See Mertztown
Brandywine Heights Area MS — 700/5-8
200 W Weis St 19562 — 610-682-5100
Kathy Johnson, prin. — Fax 682-5105

Towanda, Bradford, Pop. 2,946
Area Vocational Technical School
Supt. — None
Northern Tier Career Center — Vo/Tech
RR 1 Box 157A 18848 — 570-265-8111
Walter Becker, prin.

Towanda Area SD — 1,800/K-12
PO Box 231 18848 — 570-265-9894
Donald Butler, supt. — Fax 265-4881
www.tsd.k12.pa.us/
Towanda Area JSHS — 1,200/5-12
1 High School Dr 18848 — 570-265-3690
Steven Gobble, prin. — Fax 268-2069

Tower City, Schuylkill, Pop. 1,355
Williams Valley SD — 1,200/K-12
10330 Route 209 Rd 17980 — 717-647-2167
Diane M. Niederriter, supt. — Fax 647-2055
www.wvsd.k12.pa.us
Williams Valley JSHS — 600/7-12
10330 Route 209 Rd 17980 — 717-647-2167
John Kay, dean — Fax 647-2055

Trafford, Westmoreland, Pop. 3,147
Penn-Trafford SD
Supt. — See Harrison City
Trafford MS — 400/6-8
100 Brinton Ave 15085 — 412-372-6600
James Simpson, prin. — Fax 372-1554

Transfer, Mercer

Winner Institute of Arts & Sciences — Post-Sec.
1 Winner Rd 16154 — 724-646-2433

Trevorton, Northumberland, Pop. 2,058
Line Mountain SD — 1,300/K-12
500 W Shamokin St 17881 — 570-797-4672
Ned Sodrick, supt. — Fax 797-4688
www.linemountain.com
Other Schools – See Herndon

Trevose, Bucks

Strayer University — Post-Sec.
3600 Horizon Blvd Ste 100 19053 — 215-953-5999
Ultrasound Diagnostic School — Post-Sec.
3600 Horizon Blvd 19053 — 215-244-4906

Troy, Bradford, Pop. 1,471
Troy Area SD — 1,900/K-12
PO Box 67 16947 — 570-297-2750
Robert W. Grantier, supt. — Fax 297-1600
www.troyareasd.org/
Troy Area HS — 600/9-12
250 High St 16947 — 570-297-2176
R. Mark Strzelecki, prin. — Fax 297-2868
Troy Area MS, 350 High St 16947 — 600/5-8
Rebecca Stanfield, prin. — 570-297-4565

Martha Lloyd School — Post-Sec.
190 W Main St 16947

Tunkhannock, Wyoming, Pop. 1,847
Tunkhannock Area SD — 3,200/K-12
41 Philadelphia Ave 18657 — 570-836-3111
Steven E. Moyer, supt. — Fax 836-2942
www.tasd.net/
Tunkhannock HS — 1,000/9-12
120 W Tioga St 18657 — 570-836-8223
Michael Thornton, prin. — Fax 836-4719
Tunkhannock MS — 1,100/5-8
200 Franklin Ave 18657 — 570-836-8235
Joseph Papi, prin.

Turbotville, Northumberland, Pop. 671
Warrior Run SD — 1,900/K-12
4800 Susquehanna Trl 17772 — 570-649-5138
Daniel B. Scheaffer, supt. — Fax 649-5475
www.wrsd.org
Warrior Run HS — 600/9-12
4800 Susquehanna Trl 17772 — 570-649-5166
Patricia Cross, prin. — Fax 649-5591
Warrior Run MS — 600/5-8
4800 Susquehanna Trl 17772 — 570-649-5135
Larry Boyer, prin.

Turtle Creek, Allegheny, Pop. 5,868
Woodland Hills SD
Supt. — See Pittsburgh
Woodland Hills JHS - East — 400/7-8
126 Monroeville Ave 15145 — 412-824-2450
Janet Wilson Carter, prin. — Fax 824-6738

Tyrone, Blair, Pop. 5,398
Tyrone Area SD — 2,000/PK-12
701 Clay Ave 16686 — 814-684-0710
Dr. William Miller, supt. — Fax 684-2678
www.tyrone.k12.pa.us/
Tyrone Area HS — 700/9-12
1001 Clay Ave 16686 — 814-684-4240
Dr. Rebecca Erb, prin. — Fax 684-4245
Tyrone Area MS — 500/6-8
1001 Clay Ave 16686 — 814-684-4240
Dr. John Vendetti, prin. — Fax 684-4245

Grier S — 200/7-12
PO Box 308 16686 — 814-684-3000
— Fax 684-2177

Ulster, Bradford

North Rome Christian S — 200/K-12
RR 1 Box 190A 18850 — 570-247-2800
Lee Ann Carmichael, admin. — Fax 247-7288

Ulysses, Potter, Pop. 687
Northern Potter SD — 700/K-12
745 State Route 49 16948 — 814-848-7506
Robert C. Smith, supt. — Fax 848-7431
www.npschools.com
Northern Potter JSHS — 400/7-12
763 Northern Potter Rd 16948 — 814-848-7516
Susan Valentine, prin. — Fax 848-9671

Union City, Erie, Pop. 3,407
Union City Area SD — 1,300/K-12
107 Concord St 16438 — 814-438-3804
Sandra Myers, supt. — Fax 438-2030
ucasdweb.iu5.org
Union City HS — 400/9-12
105 Concord St 16438 — 814-438-7673
Frank McClard, prin. — Fax 438-8079
Union City MS — 300/6-8
105 Concord St 16438 — 814-438-7673
Frank McClard, prin. — Fax 438-8079

Uniontown, Fayette, Pop. 12,096
Albert Gallatin Area SD — 3,500/K-12
2625 Morgantown Rd 15401 — 724-564-7190
Walter G. Vicinelly, supt. — Fax 564-7195
www.albertgallatin.k12.pa.us/
Gallatin Area HS — 1,000/9-12
1119 Township Dr 15401 — 724-564-2024
Joetta Britvich, prin. — Fax 564-4525
Other Schools – See Mc Clellandtown, Point Marion

Area Vocational Technical School
Supt. — None
Fayette County AVTS — Vo/Tech
175 Georges Fairchance Rd 15401 — 724-437-2721
Dr. Edward Jeffreys, prin.

Laurel Highlands SD — 4,300/K-12
304 Bailey Ave 15401 — 724-437-2821
Dr. Ronald Sheba, supt. — Fax 437-8929
www.hhs.net/lhsdl
Laurel Highlands HS — 1,200/9-12
300 Bailey Ave 15401 — 724-437-4741
John K. Diamond, prin. — Fax 437-5653
Laurel Highlands MS — 600/7-8
18 Hookton Ave 15401 — 724-437-2865
Mary Macar, prin. — Fax 437-8518

Uniontown Area SD — 3,500/K-12
23 E Church St 15401 — 724-438-4501
Charles D. Machesky, supt. — Fax 437-7007
www.uniontown.k12.pa.us
Uniontown Area HS — 1,100/9-12
146 E Fayette St 15401 — 724-439-5000
Thomas Colebank, prin. — Fax 439-5004
Other Schools – See Markleysburg

Chestnut Ridge Christian Academy — 100/PK-12
115 Downer Ave 15401 — 724-439-1090
Patricia D. Cowsert, prin. — Fax 439-4540
Laurel Business Institute — Post-Sec.
11 E Penn St 15401 — 724-439-4900
Penn State Fayette Eberly Campus — Post-Sec.
PO Box 519 15401 — 724-430-4100
Wrightco Technologies Tech Training Inst — Post-Sec.
2 W Main St Ste 200 15401 — 724-439-2080

University Park, See State College

Pennsylvania State University — Post-Sec.
PO Box 3000 16802 — 814-865-4700

Upper Darby, See Darby
Upper Darby SD
Supt. — See Drexel Hill
Beverly Hills MS — 1,600/6-8
1400 Garrett Rd 19082 — 610-626-9317
Edgar Speer, prin.

PJA School — Post-Sec.
7900 W Chester Pike 19082 — 610-789-6700
Star Technical Institute — Post-Sec.
1570 Garrett Rd 19082 — 610-626-2700

Upper Saint Clair, Allegheny, Pop. 19,692
Upper St. Clair SD — 4,100/K-12
1820 McLaughlin Run Rd 15241 — 412-833-1600
Dr. James D. Lombardo, supt. — Fax 833-5535
www.uscsd.k12.pa.us
Other Schools – See Pittsburgh

Valley View, Schuylkill, Pop. 4,660
Tri-Valley SD — 1,000/K-12
110 W Main St 17983 — 570-682-9013
Jack L. Herb, supt. — Fax 682-9544
www.tri-valley.k12.pa.us
Other Schools – See Hegins

Villanova, Delaware

Academy of Notre Dame De Namur — 500/6-12
560 Sproul Rd 19085 — 610-687-0650
Maria Marino, prin. — Fax 687-1912

Devereux Foundation in Pennsylvania   Post-Sec.
444 Devereux Dr 19085   610-542-3030
Villanova University   Post-Sec.
800 E Lancaster Ave 19085   610-519-4500

Wallingford, Delaware
Wallingford-Swarthmore SD   3,400/K-12
200 S Providence Rd 19086   610-892-3470
Dr. George Slick, supt.   Fax 892-3493
www.wssd.org
Strath Haven HS   1,200/9-12
205 S Providence Rd 19086   610-892-3470
Mary Jo Yannacone, prin.   Fax 892-3494
Strath Haven MS   900/6-8
200 S Providence Rd 19086   610-892-3470
A. Ferguson Abbott, prin.   Fax 892-3492

Warfordsburg, Fulton
Southern Fulton SD   900/K-12
13083 Buck Valley Rd 17267   717-294-2203
Ralph R. Scott, supt.   Fax 294-2207
sfsd.k12.pa.us
Southern Fulton JSHS   400/7-12
13083 Buck Valley Rd 17267   717-294-3251
Todd Beatty, prin.   Fax 294-6248

Warminster, Bucks, Pop. 32,400
Centennial SD   6,300/K-12
433 Centennial Rd 18974   215-441-6000
David P. Blatt, supt.   Fax 441-8055
www.centennialsd.org/
Log College MS   800/6-8
730 Norristown Rd 18974   215-441-6075
Dr. Harry Clark, prin.
Tennent HS, 333 Centennial Rd 18974   2,000/9-12
Eileen Poroszok, prin.   215-441-6181
Other Schools – See Southampton

Archbishop Wood HS   1,200/9-12
655 York Rd 18974   215-672-5050
Mary Harkins, prin.   Fax 672-9572
Automotive Training Center   Post-Sec.
900 Johnsville Blvd 18974   877-411-8041
Empire Beauty School   Post-Sec.
435 York Rd 18974   215-443-8446
Middle Earth Academy   100/8-12
299 Jacksonville Rd 18974   215-443-0280
Elizabeth Quigley, dir.

Warren, Warren, Pop. 9,835
Area Vocational Technical School
Supt. — None
Warren County AVTS   Vo/Tech
347 E 5th Ave 16365   814-726-1260
Joseph Tassone, prin.   Fax 726-9673

Warren County SD
Supt. — See North Warren
Beaty-Warren MS   700/6-8
2 E 3rd Ave 16365   814-723-5200
Nancy Ondrasik, prin.   Fax 723-9503
Warren Area HS   900/9-12
345 E 5th Ave 16365   814-723-3370
James Miller, prin.   Fax 726-3126

Warrington, Bucks, Pop. 7,000
Central Bucks SD
Supt. — See Doylestown
Central Bucks SHS - South   2,000/10-12
1100 Folly Rd 18976   267-893-3000
W. Rodney Stone, prin.   Fax 893-5824
Tamanend MS   800/7-9
1492 Stuckert Rd 18976   267-893-2900
Alan R. Hershman, prin.   Fax 893-5818

SS. Joseph & Robert S   300/5-8
850 Euclid Ave 18976   215-343-5100
Donna Maria Meyers, prin.   Fax 343-7434

Washington, Washington, Pop. 14,858
Trinity Area SD   3,800/K-12
231 Park Ave 15301   724-225-9880
Dr. Thomas Turnbaugh, supt.   Fax 228-2640
www.trinitypride.k12.pa.us
Trinity HS, 231 Park Ave 15301   1,300/9-12
Donald Snoke, prin.   724-225-5380
Trinity MS, 50 Scenic Dr 15301   900/6-8
Peter Keruskin, prin.   724-228-2112

Washington SD   1,600/K-12
201 Allison Ave 15301   724-223-5010
Roberta DiLorenzo Ed.D., supt.   Fax 223-5024
www.washington.k12.pa.us
Washington HS   600/9-12
201 Allison Ave 15301   724-223-5080
Ronald Junko, prin.   Fax 223-5046
Washington Park MS   500/6-8
801 E Wheeling St 15301   724-223-5060
Jesse King, prin.   Fax 223-5123

Faith Christian S   100/PK-12
524 E Beau St 15301   724-222-5440
Lucy Hall, prin.   Fax 222-5442
First Love Christian Academy   50/9-12
PO Box 109 15301   724-225-3522
Kathleen Klein, pres.   Fax 229-2797
Penn Commercial Business/Technical Sch.   Post-Sec.
242 Oak Spring Rd 15301   724-222-5330
Washington & Jefferson College   Post-Sec.
60 S Lincoln St 15301   724-222-4400
Washington Hospital   Post-Sec.
155 Wilson Ave 15301   724-223-3167

Waterfall, Fulton
Forbes Road SD   500/K-12
159 Red Bird Dr 16689   814-685-3866
Larry Palmer, supt.
Forbes Road JSHS   200/7-12
159 Red Bird Dr 16689   814-685-3866
James Heroux, prin.

Waterford, Erie, Pop. 1,457
Ft. LeBoeuf SD   2,300/K-12
PO Box 810 16441   814-796-2638
Dr. Michele Campbell, supt.   Fax 796-6459
flb.fortleboeuf.net

Ft. LeBoeuf HS   800/9-12
931 N High St 16441   814-796-2616
Rick Fessler, prin.   Fax 796-2141
Ft. LeBoeuf MS   600/6-8
PO Box 516 16441   814-796-2681
Matthew Bennett, prin.   Fax 796-4712

Watsontown, Northumberland, Pop. 2,190

Maranatha Christian S   100/K-12
1485 Plotts Rd 17777   570-649-5141
Hubert Ropp, prin.
Watsontown Christian Academy   100/K-12
1225 8th Street Dr 17777   570-538-9276
H. William Wilhelm, prin.   Fax 538-9148

Wayne, Delaware
Radnor Township SD   3,300/K-12
135 S Wayne Ave 19087   610-688-8100
Dr. Gary Cooper, supt.   Fax 971-0742
www.rtsd.org/
Radnor MS   600/6-8
131 S Wayne Ave 19087   610-386-6300
William Laffey, prin.   Fax 688-2491
Other Schools – See Radnor

Tredyffrin-Easttown SD
Supt. — See Berwyn
Valley Forge MS   1,000/5-8
105 W Walker Rd 19087   610-240-1300
Matthew Gibson, prin.   Fax 240-1325

Valley Forge Military Academy   600/7-12
1001 Eagle Rd 19087   610-989-1200
Anthony McGeorge, pres.   Fax 989-1595
Valley Forge Military College   Post-Sec.
1001 Eagle Rd 19087   800-234-8362

Waynesboro, Franklin, Pop. 9,628
Waynesboro Area SD   4,100/K-12
210 Clayton Ave 17268   717-762-1191
Barry L. Dallara, supt.   Fax 762-0028
www.wasd.k12.pa.us
Waynesboro Area HS   1,200/9-12
550 E 2nd St 17268   717-762-1191
Jami Verderosa, prin.   Fax 762-3787
Waynesboro Area MS   800/7-8
702 E 2nd St 17268   717-762-1191
Larry Bricker, prin.   Fax 762-6566

Waynesburg, Greene, Pop. 4,038
Area Vocational Technical School
Supt. — None
Greene County CTC   Vo/Tech
60 Zimmerman Dr 15370   724-627-3106
Janice Quailey, prin.

Central Greene SD   2,300/K-12
PO Box 472 15370   724-627-8151
Dr. Jerome F. Bartley, supt.   Fax 627-9591
www.cgsd.org
Miller MS   600/6-8
126 E Lincoln St 15370   724-852-2722
Matt Blair, prin.   Fax 627-0637
Waynesburg Central HS   700/9-12
30 Zimmerman Dr 15370   724-852-1050
Albert Veverka, prin.   Fax 852-2109

West Greene SD   1,000/K-12
1367 Hargus Creek Rd 15370   724-499-5183
Thelma Szarell, supt.   Fax 499-5623
www.wgsd.org/
West Greene HS   300/9-12
1352 Hargus Creek Rd 15370   724-499-5191
Patricia Thomas, prin.   Fax 499-5524
West Greene MS   300/6-8
1352 Hargus Rd 15370   724-499-5051
Susie Macik, prin.   Fax 499-5492

Waynesburg College   Post-Sec.
51 W College St 15370   724-627-8191

Weatherly, Carbon, Pop. 2,613
Weatherly Area SD   700/K-12
602 6th St 18255   570-427-8681
Kathleen C. Makuch, supt.   Fax 427-8918
www.weatherlysd.org
Weatherly Area HS   200/9-12
601 6th St 18255   570-427-8521
Fax 427-4642
Weatherly Area MS   200/6-8
602 6th St 18255   570-427-8689
Deborah Popson, prin.   Fax 427-8918

Wellsboro, Tioga, Pop. 3,323
Wellsboro Area SD   1,700/K-12
2 Charles St 16901   570-724-4424
Philip Waber, supt.   Fax 724-5103
www.wellsborosd.k12.pa.us
Butler MS   500/5-8
9 Nichols St 16901   570-724-2306
David Krick, prin.   Fax 724-4143
Wellsboro Area HS   600/9-12
225 Nichols St 16901   570-724-3547
Patrick Hewitt, prin.   Fax 724-3021

Pennsylvania College of Technology   Post-Sec.
Mansfield Rd 16901   570-724-7703

West Chester, Chester, Pop. 17,722
West Chester Area SD   11,600/K-12
829 Paoli Pike 19380   484-266-1000
Dr. Alan G. Elko, supt.   Fax 266-1178
www.wcasd.k12.pa.us
Fugett MS   1,000/6-8
500 Ellis Ln 19380   484-266-2900
Dr. Eliot Larson, prin.   Fax 266-2999
Pierce MS   1,000/6-8
1314 Burke Rd 19380   484-266-2500
Anthony Barber, prin.   Fax 266-2599
Rustin HS, 1100 Shiloh Rd 19382   9-12
Dr. Phyllis Simmons, prin.   484-266-4300
Stetson MS   1,000/6-8
1060 Wilmington Pike 19382   484-266-2700
Leroy Whitehead, prin.   Fax 266-2799

West Chester East HS   1,700/9-12
450 Ellis Ln 19380   484-266-3800
Dr. Richard F. Dunlap, prin.   Fax 266-3899
West Chester Henderson HS   2,000/9-12
400 Montgomery Ave 19380   484-266-3300
Marc Bertrando, prin.   Fax 266-3399

Devereux Kanner Center   Post-Sec.
390 E Boot Rd 19380   866-532-2212
Empire Beauty School   Post-Sec.
313 W Market St 19382   610-344-7665
West Chester Christian S   200/K-12
1237 Paoli Pike 19380   610-692-3700
David Douglass, admin.   Fax 692-9480
West Chester University of Pennsylvania   Post-Sec.
S High St 19383   610-436-1000

Westfield, Tioga, Pop. 1,166
Northern Tioga SD
Supt. — See Elkland
Cowanesque Valley JSHS   400/7-12
51 N Fork Rd 16950   814-367-2233
Matthew Sottolano, prin.   Fax 367-5874

West Grove, Chester, Pop. 2,634
Avon-Grove SD   4,900/K-12
375 S Jennersville Rd 19390   610-869-2441
Dr. Augustus J. Massaro, supt.   Fax 869-4335
www.avongrove.org/
Avon-Grove HS   1,500/9-12
257 State Rd 19390   610-869-2446
Thomas Alexander, prin.   Fax 869-4511
Engle MS   900/7-8
107 Schoolhouse Rd 19390   610-869-3022
Robert Fraser, prin.   Fax 869-0827

West Lawn, Berks, Pop. 1,572
Wilson SD   5,200/K-12
2601 Grandview Blvd 19609   610-670-0180
Dr. Lawrence Mussoline, supt.   Fax 670-9101
www.wilson.k12.pa.us
Wilson Central JHS   600/7-9
2601 Grandview Blvd 19609   610-670-0180
Steven Leever, prin.   Fax 670-4783
Wilson SHS   1,300/10-12
2601 Grandview Blvd 19609   610-670-0185
E. Wayne Foley, prin.   Fax 670-9101
Other Schools – See Sinking Spring

West Middlesex, Mercer, Pop. 897
West Middlesex Area SD   1,200/K-12
3591 Sharon Rd 16159   724-634-3030
Alan Baldarelli, supt.   Fax 528-0380
www.wmasd.k12.pa.us
West Middlesex JSHS   600/7-12
3591 Sharon Rd 16159   724-634-3030
Larry Ellison, prin.   Fax 528-0380

West Mifflin, Allegheny, Pop. 21,892
West Mifflin Area SD   3,300/K-12
515 Camp Hollow Rd 15122   412-466-9131
Dr. Frank Prazenica, supt.   Fax 466-9260
www.wmasd.org
West Mifflin Area HS   1,100/9-12
91 Commonwealth Ave 15122   412-466-7220
Fax 466-4595
West Mifflin Area MS   800/6-8
371 Camp Hollow Rd 15122   412-466-3200
Clifford Bowers, prin.   Fax 466-0836

Community College of Allegheny County   Post-Sec.
1750 Clairton Rd 15122   412-469-1100
Empire Beauty School   Post-Sec.
2393 Mountain View Dr 15122   800-575-5983
Wilson Christian Academy   400/PK-12
1900 Clairton Rd 15122   412-466-1919
Mark Minkus, supt.   Fax 466-0303

Westover, Clearfield, Pop. 446
Harmony Area SD   400/PK-12
5239 Ridge Rd 16692   814-845-7918
Scott King, supt.   Fax 845-2305
www.harmonyowls.com/
Harmony Area HS   100/9-12
5239 Ridge Rd 16692   814-845-7918
Scott King, prin.   Fax 845-2305
Harmony Area MS   100/6-8
5239 Ridge Rd 16692   814-845-7655
Ted Focht, prin.   Fax 845-7811

West Sunbury, Butler, Pop. 102
Moniteau SD   1,400/K-12
1810 W Sunbury Rd 16061   724-637-2117
Dr. David Pisani, supt.   Fax 637-3862
www.moniteau.k12.pa.us
Moniteau JSHS   900/7-12
1810 W Sunbury Rd 16061   724-637-2091
Stephen Puskar, prin.   Fax 637-3862

Westtown, Chester

Westtown S   700/PK-12
PO Box 1799 19395   610-399-0123
John Baird, hdmstr.   Fax 399-3760

Wexford, Allegheny
North Allegheny SD
Supt. — See Pittsburgh
Marshall MS   800/6-8
5145 Wexford Run Rd 15090   724-934-6060
John Schwoebel, prin.   Fax 935-2474
North Allegheny SHS   1,400/11-12
10375 Perry Hwy 15090   724-934-7200
Dr. Lawrence Butterini, prin.   Fax 935-5846

Whitehall, Lehigh, Pop. 14,100
Whitehall-Coplay SD   3,900/K-12
2940 Macarthur Rd 18052   610-439-1431
John Corby, supt.   Fax 439-0124
www.whitehallcoplay.org
Whitehall-Coplay MS   1,300/5-8
2930 Macarthur Rd 18052   610-439-1439
Peter Bugbee, prin.   Fax 740-9308
Whitehall HS   1,300/9-12
3800 Mechanicsville Rd 18052   610-437-5081
James Davis, prin.   Fax 820-7520

Empire Beauty School | Post-Sec.
1634 MacArthur Rd 18052 | 610-776-8908
Intl Academy of Advanced Reflexology | Post-Sec.
1177 6th St 18052 | 215-234-0307

White Oak, Allegheny, Pop. 8,388

Mesivta of Allegheny County | 50/9-12
1400 Summitt St 15131 | 412-678-8952
Rabbi Nosson Tropper, prin. | Fax 678-8953

Wilkes Barre, Luzerne, Pop. 42,021
Area Vocational Technical School
Supt. — None
Wilkes-Barre AVTS | Vo/Tech
PO Box 1699 18705 | 570-822-4131
Dr. Thomas O'Donnell, prin.

Wilkes-Barre Area SD | 6,700/K-12
730 S Main St 18702 | 570-826-7182
Jeffrey Namey Ed.D., supt. | Fax 829-5031
www.wbasd.k12.pa.us
Coughlin HS | 1,100/9-12
80 N Washington St 18701 | 570-826-7201
Frank Michaels, prin. | Fax 826-7252
G.A.R. Memorial JSHS | 900/7-12
250 S Grant St 18702 | 570-826-7165
Dino Galella, prin. | Fax 826-7164
Meyers JSHS | 1,000/7-12
341 Carey Ave 18702 | 570-826-7145
Robert Okrasinski, prin. | Fax 820-3770
Other Schools – See Plains

Bishop Hoban HS | 600/9-12
159 S Pennsylvania Ave 18701 | 570-829-2424
Rev. Walter E. Jenkins, prin. | Fax 829-4412
King's College | Post-Sec.
133 N River St 18711 | 570-208-5900
Wilkes Barre General Hospital | Post-Sec.
575 N River St 18764 | 570-829-8111
Wilkes University | Post-Sec.
170 S Franklin St 18766 | 570-408-5000

Wilkinsburg, Allegheny, Pop. 18,518
Wilkinsburg Borough SD | 1,600/PK-12
718 Wallace Ave 15221 | 412-371-9667
Joseph Tindal, supt. | Fax 371-4058
www.wilkinsburg.k12.pa.us
Wilkinsburg HS | 400/9-12
747 Wallace Ave 15221 | 412-371-9500
Archie Perrin, prin. | Fax 371-3981
Wilkinsburg MS | 300/7-8
747 Wallace Ave 15221 | 412-244-9303
Pamela Lapczynski, prin. | Fax 871-2277

Williamsburg, Blair, Pop. 1,297
Williamsburg Community SD | 600/K-12
515 W 3rd St 16693 | 814-832-2125
Dr. Lee Swinsburg, supt. | Fax 832-3657
www.williamsburg.k12.pa.us/
Williamsburg Community JSHS | 300/7-12
515 W 3rd St 16693 | 814-832-2125
Maureen Letcher, prin. | Fax 832-0115

Williamsport, Lycoming, Pop. 29,871
Loyalsock Township SD
Supt. — See Montoursville
Loyalsock Twp. HS | 500/9-12
1801 Loyalsock Dr 17701 | 570-326-3581
Allen DiMarco, prin. | Fax 322-3952
Loyalsock Twp. MS | 400/6-8
2101 Loyalsock Dr 17701 | 570-323-9439
Timothy Fausnaught, dean | Fax 323-5303

Williamsport Area SD | 6,000/K-12
201 W 3rd St 17701 | 570-327-5500
Dr. Patricia Lowery, supt. | Fax 327-8122
www.wasd.org
Curtin MS | 500/6-8
85 Eldred St 17701 | 570-323-4785
James Dougherty, prin. | Fax 323-4974
Lycoming Valley MS | 500/6-8
1825 Hayes Ave 17701 | 570-494-1700
Robert Eichensehr, prin. | Fax 494-1706
Roosevelt MS | 500/6-8
2800 W 4th St 17701 | 570-323-6177
Geralyn Fausnaught, prin. | Fax 326-6851
Williamsport Area HS | 1,800/9-12
2990 W 4th St 17701 | 570-323-8411
Stephen Huddy, prin. | Fax 322-4150

Bishop Neumann JSHS | 200/7-12
901 Penn St 17701 | 570-323-9953
Paul Ward, prin. | Fax 321-7146
Divine Providence Hospital | Post-Sec.
1100 Grampian Blvd 17701 | 570-326-8101
Empire Beauty School | Post-Sec.
1808 E 3rd St 17701 | 570-322-8243
Lycoming College | Post-Sec.
700 College Pl 17701 | 570-321-4000
Newport Business Institute | Post-Sec.
941 W 3rd St 17701 | 570-326-2869
Pennsylvania College of Technology | Post-Sec.
1 College Ave 17701 | 570-326-3761
Williamsport Hospital | Post-Sec.
777 Rural Ave 17701 | 570-326-8101

Willow Grove, Montgomery, Pop. 16,325
Area Vocational Technical School
Supt. — None
Eastern Center for Arts & Tech | Vo/Tech
3075 Terwood Rd 19090 | 215-784-4800
Dr. Joseph Colaneri, prin. | Fax 784-4801

Upper Moreland Township SD | 2,400/K-12
2900 Terwood Rd 19090 | 215-659-6800
David Campbell Ed.D., supt. | Fax 659-3421
www.umtsd.org
Upper Moreland HS | 1,100/9-12
3000 Terwood Rd 19090 | 215-830-1500
Michael Daher, prin. | Fax 659-3421
Other Schools – See Hatboro

Willow Hill, Franklin
Fannett-Metal SD | 600/K-12
PO Box 91 17271 | 717-349-7172
Dr. Dana Baker, supt. | Fax 349-2748
Fannett-Metal JSHS | 300/6-12
PO Box 91 17271 | 717-349-2363
David Shank, prin. | Fax 349-2173

Willow Street, Lancaster, Pop. 5,817
Area Vocational Technical School
Supt. — None
Lancaster County CTC-Willow Street | Vo/Tech
PO Box 527 17584 | 717-464-7050
Dr. Timothy Bianchi, prin. | Fax 464-9518

Windber, Somerset, Pop. 4,197
Windber Area SD | 1,500/K-12
2301 Graham Ave 15963 | 814-467-5551
Dr. Joseph O. Padasak, supt. | Fax 467-4208
Windber Area HS | 500/9-12
2301 Graham Ave 15963 | 814-467-4567
Virgil Palumbo, prin. | Fax 467-0677
Windber Area MS | 400/6-8
2301 Graham Ave 15963 | 814-467-4620
Gary Buchsen, prin.

Wingate, Centre
Bald Eagle Area SD | 2,000/K-12
751 S Eagle Valley Rd 16823 | 814-355-4860
Daniel Fisher, supt. | Fax 355-1028
www.beasd.k12.pa.us
Bald Eagle Area JSHS | 1,100/7-12
751 S Eagle Valley Rd 16823 | 814-355-4868
David Reichelderfer, prin. | Fax 355-2146

Woodlyn, Delaware, Pop. 10,151

Woodlyn Christian S | 100/PK-12
112 MacDade Blvd 19094 | 610-833-2253
Nancy Dyson, dir. | Fax 833-2253

Wormleysburg, Cumberland, Pop. 2,683

Harrisburg Academy | 500/PK-12
10 Erford Rd 17043 | 717-763-7811
Dr. James Newman, hdmstr. | Fax 975-0894

Wrightsville, York, Pop. 2,187
Eastern York SD | 2,700/K-12
PO Box 150 17368 | 717-252-1555
Dr. Michael Thew, supt. | Fax 478-6000
www.easternyork.com/
Eastern York HS | 700/9-12
PO Box 2002 17368 | 717-252-1551
Jon Bilbo, prin. | Fax 252-4808
Eastern York MS | 700/6-8
PO Box 2003 17368 | 717-252-3400
Brian Kocsi, prin. | Fax 252-4891

Wyalusing, Bradford, Pop. 549
Wyalusing Area SD | 1,500/K-12
PO Box 157 18853 | 570-746-1605
Ray Fleming, supt. | Fax 746-9156
www.wyalusingrams.com/
Wyalusing Valley JSHS | 700/7-12
RR 2 Box 7 18853 | 570-746-1218
Martin Weisgold, prin.

Wyncote, Montgomery, Pop. 2,960
Cheltenham Township SD
Supt. — See Elkins Park
Cedarbrook MS | 800/7-8
300 Longfellow Rd 19095 | 215-881-6423
Iris Parker, prin.
Cheltenham HS | 1,700/9-12
500 Rices Mill Rd 19095 | 215-881-6400
Dr. Elliott Lewis, prin. | Fax 881-6406

Bishop McDevitt HS | 900/9-12
125 Royal Ave 19095 | 215-887-5575
Harry Neenhold, prin. | Fax 887-1371
Reconstructionist Rabbinical College | Post-Sec.
1299 Church Rd 19095 | 215-576-0800

Wynnewood, Montgomery, Pop. 7,800

Friends' Central S | 1,000/PK-12
1101 City Ave 19096 | 610-649-7440
David Felsen, hdmstr. | Fax 649-5669
Lankenau Hospital | Post-Sec.
100 E Lancaster Ave 19096 | 610-526-3019
Palmer Theological Seminary | Post-Sec.
6 E Lancaster Ave 19096 | 610-896-5000
St. Charles Borromeo Seminary | Post-Sec.
100 E Wynnewood Rd 19096 | 610-667-3394

Wyomissing, Berks, Pop. 11,079
Wyomissing Area SD | 1,900/K-12
630 Evans Ave 19610 | 610-374-4031
Dr. Mark T. Dietz, supt. | Fax 374-0948
www.wyoarea.org/
Wyomissing Area JSHS | 900/7-12
630 Evans Ave 19610 | 610-374-4031
William Hartman, prin. | Fax 374-6012

Berks Technical Institute | Post-Sec.
2205 Ridgewood Rd 19610 | 610-372-1722

Yardley, Bucks, Pop. 2,529
Pennsbury SD
Supt. — See Levittown
Boehm MS | 800/6-8
866 Big Oak Rd 19067 | 215-428-4220
Charles Long, prin. | Fax 428-9605
Penn MS | 1,100/6-8
1524 Derbyshire Rd 19067 | 215-428-4280
Larry Ricci, prin. | Fax 428-1549
Pennwood MS | 1,000/6-8
1523 Makefield Rd 19067 | 215-428-4237
Dr. Kevin McHugh, prin. | Fax 428-4265

Yeadon, Delaware, Pop. 11,587
William Penn SD
Supt. — See Lansdowne

Penn Wood East JHS | 700/7-9
600 Cypress St 19050 | 610-626-3223
Raymond Merriweather, prin. | Fax 284-8061

York, York, Pop. 40,081
Area Vocational Technical School
Supt. — None
York County School of Technology | Vo/Tech
2179 S Queen St 17402 | 717-741-0820
Dr. James Kraft, prin. | Fax 741-0694

Central York SD | 4,900/K-12
775 Marion Rd 17406 | 717-846-6789
Dr. Linda Estep, supt. | Fax 840-0451
www.cysd.k12.pa.us
Central York HS | 1,400/9-12
601 Mundis Mill Rd 17406 | 717-846-6789
Jay Butterfield, prin. | Fax 848-4684
Central York MS | 1,200/6-8
1950 N Hills Rd 17406 | 717-846-6789
Edmund McManama, prin.

West York Area SD | 3,100/K-12
2605 W Market St 17404 | 717-792-2796
Dr. Emilie Lonardi, supt. | Fax 792-5114
www.wyasd.k12.pa.us
West York Area HS | 900/9-12
1800 Bannister St 17404 | 717-845-6634
Janet May, prin. | Fax 845-6634
West York Area MS | 800/6-8
1700 Bannister St 17404 | 717-845-1671
Leslie Trimmer, prin. | Fax 845-1671

York CSD | 6,700/K-12
PO Box 1927 17405 | 717-845-3571
Dr. Tresa Diggs, supt. | Fax 849-1394
www.ycs.k12.pa.us
Penn HS, 101 W College Ave 17401 | 1,900/9-12
Wanda Dorm, prin. | 717-845-3571
Penn MS | 1,100/6-8
415 E Boundary Ave 17403 | 717-845-3571
Rona Kaufmann, prin. | Fax 849-1362
Smith MS | 900/6-8
701 Texas Ave 17404 | 717-845-3571
Eric Holmes, prin. | Fax 849-1418

York Suburban SD | 2,700/K-12
1800 Hollywood Dr 17403 | 717-848-2814
Dr. William Hartman, supt. | Fax 843-6899
www.yshs.k12.pa.us
York Suburban HS | 800/9-12
1800 Hollywood Dr 17403 | 717-843-3881
Michele Merkle, prin. | Fax 848-3845
York Suburban MS | 700/6-8
455 Sundale Dr 17402 | 717-755-2841
Victoria Gross, prin. | Fax 751-0496

Baltimore School of Massage-York Campus | Post-Sec.
170 Red Rock Rd 17402 | 717-268-1881
Bradley Academy for the Visual Arts | Post-Sec.
1409 Williams Rd 17402 | 717-755-2300
Christian S of York | 400/PK-12
907 Greenbriar Rd 17404 | 717-767-6842
Dr. Michael R. Learning, supt. | Fax 767-4904
Consolidated School of Business | Post-Sec.
1605 Clugston Rd 17404 | 717-764-9550
Empire Beauty School | Post-Sec.
2592 Eastern Blvd 17402 | 717-600-8111
Pennsylvania State University | Post-Sec.
1031 Edgecomb Ave 17403 | 717-771-4000
York Catholic HS | 700/7-12
601 E Springettsbury Ave 17403 | 717-846-8871
George Andrews, prin. | Fax 843-4588
York College of Pennsylvania | Post-Sec.
PO Box 15199 17405 | 717-846-7788
York Country Day S | 300/PK-12
1071 Regents Glen Blvd 17403 | 717-843-9805
Robert Shanner, hdmstr. | Fax 815-6769
York Hospital | Post-Sec.
1001 S George St 17403 | 717-851-2942
York Technical Institute | Post-Sec.
1405 Williams Rd 17402 | 717-757-1100
Yorktowne Business Institute | Post-Sec.
W 7th Ave 17404 | 717-846-5000

York Springs, Adams, Pop. 638
Bermudian Springs SD | 2,200/K-12
PO Box 501 17372 | 717-528-4113
Dr. William K. Shoemaker, supt. | Fax 528-7981
www.bermudian.org
Bermudian Springs HS | 600/9-12
PO Box 501 17372 | 717-528-4113
Russell Greenholt, prin. | Fax 528-4124
Bermudian Springs MS | 700/5-8
PO Box 501 17372 | 717-528-4113
Clifton Vanartsdalen, prin. | Fax 528-0034

Youngsville, Warren, Pop. 1,769
Warren County SD
Supt. — See North Warren
Youngsville HS | 600/8-12
227 College St 16371 | 814-563-7573
Darrell Jaskolka, prin. | Fax 563-4459

Warren County Christian S | 100/K-12
Route 6 W 16371 | 814-563-4457
Richard Kolcharno, prin. | Fax 563-7647

Youngwood, Westmoreland, Pop. 3,210

Westmoreland County Community College | Post-Sec.
400 Armbrust Rd 15697 | 724-925-4000

Zieglerville, Montgomery
Perkiomen Valley SD
Supt. — See Collegeville
Perkiomen Valley East MS | 1,100/6-8
100 Kagey Rd 19492 | 610-409-8580
Jefferey Madden, prin. | Fax 409-0625
Perkiomen Valley West MS | 1,100/6-8
220 Big Rd 19492 | 484-977-7210
Ryan Stanson-Marsh, prin. | Fax 977-7212

RHODE ISLAND

RHODE ISLAND DEPARTMENT OF EDUCATION
255 Westminster St, Providence 02903-3400
Telephone 401-222-4600
Fax 401-277-6178
Website http://www.ridoe.net

Commissioner of Education   Peter McWalters

RHODE ISLAND BOARD OF REGENTS
255 Westminster St, Providence 02903-3414

Chairperson   James Di Prete

PUBLIC, PRIVATE AND CATHOLIC SECONDARY SCHOOLS

Barrington, Bristol, Pop. 15,849
Barrington SD — 3,400/PK-12
  PO Box 95 02806 — 401-245-5000
  Ralph Malafronte, supt. — Fax 245-5003
  barringtonschools.org
Barrington HS — 1,100/9-12
  220 Lincoln Ave 02806 — 401-247-3150
  John Gray, prin. — Fax 245-6170
Barrington MS — 800/6-8
  261 Middle Hwy 02806 — 401-247-3160
  Richard Wheeler, prin. — Fax 247-3164

St. Andrew's S — 200/6-12
  63 Federal Rd 02806 — 401-246-1230
  John Martin, hdmstr. — Fax 246-0510
Zion Bible College — Post-Sec.
  27 Middle Hwy 02806 — 401-246-0900

Block Island, Washington
New Shoreham SD — 200/K-12
  PO Box 1890 02807 — 401-466-7732
  John W. Lyle, supt. — Fax 466-3249
  www.bi.k12.ri.us
Block Island S — 200/K-12
  PO Box 1890 02807 — 401-466-5600
  Marlee Lacoste, admin. — Fax 466-5610

Bristol, Bristol, Pop. 21,625
Bristol Warren Regional SD — 3,800/PK-12
  151 State St 02809 — 401-253-4000
  Edward P. Mara Ed.D., supt. — Fax 253-1740
  www2.bw.k12.ri.us/
Mt Hope HS — 1,200/9-12
  199 Chestnut St 02809 — 401-254-5980
  Margaret Vendituoli, prin. — Fax 254-5925
Other Schools – See Warren

Roger Williams University — Post-Sec.
  1 Old Ferry Rd 02809 — 401-253-1040

Central Falls, Providence, Pop. 19,287
Central Falls SD — 3,600/PK-12
  21 Hedley Ave 02863 — 401-727-7700
  Dr. Patricia Wilkins, supt. — Fax 727-7722
  www.cfschools.net/
Calcutt MS — 900/6-8
  112 Washington St 02863 — 401-727-7726
  Elizabeth Legault, prin. — Fax 724-0870
Central Falls HS — 900/9-12
  24 Summer St 02863 — 401-727-7710
  John Kennedy, prin. — Fax 727-6157

Chepachet, Providence
Foster-Glocester SD — 1,700/6-12
  PO Box D 02814 — 401-568-4175
  Mario Cirillo Ed.D., supt. — Fax 568-4178
  www.fg.k12.ri.us/
Other Schools – See North Scituate

Coventry, Kent, Pop. 31,083
Coventry SD — 6,400/PK-12
  9 Foster Dr 02816 — 401-822-9400
  Kenneth DiPietro, supt. — Fax 822-9406
  www.coventryschools.net
Career & Technical Center — Vo/Tech
  40 Reservoir Rd 02816 — 401-822-9499
  John Canole, prin. — Fax 822-9492
Coventry HS — 1,900/9-12
  40 Reservoir Rd 02816 — 401-822-9499
  Michael Hobin, prin. — Fax 822-9492
Flat River MS — 500/6-8
  1675 Flat River Rd 02816 — 401-822-9466
  Alan Yanku, prin. — Fax 822-9456
Knotty Oak MS — 400/7-8
  15 Foster Dr 02816 — 401-822-9426
  Michael Convery, prin. — Fax 822-9469

Cranston, Providence, Pop. 81,679
Cranston SD — 10,900/PK-12
  845 Park Ave 02910 — 401-270-8000
  Catherine Ciarlo, supt. — Fax 270-8703
  www.cpsed.net
Bain MS — 700/6-8
  135 Gansett Ave 02910 — 401-270-8010
  Thomas Barbieri, prin. — Fax 270-8567

Cranston Area Career & Technical Center — Vo/Tech
  100 Metropolitan Ave 02920 — 401-270-8070
  Lynda Wagner, prin. — Fax 270-8611
Cranston HS East — 1,600/9-12
  899 Park Ave 02910 — 401-270-8126
  Sean Kelly, prin. — Fax 270-8509
Cranston HS West — 1,800/9-12
  80 Metropolitan Ave 02920 — 401-270-8049
  Steven Knowlton, prin. — Fax 270-8526
Park View MS — 900/6-8
  25 Park View Blvd 02910 — 401-270-8090
  Melinda Thies, prin. — Fax 270-8527
Western Hills MS — 1,200/6-8
  400 Phenix Ave 02920 — 401-270-8030
  Norma Cole, prin. — Fax 270-8635

Katharine Gibbs School — Post-Sec.
  85 Garfield Ave 02920 — 401-861-1420

Cumberland, Providence
Cumberland SD — 5,300/PK-12
  2602 Mendon Rd 02864 — 401-658-1600
  Donna Morelle Ed.D., supt. — Fax 658-4620
  www.cumberlandschools.org/
Cumberland HS — 1,600/9-12
  2600 Mendon Rd 02864 — 401-658-2600
  Stephen R. Driscoll, prin. — Fax 658-3124
McCourt MS — 600/6-8
  35 Highland Ave 02864 — 401-725-2092
  Dr. Joyce Hindle-Koutsogiane, prin. — Fax 723-1188
North Cumberland MS — 700/6-8
  400 Nate Whipple Hwy 02864 — 401-333-6306
  Thomas Kenworthy, prin. — Fax 333-1926

East Greenwich, Kent, Pop. 11,865
East Greenwich SD — 2,300/K-12
  111 Peirce St 02818 — 401-398-1205
  Charles Meyers, supt. — Fax 886-3203
  www.egsd.net/
Cole MS — 500/7-8
  100 Cedar Ave 02818 — 401-886-3260
  Joseph Militello, prin. — Fax 886-3283
East Greenwich HS — 700/9-12
  300 Avenger Dr 02818 — 401-886-3292
  Michael Levine, prin. — Fax 885-1336

Rocky Hill S — 300/PK-12
  530 Ives Rd 02818 — 401-884-9070
  James Young, hdmstr. — Fax 885-4985

East Providence, Providence, Pop. 49,906
East Providence SD — 6,500/PK-12
  80 Burnside Ave 02915 — 401-433-6222
  Manuel Vinhateiro, supt. — Fax 433-6256
  ep.k12.ri.us/administration
East Providence Career & Technical Ctr — Vo/Tech
  1998 Pawtucket Ave 02914 — 401-435-7815
  Charles Rocha, dir. — Fax 435-7854
East Providence HS — 2,000/9-12
  2000 Pawtucket Ave 02914 — 401-435-7806
  Edward Daft, prin. — Fax 435-7864
Martin MS — 1,000/6-8
  111 Brown St 02914 — 401-435-7819
  Frank DeVall, prin. — Fax 435-7851
Other Schools – See Riverside

MTTI - MotoRing Technical Training Inst. — Post-Sec.
  54 Water St 02914 — 401-434-4840
Providence Country Day S — 300/5-12
  660 Waterman Ave 02914 — 401-438-5170
  Susan Haberlandt, hdmstr. — Fax 435-4514
St. Mary Academy-Bay View — 800/6-12
  3070 Pawtucket Ave 02915 — 401-434-0113
  Colleen Gribbin, prin. — Fax 438-5936

Esmond, Providence, Pop. 4,400
Smithfield SD — 2,700/PK-12
  49 Farnum Pike 02917 — 401-231-6606
  Robert O'Brien, supt. — Fax 232-0870
  www.ri.net/schools/Smithfield/District/
Other Schools – See Smithfield

Harrisville, Providence, Pop. 1,654
Burrillville SD
  Supt. — See Pascoag
Burrillville HS — 900/9-12
  425 East Ave 02830 — 401-568-1310
  Richard Trogisch, prin. — Fax 568-1363
Burrillville MS — 700/6-8
  2220 Broncos Hwy 02830 — 401-568-1320
  Lois Short, prin. — Fax 568-1317

Jamestown, Newport, Pop. 4,999
Jamestown SD — 500/PK-8
  55 Lawn Ave 02835 — 401-423-7010
  Katherine Sipala, supt. — Fax 423-7012
  www.jamestownri.com/school
Jamestown MS — 300/5-8
  55 Lawn Ave 02835 — 401-423-7010
  Katherine Sipala, prin. — Fax 423-7012

Johnston, Providence, Pop. 26,542
Johnston SD — 3,300/PK-12
  10 Memorial Ave 02919 — 401-233-1900
  Margaret A. Iacovelli Ph.D., supt. — Fax 233-1907
  www.ri.net/schools/johnston
Ferri MS — 900/6-8
  10 Memorial Ave 02919 — 401-233-1930
  Joan Fargnoli, prin. — Fax 233-1943
Johnston SHS — 900/9-12
  345 Cherry Hill Rd 02919 — 401-233-1920
  Dr. Elizabeth Mantelli, prin. — Fax 233-0031

Kingston, Washington, Pop. 6,504

University of Rhode Island 02881 — Post-Sec.
  — 401-874-1000

Lincoln, Providence, Pop. 18,045
Lincoln SD — 3,400/PK-12
  1624 Lonsdale Ave 02865 — 401-726-2150
  Dr. John Tindall-Gibson, supt. — Fax 726-1813
  www.lincolnps.org/
Davies Career-Technical HS — Vo/Tech
  50 Jenckes Hill Rd 02865 — 401-728-1500
  Victoria Galliard, prin. — Fax 728-8910
Lincoln HS — 1,100/9-12
  135 Old River Rd 02865 — 401-333-1850
  Robert Martin, prin. — Fax 334-8753
Lincoln MS — 600/7-8
  135 Old River Rd 02865 — 401-334-6460
  Bruce Macksoud, prin. — Fax 333-9977

Community College of Rhode Island — Post-Sec.
  1762 Louisquisset Pike 02865 — 401-333-7000
Computer-Ed Business Institute — Post-Sec.
  622 George Washington Hwy 02865 — 401-334-2430

Middletown, Newport, Pop. 3,400
Middletown SD — 2,700/PK-12
  26 Oliphant Ln 02842 — 401-849-2122
  Rosemarie Kraeger, supt. — Fax 849-0202
  www.ri.net/middletown/
Gaudet MS — 800/5-8
  1113 Aquidneck Ave 02842 — 401-846-6395
  Vincent Guillano, prin. — Fax 847-7580
Middletown HS — 800/9-12
  130 Valley Rd 02842 — 401-846-7250
  Steven Ruscito, prin. — Fax 849-7170

St. George's S — 300/9-12
  372 Purgatory Rd 02842 — 401-847-7565
  Eric Peterson, hdmstr. — Fax 842-6677

Narragansett, Washington, Pop. 3,721
Narragansett SD — 1,700/PK-12
  25 5th Ave 02882 — 401-792-9450
  — Fax 792-9439
  www.narragansett.k12.ri.us/
Narragansett HS — 500/9-12
  245 S Pier Rd 02882 — 401-792-9400
  Daniel Warner, prin. — Fax 792-9410
Narragansett Pier MS — 500/5-8
  235 S Pier Rd 02882 — 401-792-9430
  Jeffrey Sincoski, prin. — Fax 792-9436

Newport, Newport, Pop. 26,136
Newport SD — 2,800/PK-12
437 Broadway 02840 — 401-847-2100
John Ambrogi Ed.D., supt. — Fax 849-0170
www.newportrischools.org/
Newport Area Career & Technical Center — Vo/Tech
15 Wickham Rd 02840 — 401-849-3608
Joseph Martins, prin. — Fax 849-4670
Rogers HS — 800/9-12
15 Wickham Rd 02840 — 401-847-6235
Patricia DiCenso, prin. — Fax 849-3295
Thompson MS — 600/6-8
55 Broadway 02840 — 401-847-1493
Richard Tresky Ed.D., prin. — Fax 849-3426

International Yacht Restoration School — Post-Sec.
449 Thames St 02840 — 401-848-5777
Salve Regina University — Post-Sec.
100 Ochre Point Ave 02840 — 401-847-6650

North Kingstown, Washington, Pop. 2,800
North Kingstown SD — 3,700/K-12
100 Fairway Dr 02852 — 401-268-6200
James Halley, supt. — Fax 268-6405
www.nksd.net
Davisville MS — 600/6-8
200 School St 02852 — 401-541-6300
Ruthanne Logan, prin. — Fax 541-6310
North Kingstown HS — 1,500/9-12
150 Fairway Dr 02852 — 401-268-6236
Gerald Foley, prin. — Fax 268-6210
Wickford MS — 500/6-8
250 Tower Hill Rd 02852 — 401-268-6470
Kathleen Mort, prin. — Fax 268-6480

North Providence, Providence, Pop. 32,500
North Providence SD — 3,500/PK-12
2240 Mineral Spring Ave 02911 — 401-233-1100
Donna Ottaviano Ed.D., supt. — Fax 233-1106
Birchwood MS — 500/6-8
10 Birchwood Dr 02904 — 401-233-1120
Kenneth Ferrara, prin. — Fax 353-6903
North Providence HS — 1,200/9-12
1828 Mineral Spring Ave 02904 — 401-233-1150
Joseph Goho, prin. — Fax 233-1166
Ricci MS — 500/6-8
51 Intervale Ave 02911 — 401-233-1170
Patricia Hines, prin. — Fax 232-5421

St. Joseph's Hospital — Post-Sec.
200 High Service Ave 02904 — 401-456-3050

North Scituate, Providence
Foster-Glocester SD
Supt. — See Chepachet
Ponaganset HS — 900/9-12
137 Anan Wade Rd 02857 — 401-647-3377
Joseph Maruszczak, prin. — Fax 647-5743
Ponaganset MS — 800/6-8
91 Anan Wade Rd 02857 — 401-647-3361
Patricia Marcotte, prin. — Fax 647-9080
Scituate SD — 1,800/PK-12
PO Box 188 02857 — 401-647-4100
Paul Lescault, supt. — Fax 647-4102
www.scituateri.net
Scituate HS — 500/9-12
94 Trimtown Rd 02857 — 401-647-4120
David Light, prin. — Fax 647-4126
Scituate MS — 500/6-8
94 Trimtown Rd 02857 — 401-647-4123
Lawrence Filippelli, prin. — Fax 647-4104

North Smithfield, Providence, Pop. 10,497
North Smithfield SD
Supt. — See Slatersville
North Smithfield JSHS — 900/7-12
412 Greenville Rd 02896 — 401-766-2500
David Silva, prin. — Fax 765-8629

Pascoag, Providence, Pop. 5,011
Burrillville SD — 2,600/PK-12
265 Sayles Ave 02859 — 401-568-1301
Dr. Barbara Von Villas, supt. — Fax 568-4111
www.bsd-ri.net/
Other Schools – See Harrisville

Pawtucket, Providence, Pop. 74,330
Pawtucket SD — 9,600/PK-12
PO Box 388 02862 — 401-729-6315
Dr. Hans Dellith, supt. — Fax 727-1641
www.psdri.net
Goff JHS — 500/7-8
974 Newport Ave 02861 — 401-729-6500
— Fax 721-2105
Jenks JHS — 800/6-8
350 Division St 02860 — 401-729-6520
— Fax 729-6524
Shea HS — 1,200/9-12
485 East Ave 02860 — 401-729-6445
Dr. Christopher Lord, prin. — Fax 729-6454
Slater JHS — 700/6-8
281 Mineral Spring Ave 02860 — 401-729-6480
Meredith Caswell, prin. — Fax 729-6490
Tolman HS — 1,300/9-12
150 Exchange St 02860 — 401-729-6400
Fred Silva, prin. — Fax 729-6403

Bishop Keough Regional HS — 100/9-12
145 Power Rd 02860 — 401-726-0335
Jeanne Leclerc, prin. — Fax 726-0336
New England Tractor Trailer Training — Post-Sec.
600 Mshssuck Valley Ind Hwy 02860 — 401-725-1220
Newport School of Hairdressing — Post-Sec.
226 Main St 02860 — 401-725-6882
St. Raphael Academy — 500/9-12
122 Walcott St 02860 — 401-723-8100
Richard A. Rouleau, prin. — Fax 723-8740

Sawyer School — Post-Sec.
101 Main St 02860 — 401-272-8400

Peace Dale, See Wakefield
South Kingstown SD
Supt. — See Wakefield
Curtis Corner MS — 500/6-8
301 Curtis Corner Rd 02879 — 401-360-1333
Michele Humbyrd, prin. — Fax 360-1334

Portsmouth, Newport, Pop. 3,600
Portsmouth SD — 3,300/PK-12
29 Middle Rd 02871 — 401-683-1039
Susan Lusi Ph.D., supt. — Fax 683-5204
portsmouthrischools.tripod.com
Portsmouth HS — 1,000/9-12
126 Education Ln 02871 — 401-683-2124
Robert Littlefield, prin. — Fax 683-6404
Portsmouth MS — 900/5-8
125 Jepson Ln 02871 — 401-849-3700
Stephen Desposito, prin. — Fax 841-8420

Aquidneck Island Christian Academy — 100/K-12
321 E Main Rd 02871 — 401-849-5550
Stephen Bailey, admin. — Fax 849-6811
Portsmouth Abbey S — 300/9-12
285 Corys Ln 02871 — 401-683-2000
Dr. James De Vecchi, hdmstr. — Fax 683-5888

Providence, Providence, Pop. 176,365
Providence SD — 26,900/PK-12
797 Westminster St 02903 — 401-456-9100
— Fax 456-9252
www.providenceschools.org
Adelaide Avenue HS — 300/9-10
155 Harrison St 02907 — 401-456-0676
Dr. Mator Kpangbai, dir. — Fax 456-0679
Birch Vocational Center — Vo/Tech
434 Mount Pleasant Ave 02908 — 401-456-9198
Larry Roberti, admin. — Fax 453-8655
Bishop MS — 700/6-8
101 Sessions St 02906 — 401-456-9344
Earnest Cox, prin. — Fax 456-9110
Bridgham MS — 600/6-8
1655 Westminster St 02909 — 401-456-9360
Dr. Dinah Larbi, prin. — Fax 453-8632
Central HS — 1,700/9-12
70 Fricker St 02903 — 401-456-9111
Elaine Almagno, prin. — Fax 456-9113
Classical HS — 1,100/9-12
770 Westminster St 02903 — 401-456-9145
Cheryl Gomes, prin. — Fax 456-9155
Delsesto HS — 600/9-12
152 Springfield St 02909 — 401-278-0527
Albert Paranzino, prin. — Fax 278-0564
E-Cubed Academy — 9-12
812 Branch Ave 02904 — 401-456-0694
Wobberson Torchon, prin. — Fax 456-0696
Feinstein HS — 400/9-12
544 Elmwood Ave 02907 — 401-456-1706
Kenneth Perry, dir. — Fax 453-8698
Greene MS — 800/6-8
721 Chalkstone Ave 02908 — 401-456-9347
— Fax 453-8630
Hanley Career And Technology — Vo/Tech
91 Fricker St 02903 — 401-456-9136
Elaine Almagno, prin. — Fax 456-9172
Hope Arts HS — 9-12
324 Hope St 02906 — 401-456-9405
Kate Carbone, prin. — Fax 456-9329
Hope Leadership HS — 1,400/9-12
324 Hope St 02906 — 401-453-8686
Wayne Montague, prin. — Fax 456-9163
Hope Technology HS — 9-12
324 Hope St 02906 — 401-456-9164
Dr. Arthur Petrosinelli, prin. — Fax 456-9162
Hopkins MS — 600/6-8
480 Charles St 02904 — 401-456-9203
Steve Lauro, prin. — Fax 456-9226
MET S — Vo/Tech
325 Public St 02905 — 401-752-2600
— Fax 752-2612
Mt. Pleasant HS — 1,600/9-12
434 Mount Pleasant Ave 02908 — 401-456-9181
Maureen Crisafulli, prin. — Fax 453-8655
Occupational Ed Program — Vo/Tech
550 Branch Ave 02904 — 401-456-9217
Larry Roberti, coord.
Perry MS — 800/6-8
370 Hartford Ave 02909 — 401-456-9352
Gloria Jackson, admin. — Fax 453-8634
Springfield MS — 400/6-8
152 Springfield St 02909 — 401-278-0557
Albert Paranzino, prin. — Fax 278-0564
Stuart MS — 800/6-8
188 Princeton Ave 02907 — 401-456-9341
Nicole Mathis Thomas, prin. — Fax 453-8659
Williams MS — 900/6-8
278 Thurbers Ave 02905 — 401-456-9355
Roseclaire Bulgin, prin. — Fax 453-8631

Angelo School of Cosmetology Hair Design — Post-Sec.
151 Broadway 02903 — 401-272-4300
Brown S — 800/PK-12
250 Lloyd Ave 02906 — 401-831-7350
Joanne Hoffman, hdmstr. — Fax 455-0084
Brown University — Post-Sec.
1 Prospect St 02912 — 401-863-1000
Community College of Rhode Island — Post-Sec.
1 Hilton St 02905 — 401-455-6000
Community Preparatory S — 200/3-8
126 Somerset St 02907 — 401-521-9696
Daniel Corley, hdmstr. — Fax 521-9715
Johnson & Wales University — Post-Sec.
8 Abbott Park Pl 02903 — 401-598-1000
LaSalle Academy — 1,200/7-12
612 Academy Ave 02908 — 401-351-7750
Donald Kavanagh, prin. — Fax 444-1782

Lincoln S — 400/PK-12
301 Butler Ave 02906 — 401-331-9696
Julia Eells, hdmstr. — Fax 751-6670
Providence College — Post-Sec.
549 River Ave 02918 — 401-865-1000
Providence Hebrew S — 100/PK-12
450 Elmgrove Ave 02906 — 401-331-5327
Rabbi Peretz Scheinerman, dean — Fax 331-0030
Rhode Island College — Post-Sec.
600 Mount Pleasant Ave 02908 — 401-456-8000
Rhode Island Hospital — Post-Sec.
593 Eddy St 02903 — 401-444-5123
Rhode Island School of Design — Post-Sec.
2 College St 02903 — 401-454-6100
Roger Williams University — Post-Sec.
150 Washington St 02903 — 401-274-2200
Sawyer School — Post-Sec.
550 Hartford Ave 02909 — 401-272-3280
School One — 100/9-12
220 University Ave 02906 — 401-331-2497
Denise Jenkins, dir. — Fax 421-8869
Wheeler S — 800/PK-12
216 Hope St 02906 — 401-421-8100
Dan Miller, hdmstr. — Fax 751-7674
Women & Infants Hospital — Post-Sec.
101 Dudley St 02905 — 401-274-1100

Riverside, See East Providence
East Providence SD
Supt. — See East Providence
Riverside MS — 600/6-8
179 Forbes St 02915 — 401-433-6230
Michael Almeida, prin. — Fax 433-6261

Slatersville, Providence
North Smithfield SD — 2,000/PK-12
PO Box 72 02876 — 401-769-5492
Stephen F. Lindberg, supt. — Fax 769-5493
www.ri.net/schools/North_Smithfield/3classrooms/bois
v
Other Schools – See North Smithfield

Smithfield, Providence, Pop. 19,163
Smithfield SD
Supt. — See Esmond
Gallagher MS — 700/6-8
10 Indian Run Trl 02917 — 401-949-2056
Karl Smith Ed.D., prin. — Fax 949-5697
Smithfield HS — 900/9-12
90 Pleasant View Ave 02917 — 401-949-2050
Daniel Kelley, prin. — Fax 949-2052

Bryant University — Post-Sec.
1150 Douglas Pike 02917 — 401-232-6000
Masters Regional Academy — 100/7-12
915 Douglas Pike 02917 — 401-232-7061
Michael Dube, prin. — Fax 233-9267

Tiverton, Newport, Pop. 7,259
Tiverton SD — 2,200/K-12
100 N Brayton Rd 02878 — 401-624-8475
William J. Rearick, supt. — Fax 624-4086
www.tivschools.com
Tiverton HS — 700/9-12
100 N Brayton Rd 02878 — 401-624-8444
Steven Fezette, prin. — Fax 624-8495
Tiverton MS — 800/5-8
10 Quintal Dr 02878 — 401-624-6668
Patricia Aull, prin. — Fax 624-6669

Wakefield, Washington, Pop. 7,134
South Kingstown SD — 4,000/PK-12
307 Curtis Corner Rd 02879 — 401-360-1307
Robert A. Hicks Ed.D., supt. — Fax 360-1330
www.skschools.net/
Broad Rock MS — 500/6-8
351 Broad Rock Rd 02879 — 401-782-6223
Sheila Sullivan, prin. — Fax 782-6282
South Kingstown HS — 1,300/9-12
215 Columbia St 02879 — 401-360-1000
Robert McCarthy, prin. — Fax 789-5180
Other Schools – See Peace Dale

Prout S — 500/7-12
4640 Tower Hill Rd 02879 — 401-789-9262
Gary Delneo, prin. — Fax 782-2262

Warren, Bristol, Pop. 11,385
Bristol Warren Regional SD
Supt. — See Bristol
Kickemuit MS — 900/6-8
525 Child St 02885 — 401-245-2010
Michael Carbone, prin. — Fax 254-5960

Our Lady of Fatima HS — 200/7-12
360 Market St 02885 — 401-245-4449
Sr. Mary Margaret Souza, prin. — Fax 245-1380

Warwick, Kent, Pop. 87,365
Warwick SD — 12,000/PK-12
34 Warwick Lake Ave 02889 — 401-734-3100
Robert Shapiro, supt. — Fax 734-3105
www.warwickschools.org
Aldrich JHS — 700/7-8
789 Post Rd 02888 — 401-734-3500
William Sangster, prin. — Fax 734-3508
Gorton JHS — 600/7-8
69 Draper Ave 02889 — 401-734-3350
Kenneth Sheehan, prin. — Fax 734-3359
Pilgrim HS — 1,300/9-12
111 Pilgrim Pkwy 02888 — 401-734-3250
Dennis Mullen, prin. — Fax 734-3264
Toll Gate HS — 1,200/9-12
575 Centerville Rd 02886 — 401-734-3300
— Fax 734-3314
Warwick Area Career & Technical Center — Vo/Tech
575 Centerville Rd 02886 — 401-734-3150
Joseph Crowley, dir. — Fax 734-3160

Warwick Veterans Memorial HS — 1,300/9-12
  2401 W Shore Rd 02889 — 401-734-3200
  Gerry Habershaw, prin. — Fax 734-3214
Winman JHS — 700/7-8
  575 Centerville Rd 02886 — 401-734-3375
  Joanne McInerney, prin. — Fax 734-3385

———————————

Bishop Hendricken HS — 1,000/9-12
  2615 Warwick Ave 02889 — 401-739-3450
  Vincent Mancuso, prin. — Fax 732-8261
Community College of Rhode Island — Post-Sec.
  400 East Ave 02886 — 401-825-1000
New England Institute of Technology — Post-Sec.
  2500 Post Rd 02886 — 401-739-5000
Overbrook Academy — 200/6-9
  836 Warwick Neck Ave 02889 — 401-737-2850
  Heidi Seubert, prin. — Fax 737-2884
Warwick Academy of Beauty Culture — Post-Sec.
  1276 Bald Hill Rd Ste 100 02886 — 401-737-4946

Westerly, Washington, Pop. 16,477
Westerly SD — 3,700/PK-12
  15 Highland Ave 02891 — 401-348-2700
  Thomas DiPaola Ph.D., supt. — Fax 348-2707
  www.westerly.k12.ri.us
Babcock MS — 900/6-8
  15 Highland Ave 02891 — 401-348-2750
  Barbara Miller, prin. — Fax 348-2752

Westerly HS — 1,100/9-12
  23 Ward Ave 02891 — 401-596-2109
  Paula Dinoto, prin. — Fax 596-5098

West Greenwich, Kent, Pop. 3,492
Exeter-West Greenwich SD — 2,200/PK-12
  940 Nooseneck Hill Rd 02817 — 401-397-5125
  Dr. Roy M. Seitsinger, supt. — Fax 397-2407
  www.ewg.k12.ri.us
Exeter-West Greenwich Regional HS — 700/9-12
  930 Nooseneck Hill Rd 02817 — 401-397-6893
  Denise Boule', prin. — Fax 392-0134
Exeter-West Greenwich Regional JHS — 400/7-8
  930 Nooseneck Hill Rd 02817 — 401-397-6897
  Mark Thompson, prin. — Fax 392-0109

West Warwick, Kent, Pop. 29,600
West Warwick SD — 3,800/PK-12
  10 Harris Ave 02893 — 401-821-1180
  David Raiche, supt. — Fax 822-8463
  www.westwarwickpublicschools.com/
Deering MS — 900/6-8
  2 Webster Knight Dr 02893 — 401-822-8445
  Karen Wilson, prin. — Fax 822-8474
West Warwick HS — 1,100/9-12
  4 Webster Knight Dr 02893 — 401-821-6596
  Wayne Talbot, prin. — Fax 822-8473

Wood River Junction, Washington
Chariho SD — 3,900/PK-12
  455A Switch Rd 02894 — 401-364-7575
  John Pini, supt. — Fax 364-1176
  www.chariho.k12.ri.us/
Chariho Area Career & Technical Center — Vo/Tech
  459 Switch Rd 02894 — 401-364-6869
  Susan Chandler, dir. — Fax 364-1191
Chariho Regional HS — 1,200/9-12
  453 Switch Rd 02894 — 401-364-7778
  Robert Mitchell, prin. — Fax 364-1190
Chariho Regional MS — 1,100/5-8
  455b Switch Rd 02894 — 401-364-0651
  Carol Blanchette, prin. — Fax 364-1189

Woonsocket, Providence, Pop. 44,654
Woonsocket SD — 7,000/K-12
  108 High St 02895 — 401-767-4600
  Anthony D'Acchioli, supt. — Fax 767-4607
  woonsocketschools.com
Woonsocket Area Career & Tech. Center — Vo/Tech
  400 Aylsworth Ave 02895 — 401-767-4662
  Andrew Riley, prin. — Fax 767-4665
Woonsocket HS — 2,000/9-12
  777 Cass Ave 02895 — 401-767-4600
  George Nasuti, prin. — Fax 767-4748
Woonsocket MS — 1,600/6-8
  357 Park Pl 02895 — 401-767-4600
  Donna Valentine, prin. — Fax 767-4771

———————————

Good Shepherd Regional MS — 300/4-8
  1210 Mendon Rd 02895 — 401-767-5906
  Lawrence Poitras, prin. — Fax 767-5905
Mt. St. Charles Academy — 900/7-12
  800 Logee St 02895 — 401-769-0310
  Herve Richer, prin. — Fax 762-2327

SOUTH CAROLINA

SOUTH CAROLINA DEPARTMENT OF EDUCATION
1429 Senate St, Columbia 29201-3730
Telephone 803-734-8500
Fax 803-734-3389
Website ed.sc.gov/

Superintendent of Education   Inez Tenenbaum

SOUTH CAROLINA BOARD OF EDUCATION
1429 Senate St, Columbia 29201-3730

Chairperson   Mike Forrester

PUBLIC, PRIVATE AND CATHOLIC SECONDARY SCHOOLS

Abbeville, Abbeville, Pop. 5,786
Abbeville County SD — 3,700/K-12
400 Greenville St 29620 — 864-366-5427
Ivan Randolph, supt. — Fax 366-8531
www.acsd.k12.sc.us/
Abbeville County Career Center — Vo/Tech
100 Old Calhoun Falls Rd 29620 — 864-366-9069
Nick Hyduke, prin. — Fax 366-4774
Abbeville HS — 500/9-12
701 Washington St 29620 — 864-366-5916
Steve Glenn, prin. — Fax 366-4939
Wright MS — 500/6-8
111 Highway 71 29620 — 864-366-5998
Barry Jacks, prin. — Fax 366-4282
Other Schools – See Calhoun Falls, Due West

Aiken, Aiken, Pop. 26,456
Aiken County SD — 24,300/K-12
1000 Brookhaven Dr 29803 — 803-641-2428
Dr. Linda B. Eldridge, supt. — Fax 642-8903
www.aiken.k12.sc.us
Aiken HS — 1,600/9-12
449 Rutland Dr NE 29801 — 803-641-2500
Joseph Padget, prin. — Fax 641-2501
Aiken MS — 800/6-8
101 Gator Ln 29801 — 803-641-2570
Brooks Smith, prin. — Fax 641-2578
Kennedy MS — 1,000/6-8
274 E Pine Log Rd 29803 — 803-641-2470
Garen Cofer, prin. — Fax 641-2405
Schofield MS — 700/6-8
224 Kershaw St NE 29801 — 803-641-2770
Beatrice McGhee, prin. — Fax 641-2529
Silver Bluff HS — 900/9-12
64 Desoto Dr 29803 — 803-652-8100
Todd Bornshever, prin. — Fax 652-8104
South Aiken HS — 1,500/9-12
232 E Pine Log Rd 29803 — 803-641-2600
Dr. Janice Nashatker, prin. — Fax 641-2607
Other Schools – See Graniteville, Jackson, Monetta, New Ellenton, North Augusta, Wagener, Warrenville

Aiken Christian S — 100/6-12
142 Talatha Church Rd 29803 — 803-642-0286
Clark Ballard, prin. — Fax 642-0485
Aiken Preparatory S — 200/PK-12
619 Barnwell Ave NW 29801 — 803-648-3223
Deborah Boehner, hdmstr. — Fax 648-6482
Aiken Technical College — Post-Sec.
PO Box 696 29802 — 803-593-9231
Lacy Cosmetology School — Post-Sec.
3084 Whiskey Rd 29803 — 803-648-6181
University of South Carolina — Post-Sec.
471 University Pkwy 29801 — 803-648-6851

Allendale, Allendale, Pop. 3,910
Allendale County SD — 1,800/PK-12
PO Box 458 29810 — 803-584-4603
Paula Harris, supt. — Fax 584-5303
www.acs.k12.sc.us
Other Schools – See Fairfax

University of South Carolina — Post-Sec.
PO Box 617 29810 — 803-584-6314

Anderson, Anderson, Pop. 25,563
Anderson SD 5 — 12,600/PK-12
PO Box 439 29622 — 864-260-5000
Betty Bagley, supt. — Fax 260-5896
www.anderson5.net
Hanna HS — 1,600/9-12
2600 N Highway 81 29621 — 864-260-5110
Michael Sams, prin. — Fax 260-5213
Hanna-Westside Extension Campus — Vo/Tech
1225 S McDuffie St 29624 — 864-260-5160
Rick Mascaro, dir. — Fax 260-5685
Lakeside MS — 1,000/6-8
315 Pearman Dairy Rd 29625 — 864-260-5135
Martha Hanwell, prin. — Fax 260-5885
McCants MS — 1,200/6-8
2123 Marchbanks Ave 29621 — 864-260-5145
Jacky Stamps, prin. — Fax 260-5846

Southwood MS — 600/6-8
1110 Southwood St 29624 — 864-260-5205
Evelyn Murphy, prin. — Fax 964-2607
Westside HS — 1,700/9-12
806 Pearman Dairy Rd 29625 — 864-260-5230
Henry Adair, prin. — Fax 260-5007

Anderson Christian S — 200/PK-12
4523 Liberty Hwy 29621 — 864-224-7309
Dr. Michael Chivalette, admin. — Fax 224-1085
Anderson College — Post-Sec.
316 Boulevard 29621 — 864-231-2000
Anderson Memorial Hospital — Post-Sec.
800 N Fant St 29621 — 864-261-1109
Forrest Junior College — Post-Sec.
601 E River St 29624 — 864-225-7653

Andrews, Georgetown, Pop. 3,053
Georgetown County SD
Supt. — See Georgetown
Andrews HS — 800/9-12
12890 County Line Rd 29510 — 843-264-3414
Michelle Staggers, prin. — Fax 264-3326
Rosemary MS — 700/6-8
12804 County Line Rd 29510 — 843-264-9780
Michael Caviris, prin. — Fax 264-9787

Aynor, Horry, Pop. 589
Horry County SD
Supt. — See Conway
Aynor HS — 400/10-12
201 Jordanville Rd 29511 — 843-358-6261
Marion Shaw, prin. — Fax 358-7401

Ballentine, Richland
Lexington/Richland SD 5 — 15,800/PK-12
PO Box 938 29002 — 803-732-8000
Dr. Dennis McMahon, supt. — Fax 732-8017
www.lex5.k12.sc.us
Other Schools – See Chapin, Columbia, Irmo

Bamberg, Bamberg, Pop. 3,568
Bamberg SD 1 — 1,400/K-12
PO Box 526 29003 — 803-245-3053
Phyllis Schwarting, supt. — Fax 245-3056
www.bamberg1.com
Bamberg-Ehrhardt HS — 500/9-12
PO Box 89 29003 — 803-245-3030
Randall L. Maxwell, prin. — Fax 245-6502
Bamberg-Ehrhardt MS — 400/6-8
PO Box 548 29003 — 803-245-3058
Robert Kearse, prin. — Fax 245-6501

Bamberg Job Corps Center — Post-Sec.
PO Box 967 29003 — 803-245-5101

Barnwell, Barnwell, Pop. 4,958
Barnwell SD 45 — 2,700/K-12
660 Hagood Ave 29812 — 803-541-1300
Carolyne Williams, supt. — Fax 541-1348
www.barnwell45.k12.sc.us
Barnwell HS — 900/9-12
474 Jackson St 29812 — 803-541-1390
Linda Zionkowski, prin. — Fax 541-0726
Guinyard-Butler MS — 400/7-8
779 Allen St 29812 — 803-541-1370
Herman Wallace, prin. — Fax 541-1306

Batesburg, Lexington, Pop. 6,189
Lexington SD 3 — 2,200/K-12
338 W Columbia Ave 29006 — 803-532-4423
Dr. William Gummerson, supt. — Fax 532-8000
www.lex3.k12.sc.us
Batesburg-Leesville HS — 600/9-12
600 Summerland Ave 29006 — 803-532-9251
Raymond Padgett, prin. — Fax 532-3232
Batesburg-Leesville MS — 600/6-8
425 Shealy Rd 29006 — 803-532-3831
Herbert Smith, prin. — Fax 532-8021

King Academy — 300/K-12
1046 Sardis Rd 29006 — 803-532-6682
Mike Prochaska, prin. — Fax 604-0409

Beaufort, Beaufort, Pop. 12,376
Beaufort County SD — 20,000/PK-12
PO Box 309 29901 — 843-322-2300
Edna Crews, supt. — Fax 322-2371
www.beaufort.k12.sc.us/
Battery Creek HS — 1,500/9-12
1 Blue Dolphin Dr 29906 — 843-322-5500
Edmond Burns, prin. — Fax 322-5608
Beaufort HS — 1,600/9-12
84 Sea Island Pkwy, — 843-322-2000
Dan Durbin, prin. — Fax 322-2158
Beaufort MS — 600/6-8
2501 Mossy Oaks Rd 29902 — 843-322-5700
Carole Ingram, prin. — Fax 322-5723
Ladys Island MS — 700/6-8
30 Cougar Dr, — 843-322-3100
Priscilla Drake, prin. — Fax 322-3179
Smalls MS — 700/6-8
43 W K Alston Dr 29906 — 843-322-2500
Denise Smith, prin. — Fax 322-2564
Other Schools – See Bluffton, Hilton Head Island, Seabrook

Beaufort Academy — 400/PK-12
240 Sams Point Rd, — 843-524-3393
Timothy Johnson, prin. — Fax 524-1171
Beaufort Christian S — 100/K-12
378 Parris Island Gtwy 29906 — 843-525-0635
Technical College of the Lowcountry — Post-Sec.
PO Box 1288 29901 — 843-525-8324
University of South Carolina — Post-Sec.
801 Carteret St 29902 — 843-521-4100

Belton, Anderson, Pop. 4,490
Anderson SD 2
Supt. — See Honea Path
Belton MS — 500/6-8
102 Cherokee Rd 29627 — 864-338-6595
Margaret Spivey, prin. — Fax 338-3301

Bennettsville, Marlboro, Pop. 9,296
Marlboro County SD — 5,000/PK-12
PO Box 947 29512 — 843-479-4016
Dr. David A. Sherbine, supt. — Fax 479-5944
www.marlboro.k12.sc.us
Bennettsville MS — 500/6-8
701 Cheraw St 29512 — 843-479-5941
Fannie Mason, prin. — Fax 479-5943
Marlboro County HS — 1,400/9-12
951 Fayetteville Avenue Ext 29512 — 843-479-5900
Rocky Peterkin, prin. — Fax 479-5916

Bishopville, Lee, Pop. 3,688
Lee County SD — 2,900/K-12
521 Park St 29010 — 803-484-5422
Dr. Lloyd Hunter, supt. — Fax 484-9107
www.leeschoolsk12.org/home.asp
Dennis MS — 6-8
321 Roland St 29010 — 803-484-5386
Kwamine Simpson, prin. — Fax 484-5825
Lee Central HS — 800/9-12
1800 Wisacky Hwy 29010 — 803-428-4010
Leevette Malloy, prin. — Fax 428-4062
Lee County Career & Technical Center — Vo/Tech
310 Roland St 29010 — 803-484-5337
Bryan Durant, prin. — Fax 484-4171
Other Schools – See Elliott

Lee Academy — 800/K-12
630 Cousar St 29010 — 803-484-5532
Virginia Stokes, prin. — Fax 484-9491

Blacksburg, Cherokee, Pop. 1,890
Cherokee SD
Supt. — See Gaffney
Blacksburg HS — 500/9-12
201 W Ramseur Dr 29702 — 864-839-6371
Jim Touchberry, prin. — Fax 839-2960
Blacksburg MS — 600/6-8
101 London St 29702 — 864-839-6476
Virgil Hampton, prin. — Fax 839-2390

Blackville, Barnwell, Pop. 2,951
Area Vocational Schools
Supt. — None

512

Barnwell County Career Center | Vo/Tech
5214 Reynolds Rd 29817 | 803-259-5512
H. Samuel McKay, dir. | Fax 541-4701

Barnwell SD 19 | 900/K-12
PO Box 185 29817 | 803-284-2234
William Sandifer, supt. | Fax 284-4417
www.barnwell19.k12.sc.us/
Blackville-Hilda HS | 300/9-12
PO Box 245 29817 | 803-284-2280
Elliott Willingham, prin. | Fax 284-3766
Blackville-Hilda JHS | 200/7-8
PO Box 186 29817 | 803-284-3778
David Corder, prin. | Fax 284-0961

Barnwell Christian S | 50/1-12
5675 SC Highway 70 29817 | 803-259-2100
Ralph Dickerson, prin.
Davis Academy | 300/K-12
5061 Hilda Rd 29817 | 803-284-2017
Robert Len Frederick, hdmstr. | Fax 284-5544

Bluffton, Beaufort, Pop. 1,778
Beaufort County SD
Supt. — See Beaufort
Bluffton HS | 1,700/9-12
12 H E McCracken Cir 29910 | 843-706-8800
Aretha Rhone-Bush, prin.
McCracken MS | 800/6-8
250 H E McCracken Cir 29910 | 843-706-8700
Kathleen Slowiczek, prin. | Fax 706-8778

Blythewood, Richland, Pop. 273
Richland SD 2
Supt. — See Columbia
Blythewood HS | 2,000/9-12
10901 Wilson Blvd 29016 | 803-691-4090
Dr. Sharon Buddin, prin. | Fax 691-4097
Blythewood MS | 1,000/6-8
2351 Longtown Rd E 29016 | 803-691-6850
Nancy Gregory, prin. | Fax 691-6860
Kelly Mill MS | 1,200/6-8
1141 Kelly Mill Rd 29016 | 803-691-7210
Dr. Michaele Lemrow, prin. | Fax 691-7211

South Carolina Criminal Justice Academy | Post-Sec.
PO Box 1993 29016 | 803-896-7779

Boiling Springs, Spartanburg, Pop. 3,522
Spartanburg SD 2 | 8,700/K-12
4606 Parris Bridge Rd 29316 | 864-578-0128
Scott Mercer, supt. | Fax 578-8924
www.spartanburg2.k12.sc.us
Boiling Springs HS 9th Grade Campus | 500/9-9
3655 Boiling Springs Rd 29316 | 864-578-2610
Eddie L. Cole, prin. | Fax 578-2642
Boiling Springs HS | 1,300/10-12
2251 Old Furnace Rd 29316 | 864-578-8465
C. Gerald Moore, prin. | Fax 578-6825
Other Schools – See Chesnee, Inman

Bowman, Orangeburg, Pop. 1,178

Bowman Academy | 100/1-12
PO Box 98 29018 | 803-829-2770

Branchville, Orangeburg, Pop. 1,059
Orangeburg Consolidated SD 4
Supt. — See Cope
Branchville HS | 200/7-12
PO Box 188 29432 | 803-274-8875
George Benton, prin. | Fax 274-8645

Calhoun Falls, Abbeville, Pop. 2,294
Abbeville County SD
Supt. — See Abbeville
Calhoun Falls JSHS | 300/6-12
PO Box 336 29628 | 864-447-8014
Nelson Gibson, prin. | Fax 447-9379

Camden, Kershaw, Pop. 6,861
Kershaw County SD | 10,400/PK-12
PO Box 7008 29020 | 803-432-8416
Dr. Herbert Berg, supt. | Fax 425-8918
www.kershaw.k12.sc.us
Applied Technical Education Campus | Vo/Tech
874 Vocational Ln 29020 | 803-425-8982
Allen Teal, dir. | Fax 425-8983
Camden HS | 1,100/9-12
1022 Ehrenclou Dr 29020 | 803-425-8930
Edward Dean, prin. | Fax 424-2861
Camden MS | 800/6-8
416 Laurens St 29020 | 803-425-8975
Jeff Jordan, prin. | Fax 425-8954
Kershaw County Adult Education | Adult
874 Vocational Ln 29020 | 803-425-8980
Dr. Carolyn Ham, dir. | Fax 425-8988
Other Schools – See Elgin, Kershaw, Lugoff

Camden Military Academy | 300/7-12
520 Highway 1 N 29020 | 803-432-6001
Eric Boland, hdmstr. | Fax 425-1020

Campobello, Spartanburg, Pop. 453
Spartanburg SD 1 | 4,500/K-12
PO Box 218 29322 | 864-468-4542
James Littlefield, supt. | Fax 472-4118
www.spartanburg1.k12.sc.us/
Other Schools – See Inman, Landrum

Cayce, Lexington, Pop. 12,388
Lexington SD 2
Supt. — See West Columbia
Brookland-Cayce HS | 1,200/9-12
1300 State St 29033 | 803-791-5000
Scott Newman, prin. | Fax 739-4970
Busbee Creative Arts Academy | 400/6-8
501 Bulldog Blvd 29033 | 803-739-4070
Jennifer Morrow, prin. | Fax 739-4133

Columbia Beauty School | Post-Sec.
1824 Airport Blvd 29033 | 803-796-5252

Central, Pickens, Pop. 3,516
Pickens County SD
Supt. — See Easley
Daniel HS | 1,000/9-12
1819 Six Mile Hwy 29630 | 864-624-4430
Sharon Huss, prin. | Fax 624-4428
Edwards MS | 800/6-8
1157 Madden Bridge Rd 29630 | 864-624-4423
Mike Sanders, prin. | Fax 624-4426

Southern Wesleyan University | Post-Sec.
PO Box 1020 29630 | 864-644-5000

Chapin, Lexington, Pop. 647
Lexington/Richland SD 5
Supt. — See Ballentine
Chapin HS | 1,000/9-12
300 Columbia Ave 29036 | 803-345-2246
Mike Satterfield, prin. | Fax 345-7111
Chapin MS | 800/6-8
1130 Old Lexington Hwy 29036 | 803-345-1466
Jane Crawford, prin. | Fax 345-7117

Charleston, Charleston, Pop. 101,024
Charleston County SD | 80,900/PK-12
75 Calhoun St 29401 | 843-937-6300
Dr. Maria Goodloe-Johnson, supt. | Fax 937-6307
www.ccsdschools.com/
Academic Magnet HS | 500/9-12
1525 Avenue B S 29405 | 843-746-1300
Michael Tolley, prin. | Fax 746-1310
Birney MS | 700/6-8
7750 Pinehurst St 29420 | 843-764-2212
Phillip Shaw, prin. | Fax 569-5466
Burke HS | 700/9-12
244 President St 29403 | 843-579-4815
Curtis Amos, prin. | Fax 579-4855
Ft. Johnson MS | 500/6-8
1825 Camp Rd 29412 | 843-762-2740
David Parler, prin. | Fax 762-6212
James Island MS | 700/6-8
1484 Camp Rd 29412 | 843-762-2784
Phillip Davie, prin. | Fax 762-6209
Rivers MS | 300/7-8
1002 King St 29403 | 843-724-7789
Cheryl Bennett, prin. | Fax 720-3082
Toole Military Magnet S | 800/6-11
2950 Carner Ave 29405 | 843-745-7102
Anderson Townsend, prin. | Fax 566-7791
West Ashley HS | 2,200/9-12
4060 Wildcat Blvd 29414 | 843-573-1201
Bob Olson, prin. | Fax 573-1223
West Ashley MS | 800/7-8
1776 Kennerty Dr 29407 | 843-763-1546
Judy Sherman, prin. | Fax 852-6557
Williams MS | 700/5-8
640 Butte St 29414 | 843-763-1529
Carol Tempel, prin. | Fax 763-5955
Other Schools – See Hollywood, Johns Island, Mc
Clellanville, Mount Pleasant, North Charleston

Academy of Cosmetology | Post-Sec.
5117 Dorchester Rd 29418 | 843-552-3241
Ashley Hall | 600/PK-12
172 Rutledge Ave 29403 | 843-722-4088
Jill Muti, hdmstr. | Fax 720-2868
Bishop England HS | 800/9-12
363 Seven Farms Dr 29492 | 843-849-9599
David Held, prin. | Fax 849-9221
Cathedral Academy | 300/PK-12
PO Box 41129 29423 | 843-760-1192
Donna Lewis, admin. | Fax 760-1197
Charleston Cosmetology Institute | Post-Sec.
8484 Dorchester Rd 29420 | 843-552-3670
Charleston Southern University | Post-Sec.
PO Box 118087 29423 | 800-947-7474
College of Charleston | Post-Sec.
66 George St 29424 | 843-953-5500
First Baptist Church S | 500/K-12
48 Meeting St 29401 | 843-722-6646
Thomas E. Mullins, hdmstr. | Fax 720-2521
James Island Christian S | 300/PK-12
15 Crosscreek Dr 29412 | 843-795-1762
William Smith, hdmstr. | Fax 762-1619
Medical University of South Carolina | Post-Sec.
PO Box 250402 29425 | 843-792-2300
Northside Christian S | 500/PK-12
7800 Northside Dr 29420 | 843-797-2690
Dr. Cecil Beach, admin. | Fax 797-7402
Porter-Gaud S | 900/K-12
300 Albemarle Rd 29407 | 843-556-3620
Liza Lee, hdmstr. | Fax 769-9926
The Citadel | Post-Sec.
171 Moultrie St 29409 | 843-953-5000
Trident Technical College | Post-Sec.
PO Box 118067 29423 | 843-574-6111

Cheraw, Chesterfield, Pop. 5,416
Chesterfield County SD
Supt. — See Chesterfield
Cheraw HS | 900/9-12
649 Chesterfield Hwy 29520 | 843-921-1000
Henry Cobb, prin. | Fax 921-1006
Long MS | 700/6-8
1010 W Greene St 29520 | 843-921-1010
Dannie Blair, prin. | Fax 921-1017

Jesus is Lord Christian S | 200/PK-12
PO Box 639 29520 | 843-537-2033
Northeastern Technical College | Post-Sec.
PO Box 1007 29520 | 843-921-6900

Chesnee, Spartanburg, Pop. 1,010
Spartanburg SD 2
Supt. — See Boiling Springs
Chesnee HS | 700/9-12
795 S Alabama Ave 29323 | 864-461-7318
Thomas Ezell, prin. | Fax 461-4137
Chesnee MS | 500/6-8
805 S Alabama Ave 29323 | 864-461-3900
Dale Campbell, prin. | Fax 461-3950

Chester, Chester, Pop. 6,326
Chester County SD | 8,500/K-12
109 Hinton St 29706 | 803-385-6122
Larry Heath, supt. | Fax 581-0863
www.chester.k12.sc.us/
Chester County Career Center | Vo/Tech
1324 J A Cochran Byp 29706 | 803-377-1991
Lee Green, prin. | Fax 581-0912
Chester HS | 900/9-12
1330 J A Cochran Byp 29706 | 803-377-3161
Curtis Dunbar, prin. | Fax 581-2363
Chester MS | 1,000/6-8
1014 McCandless Rd 29706 | 803-377-8192
Steven Cummings, prin. | Fax 581-1875
Other Schools – See Great Falls, Richburg

Chesterfield, Chesterfield, Pop. 1,342
Chesterfield County SD | 8,000/K-12
401 West Blvd 29709 | 843-623-2175
John Williams, supt. | Fax 623-3434
www.chesterfield.k12.sc.us
Chesterfield HS | 500/9-12
401 N Page St 29709 | 843-623-2161
Scott Radkin, prin. | Fax 623-2050
Chesterfield-Ruby MS | 400/6-8
14445 Highway 9 29709 | 843-623-9401
Andrea Hampton, prin. | Fax 623-9429
Other Schools – See Cheraw, Jefferson, Mc Bee,
Pageland

Clemson, Pickens, Pop. 11,936

Clemson University | Post-Sec.
105 Sikes Hall 29634 | 864-656-3311

Clinton, Laurens, Pop. 9,010
Laurens SD 56 | 3,300/K-12
600 E Florida St 29325 | 864-833-0800
John Taylor, supt. | Fax 833-0804
www.laurens56.k12.sc.us
Bell Street MS | 600/7-8
600 Peachtree St 29325 | 864-833-0807
Maureen Tiller, prin. | Fax 833-0810
Clinton HS | 1,000/9-12
800 N Adair St 29325 | 864-833-0817
Dr. A. Keith Bridges, prin. | Fax 833-0825

Presbyterian College | Post-Sec.
503 S Broad St 29325 | 864-833-8230

Clover, York, Pop. 3,933
Clover SD 2 | 5,000/PK-12
604 Bethel St 29710 | 803-222-7191
Vicki Phelps, supt. | Fax 222-8010
www.clover2.k12.sc.us
Clover HS | 1,500/9-12
1625 Highway 55 E 29710 | 803-222-4591
Ron Wright, prin. | Fax 222-8021
Clover JHS | 900/7-8
1555 Highway 55 E 29710 | 803-222-4521
Ron Thompson, prin. | Fax 222-8034

Columbia, Richland, Pop. 117,357
Lexington/Richland SD 5
Supt. — See Ballentine
Irmo HS | 1,800/9-12
6671 Saint Andrews Rd 29212 | 803-732-8100
Eddie Walker, prin. | Fax 732-8110
Irmo MS | 1,000/7-8
6051 Wescott Rd 29212 | 803-732-8200
Marie Waldrop, prin. | Fax 732-8208

Richland SD 1 | 27,500/PK-12
1616 Richland St 29201 | 803-231-7000
Dr. Allen Coles, supt. | Fax 231-7505
www.richlandone.org/
Alcorn MS | 500/6-8
5125 Fairfield Rd 29203 | 803-735-3439
Darius Adamson, prin. | Fax 735-3487
Columbia HS | 900/9-12
1701 Westchester Dr 29210 | 803-731-8950
Francina Shack, prin. | Fax 731-8953
Crayton MS | 1,100/6-8
5000 Clemson Ave 29206 | 803-738-7224
Virginia Lacy, prin. | Fax 738-7901
Dreher HS | 1,300/9-12
701 Adger Rd 29205 | 803-253-7000
Jeanne Stiglbauer, prin. | Fax 253-7007
Eau Claire HS | 1,000/9-12
4800 Monticello Rd 29203 | 803-735-7600
Coleman Barbour, prin. | Fax 735-7629
Flora HS | 1,400/9-12
100 Falcon Dr 29204 | 803-738-7300
Kathie Greer, prin. | Fax 738-7307
Gibbes MS | 400/6-8
3602 Thurmond St 29204 | 803-343-2942
Rick Coleman, prin. | Fax 733-3040
Hand MS | 1,000/6-8
2600 Wheat St 29205 | 803-343-2947
Marisa Vickers, prin. | Fax 733-6173
Heyward Career & Technology Center | Vo/Tech
3560 Lynhaven Dr 29204 | 803-735-3343
Sherry Rivers, prin. | Fax 691-4253
Johnson Preparatory Academy | 500/9-12
2219 Barhamville Rd 29204 | 803-253-7092
Dr. James Taylor, prin. | Fax 253-5713
Keenan HS | 900/9-12
3455 Pine Belt Rd 29204 | 803-738-7232
Dr. Steve Wilson, prin. | Fax 738-7589

Perry MS — 400/6-8
2600 Barhamville Rd 29204 — 803-256-6347
Demetria Clemons, prin. — Fax 255-2262
St. Andrews MS — 900/6-8
1231 Blue Field Dr 29210 — 803-731-8910
Ken Richardson, prin. — Fax 731-8913
Sanders MS — 600/6-8
136 Alida St 29203 — 803-735-3445
Andrenna Smith, prin. — Fax 735-3679
Adult & Community Education — Adult
2612 Covenant Rd 29204 — 803-343-2935
Faye Houston, dir. — Fax 212-1453
Other Schools – See Hopkins

Richland SD 2 — 22,900/PK-12
6831 Brookfield Rd 29206 — 803-787-1910
Stephen W. Hefner Ed.D., supt. — Fax 738-7393
www.richland2.org
Dent MS — 1,100/6-8
6950 N Trenholm Rd 29206 — 803-699-2750
Randall Gary, prin. — Fax 699-2754
Richland Northeast HS — 1,700/9-12
7500 Brookfield Rd 29223 — 803-699-2800
Ralph Schmidt, prin. — Fax 699-3679
Ridge View HS — 2,300/9-12
4801 Hard Scrabble Rd 29229 — 803-699-2999
Dr. Marty Martin, prin. — Fax 699-2888
Spring Valley HS — 1,900/9-12
120 Sparkleberry Ln 29229 — 803-699-3500
Dr. Greg Owings, prin. — Fax 699-3541
Summit Parkway MS — 1,400/6-8
200 Summit Pkwy 29229 — 803-699-3580
Sig Tanner, prin. — Fax 699-3682
Wright MS — 1,300/6-8
2740 Alpine Rd 29223 — 803-736-8740
Keith Price, prin. — Fax 736-8798
Rogers Adult Continuing Center — Adult
750 Old Clemson Rd 29229 — 803-736-8787
Curtis Watson, prin. — Fax 736-8785
Other Schools – See Blythewood

Allen University — Post-Sec.
1530 Harden St 29204 — 803-376-5701
Baptist Medical Center — Post-Sec.
1519 Marion St 29201 — 803-771-5042
Benedict College — Post-Sec.
1600 Harden St 29204 — 803-256-4220
Beta Tech — Post-Sec.
7500 Two Notch Rd 29223 — 803-754-7544
Cardinal Newman HS — 400/7-12
4701 Forest Dr 29206 — 803-782-2814
Rose Tindall, prin. — Fax 782-9314
Columbia Biblical Seminary — Post-Sec.
PO Box 3122 29230 — 800-845-2721
Columbia College — Post-Sec.
1301 Columbia College Dr 29203 — 803-786-3871
Columbia International University — Post-Sec.
PO Box 3122 29230 — 803-754-4100
Covenant Christian S — 200/PK-12
2801 Stepp Dr 29204 — 803-787-0225
H. Gary Collier, prin. — Fax 782-7309
ECPI College of Technology — Post-Sec.
250 Berryhill Rd #300 29210 — 803-772-3333
Hammond S — 1,000/PK-12
854 Galway Ln 29209 — 803-776-0295
Herbert Barks, prin. — Fax 776-0122
Heathwood Hall Episcopal S — 900/PK-12
3000 S Beltline Blvd 29201 — 803-765-2309
Stephen Hickman, prin. — Fax 748-4755
Kenneth Shuler's School of Cosmetology — Post-Sec.
449 Saint Andrews Rd 29210 — 803-772-6042
Lippen Middle and HS — 500/6-12
PO Box 3999 29230 — 803-786-7200
Les Lehman, prin. — Fax 744-1387
Lutheran Theological Southern Seminary — Post-Sec.
4201 Main St 29203 — 803-786-5150
Midlands Technical College — Post-Sec.
PO Box 2408 29202 — 803-738-8324
Sloans S, 171 Starlight Dr 29210 — 200/K-12
Jay Michael Sloan, hdmstr. — 803-772-1677
Southeastern School of Neuromuscular — Post-Sec.
1420 Colonial Life Blvd #80 29210 — 803-798-8800
South University — Post-Sec.
3810 Main St 29203 — 803-799-9082
Strayer University — Post-Sec.
200 Center Point Cir # 300 29210 — 803-750-2500
University of South Carolina 29208 — Post-Sec.
803-777-7700
W.L. Bonner Bible College — Post-Sec.
4430 Argent Ct 29203 — 803-754-3950

Conway, Horry, Pop. 12,538
Horry County SD — 31,000/PK-12
PO Box 260005 29528 — 843-488-6700
Dr. Bobby Nalley, supt. — Fax 488-6722
www.hcs.k12.sc.us
Academy for Technology and Academics — Vo/Tech
5639 Highway 701 N 29526 — 843-488-6600
David Stoudenmire, prin. — Fax 488-6601
Black Water MS — 6-8
151 Bates Dr 29526 — 843-903-8440
Connie Huddle, prin. — Fax 903-8441
Conway HS — 1,500/9-12
2301 Church St 29526 — 843-488-0662
Porter Kennington, prin. — Fax 488-0686
Conway MS — 500/6-8
1104 Elm St 29526 — 843-488-6040
Mary Clark, prin. — Fax 488-0611
Whittemore Park MS — 700/6-8
1808 Rhue St 29527 — 843-488-0669
Robbie Watkins, prin. — Fax 488-0669
Other Schools – See Aynor, Galivants Ferry, Green Sea, Little River, Loris, Murrells Inlet, Myrtle Beach

Coastal Carolina University — Post-Sec.
PO Box 261954 29528 — 843-347-3161

Conway Christian S — 300/K-12
PO Box 1245 29528 — 843-365-2005
Jonathan Wright, prin. — Fax 365-2021
Horry-Georgetown Technical College — Post-Sec.
PO Box 261966 29528 — 843-349-5277

Cope, Orangeburg, Pop. 105
Orangeburg Consolidated SD 4 — 4,300/PK-12
PO Box 68 29038 — 803-534-8081
Sandra F. Tonnsen, supt. — Fax 531-5614
www.orangeburg4.com
Cope Area Career Center — Vo/Tech
PO Box 128 29038 — 803-534-7661
Mike Cory, prin. — Fax 535-4301
Other Schools – See Branchville, Cordova, Neeses

Cordova, Orangeburg, Pop. 147
Orangeburg Consolidated SD 4
Supt. — See Cope
Carver-Edisto MS — 700/6-8
PO Box 65 29039 — 803-536-0231
Renee Ritter, prin. — Fax 535-0934
Edisto HS — 800/9-12
PO Box 101 29039 — 803-534-0098
Marvin Byers, prin. — Fax 531-5615

Cowpens, Spartanburg, Pop. 2,306
Spartanburg SD 3
Supt. — See Glendale
Cowpens MS — 500/6-8
150 Foster St 29330 — 864-463-3310
Rodney Goode, prin. — Fax 463-3306

Cross, Berkeley
Berkeley County SD
Supt. — See Moncks Corner
Cross JSHS — 500/7-12
1293 Old Highway 6 29436 — 843-899-8900
Robb Streeter, prin. — Fax 899-8910

Dalzell, Sumter
Sumter SD 2
Supt. — See Sumter
Hillcrest MS — 500/6-8
PO Box 151 29040 — 803-499-3341
Robert Barth, prin. — Fax 499-3353

Sumter Academy — 600/PK-12
PO Box 869 29040 — 803-499-3378
William Hentges, hdmstr. — Fax 499-3391

Darlington, Darlington, Pop. 6,582
Darlington County SD — 12,000/K-12
PO Box 1117 29540 — 843-398-5100
Dr. Rainey H. Knight, supt. — Fax 398-2230
www.darlington.k12.sc.us
Darlington HS — 1,200/9-12
525 Spring St 29532 — 843-398-5140
Pearl Jeffords, prin. — Fax 398-2739
Darlington JHS — 900/7-8
100 Magnolia St 29532 — 843-398-5088
Aurelia Cooper, prin. — Fax 398-2575
Mayo Math Science Tech HS — 300/9-12
405 Chestnut St 29532 — 843-398-5050
Arlene Johnson, prin. — Fax 398-2647
Other Schools – See Hartsville, Lamar

Trinity Collegiate S — 100/6-12
5001 Hoffmeyer Rd 29532 — 843-395-9124
Fax 395-6495

Denmark, Bamberg, Pop. 3,168
Bamberg SD 2 — 1,100/PK-12
PO Box 345 29042 — 803-793-3346
V. Sherill Brackett, supt. — Fax 793-2006
Denmark-Olar HS — 300/9-12
PO Box 98 29042 — 803-793-3307
Hughie Peterson, prin. — Fax 793-2004
Denmark-Olar MS — 200/6-8
PO Box 383 29042 — 803-793-3383
Gwendolyn Harris, prin. — Fax 793-2038

Denmark Technical College — Post-Sec.
PO Box 327 29042 — 803-793-5149
Voorhees College — Post-Sec.
Voorhees Rd 29042 — 803-793-3351

Dillon, Dillon, Pop. 6,362
Area Vocational Schools
Supt. — None
Dillon County Applied Tech. Center — Vo/Tech
PO Box 1130 29536 — 843-774-5143
Jerry Strickland, prin. — Fax 774-7711
Dillon SD 2 — 3,800/PK-12
405 W Washington St 29536 — 843-774-1200
D. Ray Rogers, supt. — Fax 774-1203
www.dillon2.k12.sc.us
Dillon HS — 1,000/9-12
1730 Highway 301 N 29536 — 843-774-1230
Dr. Julia Von Frank, prin. — Fax 774-1234
Martin JHS — 600/7-8
301 Martin Luther King Jr 29536 — 843-774-1212
Danny Price, prin. — Fax 841-3616

Dillon Christian S — 400/K-12
PO Box 151 29536 — 843-841-1000
Dr. David Bult, hdmstr. — Fax 841-0810

Dorchester, Dorchester
Area Vocational Schools
Supt. — None
Dorchester County Career S — Vo/Tech
507 Schoolhouse Rd 29437 — 800-454-8101
James Villeponteaux, prin. — Fax 563-9038

Dorchester SD 4
Supt. — See Saint George
Woodland HS — 700/9-12
4128 Highway 78 29437 — 843-563-5956
James Peterson, prin. — Fax 563-5997

Due West, Abbeville, Pop. 1,295
Abbeville County SD
Supt. — See Abbeville
Dixie HS — 400/8-12
1 Haynes St 29639 — 864-379-2186
Tracy Carter, prin. — Fax 379-8187

Erskine College & Seminary — Post-Sec.
PO Box 176 29639 — 864-379-8838

Duncan, Spartanburg, Pop. 2,900
Spartanburg SD 5 — 6,200/K-12
PO Box 307 29334 — 864-949-2350
Scott Turner, supt. — Fax 439-0051
www.spart5.k12.sc.us
Byrnes HS — 1,800/9-12
PO Box 187 29334 — 864-949-2355
Richard McClure, prin. — Fax 949-2362
Florence Chapel MS — 7-8
290 Shoals Rd 29334 — 864-949-2310
Steve Gambrell, prin. — Fax 949-2315
Hill MS — 1,000/7-8
PO Box 277 29334 — 864-949-2370
Julia Tingen, prin. — Fax 949-2369

Easley, Pickens, Pop. 18,479
Pickens County SD — 16,200/K-12
1348 Griffin Mill Rd 29640 — 864-855-8150
Dr. Mendel Stewart, supt. — Fax 855-8159
www.pickens.k12.sc.us
Dacusville MS — 400/6-8
899 Thomas Mill Rd 29640 — 864-859-6049
Ellen Smith, prin. — Fax 850-2094
Easley HS — 1,600/9-12
PO Box 129 29641 — 864-855-8180
Betty Garrison, prin. — Fax 855-8194
Gettys MS — 1,300/6-8
105 Stewart Dr 29640 — 864-855-8170
Doug Limbaugh, prin. — Fax 855-6413
Skelton Career Center — Vo/Tech
1400 Griffin Mill Rd 29640 — 864-855-8195
Leonard Williams, dir. — Fax 855-8192
Pickens Lifelong Learning Adult Educ — Adult
200 W D Ave 29640 — 864-855-8198
Mary Gaston, dir. — Fax 850-8116
Other Schools – See Central, Liberty, Pickens

Landmark Christian Academy — 100/K-12
116 Landmark Ct 29640 — 864-859-0793
Siloam Christian S — 300/PK-12
229 Siloam Rd 29642 — 864-295-6949
Wesley Dove, admin. — Fax 295-4179

Elgin, Kershaw, Pop. 830
Kershaw County SD
Supt. — See Camden
Stover MS — 500/6-8
PO Box 1200 29045 — 803-438-7414
Dennis Reeder, prin. — Fax 438-7014

Elliott, Lee
Lee County SD
Supt. — See Bishopville
Mt. Pleasant MS — 500/6-8
PO Box 177 29046 — 803-428-3610
Linda Norton, prin. — Fax 428-3656

Estill, Hampton, Pop. 2,410
Hampton SD 2 — 1,400/K-12
PO Box 1028 29918 — 803-625-5000
Dennis Thompson, supt. — Fax 625-2573
www.hampton2.k12.sc.us
Estill HS — 400/9-12
PO Box 757 29918 — 803-625-5100
Archie Franchini, prin. — Fax 625-4695
Estill MS — 400/6-8
PO Box 817 29918 — 803-625-5200
Dr. Fayette Nick, prin. — Fax 625-3588

Henry Academy — 300/PK-12
8766 Savannah Hwy 29918 — 803-625-2440
Dr. Terry D. King, hdmstr. — Fax 625-3110

Fairfax, Allendale, Pop. 3,179
Allendale County SD
Supt. — See Allendale
Allendale-Fairfax HS — 500/9-12
3581 Allendale Fairfax Hwy 29827 — 803-584-2311
Fax 584-1787
Allendale-Fairfax MS — 400/6-8
3305 Allendale Fairfax Hwy 29827 — 803-584-3489
Fax 584-5331

Florence, Florence, Pop. 30,267
Florence SD 1 — 14,500/K-12
319 S Dargan St 29506 — 843-669-4141
Larry Jackson, supt. — Fax 673-1108
www.fsd1.org
Florence Career Ctr — Vo/Tech
126 E Howe Springs Rd 29505 — 843-664-8465
Fax 413-4688
Sneed MS — 800/7-8
1102 S Ebenezer Rd 29501 — 843-673-1199
Patricia Magee, prin. — Fax 679-6890
South Florence HS — 1,500/9-12
3200 S Irby St 29505 — 843-664-8190
Jim Slice, prin. — Fax 664-8184
Southside MS — 900/7-8
200 E Howe Springs Rd 29505 — 843-664-8467
Erik Lowry, prin. — Fax 673-5766
West Florence HS — 1,500/9-12
221 N Beltline Dr 29501 — 843-664-8472
Pamela Quick, prin. — Fax 664-8475

Williams MS | 700/7-8
1119 N Irby St 29501 | 843-664-8162
Leon McCray, prin. | Fax 664-8178
Wilson HS | 1,300/9-12
1411 E Old Marion Hwy 29506 | 843-664-8440
Gerard Edwards, prin. | Fax 664-8176

Byrnes Schools | 300/PK-12
1201 E Ashby Rd 29506 | 843-662-0131
William Bugg, hdmstr. | Fax 669-2466
Christian Assembly S | 200/K-12
401 Pamplico Hwy 29505 | 843-667-1975
Audrey Streit, prin. | Fax 664-0389
Florence Christian S | 600/PK-12
PO Box 12809 29504 | 843-662-0454
Jim Berry, prin. | Fax 661-4301
Florence-Darlington Technical College | Post-Sec.
PO Box 100548 29501 | 843-661-8324
Francis Marion University | Post-Sec.
PO Box 100547 29501 | 843-661-1362
King's Academy | 300/K-12
1015 S Ebenezer Rd 29501 | 843-661-7464
Karen Rainwater, prin. | Fax 661-7647
Maranatha Christian S | 300/PK-12
2624 W Palmetto St 29501 | 843-665-6395
Joe Postlewaite, prin. | Fax 629-0510
McLeod Regional Medical Center | Post-Sec.
555 E Cheves St 29506 | 843-667-2297

Fort Mill, York, Pop. 7,879
Lancaster County SD
Supt. — See Lancaster
Indian Land HS | 400/9-12
8361 Charlotte Hwy 29715 | 803-547-7571
Mary Bernsdorff, prin. | Fax 547-7366

York SD 4 | 6,300/K-12
120 E Elliott St 29715 | 803-548-2527
Dr. V. Keith Callicutt, supt. | Fax 547-4696
www.fort-mill.k12.sc.us
Fort Mill HS | 1,900/9-12
225 Munn Rd E 29715 | 803-548-1900
Dee Christopher, prin. | Fax 548-1911
Fort Mill MS | 700/6-8
200 Springfield Pkwy 29715 | 803-547-5553
Tommy Schmolze, prin. | Fax 548-2911
Gold Hill MS | 900/6-8
1025 Dave Gibson Blvd 29708 | 803-548-8300
Tommy Johnston, prin. | Fax 548-8322
Springfield MS | 6-8
1711 Springfield Pkwy 29715 | 803-548-8199
Keith Griffin, prin. | Fax 547-1013

Fountain Inn, Greenville, Pop. 6,440

Pleasant Grove Christian Academy | 100/PK-12
1269 S Frontage Rd 29644 | 864-862-7793
Dr. George Hopson, admin. | Fax 862-0198

Gaffney, Cherokee, Pop. 12,877
Cherokee SD | 8,900/PK-12
PO Box 460 29342 | 864-902-3500
Dr. William B. James, supt. | Fax 902-3541
www.cherokee1.k12.sc.us
Cherokee Technology Center | Vo/Tech
3206 Cherokee Ave 29340 | 864-489-3191
Ray Bedford, prin. | Fax 487-1287
Ewing MS | 500/6-8
171 E Junior High Rd 29340 | 864-489-3176
Amanda Burnette, prin. | Fax 489-8534
Gaffney HS | 2,100/9-12
149 Twin Lake Rd 29341 | 864-902-3600
Quincie Moore, prin. | Fax 902-3628
Gaffney MS | 700/6-8
805 E Frederick St 29340 | 864-902-3630
Herman Thompson, prin. | Fax 902-3637
Granard MS | 500/6-8
815 W Rutledge Ave 29341 | 864-489-6833
Charles Wright, prin. | Fax 488-1553
Limestone Learning Center - Adult | Adult
130 Leadmine St 29340 | 864-487-7152
Lisa Hanron, prin. | Fax 487-1260
Other Schools – See Blacksburg

Heritage Christian S | 100/K-12
4279 Cherokee Ave 29340 | 864-489-0788
Limestone College | Post-Sec.
1115 College Dr 29340 | 864-489-7151

Galivants Ferry, Horry
Horry County SD
Supt. — See Conway
Aynor MS | 800/6-9
400 Frye Rd 29544 | 843-358-6000
Milton Frink, prin. | Fax 358-5065

Gaston, Lexington, Pop. 1,390
Lexington SD 4
Supt. — See Swansea
Sandhills MS | 600/7-8
582 Meadowfield Rd 29053 | 803-926-1890
Angie Rye, prin. | Fax 926-1910

Georgetown, Georgetown, Pop. 8,951
Georgetown County SD | 10,600/PK-12
2018 Church St 29440 | 843-436-7000
Dr. Randy Dozier, supt. | Fax 436-7171
www.gcsd.k12.sc.us
Georgetown HS | 1,100/9-12
2500 Anthuan Maybank St 29440 | 843-546-8516
Dr. Mike Cafaro, prin. | Fax 546-8521
Georgetown MS | 900/6-8
2400 Anthuan Maybank St 29440 | 843-527-4495
Rosemary Gray, prin. | Fax 527-2290
Other Schools – See Andrews, Hemingway, Pawleys
    Island

Gilbert, Lexington, Pop. 527
Lexington County SD 1
Supt. — See Lexington
Gilbert HS | 900/9-12
840 Main St 29054 | 803-892-1100
Paul Shealy, prin. | Fax 892-1133
Gilbert MS | 700/6-8
120 Rikard Cir 29054 | 803-892-1050
Benji Ricard, prin. | Fax 892-1067

Glendale, Spartanburg
Spartanburg SD 3 | 3,100/K-12
PO Box 267 29346 | 864-579-8000
Dr. Jim Ray, supt. | Fax 579-8005
www.spa3.k12.sc.us
Other Schools – See Cowpens, Pacolet, Spartanburg

Goose Creek, Berkeley, Pop. 30,574
Berkeley County SD
Supt. — See Moncks Corner
Goose Creek HS | 1,600/9-12
1137 Red Bank Rd 29445 | 843-553-5300
John Fulmer, prin. | Fax 820-4064
Marrington MS | 300/5-8
109 Gearing St 29445 | 843-572-0313
Arnold Coull, prin. | Fax 820-4063
Sedgefield MS | 1,000/6-8
131 Charles B Gibson Blvd 29445 | 843-797-2620
Don Brown, prin. | Fax 820-5401
Stratford HS | 2,700/9-12
951 Crowfield Blvd 29445 | 843-820-4000
Jim Spencer, prin. | Fax 820-4030
Westview MS | 1,100/6-8
101 Westview Dr 29445 | 843-572-1700
Dave Barrow, prin. | Fax 820-4066

Graniteville, Aiken
Aiken County SD
Supt. — See Aiken
Leavelle-McCampbell MS | 500/6-8
82 Canal St 29829 | 803-663-4300
Al Dreyer, prin. | Fax 663-4302
Midland Valley HS | 1,200/9-12
227 Mustang Dr 29829 | 803-593-7100
Dr. Doris Hickson, prin. | Fax 593-7106

Gray Court, Laurens, Pop. 1,008
Laurens SD 55
Supt. — See Laurens
Gray Court-Owings S | 400/3-8
PO Box 187 29645 | 864-876-2171
Marilyn Ramsey, prin. | Fax 876-2965
Hickory Tavern MS | 300/6-8
163 Neely Ferry Rd 29645 | 864-575-4301
Russell Scott, prin. | Fax 575-4305

Great Falls, Chester, Pop. 2,122
Chester County SD
Supt. — See Chester
Great Falls HS | 300/9-12
411 Sunset Ave 29055 | 803-482-2210
Howard Rheiner, prin. | Fax 482-4896
Great Falls MS | 300/5-8
409 Sunset Ave 29055 | 803-482-2220
Wendell Sumter, prin. | Fax 482-6025

Greeleyville, Williamsburg, Pop. 429
Williamsburg County SD
Supt. — See Kingstree
Murray JSHS | 600/7-12
PO Box 188 29056 | 843-426-2121
Roberta Cumbee, prin. | Fax 426-2151

Green Sea, Horry
Horry County SD
Supt. — See Conway
Green Sea-Floyds JSHS | 500/7-12
5625 Highway 9 29545 | 843-392-3131
Charles Collins, prin. | Fax 392-9805

Greenville, Greenville, Pop. 55,926
Anderson SD 1
Supt. — See Williamston
Powdersville MS | 500/6-8
135 Hood Rd 29611 | 864-269-1821
Monty Oxendine, prin. | Fax 269-0795

Greenville County SD | 62,700/PK-12
PO Box 2848 29602 | 864-241-3100
Dr. Phinnize Fisher, supt. | Fax 241-3112
www.greenville.k12.sc.us/
Beck Academy | 600/6-8
302 McAlister Rd 29607 | 864-241-3268
Dr. J. Brodie Bricker, prin. | Fax 241-3282
Berea HS | 1,100/9-12
515 Berea Dr 29617 | 864-294-4200
Bill Roach, prin. | Fax 294-4221
Berea MS | 800/6-8
151 Berea Middle School Rd 29617 | 864-355-1700
Michael Sinclair, prin. | Fax 355-1777
Carolina Academy | 600/9-12
2725 Anderson Rd 29611 | 864-295-5185
Lillie Lewis, prin. | Fax 295-5175
Donaldson Career Center | Vo/Tech
100 Vocational Dr 29605 | 864-355-4683
Cheryl McClure, prin. | Fax 355-4683
Enoree Career Center | Vo/Tech
108 Scalybark Rd 29617 | 864-294-4343
John Banning, prin. | Fax 294-4341
Fine Arts Center | 11-12
1613 W Washington St 29601 | 864-241-3327
Dr. Roy Fluhrer, prin. | Fax 241-3502
Golden Strip Career Ctr | Vo/Tech
1120 E Butler Rd 29607 | 864-281-1244
Leroy Elrod, prin. | Fax 281-1247
Greenville Academy | 800/6-8
339 Lowndes Ave 29607 | 864-241-3360
Dr. Robert Palmer, prin. | Fax 241-3366
Greenville Academy | 1,300/9-12
900 Woodside Ave 29611 | 864-241-3220
Dalton Lucas, prin. | Fax 241-3227

Hampton HS | 1,200/9-12
100 Pine Knoll Dr 29609 | 864-292-7587
Lance Radford, prin. | Fax 292-7603
Hughes Academy | 900/6-8
122 Deoyley Ave 29605 | 864-299-8363
Dr. Lorraine Watson, prin. | Fax 299-8273
Lakeview MS | 500/6-8
3801 Old Buncombe Rd 29617 | 864-294-4353
Dr. Newman Sanchez, prin. | Fax 294-4236
League Academy | 700/6-8
125 Twin Lake Rd 29609 | 864-292-7688
Merry Cox, prin. | Fax 292-8681
Mann Academy | 1,300/9-12
61 Isbell Ln 29607 | 864-281-1150
Susan Hughes, prin. | Fax 281-1173
Sevier MS | 500/6-8
1004 Piedmont Park Rd 29609 | 864-292-7578
Linda Ward, prin. | Fax 292-7573
Southside HS | 1,000/9-12
100 Blassingame Rd 29605 | 864-299-8393
Paulette Payne, prin. | Fax 299-8395
Tanglewood MS | 500/6-8
44 Merriwoods Dr 29611 | 864-295-5165
Karen Kapp, prin. | Fax 295-7196
Adult Education/Lifelong Learning | Adult
206 Wilkins St 29605 | 864-241-3388
Dr. Chuck Welch, prin. | Fax 241-3548
Other Schools – See Greer, Mauldin, Piedmont,
    Simpsonville, Taylors, Travelers Rest

Academy of Hair Technology | Post-Sec.
3715 E North St Ste F 29615 | 864-322-1030
Bob Jones University | Post-Sec.
1700 Wade Hampton Blvd 29614 | 864-242-5100
Christ Church Episcopal MS | 300/6-8
555 Wenwood Rd 29607 | 864-299-1522
H. John Walter, dir. | Fax 299-8094
Christ Church Episcopal Upper S | 300/9-12
567 Wenwood Rd 29607 | 864-299-1522
Dr. Leland H. Cox, hdmstr. | Fax 299-8861
ECPI College of Technology | Post-Sec.
1001 Keys Dr # 100 29615 | 864-288-2828
Furman University | Post-Sec.
3300 Poinsett Hwy 29613 | 864-294-2000
Greenville Technical College | Post-Sec.
PO Box 5616 29606 | 864-250-8000
Hampton Park Christian S | 800/K-12
875 State Park Rd 29609 | 864-233-0556
ITT Technical Institute | Post-Sec.
6 Independence Pointe 29615 | 864-288-0777
Jones Academy | 500/9-12
1700 Wade Hampton Blvd 29614 | 864-370-1800
Dr. Sid Cates, prin. | Fax 271-7278
Jones JHS | 300/7-8
1700 Wade Hampton Blvd 29614 | 864-242-5100
R. Todd Kappel, prin. | Fax 271-7278
St. Joseph's HS | 200/9-12
100 Saint Josephs Dr 29607 | 864-234-9009
Keith Kiser, hdmstr. | Fax 234-5516
Shannon Forest Christian S | 500/PK-12
829 Garlington Rd 29615 | 864-678-5107
Brenda Hillman, hdmstr. | Fax 281-9372

Greenwood, Greenwood, Pop. 22,252
Greenwood SD 50 | 9,300/K-12
PO Box 248 29648 | 864-941-5400
William P. Steed, supt. | Fax 941-5427
www.gwd50.k12.sc.us
Brewer MS, 1000 Emerald Rd 29646 | 600/6-8
Anthony Holland, prin. | 864-941-5500
Emerald HS, 150 Bypass 225 29646 | 900/9-12
Sabra Price, prin. | 864-941-5730
Greenwood HS | 1,700/9-12
1816 Cokesbury Rd 29649 | 864-941-5600
Beth Taylor, prin.
Northside MS | 900/6-8
400 Glenwood St 29649 | 864-941-5780
Beth Pinson, prin.
Russell Career Center | Vo/Tech
601 E Northside Dr 29649 | 864-941-5750
Charles Graves, prin.
Westview MS | 800/6-8
1410 W Alexander Ave 29646 | 864-941-5400
Cynthia Storer, prin.

Cambridge Academy | 200/PK-10
103 Eastman St 29649 | 864-229-2875
| Fax 229-6712
Greenwood Christian S | 400/PK-12
2026 Woodlawn Rd 29649 | 864-229-2427
John R. Davis, admin. | Fax 943-0876
Lander University | Post-Sec.
320 Stanley Ave 29649 | 864-388-8000
Piedmont Technical College | Post-Sec.
PO Box 1467 29648 | 864-941-8324

Greer, Greenville, Pop. 19,333
Greenville County SD
Supt. — See Greenville
Blue Ridge HS | 1,300/8-12
2151 Fews Chapel Rd 29651 | 864-355-1800
Kenneth Southerlin, prin. | Fax 355-1821
Blue Ridge MS | 900/6-8
2423 E Tyger Bridge Rd 29651 | 864-355-1900
Tony Poole, prin. | Fax 355-1966
Bonds Career Center | Vo/Tech
505 N Main St 29650 | 864-848-2492
Wayne Rhodes, prin. | Fax 848-5668
Greer HS | 1,100/9-12
3000 E Gap Creek Rd 29651 | 864-848-2363
Marion Waters, prin. | Fax 848-2371
Greer MS | 900/6-8
3032 E Gap Creek Rd 29651 | 864-848-2350
Rita Mantooth, prin. | Fax 848-2352
Riverside HS | 1,300/9-12
1300 S Suber Rd 29650 | 864-848-2323
Andy Crowley, prin. | Fax 848-2407

Riverside MS | 900/6-8
615 Hammett Bridge Rd 29650 | 864-355-7900
Ron Harrison, prin. | Fax 355-7918

Hanahan, Berkeley, Pop. 12,971
Berkeley County SD
Supt. — See Moncks Corner
Hanahan HS | 900/9-12
6015 Murray Dr 29406 | 843-820-3710
James Spencer, prin. | Fax 820-3716
Hanahan MS | 500/6-8
5815 Murray Dr 29406 | 843-820-3800
Robin Rogers, prin. | Fax 820-3804

Hartsville, Darlington, Pop. 7,435
Darlington County SD
Supt. — See Darlington
Hartsville HS | 1,400/9-12
701 Lewellen Ave 29550 | 843-383-3130
Dr. Charlie Burry, prin. | Fax 857-3715
Hartsville JHS | 800/7-8
437 W Carolina Ave 29550 | 843-383-3121
Chris Rogers, prin. | Fax 857-3005

State Supported Schools
Supt. — None
Governers School Science/Math | 11-12
401 Railroad Ave 29550 | 843-383-3900

Coker College | Post-Sec.
300 E College Ave 29550 | 843-383-8000
Emmanuel Christian S | 400/PK-12
1001 N Marquis Hwy 29550 | 843-332-0164
James Tritle, admin. | Fax 332-0164

Hemingway, Williamsburg, Pop. 538
Georgetown County SD
Supt. — See Georgetown
Carvers Bay HS | 500/9-12
13002 Choppee Rd 29554 | 843-545-5837
Daryl Brown, prin. | Fax 558-6927
Carvers Bay MS | 400/6-8
13000 Choppee Rd 29554 | 843-545-0918
Darryl Stanley, prin. | Fax 558-6937

Williamsburg County SD
Supt. — See Kingstree
Hemingway AVC | Vo/Tech
1593 Hemingway Hwy 29554 | 843-558-5813
John Gardner, prin. | Fax 558-5991
Hemingway HS | 500/9-12
PO Box 1509 29554 | 843-558-9413
Grady Richardson, prin. | Fax 558-9335

Hilton Head Island, Beaufort, Pop. 34,407
Beaufort County SD
Supt. — See Beaufort
Hilton Head Island HS | 2,000/9-12
70 Wilborn Rd 29926 | 843-689-4800
Dr. Helen Ryan, prin. | Fax 689-4948
Hilton Head Island MS | 1,000/6-8
55 Wilborn Rd 29926 | 843-689-4500
Sherry DeSimone, prin. | Fax 689-4600

Hilton Head Christian Academy | 500/K-12
55 Gardner Dr 29926 | 843-681-2878
Mike Lindsay, hdmstr. | Fax 681-9758
Hilton Head Prep S | 400/1-12
8 Foxgrape Rd 29928 | 843-671-2286
Susan Groesbeck, hdmstr. | Fax 671-7624

Holly Hill, Orangeburg, Pop. 1,377
Orangeburg SD 3 | 3,000/K-12
PO Box 98 29059 | 803-496-3288
David Longshore, supt. | Fax 496-5850
www.obg3.k12.sc.us
Holly Hill MS | 700/6-8
PO Box 878 29059 | 803-496-5525
Joanne Lawton, prin. | Fax 496-7584
Lake Marion HS | 900/9-12
PO Box 339 29059 | 803-496-3818
Rose Pelzer-Brower, prin. | Fax 496-9765

Holly Hill Academy | 400/K-12
PO Box 757 29059 | 803-496-3243
John Gasque, hdmstr. | Fax 496-9778

Hollywood, Charleston, Pop. 4,223
Charleston County SD
Supt. — See Charleston
Baptist Hill HS | 500/9-12
5117 Baptist Hill Rd 29449 | 843-889-2276
Raymond Davis, prin. | Fax 889-2101
Schroder MS | 400/6-8
7224 Highway 162 29449 | 843-889-2391
Dr. Patricia Cooper, prin. | Fax 889-6539

St. Paul's Academy | 100/K-12
5139 Gibson Rd 29449 | 843-889-2702
Cliff Bell, prin. | Fax 889-6290

Honea Path, Anderson, Pop. 3,540
Anderson SD 2 | 3,700/K-12
10990 Belton Honea Path Hwy 29654 | 864-369-7364
Thomas Chapman, supt. | Fax 369-4006
www.anderson2.k12.sc.us
Belton-Honea Path HS | 1,000/9-12
11000 Belton Honea Path Hwy 29654 | 864-369-7382
Jimmy Ouzts, prin. | Fax 369-4011
Honea Path MS | 400/5-8
107 Brock Ave 29654 | 864-369-7641
John Snead, prin. | Fax 369-4034
Other Schools – See Belton

Hopkins, Richland
Richland SD 1
Supt. — See Columbia

Hopkins MS | 600/6-8
1601 Clarkson Rd 29061 | 803-695-3331
David Montgomery, prin. | Fax 695-3320
Lower Richland HS | 1,700/9-12
2615 Lower Richland Blvd 29061 | 803-695-3000
Leevette Malloy, prin. | Fax 695-3062
Southeast MS | 800/6-8
731 Horrell Hill Rd 29061 | 803-695-5700
Jeanneta Scott, prin. | Fax 695-5703

Inman, Spartanburg, Pop. 1,882
Spartanburg SD 1
Supt. — See Campobello
Chapman HS | 900/9-12
35 Oakland Ave 29349 | 864-472-2836
Ron Garner, prin. | Fax 472-6128
Mabry JHS | 400/7-8
10 W Miller St 29349 | 864-472-8402
Michael Blackwell, prin. | Fax 472-7438
Swofford Career Center | Vo/Tech
5620 Highway 11 29349 | 864-592-2790
Tommy Campbell, dir. | Fax 592-1469

Spartanburg SD 2
Supt. — See Boiling Springs
Boiling Springs JHS | 1,100/7-8
4801 Highway 9 29349 | 864-578-5954
Donald Barnette, prin. | Fax 599-5489

Irmo, Richland, Pop. 11,170
Lexington/Richland SD 5
Supt. — See Ballentine
Dutch Fork HS | 1,900/9-12
1400 Old Tamah Rd 29063 | 803-732-8050
Ron Cowden, prin. | Fax 732-8064
Dutch Fork MS | 1,100/7-8
1528 Old Tamah Rd 29063 | 803-732-8167
Roderic Taylor, prin. | Fax 732-8171

Islandton, Colleton

New Hope Christian S of Islandton | 100/K-12
PO Box 55 29929 | 843-866-2608
Mark Givens, prin.

Iva, Anderson, Pop. 1,165
Anderson SD 3 | 2,700/K-12
PO Box 118 29655 | 864-348-6196
L. Hugh Smith, supt. | Fax 348-6198
www.anderson3.k12.sc.us
Crescent HS | 700/9-12
9104 Highway 81 S 29655 | 864-352-6175
Devon Smith, prin. | Fax 348-2308
Other Schools – See Starr

Jackson, Aiken, Pop. 1,635
Aiken County SD
Supt. — See Aiken
Jackson MS | 500/6-8
8217 Atomic Rd 29831 | 803-279-3525
Marc Funderburk, prin. | Fax 471-2202

Jefferson, Chesterfield, Pop. 696
Chesterfield County SD
Supt. — See Chesterfield
New Heights MS | 600/6-8
5738 Highway 151 29718 | 843-658-6830
Lynn Jackson, prin. | Fax 658-6812

Johns Island, Charleston
Charleston County SD
Supt. — See Charleston
Haut Gap MS | 300/6-8
1861 Bohicket Rd 29455 | 843-559-6418
Deborah Fickling, prin. | Fax 559-6439
St. Johns HS | 400/9-12
1518 Main Rd 29455 | 843-559-6400
Kenneth Wilson, prin. | Fax 559-6409

Charleston Collegiate S | 300/K-12
2024 Academy Rd 29455 | 843-559-5506
Robert Shirley, prin. | Fax 559-6172

Johnsonville, Florence, Pop. 1,428
Florence SD 5 | 1,500/PK-12
PO Box 98 29555 | 843-386-2358
A. Dale Strickland, supt. | Fax 386-3139
Johnsonville HS | 400/9-12
237 S Georgetown Hwy 29555 | 843-386-2707
James Berry, prin. | Fax 386-9058
Johnsonville MS | 500/5-8
PO Box 67 29555 | 843-386-2066
Stevie Phillips, prin. | Fax 386-3786

Johnston, Edgefield, Pop. 2,323
Edgefield County SD | 3,900/K-12
3 Par Dr 29832 | 803-275-4601
Sharon Keesley, supt. | Fax 275-4426
www.edgefield.k12.sc.us
JET MS | 600/6-8
1095 Columbia Rd 29832 | 803-275-1997
Louis Scott, prin. | Fax 275-1783
Thurmond Career Center | Vo/Tech
17 Par Dr 29832 | 803-275-1767
Carroll Wates, prin. | Fax 275-1766
Thurmond HS | 1,000/9-12
1131 Columbia Rd 29832 | 803-275-1768
Greg Thompson, prin. | Fax 275-1764
Other Schools – See North Augusta

Wardlaw Academy | 200/K-12
1296 Columbia Rd 29832 | 803-275-4794
Dennis Gibson, prin. | Fax 275-4873

Jonesville, Union, Pop. 943
Union County SD
Supt. — See Union
Jonesville JSHS | 400/7-12
131 N Main St 29353 | 864-674-5272
Cindy Langley, prin. | Fax 674-5280

Kershaw, Lancaster, Pop. 1,619
Kershaw County SD
Supt. — See Camden
North Central HS | 500/9-12
3000 Lockhart Rd 29067 | 803-432-9858
Keith McAlister, prin. | Fax 425-8992
North Central MS | 500/6-8
805 Keys Ln 29067 | 803-424-2740
Burchell Richardson Ed.D., prin. | Fax 424-2742

Lancaster County SD
Supt. — See Lancaster
Jackson HS | 600/9-12
6925 Kershaw Camden Hwy 29067 | 803-475-2381
Alisa Goodman, prin. | Fax 475-7317
Jackson MS | 500/6-8
6865 Kershaw Camden Hwy 29067 | 803-475-6021
Theodore Dutton, prin. | Fax 475-8256

Kingstree, Williamsburg, Pop. 3,308
Williamsburg County SD | 5,800/K-12
PO Box 1067 29556 | 843-355-5571
Ralph Fennell, supt. | Fax 355-3213
www.wcsd.k12.sc.us/
Kingstree HS | 900/9-12
615 Martin Luther King Ave 29556 | 843-355-6525
Sam Giles, prin. | Fax 355-7730
Kingstree JHS | 500/7-8
710 3rd Ave 29556 | 843-355-6823
Tarsha Staggers, prin. | Fax 355-9207
Adult Education | Adult
400 Lexington Ave 29556 | 843-355-6887
Phillip Bookhart, dir.
Other Schools – See Greeleyville, Hemingway

Living Word Christian S | 50/K-12
644 Sumter Hwy 29556 | 843-382-2210
Wanda Gray, admin. | Fax 382-4251
Williamsburg Academy | 400/K-12
PO Box 770 29556 | 843-355-9400
Joan Thompson, prin. | Fax 355-7734
Williamsburg Technical College | Post-Sec.
601 Martin Luther King Ave 29556 | 843-354-2021

Ladson, Berkeley, Pop. 13,540
Berkeley County SD
Supt. — See Moncks Corner
College Park MS | 1,200/6-8
713 College Park Rd 29456 | 843-553-8300
Ingrid Dukes, prin. | Fax 820-4026

Dorchester SD 2
Supt. — See Summerville
Oakbrook MS | 1,000/6-8
286 Old Fort Dr 29456 | 843-873-9750
Garland Crump, prin. | Fax 821-3931

Grace Family Christian Academy | 100/PK-12
PO Box 749 29456 | 843-553-1373
Rev. Randy Wade, prin. | Fax 553-1378

Lake City, Florence, Pop. 6,536
Florence County SD 3 | 3,900/K-12
PO Box 1389 29560 | 843-374-8652
Beth Wright, supt. | Fax 374-2946
www.florence3.k12.sc.us/
Lake City HS | 1,200/9-12
PO Box 1569 29560 | 843-374-3321
Stan Yarborough, prin. | Fax 374-3138
McNair MS | 500/6-8
PO Box 1209 29560 | 843-374-8651
David Scurry, prin. | Fax 374-8504
Truluck MS | 400/6-8
PO Box 1239 29560 | 843-374-8685
Laura Hickson, prin. | Fax 374-7341

Carolina Academy | 300/K-12
351 N Country Club Rd 29560 | 843-374-5485

Lake View, Dillon, Pop. 788
Dillon SD 1 | 900/K-12
PO Box 644 29563 | 843-759-3001
Stephen Laird, supt. | Fax 759-3000
www.lakeviewschools.com
Lake View JSHS | 300/8-12
PO Box 624 29563 | 843-759-3009
Edison Arnette, prin. | Fax 759-3016

Lamar, Darlington, Pop. 1,007
Darlington County SD
Supt. — See Darlington
Lamar HS | 400/9-12
216 N Darlington St 29069 | 843-326-5543
Kathy Gainey, prin. | Fax 326-1528
Spaulding MS | 200/7-8
400 Cartersville Hwy 29069 | 843-326-5335
Fran Knotts, prin. | Fax 326-7656

Lancaster, Lancaster, Pop. 8,354
Lancaster County SD | 11,500/PK-12
PO Box 130 29721 | 803-286-6972
Dr. Patricia K. Burns, supt. | Fax 286-4865
www.lancasterscschools.org/home.asp
Buford HS | 500/9-12
4290 Tabernacle Rd 29720 | 803-286-7068
Richard E. Porter, prin. | Fax 286-8147
Buford MS | 400/6-8
1890 N Rocky River Rd 29720 | 803-285-8473
Sheri Wells, prin. | Fax 283-0423
Lancaster County Vocational S | Vo/Tech
625 Normandy Rd 29720 | 803-285-7404
 | Fax 285-2720
Lancaster HS | 1,900/9-12
617 Normandy Rd 29720 | 803-283-2001
Joseph Keenan, prin. | Fax 286-6962
Rucker MS | 700/6-8
422 Old Dixie Rd 29720 | 803-416-8555
Jonathan Phipps, prin. | Fax 285-1534

South MS   800/6-8
1551 Billings Dr 29720   803-283-8416
Joyce Crimminger, prin.   Fax 283-8417
Adult Education   Adult
610 E Meeting St 29720   803-285-7660
James Howey, dir.   Fax 285-9281
Other Schools – See Fort Mill, Kershaw

University of South Carolina   Post-Sec.
PO Box 889 29721   803-285-7471

Landrum, Spartanburg, Pop. 2,490
Spartanburg SD 1
Supt. — See Campobello
Landrum HS   400/9-12
102 Redland Rd 29356   864-457-2606
Susan Vasquez, prin.   Fax 457-3148
Landrum JHS   200/7-8
104 Redland Rd 29356   864-457-2629
John Hodge, prin.   Fax 457-5372

Latta, Dillon, Pop. 1,416
Dillon SD 3   1,400/K-12
205 King St 29565   843-752-7101
Dr. John Kirby, supt.   Fax 752-2081
www.dillon3.k12.sc.us
Latta HS   400/9-12
618 N Richardson St 29565   843-752-5751
George Liebenrood, prin.   Fax 752-2707
Latta MS   400/6-8
602 N Richardson St 29565   843-752-7117
Marth Heyward, prin.   Fax 752-2722

Laurens, Laurens, Pop. 9,819
Laurens SD 55   5,800/K-12
1029 W Main St 29360   864-984-3568
Edgar C. Taylor, supt.   Fax 984-8100
www.laurens55.k12.sc.us/
Laurens District 55 HS   1,600/9-12
5058 Highway 76 W 29360   864-682-3151
John Hendricks, prin.   Fax 682-7426
Laurens MS   400/6-8
1035 W Main St 29360   864-984-2400
Rhett Harris, prin.   Fax 984-6013
Sanders MS   300/6-8
609 Green St 29360   864-984-0354
Joe Walker, prin.   Fax 984-2452
Other Schools – See Gray Court

Lexington, Lexington, Pop. 11,746
Lexington County SD 1   18,700/K-12
PO Box 1869 29071   803-359-4178
Karen Woodward, supt.   Fax 359-8807
www.lexington1.net
Lexington HS   2,300/9-12
2463 Augusta Hwy 29072   803-359-5565
B. Creig Tyler, prin.   Fax 359-8726
Lexington MS   1,600/6-8
702 N Lake Dr 29072   803-359-6169
Laura McMahan, prin.   Fax 359-7233
Lexington Technology Center   Vo/Tech
2421 Augusta Hwy 29072   803-359-4151
Kenneth Lake, prin.   Fax 359-4073
Pleasant Hill MS   6-8
660 Rawl Rd 29072   803-996-4200
Dr. William Coon, prin.   Fax 996-4250
White Knoll HS   1,700/9-12
5643 Platt Springs Rd 29073   803-996-4500
Jo Mayer, prin.   Fax 996-4581
Other Schools – See Gilbert, Pelion, West Columbia

Columbia Adventist Academy   100/K-10
241 Riverchase Way 29072   803-796-0277
Debbie White, prin.

Liberty, Pickens, Pop. 3,002
Pickens County SD
Supt. — See Easley
Liberty HS   600/9-12
319 Summit Dr 29657   864-843-5800
Randy Gilstrap, prin.   Fax 843-5828
Liberty MS   700/5-8
310 W Main St 29657   864-843-5855
Donivan Edwards, prin.   Fax 843-5857

Little River, Horry, Pop. 3,470
Horry County SD
Supt. — See Conway
North Myrtle Beach HS   1,100/9-12
3750 Sea Mountain Hwy 29566   843-399-6171
Mike Blanton, prin.   Fax 399-6509
North Myrtle Beach MS   1,000/6-8
11240 Highway 90 29566   843-399-6136
Virginia Horton, prin.   Fax 399-2233

Lobeco, Beaufort

Agape Christian Academy   100/K-12
PO Box 719 29931   843-846-4835

Lockhart, Union, Pop. 509
Union County SD
Supt. — See Union
Lockhart JSHS   200/7-12
PO Box 220 29364   864-545-6501
Kevin Morrow, prin.   Fax 545-2175

Longs, Horry

Faith Christian Academy   100/PK-12
1760 Living Stones Ln 29568   843-399-2558
Sylvia Kenney, prin.   Fax 399-3044

Loris, Horry, Pop. 2,192
Horry County SD
Supt. — See Conway
Loris HS   800/9-12
301 Loris Lions Rd 29569   843-756-4040
Trevor Strawderman, prin.   Fax 756-5331

Loris MS   700/6-8
5209 Highway 66 29569   843-756-2181
Judy Beard, prin.   Fax 756-0522

Lugoff, Kershaw, Pop. 3,211
Kershaw County SD
Supt. — See Camden
Lugoff-Elgin HS   1,400/9-12
1284 Highway 1 S 29078   803-438-3481
Thomas Gladden, prin.   Fax 438-8005
Lugoff-Elgin MS   600/6-8
1244 Highway 1 S 29078   803-438-3591
Dave Matthews, prin.   Fax 438-8027

Mc Bee, Chesterfield, Pop. 674
Chesterfield County SD
Supt. — See Chesterfield
Mc Bee JSHS   400/7-12
PO Box 218 29101   843-335-8251
Skip Gering, prin.   Fax 335-6515

Mc Clellanville, Charleston, Pop. 334
Charleston County SD
Supt. — See Charleston
Lincoln HS   100/9-12
714 Lincoln Rd 29458   843-577-0970
Michell Glover, prin.   Fax 887-3116
Mc Clellanville MS   200/6-8
711 Pinckney St 29458   843-577-0325
William Price, prin.   Fax 887-3002

Rutledge Academy   100/K-12
1011 Old Cemetery Rd 29458   843-887-3323

Mc Cormick, McCormick, Pop. 1,736
McCormick SD   900/K-12
821 N Mine St 29835   864-852-2425
Sandra Calliham Ed.D., supt.   Fax 852-2883
www.mccormick.k12.sc.us/
Mc Cormick HS   300/9-12
516 Mims Dr 29835   864-852-2302
Fred Moore, prin.   Fax 852-3326
Mc Cormick MS   300/5-8
6979 Highway 28 S 29835   864-443-2243
Cecily Morris, prin.   Fax 443-3300

Manning, Clarendon, Pop. 3,978
Area Vocational Schools
Supt. — None
Dubose Career Center   Vo/Tech
PO Box 1249 29102   803-473-2531
Dr. Tim Hardee, prin.   Fax 473-4320
Clarendon SD 2   3,500/PK-12
PO Box 1252 29102   803-435-4435
John Tindal, supt.   Fax 435-8172
www.clarendon2.k12.sc.us
Manning HS   1,000/9-12
2155 Paxville Hwy 29102   803-435-4417
Mike Shorter, prin.   Fax 435-4404
Manning JHS   600/7-8
1101 W L Hamilton Rd 29102   803-435-8195
Preston Threatt, prin.   Fax 435-6848

Marion, Marion, Pop. 7,008
Area Vocational Schools
Supt. — None
Marion Co. Technical Education Center   Vo/Tech
PO Box 890 29571   843-423-1941
Paul Crandall, dir.   Fax 423-1943
Marion SD 1   3,100/K-12
719 N Main St 29571   843-423-1811
Dr. Cheryl Allread, supt.   Fax 423-8328
www.marion1.k12.sc.us
Johnakin MS   700/6-8
601 Gurley St 29571   843-423-8360
Gerard Edwards, prin.   Fax 423-8383
Marion HS   900/9-12
1205 S Main St 29571   843-423-2571
Alfred McFadden, prin.   Fax 423-8330
Marion SD 7
Supt. — See Rains
Creek Bridge HS   400/7-12
6641 S Highway 41 29571   843-362-3500
Burnie Bell, prin.   Fax 362-3506

Mauldin, Greenville, Pop. 17,716
Greenville County SD
Supt. — See Greenville
Mauldin HS   2,000/9-12
701 E Butler Rd 29662   864-355-6500
Ann Miller, prin.   Fax 355-6657

Moncks Corner, Berkeley, Pop. 6,019
Berkeley County SD   26,500/PK-12
PO Box 608 29461   843-899-8600
J. Floyd, supt.   Fax 899-8791
www.berkeley.k12.sc.us
Berkeley HS   1,500/9-12
406 W Main St 29461   843-899-8800
Ben Hodges Ph.D., prin.   Fax 899-8813
Berkeley MS   1,300/6-8
320 N Live Oak Dr 29461   843-899-8840
Dr. Susan Gehlmann, prin.   Fax 899-8846
Macedonia MS   600/5-8
200 Macedonia Foxes Cir 29461   843-899-8940
Janie Langley, prin.   Fax 899-8929
Other Schools – See Cross, Goose Creek, Hanahan,
Ladson, Saint Stephen

St. John Christian Academy   400/PK-12
204 W Main St 29461   843-761-8539
Rhoda Boyd, prin.   Fax 899-5514
Trident Technical College   Post-Sec.
1001 S Live Oak Dr 29461   843-899-8033

Monetta, Aiken, Pop. 219
Aiken County SD
Supt. — See Aiken

Ridge Spring-Monetta HS   200/9-12
10 J P Kneece Dr 29105   803-685-2100
William Ward, prin.   Fax 685-2108

Moore, Spartanburg
Spartanburg SD 6
Supt. — See Roebuck
Anderson Applied Technology Center   Vo/Tech
PO Box 248 29369   864-576-5020
Sherri Yarborough, prin.   Fax 576-8642
Dawkins MS   900/6-8
1300 E Blackstock Rd 29369   864-576-8088
Kenneth Kiser, prin.   Fax 595-2418

Mount Pleasant, Charleston, Pop. 54,788
Charleston County SD
Supt. — See Charleston
Cario MS   900/6-8
3500 Thomas Cario Blvd 29466   843-856-4595
Carol Bartlett, prin.   Fax 856-4599
Laing MS   500/6-8
2213 N Highway 17 29466   843-849-2809
Deborah Price, prin.   Fax 849-2895
Moultrie MS   800/6-8
645 Coleman Blvd 29464   843-849-2819
Jean Siewicki, prin.   Fax 849-2899
Wando HS   2,500/9-12
1000 Warrior Way 29466   843-849-2830
Lucy Beckham, prin.   Fax 849-2890

First Baptist Church S of Mt. Pleasant   400/K-12
681 McCants Dr 29464   843-884-3663
Chad Moore, prin.   Fax 884-9608
Trident Academy   200/K-12
1455 Wakendaw Rd 29464   843-884-7046
   Fax 881-8320

Mullins, Marion, Pop. 4,854
Marion SD 2   1,900/PK-PK, 1-
PO Box 689 29574   843-464-3700
James Hall, supt.   Fax 464-3705
www.marion2.k12.sc.us
Mullins HS   600/9-12
747 Millers Rd 29574   843-464-3710
Theodore Greene, prin.   Fax 464-3717
Palmetto MS   400/7-8
305 ONeal St 29574   843-464-3730
Tim Felder, prin.   Fax 464-3736

Pee Dee Academy   500/K-12
PO Box 449 29574   843-423-1771
Hal Townsend, prin.   Fax 423-0301

Murrells Inlet, Georgetown, Pop. 3,334
Horry County SD
Supt. — See Conway
St. James HS   1,000/9-12
10800 Highway 707 29576   843-650-5600
Joe Dowling, prin.   Fax 650-1004

Myrtle Beach, Horry, Pop. 24,691
Horry County SD
Supt. — See Conway
Academy for Arts Science & Technology   Vo/Tech
900 79th Ave N 29572   843-839-1412
Ronnie Burgess, prin.   Fax 839-1419
Carolina Forest HS   1,400/9-12
700 Gardner Lacy Rd 29579   843-236-7997
Velna Allen, prin.   Fax 236-7504
Forestbrook MS   1,000/6-8
4430 Gator Ln 29588   843-236-7300
James Bradley, prin.   Fax 236-8065
Myrtle Beach HS   1,200/9-12
3302 Robert M Grissom Pkwy 29577   843-448-7149
Nona Kerr, prin.   Fax 445-2036
Myrtle Beach MS   900/6-8
950 Seahawk Way 29577   843-448-3932
Roger Gray, prin.   Fax 448-1182
Ocean Bay MS   6-8
905 International Dr 29579   843-903-8420
Dr. Cindy Thibodeau, prin.   Fax 903-8421
St. James MS   800/6-8
9775 Saint James Rd 29588   843-650-5543
Dr. Dwight Boykin, prin.   Fax 650-5610
Socastee HS   1,400/9-12
4900 Socastee Blvd 29588   843-293-2513
Dr. Paul Browning, prin.   Fax 293-3393

Calvary Christian S   300/K-12
4511 Dick Pond Rd 29588   843-650-2829
John Gregory, prin.   215-4125
Christian Academy   100/K-10
3013 Theatre Dr 29579   843-236-6222
Todd Underwood, prin.   Fax 236-7044
Golf Academy of the Carolinas   Post-Sec.
3268 Waccamaw Blvd 29579   800-342-7342
Horry-Georgetown Technical College   Post-Sec.
743 Hemlock Ave 29577   843-477-0808
Strand College of Hair Design   Post-Sec.
423 79th Ave W 29572   843-449-1017

Neeses, Orangeburg, Pop. 407
Orangeburg Consolidated SD 4
Supt. — See Cope
Hunter-Kinard-Tyler HS   300/7-12
7066 Norway Rd 29107   803-263-4832
Titus Durin, prin.   Fax 263-4467

Newberry, Newberry, Pop. 10,608
Newberry County SD   6,100/K-12
PO Box 718 29108   803-321-2600
Walter Tobin, supt.   Fax 321-2604
www.newberry.k12.sc.us/
Newberry Career Ctr   Vo/Tech
3413 Main St 29108   803-321-2674
Donald Lawrimore, prin.   Fax 321-2676
Newberry HS   900/9-12
3113 Main St 29108   803-321-2621
Barry Rosenberg, prin.   Fax 321-2633

Newberry MS   700/6-8
125 ONeal St 29108   803-321-2640
Donivan Edwards, prin.   Fax 321-2647
Other Schools – See Prosperity, Whitmire

Newberry Academy   200/K-12
2055 Smith Rd 29108   803-276-2760
Bob Dawkins, hdmstr.   Fax 276-2401
Newberry College   Post-Sec.
2100 College St 29108   800-845-4955

New Ellenton, Aiken, Pop. 2,276
Aiken County SD
Supt. — See Aiken
New Ellenton MS   200/6-8
814 Main St S 29809   803-652-8200
Sheneque Jackson, prin.   Fax 652-8203

Ninety Six, Greenwood, Pop. 1,917
Greenwood SD 52   1,700/PK-12
605 Johnston Rd 29666   864-543-3100
Dan W. Powell Ph.D., supt.   Fax 543-3704
www.greenwood52.org
Edgewood MS   400/6-8
200 Edgewood Cir 29666   864-543-3511
Wallace Hall, prin.   Fax 543-4994
Ninety Six HS   500/9-12
601 Johnston Rd 29666   864-543-2911
Jo Anne Campbell, prin.   Fax 543-3132

North, Orangeburg, Pop. 796
Orangeburg Consolidated SD 5
Supt. — See Orangeburg
North MSHS   300/7-12
PO Box 370 29112   803-247-2541
Sterling Harris, prin.   Fax 247-5090

North Augusta, Aiken, Pop. 18,413
Aiken County SD
Supt. — See Aiken
Knox MS   700/6-8
1804 Wells Rd 29841   803-442-6300
Brenda Smith, prin.   Fax 442-6302
North Augusta HS   1,500/9-12
2000 Knobcone Ave 29841   803-442-6100
Kyle Smith, prin.   Fax 442-6127
North Augusta MS   600/6-8
725 Old Edgefield Rd 29841   803-442-6200
Barry Head, prin.   Fax 442-6202

Edgefield County SD
Supt. — See Johnston
Merriwether MS   400/6-8
PO Box 7010 29861   803-279-2511
Gaye Holmes, prin.   Fax 279-1710

Kenneth Shuler's School of Cosmetology   Post-Sec.
736 Martintown Rd 29841   803-278-1200
Victory Christian S   200/K-12
620 W Martintown Rd 29841   803-278-2138

North Charleston, Charleston, Pop. 81,577
Charleston County SD
Supt. — See Charleston
Brentwood MS   600/6-8
2685 Leeds Ave 29405   843-745-7094
Cassandra Jennings, prin.   Fax 566-1838
Charleston County S of the Arts   500/6-9
1600 Saranac St 29405   843-529-4990
Rose Myers, prin.   Fax 529-4991
Charlestowne Academy   400/K-12
5841 Rivers Ave 29406   843-746-1349
Edward Tichi, prin.   Fax 746-1354
Garrett Academy of Technology   Vo/Tech
2731 Gordon St 29405   843-745-7126
David Parson, prin.   Fax 529-3914
Morningside MS   500/6-8
1999 Singley St 29405   843-745-2000
Thomas Rylands, prin.   Fax 745-7191
North Charleston HS   1,300/9-12
1087 E Montague Ave 29405   843-745-7140
David Colwell, prin.   Fax 566-1954
Stall HS   1,000/9-12
7749 Pinehurst St 29420   843-764-2200
David Basile, prin.   Fax 764-2240

Dorchester SD 2
Supt. — See Summerville
Fort Dorchester HS   2,100/9-12
8500 Patriot Blvd 29420   843-760-4450
Timothy Payne, prin.   Fax 760-4852

Beta Tech   Post-Sec.
8088 Rivers Ave 29406   843-569-0889
ECPI College of Technology   Post-Sec.
7410 Northside Dr # G101 29420   843-414-0350
Ferndale Baptist S   200/K-12
4870 Piedmont Ave 29406   843-744-3307
Milton Ashley, prin.   Fax 554-0535
Miller-Motte Technical College   Post-Sec.
8085 Rivers Ave 29406   843-574-0101
Northwood Academy   300/6-12
2263 Otranto Rd 29406   843-764-2284
Dr. Darlene Anderson, prin.   Fax 764-3713
Southeastern School of Neuromuscular   Post-Sec.
4600 Goer Dr Ste 105 29406   843-747-1279

Orangeburg, Orangeburg, Pop. 12,758
Orangeburg Consolidated SD 5   8,700/K-12
578 Ellis Ave 29115   803-534-5454
Melvin Smoak, supt.   Fax 533-7953
www.orangeburg5.k12.sc.us/
Clark MS   900/5-8
919 Bennett St 29115   803-531-2200
Lana Williams, prin.   Fax 533-6503
Howard MS   700/5-8
1255 Belleville Rd 29115   803-534-5470
Dr. Jacqueline Vogt, prin.   Fax 535-1606

Orangeburg 5 Tech Center   Vo/Tech
3720 Magnolia St 29118   803-536-4473
Abbieqail Hugine, prin.   Fax 533-6365
Orangeburg-Wilkinson HS   1,800/9-12
601 Bruin Pkwy 29118   803-534-6180
Rodney Zimmerman, prin.   Fax 533-6310
Other Schools – See North, Rowesville

Claflin University   Post-Sec.
700 College Ave 29115   803-535-5000
Orangeburg-Calhoun Technical College   Post-Sec.
3250 Saint Matthews Rd 29118   803-536-0311
Orangeburg Prep S   800/K-12
2651 North Rd 29118   803-534-7970
Kelley Mims, prin.   Fax 535-2190
South Carolina State University   Post-Sec.
PO Box 7127 29117   803-536-7000
Southern Methodist College   Post-Sec.
PO Box 1027 29116   803-534-7826

Pacolet, Spartanburg, Pop. 2,754
Spartanburg SD 3
Supt. — See Glendale
Pacolet MS   200/6-8
850 Sunny Acres Rd 29372   864-474-4080
Cynthia James, prin.   Fax 474-4085

Pageland, Chesterfield, Pop. 2,522
Chesterfield County SD
Supt. — See Chesterfield
Central HS   700/9-12
200 Zion Church Rd 29728   843-672-6115
J.R. Green, prin.   Fax 672-2694

New Covenent Christian S   200/K-12
PO Box 188 29728   843-672-2760

Pamplico, Florence, Pop. 1,133
Florence SD 2   1,100/K-12
2121 S Pamplico Hwy 29583   843-493-2502
Steve Quick, supt.   Fax 493-1912
Hannah-Pamplico HS   300/9-12
2055 S Pamplico Hwy 29583   843-493-5781
Bernard McDaniel, prin.   Fax 493-5424

New Prospect Christian S   200/K-12
4221 Sheminally Rd 29583   843-493-2189

Pawleys Island, Georgetown, Pop. 135
Georgetown County SD
Supt. — See Georgetown
Waccamaw HS   600/9-12
2412 Kings River Rd 29585   843-237-9899
Robert Brown, prin.   Fax 237-9883
Waccamaw MS   500/6-8
247 Wildcat Way 29585   843-237-0106
Leonard Nelson, prin.   Fax 237-0237

Pelion, Lexington, Pop. 568
Lexington County SD 1
Supt. — See Lexington
Pelion HS   700/9-12
600 Lydia Dr 29123   803-894-2100
Jean Haggard, prin.   Fax 894-2101
Pelion MS   900/5-8
758 Magnolia St 29123   803-894-2050
Dr. Sandra Jowers, prin.   Fax 894-2051

Pendleton, Anderson, Pop. 2,994
Anderson SD 4   2,800/K-12
PO Box 545 29670   864-646-8000
Dr. Gary Burgess, supt.   Fax 646-8555
www.anderson4.k12.sc.us
Pendleton HS   800/9-12
PO Box 869 29670   864-646-8040
Rodney Graves, prin.   Fax 646-8066
Riverside MS   600/6-8
458 Riverside St 29670   864-646-8020
Kevin Black, prin.   Fax 646-8025

Tri-County Tech College   Post-Sec.
PO Box 587 29670   864-646-8361

Pickens, Pickens, Pop. 3,015
Pickens County SD
Supt. — See Easley
Pickens HS   1,400/9-12
111 Blue Flame Dr 29671   864-878-8730
Marion Lawson, prin.   Fax 898-5611
Pickens MS   900/6-8
467 Sparks Ln 29671   864-878-8735
Tim Mullis, prin.   Fax 878-8734

Piedmont, Greenville, Pop. 4,143
Anderson SD 1
Supt. — See Williamston
Wren HS   1,500/9-12
905 Wren School Rd 29673   864-850-5900
Robbie Binnicker, prin.   Fax 850-5929
Wren MS   700/6-8
1010 Wren School Rd 29673   864-850-5930
Robin Fulbright, prin.   Fax 850-5941

Greenville County SD
Supt. — See Greenville
Woodmont HS   1,000/9-12
150 Woodmont School Rd 29673   864-299-8300
Dr. Randy Reagan, prin.   Fax 299-8422
Woodmont MS   900/6-8
325 N Flat Rock Rd 29673   864-299-8373
Kira Geter, prin.   Fax 299-8408

Port Royal, Beaufort, Pop. 4,424

Praise Christian Academy   100/K-12
PO Box 596 29935   843-525-9321
Samuel Diaz, hdmstr.   Fax 770-0256

Prosperity, Newberry, Pop. 1,082
Newberry County SD
Supt. — See Newberry
Mid-Carolina HS   600/9-12
6794 US Highway 76 29127   803-364-2134
Lynn Cary, prin.   Fax 364-4395
Mid-Carolina MS   600/6-8
6834 US Highway 76 29127   803-364-3634
Henry Livingston, prin.   Fax 364-4877

Rains, Marion
Marion SD 7   900/K-12
PO Box 1439 29589   843-423-2891
Everette M. Dean Ed.D., supt.   Fax 423-7987
www.marion7.k12.sc.us
Other Schools – See Marion

Richburg, Chester, Pop. 327
Chester County SD
Supt. — See Chester
Lewisville HS   400/9-12
3971 Lewisville High School 29729   803-789-5131
James Knox, prin.   Fax 789-3188
Lewisville MS   400/6-8
PO Box 280 29729   803-789-5858
H.L. Erwin, prin.   Fax 789-6159

Ridgeland, Jasper, Pop. 2,591
Area Vocational Schools
Supt. — None
Academy for Career Excellence   Vo/Tech
RR 1 Box 127 29936   843-987-8107
Catherine M. Smith, dir.   Fax 987-4136

Jasper County SD   3,100/K-12
PO Box 848 29936   843-717-1100
Dr. William Singleton, supt.   Fax 717-1199
www.jcsd.net
Jasper County HS   800/9-12
PO Box 760 29936   843-717-1500
Marc Grant, prin.   Fax 717-1599
Ridgeland MS   700/5-8
PO Box 250 29936   843-717-1400
Benjamin Gadsden, prin.   Fax 717-1499

Heyward Academy   500/K-12
PO Box 2233 29936   843-726-3673
John Rogers, prin.   Fax 726-5773

Ridgeville, Dorchester, Pop. 1,790
Dorchester SD 2
Supt. — See Summerville
Givhans Community S   Adult
273 Highway 61 29472   843-832-5559
Joyce Dearing, prin.   Fax 821-3944

Rock Hill, York, Pop. 56,114
Rock Hill SD 3   16,600/PK-12
PO Box 10072 29731   803-981-1000
Dr. Randy L. Bridges, supt.   Fax 981-1094
www.rock-hill.k12.sc.us/
Castle Heights MS   900/6-8
2382 Firetower Rd 29730   803-981-1400
Kelly Kane, prin.   Fax 981-1430
Northwestern HS   2,400/9-12
2503 W Main St 29732   803-981-1200
James Blake, prin.   Fax 981-1250
Rawlinson Road MS   1,000/6-8
2631 W Main St 29732   803-981-1500
Tena Neely, prin.   Fax 981-1532
Rock Hill Applied Technology Center   Vo/Tech
2399 W Main St 29732   803-981-1100
Don Gillman, dir.   Fax 981-1125
Rock Hill HS   2,300/9-12
320 W Springdale Rd 29730   803-981-1300
Niles Chumley, prin.   Fax 981-1343
Saluda Trail MS   900/6-8
2300 Saluda Rd 29730   803-981-1800
Brenda Campbell, prin.   Fax 981-1819
South Pointe HS   9-12
801 Neely Rd 29730   803-980-2100
Al Leonard, prin.   Fax 980-2105
Sullivan MS   1,100/6-8
1825 Eden Ter 29730   803-981-1450
Dr. Bob Heath, prin.   Fax 981-1456
Adult Education   Adult
217 Orange St 29730   803-981-1375
Sandy Andrews, prin.   Fax 981-1397

Clinton Junior College   Post-Sec.
1029 Crawford Rd 29730   803-327-7402
Plaza School of Beauty Culture   Post-Sec.
946 Oakland Ave 29730   803-328-5166
Trinity Christian S   200/PK-12
505 University Dr 29730   803-366-3121
Thomas Krauter, admin.   Fax 366-8339
Westminster Catawba Christian S   600/PK-12
2650 India Hook Rd 29732   803-366-4119
Dr. John M. Blumenstein, prin.   Fax 328-5465
Winthrop University   Post-Sec.
701 W Oakland Ave 29733   803-323-2211
York Technical College   Post-Sec.
452 Anderson Rd S 29730   803-327-8000

Roebuck, Spartanburg, Pop. 1,966
Spartanburg SD 6   9,500/K-12
1390 Cavalier Way 29376   864-576-4212
Dr. Darryl Owings, supt.   Fax 574-6265
www.spartanburg6.k12.sc.us
Dorman HS   1,800/10-12
1050 Cavalier Way 29376   864-582-4347
Jerry Wyatt, prin.   Fax 587-8738
Dorman HS - Freshman Campus   800/9-9
1225 Cavalier Way 29376   864-582-3479
Cheryl Revels, prin.   Fax 342-8997
Gable MS   800/6-8
198 Otts Shoals Rd 29376   864-576-3500
Karen Bush, prin.   Fax 595-2428
Other Schools – See Moore, Spartanburg

Rowesville, Orangeburg, Pop. 369
Orangeburg Consolidated SD 5
Supt. — See Orangeburg
Bethune-Bowman MSHS 400/6-12
4857 Charleston Hwy 29133 803-516-6011
Parrie Hook, prin. Fax 516-6013

Ruffin, Colleton
Colleton County SD
Supt. — See Walterboro
Ruffin MS 300/6-8
155 Patriot Ln 29475 843-562-2291
Harry Jenkins, prin. Fax 562-8028

Saint George, Dorchester, Pop. 2,097
Dorchester SD 4 2,500/PK-12
500 Ridge St 29477 843-563-4535
Renee Mathews, supt. Fax 563-9269
www.dorchester4.k12.sc.us
Saint George MS 600/6-8
600 Minus St 29477 843-563-3171
Brooks Moore, prin. Fax 563-5936
Other Schools – See Dorchester

Dorchester Academy 500/K-12
PO Box 901 29477 843-563-9511
Phillip Rizzo, hdmstr. Fax 563-4764

Saint Matthews, Calhoun, Pop. 2,093
Calhoun SD 1,800/PK-12
PO Box 215 29135 803-655-7310
Dr. Shirley P. Martin, supt. Fax 655-7393
www.calhoun.k12.sc.us
Calhoun County HS 500/9-12
150 Saints Ave 29135 803-874-3071
Sheridan Hamilton, prin. Fax 655-5948
Ford MS 300/6-8
PO Box 287 29135 803-655-7222
Carlita Davis, prin. Fax 655-7506

Calhoun Academy 500/PK-12
PO Box 526 29135 803-874-2734
Milly McLauchlin, hdmstr. Fax 874-2734
Upward Way Christian Academy 50/K-12
3941 Old State Rd 29135 803-655-9026
Shelby Neil, admin.

Saint Stephen, Berkeley, Pop. 1,749
Berkeley County SD
Supt. — See Moncks Corner
Saint Stephen MS 300/6-8
225 Carolina Dr 29479 843-567-3128
Derrick Daniels, prin. Fax 567-8162
Timberland HS 1,000/9-12
1418 Gravel Hill Rd 29479 843-567-8110
Eugene Lemmon, prin. Fax 567-8116

Salem, Oconee, Pop. 128
Oconee County SD
Supt. — See Walhalla
Tamassee-Salem MSHS 700/6-12
PO Box 96 29676 864-944-0444
Steve Moore, prin. Fax 944-6492

Saluda, Saluda, Pop. 3,007
Saluda SD 2,200/PK-12
404 N Wise Rd 29138 864-445-8441
Pete Stone Ed.D., supt. Fax 445-9671
www.saludak-12.org
Saluda HS 500/9-12
160 Ivory Key Rd 29138 864-445-3011
Jimmy Crawford, prin. Fax 445-3542
Saluda MS 500/6-8
140 Ivory Key Rd 29138 864-445-3767
Shawn Love, prin. Fax 445-3980

Seabrook, Beaufort
Beaufort County SD
Supt. — See Beaufort
Whale Branch MS 400/6-8
2009 Trask Pkwy 29940 843-466-3000
Arlene Kennedy, prin. Fax 466-3087

Seneca, Oconee, Pop. 7,674
Oconee County SD
Supt. — See Walhalla
Hamilton Career Center Vo/Tech
100 Vocational Dr 29672 864-885-5011
Michael Pearson, prin. Fax 885-5012
Seneca HS 1,000/9-12
100 Bobcat Rdg 29678 864-885-5000
Dianne England, prin. Fax 885-5008
Seneca MS 900/6-8
810 W South 4th St 29678 864-885-5016
Kelly Pew, prin. Fax 885-5018

Oconee Christian Academy 200/PK-12
150 His Way Cir 29672 864-882-6925
Thad Cloer, dir. Fax 882-7217

Simpsonville, Greenville, Pop. 14,781
Greenville County SD
Supt. — See Greenville
Bryson MS 1,300/6-8
3657 S Industrial Dr 29681 864-355-2100
Dr. Billie McGaha, prin. Fax 355-2194
Hillcrest HS 2,200/9-12
3665 S Industrial Dr 29681 864-355-3500
Steve Chamness, prin. Fax 355-3382
Hillcrest MS 1,100/6-8
510 Garrison Rd 29681 864-355-6100
Keith Russell, prin. Fax 355-6120
Mauldin MS 1,300/6-8
1190 Holland Rd 29681 864-213-1132
Rosia Gardner, prin. Fax 213-1134

Southside Christian S 1,100/PK-12
2211 Woodruff Rd 29681 864-234-7595
Stephen Reel Ph.D., supt. Fax 234-7048

Spartanburg, Spartanburg, Pop. 38,718
Spartanburg SD 3
Supt. — See Glendale
Broome HS 900/9-12
381 Cherry Hill Rd 29307 864-579-8040
Dr. Vernon Prosser, prin. Fax 579-8050

Spartanburg SD 6
Supt. — See Roebuck
Fairforest MS 800/6-8
4120 N Blackstock Rd 29301 864-576-1270
Chuck Gordon, prin. Fax 576-2600

Spartanburg SD 7 9,100/K-12
PO Box 970 29304 864-594-4400
Lynn Batten, supt. Fax 594-4406
www.spart7.org
Carver JHS, 367 S Church St 29306 700/7-9
Charles Redmond, prin. 864-594-4435
McCracken JHS 900/7-9
300 Webber Rd 29307 864-594-4457
Jeff Stevens, prin. Fax 596-8418
Morgan Technology Center Vo/Tech
201 Zion Hill Rd 29307 864-579-2810
Wayne Chapman, prin. Fax 579-7392
Spartanburg SHS 1,500/10-12
500 Dupre Dr 29307 864-594-4410
Rodney Graves, prin. Fax 594-6142
Whitlock JHS 700/7-9
364 Successful Way 29303 864-594-4482
Virginia Jones, prin. Fax 594-6154

Converse College Post-Sec.
580 E Main St 29302 864-596-9000
Sherman College of Straight Chiropractic Post-Sec.
PO Box 1452 29304 864-578-8770
South Carolina School for Deaf and Blind Post-Sec.
355 Cedar Springs Rd 29302 864-577-7521
Spartanburg Christian Academy 600/PK-12
8740 Asheville Hwy 29316 864-578-4238
Ken Pangel, admin. Fax 542-1846
Spartanburg Day S 500/PK-12
1701 Skylyn Dr 29307 864-582-7539
Christopher A. Dorrance, hdmstr. Fax 948-0026
Spartanburg Methodist College Post-Sec.
1200 Textile Rd 29301 800-772-7286
Spartanburg Technical College Post-Sec.
PO Box 4386 29305 864-591-3600
University of South Carolina Post-Sec.
800 University Way 29303 864-503-5000
Westgate Christian S 200/K-12
1990 Old Reidville Rd 29301 864-576-4953
Fred Seiber, prin. Fax 576-7581
Wofford College Post-Sec.
429 N Church St 29303 864-597-4000

Starr, Anderson, Pop. 180
Anderson SD 3
Supt. — See Iva
Starr-Iva MS 700/6-8
1034 Rainey Rd 29684 864-352-6146
Carolyn Brown, prin. Fax 352-2095

Summerton, Clarendon, Pop. 1,033
Clarendon SD 1 1,200/K-12
PO Box 38 29148 803-485-2325
Dr. Rose Wilder, supt. Fax 485-2822
www.clarendon1.k12.sc.us
Scotts Branch HS 400/9-12
RR 3 Box 802 29148 803-478-7818
Corey Burgess, prin. Fax 478-7659
Scott's Branch IS 500/4-8
PO Box 67 29148 803-485-2043
Ernastine Oliver, prin. Fax 485-7012

Clarendon Hall S 300/K-12
PO Box 609 29148 803-485-3550
Dr. Michael Connors, prin. Fax 485-3205

Summerville, Dorchester, Pop. 31,734
Dorchester SD 2 18,000/K-12
102 Green Wave Blvd 29483 843-873-2901
Joseph Pye, supt. Fax 873-4053
www.dorchester2.k12.sc.us
Alston MS 900/6-8
500 Bryan St 29483 843-873-3890
Sam Clark, prin. Fax 821-3978
DuBose MS 900/6-8
1000 DuBose School Rd 29483 843-875-7012
Raymond Burke, prin. Fax 821-3995
Gregg MS 1,200/6-8
500 Greenwave Blvd 29483 843-871-3150
Tom McCurry, prin. Fax 821-3992
Rollings MS of the Arts 600/6-8
815 S Main St 29483 843-873-3610
Kathy Sobolewski, prin. Fax 821-3985
Summerville HS 3,300/9-12
1101 Boone Hill Rd 29483 843-873-6460
Dickey Dingle, prin. Fax 821-3989
Other Schools – See Ladson, North Charleston, Ridgeville

Faith Christian S 300/PK-12
337 Farmington Rd 29483 843-873-8464
Rev. Doug Wolfrath, prin. Fax 873-4288
Pinewood Prep S 700/K-12
1114 Orangeburg Rd 29483 843-873-1643
Glyn Cowlishaw, prin. Fax 821-4257

Sumter, Sumter, Pop. 39,790
Area Vocational Schools
Supt. — None
Sumter County Career Center Vo/Tech
2612 McCrays Mill Rd 29154 803-481-8575
John Roveri, prin. Fax 481-4232

Sumter SD 17 9,000/K-12
1109 N Pike W 29153 803-469-8536
Zona W. Jefferson Ph.D., supt. Fax 469-6006
district.sumter17.k12.sc.us/
Alice Drive MS 800/6-8
40 Miller Rd 29150 803-775-0821
Neil Baldwin, prin. Fax 778-2929
Bates MS 800/6-8
715 Estate St 29150 803-775-0711
Anthony Graham, prin. Fax 775-0715
Chestnut Oaks MS 600/6-8
1200 Oswego Hwy 29153 803-775-7272
Cornelius Leach, prin. Fax 775-7601
Sumter HS 2,500/9-12
2580 McCrays Mill Rd 29154 803-481-4480
Rutledge Dingle, prin. Fax 481-4021

Sumter SD 2 9,300/K-12
1345 Wilson Hall Rd 29150 803-469-6900
Frank Baker, supt. Fax 469-3769
www.sumter2.org
Crestwood HS 1,400/9-12
2000 Oswego Hwy 29153 803-469-6200
John Huggins, prin. Fax 469-7678
Ebenezer MS 500/6-8
3440 Ebenezer Rd 29153 803-469-8571
Marlene DeWit, prin. Fax 469-8575
Furman MS 1,000/6-8
3400 Bethel Church Rd 29154 803-481-8510
Dale Wilson, prin. Fax 481-8923
Lakewood HS 1,200/9-12
350 Old Manning Rd 29150 803-506-2704
Sherril Ray, prin. Fax 506-2708
Mayewood MS 300/6-8
4300 E Brewington Rd 29153 803-495-8014
Dr. Mary Hallums, prin. Fax 495-8016
Other Schools – See Dalzell

Central Carolina Technical College Post-Sec.
506 N Guignard Dr 29150 803-778-1961
Morris College Post-Sec.
100 W College St 29150 803-934-3200
St. Francis Xavier HS 200/9-12
15 School St 29150 803-773-0210
Dianne Trapini, prin. Fax 775-0119
Sumter Beauty College Post-Sec.
921 Carolina Ave 29150 803-773-7311
Sumter Christian S 400/K-12
420 S Pike W 29150 803-773-1902
Ron Davis, prin. Fax 775-1676
University of South Carolina Post-Sec.
200 Miller Rd 29150 803-775-6341
Wilson Hall S 800/PK-12
2801 S Wise Dr 29150 803-469-3475

Swansea, Lexington, Pop. 528
Lexington SD 4 3,700/PK-12
607 E 5th St 29160 803-568-1000
Franklin Vail, supt. Fax 568-1020
www.lexington4.net
Swansea HS 900/9-12
500 E 1st St 29160 803-568-1100
Dr. Robert Maddox, prin. Fax 568-1117
Other Schools – See Gaston

Taylors, Greenville, Pop. 19,619
Greenville County SD
Supt. — See Greenville
Eastside HS 1,300/9-12
1300 Brushy Creek Rd 29687 864-292-7715
Sheryl Taylor, prin. Fax 292-7328
Northwood MS 1,000/6-8
710 Ikes Rd 29687 864-292-7640
Richard Griffin, prin. Fax 292-7645

Tigerville, Greenville

North Greenville University Post-Sec.
PO Box 1892 29688 864-977-7000

Timmonsville, Florence, Pop. 2,335
Florence County SD 4 1,100/PK-12
220 N Pinckney St 29161 843-346-5391
Dr. Charles Gadsden, supt. Fax 346-3145
www.florence4.k12.sc.us
Johnson MS 200/6-8
304 Kemper St 29161 843-346-4685
Ronald Bowser, prin. Fax 346-5199
Timmonsville HS 300/9-12
304 Kemper St 29161 843-346-4586
Fax 346-5416

Travelers Rest, Greenville, Pop. 3,948
Greenville County SD
Supt. — See Greenville
Northwest MS 900/6-8
1606 Geer Hwy 29690 864-834-6434
Lee Givins, prin. Fax 834-6429
Travelers Rest HS 1,300/9-12
115 Wilhelm Winter St 29690 864-834-6464
Louis E. Lavely, prin. Fax 834-6804

Turbeville, Clarendon, Pop. 718
Clarendon SD 3 1,300/K-12
PO Box 270 29162 843-659-2188
Dr. Mary Rice-Crenshaw, supt. Fax 659-3204
www.clarendon3.org/
East Clarendon HS 400/9-12
PO Box 67 29162 843-659-2185
Dwayne Howell, prin. Fax 659-8933
East Clarendon MS 300/6-8
PO Box 153 29162 843-659-2187
Carol Lenderman, prin. Fax 659-2192

Union, Union, Pop. 8,431
Union County SD 4,900/K-12
PO Box 907 29379 864-429-1740
Dr. Thomas White, supt. Fax 429-1745
www.union.k12.sc.us

Sims JHS | 600/7-8
200 Sims Dr 29379 | 864-429-1755
Mickey Connolly, prin. | Fax 429-1798
Union HS | 1,100/9-12
1163 Lakeside Dr 29379 | 864-429-1750
Kristi Woodall, prin. | Fax 429-5401
Adult Education / Lifelong Learning | Adult
517 E Main St 29379 | 864-429-1770
Henry Sparrow, dir. | Fax 429-1771
Other Schools – See Jonesville, Lockhart

University of South Carolina | Post-Sec.
PO Box 729 29379 | 864-429-8728

Varnville, Hampton, Pop. 2,057
Hampton SD 1 | 3,000/PK-12
372 E Pine St 29944 | 803-943-4576
Dr. Terry Pruitt, supt. | Fax 943-5943
www.hampton1.k12.sc.us
Hampton HS | 700/9-12
115 Airport Rd 29944 | 803-943-3568
Greg Ackerman, prin. | Fax 943-5036
North District MS | 500/7-8
PO Box 368 29944 | 803-943-3507
Mark Dean, prin. | Fax 943-4074

Wagener, Aiken, Pop. 866
Aiken County SD
Supt. — See Aiken
Corbett MS | 400/5-8
10 A L Corbett Cir 29164 | 803-564-1050
Dr. Deborah Bass, prin. | Fax 564-1058
Wagener-Salley HS | 400/9-12
272 Main St S 29164 | 803-564-1100
Bryan Skipper, prin. | Fax 564-1109

Walhalla, Oconee, Pop. 3,810
Oconee County SD | 11,300/PK-12
PO Box 649 29691 | 864-886-4400
Valerie Truesdale, supt. | Fax 886-4408
www.oconee.k12.sc.us
Walhalla HS | 800/9-12
151 Razorback Ln 29691 | 864-638-4582
Evie Hughes, prin. | Fax 638-4055
Walhalla MS | 700/6-8
177 Razorback Ln 29691 | 864-638-4570
Charles Middleton, prin. | Fax 638-4576
Other Schools – See Salem, Seneca, Westminster

Walterboro, Colleton, Pop. 5,356
Colleton County SD | 6,800/PK-12
PO Box 290 29488 | 843-549-5715
Charles Gale, supt. | Fax 549-2606
www.colleton.k12.sc.us
Colleton County HS | 1,900/9-12
1379 Mighty Cougar Dr 29488 | 843-538-2904
Cliff Warren, prin. | Fax 538-8151
Colleton MS | 900/6-8
603 Colleton Loop 29488 | 843-549-2690
Shannon Stephens, prin. | Fax 549-1222
Forest Circle MS | 400/6-8
500 Forest Cir 29488 | 843-549-2361
Scott Matthews, prin. | Fax 549-5061
Thunderbolt Career & Technology Center | Vo/Tech
1069 Thunderbolt Dr 29488 | 843-538-5538
Bob McKinnon, prin. | Fax 538-3009
Other Schools – See Ruffin

Colleton Prep Academy | 500/K-12
PO Box 1426 29488 | 843-538-8959
Arthur Ellis, hdmstr. | Fax 538-8260
Family Christian Academy | 200/K-12
2107 Hampton St 29488 | 843-893-3536
Roger Quesenberry, admin. | Fax 893-2174

Ware Shoals, Greenwood, Pop. 2,352
Greenwood SD 51 | 1,300/PK-12
25 E Main St 29692 | 864-456-7496
Fay Sprouse, supt. | Fax 456-3578
www.gwd51.k12.sc.us
Ware Shoals JSHS | 600/7-12
56 S Greenwood Ave 29692 | 864-456-7923
Jane Blackwell, prin. | Fax 456-2959

Warrenville, Aiken
Aiken County SD
Supt. — See Aiken
Aiken County Career & Technical Center | Vo/Tech
2455 Jefferson Davis Hwy 29851 | 803-593-7300
Kathy Mixson, dir. | Fax 593-7115
Langley-Bath-Clearwater MS | 500/6-8
29 Lions Trl 29851 | 803-593-7260
Russell Gunter, prin. | Fax 593-7119

West Columbia, Lexington, Pop. 12,920
Lexington County SD 1
Supt. — See Lexington
White Knoll MS | 1,400/6-8
116 White Knoll Way 29170 | 803-957-4400
Nancy Turner, prin. | Fax 957-5415
Lexington SD 2 | 8,800/PK-12
715 9th St 29169 | 803-739-4001
Barry Bolen, supt. | Fax 739-4063
www.lex2.org
Airport HS | 1,400/9-12
1315 Boston Ave 29170 | 803-822-5600
Frank Jovanelly, prin. | Fax 822-5665
Fulmer MS | 700/6-8
1614 Walterboro St 29170 | 803-822-5660
Dixon Brooks, prin. | Fax 822-5664
Northside MS | 600/6-8
157 Cougar Dr 29169 | 803-739-4190
Ronny Thompkins, prin. | Fax 739-1388
Pine Ridge MS | 500/6-8
735 Pine Ridge Dr 29172 | 803-755-7400
Greg Morton, prin. | Fax 755-7449
Other Schools – See Cayce

Glenforest S | 100/K-12
1041 Harbor Dr 29169 | 803-796-7622
| Fax 796-1603
Grace Christian S | 400/K-12
416 Denham Ave 29169 | 803-794-8996
Tim Stevens, prin. | Fax 739-1204

Westminster, Oconee, Pop. 2,759
Oconee County SD
Supt. — See Walhalla
Oakway MS | 300/6-8
150 School House Rd # B 29693 | 864-972-9531
Jami Verderosa, prin. | Fax 972-0579
Westminster MS | 500/6-8
501 Westminster Hwy 29693 | 864-647-3050
Paul Ricciardi, prin. | Fax 647-1222
West-Oak HS | 900/9-12
130 Warrior Ln 29693 | 864-647-3065
Russell Claxton, prin. | Fax 647-3071

Whitmire, Newberry, Pop. 1,505
Newberry County SD
Supt. — See Newberry
Whitmire Community S | 600/K-12
2597 Highway 66 29178 | 803-694-2320
| Fax 694-3835

Williamston, Anderson, Pop. 3,817
Anderson SD 1 | 8,300/PK-12
PO Box 99 29697 | 864-847-7344
Dr. Wayne Fowler, supt. | Fax 847-3543
www.anderson1.k12.sc.us

Palmetto HS | 800/9-12
804 N Hamilton St 29697 | 864-847-7311
Dr. Mason Gary, prin. | Fax 847-3532
Palmetto MS | 700/6-8
803 N Hamilton St 29697 | 864-847-4333
Barry Knight, prin. | Fax 847-3529
Other Schools – See Greenville, Piedmont

Area Vocational Schools
Supt. — None
Career & Technology Center | Vo/Tech
702 Belton Hwy 29697 | 864-847-4121
Dr. Jerry Kirkley, dir. | Fax 847-3539

Williston, Barnwell, Pop. 3,267
Williston SD 29 | 900/K-12
12255 Main St 29853 | 803-266-7878
Alexia Clamp, supt. | Fax 266-3879
www.williston.k12.sc.us
Williston-Elko HS | 300/9-12
12233 Main St 29853 | 803-266-3110
Samuel Lax, prin. | Fax 266-5489
Williston-Elko MS | 300/5-8
12333 Main St 29853 | 803-266-3430
Dr. Eavon Hickson, prin. | Fax 266-7623

Winnsboro, Fairfield, Pop. 3,583
Fairfield County SD | 3,700/PK-12
PO Box 622 29180 | 803-635-4607
Dr. Clarence Willie, supt. | Fax 635-6578
www.fairfield.k12.sc.us/
Fairfield Career & Technology Center | Vo/Tech
1451 US Highway 321 N 29180 | 803-635-5506
Robert Sharpe, prin. | Fax 635-9958
Fairfield Central HS | 1,100/9-12
836 US Highway 321 Byp S 29180 | 803-635-1441
Nathaniel Nelson, prin. | Fax 635-3997
Fairfield MS | 600/7-8
728 US Highway 321 Byp S 29180 | 803-635-4270
Tammy Martin, prin. | Fax 635-9108

Winn Academy | 300/K-12
1796 Old Chester Rd 29180 | 803-635-5494
Elizabeth Reid, prin. | Fax 635-4310

Woodruff, Spartanburg, Pop. 4,162
Spartanburg SD 4 | 2,900/PK-12
118 McEdco Rd 29388 | 864-476-3186
Dr. W. Rallie Liston, supt. | Fax 476-8616
www.spartanburg4.org
Woodruff HS | 800/9-12
710 Cross Anchor Rd 29388 | 864-476-7045
Karen Neal, prin. | Fax 476-7224
Woodruff MS | 700/6-8
205 SJ Workman Hwy 29388 | 864-476-3150
Denise Brown, prin. | Fax 476-6036

York, York, Pop. 6,960
York SD 1 | 5,100/PK-12
PO Box 770 29745 | 803-684-9916
Russell Booker, supt. | Fax 684-1903
www.york.k12.sc.us
Johnson Technical Center | Vo/Tech
1010 Devinney Rd 29745 | 803-684-1910
Ron Roveri, prin. | Fax 684-1913
York Comprehensive HS | 1,000/10-12
1010 Devinney Rd 29745 | 803-684-2336
Diane Howell, prin. | Fax 684-1932
York JHS | 800/8-9
1280 Johnson Rd 29745 | 803-684-5008
Louvetta Dicks, prin. | Fax 684-1916

Blessed Hope Baptist S | 200/K-12
410 Blessed Hope Rd 29745 | 803-684-9819
Tommy Arrowood, prin. | Fax 684-9849

SOUTH DAKOTA

SOUTH DAKOTA DEPARTMENT OF EDUCATION
700 Governors Dr, Pierre 57501-2291
Telephone 605-773-5669
Fax 605-773-6139
Website http://www.state.sd.us/deca

Secretary of Education   Dr. Rick Melmer

SOUTH DAKOTA BOARD OF EDUCATION
700 Governors Dr, Pierre 57501-2291

President   Glenna Fouberg

PUBLIC, PRIVATE AND CATHOLIC SECONDARY SCHOOLS

Aberdeen, Brown, Pop. 24,086
Aberdeen SD 6-1 — 3,700/K-12
  314 S Main St 57401 — 605-725-7100
  Dr. Gary Harms, supt. — Fax 725-7199
  www.aberdeen.k12.sd.us
Central HS — 1,200/9-12
  2200 S Roosevelt St 57401 — 605-725-8100
  Jason Uttermark, prin. — Fax 725-8199
Holgate MS — 400/6-8
  2200 N Dakota St 57401 — 605-725-7700
  Dr. Greg Aas, prin. — Fax 725-7799
Simmons MS — 400/6-8
  1300 S 3rd St 57401 — 605-725-7900
  Jerry Heupel, prin. — Fax 725-7999

Hub Area Multi-District — 605-725-7800
  640 9th Ave SW 57401 — Fax 725-7899
  John Emmett, supt.
  www.hubarea.com
Hub Area Technical S — Vo/Tech
  640 9th Ave SW 57401 — 605-725-7800
  John Emmett, supt. — Fax 725-7899

Aberdeen Christian HS — 50/9-12
  PO Box 548 57402 — 605-226-3125
  Lynne Fuhrman, admin. — Fax 225-2873
Northern State University — Post-Sec.
  1200 S Jay St 57401 — 605-626-3011
Presentation College — Post-Sec.
  1500 N Main St 57401 — 605-225-1634
Roncalli HS — 300/7-12
  1400 N Dakota St 57401 — 605-226-2100
  Stacy Levsen, prin. — Fax 226-0616
St. Luke's Midland Regional Medical Ctr. — Post-Sec.
  305 S State St 57401 — 605-622-5230
South Dakota School Visually Handicapped — Post-Sec.
  423 17th Ave SE 57401 — 605-626-2580

Alcester, Union, Pop. 887
Alcester-Hudson SD 61-1 — 300/PK-12
  PO Box 198 57001 — 605-934-1890
  Jerry L. Joachim, supt. — Fax 934-1936
  www.alcester-hudson.k12.sd.us
Alcester-Hudson HS — 100/9-12
  PO Box 198 57001 — 605-934-1890
  LeeAnn R. Haisch, prin. — Fax 934-1936
Alcester-Hudson JHS — 100/7-8
  PO Box 198 57001 — 605-934-1890
  LeeAnn R. Haisch, prin. — Fax 934-1936

Alexandria, Hanson, Pop. 630
Hanson SD 30-1 — 400/PK-12
  PO Box 490 57311 — 605-239-4387
  John Lafave, supt. — Fax 239-4293
  www.hanson.k12.sd.us/
Hanson HS — 100/9-12
  PO Box 490 57311 — 605-239-4387
  James Bridge, prin. — Fax 239-4293
Hanson JHS — 50/7-8
  PO Box 490 57311 — 605-239-4387
  James Bridge, prin. — Fax 239-4293

Arlington, Kingsbury, Pop. 962
Arlington SD 38-1 — 300/K-12
  PO Box 359 57212 — 605-983-5597
  Chris Lund, supt. — Fax 983-4652
  www.arlington.k12.sd.us
Arlington HS — 100/9-12
  PO Box 359 57212 — 605-983-5598
  Rhonda Gross, prin. — Fax 983-4652
Arlington JHS — 100/7-8
  PO Box 359 57212 — 605-983-5598
  Rhonda Gross, prin. — Fax 983-4652

Armour, Douglas, Pop. 741
Armour SD 21-1 — 200/K-12
  PO Box 640 57313 — 605-724-2153
  Wallace Weatherford, supt. — Fax 724-2977
  www.armour.k12.sd.us/
Armour HS — 100/9-12
  PO Box 640 57313 — 605-724-2153
  Brad Preheim, prin. — Fax 724-2799
Armour MS — 100/5-8
  PO Box 640 57313 — 605-724-2698
  Wallace Weatherford, prin. — Fax 724-2799

Avon, Bon Homme, Pop. 548
Avon SD 4-1 — 300/PK-12
  PO Box 407 57315 — 605-286-3291
  Tom Oster, supt. — Fax 286-3712
  www.avon.k12.sd.us/
Avon HS — 100/9-12
  PO Box 407 57315 — 605-286-3291
  Tom Culver, prin. — Fax 286-3510
Avon JHS — 50/7-8
  PO Box 407 57315 — 605-286-3291
  Tom Culver, prin. — Fax 286-3712

Baltic, Minnehaha, Pop. 899
Baltic SD 49-1 — 300/PK-12
  PO Box 309 57003 — 605-529-5461
  Robert Sittig, supt. — Fax 529-5467
  www.baltic.k12.sd.us/
Baltic HS — 100/9-12
  PO Box 309 57003 — 605-529-5461
  James Aisenbery, prin. — Fax 529-5467
Baltic MS — 100/6-8
  PO Box 309 57003 — 605-529-5461
  James Aisenbery, prin. — Fax 529-5467

Belle Fourche, Butte, Pop. 4,577
Belle Fourche SD 9-1 — 1,300/PK-12
  2305 13th Ave 57717 — 605-723-3355
  William O'Dea, supt. — Fax 723-3366
  www.bellefourche.k12.sd.us/
Belle Fourche HS — 400/9-12
  2305 13th Ave 57717 — 605-723-3350
  Steve Willard, prin. — Fax 723-3357
Belle Fourche MS — 400/5-8
  2305 13th Ave 57717 — 605-723-3367
  Karen Wagner, prin. — Fax 723-3374

Beresford, Union, Pop. 1,956
Beresford SD 61-2 — 700/PK-12
  209 S 4th St 57004 — 605-763-5012
  Vince Schaefer, supt. — Fax 763-2205
  www.beresford.k12.sd.us/
Beresford HS — 200/9-12
  301 W Maple St 57004 — 605-763-2145
  Mike Embrock, prin. — Fax 763-5305
Beresford JHS — 100/7-8
  205 W Maple St 57004 — 605-763-2139
  Mike Embrock, prin. — Fax 763-5305

Big Stone City, Grant, Pop. 591
Big Stone CSD 25-1 — 100/PK-8
  655 Walnut St 57216 — 605-862-8108
  Ellen M. Helgeson, supt. — Fax 862-8640
  www.bigstonecity.k12.sd.us/
Big Stone City JHS — 50/7-8
  655 Walnut St 57216 — 605-862-8108
  Ellen Helgeson, prin. — Fax 862-8640

Bison, Perkins, Pop. 360
Bison SD 52-1 — 100/K-12
  PO Box 9 57620 — 605-244-5271
  Sharon Soehren, admin. — Fax 244-5275
  www.bison.k12.sd.us/
Bison HS — 50/9-12
  PO Box 9 57620 — 605-244-5961
  Sharon Soehren, prin. — Fax 244-5276
Bison JHS — 50/7-8
  PO Box 9 57620 — 605-244-5961
  Sharon Soehren, prin. — Fax 244-5276

Bonesteel, Gregory, Pop. 281
Bonesteel-Fairfax SD 26-5 — 200/PK-12
  PO Box 410 57317 — 605-654-2314
  Jess Toliver, supt. — Fax 654-2348
  www.bonesteel-fairfax.k12.sd.us/
Bonesteel-Fairfax HS — 100/9-12
  PO Box 410 57317 — 605-654-2314
  Ray Slaba, prin. — Fax 654-2348
Bonesteel-Fairfax JHS — 50/7-8
  PO Box 410 57317 — 605-654-2314
  Ray Slaba, prin. — Fax 654-2348

Bowdle, Edmunds, Pop. 542
Bowdle SD 22-1 — 100/K-12
  PO Box 563 57428 — 605-285-6272
  Richard Ulrich, supt. — Fax 285-6830
  www.bowdle.k12.sd.us
Bowdle HS — 50/9-12
  PO Box 563 57428 — 605-285-6590
  Richard Ulrich, prin. — Fax 285-6830

Bowdle JHS — 50/7-8
  PO Box 563 57428 — 605-285-6590
  Richard Ulrich, prin. — Fax 285-6830

Box Elder, Pennington, Pop. 2,884
Douglas SD 51-1 — 2,500/PK-12
  400 Patriot Dr 57719 — 605-923-0000
  Dr. Loren Scheer, supt. — Fax 923-0018
  www.dsdk12.net
Douglas HS — 700/9-12
  420 Patriot Dr 57719 — 605-923-0030
  Bud Gusso, prin. — Fax 923-0031
Douglas MS — 600/6-8
  401 Tower Rd 57719 — 605-923-0050
  Lee Thomas, prin. — Fax 923-0051

Brandon, Minnehaha, Pop. 6,522
Brandon Valley SD 49-2 — 2,700/PK-12
  301 S Splitrock Blvd 57005 — 605-582-2049
  George Gulson, supt. — Fax 582-7456
  www.brandonvalleyschools.com
Brandon Valley HS — 800/9-12
  301 S Splitrock Blvd 57005 — 605-582-3211
  Gregg Talcott, prin. — Fax 582-2652
Brandon Valley MS — 600/6-8
  700 E Holly Blvd 57005 — 605-582-3214
  Dan Pansch, prin. — Fax 582-7206

Bridgewater, McCook, Pop. 592
Bridgewater SD 43-6 — 200/PK-12
  PO Box 350 57319 — 605-729-2541
  Jason Bailey, admin. — Fax 729-2580
  www.bridgewater.k12.sd.us/
Bridgewater HS — 100/9-12
  PO Box 350 57319 — 605-729-2541
  Christena Schultz, prin. — Fax 729-2580
Bridgewater MS — 50/6-8
  PO Box 350 57319 — 605-729-2541
  Christena Schultz, prin. — Fax 729-2580

Britton, Marshall, Pop. 1,245
Britton-Hecla SD 45-4 — 500/PK-12
  PO Box 190 57430 — 605-448-2234
  Donald Kirkegaard, supt. — Fax 448-5994
  www.britton.k12.sd.us/
Britton-Hecla HS — 200/9-12
  PO Box 190 57430 — 605-448-2234
  Marcia Forrester, prin. — Fax 448-5994
Britton-Hecla JHS — 100/7-8
  PO Box 190 57430 — 605-448-2234
  Marcia Forrester, prin. — Fax 448-5994

Brookings, Brookings, Pop. 18,464
Brookings SD 5-1 — 2,700/PK-12
  2130 8th St S 57006 — 605-696-4700
  Orville Creighton, supt. — Fax 696-4704
  www.brookings.k12.sd.us/
Brookings HS — 800/9-12
  530 Elm Ave 57006 — 605-696-4100
  Douglas Beste, prin. — Fax 696-4128
Mickelson MS — 600/6-8
  1801 12th St S 57006 — 605-696-4500
  Dan Neiles, prin. — Fax 696-4506

East Central Multi-District — 605-696-4754
  700 Elm Ave 57006 — Fax 696-4765
  Fran Schoenfelder, supt.
  www.ecmdmulti.com
Select HS — Vo/Tech
  504 3rd Ave 57006 — 605-696-4766
  Gayle Klinker, prin. — Fax 696-4768

South Dakota State University — Post-Sec.
  PO Box 2201 57007 — 605-688-4151

Buffalo, Harding, Pop. 364
Harding County SD 31-1 — 300/K-12
  PO Box 367 57720 — 605-375-3241
  Kirby Baier, supt. — Fax 375-3246
  www.hardingcounty.k12.sd.us/
Harding County HS — 100/9-12
  PO Box 367 57720 — 605-375-3241
  Kirby Baier, prin. — Fax 375-3246
Harding County JHS — 50/7-8
  PO Box 367 57720 — 605-375-3241
  Kirby Baier, prin. — Fax 375-3246

Burke, Gregory, Pop. 640
Burke SD 26-2 — 200/K-12
  PO Box 382 57523 — 605-775-2644
  Kirby Baier, supt. — Fax 775-2468
Burke HS — 100/9-12
  PO Box 382 57523 — 605-775-2645
  Randy DeWolf, prin. — Fax 775-2468
Burke JHS — 50/6-8
  PO Box 382 57523 — 605-775-2645
  Randy Dewolf, prin. — Fax 775-2468

Canistota, McCook, Pop. 704
Canistota SD 43-1 — 300/K-12
  PO Box 8 57012 — 605-296-3458
  Wayne Wormstadt, supt. — Fax 296-3158
  www.canistota.k12.sd.us
Canistota HS — 100/9-12
  PO Box 8 57012 — 605-296-3458
  Kenneth Myers, prin. — Fax 296-3158
Canistota JHS — 50/7-8
  PO Box 8 57012 — 605-296-3458
  Kenneth Myers, prin. — Fax 296-3158

Canton, Lincoln, Pop. 2,955
Canton SD 41-1 — 1,000/PK-12
  800 N Main St 57013 — 605-764-2706
  Terry Majeres, supt. — Fax 764-2700
  www.canton.k12.sd.us
Canton HS — 300/9-12
  800 N Main St 57013 — 605-764-2706
  Tim Hazlett, prin. — Fax 764-2700
Canton MS — 200/6-8
  800 N Main St 57013 — 605-764-2706
  Terry Gerber, prin. — Fax 764-2700

Castlewood, Hamlin, Pop. 685
Castlewood SD 28-1 — 300/K-12
  310 E Harry St 57223 — 605-793-2497
  Keith Fodness, supt. — Fax 793-2679
  www.castlewood.k12.sd.us/
Castlewood HS — 100/9-12
  310 E Harry St 57223 — 605-793-2497
  Keith Fodness, prin. — Fax 793-2679
Castlewood JHS — 50/7-8
  310 E Harry St 57223 — 605-793-2497
  Keith Fodness, prin. — Fax 793-2679

Centerville, Turner, Pop. 876
Centerville SD 60-1 — 300/K-12
  PO Box 100 57014 — 605-563-2291
  Doug Voss, supt. — Fax 563-2615
  www.centerville.k12.sd.us
Centerville HS — 100/9-12
  PO Box 100 57014 — 605-563-2291
  Roger Hansen, prin. — Fax 563-2615
Centerville JHS — 50/7-8
  PO Box 100 57014 — 605-563-2291
  Roger Hansen, prin. — Fax 563-2615

Chamberlain, Brule, Pop. 2,279
Chamberlain SD 7-1 — 900/PK-12
  PO Box 119 57325 — 605-734-4477
  Tim Mitchell, supt. — Fax 734-4479
  www.cubs.org/
Chamberlain HS — 300/9-12
  PO Box 119 57325 — 605-734-4467
  Deb Johnson, prin. — Fax 734-4479
Chamberlain MS — 100/7-8
  PO Box 119 57325 — 605-734-4467
  Deb Johnson, prin. — Fax 734-4479

Chester, Lake
Chester Area SD 39-1 — 400/PK-12
  PO Box 159 57016 — 605-489-2416
  Mark Greguson, supt. — Fax 489-2413
  www.chester.k12.sd.us
Chester HS — 100/9-12
  PO Box 159 57016 — 605-489-2411
  Michael Reinhiller, prin. — Fax 489-2413
Chester JHS — 50/7-8
  PO Box 159 57016 — 605-489-2411
  Michael Reinhiller, prin. — Fax 489-2413

Clark, Clark, Pop. 1,215
Clark SD 12-2 — 500/PK-12
  220 N Clinton St 57225 — 605-532-3603
  Jim Holbeck, supt. — Fax 532-3600
  clark.k12.sd.us/
Clark HS — 100/9-12
  220 N Clinton St 57225 — 605-532-3605
  Jerry Hartley, prin. — Fax 532-3600
Clark JHS — 100/7-8
  220 N Clinton St 57225 — 605-532-3605
  Jerry Hartley, prin. — Fax 532-3600

Clear Lake, Deuel, Pop. 1,291
Deuel SD 19-4 — 600/PK-12
  PO Box 770 57226 — 605-874-2161
  Dean Christensen, supt. — Fax 874-8585
  www.deuel.k12.sd.us/
Clear Lake MS — 100/6-8
  PO Box 770 57226 — 605-874-2162
  Tim Steffensen, prin. — Fax 874-8585
Deuel HS — 200/9-12
  PO Box 770 57226 — 605-874-2163
  Steve Benson, prin. — Fax 874-8585

Colman, Moody, Pop. 561
Colman-Egan SD 50-5 — 300/K-12
  PO Box 1 57017 — 605-534-3534
  Roger Fritz, supt. — Fax 534-3670
  www.colman-egan.k12.sd.us
Colman-Egan HS — 100/9-12
  PO Box 1 57017 — 605-534-3534
  Terrance Stulken, prin. — Fax 534-3670
Colman-Egan JHS — 50/7-8
  PO Box 1 57017 — 605-534-3534
  Terrance Stulken, prin. — Fax 534-3670

Colome, Tripp, Pop. 322
Colome SD 59-1 — 200/K-12
  PO Box 367 57528 — 605-842-1624
  Alan Armstrong, supt. — Fax 842-0783
  www.colome.k12.sd.us/

Colome HS — 100/9-12
  PO Box 367 57528 — 605-842-1624
  Alan Armstrong, prin. — Fax 842-0783
Colome JHS — 50/7-8
  PO Box 367 57528 — 605-842-1624
  Alan Armstrong, prin. — Fax 842-0783

Colton, Minnehaha, Pop. 664
Tri-Valley SD 49-6 — 800/PK-12
  46450 252nd St 57018 — 605-446-3538
  Terry Eckstaine, supt. — Fax 446-3520
  www.tri-valley.k12.sd.us/
Tri-Valley HS — 200/9-12
  46450 252nd St 57018 — 605-446-3538
  Tim Pflanz, prin. — Fax 446-3520
Tri-Valley MS — 100/7-8
  46450 252nd St 57018 — 605-446-3538
  Tim Pflanz, prin. — Fax 446-3520

Conde, Spink, Pop. 173
Conde SD 56-1 — 100/PK-12
  PO Box 10 57434 — 605-382-5231
  Roger Youngman, supt. — Fax 382-5650
  www.conde.k12.sd.us
Conde HS — 50/9-12
  PO Box 10 57434 — 605-382-5231
  Matt Pollock, prin. — Fax 382-5650
Conde JHS — 50/7-8
  PO Box 10 57434 — 605-382-5231
  Matt Pollock, prin. — Fax 382-5650

Corsica, Douglas, Pop. 625
Corsica SD 21-2 — 200/PK-12
  PO Box 299 57328 — 605-946-5475
  Vern DeGeest, supt. — Fax 946-5607
  www.corsica.k12.sd.us
Corsica HS — 100/9-12
  PO Box 299 57328 — 605-946-5475
  Scott Muckey, prin. — Fax 946-5607
Corsica MS — 50/6-8
  PO Box 299 57328 — 605-946-5475
  Vern Degeest, prin. — Fax 946-5607

Custer, Custer, Pop. 1,860
Custer SD 16-1 — 1,300/PK-12
  147 N 5th St 57730 — 605-673-3154
  Dr. Tim Creal, supt. — Fax 673-5607
  www.csd.k12.sd.us
Custer HS — 300/9-12
  504 Bluebell Ln 57730 — 605-673-4473
  Larry Luitjens, prin. — Fax 673-4710
Custer MS — 200/6-8
  527 Montgomery St 57730 — 605-673-4540
  Larry Luitjens, prin. — Fax 673-4710

Dell Rapids, Minnehaha, Pop. 3,115
Dell Rapids SD 49-3 — 1,000/PK-12
  1216 Garfield Ave 57022 — 605-428-5473
  Thomas Ludens, supt. — Fax 428-5609
  www.dellrapids.k12.sd.us/district
Dell Rapids HS — 300/9-12
  1216 Garfield Ave 57022 — 605-428-5473
  Bruce Olson, prin. — Fax 428-5609
Dell Rapids MS — 300/5-8
  1216 Garfield Ave 57022 — 605-428-5473
  Mary Kay Swanson, prin. — Fax 428-5609

St. Mary HS — 100/7-12
  812 State Ave 57022 — 605-428-5591
  Francis Ruesink, prin. — Fax 428-5377

De Smet, Kingsbury, Pop. 1,100
De Smet SD 38-2 — 300/K-12
  PO Box 157 57231 — 605-854-3070
  Brian Heupel, supt. — Fax 854-9138
  www.desmet.k12.sd.us
De Smet HS — 100/9-12
  PO Box 157 57231 — 605-854-3423
  Larry Janish, prin. — Fax 854-9138
De Smet MS — 100/6-8
  PO Box 157 57231 — 605-854-3423
  Jim Altenburg, prin. — Fax 854-9138

Doland, Spink, Pop. 274
Doland SD 56-2 — 200/K-12
  PO Box 385 57436 — 605-635-6302
  Joel Druley, supt. — Fax 635-6504
  www.doland.k12.sd.us/
Doland HS — 50/9-12
  PO Box 385 57436 — 605-635-6241
  Scott Pudwill, prin. — Fax 635-6504
Doland JHS — 50/7-8
  PO Box 385 57436 — 605-635-6241
  Scott Pudwill, prin. — Fax 635-6504

Dupree, Ziebach, Pop. 438
Dupree SD 24-2 — 300/K-12
  PO Box 10 57623 — 605-365-5140
  Vernon Starr, supt. — Fax 365-5514
  www.dupree.k12.sd.us
Dupree HS — 100/9-12
  PO Box 10 57623 — 605-365-5140
  Carol Veit, prin. — Fax 365-5514
Dupree JHS — 50/7-8
  PO Box 10 57623 — 605-365-5140
  Carol Veit, prin. — Fax 365-5514

Eagle Butte, Dewey, Pop. 665
Eagle Butte SD 20-1 — 400/PK-12
  PO Box 260 57625 — 605-964-4911
  Brian Jones, supt. — Fax 964-4912
Eagle Butte HS — 50/9-12
  PO Box 672 57625 — 605-964-8744
  Cynthia McCrea, prin. — Fax 964-8700
Eagle Butte JHS — 50/7-8
  PO Box 672 57625 — 605-964-7841
  Jesse Mendoza, prin. — Fax 964-1224

Si Tanka University — Post-Sec.
  PO Box 220 57625 — 605-964-8011

Edgemont, Fall River, Pop. 823
Edgemont SD 23-1 — 200/K-12
  PO Box 29 57735 — 605-662-7254
  Lane Ostenson, supt. — Fax 662-7721
  edgemont.k12.sd.us
Edgemont HS — 100/9-12
  PO Box 29 57735 — 605-662-7254
  Linda Tidball, prin. — Fax 662-7721
Edgemont JHS — 50/7-8
  PO Box 29 57735 — 605-662-7254
  Linda Tidball, prin. — Fax 662-7721

Elk Point, Union, Pop. 1,795
Elk Point-Jefferson SD 61-7 — 700/PK-12
  PO Box 578 57025 — 605-356-5951
  Brian Shanks, supt. — Fax 356-5953
  www.epj.k12.sd.us/
Elk Point-Jefferson HS — 200/9-12
  PO Box 578 57025 — 605-356-5901
  Travis Aslesen, prin. — Fax 356-5999
Elk Point-Jefferson MS — 100/7-8
  PO Box 578 57025 — 605-356-5901
  Travis Aslesen, prin. — Fax 356-5999

Elkton, Brookings, Pop. 633
Elkton SD 5-3 — 400/K-12
  PO Box 190 57026 — 605-542-5361
  Gordon Fuhr, supt. — Fax 542-4441
  elktonps.org/
Elkton HS — 100/9-12
  PO Box 190 57026 — 605-542-2541
  Michael Cullen, prin. — Fax 542-4441
Elkton JHS — 100/7-8
  PO Box 190 57026 — 605-542-2541
  Michael Cullen, prin. — Fax 542-4441

Ellsworth AFB, Meade, Pop. 7,017

National American University — Post-Sec.
  1270 Ryan St 57706 — 605-923-5856

Emery, Hanson, Pop. 490
Emery SD 30-2 — 200/PK-12
  PO Box 265 57332 — 605-449-4271
  Jason Bailey, supt. — Fax 449-4270
Emery HS — 100/9-12
  PO Box 265 57332 — 605-449-4271
  Christena Schultz, prin. — Fax 449-4270
Emery JHS — 50/6-8
  PO Box 265 57332 — 605-449-4271
  Christena Schultz, prin. — Fax 449-4270

Estelline, Hamlin, Pop. 687
Estelline SD 28-2 — 300/K-12
  PO Box 306 57234 — 605-873-2201
  Dennis Rieckman, supt. — Fax 873-2102
  www.estelline.k12.sd.us
Estelline HS — 100/9-12
  PO Box 306 57234 — 605-873-2201
  Dennis Rieckman, prin. — Fax 873-2102

Ethan, Davison, Pop. 320
Ethan SD 17-1 — 200/PK-12
  PO Box 169 57334 — 605-227-4211
  Terry Mathis, supt. — Fax 227-4236
  www.ethan.k12.sd.us/
Ethan HS — 100/9-12
  PO Box 169 57334 — 605-227-4211
  Todd Cavanaugh, prin. — Fax 227-4236
Ethan MS — 100/6-8
  PO Box 169 57334 — 605-227-4211
  Todd Cavanaugh, prin. — Fax 227-4236

Eureka, McPherson, Pop. 1,025
Eureka SD 44-1 — 200/K-12
  PO Box 10 57437 — 605-284-2875
  Dr. Peggy Petersen, supt. — Fax 284-2810
  www.eureka.k12.sd.us/
Eureka HS — 100/9-12
  PO Box 10 57437 — 605-284-2521
  Bo Beck, prin. — Fax 284-2810
Eureka JHS — 50/7-8
  PO Box 10 57437 — 605-284-2521
  Bo Beck, prin. — Fax 284-2810

Faith, Meade, Pop. 499
Faith SD 46-2 — 200/K-12
  PO Box 619 57626 — 605-967-2152
  Mel Dutton, supt. — Fax 967-2153
  www.faith.k12.sd.us/
Faith HS — 100/9-12
  PO Box 619 57626 — 605-967-2152
  Mel Dutton, prin. — Fax 967-2153
Faith JHS — 50/7-8
  PO Box 619 57626 — 605-967-2152
  Michelle Becker, prin. — Fax 967-2153

Faulkton, Faulk, Pop. 739
Faulkton SD 24-2 — 400/K-12
  PO Box 308 57438 — 605-598-6266
  Joel Price, supt. — Fax 598-6666
  www.faulkton.k12.sd.us
Faulkton HS — 100/9-12
  PO Box 308 57438 — 605-598-6266
  Craig Cassens, prin. — Fax 598-6666
Faulkton JHS — 100/7-8
  PO Box 308 57438 — 605-598-6266
  Craig Cassens, prin. — Fax 598-6666

Flandreau, Moody, Pop. 2,323
Flandreau SD 50-3 — 800/K-12
  600 W Community Dr 57028 — 605-997-3263
  Rick Weber, supt. — Fax 997-2457
  www.flandreau.k12.sd.us
Flandreau HS — 200/9-12
  600 W Community Dr 57028 — 605-997-2455
  Janna Ellingson, prin. — Fax 997-2457
Flandreau MS — 200/6-8
  700 W Community Dr 57028 — 605-997-2705
  Brian Relf, prin. — Fax 997-2457

Florence, Codington, Pop. 300
Florence SD 14-1 — 200/PK-12
  PO Box 66 57235 — 605-758-2412
  Gary Leighton, supt. — Fax 758-2433
  www.florence.k12.sd.us/

Florence HS   100/9-12
   PO Box 66 57235   605-758-2412
   Gary Leighton, prin.   Fax 758-2433
Florence JHS   50/7-8
   PO Box 66 57235   605-758-2412
   Gary Leighton, prin.   Fax 758-2433

Forestburg, Sanborn
Sanborn Central SD 55-5   200/K-12
   40405 SD Highway 34 57314   605-495-4183
   Linda Whitney, supt.   Fax 495-4185
   www.artesian-letcher.com/
Sanborn Central HS   100/9-12
   40405 SD Highway 34 57314   605-495-4183
   Linda Whitney, prin.   Fax 495-4185
Sanborn Central MS   50/6-8
   40405 SD Highway 34 57314   605-495-4183
   Connie Vermeulen, prin.   Fax 495-4185

Fort Pierre, Stanley, Pop. 1,998
Stanley County SD 57-1   600/K-12
   PO Box 370 57532   605-223-7741
   Larry Jaske, supt.   Fax 223-7750
   www.stanleycounty.k12.sd.us
Stanley County HS   200/9-12
   PO Box 370 57532   605-223-7743
   Brian Doherty, prin.   Fax 223-7751
Stanley County MS   100/6-8
   PO Box 370 57532   605-223-7743
   Brian Doherty, prin.   Fax 223-7751

Frederick, Brown, Pop. 244
Frederick Area SD 6-2   200/PK-12
   PO Box 486 57441   605-329-2145
   Randall Barondeau, supt.   Fax 329-2722
Frederick HS   100/9-12
   PO Box 486 57441   605-329-2145
   Randy Barondeau, prin.   Fax 329-2722
Frederick JHS   50/7-8
   PO Box 486 57441   605-329-2145
   Randy Barondeau, prin.   Fax 329-2722

Freeman, Hutchinson, Pop. 1,265
Freeman SD 33-1   400/K-12
   PO Box 220 57029   605-925-4214
   Don Hotchkiss, supt.   Fax 925-4814
   www.freeman.k12.sd.us/
Freeman HS   100/9-12
   PO Box 220 57029   605-925-4214
   Kim Krull, prin.   Fax 925-4814
Freeman JHS   50/7-8
   PO Box 220 57029   605-925-4214
   Kim Krull, prin.   Fax 925-4814

Freeman Academy   100/5-12
   PO Box 1000 57029   605-925-4237

Garretson, Minnehaha, Pop. 1,148
Garretson SD 49-4   500/K-12
   PO Box C 57030   605-594-3451
   Robert Arend, supt.   Fax 594-3443
   www.garretson.k12.sd.us/
Garretson HS   200/9-12
   PO Box C 57030   605-594-3452
   Ryan Van Zee, prin.   Fax 594-3443
Garretson MS   100/6-8
   PO Box C 57030   605-594-3452
   Ryan Van Zee, prin.   Fax 594-3443

Gayville, Yankton, Pop. 399
Gayville-Volin SD 63-1   300/K-12
   PO Box 158 57031   605-267-4476
   Jasons Selchert, supt.   Fax 267-4294
   www.gayvillevolin.k12.sd.us/
Gayville-Volin HS   100/9-12
   PO Box 158 57031   605-267-4476
   Natasha Gault, prin.   Fax 267-4294
Gayville-Volin MS   100/6-8
   PO Box 158 57031   605-267-4476
   Natasha Gault, prin.   Fax 267-4294

Geddes, Charles Mix, Pop. 247
Geddes Community SD 11-2   100/PK-12
   PO Box 197 57342   605-337-3382
   Sandy Gant, admin.   Fax 337-3383
   www.geddes.k12.sd.us/
Geddes HS   50/9-12
   PO Box 197 57342   605-337-3382
   Sandy Gant, prin.   Fax 337-3383
Geddes JHS   50/7-8
   PO Box 197 57342   605-337-3382
   Sandy Gant, prin.   Fax 337-3383

Gettysburg, Potter, Pop. 1,257
Gettysburg SD 53-1   300/K-12
   100 E King Ave 57442   605-765-2438
   Jeff Marlette, supt.   Fax 765-2249
   www.gettysburg.k12.sd.us/
Gettysburg HS   100/9-12
   100 E King Ave 57442   605-765-2436
   Duane Sundberg, prin.   Fax 765-2249
Gettysburg JHS   100/6-8
   100 E King Ave 57442   605-765-2436
   Duane Sundberg, prin.   Fax 765-2249

Gregory, Gregory, Pop. 1,246
Gregory SD 26-4   500/K-12
   PO Box 438 57533   605-835-8771
   David Nicholas, supt.   Fax 835-8744
   www.gregory.k12.sd.us/
Gregory HS   200/9-12
   PO Box 438 57533   605-835-9672
   Michael Dacy, prin.   Fax 835-8146
Gregory MS   100/6-8
   PO Box 438 57533   605-835-9672
   Michael Dacy, prin.   Fax 835-8146

Groton, Brown, Pop. 1,338
Groton SD 6-3   600/PK-12
   PO Box 410 57445   605-397-2351
   Larry Klapperich, supt.   Fax 397-8453
   www.groton.k12.sd.us
Groton HS   200/9-12
   PO Box 410 57445   605-397-8381
   Laura Schuster, prin.   Fax 397-8453

Groton JHS   100/7-8
   PO Box 410 57445   605-397-8381
   Laura Schuster, prin.   Fax 397-8453

Harrisburg, Lincoln, Pop. 1,031
Harrisburg SD 41-2   1,000/PK-12
   200 Willow St 57032   605-743-2567
   James Hargens, supt.   Fax 743-2569
   www.harrisburg.k12.sd.us
Harrisburg HS   300/9-12
   600 S Cliff Ave 57032   605-743-2567
   Keith Huber, prin.   Fax 743-5630
Harrisburg MS   200/6-8
   200 Willow St 57032   605-743-2567
   Tim Barth, prin.   Fax 743-2569

Harrold, Hughes, Pop. 207
Harrold SD 32-1   100/K-12
   PO Box 160 57536   605-875-3298
   Ward Thelen, supt.   Fax 875-3274
Harrold HS   50/9-12
   PO Box 160 57536   605-875-3298
   Ward Thelen, prin.   Fax 875-3274
Harrold JHS   50/7-8
   PO Box 160 57536   605-875-3298
   Ward Thelen, prin.   Fax 875-3274

Hartford, Minnehaha, Pop. 1,968
West Central SD 49-7   1,200/PK-12
   PO Box 730 57033   605-528-3217
   Paul Gausman, supt.   Fax 528-3219
   www.westcentral.k12.sd.us/
West Central HS   400/9-12
   PO Box 730 57033   605-528-6236
   Mark Hofer, prin.   Fax 528-6217
West Central MS   300/6-8
   PO Box 730 57033   605-528-3799
   Guy Johnson, prin.   Fax 528-3702

Hayti, Hamlin, Pop. 368
Hamlin SD 28-3   600/PK-12
   44577 188th St 57241   605-783-3631
   Joel Jorgenson, supt.   Fax 783-3632
   www.hamlin.k12.sd.us/
Hamlin HS   200/9-12
   44577 188th St 57241   605-783-3644
   Richard Schneider, prin.   Fax 783-3360
Hamlin MS   100/7-8
   44577 188th St 57241   605-783-3631
   Richard Schneider, prin.   Fax 783-3632

Henry, Codington, Pop. 264
Henry SD 14-2   200/K-12
   PO Box 8 57243   605-532-5364
   Lee Quale, supt.   Fax 532-3795
   www.henry.k12.sd.us/
Henry HS   100/9-12
   PO Box 8 57243   605-532-5364
   Lee Quale, prin.   Fax 532-3795
Henry JHS   50/7-8
   PO Box 8 57243   605-532-5364
   Lee Quale, prin.   Fax 532-5364

Herreid, Campbell, Pop. 449
Herreid SD 10-1   100/K-12
   PO Box 276 57632   605-437-2263
   Mike Elsberry, supt.   Fax 437-2264
Herreid HS   50/9-12
   PO Box 276 57632   605-437-2263
   Mike Elsberry, prin.   Fax 437-2264
Herreid JHS   50/6-8
   PO Box 276 57632   605-437-2263
   Mike Elsberry, prin.   Fax 437-2264

Highmore, Hyde, Pop. 790
Hyde SD 34-1   300/PK-12
   PO Box 416 57345   605-852-2389
   Michael Ruth, supt.   Fax 852-2295
Highmore HS   100/9-12
   PO Box 416 57345   605-852-2275
   James Jones, prin.   Fax 852-2295
Highmore JHS   50/7-8
   PO Box 416 57345   605-852-2275
   James Jones, prin.   Fax 852-2295

Hill City, Pennington, Pop. 820
Hill City SD 51-2   500/PK-12
   PO Box 659 57745   605-574-3030
   Donald Emch, supt.   Fax 574-3031
   www.hillcity.k12.sd.us
Hill City HS   200/9-12
   PO Box 659 57745   605-574-3005
   Todd Satter, prin.   Fax 574-3040
Hill City MS   100/6-8
   PO Box 659 57745   605-574-3025
   Mark Naugle, prin.   Fax 574-3044

Hot Springs, Fall River, Pop. 4,038
Hot Springs SD 23-2   900/PK-12
   1609 University Ave 57747   605-745-4145
   Vern Hagedorn, supt.   Fax 745-4178
   www.hssd.k12.sd.us
Hot Springs HS   300/9-12
   146 N 16th St 57747   605-745-4147
   Mary Weiss, prin.   Fax 745-4061
Hot Springs MS   200/6-8
   1609 University Ave 57747   605-745-4146
   Mary Weiss, prin.   Fax 745-6387

Hoven, Potter, Pop. 464
Hoven SD 53-2   200/K-12
   PO Box 128 57450   605-948-2252
   Ron Jacobson, supt.   Fax 948-2477
Hoven HS   100/9-12
   PO Box 128 57450   605-948-2252
   Ron Jacobson, prin.   Fax 948-2477
Hoven JHS   50/7-8
   PO Box 128 57450   605-948-2252
   Ron Jacobson, prin.   Fax 948-2477

Howard, Miner, Pop. 1,000
Howard SD 48-3   400/PK-12
   500 N Section Line St 57349   605-772-5515
   Bruce Wendling, supt.   Fax 772-5516
   www.howard.k12.sd.us/default.htm

Howard HS   200/9-12
   500 N Section Line St 57349   605-772-5515
   Bruce Wendling, prin.   Fax 772-5516
Howard JHS   100/7-8
   500 N Section Line St 57349   605-772-5515
   Bruce Wendling, prin.   Fax 772-5516

Hurley, Turner, Pop. 408
Hurley SD 60-2   200/K-12
   PO Box 278 57036   605-238-5221
   Shane Voss, supt.   Fax 238-5223
Hurley HS   50/9-12
   PO Box 278 57036   605-238-5221
   Shane Voss, prin.   Fax 238-5223
Hurley JHS   50/7-8
   PO Box 278 57036   605-238-5221
   Shane Voss, prin.   Fax 238-5223

Huron, Beadle, Pop. 11,377
Huron SD 2-2   2,200/K-12
   PO Box 949 57350   605-353-6990
   Randall Zitterkopf, supt.   Fax 353-6993
   www.huron.k12.sd.us
Huron HS   700/9-12
   801 18th St SW 57350   605-353-8800
   Terry Nebelsick, prin.   Fax 353-8807
Huron MS   500/6-8
   1045 18th St SW 57350   605-353-8900
   Michael Taplett, prin.   Fax 353-8913

James Valley Christian S   200/PK-12
   1550 Dakota Ave N 57350   605-352-7737
   Paula Kleinsasser, admin.   Fax 352-9893

Ipswich, Edmunds, Pop. 913
Ipswich SD 22-6   400/PK-12
   PO Box 306 57451   605-426-6561
   Mike Steinhoff, supt.   Fax 426-6029
   www.ipswich.k12.sd.us/
Ipswich HS   100/9-12
   PO Box 306 57451   605-426-6571
   Trent Osborne, prin.   Fax 426-6029
Ipswich JHS   100/7-8
   PO Box 306 57451   605-426-6571
   Trent Osborne, prin.   Fax 426-6029

Irene, Clay, Pop. 421
Irene SD 63-2   200/PK-12
   PO Box 5 57037   605-263-3311
   Larry Johnke, supt.   Fax 263-3316
   www.irene.k12.sd.us/
Irene HS   100/9-12
   PO Box 5 57037   605-263-3313
   David Hutchison, prin.   Fax 263-3316
Irene JHS   50/7-8
   PO Box 5 57037   605-263-3313
   David Hutchison, prin.   Fax 263-3316

Iroquois, Kingsbury, Pop. 267
Iroquois SD 2-3   200/K-12
   PO Box 98 57353   605-546-2210
   Lori Wehlander, supt.   Fax 546-8540
   www.iroquois.k12.sd.us/
Iroquois HS   100/9-12
   PO Box 98 57353   605-546-2426
   Rick Soma, prin.   Fax 546-8540
Iroquois MS   50/6-8
   PO Box 98 57353   605-546-2426
   Rick Soma, prin.   Fax 546-8540

Isabel, Dewey, Pop. 237
Isabel SD 20-2   100/K-12
   PO Box 267 57633   605-466-2125
   Donald Kraemer, admin.   Fax 466-2124
   www.isabel.k12.sd.us/
Isabel HS   50/9-12
   PO Box 267 57633   605-466-2125
   Russell Budmayr, prin.   Fax 466-2124
Isabel JHS   50/7-8
   PO Box 267 57633   605-466-2125
   Russell Budmayr, prin.   Fax 466-2124

Northwest Area Schools Ed Co-op   605-466-2206
   PO Box 35 57633   Fax 466-2207
   Gerry Heck, supt.
Northwest Area Education Co-op   Vo/Tech
   PO Box 35 57633   605-466-2206
   Gerry Heck, supt.   Fax 466-2207

Kadoka, Jackson, Pop. 675
Kadoka SD 35-1   300/PK-12
   PO Box 99 57543   605-837-2175
   Mary Austad, supt.   Fax 837-2176
   www.kadoka.k12.sd.us/
Kadoka HS   100/9-12
   PO Box 99 57543   605-837-2172
   Gale Patterson, prin.   Fax 837-2176

Kennebec, Lyman, Pop. 284
Lyman SD 42-1
   Supt. — See Presho
Lyman MS   100/6-8
   PO Box 188 57544   605-869-2213
   Doug Eppard, prin.   Fax 869-2283

Kimball, Brule, Pop. 705
Kimball SD 7-2   300/K-12
   PO Box 479 57355   605-778-6232
   George Wieland, supt.   Fax 778-6393
   www.kimball.k12.sd.us
Kimball HS   100/9-12
   PO Box 479 57355   605-778-6232
   Duane Noeske, prin.   Fax 778-6393
Kimball JHS   50/7-8
   PO Box 479 57355   605-778-6231
   Duane Noeske, prin.   Fax 778-6393

Kyle, Shannon, Pop. 914

Oglala Lakota College   Post-Sec.
   PO Box 490 57752   605-455-2321

Lake Andes, Charles Mix, Pop. 790
Andes Central SD 11-1 — 400/PK-12
　PO Box 40 57356 — 605-487-7671
　Janet Varejcka, supt. — Fax 487-7051
　www.andescentral.k12.sd.us/
Andes Central HS — 100/9-12
　PO Box 40 57356 — 605-487-7671
　Rocky Brinkman, prin. — Fax 487-7051
Andes Central JHS — 50/7-8
　PO Box 40 57356 — 605-487-7671
　Rocky Brinkman, prin. — Fax 487-7051

Lake Preston, Kingsbury, Pop. 687
Lake Preston SD 38-3 — 200/K-12
　300 1st St NE 57249 — 605-847-4455
　Tim Casper, supt. — Fax 847-4311
　www.lakepreston.k12.sd.us
Lake Preston HS — 100/9-12
　300 1st St NE 57249 — 605-847-4455
　Tim Casper, prin. — Fax 847-4311
Lake Preston JHS — 50/7-8
　300 1st St NE 57249 — 605-847-4455
　Tim Casper, prin. — Fax 847-4311

Langford, Marshall, Pop. 270
Langford SD 45-2 — 200/K-12
　PO Box 127 57454 — 605-493-6454
　Monte Nipp, supt. — Fax 493-6447
　www.langford.k12.sd.us/
Langford HS — 100/9-12
　PO Box 127 57454 — 605-493-6454
　Darrel McFarland, prin. — Fax 493-6447
Langford JHS — 50/7-8
　PO Box 127 57454 — 605-493-6454
　Darrel McFarland, prin. — Fax 493-6447

Lead, Lawrence, Pop. 2,939
Lead-Deadwood SD 40-1 — 1,000/PK-12
　320 S Main St 57754 — 605-717-3890
　Dr. Dan Leikvold, supt. — Fax 717-2813
　www.lead-deadwood.k12.sd.us/
Lead-Deadwood HS — 300/9-12
　320 S Main St 57754 — 605-717-3899
　Whitney Driscoll, prin. — Fax 717-2815
Lead-Deadwood MS — 200/6-8
　234 S Main St 57754 — 605-717-3898
　Whitney Driscoll, prin. — Fax 717-2821
Other Schools – See Nemo

Lemmon, Perkins, Pop. 1,302
Lemmon SD 52-2 — 400/PK-12
　209 3rd St W 57638 — 605-374-3762
　Rick Herbel, supt. — Fax 374-3562
　www.lemmon.k12.sd.us
Lemmon HS — 100/9-12
　209 3rd St W 57638 — 605-374-3762
　Rick Herbel, prin. — Fax 374-3562
Lemmon JHS — 50/7-8
　209 3rd St W 57638 — 605-374-3762
　Rick Herbel, prin. — Fax 374-3562

Lennox, Lincoln, Pop. 1,929
Lennox SD 41-4 — 1,000/PK-12
　PO Box 38 57039 — 605-647-2202
　Dr. Roger DeGroot, supt. — Fax 647-2201
　www.lennox.k12.sd.us
Lennox HS — 400/9-12
　PO Box 38 57039 — 605-647-2203
　Tim Raabe, prin. — Fax 647-6045
Lennox MS — 200/6-8
　PO Box 38 57039 — 605-647-2204
　Grace Christianson, prin. — Fax 647-6043

Leola, McPherson, Pop. 429
Leola SD 44-2 — 300/PK-12
　PO Box 350 57456 — 605-439-3477
　Bobby Olson, supt. — Fax 439-3206
　www.leola.k12.sd.us/
Leola HS — 100/9-12
　PO Box 350 57456 — 605-439-3477
　Bobby Olson, prin. — Fax 439-3206
Leola JHS — 50/7-8
　PO Box 350 57456 — 605-439-3477
　Bobby Olson, prin. — Fax 439-3206

Mc Intosh, Corson, Pop. 302
McIntosh SD 15-1 — 200/PK-12
　PO Box 80 57641 — 605-273-4298
　Dick Schaffan, supt. — Fax 273-4531
　www.mcintosh.k12.sd.us
Mc Intosh HS — 50/9-12
　PO Box 80 57641 — 605-273-4298
　Dick Schaffan, prin. — Fax 273-4531
Mc Intosh JHS — 50/7-8
　PO Box 80 57641 — 605-273-4298
　Dick Schaffan, prin. — Fax 273-4531

Mc Laughlin, Corson, Pop. 799
Mc Laughlin SD 15-2 — 500/PK-12
　PO Box 880 57642 — 605-823-4484
　Perry Hansen, supt. — Fax 823-4886
　www.mclaughlin.k12.sd.us/
Mc Laughlin HS — 100/9-12
　PO Box 880 57642 — 605-823-4482
　Shirley Boyd, prin. — Fax 823-4886
Mc Laughlin MS — 100/6-8
　PO Box 880 57642 — 605-823-4482
　Shirley Boyd, prin. — Fax 823-4886

Madison, Lake, Pop. 6,303
Madison Central SD 39-2 — 1,200/K-12
　800 NE 9th St 57042 — 605-256-7700
　Dr. Frank Palleria, supt. — Fax 256-7711
　www.madison.k12.sd.us
Madison HS — 400/9-12
　800 NE 9th St 57042 — 605-256-7706
　Sharon Knowlton, prin. — Fax 256-7711
Madison MS — 300/6-8
　800 NE 9th St 57042 — 605-256-7717
　Keith Roskens, prin. — Fax 256-7711

Dakota State University — Post-Sec.
　820 N Washington Ave 57042 — 605-256-5112

Marion, Turner, Pop. 853
Marion SD 60-3 — 300/PK-12
　PO Box 207 57043 — 605-648-3615
　Keith McVay, supt. — Fax 648-3652
　www.marion.k12.sd.us
Marion HS — 100/9-12
　PO Box 207 57043 — 605-648-3615
　Joel Bergeson, supt. — Fax 648-3652
Marion JHS — 50/7-8
　PO Box 207 57043 — 605-648-3615
　Joel Bergeson, prin. — Fax 648-3617

Martin, Bennett, Pop. 1,049
Bennett County SD 3-1 — 500/K-12
　PO Box 580 57551 — 605-685-6697
　Wayne Semmler, supt. — Fax 685-6694
　www.bennettco.k12.sd.us/
Bennett County HS — 200/9-12
　PO Box 580 57551 — 605-685-6330
　Gary McEldowney, prin. — Fax 685-6935
Bennett County JHS — 100/7-8
　PO Box 580 57551 — 605-685-6330
　Gary McEldowney, prin. — Fax 685-6935

Mellette, Spink, Pop. 230
Northwestern Area SD 56-7 — 300/PK-12
　PO Box 46 57461 — 605-887-3467
　Ray Sauerwein, supt. — Fax 887-3101
　www.northwestern.k12.sd.us
Northwestern HS — 100/9-12
　PO Box 46 57461 — 605-887-3467
　Ray Sauerwein, prin. — Fax 887-3101
Northwestern MS — 100/6-8
　PO Box 46 57461 — 605-887-3467
　Kathy Graves, prin. — Fax 887-3101

Menno, Hutchinson, Pop. 706
Menno SD 33-2 — 300/PK-12
　PO Box 346 57045 — 605-387-5161
　Dennis Schutt, supt. — Fax 387-5171
　www.menno.k12.sd.us/
Menno HS — 100/9-12
　PO Box 346 57045 — 605-387-5161
　Dennis Schutt, prin. — Fax 387-5171
Menno MS — 100/6-8
　PO Box 346 57045 — 605-387-5161
　Terry Quam, prin. — Fax 387-5171

Midland, Haakon, Pop. 165
Midland SD 27-2 — 100/K-12
　PO Box 226 57552 — 605-843-2561
　Denise Fox, supt. — Fax 843-2562
　www.midland.k12.sd.us/
Midland HS — 50/9-12
　PO Box 226 57552 — 605-843-2561
　Denise Fox, prin. — Fax 843-2562
Midland JHS — 50/7-8
　PO Box 226 57552 — 605-843-2561
　Denise Fox, prin. — Fax 843-2562

Milbank, Grant, Pop. 3,495
Milbank SD 25-4 — 1,000/PK-12
　1001 E Park Ave 57252 — 605-432-5579
　Marlin Smart, supt. — Fax 432-4137
　www.milbank.k12.sd.us
Milbank HS — 400/9-12
　1001 E Park Ave 57252 — 605-432-5546
　Dan Snaza, prin. — Fax 432-5514
Milbank MS — 200/7-8
　1001 E Park Ave 57252 — 605-432-5510
　Dan Snaza, prin. — Fax 432-6610

Miller, Hand, Pop. 1,435
Miller Area SD 29-3 — 500/PK-12
　PO Box 257 57362 — 605-853-2614
　Michael Ruth, supt. — Fax 853-3041
　www.miller.k12.sd.us/
Miller HS — 200/9-12
　PO Box 257 57362 — 605-853-2455
　Gerry Hunter, prin. — Fax 853-3041
Miller JHS — 100/7-8
　PO Box 257 57362 — 605-853-2455
　Gerry Hunter, prin. — Fax 853-3041

Sunshine Bible Academy — 100/K-12
　400 Sunshine Dr 57362 — 605-853-3071
　Julie Hewitt, prin. — Fax 853-3072

Mission, Todd, Pop. 926
Todd County SD 66-1 — 2,100/PK-12
　PO Box 87 57555 — 605-856-4457
　Richard Bordeaux, supt. — Fax 856-2449
　www.tcsdk12.org/
Todd County HS — 500/9-12
　PO Box 726 57555 — 605-856-2324
　Victoria Sherman, prin. — Fax 856-4723
Todd County MS — 400/6-8
　PO Box 87 57555 — 605-856-2341
　Peggy Diekhoff, prin. — Fax 856-2032

Sinte Gleska University — Post-Sec.
　PO Box 105 57555 — 605-856-5880

Mitchell, Davison, Pop. 14,677
Mitchell SD 17-2 — 2,800/K-12
　800 W 10th Ave 57301 — 605-995-3010
　Joseph Graves, supt. — Fax 995-3089
　www.mitchell.k12.sd.us
Mitchell HS — 900/9-12
　920 N Capital St 57301 — 605-995-3034
　Yvonne Palli, prin. — Fax 995-3047
Mitchell MS — 600/6-8
　800 W 10th Ave 57301 — 605-995-3051
　Brad Berens, prin. — Fax 995-3037

Dakota Wesleyan University — Post-Sec.
　1200 W University Ave 57301 — 605-995-2600
Mitchell Christian S — 200/PK-12
　PO Box 1285 57301 — 605-996-8861
　Donald Mitchell, prin. — Fax 996-3642
Mitchell Technical Institute — Post-Sec.
　821 N Capital St 57301 — 605-995-3024
Queen of Peace Hospital — Post-Sec.
　5th & Foster 57301 — 605-995-2250

Mobridge, Walworth, Pop. 3,309
Mobridge SD 62-3 — 600/PK-12
　114 10th St E 57601 — 605-845-7227
　Terry Kraft, supt. — Fax 845-3455
　www.mobridge.k12.sd.us/
Mobridge HS — 200/9-12
　114 10th St E 57601 — 605-845-3460
　Tim Frederick, prin. — Fax 845-3455
Mobridge MS — 100/6-8
　114 10th St E 57601 — 605-845-2768
　Tim Frederick, prin. — Fax 845-3455

Montrose, McCook, Pop. 473
Montrose SD 43-2 — 200/K-12
　309 S Church Ave 57048 — 605-363-5026
　Dean Kueter, supt. — Fax 363-3513
　www.montroseschool.k12.sd.us/
Montrose HS — 100/9-12
　309 S Church Ave 57048 — 605-363-5025
　Kenneth Greeno, prin. — Fax 363-3513
Montrose JHS — 50/7-8
　309 S Church Ave 57048 — 605-363-5025
　Kenneth Greeno, prin. — Fax 363-3513

Mount Vernon, Davison, Pop. 465
Mount Vernon SD 17-3 — 300/K-12
　PO Box 46 57363 — 605-236-5237
　Patrick Mikkonen, supt. — Fax 236-5604
　www.mtvernon.k12.sd.us/
Mount Vernon HS — 100/9-12
　PO Box 46 57363 — 605-236-5237
　Patrick Mikkonen, prin. — Fax 236-5604
Mount Vernon MS — 100/5-8
　PO Box 46 57363 — 605-236-5237
　Al Schulz, prin. — Fax 236-5604

Murdo, Jones, Pop. 562
Jones County SD 37-3 — 200/PK-12
　PO Box 109 57559 — 605-669-2297
　Gary Knispel, supt. — Fax 669-3248
　www.jonesco.k12.sd.us
Jones County HS — 100/9-12
　PO Box 109 57559 — 605-669-2258
　Larry Ball, prin. — Fax 669-2904
Jones County MS — 50/7-8
　PO Box 109 57559 — 605-669-2258
　Larry Ball, prin. — Fax 669-2904

Nemo, Lawrence
Lead-Deadwood SD 40-1
　Supt. — See Lead
Box Elder Job Corps — Vo/Tech
　PO Box 110 57759 — 605-578-2371
　Terry Powell, prin. — Fax 578-1157

Newell, Butte, Pop. 639
Newell SD 9-2 — 400/K-12
　PO Box 99 57760 — 605-456-2393
　Tim McCann, supt. — Fax 456-2395
　www.newell.k12.sd.us
Newell HS — 200/9-12
　PO Box 99 57760 — 605-456-2393
　Tim McCann, prin. — Fax 456-2395
Newell MS — 100/6-8
　PO Box 99 57760 — 605-456-2393
　Donavan DeBoer, prin. — Fax 456-2395

New Holland, Douglas

Dakota Christian HS — 100/9-12
　PO Box 31 57364 — 605-243-2211
　Ivan Groothuis, prin. — Fax 243-2379

New Underwood, Pennington, Pop. 625
New Underwood SD 51-3 — 300/K-12
　PO Box 128 57761 — 605-754-6485
　Dr. Julie Ertz, supt. — Fax 754-6492
　www.newunderwood.k12.sd.us
New Underwood HS — 100/9-12
　PO Box 128 57761 — 605-754-6485
　Kevin Segrud, prin. — Fax 754-6492
New Underwood JHS — 50/7-8
　PO Box 128 57761 — 605-754-6485
　Kevin Segrud, prin. — Fax 754-6492

North Sioux City, Union, Pop. 2,398
Dakota Valley SD 61-8 — 900/K-12
　1150 Northshore Dr 57049 — 605-232-3190
　Al Leber, supt. — Fax 232-3198
　www.dakotavalley.k12.sd.us/
Dakota Valley HS — 200/9-12
　1150 Northshore Dr 57049 — 605-232-9595
　Jerry Rasmussen, prin. — Fax 232-9495
Dakota Valley MS — 300/5-8
　1150 Northshore Dr 57049 — 605-232-4653
　Harlan Halverson, prin. — Fax 232-0951

Oelrichs, Fall River, Pop. 144
Oelrichs SD 23-3 — 100/K-12
　PO Box 65 57763 — 605-535-2631
　Gary Reder, supt. — Fax 535-2046
　www.oelrichs.k12.sd.us
Oelrichs HS — 50/9-12
　PO Box 65 57763 — 605-535-2631
　Dr. Don Hotalling, prin. — Fax 535-2046
Oelrichs JHS — 50/7-8
　PO Box 65 57763 — 605-535-2631
　Dr. Don Hotalling, prin. — Fax 535-2046

Onida, Sully, Pop. 687
Agar-Blunt-Onida SD 58-3 — 300/K-12
　PO Box 205 57564 — 605-258-2619
　Kevin Pickner, supt. — Fax 258-2361
　www.abo.k12.sd.us
Sully Buttes HS — 100/9-12
　PO Box 205 57564 — 605-258-2618
　Keith Moore, prin. — Fax 258-2361
Sully Buttes JHS — 50/7-8
　PO Box 205 57564 — 605-258-2618
　Keith Moore, prin. — Fax 258-2361

Parker, Turner, Pop. 1,005
Parker SD 60-4 — 400/K-12
　PO Box 517 57053 — 605-297-3456
　Tracey Olson, supt. — Fax 297-4381
　parker.k12.sd.us

Parker HS
  PO Box 517 57053
  Joe Meyer, prin.
200/9-12
605-297-4473
Fax 297-4381

Parker HS
  PO Box 517 57053
  Joe Meyer, prin.
100/7-8
605-297-4473
Fax 297-4381

Parkston, Hutchinson, Pop. 1,594
Parkston SD 33-3
  102C S Chapman Dr 57366
  Shayne McIntosh, supt.
  www.parkston.k12.sd.us
800/K-12
605-928-3368
Fax 928-7284

Parkston HS
  102A S Chapman Dr 57366
  Joseph Kollmann, prin.
200/9-12
605-928-3368
Fax 928-4032

Parkston JHS
  102A S Chapman Dr 57366
  Joseph Kollmann, prin.
100/7-8
605-928-3368
Fax 928-4032

Philip, Haakon, Pop. 799
Haakon SD 27-1
  PO Box 730 57567
  Keven Morehart, supt.
  www.philip.k12.sd.us
500/PK-12
605-859-2679
Fax 859-3005

Philip HS
  PO Box 730 57567
  Jeff Rieckman, prin.
100/9-12
605-859-2680
Fax 859-3550

Philip MS
  PO Box 730 57567
  Jeff Rieckman, prin.
50/7-8
605-859-2680
Fax 859-3550

Pierre, Hughes, Pop. 13,939
Pierre SD 32-2
  211 S Poplar Ave 57501
  John Pedersen, supt.
  www.pierre.k12.sd.us
2,700/PK-12
605-773-7300
Fax 773-7304

Morse MS
  309 E Capitol Ave 57501
  Dan Elwood, prin.
700/6-8
605-773-7330
Fax 773-7338

Riggs HS
  1010 E Broadway Ave 57501
  Leroy Fugitt, prin.
800/9-12
605-773-7350
Fax 773-7360

Pine Ridge, Shannon, Pop. 2,596

Oglala Lakota Community College
  PO Box 861 57770
Post-Sec.
605-867-5857

Red Cloud Indian S
  100 Mission Dr 57770
  Fr. Paul Coelho, supt.
400/PK-12
605-867-5888
Fax 867-2528

Plankinton, Aurora, Pop. 567
Plankinton SD 1-1
  PO Box 190 57368
  Greg East, supt.
  www.plankinton.k12.sd.us
200/PK-12
605-942-7743
Fax 942-7453

Plankinton HS
  PO Box 190 57368
  Lee Ann Nussbaum, prin.
100/9-12
605-942-7743
Fax 942-7453

Plankinton JHS
  PO Box 190 57368
  Mark Sampson, prin.
50/7-8
605-942-7743
Fax 942-7453

Platte, Charles Mix, Pop. 1,329
Platte Community SD 11-3
  PO Box 140 57369
  Anton Glass, supt.
  www.platte.k12.sd.us/
600/K-12
605-337-3391
Fax 337-2549

Platte Colony S
  PO Box 140 57369
  Darrell Mueller, prin.
200/K-12
605-337-2468
Fax 337-2549

Platte HS
  PO Box 140 57369
  Steve Randall, prin.
100/9-12
605-337-3391
Fax 337-2549

Platte JHS
  PO Box 140 57369
  Steve Randall, prin.
100/7-8
605-337-3391
Fax 337-2549

Pollock, Campbell, Pop. 316
Pollock SD 10-2
  PO Box 207 57648
  Mike Elsberry, supt.
100/K-12
605-889-2831
Fax 889-2543

Pollock HS
  PO Box 207 57648
  Mike Elsberry, prin.
50/9-12
605-889-2831
Fax 889-2543

Pollock JHS
  PO Box 207 57648
  Mike Elsberry, prin.
50/7-8
605-889-2831
Fax 889-2543

Presho, Lyman, Pop. 614
Lyman SD 42-1
  PO Box 1000 57568
  Bruce Carrier, supt.
  www.lyman.k12.sd.us/
400/K-12
605-895-2579
Fax 895-2216

Lyman HS
  PO Box 1000 57568
  Bruce Carrier, prin.
100/9-12
605-895-2579
Fax 895-2216

Other Schools – See Kennebec

Ramona, Lake, Pop. 185
Oldham-Ramona SD 39-5
  PO Box 8 57054
  John Bjorkman, supt.
  www.oldhamramona.k12.sd.us
100/PK-12
605-482-8244
Fax 482-8282

Oldham-Ramona HS
  PO Box 8 57054
  John Bjorkman, prin.
50/9-12
605-482-8244
Fax 482-8282

Oldham-Ramona JHS
  PO Box 8 57054
  John Bjorkman, prin.
50/7-8
605-482-8244
Fax 482-8282

Rapid City, Pennington, Pop. 60,876
Rapid City Area SD 51-4
  300 6th St 57701
  Dr. Peter Wharton, supt.
  www.rcas.org
12,600/K-12
605-394-4031
Fax 394-2514

Central HS
  433 N Mount Rushmore Rd 57701
  Pat Jones, prin.
2,300/9-12
605-394-4023
Fax 394-4037

Dakota MS
  615 Columbus St 57701
  Brad Tucker, prin.
800/6-8
605-394-4092
Fax 394-6935

North MS
  1501 N Maple Ave 57701
  Jeanne Burckhard, prin.
600/6-8
605-394-4042
Fax 394-6120

South MS
  2 Indiana St 57701
  Larry Stevens, prin.
700/6-8
605-394-4024
Fax 394-5834

Southwest MS
  4501 Park Dr 57702
  Gordon Kendall, prin.
500/6-8
605-394-6792
Fax 355-3095

Stevens HS
  1200 44th St 57702
  Katie Bray, prin.
1,600/9-12
605-394-4051
Fax 394-1820

Western Dakota Technical Institute
  800 Mickelson Dr 57703
  Dr. Rich Gross, dir.
Vo/Tech
605-394-4034
Fax 394-1789

West MS
  1003 Soo San Dr 57702
  Doug Foley, prin.
600/6-8
605-394-4033
Fax 394-1889

Black Hills Beauty College
  623 Saint Joe St 57701
Post-Sec.
605-342-0697

National American University
  321 Kansas City St 57701
Post-Sec.
605-394-4800

Rapid City Christian HS
  PO Box 4246 57709
  David E. Berry, admin.
100/7-12
605-341-3377
Fax 341-2248

Rapid City Regional Hospital
  353 Fairmont Blvd 57701
Post-Sec.
605-341-8100

St. Thomas More HS
  300 Fairmont Blvd 57701
  Wayne Sullivan, prin.
200/9-12
605-343-8484
Fax 343-1315

South Dakota School Mines and Technology
  501 E Saint Joseph St 57701
Post-Sec.
605-394-2511

Western Dakota Technical Institute
  800 Mickelson Dr 57703
Post-Sec.
605-394-4034

Redfield, Spink, Pop. 2,345
Redfield SD 56-4
  PO Box 560 57469
  Randy Joyce, supt.
  www.redfield.k12.sd.us
700/PK-12
605-472-4524
Fax 472-4525

Redfield HS
  PO Box 560 57469
  Rob Lewis, prin.
200/9-12
605-472-4520
Fax 472-4525

Redfield JHS
  PO Box 560 57469
  Rob Lewis, prin.
100/7-8
605-472-4520
Fax 472-4525

Revillo, Grant, Pop. 144
Grant-Deuel SD 25-3
  16370 482nd Ave 57259
  Krista Atyeo-Gortmaker, supt.
  www.grant-deuel.k12.sd.us/
300/PK-12
605-623-4241
Fax 623-4215

Grant-Deuel HS
  16370 482nd Ave 57259
  Brian Fox, prin.
100/9-12
605-623-4241
Fax 623-4215

Grant-Deuel JHS
  16370 482nd Ave 57259
  Brian Fox, prin.
50/7-8
605-623-4241
Fax 623-4215

Roscoe, Edmunds, Pop. 310
Edmunds Central SD 22-5
  PO Box 317 57471
  Lew Paulson, supt.
  www.echs.k12.sd.us/
200/K-12
605-287-4251
Fax 287-4813

Edmunds Central HS
  PO Box 317 57471
  Lew Paulson, prin.
100/9-12
605-287-4251
Fax 287-4813

Edmunds Central JHS
  PO Box 317 57471
  Lew Paulson, prin.
50/7-8
605-287-4251
Fax 287-4813

Rosholt, Roberts, Pop. 434
Rosholt SD 54-4
  PO Box 106 57260
  Carolyn Eide, supt.
  www.rosholt.k12.sd.us/
200/PK-12
605-537-4283
Fax 537-4285

Rosholt HS
  PO Box 106 57260
  Carolyn Eide, prin.
100/9-12
605-537-4278
Fax 537-4285

Rosholt JHS
  PO Box 106 57260
  Carolyn Eide, prin.
50/7-8
605-537-4278
Fax 537-4285

Roslyn, Day, Pop. 211
Roslyn SD 18-2
  PO Box 196 57261
  Marc Frankenstein, supt.
  www.roslyn-eden.k12.sd.us/default.htm
200/K-12
605-486-4311
Fax 486-4635

Roslyn HS
  PO Box 196 57261
  Marc Frankenstein, prin.
100/9-12
605-486-4311
Fax 486-4635

Roslyn JHS
  PO Box 196 57261
  Marc Frankenstein, prin.
50/7-8
605-486-4311
Fax 486-4635

Rutland, Lake
Rutland SD 39-4
  PO Box 89 57057
  Carl Fahrenwald, supt.
  www.rutland.k12.sd.us
100/K-12
605-586-4352
Fax 586-4343

Rutland HS
  PO Box 89 57057
  Valerie Parsley, prin.
50/9-12
605-586-4352
Fax 586-4343

Rutland JHS
  PO Box 89 57057
  Valerie Parsley, prin.
50/7-8
605-586-4352
Fax 586-4343

Salem, McCook, Pop. 1,389
McCook Central SD 43-7
  PO Box 310 57058
  Ronald Bennett, supt.
  mccookcentral.k12.sd.us
400/PK-12
605-425-2264
Fax 425-2079

McCook Central HS
  PO Box 310 57058
  Dennis Vanoverschelde, prin.
100/9-12
605-425-2264
Fax 425-2079

McCook Central MS
  PO Box 310 57058
  Dennis Vanoverschelde, prin.
100/5-8
605-425-2264
Fax 425-2079

Scotland, Bon Homme, Pop. 846
Scotland SD 4-3
  711 4th St 57059
  Bob Graham, supt.
  www.scotland.k12.sd.us
300/PK-12
605-583-2237
Fax 583-2239

Scotland HS
  711 4th St 57059
  Robert Graham, prin.
100/9-12
605-583-2237
Fax 583-2239

Scotland MS
  711 4th St 57059
  Robert Graham, prin.
100/6-8
605-583-2237
Fax 583-2239

Selby, Walworth, Pop. 701
Selby Area SD 62-5
  PO Box 324 57472
  Frank Larson, supt.
  www.selby.k12.sd.us/
200/PK-12
605-649-7818
Fax 649-7282

Selby Area HS
  PO Box 324 57472
  Kevin Quimby, prin.
100/9-12
605-649-7818
Fax 649-7282

Selby Area JHS
  PO Box 324 57472
  Kevin Quimby, prin.
50/7-8
605-649-7818
Fax 649-7282

Sioux Falls, Minnehaha, Pop. 133,834
Sioux Falls SD 49-5
  201 E 38th St 57105
  Dr. Pam Homan, supt.
  www.sf.k12.sd.us
19,700/PK-12
605-367-7900
Fax 367-4637

Axtell Park MS
  201 N West Ave 57104
  Steve Cain, prin.
700/6-8
605-367-7647
Fax 367-8326

Edison MS
  2101 S West Ave 57105
  Steve Griffith, prin.
700/6-8
605-367-7643
Fax 367-8457

Henry MS
  2200 S 5th Ave 57105
  Steve Albrecht, prin.
1,100/6-8
605-367-7693
Fax 367-7693

Lincoln HS
  2900 S Cliff Ave 57105
  Val Fox, prin.
1,900/9-12
605-367-7990
Fax 367-8492

Memorial MS
  1401 S Sertoma Ave 57106
  Carrie Aaron, prin.
1,000/6-8
605-362-2785
Fax 362-2790

Roosevelt HS
  6600 W 41st St 57106
  Jim Denevan, prin.
1,900/9-12
605-362-2860
Fax 362-2883

Washington HS
  501 N Sycamore Ave 57110
  James Nold, prin.
2,000/9-12
605-367-7970
Fax 367-8494

Whittier MS
  930 E 6th St 57103
  Dr. Diana Messick, prin.
1,000/6-8
605-367-7620
Fax 367-8357

Augustana College
  29th And South Smt 57197
Post-Sec.
605-274-0770

Colorado Technical University
  3901 W 59th St 57108
Post-Sec.
605-361-0200

Kilian Community College
  300 E 6th St 57103
Post-Sec.
605-221-3100

McKennan Hospital
  800 E 21st St 57105
Post-Sec.
605-339-8113

National American University
  2801 S Kiwanis Ave Ste 100 57105
Post-Sec.
605-334-5430

North American Baptist Seminary
  1525 S Grange Ave 57105
Post-Sec.
605-336-6588

O'Gorman HS
  3201 S Kiwanis Ave 57105
  Kyle Groos, prin.
700/9-12
605-336-3644
Fax 336-9272

O'Gorman JHS
  3100 W 41st St 57105
  Colly Broveleit, prin.
300/7-8
605-988-0546
Fax 336-9839

Sioux Falls Christian S
  6120 S Charger Ave 57108
  Jay Woudstra, prin.
300/4-12
605-334-1422
Fax 334-6928

Sioux Valley Hospital
  PO Box 5039 57117
Post-Sec.
605-333-6424

South Dakota School for the Deaf
  2001 E 8th St 57103
Post-Sec.
605-367-5200

Southeast Technical Institute
  2301 N Career Ave 57107
Post-Sec.
605-367-7624

University of Sioux Falls
  1101 W 22nd St 57105
Post-Sec.
605-331-5000

Sisseton, Roberts, Pop. 2,594
Sisseton SD 54-2
  516 8th Ave W 57262
  Dr. Stephen Schulte, supt.
  www.sisseton.k12.sd.us/
1,200/K-12
605-698-7613
Fax 698-3032

Sisseton HS
  516 8th Ave W 57262
  Gary Evjen, prin.
400/9-12
605-698-7613
Fax 698-7353

Thollehauge MS
  516 8th Ave W 57262
  Craig Ebert, prin.
300/5-8
605-698-7613
Fax 698-7487

Sisseton Wahpeton Community College
  PO Box 689 57262
Post-Sec.
605-698-3966

South Shore, Codington, Pop. 266
South Shore SD 14-3
  PO Box 638 57263
  Scott Bartholomew, supt.
  www.southshore.k12.sd.us/
100/PK-12
605-756-4120
Fax 756-4201

South Shore HS
  PO Box 638 57263
  Scott Bartholomew, prin.
50/9-12
605-756-4120
Fax 756-4201

South Shore JHS
  PO Box 638 57263
  Scott Bartholomew, prin.
50/7-8
605-756-4120
Fax 756-4201

Spearfish, Lawrence, Pop. 8,870
Spearfish SD 40-2
  525 E Illinois St 57783
  Dave Peters, supt.
  www.spearfish.k12.sd.us
1,900/PK-PK, 1-
605-717-1229
Fax 717-1200

Spearfish HS
  1725 N Main St 57783
  Steve Morford, prin.
700/9-12
605-717-1212
Fax 717-1211

Spearfish MS
  1600 N Canyon St 57783
  Tom Riedel, prin.
500/6-8
605-717-1215
Fax 717-6926

Black Hills State University
  1200 University St 57799
Post-Sec.
605-642-6011

Stickney, Aurora, Pop. 316
Stickney SD 1-2
  PO Box 67 57375
  Robert Krietlow, supt.
  www.stickney.k12.sd.us/
200/K-12
605-732-4221
Fax 732-4281

Stickney HS | 100/9-12
PO Box 67 57375 | 605-732-4221
Robert Krietlow, prin. | Fax 732-4281
Stickney JHS | 50/8-8
PO Box 67 57375 | 605-732-4221
Robert Krietlow, prin. | Fax 732-4281

Sturgis, Meade, Pop. 6,389
Meade SD 46-1 | 3,200/K-12
1230 Douglas St 57785 | 605-347-2523
James Heinert, supt. | Fax 347-0005
meade.k12.sd.us
Brown HS | 800/9-12
12930 SD Highway 34 57785 | 605-347-2686
Tim Drone, prin. | Fax 347-0225
Sturgis Williams MS | 700/5-8
1425 Cedar St 57785 | 605-347-5232
Lonny Harter, prin. | Fax 720-0190

Summit, Roberts, Pop. 279
Summit SD 54-6 | 100/PK-12
PO Box 791 57266 | 605-398-6211
Bruce Johnson, supt. | Fax 398-6311
www.summit.k12.sd.us
Summit HS | 50/9-12
PO Box 791 57266 | 605-398-6211
Bruce Johnson, supt. | Fax 398-6311
Summit JHS | 50/7-8
PO Box 791 57266 | 605-398-6211
Bruce Johnson, prin. | Fax 398-6311

Timber Lake, Dewey, Pop. 440
Timber Lake SD 20-3 | 300/K-12
PO Box 1000 57656 | 605-865-3654
Frank Seiler, supt. | Fax 865-3294
www.tls.k12.sd.us/
Timber Lake HS | 100/9-12
PO Box 1000 57656 | 605-865-3654
Jeff Simmons, prin. | Fax 865-3294
Timber Lake MS | 100/6-8
PO Box 1000 57656 | 605-865-3654
Jeff Simmons, prin. | Fax 865-3294

Tripp, Hutchinson, Pop. 684
Tripp-Delmont SD 33-5 | 300/K-12
PO Box 430 57376 | 605-935-6766
Lynn Vlasman, supt. | Fax 935-6507
www.tridel.k12.sd.us/
Tripp-Delmont HS | 100/9-12
PO Box 430 57376 | 605-935-6766
Lynn Vlasman, prin. | Fax 935-6507
Tripp-Delmont MS | 50/6-8
PO Box 430 57376 | 605-935-6766
Lynn Vlasman, prin. | Fax 935-6507

Tulare, Spink, Pop. 206
Hitchcock - Tulare SD 56-5 | 200/K-12
PO Box 108 57476 | 605-596-4171
Barry Erickson, supt. | Fax 596-4175
Hitchcock Tulare HS | 50/9-12
PO Box 108 57476 | 605-596-4172
Dennis Smith, prin. | Fax 596-4150
Hitchcock Tulare JHS | 50/8-8
PO Box 108 57476 | 605-596-4172
Dennis Smith, prin. | Fax 596-4150

Tyndall, Bon Homme, Pop. 1,181
Bon Homme SD 4-2 | 700/PK-12
PO Box 28 57066 | 605-589-3388
Dr. Bryce Knudson, supt. | Fax 589-3468
www.bonhomme.k12.sd.us/
Bon Homme HS | 200/9-12
PO Box 28 57066 | 605-589-3387
Ed Mitzel, prin. | Fax 589-3468
Bon Homme MS | 200/6-8
PO Box 28 57066 | 605-589-3387
Ed Mitzel, prin. | Fax 589-3468

Vermillion, Clay, Pop. 10,070
Vermillion SD 13-1 | 1,400/PK-12
17 Prospect St 57069 | 605-677-7000
Dr. Mark Froke, supt. | Fax 677-7002
www.vermillion.k12.sd.us
Vermillion HS | 400/9-12
1001 E Main St 57069 | 605-677-7035
Curt Cameron, prin. | Fax 677-7042
Vermillion MS | 300/6-8
422 Princeton St 57069 | 605-677-7025
Pat Anderson, prin. | Fax 677-7028

University of South Dakota | Post-Sec.
414 E Clark St 57069 | 605-677-5011

Viborg, Turner, Pop. 815
Viborg SD 60-5 | 300/PK-12
PO Box 397 57070 | 605-766-5418
Patrick Kraning, supt. | Fax 766-5635
www.viborg.k12.sd.us/
Viborg HS | 100/9-12
PO Box 397 57070 | 605-766-5418
Pat Kraning, prin. | Fax 766-5635
Viborg JHS | 100/7-8
PO Box 397 57070 | 605-766-5418
Patrick Kraning, prin. | Fax 766-5635

Volga, Brookings, Pop. 1,435
Sioux Valley SD 5-5 | 500/PK-12
PO Box 278 57071 | 605-627-5657
Dean Johnson, supt. | Fax 627-5291
www.svschool.org
Sioux Valley HS | 200/9-12
PO Box 278 57071 | 605-627-5657
Suzanne Hegg, prin. | Fax 627-5291
Sioux Valley MS | 100/6-8
PO Box 278 57071 | 605-627-5657
Suzanne Hegg, prin. | Fax 627-5291

Wagner, Charles Mix, Pop. 1,619
Wagner Community SD 11-4 | 700/PK-12
PO Box 310 57380 | 605-384-3677
Susan Smit, supt. | Fax 384-3678
www.wagner.k12.sd.us/

Wagner HS | 200/9-12
PO Box 310 57380 | 605-384-5426
Neil Goter, prin. | Fax 384-3200
Wagner JHS | 100/7-8
PO Box 310 57380 | 605-384-5426
Steve Petry, prin. | Fax 384-3200

Wakonda, Clay, Pop. 359
Wakonda SD 13-2 | 200/PK-12
PO Box 268 57073 | 605-267-2644
Larry Johnke, supt. | Fax 267-2645
www.wakonda.k12.sd.us/
Wakonda HS | 100/9-12
PO Box 268 57073 | 605-267-2644
Dave Hutchison, prin. | Fax 267-2645
Wakonda JHS | 50/7-8
PO Box 268 57073 | 605-267-2644
Dave Hutchison, prin. | Fax 267-2645

Wakpala, Corson
Smee SD 15-3 | 200/PK-12
PO Box B 57658 | 605-845-3040
Lawrence Gauer, supt. | Fax 845-7244
www.smee.k12.sd.us
Wakpala HS | 100/9-12
PO Box B 57658 | 605-845-3040
Larry Birchem, prin. | Fax 845-7244

Wall, Pennington, Pop. 820
Wall SD 51-5 | 400/K-12
PO Box 414 57790 | 605-279-2156
Ed Wegner, supt. | Fax 279-2613
www.wall.k12.sd.us
Wall HS | 100/9-12
PO Box 414 57790 | 605-279-2156
Barbara Leiseth, prin. | Fax 279-2613
Wall MS | 100/6-8
PO Box 414 57790 | 605-279-2156
Barbara Leiseth, prin. | Fax 279-2613

Warner, Brown, Pop. 426
Warner SD 6-5 | 300/PK-12
PO Box 20 57479 | 605-225-6397
Kirk Easton, supt. | Fax 225-0007
www.warner.k12.sd.us/
Warner HS | 100/9-12
PO Box 20 57479 | 605-225-6194
Charles Welke, prin. | Fax 225-0007
Warner MS | 100/6-8
PO Box 20 57479 | 605-225-6194
Charles Welke, prin. | Fax 225-0007

Watertown, Codington, Pop. 20,191
Lake Area Multi-District
1311 3rd Ave NE 57201 | 605-882-6380
Julie LeVake, prin. | Fax 882-6381
www.lakeareamulti.k12.sd.us/
Lake Area Vocational S | Vo/Tech
1311 3rd Ave NE 57201 | 605-882-6380
Julie LeVake, prin. | Fax 882-6381

Watertown SD 14-4 | 4,000/PK-12
PO Box 730 57201 | 605-882-6312
Dr. Bob Mayer, supt. | Fax 882-6327
www.watertown.k12.sd.us/
Watertown HS | 1,300/9-12
PO Box 730 57201 | 605-882-6316
Brian Field, prin. | Fax 882-6327
Watertown JHS | 600/7-8
PO Box 730 57201 | 605-882-6370
Daniel Albertsen, prin. | Fax 886-6372

Great Plains Lutheran HS | 100/9-12
1200 Luther Ln NE 57201 | 605-886-0672
Daniel Myers, prin. | Fax 882-9089
Lake Area Technical Institute | Post-Sec.
230 11th St NE 57201 | 605-882-5284
Watertown Christian S | 100/PK-12
PO Box 1026 57201 | 605-882-0949
David Kaser, hdmstr. | Fax 882-5935

Waubay, Day, Pop. 625
Waubay SD 18-3 | 200/PK-12
202 W School Rd 57273 | 605-947-4529
Al Stewart, supt. | Fax 947-4243
www.waubay.k12.sd.us/
Waubay HS | 100/9-12
202 W School Rd 57273 | 605-947-4529
Al Stewart, prin. | Fax 947-4243
Waubay JHS | 50/7-8
202 W School Rd 57273 | 605-947-4529
Al Stewart, prin. | Fax 947-4243

Waverly, Codington
Waverly SD 14-5 | 100/PK-12
319 Mary Pl, | 605-886-9174
Loren McKinney, supt. | Fax 886-6630
www.waverly.k12.sd.us
Waverly HS | 50/9-12
319 Mary Pl, | 605-886-9174
Loren McKinney, prin. | Fax 886-6630
Waverly JHS | 50/7-8
319 Mary Pl, | 605-886-9174
Loren McKinney, prin. | Fax 886-6630

Webster, Day, Pop. 1,821
Lake Region Vocational Ed Center
1209 Main St 57274 | 605-345-4412
Debbie Henrichsen, dir. | Fax 345-3429
Lake Region Vocational Education Center | Vo/Tech
1209 Main St 57274 | 605-345-4412
Debbie Henrichsen, dir. | Fax 345-3429

Webster SD 18-4 | 500/PK-12
102 E 9th Ave 57274 | 605-345-3548
James Block, supt. | Fax 345-4421
www.webster.k12.sd.us/
Webster HS | 200/9-12
102 E 9th Ave 57274 | 605-345-4653
Jim Block, prin. | Fax 345-4421
Webster MS | 100/6-8
102 E 9th Ave 57274 | 605-345-4653
Craig Case, prin. | Fax 345-4421

Wessington Springs, Jerauld, Pop. 953
Wessington Springs SD 36-2 | 300/PK-12
PO Box 449 57382 | 605-539-9391
Darold Rounds, supt. | Fax 539-1029
www.wessingtonsprings.k12.sd.us
Wessington Springs HS | 100/9-12
PO Box 449 57382 | 605-539-9391
Darold J. Rounds, prin. | Fax 539-1029
Wessington Springs MS | 100/6-8
PO Box 449 57382 | 605-539-1754
Vicki Harmdierks, prin. | Fax 539-1029

White, Brookings, Pop. 507
Deubrook Area SD 5-6 | 400/K-12
PO Box 346 57276 | 605-629-1100
Kevin Keenaghan, supt. | Fax 629-3701
www.deubrook.com
Deubrook HS | 100/9-12
PO Box 346 57276 | 605-629-1114
Don Ray, prin. | Fax 629-3701
Deubrook JHS | 100/7-8
PO Box 346 57276 | 605-629-1114
Don Ray, prin. | Fax 629-3701

White Lake, Aurora, Pop. 390
White Lake SD 1-3 | 200/K-12
PO Box 246 57383 | 605-249-2251
Berle Johnson, supt. | Fax 249-2725
www.whitelake.k12.sd.us/
White Lake HS | 50/9-12
PO Box 246 57383 | 605-732-4221
Berle Johnson, prin. | Fax 249-2725
White Lake JHS | 50/7-8
PO Box 246 57383 | 605-249-2251
Berle Johnson, prin. | Fax 249-2725

White River, Mellette, Pop. 598
White River SD 47-1 | 400/PK-12
PO Box 273 57579 | 605-259-3311
Thomas Cameron, supt. | Fax 259-3133
www.whiteriver.k12.sd.us/
White River HS | 100/9-12
PO Box 273 57579 | 605-259-3135
Tim Hollar, prin. | Fax 259-3133
White River MS | 100/6-8
PO Box 273 57579 | 605-259-3135
Cord Angier, prin. | Fax 259-3133

Willow Lake, Clark, Pop. 277
Willow Lake SD 12-3 | 300/PK-12
PO Box 170 57278 | 605-625-5945
Leland Poppen, supt. | Fax 625-3103
www.dailypost.com/~wls
Willow Lake HS | 100/9-12
PO Box 170 57278 | 605-625-5924
Kerry Stobbs, prin. | Fax 625-3103
Willow Lake JHS | 50/7-8
PO Box 170 57278 | 605-625-5924
Kerry Stobbs, prin. | Fax 625-3103

Wilmot, Roberts, Pop. 542
Wilmot SD 54-7 | 300/PK-12
PO Box 100 57279 | 605-938-4647
Tim Graf, supt. | Fax 938-4185
www.wilmot.k12.sd.us
Wilmot HS | 100/9-12
PO Box 100 57279 | 605-938-4647
Larry Hulscher, prin. | Fax 938-4185
Wilmot JHS | 50/7-8
PO Box 100 57279 | 605-938-4647
Larry Hulscher, prin. | Fax 938-4185

Winner, Tripp, Pop. 3,001
Winner SD 59-2 | 1,000/K-12
325 S Monroe St 57580 | 605-842-0626
Mary Fisher, supt. | Fax 842-0276
www.winner.k12.sd.us
Winner HS | 300/9-12
325 S Monroe St 57580 | 605-842-2427
Mike Hanson, prin. | Fax 842-3522
Winner MS | 300/5-8
325 S Monroe St 57580 | 605-842-0880
Brian Naasz, prin. | Fax 842-0276

Wolsey, Beadle, Pop. 399
Wolsey Wessington SD 2-6 | 200/K-12
375 Ash St SE 57384 | 605-883-4221
Brian Sieh, supt. | Fax 883-4720
Wolsey Wessington HS | 100/9-12
375 Ash St SE 57384 | 605-883-4221
Brian Sieh, prin. | Fax 883-4720
Wolsey Wessington MS | 50/5-8
375 Ash St SE 57384 | 605-883-4221
Carol Rowan, prin. | Fax 883-4720

Woonsocket, Sanborn, Pop. 698
Woonsocket SD 55-4 | 200/K-12
PO Box 428 57385 | 605-796-4431
Rodrick Weber, supt. | Fax 796-4352
www.woonsocket.k12.sd.us/
Woonsocket HS | 100/9-12
PO Box 428 57385 | 605-796-4431
Rodrick Weber, prin. | Fax 796-4352

Yankton, Yankton, Pop. 13,440
Yankton SD 63-3 | 3,200/PK-12
PO Box 738 57078 | 605-665-3998
Joseph Gertsema, supt. | Fax 665-1422
www.ysd.k12.sd.us
Yankton HS | 1,100/9-12
PO Box 738 57078 | 605-665-2073
Scott Lepke, prin. | Fax 655-5948
Yankton MS | 800/6-8
PO Box 738 57078 | 605-665-2419
Wayne Kindle, prin. | Fax 665-6239

Mt. Marty College | Post-Sec.
1105 W 8th St 57078 | 605-668-1514
Sacred Heart Hospital | Post-Sec.
501 Summit St 57078 | 605-655-9371
Sacred Heart MS | 100/5-8
504 Capitol St 57078 | 605-655-1808
Tom Buckmiller, prin. | Fax 260-9787

TENNESSEE

TENNESSEE DEPARTMENT OF EDUCATION
710 James Robertson Pkwy, Nashville 37243-1219
Telephone 615-741-2731
Fax 615-532-4791
Website http://www.state.tn.us/education

Commissioner of Education   Lana Seivers

TENNESSEE BOARD OF EDUCATION
400 Deaderick St #200, Nashville 37243-1403

Chairperson   B. Fielding Rolston

PUBLIC, PRIVATE AND CATHOLIC SECONDARY SCHOOLS

Adamsville, McNairy, Pop. 2,019
McNairy County SD
  Supt. — See Selmer
Adamsville JSHS — 600/7-12
  PO Box 407 38310 — 731-632-3273
  Brian Jackson, prin. — Fax 632-3080

Afton, Greene
Greene County SD
  Supt. — See Greeneville
Chuckey-Doak HS — 500/9-12
  365 Ripley Island Rd 37616 — 423-798-2636
  George Frye, prin. — Fax 639-5761
Chuckey Doak MS — 6-8
  120 Chuckey Doak Rd 37616 — 423-787-2038
  Shelly Smith, prin. — Fax 787-2039

Alamo, Crockett, Pop. 2,385
Crockett County SD — 1,800/PK-12
  102 N Cavalier Dr 38001 — 731-696-2604
  Stan Black, supt. — Fax 696-4734
  www.ccschools.net
Crockett County HS — 700/9-12
  2014 Highway 88 38001 — 731-696-4525
  Dan Black, prin. — Fax 696-3124
Crockett County MS — 600/6-8
  497 N Cavalier Dr 38001 — 731-696-5583
  Larry Lewis, prin. — Fax 696-2034

Alcoa, Blount, Pop. 8,174
Alcoa CSD — 1,400/K-12
  524 Faraday St 37701 — 865-984-0531
  Tom Shamblin, supt. — Fax 984-5832
  www.alcoaschools.net/
Alcoa HS — 400/9-12
  532 Faraday St 37701 — 865-982-4631
  Scott Porter, prin. — Fax 380-2240
Alcoa MS — 400/5-8
  1325 Springbrook Rd 37701 — 865-982-5211
  James Kirk, prin. — Fax 380-2533

Altamont, Grundy, Pop. 1,149
Grundy County SD — 2,200/PK-12
  PO Box 97 37301 — 931-692-3467
  Dr. David Dickerson, dir. — Fax 692-2188
  volweb.utk.edu/Schools/grundyco/grundy.index.html
Other Schools – See Coalmont

Antioch, Davidson
Davidson County SD
  Supt. — See Nashville
Antioch HS — 2,400/9-12
  1900 Hobson Pike 37013 — 615-641-5400
  Dr. Margaret Bess, prin. — Fax 641-5422
Antioch MS — 1,000/5-8
  5050 Blue Hole Rd 37013 — 615-333-5642
  Jesse Pedigo, prin. — Fax 333-5053
Apollo MS — 800/5-8
  631 Richards Rd 37013 — 615-333-5025
  James Briggs, prin. — Fax 333-5029
Kennedy MS — 1,300/5-8
  2087 Hobson Pike 37013 — 615-501-7900
  Karen Bryant, prin.

Ezell-Harding Christian S — 900/PK-12
  574 Bell Rd 37013 — 615-367-0532
  Donald Hutchison, pres. — Fax 399-8747

Arlington, Shelby, Pop. 3,195
Shelby County SD
  Supt. — See Memphis
Arlington HS — 9-10
  5475 Airline Rd 38002 — 901-867-1541
  Dr. Jeff Cozzens, prin. — Fax 867-1546
Arlington MS — 800/6-8
  5470 Lamb Rd 38002 — 901-867-6015
  Patricia Prescott, prin. — Fax 867-6080
Bolton HS — 2,300/9-12
  7323 Brunswick Rd 38002 — 901-873-8150
  David Stephens, prin. — Fax 829-3650
Shadowlawn MS — 1,300/6-8
  4734 Shadowlawn Rd 38002 — 901-373-2654
  Jamie Baker, prin. — Fax 373-1363

Ashland City, Cheatham, Pop. 4,193
Cheatham County SD — 6,700/PK-12
  102 Elizabeth St 37015 — 615-792-5664
  Lynn E. Seifert, dir. — Fax 792-2551
  cheatham.k12tn.net
Cheatham County Central HS — 700/9-12
  1 Cub Cir 37015 — 615-792-5641
  — Fax 792-2090
Cheatham MS — 700/5-8
  700 Scoutview Rd 37015 — 615-792-2334
  Robin Norris, prin. — Fax 792-2337
Cheatham County Adult HS — Adult
  104 Elizabeth St 37015 — 615-746-1424
  Rita Herndon, prin. — Fax 746-1438
Other Schools – See Kingston Springs, Pleasant View

Athens, McMinn, Pop. 13,625
Athens CSD — 1,700/PK-9
  943 Crestway Dr 37303 — 423-745-2863
  Dr. Craig Rigell, supt. — Fax 745-9041
  www.athens-lea.mcminn.k12.tn.us/
Athens JHS — 400/7-9
  200 Keith Ln 37303 — 423-745-1177
  Michael Simmons, prin. — Fax 745-9679

McMinn County SD — 6,800/PK-12
  216 N Jackson St 37303 — 423-745-1612
  Dr. John Forgety, supt. — Fax 744-1641
  www.mcminn.k12.tn.us/
McMinn County HS — 1,400/9-12
  2215 Congress Pkwy S 37303 — 423-745-4142
  John Grubb, prin. — Fax 745-0584
McMinn Vocational Center — Vo/Tech
  2103 Congress Pkwy S 37303 — 423-746-4293
  Ed McCleary, prin. — Fax 744-3923
Other Schools – See Englewood

Tennessee Technology Center at Athens — Post-Sec.
  PO Box 848 37371 — 423-744-2814
Tennessee Wesleyan College — Post-Sec.
  PO Box 40 37371 — 423-745-7504

Atwood, Carroll, Pop. 995
West Carroll Special SD
  Supt. — See Trezevant
West Carroll JSHS — 600/7-12
  760 State Route 77 38220 — 731-662-7116
  Lex Suite, prin. — Fax 662-4198

Bartlett, Shelby, Pop. 42,245
Shelby County SD
  Supt. — See Memphis
Appling HS — 800/6-8
  3700 Appling Rd 38133 — 901-373-1410
  Odell Foster, prin. — Fax 373-1360
Bartlett HS — 1,800/9-12
  5688 Woodlawn St 38134 — 901-373-2620
  Mike Parnell, prin. — Fax 373-2624
Elmore Park MS — 800/6-8
  6330 Althorne Rd 38134 — 901-373-2642
  Marjorie Lowe, prin. — Fax 373-1361

Baxter, Putnam, Pop. 1,329
Putnam County SD
  Supt. — See Cookeville
Cornerstone MS — 500/5-8
  371 1st Ave S 38544 — 931-858-6601
  Garry Lee, prin. — Fax 858-6637
Upperman MS — 500/9-12
  6950 Nashville Hwy 38544 — 931-858-3112
  Herb Leftwich, prin. — Fax 858-4641

Bell Buckle, Bedford, Pop. 402

Webb S — 300/6-12
  PO Box 488 37020 — 931-389-9322
  Albert Cauz, hdmstr. — Fax 389-9101

Benton, Polk, Pop. 1,137
Polk County SD — 2,100/PK-12
  PO Box A 37307 — 423-338-4506
  James Jone, supt. — Fax 338-2691
  www.polkcountyschools.com/

Chilhowee MS — 400/6-8
  PO Box 188 37307 — 423-338-3102
  Buddy McClary, prin. — Fax 338-3158
Polk County HS — 500/9-12
  PO Box 188 37307 — 423-338-4514
  Joel Cox, prin. — Fax 338-4521
Other Schools – See Copperhill

Big Sandy, Benton, Pop. 521
Benton County SD
  Supt. — See Camden
Big Sandy S — 400/K-12
  13305 Highway 69A 38221 — 731-593-3221
  Mike Bell, prin. — Fax 593-3245

Blountville, Sullivan, Pop. 2,605
Sullivan County SD — 12,900/K-12
  PO Box 306 37617 — 423-354-1000
  Glenn Arwood, supt. — Fax 354-1004
  www.scde.k12.tn.us
Blountville MS — 400/6-8
  1651 Blountville Blvd 37617 — 423-354-1600
  Larry Hall, prin. — Fax 354-1606
Holston MS — 400/6-8
  2348 Highway 75 37617 — 423-354-1500
  Bill Miller, prin. — Fax 354-1505
Sullivan Central HS — 1,100/9-12
  131 Shipley Ferry Rd 37617 — 423-354-1200
  David Ward, prin. — Fax 354-1206
Other Schools – See Bluff City, Bristol, Kingsport

Northeast State Tech Community College — Post-Sec.
  PO Box 246 37617 — 423-323-3191

Bluff City, Sullivan, Pop. 1,576
Sullivan County SD
  Supt. — See Blountville
Bluff City MS — 400/6-8
  337 Carter St 37618 — 423-354-1801
  Jack Walling, prin. — Fax 354-1818
Sullivan East HS — 1,000/9-12
  4180 Weaver Pike 37618 — 423-354-1900
  Mary E. Rouse, prin. — Fax 354-1906

Bolivar, Hardeman, Pop. 5,689
Hardeman County SD — 4,400/K-12
  PO Box 112 38008 — 731-658-2510
  Donald Hopper Ph.D., supt. — Fax 658-2061
  www.hardemancountyschools.org
Bolivar MS — 500/6-8
  915 Pruitt St 38008 — 731-658-3656
  Hattie Price, prin. — Fax 658-6625
Central HS — 900/9-12
  313 Harris St 38008 — 731-658-3151
  Fred Kessler, prin. — Fax 658-6697
Other Schools – See Middleton

Bradford, Gibson, Pop. 1,085
Bradford Special SD — 600/K-12
  PO Box 220 38316 — 731-742-3180
  Bobby McCartney, supt. — Fax 742-3994
  www.bradfordssd.com/
Bradford JSHS — 300/7-12
  PO Box 70 38316 — 731-742-3152
  Larry W. McCartney, prin. — Fax 742-3088

Brentwood, Williamson, Pop. 28,960
Williamson County SD
  Supt. — See Franklin
Brentwood HS — 1,400/9-12
  5304 Murray Ln 37027 — 615-472-4220
  Kevin Keidel, prin. — Fax 472-4241
Brentwood MS — 900/6-8
  5324 Murray Ln 37027 — 615-472-4250
  Dr. Kay Kendrick, prin. — Fax 472-4263
Ravenwood HS — 1,100/9-12
  1724 Wilson Pike 37027 — 615-472-4800
  Dr. Pam Vaden, prin. — Fax 472-4821
Sunset MS — 6-8
  200 Sunset Trl 37027 — 615-472-5040
  Jason Pearson, prin. — Fax 472-5050
Woodland MS — 900/6-8
  1500 Volunteer Pkwy 37027 — 615-472-4930
  Priscilla Fizer, prin. — Fax 472-4941

Brentwood Academy 700/6-12
219 Granny White Pike 37027 615-373-0611
Curt Masters, hdmstr. Fax 377-3709
Currey Ingram Academy 300/K-12
6544 Murray Ln 37027 615-507-3242
Kathleen Rayburn, prin. Fax 507-3170
Montessori Academy 300/PK-12
6021 Cloverland Dr 37027 615-833-3610
Eileen Bernstorf, hdmstr. Fax 833-3680

Brighton, Tipton, Pop. 2,068
Tipton County SD
Supt. — See Covington
Brighton HS 1,000/9-12
8045 Highway 51 S 38011 901-837-5800
Grant Shipley, prin. Fax 837-5829
Brighton MS 900/6-8
7785 Highway 51 S 38011 901-837-5600
John Combs, prin. Fax 837-5625

Bristol, Sullivan, Pop. 25,021
Bristol CSD 3,600/PK-12
615 Edgemont Ave 37620 423-652-9451
Steve Dixon, supt. Fax 652-9238
www.btcs.org
Tennessee HS 1,100/9-12
1112 Edgemont Ave 37620 423-652-9494
Jim Butcher, prin. Fax 652-9327
Vance MS 600/7-8
815 Edgemont Ave 37620 423-652-9449
Rigby Kind, prin. Fax 652-9297

Sullivan County SD
Supt. — See Blountville
Holston Valley MS 200/6-8
1717 Bristol Caverns Hwy 37620 423-354-1880
Jess Lockhart, prin. Fax 354-1891

Jacobs Creek Job Corps Civilian Center Post-Sec.
984 Denton Valley Rd 37620 423-878-4021
King College Post-Sec.
1350 King College Rd 37620 423-968-1187

Brownsville, Haywood, Pop. 10,725
Haywood County SD 3,400/PK-12
900 E Main St 38012 731-772-9613
George Chapman, supt. Fax 772-3275
www.haywood.k12.tn.us
Haywood HS 900/9-12
1175 E College St 38012 731-772-1845
Robert Mitchell, prin. Fax 772-6079
Haywood JHS 600/7-8
1201 Haralson St 38012 731-772-3265
Dontye Bradford, prin. Fax 772-3352

Bruceton, Carroll, Pop. 1,508
Hollow Rock-Bruceton SD 600/K-12
PO Box 135 38317 731-586-7657
Rod Sturdivant, supt. Fax 586-7419
www.hrb.k12.tn.us
Central HS 200/9-12
PO Box 135 38317 731-586-2161
Jack McGee, prin. Fax 586-7419
Central MS 6-8
PO Box 135 38317 731-586-2161
Tim Gilmer, prin. Fax 586-7419

Byrdstown, Pickett, Pop. 910
Pickett County SD 700/K-12
141 Skyline Dr 38549 931-864-3123
Carolyn Cope, supt. Fax 864-7185
Pickett County HS 200/9-12
130 Skyline Dr 38549 931-864-3422
Patricia Reagan, prin. Fax 864-6297

Camden, Benton, Pop. 3,764
Benton County SD 2,400/K-12
197 Briarwood St 38320 731-584-6111
Randall Robertson, supt. Fax 584-8142
www.bcos.org/index/
Benton County Career/Technical Center Vo/Tech
155 Schools Dr 38320 731-584-4492
Richard Podgett, prin. Fax 584-4147
Camden Central HS 600/9-12
115 Schools Dr 38320 731-584-7254
Bill Kee, prin. Fax 584-4221
Camden JHS 500/6-8
75 Schools Dr 38320 731-584-4518
Michelle Leonard, prin. Fax 584-4493
Benton County Adult S Adult
175 Briarwood St 38320 731-584-1372
Alvin Smothers, prin. Fax 584-3215
Other Schools – See Big Sandy

Carthage, Smith, Pop. 2,246
Smith County SD 3,300/K-12
207 Main St N #B 37030 615-735-9625
Roger Lewis, supt. Fax 735-8271
boe.smithcounty.com/
Smith County HS 700/7-12
312 Fite E Ave 37030 615-735-9219
Jimmy Maynord, prin.
Smith County MS 400/5-8
133 Gordonsville Hwy 37030 615-735-8277
Ronnie Scudder, prin.
Other Schools – See Gordonsville

Cedar Hill, Robertson, Pop. 303
Robertson County SD
Supt. — See Springfield
Byrns JSHS 500/6-12
7025 Highway 41 N 37032 615-696-2251
Dr. Bill Locke, prin. Fax 696-0526

Celina, Clay, Pop. 1,364
Clay County SD 1,200/K-12
PO Box 469 38551 931-243-3310
Dr. Doug Young, dir. Fax 243-3706
www.clay-lea.k12.tn.us/

Clay County HS 300/9-12
PO Box 40 38551 931-243-2340
Brenda Kirby, prin. Fax 243-2376
Clay County Adult HS Adult
PO Box 469 38551 931-243-3310
Don Sherrell, prin.
Other Schools – See Red Boiling Springs

Centerville, Hickman, Pop. 3,940
Hickman County SD 3,800/PK-12
115 Murphree Ave 37033 931-729-3391
Dr. Jerry Nash, dir. Fax 729-3834
www.hickman.k12.tn.us
Hickman County HS 1,100/9-12
1645 Bulldog Blvd 37033 931-729-2616
Bert Mathis, prin. Fax 729-2925
Hickman County MS 500/6-8
1639 Bulldog Blvd 37033 931-729-4234
Michelle Gilbert, prin. Fax 729-5688
Other Schools – See Lyles

Chapel Hill, Marshall, Pop. 939
Marshall County SD
Supt. — See Lewisburg
Forrest MSHS 700/6-12
310 N Horton Pkwy 37034 931-364-7260
Mike Bishop, prin. Fax 364-2928

Charlotte, Dickson, Pop. 1,155
Dickson County SD
Supt. — See Dickson
Charlotte MS 400/6-8
250 Humphries St 37036 615-740-6060
Ray Lecomte, prin. Fax 789-7033
Creek Wood HS 900/9-12
3499 Highway 47 N 37036 615-740-6000
Janie Jones, prin. Fax 441-2868

Chattanooga, Hamilton, Pop. 154,887
Hamilton County SD 37,600/PK-12
6703 Bonny Oaks Dr 37421 423-209-8400
Dr. Jesse Register, supt. Fax 209-8601
www.hcde.org
Brainerd HS 900/9-12
1020 N Moore Rd 37411 423-855-2615
Frank Jones, prin. Fax 855-2651
Chattanooga HS Center for Creative Arts 500/6-12
1301 Dallas Rd 37405 423-209-5929
Gary Record, prin. Fax 209-5930
Chattanooga HS for the Arts & Sciences 700/6-12
865 E 3rd St 37403 423-209-5812
Steve Ball, prin. Fax 209-5831
Chattanooga Museum Magnet MS 300/6-8
1219 W Mississippi Ave 37405 423-209-5914
Bob Green, prin. Fax 209-5920
Dalewood MS 400/6-8
1300 Shallowford Rd 37411 423-493-0323
Linda Darden, prin. Fax 493-0327
East Lake Academy of Fine Arts 400/6-8
2700 E 34th St 37407 423-493-0334
Wendy Jung, prin. Fax 493-0343
East Ridge HS 900/9-12
4320 Bennett Rd 37412 423-867-6200
Mark Bean, prin. Fax 867-6220
East Ridge MS 800/6-8
4400 Bennett Rd 37412 423-867-6214
Steven Robinson, prin. Fax 867-6226
Howard HS of Academics & Technology Vo/Tech
2500 S Market St 37408 423-209-5868
Dr. Elaine Swafford, prin. Fax 209-5869
Lookout Valley MSHS 500/6-12
350 Lookout High St 37419 423-825-7352
Lee McDade, prin. Fax 821-7951
Orchard Knob MS 300/6-8
500 N Highland Park Ave 37404 423-493-7793
Reuben Justice, prin. Fax 493-7795
Red Bank HS 1,200/9-12
640 Morrison Springs Rd 37415 423-874-1900
Wade Kelley, prin. Fax 874-1924
Red Bank MS 600/6-8
3715 Dayton Blvd 37415 423-874-1908
Robert Alford, prin. Fax 874-1938
Tyner Academy 500/9-12
6836 Tyner Rd 37421 423-855-2635
Carol Goss, prin. Fax 855-9417
Tyner Middle Academy 400/6-8
6837 Tyner Rd 37421 423-855-2648
Charles Joynes, prin. Fax 855-2699
Other Schools – See Harrison, Hixson, Ooltewah, Sale
Creek, Signal Mountain, Soddy Daisy

Baylor S 1,000/6-12
171 Baylor School Rd 37405 423-267-8505
Bill Stacy, hdmstr. Fax 265-4276
Boyd-Buchanan S 1,000/PK-12
4626 Bonnieway Dr 37411 423-624-9064
Mary Helen Wood, prin. Fax 508-2215
Chattanooga Christian S 1,000/K-12
3354 Charger Dr 37409 423-265-6411
Don Holwerda, pres. Fax 756-4044
Chattanooga State Tech. Comm. College Post-Sec.
4501 Amnicola Hwy 37406 423-697-4400
Electronic Computer Programming College Post-Sec.
3805 Brainerd Rd 37411 423-624-0077
Girls Preparatory S 700/6-12
205 Island Ave 37405 423-634-7600
Stanley Tucker, hdmstr. Fax 634-7643
Grace Baptist Academy 800/K-12
7815 Shallowford Rd 37421 423-892-8222
David Patrick, hdmstr. Fax 892-1194
Hamilton Heights Christian Academy 100/9-12
2201 Hickory Valley Rd 37421 423-894-0597
Duke Stone, admin. Fax 894-4259
McCallie S 900/6-12
500 Dodds Ave 37404 423-624-8300
R. Kirk Walker Ph.D., prin. Fax 493-5690
Miller-Motte Technical College Post-Sec.
6020 Shallowford Rd 37421 423-510-9675

Notre Dame HS 600/9-12
2701 Vermont Ave 37404 423-624-4618
Perry Storey, prin. Fax 624-4621
Silverdale Baptist Academy 600/K-12
7236 Bonny Oaks Dr 37421 423-892-2319
Rebecca Hansard, hdmstr. Fax 648-7600
Temple Baptist Seminary Post-Sec.
1815 Union Ave 37404 423-493-4221
Tennessee Temple University Post-Sec.
1815 Union Ave 37404 423-493-4100
University of Tennessee Post-Sec.
615 McCallie Ave 37403 423-425-4111

Christiana, Rutherford
Rutherford County SD
Supt. — See Murfreesboro
Christiana MS 700/6-8
4675 Shelbyville Pike 37037 615-904-3885
John Ash, prin. Fax 904-3886

Church Hill, Hawkins, Pop. 6,119
Hawkins County SD
Supt. — See Rogersville
Church Hill MS 600/6-8
PO Box 38 37642 423-357-3051
William Christian, prin. Fax 357-9873
Volunteer HS 1,100/9-12
PO Box 247 37642 423-357-3641
James Dykes, prin. Fax 357-6694

Clarkrange, Fentress
Fentress County SD
Supt. — See Jamestown
Clarkrange HS 200/9-12
5801 S York Hwy 38553 931-863-3143
William Cody, prin. Fax 863-3981

Clarksburg, Carroll, Pop. 284
South Carroll County Special SD 400/PK-12
PO Box 219 38324 731-986-4534
Diana Collins, supt. Fax 986-4562
www.rocketsonline.org/main.html
Clarksburg S 400/K-12
PO Box 219 38324 731-986-3165
Steve Wilson, prin. Fax 986-4562

Clarksville, Montgomery, Pop. 107,953
Clarksville-Montgomery County SD 24,600/PK-12
621 Gracey Ave 37040 931-920-7808
Michael Harris, supt. Fax 648-5612
www.cmcss.net
Clarksville HS 1,200/9-12
151 Richview Rd 37043 931-648-5690
Harold Smith, prin. Fax 648-5624
Kenwood HS 1,100/9-12
251 E Pine Mountain Rd 37042 931-905-7900
Hal Bedell, prin. Fax 905-7906
Kenwood MS 1,000/6-8
241 E Pine Mountain Rd 37042 931-553-2080
Linda Medina-Griffy, prin. Fax 552-3080
New Providence MS 1,000/6-8
146 Cunningham Ln 37042 931-648-5655
Laura Barnett, prin. Fax 503-3409
Northeast HS 1,400/9-12
3701 Trenton Rd 37040 931-648-5640
Melissa Champion, prin. Fax 503-3413
Northeast MS 1,300/6-8
3703 Trenton Rd 37040 931-648-5665
Shari Salyer, prin. Fax 503-3410
Northwest HS 1,200/9-12
800 Lafayette Rd 37042 931-648-5675
Edward Stephens, prin. Fax 648-0094
Richview MS 1,000/6-8
2350 Memorial Drive Ext 37043 931-648-5620
Patrick Digby, prin. Fax 551-8111
Rossview HS 1,200/9-12
1237 Rossview Rd 37043 931-553-2070
Frank Myers, prin. Fax 503-3419
Rossview MS 1,000/6-8
2265 Cardinal Ln 37043 931-920-6150
Anna Neubauer, prin. Fax 920-6147
Adult Ed-Greenwood Complex Adult
430 Greenwood Ave 37040 931-542-5040
Betty Cook, prin.
Other Schools – See Cunningham

Austin Peay State University Post-Sec.
601 College St 37044 931-221-7011
Clarksville Academy 500/PK-12
710 N 2nd St 37040 931-647-6311
Kay Drew, prin. Fax 906-0610
Draughons Junior College Post-Sec.
1860 Wilma Rudolph Blvd 37040 931-552-7600
Miller-Motte Technical College Post-Sec.
1820 Business Park Dr 37040 931-553-0071
North Central Institute Post-Sec.
168 Jack Miller Blvd 37042 931-431-9700
North Tennessee Bible Inst. & Seminary Post-Sec.
PO Box 3797 37043 931-552-1510
Queen City College Post-Sec.
1594 Fort Campbell Blvd 37042 931-645-2361
Unity Christian Academy 50/K-12
1713 Fort Campbell Blvd 37042 931-645-6003
Jacqueline Hale, prin. Fax 645-6226

Cleveland, Bradley, Pop. 37,368
Bradley County SD 9,100/K-12
800 S Lee Hwy 37311 423-476-0620
Robert Taylor, supt. Fax 476-0485
www.bradleyschools.org
Bradley Central HS 1,600/9-12
1000 S Lee Hwy 37311 423-476-0650
Tom Losh, prin. Fax 476-0613
Lake Forest MS 1,000/6-8
610 Kile Lake Rd SE 37323 423-478-8825
Ritchie Stevenson, prin. Fax 478-8832
Ocoee MS 1,200/6-8
2250 N Ocoee St 37311 423-476-0630
Ron Spangler, prin. Fax 476-0588

Walker Valley HS | 1,100/9-12
750 Lauderdale Mem Hwy NW 37312 423-336-1383
Danny Coggin, prin. | Fax 336-1578

Cleveland CSD | 4,400/K-12
4300 Mouse Creek Rd NW 37312 423-472-9571
Dr. Frederick Denning, supt. | Fax 472-3390
www.clevelandschools.org
Cleveland HS | 1,200/9-12
850 Raider Dr NW 37312 423-478-1113
Chuck Rockholt, prin. | Fax 559-1560
Cleveland MS | 1,000/6-8
3635 Georgetown Rd NW 37312 423-479-9641
Jeffrey Elliott, prin. | Fax 479-9553

Academy of Beauty Arts | Post-Sec.
633 Mimosa Dr NW 37312 423-476-3742
Church of God Theological Seminary | Post-Sec.
PO Box 3330 37320 423-478-1131
Cleveland State Community College | Post-Sec.
PO Box 3570 37320 423-472-7141
Lee University | Post-Sec.
PO Box 3450 37320 423-614-8000
Tennessee Christian Academy | 200/PK-12
4995 N Lee Hwy 37312 423-559-8939
Dr. R.B. Thomas, hdmstr. | Fax 476-4974

Clifton, Wayne, Pop. 2,673
Wayne County SD
Supt. — See Waynesboro
Hughes S | 300/K-12
PO Box A 38425 931-676-3325
Marlon Davis, prin. | Fax 676-3903

Clinton, Anderson, Pop. 9,328
Anderson County SD | 6,700/PK-12
101 S Main St 37716 865-463-8631
V. L. Stonecipher, supt. | Fax 457-9157
www.acorns.k12.tn.us
Anderson County Career & Technical Ctr | Vo/Tech
140 Maverick Cir 37716 865-457-4205
Sid Spiva, prin. | Fax 457-1715
Anderson County HS | 900/9-12
130 Maverick Cir 37716 865-457-4716
Bob McCracken, prin. | Fax 457-3398
Clinton HS | 1,100/9-12
425 Dragon Dr 37716 865-457-2611
Linda Davis, prin. | Fax 457-8805
Clinton MS | 700/6-8
110 N Hicks St 37716 865-457-3451
Sue Voskamp, prin. | Fax 457-9486
Other Schools – See Lake City, Norris, Oliver Springs

Coalfield, Morgan
Morgan County SD
Supt. — See Wartburg
Coalfield S | 500/K-12
PO Box 98 37719 865-435-7332
Ramona Bentz, prin. | Fax 435-2646

Coalmont, Grundy, Pop. 958
Grundy County SD
Supt. — See Altamont
Grundy County HS | 700/9-12
HC 77 Box 500 37313 931-692-5400
Kenneth Colquette, prin. | Fax 692-5403

Collegedale, Hamilton, Pop. 7,129

Collegedale SDA Academy | 400/9-12
PO Box 628 37315 423-396-2124
Verle Thompson, prin. | Fax 396-3363
Southern Adventist University | Post-Sec.
PO Box 370 37315 423-238-2111

Collierville, Shelby, Pop. 35,445
Shelby County SD
Supt. — See Memphis
Collierville HS | 2,100/9-12
1101 New Byhalia Rd 38017 901-853-3310
Dr. Timothy Setterlund, prin. | Fax 853-3313
Collierville MS | 1,000/6-8
146 College St 38017 901-853-3320
Ingrid Warren, prin. | Fax 853-3327
Schilling Farms MS | 1,000/6-8
935 S Colbert St 38017 901-854-2345
Sherry Phillips, prin. | Fax 854-8200

St. George's Independent S Collierville | 500/6-12
1880 Wolf River Blvd 38017 901-457-2000
William Taylor, hdmstr. | Fax 457-2111

Collinwood, Wayne, Pop. 1,011
Wayne County SD
Supt. — See Waynesboro
Collinwood HS | 300/9-12
401 N Trojan Blvd 38450 931-724-4316
Herbert Luker, prin. | Fax 724-4488
Collinwood MS | 400/5-8
300 4th Ave N 38450 931-724-9510
Walter Butler, prin. | Fax 924-2519

Columbia, Maury, Pop. 33,305
Maury County SD | 11,500/PK-12
501 W 8th St 38401 931-388-8403
Eddie Hickman, supt. | Fax 840-4410
www.maury-lea.maury.k12.tn.us
Columbia Central HS | 1,400/9-12
921 Lion Pkwy 38401 931-381-2222
Cindy Johnson, prin. | Fax 381-6434
Cox MS | 600/6-8
633 Bear Creek Pike 38401 931-840-3902
Debbie Steen, prin. | Fax 840-3903
Spring Hill HS | 900/9-12
1 Raider Ln 38401 931-486-2207
Richard Callahan, prin. | Fax 486-3113
Whitthorne MS | 1,100/6-8
915 Lion Pkwy 38401 931-388-2558
Linda Lester, prin. | Fax 380-4684

Other Schools – See Culleoka, Hampshire, Mount Pleasant, Santa Fe

Columbia Academy | 600/K-12
1101 W 7th St 38401 931-388-5363
Phillip Wright, prin. | Fax 380-8506
Columbia State Community College | Post-Sec.
PO Box 1315 38402 931-540-2722
Hopewell Church Covenant Family S | 50/1-12
4184 Perry Hill Church Rd 38401 931-381-2605
Charles Mangum, admin. | Fax 381-8952
Zion Christian Academy | 300/K-12
6901 Old Zion Rd 38401 931-388-5731
Don Wahlman, hdmstr. | Fax 388-5842

Cookeville, Putnam, Pop. 27,052
Putnam County SD | 9,600/K-12
1400 E Spring St 38506 931-526-9777
Dr. Michael Martin, supt. | Fax 528-6942
www.putnamcountyschools.com
Cookeville HS | 1,900/9-12
2335 N Washington Ave 38501 931-520-2287
Wayne Shanks, prin. | Fax 520-2268
Trace MS | 900/7-8
230 Cavalier Dr 38501 931-520-2200
Linda Nash, prin. | Fax 520-2204
Adult Learning Center | Adult
1060B E Spring St 38501 931-528-8685
Jimmie Webber, prin. | Fax 526-8133
Other Schools – See Baxter, Monterey

Daniel 1 Academy | 100/5-12
1654 Burgess Falls Rd 38506 931-432-1496
Cynthia Holman, prin. | Fax 432-1498
MedVance Institute | Post-Sec.
1025 Highway 111 38501 931-526-3660
Middle Tennessee School of Cosmetology | Post-Sec.
880 E 10th St Ste A 38501 931-526-8735
Mister Wayne's Sch of Unisex Hair Design | Post-Sec.
170 S Willow Ave 38501 931-526-1478
Tennessee Technological University | Post-Sec.
PO Box 5006 38505 931-372-3101

Copperhill, Polk, Pop. 498
Polk County SD
Supt. — See Benton
Copper Basin JSHS | 300/7-12
266 Cougar Dr 37317 423-496-3291
Darren Danner, prin. | Fax 496-5308

Cordova, Shelby
Memphis CSD
Supt. — See Memphis
Cordova HS | 2,100/9-12
1800 Berryhill Rd 38016 901-416-4540
Dr. Larry McGhee, prin. | Fax 416-4545
Cordova MS | 700/5-8
900 N Sanga Rd 38018 901-416-2189
Joy Whitehead, prin. | Fax 416-2191

Shelby County SD
Supt. — See Memphis
Dexter MS | 600/5-8
6998 Raleigh LaGrange Rd 38018 901-373-3134
Phyllis Wynn, prin.
Mt. Pisgah MS | 1,000/5-8
1444 Pisgah Rd 38016 901-756-2386
John Gilmer, prin. | Fax 756-2306

Evangelical Christian S | 900/6-12
PO Box 1030 38088 901-754-7217
Steve Collums, hdmstr. | Fax 754-8123
First Assembly Christian S | 600/PK-12
8650 Walnut Grove Rd 38018 901-458-5543
Wendell Meadows, supt. | Fax 324-3558
ITT Technical Institute | Post-Sec.
7260 Goodlett Farms Pkwy 38016 901-381-0200
St. Benedict HS | 500/9-12
8250 Varnavas Dr 38016 901-260-2840
George Valadie, pres. | Fax 260-2850

Cornersville, Marshall, Pop. 933
Marshall County SD
Supt. — See Lewisburg
Cornersville JSHS | 400/7-12
323 S Main St 37047 931-293-6505
Bob Edens, prin. | Fax 293-6567

Corryton, Knox, Pop. 100
Knox County SD
Supt. — See Knoxville
Gibbs HS, 7628 Tazewell Pike 37721 | 900/9-12
Janice Walker, prin. | 865-689-9130

Cosby, Cocke
Cocke County SD
Supt. — See Newport
Cosby HS | 400/9-12
3320 Cosby Hwy 37722 423-487-5602
Duran Williams, prin. | Fax 487-5502

Covington, Tipton, Pop. 9,001
Tipton County SD | 10,800/PK-12
PO Box 486 38019 901-476-7148
Dr. Tim Fite, supt. | Fax 476-4870
www.tipton-county.com
Covington HS | 900/9-12
803 S College St 38019 901-475-5876
Tom Barton, prin. | Fax 476-5778
Crestview MS | 900/5-8
201 Mark Walker Dr 38019 901-475-5900
James Fields, prin. | Fax 475-2607
Other Schools – See Brighton, Munford

Tennessee Technology Center at Covington | Post-Sec.
1600 Highway 51 S 38019 901-475-2526

Cowan, Franklin, Pop. 1,757
Franklin County SD
Supt. — See Winchester
South MS | 300/7-8
601 Cumberland St W 37318 931-967-7355
Susan Carver, prin. | Fax 967-1413

Cross Plains, Robertson, Pop. 1,450
Robertson County SD
Supt. — See Springfield
East Robertson JSHS | 800/6-12
158 Kilgore Trce 37049 615-654-2191
Rick Ballard, prin. | Fax 654-4563

Crossville, Cumberland, Pop. 9,725
Cumberland County SD | 6,600/PK-12
368 4th St 38555 931-484-6135
Dr. Pattie Ragsdale, supt. | Fax 484-6491
ccschools.k12tn.net/
Cumberland County HS | 1,800/9-12
660 Stanley St 38555 931-484-6194
Roger Eichelberger, prin. | Fax 456-6872

Meridian Christian Academy | 100/PK-12
140 Rome Rd 38555 931-484-6089
Phil Asberry, prin. | Fax 484-6089
Tennessee Technology Center Crossville | Post-Sec.
PO Box 2959 38557 931-484-7502

Crump, Hardin, Pop. 1,538

Tennessee Technology Center at Crump | Post-Sec.
PO Box 89 38327 731-632-3393

Culleoka, Maury
Maury County SD
Supt. — See Columbia
Culleoka S | 1,000/K-12
2145 Quality St 38451 931-987-2511
Jeff Quirk, prin. | Fax 987-2594

Cumberland Gap, Claiborne, Pop. 195
Claiborne County SD
Supt. — See Tazewell
Cumberland Gap HS | 500/9-12
661 Old Jacksboro Rd 37724 423-869-9964
Troy R. Poore, prin. | Fax 869-4352

Cunningham, Montgomery
Clarksville-Montgomery County SD
Supt. — See Clarksville
Montgomery Central HS | 800/9-12
3955 Highway 48 37052 931-387-3201
Christy Houston, prin. | Fax 387-4578
Montgomery Central MS | 700/6-8
3941 Highway 48 37052 931-387-2575
Joe Nell Waters, prin. | Fax 387-3391

Dandridge, Jefferson, Pop. 2,205
Jefferson County SD | 7,000/PK-12
PO Box 190 37725 865-397-3194
Douglas Moody, dir. | Fax 397-3301
jc-schools.net/
Jefferson County HS | 1,900/9-12
115 W Dumplin Valley Rd 37725 865-397-3182
Dale Schneitman, prin. | Fax 397-4121
Maury MS | 600/6-8
PO Box 828 37725 865-397-3424
Jim Hodge, prin. | Fax 397-4253
Other Schools – See Jefferson City

Covenant Christian Academy | 300/1-12
3222 Chestnut Hill School 37725 865-509-3800
Dr. Douglas Mills, hdmstr. | Fax 509-3885

Dayton, Rhea, Pop. 6,371
Rhea County SD | 3,800/K-12
305 California Ave 37321 423-775-7812
Dallas Smith, supt. | Fax 775-7831
www.rheacounty.org
Other Schools – See Evensville, Spring City

Bryan College | Post-Sec.
PO Box 7000 37321 423-775-2041
Oxford Graduate School | Post-Sec.
500 Oxford Dr 37321 423-775-6596

Decatur, Meigs, Pop. 1,437
Meigs County SD | 1,800/K-12
PO Box 1039 37322 423-334-5793
Robert Greene, supt. | Fax 334-1462
www.meigscounty.net
Meigs County HS | 500/9-12
105 Abel Ave 37322 423-334-5797
Milburn Harmon, prin. | Fax 334-5798
Meigs MS | 500/6-8
564 N Main St 37322 423-334-9187
Allen Roberts, prin. | Fax 334-1353

Decaturville, Decatur, Pop. 842
Decatur County SD | 1,600/PK-12
PO Box 369 38329 731-852-2391
Dr. Michael Price, supt. | Fax 852-2960
Decatur County Riverside HS | 400/9-12
4250 Highway 641 S 38329 731-852-3941
Robert Myracle, prin. | Fax 852-3955
Other Schools – See Parsons

Denmark, Madison
Jackson-Madison County SD
Supt. — See Jackson
West MS | 500/7-8
317 Denmark Rd 38391 731-988-3810
Phinehas Hegmon, prin. | Fax 988-3810

Dickson, Dickson, Pop. 12,688
Dickson County SD | 7,700/PK-12
817 N Charlotte St 37055 615-446-7571
Charles Daniel, dir. | Fax 441-1375
www.dicksoncountyschools.org/

Dickson County HS — 1,400/9-12
509 Henslee Dr 37055 — 615-446-9003
Ed Littleton, prin. — Fax 441-4135
Dickson MS — 1,200/6-8
401 E College St 37055 — 615-446-2273
Johnny Chandler, prin. — Fax 441-4139
Other Schools – See Charlotte, White Bluff

Tennessee Technology Center at Dickson — Post-Sec.
740 Highway 46 S 37055 — 615-441-6220

Dover, Stewart, Pop. 1,471
Stewart County SD — 2,100/K-12
PO Box 433 37058 — 931-232-5176
Phillip Wallace, supt. — Fax 232-5390
www.stewartcountyschools.net
Stewart County HS — 600/9-12
PO Box 422 37058 — 931-232-5179
Chris Guynn, prin. — Fax 232-3119

Doalnara Academy — 50/K-12
802 Upper Standing Rock Rd 37058 — 931-232-8903
Ted Lee, hdmstr. — Fax 232-6362

Dresden, Weakley, Pop. 2,755
Weakley County SD — 4,700/K-12
8319 Highway 22 Ste A 38225 — 731-364-2247
Richard Barber, supt. — Fax 364-2662
www.weakleycountyschools.com
Dresden HS — 400/9-12
7150 Highway 22 38225 — 731-364-2949
Charles West, prin. — Fax 364-5328
Dresden MS — 400/5-8
759 Linden St Ste A 38225 — 731-364-2407
Jeff Kelley, prin. — Fax 364-5840
Weakley County Adult Learning Center — Adult
8250 Highway 22 38225 — 731-364-5481
Julia Rich, prin. — Fax 364-3580
Other Schools – See Gleason, Greenfield, Martin

Dunlap, Sequatchie, Pop. 4,414
Bledsoe County SD
Supt. — See Pikeville
Bledsoe County Vocational Center — Vo/Tech
RR 1 Box 1976 37327 — 423-554-3293
Jennifer Terry, dir. — Fax 554-3142

Sequatchie County SD — 1,900/PK-12
PO Box 488 37327 — 423-949-3617
Johnny Cordell, supt. — Fax 949-5257
Sequatchie County HS — 500/9-12
PO Box 759 37327 — 423-949-2154
Tommy Layne, prin. — Fax 949-4696
Sequatchie County MS — 600/5-8
PO Box 789 37327 — 423-949-4149
Donald Johnson, prin. — Fax 949-4140

Sequatchie Valley Preparatory Academy — 50/K-12
1050 Ray Hixson Rd 37327 — 423-554-4677

Dyer, Gibson, Pop. 2,415
Gibson County SD — 2,700/K-12
PO Box D 38330 — 731-692-3803
Robert Galloway, dir. — Fax 692-4375
www.gcssd.org
Gibson County HS — 600/9-12
PO Box 190 38330 — 731-692-3616
B. Booth, prin. — Fax 692-2123
Other Schools – See Medina

Dyersburg, Dyer, Pop. 17,301
Dyer County SD — 3,500/K-12
159 Everett Ave 38024 — 731-285-6712
Dr. Dwight Hedge, supt. — Fax 286-6721
www.dyercs.net
Three Oaks MS — 500/6-8
3200 Upper Finley Rd 38024 — 731-285-3100
David Lovell, prin. — Fax 285-3360
Other Schools – See Newbern

Dyersburg CSD — 3,500/K-12
PO Box 1507 38025 — 731-286-3600
Lloyd Ramer, supt. — Fax 286-2754
www.dcs.k12tn.net/dcs/index.html
Dyersburg HS — 900/9-12
125 US Highway 51 Byp W 38024 — 731-286-3630
Sam Miles, prin. — Fax 286-2209
Dyersburg MS — 800/6-8
400 Frank Maynard Dr 38024 — 731-286-3625
Tyles Davenport, prin. — Fax 286-3624

Dyersburg State Community College — Post-Sec.
1516 Lake Rd 38024 — 731-286-3200

Eagleville, Rutherford, Pop. 448
Rutherford County SD
Supt. — See Murfreesboro
Eagleville S — 600/K-12
500 Highway 99 37060 — 615-274-6336
Ronda Holton, prin. — Fax 274-6859

Eidson, Hawkins
Hawkins County SD
Supt. — See Rogersville
Clinch S — 200/K-12
1010 Clinch Valley Rd 37731 — 423-272-3110
Linda Long, prin. — Fax 272-3110

Elizabethton, Carter, Pop. 14,015
Carter County SD — 5,800/PK-12
305 Academy St 37643 — 423-547-4000
Dallas Williams, supt. — Fax 547-8338
carter.k12.tn.us
Happy Valley HS — 600/9-12
121 Warpath Ln 37643 — 423-547-4094
Dale Campbell, prin.
Happy Valley MS — 500/5-8
163 Warpath Ln 37643 — 423-547-4070
Carter Blevins, prin.

Unaka HS, 119 Robinson Ln 37643 — 300/9-12
Mickey Taylor, prin. — 423-474-4100
Carter County Adult HS — Adult
412 S Sycamore St 37643 — 423-547-4084
Paula Webster, prin.
Other Schools – See Hampton, Roan Mountain

Elizabethton CSD — 2,200/PK-12
804 S Watauga Ave 37643 — 423-547-8000
David Roper Ed.D., supt. — Fax 547-8101
www.ecschools.net
Dugger JHS — 500/6-8
306 W E St 37643 — 423-547-8025
Regina Cates, prin. — Fax 547-8021
Elizabethton HS — 800/9-12
907 Jason Witten Way 37643 — 423-547-8015
Dr. Pamela Scott, prin. — Fax 547-8016

Tennessee Technology Center Elizabethton — Post-Sec.
PO Box 789 37644 — 423-543-0070

Englewood, McMinn, Pop. 1,647
McMinn County SD
Supt. — See Athens
Central HS — 700/9-12
145 County Road 461 37329 — 423-263-5541
Roger Freeman, prin. — Fax 263-0399

Erin, Houston, Pop. 1,456
Houston County SD — 1,400/PK-12
PO Box 209 37061 — 931-289-4148
Cathy Harvey, supt. — Fax 289-5543
Houston County HS — 400/9-12
2500 State Route 149 37061 — 931-289-4447
David Bell, prin.
Houston County MS — 300/6-8
1241 W Main St 37061 — 931-289-5591
Sylvia Vinson, prin.
Houston County Adult S — Adult
1214 W Main St 37061 — 931-289-5525
Linda McDonough, prin.

Erwin, Unicoi, Pop. 5,764
Unicoi County SD — 2,400/PK-12
600 N Elm Ave 37650 — 423-743-1600
Denise Brown, dir. — Fax 743-1615
www.unicoischools.com/
Unicoi County HS — 1,000/8-12
700 S Mohawk Dr 37650 — 423-743-1632
Dr. Allen Rogers, prin. — Fax 743-1636
Unicoi County Vocational S — Vo/Tech
100 Okolona Dr 37650 — 423-743-1639
Charles Baxter, prin. — Fax 743-1671

Evensville, Rhea
Rhea County SD
Supt. — See Dayton
Rhea County HS — 1,300/9-12
405 Pierce Rd 37332 — 423-775-7821
Jerry Levengood, prin. — Fax 775-7823

Fairview, Williamson, Pop. 6,548
Williamson County SD
Supt. — See Franklin
Fairview HS — 600/9-12
2595 Fairview Blvd 37062 — 615-472-4400
Tony Donen, prin. — Fax 472-4421
Fairview MS — 500/6-8
7200 Cumberland Dr 37062 — 615-472-4430
Brian Bass, prin. — Fax 472-4441

Fayetteville, Lincoln, Pop. 6,955
Fayetteville CSD — 1,000/PK-9
110 Elk Ave S 37334 — 931-433-5542
Bill Evans, supt. — Fax 433-7499
www.fcsboe.org
Fayetteville JHS — 300/7-9
1800 Wilson Pkwy 37334 — 931-433-3158
Ron Perrin, prin. — Fax 433-4611

Lincoln County SD — 3,900/PK-12
206 Davidson St E 37334 — 931-433-3565
Stan Golden, supt. — Fax 433-7397
www.lcdoe.org
Lincoln County SHS — 1,100/10-12
1233 Huntsville Hwy 37334 — 931-433-6505
Jim Stewart, prin. — Fax 438-1490
Ninth Grade Academy — 300/9-9
900 Main Ave S 37334 — 931-433-6156
Sarah Wallace, prin. — Fax 438-2465
Lincoln County Adult HS — Adult
911 Main Ave S 37334 — 931-438-1489
Debbie Pardon, prin.

Fayetteville Beauty School — Post-Sec.
201 Main Ave S 37334 — 931-433-1305

Franklin, Williamson, Pop. 46,528
Franklin Special SD — 4,100/PK-8
507 New Highway 96 W 37064 — 615-794-6624
David L. Snowdon Ph.D., supt. — Fax 790-4716
www.fssd.org
Freedom MS — 700/7-8
750 New Highway 96 W 37064 — 615-794-0987
Kristi Jefferson, prin. — Fax 790-4742

Williamson County SD — 22,500/PK-12
1320 W Main St Ste 202 37064 — 615-472-4000
Dr. Rebecca Sharber, supt. — Fax 472-4190
www.wcs.edu
Centennial HS — 1,600/9-12
5050 Mallory Ln 37067 — 615-472-4270
Dr. Terry Shrader, prin. — Fax 472-4291
Franklin HS — 1,700/9-12
810 Hillsboro Rd 37064 — 615-472-4450
Willie Dickerson, prin. — Fax 472-4478
Grassland MS — 900/6-8
2390 Hillsboro Rd 37069 — 615-472-4500
Dr. Susan Curtis, prin. — Fax 472-4511

Middle College HS — 500/9-12
108 Everbright Ave 37064 — 615-472-4670
Harold Ford, prin. — Fax 472-4675
Page HS — 1,100/9-12
6281 Arno Rd 37064 — 615-472-4730
Dr. Andrea Anthony, prin. — Fax 472-4751
Page MS — 800/6-8
6262 Arno Rd 37064 — 615-472-4760
Josie Jacobs, prin. — Fax 472-4771
Other Schools – See Brentwood, Fairview, Thompsons Station

Battle Ground Academy — 900/K-12
PO Box 1889 37065 — 615-794-3501
Dr. John Griffith, hdmstr. — Fax 567-8360
Franklin Classical S — 100/6-12
PO Box 1601 37065 — 615-595-5337
Tina Gilchrist, prin. — Fax 595-5339
O'More College of Design — Post-Sec.
423 S Margin St 37064 — 615-794-4254
Williamson Christian College — Post-Sec.
200 Seaboard Ln 37067 — 615-771-7821

Gainesboro, Jackson, Pop. 867
Jackson County SD — 1,700/K-12
711 School Dr 38562 — 931-268-0268
Joe D. Barlow, supt. — Fax 268-3647
volweb.utk.edu/school/jackson/
Jackson County HS — 400/9-12
190 Blue Devil Ln 38562 — 931-268-9771
Dennis Tennant, prin. — Fax 268-9433
Jackson County MS — 600/4-8
170 Blue Devil Ln 38562 — 931-268-9779
Gail Myers, prin. — Fax 268-9413

Gallatin, Sumner, Pop. 25,107
Sumner County SD — 24,400/PK-12
695 E Main St 37066 — 615-451-5200
Benny Bills, dir. — Fax 451-5216
www.sumnerschools.org/
Doss MS — 600/6-8
281 Big Station Camp Blvd 37066 — 615-206-0116
Mike Brown, prin. — Fax 206-0165
Gallatin HS — 1,400/9-12
700 Dan P Herron Dr 37066 — 615-452-2621
Rufus Lassiter, prin. — Fax 451-5426
Rucker-Stewart MS — 600/6-8
350 Hancock St 37066 — 615-452-1734
Andrew Turner, prin. — Fax 451-5297
Shafer MS — 600/6-8
240 Albert Gallatin Ave 37066 — 615-452-9100
David Haltman, prin. — Fax 451-6545
Station Camp HS — 700/9-12
1040 Bison Trl 37066 — 615-451-6551
Art Crook, prin. — Fax 451-6556
Other Schools – See Hendersonville, Portland, Westmoreland, White House

College Heights Christian Academy — 300/K-12
2100 Nashville Pike 37066 — 615-452-4988
Linda Gilmore, admin. — Fax 452-4745
Volunteer State Community College — Post-Sec.
1480 Nashville Pike 37066 — 615-452-8600

Gatlinburg, Sevier, Pop. 3,870
Sevier County SD
Supt. — See Sevierville
Gatlinburg-Pittman HS — 600/9-12
150 Proffitt Rd 37738 — 865-436-5637
Don Best, prin. — Fax 436-2567

Germantown, Shelby, Pop. 37,520
Shelby County SD
Supt. — See Memphis
Germantown HS — 2,100/9-12
7653 Old Poplar Pike 38138 — 901-756-2350
Dr. Lonnie Harris, prin. — Fax 756-2356
Germantown MS — 500/6-8
7925 CD Smith Rd 38138 — 901-756-2338
Russell Joy, prin. — Fax 759-4521
Houston HS — 1,800/9-12
9755 Wolf River Blvd 38139 — 901-756-2370
John Aitken, prin. — Fax 756-2377
Houston MS — 1,000/6-8
9400 Wolf River Blvd 38139 — 901-756-2366
Mike Morrison, prin. — Fax 756-2346

Bodine S — 100/1-12
2432 Yester Oaks Dr 38139 — 901-754-1800
Rene Lee, prin. — Fax 751-8595
Mid-America Baptist Theological Seminary — Post-Sec.
PO Box 381528 38183 — 901-751-8453

Gleason, Weakley, Pop. 1,452
Weakley County SD
Supt. — See Dresden
Gleason S — 600/K-12
92-99 State Championship Dr 38229 — 731-648-5351
Randy Frazier, prin. — Fax 648-9199

Goodlettsville, Davidson, Pop. 14,229
Davidson County SD
Supt. — See Nashville
Goodlettsville MS — 600/5-8
300 S Main St 37072 — 615-859-8956
Sarah Moore, prin. — Fax 859-8961

Miller-Motte Technical College — Post-Sec.
801 Space Park N 37072 — 615-859-8090
Nossi College of Art — Post-Sec.
907 Rivergate Pkwy Ste E6 37072 — 615-851-1088

Gordonsville, Smith, Pop. 1,107
Smith County SD
Supt. — See Carthage
Gordonsville HS, 104 Main St E 38563 — 400/7-12
Steve Armistead, prin. — 615-683-8245

Gray, Washington, Pop. 1,071
Washington County SD
　Supt. — See Jonesborough
Boone HS　　　　　　　　　　　1,100/9-12
　1440 Suncrest Dr 37615　　　423-477-1600
　Dr. Suzan Baker, prin.　　　　Fax 477-1625

Greenback, Loudon, Pop. 993
Loudon County SD
　Supt. — See Loudon
Greenback S　　　　　　　　　700/K-12
　400 Chilhowee Ave 37742　　865-856-3028
　Brenda Holbrook, prin.　　　Fax 856-5427

Greenbrier, Robertson, Pop. 5,851
Robertson County SD
　Supt. — See Springfield
Greenbrier HS　　　　　　　　800/9-12
　126 Cuniff Dr 37073　　　　615-643-4526
　Gertrude Deal, prin.　　　　Fax 643-8873
Greenbrier MS　　　　　　　　600/6-8
　2450 Highway 41 S 37073　615-643-7823
　Don Jones, prin.　　　　　　Fax 643-4580

Greeneville, Greene, Pop. 15,204
Greene County SD　　　　　　6,500/PK-12
　910 W Summer St 37743　　423-639-4194
　Joe Parkins, supt.　　　　　Fax 639-1615
　pages.xtn.net/~gcs/
North Greene HS　　　　　　　400/9-12
　4675 Old Baileyton Rd 37745　423-234-1752
　Donna Waddle, prin.　　　　Fax 234-1752
South Greene HS　　　　　　　500/9-12
　7469 Asheville Hwy 37743　423-639-3790
　Cindy Bowman, prin.　　　　Fax 636-3791
Other Schools – See Afton, Mosheim

Greeneville CSD　　　　　　　2,600/K-12
　PO Box 1420 37744　　　　423-787-8000
　Lyle Ailshie, supt.　　　　　Fax 638-2540
　www.gcsschools.net
Greeneville HS　　　　　　　　800/9-12
　210 Tusculum Blvd 37745　423-787-8030
　Jerry Ayers, prin.　　　　　Fax 787-8028
Greeneville MS　　　　　　　　700/6-8
　433 E Vann Rd 37743　　　423-639-7841
　Linda Stroud, prin.　　　　Fax 639-4112
Greeneville Center for Technology　Vo/Tech
　1121 Hal Henard Rd 37743　423-639-0171
　Jerry Renner, prin.　　　　Fax 639-0176

Greeneville Adventist Academy　100/K-10
　305 Takoma Ave 37743　　423-639-2011
　Keith Nelson, prin.　　　　Fax 639-5002
Tusculum College　　　　　　Post-Sec.
　PO Box 5051 37743　　　　800-251-0256

Greenfield, Weakley, Pop. 2,133
Weakley County SD
　Supt. — See Dresden
Greenfield S　　　　　　　　600/K-12
　101 N Faxon St 38230　　731-235-3424
　Jackie Vaughan, prin.　　Fax 235-3480

Halls, Lauderdale, Pop. 2,291
Lauderdale County SD
　Supt. — See Ripley
Halls HS　　　　　　　　　　400/9-12
　800 W Tigrett St 38040　731-836-9642
　Andy Pugh, prin.　　　　Fax 836-9642
Halls JHS　　　　　　　　　200/7-8
　800 W Tigrett St 38040　731-836-5579
　Pam Sirmans, prin.　　　Fax 836-5579

Hampshire, Maury
Maury County SD
　Supt. — See Columbia
Hampshire S　　　　　　　300/K-12
　4235 Old State Rd 38461　931-285-2300
　Stan Curtis, prin.　　　　Fax 285-2612

Hampton, Carter
Carter County SD
　Supt. — See Elizabethton
Hampton HS　　　　　　　400/9-12
　766 First Ave 37658　　423-725-5200
　Danny McClain, prin.　　Fax 725-5204

Harriman, Roane, Pop. 6,663
Roane County SD
　Supt. — See Kingston
Harriman HS　　　　　　　300/9-12
　920 N Roane St 37748　865-882-1821
　Gary Powell, prin.　　　Fax 882-6479
Harriman MS　　　　　　　300/6-8
　1025 Cumberland St 37748　865-882-1727
　David R. Stevens, prin.　Fax 882-6285
Midtown Educational Center　Vo/Tech
　3096 Roane State Hwy 37748　865-882-0242
　R. Allen Williams, prin.　Fax 882-7734

Roane State Community College　Post-Sec.
　276 Patton Ln 37748　　865-354-3000
Tennessee Technology Center at Harriman　Post-Sec.
　PO Box 1109 37748　　865-882-6703

Harrison, Hamilton, Pop. 7,191
Hamilton County SD
　Supt. — See Chattanooga
Brown MS　　　　　　　　600/6-8
　5716 Highway 58 37341　423-344-1439
　John Stewart, prin.　　Fax 344-1471
Central HS　　　　　　　1,100/9-12
　5728 Highway 58 37341　423-344-1447
　Robert Sharpe, prin.　　Fax 344-1470

Harrogate, Claiborne, Pop. 3,974
Claiborne County SD
　Supt. — See Tazewell

Livesay MS　　　　　　　300/5-8
　PO Box 460 37752　　423-869-4663
　Roy Bryant, prin.　　　Fax 869-8389

Lincoln Memorial University　Post-Sec.
　PO Box 2012 37752　423-869-3611
White Academy　　　　　100/5-12
　Cumberland Gap Pkwy 37752　423-869-6295
　Dr. Sheila Clyburn, prin.　Fax 869-6425

Hartsville, Trousdale, Pop. 2,373
Trousdale County SD　　1,200/K-12
　103 Lock Six Rd 37074　615-374-2193
　Margaret Oldham, dir.　Fax 374-1108
　www.tcschools.org
Satterfield MS　　　　　300/6-8
　210 Damascus St 37074　615-374-2748
　John Kerr, prin.　　　Fax 374-2602
Trousdale County HS　　400/9-12
　262 McMurry Blvd W 37074　615-374-2201
　Toby Woodmore, prin.　Fax 374-1120

Tennessee Technology Center Hartsville　Post-Sec.
　716 McMurry Blvd 37074　615-374-2147

Henderson, Chester, Pop. 6,148
Chester County SD　　2,500/PK-12
　PO Box 327 38340　731-989-5134
　John Pipkin, supt.　　Fax 989-4755
　www.chestercountyschools.org
Chester County HS　　700/9-12
　552 E Main St 38340　731-989-8125
　Troy Kilzer, prin.　　Fax 989-8131
Chester County JHS　　400/7-8
　930 E Main St 38340　731-989-8135
　Ken West, prin.　　　Fax 989-8137

Freed-Hardeman University　Post-Sec.
　158 E Main St 38340　731-989-6000

Hendersonville, Sumner, Pop. 43,027
Sumner County SD
　Supt. — See Gallatin
Beech HS　　　　　　1,100/9-12
　3126 Long Hollow Pike 37075　615-824-6200
　Frank Cardwell, prin.　Fax 264-6553
Ellis MS　　　　　　　500/6-8
　100 Indian Lake Rd 37075　615-264-6093
　Opal Poe, prin.　　　Fax 264-5800
Hawkins MS　　　　　500/6-8
　487 Walton Ferry Rd 37075　615-824-3456
　Jeff Helbig, prin.　　Fax 264-6003
Hendersonville HS　　1,400/9-12
　123 Cherokee Rd 37075　615-824-6162
　Mike Shelton, prin.　Fax 264-6027
Hunter MS　　　　　　700/6-8
　2101 New Hope Rd 37075　615-822-4720
　Carla Easterling, prin.　Fax 264-6036
Hyde Magnet S　　　　1,100/K-12
　128 Township Dr 37075　615-264-6543
　Brad Schreiner, prin.　Fax 264-6546
Wilson Night S　　　　Adult
　102 Indian Lake Rd 37075　615-264-6085
　Cynthia Horner, prin.　Fax 264-6034

Pope John Paul II HS　300/9-12
　117 Caldwell Dr 37075　615-822-2375
　Hans Broekman, prin.　Fax 822-6226

Hermitage, See Nashville
Davidson County SD
　Supt. — See Nashville
DuPont-Tyler MS　　　700/5-8
　431 Tyler Dr 37076　615-885-8827
　Carol Cutsinger, prin.　Fax 889-4538

Hixson, See Chattanooga
Hamilton County SD
　Supt. — See Chattanooga
Hixson HS　　　　　1,000/9-12
　5705 Middle Valley Rd 37343　423-847-4800
　Eddie Gravitte, prin.　Fax 847-4801
Hixson MS　　　　　600/6-8
　5401 School Dr 37343　423-870-0600
　Jim Boles, prin.　　Fax 870-0623
Loftis MS　　　　　800/6-8
　8611 Columbus Rd 37343　423-843-4749
　Lisa Huskey, prin.　Fax 843-4758

Hohenwald, Lewis, Pop. 3,808
Lewis County SD　　2,000/K-12
　206 S Court St 38462　931-796-3264
　Benny Pace, supt.　Fax 796-5127
　www.lewis.k12.tn.us
Lewis County HS　　600/9-12
　818 W Main St 38462　931-796-4085
　Chad Moorehead, prin.　Fax 796-1172
Lewis County MS　　500/6-8
　207 S Court St 38462　931-796-4586
　Tim Watkins, prin.　Fax 796-7601

Tennessee Technology Center at Hohenwald Post-Sec.
　813 W Main St 38462　931-796-5351

Humboldt, Gibson, Pop. 9,339
Humboldt CSD　　　1,500/K-12
　1421 Osborne St 38343　731-784-2652
　Garnett Twyman, supt.　Fax 784-2480
Humboldt HS　　　400/9-12
　2600 Viking Dr 38343　731-784-2781
　Ron Canada, prin.　Fax 784-8536
Humboldt JHS　　　300/7-8
　1811 Ferrell St 38343　731-784-9514
　Lillian Shelton, prin.　Fax 784-3274

Huntingdon, Carroll, Pop. 4,251
Carroll County SD
　PO Box 799 38344　731-986-4482
　Charlotte Tucker, supt.　Fax 986-0198
　www.carrollschools.com
Carroll County Technical Center　Vo/Tech
　1235 Buena Vista Rd 38344　731-986-8908
　Mary Mays, prin.　　Fax 986-3200

Huntingdon Special SD　1,300/K-12
　585 High St 38344　731-986-2222
　Lynn Twyman, supt.　Fax 986-4365
　www.huntingdonschools.org/
Huntingdon HS　　　400/9-12
　475 Mustang Dr 38344　731-986-8223
　Mike Henson, prin.　Fax 986-4031
Huntingdon MS　　　500/4-8
　199 Browning Ave 38344　731-986-4544
　Pat Dillahunty, prin.　Fax 986-8689

Huntland, Franklin, Pop. 897
Franklin County SD
　Supt. — See Winchester
Huntland S　　　　700/PK-12
　400 Gore St 37345　931-469-7506
　Charlie Pike, prin.　Fax 469-0590

Huntsville, Scott, Pop. 988
Scott County SD　　2,600/PK-12
　PO Box 37 37756　423-663-2159
　Mike Davis, supt.　Fax 663-9682
　www.scottcounty.net
Huntsville MS　　　200/6-8
　3101 Baker Hwy 37756　423-663-2192
　Lamance Bryant, prin.　Fax 663-2967
Scott HS　　　　　700/9-12
　400 Scott High Dr 37756　423-663-2801
　Sharon Wilson, prin.　Fax 663-2368

Tennessee Technology Center Oneida/Hunts Post-Sec.
　355 Scott High Dr 37756　423-663-4900

Jacksboro, Campbell, Pop. 1,959
Campbell County SD　6,000/PK-12
　PO Box 445 37757　423-562-8377
　Dr. Judy Carr Blevins, supt.　Fax 566-7562
　www.campbell.k12.tn.us
Campbell County Comprehensive HS　1,300/9-12
　150 Cougar Ln 37757　423-562-8308
　John Turnblazer, prin.　Fax 562-2019
Jacksboro MS　　　500/6-8
　150 Eagle Cir 37757　423-562-3773
　Larry Nidiffer, prin.　Fax 562-8994
Campbell County Adult HS　Adult
　366 Alder Springs Rd 37757　423-566-5436
　Dr. Rita Goins-Claiborne, prin.　Fax 562-5219
Other Schools – See Jellico, La Follette

Tennessee Technology Center at Jacksboro　Post-Sec.
　PO Box 419 37757　423-566-9629

Jackson, Madison, Pop. 61,110
Jackson-Madison County SD　12,400/PK-12
　310 N Parkway 38305　731-664-2592
　Roy Weaver, supt.　Fax 664-2502
　www.jmcss.net/
Jackson Central-Merry HS　1,000/9-12
　332 Lane Ave 38301　731-424-2200
　Virginia Crump, prin.　Fax 423-6158
Liberty Technology Magnet HS　Vo/Tech
　3470 Ridgecrest Road Ext 38305　731-423-9086
　Johnny Reynolds, prin.　Fax 424-3445
Madison Academic Magnet S　300/9-12
　179 Allen Ave 38301　731-427-3501
　Tommy Allen, prin.　Fax 427-3587
Northeast MS　　　700/7-8
　2665 Christmasville Rd 38305　731-422-6687
　Larry Charles, prin.　Fax 423-1805
North Side HS　　　1,000/9-12
　3066 N Highland Ave 38305　731-668-3171
　Mike Martin, prin.　Fax 661-9756
Rose Hill MS　　　500/7-8
　2233 Beech Bluff Rd 38301　731-423-6170
　James Shaw, prin.　Fax 423-6171
South Side HS　　　800/9-12
　84 Harts Bridge Rd 38301　731-422-9923
　Jimmy Arnold, prin.　Fax 423-3411
Tigrett MS　　　　600/7-8
　716 Westwood Ave 38301　731-988-3840
　Nelson Piercey, prin.　Fax 988-3838
Other Schools – See Denmark

Jackson Christian S　900/PK-12
　832 Country Club Ln 38305　731-668-8055
　Dr. Michael Weimer, pres.　Fax 664-5763
Jackson State Community College　Post-Sec.
　2046 N Parkway 38301　731-424-3520
Lambuth University　　Post-Sec.
　705 Lambuth Blvd 38301　731-425-2500
Lane College　　　　Post-Sec.
　545 Lane Ave 38301　731-426-7500
McCollum & Ross The Hair School　Post-Sec.
　1433 Hollywood Dr 38301　731-427-6642
Tennessee Technology Center at Jackson　Post-Sec.
　2468 Technology Center Dr 38301　731-424-0691
Trinity Christian Academy　400/6-12
　130 Old Denmark Rd 38301　731-423-8924
　Robbie Mason, hdmstr.　Fax 427-6195
Union University　　Post-Sec.
　1050 Union University Dr 38305　731-668-1818
University S of Jackson　1,300/PK-12
　232 Mcclellan Rd 38305　731-664-6188
　Steven Maloan, hdmstr.　Fax 664-5046
West Tennessee Business College　Post-Sec.
　1186 Highway 45 Byp 38301　800-737-9822

Jamestown, Fentress, Pop. 1,844
Fentress County SD — 2,200/PK-12
  PO Box 963 38556 — 931-879-9218
  Homer Linder, supt. — Fax 879-4050
  www.fentress.k12tn.net
Fentress County Adult S — Adult
  PO Box 963 38556 — 931-752-8296
  Gerald Huddleston, prin. — Fax 879-7415
Other Schools – See Clarkrange

Jasper, Marion, Pop. 3,118
Marion County SD — 4,100/PK-12
  204 Betsy Pack Dr 37347 — 423-942-3434
  Dr. Fred Taylor, supt. — Fax 942-4210
  www.marionschools.org/
Jasper MS — 500/5-8
  601 Elm Ave 37347 — 423-942-6251
  Kim Headrick, prin. — Fax 942-0141
Marion County HS — 500/9-12
  160 Ridley Ave 37347 — 423-942-5120
  Sherry Prince, prin. — Fax 942-5544
Other Schools – See South Pittsburg, Whitwell

Jefferson City, Jefferson, Pop. 7,850
Jefferson County SD
  Supt. — See Dandridge
Jefferson MS — 700/6-8
  361 W Broadway Blvd 37760 — 865-475-6133
  Amie Lambert, prin. — Fax 475-8813

Carson-Newman College — Post-Sec.
  1646 Russell Ave 37760 — 865-471-4000

Jellico, Campbell, Pop. 2,472
Campbell County SD
  Supt. — See Jacksboro
Jellico HS — 300/9-12
  141 High School Ln 37762 — 423-784-9455
  Don Walden, prin. — Fax 784-9456

Joelton, See Nashville
Davidson County SD
  Supt. — See Nashville
Joelton MS — 500/5-8
  3500 Old Clarksville Pike 37080 — 615-876-5100
  Mary Nollner, prin. — Fax 876-5181

Johnson City, Washington, Pop. 57,394
Johnson City CSD — 6,800/PK-12
  PO Box 1517 37605 — 423-434-5200
  Dr. Richard Bales, supt. — Fax 434-5237
  www.jcschools.org
Science Hill HS — 2,400/8-12
  1509 John Exum Pkwy 37604 — 423-232-2190
  David Chupa, prin. — Fax 926-1622
Science Hill Technology Center — Vo/Tech
  501 Liberty Bell Blvd 37604 — 423-232-2200
  Kenneth Ralston, dir. — Fax 461-1695

Washington County SD
  Supt. — See Jonesborough
Boones Creek MS — 400/5-8
  4352 N Roan St 37615 — 423-283-3520
  Dr. Max Williams, prin. — Fax 283-3524

East Tennessee State University — Post-Sec.
  PO Box 70731 37614 — 423-439-1000
Emmanuel School of Religion — Post-Sec.
  1 Walker Dr 37601 — 423-926-1186
Providence Academy — 500/K-12
  2788 Carroll Creek Rd 37615 — 423-854-9819
  Jerry Williams, admin. — Fax 854-8958

Jonesborough, Washington, Pop. 4,391
Washington County SD — 8,200/K-12
  405 W College St 37659 — 423-753-1100
  Grant Rowland, supt. — Fax 753-1114
  www.wcde.org
Crockett HS — 1,400/9-12
  684 Old State Route 34 37659 — 423-753-1150
  Henry Marable, prin. — Fax 753-1167
Jonesborough MS — 500/5-8
  308 Forrest Dr 37659 — 423-753-1190
  Terry Crowe, prin. — Fax 753-1570
Other Schools – See Gray, Johnson City

Kingsport, Sullivan, Pop. 44,231
Kingsport CSD — 6,300/PK-12
  1701 E Center St 37664 — 423-378-2100
  Dr. Richard Kitzmiller, supt. — Fax 378-2120
  www.k12k.com/
Dobyns-Bennett HS — 1,800/9-12
  1800 Legion Dr 37664 — 423-378-8400
  Earl Lovelace, prin. — Fax 378-8535
Robinson MS — 700/6-8
  1517 Jessee St 37664 — 423-378-2200
  Richard Everroad, prin. — Fax 378-2220
Sevier MS — 800/6-8
  1200 Wateree St 37660 — 423-378-2450
  Dr. Carolyn McPherson, prin. — Fax 378-2430
Adult Education & Lifelong Learning — Adult
  1701 E Center St 37664 — 423-378-2130
  Tom Allen, dir. — Fax 378-2134

Sullivan County SD
  Supt. — See Blountville
Colonial Heights MS — 600/6-8
  415 Lebanon Rd 37663 — 423-354-1360
  Mike Cline, prin. — Fax 354-1365
Sullivan MS — 200/6-8
  4154 Sullivan Gardens Dr 37660 — 423-354-1780
  Clarence Marshall, prin. — Fax 354-1786
Sullivan North HS — 800/9-12
  2533 N John B Dennis Pkwy 37660 — 423-354-1400
  Richard Carroll, prin. — Fax 354-1406
Sullivan South HS — 1,000/9-12
  1236 Moreland Dr 37664 — 423-354-1300
  Greg Harvey, prin. — Fax 354-1306

Appalachian Christian S — 50/K-12
  1044 New Beason Well Rd 37660 — 423-288-3352
  Newl Dotson, admin. — Fax 288-3354

Kingston, Roane, Pop. 5,327
Roane County SD — 7,200/PK-12
  105 Bluff Rd 37763 — 865-376-5592
  Dr. Toni McGriff, supt. — Fax 376-1284
  www.roane-lea.roane.k12.tn.us/
Cherokee MS — 500/6-8
  200 Paint Rock Ferry Rd 37763 — 865-376-9281
  Joan Turbyville, prin. — Fax 376-8525
Midway HS — 200/9-12
  530 Loudon Hwy 37763 — 865-376-5645
  Tony Clower, prin. — Fax 376-8516
Roane County HS — 700/9-12
  540 W Cumberland St 37763 — 865-376-6534
  Donna Collins, prin. — Fax 376-8530
Other Schools – See Harriman, Oliver Springs, Rockwood, Ten Mile

Kingston Springs, Cheatham, Pop. 2,848
Cheatham County SD
  Supt. — See Ashland City
Harpeth HS — 600/9-12
  170 E Kingston Springs Rd 37082 — 615-952-2811
  Jenny Simpkins, prin. — Fax 952-5013
Harpeth MS — 700/5-8
  170 Harpeth View Trl 37082 — 615-952-2293
  Shannon Schwila, prin. — Fax 952-4527

Knoxville, Knox, Pop. 173,278
Knox County SD — 50,500/PK-12
  PO Box 2188 37901 — 865-594-1800
  Dr. Charles Lindsey, supt. — Fax 594-1627
  www.kcs.k12tn.net
Austin-East HS — 700/9-12
  2800 Martin Luther King Jr 37914 — 865-594-3792
  Brian Hartsell, prin.
Bearden HS — 1,900/9-12
  8352 Kingston Pike 37919 — 865-539-7800
  Barbara Jenkins, prin.
Bearden MS, 1000 Francis Rd 37909 — 1,000/6-8
  Heather Karnes, prin. — 865-539-7839
Byington-Solway Technology Center — Vo/Tech
  2700 Byington Solway Rd 37931 — 865-693-3511
  Clifford Davis, prin.
Cedar Bluff MS — 500/6-8
  707 N Cedar Bluff Rd 37923 — 865-539-7891
  Sonya Winstead, prin.
Central HS — 1,200/9-12
  5321 Jacksboro Pike 37918 — 865-689-1400
  Jon Miller, prin. — Fax 689-1403
Farragut HS — 2,300/9-12
  11237 Kingston Pike, — 865-966-9775
  Mike Reynolds, prin.
Farragut MS, 200 W End Ave, — 1,200/6-8
  Dr. Dick Dalhaus, prin. — 865-966-9756
Fulton HS, 2509 N Broadway St 37917 — 900/9-12
  Kitty Hatcher, prin. — 865-594-1240
Gresham MS, 500 Gresham Rd 37918 — 800/6-8
  Sheila Fuqua, prin. — 865-689-1430
Halls HS, 4321 E Emory Rd 37938 — 1,000/9-12
  Mark Duff, prin. — 865-922-7757
Halls MS — 1,000/6-8
  4317 E Emory Rd 37938 — 865-922-7494
  Doug Oliver, prin. — Fax 925-7439
Holston MS — 700/6-8
  600 N Chilhowee Dr 37924 — 865-594-1300
  Tom Brown, prin.
Karns HS — 1,400/9-12
  2710 Byington Solway Rd 37931 — 865-539-8670
  Clifford Davis, prin.
Karns MS — 1,000/6-8
  2925 Gray Hendrix Rd 37931 — 865-539-7732
  Danny Trent, prin.
Lincoln Park Tech/Trade Center — Vo/Tech
  535 Chickamauga Ave 37917 — 865-689-1454
  Rick Bise, prin. — Fax 689-1456
North Knox Vocational Center — Vo/Tech
  7411 Ledgerwood Rd 37938 — 865-922-7576
Northwest MS — 900/6-8
  5301 Pleasant Ridge Rd 37912 — 865-594-1345
  Ken Dunlap, prin.
South-Doyle HS — 1,200/9-12
  2020 Tipton Station Rd 37920 — 865-577-4475
  Rick Walker, prin.
South-Doyle MS — 1,100/6-8
  3900 Decatur Dr 37920 — 865-579-2133
  Jeanna Swan-Cole, prin.
Vine MS — 500/6-8
  1807 Martin Luther King Jr 37915 — 865-594-4461
  LaRoyce Beatty, prin.
West HS, 3326 Sutherland Ave 37919 — 1,300/9-12
  Sallee Reynolds, prin. — 865-594-4477
West Valley MS — 1,100/6-8
  9118 George Williams Rd 37922 — 865-539-5145
  Dr. Bill Wilson, prin.
Whittle Springs MS — 500/6-8
  2700 White Oak Ln 37917 — 865-594-4474
  Benny Perry, prin.
Knox County Evening HS — Adult
  101 E 5th Ave 37917 — 865-594-3713
  Carol Russell, prin.
Other Schools – See Corryton, Powell, Strawberry Plains

Berean Christian S — 400/K-12
  2329 Prosser Rd 37914 — 865-521-6054
  George Waller, admin. — Fax 522-5063
Christian Academy of Knoxville — 1,000/PK-12
  529 Academy Way 37923 — 865-690-4721
  Scott Sandie, prin. — Fax 690-4752
Fort Sanders School of Nursing — Post-Sec.
  9821 Cogdill Rd Ste 2 37932
Grace Christian Academy — 600/K-12
  7171 Oak Ridge Hwy 37931 — 865-691-3427
  Linda Reedy, prin. — Fax 691-1465

Huntington College of Health Sciences — Post-Sec.
  1204 Kenesaw Ave 37919 — 800-290-4226
ITT Technical Institute — Post-Sec.
  10208 Technology Dr 37932 — 865-671-2800
Johnson Bible College — Post-Sec.
  7900 Johnson Dr 37998 — 865-573-4517
Knoxville Adventist S — 100/K-10
  3615 Kingston Pike 37919 — 865-522-9929
  Ken Fuller, prin. — Fax 523-7471
Knoxville Catholic HS — 500/9-12
  9245 Fox Lonas Rd 37923 — 865-560-0313
  Richard Sompaynac Ed.D., prin. — Fax 560-0314
Pellissippi State Technical Comm. Coll. — Post-Sec.
  PO Box 22990 37933 — 865-694-6400
Reuben Allen College — Post-Sec.
  120 Center Park Dr 37922 — 865-966-0400
South College — Post-Sec.
  3904 Lonas Dr 37909 — 865-251-1800
Tennessee School for the Deaf — Post-Sec.
  2725 Island Home Blvd 37920 — 865-594-6022
Tennessee School of Beauty — Post-Sec.
  4704 Western Ave 37921 — 865-588-7878
Tennessee Technology Center at Knoxville — Post-Sec.
  1100 Liberty St 37919 — 865-546-5567
University of Tennessee — Post-Sec.
  527 Andy Holt Tower 37996 — 865-974-1000
University of Tennessee Medical Center — Post-Sec.
  1924 Alcoa Hwy 37920 — 865-546-5567
Webb S of Knoxville — 1,100/K-12
  9800 Webb School Ln 37923 — 865-693-0011
  Scott Hutchinson, pres. — Fax 691-8057

Kodak, Sevier
Sevier County SD
  Supt. — See Sevierville
Northview MS — 500/5-8
  3295 Douglas Dam Rd 37764 — 865-933-7985
  Jim Davis, prin. — Fax 933-7387

Lafayette, Macon, Pop. 4,009
Macon County SD — 3,200/K-12
  501 College St 37083 — 615-666-2125
  Mike Prock, supt. — Fax 666-7878
  www.maconcountyschools.com/
Macon County HS — 800/9-12
  PO Box 338 37083 — 615-666-4320
  Shawn Carter, prin. — Fax 666-4757
Macon Co. JHS — 700/6-8
  1003 Highway 52 Byp E 37083 — 615-666-7545
  Bobby Bransford, prin. — Fax 666-9264
Other Schools – See Red Boiling Springs

La Follette, Campbell, Pop. 8,052
Campbell County SD
  Supt. — See Jacksboro
La Follette MS — 600/6-8
  1120 Middlesboro Hwy 37766 — 423-562-8448
  Fred Kahre, prin. — Fax 562-2107

Lake City, Anderson, Pop. 1,856
Anderson County SD
  Supt. — See Clinton
Lake City MS — 300/6-8
  1132 S Main St 37769 — 865-426-2609
  Jan Moore, prin. — Fax 426-9319

La Vergne, Rutherford, Pop. 23,052
Rutherford County SD
  Supt. — See Murfreesboro
La Vergne HS — 1,500/9-12
  250 Wolverine Trl 37086 — 615-904-3870
  Melvin Daniels, prin. — Fax 904-3871
La Vergne MS — 6-8
  382 Stones River Rd 37086 — 615-904-3877
  Dirk Ash, prin. — Fax 904-3878

Lawrenceburg, Lawrence, Pop. 10,864
Lawrence County SD — 6,600/PK-12
  700 Mahr Ave 38464 — 931-762-3581
  Larry Davis, supt. — Fax 762-7299
  www.lawrenceburg.com
Coffman MS — 400/7-8
  111 Lafayette Ave 38464 — 931-762-6395
  Bernard Fuller, prin. — Fax 762-7176
Lawrence County HS — 1,100/9-12
  1800 Springer Rd 38464 — 931-762-9412
  Mickey Dunn, prin. — Fax 766-0761
Lawrence County Vo Ctr — Vo/Tech
  1906 Springer Rd 38464 — 931-762-6472
  Mickey Dunn, prin. — Fax 766-1551
Other Schools – See Loretto, Summertown

Lebanon, Wilson, Pop. 21,406
Lebanon Special SD — 2,900/PK-8
  701 Coles Ferry Pike 37087 — 615-449-6060
  Dr. Sharon Roberts, supt. — Fax 449-5673
  www.lssd.org
Baird MS — 700/7-8
  131 WJB Pride Ln 37087 — 615-444-2190
  Mark Willoughby, prin. — Fax 453-2690

Wilson County SD — 12,700/K-12
  351 Stumpy Ln 37090 — 615-444-3282
  Dr. James Duncan, dir. — Fax 449-3858
  www.wcschools.com
Lebanon HS — 1,400/9-12
  415 Harding Dr 37087 — 615-444-9610
  Don Hassler, prin. — Fax 443-1373
Wilson Central HS — 1,400/9-12
  419 Wildcat Way 37090 — 615-453-4600
  Travis Mayfield, prin. — Fax 453-4610
Wilson County Vocational Center — Vo/Tech
  418 Harding Dr 37087 — 615-444-1104
  William Moss, prin. — Fax 443-8745
Wilson County Adult HS — Adult
  207 J Branham Dr 37087 — 615-443-7199
  Pat Suddarth, lead tchr. — Fax 443-2690
Other Schools – See Mount Juliet, Watertown

Cumberland University | Post-Sec.
1 Cumberland Sq   37087 | 615-444-2562
Friendship Christian S | 700/PK-12
5400 Coles Ferry Pike   37087 | 615-449-1573
Becky Kegley, prin. | Fax 449-2769
Stylemasters Beauty Academy | Post-Sec.
223 N Cumberland St   37087 | 615-444-4908

Lenoir City, Loudon, Pop. 7,271
Lenoir City CSD | 2,000/PK-12
2145 Harrison Ave   37771 | 865-986-8058
Wayne Miller, supt. | Fax 988-6732
www.lenoircityschools.com/
Lenoir City HS | 1,100/9-12
1485 Old Highway 95   37771 | 865-986-2072
Steve Millsaps, prin. | Fax 988-2054
Lenoir City MS | 300/6-8
2141 Harrison Ave   37771 | 865-986-2038
Chip Orr, prin. | Fax 988-1964

Loudon County SD
Supt. — See Loudon
North MS | 800/5-8
421 Hickory Creek Rd   37771 | 865-986-9944
Gina Vandergriff, prin. | Fax 988-9089

Crossroads Christian Academy | 100/PK-12
1963 Martel Rd   37772 | 865-986-9823
Drew Guetterman, admin.

Lewisburg, Marshall, Pop. 10,698
Marshall County SD | 4,900/K-12
700 Jones Cir   37091 | 931-359-1581
John David Pierce, supt. | Fax 270-8816
www.mcs.k12.tn.us
Lewisburg MS | 400/7-8
500 Tiger Blvd   37091 | 931-359-1265
Randy Hubbell, prin. | Fax 359-4030
Marshall County HS | 700/9-12
597 W Ellington Pkwy   37091 | 931-359-1549
Nancy Pruitt, prin. | Fax 359-4784
Spot Lowe Vocational S | Vo/Tech
1771 Old Columbia Rd   37091 | 931-359-4911
Ray Stacey, prin. | Fax 359-3041
Other Schools – See Chapel Hill, Cornersville

Lexington, Henderson, Pop. 7,472
Henderson County SD | 3,300/K-12
PO Box 189   38351 | 731-968-3661
Susan Bunch, supt. | Fax 968-9457
www.henderson-lea.hc.k12tn.net/
Lexington HS | 800/9-12
284 White St   38351 | 731-968-2961
Chuck Patton, prin. | Fax 968-9399
Other Schools – See Reagan

Lexington CSD | 1,000/K-8
70 Dixon St   38351 | 731-967-5591
Joe T. Wood, supt. | Fax 967-0794
www.caywood.org
Lexington MS | 300/6-8
162 Monroe Ave   38351 | 731-968-8457
Angela Blankenship, prin. | Fax 968-2938

Linden, Perry, Pop. 996
Perry County SD | 1,100/K-12
333 S Mill St   37096 | 931-589-2102
David Rhodes, dir. | Fax 589-5110
www.perryboe.com/
Linden MS | 200/5-8
130 College Ave   37096 | 931-589-5000
Barry Laster, prin. | Fax 589-3685
Perry County HS | 400/9-12
401 Squirrel Hollow Dr   37096 | 931-589-2831
R. Morris, prin. | Fax 589-5063

Livingston, Overton, Pop. 3,431
Overton County SD | 3,200/K-12
302 Zachary St   38570 | 931-823-1287
Michael Gilpatrick, supt. | Fax 823-4673
www.overton.k12tn.net/
Livingston Academy HS | 800/9-12
120 Melvin Johnson Dr   38570 | 931-823-5911
Gary Ledbetter, prin. | Fax 823-8626
Livingston MS | 400/5-8
216 Bilbrey St   38570 | 931-823-5917
Rick Moles, prin. | Fax 823-7549

Tennessee Technology Center Livingston | Post-Sec.
740 Hi Tech Dr   38570 | 931-823-5525

Loretto, Lawrence, Pop. 1,691
Lawrence County SD
Supt. — See Lawrenceburg
Loretto HS | 600/9-12
525 2nd Ave S   38469 | 931-853-4324
David Daniel, prin. | Fax 853-4340

Loudon, Loudon, Pop. 4,633
Loudon County SD | 4,800/PK-12
100 River Rd   37774 | 865-458-5411
A. Edward Headlee, dir. | Fax 458-6138
k12.loudoncounty.org
Ft. Loudoun MS | 400/6-8
1703 Roberts Rd   37774 | 865-458-2026
Sherry Smith, prin. | Fax 458-6611
Loudon HS | 600/9-12
1039 Mulberry St   37774 | 865-458-4326
John Bartlett, prin. | Fax 458-0717
Other Schools – See Greenback, Lenoir City

Lyles, Hickman
Hickman County SD
Supt. — See Centerville
East Hickman MS | 500/6-8
9414 E Eagle Dr   37098 | 931-670-4237
Julia Thomasson, prin. | Fax 670-4239

Lynchburg, Moore, Pop. 5,241
Moore County SD | 900/K-12
PO Box 219   37352 | 931-759-7303
Wayne Stewart, supt. | Fax 759-6386
Moore County JSHS | 400/7-12
1502 Lynchburg Hwy   37352 | 931-759-4231
Stanley Bean, prin.

Motlow State Community College | Post-Sec.
PO Box 8500   37352 | 931-393-1500

Lynnville, Giles, Pop. 340
Giles County SD
Supt. — See Pulaski
Richland MSHS | 900/5-12
10610 Columbia Hwy   38472 | 931-527-3577
Bobbi McMasters, prin. | Fax 527-3720

Mc Ewen, Humphreys, Pop. 1,480
Humphreys County SD
Supt. — See Waverly
Mc Ewen HS | 300/9-12
335 Melrose St   37101 | 931-582-6950
Jerry Honea, prin. | Fax 582-6952
McEwen JHS | 200/6-8
360 Melrose St   37101 | 931-582-8417
Harvey Mize, prin. | Fax 582-8418

Mc Kenzie, Carroll, Pop. 5,363
Mc Kenzie CSD | 1,300/K-12
203 Bell Ave   38201 | 731-352-2246
James D. Ward, supt. | Fax 352-7550
Mc Kenzie HS | 400/9-12
23292 Highway 22   38201 | 731-352-2133
Terry Howell, prin. | Fax 352-1424
Mc Kenzie MS | 400/5-8
80 Woodrow Ave   38201 | 731-352-2792
Jon Frye, prin. | Fax 352-4709

Bethel College | Post-Sec.
325 Cherry Ave   38201 | 731-352-4000
Tennessee Technology Center at Mc Kenzie | Post-Sec.
PO Box 427   38201 | 731-352-5364

Mc Minnville, Warren, Pop. 12,060
Warren County SD | 5,900/K-12
2548 Morrison St   37110 | 931-668-4022
Dr. Jerry Hale, dir. | Fax 815-2685
www.warrenschools.com
Warren County HS | 1,600/9-12
199 Pioneer Ln   37110 | 931-668-5858
James Bennett, prin. | Fax 668-5801
Warren County MS | 800/6-8
200 Caldwell St   37110 | 931-473-6557
Betty Wood, prin. | Fax 473-2432

Georgia Career Institute | Post-Sec.
755 N Chancery St   37110
Tennessee Technology Center Mc Minnville | Post-Sec.
241 Vo Tech Dr   37110 | 931-473-5587

Madison, See Nashville
Davidson County SD
Supt. — See Nashville
Neelys Bend MS | 700/5-8
1251 Neelys Bend Rd   37115 | 615-860-1477
Ralph Tagg, prin. | Fax 612-3669

Goodpasture Christian S | 1,200/PK-12
619 W Due West Ave   37115 | 615-868-3700
Lindsey Judd, prin. | Fax 865-1766
Madison Academy | 100/9-12
PO Box 6257   37116 | 615-865-4055
Robert Stevenson M.A., prin. | Fax 865-4117
Middle Tennessee School of Anesthesia | Post-Sec.
PO Box 6414   37116 | 615-868-6503
Nashville College | Post-Sec.
1556 Crestview Dr   37115 | 615-868-2963
Volunteer Beauty Academy | Post-Sec.
1791 Gallatin Pike N   37115 | 615-860-4200

Madisonville, Monroe, Pop. 4,110
Monroe County SD | 4,800/K-12
205 Oak Grove Rd   37354 | 423-442-2373
James Millsaps, supt. | Fax 442-1389
www.monroe.k12.tn.us/
Madisonville MS | 500/6-8
175 Oak Grove Rd   37354 | 423-442-4137
Augusta Davis, prin. | Fax 442-9338
Sequoyah HS | 900/9-12
4128 Highway 411   37354 | 423-442-9230
Maurice Moser, prin. | Fax 442-5520
Other Schools – See Sweetwater, Tellico Plains, Vonore

Hiwassee College | Post-Sec.
225 Hiwassee College Dr   37354 | 423-442-2001

Manchester, Coffee, Pop. 8,929
Coffee County SD | 4,100/PK-12
1343 McArthur St   37355 | 931-723-5150
Daniel Brigman, supt. | Fax 723-5153
www.coffeecountyschools.com/
Coffee County Central HS | 1,400/9-12
100 Red Raider Dr   37355 | 931-723-5159
Joe Pedigo, prin. | Fax 723-5161
Coffee County MS | 1,000/6-8
865 McMinnville Hwy   37355 | 931-723-5177
Joey Vaughn, prin. | Fax 723-5180

Manchester CSD | 1,200/PK-9
215 E Fort St   37355 | 931-728-2316
Dr. Proter Powell, supt. | Fax 728-7075
www.manchestercitysch.org/
Westwood JHS | 400/7-9
505 E Taylor St   37355 | 931-728-2071
Richie Clark, prin. | Fax 728-0962

Martin, Weakley, Pop. 10,237
Weakley County SD
Supt. — See Dresden
Martin MS | 500/6-8
700 Fowler Rd   38237 | 731-587-2346
Nate Holmes, prin. | Fax 588-0529
Westview HS | 600/9-12
8161 Highway 45 S   38237 | 731-587-4202
David Byars, prin. | Fax 588-0806

University of Tennessee   38238 | Post-Sec.
| 731-587-7000

Maryville, Blount, Pop. 25,062
Blount County SD | 10,600/K-12
831 Grandview Dr   37803 | 865-984-1212
Alvin Hord, dir. | Fax 980-1002
www.blountk12.org
Blount HS | 1,500/9-12
219 County Farm Rd   37801 | 865-984-5500
Steve Lafon, prin. | Fax 977-0153
Blount MS | 700/6-8
1126 William Blount Dr   37801 | 865-977-5493
Alicia Lail, prin. | Fax 977-1435
Carpenters MS | 800/6-8
920 Huffstetler Rd   37803 | 865-980-1414
Rob Britt, prin. | Fax 980-1404
Eagleton MS | 400/6-8
2610 Cinema Dr   37804 | 865-982-3211
Richard Hutson, prin. | Fax 982-4203
Heritage HS | 1,400/9-12
3741 E Lamar Alexander Pkwy   37804 | 865-984-8110
Patty Mandigo, prin. | Fax 984-0147
Heritage MS | 700/6-8
3737 E Lamar Alexander Pkwy   37804 | 865-980-1300
Dr. Jesse Robinette, prin. | Fax 980-1281

Maryville CSD | 4,500/K-12
833 Lawrence Ave   37803 | 865-982-7121
Mike Dalton, supt. | Fax 977-5055
www.ci.maryville.tn.us
Maryville HS | 1,300/9-12
825 Lawrence Ave   37803 | 865-982-1132
Ken Jarnagin, prin. | Fax 983-1440
Maryville MS | 700/7-8
805 Montvale Station Rd   37803 | 865-983-2070
Lisa McGinley, prin. | Fax 977-9413

Maryville Christian S | 300/PK-12
2525 Morganton Rd   37801 | 865-681-3205
Glenn Slater, admin. | Fax 681-4086
Maryville College | Post-Sec.
502 E Lamar Alexander Pkwy   37804 | 865-981-8000

Maynardville, Union, Pop. 1,877
Union County SD | 3,000/K-12
PO Box 10   37807 | 865-992-5466
Charles E. Thomas, dir. | Fax 992-0126
www.ucps.org/
Maynard MS | 700/6-8
PO Box 669   37807 | 865-992-1030
Melissa Carter, prin. | Fax 992-1060
Union County HS | 900/9-12
PO Box 249   37807 | 865-992-5232
Linda Harrell, prin. | Fax 992-5724
Union County Adult HS | Adult
PO Box 609   37807 | 865-992-7747
Bill Robbins, prin. | Fax 992-9076

Medina, Gibson, Pop. 952
Gibson County SD
Supt. — See Dyer
Medina MS | 400/5-8
PO Box 38   38355 | 731-783-1962
Chad Jackson, prin. | Fax 783-1964

Memphis, Shelby, Pop. 645,978
Memphis CSD | 115,700/PK-12
2597 Avery Ave   38112 | 901-416-5300
Dr. Carol Johnson, supt. | Fax 325-5578
www.mcsk12.net
Airways MS | 700/6-8
2601 Ketchum Rd   38114 | 901-416-5006
Sharon Griffin, prin. | Fax 416-5009
American Way MS | 1,000/6-8
3805 American Way   38118 | 901-416-1250
Russell Heaston, prin.
Bellevue JHS | 500/7-9
575 S Bellevue Blvd   38104 | 901-416-4488
Kevin Malone, prin. | Fax 416-4490
Carver HS | 600/9-12
1591 Pennsylvania St   38109 | 901-416-7594
J.C. Williams, prin. | Fax 416-2235
Central HS | 1,300/9-12
306 S Bellevue Blvd   38104 | 901-416-4500
Gregory McCullough, prin. | Fax 416-4506
Chickasaw JHS | 400/7-9
4060 Westmont Rd   38109 | 901-416-8134
Dr. Willie Tobias, prin. | Fax 416-8139
Colonial MS | 900/6-8
4778 Sea Isle Rd   38117 | 901-416-8980
Brett Lawson, prin. | Fax 416-8996
Corry MS | 600/6-8
2230 Corry Rd   38106 | 901-416-7804
Joyce Kelly, prin. | Fax 416-7863
Craigmont HS | 1,400/9-12
3333 Covington Pike   38128 | 901-416-4312
Jim Long, prin. | Fax 416-7675
Craigmont MS | 1,100/6-8
3455 Covington Pike   38128 | 901-416-7780
Dr. Cedrick Gray, prin. | Fax 416-1454
Cypress MS | 600/6-8
2109 Howell Ave   38108 | 901-416-4524
Raymond Vasser, prin. | Fax 416-4528
East Career & Technology Center | Vo/Tech
3206 Poplar Ave   38111 | 901-416-6200
Fred Curry, prin. | Fax 416-6161

East MSHS 1,300/7-12
3206 Poplar Ave 38111 901-416-6160
Fred Curry, prin. Fax 416-6161
Fairley HS 1,100/9-12
4950 Fairley Rd 38109 901-416-8060
Clint Jackson, prin. Fax 416-8064
Fairview JHS 400/7-9
750 E Parkway S 38104 901-416-4536
Jeremiah Burks, prin. Fax 416-4539
Frayser HS 1,200/7-12
1530 Dellwood Ave 38127 901-416-3880
Dr. Charles Green, prin. Fax 416-3894
Geeter MS 600/6-8
4649 Horn Lake Rd 38109 901-416-8157
Kenneth Pinkney, prin. Fax 416-8160
Georgian Hills JHS 700/7-9
3925 Denver St 38127 901-416-3740
Rosalind Martin, prin. Fax 416-6500
Hamilton HS 1,500/9-12
1363 E Person Ave 38106 901-416-7838
Isaac White, prin. Fax 416-7829
Hamilton MS 800/6-8
1478 Wilson St 38106 901-416-7832
Willie Rhodes, prin. Fax 416-3314
Havenview MS 900/6-8
1481 Hester Rd 38116 901-416-3093
Corey Kelly, prin. Fax 416-3092
Hickory Ridge MS 900/6-8
3920 Ridgeway Rd 38115 901-416-9337
Rogenia Conley, prin. Fax 416-9210
Hillcrest HS 900/9-12
4184 Graceland Dr 38116 901-416-3104
Carolyn Shaw, prin. Fax 416-3106
Humes MS 800/6-8
659 N Manassas St 38107 901-416-3226
Michael Bates, prin. Fax 416-3228
Kansas Career & Tech Center Vo/Tech
80 W Olive Ave 38106 901-416-7300
E.C. Fields, prin. Fax 416-7315
Kingsbury Career Tech Center Vo/Tech
1328 N Graham St 38122 901-416-6000
David Johnson, prin. Fax 416-6003
Kingsbury MSHS 1,700/7-12
1270 N Graham St 38122 901-416-6060
Alex Hooker, prin. Fax 416-6054
Kirby HS 1,400/9-12
4080 Kirby Pkwy 38115 901-416-1960
Michael Smith, prin. Fax 416-1968
Kirby MS 1,100/6-8
6670 E Raines Rd 38115 901-416-1980
Eugene Lambert, prin. Fax 416-0494
Lanier MS 700/6-8
817 Brownlee Rd 38116 901-416-3128
Terrence Brown, prin. Fax 416-9875
Longview MS 500/5-8
1895 S Orleans St 38106 901-416-7420
Corey Harris, prin. Fax 416-7381
Manassas HS 300/9-12
781 Firestone Ave 38107 901-416-3244
Joe Davis, prin. Fax 416-3248
Melrose HS 1,200/9-12
2870 Deadrick Ave 38114 901-416-5974
Lavaugn Bridges, prin. Fax 416-5984
Messick Career & Technology Center Vo/Tech
703 S Greer St 38111 901-416-4840
Carol Miller, prin. Fax 416-4842
Middle College SHS 200/10-12
737 Union Ave 38103 901-416-8174
Joyce Mitchell, prin. Fax 416-8176
Mitchell Road MSHS 1,100/7-12
658 W Mitchell Rd 38109 901-789-8174
John Ware, prin. Fax 789-8176
Northside HS 1,000/9-12
1212 Vollintine Ave 38107 901-416-4582
Carolyn Currie, prin. Fax 416-4584
Oakhaven MSHS 800/7-12
3125 Ladbrook Rd 38118 901-416-2300
Marion Brewer, prin. Fax 416-2301
Overton HS 1,300/9-12
1770 Lanier Ln 38117 901-416-2136
Mike Bowlan, prin. Fax 416-2135
Price Middle College 9-9
807 Walker Ave 38126 901-947-7452
Daphne Beasley, prin. Fax 947-1800
Raleigh-Egypt HS 1,000/9-12
3970 Voltaire Ave 38128 901-416-4108
Dr. Oscar Love, prin. Fax 416-4143
Raleigh-Egypt MS 1,300/6-8
4215 Alice Ann Dr 38128 901-416-4141
Barry McGee, prin. Fax 416-4110
Ridgeway HS 1,500/9-12
2009 Ridgeway Rd 38119 901-416-8820
Michael Kyle, prin. Fax 416-2199
Ridgeway MS 1,100/6-8
6333 Quince Rd 38119 901-416-1588
Roderick Richmond, prin. Fax 416-1477
Riverview MS 600/6-8
241 Majuba Ave 38109 901-416-7340
Keith Sanders, prin. Fax 416-7343
Sheffield Career & Tech Center Vo/Tech
4350 Chuck Ave 38118 901-416-2340
John Simpson, prin. Fax 416-2394
Sheffield HS 800/9-12
4315 Sheffield Ave 38118 901-416-2370
Jimmy Holland, prin. Fax 416-2407
Sherwood MS 1,100/6-8
3480 Rhodes Ave 38111 901-416-4870
Eric Cooper, prin. Fax 416-4881
South Side HS 500/9-12
1880 Prospect St 38106 901-416-7380
Dr. Eugene Sargent, prin. Fax 416-7382
Southwest Career & Technology Center Vo/Tech
3746 Horn Lake Rd 38109 901-416-8186
Earnestine Taylor, prin. Fax 416-8188
Treadwell MSHS 800/7-12
920 N Highland St 38122 901-416-6100
Dr. John Malone, prin. Fax 416-6133

Trezevant Career & Tech Center Vo/Tech
3224 Range Line Rd 38127 901-416-3800
Milton Burchfield, prin. Fax 416-3839
Trezevant MSHS 1,300/7-12
3350 N Trezevant St 38127 901-416-3760
Ben Greene, prin. Fax 416-3761
Vance MS 500/6-8
673 Vance Ave 38126 901-416-3256
Bettye Sims, prin. Fax 416-3257
Walker MS 1,100/6-8
1900 E Raines Rd 38116 901-416-1030
Tonya McBride, prin. Fax 416-1075
Washington HS 600/9-12
715 S Lauderdale St 38126 901-416-7240
Elsie Bailey, prin. Fax 416-7228
Wells Academy 100/7-8
777 Firestone Ave 38107 901-416-3210
Verna Dobbs, prin. Fax 416-3205
Westside MSHS 700/7-12
3389 Dawn Dr 38127 901-416-3700
Jerry Smith, prin. Fax 416-3701
Westwood MSHS 800/7-12
4480 Westmont Rd 38109 901-416-8000
Tommie McCarter, prin. Fax 416-8027
Whitehaven HS 1,800/9-12
4851 Elvis Presley Blvd 38116 901-416-3000
Vincent Hunter, prin. Fax 416-3058
White Station HS 1,900/9-12
514 S Perkins Rd 38117 901-416-8880
Wanda Winnette, prin. Fax 416-8910
White Station MS 800/7-8
5465 Mason Rd 38120 901-416-2184
Terry Brown, prin. Fax 416-2187
Wooddale HS 1,500/9-12
5151 Scottsdale Ave 38118 901-416-2440
Brenda Thompson, prin. Fax 416-2476
Wooddale MS 1,400/6-8
3467 Castleman St 38118 901-416-2420
Tammi Nielsen, prin. Fax 416-2426
Other Schools – See Cordova

Shelby County SD 42,600/K-12
160 S Hollywood St 38112 901-321-2521
Bobby G. Webb Ed.D., supt.
www.scs.k12.tn.us
Southwind MS 1,000/6-8
7740 Lowrance Rd 38125 901-759-3000
Marcia Crouch, prin. Fax 759-3011
Other Schools – See Arlington, Bartlett, Collierville,
Cordova, Germantown, Millington

Baptist Memorial Coll. of Health Science Post-Sec.
1003 Monroe Ave 38104 901-575-2247
Baptist Memorial Hospital Post-Sec.
350 N Humphreys Blvd #EagB2 38103
901-227-5121
Bishop Byrne HS 300/7-12
1475 E Shelby Dr 38116 901-346-3060
Dr. Donald Edwards, prin. Fax 346-9488
Briarcrest Christian S 1,700/PK-12
6000 Briarcrest Ave 38120 901-765-4600
Bill McGee, pres. Fax 765-4667
Christian Brothers HS 900/9-12
5900 Walnut Grove Rd 38120 901-682-7801
Br. Chris Englert, prin. Fax 682-7815
Christian Brothers University Post-Sec.
650 E Parkway S 38104 901-321-3000
Concorde Career College Post-Sec.
5100 Poplar Ave Ste 132 38137 901-761-9494
Crichton College Post-Sec.
255 N Highland St 38111 901-320-9700
Elliston Baptist Academy 200/PK-12
4179 Elliston Rd 38111 901-743-4250
Kay Cotten, prin. Fax 743-4257
Gateway Christian S 1,800/K-12
4070 Macon Rd 38122 901-454-9958
Bryan Thompson, prin. Fax 323-0914
Harding Academy of Memphis 700/7-12
1100 Cherry Rd 38117 901-767-4494
Pamela Womack, pres. Fax 763-3424
Harding University Grad Sch of Religion Post-Sec.
1000 Cherry Rd 38117 800-680-0809
High-Tech Institute - Memphis Post-Sec.
5865 Shelby Oaks Cir 38134 901-387-4555
Hutchison S 800/PK-12
1740 Ridgeway Rd 38119 901-761-2220
Annette Smith, hdmstr. Fax 683-3510
Immaculate Conception HS 300/9-12
1725 Central Ave 38104 901-725-2705
Mindy Chalmers, prin. Fax 725-2701
Lausanne Collegiate S 700/PK-12
1381 W Massey Rd 38120 901-474-1000
Stuart McCathie, hdmstr. Fax 682-1696
Le Moyne-Owen College Post-Sec.
807 Walker Ave 38126 901-774-9090
Macon Road Baptist S 600/K-12
1082 Berclair Rd 38122 901-682-5420
Daniel Webb, hdmstr.
Margolin Hebrew Academy 300/K-12
390 S White Station Rd 38117 901-682-2400
Rabbi Nosson Schreiber, dean Fax 767-1871
Memphis Catholic HS 300/7-12
61 N McLean Blvd 38104 901-276-1221
James Pohlman, prin. Fax 725-1447
Memphis College of Art Post-Sec.
1930 Poplar Ave 38104 901-272-5100
Memphis Junior Academy 100/K-10
50 N Mendenhall Rd 38117 901-683-1061
Memphis Theological Seminary Post-Sec.
168 E Parkway S 38104 901-458-8232
Memphis University S 600/7-12
6191 Park Ave 38119 901-260-1300
Ellis Haguewood, hdmstr. Fax 260-1355
Methodist Hospital Post-Sec.
1265 Union Ave 38104 901-726-8274
New Wave Hair Academy Post-Sec.
3250 Coleman Rd 38128 901-323-6100

New Wave Hair Academy Post-Sec.
804 S Highland St 38111 901-320-9283
Plaza Beauty School Post-Sec.
4682 Spottswood Ave 38117 901-761-4445
Remington College Post-Sec.
2731 Nonconnah Blvd # 160 38132 901-345-1000
Rhodes College Post-Sec.
2000 N Parkway 38112 901-843-3000
St. Agnes Academy 300/9-12
4830 Walnut Grove Rd 38117 901-767-1377
Barbara Daush, pres. Fax 682-8199
St. Mary's Episcopal S 800/PK-12
60 Perkins Ext 38117 901-537-1472
Marlene Shaw, hdmstr. Fax 682-0119
Southern College of Optometry Post-Sec.
1245 Madison Ave 38104 901-722-3200
Southern Institute of Cosmetology Post-Sec.
3099 S Perkins Rd 38118 901-363-3553
Southwest Tennessee Community College Post-Sec.
5983 Macon Cv 38134 901-333-7822
State Technical Institute Post-Sec.
5983 Macon Cv 38134 901-377-4111
Strayer University Post-Sec.
2620 Thousand Oaks Blvd 38118 901-369-0835
Strayer University Post-Sec.
6211 Shelby Oaks Dr 38134 901-383-6750
Tennessee Academy of Cosmetology Post-Sec.
7041 Stage Rd Ste 101 38133 901-382-9085
Tennessee Academy of Cosmetology Post-Sec.
7020 E Shelby Dr Ste 104 38125 901-757-4166
Tennessee Technology Center at Memphis Post-Sec.
550 Alabama Ave 38105 901-543-6100
The Beauty Institute Post-Sec.
568 Colonial Rd 38117 901-761-1888
University of Memphis 38152 Post-Sec.
901-678-2000
Univ. of Tennessee Health Science Center Post-Sec.
800 Madison Ave 38163 901-448-5500
Vatterott College - Memphis Campus Post-Sec.
2655 Dividend Dr 38132 901-761-5730
Westminster Academy 300/K-12
2500 Ridgeway Rd 38119 901-380-9192
Dr. Michael Johnson, hdmstr. Fax 405-2019
William Moore College of Technology Post-Sec.
1200 Poplar Ave 38104 901-726-1977

Middleton, Hardeman, Pop. 623
Hardeman County SD
Supt. — See Bolivar
Middleton HS 600/7-12
PO Box 477 38052 731-376-8391
Troy Shaw, prin. Fax 376-8391

Milan, Gibson, Pop. 7,818
Milan Special SD 2,000/PK-12
PO Box 528 38358 731-686-0844
Jim Towater, dir. Fax 686-8781
www.milanssd.org
Milan HS 600/9-12
7060 E Van Hook St 38358 731-686-0841
Tim Warren, prin. Fax 686-9829
Milan MS 600/5-8
4040 Middle Rd 38358 731-686-7232
Lacee Mallard, prin. Fax 723-8872

Arnold's Beauty School Post-Sec.
1179 S 2nd St 38358 731-686-7351

Milligan College, Carter

Milligan College Post-Sec.
1 Milligan College 37682 423-461-8700

Millington, Shelby, Pop. 10,229
Shelby County SD
Supt. — See Memphis
Millington HS 1,500/9-12
8057 Wilkinsville Rd 38053 901-873-8100
Nancy Norwood, prin. Fax 873-8105
Millington MS 600/6-8
4964 Cuba Millington Rd 38053 901-873-8130
Michael Lowe, prin. Fax 873-8136
Woodstock MS 700/6-8
5885 Woodstock Cuba Rd 38053 901-353-8590
Eric Linsy, prin. Fax 358-9827

Faith Heritage Christian Academy 100/K-12
PO Box 157 38083 901-872-0828
M.O. Eckel, hdmstr. Fax 872-0803

Monterey, Putnam, Pop. 2,771
Putnam County SD
Supt. — See Cookeville
Burks MS 300/5-8
300 Crossville St 38574 931-839-7641
Michael Goolsby, prin. Fax 839-6683
Monterey HS 300/9-12
710 Commercial Ave S 38574 931-839-2970
Johnny Matheney, prin. Fax 839-6070

Morristown, Hamblen, Pop. 25,144
Hamblen County SD 8,900/K-12
210 E Morris Blvd 37813 423-586-7700
Dr. Dale Lynch, supt. Fax 586-7747
www.hcboe.net
Lincoln Heights MS 500/6-8
219 Lincoln Ave 37813 423-581-3200
James D. Templin, prin. Fax 585-3763
Meadowview MS 500/6-8
1623 Meadowview Ln 37814 423-581-6360
Ron Wright, prin. Fax 585-3771
Morristown-Hamblen HS East 1,200/9-12
1 Hurricane Ln 37813 423-586-2543
Gary Johnson, prin. Fax 585-3779
Morristown-Hamblen HS West 1,200/9-12
1 Trojan Trl 37813 423-581-1600
Dr. Jeff Moorhouse, prin. Fax 585-3791

West View MS 600/6-8
1 Indian Path 37813 423-581-2407
Scott Walker, prin. Fax 585-3807
Hamblen County Adult HS Adult
376 Snyder Rd 37813 423-585-3785
Tami Morelock, prin.
Other Schools – See Whitesburg

Tennessee Technology Center Morristown Post-Sec.
821 W Louise Ave 37813 423-586-5771
Walters State Community College Post-Sec.
500 S Davy Crockett Pkwy 37813 423-585-2600

Mosheim, Greene, Pop. 1,761
Greene County SD
Supt. — See Greeneville
West Greene HS 600/9-12
275 W Greene Dr 37818 423-422-4061
Larry Bible, prin. Fax 638-3180

Mountain City, Johnson, Pop. 2,445
Johnson County SD 2,200/PK-12
211 N Church St 37683 423-727-2640
Morris Woodring, dir. Fax 727-2663
www.jocoed.k12tn.net
Johnson County HS 700/9-12
510 Fairground Ln 37683 423-727-2620
Paula Norton, prin. Fax 727-2677
Johnson County MS 300/7-8
500 Fairground Ln 37683 423-727-2600
Emogene South, prin. Fax 727-2608
Johnson County Vocational S Vo/Tech
520 Fairground Ln 37683 423-727-1860
Jim Crowder, prin. Fax 727-2693

Mount Juliet, Wilson, Pop. 16,495
Wilson County SD
Supt. — See Lebanon
Mount Juliet HS 1,300/9-12
3565 N Mount Juliet Rd 37122 615-758-5606
Mel Brown, prin. Fax 758-5645
Mount Juliet MS 1,000/6-8
1003 Woodridge Pl 37122 615-754-6688
Mike Gwaltney, prin. Fax 754-7566
West Wilson MS 900/6-8
935 N Mount Juliet Rd 37122 615-758-5152
James Farley, prin. Fax 758-5283

Mt. Juliet Christian Academy 600/PK-12
735 N Mount Juliet Rd 37122 615-758-2427
Steve Norris, hdmstr. Fax 758-3662

Mount Pleasant, Maury, Pop. 4,503
Maury County SD
Supt. — See Columbia
Mount Pleasant JSHS 800/6-12
600 Greenwood St 38474 931-379-5583
Tommy Wolaver, prin. Fax 379-2093
Mt. Pleasant MS of Visual/Performing Art 300/6-8
410 Gray Ln 38474 931-379-1100
Elliotte Kinzer, prin. Fax 379-1108

Munford, Tipton, Pop. 5,249
Tipton County SD
Supt. — See Covington
Munford HS 1,300/9-12
1080 McLaughlin Dr 38058 901-837-5701
Darry Marshall, prin. Fax 837-5729
Munford MS 900/6-8
100 Education Ave 38058 901-837-1700
Glenn Turner, prin. Fax 837-5749

Murfreesboro, Rutherford, Pop. 78,074
Rutherford County SD 28,300/PK-12
2240 Southpark Dr 37128 615-893-5812
Harry Gill, supt. Fax 898-7940
www.rcs.k12.tn.us
Blackman HS 1,500/9-12
3956 Blaze Dr 37128 615-904-3850
Gail Vick, prin. Fax 904-3851
Blackman MS 1,000/6-8
3945 Blaze Dr 37128 615-904-3860
Butch Vaughn, prin. Fax 904-3861
Central MS 900/7-8
701 E Main St 37130 615-893-8262
Will Shelton, prin. Fax 898-7964
Holloway HS 100/9-12
619 S Highland Ave 37130 615-890-6004
Ivan Duggin, prin. Fax 904-7508
Oakland HS 1,300/9-12
2225 Patriot Dr 37130 615-904-3780
Butch Vaughn, prin. Fax 904-3781
Riverdale HS 1,700/9-12
802 Warrior Dr 37128 615-890-6450
Tom Nolan, prin. Fax 890-9790
Siegel HS 1,400/9-12
3300 Siegel Rd 37129 615-904-3800
Ken Nolan, prin. Fax 904-3801
Siegel MS 1,000/6-8
355 W Thompson Ln 37129 615-904-3830
Tom Delbridge, prin. Fax 904-3831
Rutherford Adult HS Adult
502 Memorial Blvd 37129 615-896-0876
Janet Fricks, prin.
Other Schools – See Christiana, Eagleville, La Vergne, Smyrna

Draughons Junior College - Murfreesboro Post-Sec.
415 Golden Bear Ct 37128 615-217-9347
Middle Tennessee Christian S 700/PK-12
100 E MTCS Rd 37129 615-893-0602
Todd Miller, prin. Fax 895-8815
Middle Tennessee State University Post-Sec.
1301 E Main St 37132 615-898-2300
Tennessee Technology Center Murfreesboro Post-Sec.
1303 Old Fort Pkwy 37129 615-898-8010

Nashville, Davidson, Pop. 545,915
Davidson County SD 66,600/PK-12
2601 Bransford Ave 37204 615-259-8400
Pedro E. Garcia Ed.D., supt. Fax 259-8492
www.mnps.org
Allen MS 100/5-8
500 Spence Ln 37210 615-291-6385
Ganet Johnson, prin. Fax 291-6066
Bailey MS 500/5-8
2000 Greenwood Ave 37206 615-262-6670
Jim Murrell, prin. Fax 262-6979
Bass MS 500/5-8
5200 Delaware Ave 37209 615-298-8065
Kathryn Dillard, prin. Fax 292-5548
Baxter MS 600/5-8
350 Hart Ln 37207 615-262-6710
Wallace McNelley, prin. Fax 262-6743
Bellevue MS 500/5-8
655 Colice Jeanne Rd 37221 615-662-3000
John Duckworth, prin. Fax 662-5728
Brick Church MS 600/5-8
2835 Brick Church Pike 37207 615-262-6665
Marvin Spears, prin. Fax 262-6966
Cameron MS 600/5-8
1034 1st Ave S 37210 615-291-6365
Beverly Walker Bell, prin. Fax 291-6072
Croft Design Center MS 800/5-8
482 Elysian Fields Rd 37211 615-332-0217
Barry Watkins, prin. Fax 332-0645
Dalewood MS 600/5-8
1460 Mcgavock Pike 37216 615-262-6680
Monae London, prin. Fax 262-6962
Donelson MS 700/5-8
110 Stewarts Ferry Pike 37214 615-884-4080
Paul Brunette, prin. Fax 884-4087
East Literature Magnet S 700/5-12
112 Gallatin Ave 37206 615-262-6947
Frances Stewart, prin. Fax 262-6656
Ewing Park MS 400/5-8
3410 Knight Dr 37207 615-876-5115
Antionette Love, prin. Fax 876-5116
Glencliff Comprehensive HS 1,300/9-12
160 Antioch Pike 37211 615-333-5070
Dr. Lora Hall, prin. Fax 333-5073
Gra-Mar MS 700/5-8
575 Joyce Ln 37216 615-262-6685
Angela Garner, prin. Fax 262-6901
Haynes Health/Medical Science Design Ctr 300/5-8
510 W Trinity Ln 37207 615-262-6688
Robert Blankenship, prin. Fax 258-3962
Head Magnet S 500/5-8
1830 Jo Johnston Ave 37203 615-329-8160
Sharon Braden, prin. Fax 321-8386
Hill MS 500/5-8
150 Davidson Rd 37205 615-353-2020
Paul G. Ketteman, prin. Fax 353-1159
Hillsboro Comprehensive HS 1,100/9-12
3812 Hillsboro Pike 37215 615-298-8400
Robert Lawson, prin. Fax 298-8402
Hillwood Comprehensive HS 1,300/9-12
400 Davidson Rd 37205 615-353-2025
Karl Lang, prin. Fax 353-2027
Hume-Fogg Magnet HS 500/9-12
700 Broadway 37203 615-291-6300
Tom Ward, prin. Fax 291-6304
Hunters Lane Comprehensive HS 1,900/9-12
1150 Hunters Ln 37207 615-860-1401
Clay Myers, prin. Fax 860-7541
King Magnet JSHS 1,000/7-12
613 17th Ave N 37203 615-329-8400
Lendozia Edwards, prin. Fax 329-8163
Litton MS 400/5-8
4601 Hedgewood Dr 37216 615-262-6700
Dr. Tonya Dennis, prin. Fax 262-6995
Maplewood Comprehensive HS 1,000/9-12
401 Walton Ln 37216 615-262-6770
Darwin Mason, prin. Fax 262-6772
McGavock Comprehensive HS 2,000/9-12
3150 Mcgavock Pike 37214 615-885-8850
Michael Tribue, prin. Fax 885-8900
McKissack MS 200/5-8
915 38th Ave N 37209 615-329-8170
Dr. Linda Miller, prin. Fax 329-8171
McMurray MS 900/5-8
520 McMurray Dr 37211 615-333-5126
Dr. Schunn Turner, prin. Fax 333-5125
Meigs Magnet MS 600/5-8
713 Ramsey St 37206 615-271-3222
Paul Fleming, prin. Fax 262-6692
Moore MS 600/5-8
4425 Granny White Pike 37204 615-298-8095
Deloris Burke, prin. Fax 298-8452
Nashville S of the Arts 900/9-12
1200 Foster Ave 37243 615-291-6600
Robert Wilson, prin. Fax 271-1767
Oliver MS 5-8
6211 Nolensville Pike 37211 615-332-3011
Karen Lefkovitz, prin.
Overton Comprehensive HS 1,500/9-12
4820 Franklin Pike 37220 615-333-5135
Dr. Monica Dillard, prin. Fax 333-5141
Pearl-Cohn Comprehensive Magnet HS 800/9-12
904 26th Ave N 37208 615-329-8150
Marva Woods, prin. Fax 329-8151
Rose Park MS 200/5-8
1025 9th Ave S 37203 615-291-6405
Wade Jones, prin. Fax 291-6337
Stratford Comprehensive HS 1,100/9-12
1800 Stratford Ave 37216 615-262-6730
Brenda Elliott, prin. Fax 262-6957
Two Rivers MS 600/5-8
2991 Mcgavock Pike 37214 615-885-8931
William Moody, prin. Fax 885-8954
Vaught MS 300/5-8
160 Rural Ave 37209 615-353-2081
Dr. Carol Garland, prin. Fax 353-2090

West End MS 400/5-8
3529 W End Ave 37205 615-298-8425
Roderick Manual, prin. Fax 298-8450
Wharton Arts Magnet MS 400/5-8
1625 Dr DB Todd Jr Blvd 37208 615-329-8180
Dr. Dorothy Gunn, prin. Fax 321-8720
Wright MS 900/5-8
180 McCall St 37211 615-333-5189
Kim Finch, prin. Fax 333-5195
Cohn Adult Learning Center Adult
4805 Park Ave 37209 615-298-8053
Barbara Crawford, prin. Fax 298-8052
Other Schools – See Antioch, Goodlettsville, Hermitage, Joelton, Madison, Old Hickory, Whites Creek

American Baptist College Post-Sec.
1800 Baptist World Ctr Dr 37207 615-256-1463
Aquinas College Post-Sec.
4210 Harding Pike 37205 615-297-7545
Belmont University Post-Sec.
1900 Belmont Blvd 37212 615-460-6000
Blair School of Music of Vanderbilt U. Post-Sec.
2400 Blakemore Ave 37212 615-322-7651
Christ Presbyterian Academy 900/K-12
2323A Old Hickory Blvd 37215 615-373-9550
Richard Anderson, hdmstr. Fax 370-0884
Davidson Academy 900/PK-12
1414 Old Hickory Blvd 37207 615-860-5300
Bill Chaney Ed.D., hdmstr. Fax 868-7918
Diamond Council of America Post-Sec.
3212 W End Ave Ste 202 37203 615-385-5301
Donelson Christian Academy 800/PK-12
300 Danyacrest Dr 37214 615-883-2926
Dr. Daniel Kellum, hdmstr. Fax 883-2998
Draughons Junior College Post-Sec.
PO Box 17386 37217 615-361-7555
Ensworth S 700/K-12
211 Ensworth Pl 37205 615-383-0661
William Moseley, hdmstr. Fax 269-4840
Father Ryan HS 1,100/9-12
700 Norwood Dr 37204 615-383-4200
James McIntyre, prin. Fax 383-9056
Fisk University Post-Sec.
1000 17th Ave N 37208 615-329-8500
Franklin Road Academy 1,000/PK-12
4700 Franklin Pike 37220 615-832-8845
Dr. Margaret Wade, hdmstr. Fax 834-4137
Free Will Baptist Bible College Post-Sec.
PO Box 50117 37205 800-763-9225
Harpeth Hall S 600/5-12
3801 Hobbs Rd 37215 615-297-9543
Ann Teaff, prin. Fax 297-0480
High-Tech Institute Post-Sec.
560 Royal Pkwy 37214 866-502-2627
International Academy of Design & Tech. Post-Sec.
1 Bridgestone Park 37214 615-232-7384
ITT Technical Institute Post-Sec.
2845 Elm Hill Pike 37214 615-889-8700
John A. Gupton College Post-Sec.
1616 Church St 37203 615-327-3927
Jon Nave University of Cosmetology Post-Sec.
5128 Charlotte Pike 37209 615-383-2255
Leslie-Grace S of Academic Excellence 50/1-12
1718 14th Ave N 37208 615-321-0886
Timothy Leslie, dir. Fax 321-2889
Lipscomb Campus S 1,400/PK-12
3901 Granny White Pike 37204 615-269-1828
Keith Nikolaus, dir. Fax 386-7633
Lipscomb University Post-Sec.
3901 Granny White Pike 37204 800-333-4358
Meharry Medical College Post-Sec.
1005 Dr DB Todd Jr Blvd 37208 615-327-6111
Montgomery Bell Academy 700/7-12
4001 Harding Rd 37205 615-298-5514
Bradford Gioia, prin. Fax 297-0271
Nashville Auto-Diesel College Post-Sec.
1524 Gallatin Ave 37206 615-226-3990
Nashville Christian S 500/K-12
7555 Sawyer Brown Rd 37221 615-356-5600
Rece Chumley, prin. Fax 352-1324
Nashville State Technical Community Coll Post-Sec.
120 White Bridge Pike 37209 615-353-3333
National College of Business & Tech. Post-Sec.
3748 Nolensville Pike 37211 615-333-3344
New Directions Hair Academy Post-Sec.
3744 Annex Ave # A-2 37209 615-353-8333
Peabody College of Vanderbilt University Post-Sec.
PO Box 327 37203 615-322-8410
Radnor Baptist Academy 200/PK-12
3112 Nolensville Pike 37211 615-832-2004
Stephen Durham, hdmstr. Fax 833-3708
Remington College Post-Sec.
441 Donelson Pike Ste 150 37214 615-889-5520
SAE Institute Nashville Post-Sec.
7 Music Cir N 37203 615-244-5848
St. Cecilia Academy 300/9-12
4210 Harding Pike 37205 615-298-4525
Sr. Mary Thomas, prin. Fax 783-0561
St. Thomas Hospital Post-Sec.
PO Box 380 37202 615-222-2111
Seminary Ext. Independent Study Inst. Post-Sec.
901 Commerce St Ste 500 37203 800-229-4612
Southeastern Career College Post-Sec.
2416 21st Ave S Ste 300 37212 615-269-9900
Strayer University Post-Sec.
30 Rachel Dr Ste 200 37214 615-871-2260
Tennessee School for the Blind Post-Sec.
115 Stewarts Ferry Pike 37214 615-231-7300
Tennessee State University Post-Sec.
3500 John A Merritt Blvd 37209 615-963-5000
Tennessee Technology Center at Nashville Post-Sec.
100 White Bridge Pike 37209 615-741-1241
Trevecca Nazarene University Post-Sec.
333 Murfreesboro Rd 37210 615-248-1200
University S of Nashville 1,000/K-12
2000 Edgehill Ave 37212 615-327-8158
Vincent Durnan, dir. Fax 321-0889

Vanderbilt University — Post-Sec.
W End Ave 37240 — 615-322-7311
Volunteer Beauty Academy — Post-Sec.
5666 Nolensville Pike 37211 — 615-331-9111
Watkins Institute-College of Art/Design — Post-Sec.
2298 Metrocenter Blvd 37228 — 615-383-4848

Newbern, Dyer, Pop. 2,996
Dyer County SD
Supt. — See Dyersburg
Dyer County HS — 900/9-12
1000 W Main St 38059 — 731-627-2229
Peggy Dodds, prin. — Fax 627-4823
Northview MS — 400/6-8
820 Williams St 38059 — 731-627-3713
Anthony Jones, prin. — Fax 627-4823

Tennessee Technology Center at Newbern — Post-Sec.
340 Washington St 38059 — 731-627-2511

Newport, Cocke, Pop. 7,203
Cocke County SD — 4,700/K-12
305 Hedrick Dr 37821 — 423-623-7821
Larry Blazer, supt. — Fax 625-3947
www.cocke-lea.cocke.k12.tn.us
Cocke County HS — 1,100/9-12
216 Hedrick Dr 37821 — 423-623-8718
Gary Williams, prin. — Fax 623-1213
Cocke County Vocational HS — Vo/Tech
210 Hedrick Dr 37821 — 423-623-6072
Larry Williams, prin. — Fax 623-6070
Other Schools – See Cosby

New Tazewell, Claiborne, Pop. 2,857
Claiborne County SD
Supt. — See Tazewell
Claiborne HS — 600/9-12
815 Davis Dr 37825 — 423-626-3532
Steve Minton, prin. — Fax 626-3555

Norris, Anderson, Pop. 1,408
Anderson County SD
Supt. — See Clinton
Norris MS — 500/6-8
PO Box 980 37828 — 865-494-7171
Joe Forgety, prin. — Fax 494-6693

Oakdale, Morgan, Pop. 239
Morgan County SD
Supt. — See Wartburg
Oakdale S — 500/K-12
225 Clifty Creek Rd 37829 — 423-369-3885
Sam Hoskins, prin. — Fax 369-2821

Oakland, Fayette, Pop. 1,385
Fayette County SD
Supt. — See Somerville
West JHS — 400/7-9
13100 Highway 194 38060 — 901-465-9213
Larry Skelton, prin. — Fax 465-1599

Oak Ridge, Anderson, Pop. 27,338
Oak Ridge CSD — 4,400/PK-12
PO Box 6588 37831 — 865-425-9001
Dr. Thomas E. Bailey, supt. — Fax 425-9070
www.ortn.edu
Jefferson MS — 700/5-8
200 Fairbanks Rd 37830 — 865-425-9301
Bruce Lay, prin. — Fax 425-9339
Oak Ridge HS — 1,500/9-12
127 Providence Rd 37830 — 865-425-9601
Becky Ervin, prin. — Fax 425-9678
Robertsville MS — 700/5-8
245 Robertsville Rd 37830 — 865-425-9201
Tom Hayes, prin. — Fax 425-9236

Old Hickory, See Nashville
Davidson County SD
Supt. — See Nashville
DuPont-Hadley MS — 600/5-8
1901 Old Hickory Blvd 37138 — 615-847-7300
Amy Downey, prin. — Fax 847-7322

Oliver Springs, Morgan, Pop. 3,284
Anderson County SD
Supt. — See Clinton
Norwood MS — 300/6-8
805 E Tri County Blvd 37840 — 865-435-7749
David Stewart, prin. — Fax 435-5426

Roane County SD
Supt. — See Kingston
Oliver Springs HS — 500/9-12
419 Kingston Ave 37840 — 865-435-7216
Jeffrey Woods, prin. — Fax 435-6774

Faith Christian Academy — 50/K-12
864 Poplar Creek Rd 37840 — 865-435-6185
Dr. Paul Cates, supt. — Fax 435-9182

Oneida, Scott, Pop. 3,659
Oneida Special SD — 1,300/PK-12
PO Box 4819 37841 — 423-569-8912
S. Henry Baggett, supt. — Fax 569-2201
www.oneidaschools.org/
Oneida HS — 400/9-12
372 N Main St 37841 — 423-569-8818
Rick Harper, prin. — Fax 569-1681
Oneida MS — 300/6-8
376 N Main St 37841 — 423-569-2475
Cheryl Butler, prin. — Fax 569-5977

Ooltewah, Hamilton, Pop. 4,903
Hamilton County SD
Supt. — See Chattanooga
Hunter MS — 900/6-8
5973 Hunter Rd 37363 — 423-344-1474
Gary Kuehn, prin. — Fax 344-1485
Ooltewah HS — 1,700/9-12
6123 Mountain View Rd 37363 — 423-238-5221
Ed Foster, prin. — Fax 238-5871

Ooltewah MS — 1,000/6-8
5100 Ooltewah Ringgold Rd 37363 — 423-238-5732
Pam Dantzler, prin. — Fax 238-5735
Hamilton County Adult HS — Adult
9050 Career Ln 37363 — 423-344-1433
Bill Warren, prin. — Fax 344-1434

Paris, Henry, Pop. 9,650
Henry County SD — 2,600/PK-12
217 Grove Blvd 38242 — 731-642-9733
Richard W. Kriesky, supt. — Fax 642-8073
www.henry.k12.tn.us
Grove S — 400/9-9
215 Grove Blvd 38242 — 731-642-4586
Mike Poteete, prin. — Fax 642-4577
Henry County HS — 1,000/10-12
315 W Wilson St 38242 — 731-642-5232
Dawn Poole, prin. — Fax 642-5240

Paris SD — 1,500/K-8
1219 Highway 641 S 38242 — 731-642-9322
Paul Doyle, supt. — Fax 642-9327
www.paris.k12.tn.us
Inman MS — 500/6-8
400 Harrison St 38242 — 731-642-8131
Mike Brown, prin. — Fax 642-8209

Tennessee Technology Center at Paris — Post-Sec.
312 S Wilson St 38242 — 731-644-7365

Parsons, Decatur, Pop. 2,428
Decatur County SD
Supt. — See Decaturville
Decatur County MS — 500/5-8
2740 Highway 641 S 38363 — 731-847-6510
Chris Villaflor, prin. — Fax 847-6572

Pigeon Forge, Sevier, Pop. 5,456
Sevier County SD
Supt. — See Sevierville
Pigeon Forge HS — 700/9-12
414 Tiger Dr 37863 — 865-774-5790
Perry Schrandt, prin. — Fax 774-5798
Pigeon Forge MS — 600/5-8
300 Wears Valley Rd 37863 — 865-453-2401
Jerry Wear, prin. — Fax 453-0799

Pikeville, Bledsoe, Pop. 1,798
Bledsoe County SD — 1,800/PK-12
PO Box 369 37367 — 423-447-2914
Thad R. Colvard, dir. — Fax 447-7135
www.bledsoe.k12.tn.us/
Bledsoe County HS — 500/9-12
RR 6 Box 5 37367 — 423-447-6851
Tommy Nipper, prin. — Fax 447-6580
Bledsoe County MS — 400/6-8
PO Box 147 37367 — 423-447-3212
Philip Kiper, prin. — Fax 447-3085
Other Schools – See Dunlap

Pleasant View, Cheatham, Pop. 3,131
Cheatham County SD
Supt. — See Ashland City
Sycamore HS — 800/9-12
1021 Old Clarksville Pike 37146 — 615-746-5013
Daniel Newton, prin. — Fax 746-3653
Sycamore MS — 900/5-8
1025 Old Clarksville Pike 37146 — 615-746-8852
Judy Bell, prin. — Fax 746-5770

Portland, Sumner, Pop. 9,786
Sumner County SD
Supt. — See Gallatin
Portland HS — 1,000/9-12
600 College St 37148 — 615-325-9201
Janet Grogan, prin. — Fax 325-5302
Portland MS — 800/6-8
604 S Broadway 37148 — 615-325-4146
Jim Butler, prin. — Fax 325-5320

Highland Academy — 100/9-12
211 Highland Circle Dr 37148 — 615-325-2036
Don Mathis, prin. — Fax 325-4824

Powell, Knox, Pop. 7,534
Knox County SD
Supt. — See Knoxville
Powell HS, 2136 W Emory Rd 37849 — 1,100/9-12
Diane Psihogios, prin. — 865-938-2171
Powell MS, 3329 W Emory Rd 37849 — 800/6-8
Glenn Marquart, prin. — 865-938-9008

Pulaski, Giles, Pop. 7,947
Giles County SD — 4,500/PK-12
270 Richland Dr 38478 — 931-363-4558
Tee Jackson, dir. — Fax 363-8975
www.giles-lea.giles.k12.tn.us
Bridgeforth MS — 400/6-8
1051 Bridgeforth Cir 38478 — 931-363-7526
J. B. Smith, prin. — Fax 424-7021
Giles County HS — 900/9-12
200 Sheila Frost Dr 38478 — 931-363-6532
Bobby Hastings, prin. — Fax 424-7010
Other Schools – See Lynnville

Highland Christian Academy — 100/K-12
1827 Mill St 38478 — 931-363-4144
Jerry Daughtry, admin.
Martin Methodist College — Post-Sec.
433 W Madison St 38478 — 800-727-1273
Tennessee Technology Center at Pulaski — Post-Sec.
PO Box 614 38478 — 931-424-4014

Reagan, Henderson
Henderson County SD
Supt. — See Lexington
Scotts Hill HS — 300/9-12
7871 Highway 100 38368 — 731-549-2900
Brian Norton, prin. — Fax 549-2909

Red Boiling Springs, Macon, Pop. 1,039
Clay County SD
Supt. — See Celina
Hermitage Springs S — 300/K-12
6000 Clay County Hwy 37150 — 615-699-2414
Donnie Cherry, prin. — Fax 699-2410

Macon County SD
Supt. — See Lafayette
Red Boiling Springs JSHS — 300/7-12
415 Hillcrest Dr 37150 — 615-699-3125
Don Jones, prin. — Fax 699-3371
Tri-County Vocational Center — Vo/Tech
PO Box 214 37150 — 615-699-2224
Jerry Spivey, prin. — Fax 669-2226

Ripley, Lauderdale, Pop. 7,745
Lauderdale County SD — 4,500/PK-12
402 S Washington St 38063 — 731-635-2941
Phillip Jackson, supt. — Fax 635-7985
www.lced.net
Lauderdale MS — 800/6-8
309 Griggs Rd 38063 — 731-635-1391
Robert England, prin. — Fax 635-0028
Ripley HS — 900/9-12
254 S Jefferson St 38063 — 731-635-2642
Robert Baker, prin. — Fax 635-7151
Other Schools – See Halls

Tennessee Technology Center at Ripley — Post-Sec.
127 Industrial Dr 38063 — 731-635-3368

Roan Mountain, Carter, Pop. 1,220
Carter County SD
Supt. — See Elizabethton
Cloudland JSHS — 400/7-12
476 Cloudland Dr 37687 — 423-772-5300
Randy Birchfield, prin. — Fax 772-5309

Rockwood, Roane, Pop. 5,389
Roane County SD
Supt. — See Kingston
Rockwood HS — 400/9-12
512 W Rockwood St 37854 — 865-354-0882
James Wilson, prin. — Fax 354-5170
Rockwood MS — 400/6-8
434 W Rockwood St 37854 — 865-354-0931
William Thompson, prin. — Fax 354-5160

Rogersville, Hawkins, Pop. 4,233
Hawkins County SD — 7,200/K-12
200 N Depot St 37857 — 423-272-7629
E. Clayton Armstrong, dir. — Fax 272-2207
www.hawkinsschools.net
Cherokee HS — 1,100/9-12
2927 Highway 66 S 37857 — 423-272-6507
Daffin Anderson, prin. — Fax 272-6598
Rogersville MS — 500/6-8
958 E Mckinney Ave 37857 — 423-272-7603
Dr. John Carroll, prin. — Fax 272-7603
Other Schools – See Church Hill, Eidson, Surgoinsville

Rutledge, Grainger, Pop. 1,215
Grainger County SD — 3,300/K-12
PO Box 38 37861 — 865-828-3611
E. Vernon Coffey Ed.D., supt. — Fax 828-4357
www.grainger.k12.tn.us/
Rutledge HS — 800/9-12
140 Pioneer Dr 37861 — 865-828-5291
Ron Cabbage, prin. — Fax 828-4828
Rutledge MS — 400/3-8
7480 Rutledge Pike 37861 — 865-828-5530
Stanley Roach, prin. — Fax 828-5797
Grainger County Adult S — Adult
PO Box 38 37861 — 865-828-5172
Edwin Jarnagin, prin. — Fax 828-4357
Other Schools – See Washburn

Sale Creek, Hamilton
Hamilton County SD
Supt. — See Chattanooga
Sale Creek MSHS — 300/6-12
211 Patterson Rd 37373 — 423-332-8819
Devota Barnes, prin. — Fax 332-8847

Santa Fe, Maury
Maury County SD
Supt. — See Columbia
Santa Fe S — 600/K-12
2629 Santa Fe Pike 38482 — 931-682-2172
Linda Rivers, prin. — Fax 682-2606

Savannah, Hardin, Pop. 7,135
Hardin County SD — 3,700/K-12
155 Guinn St 38372 — 731-925-3943
Bob Cromwell, supt. — Fax 925-7313
www.hardin.k12.tn.us
Hardin County HS — 1,000/9-12
1170 Pickwick St S 38372 — 731-925-3976
Bob McAdams, prin. — Fax 925-7407
Hardin County MS — 900/6-8
299 Lacefield Dr 38372 — 731-925-9037
Steve Haffly, prin. — Fax 925-0253

Selmer, McNairy, Pop. 4,558
McNairy County SD — 4,200/K-12
170 W Court Ave 38375 — 731-645-3267
Charles Miskelly, supt. — Fax 645-8085
www.mcnairy.org
McNairy Central HS — 700/9-12
493 McNairy Central Rd 38375 — 731-645-3226
Cecil Stroup, prin. — Fax 645-8014
Selmer MS — 500/5-8
635 E Poplar Ave 38375 — 731-645-7977
Joel Boyd, prin. — Fax 645-6377
Other Schools – See Adamsville

Styles & Profiles Beauty College — Post-Sec.
119 S 2nd St 38375 — 731-645-9728

Sevierville, Sevier, Pop. 14,167
Sevier County SD | 12,700/PK-12
  226 Cedar St 37862 | 865-453-4671
  Dr. Jack A. Parton, supt. | Fax 522-1497
  www.sevier.org
Sevier County HS | 1,500/9-12
  1200 Dolly Parton Pkwy 37862 | 865-453-5525
  Gary Roach, prin. | Fax 428-5867
Sevierville MS | 700/6-8
  520 High St 37862 | 865-453-0311
  Jayson Nave, prin. | Fax 428-2316
Whites Adult HS | Adult
  703 Whites School Rd 37876 | 865-429-1492
  Curtis Clabo, prin.
Other Schools – See Gatlinburg, Kodak, Pigeon Forge, Seymour

St. Andrew's S | 50/K-12
  3601 Lyon Springs Rd 37862 | 865-429-5437
  James Wood, hdmstr. | Fax 429-2104

Sewanee, Franklin, Pop. 2,128

St. Andrew's-Sewanee S | 300/6-12
  290 Quintard Rd 37375 | 931-598-5651
  Rev. William Wade, hdmstr. | Fax 598-0039
University of the South | Post-Sec.
  735 University Ave 37383 | 931-598-1000

Seymour, Sevier, Pop. 7,026
Sevier County SD
  Supt. — See Sevierville
Seymour HS | 900/9-12
  732 Boyds Creek Hwy 37865 | 865-577-7040
  Greg Clark, prin. | Fax 579-1492
Seymour MS | 800/6-8
  737 Boyds Creek Hwy 37865 | 865-579-0730
  Faye Nelson, prin. | Fax 579-0905

Kings Academy | 400/K-12
  202 Smothers Rd 37865 | 865-573-8321
  Steve Sharp, prin. | Fax 573-8323

Shelbyville, Bedford, Pop. 17,538
Bedford County SD | 6,700/K-12
  500 Madison St 37160 | 931-684-3284
  Mike Bone, supt. | Fax 684-1133
  www.bedfordk12tn.com/
Harris MS | 800/6-8
  570 Eagle Blvd 37160 | 931-684-5195
  Bill Pietkiewicz, prin. | Fax 685-9455
Shelbyville Central HS | 1,000/9-12
  401 Eagle Blvd 37160 | 931-684-5672
  Don Embry, prin. | Fax 684-9359
Bedford Co. Adult HS and Learning Center | Adult
  326 E Depot St 37160 | 931-684-8635
  Elaine Weaver, prin. | Fax 684-8634
Other Schools – See Unionville, Wartrace

Tennessee Technology Center Shelbyville | Post-Sec.
  1405 Madison St 37160 | 931-685-5013

Signal Mountain, Hamilton, Pop. 7,265
Hamilton County SD
  Supt. — See Chattanooga
Signal Mountain MS | 400/6-8
  315 Ault Rd 37377 | 423-886-0876
  Bob Walter, prin. | Fax 886-0894

Smithville, DeKalb, Pop. 4,109
DeKalb County SD | 2,600/PK-12
  110 S Public Sq 37166 | 615-597-4084
  Jim McCormick, supt. | Fax 597-6326
  www.smithvilletn.com/education/index.htm
DeKalb County HS | 700/9-12
  1130 W Broad St 37166 | 615-597-4094
  Kathy Hendrix, prin.
DeKalb MS, 1132 W Broad St 37166 | 500/6-8
  Randy Jennings, prin. | 615-597-7987

Smyrna, Rutherford, Pop. 30,172
Rutherford County SD
  Supt. — See Murfreesboro
Rock Springs MS | 900/6-8
  3301 Rock Springs Rd 37167 | 615-904-3825
  Dr. Pat Essary, prin. | Fax 904-3826
Smyrna HS | 1,500/9-12
  100 Bulldog Dr 37167 | 615-904-3865
  Robert Raikes, prin. | Fax 904-3866
Smyrna MS | 900/6-8
  712 Hazelwood Dr 37167 | 615-904-3845
  Dr. Linda Kennedy, prin. | Fax 904-3846

Sneedville, Hancock, Pop. 1,328
Hancock County SD | 1,000/K-12
  PO Box 629 37869 | 423-733-2591
  Mike Antrican, dir. | Fax 733-8757
  www.hancockcountyschools.com/
Hancock County MSHS | 600/6-12
  2700 Main St 37869 | 423-733-4611
  Thomas Zachary, prin. | Fax 733-1427

Soddy Daisy, Hamilton, Pop. 8,884
Hamilton County SD
  Supt. — See Chattanooga
Sequoya Technology Center | Vo/Tech
  9517 W Ridge Trail Rd 37379 | 423-843-4707
  Steve Holmes, prin. | Fax 843-4719
Soddy Daisy HS | 1,600/9-12
  618 Sequoyah Rd 37379 | 423-332-8828
  Robert Smith, prin. | Fax 332-8831
Soddy Daisy MS | 600/6-8
  200 Turner Rd 37379 | 423-332-8800
  Dr. Robert Jenkins, prin. | Fax 332-8810

Somerville, Fayette, Pop. 2,861
Fayette County SD | 3,100/PK-12
  PO Box 9 38068 | 901-465-5260
  Myles Wilson, supt. | Fax 466-3725
  www.fayette.k12.tn.us
East JHS | 300/7-9
  400 Leach Dr 38068 | 901-465-3151
  Constance Agard, prin. | Fax 465-5084
Fayette-Ware HS | 600/10-12
  PO Box 849 38068 | 901-465-9838
  Charles Earle, prin. | Fax 465-1377
Other Schools – See Oakland

Fayette Academy | 800/K-12
  PO Box 130 38068 | 901-465-3241
  Bob Archer, prin. | Fax 465-2141

South Fulton, Obion, Pop. 2,480
Obion County SD
  Supt. — See Union City
South Fulton MSHS | 400/6-12
  1302 S Fulton Dr 38257 | 731-479-1441
  Keith Frazier, prin. | Fax 479-0586

South Pittsburg, Marion, Pop. 3,164
Marion County SD
  Supt. — See Jasper
South Pittsburg JSHS | 400/7-12
  717 Elm Ave 37380 | 423-837-7561
  Margie Allison, prin. | Fax 837-4532

Richard CSD | 400/K-12
  1620 Hamilton Ave 37380 | 423-837-7282
  Grant Barham, supt. | Fax 837-0641
  www.richardhardy.org
Hardy Memorial S | 400/K-12
  1620 Hamilton Ave 37380 | 423-837-7282
  Dr. Bill Henry, prin. | Fax 837-0641

Sparta, White, Pop. 4,661
White County SD | 3,800/PK-12
  136 Baker St 38583 | 931-836-2229
  Donny Haley, supt. | Fax 836-8128
  volweb.utk.edu/school/whiteco/
White County HS | 1,100/9-12
  267 Allen Dr 38583 | 931-836-3214
  Charles Dycus, prin. | Fax 836-6295
White County MS | 1,000/6-8
  300 Turn Table Rd 38583 | 931-738-9238
  Paul Steele, prin. | Fax 738-9271
White County Vocational S | Vo/Tech
  275 Allen Dr 38583 | 931-836-8140
  Bobby Sparkman, prin. | Fax 836-2549

Spencer, Van Buren, Pop. 1,697
Van Buren County SD | 800/PK-12
  PO Box 38 38585 | 931-946-2242
  Neal O'Neal, dir. | Fax 946-2858
Van Buren County JSHS | 400/6-12
  PO Box 278 38585 | 931-946-2442
  Michael Martin, prin. | Fax 946-2733

Spring City, Rhea, Pop. 2,011
Rhea County SD
  Supt. — See Dayton
Spring City MS | 300/6-8
  751 Wassom Memorial Hwy 37381 | 423-365-9105
  Buddy Jackson, prin. | Fax 365-9102

Springfield, Robertson, Pop. 15,117
Robertson County SD | 9,000/PK-12
  2121 Woodland St 37172 | 615-384-5588
  Daniel Whitlow, supt. | Fax 384-9749
  www.robcoschools.org
Coopertown MS | 6-8
  3820 Highway 49 W 37172 | 615-382-4166
  Dr. Mike Morris, prin. | Fax 382-4171
Robertson County Technology Center | Vo/Tech
  5326 Highway 76 E 37172 | 615-384-2491
  Linda Arms, prin. | Fax 384-2491
Springfield HS | 1,000/9-12
  5240 Highway 76 E 37172 | 615-384-3516
  Rick Highsmith, prin. | Fax 384-0247
Springfield MS | 600/6-8
  715 5th Ave W 37172 | 615-384-4821
  Shirley Witley, prin. | Fax 384-7890
Other Schools – See Cedar Hill, Cross Plains, Greenbrier, White House

Strawberry Plains, Jefferson
Knox County SD
  Supt. — See Knoxville
Carter HS | 900/9-12
  210 N Carter School Rd 37871 | 865-933-3434
  Cheryl Hickman, prin.
Carter MS | 800/6-8
  204 N Carter School Rd 37871 | 865-933-3426
  Jewel Brock, prin.

Blue Springs Christian Academy | 50/K-12
  3265 Blue Springs Rd 37871 | 865-932-7603
  June Ingram, prin.

Summertown, Lawrence
Lawrence County SD
  Supt. — See Lawrenceburg
Summertown JSHS | 600/7-12
  PO Box 88 38483 | 931-964-3539
  Bryan True, prin. | Fax 964-3302

Sunbright, Morgan, Pop. 587
Morgan County SD
  Supt. — See Wartburg
Sunbright S | 600/K-12
  PO Box 129 37872 | 423-628-2244
  Rosa Dotson, prin. | Fax 628-2120

Surgoinsville, Hawkins, Pop. 1,691
Hawkins County SD
  Supt. — See Rogersville

Surgoinsville MS | 400/5-8
  1044 Main St 37873 | 423-345-2252
  Patsy Norris, prin. | Fax 345-3598

Tennessee Technology Center Morristown | Post-Sec.
  323 Phipps Bend Rd 37873 | 423-345-4130

Sweetwater, Monroe, Pop. 5,784
Monroe County SD
  Supt. — See Madisonville
Sweetwater HS | 600/9-12
  414 S High St 37874 | 423-337-7881
   | Fax 337-0685

Sweetwater CSD | 1,400/PK-8
  PO Box 231 37874 | 423-337-7051
  Dr. S. Keith Hickey, supt. | Fax 337-6773
  www.compurdy.com/scs2/
Sweetwater JHS | 400/7-8
  1013 Cannon Ave 37874 | 423-337-7336
  Wayne Key, prin. | Fax 337-7360

Tazewell, Claiborne, Pop. 2,128
Claiborne County SD | 4,400/PK-12
  PO Box 179 37879 | 423-626-3543
  Don Dobbs, supt. | Fax 626-5945
  www.claibornecountyschools.com
Soldiers Memorial MS | 500/5-8
  1510 Legion St 37879 | 423-626-3531
  Lynn Barnard, prin. | Fax 626-2151
Claiborne Adult HS | Adult
  PO Box 600 37879 | 423-626-8222
  Roger Hansard, prin. | Fax 626-5945
Other Schools – See Cumberland Gap, Harrogate, New Tazewell

Tellico Plains, Monroe, Pop. 887
Monroe County SD
  Supt. — See Madisonville
Tellico Plains HS | 500/9-12
  9180 Highway 68 37385 | 423-253-2530
  Dan Schlafer, prin. | Fax 253-2541
Tellico Plains JHS | 300/5-8
  120 Old High School Rd 37385 | 423-253-2250
  Ron Eydt, prin. | Fax 253-7824

Ten Mile, Meigs
Roane County SD
  Supt. — See Kingston
Midway MS | 200/6-8
  104 Dogtown Rd 37880 | 865-717-5464
  Naomi S. Davis, prin. | Fax 376-0948

Thompsons Station, Williamson, Pop. 914
Williamson County SD
  Supt. — See Franklin
Heritage MS | 600/6-8
  4803 Columbia Pike 37179 | 615-472-4540
  Paula Pullian, prin. | Fax 472-4553
Independence HS | 9-12
  1776 Declaration Way 37179 | 615-472-4600
  Marilyn Webb, prin. | Fax 472-4621

Tiptonville, Lake, Pop. 4,180
Lake County SD | 900/PK-12
  PO Box 397 38079 | 731-253-6601
  Joey Hassell, supt. | Fax 253-7111
  www.lake.k12.tn.us/
Lake County HS | 200/9-12
  300 Cochran St 38079 | 731-253-7733
  Bret Johnson, prin. | Fax 253-7766

Trenton, Gibson, Pop. 4,594
Trenton Special SD | 1,400/PK-12
  201 W 10th St 38382 | 731-855-1191
  Larry Ridings, supt. | Fax 855-1414
  voyager.rtd.utk.edu/~trenton/
Peabody HS | 400/9-12
  2069 US Highway 45 Byp N 38382 | 731-855-2601
  Tim Haney, prin. | Fax 855-1217
Trenton MS | 500/5-8
  2065 US Highway 45 Byp S 38382 | 731-855-2422
  Juanita Johnson, prin. | Fax 855-1826

Trezevant, Carroll, Pop. 906
West Carroll Special SD | 1,100/K-12
  PO Box 279 38258 | 731-669-5005
  Eric Williams, supt. | Fax 669-3860
  www.wcssd.org
Other Schools – See Atwood

Troy, Obion, Pop. 1,265
Obion County SD
  Supt. — See Union City
Obion County Central HS | 800/9-12
  528 N US Highway 51 38260 | 731-536-4688
  Ray Wilson, prin. | Fax 536-0277

Tullahoma, Coffee, Pop. 18,434
Tullahoma CSD | 3,500/PK-12
  510 S Jackson St 37388 | 931-454-2600
  Dr. Dan Lawson, dir. | Fax 454-2642
  www.tullahomacityschools.net/
East MS | 400/6-8
  908 Country Club Dr 37388 | 931-454-2632
  Mike Foreman, prin. | Fax 454-2660
Tullahoma HS | 1,100/9-12
  1001 N Jackson St 37388 | 931-454-2620
  Mike Landis, prin. | Fax 454-2662
West MS | 400/6-8
  90 Hermitage Dr 37388 | 931-454-2605
  Greg Carter, prin. | Fax 454-2661

Union City, Obion, Pop. 10,769
Obion County SD | 3,900/K-12
  316 S 3rd St 38261 | 731-885-9743
  Lonnie Grady, supt. | Fax 885-4902
  www.obioncountyschools.com
Career Technology Center | Vo/Tech
  1700 N 5th St 38261 | 731-885-7171
  Bill Wilder, prin. | Fax 885-4734

Other Schools – See South Fulton, Troy

Union City CSD   1,400/K-12
    PO Box 749 38281   731-885-3922
    Gary Houston, supt.   Fax 885-6033
    www.union-city-hs.obion.k12.tn.us/
Union City HS   400/9-12
    1305 High School Dr 38261   731-885-2373
    Donnie Cox, prin.   Fax 885-5011
Union City MS   300/6-8
    1111 High School Dr 38261   731-885-2901
    Dan Boykin, prin.   Fax 885-3677

Unionville, Bedford
Bedford County SD
    Supt. — See Shelbyville
Community HS   500/7-12
    3470 Highway 41A N 37180   931-294-5125
    Robert Ralston, prin.   Fax 294-5126

Vonore, Monroe, Pop. 1,263
Monroe County SD
    Supt. — See Madisonville
Vonore MS   5-8
    414 Hall St 37885   423-884-2730
    Debra Tipton, prin.   Fax 884-2731

Wartburg, Morgan, Pop. 918
Morgan County SD   3,000/K-12
    136 Flat Fork Rd 37887   423-346-6214
    Mike Davis, dir.   Fax 346-6043
    www.mcs.k12tn.net
Central HS   400/9-12
    1119 Knoxville Hwy 37887   423-346-6616
    Dallas Davis, prin.   Fax 346-5665
Central MS   100/6-8
    146 Liberty Rd 37887   423-346-2800
    Judy Hurst, prin.   Fax 346-2805
Morgan County Vo Ctr   Vo/Tech
    132 Flat Fork Rd 37887   423-346-6285
    Mitchell Heidel, prin.   Fax 346-5857
Other Schools – See Coalfield, Oakdale, Sunbright

Wartrace, Bedford, Pop. 562
Bedford County SD
    Supt. — See Shelbyville
Cascade HS   700/6-12
    1165 Bell Buckle Wartrace 37183   931-389-9389
    Terry Looper, prin.   Fax 389-6223

Washburn, Grainger
Grainger County SD
    Supt. — See Rutledge
Washburn S   600/K-12
    7925 Highway 131 37888   865-497-2557
    Lisa Setsor, prin.   Fax 497-2934

Watertown, Wilson, Pop. 1,388
Wilson County SD
    Supt. — See Lebanon
Watertown HS   500/7-12
    PO Box 67 37184   615-237-3434
    Rick Martin, prin.   Fax 237-3030

Waverly, Humphreys, Pop. 4,073
Humphreys County SD   3,200/PK-12
    2443 Highway 70 E 37185   931-296-2568
    James L. Long, supt.   Fax 296-6501
    www.hcss.org
Humphreys County Vo HS   Vo/Tech
    1327 Highway 70 W 37185   931-296-7867
    Kay Webb, dir.   Fax 296-7252
Waverly Central HS   600/9-12
    1325 Highway 70 W 37185   931-296-3911
    Richard Rawlings, prin.   Fax 296-2575
Waverly JHS   600/4-8
    520 E Main St 37185   931-296-4514
    Andy Daniels, prin.   Fax 296-6507
Other Schools – See Mc Ewen

Waynesboro, Wayne, Pop. 2,166
Wayne County SD   2,500/K-12
    PO Box 658 38485   931-722-3548
    Jerry Pigg, supt.   Fax 722-7579
    www.wayne-lea.wayne.k12.tn.us
Wayne County HS   300/9-12
    707 S Main St 38485   931-722-3238
    James Coy Anderson, prin.   Fax 722-7641
Wayne County Vo Ctr   Vo/Tech
    703 S Main St 38485   931-722-5495
    Beverly Hall, prin.   Fax 722-5496
Waynesboro MS   400/5-8
    PO Box 657 38485   931-722-5545
    Ryan Keeton, prin.   Fax 722-3953
Other Schools – See Clifton, Collinwood

Westmoreland, Sumner, Pop. 2,124
Sumner County SD
    Supt. — See Gallatin
Westmoreland HS   500/9-12
    PO Box 119 37186   615-644-2280
    DeWayne Oldham, prin.   Fax 644-3395
Westmoreland MS   400/6-8
    PO Box 69 37186   615-644-3003
    Danny Robinson, prin.   Fax 644-5584

_____

Achievement Valley Ranch   50/9-12
    45 Angela Ln 37186   615-644-4956
    Eric Larson, prin.   Fax 644-4984

White Bluff, Dickson, Pop. 2,257
Dickson County SD
    Supt. — See Dickson
James MS   300/6-8
    3030 Trace Creek Rd 37187   615-797-3201
    Louise Buchanan, prin.   Fax 797-6401

White House, Sumner, Pop. 8,256
Robertson County SD
    Supt. — See Springfield
White House-Heritage JSHS   600/6-12
    220 West Dr 37188   615-672-0311
    Kerry Baggett, prin.   Fax 672-7178

Sumner County SD
    Supt. — See Gallatin
White House HS   800/9-12
    508 Tyree Springs Rd 37188   615-672-3761
    Jeff Cordell, prin.   Fax 672-6404
White House MS   700/6-8
    2020 Highway 31 W 37188   615-672-4379
    Jerry Apple, prin.   Fax 672-6409

Gideon Academy   50/K-12
    2948 Union Rd 37188   615-672-1121
    Rick Dunnam, prin.   Fax 212-0123
Heritage - Hope Academy   50/9-12
    PO Box 570 37188   615-672-6949
    Robert Cook, hdmstr.   Fax 672-8222

Whitesburg, Hamblen
Hamblen County SD
    Supt. — See Morristown
East Ridge MS   600/6-8
    6595 Saint Clair Rd 37891   423-581-3041
    Marcia Carlyle, prin.   Fax 585-3763

Whites Creek, See Nashville
Davidson County SD
    Supt. — See Nashville
Whites Creek Comprehensive HS   900/9-12
    7277 Old Hickory Blvd 37189   615-876-5132
    Alvin Jones, prin.   Fax 876-5134

Whiteville, Hardeman, Pop. 4,465

Tennessee Technology Center Whiteville   Post-Sec.
    PO Box 489 38075   731-254-8521

Whitwell, Marion, Pop. 1,631
Marion County SD
    Supt. — See Jasper
Whitwell HS   400/9-12
    200 Tiger Trl 37397   423-658-5141
    Wesley Green, prin.   Fax 658-0313
Whitwell MS   300/5-8
    1130 Main St 37397   423-658-5635
    Linda Hooper, prin.   Fax 658-6949

Winchester, Franklin, Pop. 7,602
Franklin County SD   5,500/PK-12
    215 S College St 37398   931-967-0626
    Dr. Charles Edmonds, supt.   Fax 967-7832
    franklincountyschools.k12tn.net/
Franklin County HS   1,200/9-12
    833 Bypass Rd 37398   931-967-2821
    Harold Roberts, prin.   Fax 967-6945
North MS   500/7-8
    2990 Decherd Blvd 37398   931-967-5323
    John Butler, prin.   Fax 967-6417
Other Schools – See Cowan, Huntland

Woodbury, Cannon, Pop. 2,498
Cannon County SD   2,100/K-12
    301 W Main St 37190   615-563-5752
    Edward L. Diden, supt.   Fax 563-2716
    ccstn.net
Cannon County HS   600/9-12
    1 Lion Dr 37190   615-563-2144
    Kim Parsley, prin.   Fax 563-8068

TEXAS

TEXAS EDUCATION AGENCY
1701 Congress Ave, Austin 78701-1494
Telephone 512-463-9734
Fax 512-463-9838
Website http://www.tea.state.tx.us

Commissioner of Education   Shirley Neeley

TEXAS BOARD OF EDUCATION
1701 Congress Ave, Austin 78701-1402

Chairperson   Geraldine Miller

REGIONAL EDUCATION SERVICE CENTERS (RESC)

Region 1 ESC
Dr. Sylvia Hatton, dir.   956-984-6000
1900 W Schunior St, Edinburg   Fax 984-6299
www.esc1.net/
Region 2 ESC
Dr. Linda Villarreal, dir.   361-561-8400
209 N Water St   Fax 883-3442
Corpus Christi 78401
www.esc2.net
Region 3 ESC
Dr. Julius Cano, dir.   361-573-0731
1905 Leary Ln, Victoria 77901   Fax 576-4804
www.esc3.net/
Region 4 ESC
Dr. William McKinney, dir.   713-462-7708
7145 W Tidwell Rd, Houston 77092   Fax 744-6514
www.esc4.net/
Region 5 ESC
Dr. R. Steve Hyden, dir.   409-838-5555
2295 Delaware St   Fax 833-9755
Beaumont 77703
www.esc5.net
Region 6 ESC
Thomas Poe, dir.   936-435-8400
3332 Montgomery Rd   Fax 295-1447
Huntsville 77340
www.esc6.net/

Region 7 ESC
Elizabeth Abernethy, dir.   903-988-6700
1909 N Longview St, Kilgore 75662   Fax 988-6735
www.esc7.net/
Region 8 ESC
Harvey Hohenberger, dir.   903-572-8551
PO Box 1894   Fax 575-2611
Mount Pleasant 75456
www.reg8.net/
Region 9 ESC
Dr. Ron Preston, dir.   940-322-6928
301 Loop 11, Wichita Falls 76306   Fax 767-3836
www.esc9.net
Region 10 ESC
Dr. Jill Shugart, dir.   972-348-1700
PO Box 831300, Richardson 75083   Fax 231-3642
www.ednet10.net/
Region 11 ESC
Richard Ownby, dir.   817-740-3600
3001 North Fwy, Fort Worth 76106   Fax 740-7600
www.esc11.net
Region 12 ESC
Dr. Tom Norris, dir.   254-297-1212
PO Box 23409, Waco 76702   Fax 666-0823
www.esc12.net
Region 13 ESC
Dr. Pat Pringle, dir.   512-919-5313
5701 Springdale Rd, Austin 78723   Fax 919-5374

Region 14 ESC
Ronnie Kincaid, dir.   325-675-8600
1850 Highway 351, Abilene 79601   Fax 675-8659
www.esc14.net/
Region 15 ESC
David Smith, dir.   325-658-6571
PO Box 5199, San Angelo 76902   Fax 658-6571
www.netxv.net/
Region 16 ESC
John Bass, dir.   806-677-5000
5800 Bell St, Amarillo 79109   Fax 677-5001
www.esc16.net/
Region 17 ESC
Dr. Kyle Wargo, dir.   806-792-4000
1111 W Loop 289, Lubbock 79416   Fax 792-1523
www.esc17.net/
Region 18 ESC
Charles W. Greenawalt, dir.   432-563-2380
PO Box 60580, Midland 79711   Fax 567-3290
www.esc18.net
Region 19 ESC
Dr. James Vasquez, dir.   915-780-1919
PO Box 971127, El Paso 79997   Fax 780-6537
Region 20 ESC
Dr. Terry Smith, dir.   210-370-5200
1314 Hines, San Antonio 78208   Fax 370-5750
www.esc20.net

PUBLIC, PRIVATE AND CATHOLIC SECONDARY SCHOOLS

Abbott, Hill, Pop. 319
Abbott ISD   300/PK-12
PO Box 226 76621   254-582-9442
Terry Timmons, supt.   Fax 582-5430
www.esc12.net/abbottisd/
Abbott S   300/PK-12
PO Box 226 76621   254-582-3011
D. Beseda, prin.   Fax 582-5430

Abernathy, Hale, Pop. 2,772
Abernathy ISD   800/PK-12
505 7th St 79311   806-298-2563
Herb Youngblood, supt.   Fax 298-2400
www.abernathyisd.com
Abernathy HS   200/9-12
505 7th St 79311   806-298-2563
Gary Pugh, prin.   Fax 298-4653
Abernathy JHS   200/6-8
505 7th St 79311   806-298-2563
Harold Bufe, prin.   Fax 298-4653

Abilene, Taylor, Pop. 114,889
Abilene ISD   16,500/PK-12
PO Box 981 79604   325-677-1444
Dr. David Polnick, supt.   Fax 794-1325
www.aisd.org
Abilene HS   2,300/9-12
2800 N 6th St 79603   325-677-1731
Terry Bull, prin.   Fax 677-4127
Clack MS   700/6-8
1610 Corsicana Ave 79605   325-692-1961
Jack Nall, prin.   Fax 690-3547
Cooper HS   2,100/9-12
3639 Sayles Blvd 79605   325-691-1000
Gail Gregg, prin.   Fax 690-3402
Franklin MS   600/6-8
1200 Merchant St 79603   325-671-3791
Steve Post, prin.   Fax 671-4293
Lincoln MS   800/6-8
1699 S 1st St 79602   325-672-3279
Martin DeHoyos, prin.   Fax 671-4365
Madison MS   800/6-8
3145 Barrow St 79605   325-692-5661
Jennifer Raney, prin.   Fax 690-3584
Mann MS   600/6-8
2545 Mimosa Dr 79603   325-672-8493
Joe Alcorta, prin.   Fax 671-4405
Woodson Skill Center   Vo/Tech
342 Cockerell Dr 79601   325-671-4729
Elizabeth Dolton, lead tchr.   Fax 671-4731
Adult Learning Center   Adult
1929 S 11th St 79602   325-671-4419
Merri Lynn Rideout, dir.   Fax 671-4671

Wylie ISD   2,800/PK-12
7049 Buffalo Gap Rd 79606   325-692-4353
Don Harrison, supt.   Fax 695-3438
www.wylie.esc14.net
Wylie HS   900/9-12
4502 Antilley Rd 79606   325-690-1181
Terry Hagler, prin.   Fax 690-0320
Wylie JHS   500/7-8
4010 Beltway S 79606   325-695-1910
Tommy Vaughn, prin.   Fax 692-5786

Abilene Christian S   300/PK-12
2550 N Judge Ely Blvd 79601   325-672-9200
Billy Brant, pres.   Fax 672-1262
Abilene Christian University   Post-Sec.
ACU Box 29000 79699   325-674-2000
American Commercial College   Post-Sec.
402 Butternut St 79602   325-672-8495
Hardin-Simmons University   Post-Sec.
2200 Hickory St 79601   325-670-1000
Hendrick Medical Center   Post-Sec.
1242 N 19th St 79601   325-670-2201
McMurry University   Post-Sec.
14th and Sayles 79697   325-793-3800
Texas College of Cosmetology   Post-Sec.
117 Sayles Blvd 79605   325-677-0532

Ackerly, Dawson, Pop. 236
Sands Consolidated ISD   200/PK-12
PO Box 218 79713   432-353-4888
Wayne Blount, supt.   Fax 353-4650
sands.esc17.net
Sands S   200/PK-12
PO Box 218 79713   432-353-4888
Zelda Bilbo, prin.   Fax 353-4561

Addison, Dallas, Pop. 13,886

Greenhill S   1,300/PK-12
4141 Spring Valley Rd 75001   972-628-5400
Scott Griggs, hdmstr.   Fax 404-8217
Sterling Health Center   Post-Sec.
15070 E Beltwood Pkwy 75001   972-992-9293
Trinity Christian Academy   1,500/K-12
17001 Addison Rd 75001   972-931-8325
David Delph, admin.   Fax 931-8923

Adkins, Bexar

Salem Sayers Baptist S   100/PK-12
PO Box 397 78101   210-649-1178

Adrian, Oldham, Pop. 157
Adrian ISD   100/K-12
PO Box 189 79001   806-538-6203
David Johnson, supt.   Fax 538-6291
www.adrianisd.net

Adrian S   100/K-12
PO Box 189 79001   806-538-6203
David Johnson, prin.   Fax 538-6291

Afton, Dickens
Patton Springs ISD   100/PK-12
PO Box 32 79220   806-689-2229
Larry McClenny, supt.   Fax 689-2253
www.pattonsprings.net
Patton Springs S   100/PK-12
PO Box 32 79220   806-689-2220
Mike Norrell, prin.   Fax 689-2253

Agua Dulce, Nueces, Pop. 734
Agua Dulce ISD   300/PK-12
PO Box 250 78330   361-998-2542
Paul Czerwinski, supt.   Fax 998-2816
www.adisd.esc2.net
Agua Dulce JSHS   200/6-12
PO Box 250 78330   361-998-2214
Robyn Pesek, prin.   Fax 998-2994

Alamo, Hidalgo, Pop. 15,731
Pharr-San Juan-Alamo ISD
Supt. — See Pharr
Alamo MS   1,100/6-8
1819 W US Highway 83 78516   956-702-5887
Iris Guajardo, prin.   Fax 702-5893
Pharr-San Juan-Alamo Memorial HS   1,800/9-12
800 S Alamo Rd 78516   956-783-3600
Orlando Noyola, prin.   Fax 783-3636

Valley Christ Heritage S   100/PK-12
932 N Alamo Rd 78516   956-787-9743

Alba, Wood, Pop. 462
Alba-Golden ISD   800/PK-12
1373 County Road 2377 75410   903-768-2472
Bill Stewart, supt.   Fax 768-2130
www.agisd.com
Alba-Golden JSHS   400/6-12
1373 County Road 2377 75410   903-768-2472
Dwayne Ellis, prin.   Fax 768-2303

Albany, Shackelford, Pop. 1,922
Albany ISD   600/PK-12
PO Box 188 76430   325-762-3974
Shane Fields, supt.   Fax 762-3876
www.albany.esc14.net
Albany JSHS   300/7-12
PO Box 188 76430   325-762-3974
Thomas W. Terrell, prin.   Fax 762-3850

Aledo, Parker, Pop. 2,257
Aledo ISD   4,100/PK-12
1008 Bailey Ranch Rd 76008   817-441-8327
Don Daniel, supt.   Fax 441-5144
www.aledo.k12.tx.us

Aledo HS 1,000/9-12
1000 Bailey Ranch Rd 76008 817-441-8711
Sheryl Asay, prin. Fax 441-5136
Aledo MS 600/7-8
416 FM 1187 S 76008 817-441-5198
John Lindsay, prin. Fax 441-5133

Aledo Christian S 100/K-12
PO Box 117 76008 817-441-9062
Kay Ross, prin. Fax 441-7476

Alice, Jim Wells, Pop. 19,310
Alice ISD 5,400/K-12
1801 E Main St 78332 361-664-0981
Henry Herrera, supt. Fax 660-2113
www.aliceisd.net/home.asp
Adams MS 800/7-8
901 E 3rd St 78332 361-660-2055
Noel Estrada, prin. Fax 660-2094
Alice HS 1,600/9-12
1 Coyote Trl 78332 361-664-0126
Amy Koenning, prin. Fax 660-2128

Alice Christian S 50/PK-12
1200 N Stadium Rd 78332 361-668-6618
David Winston, prin. Fax 668-0840

Alief, Harris
Alief ISD
Supt. — See Houston
S.O.A.R. Adult
PO Box 68 77411 281-988-3499
Beth Smith, prin. Fax 983-1698

Allen, Collin, Pop. 62,400
Allen ISD 13,200/PK-12
PO Box 13 75013 972-727-0513
Jenny Preston, supt. Fax 727-0518
www.allenisd.org
Allen SHS 2,800/10-12
300 Rivercrest Blvd 75002 972-727-0400
Steve Payne, prin. Fax 727-0515
Curtis MS 1,100/7-8
1530 Rivercrest Blvd 75002 972-727-0340
Becky Kennedy, prin. Fax 727-0345
Ford MS 1,200/7-8
630 Park Place Dr 75002 972-727-0590
Sandra McCoy-Jackson, prin. Fax 727-0596
Lowery Freshman Center 1,100/9-9
120 N Jupiter Rd 75002 972-396-6975
Kelli Schreffler, prin. Fax 396-6981

Alpine, Brewster, Pop. 6,103
Alpine ISD 1,100/PK-12
704 W Sul Ross Ave 79830 432-837-7700
Mike Davis, supt. Fax 837-7740
www.alpine.esc18.net
Alpine HS 300/9-12
300 E Hendryx Dr 79830 432-837-7710
Verl O'Bryant, prin. Fax 837-7741
Alpine MS 300/5-8
801 Middle School Dr 79830 432-837-7720
Houston Hendryx, prin. Fax 837-7795

Sul Ross State University 79832 Post-Sec.
432-837-8032

Altair, Colorado
Rice Consolidated ISD 1,000/PK-12
PO Box 338 77412 979-234-3531
Michael Lanier Ph.D., supt. Fax 234-6305
www.ricecisd.org/
Rice HS 400/9-12
PO Box 338 77412 979-234-3535
Leroy Stavinoha, prin. Fax 234-5901
Other Schools – See Eagle Lake

Alto, Cherokee, Pop. 1,125
Alto ISD 700/PK-12
RR 1 Box 1000 75925 936-858-7101
LaWayne Sheffield, supt. Fax 858-2101
www.alto.esc7.net/
Alto HS 200/9-12
RR 1 Box 1000 75925 936-858-7110
Charles Weeks, prin. Fax 858-4387
Alto MS 200/5-8
RR 1 Box 1000 75925 936-858-7140
William Luttrell, prin. Fax 858-4579

Alvarado, Johnson, Pop. 3,770
Alvarado ISD 3,500/PK-12
PO Box 387 76009 817-783-6800
Dr. Chester Juroska, supt. Fax 783-3844
www.alvaradoisd.net/
Alvarado HS 1,000/9-12
PO Box 387 76009 817-783-6940
Kenneth Estes, prin. Fax 783-6944
Alvarado JHS 500/7-8
PO Box 387 76009 817-783-6840
Melodye Broods, prin. Fax 783-6844

Alvin, Brazoria, Pop. 21,978
Alvin ISD 12,100/PK-12
301 E House St 77511 281-388-1130
Dr. Greg Smith, supt. Fax 388-0566
www.alvinisd.net/
Alvin HS 3,200/9-12
301 E House St 77511 281-331-8151
Kevon Wells, prin. Fax 331-3053
Alvin JHS 700/7-8
301 E House St 77511 281-585-8491
Deborah Roberson, prin. Fax 331-5926
Harby JHS 700/7-8
301 E House St 77511 281-585-6626
Nancy Flores, prin. Fax 388-2247
Manvel JHS 400/7-8
301 E House St 77511 281-489-8257
Trisha Upchurch, prin. Fax 489-8169
Alvin Evening S Adult
301 E House St 77511 281-331-8151
Fulvia Nolte, prin.
Other Schools – See Manvel

Alvin Community College Post-Sec.
3110 Mustang Rd 77511 281-331-6111
Living Stones Christian S 200/K-12
1407 Victory Ln 77511 281-331-0086
Jessica Cedro, admin. Fax 331-6747

Alvord, Wise, Pop. 1,184
Alvord ISD 700/PK-12
PO Box 70 76225 940-427-5975
John Trice, supt. Fax 427-2313
www.alvordisd.net/
Alvord HS 200/9-12
PO Box 70 76225 940-427-9643
Carla Bullard, prin. Fax 427-9648
Alvord MS 200/6-8
PO Box 70 76225 940-427-5511
Carolyn Holloway, prin. Fax 427-2461

Amarillo, Potter, Pop. 178,612
Amarillo ISD 29,400/PK-12
7200 W Interstate 40 79106 806-326-1000
Rod Schroder, supt. Fax 354-4378
www.amaisd.org
Amarillo HS, 4225 Danbury Dr 79109 2,100/9-12
Doug Loomis, prin. 806-326-2000
Austin MS 800/6-8
1808 Wimberly Rd 79109 806-354-4450
David Vincent, prin. Fax 356-4802
Bonham MS 900/6-8
5600 W 49th Ave 79109 806-354-4550
Curtis Crump, prin. Fax 356-4865
Bowie MS 1,100/6-8
3001 E 12th Ave 79104 806-371-5580
Marilyn Jackson, prin. Fax 371-6015
Caprock HS, 3001 E 34th Ave 79103 1,600/9-12
Rebecca Harrison, prin. 806-326-2200
Crockett MS 700/6-8
4720 Floyd Ave 79106 806-354-4470
Kevin Phillips, prin. Fax 356-4873
Fannin MS 600/6-8
4627 S Rusk St 79110 806-354-4570
Tammie Villarreal, prin. Fax 354-2304
Houston MS 900/6-8
815 S Independence St 79106 806-371-5560
Angie Noel, prin. Fax 371-5818
Mann MS 800/6-8
610 N Buchanan St 79107 806-371-5600
Roscoe Guest, prin. Fax 371-5617
Palo Duro HS, 1400 N Grant St 79107 1,900/9-12
Mark Leach, prin. 806-326-2400
Tascosa HS, 3921 Westlawn St 79102 2,200/9-12
Bob Daniel, prin. 806-326-2600
Travis MS 1,000/6-8
2815 Martin Rd 79107 806-381-7200
Jay Barrett, prin. Fax 381-7342

Canyon ISD
Supt. — See Canyon
Randall HS 1,500/9-12
5800 Attebury Dr 79118 806-677-2333
Steve Williams, prin. Fax 677-2329
Westover Park JHS 800/7-8
7200 Pinnacle Dr 79119 806-677-2420
Doug Voran, prin. Fax 677-2439

Highland Park ISD 800/PK-12
PO Box 30430 79120 806-335-2823
Bill Mayfield, supt. Fax 335-3547
www.hpisd.net
Highland Park HS 200/9-12
PO Box 30430 79120 806-335-2821
Doug Rice, prin. Fax 335-3215
Highland Park MS 200/6-8
PO Box 30430 79120 806-335-2821
Shelley Collins, prin. Fax 335-3215

River Road ISD 1,400/PK-12
9500 N US Highway 287 79108 806-381-7800
Randy Owen, supt. Fax 381-1357
www.rrisd.net
River Road HS 400/9-12
9500 N US Highway 287 79108 806-383-8867
Andy Nies, prin. Fax 381-7818
River Road MS 300/6-8
7600 Pavillard Dr 79108 806-383-8721
Richard Kelley, prin. Fax 381-7815

Amarillo College Post-Sec.
PO Box 447 79178 806-371-5000
Amarillo College of Hairdressing Post-Sec.
2400 E 27th Ave 79103 806-371-7600
Arbor Christian Academy 300/K-12
5000 Hollywood Rd 79118 806-355-7207
Nancy Wilcox, admin. Fax 353-8969
Bible Heritage Christian S 200/PK-12
4100 Republic Ave 79109 806-463-2427
Dennis Rawls, admin. Fax 463-2433
Exposito School of Hair Design Post-Sec.
3710 Mockingbird Ln 79109 806-355-9111
Holy Cross Catholic Academy 100/6-12
4110 S Bonham St 79110 806-355-9637
Frank Maldonado, prin. Fax 353-9520
Northwest Texas Healthcare System Post-Sec.
PO Box 1110 79105 806-354-1110
San Jacinto Christian Academy 600/PK-12
PO Box 3428 79116 806-372-2285
Christy Creacy, prin. Fax 376-6712

Amherst, Lamb, Pop. 779
Amherst ISD 200/K-12
PO Box 248 79312 806-246-3501
Byron Shelley, supt. Fax 246-3649
Amherst S 200/K-12
PO Box 248 79312 806-246-3221
Joe Rackley, prin. Fax 246-3649

Anahuac, Chambers, Pop. 2,173
Anahuac ISD 1,400/PK-12
PO Box 369 77514 409-267-3600
Dr. Linda Kay Barnhart, supt. Fax 267-3855
www.anahuac.isd.esc4.net
Anahuac HS 400/9-12
PO Box 1560 77514 409-267-6491
Eric Humphrey, prin. Fax 267-5192
Anahuac MS 300/6-8
PO Box 849 77514 409-267-3421
Cody Abshier, prin. Fax 267-3643

Anderson, Grimes, Pop. 274
Anderson - Shiro Consolidated ISD 500/K-12
PO Box 289 77830 936-873-2802
Thomas Price, supt. Fax 873-2673
www.anderson-shirocisd.net
Anderson - Shiro Secondary S 300/5-12
PO Box 289 77830 936-873-2061
Theresa Keel, prin. Fax 873-2718

Andrews, Andrews, Pop. 9,509
Andrews ISD 3,000/PK-12
405 NW 3rd St 79714 432-523-3640
David Mitchell, supt. Fax 523-3343
andrews.esc18.net
Andrews HS 900/9-12
405 NW 3rd St 79714 432-523-3640
Rick Howell, prin. Fax 523-6807
Andrews MS 700/6-8
405 NW 3rd St 79714 432-523-3640
Penny Bane, prin. Fax 524-1904

Angleton, Brazoria, Pop. 18,625
Angleton ISD 6,400/PK-12
1900 N Downing Rd 77515 979-849-8594
Dr. Heath Burns, supt. Fax 849-3041
www.angletonisd.net/
Angleton HS 1,800/9-12
1201 W Henderson Rd 77515 979-849-8206
Larry Williams, prin. Fax 864-8675
Angleton IS 1,000/7-8
1800 N Downing Rd 77515 979-849-4318
Roy Gardner, prin. Fax 849-8652

Anna, Collin, Pop. 1,486
Anna ISD 1,100/PK-12
501 S Sherley Ave 75409 972-924-3955
Dr. Joe M. Wardell, supt. Fax 924-3321
annaisd.ednet10.net/
Anna HS 300/9-12
501 S Sherley Ave 75409 972-924-3261
Scott Wortham, prin. Fax 924-2074
Anna MS 300/6-8
501 S Sherley Ave 75409 972-924-2380
Kevin Harris, prin. Fax 924-2856

Anson, Jones, Pop. 2,412
Anson ISD 800/PK-12
1431 Commercial Ave 79501 325-823-3671
Jay Baccus, supt. Fax 823-4444
www.ansontigers.com
Anson HS 200/9-12
1509 Commercial Ave 79501 325-823-2404
Will Brewer, prin. Fax 823-2514
Anson MS 200/6-8
1120 Avenue M 79501 325-823-2771
Harper Stewart, prin. Fax 823-3667

Anthony, El Paso, Pop. 4,061
Anthony ISD 800/PK-12
610 6th St 79821 915-886-6500
Vernon Butler, supt. Fax 886-3835
www.anthonyisd.net
Anthony HS 200/9-12
610 6th St 79821 915-886-6550
Edmond Martinez, prin. Fax 886-3875
Anthony MS 200/6-8
610 6th St 79821 915-886-6530
Dr. Terry Ann Rodriguez, prin. Fax 886-3875

Anton, Hockley, Pop. 1,169
Anton ISD 300/PK-12
PO Box 309 79313 806-997-2301
Dwayne Chenault, supt. Fax 997-2062
Anton JSHS 200/7-12
PO Box 309 79313 806-997-5211
Jeff Brazil, prin. Fax 997-2062

Apple Springs, Trinity
Apple Springs ISD 200/PK-12
PO Box 125 75926 936-831-3344
Gregg Spivey, supt. Fax 831-2824
Apple Springs JSHS 100/7-12
PO Box 125 75926 936-831-2241
Cody Moree, prin. Fax 831-2824

Aquilla, Hill, Pop. 144
Aquilla ISD 200/PK-12
404 N Richards 76622 254-694-3770
James L. Gwaltney, supt. Fax 694-6237
Aquilla S 200/PK-12
404 N Richards 76622 254-694-3770
Travis Walker, prin. Fax 694-6237

Aransas Pass, San Patricio, Pop. 8,612
Aransas Pass ISD 2,100/PK-12
244 W Harrison Blvd 78336 361-758-3466
Dr. Carl A. Montoya, supt. Fax 758-2962
www.apisd.org
Aransas Pass HS 500/9-12
450 S Avenue A 78336 361-758-3248
James Crenshaw, prin. Fax 758-3251
Blunt MS 300/7-8
2103 Demory Ln 78336 361-758-2711
Bryan O'Bryant, prin. Fax 758-4690

Highland Avenue Christian S 100/1-12
1630 W Highland Ave 78336 361-758-8196
Steve Hale, prin. Fax 758-5214

Archer City, Archer, Pop. 1,893
Archer City ISD 500/PK-12
PO Box 926 76351 940-574-4536
Randel Beaver, supt. Fax 574-4051
www.esc9.net/acisd
Archer City JSHS 300/7-12
PO Box 926 76351 940-574-4713
C. Knobloch, prin. Fax 574-2636

Argyle, Denton, Pop. 2,681
Argyle ISD 1,400/PK-12
800 Eagle Dr 76226 940-464-7241
Carolyn Pierel, supt. Fax 464-7297
www.argyleisd.com
Argyle HS 400/9-12
800 Eagle Dr 76226 940-262-7777
Jeff Henry, prin. Fax 262-7783
Argyle MS 300/6-8
800 Eagle Dr 76226 940-246-2126
Sonja Ball, prin. Fax 246-2128

Liberty Christian S 1,000/PK-12
9301 Highway 377 76226 940-294-2000
Rodney Haire, dir. Fax 294-2045

Arlington, Tarrant, Pop. 355,007
Arlington ISD 61,200/PK-12
1203 W Pioneer Pkwy 76013 817-460-4611
Dr. Mac Bernd, supt. Fax 459-7299
www.aisd.net

Arlington HS 2,700/9-12
818 W Park Row Dr 76013 817-459-8100
James Adams, prin. Fax 801-6105
Bailey JHS 800/7-8
2411 Winewood Ln 76013 817-801-0700
Jimmy Walker, prin. Fax 801-0705
Barnett JHS 1,000/7-8
2101 E Sublett Rd 76018 817-419-5000
Cindy Elwood, prin. Fax 419-5005
Boles JHS 700/7-8
3900 SW Green Oaks Blvd 76017 817-561-8000
Lloyd Day, prin. Fax 561-8005
Bowie HS 2,500/9-12
2101 Highbank Dr 76018 817-472-4400
Darrell Sneed, prin. Fax 472-4444
Carter JHS 800/7-8
701 Tharp St 76010 817-801-1700
Rashel Stevens, prin. Fax 801-1705
Ferguson JHS 700/7-8
600 SE Green Oaks Blvd 76018 817-472-1600
David Tapia, prin. Fax 472-1605
Gunn JHS 600/7-8
3000 S Fielder Rd 76015 817-419-5400
Lesia Rodawalt, prin. Fax 419-5405
Houston HS 3,000/9-12
2000 Sam Houston Dr 76014 817-459-8200
Beverly McReynolds, prin. Fax 801-4505
Hutcheson JHS 900/7-8
2101 Browning Dr 76010 817-801-2400
Rose Bolden, prin. Fax 801-2415
Lamar HS 2,900/9-12
1400 W Lamar Blvd 76012 817-459-8300
Jim Jones, prin. Fax 801-6255
Martin HS 3,400/9-12
4501 W Pleasant Ridge Rd 76016 817-561-8600
Laura Jones, prin. Fax 561-8705
Nichols JHS 1,000/7-8
2201 Ascension Blvd 76006 817-801-2600
Derrell Douglas, prin. Fax 801-2605
Ousley JHS 600/7-8
950 Southeast Pkwy 76018 817-419-5700
Lora Thurston, prin. Fax 419-5705
Seguin HS 1,600/9-12
7001 Silo Rd 76002 817-375-6700
Edward Farmer, prin. Fax 375-6705
Shackelford JHS 700/7-8
2000 N Fielder Rd 76012 817-801-3600
Carolyn Galvan, prin. Fax 801-3605
Workman JHS 700/7-8
701 E Arbrook Blvd 76014 817-419-1200
David Bellile, prin. Fax 419-1205
Young JHS 900/7-8
3200 Woodside Dr 76016 817-492-3400
Mary Canon, prin. Fax 492-3405

Mansfield ISD
Supt. — See Mansfield
Coble MS 7-8
1200 Ballweg Rd 76002 817-299-6400
Darrell Douglas, prin. Fax 453-7331
Howard MS 1,200/7-8
7501 Calender Rd 76001 817-561-3828
Jimmy Neal, prin. Fax 561-3840
Summit HS 3,300/9-12
1071 Turner Warnell Rd 76001 817-473-5660
Donna Grant, prin. Fax 473-5732
Timberview HS 9-12
7700 S Watson Rd 76002 817-299-2600
Carolyn Dowler, prin. Fax 472-2980

Arlington Baptist College Post-Sec.
3001 W Division St 76012 817-461-8741
Arlington Medical Institute Post-Sec.
2301 N Collins St Ste 100 76011 817-265-0706
ATI Health Education Center Post-Sec.
701 Highlander Blvd Ste 200 76015 817-557-3337
Burton Adventist Academy 300/PK-12
4611 Kelly Elliott Rd 76017 817-572-0081
Gerald Coy, prin. Fax 561-4237
Concorde Career Institute Post-Sec.
601 Ryan Plaza Dr Ste 200 76011 817-261-1594
Fellowship Academy 200/K-10
7000 US Highway 287 S 76001 817-563-5913
Monica Collier, prin. Fax 563-5427
ITT Technical Institute Post-Sec.
551 Ryan Plaza Dr 76011 817-794-5100
Oakridge S 800/PK-12
5900 W Pioneer Pkwy 76013 817-451-4994
Andy Broadus, hdmstr. Fax 457-6681
Pantego Christian Academy 700/PK-12
2201 W Park Row Dr 76013 817-460-3315
Steve Newby, admin. Fax 459-4687
St. Albans Episcopal S 200/PK-12
2500 S Bowen Rd 76015 817-460-6071
Kathy Bonds, hdmstr. Fax 860-8305
St. Pauls Preparatory S 200/PK-12
6900 US 287 Hwy 76001 817-265-3553
Janice Wood, prin. Fax 861-7955
Tarrant County Junior College Post-Sec.
2100 Tarrant County JC Pky 76018 817-515-3100
Texas Christian Academy 100/PK-12
915 Web St 76011 817-274-5201
Jerry Jones, admin. Fax 303-4463
University of Texas Post-Sec.
PO Box 19111 76019 817-272-2011

Arp, Smith, Pop. 911
Arp ISD 900/PK-12
PO Box 70 75750 903-859-8482
Toney Lowery, supt. Fax 859-2621
www.arp.sprnet.org
Arp HS 300/9-12
PO Box 70 75750 903-859-4917
Dr. Ron Sterling, prin. Fax 859-1541
Arp JHS 200/6-8
PO Box 70 75750 903-859-4936
Dwight Thomas, prin. Fax 859-3980

Aspermont, Stonewall, Pop. 879
Aspermont ISD 200/PK-12
PO Box 549 79502 940-989-3355
John Godfrey, supt. Fax 989-3353
www.aspermont.esc14.net
Aspermont JSHS 100/7-12
PO Box 549 79502 940-989-2707
Cliff Gilmore, prin. Fax 989-3486

Athens, Henderson, Pop. 11,962
Athens ISD 3,500/PK-12
104 Hawn St 75751 903-677-6900
Vance Vaughn, supt. Fax 677-6908
www.athensisd.net
Athens HS 1,000/9-12
708 E College St 75751 903-677-6920
Todd Nix, prin. Fax 677-6925
Athens MS 500/7-8
6800 State Highway 19 S 75751 903-677-3030
Annette Faulk, prin. Fax 677-2111

Trinity Valley Community College Post-Sec.
500 S Prairieville St 75751 903-677-8822

Atlanta, Cass, Pop. 5,606
Atlanta ISD 1,900/PK-12
315 N Buckner St 75551 903-796-4194
J. D. Cox, supt. Fax 796-3487
atlantaisd.com
Atlanta HS 600/9-12
705 Rabbit Blvd 75551 903-796-4411
Mike White, prin. Fax 799-1033
Atlanta MS 400/6-8
600 High School Ln 75551 903-796-7928
Lewis Lincoln, prin. Fax 799-1021

Aubrey, Denton, Pop. 1,880
Aubrey ISD 900/PK-12
415 Tisdell Ln 76227 940-365-2721
James Monaco, supt. Fax 365-2042
www.aubrey.isd.tenet.edu/
Aubrey HS 300/9-12
510 Spring Hill Rd 76227 940-365-2433
Jeff Mulkey, prin. Fax 365-3271
Aubrey MS 300/6-8
415 Tisdell Ln 76227 940-365-2434
Delore Jones, prin. Fax 365-2627

Denton ISD
Supt. — See Denton
Navo MS, 1701 Navo Rd 76227 6-8
Shaun Perry, prin. 972-347-7500

Austin, Travis, Pop. 672,011
Austin ISD 80,800/PK-12
1111 W 6th St 78703 512-414-1700
Dr. Pascal Forgione, supt. Fax 414-1707
www.austin.isd.tenet.edu/
Akins HS 2,200/9-12
10701 S 1st St 78748 512-841-9900
Mary Alice Deike, prin. Fax 841-9903
Anderson HS 2,000/9-12
8403 Mesa Dr 78759 512-414-2538
David Kernwein, prin. Fax 338-1293
Austin HS 2,100/9-12
1715 W Cesar Chavez St 78703 512-414-2505
Barbara Spellman, prin. Fax 474-7935
Bailey MS 1,100/6-8
4020 Lost Oasis Holw 78739 512-414-4990
Julia Fletcher, prin. Fax 292-0898
Bedichek MS 900/6-8
6800 Bill Hughes Rd 78745 512-414-3265
Gail Belcher, prin. Fax 444-4382
Bowie HS 2,500/9-12
4103 Slaughter Ln W 78749 512-414-5247
Kent Ewing, prin. Fax 292-0527
Burnet MS 1,100/6-8
8401 Hathaway Dr 78757 512-414-3225
Linda Van Horne, prin. Fax 452-0695
Clifton Career Development S Vo/Tech
1519 Coronado Hills Dr 78752 512-414-3614
Tony Dishner, prin. Fax 323-2646
Covington MS 900/6-8
3700 Convict Hill Rd 78749 512-414-3276
Karon Rilling, prin. Fax 892-4547
Crockett HS 2,000/9-12
5601 Manchaca Rd 78745 512-414-2532
Barbara Gideon, prin. Fax 447-0489
Dobie MS 700/6-8
1200 E Rundberg Ln 78753 512-414-3270
Carol Chapman, prin. Fax 836-8411
Fulmore MS 1,000/6-8
201 E Mary St 78704 512-414-3207
Lucio Calzada, prin. Fax 441-3129
Health Sciences Institute of Austin 9-12
1201 Payton Gin Rd 78758 512-414-2514
Mark Kincaid, prin. Fax 832-1203
Institute of Hospitality & Culinary Arts Vo/Tech
1211 E Oltorf St 78704 512-414-4491
Mark Kincaid, dir. Fax 414-1506
International HS 9-12
1012 Arthur Stiles Rd 78721 512-414-5810
Anabel Garcia, prin. Fax 414-6819
Johnson HS 1,700/9-12
7309 Lazy Creek Dr 78724 512-414-2543
Patrick Patterson, prin. Fax 929-3955
Johnston HS 1,000/9-12
1012 Arthur Stiles Rd 78721 512-414-5810
Dr. Celina Estrada-Russell, prin. Fax 414-6819
Kealing MS 1,200/6-8
1607 Pennsylvania Ave 78702 512-414-3214
Ariel Cloud, prin. Fax 478-9133
Lamar MS 800/6-8
6201 Wynona Ave 78757 512-414-3217
Mike Atchley, prin. Fax 467-6862
Lanier HS 1,800/9-12
1201 Payton Gin Rd 78758 512-414-2514
Edmund Oropez, prin. Fax 832-1203
Martin MS 700/6-8
1601 Haskell St 78702 512-414-3243
Raffy Vizcaino, prin. Fax 320-0125
McCallum Fine Arts Academy 9-12
5600 Sunshine Dr 78756 512-414-7505
Lanier Bayliss, prin. Fax 453-2599
McCallum HS 1,700/9-12
5600 Sunshine Dr 78756 512-414-2519
Michael Garrison, prin. Fax 453-2599
Mendez MS 800/6-8
5106 Village Square Dr 78744 512-414-3284
Connie Barr, prin. Fax 442-5738
Murchison MS 1,200/6-8
3700 N Hills Dr 78731 512-414-3254
Donna Houser, prin. Fax 343-1710
O'Henry MS 900/6-8
2610 W 10th St 78703 512-414-3229
Peter Price, prin. Fax 477-7428
Paredes MS 1,300/6-8
10100 S Mary Moore Searight 78748 512-841-6800
Renette Bledsoe, prin. Fax 841-7036
Pearce MS 900/6-8
6401 N Hampton Dr 78723 512-414-3234
Ron Bolek, prin. Fax 926-6146
Porter MS 600/6-8
2206 Prather Ln 78704 512-414-3236
Judy Szilagyi, prin. Fax 441-5208
Reagan HS 1,100/9-12
7104 Berkman Dr 78752 512-414-2523
Fax 452-7089
Small MS 1,100/6-8
4801 Monterey Oaks Blvd 78749 512-841-6700
Sheila Anderson, prin. Fax 841-6703
Travis HS 1,600/9-12
1211 E Oltorf St 78704 512-414-2527
Carlos Rios, prin. Fax 707-0050
Webb MS 800/6-8
601 E Saint Johns Ave 78752 512-414-3258
Charles Hunt, prin. Fax 452-9683

Del Valle ISD
Supt. — See Del Valle
Ojeda JHS 600/7-8
4900 McKinney Falls Pkwy 78744 512-386-3500
Adelaida Olivares, prin. Fax 386-3505

Eanes ISD 7,200/PK-12
601 Camp Craft Rd 78746 512-732-9001
Dr. Nola Wellman, supt. Fax 732-9005
www.eanes.k12.tx.us
Hill Country MS 900/6-8
1300 Walsh Tarlton Ln 78746 512-732-9220
Dr. Cory Duty, prin. Fax 732-9229
Westlake HS 2,400/9-12
4100 Westbank Dr 78746 512-732-9280
Linda Rawlings, prin. Fax 732-9289
West Ridge MS 900/6-8
9201 Scenic Bluff Dr 78733 512-732-9240
Karl Wagoner, prin. Fax 732-9249

Lake Travis ISD 5,300/PK-12
3322 Ranch Rd 620 S 78738 512-533-6000
Gary Ott Ed.D., supt. Fax 533-6001
www.laketravis.txed.net
Hudson Bend MS 500/6-8
15600 Lariat Trl 78734 512-533-6400
Kim Cousins, prin. Fax 533-6401
Lake Travis HS 1,400/9-12
3324 Ranch Road 620 S 78738 512-533-6100
Charles Little, prin. Fax 533-6102
Lake Travis MS 700/6-8
3328 Ranch Road 620 S 78738 512-533-6200
Kim Brents, prin. Fax 533-6201

Leander ISD
Supt. — See Leander
Canyon Ridge MS 6-8
12601 Country Trl 78732 512-434-7650
Susan Sullivan, prin. Fax 437-7655

Pflugerville ISD
Supt. — See Pflugerville
Connally HS 1,900/9-12
13212 N Lamar Blvd 78753 512-594-0800
Daniel Garcia, prin. Fax 594-0805
Dessau MS 900/6-8
12900 Dessau Rd 78754 512-594-2600
Kathy Guerra, prin. Fax 594-2605
Westview MS 800/6-8
1805 Scofield Ln 78727 512-594-2200
Bonifacio Duran, prin. Fax 594-2205

Round Rock ISD
Supt. — See Round Rock
Canyon Vista MS 1,100/6-8
8455 Spicewood Springs Rd 78759 512-464-8100
Lisa Napper, prin. Fax 464-8210
Cedar Valley MS 1,300/6-8
8139 Racine Trl 78717 512-428-2300
Dr. John Weishaar, prin. Fax 428-2420
Deerpark MS 1,200/6-8
8849 Anderson Mill Rd 78729 512-464-6600
Toni Hicks, prin. Fax 464-6740
Grisham MS 700/6-8
10805 School House Ln 78750 512-428-2650
Dr. Malinda Grosch, prin. Fax 428-2790
McNeil HS 2,500/9-12
5720 McNeil Dr 78729 512-464-6300
Nelson Coulter, prin. Fax 464-6550
Westwood HS 2,500/9-12
12400 Mellow Meadow Dr 78750 512-464-4000
Rebecca Donald, prin. Fax 464-4020

Academy of Oriental Medicine at Austin Post-Sec.
2700 W Anderson Ln Ste 204 78757 512-454-1188
Allied Health Careers Post-Sec.
5424 W Highway 290 Ste 105 78735 512-892-5210
A New Beginning School of Massage Post-Sec.
2525 Wallingwood Dr # 1501 78746 512-306-0975
Austin Adventist Junior Academy 100/K-10
301 W Anderson Ln 78752 512-459-8976
Fax 419-7868
Austin Business College Post-Sec.
2101 S I H 35 Ste 300 78741 512-447-9415
Austin Christian Academy 100/PK-12
2120 Shiloh Dr 78745 512-292-7848
Robert Walker, prin. Fax 292-8889
Austin City Academy 50/K-12
9301 Highway 290 W 78736 512-301-0471
Stan Whitmore, prin. Fax 857-0765
Austin Community College Post-Sec.
5930 Middle Fiskville Rd 78752 512-223-7598
Austin Graduate School of Theology Post-Sec.
1909 University Ave 78705 512-476-2772
Austin Presbyterian Theological Seminary Post-Sec.
100 E 27th St 78705 512-472-6736
Austin Waldorf S 400/PK-12
8700 S View Rd 78737 512-288-5942
Joanne Andruscavage, admin. Fax 301-8997
Baldwin Beauty School #5 Post-Sec.
3005 S Lamar Blvd Ste 103 78704 512-441-6898
Baldwin Beauty School - North Post-Sec.
8440 Burnet Rd 78758 512-458-4127
Brentwood Christian S 800/PK-12
11908 N Lamar Blvd 78753 512-835-5983
Dr. Libby Weed, prin. Fax 835-2184
Capitol City Careers Post-Sec.
5424 W Highway 290 Ste 200 78735 512-892-2640
Capitol City Trade and Technical School Post-Sec.
205 E Riverside Dr 78704 512-444-3257

Concordia Academy 100/9-12
  3407 Red River St 78705 512-248-2547
Concordia University Post-Sec.
  3400 N I H 35 78705 512-486-2000
Culinary Academy of Austin Post-Sec.
  6020 Dillard Cir Ste B 78752 512-451-5743
Diego HS 500/9-12
  800 Herndon Ln 78704 512-804-1935
  Pamela Jype, prin. 512-804-1937
Episcopal Theological Seminary of the SW Post-Sec.
  PO Box 2247 78768 512-472-4133
Hill Country Christian S of Austin 500/K-12
  12124 Ranch Road 620 N 78750 512-331-7036
  Rick Peralez, hdmstr. Fax 257-4190
Huston-Tillotson University Post-Sec.
  900 Chicon St 78702 512-505-3000
Hyde Park Baptist S 800/K-12
  3901 Speedway 78751 512-465-8333
  Brian Littlefield, admin. Fax 371-1433
ITT Technical Institute Post-Sec.
  6330 E Highway 290 Ste 150 78723 512-467-6800
National Institute of Technology Post-Sec.
  9100 US Highway 290 E # 100 78754 512-928-1933
Regents S of Austin 700/K-12
  3230 Travis Country Cir 78735 512-899-8095
  Charles T. Evans, hdmstr. Fax 899-8623
St. Andrew's Episcopal S 100/9-12
  5901 Southwest Pkwy 78735 512-452-5779
St. Edward's University Post-Sec.
  3001 S Congress Ave 78704 512-448-8400
St. Michael's Academy 400/9-12
  3000 Barton Creek Blvd 78735 512-328-2323
  Sharon Scamardo, prin. Fax 328-2327
St. Stephen's Episcopal S 600/6-12
  2900 Bunny Run 78746 512-327-1213
  Rev. Roger Bowen, hdmstr. Fax 327-1311
Shoreline Christian S 300/PK-10
  15201 Burnet Rd 78728 512-310-7358
  Richard Tankersley, admin. Fax 310-1175
Southern Careers Institute Post-Sec.
  2301 S Congress Ave Ste 24A 78704 512-448-4795
Southwest Institute of Technology Post-Sec.
  5424 W Highway 290 Ste 200 78735 512-892-2640
Texas College of Traditional Chinese Med Post-Sec.
  4005 Manchaca Rd 78704 512-444-8082
Texas Culinary Academy Post-Sec.
  11400 Burnet Rd Ste 2100 78758 512-837-2665
University of Texas at Austin Post-Sec.
  0 the Univ of Texas 78712 512-471-3434

Avalon, Ellis
Avalon ISD 200/PK-12
  PO Box 455 76623 972-627-3251
  David Del Bosque, supt. Fax 627-3220
  avalon.tx.schoolwebpages.com/education/
Avalon JSHS 200/PK-12
  PO Box 455 76623 972-627-3251
  Brenda Speer, prin. Fax 627-3220

Avery, Red River, Pop. 448
Avery ISD 400/PK-12
  PO Box 97 75554 903-684-3460
  Dan Jones, supt. Fax 684-3294
  avery.esc8.net/
Avery HS 100/9-12
  PO Box 97 75554 903-684-3431
  Robert Kelsoe, prin. Fax 684-3294
Avery MS 100/5-8
  PO Box 97 75554 903-684-3079
  Bill Giles, prin. Fax 684-3294

Avinger, Cass, Pop. 452
Avinger ISD 200/K-12
  245 Conner 75630 903-562-1271
  Douglas Carter, supt. Fax 562-1271
  avinger.esc8.net/
Avinger JSHS 100/7-12
  245 Conner 75630 903-562-1355
  Kenny Abernathy, prin. Fax 562-1271

Axtell, McLennan
Axtell ISD 600/PK-12
  PO Box 429 76624 254-863-5301
  Stanley Harris, supt. Fax 863-5651
  www.axtellisd.net/
Axtell HS, PO Box 429 76624 200/9-12
  Dale Monsey, prin. 254-863-5301
Axtell MS, PO Box 429 76624 6-8
  Dale Monsey, prin. 254-863-5301

Azle, Tarrant, Pop. 10,149
Azle ISD 5,900/PK-12
  300 Roe St 76020 817-444-3235
  Dr. Edd Bigbee, supt. Fax 444-6866
  www.azle.esc11.net
Azle HS 1,800/9-12
  1200 Boyd Rd 76020 817-444-5555
  Laura Bynum, prin. Fax 444-8884
Azle JHS 500/7-8
  201 School St 76020 817-444-2564
  Stacey Summerhill, prin. Fax 270-0880
Forte JHS 500/7-8
  479 Sandy Beach Rd 76020 817-270-1133
  David McClellan, prin. Fax 270-1157

Azle Christian S 100/PK-12
  1801 S Stewart St 76020 817-444-9964
  Mike Miles, admin. Fax 444-9914

Baird, Callahan, Pop. 1,625
Baird ISD 400/PK-12
  PO Box 1147 79504 325-854-1400
  Cliff Gardner, supt. Fax 854-2058
  www.baird.esc14.net
Baird HS 100/9-12
  PO Box 1147 79504 325-854-1400
  Vick Orlando, prin. Fax 854-2808

Ballinger, Runnels, Pop. 4,002
Ballinger ISD 1,000/PK-12
  PO Box 231 76821 325-365-3588
  Scot Goen, supt. Fax 365-5920
  ballinger.netxv.net/
Ballinger HS 300/9-12
  PO Box 231 76821 325-365-3547
  Ed Wilson, prin. Fax 365-5422
Ballinger JHS 200/6-8
  PO Box 231 76821 325-365-3537
  Mike Carter, prin. Fax 365-5420

Balmorhea, Reeves, Pop. 494
Balmorhea ISD 200/PK-12
  PO Box 368 79718 432-375-2223
  Mary Lou Carrasco, supt. Fax 375-2511
  www.bisdbears.esc18.net
Balmorhea S 200/PK-12
  PO Box 368 79718 432-375-2223
  Guadalupe Molina, prin. Fax 375-2511

Bandera, Bandera, Pop. 1,097
Bandera ISD 2,700/PK-12
  PO Box 727 78003 830-796-3313
  Dr. Renee Schulze, supt. Fax 796-6238
  www.banderaisd.net
Bandera HS 900/9-12
  PO Box 727 78003 830-796-6254
  Michael Nesbit, prin. Fax 796-6251
Bandera MS 600/6-8
  PO Box 727 78003 830-796-6270
  Gary Bitzkie, prin. Fax 796-6277

Bangs, Brown, Pop. 1,625
Bangs ISD 1,100/PK-12
  PO Box 969 76823 325-752-6612
  James Hartman, supt. Fax 752-6253
  www.bangsisd.net
Bangs HS 400/9-12
  PO Box 969 76823 325-752-6822
  Sam Hancock, prin. Fax 752-7028
Bangs MS 300/6-8
  PO Box 969 76823 325-752-6088
  Gary Hounshell, prin. Fax 752-6253

Banquete, Nueces
Banquete ISD 800/PK-12
  PO Box 369 78339 361-387-2551
  Jim Rumage, supt. Fax 387-7188
  www.banqueteisd.esc2.net/
Banquete HS 300/9-12
  PO Box 369 78339 361-387-8588
  Aurelio Tamayo, prin. Fax 767-6504
Banquete JHS 200/6-8
  PO Box 369 78339 361-387-6504
  Eusebio Torres, prin. Fax 387-7051

Barksdale, Edwards
Nueces Canyon Consolidated ISD 300/K-12
  PO Box 118 78828 830-234-3514
  Russ Perry, supt. Fax 234-3435
  www.nccisd.net/
Nueces Canyon JSHS 200/7-12
  PO Box 118 78828 830-234-3524
  Scotty Carman, prin. Fax 234-4129

Bartlett, Bell, Pop. 1,685
Bartlett ISD 500/PK-12
  PO Box 170 76511 254-527-4247
  Michael Mayfield, supt. Fax 527-3340
Bartlett HS 100/9-12
  PO Box 170 76511 254-527-3351
  Gregg Devault, prin. Fax 527-3513
Bartlett MS 100/6-8
  PO Box 170 76511 254-527-3352
  Mark Anglin, prin. Fax 527-3513

Bastrop, Bastrop, Pop. 6,682
Bastrop ISD 7,400/PK-12
  906 Farm St 78602 512-321-2292
  Roderick Emanuel, supt. Fax 321-7469
  www.bastrop.isd.tenet.edu
Bastrop HS 2,000/9-12
  1614 Chambers St 78602 512-321-1151
  Garry Blasig, prin. Fax 321-7502
Bastrop MS 600/7-8
  709 Old Austin Hwy 78602 512-321-3911
  Karen Stevens, prin. Fax 321-1557
  Other Schools – See Cedar Creek

Batesville, Zavala, Pop. 1,313
Uvalde Consolidated ISD
  Supt. — See Uvalde
Batesville MS 100/5-8
  Highway 117 78829 830-376-4221
  Mary Diaz, prin. Fax 376-4223

Bay City, Matagorda, Pop. 18,573
Bay City ISD 4,200/PK-12
  520 7th St 77414 979-245-5766
  Richard Johnson, supt. Fax 245-3175
  www.bcblackcats.net
Bay City HS 1,300/9-12
  400 7th St 77414 979-245-5771
  Hal Roberts, prin. Fax 245-1220
Bay City JHS 700/7-8
  1507 Sycamore Ave 77414 979-245-6345
  Brandon Hood, prin. Fax 245-1419

Baytown, Harris, Pop. 67,251
Goose Creek ISD 19,100/PK-12
  PO Box 30 77522 281-420-4800
  Dr. Barbara A. Sultis, supt. Fax 420-4815
  www.gccisd.net/
Baytown JHS 800/6-8
  PO Box 30 77522 281-420-4560
  Steve Koester, prin. Fax 420-4908
Cedar Bayou JHS 1,000/6-8
  PO Box 30 77522 281-420-4570
  Barbara Ardoin, prin. Fax 420-4909
Gentry JHS 800/6-8
  PO Box 30 77522 281-420-4590
  Tammy Edwards, prin. Fax 420-4909
Lee HS 2,400/9-12
  PO Box 30 77522 281-420-4535
  Bruce Davis, prin. Fax 420-4548
Mann JHS 1,000/6-8
  PO Box 30 77522 281-420-4585
  Jimmy Twardowski, prin. Fax 420-4664
Sterling HS 2,400/9-12
  PO Box 30 77522 281-420-4500
  Trey Kraemer, prin. Fax 420-4974
Stuart Career Center Vo/Tech
  PO Box 30 77522 281-420-4550
  Kevin Parker, dir. Fax 420-4553
School/Community Guidance Center Adult
  PO Box 30 77522 281-420-4630
  Michelle Verdun, prin. Fax 420-4629
  Other Schools – See Highlands

Baytown Christian Academy 200/9-12
  5555 N Main St 77521 281-421-4150
  Dr. Carolyn Brock, hdmstr. Fax 421-4038

Lee College Post-Sec.
  PO Box 818 77522 281-427-5611
San Jacinto Christian Academy 200/PK-12
  301 Ilfrey St 77520 281-424-9525
  Steve Weatherly, admin. Fax 424-1600

Beaumont, Jefferson, Pop. 112,434
Beaumont ISD 19,900/PK-12
  3395 Harrison Ave 77706 409-899-9972
  Dr. Carrol A. Thomas, supt. Fax 923-1025
  www.beaumont.k12.tx.us
Austin MS 600/6-8
  3410 Austin St 77706 409-892-0193
  Dr. Aaron Covington, prin. Fax 923-5239
Central HS 1,300/9-12
  88 Jaguar Dr 77702 409-981-7100
  Patricia Lambert, prin. Fax 835-6233
King MS 500/6-8
  1400 Avenue A 77701 409-832-4431
  David Harris, prin. Fax 785-4557
Marshall MS 800/6-8
  6455 Gladys Ave 77706 409-866-4174
  Dr. Bettye Grigsby, prin. Fax 861-5211
Odom Academy 800/6-8
  2550 W Virginia St 77705 409-842-3217
  Tillie Hickman, prin. Fax 842-8604
Ozen HS 1,700/9-12
  3443 Fannett Rd 77705 409-981-7500
  James Broussard, prin. Fax 842-8501
Smith MS 600/6-8
  4415 Concord Rd 77703 409-892-3811
  Carol Batiste, prin. Fax 923-5365
South Park MS 500/6-8
  4500 Highland Ave 77705 409-838-3941
  Odis Norris, prin. Fax 785-4314
Taylor Career Center Vo/Tech
  2330 North St 77702 409-835-0153
  Thom Campbell-Amons, prin. Fax 785-4016
Vincent MS 900/6-8
  350 Eldridge Dr 77707 409-866-1491
  Richard Cantu, prin. Fax 861-5110
West Brook HS 2,400/9-12
  8750 Phelan Blvd 77706 409-981-7300
  Dr. Rodney Cavness, prin. Fax 861-1645

Hamshire-Fannett ISD
  Supt. — See Hamshire
Hamshire-Fannett MS 300/7-8
  11375 Dugat Rd 77705 409-794-2361
  Mark Martin, prin. Fax 794-3042

Baptist Hospital of Southeast Texas Post-Sec.
  PO Box 1591 77704 409-654-5351
Cathedral Christian HS 200/7-12
  8200 Highway 105 77713 409-924-0500
  Jon Cregor, prin. Fax 898-1506
Dolphin Technical Institute Post-Sec.
  4835 Concord Rd 77703 409-892-0677
Lamar Institute of Technology Post-Sec.
  855 E Lavaca St 77705 409-880-8321
Lamar University Post-Sec.
  PO Box 10009 77710 409-880-7011
Monsignor Kelly Catholic HS 600/9-12
  5950 Kelly Dr 77707 409-866-2351
  Roger Bemis, prin. Fax 866-0917
St. Elizabeth Hospital Post-Sec.
  2830 Calder St 77702 409-892-7171
Texas Careers Post-Sec.
  194 Gateway St 77701 409-833-2722

Beckville, Panola, Pop. 748
Beckville ISD 500/PK-12
  PO Box 37 75631 903-678-3311
  Devin Tate, supt. Fax 678-2157
  www.beckville.esc7.net
Beckville JSHS 200/7-12
  PO Box 37 75631 903-678-3591
  Ted Reeves, prin. Fax 678-3645

Bedford, Tarrant, Pop. 48,572
Hurst-Euless-Bedford ISD 19,500/PK-12
  1849 Central Dr 76022 817-283-4461
  Gene Buinger Ed.D., supt. Fax 354-3311
  www.hebisd.edu
Bedford JHS 900/7-9
  325 Carolyn Dr 76021 817-788-3101
  Pamela Wellman, prin. Fax 788-3105
Harwood JHS 800/7-9
  3000 Martin Dr 76021 817-354-3360
  Vicki Thurman, prin. Fax 354-3365
Technical Education Center Vo/Tech
  1849 Central Dr 76022 817-354-3542
  Lisa Karr, prin. Fax 354-3546
  Other Schools – See Euless, Hurst

Beeville, Bee, Pop. 13,007
Beeville ISD 3,700/PK-12
  2400 N Saint Marys St 78102 361-358-7111
  Dr. John Hardwick, supt. Fax 358-7837
  www.beevilleisd.net/
Jones HS 1,100/9-12
  1902 N Adams St 78102 361-362-6000
  Roger McAdoo, prin. Fax 362-6016
Moreno JHS 600/7-8
  301 N Minnesota St 78102 361-358-6262
  Jean Blankenship, prin. Fax 362-6092

Coastal Bend College Post-Sec.
  3800 Charco Rd 78102 361-358-2838

Bellaire, Harris, Pop. 16,891
Houston ISD
  Supt. — See Houston
Bellaire HS 3,300/9-12
  5100 Maple St 77401 713-295-3704
  Tim Salem, prin. Fax 295-3763
Pin Oak MS 1,100/6-8
  4601 Glenmont St 77401 713-295-6500
  Michael McDonough, prin. Fax 295-6511

Episcopal HS 600/9-12
  4650 Bissonnet St 77401 713-512-3400
  Edward Becker, hdmstr. Fax 512-3603

Bellevue, Clay, Pop. 393
Bellevue ISD 100/K-12
  PO Box 38 76228 940-928-2104
  Dean Gilstrap, supt. Fax 928-2583
  www.esc9.net/bellevue/

Bellevue JSHS
  PO Box 38 76228
  Sean McBeath, prin.
100/7-12
940-928-2104
Fax 928-2583

Bells, Grayson, Pop. 1,238
Bells ISD
  PO Box 7 75414
  Joe D. Moore, supt.
  bells.ednet10.net/
800/PK-12
903-965-7721
Fax 965-7036

Bells HS
  PO Box 7 75414
  Will Steger, prin.
200/9-12
903-965-7315
Fax 965-5205

Prichard JHS
  PO Box 7 75414
  Sara Baker, prin.
100/7-8
903-965-4835
Fax 965-7036

Bellville, Austin, Pop. 4,157
Bellville ISD
  518 S Mathews St 77418
  John Conley, supt.
  www.bellville.k12.tx.us
2,200/PK-12
979-865-3133
Fax 865-8591

Bellville HS
  850 Schumann Rd 77418
  Jim Batson, prin.
700/9-12
979-865-3681
Fax 865-7080

Bellville JHS
  1305 S Tesch 77418
  Laura Bailey, prin.
500/6-8
979-865-5966
Fax 865-7060

Faith Academy
  12177 Highway 36 S 77418
  Merlene Byler, admin.
100/PK-12
979-865-1811
Fax 865-2454

Belton, Bell, Pop. 14,883
Belton ISD
  PO Box 269 76513
  Dr. Vivian Baker, supt.
  www.bisd.net
8,800/PK-12
254-215-2000
Fax 215-2001

Belton HS
  600 Lake Rd 76513
  Bil Lawson, prin.
2,000/9-12
254-215-2200
Fax 215-2201

Belton MS
  1704 Sparta Rd 76513
  Joe Peterka, prin.
1,100/6-8
254-215-2800
Fax 215-2801

Career Studies Center
  600 Lake Rd 76513
  Ken Von Gonten, prin.
Vo/Tech
254-215-2260
Fax 215-2261

Other Schools – See Temple

University of Mary Hardin-Baylor
  UMHB Station Box 8001 76513
Post-Sec.
254-295-8642

Benavides, Duval, Pop. 1,603
Benavides ISD
  PO Box P 78341
  Dr. Ignacio Salinas, supt.
  www.benavidesisd.nu
500/PK-12
361-256-3000
Fax 256-3005

Benavides HS
  PO Box P 78341
  Olga Carrillo, prin.
200/7-12
361-256-3040
Fax 256-3043

Ben Bolt, Jim Wells
Ben Bolt-Palito Blanco ISD
  PO Box 547 78342
  Alberto Byington, supt.
  www.bbisd.esc2.net
600/PK-12
361-664-9904
Fax 668-0446

Ben Bolt MS
  PO Box 547 78342
  David Braswell, prin.
200/4-8
361-664-9568
Fax 664-5235

Ben Bolt-Palito Blanco HS
  PO Box 547 78342
  David Delgado, prin.
200/9-12
361-664-9822
Fax 664-5481

Benbrook, Tarrant, Pop. 21,000
Fort Worth ISD
  Supt. — See Fort Worth
Leonard MS
  8900 Chapin Rd 76116
  Gary Braudaway, prin.
900/7-8
817-560-5630
Fax 560-5639

Western Hills HS
  3600 Boston Ave 76116
  Donna Jeffries, prin.
1,600/9-12
817-560-5600
Fax 560-5644

Benjamin, Knox, Pop. 245
Benjamin ISD
  PO Box 166 79505
  Ben Grill, supt.
  www.esc9.net/benjamin
100/K-12
940-459-2231
Fax 459-2007

Benjamin S
  PO Box 166 79505
  C. H. Underwood, prin.
100/K-12
940-459-2231
Fax 459-2007

Ben Wheeler, Van Zandt
Martins Mill ISD
  301 FM 1861 75754
  Todd Williams, supt.
  www.martinsmill.esc7.net
500/PK-12
903-479-3872
Fax 479-3711

Martins Mill HS
  301 FM 1861 75754
  Todd Schneider, prin.
200/7-12
903-479-3234
Fax 479-3486

Big Lake, Reagan, Pop. 2,649
Reagan County ISD
  1111 E 12th St 76932
  Ron Mayfield, supt.
  rcisd.esc18.net
800/PK-12
325-884-3705
Fax 884-3021

Reagan County HS
  1111 E 12th St 76932
  Ralph Traynham, prin.
300/9-12
325-884-3714
Fax 884-5759

Reagan County MS
  500 N Pennsylvania Ave 76932
  Glenn Byrd, prin.
200/6-8
325-884-3728
Fax 884-2327

Big Sandy, Upshur, Pop. 1,322
Big Sandy ISD
  PO Box 598 75755
  Jeff Dozier, supt.
  www.bigsandyisd.org
700/PK-12
903-636-5222
Fax 636-5111

Big Sandy JSHS
  PO Box 598 75755
  Tonya Knowlton, prin.
300/6-12
903-636-5287
Fax 636-5111

Harmony ISD
  9788 State Highway 154 W 75755
  Ray Miller, supt.
  www.harmonyeagles.com
1,000/PK-12
903-725-5492
Fax 725-6737

Harmony HS
  9788 State Highway 154 W 75755
  Jed Whitaker, prin.
300/9-12
903-725-5495
Fax 725-7079

Harmony JHS
  9788 State Highway 154 W 75755
  Perry Cowan, prin.
200/6-8
903-725-5485
Fax 725-7270

Big Spring, Howard, Pop. 24,556
Big Spring ISD
  708 E 11th Pl 79720
  Michael Downes, supt.
  bsisd.esc18.net/
3,900/K-12
432-264-3600
Fax 264-3646

Big Spring HS
  708 E 11th Pl 79720
  Mike Ritchey, prin.
1,100/9-12
432-264-3641
Fax 264-4133

Big Spring JHS
  708 E 11th Pl 79720
  Coby Norman, prin.
600/7-8
432-264-4135
Fax 264-3646

Howard College
  3200 Ave C 79720
Post-Sec.
432-264-3700

Howard College
  1001 N Birdwell Ln 79720
Post-Sec.
432-264-5000

New Hope Christian S
  118 Cedar Rd 79720
  Vicki Parnell, admin.
100/PK-12
432-263-0203
Fax 263-0204

Scenic Mountain Medical Center
  1601 W 11th Pl 79720
Post-Sec.
432-263-1211

Bishop, Nueces, Pop. 3,236
Bishop Consolidated ISD
  719 E 6th St 78343
  Christina Gutierrez, supt.
  www.bishopcisd.esc2.net/
1,200/PK-12
361-584-3591
Fax 584-3593

Bishop HS
  717 E 6th St 78343
400/9-12
361-584-2547
Fax 584-2549

Luehrs JHS
  701 E 6th St 78343
  Dan True, prin.
200/7-8
361-584-3576
Fax 584-3576

Blackwell, Nolan, Pop. 348
Blackwell Consolidated ISD
  PO Box 505 79506
  J.D. Davis, supt.
  www.blackwell.esc14.net/
100/PK-12
325-282-2311
Fax 282-2027

Blackwell S
  PO Box 505 79506
  Gary Smith, prin.
100/PK-12
325-282-2311
Fax 282-2027

Blanco, Blanco, Pop. 1,583
Blanco ISD
  PO Box 340 78606
  Lynn Boyd, supt.
  www.blancoisd.org/
1,000/PK-12
830-833-4414
Fax 833-2019

Blanco HS
  PO Box 340 78606
  Tommy Bibb, prin.
300/9-12
830-833-4337
Fax 833-5028

Blanco MS
  PO Box 340 78606
  Dr. Buck Ford, prin.
200/6-8
830-833-5570
Fax 833-2507

Blanket, Brown, Pop. 397
Blanket ISD
  901 Avenue H 76432
  Davy L. Hutton, supt.
  blanket.netxv.net/
200/K-12
325-748-5311
Fax 748-3391

Blanket HS
  901 Avenue H 76432
  Buddy Hale, prin.
100/9-12
325-748-3341
Fax 748-3391

Bloomburg, Cass, Pop. 371
Bloomburg ISD
  PO Box 156 75556
  Jerry Hendrick, supt.
  bloomburg.esc8.net/
300/K-12
903-728-5216
Fax 728-5399

Bloomburg JSHS
  PO Box 156 75556
  Bill Frost, prin.
100/7-12
903-728-5216
Fax 728-5399

Blooming Grove, Navarro, Pop. 870
Blooming Grove ISD
  PO Box 258 76626
  Michael H. Baldree, supt.
  www.bgisd.org
900/PK-12
903-695-2541
Fax 695-2594

Blooming Grove HS
  PO Box 258 76626
  Donna Wood, prin.
300/9-12
903-695-2536
Fax 695-2594

Blooming Grove JHS
  PO Box 258 76626
  Doyle Bell, prin.
200/6-8
903-695-4201
Fax 695-4601

Bloomington, Victoria, Pop. 1,888
Bloomington ISD
  PO Box 158 77951
  Dr. Suzanne Wesson, supt.
  www.bisd-tx.org/
1,000/PK-12
361-897-1652
Fax 897-1214

Bloomington HS
  PO Box 158 77951
  Eric Mitchell, prin.
200/9-12
361-897-1551
Fax 897-1888

Bloomington MS
  PO Box 158 77951
  Eric Mitchell, prin.
200/7-8
361-897-2260
Fax 897-3822

Blue Ridge, Collin, Pop. 817
Blue Ridge ISD
  10688 County Road 504 75424
  Jim Shurtleff, supt.
  brisd.com
700/PK-12
972-752-5554
Fax 752-9084

Blue Ridge HS
  11020 County Road 504 75424
  Robin Ross, prin.
200/9-12
972-752-5707
Fax 752-5361

Blue Ridge S
  318 School St 75424
  Hershel Busby, prin.
200/5-8
972-752-5707
Fax 752-5363

Blum, Hill, Pop. 431
Blum ISD
  PO Box 520 76627
  Jerry Miller, supt.
  www.blumisd.net
300/PK-12
254-874-5231
Fax 874-5233

Blum JSHS
  PO Box 520 76627
  Chris Nichols, prin.
200/6-12
254-874-5231
Fax 874-5233

Boerne, Kendall, Pop. 6,849
Boerne ISD
  123 Johns Rd 78006
  Dr. John Kelly, supt.
  www.boerne-isd.net
5,300/PK-12
830-357-2000
Fax 357-2009

Boerne HS
  1 Greyhound Ln 78006
  Betty Butler, prin.
1,200/10-12
830-357-2200
Fax 357-2299

Boerne MS - North
  240 Johns Rd 78006
  Vicki Layer, prin.
600/7-9
830-357-3100
Fax 357-3199

Boerne MS - South
  10 Cascade Caverns Rd 78015
  Dr. Janey Hunt, prin.
700/7-9
830-357-3300
Fax 357-3399

Vanguard Christian Institute
  43360 IH 10 W 78006
  Walter Tracy, prin.
100/PK-12
830-537-5244
Fax 537-5785

Bogata, Red River, Pop. 1,345
Rivercrest ISD
  4100 US Highway 271 S 75417
  Fred Wade, supt.
  www.rivercrestisd.net
700/PK-12
903-632-5203
Fax 632-4691

Rivercrest HS
  4220 US Highway 271 S 75417
  Walter York, prin.
200/9-12
903-632-5204

Rivercrest JHS
  4100 US Highway 271 S 75417
  Stanley Jessee, prin.
200/6-8
903-632-0878
Fax 632-4691

Boling, Wharton, Pop. 1,119
Boling ISD
  PO Box 160 77420
  Charles Butcher, supt.
  www.bolingisd.net
1,000/PK-12
979-657-2770
Fax 657-3265

Boling HS
  PO Box 119 77420
  Wade Stidevent, prin.
300/9-12
979-657-2816
Fax 657-2026

Iago JHS
  PO Box 89 77420
  Bryan Blanar, prin.
200/6-8
979-657-2826
Fax 657-2828

Bonham, Fannin, Pop. 10,336
Bonham ISD
  PO Box 490 75418
  Dr. Linda Gist, supt.
  www.bonhamisd.org/
1,900/K-12
903-583-5526
Fax 583-8463

Bonham HS
  1002 War Path St 75418
  T. Glynn Walker, prin.
600/9-12
903-583-5567
Fax 583-5560

Rather JHS
  1200 N Main St 75418
  Karol Romans, prin.
300/7-8
903-583-7474
Fax 583-3713

Booker, Lipscomb, Pop. 1,339
Booker ISD
  PO Box 288 79005
  Mike Lee, supt.
400/PK-12
806-658-4501
Fax 658-4503

Booker JSHS, PO Box 288 79005
  Pablo De Santiago, prin.
200/5-12
806-658-4521

Borger, Hutchinson, Pop. 13,638
Borger ISD
  200 E 9th St 79007
  Clifton Stephens, supt.
  www.borgerisd.net
2,100/PK-12
806-273-6481
Fax 273-1066

Borger HS
  600 W 1st St 79007
  Bob Callaghan, prin.
800/9-12
806-273-1029
Fax 273-1036

Borger MS
  1321 S Florida St 79007
  Randal Hatfield, prin.
900/5-8
806-273-1037
Fax 273-1069

Frank Phillips College
  PO Box 5118 79008
Post-Sec.
806-274-5311

Bovina, Parmer, Pop. 1,855
Bovina ISD
  PO Box 70 79009
  Charles Carter, supt.
  www.esc16.net/bovinaisd/
600/PK-12
806-251-1336
Fax 251-1578

Bovina HS
  PO Box 70 79009
  Bill Bizzell, prin.
100/9-12
806-251-1317
Fax 251-1002

Bovina JHS
  PO Box 70 79009
  Thomas Boatwright, prin.
100/6-8
806-251-1377
Fax 251-1578

Bowie, Montague, Pop. 5,450
Bowie ISD
  PO Box 1168 76230
  Monte Barnes, supt.
  www.esc9.net/bowie
1,700/PK-12
940-872-1151
Fax 872-5979

Bowie HS
  800 N Mill St 76230
  Jeff Jackson, prin.
500/9-12
940-872-1154
Fax 872-1299

Bowie JHS
  501 E Tarrant St 76230
  Tom McEwen, prin.
400/6-8
940-872-1152
Fax 872-8921

Gold-Burg ISD
  468 Prater Rd 76230
  Dr. Ron Preston, supt.
  www.esc9.net/gold-burg/
100/K-12
940-872-3562
Fax 872-5933

Gold-Burg JSHS
  468 Prater Rd 76230
  Kenny Miller, prin.
100/6-12
940-872-3562
Fax 872-5933

Boyd, Wise, Pop. 1,247
Boyd ISD
  PO Box 92308 76023
  Charles Cox, supt.
  www.esc11.net/schools/Boyd/index.html
1,000/PK-12
940-433-2327
Fax 433-9569

Boyd HS
  PO Box 92308 76023
  Jack Williams, prin.
300/9-12
940-433-2327
Fax 433-9593

Boyd MS
  PO Box 92308 76023
  Shawn Bryans, prin.
200/7-8
940-433-2327
Fax 433-9565

Boys Ranch, Oldham
Boys Ranch ISD
  PO Box 219 79010
  Nena Mankin, supt.
  www.boysranch.isd.tenet.edu
300/K-12
806-534-2221
Fax 534-2384

Blakemore MS
  PO Box 219 79010
  Mark Peters, prin.
100/6-8
806-534-3461
Fax 534-0041

Boys Ranch HS
  PO Box 219 79010
  John Sorrell, prin.
200/9-12
806-534-0032
Fax 534-0033

Brackettville, Kinney, Pop. 1,836
Brackett ISD
  PO Box 586 78832
  Paula Renken, supt.
  www.brackett.k12.tx.us
600/PK-12
830-563-2491
Fax 563-9264

Brackett HS
  PO Box 586 78832
  Frank Taylor, prin.
200/9-12
830-563-2491
Fax 563-3213

Brackett JHS
  PO Box 586 78832
  George Burks, prin.
100/7-8
830-563-2491
Fax 563-9559

Brady, McCulloch, Pop. 5,331
Brady ISD — 1,400/PK-12
100 W Main St 76825 — 325-597-2301
Steven McCarn, supt. — Fax 597-3984
www.bradyisd.org
Brady HS — 400/9-12
100 W Main St 76825 — 325-597-2491
Liesa Land, prin. — Fax 597-0182
Brady MS — 300/6-8
100 W Main St 76825 — 325-597-8110
Eric Bierman, prin. — Fax 597-4166

Breckenridge, Stephens, Pop. 5,676
Breckenridge ISD — 1,600/PK-12
PO Box 1738 76424 — 254-559-2278
Connie M. Martin, supt. — Fax 559-2353
www.breckenridge.esc14.net
Breckenridge HS — 500/9-12
500 W Lindsey St 76424 — 254-559-2231
Bryan D. Dieterich, prin. — Fax 559-7485
Breckenridge JHS — 200/7-8
502 W Lindsey St 76424 — 254-559-6581
Brent Evans, prin. — Fax 559-1082

Bremond, Robertson, Pop. 861
Bremond ISD — 500/PK-12
PO Box 190 76629 — 254-746-7145
Dr. Timothy Peterson, supt. — Fax 746-7726
www.bremondisd.net
Bremond HS — 100/9-12
PO Box 190 76629 — 254-746-7145
Harold Schroeder, prin. — Fax 746-7726
Bremond MS — 100/6-8
PO Box 190 76629 — 254-746-7145
Morris Ogden, prin. — Fax 746-7726

Brenham, Washington, Pop. 13,999
Brenham ISD — 4,800/PK-12
PO Box 1147 77834 — 979-277-6500
David Yeager, supt. — Fax 277-6515
www.brenhamisd.net
Brenham HS — 1,600/9-12
525 A H Ehrig Dr 77833 — 979-277-6570
John Dalchau, prin. — Fax 277-6544
Brenham JHS — 700/7-8
1200 Carlee Dr 77833 — 979-277-6400
Artis Edwards, prin. — Fax 277-6407

Blinn College — Post-Sec.
902 College Ave 77833 — 979-830-4000
Brenham Christian Academy — 100/5-12
2111 S Blue Bell Rd 77833 — 979-830-8480
Diane Keller, hdmstr. — Fax 830-1687

Bridge City, Orange, Pop. 8,660
Bridge City ISD — 2,200/PK-12
1031 W Round Bunch Rd 77611 — 409-735-1602
Dr. Darrell Myers, supt. — Fax 735-1694
www.esc5.net/bcisd
Bridge City HS — 800/9-12
2690 Texas Ave 77611 — 409-735-1501
Terry Stuebing, prin. — Fax 735-1519
Bridge City MS — 600/6-8
300 Bower Dr 77611 — 409-735-1513
Randy Godsy, prin. — Fax 735-1517

Bridgeport, Wise, Pop. 5,258
Bridgeport ISD — 2,200/PK-12
2107 15th St 76426 — 940-683-5124
Richard O'Hara, supt. — Fax 683-4268
www.bridgeportisd.net
Bridgeport HS — 700/9-12
1 Maroon Dr 76426 — 940-683-4064
Tom Talley, prin. — Fax 683-4014
Bridgeport MS — 500/6-8
702 17th St 76426 — 940-683-2273
Robert Haynes, prin. — Fax 683-5812

Briscoe, Wheeler
Ft. Elliott Consolidated ISD — 200/PK-12
PO Box 138 79011 — 806-375-2454
Carl Baker, supt. — Fax 375-2327
Ft. Elliott S — 200/PK-12
PO Box 138 79011 — 806-375-2454
Sonya Holder, prin. — Fax 375-2327

Broaddus, San Augustine, Pop. 186
Broaddus ISD — 500/PK-12
PO Box 58 75929 — 936-872-3041
Dr. Jerry Meador, supt. — Fax 872-3699
www.broaddus.esc7.net
Broaddus JSHS — 200/7-12
PO Box 58 75929 — 936-872-3610
Brad Lewis, prin. — Fax 872-9020

Brock, Parker
Brock ISD — 700/K-12
100 Grindstone Rd 76087 — 817-594-7642
Richard Tedder, supt. — Fax 599-3246
www.brockisd.net
Brock HS — 200/9-12
100 Grindstone Rd 76087 — 817-594-3492
David Walden, prin. — Fax 594-2509
Brock MS — 200/6-8
100 Grindstone Rd 76087 — 817-594-3195
— Fax 594-3191

Bronte, Coke, Pop. 1,027
Bronte ISD — 300/PK-12
PO Box 670 76933 — 325-473-2511
Alan Richey, supt. — Fax 473-2313
bronte.netxv.net/
Bronte JSHS — 100/7-12
PO Box 670 76933 — 325-473-2521
Rick Howell, prin. — Fax 473-2313

Brookeland, Sabine
Brookeland ISD — 300/PK-12
RR 2 Box 18 75931 — 409-698-2677
John Lynch, supt. — Fax 698-2533
www.esc05.k12.tx.us/brookeland/
Brookeland JSHS — 100/6-12
RR 2 Box 18 75931 — 409-698-2413
Lana Comeaux, prin. — Fax 698-2891

Brookesmith, Brown
Brookesmith ISD — 200/PK-12
PO Box 706 76827 — 325-643-3023
Tom Hall, supt. — Fax 643-3378
brookesmith.netxv.net/

Brookesmith HS — 100/9-12
PO Box 706 76827 — 325-646-3791
Bryan Swartz, prin. — Fax 646-3378

Brookshire, Waller, Pop. 3,533
Royal ISD — 1,700/PK-12
2520 Durkin Rd 77423 — 281-934-2248
Norman Plemons, supt. — Fax 934-2846
www.royal.isd.esc4.net
Royal HS — 400/9-12
2520 Durkin Rd 77423 — 281-934-2215
Nathaniel Richardson, prin. — Fax 934-2866
Royal MS — 400/6-8
2500 Durkin Rd 77423 — 281-934-2241
Martin Drayton, prin. — Fax 934-2329

Brownfield, Terry, Pop. 9,237
Brownfield ISD — 1,900/PK-12
601 E Tahoka Rd 79316 — 806-637-2591
Jerry Jones, supt. — Fax 637-9208
www.brownfieldisd.net/
Brownfield HS — 600/9-12
701 Cub Dr 79316 — 806-637-4523
Philip Timmons, prin. — Fax 637-3801
Brownfield MS — 400/6-8
1001 E Broadway St 79316 — 806-637-7521
Ken Cole, prin. — Fax 637-2919

Brownsboro, Henderson, Pop. 833
Brownsboro ISD — 2,700/PK-12
PO Box 465 75756 — 903-852-3701
Elton Caldwell, supt. — Fax 852-3957
www.brownsboro.k12.tx.us
Brownsboro HS — 800/9-12
PO Box 465 75756 — 903-852-2321
Doug Williams, prin. — Fax 852-5195
Brownsboro JHS — 400/7-8
PO Box 465 75756 — 903-852-6931
Yolanda Larkin, prin. — Fax 852-5238

Brownsville, Cameron, Pop. 156,178
Brownsville ISD — 45,600/PK-12
1900 Price Rd 78521 — 956-548-8000
Michael E. Zolkoski Ph.D., supt. — Fax 548-8019
www.bisd.us/
Besteiro MS — 1,200/6-8
6280 Southmost Rd 78521 — 956-544-3900
Alma Cardenas-Rubio, prin. — Fax 544-3927
Cummings MS — 900/6-8
1800 Cummings Pl 78521 — 956-548-8630
Dora Sauceda, prin. — Fax 548-8218
Faulk MS — 900/6-8
2000 Roosevelt St 78521 — 956-548-8500
Art Rendon, prin. — Fax 982-2894
Garcia MS — 1,000/6-8
5701 FM 802 78521 — 956-832-6300
Dr. Rebecca V. Rendon, prin. — Fax 832-6304
Hanna HS — 2,500/9-12
2615 E Price Rd 78521 — 956-548-7600
Yolanda Kruger, prin. — Fax 548-7603
Lopez HS — 1,800/9-12
3205 S Dakota Ave 78521 — 956-982-7400
Maggie Gutierrez, prin. — Fax 982-7499
Lucio MS — 1,000/6-8
300 N Vermillion Ave 78521 — 956-831-4550
Rose Longoria, prin. — Fax 838-2298
Oliveira MS — 1,200/6-8
444 Land O Lakes Dr 78521 — 956-548-8530
Robert Gonzalez, prin. — Fax 544-3968
Pace HS — 2,200/9-12
314 W Los Ebanos Blvd 78520 — 956-548-7700
Jill Williams, prin. — Fax 548-7710
Perkins MS — 900/6-8
4750 Austin Rd 78521 — 956-831-8770
Victor Caballero, prin. — Fax 831-8789
Porter HS — 2,100/9-12
3500 International Blvd 78521 — 956-548-7800
Alonzo Barbosa, prin. — Fax 982-2892
Rivera HS — 2,400/9-12
6955 FM 802 78521 — 956-831-8700
Mary Tolman, prin. — Fax 831-8705
Stell MS — 1,100/6-8
1105 E Los Ebanos Blvd 78520 — 956-548-8560
Acacia Ameel, prin. — Fax 548-8666
Stillman MS — 900/6-8
2977 W Tandy Rd 78520 — 956-698-1000
Maricela Zarate, prin. — Fax 350-3231
Vela MS — 1,200/6-8
4905 Paredes Line Rd 78526 — 956-548-7770
Sylvia Senteno, prin. — Fax 548-7780
Adult Education — Adult
1625 Price Rd 78521 — 956-548-8175
Yolanda Torres, prin. — Fax 982-3017

Career Centers of Texas — Post-Sec.
1900 N Expressway 78521 — 956-547-8200
First Baptist S — 300/PK-12
1600 Boca Chica Blvd 78520 — 956-542-4854
Federico Pena, prin. — Fax 542-6188
Guadalupe Regional MS — 400/6-8
1214 Lincoln St 78521 — 956-504-5568
Cathy Thomas, prin. — Fax 504-9393
Livingway Christian S — 300/PK-12
PO Box 3731 78523 — 956-548-2223
Anne M. Moore, prin. — Fax 548-1970
St. Joseph Academy — 600/7-12
101 Saint Joseph Dr 78520 — 956-542-3581
Br. Charles Imbergamo, prin. — Fax 542-4748
South Texas Vocational-Technical Inst. — Post-Sec.
2144 Central Blvd 78520 — 956-554-3515
Texas Southmost College — Post-Sec.
80 Fort Brown St 78520 — 956-544-3879
University of Texas at Brownsville — Post-Sec.
80 Fort Brown St 78520 — 956-544-8200
Valley Christian HS — 100/9-12
PO Box 4220 78523 — 956-542-5222
Paul Hanson, prin. — Fax 544-0038

Brownwood, Brown, Pop. 19,320
Brownwood ISD — 3,600/PK-12
PO Box 730 76804 — 325-643-5644
Sue Jones, supt. — Fax 643-5640
www.brownwoodisd.com
Brownwood HS — 1,100/9-12
2100 Slayden St 76801 — 325-646-9549
Bill Faircloth, prin. — Fax 643-1965
Brownwood MS — 500/7-8
1286 76804 — 325-646-9545
Bryan Allen, prin. — Fax 646-3785

Central Texas Commercial College — Post-Sec.
PO Box 1324 76804 — 325-646-0521
Howard Payne University — Post-Sec.
1000 Fisk Ave 76801 — 325-646-2502

Bruni, Webb
Webb Consolidated ISD — 300/PK-12
PO Box 206 78344 — 361-747-5415
Dr. David Jones, supt. — Fax 747-5433
www.webb.esc1.net/
Bruni HS — 100/9-12
PO Box 206 78344 — 361-747-5415
Steven Young, prin. — Fax 747-5301
Bruni MS — 100/6-8
PO Box 206 78344 — 361-747-5415
Humberto Javier Soliz, prin. — Fax 747-5298

Bryan, Brazos, Pop. 67,774
Bryan ISD — 14,200/PK-12
101 N Texas Ave 77803 — 979-209-1000
Michael Cargill, supt. — Fax 209-1050
www.bryanisd.org
Austin MS — 1,000/6-8
801 S Ennis St 77803 — 979-209-6700
Patti Moore, prin. — Fax 209-6741
Bryan HS — 3,500/9-12
3450 Campus Dr 77802 — 979-209-2400
Carol Cune, prin. — Fax 209-2402
Long MS — 900/6-8
1106 N Harvey Mitchell Pkwy 77803 — 979-209-6500
Diana Werner, prin. — Fax 209-6566
Oliver HS for Human Sciences — 9-12
1305 Memorial Dr 77802 — 979-209-2800
Judy Hughson, dean — Fax 209-2809
Rayburn MS — 1,200/6-8
1048 N Earl Rudder Fwy 77802 — 979-209-6600
Paul Hord, prin. — Fax 209-6611
Adult Learning Center — Adult
1700 Palasota Dr 77803 — 979-209-7040
Mary Blackburn, dir. — Fax 209-7041

Allen Academy — 300/PK-12
3201 Boonville Rd 77802 — 979-776-0731
Bob Meyer, prin. — Fax 774-7769
Blinn College — Post-Sec.
PO Box 6030 77805 — 979-821-0200
Brazos Christian S — 200/PK-12
3000 W Villa Maria Rd 77807 — 979-823-1000
Robert Armstrong, hdmstr. — Fax 823-1774
Charlie & Sue's School of Hair Design — Post-Sec.
1711 Briarcrest Dr 77802 — 979-776-4375
St. Joseph Catholic S — 300/PK-12
600 S Coulter Dr 77803 — 979-822-6641
Michael Riazzi, prin. — Fax 779-2810
St. Michael's Academy — 200/PK-12
2500 S College Ave 77801 — 979-822-2715
Helen Spencer, prin. — Fax 823-4971

Bryson, Jack, Pop. 531
Bryson ISD — 300/PK-12
PO Box 309 76427 — 940-392-3281
Jack Coody, supt. — Fax 392-2086
www.brysonisd.net
Bryson S — 300/PK-12
PO Box 309 76427 — 940-392-2601
Jeff Decker, prin. — Fax 392-2086

Buckholts, Milam, Pop. 399
Buckholts ISD — 200/PK-12
PO Box 248 76518 — 254-593-3011
Kent Dutton, supt. — Fax 593-2270
Buckholts S — 200/PK-12
PO Box 248 76518 — 254-593-2744
Penny Coots, prin. — Fax 593-2270

Buda, Hays, Pop. 3,745
Hays Consolidated ISD
Supt. — See Kyle
Barton MS — 600/6-8
4950 Jack C Hays Trl 78610 — 512-268-1472
Judy Logan, prin. — Fax 268-1610
Dahlstrom MS — 600/6-8
3600 FM 967 78610 — 512-268-8441
Hilda Gartzke, prin. — Fax 295-5346
Hays HS — 2,400/9-12
4800 Jack C Hays Trl 78610 — 512-268-2911
Shirley Reich, prin. — Fax 268-1394

Buffalo, Leon, Pop. 1,884
Buffalo ISD — 800/PK-12
708 Cedar Creek Rd 75831 — 903-322-3765
Jack Thomason, supt. — Fax 322-3091
www.buffaloisd.com
Buffalo HS — 200/9-12
145 Bison Trl 75831 — 903-322-4243
Don Elsom, prin. — Fax 322-5806
Buffalo MS — 200/6-8
PO Box 1530 75831 — 903-322-4340
Lacy Freeman, prin. — Fax 322-4803

Bullard, Smith, Pop. 1,356
Bullard ISD — 1,600/PK-12
PO Box 250 75757 — 903-894-6639
Jim Wright, supt. — Fax 894-9291
www.bullardisd.net
Bullard HS — 500/9-12
PO Box 250 75757 — 903-894-3272
Leonard Speaker, prin. — Fax 894-3051
Bullard MS — 400/6-8
PO Box 250 75757 — 903-894-6533
Dwain Reynolds, prin. — Fax 894-7592

Brook Hill S — 300/PK-12
PO Box 668 75757 — 903-894-5000
Rod Fletcher, hdmstr. — Fax 894-6332

Bulverde, Comal, Pop. 4,225

Bracken Christian S — 300/PK-12
670 Boerne Rd 78163 — 830-438-3211
Craig Walker, admin. — Fax 980-2327

Buna, Jasper, Pop. 2,127
Buna ISD — 1,600/PK-12
PO Box 1087 77612 — 409-994-5101
David K. Hicks, supt. — Fax 994-4808
www.bunaisd.net
Buna HS — 400/9-12
PO Box 1087 77612 — 409-994-4811
Don Muckleroy, prin. — Fax 994-4818

Buna JHS | 300/6-8
PO Box 1087 77612 | 409-994-4860
Thomas Saunders, prin. | Fax 994-4808

Burkburnett, Wichita, Pop. 10,732
Burkburnett ISD | 3,600/PK-12
416 Glendale St 76354 | 940-569-3326
Danny W. Taylor, supt. | Fax 569-4776
www.burkburnettisd.org
Burkburnett HS | 1,000/9-12
109 W Kramer Rd 76354 | 940-569-1411
Del Hardaway, prin. | Fax 569-1512
Burkburnett MS | 800/6-8
108 S Avenue D 76354 | 940-569-3381
Sharon Scott, prin. | Fax 569-7116

Burkeville, Newton
Burkeville ISD | 400/PK-12
PO Box 218 75932 | 409-565-2201
Joe Gassiott, supt. | Fax 565-2012
www.burkeville.com
Burkeville JSHS | 200/7-12
PO Box 218 75932 | 409-565-4338
Paula Quick, prin. | Fax 565-2461

Burleson, Johnson, Pop. 25,334
Burleson ISD | 7,300/PK-12
1160 SW Wilshire Blvd 76028 | 817-447-5730
Dr. Mark Jackson, supt. | Fax 447-5737
www.burlesonisd.net
Burleson HS | 2,100/9-12
100 Elk Dr 76028 | 817-447-5700
Paul Cash, prin. | Fax 447-5796
Hughes MS | 700/6-8
316 SW Thomas St 76028 | 817-447-5750
Susan Shaha, prin. | Fax 447-5748
Kerr MS | 1,000/6-8
517 SW Johnson Ave 76028 | 817-447-5810
Paul Uttley, prin. | Fax 447-5742

Burnet, Burnet, Pop. 5,156
Burnet Consolidated ISD | 3,100/PK-12
208 E Brier Ln 78611 | 512-756-2124
Jeffrey M. Hanks, supt. | Fax 756-7498
www.burnet.txed.net
Burnet HS | 900/9-12
1000 The Green Mile Rd 78611 | 512-756-6193
Craig Spinn, prin. | Fax 756-4553
Burnet MS | 700/6-8
500 E Graves St 78611 | 512-756-6182
Rich Elsasser, prin. | Fax 756-7955

Burton, Washington, Pop. 353
Burton ISD | 400/PK-12
PO Box 37 77835 | 979-289-3131
James Palmer, supt. | Fax 289-3076
Burton JSHS | 200/7-12
PO Box 499 77835 | 979-289-3830
Karen Steenken, prin. | Fax 289-4609

Bushland, Potter
Bushland ISD | 700/PK-12
PO Box 60 79012 | 806-359-6683
John Lemons, supt. | Fax 359-6769
bushlandisd.org/
Bushland HS | 9-12
PO Box 60 79012 | 806-359-5418
Rick Davis, prin. | Fax 355-2841
Bushland MS | 200/6-8
PO Box 60 79012 | 806-359-5418
P.J. Hanna, prin. | Fax 355-2841

Byers, Clay, Pop. 526
Byers ISD | 100/K-12
PO Box 286 76357 | 940-529-6102
Steve Wolf, supt. | Fax 529-6104
www.esc9.net/byersisd/
Byers S | 100/K-12
PO Box 286 76357 | 940-529-6101
Burt Montgomery, prin. | Fax 529-6104

Bynum, Hill, Pop. 239
Bynum ISD | 200/PK-12
PO Box 68 76631 | 254-623-4251
Polly Boyd, supt. | Fax 623-4290
www.bynumisd.net/
Bynum S | 200/PK-12
PO Box 68 76631 | 254-623-4251
Kathy Collins, prin. | Fax 623-4290

Caddo Mills, Hunt, Pop. 1,193
Caddo Mills ISD | 1,200/PK-12
PO Box 160 75135 | 903-527-6056
Vicki Payne, supt. | Fax 527-4983
www.ednet10.net/caddomills/
Caddo Mills HS | 300/9-12
PO Box 160 75135 | 903-527-3164
Michael Powell, prin. | Fax 527-4772
Caddo Mills MS | 300/6-8
PO Box 160 75135 | 903-527-3161
H. Rickerson, prin. | Fax 527-2379

Caldwell, Burleson, Pop. 3,647
Caldwell ISD | 1,900/PK-12
203 N Gray St 77836 | 979-567-9000
Randall Berryhill, supt. | Fax 567-9876
www.caldwell.k12.tx.us/
Caldwell HS | 600/9-12
203 N Gray St 77836 | 979-567-9030
John Meckel, prin. | Fax 567-9032
Caldwell MS | 500/6-8
203 N Gray St 77836 | 979-567-6270
Kim McManus, prin. | Fax 567-6272

Calvert, Robertson, Pop. 1,376
Calvert ISD | 300/PK-12
PO Box 7 77837 | 979-364-2824
Morris Ogden, supt. | Fax 364-2468
www.calvertisd.com/
Calvert HS | 100/9-12
PO Box 7 77837 | 979-364-2845
Joseph Leyva, prin. | Fax 364-2043
Calvert MS | 100/7-8
PO Box 7 77837 | 979-364-2845

Cameron, Milam, Pop. 5,896
Cameron ISD | 1,600/PK-12
PO Box 712 76520 | 254-697-6591
Maxie Morgan, supt. | Fax 697-2448
www.cameronisd.net
Cameron JHS | 400/6-8
PO Box 712 76520 | 254-697-2131
Don Humphrey, prin. | Fax 605-0379

Yoe HS | 500/9-12
PO Box 712 76520 | 254-697-3902
Clint McMahon, prin. | Fax 605-0413

Campbell, Hunt, Pop. 771
Campbell ISD | 300/PK-12
409 W North St 75422 | 903-862-3259
Gene Franklin, supt. | Fax 862-2222
www.ednet10.net/campbell
Campbell JSHS | 200/7-12
409 W North St 75422 | 903-862-3257
Morris Lyon, prin. | Fax 862-3547

Canadian, Hemphill, Pop. 2,212
Canadian ISD | 600/PK-12
800 Hillside Ave 79014 | 806-323-5393
Frank Belcher, supt. | Fax 323-8143
www.canadianisd.net
Canadian HS | 200/9-12
800 Hillside Ave 79014 | 806-323-5373
Rick Berry, prin. | Fax 323-8143
Canadian MS | 100/7-8
800 Hillside Ave 79014 | 806-323-5351
Gary Laramore, prin. | Fax 323-8791

Canton, Van Zandt, Pop. 3,427
Canton ISD | 1,800/PK-12
225 W Elm St 75103 | 903-567-4179
 | Fax 567-2370
cantonisd.net
Canton HS | 500/9-12
1110 W Highway 243 75103 | 903-567-6561
Max Callahan, prin. | Fax 567-5222
Canton JHS | 400/6-8
1115 S Buffalo St 75103 | 903-567-4329
Bruce Congleton, prin. | Fax 567-1298

Canutillo, El Paso, Pop. 4,442
Canutillo ISD
Supt. — See El Paso
Canutillo HS | 1,300/9-12
PO Box 100 79835 | 915-877-7500
Max Padilla, prin. | Fax 877-7507
Canutillo MS | 800/7-8
PO Box 100 79835 | 915-877-7900
Dr. Monica Reyes-Garcia, prin. | Fax 877-7907

Canyon, Randall, Pop. 12,987
Canyon ISD | 6,900/PK-12
PO Box 899 79015 | 806-677-2600
Mike Wartes, supt. | Fax 677-2659
www.canyonisd.net
Canyon HS | 900/9-12
1701 23rd St 79015 | 806-677-2740
Shawn Neeley, prin. | Fax 677-2779
Canyon JHS | 400/7-8
910 9th Ave 79015 | 806-677-2700
Kirk Kear, prin. | Fax 677-2739
Other Schools – See Amarillo

West Texas A & M University | Post-Sec.
Wtamu Box 907 79016 | 806-651-2000

Carmine, Fayette, Pop. 229
Round Top - Carmine ISD | 200/PK-12
PO Box 385 78932 | 979-278-3252
Ronald Goehring, supt. | Fax 278-3063
www.rtcisd.net/
Round Top - Carmine HS | 100/7-12
PO Box 385 78932 | 979-278-3252
Mark Conley, prin. | Fax 278-3063

Carrizo Springs, Dimmit, Pop. 5,635
Carrizo Springs Consolidated ISD | 1,800/PK-12
300 N 7th St 78834 | 830-876-2473
Dr. Cecilia M. Moreno, supt. | Fax 876-9700
Carrizo Springs HS | 700/9-12
300 N 7th St 78834 | 830-876-5237
Adolfo F. Benavides, prin. | Fax 876-3052
Carrizo Springs JHS | 400/7-8
300 N 7th St 78834 | 830-876-2496
Sofia Morones, prin. | Fax 876-3655

Carrollton, Denton, Pop. 116,714
Carrollton-Farmers Branch ISD | 26,500/PK-12
PO Box 115186 75011 | 972-466-6100
Annette T. Griffin Ed.D., supt. | Fax 323-6675
www.cfbisd.edu
Blalack MS | 1,200/6-8
1706 E Peters Colony Rd 75007 | 972-394-3140
Les Black, prin. | Fax 323-6488
Creekview HS | 2,100/9-12
3201 Old Denton Rd 75007 | 972-939-4000
Cyndi Boyd, prin. | Fax 939-4009
Perry MS | 1,000/6-8
1709 E Belt Line Rd 75006 | 972-323-3670
Joe LaPuma, prin. | Fax 323-3696
Polk MS | 900/6-8
2001 Kelly Blvd 75006 | 972-417-8090
David Hicks, prin. | Fax 417-8089
Smith HS | 2,200/9-12
2335 N Josey Ln 75006 | 972-389-3800
Joe Pouncey, prin. | Fax 323-5866
Turner HS | 2,100/9-12
1600 S Josey Ln 75006 | 972-389-3850
Kim Holland, prin. | Fax 323-5980
Other Schools – See Dallas, Farmers Branch, Irving

Lewisville ISD
Supt. — See Flower Mound
Arbor Creek MS | 700/6-8
2109 Arbor Creek Dr 75010 | 469-713-5971
Brad Burns, prin. | Fax 350-2550
Creek Valley MS | 800/6-8
4109 Creek Valley Blvd 75010 | 214-731-2330
Dr. Glenda Edwards, prin. | Fax 395-3263
Hebron HS | 1,900/9-12
4207 Plano Pkwy 75010 | 972-862-1600
Hugh Jones, prin. | Fax 862-9095

American Heritage Academy | 400/PK-12
2660 E Trinity Mills Rd 75006 | 972-416-5437
Robert Anderson, prin. | Fax 418-5768
Carrollton Christian Academy | 500/K-12
2205 E Hebron Pkwy 75010 | 972-242-6688
Dr. Alex Ward, hdmstr. | Fax 245-0321
Prince of Peace Christian S | 800/PK-12
4000 Midway Rd 75007 | 972-447-9887
Chris Hahn, prin. | Fax 447-0877
Toni & Guy Hairdressing Academy | Post-Sec.
2810 E Trinity Mills Rd 75006 | 972-416-8396

Carthage, Panola, Pop. 6,493
Carthage ISD | 2,900/PK-12
1 Bulldog Dr 75633 | 903-693-3806
Reba Allison, supt. | Fax 693-3650
www.carthageisd.org/
Carthage HS | 900/9-12
1 Bulldog Dr 75633 | 903-693-2555
Jon Almeida, prin. | Fax 693-9752
Carthage JHS | 500/7-8
1 Bulldog Dr 75633 | 903-693-2751
Russell Porter, prin. | Fax 693-9582

Panola College | Post-Sec.
1109 W Panola St 75633 | 800-776-8153

Castroville, Medina, Pop. 2,839
Medina Valley ISD | 3,300/PK-12
8449 FM 471 S 78009 | 830-931-2243
Willard Murrey, supt. | Fax 931-4050
www.mvisd.com
Medina Valley HS | 900/9-12
8395 FM 471 S 78009 | 830-931-2514
James Chase, prin. | Fax 931-3258
Medina Valley MS | 800/6-8
8365 FM 471 S 78009 | 830-931-2243
Teresa Vielma, prin. | Fax 931-0371

Cayuga, Anderson
Cayuga ISD | 500/PK-12
PO Box 427 75832 | 903-928-2102
Dr. Rick Webb, supt. | Fax 928-2646
www.cayuga.esc7.net
Cayuga HS | 200/9-12
PO Box 427 75832 | 903-928-2294
Daniel Shead, prin. | Fax 928-2646
Cayuga MS | 100/6-8
PO Box 427 75832 | 903-928-2699
Sherri McInnis, prin. | Fax 928-2646

Cedar Creek, Bastrop
Bastrop ISD
Supt. — See Bastrop
Cedar Creek MS | 500/7-8
125 Voss Pkwy 78612 | 512-332-2626
Bruce Nelson, prin. | Fax 332-2631

Cedar Hill, Dallas, Pop. 39,260
Cedar Hill ISD | 6,800/PK-12
PO Box 248 75106 | 972-291-1581
Dr. Jim Gibson, supt. | Fax 291-5231
www.chisd.com
Cedar Hill SHS | 1,500/10-12
PO Box 248 75106 | 469-272-2000
Harry Miller, prin. | Fax 293-7125
Coleman MS, PO Box 248 75106 | 7-8
Russell Livingston, prin. | 972-293-4505
Ninth Grade Center | 9-9
PO Box 248 75106 | 469-272-2050
Delsenna Frazier, prin.
Permenter MS | 1,300/7-8
PO Box 248 75106 | 972-291-5270
Joseph Showell, prin. | Fax 291-5296

Northwood University | Post-Sec.
1114 W FM 1382 75104 | 800-927-9663
Trinity Christian S | 600/PK-12
1231 E Pleasant Run Rd 75104 | 972-291-2505
Kathleen Watts, supt. | Fax 291-4739

Cedar Park, Williamson, Pop. 41,482
Leander ISD
Supt. — See Leander
Cedar Park HS | 2,200/9-12
2150 Cypress Creek Rd 78613 | 512-435-8300
Ron Lafevers, prin. | Fax 435-8835
Cedar Park MS | 1,300/6-8
2100 Sunchase Blvd 78613 | 512-434-5025
Sandra Stewart, prin. | Fax 434-7539
Henry MS | 900/6-8
100 N Vista Ridge Pkwy 78613 | 512-435-4800
Dr. David Ellis, prin. | Fax 435-4805
Running Brushy MS | 1,000/6-8
2303 N Lakeline Blvd 78613 | 512-435-4700
Karin Johnson, prin. | Fax 435-4705
Vista Ridge HS | 900/9-12
200 S Vista Ridge Pkwy 78613 | 512-434-7300
Stu Taylor, prin. | Fax 434-7305

Summit Christian Academy of Cedar Park | 200/PK-12
2121 Cypress Creek Rd 78613 | 512-250-1369
Derek Cortez, dir. | Fax 257-1851

Celeste, Hunt, Pop. 842
Celeste ISD | 500/PK-12
PO Box 67 75423 | 903-568-4825
Collin Clark, supt. | Fax 568-4495
www.ednet10.net/celeste/cisd1/
Celeste HS | 200/9-12
PO Box 67 75423 | 903-568-4721
Ricky Beadles, prin. | Fax 568-4115
Celeste JHS | 100/6-8
PO Box 67 75423 | 903-568-4612
Paula Lyon, prin. | Fax 568-4277

Celina, Collin, Pop. 2,304
Celina ISD | 1,300/PK-12
PO Box 188 75009 | 972-382-2751
Wilburn Echols, supt. | Fax 382-3607
www.celina.k12.tx.us
Celina HS | 400/9-12
PO Box 188 75009 | 972-382-2303
Jeff Oldham, prin. | Fax 382-4830
Celina JHS | 200/7-8
PO Box 188 75009 | 972-382-2373
Jerry Moore, prin. | Fax 382-4258

Center, Shelby, Pop. 5,716
Center ISD | 2,500/PK-12
404 Mosby St 75935 | 936-598-5642
Kelly Rodgers, supt. | Fax 598-1515
www.centerisd.org/
Center HS | 700/9-12
658 Roughrider Dr 75935 | 936-598-6173
Wes Kirkham, prin. | Fax 598-1557
Center MS | 500/6-8
302 Kennedy St 75935 | 936-598-5619
James Hockenberry, prin. | Fax 598-1534

Center Point, Kerr
Center Point ISD 500/PK-12
PO Box 377 78010 830-634-2171
Dr. Lee Ann Ray, supt. Fax 634-2254
www.center-point.k12.tx.us
Center Point HS 200/9-12
PO Box 377 78010 830-634-2244
John Scott Turner, prin. Fax 634-7430
Center Point MS 100/6-8
PO Box 377 78010 830-634-2533
John Scott Turner, prin. Fax 634-7825

Centerville, Leon, Pop. 942
Centerville ISD 700/K-12
813 S Commerce St 75833 903-536-7812
Bruce Engram, supt. Fax 536-3133
www.centerville.k12.tx.us
Centerville JSHS 300/7-12
813 S Commerce St 75833 903-536-2935
Bob Loomis, prin. Fax 536-3133

Channelview, Harris, Pop. 30,600
Channelview ISD 7,700/PK-12
1403 Sheldon Rd 77530 281-452-8002
Tom Tasma, supt. Fax 452-8070
www.channelview.isd.esc4.net
Channelview HS 1,800/9-12
1100 Sheldon Rd 77530 281-457-7300
Dr. Laurie Bauer, prin. Fax 457-7346
Johnson JHS 1,200/7-8
15500 Proctor St 77530 281-452-8030
Cindi Ollis, prin. Fax 452-1022

Channing, Hartley, Pop. 357
Channing ISD 100/K-12
PO Box A 79018 806-235-3432
James Davis, supt. Fax 235-2609
Channing S 100/K-12
PO Box A 79018 806-235-3432
Robert McLain, prin. Fax 235-2609

Charlotte, Atascosa, Pop. 1,754
Charlotte ISD 500/PK-12
PO Box 489 78011 830-277-1431
Alfonso Obregon, supt. Fax 277-1551
charlotte.echalk.com
Charlotte HS 100/9-12
PO Box 489 78011 830-277-1432
David Carmichael, prin. Fax 277-1551
Charlotte JHS 100/6-8
PO Box 489 78011 830-277-1646
Rudy Gonzales, prin. Fax 277-1551

Cherokee, San Saba
Cherokee ISD 100/K-12
PO Box 100 76832 325-622-4298
Chris Perry, supt. Fax 622-4430
www.centex-edu.net/cherokee
Cherokee JSHS 100/7-12
PO Box 100 76832 325-622-4298
Chris Perry, prin. Fax 622-4430

Chester, Tyler, Pop. 262
Chester ISD 200/K-12
PO Box 28 75936 936-969-2211
C. Glen Conner, supt. Fax 969-2080
Chester JSHS, PO Box 28 75936 100/6-12
Glen Conner, prin. 936-969-2353

Chico, Wise, Pop. 1,032
Chico ISD 700/PK-12
PO Box 95 76431 940-644-2228
Thomas Ferguson, supt. Fax 644-5642
www.chicoisd.esc11.net
Chico HS 200/9-12
PO Box 95 76431 940-644-5783
Melvin Clay, prin. Fax 644-5876
Chico MS 200/6-8
PO Box 95 76431 940-644-5550
Maury Martin, prin. Fax 644-5642

Childress, Childress, Pop. 6,632
Childress ISD 1,200/PK-12
PO Box 179 79201 940-937-2501
John C. Wilson, supt. Fax 937-2938
www.childressisd.net/
Childress HS 300/9-12
800 Avenue J NW 79201 940-937-6131
Toby Tucker, prin. Fax 937-2039
Childress JHS 300/6-8
700 Commerce St 79201 940-937-3641
Marsha Meacham, prin. Fax 937-8427

Chillicothe, Hardeman, Pop. 750
Chillicothe ISD 200/K-12
PO Box 418 79225 940-852-5391
John Chapman, supt. Fax 852-5269
cisd-tx.net
Chillicothe JSHS 100/7-12
PO Box 550 79225 940-852-5391
Daniel Barker, prin. Fax 852-5465

Chilton, Falls
Chilton ISD 200/PK-12
PO Box 488 76632 254-546-1200
Benny Bobo, supt. Fax 546-1201
www.chiltonisd.org
Chilton JSHS 200/6-12
PO Box 488 76632 254-546-1200
Ray Rabroker, prin. Fax 546-1202

China, Jefferson, Pop. 1,080
Hardin-Jefferson ISD
Supt. — See Sour Lake
Henderson MS 500/6-8
PO Box 278 77613 409-981-6420
Mary Jones, prin. Fax 752-2049

China Spring, McLennan
China Spring ISD
Supt. — See Waco
China Spring HS 500/9-12
7301 N River Xing 76633 254-836-1771
Marc Faulkner, prin. Fax 836-1418
China Spring MS 300/7-8
7201 N River Xing 76633 254-836-4611
Bill Bratcher, prin. Fax 836-4777

Chireno, Nacogdoches, Pop. 396
Chireno ISD 300/K-12
PO Box 85 75937 936-362-2132
Dean Evans, supt. Fax 362-2490
www.chireno.esc7.net
Chireno HS 100/9-12
PO Box 85 75937 936-362-2132
Jamie Parmer, prin. Fax 362-2490

Christoval, Tom Green
Christoval ISD 300/K-12
PO Box 162 76935 325-896-2520
Tony Priest, supt. Fax 896-7405
Christoval JSHS 200/6-12
PO Box 162 76935 325-896-2355
Carl Wieburg, prin. Fax 896-2671

Cibolo, Guadalupe, Pop. 4,685
Schertz-Cibolo-Universal City ISD
Supt. — See Schertz
Dobie JHS 600/7-8
395 W Borgfeld Rd 78108 210-945-6000
Mike Wohlfarth, prin. Fax 945-6010
Steele HS 100/9-12
1300 FM 1103 78108 210-945-6500
Mary Pevoto, prin. Fax 945-6510

Cisco, Eastland, Pop. 3,779
Cisco ISD 800/PK-12
PO Box 1645 76437 254-442-3056
Hal Porter, supt. Fax 442-1412
www.ciscoisd.net/
Cisco HS 200/9-12
PO Box 1645 76437 254-442-3051
Craig Kent, prin. Fax 442-2516
Cisco JHS 200/6-8
PO Box 1645 76437 254-442-3004
Dee Dee Wright, prin. Fax 442-1832

Cisco Junior College Post-Sec.
RR 3 Box 3 76437 254-442-2567

Clarendon, Donley, Pop. 1,970
Clarendon ISD 500/PK-12
PO Box 610 79226 806-874-2062
Monty Hysinger, supt. Fax 874-2579
www.clarendon.k12.tx.us/
Clarendon HS 200/9-12
PO Box 610 79226 806-874-2181
Larry Jeffers, prin. Fax 874-3428
Clarendon JHS 100/6-8
PO Box 610 79226 806-874-3232
Marvin Elam, prin. Fax 874-9748

Clarendon College Post-Sec.
PO Box 968 79226 806-874-3571

Clarksville, Red River, Pop. 3,699
Clarksville ISD 1,000/PK-12
PO Box 1016 75426 903-427-3891
Joe Oliver, supt. Fax 427-5071
clarksville.esc8.net/
Cheatham MS 200/6-8
1500 W Main St 75426 903-427-3891
Pam Norwood, prin. Fax 427-4118
Clarksville HS 300/9-12
PO Box 1016 75426 903-427-3891
Charlie Martin, prin. Fax 427-5116

Claude, Armstrong, Pop. 1,262
Claude ISD 400/PK-12
PO Box 209 79019 806-226-7331
Bill D. Wood, supt. Fax 226-2244
www.region16.net/claudeisd
Claude JSHS 200/6-12
PO Box 209 79019 806-226-2191
W. Collins, prin. Fax 226-2244

Cleburne, Johnson, Pop. 27,928
Cleburne ISD 6,300/PK-12
505 N Ridgeway Dr Ste 100 76033 817-202-1100
Robert Damron, supt. Fax 202-1460
www.cleburne.k12.tx.us/
Cleburne HS 1,600/9-12
1501 Harlin Dr 76033 817-202-1200
Justin Marchel, prin. Fax 202-1470
Cleburne MS 900/7-8
1710 Country Club Rd 76033 817-202-1500
Riley Dunn, prin. Fax 202-1475

Cleburne Community Christian S 100/PK-12
PO Box 2017 76033 817-641-2857
Donald Bennett, admin. Fax 641-2863
Hill College Post-Sec.
PO Box 1899 76033 817-641-9887

Cleveland, Liberty, Pop. 7,828
Cleveland ISD 3,300/PK-12
316 E Dallas St 77327 281-592-8717
Kerry Cowart, supt. Fax 592-8283
www.clevelandisd.org
Cleveland HS 800/9-12
2000 E Houston St 77327 281-592-8752
Mike Ogden, prin. Fax 592-7485
Cleveland JHS 700/6-8
1600 E Houston St 77327 281-593-1148
Patricia Curry, prin. Fax 593-3400

Tarkington ISD 1,900/PK-12
2770 FM 163 Rd 77327 281-592-8781
John Kirchner, supt. Fax 592-3969
www.tarkingtonisd.net/
Tarkington HS 500/9-12
2770 FM 163 Rd 77327 281-592-7739
Robert Shaw, prin. Fax 592-0693
Tarkington MS 500/6-8
2770 FM 163 Rd 77327 281-592-7737
Randy O'Brien, prin. Fax 592-5241

Heritage Christian Academy 100/K-12
510 River St 77327 281-592-6430

Clifton, Bosque, Pop. 3,609
Clifton ISD 1,200/PK-12
1102 Key St 76634 254-675-2827
Gregory D. Stone, supt. Fax 675-4351
www.clifton.k12.tx.us
Clifton HS 300/9-12
1101 N Avenue Q 76634 254-675-2827
Ronnie Prueitt, prin. Fax 675-8002
Clifton MS 300/6-8
1102 Key St 76634 254-675-2827
Billy Murrell, prin. Fax 675-2005

Clint, El Paso, Pop. 981
Clint ISD
Supt. — See El Paso
Clint HS 700/9-12
12625 Alameda Ave 79836 915-926-8000
Morris Aldridge, prin. Fax 851-3895
Clint JHS 300/6-8
13100 Alameda Ave 79836 915-926-8100
Ignacio Solis, prin. Fax 851-3459

Clute, Brazoria, Pop. 10,704
Brazosport ISD 13,100/PK-12
301 W Brazoswood Dr 77531 979-730-7000
Fax 266-2409
www.brazosportisd.net
Brazoswood HS 2,600/9-12
302 W Brazoswood Dr 77531 979-730-7300
Mike Benedict, prin. Fax 266-2447
Clute IS 700/6-8
421 E Main St 77531 979-730-7230
Jay Whitehead, prin. Fax 730-7363
Other Schools – See Freeport, Lake Jackson

Clyde, Callahan, Pop. 3,444
Clyde Consolidated ISD 1,500/PK-12
PO Box 479 79510 325-893-4222
Dr. Kevin Spiller, supt. Fax 893-4024
www.clyde.esc14.net
Clyde HS 500/9-12
500 N Hays Rd 79510 325-893-2161
Teddy Merryman, prin. Fax 893-2993
Clyde JHS 200/7-8
211 S 3rd St W 79510 325-893-5788
Greg Edwards, prin. Fax 893-5255

Eula ISD 500/PK-12
6040 FM 603 79510 325-529-3186
Karen Kidd, supt. Fax 529-4461
www.eulaisd.us
Eula HS 200/9-12
6040 FM 603 79510 325-529-3605
Mike Bright, prin. Fax 529-5534
Eula MS 100/6-8
6040 FM 603 79510 325-529-4831
Tim Kelley, prin. Fax 529-4461

Coahoma, Howard, Pop. 920
Coahoma ISD 800/PK-12
PO Box 110 79511 432-394-4290
Jerry Johnson, supt. Fax 394-4302
Coahoma HS 300/9-12
PO Box 110 79511 432-394-4535
John Massey, prin. Fax 394-4031
Coahoma JHS 100/7-8
PO Box 110 79511 432-394-4615
Dean Richters, prin. Fax 394-4052

Coldspring, San Jacinto, Pop. 734
Coldspring-Oakhurst Consolidated ISD 1,800/PK-12
PO Box 39 77331 936-653-1115
V. Redden, supt. Fax 653-2197
www.cocisd.org
Coldspring-Oakhurst HS 500/9-12
PO Box 39 77331 936-653-1140
D'Wana Bryant, prin. Fax 653-3687
Lincoln JHS 400/6-8
PO Box 39 77331 936-653-1166
Malisa Hargrove, prin. Fax 653-3688

Coleman, Coleman, Pop. 4,927
Coleman ISD 1,000/PK-12
PO Box 900 76834 325-625-3575
Royce Young, supt. Fax 625-4751
coleman.netxv.net
Coleman HS 300/9-12
201 15th St 76834 325-625-2156
Kevin Hill, prin. Fax 625-4557
Coleman JHS 200/6-8
301 15th St 76834 325-625-3593
Paula Ringo, prin. Fax 625-3358

College Station, Brazos, Pop. 73,536
College Station ISD 7,900/PK-12
1812 Welsh Ave 77840 979-764-5400
Dr. Jimmy Creel, supt. Fax 764-5492
www.csisd.org
A & M Consolidated HS 2,200/9-12
1801 Harvey Mitchell Pkwy S 77840 979-764-5500
Ron Fox, prin. Fax 693-0212
A & M Consolidated MS 500/7-8
105 Holik St 77840 979-764-5575
Chris Scott, prin. Fax 764-5577
College Station MS 600/7-8
900 Rock Prairie Rd 77845 979-764-5545
Oliver Hadnot, prin. Fax 764-5557

Texas A&M University 77843 Post-Sec.
979-845-3211

Colleyville, Tarrant, Pop. 21,389
Grapevine-Colleyville ISD
Supt. — See Grapevine
Colleyville Heritage HS 2,200/9-12
5401 Heritage Ave 76034 817-358-4700
Robin Ryan, prin. Fax 358-4765
Colleyville MS 800/6-8
1100 Bogart Dr 76034 817-788-4400
Becky Prentice, prin. Fax 498-9764
Heritage MS 1,000/6-8
5300 Heritage Ave 76034 817-358-4790
Pete Valamides, prin. Fax 267-9929

Covenant Christian Academy 400/PK-12
901 Cheek Sparger Rd 76034 817-281-4333
Keith Castello, hdmstr. Fax 281-4674

Collinsville, Grayson, Pop. 1,368
Collinsville ISD 500/PK-12
PO Box 49 76233 903-429-6272
Randy Mohundro, supt. Fax 429-6665
www.collinsvilleisd.org
Collinsville JSHS 200/7-12
PO Box 49 76233 903-429-6164
Neal Harrison, prin. Fax 429-6493

Colmesneil, Tyler, Pop. 633
Colmesneil ISD 600/K-12
PO Box 37 75938 409-837-5757
Elton Hightower, supt. Fax 837-5759

Colmesneil HS — 200/9-12
PO Box 37 75938 — 409-837-2225
Ben Stewart, prin. — Fax 837-9107
Colmesneil MS — 100/6-8
PO Box 37 75938 — 409-837-5272
Walter McAlpin, prin. — Fax 837-2307

Colorado City, Mitchell, Pop. 4,007
Colorado ISD — 1,000/PK-12
PO Box 1268 79512 — 325-728-3721
Jim White, supt. — Fax 728-8471
www.ccity.esc14.net
Colorado HS — 300/9-12
1500 Lone Wolf Blvd 79512 — 325-728-3424
Jeremy Ross, prin. — Fax 728-1083
Colorado MS — 200/6-8
312 E 12th St 79512 — 325-728-2673
Mark Merrell, prin. — Fax 728-1051

Columbus, Colorado, Pop. 3,905
Columbus ISD — 1,600/PK-12
105 Cardinal Ln 78934 — 979-732-5704
Randall Hoyer, supt. — Fax 732-5960
www.columbusisd.org/
Columbus HS — 500/9-12
103 Cardinal Ln 78934 — 979-732-5746
J. Pfeffer, prin. — Fax 732-8862
Columbus JHS — 400/6-8
702 Rampart St 78934 — 979-732-2891
J. Laub, prin. — Fax 732-9081

Comanche, Comanche, Pop. 4,275
Comanche ISD — 1,300/PK-12
1414 N Austin St 76442 — 325-356-2727
Rick Howard, supt. — Fax 356-2312
www.comancheisd.net
Comanche HS — 400/9-12
N Highway 16 76442 — 325-356-2581
Ronnie Clifton, prin. — Fax 356-2658
Jeffries JHS — 300/6-8
Valley Forge Dr 76442 — 325-356-5220
Jim Baum, prin. — Fax 356-1949

Comfort, Kendall, Pop. 1,477
Comfort ISD — 1,200/PK-12
PO Box 398 78013 — 830-995-3664
John Rouse, supt. — Fax 995-2236
www.comfort.txed.net
Comfort HS — 300/9-12
PO Box 280 78013 — 830-995-3533
Bryan Clemmons, prin. — Fax 995-2261
Comfort MS — 300/6-8
PO Box 187 78013 — 830-995-3380
Mollye Williams, prin. — Fax 995-2248

Commerce, Hunt, Pop. 8,782
Commerce ISD — 1,800/PK-12
PO Box 1251 75429 — 903-886-3755
Keith Boles, supt. — Fax 886-6025
www.commerceisd.org/home.htm
Commerce HS — 500/9-12
PO Box 1251 75429 — 903-886-3756
Trish King, prin. — Fax 886-6209
Commerce MS — 400/6-8
PO Box 1251 75429 — 903-886-3795
Mitchell Curry, prin. — Fax 886-6102

Texas A&M University - Commerce — Post-Sec.
PO Box 3011 75429 — 903-886-5102

Como, Hopkins, Pop. 636
Como-Pickton Consolidated ISD — 200/PK-12
PO Box 18 75431 — 903-488-3671
Bryan Neal, supt. — Fax 488-3133
cpisd.esc8.net/
Como-Pickton HS — 200/9-12
PO Box 18 75431 — 903-488-9022
Randell Wellman, prin. — Fax 488-3133
Como-Pickton JHS — 6-8
PO Box 18 75431 — 903-488-3777
Randell Wellman, prin. — Fax 488-3133

Comstock, Val Verde
Comstock ISD — 200/K-12
PO Box 905 78837 — 432-292-4444
Kenn Norris, supt. — Fax 292-4436
Comstock S — 200/K-12
PO Box 905 78837 — 432-292-4444
Toby Ward, prin. — Fax 292-4436

Conroe, Montgomery, Pop. 39,896
Conroe ISD — 38,000/PK-12
3205 W Davis St 77304 — 936-709-7751
Dr. Don Stockton, supt. — Fax 760-7704
www.conroeisd.net/
Academy of Science & Health Professions — 9-12
3200 W Davis St 77304 — 936-525-2324
Dr. Mary Jo Parker, hdmstr. — Fax 760-6631
Academy of Science & Technology — 9-12
27330 Oak Ridge School Rd 77385 — 281-292-2615
Dr. Ron Laugen, hdmstr. — Fax 298-3292
Caney Creek HS — 1,600/9-12
16840 FM 2090 Rd 77306 — 936-231-3330
Dr. Greg Poole, prin. — Fax 231-7702
Conroe HS — 2,500/9-12
3200 W Davis St 77304 — 936-756-4416
Mike Crowl, prin. — Fax 760-6635
Moorehead JHS — 1,400/7-9
16840 FM 2090 Rd 77306 — 936-231-2400
— Fax 231-7697
Oak Ridge HS — 2,100/9-12
27330 Oak Ridge School Rd 77385 — 281-292-9800
Tommy Johnson, prin. — Fax 298-3294
Peet JHS — 900/7-8
400 Sgt Ed Holcomb Blvd N 77304 — 936-709-3700
Dr. Lloyd Swanson, prin. — Fax 538-7690
Washington JHS — 1,200/5-8
507 Dr Martin Luther King 77301 — 936-709-7400
Hartwell Brown, prin. — Fax 756-6253
York JHS — 1,000/6-8
27330 Oak Ridge School Rd 77385 — 832-592-8600
Dr. Gena Jerkins, prin. — Fax 292-1520
Other Schools – See The Woodlands

Aveda Institute — Post-Sec.
1212D S Frazier St 77301 — 936-539-6770
Calvary Baptist S — 200/PK-12
3401 N Frazier St 77303 — 936-756-0743
Becky Burchett, prin. — Fax 756-0764

Conroe SDA S — 50/PK-10
3601 S Loop 336 E 77301 — 936-756-5078
— Fax 760-4029
Covenant Christian S — 300/K-12
4503 Interstate 45 N 77304 — 936-890-8080
Dr. Charles Lloyd, admin. — Fax 890-5343
Lifestyle Christian S — 200/K-12
1201 Hillcrest Dr 77301 — 936-756-9383
Pat Maddoux, prin. — Fax 760-3003
PCAL Christian S — 50/7-12
16969 Larkspur 77385 — 936-273-4082
Karen Parish, admin. — Fax 273-4082

Converse, Bexar, Pop. 11,967
Judson ISD
Supt. — See Live Oak
Judson HS — 9-10
9695 Schaefer Rd 78109 — 210-357-0800
Don Pittman, prin. — Fax 659-8769
Judson SHS — 2,100/11-12
9142 FM 78 78109 — 210-945-1100
Dan Pittman, prin. — Fax 659-4359

Coolidge, Limestone, Pop. 872
Coolidge ISD — 300/PK-12
PO Box 70 76635 — 254-786-2206
Dr. Dan Hulen, supt. — Fax 786-4835
www.coolidge.k12.tx.us/
Coolidge HS — 100/6-12
PO Box 70 76635 — 254-786-4822
Cynthia Pollard, prin. — Fax 786-4835

Cooper, Delta, Pop. 2,175
Cooper ISD — 900/PK-12
PO Box 478 75432 — 903-395-2111
Lynn Burton, supt. — Fax 395-2117
www.cooperisd.net/
Cooper HS — 300/9-12
PO Box 429 75432 — 903-395-0509
Michael Ramsay, prin. — Fax 395-2382
Cooper JHS — 200/6-8
PO Box 478 75432 — 903-395-0509
Michael Ramsay, prin. — Fax 395-2382

Coppell, Dallas, Pop. 38,938
Coppell ISD — 10,000/PK-12
200 S Denton Tap Rd 75019 — 214-496-6000
Dr. Jeff N. Turner, supt. — Fax 496-6036
www.coppellisd.com
Coppell HS — 2,800/9-12
185 W Parkway Blvd 75019 — 214-496-6100
Brad Hunt, prin. — Fax 496-6116
Coppell MS East — 700/6-8
400 Mockingbird Ln 75019 — 214-496-6600
Karen Nix, prin. — Fax 496-6603
Coppell MS North — 800/6-8
120 Natches Trce 75019 — 214-496-7100
Dr. Juneria Berges, prin. — Fax 496-7103
Coppell MS West — 800/6-8
1301 Wrangler Cir 75019 — 214-496-8600
Vernon Edin, prin. — Fax 496-8606

Copperas Cove, Coryell, Pop. 29,988
Copperas Cove ISD — 6,900/PK-12
703 W Avenue D 76522 — 254-547-1227
Dr. Glenn Acker, supt. — Fax 547-1542
www.ccisd.com
Copperas Cove HS — 2,100/9-12
400 S 25th St 76522 — 254-547-2535
Dr. George Willey, prin. — Fax 547-9870
Copperas Cove JHS — 500/7-8
702 Sunny Ave 76522 — 254-547-6959
Christy Slagle, prin. — Fax 518-2620
Lee JHS — 600/7-8
1205 Courtney Ln 76522 — 254-542-7877
Dr. Brenda Cox, prin. — Fax 542-8103

Corinth, Denton, Pop. 16,338
Denton ISD
Supt. — See Denton
Crownover MS — 900/6-8
1901 Creekside Dr 76210 — 940-369-4700
Dianne Blair, prin. — Fax 321-0502

Lake Dallas ISD
Supt. — See Lake Dallas
Lake Dallas HS — 900/9-12
3016 Parkridge Dr 76210 — 940-497-4031
Dave Ketcher, prin. — Fax 497-3400

Corpus Christi, Nueces, Pop. 279,208
Calallen ISD — 3,900/PK-12
4205 Wildcat Dr 78410 — 361-242-5600
Arturo Almendarez, supt. — Fax 242-5620
www.calallen.k12.tx.us
Calallen HS — 1,300/9-12
4001 Wildcat Dr 78410 — 361-242-5626
Yvonne Marquez-Neth, prin. — Fax 242-5632
Calallen MS — 900/6-8
4602 Cornett Dr 78410 — 361-242-5672
Leslie Faught, prin. — Fax 242-5680

Corpus Christi ISD — 38,200/PK-12
PO Box 110 78403 — 361-886-9200
Mary Kelley, supt. — Fax 886-9109
www.corpuschristiisd.org
Baker MS — 900/6-8
3445 Pecan St 78411 — 361-878-1420
Darla Reid, prin. — Fax 878-1834
Browne MS — 800/6-8
4301 Schanen Blvd 78413 — 361-878-1426
Donna Adams, prin. — Fax 878-1836
Carroll HS — 2,300/9-12
5301 Weber Rd 78411 — 361-853-0151
Stephen Kane, prin. — Fax 857-2548
Cullen MS — 400/6-8
5225 Greely Dr 78412 — 361-994-3630
Robert Templeton, prin. — Fax 994-3624
Cunningham MS — 600/6-8
4321 Prescott St 78416 — 361-878-1432
Carlos Garza, prin. — Fax 878-1838
Driscoll MS — 800/6-8
3501 Kenwood Dr 78408 — 361-886-9365
Roland Quezada, prin. — Fax 886-9890
Grant MS — 1,100/6-8
4350 Aaron Dr 78413 — 361-878-1860
Carla Rosa-Villarreal, prin. — Fax 878-1871
Haas MS — 500/6-8
6630 McArdle Rd 78412 — 361-994-3636
Deborah Scates, prin. — Fax 994-3626

Hamlin MS — 800/6-8
3900 Hamlin Dr 78411 — 361-878-1438
Debbie McAden, prin. — Fax 878-1839
Kaffie MS — 900/6-8
5922 Brockhampton St 78414 — 361-994-3600
Nancy Benson, prin. — Fax 994-3604
King HS — 2,400/9-12
5225 Gollihar Rd 78412 — 361-994-6900
Bernadine Cervantes, prin. — Fax 994-6918
Martin MS — 700/6-8
3502 Greenwood Dr 78416 — 361-878-1400
Minerva Abrego, prin. — Fax 878-1841
Miller HS — 1,500/9-12
1 Battlin Buc Blvd 78408 — 361-884-4963
Daniel Noyola, prin. — Fax 883-1928
Moody HS — 1,800/9-12
1818 Trojan Dr 78416 — 361-854-3261
Conrado Garcia, prin. — Fax 857-8253
Ray HS — 2,200/9-12
1002 Texan Trl 78411 — 361-806-5300
Steven Gonzales, prin. — Fax 852-6528
Seale Academy of Fine Arts — 800/6-8
1707 Ayers St 78404 — 361-886-9359
Delia McLerran, prin. — Fax 886-9892
South Park MS — 600/6-8
3001 McArdle Rd 78415 — 361-878-1446
Dr. Michael Torres, prin. — Fax 878-1444
Adult Learning Center — Adult
3902 Morgan Ave 78405 — 361-886-9385
Homero Villarreal, dir. — Fax 886-9387

Flour Bluff ISD — 5,100/PK-12
2505 Waldron Rd 78418 — 361-694-9200
Julie Carbajal, supt. — Fax 694-9809
www.flourbluffschools.net
Flour Bluff HS — 1,600/9-12
2505 Waldron Rd 78418 — 361-694-9100
Eddie Chachere, prin. — Fax 694-9802
Flour Bluff JHS — 800/7-8
2505 Waldron Rd 78418 — 361-694-9300
Danny Glover, prin. — Fax 694-9803

Tuloso-Midway ISD — 3,400/PK-12
PO Box 10900 78460 — 361-903-6400
Dr. Cornelio Gonzalez, supt. — Fax 241-1554
www.tmisd.esc2.net
Tuloso-Midway Academic Career Center — Vo/Tech
PO Box 10900 78460 — 361-903-6450
Melodie McClarren, prin. — Fax 289-5642
Tuloso-Midway HS — 1,000/9-12
PO Box 10900 78460 — 361-903-6700
Ann Bartosh, prin. — Fax 241-4258
Tuloso-Midway MS — 800/6-8
PO Box 10900 78460 — 361-903-6600
Jeff Cannon, prin. — Fax 241-9829

West Oso ISD — 1,900/PK-12
5050 Rockford Dr 78416 — 361-855-5900
Dr. Crawford Helms, supt. — Fax 225-8308
www.westosoisd.esc2.net
West Oso HS — 500/9-12
5202 Bear Ln 78405 — 361-806-5960
Benito Franco, prin. — Fax 299-3111
West Oso JHS — 400/6-8
1115 Bloomington St 78416 — 361-806-5950
Joe Martinez, prin. — Fax 225-8314

Annapolis Christian Academy — 100/PK-12
3346 Airline Rd 78414 — 361-991-6004
Tim Moon, hdmstr. — Fax 992-0369
Bishop Garriga MS — 200/6-8
3114 Saratoga Blvd 78415 — 361-851-0853
Rosario Davila, prin. — Fax 853-5145
Career Centers of Texas — Post-Sec.
1620 S Padre Island Dr 78416 — 361-852-2900
Del Mar College — Post-Sec.
101 Baldwin Blvd 78404 — 361-698-1200
Incarnate Word Academy — 200/6-8
2917 Austin St 78404 — 361-883-0857
Adolfo Garza, prin. — Fax 882-9193
Incarnate Word Academy — 400/9-12
2910 S Alameda St 78404 — 361-883-0857
Gerald Lugaresi, prin. — Fax 883-2185
Institute of Cosmetic Arts and Science — Post-Sec.
1105 Airline Rd 78412 — 361-991-8868
John Paul II HS — 9-12
3036 Saratoga Blvd 78415 — 361-855-5744
Ricardo Almendarez, prin. — Fax 855-1343
Southern Careers Institute — Post-Sec.
2422 Airline Rd 78414 — 361-857-5700
South Texas Barber College — Post-Sec.
3917 Ayers St 78415 — 361-855-2297
Texas A&M University - Corpus Christi — Post-Sec.
6300 Ocean Dr 78412 — 361-825-5700

Corrigan, Polk, Pop. 1,891
Corrigan-Camden ISD — 700/PK-12
504 S Home St 75939 — 936-398-4040
Tom Bowman, supt. — Fax 398-4616
Corrigan-Camden HS — 300/9-12
504 S Home St 75939 — 936-398-2543
Andy Trekell, prin. — Fax 398-2685
Corrigan-Camden JHS — 200/7-8
504 S Home St 75939 — 936-398-2962
Ray Bostick, prin. — Fax 398-4608

Corsicana, Navarro, Pop. 25,466
Corsicana ISD — 5,500/PK-12
601 N 13th St 75110 — 903-874-7441
Don Denbow, supt. — Fax 872-2100
www.cisd.org
Collins MS — 800/7-8
1500 Dobbins Rd 75110 — 903-872-3979
Sharon McDonald, prin. — Fax 874-1423
Corsicana HS — 1,400/9-12
3701 W State Highway 22 75110 — 903-874-8211
Keith Moore, prin. — Fax 874-7403

Mildred ISD — 700/K-12
5475 S US Highway 287 75109 — 903-872-6505
Douglas Lane, supt. — Fax 872-1341
www.esc12.net/mildredisd
Mildred JSHS — 300/7-12
5475 S US Highway 287 75109 — 903-872-0392
Gerry Talley, prin. — Fax 641-0356

Navarro College — Post-Sec.
3200 W 7th Ave 75110 — 903-874-6501

Cotton Center, Hale
Cotton Center ISD 100/PK-12
PO Box 350 79021 806-879-2160
Keith Gast, supt. Fax 879-2175
cottoncenter.esc17.net
Cotton Center S 100/PK-12
PO Box 350 79021 806-879-2176
John Petree, prin. Fax 879-2175

Cotulla, LaSalle, Pop. 3,593
Cotulla ISD 1,200/PK-12
310 N Main St 78014 830-879-3073
Elizabeth Saenz, supt. Fax 879-3609
www.cotullaisd.org
Cotulla HS 300/9-12
310 N Main St 78014 830-879-2374
Ana Sulaica, prin. Fax 879-4302
Newman MS 300/6-8
310 N Main St 78014 830-879-2224
Kim Hoff, prin. Fax 879-4357

Covington, Hill, Pop. 302
Covington ISD 300/PK-12
PO Box 67 76636 254-854-2215
Diane Innis, supt. Fax 854-2272
www.covingtonisd.org/
Covington S 300/PK-12
PO Box 67 76636 254-854-2215
Hugh Ellison, prin. Fax 854-2272

Crandall, Kaufman, Pop. 3,184
Crandall ISD 2,100/PK-12
PO Box 128 75114 972-427-8000
Dr. Larry Watson, supt. Fax 427-8001
www.crandall-isd.net
Crandall HS 600/9-12
PO Box 520 75114 972-427-8030
David Greer, prin. Fax 427-8234
Raynes MS 500/6-8
PO Box 490 75114 972-427-8080
Debra Lynn, prin. Fax 427-8031

Crane, Crane, Pop. 3,093
Crane ISD 1,000/PK-12
511 W 8th St 79731 432-558-1022
Larry Lee, supt. Fax 558-1025
www.craneisd.com
Crane HS 300/9-12
511 W 8th St 79731 432-558-1030
Carlin Grammer, prin. Fax 558-1056
Crane MS 200/6-8
511 W 8th St 79731 432-558-1040
Ted Hallford, prin. Fax 558-1046

Cranfills Gap, Bosque, Pop. 343
Cranfills Gap ISD 100/PK-12
PO Box 67 76637 254-597-2505
Kevin Dyes, supt. Fax 597-0001
www.esc12.net/cranfillsgapisd/
Cranfills Gap S 100/PK-12
PO Box 67 76637 254-597-2505
Kevin Dyes, prin. Fax 597-0001

Crawford, McLennan, Pop. 767
Crawford ISD 600/K-12
200 Pirate Dr 76638 254-486-2381
Kevin Noack, supt. Fax 486-2198
www.crawfordisd.net/
Crawford HS 200/9-12
200 Pirate Dr 76638 254-486-2381
Don Harris, prin. Fax 486-2198
Crawford MS 200/5-8
200 Pirate Dr 76638 254-486-2381
Jason Ray Bunting, prin. Fax 486-2198

Crockett, Houston, Pop. 7,065
Crockett ISD 1,700/PK-12
704 E Burnett Ave 75835 936-544-2125
Dr. Bill Like, supt. Fax 544-5727
www.crockettisd.net
Crockett HS 500/9-12
704 E Burnett Ave 75835 936-544-2193
Clint McLain, prin. Fax 546-0104
Crockett JHS 300/7-8
704 E Burnett Ave 75835 936-544-2149
Debra Lamb, prin. Fax 544-4164

Crosby, Harris, Pop. 1,811
Crosby ISD 4,300/PK-12
PO Box 2009 77532 281-328-9200
Dr. Don Hendrix, supt. Fax 328-9208
www.crosbyisd.org
Crosby HS 1,200/9-12
PO Box 2009 77532 281-328-9237
Deborah Frank, prin. Fax 328-9219
Crosby MS 700/7-8
PO Box 2009 77532 281-328-9264
Patricia Kay, prin. Fax 328-9356

Crosbyton, Crosby, Pop. 1,777
Crosbyton ISD 500/PK-12
204 S Harrison St 79322 806-675-7331
Marvin Stewart, supt. Fax 675-2409
www.crosbyton.k12.tx.us
Crosbyton HS 100/9-12
204 S Harrison St 79322 806-675-7331
John-Paul Huber, prin. Fax 675-1049
Crosbyton MS 100/6-8
204 S Harrison St 79322 806-675-7331
Dennis Verkamp, prin. Fax 675-2409

Cross Plains, Callahan, Pop. 1,078
Cross Plains ISD 400/PK-12
700 N Main St 76443 254-725-6121
Jackie Tennison, supt. Fax 725-6559
www.esc14.net/schools/~cplains/default.html
Cross Plains JSHS 200/7-12
700 N Main St 76443 254-725-6121
Jimmie Cearley, prin. Fax 725-6559

Crowell, Foard, Pop. 1,080
Crowell ISD 300/PK-12
PO Box 239 79227 940-684-1403
Charles H. Hundley, supt. Fax 684-1616
www.crowellisd.net/
Crowell JSHS 100/7-12
PO Box 239 79227 940-684-1331
Amie Bell, prin. Fax 684-1978

Crowley, Tarrant, Pop. 8,831
Crowley ISD 11,800/PK-12
PO Box 688 76036 817-297-5800
Greg Gibson, supt. Fax 297-5805
www.crowley.k12.tx.us
Crowley 9th Grade Campus 400/9-9
1016 Highway 1187 76036 817-297-5845
Daphne Kahn-Wiley, prin. Fax 297-5847
Crowley HS 1,100/10-12
1005 W Main St 76036 817-297-5810
Richard Crosby, prin. Fax 297-5854
Stevens MS 900/7-8
940 N Crowley Rd 76036 817-297-5840
D.J. Molina, prin. Fax 297-5850
Other Schools – See Fort Worth

Nazarene Christian Academy 200/K-12
2001 E Main St 76036 817-297-7003
Sheila Meek, admin. Fax 297-1509

Crystal City, Zavala, Pop. 7,131
Crystal City ISD 2,200/PK-12
805 E Crockett St 78839 830-374-2367
Alberto Gonzales, supt. Fax 374-8004
www.ccjavs.net/
Crystal City HS 600/9-12
805 E Crockett St 78839 830-374-2341
Oscar Martinez, prin. Fax 374-8012
Fly JHS 500/6-8
805 E Crockett St 78839 830-374-2371
Ray Espinosa, prin. Fax 374-8060

Cuero, DeWitt, Pop. 6,659
Cuero ISD 1,900/PK-12
405 Park Heights Dr 77954 361-275-3832
Henry Lind, supt. Fax 275-2981
www.cueroisd.org
Cuero HS 700/9-12
401 Park Heights Dr 77954 361-275-6157
Michael Cavanaugh, prin. Fax 275-2430
Cuero JHS 500/6-8
502 Park Heights Dr 77954 361-275-2222
Dr. Jose Ramos, prin. Fax 275-6912

Cumby, Hopkins, Pop. 627
Cumby ISD 400/PK-12
101 Sayle St 75433 903-994-2261
Bert Vandiver, supt. Fax 994-2399
cumby.esc8.net/
Cumby HS 200/7-12
101 Sayle St 75433 903-994-2260
Don Madden, prin. Fax 994-2510

Miller Grove ISD 100/K-12
7819 Farm Road 275 S 75433 903-459-3288
Steve Johnson, supt. Fax 459-3744
millergrove.esc8.net/
Miller Grove HS 100/7-12
7819 Farm Road 275 S 75433 903-459-3288
Donna George, prin. Fax 459-3744

Cushing, Nacogdoches, Pop. 639
Cushing ISD 500/PK-12
PO Box 337 75760 936-326-4890
Stanley Wade, supt. Fax 326-4131
Cushing JSHS 200/7-12
PO Box 337 75760 936-326-4271
Michael Davis, prin. Fax 326-4131

Cypress, Harris
Cypress-Fairbanks ISD
Supt. — See Houston
Arnold MS 1,300/6-8
11111 Telge Rd 77429 281-897-4700
Susan Higgins, prin. Fax 807-8610
Carlton Pre-Vocational Center Vo/Tech
22602 Hempstead Hwy 77429 281-897-4750
Rhonda Turns, dir. Fax 517-2161
Cy-Fair HS 3,200/9-12
22602 Hempstead Hwy 77429 281-897-4600
Darlene Medford, prin. Fax 517-6530
Cypress Springs HS 3,000/9-12
7909 Fry Rd 77433 281-345-3000
Sarah Harty, prin. Fax 345-3010
Cypress Woods HS 9-12
16825 Spring Cypress Rd 77429 281-897-4000
Sue McGown, prin.
Goodson MS 1,600/6-8
17333 Huffmeister Rd 77429 281-373-2350
Phyllis Hamilton, prin. Fax 373-2355
Hamilton MS 1,400/6-8
12330 Kluge Rd 77429 281-320-7000
Sue McGown, prin. Fax 320-7021
Spillane MS, 17500 Jarvis Rd 77429 6-8
Gary Kinninger, prin. 281-213-1645

Daingerfield, Morris, Pop. 2,527
Daingerfield-Lone Star ISD 1,600/PK-12
200 Tiger Dr 75638 903-645-2239
Judy Pollan, supt. Fax 645-2137
d-lsisd.esc8.net/
Daingerfield HS 500/9-12
202 Tiger Dr 75638 903-645-3968
Gerald Singleton, prin. Fax 645-7662
Daingerfield JHS 400/6-8
200 Texas St 75638 903-645-2261
Michael Baysinger, prin. Fax 645-4010

Daisetta, Liberty, Pop. 1,081
Hull-Daisetta ISD 700/PK-12
PO Box 477 77533 936-536-6321
Steven Dozier, supt. Fax 536-6251
Hull-Daisetta HS 200/9-12
PO Box 477 77533 936-536-6321
Jay Killgo, prin. Fax 536-3839
Other Schools – See Raywood

Dalhart, Dallam, Pop. 7,153
Dalhart ISD 1,600/PK-12
315 Rock Island Ave 79022 806-244-7810
David Foote, supt. Fax 244-7822
www.dalhart.k12.tx.us
Dalhart HS 400/9-12
315 Rock Island Ave 79022 806-244-7300
David Steele, prin. Fax 244-7307
Dalhart JHS 400/6-8
315 Rock Island Ave 79022 806-244-7825
Marlin Coffman, prin. Fax 244-7835

Dallardsville, Polk
Big Sandy ISD 500/PK-12
PO Box 188 77332 936-563-1000
Kenneth Graham, supt. Fax 563-1010
www.bigsandyisd.net/
Other Schools – See Livingston

Dallas, Dallas, Pop. 1,208,318
Carrollton-Farmers Branch ISD
Supt. — See Carrollton
Long MS 900/6-8
2525 Frankford Rd 75287 972-662-4100
Nicoloas Lasker, prin. Fax 662-4101

Dallas ISD 159,600/PK-12
3700 Ross Ave 75204 972-925-3700
Michael Hinojosa Ed.D., supt. Fax 925-3201
www.dallasisd.org
Adams HS 2,600/9-12
2101 Millmar Dr 75228 972-502-4900
Karen Ramos, prin. Fax 502-4901
Adamson HS 1,300/9-12
201 E 9th St 75203 972-749-1400
Rawley Sanchez, prin. Fax 749-1401
Alternative Placement Center 9-12
4949 Village Fair Dr 75224 972-925-7000
Halice Furtado, prin. Fax 925-7001
Anderson Learning Center 800/7-8
3400 Garden Ln 75215 972-925-7900
Benita Noiel-Ashford, prin. Fax 925-7901
Atwell Law Academy 800/7-8
1303 Reynoldston Ln 75232 972-794-6400
Regina Jones-Carroll, prin. Fax 794-6401
Browne MS 1,200/7-8
3333 Sprague Dr 75233 972-502-2500
Cedric Barrett, prin. Fax 502-2501
Carter HS 1,800/9-12
1819 W Wheatland Rd 75232 214-932-5700
Deandra Hayes-Whigham, prin. Fax 932-5701
Cary MS 1,300/6-8
3978 Killion Dr 75229 972-502-7600
Santiago Camacho, prin. Fax 502-7601
Comstock MS 900/7-8
7044 Hodde St 75217 972-794-1300
Wanda Huckaby, prin. Fax 794-1301
Dallas Environmental Science Academy 200/7-8
2940 Singleton Blvd 75212 972-794-4000
Katie Watson, prin. Fax 794-4001
Edison MS 700/7-8
2940 Singleton Blvd 75212 972-794-4100
Jimmy King, prin. Fax 794-4101
Education & Social Service Magnet HS 200/9-12
1201 E 8th St 75203 972-925-5940
Fax 925-5901
Florence MS 1,100/7-8
1625 N Masters Dr 75217 972-749-6000
Bryant Joseph, prin. Fax 749-6001
Franklin MS 1,000/7-8
6920 Meadow Rd 75230 972-502-7100
Ronald Jones, prin. Fax 502-7101
Gaston MS 1,000/7-8
9565 Mercer Dr 75228 972-502-5400
Susie Stauss, prin. Fax 502-5401
Government Law & Law Enforcement HS 400/9-12
1201 E 8th St 75203 972-925-5950
Robert Giesler, prin. Fax 925-6010
Greiner Exploratory Arts Academy 1,700/7-8
501 S Edgefield Ave 75208 972-925-7100
Dorothy Gomez, prin. Fax 925-7101
Health Profession Magnet HS 500/9-12
1201 E 8th St Ste 281 75203 972-925-5930
Myrtle Walker, prin. Fax 925-5901
Hillcrest HS 1,700/9-12
9924 Hillcrest Rd 75230 972-502-6800
Marty Crawford, prin. Fax 502-6801
Hill MS 900/7-8
505 Easton Rd 75218 972-502-5700
Esther Contreras, prin. Fax 502-5701
Holmes MS 900/7-8
2001 E Kiest Blvd 75216 972-925-8500
Ronald Moore, prin. Fax 925-8501
Hood MS 1,300/7-8
7625 Hume Dr 75227 972-749-4100
Fred Davis, prin. Fax 749-4101
Hulcy MS 500/6-8
9339 S Polk St 75232 214-932-7400
Alford Tribble, prin. Fax 932-7401
Jefferson HS 1,700/9-12
4001 Walnut Hill Ln 75229 972-502-7300
Manuel Ontiveros, prin. Fax 502-7301
Kimball HS 1,800/9-12
3606 S Westmoreland Rd 75233 972-502-2100
Danny Stigers, prin. Fax 502-2101
Lincoln Humanities/Communications HS 1,200/9-12
2826 Hatcher St 75215 972-925-7600
Earl Jones, prin. Fax 925-7601
Longfellow Career Academy 400/7-8
5314 Boaz St 75209 972-749-5400
Rob Pipkin, prin. Fax 749-5401
Long MS 900/7-8
6116 Reiger Ave 75214 972-502-4700
Desiree Arias, prin. Fax 502-4701
Madison HS 600/9-12
3000 Mrtn Lthr King Jr Blvd 75215 972-925-2800
Marian Willard, prin. Fax 925-2801
Marsh MS 1,300/7-8
3838 Crown Shore Dr 75244 972-502-6600
Kyle Richardson, prin. Fax 502-6601
Molina HS 2,600/9-12
2355 Duncanville Rd 75211 972-502-1000
Francisco Ramirez, prin. Fax 502-1001
Multiple Careers Magnet HS Vo/Tech
4528 Rusk Ave 75204 972-925-2200
Bill Quinones, prin. Fax 925-2201
North Dallas HS 1,800/9-12
3120 N Haskell Ave 75204 972-925-1500
Dina Townsend, prin. Fax 925-1501
Pinkston HS 900/9-12
2200 Dennison St 75212 972-502-2700
James Colbert, prin. Fax 502-2701
Quintanilla MS 1,100/7-8
2700 Remond Dr 75211 972-502-3200
Rodney Cooksy, prin. Fax 502-3201
Roosevelt HS 800/9-12
525 Bonnie View Rd 75203 972-925-6800
Leon Dudley, prin. Fax 925-6801
Rusk MS 700/7-8
2929 Inwood Rd 75235 972-925-2000
Evangelina Kircher, prin. Fax 925-2001

Samuell HS 2,200/9-12
8928 Palisade Dr 75217 972-892-5100
Daniel Johnson, prin. Fax 892-5101
School of Business & Management 500/9-12
1201 E 8th St Ste 241 75203 972-925-5920
Edith Krutilek, prin. Fax 925-5901
Science & Engineering HS 400/9-12
1201 E 8th St 75203 972-925-5960
Richard White, prin. Fax 925-6016
Seagoville HS 1,200/9-12
15920 Seagoville Rd 75253 972-892-5900
Judie Klaus, prin. Fax 892-5901
Seagoville MS 800/7-8
950 N Woody Rd 75253 972-892-7100
Jose Cardenas, prin. Fax 892-7101
Skyline Career Development Ctr Vo/Tech
7777 Forney Rd 75227 214-502-3401
Fax 502-3401
Skyline HS 4,300/9-12
7777 Forney Rd 75227 972-502-3400
Leslie Williams, prin. Fax 502-3401
Smith HS 900/9-12
3030 Stag Rd 75241 214-932-7600
Dwain Govan, prin. Fax 932-7601
South Oak Cliff HS 1,300/9-12
3601 S Marsalis Ave 75216 214-932-7000
Donald Moten, prin. Fax 932-7001
Spence Talented/Gifted Academy 900/7-8
4001 Capitol Ave 75204 972-925-2300
Brenda Kirby, prin. Fax 925-2301
Spruce HS 1,600/9-12
9733 Old Seagoville Rd 75217 972-892-5500
Ardis McCann, prin. Fax 892-5501
Stockard MS 800/7-8
2300 S Ravinia Dr 75211 972-794-5700
Faustino Rivas, prin. Fax 794-5701
Storey MS 700/7-8
3000 Maryland Ave 75216 972-925-8700
Cassandra Asberry, prin. Fax 925-8701
Sunset HS 2,100/9-12
2120 W Jefferson Blvd 75208 972-502-1500
Emilio Castro, prin. Fax 502-1501
Townview Magnet Center 1,200/9-12
1201 E 8th St 75203 972-925-5900
Alice Black, prin. Fax 925-5901
Travis Academy 900/4-8
3001 Mckinney Ave 75204 972-794-7500
Mari Smith, prin. Fax 794-7501
Washington Performing & Visual Arts HS 700/9-12
2501 Flora St 75201 972-925-1200
Ruth Woodward, prin. Fax 925-1201
White HS 2,100/9-12
4505 Ridgeside Dr 75244 972-502-6200
Joy Barnhart, prin. Fax 502-6201
Wilson HS 1,400/9-12
100 S Glasgow Dr 75214 972-502-4400
Judy Zimny, prin. Fax 502-4401
Zumwalt MS 600/7-8
2445 E Ledbetter Dr 75216 972-749-3600
Marian Willard, prin. Fax 749-3601
Evening Academy Adult
7777 Forney Rd 75227 972-502-3458
Phillip Allen, prin. Fax 502-3463
Manns HS Adult
912 S Ervay St 75201 972-749-2200
Gene Ward, prin. Fax 749-2201

Duncanville ISD
Supt. — See Duncanville
Kennemer MS 800/7-8
7101 W Wheatland Rd 75249 972-708-3600
Daron Lee, prin. Fax 708-3636

Highland Park ISD 6,100/PK-12
7015 Westchester Dr 75205 214-780-3000
Dr. Cathy Bryce, supt. Fax 780-3099
www.hpisd.org
Highland Park HS 1,900/9-12
4220 Emerson Ave 75205 214-780-3700
Patrick Cates, prin. Fax 780-3799
Highland Park MS 1,000/7-8
3555 Granada Ave 75205 214-780-3600
Laurie Norton, prin. Fax 780-3699

Plano ISD
Supt. — See Plano
Frankford MS 1,200/6-8
7706 Osage Plaza Pkwy 75252 469-752-5200
Susan Modisette, prin. Fax 752-5201

Richardson ISD
Supt. — See Richardson
Forest Meadow JHS 800/7-8
9373 Whitehurst Dr 75243 469-593-1500
Charles Bruner, prin. Fax 593-1461
Lake Highlands Freshman Center 800/9-9
10200 White Rock Trl 75238 469-593-1300
Jayne Farmer, prin. Fax 593-1327
Lake Highlands HS 1,900/10-12
9449 Church Rd 75238 469-593-1000
Dr. Robert Iden, prin. Fax 593-1030
Lake Highlands JHS 800/7-8
10301 Kingsley Rd 75238 469-593-1600
Lorine Burrell, prin. Fax 593-1606
Liberty JHS 700/7-9
10330 Lawler Rd 75243 469-593-7888
Stephen Quisenberry, prin. Fax 593-7764
Parkhill JHS 800/7-9
16500 Shadybank Dr 75248 469-593-5600
Judy Marcum, prin. Fax 593-5500
Westwood Magnet JHS 800/7-9
7630 Arapaho Rd 75248 469-593-3600
Ron Griffen, prin. Fax 593-3508

Argosy University/Dallas Post-Sec.
8080 Park Ln Ste 400 75231 214-890-9900
Art Institute of Dallas Post-Sec.
8080 Park Ln Ste 100 75231 214-692-8080
ATI Career Training Center Post-Sec.
10003 Technology Blvd W 75220 214-902-8191
ATI Technical Training Center Post-Sec.
6627 Maple Ave 75235 214-352-2222
Aviation Institute of Maintenance Post-Sec.
7555 Lemmon Ave 75209 214-333-9711
Baylor University Medical Center Post-Sec.
3500 Gaston Ave 75246 214-820-2731
Bill Priest Inst. Economic Development Post-Sec.
1402 Corinth St 75215 214-860-5900

Bishop Dunne HS 500/7-12
3900 Rugged Dr 75224 214-339-6561
Kate Dailey, prin. Fax 339-1438
Bishop Lynch HS 1,100/9-12
9750 Ferguson Rd 75228 214-324-3607
Evelyn Grubbs, prin. Fax 324-3600
Brown Mackie College 972-279-4446
8080 Park Ln Ste 315 75231
Central Texas Commercial College 214-368-3680
9400 N Central Expy Ste 200 75231
Court Reporting Institute of Dallas 214-350-9722
1341 W Mockingbird Ln # 200 75247
Covenant S 200/K-12
3877 Walnut Hill Ln 75229 214-358-5818
Brad Ryden, hdmstr. Fax 358-5809
Dallas Academy 100/K-12
950 Tiffany Way 75218 214-324-1481
James Richardson, prin. Fax 327-8537
Dallas Baptist University Post-Sec.
3000 Mountain Creek Pkwy 75211 214-333-7100
Dallas Barber and Stylist College Post-Sec.
9357 Forest Ln 75243 214-360-9570
Dallas Christian College Post-Sec.
2700 Christian Pkwy 75234 800-688-1029
Dallas Institute of Funeral Service Post-Sec.
3909 S Buckner Blvd 75227 214-388-5466
Dallas Theological Seminary Post-Sec.
3909 Swiss Ave 75204 214-824-3094
El Centro College Post-Sec.
801 Main St 75202 214-860-2037
Episcopal S of Dallas 500/5-12
4100 Merrell Rd 75229 214-353-5812
Rev. Stephen Swann, hdmstr. Fax 353-5865
Everest College Post-Sec.
6060 N Central Expy Ste 101 75206 214-234-4850
Fairhill S 200/1-12
16150 Preston Rd 75248 972-233-1026
Jane Sego, dir. Fax 233-8205
First Baptist Academy 700/K-12
PO Box 868 75221 214-969-7861
Jake Walters, hdmstr. Fax 969-7797
Graduate Institute of Applied Linguistic 972-708-7340
7500 W Camp Wisdom Rd 75236
Hockaday S 1,000/PK-12
11600 Welch Rd 75229 214-363-6311
Jeanne Whitman, hdmstr. Fax 363-0942
Interactive Learning Systems 214-637-3377
8585 N Stemmons Fwy Ste C15 75247
Jesuit College Preparatory S 1,000/9-12
12345 Inwood Rd 75244 972-387-8700
Michael Earsing, prin. Fax 661-9349
Jones Beauty College 214-956-0088
10909 Webbs Chapel Rd # 129 75229
KD Studio - Actors Conservatory 214-638-0484
2600 N Stemmons Fwy Ste 117 75207
Lakehill Prep S 400/K-12
2720 Hillside Dr 75214 214-826-2931
Roger Perry, hdmstr. Fax 826-4623
Lobias Murray Christian Academy 200/K-12
330 E Ann Arbor Ave 75216 214-372-6466
Sharon Smith, prin. Fax 376-6763
Lutheran HS 300/7-12
8494 Stults Rd 75243 214-349-8912
Patricia Klekamp, prin. Fax 340-3095
Mesorah S 50/9-12
6921 Frankford Rd 75252 972-599-0031
Rabbi Avraham Kosowsky, hdmstr. Fax 599-0033
Metropolitan Christian S 300/PK-12
8501 Bruton Rd 75217 214-388-4426
Terry Carpenter, hdmstr. Fax 381-2574
MJ's Beauty Academy 214-374-7500
3939 S Polk St Ste 505 75224
Mountain View College 214-860-8680
4849 W Illinois Ave 75211
Neilson Beauty College Post-Sec.
416 W Jefferson Blvd 75208 214-941-8756
New Vision Christian Academy 50/K-12
4710 W Illinois Ave 75211 214-333-2147
Juan Bell, prin. Fax 333-8286
Ogle School of Hair Design 214-821-0819
6333 E Mockingbird Ln #201 75214
Parish Episcopal S 1,000/PK-12
4101 Sigma Rd 75244 972-239-8011
Gloria Snyder, hdmstr. Fax 991-1237
Parker College of Chiropractic Post-Sec.
2500 Walnut Hill Ln 75229 972-438-6932
Paul Quinn College 214-376-1000
3837 Simpson Stuart Rd 75241
PCI Health Training Center 214-630-0568
8101 John W Carpenter Fwy 75247
Presbyterian Hospital 214-345-7558
8200 Walnut Hill Ln 75231
Richland College 972-238-6100
12800 Abrams Rd 75243
St. Marks S of Texas 800/1-12
10600 Preston Rd 75230 214-346-8000
Arnold Holtberg, hdmstr. Fax 346-8002
Shelton S 800/PK-12
15720 Hillcrest Rd 75248 972-774-1772
Dr. Joyce Pickering, dir. Fax 991-3977
Southeastern Career Institute Post-Sec.
12005 Ford Rd Ste 100 75234 972-385-1446
Southern Methodist University Post-Sec.
PO Box 750181 75275 214-768-2000
Southwest Adventist Jr. Academy 100/K-10
1600 Bonnie View Rd 75203 214-948-1666
Fax 948-1668
Texas A&M Univ.-Baylor Coll. Dentistry Post-Sec.
3302 Gaston Ave 75246 214-828-8100
Texas Barber Colleges & Hairstyling Sch 214-943-7255
5148 S Lancaster Rd Ste A 75241
The Criswell College 800-899-0012
4010 Gaston Ave 75246
Tyler Street Christian Academy 200/PK-12
915 W 9th St 75208 214-941-9717
Karen Egger, supt. Fax 941-0324
Ultrasound Diagnostic School 214-638-6400
2998 N Stemmons Fwy # B 75247
University of Texas S.W. Medical Center 214-648-3111
5323 Harry Hines Blvd 75390
Ursuline Academy 800/9-12
4900 Walnut Hill Ln 75229 469-232-1800
Elizabeth Bourgeois, prin. Fax 232-1836
Velma B's Beauty Academy 214-942-1541
1511 S Ewing Ave 75216
Wade College Dallas Market Center 800-624-4850
PO Box 421149 75342
Westwood College of Technology Post-Sec.
8390 LBJ Fwy 75243 214-570-0100

White Rock Montessori 200/PK-10
1601 Oates Dr 75228 214-324-5580
Sue Henry, prin. Fax 324-5671
Winston S 200/1-12
5707 Royal Ln 75229 214-691-6950
Pam Murfin, hdmstr. Fax 691-1509
Yavneh Academy 50/9-12
12324 Merit Dr 75251 214-295-3500
Donald O'Quinn, prin. Fax 788-1947

Danbury, Brazoria, Pop. 1,646
Danbury ISD 700/PK-12
PO Box 378 77534 979-922-1218
Eric Grimmett, supt. Fax 922-8246
www.danbury.isd.esc4.net
Danbury HS 200/9-12
PO Box 377 77534 979-922-1226
Gordon Smith, prin. Fax 922-1051
Danbury MS 100/7-8
PO Box 586 77534 979-922-1226
Gordon Smith, prin. Fax 922-1051

Dawson, Navarro, Pop. 878
Dawson ISD 500/PK-12
199 N School Ave 76639 254-578-1031
Hugh Ellis, supt. Fax 578-1721
www.dawsonisd.org/
Dawson HS 200/7-12
199 N School Ave 76639 254-578-1031
Ronnie Shiflet, prin. Fax 578-1721

Dayton, Liberty, Pop. 6,363
Dayton ISD 4,300/PK-12
PO Box 248 77535 936-258-2667
Greg Hayman, supt. Fax 258-5616
www.daytonisd.net/
Dayton HS 1,400/9-12
PO Box 248 77535 936-258-2510
Laurie Elliott, prin. Fax 257-4047
Wilson JHS 900/7-8
PO Box 248 77535 936-258-2309
Oran Hamilton, prin. Fax 257-4109

Decatur, Wise, Pop. 5,743
Decatur ISD 2,800/PK-12
501 E Collins St 76234 940-627-3215
Gerard Gindt Ed.D., supt. Fax 627-3141
www.decatur.esc11.net
Decatur HS 900/9-12
1201 W Thompson St 76234 940-627-2155
Melinda Reeves, prin. Fax 627-3669
Decatur MS 500/7-8
1200 W Eagle Dr 76234 940-627-2384
Linda Whiddon, prin. Fax 627-2497

Deer Park, Harris, Pop. 28,844
Deer Park ISD 11,100/PK-12
203 Ivy Ave 77536 832-668-7000
Arnold Adair, supt. Fax 930-1945
www.dpisd.org
Bonnette JHS 700/6-8
5010 W Pasadena Blvd 77536 832-668-7700
Judy Connors, prin. Fax 930-4756
Deer Park HS - North Campus 9-9
402 Ivy Ave 77536 832-668-7300
Grover Belcher, prin. Fax 930-4840
Deer Park HS - South Campus 2,600/10-12
710 W San Augustine St 77536 832-668-7200
Ronda Kouba, prin. Fax 930-4894
Deer Park JHS 800/6-8
410 E 9th St 77536 832-668-7500
Victor White, prin. Fax 930-4726
Other Schools – See Pasadena

De Kalb, Bowie, Pop. 1,781
De Kalb ISD 900/PK-12
101 Maple St 75559 903-667-2566
James Brewer, supt. Fax 667-3791
www.dekalbisd.net
De Kalb HS 300/9-12
101 Maple St 75559 903-667-2422
Stephanie Sparks, prin. Fax 667-4086
De Kalb MS 300/5-8
101 Maple St 75559 903-667-2834
Donna McDaniel, prin. Fax 667-5509

De Leon, Comanche, Pop. 2,346
De Leon ISD 700/PK-12
601 S Houston St 76444 254-893-5095
Mary Jane Atkins, supt. Fax 893-3101
www.deleon.esc14.net
De Leon HS 200/9-12
601 S Houston St 76444 254-893-6222
Mark Lewis, prin. Fax 893-4985
Perkins MS 200/6-8
601 S Houston St 76444 254-893-6111
Scott Carlisle, prin. Fax 893-7918

Dell City, Hudspeth, Pop. 397
Dell City ISD 100/K-12
PO Box 37 79837 915-964-2663
Tanya Lewis, supt. Fax 964-2473
Dell City S 100/K-12
PO Box 37 79837 915-964-2495
Tanya Lewis, prin. Fax 964-2473

Del Rio, Val Verde, Pop. 35,136
San Felipe-Del Rio Consolidated ISD 9,800/PK-12
PO Box 428002 78842 830-778-4000
Roberto Fernandez, supt. Fax 774-9892
www.sfdr-cisd.org
Del Rio Freshman S 700/9-9
PO Box 428002 78842 830-778-4400
Jorge Garza, prin. Fax 774-9873
Del Rio HS 1,800/10-12
PO Box 428002 78842 830-778-4329
Jorge Garza, prin. Fax 774-9320
Del Rio MS 1,000/7-8
PO Box 428002 78842 830-778-4530
Alfonso Ozuna, prin. Fax 778-4550

Amistad Christian HS 50/9-12
901 Amistad Blvd 78840 830-775-0870
Lynn Garcia, admin. Fax 774-0020

Del Valle, Travis
Del Valle ISD 7,600/PK-12
5301 Ross Rd 78617 512-386-3000
Bernard Blanchard, supt. Fax 386-3015
www.del-valle.k12.tx.us

Del Valle HS | 1,800/9-12
5201 Ross Rd 78617 | 512-386-3200
Jean MacInnis, prin. | Fax 386-3205
Del Valle JHS | 600/7-8
5500 Ross Rd 78617 | 512-386-3400
Kenneth Storm, prin. | Fax 386-3405
Other Schools – See Austin

Denison, Grayson, Pop. 23,335
Denison ISD | 4,600/PK-12
1201 S Rusk Ave 75020 | 903-462-7000
Henry Scott, supt. | Fax 462-7002
denisonisd.net
Denison HS | 1,300/9-12
1901 S Mirick Ave 75020 | 903-462-7125
Cavin Boettger, prin. | Fax 462-7217
McDaniel MS | 1,100/6-8
400 S Lillis Ln 75020 | 903-462-7200
Alvis Dunlap, prin. | Fax 462-7328

Grayson County College | Post-Sec.
6101 Grayson Dr 75020 | 903-465-6030

Denton, Denton, Pop. 93,435
Denton ISD | 15,800/PK-12
1307 N Locust St 76201 | 940-369-0000
Dr. Ray Braswell, supt. | Fax 369-4982
www.dentonisd.org
Calhoun MS | 700/6-8
709 W Congress St 76201 | 940-369-2400
Anthony Sims, prin. | Fax 369-4939
Denton HS | 1,900/9-12
1007 Fulton St 76201 | 940-369-2000
Darrell Muncy, prin. | Fax 369-4953
Guyer HS | 9-12
7501 Teasley Ln 76210 | 940-369-1000
Barbara Fischer, prin. | Fax 369-4965
LaGrone Advanced Technology Complex | Vo/Tech
1504 Long Rd 76207 | 940-369-4850
Marty Thompson, dean | Fax 369-4971
McMath MS | 1,000/6-8
1900 Jason Dr 76205 | 940-369-3300
Dr. Debra Nobles, prin. | Fax 369-4946
Ryan HS | 2,000/9-12
5101 E McKinney St 76208 | 940-369-3000
Vernon Reeves, prin. | Fax 369-4960
Strickland MS | 900/6-8
324 E Windsor Dr 76209 | 940-369-4200
Mike Vance, prin. | Fax 369-4950
Other Schools – See Aubrey, Corinth

Denton Calvary Academy | 200/1-12
PO Box 2414 76202 | 940-320-1944
Eddie Baca, admin. | Fax 591-9311
International Business College | Post-Sec.
2006 W University Dr 76201 | 940-380-0024
Selwyn S | 300/PK-12
3333 W University Dr 76207 | 940-382-6771
Robert M. Estes, hdmstr. | Fax 383-0704
Texas Woman's University | Post-Sec.
PO Box 425589 76204 | 940-898-2000
University of North Texas | Post-Sec.
PO Box 305309 76203 | 940-565-2000

Denver City, Yoakum, Pop. 3,923
Denver City ISD | 1,300/PK-12
501 Mustang Dr 79323 | 806-592-5900
Howard Pollard, supt. | Fax 592-5909
www.dcisd.org
Denver City HS | 400/9-12
601 Mustang Dr 79323 | 806-592-5950
Gary Davis, prin. | Fax 592-5959
Gravitt JHS | 300/6-8
419 Mustang Dr 79323 | 806-592-5940
Howard Wright, prin. | Fax 592-5949

De Soto, Dallas, Pop. 39,440
De Soto ISD | 7,700/PK-12
200 E Belt Line Rd, | 972-223-6666
Alton Frailey, supt. | Fax 274-8029
www.desotoisd.org
De Soto East JHS | 700/7-8
601 E Belt Line Rd, | 972-223-0690
Melvlyn Lowe, prin. | Fax 274-8156
De Soto HS Freshman Campus | 700/9
620 S Westmoreland Rd, | 972-274-1818
Jim Yakubovsky, prin. | Fax 274-2501
De Soto SHS | 1,600/10-12
600 Eagle Dr, | 972-230-0726
Aubrey Todd, prin. | Fax 274-8115
De Soto West JHS | 700/7-8
800 N Westmoreland Rd, | 972-230-1820
Skip McCambridge, prin. | Fax 274-8183

Canterbury Episcopal S | 300/K-12
1708 N Westmoreland Rd, | 972-572-7200
Dick Cadigan, prin. | Fax 572-7400

Detroit, Red River, Pop. 752
Detroit ISD | 500/PK-12
110 E Garner St 75436 | 903-674-6131
Darrel Adkison, supt. | Fax 674-2478
detroitisd.esc8.net/
Detroit HS | 100/9-12
110 E Garner St 75436 | 903-674-2646
Kathy Garrison, prin. | Fax 674-2815
Detroit JHS | 100/6-8
110 E Garner St 75436 | 903-674-2646
Pat Travis, prin. | Fax 674-2206

Devers, Liberty, Pop. 432
Devers ISD | 100/PK-8
PO Box 488 77538 | 936-549-7135
Danny J. Grimes, supt. | Fax 549-7595
Devers JHS, PO Box 488 77538 | 6-8
Danny Grimes, prin. | 936-549-7135

Devine, Medina, Pop. 4,324
Devine ISD | 2,000/PK-12
205 W College Ave 78016 | 830-663-3611
Rickey Williams, supt. | Fax 663-6706
www.devineisd.org
Devine HS | 600/9-12
1225 W Hondo Ave 78016 | 830-663-6780
Don Beck, prin. | Fax 663-6792
Devine MS | 500/6-8
400 Cardinal Dr 78016 | 830-663-6760
Lori Marek, prin. | Fax 663-6769

Deweyville, Newton, Pop. 1,218
Deweyville ISD | 800/PK-12
PO Box 259 77614 | 409-746-2731
Rick Summers, supt. | Fax 746-3360
www.esc05.k12.tx.us/dewisd/
Deweyville HS | 200/9-12
PO Box 259 77614 | 409-746-3173
Richard Sessions, prin. | Fax 746-9343
Deweyville MS | 200/6-8
PO Box 109 77614 | 409-746-2924
Darryl Dans, prin. | Fax 746-2753

D Hanis, Medina
D'Hanis ISD | 200/K-12
PO Box 307 78850 | 830-363-7216
Pam Seipp, supt. | Fax 363-7390
dhanis.tx.schoolwebpages.com
D'Hanis MSHS | 200/6-12
PO Box 307 78850 | 830-363-7216
Michael Poppell, prin. | Fax 363-7390

Diana, Upshur
New Diana ISD | 800/K-12
PO Box 26 75640 | 903-663-8000
Patrick T. Clark, supt. | Fax 663-9565
www.newdianaisd.net/
New Diana HS | 300/9-12
PO Box 26 75640 | 903-663-8001
Stevie Ford, prin. | Fax 663-2200
New Diana MS | 200/6-8
PO Box 26 75640 | 903-663-8002
Connie Robinson, prin. | Fax 663-1812

Diboll, Angelina, Pop. 5,439
Diboll ISD | 1,900/PK-12
PO Box 550 75941 | 936-829-4718
Bobby Baker, supt. | Fax 829-5558
www.dibollisd.com
Diboll HS | 500/9-12
1000 Lumberjack St 75941 | 936-829-5626
Brent Hawkins, prin. | Fax 829-5708
Diboll JHS | 400/6-8
403 Dennis St 75941 | 936-829-5225
Mark Kettering, prin. | Fax 829-5848

Dickinson, Galveston, Pop. 17,847
Dickinson ISD | 6,000/PK-12
PO Box Z 77539 | 281-229-6000
Leland Williams, supt. | Fax 229-6011
www.dickinsonisd.org
Dickinson HS | 1,600/9-12
3800 Baker Dr 77539 | 281-229-6400
Michael La Touche, prin. | Fax 229-6401
McAdams JHS | 1,000/7-8
4007 Video St 77539 | 281-229-7100
Ernest Hubert, prin. | Fax 229-7101

Living Faith Academy | 100/K-12
3700 Deats Rd 77539 | 281-309-0799
Dylis Mulder, prin. | Fax 309-0610
Pine Drive Christian S | 400/PK-12
705 FM 517 Rd E 77539 | 281-534-4881
Larry Bowles, admin. | Fax 534-4318

Dilley, Frio, Pop. 4,203
Dilley ISD | 800/PK-12
245 W FM 117 78017 | 830-965-1912
Jack Seals, supt. | Fax 965-4069
www.dilleyisd.net
Dilley HS | 200/9-12
245 W FM 117 78017 | 830-965-1814
David Kyser, prin. | Fax 965-1276
Harper MS | 200/6-8
245 W FM 117 78017 | 830-965-2195
Nobert Rodriquez, prin. | Fax 965-2171

Dime Box, Lee
Dime Box ISD | 200/PK-12
PO Box 157 77853 | 979-884-2324
Clayton Waits, supt. | Fax 884-0106
www.esc13.net/dimebox/
Dime Box S | 200/PK-12
PO Box 157 77853 | 979-884-3366
Vivian Bage, prin. | Fax 884-0106

Dimmitt, Castro, Pop. 4,142
Dimmitt ISD | 1,200/PK-12
608 W Halsell St 79027 | 806-647-3101
Charles Miller, supt. | Fax 647-5433
www.dimmittisd.net
Dimmitt HS | 300/9-12
1505 Western Cir 79027 | 806-647-3105
George Rasor, prin. | Fax 647-5795
Dimmitt MS | 400/4-8
805 W Jones St 79027 | 806-647-3108
Michael Graham, prin. | Fax 647-2996

Dodd City, Fannin, Pop. 431
Dodd City ISD | 300/PK-12
602 N Main St 75438 | 903-583-7585
Craig Reed, supt. | Fax 583-9545
doddcity.ednet10.net
Dodd City S | 300/PK-12
602 N Main St 75438 | 903-583-7585
Lesia Bridges, prin. | Fax 583-9545

Donna, Hidalgo, Pop. 15,562
Donna ISD | 11,600/PK-12
116 N 10th St 78537 | 956-464-1600
Joe Gonzalez, supt. | Fax 464-1752
www.donnaisd.net
Donna SHS | 1,600/10-12
116 N 10th St 78537 | 956-464-1700
Fernando Castillo, prin. | Fax 464-1629
Sauceda MS | 6-8
116 N 10th St 78537 | 956-464-1360
Nancy Castillo, prin. | Fax 464-1349
Solis MS | 1,200/6-8
116 N 10th St 78537 | 956-464-1650
| Fax 464-1786
Todd 9th Grade Campus | 800/9-9
116 N 10th St 78537 | 956-464-1800
David C. Villarreal, prin. | Fax 464-1824
Veterans MS | 1,300/6-8
116 N 10th St 78537 | 956-464-1350
Jose Javier Villanueva, prin. | Fax 464-1356

Douglass, Nacogdoches
Douglass ISD | 400/PK-12
PO Box 38 75943 | 936-569-9804
Lowell McCuistion, supt. | Fax 569-9446
www.douglass.esc7.net

Douglass S | 400/PK-12
PO Box 38 75943 | 936-569-9804
Jay Tullos, prin. | Fax 569-9446

Dripping Springs, Hays, Pop. 1,645
Dripping Springs ISD | 3,500/PK-12
PO Box 479 78620 | 512-858-3100
Mary Ward, supt. | Fax 858-4232
www.dripping-springs.k12.tx.us/
Dripping Springs HS | 1,100/9-12
PO Box 479 78620 | 512-858-6400
Greg Jung, prin. | Fax 858-1656
Dripping Springs MS | 800/6-8
PO Box 479 78620 | 512-858-4902
Tyler Damron, prin. | Fax 858-7213

Driscoll, Nueces, Pop. 820
Driscoll ISD | 300/PK-8
PO Box 238 78351 | 361-387-7349
Ron Thomas, supt. | Fax 387-6088
www.driscollisd.esc2.net
Driscoll MS | 100/6-8
PO Box 238 78351 | 361-387-7349
Cynthia Garcia, prin. | Fax 387-6088

Dublin, Erath, Pop. 3,672
Dublin ISD | 1,300/PK-12
PO Box 169 76446 | 254-445-3341
Roy Neff, supt. | Fax 445-3345
www.dublin.k12.tx.us
Dublin HS | 400/9-12
PO Box 169 76446 | 254-445-0362
Vicky Stone, prin. | Fax 445-1706
Dublin JHS | 300/6-8
PO Box 169 76446 | 254-445-2555
John Grimland, prin. | Fax 445-2607

Dumas, Moore, Pop. 13,724
Dumas ISD | 4,100/PK-12
PO Box 615 79029 | 806-935-6461
Larry Appel, supt. | Fax 935-6275
www.dumas-k12.net/
Dumas HS | 1,100/9-12
PO Box 615 79029 | 806-935-4151
Bob Callahan, prin. | Fax 934-1433
Dumas JHS | 600/7-8
PO Box 615 79029 | 806-935-4155
Danny Potter, prin. | Fax 934-1434

Duncanville, Dallas, Pop. 35,670
Duncanville ISD | 11,100/PK-12
802 S Main St 75137 | 972-708-2000
Kenneth English, supt. | Fax 708-2020
www.duncanvilleisd.org
Byrd MS | 900/7-8
1040 W Wheatland Rd 75116 | 972-708-3400
Gabe Trujillo, prin. | Fax 708-3434
Duncanville HS | 2,500/9-12
900 W Camp Wisdom Rd 75116 | 972-708-3700
Mike Chrietzberg, prin. | Fax 708-3737
Reed MS | 1,000/7-8
530 E Freeman St 75116 | 972-708-3500
Andre Smith, prin. | Fax 708-3535
Other Schools – See Dallas

ChristWay Academy | 100/PK-12
419 N Cedar Ridge Dr 75116 | 972-296-6525
Daryl Johnston, admin. | Fax 780-7273
Masters Academy | 50/5-12
PO Box 381174 75138 | 972-780-2616
Elderine Wyrick, dir. | Fax 283-0296
State Beauty Academy | Post-Sec.
663 Oriole Blvd 75116 | 972-298-0100

Eagle Lake, Colorado, Pop. 3,696
Rice Consolidated ISD
Supt. — See Altair
Eagle Lake JHS | 100/6-8
600 Johnnie D Hutchins 77434 | 979-234-3501
Mike Keenon, prin. | Fax 234-5027

Eagle Pass, Maverick, Pop. 24,462
Eagle Pass ISD | 13,000/PK-12
1420 Eidson Rd 78852 | 830-773-5181
Jesus Sanchez, supt. | Fax 773-7252
Eagle Pass HS 9th-10th Grade Campus | 2,000/9-10
1420 Eidson Rd 78852 | 830-773-2381
Rudolph Bowles, prin. | Fax 758-1795
Eagle Pass JHS | 900/7-8
1420 Eidson Rd 78852 | 830-758-7037
Maria Sumpter, prin. | Fax 757-1278
Eagle Pass SHS CC Winn Campus | 1,400/11-12
1420 Eidson Rd 78852 | 830-757-0828
Jesus A. Diaz-Wever, prin. | Fax 757-3268
Memorial JHS | 1,100/7-8
1420 Eidson Rd 78852 | 830-758-7053
Oscar Castillon, prin. | Fax 773-8900

SW School of Business & Tech Careers | Post-Sec.
272 Commercial St 78852 | 830-773-1373

Early, Brown, Pop. 2,704
Early ISD | 1,300/PK-12
PO Box 3315, Brownwood TX 76803 | 325-646-7934
Brett A. Koch, supt. | Fax 646-9238
www.earlyisd.net/
Early HS | 400/9-12
PO Box 3315, Brownwood TX 76803 | 325-643-4593
Wes Beck, prin. | Fax 646-4061
Early MS | 300/6-8
PO Box 3315, Brownwood TX 76803 | 325-643-5665
Randy Lancaster, prin. | Fax 646-9972

Earth, Lamb, Pop. 1,096
Springlake-Earth ISD | 400/K-12
PO Box 130 79031 | 806-257-3310
Gary Bigham, supt. | Fax 257-3927
www.springlake-earth.org
Springlake HS | 100/9-12
PO Box 130 79031 | 806-257-3819
Robert Conkin, prin. | Fax 257-3370

East Bernard, Wharton, Pop. 1,544
East Bernard ISD | 900/PK-12
723 College St 77435 | 979-335-7519
Garland Calhoun, supt. | Fax 335-6561
www.ebisd.org/
East Bernard HS | 300/9-12
723 College St 77435 | 979-335-7519
Buck Wenglar, prin. | Fax 335-6085

East Bernard JHS — 300/5-8
723 College St 77435 — 979-335-7519
Emmett Tugwell, prin. — Fax 335-6085

Eastland, Eastland, Pop. 3,799
Eastland ISD — 1,200/PK-12
PO Box 31 76448 — 254-631-5120
Donald W. Hughes, supt. — Fax 631-5126
Eastland HS, PO Box 31 76448 — 400/9-12
Joel Lawson, prin. — 254-631-5000
Eastland MS, PO Box 31 76448 — 300/6-8
Rickie Pack, prin. — 254-631-5040

Ector, Fannin, Pop. 618
Ector ISD — 300/K-12
PO Box 128 75439 — 903-961-2355
Gary Bohannon, supt. — Fax 961-2110
ector.ednet10.net
Ector ISD — 100/7-12
PO Box 128 75439 — 903-961-2076
Shannon Baker, prin. — Fax 961-2356

Edcouch, Hidalgo, Pop. 4,165
Edcouch-Elsa ISD — 5,000/PK-12
PO Box 127 78538 — 956-262-6000
Michael Sandroussi, supt. — Fax 262-6032
www.eeisd.org
Other Schools – See Elsa

Eddy, McLennan, Pop. 1,113
Bruceville-Eddy ISD — 900/PK-12
1 Eagle Dr 76524 — 254-859-5832
Gary Herbert, supt. — Fax 859-4023
www.brucevilleeddyisd.net
Bruceville-Eddy HS — 200/10-12
1 Eagle Dr 76524 — 254-859-5525
Richard Kilgore, prin. — Fax 859-5001
Bruceville-Eddy MS, 1 Eagle Dr 76524 — 200/7-9
Mike Hawkins, prin. — 254-859-5525

Eden, Concho, Pop. 2,471
Eden Consolidated ISD — 300/K-12
PO Box 988 76837 — 325-869-4121
Bill Alcorn, supt. — Fax 869-5210
Eden JSHS — 100/7-12
PO Box 988 76837 — 325-869-5180
Tim Siler, prin. — Fax 869-5023

Edgewood, Van Zandt, Pop. 1,404
Edgewood ISD — 900/PK-12
PO Box 6 75117 — 903-896-4332
Jack Shellnutt, supt. — Fax 896-7056
www.edgewood.esc7.net
Edgewood HS — 300/9-12
PO Box 6 75117 — 903-896-4856
Blake Cooper, prin. — Fax 896-1050
Edgewood MS — 200/6-8
PO Box 6 75117 — 903-896-1530
Terry Phillips, prin. — Fax 896-7056

Edinburg, Hidalgo, Pop. 55,302
Edinburg Consolidated ISD — 23,700/PK-12
PO Box 990 78540 — 956-289-2300
Eugenio Gutierrez, supt. — Fax 383-3576
www.ecisd.us/
Economedes HS — 2,100/9-12
PO Box 990 78540 — 956-385-3000
Anibal Gorena, prin. — Fax 385-3050
Edinburg HS — 2,100/9-12
PO Box 990 78540 — 956-289-2400
Maria Guerra, prin. — Fax 386-1225
Edinburg North HS — 1,900/9-12
PO Box 990 78540 — 956-316-7654
Ramiro Guerra, prin. — Fax 316-7712
Edinburg South MS — 900/7-8
PO Box 990 78540 — 956-316-7750
Hector Gonzalez, prin. — Fax 316-8817
Garza MS — 1,500/6-8
PO Box 990 78540 — 956-316-3100
Cipriano Pena, prin. — Fax 316-3109
Memorial MS — 900/7-8
PO Box 990 78540 — 956-316-7575
Ruben Gonzalez, prin. — Fax 316-7581

South Texas ISD
Supt. — See Mercedes
South Texas Business Educ &Tech Academy — 700/7-12
510 S Sugar Rd 78539 — 956-383-1684
Adan Farias, prin. — Fax 383-8544

Rio Grande Bible Institute — Post-Sec.
4300 S US Highway 281 78539 — 956-380-8100
University of Texas-Pan American — Post-Sec.
1201 W University Dr 78539 — 956-381-2011

Edna, Jackson, Pop. 5,838
Edna ISD — 1,500/PK-12
PO Box 919 77957 — 361-782-3573
Robert Wells, supt. — Fax 781-1002
www.ednaisd.org
Edna HS — 500/9-12
PO Box 919 77957 — 361-782-5255
Richard Wright, prin. — Fax 781-1014
Pumphrey JHS — 400/6-8
PO Box 919 77957 — 361-782-2351
Demetric Wells, prin. — Fax 781-1025

El Campo, Wharton, Pop. 10,842
El Campo ISD — 3,500/PK-12
700 W Norris St 77437 — 979-543-6771
Robert Mark Poole, supt. — Fax 543-1670
www.ecisd.org/
El Campo HS — 1,100/9-12
600 W Norris St 77437 — 979-543-6341
Diann Srubar, prin. — Fax 543-2528
El Campo MS — 800/6-8
1401 MLK Blvd 77437 — 979-543-6362
Rodney Montello, prin. — Fax 541-5210

Eldorado, Schleicher, Pop. 1,871
Schleicher County ISD — 600/PK-12
PO Box W 76936 — 325-853-2514
George Blanch, supt. — Fax 853-2695
www.scisd.net
Eldorado HS — 200/9-12
PO Box W 76936 — 325-853-2549
Bob Wanoreck, prin. — Fax 853-2710
Eldorado MS — 200/5-8
PO Box W 76936 — 325-853-3028
Kara Sue Garlitz, prin. — Fax 853-2895

Electra, Wichita, Pop. 3,055
Electra ISD — 600/PK-12
PO Box 231 76360 — 940-495-3683
Gary Nightingale, supt. — Fax 495-3945
www.electraisd.net
Electra HS — 200/9-12
400 E Roosevelt Ave 76360 — 940-495-2218
Nora Curry, prin. — Fax 495-3303
Electra JHS — 200/5-8
621 S Bailey St 76360 — 940-495-2533
Gene Jarvis, prin. — Fax 495-4636

Elgin, Bastrop, Pop. 7,218
Elgin ISD — 3,100/PK-12
PO Box 351 78621 — 512-281-3434
Bill Graves, supt. — Fax 281-5388
www.elginisd.org
Elgin HS — 900/9-12
PO Box 311 78621 — 512-281-3438
Roberto Vasquez, prin. — Fax 281-9804
Elgin MS — 700/6-8
902 W 2nd St 78621 — 512-281-3382
Ehrikka Hodge, prin. — Fax 281-9781

Elkhart, Anderson, Pop. 1,246
Elkhart ISD — 1,200/PK-12
301 E Parker 75839 — 903-764-2952
J. Glenn Hambrick, supt. — Fax 764-2466
Elkhart HS — 400/9-12
301 E Parker 75839 — 903-764-5161
Tim Ratcliff, prin. — Fax 764-2466
Elkhart MS — 300/6-8
301 E Parker 75839 — 903-764-2459
Ron Mays, prin. — Fax 764-2466

Slocum ISD — 400/PK-12
5765 E State Highway 294 75839 — 903-478-3624
Fred Fulton, supt. — Fax 478-3030
www.slocum.esc7.net
Slocum JSHS — 200/7-12
5765 E State Highway 294 75839 — 903-478-3624
Ronnie Shepperd, prin. — Fax 478-3030

Elmaton, Matagorda
Tidehaven ISD — 900/PK-12
PO Box 129 77440 — 361-588-6321
Tom Jones, supt. — Fax 588-7109
www.tidehavenisd.com
Tidehaven HS — 300/9-12
PO Box 159 77440 — 361-588-6810
Kathy Boyett, prin. — Fax 588-6966
Tidehaven IS — 200/6-8
PO Box 130 77440 — 361-588-6600
Debra Taska, prin. — Fax 588-6600

El Paso, El Paso, Pop. 584,113
Canutillo ISD — 4,800/PK-12
7965 Artcraft Rd 79932 — 915-877-7400
Charles Hart, supt. — Fax 877-7414
www.canutillo-isd.org
Other Schools – See Canutillo

Clint ISD — 8,700/PK-12
14521 Horizon Blvd 79928 — 915-926-4000
Ricardo Estrada, supt. — Fax 926-4009
www.clintweb.net
East Montana MS — 900/6-8
3490 Ascension Rd 79938 — 915-926-5200
Robert Mendoza, prin. — Fax 855-0821
Horizon HS — 900/9-12
14651 Horizon Blvd 79928 — 915-926-4200
Holly Fields, prin. — Fax 852-0357
Horizon MS — 6-8
14510 McMahon Ave 79928 — 915-926-4700
Josie Perez, prin. — Fax 852-9274
Mountain View HS — 1,000/9-12
14964 Greg Dr 79938 — 915-926-5000
Ramon Aguilar, prin. — Fax 855-2503
Other Schools – See Clint

El Paso ISD — 63,700/PK-12
PO Box 20100 79998 — 915-779-3781
Robert Ortega, supt. — Fax 779-6613
www.episd.org
Andress HS — 1,900/9-12
5400 Sun Valley Dr 79924 — 915-832-8600
James Anderson, prin. — Fax 757-6443
Austin HS — 1,400/9-12
3500 Memphis Ave 79930 — 915-587-2000
Archangelo Pokluda, prin. — Fax 566-7360
Bassett MS — 1,000/6-8
4400 Elm St 79930 — 915-231-2260
Oscar Santaella, prin. — Fax 565-1562
Bowie HS — 1,200/9-12
801 S San Marcial St 79905 — 915-496-8200
Lionel Rubio, prin. — Fax 532-1918
Burges HS — 1,400/9-12
7800 Edgemere Blvd 79925 — 915-780-1100
Ernest Watts, prin. — Fax 771-6914
Canyon Hills MS — 1,000/6-8
8930 Eclipse St 79904 — 915-231-2240
Zack Gray, prin. — Fax 757-8067
Center for Career & Technology Education — Vo/Tech
1170 N Walnut St 79930 — 915-545-5900
Eric Winkelman, prin. — Fax 544-5976
Chapin HS — 1,600/9-12
7000 Dyer St 79904 — 915-832-6730
Dr. Carla Gonzales, prin. — Fax 565-9716
Charles MS — 600/6-8
4909 Trojan Dr 79924 — 915-849-3940
Jan Cieslik, prin. — Fax 821-0505
Cordova MS — 1,000/6-8
2231 Arizona Ave 79930 — 915-546-9012
Patsy Smith, prin. — Fax 577-0848
Coronado HS — 2,500/9-12
100 Champions Pl 79912 — 915-834-2460
Maria Morales, prin. — Fax 587-6458
El Paso HS — 1,100/9-12
800 E Schuster Ave 79902 — 915-496-8300
John Roskosky, prin. — Fax 532-2008
Franklin HS — 2,600/9-12
900 N Resler Dr 79912 — 915-832-6600
Carla Gasway, prin. — Fax 587-4094
Guillen MS — 1,000/6-8
900 S Cotton St 79901 — 915-496-4620
Rosa Lovelace, prin. — Fax 532-1143
Henderson MS — 1,100/6-8
5505 Robert Alva Ave 79905 — 915-887-3080
Lydia Muniz, prin. — Fax 772-3425

Hornedo MS — 1,700/6-8
825 E Redd Rd 79912 — 915-231-2200
Victoria York, prin. — Fax 587-5059
Irvin HS — 1,700/9-12
9465 Roanoke Dr 79924 — 915-587-3500
Mark Rupcich, prin. — Fax 757-6450
Jefferson HS — 1,100/9-12
4700 Alameda Ave 79905 — 915-496-8010
Samuel Villarreal, prin. — Fax 532-2033
Lincoln MS — 1,200/6-8
500 Mulberry Ave 79932 — 915-231-2180
Sandy Whitney, prin. — Fax 581-1371
Magoffin MS — 800/6-8
4931 Hercules Ave 79904 — 915-231-2160
Ione Grimm, prin. — Fax 759-0515
Morehead MS — 1,200/6-8
5625 Confetti Dr 79912 — 915-231-2140
James Lamonica, prin. — Fax 587-5355
Occupational Center — Vo/Tech
5300 Warriors Dr 79932 — 915-587-9680
Toni Bowermaster, prin. — Fax 584-2940
Richardson MS — 800/6-8
11350 Loma Franklin Dr 79934 — 915-822-8829
Dianne Jones, prin. — Fax 822-8812
Ross MS — 800/6-8
6101 Hughey Cir 79925 — 915-887-3060
John Tanner, prin. — Fax 771-6792
Silva Health Magnet HS — 700/9-12
121 Val Verde St 79905 — 915-496-8100
Sam Villarreal, prin. — Fax 533-3695
Sunset HS — 200/9-12
2300 Murchison 79930 — 915-543-6000
Vera Cancellare, prin. — Fax 545-2836
Terrace Hills MS — 700/6-8
4835 Blossom Ave 79924 — 915-231-2120
Milton Jones, prin. — Fax 759-0615
Wiggs MS — 800/6-8
1300 Circle Dr 79902 — 915-231-2100
Armando Aguirre, prin. — Fax 533-2902
San Jacinto Adult Learning Center — Adult
1216 N Olive Ave 79901 — 915-533-9072
Blanca Andrade, admin. — Fax 544-7163

Socorro ISD — 32,300/PK-12
PO Box 292800 79929 — 915-937-0000
Dr. Robert J. Duron, supt. — Fax 860-7137
www.sisd.net
Americas HS — 2,900/9-12
12101 Pellicano Dr 79936 — 915-937-2800
Mary Ross, prin. — Fax 856-6898
Clarke MS — 1,300/6-8
1515 Bob Hope Dr 79936 — 915-937-5600
Bonnie Gonzalez, prin. — Fax 857-3765
Ensor MS — 700/5-8
13600 Ryderwood Ave 79928 — 915-937-6000
Rosa Hood, prin. — Fax 851-7590
Montwood HS — 2,700/9-12
12000 Montwood Dr 79936 — 915-937-2400
Juni Matthews, prin. — Fax 849-2077
Montwood MS — 900/6-8
11710 Pebble Hills Blvd 79936 — 915-937-5800
Libby Tidwell, prin. — Fax 856-9909
Sanchez MS — 900/6-8
321 N Rio Vista Rd 79927 — 915-872-7000
Clarise Jones, prin. — Fax 859-6636
Slider MS — 1,100/6-8
11700 School Ln 79936 — 915-937-5400
Mitchell Ferguson, prin. — Fax 857-5804
Socorro HS — 2,700/9-12
10150 Alameda Ave 79927 — 915-937-2000
Oscar Troncoso, prin. — Fax 859-0206
Socorro MS — 800/6-8
321 Bovee Rd 79927 — 915-937-5000
David Pena, prin. — Fax 858-2672
Sun Ridge MS — 500/6-8
2210 Sun Country Dr 79938 — 915-937-5600
Joe Keith, prin. — Fax 851-7730

Ysleta ISD — 46,200/PK-12
9600 Sims Dr 79925 — 915-434-0000
Hector Montenegro, supt. — Fax 591-4144
www.yisd.net
Bel Air HS — 2,300/9-12
731 N Yarbrough Dr 79915 — 915-434-2000
Lionel Nava, prin. — Fax 593-6110
Camino Real MS — 700/6-8
9393 Alameda Ave 79907 — 915-434-4300
Dolores Chaparro, prin. — Fax 858-3743
Del Valle HS — 1,900/9-12
950 Bordeaux Dr 79907 — 915-434-3000
Paul Pearson, prin. — Fax 858-1427
Desert View MS — 600/7-8
1641 Billie Marie Dr 79936 — 915-434-5300
Ricardo Lopez, prin. — Fax 591-9327
Eastwood HS — 2,100/9-12
2430 Mcrae Blvd 79925 — 915-434-4000
Frank Burton, prin. — Fax 594-8014
Eastwood MS — 800/7-8
2612 Chaswood St 79935 — 915-434-4300
Barbara Trousdale, prin. — Fax 591-9426
Hanks HS — 2,400/9-12
2001 N Lee Trevino Dr 79936 — 915-434-5000
Dr. Eileen Wade, prin. — Fax 598-9621
Hillcrest MS — 700/7-8
8040 Yermoland Dr 79907 — 915-434-2200
Paul Covey, prin. — Fax 591-9439
Indian Ridge MS — 600/7-8
11201 Pebble Hills Blvd 79936 — 915-434-5400
Grace Martinez, prin. — Fax 591-9447
Parkland HS — 1,200/9-12
5932 Quail Ave 79924 — 915-434-6000
Miles Hume, prin. — Fax 434-6291
Parkland MS — 700/7-8
6045 Nova Way 79924 — 915-434-6300
Roger Parks, prin. — Fax 757-6608
Ranchland Hills MS — 500/7-8
7615 Yuma Dr 79915 — 915-434-2300
Felipe de Jesus Barraza, prin. — Fax 592-0036
Rio Bravo MS — 400/6-8
525 Greggerson Dr 79907 — 915-434-8400
Michael Martinez, prin. — Fax 872-0269
Riverside HS — 1,400/9-12
301 Midway Dr 79915 — 915-434-7000
Ismael Villafane, prin. — Fax 779-6983
Riverside MS — 700/7-8
7615 Mimosa Ave 79915 — 915-434-7300
James Mesta, prin. — Fax 772-7549
Valley View MS — 700/7-8
8660 N Loop Dr 79907 — 915-434-3300
Victor Montes, prin. — Fax 858-3615

Ysleta HS — 1,900/9-12
  8600 Alameda Ave 79907 — 915-434-8000
  Gerard Lee, prin. — Fax 858-3299
Ysleta MS — 600/6-8
  8691 Independence Dr 79907 — 915-434-8200
  Irene Medina, prin. — Fax 858-0261

Bethel Temple Christian S — 200/PK-12
  6301 Alabama St 79904 — 915-565-2222
  Marsha Hodge-Cardenas, admin. — Fax 565-2223
Border Institute of Technology — Post-Sec.
  9611 Acer Ave 79925 — 915-593-7328
Business Skills Institute — Post-Sec.
  7850 Paseo Del Norte #216 79912 — 915-845-7772
Career Centers of Texas — Post-Sec.
  8360 Burnham Rd Ste 100 79907 — 915-595-1935
Cathedral HS — 700/9-12
  1309 N Stanton St 79902 — 915-532-3238
  Sam Govea, prin. — Fax 533-8248
Computer Career Center — Post-Sec.
  6101 Montana Ave 79925 — 915-779-8031
David L. Carrasco Job Corps Center — Post-Sec.
  11155 Gateway Blvd W 79935 — 915-594-0022
El Paso Community College — Post-Sec.
  PO Box 20500 79998 — 915-831-2000
El Paso Country Day S — 200/PK-12
  220 E Cliff Dr 79902 — 915-533-4492
  Rose Ann Martinez, prin. — Fax 533-9626
Faith Christian Academy — 500/K-12
  8960 Escobar Dr 79907 — 915-594-3305
  Cesar Ramirez, prin. — Fax 593-5474
Father Yermo HS — 100/9-12
  250 Washington St 79905 — 915-533-3185
  Sr. Elia Hernandez, prin. — Fax 544-0738
Immanuel Christian S — 700/PK-12
  1201 Hawkins Blvd 79925 — 915-778-6160
  Donene O'Dell, admin. — Fax 772-8207
International Business College — Post-Sec.
  5700 Cromo Dr 79912 — 915-842-0422
International Business College — Post-Sec.
  1155 N Zaragoza Rd 79907 — 915-859-3986
Jesus Chapel S — 200/K-12
  10200 Album Ave 79925 — 915-593-1153
  Alba Wilcox, prin. — Fax 593-1113
Loretto Academy — 500/6-12
  1300 Hardaway St 79903 — 915-566-8400
  Abe Ramirez, prin. — Fax 564-0563
North Loop Christian Academy — 100/K-12
  8617 N Loop Dr 79907 — 915-859-9435
  Mary Greenup, prin. — Fax 872-9435
Patterson Institute — 400/9-12
  517 S Florence St 79901 — 915-533-8286
  Hector Lachica, prin. — Fax 533-5236
Pipo Academy of Hair Design — Post-Sec.
  3000 Pershing Dr 79903 — 915-565-3491
Radford S — 100/PK-12
  2001 Radford St 79903 — 915-565-2737
Tri-State Cosmetology Institute — Post-Sec.
  3910 Doniphan Dr Ste C 79922 — 915-585-8777
Tri-State Cosmetology Institute — Post-Sec.
  6800 Gateway Blvd E Ste 4A 79915 — 915-778-1741
University of Texas at El Paso — Post-Sec.
  500 W University Ave 79968 — 915-747-5000
Western Technical College — Post-Sec.
  9624 Plaza Cir 79927 — 915-760-8123
Western Technical College — Post-Sec.
  9451 Diana Dr 79924 — 915-566-9621

Elsa, Hidalgo, Pop. 6,174
Edcouch-Elsa ISD
  Supt. — See Edcouch
Edcouch-Elsa HS — 1,400/9-12
  N Yellowjacket Dr 78543 — 956-262-6074
  Carmen Garcia, prin. — Fax 262-6060
Truan JHS — 700/7-8
  E 9th St 78543 — 956-262-6082
  Fred Aguilar, prin. — Fax 262-6079

Elysian Fields, Harrison
Elysian Fields ISD — 1,000/PK-12
  PO Box 120 75642 — 903-633-2420
  Dr. Bob Browning, supt. — Fax 633-2498
  www.elysian-fields.k12.tx.us/
Elysian Fields HS — 400/9-12
  PO Box 120 75642 — 903-633-2455
  David Carter, prin. — Fax 633-2498
Elysian Fields JHS — 200/6-8
  PO Box 120 75642 — 903-633-2306
  Maynard Chapman, prin. — Fax 633-2326

Emory, Rains, Pop. 1,213
Rains ISD — 1,600/PK-12
  PO Box 247 75440 — 903-473-2222
  David Seago, supt. — Fax 473-3053
  www.rains.k12.tx.us/
Rains HS — 500/9-12
  PO Box 247 75440 — 903-473-2222
  Steve Steadham, prin. — Fax 473-5584
Rains JHS — 400/6-8
  PO Box 247 75440 — 903-473-2222
  Denise Flagg, prin. — Fax 473-5162

Ennis, Ellis, Pop. 18,319
Ennis ISD — 5,300/PK-12
  PO Box 1420 75120 — 972-875-9027
  Mike Harper, supt. — Fax 875-8667
  www.ednet10.net/ennis/
Ennis HS — 1,500/9-12
  1405 W Lake Bardwell Dr 75119 — 972-875-9011
  John Doslich, prin. — Fax 875-7027
Ennis JHS — 800/7-8
  501 N Gaines St 75119 — 972-875-3779
  Floyd Tolston, prin. — Fax 875-1433

St. John S — 300/K-12
  701 S Paris St 75119 — 972-878-5411
  Christopher Rebuck, prin. — Fax 875-2226

Era, Cooke
Era ISD — 200/K-12
  PO Box 98 76238 — 940-665-5961
  Jeremy Thompson, supt. — Fax 665-5311
  www.eraisd.net
Era JSHS — 200/6-12
  PO Box 98 76238 — 940-665-5961
  Jerry Skelton, prin. — Fax 665-5311

Euless, Tarrant, Pop. 50,118
Hurst-Euless-Bedford ISD
  Supt. — See Bedford

Central JHS — 900/7-9
  3191 W Pipeline Rd 76040 — 817-354-3350
  Dr. June Jacoby, prin. — Fax 354-3357
Euless JHS — 800/7-9
  306 Airport Fwy 76039 — 817-354-3340
  David Robbins, prin. — Fax 354-3345
Trinity SHS — 2,100/10-12
  500 N Industrial Blvd 76039 — 817-571-0271
  Andy Cargile, prin. — Fax 354-3322

Eustace, Henderson, Pop. 841
Eustace ISD — 1,500/PK-12
  PO Box 188 75124 — 903-425-5151
  Dr. Coy Holcombe, supt. — Fax 425-5147
  www.eustaceisd.net/
Eustace HS — 400/9-12
  PO Box 188 75124 — 903-425-5161
  Stan Sowers, prin. — Fax 425-5227
Eustace MS — 400/6-8
  PO Box 188 75124 — 903-425-5171
  Karyn Mullen, prin. — Fax 425-5146

Evadale, Jasper, Pop. 1,422
Evadale ISD — 400/PK-12
  PO Box 497 77615 — 409-276-1337
  David Kennedy, supt. — Fax 276-1908
  www.esc5.net/evadale/
Evadale HS — 100/9-12
  PO Box 497 77615 — 409-276-1337
  Byron Terrier, prin. — Fax 276-1050

Evant, Coryell, Pop. 392
Evant ISD — 300/PK-12
  PO Box 339 76525 — 254-471-5536
  Terry Pilgrim, supt. — Fax 471-5629
  www.centex-edu.net/evant/evant_i_s_d_home_page.htm
Evant S — 300/PK-12
  PO Box 339 76525 — 254-471-5536
  Linda Petty, prin. — Fax 471-5629

Everman, Tarrant, Pop. 5,849
Everman ISD — 3,200/PK-12
  608 Townley Dr 76140 — 817-568-3500
  Jeri Pfeifer, supt. — Fax 568-3508
  www.eisd.org
Everman HS — 1,100/9-12
  1 Bulldog Rd 76140 — 817-568-3550
  Kathy Culbertson, prin. — Fax 568-3570
Everman JHS — 600/7-8
  8901 Oak Grove Rd 76140 — 817-568-3530
  Anthony Price, prin. — Fax 568-3594

Fabens, El Paso, Pop. 5,599
Fabens ISD — 2,900/PK-12
  PO Box 697 79838 — 915-764-2025
  Poncho Garcia, supt. — Fax 764-3115
  www.fabensisd.net/
Fabens HS — 800/9-12
  PO Box 697 79838 — 915-764-2246
  Robert Sepulveda, prin. — Fax 764-4953
Fabens MS — 700/6-8
  PO Box 697 79838 — 915-764-7051
  Luis Liano, prin. — Fax 764-7263

Fairfield, Freestone, Pop. 3,398
Fairfield ISD — 1,700/PK-12
  615 Post Oak Rd 75840 — 903-389-2532
  Tony Price, supt. — Fax 389-7050
  www.fairfield.k12.tx.us
Fairfield HS — 500/9-12
  631 Post Oak Rd 75840 — 903-389-4177
  Von Wade, prin. — Fax 389-5453
Fairfield JHS — 500/5-8
  701 Post Oak Rd 75840 — 903-389-4210
  Elton Moore, prin. — Fax 389-5454

Falfurrias, Brooks, Pop. 5,100
Brooks County ISD — 1,600/PK-12
  PO Box 589 78355 — 361-325-5681
  Joe R. Trevino, supt. — Fax 325-1913
  www.bcisd.esc2.net
Falfurrias HS — 500/9-12
  PO Box 589 78355 — 361-325-5681
  Dr. Cynthia Perez, prin. — Fax 325-9284
Falfurrias JHS — 400/6-8
  PO Box 589 78355 — 361-325-5681
  Israel Escobar, prin. — Fax 325-2220

Falls City, Karnes, Pop. 589
Falls City ISD — 300/K-12
  PO Box 399 78113 — 830-254-3551
  Linda Bettin, supt. — Fax 254-3354
  www.fcisd.net/
Falls City JSHS — 200/7-12
  PO Box 399 78113 — 830-254-3551
  Sam Swierc, prin. — Fax 254-3354

Farmers Branch, Dallas, Pop. 27,025
Carrollton-Farmers Branch ISD
  Supt. — See Carrollton
Field MS — 1,000/6-8
  13551 Dennis Ln 75234 — 972-969-9500
  Lance Campbell, prin. — Fax 969-9528

Brookhaven College — Post-Sec.
  3939 Valley View Ln 75244 — 972-860-4700

Farmersville, Collin, Pop. 3,252
Farmersville ISD — 1,500/PK-12
  501A Highway 78 N 75442 — 972-782-6601
  Jeff Adams, supt. — Fax 784-7293
  www.farmersvilleisd.net/
Farmersville HS — 400/9-12
  499 Highway 78 N 75442 — 972-548-0576
  Scott Moss, prin. — Fax 529-3750
Farmersville JHS — 400/6-8
  501 Highway 78 N 75442 — 972-782-6202
  Wayne Callaway, prin. — Fax 782-7029

Farwell, Parmer, Pop. 1,331
Farwell ISD — 500/PK-12
  PO Box F 79325 — 806-481-3371
  Larry Gregory, supt. — Fax 481-9275
  www.farwellschools.org
Farwell HS — 100/9-12
  PO Box F 79325 — 806-481-3351
  Gary Cates, prin. — Fax 481-3531
Farwell JHS — 100/6-8
  PO Box F 79325 — 806-481-9260
  Jimmy Mace, prin. — Fax 481-9258

Fayetteville, Fayette, Pop. 264
Fayetteville ISD — 200/K-12
  PO Box 129 78940 — 979-378-4242
  Roy Green, supt. — Fax 378-4246
  www.esc13.net/fayetteville/fayetteville/home.htm
Fayetteville JSHS — 100/6-12
  PO Box 129 78940 — 979-378-4242
  Roy Green, supt. — Fax 378-4246

Ferris, Ellis, Pop. 2,275
Ferris ISD — 2,300/PK-12
  PO Box 459 75125 — 972-544-3858
  Michael Bodine, supt. — Fax 544-2784
  www.ferrisisd.org
Ferris HS — 600/9-12
  PO Box 461 75125 — 972-544-3737
  Jana Giles, prin. — Fax 544-2029
Ferris JHS — 300/7-8
  PO Box 459 75125 — 972-544-2279
  Marty Renner, prin. — Fax 544-2281

Flatonia, Fayette, Pop. 1,421
Flatonia ISD — 600/PK-12
  PO Box 189 78941 — 361-865-2941
  William Clements, supt. — Fax 865-2940
  www.esc13.net/flatonia/
Flatonia HS — 200/9-12
  PO Box 189 78941 — 361-865-2944
  Kathy Orsak, prin. — Fax 865-2940

Florence, Williamson, Pop. 1,110
Florence ISD — 1,000/PK-12
  PO Box 489 76527 — 254-793-2850
  John VanDever Ed.D., supt. — Fax 793-3055
  www.florence.k12.tx.us
Florence HS — 300/9-12
  PO Box 489 76527 — 254-793-2495
  Marilyn Hill, prin. — Fax 793-3784
Florence MS — 200/6-8
  PO Box 489 76527 — 254-793-2504
  Sheri Hawthorn, prin. — Fax 793-3054

Floresville, Wilson, Pop. 6,475
Floresville ISD — 3,500/PK-12
  908 10th St 78114 — 830-393-5300
  David Vinson, supt. — Fax 393-5399
  www.fisd.us
Floresville HS — 1,100/9-12
  1000 10th St 78114 — 830-393-5370
  Jim Davidson, prin. — Fax 393-5719
Floresville MS — 800/6-8
  2601 B St 78114 — 830-393-5350
  Sherri Bays, prin. — Fax 393-5339

Flower Mound, Denton, Pop. 60,621
Lewisville ISD — 43,500/PK-12
  1800 Timber Creek Rd 75028 — 972-539-1551
  Dr. Jerry Roy, supt. — Fax 539-0239
  www.lisd.net
Downing MS — 500/6-8
  5555 Bridlewood Blvd 75028 — 469-713-5962
  Lisa Lingren, prin. — Fax 350-1450
Flower Mound HS — 2,600/9-12
  3411 Peters Colony Rd 75022 — 972-539-6634
  Jack Clark, prin. — Fax 691-5826
Forestwood MS — 1,100/6-8
  2810 Morriss Rd 75028 — 469-713-5972
  Dave Tickner, prin. — Fax 350-2750
Lamar MS — 700/6-8
  4000 Timber Creek Rd 75028 — 469-713-5966
  Mike Fields, prin. — Fax 350-5050
Marcus HS — 2,500/9-12
  5707 Morriss Rd 75028 — 972-539-1591
  Kevin Rogers, prin. — Fax 355-7513
McKamy MS — 900/6-8
  2401 Old Settlers Rd 75022 — 469-713-5991
  Gary Shafferman, prin. — Fax 350-3250
Shadow Ridge MS — 6-8
  2050 Aberdeen Dr 75028 — 469-713-5984
  Gary Goldsmith, prin. — Fax 350-1550
Other Schools – See Carrollton, Highland Village, Lewisville, The Colony

Floydada, Floyd, Pop. 3,433
Floydada ISD — 1,000/PK-12
  226 W California St 79235 — 806-983-3498
  Jerry Vaughn, supt. — Fax 983-5739
  www.floydadaisd.esc17.net
Floydada HS — 300/9-12
  618 Whirlwind Alley 79235 — 806-983-4970
  Wayne Morren, prin. — Fax 983-5739
Floydada MS — 200/6-8
  910 S 5th St 79235 — 806-983-2161
  Jim Bob Hobbs, prin. — Fax 983-5739

Follett, Lipscomb, Pop. 412
Follett ISD — 200/K-12
  PO Box 28 79034 — 806-653-2301
  Mollie Howell, supt. — Fax 653-2036
  www.follettisd.net
Follett S — 200/K-12
  PO Box 28 79034 — 806-653-4241
  Jeff Northern, prin. — Fax 653-2036

Forestburg, Montague
Forestburg ISD — 100/K-12
  PO Box 415 76239 — 940-964-2323
  Dr. Fonda Huneycutt, supt. — Fax 964-2531
  www.nortexinfo.net/fbisd/
Forestburg S — 100/K-12
  PO Box 415 76239 — 940-964-2323
  Dr. Sid Brannan, prin. — Fax 964-2531

Forney, Kaufman, Pop. 7,565
Forney ISD — 3,700/K-12
  600 S Bois d Arc St 75126 — 972-564-4055
  Michael Smith, supt. — Fax 564-7007
  www.forney-isd.org
Forney HS — 900/9-12
  800 Fm 741 75126 — 972-564-3890
  Bobby Milliorn, prin. — Fax 564-5616
Forney MS — 600/7-8
  811 S Bois d Arc St 75126 — 972-564-3967
  Leslie Mauk, prin. — Fax 564-7022

Forsan, Howard, Pop. 221
Forsan ISD — 700/K-12
  PO Box A 79733 — 432-457-2223
  Randy Johnson, supt. — Fax 457-2225
  forsan.esc18.net

Forsan JSHS 400/6-12
PO Box A 79733 432-457-2223
Keith Stone, prin. Fax 457-2225

Fort Davis, Jeff Davis
Ft. Davis ISD 300/PK-12
PO Box 1339 79734 432-426-4440
Robert Sanford, supt. Fax 426-3841
fdisd.esc18.net/
Fort Davis JSHS 100/7-12
PO Box 1339 79734 432-426-4444
David Rueda, prin. Fax 426-4449

Fort Hancock, Hudspeth
Fort Hancock ISD 200/K-12
PO Box 98 79839 915-769-3811
Jose Franco, supt. Fax 769-3940
www.forthancockisd.net/
Fort Hancock HS 100/9-12
PO Box 98 79839 915-769-3867
Randy Speer, prin. Fax 769-0044
Fort Hancock MS 6-8
PO Box 98 79839 915-769-3811
Tootsie Farris, dir. Fax 769-0045

Fort Hood, Bell, Pop. 33,700
Killeen ISD
Supt. — See Killeen
Murphy MS 6-8
53393 Sun Dance Dr 76544 254-200-6530
Minerva Trujillo, prin. Fax 616-5245
Smith MS 800/6-8
51000 Tank Destroyer Blvd 76544 254-501-1050
Sandra Forsythe, prin. Fax 532-1247

Fort Stockton, Pecos, Pop. 7,387
Fort Stockton ISD 2,300/PK-12
101 W Division St 79735 432-336-4000
Ron Mayfield, supt. Fax 336-4008
www.fort-stockton.k12.tx.us
Fort Stockton HS 700/9-12
101 W Division St 79735 432-336-4101
Alice Duerksen, prin. Fax 336-4113
Fort Stockton MS 500/6-8
101 W Division St 79735 432-336-4131
Judy Espino, prin. Fax 336-4136

Fort Worth, Tarrant, Pop. 585,122
Castleberry ISD 2,900/PK-12
315 Churchill Rd 76114 817-252-2000
Gary S. Jones, supt. Fax 738-1062
www.castleberryisd.net
Castleberry HS 800/9-12
215 Churchill Rd 76114 817-252-2100
Laina McDonald, prin. Fax 252-2575
Marsh MS 800/6-8
415 Hagg Dr 76114 817-252-2200
Stephanie Romeo, prin. Fax 738-3454

Crowley ISD
Supt. — See Crowley
Crowley MS 1,000/7-8
3800 W Risinger Rd 76123 817-370-5650
Dan Peterson, prin. Fax 370-5656
North Crowley 9th Grade Campus 500/9-9
4630 McPherson Blvd 76123 817-297-5896
Brandon Neeley, prin. Fax 297-5878
North Crowley HS 1,400/10-12
9100 S Hulen St 76123 817-263-1250
Trent Lovette, prin. Fax 263-1282

Eagle Mtn.-Saginaw ISD 8,400/PK-12
1200 Old Decatur Rd 76179 817-232-0880
Dr. Cole Pugh, supt. Fax 847-6124
www.emsisd.com
Boswell HS 2,200/9-12
5805 W Bailey Boswell Rd 76179 817-237-3314
Terry Houston, prin. Fax 238-8706
Creekview MS 6-8
6716 Bob Hanger St 76179 817-237-4261
Anthe Anagnostis, prin. Fax 237-2387
Highland MS 1,000/6-8
1001 E Bailey Boswell Rd 76131 817-847-5143
Clete Welch, prin. Fax 847-1922
Wayside MS 900/6-8
1300 Old Decatur Rd 76179 817-232-0541
Dan Jordan, prin. Fax 232-2391
Other Schools – See Saginaw

Fort Worth ISD 76,100/PK-12
100 N University Dr 76107 817-871-2000
Dr. Melody Johnson, supt. Fax 871-2112
www.fortworthisd.org
Arlington Heights HS 1,800/9-12
4501 West Fwy 76107 817-377-7200
Neta Alexander, prin. Fax 377-7266
Carter-Riverside HS 1,100/9-12
3301 Yucca Ave 76111 817-838-1500
Maria Sanchez, prin. Fax 838-1517
Daggett MS 500/6-8
1108 Carlock St 76110 817-922-6550
Rhonda Fields, prin. Fax 922-6996
Diamond Hill-Jarvis HS 900/9-12
1411 Maydell St 76106 817-740-5400
Juanita Ornelas, prin. Fax 740-5402
Dunbar HS 1,200/9-12
5700 Ramey Ave 76112 817-496-7400
Ingrid Williams, prin. Fax 496-7446
Dunbar MS 700/7-8
2501 Stalcup Rd 76119 817-496-7430
Patricia Williams, prin. Fax 496-7697
Eastern Hills HS 1,600/9-12
5701 Shelton St 76112 817-496-7600
Richard Dean Pritchett, prin. Fax 496-7603
Elder MS 1,100/6-8
709 NW 21st St 76106 817-740-5450
Virginia Dean, prin. Fax 740-5468
Forest Oak MS 700/6-8
3221 Pecos St 76119 817-531-6330
Gerald Batty, prin. Fax 531-4342
Handley MS 700/6-8
2801 Patino Rd 76112 817-496-7450
Sherian Hayward M.Ed., prin. Fax 496-7653
James MS 1,100/6-8
1101 Nashville Ave 76105 817-531-6230
Renae Ruffin, prin. Fax 531-6114
Kirkpatrick MS 500/6-8
3201 Refugio Ave 76106 817-740-5350
Jorge Mendoza, prin. Fax 740-5363
McLean MS 800/6-8
3816 Stadium Dr 76109 817-922-6830
Nancy Weisskopf, prin. Fax 922-4498
Meacham MS 800/6-8
3600 Weber St 76106 817-740-5330
Manuel Cantu, prin. Fax 740-4546
Meadowbrook MS 1,100/6-8
2001 Ederville Rd S 76103 817-531-6250
David Trimble, prin. Fax 531-7709
Metro Opportunity S Vo/Tech
2720 Cullen 76107 817-852-1160
Linda Ballenger, prin. Fax 852-1183
Monnig MS 600/6-8
3136 Bigham Blvd 76116 817-377-7250
Stephen Griffin, prin. Fax 377-7024
Morningside MS 600/6-8
2751 Mississippi Ave 76104 817-922-6680
Andrew Chambers, prin. Fax 922-6869
North Side HS 1,600/9-12
2211 Mckinley Ave 76106 817-740-5300
Cathleen Richardson, prin. Fax 740-5302
Paschal HS 2,200/9-12
3001 Forest Park Blvd 76110 817-922-6600
Dr. Sharon Meng, prin. Fax 922-6661
Polytechnic HS Vo/Tech
1300 Conner Ave 76105 817-531-6200
Joe Scott, prin. Fax 531-6267
Riverside MS 900/6-8
1600 Bolton St 76111 817-838-1530
Daniel Scroggins, prin. Fax 838-1534
Rosemont MS 800/7-8
1501 W Seminary Dr 76115 817-922-6650
Elodia Escamilla, prin. Fax 922-4491
South Hills HS 1,400/9-12
6101 Mccart Ave 76133 817-263-1600
Glynna Torres, prin. Fax 263-1607
Southwest HS 1,500/9-12
4100 Altamesa Blvd 76133 817-370-5800
Laura Williams, prin. Fax 370-5833
Stripling MS 800/6-8
2100 Clover Ln 76107 817-377-7230
Cynthia Hernandez, prin. Fax 377-7030
Trimble Technical HS Vo/Tech
1003 W Cannon St 76104 817-871-3400
Omar Ramos, prin. Fax 871-3420
Wedgwood MS 1,000/7-8
3909 Wilkie Way 76133 817-370-5830
Linda Villarreal, prin. Fax 370-5733
Wyatt HS 1,100/9-12
2400 E Seminary Dr 76119 817-531-6300
Steven Johnson, prin. Fax 531-6326
Other Schools – See Benbrook

Keller ISD
Supt. — See Keller
Fossil Hill MS 900/7-8
3821 Staghorn Cir S 76137 817-744-3050
David Hadley, prin. Fax 847-6990
Hillwood MS 1,000/7-8
8250 Parkwood Hill Blvd 76137 817-744-3350
Jim Joros, prin. Fax 581-1810

White Settlement ISD 4,500/PK-12
401 S Cherry Ln 76108 817-367-1350
Dr. Susan Simpson, supt. Fax 367-1351
www.wsisd.com/
Ninth Grade Center 9-9
1025 West Loop 820 N 76108 817-367-1250
Mike Wallace, prin.
Other Schools – See White Settlement

All Saints' Episcopal S 800/K-12
9700 Saints Cir 76108 817-246-2413
Thaddeus Bird, hdmstr. Fax 560-5720
Bethesda Christian S 400/PK-12
4700 N Beach St 76137 817-281-6446
Vicki Vaughn, prin. Fax 281-1560
Calvary Christian Academy 300/PK-12
1401 Oakhurst Scenic Dr 76111 817-332-3351
Sue Tidwell, prin. Fax 332-4621
Career Centers of Texas Post-Sec.
2001 Beach St 76103 817-688-1132
Cassata Learning Center 400/9-12
1400 Hemphill St 76104 817-926-1745
Bill Hardisty, prin. Fax 926-3132
Christian Life Preparatory S 200/K-12
6250 South Fwy 76134 817-293-1500
Fax 293-1500
College of Saint Thomas More Post-Sec.
3020 Lubbock Ave 76109 817-923-8459
Ft. Worth Adventist Jr Academy 100/PK-10
3040 Sycamore School Rd 76133 817-370-7177
Fax 370-8455
Fort Worth Beauty School Post-Sec.
6785 Camp Bowie Blvd # 100 76116 817-924-4289
Fort Worth Christian S 800/PK-12
7517 Bogart Dr 76180 817-281-6504
Brian Miller, prin. Fax 281-7063
Fort Worth Country Day S 1,100/K-12
4200 Country Day Ln 76109 817-732-7718
Evan D. Peterson, hdmstr. Fax 377-3425
Glenview Christian S 200/PK-12
4805 NE Loop 820 76137 817-281-5155
Jerome Chenausky, admin. Fax 514-0760
Harris Hospital Post-Sec.
1301 Pennsylvania Ave 76104 817-878-2106
Harvest Christian S 200/K-12
7501 Crowley Rd 76134 817-568-0021
John Winner, prin. Fax 568-1395
Hill S of Ft. Worth 200/2-12
4817 Odessa Ave 76133 817-923-9482
Gregory Owens, prin. Fax 923-4894
JPS Inst. for Health Career Development Post-Sec.
2400 Circle Dr 76119 817-920-7380
Key S 100/PK-12
3947 E Loop 820 S 76119 817-446-3738
Lake Country Christian S 400/PK-12
8777 Boat Club Rd 76179 817-236-8703
Nancy Purtell, admin. Fax 236-1103
Meadowbrook Legacy Christian Academy 200/K-12
6801 Meadowbrook Dr 76112 817-457-2345
Terry Gaillard, prin. Fax 457-2347
Nolan JSHS 1,000/7-12
4501 Bridge St 76103 817-457-2920
Br. Richard Thompson, prin. Fax 496-9775
Ogle School of Hair Design Post-Sec.
5063 Old Granbury Rd 76133 817-294-2950
Remington College Post-Sec.
300 E Loop 820 76112 817-451-0017
Southwest Christian Prep S 400/7-12
7001 Benbrook Lake Dr 76123 817-294-9596
Scott Barron, hdmstr. Fax 294-9603
Southwestern Baptist Theological Sem. Post-Sec.
PO Box 22000 76122 817-923-1921
Tarrant County Junior College Post-Sec.
5301 Campus Dr 76119 817-515-4100
Tarrant County Junior College Post-Sec.
4801 Marine Creek Pkwy 76179 817-515-7100
Temple Christian S of Ft. Worth 900/PK-12
6824 Randol Mill Rd 76120 817-457-0770
Dorothy Stringer, supt. Fax 457-0777
Texas Christian University Post-Sec.
TCU Box 297013 76129 817-257-7000
Texas Wesleyan University Post-Sec.
1201 Wesleyan St 76105 800-580-8980
Trinity Valley S 900/K-12
7500 Dutch Branch Rd 76132 817-321-0100
Gerald Kramer, hdmstr. Fax 321-0105
University of N Texas Health Science Ctr Post-Sec.
3500 Camp Bowie Blvd 76107 817-735-2000
Westwood College Post-Sec.
4232 North Fwy 76137 817-685-9994

Franklin, Robertson, Pop. 1,450
Franklin ISD 1,000/PK-12
PO Box 909 77856 979-828-1900
Timothy Lowry, supt. Fax 828-1910
www.franklinisd.net/fisdwebpage/
Franklin HS 300/9-12
PO Box 909 77856 979-828-3236
Stacy Ely, prin. Fax 828-3364
Franklin MS 300/5-8
PO Box 909 77856 979-828-5434
Randel Mayfield, prin. Fax 828-3134

Frankston, Anderson, Pop. 1,215
Frankston ISD 800/PK-12
PO Box 428 75763 903-876-2556
Austin Thacker, supt. Fax 876-4558
www.frankston.esc7.net
Frankston HS 200/9-12
PO Box 428 75763 903-876-3219
Nicci Cook, prin. Fax 876-4558
Frankston MS 200/6-8
PO Box 428 75763 903-876-2215
Chris White, prin. Fax 876-4558

Fredericksburg, Gillespie, Pop. 9,955
Fredericksburg ISD 2,800/PK-12
234 Friendship Ln 78624 830-997-9551
Marc Williamson, supt. Fax 997-6164
www.fisd.org/
Fredericksburg HS 1,000/9-12
1107 S State Highway 16 78624 830-997-7551
Lynn Blackwell, prin. Fax 997-8583
Fredericksburg MS 600/6-8
110 W Travis St 78624 830-997-7657
Kevan Webb, prin. Fax 997-1927

Fredericksburg Christian S 50/K-12
1208 N Milam St 78624 830-997-9193
Linda Williams, prin.
Heritage S 200/K-12
PO Box 1217 78624 830-997-6597
Nancy Hierholzer, prin. Fax 997-4900

Freeport, Brazoria, Pop. 12,715
Brazosport ISD
Supt. — See Clute
Brazosport HS 1,100/9-12
PO Box Z 77542 979-730-7260
Gary Jones, prin. Fax 237-6310
Freeport IS 600/7-8
PO Box Z 77542 979-730-7240
Clara Sale-Davis, prin. Fax 237-6329

Freer, Duval, Pop. 3,129
Freer ISD 900/PK-12
PO Box 240 78357 361-394-6025
Edgar Camacho, supt. Fax 394-5005
www.freerisd.esc2.net
Freer HS 300/9-12
PO Box 240 78357 361-394-6717
Ramon Pulido, prin. Fax 394-5012
Freer JHS 200/6-8
PO Box 240 78357 361-394-7102
Linda Garza, prin. Fax 394-5016

Friendswood, Galveston, Pop. 32,460
Clear Creek ISD
Supt. — See League City
Brookside IS 1,200/6-8
3535 E Parkwood 77546 281-482-9710
Deanna Daws, prin. Fax 992-7858
Clear Brook HS 2,700/9-12
4607 FM 2351 Rd 77546 281-284-2100
Kristi Lamell, prin. Fax 284-2105
West Brook IS 6-8
302 W El Dorado Blvd 77546 281-284-3800
Marlene Skiba, prin. Fax 284-3805

Friendswood ISD 5,500/K-12
302 Laurel Dr 77546 281-482-1267
Trish Hanks, supt. Fax 996-2513
www.fisdk12.net
Friendswood HS 1,800/9-12
702 Greenbriar Ave 77546 281-482-3413
Myrlene Kennedy, prin. Fax 996-2523
Friendswood JHS 900/7-8
402 Laurel Dr 77546 281-482-7818
Robin Lowe, prin. Fax 996-2529

Texas School of Business Post-Sec.
3208 W Parkwood Ave 77546 281-648-0880

Friona, Parmer, Pop. 3,807
Friona ISD 1,300/PK-12
909 E 11th St 79035 806-250-2747
Jim Parker, supt. Fax 250-3805
www.frionaisd.com
Friona HS 400/9-12
909 E 11th St 79035 806-250-3951
Denver Crum, prin. Fax 259-2281
Friona JHS 300/6-8
909 E 11th St 79035 806-250-2788
Kevin Wiseman, prin. Fax 250-8155

Frisco, Collin, Pop. 55,126
Frisco ISD — 13,100/K-12
6942 Maple St 75034 — 469-633-6000
Rick Reedy, supt. — Fax 633-6050
www.friscoisd.org
Clark MS — 600/6-8
4600 Colby Dr 75035 — 469-633-4600
Mary Dowd, prin. — Fax 633-4650
Frisco Centennial HS — 700/9-12
6901 Coit Rd 75035 — 469-633-5600
Randy Spain, prin. — Fax 633-5650
Frisco HS — 1,900/9-12
6401 Parkwood Dr 75034 — 469-633-5500
Rick Burnett, prin. — Fax 633-5550
Griffin MS — 6-8
3703 Eldorado Pkwy 75034 — 469-633-4900
Elizabeth Holcomb, prin. — Fax 633-4950
Pioneer Heritage MS — 700/6-8
1649 High Shoals Dr 75034 — 469-633-4700
Katie Kordel, prin. — Fax 633-4750
Roach MS — 6-8
12499 Independence Pkwy 75035 — 469-633-5000
Terri Gladden, prin. — Fax 633-5010
Staley MS — 600/6-8
6927 Stadium Ln 75034 — 469-633-4500
Dennis McDonald, prin. — Fax 633-4550
Wakeland HS — 9-12
10700 Legacy Dr 75034 — 469-633-5700
Mike Farish, prin.
Wester MS — 800/6-8
12293 Shepherds Hill Ln 75035 — 469-633-4800
Kenny Chandler, prin. — Fax 633-4850
Other Schools – See Plano

Legacy Christian Academy — 600/PK-12
5000 Academy Dr 75034 — 469-633-1330
Jody Capehart, hdmstr. — Fax 633-1348

Fritch, Hutchinson, Pop. 2,148
Sanford ISD — 1,000/PK-12
PO Box 1290 79036 — 806-857-3122
Daymun White, supt. — Fax 857-3795
www.sanfordisd.org
Sanford-Fritch HS — 300/9-12
PO Box 1290 79036 — 806-857-3121
Jim McClellon, prin. — Fax 857-9147
Sanford-Fritch JHS — 200/6-8
PO Box 1290 79036 — 806-857-9268
Edith Allen, prin. — Fax 857-9431

Frost, Navarro, Pop. 679
Frost ISD — 400/PK-12
PO Box K 76641 — 903-682-2711
Jim Revill, supt. — Fax 682-2107
Frost JSHS — 200/7-12
PO Box K 76641 — 903-682-2541
Gordon Lockett, prin. — Fax 682-2107

Fruitvale, Van Zandt, Pop. 437
Fruitvale ISD — 400/PK-12
PO Box 77 75127 — 903-896-1191
Stan Surratt, supt. — Fax 896-1011
www.fruitvaleisd.com
Fruitvale HS — 100/9-12
PO Box 77 75127 — 903-896-4363
Del Goggans, prin. — Fax 896-1011
Fruitvale MS — 100/6-8
PO Box 77 75127 — 903-896-4363
Loyd Nations, prin. — Fax 896-4363

Gail, Borden
Borden County ISD — 200/K-12
PO Box 95 79738 — 806-756-4313
Jimmy Thomas, supt. — Fax 756-4310
www.bcisd.net/
Borden S — 200/K-12
PO Box 95 79738 — 806-756-4314
Bart McMeans, prin. — Fax 756-4310

Gainesville, Cooke, Pop. 16,040
Callisburg ISD — 1,000/PK-12
148 Dozier St 76240 — 940-665-0540
Dr. Charles Holloway, supt. — Fax 668-2706
Callisburg HS — 600/7-12
148 Dozier St 76240 — 940-665-0961
Skipper Waller, prin. — Fax 665-2849

Gainesville ISD — 2,900/PK-12
800 S Morris St 76240 — 940-665-4362
Mike Rosenberg, supt. — Fax 665-4473
www.gainesvilleisd.com/
Gainesville HS — 800/9-12
1201 S Lindsay St 76240 — 940-665-5528
Bill Gravitt, prin. — Fax 665-7975
Gainesville JHS — 400/7-8
421 N Denton St 76240 — 940-665-4062
Juan Lopez, prin. — Fax 665-1432

North Central Texas College — Post-Sec.
1525 W California St 76240 — 940-668-4222

Galena Park, Harris, Pop. 10,443
Galena Park ISD
Supt. — See Houston
Galena Park HS — 1,600/9-12
1000 Keene St 77547 — 832-386-2800
Marsha Masi, prin. — Fax 386-2802
Galena Park MS — 1,000/6-8
400 Keene St 77547 — 832-386-1700
Tony Mayeux, prin. — Fax 386-1738
Sheffield Career Center — Vo/Tech
1001 Parkside Dr 77547 — 832-386-2802
Janis Tomlinson, prin. — Fax 386-2851

Galveston, Galveston, Pop. 56,667
Galveston ISD — 9,100/PK-12
PO Box 660 77553 — 409-766-5100
Lynn Hale, supt. — Fax 766-5106
www.gisd.org
Austin MS — 500/6-8
5101 Avenue U 77551 — 409-765-9373
Canzetta Hollis, prin. — Fax 765-5946
Ball HS — 2,500/9-12
4115 Avenue O 77550 — 409-766-5715
Diane Reaume, prin. — Fax 766-5738
Central MS — 6-8
3014 Avenue I 77550 — 409-765-2101
Connie Hebert, prin. — Fax 765-2141
Weis MS — 800/6-8
7100 Stewart Rd 77551 — 409-740-5100
Manuel Garza, prin. — Fax 744-8936

Galveston College — Post-Sec.
4015 Avenue Q 77550 — 409-763-6551
O'Connell HS — 200/9-12
1320 Tremont St 77550 — 409-765-6551
Bill Doughty, prin. — Fax 765-5536
Texas A&M at Galveston — Post-Sec.
PO Box 1675 77553 — 409-740-4400
University of Texas Medical Branch — Post-Sec.
301 University Blvd 77555 — 409-761-1215

Ganado, Jackson, Pop. 1,874
Ganado ISD — 600/PK-12
PO Box 1200 77962 — 361-771-3482
Jeff Black, supt. — Fax 771-2280
www.ganadoisd.org/
Ganado JSHS — 300/7-12
PO Box 1200 77962 — 361-771-3430
Andy Bridges, prin. — Fax 771-2280

Garden City, Glasscock
Glasscock County ISD — 300/PK-12
PO Box 9 79739 — 432-354-2230
Steve Long, supt. — Fax 354-2503
Glasscock County JSHS — 100/7-12
PO Box 9 79739 — 432-354-2244
John Petree, prin. — Fax 354-2503

Gardendale, Ector, Pop. 1,103

Gardendale Christian S — 200/K-12
PO Box 345 79758 — 432-561-9024

Garland, Dallas, Pop. 218,027
Garland ISD — 54,600/PK-12
PO Box 469026 75046 — 972-494-8201
Dr. Curtis Culwell, supt. — Fax 485-4928
www.garlandisd.net
Austin Academy for Excellence MS — 1,000/6-8
1125 Beverly Dr 75040 — 972-926-2620
Dr. Ann Poore, prin. — Fax 926-2628
Bussey MS — 1,000/6-8
1204 Travis St 75040 — 972-494-8391
Harry Farley, prin. — Fax 494-8971
Classical Center at Brandenburg MS — 1,000/6-8
626 Nickens Rd 75043 — 972-926-2630
Carra King, prin. — Fax 926-2633
Garland HS — 2,400/9-12
310 S Garland Ave 75040 — 972-494-8492
John Morris, prin. — Fax 494-8415
Houston MS — 600/6-8
2232 Sussex Dr 75041 — 972-926-2640
Don Hernandez, prin. — Fax 926-2647
Hudson MS — 1,200/6-8
4405 Hudson Park 75048 — 972-675-3070
Michelle Baker, prin. — Fax 675-3077
Jackson Technology MS — 1,100/6-8
1310 Bobbie Ln 75042 — 972-494-8362
Richard Cozby, prin. — Fax 494-8802
Lakeview Centennial HS — 2,000/9-12
3505 Hayman Rd 75043 — 972-240-3740
Wendell Brown, prin. — Fax 240-3750
Lyles MS — 1,000/6-8
4655 S Country Club Rd 75043 — 972-240-3720
Janice Howard, prin. — Fax 240-3723
Naaman Forest HS — 2,200/9-12
4843 Naaman Forest Blvd 75040 — 972-675-3091
Steve Baker, prin. — Fax 675-3100
North Garland HS — 2,400/9-12
2109 W Buckingham Rd 75042 — 972-675-3120
Dr. Susie Fegraeus, prin. — Fax 675-3145
O'Banion MS — 1,100/6-8
700 Birchwood Dr 75043 — 972-279-6103
John Tucci, prin. — Fax 613-9532
Sellers MS — 800/6-8
1009 Mars Dr 75040 — 972-494-8337
William Woods, prin. — Fax 494-8607
South Garland HS — 2,200/9-12
600 Colonel Dr 75043 — 972-926-2700
Charlie Rose, prin. — Fax 926-2727
Webb MS — 1,200/6-8
1610 Spring Creek Dr 75040 — 972-675-3080
Jim Lewis, prin. — Fax 675-3089
Garland Evening S — Adult
310 S Garland Ave 75040 — 972-494-8162
David Benson, prin. — Fax 494-8977
Other Schools – See Rowlett, Sachse

Amberton University — Post-Sec.
1700 Eastgate Dr 75041 — 972-279-6511
Garland Christian Academy — 500/K-12
1522 Lavon Dr 75040 — 972-487-0043
Dr. John McCartt, supt. — Fax 276-4079
International Beauty College #3 — Post-Sec.
1225 Belt Line Rd Ste 7 75040 — 972-530-1103
National Beauty College — Post-Sec.
149 W Kingsley Rd Ste 230 75041 — 972-278-2020
Remington College — Post-Sec.
1800 Eastgate Dr 75041 — 972-686-7878

Garrison, Nacogdoches, Pop. 832
Garrison ISD — 700/PK-12
459 N US Highway 59 75946 — 936-347-7000
Arnie Kelley, supt. — Fax 347-2529
www.garrisonisd.com
Garrison HS — 200/9-12
459 N US Highway 59 75946 — 936-347-7030
Darren Webb, prin. — Fax 347-2529
Garrison MS — 200/6-8
459 N US Highway 59 75946 — 936-347-7020
Virgil Wedgeworth, prin. — Fax 347-7004

Gary, Panola
Gary ISD — 300/K-12
PO Box 189 75643 — 903-685-2291
Todd Greer, supt. — Fax 685-2639
www.gary.esc7.net
Gary S — 300/K-12
PO Box 189 75643 — 903-685-2291
Todd Greer, supt. — Fax 685-2639

Gatesville, Coryell, Pop. 15,373
Gatesville ISD — 2,600/PK-12
311 S Lovers Ln 76528 — 254-865-7251
Ricky Copp, supt. — Fax 865-2279
www.gatesvilleisd.org/
Gatesville HS — 800/9-12
311 S Lovers Ln 76528 — 254-865-8281
Michael Barr, prin. — Fax 865-2293

Gatesville JHS — 400/7-8
311 S Lovers Ln 76528 — 254-865-8271
Bobby Cole, prin. — Fax 865-2252

Coryell Cosmetology College — Post-Sec.
608 E Leon St 76528 — 254-248-1716

Georgetown, Williamson, Pop. 34,815
Georgetown ISD — 8,700/PK-12
603 Lakeway Dr 78628 — 512-943-5000
Joe Dan Lee, supt. — Fax 943-5002
www.georgetown.txed.net
Benold MS — 600/6-8
3407 Northwest Blvd 78628 — 512-943-5090
Leslie Michalik, prin. — Fax 943-5099
Forbes MS — 600/6-8
1911 NE Inner Loop 78626 — 512-943-5150
Leonard Rhoads, prin. — Fax 943-5159
Georgetown HS — 1,800/10-12
2211 N Austin Ave 78626 — 512-943-5100
Randy Weisinger, prin. — Fax 943-5109
Georgetown Ninth Grade S — 700/9-9
2295 S Austin Ave 78626 — 512-943-5130
Dwayne Lenox, prin. — Fax 943-5139
Tippit MS — 800/6-8
1601 Leander Rd 78628 — 512-943-5040
Carlos Cantu, prin. — Fax 943-5049

Covenant Christian Academy — 100/PK-12
1521 Northwest Blvd 78628 — 512-863-6946
Terry L. Wright, prin. — Fax 863-4756
Southwestern University — Post-Sec.
PO Box 770 78627 — 512-863-6511

George West, Live Oak, Pop. 2,416
George West ISD — 1,100/PK-12
913 Houston St 78022 — 361-449-1914
James Stansberry, supt. — Fax 449-1426
www.gwisd.esc2.net/
George West HS — 400/9-12
1013 Houston St 78022 — 361-449-1914
Cris Luna, prin. — Fax 449-3128
George West JHS — 200/7-8
900 Houston St 78022 — 361-449-1914
Pat James, prin. — Fax 449-3909

Giddings, Lee, Pop. 5,386
Giddings ISD — 1,800/PK-12
PO Box 389 78942 — 979-542-2854
Michael Kuhrt, supt. — Fax 542-9264
www.giddings.txed.net
Giddings HS — 600/9-12
PO Box 389 78942 — 979-542-3351
Andy Masek, prin. — Fax 542-5312
Giddings MS — 200/7-8
PO Box 389 78942 — 979-542-2057
Shane Holman, prin. — Fax 542-3941

Gilmer, Upshur, Pop. 5,025
Gilmer ISD — 2,300/PK-12
500 S Trinity St 75644 — 903-843-2525
Rick Albritton, supt. — Fax 843-5279
www.gilmerisd.org
Bruce JHS — 500/6-8
111 Bruce St 75645 — 903-843-3051
Greg Watson, prin. — Fax 843-6108
Gilmer HS — 600/9-12
850 Buffalo St 75644 — 903-843-3021
Gary Whitwell, prin. — Fax 843-2171

Union Hill ISD — 300/PK-12
2197 FM 2088 75644 — 903-762-2140
Sharon Richardson, supt. — Fax 762-6845
www.uhisd.org/
Union Hill HS — 200/6-12
2197 FM 2088 75644 — 903-762-2138
Cathy Schmidt, prin. — Fax 762-6845

Gladewater, Gregg, Pop. 6,155
Gladewater ISD — 2,300/PK-12
500 W Quitman Ave 75647 — 903-845-6991
Guy Yarborough, supt. — Fax 845-6994
www.gladewaterisd.com
Gladewater HS — 700/9-12
2201 W Gay Ave 75647 — 903-845-5591
Sam Chenoweth, prin. — Fax 845-3694
Gladewater MS — 500/6-8
700 Melba Ave 75647 — 903-845-2223
James Griffin, prin. — Fax 844-1738

Sabine ISD — 1,300/PK-12
5424 FM 1252 W 75647 — 903-984-8564
Stacey Bryce, supt. — Fax 984-6108
Sabine HS — 400/9-12
5424 FM 1252 W 75647 — 903-984-8587
Eddie Shawn, prin. — Fax 986-1103
Sabine MS — 300/6-8
5424 FM 1252 W 75647 — 903-984-4767
Durwin Cooley, prin. — Fax 984-8823

Union Grove ISD — 700/PK-12
PO Box 1447 75647 — 903-845-5509
Richard Cooper, supt. — Fax 845-6178
www.ungr.sprnet.org
Union Grove HS — 300/7-12
PO Box 1447 75647 — 903-845-5656
Kevin Whitman, prin. — Fax 845-3003

Glenn Heights, Dallas, Pop. 8,100

Community Christian Academy — 50/K-12
1931 S Hampton Rd 75154 — 972-274-0015
Dr. Nancie S. Rowe, admin. — Fax 274-0078

Glen Rose, Somervell, Pop. 2,373
Glen Rose ISD — 1,600/PK-12
PO Box 2129 76043 — 254-897-2517
Wayne Rotan, supt. — Fax 897-3651
www.grisd.net
Glen Rose HS — 500/9-12
PO Box 2129 76043 — 254-898-3800
Tommy Corcoran, prin. — Fax 897-9871
Glen Rose JHS — 400/6-8
PO Box 2129 76043 — 254-898-3700
Shirley Craft, prin. — Fax 897-4059

Godley, Johnson, Pop. 944
Godley ISD 1,300/PK-12
512 W Links Dr 76044 817-389-2536
Paul Smithson, supt. Fax 389-2543
www.godleyisd.com/
Godley HS 400/9-12
9401 N Highway 171 76044 817-389-2265
Ralph Davis, prin. Fax 389-4455
Godley MS 300/6-8
409 N Pearson St 76044 817-389-2121
David Williams, prin. Fax 389-4357

Goldthwaite, Mills, Pop. 1,760
Goldthwaite ISD 600/PK-12
PO Box 608 76844 325-648-3531
Dr. Gary Long, supt. Fax 648-2456
www.centex-edu.net/goldthwaiteisd
Goldthwaite HS 200/9-12
PO Box 608 76844 325-648-3081
Vince Gilbert, prin. Fax 648-2325
Goldthwaite MS, PO Box 608 76844 100/6-8
Brad Jones, prin. 325-648-3630

Goliad, Goliad, Pop. 2,015
Goliad ISD 1,300/PK-12
PO Box 830 77963 361-645-3259
Sam Atwood, supt. Fax 645-3614
www.goliadisd.org
Goliad HS 400/9-12
PO Box 830 77963 361-645-3257
David Hill, prin. Fax 645-8039
Goliad MS 300/6-8
PO Box 830 77963 361-645-3146
Emilio Vargas, prin. Fax 645-8040

Gonzales, Gonzales, Pop. 7,320
Gonzales ISD 2,600/PK-12
926 Saint Lawrence St 78629 830-672-9551
Dr. Steven Ebell, supt. Fax 672-7159
www.gonzales.txed.net
Gonzales HS 700/9-12
1801 N Sarah DeWitt Dr 78629 830-672-7535
Ronald Bragg, prin. Fax 672-8273
Gonzales JHS 400/7-8
426 N College St 78629 830-672-8641
Tony Dominguez, prin. Fax 672-6466

Goodrich, Polk, Pop. 270
Goodrich ISD 300/K-12
PO Box 789 77335 936-365-1112
William Gorham, supt. Fax 365-3518
www.goodrichisd.net
Goodrich JSHS 100/6-12
PO Box 789 77335 936-365-1121
Malissa Williams, prin. Fax 365-3518

Gordon, Palo Pinto, Pop. 455
Gordon ISD 200/K-12
PO Box 47 76453 254-693-5582
Jon Hartgraves, supt. Fax 693-5503
www.gordonisd.net
Gordon S 200/K-12
PO Box 47 76453 254-693-5342
William Cochran, prin. Fax 693-5503

Goree, Knox, Pop. 296
Munday Consolidated ISD
Supt. — See Munday
Munday JHS 100/7-8
PO Box 156 76363 940-422-5233
Kristi Bufkin, prin. Fax 422-4429

Gorman, Eastland, Pop. 1,258
Gorman ISD 400/PK-12
PO Box 8 76454 254-734-3171
David Perry, supt. Fax 734-3393
www.gorman.esc14.net/
Gorman HS 200/7-12
PO Box 8 76454 254-734-2614
Ricky Panter, prin. Fax 734-3425

Graford, Palo Pinto, Pop. 598
Graford ISD 400/PK-12
400 W Division Ave 76449 940-664-3101
Chance Welch, supt. Fax 664-2123
www.grafordisd.net
Graford JSHS 200/7-12
400 W Division Ave 76449 940-664-3161
Don Hise, prin. Fax 664-2026

Graham, Young, Pop. 8,651
Graham ISD 2,400/PK-12
400 3rd St 76450 940-549-0595
Beau Rees, supt. Fax 549-8656
www.grahamisd.com
Graham HS 700/9-12
1000 Brazos St 76450 940-549-4030
Clay Wright, prin. Fax 549-4031
Graham JHS 500/6-8
1000 2nd St 76450 940-549-2002
Don Davis, prin. Fax 549-6991

Granbury, Hood, Pop. 6,403
Granbury ISD 5,500/PK-12
600 W Pearl St 76048 817-408-4000
William Harris, supt. Fax 408-4014
www.granbury.k12.tx.us
Acton MS 600/6-8
1300 James Rd 76049 817-408-4800
Bobby Mabery, prin. Fax 408-4849
Crossland 9th Grade Ctr. 100/9-9
217 N Jones St 76048 817-408-4700
Lynn Pool, prin. Fax 408-4749
Granbury MS 600/6-8
2000 Crossland Rd 76048 817-408-4850
Jimmy Dawson, prin. Fax 408-4899
Granbury SHS 1,300/10-12
2000 W Pearl St 76048 817-408-4600
Marsha Grissom, prin. Fax 408-4699

Happy Hill Farm Academy 100/K-12
3846 N Highway 144 76048 254-897-4822
Dru Pruitt, prin. Fax 897-7650

Grandfalls, Ward, Pop. 368
Grandfalls-Royalty ISD 100/PK-12
PO Box 10 79742 432-547-2266
Billy Collins, supt. Fax 547-2960
www.grisd.com/
Grandfalls-Royalty S 100/PK-12
PO Box 10 79742 432-547-2266
J.D. Stocks, prin. Fax 547-2960

Grand Prairie, Dallas, Pop. 136,671
Grand Prairie ISD 20,200/PK-12
PO Box 531170 75053 972-264-6141
Dr. David Barbosa, supt. Fax 237-5440
www.gpisd.org
Adams MS 700/6-8
833 W Tarrant Rd 75050 972-262-1934
Calvin Harrison, prin. Fax 522-3099
Arnold MS 1,000/6-8
1204 E Marshall Dr 75051 972-642-5137
Rich Laffey, prin. Fax 343-7499
Grand Prairie HS 9th Grade Center 9-9
102 High School Dr 75050 972-237-5603
Sal Sosa, prin. Fax 343-6399
Grand Prairie SHS 2,000/10-12
101 Highschool Dr 75050 972-809-5711
Rose-Levy Brenner, prin. Fax 809-5775
Jackson MS 1,100/6-8
3504 Corn Valley Rd 75052 972-264-2704
Michael Brinkley, prin. Fax 343-7599
Kennedy MS 700/6-8
2205 SE 4th St 75051 972-264-8651
Leslee Shepherd, prin. Fax 522-3699
Lee MS 700/6-8
401 E Grand Prairie Rd 75051 972-262-6785
Rosalinda Brewington, prin. Fax 343-6099
Reagan MS 6-8
4616 Bardin Rd 75052 972-522-7300
John Walsh, prin. Fax 522-7399
South Grand Prairie HS 9th Grade Campus 9-9
305 W Warrior Trl 75052 972-264-1769
Vicki Villarreal, prin. Fax 343-7698
South Grand Prairie SHS 2,000/10-12
301 W Warrior Trl 75052 972-343-1500
Vicki Bridges, prin. Fax 642-7902
Truman MS 900/6-8
1501 Coffeyville Trl 75052 972-641-7676
Charles Lester, prin. Fax 641-8666

AIMS Academy Post-Sec.
1106 N Highway 360 #305 75050 972-988-3202
Arlington Career Institute Post-Sec.
901 E Avenue K 75050 972-647-1607
Jones Beauty College #2 Post-Sec.
311A W Pioneer Pkwy 75051 214-956-0088
Lincoln Technical Institute Post-Sec.
2501 Arkansas Ln 75052 972-660-5701
Mid Cities Barber College Post-Sec.
2345 SW 3rd St Ste 101 75051 972-642-1892
Shady Grove Christian Academy 200/K-12
1829 W Shady Grove Rd 75050 972-313-2431
Russell Kested, hdmstr. Fax 313-2483

Grand Saline, Van Zandt, Pop. 3,125
Grand Saline ISD 1,200/PK-12
400 Stadium Dr 75140 903-962-7546
Gerald Gilbert, supt. Fax 962-7464
www.gsisd.esc7.net
Grand Saline HS 300/9-12
500 Stadium Dr 75140 903-962-7533
Gary Redding, prin. Fax 962-7482
Grand Saline MS 200/6-8
400 Stadium Dr 75140 903-962-7537
J. W. Witt, prin. Fax 962-7474

Grandview, Johnson, Pop. 1,492
Grandview ISD 1,200/PK-12
PO Box 310 76050 817-866-2450
Keith Scharnhorst, supt. Fax 866-3351
www.gvisd.org
Grandview HS 300/9-12
PO Box 310 76050 817-866-3320
Joe Perrin, prin. Fax 866-3351
Grandview JHS 300/6-8
PO Box 310 76050 817-866-2492
Jeff Hudson, prin. Fax 866-3912

Granger, Williamson, Pop. 1,307
Granger ISD 400/K-12
PO Box 578 76530 512-859-2613
James Bartosh, supt. Fax 859-2446
www.grangerisd.net
Granger S 400/K-12
PO Box 578 76530 512-859-2173
Johnnie Thornton, prin. Fax 859-2446

Grapeland, Houston, Pop. 1,434
Grapeland ISD 600/PK-12
PO Box 249 75844 936-687-4619
E. D. Sumrall, supt. Fax 687-4624
Grapeland HS 200/9-12
PO Box 249 75844 936-687-4661
Don Jackson, prin. Fax 687-9739
Grapeland JHS 100/7-8
PO Box 249 75844 936-687-2351
Joe Young, prin. Fax 687-4624

Grapevine, Tarrant, Pop. 46,891
Carroll ISD 7,300/PK-12
3051 Dove Rd 76051 817-949-8222
Diane Frost Ph.D., supt. Fax 949-8228
www.southlakecarroll.edu
Other Schools – See Southlake

Grapevine-Colleyville ISD 13,900/PK-12
3051 Ira E Woods Ave 76051 817-251-5501
Dr. Kay Waggoner, supt. Fax 481-2907
www.gcisd-k12.org
Cross Timbers MS 800/6-8
2301 Pool Rd 76051 817-251-5320
Linda Tidmore, prin. Fax 424-4296
Grapevine HS 2,000/9-12
3223 Mustang Dr 76051 817-251-5210
Jerry Hollingsworth, prin. Fax 481-5957
Grapevine MS 800/6-8
301 Pony Pkwy 76051 817-251-5660
Tim Hughes, prin. Fax 424-1626
Other Schools – See Colleyville

Faith Christian S 700/PK-12
730 E Worth St 76051 817-442-9144
Dr. Ed Smith, prin. Fax 442-9904

Greenville, Hunt, Pop. 24,838
Greenville ISD 5,200/PK-12
PO Box 1022 75403 903-457-2500
Lloyd Graham, supt. Fax 457-2504
www.greenvilleisd.com
Greenville HS 1,400/9-12
3515 Lions Lair Rd 75402 903-457-2550
Don Jefferies, prin. Fax 455-5158
Greenville MS 700/7-8
3611 Texas St 75401 903-457-2620
Mike Clyde, prin. Fax 457-2628

Greenville Christian S 300/PK-12
8420 Jack Finney Blvd 75402 903-454-1111
Julie Robinson, hdmstr. Fax 455-8470

Gregory, San Patricio, Pop. 2,275
Gregory-Portland ISD 4,300/PK-12
608 College St 78359 361-777-1091
Dr. Paul Clore, supt. Fax 777-1093
www.g-pisd.org
Other Schools – See Portland

Groesbeck, Limestone, Pop. 4,348
Groesbeck ISD 1,700/PK-12
PO Box 559 76642 254-729-4100
John Key, supt. Fax 729-5167
www.groesbeck.k12.tx.us
Groesbeck HS 500/9-12
1202 N Ellis St 76642 254-729-4101
Kent Reynolds, prin. Fax 729-5458
Groesbeck MS 400/6-8
410 Elwood Enge Dr 76642 254-729-4102
Ladena King, prin. Fax 729-8763

Groom, Carson, Pop. 582
Groom ISD 100/K-12
PO Box 598 79039 806-248-7557
Terry Lee Stevens, supt. Fax 248-7949
www.groomisd.net
Groom S 100/K-12
PO Box 598 79039 806-248-7474
Terry Stevens, prin. Fax 248-7949

Groves, Jefferson, Pop. 15,333
Port Neches-Groves ISD
Supt. — See Port Neches
Groves MS 500/6-8
5201 Wilson St 77619 409-962-0225
Ken Cummings, prin. Fax 963-1898

Groveton, Trinity, Pop. 1,124
Centerville ISD 200/PK-12
10327 N State Highway 94 75845 936-642-1597
Craig Quincy Davis, supt. Fax 642-2810
www.centervilleisd.net/site/
Centerville JSHS 100/7-12
10327 N State Highway 94 75845 936-642-1597
Charles Brantner, prin. Fax 642-2810

Groveton ISD 700/K-12
PO Box 728 75845 936-642-1473
Joe Driskell, supt. Fax 642-1628
www.grovetonisd.net
Groveton JSHS 300/7-12
PO Box 700 75845 936-642-1128
Johnny Rhea, prin. Fax 642-1616

Grulla, Starr, Pop. 1,613
Rio Grande City ISD
Supt. — See Rio Grande City
Grulla MS 700/6-8
PO Box 338 78548 956-487-5558
Pablo Martinez, prin. Fax 487-5633

Gruver, Hansford, Pop. 1,123
Gruver ISD 400/PK-12
PO Box 650 79040 806-733-2001
David Teal, supt. Fax 733-5416
www.gruverisd.net
Gruver HS 100/9-12
PO Box 747 79040 806-733-2477
Mike King, prin. Fax 733-2596
Gruver JHS 100/5-8
PO Box 709 79040 806-733-2081
Mathew Branstine, prin. Fax 733-5523

Gunter, Grayson, Pop. 1,487
Gunter ISD 800/PK-12
PO Box 109 75058 903-433-4750
R. Cohagan, supt. Fax 433-1053
www.gunterisd.org
Gunter HS 200/9-12
PO Box 109 75058 903-433-1542
Jim Watson, prin. Fax 433-1492
Gunter MS 300/5-8
PO Box 109 75058 903-433-1545
Diana Ferguson, prin. Fax 433-9306

Gustine, Comanche, Pop. 438
Gustine ISD 200/PK-12
503 W Main St 76455 325-667-7981
Steve Nash, supt. Fax 667-7281
www.gustine.esc14.net/
Gustine S 200/PK-12
503 W Main St 76455 325-667-7303
Ken Baugh, prin. Fax 667-7281

Guthrie, King
Guthrie Common SD 100/PK-12
PO Box 70 79236 806-596-4466
Dan Pickering, supt. Fax 596-4519
www.guthriejags.com/
Guthrie S 100/PK-12
PO Box 70 79236 806-596-4466
Roddy Shipman, prin. Fax 596-4519

Hale Center, Hale, Pop. 2,161
Hale Center ISD 600/PK-12
PO Box 1210 79041 806-839-2451
Rick Teran, supt. Fax 839-2195
www.hale-center.k12.tx.us/
Carr MS 200/5-8
PO Box 1210 79041 806-839-2141
Christian Rabone, prin. Fax 839-4417
Hale Center HS 200/9-12
PO Box 1210 79041 806-839-2452
Keith Langfitt, prin. Fax 839-2059

Hallettsville, Lavaca, Pop. 2,527
Hallettsville ISD 1,000/K-12
PO Box 368 77964 361-798-2242
Joseph T. Patek, supt. Fax 798-5902
www.hisdbrahmas.org
Hallettsville HS 400/9-12
200 N Ridge St 77964 361-798-2242
Lynn Cook, prin. Fax 798-9297

Hallettsville JHS — 300/5-8
410 S Russell St 77964 — 361-798-2242
Sophie Teltschik, prin. — Fax 798-3573

Sacred Heart S — 300/K-12
313 S Texana St 77964 — 361-798-4251
David Smolik, prin. — Fax 798-4970

Hallsville, Harrison, Pop. 2,813
Hallsville ISD — 3,500/PK-12
PO Box 810 75650 — 903-668-5990
Greg Wright, supt. — Fax 668-5990
www.hisd.com
Hallsville HS — 1,200/9-12
PO Box 810 75650 — 903-668-5990
Dr. Brian Morris, prin. — Fax 668-5990
Hallsville JHS — 700/7-8
PO Box 810 75650 — 903-668-5990
Eve Ford, prin. — Fax 668-5990

Haltom City, Tarrant, Pop. 40,475
Birdville ISD — 22,500/PK-12
6125 E Belknap St 76117 — 817-847-5700
Stephen F. Waddell Ed.D., supt. — Fax 838-7261
www.birdville.k12.tx.us
Haltom HS — 2,600/9-12
5501 Haltom Rd 76137 — 817-547-6000
Jim Vaszauskas, prin. — Fax 547-6352
Haltom MS — 800/6-8
5000 Hires Ln 76117 — 817-547-4000
Susan Taylor, prin. — Fax 831-5778
North Oaks MS — 600/6-8
4800 Jordan Park Dr 76117 — 817-547-4600
Terri Thompson, prin. — Fax 581-5352
Other Schools – See North Richland Hills, Richland Hills, Watauga

Hamilton, Hamilton, Pop. 2,938
Hamilton ISD — 900/PK-12
PO Box 392 76531 — 254-386-3149
Sam Bell, supt. — Fax 386-8885
www.hamilton.k12.tx.us
Hamilton HS — 300/9-12
PO Box 392 76531 — 254-386-8167
James Hopper, prin. — Fax 386-4677
Hamilton MS — 200/6-8
PO Box 392 76531 — 254-386-8168
Brenda Smith, prin. — Fax 386-8885

Hamlin, Jones, Pop. 2,096
Hamlin ISD — 500/PK-12
PO Box 338 79520 — 325-576-2722
James Bible, supt. — Fax 576-2152
www.hamlin.esc14.net
Hamlin HS — 100/9-12
450 SW Avenue F 79520 — 325-576-3625
Tony Daniel, prin. — Fax 576-3926
Hamlin MS — 100/6-8
250 SW Avenue F 79520 — 325-576-2933
Chad Worrell, prin. — Fax 576-2317

Hamshire, Jefferson
Hamshire-Fannett ISD — 1,800/PK-12
PO Box 223 77622 — 409-243-2517
Marianne Kondo, supt. — Fax 243-3437
www.hfisd.net/
Hamshire-Fannett HS — 600/9-12
PO Box 223 77622 — 409-243-2512
Dwaine Augustine, prin. — Fax 243-2518
Other Schools – See Beaumont

Happy, Swisher, Pop. 629
Happy ISD — 200/K-12
PO Box 458 79042 — 806-558-5331
Ken Plumlee, supt. — Fax 558-2070
www.happyisd.net
Happy HS, PO Box 458 79042 — 100/7-12
Cindy McCuaig, prin. — 806-558-5311

Hardin, Liberty, Pop. 796
Hardin ISD — 1,100/PK-12
PO Box 330 77561 — 936-298-2112
Craig Ringer, supt. — Fax 298-9161
www.hardin.isd.esc4.net/
Hardin HS — 400/9-12
PO Box 330 77561 — 936-298-2118
Dr. D'Ann Cathriner, prin. — Fax 298-3612
Hardin MS — 200/7-8
PO Box 330 77561 — 936-298-2054
Dr. Michael Bearden, prin. — Fax 298-3264

Harker Heights, Bell, Pop. 18,365
Killeen ISD
Supt. — See Killeen
Eastern Hills MS — 800/6-8
300 Indian Trl 76548 — 254-501-1100
Sharon Miller, prin. — Fax 680-6606
Harker Heights HS — 2,100/9-12
1001 E FM 2410 Rd 76548 — 254-501-0800
Ralph Bray, prin. — Fax 698-5267
Union Grove MS — 100/6-8
101 E Iowa Dr 76548 — 254-200-6580
Ron Gray, prin. — Fax 690-5042

Harleton, Harrison
Harleton ISD — 600/PK-12
PO Box 510 75651 — 903-777-2372
Rickey Logan, supt. — Fax 777-2406
harletonisd.net
Harleton HS — 200/9-12
PO Box 710 75651 — 903-777-2711
Debbie Connor, prin. — Fax 777-2547
Harleton JHS — 200/6-8
PO Box 610 75651 — 903-777-3010
Clint Coyne, prin. — Fax 777-3009

Harlingen, Cameron, Pop. 60,769
Harlingen Consolidated ISD — 21,500/PK-12
1409 E Harrison Ave 78550 — 956-427-3400
Dr. Linda Wade, supt. — Fax 427-3589
www.harlingen.isd.tenet.edu
Coakley MS — 900/6-8
1402 S 6th St 78550 — 956-427-3000
Kevin Brackmeyer, prin. — Fax 427-3006
Gutierrez MS — 1,100/6-8
3205 Wilson Rd 78552 — 956-430-4400
Dr. Marsha Marchbanks, prin. — Fax 430-4480
Harlingen HS — 2,500/9-12
1201 Marshall St 78550 — 956-427-3600
Leeroy Zepeda, prin. — Fax 427-3792

Harlingen HS South — 1,900/9-12
1701 Dixieland Rd 78552 — 956-427-3800
Guadalupe Nava, prin. — Fax 427-3995
Memorial MS — 900/6-8
300 N 13th St 78550 — 956-427-3020
Alex Gonzalez, prin. — Fax 427-3024
Vela MS — 6-8
801 S Palm Blvd 78552 — 956-427-3479
Dr. Alicia Torres, prin. — Fax 427-3549
Vernon MS — 800/6-8
125 S 13th St 78550 — 956-427-3040
Gracie Gutierrez, prin. — Fax 427-3046

Calvary Christian S — 400/PK-10
1815 N 7th St 78550 — 956-425-1882
Karen Zeissel, prin. — Fax 412-0324
Marine Military Academy — 400/8-12
320 Iwo Jima Blvd 78550 — 956-423-6006
General Stephen Cheney, pres. — Fax 423-7716
Texas State Technical College — Post-Sec.
1901 Loop 499 78550 — 956-364-4001
University of Cosmetology Arts & Science — Post-Sec.
913 N 13th St 78550 — 956-412-1212

Harper, Gillespie
Harper ISD — 500/PK-12
PO Box 68 78631 — 830-864-4044
Pari Whitten, supt. — Fax 864-4060
www.harper.txed.net/
Harper HS — 200/9-12
PO Box 68 78631 — 830-864-4044
Chris Stevenson, prin. — Fax 864-4748
Harper MS — 100/6-8
PO Box 68 78631 — 830-864-4044
Chris Stevenson, prin. — Fax 864-4748

Harrold, Wilbarger
Harrold ISD — 100/K-12
PO Box 400 76364 — 940-886-2213
David Thweatt, supt. — Fax 886-2215
www.esc9.net/harroldisd/
Harrold S — 100/K-12
PO Box 400 76364 — 940-886-2213
Craig Templeton, prin. — Fax 886-2215

Hart, Castro, Pop. 1,149
Hart ISD — 300/PK-12
PO Box 490 79043 — 806-938-2143
Digger Elam, supt. — Fax 938-2610
www.region16.net/hartisd
Hart JSHS — 100/7-12
PO Box 490 79043 — 806-938-2141
Don Sanders, prin. — Fax 938-2610

Hartley, Hartley
Hartley ISD — 200/K-12
PO Box 408 79044 — 806-365-4458
Jimmy Hoyle, supt. — Fax 365-4459
www.hartleytx.com/hartleyisd
Hartley S — 200/K-12
PO Box 408 79044 — 806-365-4458
Rick McCarty, prin. — Fax 365-4459

Haskell, Haskell, Pop. 2,909
Haskell CISD — 500/PK-12
PO Box 937 79521 — 940-864-2602
Eddie Bland, supt. — Fax 864-8096
www.haskell.esc14.net/
Haskell HS, PO Box 937 79521 — 200/9-12
Bryan McCulloch, prin. — 940-864-8535
Other Schools – See Rochester

Paint Creek ISD — 100/K-12
4485 FM 600 79521 — 940-864-2471
Don Ballard, supt. — Fax 864-8038
www.paintcreek.esc14.net
Paint Creek S — 100/K-12
4485 FM 600 79521 — 940-864-2471
James Horton, prin. — Fax 864-8038

Hawkins, Wood, Pop. 1,424
Hawkins ISD — 700/PK-12
PO Box 1430 75765 — 903-769-2181
Dan Rose, supt. — Fax 769-0505
www.hawkinsisd.org
Hawkins HS — 200/9-12
PO Box 1430 75765 — 903-769-0571
Charles Leffall, prin. — Fax 769-0573
Hawkins MS — 200/6-8
PO Box 1430 75765 — 903-769-0552
David Ledkins, prin. — Fax 769-0583

Jarvis Christian College — Post-Sec.
PO Box 1470 75765 — 903-769-5700

Hawley, Jones, Pop. 624
Hawley ISD — 700/PK-12
PO Box 440 79525 — 325-537-2214
Bobby Matthews, supt. — Fax 537-2265
www.hawley.esc14.net
Hawley HS — 200/9-12
PO Box 440 79525 — 325-537-2722
Christy Ames, prin. — Fax 537-2265
Hawley MS — 200/6-8
PO Box 440 79525 — 325-537-2070
Whitney Hill, prin. — Fax 537-2265

Hearne, Robertson, Pop. 4,657
Hearne ISD — 1,200/PK-12
900 Wheelock St 77859 — 979-279-3200
David C. Deaver, supt. — Fax 279-3631
www.hearne.k12.tx.us/
Hearne HS — 300/9-12
1201 W Brown St 77859 — 979-279-2332
Norris McDaniel, prin. — Fax 279-8006
Hearne JHS — 200/7-8
401 Wheelock St 77859 — 979-279-2449
Leon Jackson, prin. — Fax 279-8033
Adult Learning Center — Adult
1210 Hackberry St 77859 — 979-279-8020
Karan Elliott, prin. — Fax 279-8017

Hebbronville, Jim Hogg, Pop. 4,465
Jim Hogg County ISD — 1,100/PK-12
PO Box 880 78361 — 361-527-3203
Pedro Lopez, supt. — Fax 527-4823
Hebbronville HS — 400/9-12
PO Box 880 78361 — 361-527-5751
Arnulfo Guerra, prin. — Fax 527-5989

Hebbronville JHS — 200/6-8
PO Box 880 78361 — 361-527-4815
Fantina Garcia, prin. — Fax 527-5986

Hedley, Donley, Pop. 386
Hedley ISD — 200/PK-12
PO Box 69 79237 — 806-856-5323
Bryan Hill, supt. — Fax 856-5372
Hedley S — 200/PK-12
PO Box 69 79237 — 806-856-5323
Bryan Hill, prin. — Fax 856-5372

Helotes, Bexar, Pop. 5,239
Northside ISD
Supt. — See San Antonio
O'Connor HS — 3,000/9-12
12221 Leslie Rd 78023 — 210-397-4800
Larry Martin, prin. — Fax 695-4804

Hemphill, Sabine, Pop. 1,076
Hemphill ISD — 1,000/PK-12
PO Box 1950 75948 — 409-787-3371
Mike Terry, supt. — Fax 787-4005
www.hemphill.esc7.net
Hemphill HS — 300/9-12
PO Box 1950 75948 — 409-787-3371
Marc Griffin, prin. — Fax 787-1259
Hemphill MS — 300/5-8
PO Box 1950 75948 — 409-787-3371
C.J. O'Neal, prin. — Fax 787-4005

Hempstead, Waller, Pop. 6,051
Hempstead ISD — 1,400/PK-12
PO Box 1007 77445 — 979-826-3304
Anneta Buenger, supt. — Fax 826-5510
www.hempstead.isd.esc4.net
Hempstead HS — 400/9-12
PO Box 1007 77445 — 979-826-3331
Michael Lawson, prin. — Fax 826-4779
Hempstead MS — 300/6-8
PO Box 1007 77445 — 979-826-2530
Sarah Garrison, prin. — Fax 826-5583

Henderson, Rusk, Pop. 11,069
Henderson ISD — 3,500/PK-12
PO Box 728 75653 — 903-657-8511
Tommy Alexander, supt. — Fax 657-9271
www.hendersonisd.org/
Henderson HS — 1,100/9-12
PO Box 728 75653 — 903-657-1483
Stacey Sullivan, prin. — Fax 657-7604
Henderson MS — 800/6-8
PO Box 728 75653 — 903-657-1491
Kelly Teems, prin. — Fax 657-6499

Henrietta, Clay, Pop. 3,321
Henrietta ISD — 1,000/PK-12
1801 E Crafton St 76365 — 940-538-7500
Jeff McClure, supt. — Fax 538-7505
www.henrietta.isd.net
Henrietta HS — 300/9-12
1700 E Crafton St 76365 — 940-538-7530
Jerre Gibbons, prin. — Fax 538-7535
Henrietta JHS — 200/6-8
308 E Gilbert St 76365 — 940-538-7520
Gary Parrish, prin. — Fax 538-7525

Midway ISD — 100/PK-12
12142 State Highway 148 S 76365 — 940-476-2215
Hollis Adams, supt. — Fax 476-2226
www.esc9.net/midway
Midway S — 100/PK-12
RR 2 Box 179 76365 — 940-476-2222
Peggy Demoss, prin. — Fax 476-2226

Hereford, Deaf Smith, Pop. 14,428
Hereford ISD — 3,600/K-12
601 N 25 Mile Ave 79045 — 806-363-7600
Dr. Michael Stevens, supt. — Fax 363-7699
www.herefordisd.net
Hereford HS, 200 Avenue F 79045 — 1,100/9-12
Richard Sauceda, prin. — 806-363-7620
Hereford JHS, 704 La Plata St 79045 — 900/6-8
Amy Lopez, prin. — 806-363-7630

Community Christian S — 50/5-12
PO Box 487 79045 — 806-364-8867
Jan Wilks, prin. — Fax 364-0084

Hermleigh, Scurry
Hermleigh ISD — 200/K-12
1026 School Ave 79526 — 325-863-2772
Gary Rotan, supt. — Fax 863-2713
www.hermleigh.esc14.net/
Hermleigh S — 200/K-12
1026 School Ave 79526 — 325-863-2451
Clarence Spieker, prin. — Fax 863-2713

Hewitt, McLennan, Pop. 12,261
Midway ISD
Supt. — See Waco
Midway MS — 1,000/7-8
800 Hewitt Dr 76643 — 254-761-5680
Joe Kucera, prin. — Fax 761-5775

Hico, Hamilton, Pop. 1,345
Hico ISD — 700/PK-12
PO Box 218 76457 — 254-796-2181
Rod Townsend, supt. — Fax 796-2446
www.hico-isd.net
Hico HS — 200/9-12
PO Box 218 76457 — 254-796-2184
Jon Hartgraves, prin. — Fax 796-2446
Hico JHS — 200/6-8
PO Box 218 76457 — 254-796-2182
Delores Helms, prin. — Fax 796-9830

Hidalgo, Hidalgo, Pop. 9,110
Hidalgo ISD — 3,200/PK-12
PO Box D 78557 — 956-843-3300
Daniel King Ph.D., supt. — Fax 843-3343
hidalgo.tx.schoolwebpages.com
Diaz JHS — 700/6-8
PO Box D 78557 — 956-843-3140
Dr. M. Vidaurri, prin. — Fax 843-3198
Hidalgo HS — 900/9-12
PO Box D 78557 — 956-843-3160
Edward Blaha, prin. — Fax 843-3322

Higgins, Lipscomb, Pop. 434
Higgins ISD 100/K-12
PO Box 218 79046 806-852-2171
Hope Appel, supt. Fax 852-3502
Higgins S 100/K-12
PO Box 218 79046 806-852-2631
Hope Appel, prin. Fax 852-3502

High Island, Galveston
High Island ISD 300/K-12
PO Box 246 77623 409-286-5317
Michael Sims, supt. Fax 286-5351
www.esc05.k12.tx.us/hiisd/hiweb.html
High Island HS 100/9-12
PO Box 246 77623 409-286-5314
Mike Sims, prin. Fax 286-2120
High Island MS 100/6-8
PO Box 246 77623 409-286-5314
Mike Sims, prin. Fax 286-2120

Highlands, Harris, Pop. 6,632
Goose Creek ISD
Supt. — See Baytown
Highlands JHS 700/6-8
1212 E Wallisville Rd 77562 281-420-4695
Steve Herring, prin. Fax 426-4301

Chinquapin S 100/7-12
2615 E Wallisville Rd 77562 281-426-5551

Highland Village, Denton, Pop. 14,080
Lewisville ISD
Supt. — See Flower Mound
Briarhill MS 900/6-8
2100 Briarhill Blvd 75077 469-713-5975
Mechelle Bryson, prin. Fax 350-3350

Hillsboro, Hill, Pop. 8,705
Hillsboro ISD 1,800/PK-12
121 E Franklin St 76645 254-582-8585
Jerry Maze, supt. Fax 582-4165
www.hillsboroisd.org
Hillsboro HS 500/9-12
1600 Abbott Ave 76645 254-582-4100
Nina LeBlanc, prin. Fax 582-4108
Hillsboro JHS 300/7-8
210 E Walnut St 76645 254-582-4120
Mark Edens, prin. Fax 582-4122

Hill College Post-Sec.
PO Box 619 76645 254-582-2555

Hitchcock, Galveston, Pop. 7,176
Hitchcock ISD 1,200/PK-12
8117 Highway 6 77563 409-986-5514
Barbara Wilson, supt. Fax 986-5141
www.hitchcockisd.org
Crosby MS 400/5-8
7801 Neville Ave 77563 409-986-5528
Randy Dowdy, prin. Fax 986-9254
Hitchcock HS 300/9-12
6625 FM 2004 Rd 77563 409-986-5581
Cassandra Hart, prin. Fax 986-9339

Holland, Bell, Pop. 1,101
Holland ISD 500/PK-12
PO Box 217 76534 254-657-0175
Cindy Gunn, supt. Fax 657-0172
www.holland.k12.tx.us
Bowman MS 100/6-8
PO Box 217 76534 254-657-2224
Mike Mazoch, prin. Fax 657-2250
Holland HS 100/9-12
PO Box 217 76534 254-657-2523
Britt Gordon, prin. Fax 657-2250

Holliday, Archer, Pop. 1,710
Holliday ISD 900/PK-12
PO Box 689 76366 940-586-1281
Clarke Boyd, supt. Fax 586-1492
www.esc9.net/holliday
Holliday HS 300/9-12
PO Box 947 76366 940-586-1624
Kent Lemons, prin. Fax 586-9501
Holliday MS 200/6-8
PO Box 977 76366 940-586-1314
Kelly Carver, prin. Fax 586-1492

Hondo, Medina, Pop. 8,208
Hondo ISD 2,100/PK-12
PO Box 308 78861 830-426-3027
Clyde Parsons, supt. Fax 426-7683
www.hondo.k12.tx.us
Hondo HS 600/9-12
2603 Avenue H 78861 830-426-3341
Larry Carroll, prin. Fax 426-7690
McDowell JHS 500/6-8
1602 27th St S 78861 830-426-2261
Michael Neuman, prin. Fax 426-7624

Honey Grove, Fannin, Pop. 1,788
Honey Grove ISD 700/PK-12
540 6th St 75446 903-378-2264
Jan M. Cummins, supt. Fax 378-2991
www.honeygroveisd.net/
Honey Grove HS 200/9-12
540 6th St 75446 903-378-2264
Jeffry Clark, prin. Fax 378-3050
Honey Grove MS 200/6-8
540 6th St 75446 903-378-2264
Robert Milton, prin. Fax 378-2095

Hooks, Bowie, Pop. 2,935
Hooks ISD 1,100/PK-12
PO Box 39 75561 903-547-6077
Kathy Allen, supt. Fax 547-2943
www.esc8.net/hooks
Hooks HS, PO Box 1447 75561 400/9-12
Lynne Hopper, prin. 903-547-2215
Hooks JHS, PO Box 249 75561 300/5-8
Shane Krueger, prin. 903-547-2568

Houston, Harris, Pop. 2,009,690
Aldine ISD 55,500/PK-12
14910 Aldine Westfield Rd 77032 281-449-1011
Nadine Kujawa, supt. Fax 449-4911
www.aldine.k12.tx.us
Aldine MS 900/7-8
14908 Aldine Westfield Rd 77032 281-985-6580
Todd Davis, prin. Fax 985-6480
Aldine Ninth Grade S 900/9-9
10650 North Fwy 77037 281-878-6800
Jeanie Outhouse, prin. Fax 878-6824
Aldine SHS 2,100/10-12
11101 Airline Dr 77037 281-448-5231
Cecil Hutson, prin. Fax 878-0641
Carver HS 600/9-12
2100 S Victory Dr 77088 281-878-0310
Willie Pickens, prin. Fax 591-8579
Drew Academy 900/6-8
1910 W Little York Rd 77091 281-878-0360
Fred Walker, prin. Fax 447-4694
Eisenhower Ninth Grade S 900/9-9
3550 W Gulf Bank Rd 77088 281-878-7700
Melvin McGowen, prin. Fax 878-7736
Eisenhower SHS 2,200/10-12
7922 Antoine Dr 77088 281-878-0900
Alonzo Reynolds, prin. Fax 448-2936
Grantham Academy 1,200/7-8
13300 Chrisman Rd 77039 281-985-6590
Kenneth Hodgkinson, prin. Fax 985-6595
Hambrick MS 1,000/7-8
4600 Aldine Mail Rd 77039 281-985-6570
Holly Fisackerly, prin. Fax 442-9036
Hoffman MS 1,200/7-8
6101 W Little York Rd 77091 713-613-7670
Rhonda Johnson, prin. Fax 613-7675
MacArthur Ninth Grade S 900/9-9
12111 Gloger St 77039 281-985-7400
Therese Samperi, prin. Fax 985-7423
MacArthur SHS 1,800/10-12
4400 Aldine Mail Rd 77039 281-985-6330
Nancy Blackwell, prin. Fax 985-6294
Nimitz 9th Grade S 800/9-9
2425 WW Thorne Blvd 77073 281-209-8200
Ann-Marie Hazzan, prin. Fax 209-8220
Nimitz SHS 1,900/10-12
2005 WW Thorne Blvd 77073 281-443-7480
Ken Knippel, prin. Fax 233-4331
Shotwell MS 1,000/7-8
6515 Trail Valley Way 77086 281-878-0960
Wanda Walker, prin. Fax 591-8564
Stovall MS 1,100/7-8
11201 Airline Dr 77037 281-878-0670
Watson Wright, prin. Fax 448-0636
Other Schools – See Humble

Alief ISD 43,800/PK-12
12302 High Star Dr 77072 281-498-8110
Louis B. Stoerner, supt. Fax 575-1923
www.aliefisd.net/
Albright MS 1,300/7-8
6315 Winkleman Rd 77083 281-983-8411
Walter Jackson, prin. Fax 983-8443
Alief MS 1,200/6-8
4415 Cook Rd 77072 281-983-8422
Maggie Cuellar, prin. Fax 983-8053
Alief Taylor HS 2,900/9-12
7555 Howell Sugar Land Rd 77083 281-988-3500
Manette Schaller, prin. Fax 561-7214
Elsik HS 2,600/10-12
12601 High Star Dr 77072 281-498-8110
Linda Graessle, prin. Fax 530-7058
Elsik Ninth Grade Center 9-9
6767 S Dairy Ashford St 77072 281-988-3239
Gregory Freeman, prin. Fax 988-3319
Hastings HS 2,600/10-12
4410 Cook Rd 77072 281-498-8110
Rhonda McWilliams, prin. Fax 561-5763
Hastings Ninth Grade Center 9-9
6750 Cook Rd 77072 281-988-3139
Gina Tomas, prin. Fax 988-3419
Holub MS 1,200/7-8
9515 S Dairy Ashford St 77099 281-983-8433
Pat Brown, prin. Fax 983-8398
Kerr HS 700/9-12
8150 Howell Sugar Land Rd 77083 281-983-8484
Pat McCutcheon, prin. Fax 983-8014
Killough MS 1,000/7-8
7600 Synott Rd 77083 281-983-8444
Luis Olivas, prin. Fax 983-8067
O'Donnell MS 1,500/6-8
14041 Alief Clodine Rd 77082 281-495-6000
Tyrone Sylvester, prin. Fax 568-5029
Olle MS 1,100/7-8
9200 Boone Rd 77099 281-983-8455
Jackie Armwood, prin. Fax 983-8077
Other Schools – See Alief

Clear Creek ISD
Supt. — See League City
Clear Lake 9th Grade Center 9-9
2903 Falcon Pass 77062 281-284-1900
Brett Lemley, prin. Fax 284-1905
Clear Lake HS 3,500/9-12
2929 Bay Area Blvd 77058 281-284-1900
Dr. Christopher Moran, prin. Fax 284-1905
Clear Lake IS 1,100/6-8
15545 El Camino Real 77062 281-488-1296
Dean Muths, prin. Fax 488-8795
Space Center IS 1,200/6-8
17400 Saturn Ln 77058 281-284-3300
Susan Stuart, prin. Fax 284-3305

Cypress-Fairbanks ISD 75,500/PK-12
PO Box 692003 77269 281-897-4000
David Anthony Ed.D., supt. Fax 897-4125
www.cfisd.net
Aragon MS 1,600/6-8
16823 West Rd 77095 281-856-5100
Vicki McComas, prin. Fax 856-5105
Bleyl MS 1,400/6-8
10800 Mills Rd 77070 281-897-4340
Dr. Donna Poland, prin. Fax 897-4353
Campbell MS 1,300/6-8
11415 Bobcat Rd 77064 281-897-4300
Dr. Robert Hatcher, prin. Fax 807-8634
Cook MS 1,400/6-8
9111 Wheatland Dr 77064 281-897-4400
Dr. Robert Borneman, prin. Fax 897-3850
Cypress Creek HS 2,900/9-12
9815 Grant Rd 77070 281-897-4200
Jim Wells, prin. Fax 897-4193
Cypress Falls HS 3,200/9-12
9811 Huffmeister Rd 77095 281-856-1000
Dr. Robert Worthy, prin. Fax 856-1445
Cypress Ridge HS 2,400/9-12
7900 N Eldridge Pkwy 77041 713-807-8000
Claudio Garcia, prin. Fax 807-8005
Dean MS 1,400/6-8
14104 Reo St 77040 713-460-6153
Mike Smith, prin. Fax 460-6197
Jersey Village HS 3,100/9-12
7600 Solomon St 77040 713-896-3400
Ralph Funk, prin. Fax 896-3438
Kahla MS 6-8
16212 W Little York Rd 77084 281-345-3260
Marvin Webster, prin.
Labay MS 1,400/6-8
15435 Willow River Dr 77095 281-463-5800
Dr. Cheryl Johns, prin. Fax 463-5804
Langham Creek HS 3,200/9-12
17610 FM 529 Rd 77095 281-463-5400
Tom Strother, prin. Fax 345-3509
Truitt MS 1,400/6-8
6600 Addicks Satsuma Rd 77084 281-856-1100
Robert Hull, prin. Fax 856-1104
Watkins MS 1,500/6-8
4800 Cairnvillage St 77084 281-463-5850
Diana Lewis, prin. Fax 463-5508
Other Schools – See Cypress, Katy

Fort Bend ISD
Supt. — See Sugar Land
Hodges Bend MS 1,800/6-8
16510 Bissonnet St 77083 281-634-3000
Corliss Rogers, prin. Fax 634-3028
McAuliffe MS 1,400/6-8
16650 S Post Oak Rd 77053 281-634-3360
Isaac Malbrough, prin. Fax 634-3393
Willowridge HS 1,800/9-12
16301 Chimney Rock Rd 77053 281-634-2450
Billy Polk, prin. Fax 634-2513

Galena Park ISD 21,600/PK-12
14705 Woodforest Blvd 77015 832-386-1000
Dr. Mark Henry, supt. Fax 386-1298
www.galenaparkisd.com
Cunningham MS 1,400/6-8
14110 Wallisville Rd 77049 713-450-9000
Thad M. Gittens, prin. Fax 450-9014
North Shore HS 2,100/9-10
13501 Hollypark Dr 77015 713-453-7183
John Moore, prin. Fax 450-7335
North Shore MS 1,700/6-8
120 Castlegory Rd 77015 832-386-2600
Paul Drexler, prin. Fax 450-7006
North Shore SHS 1,600/11-12
353 N Castlegory Rd 77049 281-459-4494
Kenneth Wallace, prin. Fax 459-2967
Woodland Acres MS 400/6-8
12947 Myrtle Ln 77015 713-450-7300
Michelle Chae, prin. Fax 450-7304
Other Schools – See Galena Park

Houston ISD 194,200/PK-12
3830 Richmond Ave 77027 713-556-6005
Dr. Abelardo Saavedra, supt. Fax 892-6061
www.houstonisd.org/
Attucks MS 900/6-8
4330 Bellfort St 77051 713-732-3670
Renaldo Wallace, prin. Fax 732-3677
Austin HS 2,000/9-12
1700 Dumble St 77023 713-924-1600
Linda M. Llorente, prin. Fax 923-3157
Black MS 700/6-8
1575 Chantilly Ln 77018 713-613-2505
Suzanne Mihaloglou, prin. Fax 613-2233
Burbank MS 1,400/6-8
315 Berry Rd 77022 713-696-2720
Charlotte Parker, prin. Fax 696-2723
Carnegie Vanguard HS 200/9-12
10401 Scott St 77051 713-732-3690
Ramon Moss, prin. Fax 732-3695
Carter Career Center Vo/Tech
1700 Gregg St 77020 713-226-2651
Rhonda Cotton, prin. Fax 226-2666
Challenge Early College HS 9-12
5601 West Loop S 77081 713-664-9712
Justin Fuentes, prin. Fax 664-9780
Chavez HS 2,300/9-12
8501 Howard Dr 77017 713-495-6950
Dan P. Martinez, prin. Fax 495-6986
Clifton MS 1,100/6-8
6001 Golden Forest Dr 77092 713-613-2516
Beverly Teal, prin. Fax 613-2523
Cullen MS 700/6-8
6900 Scott St 77021 713-746-8180
Ronald Mumphery, prin. Fax 746-8181
Davis HS 1,700/9-12
1101 Quitman St 77009 713-226-4900
Diana Mulet, prin. Fax 226-4999
Deady MS 1,100/6-8
2500 Broadway St 77012 713-845-7411
James D. Troutman, prin. Fax 845-5645
DeBakey Health Professions HS 700/9-12
3100 Shenandoah St 77021 713-741-2410
Charlesetta Deason, prin. Fax 746-5211
Dowling MS 1,600/6-8
14000 Stancliff St 77045 713-434-5603
Barrett Brooks, prin. Fax 434-5608
Edison MS 1,000/6-8
6901 Avenue I 77011 713-924-1800
George Martin, prin. Fax 924-1316
Empowerment College Preparatory HS 9-12
3730 S Acres Dr 77047 713-732-9231
Misha Lesley, prin.
Fleming MS 600/6-8
4910 Collingsworth St 77026 713-671-4170
Wiley Johnson, prin. Fax 671-4176
Fondren MS 900/6-8
6333 S Braeswood Blvd 77096 713-778-3360
Barbara Neal, prin. Fax 778-3362
Fonville MS 1,200/6-8
725 E Little York Rd 77076 713-696-2825
Efrain Olivo, prin. Fax 696-2829
Furr HS 1,100/9-12
520 Mercury Dr 77013 713-675-1118
Bertie Simmons, prin. Fax 671-3612
Grady MS 600/6-8
5215 San Felipe St 77056 713-625-1411
Teresa Stoger, prin. Fax 625-1415
Gregory-Lincoln Education Center 500/6-8
1101 Taft St 77019 713-942-1400
Johnnie Jackson, prin. Fax 942-1406
Hamilton MS 1,200/6-8
139 E 20th St 77008 713-802-4725
Roger A. Bunnell, prin. Fax 802-4731

Hartman MS 1,500/6-8
7111 Westover St 77087 713-845-7435
Joseph Addison, prin. Fax 847-4706
Henry MS 1,200/6-8
10702 E Hardy Rd 77093 713-696-2650
Cynthia Banda, prin. Fax 696-2657
Hogg MS 900/6-8
1100 Merrill St 77009 713-802-4700
Imelda Medrano, prin. Fax 802-4708
Holland MS 800/6-8
1600 Gellhorn Dr 77029 713-671-3860
Brian McDonald, prin. Fax 671-3874
Houston HS 2,900/9-12
9400 Irvington Blvd 77076 713-696-8970
Aida Tello, prin. Fax 696-8984
HS for Law Enforcement/Criminal Justice 700/9-12
4701 Dickson St 77007 713-867-5100
Carol Mosteit, prin. Fax 802-4600
HS for Performing & Visual Arts 700/9-12
4001 Stanford St 77006 713-942-1960
Herbert Karpicke, prin. Fax 942-1968
Jackson MS 1,200/6-8
5100 Polk St 77023 713-924-1760
Flor E. Blanco-Perfetti, prin. Fax 924-1768
Johnston MS 1,300/6-8
10410 Manhattan Dr 77096 713-726-3616
Linda Balkin, prin. Fax 726-3622
Jones HS 1,100/9-12
7414 Saint Lo Rd 77033 713-733-1111
Adele Rogers, prin. Fax 732-3450
Jordan HS for Careers Vo/Tech
5800 Eastex Fwy 77026 713-636-6900
Rever Givens, prin. Fax 636-6917
Kashmere HS 900/9-12
6900 Wileyvale Rd 77028 713-631-2185
Willie Spencer, prin. Fax 636-6433
Key MS 900/6-8
4000 Kelley St 77026 713-636-6000
Mable Caleb, prin. Fax 636-6008
Lamar HS 3,300/9-12
3325 Westheimer Rd 77098 713-522-5960
James McSwain, prin. Fax 535-3769
Las Americas MS 100/6-8
5909 Glenmont Dr 77081 713-661-1670
Marie Moreno, prin. Fax 660-9259
Lee HS 2,200/9-12
6529 Beverlyhill St 77057 713-787-1700
Steven Amstutz, prin. Fax 787-1723
Long MS 1,500/6-8
6501 Bellaire Blvd 77074 713-778-3380
Diana De La Rosa, prin. Fax 778-3387
Madison HS 2,100/9-12
13719 White Heather Dr 77045 713-433-9801
Gloria Legington, prin. Fax 434-5242
Marshall MS 1,100/6-8
1115 Noble St 77009 713-226-2600
Juan Gonzales, prin. Fax 226-2605
McReynolds MS 700/6-8
5910 Market St 77020 713-671-3650
Jorge Arredondo, prin. Fax 671-3657
Middle College for Tech. Careers at TSU Vo/Tech
5655 Selinsky Rd 77048 713-523-9097
LaShawn Porter, prin. Fax 523-9202
Milby HS 2,100/9-12
1601 Broadway St 77012 713-928-7401
Richard Barajas, prin. Fax 928-7474
Ortiz MS 1,000/6-8
6767 Telephone Rd 77061 713-845-5650
Yolanda Alleman, prin. Fax 845-5646
Pershing MS 1,700/6-8
7000 Braes Blvd 77025 713-295-5240
Bryce Amos, prin. Fax 295-5252
Reagan HS 1,700/9-12
413 E 13th St 77008 713-861-5694
Robert Pambello, prin. Fax 867-0876
Revere MS 1,300/6-8
10502 Briar Forest Dr 77042 713-917-3500
Kenneth Estrella, prin. Fax 917-3505
Ryan MS, 2610 Elgin St 77004 700/6-8
Edward Thompson, prin. 713-942-1932
Scarborough HS 800/9-12
4141 Costa Rica Rd 77092 713-613-2200
Lucy Anderson, prin. Fax 613-2205
Sharpstown HS 1,700/9-12
7504 Bissonnet St 77074 713-771-7215
David Kendler, prin. Fax 773-6103
Sharpstown MS 1,400/6-8
8330 Triola Ln 77036 713-778-3440
Jeffrey Amerson, prin. Fax 778-3444
Sterling HS 1,200/9-12
11625 Martindale Rd 77048 713-991-0510
Marcellars Mason, prin. Fax 991-8111
Stevenson MS 1,200/6-8
9595 Winkler Dr 77017 713-943-5700
Jane Crump, prin. Fax 943-5711
Thomas MS 800/6-8
5655 Selinsky Rd 77048 713-732-3500
Bill Sorrells, prin. Fax 732-3511
Waltrip HS 1,800/9-12
1900 W 34th St 77018 713-688-1361
Steven Siebenaler, prin. Fax 957-7743
Washington HS 1,300/9-12
119 E 39th St 77018 713-692-5947
Franklin Wesley, prin. Fax 696-6657
Welch MS 1,300/6-8
11544 S Gessner Dr 77071 713-778-3300
Ruby J. Andrews, prin. Fax 995-6067
West Briar MS 1,400/6-8
13733 Brimhurst Dr 77077 281-368-2140
Geoffrey Ohl, prin. Fax 368-2194
Westbury HS 1,900/9-12
11911 Chimney Rock Rd 77035 713-723-6015
Eric Coleman, prin. Fax 726-2165
Westside HS 2,800/9-12
14201 Briar Forest Dr 77077 281-920-8000
Paul Castro, prin. Fax 920-8059
Wheatley HS 800/9-12
4900 Market St 77020 713-671-3900
Bruce Goffney, prin. Fax 671-3951
Worthing HS 1,300/9-12
9215 Scott St 77051 713-733-3433
Robert Dean, prin. Fax 731-5537
Yates HS 1,400/9-12
3703 Sampson St 77004 713-748-5400
George August, prin. Fax 746-8206
Kay On Going Education Center Adult
4425 N Shepherd Dr 77018 713-696-7350
Linda Bundage, prin. Fax 696-7356
Other Schools – See Bellaire

Katy ISD
Supt. — See Katy
Mayde Creek HS 3,400/9-12
19202 Groeschke Rd 77084 281-237-3000
O.D. Tompkins, prin. Fax 644-1715
Mayde Creek JHS 1,200/6-8
2700 Greenhouse Rd 77084 281-237-3900
Richard Hull, prin. Fax 644-1650

Klein ISD
Supt. — See Klein
Klein Forest HS 3,200/9-12
11400 Misty Valley Dr 77066 832-484-4500
Bill Lakin, prin. Fax 484-7801
Klein IS 1,200/6-8
4710 W Mount Houston Rd 77088 832-249-4900
Anthony Indelicato, prin. Fax 249-4046
Wunderlich IS 1,300/6-8
11800 Misty Valley Dr 77066 832-249-5200
Patricia Crittendon, prin. Fax 249-4050

North Forest ISD 11,100/PK-12
PO Box 23278 77228 713-633-1600
James Simpson Ph.D., supt. Fax 491-1097
northforest.schoolnet.com/
Forest Brook HS 1,100/9-12
7525 Tidwell Rd 77016 713-631-7720
Marshall Dupas, prin. Fax 635-6309
Kirby MS 700/7-8
9706 Mesa Dr 77078 713-633-0670
Rubye Gilbert, prin. Fax 636-7895
Oak Village MS 600/7-8
6602 Winfield Rd 77050 281-449-6561
Robert Coates, prin. Fax 671-7650
Smiley Career & Technology S Vo/Tech
10726 Mesa Dr 77078 713-636-6753
Leslie Berry, prin. Fax 636-8119
Smiley HS 1,600/9-12
10725 Mesa Dr 77078 713-636-4300
Norris Rhines, prin. Fax 636-8116

Pasadena ISD
Supt. — See Pasadena
Beverly Hills IS 1,100/6-8
11111 Beamer Rd 77089 713-740-0420
Stephanie Wright, prin. Fax 740-4051
Dobie HS 2,700/9-12
10220 Blackhawk Blvd 77089 281-481-3000
Steve Jamail, prin. Fax 929-3816
Thompson IS 1,100/6-8
11309 Sagedowne Ln 77089 713-740-0510
Dr. Gregory Jones, prin. Fax 740-4083

Sheldon ISD 5,200/PK-12
11411 C E King Pkwy 77044 281-727-2000
Dr. G. Steve Mills, supt. Fax 727-2085
www.sheldonisd.com/
King HS 1,100/9-12
8540 C E King Pkwy 77044 281-727-3500
Cindy Worley, prin. Fax 459-7346
King MS 700/7-8
8530 C E King Pkwy 77044 281-727-4300
Donna Ullrich, prin. Fax 459-7452

Spring Branch ISD 32,600/PK-12
955 Campbell Rd 77024 713-464-1511
Duncan Klussmann Ed.D., supt. Fax 365-4071
www.springbranchisd.com/
Harold Guthrie Career Center Vo/Tech
10660 Hammerly Blvd 77043 713-365-4610
Joe Kolenda, prin. Fax 365-4621
Landrum MS 800/6-8
2200 Ridgecrest Dr 77055 713-365-4020
Jennifer Parker, prin. Fax 365-4040
Memorial HS 2,200/9-12
935 Echo Ln 77024 713-365-5110
Stephen Shorter, prin. Fax 365-5138
Memorial MS 1,000/6-8
12550 Vindon Dr 77024 713-365-5400
Bob Price, prin. Fax 365-5411
Northbrook HS 2,100/9-12
1 Raider Cir 77080 713-365-4430
Randolph Adami, prin. Fax 365-4416
Northbrook MS 700/6-8
3030 Rosefield Dr 77080 713-329-6510
Laura Schulmann, prin. Fax 329-6523
Spring Branch MS 1,100/6-8
1000 Piney Point Rd 77024 713-365-5500
Cathryn White, prin. Fax 365-5515
Spring Forest MS 900/6-8
14240 Memorial Dr 77079 281-560-7500
Marianne Cribbin, prin. Fax 560-7509
Spring Oaks MS 900/6-8
2150 Shadowdale Dr 77043 713-365-4515
David Sablatura, prin. Fax 365-4522
Spring Woods HS 2,200/9-12
2045 Gessner Dr 77080 713-365-4475
Wayne Schaper, prin. Fax 365-4474
Spring Woods MS 800/6-8
9810 Neuens Rd 77080 713-365-4110
Cynthia Chai, prin. Fax 365-4115
Stratford HS 2,100/9-12
14555 Fern Dr 77079 281-560-7550
Ann Kucera, prin. Fax 560-7578

Spring ISD 23,900/PK-12
16717 Ella Blvd 77090 281-586-1100
Ralph Draper, supt. Fax 586-1134
www.springisd.org
Bammel MS 700/6-8
16711 Ella Blvd 77090 281-586-2600
Patricia Crittendon, prin. Fax 586-2621
Claughton MS 1,300/6-8
3000 Spears Rd 77067 281-355-3101
Delic Loyde, prin. Fax 355-3104
DeKaney HS 9-12
22351 Imperial Valley Dr 77073
Bill Lakin, prin.
Wells MS 1,000/6-8
4033 Gladeridge Dr 77068 281-586-2630
Cornelius Phelps, prin. Fax 586-2637
Westfield HS 2,700/10-12
16713 Ella Blvd 77090 281-586-1300
Julie Guillory, prin. Fax 587-3998
Westfield Ninth Grade Center 9-9
16713 Ella Blvd 77090 832-446-1401
Eric Wiestruck, prin. Fax 446-1402
Other Schools – See Spring

Academy of Hair Design Post-Sec.
744 FM 1960 Rd W Ste G 77090 281-893-0980
Alexander-Smith Academy 100/9-12
10255 Richmond Ave 77042 713-266-0920
Alfred G. Glassell School of Art Post-Sec.
PO Box 6826 77265 713-639-7500
American College of Acupuncture Post-Sec.
9100 Park West Dr 77063 713-780-9777
Art Institute of Houston Post-Sec.
1900 Yorktown St 77056 713-623-2040
Art Institute of Houston - Culinary Post-Sec.
1900 Yorktown St 77056 800-275-4244
Astrodome Dental Career Center Post-Sec.
2646 South Loop W Ste 415 77054 713-664-5300
Awty International S 1,100/PK-12
7455 Awty School Ln 77055 713-686-4850
Dr. David Watson, hdmstr. Fax 686-4956
Banff S 200/PK-12
13726 Cutten Rd 77069 281-444-9326
Deborah Wasser, prin. Fax 444-3632
Baylor College of Medicine Post-Sec.
1 Baylor Plz 77030 713-798-4951
Behold! Beauty Academy Post-Sec.
9937 Homestead Rd 77016 713-635-5252
Ben Taub Hospital Post-Sec.
2525 Holly Hall St 77054 713-746-6400
Beren Academy 400/PK-12
11333 Cliffwood Dr 77035 713-723-7170
Virginia McCracken, hdmstr. Fax 723-8343
Bradford School of Business Post-Sec.
4669 Southwest Fwy Ste 300 77027 713-629-1500
Briarwood S 300/K-12
12207 Whittington Dr 77077 281-493-1070
Carole Wills, hdmstr. Fax 493-1343
Careers Unlimited Post-Sec.
10058 Long Point Rd 77055 713-464-0770
Carethers Adventist S 100/PK-10
5878 Bellfort St 77033 713-733-1351
Fax 738-7283
Center for Advanced Legal Studies Post-Sec.
3910 Kirby Dr Ste 200 77098 713-529-2778
Central Christian Academy 100/K-12
2217 Bingle Rd 77055 713-468-3248
Scott Jacobs, admin. Fax 468-7322
Clear Lake Christian S 300/K-12
14325 Crescent Landing Dr 77062 281-488-4883
Bruce Guillot, admin. Fax 480-3287
College of Biblical Studies Post-Sec.
7000 Regency Square # 110 77036 713-785-5995
Commonwealth Institute / Funeral Service Post-Sec.
415 Barren Springs Dr 77090 281-873-0262
Court Reporting Institute of Houston Post-Sec.
13101 Northwest Fwy Ste 100 77040 713-996-8300
Culinary Institute Post-Sec.
7070 Allensby St 77022 713-692-0077
Cypress Community Christian S 600/K-12
11123 Cypress N Houston Rd 77065 281-469-8829
Dr. Glenn Holzman, admin. Fax 469-6040
DeVry University Post-Sec.
2000 West Loop S Ste 150 77027 713-850-0888
DeVry University Post-Sec.
11125 Equity Dr 77041 713-973-3200
Duchesne Academy HS 300/9-12
10202 Memorial Dr 77024 713-468-8211
Dr. Rae Flory, prin. Fax 465-9809
Duchesne Academy MS 200/5-8
10202 Memorial Dr 77024 713-468-8211
Sr. Ann Caire, prin. Fax 465-9809
Emery/Weiner S 400/6-12
9825 Stella Link Rd 77025 832-204-5900
Stuart J. Dow, hdmstr. Fax 204-5910
Family Christian Academy 300/K-12
14718 Woodford Dr 77015 713-455-4483
Robert Anderson, prin. Fax 455-2918
Franklin Beauty School #2 Post-Sec.
4965 Martin Luther King 77021 713-645-9060
Gulf Coast Regional Blood Center Post-Sec.
1400 La Concha Ln 77054 713-790-1200
Houston Baptist University Post-Sec.
7502 Fondren Rd 77074 281-649-3000
Houston Christian HS 400/9-12
2700 W Sam Houston Pkwy N 77043 713-580-6000
Dr. Steve Livingston, hdmstr. Fax 580-6001
Houston Community College Post-Sec.
PO Box 667517 77266 713-718-5000
Houston Graduate School of Theology Post-Sec.
2501 Central Pkwy Ste A19 77092 713-942-9505
Houston Learning Academy - Galleria 50/9-12
3333 Bering Dr 77057 713-974-6658
Erik Srnka, dir. Fax 785-9043
Houston Learning Academy - North 50/9-12
13029 Champions Dr 77069 281-537-6433
Bill Snead, prin. Fax 537-2361
Houstons Training and Education Center Post-Sec.
7457 Harwin Dr Ste 190 77036 713-783-2221
Houston Training School Post-Sec.
709 Shotwell St 77020 713-675-4300
Houston Training School Post-Sec.
6630 Gulf Fwy 77087
ICC Technical Institute Post-Sec.
3333 Fannin St Ste 203 77004 713-522-7799
Incarnate Word Academy 200/9-12
609 Crawford St 77002 713-227-3637
Mary Getschow, prin. Fax 227-1014
Institute of Cosmetology Post-Sec.
7011 Harwin Dr Ste 100 77036 713-783-9988
Interactive Learning Systems Post-Sec.
6200 Hillcroft St Ste 200 77081 713-771-5336
Interactive Learning Systems Post-Sec.
256 N Sam Houston Pkwy E 77060 281-931-7717
ITT Technical Institute Post-Sec.
2950 S Gessner Rd Ste 100 77063 713-952-2294
ITT Technical Institute Post-Sec.
2222 Bay Area Blvd 77058 281-486-2630
ITT Technical Institute Post-Sec.
15621 Blue Ash Dr Ste 160 77090 281-873-0512
Jay's Technical Institute Post-Sec.
10754 S Gessner Dr 77071 713-772-2410
Kinkaid S 1,300/PK-12
201 Kinkaid School Dr 77024 713-782-1640
Donald North, hdmstr. Fax 782-3543
Lutheran HS North 300/9-12
1130 W 34th St 77018 713-880-3131
Bruce Schaller, prin. Fax 880-5447
Lutheran South Academy 600/K-12
12555 Ryewater Dr 77089 281-464-8299
Dr. Wayne Kramer, hdmstr. Fax 464-6119
MedVance Institute Post-Sec.
6220 W Park #180 77057 713-266-6594

Memorial Hall S 100/K-12
3721 Dacoma St 77092 713-688-5566
Memorial Hospital System Post-Sec.
7737 Southwest Fwy 77074 713-776-5100
Methodist Hospital Post-Sec.
6565 Fannin St 77030 713-441-2599
Mt. Carmel HS 200/9-12
6700 Mount Carmel St 77087 713-649-2745
Lucille Maggi, prin. Fax 649-6851
MTI College of Business & Technology Post-Sec.
11420 East Fwy 77029 713-979-1800
MTI College of Business & Technology Post-Sec.
7277 Regency Square Blvd 77036 713-974-7181
National Institute of Technology Post-Sec.
255 Northpoint Dr # 100 77060 281-447-7037
National Institute of Technology Post-Sec.
4150 Westheimer Rd Ste 200 77027 713-629-1637
National Institute of Technology Post-Sec.
7151 Office City Dr 77087 713-645-7404
New Heights Christian Academy 100/K-12
1422 Dorothy St 77008 713-861-9101
North Harris Montgomery Comm. College Post-Sec.
250 N Sam Houston Pkwy E 77060 281-260-3500
Northland Christian S 700/PK-12
4363 Sylvanfield Dr 77014 281-440-1060
Dr. Harley Tefertiller, supt. Fax 440-7572
Northwest Educational Center Post-Sec.
2910 Antoine Dr Ste B100 77092 713-680-2929
Oaks Adventist Christian S 100/PK-12
11903C Tanner Rd 77041 713-896-0071
Robert Schimp, prin. Fax 896-0721
Page Parkes Center of Modeling & Acting Post-Sec.
1535 West Loop S Ste 100 77027 713-807-8200
Polytechnic Institute Post-Sec.
5206 Airline Dr 77022 713-694-6027
Prairie View A&M University Post-Sec.
6436 Fannin St 77030 713-797-7000
Remington College Post-Sec.
3110 Hayes Rd 77082 281-899-1240
Rice University Post-Sec.
6100 Main St 77005 713-348-0001
Royal Beauty Careers Post-Sec.
5020 FM 1960 Rd W Ste A12 77069 281-580-2554
St. Agnes Academy 800/9-12
9000 Bellaire Blvd 77036 713-219-5400
Sr. Jane Meyer, prin. Fax 219-5499
St. John's S 1,200/K-12
2401 Claremont Ln 77019 713-850-0222
John Allman, hdmstr. Fax 622-2309
St. Peter the Apostle MS 100/6-8
6220 La Salette St 77021 713-747-9484
Sr. Maria Goretti-Babatunde, prin. Fax 842-7055
St. Pius X HS 700/9-12
811 W Donovan St 77091 713-692-3581
Sr. Donna Pollard, prin. Fax 692-5725
St. Stephen's Episcopal S Houston 200/PK-12
1815 Sul Ross St 77098 713-821-9100
Rod Kehl, hdmstr. Fax 521-0785
St. Thomas' Episcopal S 600/K-12
4900 Jackwood St 77096 713-666-3111
Michael F. Cusack, hdmstr. Fax 668-3887
St. Thomas HS 600/9-12
4500 Memorial Dr 77007 713-864-6348
Rev. Ronald Schwenzer, prin. Fax 864-5750
Sanford-Brown Institute Houston Post-Sec.
10500 Forum Place Dr 77036 713-779-1110
San Jacinto College Post-Sec.
5800 Uvalde Rd 77049 281-458-4050
San Jacinto College Post-Sec.
13735 Beamer Rd 77089 281-484-1900
School of Automotive Machinists Post-Sec.
1911 Antoine Dr 77055 713-683-3817
School of the Woods 400/PK-12
1321 Wirt Rd 77055 713-686-8811
Sherry Herron, hdmstr. Fax 686-1936
Sebring Career School Post-Sec.
7060 Bissonnet St 77074 713-772-0702
Second Baptist S 1,100/PK-12
6410 Woodway Dr 77057 713-365-2310
Brett Jacobsen, supt. Fax 365-2355
Seton Catholic JHS 300/6-8
801 Roselane St 77037 281-447-2132
Patrick Clark, prin. Fax 447-1825
Shady Acres Christian S 50/1-12
7330 Vogel Rd 77088 281-999-2040
Marsha Farley, prin. Fax 999-2040
South Texas College of Law Post-Sec.
1303 San Jacinto St 77002 713-646-1510
Southwest Christian Academy 200/PK-12
7400 Eldridge Pkwy 77083 281-561-7400
Paula Thurmond, prin. Fax 240-9606
Southwestern Professional Institute Post-Sec.
3033 Chimney Rock Rd #200 77056 713-781-5908
Strake Jesuit College Prep S 800/9-12
8900 Bellaire Blvd 77036 713-774-7651
Richard Nevle, prin. Fax 774-6427
Sweetwater Christian S 200/K-12
350 Century Plaza Dr 77073 281-209-9130
David Kelly, admin. Fax 443-3766
Sylvia's International School of Beauty Post-Sec.
434 W Parker Rd 77091 713-697-1200
Texas Barber Colleges & Hairstyling Sch Post-Sec.
9275 Richmond Ave Ste 180 77063 713-953-0262
Texas Christian S 200/PK-12
17810 Kieth Harrow Blvd 77084 281-550-6060
Herc Palmquist, admin. Fax 550-2400
Texas Heart Institute Post-Sec.
PO Box 20345 77225 713-791-4026
Texas School of Business Post-Sec.
711 E Airtex Dr 77073 281-443-8900
Texas School of Business Southwest Post-Sec.
6363 Richmond Ave Ste 300 77057 713-975-7527
Texas Southern University Post-Sec.
3100 Cleburne St 77004 713-313-7011
Texas Woman's University Post-Sec.
1130 John Freeman St 77030 713-794-2376
The Ocean Corporation Post-Sec.
10840 Rockley Rd 77099 281-530-0202
Trend Barber College Post-Sec.
7725 W Bellfort St 77071 713-721-0000
Ultrasound Diagnostic School Post-Sec.
10500 Forum Place Dr #200 77036 713-664-9632
Universal Technical Institute Post-Sec.
721 Lockhaven Dr 77073 281-443-6262
University of Houston Post-Sec.
4800 Calhoun Rd 77204 713-743-1000
University of Houston-Clear Lake Post-Sec.
2700 Bay Area Blvd 77058 281-283-7600
University of Houston-Downtown Post-Sec.
1 Main St 77002 713-221-8000
University of St. Thomas Post-Sec.
3800 Montrose Blvd 77006 713-522-7911
University of Texas Anderson Cancer Ctr. Post-Sec.
1515 Holcombe Blvd 77030 713-792-6000
University of TX Health Science Center Post-Sec.
PO Box 20036 77225 713-500-4472
University of Texas-Houston Post-Sec.
6901 Bertner St 77030 713-500-2100
Veterans Affairs Medical Center Post-Sec.
2002 Holcombe Blvd 77030 713-794-7100
Westbury Christian S 600/PK-12
10420 Hillcroft St 77096 713-723-8377
Westwood Aviation Institute Post-Sec.
8880 Telephone Rd 77061 800-776-7423
Westwood College - Houston South Post-Sec.
7322 Southwest Fwy Ste 1900 77074 713-777-4433

Howe, Grayson, Pop. 2,670
Howe ISD 1,000/PK-12
105 W Tutt St 75459 903-532-5518
Randy Hancock, supt. Fax 532-9378
www.howeisd.net
Howe HS 300/9-12
200 Ponderosa Rd 75459 903-532-5222
Kevin Wilson, prin. Fax 532-5563
Howe MS 300/5-8
300 Beatrice St 75459 903-532-6013
Clay Wilson, prin. Fax 537-0113

Hubbard, Hill, Pop. 1,653
Hubbard ISD 500/PK-12
PO Box 218 76648 254-576-2564
Walter Padgett, supt. Fax 576-5019
www.hubbardisd.com/
Hubbard HS 200/9-12
PO Box 218 76648 254-576-2549
Bill Shepard, prin. Fax 576-2477
Hubbard MS 100/6-8
PO Box 218 76648 254-576-2758
Bill Shepard, prin. Fax 576-5017

Huffman, Harris
Huffman ISD 2,900/PK-12
24302 FM 2100 Rd 77336 281-324-1871
Steven Myers, supt. Fax 324-3293
www.huffmanisd.net
Hargrave HS 900/9-12
25400 Willy Ln 77336 281-324-1845
Robert Schnuriger, prin. Fax 324-3368
Huffman MS 700/6-8
3407 Huffman Eastgate Rd 77336 281-324-2598
Shirley Hitt, prin. Fax 324-2710

Hughes Springs, Cass, Pop. 1,849
Hughes Springs ISD 1,000/PK-12
PO Box 398 75656 903-639-3800
Freddy Wade, supt. Fax 639-2624
www.hsisd.net
Hughes Springs HS 300/9-12
PO Box 399 75656 903-639-3841
Rick Ogden, prin. Fax 639-3928
Hughes Springs JHS 200/6-8
PO Box 1389 75656 903-639-3812
Rex Stone, prin. Fax 639-3929

Humble, Harris, Pop. 14,753
Aldine ISD
Supt. — See Houston
Teague MS 1,300/7-8
21700 Rayford Rd 77338 281-233-4310
Michael Gallien, prin. Fax 233-4318

Humble ISD 25,300/PK-12
PO Box 2000 77347 281-641-1000
Dr. Guy M. Sconzo, supt. Fax 641-1050
www.humble.k12.tx.us
Atascocita HS 9-12
13300 Will Clayton Pkwy 77346 281-641-7500
Lawrence Kohn, prin.
Atascocita MS 1,300/6-8
18810 W Lake Houston Pkwy 77346 281-641-4600
Ron Westerfeld, prin. Fax 641-4617
Career & Technology Education Center Vo/Tech
9155 Will Clayton Pkwy 77338 281-641-7950
Bodie Wagener, prin. Fax 641-7967
Humble 9th Grade Campus 9-9
1131 Wilson Rd 77338 281-641-6000
Penne Leifer, prin. Fax 641-6017
Humble MS 1,200/6-8
11207 Will Clayton Pkwy 77346 281-641-4000
Larry Johnson, prin. Fax 641-4017
Humble SHS 3,000/10-12
1700 Wilson Rd 77338 281-641-6300
Dr. Raul Font, prin. Fax 641-6517
Timberwood MS 1,100/6-8
18450 Timber Forest Dr 77346 281-641-3800
Carol Atwood, prin. Fax 641-3817
Other Schools – See Kingwood

Christian Life Center Academy 200/PK-12
600 Charles St 77338 281-319-0077
Chelliah Soundar, admin. Fax 446-5501
Houston Learning Academy - Humble 50/9-12
5334 FM 1960 Rd E 77346 281-852-2022
Humble Christian S 300/PK-12
16202 Old Humble Rd 77396 281-441-1313
Ted Howell, admin. Fax 441-1329

Hunt, Kerr
Hunt ISD 200/PK-12
PO Box 259 78024 830-238-4893
David Kelm, supt. Fax 238-4691
www.huntisd.com
Hunt S 200/PK-12
PO Box 259 78024 830-238-4893
David Kelm, prin. Fax 238-4691

Huntington, Angelina, Pop. 2,088
Huntington ISD 1,600/PK-12
PO Box 328 75949 936-876-4287
Shirley Davis, supt. Fax 876-3212
www.huntington.esc7.net/
Huntington HS 500/9-12
PO Box 328 75949 936-876-4150
Pete Jackson, prin. Fax 876-3057
Huntington MS 400/6-8
PO Box 328 75949 936-876-4722
Glenn Frank, prin. Fax 876-4009

Huntsville, Walker, Pop. 35,567
Huntsville ISD 6,700/PK-12
441 FM 2821 Rd E 77320 936-295-3421
Dr. Richard Montgomery, supt. Fax 291-3444
www.huntsville-isd.org
Huntsville HS 1,900/9-12
441 FM 2821 Rd E 77320 936-293-2626
Pat Taliaferro, prin. Fax 293-2670
Mance Park JHS 900/7-8
441 FM 2821 Rd E 77320 936-293-2755
Tommy Hooker, prin. Fax 293-2759

Alpha Omega Academy 200/K-12
PO Box 8419 77340 936-438-8833
Paul Davidhizar, hdmstr. Fax 438-8844
Heritage Christian Academy 200/K-12
2407 Sam Houston Ave 77340 936-291-0203
Pam Bouldin, prin. Fax 291-9203
Sam Houston State University Post-Sec.
PO Box 2026 77341 936-294-1111

Hurst, Tarrant, Pop. 37,141
Hurst-Euless-Bedford ISD
Supt. — See Bedford
Bell SHS 1,900/10-12
1601 Brown Trl 76054 817-282-2551
Jim Bannister, prin. Fax 285-3200
Hurst JHS 900/7-9
500 Harmon Rd 76053 817-285-3220
Sherilynn Colten, prin. Fax 285-3225

Brown Mackie College Post-Sec.
301 NE Loop 820 76053 817-589-0505
Ogle School of Hair Design Post-Sec.
720 Arcadia St Ste B 76053 817-284-9231
Tarrant County Junior College Post-Sec.
828 W Harwood Rd 76054 817-515-6100

Hutto, Williamson, Pop. 4,036
Hutto ISD 1,700/PK-12
PO Box 430 78634 512-759-3771
Dr. David Borrer, supt. Fax 759-4796
www.hutto.txed.net
Hutto HS 500/9-12
PO Box 430 78634 512-759-4700
Manuel Lunoff, prin. Fax 759-4757
Hutto MS 500/6-8
PO Box 430 78634 512-759-4541
Don Kuempel, prin. Fax 759-4753

Idalou, Lubbock, Pop. 2,138
Idalou ISD 800/PK-12
PO Box 1338 79329 806-892-2552
Jim Waller, supt. Fax 892-3204
www.llano.net/idalou
Idalou HS 300/9-12
PO Box 1558 79329 806-892-2123
Steve Bigham, prin. Fax 892-2690
Idalou MS 300/5-8
PO Box 1353 79329 806-892-2133
Steve Gunter, prin. Fax 892-2388

Imperial, Pecos
Buena Vista ISD 100/PK-12
PO Box 310 79743 432-536-2225
David Dillard, supt. Fax 536-2469
www.bvisd.esc18.net/
Buena Vista S 100/PK-12
PO Box 310 79743 432-536-2225
Letha Dulaney, prin. Fax 536-2469

Ingleside, San Patricio, Pop. 9,203
Ingleside ISD 2,300/PK-12
PO Box 1320 78362 361-776-7631
Troy Mircovich, supt. Fax 776-0267
www.inglesideisd.org
Ingleside HS 600/9-12
2807 Mustang Dr 78362 361-776-2712
Steve Snyder, prin. Fax 776-5200
Taylor JHS 400/7-8
2739 Mustang Dr 78362 361-776-2232
James Bonorden, prin. Fax 776-2192

Ingram, Kerr, Pop. 1,813
Ingram ISD 1,500/PK-12
510 College St 78025 830-367-5517
Bruce Faust, supt. Fax 367-5631
www.ingramisd.net
Ingram MS 400/6-8
510 College St 78025 830-367-4012
Jill Dworsky, prin. Fax 367-7335
Ingram-Tom Moore HS 500/9-12
510 College St 78025 830-367-4111
Pamela Morris, prin. Fax 367-7332

Iola, Grimes
Iola ISD 500/PK-12
PO Box 159 77861 936-394-2361
Douglas Devine, supt. Fax 394-2132
www.esc6.net/~iola/
Iola JSHS 200/7-12
PO Box 159 77861 936-394-2361
Jeff Dyer, prin. Fax 394-4700

Iowa Park, Wichita, Pop. 6,318
Iowa Park Consolidated ISD 1,800/PK-12
PO Box 898 76367 940-592-4193
Jerry Baird, supt. Fax 592-2136
www.ipcisd.net/
George MS 500/6-8
412 E Cash St 76367 940-592-2196
Steven Moody, prin. Fax 592-2801
Iowa Park HS 600/9-12
1513 W Highway St 76367 940-592-2144
James Skeeler, prin. Fax 592-2583

Ira, Scurry
Ira ISD 200/K-12
PO Box 240 79527 325-573-2629
Dr. Larry Devitt, supt. Fax 573-5825
www.ira.esc14.net
Ira S 200/K-12
PO Box 240 79527 325-573-2628
Dr. Larry Devitt, prin. Fax 573-5825

Iraan, Pecos, Pop. 1,184
Iraan-Sheffield ISD 400/PK-12
PO Box 486 79744 432-639-2512
Kevin Allen, supt. Fax 639-2501
isisd.esc18.net

Iraan HS | 200/9-12
PO Box 486 79744 | 432-639-2722
Benny Hernandez, prin. | Fax 639-2501
Iraan JHS | 100/6-8
PO Box 486 79744 | 432-639-2867
Benny Hernandez, prin. | Fax 639-2501

Iredell, Bosque, Pop. 365
Iredell ISD | 100/PK-12
PO Box 39 76649 | 254-364-2411
David Mims, supt. | Fax 364-2206
www.iredell-isd.com
Iredell S | 100/PK-12
PO Box 39 76649 | 254-364-2411
David Mims, prin. | Fax 364-2206

Irving, Dallas, Pop. 194,455
Carrollton-Farmers Branch ISD
Supt. — See Carrollton
Bush MS | 600/6-8
515 Cowboys Pkwy 75063 | 972-868-3000
Lynda Opitz, prin. | Fax 868-3023
Ranchview HS | 800/9-12
8401 Valley Ranch Pkwy E 75063 | 214-296-6400
Dr. Barry Dodson, prin. | Fax 256-6504

Irving ISD | 31,200/PK-12
PO Box 152637 75015 | 972-215-5000
Jack Singley, supt. | Fax 215-5201
www.irvingisd.net
Austin MS | 900/6-8
825 E Union Bower Rd 75061 | 972-721-3100
Cynthia Bean, prin. | Fax 721-3105
Bowie MS | 1,000/6-8
600 E 6th St 75060 | 972-721-3300
Joe Moreno, prin. | Fax 721-3044
Crockett MS | 1,000/6-8
2431 Hancock St 75061 | 972-313-4700
John Rose, prin. | Fax 313-4770
de Zavala MS | 1,000/6-8
707 W Pioneer Dr 75061 | 972-273-8900
Sebastian Bozas, prin. | Fax 273-8924
Houston MS | 1,000/6-8
3033 Country Club Dr W 75038 | 972-261-2300
Rick Nolly, prin. | Fax 261-2399
Irving HS | 2,500/9-12
900 N O Connor Rd 75061 | 972-273-8300
Linda Kimm, prin. | Fax 273-8319
Lamar MS | 1,100/6-8
219 Crandall Rd 75060 | 972-313-4400
Cindy Goodsell, prin. | Fax 313-4499
MacArthur HS | 2,500/9-12
3700 N Macarthur Blvd 75062 | 972-261-2100
Tracie Fraley, prin. | Fax 261-2299
Nimitz HS | 2,600/9-12
100 W Oakdale Rd 75060 | 972-273-8600
Samuel Bean, prin. | Fax 273-8610
Ratterree Career Development Center | Vo/Tech
2121 S MacArthur Blvd 75060 | 972-313-4821
Lea Bailey, prin. | Fax 313-4823
Travis MS | 1,000/6-8
1600 Finley Rd 75062 | 972-261-2400
Terry Cooper, prin. | Fax 261-2450

Cistercian Preparatory S | 300/5-12
PO Box 140699 75014 | 469-499-5400
Fr. Peter Verhalen, hdmstr. | Fax 499-5440
DeVry University | Post-Sec.
4800 Regent Blvd 75063 | 972-929-6777
Highlands S | 500/PK-12
1451 E Northgate Dr 75062 | 972-554-1980
 | Fax 721-1691
High-Tech Institute | Post-Sec.
4250 N Belt Line Rd 75038 | 972-871-2824
International Beauty College #4 | Post-Sec.
2716 W Irving Blvd 75061 | 972-513-1176
Irving Christian Academy | 100/PK-12
1400 W Grauwyler Rd 75061 | 972-259-8778
Joann Fuller, admin. | Fax 253-2172
North Lake College | Post-Sec.
5001 N Macarthur Blvd 75038 | 972-273-3000
University of Dallas | Post-Sec.
1845 E Northgate Dr 75062 | 972-721-5000

Italy, Ellis, Pop. 2,057
Italy ISD | 700/PK-12
300 College 76651 | 972-483-1815
Wilburn Roesler, supt. | Fax 483-6152
www.italyisd.org/
Italy JSHS | 300/7-12
300 College 76651 | 972-483-7411
Don Clingenpeel, prin. | Fax 483-1500

Itasca, Hill, Pop. 1,585
Itasca ISD | 700/PK-12
123 N College St 76055 | 254-687-2922
Dr. E. Ray Freeman, supt. | Fax 687-2637
www.itasca.k12.tx.us
Itasca HS | 200/9-12
123 N College St 76055 | 254-687-2922
Glenn Pittman, prin. | Fax 687-2637
Itasca JHS | 200/5-8
123 N College St 76055 | 254-687-2922
Barry Durham, prin. | Fax 687-2637

Ivanhoe, Fannin
Sam Rayburn ISD | 400/PK-12
9363 E FM 273 75447 | 903-664-2255
Steve Arthur, supt. | Fax 664-2406
samrayburn.ednet10.net/
Rayburn JSHS | 200/7-12
9363 E FM 273 75447 | 903-664-2165
Lance Campbell, prin. | Fax 664-2406

Jacksboro, Jack, Pop. 4,575
Jacksboro ISD | 1,000/PK-12
812 W Belknap St 76458 | 940-567-5544
Dennis Bennett, supt. | Fax 567-2214
www.jacksboroisd.net/
Jacksboro HS | 300/9-12
812 W Belknap St 76458 | 940-567-5171
Brad Burnett, prin. | Fax 567-6028
Lowrance MS | 200/6-8
117 N 4th St 76458 | 940-567-2613
Steven Monkres, prin. | Fax 567-2681

Jacksonville, Cherokee, Pop. 13,974
Jacksonville ISD | 4,600/PK-12
PO Box 631 75766 | 903-586-6511
Stuart Bird, supt. | Fax 586-3133
www.jacksonvilleisd.org

Jacksonville HS | 1,200/9-12
PO Box 631 75766 | 903-586-3661
Duane Barber, prin. | Fax 586-8229
Jacksonville MS | 600/7-8
PO Box 631 75766 | 903-586-3686
Lisa Hancock, prin. | Fax 586-8071

Baptist Missionary Theological Seminary | Post-Sec.
1530 E Pine St 75766 | 903-586-2501
Jacksonville College | Post-Sec.
105 B J Albritton Dr 75766 | 903-586-2518
Lon Morris College | Post-Sec.
800 College Ave 75766 | 903-589-4000

Jarrell, Williamson, Pop. 1,396
Jarrell ISD | 700/PK-12
PO Box 9 76537 | 512-746-2124
Dr. Jamie Mattison, supt. | Fax 746-2518
www.esc13.net/jarrell
Jarrell HS | 200/9-12
PO Box 9 76537 | 512-746-4180
Freddie McFarland, prin. | Fax 746-4280
Jarrell MS | 200/6-8
PO Box 9 76537 | 512-746-2259
Freddie McFarland, prin. | Fax 746-4280

Jasper, Jasper, Pop. 7,541
Jasper ISD | 3,100/PK-12
128 Park Ln 75951 | 409-384-2401
Eddie Dunn Ed.D., supt. | Fax 382-1084
www.jasperisd.net
Jasper HS | 900/9-12
400 Bulldog Ave 75951 | 409-384-3242
Dr. Dean Miller, prin. | Fax 382-1310
Jasper JHS | 500/7-8
211 2nd St 75951 | 409-384-3585
Mervin Cleveland, prin. | Fax 382-1160

Jayton, Kent, Pop. 462
Jayton-Girard ISD | 100/PK-12
PO Box 168 79528 | 806-237-2991
Gary Harrell, supt. | Fax 237-2670
www.jaytonjaybirds.com
Jayton S | 100/PK-12
PO Box 168 79528 | 806-237-2991
Troy Parton, prin. | Fax 237-2670

Jefferson, Marion, Pop. 1,994
Jefferson ISD | 1,200/PK-12
1600 Martin Luther King Dr 75657 | 903-665-2461
Richard Cook, supt. | Fax 665-7367
jefferson.esc8.net/
Jefferson HS | 400/9-12
1 Bulldog Dr 75657 | 903-665-2461
Don Prather, prin. | Fax 665-2146
Jefferson JHS | 400/5-8
804 N Alley St 75657 | 903-665-2461
John McCoy, prin. | Fax 665-8914

Jefferson Christian Academy | 100/9-12
3060 FM 728 75657 | 903-665-3973
 | Fax 665-5978

Jewett, Leon, Pop. 905
Leon ISD | 700/PK-12
PO Box 157 75846 | 903-626-4532
Jay Winn, supt. | Fax 626-4954
Leon HS | 200/9-12
PO Box 157 75846 | 903-626-4444
David Jones, prin. | Fax 626-5090
Leon JHS | 200/6-8
PO Box 157 75846 | 903-626-4937
John Davis, prin. | Fax 626-4954

Joaquin, Shelby, Pop. 930
Joaquin ISD | 700/PK-12
11109 US Highway 84 E 75954 | 936-269-3128
Phil Worsham, supt. | Fax 269-3615
www.joaquinisd.net/
Joaquin HS | 200/9-12
11109 US Highway 84 E 75954 | 936-269-3122
Mid Johnson, prin. | Fax 269-9123
Joaquin JHS | 100/7-8
11109 US Highway 84 E 75954 | 936-269-3090
Mid Johnson, prin. | Fax 269-9123

Johnson City, Blanco, Pop. 1,274
Johnson City ISD | 700/PK-12
PO Box 498 78636 | 830-868-7410
David Shanley, supt. | Fax 868-7375
www.johnsoncity.txed.net
Johnson HS | 200/9-12
PO Box 498 78636 | 830-868-4025
A'Lann Truelock, prin. | Fax 868-9244
Johnson MS | 200/5-8
PO Box 498 78636 | 830-868-9025
Julie Storer, prin. | Fax 868-7375

Joinerville, Rusk
West Rusk ISD
Supt. — See New London
West Rusk JHS | 200/6-8
Highway 64 75658 | 903-895-4613
Janis Underwood, prin. | Fax 895-2267

Jonesboro, Coryell
Jonesboro ISD | 200/K-12
PO Box 125 76538 | 254-463-2111
Randy Savage, supt. | Fax 463-2275
www.jonesboro-isd.com
Jonesboro S | 200/K-12
PO Box 125 76538 | 254-463-2111
Larry Robinson, prin. | Fax 463-2275

Joshua, Johnson, Pop. 5,161
Joshua ISD | 5,500/PK-12
PO Box 40 76058 | 817-202-2500
Ray Dane, supt. | Fax 641-2738
www.joshuaisd.org
Joshua HS | 1,200/9-12
909 S Broadway St 76058 | 817-202-2500
Mick Cochran, prin. | Fax 556-3403
Loflin MS | 700/7-8
520 Stadium Dr 76058 | 817-202-2500
Dr. Delayne Sprinkles, prin. | Fax 202-9140

Jourdanton, Atascosa, Pop. 4,052
Jourdanton ISD | 1,200/PK-12
200 Zanderson Ave 78026 | 830-769-3548
Dr. Lana Collavo, supt. | Fax 769-3272
www.jourdanton.k12.tx.us

Jourdanton HS | 400/9-12
200 Zanderson Ave 78026 | 830-769-2350
Keith Chapman, prin. | Fax 769-3272
Jourdanton JHS | 300/6-8
200 Zanderson Ave 78026 | 830-769-2234
Robert Rutkowski, prin. | Fax 769-3272

Junction, Kimble, Pop. 2,649
Junction ISD | 800/PK-12
1700 College St 76849 | 325-446-3510
Tony Peter, supt. | Fax 446-4413
junction.netxv.net
Junction HS | 300/9-12
1700 College St 76849 | 325-446-3326
Mary Murr, prin. | Fax 446-8206
Junction MS | 200/6-8
1700 College St 76849 | 325-446-2464
James Armstrong, prin. | Fax 446-2255

Justin, Denton, Pop. 2,409
Northwest ISD | 6,900/PK-12
2001 Texan Dr 76247 | 817-490-6473
Dr. Karen Rue, supt. | Fax 215-0170
northwest.k12.tx.us
Northwest HS | 1,800/9-12
2301 Texan Dr 76247 | 817-215-0200
Gene Suttle, prin. | Fax 215-0262
Pike MS | 800/6-8
2200 Texan Dr 76247 | 817-215-0400
Damon Edwards, prin. | Fax 215-0425
Other Schools – See Rhome, Trophy Club

Karnack, Harrison
Karnack ISD | 300/PK-12
PO Box 259 75661 | 903-679-3121
Cozzetta Robinson, supt. | Fax 679-4252
www.karnack.esc7.net/
Karnack JSHS | 100/7-12
PO Box 259 75661 | 903-679-3113
Joe Chisum, prin. | Fax 679-4264

Karnes City, Karnes, Pop. 3,397
Karnes City ISD | 1,000/PK-12
PO Box 38 78118 | 830-780-2321
Bernard Zarosky, supt. | Fax 780-3823
www.kcisd.net
Karnes City HS | 300/9-12
400 E Highway 123 78118 | 830-780-2321
Harold Steele, prin. | Fax 780-4352
Karnes City JHS | 200/6-8
410 E Highway 123 78118 | 830-780-2321
Ron Baker, prin. | Fax 780-4382

Katy, Harris, Pop. 12,726
Cypress-Fairbanks ISD
Supt. — See Houston
Thornton MS | 1,500/6-8
19802 Kieth Harrow Blvd 77449 | 281-856-1500
Barbara Crook, prin. | Fax 856-1548

Katy ISD | 41,600/PK-12
PO Box 159 77492 | 281-396-6000
Dr. Leonard Merrell, supt. | Fax 644-1800
www.katyisd.org/
Beckendorff JHS | 6-8
8200 S Fry Rd 77494 | 281-237-8800
David Truitt, prin. | Fax 644-1635
Beck JHS | 1,500/6-8
5200 S Fry Rd 77450 | 281-237-3300
James Cross, prin. | Fax 644-1630
Cinco Ranch HS | 3,200/9-12
23440 Cinco Ranch Blvd 77494 | 281-237-7000
Bonnie Brasic, prin. | Fax 644-1734
Cinco Ranch JHS | 1,100/6-8
23420 Cinco Ranch Blvd 77494 | 281-237-7300
Dr. Steven Robertson, prin. | Fax 644-1640
Katy HS | 3,200/9-12
6331 Highway Blvd 77494 | 281-237-6700
Joe Kelley, prin. | Fax 644-1700
Katy JHS | 1,100/6-8
5350 Franz Rd 77493 | 281-237-6800
Scott Sheppard, prin. | Fax 644-1645
McDonald JHS | 800/6-8
3635 Lakes of Bridgewater D 77449 | 281-237-5300
Ed Keeney, prin. | Fax 644-1655
McMeans JHS | 1,100/6-8
21000 Westheimer Pkwy 77450 | 281-237-8000
Dr. Susan Rice, prin. | Fax 644-1660
Memorial Parkway JHS | 1,100/6-8
21203 Highland Knolls Dr 77450 | 281-237-5800
Joe Graham, prin. | Fax 644-1665
Miller Career Center | Vo/Tech
1734 Katyland Dr 77493 | 281-237-6300
Anna Webb-Storey, prin. | Fax 644-1775
Morton Ranch HS | 9-12
21000 Franz Rd 77449 | 281-237-7800
Joe Cammarata, prin. | Fax 644-1746
Morton Ranch JHS | 1,200/6-8
2498 N Mason Rd 77449 | 281-237-7400
Becky Bracewell, prin. | Fax 644-1670
Opportunity Awareness Center | Vo/Tech
1732 Katyland Dr 77493 | 281-237-6350
Dr. Patricia Bing, prin. | Fax 644-1780
Seven Lakes HS | 9-12
9251 S Fry Rd 77494 | 281-237-2800
Christie Whitbeck, prin. | Fax 644-1785
Taylor HS | 2,700/9-12
20700 Kingsland Blvd 77450 | 281-237-3100
James McDonald, prin. | Fax 644-1760
West Memorial JHS | 800/6-8
22311 Provincial Blvd 77450 | 281-237-6400
Patricia Shafer, prin. | Fax 644-1675
Other Schools – See Houston

Faith West Academy | 500/PK-12
2225 Porter Rd 77493 | 281-391-5683
Raul Hinojosa, hdmstr. | Fax 391-2606
Houston Learning Academy - Katy | 50/9-12
180 Applewhite Dr 77450 | 281-693-4151
Lawrence Ermis, prin. | Fax 693-1255
Pope John XXIII HS | 200/9-12
1800 N Grand Pkwy 77449 | 281-693-1000
Lynn Veazey, prin. | Fax 693-1000

Kaufman, Kaufman, Pop. 7,502
Kaufman ISD | 3,400/PK-12
1000 S Houston St 75142 | 972-932-2622
Dr. Bruce Wood, supt. | Fax 932-3325
www.kaufmanisd.net/

Kaufman HS
3205 S Houston St 75142 — 800/9-12 — 972-932-2811
Mark Albin, prin. — Fax 932-1948
Norman JHS
3701 S Houston St 75142 — 500/7-8 — 972-932-2410
Jeri Ann Campbell, prin. — Fax 932-7771

Trinity Valley Community College
800 W Highway 243 75142 — Post-Sec. — 972-932-4309

Keene, Johnson, Pop. 5,514
Keene ISD — 900/PK-12
PO Box 656 76059 — 817-556-9082
Wanda Smith, supt. — Fax 556-2087
www.keeneisd.org/
Keene HS — 200/9-12
PO Box 656 76059 — 817-641-4843
Kevin Sellers, prin. — Fax 556-2087
Keene JHS — 200/6-8
PO Box 656 76059 — 817-641-2931
Billie Hopps, prin. — Fax 641-4035

Chisholm Trail Academy
PO Box 717 76059 — 100/9-12 — 817-641-6626
Mike Furr, prin. — Fax 556-2009
Southwestern Adventist University
PO Box 567 76059 — Post-Sec. — 817-645-3921

Keller, Tarrant, Pop. 33,951
Keller ISD — 22,400/PK-12
350 Keller Pkwy 76248 — 817-744-1000
Dr. James Veitenheimer, supt. — Fax 337-3261
www.kellerisd.net
Central HS — 1,700/9-12
9450 Ray White Rd 76248 — 817-744-2000
David Hinson, prin. — Fax 744-2252
Fossil Ridge HS — 2,400/9-12
4101 Thompson Rd 76248 — 817-744-1700
Todd Tunnell, prin. — Fax 337-3407
Indian Springs MS — 600/7-8
305 Bursey Rd 76248 — 817-744-3200
Don Cotten, prin. — Fax 431-4432
Keller HS — 2,600/9-12
601 Pate Orr Rd N 76248 — 817-744-1400
Mike Kreis, prin. — Fax 337-3316
Keller MS — 900/7-8
300 College Ave 76248 — 817-744-2900
Debi LaMarr, prin. — Fax 337-3500
Other Schools – See Fort Worth

Kemp, Kaufman, Pop. 1,221
Kemp ISD — 1,700/PK-12
202 W 17th St 75143 — 903-498-1314
Larry Davis, supt. — Fax 498-1315
kemp.ednet10.net
Kemp HS — 500/9-12
1 Yellow Jacket Dr 75143 — 903-498-1322
Mary Lyons, prin. — Fax 498-1375
Kemp JHS — 300/7-8
202 W 17th St 75143 — 903-498-1343
Amelia Hood, prin. — Fax 498-1359

Kenedy, Karnes, Pop. 3,413
Kenedy ISD — 900/PK-12
401 FM 719 78119 — 830-583-4100
Dr. Richard Irizarry, supt. — Fax 583-9950
www.kenedy.isd.tenet.edu
Kenedy HS — 300/9-12
401 FM 719 78119 — 830-583-4100
Rickey DeLeon, prin. — Fax 583-9126
Kenedy MS — 200/6-8
401 FM 719 78119 — 830-583-4100
Candace Angell, prin. — Fax 583-9950

Kennard, Houston, Pop. 316
Kennard ISD — 300/PK-12
PO Box 38 75847 — 936-655-2008
Gene Glover, supt. — Fax 655-2327
www.kennardisd.net/
Kennard JSHS — 100/7-12
PO Box 38 75847 — 936-655-2121
James Applewhite, prin. — Fax 655-2327

Kennedale, Tarrant, Pop. 6,399
Kennedale ISD — 2,700/K-12
PO Box 467 76060 — 817-483-3600
Gary Dugger, supt. — Fax 483-3610
www.kennedale.net
Kennedale HS — 900/9-12
PO Box 1208 76060 — 817-563-3700
Richard Edwards, prin. — Fax 563-3718
Kennedale JHS — 500/7-8
PO Box 489 76060 — 817-483-3640
Sandra Knox, prin. — Fax 483-3655

Kerens, Navarro, Pop. 1,747
Kerens ISD — 700/PK-12
PO Box 310 75144 — 903-396-2924
Dr. Vance Vaughn, supt. — Fax 396-2334
www.kerens.k12.tx.us/
Kerens S — 700/PK-12
PO Box 310 75144 — 903-396-2931
David Atkeisson, prin. — Fax 396-2334

Kermit, Winkler, Pop. 5,367
Kermit ISD — 1,300/PK-12
601 S Poplar St 79745 — 432-586-1000
Santos L. Lujan, supt. — Fax 586-1016
kisd.esc18.net
Kermit HS — 400/9-12
601 S Poplar St 79745 — 432-586-1050
Paul Abundez, prin. — Fax 586-1055
Kermit JHS — 300/6-8
601 S Poplar St 79745 — 432-586-1040
Joe Young, prin. — Fax 586-1045

Kerrville, Kerr, Pop. 21,343
Kerrville ISD — 4,700/PK-12
1009 Barnett St 78028 — 830-257-2200
Dan Troxell Ph.D., supt. — Fax 257-2249
www.kerrvilleisd.net
Peterson MS — 800/7-8
605 Tivy St 78028 — 830-257-2204
Sharon Mock, prin. — Fax 257-1300
Tivy HS — 1,300/9-12
3250 Loop 534 78028 — 830-257-2212
Robert Jolly, prin. — Fax 895-3575

Conlee's College of Cosmetology
402 Quinlan St 78028 — Post-Sec. — 830-896-2380

Our Lady of the Hills Catholic HS
575 Peterson Farm Rd 78028 — 500/9-12 — 830-895-0501
Barry Neuberger, prin. — Fax 895-3470
Schreiner University — Post-Sec.
2100 Memorial Blvd 78028 — 800-343-4919

Kilgore, Gregg, Pop. 11,472
Kilgore ISD — 3,700/PK-12
301 N Kilgore St 75662 — 903-984-2073
Jerry Roberts, supt. — Fax 983-3212
www.kisd.org/
Kilgore HS — 1,100/9-12
301 N Kilgore St 75662 — 903-984-5591
Robert Wheeley, prin. — Fax 984-0571
Laird MS — 800/6-8
301 N Kilgore St 75662 — 903-984-5072
Jody Clements, prin. — Fax 984-6225

Kilgore College
1100 Broadway Blvd 75662 — Post-Sec. — 903-984-8531

Killeen, Bell, Pop. 96,159
Killeen ISD — 32,500/PK-12
PO Box 967 76540 — 254-501-0006
Dr. Jim Hawkins, supt. — Fax 526-3103
www.killeenisd.org
CATE — Vo/Tech
3004 Atkinson Ave 76543 — 254-501-0563
Laurel Blair, prin. — Fax 519-7737
Ellison HS — 1,800/9-12
909 E Elms Rd 76542 — 254-501-0600
Marvin Rainwater, prin. — Fax 501-0697
Fairway MS — 700/6-8
701 Whitlow Dr 76541 — 254-501-1000
Teresa Daugherty, prin. — Fax 519-5599
Killeen HS — 1,600/9-12
500 N 38th St 76543 — 254-501-0400
Michael Sibberson, prin. — Fax 680-2424
Liberty Hill MS — 1,000/6-8
4500 Kit Carson Trl 76542 — 254-501-1370
Michael Berger, prin. — Fax 953-4367
Live Oak Ridge MS — 700/6-8
2600 Robinett Rd 76549 — 254-501-2490
Brenda Alexander, prin. — Fax 554-2170
Manor MS — 700/6-8
1700 S W S Young Dr 76543 — 254-501-1310
Floristine Gray, prin. — Fax 680-7029
Nolan MS — 800/6-8
505 E Jasper Dr 76541 — 254-501-1150
Mike Burch, prin. — Fax 519-5598
Palo Alto MS — 900/6-8
2301 W Elms Rd 76549 — 254-501-1000
Dee Levens, prin. — Fax 519-5577
Rancier MS — 700/6-8
3301 Hilliard Ave 76543 — 254-501-1250
Corbett Lawler, prin. — Fax 680-6601
Shoemaker HS — 2,100/9-12
3302 S Clear Creek Rd 76549 — 254-501-0900
Janet Addair, prin. — Fax 520-1118
Other Schools – See Fort Hood, Harker Heights

American Preparatory S — 100/9-12
PO Box 1800 76540 — 254-526-1390
Central Texas College — Post-Sec.
PO Box 1800 76540 — 254-526-1104
Killeen Adventist Junior Academy — 100/PK-10
3412 Lake Rd 76543 — 254-699-9466
Fax 699-0519

Kingsville, Kleberg, Pop. 25,270
Kingsville ISD — 4,500/PK-12
PO Box 871 78364 — 361-592-3387
Dr. Rudy Lopez, supt. — Fax 595-7805
www.kvisd.esc2.net
King HS — 1,200/9-12
PO Box 871 78364 — 361-592-6401
Dr. Michael McClure, prin. — Fax 595-9170
Memorial MS — 600/7-8
PO Box 871 78364 — 361-595-5771
Roel Gonzalez, prin. — Fax 592-4198

Ricardo ISD — 500/PK-8
138 W County Road 2160 78363 — 361-592-6465
Dr. Don Jones, supt. — Fax 592-3101
www.ricardoisd.us
Ricardo MS — 200/6-8
138 W County Road 2160 78363 — 361-592-6465
Karen Unterbrink, prin. — Fax 593-0707

Santa Gertrudis ISD — 300/PK-12
PO Box 592 78364 — 361-592-7582
Jon C. Orozco, supt. — Fax 592-2836
www.sgisd.esc2.net
Academy HS — 200/9-12
PO Box 592 78364 — 361-592-0058
Mike Gonzalez, prin. — Fax 592-5335

Presbyterian Pan American S — 100/9-12
PO Box 1578 78364 — 361-592-4307
Texas A&M University — Post-Sec.
700 University Blvd 78363 — 361-593-2111

Kingwood, Harris, Pop. 37,397
Humble ISD
Supt. — See Humble
Creekwood MS — 1,000/6-8
3603 W Lake Houston Pkwy 77339 — 281-641-4400
Walt Winicki, prin. — Fax 641-4417
Kingwood 9th Grade Campus — 9-9
4015 Woodland Hills Dr 77339 — 281-641-6600
Larry Cooper, prin. — Fax 641-6617
Kingwood MS — 1,000/6-8
2407 Pine Terrace Dr 77339 — 281-641-4200
Robert Atteberry, prin. — Fax 641-4217
Kingwood SHS — 2,800/10-12
2701 Kingwood Dr 77339 — 281-641-6900
Melissa Hayhurst, prin. — Fax 641-7217
Riverwood MS — 1,000/6-8
2910 High Valley Dr 77345 — 281-641-4800
Greg Joseph, prin. — Fax 641-4817

Kingwood Christian Academy — 200/PK-12
1365 Northpark Dr 77339 — 281-354-1197
Joan Baker, admin. — Fax 354-5798
Kingwood College — Post-Sec.
20000 Kingwood Dr 77339 — 281-359-1600
Northeast Christian Academy — 300/PK-12
1711 Hamblen Rd 77339 — 281-359-1090
Earl Garland, prin. — Fax 359-5560

Kirbyville, Jasper, Pop. 2,037
Kirbyville Consolidated ISD — 1,600/PK-12
206 E Main St 75956 — 409-423-7520
Dr. Joseph Burns, supt. — Fax 423-2367
kirbyvillecisd.org
Kirbyville HS — 500/9-12
100 E Wildcat Dr 75956 — 409-423-7500
David Pitts, prin. — Fax 423-5313
Kirbyville JHS — 200/7-8
2200 S Margaret Ave 75956 — 409-420-0692
Gary Fairchild, prin. — Fax 423-6654

Klein, Harris, Pop. 12,000
Klein ISD — 35,500/PK-12
7200 Spring Cypress Rd 77379 — 832-249-4000
Dr. Jim Cain, supt. — Fax 249-4055
www.kleinisd.net
Doerre IS — 1,200/6-8
18218 Theiss Mail Route Rd 77379 — 832-249-5700
Cecilia Saccomanno, prin. — Fax 249-4054
Kleb IS — 1,200/6-8
7425 Louetta Rd 77379 — 832-249-5500
Pam Bourgeois, prin. — Fax 249-4053
Klein HS — 3,500/9-12
16715 Stuebner Airline Rd 77379 — 832-484-4000
Pat Huff, prin. — Fax 484-7820
Strack IS — 1,100/6-8
18027 Kuykendahl Rd Ste S 77379 — 832-249-5400
Larry Whitehead, prin. — Fax 249-4051
Other Schools – See Houston, Spring

Knippa, Uvalde
Knippa ISD — 200/PK-12
PO Box 99 78870 — 830-934-2176
Dr. David Rueda, supt. — Fax 934-2490
www.knippa.k12.tx.us/
Knippa S, PO Box 99 78870 — 200/PK-12
Rebecca Suttles, prin. — 830-934-2177

Knox City, Knox, Pop. 1,131
Knox City-O'Brien ISD — 300/PK-12
606 E Main St 79529 — 940-658-3521
Louis Baty, supt. — Fax 658-3379
www.esc9.net/knoxcity/
Knox City HS — 100/9-12
606 E Main St 79529 — 940-658-3565
Mack Lowe, prin. — Fax 658-3379
Other Schools – See O Brien

Kopperl, Bosque
Kopperl ISD — 300/PK-12
PO Box 67 76652 — 254-889-3502
Bill Brister, supt. — Fax 889-3443
www.esc12.net/kopperlisd
Kopperl S — 300/PK-12
PO Box 67 76652 — 254-889-3502
Ken Barrow, supt. — Fax 889-3443

Kountze, Hardin, Pop. 2,128
Kountze ISD — 1,400/PK-12
PO Box 460 77625 — 409-246-3352
Dianne Daniels, supt. — Fax 246-3217
kountzeisd.org
Kountze HS — 400/9-12
PO Box 460 77625 — 409-246-3474
Patti Carraway, prin. — Fax 246-8180
Kountze MS — 300/6-8
PO Box 460 77625 — 409-246-3551
John Ferguson, prin. — Fax 246-3857

Kress, Swisher, Pop. 802
Kress ISD — 200/K-12
PO Box 970 79052 — 806-684-2652
Doug Setliff, supt. — Fax 684-2687
www.kressonline.net
Kress JSHS — 100/7-12
PO Box 970 79052 — 806-684-2651
Leah Zeigler, prin. — Fax 684-2687

Krum, Denton, Pop. 2,632
Krum ISD — 1,200/PK-12
809 E McCart St 76249 — 940-482-6000
Troy Hamm, supt. — Fax 482-3929
www.krumisd.net
Krum HS — 300/9-12
809 E McCart St 76249 — 940-482-6000
Mike Pierson, prin. — Fax 482-2997
Krum MS — 300/6-8
809 E McCart St 76249 — 940-482-6000
John Murtell, prin. — Fax 482-6299

Kyle, Hays, Pop. 11,248
Hays Consolidated ISD — 9,200/PK-12
21003 I H 35 78640 — 512-268-2141
Dr. Kirk London, supt. — Fax 268-2147
www.hayscisd.net
Chapa MS, 3311 Dacy Ln 78640 — 6-8
Lisa Islas, prin. — 512-268-8500
Lehman HS — 900/8-12
1700 Lehman Rd 78640 — 512-268-8454
Elsa Hinojosa, prin. — Fax 268-2146
Other Schools – See Buda

Ladonia, Fannin, Pop. 678
Fannindel ISD — 200/PK-12
601 W Main St 75449 — 903-367-7251
Beverly Felts, supt. — Fax 367-7252
www.esc8.net/fannindel/
Fannindel HS — 100/7-12
601 W Main St 75449 — 903-367-7251
Michael Lide, prin. — Fax 367-7252

La Feria, Cameron, Pop. 6,436
La Feria ISD — 2,700/PK-12
PO Box 1159 78559 — 956-797-2612
Luis Garza, supt. — Fax 797-3737
www.esconett.org/laferiaisd/
Green JHS — 400/7-8
501 N Canal St 78559 — 956-797-1512
Michael Torres, prin. — Fax 797-2157
La Feria HS — 700/9-12
901 N Canal St 78559 — 956-797-1353
Rebecca Stirzaker, prin. — Fax 797-9374

Lago Vista, Travis, Pop. 5,167
Lago Vista ISD — 1,100/PK-12
PO Box 98 78645 — 512-267-8300
Dr. Barbara Qualls, supt. — Fax 267-8304
www.lagovista.txed.net/
Lago Vista HS — 300/9-12
PO Box 4929 78645 — 512-267-8315
Donna Larkin, prin. — Fax 267-8330

Lago Vista MS | 300/6-8
PO Box 4929 78645 | 512-267-8305
Paul Bixler, prin. | Fax 267-8329

La Grange, Fayette, Pop. 4,581
La Grange ISD | 1,900/PK-12
PO Box 100 78945 | 979-968-7000
Erwin Sladek, supt. | Fax 968-8155
www.la-grange.k12.tx.us
La Grange HS | 600/9-12
PO Box 100 78945 | 979-968-4800
William Wagner, prin. | Fax 968-6744
La Grange MS | 300/7-8
PO Box 100 78945 | 979-968-4747
Neal Miller, prin. | Fax 968-8155

Laird Hill, Rusk
Leveretts Chapel ISD | 200/PK-12
PO Box 669 75666 | 903-834-3181
Donna Johnson, supt. | Fax 834-6602
www.lcisd.esc7.net/
Other Schools – See Overton

La Joya, Hidalgo, Pop. 4,235
La Joya ISD | 21,700/PK-12
201 E Expressway 83 78560 | 956-580-5000
Filomena Leo, supt. | Fax 580-5444
www.lajoyaisd.com
Carter HS | 1,300/9-10
603 N Coyote Dr 78560 | 956-584-4839
Mary Ann Contreras, prin. | Fax 584-4848
De Zavala MS | 1,000/6-8
603 Tabasco Rd 78560 | 956-580-5472
Gisela Saenz, prin. | Fax 580-5494
Juarez-Lincoln HS | 1,600/9-10
801 N Coyote Dr 78560 | 956-580-5900
Diana Vela, prin. | Fax 580-5918
La Joya SHS | 1,800/11-12
604 N Coyote Dr 78560 | 956-580-5100
Judith Solis, prin. | Fax 580-5103
Schunior MS | 6-8
200 W Expressway 83 78560 | 956-580-8500
Antonio Uresti, prin. | Fax 580-8509
Other Schools – See Mission, Palmview

Lake Dallas, Denton, Pop. 6,779
Lake Dallas ISD | 3,600/PK-12
PO Box 548 75065 | 940-497-4039
Thomas Davenport, supt. | Fax 497-3737
www.ldisd.net
Lake Dallas MS | 600/7-8
PO Box 548 75065 | 940-497-4037
Randy Charles, prin. | Fax 497-4028
Other Schools – See Corinth

Lake Jackson, Brazoria, Pop. 26,950
Brazosport ISD
Supt. — See Clute
Lake Jackson IS | 900/7-8
100 Oyster Creek Dr 77566 | 979-730-7250
Steve Snell, prin. | Fax 292-2804

Brazosport Christian S | 300/PK-12
200B Willow Dr 77566 | 979-297-0563
Dan McDowell, admin. | Fax 297-8455
Brazosport College | Post-Sec.
500 College Dr 77566 | 979-230-3000

Lake Worth, Tarrant, Pop. 4,676
Lake Worth ISD | 2,400/PK-12
6800 Telephone Rd 76135 | 817-306-4200
Dr. Janice Cooper, supt. | Fax 237-5131
www.lake-worth.k12.tx.us/
Howry MS | 500/6-8
4000 Dakota Trl 76135 | 817-306-4240
Kathy Harmon, prin. | Fax 232-3687
Lake Worth HS | 600/9-12
4210 Boat Club Rd 76135 | 817-306-4230
John Hebert, prin. | Fax 237-0697

La Marque, Galveston, Pop. 13,788
La Marque ISD | 3,700/9-12
PO Box 7 77568 | 409-938-4251
Dr. Adrain B. Johnson, supt. | Fax 908-5012
www.la-marque.isd.tenet.edu
La Marque HS | 1,100/9-12
PO Box 7 77568 | 409-938-4261
Travis Weatherspoon, prin. | Fax 908-5036
La Marque MS | 800/6-8
PO Box 7 77568 | 409-938-4286
Rita Goudeau, prin. | Fax 908-5071

Lamesa, Dawson, Pop. 9,462
Klondike ISD | 200/PK-12
2911 County Road H 79331 | 806-462-7334
Steve McLaren, supt. | Fax 462-7333
klondike.esc17.net
Klondike S | 200/PK-12
2911 County Road H 79331 | 806-462-7332
Steve McLaren, prin. | Fax 462-7323

Lamesa ISD | 2,100/PK-12
PO Box 261 79331 | 806-872-5461
Keith Bryant, supt. | Fax 872-6220
www.lamesa.esc17.net
Lamesa HS | 600/9-12
PO Box 261 79331 | 806-872-8385
Joe Nicks, prin. | Fax 872-6608
Lamesa MS | 400/6-8
PO Box 261 79331 | 806-872-8301
Chris Riggins, prin. | Fax 872-2949

Lampasas, Lampasas, Pop. 7,426
Lampasas ISD | 3,500/PK-12
207 W 8th St 76550 | 512-556-6224
Rex Daniels, supt. | Fax 556-8711
www.lampasas.k12.tx.us
Lampasas HS | 1,000/9-12
902 S Broad St 76550 | 512-556-3614
Steve Zipkes, prin. | Fax 556-9962
Lampasas MS | 800/6-8
207 E Avenue A 76550 | 512-556-3101
Dwain Brock, prin. | Fax 556-0245

Lancaster, Dallas, Pop. 27,814
Lancaster ISD | 4,800/PK-12
PO Box 400 75146 | 972-227-4141
Dr. Larry D. Lewis, supt. | Fax 227-1102
www.lancasterisd.org
Lancaster HS | 1,400/9-12
822 W Pleasant Run Rd 75146 | 972-227-2418
Phillip Randall, prin. | Fax 218-3080

Lancaster JHS | 800/7-8
1109 W Main St 75146 | 972-227-4804
Stephaney Norman, prin. | Fax 218-3059

Cedar Valley College | Post-Sec.
3030 N Dallas Ave 75134 | 972-860-8200

Laneville, Rusk
Laneville ISD | 200/PK-12
PO Box 127 75667 | 903-863-5353
Ron Tidwell, supt. | Fax 863-2736
Laneville S | 200/PK-12
PO Box 127 75667 | 903-863-5354
Carolyn Reeves, prin. | Fax 863-2376

La Porte, Harris, Pop. 33,263
La Porte ISD | 7,600/PK-12
1002 San Jacinto St 77571 | 281-604-7000
Dr. Michael Say, supt. | Fax 604-7020
www.lpisd.org
La Porte HS | 2,300/9-12
1002 San Jacinto St 77571 | 281-604-7501
David Drake, prin. | Fax 604-7503
La Porte JHS | 600/7-8
1002 San Jacinto St 77571 | 281-604-6604
Dr. Mike Thomas, prin. | Fax 604-6605
Lomax JHS | 500/7-8
1002 San Jacinto St 77571 | 281-604-6701
Leigh Wall, prin. | Fax 604-6730

La Pryor, Zavala, Pop. 1,343
La Pryor ISD | 500/PK-12
PO Box 519 78872 | 830-365-4000
Eddie Ramirez, supt. | Fax 365-4006
www.lapryor.net
La Pryor HS | 200/7-12
PO Box 519 78872 | 830-365-4007
Victor Baron, prin. | Fax 365-4026

Laredo, Webb, Pop. 197,488
Laredo ISD | 24,600/PK-12
1702 Houston St 78040 | 956-795-3200
Daniel Garcia Ph.D., supt. | Fax 795-3405
www.laredoisd.org/
Christen MS | 1,500/6-8
2001 Santa Maria Ave 78040 | 956-795-3725
Clementina Cuellar, prin. | Fax 795-3732
Cigarroa HS | 1,500/9-12
2600 Zacatecas St 78046 | 956-795-3800
Mario Guzman, prin. | Fax 795-3814
Cigarroa MS | 1,400/6-8
2600 Palo Blanco St 78046 | 956-795-3700
| Fax 795-3711
Lamar MS | 1,400/6-8
1818 N Arkansas Ave 78043 | 956-795-3750
Virginia Salinas, prin. | Fax 795-3766
Martin HS | 1,900/9-12
2002 San Bernardo Ave 78040 | 956-795-3850
Roberto Gonzalez, prin. | Fax 795-3860
Memorial MS | 700/6-8
2002 Marcella Ave 78040 | 956-795-3775
Adriana Padilla, prin. | Fax 795-3780
Nixon HS | 2,200/9-12
2000 E Plum St 78043 | 956-795-3849
Sylvia Rios, prin. | Fax 795-3844
Trevino S of Communications & Fine Arts | 9-12
1701 Victoria St 78040 | 956-795-3325
Jose Cerda, dir. | Fax 795-3330

United ISD | 33,600/PK-12
201 Lindenwood Dr 78045 | 956-717-6201
Roberto J. Santos, supt. | Fax 764-6415
www.uisd.net
Alexander Health & Science Magnet S | 9-12
3600 E Del Mar Blvd 78041 | 956-473-5866
Yvonne Gutierrez Valdez, dir. | Fax 473-5998
Alexander HS | 2,000/9-12
3600 E Del Mar Blvd 78041 | 956-473-5800
Sandra Alvarez, prin. | Fax 473-5999
Clark MS | 700/6-8
500 W Hillside Rd 78041 | 956-473-7500
Dolores Barrera, prin. | Fax 473-7599
Garcia MS | 600/6-8
499 Pena Dr 78046 | 956-473-5000
Gerardo Gonzalez, prin. | Fax 473-5099
Gonzalez MS | 800/6-8
5208 Santa Claudia 78043 | 956-473-7000
Adriana Ramirez, prin. | Fax 473-7099
Johnson HS | 1,600/9-12
5626 Cielito Lindo 78046 | 956-473-5100
Oscar Perez, prin. | Fax 473-5399
Los Obispos MS | 1,100/6-8
4801 S Ejido Ave 78046 | 956-473-7800
Annabel Rubio, prin. | Fax 473-1899
Trautmann MS | 1,200/6-8
8501 Curly Ln 78045 | 956-473-7400
Raymundo Gonzalez, prin. | Fax 473-7499
United Engineering Magnet HS | 9-12
8800 McPherson Rd 78045 | 956-473-5627
David Canales, dir. | Fax 473-1981
United HS | 2,500/9-12
8800 McPherson Rd 78045 | 956-473-5600
Alberto Aleman, prin. | Fax 473-1980
United MS | 700/6-8
700 E Del Mar Blvd 78041 | 956-473-7300
Alberto Ibarra, prin. | Fax 473-7399
United South HS | 1,900/9-12
4001 Los Presidentes Ave 78046 | 956-473-5400
Roylin Wilson, prin. | Fax 473-5599
United South Magnet S for Business | 1,300/9-12
4001 Los Presidentes Ave 78046 | 956-726-6419
Maggie Martinez, dir. | Fax 726-6480
United South MS | 900/6-8
3707 Los Presidentes Ave 78046 | 956-473-7700
Selma Santos, prin. | Fax 473-7799
Washington MS | 900/6-8
10306 Riverbank Dr 78045 | 956-473-7600
David Gonzalez, prin. | Fax 473-7699

Laredo Beauty College | Post-Sec.
3020 N Meadow Ave 78040 | 956-723-2059
Laredo Community College | Post-Sec.
1 W End Washington St 78040 | 956-722-0521
St. Augustine HS | 600/6-12
1300 Galveston St 78040 | 956-724-8131
Sr. Carol Mucha, prin. | Fax 725-9241
Southern Careers Institute | Post-Sec.
4805 Maher Ave 78041 | 956-723-2345
Texas A&M International University | Post-Sec.
5201 University Blvd 78041 | 956-326-2000

Texas Careers | Post-Sec.
6410 McPherson Ave 78041 | 956-717-5909

La Rue, Henderson
La Poynor ISD | 500/K-12
13155 US Highway 175 E, | 903-876-4057
Eugene Buford, supt. | Fax 876-4541
www.lapoynor.esc7.net
La Poynor HS | 100/9-12
13155 US Highway 175 E, | 903-876-2373
Trent Cook, prin. | Fax 876-4541
La Poynor JHS | 100/6-8
13155 US Highway 175 E, | 903-876-1085
Lana Miller, prin. | Fax 876-4541

Latexo, Houston, Pop. 275
Latexo ISD | 400/K-12
PO Box 975 75849 | 936-544-5664
Dr. Roy H. Tucker, supt. | Fax 544-5332
www.latexoisd.net
Latexo JSHS | 200/7-12
PO Box 975 75849 | 936-544-5638
Albert Harris, prin. | Fax 544-8456

La Vernia, Wilson, Pop. 1,005
La Vernia ISD | 2,400/PK-12
13600 US Highway 87 W 78121 | 830-779-2181
Dr. Tom Harvey, supt. | Fax 779-2304
www.la-vernia.k12.tx.us
La Vernia HS | 700/9-12
225 FM 775 78121 | 830-779-2181
John Burks, prin. | Fax 779-3218
La Vernia IMS | 400/7-8
110 D L Vest 78121 | 830-779-2181
Sam Hughes, prin. | Fax 779-2728

La Villa, Hidalgo, Pop. 1,412
La Villa ISD | 700/PK-12
PO Box 9 78562 | 956-262-4755
Dr. Norma Salaiz, supt. | Fax 262-7323
www.lavillaisd.org
La Villa HS | 200/9-12
PO Box 9 78562 | 956-262-4715
Robert Munoz, prin. | Fax 262-9798
La Villa MS | 100/6-8
PO Box 9 78562 | 956-262-4760
Irasema Gonzalez, prin. | Fax 262-5243

Lazbuddie, Parmer
Lazbuddie ISD | 200/PK-12
PO Box 9 79053 | 806-965-2156
Karl Vaughn, supt. | Fax 965-2892
www.lazbuddieisd.org
Lazbuddie S | 200/PK-12
PO Box 9 79053 | 806-965-2152
John Jones, prin. | Fax 965-2892

League City, Galveston, Pop. 54,775
Clear Creek ISD | 32,000/PK-12
PO Box 799 77574 | 281-284-0000
Dr. Sandra Mossman, supt. | Fax 284-0005
www.ccisd.net
Clear Creek 9th Grade Center | 9-9
2451 E Main St 77573 | 281-284-2300
Joseph Ruiz, prin. | Fax 284-2305
Clear Creek HS | 3,300/9-12
2305 E Main St 77573 | 281-284-1700
Fred Hayes Ph.D., prin. | Fax 284-1705
Creekside IS | 700/6-8
4320 W Main St 77573 | 281-284-3500
Pete Caterina, prin. | Fax 284-3505
League City IS | 1,100/6-8
2588 Webster St 77573 | 281-284-3400
Scott Bockart, prin. | Fax 284-3405
Victory Lakes IS | 600/6-8
2880 W Walker St 77573 | 281-284-3700
Barry Beck, prin. | Fax 284-3705
Other Schools – See Friendswood, Houston, Seabrook

Bay Area Christian S | 600/K-12
4800 W Main St 77573 | 281-332-4814
Freddie Cullins, prin. | Fax 316-2001
Devereux-Texas Treatment Network | Post-Sec.
1150 Devereux Dr 77573 | 800-373-0011

Leakey, Real, Pop. 387
Leakey ISD | 300/PK-12
PO Box 1129 78873 | 830-232-5595
Fred McNiel, supt. | Fax 232-5535
www.leakey.k12.tx.us/
Leakey S | 300/PK-12
PO Box 1129 78873 | 830-232-5595
Lori Gonzalez, prin. | Fax 232-5535

Leander, Williamson, Pop. 13,846
Leander ISD | 18,700/PK-12
PO Box 218 78646 | 512-434-5000
Tom Glenn, supt. | Fax 434-5398
www.leanderisd.org
Leander HS | 2,100/9-12
3301 S Bagdad Rd 78641 | 512-435-8000
Todd Washburn, prin. | Fax 435-8011
Leander MS | 1,000/6-8
410 S West Dr 78641 | 512-434-7800
Sandy Trujillo, prin. | Fax 434-7805
Other Schools – See Austin, Cedar Park

Lefors, Gray, Pop. 537
Lefors ISD | 200/PK-12
PO Box 390 79054 | 806-835-2533
Garry Jameson, supt. | Fax 835-2238
www.region16.net/leforsisd/
Lefors S, PO Box 390 79054 | 200/PK-12
Ronnie Miller, prin. | 806-835-2533

Leggett, Polk
Leggett ISD | 300/PK-12
PO Box 68 77350 | 936-398-2804
Bennett Geeslin, supt. | Fax 398-2078
Leggett JSHS | 100/7-12
PO Box 68 77350 | 936-398-2412
Lara Kelley, prin. | Fax 398-0889

Lenorah, Martin
Grady ISD | 300/PK-12
3500 FM 829 79749 | 432-459-2444
John Tubb, supt. | Fax 459-2729
gradyisd.esc18.net/
Grady S | 300/PK-12
3500 FM 829 79749 | 432-459-2445
Richard Gibson, prin. | Fax 459-2729

Leonard, Fannin, Pop. 1,953
Leonard ISD 800/PK-12
1 Tiger Aly 75452 903-587-2318
Larry LaFavers, supt. Fax 587-2845
www.leonardisd.net
Leonard HS 200/9-12
1 Tiger Aly 75452 903-587-3556
John Kent, prin. Fax 587-8011
Leonard JHS 200/6-8
1 Tiger Aly 75452 903-587-2315
Beryl Sears, prin. Fax 587-2228

Levelland, Hockley, Pop. 12,904
Levelland ISD 3,100/PK-12
704 11th St 79336 806-894-9628
John Booth, supt. Fax 894-2583
www.levelland.isd.tenet.edu
Levelland HS 900/9-12
704 11th St 79336 806-894-8515
Virdie Montgomery, prin. Fax 894-6029
Levelland JHS 400/7-8
704 11th St 79336 806-894-6355
Mel Gierhart, prin. Fax 894-8935

South Plains College Post-Sec.
1401 College Ave 79336 806-894-9611

Lewisville, Denton, Pop. 87,127
Lewisville ISD
Supt. — See Flower Mound
Delay MS 600/6-8
136 W Purnell Rd 75057 972-436-6525
Pam Flores, prin. Fax 420-7122
Durham MS 600/6-8
2075 S Edmonds Ln 75067 469-713-5963
Alan Cassel, prin. Fax 350-1650
Hedrick MS 700/6-8
1526 Bellaire Blvd 75067 972-436-4536
Pete Taggart, prin. Fax 221-7462
Huffines MS 1,000/6-8
1440 N Valley Pkwy 75077 469-713-5990
Beth Brockman, prin. Fax 350-4950
Jackson Career Center Vo/Tech
1597 S Edmonds Ln 75067 972-221-0909
Alan Strong, prin. Fax 436-5912
Killough North HS 9-9
1301 Summit Ave 75077 469-713-5987
Andy Plunkett, prin. Fax 350-4550
Lewisville HS 2,300/9-12
1098 W Main St 75067 972-221-3535
Royce Cooper, prin. Fax 436-8658
Lewisville North HS 900/9-9
2103 Savage Ln 75057 972-436-7581
Andy Plunkett, prin. Fax 221-7289

Temple Christian Academy 300/PK-12
1010 Bellaire Blvd 75067 972-436-3480
Tom Wing, prin. Fax 219-5639

Lexington, Lee, Pop. 1,262
Lexington ISD 1,000/PK-12
8731 N Highway 77 78947 979-773-2254
Chuck Holt, supt. Fax 773-4455
www.lexington.isd.tenet.edu
Lexington HS 300/9-12
3rd & Burns St 78947 979-773-2255
Rebecca Otte French, prin. Fax 773-4455
Lexington MS 200/6-8
3rd & Burns St 78947 979-773-2255
Steven Coston, prin. Fax 773-4455

Liberty, Liberty, Pop. 8,261
Liberty ISD 2,300/PK-12
1600 Grand Ave 77575 936-336-7213
Mona Chadwick, supt. Fax 336-2283
www.libertyisd.net
Liberty HS 700/9-12
2615 Jefferson Dr 77575 936-336-6483
David Taylor, prin. Fax 336-3931
Liberty MS 500/6-8
2515 Jefferson Dr 77575 936-336-3582
Bruce Lacefield, prin. Fax 336-1021

Liberty Hill, Williamson, Pop. 1,485
Liberty Hill ISD 1,800/PK-12
PO Box 68 78642 512-260-5580
Dr. Dean Andrews, supt. Fax 260-5581
www.libertyhill.txed.net
Liberty Hill HS 500/9-12
PO Box 68 78642 512-260-5500
Dalton West, prin. Fax 260-5510
Liberty Hill MS 400/6-8
PO Box 68 78642 512-515-5636
Lila West, prin. Fax 778-5937

Lindale, Smith, Pop. 3,592
Lindale ISD 3,100/PK-12
PO Box 370 75771 903-881-4001
Jane Ann Morrison, supt. Fax 882-8641
www.lind.sprnet.org
Lindale HS 900/9-12
PO Box 370 75771 903-881-4051
Jamie Holder, prin. Fax 882-2813
Lindale JHS 500/7-8
PO Box 370 75771 903-881-4150
Vicki Thrasher, prin. Fax 882-2842

Linden, Cass, Pop. 2,198
Linden-Kildare Consolidated ISD 900/PK-12
205 Kildare Rd 75563 903-756-5027
John York, supt. Fax 756-7242
www.lkcisd.net
Linden-Kildare HS 300/9-12
205 Kildare Rd 75563 903-756-7026
Hoby Holder, prin. Fax 756-8512
Linden-Kildare JHS 200/6-8
205 Kildare Rd 75563 903-756-5381
Jerry Hankins, prin. Fax 756-8832

Lindsay, Cooke, Pop. 881
Lindsay ISD 500/K-12
PO Box 145 76250 940-668-8923
Jerry Metzler, supt. Fax 668-2662
www.esc11.net/schools/lindsay/index.htm
Lindsay HS 200/7-12
PO Box 145 76250 940-668-8474
Larry Smith, prin. Fax 665-1637

Lingleville, Erath
Lingleville ISD 300/PK-12
PO Box 134 76461 254-968-2596
Dennis Hughes, supt. Fax 965-5821
www.lingleville.k12.tx.us/
Lingleville S 300/PK-12
PO Box 134 76461 254-968-2596
Dennis Hughes, prin. Fax 965-5821

Lipan, Hood, Pop. 457
Lipan ISD 300/PK-12
211 N Kickapoo St 76462 254-646-2266
Dr. Dennis McNaughten, supt. Fax 646-3499
Lipan S 300/PK-12
211 N Kickapoo St 76462 254-646-2266
Kim Gibbs, prin. Fax 646-3499

Little Elm, Denton, Pop. 12,003
Little Elm ISD 3,500/PK-12
500 Lobo Ln 75068 972-292-1847
Steve Murray, supt. Fax 294-1107
www.leisd.ws/
Lakeside JHS 500/7-8
400 Lobo Ln 75068 972-292-3200
Camille Porter, prin. Fax 292-3009
Little Elm HS 700/9-12
1900 Walker Ln 75068 972-292-1840
Gerry Talley, prin. Fax 292-3505

Littlefield, Lamb, Pop. 6,432
Littlefield ISD 1,500/PK-12
1207 E 14th St 79339 806-385-3844
Jerry Blakely, supt. Fax 385-6297
www.littlefield.k12.tx.us
Littlefield HS 400/9-12
1207 E 14th St 79339 806-385-5683
Ricky Hobbs, prin. Fax 385-3603
Littlefield JHS 300/6-8
1207 E 14th St 79339 806-385-3922
Shawn Mason, prin. Fax 385-5603

Little River, Bell, Pop. 1,512
Academy ISD 900/PK-12
704 E Main St 76554 254-982-4304
Randy Hendricks, supt. Fax 982-0023
www.academy.k12.tx.us/
Academy HS 300/9-12
602 E Main St 76554 254-982-4201
Joe Craig, prin. Fax 982-4420
Academy JHS 300/5-8
501 E Main St 76554 254-982-4620
Stephen Ash, prin. Fax 982-4776

Live Oak, Bexar, Pop. 9,786
Judson ISD 15,700/PK-12
8012 Shin Oak Dr 78233 210-945-5400
Dr. Ed Lyman, supt. Fax 945-6900
www.judsonisd.org
Other Schools – See Converse, San Antonio, Universal City

Livingston, Polk, Pop. 6,317
Big Sandy ISD
Supt. — See Dallardsville
Big Sandy S 500/PK-12
FM 1276 77351 936-563-1000
Kevin Foster, prin. Fax 563-1010

Livingston ISD 4,000/PK-12
PO Box 1297 77351 936-328-2100
Dr. Carol Ann Bonds, supt. Fax 328-2109
www.livingstonisd.com
Livingston JHS 900/7-9
1801 Highway 59 Loop N 77351 936-328-2120
John Omelan, prin. Fax 328-2139
Livingston SHS 900/10-12
1 Lion Ave 77351 936-328-2240
Jason Mixon, prin. Fax 328-2231

Llano, Llano, Pop. 3,464
Llano ISD 1,900/PK-12
200 E Lampasas St 78643 325-247-4747
Dennis Hill, supt. Fax 247-5623
www.llano.k12.tx.us
Llano HS 500/9-12
2509 S State Highway 16 78643 325-248-2200
Earl Jarrett, prin. Fax 247-2122
Llano JHS 400/6-8
400 Highway 71 E 78643 325-247-4659
Candace Hughs, prin. Fax 247-5916

Lockhart, Caldwell, Pop. 13,064
Lockhart ISD 4,500/PK-12
PO Box 120 78644 512-398-0000
Dr. John Hall, supt. Fax 398-0025
www.lockhartisd.org
Lockhart HS 900/10-12
1 Lion Country Dr 78644 512-398-0300
Larry Ramirez, prin. Fax 398-0302
Lockhart HS Freshman Campus 400/9-9
419 Bois D Arc St 78644 512-398-0170
John Henk, prin. Fax 398-0172
Lockhart JHS 1,000/6-8
1015 City Line Rd 78644 512-398-0770
Susan Brooks, prin. Fax 398-0772

Lockney, Floyd, Pop. 1,960
Lockney ISD 600/PK-12
PO Box 428 79241 806-652-2115
Phil Cotham, supt. Fax 652-2729
www.lockney.isd.tenet.edu/
Lockney HS 200/9-12
PO Box 1058 79241 806-652-3325
Dean Thompson, prin. Fax 652-4945
Lockney JHS, PO Box 550 79241 200/6-8
Todd Hallmark, prin. 806-652-2236

Lohn, McCulloch
Lohn ISD 100/PK-12
PO Box 277 76852 325-344-5749
Leon Freeman, supt. Fax 344-5789
www.centex-edu.net/lohn
Lohn S 100/PK-12
PO Box 277 76852 325-344-5749
Clay Burns, prin. Fax 344-5789

Lolita, Jackson
Industrial ISD
Supt. — See Vanderbilt
Industrial JHS 200/6-8
PO Box 218 77971 361-874-4343
Jim Green, prin. Fax 874-4314

Lometa, Lampasas, Pop. 837
Lometa ISD 300/PK-12
PO Box 250 76853 512-752-3384
David Rice, supt. Fax 752-8531
www.centex-edu.net/lometa/
Lometa S 300/PK-12
PO Box 250 76853 512-752-3384
Kip Bullock, prin. Fax 752-3424

Lone Oak, Hunt, Pop. 546
Lone Oak ISD 800/PK-12
PO Box 38 75453 903-662-5427
Eddie White, supt. Fax 662-5290
loisd.echalk.com/
Lone Oak HS 300/9-12
8205 Highway 69 S 75453 903-662-0981
Curt Hale, prin. Fax 662-0984
Lone Oak MS 300/5-8
8161 Highway 69 S 75453 903-662-5121
Kim White, prin.

Longview, Gregg, Pop. 74,902
Longview ISD 7,700/PK-12
PO Box 3268 75606 903-381-2200
Dr. Dana Marable, supt. Fax 753-5389
www.lisd.org
Forest Park MS 600/6-8
PO Box 3268 75606 903-758-9971
Margaret Davis, prin. Fax 758-6964
Foster MS 700/6-8
PO Box 3268 75606 903-753-1692
Sedric Clark, prin. Fax 758-1571
Judson MS 600/6-8
PO Box 3268 75606 903-663-0206
Brian Kasper, prin. Fax 663-0275
Longview HS 2,200/9-12
PO Box 3268 75606 903-663-1301
Milton Wallace, prin. Fax 663-7180

Pine Tree ISD 4,600/PK-12
PO Box 5878 75608 903-295-5000
Lynn Whitaker, supt. Fax 295-5004
www.ptisd.org
Pine Tree JHS 800/8-9
PO Box 5878 75608 903-295-5081
Jerald Jeter, prin. Fax 295-5082
Pine Tree SHS 1,100/10-12
PO Box 5878 75608 903-295-5031
Jason Mixon, prin. Fax 295-5029

Spring Hill ISD 1,700/PK-12
3101 Spring Hill Rd 75605 903-759-4404
D. Michael Crossland, supt. Fax 297-0141
www.springhill.esc7.net
Spring Hill HS 500/9-12
3101 Spring Hill Rd 75605 903-323-7738
Mike Gilbert, prin. Fax 323-7766
Spring Hill JHS 300/7-8
3101 Spring Hill Rd 75605 903-323-7718
David Reed, prin. Fax 323-7765

Advanced Christian Training S 50/K-12
100 Kings Ln 75605 903-759-8335
Genevieve Germany, dir.
Christian Heritage S 200/K-12
2715 FM 1844 75605 903-663-4151
Connie Puryear, admin. Fax 663-4587
East Texas Christian S 200/PK-12
PO Box 8053 75607 903-757-7891
Philip Brown, prin. Fax 236-4968
Le Tourneau University Post-Sec.
PO Box 7001 75607 903-233-3000
Longview Christian S 200/K-12
2101 W Marshall Ave 75604 903-297-3501
Mark Clark, admin. Fax 663-4448
Star College of Cosmetology Post-Sec.
700 E Whaley St 75601 903-758-8611
Trinity S of Texas 300/PK-12
215 N Teague St 75601 903-753-0612
Rev. Charlene Miller, hdmstr. Fax 753-4812

Loop, Gaines
Loop ISD 100/PK-12
PO Box 917 79342 806-487-6411
Phil Mitchell, supt. Fax 487-6416
www.loopisd.net/
Loop S 100/PK-12
PO Box 917 79342 806-487-6411
Ray Conner, prin. Fax 487-6416

Loraine, Mitchell, Pop. 616
Loraine ISD 200/PK-12
PO Box 457 79532 325-737-2235
Eric Stoddard, supt. Fax 737-2019
www.loraine.esc14.net/
Loraine S 200/PK-12
PO Box 457 79532 325-737-2225
Cindy Tribble, prin. Fax 737-2603

Lorena, McLennan, Pop. 1,503
Lorena ISD 1,300/PK-12
PO Box 97 76655 254-857-3239
Don Ickles, supt. Fax 857-4533
www.lorenaisd.net
Lorena HS 500/9-12
PO Box 97 76655 254-857-4604
Randy Blanchard, prin. Fax 857-3883
Lorena MS 500/5-8
PO Box 97 76655 254-857-4621
Sandra Talbert, prin. Fax 857-3419

Lorenzo, Crosby, Pop. 1,304
Lorenzo ISD 300/PK-12
PO Box 520 79343 806-634-5591
Dick Van Hoose, supt. Fax 634-5928
lorenzo.esc17.net/
Lorenzo JSHS 100/7-12
PO Box 520 79343 806-634-5592
Joe Christian, prin. Fax 634-5788

Los Fresnos, Cameron, Pop. 4,960
Los Fresnos Consolidated ISD 7,500/PK-12
PO Box 309 78566 956-233-4407
Dr. Sylvia P. Atkinson, supt. Fax 233-4031
www.lfcisd.net
Liberty Memorial MS 6-8
PO Box 309 78566 956-233-3900
Ms. Marty Vasquez, prin. Fax 233-1074
Los Cuates MS 800/6-8
PO Box 309 78566 956-233-6250
Pablo Leal, prin. Fax 233-6265

Los Fresnos HS 2,000/9-12
PO Box 309 78566 956-233-3300
Dawn Hall, prin. Fax 233-3510
Reseca MS 900/6-8
PO Box 309 78566 956-233-6210
Steve Rosales, prin. Fax 233-6209

Louise, Wharton
Louise ISD 500/PK-12
PO Box 97 77455 979-648-2982
Andrew Peters, supt. Fax 648-2520
louiseisd.org
Louise JSHS 200/7-12
PO Box 97 77455 979-648-2202
Diana Blumrick, prin. Fax 648-2142

Lovelady, Houston, Pop. 611
Lovelady ISD 600/PK-12
PO Box 99 75851 936-636-7616
John Reynolds, supt. Fax 636-2212
www.loveladyisd.net
Lovelady HS 200/9-12
PO Box 280 75851 936-636-7636
Mark Parker, prin. Fax 636-2305

Lubbock, Lubbock, Pop. 206,481
Frenship ISD
Supt. — See Wolfforth
Terra Vista MS 6-8
1111 Upland Ave 79416 806-796-0076
Brent Lowrey, prin.

Lubbock ISD 27,900/PK-12
1628 19th St 79401 806-766-1000
Wayne Havens, supt. Fax 766-1210
www.lubbockisd.org
Alderson MS 400/6-8
219 Walnut Ave 79403 806-766-1500
George Love, prin. Fax 766-1490
Atkins JHS 500/7-9
5401 Avenue U 79412 806-766-1522
Miles Walston, prin. Fax 766-2226
Cavazos JHS 800/7-9
210 University Ave 79415 806-766-6600
Mike Worth, prin. Fax 766-6627
Coronado SHS 1,700/10-12
3307 Vicksburg Ave 79410 806-766-0600
Eric McKnight, prin. Fax 766-0560
Dunbar MS 600/6-8
2010 E 26th St 79404 806-766-1300
Royce Avery, prin. Fax 766-1320
Estacado HS 800/9-12
1504 E Itasca St 79403 806-766-1400
Paul Frazier, prin. Fax 766-1952
Evans JHS 700/7-9
4211 58th St 79413 806-766-0722
Leslie Soto, prin. Fax 766-0570
Hutchinson JHS 800/7-9
3102 Canton Ave 79410 806-766-0755
Mike Bustillos, prin. Fax 766-0538
Irons JHS 700/7-9
5214 79th St 79424 806-766-2044
Lynn Akin, prin. Fax 766-2070
Lubbock SHS 1,700/10-12
2004 19th St 79401 806-766-1444
Doyle Vogler, prin. Fax 766-1469
MacKenzie JHS 600/7-9
5402 12th St 79416 806-766-0777
John Carter, prin. Fax 766-0510
Martin ATC Vo/Tech
3201 Avenue Q 79411 806-766-6651
Bill Landis, dir. Fax 766-6675
Monterey SHS 1,600/10-12
3211 47th St 79413 806-766-0700
Al Griggs, prin. Fax 766-0509
Slaton JHS 800/7-9
1602 32nd St 79411 806-766-1555
Robert Guerrero, prin. Fax 766-1571
Wilson JHS 600/7-9
4402 31st St 79410 806-766-0799
Cindy Wallace, prin. Fax 766-0814

Lubbock-Cooper ISD 2,600/PK-12
16302 Loop 493 79423 806-863-2282
Pat Henderson, supt. Fax 863-3130
www.lcisd.net
Lubbock-Cooper HS 600/9-12
16302 Loop 493 79423 806-863-2282
Steve Naurkal, prin. Fax 863-2877
Lubbock-Cooper JHS 600/6-8
16302 Loop 493 79423 806-863-2282
Kevin Hahn, prin. Fax 863-2654

Roosevelt ISD 1,200/PK-12
1406 County Road 3300 79403 806-842-3282
Berhl Robertson, supt. Fax 842-3266
www.roosevelt.esc17.net
Roosevelt HS 300/9-12
1406 County Road 3300 79403 806-842-3283
Ricardo Garcia, prin. Fax 842-3931
Roosevelt JHS 300/6-8
1406 County Road 3300 79403 806-842-3218
Kayla Morrison, prin. Fax 842-3337

American Commercial College Post-Sec.
2007 34th St 79411 806-747-4339
Christ the King S 300/PK-12
4011 54th St 79413 806-795-8283
Christine Wanjura, prin. Fax 795-9715
Covenant Sch. of Nursing & Allied Health Post-Sec.
2002 Miami Ave 79410 806-797-0955
International Business College Post-Sec.
5020 50th St Unit 108 79414 806-797-1933
Lubbock Christian S 400/PK-12
2604 Dover Ave 79407 806-796-8700
Peter Dahlstrom, supt. Fax 791-3569
Lubbock Christian University Post-Sec.
5601 19th St 79407 806-796-8800
Lubbock Hair Academy Post-Sec.
2844 34th St 79410 806-795-0806
Methodist Hospital Post-Sec.
3615 19th St 79410 806-792-1011
South Plains College Post-Sec.
9730 Reese Blvd 79416 806-894-9611
Texas Careers Post-Sec.
1421 9th St 79401 806-765-7051
Texas Tech University Post-Sec.
1 Texas Tech University 79409 806-742-2011
Texas Tech University Health Science Ctr Post-Sec.
79430 806-743-3111

Trinity Christian HS 300/7-12
6701 University Ave 79413 806-791-6583
David Pruett, supt. Fax 745-8641

Lucas, Collin, Pop. 3,501

Lucas Christian Academy 300/1-12
415 W Lucas Rd, 972-429-4362
Carl Bindhammer, admin. Fax 429-5141

Lueders, Jones, Pop. 283
Lueders-Avoca ISD 200/PK-12
334 S McHarg St 79533 325-228-4211
Billie McKeever, supt. Fax 228-4513
laisd.com
Lueders-Avoca HS 100/9-12
8762 CR 604, 325-773-2785
John Jensen, prin. Fax 773-3072

Lufkin, Angelina, Pop. 33,162
Hudson ISD 2,300/PK-12
6735 Ted Trout Dr 75904 936-875-3351
Mary Ann Whiteker, supt. Fax 875-9209
www.hudsonisd.org
Hudson HS 700/9-12
6735 Ted Trout Dr 75904 936-875-9232
Donny Webb, prin. Fax 875-9307
Hudson MS 700/5-8
6735 Ted Trout Dr 75904 936-875-9292
Stanley Tupman, prin. Fax 875-9317

Lufkin ISD 8,300/PK-12
PO Box 1407 75902 936-634-6696
Roy Knight, supt. Fax 634-8864
www.lufkinisd.org
Lufkin HS 2,200/9-12
309 S Medford Dr 75901 936-632-7721
Mark Smith, prin. Fax 632-8132
Lufkin MS 1,800/6-8
900 E Denman Ave 75901 936-630-4444
Vickie Evans, prin. Fax 632-4444

Academy of Hair Design Post-Sec.
512 S Chestnut St 75901 936-634-8440
Angelina College Post-Sec.
PO Box 1768 75902 936-639-1301

Luling, Caldwell, Pop. 5,291
Luling ISD 1,600/PK-12
212 E Bowie St 78648 830-875-3191
Mark Weisner, supt. Fax 875-3193
www.luling.txed.net
Luling HS 400/9-12
218 E Travis St 78648 830-875-2458
James Matthews, prin. Fax 875-2751
Luling JHS 400/6-8
214 E Bowie St 78648 830-875-2121
Brian Thompson, prin. Fax 875-5482

Lumberton, Hardin, Pop. 9,122
Lumberton ISD 3,500/PK-12
121 S Main St 77657 409-923-7580
Gus Hollomon, supt. Fax 755-7848
www.lumberton.k12.tx.us
Lumberton HS 1,000/9-12
103 LHS Dr 77657 409-923-7890
Mike Smith, prin. Fax 755-6576
Lumberton MS 600/7-8
123 S Main St 77657 409-923-7581
Robin Perez, prin. Fax 751-0641

Lyford, Willacy, Pop. 1,962
Lyford Consolidated ISD 1,300/PK-12
PO Box 220 78569 956-347-3521
Jack Damron, supt. Fax 347-5201
www.lyfordcisd.net
Lyford HS 400/9-12
PO Box 220 78569 956-347-3909
Isabel Solis, prin. Fax 347-5034
Lyford MS 300/6-8
PO Box 220 78569 956-347-3910
Dana Yates, prin. Fax 347-2351

Lytle, Atascosa, Pop. 2,576
Lytle ISD 1,500/PK-12
PO Box 745 78052 830-709-5100
Michelle Carroll Smith, supt. Fax 709-5104
www.lytleisd.com
Lytle HS 400/9-12
PO Box 190 78052 830-709-5105
Rosa Mares, prin. Fax 709-5107
Lytle JHS 300/6-8
PO Box 825 78052 830-709-5115
Jesse Vela, prin. Fax 709-5119

Mabank, Kaufman, Pop. 2,426
Mabank ISD 3,400/PK-12
124 E Market St 75147 903-887-9311
Dr. Russell D. Marshall, supt. Fax 887-9399
www.mabankisd.net
Mabank HS 900/9-12
124 E Market St 75147 903-887-9333
Tommy Wallis, prin. Fax 887-9303
Mabank MS 800/6-8
124 E Market St 75147 903-887-9360
Gary Jacobs, prin. Fax 887-0361
Mabank AEP Adult
124 E Market St 75147 903-880-1320
Zan Tidmore, prin. Fax 880-1324

Mc Allen, Hidalgo, Pop. 113,877
McAllen ISD 23,500/PK-12
2000 N 23rd St 78501 956-618-6000
Yolanda Chapa, supt. Fax 631-7206
www.mcallenisd.org/
Brown MS 900/6-8
2700 S Ware Rd 78503 956-632-8700
Yvette Cavazos, prin. Fax 632-8709
Cathey MS 900/6-8
1800 N Cynthia St 78501 956-971-4300
Priscila Hinojosa, prin. Fax 632-2811
De Leon MS 1,000/6-8
4201 N 29th Ln 78504 956-632-8800
Joanetta Ellis, prin. Fax 632-8805
Lincoln MS 800/6-8
1601 N 27th St 78501 956-971-4200
Rosalinda Martinez, prin. Fax 971-4273
Mc Allen HS 2,000/9-12
2021 La Vista Ave 78501 956-632-3100
Delia Longoria, prin. Fax 632-3114

Memorial HS 2,000/9-12
101 E Hackberry Ave 78501 956-632-5201
Jose Saenz, prin. Fax 632-5226
Morris MS 800/6-8
1400 Trenton Rd 78504 956-618-7300
Jose Perez, prin. Fax 632-3666
Rowe HS 1,900/9-12
2101 N Ware Rd 78501 956-632-5100
Joe Puente, prin. Fax 632-8850
Travis MS 800/6-8
600 E Houston Ave 78501 956-971-4242
Trecia Munal, prin. Fax 632-8454

Sharyland ISD
Supt. — See Mission
Sharyland Worth JHS 600/7-8
5100 Dove Ave 78504 956-686-1415
David Guel, prin. Fax 668-0425

Kings Way Missionary Institute Post-Sec.
401 S 35th St 78501 956-682-6187
San Antonio College Medical Dental Asst. Post-Sec.
1500 S Jackson Rd 78503 956-630-1499
South Texas Christian Academy 100/PK-12
7001 N Ware Rd 78504 956-682-1117
Fax 682-7398
South Texas College Post-Sec.
3201 Pecan Blvd 78501 956-631-4922
South Texas Vocational-Technical Inst. Post-Sec.
2400 Daffodil Ave 78501 956-631-1107
University of Cosmetology Arts & Science Post-Sec.
PO Box 720391 78504 956-687-9444

Mc Camey, Upton, Pop. 2,028
McCamey ISD 500/PK-12
PO Box 1069 79752 432-652-3666
Jerry Stinson, supt. Fax 652-4219
mcisd.esc18.net/
Mc Camey HS 200/9-12
PO Box 1069 79752 432-652-3666
Donny Wiley, prin. Fax 652-4245
Mc Camey MS 200/5-8
PO Box 1069 79752 432-652-3666
Scott Allen, prin. Fax 652-4246

Mc Gregor, McLennan, Pop. 4,940
McGregor ISD 1,100/PK-12
PO Box 356 76657 254-840-2828
Kevin Houchin, supt. Fax 840-4077
www.mcgregor-isd.org
Isbill JHS 300/5-8
PO Box 356 76657 254-840-3251
Paul Miller, prin. Fax 840-4077
Mc Gregor HS 300/9-12
PO Box 356 76657 254-840-2853
James Lenamon, prin. Fax 840-4077

Mc Kinney, Collin, Pop. 73,081
McKinney ISD 16,100/PK-12
1 Duvall St 75069 469-742-4000
Tom Crowe, supt. Fax 742-4071
www.mckinneyisd.net
Dowell MS 1,300/6-8
301 Ridge Rd 75070 469-742-6700
Eartha Linson, prin. Fax 742-6701
Evans MS 6-8
6998 Eldorado Pkwy 75070 469-742-7100
Todd Young, prin. Fax 742-7101
Faubion MS 1,100/6-8
2000 Rollins St 75069 469-742-6900
Patty Jackson, prin. Fax 742-6901
Johnson MS 1,200/6-8
3400 Community Blvd 75071 469-742-4900
Dr. Melinda DeFelice, prin. Fax 742-4901
McKinney Boyd HS 9-12
600 Lake Forest Dr 75070 469-452-4900
Rick McDaniel, prin. Fax 452-4901
McKinney Boyd HS 9-12
600 Lake Forest Dr 75070 469-742-4000
Rick McDaniel, prin.
McKinney HS 1,900/9-12
1400 Wilson Creek Pkwy 75069 469-742-5700
Donna Rother, prin. Fax 742-5701
McKinney North HS 1,900/9-12
2550 Wilmeth Rd 75071 469-742-4300
Linda Theret, prin. Fax 742-4301

International Business School Post-Sec.
1434 N Central Expy Ste 116 75070 972-548-0774
Mc Kinney Christian Academy 400/K-12
3601 Bois D Arc Rd 75071 972-548-4855
Todd Clingman, hdmstr. Fax 548-9243

Mc Lean, Gray, Pop. 764
McLean ISD 100/PK-12
PO Box 90, 806-779-2301
Jimmy Hannon, supt. Fax 779-2248
McLean HS 9-12
PO Box 90, 806-779-2571
Rhonda Patterson, prin. Fax 779-2315

Mc Leod, Cass
Mc Leod ISD 500/K-12
PO Box 350 75565 903-796-7181
Cathy May, supt. Fax 796-8443
www.mcleodisd.net
Mc Leod HS 200/9-12
PO Box 350 75565 903-796-7181
Teal Lambert, prin. Fax 796-8443
Mc Leod MS 100/6-8
PO Box 350 75565 903-796-7181
Teal Lambert, prin. Fax 796-8443

Madisonville, Madison, Pop. 4,192
Madisonville Consolidated ISD 2,000/PK-12
PO Box 879 77864 936-348-2797
Karen Ritcher, supt. Fax 348-2751
www.madisonvillecisd.org
Madisonville HS 600/9-12
PO Box 879 77864 936-348-2721
Keith Smith, prin. Fax 348-5753
Madisonville JHS 300/6-8
PO Box 819 77864 936-348-3587
James Sanders, prin. Fax 348-5603

Magnolia, Montgomery, Pop. 1,214
Magnolia ISD 9,100/PK-12
PO Box 88 77353 281-356-3571
Michael Holland, supt. Fax 356-1328
www.magnoliaisd.org

Bear Branch JHS 600/7-8
PO Box 606 77353 281-356-6088
Gerald Evans, prin. Fax 252-2060
Magnolia HS 2,500/9-12
PO Box 428 77353 281-356-3572
Jeff Springer, prin. Fax 252-2092
Magnolia JHS 900/7-8
PO Box 476 77353 281-356-1327
Mark Weatherly, prin. Fax 252-2125
Magnolia West HS, PO Box 426 77353 9-12
Rob Stewart, prin. 281-356-3571

Malakoff, Henderson, Pop. 2,319
Cross Roads ISD 600/PK-12
14434 FM 59 75148 903-489-2001
Clay Tompkins, supt. Fax 489-2527
www.crossroadsisd.org/
Cross Roads HS 200/9-12
14434 FM 59 75148 903-489-1275
Charles Taylor, prin. Fax 489-0054
Cross Roads JHS 100/6-8
14434 FM 59 75148 903-489-2667
Glenda Wisenbaker, prin. Fax 489-1843

Malakoff ISD 1,200/PK-12
813 E Royall Blvd 75148 903-489-1152
Larry Hulsey, supt. Fax 489-2566
www.malakoff.esc7.net
Malakoff HS 300/9-12
15201 FM 3062 75148 903-489-1527
Russell Grant, prin. Fax 489-0971
Malakoff MS 300/6-8
106 N Cedar St 75148 903-489-0264
George Hull, prin. Fax 489-1812

Manor, Travis, Pop. 1,169
Manor ISD 3,200/PK-12
PO Box 359 78653 512-278-4000
Mark Diaz Ed.D., supt. Fax 278-4017
www.manorisd.net
Manor HS 800/9-12
PO Box 679 78653 512-278-4030
Carlton Tucker, prin. Fax 278-4033
Manor MS 700/6-8
PO Box 388 78653 512-278-4065
Don Wise, prin. Fax 278-4285

Mansfield, Tarrant, Pop. 33,123
Mansfield ISD 20,800/PK-12
605 E Broad St 76063 817-473-5600
Vernon Newsom, supt. Fax 473-5611
www.mansfieldisd.org
Barber Career Tech Center Vo/Tech
1120 W Debbie Ln 76063 817-299-1900
Jerri McNair, prin. Fax 453-6839
Brooks Wester MS 1,300/7-8
1520 W Walnut Creek Dr 76063 817-453-7200
Scott Shafer, prin. Fax 453-7213
Jones MS 7-8
4500 E Broad St 76063 817-276-6200
Lamar Goree, prin. Fax 453-7380
Mansfield HS 2,500/9-12
3001A E Broad St 76063 817-473-5750
Steven Gast, prin. Fax 473-5424
Worley MS 900/7-8
500 Pleasant Ridge Dr 76063 817-473-5668
Christie Alfred, prin. Fax 473-5623
Other Schools – See Arlington

Manvel, Brazoria, Pop. 3,234
Alvin ISD
Supt. — See Alvin
Manvel HS 9-12
19601 Highway 6 77578 281-692-0700
Darrell Alexander, prin. Fax 692-0852

Heritage Christian Academy 100/PK-12
PO Box 848 77578 281-489-9746
Angi Fox, prin. Fax 997-7218

Marathon, Brewster
Marathon ISD 100/PK-12
PO Box 416 79842 432-386-4431
Conrad Arriola, supt. Fax 386-4395
www.marathonisd.com/
Marathon S 100/PK-12
PO Box 416 79842 432-386-4431
Conrad Arriola, prin. Fax 386-4395

Marble Falls, Burnet, Pop. 5,503
Marble Falls ISD 4,400/PK-12
2001 Broadway St 78654 830-693-4357
Dr. Ryder Warren, supt. Fax 693-5685
www.mfisd.txed.net
Marble Falls HS 1,100/9-12
2101 Mustang Dr 78654 830-693-4375
Buck Gilcrease, prin. Fax 693-6079
Marble Falls MS 800/6-8
1511 Pony Dr 78654 830-693-4439
Brandon Stiewig, prin. Fax 693-7788

Faith Academy of Marble Falls 200/1-12
PO Box 1240 78654 830-798-1333
Aaron Weast, admin. Fax 798-1332

Marfa, Presidio, Pop. 2,029
Marfa ISD 500/PK-12
PO Box T 79843 432-729-4252
Kenn K. Franklin, supt. Fax 729-4310
www.marfa.esc18.net
Marfa JSHS 200/7-12
PO Box T 79843 432-729-4252
Brian Hermosillo, prin. Fax 729-4053

Marion, Guadalupe, Pop. 1,128
Marion ISD 1,400/PK-12
PO Box 189 78124 830-914-2803
Dennis Dreyer, supt. Fax 420-2300
www.marion.txed.net
Marion HS 400/9-12
PO Box 189 78124 830-914-2803
Daryl Wendel, prin. Fax 420-3639
Marion MS 400/6-8
PO Box 189 78124 830-914-2803
Johanna Lopez, prin. Fax 420-2300

Marlin, Falls, Pop. 6,340
Marlin ISD 1,400/PK-12
130 Coleman St 76661 254-883-3585
Dr. Eli Casey, supt. Fax 883-6612
www.marlinisd.org

Marlin HS 500/9-12
1400 Capps St 76661 254-883-2394
William Almond, prin. Fax 883-3470
Marlin MS 300/6-8
678 Success Dr 76661 254-883-9241
Jo Ann Garrison, prin. Fax 883-2839

Marshall, Harrison, Pop. 23,938
Marshall ISD 5,900/PK-12
PO Box 879 75671 903-927-8701
Ken Franklin, supt. Fax 935-0203
www.marshallisd.com
Marshall HS 1,600/9-12
1900 Maverick Dr 75670 903-927-8800
William Spivey, prin. Fax 938-7052
Marshall JHS 900/7-8
700 W Houston St 75670 903-927-8830
Tony Thomas, prin. Fax 927-8837

East Texas Baptist University Post-Sec.
1209 N Grove St 75670 903-935-7963
Texas State Technical College Marshall Post-Sec.
2400 E End Blvd S 75672 903-935-1010
Wiley College Post-Sec.
711 Wiley Ave 75670 903-927-3300

Mart, McLennan, Pop. 2,233
Mart ISD 600/PK-12
PO Box 120 76664 254-876-2523
Leonard Williams, supt. Fax 876-3028
www.martisd.org/
Mart HS 200/9-12
PO Box 120 76664 254-876-2574
Todd Gooden, prin. Fax 876-2575
Mart MS 200/5-8
PO Box 120 76664 254-876-2762
Linda Delaney, prin. Fax 876-2792

Martinsville, Nacogdoches
Martinsville ISD 200/PK-12
PO Box 100 75958 936-564-3455
Allen D. Garner, supt. Fax 569-0498
www.martinsville.esc7.net
Martinsville JSHS 200/7-12
PO Box 100 75958 936-564-3455
Charles Farrell, prin. Fax 569-0498

Mason, Mason, Pop. 2,168
Mason ISD 400/PK-12
PO Box 410 76856 325-347-1144
Matt Underwood, supt. Fax 347-5877
www.masonisd.net/
Mason HS 200/9-12
PO Box 410 76856 325-347-1122
Casey Callahan, prin. Fax 347-8247
Mason JHS 5-8
PO Box 410 76856 325-347-1122
Doug Bawcom, prin. Fax 347-5461

Matador, Motley, Pop. 679
Motley County ISD 200/PK-12
PO Box 310 79244 806-347-2676
Randy Brown, supt. Fax 347-2871
www.motleyco.org
Motley S 200/PK-12
PO Box 310 79244 806-347-2676
Marilyn Hicks, prin. Fax 347-2871

Mathis, San Patricio, Pop. 5,159
Mathis ISD 1,900/PK-12
PO Box 1179 78368 361-547-3378
Dr. Luis Baldemar Gonzalez, supt. Fax 547-4198
www.mathisisd.esc2.net
Mathis HS 600/9-12
PO Box 1179 78368 361-547-3322
Joyce St John, prin. Fax 547-4139
McCraw JHS 300/7-8
PO Box 1179 78368 361-547-2381
Valora Ann Bartosh, prin. Fax 547-4156

Maud, Bowie, Pop. 1,018
Maud ISD 500/PK-12
PO Box 1028 75567 903-585-2219
Robert Stinnett, supt. Fax 585-5451
www.maud.esc8.net
Maud S 500/PK-12
PO Box 1028 75567 903-585-2219
Roy Crow, prin. Fax 585-5451

May, Brown
May ISD 300/K-12
PO Box 30 76857 254-259-2091
Donald Rhodes, supt. Fax 259-3514
www.mayisd.com
May JSHS 100/7-12
PO Box 30 76857 254-259-2131
Steven Howard, prin. Fax 259-2706

Maypearl, Ellis, Pop. 828
Maypearl ISD 900/PK-12
PO Box 40 76064 972-435-2116
Arvell Lynn Dehart, supt. Fax 435-2340
maypearl.ednet10.net/
Maypearl HS 300/9-12
PO Box 40 76064 972-435-2581
Tim Wright, prin. Fax 435-1701
Maypearl JHS, PO Box 40 76064 100/7-8
Tonya Routson, prin. 972-435-2170

Meadow, Terry, Pop. 636
Meadow ISD 100/PK-12
400 Morehead St 79345 806-539-2246
Jim Kirkland, supt. Fax 539-2529
meadow.esc17.net
Meadow HS 100/7-12
400 Morehead St 79345 806-539-2222
Cody Carroll, prin. Fax 539-2529

Medina, Bandera
Medina ISD 300/K-12
PO Box 1470 78055 830-589-2855
Randy Moczygemba, supt. Fax 589-7150
www.medinaisd.org
Medina HS 200/7-12
PO Box 1470 78055 830-589-2851
Ross Hord, prin. Fax 589-7150

Megargel, Archer, Pop. 254
Megargel ISD 100/PK-12
PO Box 39 76370 940-562-2431
Don Berry, supt. Fax 562-2108

Megargel S 100/PK-12
PO Box 39 76370 940-563-2431
John Robertson, prin. Fax 563-2108

Melissa, Collin, Pop. 1,884
Melissa ISD 400/PK-12
1904 Cooper St 75454 972-837-2411
Loyd Jason Smith, supt. Fax 837-4233
www.melissaisd.org
Melissa HS 7-12
3150 Cardinal Dr 75454 972-837-4216
Tonya Fleming, prin. Fax 837-4381

Memphis, Hall, Pop. 2,502
Memphis ISD 500/PK-12
PO Box 460 79245 806-259-2443
Glen Howl, supt. Fax 259-2515
Memphis HS 100/9-12
PO Box 460 79245 806-259-2525
Toby Tyler, prin. Fax 259-3026
Memphis MS 100/6-8
PO Box 460 79245 806-259-3400
Patrick Shaffer, prin. Fax 259-2051

Menard, Menard, Pop. 1,652
Menard ISD 400/K-12
PO Box 729 76859 325-396-2404
David Hutton, supt. Fax 396-2143
Menard HS 100/9-12
PO Box 729 76859 325-396-2513
Amy Bannowsky, prin. Fax 396-2053
Menard JHS 100/6-8
PO Box 729 76859 325-396-2348
Martha Ellis, prin. Fax 396-2761

Mercedes, Hidalgo, Pop. 14,128
Mercedes ISD 4,900/PK-12
PO Box 419 78570 956-514-2000
Dr. Janice Wiley, supt. Fax 514-2032
www.mercedes.k12.tx.us
Mercedes HS 1,200/9-12
1200 Florida St 78570 956-514-2100
Liz De La Rosa, prin. Fax 514-2111
Mercedes JHS 700/7-8
PO Box 419 78570 956-514-2200
Rafael Leal, prin. Fax 514-2233

South Texas ISD 2,100/7-12
100 Med High Dr 78570 956-565-2454
Marla Guerra Ed.D., supt. Fax 565-9129
www.stisd.net
Science Academy of South Texas 600/9-12
900 Med High Dr 78570 956-565-2454
Edward Argueta, prin. Fax 565-9112
South Texas HS for Health Professions 700/9-12
700 Med High Dr 78570 956-565-2454
Lucy Fernandez, prin. Fax 565-4039
Other Schools – See Edinburg, San Benito

Meridian, Bosque, Pop. 1,503
Meridian ISD 600/PK-12
PO Box 349 76665 254-435-2081
Billy Jack Henderson, supt. Fax 435-2025
www.meridianisd.org
Meridian JSHS 300/7-12
PO Box 349 76665 254-435-2723
Chance Welch, prin. Fax 435-2199

Merit, Hunt
Bland ISD 600/PK-12
PO Box 216 75458 903-776-2239
Bryan E. Clark, supt. Fax 776-2240
www.blandisd.net
Bland HS 200/9-12
PO Box 216 75458 903-776-2161
Brian Garner, prin. Fax 776-2426
Bland MS 200/5-8
PO Box 216 75458 903-776-2373
Stephen Chick, prin. Fax 776-2853

Merkel, Taylor, Pop. 2,599
Merkel ISD 1,400/PK-12
PO Box 430 79536 325-928-5813
Bill Hood, supt. Fax 928-3910
www.merkel.esc14.net
Merkel HS 400/9-12
PO Box 430 79536 325-928-4667
Ronny Wright, prin. Fax 928-4684
Merkel MS 300/6-8
PO Box 430 79536 325-928-5511
Duane Hyde, prin. Fax 928-3138

Mertzon, Irion, Pop. 828
Irion County ISD 400/PK-12
PO Box 469 76941 325-835-6111
Stephen Peters, supt. Fax 835-2017
Irion County MSHS 200/7-12
PO Box 469 76941 325-835-2881
Billy Barnett, prin. Fax 835-2298

Mesquite, Dallas, Pop. 129,270
Mesquite ISD 34,100/PK-12
405 E Davis St 75149 972-288-6411
Dr. Linda Henrie, supt. Fax 882-7787
www.mesquiteisd.org
Agnew MS 1,000/7-8
729 Wilkinson Dr 75149 972-882-5750
Connie Boone, prin. Fax 882-5760
Berry MS 1,100/7-8
2675 Bear Dr 75181 972-882-5850
Sharon Rankin, prin. Fax 882-5888
Horn HS 1,900/9-12
3300 E Cartwright Rd 75181 972-882-5200
Bruce Perkins, prin. Fax 882-5291
Kimbrough MS 800/7-8
3900 N Galloway Ave 75150 972-882-5900
Dr. Alane Malone, prin. Fax 882-5942
McDonald MS 1,000/7-8
2930 N Town East Blvd 75150 972-882-5700
Cathy Swann, prin. Fax 882-5710
Mesquite HS 2,400/9-12
300 E Davis St 75149 972-882-7800
Linda Marshall, prin. Fax 882-7876
New MS 700/6-8
3700 S Belt Line Rd 75181 972-882-5600
Ed Burns, prin. Fax 882-5620
North Mesquite HS 2,500/9-12
18201 Lyndon B Johnson Fwy 75150 972-882-7900
Susie Court, prin. Fax 882-7908
Poteet HS 1,600/9-12
3300 Poteet Dr 75150 972-882-5300
Andrew Bauer, prin. Fax 882-5353

Vanston MS — 700/7-8
3230 Karla Dr 75150 — 972-882-5801
Sandra Bibb, prin. — Fax 882-5848
West Mesquite HS — 1,700/9-12
2500 Memorial Blvd 75149 — 972-882-7600
Martha Jo Talbot, prin. — Fax 882-7611
Wilkinson MS — 800/6-8
2100 Crest Park Dr 75149 — 972-882-5950
Ron Richardson, prin. — Fax 882-5988

Dallas Christian S — 800/K-12
1515 Republic Pkwy 75150 — 972-270-5495
Terry Harlow, pres. — Fax 270-7581
Eastfield College — Post-Sec.
3737 Motley Dr 75150 — 214-860-7002
Metroplex Beauty School — Post-Sec.
519 N Galloway Ave 75149 — 972-288-5485

Mexia, Limestone, Pop. 6,710
Mexia ISD — 2,200/PK-12
PO Box 2000 76667 — 254-562-4000
Charlene Simpson, supt. — Fax 562-4007
www.mexia.k12.tx.us/
Mexia HS — 600/9-12
PO Box 2000 76667 — 254-562-4010
John Turpin, prin. — Fax 562-2142
Mexia JHS — 500/6-8
PO Box 2000 76667 — 254-562-4020
Greg Goodrum, prin. — Fax 562-5053

Miami, Roberts, Pop. 545
Miami ISD — 200/K-12
PO Box 368 79059 — 806-868-3971
Allan Dinsmore, supt. — Fax 868-3171
www.miamiisd.net
Miami S — 200/K-12
PO Box 368 79059 — 806-868-3971
Donna Gill, prin. — Fax 868-3171

Midland, Midland, Pop. 96,573
Greenwood ISD — 1,500/PK-12
2700 FM 1379 79706 — 432-685-7800
Glenn Barber, supt. — Fax 685-7804
www.greenwood.esc18.net/
Brooks MS — 200/7-8
2700 FM 1379 79706 — 432-685-7837
Byron Moreland, prin. — Fax 685-7838
Greenwood HS — 500/9-12
2700 FM 1379 79706 — 432-685-7805
Scott Knippa, prin. — Fax 685-7814

Midland ISD — 18,900/PK-12
615 W Missouri Ave 79701 — 432-689-1000
Dr. Robert E. Nicks, supt. — Fax 689-1976
www.midlandisd.net/
Abell JHS — 800/7-8
3201 Heritage Blvd 79707 — 432-689-6200
Debbie Jordan, prin. — Fax 689-6217
Alamo JHS — 900/7-8
3800 Storey Ave 79703 — 432-689-1700
Jeff Horner, prin. — Fax 689-1712
Coleman HS — 200/9-12
1600 E Golf Course Rd 79701 — 432-689-5000
Greg McDaniel, prin. — Fax 689-5016
Goddard JHS — 900/7-8
2500 Haynes Dr 79705 — 432-689-1300
Rick Wood, prin. — Fax 689-1321
Lee Freshman HS — 800/9-9
1400 E Oak Ave 79705 — 432-689-1250
Larry Winget, prin. — Fax 689-1253
Lee SHS — 2,200/10-12
3500 Neely Ave 79707 — 432-689-1600
Patrick Jones, prin. — Fax 689-1647
Midland Freshman HS — 800/9-9
100 E Gist Ave 79701 — 432-689-1200
Elise Kail, prin. — Fax 689-1209
Midland SHS — 100/10-12
906 W Illinois Ave 79701 — 432-689-1100
Linda Jolly, prin. — Fax 689-1144
San Jacinto JHS — 800/7-8
1400 N N St 79701 — 432-689-1350
Stephanie Howard, prin. — Fax 689-1385

International Business School — Post-Sec.
3305 Andrews Hwy 79703 — 432-694-7584
Midland Christian S — 1,000/PK-12
2001 Culver Dr 79705 — 432-694-1661
Eddie Lee, supt. — Fax 694-5281
Midland College — Post-Sec.
3600 N Garfield St 79705 — 432-685-4500
Trinity S of Midland — 500/PK-12
3500 W Wadley Ave 79707 — 432-697-3201
Rhonda Durham, hdmstr. — Fax 697-7403

Midlothian, Ellis, Pop. 10,942
Midlothian ISD — 7,300/PK-12
100 Walter Stephenson Rd 76065 — 972-775-8296
Dr. J.D. Kennedy, supt. — Fax 775-1757
www.midlothian-isd.net
Midlothian HS North Campus — 900/9-10
911 S 9th St 76065 — 972-775-8237
James Smith, prin. — Fax 775-3178
Midlothian HS South Campus — 700/11-12
923 S 9th St 76065 — 972-775-8226
James Smith, prin. — Fax 775-3321
Seale MS — 1,300/6-8
700 George Hopper Rd 76065 — 972-775-6145
Robin Bullock, prin. — Fax 775-1502
Walnut Grove MS — 6-8
990 N Walnut Grove Rd 76065 — 972-775-5355
Brian Blackwell, prin. — Fax 775-8127

Milano, Milam, Pop. 413
Milano ISD — 400/PK-12
PO Box 145 76556 — 512-455-2533
Tommy Hancock, supt. — Fax 455-9311
Milano HS — 100/9-12
PO Box 145 76556 — 512-455-9333
Joe Mobley, prin. — Fax 455-9336
Milano JHS — 100/6-8
PO Box 145 76556 — 512-455-6701
Clay Tarpley, prin. — Fax 455-9311

Miles, Runnels, Pop. 819
Miles ISD — 400/PK-12
PO Box 308 76861 — 325-468-2861
Robert Gibson, supt. — Fax 468-2179
www.netxv.net/milesisd/index.htm
Miles JSHS — 200/7-12
PO Box 308 76861 — 325-468-2861
Merl Brandon, prin. — Fax 468-2179

Milford, Ellis, Pop. 705
Milford ISD — 200/K-12
PO Box 545 76670 — 972-493-2911
Alan Oakley, supt. — Fax 493-2429
www.milfordisd.org
Milford S — 200/K-12
PO Box 545 76670 — 972-493-2921
Marilee Byrne, prin. — Fax 493-4600

Millsap, Parker, Pop. 375
Millsap ISD — 800/PK-12
305 Pine St 76066 — 940-682-3101
Bob Lee, supt. — Fax 682-4476
www.millsapisd.net
Millsap HS — 300/9-12
600 Bulldog Dr 76066 — 940-682-3182
Matt Adams, prin. — Fax 682-4035
Millsap MS — 200/6-8
305 Pine St 76066 — 940-682-3161
Zoe Hurley, prin. — Fax 682-4476

Mineola, Wood, Pop. 4,840
Mineola ISD — 1,600/PK-12
1000 W Loop 564 75773 — 903-569-2448
Mary Lookadoo, supt. — Fax 569-5155
www.mineolaisd.net
Mineola HS — 400/9-12
1000 W Loop 564 75773 — 903-569-3000
Ricky Stephens, prin. — Fax 569-1930
Mineola MS — 400/6-8
1000 W Loop 564 75773 — 903-569-5338
Bob Simmons, prin. — Fax 569-5339

Mineral Wells, Palo Pinto, Pop. 16,970
Mineral Wells ISD — 3,700/PK-12
906 SW 5th Ave 76067 — 940-325-6404
Ray M. Crass, supt. — Fax 325-6378
www.mwisd.net/
Mineral Wells HS — 1,000/9-12
3801 Ram Blvd 76067 — 940-325-4408
John Corsi, prin. — Fax 325-7623
Mineral Wells JHS — 600/7-8
1301 SE 14th Ave 76067 — 940-325-0711
Jay Walsworth, prin. — Fax 328-0450

Mission, Hidalgo, Pop. 54,619
La Joya ISD
Supt. — See La Joya
Chavez ISD — 1,000/6-8
78 Showers Rd 78572 — 956-580-6180
Daniel Villareal, prin. — Fax 580-6169
Garcia MS — 800/6-8
900 Paula St, — 956-584-0800
Alfonso Solis, prin. — Fax 584-0817
Memorial MS — 800/6-8
2610 Moore Field Rd, — 956-580-6087
Rolando Rios, prin. — Fax 580-6084

Mission Consolidated ISD — 14,100/PK-12
1201 Bryce Dr 78572 — 956-323-5505
Oscar Rodriguez, supt. — Fax 323-5891
www.mcisd.net/
Alton Memorial JHS — 600/7-8
1201 Bryce Dr 78572 — 956-323-5000
Sylvia Garcia, prin. — Fax 323-5045
Mission HS — 1,700/9-12
1201 Bryce Dr 78572 — 956-323-5700
Ms. San Juanita Connelly, prin. — Fax 323-5890
Mission JHS — 700/7-8
1201 Bryce Dr 78572 — 956-323-3300
Rogelio Rivera, prin. — Fax 323-3338
Veterans Memorial HS — 1,600/9-12
1201 Bryce Dr 78572 — 956-323-3000
Joe Reyes, prin. — Fax 323-3280
White JHS — 700/7-8
1201 Bryce Dr 78572 — 956-323-3600
Pete Garcia, prin. — Fax 323-3631

Sharyland ISD — 7,300/PK-12
1106 N Shary Rd 78572 — 956-580-5200
Dr. Sandra Reed, supt. — Fax 580-5225
www.sharyland.k12.tx.us/index.html
Gray JHS — 1,100/7-8
1106 N Shary Rd 78572 — 956-580-5333
Cynthia Sandoval, prin. — Fax 580-5346
Sharyland HS — 1,900/9-12
1106 N Shary Rd 78572 — 956-580-5300
Hector Madrigal, prin. — Fax 580-5311
Other Schools – See Mc Allen

Missouri City, Fort Bend, Pop. 62,570
Fort Bend ISD
Supt. — See Sugar Land
Elkins HS — 2,100/9-12
7007 Knights Ct 77459 — 281-634-2600
Diana Sustaita, prin. — Fax 634-2674
Hightower HS — 2,000/9-12
3333 Hurricane Ln 77459 — 281-634-5240
Patricia Paquin, prin. — Fax 634-5333
Lake Olympia MS — 1,700/6-8
3100 Lake Olympia Pkwy 77459 — 281-634-3520
Dr. LaRoyce Sublett, prin. — Fax 634-3549
Marshall HS — 1,700/9-12
1220 Buffalo Run 77489 — 281-634-6630
Bob Banks, prin. — Fax 634-6650
Missouri City MS — 1,200/6-8
200 Louisiana St 77489 — 281-634-3440
Jerry Jones, prin. — Fax 634-3473
Quail Valley MS — 1,100/6-8
3019 FM 1092 Rd 77459 — 281-634-3600
Bruce Drennan, prin. — Fax 634-3632

Monahans, Ward, Pop. 6,397
Monahans-Wickett-Pyote ISD — 2,000/PK-12
606 S Betty Ave 79756 — 432-943-6711
Keith Richardson, supt. — Fax 943-2307
mwpisd.esc18.net
Monahans HS — 600/9-12
809 S Betty Ave 79756 — 432-943-2519
Kellye Riley, prin. — Fax 943-3327
Walker JHS — 300/7-8
800 S Faye Ave 79756 — 432-943-4622
John Horak, prin. — Fax 943-3723

Mont Belvieu, Chambers, Pop. 2,472
Barbers Hill ISD — 3,000/PK-12
PO Box 1108 77580 — 281-576-2221
G. Wayne Rotan, supt. — Fax 576-5879
www.barbershill.isd.esc4.net

Barbers Hill HS — 800/9-12
PO Box 1108 77580 — 281-576-3400
Susan Haynie, prin. — Fax 576-3356
Barbers Hill MS — 500/7-8
PO Box 1108 77580 — 281-576-3351
Cindy Price, prin. — Fax 576-3353

Monte Alto, Hidalgo
Monte Alto ISD — 500/PK-8
RR 1 Box 116 78538 — 956-262-1381
Andres Martinez, supt. — Fax 262-1535
www.monte-alto.k12.tx.us
Monte Alto MS — 200/6-8
RR 1 Box 116 78538 — 956-262-1374
Roel Zamora, prin. — Fax 262-1377

Montgomery, Montgomery, Pop. 531
Montgomery ISD — 4,600/PK-12
PO Box 1475 77356 — 936-582-1333
Dr. Bob Smith, supt. — Fax 582-6447
www.misd.org
Montgomery HS — 1,300/9-12
22825 Highway 105 W 77356 — 936-597-6401
Bobby Morris, prin. — Fax 597-6415
Montgomery JHS — 700/7-8
22627 Highway 105 W 77356 — 936-597-6466
Duane McFadden, prin. — Fax 597-6485

Moody, McLennan, Pop. 1,399
Moody ISD — 700/PK-12
107 Cora Lee Ln 76557 — 254-853-2172
Allen Law, supt. — Fax 853-2886
www.moodyisd.org
Moody HS — 200/9-12
107 Cora Lee Ln 76557 — 254-853-3622
Ed Husk, prin. — Fax 853-3822
Moody MS, 107 Cora Lee Ln 76557 — 200/5-8
Clayton Brantley, prin. — 254-853-2182

Moran, Shackelford, Pop. 230
Moran ISD — 100/PK-12
PO Box 98 76464 — 325-945-3101
Dottie Norwood, supt. — Fax 945-2741
Moran S — 100/PK-12
PO Box 98 76464 — 325-945-3101
Scott South, prin. — Fax 945-2741

Morgan, Bosque, Pop. 508
Morgan ISD — 100/PK-12
PO Box 300 76671 — 254-635-2311
Charles McGehee, supt. — Fax 635-2224
Morgan S — 100/PK-12
PO Box 300 76671 — 254-635-2311
Pamela Miller, prin. — Fax 635-2224

Morton, Cochran, Pop. 2,088
Morton ISD — 500/PK-12
500 Champion Dr 79346 — 806-266-5505
Fredda Schooler, supt. — Fax 266-5449
www.mortonisd.net/
Morton HS — 100/9-12
500 Champion Dr 79346 — 806-266-5524
Vicki Rice, prin. — Fax 266-5780
Morton JHS — 100/6-8
500 Champion Dr 79346 — 806-266-5505
H. Kirkland, prin. — Fax 266-5739

Moulton, Lavaca, Pop. 940
Moulton ISD — 300/K-12
PO Box C 77975 — 361-596-4609
Edward Pustka, supt. — Fax 596-7578
www.moultonisd.net
Moulton JSHS — 200/7-12
PO Box C 77975 — 361-596-4691
Tom Weaaks, prin. — Fax 596-7578

Mount Enterprise, Rusk, Pop. 522
Mount Enterprise ISD — 400/PK-12
301 W 3rd St N 75681 — 903-822-3721
Paul Moore, supt. — Fax 822-3633
www.meisd.esc7.net
Mount Enterprise JSHS — 200/7-12
301 W 3rd St N 75681 — 903-822-3721
Bobby Briscoe, prin. — Fax 822-3633

Mount Pleasant, Titus, Pop. 14,266
Chapel Hill ISD — 800/PK-12
PO Box 1257 75456 — 903-572-8096
Marc Levesque, supt. — Fax 572-1086
www.chapelhillisd.org/
Chapel Hill HS — 300/9-12
PO Box 1257 75456 — 903-572-8096
Sandi Luttrell, prin. — Fax 572-9747
Chapel Hill JHS — 100/7-8
PO Box 1257 75456 — 903-572-3925
Sandi Luttrell, prin. — Fax 572-9747

Mount Pleasant ISD — 6,100/PK-12
PO Box 1117 75456 — 903-575-2000
Terry Myers, supt. — Fax 575-2014
www.mpisd.net
Mount Pleasant HS — 1,300/9-12
PO Box 1117 75456 — 903-575-2020
David Davis, prin. — Fax 575-2036
Mount Pleasant JHS — 700/7-8
PO Box 1117 75456 — 903-575-2110
Fax 575-2117

Northeast Texas Community College — Post-Sec.
PO Box 1307 75456 — 903-572-1911

Mount Vernon, Franklin, Pop. 2,366
Mt. Vernon ISD — 1,500/PK-12
PO Box 98 75457 — 903-537-2546
Richard Flanagan, supt. — Fax 537-4784
mvisd.esc8.net/
Mount Vernon HS — 500/9-12
PO Box 1139 75457 — 903-537-3700
David Pierce, prin. — Fax 537-2536
Mount Vernon JHS — 300/7-8
PO Box 1139 75457 — 903-537-2267
Danny Willis, prin. — Fax 537-3601

Muenster, Cooke, Pop. 1,645
Muenster ISD — 500/PK-12
PO Box 608 76252 — 940-759-2281
David Manley, supt. — Fax 759-5200
www.esc11.net/schools/Muenster/
Muenster HS — 300/7-12
PO Box 608 76252 — 940-759-4614
Philip Newton, prin. — Fax 759-2284

Sacred Heart S 300/PK-12
PO Box 588 76252 940-759-2511
Chad Riley, prin. Fax 759-4422

Muleshoe, Bailey, Pop. 4,556
Muleshoe ISD 1,500/PK-12
514 W Avenue G 79347 806-272-7400
Gene Sheets, supt. Fax 272-4120
www.muleshoeisd.net
Muleshoe HS, 514 W Avenue G 79347 400/9-12
David Jenkins, prin. 806-272-7303
Watson JHS, 514 W Avenue G 79347 300/6-8
David Dominguez, prin. 806-272-7349

Mullin, Mills, Pop. 173
Mullin ISD 100/PK-12
PO Box 128 76864 325-985-3374
C.L. Hammond, supt. Fax 985-3915
www.centex-edu.net/mullin/
Mullin HS 100/7-12
PO Box 128 76864 325-985-3374
Steven Ray Coston, prin. Fax 985-3372

Mumford, Robertson
Mumford ISD 400/PK-12
PO Box 268 77867 979-279-3678
Pete Bienski, supt. Fax 279-5044
www.mumford.k12.tx.us
Mumford JSHS 100/7-12
PO Box 268 77867 979-279-3678
Pete Bienski, prin. Fax 279-5044

Munday, Knox, Pop. 1,410
Munday Consolidated ISD 500/PK-12
PO Box 300 76371 940-422-4241
Robert Dillard, supt. Fax 422-5331
www.esc9.net/munday
Munday HS 100/9-12
PO Box 300 76371 940-422-4321
Kevin White, prin. Fax 422-5331
Other Schools – See Goree

Murphy, Collin, Pop. 7,991
Plano ISD
Supt. — See Plano
Murphy MS 800/6-8
620 N Murphy Rd 75094 469-752-7000
Bonnie Manley, prin. Fax 752-7001

Nacogdoches, Nacogdoches, Pop. 30,441
Central Heights ISD 800/PK-12
10317 US Highway 259 75965 936-564-2681
Earl W. Adams, supt. Fax 569-6889
www.centralhts.org
Central Heights JSHS 300/7-12
10317 US Highway 259 75965 936-552-3408
Andy Binford, prin. Fax 569-6889

Nacogdoches ISD 9,200/PK-12
PO Box 631521 75963 936-569-5000
Dr. Anthony Riehl, supt. Fax 569-5797
www.nacogdoches.k12.tx.us
McMichael MS 6-8
PO Box 631521 75963 936-552-0519
Dennis Williams, prin. Fax 552-0523
Moses MS 1,400/6-8
PO Box 631521 75963 936-569-5001
Steve Green, prin. Fax 569-5031
Nacogdoches HS 1,900/9-12
PO Box 631521 75963 936-564-2466
Liz Ballenger, prin. Fax 560-8162

Northwood Baptist Academy 100/7-12
3224 NE Stallings Dr 75965 936-564-0243
Star College of Cosmetology Post-Sec.
705 N University Dr 75961 936-462-7232
Stephen F. Austin State University Post-Sec.
PO Box 6078 75962 936-468-2011

Natalia, Medina, Pop. 1,764
Natalia ISD 1,200/PK-12
PO Box 548 78059 830-663-4416
Joey Moczygemba, supt. Fax 663-4186
Natalia HS 300/9-12
PO Box 548 78059 830-663-4417
Oswaldo Garcia, prin. Fax 663-6410
Natalia JHS 300/6-8
PO Box 548 78059 830-663-4027
Henry Booth, prin. Fax 663-2347

Navasota, Grimes, Pop. 7,235
Navasota ISD 3,000/PK-12
PO Box 511 77868 936-825-4200
David Faltys, supt. Fax 825-4297
www.navasotaisd.org
Navasota HS 800/9-12
PO Box 511 77868 936-825-4250
Fred Brent, prin. Fax 825-8539
Navasota JHS 700/6-8
PO Box 511 77868 936-825-4225
Cindy DeMott, prin. Fax 825-4260

Nazareth, Castro, Pop. 347
Nazareth ISD 200/K-12
PO Box 189 79063 806-945-2231
Marshall Harrison, supt. Fax 945-2431
Nazareth S 200/K-12
PO Box 189 79063 806-945-2231
Deborah Clinton, prin. Fax 945-2431

Neches, Anderson
Neches ISD 300/K-12
PO Box 310 75779 903-584-3311
Gary Holcomb, supt. Fax 584-3686
www.neches.esc7.net
Neches JSHS 100/7-12
PO Box 310 75779 903-584-3443
Joe Ellis, prin. Fax 584-3686

Nederland, Jefferson, Pop. 16,928
Nederland ISD 5,000/PK-12
220 N 17th St 77627 409-724-2391
Beverly Gail Krohn, supt. Fax 724-4280
www.nederland.k12.tx.us
Central MS 800/5-8
220 N 17th St 77627 409-727-5765
Charles Jehlen, prin. Fax 724-4275
Nederland HS 1,500/9-12
220 N 17th St 77627 409-727-2741
Randy Lupton, prin. Fax 726-2679

Wilson MS 800/5-8
220 N 17th St 77627 409-727-6224
Stuart Kieschnick, prin. Fax 726-2699

Faris Computer School Post-Sec.
1119 Kent Ave 77627 409-722-4072

Needville, Fort Bend, Pop. 2,987
Needville ISD 2,500/PK-12
PO Box 412 77461 979-793-4308
Gary Gazaway, supt. Fax 793-3823
www.needvilleisd.com
Needville HS 700/9-12
PO Box 412 77461 979-793-4158
Ron Bragg, prin. Fax 793-5590
Needville JHS 400/7-8
PO Box 412 77461 979-793-4250
Otis Harr, prin. Fax 793-4575

Nevada, Collin, Pop. 598
Community ISD 1,400/PK-12
PO Box 400 75173 972-853-2474
Bud Nauyokas, supt. Fax 843-2392
www.community.isd.tenet.edu
Community HS 400/9-12
PO Box 400 75173 972-853-2192
Terry Sowers, prin. Fax 853-2834
Community MS 400/6-8
PO Box 400 75173 972-853-2141
John Reves, prin. Fax 843-2392

New Boston, Bowie, Pop. 4,633
New Boston ISD 1,400/PK-12
600 N McCoy Blvd 75570 903-628-2521
Jerry May, supt. Fax 628-2235
nbisd.esc8.net/
New Boston HS 500/9-12
1 W Lion Dr 75570 903-628-6551
Roger Busse, prin. Fax 628-3695
New Boston MS 400/5-8
1215 N Highway 8 75570 903-628-6588
Glenn Barfield, prin. Fax 628-5132

New Braunfels, Comal, Pop. 42,693
Comal ISD 11,500/PK-12
1421 N Business IH 35 78130 830-221-2000
Dr. Marc Walker, supt. Fax 221-2001
www.comalisd.org
Canyon HS 1,400/9-12
1510 N IH 35 78130 830-221-2400
Robert Wiegand, prin. Fax 221-2401
Canyon MS 900/6-8
2014 FM 1101 78130 830-221-2300
Patti Vlieger, prin. Fax 221-2301
Other Schools – See Spring Branch

New Braunfels ISD 6,200/PK-12
PO Box 311688 78131 830-643-5700
Ron Reaves, supt. Fax 643-5701
www.newbraunfels.txed.net/
New Braunfels HS 1,800/9-12
2551 Loop 337 78130 830-627-6000
Robert Rodriguez, prin. Fax 627-6001
New Braunfels MS 1,000/7-8
656 S Guenther Ave 78130 830-627-6270
Dr. Demetria Cummins, prin. Fax 627-6271

New Braunfels Christian Academy 500/PK-12
995 Mission Hills Dr 78130 830-629-6222
Richard Ramirez, hdmstr. Fax 629-8049

New Caney, Montgomery, Pop. 3,000
New Caney ISD 6,700/PK-12
21580 Loop 494 77357 281-577-8600
Richard Cowan, supt. Fax 354-2639
www.newcaneyisd.org
Keefer Crossing MS 700/6-8
20350 FM 1485 Rd 77357 281-577-8840
Steve Freeman, prin. Fax 399-9859
New Caney HS 1,200/10-12
21650 Loop 494 77357 281-577-2000
John Yonker, prin. Fax 354-0186
Other Schools – See Porter

Newcastle, Young, Pop. 572
Newcastle ISD 200/PK-12
PO Box 129 76372 940-846-3551
Gordon Grubbs, supt. Fax 846-3452
esc9.net/newcastle
Newcastle HS 100/7-12
PO Box 129 76372 940-846-3531
Cathy Creel, prin. Fax 846-3452

New Deal, Lubbock, Pop. 732
New Deal ISD 700/PK-12
PO Box 280 79350 806-746-5833
Jimmy Noland, supt. Fax 746-5707
www.newdealisd.net
New Deal HS 200/9-12
PO Box 250 79350 806-746-5933
Steven McCray, prin. Fax 746-5544
New Deal MS 200/5-8
PO Box 308 79350 806-746-6633
Jerry Adams, prin. Fax 746-5244

New Home, Lynn, Pop. 312
New Home ISD 200/K-12
PO Box 248 79383 806-924-7542
Leland Zant, supt. Fax 924-7520
New Home S 200/K-12
PO Box 248 79383 806-924-7543
Shane Fiedler, prin. Fax 924-7520

New London, Rusk, Pop. 992
West Rusk ISD 800/PK-12
PO Box 168 75682 903-895-4503
Will S. Jones Ed.D., supt. Fax 895-2267
www.westrusk.esc7.net
West Rusk HS 200/9-12
PO Box 168 75682 903-895-4428
Susan Brown, prin. Fax 895-2267
Other Schools – See Joinerville

New Summerfield, Cherokee, Pop. 1,040
New Summerfield ISD 400/PK-12
PO Box 6 75780 903-726-3300
Tony Murray, supt. Fax 726-3405
www.nsisd.sprnet.org/
New Summerfield S 400/PK-12
PO Box 6 75780 903-726-3306
Debra Sikes, prin. Fax 726-3405

Newton, Newton, Pop. 2,437
Newton ISD 1,400/PK-12
414 Main St 75966 409-379-8137
Gene Isabell, supt. Fax 379-2189
newtonisd.com
Newton HS 400/9-12
414 Main St 75966 409-379-4731
Johnny Metz, prin. Fax 379-3321
Newton MS 300/6-8
414 Main St 75966 409-379-8324
Howell Wright, prin. Fax 379-5082

New Waverly, Walker, Pop. 942
New Waverly ISD 800/PK-12
355 Front St 77358 936-344-6751
Dr. Clay Webb, supt. Fax 344-2438
www.new-waverly.k12.tx.us
New Waverly HS 200/9-12
355 Front St 77358 936-344-6451
Chris McKinley, prin. Fax 344-6113
New Waverly JHS 200/6-8
355 Front St 77358 936-344-2246
Truman Goodwin, prin. Fax 344-8313

Gulf Coast Trades Center Post-Sec.
PO Box 515 77358 936-344-6677

Nixon, Gonzales, Pop. 2,215
Nixon-Smiley Consolidated ISD 1,000/PK-12
PO Box 400 78140 830-582-1536
Cathy Booth Ph.D., supt. Fax 582-1920
www.esc13.net/nixon
Nixon-Smiley HS 300/9-12
PO Box 400 78140 830-582-1536
Hensley Cone, prin. Fax 582-2168
Other Schools – See Smiley

Nocona, Montague, Pop. 3,228
Nocona ISD 900/PK-12
220 Clay St 76255 940-825-3267
Harold Reynolds, supt. Fax 825-4945
www.esc9.net/nocona
Nocona HS 300/9-12
220 Clay St 76255 940-825-3264
Robert Ulibarri, prin. Fax 825-7270
Nocona MS 200/6-8
220 Clay St 76255 940-825-3121
Norman Waters, prin. Fax 826-6151

Prairie Valley ISD 100/PK-12
RR 3 Box 550 76255 940-825-4425
W. Tucker, supt. Fax 825-4650
www.esc9.net/pvisd/
Prairie Valley S 100/6-12
RR 3 Box 550 76255 940-825-4425
Leslie Christian, prin. Fax 825-4650

Nordheim, DeWitt, Pop. 323
Nordheim ISD 100/K-12
500 Broadway 78141 361-938-5211
Sonya Little, supt. Fax 938-5266
www.nordheimisd.org
Nordheim S 100/K-12
500 Broadway 78141 361-938-5211
Sonya Little, prin. Fax 938-5266

Normangee, Leon, Pop. 750
Normangee ISD 600/PK-12
PO Box 219 77871 936-396-3111
Gary Adams, supt. Fax 396-3112
www.normangeeisd.org
Normangee JSHS 300/7-12
PO Box 219 77871 936-396-6111
Kendall Todd, prin. Fax 396-6879

North Richland Hills, Tarrant, Pop. 60,238
Birdville ISD
Supt. — See Haltom City
Birdville HS 1,900/9-12
9100 Mid Cities Blvd 76180 817-547-8000
Lane Ledbetter, prin. Fax 547-8009
North Richland MS 800/6-8
4800 Rufe Snow Dr 76180 817-547-4200
Ernie Valamides, prin. Fax 581-5372
North Ridge MS 900/6-8
7332 Douglas Ln 76180 817-547-5200
Carla Saddler-Rix, prin. Fax 581-5460
Richland HS 2,000/9-12
5201 Holiday Ln 76180 817-547-7000
Randy Cobb, prin. Fax 581-5454
Smithfield MS 900/6-8
8400 Main St 76180 817-547-5000
Jeff Russell, prin. Fax 581-5480

ATI Career Training Center Post-Sec.
6351 Grapevine Hwy Ste 100 76180 817-284-1141

North Zulch, Madison
North Zulch ISD 300/PK-12
PO Box 158 77872 936-399-4151
Roy E. Gilbert, supt. Fax 399-2025
www.northzulchisd.net
North Zulch JSHS 200/7-12
PO Box 158 77872 936-399-2821
Tim Waldrip, prin. Fax 399-2038

Novice, Coleman, Pop. 136
Novice ISD 100/PK-12
PO Box 205 79538 325-625-4069
Charles Bryant, supt. Fax 625-3915
Novice S 100/PK-12
PO Box 205 79538 325-625-4500
Charles Bryant, prin. Fax 625-3915

Oakwood, Leon, Pop. 489
Oakwood ISD 200/PK-12
631 N Holly St 75855 903-545-2666
Kevin Woolley, supt. Fax 545-2310
Oakwood JSHS 100/6-12
631 N Holly St 75855 903-545-2140
Kenneth Barnett, prin. Fax 545-2310

O Brien, Haskell, Pop. 148
Knox City-O'Brien ISD
Supt. — See Knox City
O'Brien MS 100/5-8
711 9th St 79539 940-658-3731
Russ Chisum, prin. Fax 658-3379

Odem, San Patricio, Pop. 2,457
Odem-Edroy ISD 1,200/PK-12
PO Box 727 78370 361-368-2561
Manuel Lunoff, supt. Fax 368-2879
www.oeisd.org/
Odem HS 300/9-12
PO Box 1050 78370 361-368-3401
Reymundo Gonzalez, prin. Fax 368-3781
Odem JHS 300/6-8
PO Box 1407 78370 361-368-8121
Debra Litton, prin. Fax 368-2033

Odessa, Ector, Pop. 91,113
Ector County ISD 25,000/PK-12
PO Box 3912 79760 432-334-7100
Wendell Sollis, supt. Fax 335-8984
www.ector-county.k12.tx.us/
Bonham JHS 800/7-9
PO Box 3912 79760 432-368-2811
Steve Brown, prin. Fax 362-8514
Bowie JHS 1,000/7-9
PO Box 3912 79760 432-337-8361
Karla Wright, prin. Fax 334-0879
Career Center Vo/Tech
PO Box 3912 79760 432-337-3377
Curtis Britt, prin. Fax 334-3712
Crockett JHS 900/7-9
PO Box 3912 79760 432-332-1451
Ismael Lujan, prin. Fax 332-1567
Ector JHS 1,400/7-9
PO Box 3912 79760 432-334-5269
Roy Garcia, prin. Fax 337-3472
Hood JHS 700/7-10
PO Box 3912 79760 432-362-2371
Tommie Robinson, prin. Fax 368-2221
Nimitz JHS 1,000/7-9
PO Box 3912 79760 432-366-2891
Stacy Jones, prin. Fax 368-2239
Odessa HS 2,200/9-12
PO Box 3912 79760 432-337-6655
Ron Leach, prin. Fax 332-6014
Permian HS 2,000/9-12
PO Box 3912 79760 432-366-3652
Fax 368-2209

American Commercial College Post-Sec.
5119 Twin Towers Blvd 79762 432-362-6768
Odessa College Post-Sec.
201 W University Blvd 79764 432-335-6400
University of Texas of the Permian Basin Post-Sec.
4901 E University Blvd 79762 432-552-2020

O Donnell, Lynn, Pop. 1,070
O'Donnell ISD 400/PK-12
PO Box 487, 806-428-3241
Fax 428-3395
odonnell.esc17.net
O'Donnell HS 100/9-12
PO Box 487, 806-428-3247
Mike Read, prin. Fax 428-3759
O'Donnell JHS 100/6-8
PO Box 487, 806-428-3248
Mike Read, prin. Fax 428-3347

Oglesby, Coryell, Pop. 459
Oglesby ISD 200/K-12
PO Box 158 76561 254-456-2271
Edna Biggerstaff, supt. Fax 456-2522
www.oglesbyisd.net
Oglesby S 200/K-12
PO Box 158 76561 254-456-2241
Joshua Carty, prin. Fax 456-2522

Olney, Young, Pop. 3,340
Olney ISD 700/PK-12
809 W Hamilton St 76374 940-564-3519
Tom Bailey, supt. Fax 564-5205
www.esc9.net/olney
Olney HS 200/9-12
704 W Grove St 76374 940-564-5637
Elaine Reno, prin. Fax 564-5733
Olney JHS 200/6-8
300 S Avenue H 76374 940-564-3517
Terry Dunlap, prin. Fax 564-8824

Olton, Lamb, Pop. 2,305
Olton ISD 800/PK-12
PO Box 388 79064 806-285-2641
Mike Jackson, supt. Fax 285-2724
www.oltonisd-esc17.net/
Olton HS 200/9-12
PO Box 667 79064 806-285-2691
Clay Richerson, prin. Fax 285-2724
Olton JHS 200/6-8
PO Box 509 79064 806-285-2681
Bub McIver, prin. Fax 285-3348

Omaha, Morris, Pop. 981
Pewitt Consolidated ISD 900/PK-12
PO Box 1106 75571 903-884-2804
David Fitts, supt. Fax 884-2866
pewitt.esc8.net/
Pewitt HS 300/9-12
PO Box 1106 75571 903-884-2293
Bill Harp, prin. Fax 884-3111
Pewitt JHS 200/6-8
PO Box 1106 75571 903-884-2505
Ronnie Herron, prin. Fax 884-3111

Onalaska, Polk, Pop. 1,305
Onalaska ISD 800/PK-12
PO Box 2289 77360 936-646-1000
Kerry Cowart, supt. Fax 646-2605
www.onalaskaisd.net
Onalaska JSHS 300/7-12
PO Box 2289 77360 936-646-1020
Charles Hebert, prin. Fax 646-1022

Orange, Orange, Pop. 18,073
Little Cypress-Mauriceville Cons. ISD 3,700/PK-12
6586 FM 1130 77632 409-883-2232
Pauline Hargrove, supt. Fax 883-3509
www.lcmcisd.org/
Little Cypress JHS 500/6-8
6765 FM 1130 77632 409-883-2317
Keith Lindsey, prin. Fax 883-5044
Little Cypress-Mauriceville HS 1,200/9-12
7327 Highway 87 N 77632 409-886-5821
James Armstrong, prin. Fax 886-5762
Mauriceville MS 400/6-8
19952 FM 1130 77632 409-745-1958
Stacey Brister, prin. Fax 745-3383

West Orange-Cove Consolidated ISD 2,300/PK-12
PO Box 1107 77631 409-882-5500
Dr. O. Taylor Collins, supt. Fax 882-5467
www.woccisd.net
Career Center Vo/Tech
PO Box 1107 77631 409-882-5412
Mike Mason, dir. Fax 882-5573
West Orange-Stark HS 900/9-12
PO Box 1107 77631 409-882-5570
Mike Mason, prin. Fax 882-5573
West Orange-Stark MS 700/6-8
PO Box 1107 77631 409-882-5520
Anitrea Goodwin, prin. Fax 882-5545

Baptist Hospital Post-Sec.
608 Strickland Dr 77630 409-883-9361
Community Christian S 300/PK-12
3400 Martin Luther King Jr 77632 409-883-4531
Catherine Stewart, prin. Fax 883-8855
Lamar State College-Orange Post-Sec.
410 W Front St 77630 409-883-7750

Orangefield, Orange
Orangefield ISD 1,600/PK-12
PO Box 228 77639 409-735-5337
Mike Gentry, supt. Fax 735-2080
www.orangefieldisd.com/
Orangefield HS 500/9-12
PO Box 228 77639 409-735-3851
Stephen Patterson, prin. Fax 697-2301
Orangefield JHS 500/5-8
PO Box 228 77639 409-735-6737
Jacqueline Kyle, prin. Fax 792-9605

Orange Grove, Jim Wells, Pop. 1,356
Orange Grove ISD 1,600/PK-12
PO Box 534 78372 361-384-2495
Earl H. Luce, supt. Fax 384-2148
www.ogisd.esc2.net/
Orange Grove HS 500/9-12
PO Box 534 78372 361-384-2330
Bryan Henderson, prin. Fax 384-0206
Orange Grove JHS 400/6-8
PO Box 534 78372 361-384-2323
Tommy Moses, prin. Fax 384-9579

Ore City, Upshur, Pop. 1,154
Ore City ISD 800/PK-12
PO Box 100 75683 903-968-3300
Tom Barnett, supt. Fax 968-3797
www.ocisd.net
Ore City HS 200/9-12
PO Box 100 75683 903-968-3300
Scot Wright, prin. Fax 968-8726
Ore City JHS 200/6-8
PO Box 100 75683 903-968-3300
Neil Hinson, prin. Fax 968-4913

Overton, Rusk, Pop. 2,301
Leveretts Chapel ISD
Supt. — See Laird Hill
Leveretts Chapel HS 100/9-12
8956 State Highway 42/135 N 75684 903-834-3181
Luther Cockerham, prin. Fax 834-6602

Overton ISD 500/PK-12
PO Box 130 75684 903-834-6145
Dr. Mark Stretcher, supt. Fax 834-6755
www.overton.esc7.net
Overton JSHS 200/7-12
PO Box 130 75684 903-834-6143
Jim Fenton, prin. Fax 834-6146

Ovilla, Dallas, Pop. 3,670

Ovilla Christian S 400/PK-12
3251 Ovilla Rd 75154 972-617-1177
Michael Partain, admin. Fax 617-2275

Ozona, Crockett, Pop. 3,181
Crockett County Consolidated SD 800/PK-12
PO Box 400 76943 325-392-5501
John King, supt. Fax 392-5177
www.ozonaschools.net
Ozona HS 300/9-12
PO Box 400 76943 325-392-5501
Dan Webb, prin. Fax 392-5177
Ozona MS 200/6-8
PO Box 400 76943 325-392-5501
J. Douglas Guynes, prin. Fax 392-5177

Paducah, Cottle, Pop. 1,372
Paducah ISD 200/K-12
PO Box P 79248 806-492-3524
John Brinson, supt. Fax 492-2432
Paducah HS 100/9-12
810 Goodwin 79248 806-492-2009
Steve Paschall, prin. Fax 492-2193

Paint Rock, Concho, Pop. 300
Paint Rock ISD 200/PK-12
PO Box 277 76866 325-732-4314
Brett Starkweather, supt. Fax 732-4384
paintrock.netxv.net/
Paint Rock S 200/PK-12
PO Box 277 76866 325-732-4314
Erbey Valdez, prin. Fax 732-4384

Palacios, Matagorda, Pop. 5,270
Palacios ISD 1,700/PK-12
1209 12th St 77465 361-972-5491
Paul Smith, supt. Fax 972-3567
www.palacios.k12.tx.us
Palacios HS 500/9-12
100 Shark Dr 77465 361-972-2571
Valerie Segovia, prin. Fax 972-6287
Palacios JHS 200/7-8
200 Shark Dr 77465 361-972-2417
Alton Perry, prin. Fax 972-6372

Palestine, Anderson, Pop. 17,808
Palestine ISD 3,000/PK-12
1600 S Loop 256 75801 903-731-8000
Jerry K. Mayo, supt. Fax 729-5588
www.palestine.esc7.net/
Palestine HS 900/9-12
1600 S Loop 256 75801 903-731-8005
Richard Scoggin, prin. Fax 731-9326
Palestine MS 800/6-8
233 Ben Milam Dr 75801 903-731-8008
Peggy Herrington, prin. Fax 731-8010

Westwood ISD 1,800/PK-12
PO Box 260 75802 903-729-1776
Marvin Thompson, supt. Fax 729-3696
www.westwoodisd.net
Westwood HS 500/9-12
PO Box 260 75802 903-729-1773
Judith Thomason, prin. Fax 729-8695
Westwood JHS 300/7-8
PO Box 260 75802 903-723-0423
Ronnie Shepperd, prin. Fax 723-6765

Anderson County Beauty College Post-Sec.
217 W Oak St 75801 903-729-0801

Palmer, Ellis, Pop. 1,950
Palmer ISD 1,100/PK-12
PO Box 790 75152 972-449-3389
Dian Cooper, supt. Fax 845-2112
www.palmer-isd.org
Palmer HS 300/9-12
PO Box 790 75152 972-449-3487
Phil Seay, prin. Fax 845-3517
Palmer MS 200/6-8
PO Box 790 75152 972-449-3319
Renee Warner, prin. Fax 845-3380

Palmview, Hidalgo, Pop. 4,344
La Joya ISD
Supt. — See La Joya
Richards MS 800/6-8
7005 Ann Richards Rd 78572 956-519-5710
Melba Lozano, prin. Fax 519-5726

Pampa, Gray, Pop. 16,897
Pampa ISD 3,300/PK-12
321 W Albert St 79065 806-669-4700
Barry Haenisch, supt. Fax 665-0506
www.pampaisd.net
Pampa HS 900/9-12
111 E Harvester Ave 79065 806-669-4800
Danny Seabourn, prin. Fax 669-4739
Pampa JHS 800/6-8
2401 Charles St 79065 806-669-4901
Randy Stephenson, prin. Fax 669-4742

Panhandle, Carson, Pop. 2,574
Panhandle ISD 700/PK-12
PO Box 1030 79068 806-537-3568
Gary Laramore, supt. Fax 537-5553
www.panhandleisd.net
Panhandle HS 200/9-12
PO Box 1030 79068 806-537-3897
Greg Slover, prin. Fax 537-3476
Panhandle JHS 200/6-8
PO Box 1030 79068 806-537-3541
John Strother, prin. Fax 537-5725

Pantego, Tarrant, Pop. 2,348

Ogle School of Hair Design Post-Sec.
2200 W Park Row Dr Ste 106 76013 817-277-6341

Paradise, Wise, Pop. 502
Paradise ISD 1,000/PK-12
338 School House Rd 76073 940-969-2501
Robert Criswell, supt. Fax 969-5008
www.pisd.net
Paradise HS 300/9-12
338 School House Rd 76073 940-969-2501
Patti Seckman, prin. Fax 969-5009
Paradise MS 200/7-8
338 School House Rd 76073 940-969-2501
Scott McPherson, prin. Fax 969-5025

Paris, Lamar, Pop. 26,523
Chisum ISD 900/PK-12
3250 S Church St 75462 903-737-2830
Diane Stegall, supt. Fax 737-2831
chisum.esc8.net/
Chisum HS 300/9-12
3250 S Church St 75462 903-737-2800
Tommy Chalaire, prin. Fax 737-2801
Chisum MS 200/6-8
3250 S Church St 75462 903-737-2806
Cliff Chadwick, prin. Fax 737-2805

North Lamar ISD 3,200/PK-12
3201 Lewis Ln 75460 903-737-2000
James Dawson, supt. Fax 737-2008
www.northlamar.net
North Lamar HS 900/9-12
3201 Lewis Ln 75460 903-737-2011
Glen Martin, prin. Fax 737-2018
Stone MS 800/6-8
3201 Lewis Ln 75460 903-737-2041
Steve Sparks, prin. Fax 737-2089

Paris ISD 3,800/PK-12
1920 Clarksville St 75460 903-737-7473
Paul Trull, supt. Fax 737-7484
www.parisisd.net
Paris HS 900/9-12
2400 Jefferson Rd 75460 903-737-7400
Gary Preston, prin. Fax 737-7515
Travis MS 300/8-8
3270 Graham St 75460 903-737-7434
Billie Viehe, prin. Fax 737-7534

Paris Junior College Post-Sec.
2400 Clarksville St 75460 903-785-7661
Trinity Christian Academy 100/PK-12
2060 FM 79 75460 903-789-9557
Alice Newbourn, admin. Fax 785-7372

Pasadena, Harris, Pop. 144,413
Deer Park ISD
Supt. — See Deer Park
Deepwater JHS 600/6-8
501 Glenmore Dr 77503 832-668-7600
Stephen Harrell, prin. Fax 475-6138
Fairmont JHS 700/6-8
4911 Holly Bay Ct 77505 832-668-7800
Gay Dalton, prin. Fax 998-4456

Pasadena ISD 47,000/PK-12
  1515 Cherrybrook Ln 77502 713-740-0000
  Kirk Lewis, supt. Fax 475-7912
  www.pasadenaisd.org
  Bondy IS, 5101 Keith Ave 77505 1,000/6-8
  Dan Cannolly, prin. 713-740-0430
  Card Career & Technical Center Vo/Tech
  4320 Crenshaw Rd 77504 713-740-0802
  Mickey Ohlendorf, dir. Fax 740-4081
  Jackson IS 1,200/6-8
  1020 Thomas Ave 77506 713-740-0440
  Mindy Evans, prin. Fax 740-4109
  Miller IS 1,000/6-8
  1002 Fairmont Pkwy 77504 713-740-0450
  Joe Saavedra, prin. Fax 740-4106
  Park View IS 1,000/6-8
  3003 Dabney Dr 77502 713-740-0460
  Rob Hasson, prin. Fax 740-4115
  Pasadena HS 2,800/9-12
  206 Shaver St 77506 713-740-0310
  Morris Fuselier, prin. Fax 740-4085
  Pasadena Memorial HS 1,400/9-12
  4410 Crenshaw Rd 77504 281-991-2440
  Billye Smith, prin. Fax 991-2450
  Queens IS 1,000/6-8
  1112 Queens Rd 77502 713-740-0470
  Troy Jones, prin. Fax 740-4101
  Rayburn HS 2,300/9-12
  2121 Cherrybrook Ln 77502 713-477-3601
  Troy McCarley, prin. Fax 920-8267
  San Jacinto IS 900/6-8
  3102 San Augustine Ave 77503 713-740-0400
  David Post, prin.
  Southmore IS 900/6-8
  1200 Houston Ave 77502 713-740-0550
  Lana Stahl, prin.
  Tegeler Career Center Vo/Tech
  4949 Burke Rd 77504 713-740-0410
  Jean Cain, prin. Fax 740-4077
  Community Evening S Adult
  1838A E Sam Houston Pkwy S 77503 713-740-0298
  Tom Swan, admin. Fax 740-4048
  Other Schools – See Houston, South Houston

  Faith Christian Academy 200/K-12
  3519 Burke Rd 77504 713-943-9978
  Dr. Joyce Ellis, prin. Fax 944-4416
  First Baptist Christian Academy 500/PK-12
  7500 Fairmont Pkwy 77505 281-991-9191
  Joyce Harding, admin. Fax 991-7092
  Harvest Christian Academy 200/K-12
  1117 Main St 77506 713-472-7228
  Patricia Gehret, prin. Fax 472-4677
  Interactive Learning Systems Post-Sec.
  1001 Southmore Ave 77502 713-920-1120
  Pasadena Academy Post-Sec.
  2155 Red Bluff Rd 77506 713-473-1777
  San Jacinto College Post-Sec.
  8060 Spencer Hwy 77505 281-476-1501
  Texas Chiropractic College Post-Sec.
  5912 Spencer Hwy 77505 281-487-1170

Pattonville, Lamar
Prairiland ISD 1,000/PK-12
  RR 1 Box 200 75468 903-652-6476
  James R. Morton, supt. Fax 652-3738
  www.prairiland.net
  Prairiland HS 300/9-12
  RR 1 Box 200 75468 903-652-5681
  Jeff Ballard, prin. Fax 652-6400
  Prairiland JHS, 466 196 S 75468 6-8
  Jason Hostetler, prin. 903-652-5681

Pearland, Brazoria, Pop. 47,903
Pearland ISD 13,000/PK-12
  PO Box 7 77588 281-485-3203
  Dr. Bonny Cain, supt. Fax 412-1231
  www.pearlandisd.org
  Pearland East JHS 600/7-8
  2315 Old Alvin Rd 77581 281-485-2481
  Lonnie Leal, prin. Fax 412-1203
  Pearland HS 2,500/10-12
  3775 S Main St 77581 281-997-7445
  Dr. Nyla Watson, prin. Fax 412-1113
  Pearland Ninth Grade Center 1,000/9-9
  4717 Bailey Rd 77584 281-727-1600
  David Moody, prin. Fax 727-1660
  Pearland South JHS 800/7-8
  4719 Bailey Rd 77584 281-727-1500
  Bradley Brown, prin. Fax 727-1580
  Pearland West JHS 700/7-8
  2337 Galveston Ave 77581 281-412-1222
  Pam Wilson, prin. Fax 412-1228

  Eagle Heights Christian Academy 300/PK-12
  3005 Pearland Pkwy 77581 281-485-6330
  John Stahl, prin. Fax 485-8682

Pearsall, Frio, Pop. 7,132
Pearsall ISD 2,300/PK-12
  318 Berry Ranch Rd 78061 830-334-8001
  Mario Sotelo, supt. Fax 334-8007
  www.pearsall.k12.tx.us
  Pearsall HS 600/9-12
  1990 Maverick Dr 78061 830-334-8011
  Margaret McCloskey, prin. Fax 334-5018
  Pearsall JHS 500/6-8
  607 E Alabama St 78061 830-334-8021
  Julian Hernandez, prin. Fax 334-8025

Pecos, Reeves, Pop. 8,752
Pecos-Barstow-Toyah ISD 2,300/PK-12
  PO Box 869 79772 432-447-7201
  Ray Matthews, supt. Fax 447-3076
  pbtisd.esc18.net/
  Crockett IS 400/7-8
  PO Box 869 79772 432-447-7251
  Victor Tarin, prin. Fax 447-4853
  Pecos HS 700/9-12
  PO Box 869 79772 432-447-7222
  Steve Lucas, prin. Fax 447-9055
  Lamar AEP Adult
  PO Box 869 79772 432-447-7265
  Jimmy Dutchover, admin. Fax 445-3814

Penelope, Hill, Pop. 225
Penelope ISD 200/PK-12
  PO Box 68 76676 254-533-2215
  Harley Johnson, supt. Fax 533-2262

  Penelope S 200/PK-12
  PO Box 68 76676 254-533-2215
  Gordon Vogel, prin. Fax 533-2262

Perrin, Jack
Perrin-Whitt Consolidated ISD 300/K-12
  216 N Benson St 76486 940-798-3718
  Darren Francis, supt. Fax 798-3071
  www.pwcisd.net
  Perrin JSHS 200/7-12
  216 N Benson St 76486 940-798-3845
  Carolyn Warterfield, prin. Fax 798-3071

Perryton, Ochiltree, Pop. 7,775
Perryton ISD 2,000/PK-12
  PO Box 1048 79070 806-435-5478
  Robin Adkins, supt. Fax 435-4689
  www.perrytonisd.com
  Perryton HS 500/9-12
  PO Box 1048 79070 806-435-3633
  Isabell Weynand, prin. Fax 435-2602
  Perryton JHS 500/6-8
  PO Box 1048 79070 806-435-3601
  Charles McLarty, prin. Fax 435-3624

  Victory Christian Academy 100/PK-12
  PO Box 1267 79070 806-435-3476
  Kathy Sparks, prin. Fax 435-9256

Petersburg, Hale, Pop. 1,233
Petersburg ISD 300/PK-12
  PO Box 160 79250 806-667-3585
  Joey Nichols, supt. Fax 667-3463
  www.petersburgisd.net
  Petersburg JSHS 200/7-12
  PO Box 160 79250 806-667-3574
  Dwain Milam, prin. Fax 667-3463

Petrolia, Clay, Pop. 802
Petrolia ISD 500/PK-12
  PO Box 176 76377 940-524-3555
  Derrith Welch, supt. Fax 524-3370
  www.esc9.net/petrolia
  Petrolia HS 200/9-12
  PO Box 176 76377 940-524-3264
  Tommy Cummings, prin. Fax 524-3215
  Petrolia JHS 100/6-8
  PO Box 176 76377 940-524-3433
  Wade Wesley, prin. Fax 524-3202

Pettus, Bee
Pettus ISD 400/K-12
  PO Box D 78146 361-375-2296
  Tucker Rackley, supt. Fax 375-2295
  www.pettusisd.esc2.net
  Pettus HS 200/7-12
  PO Box D 78146 361-375-2296
  Dr. Susan Warner, prin. Fax 375-2295

Pflugerville, Travis, Pop. 24,661
Pflugerville ISD 17,300/PK-12
  1401 Pecan St W 78660 512-594-0000
  Charles Dupre, supt. Fax 594-0005
  www.pflugervilleisd.net
  Hendrickson HS 1,200/9-12
  2905 FM 685 78660 512-594-1100
  Dr. Lori Einfalt, prin. Fax 594-1105
  Kelly Lane MS 6-8
  18900 Falcon Pointe Blvd 78660 512-594-2800
  Rachelle Warren, prin. Fax 594-2805
  Park Crest MS 1,100/6-8
  1500 N Railroad Ave 78660 512-594-2400
  Steve Fuller, prin. Fax 594-2405
  Pflugerville HS 2,200/9-12
  1301 Pecan St W 78660 512-594-0500
  Larry Bradley, prin. Fax 594-0505
  Pflugerville MS 1,000/6-8
  1600 Settlers Valley Dr 78660 512-594-2000
  Mary Kimmins, prin. Fax 594-2005
  Other Schools – See Austin

Pharr, Hidalgo, Pop. 54,452
Pharr-San Juan-Alamo ISD 26,800/PK-12
  PO Box 1150 78577 956-702-5600
  Arturo Guajardo, supt. Fax 702-5648
  www.psja.k12.tx.us/
  Johnson MS 1,200/6-8
  500 E Sioux Rd 78577 956-702-5657
  Juan Serna, prin. Fax 702-5661
  Liberty MS 1,300/6-8
  1212 Fir Rdg 78577 956-702-5826
  Marisela Zepeda, prin. Fax 783-2820
  Pharr-San Juan-Alamo North HS 2,100/9-12
  500 E Nolana Loop 78577 956-783-3300
  Antonio Lozano, prin. Fax 783-3307
  Other Schools – See Alamo, San Juan

  Valley View ISD 3,000/PK-12
  RR 1 Box 122 78577 956-843-8825
  Leonel Galaviz, supt. Fax 843-8688
  www.valley-view-pharr.k12.tx.us
  Valley View HS 700/9-12
  RR 1 Box 122 78577 956-843-9222
  Kelly VanHee, prin. Fax 843-9368
  Valley View MS 700/6-8
  RR 1 Box 122 78577 956-843-2452
  Ramiro Balderas, prin. Fax 843-7992

  Oratory Academy 300/PK-12
  1407 W Moore Rd 78577 956-781-3056
  Fr. Mario Aviles, prin. Fax 702-3047
  Southern Careers Institute Post-Sec.
  1414 N Jackson Rd 78577 956-687-1415
  Vanguard Institute of Technology Post-Sec.
  3107 N Sugar Rd 78577 956-787-4388

Pilot Point, Denton, Pop. 3,859
Pilot Point ISD 1,500/PK-12
  829 S Harrison St 76258 940-686-5221
  Cloyce Purcell, supt. Fax 686-5220
  www.pilotpointisd.com
  Pilot Point HS 400/9-12
  1300 N Washington St 76258 940-686-2189
  Lori Sitzes, prin. Fax 686-5314
  Pilot Point MS - J. Earl Selz Campus 200/7-8
  828 S Harrison St 76258 940-686-2176
  Larry Shuman, prin. Fax 686-2711

Pineland, Sabine, Pop. 925
West Sabine ISD 600/K-12
  PO Box 869 75968 409-584-2655
  Malcolm Nash, supt. Fax 584-2139
  www.westsabine.esc7.net
  West Sabine JSHS 300/7-12
  PO Box 869 75968 409-584-2525
  Ronald Barlow, prin. Fax 584-2695

Pittsburg, Camp, Pop. 4,370
Pittsburg ISD 2,300/PK-12
  PO Box 1189 75686 903-856-3628
  Melinda Jones, supt. Fax 856-0269
  pittsburg.esc8.net
  Pittsburg HS 600/9-12
  300 N Texas St 75686 903-856-3646
  Dennis Glenn, prin. Fax 855-3325
  Pittsburg MS 400/7-8
  313 Broach St 75686 903-856-6432
  Grover Bishop, prin. Fax 855-3357

Plains, Yoakum, Pop. 1,431
Plains ISD 500/PK-12
  PO Box 479 79355 806-456-7401
  James Haynes, supt. Fax 456-4325
  plainsisd.esc17.net
  Plains HS, PO Box 479 79355 100/9-12
  Steven O'Quinn, prin. 806-456-7498
  Plains MS, PO Box 479 79355 100/5-8
  Michael Michaleson, prin. 806-456-7490

Plainview, Hale, Pop. 21,889
Plainview ISD 6,000/PK-12
  PO Box 1540 79073 806-296-6392
  Dr. Ron Miller, supt. Fax 296-4014
  www.plainview.k12.tx.us
  Estacado JHS 400/8-8
  2500 W 20th St 79072 806-296-4165
  Dr. Dana West, prin. Fax 296-4169
  Plainview HS 1,500/9-12
  1501 Quincy St 79072 806-296-4051
  Lisa Kersh, prin. Fax 296-4069

  Plainview Christian Academy 200/PK-12
  310 S Ennis St 79072 806-296-6034
  Brenda Williams, prin. Fax 296-0074
  Wayland Baptist University Post-Sec.
  1900 W 7th St 79072 806-296-5521

Plano, Collin, Pop. 241,991
  Frisco ISD
  Supt. — See Frisco
  Liberty HS 9-12
  3801 McDermott Rd 75025 469-633-5800
  Mike Waldrip, prin.

  Plano ISD 51,800/PK-12
  2700 W 15th St 75075 469-752-8100
  Dr. Douglas Otto, supt. Fax 752-8096
  www.pisd.edu
  Armstrong MS 700/6-8
  3805 Timberline Dr 75074 469-752-4600
  Donella Chennault, prin. Fax 752-4601
  Bowman MS 1,000/6-8
  2501 Jupiter Rd 75074 469-752-4800
  Tonya Horton, prin. Fax 752-4801
  Carpenter MS 1,100/6-8
  1501 Cross Bend Rd 75023 469-752-5000
  Shauna Koehne, prin. Fax 752-5001
  Clark HS 1,300/9-10
  523 W Spring Creek Pkwy 75023 469-752-7200
  Stephanie Schmoker, prin. Fax 752-7201
  Haggard MS 800/6-8
  2401 Westside Dr 75075 469-752-5400
  Julie-Anne Dean, prin. Fax 752-5401
  Hendrick MS 800/6-8
  7400 Red River Dr 75025 469-752-5600
  Sheila Spencer, prin. Fax 752-5601
  Jasper HS 2,000/9-10
  6800 Archgate Dr 75024 469-752-7400
  Michael Novotny, prin. Fax 752-7401
  Plano East SHS 2,500/11-12
  3000 Los Rios Blvd 75074 469-752-9000
  Karen McDonald, prin. Fax 752-9001
  Plano SHS 2,300/11-12
  2200 Independence Pkwy 75075 469-752-9300
  Dr. Doyle Dean, prin. Fax 752-9301
  Plano West SHS 1,800/11-12
  5601 W Parker Rd 75093 469-752-9600
  Phil Saviano, prin. Fax 752-9601
  Renner MS 1,200/6-8
  5701 W Parker Rd 75093 469-752-5800
  Mike Collinsworth, prin. Fax 752-5801
  Rice MS 1,100/6-8
  8500 Gifford Dr 75025 469-752-6000
  Carol Johnson, prin. Fax 752-6001
  Robinson MS 1,100/6-8
  6701 Preston Meadow Dr 75024 469-752-6200
  Kary Cooper, prin. Fax 752-6201
  Schimelpfenig MS 1,000/6-8
  2400 Maumelle Dr 75023 469-752-6400
  Olga Sanchez-Grosscup, prin. Fax 752-6401
  Shepton HS 1,500/9-10
  5505 W Plano Pkwy 75093 469-752-7600
  Kathy King, prin. Fax 752-7601
  Vines HS 1,300/9-10
  1401 Highedge Dr 75075 469-752-7800
  Roxanne Burleson, prin. Fax 752-7801
  Williams HS 1,600/9-10
  1717 17th St 75074 469-752-8300
  Sara Bonser, prin. Fax 752-8301
  Wilson MS 1,100/6-8
  1001 Custer Rd 75075 469-752-6700
  George King, prin. Fax 752-6701
  Other Schools – See Dallas, Murphy

  Bethany Christian S 100/PK-12
  3300 W Parker Rd 75075 972-596-5811
  Dr. Marvin Effa, prin. Fax 596-5814
  Collin County Community College Post-Sec.
  4800 Preston Park Blvd 75093 972-881-5790
  DeVry University Post-Sec.
  2301 W Plano Pkwy Ste 101 75075 972-943-8041
  John Paul II HS 200/9-12
  900 Coit Rd 75075 972-867-0005
  Thomas Poore, prin. Fax 867-7557
  Plano Christian Academy 50/1-12
  1501 H Ave 75074 972-422-1722
  Scott Harris, admin. Fax 422-5497

Prestonwood Christian Academy 1,400/PK-12
6801 W Park Blvd 75093 972-820-5300
Larry Taylor, hdmstr. Fax 820-5068

Pleasanton, Atascosa, Pop. 8,999
Pleasanton ISD 3,500/PK-12
831 Stadium Dr 78064 830-569-1200
Alton Fields, supt. Fax 569-2171
www.pisd.us
Pleasanton HS 1,000/9-12
831 Stadium Dr 78064 830-569-1250
Kenneth Whiteker, prin. Fax 569-1259
Pleasanton JHS 500/7-8
831 Stadium Dr 78064 830-569-1280
Deborah Garcia, prin. Fax 569-2514

Pollok, Angelina
Central ISD 1,700/PK-12
7622 N US Highway 69 75969 936-853-2216
Vernis Rogers, supt. Fax 853-2215
www.centralisd.com
Central HS 400/9-12
7622 N US Highway 69 75969 936-853-2167
Ronald Lindgren, prin. Fax 853-2208
Central JHS 400/6-8
7622 N US Highway 69 75969 936-853-2115
David Flowers, prin. Fax 853-2348

Ponder, Denton, Pop. 684
Ponder ISD 800/PK-12
PO Box 278 76259 940-479-8200
Bruce Yeager, supt. Fax 479-8209
www.ponderisd.net
Ponder HS 400/7-12
PO Box 278 76259 940-479-8210
Chance Allen, prin. Fax 479-8219
Ponder JHS 6-8
PO Box 278 76259 940-479-8220
Ted Heers, prin. Fax 479-8229

Poolville, Parker
Poolville ISD 500/K-12
PO Box 96 76487 817-594-4452
Terry Hamilton, supt. Fax 594-2651
www.poolville.net
Poolville HS 100/9-12
101 Lone Star Rd 76487 817-599-5134
Jimmie Dobbs, prin. Fax 599-5171
Poolville JHS 100/6-8
PO Box 96 76487 817-594-4539
Tony Phillips, prin. Fax 594-0081

Port Aransas, Nueces, Pop. 3,534
Port Aransas ISD 600/PK-12
100 S Station St 78373 361-749-1205
Billy Wiggins, supt. Fax 749-1215
www.port-aransas.k12.tx.us
Brundrett MS 100/6-8
100 S Station St 78373 361-749-1209
Travis Longanecker, prin. Fax 749-1218
Port Aransas HS 200/9-12
100 S Station St 78373 361-749-1206
Jim Moss, prin. Fax 749-1219

Port Arthur, Jefferson, Pop. 57,042
Port Arthur ISD 9,300/PK-12
PO Box 1388 77641 409-989-6244
Dr. James Weeks, supt. Fax 989-6268
www.paisd.org
Austin MS 500/6-8
2441 61st St 77640 409-736-1521
Dr. Edna Edwards, prin. Fax 736-0267
Edison MS 1,000/6-8
3501 12th St 77642 409-985-4311
Sharon Dozier-Davis, prin. Fax 985-6945
Memorial 9th Grade Campus 700/9-9
1023 Abe Lincoln Ave 77640 409-985-2551
Bannister Baptiste, prin. Fax 985-3376
Memorial HS 1,900/10-12
2200 Jefferson Dr 77642 409-962-8451
Raymond Polk, prin. Fax 963-3862
Stillwell Technical Center Vo/Tech
4801 9th Ave 77642 409-983-3286
Martha Harris, prin. Fax 983-2204

Academy of Hair Design Post-Sec.
3141 College St #A10 77642 409-813-3100
Lamar State College-Port Arthur Post-Sec.
PO Box 310 77641 409-983-4921
United Christian Academy 100/7-12
2700 25th St 77640 409-985-8803
Rev. Darrell McCoy, prin. Fax 985-8804

Porter, Montgomery, Pop. 7,000
New Caney ISD
Supt. — See New Caney
New Caney 9th Grade Campus 9-9
22784 Highway 59 77365 281-354-4137
Charlotte Montgomery, prin. Fax 354-8725
White Oak MS 900/6-8
24161 Briar Berry Ln 77365 281-577-8800
Paula Burk, prin. Fax 354-5186

Port Isabel, Cameron, Pop. 5,199
Point Isabel ISD 2,600/PK-12
PO Box AH 78578 956-943-0000
Dr. Estella Pineda, supt. Fax 943-0014
www.pi-isd.net/
Port Isabel HS 600/9-12
PO Box AH 78578 956-943-0030
Lorene Villarreal, prin. Fax 943-0048
Port Isabel JHS 600/6-8
PO Box AH 78578 956-943-0060
Joel Garcia, prin. Fax 943-0055

Portland, San Patricio, Pop. 15,489
Gregory-Portland ISD
Supt. — See Gregory
Gregory-Portland HS 1,300/9-12
4601 Wildcat Dr 78374 361-777-4251
Barbara Cade, prin. Fax 777-4272
Gregory-Portland JHS 700/7-8
4600 Wildcat Dr 78374 361-643-2552
Patricia Arnold, prin. Fax 643-3187

Port Lavaca, Calhoun, Pop. 11,865
Calhoun County ISD 4,200/PK-12
525 N Commerce St 77979 361-552-9728
Larry Nichols, supt. Fax 551-2648
www.calcoisd.org

Calhoun HS 1,100/9-12
201 Sandcrab Blvd 77979 361-552-3775
Edward Presley, prin. Fax 551-2620
Travis MS 800/6-8
705 N Nueces St 77979 361-552-3784
Scott Norris, prin. Fax 551-2692

Port Neches, Jefferson, Pop. 13,269
Port Neches-Groves ISD 4,700/PK-12
620 Avenue C 77651 409-722-4244
Dr. Lani Randall, supt. Fax 724-7864
www.pngisd.org
Port Neches-Groves HS 1,500/9-12
1401 Merriman St 77651 409-729-7644
Roy Esquivel, prin. Fax 722-7371
Port Neches MS 500/6-8
2031 Llano St 77651 409-722-8115
Marc Keith, prin. Fax 727-8342
Other Schools – See Groves

Post, Garza, Pop. 3,817
Post ISD 1,000/PK-12
PO Box 70 79356 806-495-3343
Marlin Marcum, supt. Fax 495-2945
www.post.k12.tx.us
Post HS 300/9-12
PO Box 70 79356 806-495-2770
Johnny McGregor, prin. Fax 495-2792
Post MS 200/6-8
PO Box 70 79356 806-495-2874
Judy Miers, prin. Fax 495-2426

Poteet, Atascosa, Pop. 3,528
Poteet ISD 1,300/PK-12
PO Box 138 78065 830-742-3567
Dr. Douglas Killian, supt. Fax 742-3332
www.poteet.k12.tx.us
Poteet HS 500/9-12
PO Box 138 78065 830-742-3522
Tim Coyle, prin. Fax 742-8497
Poteet JHS 300/7-8
PO Box 138 78065 830-742-3571
Mary Garcia, prin. Fax 742-8495

Poth, Wilson, Pop. 2,002
Poth ISD 700/PK-12
PO Box 250 78147 830-484-3330
David Wehmeyer, supt. Fax 484-2961
www.pothisd.us
Poth HS 200/9-12
PO Box 250 78147 830-484-3322
Frank Hosek, prin. Fax 484-3304
Poth JHS 200/6-8
PO Box 250 78147 830-484-3323
Scott Caloss, prin. Fax 484-3682

Pottsboro, Grayson, Pop. 1,715
Pottsboro ISD 1,400/PK-12
PO Box 555 75076 903-786-3051
Dr. Kyle Collier, supt. Fax 786-9085
www.pottsboroisd.org/
Pottsboro HS 400/9-12
PO Box 555 75076 903-786-2470
Paul Holliday, prin. Fax 786-6349
Pottsboro MS 400/6-8
PO Box 555 75076 903-786-9702
Wendi Russell, prin. Fax 786-4902

Prairie Lea, Caldwell
Prairie Lea ISD 200/PK-12
PO Box 9 78661 512-488-2070
Jesus Lopez III, supt. Fax 488-9006
Prairie Lea S 200/PK-12
PO Box 9 78661 512-488-2328
Darren Kesselus, prin. Fax 488-2425

Prairie View, Waller, Pop. 4,540

Prairie View A&M University Post-Sec.
PO Box 188 77446 936-857-3311

Premont, Jim Wells, Pop. 2,825
Premont ISD 900/PK-12
PO Box 530 78375 361-348-3915
David Garza, supt. Fax 348-2882
www.premontisd.net
Premont HS 400/9-12
PO Box B 78375 361-348-3915
Rebecca T. Pulido, prin. Fax 348-2914
Premont JHS 200/6-8
PO Box 769 78375 361-348-3915
Dr. Terry Oberg, prin. Fax 348-2751

Presidio, Presidio, Pop. 4,575
Presidio ISD 1,500/PK-12
PO Box 1401 79845 432-229-3215
Dr. Douglas Karr, supt. Fax 229-4228
www.presidio.esc18.net
Franco MS 300/6-8
PO Box 1401 79845 432-229-3113
Teresa Porras, prin. Fax 229-4087
Presidio HS 500/9-12
PO Box 1401 79845 432-229-3365
Murphy Quick, prin. Fax 229-4625

Price, Rusk
Carlisle ISD 200/PK-12
PO Box 187 75687 903-861-3801
Michael Payne, supt. Fax 861-3932
www.carl.sprnet.org/cisd2.htm
Carlisle HS 200/7-12
PO Box 187 75687 903-861-3811
Cathy Amonett, prin. Fax 861-0100

Priddy, Mills
Priddy ISD 100/K-12
PO Box 40 76870 325-966-3323
Robby Stuteville, supt. Fax 966-3380
www.centex-edu.net/priddy/
Priddy S 100/K-12
PO Box 40 76870 325-966-3323
Bob Rauch, prin. Fax 966-3380

Princeton, Collin, Pop. 3,789
Princeton ISD 2,300/PK-12
321 Panther Pkwy 75407 469-952-5400
Philip Anthony, supt. Fax 736-3505
www.princetonisd.net
Clark JHS 400/7-8
301 Panther Pkwy 75407 972-736-3503
Greg Tabor, prin. Fax 736-5903

Princeton HS 700/9-12
1000 E Princeton Dr 75407 469-952-5400
Robert Lovelady, prin. Fax 736-5902

Progreso, Hidalgo, Pop. 5,043
Progreso ISD 2,700/PK-12
PO Box 610 78579 956-565-3002
Dr. Fernando Castillo, supt. Fax 565-2128
www.progreso-isd.net/
Progreso HS 500/9-12
PO Box 610 78579 956-565-4142
Manual Garcia, prin. Fax 565-6029
Thompson MS 600/5-8
PO Box 610 78579 956-565-6539
Mischellene Pemelton, prin. Fax 565-1718

Prosper, Collin, Pop. 2,920
Prosper ISD 900/PK-12
PO Box 100 75078 972-346-3316
Drew Watkins, supt. Fax 346-9247
www.prosper-isd.net
Prosper HS 400/9-12
PO Box 490 75078 972-346-2455
Mike Brown, prin. Fax 346-9246
Prosper MS 400/6-8
PO Box 100 75078 972-346-9114
Andy Baker, prin. Fax 346-9248

Quanah, Hardeman, Pop. 2,826
Quanah ISD 600/PK-12
PO Box 150 79252 940-663-2281
Terry Allen, supt. Fax 663-2875
www.qisd.net
Quanah HS 200/9-12
PO Box 150 79252 940-663-2791
Jack Campsey, prin. Fax 663-6447
Travis MS 100/7-8
PO Box 150 79252 940-663-2226
Mike Hale, prin. Fax 663-6361

Queen City, Cass, Pop. 1,586
Queen City ISD 1,100/PK-12
PO Box 128 75572 903-796-8256
Rob Barnwell, supt. Fax 796-0248
www.qcisd.net
Queen City HS 300/9-12
PO Box 128 75572 903-796-8259
Charlotte Williams, prin. Fax 796-8258
Upchurch MS 300/5-8
PO Box 128 75572 903-796-6412
Steve Holmes, prin. Fax 796-0834

Quinlan, Hunt, Pop. 1,437
Boles ISD 500/PK-12
7071 FM 2101 75474 903-883-4464
Dr. Graham Sweeney, supt. Fax 883-4531
boles.ednet10.net
Boles HS 200/9-12
7071 FM 2101 75474 903-883-2918
Carol Brown, prin. Fax 883-4531
Boles MS 200/5-8
7071 FM 2101 75474 903-883-4464
Mikayle Moreland, prin. Fax 883-4531
Quinlan ISD 2,900/PK-12
301 E Main St 75474 903-356-3293
Larry Johnson, supt. Fax 356-2339
www.quinlanisd.net
Ford HS 900/9-12
10064 Business Highway 34 S 75474 903-356-2155
Beverly Newcomb, prin. Fax 356-3558
Thompson MS 700/6-8
423 Panther Path 75474 903-356-2154
Michael Tull, prin. Fax 356-2414

Quitman, Wood, Pop. 2,126
Quitman ISD 1,100/PK-12
1101 E Goode St 75783 903-763-5000
Bill Travis, supt. Fax 763-2710
www.quitmanisd.net/
Quitman HS 300/9-12
1101 E Goode St 75783 903-763-5000
Tony Gilbreath, prin. Fax 763-2589
Quitman JHS 200/7-8
1101 E Goode St 75783 903-763-5000
Andrea Middendorf, prin. Fax 763-2589

Ralls, Crosby, Pop. 2,144
Ralls ISD 700/PK-12
810 Avenue I 79357 806-253-2509
Dagobert Azam, supt. Fax 253-2508
Ralls HS 200/9-12
810 Avenue I 79357 806-253-2571
Deanna Logan, prin. Fax 253-2609
Ralls MS 100/6-8
810 Avenue I 79357 806-253-2549
Michael Allbright, prin. Fax 253-4031

Randolph AFB, Bexar
Randolph Field ISD 1,100/PK-12
Building 1225 78148 210-357-2300
Dr. Barbara Maddox, supt. Fax 357-2469
www.randolph-field.k12.tx.us
Randolph HS 300/9-12
Building 1225 78148 210-357-2400
Bruce Cannon, prin. Fax 357-2475
Randolph MS 300/6-8
Building 1225 78148 210-357-2400
Bruce Cannon, prin. Fax 357-2475

Ranger, Eastland, Pop. 2,544
Ranger ISD 500/PK-12
1842 E Loop 254 76470 254-647-1187
Doyle Russell, supt. Fax 647-5215
www.ranger.esc14.net
Ranger JSHS 200/6-12
1842 E Loop 254 76470 254-647-3216
Tooter Draper, prin. Fax 647-1895

Ranger College Post-Sec.
1100 College Cir 76470 254-647-3234

Rankin, Upton, Pop. 747
Rankin ISD 200/PK-12
PO Box 90 79778 432-693-2461
Tena Gray, supt. Fax 693-2353
www.rankin.k12.tx.us
Rankin JSHS 100/7-8
PO Box 90 79778 432-693-2451
Paula Hill, prin. Fax 693-2453

Raymondville, Willacy, Pop. 9,512
Raymondville ISD ... 2,500/PK-12
1 Bearkat Blvd 78580 ... 956-689-2471
Eloy Castaneda, supt. ... Fax 689-5869
www.raymondvilleisd.org/
Green MS ... 600/6-8
1 Bearkat Blvd 78580 ... 956-689-2471
Max Lundstrom, prin. ... Fax 689-5330
Raymondville HS ... 600/9-12
1 Bearkat Blvd 78580 ... 956-689-2471
Gilbert Galvan, prin. ... Fax 689-8152

Raywood, Liberty
Hull-Daisetta ISD
Supt. — See Daisetta
Hull-Daisetta JHS ... 200/6-8
F M 160 77582 ... 936-536-6321
Frederick Freeman, prin. ... Fax 587-4093

Red Oak, Ellis, Pop. 5,871
Red Oak ISD ... 4,800/PK-12
PO Box 9000 75154 ... 972-617-2941
Craig Stockstill, supt. ... Fax 617-4333
www.redoakisd.org
Red Oak HS ... 1,500/9-12
PO Box 9000 75154 ... 972-617-3535
Bobby Stults, prin. ... Fax 617-4355
Red Oak JHS ... 800/7-8
PO Box 9000 75154 ... 972-617-0066
Morris Watson, prin. ... Fax 617-4377

Redwater, Bowie, Pop. 882
Redwater ISD ... 1,100/PK-12
PO Box 347 75573 ... 903-671-3481
Dr. Max Thompson, supt. ... Fax 671-2019
redwater.esc8.net/
Redwater HS, PO Box 347 75573 ... 300/9-12
Amy Roberts, prin. ... 903-671-3421
Redwater JHS ... 200/7-8
PO Box 347 75573 ... 903-671-3227
Bebe Hayes, prin. ... Fax 671-2019

Refugio, Refugio, Pop. 2,793
Refugio ISD ... 700/K-12
212 W Vance St 78377 ... 361-526-2325
Dr. John S. Sutton, supt. ... Fax 526-2326
www.refugioisd.net/
Refugio JHSH ... 400/7-12
212 W Vance St 78377 ... 361-526-2344
David Solomon, prin. ... Fax 526-1075

Rhome, Wise, Pop. 739
Northwest ISD
Supt. — See Justin
Chisholm Trail MS ... 300/6-8
583 FM 3433 76078 ... 817-215-0600
Dr. Philo Waters, prin. ... Fax 215-0648

Rice, Ellis, Pop. 884
Rice ISD ... 600/PK-12
1302 SW McKinney St 75155 ... 903-326-4287
Judith Pritchett, supt. ... Fax 326-4164
www.rice-isd.org
Rice JSHS ... 400/6-12
1400 S McKinney St 75155 ... 903-326-4502
Tom Herrin, prin. ... Fax 326-5042

Richards, Grimes
Richards ISD ... 200/K-12
PO Box 308 77873 ... 936-851-2364
Martey Ainsworth, supt. ... Fax 851-2210
Richards JSHS ... 100/7-12
PO Box 308 77873 ... 936-851-2364
Willow Walker, prin. ... Fax 851-2210

Richardson, Dallas, Pop. 99,536
Richardson ISD ... 35,700/PK-12
400 S Greenville Ave 75081 ... 469-593-0000
Patti Kieker, supt. ... Fax 593-0402
www.risd.org
Apollo JHS ... 1,000/7-9
1600 Apollo Rd 75081 ... 469-593-7900
Jack Noteware, prin. ... Fax 593-7911
Berkner HS ... 2,200/10-12
1600 E Spring Valley Rd 75081 ... 469-593-7000
Dave Casey, prin. ... Fax 593-7211
Pearce HS ... 1,500/10-12
1600 N Coit Rd 75080 ... 469-593-5000
Karen Neal, prin. ... Fax 593-5169
Richardson Arts Law & Science Magnet HS 1,300/10-12
1250 W Belt Line Rd 75080 ... 469-593-3038
Debbie Deaton, prin. ... Fax 593-3082
Richardson HS ... 1,500/10-12
1250 W Belt Line Rd 75080 ... 469-593-3000
Bob DeVoll, prin. ... Fax 593-3010
Richardson JHS ... 600/7-9
450 Abrams Rd 75081 ... 469-593-7600
Ron Griffen, prin. ... Fax 593-7686
Richardson-North JHS ... 900/7-9
1820 N Floyd Rd 75080 ... 469-593-5400
Charles Pickitt, prin. ... Fax 593-5434
Richardson-West JHS Tech Magnet ... 800/7-9
1309 Holly Dr 75080 ... 469-593-3700
Walter Kelly, prin. ... Fax 593-3666
Other Schools – See Dallas

Alexander S ... 100/8-12
409 International Pkwy 75081 ... 972-690-9210
Andrew Cody, prin. ... Fax 690-9284
Canyon Creek Christian Academy ... 500/PK-12
2800 Custer Pkwy 75080 ... 972-231-4890
Dr. Steve Lawrence, admin. ... Fax 234-8414
Compu Tech Consultants School ... Post-Sec.
811 S Central Expy Ste 500 75080 ... 214-570-0404
ITT Technical Institute ... Post-Sec.
2101 Waterview Pkwy 75080 ... 972-279-0500
PCI Health Training Center ... Post-Sec.
1300 International Pkwy 75081 ... 214-630-0568
Richardson Adventist S ... 100/1-10
1201 W Belt Line Rd 75080 ... 972-238-1183
... Fax 644-3488
University of Texas at Dallas ... Post-Sec.
PO Box 830688 75083 ... 972-690-2111

Richland Hills, Tarrant, Pop. 8,184
Birdville ISD
Supt. — See Haltom City
Richland MS ... 500/6-8
7400 Hovenkamp Ave 76118 ... 817-547-4400
Cheri Sizemore, prin. ... Fax 595-5139

Richland Springs, San Saba, Pop. 337
Richland Springs ISD ... 200/K-12
700 US Highway 190 W 76871 ... 325-452-3524
Travis Winn, supt. ... Fax 452-3230
www.rscoyotes.net
Richland Springs S ... 200/K-12
700 US Highway 190 W 76871 ... 325-452-3434
Don Fowler, prin. ... Fax 452-3580

Richmond, Fort Bend, Pop. 12,752
Fort Bend ISD
Supt. — See Sugar Land
Bush HS ... 2,100/9-12
6707 FM 1464 Rd 77469 ... 281-634-6060
Shirley Rose, prin. ... Fax 634-6066
Travis HS ... 9-12
11111 Harlem Rd 77469 ... 281-634-7020
Jeryl Kyle, prin. ... Fax 634-7010

Lamar Consolidated ISD
Supt. — See Rosenberg
Briscoe JHS ... 1,200/6-8
4300 FM 723 Rd 77469 ... 281-762-4300
Mike Semmler, prin. ... Fax 762-4315
Foster HS ... 1,500/9-12
4400 FM 723 Rd 77469 ... 281-762-4000
Gene Tomas, prin. ... Fax 762-4015

Grand Parkway Christian Academy ... 200/PK-10
12000 FM 1464 Rd 77469 ... 281-240-4722
Karen Bowen, prin. ... Fax 240-6576

Riesel, McLennan, Pop. 991
Riesel ISD ... 600/PK-12
600 Frederick St 76682 ... 254-896-6411
Steve Clugston, supt. ... Fax 896-2981
www.rieselisd.org
Riesel JSHS ... 300/7-12
600 Frederick St 76682 ... 254-896-3171
David Wren, prin. ... Fax 896-2981

Rio Grande City, Starr, Pop. 12,985
Rio Grande City ISD ... 8,700/PK-12
1 S Fort Ringgold St 78582 ... 956-716-6702
Roel Gonzalez, supt. ... Fax 487-8506
www.rgccisd.org/
Ringgold MS ... 1,500/6-8
212 Crockett St 78582 ... 956-716-6851
Adolfo Pena, prin. ... Fax 716-6807
Rio Grande City 9th Grade Campus ... 9-9
1 S Fort Ringgold St 78582 ... 956-488-6000
Joel Trigo, prin.
Rio Grande City SHS ... 1,500/10-12
144 N FM 3167 78582 ... 956-488-6000
Jorge Recio, prin. ... Fax 488-6050
Other Schools – See Grulla

Rio Hondo, Cameron, Pop. 2,057
Rio Hondo ISD ... 2,200/PK-12
215 W Colorado St 78583 ... 956-748-1000
Anneliese McMinn, supt. ... Fax 748-1038
www.riohondoisd.net
Rio Hondo HS ... 600/9-12
215 W Colorado St 78583 ... 956-748-1200
Juan Montez, prin. ... Fax 748-1204
Rio Hondo JHS ... 500/6-8
215 W Colorado St 78583 ... 956-748-1150
Kristopher McKinney, prin. ... Fax 748-1168

Rio Vista, Johnson, Pop. 694
Rio Vista ISD ... 900/PK-12
PO Box 369 76093 ... 817-373-2241
Dr. Rock McNulty, supt. ... Fax 373-2076
www.rvisd.net
Rio Vista HS ... 300/9-12
PO Box 369 76093 ... 817-373-2669
Tim Wright, prin. ... Fax 373-3047
Rio Vista MS ... 200/5-8
PO Box 369 76093 ... 817-373-2009
Gary Peacock, prin. ... Fax 373-3046

Rising Star, Eastland, Pop. 845
Rising Star ISD ... 200/PK-12
PO Box 37 76471 ... 254-643-2717
Johnny Singleton, supt. ... Fax 643-1922
Rising Star JSHS ... 100/7-12
PO Box 37 76471 ... 254-643-3521
Buddy Hale, prin. ... Fax 643-5408

Riviera, Kleberg
Riviera ISD ... 500/PK-12
203 Seahawk Dr 78379 ... 361-296-3101
Dr. Cynthia Clary, supt. ... Fax 296-3104
www.rivieraisd.esc2.net
De La Paz MS ... 100/6-8
203 Seahawk Dr 78379 ... 361-296-3610
Therese Crocker, prin. ... Fax 296-3890
Kaufer HS ... 200/9-12
203 Seahawk Dr 78379 ... 361-296-3607
Brian Roberts, prin. ... Fax 296-3108

Robert Lee, Coke, Pop. 1,115
Robert Lee ISD ... 300/PK-12
1323 W Hamilton St 76945 ... 325-453-4555
Max Gordon, supt. ... Fax 453-2326
robertlee.netxv.net/
Robert Lee HS ... 100/7-12
1323 W Hamilton St 76945 ... 325-453-4557
Jill Lankford, prin. ... Fax 453-2326

Robinson, McLennan, Pop. 8,392
Robinson ISD ... 2,100/PK-12
500 W Lyndale Ave 76706 ... 254-662-0194
Micheal Hope, supt. ... Fax 662-0215
www.robinson.k12.tx.us
Robinson HS ... 700/9-12
500 W Lyndale Ave 76706 ... 254-662-3840
Tim VanCleave, prin. ... Fax 662-4007
Robinson JHS ... 500/6-8
500 W Lyndale Ave 76706 ... 254-662-3843
Barry Gann, prin. ... Fax 662-1845

Robstown, Nueces, Pop. 12,637
Robstown ISD ... 4,000/PK-12
801 N 1st St 78380 ... 361-767-6600
Dr. Roberto E. Garcia, supt. ... Fax 387-6311
www.robstownisd.org/
Robstown HS ... 1,000/9-12
609 Highway 44 78380 ... 361-387-5999
Roel Lara, prin. ... Fax 387-8960

Seale JHS ... 500/7-8
401 E Avenue G 78380 ... 361-767-6631
Raul Garza, prin. ... Fax 387-0202

Roby, Fisher, Pop. 645
Roby Consolidated ISD ... 300/PK-12
PO Box 519 79543 ... 325-776-2222
Wesley Hays, supt. ... Fax 776-2823
www.roby.esc14.net/
Roby HS ... 100/9-12
PO Box 519 79543 ... 325-776-2223
Gary O'Daniel, prin. ... Fax 776-2823

Rochelle, McCulloch
Rochelle ISD ... 200/K-12
PO Box 167 76872 ... 325-243-5224
Steve Butler, supt. ... Fax 243-5216
www.centex-edu.net/~rochelle/
Rochelle S ... 200/K-12
PO Box 167 76872 ... 325-243-5224
Scott Edmondson, prin. ... Fax 243-5216

Rochester, Haskell, Pop. 359
Haskell CISD
Supt. — See Haskell
Rochester JHS, PO Box 140 79544 ... 7-8
Reida Penman, prin. ... 940-743-3260

Rockdale, Milam, Pop. 6,024
Rockdale ISD ... 1,900/PK-12
PO Box 632 76567 ... 512-430-6000
Walter Pond, supt. ... Fax 446-3460
www.rockdale.txed.net/risd
Rockdale HS ... 500/9-12
PO Box 632 76567 ... 512-430-6140
Allen Sanders, prin. ... Fax 446-3512
Rockdale JHS ... 400/6-8
PO Box 632 76567 ... 512-430-6100
Richard Kolek, prin. ... Fax 446-2597

Rockport, Aransas, Pop. 8,469
Aransas County ISD ... 3,400/PK-12
PO Box 907 78381 ... 361-790-2212
P. Wayne Johnson, supt. ... Fax 790-2299
www.acisd.org
Rockport-Fulton HS ... 1,000/9-12
PO Box 907 78381 ... 361-790-2220
Tisha Piwetz, prin. ... Fax 790-2206
Rockport-Fulton MS ... 800/6-8
PO Box 907 78381 ... 361-790-2230
Kim James, prin. ... Fax 790-2030

Rocksprings, Edwards, Pop. 1,216
Rocksprings ISD ... 400/PK-12
PO Box 157 78880 ... 830-683-4137
Ms. Henri Gearing, supt. ... Fax 683-4141
www.rockspringsisd.net
Rocksprings HS ... 100/9-12
PO Box 157 78880 ... 830-683-4136
Jeff Dabney, prin. ... Fax 683-4141

Rockwall, Rockwall, Pop. 24,624
Rockwall ISD ... 9,900/PK-12
1050 Williams St 75087 ... 972-771-0605
Dr. Gene Burton, supt. ... Fax 771-2637
www.rockwallisd.com
Cain MS ... 700/7-8
6620 FM 3097 75032 ... 972-772-1170
Sarah Watkins, prin. ... Fax 772-2414
Rockwall-Heath HS ... 9-10
801 Laurence Dr 75032 ... 972-772-2474
Dr. Charles Nix, prin. ... Fax 698-2608
Rockwall HS ... 2,100/10-12
901 Yellow Jacket Ln 75087 ... 972-771-7339
Dr. Mark Le Master, prin. ... Fax 772-2016
Utley Freshman Center ... 800/9-9
1201 Townsend Dr 75087 ... 972-771-5281
Randy Cordial, prin. ... Fax 772-1164
Williams MS ... 900/7-8
625 E FM 552 75087 ... 972-771-8313
Billy Pringle, prin. ... Fax 772-2043

Heritage Christian Academy ... 300/PK-12
1408 S Goliad St 75087 ... 972-772-3003
Kevin Fields, hdmstr. ... Fax 772-0029

Rogers, Bell, Pop. 1,081
Rogers ISD ... 900/PK-12
1 Eagle Dr 76569 ... 254-642-3802
Katie Ryan, supt. ... Fax 642-3851
www.rogers.k12.tx.us
Rogers HS ... 300/9-12
1 Eagle Dr 76569 ... 254-642-3224
Robert Chappell, prin. ... Fax 642-3037
Rogers MS ... 200/6-8
1 Eagle Dr 76569 ... 254-642-3011
Genie Allison, prin. ... Fax 642-0033

Roma, Starr, Pop. 10,315
Roma ISD ... 6,200/PK-12
PO Box 187 78584 ... 956-849-1377
Jesus O. Guerra, supt. ... Fax 849-3118
www.romaisd.com/
Roma HS ... 1,500/9-12
PO Box 187 78584 ... 956-849-1333
Noe Muniz, prin. ... Fax 849-2955
Roma MS ... 1,000/7-8
PO Box 187 78584 ... 956-849-1434
Teresa Ramirez, prin. ... Fax 849-1895

Ropesville, Hockley, Pop. 522
Ropes ISD ... 400/PK-12
304 Ranch Rd 79358 ... 806-562-4031
Gary E. Lehnen, supt. ... Fax 562-4059
www.ropesisd.com/
Ropes S ... 400/PK-12
304 Ranch Rd 79358 ... 806-562-4031
Joel Willmon, prin. ... Fax 562-4059

Roscoe, Nolan, Pop. 1,301
Highland ISD ... 200/PK-12
6625 FM 608 79545 ... 325-766-3652
Guy Nelson, supt. ... Fax 766-2281
Highland S ... 200/PK-12
6625 FM 608 79545 ... 325-766-3652
Duane Hyde, prin. ... Fax 766-3869

Roscoe ISD
PO Box 579 79545   400/PK-12
Kim Alexander, supt.   325-766-3629
www.roscoe.esc14.net   Fax 766-3138
Roscoe JSHS, PO Box 10 79545   200/7-12
Frank Young, prin.   325-766-3327

Rosebud, Falls, Pop. 1,430
Rosebud-Lott ISD   900/PK-12
PO Box 638 76570   254-583-4510
Howell Wright, supt.   Fax 583-2602
www.rosebudlottisd.org/
Rosebud-Lott HS   300/9-12
PO Box 638 76570   254-583-7967
Walter Key, prin.   Fax 583-1130
Rosebud-Lott JHS   100/7-8
PO Box 638 76570   254-583-7967
Walter Key, prin.   Fax 583-1130

Rosenberg, Fort Bend, Pop. 27,808
Lamar Consolidated ISD   17,700/PK-12
3911 Avenue I 77471   281-341-3100
Dr. Thomas Randle, supt.   Fax 341-3598
www.lcisd.org
George ISD   800/7-8
4601 Airport Ave 77471   281-341-3399
Kelly Waters, prin.   Fax 341-3410
Lamar Consolidated HS   1,600/9-12
4606 Mustang Ave 77471   281-341-3434
Richard DuBroc, prin.   Fax 341-3420
Lamar JHS   1,000/7-8
4814 Mustang Ave 77471   281-341-3388
Victoria Bedo, prin.   Fax 341-3370
Terry HS   1,600/9-12
5500 Avenue N 77471   281-341-3500
Tom Rowland, prin.   Fax 341-3590
Community Center   Adult
1000 E Stadium Dr 77471   281-341-3553
Bobby Stanley, admin.   Fax 341-3559
Other Schools – See Richmond

Rotan, Fisher, Pop. 1,515
Rotan ISD   400/PK-12
102 N McKinley Ave 79546   325-735-2332
Mickey Early, supt.   Fax 735-2686
www.rotan.org
Rotan HS   100/9-12
102 N McKinley Ave 79546   325-735-3041
Bob Spikes, prin.   Fax 735-2686
Rotan JHS   100/5-8
102 N McKinley Ave 79546   325-735-3162
Mickey Early, prin.   Fax 735-2686

Round Rock, Williamson, Pop. 77,946
Round Rock ISD   35,300/PK-12
1311 Round Rock Ave 78681   512-464-5000
Jesus Chavez Ph.D., supt.   Fax 464-5090
www.roundrockisd.org
Chisholm Trail MS   1,100/6-8
500 Oakridge Dr 78681   512-428-2500
Diana Negrete, prin.   Fax 428-2629
Fulkes MS   700/6-8
300 W Anderson Ave 78664   512-428-3100
Terrence Eaton, prin.   Fax 428-3240
Hopewell MS   1,100/6-8
1535 Gulf Way 78664   512-464-5200
Rosena Malone, prin.   Fax 464-5349
Ridgeview MS   1,000/6-8
2000 Via Sonoma Trl 78664   512-424-8400
Ann O'Doherty, prin.   Fax 424-8540
Round Rock HS   1,900/9-12
300 N Lake Creek Dr 78681   512-464-6000
Mark Gesch, prin.   Fax 464-6190
Round Rock Opportunity Center   Vo/Tech
931 Luther Peterson 78664   512-428-2900
Rene Posey, prin.   Fax 428-2943
Stony Point 9th Grade Center   800/9-9
1901 Sunrise Rd 78664   512-424-8800
Albert Hernandez, prin.   Fax 424-8940
Stony Point SHS   2,000/10-12
1801 Bowman Rd 78664   512-428-7000
T.J. Dilworth, prin.   Fax 428-7280
Other Schools – See Austin

Central Texas Beauty College #2   Post-Sec.
1350 E Palm Valley Rd #A 78664   512-244-2235
Round Rock Christian Academy   400/PK-12
301 N Lake Creek Dr 78681   512-255-4491
Susan Owen, prin.   Fax 255-6043

Rowlett, Dallas, Pop. 51,102
Garland ISD
Supt. — See Garland
Coyle MS   1,200/6-8
4500 Skyline Dr 75088   972-475-3711
Dretha Burris, prin.   Fax 412-7222
Rowlett HS   2,600/9-12
4700 Kirby Rd 75088   972-463-1712
Dr. Marlene Hammerle, prin.   Fax 412-2951
Schrade MS   1,300/6-8
6201 Danridge Rd 75089   972-463-8790
Jim Thomas, prin.   Fax 463-8793

Rockwall Christian Academy   300/PK-12
6005 Dalrock Rd 75088   972-412-8266
Jeanne Zakem, supt.   Fax 463-3746
Rowlett Christian Academy   100/PK-12
8200 Schrade Rd 75088   972-412-7761
Dena Gregory, admin.   Fax 412-2320

Roxton, Lamar, Pop. 700
Roxton ISD   200/PK-12
PO Box 307 75477   903-346-3213
Dr. Kenneth Hall, supt.   Fax 346-3356
roxton.esc8.net
Roxton HS   100/7-12
PO Box 307 75477   903-346-3213
David Taylor, prin.   Fax 346-3356

Royse City, Rockwall, Pop. 4,129
Royse City ISD   2,900/PK-12
PO Box 479 75189   972-635-2413
Mike Harris, supt.   Fax 635-7037
www.rcisd.org
Royse City HS   700/9-12
PO Box 479 75189   972-636-9991
Tony Gauntt, prin.   Fax 635-2906
Royse City MS   400/7-8
PO Box 479 75189   972-635-9544
Andy Molck, prin.   Fax 635-2531

Rule, Haskell, Pop. 656
Rule ISD   200/PK-12
1100 Union Ave 79547   940-997-2521
David Parr, supt.   Fax 997-2446
www.rule.esc14.net
Rule S   200/PK-12
1100 Union Ave 79547   940-997-2246
Jimmy New, prin.   Fax 997-2446

Runge, Karnes, Pop. 1,070
Runge ISD   300/PK-12
PO Box 158 78151   830-239-4315
Ernest Havner, supt.   Fax 239-4816
www.rungeisd.org
Runge JSHS   100/7-12
PO Box 158 78151   830-239-4864
Scott Cutler, prin.   Fax 239-4816

Rusk, Cherokee, Pop. 5,212
Rusk ISD   2,000/PK-12
203 E 7th St 75785   903-683-5401
Dr. James Largent, supt.   Fax 683-2104
www.ruskisd.net
Rusk HS   500/9-12
203 E 7th St 75785   903-683-5401
Ricky Hassell, prin.   Fax 683-6090
Rusk JHS   500/6-8
203 E 7th St 75785   903-683-2502
Carlene Clayton, prin.   Fax 683-4363

Sabinal, Uvalde, Pop. 1,637
Sabinal ISD   600/PK-12
PO Box 338 78881   830-988-2472
Scott Dahlin, supt.   Fax 988-7151
www.sabinal.k12.tx.us
Sabinal HS   200/9-12
PO Box 338 78881   830-988-2475
Sean Johnston, prin.   Fax 988-7170
Sabinal JHS   100/7-8
PO Box 338 78881   830-988-2475
Sean Johnston, prin.   Fax 988-7170

Sabine Pass, Jefferson
Sabine Pass ISD   200/PK-12
PO Box 1148 77655   409-971-2321
Walter Lloyd Fenn, supt.   Fax 971-2120
www.spisd.com
Sabine Pass S   200/PK-12
PO Box 1148 77655   409-971-2321
Kristi Heid, prin.   Fax 971-2120

Sachse, Collin, Pop. 14,550
Garland ISD
Supt. — See Garland
Sachse HS   1,800/9-12
3901 Miles Rd 75048   972-414-7450
Steve Hammerle, prin.   Fax 414-7458

Sadler, Grayson, Pop. 422
S & S Consolidated ISD   900/PK-12
PO Box 837 76264   903-564-6051
Bill Gentzel, supt.   Fax 564-3492
www.ednet10.net/sands
S & S Consolidated HS   300/9-12
PO Box 837 76264   903-564-3768
Jay Roberts, prin.   Fax 564-7308
S & S Consolidated MS   200/6-8
PO Box 837 76264   903-564-7626
Dr. Mack Pate, prin.   Fax 564-7857

Saginaw, Tarrant, Pop. 16,127
Eagle Mtn.-Saginaw ISD
Supt. — See Fort Worth
Saginaw HS   9-12
800 N Blue Mound Rd 76131   817-306-0914
Ric Canterbury, prin.   Fax 306-1344

Saint Jo, Montague, Pop. 969
Saint Jo ISD   300/PK-12
PO Box L 76265   940-995-2668
Rick Moss, supt.   Fax 995-2026
www.saintjoisd.net
Saint Jo JSHS   200/7-12
PO Box L 76265   940-995-2532
Larry Jones, prin.   Fax 995-2087

Salado, Bell, Pop. 1,956
Salado ISD   1,100/PK-12
PO Box 98 76571   254-947-5479
Robin Battershell, supt.   Fax 947-5605
www.saladoisd.org
Salado HS   300/9-12
PO Box 98 76571   254-947-5429
Kay Matthews, prin.   Fax 947-6984
Salado IS   400/5-8
PO Box 98 76571   254-947-1700
Joe Palmer, prin.   Fax 947-6954

Saltillo, Hopkins
Saltillo ISD   300/PK-12
PO Box 269 75478   903-537-2386
Paul Jones, supt.   Fax 537-2191
www.esc8.net/saltillo
Saltillo S   300/PK-12
PO Box 269 75478   903-537-2386
Jack Arnwine, prin.   Fax 537-2191

Samnorwood, Collingsworth
Samnorwood ISD   100/PK-12
PO Box 765 79077   806-256-2039
Shawn Read, supt.   Fax 256-3974
Samnorwood S   100/PK-12
PO Box 765 79077   806-256-2039
Gerry Nickell, prin.   Fax 256-3974

San Angelo, Tom Green, Pop. 87,922
Grape Creek ISD   1,200/PK-12
8189 US Highway 87 N 76901   325-658-7823
Frank Walter, supt.   Fax 658-8719
www.grapecreek.org
Grape Creek HS   400/9-12
8189 US Highway 87 N 76901   325-653-1852
Chris duBois, prin.   Fax 653-3568
Grape Creek MS   300/6-8
8189 US Highway 87 N 76901   325-655-1735
Greg Baucom, prin.   Fax 657-2997

San Angelo ISD   13,000/PK-12
1621 University Ave 76904   325-947-3700
Fax 947-3771
www.saisd.org
Central Freshman Campus   200/9-9
218 N Oakes St 76903   325-659-3576
Keeva Frazier, prin.   Fax 659-3583
Central SHS   2,400/10-12
100 Cottonwood St 76901   325-659-3400
Joe Coleman, prin.   Fax 659-3413
Glenn MS   600/7-8
2201 University Ave 76904   325-947-3841
Bill Waters, prin.   Fax 947-3847
Lake View HS   1,200/9-12
900 E 43rd St 76903   325-659-3661
Don Levinski, prin.   Fax 653-8661
Lee MS   600/7-8
2500 Sherwood Way 76901   325-947-3871
J. D. Koehn, prin.   Fax 947-3890
Lincoln MS   1,000/6-8
255 E 50th St 76903   325-659-3550
Ron Cline, prin.   Fax 659-3559

American Commercial College   Post-Sec.
3177 Executive Dr 76904   325-942-6797
Angelo State University   Post-Sec.
ASU Station 11014 76909   325-942-2041
Cornerstone Christian S   200/PK-12
1502 N Jefferson St 76901   325-655-3439
Grady Roe, admin.   Fax 658-8998
Howard College   Post-Sec.
3197 Executive Dr 76904   325-944-9585
Shannon West Texas Memorial Hospital   Post-Sec.
120 E Harris Ave 76903   325-653-6741
Texas College of Cosmetology   Post-Sec.
918 N Chadbourne St 76903   325-677-0532

San Antonio, Bexar, Pop. 1,214,725
Alamo Heights ISD   4,400/PK-12
7101 Broadway St 78209   210-824-2483
Dr. Jerry Christian, supt.   Fax 822-2221
www.ahisd.net
Alamo Heights HS   1,300/9-12
6900 Broadway St 78209   210-820-8850
Dr. Linda Foster, prin.   Fax 832-5777
Alamo Heights JHS   1,100/6-8
7607 N New Braunfels Ave 78209   210-824-3231
Stephanie Kershner, prin.   Fax 832-5825

East Central ISD   7,800/PK-12
6634 New Sulphur Springs Rd 78263   210-648-7861
Gary Patterson, supt.   Fax 648-0931
www.ecisd.net/
East Central Heritage MS   1,200/7-8
8004 New Sulphur Springs Rd 78263   210-648-4546
Stevie Gonzales, prin.   Fax 648-3501
East Central HS   2,200/9-12
7173 FM 1628 78263   210-649-2951
Paul Rutledge, prin.   Fax 649-2752

Edgewood ISD   11,300/PK-12
5358 W Commerce St 78237   210-444-4500
Richard M. Bocanegra, supt.   Fax 444-4602
www.eisd.net/
Brentwood MS   600/6-8
1626 Thompson Pl 78226   210-444-7675
Lourdes Calderon, prin.   Fax 444-7698
Garcia MS   600/6-8
3306 Ruiz St 78228   210-444-8075
Anne Lackner, prin.   Fax 444-8098
Kennedy HS   1,500/9-12
1922 S General McMullen Dr 78226   210-444-8040
Owen J. Kelly, prin.   Fax 444-8020
Memorial HS   1,400/9-12
1227 Memorial St 78228   210-444-8300
George Colon, prin.   Fax 444-8336
Truman MS   500/6-8
1018 NW 34th St 78228   210-444-8425
Sharon Luce, prin.   Fax 444-8448
Wrenn MS   600/6-8
627 S Acme Rd 78237   210-444-8475
Patricia Zambrano, prin.   Fax 444-8498

Ft. Sam Houston ISD   1,300/PK-12
1902 Winans Rd 78234   210-368-8701
Dr. Gail E. Siller, supt.   Fax 368-8741
www.fort-sam-houston.k12.tx.us
Cole JSHS   500/7-12
1900 Winans Rd 78234   210-368-8730
Roland Rios, prin.   Fax 368-8731

Harlandale ISD   13,400/PK-12
102 Genevieve Dr 78214   210-921-4300
Dr. Guillermo Zavala, supt.   Fax 921-4334
www.harlandale.k12.tx.us
Harlandale HS   1,900/9-12
114 E Gerald Ave 78214   210-977-1000
Rey Madrigal, prin.   Fax 924-2335
Harlandale MS   900/6-8
300 W Huff Ave 78214   210-921-4507
Kathryn Pena, prin.   Fax 977-8764
Kingsborough MS   700/6-8
422 E Ashley Rd 78221   210-921-4428
William Hall, prin.   Fax 977-9463
Leal MS   800/6-8
743 W Southcross Blvd 78211   210-921-4570
Robert Villafranca, prin.   Fax 977-8764
McCollum HS   1,700/9-12
500 W Formosa Blvd 78221   210-921-4500
David Stelmazewski, prin.   Fax 921-9673
Wells MS   800/6-8
422 W Hutchins Pl 78221   210-921-4774
Diana Casas, prin.   Fax 923-5126

Judson ISD
Supt. — See Live Oak
Kirby MS   1,300/6-8
5441 Seguin Rd 78219   210-661-1140
Sharon Roddy, prin.   Fax 669-9275
Metzger MS   6-8
7475 Binz Engleman Rd 78244   210-662-2210
Dawn Brown, prin.   Fax 662-8390
Wagner HS   9-11
3000 N Foster Rd 78244   210-662-5000
Joe Gonzalez, prin.   Fax 662-9896
Woodlake Hills MS   1,600/6-8
6625 Woodlake Pkwy 78244   210-661-1110
Verna Ruffin, prin.   Fax 666-0169

Lackland ISD 1,000/PK-12
2460 Kenly Ave Bldg 8265 78236 210-357-5000
Dr. David Splitek, supt. Fax 357-5050
www.lacklandisd.net/
Stacey JSHS 300/7-12
2460 Kenly Ave Bldg 8265 78236 210-357-5100
Burnie Roper, prin. Fax 357-5109

North East ISD 55,600/PK-12
8961 Tesoro Dr 78217 210-804-7000
Dr. Richard Middleton, supt. Fax 804-7017
www.neisd.net
Bradley MS 1,400/6-8
14819 Heimer Rd 78232 210-491-8300
Terry Peel, prin. Fax 491-8314
Bush MS 1,400/6-8
1500 Evans Rd 78258 210-491-8450
Randy Hoyer, prin. Fax 491-8471
Churchill HS 2,700/9-12
12049 Blanco Rd 78216 210-442-0800
Joe Reasons, prin. Fax 442-0879
Driscoll MS 1,500/6-8
17150 Jones Maltsberger Rd 78247 210-491-6450
Jackie Lipski, prin. Fax 491-6467
Eisenhower MS 1,200/6-8
8231 Blanco Rd 78216 210-442-0500
Gary Chambers, prin. Fax 442-0537
Garner MS 900/6-8
4302 Harry Wurzbach Rd 78209 210-805-5100
Peggy Clemons, prin. Fax 805-5138
Harris MS, 5300 Knollcreek 78247 6-8
Peggy Clemmons, prin. 210-805-5348
International HS of America 400/9-12
1400 Jackson Keller Rd 78213 210-442-0404
Kristopher Wickerham, prin. Fax 442-0409
Jackson MS 1,000/6-8
4538 Vance Jackson Rd 78230 210-442-0550
Tom Defosset, prin. Fax 442-0580
Krueger MS 1,100/6-8
438 Lanark Dr 78218 210-650-1350
Phyllis Hickey, prin. Fax 650-1374
Lee HS 2,000/9-12
1400 Jackson Keller Rd 78213 210-442-0300
Michael Keranen, prin. Fax 442-0325
MacArthur HS 2,500/9-12
2923 E Bitters Rd 78217 210-650-1100
Bobbie Turnbo, prin. Fax 650-1195
Madison HS 2,900/9-12
5005 Stahl Rd 78247 210-637-4400
Chris Thompson, prin. Fax 637-4435
Nimitz Academy 900/6-8
5426 Blanco Rd 78216 210-442-0450
Thalia Chaney, prin. Fax 442-0489
Reagan HS 3,100/9-12
19000 Ronald Reagan 78258 210-482-2200
Bill Boyd, prin. Fax 482-2222
Roosevelt HS 2,400/9-12
5110 Walzem Rd 78218 210-650-1200
Robert Todd, prin. Fax 650-1291
Tejeda MS 1,200/6-8
2909 E Evans Rd 78259 210-482-2260
Nalzane White, prin. Fax 482-2277
White MS 1,000/6-8
7800 Midcrown Dr 78218 210-650-1400
Fax 650-1443
Wood MS 1,300/6-8
14800 Judson Rd 78233 210-650-1300
Kaye Fenn, prin. Fax 650-1309

Northside ISD 70,900/PK-12
5900 Evers Rd 78238 210-397-8500
Kay Cavanaugh, admin. Fax 706-8772
www.nisd.net
Business Careers HS 9-12
6500 Ingram Rd 78238 210-397-7070
Geri Berger, prin. Fax 706-7076
Clark HS 2,700/9-12
5150 De Zavala Rd 78249 210-397-5150
Brian Woods, prin. Fax 561-5211
Communications Arts HS 9-12
11600 W FM 471 78253 210-397-6043
James Buchanan, prin. Fax 688-6092
Connally MS 1,400/6-8
8661 Silent Sunrise 78250 210-397-1000
Linda Garcia, prin. Fax 257-1004
Health Careers HS 800/9-12
4646 Hamilton Wolfe Rd 78229 210-397-5400
Jacqueline Horras, prin. Fax 617-5423
Hobby MS 1,000/6-8
11843 Vance Jackson Rd 78230 210-397-6300
Ray Moncus, prin. Fax 690-6332
Holmes HS 2,100/9-12
6500 Ingram Rd 78238 210-397-7000
Corinne Saldana, prin. Fax 706-7030
Jay HS 3,200/9-12
7611 Marbach Rd 78227 210-397-2700
Gerardo Marquez, prin. Fax 678-2753
Jay Science and Engineering Academy 9-12
7611 Marbach Rd 78227 210-397-2700
Peggy Greff, prin. Fax 678-2753
Jones MS 1,100/6-8
1256 Pinn Rd 78227 210-397-2100
Erika Foerster, prin. Fax 678-2113
Jordan MS 1,700/6-8
1725 Richland Hills Dr 78251 210-397-6150
Jennifer Alvarez, prin. Fax 523-4876
Luna MS 6-8
200 Grosenbacher Rd N 78253 210-397-5300
Lynn Pierson, prin.
Marshall HS 2,500/9-12
8000 Lobo Ln 78240 210-397-7100
Steven Daniel, prin. Fax 706-7175
Neff MS 1,000/6-8
5227 Evers Rd 78238 210-397-4100
Sylvia Wade, prin. Fax 523-4566
Northside Vocational Transition S Vo/Tech
4711 Sid Katz Dr 78229 210-397-2401
David Lamoureux, prin. Fax 615-2411
Pease MS 1,200/6-8
201 Hunt Ln 78245 210-397-2950
Kevin Kearns, prin. Fax 678-2974
Rawlinson MS 900/6-8
14100 Vance Jackson Rd 78249 210-397-4900
Nancy Pena, prin. Fax 767-4055
Rayburn MS 800/6-8
1400 Cedarhurst Dr 78227 210-397-2150
Eric Tobias, prin. Fax 678-2181
Rudder MS 1,100/6-8
6558 Horn Blvd 78240 210-397-5000
Scott Zolinski, prin. Fax 561-5022
Stevens HS 9-12
600 N Ellison Dr 78251 210-397-6450
Harold Maldonado, prin. Fax 706-8772
Stevenson MS 1,600/6-8
8403 Tezel Rd 78254 210-397-7300
Glenda Munson, prin. Fax 706-7336
Stinson MS 1,500/6-8
13200 Skyhawk Dr 78249 210-397-3600
Willie Frantzen, prin. Fax 561-3609
Sul Ross MS 1,000/6-8
3630 Callaghan Rd 78228 210-397-6350
Deonna Dean, prin. Fax 431-6383
Taft HS 2,700/9-12
11600 W FM 471 78253 210-397-6000
Tommy Garcia, prin. Fax 688-6091
Warren HS 2,500/9-12
9411 W Military Dr 78251 210-397-4200
Patty Denham-Hill, prin. Fax 257-4246
Zachry MS 1,600/6-8
9410 Timber Path 78250 210-397-7400
Javier Martinez, prin. Fax 706-7432
Northside Evening HS Adult
6500 Ingram Rd 78238 210-397-7060
Ruben Perez, prin. Fax 706-7060
Other Schools – See Helotes

San Antonio ISD 56,500/PK-12
141 Lavaca St 78210 210-299-5500
Dr. Ruben Olivarez, supt. Fax 299-5580
www.saisd.net
Brackenridge HS 1,900/9-12
400 Eagleland Dr 78210 210-533-8144
Linda Marsh, prin. Fax 534-9770
Burbank HS 1,300/9-12
1002 Edwards 78204 210-532-4241
Andrew Rodriguez, prin. Fax 533-4394
Connell MS 700/6-8
400 Hot Wells Blvd 78223 210-534-6511
Eduardo Elizondo, prin. Fax 534-6589
Cooper MS 400/6-8
1700 Tampico St 78207 210-223-9031
Beatrice Hammodeh, prin. Fax 223-9598
Davis MS 800/6-8
4702 E Houston St 78220 210-662-8184
Ruben Fernandez, prin. Fax 662-8189
Edison HS 1,700/9-12
701 Santa Monica 78212 210-733-9147
Charles Munoz, prin. Fax 738-2408
Fox Tech HS Vo/Tech
637 N Main Ave 78205 210-226-5103
Nancy York, prin. Fax 224-8792
Harris MS 500/6-8
325 Pruitt Ave 78204 210-226-4952
Moises Ortiz, prin. Fax 226-9448
Highlands HS 2,200/9-12
3118 Elgin Ave 78210 210-333-0421
Lisa Contreras, prin. Fax 337-2567
Houston HS 1,100/9-12
4635 E Houston St 78220 210-661-4134
Melonie Hammons, prin. Fax 666-2915
Irving MS 900/6-8
1300 Delgado St 78207 210-734-2937
Anita Chavera, prin. Fax 734-0941
Jefferson HS 1,900/9-12
723 Donaldson Ave 78201 210-736-1981
David Udovich, prin. Fax 738-2406
Lanier HS 1,500/9-12
1514 W Durango Blvd 78207 210-223-2926
Richard Solis, prin. Fax 224-9516
Longfellow MS 700/6-8
1130 E Sunshine Dr 78228 210-433-0311
Liz Solis, prin. Fax 433-0375
Lowell MS 500/6-8
919 Thompson Pl 78226 210-223-4741
Armando Rene Gutierrez, prin. Fax 223-6248
Mann MS 600/6-8
2123 W Huisache Ave 78201 210-732-4851
Linda Nance, prin. Fax 732-7999
Page MS 600/6-8
401 Berkshire Ave 78210 210-533-7331
Gary Pollock, prin. Fax 533-7369
Poe MS 900/6-8
814 Aransas Ave 78210 210-534-6331
Lorna Klokkenga, prin. Fax 534-7299
Rhodes MS 700/6-8
3000 Tampico St 78207 210-433-5092
Edward Garcia, prin. Fax 433-7299
Rogers MS 800/6-8
314 Galway St 78223 210-333-7551
Kathy Tackett, prin. Fax 333-7954
Tafolla MS 900/6-8
1303 W Durango Blvd 78207 210-227-3383
Sylvia Lopez, prin. Fax 227-7044
Twain MS 700/6-8
2411 San Pedro Ave 78212 210-732-4641
Janet Mansmann, prin. Fax 738-0518
Wheatley MS 600/6-8
415 Gabriel 78202 210-227-3921
Everett Fuller, prin. Fax 227-9972
Whittier MS 800/6-8
2101 Edison Dr 78201 210-735-7181
Linda Sanchez, prin. Fax 735-0704

South San Antonio ISD 9,900/PK-12
2515 Bobcat Ln 78224 210-977-7000
Ron Durbon, supt. Fax 977-7021
www.southsanisd.net
Dwight MS 800/6-8
2454 W Southcross Blvd 78211 210-977-7300
Tommy Fonseca, prin. Fax 977-7316
Kazen MS 800/6-8
1520 Gillette Blvd 78224 210-977-7150
Steve Veazey, prin. Fax 977-7155
Shepard MS 600/6-8
5558 Ray Ellison Blvd 78242 210-623-1875
Blanca Gonzalez, prin. Fax 623-1880
South San Antonio Career Ed Vo/Tech
2615 Navajo St 78224 210-977-7350
Bob Norman, prin. Fax 977-7356
South San Antonio HS 1,800/9-12
2515 Bobcat Ln 78224 210-977-7400
Victor Ortiz, prin. Fax 977-7430
South San Antonio HS West 600/9-12
5622 Ray Ellison Blvd 78242 210-623-1800
Priscilla Mihalic, prin. Fax 623-1812
Zamora MS 6-8
2515 Bobcat Ln 78224 210-977-7000
Fax 977-7021
Southside ISD 5,200/PK-12
1460 Martinez Losoya Rd 78221 210-882-1600
Dr. Mard A. Herrick, supt. Fax 626-0101
www.southside.k12.tx.us
Southside HS 1,200/9-12
1460 Martinez Losoya Rd 78221 210-882-1606
Martha Quijano, prin. Fax 626-0119
Southside MS 1,100/6-8
1460 Martinez Losoya Rd 78221 210-882-1601
R. Chris Christian, prin. Fax 626-0113

Southwest ISD 9,700/PK-12
11914 Dragon Ln 78252 210-622-4300
Dr. Velma Villegas, supt. Fax 622-4301
www.swisd.net/
McAuliffe JHS 700/7-8
11914 Dragon Ln 78252 210-623-6260
Michael Wagner, prin. Fax 623-6261
Scobee JHS 800/7-8
11914 Dragon Ln 78252 210-645-7500
Lisa Klein, prin. Fax 645-7501
Southwest HS 2,600/9-12
11914 Dragon Ln 78252 210-622-4500
Charlene Walden, prin. Fax 622-4501

Antonian College Preparatory HS 600/9-12
6425 West Ave 78213 210-344-9265
Gilbert Saenz, prin. Fax 344-9267
Atonement Academy 200/PK-12
15415 Red Robin Rd 78255 210-695-2944
Richard Arndt, hdmstr. Fax 695-9679
Baptist Health System Post-Sec.
215 E Quincy St 78215 210-297-1040
Baptist University of the Americas Post-Sec.
8019 S Panam Expy 78224 800-721-1396
Believers Academy 200/K-12
13714 Lookout Rd 78233 210-656-2999
Rollin Mayes, hdmstr. Fax 656-1226
Blessed Hope Academy 100/10-12
12721 Mountain Air 78249 210-697-9191
Alice Ashcraft, dir. Fax 690-9299
Cancer Therapy and Research Center Post-Sec.
7979 Wurzbach Rd 78229 210-616-6669
Career Advancement & Applied Technology Post-Sec.
9350 S Presa St 78223 210-633-1000
Career Point Institute Post-Sec.
485 Spencer Ln 78201 210-732-3000
Career Quest Post-Sec.
5430 Frdrcksburg Rd #310 78229 210-366-2701
Castle Hills First Baptist S 300/K-12
2220 NW Military Hwy 78213 210-377-8485
Jim Bazar, hdmstr. Fax 377-8473
Central Catholic HS 500/9-12
1403 N Saint Marys St 78215 210-225-6794
Pat Cunningham, prin. Fax 227-9353
Christian Academy of San Antonio 500/PK-12
325 Castroville Rd 78207 210-436-2277
Yolanda Molina, prin. Fax 436-2210
Christian Heritage S 400/PK-12
16316 San Pedro Ave 78232 210-496-1644
Joel Arnold, prin. Fax 496-1993
Christian Military Academy 100/6-12
6500 N IH 35 78218 210-653-2262
Trina Cardenas, admin. Fax 653-9262
Cornerstone Christian S 700/PK-12
4802 Vance Jackson Rd 78230 210-979-9203
Alan Hulme, admin. Fax 979-0310
Ewing Educational Center 50/K-12
PO Box 290309 78280 210-732-7550
Billy G. Burchfield, prin. Fax 732-7559
Galen Health Institute School of Nursing Post-Sec.
4440 Piedras Dr S Ste 200 78228 210-733-3056
Gateway Christian S 100/PK-12
6623 Five Palms Dr 78242 210-674-5703
Roger Gaines, prin. Fax 674-6811
Hallmark Institute of Aeronautics Post-Sec.
8901 Wetmore Rd 78216 210-826-1000
Hallmark Institute of Technology Post-Sec.
10401 W IH 10 78230 210-690-9000
Harvest Academy 400/PK-12
1270 N Loop 1604 E 78232 210-490-2277
Jim Fleetwood, prin. Fax 490-3262
Healy-Murphy Center HS 200/9-12
618 Live Oak 78202 210-223-2944
Janie Whiteley, prin. Fax 224-1033
Holy Cross HS 500/6-12
426 N San Felipe Ave 78228 210-433-9395
Br. Stanley Culotta, pres. Fax 433-1666
Incarnate Word HS 600/9-12
727 E Hildebrand Ave 78212 210-829-3100
B. J. Nelsen, prin. Fax 829-3120
International Bible Center Post-Sec.
2369 Benrus Blvd 78228 210-434-5541
ITT Technical Institute Post-Sec.
5700 Northwest Pkwy 78249 210-694-4612
Keystone S 400/K-12
119 E Craig Pl 78212 210-735-4022
Hugh McIntosh, hdmstr. Fax 734-5508
Laurel Ridge S 100/K-12
17720 Corporate Woods Dr 78259 210-491-9400
Lutheran HS of San Antonio 100/9-12
6487 Whitby Rd 78240 210-694-4962
Fax 694-9150
Mims Classic Beauty College Post-Sec.
5121 Blanco Rd 78216 210-344-2041
National Institute of Technology Post-Sec.
6550 1st Park Ten Blvd #210 78213 210-732-7800
New Life Christian Academy 200/K-12
6622 Highway 90 W 78227 210-679-6001
Anthony Jackson, prin. Fax 679-6080
Northwest Vista College Post-Sec.
3535 N Ellison Dr 78251 210-348-2001
Oblate School of Theology Post-Sec.
285 Oblate Dr 78216 210-341-1366
Our Lady of the Lake University Post-Sec.
411 SW 24th St 78207 210-434-6711
Palo Alto College Post-Sec.
1400 W Villaret Blvd 78224 210-921-5000
Providence MSHS 500/6-12
1215 N Saint Marys St 78215 210-224-6651
Anne Bristol, prin. Fax 224-6214
Rainbow Hills Baptist S 300/PK-12
2255 Horal St 78227 210-674-0490
Rev. Dennis Wall, chncllr. Fax 674-3615
St. Anthony HS 200/9-12
3200 McCullough Ave 78212 210-832-5600
Joseph Hannon, prin. Fax 832-5615
St. Gerard HS 200/9-12
521 S New Braunfels Ave 78203 210-533-8061
Katheryn Stanbridge, prin. Fax 533-3697

St. Mary's Hall 900/PK-12
  9401 Starcrest Dr 78217 210-483-9100
  Bob Windham, hdmstr. Fax 483-9299
St. Mary's University of San Antonio Post-Sec.
  1 Camino Santa Maria St 78228 210-436-3011
St. Phillip's College Post-Sec.
  1801 Martin Luther King Dr 78203 210-531-3200
San Antonio Beauty College #3 Post-Sec.
  4130 Naco Perrin Blvd 78217 210-654-9734
San Antonio Beauty College #4 Post-Sec.
  2423 Jamar St # 2 78226 210-433-7222
San Antonio Christian HS 300/9-12
  19202 Redland Rd # F 78259 210-340-1864
  Joseph Todd Holzmann, prin. Fax 530-9624
San Antonio Christian MS 200/6-8
  19202 Redland Rd # F 78259 210-340-1864
  Dr. Thomas Erbaugh, prin. Fax 348-6030
San Antonio College Post-Sec.
  1300 San Pedro Ave 78212 210-733-2000
San Antonio College Medical Dental Asst. Post-Sec.
  7142 San Pedro Ave Ste 100 78216 800-840-3101
Sendero Christian Academy 400/PK-12
  5408 Daughtry Dr 78238 210-543-7218
  Roberto Lara, admin. Fax 543-7368
Southern Careers Institute Post-Sec.
  1405 N Main Ave Ste 100 78212 210-271-0096
Sunnybrook Christian Academy 300/PK-12
  1620 Pinn Rd 78227 210-674-8000
  Trudie Perez, admin. Fax 673-4603
SW School of Business & Tech Careers Post-Sec.
  602 W Southcross Blvd 78221 210-921-0951
SW School of Business & Tech Careers Post-Sec.
  2402 San Pedro Ave 78212 210-731-8449
Texas Beauty College Post-Sec.
  6151 NW Loop 410 Ste 201 78238 210-647-5100
Texas Careers Post-Sec.
  1015 Jackson-Keller Rd #102 78213 210-308-8584
TMI - The Episcopal S of Texas 300/6-12
  20955 W Tejas Trl 78257 210-698-7171
  James Freeman, hdmstr. Fax 698-0715
Trinity Christian Academy 200/K-12
  5401 N Loop 1604 E 78247 210-653-2800
  Susan Oldfield, prin. Fax 653-0303
Trinity University Post-Sec.
  715 Stadium Dr 78212 210-999-7011
University Hospital Post-Sec.
  4502 Medical Dr 78229 210-616-2000
University of Texas at San Antonio Post-Sec.
  6900 N Loop 1604 W 78249 210-458-4011
University of Texas Health Science Ctr. Post-Sec.
  7703 Floyd Curl Dr 78229 210-567-7000
University of the Incarnate Word Post-Sec.
  4301 Broadway St 78209 210-829-6000
Winston S 200/K-12
  8565 Ewing Halsell Dr 78229 210-615-6544
  Dr. Charles Karulak, prin. Fax 615-6627

San Augustine, San Augustine, Pop. 2,475
San Augustine ISD 900/PK-12
  702 High School Dr 75972 936-275-2306
  Marshall McMillan, supt. Fax 275-9776
  www.san-augustine.k12.tx.us
San Augustine HS 300/9-12
  702 High School Dr 75972 936-275-9603
  George Cox, prin. Fax 275-9829
San Augustine IS 300/5-8
  1002 Barrett St 75972 936-275-2318
  Warren Norvell, prin. Fax 275-2962

San Benito, Cameron, Pop. 24,208
San Benito Consolidated ISD 9,800/PK-12
  240 N Crockett St 78586 956-361-6110
  Antonio Limon, supt. Fax 361-6115
  www.sanbenito.k12.tx.us
Cabaza MS 1,000/6-8
  2901 Shafer Rd 78586 956-361-6600
  Mary Alice Martinez, prin. Fax 361-6608
Jordan MS 1,200/6-8
  700 N McCullough St 78586 956-361-6650
  Joel Wood, prin. Fax 361-6658
San Benito HS 1,500/10-12
  450 S Williams Rd 78586 956-361-6500
  Jesus Amaya, prin. Fax 361-6508
San Benito Riverside MS 6-8
  35428 Padilla St 78586 956-361-6110
San Benito Veterans Memorial Academy 900/9-9
  2115 N Williams Rd 78586 956-361-6000
  Elaine Sandell, prin. Fax 361-6008

South Texas ISD
  Supt. — See Mercedes
South Texas Acad of Medical Technology 100/9-12
  151 N Helen Moore Rd 78586 956-399-4331
  Harry Goette, prin. Fax 399-3570

Sanderson, Terrell, Pop. 1,128
Terrell County ISD 200/PK-12
  PO Box 747 79848 432-345-2515
  Gary Hamilton, supt. Fax 345-2670
  www.terrell.esc18.net
Sanderson HS 100/9-12
  PO Box 747 79848 432-345-2282
  Gary Hamilton, prin. Fax 345-2404
Sanderson JHS 50/6-8
  PO Box 747 79848 432-345-2601
   Fax 345-2670

San Diego, Duval, Pop. 4,633
San Diego ISD 1,500/PK-12
  609 W Labbe St 78384 361-279-3382
  Luis A. Pizzini, supt. Fax 279-2267
  www.sdisd.esc2.net
Jaime JHS 400/6-8
  609 W Labbe St 78384 361-279-3382
  Sam Bueno, prin. Fax 279-3139
San Diego HS 500/9-12
  609 W Labbe St 78384 361-279-3544
  Nora Casarez, prin. Fax 279-5098

San Elizario, El Paso, Pop. 4,385
San Elizario ISD 3,300/PK-12
  PO Box 920 79849 915-872-3900
  Mike Quatrini, supt. Fax 872-3903
  www.seisd.net
San Elizario HS 1,000/9-12
  PO Box 920 79849 915-872-3970
  Joe Keith, prin. Fax 872-3971
San Elizario MS 800/6-8
  PO Box 920 79849 915-872-3960
  Linda Rodriguez, prin. Fax 872-3961

Sanger, Denton, Pop. 5,122
Sanger ISD 2,200/PK-12
  PO Box 2399 76266 940-458-7438
  Jack Biggerstaff, supt. Fax 458-5140
  sisd.sangerisd.net
Sanger HS 600/9-12
  100 Indian Ln 76266 940-458-7497
  Mary Edwards, prin. Fax 458-4637
Sanger MS 400/7-8
  105 Berry St 76266 940-458-7916
  Bob Danley, prin. Fax 458-5111

San Isidro, Starr
San Isidro ISD 300/PK-12
  PO Box 10 78588 956-481-3110
  Miguel Garcia, supt. Fax 481-3950
San Isidro HS 100/9-12
  PO Box 10 78588 956-481-3110
  Miguel Garcia, prin. Fax 481-3950

San Juan, Hidalgo, Pop. 28,894
Pharr-San Juan-Alamo ISD
  Supt. — See Pharr
Austin MS 900/6-8
  804 S Stewart Rd 78589 956-702-5849
  Elias Hernandez, prin. Fax 702-5858
Pharr-San Juan-Alamo HS 2,200/9-12
  805 Ridge Rd 78589 956-783-2200
  Rene Ramirez, prin. Fax 783-2293
San Juan MS 1,100/6-8
  1229 S I Rd 78589 956-783-3800
  Corina Ramirez, prin. Fax 783-3811

San Marcos, Hays, Pop. 43,007
San Marcos Consolidated ISD 7,200/PK-12
  4020 Monterrey Oak 78667 512-393-6700
  Dr. Sylvester Perez, supt. Fax 393-6709
  www.smcisd.net/
Goodnight JHS 600/7-8
  1805 Peter Garza Dr 78666 512-393-6550
  Steve Dow, prin. Fax 393-6560
Miller JHS 500/7-8
  301 Foxtail Run 78666 512-393-6660
  Jon Orozco, prin. Fax 393-6602
San Marcos HS 1,900/9-12
  1301 N State Highway 123 78666 512-393-6800
  Dr. Chad Kelly, prin. Fax 392-8927

Gary Job Corps Center Post-Sec.
  PO Box 967 78667 512-396-6561
San Marcos Adventist Academy 50/PK-10
  1523 Ranch Rd 12 78666 512-392-9475
   Fax 392-2693
San Marcos Baptist Academy 200/7-12
  2801 Ranch Rd 12 78666 512-753-8000
  Robert Bryant, prin. Fax 753-8031
Texas State University - San Marcos Post-Sec.
  601 University Dr 78666 512-245-2111

San Perlita, Willacy, Pop. 682
San Perlita ISD 200/PK-12
  PO Box 37 78590 956-248-5563
  Marco Lara, supt. Fax 248-5561
  www.spisd.org
San Perlita HS 100/9-12
  PO Box 37 78590 956-248-5250
  Doyle Todd, prin. Fax 248-5103
San Perlita MS 50/7-8
  PO Box 37 78590 956-248-5250
  Doyle Todd, prin. Fax 248-5103

San Saba, San Saba, Pop. 2,635
San Saba ISD 800/PK-12
  808 W Wallace St 76877 325-372-3771
  Johnny Clawson, supt. Fax 372-5977
  www.san-saba.net
San Saba JHS 200/9-12
  808 W Wallace St 76877 325-372-3786
  Kevy Allred, prin. Fax 372-3478
San Saba MS 200/5-8
  808 W Wallace St 76877 325-372-3200
  Dave Underwood, prin. Fax 372-5228

Santa Anna, Coleman, Pop. 1,029
Santa Anna ISD 300/K-12
  701 Bowie St 76878 325-348-3136
  Roger Walker, supt. Fax 348-3141
  santaanna.netxv.net/
Santa Anna HS 100/7-12
  701 Bowie St 76878 325-348-3137
  David Robinett, prin. Fax 348-3149

Santa Fe, Galveston, Pop. 10,259
Santa Fe ISD 4,500/PK-12
  PO Box 370 77510 409-925-3526
  Dr. Jon Whittemore, supt. Fax 925-4002
  www.sfisd.org/
Santa Fe HS 1,300/9-12
  PO Box 370 77510 409-925-3526
  Mike VanEssen, prin. Fax 925-0658
Santa Fe JHS 800/7-8
  PO Box 370 77510 409-925-3526
  Dr. Joan Bowman, prin. Fax 925-4002

Santa Maria, Cameron, Pop. 500
Santa Maria ISD 600/PK-12
  PO Box 448 78592 956-565-6308
  Homero Garcia, supt. Fax 565-4422
Santa Maria HS 200/9-12
  PO Box 448 78592 956-565-9144
  Francisco Garcia, prin. Fax 514-1968
Santa Maria MS, PO Box 448 78592 200/5-8
  David Almaguer, prin. 956-565-6309

Santa Rosa, Cameron, Pop. 2,910
Santa Rosa ISD 1,200/PK-12
  PO Box 368 78593 956-636-1813
  Carlos Guerra, prin. Fax 636-2168
  www.santarosaisd.org
Nelson MS 300/6-8
  PO Box 368 78593 956-636-1246
  Andres Contreras, prin. Fax 636-1725
Santa Rosa HS 300/9-12
  PO Box 368 78593 956-636-1811
  Eberto Mirelos, prin. Fax 636-1139

Santo, Palo Pinto
Santo ISD 500/PK-12
  PO Box 67 76472 940-769-2835
  G. Gilbert, supt. Fax 769-3116
  www.santoisd.net/

Santo JSHS 300/6-12
  PO Box 67 76472 940-769-3847
  Mike Scott, prin. Fax 769-2796

Saratoga, Hardin
West Hardin County Consolidated ISD 700/PK-12
  39227 Highway 105 77585 936-274-5061
  T. Brad Lane, supt. Fax 274-4321
  www.esc5.net/whccisd
West Hardin HS 200/9-12
  39227 Highway 105 77585 936-274-5061
  Wilt Alexander, prin. Fax 274-5671
West Hardin JHS 100/6-8
  39227 Highway 105 77585 936-274-5061
  Fran Bledsoe, prin. Fax 274-5671

Savoy, Fannin, Pop. 878
Savoy ISD 300/PK-12
  302 W Hayes St 75479 903-965-5262
  Brian Neal, supt. Fax 965-7282
  www.savoyisd.org
Savoy JSHS 200/7-12
  302 W Hayes St 75479 903-965-6404
  Kelly Mercy, prin. Fax 965-5608

Schertz, Guadalupe, Pop. 23,690
Schertz-Cibolo-Universal City ISD 7,400/PK-12
  1060 Elbel Rd 78154 210-945-6200
  Belinda Pustka, supt. Fax 945-6252
  www.scuc.txed.net
Clemens HS 2,200/9-12
  1001 Elbel Rd 78154 210-945-6100
  Jeff Bryan, prin. Fax 945-6171
Corbett JHS 600/7-8
  301 Main 78154 210-945-6350
  Jay Muennink, prin. Fax 945-6360
Other Schools – See Cibolo

Schulenburg, Fayette, Pop. 2,752
Schulenburg ISD 800/PK-12
  517 North St 78956 979-743-3448
  Dr. Dale Pitts, supt. Fax 743-4721
  www.schulenburg.txed.net
Schulenburg HS 400/7-12
  150 College St 78956 979-743-3605
  Gary McNeal, prin. Fax 743-4721

Blinn College Post-Sec.
  100 Ranger Dr 78956 979-743-5003

Scurry, Kaufman
Scurry-Rosser ISD 800/PK-12
  10705 S State Highway 34 75158 972-452-8823
  Micheal French, supt. Fax 452-8586
  www.scurry-rosser.com/
Scurry-Rosser HS 200/9-12
  8321 S State Highway 34 75158 972-452-8823
  Dan Taylor, prin. Fax 452-8902
Scurry-Rosser MS 300/5-8
  10729 S State Highway 34 75158 972-452-8823
  Chris Couch, prin. Fax 452-8586

Seabrook, Harris, Pop. 10,822
Clear Creek ISD
  Supt. — See League City
Seabrook IS 1,000/6-8
  2401 Meyer Rd 77586 281-284-3100
  David Williams, prin. Fax 284-3105

Seagraves, Gaines, Pop. 2,296
Seagraves ISD 500/PK-12
  PO Box 577 79359 806-387-2035
  Wynn Robinson, supt. Fax 387-2451
  seagraves.esc17.net/
Seagraves HS 200/9-12
  PO Box 1505 79359 806-387-2520
  Eric Beam, prin. Fax 387-2944
Seagraves MS 100/6-8
  PO Box 938 79359 806-387-2646
  Clay Mahler, prin. Fax 387-2451

Sealy, Austin, Pop. 5,771
Sealy ISD 2,400/PK-12
  939 Tiger Ln 77474 979-885-3516
  Charles Uselton, supt. Fax 885-6457
  www.sealyisd.com
Sealy HS 700/9-12
  2372 Championship Dr 77474 979-885-3515
  David Hill, prin. Fax 987-3398
Sealy JHS 500/6-8
  939 Tiger Ln 77474 979-885-3292
  Scott Kana, prin. Fax 885-6457

Blinn College Post-Sec.
  3701 Outlet Center Dr 77474 979-627-7997

Seguin, Guadalupe, Pop. 23,186
Navarro ISD 1,300/PK-12
  6450 N State Highway 123 78155 830-372-1930
  Dr. David Harriger, supt. Fax 372-1853
  www.navarroisd.us
Navarro HS 400/9-12
  6450 N State Highway 123 78155 830-372-1931
  Mary Springs, prin. Fax 379-3135
Navarro MS 400/5-8
  300 Link Rd 78155 830-372-1943
  Luke Morales, prin. Fax 379-3170

Seguin ISD 7,900/PK-12
  1221 E Kingsbury St 78155 830-372-5771
  Dr. Irene Garza, supt. Fax 379-0392
  www.seguin.k12.tx.us
Barnes MS 500/7-8
  1539 Joe Carrillo Blvd 78155 830-379-4717
  Rey Garcia, prin. Fax 379-4239
Briesemeister MS 600/7-8
  1616 W Court St 78155 830-379-0600
  G. Moreno, prin. Fax 379-0615
Seguin HS 2,000/9-12
  815 Lamar 78155 830-372-5770
   Fax 372-9851

Lifegate Christian S 100/K-12
  395 Lifegate Ln 78155 830-372-0850
  Tina Lee, prin. Fax 372-0895
Seguin Beauty College Post-Sec.
  102 E Court St 78155 830-372-0935
Texas Lutheran University Post-Sec.
  1000 W Court St 78155 830-372-8000

Seminole, Gaines, Pop. 5,839
Seminole ISD — 2,200/PK-12
207 SW 6th St 79360 — 432-758-3662
Doug Harriman, supt. — Fax 758-9833
www.seminole.k12.tx.us
Seminole HS — 600/9-12
2100 NW Avenue D 79360 — 432-758-5873
Don Worth, prin. — Fax 758-8146
Seminole JHS — 500/6-8
601 SW Avenue B 79360 — 432-758-9431
Cary Moring, prin. — Fax 758-5795

Seven Points, Henderson, Pop. 1,229

Lake Pointe Christian Academy — 50/PK-12
1724 N Tool Dr 75143 — 903-432-4476
Rev. Curtis Baker, admin. — Fax 432-1898

Seymour, Baylor, Pop. 2,773
Seymour ISD — 700/PK-12
409 W Idaho St 76380 — 940-889-3525
Dr. John Baker, supt. — Fax 889-5340
www.esc9.net/seymourisd
Seymour HS — 200/9-12
409 W Idaho St 76380 — 940-888-2947
John Kaufman, prin. — Fax 889-1045
Seymour MS — 200/5-8
409 W Idaho St 76380 — 940-889-4548
Dr. Greg Roach, prin. — Fax 889-4962

Shallowater, Lubbock, Pop. 2,187
Shallowater ISD — 1,300/PK-12
1100 Avenue K 79363 — 806-832-4531
Phil Warren, supt. — Fax 832-4350
www.shallowaterisd.net
Shallowater HS — 400/9-12
1100 Avenue K 79363 — 806-832-4535
Tom Johnson, prin. — Fax 832-4523
Shallowater MS — 300/6-8
1100 Avenue K 79363 — 806-832-4531
Rick DeMasters, prin. — Fax 832-5543

Shamrock, Wheeler, Pop. 1,828
Shamrock ISD — 300/PK-12
100 S Illinois St 79079 — 806-256-3492
Ray Cogburn, supt. — Fax 256-3628
www.shamrockisd.net
Shamrock HS — 100/9-12
100 S Illinois St 79079 — 806-256-2241
Kenneth Shields, prin. — Fax 256-3628

Shelbyville, Shelby
Shelbyville ISD — 700/PK-12
PO Box 325 75973 — 936-598-2641
Dr. Ray West, supt. — Fax 598-6842
www.shelbyville.k12.tx.us
Shelbyville S — 700/PK-12
PO Box 325 75973 — 936-598-7323
Rudy Eddington, prin. — Fax 598-6842

Shepherd, San Jacinto, Pop. 2,186
Shepherd ISD — 1,900/PK-12
1401 S Byrd Ave 77371 — 936-628-3396
Michael Jansen, supt. — Fax 628-3841
www.shepherdisd.net/
Shepherd HS — 600/9-12
1401 S Byrd Ave 77371 — 936-628-3371
Michael Faulk, prin. — Fax 628-3841
Shepherd MS — 400/6-8
1401 S Byrd Ave 77371 — 936-628-3377
Jan Page, prin. — Fax 628-3841

Sherman, Grayson, Pop. 36,261
Sherman ISD — 6,000/PK-12
PO Box 1176 75091 — 903-891-6400
Rodney Hutto, supt. — Fax 891-6407
www.shermanisd.net
Piner MS — 1,000/7-8
402 W Pecan St 75090 — 903-891-6470
David Parker, prin. — Fax 891-6475
Sherman HS — 1,600/9-12
2201 E Lamar St 75090 — 903-891-6440
Thomas O'Neal, prin. — Fax 891-6446

Austin College — Post-Sec.
900 N Grand Ave 75090 — 903-813-2000
International Business School — Post-Sec.
4107 Texoma Pkwy 75090 — 903-893-6604
Texoma Christian S — 400/PK-12
3500 W Houston St 75092 — 903-893-7076
Dr. Eric Stricker, hdmstr. — Fax 891-8486

Shiner, Lavaca, Pop. 2,044
Shiner ISD — 500/PK-12
PO Box 804 77984 — 361-594-3121
Trey Lawrence, supt. — Fax 594-3925
www.shinerisd.net
Shiner JSHS — 200/7-12
PO Box 804 77984 — 361-594-3131
Trey Lawrence, prin. — Fax 594-4295

Shiner Catholic S — 300/PK-12
PO Box 725 77984 — 361-594-2313
Robert Whitworth, prin. — Fax 594-8599

Sidney, Comanche
Sidney ISD — 100/PK-12
PO Box 190 76474 — 254-842-5500
Doug Bowden, supt. — Fax 842-5731
www.sidney.esc14.net/
Sidney S — 100/PK-12
PO Box 190 76474 — 254-842-5500
Aletha Patterson, prin. — Fax 842-5731

Sierra Blanca, Hudspeth
Sierra Blanca ISD — 100/K-12
PO Box 308 79851 — 915-369-3741
Dr. Joseph Gallegos, supt. — Fax 369-2605
www.sierrablancaisd.com/
Sierra Blanca S — 100/K-12
PO Box 308 79851 — 915-369-2781
Juanita Snyder, prin. — Fax 369-2605

Silsbee, Hardin, Pop. 6,498
Silsbee ISD — 2,800/K-12
415 W Avenue N 77656 — 409-385-5286
James M. McGowan, supt. — Fax 385-6530
www.silsbee.k12.tx.us
Edwards-Johnson Memorial Silsbee MS — 700/6-8
1140 Highway 327 E 77656 — 409-385-2291
Kevin Wharton, prin. — Fax 386-5792

Silsbee HS — 900/9-12
1575 US Highway 96 N 77656 — 409-385-5574
Mike Day, prin. — Fax 385-9115

Silverton, Briscoe, Pop. 718
Silverton ISD — 200/PK-12
PO Box 608 79257 — 806-823-2476
Jerry Birdsong, supt. — Fax 823-2276
www.silvertonisd.net
Silverton S — 200/PK-12
PO Box 608 79257 — 806-823-2476
Sheryl Weaver, prin. — Fax 823-2276

Simms, Bowie
Simms ISD — 600/PK-12
PO Box 9 75574 — 903-543-2219
Rex Burks, supt. — Fax 543-2512
simms.esc8.net
Bowie HS — 100/9-12
PO Box 9 75574 — 903-543-2275
Brian Gray, prin. — Fax 543-2512
Bowie JHS — 100/6-8
PO Box 9 75574 — 903-543-2275
Brian Gray, prin. — Fax 543-2512

Sinton, San Patricio, Pop. 5,549
Sinton ISD — 2,100/PK-12
PO Box 1337 78387 — 361-364-6800
Mike Roberts, supt. — Fax 364-6905
www.sintonisd.net
Sinton HS — 600/9-12
400 N Pirate Blvd 78387 — 361-364-6652
David Patterson, prin. — Fax 364-6668
Smith JHS — 300/7-8
900 S San Patricio St 78387 — 361-364-6840
Stephen VanMatre, prin. — Fax 364-6856

Skidmore, Bee
Skidmore-Tynan ISD — 700/PK-12
PO Box 409 78389 — 361-287-3426
Dr. Brett Belmarez, supt. — Fax 287-3442
www.stisd.esc2.net
Skidmore-Tynan HS — 200/9-12
PO Box 409 78389 — 361-287-3426
Patricia Holubec, prin. — Fax 287-0146
Skidmore-Tynan JHS — 200/6-8
PO Box 409 78389 — 361-287-3426
Lawrence Carranco, prin. — Fax 287-0714

Slaton, Lubbock, Pop. 6,022
Slaton ISD — 1,400/PK-12
140 E Panhandle St 79364 — 806-828-6591
James Taliaferro, supt. — Fax 828-5506
www.slaton.esc17.net/
Slaton HS — 400/9-12
105 N 20th St 79364 — 806-828-5833
Chris Kennedy, prin. — Fax 828-1229
Slaton JHS — 300/6-8
300 W Jean St 79364 — 806-828-6583
Louie Spinks, prin. — Fax 828-2080

Slidell, Wise
Slidell ISD — 300/PK-12
PO Box 69 76267 — 940-466-3118
Greg Enis, supt. — Fax 466-3062
www.slidellisd.net/
Slidell JSHS — 100/7-12
PO Box 69 76267 — 940-466-3118
Jereme Dietz, prin. — Fax 466-3607

Smiley, Gonzales, Pop. 470
Nixon-Smiley Consolidated ISD
Supt. — See Nixon
Nixon-Smiley MS — 300/5-8
500 Anglin Rd 78159 — 830-587-6401
Gary Tausch, prin. — Fax 587-6558

Smithville, Bastrop, Pop. 4,391
Smithville ISD — 1,900/PK-12
PO Box 479 78957 — 512-237-2487
Gary Sage, supt. — Fax 237-2775
www.smithvilleisd.org
Smithville HS — 500/9-12
PO Box 479 78957 — 512-237-2451
Jim Manning, prin. — Fax 237-5643
Smithville JHS — 400/6-8
PO Box 479 78957 — 512-237-2407
Mary Liz Singleton, prin. — Fax 237-5624

Smyer, Hockley, Pop. 483
Smyer ISD — 400/PK-12
PO Box 206 79367 — 806-234-2935
Dane A. Kerns, supt. — Fax 234-2411
www.smyer-isd.org
Smyer JSHS — 200/7-12
PO Box 206 79367 — 806-234-3871
Bruce Cunningham, prin. — Fax 234-2411

Snook, Burleson, Pop. 584
Snook ISD — 500/PK-12
PO Box 87 77878 — 979-272-8307
Jim Copeland, supt. — Fax 272-5041
www.snookisd.com
Snook JSHS — 200/7-12
PO Box 87 77878 — 979-272-8307
Robert Reyes, prin. — Fax 272-5041

Snyder, Scurry, Pop. 10,536
Snyder ISD — 2,800/PK-12
2901 37th St 79549 — 325-573-5401
James R. Collins, supt. — Fax 573-9025
www.snyder.esc14.net
Snyder HS — 700/9-12
2901 37th St 79549 — 325-573-6301
Larry Scott, prin. — Fax 573-9500
Snyder JHS — 600/6-8
2901 37th St 79549 — 325-573-6356
Kellye Starnes, prin. — Fax 574-6024

Western Texas College — Post-Sec.
6200 College Ave 79549 — 325-573-8511

Somerset, Bexar, Pop. 1,721
Somerset ISD — 3,000/PK-12
PO Box 279 78069 — 866-852-9858
Mary Ellen Morin, supt. — Fax 852-9860
www.somerset.k12.tx.us
Somerset HS — 900/9-12
PO Box 279 78069 — 866-852-9861
Gilbert Olivarri, prin. — Fax 667-2608

Somerset JHS — 700/6-8
PO Box 279 78069 — 866-852-9862
Saul Hinojosa, prin. — Fax 448-2738

Somerville, Burleson, Pop. 1,741
Somerville ISD — 700/PK-12
PO Box 997 77879 — 979-596-2153
Charles Camarillo, supt. — Fax 596-1778
Somerville HS — 200/9-12
PO Box 997 77879 — 979-596-1534
Sandi Belcher, prin. — Fax 596-1778
Somerville JHS — 200/6-8
PO Box 997 77879 — 979-596-1461
Susan Jackson, prin. — Fax 596-2004

Sonora, Sutton, Pop. 2,953
Sonora ISD — 900/PK-12
807 S Concho Ave 76950 — 325-387-2220
Doug Bawcom, supt. — Fax 387-5090
www.sonoraisd.net/
Sonora HS — 300/9-12
807 S Concho Ave 76950 — 325-387-6533
Raul Chavarria, prin. — Fax 387-5348
Sonora JHS — 300/5-8
807 S Concho Ave 76950 — 325-387-3023
John Berry, prin. — Fax 387-2007

Sour Lake, Hardin, Pop. 1,693
Hardin-Jefferson ISD — 2,200/PK-12
PO Box 490 77659 — 409-981-6400
Elizabeth Treadway, supt. — Fax 287-2283
www.hjisd.net/
Hardin-Jefferson HS — 700/9-12
PO Box 639 77659 — 409-981-6430
Dr. Jamey Harrison, prin. — Fax 287-2558
Other Schools — See China

South Houston, Harris, Pop. 16,058
Pasadena ISD
Supt. — See Pasadena
South Houston HS — 2,300/9-12
3820 S Shaver St 77587 — 713-740-0350
Deborah Aubin, prin.
South Houston IS — 1,100/6-8
900 College Ave 77587 — 713-740-0490
Joe McCorvey, prin. — Fax 740-4097

Circle J Beauty School — Post-Sec.
1611 Spencer Hwy Ste E 77587 — 713-946-5055

Southlake, Tarrant, Pop. 24,192
Carroll ISD
Supt. — See Grapevine
Carroll HS — 1,200/9-10
800 N White Chapel Blvd 76092 — 817-949-5600
Rick Westfall, prin. — Fax 949-5656
Carroll MS — 600/7-8
1101 E Dove Rd 76092 — 817-949-5400
Kenneth Anderson, prin. — Fax 949-5454
Carroll SHS — 1,000/11-12
1501 W Southlake Blvd 76092 — 817-949-5800
Dr. Danniel Presley, prin. — Fax 949-5858
Dawson MS — 700/7-8
400 S Kimball Ave 76092 — 817-949-5500
Trudie Jackson, prin. — Fax 949-5555

Southland, Garza
Southland ISD — 200/K-12
RR 2 Box 103 79364 — 806-996-5599
Oran Hamilton, supt. — Fax 996-5342
Southland S — 200/K-12
RR 2 Box 103 79364 — 806-996-5339
Tohy Miller, prin. — Fax 996-5595

Spade, Lamb
Spade ISD — 100/PK-12
PO Box 129 79369 — 806-233-2030
Donette Sabins, supt. — Fax 233-2035
Spade S — 100/PK-12
PO Box 69 79369 — 806-233-2131
Joel Rodgers, prin. — Fax 233-2118

Spearman, Hansford, Pop. 2,928
Spearman ISD — 800/PK-12
403 E 11th Ave 79081 — 806-659-3233
Rodney Sumner, supt. — Fax 659-2079
www.spearmanisd.com
Spearman HS — 200/9-12
403 E 11th Ave 79081 — 806-659-2584
Bill Belger, prin. — Fax 659-3824
Spearman MS — 200/6-8
505 Townsend St 79081 — 806-659-2563
Bill Wiggins, prin. — Fax 659-3933

Splendora, Montgomery, Pop. 1,398
Splendora ISD — 3,600/PK-12
23419 FM 2090 Rd 77372 — 281-689-3129
Leon Cubillas, supt. — Fax 689-7509
www.splendoraisd.org/
Splendora HS — 800/9-12
23747 FM 2090 Rd 77372 — 281-689-8008
David Parker, prin. — Fax 689-8675
Splendora JHS — 500/7-8
23411 FM 2090 Rd 77372 — 281-689-6343
Will Gollihar, prin. — Fax 689-8702

Spring, Harris, Pop. 37,100
Klein ISD
Supt. — See Klein
Hildebrandt IS — 1,400/6-8
22800 Hildebrandt Rd 77389 — 832-249-5100
Scott Crowe, prin. — Fax 249-4048
Klein Collins HS — 2,600/9-12
20811 Ella Blvd 77388 — 832-484-5500
Randy Kirk, prin. — Fax 484-7811
Klein Oak HS — 1,900/9-12
22603 Northcrest Dr 77389 — 832-484-5000
Kelly Schumacher, prin. — Fax 484-7831
Schindewolf IS — 1,200/6-8
20903 Ella Blvd 77388 — 832-249-5900
Debbie Hamilton, prin. — Fax 249-4066

Spring ISD
Supt. — See Houston
Bailey MS — 6-8
3377 James C Leo Dr 77373
Veronica Vijil, prin.
Dueitt MS — 1,100/6-8
1 Eagle Xing 77373 — 281-355-3100
Kelly Ingram, prin. — Fax 249-2210

Spring HS
19428 Interstate 45 77373 — 3,000/9-12 — 281-353-3465
Gloria Marshall, prin. — Fax 355-2112
Twin Creeks MS — 1,400/6-8
27100 Cypresswood Dr 77373 — 281-355-3130
Charlie Rooke, prin. — Fax 249-2240

Success Institute of Business — Post-Sec.
16120 Stuebner Airline #104 77379 — 713-682-2262

Spring Branch, Comal
Comal ISD
Supt. — See New Braunfels
Smithson Valley HS — 2,100/9-12
14001 State Highway 46 W 78070 — 830-885-1000
Chris Trotter, prin. — Fax 885-1001
Smithson Valley MS — 600/6-8
6101 FM 311 78070 — 830-885-1200
Link Fuller, prin. — Fax 885-1201
Spring Branch MS — 800/6-8
21053 State Highway 46 W 78070 — 830-885-1150
Jo Beth Jimerson, prin. — Fax 885-1151

Springtown, Parker, Pop. 2,451
Springtown ISD — 3,500/PK-12
101 E 2nd St 76082 — 817-523-7243
Lonnie Seipp, supt. — Fax 523-5766
www.springtownisd.net
Springtown HS — 1,100/9-12
915 W Highway 199 76082 — 817-220-3888
Mike Kelley, prin. — Fax 523-5290
Springtown MS — 600/7-8
500 Po Jo Dr 76082 — 817-220-7455
Mark Wilson, prin. — Fax 220-2395

Spur, Dickens, Pop. 1,060
Spur ISD — 100/PK-12
PO Box 250 79370 — 806-271-3272
Bobby Azam, supt. — Fax 271-4575
www.spurbulldogs.com/
Spur MSHS — 100/6-12
PO Box 250 79370 — 806-271-3385
Kevin Brendle, prin. — Fax 271-4575

Spurger, Tyler
Spurger ISD — 500/PK-12
PO Box 38 77660 — 409-429-3464
Angela M. Matterson, supt. — Fax 429-3770
www.spurger.k12.tx.us
Spurger HS — 200/7-12
PO Box 38 77660 — 409-429-3464
Summer Carter, prin. — Fax 429-3770

Stafford, Fort Bend, Pop. 18,295
Stafford Municipal SD — 2,900/PK-12
1625 Staffordshire Rd 77477 — 281-261-9200
Lloyd Graham, supt. — Fax 261-9249
www.stafford.msd.esc4.net
Stafford HS — 800/9-12
1625 Staffordshire Rd 77477 — 281-261-9239
Rebecca Benedict, prin. — Fax 261-9347
Stafford MS — 400/7-8
1625 Staffordshire Rd 77477 — 281-261-9215
Mike Clyde, prin. — Fax 261-9349

Houston Learning Academy - Stafford — 50/9-12
3964 Bluebonnet Dr 77477 — 281-240-6060
Diana Monn, prin. — Fax 240-0022

Stamford, Jones, Pop. 3,374
Stamford ISD — 700/PK-12
507 S Orient St 79553 — 325-773-2705
Susan Graham, supt. — Fax 773-5684
www.stamford.esc14.net
Stamford HS — 200/9-12
507 S Orient St 79553 — 325-773-2701
Richard Holloway, prin. — Fax 773-4015
Stamford MS — 200/6-8
507 S Orient St 79553 — 325-773-2651
Susan Mueller, prin. — Fax 773-4052

Stanton, Martin, Pop. 2,428
Stanton ISD — 700/PK-12
PO Box 730 79782 — 432-756-2244
David L. Carr, supt. — Fax 756-2052
www.esc18.net/stanton/stanton.htm
Stanton HS — 200/9-12
PO Box 730 79782 — 432-756-3326
Mark Cotton, prin. — Fax 756-2052
Stanton MS — 200/6-8
PO Box 730 79782 — 432-756-2544
Timothy Outlaw, prin. — Fax 756-2052

Star, Mills
Star ISD — 100/K-12
PO Box 838 76880 — 325-948-3661
Roger Hashem, supt. — Fax 948-3398
www.centex-edu.net/star
Star S — 100/K-12
PO Box 838 76880 — 325-948-3661
Marion Ferguson, prin. — Fax 948-3398

Stephenville, Erath, Pop. 15,216
Huckabay ISD — 200/K-12
200 County Road 421 76401 — 254-968-8476
Cheryl Floyd, prin. — Fax 965-3740
www.huckabay.k12.tx.us
Huckabay S — 200/K-12
200 County Road 421 76401 — 254-968-5274
Cheryl Floyd, prin. — Fax 965-3140

Stephenville ISD — 3,500/PK-12
2655 W Overhill Dr 76401 — 254-968-7990
Dr. Darrell Floyd, supt. — Fax 968-5942
www.sville.us
Stephenville HS — 1,100/9-12
2650 W Overhill Dr 76401 — 254-968-4141
Travis Stilwell, prin. — Fax 968-4897
Stephenville JHS — 600/7-8
2798 W Frey St 76401 — 254-968-6967
Paul Henderson, prin. — Fax 965-7018

Stephenville Beauty College — Post-Sec.
951 S Lillian St 76401 — 254-968-2111
Tarleton State University — Post-Sec.
PO Box T0030 76402 — 254-968-9000

Sterling City, Sterling, Pop. 1,044
Sterling City ISD — 300/K-12
PO Box 786 76951 — 325-378-4781
Ronnie Krejci, supt. — Fax 378-2283

Sterling City HS — 100/9-12
PO Box 786 76951 — 325-378-5821
Sharla Arp, prin. — Fax 378-2087
Sterling City JHS — 100/6-8
PO Box 786 76951 — 325-378-5821
Glenn Coles, prin. — Fax 378-2283

Stinnett, Hutchinson, Pop. 1,884
Plemons-Stinnett-Phillips Cons ISD — 700/PK-12
PO Box 3440 79083 — 806-878-2858
Rodney Schneider, supt. — Fax 878-3585
www.pspcisd.net
West Texas HS — 200/9-12
PO Box 3440 79083 — 806-878-2456
Steven Scott, prin. — Fax 878-2456
West Texas MS — 100/6-8
PO Box 3440 79083 — 806-878-2247
Kevin Freriks, prin. — Fax 878-3434

Stockdale, Wilson, Pop. 1,489
Stockdale ISD — 800/K-12
PO Box 7 78160 — 830-996-3551
Reece Blincoe, supt. — Fax 996-1071
www.stockdale.k12.tx.us
Stockdale HS — 200/9-12
PO Box 7 78160 — 830-996-3103
Sandy Lynn, prin. — Fax 996-1071
Stockdale JHS — 200/6-8
PO Box 7 78160 — 830-996-3153
Roxanne Seidel, prin. — Fax 996-1071

Stratford, Sherman, Pop. 2,003
Stratford ISD — 600/PK-12
PO Box 108 79084 — 806-366-3300
Tim Gilliland, supt. — Fax 366-3304
www.stratfordisd.net
Stratford HS — 200/9-12
PO Box 108 79084 — 806-366-3330
Steve Haynes, prin. — Fax 366-3304
Stratford JHS — 200/5-8
PO Box 108 79084 — 806-366-3320
Clint Seward, prin. — Fax 366-3304

Strawn, Palo Pinto, Pop. 743
Strawn ISD — 200/K-12
PO Box 428 76475 — 254-672-5313
Andrew Lindsey, supt. — Fax 672-5662
Strawn S — 200/K-12
PO Box 428 76475 — 254-672-5776
Melanie Cormack, prin. — Fax 672-5662

Sudan, Lamb, Pop. 1,040
Sudan ISD — 400/K-12
PO Box 249 79371 — 806-227-2431
Hollis Lowrance, supt. — Fax 227-2146
www.sudanisd.net
Sudan JSHS — 100/8-12
PO Box 249 79371 — 806-227-2336
Ronald Beard, prin. — Fax 227-2146

Sugar Land, Fort Bend, Pop. 70,815
Fort Bend ISD — 61,200/PK-12
16431 Lexington Blvd 77479 — 281-634-1000
Betty Baitland Ed.D., supt. — Fax 634-1700
www.fortbend.k12.tx.us
Austin HS — 2,700/9-12
3434 Pheasant Creek Dr 77478 — 281-634-2000
Mike Leach, prin. — Fax 634-2074
Clements HS — 2,400/9-12
4200 Elkins Rd 77479 — 281-634-2150
Michael McKie, prin. — Fax 634-2168
Dulles HS — 2,400/9-12
550 Dulles Ave 77478 — 281-634-5600
Lance Hindt, prin. — Fax 634-5681
Dulles MS — 1,500/6-8
500 Dulles Ave 77478 — 281-634-5750
Michael Heinzen, prin. — Fax 634-5781
First Colony MS — 1,100/6-8
3225 Austin Pkwy 77479 — 281-634-3240
Lee Crews, prin. — Fax 634-3267
Fort Settlement MS — 1,100/6-8
5440 Elkins Rd 77479 — 281-634-6440
Karon Crockett, prin. — Fax 634-6456
Garcia MS — 1,500/6-8
18550 Old Richmond Rd 77478 — 281-634-3160
Dr. Charles Michel, prin. — Fax 634-3207
Kempner HS — 2,500/9-12
14777 Voss Rd 77478 — 281-634-2300
Dr. James May, prin. — Fax 634-2378
Sartartia MS — 1,200/6-8
8125 Homeward Way 77479 — 281-634-6310
Jeryl Jean Kyle, prin. — Fax 634-6373
Sugar Land MS — 1,500/6-8
321 7th St 77478 — 281-634-3080
Lisa Padron, prin. — Fax 634-3108
Technical Education Center — Vo/Tech
540 Dulles Ave 77478 — 281-634-5671
Kennith Kendziora, admin. — Fax 634-5700
Other Schools – See Houston, Missouri City, Richmond

Ft. Bend Baptist Academy — 200/6-8
13303 Southwest Fwy #150 77478 — 281-263-9191
Ronald Bell, prin. — Fax 242-7195
Ft. Bend Baptist Academy — 300/9-12
1250 7th St 77478 — 281-263-9175
David Hook, prin. — Fax 263-9199

Sulphur Bluff, Hopkins
Sulphur Bluff ISD — 100/PK-12
PO Box 30 75481 — 903-945-2460
Mark Keahey, supt. — Fax 945-2459
www.esc8.net/sbisd/
Sulphur Bluff S — 100/7-12
PO Box 30 75481 — 903-945-2460
Gwen Crutcher, prin. — Fax 945-2459

Sulphur Springs, Hopkins, Pop. 14,787
North Hopkins ISD — 400/PK-12
1994 Farm Road 71 W 75482 — 903-945-2192
Tom Long, supt. — Fax 945-2531
www.northhopkins.net/
North Hopkins JSHS — 200/7-12
1994 Farm Road 71 W 75482 — 903-945-2192
Steve Drummond, prin. — Fax 945-2531

Sulphur Springs ISD — 4,100/PK-12
631 Connally St 75482 — 903-885-2153
Patsy Bolton, supt. — Fax 439-6162
www.ssisd.net/
Sulphur Springs HS — 1,200/9-12
1200 Connally St 75482 — 903-885-2158
Chuck King, prin. — Fax 439-6116
Sulphur Springs MS — 900/6-8
829 Bell St 75482 — 903-885-7741
Glenn Wilson, prin. — Fax 439-6126

Sundown, Hockley, Pop. 1,539
Sundown ISD — 500/PK-12
PO Box 1110 79372 — 806-229-3021
Mike Motheral, supt. — Fax 229-2004
www.sundownisd.com
Sundown HS — 100/9-12
PO Box 1110 79372 — 806-229-2511
Jack Gaskins, prin. — Fax 229-2004
Sundown JHS — 100/6-8
PO Box 1110 79372 — 806-229-4691
Eddie Carter, prin. — Fax 229-2004

Sunnyvale, Dallas, Pop. 3,598

Grace Fellowship Christian S — 100/K-12
3052 N Belt Line Rd 75182 — 972-226-4499
Edris Carr, prin. — Fax 226-0242

Sunray, Moore, Pop. 1,944
Sunray ISD — 500/PK-12
PO Box 240 79086 — 806-948-4411
Michael Brown, supt. — Fax 948-5274
Sunray HS — 100/9-12
PO Box 240 79086 — 806-948-5515
Judy Stewart, prin. — Fax 948-5399
Sunray MS — 200/5-8
PO Box 240 79086 — 806-948-4444
Sid Whiteley, prin. — Fax 948-4208

Sweeny, Matagorda, Pop. 3,658
Sweeny ISD — 2,100/PK-12
1310 N Elm St 77480 — 979-491-8000
Randy Miksch, supt. — Fax 491-8030
www.sweeny.isd.esc4.net/
Sweeny HS — 600/9-12
1310 N Elm St 77480 — 979-491-8100
Michael Heinroth, prin. — Fax 491-8171
Sweeny JHS — 500/6-8
1310 N Elm St 77480 — 979-491-8200
Raymond Washington, prin. — Fax 491-8274

Sweetwater, Nolan, Pop. 10,892
Sweetwater ISD — 2,100/PK-12
207 Musgrove St 79556 — 325-235-8601
Ronny Beard, supt. — Fax 235-5561
www.esc14.net/sweetwaterisd/sisd.htm
Sweetwater HS — 600/9-12
1205 Ragland St 79556 — 325-235-4371
Jan Baker, prin. — Fax 235-4861
Sweetwater MS — 500/6-8
305 Lamar St 79556 — 325-236-6303
Kent Ruffin, prin. — Fax 236-6941

Texas State Technical College — Post-Sec.
300 Homer K Taylor Dr 79556 — 325-235-7300

Taft, San Patricio, Pop. 3,423
Taft ISD — 1,400/PK-12
400 College St 78390 — 361-528-2636
Don Madden, supt. — Fax 528-2223
www.taftisd.net
Taft HS — 400/9-12
502 Rincon Rd 78390 — 361-528-2636
Dr. Charles Climer, prin. — Fax 528-3918
Taft JHS — 300/6-8
727 McIntyre Ave 78390 — 361-528-2636
Ricardo Trevino, prin. — Fax 528-5477

Tahoka, Lynn, Pop. 2,723
Tahoka ISD — 700/PK-12
PO Box 1230 79373 — 806-561-4105
Jimmy Parker, supt. — Fax 561-4160
www.tahoka.esc17.net
Tahoka HS — 200/9-12
PO Box 1500 79373 — 806-561-4538
Robert Webb, prin. — Fax 561-6082
Tahoka MS — 100/7-8
PO Box 1500 79373 — 806-561-4538
Glo Hays, prin. — Fax 561-6082

Tatum, Rusk, Pop. 1,175
Tatum ISD — 1,200/PK-12
PO Box 808 75691 — 903-947-6482
Dee Hartt Ed.D., supt. — Fax 947-3295
www.tatumisd.org/
Tatum HS — 400/9-12
PO Box 808 75691 — 903-947-6486
Debbie Maxey, prin. — Fax 947-6206
Tatum MS — 200/7-8
PO Box 808 75691 — 903-947-6487
Bob Garcia, prin. — Fax 947-2322

Taylor, Williamson, Pop. 14,204
Taylor ISD — 2,700/PK-12
602 W 12th St 76574 — 512-365-1391
Bruce Scott Ed.D., supt. — Fax 365-3800
www.taylorisd.org
Taylor HS — 900/9-12
3101 N Main St 76574 — 512-365-1291
Kim Mason, prin. — Fax 365-9334
Taylor MS — 700/6-8
304 Carlos Parker Blvd NW 76574 — 512-365-8591
Ester Allgower, prin. — Fax 365-8589

Teague, Freestone, Pop. 4,638
Teague ISD — 1,100/PK-12
420 N 10th Ave 75860 — 254-739-3071
Ned Burns, supt. — Fax 739-5223
www.teagueisd.org/
Teague HS — 400/9-12
E Highway 84 75860 — 254-739-2532
Darrell Evans, prin. — Fax 739-2724
Teague JHS — 200/7-8
E Highway 84 75860 — 254-739-3011
Donnie Osborn, prin. — Fax 739-5896

Temple, Bell, Pop. 54,975
Belton ISD
Supt. — See Belton

Lake Belton MS | 1,100/6-8
8818 Tarver Dr 76502 | 254-215-2900
Kathy Cook, prin. | Fax 215-2901

Temple ISD | 8,300/PK-12
PO Box 788 76503 | 254-215-8473
Beto Gonzalez, supt. | Fax 215-6783
www.tisd.org
Bonham MS | 500/6-8
4600 Midway Dr 76502 | 254-215-6600
Judy Hundley, prin. | Fax 215-6634
Lamar MS | 700/6-8
2120 N 1st St 76501 | 254-215-6444
Jennifer Mathesen, prin. | Fax 215-6483
Temple HS | 2,100/9-12
415 N 31st St 76504 | 254-215-7000
J. J. Villarreal, prin. | Fax 899-2926
Travis MS | 700/6-8
1500 S 19th St 76504 | 254-215-6300
Eddy McNamara, prin. | Fax 215-6352

Central Texas Beauty College | Post-Sec.
2010 S 57th St 76504 | 254-773-9911
Central Texas Christian S | 500/PK-12
4141 W FM 93 76502 | 254-939-5700
Ed Thomas, admin. | Fax 939-5733
Holy Trinity Catholic HS | 50/9-12
418 N 11th St 76501 | 254-771-0787
Robin Couvillon, prin. | Fax 771-2285
Scott & White Memorial Hospital & Clinic | Post-Sec.
2401 S 31st St 76508 | 254-724-5177
Temple College | Post-Sec.
2600 S 1st St 76504 | 254-298-8300

Tenaha, Shelby, Pop. 1,081
Tenaha ISD | 400/PK-12
PO Box 318 75974 | 936-248-5000
Don Fallin, supt. | Fax 248-3902
www.tenahaisd.com/
Tenaha HS | 100/9-12
PO Box 318 75974 | 936-248-3931
Tom H. Jones, prin. | Fax 248-4009
Tenaha MS | 100/6-8
PO Box 318 75974 | 936-248-3484
 | Fax 248-3902

Terlingua, Brewster
Terlingua Common SD | 200/PK-12
PO Box 256 79852 | 432-371-2281
Kathy Killingsworth, supt. | Fax 371-2245
Big Bend HS | 100/9-12
PO Box 256 79852 | 432-371-2281
Kathy Killingsworth, prin. | Fax 371-2245

Terrell, Kaufman, Pop. 15,771
Terrell ISD | 4,100/PK-12
700 N Catherine St 75160 | 972-563-7504
Walt Davis, supt. | Fax 563-1406
www.terrellisd.com/
Furlough MS | 600/7-8
1351 Colquitt Rd 75160 | 972-563-7501
Danielle Banz, prin. | Fax 563-5721
Terrell HS | 1,200/9-12
400 Poetry Rd 75160 | 972-563-7525
Bob Densmore, prin. | Fax 563-6318

Poetry Community Christian S | 200/K-12
18688 FM 986 75160 | 972-563-7227
Anne Puidk Horan, admin. | Fax 563-0025
Southwestern Christian College | Post-Sec.
PO Box 10 75160 | 972-524-3341
Terrell Christian Academy | 100/K-12
805 Johnson St 75160 | 972-563-5291
Keith Honey, admin. | Fax 551-0266

Texarkana, Bowie, Pop. 35,199
Liberty-Eylau ISD | 2,700/PK-12
2901 Leopard Dr 75501 | 903-832-1535
Scott Niven, supt. | Fax 838-9444
www.leisd.net
Liberty-Eylau HS | 700/9-12
2905 Leopard Dr 75501 | 903-832-1535
Bill Hastings, prin. | Fax 831-6113
Liberty-Eylau MS | 800/5-8
5555 Leopard Dr 75501 | 903-838-5555
Christy Tidwell, prin. | Fax 832-6700

Pleasant Grove ISD | 1,900/PK-12
8500 N Kings Hwy 75503 | 903-831-4086
Margaret Davis, supt. | Fax 831-4435
www.pgisd.net
Pleasant Grove HS | 600/9-12
5406 McKnight Rd 75503 | 903-832-8005
Jason Marshall, prin. | Fax 832-5381
Pleasant Grove MS | 600/5-8
5605 Cooks Ln 75503 | 903-831-4295
Jeanie Davis, prin. | Fax 831-5501

Red Lick ISD | 400/K-8
3511 N FM 2148 75503 | 903-838-8230
Dr. Richard Hervey, supt. | Fax 831-6134
www.redlickisd.com
Red Lick MS | 100/6-8
3511 N FM 2148 75503 | 903-838-8230
Phyllis Deese, prin. | Fax 831-6134

Texarkana ISD | 5,600/PK-12
4241 Summerhill Rd 75503 | 903-794-3651
F. Larry Sullivan Ed.D., supt. | Fax 792-2632
www.txkisd.net
Texas HS | 1,400/9-12
2112 Kennedy Ln 75503 | 903-794-3891
Paul Norton, prin. | Fax 792-8971
Texas MS | 1,300/6-8
2100 College Dr 75503 | 903-793-5631
George Moore, prin. | Fax 792-2935

Career Academy | Post-Sec.
32 Oaklawn Vlg 75501 | 903-832-1021
Texarkana College | Post-Sec.
2500 N Robison Rd 75501 | 903-838-4541
Texas A&M University - Texarkana | Post-Sec.
PO Box 5518 75505 | 903-223-3000
Wadley Regional Medical Center | Post-Sec.
1000 Pine St 75501 | 903-798-8000

Texas City, Galveston, Pop. 43,233
Texas City ISD | 5,800/PK-12
PO Box 1150 77592 | 409-942-2713
Richard Ettredge, supt. | Fax 942-2655
www.texascity.isd.tenet.edu
Blocker MS | 1,000/7-8
500 14th Ave N 77590 | 409-942-2756
R. Carter, prin. | Fax 942-2755
Texas City HS | 1,500/9-12
1800 9th Ave N 77590 | 409-942-2645
Mike Rhodes, prin. | Fax 942-2672

College of the Mainland | Post-Sec.
1200 N Amburn Rd 77591 | 409-938-1211

Texline, Dallam, Pop. 507
Texline ISD | 100/K-12
PO Box 60 79087 | 806-362-4667
Paul Evans, supt. | Fax 362-4538
Texline S | 100/K-12
PO Box 60 79087 | 806-362-4284
Ron Van Vranken, prin. | Fax 362-4538

The Colony, Denton, Pop. 35,189
Lewisville ISD
Supt. — See Flower Mound
Griffin MS | 800/6-8
5105 N Colony Blvd 75056 | 469-713-5973
Cynthia Williams, prin. | Fax 350-2950
Lakeview MS | 900/6-8
4300 Keys Dr 75056 | 469-713-5974
Dr. Steve Nauman, prin. | Fax 350-3150
The Colony HS | 1,900/9-12
4301 Blair Oaks Dr 75056 | 972-625-9000
Becky MacDonald, prin. | Fax 625-9015

The Woodlands, Montgomery, Pop. 63,000
Conroe ISD
Supt. — See Conroe
Knox JHS | 1,200/7-8
12104 Sawmill Rd 77380 | 832-592-8300
Gale Drummond, prin. | Fax 592-8410
McCullough JHS | 7-8
3800 S Panther Creek Dr 77381 | 832-592-5100
Chris McCord, prin. | Fax 592-5116
The Woodlands College Park HS | 9-12
3701 College Park Dr 77384 | 936-709-3000
Mark Murrell, prin. | Fax 709-3019
The Woodlands HS | 1,300/9-9
10010 Branch Crossing Dr 77382 | 832-592-8200
Marguerite Weatherall, prin. | Fax 592-8202
The Woodlands SHS | 2,700/10-12
6101 Research Forest Dr 77381 | 936-273-4837
Dr. Gregg Colsdien, prin. | Fax 273-8599

Cooper S | 900/K-12
1 John Cooper Dr 77381 | 281-367-0900
Michael Maher, hdmstr. | Fax 292-9201
Woodlands Christian Academy | 400/PK-12
5800 Alden Woods 77384 | 936-273-2555
John Echols, hdmstr. | Fax 271-3115

Thorndale, Milam, Pop. 1,309
Thorndale ISD | 500/K-12
PO Box 870 76577 | 512-898-2538
Gene Solis, supt. | Fax 898-5356
www.thorndale.txed.net/
Thorndale HS | 200/9-12
PO Box 870 76577 | 512-898-2321
Davis Denny, prin. | Fax 898-5558
Thorndale MS | 100/6-8
PO Box 870 76577 | 512-898-2670
Heather Klotz, prin. | Fax 898-5505

Thrall, Williamson, Pop. 813
Thrall ISD | 500/K-12
201 S Bounds St 76578 | 512-898-0062
Keith Brown, supt. | Fax 898-5349
www.thrallisd.com
Thrall MSHS | 300/6-12
201 S Bounds St 76578 | 512-898-5193
Deana Steeber, prin. | Fax 898-2132

Three Rivers, Live Oak, Pop. 1,782
Three Rivers ISD | 700/K-12
108 N School Rd 78071 | 361-786-3626
Mac Johanson, supt. | Fax 786-2555
www.trisd.esc2.net
Three Rivers HS | 200/9-12
108 N School Rd 78071 | 361-786-3531
Kenneth Rohrbach, prin. | Fax 786-3533
Three Rivers MS | 200/6-8
108 N School Rd 78071 | 361-786-3803
Hortensia Brooks, prin. | Fax 786-2555

Throckmorton, Throckmorton, Pop. 827
Throckmorton ISD | 200/PK-12
210 College St 76483 | 940-849-2411
Scott Hogue, supt. | Fax 849-3345
www.esc9.net/tisd
Throckmorton HS | 100/9-12
210 College St 76483 | 940-849-2421
John Powers, prin. | Fax 849-3345

Tilden, McMullen
McMullen County ISD | 200/PK-12
PO Box 359 78072 | 361-274-3315
Frank Franklin, supt. | Fax 274-3665
McMullen County S | 200/PK-12
PO Box 359 78072 | 361-274-3371
Dr. Jay Smith, prin. | Fax 274-3580

Timpson, Shelby, Pop. 1,118
Timpson ISD | 600/PK-12
PO Box 370 75975 | 936-254-2463
Dr. Leland Moore, supt. | Fax 254-3878
www.timpson.k12.tx.us
Timpson HS | 200/9-12
PO Box 370 75975 | 936-254-3125
Kelly Parker, prin. | Fax 254-3263
Timpson MS | 100/6-8
PO Box 370 75975 | 936-254-2078
Calvin Smith, prin. | Fax 254-2355

Tivoli, Refugio
Austwell-Tivoli ISD | 200/K-12
207 Redfish St 77990 | 361-286-3212
Dr. Antonio Aguirre, supt. | Fax 286-3637
www.atisd.net

Austwell-Tivoli JSHS | 100/7-12
207 Redfish St 77990 | 361-286-3582
Tracy Gleghorn, prin. | Fax 286-3637

Tolar, Hood, Pop. 593
Tolar ISD | 500/PK-12
PO Box 368 76476 | 254-835-4718
Jack Davis, supt. | Fax 835-4704
www.tolar.esc11.net
Tolar HS | 200/9-12
PO Box 368 76476 | 254-835-4316
Bruce Gibbs, prin. | Fax 835-4237
Tolar JHS | 6-8
PO Box 368 76476 | 254-835-5207
Harold Roan, prin. | Fax 835-5208

Tomball, Harris, Pop. 9,784
Tomball ISD | 8,500/PK-12
221 W Main St 77375 | 281-357-3100
John Neubauer, supt. | Fax 357-3128
www.tomballisd.net
Tomball HS | 2,500/9-12
30330 Quinn Rd 77375 | 281-357-3220
Gary Moss, prin. | Fax 357-3248
Tomball JHS | 600/7-8
30403 Quinn Rd 77375 | 281-357-3000
Dan Johnson, prin. | Fax 357-3027
Willow Wood JHS | 700/7-8
11770 Gregson Rd 77377 | 281-357-3030
Dr. Kate Caffery, prin. | Fax 357-3044

Concordia Lutheran HS | 400/9-12
700 E Main St 77375 | 281-351-2547
Joel R. Bode, prin. | Fax 255-8806
Rosehill Christian S | 300/PK-12
19830 FM 2920 Rd 77377 | 281-351-8114
Dean Unsicker, admin. | Fax 516-3418

Tom Bean, Grayson, Pop. 976
Tom Bean ISD | 800/K-12
PO Box 128 75489 | 903-546-6076
Dr. Jerry Stout, supt. | Fax 546-6104
www.tombean-isd.org
Tom Bean HS | 300/9-12
PO Box 128 75489 | 903-546-6319
Sheryl Miller, prin. | Fax 546-6319
Tom Bean MS | 200/6-8
PO Box 128 75489 | 903-546-6161
Roger Ellis, prin. | Fax 546-6161

Tornillo, El Paso
Tornillo ISD | 1,200/PK-12
PO Box 170 79853 | 915-764-2366
Paul Vranish, supt. | Fax 764-2120
www.tisd.us/
Tornillo HS | 300/9-12
PO Box 170 79853 | 915-764-2040
Ray Cobos, prin. | Fax 764-3482
Tornillo JHS | 200/7-8
PO Box 170 79853 | 915-764-5701
James Blake, prin. | Fax 764-2020

Trent, Taylor, Pop. 312
Trent ISD | 100/PK-12
PO Box 105 79561 | 325-862-6400
Greg Priddy, supt. | Fax 862-6448
www.esc14.net/data/trent.pdf
Trent S | 100/PK-12
PO Box 105 79561 | 325-862-6125
Greg Priddy, prin. | Fax 862-6448

Trenton, Fannin, Pop. 673
Trenton ISD | 500/PK-12
PO Box 5 75490 | 903-989-2245
Jerry Don Cook, supt. | Fax 989-2767
www.trentonisd.com
Trenton HS | 200/9-12
PO Box 5 75490 | 903-989-2242
Rick Foreman, prin. | Fax 989-2767
Trenton MS | 100/6-8
PO Box 5 75490 | 903-989-2243
Rick Largent, prin. | Fax 989-5173

Trinidad, Henderson, Pop. 1,116
Trinidad ISD | 300/PK-12
PO Box 349 75163 | 903-778-2673
Michael Green, supt. | Fax 778-4120
www.trinidad.k12.tx.us/
Trinidad S | 300/PK-12
PO Box 349 75163 | 903-778-2415
Corey Jenkins, prin. | Fax 778-4120

Trinity, Trinity, Pop. 2,750
Trinity ISD | 1,200/PK-12
PO Box 752 75862 | 936-594-3569
Dr. Douglas E. Moore, supt. | Fax 594-8425
www.trinity.k12.tx.us
Trinity HS | 400/9-12
PO Box 752 75862 | 936-594-3560
Jeremy Glenn, prin. | Fax 594-2162
Trinity JHS | 300/6-8
PO Box 752 75862 | 936-594-2321
James Spurlin, prin. | Fax 594-8425

Trophy Club, Denton, Pop. 7,194
Northwest ISD
Supt. — See Justin
Medlin MS | 600/6-8
601 Parkview Dr 76262 | 817-215-0500
Robin Ellis, prin. | Fax 215-0548

Troup, Smith, Pop. 2,007
Troup ISD | 1,000/PK-12
PO Box 578 75789 | 903-842-3067
Marvin Beaty, supt. | Fax 842-4563
www.troupisd.org
Troup HS | 300/9-12
PO Box 578 75789 | 903-842-3065
Derek Driver, prin. | Fax 842-4563
Troup MS | 200/6-8
PO Box 578 75789 | 903-842-3081
Ava Johnson, prin. | Fax 842-4563

Troy, Bell, Pop. 1,365
Troy ISD | 1,300/PK-12
PO Box 409 76579 | 254-938-2595
Kerry Hansen, supt. | Fax 938-7323
www.troy.k12.tx.us
Troy HS | 400/9-12
PO Box 409 76579 | 254-938-2561
Wayne Cooper, prin. | Fax 938-2328

Troy MS   300/6-8
PO Box 409 76579   254-938-2543
Jimmy Cox, prin.   Fax 938-2880

Tulia, Swisher, Pop. 4,869
Tulia ISD   1,100/PK-12
702 NW 8th St 79088   806-995-4591
Dr. Ken Miller, supt.   Fax 995-3169
www.tuliaisd.net
Tulia HS   400/9-12
501 Hornet Pl 79088   806-995-2759
Bobby Hudson, prin.   Fax 995-4413
Tulia JHS   300/6-8
421 NE 3rd St 79088   806-995-4842
Dennis Holt, prin.   Fax 995-4498

Turkey, Hall, Pop. 507
Turkey-Quitaque ISD   300/K-12
PO Box 397 79261   806-455-1411
Jerry Smith, supt.   Fax 455-1718
Valley S   300/K-12
PO Box 397 79261   806-455-1411
Jon Davidson, prin.   Fax 455-1718

Tuscola, Taylor, Pop. 720
Jim Ned Consolidated ISD   1,000/PK-12
PO Box 9 79562   325-554-7500
Kent LeFevre, supt.   Fax 554-7740
www.jimned.esc14.net/
Jim Ned HS   400/9-12
PO Box 9 79562   325-554-7755
Paul Lippe, prin.   Fax 554-7550
Jim Ned MS   300/6-8
PO Box 9 79562   325-554-7870
Bob Easterling, prin.   Fax 554-7750

Tyler, Smith, Pop. 88,316
Chapel Hill ISD   3,100/PK-12
11134 County Road 2249 75707   903-566-2441
Joe Stubblefield, supt.   Fax 566-8469
www.sprnet.org/chisd
Chapel Hill HS   900/9-12
13172 State Highway 64 E 75707   903-566-2311
Randell Jarvis, prin.   Fax 566-5343
Chapel Hill MS   700/6-8
13174 State Highway 64 E 75707   903-566-1491
Lisa McCreary, prin.   Fax 566-6441

Tyler ISD   17,200/PK-12
PO Box 2035 75710   903-262-1000
Dr. David Simmons, supt.   Fax 262-1178
www.tylerisd.org
Boulter Creative Arts Magnet S   500/6-8
2926 Garden Valley Rd 75702   903-262-1390
Vanessa A. Choice, prin.   Fax 262-1392
Dogan MS   500/6-8
2621 N Border Ave 75702   903-262-1450
H. T. Sanchez, prin.   Fax 262-1451
Hogg MS   600/6-8
920 S Broadway Ave 75701   903-262-1500
Shauna Hittle, prin.   Fax 262-1501
Hubbard MS   900/6-8
1300 Hubbard Dr 75703   903-262-1560
Tammy VanSchoubroek, prin.   Fax 262-1566
Lee HS   2,600/9-12
411 E Southeast Loop 323 75701   903-262-2625
Rick McDaniel, prin.   Fax 262-2630
Moore MST Magnet MS   800/6-8
1200 S Tipton Ave 75701   903-262-1640
Claude Lane, prin.   Fax 262-1641
Stewart MS   500/6-8
2800 W Shaw St 75701   903-262-1710
Dr. Sharon Ross, prin.   Fax 262-1711
Tyler HS   1,900/9-12
1120 N Northwest Loop 323 75702   903-262-2850
Michael McFarland, prin.   Fax 262-2852

All Saints Episcopal S   700/PK-12
2695 S Southwest Loop 323 75701   903-579-6000
    Fax 579-6002
Bishop Gorman MSHS   400/6-12
1405 E Southeast Loop 323 75701   903-561-2424
Jim Franz, prin.   Fax 561-2645
Careers Unlimited   Post-Sec.
335 S Bonner Ave 75702   903-593-4424
Christian Heritage S   200/K-12
961 County Road 1143 75704   903-593-2702
James Kilkenny, hdmstr.   Fax 531-2226
East Texas Christian Academy   200/PK-12
1797 Shiloh Rd 75703   903-561-8642
Scott Fossey, pres.   Fax 561-9620
Good Shepherd Reformed Episcopal S   200/PK-12
2525 Old Jacksonville Rd 75701   903-592-4045
Fr. Walter Banek, hdmstr.   Fax 596-7149
Grace Community S   500/6-12
3001 University Blvd 75701   903-566-5661
John Ferguson, admin.   Fax 566-5639
Star College of Cosmetology   Post-Sec.
520 E Front St 75702   903-596-7860
Texas College   Post-Sec.
2404 N Grand Ave 75702   903-593-8311
Tyler Junior College   Post-Sec.
PO Box 9020 75711   903-510-2200
University of Texas at Tyler   Post-Sec.
3900 University Blvd 75701   800-888-9537

Universal City, Bexar, Pop. 15,428
Judson ISD
Supt. — See Live Oak
Kitty Hawk MS   1,400/6-8
840 Old Cimmaron Trl 78148   210-945-1220
Yvonne Anglada, prin.   Fax 659-0687

First Baptist Academy of Universal City   400/PK-10
1401 Pat Booker Rd 78148   210-658-5331
Cissy Stubblefield, admin.   Fax 658-7024

Utopia, Uvalde
Utopia ISD   200/K-12
PO Box 880 78884   830-966-1928
John Walts, supt.   Fax 966-6162
www.utopia.k12.tx.us
Utopia S   200/K-12
PO Box 880 78884   830-966-3339
James D. Phillips, prin.   Fax 966-6162

Uvalde, Uvalde, Pop. 16,391
Uvalde Consolidated ISD   5,300/PK-12
PO Box 1909 78802   830-278-6655
Ramon Abarca, supt.   Fax 591-4909
www.uvalde-cons.k12.tx.us

Uvalde HS   1,400/9-12
PO Box 1909 78802   830-591-2950
Hal Harrell, prin.   Fax 591-2961
Uvalde JHS   700/7-8
PO Box 1909 78802   830-591-2980
Don Wise, prin.   Fax 591-2975
Other Schools – See Batesville

Southwest Texas Junior College   Post-Sec.
2401 Garner Field Rd 78801   830-278-4401
SW School of Business & Tech Careers   Post-Sec.
122 W North St 78801

Valentine, Jeff Davis, Pop. 186
Valentine ISD   100/PK-12
PO Box 188 79854   432-467-2671
Glen Nix, supt.   Fax 467-2004
valentineisd.esc18.net
Valentine S   100/PK-12
PO Box 188 79854   432-467-2671
Cherri Franklin, prin.   Fax 467-2004

Valera, Coleman
Panther Creek Consolidated ISD   200/PK-12
129 Private Rd 3421 76884   325-357-4506
Dan Harris, supt.   Fax 357-4470
www.panthercountry.net/
Panther Creek JSHS   100/6-12
129 Private Rd 3421 76884   325-357-4449
David Low, prin.   Fax 357-4470

Valley Mills, Bosque, Pop. 1,136
Valley Mills ISD   600/PK-12
PO Box 518 76689   254-932-5210
Dr. John Spies, supt.   Fax 932-6601
Valley Mills HS   200/9-12
PO Box 518 76689   254-932-5251
Randy Anderson, prin.   Fax 932-6601
Valley Mills JHS   100/7-8
PO Box 518 76689   254-932-5251
Randy Anderson, prin.   Fax 932-6601

Valley View, Cooke, Pop. 788
Valley View ISD   600/K-12
200 Newton St 76272   940-726-3659
Gordon D. Taylor, supt.   Fax 726-3614
www.vvisd.net
Valley View HS   200/9-12
200 Newton St 76272   940-726-3522
Clay Montgomery, prin.   Fax 726-3862
Valley View MS   200/5-8
200 Newton St 76272   940-726-3244
Matthew Chalmers, prin.   Fax 726-3862

Van, Van Zandt, Pop. 2,488
Van ISD   2,200/PK-12
PO Box 697 75790   903-963-8328
Joddie White, supt.   Fax 963-3904
www.van.sprnet.org
Van HS   700/9-12
PO Box 697 75790   903-963-8623
Keith Murphy, prin.   Fax 963-5591
Van JHS   500/6-8
PO Box 697 75790   903-963-8321
Don Dunn, prin.   Fax 963-3277

Van Alstyne, Grayson, Pop. 2,605
Van Alstyne ISD   1,300/PK-12
PO Box 518 75495   903-482-8802
Bill Lytle, supt.   Fax 482-6086
www.vanalstyneisd.org
Van Alstyne HS   400/9-12
2001 N Waco St 75495   903-482-8803
John Williamson, prin.   Fax 482-8885
Van Alstyne JHS   200/7-8
PO Box 699 75495   903-482-8804
Jim Martin, prin.   Fax 482-9234

Vanderbilt, Jackson
Industrial ISD   900/PK-12
PO Box 369 77991   361-284-3226
Anthony Williams Ed.D., supt.   Fax 284-3349
www.iisd1.org
Industrial HS   300/9-12
PO Box 399 77991   361-284-3216
    Fax 284-3328
Other Schools – See Lolita

Van Horn, Culberson, Pop. 2,271
Culberson County-Allamore ISD   700/PK-12
PO Box 899 79855   432-283-2245
Anne E. Pemberton, supt.   Fax 283-9062
www.ccaisd.net/
Van Horn HS   200/9-12
PO Box 899 79855   432-283-2245
George Elliott, prin.   Fax 283-9062
Van Horn JHS   200/6-8
PO Box 899 79855   432-283-2245
Donna Young, prin.   Fax 283-9062

Van Vleck, Matagorda, Pop. 1,534
Van Vleck ISD   1,000/PK-12
302 S 4th St 77482   979-245-8518
Dr. Juan Antonio Jasso, supt.   Fax 245-1214
www.vvisd.org
Herman MS   200/6-8
901 1st St 77482   979-245-6401
John O'Brien, prin.   Fax 245-8538
Van Vleck HS   300/9-12
302 S 4th St 77482   979-245-4664
Larry Meche, prin.   Fax 244-3485

Vega, Oldham, Pop. 921
Vega ISD   300/K-12
PO Box 190 79092   806-267-2123
Steve Hopper, supt.   Fax 267-2146
www.region16.net/vegaisd
Vega HS   200/7-12
PO Box 190 79092   806-267-2126
Ashley Hartsell, prin.   Fax 267-2146

Venus, Johnson, Pop. 2,094
Venus ISD   1,800/PK-12
PO Box 364 76084   972-366-3448
Johnnie Hauerland, supt.   Fax 366-8742
www.venusisd.net/
Venus HS   500/9-12
PO Box 364 76084   972-366-8815
Robert White, prin.   Fax 366-8919
Venus MS   400/6-8
PO Box 364 76084   972-366-3358
Cynthia McCallum, prin.   Fax 366-1740

Veribest, Tom Green
Veribest ISD   300/PK-12
PO Box 475 76886   325-655-4912
Jeffrey Brasher, supt.   Fax 655-3355
veribest.netxv.net/
Veribest HS   100/9-12
PO Box 475 76886   325-655-2851
Aaron Hood, prin.   Fax 655-3355

Vernon, Wilbarger, Pop. 10,902
Northside ISD   200/K-12
18040 US Highway 283 76384   940-552-2551
Ed Donahue, supt.   Fax 553-4919
www.esc9.net/northside
Northside S   200/K-12
18040 US Highway 283 76384   940-552-2551
Doug Gore, prin.   Fax 553-4919
Vernon ISD   2,300/PK-12
1713 Wilbarger St 76384   940-553-1900
Tom Woody, supt.   Fax 553-3802
vernonisd.org/
Vernon HS   700/9-12
2102 Yucca Ln 76384   940-553-3377
Kenny Railsback, prin.   Fax 553-4531
Vernon MS   500/6-8
2200 Yamparika St 76384   940-552-6231
William Belew, prin.   Fax 552-0504

Vernon College   Post-Sec.
4400 College Dr 76384   940-552-6291

Victoria, Victoria, Pop. 61,410
Victoria ISD   14,300/PK-12
PO Box 1759 77902   361-576-3131
Bob Moore, supt.   Fax 788-9643
www.visd.com
Crain MS   1,000/6-8
2706 N Azalea St 77901   361-573-7453
Lisa Blundell, prin.   Fax 788-9566
Howell MS   1,100/6-8
2502 Fannin Dr 77901   361-578-1561
Debbie Crick, prin.   Fax 788-9547
Memorial HS Stroman Campus   200/9-9
3002 E North St 77901   361-578-2711
Nancy McCord, prin.   Fax 788-9800
Memorial SHS   2,800/10-12
1110 Sam Houston Dr 77901   361-575-7451
Nancy McCord, prin.   Fax 788-9701
Profit Magnet HS   9-12
104 Profit Dr 77901   361-788-9650
Michelle Callis, dir.   Fax 788-9649
Victoria Career Development S   Vo/Tech
104 Profit Dr 77901   361-788-9288
Nancy McCord, prin.   Fax 788-9656
Welder Magnet MS   1,100/6-8
1604 E North St 77901   361-575-4553
Calvin Singleton, prin.   Fax 788-9629

Citizens Medical Center   Post-Sec.
2701 Hospital Dr 77901   361-573-9181
Devereux-Texas Treatment Network   Post-Sec.
120 David Wade Dr 77902   800-383-5000
Faith Academy   200/PK-12
PO Box 4824 77903   361-572-2484
Dr. Chris Royael, admin.   Fax 573-5058
St. Joseph HS   400/9-12
110 E Red River St 77901   361-573-2446
William H. McArdle, prin.   Fax 573-4221
Texas Vocational School   Post-Sec.
1921 E Red River St 77901   361-575-4768
University of Houston-Victoria   Post-Sec.
3007 N Ben Wilson St 77901   361-570-4848
Victoria Beauty School   Post-Sec.
1508 N Laurent St 77901   361-575-4526
Victoria College   Post-Sec.
2200 E Red River St 77901   361-573-3291

Vidor, Orange, Pop. 11,283
Vidor ISD   5,300/PK-12
120 E Bolivar St 77662   409-769-2143
Robert E. Madding, supt.   Fax 769-0093
www.vidor.k12.tx.us
Vidor HS   1,400/9-12
500 Orange St 77662   409-769-5418
Dr. Lynn Hancock, prin.   Fax 769-6767
Vidor JHS   800/7-8
945 N Tram Rd 77662   409-769-2461
Debra Jordan, prin.   Fax 769-6754

Waco, McLennan, Pop. 116,887
Bosqueville ISD   500/PK-12
7636 Rock Creek Rd 76708   254-757-3113
Stephanie Kucera, supt.   Fax 752-4909
www.bosqueville.k12.tx.us
Bosqueville JSHS   200/7-12
7636 Rock Creek Rd 76708   254-757-3113
Gregg McCarthy, prin.   Fax 752-0326

China Spring ISD   1,800/PK-12
6301 Sylvia St 76708   254-836-1115
George Kazanas, supt.   Fax 836-0559
www.chinaspringisd.net
Other Schools – See China Spring

Connally ISD   2,700/PK-12
200 Cadet Way 76705   254-296-6460
Bruce Shores, supt.   Fax 412-5530
www.connally.org/
Connally HS   700/9-12
900 N Lacy Dr 76705   254-296-6700
Joe Crownover, prin.   Fax 412-5549
Connally JHS   400/7-8
100 Hancock Dr 76705   254-296-7700
Keith Pate, prin.   Fax 829-2354

La Vega ISD   2,600/PK-12
3100 Bellmead Dr 76705   254-799-4963
Dr. Monte Geren, supt.   Fax 799-8642
www.lavegaisd.org
La Vega HS   700/9-12
555 N Loop 340 76705   254-799-4951
Jerry Brem, prin.   Fax 799-0720
La Vega JHS George Dixon Campus   400/7-8
4401 Orchard Ln 76705   254-799-2428
Bryant Adams, prin.   Fax 799-8943

Midway ISD 5,700/PK-12
1205 Foundation Dr 76712 254-761-5610
Randy Albers Ed.D., supt. Fax 666-7785
www.midwayisd.org/
Midway HS 1,900/9-12
8200 Mars Dr 76712 254-761-5650
Sharron Zachry, prin. Fax 761-5770
Other Schools – See Hewitt

Waco ISD 15,400/PK-12
PO Box 27 76703 254-755-9463
Dr. Jerry Major, supt. Fax 755-9690
www.wacoisd.org
Brazos MS 400/6-8
2415 Cumberland Ave 76707 254-754-5491
H. T. Sanchez, prin. Fax 750-3576
Carver Academy 600/6-8
1601 J J Flewellen Rd 76704 254-757-0787
Pamela Correa, prin. Fax 750-3442
Chavez MS 400/6-8
700 S 15th St 76706 254-750-3736
Alfredo Loredo, prin. Fax 750-3739
Lake Air MS 600/6-8
4601 Cobbs Dr 76710 254-772-1910
Dr. Louise Powell, prin. Fax 741-4945
Moore Academy 700/9-12
500 N University Parks Dr 76701 254-753-6486
Dr. Debra Bishop, prin. Fax 750-3464
Tennyson MS 500/6-8
6100 Tennyson Dr 76710 254-772-1440
Robin Wilson, prin. Fax 741-4970
University HS 1,100/9-12
2600 Bagby Ave 76711 254-756-1843
Nolan Correa, prin. Fax 750-3709
University MS 400/6-8
1820 Irving Lee St 76711 254-753-1533
Dr. Rene Garganta, prin. Fax 750-3486
Waco HS 2,000/9-12
2020 N 42nd St 76710 254-776-1150
Donald Garrett, prin. Fax 741-4815
Wiley MS 300/6-8
1030 E Live Oak St 76704 254-752-9691
E. Dean Frederick, prin. Fax 750-3434

Baylor University Post-Sec.
Po Box 97008 76798 254-710-1011
Hillcrest Baptist Medical Center Post-Sec.
3000 Herring Ave 76708 254-756-8551
McLennan Community College Post-Sec.
1400 College Dr 76708 254-299-8000
Reicher Catholic HS 200/9-12
2102 N 23rd St 76708 254-752-8349
Molly Maloy, prin. Fax 752-8408
Texas Christian Academy 300/PK-12
4600 Sanger Ave 76710 254-772-5474
Albert Beck, hdmstr. Fax 772-4485
Texas State Technical College - Waco Post-Sec.
3801 Campus Dr 76705 254-799-3611
Vanguard College Preparatory S 200/7-12
2517 Mount Carmel Dr 76710 254-772-8111
Fred Niell, hdmstr. Fax 772-8263

Waelder, Gonzales, Pop. 978
Waelder ISD 300/K-12
PO Box 247 78959 830-788-7161
Jim Haley, supt. Fax 788-7429
Waelder JSHS 100/6-12
PO Box 247 78959 830-788-7151
L.D. Johnson, prin. Fax 788-7323

Wall, Tom Green
Wall ISD 1,000/K-12
PO Box 259 76957 325-651-7790
Walter Holik, supt. Fax 651-5081
www.wall.netxv.net
Miles Vocational Training Vo/Tech
PO Box 259 76957 325-651-7521
Keith Mahler, prin. Fax 651-9419
Wall HS 300/9-12
PO Box 259 76957 325-651-7521
Keith Mahler, prin. Fax 651-9419
Wall MS 200/6-8
PO Box 259 76957 325-651-7648
Ryan Snowden, prin. Fax 651-9664

Waller, Waller, Pop. 2,061
Waller ISD 4,800/PK-12
2214 Waller St 77484 936-931-3685
Richard T. McReavy, supt. Fax 372-5576
www.waller.isd.esc4.net/
Waller HS 1,400/9-12
20950 Fields Store Rd 77484 936-372-3654
Kelly Baehren, prin. Fax 372-4114
Waller JHS 800/7-8
2402 Waller St 77484 936-931-1353
Troy Mooney, prin. Fax 931-4044

Wallis, Austin, Pop. 1,232
Brazos ISD 900/PK-12
PO Box 819 77485 979-478-6551
Dr. Mike Bergman, supt. Fax 478-6413
www.brazosisd.net/
Brazos HS 300/9-12
PO Box 458 77485 979-478-6832
Lyle Ebner, prin. Fax 478-7161
Brazos MS 200/6-8
PO Box 879 77485 979-478-6411
Jackie Ellis, prin. Fax 478-7211

Walnut Springs, Bosque, Pop. 786
Walnut Springs ISD 300/PK-12
PO Box 63 76690 254-797-2133
Randy Edwards, supt. Fax 797-2191
Walnut Springs S 300/PK-12
PO Box 63 76690 254-797-2132
Chris Hestilow, prin. Fax 797-2191

Warren, Tyler
Warren ISD 1,100/PK-12
PO Box 69 77664 409-547-2241
Mike Pate, supt. Fax 547-3405
Warren HS 300/9-12
PO Box 190 77664 409-547-2243
James Swinney, prin. Fax 547-0214
Warren JHS 300/6-8
PO Box 205 77664 409-547-2246
Ernestine Mitchell, prin. Fax 547-2740

Waskom, Harrison, Pop. 2,104
Waskom ISD 800/PK-12
PO Box 748 75692 903-687-3361
Jimmy E. Cox, supt. Fax 687-3253
www.waskomisd.net
Waskom HS, PO Box 748 75692 200/9-12
Rick Baker, prin. 903-687-3362
Waskom MS, PO Box 748 75692 200/6-8
Penny Champion, prin. 903-687-3402

Watauga, Tarrant, Pop. 23,593
Birdville ISD
Supt. — See Haltom City
Watauga MS 700/6-8
6300 Maurie Dr 76148 817-547-4800
Michael Jasso, prin. Fax 581-5369

Harvest Christian Academy 600/PK-12
7200 Denton Hwy 76148 817-485-1660
Judy Dodson, hdmstr. Fax 514-6279

Water Valley, Tom Green
Water Valley ISD 300/PK-12
PO Box 250 76958 325-484-2478
David Howard, supt. Fax 484-3359
www.watervalley.netxv.net
Water Valley JSHS 100/7-12
PO Box 250 76958 325-484-2424
Richard Bain, prin. Fax 484-3359

Waxahachie, Ellis, Pop. 23,915
Waxahachie ISD 5,800/PK-12
411 N Gibson St 75165 972-923-4631
Dr. James E. Wilcox, supt. Fax 923-4759
www.wisd.org
Waxahachie HS 1,200/10-12
1000 N Highway 77 75165 972-923-4600
David Nix, prin. Fax 923-4617
Waxahachie JHS 1,000/7-8
2401 Brown St 75165 972-923-4680
Robert Woodhouse, prin. Fax 923-4687
Waxahatchie 9th Grade Academy 500/9-9
275 Indian Dr 75165 972-923-4780
John Aune, prin. Fax 923-4782

Cornerstone Christian S 300/PK-12
701 W Highway 287 Byp 75165 972-937-5611
Liz Matteson, prin. Fax 938-0078
Southwestern Assemblies of God Univ. Post-Sec.
1200 Sycamore St 75165 972-937-4010
Waxahachie Preparatory Academy 200/K-12
PO Box P 75168 972-937-0440
John Cullen, prin. Fax 937-5033

Weatherford, Parker, Pop. 21,420
Peaster ISD 900/PK-12
8512 FM Road 920 76088 817-341-5000
Philip Bledsoe, supt. Fax 341-5003
www.peaster.net
Peaster HS 300/9-12
8512 FM Road 920 76088 817-341-5000
Mark Burress, prin. Fax 341-5027
Peaster MS 200/6-8
8512 FM Road 920 76088 817-341-5000
Ed Daugherty, prin. Fax 341-5052
Weatherford ISD 7,000/PK-12
1100 Longhorn Dr 76086 817-598-2800
Dr. Deborah Cron, supt. Fax 598-2835
www.weatherfordisd.com
Hall MS 600/7-8
902 Charles St 76086 817-598-2822
Linda Roy, prin. Fax 598-2854
Ninth Grade Center 600/9-9
1007 S Main St 76086 817-598-2847
Jim Vaszauskas, prin. Fax 598-2928
Tison MS 500/7-8
102 Meadowview Rd 76087 817-598-2960
Dr. Nita Ellis, prin. Fax 598-2963
Weatherford HS 1,400/10-12
2121 Bethel Rd 76087 817-598-2858
Dr. Chip Evans, prin. Fax 598-2881

Weatherford College Post-Sec.
225 College Park Dr 76086 817-594-5471

Weimar, Colorado, Pop. 1,995
Weimar ISD 700/PK-12
506 W Main St 78962 979-725-9506
Mike Wallace Ed.D., supt. Fax 725-8737
www.weimarisd.org/
Weimar HS 200/9-12
506 W Main St 78962 979-725-9504
Dr. Mike Laird, prin. Fax 725-8737
Weimar JHS 200/6-8
101 N West St 78962 979-725-9515
Nancy Schapp, prin. Fax 725-8383

Welch, Dawson
Dawson ISD 200/PK-12
PO Box 180 79377 806-489-7461
Tim Seymore, supt. Fax 489-7463
Dawson S 200/PK-12
PO Box 180 79377 806-489-7461
Marva Hogue, prin. Fax 489-7463

Wellington, Collingsworth, Pop. 2,129
Wellington ISD 600/PK-12
609 15th St 79095 806-447-2512
Carl Taylor, supt. Fax 447-5124
www.wellingtonisd.net
Wellington HS 200/9-12
811 15th St 79095 806-447-2527
Danny Chisum, prin. Fax 447-9012
Wellington JHS 100/6-8
1504 Amarillo St 79095 806-447-5726
Don Hinsley, prin. Fax 447-5089

Wellman, Terry, Pop. 200
Wellman-Union ISD 100/K-12
PO Box 129 79378 806-637-4910
Leslie Vann, supt. Fax 637-2585
wellman.esc17.net
Wellman-Union HS 100/6-12
PO Box 129 79378 806-637-4619
Russell Schaub, prin. Fax 637-2585

Wells, Cherokee, Pop. 784
Wells ISD 200/PK-12
PO Box 469 75976 936-867-4466
Dale Morton, supt. Fax 867-4466
www.wells.esc7.net
Wells HS 9-12
PO Box 469 75976 936-867-4400
Bradley Hines, prin. Fax 867-4466

Weslaco, Hidalgo, Pop. 30,416
Weslaco ISD 15,000/PK-12
PO Box 266 78599 956-969-6500
Richard Rivera, supt. Fax 969-2664
www.wisd.us
Central MS 900/6-8
503 E 6th St 78596 956-969-6710
Lauren Arce, prin. Fax 969-0779
Cuellar MS 700/6-8
1201 S Bridge Ave 78596 956-969-6720
Mario Hernandez, prin. Fax 973-9797
Garza MS 900/6-8
1111 W Sugar Cane Dr 78596 956-969-6774
Daniel Budimir, prin. Fax 447-0484
Hoge MS 800/6-8
2302 N International Blvd 78596 956-969-6730
Patricia Munoz, prin. Fax 514-0903
Weslaco East HS 1,600/9-12
810 S Pleasantview Dr 78596 956-969-6950
Sue Peterson, prin. Fax 968-8693
Weslaco HS 2,000/9-12
1005 W Pike Blvd 78596 956-969-6700
Isidoro Nieto, prin. Fax 968-8008

Advanced Barber College and Hair Design Post-Sec.
2818 S International Blvd 78596 956-969-0341
South Texas Vocational-Technical Inst. Post-Sec.
2419 E Hagger Ave 78596 956-969-1564
Valley Grande Academy 100/9-12
PO Box 1126 78599 956-968-0573
Fax 968-9814

West, McLennan, Pop. 2,699
West ISD 1,500/PK-12
801 N Reagan St 76691 254-826-7500
Rob Hart Ed.D., supt. Fax 826-7503
www.westisd.net
West HS 500/9-12
801 N Reagan St 76691 254-826-7510
Phyllis Ramsey, prin. Fax 826-7514
West MS 300/6-8
801 N Reagan St 76691 254-826-7520
Grady Fulbright, prin. Fax 826-7524

Westbrook, Mitchell, Pop. 193
Westbrook ISD 200/PK-12
PO Box 99 79565 325-644-2311
Todd Burleson, supt. Fax 644-5101
www.westbrookisd.com
Westbrook S 200/PK-12
PO Box 99 79565 325-644-2311
Doc Rowell, prin. Fax 644-5101

West Columbia, Brazoria, Pop. 4,284
Columbia-Brazoria ISD 3,100/PK-12
PO Box 158 77486 979-345-5147
Carol Bertholf, supt. Fax 345-4890
www.cbisd.org
Columbia HS 900/9-12
PO Box 158 77486 979-345-5147
Steve Galloway, prin. Fax 345-6785
West Columbia JHS 500/7-8
PO Box 158 77486 979-345-4131
Chuck Rylander, prin. Fax 345-6871

Columbia Christian S 100/PK-12
725 W Brazos Ave 77486 979-345-2434
Joshua Davenport, prin. Fax 345-5134

Wharton, Wharton, Pop. 9,337
Wharton ISD 2,500/PK-12
2100 N Fulton St 77488 979-532-6201
Don Hillis, supt. Fax 532-6228
www.wharton.isd.tenet.edu/
Wharton HS 700/9-12
1 Tiger Ave 77488 979-532-6800
Don Jennings, prin. Fax 532-6807
Wharton JHS 400/7-8
1120 N Rusk St 77488 979-532-6840
Larry Boyette, prin. Fax 532-6849

Wharton County Junior College Post-Sec.
911 E Boling Hwy 77488 979-532-4560

Wheeler, Wheeler, Pop. 1,247
Wheeler ISD 300/PK-12
PO Box 1010 79096 806-826-5241
Roy Baker, supt. Fax 826-3118
www.thestangs.com/
Wheeler S, PO Box 1010 79096 300/PK-12
Toby Tucker, prin. 806-826-5534

White Deer, Carson, Pop. 1,060
White Deer ISD 400/K-12
PO Box 517 79097 806-883-2311
Danny Ferrell, supt. Fax 883-2321
www.pan-tex.net/wdisd
White Deer HS 100/9-12
PO Box 248 79097 806-883-6414
Tom Norrell, prin. Fax 883-5029

Whiteface, Cochran, Pop. 437
Whiteface Consolidated ISD 400/PK-12
PO Box 7 79379 806-287-1154
Elbert Wuthrich, supt. Fax 287-1131
www.whiteface.k12.tx.us
Whiteface JSHS 200/7-12
PO Box 67 79379 806-287-1104
James German, prin. Fax 287-1131

Whitehouse, Smith, Pop. 6,582
Whitehouse ISD 4,100/PK-12
106 Wildcat Dr 75791 903-839-5500
Dennis Miller, supt. Fax 839-5515
www.whitehouseisd.org
Whitehouse HS, 901 E Main St 75791 1,200/9-12
Tony Black, prin. 903-839-5551
Whitehouse JHS 600/7-8
108 Wildcat Dr 75791 903-839-5560
David Smith, prin.

White Oak, Gregg, Pop. 5,858
White Oak ISD 1,300/PK-12
200 S White Oak Rd 75693 903-291-2200
Jack R. Hale, supt. Fax 291-2222
www.woisd.net
White Oak HS 400/9-12
200 S White Oak Rd 75693 903-291-2000
Don Noll, prin. Fax 291-2034
White Oak MS 300/6-8
200 S White Oak Rd 75693 903-291-2050
Ronnie Hinkle, prin. Fax 291-2035

Whitesboro, Grayson, Pop. 3,961
Whitesboro ISD 1,600/PK-12
115 4th St 76273 903-564-4200
Ray Lea, supt. Fax 564-9303
www.whitesboroisd.org
Whitesboro HS 500/9-12
1 Bearcat Dr 76273 903-564-4208
Rendell Cole, prin. Fax 564-4288
Whitesboro MS 400/6-8
600 4th St 76273 903-564-4240
Patty Mitchell, prin. Fax 564-5939

White Settlement, Tarrant, Pop. 15,553
White Settlement ISD
Supt. — See Fort Worth
Brewer HS 900/10-12
1000 S Cherry Ln 76108 817-367-1200
Julio Toro, prin. Fax 367-1242
Brewer MS 800/7-8
1000 S Cherry Ln 76108 817-367-1267
Christie Beaty, prin. Fax 367-1268

Whitewright, Grayson, Pop. 1,768
Whitewright ISD 800/PK-12
PO Box 888 75491 903-364-2155
Robert O'Connor, supt. Fax 364-2839
Whitewright HS 300/9-12
PO Box 888 75491 903-364-2535
Bobby Worthy, prin. Fax 364-2579
Whitewright MS 200/6-8
PO Box 888 75491 903-364-2151
Reid Pittman, prin. Fax 364-5263

Whitharral, Hockley
Whitharral ISD 200/K-12
PO Box 225 79380 806-299-1184
Ed Sharp, supt. Fax 299-1257
www.whitharral.k12.tx.us/
Whitharral S 200/K-12
PO Box 225 79380 806-299-1135
Carla Kristinek, prin. Fax 299-1257

Whitney, Hill, Pop. 1,987
Whitney ISD 1,500/PK-12
PO Box 518 76692 254-694-2254
Lee Coffman, supt. Fax 694-2064
www.whitney.k12.tx.us
Whitney HS 400/9-12
PO Box 518 76692 254-694-3457
Curt Haley, prin. Fax 694-4206
Whitney JHS, PO Box 518 76692 400/6-8
Wayne Redding, prin. 254-694-3446

Wichita Falls, Wichita, Pop. 102,340
City View ISD 1,100/PK-12
1025 City View Dr 76306 940-855-4042
Michael Smith, supt. Fax 851-8889
www.cityview-isd.net/
City View JSHS 400/7-12
1600 City View Dr 76306 940-855-7511
Steve Harris, prin. Fax 851-5027

Wichita Falls ISD 14,700/PK-12
PO Box 97533 76307 940-720-3273
Dr. Dawson Orr, supt. Fax 720-3167
www.wfisd.net
Barwise JHS 600/7-8
3807 Kemp Blvd 76308 940-720-3035
Linda Muehlberger, prin. Fax 692-2372
Carrigan Vocational Center Vo/Tech
1609 Blonde St 76301 940-720-3224
Rhonda Hall, prin. Fax 720-3368
Hirschi HS 900/9-12
3106 Borton St 76306 940-716-2800
Wanda Jackson, prin. Fax 716-2835
Kirby JHS 600/7-8
1715 Loop 11 76306 940-716-2900
Dee Palmore, prin. Fax 716-2915
McNiel JHS 700/7-8
4712 Barnett Rd 76310 940-720-3030
Carol English, prin. Fax 720-3032
Rider HS 1,600/9-12
4611 Cypress Ave 76310 940-720-3000
Nat Lunn, prin. Fax 720-3002
Wichita Falls HS 1,500/9-12
2149 Avenue H 76309 940-720-3177
Dr. Robert Mobley, prin. Fax 767-4248
Zundelowitz JHS 400/7-8
1706 Polk St 76309 940-720-3170
Chad Brewster, prin. Fax 720-3172

Agape Christian S 100/K-12
5600 Burkburnett Rd 76306 940-851-6727
John Meade, prin. Fax 851-6592
American Commercial College Post-Sec.
4317 Barnett Rd 76310 940-691-0454
Midwestern State University Post-Sec.
3410 Taft Blvd 76308 940-397-4000
Notre Dame S 300/PK-12
2821 Lansing Blvd 76309 940-692-6041
Dr. Robert McBee, prin. Fax 692-2811
United Regional Health Care System Post-Sec.
1600 11th St 76301 940-764-3187

Willis, Montgomery, Pop. 4,225
Willis ISD 6,000/PK-12
204 W Rogers St 77378 936-856-1200
Dr. Brian Zemlicka, supt. Fax 856-5182
wisd.willis.k12.tx.us
Brabham MS 6-8
10000 FM 830 Rd 77318 936-890-2312
Sheryl Burlison, prin. Fax 856-2910
Lucas MS 900/6-8
1304 N Campbell St 77378 936-856-1274
Tiffany Forester, prin. Fax 856-1065
Willis HS 1,400/9-12
1201 FM 830 Rd 77378 936-856-1250
Ben Cooper, prin. Fax 856-3391

Willow Park, Parker, Pop. 3,208

Trinity Christian Academy 400/PK-12
4954 E Interstate 20 Svc Rd 76087 817-441-7901
Dr. Marsha Barber, admin. Fax 441-7912

Wills Point, Van Zandt, Pop. 3,661
Wills Point ISD 2,700/PK-12
338 W North Commerce St 75169 903-873-3161
William Stewart, supt. Fax 873-2462
www.ednet10.net/willspoint/
Wills Point HS 800/9-12
1800 W South Commerce St 75169 903-873-2371
Jim Lamb, prin. Fax 873-6008
Wills Point JHS 400/7-8
200 Tiger Dr 75169 903-873-4924
Thomas Harp, prin. Fax 873-4873

Wilson, Lynn, Pop. 499
Wilson ISD 200/PK-12
PO Box 9 79381 806-628-6271
Mike Jones, supt. Fax 628-6441
wilson.esc17.net/
Wilson S 200/PK-12
PO Box 9 79381 806-628-6261
Larry Williams, prin. Fax 628-6441

Wimberley, Hays, Pop. 2,710
Wimberley ISD 1,900/PK-12
14401 Ranch Rd 12 78676 512-847-2414
Dr. Marian Strauss, supt. Fax 847-2142
www.wimberley.txed.net/
Wimberley HS 600/9-12
100 Carney Ln 78676 512-847-5729
Dwain York, prin. Fax 847-7269
Wimberley JHS 400/6-8
200 Texan Blvd 78676 512-847-2181
Dee Howard, prin. Fax 847-7897

Windthorst, Archer, Pop. 451
Windthorst ISD 500/PK-12
PO Box 190 76389 940-423-6688
Anne Poplin, supt. Fax 423-6505
www.esc9.net/windthorst
Windthorst JSHS 200/7-12
PO Box 190 76389 940-423-6680
Leonard Schenk, prin. Fax 423-6505

Wink, Winkler, Pop. 885
Wink-Loving ISD 300/PK-12
PO Box 637 79789 432-527-3880
John Benham, supt. Fax 527-3505
wlisd.esc18.net
Wink JSHS 200/7-12
PO Box 637 79789 432-527-3880
Danny Carrillo, prin. Fax 527-3505

Winnie, Chambers, Pop. 2,238
East Chambers ISD 1,200/PK-12
1955 State Highway 124 77665 409-296-6100
Scott Campbell, supt. Fax 296-3528
www.eastchambers.net
East Chambers HS 300/9-12
234 E Buccaneer Dr 77665 409-296-6100
Steve Franzen, prin. Fax 296-9596
East Chambers JHS 200/7-8
1931 State Highway 124 77665 409-296-6100
Lou Ann Rainey, prin. Fax 296-2724

Winnsboro, Wood, Pop. 3,745
Winnsboro ISD 1,500/PK-12
207 E Pine St 75494 903-342-3737
Dr. Mark Bosold, supt. Fax 342-3380
www.winnsboroisd.org
Memorial MS 400/5-8
505 S Chestnut St 75494 903-342-5711
Nan Saucier, prin. Fax 342-6689
Winnsboro HS 400/9-12
409 Newsome St 75494 903-342-3641
Susan Morton, prin. Fax 342-3645

Winona, Smith, Pop. 597
Winona ISD 1,000/PK-12
PO Box 218 75792 903-939-4001
Rodney Fausett, supt. Fax 877-9387
Winona HS 300/9-12
PO Box 218 75792 903-939-4100
Brent Rumbo, prin. Fax 877-2451
Winona MS 200/6-8
PO Box 218 75792 903-939-4040
Oscar Rendon, prin. Fax 877-9150

Winters, Runnels, Pop. 2,739
Winters ISD 700/PK-12
603 N Heights St 79567 325-754-5574
Danny Clack, supt. Fax 754-5374
www.wintersisd.org/
Winters HS 200/9-12
603 N Heights St 79567 325-754-5516
Allan Gillespie, prin. Fax 754-5085
Winters JHS 100/7-8
603 N Heights St 79567 325-754-5518
David Evans, prin. Fax 754-5085

Woden, Nacogdoches
Woden ISD 900/PK-12
PO Box 100 75978 936-564-2073
L. Wayne Mason, supt. Fax 564-1250
www.woden.esc7.net/
Woden HS 300/9-12
PO Box 100 75978 936-564-7903
Mike King, prin. Fax 462-4962
Woden JHS, PO Box 100 75978 200/6-8
Keith Lowery, prin. 936-564-2481

Wolfe City, Hunt, Pop. 1,631
Wolfe City ISD 600/PK-12
PO Box L 75496 903-496-2283
Rick Loesch, supt. Fax 496-7905
www.wcisd.net
Wolfe City HS 200/9-12
505 W Dallas St 75496 903-496-2891
Chris Sheets, prin. Fax 496-7124
Wolfe City MS 100/6-8
505 W Dallas St 75496 903-496-7333
Chris Sheets, prin. Fax 496-7905

Wolfforth, Lubbock, Pop. 2,725
Frenship ISD 6,500/PK-12
PO Box 100 79382 806-866-9541
John R. Thomas, supt. Fax 866-4135
www.frenship.us
Frenship HS 1,300/9-12
PO Box 100 79382 806-866-4440
Kim Spicer, prin. Fax 866-9370
Frenship MS 1,200/6-8
PO Box 100 79382 806-866-4464
Jerry Jerabek, prin. Fax 866-2181
Other Schools – See Lubbock

Woodsboro, Refugio, Pop. 1,631
Woodsboro ISD 500/PK-12
PO Box 770 78393 361-543-4518
Steven Self, supt. Fax 543-4856
www.wisd.net
Woodsboro HS 100/9-12
PO Box 770 78393 361-543-4521
Brian Hicks, prin. Fax 543-5140
Woodsboro JHS, PO Box 770 78393 100/6-8
Mary P. Vickery, prin. 361-543-4622

Woodson, Throckmorton, Pop. 274
Woodson ISD 100/PK-12
PO Box 287 76491 940-345-6528
Dan Bellah, supt. Fax 345-6549
www.esc9.net/woodson/
Woodson S 100/PK-12
PO Box 287 76491 940-345-6521
Gordon Thomas, prin. Fax 345-6549

Woodville, Tyler, Pop. 2,329
Woodville ISD 1,300/PK-12
505 N Charlton St 75979 409-283-3752
Dr. Eric Wright, supt. Fax 283-7962
www.esc05.k12.tx.us/woodville
Woodville HS 400/9-12
505 N Charlton St 75979 409-283-3714
Roschelle Springfield, prin. Fax 331-3427
Woodville MS 300/6-8
505 N Charlton St 75979 409-283-7109
Dr. Sherry Kenner, prin. Fax 331-3418

Wortham, Freestone, Pop. 1,084
Wortham ISD 400/PK-12
PO Box 247 76693 254-765-3080
Albert Armer, supt. Fax 765-3473
www.esc12.net/worthamisd
Wortham HS 100/9-12
PO Box 247 76693 254-765-3094
Lynn Jantzen, prin. Fax 765-3473
Wortham MS 100/6-8
PO Box 247 76693 254-765-3094
Lynn Jantzen, prin. Fax 765-3473

Wylie, Dallas, Pop. 21,720
Wylie ISD 6,500/PK-12
PO Box 490 75098 972-429-3000
Dr. H. John Fuller, supt. Fax 442-5368
www.wylieisd.net
Burnett JHS 800/7-8
PO Box 490 75098 972-429-3200
Mike Williams, prin. Fax 429-7999
McMillan JHS 800/7-8
PO Box 490 75098 972-429-3225
Jon Peters, prin. Fax 941-6372
Wylie HS 1,700/9-12
PO Box 490 75098 972-429-3100
Gary Brown, prin. Fax 429-3077

Wylie Preparatory Academy 100/1-12
PO Box 2273 75098 972-442-1388
Jim Sullenger, prin. Fax 429-3568

Yantis, Wood, Pop. 349
Yantis ISD 400/PK-12
105 W Oak St 75497 903-383-2463
Jim Richardson, supt. Fax 383-7620
www.yantisisd.net
Yantis HS 200/6-12
105 W Oak St 75497 903-383-2463
Richard Kirby, prin. Fax 383-3075

Yoakum, Lavaca, Pop. 5,734
Yoakum ISD 1,400/PK-12
PO Box 737 77995 361-293-3162
Michael Poynor, supt. Fax 293-6678
www.yoakumisd.net/
Yoakum HS 500/9-12
PO Box 737 77995 361-293-3442
Chris Kvinta, prin. Fax 293-2145
Yoakum JHS 300/6-8
PO Box 737 77995 361-293-3111
Pat Brewer, prin. Fax 293-5787

Yorktown, DeWitt, Pop. 2,238
Yorktown ISD 700/PK-12
PO Box 487 78164 361-564-2252
Deborah Kneese, supt. Fax 564-2254
www.yisd.org
Yorktown HS 200/9-12
PO Box 487 78164 361-564-2252
David Plymale, prin. Fax 564-2274
Yorktown JHS 200/6-8
PO Box 487 78164 361-564-2252
Sylvia Hernandez, prin. Fax 564-2289

Zapata, Zapata, Pop. 7,119
Zapata County ISD 3,200/PK-12
PO Box 158 78076 956-765-6546
Romeo Rodriguez, supt. Fax 765-8350
www.zcisd.org
Zapata HS 800/9-12
PO Box 3750 78076 956-765-0280
Jose Flores, prin. Fax 765-0274
Zapata MS 700/6-8
PO Box 3636 78076 956-765-6542
Jose Morales, prin. Fax 765-9204

Zavalla, Angelina, Pop. 653
Zavalla ISD 400/PK-12
PO Box 45 75980 936-897-2271
Dr. Kathy Ray, supt. Fax 897-2674
www.zavalla.esc7.net
Zavalla JSHS 200/6-12
PO Box 45 75980 936-897-2301
Clark Bynum, prin. Fax 897-2674

Zephyr, Brown
Zephyr ISD 200/K-12
11625 County Road 281 76890 325-739-5331
David Whisenhunt, supt. Fax 739-2126
Zephyr JSHS 100/7-12
11625 County Road 281 76890 325-739-5331
Gary Bufe, prin. Fax 739-2126

UTAH

UTAH OFFICE OF EDUCATION
PO Box 144200, Salt Lake City 84114-4200
Telephone 801-538-7500
Fax 801-538-7768
Website http://www.usoe.k12.ut.us

Superintendent of Public Instruction   Patti Harrington

UTAH BOARD OF EDUCATION
250 E 500 S, Salt Lake City 84111-3284

Chairperson   Kim Burningham

REGIONAL SERVICE CENTERS (RSC)

Central Utah Educational Services
Glen Taylor, dir. — 435-896-4469
195 E 500 N, Richfield 84701 — Fax 896-4767

Northeastern Utah Educational Services
Gerold R. Erickson, dir. — 435-654-1921
755 S Main St, Heber City 84032 — Fax 654-2403

Southeast Educational Service Center
Thomas Roush, dir. — 435-637-1173
685 E 200 S, Price 84501 — Fax 637-1178
Southwest Educational Development Ctr
Randy Johnson, dir. — 435-586-2865
520 W 800 S, Cedar City 84720 — Fax 586-2868

PUBLIC, PRIVATE AND CATHOLIC SECONDARY SCHOOLS

Alpine, Utah, Pop. 7,937
Alpine SD
Supt. — See American Fork
Timberline MS — 900/7-9
500 W Canyon Crest Rd 84004 — 801-763-7005
Terry Hill, prin. — Fax 763-7045

Altamont, Duchesne, Pop. 178
Duchesne SD
Supt. — See Duchesne
Altamont JSHS — 200/7-12
PO Box 130 84001 — 435-738-1345
Mary Ellen Kettle, prin. — Fax 738-1370

American Fork, Utah, Pop. 22,876
Alpine SD — 50,000/K-12
575 N 100 E 84003 — 801-756-8400
Dr. Vernon Henshaw, supt. — Fax 756-8516
www.alpine.k12.ut.us/
American Fork JHS — 1,400/7-9
20 W 1120 N 84003 — 801-756-8543
Theron Murphy, prin. — Fax 756-8407
American Fork SHS — 1,400/10-12
510 N 600 E 84003 — 801-756-8547
Carolyn Merrill, prin. — Fax 756-8575
Other Schools – See Alpine, Highland, Lehi, Lindon,
Orem, Pleasant Grove

Beaver, Beaver, Pop. 2,511
Beaver SD — 1,500/K-12
PO Box 31 84713 — 435-438-2291
Henry Jolley, supt. — Fax 438-5898
www.beaver.k12.ut.us
Beaver JSHS — 400/7-12
PO Box 71 84713 — 435-438-2301
David Green, prin. — Fax 438-1519
Other Schools – See Milford

Bicknell, Wayne, Pop. 337
Wayne SD — 500/K-12
PO Box 127 84715 — 435-425-3813
Jessie Pace, supt. — Fax 425-3806
www.wayne.k12.ut.us
Wayne HS — 200/9-12
PO Box 217 84715 — 435-425-3411
Charles Nelson, prin. — Fax 425-3480
Wayne MS — 100/6-8
PO Box 128 84715 — 435-425-3421
Mary Bray, lead tchr. — Fax 425-3130

Big Water, Kane, Pop. 416
Kane SD
Supt. — See Kanab
Big Water HS — 7-12
PO Box 410126 84741 — 435-675-5821
Gary Young, prin. — Fax 675-5821

Blanding, San Juan, Pop. 3,035
San Juan SD — 3,000/K-12
200 N Main St 84511 — 435-678-1200
Dr. Douglas E. Wright, supt. — Fax 678-1204
www.sanjuan.k12.ut.us
Lyman MS — 300/6-8
535 N 100 E 84511 — 435-678-1398
Chas DeWitt, prin. — Fax 678-1399
San Juan HS — 400/9-12
311 N 100 E 84511 — 435-678-1301
Bob Peterson, prin. — Fax 678-1396
Other Schools – See Montezuma Creek, Monticello,
Monument Valley

Bountiful, Davis, Pop. 41,401
Davis SD
Supt. — See Farmington

Bountiful JHS — 700/7-9
30 W 400 N 84010 — 801-402-6000
Steve Lindsay, prin. — Fax 402-6001
Bountiful SHS — 1,300/10-12
695 Orchard Dr 84010 — 801-402-3900
Ryck Astle, prin. — Fax 402-3901
Millcreek JHS — 600/7-9
245 E 1000 S 84010 — 801-402-6200
David Tanner, prin. — Fax 402-6201
Mueller Park JHS — 700/7-9
955 E 1800 S 84010 — 801-402-6300
Dr. Doug Beer, prin. — Fax 402-6301
South Davis JHS — 900/7-9
298 W 2600 S 84010 — 801-402-6400
Bryan Nielsen, prin. — Fax 402-6401
Viewmont SHS — 1,800/10-12
120 W 1000 N 84010 — 801-402-4200
Scott Tennis, prin. — Fax 402-4201

Brigham City, Box Elder, Pop. 17,334
Box Elder SD — 11,500/K-12
960 S Main St 84302 — 435-734-4800
Martell Menlove, supt. — Fax 734-4833
www.besd.net
Box Elder MS — 1,000/8-9
18 S 500 E 84302 — 435-734-4880
Mike Madeo, prin. — Fax 734-4885
Box Elder SHS — 1,300/10-12
380 S 600 W 84302 — 435-734-4840
Darrell Eddington, prin. — Fax 734-4846
Young Alternative HS — Adult
230 W 200 S 84302 — 435-734-4834
Steve Chadaz, prin. — Fax 734-4860
Other Schools – See Garland, Grouse Creek, Park Valley

Northridge Learning Center — 100/K-12
44 S Main St 84302 — 435-734-2550
— Fax 723-3903

Castle Dale, Emery, Pop. 1,618
Emery County SD
Supt. — See Huntington
Emery SHS — 500/10-12
PO Box 499 84513 — 435-381-2689
Gwen Callahan, prin. — Fax 381-5370

Cedar City, Iron, Pop. 21,946
Iron SD — 6,600/K-12
2077 W Royal Hunte Dr 84720 — 435-586-2804
James S. Johnson, supt. — Fax 586-2815
www.iron.k12.ut.us
Canyon View HS — 900/9-12
166 W 1925 N 84720 — 435-586-2813
Jennifer Wood, prin. — Fax 586-2849
Canyon View MS — 6-8
1865 N Main St 84720 — 435-586-2830
Conrad Aitken, prin. — Fax 586-2837
Cedar HS — 900/9-12
703 W 600 S 84720 — 435-586-2820
Kevin Garrett, prin. — Fax 586-2826
Cedar MS — 800/6-8
2215 W Royal Hunte Dr 84720 — 435-586-2810
Kendall Benson, prin. — Fax 586-2829
Adult HS/Southwest Education Academy — Adult
510 W 800 S 84720 — 435-586-2870
Dennis Heaton, prin. — Fax 586-2815
Other Schools – See Parowan

Southern Utah University — Post-Sec.
351 W Center St 84720 — 435-586-7715
Southwest Applied Technology College — Post-Sec.
510 W 800 S 84720 — 435-586-2899

Centerville, Davis, Pop. 14,748
Davis SD
Supt. — See Farmington
Centerville JHS — 1,000/7-9
625 S Main St 84014 — 801-402-6100
Craig Hansen, prin. — Fax 402-6101

Clearfield, Davis, Pop. 27,146
Davis SD
Supt. — See Farmington
Clearfield SHS — 1,900/10-12
931 S 1000 E 84015 — 801-402-8200
Mike Timothy, prin. — Fax 402-8336
North Davis JHS — 900/7-9
835 S State St 84015 — 801-402-6500
Curtis Stromberg, prin. — Fax 402-6501

Certified Careers Institute — Post-Sec.
775 S 2000 E 84015 — 801-774-9900

Coalville, Summit, Pop. 1,426
North Summit SD — 1,000/PK-12
PO Box 497 84017 — 435-336-5654
Steven Carlson, supt. — Fax 336-2401
www.nsummit.k12.ut.us
North Summit HS — 300/9-12
PO Box 497 84017 — 435-336-5656
Jerre Holmes, prin. — Fax 336-0309
North Summit MS — 300/5-8
PO Box 497 84017 — 435-336-5678
Lloyd Marchant, prin. — Fax 336-4474

Cottonwood Heights, Salt Lake, Pop. 27,500
Jordan SD
Supt. — See Sandy
Brighton SHS — 2,000/10-12
2220 Bengal Blvd, — 801-256-5200
Robert Sproul, prin. — Fax 256-5270

Delta, Millard, Pop. 3,186
Millard SD — 3,300/K-12
285 E 450 N 84624 — 435-864-5600
David W. Taylor, supt. — Fax 864-5684
www.millard.k12.ut.us
Delta HS — 700/9-12
50 W 300 N 84624 — 435-864-5610
Dean Fowles, prin. — Fax 864-5619
Delta MS — 500/6-8
251 E 300 N 84624 — 435-864-5660
David Styler, prin. — Fax 864-5669
Delta Tech Ctr — Vo/Tech
305 E 200 N 84624 — 435-864-5710
LaVoy Starley, prin. — Fax 864-5719
Other Schools – See Fillmore

Draper, Salt Lake, Pop. 31,020

Ameritech College — Post-Sec.
12257 Business Park Dr #108 84020 — 801-816-1444
Juan Diego Catholic HS — 300/9-12
300 E 11800 S 84020 — 801-984-7602
Gabriel Colosimo, prin. — Fax 984-7601
Oxford Learning Source — 50/PK-12
1259 Draper Pkwy 84020 — 801-501-0228
Shelly Siebach, dir. — Fax 501-0296
Pine Ridge Academy — 50/7-12
PO Box 909 84020 — 801-562-1717
Lisa Wisham, dir. — Fax 572-8220
St. John the Baptist MS — 300/6-8
300 E 11800 S 84020 — 801-984-7613
Nikki Ward, prin. — Fax 984-7649

Duchesne, Duchesne, Pop. 1,447
Duchesne SD — 3,900/K-12
PO Box 446 84021 — 435-738-1240
John Aland, supt. — Fax 738-1254
www.dcsd.org
Duchesne JSHS — 300/7-12
PO Box 330 84021 — 435-738-1260
Stan Young, prin. — Fax 738-1285
Other Schools – See Altamont, Roosevelt, Tabiona

Dugway, Tooele, Pop. 1,761
Tooele County SD
Supt. — See Tooele
Dugway JSHS — 100/7-12
Bldg 5020 5th St 84022 — 435-831-4566
Karen Swenson, prin. — Fax 831-4951

Eden, Weber
Weber SD
Supt. — See Ogden
Snowcrest JHS — 300/7-9
2755 N Highway 162 84310 — 801-476-5360
Rob Stillwell, prin. — Fax 476-5399

Enterprise, Washington, Pop. 1,298
Washington County SD
Supt. — See Saint George
Enterprise JSHS — 300/7-12
PO Box 460 84725 — 435-878-2248
Russell Holmes, prin. — Fax 878-2479

Ephraim, Sanpete, Pop. 4,962
South Sanpete SD
Supt. — See Manti
Ephraim MS — 400/6-8
555 S 100 E 84627 — 435-283-4037
Kent Larsen, prin. — Fax 283-4885

Snow College — Post-Sec.
150 College Ave 84627 — 435-283-7000

Escalante, Garfield, Pop. 771
Garfield SD
Supt. — See Panguitch
Escalante HS — 100/7-12
PO Box 228 84726 — 435-826-4205
Angie Alvey, prin. — Fax 826-4231

Eureka, Juab, Pop. 772
Tintic SD — 300/PK-12
PO Box 210 84628 — 435-433-6363
Ron Barlow, supt. — Fax 433-6643
www.tintic.k12.ut.us
Tintic JSHS — 100/7-12
PO Box 230 84628 — 435-433-6939
Gordon Grimstead, prin. — Fax 433-6845
Other Schools – See Trout Creek

Farmington, Davis, Pop. 13,407
Davis SD — 57,400/PK-12
PO Box 588 84025 — 801-402-5261
Dr. W. Bryan Bowles, supt. — Fax 402-5249
www.davis.k12.ut.us
Farmington JHS — 1,100/7-9
150 S 200 W 84025 — 801-402-6900
Bill Fullmer, prin. — Fax 402-6901
Other Schools – See Bountiful, Centerville, Clearfield, Kaysville, Layton, Sunset, Syracuse, West Point, Woods Cross

Ferron, Emery, Pop. 1,576
Emery County SD
Supt. — See Huntington
San Rafael JHS — 300/7-9
PO Box 790 84523 — 435-384-2335
Garth Johnson, prin. — Fax 384-3354

Fillmore, Millard, Pop. 2,220
Millard SD
Supt. — See Delta
Fillmore MS — 300/5-8
435 S 500 W 84631 — 435-743-5660
Kerry Watson, prin. — Fax 743-5669
Millard HS — 300/9-12
200 W Eagle Ave 84631 — 435-743-5610
Dennis Alldredge, prin. — Fax 743-5619

Garland, Box Elder, Pop. 1,964
Box Elder SD
Supt. — See Brigham City
Bear River MS — 700/8-9
300 E 1500 S 84312 — 435-257-2540
Calvin Bingham, prin. — Fax 257-3945
Bear River SHS — 1,000/10-12
1450 S Main St 84312 — 435-257-2500
Gary Allen, prin. — Fax 257-3899

Grantsville, Tooele, Pop. 6,824
Tooele County SD
Supt. — See Tooele
Grantsville HS — 800/9-12
155 Cowboy Dr 84029 — 435-884-4500
Leon Jones, prin. — Fax 884-4502
Grantsville MS — 500/7-8
318 S Hale St 84029 — 435-884-4510
Keith Davis, prin. — Fax 884-4513

Green River, Emery, Pop. 958
Emery County SD
Supt. — See Huntington
Green River JSHS — 100/7-12
PO Box 450 84525 — 435-564-3461
Nolan Johnson, prin. — Fax 564-3508

Grouse Creek, Box Elder
Box Elder SD
Supt. — See Brigham City
Grouse Creek S — 800/K-10
1 W Buckaroo Blvd 84313 — 435-747-7321
Duane Runyan, prin. — Fax 747-7182

Gunnison, Sanpete, Pop. 2,484
South Sanpete SD
Supt. — See Manti
Gunnison Valley HS — 300/9-12
PO Box 460 84634 — 435-528-7256
Kirk Anderson, prin. — Fax 528-3556
Gunnison Valley MS — 200/6-8
PO Box 1090 84634 — 435-528-5337
Alan Peterson, prin. — Fax 528-5397

Harrisville, Weber, Pop. 4,452
Weber SD
Supt. — See Ogden
Orion JHS — 700/7-9
370 W 2000 N 84404 — 801-452-4700
Steve Elsnab, prin. — Fax 452-4777

Heber City, Wasatch, Pop. 5,299
Wasatch SD — 4,000/K-12
101 E 200 N 84032 — 435-654-0280
Terry Shoemaker, supt. — Fax 654-4714
www.wasatch.edu/
Wasatch HS — 900/10-12
64 E 600 S 84032 — 435-654-0640
Paul Sweat, prin. — Fax 654-3011
Wasatch Mountain JHS — 600/8-9
200 E 800 S 84032 — 435-654-0550
James Judd, prin. — Fax 654-0622

Helper, Carbon, Pop. 1,911
Carbon SD
Supt. — See Price
Helper JHS — 200/7-9
130 Uintah St 84526 — 435-472-5441
Tom Montoya, prin. — Fax 472-3502

Northridge Learning Center — 100/K-12
202 S Main St 84526 — 435-472-0870
Fax 472-0806

Herriman, Salt Lake, Pop. 5,632
Jordan SD
Supt. — See Sandy
Fort Herriman MS — 7-9
14058 Mirabella Dr, — 801-412-2450
Michael Sirois, prin.

Highland, Utah, Pop. 9,642
Alpine SD
Supt. — See American Fork
Lone Peak SHS — 1,600/10-12
10189 N 4800 W 84003 — 801-763-7050
Kenneth Koop, prin. — Fax 763-7064
Mountain Ridge JHS — 1,100/7-9
5525 W 10400 N 84003 — 801-763-7010
Paula Fugal, prin. — Fax 763-7018

Huntington, Emery, Pop. 2,087
Emery County SD — 2,400/K-12
PO Box 120 84528 — 435-687-9846
Kirk Sitterud, supt. — Fax 687-9849
www.emery.k12.ut.us
Canyon View JHS — 200/7-9
PO Box 250 84528 — 435-687-2265
Larry Davis, prin. — Fax 687-9546
Other Schools – See Castle Dale, Ferron, Green River

Hurricane, Washington, Pop. 9,465
Washington County SD
Supt. — See Saint George
Hurricane MS — 800/6-8
395 N 200 W 84737 — 435-635-4634
Larry Bergeson, prin. — Fax 635-4663
Hurricane SHS — 700/10-12
345 W Tiger Blvd 84737 — 435-635-3280
Roy Hoyt, prin. — Fax 635-3287

Hyrum, Cache, Pop. 6,305
Cache SD
Supt. — See Logan
Mountain Crest SHS — 1,400/10-12
255 S 800 E 84319 — 435-245-6093
Jack Robinson, prin. — Fax 245-3818
South Cache JHS — 1,000/8-9
10 S 400 W 84319 — 435-245-6433
Teri Cutler, prin. — Fax 245-6662

Junction, Piute, Pop. 170
Piute SD — 300/PK-12
PO Box 69 84740 — 435-577-2912
Dr. Lewis S. Mullins, supt. — Fax 577-2561
Piute JSHS — 100/7-12
550 N 100 W 84740 — 435-577-2881
Scott Bagley, prin. — Fax 577-2512

Kamas, Summit, Pop. 1,429
South Summit SD — 1,300/PK-12
375 E 300 S 84036 — 435-783-4301
Timothy W. Smith, supt. — Fax 783-4501
www.ssummit.k12.ut.us/
South Summit HS — 400/9-12
45 S 300 E 84036 — 435-783-4313
Gary Twitchell, prin. — Fax 783-4765
South Summit MS — 300/6-8
355 E 300 S 84036 — 435-783-4341
Barry Walker, prin. — Fax 783-2787

Kanab, Kane, Pop. 3,490
Kane SD — 1,200/K-12
746 S 175 E 84741 — 435-644-2555
Robert Johnson, supt. — Fax 644-2509
www.kane.k12.ut.us
Kanab HS — 300/9-12
59 Cowboy Dr 84741 — 435-644-5821
Doug Jacobs, prin. — Fax 644-5242
Kanab MS — 100/7-8
690 Cowboy Way 84741 — 435-644-5800
Doug Jacobs, prin. — Fax 644-5121
Other Schools – See Big Water, Lake Powell, Orderville

Kaysville, Davis, Pop. 21,386
Davis SD
Supt. — See Farmington
Davis Applied Technology Center — Vo/Tech
550 E 300 S 84037 — 801-593-2500
Mike Bouwhuis, dir. — Fax 593-2400
Davis SHS — 2,200/10-12
325 S Main St 84037 — 801-402-8800
Rulon Homer, prin. — Fax 402-8801
Fairfield HS — 1,000/7-9
951 N Fairfield Rd 84037 — 801-402-7000
Kathy Washburn, prin. — Fax 402-7001
Kaysville JHS — 1,100/7-9
100 E 350 S 84037 — 801-402-7200
Dr. Ken Hadlock, prin. — Fax 402-7201

David Applied Technology College — Post-Sec.
550 E 300 S 84037 — 801-593-2500

Kearns, Salt Lake, Pop. 34,900
Granite SD
Supt. — See Salt Lake City
Jefferson JHS — 1,200/7-9
5850 S 5600 W 84118 — 801-964-7970
Karl Moody, prin. — Fax 964-4250
Kearns JHS — 1,000/7-9
4040 W 5305 S 84118 — 801-646-5204
Kandace Barber, prin. — Fax 646-5206
Kearns SHS — 1,900/10-12
5525 Cougar Ln 84118 — 801-646-5380
David Stevens, prin. — Fax 646-5392

Koosharem, Sevier, Pop. 272

Sorenson's Ranch S — 100/7-12
PO Box 440219 84744 — 435-638-7318
Shane Sorenson, dir. — Fax 638-7582

Lake Powell, San Juan, Pop. 15
Kane SD
Supt. — See Kanab
Lake Powell HS — 7-12
PO Box 4345 84533 — 435-684-2268
Gordon Miller, prin. — Fax 684-3821

Laketown, Rich, Pop. 185
Rich SD
Supt. — See Randolph
Rich MS — 100/6-8
PO Box 129 84038 — 435-946-3359
Kip Motta, prin. — Fax 946-3366

La Verkin, Washington, Pop. 3,731

Cross Creek Academy — 400/6-12
150 N State St 84745 — 435-635-0600
Andrea Gardner, admin. — Fax 635-1099

Layton, Davis, Pop. 60,769
Davis SD
Supt. — See Farmington
Central Davis JHS — 1,000/7-9
663 Church St 84041 — 801-402-7100
Karyn Bertelsen, prin. — Fax 402-7101
Layton HS — 1,700/10-12
440 Lancer Ln 84041 — 801-402-4800
Paul Smith, prin. — Fax 402-4801
North Layton JHS — 1,000/7-9
1100 W 2000 N 84041 — 801-402-6600
David Turner, prin. — Fax 402-6601
Northridge SHS — 2,100/10-12
2430 N 400 W 84041 — 801-402-8500
Dr. Steve Hill, prin. — Fax 402-8501

Fran Brown College of Beauty — Post-Sec.
521 W 600 N 84041 — 801-546-6166
Layton Christian Academy — 500/PK-12
2352 E Highway 193 84040 — 801-771-7141
Greg Miller, admin. — Fax 771-0170
Northridge Learning Center — 200/K-12
2405 N Hillfield Rd 84041 — 801-776-4532
Dixie Dorius Evans, dir. — Fax 776-0638

Lehi, Utah, Pop. 23,266
Alpine SD
Supt. — See American Fork
Lehi JHS — 1,700/7-9
700 Cedar Hollow Rd 84043 — 801-768-7010
Kevin Cox, prin. — Fax 768-7016
Lehi SHS — 1,300/10-12
180 N 500 E 84043 — 801-768-7000
Chuck Bearce, prin. — Fax 768-7007
Willow Creek MS — 7-9
2275 W 300 N 84043 — 801-766-5273
Fred Openshaw, prin. — Fax 766-5168

Lindon, Utah, Pop. 8,680
Alpine SD
Supt. — See American Fork
Oak Canyon JHS — 1,400/7-9
111 S 725 E 84042 — 801-785-8760
David Smith, prin. — Fax 785-8768

Loa, Wayne, Pop. 504

Aspen Ranch S — 100/8-12
PO Box 369 84747 — 435-836-2080
Lisa Lewis, prin. — Fax 836-2085

Logan, Cache, Pop. 43,675
Cache SD — 12,900/K-12
2063 N 1200 E 84341 — 435-752-3925
Dr. Steven Norton, supt. — Fax 753-2168
www.cache.k12.ut.us/
Other Schools – See Hyrum, Richmond, Smithfield

Logan CSD 5,600/K-12
101 W Center St 84321 435-755-2300
Richard Jensen, supt. Fax 755-2311
www.lcsd.logan.k12.ut.us
Logan HS 1,600/9-12
162 W 100 S 84321 435-755-2380
Pat Hansen, prin. Fax 755-2387
Mt. Logan MS 1,300/6-8
875 N 200 E 84321 435-755-2370
Daniel Johnson, prin. Fax 755-2370

Beau La Reine College of Beauty Culture Post-Sec.
PO Box 6504 84341 435-752-8688
Bridgerland Applied Technology Center Post-Sec.
1301 N 600 W 84321 435-753-6780
New Horizons Beauty College Post-Sec.
550 N Main St Ste 115 84321 435-753-9779
Stevens Henager College Post-Sec.
755 Main St 84321 435-713-4777
Utah State University 84322 Post-Sec.
435-797-1000

Magna, Salt Lake, Pop. 17,829
Granite SD
Supt. — See Salt Lake City
Brockbank JHS 1,000/7-9
2935 S 8560 W 84044 801-646-5134
Terri VanWinkle, prin. Fax 646-5135
Cyprus SHS 1,400/10-12
8623 W 3000 S 84044 801-646-5300
Mark Manning, prin. Fax 646-5303
Matheson JHS 1,000/7-9
3650 Montclair St 84044 801-646-5290
Alan Bailey, prin. Fax 646-5299

Vista S 50/7-12
PO Box 69 84044 801-250-9762
Ron Crossman, prin. Fax 250-8483

Manila, Daggett, Pop. 297
Daggett SD 200/K-12
PO Box 249 84046 435-784-3174
Bruce Northcott, supt. Fax 784-3549
www.dsdf.org
Manila JSHS 100/7-12
PO Box 249 84046 435-784-3174
Bruce Northcott, prin. Fax 784-3271

Manti, Sanpete, Pop. 3,070
South Sanpete SD 2,800/PK-12
39 S Main St 84642 435-835-2261
Don Hill, supt. Fax 835-2265
www.ssanpete.k12.ut.us
Manti HS 500/9-12
100 W 500 N 84642 435-835-2281
Brenan Jackson, prin. Fax 835-2285
Other Schools – See Ephraim, Gunnison

Midvale, Salt Lake, Pop. 27,166
Jordan SD
Supt. — See Sandy
Hillcrest SHS 1,700/10-12
7350 S 900 E 84047 801-256-5400
Sue Malone, prin. Fax 256-5488
Midvale MS 700/7-9
7852 Pioneer St 84047 801-412-2150
Anthony Godfrey, prin. Fax 412-2190

Kendall's Academy of Beauty Arts/Science Post-Sec.
7353 S 900 E 84047 801-561-5610

Milford, Beaver, Pop. 1,438
Beaver SD
Supt. — See Beaver
Milford JSHS 200/7-12
PO Box 159 84751 435-387-2751
John Nielsen, prin. Fax 387-2494

Moab, Grand, Pop. 4,845
Grand SD 1,500/PK-12
264 S 400 E 84532 435-259-5317
Ron Ferguson, supt. Fax 259-6212
www.grand.k12.ut.us
Grand County HS 500/9-12
608 S 400 E 84532 435-259-8931
Tom Brown, prin. Fax 259-4191
Grand County MS 200/7-8
439 S 100 E 84532 435-259-7158
Melinda Snow, prin. Fax 259-6221

Monroe, Sevier, Pop. 1,819
Sevier SD
Supt. — See Richfield
South Sevier HS 400/9-12
430 W 100 S 84754 435-527-4651
Bruce Douglas, prin. Fax 527-4653
South Sevier MS 300/6-8
300 E Center St 84754 435-527-4607
William Jolley, prin. Fax 527-4636

Montezuma Creek, San Juan, Pop. 345
San Juan SD
Supt. — See Blanding, UT
Whitehorse HS 300/7-12
PO Box 660 84534 435-678-1209
John Fahey, prin. Fax 678-1854

Monticello, San Juan, Pop. 1,900
San Juan SD
Supt. — See Blanding, UT
Monticello JSHS 300/7-12
PO Box 69 84535 435-587-1130
Scott Shakespeare, prin. Fax 587-1150

Monument Valley, San Juan
San Juan SD
Supt. — See Blanding, UT
Monument Valley JSHS 200/7-12
PO Box 360008 84536 435-678-1208
Patricia Seltzer, prin. Fax 678-1258

Morgan, Morgan, Pop. 2,711
Morgan SD 1,900/K-12
PO Box 530 84050 801-829-3411
Ronald Wolff, supt. Fax 829-3531
www.morgan.k12.ut.us
Morgan HS 700/9-12
PO Box 917 84050 801-829-3418
Ken Adams, prin. Fax 829-6553
Morgan MS 600/5-8
PO Box 470 84050 801-829-3467
Tom McFarland, prin. Fax 829-0645

Moroni, Sanpete, Pop. 1,296
North Sanpete SD
Supt. — See Mount Pleasant
North Sanpete MS 400/7-8
PO Box 307 84646 435-436-8206
Randy Shelley, prin. Fax 436-8208

Mount Pleasant, Sanpete, Pop. 2,735
North Sanpete SD 2,300/PK-12
220 E 700 S 84647 435-462-2485
Courtney Syme, supt. Fax 462-2480
www.nsanpete.k12.ut.us
North Sanpete HS 700/9-12
390 E 700 S 84647 435-462-2452
John Ericksen, prin. Fax 462-3112
Other Schools – See Moroni

Wasatch Academy 200/9-12
120 S 100 W 84647 435-462-1400
Joseph Loftin, hdmstr. Fax 462-1450

Murray, Salt Lake, Pop. 43,617
Murray CSD 6,200/K-12
147 E 5065 S 84107 801-264-7400
Richard Tranter, supt. Fax 264-7456
www.murrayschools.org/
Hillcrest JHS 800/7-9
126 E 5300 S 84107 801-264-7442
David Dunn, prin. Fax 264-4820
Murray SHS 1,400/10-12
5440 S State St 84107 801-264-7460
Scott Bushnell, prin. Fax 264-7499
Riverview JHS 700/7-9
751 Tripp Ln 84123 801-264-7446
Shauna Ballou, prin. Fax 264-7458

Eagle Gate College Post-Sec.
5588 Green St 84123 801-268-9271
ITT Technical Institute Post-Sec.
920 Levoy Dr 84123 801-263-3313
Mt. Vernon Academy 50/K-12
184 E Vine St 84107 801-266-5521
Nancy Woodward, prin. Fax 269-8080
Stevens Henager College Post-Sec.
383 W Vine St 84123 801-262-7600

Nephi, Juab, Pop. 4,962
Juab SD 2,600/K-12
346 E 600 N 84648 435-623-1940
Kirk Wright, supt. Fax 623-1941
www.juab.k12.ut.us
Juab HS 500/9-12
802 N 650 E 84648 435-623-1764
M. Richard Durbin, prin. Fax 623-1772
Juab JHS 300/7-8
555 E 800 N 84648 435-623-1541
Ken Rowley, prin. Fax 623-4995

Oakley, Summit, Pop. 1,125

Oakley S 100/9-12
PO Box 357 84055 435-783-5001
James Meyer, dir. Fax 783-5010

Ogden, Weber, Pop. 78,293
Ogden City SD 12,300/K-12
1950 Monroe Blvd 84401 801-737-7300
Noel Zabriskie, supt. Fax 627-7654
www.ogdensd.org
Central MS 600/6-8
2563 Monroe Blvd 84401 801-737-8500
Mark Peterson, prin. Fax 627-7650
Highland MS 700/6-8
325 Gramercy Ave 84404 801-737-7700
Sondra Jolovich-Motes, prin. Fax 625-8860
Lomond HS 1,500/9-12
800 Jackson Ave 84404 801-737-7900
Ben Smith, prin. Fax 625-1138
Mound Fort MS 600/6-8
1400 Mound Fort Dr 84404 801-737-7800
Kevin Kuykendall, prin. Fax 625-8993
Mt. Ogden MS 1,000/6-8
3260 Harrison Blvd 84403 801-737-8600
Brenda Ruffier, prin. Fax 627-7641
Ogden HS 1,600/9-12
2828 Harrison Blvd 84403 801-737-8673
Ed Jenson, prin. Fax 392-7338
Adult Education S Adult
1950 Monroe Blvd 84401 801-737-7458

Weber SD 27,400/K-12
5320 S 500 E 84405 801-476-7500
Michael Jacobsen, supt. Fax 476-8139
www.weber.k12.ut.us/
Bonneville SHS 1,300/10-12
251 E 4800 S 84405 801-452-4050
Leslie Meyer, prin. Fax 452-4099
North Ogden JHS 700/7-9
575 E 2900 N 84414 801-452-4800
Don Tanner, prin. Fax 452-4849
South Ogden JHS 800/7-9
4300 Madison Ave 84403 801-452-4460
Bill Gritz, prin. Fax 452-4499
Wahlquist JHS 700/7-9
1033 N 1200 W 84404 801-452-4640
James Shaw, prin. Fax 452-4679
Weber SHS 1,600/10-12
3650 N 500 W 84414 801-476-3700
Alan Stokes, prin. Fax 476-3799
Other Schools – See Eden, Harrisville, Plain City, Roy, Washington Terrace, West Haven

---

Ogden-Weber Applied Technology College Post-Sec.
200 N Washington Blvd 84404 801-627-8300
St. Joseph's HS 200/9-12
1790 Lake St 84401 801-394-1515
Louise Price, prin. Fax 394-6428
Stacey's Hands of Champions Beauty Coll Post-Sec.
3721 S 250 W 84405 801-394-5718
Stevens Henager College Post-Sec.
PO Box 9428 84409 801-394-7791
Utah Schools for the Deaf and the Blind Post-Sec.
742 Harrison Blvd 84404 801-629-4700
Weber State University Post-Sec.
1001 University Cir 84408 801-626-6000

Orderville, Kane, Pop. 593
Kane SD
Supt. — See Kanab
Valley HS 200/7-12
PO Box 128 84758 435-648-2278
William Sorbe, prin. Fax 648-2366

Orem, Utah, Pop. 87,599
Alpine SD
Supt. — See American Fork
Canyon View JHS 1,200/7-9
625 E 950 N 84097 801-227-8748
Amelia Schwartz, prin. Fax 227-8706
Lakeridge JHS 1,200/7-9
951 S 400 W 84058 801-227-8752
Dr. Jim McCoy, prin. Fax 227-2490
Mountain View SHS 1,500/10-12
665 W Center St 84057 801-227-8759
Rick Clark, prin. Fax 227-8764
Orem JHS 1,000/7-9
765 N 600 W 84057 801-227-8756
Steven Stewart, prin. Fax 227-8796
Orem SHS 1,400/10-12
175 S 400 E 84097 801-227-8765
Jane Lindhout, prin. Fax 227-8774
Timpanogos SHS 1,500/10-12
1450 N 200 E 84057 801-223-3120
Brad Kendall, prin. Fax 223-3134

Careers Unlimited Post-Sec.
University Mall # I-163 84097 801-687-1271
Evan's Hairstyling College Post-Sec.
798 W 400 N 84057 801-224-6034
Mountainland Applied Technology College Post-Sec.
987 S Geneva Rd 84058 801-863-7662
Provo Canyon S 200/7-12
1350 E 750 N 84097 801-227-2100
Nicholas Pakidko, prin. Fax 223-7130
Stevens Henager College Post-Sec.
1476 Sandhill Rd 84058 801-375-5455
Utah Valley State College Post-Sec.
800 W University Pkwy 84058 801-222-8000

Panguitch, Garfield, Pop. 1,525
Garfield SD 900/K-12
PO Box 398 84759 435-676-8821
Dr. George Park, supt. Fax 676-8266
www.garfield.k12.ut.us
Panguitch HS 200/9-12
PO Box 393 84759 435-676-8805
Betty Ann Rember, prin. Fax 676-8521
Panguitch MS 100/7-8
PO Box 393 84759 435-676-8225
Betty Ann Rember, prin. Fax 676-2518
Other Schools – See Escalante, Tropic

Park City, Summit, Pop. 7,854
Park City SD 3,400/K-12
2700 Kearns Blvd 84060 435-645-5600
Dave Adamson, supt. Fax 645-5609
www.parkcity.k12.ut.us
Park City SHS 900/10-12
1750 Kearns Blvd 84060 435-645-5650
Hilary Hays, prin. Fax 645-5658
Treasure Mountain International S 500/8-9
2530 Kearns Blvd 84060 435-645-5640
Bob O'Connor, prin. Fax 645-5644

Park Valley, Box Elder
Box Elder SD
Supt. — See Brigham City
Park Valley S 700/K-10
788 Education Dr 84329 435-871-4411
Brian Anderson, prin. Fax 871-4444

Parowan, Iron, Pop. 2,518
Iron SD
Supt. — See Cedar City
Parowan HS 400/7-12
168 N Main St 84761 435-477-3366
Scott Doubek, prin. Fax 477-3743

Payson, Utah, Pop. 14,761
Nebo SD
Supt. — See Spanish Fork
Payson JHS 1,100/8-9
1025 S Highway 91 84651 801-465-6015
Clark Clayson, prin. Fax 465-6023
Payson SHS 1,400/10-12
1050 S Main St 84651 801-465-6025
John Penrod, prin. Fax 465-6067

Plain City, Weber, Pop. 3,932
Weber SD
Supt. — See Ogden
Fremont SHS 1,800/10-12
1900 N 4700 W 84404 801-452-4000
Jeff Meyer, prin. Fax 452-4049

Pleasant Grove, Utah, Pop. 23,901
Alpine SD
Supt. — See American Fork
Pleasant Grove JHS 1,200/7-9
810 N 100 E 84062 801-785-8707
Blaine Edman, prin. Fax 785-8743
Pleasant Grove SHS 1,600/10-12
700 E 200 S 84062 801-785-8700
Jess Christen, prin. Fax 785-8744

Price, Carbon, Pop. 8,229
Carbon SD 3,300/K-12
PO Box 1438 84501 435-637-1732
Dr. David A. Armstrong, supt. Fax 637-9417
www.carbon.k12.ut.us
Carbon SHS 800/10-12
750 E 400 N 84501 435-637-2463
Robert Cox, prin. Fax 637-4127
Mont Harmon JHS 600/7-9
60 W 400 N 84501 435-637-0510
Todd Lauritsen, prin. Fax 637-6074
Adult Education Adult
PO Box 1438 84501 435-637-1732
Judy Mainord, prin. Fax 637-4019
Other Schools – See Helper

College of Eastern Utah Post-Sec.
451 E 400 N 84501 435-637-2120
Southeast Applied Technology College Post-Sec.
375 S Carbon Ave 84501 435-613-1438

Provo, Utah, Pop. 105,410
Provo CSD 11,400/K-12
280 W 940 N 84604 801-374-4800
Dr. Randall J. Merrill, supt. Fax 374-4808
www.provo.edu
Centennial MS 700/7-8
305 E 2320 N 84604 801-374-4621
Mitch Swenson, prin. Fax 374-4626
Dixon MS 600/7-8
750 W 200 N 84601 801-374-4980
Rosanna Ungerman, prin. Fax 374-4884
Provo HS 1,800/9-12
1125 N University Ave 84604 801-373-6550
Sam Ray, prin. Fax 374-4880
Timpview HS 1,600/9-12
3570 N 650 E 84604 801-221-9720
George Bayles, prin. Fax 224-4210

American Inst. of Medical-Dental Tech. Post-Sec.
1675 N Freedom Blvd 84604 801-377-2900
Brigham Young University 84602 Post-Sec.
801-378-5000
Dallas Roberts Academy of Hair Design Post-Sec.
1700 N State St Ste 18 84604 801-375-1501
Discovery Academy 100/7-12
105 N 500 W 84601 801-374-2121
Joel Gardener, prin. Fax 373-4451
Heritage S 50/7-12
PO Box 5600 84604 801-226-4621
Bruce Knowlton, prin. Fax 226-4630
Meridian S 200/PK-12
931 E 300 N 84606 801-374-5480
David H. Hennessey Ph.D., hdmstr. Fax 374-5491
Provo College Post-Sec.
1450 W 820 N 84601 801-375-1861
Utah Valley Regional Medical Center Post-Sec.
1034 N 500 W 84604 801-373-7850
Von Curtis Academy of Hair Design Post-Sec.
480 N 900 E 84606 801-374-5111

Randolph, Rich, Pop. 478
Rich SD 500/K-12
PO Box 67 84064 435-793-2135
Dale Lamborn, supt. Fax 793-2136
www.rich.k12.ut.us
Rich HS 100/9-12
PO Box 278 84064 435-793-2365
Rick Larsen, prin. Fax 793-2375
Other Schools – See Laketown

Richfield, Sevier, Pop. 6,936
Sevier SD 4,200/PK-12
180 E 600 N 84701 435-896-8214
Brent Thorne, supt. Fax 896-8804
www.sevier.k12.ut.us
Red Hills MS 500/6-8
400 S 600 W 84701 435-896-6421
Brent Gubler, prin. Fax 896-6423
Richfield HS 600/9-12
510 W 100 S 84701 435-896-8247
Randall Brown, prin. Fax 896-8246
Other Schools – See Monroe, Salina

Richmond, Cache, Pop. 2,045
Cache SD
Supt. — See Logan
North Cache JHS 1,100/8-9
157 W 600 S 84333 435-258-2452
Larry Larson, prin. Fax 258-5437

Riverdale, Weber, Pop. 7,791

Christian Heritage HS 300/7-12
5120 S 1050 W 84405 801-393-4475
Mike Hoff, prin. Fax 393-6698

Riverton, Salt Lake, Pop. 29,244
Jordan SD
Supt. — See Sandy
Oquirrh Hills MS 1,200/7-9
12949 S 2700 W 84065 801-412-2350
G. Norma Villar, prin. Fax 412-2370
Riverton SHS 2,200/10-12
12476 S 2700 W 84065 801-256-5800
Stephen Park, prin. Fax 256-5880
South Hills MS 1,300/7-9
13508 S 4000 W 84065 801-412-2400
Janette Milano, prin. Fax 412-2430

Roosevelt, Duchesne, Pop. 4,404
Duchesne SD
Supt. — See Duchesne
Roosevelt JHS 400/7-8
265 N 300 W #425-1 84066 435-725-4585
David Brotherson, prin. Fax 725-4622
Union HS 800/9-12
135 N Union St #124-3 84066 435-725-4525
Brent Feldsted, prin. Fax 725-4576

Uintah SD
Supt. — See Vernal
West JHS 200/6-9
RR 2 Box 2466 84066 435-722-4563
Deena Millecam, prin. Fax 722-4565

Uintah Basin Applied Technology College Post-Sec.
1100 E Lagoon St 84066 435-722-4523

Roy, Weber, Pop. 35,249
Weber SD
Supt. — See Ogden
Roy JHS 900/7-9
5400 S 2100 W 84067 801-476-5260
Sue Sweet, prin. Fax 476-5299
Roy SHS 1,400/10-12
2150 W 4800 S 84067 801-476-3600
Lee Dickemore, prin. Fax 476-3699
Sand Ridge JHS 700/7-9
2075 W 4600 S 84067 801-476-5320
Richard Rhees, prin. Fax 476-5359

Saint George, Washington, Pop. 56,382
Washington County SD 19,500/K-12
121 W Tabernacle St 84770 435-673-3553
Max H. Rose Ph.D., supt. Fax 673-3216
www.wash.k12.ut.us
Dixie MS 1,200/7-9
825 S 100 E 84770 435-628-0441
Jim McKim, prin. Fax 674-6467
Dixie SHS 1,000/10-12
350 E 700 S 84770 435-673-4682
Craig Hammer, prin. Fax 673-2384
Millcreek SHS 200/10-12
2450 E Riverside Dr 84790 435-628-2462
Terry Ogborn, prin. Fax 628-8206
Pine View MS 800/8-9
2145 E 130 N 84790 435-628-7915
Ray Brooks, prin. Fax 634-0470
Pine View SHS 1,200/10-12
2850 E 750 N 84790 435-628-5255
Rich Palmer, prin. Fax 628-0327
Snow Canyon MS 800/8-9
1215 Lava Flow Dr 84770 435-674-6474
John Goldhardt, prin. Fax 628-6904
Snow Canyon SHS 1,100/10-12
1385 Lava Flow Dr 84770 435-634-1967
Warren Brooks, prin. Fax 634-1130
Other Schools – See Enterprise, Hurricane

Cinnamon Hills S 100/6-12
770 E Saint George Blvd 84770 435-674-0984
David Broadhead, prin. Fax 674-4628
Dixie State College of Utah Post-Sec.
225 S 700 E 84770 435-652-7500
Evan's Hairstyling College Post-Sec.
955 E Tabernacle St 84770 435-673-6128
Hairitage Hair Academy Post-Sec.
900 S Bluff St Ste 9 84770 435-673-5233
Hatch Academy 50/K-12
PO Box 910400 84791 435-673-6474
Brent Arnold, dir. Fax 673-5339
Sun Hawk Academy 100/7-12
948 N 1300 W 84770 435-656-3211
Brent Arnold, prin. Fax 656-3213

Salina, Sevier, Pop. 2,378
Sevier SD
Supt. — See Richfield
North Sevier HS 300/9-12
350 W 400 N 84654 435-529-3717
Steve Camp, prin. Fax 529-7910
North Sevier MS 200/6-8
135 N 100 W 84654 435-529-3841
Jill Porter, prin. Fax 529-7377

Salt Lake City, Salt Lake, Pop. 179,894
Granite SD 68,400/PK-12
2500 S State St 84115 801-646-5000
Dr. Stephen Ronnenkamp, supt. Fax 646-4128
www.granite.k12.ut.us
Bennion JHS 1,000/7-9
6055 S 2700 W 84118 801-646-5114
Dr. Mary Rhodes, prin. Fax 646-5119
Bonneville JHS 900/7-9
5330 S 1600 E 84117 801-646-5124
Joel Danning, prin. Fax 646-5127
Churchill JHS 700/7-9
3450 Oakview Dr 84124 801-646-5144
Bryce Hollbrook, prin. Fax 646-5147
Cottonwood SHS 1,500/10-12
5715 S 1300 E 84121 801-646-5264
Garrett Muse, prin. Fax 646-5266
Eisenhower JHS 1,200/7-9
4351 S Redwood Rd 84123 801-646-5154
Nancy Jadallah, prin. Fax 646-5156
Evergreen JHS 800/7-9
3401 S 2000 E 84109 801-481-7215
Lynn Boehme, prin. Fax 481-7281
Granite Park JHS 700/7-9
3031 S 200 E 84115 801-481-7139
Robert McDaniel, prin. Fax 263-6138
Granite SHS 1,000/10-12
3305 S 500 E 84106 801-646-5340
Stephen Hess, prin. Fax 646-5353
Olympus JHS 800/7-9
2217 E 4800 S 84117 801-646-5224
Ben Lems, prin. Fax 646-5227
Olympus SHS 1,500/10-12
4055 S 2300 E 84124 801-646-5400
Paul Hansen, prin. Fax 646-5403
Skyline SHS 1,500/10-12
3251 E 3760 S 84109 801-646-5420
Kathy Clark, prin. Fax 646-5422
Taylorsville SHS 1,900/10-12
5225 S Redwood Rd 84123 801-646-5455
Jerry Haslam, prin. Fax 646-5457
Wasatch JHS 900/7-9
3450 Oakview Dr 84124 801-646-5244
Doug Bingham, prin. Fax 646-5246
Granite Peaks Adult & Comm Education Adult
464 E 3700 S 84115 801-646-4666
Dr. Claudia Thorum, prin. Fax 646-4667
Other Schools – See Kearns, Magna, West Valley

Jordan SD
Supt. — See Sandy
Butler MS 1,100/7-9
7530 S 2700 E 84121 801-412-2250
Marsha Morgan, prin. Fax 412-2277

Salt Lake City SD 22,200/K-12
440 E 100 S 84111 801-578-8599
Dr. McKell Withers, supt. Fax 578-8248
www.slc.k12.ut.us
Bryant MS 600/7-8
40 S 800 E 84102 801-578-8118
Francis Battle, prin. Fax 578-8125
Clayton MS 600/7-8
1471 S 1800 E 84108 801-481-4810
Rosemary Baron, prin. Fax 481-4884
East HS 1,900/9-12
840 S 1300 E 84102 801-583-1661
Dr. Robyn Roberts, prin. Fax 584-2927
Glendale MS 500/7-8
1400 Goodwin Ave 84116 801-974-8319
Ernie Nix, prin. Fax 974-8356
Highland HS 1,700/9-12
2166 S 1700 E 84106 801-484-4343
Paul Schulte, prin. Fax 481-4893
Hillside MS 600/7-8
2375 Garfield Ave 84108 801-481-4828
Jane Larson, prin. Fax 481-4831
Northwest MS 700/7-8
1730 W 1700 N 84116 801-578-8547
Cherrie Brinlee, prin. Fax 578-8558
West HS 2,100/9-12
241 N 300 W 84103 801-578-8500
Margery Parker, prin. Fax 578-8516

Anchor Christian Academy 100/K-12
1880 E 5600 S 84121 801-272-9405
Wayne Musson, prin.
California College for Health Sciences Post-Sec.
5295 Commerce Dr 84107 800-221-7374
Cameo College of Essential Beauty Post-Sec.
1600 S State St 84115 801-484-6173
Certified Careers Institute Post-Sec.
1385 W 2200 S Ste 100 84119 801-973-7008
Hairitage College of Beauty Post-Sec.
5414 S 900 E 84117 801-266-4693
Intermountain Christian S 300/PK-12
6515 Lion Ln 84121 801-942-8811
Rob Brown, admin. Fax 942-8813
Judge Memorial Catholic HS 900/9-12
650 S 1100 E 84102 801-363-8895
James Hamburge, prin. Fax 521-3920
Kendall's Academy of Beauty Arts/Science Post-Sec.
2230 S 700 E 84106 801-486-0101
L.D.S. Business College Post-Sec.
95 North 300 West 84101 801-524-8100
Myotherapy College of Utah Post-Sec.
2120 S 1300 E Ste 102 84106 801-484-7624
Odyssey House S 50/8-12
607 E 200 S 84102 801-578-8613
James Anderson, prin. Fax 578-8613
Oxford Learning Source 50/PK-12
2290 E 4500 S 84117 801-942-4449
Millicent Jacobsen, dir. Fax 495-2992
Realms of Inquiry S 100/PK-12
1140 S 900 E 84105 801-467-5911
Laurie Bragg, hdmstr. Fax 467-5932
Rowland Hall St. Marks S 900/PK-12
720 Guardsman Way 84108 801-355-7485
Alan Sparrow, hdmstr. Fax 363-5521
Salt Lake Community College Post-Sec.
PO Box 30808 84130 801-957-4111
Salt Lake Lutheran HS 100/9-12
4020 S 900 E 84124 801-266-6676
Charles Gebhardt, prin. Fax 266-1953
Skin Works School of Advanced Skin Care Post-Sec.
2121 Nowell Cir 84115 801-530-0001
Tooele Applied Technology College Post-Sec.
1655 E 3300 S 84106 801-493-8700
University of Utah Post-Sec.
1460 E 201 S 84112 801-581-7200
Valley Christian S 100/K-12
3818 W 4700 S 84118 801-968-8107
Kevin Bowles, prin. Fax 968-8182
Veterans Affairs Medical Center Post-Sec.
500 Foothill Dr 84148 801-582-1565
Western Governors University Post-Sec.
4001 S 700 E Ste 700 84107 801-274-3280
Westminster College Post-Sec.
1840 S 1300 E 84105 801-484-7651
Woodland Hills S 200/7-12
5858 S 900 E 84121 801-266-1262
Pat Murdoch, dir. Fax 266-5876

Sandy, Salt Lake, Pop. 89,319
Jordan SD 72,700/K-12
9361 S 300 E 84070 801-567-8100
Barry L. Newbold Ed.D., supt. Fax 567-8064
www.jordandistrict.org/

Albion MS   1,100/7-9
  2755 Newcastle Dr 84093   801-412-2700
  Larry Odom, prin.   Fax 412-2720
Alta SHS   2,500/10-12
  11055 S 1000 E 84094   801-256-5000
  Mont Winderberg, prin.   Fax 256-5081
Crescent View MS   1,400/7-9
  11150 S 300 E 84070   801-412-2750
  Sherry H. Devenberg, prin.   Fax 412-2780
Eastmont MS   1,000/7-9
  10100 S 1300 E 84094   801-412-2000
  Ann White, prin.   Fax 412-2040
Indian Hills MS   1,200/7-9
  1180 Sanders Rd 84094   801-412-2550
  Floyd Stensrud, prin.   Fax 412-2580
Jordan Applied Technology Center   Vo/Tech
  825 E 9085 S 84094   801-256-5700
  Ronald Sing, prin.   Fax 256-5710
Jordan SHS   2,000/10-12
  95 Beetdigger Blvd 84070   801-256-5500
  Mark Montague, prin.   Fax 256-5556
Mt. Jordan MS   700/7-9
  9360 S 300 E 84070   801-412-2050
  Eduardo Alba, prin.   Fax 412-2055
Union MS   1,100/7-9
  615 E 8000 S 84070   801-412-2200
  Mary Anderson, prin.   Fax 412-2227
Other Schools – See Cottonwood Heights, Herriman,
  Midvale, Riverton, Salt Lake City, South Jordan, West
  Jordan

Francois D. Hair Design Academy   Post-Sec.
  111 W 9000 S 84070   801-561-2244
Oxford Learning Source   50/PK-12
  1842 E 9400 S 84093   801-942-4449
  Millicent Jacobsen, dir.   Fax 495-2992
Waterford S   1,000/PK-12
  1480 E 9400 S 84093   801-572-1780
  Nancy Heuston, hdmstr.   Fax 572-1787

Smithfield, Cache, Pop. 7,877
Cache SD
  Supt. — See Logan
Sky View SHS   1,500/10-12
  520 S 250 E 84335   435-563-6273
  Dee Ashcroft, prin.   Fax 563-9534

South Jordan, Salt Lake, Pop. 33,589
Jordan SD
  Supt. — See Sandy
Bingham SHS   2,100/10-12
  2160 W Miners Mile 84095   801-256-5100
  Jolene Jolley, prin.   Fax 256-5151
Elk Ridge MS   1,300/7-9
  3659 W 9800 S 84095   801-412-2800
  Gary Garcia, prin.   Fax 412-2830
South Jordan MS   1,400/7-9
  10245 S 2700 W 84095   801-412-2900
  Diana Kline, prin.   Fax 412-2930

Spanish Fork, Utah, Pop. 23,000
Nebo SD   24,100/PK-12
  350 S Main St 84660   801-354-7400
  Chris Sorensen, supt.   Fax 798-4010
  www.nebo.edu
Spanish Fork JHS   1,200/8-9
  600 S 820 E 84660   801-798-4075
  John DeGraffenried, prin.   Fax 798-4097
Spanish Fork SHS   1,700/10-12
  99 N 300 W 84660   801-798-4060
  Tim Braithwaite, prin.   Fax 798-0483
Other Schools – See Payson, Springville

New Haven S   50/7-12
  2152 E 7200 S 84660   801-794-1218
  James Young, prin.   Fax 794-9558

Springville, Utah, Pop. 21,929
Nebo SD
  Supt. — See Spanish Fork
Springville JHS   1,100/8-9
  165 S 700 E 84663   801-489-2880
  Everett Kelepolo, prin.   Fax 489-2838
Springville SHS   1,400/10-12
  1205 E 900 S 84663   801-489-2870
  Ann Anderson, prin.   Fax 489-2806

Sunset, Davis, Pop. 5,068
Davis SD
  Supt. — See Farmington
Sunset JHS   1,000/7-9
  1610 N 250 W 84015   801-402-6700
  Dr. James Schmidt, prin.   Fax 402-6701

Syracuse, Davis, Pop. 14,159
Davis SD
  Supt. — See Farmington
Syracuse JHS   900/7-9
  1450 S 2000 W 84075   801-402-6800
  Dr. Robin Bowden, prin.   Fax 402-6801

Island View S   100/7-9
  2650 W 2700 S 84075   801-773-0200
  Jan Whimpey, prin.   Fax 773-0208

Tabiona, Duchesne, Pop. 150
Duchesne SD
  Supt. — See Duchesne
Tabiona HS   100/7-12
  PO Box 470 84072   435-738-1320
  Robert Park, prin.   Fax 738-1332

Tooele, Tooele, Pop. 27,052
Tooele County SD   10,500/K-12
  92 Lodestone Way 84074   435-833-1900
  Michael Johnsen, supt.   Fax 833-1912
  www.tooele.k12.ut.us
Tooele HS   1,500/9-12
  301 W Vine St 84074   435-833-1978
  Michael Westover, prin.   Fax 833-1984
Tooele JHS   900/7-8
  412 W Vine St 84074   435-833-1921
  Kendall Topham, prin.   Fax 833-1923
Tooele Valley HS   200/9-12
  Tooele Army Depot Bldg S110 84074   435-833-1928
  Terry Linares, prin.   Fax 833-1929
Other Schools – See Dugway, Grantsville, Wendover

Tropic, Garfield, Pop. 479
Garfield SD
  Supt. — See Panguitch
Bryce Valley HS   100/7-12
  PO Box 70 84776   435-679-8835
  Earl Slack, prin.   Fax 679-8539

Trout Creek, Juab
Tintic SD
  Supt. — See Eureka
West Desert JSHS   50/7-12
  PO Box 440 84083   435-693-3112
  Edgar Alder, prin.   Fax 693-3109

Vernal, Uintah, Pop. 7,892
Uintah SD   7,200/PK-12
  635 W 200 S 84078   435-781-3100
  Wayne Gurney, supt.   Fax 781-3107
  www.uintah.net/
Uintah SHS   1,100/10-12
  1880 W 500 N 84078   435-781-3110
  Robert Stearmer, prin.   Fax 781-3117
Vernal JHS   700/8-9
  161 N 1000 W 84078   435-781-3130
  Kent Bunderson, prin.   Fax 781-3134
Other Schools – See Roosevelt

Washington Terrace, Weber, Pop. 8,455
Weber SD
  Supt. — See Ogden
Bell JHS   600/7-9
  165 W 5100 S 84405   801-452-4600
  Corey Jenkins, prin.   Fax 452-4639

Wendover, Tooele, Pop. 1,620
Tooele County SD
  Supt. — See Tooele
Wendover JSHS   200/7-12
  PO Box 610 84083   435-665-2343
  Stephen Lawrence, prin.   Fax 665-7706

West Haven, Weber, Pop. 4,991
Weber SD
  Supt. — See Ogden
Rocky Mountain JHS   1,000/7-9
  4350 W 4800 S 84401   801-476-5220
  Craig Jessop, prin.   Fax 476-5259

West Jordan, Salt Lake, Pop. 84,701
Jordan SD
  Supt. — See Sandy
Copper Hills SHS   1,800/10-12
  5445 New Bingham Hwy 84088   801-256-5300
  Tom Worlton, prin.   Fax 256-5393
Jensen MS   1,100/7-9
  8105 S 3200 W 84088   801-412-2850
  Joanne Ackerman, prin.   Fax 412-2875
Jordan Applied Technology Center   Vo/Tech
  9301 Wights Fort Rd 84088   801-256-5900
  Todd Quamberg, prin.   Fax 256-5930
Sunset Ridge MS   7-9
  6881 W 8200 S 84088   801-412-2475
  Catherine Jensen, prin.
West Hills MS   1,400/7-9
  8270 Grizzly Way 84088   801-412-2300
  Kim Baker, prin.   Fax 412-2327
West Jordan MS   1,100/7-9
  7550 S 1700 W 84084   801-412-2100
  Joanne Mattes, prin.   Fax 412-2140
West Jordan SHS   2,100/10-12
  8136 S 2700 W 84088   801-256-5600
  Paul Argyle, prin.   Fax 256-5670

Copperhills Youth Center   50/6-12
  5899 Rivendell Dr 84088   801-561-3377
  Seema Mehta, prin.   Fax 561-3393
Hawthorne Academy   50/9-12
  PO Box 9327 84088   801-255-3651
  Kraig Munsert, dir.   Fax 255-3957
Utah Career College   Post-Sec.
  1902 W 7800 S 84088   801-304-4224
West Ridge Academy   100/6-12
  5500 Bagley Park Rd 84088   801-282-1034
  Paul Keene, prin.   Fax 282-1009

West Point, Davis, Pop. 6,472
Davis SD
  Supt. — See Farmington
West Point JHS   1,000/7-9
  2775 W 550 N 84015   801-402-8100
  Dr. Jane Muna, prin.   Fax 402-8101

West Valley, Salt Lake, Pop. 111,254
Granite SD
  Supt. — See Salt Lake City
Granger SHS   1,400/10-12
  3690 S 3600 W 84119   801-646-5320
  Dr. Parley Jacobs, prin.   Fax 646-5322
Hunter JHS   1,000/7-9
  6131 W 3785 S 84128   801-646-5184
  Lori Gardner, prin.   Fax 646-5185
Hunter SHS   2,200/10-12
  4200 S 5600 W 84120   801-646-5360
  Maile Loo, prin.   Fax 646-5374
Kennedy JHS   1,200/7-9
  4495 S 4800 W 84120   801-964-7640
  Howard Sagers, prin.   Fax 964-7642
Valley JHS   900/7-9
  4195 S 3200 W 84119   801-964-7635
  Tim Frost, prin.   Fax 964-4238
West Lake JHS   1,100/7-9
  3400 S 3450 W 84119   801-646-5254
  Art Cox, prin.   Fax 646-5259

Mountain West College   Post-Sec.
  3280 W 3500 S 84119   801-840-4800
Premier Hair Academy   Post-Sec.
  4062 S 4000 W 84120   801-966-8414

Woods Cross, Davis, Pop. 7,466
Davis SD
  Supt. — See Farmington
Woods Cross SHS   1,200/10-12
  2200 S 600 W 84010   801-402-4500
  Vickie Ingram, prin.   Fax 402-4501

Benchmark S   50/8-12
  592 W 1350 S 84010   801-299-5300
  Michelle Brown, dir.   Fax 296-2163

VERMONT

VERMONT DEPARTMENT OF EDUCATION
120 State St, Montpelier 05620-0002
Telephone 802-828-3135
Fax 802-828-3140
Website http://www.state.vt.us/educ/

Commissioner of Education   Richard Cate

VERMONT BOARD OF EDUCATION
120 State St, Montpelier 05620-0002

Chairperson   Diane Mueller

PUBLIC, PRIVATE AND CATHOLIC SECONDARY SCHOOLS

Arlington, Bennington, Pop. 1,311
Battenkill Valley Supervisory SD — 400/K-12
530 E Arlington Rd # A 05250 — 802-375-9744
Charles F. Sweetman, supt. — Fax 375-2368
Arlington Memorial HS — 300/6-12
529 E Arlington Rd 05250 — 802-375-2589
Kerry Czismesia, prin. — Fax 375-1547

Ascutney, Windsor
Windsor Southeast Supervisory Union
Supt. — See Windsor
Weathersfield MS — 200/4-8
PO Box 279 05030 — 802-674-5400
Mario Bevacqua, prin. — Fax 674-9326

Barre, Washington, Pop. 9,166
Barre Supervisory Union — 3,000/PK-12
120 Ayers St 05641 — 802-476-5011
Dorothy Anderson, supt. — Fax 476-4944
Barre Technical Center — Vo/Tech
155 Ayers St 05641 — 802-476-6237
— Fax 476-4045
Spaulding HS — 1,000/9-12
155 Ayers St 05641 — 802-476-4811
Cynthia Donlon, prin. — Fax 479-4535

Washington Central Supervisory Union — 1,600/PK-12
22 E View Ln 05641 — 802-229-0553
Robbe Brook, supt. — Fax 229-2761
www.wcsuonline.org
Other Schools – See Montpelier

Central Vermont SDA S — 50/K-12
317 Vine St 05641 — 802-479-0868
Sherrie Wall, prin. — Fax 479-4311

Bellows Falls, Windham, Pop. 3,086
Windham Northeast Supervisory Union — 1,300/K-12
8A Atkinson St 05101 — 802-463-9958
Johanna Harpster, supt. — Fax 463-9705
www.wnesu.org
Bellows Falls MS — 300/5-8
11-17 School St 05101 — 802-463-4366
Marcy Henry, prin. — Fax 463-9738
Bellows Falls Union HS — 400/9-12
RR 5 S 05101 — 802-463-3944
Christopher Hodsden, prin. — Fax 463-9322

Bennington, Bennington, Pop. 9,532
Southwest Vermont Supervisory Union — 3,600/K-12
246 S Stream Rd 05201 — 802-447-7501
Wesley L. Knapp, supt. — Fax 447-0475
www.svsu.org
Mt. Anthony Union HS — 1,200/9-12
301 Park St 05201 — 802-447-7511
Suzanne Maguire, prin. — Fax 442-1260
Mt. Anthony Union MS — 600/7-8
747 East Rd 05201 — 802-447-7541
David Adams, prin. — Fax 442-1262
SW VT Career Development Center — Vo/Tech
321 Park St 05201 — 802-447-0220
Donna Oyama, prin. — Fax 442-1745

Bennington College — Post-Sec.
1 College Dr 05201 — 800-833-6845
Bennington S, 192 Fairview St 05201 — 100/6-12
Jeffrey LaBonte, prin. — 802-447-1557
Grace Christian S — 200/PK-12
104 Kocher Dr 05201 — 802-447-2233
Joyce Lloyd, admin. — Fax 442-8403
Southern Vermont College — Post-Sec.
982 Mansion Dr 05201 — 802-442-5427

Bethel, Windsor
Windsor Northwest Supervisory Union — 700/PK-12
PO Box 37 05032 — 802-234-5364
Timothy Mock, supt. — Fax 234-6730
Whitcomb JSHS — 200/7-12
273 Pleasant St 05032 — 802-234-9966
William Elberty, prin. — Fax 234-5779
Other Schools – See Rochester

Bradford, Orange, Pop. 824
Orange East Supervisory Union — 1,400/K-12
PO Box 396 05033 — 802-222-5216
Wendy Hovey, supt. — Fax 222-4451
www.orangeeast.k12.vt.us/
Oxbow HS — 500/7-12
36 Oxbow Dr 05033 — 802-222-5214
Charles Brown, prin. — Fax 222-5847
River Bend Career & Tech Center — Vo/Tech
PO Box 618 05033 — 802-222-5212
Ted Guilemette, dir. — Fax 222-9002

Brandon, Rutland, Pop. 1,902
Rutland Northeast Supervisory Union — 1,800/PK-12
49 Court Dr 05733 — 802-247-5757
William Mathis, supt. — Fax 247-5548
www.rnesu.k12.vt.us/
Otter Valley Union JSHS — 700/7-12
2997 Franklin St 05733 — 802-247-6833
Dana Cole-Levesque, prin. — Fax 247-4627

Brattleboro, Windham, Pop. 8,612
Windham Southeast Supervisory Union — 2,900/K-12
53 Green St 05301 — 802-254-3731
Ron Stahley, supt. — Fax 254-3733
www.wssu.k12.vt.us
Brattleboro Area MS — 300/7-8
109 Sunny Acres St 05301 — 802-451-3500
Ingrid Chrisco, prin. — Fax 254-7672
Brattleboro Union HS — 1,000/9-12
131 Fairground Rd 05301 — 802-451-3400
James Day, prin. — Fax 257-8922
Windham Regional Career Center — Vo/Tech
131 Fairground Rd 05301 — 802-257-7335
Dr. Ed Bouquillon, prin. — Fax 257-3079

Austine School for the Deaf — Post-Sec.
60 Austine Dr 05301 — 802-258-9522
School for International Training — Post-Sec.
PO Box 676 05302 — 802-257-7751

Bristol, Addison, Pop. 1,841
Addison Northeast Supervisory Union — 1,900/K-12
10 Orchard Terrace Park 05443 — 802-453-3657
Evelyn Howard, supt. — Fax 453-2029
www.mtabe.k12.vt.us
Mt. Abraham Union JSHS 28 — 1,000/7-12
7 Airport Dr 05443 — 802-453-2333
Paulette Bogan, prin. — Fax 453-4359

Burlington, Chittenden, Pop. 39,148
Burlington SD — 3,600/PK-12
150 Colchester Ave 05401 — 802-865-5332
Jeanne Collins, supt. — Fax 864-8501
www.bsdvt.org/
Burlington HS — 1,100/9-12
52 Institute Rd, — 802-864-8411
Amy Mellencamp, prin. — Fax 864-8408
Burlington Technical Center — Vo/Tech
52 Institute Rd, — 802-864-8426
Mark Aliquo, dir. — Fax 864-8521
Edmunds MS — 400/6-8
275 Main St 05401 — 802-864-8486
Bonnie Johnson-Aten, prin. — Fax 864-2218
Hunt MS — 500/6-8
1364 North Ave, — 802-864-8469
Linda Carroll, prin. — Fax 864-8467

Burlington College — Post-Sec.
95 North Ave 05401 — 802-862-9616
Champlain College — Post-Sec.
PO Box 670 05402 — 802-860-2700
Fletcher Allen Health Care — Post-Sec.
111 Colchester Ave 05401 — 802-847-5133
Rock Point S — 50/9-12
1 Rock Point Rd, 05408 — 802-863-1104
John Rouleau, hdmstr. — Fax 863-6628
University of Vermont — Post-Sec.
194 S Prospect St 05401 — 802-656-3131

Cabot, Washington, Pop. 242
Washington NE Supervisory Union
Supt. — See Plainfield

Cabot S — 200/PK-12
PO Box 98 05647 — 802-563-2289
Paul Fassler, prin. — Fax 563-2022

Canaan, Essex
Essex North Supervisory Union — 300/K-12
PO Box 100 05903 — 802-266-3330
Daniel French, supt. — Fax 266-7085
www.essexnorth.org/
Canaan S — 300/K-12
99 School St 05903 — 802-266-8910
Mary Kelley, prin. — Fax 266-7068

Castleton, Rutland
Addison-Rutland Supervisory Union
Supt. — See Fair Haven
Castleton Village S — 100/7-8
PO Box 68 05735 — 802-468-2203
Albert J. Rousse, prin. — Fax 468-5131

Castleton State College 05735 — Post-Sec.
— 800-639-8521

Charlotte, Chittenden

Lake Champlain Waldorf HS — 100/9-12
735 Ferry Rd 05445 — 802-425-6195
— Fax 425-6207

Chelsea, Orange
Orange-Windsor Supervisory Union
Supt. — See South Royalton
Chelsea S — 200/K-12
6 School St 05038 — 802-685-4551
Karl Stein, prin. — Fax 685-3310

Chester, Windsor, Pop. 1,057
Windsor Southwest Supervisory Union — 1,100/K-12
89 VT Route 103 S 05143 — 802-875-3365
Edward Brown, supt. — Fax 875-3313
Green Mountain Union JSHS — 400/7-12
716 VT Route 103 S 05143 — 802-875-2146
Carol Gilbert, prin. — Fax 875-3183

Colchester, Chittenden
Colchester SD — 2,400/PK-12
PO Box 27 05446 — 802-658-4047
Armando Vilaseca, supt. — Fax 863-4774
www.colchester.k12.vt.us
Colchester HS — 700/9-12
PO Box 900 05446 — 802-658-1570
Joyce Stone, prin. — Fax 864-0450
Colchester MS — 600/6-8
PO Box 30 05446 — 802-655-1772
John Barone, prin. — Fax 655-4495

St. Michael's College — Post-Sec.
1 Winooski Park # 7 05439 — 802-654-2000

Concord, Essex
Essex-Caledonia Supervisory Union — 600/PK-12
PO Box 255 05824 — 802-695-3373
Dr. Mariann Bertolini, supt. — Fax 695-1334
Concord S — 200/PK-12
173 School St 05824 — 802-695-2550
Phyllis Perkins, prin. — Fax 695-3311

Craftsbury Common, Orleans
Orleans Southwest Supervisory Union
Supt. — See Hardwick
Craftsbury Academy — 100/7-12
PO Box 73, — 802-586-2541
Chris Young, prin. — Fax 586-7524

Sterling College — Post-Sec.
PO Box 72 05827 — 802-586-7711

Derby, Orleans, Pop. 725
Orleans-Essex North Supervisory Union
Supt. — See Newport
North Country Union JHS — 300/7-8
57 Junior High Dr 05829 — 802-766-2276
Nicole Larose, prin. — Fax 766-2287

586

Dorset, Bennington

Long Trail S | 200/6-12
1045 Kirby Hollow Rd 05251 | 802-867-5717
David Wilson, hdmstr. | Fax 867-4525

Duxbury, See Waterbury
Washington West Supervisory Union
Supt. — See Waitsfield
Crossett Brook MS | 300/5-8
5672 VT Route 100 05676 | 802-244-6100
Kenneth Page, prin. | Fax 244-6899

East Burke, Caledonia

Burke Mountain Academy | 100/8-12
PO Box 78 05832 | 802-626-5607
Kirk Dwyer, hdmstr. | Fax 626-3784

Enosburg Falls, Franklin, Pop. 1,492
Franklin Northeast Supervisory Union
Supt. — See Richford
Cold Hollow Career Center | Vo/Tech
PO Box 530 05450 | 802-933-4003
Jane Greenwood, prin. | Fax 933-2431
Enosburg Falls HS | 300/9-12
PO Box 417 05450 | 802-933-7777
Edward Grossman, prin. | Fax 933-5375
Enosburg Falls MS | 6-8
PO Box 417 05450 | 802-933-7777
Sandra Schroeder, prin. | Fax 933-5375

Essex Junction, Chittenden, Pop. 8,717
Chittenden Central Supervisory Union | 2,900/PK-12
21 New England Dr 05452 | 802-879-5579
Michael Deweese, supt. | Fax 878-1370
www.ejhs.k12.vt.us/ccsu/
Center for Technology/Essex | Vo/Tech
3 Educational Dr 05452 | 802-879-5562
Kathy Finck, prin. | Fax 879-5593
Essex Junction HS | 1,600/9-12
2 Educational Dr 05452 | 802-879-7121
Robert Reardon, prin. | Fax 879-5503
Lawton MS | 400/6-8
104 Maple St 05452 | 802-878-1388
Edward R. Wilkens, prin. | Fax 879-8175

Essex Town SD | 1,400/PK-8
58 Founders Rd 05452 | 802-878-8168
Jay Nichols, supt. | Fax 878-5190
www.etsdvt.org
Essex MS | 500/6-8
60 Founders Rd 05452 | 802-879-7173
Ned Kirsch, prin. | Fax 879-1363

Essex Technical Center | Post-Sec.
3 Educational Dr 05452
New England Culinary Institute | Post-Sec.
48 1/2 Park St 05452 | 802-872-3400

Fairfax, Franklin
Franklin West Supervisory Union | 1,700/PK-12
PO Box 108 05454 | 802-849-2283
Philip Higgins, supt. | Fax 849-2865
Bellows Free Academy | 900/PK-12
75 Hunt St 05454 | 802-849-6711
D. Scott Lang, prin. | Fax 849-6711

Fair Haven, Rutland, Pop. 2,432
Addison-Rutland Supervisory Union | 1,800/PK-12
49 Main St 05743 | 802-265-4905
Ronald C. Ryan, supt. | Fax 265-2158
Fair Haven Union HS | 600/9-12
33 Mechanic St 05743 | 802-265-4966
Felice Clauder, prin. | Fax 265-3602
Other Schools – See Castleton

Hardwick, Caledonia
Orleans Southwest Supervisory Union | 1,100/K-12
PO Box 338 05843 | 802-472-6531
Mark Andrews, supt. | Fax 472-6250
ossu35.tripod.com/index.htm
Hazen Union JSHS | 400/7-12
PO Box 368 05843 | 802-472-6511
Peter Martenson, prin. | Fax 472-3327
Other Schools – See Craftsbury Common

Hinesburg, Chittenden
Chittendon South Supervisory Union
Supt. — See Shelburne
Champlain Valley Union HS 15 | 1,300/9-12
369 CVU Rd 05461 | 802-482-7100
Sean McMannon, prin. | Fax 482-7108

Hyde Park, Lamoille, Pop. 430
Lamoille North Supervisory Union | 1,600/PK-12
95 Cricket Hill Rd 05655 | 802-888-3142
Terry D. Bailey Ed.D., supt. | Fax 888-7908
Green Mountain Technology & Career Ctr | Vo/Tech
PO Box 600 05655 | 802-888-4447
Joe Teagarden, prin. | Fax 888-7838
Lamoille Union HS | 600/9-12
736 VT 15 W 05655 | 802-888-4261
Sharon Fortune, prin. | Fax 888-2997
Lamoille Union MS | 7-8
736 VT 15 W 05655 | 802-851-1300
Paul Lowe, prin. | Fax 851-1397

Jericho, Chittenden, Pop. 1,405
Chittenden East Supervisory Union
Supt. — See Richmond
Browns River MS | 500/5-8
20 River Rd 05465 | 802-899-3711
Nancy Guyette, prin. | Fax 899-4281
Mt. Mansfield Union HS | 1,100/9-12
211 Browns Trace Rd 05465 | 802-899-4690
Jennifer Botzojorns, prin. | Fax 899-2904

Johnson, Lamoille, Pop. 1,427

Johnson State College | Post-Sec.
337 College Hl 05656 | 802-635-2356

Ludlow, Windsor, Pop. 939
Rutland-Windsor Supervisory Union | 500/K-12
8 High St 05149 | 802-228-2541
Dr. Frank Perotti, supt. | Fax 228-8359
www.rwsu.org/
Black River JSHS | 300/7-12
43 Main St 05149 | 802-228-4721
John Barth, prin. | Fax 228-7233

Lyndon Center, Caledonia

Lyndon Institute | 600/9-12
PO Box 127 05850 | 802-626-3357
Richard Hilton, prin. | Fax 626-9164

Lyndonville, Caledonia, Pop. 1,213

Lyndon State College | Post-Sec.
PO Box 919 05851 | 802-626-6200

Manchester, Bennington, Pop. 669

Burr and Burton Academy | 600/9-12
PO Box 498 05254 | 802-362-1775
Charles Scranton, hdmstr. | Fax 362-0574

Marlboro, Windham

Marlboro College | Post-Sec.
PO Box A 05344 | 802-257-4333

Middlebury, Addison, Pop. 6,007
Addison Central Supervisory Union | 2,100/PK-12
49 Charles Ave 05753 | 802-382-1274
William Lee Sease, supt. | Fax 388-0024
www.acsu.k12.vt.us/
Hannaford Career Center | Vo/Tech
51 Charles Ave 05753 | 802-382-1012
D. Lynn Coale, prin. | Fax 388-2591
Middlebury Union HS | 800/9-12
73 Charles Ave 05753 | 802-382-1500
William Lawson, prin. | Fax 382-1101
Middlebury Union MS | 300/7-8
48 Deerfield Ln 05753 | 802-382-1600
Inga Duktig, prin. | Fax 382-1215

Middlebury College 05753 | Post-Sec.
| 802-443-5000

Milton, Chittenden, Pop. 1,557
Milton Town SD | 1,900/PK-12
42 Herrick Ave 05468 | 802-893-3210
Holden Waterman, supt. | Fax 893-3213
www.milton.k12.vt.us
Milton HS | 500/9-12
17 Rebecca Lander Dr 05468 | 802-893-3230
Anne Blake, prin. | Fax 893-3247
Milton JHS | 300/7-8
17 Rebecca Lander Dr 05468 | 802-893-3230
Wes McClellan, prin. | Fax 893-3247

Montpelier, Washington, Pop. 7,945
Montpelier SD | 1,100/K-12
58 Barre St 05602 | 802-223-9796
John Everitt, supt. | Fax 223-9795
www.mpsvt.org
Main Street MS | 300/6-8
170 Main St 05602 | 802-223-3404
Laura Singer, prin. | Fax 223-9220
Montpelier HS | 400/9-12
5 High School Dr 05602 | 802-225-8000
Peter Evans, prin. | Fax 223-9227

Washington Central Supervisory Union
Supt. — See Barre
Union 32 JSHS | 900/7-12
930 Gallison Hill Rd 05602 | 802-229-0321
Dot Blake, prin. | Fax 223-7411

New England Culinary Institute | Post-Sec.
250 Main St 05602 | 802-223-6324
Union Institute & University | Post-Sec.
36 College St 05602 | 802-828-8740
Woodbury College | Post-Sec.
660 Elm St 05602 | 802-229-0516

Morrisville, Lamoille, Pop. 2,063
Lamoille South Supervisory Union | 1,600/K-12
PO Box 340 05661 | 802-888-4541
Alice Angney, supt. | Fax 888-6710
Peoples Academy | 400/9-12
202 Copley Ave 05661 | 802-888-4600
Otho Thompson, prin. | Fax 888-6726
Peoples Academy MS | 300/6-8
202 Copley Ave 05661 | 802-888-1402
Otho Thompson, prin. | Fax 888-6488
Other Schools – See Stowe

Newport, Orleans, Pop. 5,092
Orleans-Essex North Supervisory Union | 3,000/K-12
338 Highland Ave Ste 4 05855 | 802-334-5847
Dr. Rodman Weston, supt. | Fax 334-6528
www.northcountryschools.org
North Country Career Center | Vo/Tech
PO Box 705 05855 | 802-334-5469
Robert Fitts, prin. | Fax 334-3492
North Country Union HS | 1,000/9-12
209 Veterans Ave 05855 | 802-334-7921
William Rivard, prin. | Fax 334-1618
Other Schools – See Derby

United Christian Academy | 100/K-12
65 School St 05855 | 802-334-3112
Dr. Richard E O'Hara, hdmstr. | Fax 334-2305

North Clarendon, Rutland
Rutland South Supervisory Union | 1,200/K-12
PO Box 87 05759 | 802-775-3264
Walter Goetz, supt. | Fax 775-8063
www.rssu.org
Mill River Union JSHS | 700/7-12
PO Box 6 05759 | 802-775-1925
Bruce Gee, prin. | Fax 775-6447

Northfield, Washington, Pop. 3,178
Washington South Supervisory Union | 900/PK-12
37 Cross St 05663 | 802-485-7755
David Bickford, supt. | Fax 485-3348
wssu.org
Northfield MSHS | 500/6-12
37 Cross St 05663 | 802-485-4500
Tom Marshall, prin. | Fax 485-4440

Norwich University | Post-Sec.
158 Harmon Dr 05663 | 800-468-6679

Orleans, Orleans, Pop. 845
Orleans Central Supervisory Union | 1,200/K-12
PO Box 207 05860 | 802-754-6945
Ronald D. Paquette Ed.D., supt. | Fax 754-2781
www.ocsu.org/
Lake Region Union HS 24 | 400/9-12
317 Lake Region Rd 05860 | 802-754-6521
Steve Urgensen, prin. | Fax 754-2780

Plainfield, Washington
Washington NE Supervisory Union | 700/PK-12
6328 US Route 2 05667 | 802-426-3245
George Burlison, supt. | Fax 426-3801
Twinfield Union S | 500/PK-12
106 Nasmith Brook Rd 05667 | 802-426-3213
Owen Bradley, prin. | Fax 426-4085
Other Schools – See Cabot

Goddard College | Post-Sec.
123 Pitkin Rd 05667 | 802-454-8311

Poultney, Rutland, Pop. 1,558
Rutland Southwest Supervisory Union | 900/PK-12
168 York St 05764 | 802-287-5286
Maynard Baldwin, supt. | Fax 287-2284
www.rswsu.org
Poultney HS | 300/7-12
154 E Main St 05764 | 802-287-5861
Jean Oakman, prin. | Fax 287-2304

Green Mountain College | Post-Sec.
1 College Cir 05764 | 802-287-8000

Proctor, Rutland
Rutland Central Supervisory Union
Supt. — See Rutland
Proctor JSHS | 200/7-12
4 Park St 05765 | 802-459-3353
Christopher J. Sousa, prin. | Fax 459-6323

Putney, Windham

Landmark College | Post-Sec.
River Rd S 05346 | 802-387-4767
Putney S | 200/9-12
418 Houghton Brook Rd 05346 | 802-387-5566
Brian Morgan, dir. | Fax 387-6259

Randolph, Orange
Orange Southwest Supervisory Union | 1,200/K-12
24 Central St 05060 | 802-728-5052
Brent Kay, supt. | Fax 728-4844
www.orangesw.k12.vt.us/
Randolph TCC | Vo/Tech
17 Forest St 05060 | 802-728-9595
Bill Sugarman, prin. | Fax 728-9596
Randolph Union JSHS | 600/7-12
15 Forest St 05060 | 802-728-3397
John Holmes, prin. | Fax 728-6703

Randolph Center, Orange

Vermont Technical College | Post-Sec.
PO Box 500 05061 | 802-728-1000

Richford, Franklin, Pop. 1,417
Franklin Northeast Supervisory Union | 1,600/K-12
PO Box 130 05476 | 802-848-7661
Mary Sherrer, supt. | Fax 848-3531
Richford JSHS | 300/7-12
1 Corliss Hts 05476 | 802-848-7416
Cynthia Hinrichsen, prin. | Fax 848-3210
Other Schools – See Enosburg Falls

Richmond, Chittenden
Chittenden East Supervisory Union | 3,000/K-12
PO Box 282 05477 | 802-434-2128
James Massingham, supt. | Fax 434-2196
www.cesu.k12.vt.us
Camels Hump MS | 400/5-8
173 School St 05477 | 802-434-2188
Mark Carbone, prin. | Fax 434-2192
Other Schools – See Jericho

Rochester, Windsor
Windsor Northwest Supervisory Union
Supt. — See Bethel
Rochester S | 300/K-12
222 S Main St 05767 | 802-767-3161
Bob Gray, prin. | Fax 767-1130

Rutland, Rutland, Pop. 17,103
Rutland Central Supervisory Union 1,100/PK-12
257 S Main St 05701 802-775-4342
Karen White, supt. Fax 775-7319
www.rcsu.org
Other Schools – See Proctor, West Rutland

Rutland City SD 2,800/K-12
6 Church St 05701 802-773-1900
Mary Moran, supt. Fax 773-1927
rutlandhs.k12.vt.us
Rutland HS 1,100/9-12
22 Stratton Rd 05701 802-773-1955
Peter Folaros, prin. Fax 770-1020
Rutland MS 400/7-8
65 Library Ave 05701 802-773-1960
Wilfred Cunningham, prin. Fax 773-1914
Stafford Tech Ctr Vo/Tech
8 Stratton Rd 05701 802-773-1990
Lyle Jepson, prin. Fax 770-1066

College of Saint Joseph Post-Sec.
71 Clement Rd 05701 802-773-5900
Mt. St. Joseph Academy 200/9-12
127 Convent Ave 05701 802-775-0151
Sr. Kathryn Gallagher, prin. Fax 775-0424
Rutland Area Christian S 100/PK-12
112 Lincoln Ave 05701 802-775-0709
Ron Comfort, hdmstr. Fax 786-0111
Rutland Regional Medical Center Post-Sec.
160 Allen St 05701 802-775-7111

Saint Albans, Franklin, Pop. 7,565
Franklin Central Supervisory Union 2,900/PK-12
28 Catherine St 05478 802-524-2600
Marilyn Grunewald, supt. Fax 524-1540
www.sover.net/~fcsu/
Bellows Free Academy 1,200/PK-12
71 S Main St 05478 802-527-6555
Ned Caron, prin. Fax 527-6402
Northwest Technical Center Vo/Tech
71 S Main St 05478 802-527-0614
Ned Caron, prin. Fax 527-6469

DLI Distance Learning International Post-Sec.
PO Box 846 05478 800-489-4114

Saint Johnsbury, Caledonia, Pop. 6,424

St. Johnsbury Academy 1,000/9-12
PO Box 906 05819 802-748-8171
Thomas Lovett, hdmstr. Fax 748-5463

Saxtons River, Windham, Pop. 515

Vermont Academy 300/9-12
PO Box 500 05154 802-869-6200
James Mooney, prin. Fax 869-6242

Sharon, Windsor

Sharon Academy, PO Box 207 05065 200/7-12
Judy Moore, prin. 802-763-2531

Shelburne, Chittenden
Chittendon South Supervisory Union 4,400/PK-12
5420 Shelburne Rd Ste 300 05482 802-383-1234
Dr. Brian O'Regan, supt. Fax 383-1242
www.cssu.org/
Other Schools – See Hinesburg

Lake Champlain Waldorf S 300/PK-12
PO Box 250 05482 802-985-2827
Ellen Coogan, contact Fax 985-2834

South Burlington, Chittenden, Pop. 16,285
South Burlington SD 2,700/K-12
550 Dorset St 05403 802-652-7250
Gail Durckel Ed.D., supt. Fax 652-7257
www.sbschools.net
South Burlington HS 1,000/9-12
550 Dorset St 05403 802-652-7000
Patrick Burke, prin. Fax 652-7006
Tuttle MS 600/6-8
500 Dorset St 05403 802-652-7100
Joseph O'Brien, prin. Fax 652-7152

O'Briens Training Center Post-Sec.
1475 Shelburne Rd 05403 802-658-9591
Rice Memorial HS 500/9-12
99 Proctor Ave 05403 802-862-6521
Dr. Alan Crowley, prin. Fax 864-9931

South Duxbury, Washington
Washington West Supervisory Union
Supt. — See Waitsfield

Harwood Union HS 800/7-12
458 VT Route 100 05660 802-244-5186
Duane Pierson, prin. Fax 882-1199

South Royalton, Windsor
Orange-Windsor Supervisory Union 1,100/PK-12
PO Box 240 05068 802-763-8840
Stephen Metcalf, supt. Fax 763-3235
South Royalton S 400/PK-12
223 S Windsor St 05068 802-763-8844
Shaun Pickett, prin. Fax 763-3233
Other Schools – See Chelsea

Vermont Law School Post-Sec.
PO Box 96 05068 802-763-8303

Springfield, Windsor, Pop. 4,207
Springfield SD 1,500/K-12
60 Park St 05156 802-885-5141
Rose Rooth, supt. Fax 885-8169
www.springfield.k12.vt.us
Riverside MS 300/6-8
13 Fairground Rd 05156 802-885-8490
Judy Pullinen, prin. Fax 885-8442
River Valley Technical Center Vo/Tech
307 South St 05156 802-885-8300
Carl Mock, prin. Fax 885-8454
Springfield HS 600/9-12
303 South St 05156 802-885-7900
Dr. Judson Bolles, prin. Fax 885-4459

Stowe, Lamoille, Pop. 500
Lamoille South Supervisory Union
Supt. — See Morrisville
Stowe HS 200/9-12
413 Barrows Rd 05672 802-253-7229
Richard Kraemer, prin. Fax 253-6911
Stowe MS 6-8
413 Barrows Rd 05672 802-253-6913
Nancy Shiok, prin. Fax 253-5314

Stratton Mountain, Windham, Pop. 50

Stratton Mountain S 100/7-12
7 World Cup Cir 05155 802-297-1886
Christopher Kaltsas, prin. Fax 297-0020

Swanton, Franklin, Pop. 2,578
Franklin Northwest Supervisory Union 2,400/K-12
100 Robin Hood Dr 05488 802-868-4967
John McCarthy, supt. Fax 868-4265
www.missisquoi.k12.vt.us/fnwtitl4.html
Missisquoi Valley Union MSHS 1,100/7-12
100 Thunderbird Dr 05488 802-868-7311
Chaunce Benedict, prin. Fax 868-3129

Thetford, Orange

Thetford Academy, PO Box 190 05074 400/7-12
Martha Rich, prin. 802-785-4805

Townshend, Windham
Windham Central Supervisory Union 1,000/K-12
1219 Vt Route 30 05353 802-365-9510
James Peters, supt. Fax 365-7934
www.wcsu.k12.vt.us
Leland-Gray Union HS 400/7-12
PO Box 128 05353 802-365-7355
Lloyd Szulborski, prin. Fax 365-4126

Vergennes, Addison, Pop. 2,789
Addison Northwest Supervisory Union 1,000/K-12
48 Green St Ste 1 05491 802-877-3332
Thomas F. O'Brien, supt. Fax 877-3628
www.anwsu.org
Vergennes Union JHS 7-9
50 Monkton Rd 05491 802-877-2938
Manya Bouteneff, prin. Fax 877-2558
Vergennes Union SHS 300/10-12
50 Monkton Rd 05491 802-877-2938
Edwin Webbley, prin. Fax 877-2558

Champlain Valley Christian S 100/K-12
73B Church St 05491 802-877-3640
Bruce Davis, admin. Fax 877-1103

Waitsfield, Washington
Washington West Supervisory Union 2,200/PK-12
1673 Main St Ste A 05673 802-496-2272
Robert McNamara, supt. Fax 496-6515
www.harwood.org
Other Schools – See Duxbury, South Duxbury

Green Mountain Valley S 100/9-12
271 Moulton Rd 05673 802-496-2150
David Gavett, prin.

Waterbury, Washington, Pop. 1,701

Community College of Vermont Post-Sec.
PO Box 120 05676 802-241-3535

Wells River, Orange, Pop. 329
Blue Mountain SD 400/PK-12
2420 Route 302 05081 802-757-2766
Dr. Gordon Schnare, supt. Fax 757-2790
www.bmuschool.org
Blue Mountain Union S 21 400/PK-12
2420 Route 302 05081 802-757-2711
Carol A. Curtis, supt. Fax 757-3894

West Rutland, Rutland, Pop. 2,246
Rutland Central Supervisory Union
Supt. — See Rutland
West Rutland S 400/PK-12
713 Main St 05777 802-438-2288
Joseph Bowen, prin. Fax 438-5708

White River Junction, Windsor, Pop. 2,521
Hartford SD 1,900/PK-12
73 Highland Ave 05001 802-295-8600
Carl Mock, supt. Fax 295-8602
www.hartfordsd.com/
Hartford Area Career & Technology Center Vo/Tech
1 Gifford Rd 05001 802-295-8630
Michael Redington, prin. Fax 295-8631
Hartford HS 800/9-12
37 Highland Ave 05001 802-295-8620
Joseph Collea, prin. Fax 295-8611
Hartford Memorial MS 400/6-8
245 Highland Ave 05001 802-295-8640
John Grant, prin. Fax 295-8602

Mid-Vermont Christian S 200/PK-12
399 W Gilson Ave 05001 802-295-6800
Robert Bracy, hdmstr. Fax 295-3748

Williamstown, Orange
Orange North Supervisory Union 800/PK-12
111 Brush Hill Rd 05679 802-433-5818
Douglas R. Shiok, supt. Fax 433-5825
Williamstown MSHS 300/6-12
120 Hebert Rd 05679 802-433-5350
Kathleen Morris-Kortz, prin. Fax 433-1037

Williston, Chittenden

Pine Ridge S 100/9-12
9505 Williston Rd 05495 802-434-2161
Douglas Dague, hdmstr. Fax 434-5512
Trinity Baptist S 100/K-12
280 Trinity Dr 05495 802-878-8118
Mitch Bilbe, prin. Fax 879-5272
Vermont College of Cosmetology Post-Sec.
400 Cornerstone Dr Ste 220 05495 802-863-4666

Wilmington, Windham
Windham Southwest Supervisory Union 700/PK-12
211 Route 9 W 05363 802-464-1300
M. Wright, supt. Fax 464-1303
Twin Valley HS 200/9-12
1 School St 05363 802-464-5255
Frank Spencer, prin. Fax 464-5903

Windsor, Windsor, Pop. 3,714
Windsor Southeast Supervisory Union 1,400/PK-12
105 Main St Ste 200 05089 802-674-2144
Fax 674-6357
Windsor JSHS 500/7-12
19 Ascutney St 05089 802-674-6344
Henry Rupertsberger, prin. Fax 674-9802
Other Schools – See Ascutney

Winooski, Chittenden, Pop. 6,387
Winooski SD 800/PK-12
60 Normand St 05404 802-655-0485
Bruce Chattman, supt. Fax 655-7602
www.winooski.k12.vt.us
Winooski HS 200/9-12
80 Normand St 05404 802-655-3531
Steve Perkins, prin. Fax 655-6538
Winooski MS 200/6-8
80 Normand St 05404 802-655-3530
Mary Woodruff, prin. Fax 655-6538

Woodstock, Windsor, Pop. 960
Windsor Central Supervisory Union 1,200/PK-12
496 Woodstock Rd Ste 2 05091 802-457-1213
Meg Gallagher, supt. Fax 457-2989
www.wcsu.net/
Woodstock Union HS 400/9-12
496 Woodstock Rd Ste 1 05091 802-457-1317
Johanna Harpster, prin. Fax 457-1850
Woodstock Union MS 200/7-8
496 Woodstock Rd Ste 1 05091 802-457-1330
Dana Peterson, prin. Fax 457-5048

VIRGINIA

VIRGINIA DEPARTMENT OF EDUCATION
PO Box 2120, Richmond 23218-2120
Telephone 804-225-2020
Fax 804-371-2099
Website http://www.pen.k12.va.us

Superintendent of Public Instruction   Patricia Wright

VIRGINIA BOARD OF EDUCATION
PO Box 2120, Richmond 23218-2120

President   Thomas Jackson

PUBLIC, PRIVATE AND CATHOLIC SECONDARY SCHOOLS

Abingdon, Washington, Pop. 7,750
Regional Academic Governors SD
 Supt. — See Richmond
Holton Governor's S 10-12
 PO Box 1987 24212 276-619-4326
 Danny Dixon, dir. Fax 619-4328

Washington County SD 7,300/PK-12
 812 Thompson Dr 24210 276-739-3003
 Dr. Alan Lee, supt. Fax 623-4137
 www.wcs.k12.va.us
Abingdon HS 1,000/9-12
 705 Thompson Dr 24210 276-739-3200
 Jeff Noe, prin. Fax 628-1897
Neff Center for Science & Tech Vo/Tech
 255 Stanley St 24210 276-628-1870
 Doug Sparks, prin. Fax 623-4126
Stanley MS 700/6-8
 297 Stanley St 24210 276-739-3300
 Gary McCool, prin. Fax 676-1945
Washington County Technical S Vo/Tech
 850 Thompson Dr 24210 276-739-3140
 Douglas Sparks, prin. Fax 623-4197
Other Schools – See Bristol, Damascus, Glade Spring

Virginia Highlands Community College Post-Sec.
 PO Box 828 24212 276-676-5484
Washington County Adult Skill Center Post-Sec.
 848 Thompson Dr 24210 276-676-1948

Accomac, Accomack, Pop. 543
Accomack County SD 4,100/K-12
 PO Box 330 23301 757-787-5754
 W. Richard Bull, supt. Fax 787-2951
 sbo.accomack.k12.va.us
Other Schools – See Chincoteague, Oak Hall, Onley, Tangier

Afton, Nelson

Afton Christian S 100/K-12
 9357 Critzers Shop Rd 22920 540-456-6853
 Debbie Beaver, hdmstr. Fax 456-6236

Alberta, Brunswick, Pop. 307

Southside Virginia Community College Post-Sec.
 109 Campus Dr 23821 434-949-1000

Aldie, Loudoun
Loudoun County SD
 Supt. — See Ashburn
Mercer MS 6-8
 42149 Greenstone Dr 20105 703-444-8061
 Frederic Gauriloff, prin.

Alexandria, Alexandria, Pop. 128,923
Alexandria CSD 10,100/K-12
 2000 N Beauregard St 22311 703-824-6600
 Rebecca Perry, supt. Fax 824-6699
 www.acps.k12.va.us
Hammond MS 1,300/6-8
 4646 Seminary Rd 22304 703-461-4100
 Kristen Clark, prin. Fax 461-4111
Howard S 9-9
 3801 W Braddock Rd 22302 703-824-6750
 Fax 824-6781
Secondary Training & Education Program Vo/Tech
 3330 King St 22302 703-824-6631
 Carolyn Lewis, prin. Fax 931-0652
Washington MS 1,100/6-8
 1005 Mount Vernon Ave 22301 703-706-4500
 Grace Taylor, prin. Fax 706-4507
Williams HS 2,100/10-12
 3330 King St 22302 703-824-6800
 John Porter, prin. Fax 824-6826

Fairfax County SD
 Supt. — See Fairfax
Edison HS 1,800/9-12
 5801 Franconia Rd 22310 703-924-8000
 Gregory Croghan, prin. Fax 924-8097
Glasgow MS 1,100/6-8
 4101 Fairfax Pkwy 22312 703-813-8700
 Deirdre Lavery, prin. Fax 813-8797

Hayfield JSHS 3,900/7-12
 7630 Telegraph Rd 22315 703-924-7400
 Bill Oehrlein, prin. Fax 924-7497
Holmes MS 800/6-8
 6525 Montrose St 22312 703-658-5900
 Roberto Pamas, prin. Fax 658-5997
Jefferson Science & Tech HS 1,700/9-12
 6560 Braddock Rd 22312 703-750-8300
 Elizabeth Lodal, prin. Fax 750-5010
Landmark Career Academy Vo/Tech
 5801 Duke St 22304 703-658-6451
 Jan McKee, prin. Fax 658-6497
Mt. Vernon HS 1,800/9-12
 8515 Old Mount Vernon Rd 22309 703-619-3100
 Eric Brent, prin. Fax 619-3197
Pulley Vocational Center Vo/Tech
 6500 Quander Rd 22307 703-718-2700
 Fax 718-2797
Sandburg MS 1,200/7-8
 8428 Fort Hunt Rd 22308 703-799-6100
 Donna Pasteur, prin. Fax 799-6197
Twain MS 1,100/7-8
 4700 Franconia Rd 22310 703-313-3700
 Carol Robinson, prin. Fax 313-3797
West Potomac HS 2,100/9-12
 6500 Quander Rd 22307 703-718-2500
 Rima Vesilind, prin. Fax 718-2597
Whitman MS 1,000/7-8
 2500 Parkers Ln 22306 703-660-2400
 Otha Davis, prin. Fax 660-2497

Alexandria Friends S 50/9-12
 25 S Quaker Ln 22314 703-461-7222
 William Stewart, hdmstr. Fax 461-7003
Bishop Ireton HS 800/9-12
 201 Cambridge Rd 22314 703-751-7606
 Rev. Matthew Hillyard, prin. Fax 212-8173
Episcopal HS 400/9-12
 1200 N Quaker Ln 22302 703-933-3000
 F. Robertson Hershey, hdmstr. Fax 933-3017
Northern Virginia Community College Post-Sec.
 3001 N Beauregard St 22311 703-845-6200
Protestant Episcopal Theologcl. Seminary Post-Sec.
 3737 Seminary Rd 22304 703-370-6600
St. Stephen's & St. Agnes S 300/6-8
 4401 W Braddock Rd 22304 703-751-2741
 Fax 578-0193
St. Stephen's & St. Agnes S 400/9-12
 1000 Saint Stephens Rd 22304 703-751-2700
 Joan Holden, hdmstr. Fax 751-7142
TESST Electronic School Post-Sec.
 6315 Bren Mar Dr 22312 703-354-1005
Thornton Friends S 50/9-12
 3830 Seminary Rd 22304 703-461-8880
 Michael DeHart, hdmstr. Fax 461-3697

Altavista, Campbell, Pop. 3,339
Campbell County SD
 Supt. — See Rustburg
Altavista JSHS 800/6-12
 904 Bedford Ave 24517 434-369-4768
 Clayton Stanley, prin. Fax 369-5191

Amelia Court House, Amelia
Amelia County SD 1,700/PK-12
 8701 Otterburn Rd Ste 101 23002 804-561-2621
 Dr. David M. Gangel, supt. Fax 561-3057
 eclipse.achs.amelia.k12.va.us/public/
Amelia County HS 500/9-12
 8500 Otterburn Rd 23002 804-561-2101
 Karl Leap, prin. Fax 561-4567
Amelia County MS 400/6-8
 8740 Otterburn Rd 23002 804-561-4422
 Tammy Maxey, prin. Fax 561-6525

Amherst, Amherst, Pop. 2,220
Amherst County SD 4,500/K-12
 PO Box 1257 24521 434-946-9387
 John Walker Ed.D., supt. Fax 946-9346
 www.amherst.k12.va.us
Amherst County HS 1,400/9-12
 139 Lancer Ln 24521 434-946-2898
 Ernie Guill, prin. Fax 946-2263
Amherst MS 500/6-8
 165 Gordons Fairgrounds Rd 24521 434-946-0691
 Christie Cundiff, prin. Fax 946-0258

Other Schools – See Madison Heights

Annandale, Fairfax, Pop. 55,800
Fairfax County SD
 Supt. — See Fairfax
Annandale HS 2,600/9-12
 4700 Medford Dr 22003 703-642-4100
 John Ponton, prin. Fax 642-4197
Poe MS 1,200/6-8
 7000 Cindy Ln 22003 703-813-3800
 June Monterio, prin. Fax 813-3897

Northern Virginia Community College Post-Sec.
 4001 Wakefield Chapel Rd 22003 703-323-3000
Springfield Beauty Academy Post-Sec.
 4223 Annandale Rd 22003 703-256-5662

Appalachia, Wise, Pop. 1,756
Wise County SD
 Supt. — See Wise
Appalachia HS 200/8-12
 205 Lee St 24216 276-565-0214
 George Barton, prin. Fax 565-0922

Appomattox, Appomattox, Pop. 1,725
Appomattox County SD 2,300/PK-12
 PO Box 548 24522 434-352-8251
 Dr. Walter Krug, supt. Fax 352-0883
 www.appomattox.k12.va.us
Appomattox HS 700/9-12
 198 Evergreen Ave 24522 434-352-7146
 Dr. Greg Wheeler, prin. Fax 352-0822
Appomattox MS 500/6-8
 2020 Church St 24522 434-352-8257
 Robert Kerns, prin. Fax 352-5621

Arlington, Arlington, Pop. 189,927
Arlington County SD 19,400/PK-12
 1426 N Quincy St 22207 703-228-6000
 Dr. Robert G. Smith, supt. Fax 228-6188
 www.arlington.k12.va.us
Career Center Continuation HS Vo/Tech
 816 S Walter Reed Dr 22204 703-228-5800
 Gerald Caputo, prin. Fax 228-5815
Gunston MS 600/6-8
 2700 S Lang St 22206 703-228-6900
 Margaret Gill, prin. Fax 519-9183
Jefferson MS 700/6-8
 125 S Old Glebe Rd 22204 703-228-5900
 Sharon Monde, prin. Fax 979-3744
Kenmore MS 800/6-8
 200 S Carlin Springs Rd 22204 703-228-6800
 John Word, prin. Fax 998-3069
Swanson MS 800/6-8
 5800 Washington Blvd 22205 703-228-5500
 Chrystal Forrester, prin. Fax 536-2775
Wakefield HS 1,900/9-12
 4901 S Chesterfield Rd 22206 703-228-6700
 Doris Jackson, prin. Fax 575-8832
Washington-Lee HS 1,800/9-12
 1300 N Quincy St 22201 703-228-6200
 Gregg Robertson, prin. Fax 524-9814
Williamsburg MS 1,000/6-8
 3600 N Harrison St 22207 703-228-5450
 Kathleen Francis, prin. Fax 536-2870
Yorktown HS 1,800/9-12
 5201 28th St N 22207 703-228-5400
 Raymond Pasi, prin. Fax 228-5409
HS Continuation - Arlington Mill Adult
 4975 Columbia Pike 22204 703-228-5350
 Barbara Thompson, prin. Fax 575-8666
HS Continuation - Langston Adult
 2121 N Culpeper St 22207 703-228-5295
 Cleveland James, prin. Fax 807-0614

ACT College Post-Sec.
 1100 Wilson Blvd Ste M780 22209 703-527-6660
Argosy University/Washington DC Post-Sec.
 1550 Wilson Blvd Ste 600 22209 703-526-5800
Art Institute of Washington Post-Sec.
 1820 Fort Myer Dr 22209 703-358-9550
Bishop Denis J. O'Connell HS 1,500/9-12
 6600 Little Falls Rd 22213 703-237-1400
 Dick Martin, prin. Fax 237-1412
DeVry University Post-Sec.
 2341 Jefferson Davis Hwy 22202 866-338-7932

DeVry University — Post-Sec.
2450 Crystal Dr 22202 — 703-415-0600
Graham Webb Intl. Academy of Hair — Post-Sec.
1621 N Kent St # 1617LL 22209 — 703-243-9322
Marymount University — Post-Sec.
2807 N Glebe Rd 22207 — 703-522-5600
University of Management and Technology — Post-Sec.
1901 Fort Myer Dr Ste 700 22209 — 703-516-0035

Ashburn, Loudoun, Pop. 3,393
Loudoun County SD — 41,400/PK-12
21000 Education Ct 20148 — 571-252-1000
Dr. Edgar Hatrick, supt. — Fax 252-1669
www.loudoun.k12.va.us
Briar Woods HS — 9-12
22525 Belmont Ridge Rd 20148 — 571-223-2344
Edward Starzenski, prin.
Broad Run HS — 1,500/9-12
21670 Ashburn Rd 20147 — 703-771-6620
Dr. Edgar Markley, prin. — Fax 771-6636
Eagle Ridge MS — 600/6-8
42901 Waxpool Rd 20148 — 703-779-8970
Janice Koslowski, prin. — Fax 779-8977
Farmwell Station MS — 1,300/6-8
44281 Gloucester Pkwy 20147 — 703-771-6491
Sherryl Loya, prin. — Fax 771-6495
Stone Bridge HS — 1,600/9-12
43100 Hay Rd 20147 — 703-779-8900
James Person, prin. — Fax 779-8908
Other Schools – See Aldie, Hamilton, Leesburg, Purcellville, South Riding, Sterling

Christian Fellowship S — 400/PK-12
21673 Beaumeade Cir #600 20147 — 703-729-5968
Kevin Jeter, hdmstr. — Fax 729-6635
Strayer University — Post-Sec.
45150 Russell Branch Pkwy 20147 — 703-729-8800

Ashland, Hanover, Pop. 6,876
Hanover County SD — 18,000/K-12
200 Berkley St 23005 — 804-365-4500
Dr. Stewart Roberson, supt. — Fax 365-4680
www.hcps.us
Henry HS — 1,600/9-12
12449 W Patrick Henry Rd 23005 — 804-365-8000
Paul Vecchione, prin. — Fax 365-8027
Liberty MS — 1,200/6-8
13496 Liberty School Rd 23005 — 804-365-8060
Donald E. Latham, prin. — Fax 365-8061
Other Schools – See Mechanicsville

Randolph-Macon College — Post-Sec.
PO Box 5005 23005 — 804-752-7200

Bassett, Henry, Pop. 1,579
Henry County SD
Supt. — See Collinsville
Bassett HS — 700/9-12
85 Riverside Dr 24055 — 276-629-1731
A. Dean Randall, prin. — Fax 629-9329

Bastian, Bland
Bland County SD — 900/K-12
361 Bears Trl 24314 — 276-688-3361
Don Hodock, supt. — Fax 688-4659
www.bland.k12.va.us
Other Schools – See Bland, Rocky Gap

Bealeton, Fauquier
Fauquier County SD
Supt. — See Warrenton
Cedar-Lee MS — 700/6-8
11138 Marsh Rd 22712 — 540-439-3207
Steven Parker, prin. — Fax 439-2051
Liberty HS — 1,500/9-12
6300 Independence Ave 22712 — 540-439-6300
Roger Lee, prin. — Fax 439-3397

Bedford, Bedford, Pop. 6,339
Bedford County SD — 11,000/K-12
PO Box 748 24523 — 540-586-1045
Dr. James Blevins, supt. — Fax 586-7703
www.bedford.k12.va.us
Bedford MS — 600/7-8
503 Longwood Ave 24523 — 540-586-7735
Rhetta Watkins, prin. — Fax 586-4957
Bedford Science and Technology Center — Vo/Tech
600 Edmund St 24523 — 540-586-3933
Charles Coles, prin. — Fax 586-7711
Liberty HS — 1,000/9-12
100 Minute Man Dr 24523 — 540-586-2541
Dr. Cherie Whitehurst, prin. — Fax 586-7720
Other Schools – See Forest, Moneta

Ben Hur, Lee
Lee County SD
Supt. — See Jonesville
Lee County Career & Technical Center — Vo/Tech
PO Box 100 24218 — 276-346-1960
Randal A. Ingle, prin. — Fax 346-2831

Berryville, Clarke, Pop. 3,030
Clarke County SD — 2,100/PK-12
309 W Main St 22611 — 540-955-6100
Eleanor Smalley, supt. — Fax 955-6109
www.clarke.k12.va.us
Clarke County HS — 600/9-12
240 Westwood Rd 22611 — 540-955-6130
Francis Ball, prin. — Fax 955-6139
Johnson-Williams MS — 500/6-8
200 Swan Ave 22611 — 540-955-6160
Evan Robb, prin. — Fax 955-6169

Big Stone Gap, Wise, Pop. 5,839
Wise County SD
Supt. — See Wise
Powell Valley HS — 500/9-12
1 Avenue of Champions 24219 — 276-523-1290
David Lee, prin. — Fax 523-6804
Powell Valley MS — 600/5-8
3137 2nd Ave E 24219 — 276-523-0195
Alice Williams, prin. — Fax 523-4762

King's Christian Academy — 50/PK-12
PO Box 339 24219 — 276-523-0004
Allison Giles, admin. — Fax 523-0004
Mountain Empire Community College — Post-Sec.
3441 Mountain Empire Rd 24219 — 276-523-2400

Blacksburg, Montgomery, Pop. 40,066
Montgomery County SD
Supt. — See Christiansburg
Blacksburg HS — 1,200/9-12
520 Patrick Henry Dr 24060 — 540-951-5706
Michael Hurst, prin. — Fax 951-5714
Blacksburg MS — 900/6-8
3109 Prices Fork Rd 24060 — 540-951-5800
G. Daniel Knott, prin. — Fax 951-5808

Dayspring Christian Academy — 200/K-12
PO Box 24063 — 540-552-7777
Doug Hampton, admin. — Fax 552-7778
Virginia College of Osteopathic Medicine — Post-Sec.
2265 Kraft Dr 24060 — 540-231-4000
Virginia Polytechnic Inst. & State Univ. — Post-Sec.
24061 — 540-231-6000

Blackstone, Nottoway, Pop. 3,593

Kenston Forest S — 400/PK-12
75 Ridge Rd 23824 — 434-292-7218
Alan Barr, hdmstr. — Fax 292-7455

Bland, Bland
Bland County SD
Supt. — See Bastian
Bland HS — 200/8-12
31 Rocket Dr 24315 — 276-688-3621
Kevin Siers, prin. — Fax 688-4451

Bluefield, Tazewell, Pop. 4,996
Tazewell County SD
Supt. — See Tazewell
Graham HS — 500/9-12
210 Valleydale St 24605 — 276-326-1235
John O'Neal, prin. — Fax 326-1128
Graham MS — 400/6-8
1 Academic Cir 24605 — 276-326-1101
Kathy Tabor, prin. — Fax 322-1409

Bluefield College — Post-Sec.
3000 College Dr 24605 — 276-326-3682
National College of Business & Tech. — Post-Sec.
100 Logan St 24605 — 276-326-3621

Bowling Green, Caroline, Pop. 946
Caroline County SD — 3,700/K-12
16221 Richmond Tpke 22427 — 804-633-5088
Stanley O. Jones, supt. — Fax 633-5563
www.caroline.k12.va.us
Other Schools – See Milford

Boydton, Mecklenburg, Pop. 469
Mecklenburg County SD — 4,700/PK-12
PO Box 190 23917 — 434-738-6111
Dr. Frank J. Polakiewicz, supt. — Fax 738-6679
www.meck.k12.va.us
Other Schools – See Skipwith, South Hill

Bridgewater, Rockingham, Pop. 5,273
Rockingham County SD
Supt. — See Harrisonburg
Ashby HS — 1,100/9-12
800 N Main St 22812 — 540-828-2008
Steven Walk, prin. — Fax 828-4764

Bridgewater College — Post-Sec.
402 E College St 22812 — 540-828-8000

Bristol, Bristol, Pop. 17,206
Bristol CSD — 2,300/K-12
222 Oak St 24201 — 276-821-5600
Dr. Douglas Arnold, supt. — Fax 821-5601
www.bvps.org/
Virginia HS — 700/9-12
1200 Long Crescent Dr 24201 — 276-821-5858
Ina Danko, prin. — Fax 821-5851
Virginia MS — 600/6-8
501 Piedmont Ave 24201 — 276-821-5660
Gary Ritchie, prin. — Fax 821-5661

Washington County SD
Supt. — See Abingdon
Battle HS — 600/9-12
21264 Battle Hill Dr 24202 — 276-642-5300
Judy Wilson, prin. — Fax 645-2386
Wallace MS — 500/6-8
13077 Wallace Pike 24202 — 276-642-5400
Dr. Fred Keller, prin. — Fax 645-2365

Graham Bible College — Post-Sec.
PO Box 1630 24203 — 423-968-4201
National College of Business & Tech. — Post-Sec.
300A Piedmont Ave 24201 — 276-669-5333
Virginia Intermont College — Post-Sec.
1013 Moore St 24201 — 276-669-6101

Bristow, Prince William
Prince William County SD
Supt. — See Manassas
Marsteller MS — 1,200/6-8
14000 Sudley Manor Dr 20136 — 703-393-7608
Roberta Knetter, prin. — Fax 530-6327

Broadway, Rockingham, Pop. 2,415
Rockingham County SD
Supt. — See Harrisonburg
Broadway HS — 1,000/9-12
269 Gobbler Dr 22815 — 540-896-7081
Dr. Stephen Leaman, prin. — Fax 896-2640
Hillyard MS — 800/6-8
226 Hawks Hill Dr 22815 — 540-896-8961
Douglas Alderfer, prin. — Fax 896-6641

Buchanan, Botetourt, Pop. 1,237
Botetourt County SD
Supt. — See Fincastle
James River HS — 500/9-12
9906 Springwood Rd 24066 — 540-254-1121
James Talbott, prin. — Fax 254-2765

Buckingham, Buckingham, Pop. 370
Buckingham County SD — 2,200/K-12
PO Box 24 23921 — 434-969-6100
Larry A. Massie, supt. — Fax 969-1176
www.bchs.k12.va.us
Buckingham County HS — 700/9-12
HC 2 Box 376 23921 — 434-969-6160
Claude Morris, prin. — Fax 969-3209
Buckingham County MS — 600/6-8
HC 02 Box 374-A 23921 — 434-983-2102
Bruce Cook, prin. — Fax 983-1002

Buena Vista, Buena Vista, Pop. 6,320
Buena Vista CSD — 1,100/K-12
2329 Chestnut Ave Ste A 24416 — 540-261-2129
Dr. Joseph King, supt. — Fax 261-2967
www.buena-vista.k12.va.us
McCluer HS — 300/9-12
100 Bradford Dr 24416 — 540-261-2128
Haywood Hand, prin. — Fax 261-1828
McCluer MS — 300/5-8
2329 Chestnut Ave 24416 — 540-261-7340
Lori Teague, prin. — Fax 261-3292

Southern Virginia University — Post-Sec.
1 University Hill Dr 24416 — 540-261-8400

Burke, Fairfax, Pop. 57,700
Fairfax County SD
Supt. — See Fairfax
Lake Braddock JSHS — 4,000/7-12
9200 Burke Lake Rd 22015 — 703-426-1000
Linda Burke, prin. — Fax 426-1093

Carson, Prince George
Jointly Operated Vo Tech SD
Supt. — None
Rowanty Vocational Tech Center — Vo/Tech
20000 Rowanty Rd 23830 — 434-246-5741
Tom Cope, prin. — Fax 246-5721

Castlewood, Russell, Pop. 3,036
Russell County SD
Supt. — See Lebanon
Castlewood HS — 300/8-12
Highway 58 24224 — 276-762-9449
Scotty Fletcher, prin. — Fax 762-9418

Centreville, Fairfax, Pop. 56,700
Fairfax County SD
Supt. — See Fairfax
Stone MS — 1,200/7-8
5500 Sully Park Dr 20120 — 703-631-5500
Kenneth Gaudreault, prin. — Fax 631-5598

Chantilly, Fairfax, Pop. 44,300
Fairfax County SD
Supt. — See Fairfax
Chantilly HS — 2,600/9-12
4201 Stringfellow Rd 20151 — 703-222-8100
James Kacur, prin. — Fax 222-8197
Franklin MS — 1,000/7-8
3300 Lees Corner Rd 20151 — 703-904-5100
Michelle Peyser, prin. — Fax 904-5197
Rocky Run MS — 800/7-8
4400 Stringfellow Rd 20151 — 703-802-7700
Dan Parris, prin. — Fax 802-7797
Westfield HS — 3,000/9-12
4700 Stonecroft Blvd 20151 — 703-488-6300
Michael Campbell, prin. — Fax 488-6397

Charles City, Charles City
Charles City County SD — 900/K-12
10910 Courthouse Rd 23030 — 804-652-4612
Dr. Janet Crawley, supt. — Fax 829-6723
208.31.123.10/
Charles City County HS — 300/9-12
10039 Courthouse Rd 23030 — 804-829-9249
Pamela Boyd, prin. — Fax 829-2644
Charles City County MS — 200/6-8
10035 Courthouse Rd 23030 — 804-829-9252
Dr. Earlinda Fauntleroy, prin. — Fax 829-2363

Charlotte Court House, Charlotte, Pop. 453
Charlotte County SD — 2,300/PK-12
PO Box 790 23923 — 434-542-5151
Melody D. Hackney, supt. — Fax 542-4261
www.ccps.k12.va.us
Central MS — 600/6-8
PO Box 748 23923 — 434-542-4536
Bonita Hamlett, prin. — Fax 542-4630
Randolph-Henry HS — 700/9-12
PO Box 668 23923 — 434-542-4111
Gloria Talbott, prin. — Fax 542-4114

Charlottesville, Charlottesville, Pop. 39,162
Albemarle County SD — 12,300/K-12
401 McIntire Rd 22902 — 434-972-4055
Dr. Pamela Moran, supt. — Fax 296-5869
www.k12albemarle.org/
Albemarle HS — 1,600/9-12
2775 Hydraulic Rd 22901 — 434-975-9300
Dr. Matthew Haas, prin. — Fax 974-4335
Burley MS — 400/6-8
901 Rose Hill Dr 22903 — 434-295-5101
Dr. L. Bernard Hairston, prin. — Fax 984-4975
Jouett MS — 600/6-8
210 Lambs Ln 22901 — 434-975-9320
David B. Rogers, prin. — Fax 975-9325
Monticello HS — 1,100/9-12
1400 Independence Way 22902 — 434-244-3100
John W. Haun, prin. — Fax 244-3104
Sutherland MS — 700/6-8
2801 Powell Creek Dr 22911 — 434-975-0599
Kathryn L. Baylor, prin. — Fax 975-0852

Walton MS | 600/6-8
4217 Red Hill Rd 22903 | 434-977-5615
Eric D. Johnson, prin. | Fax 296-6648
Other Schools – See Crozet

Charlottesville CSD | 4,400/PK-12
1562 Dairy Rd 22903 | 434-245-2400
Robert Thompson, supt. | Fax 245-2603
www.ccs.k12.va.us
Buford MS | 600/7-8
617 9th St SW 22903 | 434-245-2411
Timothy J. Flynn, prin. | Fax 245-2611
Charlottesville HS | 1,300/9-12
1400 Melbourne Rd 22901 | 434-245-2410
Kenneth H. Leatherwood, prin. | Fax 245-2610

Jointly Operated Vo Tech SD
Supt. — None
Charlottsville-Albemarle Tech Center | Vo/Tech
1000 Rio Rd E 22901 | 434-973-4461
J. Joseph Johnson, dir. | Fax 973-4876

Albemarle Christian Academy | 100/PK-12
PO Box 6839 22906 | 434-973-6571
Covenant S | 700/PK-12
175 Hickory St 22902 | 434-220-7329
Ronald Sykes, hdmstr. | Fax 220-7320
International Beauty School | Post-Sec.
2024 Holiday Dr 22901 | 434-296-0159
Miller S of Albemarle | 200/6-12
1000 Samuel Miller Loop 22903 | 434-823-4805
Lindsay Barnes, hdmstr. | Fax 823-6617
National College of Business & Tech. | Post-Sec.
1819 Emmet St N 22901 | 434-295-0136
Piedmont Virginia Community College | Post-Sec.
501 College Dr 22902 | 434-977-3900
RSHT Training Center | Post-Sec.
702 Charlton Ave Ste A 22903 | 434-245-0400
St. Anne's Belfield S | 800/PK-12
2132 Ivy Rd 22903 | 434-296-5106
Rev. George Conway, hdmstr. | Fax 979-1486
Tandem Friends S | 200/5-12
279 Tandem Ln 22902 | 434-296-1303
Paul Perkinson, hdmstr. | Fax 296-1886
University of Virginia | Post-Sec.
PO Box 400160 22904 | 434-924-0311
Virginia School of Massage | Post-Sec.
2008 Morton Dr 22903 | 434-293-4031

Chatham, Pittsylvania, Pop. 1,297
Pittsylvania County SD | 9,300/PK-12
PO Box 232 24531 | 434-432-2761
James E. McDaniel, supt. | Fax 432-9560
www.pcs.k12.va.us
Chatham HS | 700/9-12
100 Chatham Cavalier Cir 24531 | 434-432-8305
Stephen Welch, prin. | Fax 432-8351
Chatham MS | 500/6-8
11650 US Highway 29 24531 | 434-432-2169
Danny Bowman, prin.
Pittsylvania Career Tech | Vo/Tech
11700 U S Highway 29 24531 | 434-432-9416
Jimmie Tickle, prin. | Fax 432-0516
Other Schools – See Dry Fork, Gretna, Ringgold

Chatham Hall S | 100/9-12
800 Chatham Hall Cir 24531 | 434-432-2941
Gary Fountain, prin. | Fax 432-1002
Hargrave Military Academy | 400/7-12
200 Military Dr 24531 | 434-432-2481
Wheeler Baker, pres. | Fax 432-3129

Chesapeake, Chesapeake, Pop. 210,834
Chesapeake CSD | 39,400/K-12
PO Box 16496 23328 | 757-547-0165
Dr. W. Randolph Nichols, supt. | Fax 547-0196
eclipse.cps.k12.va.us
Chesapeake Center Science & Tech | Vo/Tech
1617 Cedar Rd 23322 | 757-547-0134
William Joe, prin. | Fax 547-2391
Crestwood MS | 700/6-8
1420 Great Bridge Blvd 23320 | 757-494-7560
Paul A. Joseph, prin. | Fax 494-7599
Deep Creek HS | 2,000/9-12
2900 Margaret Booker Dr 23323 | 757-558-5302
Nathan Hardee, prin. | Fax 558-5305
Deep Creek MS | 600/6-8
1955 Deal Dr 23323 | 757-558-5321
J. Coppage-Miller, prin. | Fax 558-5320
Great Bridge HS | 2,100/9-12
301 Hanbury Rd W 23322 | 757-482-5191
Clifton Randolph, prin. | Fax 482-5559
Great Bridge MS | 1,400/6-8
441 Battlefield Blvd S 23322 | 757-482-5128
Beverly Oliver, prin. | Fax 482-0210
Greenbrier MS | 900/6-8
1016 Greenbrier Pkwy 23320 | 757-548-5309
Dr. Jean Infantino, prin. | Fax 548-8921
Hickory HS | 2,400/9-12
1996 Hawk Blvd 23322 | 757-421-4295
Linda Byrd, prin. | Fax 421-2190
Hickory MS | 1,900/6-8
1997 Hawk Blvd 23322 | 757-421-0468
Dr. Woodley Koonce, prin. | Fax 421-0475
Indian River HS | 1,800/9-12
1969 Braves Trl 23325 | 757-578-7000
James Frye, prin. | Fax 578-7004
Indian River MS | 900/6-8
2300 Old Greenbrier Rd 23325 | 757-578-7030
Naomi Epps, prin. | Fax 578-7036
Jolliff MS | 700/6-8
1021 Jolliff Rd 23321 | 757-465-5246
Dr. Lee Fowler, prin. | Fax 465-1646
Owens MS | 1,100/6-8
2801 Cedar Rd 23323 | 757-558-5382
John Sykes, prin. | Fax 558-5386
Smith HS | 2,100/9-12
1994 Tiger Dr 23320 | 757-548-0696
Dr. Janet Andrejco, prin. | Fax 548-0531

Smith MS | 1,100/6-8
2500 Rodgers St 23324 | 757-494-7590
Dr. Linda Scott, prin. | Fax 494-7680
Western Branch HS | 2,100/9-12
1968 Bruin Pl 23321 | 757-638-7900
Arthur Brandriff, prin. | Fax 638-7904
Western Branch MS | 900/6-8
4201 Hawksley Dr 23321 | 757-638-7920
Craig Jones, prin. | Fax 638-7926

Atlantic Shores Christian S | 400/7-12
1217 Centerville Tpke N 23320 | 757-479-9598
Keith Hall, admin. | Fax 479-5311
Greenbrier Christian Academy | 700/PK-12
311 Kempsville Rd 23320 | 757-547-9595
H. Ron White, supt. | Fax 547-9569
Sentara School of Health Professions | Post-Sec.
1441 Crossways Blvd Ste 105 23320 | 757-388-2900
StoneBridge S | 500/PK-12
PO Box 9247 23321 | 757-488-2214
Dr. Jim Arcieri, hdmstr. | Fax 465-7637
Strayer University | Post-Sec.
700 Independence Pkwy # 400 23320 | 757-382-9900
Tidewater Adventist Academy | 100/K-12
1136 Centerville Tpke N 23320 | 757-479-0002
Donna Steen, prin. | Fax 479-0008
Tidewater Community College | Post-Sec.
1428 Cedar Rd 23322 | 757-547-9271
Tidewater Tech | Post-Sec.
932 Ventures Way 23320 | 757-549-2121

Chester, Chesterfield, Pop. 14,986
Chesterfield County SD
Supt. — See Chesterfield
Carver MS | 1,400/6-8
3800 Cougar Trl 23831 | 804-524-3620
Donald Ashburn, prin. | Fax 520-0189
Chester MS | 800/6-8
3900 W Hundred Rd 23831 | 804-768-6145
James Copp, prin. | Fax 768-6152
Dale MS | 2,100/9-12
3626 W Hundred Rd 23831 | 804-768-6245
Robert Stansberry, prin. | Fax 796-5062

Evangel Christian S | 200/PK-12
16801 Harrow Gate Rd 23831 | 804-526-5941
Ada Dowdy, prin. | Fax 526-3582
John Tyler Community College | Post-Sec.
13101 Jefferson Davis Hwy 23831 | 800-522-3490

Chesterfield, Chesterfield
Chesterfield County SD | 56,600/PK-12
PO Box 10 23832 | 804-748-1405
Dr. Billy Cannaday, supt. | Fax 796-7178
www.chesterfield.k12.va.us
Bird HS | 1,900/9-12
10301 Courthouse Rd 23832 | 804-768-6110
Joseph Tylus, prin. | Fax 768-6117
Chesterfield Technical S | Vo/Tech
10101 Courthouse Rd 23832 | 804-768-6160
Michael Rose, prin. | Fax 768-6164
Cosby HS | 1,700/9-12
10101 Courthouse Rd 23832 | 804-768-6160
Brenda Mayo, prin. | Fax 768-6160
Other Schools – See Chester, Ettrick, Matoaca,
Midlothian, Richmond

Richmond Christian S | 500/K-12
6511 Belmont Rd 23832 | 804-276-3193
| Fax 276-9106

Chilhowie, Smyth, Pop. 1,796
Smyth County SD
Supt. — See Marion
Chilhowie HS | 400/9-12
PO Box 2280 24319 | 276-646-8966
Stephen D. Reedy, prin. | Fax 646-5951
Chilhowie MS | 300/6-8
PO Box 5018 24319 | 276-646-3942
Sue Tilson, prin. | Fax 646-0210

Chincoteague, Accomack, Pop. 4,358
Accomack County SD
Supt. — See Accomac
Chincoteague HS | 400/6-12
4586 Main St 23336 | 757-336-6166
Warren Holland, prin. | Fax 336-1902

Christchurch, Middlesex

Christchurch S | 200/8-12
49 Seahorse Ln 23031 | 804-758-2306
John Byers, hdmstr. | Fax 758-0721

Christiansburg, Montgomery, Pop. 17,756
Montgomery County SD | 9,500/PK-12
200 Junkin St 24073 | 540-382-5100
Dr. Tiffany Anderson, supt. | Fax 381-6127
www.mcps.org
Christiansburg HS | 1,000/9-12
100 Independence Blvd 24073 | 540-382-5178
Corie Franklin, prin. | Fax 381-6525
Christiansburg MS | 800/6-8
1205 Buffalo Dr 24073 | 540-394-2180
Annette Perkins, prin. | Fax 394-2197
Other Schools – See Blacksburg, Elliston, Riner,
Shawsville

Pathway Christian Academy | 100/K-12
896 Life Dr 24073 | 540-394-7300
Lonna Burton, admin.

Clifton, Fairfax, Pop. 200
Fairfax County SD
Supt. — See Fairfax
Centreville HS | 2,100/9-12
6001 Union Mill Rd 20124 | 703-802-5400
Peter Noonan, prin. | Fax 802-5497
Liberty MS | 1,200/7-8
6801 Union Mill Rd 20124 | 703-988-8100
Peggy Kelly, prin. | Fax 988-8197

Clifton Forge, Clifton Forge, Pop. 4,716
Regional Academic Governors SD
Supt. — See Richmond
Jackson River Governor's HS | 11-12
PO Box 1000 24422 | 540-863-2841
Dr. Susan Rollinson, dir. | Fax 863-2915

Dabney S. Lancaster Community College | Post-Sec.
PO Box 1000 24422 | 540-863-2800

Clinchco, Dickenson, Pop. 411
Dickenson County SD
Supt. — See Clintwood
Dickenson County Career Center | Vo/Tech
RR 1 Box 325 24226 | 276-835-9384
Brian Baker, prin. | Fax 835-9386

Clinchport, Scott, Pop. 75
Scott County SD
Supt. — See Gate City
Rye Cove HS | 300/8-12
RR 4 24244 | 276-940-2701
James Meade, prin. | Fax 940-2277

Clintwood, Dickenson, Pop. 1,514
Dickenson County SD | 2,600/PK-12
PO Box 1127 24228 | 276-926-4643
Damon Rasnick, supt. | Fax 926-6374
www.dickenson.k12.va.us
Clintwood HS | 300/9-12
PO Box 577 24228 | 276-926-8400
Bill Castle, prin. | Fax 926-6154
Other Schools – See Clinchco, Haysi, Nora

Cloverdale, Botetourt, Pop. 1,689
Botetourt County SD
Supt. — See Fincastle
Read Mountain MS | 700/6-8
182 Orchard Hill Dr 24077 | 540-966-8655
Julie Baker, prin. | Fax 966-8656

Coeburn, Wise, Pop. 1,967
Wise County SD
Supt. — See Wise
Coeburn HS | 400/9-12
PO Box 2036 24230 | 276-395-3389
Dante Lee, prin. | Fax 395-5167
Coeburn MS | 400/5-8
PO Box 670 24230 | 276-395-2135
Walt Padgett, prin. | Fax 395-5453

Flatwoods Civilian Conservation Center | Post-Sec.
2803 Dungannon Rd 24230 | 276-395-3384

Collinsville, Henry, Pop. 7,280
Henry County SD | 5,800/PK-12
PO Box 8958 24078 | 276-634-4712
Dr. Sharon D. Dodson, supt. | Fax 638-8990
www.henry.k12.va.us
Fieldale-Collinsville MS | 500/6-8
645 Miles Rd 24078 | 276-647-3841
Moriah Dollarhite, prin. | Fax 647-4090
Other Schools – See Bassett, Martinsville, Ridgeway

Regional Academic Governors SD
Supt. — See Richmond
Piedmont Governor's S for Math/Sci/Tech | 100/11-12
PO Box 728 24078 | 276-632-5079
Brian Pace, prin. | Fax 656-0234

Colonial Beach, Westmoreland, Pop. 3,241
Colonial Beach SD | 600/K-12
16 Irving Ave N 22443 | 804-224-0906
Dr. Alice H. Howard, supt. | Fax 224-8357
www.cbschools.net
Colonial Beach HS | 200/8-12
100 1st St 22443 | 804-224-7166
David Bridges, prin. | Fax 224-7465

Colonial Heights, Colonial Heights, Pop. 17,286
Colonial Heights CSD | 2,800/K-12
512 Boulevard 23834 | 804-524-3400
Dr. Joseph O. Cox, supt. | Fax 526-4524
www.colonialhts.net
Colonial Heights HS | 900/9-12
3600 Conduit Rd 23834 | 804-524-3405
John Keeler, prin. | Fax 520-7222
Colonial Heights MS | 700/6-8
500 Conduit Rd 23834 | 804-524-3420
Roger Green, prin. | Fax 526-9288

Council, Buchanan
Buchanan County SD
Supt. — See Grundy
Council HS | 100/9-12
HC 4 Box 230 24260 | 276-859-2627
Deborah Estep, prin. | Fax 859-6227

Courtland, Southampton, Pop. 1,240
Southampton County SD | 3,000/PK-12
PO Box 96 23837 | 757-653-2692
Charles Turner, supt. | Fax 653-9422
www.southampton.k12.va.us/
Southampton HS | 900/9-12
23350 Southampton Pkwy 23837 | 757-653-2751
Allene Atkinson, prin. | Fax 653-0414
Southampton MS | 700/6-8
23350 Southampton Pkwy 23837 | 757-653-9250
Angela Goodloe, prin. | Fax 653-7251
Southampton Technical Career Center | Vo/Tech
23350 Southampton Pkwy 23837 | 757-653-9170
Linda Adams, admin. | Fax 653-9404

Southampton Academy | 400/PK-12
26495 Old Plank Rd 23837 | 757-653-2512
Craig Jones, hdmstr. | Fax 653-0011

Covington, Covington, Pop. 6,284
Alleghany County SD | 2,800/PK-12
110 Rosedale Ave Ste A 24426 | 540-965-1800
Robert P. Grimesey, supt. | Fax 965-1804
www.alleghany.k12.va.us/

Alleghany HS | 800/9-12
210 Mountaineer Dr 24426 | 540-863-1700
R. Kenneth Higgins, prin. | Fax 863-1705
Clifton MS | 700/6-8
1000 Riverview Farm Rd 24426 | 540-863-1726
Brenda Siple, prin. | Fax 863-1731

Covington CSD | 900/PK-12
340 E Walnut St 24426 | 540-965-1400
Edward Graham, supt. | Fax 965-1404
www.covington.k12.va.us/
Covington JSHS | 400/8-12
530 S Lexington Ave 24426 | 540-965-1410
Ruth Fuhrman, prin.

Jointly Operated Vo Tech SD
Supt. — None
Jackson River Tech Center | Vo/Tech
105 E Country Club Ln 24426 | 540-862-1308
Thomas Beirne, prin. | Fax 862-3592

Crewe, Nottoway, Pop. 2,309
Nottoway County SD
Supt. — See Nottoway
Nottoway HS | 700/9-12
5267 Old Nottoway Rd 23930 | 434-292-5373
Anne Stinson, prin. | Fax 292-3021
Nottoway MS | 400/7-8
5279 Old Nottoway Rd 23930 | 434-292-5375
George Smith, prin. | Fax 292-7479

Crozet, Albemarle, Pop. 2,256
Albemarle County SD
Supt. — See Charlottesville
Henley MS | 700/6-8
5880 Rockfish Gap Tpke 22932 | 434-823-4393
Donald Vale, prin. | Fax 823-2711
Western Albemarle HS | 1,100/9-12
5941 Rockfish Gap Tpke 22932 | 434-823-8700
Dr. Anne Coughlin, prin. | Fax 823-8711

Culpeper, Culpeper, Pop. 10,442
Culpeper County SD | 6,200/K-12
450 Radio Ln 22701 | 540-825-3677
Dr. David A. Cox, supt. | Fax 829-2111
www.culpeperschools.org
Binns MS | 800/6-8
205 E Grandview Ave 22701 | 540-825-6894
Sherri Harkness, prin. | Fax 829-9926
Culpeper County HS | 1,800/9-12
14240 Achievement Dr 22701 | 540-825-8310
Dr. Eric Porter, prin. | Fax 829-6615
Culpeper County MS | 700/6-8
14300 Achievement Dr 22701 | 540-825-4140
William W. Zierden, prin. | Fax 825-7543

Cumberland, Cumberland
Cumberland County SD | 1,400/PK-12
PO Box 170 23040 | 804-492-4212
James Thornton, supt. | Fax 492-4818
www.cucps.k12.va.us
Cumberland HS | 400/9-12
PO Box 140 23040 | 804-492-4808
Larry Bryan, prin. | Fax 492-3138
Cumberland MS | 400/6-8
PO Box 184 23040 | 804-492-9627
Alvin Beasley, prin. | Fax 492-9326

Daleville, Botetourt, Pop. 1,163
Botetourt County SD
Supt. — See Fincastle
Lord Botetourt HS | 1,000/9-12
1435 Roanoke Rd 24083 | 540-992-1261
Alan Brenner, prin. | Fax 992-8381

Damascus, Washington, Pop. 1,091
Washington County SD
Supt. — See Abingdon
Damascus MS | 200/6-8
32101 Government Rd 24236 | 276-475-4000
Janet Lester, prin. | Fax 475-4032
Holston HS | 300/9-12
21308 Monroe Rd 24236 | 276-739-4000
Jimmy King, prin. | Fax 475-4024

Danville, Danville, Pop. 46,988
Danville CSD | 7,300/PK-12
PO Box 9600 24543 | 434-799-6400
Sue Davis Ed.D., supt. | Fax 799-5267
web.dps.k12.va.us
Bonner MS | 700/6-8
300 Apollo Ave 24540 | 434-799-6446
Dr. J. David Cochran, prin. | Fax 797-8867
Galileo Magnet HS | 200/9-12
230 Ridge St 24541 | 434-773-8186
Wilfred Lawrence, prin. | Fax 773-8188
Gibson MS | 500/6-8
1215 Industrial Ave 24541 | 434-799-6426
John Thacker, prin. | Fax 797-8857
Washington HS | 1,900/9-12
701 Broad St 24541 | 434-799-6410
Dr. Ron Sieber, prin. | Fax 799-5251
Westwood MS | 500/6-8
500 Apollo Ave 24540 | 434-797-8860
Wanda Fields, prin. | Fax 797-8874

Averett University | Post-Sec.
420 W Main St 24541 | 434-791-5600
Danville Community College | Post-Sec.
1008 S Main St 24541 | 434-797-2222
Danville Regional Medical Center | Post-Sec.
142 S Main St 24541 | 434-799-4510
National College of Business & Tech. | Post-Sec.
734 Main St 24541 | 434-793-6822
Westover Christian Academy | 600/PK-12
5665 Riverside Dr 24541 | 434-822-0800
Donald Criss, admin. | Fax 822-0441

Dayton, Rockingham, Pop. 1,333
Rockingham County SD
Supt. — See Harrisonburg

Pence MS | 800/6-8
375 Bowman Rd 22821 | 540-879-2535
Mary Shifflett, prin. | Fax 879-2179

Dendron, Surry, Pop. 292
Surry County SD
Supt. — See Surry
Jackson MS | 300/5-8
4255 New Design Rd 23839 | 757-267-2810
Elaine J. Pearson, prin. | Fax 267-0809
Surry County HS | 400/9-12
1675 Hollybush Rd 23839 | 757-267-2211
Rita Holmes, prin. | Fax 267-2978

Dinwiddie, Dinwiddie
Dinwiddie County SD | 4,500/K-12
PO Box 7 23841 | 804-469-4190
Dr. Charles Maranzano, supt. | Fax 469-4197
www.dinwiddie.k12.va.us
Dinwiddie County HS | 1,300/9-12
PO Box 299 23841 | 804-469-4280
Barbara T. Pittman, prin.
Dinwiddie County MS | 1,200/6-8
PO Box 340 23841 | 804-469-4380
Alfred Cappellanti, prin.

Dry Fork, Pittsylvania
Pittsylvania County SD
Supt. — See Chatham
Tunstall HS, 100 Trojan Cir 24549 | 900/9-12
Hattie Hairston, prin. | 434-724-7111
Tunstall MS | 600/6-8
1160 Tunstall High Rd 24549 | 434-724-7086
Rebecca Stevens, prin. | Fax 724-7907

Dublin, Pulaski, Pop. 2,232
Pulaski County SD
Supt. — See Pulaski
Dublin MS | 600/6-8
650 Giles Ave 24084 | 540-643-0367
Robin Keener, prin. | Fax 674-0813
Pulaski County HS | 1,500/9-12
5414 Cougar Trail Rd 24084 | 540-643-0747
Rodney Reedy, prin. | Fax 674-4722

Regional Academic Governors SD
Supt. — See Richmond
SW VA Governor's S Science Math & Tech | 11-12
PO Box 1739 24084 | 540-674-1980
Margaret Duncan, dir. | Fax 674-2552

New River Community College | Post-Sec.
PO Box 1127 24084 | 540-674-3600

Dumfries, Prince William, Pop. 4,934
Prince William County SD
Supt. — See Manassas
Potomac HS | 1,800/9-12
3401 Four Year Trl 22026 | 703-441-4200
Rodger Jones, prin. | Fax 441-4497
Potomac MS | 6-8
3130 Four Year Trl 22026 | 703-221-4996
Benita Stephens, prin.

Eastville, Northampton, Pop. 199
Northampton County SD
Supt. — See Machipongo
Northampton HS | 700/9-12
PO Box 38 23347 | 757-678-8040
Dr. Daryl Unnasch, prin. | Fax 678-5244

Elkton, Rockingham, Pop. 2,027
Rockingham County SD
Supt. — See Harrisonburg
Elkton MS | 300/6-8
21063 Blue and Gold Dr 22827 | 540-298-1228
Ramona Pence, prin. | Fax 298-0029

Elliston, Montgomery, Pop. 1,243
Montgomery County SD
Supt. — See Christiansburg
Eastern Montgomery HS | 300/9-12
4695 Crosier Rd 24087 | 540-268-3010
Nelson Simpkins, prin. | Fax 268-3012

Emory, Washington, Pop. 2,248

Emory & Henry College | Post-Sec.
PO Box 10 24327 | 276-944-4121

Emporia, Emporia, Pop. 5,656
Greensville County SD | 2,700/PK-12
105 Ruffin St 23847 | 434-634-3748
Dr. Philip Worrell, supt. | Fax 634-3495
www.greensville.k12.va.us/
Greensville County HS | 800/9-12
403 Harding St 23847 | 434-634-2195
Alvera Parrish, prin.
Wyatt MS, 206 Slagles Lake Rd 23847 | 400/7-8
John Conley, prin. | 434-634-5159

Ettrick, Chesterfield, Pop. 5,290
Chesterfield County SD
Supt. — See Chesterfield
Matoaca HS | 1,300/9-12
6001 Hickory Rd 23803 | 804-590-3110
Stephen Cunningham, prin. | Fax 590-3022

Ewing, Lee
Lee County SD
Supt. — See Jonesville
Walker HS | 400/8-12
PO Box 39 24248 | 276-445-4111
Terry Welch, prin. | Fax 445-3046

Exmore, Northampton, Pop. 1,434

Broadwater Academy | 500/PK-12
PO Box 546 23350 | 757-442-9041
Kendall Berry, prin. | Fax 442-9615

Fairfax, Fairfax, Pop. 22,031
Fairfax County SD | 160,400/K-12
10700 Page Ave 22030 | 703-246-2631
Jack Dale, supt. | Fax 691-2876
www.fcps.edu
Fairfax HS | 2,100/9-12
3500 Old Lee Hwy 22030 | 703-219-2200
Scott Brabrand, prin. | Fax 219-2297
Frost MS | 1,100/7-8
4101 Pickett Rd 22032 | 703-426-5700
Marti Jo Jackson, prin. | Fax 426-5797
Lanier MS | 900/7-8
3710 Bevan Dr 22030 | 703-934-2400
Rodney Moore, prin. | Fax 934-2497
Robinson JSHS | 4,400/7-12
5035 Sideburn Rd 22032 | 703-426-2100
Dan Meier, prin. | Fax 426-2197
Woodson HS | 1,900/9-12
9525 Main St 22031 | 703-503-4600
Robert Elliott, prin. | Fax 503-4697
Other Schools – See Alexandria, Annandale, Burke,
Centreville, Chantilly, Clifton, Falls Church, Herndon,
Lorton, Mc Lean, Reston, Springfield, Vienna

Fair Oaks Academy | 400/PK-12
4601 W Ox Rd 22030 | 703-631-1467
Janice Iddins, admin. | Fax 631-3007
George Mason University | Post-Sec.
4400 University Dr 22030 | 703-993-2400
Paul VI HS | 1,000/9-12
10675 Lee Hwy 22030 | 703-352-0925
Philip Robey, prin. | Fax 273-9845
Reformed Theological Seminary | Post-Sec.
12500 Fair Lakes Cir # 325 22033 | 703-222-7871
Trinity Christian S | 500/1-12
11204 Braddock Rd 22030 | 703-273-8787
David Vanderpoel Ph.D., hdmstr. | Fax 352-8522
Way of Faith Christian Academy | 200/K-12
8800 Arlington Blvd 22031 | 703-573-7221
Ellen Blackwell, dir. | Fax 573-7248

Fairfield, Rockbridge
Rockbridge County SD
Supt. — See Lexington
Rockbridge MS | 200/6-8
PO Box 328 24435 | 540-348-5445
John Morris, prin. | Fax 348-1016

Falls Church, Falls Church, Pop. 10,485
Fairfax County SD
Supt. — See Fairfax
Davis Career Center | Vo/Tech
7731 Leesburg Pike 22043 | 703-714-5600
Aaron Engley, admin. | Fax 714-5697
Falls Church HS | 1,500/9-12
7521 Jaguar Trl 22042 | 703-207-4000
Janice Lloyd, prin. | Fax 207-4097
Jackson MS | 1,100/7-8
3020 Gallows Rd 22042 | 703-204-8100
Carol Robinson, prin. | Fax 204-8197
Longfellow MS | 1,100/7-8
2000 Westmoreland St 22043 | 703-533-2600
Vince Lynch, prin. | Fax 533-2697
Marshall HS | 1,300/9-12
7731 Leesburg Pike 22043 | 703-714-5400
Jay Pearson, prin. | Fax 714-5497
Stuart HS | 1,500/9-12
3301 Peace Valley Ln 22044 | 703-824-3900
Mel Riddile, prin. | Fax 824-3997

Falls Church CSD | 1,900/K-12
803 W Broad St Ste 300 22046 | 703-248-5600
Lois F. Berlin, supt. | Fax 248-5613
www.fccps.k12.va.us
Mason HS | 800/8-12
7124 Leesburg Pike 22043 | 703-248-5550
Robert Snee, prin. | Fax 248-5533

Child Development Ctr. of Northern VA | Post-Sec.
111 N Cherry St 22046
Fairfax Hospital | Post-Sec.
3300 Gallows Rd 22042 | 703-698-3371
Heritage Institute | Post-Sec.
350 S Washington St 22046 | 703-773-5050
Potomac Academy of Hair Design | Post-Sec.
350 S Washington St 22046 | 703-532-5050
Stratford University | Post-Sec.
7777 Leesburg Pike Ste 100S 22043 | 703-821-8570

Falmouth, Stafford, Pop. 3,541
Stafford County SD
Supt. — See Stafford
Drew MS | 800/6-8
501 Cambridge St 22405 | 540-371-1415
Joseph Soldan, prin. | Fax 371-1447
Gayle MS | 1,100/6-8
100 Panther Dr 22406 | 540-373-0383
Michael Wondree, prin. | Fax 373-8856
Stafford HS | 1,900/9-12
33 Stafford Indians Ln 22405 | 540-371-7200
Tricia Jacobs, prin. | Fax 371-2389

Farmville, Prince Edward, Pop. 6,959
Prince Edward County SD | 2,800/K-12
35 Eagle Dr 23901 | 434-315-2100
Dr. Margaret Blackmon, supt. | Fax 392-1911
www.pecps.k12.va.us
Prince Edward County HS | 900/9-12
35 Eagle Dr 23901 | 434-315-2130
Odessa Pride, prin. | Fax 392-1901
Prince Edward MS | 900/5-8
35 Eagle Dr 23901 | 434-315-2120
Dr. Michael McClellan, prin. | Fax 392-4286

Fuqua S | 500/PK-12
PO Box 328 23901 | 434-392-4131
Ruth Murphy, pres. | Fax 392-5062
Longwood University | Post-Sec.
201 High St 23909 | 434-395-2000

New Life Christian Academy 100/PK-12
9 Mahan Rd 23901 434-392-6236
Betty Weaver, admin. Fax 392-4462

Ferrum, Franklin, Pop. 1,514

Ferrum College Post-Sec.
PO Box 1000 24088 800-868-9797

Fincastle, Botetourt, Pop. 354

Botetourt County SD 4,800/PK-12
143 Poor Farm Rd 24090 540-473-8263
Dr. Anthony Brads, supt. Fax 473-8298
www.bcps.k12.va.us
Botetourt Technical Education Center Vo/Tech
253 Poor Farm Rd 24090 540-473-8216
Chester Adams, prin. Fax 473-8376
Central Academy MS 400/6-8
367 Poor Farm Rd 24090 540-473-8333
Vaneta McAlexander, prin. Fax 473-8398
Other Schools – See Buchanan, Cloverdale, Daleville

Fishersville, Augusta, Pop. 3,230

Augusta County SD 10,700/K-12
6 John Lewis Rd 22939 540-245-5100
Gary McQuain, supt. Fax 245-5115
www.augusta.k12.va.us
Wilson Memorial HS 700/9-12
189 Hornet Rd 22939 540-886-4286
Doug Shifflett, prin. Fax 886-4611
Wilson MS 6-8
232 Hornet Rd 22939 540-245-5185
Donald Curtis, prin. Fax 245-5189
Other Schools – See Fort Defiance, Staunton, Stuarts
Draft, Swoope

Jointly Operated Vo Tech SD
Supt. — None
Valley Vocational Tech Center Vo/Tech
49 Hornet Rd 22939 540-245-5002
G. John Avoli, prin. Fax 885-0407

Regional Academic Governors SD
Supt. — See Richmond
Shenandoah Valley Governor's S 100/11-12
49 Hornet Rd 22939 540-245-5088
Linda Cauley, dir. Fax 886-6476

Augusta Medical Center Post-Sec.
PO Box 1000 22939 540-332-4539
Woodrow Wilson Rehabilitation Center Post-Sec.
PO Box 1500 22939 540-332-7265

Floyd, Floyd, Pop. 428

Floyd County SD 2,100/K-12
140 Harris Hart Rd NE 24091 540-745-9400
Terry E. Arbogast Ed.D., supt. Fax 745-9496
www.floyd.k12.va.us
Floyd JSHS 800/8-12
721 Baker St 24091 540-745-9450
Barry Hollandsworth, prin. Fax 745-9481

Forest, Bedford, Pop. 5,624

Bedford County SD
Supt. — See Bedford
Forest MS 1,000/6-8
100 Ashwood Dr 24551 434-525-6630
Michelle Morgan, prin. Fax 525-1284
Jefferson Forest HS 1,300/9-12
1 Cavalier Cir 24551 434-525-2674
Anthony H. Francis, prin. Fax 525-0106

Timberlake Christian Schools 500/PK-12
202 Horizon Dr 24551 434-237-5943
Randl J. Spear, supt. Fax 239-3319

Fork Union, Fluvanna

Fluvanna County SD
Supt. — See Palmyra
Fluvanna MS 800/6-8
9172 James Madison Hwy 23055 434-842-2222
Kathi Driver, prin. Fax 842-5150

Fork Union Military Academy 500/6-12
PO Box 278 23055 434-842-3212
John Jackson, prin. Fax 842-4300

Fort Defiance, Augusta

Augusta County SD
Supt. — See Fishersville
Fort Defiance HS 900/9-12
195 Fort Defiance Rd 24437 540-245-5050
Larry Landes, prin. Fax 245-5054
Stewart MS 900/6-8
118 Fort Defiance Rd 24437 540-245-5046
Bill Roberts, prin. Fax 245-5049

Franklin, Franklin, Pop. 8,254

Franklin CSD 1,400/PK-12
207 W 2nd Ave 23851 757-569-8111
Dr. Alline Farmer, supt. Fax 516-1015
www.franklincity.k12.va.us
Franklin HS 400/9-12
310 Crescent Dr 23851 757-562-5187
Samuel Jones, prin. Fax 562-3656
King MS 400/6-8
501 Charles St 23851 757-562-4631
Jo Ann Murray, prin. Fax 562-0231

Paul D. Camp Community College Post-Sec.
100 N College Dr 23851 757-569-6700

Fredericksburg, Fredericksburg, Pop. 20,189

Fredericksburg CSD 1,900/K-12
817 Princess Anne St 22401 540-372-1130
Dale Sander, supt. Fax 372-1111
www.cityschools.com
Monroe MS 700/9-12
2300 Washington Ave 22401 540-372-1100
Daryl Chesley, prin. Fax 373-8643

Walker-Grant MS 600/6-8
1 Learning Ln 22401 540-372-1145
Dennis Keffer, prin. Fax 891-5449

Regional Academic Governors SD
Supt. — See Richmond
Commonwealth Governor's HS 9-12
12301 Spotswood Furnace Rd 22407 540-548-1278
Dr. David Baker, dir. Fax 548-1736

Spotsylvania County SD 21,200/PK-12
8020 River Stone Dr 22407 540-834-2500
Dr. Jerry W. Hill, supt. Fax 834-2556
www.spotsylvania.k12.va.us
Battlefield MS 700/6-8
11120 Leavells Rd 22407 540-786-4400
Sheila B. Smith, prin. Fax 786-7109
Chancellor HS 1,600/9-12
6300 Harrison Rd 22407 540-786-2606
Jacqueline Bass-Fortune, prin. Fax 786-1176
Chancellor MS 900/6-8
6320 Harrison Rd 22407 540-786-8099
Shirley Eye, prin. Fax 785-9392
Freedom MS 800/6-8
7315 North Station Rd 22407 540-548-1030
Alan C. Jacobs, prin. Fax 786-0782
Massaponax HS 1,900/9-12
8201 Jefferson Davis Hwy 22407 540-710-0419
Joseph Rodkey, prin. Fax 710-1596
Riverbend HS 9-12
12301 Spotswood Furnace Rd 22407 540-548-4051
Steven Fitch, prin. Fax 548-2964
Other Schools – See Spotsylvania

Career Training Solutions Post-Sec.
100 Riverside Pkwy Ste 123 22406 540-373-2200
Fredericksburg Academy 400/PK-12
10800 Academy Dr 22408 540-898-0020
Donald Reed, hdmstr. Fax 898-8951
Fredericksburg Christian HS 300/9-12
9400 Thornton Rolling Rd 22408 540-371-3852
Sharon E. Roper, prin. Fax 371-4121
Fredericksburg Christian MS 300/4-8
2231 Jefferson Davis Hwy 22401 540-373-5357
Warren Aldrich, prin. Fax 899-6211
Mary Washington Hospital Post-Sec.
1001 Sam Perry Blvd 22401 540-899-1565
University of Mary Washington Post-Sec.
1301 College Ave 22401 540-654-1000

Front Royal, Warren, Pop. 14,160

Warren County SD 5,000/K-12
210 N Commerce Ave 22630 540-635-2171
Pamela McInnis, supt. Fax 636-4195
www.wcps.k12.va.us
Warren County HS 1,100/10-12
240 Luray Ave 22630 540-635-4144
Melinda Calhoun, prin. Fax 635-2009
Warren County JHS 800/8-9
155 Westminster Dr 22630 540-636-3199
Andrew Keller, prin. Fax 636-3244

Christendom College Post-Sec.
134 Christendom Dr 22630 540-636-2900
Notre Dame Grad Sch of Christendom Coll. Post-Sec.
134 Christendom Dr 22630 800-877-5456
Randolph-Macon Academy 400/6-12
200 Academy Dr 22630 540-636-5200
Henry Hobgood, pres. Fax 636-5344
Royal Christian Academy 200/PK-12
1111 N Shenandoah Ave 22630 540-636-7940
Nellie Adkins, prin. Fax 636-7213

Gainesville, Prince William

Prince William County SD
Supt. — See Manassas
Bull Run MS 1,000/6-8
6308 Catharpin Rd 20155 703-753-9969
William Bixby, prin. Fax 753-9610

Galax, Galax, Pop. 6,655

Galax CSD 1,300/K-12
223 Long St 24333 276-236-2911
Samuel Cook, supt. Fax 236-5776
www.gcps.k12.va.us/
Galax JSHS 500/8-12
200 Maroon Tide Dr 24333 276-236-2991
William Sturgill, prin.

Gate City, Scott, Pop. 2,090

Scott County SD 3,700/K-12
261 E Jackson St 24251 276-386-6118
James Scott, supt. Fax 386-2684
scott.k12.va.us/
Gate City HS 500/10-12
127 Beech St 24251 276-386-7522
Michael Brickey, prin. Fax 386-2695
Gate City MS 500/7-9
125 Beech St 24251 276-386-6065
John Ferguson, prin. Fax 386-2556
Scott County Career & Technical Center Vo/Tech
150 Broadwater Ave 24251 276-386-6515
Ralph Quesinberry, prin. Fax 386-2852
Other Schools – See Clinchport, Nickelsville

Glade Spring, Washington, Pop. 1,547

Washington County SD
Supt. — See Abingdon
Glade Spring MS 300/6-8
33474 Stagecoach Rd 24340 276-429-4200
Sharon Rainey, prin. Fax 429-4211
Henry HS 500/9-12
31437 Hillman Hwy 24340 276-739-3700
Keith Perrigan, prin. Fax 944-2125

Glen Allen, Henrico, Pop. 9,010

Henrico County SD
Supt. — See Richmond
Deep Run HS 1,300/9-12
4801 Twin Hickory Rd 23059 804-364-8000
Dr. Aaron C. Spence, prin. Fax 364-0887

Hungary Creek MS 6-8
4909 Francistown Rd 23060 804-527-2640
Elizabeth Armbruster, prin.
Short Pump MS 1,600/6-8
4701 Pouncey Tract Rd 23059 804-360-0800
Dr. Mark E. Chamberlain, prin. Fax 360-0808
Adult Education Center at Mountain Adult
2202 Mountain Rd 23060 804-261-5070
Elaine Callahan, prin.

ECPI Technical College Post-Sec.
4305 Cox Rd 23060 804-934-0100

Gloucester, Gloucester

Gloucester County SD 6,200/PK-12
6489 Main St 23061 804-693-5300
Dr. Howard B. Kiser, supt. Fax 693-1426
gets.gc.k12.va.us/
Gloucester HS, 6680 Short Ln 23061 2,000/9-12
Dr. Layton Beverage, prin. 804-693-2526
Page MS 600/6-8
5628 George Washington Mem 23061 804-693-2540
Dr. Barbara Anderson, prin. Fax 693-6595
Peasley MS 900/6-8
2885 Hickory Fork Rd 23061 804-693-1499
Daniel Fary, prin. Fax 693-1497

Gloucester Point, Gloucester, Pop. 8,509

College of William and Mary Post-Sec.
PO Box 1346 23062 804-642-7000

Goochland, Goochland

Goochland County SD 2,100/K-12
PO Box 169 23063 804-556-5316
Frank E. Morgan, supt. Fax 556-3847
www.glnd.k12.va.us
Goochland HS 800/8-12
3250 River Rd W 23063 804-556-5322
Jon Bennett, prin. Fax 556-6485

Gretna, Pittsylvania, Pop. 1,226

Pittsylvania County SD
Supt. — See Chatham
Gretna HS, PO Box 398 24557 700/9-12
Deborah D. Powell, prin. 434-656-2246
Gretna MS, 201 Coffey St 24557 600/6-8
Vera F. Glass, prin. 434-656-2217

Grundy, Buchanan, Pop. 1,030

Buchanan County SD 3,600/PK-12
PO Box 833 24614 276-935-4551
Tommy P. Justus, supt. Fax 935-6091
www.buc.k12.va.us
Buchanan County Tech & Career Center Vo/Tech
RR 5 Box 110 24614 276-935-4541
Donna Dotson, prin. Fax 935-4682
Grundy HS 500/9-12
RR 5 Box 23 24614 276-935-2106
James Branham, prin. Fax 935-8602
Other Schools – See Council, Hurley, Pilgrims Knob

Appalachian School of Law Post-Sec.
PO Box 2825 24614 800-895-7411

Halifax, Halifax, Pop. 1,321

Halifax County SD 5,900/K-12
PO Box 1849 24558 434-476-2171
Paul D. Stapleton, supt. Fax 476-1858
www.halifax.k12.va.us
Halifax County Career Center Vo/Tech
PO Box 1849 24558 434-476-5515
Charles Lowery, prin. Fax 476-5527
Other Schools – See South Boston

Hamilton, Loudoun, Pop. 654

Loudoun County SD
Supt. — See Ashburn
Harmony IS 900/8-9
38174 W Colonial Hwy 20158 540-338-0800
Sherron Gladden, prin. Fax 338-0805

Catholic Distance University Post-Sec.
120 E Colonial Hwy 20158 540-338-2700

Hampden Sydney, Prince Edward, Pop. 1,240

Hampden-Sydney College Post-Sec.
PO Box 128 23943 434-223-6000

Hampton, Hampton, Pop. 146,878

Hampton CSD 22,500/PK-12
1 Franklin St 23669 757-727-2000
Dr. Patrick Russo, supt. Fax 727-2002
www.sbo.hampton.k12.va.us
Bethel HS 2,100/9-12
1067 Big Bethel Rd 23666 757-825-4400
John Bailey, prin. Fax 825-4464
Davis MS 1,100/6-8
1435 Todds Ln 23666 757-825-4520
David Leech, prin. Fax 825-4533
Eaton MS 900/6-8
2108 Cunningham Dr 23666 757-825-4540
Raymond Haynes, prin. Fax 825-4551
Hampton HS 1,600/9-12
1491 W Queen St 23669 757-825-4430
Myra Chambers, prin. Fax 825-4711
Jones Magnet MS 600/6-8
1819 Nickerson Blvd 23663 757-850-7900
Sue Edwards, prin. Fax 850-5395
Kecoughtan HS 1,900/9-12
522 Woodland Rd 23669 757-850-5000
Arnold Baker, prin. Fax 850-5153
Lindsay MS 1,000/6-8
1636 Briarfield Rd 23661 757-825-4560
Carol Mann, prin. Fax 825-4839
Phoebus HS 1,400/9-12
100 Ireland St 23663 757-727-1000
Michael Cromartie, prin. Fax 727-0981

Spratley MS | 900/6-8
339 Woodland Rd 23669 | 757-850-5032
Rashard Wright, prin. | Fax 850-5186
Syms MS | 1,100/6-8
170 Fox Hill Rd 23669 | 757-850-5050
John Caggiano, prin. | Fax 850-5413

Regional Academic Governors SD
Supt. — See Richmond
New Horizons Governor's S Science/Tech. | 100/11-12
520 Butler Farm Rd 23666 | 757-766-1100
Dr. Donna Poland, dir. | Fax 766-3591

Crescent Cosmetology University | Post-Sec.
34 Holloway Dr 23666 | 757-826-4609
Faith Outreach Education Center | 100/PK-12
3105 Mercury Blvd 23666 | 757-838-8949
Crystal Caskie, prin. | Fax 838-4434
Hampton Christian HS | 300/7-12
2419 N Armistead Ave 23666 | 757-838-7427
Kathleen Mallory, prin. | Fax 827-8067
Hampton University 23669 | Post-Sec.
| 757-727-5000
Peninsula Academy | Post-Sec.
2244 Executive Dr 23666
Thomas Nelson Community College | Post-Sec.
PO Box 9407 23670 | 757-825-2700
Virginia School for the Deaf and Blind | Post-Sec.
700 Shell Rd 23661 | 757-247-2058
Virginia School of Hair Design | Post-Sec.
101 W Queens Way 23669 | 757-722-0211

Harrisonburg, Harrisonburg, Pop. 41,170
Harrisonburg CSD | 4,000/K-12
317 S Main St 22801 | 540-434-9916
Donald Ford, supt. | Fax 434-5196
www.harrisonburg.k12.va.us
Harrisonburg HS | 1,200/9-12
1001 Garbers Church Rd 22801 | 540-433-2651
Irene Reynolds, prin. | Fax 433-3595
Harrison MS | 1,000/6-8
1311 W Market St 22801 | 540-434-1949
Elisabeth Dunnenberger, prin. | Fax 434-4052

Jointly Operated Vo Tech SD
Supt. — None
Massanutten Tech Center | Vo/Tech
325 Pleasant Valley Rd 22801 | 540-434-5961
Marshall Price, prin. | Fax 434-1402

Rockingham County SD | 11,200/PK-12
100 Mount Clinton Pike 22802 | 540-564-3200
Dr. John Kidd, supt. | Fax 564-3241
www.rockingham.k12.va.us/
Other Schools – See Bridgewater, Broadway, Dayton,
Elkton, Penn Laird

Eastern Mennonite HS | 300/6-12
801 Parkwood Dr 22802 | 540-432-4500
Paul Leaman, prin. | Fax 432-4528
Eastern Mennonite University | Post-Sec.
1200 Park Rd 22802 | 540-432-4000
Good Shepherd S | 200/PK-12
342 Neff Ave 22801 | 540-564-1744
James Madison University | Post-Sec.
800 S Main St 22807 | 540-568-6211
National College of Business & Tech. | Post-Sec.
51 Burgess Rd Ste B 22801 | 540-432-0943
Rockingham Memorial Hospital | Post-Sec.
235 Cantrell Ave 22801 | 540-564-5407

Haymarket, Prince William, Pop. 960
Prince William County SD
Supt. — See Manassas
Battlefield HS | 9-12
15000 Graduation Dr 20169 | 571-261-4400
Amy Ethridge, prin. | Fax 261-3719

Haysi, Dickenson, Pop. 179
Dickenson County SD
Supt. — See Clintwood
Haysi HS | 300/9-12
PO Box G 24256 | 276-865-5126
Larry Compton, prin. | Fax 865-5240

Heathsville, Northumberland
Northumberland County SD
Supt. — See Lottsburg
Northumberland HS | 500/9-12
PO Box 40 22473 | 804-580-5192
Larry Shumaker, prin.
Northumberland MS | 400/6-8
PO Box 100 22473 | 804-580-5753
Robert Bailey, prin.

Herndon, Fairfax, Pop. 21,721
Fairfax County SD
Supt. — See Fairfax
Carson MS | 1,100/7-8
13618 McLearen Rd 20171 | 703-925-3600
August Frattali, prin. | Fax 925-3697
Herndon HS | 2,300/9-12
700 Bennett St 20170 | 703-810-2200
Frances Ivey, prin. | Fax 810-2262
Herndon MS | 1,200/7-8
901 Locust St 20170 | 703-904-4800
Frank Jenkins, prin. | Fax 904-4897

AKS Massage School | Post-Sec.
462 Herndon Pkwy Ste 208 20170 | 703-464-0333

Highland Springs, Henrico, Pop. 13,823
Henrico County SD
Supt. — See Richmond
Highland Springs HS | 1,700/9-12
15 S Oak Ave 23075 | 804-328-4000
Albert M. Ciarochi, prin. | Fax 328-4019
Highland Springs Technical Center | Vo/Tech
100 Tech Dr 23075 | 804-328-4075
Thomas Collier, prin. | Fax 328-4074

Adult Education Center | Adult
201 E Nine Mile Rd 23075 | 804-328-4095
Elaine Callahan, prin.

Hillsville, Carroll, Pop. 2,760
Carroll County SD | 4,000/K-12
605 Pine St Ste 9 24343 | 276-728-3191
Oliver McBride, supt. | Fax 728-3195
www.ccpsd.k12.va.us
Carroll County HS | 800/10-12
100 Cavs Ln 24343 | 276-728-2125
Robbie Patton, prin. | Fax 728-9067
Carroll County IS | 700/8-9
1036 N Main St 24343 | 276-728-2382
Dr. Kevin Harris, prin. | Fax 728-4089

New Life Christian S International | 100/K-12
PO Box 1268 24343 | 276-730-0706
Leon Goad, admin. | Fax 730-0705

Honaker, Russell, Pop. 922
Russell County SD
Supt. — See Lebanon
Honaker HS | 500/8-12
PO Box 764 24260 | 276-873-6363
Tony Bush, prin. | Fax 873-7252

Hopewell, Hopewell, Pop. 22,391
Hopewell CSD | 3,900/K-12
103 N 12th Ave 23860 | 804-541-6400
Dr. Winston Odom, supt. | Fax 541-6401
www.hopewell.k12.va.us
Hopewell HS | 1,000/9-12
400 S Mesa Dr 23860 | 804-541-6402
Gayle Keith, prin. | Fax 541-6403
Woodson MS | 1,000/6-8
1000 Winston Churchill Dr 23860 | 804-541-6404
Cheryl Webb, prin. | Fax 541-6405

Hot Springs, Bath
Bath County SD
Supt. — See Warm Springs
Bath County HS | 300/8-12
RR 1 Box 575 24445 | 540-839-2431
Pete Pitard, prin. | Fax 839-3290

Hurley, Buchanan
Buchanan County SD
Supt. — See Grundy
Hurley HS | 200/9-12
RR 1 Box 249 24620 | 276-566-8334
Richie T. Blankenship, prin. | Fax 566-7127

Hurt, Pittsylvania, Pop. 1,252

Faith Christian Academy | 100/PK-12
PO Box 670 24563 | 434-324-8276
Lisa Moore, prin. | Fax 324-8279

Independence, Grayson, Pop. 936
Grayson County SD | 2,200/K-12
PO Box 888 24348 | 276-773-2832
Jerry Cock, supt. | Fax 773-2939
www.grayson.k12.va.us
Fries MS, PO Box 155 24348 | 100/6-8
Elizabeth Brown, prin. | 276-744-7548
Grayson County Career & Technical Center | Vo/Tech
PO Box 707 24348 | 276-773-2951
Diane Haynes, prin. | Fax 773-2396
Grayson County HS | 700/9-12
PO Box 828 24348 | 276-773-2131
Diane Haynes, prin. | Fax 773-2682
Independence MS | 400/6-8
PO Box 155 24348 | 276-773-3020
Bobby Cheeks, prin. | Fax 773-0479
Other Schools – See Whitetop

Isle of Wight, Isle of Wight
Isle of Wight County SD | 4,300/PK-12
PO Box 78 23397 | 757-357-4393
Michael W. McPherson Ed.D., supt. | Fax 357-0849
www.iwcs.k12.va.us
Other Schools – See Smithfield, Windsor

Isle of Wight Academy | 500/PK-12
PO Box 105 23397 | 757-357-3866
Benjamin Vaughan, hdmstr. | Fax 357-6886

Jetersville, Amelia
Jointly Operated Vo Tech SD
Supt. — None
Amelia-Nottoway Vo Tech Ctr | Vo/Tech
148 Votech Rd 23083 | 434-645-7854
Richard Glowinski, prin. | Fax 645-1044

Nottoway County SD
Supt. — See Nottoway
Piedmont Alternative S | Vo/Tech
128 Votech Rd 23083 | 434-645-7471
| Fax 645-1044

Jonesville, Lee, Pop. 987
Lee County SD | 3,700/K-12
5 Park St 24263 | 276-346-2107
Fref Marion, supt. | Fax 346-0307
www.leectysch.com/
Jonesville MS | 300/5-8
RR 1 Box 104H 24263 | 276-346-1011
Connie Daugherty, prin. | Fax 346-1411
Lee HS | 800/9-12
RR 2 Box 740 24263 | 276-346-0173
Ronald Earley, prin. | Fax 346-4032
Other Schools – See Ben Hur, Ewing, Pennington Gap

Kenbridge, Lunenburg, Pop. 1,328
Lunenburg County SD | 1,700/PK-12
1009 Main St 23944 | 434-676-2467
Wayne Staples, supt. | Fax 676-1000
Other Schools – See Victoria

Keysville, Charlotte, Pop. 790
Regional Academic Governors SD
Supt. — See Richmond

Governor's S of Southside VA | 100/11-12
200 Daniel Rd 23947 | 434-736-0616
Catherine Cottrell, dir. | Fax 736-0719

Southside Virginia Community College | Post-Sec.
200 Daniel Rd 23947 | 434-736-2018

Kilmarnock, Lancaster, Pop. 1,235
Lancaster County SD | 1,400/PK-12
PO Box 2000 22482 | 804-435-3183
Randolph H. Latimore Ed.D., supt. | Fax 435-3309
www.lcs.k12.va.us
Lancaster MS, 191 School St 22482 | 500/4-8
Craig Kauffman, prin. | 804-435-1681
Other Schools – See Lancaster

King and Queen Court House, King and Queen
King & Queen County SD | 800/K-12
PO Box 97 23085 | 804-785-5981
Dr. Richard Layman, supt. | Fax 785-5686
www.kqps.net
Central HS | 300/8-12
17024 The Trl 23085 | 804-785-6102
Veronica Simms, prin. | Fax 785-5129

King George, King George
King George County SD | 3,400/K-12
PO Box 1239 22485 | 540-775-5833
Dr. Candace Brown, supt. | Fax 775-2165
www.kgcs.k12.va.us
King George HS | 1,000/9-12
8246 Dahlgren Rd 22485 | 540-775-3055
Todd Satterwhite, prin. | Fax 775-5345
King George MS | 500/7-8
8562 Dahlgren Rd 22485 | 540-775-2331
Peter Vernimb, prin. | Fax 775-0263

King William, King William
King William County SD | 1,900/PK-12
PO Box 185 23086 | 804-769-3434
Dr. Brenda Cowlbeck, supt. | Fax 769-3312
www.kwcps.k12.va.us
Hamilton-Holmes MS | 500/6-8
18444 King William Rd 23086 | 804-769-3316
Stacey B. Johnson, prin.
King William HS, 80 Cavalier Dr 23086 | 500/9-12
Charles Clare, prin. | 804-769-2708

Lancaster, Lancaster
Lancaster County SD
Supt. — See Kilmarnock
Lancaster HS, PO Box 790 22503 | 400/9-12
Sandra Spears, prin. | 804-462-5177

Lawrenceville, Brunswick, Pop. 1,231
Brunswick County SD | 2,400/PK-12
PO Box 309 23868 | 434-848-3138
Dale Baird, supt. | Fax 848-4001
www.brun.k12.va.us
Brunswick SHS | 500/10-12
2171 Lawrenceville Plank Rd 23868 | 434-848-2716
R. Gerald Burke, prin. | Fax 848-6303
Russell JHS | 600/7-9
19400 Christanna Hwy 23868 | 434-848-2132
Arthur Jarrett, prin. | Fax 848-6201

Brunswick Academy | 500/PK-12
2100 Planters Rd 23868 | 434-848-2220
Jean Grizzard, hdmstr. | Fax 848-4729
St. Paul's College | Post-Sec.
406 Windsor Ave 23868 | 434-848-3111

Lebanon, Russell, Pop. 3,218
Russell County SD | 3,600/K-12
PO Box 8 24266 | 276-889-6500
Lorraine Turner, supt. | Fax 889-6508
www.russell.k12.va.us
Lebanon HS | 600/9-12
PO Box 217 24266 | 276-889-6539
Nelson Dodi, prin. | Fax 889-0622
Lebanon MS | 200/7-8
PO Box 577 24266 | 276-889-6548
Joey Long, prin. | Fax 889-4262
Russell County Career & Technology Ctr | Vo/Tech
PO Box 849 24266 | 276-889-6550
Brian Hooker, prin. | Fax 889-4470
Other Schools – See Castlewood, Honaker

Leesburg, Loudoun, Pop. 33,319
Loudoun County SD
Supt. — See Ashburn
Belmont Ridge MS | 1,000/6-8
19045 Upper Belmont Pl 20176 | 703-669-1450
Theresa N. Redd, prin.
Harper Park MS | 1,200/6-8
701 Potomac Station Dr NE 20176 | 703-779-8860
William Shipp, prin. | Fax 779-8867
Heritage HS | 1,100/9-12
520 Evergreen Mill Rd SE 20175 | 703-669-1400
Margaret Huckaby, prin. | Fax 669-1410
Loudoun County HS | 1,100/9-12
415 Dry Mill Rd SW 20175 | 703-771-6580
William Oblas, prin. | Fax 771-6595
Monroe Technology Center | Vo/Tech
715 Childrens Center Rd SW 20175 | 703-771-6560
Wagner B. Grier, prin. | Fax 771-6563
Simpson MS | 1,000/6-8
490 Evergreen Mill Rd SE 20175 | 703-771-6640
John Bannister, prin. | Fax 771-6643
Smart's Mill MS, 850 N King St 20176 | 6-8
Eric L. Steward, prin. | 703-669-1480

Lexington, Lexington, Pop. 7,076
Lexington CSD | 500/K-8
300A White St 24450 | 540-463-7146
Daniel Lyons, supt. | Fax 464-5230
www.lexedu.org/
Lyburn-Downing MS | 200/6-8
302 Diamond St 24450 | 540-463-3532
Richard Dowd, prin.

Rockbridge County SD — 2,900/K-12
  1972 Big Spring Dr 24450 — 540-463-7386
  John Burks, supt. — Fax 463-7823
  www.rcs.rang.k12.va.us
Maury River MS — 400/6-8
  600 Waddell St 24450 — 540-463-3129
  Lena Beason, prin. — Fax 464-4838
Rockbridge County HS — 1,100/9-12
  143 Greenhouse Rd 24450 — 540-463-5555
  Andy Bryan, prin. — Fax 463-6152
Other Schools – See Fairfield

Virginia Military Institute 24450 — Post-Sec.
  — 540-464-7000
Washington & Lee University 24450 — Post-Sec.
  — 540-463-8400

Locust Grove, Orange
Orange County SD
  Supt. — See Orange
Locust Grove MS — 500/6-8
  31208 Constitution Hwy 22508 — 540-661-4550
  Eric Barna, prin. — Fax 661-4447

Germanna Community College — Post-Sec.
  2130 Germanna Hwy 22508 — 540-727-3000

Locust Hill, Middlesex
Middlesex County SD
  Supt. — See Saluda
St. Clare Walker MS — 400/6-8
  PO Box 9 23092 — 804-758-2561
  Joe Fears, prin. — Fax 758-0834

Lorton, Fairfax, Pop. 15,385
Fairfax County SD
  Supt. — See Fairfax
South County JSHS — 7-12
  8501 Silverbrook Rd 22079 — 703-446-1600
  Dale Rumberger, prin. — Fax 446-1697

Lottsburg, Northumberland
Northumberland County SD — 1,500/PK-12
  2172 Northumberland Hwy 22511 — 804-529-6134
  Clint Stables, supt. — Fax 529-6449
Other Schools – See Heathsville

Lovingston, Nelson
Nelson County SD — 2,000/PK-12
  PO Box 276 22949 — 434-263-7100
  Dr. Roger Dale Collins, supt. — Fax 263-7115
  www.nelson.k12.va.us
Nelson County HS — 600/9-12
  6919 Thomas Nelson Hwy 22949 — 434-263-8317
  Mike Jamerson, prin. — Fax 263-5987
Nelson MS — 500/6-8
  6925 Thomas Nelson Hwy 22949 — 434-263-4801
  Joe Johnson, prin. — Fax 263-4483

Luray, Page, Pop. 4,892
Page County SD — 3,600/PK-12
  735 W Main St 22835 — 540-743-6533
  Dr. Randall W. Thomas, supt. — Fax 743-7784
  eclipse.pagecounty.k12.va.us/~pcps/index.html
Luray HS, 14 Luray Ave 22835 — 800/8-12
  David Ponn, prin. — 540-743-3800
Page County Technical Ctr — Vo/Tech
  525 Middleburg Rd 22835 — 540-778-7282
  Philip Secrist, prin.
Other Schools – See Shenandoah

Lynchburg, Lynchburg, Pop. 65,113
Campbell County SD
  Supt. — See Rustburg
Brookville HS — 1,000/9-12
  100 Laxton Rd 24502 — 434-239-2636
  James Whorley, prin. — Fax 239-6706
Brookville MS — 800/6-8
  320 Bee Dr 24502 — 434-239-9267
  Robert Bailey, prin. — Fax 237-8974

Lynchburg CSD — 9,500/PK-12
  PO Box 1599 24505 — 434-522-3700
  Dr. Paul McKendrick, supt. — Fax 846-1500
  www.lynchburg.org
Central VA Governor's S Science & Tech. — 600/11-12
  3020 Wards Ferry Rd 24502 — 434-582-1104
  Dr. Thomas Morgan, prin. — Fax 239-4140
Dunbar MS for Innovation — 700/6-8
  1200 Polk St 24504 — 434-522-3740
  Brian Wray, prin. — Fax 522-3727
Glass HS — 1,700/9-12
  2111 Memorial Ave 24501 — 434-522-3712
  Susan Morrison, prin. — Fax 522-3741
Heritage HS — 1,200/9-12
  3020 Wards Ferry Rd 24502 — 434-582-1147
  Robert Miller, prin. — Fax 582-1137
Linkhorne MS — 800/6-8
  2525 Linkhorne Dr 24503 — 434-384-5150
  Robert Kerns, prin. — Fax 384-2810
Sandusky MS — 600/6-8
  805 Chinook Pl 24502 — 434-582-1120
  James E. Sales, prin. — Fax 582-1183
Adult Learning Center — Adult
  1015 Miller Park Sq 24501 — 434-522-2319
  Linda Cole, prin. — Fax 522-2320

Centra Health — Post-Sec.
  1920 Atherholt Rd 24501 — 434-947-4705
Central Virginia Community College — Post-Sec.
  3506 Wards Rd 24502 — 434-832-7600
Doss Junior Academy — 100/K-10
  19 George St 24502 — 434-237-1899
  Tammy Tomlin, prin. — Fax 237-0820
Holy Cross S — 300/PK-12
  2125 Langhorne Rd 24501 — 434-847-5436
  John Jones, prin. — Fax 847-4156
Liberty Christian Academy — 1,000/PK-12
  1000 Mountain View Rd 24502 — 434-832-2000
  Harvey Klamm, supt. — Fax 832-2027
Liberty University — Post-Sec.
  PO Box 20000 24506 — 434-582-2000

Lynchburg College — Post-Sec.
  1501 Lakeside Dr 24501 — 434-544-8100
Lynchburg General Hosp School of Nursing — Post-Sec.
  1901 Tate Springs Rd 24501 — 434-947-3070
Miller-Motte Technical College — Post-Sec.
  1011 Creekside Ln 24502 — 877-333-6622
National College of Business & Tech. — Post-Sec.
  104 Candlewood Ct 24502 — 434-239-3500
Ralph's Virginia School of Cosmetology — Post-Sec.
  3225 Old Forest Rd Ste 5 24501 — 434-385-7722
Randolph-Macon Woman's College — Post-Sec.
  2500 Rivermont Ave 24503 — 434-947-8000
Virginia Episcopal S — 200/9-12
  PO Box 408 24505 — 434-385-3600
  Philip Hadley, hdmstr. — Fax 385-3603
Virginia University of Lynchburg — Post-Sec.
  2058 Garfield Ave 24501 — 434-528-5276

Machipongo, Northampton
Northampton County SD — 2,100/K-12
  7207 Young St 23405 — 757-678-5151
  Dr. Mary K English, supt. — Fax 678-7267
  www.ncps.k12.va.us
Northampton MS — 500/6-8
  7247 Young St 23405 — 757-678-8070
  Irma Berry, prin. — Fax 678-7645
TECH Center — Vo/Tech
  7207 Young St 23405 — 757-678-8004
  Dr. David van de Graaff, prin. — Fax 678-7267
Other Schools – See Eastville

Mc Lean, Fairfax, Pop. 39,100
Fairfax County SD
  Supt. — See Fairfax
Cooper MS — 900/7-8
  977 Balls Hill Rd 22101 — 703-442-5800
  Arlene Randall, prin. — Fax 442-5897
Langley HS — 2,000/9-12
  6520 Georgetown Pike 22101 — 703-287-2700
  William Clendaniel, prin. — Fax 287-2797
Mc Lean HS — 1,700/9-12
  1633 Davidson Rd 22101 — 703-714-5700
  Paul Wardinski, prin. — Fax 714-5797

Keller Graduate School — Post-Sec.
  1751 Pinnacle Dr Ste 250 22102 — 703-556-9669
Madeira S — 300/9-12
  8328 Georgetown Pike 22102 — 703-556-8200
  Elisabeth Griffith, hdmstr. — Fax 893-3289
Oakcrest S — 200/6-12
  850 Balls Hill Rd 22101 — 703-790-5450
  Ellen Cavanagh, prin. — Fax 790-5380
Potomac S — 900/K-12
  PO Box 430 22101 — 703-356-4101
  Geoffrey Jones, hdmstr. — Fax 883-9031

Madison, Madison, Pop. 211
Madison County SD — 1,900/K-12
  PO Box 647 22727 — 540-948-3780
  Dr. Brenda Tanner, supt. — Fax 948-6988
  www.madisonschools.k12.va.us
Madison County HS — 600/9-12
  68 Mountaineer Ln 22727 — 540-948-3785
  J. Marcus Carraway, prin. — Fax 948-4425
Wetsel MS — 500/6-8
  186 Mountaineer Ln 22727 — 540-948-3783
  Robert Otto, prin. — Fax 948-4809

Madison Heights, Amherst, Pop. 11,700
Amherst County SD
  Supt. — See Amherst
Monelison MS — 700/6-8
  257 Trojan Rd 24572 — 434-846-1307
  Kathleen M. Pierce, prin. — Fax 846-5318

Temple Christian S — 300/PK-12
  PO Box 970 24572 — 434-846-0024
  Marty Swear, admin. — Fax 846-1807

Manassas, Manassas, Pop. 37,166
Manassas CSD — 6,700/K-12
  9000 Tudor Ln 20110 — 703-257-8808
  Dr. Sidney Zullinger, supt. — Fax 257-8807
  www.manassas.k12.va.us
Metz JHS — 1,600/6-8
  9700 Fairview Ave 20110 — 703-257-8600
  Melissa Saunders, prin. — Fax 258-8615
Osbourn HS — 2,000/9-12
  9005 Tudor Ln 20110 — 703-257-8500
  John Conti, prin. — Fax 530-0937

Prince William County SD — 63,800/PK-12
  PO Box 389 20108 — 703-791-7200
  Steven L. Walts Ph.D., supt. — Fax 791-7309
  www.pwcs.edu
Benton MS — 1,100/6-8
  7411 Hoadly Rd 20112 — 703-791-0727
  Linda Leibert, prin. — Fax 791-0977
Jackson MS — 2,900/9-12
  8820 Rixlew Ln 20109 — 703-365-2900
  David Huckestein, prin. — Fax 365-6984
Osbourn Park HS — 2,700/9-12
  8909 Euclid Ave 20111 — 703-365-6500
  Timothy Healey, prin. — Fax 365-6798
Parkside MS — 1,100/6-8
  8602 Mathis Ave 20110 — 703-361-3106
  Marie Bowe-Quick Ed.D., prin. — Fax 361-8993
Saunders MS — 1,200/6-8
  13557 Spriggs Rd 20112 — 703-670-9188
  Pat Puttre, prin. — Fax 670-3078
Stonewall MS — 1,000/6-8
  10100 Lomond Dr 20109 — 703-361-3185
  John G. Miller, prin. — Fax 368-1266
Other Schools – See Bristow, Dumfries, Gainesville,
  Haymarket, Nokesville, Triangle, Woodbridge

American Military University — Post-Sec.
  10648 Wakeman Ct 20110 — 703-330-5398
ECPI College of Technology — Post-Sec.
  10021 Balls Ford Rd # 100 20109 — 703-330-5300

Emmanuel Christian S — 300/PK-12
  8302 Spruce St 20111 — 703-369-3950
  Allen Edgar, prin. — Fax 330-9285
Heritage Institute — Post-Sec.
  8255 Shoppers Sq 20111 — 703-361-7775
Northern Virginia Community College — Post-Sec.
  6901 Sudley Rd 20109 — 703-368-0184
Seton S — 200/7-12
  9314 Maple St 20110 — 703-368-3220
  Anne Carroll, prin. — Fax 393-1199
Strayer University — Post-Sec.
  9990 Battleview Pkwy 20109 — 703-330-8400
University of Northern Virginia — Post-Sec.
  10021 Balls Ford Rd 20109 — 703-392-0771

Manassas Park, Manassas Park, Pop. 10,990
Manassas Park CSD — 2,300/PK-12
  1 Park Center Ct #A 20111 — 703-335-8850
  Dr. Thomas DeBolt, supt. — Fax 361-4583
  www.mpark.net
Manassas Park HS — 600/9-12
  8200 Euclid Ave 20111 — 703-361-9131
  Dr. C. Bruce McDade, prin.
Manassas Park MS — 500/6-8
  8202 Euclid Ave 20111 — 703-361-1510
  Elizabeth Purcell, prin.

Marion, Smyth, Pop. 6,208
Smyth County SD — 5,100/PK-12
  121 Bagley Cir Ste 300 24354 — 276-783-3791
  Jim R. Sullivan, supt. — Fax 783-3291
  www.scsb.org
Marion HS — 800/9-12
  848 Stage St 24354 — 276-783-4731
  Dale Holt, prin. — Fax 783-4117
Marion MS — 600/6-8
  134 Wilden St 24354 — 276-783-4466
  Kyle Rhodes, prin. — Fax 783-4952
Smyth Career & Technology Center — Vo/Tech
  147 Fox Valley Rd 24354 — 276-646-8117
  Edward L. Worley, prin. — Fax 646-4009
Other Schools – See Chilhowie, Saltville

Blue Ridge Job Corps Center — Post-Sec.
  245 W Main St 24354 — 276-783-7221

Marshall, Fauquier
Fauquier County SD
  Supt. — See Warrenton
Marshall MS — 600/6-8
  PO Box 117 20116 — 540-364-1551
  Christine Moschetti, prin. — Fax 364-4699

Fresta Valley Christian S — 300/PK-12
  6428 Wilson Rd 20115 — 540-364-1929
  Stacy Lam, prin. — Fax 364-4603

Martinsville, Martinsville, Pop. 15,121
Henry County SD
  Supt. — See Collinsville
Laurel Park MS — 500/6-8
  280 Laurel Park Ave 24112 — 276-632-7216
  Wayne Moore, prin. — Fax 632-4865
Martinsville CSD — 2,500/PK-12
  202 Cleveland Ave 24112 — 276-403-5820
  Dr. Scott Kizner, supt. — Fax 403-5830
  www.martinsville.k12.va.us/
Martinsville HS — 800/9-12
  351 Commonwealth Blvd E 24112 — 276-632-9755
  Thomas Fitzgibbons, prin. — Fax 632-1516
Martinsville MS — 700/6-8
  201 Brown St 24112 — 276-634-5728
  Paulette Simington, prin. — Fax 638-4140

Carlisle S — 400/PK-12
  PO Box 5388 24115 — 276-632-7288
  Simon Owen-Williams, prin. — Fax 632-9545
National College of Business & Tech. — Post-Sec.
  10 Church St 24114 — 276-632-5621
Patrick Henry Community College — Post-Sec.
  PO Box 5311 24115 — 276-638-8777

Mathews, Mathews
Mathews County SD — 1,300/K-12
  PO Box 369 23109 — 804-725-3909
  David J. Holleran Ed.D., supt. — Fax 725-3951
  www.mathews.k12.va.us
Hunter MS — 400/5-8
  PO Box 339 23109 — 804-725-2434
  Dino A. Papas, prin. — Fax 725-2337
Mathews HS — 400/9-12
  PO Box 38 23109 — 804-725-3702
  Mary B. Whitley, prin. — Fax 725-5778

Matoaca, Chesterfield
Chesterfield County SD
  Supt. — See Chesterfield
Matoaca MS — 700/6-8
  20300 Halloway Ave 23803 — 804-590-3130
  Jeff McGee, prin. — Fax 590-3136

Max Meadows, Wythe
Wythe County SD
  Supt. — See Wytheville
Ft. Chiswell HS — 500/9-12
  1 Pioneer Trl 24360 — 276-637-3437
  LaDonna Meade, prin. — Fax 637-6316
Ft. Chiswell MS — 400/6-8
  101 Pioneer Trl 24360 — 276-637-4400
  Richard D. Thomas, prin. — Fax 637-4452

Mechanicsville, Hanover, Pop. 22,027
Hanover County SD
  Supt. — See Ashland
Atlee HS — 1,400/9-12
  9414 Atlee Station Rd 23116 — 804-723-2100
  Vincent L. D'Agostino, prin. — Fax 723-2134
Chickahominy MS — 1,100/6-8
  9450 Atlee Station Rd 23116 — 804-723-2160
  S. Scott Baker, prin. — Fax 723-2191

Hanover HS   900/9-12
10307 Chamberlayne Rd 23116   804-723-3700
Dr. Carol S. Cash, prin.   Fax 723-3759
Jackson MS   1,300/6-8
8021 Lee Davis Rd 23111   804-723-2260
Robert D. Staley, prin.   Fax 723-2261
Lee-Davis HS   1,500/9-12
7052 Mechanicsville Tpke 23111   804-723-2200
Stanley B. Jones, prin.   Fax 723-2202
Oak Knoll MS   900/6-8
10295 Chamberlayne Rd 23116   804-365-4740
Sue Richardson, prin.   Fax 365-4741

Melfa, Accomack, Pop. 446

Eastern Shore Community College   Post-Sec.
29300 Lankford Hwy 23410   757-787-5900

Middleburg, Loudoun, Pop. 760

Foxcroft S   200/9-12
PO Box 5555 20118   540-687-5555
Mary Leipheimer, prin.   Fax 687-3675
Notre Dame Academy   300/9-12
35321 Notre Dame Ln 20117   540-687-5581
Ed Hoffman, prin.   Fax 687-3103

Middletown, Frederick, Pop. 1,058

Lord Fairfax Community College   Post-Sec.
173 Skirmisher Ln 22645   800-906-5322

Midlothian, Chesterfield

Chesterfield County SD
Supt. — See Chesterfield
Bailey Bridge MS   1,600/6-8
12501 Bailey Bridge Rd 23112   804-739-6200
Donald Skeen, prin.   Fax 739-6211
Clover Hill HS   2,100/9-12
13900 Hull Street Rd 23112   804-739-6230
Deborah Marks, prin.   Fax 739-6239
James River HS   1,900/9-12
3700 James River Rd 23113   804-378-2420
John Titus, prin.   Fax 379-2695
Manchester HS   2,400/9-12
12601 Bailey Bridge Rd 23112   804-739-6275
Pete Koste, prin.   Fax 739-6340
Midlothian HS   1,700/9-12
401 Charter Colony Pkwy 23114   804-378-2440
Christine Wilson, prin.   Fax 378-2450
Midlothian MS   1,400/6-8
13501 Midlothian Tpke 23113   804-378-2460
Patrick Stanfield, prin.   Fax 378-7556
Robious MS   1,100/6-8
2701 Robious Crossing Dr 23113   804-378-2510
Jeff Ellick, prin.   Fax 378-2519
Swift Creek MS   1,400/6-8
3700 Old Hundred Rd S 23112   804-739-6315
Mary Robinson, prin.   Fax 739-6322

Empire Beauty School   Post-Sec.
10807 Hull Street Rd 23112   800-575-5983
Heritage Christian Academy   100/6-12
10700 Academy Dr 23112   804-745-2387
Clarinda Cole, prin.   Fax 745-8178

Milford, Caroline

Caroline County SD
Supt. — See Bowling Green
Caroline HS   1,100/9-12
19155 Rogers Clark Blvd 22514   804-633-9886
Pat Taylor-Smith, prin.   Fax 633-2435
Caroline MS   900/6-8
13325 Devils Three Jump Rd 22514   804-633-6561
Reginald Underwood, prin.   Fax 633-9014

Mineral, Louisa, Pop. 445

Louisa County SD   4,300/PK-12
PO Box 7 23117   540-894-5115
Dr. David Melton, supt.   Fax 894-0252
www.lcps.k12.va.us
Louisa HS   1,300/9-12
PO Box 328 23117   540-894-5436
Michael Wills, prin.   Fax 894-0534
Louisa MS   1,100/6-8
PO Box 448 23117   540-894-5457
LuAnne Unruh, prin.   Fax 894-5096

Moneta, Bedford

Bedford County SD
Supt. — See Bedford
Staunton River HS   1,100/9-12
1095 Golden Eagle Dr 24121   540-297-7151
Michael Kelly, prin.   Fax 297-4514
Staunton River MS   900/6-8
1293 Golden Eagle Dr 24121   540-297-4152
Linwood Roberts, prin.   Fax 297-4076

Monroe, Amherst

Old Dominion Job Corps Center   Post-Sec.
1073 Father Judge Rd 24574   434-929-4081

Monterey, Highland, Pop. 155

Highland County SD   300/K-12
PO Box 250 24465   540-468-2240
Percy C. Nowlin, supt.   Fax 468-2940
www.highland.k12.va.us/highland/site/default.asp
Highland JSHS, PO Box 430 24465   200/6-12
Randolph Hooke, prin.   540-468-2129

Montross, Westmoreland, Pop. 313

Westmoreland County SD   2,000/PK-12
141 Opal Ln 22520   804-493-8018
A. Elaine Fogliani, supt.   Fax 493-9323
www.wmlcps.org/
Montross MS   500/6-8
8884 Menokin Rd 22520   804-493-9818
Eric Jones, prin.   Fax 493-0918

Washington & Lee HS   700/9-12
16380 Kings Hwy 22520   804-493-8015
Chastine Williams, prin.   Fax 493-0243

Mount Jackson, Shenandoah, Pop. 1,720

Regional Academic Governors SD
Supt. — See Richmond
Massanutten Governor's S   11-12
6375 Main St 22842   540-477-3226
Catherine Glenn, prin.

Shenandoah County SD
Supt. — See Woodstock
Triplett Vo-Tech, 6375 Main St 22842   Vo/Tech
Lee Sterner, prin.   540-477-3161

Mouth of Wilson, Grayson

Oak Hill Academy   200/8-12
2635 Oak Hill Rd 24363   276-579-2619
Dr. Michael D. Groves, pres.   Fax 579-4722

Narrows, Giles, Pop. 2,151

Giles County SD
Supt. — See Pearisburg
Narrows HS   400/8-12
1 Green Wave Ln 24124   540-726-2384
Robert N. Stump, prin.   Fax 726-2775

Naruna, Campbell

Campbell County SD
Supt. — See Rustburg
Campbell JSHS   700/6-12
PO Box 7 24576   434-376-2015
Robert Arnold, prin.   Fax 376-5859

New Castle, Craig, Pop. 176

Craig County SD   700/K-12
PO Box 245 24127   540-864-5191
  Fax 864-6885
www.craig.k12.va.us/
Craig County JSHS   400/6-12
RR 3 Box 1007 24127   540-864-5185
Greg Stick, prin.   Fax 864-5636

Newington, Fairfax, Pop. 17,965

Strayer University   Post-Sec.
PO Box 487 22122   703-339-1850

New Kent, New Kent

New Kent County SD   2,500/K-12
PO Box 110 23124   804-966-9650
J. Geiger, supt.   Fax 966-9879
www.nkcps.k12.va.us
New Kent County HS   800/9-12
PO Box 300 23124   804-966-9671
Yvonne Jones, prin.   Fax 966-2773
New Kent County MS   700/6-8
PO Box 190 23124   804-966-9655
Howard Ormond, prin.   Fax 966-2703

New Market, Shenandoah, Pop. 1,782

Shenandoah Valley Academy   200/9-12
234 W Lee Hwy 22844   540-740-3161
John Nafie, prin.   Fax 740-3336

Newport News, Newport News, Pop. 181,647

Jointly Operated Vo Tech SD
Supt. — None
New Horizons Technical Ctr - Woodside   Vo/Tech
13400 Woodside Ln 23608   757-874-4444
Roger Tomlinson, prin.   Fax 872-8951

Newport News CSD   33,900/PK-12
12465 Warwick Blvd 23606   757-591-4500
Dr. Marcus J. Newsome, supt.   Fax 599-8270
www.sbo.nn.k12.va.us
Achievable Dream MS   200/6-8
726 16th St 23607   757-928-6727
Frederick Cheeks, prin.   Fax 247-1720
Aviation Academy   Vo/Tech
902B Bland Blvd 23602   757-886-2745
John Hutchinson, dir.   Fax 877-5647
Crittenden MS   1,300/6-8
6158 Jefferson Ave 23605   757-591-4900
Stephanie Bourgeois, prin.   Fax 838-8261
Denbigh HS   1,900/9-12
259 Denbigh Blvd 23608   757-886-7700
Michael Evans, prin.   Fax 872-6542
Dozier MS   1,000/6-8
432 Industrial Park Dr 23608   757-888-3300
Carol Lambiotte, prin.   Fax 887-3662
Gildersleeve MS   1,300/6-8
1 Minton Dr 23606   757-591-4862
Susan Tilley, prin.   Fax 596-2059
Heritage HS   1,700/9-12
5800 Marshall Ave 23605   757-928-6100
Timothy Sweeney, prin.   Fax 247-9058
Hines MS   1,300/6-8
561 McLawhorne Dr 23601   757-591-4878
Benjamin A. Hogan, prin.   Fax 591-0119
Huntington MS   900/6-8
3401 Orcutt Ave 23607   757-928-6846
Michele D. Mitchell, prin.   Fax 245-8451
Menchville HS   2,000/9-12
275 Menchville Rd 23602   757-886-7722
Robert Surry, prin.   Fax 875-0648
Passage MS   1,200/6-8
400 Atkinson Way 23608   757-886-7600
Kipp Rogers, prin.   Fax 886-7661
Reservoir MS   600/6-8
15638 Warwick Blvd 23608   757-888-3310
Angela Seiders, prin.   Fax 888-2066
Warwick HS   1,800/9-12
51 Copeland Ln 23601   757-591-4700
Varinda Robinson, prin.   Fax 596-7415
Washington MS   1,000/6-8
3700 Chestnut Ave 23607   757-928-6830
Deborah L. Fields, prin.

Woodside HS   1,900/9-12
13450 Woodside Ln 23608   757-886-7530
Stephanie Hautz, prin.   Fax 877-0480

Apprentice Sch. - Northrop Grumman   Post-Sec.
4101 Washington Ave 23607   757-880-3717
Christopher Newport University   Post-Sec.
1 University Pl 23606   757-594-7000
Denbigh Baptist Christian S   500/PK-12
13010 Mitchell Point Rd 23602   757-249-2654
Wayne Embry, admin.   Fax 249-9480
ECPI College of Technology   Post-Sec.
1001 Omni Blvd Ste 100 23606   757-838-9191
Hampton Roads Academy   500/6-12
739 Academy Ln 23602   757-884-9100
Thomas Harvey, hdmstr.   Fax 884-9137
Kee Business College   Post-Sec.
803 Diligence Dr 23606   757-873-1111
Medical Careers Institute   Post-Sec.
1001 Omni Blvd Ste 200 23606   757-873-2423
Peninsula Catholic HS   300/8-12
600 Harpersville Rd 23601   757-596-7247
Francine Conway, prin.   Fax 591-9718
Riverside School of Health Careers   Post-Sec.
316 Main St 23601   757-240-2200
Tidewater Tech   Post-Sec.
616 Denbigh Blvd 23608   757-874-2121

Nickelsville, Scott, Pop. 440

Scott County SD
Supt. — See Gate City
Twin Springs HS   300/8-12
RR 1 24271   276-479-2185
Michael V. Lane, prin.   Fax 479-3103

Nokesville, Prince William

Prince William County SD
Supt. — See Manassas
Brentsville District HS   1,000/9-12
12109 Aden Rd 20181   703-594-2161
Thomas Gill, prin.   Fax 594-2365

Nora, Dickenson

Dickenson County SD
Supt. — See Clintwood
Ervinton JSHS   200/8-12
RR 1 Box 76 24272   276-835-8604
Rodney Compton, prin.   Fax 835-1242

Norfolk, Norfolk, Pop. 241,727

Norfolk CSD   36,600/PK-12
PO Box 1357 23501   757-628-3830
Dr. Stephen Jones, supt.   Fax 628-3820
www.nps.k12.va.us/
Azalea Gardens MS   900/6-8
7721 Azalea Garden Rd 23518   757-531-3000
Sharon Byrdsong, prin.   Fax 531-3013
Blair MS   1,300/6-8
730 Spotswood Ave 23517   757-628-2400
Sarah Bell-McKown, prin.   Fax 628-2422
Coronado S   Vo/Tech
1025 Widgeon Rd 23513   757-852-4630
Yvette Williams, admin.   Fax 852-4632
Granby HS   2,300/9-12
7101 Granby St 23505   757-451-4110
Edward L. Daughtrey, prin.   Fax 451-4118
Lafayette-Winona MS   1,000/6-8
1701 Alsace Ave 23509   757-628-2477
Clifton L. Harrison, prin.   Fax 628-2486
Lake Taylor HS   1,500/9-12
1384 Kempsville Rd 23502   757-892-3200
Dr. Noah Rogers, prin.   Fax 892-3210
Lake Taylor MS   1,000/6-8
1380 Kempsville Rd 23502   757-892-3230
Inez Blount-Mason, prin.   Fax 892-3240
Madison Career Center   Vo/Tech
3700 Bowdens Ferry Rd 23508   757-628-3403
Dr. Julia Avery Muse, prin.   Fax 628-3406
Maury HS   2,000/9-12
322 Shirley Ave 23517   757-628-3344
Michael J. Caprio, prin.   Fax 628-3359
Norfolk Technical Vocational Center   Vo/Tech
1330 N Military Hwy 23502   757-892-3300
William Davis, prin.   Fax 892-3305
Northside MS   1,200/6-8
8720 Granby St 23503   757-531-3150
Andrea Tottossy, prin.   Fax 531-3144
Norview HS   1,500/9-12
6501 Chesapeake Blvd 23513   757-852-4500
Marjorie Stealey, prin.   Fax 852-4511
Norview MS   1,200/6-8
6325 Sewells Point Rd 23513   757-852-4600
Dr. Joseph Melvin, prin.   Fax 852-4590
Rosemont MS   800/6-8
1330 Branch Rd 23513   757-852-4610
Jeanne Kruger, prin.   Fax 852-4615
Ruffner Academy   1,100/6-8
610 May Ave 23504   757-628-2466
Kenyetta Goshen, prin.   Fax 628-2465
Washington HS   1,400/9-12
1111 Park Ave 23504   757-628-3575
Cynthia J. Watson, prin.   Fax 628-3566

Regional Academic Governors SD
Supt. — See Richmond
Governor's S for the Arts   100/9-12
Old Dominion University 23529   757-451-4711
Leon Hughes, dir.   Fax 451-4715

Calvary Christian S   400/PK-12
2331 E Little Creek Rd 23518   757-480-4400
Olivia Dabney, admin.   Fax 480-5689
De Paul Medical Center   Post-Sec.
150 Kingsley Ln 23505   757-489-5120
Eastern Virginia Medical School   Post-Sec.
PO Box 1980 23501   757-446-5600
Ghent Beauty Academy   Post-Sec.
2811 Lafayette Blvd 23509   757-855-2103
ITT Technical Institute   Post-Sec.
863 Glenrock Rd Ste 100 23502   757-466-1260

Norfolk Academy ... 1,200/1-12
1585 Wesleyan Dr 23502 ... 757-461-6236
Dennis G. Manning, hdmstr. ... Fax 455-3181
Norfolk Christian HS ... 200/9-12
255 Thole St 23505 ... 757-423-5770
Ed White, prin. ... Fax 440-5388
Norfolk Christian MS ... 200/6-8
255 Thole St 23505 ... 757-423-5770
Dr. Jane Duffy, prin. ... Fax 440-5388
Norfolk Collegiate S ... 400/6-12
7336 Granby St 23505 ... 757-480-2885
William King, hdmstr. ... Fax 588-8655
Norfolk Skills Center ... Post-Sec.
922 W 21st St 23517 ... 757-628-3300
Norfolk State University ... Post-Sec.
700 Park Ave 23504 ... 757-823-8600
Old Dominion University ... Post-Sec.
1 Old Dominion Univ 23529 ... 757-683-3000
Tidewater Community College ... Post-Sec.
121 College Pl 23510 ... 757-822-1030
Tidewater Tech ... Post-Sec.
7020 N Military Hwy 23518 ... 757-853-2121
Virginia Wesleyan College ... Post-Sec.
1584 Wesleyan Dr 23502 ... 757-455-3200
Wards Corner Beauty Academy ... Post-Sec.
7525 Tidewater Dr Ste 45 23505 ... 757-583-3300

Norton, Norton, Pop. 3,909
Norton CSD ... 700/PK-12
PO Box 498 24273 ... 276-679-2330
John Sessoms, supt. ... Fax 679-4315
www.nortoncityschools.org/
Burton HS ... 200/8-12
109 11th St 24273 ... 276-679-2554
Scott Keith, prin. ... Fax 679-2664

Nottoway, Nottoway
Nottoway County SD ... 2,700/K-12
10321 E Colonial Hwy 23955 ... 434-645-9596
Dr. Gwen E. Edwards, supt. ... Fax 645-1266
www.nottowayschools.org
Other Schools – See Crewe, Jetersville

Oak Hall, Accomack
Accomack County SD
Supt. — See Accomac
Arcadia HS ... 600/9-12
PO Box 69 23416 ... 757-824-5613
Alma Brim, prin. ... Fax 824-0767
Arcadia MS ... 6-8
PO Box 220 23416 ... 757-824-4862
Eddie Lawrence, prin. ... Fax 824-6618
Badger Technical Center North ... Vo/Tech
PO Box 69 23416 ... 757-824-4659
Alma Brim, prin. ... Fax 824-0767

Oakton, Fairfax, Pop. 24,610

Flint Hill S ... 900/PK-12
3320 Jermantown Rd 22124 ... 703-584-2300
John Thomas, hdmstr. ... Fax 584-2417

Onley, Accomack, Pop. 495
Accomack County SD
Supt. — See Accomac
Badger Technical Center South ... Vo/Tech
26350B Lankford Hwy 23418 ... 757-787-4514
Dennis Custis, prin. ... Fax 787-2194
Nandua HS ... 700/9-12
26350 Lankford Hwy 23418 ... 757-787-4514
Dennis Custis, prin. ... Fax 787-2194
Nandua MS ... 6-8
20330 Warrior Dr 23418 ... 757-787-7037
Jessie Duncill, prin. ... Fax 787-8807

Orange, Orange, Pop. 4,258
Orange County SD ... 4,100/K-12
437 Waugh Blvd 22960 ... 540-661-4550
William Crawford, supt. ... Fax 661-4599
www.ocss-va.org
Orange County HS ... 1,200/9-12
201 Selma Rd 22960 ... 540-661-4300
Gena Keller, prin. ... Fax 661-4299
Prospect Heights MS ... 500/6-8
202 Dailey Dr 22960 ... 540-661-4400
Pete Gretz, prin. ... Fax 661-4399
Other Schools – See Locust Grove

Palmyra, Fluvanna
Fluvanna County SD ... 3,300/K-12
PO Box 419 22963 ... 434-589-8208
Thomas W.D. Smith, supt. ... Fax 589-2248
www.fluco.org
Fluvanna County HS ... 1,000/9-12
3717 Central Plains Rd 22963 ... 434-589-3666
James Barlow, prin. ... Fax 589-3137
Other Schools – See Fork Union

Regional Academic Governors SD
Supt. — See Richmond
Blue Ridge Governor's HS ... 100/9-12
PO Box 419 22963 ... 434-589-8208
Marc Carraway, dir. ... Fax 589-2248

Pearisburg, Giles, Pop. 2,793
Giles County SD ... 2,500/K-12
151 School Rd 24134 ... 540-921-1421
Dr. Terry Arbogast, supt. ... Fax 921-1424
sbo.gilesk12.org/
Giles County Technology Center ... Vo/Tech
PO Box 479 24134 ... 540-921-1166
Forest Fowler, prin. ... Fax 921-3906
Giles HS ... 700/8-12
1825 Wenonah Ave 24134 ... 540-921-1711
Gregory A. Brown, prin. ... Fax 921-9841
Other Schools – See Narrows

Pennington Gap, Lee, Pop. 1,769
Lee County SD
Supt. — See Jonesville
Pennington MS ... 400/5-8
201 Middle School Dr 24277 ... 276-546-1453
Harry Reasor, prin. ... Fax 546-3515

Penn Laird, Rockingham
Rockingham County SD
Supt. — See Harrisonburg
Montevideo MS ... 700/6-8
7648 McGaheysville Rd 22846 ... 540-289-3401
Robert Scott, prin. ... Fax 289-3601
Spotswood HS ... 1,200/9-12
368 Blazer Dr 22846 ... 540-289-3100
Tim Woodward, prin. ... Fax 289-3301

Petersburg, Petersburg, Pop. 33,091
Petersburg CSD ... 5,300/PK-12
255 E South Blvd 23805 ... 804-732-0510
Lloyd Hamlin, supt. ... Fax 732-0514
www.petersburg.k12.va.us/home.asp
Johns MS ... 700/6-8
3101 Homestead Dr 23805 ... 804-862-7020
Paul Britt, prin. ... Fax 862-5434
Peabody MS ... 700/6-8
725 Wesley St 23803 ... 804-862-7075
Dr. Virginia Berry, prin. ... Fax 733-6091
Petersburg HS ... 1,400/9-12
3101 Johnson Rd 23805 ... 804-862-7095
Thomas Whittle, prin. ... Fax 733-5897

Regional Academic Governors SD
Supt. — See Richmond
Appomattox Reg. Governor's S Arts/Tech ... 100/9-12
512 W Washington St 23803 ... 804-722-0200
Dr. James Ruffa, dir. ... Fax 722-0201

Restoration Military Academy ... 50/PK-12
PO Box 2489 23804 ... 804-862-9571
Sonya Brown, dir. ... Fax 530-1019
Richard Bland College ... Post-Sec.
11301 Johnson Rd 23805 ... 804-862-6100
Southside Regional Medical Center ... Post-Sec.
801 S Adams St 23803 ... 804-862-5800
Virginia State University ... Post-Sec.
1 Hayden Dr 23806 ... 804-524-5000

Pilgrims Knob, Buchanan
Buchanan County SD
Supt. — See Grundy
Twin Valley HS ... 200/9-12
PO Box 190 24634 ... 276-259-7818
Janie West, prin. ... Fax 259-6147

Pocahontas, Tazewell, Pop. 420
Tazewell County SD
Supt. — See Tazewell
Pocahontas JSHS ... 200/6-12
PO Box 308 24635 ... 276-945-5988
Chris Stacy, prin. ... Fax 945-2722

Poquoson, Poquoson, Pop. 11,844
Poquoson CSD ... 2,500/K-12
PO Box 2068 23662 ... 757-868-3055
Jonathan Lewis, supt. ... Fax 868-3107
www.sbo.poquoson.k12.va.us
Poquoson HS ... 900/9-12
51 Odd Rd 23662 ... 757-868-7123
Donald Bock, prin. ... Fax 868-3141
Poquoson MS ... 600/6-8
985 Poquoson Ave 23662 ... 757-868-6031
Ken Crum, prin. ... Fax 868-4220

Portsmouth, Portsmouth, Pop. 99,617
Portsmouth CSD ... 18,900/PK-12
PO Box 998 23705 ... 757-393-8751
Dr. David C. Stuckwisch, supt. ... Fax 393-5236
www.pps.k12.va.us
Churchland HS ... 1,800/9-12
4301 Cedar Ln 23703 ... 757-686-2500
Dr. Susan Bechtol, prin. ... Fax 686-2504
Churchland MS ... 700/7-8
4051 River Shore Rd 23703 ... 757-686-2512
Dr. Karen Giacometti, prin. ... Fax 686-2515
Cradock MS ... 400/7-8
21 Alden Ave 23702 ... 757-393-8788
Dr. Eric Fischer, prin. ... Fax 393-5020
Norcom HS ... 1,300/9-12
1801 London Blvd 23704 ... 757-393-5442
Lynn Briley, prin. ... Fax 393-5449
Waters MS ... 500/7-8
600 Roosevelt Blvd 23701 ... 757-558-2813
... Fax 485-2829
Wilson HS ... 1,300/9-12
1401 Elmhurst Ln 23701 ... 757-465-2907
Timothy Johnson, prin. ... Fax 405-1335
EXCEL Campus ... Adult
1401 Elmhurst Ln 23701 ... 757-465-2958
Dr. Rosalynn Sanderlin, prin. ... Fax 465-2913

Alliance Christian S ... 200/PK-12
5809 Portsmouth Blvd 23701 ... 757-488-5552
Duane Renard, admin. ... Fax 488-3192
Hicks Academy of Beauty Culture ... Post-Sec.
904 Loudoun Ave 23707 ... 757-399-2400
Portsmouth Christian S ... 800/PK-12
3214 Elliott Ave 23702 ... 757-393-0725
Bruce Devers, admin. ... Fax 397-7487
Tidewater Community College ... Post-Sec.
State Route 135 23703 ... 757-484-2121

Pound, Wise, Pop. 1,085
Wise County SD
Supt. — See Wise
Pound HS ... 300/9-12
11531 Wildcat Dr 24279 ... 276-796-4432
Greg Mullins, prin. ... Fax 796-5983

Powhatan, Powhatan
Powhatan County SD ... 4,000/K-12
2320 Skaggs Rd 23139 ... 804-598-5700
Margaret Meara, supt. ... Fax 598-5705
www.powhatan.k12.va.us
Powhatan HS ... 1,200/9-12
1800 Judes Ferry Rd 23139 ... 804-598-5710
Richard Cole, prin. ... Fax 598-0036

Powhatan JHS ... 600/7-8
4135 Old Buckingham Rd 23139 ... 804-598-5782
Richard Stewart, prin.
Powhatan Vo-Tech ... Vo/Tech
1800 Judes Ferry Rd 23139 ... 804-598-5700
Kathryn Garrett, prin.

Blessed Sacrament S ... 500/PK-12
2501 Academy Rd 23139 ... 804-598-4211
Dr. Lou Hopewell, pres. ... Fax 598-1053

Prince George, Prince George
Prince George County SD ... 6,100/PK-12
PO Box 400 23875 ... 804-733-2700
Dr. R. Francis Moore, supt. ... Fax 733-2737
pgs.k12.va.us
Clements JHS ... 1,000/8-9
7800 Laurel Spring Rd 23875 ... 804-733-2730
Peter Fisher, prin. ... Fax 733-3783
Prince George SHS ... 1,300/10-12
7801 Laurel Spring Rd 23875 ... 804-733-2720
Dave Clark, prin. ... Fax 861-4530

Pulaski, Pulaski, Pop. 9,173
Pulaski County SD ... 4,300/PK-12
202 N Washington Ave 24301 ... 540-643-0200
Donald E. Stowers Ed.D., supt. ... Fax 980-4147
www.pcva.us
Pulaski MS ... 600/6-8
500 Pico Ter 24301 ... 540-643-0767
Joseph Reed, prin. ... Fax 980-8571
Other Schools – See Dublin

Purcellville, Loudoun, Pop. 4,244
Loudoun County SD
Supt. — See Ashburn
Blue Ridge MS ... 1,200/6-8
551 E A St 20132 ... 540-338-6820
Roberta Griffith, prin. ... Fax 338-6823
Loudoun Valley HS ... 1,600/9-12
340 N Maple Ave 20132 ... 540-338-6800
Susan Ross, prin. ... Fax 338-6815

Patrick Henry College ... Post-Sec.
1 Patrick Henry Cir 20132 ... 540-338-1776

Quicksburg, Shenandoah
Shenandoah County SD
Supt. — See Woodstock
Jackson HS, 150 Stonewall Ln 22847 ... 500/9-12
Karen Whetzel, prin. ... 540-477-2732
North Fork MS ... 400/6-8
1018 Caverns Rd 22847 ... 540-477-2953
David Hinegardner, prin.

Radford, Radford, Pop. 15,006
Radford CSD ... 1,500/PK-12
PO Box 24143 ... 540-731-3647
Randall Wright, supt. ... Fax 731-4419
www.rcps.org/
Dalton IS ... 300/7-8
60 Dalton Dr 24141 ... 540-731-3651
Walter Smith, prin. ... Fax 731-5033
Radford HS ... 500/9-12
50 Dalton Dr 24141 ... 540-731-3649
James Martin, prin. ... Fax 731-4427

Radford University ... Post-Sec.
PO Box 6903 24142 ... 540-831-5000

Reston, Fairfax, Pop. 58,200
Fairfax County SD
Supt. — See Fairfax
Hughes MS ... 900/7-8
11401 Ridge Heights Rd 20191 ... 703-715-3600
Deborah Jackson, prin. ... Fax 715-3697
South Lakes HS ... 1,700/9-12
11400 S Lakes Dr 20191 ... 703-715-4500
Bruce Butler, prin. ... Fax 715-4597

Richlands, Tazewell, Pop. 4,095
Tazewell County SD
Supt. — See Tazewell
Richlands HS ... 800/9-12
249 Front St 24641 ... 276-964-4602
Karen A. Webb, prin. ... Fax 963-1049
Richlands MS ... 700/6-8
293 Front St 24641 ... 276-963-5370
Lynn Lawson, prin. ... Fax 963-0210

Southwest Virginia Community College ... Post-Sec.
PO Box SVCC 24641 ... 276-964-2555

Richmond, Richmond, Pop. 194,729
Chesterfield County SD
Supt. — See Chesterfield
Falling Creek MS ... 1,200/6-8
4724 Hopkins Rd 23234 ... 804-743-3640
Sarah Fraher, prin. ... Fax 743-3644
Manchester MS ... 1,500/6-8
7401 Hull Street Rd 23235 ... 804-674-1385
Carolyn Tisdale, prin. ... Fax 674-1394
Meadowbrook HS ... 1,600/9-12
4901 Cogbill Rd 23234 ... 804-743-3675
C.W. Fletcher, prin. ... Fax 743-3686
Monacan HS ... 1,700/9-12
11501 Smoketree Dr 23236 ... 804-378-2480
David Sovine, prin. ... Fax 378-2485
Providence MS ... 1,100/6-8
900 Starlight Ln 23235 ... 804-674-1355
Harold Saunders, prin. ... Fax 674-1361
Salem Church MS ... 1,200/6-8
9700 Salem Church Rd 23237 ... 804-768-6225
Kenneth Butta, prin. ... Fax 768-6230

Henrico County SD ... 44,700/PK-12
PO Box 23120 23223 ... 804-652-3600
Fred S. Morton, supt. ... Fax 652-3856
www.henrico.k12.va.us
Brookland MS ... 1,400/6-8
9200 Lydell Dr 23228 ... 804-261-5000
Dallas Dance, prin. ... Fax 261-5003

Byrd MS 1,000/6-8
9400 Quioccasin Rd 23238 804-750-2630
Anne Poates, prin. Fax 750-2629
Fairfield MS 1,300/6-8
5121 Nine Mile Rd 23223 804-328-4020
Deborah Jones, prin. Fax 328-4031
Freeman HS 1,600/9-12
8701 Three Chopt Rd 23229 804-673-3700
Dr. Edward Pruden, prin. Fax 673-3713
Godwin HS 2,000/9-12
2101 Pump Rd 23238 804-750-2600
Terry G. Moore, prin. Fax 750-2611
Henrico HS 1,500/9-12
302 Azalea Ave 23227 804-228-2700
William H. Parker, prin. Fax 228-2715
Hermitage HS 2,100/9-12
8301 Hungary Spring Rd 23228 804-756-3000
Robert B. Tyson, prin. Fax 672-1501
Hermitage Technical Center Vo/Tech
8301 Hungary Spring Rd 23228 804-756-3020
Victor Sorrell, prin. Fax 756-3025
Moody MS 1,000/6-8
7800 Woodman Rd 23228 804-261-5015
E. Earl Binns, prin. Fax 261-5024
Mount Vernon MS 100/6-8
7850 Carousel Ln 23294 804-527-4660
Ronald Rodriguez, prin. Fax 527-4665
Pocahontas MS 900/6-8
12000 Three Chopt Ln 23233 804-364-0830
Raymond E. Honeycutt, prin.
Rolfe MS 1,400/6-8
6901 Messer Rd 23231 804-226-8730
A. Katrise Perera, prin. Fax 226-8739
Tuckahoe MS 1,200/6-8
9000 Three Chopt Rd 23229 804-673-3720
Dr. Kurt E. Hulett, prin. Fax 673-3731
Tucker HS 1,600/9-12
2910 N Parham Rd 23294 804-527-4600
Gwen E. Miller, prin. Fax 527-4618
Varina HS 1,700/9-12
7053 Messer Rd 23231 804-226-8700
Tracie Omohundro, prin. Fax 226-8706
Wilder MS 900/6-8
6900 Wilkinson Rd 23227 804-515-1100
Christie Forrest, prin. Fax 515-1110
Other Schools – See Glen Allen, Highland Springs

Regional Academic Governors SD 900/9-12
PO Box 2120 23218 804-225-2755
Governor's S for Gov & Intl Studies 100/9-12
1000 N Lombardy St 23220 804-354-6800
Doug Hunt, dir. Fax 354-6939
Other Schools – See Abingdon, Clifton Forge, Collinsville, Dublin, Fishersville, Fredericksburg, Hampton, Keysville, Mount Jackson, Norfolk, Palmyra, Petersburg, Roanoke, Tappahannock

Richmond CSD 23,700/PK-12
301 N 9th St 23219 804-780-7700
Deborah Jewell-Sherman Ed.D., supt. Fax 780-4122
www.richmond.k12.va.us
Armstrong HS 700/9-12
2300 Cool Ln 23223 804-780-4449
Carl Vaughan, prin. Fax 780-4538
Binford MS 500/6-8
1701 Floyd Ave 23220 804-780-6231
Brenda B. Walton, prin. Fax 780-6057
Boushall MS 800/6-8
3400 Hopkins Rd 23234 804-780-5016
A. Parke Land, prin. Fax 780-5396
Brown MS 700/6-8
6300 Jahnke Rd 23225 804-319-3013
Colleen Boyd, prin. Fax 319-3009
Chandler MS 600/6-8
201 E Brookland Park Blvd 23222 804-780-4332
Melvin L. Rose, prin. Fax 780-4423
Elkhardt MS 500/6-8
6300 Hull Street Rd 23224 804-745-3600
Amanda Johnson, prin. Fax 674-5518
Franklin Military Academy 200/9-12
701 N 37th St 23223 804-780-8526
Sterling Stokes, prin. Fax 780-8054
Henderson MS 600/6-8
4319 Old Brook Rd 23227 804-780-8288
Dionne Ward, prin. Fax 228-5353
Hill MS 500/6-8
3400 Patterson Ave 23221 804-780-6107
Michael Kight, prin. Fax 780-8754
Huguenot HS 1,200/9-12
7945 Forest Hill Ave 23225 804-320-7967
J. Austin Brown, prin. Fax 560-9103
Jefferson HS 700/9-12
4100 W Grace St 23230 804-780-6028
Barbara Ulschmid, prin. Fax 780-6295
King MS 500/6-8
1000 Mosby St 23223 804-780-8011
Aaron L. Dixon, prin. Fax 780-5590
Marshall HS 900/9-12
4225 Old Brook Rd 23227 804-780-6052
Beverly Britt, prin. Fax 780-4991
Open HS 200/9-12
600 S Pine St 23220 804-780-4661
Priscilla Green, prin. Fax 780-4865
Richmond Community HS 200/9-12
5800 Patterson Ave 23226 804-285-1015
Howard Hopkins Ed.D., prin. Fax 282-1303
Richmond Technical Center North Vo/Tech
2015 Seddon Way 23230 804-780-6272
N. Mauricee Holmes, prin. Fax 254-2915
Richmond Technical Center South Vo/Tech
2020 Westwood Ave 23230 804-780-6237
N. Mauricee Holmes, prin. Fax 780-6061
Thompson MS 700/6-8
7825 Forest Hill Ave 23225 804-272-7554
Thomas H. Beatty, prin. Fax 560-5115
Wythe HS 1,100/9-12
4314 Crutchfield St 23225 804-780-5037
Earl M. Pappy, prin. Fax 780-5043
Adult Career Development Center Adult
119 W Leigh St 23220 804-780-4388
Martha Suber, prin. Fax 780-8184

Banner Christian S 100/K-12
PO Box 74010 23236 804-276-5200
Patricia Burkett, hdmstr. Fax 276-7620
Baptist Theological Seminary Post-Sec.
3400 Brook Rd 23227 888-345-2877
Benedictine HS 300/9-12
304 N Sheppard St 23221 804-342-1300
John McGinty, hdmstr. Fax 355-2407
Beta Tech Post-Sec.
7914 Midlothian Tpke 23235 804-330-0111
Beta Tech West Post-Sec.
7001 W Broad St 23294 804-672-2300
Braxton School Post-Sec.
3600 W Broad St Ste 190 23230 804-353-4458
Bryant & Stratton College Post-Sec.
8141 Hull Street Rd 23235 804-745-2444
Buford Academy Post-Sec.
PO Box 26665 23261
Collegiate S 1,500/K-12
103 N Mooreland Rd 23229 804-740-7077
Keith Evans, hdmstr. Fax 741-9797
Descending Dove Christian S 100/K-12
1941 Celia Cres 23236 804-901-2401
Brenda Robertson, dir. Fax 276-6522
ECPI Technical College Post-Sec.
800 Moorefield Park Dr 23236 804-330-5533
Grove Avenue Baptist Christian S 200/PK-12
8701 Ridge Rd 23229 804-741-2860
Clay Fogler, admin. Fax 754-8534
ITT Technical Institute Post-Sec.
300 Gateway Centre Pkwy 23235 804-330-4992
J. Sargeant Reynolds Community College Post-Sec.
PO Box 85622 23285 804-371-3000
Medical Careers Institute Post-Sec.
800 Moorefield Park Dr #302 23236 804-521-0400
New Community S 100/6-12
4211 Hermitage Rd 23227 804-266-2494
Julia Ann Greenwood, hdmstr. Fax 264-3281
Richmond Adventist Academy 100/K-12
3809 Patterson Ave 23221 804-353-0036
Fax 358-8797
RSHT Training Center Post-Sec.
1601 Willow Lawn Dr Ste 320 23230 804-288-1000
Rudlin Torah Academy 100/K-12
12285 Patterson Ave 23238 804-784-9050
Rabbi Hal Klestzick, prin. Fax 784-9005
St. Catherine's S 800/PK-12
6001 Grove Ave 23226 804-288-2804
Auguste Bannard, prin. Fax 285-8169
St. Christopher's S 900/PK-12
711 Saint Christophers Rd 23226 804-282-3185
Charles M. Stillwell, hdmstr. Fax 285-3914
St. Gertrude HS 300/9-12
3215 Stuart Ave 23221 804-358-9114
Sr. Charlotte Lange, prin. Fax 355-5682
St. Mary's Hospital Post-Sec.
5801 Bremo Rd 23226 804-285-2011
Steward S 600/K-12
11600 Gayton Rd 23238 804-740-3394
Kenneth H. Seward, prin. Fax 740-1464
Trinity Episcopal HS 300/8-12
3850 Pittaway Dr 23235 804-272-5864
Thomas Aycock, hdmstr. Fax 323-1335
Union Theological Sem. & Presbyterian Post-Sec.
3401 Brook Rd 23227 800-229-2990
University of Richmond 23173 Post-Sec.
804-289-8000
Veritas Classical Christian S 200/K-10
6627B Jahnke Rd 23225 804-272-9517
Dean Luckenbaugh, hdmstr. Fax 272-9518
Victory Christian Academy 200/K-12
8491 Chamberlayne Rd 23227 804-262-8256
Cynthia Trotman, prin. Fax 266-7127
Virginia Commonwealth University Post-Sec.
901 W Franklin St 23284 804-828-0100
Virginia Home for Boys Post-Sec.
8716 W Broad St 23294
Virginia School of Technology Post-Sec.
9210 Arboretum Pkwy Ste 100 23236 804-323-1020
Virginia Union University Post-Sec.
1500 N Lombardy St 23220 804-257-5600
Yeshiva of Virginia 100/9-12
6801 Patterson Ave 23226 804-288-7610
Rabbi Chaim Chait, prin. Fax 784-9005

Ridgeway, Henry, Pop. 807
Henry County SD
Supt. — See Collinsville
Magna Vista HS 800/9-12
701 Magna Vista School Rd 24148 276-956-3147
Eugene Kotulka, prin. Fax 956-1401

Riner, Montgomery
Montgomery County SD
Supt. — See Christiansburg
Auburn HS 400/9-12
4163 Riner Rd 24149 540-382-5160
Carl Pauli, prin. Fax 381-6110
Auburn MS 300/6-8
4069 Riner Rd 24149 540-382-5165
Leonard Session, prin. Fax 381-6562

Ringgold, Pittsylvania
Pittsylvania County SD
Supt. — See Chatham
Dan River HS 600/9-12
100 Dan River Wildcat Cir 24586 434-822-7081
Martin E. Ringstaff, prin.
Dan River MS 600/6-8
5875 Kentuck Rd 24586 434-822-6027
D. Edward Raper, prin. Fax 822-6548

Roanoke, Roanoke, Pop. 92,863
Regional Academic Governors SD
Supt. — See Richmond
Roanoke Valley Governor's S Science/Tech 100/9-12
2104 Grandin Rd SW 24015 540-853-2116
Dr. Evan Glazer, dir. Fax 853-1056

Roanoke CSD 13,300/PK-12
PO Box 13145 24031 540-853-2381
Marvin Thompson, supt. Fax 853-2951
www.rcps.info
Addison Aerospace Magnet MS 500/6-8
1220 5th St NW 24016 540-853-2681
Anastasia Slack, prin. Fax 853-2842
Breckinridge MS 500/6-8
3901 Williamson Rd NW 24012 540-853-2251
Asia Jones, prin. Fax 853-6505
Fleming HS 1,400/9-12
3649 Ferncliff Ave NW 24017 540-853-2781
Susan Willis, prin. Fax 563-1984
Henry HS 1,800/9-12
2102 Grandin Rd SW 24015 540-853-2255
Gary Leah, prin. Fax 853-1575
Jackson MS 500/6-8
1004 Montrose Ave SE 24013 540-853-6040
Stephanie Hogan, prin. Fax 853-6027
Madison MS 500/6-8
1160 Overland Rd SW 24015 540-853-2351
Debra Dietrich, prin. Fax 853-1050
Ruffner MS 600/6-8
3601 Ferncliff Ave NW 24017 540-853-2605
Catherine Lassiter, prin. Fax 853-1350
Wilson MS 600/6-8
1813 Carter Rd SW 24015 540-853-2358
Connie Ratcliffe, prin. Fax 853-2004

Roanoke County SD 14,400/K-12
5937 Cove Rd 24019 540-562-3700
Dr. Lorraine Lange, supt. Fax 562-3994
www.rcs.k12.va.us
Cave Spring HS 800/9-12
3712 Chaparral Dr 24018 540-772-7550
Martha Cobble, prin. Fax 772-2107
Cave Spring MS 600/6-8
4880 Brambleton Ave 24018 540-772-7560
Steven Boyer, prin. Fax 772-2195
Hidden Valley HS 1,000/9-12
5000 Titan Trl 24018 540-776-7320
Rhonda Stegall, prin. Fax 776-7322
Hidden Valley MS 800/6-8
4902 Hidden Valley School 24018 540-772-7570
Ken Nicely, prin. Fax 772-7519
Northside HS 1,000/9-12
6758 Northside High School 24019 540-561-8155
Frank Dent, prin. Fax 561-8160
Northside MS 800/6-8
6810 Northside High School 24019 540-561-8145
Fax 561-8152
Other Schools – See Salem, Vinton

BarPalma Beauty Careers Academy Post-Sec.
3535 Franklin Rd SW Ste D 24014 540-343-0153
Carilion Health Systems Post-Sec.
PO Box 13727 24036 540-981-7347
ECPI Technical College Post-Sec.
5234 Airport Rd NW 24012 540-563-8080
Faith Christian S 200/K-12
4873 Brambleton Ave Ste A 24018 540-769-5200
Samuel P. Cox, admin. Fax 769-6030
Hollins University Post-Sec.
PO Box 9707 24020 540-362-6000
Jefferson College of Health Sciences Post-Sec.
PO Box 13186 24031 540-985-8483
National College of Business & Tech. Post-Sec.
PO Box 6400 24017 540-986-1800
North Cross S 500/PK-12
4254 Colonial Ave 24018 540-989-6641
Paul Stellato, hdmstr. Fax 989-7299
Roanoke Catholic S 600/PK-12
621 N Jefferson St 24016 540-982-3532
Ray Correia, pres. Fax 345-0785
Roanoke Valley Christian S 300/K-12
PO Box 7010 24019 540-366-2432
Rick Brown, admin. Fax 366-9719
TAP Center for Employment Training Post-Sec.
108 N Jefferson St Ste 303 24016 540-767-6222
Virginia Western Community College Post-Sec.
PO Box 14007 24038 540-857-7311

Rocky Gap, Bland
Bland County SD
Supt. — See Bastian
Rocky Gap HS 200/8-12
PO Box 9 24366 276-928-1100
Robert Morehead, prin. Fax 928-1988

Rocky Mount, Franklin, Pop. 4,542
Franklin County SD 7,100/PK-12
25 Bernard Rd 24151 540-483-5138
Larry E. Hixson, supt. Fax 483-5806
www.frco.k12.va.us
Franklin County HS 2,100/9-12
700 Tanyard Rd 24151 540-483-0221
William Gibson, prin. Fax 483-5306
Franklin MS West 900/7-8
225 Middle School Rd 24151 540-483-5105
Derrick Scarborough, prin. Fax 483-5501
Gereau CATCE Vo/Tech
150 Technology Dr 24151 540-483-5446
Kevin Bezy, prin. Fax 483-5788

Christian Heritage Academy 200/PK-12
625 Glennwood Dr 24151 540-483-5855
Charlotte Hamilton, admin. Fax 483-9355

Rural Retreat, Wythe, Pop. 1,339
Wythe County SD
Supt. — See Wytheville
Rural Retreat HS 400/9-12
321 E Buck Ave 24368 276-686-4143
Michael Neal, prin. Fax 686-4601
Rural Retreat MS 300/6-8
321 E Buck Ave 24368 276-686-5200
G. Wesley Poole, prin. Fax 686-4944

Rustburg, Campbell
Campbell County SD 8,700/K-12
PO Box 99 24588 434-332-3458
Dr. George Nolley, supt. Fax 528-1655
www.campbell.k12.va.us
Campbell Technical Center Vo/Tech
194 Dennis Riddle Dr 24588 434-821-6213
Robert Ashwell, prin. Fax 821-2808
Rustburg HS 800/9-12
PO Box 830 24588 434-332-5171
Denton Sisk, prin. Fax 332-1187
Rustburg MS 900/5-8
PO Box 130 24588 434-332-5141
Haywood McCrickard, prin. Fax 332-2058
Other Schools – See Altavista, Lynchburg, Naruna

Clearview Christian S 100/PK-12
PO Box 386 24588 434-845-0637
Terry Cook, admin. Fax 845-4778

Ruther Glen, Caroline

Carmel Christian S 100/PK-12
PO Box 605 22546 804-448-3288
Harold Stills, admin. Fax 448-3146

Saint George, Greene

Blue Ridge S 200/9-12
Bacon Hollow Rd, 434-985-2811
David Bouton, hdmstr. Fax 985-7215

Saint Paul, Wise, Pop. 969
Wise County SD
Supt. — See Wise
Saint Paul HS 200/8-12
PO Box 976 24283 276-762-5221
Tom Fletcher, prin. Fax 762-5580

Salem, Salem, Pop. 24,603
Roanoke County SD
Supt. — See Roanoke
Burton Technical Center Vo/Tech
1760 Roanoke Blvd 24153 540-857-5000
Andrew McClung, prin. Fax 857-5061
Glenvar HS 500/9-12
4549 Malus Dr 24153 540-387-6536
Curtis Hicks, prin. Fax 387-6347
Glenvar MS 400/6-8
4555 Malus Dr 24153 540-387-6322
Juliette Meyers, prin. Fax 387-6283

Salem CSD 3,900/PK-12
510 S College Ave 24153 540-389-0130
Dr. N. Wayne Tripp, supt. Fax 389-4135
www.salem.k12.va.us
Lewis MS 1,000/6-8
616 S College Ave 24153 540-387-2513
Jerome Campbell, prin. Fax 389-8914
Salem HS 1,200/9-12
400 Spartan Dr 24153 540-387-2437
Caleb Hall, prin. Fax 387-2543

National College of Business & Tech. Post-Sec.
1813 E Main St 24153 540-986-1800
Roanoke College Post-Sec.
221 College Ln 24153 540-375-2500

Saltville, Smyth, Pop. 2,268
Smyth County SD
Supt. — See Marion
Northwood HS 300/9-12
PO Box Y 24370 276-496-7751
Steven Johnston, prin. Fax 496-3216
Northwood MS 300/6-8
156 Long Hollow Rd 24370 276-624-3341
Jeffrey Comer, prin. Fax 624-3535

Saluda, Middlesex
Middlesex County SD 1,300/PK-12
PO Box 205 23149 804-758-2277
Dr. Oliver Spencer, supt. Fax 758-3727
www.mcps.k12.va.us/
Middlesex HS 400/9-12
PO Box 206 23149 804-758-2132
Chris Valdrighi, prin. Fax 758-2786
Other Schools – See Locust Hill

Rappahannock Community College Post-Sec.
12745 College Dr 23149 804-758-6700

Shawsville, Montgomery, Pop. 1,260
Montgomery County SD
Supt. — See Christiansburg
Shawsville MS 300/6-8
PO Box 7 24162 540-268-2262
Rebecca Kahila, prin. Fax 268-1868

Shenandoah, Page, Pop. 1,874
Page County SD
Supt. — See Luray
Page County HS 700/8-12
5550 US Highway 340 22849 540-652-8712
Dr. Morgan Phenix, prin.

Skipwith, Mecklenburg
Mecklenburg County SD
Supt. — See Boydton
Bluestone HS 700/9-12
6825 Skipwith Rd 23968 434-372-5177
Lindell Palmer, prin. Fax 372-5217
Bluestone MS 600/6-8
250 Middle School Rd 23968 434-372-3266
Carole Nelson, prin. Fax 372-3362

Smithfield, Isle of Wight, Pop. 6,703
Isle of Wight County SD
Supt. — See Isle of Wight
Smithfield HS 1,100/9-12
14171 Turner Dr 23430 757-357-3108
Rebecca Mercer, prin. Fax 357-7253
Smithfield MS 600/7-8
14175 Turner Dr 23430 757-365-4100
Dr. Garett Smith, prin. Fax 365-4222

James River Christian Academy 200/PK-12
14353 Benns Church Blvd 23430 757-357-3707
Ray Owens, admin. Fax 365-4195

South Boston, Halifax, Pop. 8,222
Halifax County SD
Supt. — See Halifax
Halifax HS 1,600/9-12
PO Box 310 24592 434-572-4977
Albert Randolph, prin. Fax 572-2675
Halifax MS 1,000/7-8
1011 Middle School Cir 24592 434-572-4100
Gail Bosiger, prin. Fax 572-4106

South Hill, Mecklenburg, Pop. 4,628
Mecklenburg County SD
Supt. — See Boydton
Park View HS 700/9-12
205 Park View Cir 23970 434-447-3435
George Taylor, prin. Fax 447-7876
Park View MS 600/6-8
365 Dockery Rd 23970 434-447-3761
James Powell, prin. Fax 447-4920

South Riding, See Fairfax
Loudoun County SD
Supt. — See Ashburn
Freedom HS 9-12
25450 Riding Center Dr 20152 703-444-8080
Christine M. Forester, prin.

Spotsylvania, Spotsylvania
Spotsylvania County SD
Supt. — See Fredericksburg
Courtland HS 1,500/9-12
6701 Smith Station Rd 22553 540-898-4445
Michael Bedwell, prin. Fax 898-4458
Ni River MS 800/6-8
11632 Catharpin Rd 22553 540-785-3990
Stephen Covert, prin. Fax 785-0658
Post Oak MS 6-8
6959 Courthouse Rd 22553 540-582-7517
Chester Mummau, prin. Fax 582-7510
Spotsylvania HS 1,500/9-12
6975 Courthouse Rd 22553 540-582-3882
David Eshelman, prin. Fax 582-3890
Spotsylvania MS 900/6-8
8801 Courthouse Rd 22553 540-582-6341
Mark Beckett, prin. Fax 582-3207
Spotsylvania Vocational Ctr Vo/Tech
6713 Smith Station Rd 22553 540-898-2655
Lee Browning, prin. Fax 891-1784
Thornburg MS 800/6-8
6929 N Roxbury Mill Rd 22553 540-582-7600
Kirk Tower, prin. Fax 582-7606

Springfield, Fairfax, Pop. 23,706
Fairfax County SD
Supt. — See Fairfax
Irving MS 1,200/7-8
8100 Old Keene Mill Rd 22152 703-912-4500
Danny Little, prin. Fax 912-4597
Key MS 1,000/7-8
6402 Franconia Rd 22150 703-313-3900
Sharon Eisenberg, prin. Fax 313-3997
Lee HS 2,100/9-12
6540 Franconia Rd 22150 703-924-8300
Donald Thurston, prin. Fax 924-8397
West Springfield HS 2,300/9-12
6100 Rolling Rd 22152 703-913-3800
David Smith, prin. Fax 913-3897

Accotink Academy Post-Sec.
8519 Tuttle Rd 22152
Word of Life Christian Academy 400/PK-12
5225 Backlick Rd 22151 703-354-4222
Michael Burroughs, admin. Fax 750-1306

Stafford, Stafford
Stafford County SD 24,700/PK-12
31 Stafford Ave 22554 540-658-6000
Jean Murray Ed.D., supt. Fax 658-5963
www.pen.k12.va.us/Div/Stafford/
Brooke Point HS 1,900/9-12
1700 Courthouse Rd 22554 540-658-6080
Cynthia Holder, prin. Fax 658-6072
Colonial Forge HS 1,800/9-12
550 Courthouse Rd 22554 540-658-6115
Dr. Lisa Martin, prin. Fax 658-6120
Mountain View HS 9-12
2135 Mountain View Rd, 540-658-6840
James Stemple, prin. Fax 658-6860
North Stafford HS 1,900/9-12
839 Garrisonville Rd 22554 540-658-6150
Thomas Nichols, prin. Fax 658-6158
Poole MS 1,100/6-8
800 Eustace Rd 22554 540-658-6190
Mary Grace McGraw, prin. Fax 658-6176
Stafford MS 1,200/6-8
101 Spartan Dr 22554 540-658-6210
Steven Butters, prin. Fax 658-6204
Thompson MS 1,100/6-8
75 Walpole St 22554 540-658-6420
Gwendolyn Payne, prin. Fax 658-6430
Wright MS 800/6-8
100 Wood Dr, 540-658-6240
William Boatwright, prin. Fax 658-6238
Other Schools – See Falmouth

Grace Preparatory S 100/6-12
200 Onville Rd, 540-657-4500
Kristine Lisech, admin.

Stanardsville, Greene, Pop. 494
Greene County SD 2,700/PK-12
PO Box 1140 22973 434-985-5254
Raymond Dingledine, supt. Fax 985-4686
www.greenecountyschools.com
Greene County Technical Education Center Vo/Tech
PO Box 510 22973 434-985-5239
Harry Daniel, prin. Fax 985-2071
Monroe HS 800/9-12
254 Monroe Dr 22973 434-985-5273
Mike Jamerson, prin. Fax 985-1461
Monroe MS 700/6-8
PO Box 1080 22973 434-985-5240
Deborah DuPell, prin. Fax 985-1359

Staunton, Staunton, Pop. 23,848
Augusta County SD
Supt. — See Fishersville
Beverley Manor MS 800/6-8
58 Cedar Green Rd 24401 540-886-5806
Nancy Miller, prin. Fax 886-4019
Riverheads HS 500/9-12
19 Howardsville Rd 24401 540-337-1921
P. Steve Barnett, prin. Fax 337-0258

Staunton CSD 2,800/K-12
PO Box 900 24402 540-332-3920
Harry Lunsford, supt. Fax 332-3924
www.staunton.k12.va.us
Lee HS, 1200 N Coalter St 24401 800/9-12
Dr. John Fahey, prin. 540-332-3926
Shelburne MS 600/6-8
300 Grubert Ave 24401 540-332-3930
Barbara L. Smallwood, prin.

Grace Christian HS 100/8-12
19 S Market St 24401 540-886-9109
Debbie Harper, admin. Fax 886-5958
Guardian Angel Academy 100/K-12
300 Churchville Ave 24401 540-887-5900
Mary Thompson, prin. Fax 887-5905
Mary Baldwin College 24401 Post-Sec.
800-468-2262
Richards Jr Academy 100/K-10
414 Sterling St 24401 540-886-4984
Steve Wilson, prin. Fax 886-7087
Staunton School of Cosmetology Post-Sec.
PO Box 2385 24402 540-885-0808
Stuart Hall 200/6-12
PO Box 210 24402 540-885-0356
Mark Eastham, hdmstr. Fax 886-2275
Virginia School for the Deaf and Blind Post-Sec.
24401

Stephens City, Frederick, Pop. 1,195
Frederick County SD
Supt. — See Winchester
Aylor MS 1,000/6-8
901 Aylor Rd 22655 540-869-3736
Donald Williams, prin. Fax 867-2756
Sherando HS 1,300/9-12
185 Warrior Dr 22655 540-869-0060
John Nelson, prin. Fax 869-5183

Shenandoah Valley Christian Academy 300/PK-12
PO Box 1360 22655 540-869-4600
Robert Quinn, supt. Fax 869-4662

Sterling, Loudoun, Pop. 20,512
Loudoun County SD
Supt. — See Ashburn
Dominion HS 1,000/9-12
21326 Augusta Dr 20164 703-444-8025
Dr. W. John Brewer, prin.
Park View HS 1,400/9-12
400 W Laurel Ave 20164 703-444-7500
Dr. Virginia Minshew, prin. Fax 444-7521
Potomac Falls HS 1,400/9-12
46400 Algonkian Pkwy 20165 703-444-7542
David Spage, prin. Fax 444-7526
River Bend MS 1,100/6-8
46240 Algonkian Pkwy 20165 703-444-7574
Bennett P. Lacy, prin. Fax 444-7578
Seneca Ridge MS 900/6-8
98 Seneca Ridge Dr 20164 703-444-7480
Mark McDermott, prin. Fax 444-7567
Sterling MS 1,000/6-8
201 W Holly Ave 20164 703-444-7490
Michael Williams, prin. Fax 444-7492

Faith Christian S 200/PK-12
21393 Potomac View Rd # 100 20164 703-430-0499
Randy Luckette, hdmstr. Fax 430-4235
Northern Virginia Community College Post-Sec.
1000 Harry Flood Byrd Hwy 20164 703-323-3000

Strasburg, Shenandoah, Pop. 4,153
Shenandoah County SD
Supt. — See Woodstock
Signal Knob MS 500/6-8
687 Sandy Hook Rd 22657 540-465-3422
Charles Everett, prin.
Strasburg HS, 250 Ram Dr 22657 600/9-12
Mike Dorman, prin. 540-465-5195

Stuart, Patrick, Pop. 930
Patrick County SD 2,600/K-12
PO Box 346 24171 276-694-3163
Judy Lacks, supt. Fax 694-3170
www.patrick-county.org
Patrick County HS 1,000/8-12
215 Cougar Ln 24171 276-694-7137
E.G. Bradshaw, prin. Fax 694-6997

Stuarts Draft, Augusta, Pop. 5,087
Augusta County SD
Supt. — See Fishersville
Stuarts Draft HS 800/9-12
1028 Augusta Farms Rd 24477 540-946-7600
T. Nate Collins, prin. Fax 946-7605

Stuarts Draft MS | 900/6-8
1088 Augusta Farms Rd 24477 | 540-946-7611
Betsy Agee, prin. | Fax 946-7613

Suffolk, Suffolk, Pop. 73,515
Jointly Operated Vo Tech SD
Supt. — None
Pruden Center for Industry/Technology | Vo/Tech
4169 Pruden Blvd 23434 | 757-539-7407
Peggy Wade, prin.

Suffolk CSD | 14,900/PK-12
PO Box 1549 23439 | 757-925-6750
Dr. Milton Liverman, supt. | Fax 925-6751
www.sps.k12.va.us
Forest Glen MS | 500/6-8
200 Forest Glen Dr 23434 | 757-925-5550
Melvin Bradshaw, prin. | Fax 925-5557
Kennedy MS | 800/6-8
2325 E Washington St 23434 | 757-925-5560
Vivian Covington, prin. | Fax 925-5594
King's Fork HS | 1,800/9-12
351 Kings Fork Rd 23434 | 757-923-5240
Daniel Ward, prin.
King's Fork MS | 1,100/6-8
350 Kings Fork Rd 23434 | 757-925-5750
Talmadge Darden, prin. | Fax 925-5754
Lakeland HS | 2,000/9-12
214 Kenyon Rd 23434 | 757-925-5530
Thomas Whitley, prin. | Fax 925-5599
Nansemond River HS | 1,700/9-12
3301 Nansemond Pkwy 23434 | 757-538-5420
T. McLemore, prin. | Fax 538-5430
Yeates MS | 800/6-8
4901 Bennetts Pasture Rd 23435 | 757-538-5400
Daniel O'Leary, prin. | Fax 538-5416

Nansemond-Suffolk Academy | 1,000/PK-12
3373 Pruden Blvd 23434 | 757-539-8789
Shane Foster, hdmstr. | Fax 934-8363
Suffolk Beauty Academy | Post-Sec.
860 Portsmouth Blvd 23434 | 757-934-0656

Surry, Surry, Pop. 260
Surry County SD | 1,100/PK-12
PO Box 317 23883 | 757-294-5229
Dr. Marion H. Wilkins, supt. | Fax 294-5263
www.surryschools.net/
Other Schools – See Dendron

Sussex, Sussex
Sussex County SD | 1,400/K-12
PO Box 1368 23884 | 434-246-1099
Charles H. Harris, supt. | Fax 246-8214
www.sussex.k12.va.us/
Sussex Central HS | 400/9-12
PO Box 1307 23884 | 434-246-6051
Gurnery Ramsey, prin.
Sussex Central MS | 400/6-8
PO Box 1387 23884 | 434-246-2251
Nancy Coner, prin.

Sweet Briar, Amherst

Sweet Briar College 24595 | Post-Sec.
| 434-381-6100

Swoope, Augusta
Augusta County SD
Supt. — See Fishersville
Buffalo Gap HS | 600/9-12
1800 Buffalo Gap Hwy 24479 | 540-337-6021
William Deardorff, prin. | Fax 337-6236

Tangier, Accomack, Pop. 692
Accomack County SD
Supt. — See Accomac
Tangier S | 100/K-12
PO Box 245 23440 | 757-891-2234
Nina Pruitt, prin. | Fax 891-2572

Tappahannock, Essex, Pop. 2,155
Essex County SD | 1,700/PK-12
PO Box 756 22560 | 804-443-4366
Thomas M. Saville, supt. | Fax 443-4498
www.essex.k12.va.us
Essex HS | 500/9-12
PO Box 1006 22560 | 804-443-4301
Lawrence Lenz, prin. | Fax 443-4272
Essex MS | 500/5-8
PO Box 609 22560 | 804-443-3040
Wanda Wallace-Durham, prin. | Fax 445-1079

Regional Academic Governors SD
Supt. — See Richmond
Chesapeake Bay Governor's S | 11-12
PO Box 756 22560 | 804-443-0267
Patricia Griffin, dir. | Fax 443-4498

St. Margaret's S | 200/8-12
PO Box 158 22560 | 804-443-3357
Margaret Broad, hdmstr. | Fax 443-1832

Tazewell, Tazewell, Pop. 4,115
Tazewell County SD | 7,000/PK-12
PO Box 927 24651 | 276-988-5511
Dr. Brenda B. Lawson, supt. | Fax 988-6765
tazewell.k12.va.us
Tazewell County Career Technical Center | Vo/Tech
114 Maplewood Dr 24651 | 276-988-2529
Dr. Barry Yost, prin. | Fax 988-5494
Tazewell HS | 600/9-12
627 E Fincastle St 24651 | 276-988-6502
B. Keith Hovis, prin. | Fax 988-3263
Tazewell MS | 500/6-8
100 Bull Dog Ave 24651 | 276-988-6513
Kristina Welch, prin. | Fax 988-6514
Other Schools – See Bluefield, Pocahontas, Richlands

Toano, James City
Williamsburg-James City County SD
Supt. — See Williamsburg

Toano MS | 800/6-8
7817 Richmond Rd 23168 | 757-566-4251
Lynda Poller, prin. | Fax 566-3006

Triangle, Prince William, Pop. 4,740
Prince William County SD
Supt. — See Manassas
Graham Park MS | 1,300/6-8
3613 Graham Park Rd 22172 | 703-221-2118
Gary Anderson, prin. | Fax 221-1079

Calvary Christian S | 200/PK-12
4345 Inn St 22172 | 703-221-2016
John Wallace, admin. | Fax 221-7698

Victoria, Lunenburg, Pop. 1,783
Lunenburg County SD
Supt. — See Kenbridge
Central HS | 600/9-12
131 K V Rd 23974 | 434-696-2137
C. B. Haskins, prin. | Fax 696-1322
Lunenburg MS | 400/6-8
583 Tomlinson Rd 23974 | 434-696-2161
Nancy Chappell, prin. | Fax 696-2162

Vienna, Fairfax, Pop. 14,868
Fairfax County SD
Supt. — See Fairfax
Kilmer MS | 1,000/7-8
8100 Wolftrap Rd 22182 | 703-846-8800
Deborah Hernandez, prin. | Fax 846-8897
Madison HS | 1,700/9-12
2500 James Madison Dr 22181 | 703-319-2300
Mark Merrell, prin. | Fax 319-2397
Oakton HS | 2,300/9-12
2900 Sutton Rd 22181 | 703-319-2700
John Banbury, prin. | Fax 319-2797
Thoreau MS | 800/7-8
2505 Cedar Ln 22180 | 703-846-8000
Mark Greenfelder, prin. | Fax 846-8097

Fairfax Christian S | 300/PK-12
1624 Hunter Mill Rd 22182 | 703-759-5100
Jo Thoburn, admin. | Fax 759-2143
Gibbs College - Northern Virginia | Post-Sec.
1980 Gallows Rd 22182 | 703-556-8888

Vinton, Roanoke, Pop. 7,749
Roanoke County SD
Supt. — See Roanoke
Byrd HS | 1,100/9-12
2902 E Washington Ave 24179 | 540-890-3090
Richard Turner, prin. | Fax 890-7568
Byrd MS | 900/6-8
2910 E Washington Ave 24179 | 540-890-1035
Steve Spangler, prin. | Fax 890-0703
Roanoke County Career Center | Vo/Tech
100 Highland Rd 24179 | 540-857-5004
Becky Rowe, prin. | Fax 857-5066

Parkway Christian Academy | 100/PK-12
2525 Feather Rd 24179 | 540-890-2400
Troy Dixon, prin. | Fax 890-0242

Virginia Beach, Virginia Beach, Pop. 439,467
Virginia Beach CSD | 75,800/PK-12
PO Box 6038 23456 | 757-263-1000
Dr. James Merrill, supt. | Fax 263-1397
www.vbschools.com/
Advanced Technology Center | Vo/Tech
1800 College Cres. | 757-468-8960
William Johnsen, dir. | Fax 468-4235
Bayside HS | 2,100/9-12
4960 Haygood Rd 23455 | 757-473-5050
Dr. Eugene Soltner, prin. | Fax 473-5123
Bayside MS | 1,300/6-8
965 Newtown Rd 23462 | 757-473-5080
Dr. Barbara Cooper, prin. | Fax 473-5185
Brandon MS | 1,500/6-8
1700 Pope St 23464 | 757-366-4545
Dr. Catherine S. Rogers, prin. | Fax 366-4550
Corporate Landing MS | 1,800/6-8
1597 Corporate Landing Pkwy 23454 | 757-437-6199
Rodney J. Burnsworth, prin. | Fax 437-6487
Cox HS | 2,100/9-12
2425 Shorehaven Dr 23454 | 757-496-6767
Dr. Brian K. Matney, prin. | Fax 496-6731
First Colonial HS | 2,100/9-12
1272 Mill Dam Rd 23454 | 757-496-6711
Dr. Hazel Jesse, prin. | Fax 496-6719
Great Neck MS | 1,200/6-8
1848 N Great Neck Rd 23454 | 757-496-6770
Dr. John Smith, prin. | Fax 496-6774
Green Run HS | 1,900/9-12
1700 Dahlia Dr, | 757-431-4040
George Parker, prin. | Fax 431-4153
Independence MS | 1,600/6-8
1370 Dunstan Ln 23455 | 757-460-7500
Peggy W. Peebles, prin. | Fax 363-0874
Kellam HS | 2,400/9-12
2323 Holland Rd, | 757-427-3232
Bruce Biehl, prin. | Fax 427-6265
Kemps Landing Magnet MS | 600/6-8
4722 Jericho Rd 23462 | 757-473-5665
Randi Reigel-Riesbeck, prin. | Fax 473-5106
Kempsville HS | 2,100/9-12
5194 Chief Trl 23464 | 757-474-8400
Dr. Louis Tonelson, prin. | Fax 474-8404
Kempsville MS | 1,300/6-8
860 Churchill Dr 23464 | 757-474-8444
Kay Thomas, prin. | Fax 474-8449
Landstown HS | 2,200/9-12
2001 Concert Dr 23456 | 757-468-3800
Brian Baxter, prin. | Fax 468-1860
Landstown MS | 1,700/6-8
2204 Recreation Dr 23456 | 757-430-2412
Timothy Albert, prin. | Fax 430-3247
Larkspur MS | 2,000/6-8
4696 Princess Anne Rd 23462 | 757-474-8525
Dr. Dianne Cunningham, prin. | Fax 474-8598

Lynnhaven MS | 1,400/6-8
1250 Bayne Dr 23454 | 757-496-6790
Dr. Michael D. Kelly, prin. | Fax 496-6793
Ocean Lakes HS | 2,400/9-12
885 Schumann Dr 23454 | 757-721-4110
Cheryl Askew, prin. | Fax 721-4309
Plaza MS | 1,200/6-8
3080 S Lynnhaven Rd 23452 | 757-431-4060
Andrea Warren, prin. | Fax 431-5331
Princess Anne MS | 1,500/6-8
2509 Seaboard Rd 23456 | 757-427-5325
Lauralee Grim, prin. | Fax 430-0972
Princess Ann HS | 2,300/9-12
4400 Virginia Beach Blvd 23462 | 757-473-5000
Patricia Griffin, prin. | Fax 473-5004
Salem HS | 1,900/9-12
1993 Sundevil Dr 23464 | 757-474-8484
Donald Robertson, prin. | Fax 467-3976
Salem MS | 1,200/6-8
2380 Lynnhaven Pkwy 23464 | 757-474-8411
Shea Paisley, prin. | Fax 474-8467
Tallwood HS | 2,100/9-12
1668 Kempsville Rd 23464 | 757-474-8555
Johnia Caldwell, prin. | Fax 479-5534
Technical & Career Education Center | Vo/Tech
2925 N Landing Rd 23456 | 757-427-5300
David Swanger, prin. | Fax 427-5558
Virginia Beach MS | 800/6-8
600 25th St 23451 | 757-437-4892
Rita Simpson, prin. | Fax 437-4708
Adult Learning Center | Adult
4160 Virginia Beach Blvd 23452 | 757-473-5091
Bonnie Mizenko, dir. | Fax 306-0999

Advanced Technology Institute | Post-Sec.
5700 Southern Blvd # 100 23462 | 757-490-1241
Atlantic University | Post-Sec.
215 67th St 23451 | 800-428-1512
Aviation Institute of Maintenance | Post-Sec.
1429 Miller Store Rd 23455 | 757-363-2121
Bishop Sullivan Catholic HS | 500/9-12
4552 Princess Anne Rd 23462 | 757-467-2881
Dennis Rolce, prin. | Fax 467-0284
Bryant & Stratton College | Post-Sec.
301 Centre Pointe Dr 23462 | 757-499-7900
Cape Henry Collegiate S | 1,000/PK-12
1320 Mill Dam Rd 23454 | 757-481-2446
Dr. John P. Lewis, prin. | Fax 481-9194
Coastal Christian Academy | 50/PK-12
640 Kempsville Rd 23464 | 757-495-5200
Rev. Anne Giminez, prin. | Fax 467-5298
ECPI College of Technology | Post-Sec.
5555 Greenwich Rd Ste 300 23462 | 757-671-7171
Medical Careers Institute | Post-Sec.
5501 Greenwich Rd 23462 | 757-497-8400
Regent University | Post-Sec.
1000 Regent University Dr 23464 | 757-226-4000
Rudy & Kelly Academy of Hair & Nails | Post-Sec.
5606 Princess Anne Rd 23462 | 757-473-0994
Tidewater Community College | Post-Sec.
1700 College Cres, | 757-468-6348
Tidewater Tech | Post-Sec.
2697 Dean Dr Ste 100 23452 | 757-340-2121
Victory Innovative Christian Academy | 50/1-12
3900 Bonney Rd Ste 113 23452 | 757-747-9295
Darrell Brown, prin. | Fax 747-9295
Virginia Beach Friends S | 200/PK-12
1537 Laskin Rd 23451 | 757-428-7534
Jonathan K. Alden, hdmstr. | Fax 428-7511
Virginia School of Technology | Post-Sec.
100 Constitution Dr Ste 101 23462 | 757-499-5447
World College | Post-Sec.
5193 Shore Dr Ste 105 23455 | 757-464-4600

Wakefield, Sussex, Pop. 984

Tidewater Academy | 300/PK-12
PO Box 536 23888 | 757-899-5401
Dr. David Pitre, prin. | Fax 899-2521

Warm Springs, Bath
Bath County SD | 800/K-12
PO Box 67 24484 | 540-839-2722
Dr. K. David Smith, supt. | Fax 839-3040
www.bath.k12.va.us
Other Schools – See Hot Springs

Warrenton, Fauquier, Pop. 7,840
Fauquier County SD | 11,000/PK-12
320 Hospital Dr Ste 40 20186 | 540-351-1000
Dr. J. David Martin, supt. | Fax 347-1026
www.fcps1.org
Auburn MS | 600/6-8
7270 Riley Rd 20187 | 540-428-3750
Jim Angelo, prin. | Fax 428-3760
Fauquier HS | 1,600/9-12
705 Waterloo Rd 20186 | 540-347-6100
Roger Sites, prin. | Fax 347-6110
Taylor MS | 700/6-8
350 E Shirley Ave 20186 | 540-347-6140
Ruth Nelson, prin. | Fax 347-6145
Warrenton MS | 600/6-8
244 Waterloo St 20186 | 540-347-6160
Wallicia Gill, prin. | Fax 347-6169
Other Schools – See Bealeton, Marshall

Fireside Christian S | 100/PK-12
4295 Aiken Dr 20187 | 540-349-4989
Karen Morris, prin. | Fax 349-3177
Highland S | 500/PK-12
597 Broadview Ave 20186 | 540-347-1221
Hank Berg, prin. | Fax 341-7164

Warsaw, Richmond, Pop. 1,379
Jointly Operated Vo Tech SD
Supt. — None
Northern Neck Technical Center | Vo/Tech
PO Box 787 22572 | 804-333-4940
Harold Randolph Long, prin. | Fax 333-0538

Richmond County SD   1,200/K-12
   PO Box 1507   22572   804-333-3681
   Robert Luttrell, supt.   Fax 333-5586
   www.richmond-county.k12.va.us/
Rappahannock HS   400/9-12
   PO Box 550   22572   804-333-3551
   Jack Cooley, prin.   Fax 333-5186
Richmond County IS   300/6-8
   PO Box 519   22572   804-333-3560
   Daniel Bowling, prin.   Fax 333-5387

Rappahannock Community College   Post-Sec.
   52 Campus Dr   22572   804-333-6700

Washington, Rappahannock, Pop. 178
Rappahannock County SD   1,000/K-12
   6 School House Rd   22747   540-987-8773
   Robert T. Chappell, supt.   Fax 987-8896
   www.rappahannock.k12.va.us
Rappahannock County HS   400/8-12
   12576 Lee Hwy   22747   540-987-8575
   Roger Mello, prin.   Fax 987-9331

Waynesboro, Waynesboro, Pop. 20,388
Waynesboro CSD   3,000/K-12
   301 Pine Ave   22980   540-946-4600
   T. Lowell Lemons, supt.   Fax 946-4608
   www.waynesboro.k12.va.us
Collins MS, 1625 Ivy St   22980   700/6-8
   Julie Zook, prin.   540-946-4635
Waynesboro HS   800/9-12
   1200 W Main St   22980   540-946-4616
   Sue Wright, prin.

Fishburne Military S   100/8-12
   PO Box 988   22980   540-946-7700
   William Alexander, supt.   Fax 946-7702

West Point, King William, Pop. 2,974
West Point CSD   800/K-12
   PO Box T   23181   804-843-4368
   Dr. K. Jane Massey, supt.   Fax 843-4421
   wpps.k12.va.us
West Point HS   300/9-12
   2700 Mattaponi Ave   23181   804-843-3630
   Mark Dorsey, prin.   Fax 843-3406
West Point MS   200/6-8
   2700 Mattaponi Ave   23181   804-843-3630
   Todd Perelli, prin.   Fax 843-3406

Weyers Cave, Augusta

Blue Ridge Community College   Post-Sec.
   PO Box 80   24486   540-234-9261

Whitetop, Grayson
Grayson County SD
   Supt. — See Independence
Mt. Rogers S   100/K-12
   11337 Highlands Pkwy   24292   276-388-3489
   Bruce Thomas, prin.   Fax 388-3103

Williamsburg, Williamsburg, Pop. 11,605
Williamsburg-James City County SD   9,100/K-12
   101 Mounts Bay Rd Bldg D   23185   757-253-6777
   Gary Mathews, supt.   Fax 229-3027
   www.wjcc.k12.va.us/
Berkeley MS   800/6-8
   1118 Ironbound Rd   23188   757-229-8051
   Sammy Fudge, prin.   Fax 229-6133
Blair MS   600/6-8
   117 Ironbound Rd   23185   757-229-1341
   Byron Bishop, prin.   Fax 229-7057
Jamestown HS   1,300/9-12
   3751 John Tyler Hwy   23185   757-259-3600
   Chuck Wagner, prin.   Fax 259-3759
LaFayette HS   1,500/9-12
   4460 Longhill Rd   23188   757-565-0373
   Anita Swinton, prin.   Fax 565-4268
Other Schools – See Toano

York County SD
   Supt. — See Yorktown
Bruton HS   700/9-12
   185 East Rochambeau Dr   23188   757-220-4050
   Catherine Jones Ed.D., prin.   Fax 220-4090
Queens Lake MS   500/6-8
   124 W Queens Dr   23185   757-220-4080
   Kendra Crump Ed.D., prin.   Fax 220-4074
School of the Arts   9-12
   185 E Rochambeau Dr   23188   757-220-4095
   Elizabeth Wigley, prin.

College of William and Mary   Post-Sec.
   PO Box 8795   23187   757-221-4000
Walsingham Academy Upper S   300/8-12
   PO Box 8702   23187   757-229-6026
   Peter Bender, prin.   Fax 259-1401

Williamsburg Christian Academy   300/PK-12
   101 School House Ln   23188   757-220-1978
   Gwendolyn Martin, prin.   Fax 741-4009

Winchester, Winchester, Pop. 24,434
Frederick County SD   11,500/K-12
   1415 Amherst St   22601   540-662-3888
   Patricia Taylor, supt.   Fax 722-2788
   www.frederick.k12.va.us
Byrd MS   6-8
   134 Rosa Ln   22602   540-662-0500
   Mark Whittle, prin.   Fax 662-7790
Frederick County MS   800/6-8
   441 Linden Dr   22601   540-667-4233
   Sharon Riggleman, prin.   Fax 667-2392
Howard Center   Vo/Tech
   156 Dowell J Cir   22602   540-722-2134
   Charlotte Casey, dir.   Fax 662-9112
Millbrook HS   1,000/9-12
   251 First Woods Dr   22603   540-545-2800
   Joseph Swack, prin.   Fax 545-7962
Wood HS   1,100/9-12
   161 Apple Pie Ridge Rd   22603   540-667-5226
   Joseph Salyer, prin.   Fax 667-3154
Wood MS   1,100/6-8
   1313 Amherst St   22601   540-667-7500
   Teresa Miller, prin.   Fax 667-7500
Other Schools – See Stephens City

Winchester CSD   3,400/K-12
   PO Box 551   22604   540-667-4253
   Dennis Kellison, supt.   Fax 722-3583
   www.wps.k12.va.us
Handley HS   1,100/9-12
   PO Box 910   22604   540-662-3471
   Doug Joyner, prin.   Fax 722-6722
Morgan HS   1,000/5-8
   48 S Purcell Ave   22601   540-667-7171
   Adam Burket, prin.   Fax 723-8897

Crossroads Christian Academy   100/K-12
   PO Box 4339   22604   540-722-8660
   Greg Roberts, prin.   Fax 722-8667
Grafton School   Post-Sec.
   PO Box 2500   22604   540-542-0200
Mountain View Christian Academy   300/K-12
   153 Narrow Ln   22602   540-868-1231
   Minta Hardman, admin.   Fax 869-8976
Shenandoah University   Post-Sec.
   1460 University Dr   22601   540-665-4500
Winchester Memorial Hospital   Post-Sec.
   PO Box 3340   22604   540-722-8000

Windsor, Isle of Wight, Pop. 2,375
Isle of Wight County SD
   Supt. — See Isle of Wight
Windsor HS   500/9-12
   24 Church St   23487   757-242-6172
   William Owen, prin.   Fax 242-4948
Windsor MS   400/6-8
   23320 N Court St   23487   757-242-3229
   Calvin Bullock, prin.   Fax 242-3405

Wise, Wise, Pop. 3,240
Wise County SD   6,800/PK-12
   PO Box 1217   24293   276-328-8017
   Michael Basham, supt.   Fax 328-3350
   www.wise.k12.va.us
Addington MS   500/5-8
   PO Box 977   24293   276-328-8821
   James Bryant, prin.   Fax 328-2044
Kelly HS   500/9-12
   PO Box 796   24293   276-328-8015
   Charles Collins, prin.   Fax 328-8316
Wise County Career-Technical Center   Vo/Tech
   PO Box 1218   24293   276-328-6113
   Larry Hamilton, prin.   Fax 328-4443
Other Schools – See Appalachia, Big Stone Gap,
   Coeburn, Pound, Saint Paul

University of Virginia College at Wise   Post-Sec.
   1 College Ave   24293   276-328-0100

Woodberry Forest, Madison

Woodberry Forest S   400/9-12
   PO Box 10   22989   540-672-3900
   Dennis Campbell, hdmstr.   Fax 672-0928

Woodbridge, Prince William, Pop. 33,300
Prince William County SD
   Supt. — See Manassas
Beville MS   1,200/6-8
   4901 Dale Blvd   22193   703-878-2593
   Dominick Graziano, prin.   Fax 730-1274
Forest Park HS   2,600/9-12
   15721 Spriggs Rd   22193   703-583-3200
   William L. Brown, prin.   Fax 583-6867

Freedom HS   9-12
   15201 Neabsco Mills Rd   22191   703-583-1405
   Dorothy McCabe Ed.D., prin.   Fax 583-2394
Gar-Field HS   2,800/9-12
   14000 Smoketown Rd   22192   703-730-7000
   Roger Dallek, prin.   Fax 730-7197
Godwin MS   1,200/6-8
   14800 Darbydale Ave   22193   703-670-6166
   William Reid, prin.   Fax 670-9888
Hylton HS   2,300/9-12
   14051 Spriggs Rd   22193   703-580-4000
   Carolyn Custard, prin.   Fax 580-4299
Lake Ridge MS   1,100/6-8
   12350 Mohican Rd   22192   703-494-5154
   Jo Fitzgerald, prin.   Fax 494-8246
Lynn MS   1,300/6-8
   2451 Longview Dr   22191   703-494-5157
   John Thomas Payne, prin.   Fax 491-5141
Rippon MS   1,200/6-8
   15101 Blackburn Rd   22191   703-491-2171
   Benita Stephens Ed.D., prin.   Fax 491-2487
Woodbridge HS   2,700/9-12
   3001 Old Bridge Rd   22192   703-497-8000
   Alan Ross, prin.   Fax 497-8117
Woodbridge MS   1,000/6-8
   2201 York Dr   22191   703-494-3181
   Judy Warme, prin.   Fax 491-1441

Northern Virginia Community College   Post-Sec.
   15200 Neabsco Mills Rd   22191   703-670-2191
Richard Milburn High School   Post-Sec.
   3421 Commission Ct Ste 201   22192   703-494-0147

Woodstock, Shenandoah, Pop. 4,071
Shenandoah County SD   5,800/K-12
   600 N Main St Ste 200   22664   540-459-6222
   H.D. Northern, supt.   Fax 459-6707
   shenandoah.va.schoolwebpages.com
Central HS, 217 Susan Ave   22664   700/9-12
   Mike McCormick, prin.   540-459-2161
Muhlenberg MS   600/6-8
   1251 Susan Ave   22664   540-459-2941
   Gina Stetter, prin.
Other Schools – See Mount Jackson, Quicksburg,
   Strasburg

Massanutten Military Academy   100/6-12
   614 S Main St   22664   540-459-2167
   Roy Zinser, pres.   Fax 459-5421

Wytheville, Wythe, Pop. 7,865
Wythe County SD   4,300/K-12
   1570 W Reservoir St   24382   276-228-5411
   Dr. Albert Armentrout, supt.   Fax 228-9192
   wcps.wythe.k12.va.us
Scott Memorial MS   400/6-8
   950 S 7th St   24382   276-228-2851
   Sidney Crockett, prin.   Fax 228-8261
Wythe Co. Technical Center   Vo/Tech
   1505 W Spiller St   24382   276-228-5481
   Debbie Stone, prin.   Fax 228-8254
Wythe HS   500/9-12
   1 Maroon Way   24382   276-228-3157
   Ron McMurray, prin.   Fax 228-4124
Other Schools – See Max Meadows, Rural Retreat

Wytheville Community College   Post-Sec.
   1000 E Main St   24382   276-223-4700

Yorktown, York
York County SD   12,400/K-12
   302 Dare Rd   23692   757-898-0300
   Steve Staples, supt.   Fax 890-0771
   www.yorkcountyschools.org
Grafton HS   1,300/9-12
   403 Grafton Dr   23692   757-898-0530
   Stephanie Guy, prin.   Fax 898-0533
Grafton MS   1,000/6-8
   405 Grafton Dr   23692   757-898-0525
   Edward Holler Ed.D., prin.   Fax 898-0534
Tabb HS   1,200/9-12
   4431 Big Bethel Rd   23693   757-867-7400
   Laura Abel, prin.   Fax 867-7414
Tabb MS   1,000/6-8
   300 Yorktown Rd   23693   757-898-0320
   Dr. Barry Beers, prin.   Fax 867-7425
York HS   1,000/9-12
   9300 George Washington Mem   23692   757-898-0354
   Royce Hart, prin.   Fax 898-8235
Yorktown MS   700/6-8
   11201 George Washington Mem   23692
      757-898-0360
   Michael Cataldo, prin.   Fax 898-0412
Other Schools – See Williamsburg

Summit Christian Academy   100/7-12
   4209 Big Bethel Rd   23693   757-867-7005
   Joel Staggers, hdmstr.   Fax 867-8590

WASHINGTON

WASHINGTON DEPARTMENT OF EDUCATION
PO Box 47200, Olympia 98504-7200
Telephone 360-725-6000
Fax 360-753-6712
Website http://www.k12.wa.us

Superintendent of Public Instruction   Terry Bergeson

WASHINGTON BOARD OF EDUCATION
PO Box 47206, Olympia 98504-7206

President   Carolyn Tolas

EDUCATIONAL SERVICE DISTRICTS (ESD)

North Central ESD 171
Dr. Richard McBride, supt.   509-665-2610
PO Box 1847, Wenatchee 98807   Fax 662-9027
www.ncesd.org
Northwest ESD 189
Dr. Gerald Jenkins, supt.   360-299-4000
1601 R Ave, Anacortes 98221   Fax 299-4070
www.esd189.org
ESD 113
Dr. Bill Keim, supt.   360-586-2933
601 McPhee Rd SW   Fax 586-4658
Olympia 98502
www.esd113.k12.wa.us

Olympic ESD 114
Dr. Walt Bigby, supt.   360-479-0993
105 National Ave N   Fax 478-6869
Bremerton 98312
www.oesd.wednet.edu
ESD 123
Bruce Hawkins, supt.   509-547-8441
3918 W Court St, Pasco 99301   Fax 544-5795
www.esd123.org
Puget Sound ESD
Dr. Monte Bridges, supt.   800-664-4549
800 Oakesdale Ave SW   Fax 917-7610
Renton 98057
www.psesd.org

ESD 101
Dr. Terry Munther, supt.   509-789-3800
4202 S Regal St, Spokane 99223 Fax 789-3780
www.esd101.net
ESD 112
Dr. Twyla Barnes, supt.   360-750-7500
2500 NE 65th Ave   Fax 750-9706
Vancouver 98661
www.esd112.org
ESD 105
Dr. Jane Gutting, supt.   509-575-2885
33 S 2nd Ave, Yakima 98902   Fax 575-2918
www.esd105.wednet.edu

PUBLIC, PRIVATE AND CATHOLIC SECONDARY SCHOOLS

Aberdeen, Grays Harbor, Pop. 16,207
Aberdeen SD 5   3,600/PK-12
216 N G St 98520   360-538-2000
Martin Kay, supt.   Fax 538-2014
www.asd5.org
Aberdeen HS   1,100/9-12
414 N I St 98520   360-538-2040
David Tobin, prin.   Fax 538-2046
Miller JHS   600/7-8
100 E Lindstrom St 98520   360-538-2100
Dennis Eygabroad, prin.   Fax 538-2106

Wishkah Valley SD 117   200/K-12
4640 Wishkah Rd 98520   360-532-3128
Tom Manke, supt.   Fax 533-4638
www.wishkah.org
Wishkah Valley S   200/K-12
4640 Wishkah Rd 98520   360-532-3128
Joel Tyndell, prin.   Fax 533-4638

Grays Harbor College   Post-Sec.
1620 Edward P Smith Dr 98520   360-532-9020

Adna, Lewis
Adna SD 226   600/PK-12
PO Box 118 98522   360-748-0362
Edward J. Rothlin, supt.   Fax 748-9217
www.adna.k12.wa.us
Adna JSHS   300/6-12
PO Box 148 98522   360-748-0315
Richard DuBois, prin.   Fax 748-1625

Amanda Park, Grays Harbor
Lake Quinault SD 97   300/K-12
PO Box 38 98526   360-288-2260
John Jones, supt.   Fax 288-2732
www.lakequinaultschools.org
Lake Quinault HS   100/9-12
PO Box 38 98526   360-288-2414
Beth Daneker, prin.   Fax 288-2209

Amboy, Clark
Battle Ground SD 119
Supt. — See Brush Prairie
Amboy MS   600/5-8
22115 NE Chelatchie Rd 98601   360-885-6050
Shayla Ebner, prin.   Fax 885-6055

Anacortes, Skagit, Pop. 15,474
Anacortes SD 103   2,900/K-12
2200 M Ave 98221   360-293-1200
Chris Borgen, supt.   Fax 293-1222
www.asd103.org/
Anacortes HS   900/9-12
1600 20th St 98221   360-293-2166
Donna Zickuhr, prin.   Fax 293-0744
Anacortes MS   500/7-8
2200 M Ave 98221   360-293-1230
Susan Willet, prin.   Fax 293-1231

Arlington, Snohomish, Pop. 13,911
Arlington SD 16   4,900/PK-12
315 N French Ave 98223   360-618-6200
Linda Byrnes, supt.   Fax 618-6221
www.asd.wednet.edu

Arlington HS   1,500/9-12
18821 Crown Ridge Blvd 98223   360-618-6300
Kurt Criscione, prin.   Fax 618-6310
Haller MS   6-8
600 E 1st St 98223   360-618-6400
Eric DeJong, prin.   Fax 618-6402
Post MS   900/6-8
1220 E 5th St 98223   360-435-3458
Brian Beckley, prin.   Fax 435-1242

Academy Northwest / Family Academy 300/K-12
23420 Jordan Rd 98223   360-435-9423
Diana McAlister, admin.
Arlington Christian S   100/PK-12
PO Box 3337 98223   360-652-2988
Ruth Graber, admin.   Fax 652-2921
Masters Touch Christian S   100/K-12
135 S French Ave 98223   360-403-8351
Kathy Troll, prin.   Fax 403-4821

Asotin, Asotin, Pop. 1,098
Asotin-Anatone SD 420   600/K-12
PO Box 489 99402   509-243-1100
Paul Boeckman, supt.   Fax 243-4251
www.aasd.wednet.edu/index.htm
Asotin JSHS   300/7-12
PO Box 489 99402   509-243-4151
Dale Bonfield, prin.   Fax 243-4090

Auburn, King, Pop. 44,655
Auburn SD 408   13,700/K-12
915 4th St NE 98002   253-931-4900
Linda Cowan, supt.   Fax 931-8006
www.auburn.wednet.edu
Auburn HS   2,400/9-12
800 4th St NE 98002   253-931-4880
Paul Harvey, prin.   Fax 931-4701
Auburn Mountainview HS   9-12
28900 124th Ave SE 98092   253-804-4539
Bob Odman, prin.
Auburn Riverside HS   1,900/9-12
501 Oravetz Rd SE 98092   253-804-5154
Bruce Phillips, prin.
Cascade MS   800/6-8
1015 24th St NE 98002   253-931-4995
Dennis Grad, prin.   Fax 833-7580
Mt. Baker MS, 620 37th St SE 98002 800/6-8
Louanne Decker, prin.   253-804-4554
Olympic MS   900/6-8
1825 K St SE 98002   253-931-4969
Paul Douglas, prin.   Fax 939-2753
Rainier MS   900/6-8
30620 116th Ave SE 98092   253-931-4843
Ben Talbert, prin.

Federal Way SD 210
Supt. — See Federal Way
Jefferson HS   1,900/9-12
4248 S 288th St 98001   253-945-5600
Mark Marshall, prin.   Fax 945-5656
Kilo MS   1,000/6-8
4400 S 308th St 98001   253-945-4700
Debbie Brewer, prin.   Fax 945-4747

Auburn Adventist Academy   400/9-12
5000 Auburn Way S 98092   253-939-5000
Keith Hallam, prin.   Fax 351-9806
Green River Community College   Post-Sec.
12401 SE 320th St 98092   253-833-9111
Northwest Aviation College   Post-Sec.
506 23rd St NE 98002   253-854-4960
Ranier Christian HS   100/9-12
19830 SE 328th Pl 98092   253-735-1413
Ted Madden, prin.   Fax 887-8234

Bainbridge Island, Kitsap, Pop. 21,701
Bainbridge Island SD 303   4,500/PK-12
8489 Madison Ave NE 98110   206-842-4714
Dr. Ken Crawford, supt.   Fax 842-2928
www.bainbridge.wednet.edu
Bainbridge HS   1,400/9-12
9330 NE High School Rd 98110   206-842-2634
Brent Peterson, prin.   Fax 780-1260
Eagle Harbor HS   100/9-12
9530 NE High School Rd 98110   206-780-1646
Catherine Camp, prin.   Fax 855-0511
Woodward MS   600/7-8
9125 Sportsman Club Rd NE 98110 206-842-4787
Matt Vandeleur, prin.   Fax 780-4525

Battle Ground, Clark, Pop. 12,731
Battle Ground SD 119
Supt. — See Brush Prairie
Battle Ground HS   2,100/9-12
300 W Main St 98604   360-885-6500
Tim Lexow, prin.   Fax 687-6590
Lewisville MS   800/6-8
406 NW 5th Ave 98604   360-885-6350
Linda Allen, prin.   Fax 885-6355
Maple Grove MS   700/5-8
12500 NE 199th St 98604   360-885-6700
Ann Perrin, prin.   Fax 885-6747

Columbia Adventist Academy   100/9-12
11100 NE 189th St 98604   360-687-3161
Gary Brown, prin.   Fax 687-9856

Belfair, Mason
North Mason SD 403   2,400/K-12
71 E Campus Dr 98528   360-277-2300
Thomas J. Kelly, supt.   Fax 277-2320
www.nmsd.wednet.edu/
Hawkins MS   400/7-8
300 E Campus Dr 98528   360-277-2302
Josh Joslin, prin.   Fax 277-2324
North Mason HS   800/9-12
200 E Campus Dr 98528   360-277-2303
Ted Jansen, prin.   Fax 277-2323

Bellevue, King, Pop. 112,344
Bellevue SD 405   14,600/K-12
PO Box 90010 98009   425-456-4000
Dr. Michael Riley, supt.   Fax 456-4176
www.bsd405.org
Bellevue HS   1,300/9-12
10416 Wolverine Way 98004   425-456-7000
Michael Bacigalupi, prin.   Fax 456-7005

Chinook MS | 800/6-8
2001 98th Ave NE 98004 | 425-456-6300
Frank Atkinson, prin. | Fax 456-6304
Highland MS | 500/6-8
15027 Bel Red Rd 98007 | 425-456-6400
David Wellington, prin. | Fax 456-6499
Interlake HS | 800/9-12
16245 NE 24th St 98008 | 425-456-7200
Sharon Collins, prin. | Fax 456-7215
International S | 500/6-12
445 128th Ave SE 98005 | 425-456-6500
Peter Bang-Knudsen, prin. | Fax 456-6565
Newport HS | 1,300/9-12
4333 Factoria Blvd SE 98006 | 425-456-7400
Patricia Siegwarth, prin. | Fax 456-7530
Odle MS | 700/6-8
14401 NE 8th St 98007 | 425-456-6600
Laurie Harvey, prin. | Fax 456-6616
Sammamish HS | 1,200/9-12
100 140th Ave SE 98005 | 425-456-7600
Spencer Welch, prin. | Fax 456-7630
Tillicum MS | 600/6-8
16020 SE 16th St 98008 | 425-456-6700
Tom Duenwald, prin. | Fax 456-6770
Tyee MS | 800/6-8
13630 SE Allen Rd 98006 | 425-456-6800
Jerry Schaefer, prin. | Fax 456-6801

Bellevue Christian JSHS | 500/7-12
1601 98th Ave NE 98004 | 425-454-4028
Bill Safstrom, prin. | Fax 454-4418
Bellevue Community College | Post-Sec.
3000 Landerholm Cir SE 98007 | 425-564-1000
Bellvue Beauty School | Post-Sec.
14045 NE 20th St 98007 | 425-643-0270
City University | Post-Sec.
11900 NE 1st St 98005 | 425-637-1010
Dartmoor S | 100/1-12
13401 Bel Red Rd 98005 | 425-603-1975
Dori Bower, dir. | Fax 603-0038
DeVry University | Post-Sec.
500 108th Ave NE Ste 320 98004 | 425-455-2242
Eastside Catholic HS | 500/9-12
11650 SE 60th St 98006 | 425-644-7737
Greg Marsh, prin. | Fax 644-8127
Forest Ridge HS | 400/5-12
4800 139th Ave SE 98006 | 425-641-0700
Dr. Mary Magano Smith, prin. | Fax 643-3881

Bellingham, Whatcom, Pop. 71,289
Bellingham SD 501 | 10,400/PK-12
1306 Dupont St 98225 | 360-676-6400
Dr. Dale Kinsley, supt. | Fax 676-2793
www.bham.wednet.edu
Bellingham HS | 1,100/9-12
2020 Cornwall Ave 98225 | 360-676-6575
Steve Clarke, prin. | Fax 647-6803
Fairhaven MS | 600/6-8
110 Parkridge Rd 98225 | 360-676-6450
Deirdre O'Neill, prin. | Fax 647-6887
Kulshan MS | 600/6-8
1250 Kenoyer Dr, | 360-676-4886
Gordon Grissom, prin. | Fax 647-6892
Sehome HS | 1,100/9-12
2700 Bill Mcdonald Pkwy 98225 | 360-676-6481
Phyllis Textor, prin. | Fax 647-6819
Shuksan MS | 600/6-8
2713 Alderwood Ave 98225 | 360-676-6454
Dr. Christine Stevens, prin. | Fax 647-6879
Squalicum HS | 1,200/9-12
3773 E McLeod Rd 98226 | 360-676-6471
Dr. David Engle, prin. | Fax 676-6561
Whatcom MS | 700/6-8
810 Halleck St 98225 | 360-676-6460
Jeffrey Coulter, prin. | Fax 647-6899

Meridian SD 505 | 1,500/K-12
214 W Laurel Rd 98226 | 360-398-7111
Dr. Burton Dickerson, supt. | Fax 398-8966
www.meridian.wednet.edu
Meridian HS | 500/9-12
194 W Laurel Rd 98226 | 360-398-8111
David Shockley, prin. | Fax 398-7720
Other Schools – See Lynden

Bellingham Beauty School | Post-Sec.
4192 Meridian St 98226 | 360-734-1090
Bellingham Technical College | Post-Sec.
3028 Lindbergh Ave 98225 | 360-738-0221
Northwest Indian College | Post-Sec.
2522 Kwina Rd 98226 | 360-676-2772
Western Washington University | Post-Sec.
516 High St 98225 | 360-650-3000
Whatcom Community College | Post-Sec.
237 W Kellogg Rd 98226 | 360-676-2170

Benton City, Benton, Pop. 2,879
Kiona-Benton City SD 52 | 1,700/PK-12
1107 Grace 99320 | 509-588-2000
Gary Schuman, supt. | Fax 588-5580
www.owt.com/kibe/
Kiona-Benton City HS | 500/9-12
1107 Grace 99320 | 509-588-2140
Rick Linehan, prin. | Fax 588-2651
Kiona-Benton City MS | 400/6-8
1107 Grace 99320 | 509-588-2040
Vance Wing, prin. | Fax 588-2905

Bickleton, Klickitat
Bickleton SD 203 | 100/K-12
PO Box 10 99322 | 509-896-5473
Ric Palmer, supt. | Fax 896-2071
Bickleton S | 100/K-12
PO Box 10 99322 | 509-896-5473
Ric Palmer, prin. | Fax 896-2071

Blaine, Whatcom, Pop. 4,003
Blaine SD 503 | 2,100/PK-12
765 H St 98230 | 360-332-5881
Dr. Mary Lynne Derrington, supt. | Fax 332-7568
www.blaine.k12.wa.us
Blaine HS | 700/9-12
1055 H St 98230 | 360-332-6045
Dan Newell, prin. | Fax 332-7568
Blaine MS | 500/6-8
975 H St 98230 | 360-332-8226
Darren Benson, prin. | Fax 332-7568

Bonney Lake, Pierce, Pop. 13,215
Sumner SD 320
Supt. — See Sumner
Bonney Lake HS | 9-12
10920 199th Avenue Ct E, | 253-891-5725
Linda Masteller, prin. | Fax 891-5797
Lakeridge MS | 500/6-8
5909 Myers Rd, | 253-891-5100
Steve Fulkerson, prin. | Fax 891-5145
Mountain View MS | 600/6-8
10921 199th Avenue Ct E, | 253-891-5200
Laurie Dent-Cleveland, prin. | Fax 891-5245

Bothell, King, Pop. 30,568
Northshore SD 417 | 19,600/PK-12
3330 Monte Villa Pkwy 98021 | 425-489-6000
Karen Forys Ph.D., supt. | Fax 489-6005
www.nsd.org
Bothell SHS | 1,600/10-12
18125 92nd Ave NE 98011 | 425-489-6100
Bob Stewart, prin. | Fax 489-6179
Canyon Park JHS | 800/7-9
23723 23rd Ave SE 98021 | 425-489-6476
Sharon Lehwalder, prin. | Fax 402-5549
Northshore JHS | 900/7-9
12101 NE 160th St 98011 | 425-489-6411
Gretchen Schaefer, prin. | Fax 402-7653
Skyview JHS | 900/7-9
21404 35th Ave SE 98021 | 425-489-6040
Mike Anderson, prin. | Fax 402-5217
Other Schools – See Kenmore, Woodinville

Bastyr University | Post-Sec.
14500 Juanita Dr NE 98028 | 425-823-1300
Cedar Park Christian S | 1,200/PK-12
16300 112th Ave NE 98011 | 425-488-9778
Clint Behrends, supt. | Fax 483-5765
Mars Hill Graduate School | Post-Sec.
2525 220th St SE Ste 100 98021 | 425-415-0505

Bremerton, Kitsap, Pop. 39,597
Bremerton SD 100-C | 5,500/PK-12
134 Marion Ave N 98312 | 360-478-5151
Dr. Elizabeth M. Hyde, supt. | Fax 478-6082
www.bremertonschools.org
Bremerton Freshman Academy | 400/9-9
1300 E 30th St 98310 | 360-478-5104
Aaron Leavell, prin. | Fax 478-0787
Bremerton HS | 1,200/10-12
1500 13th St 98337 | 360-478-6033
Aaron Leavell, prin. | Fax 478-5061
Mountain View MS | 1,000/6-8
2400 Perry Ave 98310 | 360-478-5130
Jerry Willson, prin. | Fax 478-5144
Mountain View MS Sheridan Campus | 8-8
1300 E 30th St 98310 | 360-478-5025
Jerry Willson, prin. | Fax 478-6070
West Sound Technical Skills Center | Vo/Tech
101 National Ave N 98312 | 360-478-5083
Kathrin Carr, dir. | Fax 478-5090

Central Kitsap SD 401
Supt. — See Silverdale
Fairview JHS | 800/7-9
8107 Central Valley Rd NW 98311 | 360-662-2600
Kathy Wales, prin. | Fax 662-2601
Olympic HS | 1,100/10-12
7070 Stampede Blvd NW 98311 | 360-662-2700
Robert Barnes, prin. | Fax 662-2701

Kings West JSHS | 200/7-12
4012 Chico Way NW 98312 | 360-377-7700
Dr. Eric Rasmussen, supt. | Fax 377-7795
Olympic College | Post-Sec.
1600 Chester Ave 98337 | 360-792-6050

Brewster, Okanogan, Pop. 2,154
Brewster SD 111 | 1,000/PK-12
PO Box 97 98812 | 509-689-3418
James Kelly, supt. | Fax 689-2892
www.brewster.wednet.edu
Brewster JSHS | 400/7-12
PO Box 97 98812 | 509-689-3449
Randy Phillips, prin. | Fax 689-2580

Bridgeport, Douglas, Pop. 2,051
Bridgeport SD 75 | 600/PK-12
PO Box 1060 98813 | 509-686-5656
Gene Schmidt, supt. | Fax 686-2221
www.bridgeport.wednet.edu
Bridgeport HS | 100/9-12
PO Box 1090 98813 | 509-686-8770
Steve Pointer, prin. | Fax 686-9622
Bridgeport MS | 200/6-8
PO Box 1060 98813 | 509-686-9501
Diane Hull, prin. | Fax 686-4052

Brier, Snohomish, Pop. 6,361
Edmonds SD 15
Supt. — See Lynnwood
Brier Terrace MS | 700/7-8
22200 Brier Rd 98036 | 425-431-7834
Bill Fritz, prin. | Fax 431-7836

Brush Prairie, Clark, Pop. 2,650
Battle Ground SD 119 | 11,300/K-12
11104 NE 149th St 98606 | 360-885-5300
Shonny Bria Ph.D., supt. | Fax 885-5310
www.bgsd.k12.wa.us/
Prairie HS | 1,500/9-12
11500 NE 117th Ave 98606 | 360-885-5000
Jason Perrins, prin. | Fax 885-5050
Other Schools – See Amboy, Battle Ground, Vancouver

Hockinson SD 98 | 1,700/K-12
17912 NE 159th St 98606 | 360-448-6400
Delcine Mesa-Johnson, supt. | Fax 448-6409
www.hock.k12.wa.us/
Hockinson HS | 300/9-12
16818 NE 159th St 98606 | 360-448-6450
Sandra Yager, prin. | Fax 448-6459
Hockinson MS | 600/6-8
15916 NE 182nd Ave 98606 | 360-448-6440
Peter Rosenkranz, prin. | Fax 448-6449

Buckley, Pierce, Pop. 4,502
White River SD 416 | 3,400/K-12
PO Box 2050 98321 | 360-829-0600
Tom Lockyer, supt. | Fax 829-3843
www.whiteriver.wednet.edu
White River HS | 800/9-12
PO Box 1683 98321 | 360-829-3352
Michael Hagadone, prin. | Fax 829-3351
White River MS | 700/6-8
PO Box 2180 98321 | 360-829-3353
Teresa Sinay, prin. | Fax 829-3364
Other Schools – See Wilkeson

Rainier School, PO Box 600 98321 | Post-Sec.

Burbank, Walla Walla, Pop. 1,745
Columbia SD 400 | 1,000/PK-12
755 Maple St 99323 | 509-547-2136
Ben Small, supt. | Fax 546-0603
www.cbvcp.com/columbiasd
Columbia HS | 300/9-12
787 Maple St 99323 | 509-545-8573
Kyle Miller, prin. | Fax 545-6553
Columbia MS | 200/6-8
835 Maple St 99323 | 509-545-8571
Mike Taylor, prin. | Fax 547-4277

Burien, King, Pop. 31,116
Highline SD 401 | 17,300/K-12
PO Box 66100 98166 | 206-433-0111
John P. Welch, supt. | Fax 433-2351
www.hsd401.org
Highline HS | 1,600/9-12
225 S 152nd St 98148 | 206-433-2511
Patricia Dunn, prin. | Fax 433-2235
Sylvester MS | 700/7-8
16222 Sylvester Rd SW 98166 | 206-433-2401
Vicki Fisher, prin. | Fax 433-2530
Other Schools – See Des Moines, SeaTac, Seattle

Kennedy Memorial HS | 900/9-12
140 S 140th St 98168 | 206-246-0500
Michael L. Prato, prin. | Fax 242-0831
Three Tree Montessori S | 100/PK-12
220 SW 160th St 98166 | 206-242-5100
Connie Blair, dir. | Fax 242-5112

Burlington, Skagit, Pop. 7,710
Burlington-Edison SD 100 | 3,600/K-12
927 E Fairhaven Ave 98233 | 360-757-3311
Richard Jones, supt. | Fax 755-9198
www.be.wednet.edu/
Burlington-Edison HS | 1,100/9-12
301 N Burlington Blvd 98233 | 360-757-4074
Beth VanderVeen, prin. | Fax 757-3350

Skagit Adventist S | 100/K-10
530 N Section St 98233 | 360-755-9261
| Fax 755-9931

Camas, Clark, Pop. 14,976
Camas SD 117 | 4,800/K-12
1919 NE Ione St 98607 | 360-817-4400
Dr. Mike Nerland, supt. | Fax 817-4401
www.camas.wednet.edu/
Camas HS | 1,400/9-12
26900 SE 15th St 98607 | 360-817-4441
Richard Zimmerman, prin. | Fax 817-4442
Liberty MS, 1612 NE Garfield St 98607 | 6-8
Marilyn Boerke, prin. | 360-817-4400
Skyridge MS | 800/6-8
5220 NW Parker St 98607 | 360-817-4455
Ray Bell, prin. | Fax 817-4456

Carnation, King, Pop. 1,843
Riverview SD 407 | 2,700/K-12
32240 NE 50th St 98014 | 425-844-4500
Conrad Robertson, supt. | Fax 844-4502
www.riverview.wednet.edu
Tolt MS | 700/6-8
3740 Tolt Ave 98014 | 425-844-4600
Janet Gavigan, prin. | Fax 844-4602
Other Schools – See Duvall

Cashmere, Chelan, Pop. 2,960
Cashmere SD 222 | 1,500/PK-12
210 S Division St 98815 | 509-782-3355
Glenn Johnson, supt. | Fax 782-4747
www.cashmere.wednet.edu
Cashmere HS | 500/9-12
329 Tigner Rd 98815 | 509-782-2914
Sam Willsey, prin. | Fax 782-2891
Cashmere MS | 500/5-8
300 Tigner Rd 98815 | 509-782-2001
Russ Elliott, prin. | Fax 782-2547

Castle Rock, Cowlitz, Pop. 2,093
Castle Rock SD 401 — 1,500/PK-12
600 Huntington Ave S 98611 — 360-501-2940
Richard Wilde, supt. — Fax 501-3140
www.castlerock.wednet.edu
Castle Rock HS — 400/9-12
5180 Westside Hwy 98611 — 360-501-2930
Henry Karnotski, prin. — Fax 501-2999
Castle Rock MS — 400/6-8
615 Front Ave SW 98611 — 360-501-2920
Faye Ashland, prin. — Fax 501-3125

Cathlamet, Wahkiakum, Pop. 540
Wahkiakum SD 200 — 400/K-12
PO Box 398 98612 — 360-795-3971
Bob Garrett, supt. — Fax 795-0545
Wahkiakum HS — 200/9-12
PO Box 398 98612 — 360-795-3271
Loren Davis, prin. — Fax 795-0545
Wahkiakum MS — 6-8
PO Box 398 98612 — 360-795-3261
Theresa Libby, prin. — Fax 795-3205

Centralia, Lewis, Pop. 14,981
Centralia SD 401 — 3,400/K-12
PO Box 610 98531 — 360-330-7600
Dr. Doug Kernutt, supt. — Fax 330-7604
www.centralia.wednet.edu
Centralia HS — 1,100/9-12
813 Eshom Rd 98531 — 360-330-7605
Tom Boehme, prin. — Fax 330-7616
Centralia MS — 500/7-8
901 Johnson Rd 98531 — 360-330-7619
Steve Warren, prin. — Fax 330-7622

Centralia College — Post-Sec.
600 W Locust St 98531 — 360-736-9391

Chattaroy, Spokane
Riverside SD 416 — 1,800/PK-12
34515 N Newport Hwy 99003 — 509-464-8201
Galen Hansen, supt. — Fax 464-8206
www.riversidesd.org
Riverside HS — 600/9-12
4120 E Deer Park Milan Rd 99003 — 509-464-8550
John McCoy, prin. — Fax 464-8556
Riverside MS — 500/6-8
3814 E Deer Park Milan Rd 99003 — 509-464-8450
James McConnell, prin. — Fax 464-8447

Chehalis, Lewis, Pop. 7,105
Chehalis SD 302 — 2,800/K-12
310 SW 16th St 98532 — 360-807-7200
Dr. Greg Kirsch, supt. — Fax 748-8899
www.chehalis.k12.wa.us
Chehalis MS — 600/6-8
1060 SW 20th St 98532 — 360-807-7230
James Budgett, prin. — Fax 740-1849
West HS — 900/9-12
342 SW 16th St 98532 — 360-807-7235
Dr. Linda Smith, prin. — Fax 748-3664

Lewis County Adventist S — 100/PK-10
2104 S Scheuber Rd 98532 — 360-748-3213
Dan Baker, prin. — Fax 748-6399

Chelan, Chelan, Pop. 3,563
Lake Chelan SD 129 — 1,300/K-12
PO Box 369 98816 — 509-682-3515
Dr. Jim Busey, supt. — Fax 682-5842
www.chelanschools.org
Chelan HS — 400/9-12
PO Box 369 98816 — 509-682-4061
Tim Berndt, prin. — Fax 682-5001
Chelan MS — 300/6-8
PO Box 369 98816 — 509-682-4073
Barry DePaoli, prin. — Fax 682-5001

Cheney, Spokane, Pop. 9,743
Cheney SD 360 — 3,400/PK-12
520 4th St 99004 — 509-559-4599
Michael Dunn, supt. — Fax 559-4508
www.cheneysd.org
Cheney HS — 1,100/9-12
460 N 6th St 99004 — 509-559-4000
Thomas Gresch, prin. — Fax 559-4005
Cheney MS — 800/6-8
2716 N 6th St 99004 — 509-559-4400
Erika Burden, prin. — Fax 559-4479

Eastern Washington University 99004 — Post-Sec.
— 509-359-6200

Chewelah, Stevens, Pop. 2,199
Chewelah SD 36 — 1,100/K-12
PO Box 47 99109 — 509-935-8671
Marcus Morgan, supt. — Fax 935-8605
www.chewelah.k12.wa.us
Jenkins HS — 400/9-12
PO Box 138 99109 — 509-935-8671
John Polm, prin. — Fax 935-9206
Jenkins MS — 300/6-8
PO Box 1099 99109 — 509-935-8671
C. Jean Homer, prin. — Fax 935-4404

Chimacum, Jefferson
Chimacum SD 49 — 1,300/PK-12
PO Box 278 98325 — 360-385-3922
Mike Blair, supt. — Fax 732-4336
www.csd49.org
Chimacum HS — 500/9-12
PO Box 460 98325 — 360-732-4481
Rex Whipple, prin. — Fax 732-7359
Chimacum MS — 300/6-8
PO Box 250 98325 — 360-732-4219
Whitney Meissner, prin. — Fax 732-6859

Clallam Bay, Clallam
Cape Flattery SD 401
Supt. — See Sekiu
Clallam Bay S — 200/K-12
PO Box 337 98326 — 360-963-2324
Kandy Ritter, prin. — Fax 963-2228

Clarkston, Asotin, Pop. 7,211
Clarkston SD J 250-185 — 2,600/K-12
PO Box 70 99403 — 509-758-2531
Pete Lewis, supt. — Fax 758-3326
www.csdk12.org
Adams HS — 800/9-12
PO Box 370 99403 — 509-758-5591
Van Cummings, prin. — Fax 758-2831
Lincoln MS — 400/7-8
1945 4th Ave 99403 — 509-758-5506
Bob Burrus, prin. — Fax 758-7838

Cle Elum, Kittitas, Pop. 1,792
Cle Elum-Roslyn SD 404 — 900/K-12
2690 State Route 903 98922 — 509-649-2393
Mark Flatau, supt. — Fax 649-2404
Cle Elum-Roslyn HS — 300/9-12
2692 State Route 903 98922 — 509-649-2291
Boyd Keyser, prin. — Fax 649-3563
Strom MS — 200/6-8
2694 State Route 903 98922 — 509-649-3560
Kim Headrick, prin. — Fax 649-3634

Colbert, Spokane

Northwest Christian S — 300/7-12
5104 E Bernhill Rd 99005 — 509-238-4005
Jack Hancock, hdmstr. — Fax 238-2242

Colfax, Whitman, Pop. 2,793
Colfax SD 300 — 700/K-12
1110 N Morton St 99111 — 509-397-3042
Michael Morgan, supt. — Fax 397-5835
www.colfax.k12.wa.us
Colfax HS — 300/9-12
1110 N Morton St 99111 — 509-397-4368
Kevin Ore, prin. — Fax 397-2414

College Place, Walla Walla, Pop. 8,446
College Place SD 250 — 900/K-8
107 SE 2nd St 99324 — 509-525-4827
Timothy Payne, supt. — Fax 525-3741
www.cpps.org
Sager MS — 200/7-8
1755 S College Ave 99324 — 509-525-5300
Eric Price, prin. — Fax 525-5305

Walla Walla College — Post-Sec.
204 S College Ave 99324 — 509-527-2615
Walla Walla Valley Academy — 200/9-12
300 SW Academy Way 99324 — 509-525-1050
John M. Deming, prin. — Fax 525-1056

Colton, Whitman, Pop. 383
Colton SD 306 — 200/K-12
706 Union St 99113 — 509-229-3385
C. Foley, supt. — Fax 229-3374
www.colton.k12.wa.us/
Colton S, 706 Union St 99113 — 200/K-12
Nate Smith, prin. — 509-229-3386

Colville, Stevens, Pop. 4,960
Colville SD 115 — 2,100/K-12
217 S Hofstetter St 99114 — 509-684-7850
Ken Emmil, supt. — Fax 684-7855
www.colsd.org
Colville HS — 700/9-12
154 Highway 20 E 99114 — 509-684-7800
Kevin Knight, prin. — Fax 684-7809
Colville JHS — 300/7-8
990 S Cedar St 99114 — 509-684-7820
Paul Dumas, prin. — Fax 684-7825

Colville Valley Junior Academy — 50/K-10
139 E Cedar Loop 99114 — 509-684-6830
Laurie Hosey, prin. — Fax 684-1084

Concrete, Skagit, Pop. 789
Concrete SD 11 — 800/K-12
45389 Airport Way 98237 — 360-853-8141
Mike Parker, supt. — Fax 853-7521
www.concrete.k12.wa.us
Concrete HS — 200/9-12
7830 S Superior Ave 98237 — 360-853-8143
Don Beazizo, prin. — Fax 853-8110
Concrete MS — 100/7-8
45389 Airport Way 98237 — 360-853-8116
Don Beazizo, prin. — Fax 853-7521

Connell, Franklin, Pop. 3,178
North Franklin SD J 51-162 — 1,900/K-12
PO Box 829 99326 — 509-234-2021
Michael Kirby, supt. — Fax 234-9200
www.nfsd.k12.wa.us
Connell HS — 500/9-12
PO Box 829 99326 — 509-234-2911
Pat Ena, prin. — Fax 234-9226
Olds JHS — 300/7-8
PO Box 829 99326 — 509-234-3931
Mary Nipper, prin. — Fax 234-8171

Cosmopolis, Grays Harbor, Pop. 1,607
North River SD 200 — 100/K-12
2867 N River Rd 98537 — 360-532-3079
David Pickering, supt. — Fax 532-1738
www.nr.k12.wa.us/
North River S — 100/K-12
2867 N River Rd 98537 — 360-532-3079
David Pickering, prin. — Fax 532-1738

Coulee City, Grant, Pop. 612
Coulee-Hartline SD 151 — 200/K-12
PO Box 428 99115 — 509-632-8642
Dr. Edward Fisk, supt. — Fax 632-5166
www.achsd.org
Other Schools – See Hartline

Coulee Dam, Okanogan, Pop. 1,080
Grand Coulee Dam SD 301J — 900/K-12
110 Stevens Ave 99116 — 509-633-2143
Bob Ranells, supt. — Fax 633-2530
www.gcdsd.org
Lake Roosevelt HS — 300/9-12
500 Civic Way 99116 — 509-633-1442
Terry Cosentino, prin. — Fax 633-0356
Other Schools – See Grand Coulee

Coupeville, Island, Pop. 1,797
Coupeville SD 204 — 1,100/K-12
2 S Main St 98239 — 360-678-4522
Bill Myhr, supt. — Fax 678-4834
pride.coup.wednet.edu
Coupeville HS — 400/9-12
501 S Main St 98239 — 360-678-4409
Sheldon Rosenkrance, prin. — Fax 678-0540
Coupeville MS — 300/6-8
501 S Main St 98239 — 360-678-4409
David Ebersole, prin. — Fax 678-0540

Covington, King, Pop. 15,294
Kent SD 415
Supt. — See Kent
Cedar Heights MS — 700/7-8
19640 SE 272nd St 98042 — 253-373-7620
Angela Grutko, prin. — Fax 373-7628
Kentwood SHS — 1,600/9-12
25800 164th Ave SE 98042 — 253-373-7680
Doug Hostetter, prin. — Fax 373-7326
Mattson MS — 700/7-8
16400 SE 251st St 98042 — 253-373-7670
Steve Beck, prin. — Fax 373-7673

Tahoma SD 409
Supt. — See Maple Valley
Tahoma SHS — 1,400/10-12
18200 SE 240th St 98042 — 425-413-6200
Terry Duty, prin. — Fax 413-6333

Cowiche, Yakima
Highland SD 203 — 1,200/K-12
PO Box 38 98923 — 509-678-4173
Gary Masten, supt. — Fax 678-4177
www.highland.wednet.edu/
Highland HS — 200/10-12
PO Box 38 98923 — 509-678-4161
Greg George, prin. — Fax 678-4140
Highland JHS, PO Box 38 98923 — 300/7-9
Greg George, prin. — 509-678-7200

Creston, Lincoln, Pop. 230
Creston SD 73 — 100/K-12
PO Box 17 99117 — 509-636-2721
Michael Crowell, supt. — Fax 636-2910
www.creston.wednet.edu
Creston JSHS — 100/7-12
PO Box 17 99117 — 509-636-2721
Michael Crowell, prin. — Fax 636-2910

Curlew, Ferry
Curlew SD 50 — 200/K-12
PO Box 370 99118 — 509-779-4931
Steve McCullough, supt. — Fax 779-4938
www.curlew.wednet.edu/default.htm
Curlew S — 200/K-12
PO Box 370 99118 — 509-779-4931
Brett Simpson, prin. — Fax 779-4938

Cusick, Pend Oreille, Pop. 215
Cusick SD 59 — 300/K-12
305 Monumental Rd 99119 — 509-445-1125
Dan Read, supt. — Fax 445-1598
www.cusick.wednet.edu/
Cusick JSHS — 100/7-12
305 Monumental Rd 99119 — 509-445-1125
Dustin Andres, prin. — Fax 445-1598

Darrington, Snohomish, Pop. 1,324
Darrington SD 330 — 600/K-12
PO Box 27 98241 — 360-436-1323
Larry Johnson, supt. — Fax 436-2045
www.dsd.k12.wa.us
Darrington MSHS — 300/7-12
PO Box 27 98241 — 360-436-1140
Dave Holmer, prin. — Fax 436-1089

Davenport, Lincoln, Pop. 1,710
Davenport SD 207 — 500/PK-12
801 7th St 99122 — 509-725-1481
Gary Greene, supt. — Fax 725-2260
www.davenport.wednet.edu/
Davenport JSHS — 200/7-12
801 7th St 99122 — 509-725-4021
Mike Perry, prin. — Fax 725-2260

Dayton, Columbia, Pop. 2,690
Dayton SD 2 — 600/PK-12
609 S 2nd St 99328 — 509-382-2543
Richard Stewart, supt. — Fax 382-2081
www.dayton.wednet.edu/
Dayton HS — 200/9-12
614 S 3rd St 99328 — 509-382-4775
Jude Cornaggia, prin. — Fax 382-2081
Dayton MS — 100/7-8
609 S 2nd St 99328 — 509-382-2522
Katie Leid, prin. — Fax 381-2081

Deer Park, Spokane, Pop. 3,066
Deer Park SD 414 — 2,000/K-12
PO Box 490 99006 — 509-464-5500
Mick Miller, supt. — Fax 464-5510
www.dpsd.org

Deer Park HS 600/9-12
PO Box 550 99006 509-464-5900
Trip Goodall, prin. Fax 464-5910
Deer Park MS 500/6-8
PO Box 882 99006 509-464-5800
Brent Seedall, prin. Fax 464-5810

Deming, Whatcom
Mt. Baker SD 507 2,800/K-12
PO Box 95 98244 360-383-2000
Dr. Richard Gantman, supt. Fax 383-2009
www.mtbaker.wednet.edu
Mt. Baker HS 800/9-12
PO Box 95 98244 360-383-2015
Steve King, prin. Fax 383-2029
Mt. Baker JHS 400/7-8
PO Box 95 98244 360-383-2030
Charles Burleigh, prin. Fax 383-2039

Des Moines, King, Pop. 29,039
Highline SD 401
Supt. — See Burien
Mount Rainier HS 1,400/9-12
615 S 200th St 98198 206-433-2441
Toni Pace, prin. Fax 433-2423
Pacific MS 700/7-8
22705 24th Ave S 98198 206-433-2581
Cecilia Beaman, prin. Fax 433-2451

Evergreen Lutheran HS 100/9-12
2021 S 260th St 98198 253-946-4488
Greg Thiesfeldt, prin. Fax 529-9475
Highline Community College Post-Sec.
PO Box 98000 98198 206-878-3710

Duvall, King, Pop. 5,568
Riverview SD 407
Supt. — See Carnation
Cedarcrest HS 800/9-12
29000 NE 150th St 98019 425-844-4800
Clarence Lavarias, prin. Fax 844-4802

Easton, Kittitas
Easton SD 28 100/PK-12
PO Box 8 98925 509-656-2317
Suellen White, supt. Fax 656-2585
www.easton.wednet.edu
Easton S 100/PK-12
PO Box 8 98925 509-656-2317
Fax 656-2585

Eastsound, San Juan
Orcas Island SD 137 500/K-12
557 School Rd 98245 360-376-2284
Dr. Jeff Van Handel, supt. Fax 376-2283
www.orcasislandschools.org
Orcas Island HS 200/9-12
715 School Rd 98245 360-376-2287
Barbara Kline, prin. Fax 376-6078
Orcas Island MS 100/7-8
715 School Rd 98245 360-376-2287
Barbara Kline, prin. Fax 376-6078

Orcas Christian Day S 100/1-12
PO Box 669 98245 360-376-6683
Fax 376-7642

East Wenatchee, Douglas, Pop. 8,590
Eastmont SD 206 4,800/K-12
460 9th St NE 98802 509-884-7169
Dr. Harry P. Vanikiotis, supt. Fax 884-4210
www.eastmont206.com/distoff/main/
Eastmont JHS 900/8-9
905 8th St NE 98802 509-884-2407
John Westerman, prin. Fax 884-1988
Eastmont SHS 1,100/10-12
955 3rd St NE 98802 509-884-6665
Mark Marney, prin. Fax 884-8805
Other Schools – See Wenatchee

Eatonville, Pierce, Pop. 2,207
Eatonville SD 404 2,100/K-12
PO Box 698 98328 360-879-1000
Raymond F. Arment, supt. Fax 879-1086
cruiser.eatonville.wednet.edu/
Eatonville HS 700/9-12
PO Box 699 98328 360-879-1200
Garth Steedman, prin. Fax 879-1284
Eatonville MS 500/6-8
PO Box 910 98328 360-879-1400
Kim Andersen, prin. Fax 879-1480

Edgewood, Pierce, Pop. 9,526
Puyallup SD 3
Supt. — See Puyallup
Edgemont JHS 400/7-9
2300 110th Ave E 98372 253-841-8727
Sandra Jacobson, prin. Fax 840-8883

Edmonds, Snohomish, Pop. 39,882
Edmonds SD 15
Supt. — See Lynnwood
Edmonds-Woodway HS 1,800/9-12
7600 212th St SW 98026 425-431-7900
Alan Weiss, prin. Fax 431-7929

Solomon Christian S 100/7-12
8021 230th St SW 98026 425-640-9000
Richard Lee, prin. Fax 778-1393

Edwall, Lincoln

Christian Heritage S 100/K-12
PO Box 118 99008 509-236-2224
Marty Klein, admin. Fax 236-2224

Ellensburg, Kittitas, Pop. 16,257
Ellensburg SD 401 2,900/K-12
1300 E 3rd Ave 98926 509-925-8000
John Glenewinkel, supt. Fax 925-8025
wonders.eburg.wednet.edu/
Ellensburg HS 1,000/9-12
1203 E Capitol Ave 98926 509-925-8300
Jeff Ellersick, prin. Fax 925-8305
Morgan MS 700/6-8
400 E 1st Ave 98926 509-925-8200
Gary Ristine, prin. Fax 925-8202

Central Washington University Post-Sec.
400 E University Way 98926 509-963-1111

Elma, Grays Harbor, Pop. 3,131
Elma SD 68 2,000/K-12
1235 Monte Elma Rd 98541 360-482-2822
Tami Hickle, supt. Fax 482-2092
www.eagles.edu
Elma HS 700/9-12
1235 Monte Elma Rd 98541 360-482-3121
Deborah Parriott, prin. Fax 482-1200
Elma MS 400/6-8
1235 Monte Elma Rd 98541 360-482-2237
Greg Scroggins, prin. Fax 482-4872

Mary M. Knight SD 311 200/PK-12
2987 W Matlock Brady Rd 98541 360-426-6767
Carol Ersland, supt. Fax 427-5516
mary.wa.schoolwebpages.com
Knight JSHS 100/7-12
2987 W Matlock Brady Rd 98541 360-426-6767
Carol Ersland, prin. Fax 427-5516

Endicott, Whitman, Pop. 336
Endicott SD 308 100/K-8
308 School Dr 99125 509-657-3523
Rick Winters, supt. Fax 657-3521
www.sje.wednet.edu
Endicott-St. John MS 7-8
308 School Dr 99125 509-657-3523
Suzanne Schmick, prin. Fax 657-3521

Entiat, Chelan, Pop. 987
Entiat SD 127 400/K-12
2650 Entiat Way 98822 509-784-1800
Dennis Chambers, supt. Fax 784-2986
www.entiatschools.org
Entiat JSHS 200/7-12
2650 Entiat Way 98822 509-784-1911
Dan English, prin. Fax 784-2986

Enumclaw, King, Pop. 10,941
Enumclaw SD 216 5,200/K-12
2929 McDougall Ave 98022 360-802-7100
Arthur Jarvis, supt. Fax 802-7123
www.enumclaw.wednet.edu/
Enumclaw HS 1,600/9-12
226 Semanski St 98022 360-802-7669
David Dorn, prin. Fax 802-7676
Enumclaw MS 600/6-8
550 Semanski St 98022 360-802-7150
Steve Rabb, prin. Fax 802-7224
Thunder Mountain MS 700/6-8
42018 264th Ave SE 98022 360-802-7492
Darin Adams, prin. Fax 802-7500

Ephrata, Grant, Pop. 7,069
Ephrata SD 165 2,500/K-12
499 C St NW 98823 509-754-2474
Dr. Jerry Simon, supt. Fax 754-4712
www.ephrataschools.org
Ephrata HS 700/9-12
333 4th Ave NW 98823 509-754-2043
Dan Martell, prin. Fax 754-5285
Ephrata MS, 384 A St SE 98823 400/7-8
Rick Allstot, prin. 509-754-4659

New Life Christian S 100/PK-12
911 E Division Ave 98823 509-754-5558
JoAnn Henke, admin. Fax 754-3540

Everett, Snohomish, Pop. 96,643
Everett SD 2 18,000/PK-12
PO Box 2098, 425-385-4000
Carol A. Whitehead Ed.D., supt. Fax 385-4012
www.everett.k12.wa.us
Cascade HS 1,900/9-12
801 E Casino Rd 98203 425-385-6000
Jim Dean, prin. Fax 385-6002
Eisenhower MS 800/6-8
10200 25th Ave SE 98208 425-385-7500
David Jones, prin. Fax 385-7502
Everett HS 1,700/9-12
2416 Colby Ave 98201 425-385-4400
Catherine Matthews, prin. Fax 385-4402
Evergreen MS 900/6-8
7621 Beverly Ln 98203 425-385-5700
Joyce Stewart, prin. Fax 385-5702
Gateway MS 900/6-8
15404 Silver Firs Dr 98208 425-385-6600
Cathy Woods, prin. Fax 385-6602
North MS 700/6-8
2514 Rainier Ave 98201 425-385-4800
Kelly Shepherd, prin. Fax 385-4802
Other Schools – See Mill Creek

Lake Stevens SD 4
Supt. — See Lake Stevens
Lake Stevens MS 900/6-8
1031 91st Ave SE 98205 425-335-1544
John Gebert, prin. Fax 335-1564

Mukilteo SD 6 13,400/K-12
9401 Sharon Dr 98204 425-356-1274
Marci L. Larsen, supt. Fax 356-1310
www.mukilteo.wednet.edu
Explorer MS 800/6-8
9600 Sharon Dr 98204 425-356-1240
Mark Flotlin, prin. Fax 356-1288
Mariner HS 1,900/9-12
200 120th St SW 98204 425-356-1700
Brent Kline, prin. Fax 356-1717
Sno-Isle Vo Skills Ctr Vo/Tech
9001 Airport Rd 98204 425-348-2220
Steve Burch, prin. Fax 356-2201
Voyager MS 800/6-8
11711 4th Ave W 98204 425-356-1730
Alison Brynelson, prin. Fax 290-3747
Other Schools – See Mukilteo

Archbishop Thomas Murphy HS 300/9-12
12911 39th Ave SE 98208 425-379-6363
Dr. Kristine Smith, prin. Fax 385-2875
Bryman College Post-Sec.
906 SE Evrtt Mall Way #600 98208 425-789-7960
Cedar Park Christian S 300/PK-12
13000 21st Dr SE 98208 425-337-6992
Curt Frunz, prin. Fax 357-9399
Everett Beauty Academy Post-Sec.
607 SE Everett Mall Way #5 98208 425-353-8193
Everett Community College Post-Sec.
2000 Tower St 98201 425-388-9100
Henry Cogswell College Post-Sec.
3002 Colby Ave 98201 425-258-3351
ITT Technical Institute Post-Sec.
1615 75th St SW Ste 220 98203 425-583-0200
Montessori S of Snohomish County 200/PK-12
1804 Puget Dr 98203 425-355-1311
Kathleen Gunnell, admin.
Puget Sound Christian College Post-Sec.
PO Box 13108 98206 425-257-3090
Western Pacific Truck School Post-Sec.
9901 Evergreen Way 98204 425-486-7117

Everson, Whatcom, Pop. 2,072
Nooksack Valley SD 506 1,800/PK-12
3326 E Badger Rd 98247 360-988-4754
Mark Johnson, supt. Fax 988-8983
www.nooksackschools.org
Nooksack Valley HS 600/9-12
3326 E Badger Rd 98247 360-988-2641
Robert Prosch, prin. Fax 988-7058
Nooksack Valley MS 500/6-8
404 W Columbia St 98247 360-966-7561
Cindy Stockwell, prin. Fax 966-7805

Fall City, King, Pop. 1,582
Snoqualmie Valley SD 410
Supt. — See Snoqualmie
Chief Kanim MS 500/6-8
PO Box 639 98024 425-831-8225
Kirk Dunckel, prin. Fax 831-8290

Federal Way, King, Pop. 81,711
Federal Way SD 210 22,700/PK-12
31405 18th Ave S 98003 253-945-2000
Tom Murphy, supt. Fax 945-2001
www.fwps.org
Beamer HS 1,400/9-12
35999 16th Ave S 98003 253-945-2570
Joshua Garcia, prin. Fax 945-2599
Decatur HS 1,700/9-12
2800 SW 320th St 98023 253-945-5200
Tom Leacy, prin. Fax 945-5252
Federal Way HS 1,700/9-12
30611 16th Ave S 98003 253-945-5400
Randy Kaczar, prin. Fax 945-5454
Illahee MS 1,000/6-8
36001 1st Ave S 98003 253-945-4600
Stacy Lucas, prin. Fax 945-4646
Lakota MS 800/6-8
1415 SW 314th St 98023 253-945-4800
Pam Tuggle, prin. Fax 945-4848
Sacajawea MS 900/6-8
1101 S Dash Point Rd 98003 253-945-4900
Dr. Brenda McBrayer, prin. Fax 945-4949
Saghalie MS 700/6-8
33914 19th Ave SW 98023 253-945-5000
Damon Hunter, prin. Fax 945-5050
Truman HS Adult
31455 28th Ave S 98003 253-945-5800
Judith Kraft, prin. Fax 945-5858
Other Schools – See Auburn, Kent

DeVry University Post-Sec.
3600 S 344th Way 98001 253-943-2800
Gene Juarez Academy of Beauty Post-Sec.
2222 S 314th St 98003 253-839-6483
Life Academy of Puget Sound 100/K-12
414 SW 312th St 98023 253-839-7378
Sue Austin, admin. Fax 839-1031

Ferndale, Whatcom, Pop. 9,591
Ferndale SD 502 5,100/PK-12
PO Box 698 98248 360-383-9200
Dr. Roger Lehnert, supt. Fax 383-9201
www.ferndale.wednet.edu
Ferndale HS 1,500/9-12
PO Box 428 98248 360-383-9240
Dawn Fairchild, prin. Fax 383-9242
Horizon MS 400/7-8
PO Box 1769 98248 360-383-9850
David Hutchinson, prin. Fax 383-9852
Vista MS 500/7-8
PO Box 1328 98248 360-383-9370
Mary Kanikeberg, prin. Fax 383-9372
Windward HS 9-12
PO Box 428 98248 360-383-9150
Jill Iwasaki, prin. Fax 383-9152

Forks, Clallam, Pop. 3,176
Quillayute Valley SD 402 — 1,200/K-12
  411 S Spartan Ave 98331 — 360-374-6262
  Frank Walter, supt. — Fax 374-6990
  www.forks.wednet.edu
Forks HS — 300/9-12
  261 S Spartan Ave 98331 — 360-374-6262
  Steve Quick, prin. — Fax 374-9657
Forks MS — 300/6-8
  121 S Spartan Ave 98331 — 360-374-6262
  Raymond Marshall, prin. — Fax 374-2362

Friday Harbor, San Juan, Pop. 2,003
San Juan Island SD 149 — 1,200/K-12
  PO Box 458 98250 — 360-378-4133
  Michael D. Soltman, supt. — Fax 378-6276
  www.sjisd.wednet.edu
Friday Harbor HS — 400/9-12
  PO Box 458 98250 — 360-378-5215
  Marilyn Luckman, prin. — Fax 378-2647
Friday Harbor MS — 200/6-8
  PO Box 458 98250 — 360-378-5214
  Ann Spratt, prin. — Fax 378-9750

Garfield, Whitman, Pop. 629
Garfield SD 302 — 200/PK-12
  PO Box 398 99130 — 509-635-1331
  Bill LaMunyan, supt. — Fax 635-1332
  www.garpal.wednet.edu
Garfield/Palouse MS — 100/6-8
  PO Box 398 99130 — 509-635-1331
  Bill LaMunyan, prin. — Fax 635-1332

Gig Harbor, Pierce, Pop. 6,616
Peninsula SD 401 — 9,600/PK-12
  14015 62nd Ave NW 98332 — 253-530-1000
  Terry Bouck, supt. — Fax 530-1010
  www.peninsula.wednet.edu
Gig Harbor HS — 1,700/9-12
  5101 Rosedale St NW 98335 — 253-530-1400
  Greg Schellenberg, prin. — Fax 530-1420
Goodman MS — 500/6-8
  3701 38th Ave NW 98335 — 253-530-1600
  Doris Bolender, prin. — Fax 858-5515
Harbor Ridge MS — 600/6-8
  9010 Prentice Ave 98332 — 253-530-1900
  Connie West, prin. — Fax 530-1920
Kopachuck MS — 600/6-8
  10414 56th St NW 98335 — 253-530-4100
  David Clombini, prin. — Fax 265-8810
Peninsula HS — 1,500/9-12
  14105 Purdy Dr NW 98332 — 253-857-3530
  Grant Hosford, prin. — Fax 857-8133
Other Schools – See Lakebay

Glenwood, Klickitat
Glenwood SD 401 — 100/K-12
  PO Box 12 98619 — 509-364-3595
  Shane Couch, supt. — Fax 364-3689
  www.glenwood.k12.wa.us/schoolinfo.HTM
Glenwood S — 100/K-12
  PO Box 12 98619 — 509-364-3565
  Calvin McRae, prin. — Fax 364-3689

Goldendale, Klickitat, Pop. 3,736
Goldendale SD 404 — 1,200/K-12
  603 S Roosevelt Ave 98620 — 509-773-5177
  Dr. Marie Phillips, supt. — Fax 773-6028
  www.golden.wednet.edu
Goldendale HS — 400/9-12
  525 E Simcoe Dr 98620 — 509-773-5846
  Mike Lindhe, prin. — Fax 773-6900
Goldendale MS — 400/5-8
  520 E Collins St 98620 — 509-773-4323
  Dave Barta, prin. — Fax 773-4579

Graham, Pierce
Bethel SD 403
  Supt. — See Spanaway
Cougar Mountain JHS — 900/7-9
  5108 260th St E 98338 — 253-683-8000
  Cliff Anderson, prin. — Fax 683-8098
Frontier JHS — 900/7-9
  22110 108th Ave E 98338 — 253-683-8300
  Tom Mitchell, prin. — Fax 683-8398
Graham-Kapowsin HS — 10-12
  22100 108th Ave E 98338 — 253-683-6100
  Jennifer Bethman, prin. — Fax 683-6198

Grand Coulee, Grant, Pop. 907
Grand Coulee Dam SD 301J
  Supt. — See Coulee Dam
Grand Coulee Dam MS — 200/5-8
  PO Box J 99133 — 509-633-1520
  Dawn Millard, prin. — Fax 633-2257

Grandview, Yakima, Pop. 8,515
Grandview SD 200 — 3,000/K-12
  913 W 2nd St 98930 — 509-882-8500
  Kevin Chase, supt. — Fax 882-2029
  www.grandview.wednet.edu
Grandview HS — 800/9-12
  1601 W 5th St 98930 — 509-882-8750
  Arcella Hall, prin. — Fax 882-8739
Grandview MS — 700/6-8
  1401 W 2nd St 98930 — 509-882-8600
  Matt Mallery, prin. — Fax 882-8665

Granger, Yakima, Pop. 2,727
Granger SD 204 — 1,300/PK-12
  PO Box 400 98932 — 509-854-1515
  Timothy J. Dunn, supt. — Fax 854-1126
  www.gsd.wednet.edu
Granger HS — 300/9-12
  PO Box 400 98932 — 509-854-1115
  Richard Esparza, prin. — Fax 854-2757
Granger MS — 400/5-8
  PO Box 400 98932 — 509-854-1003
  Paul Nelson, prin. — Fax 854-1083

Granite Falls, Snohomish, Pop. 2,645
Granite Falls SD 332 — 3,100/K-12
  307 N Alder St 98252 — 360-691-7717
  Joel Thaut, supt. — Fax 691-4459
  www.gfalls.wednet.edu
Granite Falls HS — 700/9-12
  405 N Alder St 98252 — 360-691-7713
  Larry Brown, prin. — Fax 691-3704
Granite Falls MS — 600/6-8
  205 N Alder St 98252 — 360-691-7710
  Larry Panagos, prin. — Fax 691-3726

Greenacres, Spokane, Pop. 4,626
Central Valley SD 356 — 11,100/PK-12
  19307 E Cataldo Ave 99016 — 509-228-5400
  Mike Pearson, supt. — Fax 228-5439
  www.cvsd.org
Greenacres MS — 600/6-8
  17409 E Sprague Ave 99016 — 509-228-4860
  Vern DiGiovanni, prin. — Fax 228-4869
Other Schools – See Spokane, Veradale

Harrington, Lincoln, Pop. 417
Harrington SD 204 — 200/K-12
  PO Box 204 99134 — 509-253-4331
  Randy Behrens, supt. — Fax 456-6306
  www.harrsd.k12.wa.us
Harrington HS — 100/7-12
  PO Box 204 99134 — 509-253-4331
  Randy Behrens, prin. — Fax 456-6306

Hartline, Grant, Pop. 136
Coulee-Hartline SD 151
  Supt. — See Coulee City
Almira/Coulee-Hartline HS — 100/9-12
  PO Box 98 99135 — 509-639-2611
  Scott Brown, prin. — Fax 639-2353

Hoquiam, Grays Harbor, Pop. 8,925
Hoquiam SD 28 — 2,100/K-12
  305 Simpson Ave 98550 — 360-538-8200
  Tim McCarthy, supt. — Fax 538-8202
  www.hoquiam.k12.wa.us
Hoquiam HS — 700/9-12
  501 W Emerson Ave 98550 — 360-538-8210
  Mark VandenHazel, prin. — Fax 538-8212
Hoquiam MS — 400/7-8
  200 Spencer St 98550 — 360-538-8220
  Tony Miles, prin. — Fax 538-8222

Hunters, Stevens
Columbia SD 206 — 200/PK-12
  PO Box 7 99137 — 509-722-3311
  B. Paul Turner, supt. — Fax 722-3310
  www.columbia206.k12.wa.us/
Columbia S — 200/PK-12
  PO Box 7 99137 — 509-722-3311
  Chuck Wyborney, prin. — Fax 722-3310

Ilwaco, Pacific, Pop. 944
Ocean Beach SD 101 — 1,500/K-12
  PO Box I 98624 — 360-642-3739
  Rainer Houser, supt. — Fax 642-1298
  www.ocean.k12.wa.us
Ilwaco JSHS — 500/7-12
  PO Box F 98624 — 360-642-3731
  Lisa Nelson, prin. — Fax 642-1224

Inchelium, Ferry, Pop. 393
Inchelium SD 70 — 200/K-12
  PO Box 285 99138 — 509-722-6181
  Ron L. Washington, supt. — Fax 722-6192
  www.inchelium.wednet.edu
Inchelium S — 200/K-12
  PO Box 285 99138 — 509-722-6181
  Virginia Elkington, prin. — Fax 722-6192

Ione, Pend Oreille, Pop. 487
Selkirk SD 70
  Supt. — See Metaline Falls
Selkirk JSHS — 200/7-12
  10372 Highway 31 99139 — 509-446-3505
  Larry Reed, prin. — Fax 446-2408

Issaquah, King, Pop. 14,662
Issaquah SD 411 — 13,900/PK-12
  565 NW Holly St 98027 — 425-837-7000
  Janet Barry, supt. — Fax 837-7005
  www.issaquah.wednet.edu
Beaver Lake MS — 900/6-8
  25025 SE 32nd St 98029 — 425-837-4150
  Josh Almy, prin. — Fax 837-4195
Issaquah HS — 1,100/10-12
  700 2nd Ave SE 98027 — 425-837-6000
  Paula Phelps, prin. — Fax 837-6078
Issaquah MS — 900/6-8
  400 1st Ave SE 98027 — 425-837-6800
  Corrine DeRosa, prin. — Fax 837-6855
Pacific Cascade Freshman Campus — 9-9
  24635 SE Issaquah Fall City 98029 — 425-837-5900
  Dana Bailey, prin.
Pine Lake MS — 900/6-8
  3200 228th Ave SE 98075 — 425-837-5700
  Roy Adler, prin. — Fax 837-5762
Skyline HS — 1,200/10-12
  1122 228th Ave SE 98075 — 425-837-7700
  Ed Young, prin. — Fax 837-7705
Other Schools – See Renton

Trinity Lutheran College — Post-Sec.
  4221 228th Ave SE 98029 — 425-392-0400

Joyce, Clallam
Crescent SD 313 — 100/K-12
  PO Box 20 98343 — 360-928-3311
  Douglas Kubalek, supt. — Fax 928-3066
  www.crescent.wednet.edu
Crescent JSHS — 100/7-12
  PO Box 20 98343 — 360-928-3311
  Doug Kubalek, prin. — Fax 928-3066

Kahlotus, Franklin, Pop. 242
Kahlotus SD 56 — 50/K-12
  PO Box 69 99335 — 509-282-3338
  Warren Reeves, supt. — Fax 282-3339
Kahlotus JSHS — 50/7-12
  PO Box 69 99335 — 509-282-3338
  Ron Hopkins, prin. — Fax 282-3339

Kalama, Cowlitz, Pop. 1,893
Kalama SD 402 — 1,000/K-12
  548 China Garden Rd 98625 — 360-673-5282
  James Sutton, supt. — Fax 673-5228
  www.kalama.k12.wa.us
Kalama JSHS — 600/6-12
  548 China Garden Rd 98625 — 360-673-5212
  Mike Hamilton, prin. — Fax 673-1280

Kelso, Cowlitz, Pop. 11,744
Kelso SD 458 — 4,600/PK-12
  601 Crawford St 98626 — 360-501-1900
  Glenys Hill, supt. — Fax 501-1902
  www.kelso.wednet.edu
Coweeman MS — 500/6-8
  2000 Allen St 98626 — 360-501-1750
  Adele Marshall, prin. — Fax 501-1782
Huntington JHS — 500/6-8
  500 Redpath St 98626 — 360-501-1700
  Elaine Cockrell, prin. — Fax 501-1723
Kelso HS — 1,400/9-12
  1904 Allen St 98626 — 360-501-1800
  Pat Spear, prin. — Fax 501-1843

Cornerstone Community Christian S — 100/7-12
  PO Box 33 98626 — 360-636-1600
  Wayne Hayes, admin. — Fax 577-5955

Kenmore, King, Pop. 19,032
Northshore SD 417
  Supt. — See Bothell
Inglemoor SHS — 1,900/10-12
  15500 Simonds Rd NE 98028 — 425-489-6500
  Vicki Sherwood, prin. — Fax 489-6593
Kenmore JHS — 800/7-9
  20323 66th Ave NE 98028 — 425-489-6211
  Tim Gordon, prin. — Fax 402-5314

Kennewick, Benton, Pop. 59,334
Finley SD 53 — 1,000/PK-12
  224606 E Game Farm Rd 99337 — 509-586-3217
  Suzanne Feeney, supt. — Fax 586-4408
  www.finleysd.org
Finley MS — 300/6-8
  37208 S Finley Rd 99337 — 509-586-7561
  Rod Bryson, prin. — Fax 582-8452
River View HS — 300/9-12
  36509 S Lemon Dr 99337 — 509-582-2158
  Bob Miller, prin. — Fax 586-9297

Kennewick SD 17 — 14,200/K-12
  524 S Auburn St 99336 — 509-222-5000
  Dr. Paul Rosier, supt. — Fax 222-5050
  www.ksd.org
Desert Hills MS — 900/6-8
  6011 W 10th Pl 99338 — 509-222-6600
  Steve Jones, prin. — Fax 222-6601
Highlands MS — 800/6-8
  425 S Tweedt St 99336 — 509-222-6700
  Bill Parks, prin. — Fax 222-6701
Horse Heaven Hills MS — 900/6-8
  3500 S Vancouver St 99337 — 509-222-6800
  Susan Denslow, prin. — Fax 222-6801
Kamiakin HS — 1,400/9-12
  600 N Arthur St 99336 — 509-222-7000
  David Bond, prin. — Fax 222-7001
Kennewick HS — 1,600/9-12
  500 S Dayton St 99336 — 509-222-7100
  Jack Anderson, prin. — Fax 222-7101
Park MS — 800/6-8
  1011 W 10th Ave 99336 — 509-222-6900
  Rob Phillips, prin. — Fax 222-6901
Southridge HS — 1,400/9-12
  3320 S Union Loop 99338 — 509-222-7200
  Ron Williamson, prin. — Fax 222-7201
Tri-Tech Vocational Skills Center — Vo/Tech
  5929 W Metaline Ave 99336 — 509-222-7300
  Gerry Ringwood, prin. — Fax 222-7301

Kent, King, Pop. 81,567
Federal Way SD 210
  Supt. — See Federal Way
Totem MS — 800/6-8
  26630 40th Ave S 98032 — 253-945-5100
  Jeanette Crute-Bullock, prin. — Fax 945-5151

Kent SD 415 — 24,200/K-12
  12033 SE 256th St 98030 — 253-373-7000
  Dr. Barbara Grohe, supt. — Fax 373-7231
  www.kent.k12.wa.us
Kentlake SHS — 1,300/9-12
  21401 SE 300th St 98042 — 253-373-4900
  Diana Pratt, prin. — Fax 373-4908
Kent-Meridian SHS — 1,300/9-12
  10020 SE 256th St, 98030 — 253-373-7405
  David Dorn, prin. — Fax 373-7411
Kentridge SHS — 1,600/9-12
  12430 SE 208th St 98031 — 253-373-7345
  Mike Albrecht, prin. — Fax 373-7363
Meridian MS — 700/7-8
  23480 120th Ave SE 98031 — 253-373-7383
  Doug Boushey, prin. — Fax 373-7395
Mill Creek MS — 500/7-8
  620 Central Ave N 98032 — 253-373-7448
  Dennis Duffy, prin. — Fax 373-7478
Sequoia MS — 700/7-8
  11000 SE 264th St, 98031 — 253-373-7542
  Beverlie Duff, prin. — Fax 373-7554
Other Schools – See Covington, Renton

Rainier Christian MS 100/7-8
26201 180th Ave SE 98042 253-639-7715
Ed Parr, admin. Fax 639-3184

Kettle Falls, Stevens, Pop. 1,545
Kettle Falls SD 212 800/K-12
PO Box 458 99141 509-738-6625
Greg Goodnight, supt. Fax 738-6375
www.kettlefalls.wednet.edu/
Kettle Falls HS 300/9-12
PO Box 458 99141 509-738-6388
James Hill, prin. Fax 738-2670
Kettle Falls MS 200/5-8
PO Box 458 99141 509-738-6014
Tom Graham, prin. Fax 738-2401

Kingston, Kitsap, Pop. 1,270
North Kitsap SD 400
Supt. — See Poulsbo
Kingston JHS 800/7-9
9000 NE West Kingston Rd 98346 360-394-4900
Ed Serra, prin. Fax 394-4901

Kirkland, King, Pop. 45,573
Lake Washington SD 414
Supt. — See Redmond
Finn Hill JHS 500/7-9
8040 NE 132nd St 98034 425-821-6544
Victor Scarpelli, prin. Fax 814-2955
Juanita SHS 1,100/10-12
10601 NE 132nd St 98034 425-823-7600
Jane Todd, prin. Fax 823-7637
Kamiakin JHS 700/7-9
14111 132nd Ave NE 98034 425-823-6750
Joe Joss, prin. Fax 823-2921
Kirkland JHS 500/7-9
430 18th Ave 98033 425-822-6224
Deborah McCarson, prin. Fax 889-1589
Lake Washington SHS 1,200/10-12
12033 NE 80th St 98033 425-828-3371
Mark Robertson, prin. Fax 828-3390

Lake Washington Technical College Post-Sec.
11605 132nd Ave NE 98034 425-739-8100
Northwest University Post-Sec.
PO Box 579 98083 425-822-8266
Puget Sound Adventist Academy 100/9-12
5320 108th Ave NE 98033 425-822-7554
Doug White, prin. Fax 828-0856

Kittitas, Kittitas, Pop. 1,098
Kittitas SD 403 600/K-12
PO Box 599 98934 509-968-3014
Jerry Harding, supt. Fax 968-4730
www.kittitas.wednet.edu
Kittitas HS 300/6-12
PO Box 599 98934 509-968-3902
Monty Sabin, prin. Fax 968-4730

Klickitat, Klickitat
Klickitat SD 402 100/K-12
PO Box 37 98628 509-369-4145
Ron Hackbarth, supt. Fax 369-3422
Klickitat JSHS 7-12
PO Box 37 98628 509-369-4145
Jerry Lynch, prin. Fax 369-3422

La Center, Clark, Pop. 1,788
La Center SD 101 1,300/K-12
PO Box 1840 98629 360-263-2131
Mark Mansell, supt. Fax 263-1140
www.lacenterschools.org
La Center HS 500/9-12
PO Box 98629 360-263-1700
Dave Holmes, prin. Fax 263-1705
La Center MS 300/6-8
PO Box 1750 98629 360-263-2136
Bill Penrose, prin. Fax 263-5936

Lacey, Thurston, Pop. 32,781
North Thurston SD 3 12,800/PK-12
305 College St NE 98516 360-412-4400
Dr. James Koval, supt. Fax 412-4410
www.nthurston.k12.wa.us
Chinook MS 700/7-8
4301 6th Ave NE 98516 360-412-4760
Monica Sweet, prin. Fax 412-4769
Komachin MS 700/7-8
3650 College St SE 98503 360-412-4740
Fax 412-4749
Nisqually MS 600/7-8
8100 Steilacoom Rd SE 98503 360-412-4770
Karen Owen, prin. Fax 493-2756
North Thurston HS 1,400/9-12
600 Sleater Kinney Rd NE 98506 360-412-4800
Steve Rood, prin. Fax 412-4819
River Ridge HS 1,200/9-12
350 River Ridge Dr SE 98513 360-412-4820
Brian Hunter, prin. Fax 412-4839
Timberline HS 1,300/9-12
6120 Mullen Rd SE 98503 360-412-4860
Dave Lehnis, prin. Fax 412-4879

Northwest Christian HS 200/9-12
4710 Park Center Ave NE 98516 360-491-2966
Al Lynch, prin. Fax 491-3086
St. Martin's University Post-Sec.
5300 Pacific Ave SE 98503 360-491-4700

La Conner, Skagit, Pop. 769
La Conner SD 311 600/K-12
PO Box 2103 98257 360-466-3171
Tim Bruce, supt. Fax 466-3523
lcsd.wednet.edu/index.htm
La Conner HS, PO Box 2103 98257 360-466-3173
Kurt Schonberg, prin.
La Conner MS, PO Box 2103 98257 200/6-8
K. C. Knudson, prin. 360-466-4113

La Crosse, Whitman, Pop. 370
LaCrosse SD 126 200/K-12
PO Box 218 99143 509-549-3591
Gary Wargo, supt. Fax 549-3529
www.lax.wednet.edu
LaCrosse JSHS 100/7-12
PO Box 218 99143 509-549-3592
Doug Curtis, prin. Fax 549-3529

Lakebay, Pierce
Peninsula SD 401
Supt. — See Gig Harbor
Key Peninsula MS 600/6-8
5510 Key Peninsula Hwy N 98349 253-530-4200
Sharon Shaffer, prin. Fax 530-4220

Lake Stevens, Snohomish, Pop. 7,015
Lake Stevens SD 4 7,200/PK-12
12309 22nd St NE 98258 425-335-1500
David Burgess, supt. Fax 335-1549
www.lkstevens.wednet.edu
Lake Stevens HS 2,100/9-12
2908 113th Ave NE 98258 425-335-1515
Ken Collins, prin. Fax 335-1524
North Lake MS 900/6-8
2202 123rd Ave NE 98258 425-335-1530
Gary Taber, prin. Fax 335-1576
Other Schools – See Everett

Lakewood, Snohomish, Pop. 58,789
Clover Park SD 400 12,700/PK-12
10903 Gravelly Lake Dr SW 98499 253-583-5000
Dr. Doris McEwen Walker, supt. Fax 583-5198
www.cloverpark.k12.wa.us/
Clover Park HS 1,500/9-12
11023 Gravelly Lake Dr SW 98499 253-583-5500
John Seaton, prin. Fax 583-5508
Hudtloff MS 700/6-8
7702 Phillips Rd SW 98498 253-583-5400
Moureen David, prin. Fax 583-5408
Lakes HS 1,500/9-12
10320 Farwest Dr SW 98498 253-583-5550
Georgia Dewhurst, prin. Fax 583-5558
Lochburn MS 700/6-8
5431 Steilacoom Blvd SW 98499 253-583-5420
Helen Wilson, prin. Fax 583-5428
Mann MS 600/6-8
11509 Holden Rd SW 98498 253-583-5440
John Miller, prin. Fax 583-5448
Woodbrook MS 800/6-8
14920 Spring St SW 98439 253-583-5460
Nancy LaChapelle, prin. Fax 583-5468

Clover Park Technical College Post-Sec.
4500 Steilacoom Blvd SW 98499 253-589-5800
Pierce College Post-Sec.
9401 Farwest Dr SW 98498 253-964-6500

Lamont, Whitman, Pop. 104
Lamont SD 264 50/6-8
602 Main St 99017 509-257-2463
Mark Stedman, supt. Fax 257-2316
Lamont MS 50/6-8
602 Main St 99017 509-257-2463
Joseph Whipple, prin. Fax 257-2316

Langley, Island, Pop. 1,011
South Whidbey SD 206 2,200/K-12
PO Box 346 98260 360-221-6100
Robert Brown, supt. Fax 221-3835
www.sw.wednet.edu
Langley MS 500/6-8
PO Box 370 98260 360-221-5100
Darrell Posch, prin. Fax 221-8545
South Whidbey HS 800/9-12
PO Box 390 98260 360-221-4300
Mike Johnson, prin. Fax 221-5797

Leavenworth, Chelan, Pop. 2,120
Cascade SD 228 1,500/PK-12
330 Evans St 98826 509-548-5885
Rob Clark, supt. Fax 548-6149
www.cascade.wednet.edu/
Cascade HS 500/9-12
10190 Chumstick Hwy 98826 509-548-5277
Bill Wadlington, prin. Fax 548-7458
Icicle River MS 300/6-8
10195 Titus Rd 98826 509-548-4042
Kenny Renner-Singer, prin. Fax 548-6646

Upper Valley Christian S 100/K-12
111 Ski Hill Dr 98826 509-548-5292
John Bangsund, admin. Fax 548-5293

Lind, Adams, Pop. 573
Lind SD 158 200/PK-12
PO Box 340 99341 509-677-3481
David Thomas, supt. Fax 677-3463
www.lind.k12.wa.us
Lind JSHS 100/7-12
PO Box 340 99341 509-677-3408
John McGregor, prin. Fax 677-3420

Longview, Cowlitz, Pop. 35,741
Longview SD 122 7,500/PK-12
2715 Lilac St 98632 360-575-7000
Dr. Nicholas Seaver, supt. Fax 575-7022
www.longview.k12.wa.us
Cascade MS, 2821 Parkview Dr 98632 900/6-8
Bruce Holway, prin. 360-577-2703
Long HS 1,100/9-12
2903 Nichols Blvd 98632 360-575-7225
Rolland Johnson, prin. Fax 577-2828
Monticello MS, 1225 28th Ave 98632 900/6-8
Bill Marshall, prin. 360-575-7050
Morris HS, 1602 Mark Morris Ct 98632 1,100/9-12
Chris Fritsch, prin. 360-575-7100
Mt. Solo MS, 5300 Mt Solo Rd 98632 6-8
Lori Cournyer, prin. 360-577-2800

Lower Columbia College Post-Sec.
PO Box 3010 98632 360-577-2300
Stylemasters College of Hair Design Post-Sec.
1224 Commerce Ave 98632 360-636-2720

Lopez Island, San Juan
Lopez Island SD 144 300/K-12
86 School Rd 98261 360-468-2202
Bill Evans, supt. Fax 468-2212
www.lopez.k12.wa.us
Lopez Island HS 200/6-12
86 School Rd 98261 360-468-2219
Roland MacNichol, prin.

Lyle, Klickitat
Lyle SD 406 400/K-12
PO Box 368 98635 509-365-2191
Martin Huffman, supt. Fax 365-5000
Lyle HS 100/9-12
PO Box 368 98635 509-365-2211
Phill Williams, prin. Fax 365-2665
Lyle MS 100/7-8
PO Box 368 98635 509-365-2211
Phil Williams, prin. Fax 365-2665

Lynden, Whatcom, Pop. 10,039
Lynden SD 504 2,600/K-12
1203 Bradley Rd 98264 360-354-4443
Dennis L. Carlson Ed.D., supt. Fax 354-7662
www.lynden.wednet.edu
Lynden HS 900/9-12
1201 Bradley Rd 98264 360-354-4401
Jeff Baglio, prin. Fax 354-0991
Lynden MS 600/6-8
516 Main St 98264 360-354-2952
Kris Petersen, prin. Fax 354-6631

Meridian SD 505
Supt. — See Bellingham
Meridian MS 400/6-8
861 Ten Mile Rd 98264 360-398-2291
Gerald Sanderson, prin. Fax 398-8131

Cornerstone Christian S 100/1-12
8872 Northwood Rd 98264 360-318-0663
Otto Bouwman, prin. Fax 318-8175
Lynden Christian HS 500/9-12
515 Drayton St 98264 360-354-3221
Keith Lambert, prin. Fax 354-1047
Lynden Christian MS 300/5-8
503 Nooksack Ave 98264 360-354-3358
Sheryl Holwerda, prin. Fax 354-6690

Lynnwood, Snohomish, Pop. 33,704
Edmonds SD 15 20,400/PK-12
20420 68th Ave W 98036 425-431-7000
Nick J. Brossoit Ed.D., supt. Fax 431-7182
www.edmonds.wednet.edu
Alderwood MS 800/7-8
20000 28th Ave W 98036 425-431-7579
Mike VanOrden, prin. Fax 431-7580
College Place MS 700/7-8
7501 208th St SW 98036 425-431-7451
Thea Gardner, prin. Fax 431-7449
Lynnwood HS 1,400/9-12
3001 184th St SW 98037 425-431-7520
David Golden, prin. Fax 431-7527
Meadowdale HS 1,600/9-12
6002 168th St SW 98037 425-431-7650
Dale Cote, prin. Fax 431-7655
Meadowdale MS 700/7-8
6500 168th St SW 98037 425-431-7707
Christine Avery, prin. Fax 431-7714
Other Schools – See Brier, Edmonds, Mountlake Terrace

Bryman College Post-Sec.
19020 33rd Ave W Ste 250 98036 425-778-9894
Edmonds Community College Post-Sec.
20000 68th Ave W 98036 425-640-1500

Mabton, Yakima, Pop. 2,038
Mabton SD 120 900/K-12
PO Box 37 98935 509-894-4852
Sandra Pasiero-Davis, supt. Fax 894-4769
www.mabton.wednet.edu
Mabton JSHS 400/7-12
PO Box 38 98935 509-894-4951
Keith Morris, prin. Fax 894-4761

Mansfield, Douglas, Pop. 322
Mansfield SD 207 100/PK-12
PO Box 188 98830 509-683-1012
Larry Keller, supt. Fax 683-1281
www.mansfield.wednet.edu/
Mansfield S 100/PK-12
PO Box 188 98830 509-683-1012
Larry Keller, prin. Fax 683-1281

Manson, Chelan
Manson SD 19 700/PK-12
PO Box A 98831 509-687-3140
Steve McKenna, supt. Fax 687-9877
www.manson.org
Manson JSHS 300/7-12
PO Box A 98831 509-687-9585
Marsha Hanson, prin. Fax 687-6109

Maple Valley, King, Pop. 14,119
Tahoma SD 409 6,300/K-12
25720 Maple Valley Black Di 98038 425-413-3400
Mike Maryanski, supt. Fax 413-3455
www.tahoma.wednet.edu
Other Schools – See Covington, Ravensdale

Marysville, Snohomish, Pop. 28,260
Lakewood SD 306 2,600/PK-12
17110 16th Dr NE 98271 360-652-4500
Larry Francois, supt. Fax 652-4502
www.lwsd.wednet.edu

Lakewood HS 800/9-12
17023 11th Ave NE 98271 360-652-4505
Kevin Allen, prin. Fax 652-4507
Lakewood MS 600/6-8
16800 16th Dr NE 98271 360-652-4510
Crystal Knight, prin. Fax 652-4512

Marysville SD 25 10,300/PK-12
4220 80th St NE 98270 360-653-7058
Dr. Larry Nyland, supt. Fax 653-9707
www.msvl.k12.wa.us
Cedarcrest MS 900/6-8
6400 88th St NE 98270 360-653-0850
Susan Bell, prin. Fax 658-9699
Marysville JHS 900/8-9
1605 7th St 98270 360-653-0610
Judy Albertson, prin. Fax 659-2780
Marysville-Pilchuck SHS 2,200/10-12
5611 108th St NE 98271 360-653-0600
Tracy Suchan Toothaker, prin. Fax 659-1364

Grace Academy 400/PK-12
8521 67th Ave NE 98270 360-659-8517
Timothy Lugg, prin. Fax 653-5899

Mattawa, Grant, Pop. 3,170
Wahluke SD 73 1,800/PK-12
PO Box 907 99349 509-932-4565
Dr. William Miller, supt. Fax 932-4571
www.wsd73.wednet.edu
Schott MS 400/6-8
PO Box 907 99349 509-932-4455
Lester McCormick, prin. Fax 932-4282
Sentinel Technical Center Vo/Tech
PO Box 907 99349 509-932-3133
Dale Hedman, prin. Fax 932-3320
Wahluke HS 400/9-12
PO Box 907 99349 509-932-4477
Dale Hedman, prin. Fax 932-4241

Mead, Spokane
Mead SD 354 8,600/K-12
12828 N Newport Hwy 99021 509-465-6000
Thomas Rockefeller, supt. Fax 465-6020
www.mead.k12.wa.us
Mead MS 600/7-8
12509 N Market St 99021 509-465-7400
Craig Busch, prin. Fax 465-7420
Mount Spokane HS 1,300/9-12
6015 E Mt Spokane Park Dr 99021 509-465-7200
John Hook, prin. Fax 465-7220
Other Schools – See Spokane

Medical Lake, Spokane, Pop. 4,003
Medical Lake SD 326 2,300/PK-12
PO Box 128 99022 509-565-3100
Dr. Pam Veltri, supt. Fax 565-3102
www.mlsd.org/
Medical Lake HS 700/9-12
PO Box 128 99022 509-565-3200
Scott Blasingame, prin. Fax 565-3201
Medical Lake MS 300/7-8
PO Box 128 99022 509-565-3300
Mike Dahmen, prin. Fax 565-3301

Lakeland Village School Post-Sec.
PO Box 200 99022

Menlo, Pacific
Willapa Valley SD 160 300/K-12
PO Box 128 98561 360-942-5855
Dr. Paula Akerlund, supt. Fax 942-3216
www.willapa.wednet.edu
Menlo MS, PO Box 128 98561 6-8
Rob Friese, prin. 360-942-2006
Willapa Valley HS, PO Box 128 98561 200/9-12
Rob Friese, prin. 360-942-2006

Mercer Island, King, Pop. 22,351
Mercer Island SD 400 4,100/K-12
4160 86th Ave SE 98040 206-236-3330
Dr. Cynthia Sickman Simms, supt. Fax 236-3333
www.misd.k12.wa.us
Islander MS 1,100/6-8
8225 SE 72nd St 98040 206-236-3400
Sharon Gillaspie, prin. Fax 236-3408
Mercer Island HS 1,400/9-12
9100 SE 42nd St 98040 206-236-3345
John Harrison, prin. Fax 236-3358

ETC Preparatory Academy 100/K-12
8005 SE 28th St Ste 102 98040 206-236-1095
Meredith Oullette, dir. Fax 236-0998
Northwest Yeshiva HS 100/9-12
5017 90th Ave SE 98040 206-232-5272
Rabbi Bernie Fox, dean Fax 232-2711

Metaline Falls, Pend Oreille, Pop. 226
Selkirk SD 70 400/PK-12
PO Box 129 99153 509-446-2951
Nancy Lotze, supt. Fax 446-2929
www.selkirk.k12.wa.us
Other Schools – See Ione

Mill Creek, Snohomish, Pop. 12,832
Everett SD 2
Supt. — See Everett
Heatherwood MS 800/6-8
1419 Trillium Blvd SE 98012 425-385-6300
Greg Gelderman, prin. Fax 385-6302
Jackson HS 1,700/9-12
1508 136th St SE 98012 425-385-7000
Terry Cheshire, prin. Fax 385-7002

Monroe, Snohomish, Pop. 14,798
Monroe SD 103 5,900/K-12
200 E Fremont St 98272 360-794-7777
Dr. Bill Prenevost, supt. Fax 794-3029
www.monroe.wednet.edu
Monroe HS 1,300/9-12
17001 Tester Rd 98272 360-863-4000
Lou Imbesi, prin. Fax 805-0528
Monroe MS 500/6-8
351 Short Columbia St 98272 360-794-3020
Cyndy McCartney, prin. Fax 805-3233
Park Place MS 700/6-8
1408 W Main St 98272 360-794-3010
JoAnn Carbonetti, prin. Fax 794-7833
Other Schools – See Snohomish

Montesano, Grays Harbor, Pop. 3,318
Montesano SD 66 1,300/PK-12
302 N Church St 98563 360-249-3942
Dr. Marti Harruff, supt. Fax 249-3391
www.monte.wednet.edu
Montesano JSHS 700/7-12
303 N Church St 98563 360-249-4041
David Lipe, prin. Fax 249-4459
Community Education Adult
302 N Church St 98563 360-249-5781
Judy Thompson, coord. Fax 249-3391

Morton, Lewis, Pop. 1,062
Morton SD 214 500/K-12
PO Box H 98356 360-496-5300
John Flaherty, supt. Fax 586-3208
www.morton.wednet.edu
Morton JSHS 300/6-12
PO Box F 98356 360-496-5137
Joshua Brooks, prin. Fax 586-3208

Moses Lake, Grant, Pop. 16,147
Moses Lake SD 161 6,600/K-12
920 W Ivy Ave 98837 509-766-2650
Steven Chestnut, supt. Fax 766-2678
www.moseslakeschools.org
Chief Moses MS 800/6-8
1111 E Nelson Rd 98837 509-766-2661
Mark Johnson, prin. Fax 766-2680
Frontier MS 700/6-8
517 W 3rd Ave 98837 509-766-2662
Chris Lupo, prin. Fax 766-2663
Moses Lake HS 1,800/9-12
803 Sharon Ave E 98837 509-766-2666
Dave Balcom, prin. Fax 766-2682

Big Bend Community College Post-Sec.
7662 Chanute St NE 98837 509-762-5351
Moses Lake Christian Academy 300/PK-12
1001 N Grape Dr 98837 509-765-9704
LeAnne Parton, admin. Fax 765-3698

Mossyrock, Lewis, Pop. 500
Mossyrock SD 206 500/K-12
PO Box 478 98564 360-983-3181
Dr. Karen Ernest, supt. Fax 983-8111
viking.mossyrock.k12.wa.us
Mossyrock HS 200/9-12
PO Box 454 98564 360-983-3183
Jim Forrest, prin. Fax 983-3188
Mossyrock JHS 7-8
PO Box 454 98564 360-983-3183
Jim Forrest, prin. Fax 983-3188

Mountlake Terrace, Snohomish, Pop. 20,606
Edmonds SD 15
Supt. — See Lynnwood
Mountlake Terrace HS 1,800/9-12
21801 44th Ave W 98043 425-431-7776
Greg Schwab, prin. Fax 431-7771

North Sound Christian HS 200/7-12
23607 54th Ave W 98043 425-774-7773
Debbie Schindler, admin. Fax 774-3218

Mount Vernon, Skagit, Pop. 27,935
Mount Vernon SD 320 5,800/K-12
124 E Lawrence St 98273 360-428-6110
Carl Bruner, supt. Fax 428-6172
www.mv.k12.wa.us
LaVenture MS 400/7-8
1200 N Laventure Rd 98273 360-428-6116
Tara Dowd, prin. Fax 428-6189
Mount Baker MS 500/7-8
2310 E Section St 98274 360-428-6127
Beth Ashley, prin. Fax 428-6155
Mount Vernon HS 1,800/9-12
314 N 9th St 98273 360-428-6100
David Anderson, prin. Fax 428-6152

Mt. Vernon Beauty School Post-Sec.
615 S 1st St 98273 360-336-6553
Mt. Vernon Christian S 300/K-12
820 W Blackburn Rd 98273 360-424-9157
Patrick DeJong, prin. Fax 424-9256
Skagit Valley College Post-Sec.
2405 E College Way 98273 360-416-7600

Mukilteo, Snohomish, Pop. 19,169
Mukilteo SD 6
Supt. — See Everett
Harbour Pointe MS 900/6-8
5000 Harbour Pointe Blvd 98275 425-356-6658
Nikki Cannen, prin. Fax 356-6660
Kamiak HS 2,100/9-12
10801 Harbour Pointe Blvd 98275 425-356-6620
Keith Rittel, prin. Fax 356-6635
Olympic View MS 900/6-8
2602 Mukilteo Speedway 98275 425-356-1308
Nancy Coogan, prin. Fax 356-1332

Naches, Yakima, Pop. 669
Naches Valley SD JT3 1,400/K-12
PO Box 99 98937 509-653-2220
Duane Lyons, supt. Fax 653-1211
www.naches.wednet.edu
Naches Valley HS 500/9-12
PO Box 159 98937 509-653-2342
Rich Rouleau, prin. Fax 653-2921
Naches Valley MS 500/5-8
PO Box 39 98937 509-653-2725
Todd Hilmes, prin. Fax 653-2729

Nile Christian S / Hope Academy 50/K-12
370 Flying H Loop 98937 509-658-2990
Bruce Gillespie, prin. Fax 658-2009

Napavine, Lewis, Pop. 1,419
Napavine SD 14 700/PK-12
PO Box 840 98565 360-262-3303
George Crawford, supt. Fax 262-9737
www.napa.k12.wa.us
Napavine JSHS 300/7-12
PO Box 357 98565 360-262-3301
Douglas Skinner, prin. Fax 262-9541

Naselle, Pacific
Naselle-Grays River Valley SD 155 400/K-12
793 State Route 4 98638 360-484-7123
Alan Bennett, supt. Fax 484-3191
www.naselle.wednet.edu
Naselle-Grays River Valley S 400/K-12
793 State Route 4 98638 360-484-7121
Karen Wirkkala, prin. Fax 484-3191

Neah Bay, Clallam, Pop. 916
Cape Flattery SD 401
Supt. — See Sekiu
Neah Bay S 300/K-12
PO Box 86 98357 360-645-2221
Ann Renker, prin. Fax 645-2574

Newman Lake, Spokane
East Valley SD 361
Supt. — See Spokane
Mountain View MS 500/6-8
6011 N Chase Rd 99025 509-226-1379
Jim McAdam, prin. Fax 226-3082

Newport, Pend Oreille, Pop. 2,105
Newport SD 56-415 1,300/PK-12
PO Box 70 99156 509-447-3167
Teresa von Marbod, supt. Fax 447-2553
www.newport.wednet.edu
Halstead MS 400/5-8
PO Box 70 99156 509-447-2426
Janet Burcham, prin. Fax 447-4914
Newport HS 400/9-12
PO Box 70 99156 509-447-2481
Steve McCoy, prin. Fax 447-4354

Nine Mile Falls, Spokane
Nine Mile Falls SD 325 1,600/PK-12
10110 W Charles Rd 99026 509-340-4300
Michael Green, supt. Fax 340-4301
www.9mile.org
Lakeside HS 600/9-12
5909 Highway 291 99026 509-340-4200
Bob Anacker, prin. Fax 340-4201
Lakeside MS 400/6-8
6169 Highway 291 99026 509-340-4100
Jeff Baerwald, prin. Fax 340-4101

Northport, Stevens, Pop. 332
Northport SD 211 200/K-12
PO Box 1280 99157 509-732-4441
Patsy Guglielmino, supt. Fax 233-2815
www.northportschools.org
Northport HS 100/9-12
PO Box 1280 99157 509-732-4430
Patsy Guglielmino, prin. Fax 233-2815

Oakesdale, Whitman, Pop. 415
Oakesdale SD 324 100/K-12
PO Box 228 99158 509-285-5296
Steven Deal, supt. Fax 285-5121
www.oakesdale.wednet.edu
Oakesdale HS 50/9-12
PO Box 228 99158 509-285-5296
Karl Ostheller, prin. Fax 285-5121

Oak Harbor, Island, Pop. 21,071
Oak Harbor SD 201 6,000/PK-12
350 S Oak Harbor St 98277 360-279-5000
Dr. Rick Schulte, supt. Fax 279-5070
www.ohsd.net
North Whidbey MS 700/6-8
67 NE Izett St 98277 360-279-5500
Dale Leach, prin. Fax 675-1420
Oak Harbor HS 1,700/9-12
950 NW 2nd Ave 98277 360-279-5400
Dwight Lundstrom, prin. Fax 679-4846
Oak Harbor MS 600/6-8
150 SW 6th Ave 98277 360-279-5300
Peggy Ellis, prin. Fax 279-5399

Oakville, Grays Harbor, Pop. 671
Oakville SD 400 300/K-12
PO Box H 98568 360-273-0171
Brian Metke, supt. Fax 273-6724
Oakville JSHS 100/7-12
PO Box H 98568 360-273-5947
Kevin Acuff, prin. Fax 273-8229

Ocean Shores, Grays Harbor, Pop. 4,125
North Beach SD 64 700/K-12
PO Box 159 98569 360-289-2447
Stanley Pinnick, supt. Fax 289-2492
www.northbeach.k12.wa.us
North Beach HS 200/9-12
PO Box 969 98569 360-289-3888
Roger Lee, prin. Fax 289-0996
North Beach MS 200/6-8
PO Box 969 98569 360-289-2666
Roger Lee, prin. Fax 289-0996

Odessa, Lincoln, Pop. 940
Odessa SD 105-157-166 J   300/K-12
   PO Box 248 99159   509-982-2668
   Douglas L. Johnson, supt.   Fax 982-0163
   www.odessa.wednet.edu/
Odessa JSHS   200/6-12
   PO Box 248 99159   509-982-2111
   Ken C. Schutz, prin.   Fax 982-0163

Okanogan, Okanogan, Pop. 2,389
Okanogan SD 105   1,000/K-12
   PO Box 592 98840   509-422-3629
   Dr. Richard Johnson, supt.   Fax 422-1525
   www.oksd.wednet.edu
Okanogan HS   300/9-12
   PO Box 592 98840   509-422-3770
   Tom Monroe, prin.   Fax 422-4457
Okanogan MS   200/6-8
   PO Box 592 98840   509-422-2680
   Brett Baum, prin.   Fax 422-0068

Olympia, Thurston, Pop. 43,963
Olympia SD 111   8,900/K-12
   1113 Legion Way SE 98501   360-596-6100
   Bill Lahmann, supt.   Fax 596-6111
   osd.wednet.edu
Capital HS   1,600/9-12
   2707 Conger Ave NW 98502   360-596-8000
   Teri Ploff, prin.   Fax 596-8001
Jefferson MS   400/6-8
   2200 Conger Ave NW 98502   360-596-3200
   Michael Cimino, prin.   Fax 596-3201
Marshall MS   400/6-8
   3939 20th Ave NW 98502   360-596-7600
   Kevin Evoy, prin.   Fax 596-7601
Olympia HS   1,800/9-12
   1302 North St SE 98501   360-596-7000
   Matt Grant, prin.   Fax 596-7001
Reeves MS   400/6-8
   2200 Quince St NE 98506   360-596-3400
   Martha Roth, prin.   Fax 596-3401
Washington MS   700/6-8
   3100 Cain Rd SE 98501   360-596-3000
   Joni Wolpert, prin.   Fax 596-3001

Tumwater SD 33
   Supt. — See Tumwater
West Black Hills HS   900/9-12
   7741 Littlerock Rd SW 98512   360-709-7800
   Jim Hainer, prin.   Fax 709-7802

Evergreen State College   Post-Sec.
   2700 Evergreen Pkwy NW 98505   360-866-6000
Nova S   100/6-8
   2020 22nd Ave SE 98501   360-491-7097
   Lisa Iverson, admin.   Fax 491-0775
Sunrise Beach S   50/K-12
   6101 Mink St NW 98502   360-866-1343
   Roxanne Cox, admin.   Fax 866-1824

Omak, Okanogan, Pop. 4,730
Omak SD 19   1,700/PK-12
   PO Box 833 98841   509-826-0320
   R. Robert Risinger, supt.   Fax 826-7689
   www.omaksd.wednet.edu
Omak HS   500/9-12
   PO Box 833 98841   509-826-5150
   John Belcher, prin.   Fax 826-8515
Omak MS   400/6-8
   PO Box 833 98841   509-826-2320
   John Belcher, prin.   Fax 826-7696

Wenatchee Valley College   Post-Sec.
   PO Box 2058 98841   509-422-7805

Onalaska, Lewis
Onalaska SD 300   900/K-12
   540 Carlisle Ave 98570   360-978-4111
   Dale McDaniel, supt.   Fax 978-4185
   www.onysd.wednet.edu
Onalaska HS   300/K-12
   540 Carlisle Ave 98570   360-978-4113
   Bill Huizinga, prin.   Fax 978-5040

Oroville, Okanogan, Pop. 1,591
Oroville SD 410   700/PK-12
   816 Juniper St 98844   509-476-2281
   Dr. Ernie Bartelson, supt.   Fax 476-2190
   www.oroville.wednet.edu/
Oroville JSHS   400/7-12
   816 Juniper St 98844   509-476-3612
   Steve Quick, prin.   Fax 476-3224

Orting, Pierce, Pop. 4,387
Orting SD 344   1,900/K-12
   120 Washington Ave N 98360   360-893-6500
   Jeff Davis, supt.   Fax 893-2300
   www.orting.wednet.edu
Orting HS   500/9-12
   320 Washington Ave N 98360   360-893-2246
   Gerald Black, prin.   Fax 893-5701
Orting MS   500/6-8
   121 Whitesell St E 98360   360-893-3565
   Patrick Kelly, prin.   Fax 893-2919

Othello, Adams, Pop. 6,003
Othello SD 147-163-55   3,100/K-12
   615 E Juniper St 99344   509-488-2659
   George Juarez, supt.   Fax 488-5876
   www.othello.wednet.edu
McFarland JHS   500/7-8
   790 S 10th Ave 99344   509-488-3326
   Dennis Adams, prin.   Fax 488-4844
Othello HS   800/9-12
   340 S 7th Ave 99344   509-488-3351
   William Duncanson, prin.   Fax 488-4600

Palouse, Whitman, Pop. 986
Palouse SD 301   200/PK-12
   600 E Alder St 99161   509-878-1921
   Bev Fox, supt.   Fax 878-1948
   www.garpal.wednet.edu
Garfield-Palouse HS   100/9-12
   600 E Alder St 99161   509-878-1921
   Steven Heeg, prin.   Fax 878-1675

Pasco, Franklin, Pop. 38,233
Pasco SD 1   10,200/K-12
   1215 W Lewis St 99301   509-543-6700
   Saundra L. Hill, supt.   Fax 546-2685
   www.pasco.wednet.edu
McLoughlin MS   900/6-8
   2803 N Rd 88 99301   509-547-4542
   Michelle Whitney, prin.   Fax 543-6797
Ochoa MS   800/6-8
   1801 E Sheppard St 99301   509-543-6742
   Jackie Ramirez, prin.   Fax 543-6744
Pasco HS   2,500/9-12
   1108 N 10th Ave 99301   509-547-5581
   Raul Sital, prin.   Fax 546-2684
Stevens MS   800/6-8
   1120 N 10th Ave 99301   509-543-6798
   Robert Elizondo, prin.   Fax 546-2854

Clare's Beauty College   Post-Sec.
   104 N 4th Ave 99301   509-547-8871
Columbia Basin College   Post-Sec.
   2600 N 20th Ave 99301   509-547-0511
Kingspoint Christian S   100/PK-12
   7900 W Court St 99301   509-547-6498
   Georgia Perkins, admin.   Fax 547-6788
Tri Cities Preparatory S   50/9-10
   9612 Saint Thomas Dr 99301   509-546-2465
   Steve Potter, prin.   Fax 546-2490
Tri-City Junior Academy   100/K-10
   4115 W Henry St 99301   509-547-8092
   Anthony Oucharek, prin.   Fax 547-8516

Pateros, Okanogan, Pop. 622
Pateros SD 122   300/K-12
   PO Box 98 98846   509-923-2751
   Neal Powell Ph.D., supt.   Fax 923-2283
   www.pateros.org
Pateros S, PO Box 98 98846   509-923-2343
   Gary Weitz, prin.

Pe Ell, Lewis, Pop. 669
Pe Ell SD 301   300/K-12
   PO Box 368 98572   360-291-3244
   Scott Fenter, supt.   Fax 291-3823
Pe Ell S   300/K-12
   PO Box 368 98572   360-291-3244
   F. Patrick Meehan, prin.   Fax 291-3823

Pomeroy, Garfield, Pop. 1,502
Pomeroy SD 110   400/K-12
   PO Box 950 99347   509-843-3393
   James Kowalkowski, supt.   Fax 843-3046
   www.psd.wednet.edu
Pomeroy JSHS   200/7-12
   PO Box 950 99347   509-843-1331
   Kim Spacek, prin.   Fax 843-8245

Port Angeles, Clallam, Pop. 18,516
Port Angeles SD 121   4,400/K-12
   216 E 4th St 98362   360-457-8575
   Gary D. Cohn, supt.   Fax 457-4649
   www.portangelesschools.org/
North Olympic Peninsula Skills Center   Vo/Tech
   905 W 9th St 98363   360-565-1533
   Dr. Clyde Rasmussen, prin.
Port Angeles HS   1,500/9-12
   304 E Park Ave 98362   360-452-7602
   Scott Harker, prin.   Fax 452-0256
Roosevelt MS   500/6-8
   106 Monroe Rd 98362   360-452-8973
   Brad Boudreau, prin.   Fax 452-4011
Stevens MS   600/6-8
   1139 W 14th St 98363   360-452-5590
   Charles Lisk, prin.   Fax 457-5709

Olympic Christian S   200/PK-12
   43 OBrien Rd 98362   360-457-4640
   Brian Clark, prin.   Fax 457-4612
Peninsula College   Post-Sec.
   1502 E Lauridsen Blvd 98362   360-452-9277

Port Hadlock, Jefferson, Pop. 2,742

Northwest School of Wooden Boatbuilding   Post-Sec.
   42 N Water St 98339   360-385-4948

Port Orchard, Kitsap, Pop. 7,903
South Kitsap SD 402   11,100/K-12
   1962 Hoover Ave SE 98366   360-874-7000
   Dr. Beverly Cheney, supt.   Fax 874-7068
   www.skitsap.wednet.edu
Cedar Heights JHS   800/7-9
   2220 Pottery Ave 98366   360-874-6020
   Bruce Dearborn, prin.   Fax 874-6420
Sedgewick JHS   900/7-9
   8995 SE Sedgwick Rd 98366   360-874-6090
   Jay Villars, prin.   Fax 874-6430
South Kitsap SHS   2,500/10-12
   425 Mitchell Ave 98366   360-874-5600
   Dave Colombini, prin.   Fax 874-5892
Whitman JHS   900/7-9
   1887 Madrona Dr SE 98366   360-874-6100
   Brian Carlson, prin.   Fax 874-6440

Bryman College   Post-Sec.
   3649 W Frontage Rd 98367   360-473-1120
Burley Christian S   100/PK-12
   14687 Olympic Dr SE 98367   253-851-8619
   Dennis Myers, admin.   Fax 857-0093

South Kitsap Christian S   200/PK-12
   1780 Lincoln Ave SE 98366   360-876-5595
   Sandy Jennings, admin.   Fax 876-2206

Port Townsend, Jefferson, Pop. 8,685
Port Townsend SD 50   1,500/K-12
   450 Fir St 98368   360-379-4502
   Thomas Opstad, supt.   Fax 385-3617
   www.ptsd.wednet.edu
Blue Heron MS   400/6-8
   3939 San Juan Ave 98368   360-379-4540
   Mark Decker, prin.   Fax 379-4548
Port Townsend HS   600/9-12
   1500 Van Ness St 98368   360-379-4520
   Carrie Ehrhardt, prin.   Fax 379-4505

Poulsbo, Kitsap, Pop. 7,336
North Kitsap SD 400   6,600/PK-12
   18360 Caldart Ave NE 98370   360-779-8704
   Dr. Eugene Medina, supt.   Fax 697-3175
   www.nksd.wednet.edu
Kingston HS 98370   9-12
   Bruce Saari, prin.   360-394-2623
North Kitsap SHS   1,400/10-12
   1780 NE Hostmark St 98370   360-779-4408
   Roy Herrera, prin.   Fax 598-8406
Poulsbo JHS   800/7-9
   2003 NE Hostmark St 98370   360-779-4453
   Wally Lis, prin.   Fax 598-1041
Other Schools – See Kingston

Northwest College of Art   Post-Sec.
   16464 State Highway 305 NE 98370   360-779-9993

Prescott, Walla Walla, Pop. 325
Prescott SD 402-37   300/K-12
   PO Box 65 99348   509-849-2216
   Scott Harris, supt.   Fax 849-2800
   www.prescott.k12.wa.us/
Prescott JSHS, PO Box 65 99348   100/7-12
   Ron Woodruff, prin.   509-849-2215

Prosser, Benton, Pop. 5,053
Prosser SD 116   2,800/K-12
   823 Park Ave 99350   509-786-3323
   Dr. Ray Tolcacher, supt.   Fax 786-2062
   www.prosserschools.org
Housel MS   700/6-8
   2001 Highland Dr 99350   509-786-1732
   Steven Ellis, prin.   Fax 786-2814
Prosser HS   800/9-12
   1203 Prosser Ave 99350   509-786-1224
   Kevin Lusk, prin.   Fax 786-4227

Pullman, Whitman, Pop. 25,237
Pullman SD 267   2,300/K-12
   240 SE Dexter St 99163   509-332-3581
   Dr. Thomas Rockefeller, supt.   Fax 334-0375
   www.psd267.wednet.edu
Lincoln MS   500/6-8
   315 SE Crestview St 99163   509-334-3411
   Bill Motsenbocker, prin.   Fax 334-9678
Pullman HS   700/9-12
   510 NW Larry St 99163   509-332-1551
   Dave Harrington, prin.   Fax 332-6868

Pullman Christian S   100/K-12
   345 SW Kimball Dr 99163   509-332-3545
   Sherri Goetze, prin.   Fax 332-5433
Washington State University   Post-Sec.
   1 SE Stadium Way 99164   509-335-3564

Puyallup, Pierce, Pop. 35,641
Puyallup SD 3   20,200/PK-12
   PO Box 370 98371   253-841-1301
   Dr. Tony Apostle, supt.   Fax 840-8959
   www.puyallup.k12.wa.us
Aylen JHS   900/7-9
   101 15th St SW 98371   253-841-8723
   Christine Moloney, prin.   Fax 840-8856
Ballou JHS   900/7-9
   9916 136th St E 98373   253-841-8725
   Gerald Denman, prin.   Fax 840-8819
Emerald Ridge SHS   1,400/10-12
   12405 184th St E 98374   253-435-6300
   Brian Lowney, prin.   Fax 435-6310
Ferrucci JHS   800/7-9
   3213 Wildwood Park Dr 98374   253-841-8756
   Mark Vetter, prin.   Fax 840-8855
Kalles JHS   900/7-9
   515 3rd St SE 98372   253-841-8729
   Mario Casello, prin.   Fax 840-8984
Puyallup SHS   1,600/10-12
   105 7th St SW 98371   253-841-8711
   Mike Joyner, prin.   Fax 841-8624
Rogers SHS   1,600/10-12
   12801 86th Ave E 98373   253-841-8717
   Scott Brittain, prin.   Fax 840-8802
Stahl JHS   1,100/7-9
   9610 168th Street Ct E 98375   253-840-8881
   John Bustad, prin.   Fax 840-8992
Other Schools – See Edgewood

BJ's Beauty & Barber College   Post-Sec.
   12020 Meridian E Ste K 98373   253-848-1595
Cascade Christian JSHS   500/7-12
   811 21st St SE 98372   253-445-9706
   Terry Broberg, prin.   Fax 445-0859
Pierce College   Post-Sec.
   1601 39th Ave SE 98374   253-840-8470

Quilcene, Jefferson
Quilcene SD 48   300/K-12
   PO Box 40 98376   360-765-3363
   David Andersen, supt.   Fax 765-4183
   www.quilcene.wednet.edu
Quilcene S   300/K-12
   PO Box 40 98376   360-765-3363
   David Andersen, prin.   Fax 765-4183

Quincy, Grant, Pop. 5,325
Quincy SD 144-101 — 2,400/K-12
  119 J St SW 98848 — 509-787-4571
  Roger Fox, supt. — Fax 787-4336
  www.qsd.wednet.edu
Quincy HS — 700/9-12
  16 6th Ave SE 98848 — 509-787-3501
  Jack Peasley, prin. — Fax 787-8989
Quincy High Tech HS — Vo/Tech
  404 1st Ave SW 98848 — 509-787-1678
  Garry Stidman, prin. — Fax 787-1680
Quincy JHS — 400/7-8
  417 C St SE 98848 — 509-787-4435
  Scott Ramsey, prin. — Fax 787-8949

Rainier, Thurston, Pop. 1,634
Rainier SD 307 — 900/K-12
  PO Box 98 98576 — 360-446-2207
  Dennis Friedrich, supt. — Fax 446-2918
  www.rainier.wednet.edu
Rainier HS — 300/9-12
  PO Box 98 98576 — 360-446-2205
  Jennifer Shaw, prin. — Fax 446-2208
Rainier MS, PO Box 98 98576 — 200/7-8
  Paulette Johnson, prin. — 360-446-2206

Randle, Lewis
White Pass SD 303 — 500/PK-12
  PO Box 188 98377 — 360-497-3791
  Brian Talbott, supt. — Fax 497-2560
  www.wpsd.wednet.edu
White Pass JSHS — 400/7-12
  516 Silverbrook Rd 98377 — 360-497-5816
  Karen Larsen, prin. — Fax 497-7773

Ravensdale, King, Pop. 3,778
Tahoma SD 409
  Supt. — See Maple Valley
Tahoma JHS — 1,100/8-9
  25600 SE Summit-Landsburg R 98051
  — 425-413-5600
  Rob Morrow, prin. — Fax 413-5500

Raymond, Pacific, Pop. 2,961
Raymond SD 116 — 500/K-12
  1016 Commercial St 98577 — 360-942-3415
  Stephen A. Holland, supt. — Fax 942-3416
  raymondschools.org
Raymond JSHS — 300/7-12
  1016 Commercial St 98577 — 360-942-2474
  Ron Bell, prin. — Fax 942-2504

Reardan, Spokane, Pop. 604
Reardan-Edwall SD 9 — 700/K-12
  PO Box 225 99029 — 509-796-2701
  Doug Asbjornsen, supt. — Fax 796-4954
  www.reardan.net
Reardan JSHS, PO Box 225 99029 — 300/7-12
  Gene Nelson, prin. — 509-796-2711

Redmond, King, Pop. 46,391
Lake Washington SD 414 — 22,900/K-12
  PO Box 97039 98073 — 425-702-3200
  Dr. Don Saul, supt. — Fax 702-3213
  www.lkwash.wednet.edu
Eastlake SHS — 1,300/10-12
  400 228th Ave NE 98074 — 425-836-6600
  Rondel Hardie, prin. — Fax 836-6609
Evergreen JHS — 700/7-9
  6900 208th Ave NE 98053 — 425-868-2600
  Jan Olson, prin. — Fax 868-2613
Inglewood JHS — 1,200/7-9
  24120 NE 8th St 98074 — 425-868-2300
  Tim Stonich, prin. — Fax 868-0628
Redmond JHS — 900/7-9
  10055 166th Ave NE 98052 — 425-885-7034
  Prato Barone, prin. — Fax 556-9806
Redmond SHS — 1,400/10-12
  17272 NE 104th St 98052 — 425-498-7130
  Brian Hunter, prin. — Fax 498-7169
Rose Hill JHS — 600/7-9
  13505 NE 75th St 98052 — 425-881-2079
  David Larson, prin. — Fax 556-0629
Explorer Community S — Adult
  7040 208th Ave NE 98053 — 425-868-2615
  Ellen Challenger, prin. — Fax 836-4658
Other Schools – See Kirkland

Bear Creek S — 600/K-12
  8905 208th Ave NE 98053 — 425-898-1720
  Nancy Price, hdmstr. — Fax 898-1430
DigiPen Institute of Technology — Post-Sec.
  5001 150th Ave NE 98052 — 425-558-0299
Overlake S — 500/5-12
  20301 NE 108th St 98053 — 425-868-1000
  Dr. Francisco Grijalva, hdmstr. — Fax 868-6770

Renton, King, Pop. 54,028
Issaquah SD 411
  Supt. — See Issaquah
Liberty HS — 1,200/9-12
  16655 SE 136th St 98059 — 425-837-4800
  Kevin Davis, prin. — Fax 837-4905
Maywood MS — 900/6-8
  14490 168th Ave SE 98059 — 425-837-6900
  Patrick Murphy, prin. — Fax 837-6910

Kent SD 415
  Supt. — See Kent
Meeker MS — 600/7-8
  12600 SE 192nd St 98058 — 253-373-7284
  Jeff Pelzel, prin. — Fax 373-7560
Northwood MS — 600/7-8
  17007 SE 184th St 98058 — 253-373-7780
  Colleen Nelson, prin. — Fax 373-7788

Renton SD 403 — 12,700/K-12
  300 SW 7th St 98057 — 425-204-2340
  Dr. Mary Alice Heuschel, supt. — Fax 204-2456
  www.renton.wednet.edu
Hazen HS — 1,200/9-12
  1101 Hoquiam Ave NE 98059 — 425-204-4200
  Sue Beeson, prin. — Fax 204-4220
Lindbergh HS — 1,200/9-12
  16426 128th Ave SE 98058 — 425-204-3200
  Tres Genger, prin. — Fax 204-3220
McKnight MS — 1,000/6-8
  1200 Edmonds Ave NE 98056 — 425-204-3600
  Mary Merritt, prin. — Fax 204-3680
Nelson MS — 1,100/6-8
  2403 Jones Ave S 98055 — 425-204-3000
  Dr. James Noddings, prin. — Fax 204-3079
Renton HS — 1,000/9-12
  400 S 2nd St 98057 — 425-204-3400
  Kathryn Hutchinson, prin. — Fax 204-3412
Other Schools – See Seattle

Bryman College — Post-Sec.
  981 Powell Ave SW 98055 — 425-255-3281
Pima Medical Institute — Post-Sec.
  555 S Renton Village Pl 98055 — 425-228-9600
Renton Technical College — Post-Sec.
  3000 NE 4th St 98056 — 425-235-2352

Republic, Ferry, Pop. 985
Republic SD 309 — 400/K-12
  30306 E Highway 20 99166 — 509-775-3173
  Dan Chaplik, supt. — Fax 775-3712
  www.republic.wednet.edu
Republic HS — 200/9-12
  30306 E Highway 20 99166 — 509-775-3171
  Nancy Giddings, prin. — Fax 775-1098
Republic JHS — 7-8
  30306 E Highway 20 99166 — 509-775-3171
  Shawn Anderson, prin. — Fax 775-1098

Richland, Benton, Pop. 42,537
Richland SD 400 — 8,800/K-12
  615 Snow Ave 99352 — 509-967-6000
  Dr. Richard Semler, supt. — Fax 942-2401
  www.rsd.edu
Carmichael MS — 800/6-8
  620 Thayer Dr 99352 — 509-942-2468
  Tim Praino, prin. — Fax 942-2471
Chief Joseph MS — 800/6-8
  504 Wilson St, — 509-942-2487
  Jon Lobdell, prin. — Fax 942-2492
Hanford HS — 1,300/9-12
  450 Hanford St, — 509-371-2600
  Todd Baddley, prin. — Fax 371-2601
Richland HS — 1,900/9-12
  930 Long Ave 99352 — 509-942-2500
  Sergio Fossa, prin. — Fax 942-2512
Other Schools – See West Richland

Liberty Christian S of the Tri-Cities — 600/PK-12
  2200 Williams Blvd, — 509-946-0602
  Terry Campbell, admin. — Fax 943-5623

Ridgefield, Clark, Pop. 2,230
Ridgefield SD 122 — 1,800/K-12
  2724 S Hillhurst Rd 98642 — 360-619-1300
  Mary Vagner, supt. — Fax 619-1397
  www.ridge.k12.wa.us
Ridgefield HS — 600/9-12
  2630 S Hillhurst Rd 98642 — 360-619-1320
  Dan Winter, prin. — Fax 619-1395
View Ridge MS — 300/7-8
  510 Pioneer St 98642 — 360-619-1400
  Gary Dietderich, prin. — Fax 619-1459

Ritzville, Adams, Pop. 1,709
Ritzville SD 160-67 — 300/PK-12
  209 E Wellsandt Rd 99169 — 509-659-1660
  Richard Graham, supt. — Fax 659-0927
  www.ritzville.wednet.edu
Ritzville HS — 100/9-12
  209 E Wellsandt Rd 99169 — 509-659-1720
  David Funk, prin. — Fax 659-5140

Rochester, Thurston, Pop. 1,250
Rochester SD 401 — 2,000/K-12
  PO Box 457 98579 — 360-273-5536
  James Anderson, supt. — Fax 273-5547
  www.rochester.wednet.edu/
Rochester HS — 600/9-12
  19800 Carper Rd SW 98579 — 360-273-5534
  Greg McDaniel, prin. — Fax 273-2570
Rochester MS — 500/6-8
  PO Box 398 98579 — 360-273-5958
  Linda Shotwell, prin. — Fax 273-2045

Rockford, Spokane, Pop. 489
Freeman SD 358 — 600/K-12
  15001 S Jackson Rd 99030 — 509-291-3695
  William Thurston, supt. — Fax 291-3636
  www.freemansd.org
Freeman HS — 300/9-12
  14626 S Jackson Rd 99030 — 509-291-3721
  Patrick Kane, prin. — Fax 291-7337
Freeman MS — 6-8
  14917 S Jackson Rd 99030 — 509-291-7301
  Jim Straw, prin.

Rosalia, Whitman, Pop. 631
Rosalia SD 320 — 300/K-12
  916 S Josephine Ave 99170 — 509-523-3061
  Dr. Thomas Crowley, supt. — Fax 523-3861
  www.rosalia.wednet.edu
Rosalia S — 300/K-12
  916 S Josephine Ave 99170 — 509-523-3061
  Darrell Kuhn, prin. — Fax 523-3861

Royal City, Grant, Pop. 1,895
Royal SD 160 — 1,400/K-12
  PO Box 486 99357 — 509-346-2222
  David James, supt. — Fax 346-8746
  www.royal.wednet.edu/
Royal HS — 300/9-12
  PO Box 486 99357 — 509-346-2256
  Jack Hill, prin. — Fax 346-9739
Royal MS — 400/6-8
  PO Box 486 99357 — 509-346-2268
  David Jaderlund, prin. — Fax 346-2269

Saint John, Whitman, Pop. 552
St. John SD 322 — 200/K-12
  PO Box 58 99171 — 509-648-3336
  Rick Winters, supt. — Fax 648-3451
  www.sje.wednet.edu/index.html
St. John-Endicott HS — 100/9-12
  PO Box 58 99171 — 509-648-3336
  Marc Thielman, prin.

SeaTac, King, Pop. 25,014
Highline SD 401
  Supt. — See Burien
Academy of Citizenship & Empowerment HS 1,200/9-12
  4424 S 188th St 98188 — 206-433-2342
  Stacy Spector, prin. — Fax 998-7238
Chinook MS — 600/7-8
  18650 42nd Ave S 98188 — 206-433-2231
  Todd Moorhead, prin. — Fax 433-2308
Global Connections HS — 9-12
  4424 S 188th St 98188 — 206-433-2343
  Rick Harwood, prin. — Fax 433-2227
Odyssey HS — 9-12
  4424 S 188th St 98188 — 206-433-2344
  Joan Ferrigno, prin. — Fax 988-7239

Seattle Christian S — 700/K-12
  18301 Military Rd S 98188 — 206-246-8241
  Dr. Greg Johnson, supt. — Fax 246-9066

Seattle, King, Pop. 569,101
Highline SD 401
  Supt. — See Burien
Aviation HS — 9-12
  6770 E Marginal Way S 98108 — 206-716-0006
  Reba Gilman, prin. — Fax 716-0020
Cascade MS — 600/7-8
  11212 10th Ave SW 98146 — 206-433-2551
  Patricia Larson, prin. — Fax 433-2296
Evergreen HS — 1,200/9-12
  830 SW 116th St 98146 — 206-433-2311
  Gail Barnum, prin. — Fax 433-2488
Sea Tac Occupational Skills Ctr — Vo/Tech
  18010 8th Ave S 98148 — 206-433-2524
  Dr. Sue Shields, prin. — Fax 433-2405

Renton SD 403
  Supt. — See Renton
Dimmitt MS — 900/6-8
  12320 80th Ave S 98178 — 425-204-2800
  Dan Sakaue, prin. — Fax 204-2812

Seattle SD 1 — 47,600/PK-12
  PO Box 34165 98124 — 206-252-0000
  Raj Manhas, supt. — Fax 252-0102
  www.seattleschools.org
Ballard HS — 1,600/9-12
  1418 NW 65th St 98117 — 206-252-1000
  Phil Brockman, prin. — Fax 252-1001
Center S — 300/9-12
  305 Harrison St 98109 — 206-252-9850
  Brian Vance, prin. — Fax 252-9851
Chief Sealth HS — 1,000/9-12
  2600 SW Thistle St 98126 — 206-252-8550
  John Boyd, prin. — Fax 252-8551
Cleveland HS — 700/9-12
  5950 Delridge Way SW 98106 — 206-252-7800
  Donna Marshall, prin. — Fax 252-7801
Denny MS — 800/6-8
  8402 30th Ave SW 98126 — 206-252-9000
  Jeff Clarke, prin. — Fax 252-9001
Eckstein MS — 1,300/6-8
  3003 NE 75th St 98115 — 206-252-5010
  Marnie Campbell, prin. — Fax 252-5011
Franklin HS — 1,600/9-12
  3013 S Mount Baker Blvd 98144 — 206-252-6150
  Jennifer Wiley, prin. — Fax 252-6151
Garfield HS — 1,700/9-12
  400 23rd Ave 98122 — 206-252-2270
  Ted Howard, prin. — Fax 252-2271
Hale HS — 1,100/9-12
  10750 30th Ave NE 98125 — 206-252-3680
  Lisa Hechtman, prin. — Fax 262-3681
Hamilton International MS — 800/6-8
  1610 N 41st St 98103 — 206-252-5810
  Terry Acena, prin. — Fax 252-5811
Ingraham HS — 1,200/9-12
  1819 N 135th St 98133 — 206-252-3880
  Martin Floe, prin. — Fax 252-3881
Kurose MS — 700/6-8
  3928 S Graham St 98118 — 206-252-7700
  Bi Hoa Caldwell, prin. — Fax 252-7701
Madison MS — 900/6-8
  3429 45th Ave SW 98116 — 206-252-9200
  Jill Hudson, prin. — Fax 252-9201
McClure MS — 600/6-8
  1915 1st Ave W 98119 — 206-252-1900
  Kathy Bledsoe, prin. — Fax 252-1901
Meany MS — 400/6-8
  301 21st Ave E 98112 — 206-252-2500
  Princess Shareef, prin. — Fax 252-2501
Mercer MS — 800/6-8
  1600 S Columbian Way 98108 — 206-252-8000
  Andhra Lutz, prin. — Fax 252-8001
Rainier Beach HS — 600/9-12
  8815 Seward Park Ave S 98118 — 206-252-6350
  Robert Gary, prin. — Fax 252-6351

Roosevelt HS | 1,700/9-12
4400 Interlake Ave N 98103 | 206-252-4810
Chuck Chinn, prin. | Fax 252-4811
Washington MS | 1,100/6-8
2101 S Jackson St 98144 | 206-252-2600
Jon Halfaker, prin. | Fax 252-2601
West Seattle HS | 1,100/9-12
3000 California Ave SW 98116 | 206-252-8800
Susan Derse, prin. | Fax 252-8801
Whitman MS | 1,100/6-8
9201 15th Ave NW 98117 | 206-252-1200
Robert Kogane, prin. | Fax 252-1201
Seattle Evening HS | Adult
520 NE Ravenna Blvd 98115 | 206-252-4680
Marella Francois, prin. | Fax 252-4681

Antioch University | Post-Sec.
2326 6th Ave 98121 | 206-441-5352
Argosy University/Seattle | Post-Sec.
2601A Elliott Ave 98121 | 206-283-4500
Art Institute of Seattle | Post-Sec.
2323 Elliott Ave 98121 | 206-448-0900
Bakke Graduate University of Ministry | Post-Sec.
1013 8th Ave 98104 | 206-264-9100
Billings MS | 100/6-8
7217 Woodlawn Ave NE 98115 | 206-547-4614
Ted Kalmus, hdmstr. | Fax 545-8505
Bishop Blanchet HS | 1,100/9-12
8200 Wallingford Ave N 98103 | 206-527-7711
Kent Hickey, prin. | Fax 527-7712
Bush S | 600/K-12
3400 E Harrison St 98112 | 206-322-7978
Frank Magusin, hdmstr. | Fax 860-3876
Christian Faith S | 500/K-12
PO Box 98600 98198 | 206-878-6036
Jim Davis, hdmstr. | Fax 878-3610
Cornish College of the Arts | Post-Sec.
1000 Lenora St 98121 | 206-726-5151
Court Reporting Institute | Post-Sec.
929 N 130th St Ste 2 98133 | 206-363-8300
Divers Institute of Technology | Post-Sec.
PO Box 70667 98127 | 206-783-5542
Gene Juarez Academy of Beauty | Post-Sec.
10715 8th Ave NE 98125 | 206-365-6900
Greenwood Academy of Hair Design | Post-Sec.
8501 Greenwood Ave N 98103 | 206-782-0220
Holy Names Academy | 600/9-12
728 21st Ave E 98112 | 206-323-4272
Elizabeth Swift, prin. | Fax 323-5254
Lakeside MS | 300/5-8
13510 1st Ave NE 98125 | 206-368-3630
Bernie Noe, hdmstr. | Fax 440-2777
Lakeside Upper S | 500/9-12
14050 1st Ave NE 98125 | 206-368-3600
Bernie Noe, hdmstr.
Menachem Mendel Seattle Cheder | 100/PK-10
4541 19th Ave NE 98105 | 206-523-9766
Rabbi Charytan, prin. | Fax 524-6105
Northgate Christian Academy | 50/K-12
10510 Stone Ave N 98133 | 206-525-5699
North Seattle Community College | Post-Sec.
9600 College Way N 98103 | 206-527-3600
Northwest S | 400/6-12
1415 Summit Ave 98122 | 206-682-7309
Ellen Taussig, hdmstr. | Fax 467-7353
O'Dea HS | 500/9-12
802 Terry Ave 98104 | 206-622-6596
Br. Dominic Murray, prin. | Fax 340-4110
Photographic Center Northwest | Post-Sec.
900 12th Ave 98122 | 206-720-7222
Pima Medical Institute | Post-Sec.
9709 3rd Ave NE Ste 400 98115 | 206-322-6100
Pima Medical Institute | Post-Sec.
9709 3rd Ave NE Ste 400 98115 | 206-322-6100
Seattle Academy of Arts & Sciences | 200/6-8
1432 15th Ave 98122 | 206-323-6600
Jean Orvis, dir. | Fax 323-6618
Seattle Academy of Arts & Sciences | 300/9-12
1201 E Union St 98122 | 206-323-6600
Jean Orvis, dir. | Fax 323-6618
Seattle Central Community College | Post-Sec.
1701 Broadway 98122 | 206-587-3800
Seattle Girls' S | 100/5-8
PO Box 22576 98122 | 206-709-2228
Marja Brandon, hdmstr. | Fax 329-1580
Seattle Institute of Oriental Medicine | Post-Sec.
916 NE 65th St # B 98115 | 206-517-4541
Seattle Lutheran HS | 100/9-12
4141 41st Ave SW 98116 | 206-937-7722
Bruce Biesenthal, dir. | Fax 937-6781
Seattle Pacific University | Post-Sec.
3307 3rd Ave W 98119 | 206-281-2000
Seattle Preparatory S | 700/9-12
2400 11th Ave E 98102 | 206-324-0400
Rev. Michael Tyrrell, prin. | Fax 577-2198
Seattle University | Post-Sec.
900 Broadway 98122 | 206-296-6000
Seattle University School of Law | Post-Sec.
900 Broadway 98122 | 206-398-4200
South Seattle Community College | Post-Sec.
6000 16th Ave SW 98106 | 206-764-5300
University of Washington 98195 | Post-Sec.
 | 206-543-2100
University Prep Academy | 400/6-12
8000 25th Ave NE 98115 | 206-525-2714
Erica Hamlin, hdmstr. | Fax 525-9659
Wolf HS | 50/9-12
160 John St 98109 | 206-522-2644
Carol Oliver, coord. | Fax 522-2631

Sedro Woolley, Skagit, Pop. 7,506
Sedro Woolley SD 101 | 4,100/K-12
801 Trail Rd 98284 | 360-855-3500
Mark Venn, supt. | Fax 855-3574
www.swsd.k12.wa.us

Cascade MS | 700/7-8
201 N Township St 98284 | 360-855-3520
Michelle Kuss-Cybula, prin. | Fax 855-3521
Sedro Woolley HS | 1,200/9-12
1235 3rd St 98284 | 360-855-3510
Mike Schweigert, prin. | Fax 855-3517

Sekiu, Clallam
Cape Flattery SD 401 | 500/K-12
PO Box 109 98381 | 360-963-2329
Gene Laes, supt. | Fax 963-2373
www.capeflattery.wednet.edu
Other Schools – See Clallam Bay, Neah Bay

Selah, Yakima, Pop. 6,573
Selah SD 119 | 3,400/K-12
105 W Bartlett Ave 98942 | 509-697-0706
Dr. Larry Parsons, supt. | Fax 697-0823
www.selah.k12.wa.us
Selah HS | 700/10-12
801 N 1st St 98942 | 509-697-0800
Jerry Holsten, prin. | Fax 697-0811
Selah JHS | 600/8-9
411 N 1st St 98942 | 509-697-0500
Marc Gallaway, prin. | Fax 697-0696

Sequim, Clallam, Pop. 4,704
Sequim SD 323 | 2,900/K-12
503 N Sequim Ave 98382 | 360-582-3260
Garn Christensen, supt. | Fax 683-6303
www.sequim.k12.wa.us/
Sequim HS | 1,000/9-12
601 N Sequim Ave 98382 | 360-582-3600
Shawn Langston, prin. | Fax 681-8688
Sequim MS | 700/6-8
301 W Hendrickson Rd 98382 | 360-582-3500
Brian Jones, prin. | Fax 582-9486

Shelton, Mason, Pop. 8,789
Pioneer SD 402 | 800/PK-8
611 E Agate Rd 98584 | 360-426-9115
Richard Sirokman, supt. | Fax 426-1036
www.psd402.org
Pioneer MS | 500/4-8
611 E Agate Rd 98584 | 360-426-8291
Bill Lanning, prin. | Fax 426-1036

Shelton SD 309 | 3,500/PK-12
700 S 1st St 98584 | 360-426-1687
Joan Zook, supt. | Fax 427-8610
www.sheltonschools.org
Oakland Bay JHS | 400/8-9
3301 N Shelton Springs Rd 98584 | 360-426-7991
Sheryal Balding, prin. | Fax 427-2940
Shelton HS | 1,500/9-12
3737 N Shelton Springs Rd 98584 | 360-426-4471
Wanda Berndtson, prin. | Fax 427-6141
Choice HS | Adult
807 W Pine St 98584 | 360-426-7664
Gordy Hansen, prin. | Fax 462-1203

Mason County Christian S | 200/PK-12
470 E Eagle Ridge Dr 98584 | 360-426-7616
David Roller, supt. | Fax 426-6582

Shoreline, King, Pop. 52,380
Shoreline SD 412 | 9,400/PK-12
18560 1st Ave NE 98155 | 206-367-6111
Dr. James Welsh, supt. | Fax 361-4204
www.shorelineschools.org
Einstein MS | 800/7-8
19343 3rd Ave NW 98177 | 206-368-4730
Bill Dunbar, prin. | Fax 368-4735
Kellogg MS | 700/7-8
16045 25th Ave NE 98155 | 206-368-4783
Lori Longo, prin. | Fax 368-4780
Shorecrest HS | 1,500/9-12
15343 25th Ave NE 98155 | 206-361-4286
Brian Schultz, prin. | Fax 361-4284
Shorewood HS | 1,800/9-12
17300 Fremont Ave N 98133 | 206-361-4372
John Green, prin. | Fax 368-4711

King's HS | 400/9-12
19303 Fremont Ave N 98133 | 206-546-7245
Randy Hibbard, prin. | Fax 546-7214
King's JHS | 200/7-8
19303 Fremont Ave N 98133 | 206-546-7243
Jordana Halkett, prin. | Fax 546-7250
Shoreline Christian S | 300/PK-12
2400 NE 147th St 98155 | 206-364-7777
Timothy Visser, prin. | Fax 364-0349
Shoreline Community College | Post-Sec.
16101 Greenwood Ave N 98133 | 206-546-4101

Silverdale, Kitsap, Pop. 7,660
Central Kitsap SD 401 | 12,800/K-12
PO Box 8 98383 | 360-662-1610
Gregory Lynch, supt. | Fax 662-1611
www.cksd.wednet.edu
Career & Technical Education | Vo/Tech
PO Box 8 98383 | 360-662-1800
Bruce McBurney, dir. | Fax 662-1801
Central Kitsap HS | 1,400/10-12
PO Box 8 98383 | 360-662-2400
John Cervinsky, prin. | Fax 662-2401
Central Kitsap JHS | 1,000/7-9
PO Box 8 98383 | 360-662-2300
Barbara Gilchrist, prin. | Fax 662-2301
Klahowya Secondary S | 1,000/7-12
PO Box 8 98383 | 360-662-4000
Ryan Stevens, prin. | Fax 662-4001
Ridgetop JHS | 800/7-9
PO Box 8 98383 | 360-662-2900
Chris Wyatt, prin. | Fax 662-2901
Other Schools – See Bremerton

Skykomish, King, Pop. 207
Skykomish SD 404 | 100/K-12
PO Box 325 98288 | 360-677-2623
Desiree L. Gould, supt. | Fax 677-2418
Skykomish SHS | 50/7-12
PO Box 325 98288 | 360-677-2623
Desiree L. Gould, prin. | Fax 677-2418

Snohomish, Snohomish, Pop. 8,620
Monroe SD 103
Supt. — See Monroe
Hidden River MS | 300/6-8
9224 Paradise Lake Rd 98296 | 360-863-4100
Janna Dmochowsky, prin. | Fax 668-5222

Snohomish SD 201 | 8,100/K-12
1601 Avenue D 98290 | 360-563-7300
William A. Mester Ph.D., supt. | Fax 563-7373
www.sno.wednet.edu
Centennial MS | 700/7-8
3000 S Machias Rd 98290 | 360-563-4525
Scott Peacock, prin. | Fax 563-4585
Snohomish Freshman Campus | 50/9-9
601 Glen Ave 98290 | 360-563-4300
Jeff Michaelson, prin. | Fax 563-4360
Snohomish SHS | 2,000/10-12
1316 5th St 98290 | 360-563-4000
Diana Plumis, prin. | Fax 563-4183
Valley View MS | 800/7-8
14308 Broadway Ave 98296 | 360-563-4225
Nancy Rhoades, prin. | Fax 563-4236

Peaceful Glen Christian S | 100/PK-12
PO Box 710 98291 | 360-563-0131
Kathleen Biehl, prin.

Snoqualmie, King, Pop. 4,742
Snoqualmie Valley SD 410 | 4,700/K-12
PO Box 400 98065 | 425-831-8000
Joe Aune, supt. | Fax 831-8040
www.snoqualmie.k12.wa.us
Cascade View ES | K-12
34816 SE Ridge St 98065 | 425-831-4100
Tim Nootenboom, prin. | Fax 831-4110
Mount Si HS | 1,400/9-12
8651 Meadowbrook Way SE 98065 | 425-831-8100
Randy Taylor, prin. | Fax 831-8222
Snoqualmie MS | 600/6-8
9200 Railroad Ave SE 98065 | 425-831-8450
Ruth Moen, prin. | Fax 831-8440
Other Schools – See Fall City

Soap Lake, Grant, Pop. 1,777
Soap Lake SD 156 | 300/PK-12
PO Box 158 98851 | 509-246-1822
John Adkins, supt. | Fax 246-0669
Soap Lake HS | 100/9-12
PO Box 878 98851 | 509-246-1201
Dan Andrews, prin. | Fax 246-0669
Soap Lake MS, PO Box 878 98851 | 6-8
Shane Couch, prin. | 509-246-1201

South Bend, Pacific, Pop. 1,804
South Bend SD 118 | 700/PK-12
PO Box 437 98586 | 360-875-6041
Mike Morris, supt. | Fax 875-6062
www.southbend.wednet.edu/
South Bend JSHS | 300/7-12
PO Box 437 98586 | 360-875-5707
Michael Rogers, prin. | Fax 875-6036

Spanaway, Pierce, Pop. 15,001
Bethel SD 403 | 17,100/PK-12
516 176th St E 98387 | 253-683-6000
Tom Seigel, supt. | Fax 683-6059
www.bethelsd.org
Bethel JHS | 1,000/7-9
22001 38th Ave E 98387 | 253-683-7200
Paul Rempfer, prin. | Fax 683-7298
Bethel SHS | 1,900/10-12
22215 38th Ave E 98387 | 253-683-7000
Wanda Riley, prin. | Fax 683-7098
Cedarcrest JHS | 900/7-9
19120 13th Avenue Ct E 98387 | 253-683-7500
Cheryl A. Barnett, prin. | Fax 683-7598
Spanaway Lake SHS | 1,800/10-12
1305 168th St E 98387 | 253-683-5600
Michelle Ledbetter, prin. | Fax 683-5698
Other Schools – See Graham, Tacoma

Spangle, Spokane, Pop. 238
Liberty SD 362 | 500/K-12
29818 S North Pine Creek Rd 99031 | 509-245-3223
Duane Reidenbach, supt. | Fax 245-3288
www.liberty.wednet.edu/
Liberty HS | 200/9-12
6404 E Spangle Waverly Rd 99031 | 509-245-3229
Steve Boosinger, prin. | Fax 245-3205

Upper Columbia Academy | 300/9-12
3025 E Spangle Waverly Rd 99031 | 509-245-3600
Jeff Bovee, prin. | Fax 245-3643

Spokane, Spokane, Pop. 196,624
Central Valley SD 356
Supt. — See Greenacres
Bowdish MS | 500/6-8
2109 S Skipworth Rd 99206 | 509-228-4700
Dave Bouge, prin. | Fax 228-4714
Horizon MS | 500/6-8
3915 S Pines Rd 99206 | 509-228-4940
Denis Rusca, prin. | Fax 228-4983
North Pines MS | 500/6-8
701 N Pines Rd 99206 | 509-228-5020
Gordon Grassi, prin. | Fax 228-5029
University HS | 1,800/9-12
12420 E 32nd Ave 99216 | 509-228-5240
Daryl Hart, prin. | Fax 228-5249

East Valley SD 361 — 4,300/K-12
12325 E Grace Ave 99216 — 509-924-1830
Christine Burgess, supt. — Fax 927-9500
www.evsd.org
East Valley HS — 1,400/9-12
15711 E Wellesley Ave 99216 — 509-927-3200
Jeffrey Miller, prin. — Fax 921-6830
East Valley MS — 600/6-8
4920 N Progress Rd 99216 — 509-924-9383
Doris Hoffman, prin. — Fax 927-3214
Other Schools – See Newman Lake

Mead SD 354
Supt. — See Mead
Mead HS — 1,600/9-12
302 W Hastings Rd 99218 — 509-465-7000
Bruce Olgard, prin. — Fax 465-7020
Northwood MS — 800/7-8
13120 N Pittsburg St 99208 — 509-465-7500
Dave Stenersen, prin. — Fax 465-7520

Spokane SD 81 — 30,300/PK-12
200 N Bernard St 99201 — 509-354-5900
Brian L. Benzel Ph.D., supt. — Fax 354-5965
www.spokaneschools.org
Chase MS — 900/7-8
4747 E 37th Ave 99223 — 509-354-5000
John Andes, prin. — Fax 354-5100
Ferris HS — 1,800/9-12
3020 E 37th Ave 99223 — 509-354-6000
Erik Ohlund, prin. — Fax 354-6161
Garry MS — 700/7-8
725 E Joseph Ave 99208 — 509-354-5200
Brenda Meenach, prin. — Fax 354-5212
Glover MS — 900/7-8
2404 W Longfellow Ave 99205 — 509-354-5400
Roberta Kramer, prin. — Fax 354-5399
Lewis & Clark HS — 2,000/9-12
521 W 4th Ave 99204 — 509-354-7000
Jon Swett, prin. — Fax 354-6969
North Central HS — 1,500/9-12
1600 N Howard St 99205 — 509-354-6300
Steven Gering, prin. — Fax 354-6303
Rogers HS — 1,800/9-12
1622 E Wellesley Ave 99207 — 509-354-6600
Carol Meyer, prin. — Fax 354-6665
Sacajawea MS — 1,000/7-8
401 E 33rd Ave 99203 — 509-354-5500
Paula Ronhaar, prin. — Fax 354-5505
Salk MS — 800/7-8
6411 N Alberta St 99208 — 509-354-5600
Mark Gorman, prin. — Fax 354-5542
Shadle Park HS — 1,700/9-12
4327 N Ash St 99205 — 509-354-6700
Herb Rotchford, prin. — Fax 354-6710
Shaw MS — 800/7-8
4106 N Cook St 99207 — 509-354-5800
Christine Lynch, prin. — Fax 354-5899
Spokane Area Professional Tech Skill Ctr — Vo/Tech
4141 N Regal St 99207 — 509-354-7470
Don Howell, prin. — Fax 354-7474

West Valley SD 363 — 2,900/PK-12
PO Box 11739 99211 — 509-924-2150
Dr. Polly Crowley, supt. — Fax 922-5295
www.wvsd.com
Centennial MS — 600/6-8
915 N Ella Rd 99212 — 509-922-5482
Pam Francis, prin. — Fax 891-9520
Spokane Valley HS — 100/9-12
2011 N Hutchinson Rd 99212 — 509-922-5475
Larry Bush, prin. — Fax 922-5477
West Valley City MS — 200/5-8
8920 E Valleyway Ave 99212 — 509-921-2836
Tom Moore, prin. — Fax 921-2849
West Valley HS — 800/9-12
8301 E Buckeye Ave 99212 — 509-922-5488
Gary Neal, prin. — Fax 928-3676

———————————

All Saints MS — 200/5-8
1428 E 33rd Ave 99203 — 509-624-5712
Katherine Hicks, prin. — Fax 624-7752
Apollo College — Post-Sec.
10102 E Knox Ave 99206 — 509-532-8888
Cornerstone Christian Academy — 100/K-10
1801 E 29th Ave 99203 — 509-835-1235
Christina Hilderbrand, admin.
Glen Dow Academy of Hair Design — Post-Sec.
309 W Riverside Ave 99201 — 509-624-3244
Gonzaga Prep S — 1,000/9-12
1224 E Euclid Ave 99207 — 509-483-8511
Kevin Booth, prin. — Fax 483-3124
Gonzaga University — Post-Sec.
502 E Boone Ave 99258 — 509-328-4220
Gonzaga University 99258 — Post-Sec.
509-323-5546
Holy Family Hospital — Post-Sec.
5633 N Lidgerwood St 99208 — 509-482-2450
Inland Northwest HVAC Training Center — Post-Sec.
811 E Sprague Ave Ste 6 99202 — 509-747-8810
Intercollegiate Center/Nursing Education — Post-Sec.
2917 W Fort Gorge Wright Dr 99204 — 509-324-7360
ITT Technical Institute — Post-Sec.
13518 E Indiana Ave 99216 — 509-926-2900
Oaks-A Classical Christian Academy — 300/K-12
4224 E 4th Ave 99202 — 509-536-5955
Bruce Williams, prin. — Fax 536-7877
Sacred Heart Medical Center — Post-Sec.
101 W 8th Ave 99204 — 509-455-3040
St. George's S — 400/K-12
2929 W Waikiki Rd 99208 — 509-466-1636
Mo Copeland, hdmstr. — Fax 467-3258
Spokane Community College — Post-Sec.
1810 N Greene St 99217 — 509-533-7000
Spokane Falls Community College — Post-Sec.
3410 W Fort George Wright 99224 — 509-533-3500

Spokane Junior Academy — 100/K-10
1505 W Cleveland Ave 99205 — 509-325-1985
Donald Bryan, prin. — Fax 324-8904
Valley Christian S — 400/K-12
10212 E 9th Ave 99206 — 509-924-9131
Wes Evans, admin. — Fax 924-2971
Whitworth College — Post-Sec.
300 W Hawthorne Rd 99251 — 800-533-4668

Sprague, Lincoln, Pop. 487
Sprague SD 8 — 100/K-12
PO Box 305 99032 — 509-257-2591
Mark Stedman, supt. — Fax 257-2539
www.sprague.wednet.edu
Sprague HS, PO Box 305 99032 — 50/9-12
Patrick Whipple, prin. — 509-257-2511

Springdale, Stevens, Pop. 287
Mary Walker SD 207 — 500/PK-12
PO Box 159 99173 — 509-258-4534
Kevin Jacka, supt. — Fax 258-4707
www.marywalker.org/
Springdale MS — 100/7-8
PO Box 159 99173 — 509-258-7357
Helen Hindley, prin. — Fax 258-7756
Walker HS — 100/9-12
PO Box 159 99173 — 509-258-4533
Matthew Cobb, prin. — Fax 258-4555

Stanwood, Snohomish, Pop. 4,515
Stanwood-Camano SD 401 — 5,300/K-12
26920 Pioneer Hwy 98292 — 360-629-1200
Dr. Jean Shumate, supt. — Fax 629-1242
www.stanwood.wednet.edu
Church Creek Campus — 9-9
7600 272nd St NW 98292 — 360-629-1400
Fax 629-1410
Port Susan MS — 700/6-8
7506 267th Pl NW 98292 — 360-629-1360
Cinco Delgado, prin. — Fax 629-1365
Stanwood HS — 1,700/9-12
7400 272nd St NW 98292 — 360-629-1300
Jan Schuette, prin. — Fax 629-1310
Stanwood MS — 700/6-8
9405 271st St NW 98292 — 360-629-1350
Barbara Marsh, prin. — Fax 629-1354

Steilacoom, Pierce, Pop. 6,165
Steilacoom Historical SD 1 — 2,400/K-12
510 Chambers St 98388 — 253-983-2200
Dr. Arthur Himmler, supt. — Fax 584-7198
www.steilacoom.k12.wa.us
Pioneer MS — 500/6-8
511 Chambers St 98388 — 253-983-2400
Dan Luce, prin. — Fax 589-4892
Steilacoom HS — 700/9-12
54 Sentinel Dr 98388 — 253-983-2300
Janice McCrimmon, prin. — Fax 584-6255

Stevenson, Skamania, Pop. 1,233
Stevenson-Carson SD 303 — 1,100/K-12
PO Box 850 98648 — 509-427-5674
Jim Saltness, supt. — Fax 427-4028
www.scsd.k12.wa.us
Stevenson HS — 400/9-12
PO Box 850 98648 — 509-427-5631
Brian Howe, prin. — Fax 427-5639
Wind River MS — 200/7-8
PO Box 850 98648 — 509-427-8952
Kathleen Browning, prin. — Fax 427-8614

Sultan, Snohomish, Pop. 3,684
Sultan SD 311 — 2,200/K-12
514 4th St 98294 — 360-793-9800
Al Robinson, supt. — Fax 793-9890
www.sultan.k12.wa.us
Sultan HS — 600/9-12
13715 310th Ave SE 98294 — 360-793-9860
Robert Shacklett, prin. — Fax 793-9864
Sultan MS — 600/6-8
301 High Ave 98294 — 360-793-9850
Robin Briganti, prin. — Fax 793-9859

Sumner, Pierce, Pop. 9,026
Dieringer SD 343 — 1,100/K-8
1320 178th Ave E, — 253-862-2537
Judy Neumeier-Martinson, supt. — Fax 862-8472
www.dieringer.wednet.edu
North Tapps MS — 400/6-8
20029 12th St E, — 253-862-2776
Pat Keaton, prin. — Fax 862-2587

Sumner SD 320 — 7,100/K-12
1202 Wood Ave 98390 — 253-891-6000
Dr. Donald Eismann, supt. — Fax 891-6097
www.sumner.wednet.edu
Sumner HS — 1,900/9-12
1707 Main St 98390 — 253-891-5500
Bill Gaines, prin. — Fax 891-5585
Sumner MS — 600/6-8
1508 Willow St 98390 — 253-891-5000
Chuck Eychaner, prin. — Fax 891-5045
Other Schools – See Bonney Lake

Sunnyside, Yakima, Pop. 14,080
Sunnyside SD 201 — 7,500/K-12
1110 S 6th St 98944 — 509-836-6532
Dr. Richard D. Cole, supt. — Fax 837-0535
www.sunnyside.wednet.edu
Harrison MS — 1,300/6-8
810 S 16th St 98944 — 509-837-3601
Janie Hernandez, prin. — Fax 837-0450
Sierra Vista MS, 916 N 16th St 98944 — 6-8
Doug Rogers, prin. — 509-836-6532
Sunnyside HS — 1,300/9-12
1801 N Edison Ave 98944 — 509-837-2601
Brian Hart, prin. — Fax 837-0494

———————————

Professional Beauty School — Post-Sec.
214 S 6th St 98944 — 509-837-4040

Sunnyside Christian HS — 100/9-12
1820 Sheller Rd 98944 — 509-837-3044
Dean Wagenaar, prin. — Fax 837-8895

Tacoma, Pierce, Pop. 196,790
Bethel SD 403
Supt. — See Spanaway
Spanaway JHS — 900/7-9
15701 B St E 98445 — 253-683-5400
Roger Samples, prin. — Fax 683-5498

Fife SD 417 — 3,200/K-12
5802 20th St E 98424 — 253-517-1000
Dr. Stephen D. McCammon, supt. — Fax 517-1055
www.fifeschools.com
Columbia JHS — 600/8-9
2901 54th Ave E 98424 — 253-517-1600
J. Nelson, prin. — Fax 517-1605
Fife SHS — 800/10-12
5616 20th St E 98424 — 253-517-1100
John McCrossin, prin. — Fax 517-1105

Franklin Pierce SD 402 — 7,400/PK-12
315 129th St S 98444 — 253-537-0211
Steve Rasmussen, supt. — Fax 536-5406
www.fp.k12.wa.us
Ford MS — 1,000/6-8
1602 104th St E 98445 — 253-535-9883
Gary Benson, prin. — Fax 539-2496
Keithley MS — 800/6-8
12324 12th Ave S 98444 — 253-535-9884
Joyce Knowles, prin. — Fax 539-2495
Pierce HS — 1,200/9-12
11002 18th Ave E 98445 — 253-535-9880
Eric Hogan, prin. — Fax 535-2691
Washington HS — 1,000/9-12
12420 Ainsworth Ave S 98444 — 253-535-9881
James Ridgeway, prin. — Fax 539-2484

Tacoma SD 10 — 32,400/PK-12
PO Box 1357 98401 — 253-571-1000
James Shoemake Ed.D., supt. — Fax 571-2550
www.tacomaschools.org/
Baker MS — 800/6-8
8320 S I St 98408 — 253-571-5000
Harold H. Wright, prin. — Fax 571-5090
Foss HS — 1,900/9-12
2112 S Tyler St 98405 — 253-571-2000
Sharon Schauss, prin. — Fax 571-7466
Gault MS — 500/6-8
1115 E Division Ln 98404 — 253-571-1405
Miguel Villahermosa, prin. — Fax 571-1478
Giaudrone MS — 700/6-8
4902 S Alaska St 98408 — 253-571-5811
Gaile McLaurin, prin. — Fax 683-5812
Gray MS — 700/6-8
3109 S 60th St 98409 — 253-571-1860
Yvonne Bullock, prin. — Fax 571-1890
Hunt MS — 700/6-8
6501 S 10th St 98465 — 253-571-2335
Katherine Boyd, prin. — Fax 571-2351
Lee MS — 700/6-8
602 N Sprague Ave 98403 — 253-571-1395
Harjeet Sandhu, prin. — Fax 571-1466
Lincoln HS — 1,700/9-12
701 S 37th St 98418 — 253-571-2000
Patrick Erwin, prin. — Fax 571-6789
Mason MS — 800/6-8
3901 N 28th St 98407 — 253-571-2256
Patrice Sulkosky, prin. — Fax 571-2294
McIlvaigh MS — 500/6-8
1801 E 56th St 98404 — 253-571-2080
Daniel Dizon, prin. — Fax 571-2179
Meeker MS — 800/6-8
4402 Nassau Ave NE 98422 — 253-571-1377
Adrian Hartness, prin. — Fax 571-1266
Mount Tahoma HS — 1,600/9-12
4634 S 74th St 98409 — 253-571-3800
Greg Eisnaugle, prin. — Fax 571-3801
Stadium HS — 1,700/9-12
6229 S Tyler St 98409 — 253-571-1325
Jonathan Kellett, prin. — Fax 571-1463
Stewart MS — 600/6-8
5010 Pacific Ave 98408 — 253-571-2085
Howard King, prin. — Fax 571-2134
Truman MS — 800/6-8
5801 N 35th St 98407 — 253-571-2245
Patricia Robinson, prin. — Fax 571-2293
Wilson HS — 1,700/9-12
1202 N Orchard St 98406 — 253-571-6000
Dan Besett, prin. — Fax 571-6022

———————————

Bates Technical College — Post-Sec.
1101 Yakima Ave 98405 — 253-680-7000
Bellarmine Prep S — 1,000/9-12
2300 S Washington St 98405 — 253-838-9979
Chris Gavin, prin. — Fax 756-3887
BJ's Beauty & Barber College — Post-Sec.
5239 S Tacoma Way 98409 — 253-473-4320
Bryman College — Post-Sec.
2156 Pacific Ave 98402 — 253-207-4000
Covenant HS — 100/9-12
620 S Shirley St 98465 — 253-759-9570
Richard Hannula, prin. — Fax 752-5992
Crown College — Post-Sec.
8739 S Hosmer St 98444 — 253-531-3123
Faith Evangelical Lutheran Seminary — Post-Sec.
3504 N Pearl St 98407 — 253-752-2020
Life Christian S — 1,100/PK-12
1717 S Union Ave 98405 — 253-756-5317
Ross Hjelseth, hdmstr. — Fax 761-9798
Mount Rainier Lutheran HS — 253-284-4433
7306 Waller Rd E 98443
Dr. Robert Malzahn, dir. — Fax 284-4435
Northwest Baptist Seminary — Post-Sec.
4301 N Stevens St 98407 — 253-759-6104
Pacific Lutheran University — Post-Sec.
12180 Park Ave S 98447 — 253-531-6900

Tacoma Baptist S — 400/PK-12
2052 S 64th St 98409 — 253-475-7226
Robert White, admin. — Fax 471-9949
Tacoma Community College — Post-Sec.
6501 S 19th St 98466 — 253-566-5000
University of Puget Sound — Post-Sec.
1500 N Warner St 98416 — 253-879-3100
Western Pacific Truck School — Post-Sec.
11020 S Tacoma Way 98499 — 253-581-6494
Wright S — 500/PK-12
827 N Tacoma Ave 98403 — 253-272-2216
Dr. Jayasri Ghosh, hdmstr. — Fax 572-3616

Taholah, Grays Harbor, Pop. 788
Taholah SD 77 — 200/PK-12
PO Box 249 98587 — 360-276-4729
Leon Strom, supt. — Fax 276-4370
www.taholah.k12.wa.us/
Taholah S — 200/PK-12
PO Box 249 98587 — 360-276-4514
Rick Lindblad, prin. — Fax 276-4370

Tekoa, Whitman, Pop. 807
Tekoa SD 265 — 200/PK-12
PO Box 869 99033 — 509-284-3281
Sergio Hernandez, supt. — Fax 284-2045
www.tekoa.wednet.edu
Tekoa JSHS — 100/7-12
PO Box 869 99033 — 509-284-3401
Wayne Roellich, prin. — Fax 284-5802

Tenino, Thurston, Pop. 1,541
Tenino SD 402 — 1,400/PK-12
PO Box 4024 98589 — 360-264-3400
Dr. Steven Smedley, supt. — Fax 264-3438
www.tenino.k12.wa.us
Tenino HS — 500/9-12
PO Box 4024 98589 — 360-264-3500
Jeff Johnson, prin. — Fax 264-3538
Tenino MS — 300/6-8
PO Box 4024 98589 — 360-264-3600
Tony Howard, prin. — Fax 264-3638

Thorp, Kittitas
Thorp SD 400 — 200/K-12
PO Box 150 98946 — 509-964-2107
Dr. Virginia Erion, supt. — Fax 964-2313
www.thorp.wednet.edu
Thorp S — 200/K-12
PO Box 150 98946 — 509-964-2107
Sim Egbert, prin. — Fax 964-2313

Toledo, Lewis, Pop. 664
Toledo SD 237 — 1,000/PK-12
PO Box 469 98591 — 360-864-6325
Sharon Bower, supt. — Fax 864-6326
www.toledo.k12.wa.us
Toledo HS — 300/9-12
PO Box 820 98591 — 360-864-2391
Shawn Corrigan, prin. — Fax 864-2396
Toledo MS — 300/6-8
PO Box 668 98591 — 360-864-2395
Bill Waag, prin. — Fax 864-8147

Tonasket, Okanogan, Pop. 962
Tonasket SD 404 — 1,100/PK-12
35 Highway 20 98855 — 509-486-2126
Randall Hauff, supt. — Fax 486-1263
www.tonasket.wednet.edu
Tonasket HS — 400/9-12
35 Highway 20 98855 — 509-486-2161
Jeff Hardesty, prin. — Fax 486-4382
Tonasket MS — 300/6-8
35 Highway 20 98855 — 509-486-2147
Ed Morgan, prin. — Fax 486-1576

Toppenish, Yakima, Pop. 9,108
Toppenish SD 202 — 2,800/K-12
306 Bolin Dr 98948 — 509-865-4455
Steve Myers, supt. — Fax 865-2067
www.toppenish.wednet.edu/
Toppenish HS — 700/9-12
141 Ward Rd 98948 — 509-865-3370
Walt Wegener, prin. — Fax 865-3244
Toppenish MS — 900/6-8
104 Goldendale Ave 98948 — 509-865-2730
Leonor de Maldonado, prin. — Fax 865-7503

Heritage University — Post-Sec.
3240 Fort Rd 98948 — 509-865-8500

Touchet, Walla Walla
Touchet SD 300 — 300/K-12
PO Box 135 99360 — 509-394-2352
Dan McDonald, supt. — Fax 394-2952
www.touchet.org/
Touchet S — 300/K-12
PO Box 135 99360 — 509-394-2352
Larry Smith, prin. — Fax 394-2952

Toutle, Cowlitz
Toutle Lake SD 130 — 600/K-12
5050 Spirit Lake Hwy 98649 — 360-274-6182
Scott Grabenhorst, supt. — Fax 274-7608
www.toutlesd.k12.wa.us
Toutle Lake JSHS — 300/7-12
5050 Spirit Lake Hwy 98649 — 360-274-6132
Larry Hearst, prin. — Fax 274-7608

Trout Lake, Klickitat
Trout Lake SD R-400 — 200/K-12
PO Box 488 98650 — 509-395-2571
Doug Dearden, supt. — Fax 395-2399
www.troutlake.k12.wa.us/default.htm
Trout Lake JSHS — 100/5-12
PO Box 488 98650 — 509-395-2571
Doug Dearden, prin. — Fax 395-2399

Tukwila, King, Pop. 17,081
Tukwila SD 406 — 2,600/K-12
4640 S 144th St 98168 — 206-901-8000
Dr. James Quezon Hammond, supt. — Fax 901-8016
www.tukwila.wednet.edu
Foster HS — 700/9-12
4242 S 144th St 98168 — 206-901-7900
Willie Fisher, prin. — Fax 901-7907
Showalter MS — 600/6-8
4628 S 144th St 98168 — 206-901-7800
Brett Christopher, prin. — Fax 901-7807

ITT Technical Institute — Post-Sec.
12720 Gateway Dr Ste 100 98168 — 206-244-3300

Tumwater, Thurston, Pop. 13,162
Tumwater SD 33 — 5,900/K-12
419 Linwood Ave SW 98512 — 360-709-7000
Terry Borden, supt. — Fax 709-7002
www.tumwater.k12.wa.us
Bush MS — 500/7-8
2120 83rd Ave SW 98512 — 360-709-7400
Linda O'Shaughnessy, prin. — Fax 709-7402
New Market Vocational Skills Center — Vo/Tech
7299 New Market St SW 98501 — 360-570-4500
John Aultman, prin. — Fax 570-4502
Tumwater HS — 1,000/9-12
700 Israel Rd SW 98501 — 360-709-7600
Scott Seaman, prin. — Fax 709-7602
Tumwater MS — 500/7-8
6335 Littlerock Rd SW 98512 — 360-709-7500
John Wilcox, prin. — Fax 709-7502
Other Schools – See Olympia

South Puget Sound Community College — Post-Sec.
2011 Mottman Rd SW 98512 — 360-754-7711

Union Gap, Yakima, Pop. 5,710

La Salle HS — 200/9-12
3000 Lightning Way 98903 — 509-225-2900
Br. James Joost, prin. — Fax 225-2950

University Place, Pierce, Pop. 30,638
University Place SD 83 — 5,300/K-12
3717 Grandview Dr W 98466 — 253-566-5600
Patricia Baker, supt. — Fax 566-5607
www.upsd.wednet.edu
Curtis JHS — 1,000/8-9
8901 40th St W 98466 — 253-566-5670
Susan Follmer, prin. — Fax 566-5644
Curtis SHS — 1,400/10-12
8425 40th St W 98466 — 253-566-5710
Gary Martin, prin. — Fax 566-5626

Wright Academy — 700/PK-12
7723 Chambers Creek Rd W 98467 — 253-620-8300
Robert Camner, prin. — Fax 620-8431

Vancouver, Clark, Pop. 151,654
Battle Ground SD 119
Supt. — See Brush Prairie
Laurin MS — 500/5-8
13601 NE 97th Ave 98662 — 360-885-5200
Bill Penrose, prin. — Fax 885-5205
Pleasant Valley MS — 500/5-8
14320 NE 50th Ave 98686 — 360-885-5500
Ward Holcomb, prin. — Fax 885-5510
Evergreen SD 114 — 24,300/K-12
PO Box 8910 98668 — 360-604-4000
Dr. Robert Corley, supt. — Fax 892-5307
www.egreen.wednet.edu
Cascade MS — 800/6-8
13900 NE 18th St 98684 — 360-604-3600
Gary Price, prin. — Fax 604-3602
Clark County Vocational Skills Center — Vo/Tech
12200 NE 28th St 98682 — 360-604-1050
Dennis Kampe, prin. — Fax 604-1052
Covington MS — 800/6-8
11200 NE Rosewood Ave 98662 — 360-604-6300
Byron Molle, prin. — Fax 604-6302
Evergreen HS — 2,200/9-12
14300 NE 18th St 98684 — 360-604-3700
Jim Hudson, prin. — Fax 604-3702
Frontier MS — 1,000/6-8
7600 NE 166th Ave 98682 — 360-604-3200
Lisa Wagner, prin. — Fax 604-3202
Heritage HS — 2,200/9-12
7825 NE 130th Ave 98682 — 360-604-3400
Ann Sosky, prin. — Fax 604-3402
Mountain View HS — 2,100/9-12
1500 SE Blairmont Dr 98683 — 360-604-6100
Mark Ross, prin. — Fax 604-6102
Pacific MS — 1,100/6-8
2017 NE 172nd Ave 98684 — 360-604-6500
Roland Brosius, prin. — Fax 604-6502
Shahala MS — 900/6-8
601 SE 192nd Ave 98683 — 360-604-3800
Renee Bernazzani, prin. — Fax 604-3802
Wy' East MS — 1,000/6-8
1112 SE 136th Ave 98683 — 360-604-6400
Gary Tichenor, prin. — Fax 604-6402

Vancouver SD 37 — 22,100/PK-12
PO Box 8937 98668 — 360-313-1000
John Erickson Ph.D., supt. — Fax 313-1001
www.vansd.org
Alki MS — 1,200/6-8
1800 NW Bliss Rd 98685 — 360-313-3200
Karla Schlosser, prin. — Fax 313-3201
Columbia River HS — 1,300/9-12
800 NW 99th St 98665 — 360-313-3900
Mike Stromme, prin. — Fax 313-3901
Discovery MS — 700/6-8
800 E 40th St 98663 — 360-313-3300
Susan Cone, prin. — Fax 313-3301

Fir Grove Childrens Center — 100/K-12
2920 Falk Rd 98661 — 360-313-1800
Mike Palshis, prin. — Fax 313-1801
Ft. Vancouver HS — 1,600/9-12
5700 E 18th St 98661 — 360-313-4000
Nancy Faaren, prin. — Fax 313-4001
Gaiser MS — 1,000/6-8
3000 NE 99th St 98665 — 360-313-3400
Betty Roberts, prin. — Fax 313-3401
Hudson's Bay HS — 1,500/9-12
1206 E Reserve St 98661 — 360-313-4400
Kathy Everidge, prin. — Fax 313-4401
Jefferson MS — 6-8
3000 NW 119th St 98685 — 360-313-3700
Marianne Thompson, prin. — Fax 313-3701
Lee MS — 900/6-8
8500 NW 9th Ave 98665 — 360-313-3500
Janet Gillingham, prin. — Fax 313-3501
McLoughlin MS — 900/6-8
5802 MacArthur Blvd 98661 — 360-313-3600
Richard Reeves, prin. — Fax 313-3601
School of Arts & Academics — 600/6-12
3101 Main St 98663 — 360-313-4600
Chris Olsen, prin. — Fax 313-4601
Skyview HS — 1,800/9-12
1300 NW 139th St 98685 — 360-313-4200
Ed Little, prin. — Fax 313-4201

Clark College — Post-Sec.
1800 E McLoughlin Blvd 98663 — 360-992-2000
E. Fries School of Piano Tuning & Tech. — Post-Sec.
2510 E Evergreen Blvd 98661 — 360-693-1511
International Air & Hospitality Academy — Post-Sec.
2901 E Mill Plain Blvd 98661 — 360-695-2500
New Generation Christian S — 100/K-12
PO Box 820289 98682 — 360-944-3905
Dave Webb, prin. — Fax 254-5567
Phagans' Orchards Beauty School — Post-Sec.
10411 NE 4th Plain Blvd 109 98662 — 360-254-9519
Vancouver Christian HS — 100/9-12
PO Box 87625 98687 — 360-735-7915
Roger Miller, admin. — Fax 735-8049
Washington State School for the Blind — Post-Sec.
2214 E 13th St 98661
Washington State School for the Deaf — Post-Sec.
611 Grand Blvd 98661
Western Business College — Post-Sec.
120 NE 136th Ave Ste 130 98684 — 360-254-3282

Vashon, King
Vashon Island SD 402 — 1,500/PK-12
18850 103rd Ave SW 98070 — 206-463-2121
Dr. Mimi Walker, supt. — Fax 463-6262
www.vashonsd.org
McMurray MS — 400/6-8
9329 SW Cemetery Rd 98070 — 206-463-9168
Greg Allison, prin. — Fax 463-9707
Vashon Island HS — 500/9-12
20120 Vashon Hwy SW 98070 — 206-463-9171
Susan Hanson, prin. — Fax 463-1944

Veradale, Spokane, Pop. 7,836
Central Valley SD 356
Supt. — See Greenacres
Central Valley HS — 1,700/9-12
821 S Sullivan Rd 99037 — 509-228-5100
Mike Hittle, prin. — Fax 228-5109
Evergreen MS — 500/6-8
14221 E 16th Ave 99037 — 509-228-4780
Dave Feldhusen, prin. — Fax 228-4789

Waitsburg, Walla Walla, Pop. 1,227
Waitsburg SD 401-100 — 400/K-12
PO Box 217 99361 — 509-337-6301
Dr. Carol Clarke, supt. — Fax 337-6042
www.waitsburgsd.org
Preston Hall MS — 100/6-8
PO Box 217 99361 — 509-337-9474
Ben Christensen, prin. — Fax 337-6170
Waitsburg HS — 100/9-12
PO Box 217 99361 — 509-337-6351
Ken Beasley, prin. — Fax 337-6551

Walla Walla, Walla Walla, Pop. 30,134
Walla Walla SD 140 — 5,700/K-12
364 S Park St 99362 — 509-527-3000
Dr. Richard Carter, supt. — Fax 529-7713
www.wwps.org
Garrison MS — 600/6-8
906 Chase St 99362 — 509-527-3040
Jim Sporleder, prin. — Fax 527-3048
Pioneer MS — 700/6-8
450 Bridge St 99362 — 509-527-3050
Dana Jones, prin. — Fax 526-5212
Walla Walla HS — 1,900/9-12
800 Abbott Rd 99362 — 509-527-3020
Darcy Weisner, prin. — Fax 527-3034

DeSales HS — 200/6-12
919 E Sumach St 99362 — 509-525-3030
John Lesko, prin. — Fax 527-0361
Walla Walla Community College — Post-Sec.
500 Tausick Way 99362 — 509-527-4283
Whitman College — Post-Sec.
345 Boyer Ave 99362 — 509-527-5111

Wapato, Yakima, Pop. 4,575
Wapato SD 207 — 3,200/K-12
PO Box 38 98951 — 509-877-4181
Art Edgerly, supt. — Fax 877-6077
www.wapato.k12.wa.us/
Wapato HS — 700/9-12
PO Box 38 98951 — 509-877-3138
Bob Anacker, prin. — Fax 877-4334
Wapato MS — 800/6-8
PO Box 38 98951 — 509-877-2173
Kelly Garza, prin. — Fax 877-6232

Warden, Grant, Pop. 2,611
Warden SD 146-161 — 1,000/PK-12
  101 W Beck Way 98857 — 509-349-2366
  Larry Blades, supt. — Fax 349-2367
  www.warden.wednet.edu
Warden HS — 300/9-12
  101 W Beck Way 98857 — 509-349-2581
  Leonard Lusk, prin. — Fax 349-2531
Warden MS — 200/6-8
  101 W Beck Way 98857 — 509-349-2581
  Mike Villarreal, prin. — Fax 349-2531

Washougal, Clark, Pop. 9,541
Washougal SD 112-6 — 2,700/K-12
  4855 Evergreen Way 98671 — 360-954-3000
  Robert Donaldson, supt. — Fax 835-7776
  www.washougal.k12.wa.us
Canyon Creek MS — 200/6-8
  9731 Washougal River Rd 98671 — 360-954-3500
  Sandi Christensen, prin. — Fax 837-1500
Jemtegaard MS — 400/6-8
  35300 SE Evergreen Blvd 98671 — 360-954-3400
  Doug Bright, prin. — Fax 835-9145
Washougal HS — 800/9-12
  1201 39th St 98671 — 360-954-3100
  Ronald Carlson, prin. — Fax 835-3968
Washougal Community Education — Adult
  4855 Evergreen Way 98671 — 360-954-3838
  Jan Storm, prin. — Fax 335-0320

Washtucna, Adams, Pop. 259
Washtucna SD 109-43 — 100/K-12
  PO Box 688 99371 — 509-646-3237
  Chris Gregory, supt. — Fax 646-3249
Washtucna S — 100/K-12
  100 School St 99371 — 509-646-3401
  Glenn Martin, prin. — Fax 646-3249

Waterville, Douglas, Pop. 1,147
Waterville SD 209 — 400/K-12
  PO Box 490 98858 — 509-745-8584
  Mark Heid, supt. — Fax 745-9073
  www.waterville.wednet.edu/
Waterville JSHS — 200/6-12
  PO Box 490 98858 — 509-745-8583
  Jay Tyus, prin. — Fax 745-9073

Wellpinit, Stevens
Wellpinit SD 49 — 400/K-12
  PO Box 390 99040 — 509-258-4535
  Tim Ames, supt. — Fax 258-7378
  www.wellpinit.wednet.edu
Wellpinit HS — 100/9-12
  PO Box 390 99040 — 509-258-4535
  Terry Bartolino, prin. — Fax 258-7378
Wellpinit MS — 100/6-8
  PO Box 390 99040 — 509-258-4535
  Terry Bartolino, prin. — Fax 258-7378

Wenatchee, Chelan, Pop. 28,636
Eastmont SD 206
  Supt. — See East Wenatchee
North Central Washington Skills Center — Vo/Tech
  327 E Penny Rd Ste D 98801 — 509-662-8827
  John Linder, prin. — Fax 662-5993

Wenatchee SD 246 — 7,300/K-12
  PO Box 1767 98807 — 509-663-8161
  Brian Flones, supt. — Fax 663-3082
  home.wsd.wednet.edu
Foothills MS, 1410 Maple St 98801 — 600/6-8
  John Waldren, prin. — 509-664-8961
Orchard MS — 500/6-8
  1024 Orchard Ave 98801 — 509-662-7745
  Mike Hopkins, prin.
Pioneer MS, 1620 Russell St 98801 — 600/6-8
  Mark Helm, prin. — 509-663-7171
Wenatchee HS — 2,000/9-12
  1101 Millerdale Ave 98801 — 509-663-8117
  Michele Wadeikis, prin. — Fax 663-2573

Academy of Hair Design — Post-Sec.
  208 S Wenatchee Ave 98801 — 509-662-9082
Cascade Christian Academy — 200/K-12
  600 N Western Ave 98801 — 509-662-2723
  Mark Witas, prin. — Fax 662-5892
River Academy — 100/PK-12
  PO Box 4485 98807 — 509-665-2415
   — Fax 662-9235
SkillSource Office & Technology Center — Post-Sec.
  234 N Mission St 98801 — 509-665-0313
Wenatchee Valley College — Post-Sec.
  1300 5th St 98801 — 509-682-6800

Westport, Grays Harbor, Pop. 2,188
Ocosta SD 172 — 700/PK-12
  2580 S Montesano St 98595 — 360-268-9125
  Mark Jacobson, supt. — Fax 268-2540
  www.ocosta.wednet.edu
Ocosta JSHS — 400/7-12
  2580 S Montesano St 98595 — 360-268-9125
  Mike Church, prin. — Fax 268-0908

West Richland, Benton, Pop. 9,290
Richland SD 400
  Supt. — See Richland
Enterprise MS — 6-8
  5200 Paradise Dr 99353 — 509-967-6200
  Mary McConnell, prin. — Fax 967-5685

White Salmon, Klickitat, Pop. 2,244
White Salmon Valley SD 405-17 — 1,200/K-12
  PO Box 157 98672 — 509-493-1500
  Dale Palmer, supt. — Fax 493-2275
  schools.gorge.net/whitesalmon
Columbia HS — 400/9-12
  PO Box 1339 98672 — 509-493-1970
  Malcolm Dennis, prin. — Fax 493-4182
Henkle MS — 400/5-8
  480 NW Loop Rd 98672 — 509-493-1502
  Rick George, prin. — Fax 493-3385

White Swan, Yakima, Pop. 2,669
Mount Adams SD 209 — 1,100/PK-12
  PO Box 578 98952 — 509-874-2611
  Mary Hall Ed.D., supt. — Fax 874-2960
  www.mtadams.wednet.edu
Mount Adams MS — 300/6-8
  PO Box 578 98952 — 509-874-2324
  Henry Strom, prin. — Fax 874-2646
White Swan HS — 300/9-12
  PO Box 578 98952 — 509-874-2324
  Tracy Savage, prin. — Fax 874-2646

Wilbur, Lincoln, Pop. 898
Wilbur SD 200 — 200/K-12
  PO Box 1090 99185 — 509-647-2221
  Steve Gaub, supt. — Fax 647-2509
  www.wilbur.wednet.edu/
Wilbur JSHS — 100/7-12
  PO Box 1090 99185 — 509-647-5602
  Tom Johnson, prin. — Fax 647-2509

Wilkeson, Pierce, Pop. 396
White River SD 416
  Supt. — See Buckley
Glacier MS — 200/6-8
  PO Box 1976, — 360-829-3395
  Andy McGrath, prin. — Fax 829-3391

Wilson Creek, Grant, Pop. 232
Wilson Creek SD 167-202 — 100/K-12
  PO Box 46 98860 — 509-345-2541
  Bob Nolan, supt. — Fax 345-2288
  www.wilsoncreek.org
Wilson Creek JSHS, PO Box 46 98860 — 100/7-12
  Linda McKay, prin. — 509-345-2541

Winlock, Lewis, Pop. 1,183
Winlock SD 232 — 700/PK-12
  311 NW Fir St 98596 — 360-785-3582
  Richard Conley, supt. — Fax 785-3583
Winlock HS — 200/9-12
  241 N Military Rd 98596 — 360-785-3537
  John Stemkoski, prin. — Fax 785-3538
Winlock MS — 200/6-8
  241 N Military Rd 98596 — 360-785-3046
  Marshall Mayer, prin. — Fax 785-3047

Winthrop, Okanogan, Pop. 345
Methow Valley SD 350 — 700/PK-12
  18 Twin Lakes Rd 98862 — 509-996-9205
  Dr. Louis Gates, supt. — Fax 996-9208
  www.methow.org
Liberty Bell JSHS — 400/7-12
  18 Twin Lakes Rd 98862 — 509-996-2215
  Deborah Dekalb, prin. — Fax 996-3609

Wishram, Klickitat
Wishram SD 94 — 100/PK-12
  PO Box 8 98673 — 509-748-2551
  Duane Grams, supt. — Fax 748-2127
Wishram S — 100/PK-12
  PO Box 8 98673 — 509-748-2551
  Duane Grams, prin. — Fax 748-2127

Woodinville, King, Pop. 9,632
Northshore SD 417
  Supt. — See Bothell
Leota JHS — 700/7-9
  19301 168th Ave NE 98072 — 425-402-5400
  Scott Farquhar, prin. — Fax 402-5412
Timbercrest JHS — 700/7-9
  19115 215th Way NE, — 425-806-7000
  Larry Little, prin. — Fax 806-7011
Woodinville SHS — 1,500/10-12
  19819 136th Ave NE 98072 — 425-489-6700
  Vicki Puckett, prin. — Fax 489-6787

Chrysalis S — 300/K-12
  14241 NE Woodinville Duvall 98072 — 425-481-2228
  Karen Fogle, dir. — Fax 486-8107
Kirkland Beauty School — Post-Sec.
  17311 140th Ave NE 98072 — 425-487-0437

Woodland, Cowlitz, Pop. 4,007
Woodland SD 404 — 2,000/PK-12
  800 3rd St 98674 — 360-225-9451
  Dr. William Hundley, supt. — Fax 225-8956
  www.woodland.wednet.edu
Woodland HS — 600/9-12
  757 Park St 98674 — 360-225-8201
  John Shoup, prin. — Fax 225-8814
Woodland MS — 300/7-8
  755 Park St 98674 — 360-225-9416
  Carl Thomson, prin. — Fax 225-6725

West Coast Training — Post-Sec.
  PO Box 970 98674 — 360-225-6787

Yakima, Yakima, Pop. 80,223
East Valley SD 90 — 2,400/K-12
  2002 Beaudry Rd 98901 — 509-573-7300
  John J. Schieche, supt. — Fax 573-7340
  www.evsd90.wednet.edu
East Valley Central MS — 400/7-8
  2010 Beaudry Rd 98901 — 509-573-7500
  Jeri Young, prin. — Fax 573-7540
East Valley HS — 700/9-12
  1900 Beaudry Rd 98901 — 509-573-7400
  Mark Hummel, prin. — Fax 573-7440

West Valley SD 208 — 4,600/K-12
  8902 Zier Rd 98908 — 509-972-6000
  Dr. Peter Ansingh, supt. — Fax 972-6001
  www.wvsd208.org
West Valley JHS — 800/8-9
  7505 Zier Rd 98908 — 509-966-5800
  Steve Smith, prin. — Fax 972-5801
West Valley SHS — 1,100/10-12
  9206 Zier Rd 98908 — 509-972-5900
  Jean Seibert, prin. — Fax 972-5901

Yakima SD 7 — 15,100/PK-12
  104 N 4th Ave 98902 — 509-573-7000
  Benjamin Soria, supt. — Fax 573-7189
  www.ysd.wednet.edu
Davis HS — 1,700/9-12
  212 S 6th Ave 98902 — 509-573-2500
  Lee Maras, prin. — Fax 573-2525
Eisenhower HS — 1,900/9-12
  702 S 40th Ave 98908 — 509-573-2600
  Stacey Locke, prin. — Fax 573-2626
Franklin MS — 800/6-8
  410 S 19th Ave 98902 — 509-573-2100
  Bill Hilton, prin. — Fax 573-2121
Lewis & Clark MS — 700/6-8
  1114 W Pierce St 98902 — 509-573-2200
  Lois Betzing, prin. — Fax 573-2222
Washington MS — 700/6-8
  510 S 9th St 98901 — 509-573-2300
  Lorenzo Alvarado, prin. — Fax 573-2323
Wilson MS — 800/6-8
  902 S 44th Ave 98908 — 509-573-2400
  Ernesto Araiza, prin. — Fax 573-2424
Yakima Valley Technical Skills Center — Vo/Tech
  1116 S 15th Ave 98902 — 509-573-5000
  Craig Dwight, dir. — Fax 573-5023

McAuliffe Academy — 400/K-12
  402 E Yakima Ave Ste 1100 98901 — 509-575-4989
  Glen Blomgren, dir. — Fax 575-4976
Perry Technical Institute — Post-Sec.
  2011 W Washington Ave 98903 — 509-453-0374
Professional Beauty School — Post-Sec.
  PO Box 9243 98909 — 509-877-6443
Riverside Christian S — 500/PK-12
  721 Keys Rd 98901 — 509-965-2602
  Rick Van Beek, supt. — Fax 966-7031
Yakima Adventist Christian S — 100/K-10
  1200 City Reservoir Rd 98908 — 509-966-1933
  P.K. Frey, prin. — Fax 966-3907
Yakima Valley Community College — Post-Sec.
  PO Box 22520 98907 — 509-574-4600

Yelm, Thurston, Pop. 4,085
Yelm SD 2 — 5,100/PK-12
  PO Box 476 98597 — 360-458-1900
  Dr. Alan Burke, supt. — Fax 458-6178
  www.ycs.wednet.edu
Yelm HS — 1,400/9-12
  PO Box 476 98597 — 360-458-7777
  Pete Diklich, prin. — Fax 458-6198
Yelm MS — 800/7-8
  PO Box 476 98597 — 360-458-3600
  Lorene Rang, prin. — Fax 458-6122

Zillah, Yakima, Pop. 2,505
Zillah SD 205 — 1,300/PK-12
  1301 Cutler Way 98953 — 509-829-5911
  Kevin McKay, supt. — Fax 829-6290
  www.zillahschools.org/
Zillah HS — 400/9-12
  1602 2nd Ave 98953 — 509-829-5565
  Mike Torres, prin. — Fax 829-5285
Zillah MS — 200/7-8
  1301 Cutler Way 98953 — 509-829-5511
  Michael Harrington, prin. — Fax 829-6290

WEST VIRGINIA

WEST VIRGINIA DEPARTMENT OF EDUCATION
1900 Kanawha Blvd E, Charleston 25305-0009
Telephone 304-558-2681
Fax 304-558-0048
Website wvde.state.wv.us

State Superintendent of Schools   Steve Paine

WEST VIRGINIA BOARD OF EDUCATION
1900 Kanawha Blvd E, Charleston 25305-0009

President   Barbara Fish

REGIONAL EDUCATION SERVICE AGENCIES (RESA)

RESA I
Carol Morgan, dir.   304-256-4712
400 Neville St, Beckley 25801   Fax 256-4683
resa1.k12.wv.us/
RESA II
Rick Powell, dir.   304-529-6205
2001 McCoy Rd, Huntington 25701   Fax 529-6209
resa2.k12.wv.us/
RESA III
Charles Nichols, dir.   304-766-7655
501 22nd St, Dunbar 25064   Fax 766-7915
resa3.k12.wv.us

RESA IV
Elmer Pritt, dir., 404 Old Main Dr   304-872-6440
Summersville 26651   Fax 872-6442
resa4.k12.wv.us/
RESA V
Ron Nichols, dir.   304-485-6513
2507 9th Ave, Parkersburg 26101   Fax 485-6515
resa5.k12.wv.us/
RESA VII
Gabriel Devono, dir.   304-624-6554
1201 N 15th St, Clarksburg 26301   Fax 624-5223
resa7.k12.wv.us/

RESA VIII
John Hough, dir., 109 S College St   304-267-3595
Martinsburg 25401   Fax 267-3599
resa8.k12.wv.us/
RESA VI
Nick P. Zervos, dir.   304-243-0440
30 G C and P Rd, Wheeling 26003   Fax 243-0443
resa6.k12.wv.us/

PUBLIC, PRIVATE AND CATHOLIC SECONDARY SCHOOLS

Ansted, Fayette, Pop. 1,590
Fayette County SD
Supt. — See Fayetteville
Ansted MS   200/5-8
PO Box 766 25812   304-658-5170
Chris Pinnick, prin.   Fax 658-5170

Ashton, Mason
Mason County SD
Supt. — See Point Pleasant
Hannan JSHS   300/7-12
6770 Ashton Upland Rd 25503   304-576-2571
Tom McNeely, prin.   Fax 743-4513

Athens, Mercer, Pop. 1,083

Concord University 24712   Post-Sec.
    304-384-3115

Avondale, McDowell
McDowell County SD
Supt. — See Welch
Sandy River MS   300/6-8
PO Box 419 24811   304-938-2407
William Campbell, prin.   Fax 938-2418

Baker, Hardy
Hardy County SD
Supt. — See Moorefield
East Hardy HS   200/9-12
PO Box 120 26801   304-897-5948
David Jones, prin.   Fax 897-6261
East Hardy MS   200/5-8
PO Box 260 26801   304-897-5970
Rebecca Brill, prin.   Fax 897-6653

Barboursville, Cabell, Pop. 3,186
Cabell County SD
Supt. — See Huntington
Barboursville MS   800/6-8
1400 Central Ave 25504   304-733-3003
Leo Lake, prin.   Fax 733-3009

Covenant S   300/K-12
5800 Route 60 E 25504   304-736-0000
H. Keener Fry, hdmstr.   Fax 736-5213

Beaver, Raleigh, Pop. 1,244

Victory Baptist Academy   100/K-12
PO Box 549 25813   304-255-4535

Beckley, Raleigh, Pop. 16,994
Raleigh County SD   11,500/PK-12
105 Adair St 25801   304-256-4500
Charlotte Hutchens Ed.D., supt.   Fax 256-4707
boe.rale.k12.wv.us
Academy of Careers and Technology   Vo/Tech
390 Stanaford Rd 25801   304-256-4615
    Fax 256-4674
Beckley-Stratton MS   800/6-8
401 Grey Flats Rd 25801   304-256-4616
Judy Thomas, prin.   Fax 256-4616
Park MS   400/6-8
212 Park Ave 25801   304-256-4586
Joe Wright, prin.   Fax 256-4709
Wilson HS   1,400/9-12
400 Stanaford Rd 25801   304-256-4646
Bob Maynard, prin.   Fax 256-4642

Other Schools – See Coal City, Glen Daniel, Shady
Spring, Sophia

Beckley Beauty Academy   Post-Sec.
109 S Fayette St 25801   304-253-8326
Mountain State University   Post-Sec.
PO Box 9003 25802   304-253-7351
New River Community & Technical College   Post-Sec.
167 Dye Dr 25801   304-255-5812
Trinity Christian Academy   100/PK-12
PO Box 1123 25802   304-254-9600
J.S. Peterson, admin.   Fax 254-9655
Valley College of Technology   Post-Sec.
713 S Oakwood Ave 25801   304-252-9547
Veterans Administration Hospital   Post-Sec.
200 Veterans Ave 25801   304-255-2121

Belington, Barbour, Pop. 1,816
Barbour County SD
Supt. — See Philippi
Belington MS   200/6-8
RR 2 Box 343 26250   304-823-1281
H. Moke Post, prin.   Fax 823-2403

Belle, Kanawha, Pop. 1,201
Kanawha County SD
Supt. — See Charleston
DuPont MS   400/6-8
301 W 34th St 25015   304-348-1978
David L. Miller, prin.   Fax 348-1138
Riverside HS   1,200/9-12
1 Warrior Way 25015   304-348-1996
Paula Potter, prin.   Fax 348-1921

Belmont, Pleasants, Pop. 1,028
Pleasants County SD
Supt. — See Saint Marys
Pleasants County MS   400/5-8
510 Riverview Dr 26134   304-665-2415
Mike Wells, prin.   Fax 665-2451

Berkeley Springs, Morgan, Pop. 756
Morgan County SD   2,000/PK-12
247 Harrison Ave 25411   304-258-2430
David Temple, supt.   Fax 258-9146
www.morganschools.net
Berkeley Springs HS   700/9-12
149 Concord Ave 25411   304-258-2876
George Ward, prin.   Fax 258-5058
Warm Springs MS   600/6-8
1415 Fairfax St 25411   304-258-1500
Gene Brock, prin.   Fax 258-4600
Other Schools – See Paw Paw

Berkeley Springs SDA S   50/K-10
3606 Valley Rd 25411   304-258-3581
    Fax 258-8344

Bethany, Brooke, Pop. 977

Bethany College 26032   Post-Sec.
    304-829-7000

Blacksville, Monongalia, Pop. 174
Monongalia County SD
Supt. — See Morgantown
Clay-Battelle JSHS   400/7-12
PO Box A 26521   304-432-8208
Karen Stiles, prin.   Fax 432-8189

Bluefield, Mercer, Pop. 11,124
Mercer County SD
Supt. — See Princeton
Bluefield HS   700/9-12
535 W Cumberland Rd 24701   304-325-9116
Joe Turner, prin.   Fax 325-0529
Bluefield MS   600/6-8
2002 Stadium Dr 24701   304-325-2481
Todd Browning, prin.   Fax 325-2156

Bluefield Regional Medical Center   Post-Sec.
500 Cherry St 24701   304-327-1701
Bluefield State College   Post-Sec.
219 Rock St 24701   304-327-4000
Valley View SDA S   50/K-12
PO Box 6312 24701   304-325-8679
Rosalie Stockil, prin.

Bradley, Raleigh, Pop. 2,144

Appalachian Bible College   Post-Sec.
PO Box ABC 25818   800-678-9222

Branchland, Lincoln
Lincoln County SD
Supt. — See Hamlin
Guyan Valley JSHS   600/7-12
700 State Route 10 25506   304-824-3235
Frank Barnett, prin.   Fax 824-3459

Bridgeport, Harrison, Pop. 7,470
Harrison County SD
Supt. — See Clarksburg
Bridgeport HS   800/9-12
515 Johnson Ave 26330   304-842-3693
Lindy Bennett, prin.   Fax 842-6288
Bridgeport MS   700/6-8
413 Johnson Ave 26330   304-842-6251
Carole Crawford, prin.   Fax 842-6275

Webster College   Post-Sec.
176 Thompson Dr 26330   304-363-8824

Buckeye, Pocahontas
Pocahontas County SD
Supt. — See Marlinton
Marlinton MS   300/5-8
RR 2 Box 52S 24924   304-799-6773
Cyrus Lester, prin.   Fax 799-7278

Buckhannon, Upshur, Pop. 5,753
Upshur County SD   3,900/K-12
102 Smithfield St 26201   304-472-5480
Dr. Charles L. Chandler, supt.   Fax 472-0258
boe.upsh.k12.wv.us
Buckhannon-Upshur HS   1,100/9-12
50 B U Dr 26201   304-472-3720
Donald Swisher, prin.   Fax 472-0772
Buckhannon-Upshur MS   900/6-8
RR 6 Box 303 26201   304-472-1520
Jack Reger, prin.   Fax 472-6864
Eberle Tech Ctr   Vo/Tech
RR 5 Box 2 26201   304-472-1259
Mike Cutright, prin.   Fax 472-3418

West Virginia Wesleyan College   Post-Sec.
59 College Ave 26201   304-473-8000

Buffalo, Putnam, Pop. 1,188
Putnam County SD
Supt. — See Winfield
Buffalo HS 300/9-12
3317 Buffalo Rd 25033 304-937-2661
Richard Grim, prin. Fax 937-3470

Bunker Hill, Berkeley
Berkeley County SD
Supt. — See Martinsburg
Musselman MS 1,000/6-8
105 Pride Ave 25413 304-229-1965
James Holland, prin. Fax 229-1967

Cameron, Marshall, Pop. 1,161
Marshall County SD
Supt. — See Moundsville
Cameron JSHS 400/7-12
61 Maple Ave 26033 304-686-3336
Marilyn McWhorler, prin. Fax 686-3510

Capon Bridge, Hampshire, Pop. 205
Hampshire County SD
Supt. — See Romney
Capon Bridge MS 400/6-8
PO Box 147 26711 304-856-2534
Jeff Meadows, prin. Fax 856-3192

Center Point, Doddridge

Mountain State Academy 100/K-12
PO Box 10 26339 304-266-7794
Fax 659-2666

Ceredo, Wayne, Pop. 1,637
Wayne County SD
Supt. — See Wayne
Ceredo-Kenova MS 300/6-8
PO Box 705 25507 304-453-3588
Barry Scragg, prin. Fax 453-4420

Chapmanville, Logan, Pop. 1,168
Logan County SD
Supt. — See Logan
Chapmanville HS 500/9-12
200 Vance St 25508 304-855-4522
Terry M. Elkins, prin. Fax 855-1911
Chapmanville MS 600/5-8
300 Vance St 25508 304-855-8378
Martina Mills, prin. Fax 855-1307

Charleston, Kanawha, Pop. 51,394
Kanawha County SD 28,200/PK-12
200 Elizabeth St 25311 304-348-7732
Ronald Duerring Ed.D., supt. Fax 348-7735
kcs.kana.k12.wv.us/
Adams MS 700/6-8
2002 Presidential Dr 25314 304-348-6652
Thomas Kidd, prin. Fax 348-6592
Capital HS 1,400/PK-PK, 9-
1500 Greenbrier St 25311 304-348-6500
Clinton Giles, prin. Fax 348-6509
Carver Career & Tech Ed Ctr Vo/Tech
4799 Midland Dr 25306 304-348-1965
James Casdorph, prin. Fax 348-1938
Garnet Adult Center Vo/Tech
422 Dickinson St 25301 304-348-6195
Sharon Miller, prin. Fax 348-6198
Jackson MS 700/6-8
5445 Big Tyler Rd 25313 304-776-3310
Lisa Woo, prin. Fax 776-3305
Jackson MS 600/6-8
812 Park Ave 25302 304-348-6123
George Aulenbacher, prin. Fax 348-1999
Mann MS 500/6-8
4300 Maccorkle Ave SE 25304 304-348-1971
James Blackwell, prin. Fax 348-6591
Sissonville HS 700/9-12
6100 Sissonville Dr 25312 304-348-1954
Calvin McKinney, prin. Fax 348-6565
Tyler MS 6-8
4277 Washington St W 25313 304-348-6133
Wayman Wilson, prin.
Washington HS 900/9-12
1522 Tennis Club Rd 25314 304-348-7729
James Vickers, prin. Fax 344-4947
Other Schools – See Belle, Clendenin, Dunbar, East Bank, Elkview, Nitro, Saint Albans, Sissonville, South Charleston

---

Camcare Health Education & Research Inst Post-Sec.
3200 Maccorkle Ave SE 25304 304-348-5570
Carver Career and Tech Education Center Post-Sec.
4799 Midland Dr 25306 304-348-1965
Charleston Catholic HS 500/6-12
1033 Virginia St E 25301 304-342-8415
Debra Sullivan, prin. Fax 342-1259
Charleston School of Beauty Culture Post-Sec.
210 Capitol St 25301 304-346-9603
Cross Lanes Christian S 300/K-12
5330 Floradale Dr 25313 304-776-5020
Fairhaven Christian S 100/K-12
689 Fairhaven Dr 25306 304-925-5954
Garnet Career Center Post-Sec.
422 Dickinson St 25301 304-348-6195
University of Charleston Post-Sec.
2300 Maccorkle Ave SE 25304 304-357-4800
West Virginia Junior College Post-Sec.
1000 Virginia St E 25301 304-345-2820

Charles Town, Jefferson, Pop. 3,180
Jefferson County SD 7,200/PK-12
PO Box 987 25414 304-725-9741
Dr. Steven Nichols, supt. Fax 725-6487
boe.jeff.k12.wv.us
Charles Town MS 900/6-8
193 High St 25414 304-725-7821
Charles Hampton, prin. Fax 728-7526
Other Schools – See Harpers Ferry, Shenandoah Junction, Shepherdstown

---

American Public University Post-Sec.
111 W Congress St 25414 877-468-6268

Charmco, Greenbrier
Greenbrier County SD
Supt. — See Lewisburg
Greenbrier West HS 500/9-12
PO Box 325 25958 304-438-6191
Randall Patterson, prin. Fax 438-9189

Clarksburg, Harrison, Pop. 16,425
Harrison County SD 11,500/PK-12
PO Box 1370 26302 304-624-3300
Carl H. Friebel Ed.D., supt. Fax 624-3361
www.harcoboe.com
Byrd HS 900/9-12
1 Eagle Way 26301 304-624-2453
Leon Pilewski, prin. Fax 624-3211
Gore MS 300/6-8
RR 3 Box 43B 26301 304-624-3260
Fax 624-3245
Irving MS 700/6-8
443 Lee Ave 26301 304-624-3271
Douglas Hogue, prin. Fax 624-3388
Liberty HS 700/9-12
1 Mountaineer Dr 26301 304-624-3264
Dennis Zahradnik, prin. Fax 623-3159
United Technical Ctr Vo/Tech
RR 3 Box 43C 26301 304-624-3280
Joan Smith, prin. Fax 622-6138
Other Schools – See Bridgeport, Lost Creek, Lumberport, Salem, Shinnston

---

Clarksburg Beauty Academy Post-Sec.
120 S 3rd St 26301 304-624-6475
Emmanuel Christian S 200/PK-12
1318 N 16th St 26301 304-624-6125
Notre Dame HS 200/7-12
127 E Pike St 26301 304-623-1026
Dr. Carroll Morrison, prin. Fax 623-1026
United Hospital Center Post-Sec.
PO Box 2308 26302 304-624-2332

Clay, Clay, Pop. 584
Clay County SD 2,100/PK-12
PO Box 120 25043 304-587-4266
Jerry Linkinoggor, supt. Fax 587-4181
www.claycountyschools.org
Clay County HS 600/9-12
1 Panther Dr 25043 304-587-4226
Phillip Dobbins, prin. Fax 587-7698
Clay County MS 500/6-8
PO Box 489 25043 304-587-2343
Joan Haynie, prin. Fax 587-2759

Clear Fork, Wyoming
Wyoming County SD
Supt. — See Pineville
Westside HS 600/9-12
HC 65 Box 275 24822 304-682-8965
Deborah Marsh, prin. Fax 682-6273

Clendenin, Kanawha, Pop. 1,067
Kanawha County SD
Supt. — See Charleston
Hoover HS 700/9-12
275 Elk River Rd S 25045 304-965-3394
Roy G. Jones, prin. Fax 965-1871

Coal City, Raleigh, Pop. 1,876
Raleigh County SD
Supt. — See Beckley
Independence HS 700/9-12
PO Box 1595 25823 304-683-3228
Bob Meadows, prin. Fax 683-4393

Cowen, Webster, Pop. 511
Webster County SD
Supt. — See Webster Springs
Glade MS 300/5-8
25 Mill St 26206 304-226-5353
James D. Holbrook, prin. Fax 226-3666

Craigsville, Nicholas, Pop. 1,955
Nicholas County SD
Supt. — See Summersville
Nicholas County Career and Technical Ctr Vo/Tech
HC 59 Box 311 26205 304-742-5416
Vicki Nutter, prin. Fax 742-3953

Crawley, Greenbrier
Greenbrier County SD
Supt. — See Lewisburg
Western Greenbrier MS 300/6-8
HC 40 Box 14 24931 304-392-6446
Christi Chambers, prin. Fax 392-6785

Cross Lanes, Kanawha, Pop. 10,878

National Institute of Technology Post-Sec.
5514 Big Tyler Rd 25313 304-776-6290

Crum, Wayne
Wayne County SD
Supt. — See Wayne
Crum MS 200/6-8
PO Box 9 25669 304-393-3200
Jim Fletcher, prin. Fax 393-4429

Danville, Boone, Pop. 548
Boone County SD
Supt. — See Madison
Boone County Career & Tech Ctr Vo/Tech
3505 Daniel Boone Pkwy 25053 304-369-4585
Keith Phipps, prin. Fax 369-3692

Boone County Career Center Post-Sec.
HC 81 Box 50B 25053 304-369-4585

Delbarton, Mingo, Pop. 451
Mingo County SD
Supt. — See Williamson
Burch HS 300/9-12
RR 2 Box 521-A 25670 304-475-2700
Jada Hunter, prin. Fax 475-5106
Mingo County Vocational Technical Center Vo/Tech
RR 2 Box 52A 25670 304-475-3347
Robert Starr, prin. Fax 475-3797

Regional Christian S 100/PK-12
PO Box 236 25670 304-475-3468
Michael Edds, hdmstr. Fax 475-5287

Dunbar, Kanawha, Pop. 7,868
Kanawha County SD
Supt. — See Charleston
Dunbar MS 400/6-8
325 27th St 25064 304-766-0363
Lynda Gilkeson, prin. Fax 766-0365
Franklin Career & Tech Ed Vo/Tech
500 28th St 25064 304-766-0369
Thomas Reed Owens, prin. Fax 766-0371

Dunmore, Pocahontas
Pocahontas County SD
Supt. — See Marlinton
Pocahontas County HS 400/9-12
RR 1 Box 133A 24934 304-799-6565
Thomas Sanders, prin. Fax 799-6893

East Bank, Kanawha, Pop. 896
Kanawha County SD
Supt. — See Charleston
East Bank MS 500/6-8
PO Box 499 25067 304-595-2311
Candy Strader, prin. Fax 595-4676

Eleanor, Putnam, Pop. 1,426
Putnam County SD
Supt. — See Winfield
Putnam County Technical Center Vo/Tech
101 Roosevelt Blvd 25070 304-586-3494
Robert Manley, prin. Fax 586-4467
Washington MS 300/6-8
PO Box 660 25070 304-586-2875
Joann Stewart, prin. Fax 586-3037

Elizabeth, Wirt, Pop. 971
Wirt County SD 1,000/PK-12
PO Box 189 26143 304-275-4279
Dan Metz, supt. Fax 275-4581
Wirt County HS 300/9-12
PO Box 219 26143 304-275-4241
Ken Heiney, prin. Fax 275-3271
Wirt County MS 300/5-8
PO Box 699 26143 304-275-3977
J. D. Hoover, prin. Fax 275-4257

Elkins, Randolph, Pop. 6,976
Randolph County SD 4,400/PK-12
40 11th St 26241 304-636-9150
Susan Hinzman, supt. Fax 636-9157
boe.rand.k12.wv.us
Elkins HS 900/9-12
100 Kennedy Dr 26241 304-636-9170
Thomas Pritt, prin. Fax 636-9168
Elkins JHS 800/6-8
308 Robert E Lee Ave 26241 304-636-9176
David Roth, prin. Fax 636-9178
Randolph County Vo Tech Center Vo/Tech
200 Kennedy Dr 26241 304-636-9195
Don Johnson, prin. Fax 636-9169
Other Schools – See Harman, Mill Creek, Pickens

Davis & Elkins College Post-Sec.
100 Campus Dr 26241 304-637-1900
Highland Adventist S 50/K-12
205 Wilson St 26241 304-636-0811
Cheryl Jacko, prin. Fax 636-0811

Elkview, Kanawha, Pop. 1,047
Kanawha County SD
Supt. — See Charleston
Elkview MS 800/6-8
5090 Elk River Rd 25071 304-348-1947
Rick Messinger, prin. Fax 348-6590

Elk Valley Christian S 200/PK-12
5110 Elk River Rd 25071 304-965-7063
Barbara Hamm, prin. Fax 965-7064

Ellenboro, Ritchie, Pop. 377
Ritchie County SD
Supt. — See Harrisville
Ritchie County HS 500/9-12
107 Ritchie Co School Rd 26346 304-869-3526
April Haught, prin. Fax 869-3526
Ritchie Co. MS 400/6-8
105 Ritchie Co School Rd 26346 304-869-3512
April Haught, prin. Fax 869-3512

Fairmont, Marion, Pop. 18,984
Marion County SD 8,200/PK-12
200 Gaston Ave 26554 304-367-2100
Dr. James B. Phares, supt. Fax 367-2111
www.marionboe.com/index.asp?process=schools
East Fairmont HS 900/9-12
1993 Airport Rd 26554 304-367-2140
Tom Dragich, prin. Fax 367-2180
East Fairmont JHS 400/7-8
1 Orion Ln 26554 304-367-2123
David Nuzum, prin. Fax 367-2179
Fairmont HS 800/9-12
1 Loop Park Dr 26554 304-367-2150
Chad Norman, prin. Fax 366-5980
Miller JHS 400/7-8
2 Pennsylvania Ave 26554 304-367-2147
Stephen Higgins, prin. Fax 367-2169
Marion County Adult & Community Educ. Adult
601 Locust Ave 26554 304-363-7323
Roman Prezioso, prin. Fax 366-2483
Other Schools – See Fairview, Farmington, Mannington, Monongah

Calvary Christian S — 100/K-12
28 Fellowship Dr 26554 — 304-363-8008
Fairmont State University — Post-Sec.
1201 Locust Ave 26554 — 304-367-4000

Fairview, Marion, Pop. 435
Marion County SD
Supt. — See Fairmont
Fairview MS, 17 Jesses Run Rd 26570 — 200/5-8
Steve Rodriguez, prin. — 304-449-1312

Farmington, Marion, Pop. 382
Marion County SD
Supt. — See Fairmont
Marion County Technical Center — Vo/Tech
RR 1 Box 100A 26571 — 304-986-3590
Roger Perdue, prin. — Fax 986-3440
North Marion HS — 900/9-12
RR 1 Box 100 26571 — 304-986-3063
Judd Ashcraft, prin. — Fax 986-3086

Fayetteville, Fayette, Pop. 2,706
Fayette County SD — 6,600/PK-12
111 Fayette Ave 25840 — 304-574-1176
Helen Whitehair, supt. — Fax 574-3643
boe.faye.k12.wv.us
Fayetteville HS — 300/9-12
515 W Maple Ave 25840 — 304-574-0560
Bryan Parsons, prin. — Fax 574-0118
Fayetteville MS — 300/6-8
135 High St 25840 — 304-574-2449
Susan Bossie-Maddox, prin. — Fax 574-3476
Other Schools – See Ansted, Hico, Lookout, Meadow Bridge, Mount Hope, Oak Hill, Smithers

Follansbee, Brooke, Pop. 2,992
Brooke County SD
Supt. — See Wellsburg
Follansbee MS — 700/5-8
Main and Mark Ave 26037 — 304-527-1942
Joe Starcher, prin. — Fax 527-1954

Fort Gay, Wayne, Pop. 820
Wayne County SD
Supt. — See Wayne
Fort Gay MS — 300/6-8
PO Box 460 25514 — 304-648-5404
Donita Webb, prin. — Fax 648-7082
Tolsia HS — 400/9-12
1 Rebel Dr 25514 — 304-648-5566
Matthew Stanley, prin. — Fax 648-5447

Franklin, Pendleton, Pop. 837
Pendleton County SD — 1,200/PK-12
PO Box 888 26807 — 304-358-2207
Doug Lambert, supt. — Fax 358-2936
pendletoncountyschools.com/
Pendleton County MSHS — 600/7-12
PO Box 40 26807 — 304-358-2573
Doug Lambert, prin. — Fax 358-7701

Gilbert, Mingo, Pop. 408
Mingo County SD
Supt. — See Williamson
Gilbert HS — 400/7-12
PO Box 366 25621 — 304-664-8197
Gary Justice, prin. — Fax 664-8249

Glen Dale, Marshall, Pop. 1,505
Marshall County SD
Supt. — See Moundsville
Marshall HS — 1,400/9-12
1300 Wheeling Ave 26038 — 304-843-4444
David Takach, prin. — Fax 843-4419

Glen Daniel, Raleigh
Raleigh County SD
Supt. — See Beckley
Liberty HS — 600/9-12
PO Box 265 25844 — 304-934-5307
Clyde Stepp, prin. — Fax 934-5307
Trap Hill MS — 500/6-8
665 Coal River Rd 25844 — 304-934-5392
Marsha Smith, prin. — Fax 934-5393

Glenville, Gilmer, Pop. 1,501
Gilmer County SD — 1,000/PK-12
201 N Court St 26351 — 304-462-7386
Edward Toman, supt. — Fax 462-5103
gilmercountyschools.org/
Gilmer County JSHS — 500/7-12
300 Pine St 26351 — 304-462-7960
Karen Finamore, prin. — Fax 462-7059

Glenville State College — Post-Sec.
200 High St 26351 — 304-462-7361

Grafton, Taylor, Pop. 5,351
Taylor County SD — 2,400/PK-12
1 Prospect St 26354 — 304-265-2497
Jane Reynolds, supt. — Fax 265-2508
www.wvonline.com/taylorcounty
Grafton HS — 700/9-12
400 Riverside Dr 26354 — 304-265-3046
Orville Wright, prin. — Fax 265-2156
Taylor County MS — 800/5-8
RR 2 Box 148A 26354 — 304-265-0722
James Reneau, prin. — Fax 265-4623
Taylor County Vo Ctr — Vo/Tech
115 Luby St 26354 — 304-265-1050
Mary Tucker, prin. — Fax 265-1058

Grantsville, Calhoun, Pop. 537
Calhoun County SD
Supt. — See Mount Zion
Calhoun Gilmer Career Ctr — Vo/Tech
RR 1 Box 542A 26147 — 304-354-6151
John Bennett, dir. — Fax 354-6154

Griffithsville, Lincoln
Lincoln County SD
Supt. — See Hamlin

Duval JSHS — 400/7-12
PO Box 67 25521 — 304-524-2101
Tom Hughes, prin. — Fax 524-2732

Hambleton, Tucker, Pop. 245
Tucker County SD
Supt. — See Parsons
Tucker County Career Center — Vo/Tech
RR 1 Box 153 26269 — 304-478-3111
Joe Michael, prin.
Tucker County HS — 400/9-12
RR 1 Box 153 26269 — 304-478-2651
Joe Michael, prin. — Fax 478-4357

Hamlin, Lincoln, Pop. 1,096
Lincoln County SD — 3,800/PK-12
10 Marlin Ave 25523 — 304-824-3033
William Grizzell, supt. — Fax 824-7947
boe.linc.k12.wv.us/
Hamlin JSHS — 400/7-12
General Delivery 25523 — 304-824-3036
Eddie Smith, prin. — Fax 824-5575
Yeager Career Center — Vo/Tech
10 Marlin Ave 25523 — 304-824-5449
Dana Snyder, prin. — Fax 824-5559
Other Schools – See Branchland, Griffithsville, Harts

Harman, Randolph, Pop. 124
Randolph County SD
Supt. — See Elkins
Harman S — 200/K-12
PO Box 130 26270 — 304-227-4114
Debbie Schmidlen, prin. — Fax 227-3610

Harpers Ferry, Jefferson, Pop. 302
Jefferson County SD
Supt. — See Charles Town
Harpers Ferry MS — 500/6-8
1710 W Washington St 25425 — 304-535-6357
Joseph Spurgas, prin. — Fax 535-6986

Harpers Ferry Job Corps — Post-Sec.
146 Buffalo Dr 25425 — 304-728-5772

Harrisville, Ritchie, Pop. 1,868
Ritchie County SD — 1,700/PK-12
134 S Penn Ave 26362 — 304-643-2991
Dr. Richard Butler, supt. — Fax 643-2994
Other Schools – See Ellenboro

Harts, Lincoln, Pop. 2,332
Lincoln County SD
Supt. — See Hamlin
Harts JSHS — 300/7-12
RR 1 Box 130 25524 — 304-855-4881
Peggy Adkins, prin. — Fax 855-7945

Hedgesville, Berkeley, Pop. 236
Berkeley County SD
Supt. — See Martinsburg
Hedgesville HS — 1,400/9-12
109 Ridge Rd N 25427 — 304-754-3354
Don Dellinger, prin. — Fax 754-7445
Hedgesville MS — 1,000/6-8
101 Poplar St 25427 — 304-754-3313
Charles Scott, prin. — Fax 754-6613

Hico, Fayette
Fayette County SD
Supt. — See Fayetteville
Midland Trail HS — 300/9-12
PO Box 89 25854 — 304-658-5184
Diane Blume, prin. — Fax 658-5185

Hilltop, Fayette, Pop. 250

Mountainview Christian S — 200/PK-12
2 Mountain View Rd 25855 — 304-465-0502
Rev. Rudell Bloomfield, prin. — Fax 465-5484

Hinton, Summers, Pop. 2,746
Summers County SD — 1,600/PK-12
116 Main St 25951 — 304-466-6000
Vicki Hinerman, supt. — Fax 466-6008
boe.summ.k12.wv.us
Summers County HS — 500/9-12
HC 74 Box 11A 25951 — 304-466-6040
Garrett Crowder, prin. — Fax 466-6044
Summers MS — 400/6-8
400 Temple St 25951 — 304-466-6030
Robert Rodes, prin. — Fax 466-2271

Hundred, Wetzel, Pop. 328
Wetzel County SD
Supt. — See New Martinsville
Hundred HS — 100/9-12
PO Box 830 26575 — 304-775-5221
Samuel M. Snyder, prin. — Fax 775-2922

Huntington, Cabell, Pop. 49,533
Cabell County SD — 12,200/PK-12
2850 5th Ave 25702 — 304-528-5000
William Smith, supt. — Fax 528-5080
boe.cabe.k12.wv.us
Beverly Hills MS — 600/6-8
2901 Saltwell Rd 25705 — 304-528-5102
Gary Cook, prin. — Fax 528-5197
Cabell County Career Technology Center — Vo/Tech
1035 Norway Ave 25705 — 304-528-5172
Bob McClain, prin. — Fax 528-5110
Cammack MS — 400/6-8
200 10th Ave 25701 — 304-528-5116
Mary A. Freeman, prin. — Fax 528-5199
Enslow MS — 300/6-8
2613 Collis Ave 25702 — 304-528-5121
Georgia Thornton, prin. — Fax 528-5097
Huntington HS — 1,700/9-12
1 Highlander Way 25701 — 304-528-6400
Greg Webb, prin. — Fax 528-6422
West MS — 200/6-8
1001 Jefferson Ave 25704 — 304-528-5180
Joe Brison, prin. — Fax 528-5215

Other Schools – See Barboursville, Milton, Ona
Wayne County SD
Supt. — See Wayne
Spring Valley HS — 1,000/9-12
1 Timberwolfe Dr 25704 — 304-429-1699
Paula Staley, prin. — Fax 429-7315
Vinson MS — 300/6-8
3851 Piedmont Rd 25704 — 304-429-1641
Tammy Brumfield, prin. — Fax 429-6162

Cabell Huntington Hospital — Post-Sec.
1340 Hal Greer Blvd 25701 — 304-526-2111
Grace Christian S — 400/PK-12
1111 Adams Ave 25704 — 304-522-8635
Dr. Dan Brokke, admin. — Fax 522-3240
Huntington Junior College — Post-Sec.
900 5th Ave 25701 — 304-697-7550
Huntington School of Beauty Culture — Post-Sec.
5185 US Route 60 Rm 115 25705 — 304-736-6289
Marshall University — Post-Sec.
400 Hal Greer Blvd 25755 — 304-696-3170
St. Joseph Catholic HS — 100/7-12
600 13th St 25701 — 304-525-5096
Patrick Finneran, prin. — Fax 525-0781
St. Mary's Medical Center — Post-Sec.
2900 1st Ave 25702 — 304-526-1270

Hurricane, Putnam, Pop. 5,623
Putnam County SD
Supt. — See Winfield
Hurricane HS — 1,000/9-12
3350 Teays Valley Rd 25526 — 304-562-3991
Joyce Vessey Swanson, prin. — Fax 562-5460
Hurricane MS — 900/6-8
518 Midland Trl 25526 — 304-562-9271
Greg LeMaster, prin. — Fax 562-7163

Calvary Baptist Academy — 100/K-12
3655 Teays Valley Rd 25526 — 304-757-6768

Iaeger, McDowell, Pop. 330
McDowell County SD
Supt. — See Welch
Iaeger HS — 500/9-12
PO Box 779 24844 — 304-938-2431
Doug Addair, prin. — Fax 938-5158

Institute, Kanawha

WV State Community & Technical College — Post-Sec.
PO Box 1000 25112 — 304-766-3118
West Virginia State University — Post-Sec.
PO Box 1000 25112 — 304-766-3000

Inwood, Berkeley, Pop. 1,360
Berkeley County SD
Supt. — See Martinsburg
Musselman HS — 1,200/9-12
126 Excellence Way 25428 — 304-229-1950
Ronald Stephens, prin. — Fax 229-1959

Kenova, Wayne, Pop. 3,358
Wayne County SD
Supt. — See Wayne
Buffalo MS — 400/6-8
298 Buffalo Creek Rd 25530 — 304-429-6062
John Waugaman, prin. — Fax 429-7245

Keyser, Mineral, Pop. 5,515
Mineral County SD — 4,500/PK-12
1 Baker Pl 26726 — 304-788-4200
Skip Hackworth, supt. — Fax 788-4204
boe.mine.k12.wv.us/
Keyser HS — 800/9-12
RR 4 Box 110 26726 — 304-788-4230
John Haines, prin. — Fax 788-4234
Mineral County Technical Center — Vo/Tech
600 Harley O Staggers Sr Dr 26726 — 304-788-4240
Alan Whetzel, prin. — Fax 788-4243
Other Schools – See Ridgeley

Potomac State College of West Virginia U — Post-Sec.
101 Fort Ave Bldg 1 26726 — 304-788-6800

Kingwood, Preston, Pop. 2,928
Preston County SD — 4,700/PK-12
PO Box 566 26537 — 304-329-0580
John Lofink, supt. — Fax 329-0720
www.prestonboe.com
Central Preston MS — 300/6-8
100 E High St 26537 — 304-329-0033
Thomas Strahin, prin. — Fax 329-2389
Preston HS — 1,400/9-12
400 Preston Dr 26537 — 304-329-0400
Douglas Riley, prin. — Fax 329-3899
Other Schools – See Masontown, Tunnelton

Integrity Christian S — 50/K-12
PO Box 457 26537 — 304-329-2498
Teresa Lewis, prin. — Fax 329-2498

Le Roy, Jackson
Jackson County SD
Supt. — See Ripley
Roane-Jackson Tech Ctr — Vo/Tech
4800 Spencer Rd 25252 — 304-372-7335
Dennis Carpenter, prin. — Fax 372-7336

Lewisburg, Greenbrier, Pop. 3,577
Greenbrier County SD — 5,000/PK-12
202 Chestnut St 24901 — 304-647-6470
John D. Curry, supt. — Fax 647-6490
boe.gree.k12.wv.us/
Greenbrier East HS — 1,100/9-12
1 Spartan Ln 24901 — 304-647-6464
Jeff Bryant, prin. — Fax 645-2698
Other Schools – See Charmco, Crawley, Ronceverte

Greenbrier Adventist Junior Academy 50/K-10
235 N Court St 24901 304-647-9750
West Virginia Sch./Osteopathic Medicine Post-Sec.
400 N Lee St 24901 304-645-6270

Lindside, Monroe
Monroe County SD
Supt. — See Union
Monroe County Technical Center Vo/Tech
RR 1 Box 97 24951 304-753-9971
Fax 753-9792
Monroe HS 600/9-12
RR 1 Box 97-1A 24951 304-753-5182
Christine Parker, prin. Fax 753-5184

Logan, Logan, Pop. 1,551
Logan County SD 6,100/PK-12
PO Box 477 25601 304-792-2060
David Godby, supt. Fax 752-3711
lc2.boe.loga.k12.wv.us/
Logan HS 700/9-12
1 Wildcat Way 25601 304-752-6606
Robert Lucas, prin. Fax 752-6614
Logan MS 900/5-8
14 Wildcat Way 25601 304-752-1804
Ernestine Sutherland, prin. Fax 752-0207
Willis Vo-Tech Center Vo/Tech
PO Box 1747 25601 304-752-4687
Clarence Elkins, prin. Fax 752-2943
Other Schools – See Chapmanville, Man

Lookout, Fayette
Fayette County SD
Supt. — See Fayetteville
Nuttall MS 200/5-8
PO Box 130 25868 304-574-0429
Lee Jones, prin. Fax 574-0491

Lost Creek, Harrison, Pop. 480
Harrison County SD
Supt. — See Clarksburg
South Harrison HS 400/9-12
RR 1 Box 58 26385 304-745-3315
Philip Brown, prin. Fax 745-4292
South Harrison MS 300/6-8
RR 1 Box 58B 26385 304-745-5582
Phil Brown, prin. Fax 745-5587

Lumberport, Harrison, Pop. 943
Harrison County SD
Supt. — See Clarksburg
Lumberport MS 500/6-8
PO Box 309 26386 304-584-4090
Anthony Fratto, prin. Fax 584-4602

Mc Mechen, Marshall, Pop. 2,019

Bishop Donahue HS 100/9-12
325 Logan St 26040 304-233-3850
Daniel Angalich, prin. Fax 233-8677

Madison, Boone, Pop. 2,671
Boone County SD 4,500/PK-12
69 Avenue B 25130 304-369-3131
Steve Pauley, supt. Fax 369-6789
www.boonecountyboe.org
Madison MS 600/6-8
404 Riverside Dr W 25130 304-369-4464
Gary Bell, prin. Fax 369-5800
Scott HS 600/9-12
1 Skyhawk Pl 25130 304-369-3011
Leonard Bolton, prin. Fax 369-6564
Other Schools – See Danville, Seth, Van

Man, Logan, Pop. 734
Logan County SD
Supt. — See Logan
Man HS 500/9-12
800 E McDonald Ave 25635 304-583-6521
Sandy Manning, prin. Fax 583-6566

Mannington, Marion, Pop. 2,085
Marion County SD
Supt. — See Fairmont
Mannington MS 400/5-8
113 Clarksburg St 26582 304-986-1050
Mike Call, prin.

Marlinton, Pocahontas, Pop. 1,226
Pocahontas County SD 1,400/PK-12
926 5th Ave 24954 304-799-4505
Dr. Patrick Law, supt. Fax 799-4499
Other Schools – See Buckeye, Dunmore

Martinsburg, Berkeley, Pop. 15,309
Berkeley County SD 15,300/PK-12
401 S Queen St 25401 304-267-3500
Manny Arvon, supt. Fax 267-3524
boe.berk.k12.wv.us
Martinsburg HS 1,400/9-12
701 S Queen St 25401 304-267-3530
Kenneth Pack, prin. Fax 267-3536
Martinsburg North MS 700/6-8
250 East Rd, 304-267-3540
David Rudy, prin. Fax 264-5066
Martinsburg South MS 700/6-8
Bulldog Blvd 25401 304-267-3545
David Rogers, prin. Fax 264-5062
Rumsey Technical Institute Vo/Tech
3274 Hedgesville Rd, 304-754-7925
Vicki Jenkins, dir. Fax 754-7933
Spring Mills MS 6-8
255 Campus Dr, 304-274-5030
Marc Arvon, prin. Fax 274-3598
Other Schools – See Bunker Hill, Hedgesville, Inwood

CTC of Shepherd Post-Sec.
400 W Stephen St 25401 304-260-4380
Faith Christian Academy 300/PK-12
138 Greensburg Rd, 304-263-0011
Eric Kerns, admin. Fax 267-0638

International Beauty School Post-Sec.
201 W King St 25401 304-263-4929
Martinsburg Christian Academy 100/K-12
2247 Williamsport Pike, 304-267-6368
Valley College of Technology Post-Sec.
287 Aikens Ctr 25401 304-263-0979

Mason, Mason, Pop. 1,065
Mason County SD
Supt. — See Point Pleasant
Wahama JSHS 400/7-12
PO Box 348 25260 304-773-5539
Fax 773-5216

Masontown, Preston, Pop. 642
Preston County SD
Supt. — See Kingwood
West Preston MS 200/6-8
PO Box 70 26542 304-864-5221
Karen Finamore, prin. Fax 864-5298

Matewan, Mingo, Pop. 512
Mingo County SD
Supt. — See Williamson
Matewan HS 200/9-12
PO Box 540 25678 304-426-6555
Marcella Charles, prin. Fax 426-6292
Matewan MS 200/5-8
PO Box 535 25678 304-426-8569
Cindy Calfee, prin. Fax 426-4480

Meadow Bridge, Fayette, Pop. 316
Fayette County SD
Supt. — See Fayetteville
Meadow Bridge JSHS 300/7-12
PO Box 10 25976 304-484-7917
Al Martine, prin. Fax 484-7921

Middlebourne, Tyler, Pop. 862
Tyler County SD 1,600/PK-12
PO Box 25 26149 304-758-2145
Anne Seaver, supt. Fax 758-4566
Other Schools – See Sistersville

Mill Creek, Randolph, Pop. 660
Randolph County SD
Supt. — See Elkins
Tygarts Valley JSHS 500/7-12
PO Box 68 26280 304-335-4575
Wilbert Smith, prin. Fax 335-6963

Milton, Cabell, Pop. 2,273
Cabell County SD
Supt. — See Huntington
Milton MS 700/6-8
1302 W Main St 25541 304-743-7308
Dan Gleason, prin. Fax 743-7324

Monongah, Marion, Pop. 912
Marion County SD
Supt. — See Fairmont
Monongah MS, 1 Camden Rd 26554 300/5-8
James Pulice, prin. 304-367-2164

Montcalm, Mercer, Pop. 1,023
Mercer County SD
Supt. — See Princeton
Montcalm HS 300/7-12
PO Box 330 24737 304-589-3719
Brenda Ash, prin. Fax 589-7140

Montgomery, Fayette, Pop. 1,981

West Virginia University Inst of Tech. Post-Sec.
405 Fayette Pike 25136 304-442-3071

Moorefield, Hardy, Pop. 2,409
Hardy County SD 2,000/PK-12
510 Ashby St 26836 304-530-2348
Ronald Whetzel, supt. Fax 530-2340
www.hardycountyschools.com/
Moorefield HS 400/9-12
401 N Main St 26836 304-530-6034
Douglas Hines, prin. Fax 530-7569
Moorefield MS 500/5-8
303 Caledonia Dr 26836 304-434-3000
Fax 434-3003
Other Schools – See Baker

Morgantown, Monongalia, Pop. 27,969
Monongalia County SD 10,200/PK-12
13 S High St 26501 304-291-9210
Frank Devono, supt. Fax 291-3015
boe.mono.k12.wv.us
Cheat Lake MS 600/5-8
160 Crosby Rd 26508 304-594-1165
Joanne Hines, prin. Fax 594-1677
Monongalia County Tech Education Center Vo/Tech
1000 Mississippi St 26501 304-291-9240
Marlene Lawrence, prin. Fax 291-9247
Morgantown HS 1,700/9-12
109 Wilson Ave 26501 304-291-9260
John George, prin. Fax 291-9263
South MS 800/6-8
500 E Parkway Dr 26501 304-291-9340
Dennis Gallon, prin. Fax 291-9306
Suncrest MS 400/6-8
360 Baldwin St 26505 304-291-9335
James Napolillo, prin. Fax 284-9362
University MS 1,300/9-12
991 Price St 26505 304-291-9270
James Forst, prin. Fax 291-9248
Westwood MS 500/6-8
670 River Rd 26501 304-291-9300
Leonard Honey, prin. Fax 284-9368
Adult Basic Education Adult
1000 Mississippi St 26501 304-291-9240
Johnnie Hamilton, prin. Fax 291-9247
Other Schools – See Blacksville

Lighthouse Christian Academy 50/6-12
275 Canyon Rd 26508 304-594-3717
Christy Johnson, prin. Fax 594-3717
Monongalia County Tech Education Center Post-Sec.
1000 Mississippi St 26501 304-291-9240
Morgantown Beauty College Post-Sec.
276 Walnut St 26505 304-292-8475
Trinity Christian S 300/PK-12
200 Trinity Way 26505 304-291-4659
Michael Staud, supt. Fax 291-4660
West Virginia Junior College Post-Sec.
148 Willey St 26505 304-296-8282
West Virginia University Post-Sec.
PO Box 6001 26506 304-293-0111
West Virginia University Hospital Post-Sec.
PO Box 8150 26506 304-598-4000

Moundsville, Marshall, Pop. 9,745
Marshall County SD 5,300/PK-12
PO Box 578 26041 304-843-4400
Alfred N. Renzella, supt. Fax 843-4409
boe.mars.k12.wv.us
Moundsville JHS 400/7-8
223 Tomlinson Ave 26041 304-843-4440
M. Jan Madden, prin. Fax 843-4446
Other Schools – See Cameron, Glen Dale, Wheeling

Mount Gay Shamrock, Logan, Pop. 3,377

Southern WV Community & Technical Coll. Post-Sec.
PO Box 2900 25637 304-792-7160

Mount Hope, Fayette, Pop. 1,428
Fayette County SD
Supt. — See Fayetteville
Mount Hope MSHS 400/5-12
110 High School Dr 25880 304-877-2121
David Null, prin. Fax 877-6354

Mount Zion, Calhoun
Calhoun County SD 1,200/PK-12
HC 89 Box 119 26151 304-354-7011
Ron Blankenship, supt. Fax 354-7420
boe.calh.k12.wv.us
Calhoun County MSHS 700/5-12
HC 89 Box 119 26151 304-354-6148
Michael Offutt, prin. Fax 354-7382
Other Schools – See Grantsville

Mullens, Wyoming, Pop. 1,674
Wyoming County SD
Supt. — See Pineville
Mullens MS 200/5-8
801 Moran Ave 25882 304-294-5757
Stephen Kirby, prin. Fax 294-5757

New Cumberland, Hancock, Pop. 1,049
Hancock County SD 4,000/PK-12
PO Box 1300 26047 304-564-3411
Danny Kaser, supt. Fax 564-3990
www.hancockschools.org
Oak Glen HS 600/9-12
195 Golden Bear Dr 26047 304-564-3500
Wayne Neely, prin. Fax 387-2079
Oak Glen MS 500/5-8
39 Golden Bear Dr 26047 304-387-2363
Donna Popovich, prin.
Rockefeller Career Center Vo/Tech
95 Rockyside Rd 26047 304-564-3337
George Danford, dir. Fax 564-4058
Other Schools – See Weirton

New Martinsville, Wetzel, Pop. 5,823
Wetzel County SD 3,200/PK-12
333 Foundry St 26155 304-455-2441
Paul E. Barcus Ed.D., supt. Fax 455-3446
www.wetzelcountyschools.com
Magnolia HS 500/9-12
601 Maple Ave 26155 304-455-1990
Timothy Haught, prin. Fax 455-5536
Other Schools – See Hundred, Paden City, Pine Grove

New Richmond, Wyoming
Wyoming County SD
Supt. — See Pineville
Wyoming East HS 600/9-12
PO Box 390 24867 304-294-5200
Barry Wayne Smith, prin. Fax 294-5900

Nitro, Kanawha, Pop. 6,708
Kanawha County SD
Supt. — See Charleston
Nitro HS 900/9-12
1301 Park Ave 25143 304-755-4321
Paul McClanahan, prin. Fax 755-4345

Nutter Fort Stonewood, Harrison, Pop. 1,800

West Virginia Business College Post-Sec.
116 Pennsylvania Ave 26301 304-624-7695

Oak Hill, Fayette, Pop. 7,486
Fayette County SD
Supt. — See Fayetteville
Collins MS 800/5-8
601 Jones Ave 25901 304-469-3711
David Perry, prin. Fax 465-1352
Fayette Institute of Technology Vo/Tech
300 Oyler Ave 25901 304-469-2911
Barry Crist, prin. Fax 469-6963
Oak Hill HS 700/9-12
350 Oyler Ave 25901 304-469-3551
Fred McLain, prin. Fax 465-1769

Oceana, Wyoming, Pop. 1,500
Wyoming County SD
Supt. — See Pineville
Oceana MS 300/5-8
HC 65 Box 520 24870 304-682-6296
Richard Cook, prin. Fax 682-6296

Omar, Logan

Beth Haven Christian S 100/PK-12
PO Box 620 25638 304-946-4447
Regina Vance, prin. Fax 946-4447

Ona, Cabell
Cabell County SD
Supt. — See Huntington
Cabell Midland HS 1,800/9-12
2300 US Route 60 25545 304-743-7400
Karen Oldham, prin. Fax 743-7577

Paden City, Wetzel, Pop. 2,771
Wetzel County SD
Supt. — See New Martinsville
Paden City HS 200/7-12
201 N 4th Ave 26159 304-337-2266
Warren Grace, prin. Fax 337-2290

Parkersburg, Wood, Pop. 32,100
Wood County SD 13,800/PK-12
1210 13th St 26101 304-420-9663
William Niday, supt. Fax 420-9513
www.netassoc.net/wcboe/
Blennerhassett JHS 700/7-9
RR 4 Box 475A 26101 304-863-3356
Steve Angel, prin. Fax 863-3357
Caperton Center for Applied Tech Vo/Tech
300 Campus Dr 26104 304-424-8365
Joe Smith, prin. Fax 424-8366
Edison JHS 700/7-9
1201 Hillcrest St 26101 304-420-9525
Jean Mewshaw, prin. Fax 420-9527
Hamilton JHS 600/7-9
3501 Cadillac Dr 26104 304-420-9547
Mike Windland, prin. Fax 420-9567
Parkersburg SHS 1,400/10-12
2101 Dudley Ave 26101 304-420-9595
Ralph Board, prin. Fax 420-9604
Parkersburg South SHS 1,200/10-12
1511 Blizzard Dr 26101 304-420-9610
Tom Eschbacher, prin. Fax 420-9607
Van Devender JHS 400/7-9
918 31st St 26104 304-420-9645
Steve Taylor, prin. Fax 420-9647
Wood County Technical Center Vo/Tech
1515 Blizzard Dr 26101 304-420-9501
Doug Kiger, prin. Fax 485-1048
Other Schools – See Vienna, Williamstown

Camden Clark Memorial Hospital Post-Sec.
800 Garfield Ave 26101 304-424-2204
Mountain State College Post-Sec.
1508 Spring St 26101 304-485-5487
Parkersburg Catholic HS 200/7-12
3201 Fairview Ave 26104 304-485-6341
Marie Held, prin. Fax 485-4697
Parkersburg Christian S 100/K-12
1093 Core Rd 26104 304-485-6654
Valley Beauty School Post-Sec.
707 Market St 26101 304-422-2226
West Virginia University at Parkersburg Post-Sec.
300 Campus Dr 26104 304-424-8000

Parsons, Tucker, Pop. 1,451
Tucker County SD 1,200/PK-12
501 Chestnut St 26287 304-478-2771
Rick Hicks, supt. Fax 478-3422
www.tuckercountyschools.com
Other Schools – See Hambleton

Paw Paw, Morgan, Pop. 513
Morgan County SD
Supt. — See Berkeley Springs
Paw Paw JSHS 100/7-12
36 Pirate Cir 25434 304-947-7425
Michelle Fleming, prin. Fax 947-5513

Petersburg, Grant, Pop. 2,585
Grant County SD 2,000/PK-12
204 Jefferson Ave 26847 304-257-1011
Dr. Marsha Lambert, supt. Fax 257-2453
www.grantcountyschools.com
Petersburg JSHS 800/7-12
207 Jefferson Ave 26847 304-257-1444
Dennis Albright, prin. Fax 257-5243
South Branch Career & Technical Center Vo/Tech
401 Pierpont St 26847 304-257-1331
Robert Sisk, dir. Fax 257-2270

Peterstown, Monroe, Pop. 501
Monroe County SD
Supt. — See Union
Peterstown MS 300/5-8
36 College Dr 24963 304-753-4322
James Gore, prin. Fax 772-4322

Philippi, Barbour, Pop. 2,822
Barbour County SD 2,600/PK-12
105 S Railroad St 26416 304-457-3030
R. Matthew Kittle, supt. Fax 457-3559
bcnetnt1.ab.edu/Barbour/Barbour+Schools.nsf
Barbour County Vocational Center Vo/Tech
RR 2 Box 268 26416 304-457-4807
Kenna Barger, dir. Fax 457-3009
Barbour HS 700/9-12
RR 2 Box 268a 26416 304-457-1360
Garry Tenney, prin. Fax 457-2658
Philippi MS 400/6-8
RR 3 Box 40 26416 304-457-2999
James Sprouse, prin. Fax 457-2561
Other Schools – See Belington

Alderson-Broaddus College 26416 Post-Sec.
304-457-1700

Pickens, Randolph
Randolph County SD
Supt. — See Elkins

Pickens S 100/K-12
Route 45 26230 304-924-5525
Diane Butler, prin. Fax 924-6460

Pine Grove, Wetzel, Pop. 542
Wetzel County SD
Supt. — See New Martinsville
Valley HS 200/9-12
1 Lumberjack Ln 26419 304-889-3151
Tammy Wells, prin. Fax 889-2534

Pineville, Wyoming, Pop. 684
Wyoming County SD 4,400/PK-12
PO Box 69 24874 304-732-6262
Frank Blackwell, supt. Fax 732-7226
boe.wyom.k12.wv.us/
Pineville MS 300/7-9
PO Box 470 24874 304-732-6442
Ronnie Ellison, prin. Fax 732-6442
Wyoming County Career & Technical Center Vo/Tech
HC 72 Box 200 24874 304-732-8050
Glennis Paul McNair, prin. Fax 732-8332
Other Schools – See Clear Fork, Mullens, New
Richmond, Oceana

Poca, Putnam, Pop. 1,009
Putnam County SD
Supt. — See Winfield
Poca HS 500/9-12
RR 1 Box 5B 25159 304-755-5001
Vic Donalson, prin. Fax 755-5009
Poca MS 400/6-8
PO Box 647 25159 304-755-7343
Dale Eggleton, prin. Fax 755-8930

Point Pleasant, Mason, Pop. 4,572
Mason County SD 3,900/PK-12
1200 Main St 25550 304-675-4540
Dr. Larry Parsons, supt. Fax 675-7226
boe.maso.k12.wv.us/
Mason County Career Center Vo/Tech
Ohio River Rd 25550 304-675-3039
Ruth Caplinger, dir. Fax 675-3413
Point Pleasant HS 700/9-12
RR 1 Box 4 25550 304-675-1350
Rick Northup, prin. Fax 675-7480
Point Pleasant MS 400/7-8
2312 Jackson Ave 25550 304-675-3820
Rita Cooper, prin. Fax 675-7950
Other Schools – See Ashton, Mason

Christ Academy, PO Box 224 25550 50/K-12
Cynthia Langona, admin. 304-675-1559

Princeton, Mercer, Pop. 6,201
Mercer County SD 9,200/PK-12
1403 Honaker Ave 24740 304-487-1551
Deborah Akers Ed.D., supt. Fax 425-5844
boe.merc.k12.wv.us/
Mercer County Technical Education Ctr Vo/Tech
1397 Stafford Dr 24740 304-425-9551
William Sherwood, prin. Fax 425-0833
Pikeview HS 600/9-12
3566 Eads Mill Rd 24740 304-384-7586
Ben Disibbio, prin. Fax 384-7901
Princeton HS 1,000/9-12
1321 Stafford Dr 24740 304-425-8101
Dr. Stephen Akers, prin. Fax 425-2823
Princeton JHS 600/6-8
300 N Johnston St 24740 304-425-7517
Danny Buckner, prin. Fax 487-2250
Other Schools — See Bluefield, Montcalm

Mercer Christian Academy 200/K-12
314 Oakvale Rd # A 24740 304-487-1603
Bob Brooks, prin. Fax 487-1263
Valley College of Technology Post-Sec.
616 Harrison St 24740 304-425-2323

Prosperity, Raleigh, Pop. 1,322

Greater Beckley Christian S 200/K-12
PO Box 670 25909 304-255-1571
John O'Neal, prin. Fax 255-2675

Rainelle, Greenbrier, Pop. 1,513

Rainelle Christian Academy 100/K-12
PO Box 784 25962 304-438-8874

Ravenswood, Jackson, Pop. 4,007
Jackson County SD
Supt. — See Ripley
Ravenswood HS 500/9-12
100 Plaza Dr 26164 304-273-9301
Kent Kennedy, prin. Fax 273-9556
Ravenswood MS 400/6-8
409 Sycamore St 26164 304-273-5480
Gary Higginbotham, prin. Fax 273-5746

Heritage Christian Academy 100/K-12
PO Box 427 26164 304-273-9463

Richwood, Nicholas, Pop. 2,361
Nicholas County SD
Supt. — See Summersville
Richwood HS 300/10-12
1 Valley Ave 26261 304-846-2591
Bill Hutchinson, prin. Fax 846-2684
Richwood JHS 400/7-9
2 Valley Ave 26261 304-846-2638
Mark Skaggs, prin. Fax 846-2639

Ridgeley, Mineral, Pop. 713
Mineral County SD
Supt. — See Keyser
Frankfort HS 600/9-12
RR 3 Box 169 26753 304-726-4767
Jeffrey H. Marsh, prin. Fax 726-8597

Frankfort MS 600/5-8
RR 3 Box 170 26753 304-726-4341
Susan Ray, prin. Fax 726-4339

Ripley, Jackson, Pop. 3,263
Jackson County SD 5,100/PK-12
PO Box 770 25271 304-372-7300
Blaine Hess, supt. Fax 372-7312
boe.jack.k12.wv.us
Ripley HS 1,000/9-12
2 School St 25271 304-372-7355
Todd Layhew, prin. Fax 372-7334
Ripley MS 700/6-8
RR 2 Box 75A 25271 304-372-7350
Gail Varney, prin. Fax 372-7332
Other Schools – See Le Roy, Ravenswood

Romney, Hampshire, Pop. 1,969
Hampshire County SD 3,600/PK-12
46 S High St 26757 304-822-3528
Cynthia Kolsun, supt. Fax 822-5382
boe.hamp.k12.wv.us/Schools.htm
Hampshire HS 1,000/9-12
HC 63 Box 1970 26757 304-822-5016
Bill Cottrill, prin. Fax 822-5760
Romney MS 500/6-8
111 School St 26757 304-822-5014
John Watson, prin. Fax 822-5744
Other Schools – See Capon Bridge

West Virginia Schools/Deaf and Blind Post-Sec.
26757

Ronceverte, Greenbrier, Pop. 1,536
Greenbrier County SD
Supt. — See Lewisburg
Eastern Greenbrier MS 700/6-8
RR 1 Box 150 24970 304-647-6498
Doug Clemons, prin. Fax 647-3087
Seneca Trail Christian Academy 100/K-12
RR 2 Box 269 24970 304-647-4878

Saint Albans, Kanawha, Pop. 11,167
Kanawha County SD
Supt. — See Charleston
Hayes MS 500/6-8
830 Strawberry Rd 25177 304-722-0222
Scott Monty, prin. Fax 722-0247
McKinley JHS 400/6-8
3000 Kanawha Ter 25177 304-722-0218
Melissa H. Ruddle, prin. Fax 722-0246
Saint Albans HS 1,000/9-12
2100 Kanawha Ter 25177 304-722-0212
Tom Williams, prin. Fax 722-0211

Mountaineer Beauty College Post-Sec.
PO Box 547 25177 304-727-9999

Saint Marys, Pleasants, Pop. 1,979
Pleasants County SD 1,300/PK-12
PO Box 210 26170 304-684-2215
Thomas E. Long, supt. Fax 684-3569
boe.plea.k12.wv.us
PRT Technical Center Vo/Tech
PO Box 29 26170 304-684-2464
Jim Ankrom, prin. Fax 684-2544
Saint Marys HS 400/9-12
1002 2nd St 26170 304-684-2421
Charles Heinlein, prin. Fax 684-3859
Other Schools – See Belmont

Salem, Harrison, Pop. 1,779
Harrison County SD
Supt. — See Clarksburg
Salem MS 200/6-8
RR 1 Box 10A 26426 304-782-1131
Pamela Leggett, prin. Fax 782-1293

Salem International University Post-Sec.
PO Box 500 26426 304-782-5011

Scott Depot, Putnam

Teays Valley Christian S 300/K-12
4345 Teays Valley Rd 25560 304-757-9550
Jack Davis, prin. Fax 757-0529

Seth, Boone
Boone County SD
Supt. — See Madison
Sherman HS 400/9-12
PO Box AB 25181 304-837-3301
Theresa Lonker, prin. Fax 837-7529
Sherman JHS 200/7-8
PO Box AA 25181 304-837-3694
David Price, prin. Fax 837-7603

Shady Spring, Raleigh, Pop. 1,929
Raleigh County SD
Supt. — See Beckley
Shady Spring HS 700/9-12
PO Box 2001 25918 304-256-4647
Danny Moye, prin. Fax 256-4771
Shady Spring MS 600/6-8
500 Flat Top Rd 25918 304-256-4570
Gary Nichols, prin. Fax 256-4612

Shenandoah Junction, Jefferson
Jefferson County SD
Supt. — See Charles Town
Jefferson HS 9th Grade Campus 9-9
1209 Shenandoah Junction Rd 25442
Ralph Dinges, prin. 304-728-4518
Jefferson HS 1,500/10-12
4141 Flowing Springs Rd 25442 304-725-8491
Fax 728-6590

Shepherdstown, Jefferson, Pop. 1,140
Jefferson County SD
Supt. — See Charles Town

Shepherdstown MS   400/6-8
  54 Minden Ave 25443   304-876-6120
  Judy Marcus, prin.   Fax 876-1826

Shepherd University   Post-Sec.
  PO Box 3210 25443   304-876-5000

Shinnston, Harrison, Pop. 2,233
Harrison County SD
  Supt. — See Clarksburg
Lincoln HS   600/9-12
  RR 1 Box 300 26431   304-592-2248
  Brad Underwood, prin.   Fax 592-3415

Sissonville, Kanawha, Pop. 4,290
Kanawha County SD
  Supt. — See Charleston
Sissonville MS   500/6-8
  8316 Old Mill Rd 25320   304-348-1993
  John Baird, prin.   Fax 348-6594

Sistersville, Tyler, Pop. 1,533
Tyler County SD
  Supt. — See Middlebourne
Tyler Consolidated HS   500/9-12
  1993 Silver Knight Dr 26175 304-758-9000
  Sandra Weese, prin.   Fax 758-9006
Tyler Consolidated MS   400/6-8
  1993 Silver Knight Dr 26175 304-758-9000
  Norris Stombock, prin.   Fax 758-9006

Smithers, Fayette, Pop. 869
Fayette County SD
  Supt. — See Fayetteville
Valley HS   200/9-12
  PO Box 459 25186   304-442-8284
  H. Ray Londeree, prin.   Fax 442-5865

Sophia, Raleigh, Pop. 1,281
Raleigh County SD
  Supt. — See Beckley
Independence MS   600/6-8
  PO Box 1171 25921   304-683-4542
  Terry Poe, prin.   Fax 683-4552

South Charleston, Kanawha, Pop. 12,933
Kanawha County SD
  Supt. — See Charleston
South Charleston HS   1,100/9-12
  1 Eagle Way 25309   304-766-0352
  William Walton, prin.   Fax 768-4663
South Charleston MS   400/6-8
  400 3rd Ave 25303   304-348-1918
  Henry Graves, prin.   Fax 744-4869

Spencer, Roane, Pop. 2,283
Roane County SD   2,600/PK-12
  PO Box 609 25276   304-927-6400
  Stephen Goffreda, supt.   Fax 927-6402
  www.roanecountyschools.com/
Roane County HS   700/9-12
  1 Raider Way 25276   304-927-6420
  David Tupper, prin.   Fax 927-6404
Spencer MS   500/5-8
  102 Chapman Ave 25276   304-927-6415
  William Chapman, prin.   Fax 927-6416

Summersville, Nicholas, Pop. 3,300
Nicholas County SD   4,300/PK-12
  400 Old Main Dr 26651   304-872-3611
  Luther Baker, supt.   Fax 872-4626
  boe.nich.k12.wv.us
Nicholas County SHS   700/10-12
  30 Grizzley Ln 26651   304-872-2141
  Pat Metheney, prin.   Fax 872-3026
Summersville JHS   700/7-9
  40 Grizzley Ln 26651   304-872-5092
  Freddy Amick, prin.   Fax 872-6314
Other Schools – See Craigsville, Richwood

New Life Christian Academy   200/PK-12
  899 Broad St 26651   304-872-1148
  Margaret Campbell, admin.   Fax 872-7477

Sutton, Braxton, Pop. 993
Braxton County SD   2,600/PK-12
  411 N Hill Rd 26601   304-765-7101
  Carolyn D. Long, supt.   Fax 765-7148
  www.wvonline.com/bcs/
Braxton County HS   800/9-12
  200 Jerry Burton Dr 26601   304-765-7331
  James Lambert, prin.   Fax 765-7976
Braxton Co. MS   800/5-8
  100 Carter Braxton Dr 26601 304-765-2644
  Denver Drake, prin.   Fax 765-2696

Tunnelton, Preston, Pop. 339
Preston County SD
  Supt. — See Kingwood
South Preston MS   200/6-8
  PO Box 400 26444   304-568-2331
  Darrell Martin, prin.   Fax 568-2759

Union, Monroe, Pop. 551
Monroe County SD   2,000/PK-12
  PO Box 330 24983   304-772-3094
  Dr. Lyn Guy, supt.   Fax 772-5020
  www.monroecountyschoolswv.org
Other Schools – See Lindside, Peterstown

Upperglade, Webster
Webster County SD
  Supt. — See Webster Springs
Webster County HS   500/9-12
  1 Highlander Dr 26266   304-226-5772
  Paula Varney, prin.   Fax 226-5792

Van, Boone
Boone County SD
  Supt. — See Madison
Van JSHS   300/6-12
  PO Box 100 25206   304-245-8237
  Rod Cummings, prin.   Fax 245-8695

Vienna, Wood, Pop. 10,884
Wood County SD
  Supt. — See Parkersburg
Jackson JHS   600/7-9
  1601 34th St 26105   304-420-9551
  Richard Summers, prin.   Fax 295-9954

Ohio Valley University   Post-Sec.
  1 Campus View Dr 26105   877-446-8668

War, McDowell, Pop. 719
McDowell County SD
  Supt. — See Welch
Big Creek HS   300/9-12
  PO Box 790 24892   304-875-2287
  Roger Smith, prin.   Fax 875-4208

Wayne, Wayne, Pop. 1,154
Wayne County SD   7,400/PK-12
  PO Box 70 25570   304-272-5116
  Gary Adkins, supt.   Fax 272-6500
  boe.wayn.k12.wv.us/
Wayne HS   600/9-12
  100 Pioneer Rd 25570   304-272-5639
  Dr. Kevin Smith, prin.   Fax 272-6439
Wayne MS   500/6-8
  200 Pioneer Rd 25570   304-272-3227
  Loren Perry, prin.   Fax 272-5811
Other Schools – See Ceredo, Crum, Fort Gay,
  Huntington, Kenova

Webster Springs, Webster, Pop. 836
Webster County SD   1,700/PK-12
  315 S Main St 26288   304-847-5638
  Kay Carpenter, supt.   Fax 847-2538
  glade.webs.k12.wv.us/websterbdoff.htm
Other Schools – See Cowen, Upperglade

Weirton, Hancock, Pop. 19,838
Hancock County SD
  Supt. — See New Cumberland
Weir HS   700/9-12
  100 Red Rider Rd 26062   304-748-7600
  Marty Hudek, prin.   Fax 748-7602
Weir MS   700/5-8
  125 Sinclair Ave 26062   304-748-6080
  Dawn Petrovich, prin.   Fax 748-0847

Madonna HS   100/9-12
  150 Michael Ave 26062   304-723-0545
  Dr. Cathy Sistilli, prin.   Fax 723-0564
West Virginia Northern Community College   Post-Sec.
  150 Park Ave 26062   304-723-2210

Welch, McDowell, Pop. 2,485
McDowell County SD   3,800/PK-12
  30 Central Ave 24801   304-436-8441
  Dr. Mark Manchin, supt.   Fax 436-4008
  boe.mcdo.k12.wv.us
McDowell County Vocational Tech Ctr   Vo/Tech
  PO Box V 24801   304-436-3488
  Ron Estep, prin.   Fax 436-8063
Mount View HS   500/9-12
  950 Mount View Rd 24801   304-436-2939
  Dan Zirkle, prin.   Fax 436-4714
Mount View MS   300/7-8
  960 Mount View Rd 24801   304-436-4657
  Alvin Cline, prin.   Fax 436-3472
Adult Learning Center   Adult
  PO Box 556 24801   304-436-6580
  Everett Sparks, coord.   Fax 436-6580
Other Schools – See Avondale, Iaeger, War

Wellsburg, Brooke, Pop. 2,840
Brooke County SD   3,400/K-12
  1201 Pleasant Ave 26070   304-737-3481
  Mary Hervey DeGarmo, supt.   Fax 737-3480
  bhs.broo.k12.wv.us/Brk-Schs/
Brooke HS   1,100/9-12
  Bruin Dr 26070   304-527-1410
  Joyce Rea, prin.   Fax 527-3604
Wellsburg MS   500/5-8
  1447 Main St 26070   304-737-2922
  Toni Ann Shute, prin.   Fax 737-2976
Other Schools – See Follansbee

West Liberty, Ohio, Pop. 1,204

West Liberty State College   Post-Sec.
  PO Box 295 26074   304-336-5000

Weston, Lewis, Pop. 4,239
Lewis County SD   2,700/PK-12
  239 Court Ave 26452   304-269-8300
  Dr. Joseph L. Mace, supt.   Fax 269-8305
  boe.lewi.k12.wv.us/
Bland MS   900/5-8
  358 Court Ave 26452   304-269-8325
  Grace Talhammer, prin.   Fax 269-8310
Lewis County HS   800/9-12
  205 Minuteman Dr 26452   304-269-8315
  Timothy Derico, prin.   Fax 269-8319

West Union, Doddridge, Pop. 807
Doddridge County SD   1,300/PK-12
  104 Sistersville Pike 26456 304-873-2300
  Janice Michels, supt.   Fax 873-2210
Doddridge County HS   400/9-12
  201 Stuart St 26456   304-873-2521
  Bonnie Allman, prin.   Fax 873-1873
Doddridge County MS   400/5-8
  RR 2 Box 35C 26456   304-873-2390
  Betsy Yeager, prin.   Fax 873-2541

Wheeling, Ohio, Pop. 30,096
Marshall County SD
  Supt. — See Moundsville
Sherrard JHS   400/7-8
  1000 Fairmont Pike 26003   304-233-3331
  James Asplund, prin.   Fax 233-6418

Ohio County SD   5,400/K-12
  2203 National Rd 26003   304-243-0300
  Lawrence Miller, supt.   Fax 243-0328
  wphs.ohio.k12.wv.us/ocbe/
Bridge Street MS   400/6-8
  19 Junior Ave 26003   304-243-0381
  Lori Wiggins, prin.   Fax 243-0385
Triadelphia MS   500/6-8
  1636 National Rd 26003   304-243-0387
  Dr. Mary Lee Porter, prin.   Fax 243-0392
Wheeling MS   200/6-8
  3500 Chapline St 26003   304-243-0425
  Andy Garber, prin.   Fax 243-0426
Wheeling Park HS   1,800/9-12
  1976 Park View Rd 26003   304-243-0400
  Christine Carder, prin.   Fax 243-0449

Central Catholic HS   400/9-12
  75 14th St 26003   304-233-1660
  Dr. Joseph Viglietta, prin.   Fax 233-3187
Linsly S   400/5-12
  60 Knox Ln 26003   304-233-3260
  Reno Diorio, prin.   Fax 232-1975
Mt. de Chantal Visitation Academy   200/PK-12
  410 Washington Ave 26003   304-233-3771
  Dr. Becky Johnen, prin.   Fax 233-8598
Ohio Valley Medical Center   Post-Sec.
  2000 Eoff St 26003   304-234-8294
Scott College of Cosmetology   Post-Sec.
  1502 Market St 26003   304-232-7798
Speiro Academy   100/K-12
  135 Stewarts Hill Rd 26003   304-243-0001
  Susan Olinda Cline, prin.   Fax 845-4047
West Virginia Business College Post-Sec.
  1052 Main St 26003   304-232-0361
West Virginia Northern Community College   Post-Sec.
  1704 Market St 26003   304-233-5900
Wheeling Hospital   Post-Sec.
  1 Medical Park 26003   304-243-3000
Wheeling Jesuit University   Post-Sec.
  316 Washington Ave 26003   304-243-2000

Williamson, Mingo, Pop. 3,217
Mingo County SD   4,200/PK-12
  RR 2 Box 310 25661   304-235-3333
  Brenda Skibo, supt.   Fax 235-3410
  boe.ming.k12.wv.us
Tug Valley HS   400/9-12
  555 Panther Ave 25661   304-235-2266
  Thomas Newsome, prin.   Fax 235-2636
Williamson HS   200/9-12
  801 Alderson St 25661   304-235-2518
  Jeffrey Marion Reynolds, prin. Fax 235-6590
Williamson MS   200/5-8
  801 Alderson St 25661   304-235-3430
  Jim Saunders, prin.   Fax 235-5567
Other Schools – See Delbarton, Gilbert, Matewan

Southern WV Community & Technical Coll.   Post-Sec.
  25661   304-235-2800

Williamstown, Wood, Pop. 2,928
Wood County SD
  Supt. — See Parkersburg
Williamstown JSHS   600/7-12
  219 W 5th St 26187   304-375-6151
  Jack Mental, prin.   Fax 375-6194

Winfield, Putnam, Pop. 1,930
Putnam County SD   8,700/PK-12
  9 Courthouse Dr 25213   304-586-0500
  Harold Hatfiled, supt.   Fax 586-0553
  www.putnamschools.com
Winfield HS   800/9-12
  3022 Winfield Rd 25213   304-586-3279
  William H. Hughes, prin.   Fax 586-3601
Winfield MS   600/6-8
  3280 Winfield Rd 25213   304-586-3072
  Clarence Woodworth, prin.   Fax 586-0920
Other Schools – See Buffalo, Eleanor, Hurricane, Poca

WISCONSIN

WISCONSIN DEPARTMENT PUBLIC INSTRUCTION
PO Box 7841, Madison 53707-7841
Telephone 608-266-3390
Fax 608-267-1052
Website http://www.dpi.state.wi.us

Superintendent of Public Instruction   Elizabeth Burmaster

COOPERATIVE EDUCATIONAL SERVICE AGENCIES (CESA)

CESA 1
Timothy Gavigan, admin.   262-787-9500
19601 W Bluemound Rd   Fax 787-9501
Brookfield 53045
www.cesa1.k12.wi.us
CESA 2
Gary Albrecht, admin.   608-758-6232
448 E High St, Milton 53563   Fax 868-4864
www.cesa2.k12.wi.us
CESA 3
Gary Rooney, admin.   608-822-3276
1300 Industrial Dr   Fax 822-3828
Fennimore 53809
www.cesa3.k12.wi.us
CESA 4
Jerry Freimark, admin.   608-786-4800
923 E Garland St   Fax 786-4801
West Salem 54669
www.cesa4.k12.wi.us

CESA 5
Don Stevens, admin.   608-742-8811
PO Box 564, Portage 53901   Fax 742-2384
www.cesa5.k12.wi.us
CESA 6
Joan Wade, admin.   920-233-2372
PO Box 2568, Oshkosh 54903   Fax 424-3478
www.cesa6.k12.wi.us
CESA 7
Carol Gerhardt, admin.   920-492-5960
595 Baeten Rd, Green Bay 54304 Fax 492-5965
www.cesa7.k12.wi.us
CESA 8
Bob Kellogg, admin.   920-855-2114
PO Box 320, Gillett 54124   Fax 855-2299
www.cesa8.k12.wi.us

CESA 9
Jerome Fiene, admin.   715-453-2141
PO Box 449, Tomahawk 54487   Fax 453-7519
www.cesa9.k12.wi.us
CESA 10
Larry D. Annett, admin.   715-723-0341
725 W Park Ave   Fax 720-2070
Chippewa Falls 54729
www.cesa10.k12.wi.us
CESA 11
Robert Rykal, admin.   715-986-2020
225 Ostermann Dr   Fax 986-2040
Turtle Lake 54889
www.cesa11.k12.wi.us
CESA 12
Fred Schlichting, admin.   715-682-2363
618 Beaser Ave, Ashland 54806 Fax 682-7244
www.cesa12.k12.wi.us

PUBLIC, PRIVATE AND CATHOLIC SECONDARY SCHOOLS

Abbotsford, Clark, Pop. 1,944
Abbotsford SD   600/PK-12
PO Box 70 54405   715-223-6715
Reed Welsh, supt.   Fax 223-4239
www.abbotsford.k12.wi.us
Abbotsford JSHS   400/6-12
PO Box 70 54405   715-223-2386
Jerry Zanotelli, prin.   Fax 223-4239

Adams, Adams, Pop. 1,840
Adams-Friendship Area SD
Supt. — See Friendship
Adams-Friendship HS   600/9-12
1109 E North St 53910   608-339-3921
Tim Hodkiewicz, prin.   Fax 339-2569
Adams-Friendship MS   500/6-8
420 N Main St 53910   608-339-4064
Garret Gould, prin.   Fax 339-2434

Albany, Green, Pop. 1,148
Albany SD   400/PK-12
PO Box 349 53502   608-862-3225
David Westhoff, supt.   Fax 862-3230
www.albany.k12.wi.us
Albany HS   100/9-12
PO Box 349 53502   608-862-3135
                               Fax 862-3230
Albany MS   100/6-8
PO Box 349 53502   608-862-3135
Tina Van Meer, prin.   Fax 862-3230

Algoma, Kewaunee, Pop. 3,231
Algoma SD   500/PK-12
1715 Division St 54201   920-487-7001
Ronald Welch, supt.   Fax 487-7016
www.alghs.k12.wi.us
Algoma S   500/PK-12
1715 Division St 54201   920-487-7010
William Bush, prin.   Fax 487-7015

Alma, Buffalo, Pop. 906
Alma SD   400/PK-12
S1618 State Rd 35 54610   608-685-4416
Steven Sedlmayr, supt.   Fax 685-4446
www.alma.k12.wi.us
Alma HS   100/9-12
S1618 State Rd 35 54610   608-685-4416
Bert Plucker, prin.   Fax 685-4446

Alma Center, Jackson, Pop. 451
SD of Alma Center-Humbird-Merrillan 600/PK-12
PO Box 308 54611   715-964-8271
Robert C. Lambert, supt.   Fax 964-1005
www.achm.k12.wi.us
Lincoln HS   200/9-12
PO Box 308 54611   715-964-5311
Jeffrey Arzt, prin.   Fax 964-1005
Lincoln JHS   100/7-8
PO Box 308 54611   715-964-5311
Jeffrey Arzt, prin.   Fax 964-1005

Almond, Portage, Pop. 438
Almond-Bancroft SD   500/PK-12
1336 Elm St 54909   715-366-2941
Joe Garza, admin.   Fax 366-2940
www.abschools.k12.wi.us
Almond-Bancroft JSHS   300/6-12
1336 Elm St 54909   715-366-2940
Jeff Rykal, prin.   Fax 366-2943

Altoona, Eau Claire, Pop. 6,545
Altoona SD   1,400/PK-12
1903 Bartlett Ave 54720   715-839-6032
Gregory Fahrman, supt.   Fax 839-6066
www.altoona.k12.wi.us
Altoona HS   400/9-12
711 7th St W 54720   715-839-6031
Jeff Pepowski, prin.   Fax 839-6028
Altoona MS   400/5-8
1903 Bartlett Ave 54720   715-839-6030
Jack Wagener, prin.   Fax 839-6099

Otter Creek Christian Academy 50/1-10
919 10th St W 54720   715-834-1782
Richard Bauer, prin.

Amery, Polk, Pop. 2,865
Amery SD   1,900/PK-12
543 Minneapolis Ave S 54001   715-268-0272
Stephen Schiell, supt.   Fax 268-7300
www.amerysd.k12.wi.us
Amery HS   600/9-12
555 Minneapolis Ave S 54001   715-268-0233
Mike Goodrum, prin.   Fax 268-7792
Amery MS   400/6-8
501 Minneapolis Ave S 54001   715-268-0303
Thomas Bensen, prin.   Fax 268-4967

Amherst, Portage, Pop. 971
Tomorrow River SD   900/PK-12
357 N Main St 54406   715-824-5521
John Haugen, supt.   Fax 824-7177
www.amherst.k12.wi.us
Amherst HS   300/9-12
357 N Main St 54406   715-824-5522
Peter Sippel, prin.   Fax 824-5454
Amherst MS   100/7-8
357 N Main St 54406   715-824-5522
Michael Toelle, prin.   Fax 824-5454

Antigo, Langlade, Pop. 8,340
Antigo SD   2,900/PK-12
120 S Dorr St 54409   715-627-4355
Larry Nelson, supt.   Fax 623-3279
www.antigoschools.k12.wi.us
Antigo HS   1,100/9-12
1900 10th Ave 54409   715-623-7611
Thomas Zamzow, prin.   Fax 623-7624
Antigo MS   600/6-8
815 7th Ave 54409   715-623-4173
Douglas Knol, prin.   Fax 627-4982

Appleton, Outagamie, Pop. 70,354
Appleton Area SD   13,700/PK-12
PO Box 2019 54912   920-832-6161
Dr. Thomas Scullen, supt.   Fax 832-1725
www.aasd.k12.wi.us
Appleton East HS   1,500/9-12
2121 E Emmers Dr 54915   920-832-6212
Ben Vogel, prin.   Fax 832-4880
Appleton North HS   1,800/9-12
5000 N Ballard Rd 54913   920-832-4300
Barry O'Connor, prin.   Fax 832-4301
Appleton West HS   1,500/9-12
610 N Badger Ave 54914   920-832-6219
Greg Hartjes, prin.   Fax 832-4198

Einstein MS   400/7-8
324 E Florida Ave 54911   920-832-6240
James Huggins, prin.   Fax 832-6164
Madison MS   700/7-8
2020 S Carpenter St 54915   920-832-6276
Chris VanderHeyden, prin.   Fax 832-6337
Roosevelt MS   500/7-8
318 E Brewster St 54911   920-832-6294
Al Brant, prin.   Fax 832-4605
Wilson MS   500/7-8
225 N Badger Ave 54914   920-832-6226
John Magas, prin.   Fax 832-4857

Fox Valley Lutheran HS   600/9-12
5300 N Meade St 54913   920-739-4441
Paul Hartwig, prin.   Fax 739-4418
Fox Valley Technical College   Post-Sec.
PO Box 2277 54912   920-735-5600
Gill-Tech Academy of Hair Design Post-Sec.
423 W College Ave 54911   920-739-8684
Lawrence University   Post-Sec.
PO Box 599 54912   920-832-7000
St. Elizabeth Hospital   Post-Sec.
1506 S Oneida St 54915   920-738-2015
St. Joseph MS   500/6-8
2626 N Oneida St 54911   920-730-8849
Joseph Linsmeier, prin.   Fax 730-4147
Xavier HS   500/9-12
1600 W Prospect Ave 54914   920-733-6632
Matt Reynebeau, prin.   Fax 733-5513

Arcadia, Trempealeau, Pop. 2,332
Arcadia SD   900/PK-12
756 Raider Dr 54612   608-323-3315
Jon Turnell, supt.   Fax 323-2256
www.arcadia.k12.wi.us/
Arcadia HS   300/9-12
756 Raider Dr 54612   608-323-3334
Louie Ferguson, prin.   Fax 323-2256

Argyle, Lafayette, Pop. 810
Argyle SD   300/PK-12
PO Box 256 53504   608-543-3318
Michael Manning, supt.   Fax 543-3868
www.argyle.k12.wi.us
Argyle MSHS   200/6-12
PO Box 256 53504   608-543-3318
Gerry Benish, prin.   Fax 543-3868

Arkansaw, Pepin
Durand SD
Supt. — See Durand
Arkansaw MS   300/5-8
N6290 N H St 54721   715-285-5315
                               Fax 285-5684

Ashland, Ashland, Pop. 8,397
Ashland SD   2,300/PK-12
2000 Beaser Ave 54806   715-682-7080
Kenneth Kasinski, supt.   Fax 682-7097
www.ashland.k12.wi.us
Ashland HS   800/9-12
1900 Beaser Ave 54806   715-682-7089
Thomas Goudreau, prin.   Fax 682-2075
Ashland MS   500/6-8
203 11th St E 54806   715-682-7087
Robert Morelan, prin.   Fax 682-7944

621

Northland College
1411 Ellis Ave 54806
Post-Sec.
715-682-1699

Athens, Marathon, Pop. 1,072
Athens SD
PO Box F 54411
500/PK-12
715-257-7511
Frank Harrington, supt.
Fax 257-7502
www.athens.k12.wi.us
Athens HS
PO Box F 54411
200/9-12
715-257-7511
Timothy Micke, prin.
Fax 257-7651
Athens MS
PO Box F 54411
100/6-8
715-257-7511
Timothy Micke, prin.
Fax 257-7651

Auburndale, Wood, Pop. 727
Auburndale SD
PO Box 139 54412
900/PK-12
715-652-2117
John Timmerman, supt.
Fax 652-2836
www.aubschools.com
Auburndale JSHS
PO Box 190 54412
500/7-12
715-652-2115
Kevin Yeske, prin.
Fax 652-6322

Augusta, Eau Claire, Pop. 1,406
Augusta SD
E19320 Bartig Rd 54722
600/PK-12
715-286-3300
Stephen LaFave, supt.
Fax 286-3336
www.augusta.k12.wi.us
Augusta JSHS
E19320 Bartig Rd 54722
300/6-12
715-286-3352
Tom Crowe, dean
Fax 286-3393

Baldwin, Saint Croix, Pop. 3,089
Baldwin-Woodville Area SD
550 US Highway 12 54002
1,400/PK-12
715-684-3411
Russell J. Helland, supt.
Fax 684-3168
www.bwsd.k12.wi.us/
Baldwin-Woodville HS
1000 13th Ave 54002
400/9-12
715-684-3321
Eric Russell, prin.
Fax 684-5160
Other Schools – See Woodville

Balsam Lake, Polk, Pop. 977
Unity SD
PO Box 307 54810
1,100/PK-12
715-825-3515
Terry Schmidt, supt.
Fax 825-3517
www.unity.k12.wi.us/
Unity HS
PO Box 307 54810
400/9-12
715-825-2131
William Alleva, prin.
Fax 825-4430
Unity MS
PO Box 307 54810
300/6-8
715-825-2101
Brandon Robinson, prin.
Fax 825-4410

Bangor, LaCrosse, Pop. 1,395
Bangor SD
PO Box 99 54614
600/K-12
608-486-2331
Roger Foegen, supt.
Fax 486-4587
www.bangor.k12.wi.us
Bangor MSHS
PO Box 99 54614
400/6-12
608-486-2331
Don Addington, prin.
Fax 486-4587

Baraboo, Sauk, Pop. 10,768
Baraboo SD
101 2nd Ave 53913
2,800/PK-12
608-355-3950
Lance Alwin, supt.
Fax 355-3960
www.baraboo.k12.wi.us
Baraboo HS
1201 Draper St 53913
1,000/9-12
608-355-3940
Machell Schwarz, prin.
Fax 355-3962
Young MS
1531 Draper St 53913
700/6-8
608-355-3930
Robert Meicher, prin.
Fax 355-3998

University of Wisconsin Baraboo/Sauk Co.
1006 Connie Rd 53913
Post-Sec.
608-356-8351

Barneveld, Iowa, Pop. 1,088
Barneveld SD
PO Box 98 53507
400/PK-12
608-924-4711
Joe Bertone, supt.
Fax 924-1646
www.barneveld.k12.wi.us
Barneveld S
PO Box 98 53507
400/PK-12
608-924-4711
Kevin Knudson, prin.
Fax 924-1646

Barron, Barron, Pop. 3,308
Barron Area SD
100 W River Ave 54812
1,400/PK-12
715-537-5612
Monti Hallberg, supt.
Fax 537-5161
www.barron.k12.wi.us/
Barron HS
1050 E Woodland Ave 54812
500/9-12
715-537-5627
Kirk Haugestuen, prin.
Fax 537-1603
Riverview MS
135 W River Ave 54812
300/6-8
715-537-5641
John Gevens, prin.
Fax 637-5373

Bayfield, Bayfield, Pop. 608
Bayfield SD
PO Box 5001 54814
500/PK-12
715-779-3201
Mark A. Jansen, supt.
Fax 779-5268
www.bayfield.k12.wi.us
Bayfield HS
PO Box 5001 54814
200/9-12
715-779-3201
Robert Kent, prin.
Fax 779-5226
Bayfield MS
PO Box 5001 54814
100/6-8
715-779-3201
Michael J. Malyuk, prin.
Fax 779-5226

Beaver Dam, Dodge, Pop. 14,949
Beaver Dam SD
705 McKinley St 53916
3,300/K-12
920-885-7300
Donald Childs, supt.
Fax 885-7305
www.beaverdam.k12.wi.us
Beaver Dam HS
500 Gould St 53916
1,200/9-12
920-885-7313
Chris Ligocki, prin.
Fax 885-7317

Beaver Dam MS
108 4th St 53916
700/6-8
920-885-7365
Richard Brouillard, prin.
Fax 885-7415

Moraine Park Technical College
700 Gould St 53916
Post-Sec.
920-887-1101
Wayland Academy
101 N University Ave 53916
200/9-12
920-885-3373
Robert L. Esten, pres.
Fax 885-2032

Belleville, Dane, Pop. 2,011
Belleville SD
PO Box 230 53508
900/PK-12
608-424-3315
Dr. Randy Freese, supt.
Fax 424-3486
www.belleville.k12.wi.us/
Belleville HS
635 W Church St 53508
300/9-12
608-424-1902
Rick Conroy, prin.
Fax 424-3692
Belleville MS
625 W Church St 53508
200/7-8
608-424-1902
Rick Conroy, prin.
Fax 424-3692

Belmont, Lafayette, Pop. 905
Belmont Community SD
PO Box 348 53510
300/K-12
608-762-5131
Johannus Benkers, supt.
Fax 762-5129
www.belmont.k12.wi.us
Belmont JSHS
PO Box 348 53510
200/7-12
608-762-5131
Ron Shefchik, prin.
Fax 762-5129

Beloit, Rock, Pop. 35,505
Beloit SD
1633 Keeler Ave 53511
6,800/PK-12
608-361-4000
Bette Lang, supt.
Fax 361-4122
www.sdb.k12.wi.us
Aldrich MS
1859 Northgate Dr 53511
800/6-8
608-361-3605
David Luebke, prin.
Fax 361-3620
McNeel MS
1524 Frederick St 53511
900/6-8
608-361-3800
Chris Wesling, prin.
Fax 361-3820
Memorial HS
1225 4th St 53511
1,900/9-12
608-361-3005
Richard Jancek, prin.
Fax 361-3080

Beloit-Turner SD
1237 E Inman Pkwy 53511
1,200/PK-12
608-364-6372
Charles Melvin, supt.
Fax 364-6373
www.fjturner.k12.wi.us
Turner HS
1231 E Inman Pkwy 53511
400/9-12
608-364-6370
Dennis McCarthy, prin.
Fax 365-4768
Turner MS
1237 E Inman Pkwy 53511
300/6-8
608-364-6367
Randall McClellan, prin.
Fax 364-6369

Beloit College
700 College St 53511
Post-Sec.
608-363-2000
Rock County Christian HS
916 Bushnell St 53511
100/6-12
608-365-7378
Tim Befus, admin.
Fax 365-7382

Benton, Lafayette, Pop. 992
Benton SD
PO Box 7 53803
300/PK-12
608-759-4002
Gary Neis, admin.
Fax 759-3805
www.benton.k12.wi.us
Benton JSHS
PO Box 7 53803
100/7-12
608-759-4002
Gary Neis, prin.
Fax 759-3805

Berlin, Green Lake, Pop. 5,303
Berlin Area SD
295 E Marquette St 54923
1,700/PK-12
920-361-2004
Jerry Runice, supt.
Fax 361-2170
www.berlin.k12.wi.us
Berlin HS
222 Memorial Dr 54923
600/9-12
920-361-2000
Robert Eidahl, prin.
Fax 361-2005
Berlin MS
289 E Huron St 54923
400/6-8
920-361-2441
Diane Toraason, prin.
Fax 361-2945

Birchwood, Washburn, Pop. 538
Birchwood SD
300 S Wilson St 54817
300/PK-12
715-354-3471
Frank Helquist, supt.
Fax 354-3469
www.birchwood.k12.wi.us/
Birchwood HS
300 S Wilson St 54817
100/9-12
715-354-3471
Jeff Stanley, supt.
Fax 354-3469

Black River Falls, Jackson, Pop. 3,578
Black River Falls SD
301 N 4th St 54615
1,900/PK-12
715-284-4357
Dennis Richards, supt.
Fax 284-7064
www.brf.org
Black River Falls HS
1200 Pierce St 54615
700/9-12
715-284-4324
Robert Lecheler, prin.
Fax 284-7626
Black River Falls MS
1202 Pierce St 54615
400/6-8
715-284-5315
David Roou, prin.
Fax 284-0364

Blair, Trempealeau, Pop. 1,271
Blair-Taylor SD
PO Box 125 54616
700/PK-12
608-989-2881
Guy Leavitt, supt.
Fax 989-2451
btsd.k12.wi.us
Blair-Taylor MSHS
PO Box 107 54616
300/7-12
608-989-2525
Jeff Eide, prin.
Fax 989-9161

Blanchardville, Lafayette, Pop. 796
Pecatonica Area SD
PO Box 117 53516
500/PK-12
608-523-4248
Nancy Hendrickson, supt.
Fax 523-4286
www.pecatonica.k12.wi.us

Pecatonica JSHS
PO Box 117 53516
300/7-12
608-523-4285
David McSherry, prin.
Fax 523-4286

Bloomer, Chippewa, Pop. 3,284
Bloomer SD
1310 17th Ave 54724
1,000/PK-12
715-568-2800
Douglas Martin, supt.
Fax 568-5315
www.bloomer.k12.wi.us
Bloomer HS
1310 17th Ave 54724
400/9-12
715-568-5300
Brent Ashland, prin.
Fax 568-5304
Bloomer MS
600 Jackson St 54724
200/6-8
715-568-1025
Barry Kamrath, prin.
Fax 568-3687

Bloomington, Grant, Pop. 683
River Ridge SD
Supt. — See Patch Grove
River Ridge MS
545 Mill St 53804
200/5-8
608-994-2711
Michael Murphy, prin.
Fax 994-2714

Bonduel, Shawano, Pop. 1,404
Bonduel SD
PO Box 310 54107
1,000/PK-12
715-758-4860
Peter Behnke, supt.
Fax 758-4869
www.bonduel.k12.wi.us
Bonduel HS
PO Box 310 54107
300/9-12
715-758-4850
Gary Berger, prin.
Fax 758-4859
Bonduel MS
PO Box 310 54107
200/6-8
715-758-4840
Connie Rutledge, prin.
Fax 758-4849

Boscobel, Grant, Pop. 3,191
Boscobel Area SD
1110 Park St 53805
1,000/PK-12
608-375-4164
David U'Ren, supt.
Fax 375-2378
www.boscobel.k12.wi.us
Boscobel HS
300 Brindley St 53805
300/9-12
608-375-4161
William Mercer, prin.
Fax 375-2640
Boscobel MS
300 Brindley St 53805
200/7-8
608-375-4161
William Mercer, prin.
Fax 375-2640

Bowler, Shawano, Pop. 335
Bowler SD
PO Box 8 54416
500/PK-12
715-793-4307
Dr. Stephen Smith, supt.
Fax 793-1302
www.bowler.k12.wi.us
Bowler JSHS
PO Box 8 54416
200/7-12
715-793-4301
Barry Wolff, dean
Fax 793-1302

Boyceville, Dunn, Pop. 1,048
Boyceville Community SD
1003 Tiffany St 54725
900/PK-12
715-643-4311
Dennis Rettke, supt.
Fax 643-3127
www.boyceville.k12.wi.us
Boyceville MSHS
1003 Tiffany St 54725
400/7-12
715-643-4321
William Fisher, prin.
Fax 643-2209

Brillion, Calumet, Pop. 2,940
Brillion SD
315 S Main St 54110
900/PK-12
920-756-2368
Dominick Madison, supt.
Fax 756-3705
www.brillion.k12.wi.us
Brillion HS
W1101 County Hwy HR 54110
300/9-12
920-756-9238
Paul Nistler, prin.
Fax 756-9427
Brillion MS
315 S Main St 54110
200/6-8
920-756-2166
Paul Cooney, prin.
Fax 756-3705

Brodhead, Green, Pop. 3,095
Brodhead SD
2501 W 5th Ave 53520
1,200/PK-12
608-897-2141
Charles J. Deery, supt.
Fax 897-2770
www.brodhead.k12.wi.us
Brodhead HS
2501 W 5th Ave 53520
400/9-12
608-897-2155
Leonard Lueck, prin.
Fax 897-3026
Brodhead MS
2100 W 9th Ave 53520
300/6-8
608-897-2184
Charles Urness, prin.
Fax 897-2789

Brookfield, Waukesha, Pop. 39,637
Elmbrook SD
PO Box 1830 53008
7,600/PK-12
262-781-3030
Matthew Gibson, supt.
Fax 783-0983
www.elmbrook.k12.wi.us
Central HS
16900 Gebhardt Rd 53005
1,400/9-12
262-785-3910
Don La Bonte, prin.
Fax 785-3993
East HS
3305 Lilly Rd 53005
1,300/9-12
262-781-3500
Brett Bowers, prin.
Fax 781-8314
Wisconsin Hills MS
18700 W Wisconsin Ave 53045
900/6-8
262-785-3960
Robyn Martino, prin.
Fax 785-3967
Other Schools – See Elm Grove

Brookfield Academy
3460 N Brookfield Rd 53045
700/PK-12
262-783-3200
Robert Solsrud, hdmstr.
Fax 783-3213
Ottawa University - Milwaukee
300 N Corporate Dr Ste 110 53045
Post-Sec.
262-879-0200

Brown Deer, Milwaukee, Pop. 12,031
Brown Deer SD
8200 N 60th St 53223
1,800/PK-12
414-371-6700
Bruce Connolly, supt.
Fax 371-6751
www.bdsd.k12.wi.us
Brown Deer HS
8060 N 60th St 53223
700/9-12
414-371-7000
James Piatt, prin.
Fax 371-7001

Brown Deer MS
5757 W Dean Rd 53223
Blake Peuse, prin.
600/5-8
414-371-6900
Fax 371-6901

Bruce, Rusk, Pop. 752
Bruce SD
104 W Washington Ave 54819
Debra Brown, supt.
www.bruce.k12.wi.us
600/PK-12
715-868-2533
Fax 868-2534
Bruce HS
104 W Washington Ave 54819
Larry Villiard, prin.
200/9-12
715-868-2585
Fax 868-2534
Bruce MS
104 W Washington Ave 54819
Larry Villiard, prin.
100/7-8
715-868-2585
Fax 868-2534

Brussels, Door
Southern Door SD
8240 State Highway 57 54204
Joseph Innis, supt.
www.southerndoor.k12.wi.us
1,300/PK-12
920-825-7311
Fax 825-7311
Southern Door HS
8240 State Highway 57 54204
Lois Mahaffey, prin.
400/9-12
920-825-7333
Fax 825-7081
Southern Door MS
8240 State Highway 57 54204
Gary Langenberg, prin.
300/6-8
920-825-7321
Fax 825-7692

Burlington, Racine, Pop. 10,836
Burlington Area SD
100 N Kane St 53105
Ronald Jandura, supt.
www.basd.k12.wi.us
3,600/PK-12
262-763-0210
Fax 763-0215
Burlington HS
400 Mc Canna Pkwy 53105
Barbara Kopack-Hill, prin.
1,400/9-12
262-763-0200
Fax 763-0216
Karcher MS
225 Robert St 53105
Mark Sheldon, prin.
600/7-8
262-763-0190
Fax 767-5580

Catholic Central HS
148 McHenry St 53105
Ralph Lynch, prin.
200/9-12
262-763-1510
Fax 763-1509

Butternut, Ashland, Pop. 392
Butternut SD
PO Box 247 54514
Bruce LaRose, supt.
www.butternut.k12.wi.us
200/PK-12
715-769-3434
Fax 769-3712
Butternut S
PO Box 247 54514
Bruce LaRose, prin.
200/PK-12
715-769-3434
Fax 769-3712

Cadott, Chippewa, Pop. 1,308
Cadott Community SD
PO Box 310 54727
Guy Habeck, supt.
www.cadott.k12.wi.us
900/PK-12
715-289-3795
Fax 289-3748
Cadott HS
PO Box 310 54727
Matthew McDonough, prin.
300/9-12
715-289-4211
Fax 289-3085
Cadott JHS
PO Box 310 54727
Matthew McDonough, prin.
100/7-8
715-289-4211
Fax 289-3085

Cambria, Columbia, Pop. 782
Cambria-Friesland SD
410 E Edgewater St 53923
Jeff Walker, supt.
www.cf.k12.wi.us
500/PK-12
920-348-5548
Fax 348-5119
Cambria-Friesland MSHS
410 E Edgewater St 53923
Rick Hammes, prin.
300/6-12
920-348-5135
Fax 348-5119

Cambridge, Dane, Pop. 1,172
Cambridge SD
403 Blue Jay Way 53523
Ronald Dayton, supt.
www.cambridge.k12.wi.us
1,000/PK-12
608-423-4345
Fax 423-9869
Cambridge HS
403 Blue Jay Way 53523
Robert Rosen, prin.
300/9-12
608-423-3262
Fax 423-9598
Nikolay MS
211 South St 53523
George Smith, prin.
200/6-8
608-423-7335
Fax 423-4499

Cameron, Barron, Pop. 1,609
Cameron SD
PO Box 378 54822
Randal Braun, supt.
www.cameron.k12.wi.us
900/PK-12
715-458-4560
Fax 458-0041
Cameron HS
PO Box 378 54822
Joseph Leschisin, prin.
300/9-12
715-458-4510
Fax 458-4236
Cameron MS
PO Box 378 54822
Thomas Spanel, prin.
300/5-8
715-458-4563
Fax 458-3436

Campbellsport, Fond du Lac, Pop. 1,914
Campbellsport SD
114 W Sheboygan St 53010
Dan Olson, supt.
www.csd.k12.wi.us
1,500/PK-12
920-533-8381
Fax 533-5726
Campbellsport HS
114 W Sheboygan St 53010
Tom Hercules, prin.
600/9-12
920-533-4811
Fax 533-3521
Campbellsport JHS
114 W Sheboygan St 53010
Michael Maxson, prin.
300/7-8
920-533-3411
Fax 533-5726

Casco, Kewaunee, Pop. 559
Luxemburg-Casco SD
Supt. — See Luxemburg
Luxemburg-Casco MS
619 Church Ave 54205
John LeClair, prin.
300/7-8
920-837-2205
Fax 837-7517

Cashton, Monroe, Pop. 1,019
Cashton SD
PO Box 129 54619
Norbert Resheske, supt.
www.cashton.k12.wi.us
500/PK-12
608-654-5131
Fax 654-5136
Cashton JSHS, PO Box 129 54619
Bradford Saron, prin.
300/7-12
608-654-5131

Cassville, Grant, Pop. 1,053
Cassville SD
715 E Amelia St 53806
Dorance Hefte, supt.
www.cassvillesd.k12.wi.us
300/PK-12
608-725-5116
Fax 725-2353
Cassville JSHS
715 E Amelia St 53806
Linda Layer, prin.
200/7-12
608-725-5116
Fax 725-2353

Cazenovia, Richland, Pop. 326
Weston SD
E2511A County Rd S 53924
John Klang, supt.
www.weston.k12.wi.us
400/PK-12
608-986-2151
Fax 986-2205
Weston HS
E2511A County Rd S 53924
John Klang, prin.
100/9-12
608-986-2151
Fax 986-2205
Weston MS
E2511A County Rd S 53924
John Klang, prin.
100/6-8
608-986-2151
Fax 986-2205

Cedarburg, Ozaukee, Pop. 11,169
Cedarburg SD
W68N611 Evergreen Blvd 53012
Dr. Daryl Herrick, supt.
www.cedarburg.k12.wi.us
3,100/K-12
262-376-6100
Fax 376-6110
Cedarburg HS
W68N611 Evergreen Blvd 53012
Jay Grieger, prin.
1,200/9-12
262-376-6200
Fax 376-6210
Webster MS
W75N624 Wauwatosa Rd 53012
Robert Klimpke, prin.
700/6-8
262-376-6500
Fax 376-6510

Cedar Grove, Sheboygan, Pop. 1,928
Cedar Grove-Belgium SD
321 N 2nd St 53013
Michael Salkowski, supt.
www.cedargrovebelgium.k12.wi.us/
1,000/PK-12
920-668-8686
Fax 668-8605
Cedar Grove-Belgium HS
321 N 2nd St 53013
John Hocking, prin.
300/9-12
920-668-8686
Fax 668-8605
Cedar Grove-Belgium MS
321 N 2nd St 53013
Jeanne Courneene, prin.
300/5-8
920-668-8518
Fax 668-8566

Chetek, Barron, Pop. 2,157
Chetek SD
1001 Knapp St 54728
Al Brown, supt.
www.chetek.k12.wi.us/
1,000/K-12
715-924-2226
Fax 924-2376
Chetek HS
1001 Knapp St 54728
Ed Harris, prin.
400/9-12
715-924-3137
Fax 924-2921
Chetek MS
1001 Knapp St 54728
Bryan Yenter, prin.
300/6-8
715-924-3136
Fax 924-2921

Chilton, Calumet, Pop. 3,646
Chilton SD
530 W Main St 53014
Steve Patz, supt.
www.chilton.k12.wi.us
1,300/PK-12
920-849-8109
Fax 849-4539
Chilton HS
530 W Main St 53014
Timothy Schaid, prin.
500/9-12
920-849-2358
Fax 849-3998
Chilton MS
421 Court St 53014
Robert Knadle, prin.
400/5-8
920-849-9152
Fax 849-7210

Chippewa Falls, Chippewa, Pop. 12,708
Chippewa Falls Area SD
1130 Miles St 54729
Michael Schoch, supt.
cfsd.chipfalls.k12.wi.us/
4,500/PK-12
715-726-2417
Fax 726-2781
Chippewa Falls HS
735 Terrill St 54729
James Sauter, prin.
1,500/9-12
715-726-2406
Fax 726-2792
Chippewa Falls MS
750 Tropicana Blvd 54729
Janet Etmund, prin.
1,100/6-8
715-726-2400
Fax 726-2789

McDonell Central HS
1316 Bel Air Blvd 54729
John Flanagan, prin.
200/9-12
715-723-9126
Fax 723-1501
Notre Dame MS
22 S Prairie St 54729
Sue Goslyn, prin.
200/6-8
715-723-4777
Fax 723-3353

Clayton, Polk, Pop. 531
Clayton SD
PO Box 130 54004
Maurice Veilleux, supt.
www.claytonsd.k12.wi.us
400/PK-12
715-948-2163
Fax 948-2362
Clayton HS
PO Box 130 54004
Maurice Veilleux, prin.
100/9-12
715-948-2163
Fax 948-2362
Clayton MS
PO Box 130 54004
Maurice Veilleux, prin.
100/6-8
715-948-2163
Fax 948-2362

Clear Lake, Polk, Pop. 1,079
Clear Lake SD
1101 3rd St SW 54005
Mark Heyerdahl, supt.
www.clearlake.k12.wi.us
700/PK-12
715-263-2114
Fax 263-2933
Clear Lake HS
1101 3rd St SW 54005
Wayne Whitwam, prin.
200/9-12
715-263-2113
Fax 263-3550
Clear Lake JHS
1101 3rd St SW 54005
Wayne Whitwam, prin.
100/7-8
715-263-2113
Fax 263-3550

Cleveland, Manitowoc, Pop. 1,399

Lakeshore Technical College
1290 North Ave 53015
Post-Sec.
920-693-8213

Clinton, Rock, Pop. 2,755
Clinton Community SD
PO Box 566 53525
Rebecca Nodorft, supt.
www.clinton.k12.wi.us
1,200/PK-12
608-676-5482
Fax 676-4444
Clinton HS
PO Box 566 53525
Steve Ferger, prin.
400/9-12
608-676-2223
Fax 676-4444
Clinton MS
PO Box 559 53525
Carol Langley, prin.
400/5-8
608-676-2275
Fax 676-5176

Clintonville, Waupaca, Pop. 4,568
Clintonville SD
45 W Green Tree Rd 54929
Tom O'Toole, supt.
www.clintonville.k12.wi.us
1,400/PK-12
715-823-7215
Fax 823-1315
Clintonville HS
64 W Green Tree Rd 54929
Joe Stutting, prin.
600/9-12
715-823-7215
Fax 823-1481
Clintonville MS
255 N Main St 54929
Barbara Sparish, prin.
400/5-8
715-823-7215
Fax 823-1443

Colby, Clark, Pop. 1,666
Colby SD
PO Box 139 54421
J. Terry Downen, supt.
www.colby.k12.wi.us
1,100/PK-12
715-223-2301
Fax 223-4539
Colby HS
PO Box 110 54421
Nancy Marcott, prin.
400/9-12
715-223-2338
Fax 223-4388
Colby MS
PO Box 110 54421
James Hagen, prin.
200/6-8
715-223-8869
Fax 223-6754

Coleman, Marinette, Pop. 716
Coleman SD
PO Box 259 54112
Paula Hansen, supt.
www.coleman.k12.wi.us
800/PK-12
920-897-4011
Fax 897-2015
Coleman HS
PO Box 259 54112
Kelly Casper, prin.
300/9-12
920-897-2291
Fax 897-2015

Faith Christian S
233 W Main St 54112
Mark Widmer, admin.
100/K-12
920-897-3380
Fax 897-4880

Colfax, Dunn, Pop. 1,097
Colfax SD
601 University Ave 54730
Lee Bjurquist, supt.
www.colfax.k12.wi.us/
900/PK-12
715-962-3773
Fax 962-4024
Colfax HS
601 University Ave 54730
Dennis Geissler, prin.
300/9-12
715-962-3155
Fax 962-4024

Columbus, Columbia, Pop. 4,844
Columbus SD
200 W School St 53925
Mark Jansen, supt.
www.columbus.k12.wi.us
1,200/PK-12
920-623-5950
Fax 623-5958
Columbus HS
1164 Farnham St 53925
Connie Valenza, prin.
500/9-12
920-623-5956
Fax 623-5959
Columbus MS
400 S Dickason Blvd 53925
Doug Waitrovich, prin.
400/4-8
920-623-5954
Fax 623-5742

Wisconsin Academy
N2355 Du Borg Rd 53925
Derral Reeve, prin.
100/9-12
920-623-3300
Fax 623-3318

Cornell, Chippewa, Pop. 1,417
Cornell SD
PO Box 517 54732
Paul M. Schley, supt.
www.cornell.k12.wi.us
600/PK-12
715-239-6577
Fax 239-6467
Cornell JSHS
PO Box 517 54732
David Elliott, prin.
300/7-12
715-239-6464
Fax 239-6467

Crandon, Forest, Pop. 1,874
Crandon SD
9750 US Highway 8 W 54520
Dr. Richard Peters, supt.
www.crandon.k12.wi.us
1,000/PK-12
715-478-3339
Fax 478-5130
Crandon HS
9750 US Highway 8 W 54520
John Gruber, prin.
300/9-12
715-478-3583
Fax 478-5570
Crandon MS
9750 US Highway 8 W 54520
Glen Pfeifer, prin.
300/6-8
715-478-3713
Fax 478-5570

Crivitz, Marinette, Pop. 1,037
Crivitz SD
PO Box 130 54114
Charles Poches, supt.
www.crivitz.k12.wi.us
900/PK-12
715-854-2721
Fax 854-3755
Crivitz HS
PO Box 130 54114
Vic Gehm, prin.
300/9-12
715-854-2721
Fax 854-3755
Crivitz MS
PO Box 130 54114
Eugene Chapman, prin.
200/7-8
715-854-2721
Fax 854-2050

Cross Plains, Dane, Pop. 3,295
Middleton-Cross Plains Area SD
Supt. — See Middleton
Glacier Creek MS
2800 Military Rd 53528
Tim Keeler, prin.
600/6-8
608-829-9420
Fax 798-5425

Cuba City, Grant, Pop. 2,131
Cuba City SD — 600/PK-12
101 N School St 53807 — 608-744-2847
Sam McGrew, supt. — Fax 744-2324
www.cubacity.k12.wi.us
Cuba City HS — 300/9-12
101 N School St 53807 — 608-744-8888
Tim Hazen, prin. — Fax 744-2324

Cudahy, Milwaukee, Pop. 18,300
Cudahy SD — 2,800/PK-12
2915 E Ramsey Ave 53110 — 414-294-7400
James Heiden, supt. — Fax 769-2319
www.cudahy.k12.wi.us/
Cudahy HS — 900/9-12
4950 S Lake Dr 53110 — 414-294-2700
Kay Marks, prin. — Fax 769-2379
Cudahy MS — 400/7-8
5530 S Barland Ave 53110 — 414-294-2830
Gene Bibis, prin. — Fax 489-3010

Cumberland, Barron, Pop. 2,302
Cumberland SD — 1,200/PK-12
1010 8th Ave 54829 — 715-822-5124
Donald Groth, supt. — Fax 822-5136
www.cumberland.k12.wi.us/
Cumberland HS — 400/9-12
1000 8th Ave 54829 — 715-822-5121
Ritchie Narges, prin. — Fax 822-5138
Cumberland MS — 400/5-8
980 8th Ave 54829 — 715-822-5122
Jim Sciacca, prin. — Fax 822-5132

Darlington, Lafayette, Pop. 2,391
Darlington Community SD — 900/PK-12
11630 Center Hill Rd 53530 — 608-776-2006
Joseph Galle, supt. — Fax 776-3407
www.darlington.k12.wi.us
Darlington HS — 300/9-12
11838 Center Hill Rd 53530 — 608-776-4001
Dan Myers, prin. — Fax 776-2378

Deerfield, Dane, Pop. 1,989
Deerfield Community SD — 700/PK-12
300 Simonson Blvd 53531 — 608-764-8261
Ruthann Faber, supt. — Fax 764-5433
www.deerfield.k12.wi.us
Deerfield HS — 200/9-12
300 Simonson Blvd 53531 — 608-764-8261
David Podmolik, prin. — Fax 764-5433
Deerfield MS — 100/7-8
300 Simonson Blvd 53531 — 608-764-8261
Michelle Jensen, prin. — Fax 764-5433

De Forest, Dane, Pop. 6,262
De Forest Area SD — 3,200/PK-12
520 E Holum St 53532 — 608-842-6500
Jon Bales, supt. — Fax 842-6576
www.deforest.k12.wi.us
De Forest Area HS — 1,000/9-12
815 Jefferson St 53532 — 608-842-6600
Tim Onsager, prin. — Fax 842-6615
De Forest Area MS — 1,000/5-8
404 Yorktown Rd 53532 — 608-842-6000
Ann Higgins, prin. — Fax 842-6015

Delafield, Waukesha, Pop. 6,705
St. Johns Northwestern Military Academy — 300/7-12
1101 Genesee St 53018 — 262-646-7111
Jack Albert, pres. — Fax 646-4796

Delavan, Walworth, Pop. 8,304
Delavan-Darien SD — 2,800/PK-12
324 Beloit St 53115 — 262-728-2642
James Sorensen, supt. — Fax 728-5954
www.ddschools.org
Delavan-Darien HS — 900/9-12
150 Cumming St 53115 — 262-728-2642
Mike Cipriano, prin. — Fax 728-9713
Phoenix MS — 600/6-8
414 Beloit St 53115 — 262-728-2642
Deborah Bissett, prin. — Fax 728-0359

Wisconsin School for the Deaf — Post-Sec.
309 W Walworth Ave 53115

Denmark, Brown, Pop. 2,002
Denmark SD — 1,600/PK-12
450 N Wall St 54208 — 920-863-4000
Tony Klaubauf, supt. — Fax 863-4015
www.denmark.k12.wi.us
Denmark HS — 500/9-12
450 N Wall St 54208 — 920-863-4200
Kevin Kilstofte, prin. — Fax 863-8856
Denmark MS — 400/6-8
450 N Wall St 54208 — 920-863-4100
Dyan Pasono, prin. — Fax 863-3184

De Pere, Brown, Pop. 22,229
De Pere SD — 3,200/PK-12
1700 Chicago St 54115 — 920-337-1032
Benjamin Villarruel, supt. — Fax 337-1033
www.depere.k12.wi.us
De Pere HS — 1,000/9-12
1700 Chicago St 54115 — 920-337-1020
Matthew Weller, prin. — Fax 337-1041
De Pere MS — 500/7-8
700 Swan Rd 54115 — 920-337-1024
Curt Albers, prin. — Fax 337-1049

West De Pere SD — 2,000/PK-12
930 Oak St 54115 — 920-337-1393
Lanny J. Tibaldo, supt. — Fax 337-1398
www.wdpsd.com
West De Pere HS — 700/9-12
665 Grant St 54115 — 920-338-5200
Russell Gerke, prin. — Fax 338-5310

West De Pere MS — 600/5-8
1177 S 9th St 54115 — 920-337-1099
James Finley, prin. — Fax 337-1380

St. Norbert College — Post-Sec.
100 Grant St 54115 — 800-236-4878

De Soto, Vernon, Pop. 366
De Soto Area SD — 600/PK-12
615 Main St 54624 — 608-648-0102
Michael Davis, supt. — Fax 648-3959
www.desoto.k12.wi.us
De Soto HS — 200/9-12
615 Main St 54624 — 608-648-0100
Martin Kirchhof, prin. — Fax 648-0117
De Soto MS — 100/6-8
615 Main St 54624 — 608-648-0104
Martin Kirchhof, prin. — Fax 648-0117

Dodgeville, Iowa, Pop. 4,625
Dodgeville SD — 1,300/PK-12
400 N Johnson St 53533 — 608-935-3307
Diane Messer, supt. — Fax 935-3021
dsd.k12.wi.us
Dodgeville HS — 400/9-12
912 W Chapel St 53533 — 608-935-3307
Jeff Athey, prin. — Fax 935-9540
Dodgeville MS — 300/6-8
951 W Chapel St 53533 — 608-935-3307
Bruce Rundle, prin. — Fax 935-9643

Dousman, Waukesha, Pop. 1,819
Kettle Moraine SD
Supt. — See Wales
Kettle Moraine MS — 1,000/6-8
301 E Ottawa Ave 53118 — 262-965-6500
Ryan Krohn, prin. — Fax 965-6506

Drummond, Bayfield
Drummond SD — 500/PK-12
PO Box 40 54832 — 715-739-6669
Henry Lamkin, supt. — Fax 739-6345
www.dasd.k12.wi.us
Drummond HS — 200/9-12
PO Box 40 54832 — 715-739-6231
Lesley Boyer, prin. — Fax 739-6345
Drummond MS — 100/7-8
PO Box 40 54832 — 715-739-6231
Lesley Boyer, prin. — Fax 739-6345

Dunbar, Marinette
Northland Baptist Bible College — Post-Sec.
W10085 Pike Plains Rd 54119 — 715-324-6900

Durand, Pepin, Pop. 1,936
Durand SD — 1,100/PK-12
604 7th Ave E 54736 — 715-672-8919
Jerry Walters, supt. — Fax 672-8900
www.durand.k12.wi.us
Durand HS — 400/9-12
604 7th Ave E 54736 — 715-672-8917
Bill Clouse, prin. — Fax 672-8930
Other Schools – See Arkansaw

St. Mary S — 100/4-8
901 W Prospect St 54736 — 715-672-5617
Bernard Huettl, prin. — Fax 672-3931

Eagle River, Vilas, Pop. 1,565
Northland Pines SD — 1,500/PK-12
1780 Pleasure Island Rd 54521 — 715-479-6487
Mike Richie, supt. — Fax 479-7633
www.npsd.k12.wi.us/
Northland Pines HS — 600/9-12
1800 Pleasure Island Rd 54521 — 715-479-4473
Pat Sullivan, prin. — Fax 479-5808
Northland Pines MS — 400/6-8
1700 Pleasure Island Rd 54521 — 715-479-6479
Jacqueline Coghlan, prin. — Fax 479-7303

East Troy, Walworth, Pop. 4,046
East Troy Community SD — 1,700/K-12
2043 Division St 53120 — 262-642-6710
Robert Spence, supt. — Fax 642-6712
www.easttroy.k12.wi.us
East Troy HS — 600/9-12
3128 Graydon Ave 53120 — 262-642-6760
John Stockowitz, prin. — Fax 642-6776
East Troy MS — 400/6-8
3143 Graydon Ave 53120 — 262-642-6740
Michael Willeman, prin. — Fax 642-6743

Eau Claire, Eau Claire, Pop. 62,496
Eau Claire Area SD — 10,100/PK-12
500 Main St 54701 — 715-852-3000
Dr. William Klaus, supt. — Fax 852-3004
www.ecasd.k12.wi.us
Delong MS — 900/6-8
2000 Vine St 54703 — 715-852-4900
Dr. Deb Hansen, prin. — Fax 852-4904
Memorial HS — 1,800/9-12
2225 Keith St 54701 — 715-852-6300
Tim Leibham, prin. — Fax 852-6304
North HS — 1,600/9-12
1801 Piedmont Rd 54703 — 715-852-6600
Dave Valk, prin. — Fax 852-6604
Northstar MS — 600/6-8
2711 Abbe Hill Dr 54703 — 715-852-5100
Tom Fiedler, prin. — Fax 852-5104
South MS — 900/6-8
2115 Mitscher Ave 54701 — 715-852-5200
John Wallace, prin. — Fax 852-5204

Chippewa Valley Technical College — Post-Sec.
620 W Clairemont Ave 54701 — 715-833-6200
Eau Claire Academy — 100/3-12
PO Box 1168 54702 — 715-834-6681
Laurie Van Beek, prin. — Fax 834-9954

Immanuel Lutheran College HS — 100/9-12
501 Grover Rd 54701 — 715-836-6621
Jeffrey Schierenbeck, prin. — Fax 836-6634
Professional Hair Design Academy — Post-Sec.
3408 Mall Dr 54701 — 715-835-2345
Regis HS — 300/9-12
2100 Fenwick Ave 54701 — 715-830-2271
Cynthia Hofacker, prin. — Fax 830-5461
Regis MS — 100/7-8
2100 Fenwick Ave 54701 — 715-830-2272
William Uelmen, prin. — Fax 830-5461
Sacred Heart Hospital — Post-Sec.
900 W Clairemont Ave 54701 — 715-839-4131
University of Wisconsin — Post-Sec.
PO Box 4004 54702 — 715-836-2637

Edgar, Marathon, Pop. 1,354
Edgar SD — 600/PK-12
PO Box 196 54426 — 715-352-2351
Mark Lacke, supt. — Fax 352-3198
www.edgar.k12.wi.us/edgar/
Edgar HS — 200/9-12
PO Box 196 54426 — 715-352-2352
Bob Houts, prin. — Fax 352-3198
Edgar MS — 100/6-8
PO Box 198 54426 — 715-352-2727
Lisa Witt, prin. — Fax 352-3022

Edgerton, Rock, Pop. 4,926
Edgerton SD — 1,900/PK-12
200 Elm High Dr 53534 — 608-884-9402
Dr. Norman Fjelstad, supt. — Fax 884-9327
www.edgerton.k12.wi.us
Edgerton HS — 600/9-12
200 Elm High Dr 53534 — 608-884-9402
James Halberg, prin. — Fax 884-7969
Edgerton MS — 500/6-8
300 Elm High Dr 53534 — 608-884-9402
Kenneth Haugom, prin. — Fax 884-2279

Oaklawn Academy — 200/6-8
432 Liguori Rd 53534 — 608-884-3425
Javier Valenzuela, prin. — Fax 884-8175

Elcho, Langlade
Elcho SD — 400/PK-12
PO Box 800 54428 — 715-275-3205
Christopher Thomalla, supt. — Fax 275-4388
www.elcho.k12.wi.us
Elcho HS, PO Box 800 54428 — 100/9-12
Jason Tadlock, prin. — 715-275-3707

Elkhart Lake, Sheboygan, Pop. 1,034
Elkhart Lake - Glenbeulah SD — 400/PK-12
PO Box K 53020 — 920-876-3381
Jerry Smith, supt. — Fax 876-3511
www.elgs.com/
Elkhart Lake - Glenbeulah HS — 200/9-12
PO Box K 53020 — 920-876-3381
John Porior, prin. — Fax 876-3511
Elkhart Lake - Glenbeulah MS — 200/5-8
PO Box 518 53020 — 920-876-3307
Ann Buechel Haack, prin. — Fax 876-3105

Elkhorn, Walworth, Pop. 8,245
Elkhorn Area SD — 3,400/K-12
3 N Jackson St 53121 — 262-723-3160
Gregory Wescott, supt. — Fax 723-4652
www.elkhorn.k12.wi.us
Elkhorn Area HS — 800/9-12
482 E Geneva St 53121 — 262-723-4920
Gary Baumann, prin. — Fax 723-8092
Elkhorn Area MS — 600/6-8
627 E Court St 53121 — 262-723-6800
John Gendron, prin. — Fax 723-4967

Gateway Technical College — Post-Sec.
400 County Road H 53121 — 262-741-8200

Elk Mound, Dunn, Pop. 826
Elk Mound Area SD — 900/PK-12
405 University St 54739 — 715-879-5066
Ronald Walsh, supt. — Fax 879-5846
www.elkmound.k12.wi.us
Elk Mound HS — 300/9-12
405 University St 54739 — 715-879-5521
Paul Weber, prin. — Fax 879-5846
Elk Mound MS — 300/5-8
302 University St 54739 — 715-879-5595
Eric Wright, prin. — Fax 879-5846

Ellsworth, Pierce, Pop. 3,013
Ellsworth Community SD — 1,800/PK-12
PO Box 1500 54011 — 715-273-3900
Dan Kaler, supt. — Fax 273-5775
www.ellsworth.k12.wi.us
Ellsworth HS — 600/9-12
PO Box 1500 54011 — 715-273-3904
Charles Buckel, prin. — Fax 273-6824
Ellsworth MS — 400/6-8
PO Box 1500 54011 — 715-273-3908
Steve Broton, prin. — Fax 273-6834

Elm Grove, Waukesha, Pop. 6,290
Elmbrook SD
Supt. — See Brookfield
Pilgrim Park MS — 900/6-8
1500 Pilgrim Pkwy 53122 — 262-785-3920
Don Galster, prin. — Fax 785-3933

Elmwood, Pierce, Pop. 812
Elmwood SD — 400/PK-12
213 S Scott St 54740 — 715-639-2711
Barry Rose, supt. — Fax 639-3110
www.elmwood.k12.wi.us
Elmwood HS — 100/9-12
213 S Scott St 54740 — 715-639-2721
Barry Rose, prin. — Fax 639-3110

Elmwood MS | 100/7-8
213 S Scott St 54740 | 715-639-2721
Shawn Madden, prin. | Fax 639-3110

Elroy, Juneau, Pop. 1,535
Royall SD | 700/PK-12
PO Box 125 53929 | 608-462-2600
Scott A. Sarnow, supt. | Fax 462-2618
www.royall.k12.wi.us
Royall MSHS | 400/6-12
PO Box 125 53929 | 608-462-2602
Kevin Hoff, prin. | Fax 462-2604

Evansville, Rock, Pop. 4,289
Evansville Community SD | 1,700/PK-12
340 Fair St 53536 | 608-882-5224
Heidi Carvin, supt. | Fax 882-6564
www.evansville.k12.wi.us
Evansville HS | 500/9-12
640 S 5th St 53536 | 608-882-4600
Jamie Gillespie, prin. | Fax 882-6157
McKenna MS | 400/6-8
307 S 1st St 53536 | 608-882-4780
Jerry Roth, prin. | Fax 882-5744

Fall Creek, Eau Claire, Pop. 1,235
Fall Creek SD | 900/PK-12
336 E Hoover Ave 54742 | 715-877-2123
Gerry Nolan, supt. | Fax 877-2911
www.fallcreek.k12.wi.us
Fall Creek HS | 300/9-12
336 E Hoover Ave 54742 | 715-877-2809
Rob Taylor, prin. | Fax 877-2911
Fall Creek MS | 300/5-8
336 E Hoover Ave 54742 | 715-877-2511
Brian Schulner, prin. | Fax 877-2911

Fall River, Columbia, Pop. 1,133
Fall River SD | 400/PK-12
PO Box 116 53932 | 920-484-3327
Heidi A. Schmidt, supt. | Fax 484-3600
www.fallriver.k12.wi.us
Fall River HS | 200/6-12
PO Box 116 53932 | 920-484-3327
Bradley Johnsrud, prin. | Fax 484-3600

Fennimore, Grant, Pop. 2,349
Fennimore Community SD | 800/PK-12
1397 9th St 53809 | 608-822-3243
Richard Feutz, supt. | Fax 822-3250
www.fennimore.k12.wi.us
Fennimore JSHS | 400/7-12
510 7th St 53809 | 608-822-3245
Dan Bredeson, prin. | Fax 822-3247

Southwest Wisconsin Technical College | Post-Sec.
1800 Bronson Blvd 53809 | 608-822-3262

Fish Creek, Door
Gibraltar Area SD | 600/PK-12
3924 State Highway 42 54212 | 920-868-3284
Stephen Seyfer, supt. | Fax 868-2714
www.gibraltar.k12.wi.us
Gibraltar HS | 200/9-12
3924 State Highway 42 54212 | 920-868-3284
Kirk Knutson, prin. | Fax 868-2714
Gibraltar MS | 100/6-8
3924 State Highway 42 54212 | 920-868-3284
Kirk Knutson, prin. | Fax 868-2714

Fitchburg, Dane, Pop. 21,736
Verona Area SD
Supt. — See Verona
Savanna Oaks MS | 500/6-8
5890 Lacy Rd 53711 | 608-845-4000
Stephanie Edwards, prin. | Fax 845-4020

Florence, Florence
Florence SD | 700/PK-12
PO Box 440 54121 | 715-528-3217
Jan Dooley, supt. | Fax 528-5338
www.florence.k12.wi.us
Florence HS | 300/9-12
PO Box 440 54121 | 715-528-3215
Brandon Jerue, admin. | Fax 528-5330
Florence MS | 200/6-8
PO Box 440 54121 | 715-528-3215
Brandon Jerue, admin. | Fax 528-5338

Fond du Lac, Fond du Lac, Pop. 42,095
Fond du Lac SD | 7,100/K-12
72 W 9th St 54935 | 920-929-2900
Gregory R. Maass Ph.D., supt. | Fax 929-6804
www.fonddulac.k12.wi.us
Fond du Lac HS | 2,400/9-12
801 Campus Dr 54935 | 920-929-2740
Mary Fran Merwin, prin. | Fax 929-6964
Sabish MS | 600/6-8
100 N Peters Ave 54935 | 920-929-2800
Kelly Noble, prin. | Fax 929-2807
Theisen MS | 600/6-8
525 E Pioneer Rd 54935 | 920-929-2850
Kim Pahlow, prin. | Fax 929-2854
Woodworth MS | 500/6-8
101 Morningside Dr 54935 | 920-929-6900
Steven Hill, prin. | Fax 929-6944

FACES MS | 200/6-8
PO Box 2138 54936 | 920-921-9610
Susan Zackerl, prin. | Fax 921-0457
Fond du Lac Christian S | 100/K-12
720 Rienzi Rd 54935 | 920-924-2177
Wendy Lundberg, prin. | Fax 322-9459
Marian College of Fond du Lac | Post-Sec.
45 S National Ave 54935 | 920-923-7600
Moraine Park Technical College | Post-Sec.
235 N National Ave 54935 | 920-922-8611
St. Mary Springs HS | 400/9-12
255 County Road K 54935 | 920-921-4870
Tom Wonderling, prin. | Fax 921-2786

University of Wisconsin Center | Post-Sec.
400 University Dr 54935 | 920-929-3606
Winnebago Lutheran Academy | 300/9-12
475 E Merrill Ave 54935 | 920-921-4930
Randall Westphal, prin. | Fax 921-4280

Fort Atkinson, Jefferson, Pop. 11,781
Fort Atkinson SD | 2,600/PK-12
201 Park St 53538 | 920-563-7807
James Fitzpatrick, supt. | Fax 563-7809
www.fortschools.org
Fort Atkinson HS | 900/9-12
925 Lexington Blvd 53538 | 920-563-7811
Jeff Zaspel, prin. | Fax 563-7810
Fort Atkinson MS | 600/6-8
310 S 4th St E 53538 | 920-563-7833
Robert Abbott, prin. | Fax 563-7838

Fountain City, Buffalo, Pop. 940
Cochrane-Fountain City SD | 700/PK-12
S2770 State Highway 35 54629 | 608-687-7771
Steven Mieden, supt. | Fax 687-3312
www.cfc.k12.wi.us
Cochrane-Fountain City JSHS | 400/7-12
S2770 State Highway 35 54629 | 608-687-4391
John Zurbuchen, prin. | Fax 687-6412

Franklin, Milwaukee, Pop. 31,994
Franklin SD | 3,900/K-12
8255 W Forest Hill Ave 53132 | 414-529-8220
Bill Szakacs, supt. | Fax 529-8230
www.franklin.k12.wi.us
Forest Park MS | 600/7-8
8225 W Forest Hill Ave 53132 | 414-529-8250
Matthew Lesar, prin. | Fax 529-8249
Franklin HS | 1,400/9-12
8222 S 51st St 53132 | 414-423-4640
Michael Cady, prin. | Fax 421-0558

Frederic, Polk, Pop. 1,253
Frederic SD | 600/PK-12
1437 Clam Falls Dr 54837 | 715-327-5630
Gerald Tischer, supt. | Fax 327-5609
www.frederic.k12.wi.us/
Frederic JSHS | 300/6-12
1437 Clam Falls Dr 54837 | 715-327-4223
Raymond Draxler, prin. | Fax 327-8655

Fredonia, Ozaukee, Pop. 2,102
Northern Ozaukee SD | 900/PK-12
401 Highland Dr 53021 | 262-692-2489
William Harbron, supt. | Fax 692-6257
www.nosd.edu
Ozaukee HS | 300/9-12
401 Highland Dr 53021 | 262-692-2453
Kevin Parker, prin. | Fax 692-6257
Ozaukee MS | 200/5-8
401 Highland Dr 53021 | 262-692-2463
Pam Warner, prin. | Fax 692-2313

Freedom, Outagamie
Freedom Area SD | 1,600/PK-12
PO Box 1008 54131 | 920-788-7944
Lois Cuff, supt. | Fax 788-7949
www.freedomschools.k12.wi.us
Freedom HS | 500/9-12
PO Box 1003 54131 | 920-788-7940
Dannette Arndt, prin. | Fax 788-7700
Freedom MS | 300/6-8
PO Box 1002 54131 | 920-788-7945
Ken Fisher, prin. | Fax 788-7701

Friendship, Adams, Pop. 772
Adams-Friendship Area SD | 2,100/PK-12
201 W 6th St 53934 | 608-339-3213
Steven Lavallee, supt. | Fax 339-6213
af.k12.wi.us
Other Schools – See Adams

Galesville, Trempealeau, Pop. 1,408
Galesville-Ettrick-Trempealeau SD | 1,400/PK-12
PO Box 4000 54630 | 608-582-2291
Craig Gerlach, supt. | Fax 582-4263
www.getschools.k12.wi.us
Coulee Region HS | 9-12
16935 N Main St 54630 | 608-582-2200
Chuck Forster, prin. | Fax 582-4263
Gale-Ettrick-Tremp HS | 500/9-12
PO Box 4000 54630 | 608-582-2291
Chuck Forster, prin. | Fax 582-4263
Other Schools – See Trempealeau

Genoa City, Walworth, Pop. 2,394
Genoa City J2 SD | 600/K-8
PO Box 250 53128 | 262-279-1051
Bill Lehner, supt. | Fax 279-1052
Brookwood MS | 300/5-8
PO Box 250 53128 | 262-279-1053
Kellie Bohn, prin. | Fax 279-1052

Germantown, Washington, Pop. 18,973
Germantown SD | 3,700/PK-12
N104W13840 Donges Bay Rd 53022 | 262-253-3900
Victor Rossetti, supt. | Fax 251-6999
www.germantown.k12.wi.us
Germantown HS | 1,300/9-12
W180N11501 River Ln 53022 | 262-253-3400
Jim Blackburn, prin. | Fax 253-3494
Kennedy MS | 900/6-8
W160N11836 Crusader Ct 53022 | 262-253-3450
Steven Bold, prin. | Fax 253-3499

Gillett, Oconto, Pop. 1,222
Gillett SD | 800/PK-12
PO Box 227 54124 | 920-855-2137
Stuart Rivard, supt. | Fax 855-1557
www.gillett.k12.wi.us
Gillett HS | 300/9-12
PO Box 227 54124 | 920-855-2137
Sam Santacroce, prin. | Fax 855-6600

Gillett MS | 200/6-8
PO Box 227 54124 | 920-855-2138
Sam Santacroce, prin. | Fax 855-6600

Gilman, Taylor, Pop. 469
Gilman SD | 500/PK-12
325 N 5th Ave 54433 | 715-447-8216
Drew Johnson, supt. | Fax 447-8731
www.gilman.k12.wi.us
Gilman S | 500/PK-12
325 N 5th Ave 54433 | 715-447-8211
Dawn Randall, prin. | Fax 447-8731

Gilmanton, Buffalo
Gilmanton SD | 200/PK-12
PO Box 28 54743 | 715-946-3158
William Perry, supt. | Fax 946-3474
www.ghs.k12.wi.us
Gilmanton JSHS | 100/7-12
PO Box 28 54743 | 715-946-3158
William Perry, prin. | Fax 946-3474

Glendale, Milwaukee, Pop. 13,181
Glendale-River Hills SD | 1,000/PK-8
2600 W Mill Rd 53209 | 414-351-7170
Dr. Frances B. Smith, supt. | Fax 434-0109
www.glendale.k12.wi.us
Glen Hills MS | 500/5-8
2600 W Mill Rd 53209 | 414-351-7160
Larry Smalley, prin. | Fax 351-8100
Maple Dale-Indian Hill SD | 500/PK-8
2600 W Mill Rd 53209 | 414-351-7170
Dr. Frances Smith, supt. | Fax 434-0109
www.mapledale.k12.wi.us
Other Schools – See Milwaukee

Nicolet UNHSD | 1,400/9-12
6701 N Jean Nicolet Rd 53217 | 414-351-7520
Dr. Elliott Moeser, supt. | Fax 351-7526
nicolet.k12.wi.us
Nicolet Union HS | 1,400/9-12
6701 N Jean Nicolet Rd 53217 | 414-351-1700
Dr. Elliott Moeser, prin. | Fax 351-7526

Glenwood City, Saint Croix, Pop. 1,200
Glenwood City SD | 800/K-12
PO Box 339 54013 | 715-265-4757
Timothy J. Emholtz, supt. | Fax 265-4214
www.gcsd.k12.wi.us/
Glenwood City HS | 300/9-12
PO Box 339 54013 | 715-265-4266
Timothy Johnson, prin. | Fax 265-7129
Glenwood City JHS | 100/7-8
PO Box 339 54013 | 715-265-4266
Timothy Johnson, prin.

Glidden, Ashland
Glidden SD | 200/PK-12
RR 1 Box 1 54527 | 715-264-2141
Mark W. Luoma, supt. | Fax 264-3413
www.glidden.k12.wi.us
Glidden S | 200/PK-12
RR 1 Box 1 54527 | 715-264-2141
Mark Luoma, prin. | Fax 264-3413

Goodman, Marinette
Goodman-Armstrong Creek SD | 200/PK-12
PO Box 160 54125 | 715-336-2575
Dennis Christian, supt. | Fax 336-2576
www.goodman.k12.wi.us
Goodman JSHS | 100/7-12
PO Box 160 54125 | 715-336-2575
Jeff Reeder, prin. | Fax 336-2576

Grafton, Ozaukee, Pop. 11,356
Grafton SD | 2,000/PK-12
1900 Washington St 53024 | 262-376-5400
Jeffrey Pechura, supt. | Fax 376-5599
www.grafton.k12.wi.us/
Grafton HS | 800/9-12
1950 Washington St 53024 | 262-376-5500
Ken McCormick, prin. | Fax 376-5510
Long MS | 400/6-8
700 Hickory St 53024 | 262-376-5800
Tom Engle, prin. | Fax 376-5810

Granton, Clark, Pop. 402
Granton Area SD | 300/K-12
217 N Main St 54436 | 715-238-7292
Gerald Nelson, supt. | Fax 238-7288
www.granton.k12.wi.us/
Granton HS | 100/9-12
217 N Main St 54436 | 715-238-7175
Craig Anderson, prin. | Fax 238-7827

Grantsburg, Burnett, Pop. 1,410
Grantsburg SD | 1,000/PK-12
480 E James Ave 54840 | 715-463-5499
Joni Burgin, supt. | Fax 463-2534
www.gk12.net/
Grantsburg HS | 300/9-12
480 E James Ave 54840 | 715-463-2531
Jeff Bush, prin. | Fax 463-5068
Grantsburg MS | 400/4-8
480 E James Ave 54840 | 715-463-2455
Brad Jones, prin. | Fax 463-3209

Gratiot, Lafayette, Pop. 256
Black Hawk SD
Supt. — See South Wayne
Black Hawk MS | 200/5-8
PO Box 457 53541 | 608-922-6457
Kevin Shetler, prin. | Fax 922-3376

Green Bay, Brown, Pop. 101,467
Ashwaubenon SD | 3,100/PK-12
1055 Griffiths Ln 54304 | 920-492-2900
Sue Alberti, supt. | Fax 492-2911
www.ashwaubenon.k12.wi.us

Ashwaubenon HS | 1,100/9-12
2391 S Ridge Rd 54304 | 920-492-2950
Mark Sheedy, prin. | Fax 492-2912
Parkview MS | 800/6-8
955 Willard Dr 54304 | 920-492-2940
Rae Bennett, prin. | Fax 492-2944

Green Bay Area SD | 20,400/PK-12
PO Box 23387 54305 | 920-448-2000
Daniel Nerad, supt. | Fax 448-3562
www.greenbay.k12.wi.us
East HS | 1,400/9-12
1415 E Walnut St 54301 | 920-448-2090
Ed Dorff, prin. | Fax 448-2166
Edison MS | 1,200/6-8
442 Alpine Dr 54302 | 920-391-2450
Rodney Bohm, prin. | Fax 391-2531
Franklin MS | 900/6-8
1234 W Mason St 54303 | 920-492-2670
Matthew Weller, prin. | Fax 492-5563
Lombardi MS | 1,000/6-8
1520 S Point Rd 54313 | 920-492-2625
Nancy Croy, prin. | Fax 492-5564
Preble HS | 2,100/9-12
2222 Deckner Ave 54302 | 920-391-2400
Christopher Wagner, prin. | Fax 391-2530
Southwest HS | 1,500/9-12
1331 Packerland Dr 54304 | 920-492-2650
Bryan Davis, prin. | Fax 492-5561
Washington MS | 1,000/6-8
314 S Baird St 54301 | 920-448-2095
Amy Bindas, prin. | Fax 448-3551
West HS | 1,300/9-12
966 Shawano Ave 54303 | 920-492-2600
Luke Valitchka, prin. | Fax 492-2641

Howard-Suamico SD | 4,700/PK-12
2700 Lineville Rd 54313 | 920-662-7878
Donald Childs, supt. | Fax 662-9777
www.hssd.k12.wi.us
Bay Port HS | 1,500/9-12
2710 Lineville Rd 54313 | 920-662-7000
Michael Frieder, prin. | Fax 662-7291
Bay View MS | 800/7-8
1217 Cardinal Ln 54313 | 920-662-8196
Steve Meyers, prin. | Fax 662-7979

Bay City Baptist S | 100/PK-12
1840 Bond St 54303 | 920-499-5561
Ray Anderson, prin. | Fax 499-5619
Bellin College of Nursing | Post-Sec.
PO Box 23400 54305 | 920-433-5803
Bellin Hospital | Post-Sec.
PO Box 23400 54305 | 920-433-3673
Martin's College of Cosmetology | Post-Sec.
2575 W Mason St 54303 | 920-494-1430
Northeastern Wisconsin Lutheran HS | 100/9-12
1311 S Robinson Ave 54311 | 920-469-6810
Stephen Siekmann, prin. | Fax 469-2200
Northeast Wisconsin Technical College | Post-Sec.
PO Box 19042 54307 | 920-498-5400
Notre Dame De La Baie Academy | 700/9-12
610 Maryhill Dr 54303 | 920-429-6100
Dr. Mark Schmidt, prin. | Fax 429-6168
St. Vincent Hospital | Post-Sec.
PO Box 13508 54307 | 920-433-8155
University of Wisconsin | Post-Sec.
2420 Nicolet Dr 54311 | 920-465-2000
Wisconsin College of Cosmetology | Post-Sec.
2960 Allied St 54304 | 920-336-8888

Greendale, Milwaukee, Pop. 14,183
Greendale SD | 2,300/PK-12
5900 S 51st St 53129 | 414-423-2700
William Hughes, supt. | Fax 423-2723
www.greendale.k12.wi.us
Greendale HS | 900/9-12
6801 Southway 53129 | 414-423-0110
Peter DeRubeis, prin. | Fax 423-1667
Greendale MS | 500/6-8
6800 Schoolway 53129 | 414-423-2800
Steve Lodes, prin. | Fax 423-2806

Martin Luther HS | 400/9-12
5201 S 76th St 53129 | 414-421-4000
Carl Eisman, admin. | Fax 421-4071

Greenfield, Milwaukee, Pop. 36,101
Greenfield SD | 3,400/PK-12
8500 W Chapman Ave 53228 | 414-529-9090
Louis Birchbauer, supt. | Fax 529-9478
www.greenfield.k12.wi.us
Greenfield HS | 1,200/9-12
4800 S 60th St 53220 | 414-281-6200
John Thomsen, prin. | Fax 281-8860
Greenfield MS | 700/6-8
3200 W Barnard Ave 53221 | 414-282-4700
Todd Bugnacki, prin. | Fax 282-1017

Whitnall SD | 2,500/PK-12
5000 S 116th St 53228 | 414-525-8400
Karen Petric, supt. | Fax 525-8401
www.whitnall.com
Whitnall HS | 1,000/9-12
5000 S 116th St 53228 | 414-525-8500
Joel Eul, prin. | Fax 525-8501
Whitnall MS | 600/6-8
5025 S 116th St 53228 | 414-525-8650
John Lehnen, prin. | Fax 525-8651

Green Lake, Green Lake, Pop. 1,115
Green Lake SD | 400/PK-12
PO Box 369 54941 | 920-294-6411
Nancy Burns, supt. | Fax 294-6589
www.greenlakeschools.com
Green Lake JSHS | 200/7-12
PO Box 369 54941 | 920-294-6411
Nancy Burns, prin. | Fax 294-6589

Greenville, Outagamie
Hortonville SD
Supt. — See Hortonville
Greenville MS | 300/6-8
N1450 Fawn Ridge Dr 54942 | 920-757-7140
Bruce Carew, prin. | Fax 757-7141

Greenwood, Clark, Pop. 1,092
Greenwood SD | 500/PK-12
306 W Central Ave 54437 | 715-267-6101
Marsha Hochhalter, supt. | Fax 267-6113
www.greenwood.k12.wi.us/
Greenwood MSHS | 300/7-12
306 W Central Ave 54437 | 715-267-6101
David Schaller, prin. | Fax 267-6113

Gresham, Shawano, Pop. 587
Shawano-Gresham SD
Supt. — See Shawano
Gresham HS | 100/9-12
501 Schabow St 54128 | 715-787-3211
Robert Klopke, prin. | Fax 787-3951

Hales Corners, Milwaukee, Pop. 7,688

Hales Corners Lutheran MS | 100/6-8
12300 W Janesville Rd 53130 | 414-529-6700
Albert Amling, prin. | Fax 529-6712
Sacred Heart School of Theology | Post-Sec.
PO Box 429 53130 | 414-425-8300

Hammond, Saint Croix, Pop. 1,643
St. Croix Central SD | 1,100/PK-12
1751 Broadway St 54015 | 715-796-5383
Dan Woll, supt. | Fax 796-5662
www.scc.k12.wi.us
St. Croix HS | 300/9-12
1751 Broadway St 54015 | 715-796-5383
Glenn Webb, prin. | Fax 796-5662
St. Croix MS | 200/7-8
PO Box 118 54015 | 715-796-2256
Scott Woodington, prin. | Fax 796-2460

Hartford, Washington, Pop. 11,852
Hartford J1 SD | 1,600/PK-8
675 E Rossman St 53027 | 262-673-3155
Dr. Mark Smits, admin. | Fax 673-3548
www.hartfordjt1.k12.wi.us
Central MS | 600/6-8
1100 Cedar St 53027 | 262-673-8040
Wayne Thuecks, prin. | Fax 673-7596

Hartford UNHSD | 1,700/9-12
805 Cedar St 53027 | 262-673-8950
Jeff Tortomasi, supt. | Fax 673-8943
www.huhs.org
Hartford Union HS | 1,700/9-12
805 Cedar St 53027 | 262-673-8950
Mary Koehl, prin. | Fax 673-8943

Hartland, Waukesha, Pop. 8,558
Arrowhead UNHSD | 1,200/9-12
700 North Ave 53029 | 262-369-3611
David Lodes Ph.D., supt. | Fax 367-7406
www.arrowheadschools.org
Arrowhead Union HS - North Campus | 11-12
800 North Ave 53029 | 262-369-3612
Bonnie Laugerman Ed.D., prin. | Fax 369-0996
Arrowhead Union HS - South Campus | 1,200/9-10
700 North Ave 53029 | 262-369-3611
Gregg Wieczorek, prin. | Fax 367-4693

Hartland-Lakeside J3 SD | 1,400/PK-8
800 N Shore Dr 53029 | 262-369-6700
John Ehle, supt. | Fax 369-6755
www.hartlake.org
North Shore MS | 500/6-8
800 N Shore Dr 53029 | 262-369-6767
Dale Fisher, prin. | Fax 369-6766

University Lake S | 300/PK-12
PO Box 290 53029 | 262-367-6011
Bradley F. Ashley, hdmstr. | Fax 367-3146

Hayward, Sawyer, Pop. 2,245
Hayward Community SD | 1,900/PK-12
PO Box 860 54843 | 715-634-2616
Michael Cox, supt. | Fax 634-3560
www.hayward.k12.wi.us
Hayward HS | 600/9-12
PO Box 860 54843 | 715-634-2616
William Mestelle, prin. | Fax 634-2761
Hayward MS | 500/6-8
PO Box 860 54843 | 715-634-2619
Jane Gillis, prin. | Fax 634-9953

Lac Courte Oreilles Ojibwa Comm College | Post-Sec.
13466 W Trepania Rd 54843 | 715-634-4790
Northern Lights Christian Academy | 50/K-12
PO Box 757 54843 | 715-634-5040
Sandra Warner, admin. | Fax 634-7373

Hazel Green, Grant, Pop. 1,188
Southwestern Wisconsin SD | 600/PK-12
PO Box 368 53811 | 608-854-2261
James Egan, supt. | Fax 854-2305
www.swsd.k12.wi.us
Southwestern Wisconsin HS | 200/9-12
PO Box 368 53811 | 608-854-2261
Janet Kunert, prin. | Fax 854-2315

Highland, Iowa, Pop. 834
Highland SD | 300/PK-12
PO Box 2850 53543 | 608-929-4525
David Romstad, supt. | Fax 929-4527
www.highland.k12.wi.us
Highland HS | 200/6-12
1030 Cardinal Dr 53543 | 608-929-4525
Mitch Wainwright, prin. | Fax 929-4527

Hilbert, Calumet, Pop. 1,096
Hilbert SD | 500/PK-12
PO Box 390 54129 | 920-853-3558
Dr. Debra Hunt, supt. | Fax 853-7030
www.hilbert.k12.wi.us
Hilbert HS | 200/9-12
PO Box 390 54129 | 920-853-3558
Dr. Debra Hunt, prin. | Fax 853-7030
Hilbert MS | 100/7-8
PO Box 390 54129 | 920-853-3558
Martha Albers, prin. | Fax 853-7030

Hillsboro, Vernon, Pop. 1,304
Hillsboro SD | 600/PK-12
PO Box 526 54634 | 608-489-2221
Ron Benish, supt. | Fax 489-2811
www.hillsboro.k12.wi.us
Hillsboro JSHS | 300/7-12
PO Box 526 54634 | 608-489-2221
Greg Zimmerman, prin. | Fax 489-2811

Holcombe, Chippewa
Lake Holcombe SD | 500/PK-12
27331 262nd Ave 54745 | 715-595-4241
Tom Goulet, supt. | Fax 595-6383
lakeholcombe.k12.wi.us
Holcombe HS | 200/9-12
27331 262nd Ave 54745 | 715-595-4241
Mark Porter, prin. | Fax 595-6383

Holmen, LaCrosse, Pop. 6,976
Holmen SD | 3,100/PK-12
PO Box 580 54636 | 608-526-6610
Fred Frick, supt. | Fax 526-1333
www.holmen.k12.wi.us
Holmen HS | 900/9-12
PO Box 430 54636 | 608-526-3372
Bernie Ferry, prin. | Fax 526-9446
Holmen MS | 700/6-8
PO Box 490 54636 | 608-526-3391
Roger Kordus, prin. | Fax 526-6716

Horicon, Dodge, Pop. 3,690
Horicon SD | 1,000/PK-12
611 Mill St 53032 | 920-485-2898
James A. McCartney, supt. | Fax 485-3601
www.horicon.k12.wi.us
Horicon HS | 400/9-12
841 Gray St 53032 | 920-485-4441
Jeffrey Higgins, prin. | Fax 485-3244
Van Brunt MS | 200/6-8
611 Mill St 53032 | 920-485-4423
Scott Miller, prin. | Fax 485-4318

Hortonville, Outagamie, Pop. 2,470
Hortonville SD | 3,000/PK-12
PO Box 70 54944 | 920-779-7900
Gregory Joseph, supt. | Fax 779-7903
www.hasd.org
Hortonville HS | 1,000/9-12
PO Box 220 54944 | 920-779-7933
Bob McIntosh, prin. | Fax 779-7935
Hortonville MS | 400/6-8
PO Box 70 54944 | 920-779-7922
John Brattlund, prin. | Fax 779-7923
Other Schools – See Greenville

Howards Grove, Sheboygan, Pop. 2,880
Howards Grove SD | 1,000/K-12
403 Audubon Rd 53083 | 920-565-4454
John Eickholt, supt. | Fax 565-4461
Howards Grove HS | 400/9-12
401 Audubon Rd 53083 | 920-565-4450
Mark Holzman, prin. | Fax 565-4451
Howards Grove MS | 300/5-8
506 Kennedy Ave 53083 | 920-565-4452
Andy Hansen, prin. | Fax 565-4460

Hudson, Saint Croix, Pop. 10,240
Hudson SD | 4,600/PK-12
1401 Vine St 54016 | 715-377-3700
Mary Bowen-Eggebraaten, supt. | Fax 377-3701
www.hudson.k12.wi.us
Hudson HS | 1,500/9-12
1501 Vine St 54016 | 715-377-3800
Ed Lucas, prin. | Fax 377-3801
Hudson MS | 1,100/6-8
1300 Carmichael Rd 54016 | 715-377-3820
Dan Koch, prin. | Fax 377-3821

Hurley, Iron, Pop. 1,734
Hurley SD | 800/PK-12
5503 W Rangeview Dr 54534 | 715-561-4900
Christopher Patritto, supt. | Fax 561-4953
www.hurley.k12.wi.us
Hurley JSHS | 400/6-12
5503 W Rangeview Dr 54534 | 715-561-4900
Elizabeth Jorgensen, prin. | Fax 561-4157

Hustisford, Dodge, Pop. 1,119
Hustisford SD | 400/PK-12
PO Box 326 53034 | 920-349-8109
Ed Van Ravenstein, supt. | Fax 349-3716
www.hustisford.k12.wi.us
Hustisford JSHS | 200/7-12
PO Box 326 53034 | 920-349-3261
Jeremy Biehl, prin. | Fax 349-8495

Independence, Trempealeau, Pop. 1,249
Independence SD | 300/PK-12
23786 Indee Blvd 54747 | 715-985-3172
Dave Laehn, supt. | Fax 985-2303
www.indps.k12.wi.us
Independence HS | 100/9-12
23786 Indee Blvd 54747 | 715-985-3172
Dave Laehn, prin. | Fax 985-2303

Iola, Waupaca, Pop. 1,262

Iola-Scandinavia SD | 800/PK-12
450 Division St 54945 | 715-445-2411
Joseph Price, supt. | Fax 445-4468
www.iola.k12.wi.us/
Iola-Scandinavia JSHS | 400/7-12
540 S Jackson St 54945 | 715-445-2411
Sara Anderson, prin. | Fax 445-5119

Jackson, Washington, Pop. 5,676

Kettle Moraine Lutheran HS | 400/9-12
3399 Division Rd 53037 | 262-677-4051
Stephen Granberg, prin. | Fax 677-4290
Living Word Lutheran HS | 50/9-12
2230 Living Word Ln 53037 | 262-677-9353
Dr. Cary Stelmachowicz, prin. | Fax 677-8357

Janesville, Rock, Pop. 61,145

Janesville SD | 10,600/PK-12
527 S Franklin St, | 608-743-5000
Thomas Evert, supt. | Fax 743-5110
janesville.k12.wi.us/sdj
Craig HS | 1,800/9-12
401 S Randall Ave 53545 | 608-743-5200
Michael Kuehne, prin. | Fax 743-5150
Edison MS | 700/6-8
1649 S Chatham St 53546 | 608-743-5900
Steve Sperry, prin. | Fax 743-5910
Franklin MS | 700/6-8
450 N Crosby Ave, | 608-743-6000
Kim Ehrhardt, prin. | Fax 743-6010
Marshall MS | 1,000/6-8
25 S Pontiac Dr 53545 | 608-743-6200
Steven Salerno, prin. | Fax 743-6210
Parker HS | 1,800/9-12
3125 Mineral Point Ave, | 608-743-5600
Dale Carlson, prin. | Fax 743-5550

Blackhawk Technical College | Post-Sec.
PO Box 5009 53547 | 608-758-6900
Oakhill Christian S | 100/K-12
1650 S Oakhill Ave 53546 | 608-754-2759
Charlene Meiklejohn, admin. | Fax 754-2159
University of Wisconsin Center | Post-Sec.
2909 Kellogg Ave 53546 | 608-755-2823
WI School for Visually Handicapped | Post-Sec.
1700 W State St 53546 | 608-758-6100

Jefferson, Jefferson, Pop. 7,388

Jefferson SD | 1,700/PK-12
206 S Taft Ave 53549 | 920-675-1000
Michael Swartz, supt. | Fax 675-1020
www.jefferson.k12.wi.us
Jefferson HS | 600/9-12
700 W Milwaukee St 53549 | 920-675-1100
Richard Lovett, prin. | Fax 675-1120
Jefferson MS | 400/6-8
501 S Taft Ave 53549 | 920-675-1300
Mark Rollefson, prin. | Fax 675-1320

St. Coletta School, RR 1 Box 43 53549 | Post-Sec.

Johnson Creek, Jefferson, Pop. 1,761

Johnson Creek SD | 600/PK-12
PO Box 39 53038 | 920-699-2811
C. Scott Huth, supt. | Fax 699-2801
www.johnsoncreek.k12.wi.us/
Johnson Creek HS | 300/7-12
PO Box 39 53038 | 920-699-3481
Eric Ranzen, prin. | Fax 699-3566

Juda, Green

Juda SD | 300/PK-12
N2385 Spring St 53550 | 608-934-5251
Gary Scheuerell, supt. | Fax 934-5254
www.juda.k12.wi.us
Juda HS | 100/9-12
N2385 Spring St 53550 | 608-934-5251
Gary Scheuerell, prin. | Fax 934-5254

Juneau, Dodge, Pop. 2,472

Dodgeland SD | 600/PK-12
401 S Western Ave 53039 | 920-386-4404
Joseph G. Reed, supt. | Fax 386-4498
www.dodgeland.k12.wi.us
Dodgeland HS | 200/9-12
401 S Western Ave 53039 | 920-386-4404
Steven Schiller, prin. | Fax 386-2601
Dodgeland MS | 6-8
401 S Western Ave 53039 | 920-386-4404
Michelle Weidemann, prin. | Fax 386-2601

Kansasville, Racine

Providence Catholic S - West Campus | 100/5-8
1714 240th Ave 53139 | 262-878-2713

Kaukauna, Outagamie, Pop. 14,121

Kaukauna Area SD | 3,700/PK-12
112 Main Ave 54130 | 920-766-6100
Lloyd McCabe, supt. | Fax 766-6104
www.kaukauna.k12.wi.us
Kaukauna HS | 1,300/9-12
1701 County Road CE 54130 | 920-766-6113
Joe Lewis, prin. | Fax 766-6157
River View MS | 800/6-8
101 Oak St 54130 | 920-766-6111
Mark Elworthy, prin. | Fax 766-6109

Holy Cross S | 300/3-8
220 Doty St 54130 | 920-766-0186
Elizabeth Watson, prin. | Fax 759-2428

Kenosha, Kenosha, Pop. 92,871

Kenosha SD | 19,900/PK-12
PO Box 340 53141 | 262-653-6320
R. Scott Pierce, supt. | Fax 653-7672
www.kusd.edu/

Bradford HS | 2,000/9-12
3700 Washington Rd 53144 | 262-653-6200
Jean Schlais, prin. | Fax 653-5948
Bullen MS | 800/6-8
2804 39th Ave 53144 | 262-597-4460
Bill Haithcock, prin. | Fax 597-4487
Indian Trail Academy | 1,100/9-12
6800 60th St 53144 | 262-653-0317
Richard Aiello, prin. | Fax 653-9956
Lakeview Technology Academy | Vo/Tech
9449 88th Ave 53158 | 262-947-8155
William Hittman, prin. | Fax 947-8159
Lance MS | 1,000/6-8
4515 80th St 53142 | 262-942-2240
Bethany Ormseth, prin. | Fax 942-2184
Lincoln MS | 800/6-8
6729 18th Ave 53143 | 262-653-6296
Margaret Modory, prin. | Fax 653-5966
Mahone MS | 900/6-8
6900 60th St 53144 | 262-605-8100
Brian Edwards, prin. | Fax 605-6851
McKinley MS | 700/6-8
5710 32nd Ave 53144 | 262-653-6367
Sharon Miller, prin. | Fax 653-6089
Reuther Central HS | 600/9-12
913 57th St 53140 | 262-653-6160
Daniel Tenuta, prin. | Fax 653-6281
Tremper HS | 2,300/9-12
8560 26th Ave 53143 | 262-942-2200
Ed Kupka, prin. | Fax 942-2187
Washington MS | 700/6-8
811 Washington Rd 53140 | 262-653-6291
Elizabeth Sabo, prin. | Fax 653-6056

Carthage College | Post-Sec.
2001 Alford Park Dr 53140 | 262-551-8500
Christian Life S | 800/PK-12
10700 75th St 53142 | 262-694-3900
Paul Blount, admin. | Fax 694-3312
Gateway Technical College | Post-Sec.
3520 30th Ave 53144 | 262-564-2200
St. Joseph HS | 500/7-12
2401 69th St 53143 | 262-654-8651
Robert Freund, prin. | Fax 654-1615
University of Wisconsin | Post-Sec.
PO Box 2000 53141 | 262-595-2345

Keshena, Menominee, Pop. 685

Menominee Indian SD | 900/K-12
PO Box 1330 54135 | 715-799-3824
Wendell Waukau, supt. | Fax 799-4659
www.misd.k12.wi.us
Menominee Indian HS | 300/9-12
PO Box 850 54135 | 715-799-3846
Charles Raasch, prin. | Fax 799-5558
Other Schools – See Neopit

College of Menominee Nation | Post-Sec.
PO Box 1179 54135 | 715-799-5600

Kewaskum, Washington, Pop. 3,436

Kewaskum SD | 1,800/PK-12
PO Box 37 53040 | 262-626-8427
Scott Peterson, supt. | Fax 626-2961
www.kewaskumschools.org
Kewaskum HS | 700/9-12
PO Box 426 53040 | 262-626-8427
Christine Horbas, prin. | Fax 626-4214
Kewaskum MS | 400/6-8
PO Box 432 53040 | 262-626-8427
Ken Soerens, prin. | Fax 626-4014

Kewaunee, Kewaunee, Pop. 2,863

Kewaunee SD | 800/PK-12
915 2nd St 54216 | 920-388-3230
Barbara Lundgren, supt. | Fax 388-5174
www.kewaunee.k12.wi.us
Kewaunee HS | 400/9-12
911 3rd St 54216 | 920-388-2951
Michael Holtz, prin. | Fax 388-5165
Kewaunee MS | 5-8
921 3rd St 54216 | 920-388-2458
Marge Weichelt, prin. | Fax 388-5696

Kiel, Manitowoc, Pop. 3,480

Kiel Area SD | 1,400/PK-12
PO Box 201 53042 | 920-894-2266
Jerry Schutz, supt. | Fax 894-5100
www.kiel.k12.wi.us/
Kiel HS | 600/9-12
210 Raider Hts 53042 | 920-894-2263
Dario Talerico, prin. | Fax 894-5101
Kiel MS | 400/5-8
PO Box 197 53042 | 920-894-2264
David Slosser, prin. | Fax 894-5121

Kieler, Grant

Immaculate Conception S | 100/4-8
PO Box 129 53812 | 608-568-7220
Beverly Florence, prin. | Fax 568-3811

Kimberly, Outagamie, Pop. 6,237

Kimberly Area SD | 3,800/PK-12
217 E Kimberly Ave 54136 | 920-788-7900
Mel Lightner, supt. | Fax 788-7919
www.kimberly.k12.wi.us
Gerritts MS | 800/6-8
545 S John St 54136 | 920-788-7905
Cathy Clarksen, prin. | Fax 788-7914
Kimberly HS | 1,100/9-12
W2662 Kennedy Ave 54136 | 920-687-3024
Michael Rietveld, prin. | Fax 687-3029

Kohler, Sheboygan, Pop. 1,945

Kohler SD | 500/PK-12
333 Upper Rd 53044 | 920-459-2920
Jeffrey Dickert, supt. | Fax 459-2940
www.kohler.k12.wi.us

Kohler JSHS | 200/7-12
333 Upper Rd 53044 | 920-459-2921
Lance Northey, prin. | Fax 459-2930

La Crosse, LaCrosse, Pop. 51,001

La Crosse SD | 7,100/PK-12
807 East Ave S 54601 | 608-789-7600
Gerald R. Kember, supt. | Fax 789-7960
www.lacrosseschools.com/
Central HS | 1,400/9-12
1801 Losey Blvd S 54601 | 608-789-7900
Thomas Barth, prin. | Fax 789-7931
Lincoln MS | 300/6-8
510 9th St S 54601 | 608-789-7780
Larry D. Myhra, prin. | Fax 789-7181
Logan HS | 1,000/9-12
1500 Ranger Dr 54603 | 608-789-7700
Scott L. Mihalovic, prin. | Fax 789-7711
Logan MS | 600/6-8
1450 Avon St 54603 | 608-789-7740
Troy Harcey, prin. | Fax 789-7754
Longfellow MS | 600/6-8
1900 Denton St 54601 | 608-789-7670
Penny Reedy, prin. | Fax 789-7975

Aquinas HS | 400/9-12
315 11th St S 54601 | 608-784-0287
Phillip Hahn, prin. | Fax 782-8851
Aquinas MS South Campus | 200/7-8
315 11th St S 54601 | 608-784-0156
Patricia Kosmatka, prin. | Fax 784-0229
Gunderson Medical Foundation | Post-Sec.
1836 South Ave 54601 | 608-782-7300
Scientific College of Beauty/Barbering | Post-Sec.
326 Pearl St 54601 | 608-784-4702
University of Wisconsin - LaCrosse | Post-Sec.
1725 State St 54601 | 608-785-8000
Viterbo University | Post-Sec.
815 9th St S 54601 | 608-796-3000
Western Wisconsin Technical College | Post-Sec.
PO Box 908 54601 | 608-785-9200

Ladysmith, Rusk, Pop. 3,835

Ladysmith-Hawkins SD | 1,100/PK-12
1700 Edgewood Ave E 54848 | 715-532-5277
James Schuchardt, supt. | Fax 532-7445
www.lhsd.k12.wi.us/
Ladysmith HS | 300/9-12
1700 Edgewood Ave E 54848 | 715-532-5531
Robert King, prin. | Fax 532-5961
Ladysmith MS | 200/6-8
115 E 6th St S 54848 | 715-532-5252
Kurt Lindau, prin. | Fax 532-7455

La Farge, Vernon, Pop. 773

La Farge SD | 300/PK-12
301 W Adams St 54639 | 608-625-0103
Al Szepi, admin. | Fax 625-0118
www.lafarge.k12.wi.us/
La Farge HS | 100/9-12
301 W Adams St 54639 | 608-625-2400
Jack Sulik, prin. | Fax 625-0152
La Farge MS | 100/6-8
301 W Adams St 54639 | 608-625-2400
Jack Sulik, prin. | Fax 625-0152

Lake Geneva, Walworth, Pop. 7,369

Lake Geneva J1 SD | 1,700/K-8
208 E South St 53147 | 262-348-1000
James Gottinger, supt. | Fax 248-9704
www.lakegenevaschools.com
Lake Geneva MS | 600/6-8
600 N Bloomfield Rd 53147 | 262-348-3000
Donna Jaeger, prin. | Fax 348-3092
Lake Geneva-Genoa City UHSD | 1,300/9-12
208 E South St 53147 | 262-348-1000
James Gottinger, supt. | Fax 248-9704
www.lakegenevaschools.com
Badger HS | 1,300/9-12
220 E South St 53147 | 262-348-2000
Steve McNeal, prin. | Fax 248-6178

Lake Mills, Jefferson, Pop. 4,875

Lake Mills Area SD | 1,200/PK-12
120 E Lake Park Pl 53551 | 920-648-2215
Dean Sanders, supt. | Fax 648-5795
www.lakemills.k12.wi.us
Lake Mills HS | 400/9-12
615 Catlin Dr 53551 | 920-648-2355
Robert Gilpatrick, prin. | Fax 648-2357
Lake Mills MS | 300/6-8
318 College St 53551 | 920-648-2358
Doris Thompson, prin. | Fax 648-8928

Lakeside Lutheran HS | 400/9-12
231 Woodland Beach Rd 53551 | 920-648-2321
James Grasby, prin. | Fax 648-5625

Lancaster, Grant, Pop. 3,981

Lancaster Community SD | 1,000/PK-12
925 W Maple St 53813 | 608-723-2175
Robert Wagner, supt. | Fax 723-6397
www.lancastersd.k12.wi.us
Lancaster HS | 400/9-12
806 E Elm St 53813 | 608-723-2173
Gary Swanstrom, prin. | Fax 723-2441
Lancaster MS | 300/6-8
802 E Elm St 53813 | 608-723-6425
Gary Swanstrom, prin. | Fax 723-6731

Land O Lakes, Vilas

Conserve S | 600/9-12
5400 N Black Oak Lake Rd 54540 | 715-547-1300
Stefan Anderson, hdmstr. | Fax 547-1386

Laona, Forest
Laona SD ... 300/PK-12
PO Box 100 54541 ... 715-674-2143
Storm Carroll, supt. ... Fax 674-5904
www.laona.k12.wi.us
Laona JSHS ... 100/7-12
PO Box 100 54541 ... 715-674-2143
James Hansen, prin. ... Fax 674-5904

Lena, Oconto, Pop. 516
Lena SD ... 500/PK-12
PO Box 48 54139 ... 920-829-5703
Robert Werley, supt. ... Fax 829-5122
www.lena.k12.wi.us
Lena HS ... 200/9-12
PO Box 48 54139 ... 920-829-5244
David Honish, prin. ... Fax 829-5122
Lena MS ... 100/5-8
PO Box 48 54139 ... 920-829-5244
David Honish, prin. ... Fax 829-5122

Little Chute, Outagamie, Pop. 10,737
Little Chute Area SD ... 1,500/PK-12
325 Meulemans St #A 54140 ... 920-788-7605
David Botz, supt. ... Fax 788-7603
www.littlechute.k12.wi.us
Little Chute HS ... 600/9-12
1402 Freedom Rd 54140 ... 920-788-7600
Daniel Valentyn, prin. ... Fax 788-7841
Little Chute MS ... 300/6-8
325 Meulemans St 54140 ... 920-788-7607
Lori A Van Handel, prin. ... Fax 788-7603

Livingston, Iowa, Pop. 583
Iowa-Grant SD ... 900/PK-12
498 County Road IG 53554 ... 608-943-6311
Terrance Slack, supt. ... Fax 943-8438
www.igs.k12.wi.us
Iowa-Grant HS ... 400/9-12
462 County Road IG 53554 ... 608-943-6312
Mitch Munson, prin. ... Fax 943-8438

Lodi, Columbia, Pop. 2,957
Lodi SD ... 1,700/PK-12
115 School St 53555 ... 608-592-3851
Michael Shimshak, supt. ... Fax 592-3852
www.lodi.k12.wi.us
Lodi HS ... 500/9-12
1100 Sauk St 53555 ... 608-592-3853
Laura Love, prin. ... Fax 592-1045
Lodi MS ... 400/6-8
900 Sauk St 53555 ... 608-592-3854
... Fax 592-1035

Lomira, Dodge, Pop. 2,373
Lomira SD ... 1,100/PK-12
1030 4th St 53048 ... 920-269-4396
Jeffrey R. McCartney, supt. ... Fax 269-4996
www.lomira.k12.wi.us/
Lomira HS ... 400/9-12
1030 4th St 53048 ... 920-269-4396
Shannon M. Stein, prin. ... Fax 269-4996
Lomira JHS ... 200/7-8
1030 4th St 53048 ... 920-269-4396
Robert P. Lloyd, prin. ... Fax 269-4996

Loyal, Clark, Pop. 1,301
Loyal SD ... 700/PK-12
PO Box 10 54446 ... 715-255-8552
Graeme Williams, supt. ... Fax 255-8553
www.loyal.k12.wi.us
Loyal HS ... 200/9-12
PO Box 10 54446 ... 715-255-8511
Walter Leipart, prin. ... Fax 255-8553
Loyal JHS ... 100/7-8
PO Box 10 54446 ... 715-255-8511
Walter Leipart, prin. ... Fax 255-8553

Luck, Polk, Pop. 1,223
Luck SD ... 600/K-12
810 S 7th St 54853 ... 715-472-2151
Rick Palmer, supt. ... Fax 472-2159
www.lucksd.k12.wi.us
Luck JSHS ... 300/7-12
810 S 7th St 54853 ... 715-472-2152
Mark Gobler, prin. ... Fax 472-2159

Luxemburg, Kewaunee, Pop. 2,078
Luxemburg-Casco SD ... 1,900/PK-12
PO Box 70 54217 ... 920-845-2391
Patrick Saunders, supt. ... Fax 845-5871
www.luxcasco.k12.wi.us/
Luxemburg-Casco HS ... 700/9-12
PO Box 410 54217 ... 920-845-2336
Steve Okoniewski, prin. ... Fax 845-2280
Other Schools – See Casco

Mc Farland, Dane, Pop. 5,724
Mc Farland SD ... 2,000/PK-12
5101 Farwell St 53558 ... 608-838-3169
Scott Brown, admin. ... Fax 838-3074
www.mcfarland.k12.wi.us/
Indian Mound MS ... 500/6-8
6330 Exchange St 53558 ... 608-838-8980
Roberta Felker, prin. ... Fax 838-4588
Mc Farland HS ... 600/9-12
5103 Farwell St 53558 ... 608-838-3166
James Hickey, prin. ... Fax 838-4562

Madison, Dane, Pop. 218,432
Madison Metro SD ... 24,200/PK-12
545 W Dayton St 53703 ... 608-663-1879
Art Rainwater, supt. ... Fax 204-0341
www.madison.k12.wi.us
Black Hawk MS ... 400/6-8
1402 Wyoming Way 53704 ... 608-204-4360
Mary Kelley, prin. ... Fax 204-0368
Cherokee Heights MS ... 600/6-8
4301 Cherokee Dr 53711 ... 608-204-1240
Karen Seno, prin. ... Fax 204-0378

East HS ... 2,100/9-12
2222 E Washington Ave 53704 ... 608-204-1600
Alan Harris, prin. ... Fax 204-0388
Hamilton MS ... 700/6-8
4801 Waukesha St 53705 ... 608-204-4620
Henry Schmelz, prin. ... Fax 204-0417
Jefferson MS ... 500/6-8
101 S Gammon Rd 53717 ... 608-663-6403
John Burmaster, prin. ... Fax 442-2193
LaFollette HS ... 1,700/9-12
702 Pflaum Rd 53716 ... 608-204-3600
Michael Meissen, prin. ... Fax 204-0435
Memorial HS ... 2,200/9-12
201 S Gammon Rd 53717 ... 608-663-5990
Bruce Dahmen, prin. ... Fax 442-2197
O'Keeffe MS ... 400/6-8
510 S Thornton Ave 53703 ... 608-204-6820
Pat Delmore, prin. ... Fax 204-0561
Sennett MS ... 700/6-8
502 Pflaum Rd 53716 ... 608-204-1920
Colleen Lodholz, prin. ... Fax 204-0495
Sherman MS ... 600/6-8
1610 Ruskin St 53704 ... 608-204-2100
Ann Yehle, prin. ... Fax 204-0501
Spring Harbor MS ... 200/6-8
1110 Spring Harbor Dr 53705 ... 608-204-1100
Gail Anderson, prin. ... Fax 204-0509
Toki MS ... 600/6-8
5606 Russett Rd 53711 ... 608-204-4740
Joe Gothard, prin. ... Fax 204-0523
West HS ... 2,100/9-12
30 Ash St 53726 ... 608-204-4100
Ed Holmes, prin. ... Fax 204-0529
Whitehorse MS ... 400/6-8
218 Schenk St 53714 ... 608-204-4480
Anne Nolan, prin. ... Fax 204-0538

Abundant Life Christian S ... 400/K-12
4901 E Buckeye Rd 53716 ... 608-221-1520
Bill Zehner, admin. ... Fax 221-8572
Edgewood College ... Post-Sec.
1000 Edgewood College Dr 53711 ... 800-444-4861
Edgewood HS ... 600/9-12
2219 Monroe St 53711 ... 608-257-1023
Robert Growney, prin. ... Fax 257-9133
Herzing College ... Post-Sec.
5218 E Terrace Dr 53718 ... 608-249-6611
Madison Area Technical College ... Post-Sec.
3550 Anderson St 53704 ... 608-246-6282
Madison Cosmetology College ... Post-Sec.
310 Westgate Mall 53711 ... 608-271-4206
Madison Media Institute ... Post-Sec.
2702 Agriculture Dr 53718 ... 608-663-2000
Martin's College of Cosmetology ... Post-Sec.
6414 Odana Rd 53719 ... 608-270-0188
St Ambose Academy ... 50/7-12
602 Everglade Dr 53717 ... 608-827-5863
John Gillette, prin.
State Laboratory of Hygiene ... Post-Sec.
465 Henry Mall 53706 ... 608-262-2802
University of Wisconsin ... Post-Sec.
716 Langdon St 53706 ... 608-262-1234

Manawa, Waupaca, Pop. 1,356
Manawa SD ... 900/PK-12
800 Beech St 54949 ... 920-596-2525
Larry Brown, supt. ... Fax 596-5308
www.manawa.k12.wi.us
Little Wolf HS ... 300/9-12
515 E 4th St 54949 ... 920-596-2524
Duane Braun, prin. ... Fax 596-2655
Manawa MS ... 300/5-8
800 Beech St 54949 ... 920-596-2551
James Quinn, prin. ... Fax 596-5320

Manitowoc, Manitowoc, Pop. 34,080
Manitowoc SD ... 5,300/PK-12
PO Box 1657 54221 ... 920-683-4777
Mark Swanson, supt. ... Fax 686-4780
www.mpsd.k12.wi.us
Lincoln SHS ... 1,400/10-12
1433 S 8th St 54220 ... 920-683-4861
Keith Shaw, prin. ... Fax 683-4845
Washington JHS ... 700/7-9
2101 Division St 54220 ... 920-683-4757
Kathleen Lemberger, prin. ... Fax 683-7989
Wilson JHS ... 700/7-9
1201 N 11th St 54220 ... 920-683-4759
Darlene Wotachek, prin. ... Fax 683-7988

Manitowoc Lutheran HS ... 300/9-12
4045 Lancer Cir 54220 ... 920-682-0215
Dennis Steinbrenner, prin. ... Fax 682-2363
Martin's College of Cosmetology ... Post-Sec.
1034 S 18th St 54220 ... 920-684-3028
Roncalli HS ... 300/9-12
2000 Mirro Dr 54220 ... 920-682-8801
Tim Olson, prin. ... Fax 686-8110
St. Francis Cabrini MS ... 200/6-8
2109 Marshall St 54220 ... 920-683-6884
James Clark, prin. ... Fax 683-6881
Silver Lake College ... Post-Sec.
2406 S Alverno Rd 54220 ... 920-684-6691
University of Wisconsin Center ... Post-Sec.
705 Viebahn St 54220 ... 920-683-4707

Maple, Douglas
Maple SD ... 1,400/K-12
PO Box 188 54854 ... 715-363-2431
Gregg Lundberg, supt. ... Fax 363-2191
www.maple.k12.wi.us
Northwestern HS ... 400/9-12
PO Box 188 54854 ... 715-363-2434
Steve High, prin. ... Fax 363-2523
Other Schools – See Poplar

Marathon, Marathon, Pop. 1,642
Marathon City SD ... 700/PK-12
PO Box 37 54448 ... 715-443-2228
Donald Viegut, supt. ... Fax 443-2611
www.marathon.k12.wi.us
Marathon HS ... 300/9-12
PO Box 37 54448 ... 715-443-2226
David Beranek, prin. ... Fax 443-2611

Marinette, Marinette, Pop. 11,420
Marinette SD ... 2,400/K-12
2139 Pierce Ave 54143 ... 715-735-1406
Dr. Nancy Hipskind, supt. ... Fax 732-7930
www.marinette.k12.wi.us
Marinette HS ... 800/9-12
2135 Pierce Ave 54143 ... 715-732-7920
Tim Stauss, prin. ... Fax 732-7929
Marinette MS ... 700/5-8
1011 Water St 54143 ... 715-732-7900
Wendy Dzurick, prin. ... Fax 732-7939

Holy Family S ... 100/5-8
1200 Main St 54143 ... 715-735-7174
... Fax 735-7146
Northeast Wisconsin Technical College ... Post-Sec.
1601 University Dr 54143 ... 715-735-9361
St. Thomas Aquinas Academy ... 100/9-12
1200 Main St 54143 ... 715-735-7481
Marge Bruemmer, prin. ... Fax 735-3375
University of Wisconsin-Marinette ... Post-Sec.
750 W Bay Shore St 54143 ... 715-735-7470

Marion, Waupaca, Pop. 1,272
Marion SD ... 700/PK-12
1001 N Main St 54950 ... 715-754-2511
Earl G. Knitt, supt. ... Fax 754-4508
www.marion.k12.wi.us
Marion JSHS ... 300/7-12
105 School St 54950 ... 715-754-5273
Keary Mattson, prin. ... Fax 754-1350

Markesan, Green Lake, Pop. 1,376
Markesan SD ... 900/PK-12
PO Box 248 53946 ... 920-398-2373
Susan Alexander, supt. ... Fax 398-3281
www.markesan.k12.wi.us
Markesan HS ... 300/9-12
PO Box 248 53946 ... 920-398-2373
Christopher Telfer, prin. ... Fax 398-3281
Markesan MS ... 200/7-8
PO Box 248 53946 ... 920-398-2373
Christopher Telfer, prin. ... Fax 398-3281

Marshall, Dane, Pop. 3,569
Marshall SD ... 1,200/PK-12
PO Box 76 53559 ... 608-655-3466
Barb Sramek, supt. ... Fax 655-4481
www.marshall.k12.wi.us
Marshall HS ... 300/9-12
PO Box 76 53559 ... 608-655-1310
Dennis Riley, prin. ... Fax 655-3046
Marshall MS ... 200/7-8
PO Box 76 53559 ... 608-655-1571
Mark Mueller, prin. ... Fax 655-1591

Marshfield, Wood, Pop. 18,670
Marshfield SD ... 4,100/PK-12
1010 E 4th St 54449 ... 715-387-1101
Bruce King, supt. ... Fax 387-0133
www.marshfield.k12.wi.us/
Marshfield HS ... 1,500/9-12
1401 E Becker Rd 54449 ... 715-387-8464
John Blankush, prin. ... Fax 384-3589
Marshfield MS ... 600/7-8
900 E 4th St 54449 ... 715-387-1249
David Schoepke, prin. ... Fax 384-9269

Columbus HS ... 200/9-12
710 S Columbus Ave 54449 ... 715-387-1177
Gary Catalano, prin. ... Fax 384-4535
Columbus MS ... 100/6-8
710 S Columbus Ave 54449 ... 715-387-1177
Barbara Billings, prin. ... Fax 384-4535
Marshfield Christian S ... 100/K-12
PO Box 1077 54449 ... 715-387-8639
Roger Gerstenberger, admin. ... Fax 389-2778
Marshfield Clinic/St. Josephs Hospital ... Post-Sec.
611 Saint Joseph Ave 54449 ... 715-387-7440
Mid-State Technical College ... Post-Sec.
2600 W 5th St 54449 ... 715-387-2538
St. Joseph Hospital/Marshfield Clinic ... Post-Sec.
611 Saint Joseph Ave 54449 ... 715-387-1713
Univ. of Wisconsin - Marshfield/Wood Co. ... Post-Sec.
2000 W 5th St 54449 ... 715-389-6530

Mauston, Juneau, Pop. 4,017
Mauston SD ... 1,600/PK-12
510 Grayside Ave 53948 ... 608-847-5451
Bruce Anderson, supt. ... Fax 847-4635
www.mauston.k12.wi.us
Mauston HS ... 600/9-12
800 Grayside Ave 53948 ... 608-847-4410
William Bomber, prin. ... Fax 847-4802
Olson MS ... 400/6-8
508 Grayside Ave 53948 ... 608-847-6603
Tom Reisenauer, prin. ... Fax 847-4925

Mayville, Dodge, Pop. 4,979
Mayville SD ... 1,100/PK-12
234 N John St 53050 ... 920-387-7963
Ronald Bieri, supt. ... Fax 387-7979
www.mayville.k12.wi.us
Mayville HS ... 500/9-12
500 N Clark St 53050 ... 920-387-7960
Lee Zarnott, prin. ... Fax 387-7977
Mayville MS ... 500/3-8
445 N Henninger St 53050 ... 920-387-7970
Robert Clark, prin. ... Fax 387-7974

Mazomanie, Dane, Pop. 1,479
Wisconsin Heights SD 1,100/PK-12
10173 US Highway 14 53560 608-767-2595
Larry Black, supt. Fax 767-3579
www.wisheights.k12.wi.us
Wisconsin Heights HS 400/9-12
10173 US Highway 14 53560 608-767-2586
Vince Breunig, prin. Fax 767-2062
Wisconsin Heights MS 300/6-8
10173 US Highway 14 53560 608-767-2596
Patricia Larson, prin. Fax 767-3579

Medford, Taylor, Pop. 4,215
Medford Area SD 2,200/PK-12
124 W State St 54451 715-748-4620
Steve Russ, supt. Fax 748-6839
www.medford.k12.wi.us
Medford HS 800/9-12
1015 W Broadway Ave 54451 715-748-5951
Jill Schafer, prin. Fax 748-6438
Medford MS 600/5-8
509 Clark St 54451 715-748-2516
Al Leonard, prin. Fax 748-1213

Mellen, Ashland, Pop. 828
Mellen SD 300/PK-12
PO Box 500 54546 715-274-3601
Jeffrey Ehrhardt, supt. Fax 274-3715
www.mellen.k12.wi.us
Mellen S 300/PK-12
PO Box 500 54546 715-274-3601
Thomas Kriesel, prin. Fax 274-3715

Melrose, Jackson, Pop. 527
Melrose-Mindoro SD 900/PK-12
N181 State Road 108 54642 608-488-2201
Ron Perry, supt. Fax 488-2805
www.mel-min.k12.wi.us
Melrose-Mindoro HS 200/9-12
N181 State Road 108 54642 608-488-2201
Del DeBerg, prin. Fax 488-2805

Menasha, Winnebago, Pop. 16,259
Menasha JSD 3,500/PK-12
PO Box 360 54952 920-967-1400
Keith Fuchs, supt. Fax 751-5038
www.mjsd.k12.wi.us
Maplewood MS 800/6-8
1600 Midway Rd 54952 920-967-1600
Bev Sturke, prin. Fax 832-5837
Menasha HS 1,100/9-12
420 7th St 54952 920-967-1800
Lawrence Haase, prin. Fax 751-5223

Seton Catholic MS 200/6-8
312 Nicolet Blvd 54952 920-727-0279
Monica Bausom, prin. Fax 727-1215
University of Wisconsin Center Post-Sec.
1478 Midway Rd 54952 920-832-2620

Menomonee Falls, Waukesha, Pop. 33,727
Menomonee Falls SD 4,400/K-12
N84W16579 Menomonee Ave 53051 262-255-8440
Keith A. Marty, supt. Fax 255-8461
www.sdmf.k12.wi.us
Menomonee Falls SHS 1,100/10-12
W142N8101 Merrimac Dr 53051 262-255-8444
William C. Hintz, prin. Fax 255-8377
North JHS 800/8-9
N88W16750 Garfield Dr 53051 262-255-8450
Barbara Tays, prin. Fax 255-8475

Bethlehem Lutheran S - South 100/5-8
N84W15252 Menomonee Ave 53051 262-251-3120
Daryl Weber, prin. Fax 251-4679
Calvary Baptist S 300/K-12
N84W16971 Menomonee Ave 53051 262-251-0328
Steven Lafferty, admin. Fax 251-0312
Falls Baptist Academy 200/K-12
N69W12703 Appleton Ave 53051 262-251-7051
John Flanders, admin. Fax 251-7043

Menomonie, Dunn, Pop. 15,155
Menomonie Area SD 3,200/PK-12
215 Pine Ave NE 54751 715-232-1642
Jesse Harness, supt. Fax 232-1317
msd.k12.wi.us
Menomonie HS 1,200/9-12
1715 5th St W 54751 715-232-2606
Thomas Wiatr, prin. Fax 232-2629
Menomonie MS 700/6-8
920 21st St SE 54751 715-232-1673
Dudley Markham, prin. Fax 232-5486

University of Wisconsin Post-Sec.
124 Bowman Hall 54751 715-232-1123

Mequon, Ozaukee, Pop. 23,449
Mequon-Thiensville SD 3,800/PK-12
5000 W Mequon Rd 53092 262-238-8503
Robert J. Slotterback, supt. Fax 238-8520
www.mtsd.k12.wi.us
Homestead HS 1,600/9-12
5000 W Mequon Rd 53092 262-238-5646
Mark Roherty, prin. Fax 238-5633
Lake Shore MS 500/6-8
11036 N Range Line Rd 53092 262-238-7613
Michael Dietz, prin. Fax 238-7650
Steffen MS 500/6-8
6633 W Steffen Dr 53092 262-238-4706
Deborah Anderson, prin. Fax 238-4740

Concordia University Post-Sec.
12800 N Lake Shore Dr 53097 262-243-5700
Milwaukee Area Technical College Post-Sec.
5555 W Highland Rd 53092 262-238-2200

Mercer, Iron
Mercer SD 200/PK-12
PO Box 567 54547 715-476-2154
Ron Vaughn, supt. Fax 476-2587
www.mercer.k12.wi.us
Mercer S 200/PK-12
PO Box 567 54547 715-476-2154
Ron Vaughn, prin. Fax 476-2587

Merrill, Lincoln, Pop. 10,164
Merrill Area SD 3,200/PK-12
1111 N Sales St 54452 715-536-4581
Sally Sarnstrom, supt. Fax 536-1788
www.maps.k12.wi.us
Merrill HS 1,200/9-12
1201 N Sales St 54452 715-536-4594
Shannon Murray, prin. Fax 536-5504
Prairie River MS 700/6-8
106 Polk St 54452 715-536-9593
Gerald Beyer, prin. Fax 536-6378

Merton, Waukesha, Pop. 2,216
Merton Community SD 900/PK-8
PO Box 15 53056 262-538-1130
Mark Flynn, supt. Fax 538-4978
www.merton.k12.wi.us
Merton IS 500/4-8
PO Box 15 53056 262-538-1130
Jon Wagner, prin. Fax 538-4978

Middleton, Dane, Pop. 16,189
Middleton-Cross Plains Area SD 5,400/PK-12
7106 South Ave 53562 608-829-9000
William Reis, supt. Fax 836-1536
www.mcpasd.k12.wi.us
Kromrey MS 600/6-8
7009 Donna Dr 53562 608-829-9530
Mike Nummerdor, prin. Fax 831-8388
Middleton HS 1,700/9-12
2100 Bristol St 53562 608-829-9660
Denise Herrmann, prin. Fax 831-1995
Other Schools – See Cross Plains

Milton, Rock, Pop. 5,335
Milton SD 3,000/PK-12
430 E High St 53563 608-868-9200
Peg Ekedahl, supt. Fax 868-9215
www.milton.k12.wi.us
Milton HS 1,000/9-12
114 W High St 53563 608-868-9300
Randy Refsland, prin. Fax 868-9399
Milton MS 500/7-8
20 E Madison Ave 53563 608-868-9350
Bob Parker, prin. Fax 868-9269

Milwaukee, Milwaukee, Pop. 586,941
Fox Point Bayside SD 900/PK-8
7300 N Lombardy Rd 53217 414-247-4167
Gary W. Petersen, supt. Fax 351-7164
www.foxbay.k12.wi.us
Bayside MS 400/5-8
601 E Ellsworth Ln 53217 414-351-7486
John Roubik, prin. Fax 247-8963

Maple Dale-Indian Hill SD
Supt. — See Glendale
Maple Dale S 400/3-8
8377 N Port Washington Rd 53217 414-351-7380
Mary Dean, prin. Fax 351-8104

Milwaukee SD 76,600/PK-12
PO Box 2181 53201 414-475-8001
William G. Andrekopoulos, supt. Fax 475-8595
www.milwaukee.k12.wi.us
Bay View HS 1,800/9-12
2751 S Lenox St 53207 414-294-2400
Barbara Goss, prin. Fax 294-2415
Bell MS 900/6-8
6506 W Warnimont Ave 53220 414-604-7800
Suzanne Kirby, admin. Fax 604-7815
Bradley Tech & Trade HS Vo/Tech
700 S 4th St 53204 414-212-2400
Edward Kovochich, prin. Fax 212-2415
Burroughs MS 900/6-8
6700 N 80th St 53223 414-393-3500
Ramelann Kalagian, prin. Fax 393-3515
Custer HS 1,200/9-12
5075 N Sherman Blvd 53209 414-393-4900
Kathy Bonds, prin. Fax 393-4915
Edison MS 500/6-8
5372 N 37th St 53209 414-616-5400
Jennie Dorsey, prin. Fax 616-5415
Foster & Williams HS 9-12
4141 N 64th St 53216 414-393-3800
Charles Marks, prin.
Grand Ave MS 700/6-8
2430 W Wisconsin Ave 53233 414-934-4200
Ed Szopinski, prin. Fax 934-4215
Hamilton HS 2,100/9-12
6215 W Warnimont Ave 53220 414-327-9300
Milford Moffett, prin. Fax 327-9315
King HS 1,400/9-12
1801 W Olive St 53209 414-267-0700
Andrew Meuler, prin. Fax 267-0715
Kosciuszko MS 600/6-8
971 W Windlake Ave 53204 414-902-7200
Cheryl Clancy, prin. Fax 902-7215
Lincoln MS of the Arts 800/6-8
820 E Knapp St 53202 414-212-3300
Maria Sanchez, admin. Fax 212-3315
Madison HS 1,500/9-12
8135 W Florist Ave 53218 414-393-6100
Janie Hatton, prin. Fax 393-6262
Marshall HS 1,400/9-12
4141 N 64th St 53216 414-393-2300
Nancy Connor, prin. Fax 393-2315
Milwaukee Education Center MS 800/6-8
227 W Pleasant St 53212 414-212-2900
Jessie Rodriguez, admin. Fax 212-2967
Milwaukee HS of the Arts 900/9-12
2300 W Highland Ave 53233 414-934-7000
Eugene Humphrey, prin. Fax 934-7015
Milwaukee S of Languages 800/6-10
8400 W Burleigh St 53222 414-393-5700
Grace Thomsen, prin. Fax 393-5715
Milwaukee Village S 100/6-8
1011 W Center St 53206 414-267-5181
Willie Killins, admin. Fax 267-5184
Morse MS 1,100/6-8
4601 N 84th St 53225 414-616-5800
Rogers Onick, prin. Fax 616-5815
Muir MS 700/6-8
5496 N 72nd St 53218 414-393-3100
D. Rose Coppins, prin. Fax 393-3115
North Division HS 100/12-12
1011 W Center St 53206 414-267-4900
Reginald Lawrence, prin. Fax 267-4915
Pulaski HS 1,600/9-12
2500 W Oklahoma Ave 53215 414-902-8900
Ada Rivera, prin. Fax 902-8915
Riverside HS 1,600/9-12
1615 E Locust St 53211 414-906-4900
Daniel Donder, prin. Fax 906-4915
Ronald Wilson Reagan HS 500/9-12
4965 S 20th St 53221 414-304-6100
Julia D'Amato, prin. Fax 304-6115
Roosevelt MS 800/6-8
800 W Walnut St 53205 414-267-8800
Tom Matthews, prin. Fax 267-8815
Scott for the Health Sciences MS 800/6-8
1017 N 12th St 53233 414-934-4000
Willie Hickman, prin. Fax 934-4015
South Division HS 1,700/9-12
1515 W Lapham Blvd 53204 414-902-8300
Charles Siebert, prin. Fax 902-8315
Vincent HS 1,500/9-12
7501 N Granville Rd 53224 262-236-1200
Gloria Erkins, prin. Fax 236-1254
Washington HS of Expeditonary Lrng 9-12
2525 N Sherman Blvd 53210 414-875-5906
Greg Ogunbowale, prin.
Washington HS of Info Technology 1,500/9-12
2525 N Sherman Blvd 53210 414-875-5900
Winnifred Aitch, prin. Fax 875-5915
Washington HS of Law-Ed-Public Service 9-12
2525 N Sherman Blvd 53210 414-875-5900
Arnita Antao, prin.
Webster MS 900/6-8
6850 N 53rd St 53223 414-393-5900
Minnie Novy, prin. Fax 393-5915

Alverno College Post-Sec.
PO Box 343922 53234 414-382-6000
Atlas Preparatory Academy 600/K-10
2911 S 32nd St 53215 414-385-0771
Michelle Lukacs, prin. Fax 385-0773
Aurora Health Care Post-Sec.
3000 W Montana St 53215 414-647-3000
Believers in Christ Christian Academy 300/PK-12
4065 N 25th St 53209 414-444-1146
Candace Covington, prin. Fax 444-5378
Blood Center of SE Wisconsin Post-Sec.
1701 W Wisconsin Ave 53233 414-937-6338
Bryant & Stratton College Post-Sec.
310 W Wisconsin Ave 53203 414-276-5200
Cardinal Stritch University Post-Sec.
6801 N Yates Rd 53217 414-410-4000
Columbia College of Nursing Post-Sec.
2121 E Newport Ave 53211 414-961-3530
Columbia Hospital Post-Sec.
2025 E Newport Ave 53211 414-961-3800
DeVry University Post-Sec.
100 E Wsconsin Ave #2550 53202 414-278-7677
Divine Savior-Holy Angels HS 600/9-12
4257 N 100th St 53222 414-466-3706
Sr. Virginia Honish, prin. Fax 466-0590
Early View Academy of Excellence 300/PK-10
7132 W Good Hope Rd 53223 414-431-0001
Annie Oliver, prin. Fax 431-0046
Froedtert Memorial Lutheran Hospital Post-Sec.
PO Box 26099 53226 414-259-2606
Heritage Christian S 600/PK-12
1300 S 109th St 53214 414-259-1231
Thomas Wittkamper, supt. Fax 257-2548
Holy Redeemer Christian Academy 400/PK-12
3500 W Mother Daniels Way 53209 414-466-1800
Alton Townsel, admin. Fax 466-4930
Holy Wisdom Academy West Campus 200/4-8
3344 S 16th St 53215 414-383-3453
Richard Mason, prin. Fax 672-2645
Hope MS, 510 E Burleigh St 53212 100/6-8
Patrick Hurley, prin. 414-517-5814
Hope S 100/9-12
3229 N Martin L King Dr 53212 414-264-4476
Tommie Myles, admin. Fax 264-4592
ITT Technical Institute Post-Sec.
6300 W Layton Ave 53220 414-282-9494
Lakeside School of Massage Therapy Post-Sec.
1726 N 1st St 53212 414-372-4345
Marquette University Post-Sec.
PO Box 1881 53201 414-288-7700
Marquette University HS 1,000/9-12
3401 W Wisconsin Ave 53208 414-933-7220
Fr. John Belmonte, prin. Fax 937-8588
Medical College of Wisconsin Post-Sec.
PO Box 26509 53226 414-456-8296
Messmer HS 500/9-12
742 W Capitol Dr 53206 414-264-5440
Jeff Monday, prin. Fax 264-0672
Milwaukee Area Technical College Post-Sec.
700 W State St 53233 414-297-6600
Milwaukee Institute of Art & Design Post-Sec.
273 E Erie St 53202 414-291-8070
Milwaukee Lutheran HS 800/9-12
9700 W Grantosa Dr 53222 414-461-6000
Paul Bahr, prin. Fax 461-2733

Milwaukee School of Engineering   Post-Sec.
1025 N Broadway 53202   414-277-7300
Milwaukee SDA S   50/1-10
10900 W Mill Rd 53225   414-353-3520
Alberto Torres, admin.   Fax 353-1451
Mohammed S   200/PK-12
317 W Wright St 53212   414-263-6772
Basimah Abdullah, admin.   Fax 263-6852
Mt. Mary College   Post-Sec.
2900 N Menomonee River Pkwy 53222
    414-258-4810
Multicultural Community Services   200/3-12
5161 N Hopkins St 53209   414-527-1010
Nancy Peters, pres.   Fax 527-4518
Nativity Jesuit MS   50/6-8
1515 S 29th St 53215   414-645-1060
Rosarios Sanchez, prin.   Fax 645-0505
Noach S   100/K-12
750 N Lincoln Memorial Dr 53202   414-431-0146
Dr. Brenda Noach-Ewing, admin.   Fax 431-2171
Notre Dame MS   100/5-8
1420 W Scott St 53204   414-671-3000
Mary Garcia-Velez, prin.   Fax 671-3170
Pius XI HS   1,500/9-12
135 N 76th St 53213   414-290-7000
Richard Pendergast, prin.   Fax 290-7001
Prince of Peace S   200/4-8
1114 S 25th St 53204   414-383-2157
    Fax 645-8918
St. Aemilian Lakeside S   100/1-10
8901 W Capitol Dr 53222   414-463-1880
Tami Trulock, admin.   Fax 463-2770
St. Francis Hospital   Post-Sec.
3237 S 16th St 53215   414-647-5106
St. Francis Seminary   Post-Sec.
3257 S Lake Dr 53235   414-747-6400
St. Joan Antida HS   400/9-12
1341 N Cass St 53202   414-272-8423
Sioux Henzig, prin.   Fax 272-3135
St. Luke's Medical Center   Post-Sec.
2900 W Oklahoma Ave 53215   414-649-7500
St. Rafael the Archangel S - South   100/5-8
2251 S 31st St 53215   414-645-1300
Carolyn Ettlie, prin.   Fax 645-1415
St. Thomas Aquinas Academy - West   400/4-8
341 E Norwich St 53207   414-744-1214
Julie Ann Robinson, prin.   Fax 482-3025
Salam S   400/PK-10
4707 S 13th St 53221   414-282-0504
Dr. Abdul-Mun'im Jitmoud, admin.   Fax 282-6959
Thomas More HS   700/9-12
2601 E Morgan Ave 53207   414-481-8370
James Griswold, prin.   Fax 481-3382
Torah Academy   50/9-12
6789 N Green Bay Ave 53209   414-352-6789
Sara Rauch, prin.   Fax 352-6646
University of Wisconsin   Post-Sec.
PO Box 413 53201   414-229-1122
University S   1,100/PK-12
2100 W Fairy Chasm Rd 53217   414-352-6000
Ward Ghory, hdmstr.   Fax 352-8076
Vici Beauty School   Post-Sec.
11010 W Hampton Ave 53225   414-464-5002
Wisconsin Conservatory of Music   Post-Sec.
1584 N Prospect Ave 53202   414-276-5760
Wisconsin Institute for Torah Study   100/9-12
3288 N Lake Dr 53211   414-963-9317
Earl Lebakken, prin.   Fax 963-1519
Wisconsin Lutheran College   Post-Sec.
8800 W Bluemound Rd 53226   414-443-8800
Wisconsin Lutheran HS   900/9-12
330 Glenview Ave 53213   414-453-4567
Ned Goede, prin.   Fax 453-3001
WI School of Professional Psychology   Post-Sec.
9120 W Hampton Ave Ste 212 53225 414-464-9777
Zablocki VA Medical Center   Post-Sec.
5000 W National Ave 53295   414-384-2000

Mineral Point, Iowa, Pop. 2,510
Mineral Point SD   800/PK-12
705 Ross St 53565   608-987-3924
Vincent Smith, supt.   Fax 987-3766
www.mp.k12.wi.us
Mineral Point HS   300/9-12
705 Ross St 53565   608-987-2321
Ted Evans, prin.   Fax 987-3766
Mineral Point MS   200/6-8
705 Ross St 53565   608-987-2371
Ted Evans, prin.   Fax 987-3766

Minocqua, Oneida
Lakeland UNHSD   1,000/9-12
9573 State Highway 70 54548   715-358-8480
Michael Dailey, supt.   Fax 356-1892
www.luhs.k12.wi.us
Lakeland HS   1,000/9-12
9573 State Highway 70 54548   715-356-5252
Todd Kleinhans, prin.   Fax 356-1892

Minong, Washburn, Pop. 572
Northwood SD   400/PK-12
N14463 Highway 53 54859   715-466-2297
Donald H. Anderson, supt.   Fax 466-5149
northwood.k12.wi.us
Northwood S   400/PK-12
N14463 Highway 53 54859   715-466-2297
Clendon Gustafson, prin.   Fax 466-5149

Mishicot, Manitowoc, Pop. 1,408
Mishicot SD   1,100/PK-12
PO Box 280 54228   920-755-4633
Stephen Cromell, supt.   Fax 755-2390
www.mishicot.k12.wi.us
Mishicot HS   400/9-12
PO Box 280 54228   920-755-4633
Deborah Knox, prin.   Fax 755-2390
Mishicot MS   300/6-8
PO Box 280 54228   920-755-4633
Colleen Timm, prin.   Fax 755-2390

Mondovi, Buffalo, Pop. 2,640
Mondovi SD   1,100/PK-12
337 N Jackson St 54755   715-926-3684
Cheryl Gullicksrud, supt.   Fax 926-3617
www.mondovi.k12.wi.us/
Mondovi HS   300/9-12
337 N Jackson St 54755   715-926-3656
Mike Bruning, prin.   Fax 926-3617
Mondovi MS   300/6-8
337 N Jackson St 54755   715-926-3457
Michael Erickson, prin.   Fax 926-3617

Monona, Dane, Pop. 7,987
Monona Grove SD   3,000/PK-12
5301 Monona Dr 53716   608-221-7660
Gary Schumacher, supt.   Fax 221-7688
www.mononagrove.org
Monona Grove HS   900/9-12
4400 Monona Dr 53716   608-221-7666
Paul Brost, prin.   Fax 221-7690
Winnequah MS   700/6-8
800 Greenway Rd 53716   608-221-7676
Patti McGinnis, prin.   Fax 221-7694

Monroe, Green, Pop. 10,676
Monroe SD   2,500/PK-12
925 16th Ave #3 53566   608-328-7171
Craig Jefson, supt.   Fax 328-7214
www.monroeschools.com
Monroe HS   900/9-12
1600 26th St 53566   608-328-7117
Mark Burandt, prin.   Fax 328-7230
Monroe MS   600/6-8
1510 13th St 53566   608-328-7120
William Van Meer, prin.   Fax 328-7224

Four Seasons Salon and Day Spa School   Post-Sec.
128 W 8th St Ste 8 53566   608-325-4007

Montello, Marquette, Pop. 1,442
Montello SD   800/PK-12
222 Forest Ln 53949   608-297-7617
Randy Guttenberg, supt.   Fax 297-7726
www.montello.k12.wi.us
Montello JSHS   400/7-12
222 Forest Ln 53949   608-297-2126
Jeffrey Holmes, prin.   Fax 297-7726

Monticello, Green, Pop. 1,130
Monticello SD   400/PK-12
334 S Main St 53570   608-938-4194
Karen Ballin, supt.   Fax 938-1062
Monticello HS   100/9-12
334 S Main St 53570   608-938-4194
Kenneth Colle, prin.   Fax 938-1062
Monticello MS   100/6-8
334 S Main St 53570   608-938-4194
Kenneth Colle, prin.   Fax 938-1062

Mosinee, Marathon, Pop. 4,062
Mosinee SD   2,000/PK-12
591 W State Highway 153 54455   715-693-2530
Jerry L. Rosso, supt.   Fax 693-7272
www.mosineeschools.org
Mosinee HS   700/9-12
1000 High St 54455   715-693-2550
James Debroux, prin.   Fax 693-1152
Mosinee MS   800/4-8
700 High St 54455   715-693-3660
Ronald Mueller, prin.   Fax 693-6655

Northland Lutheran HS   100/9-12
2107 Tower Rd 54455   715-359-3400
Rick Grundman, prin.   Fax 241-9203
WI Valley Lutheran HS   50/9-12
601 Maple Ridge Rd 54455   715-693-2693
Jim Rawlings, prin.   Fax 693-5962

Mount Calvary, Fond du Lac, Pop. 936

St. Lawrence Seminary HS   200/9-12
301 Church St 53057   920-753-7500
David Bartel, prin.   Fax 753-2907

Mount Horeb, Dane, Pop. 6,074
Mount Horeb Area SD   2,100/PK-12
1304 E Lincoln St 53572   608-437-2400
Wayne Anderson, supt.   Fax 437-5597
www.mhasd.k12.wi.us
Mount Horeb HS   600/9-12
305 S 8th St 53572   608-437-2400
Michael Lancaster, prin.   Fax 437-4926
Mount Horeb MS   500/6-8
900 E Garfield St 53572   608-437-2400
Jeff Rasmussen, prin.   Fax 437-6227

Mukwonago, Waukesha, Pop. 6,562
Mukwonago SD   5,000/K-12
423 Division St 53149   262-363-6300
Paul Strobel, supt.   Fax 363-6272
www.mukwonago.k12.wi.us
Mukwonago HS   1,700/9-12
605 W School Rd 53149   262-363-6200
Dale Henry, prin.   Fax 363-6239
Park View MS   800/7-8
930 N Rochester St 53149   262-363-6292
David Arnott, prin.   Fax 363-6320

Norris SD   100/7-12
W247S10395 Center Dr 53149   262-662-5911
Sara Trampf, supt.   Fax 662-5502
www.norriscenter.org/
Norris JSHS   100/7-12
W247S10395 Center Dr 53149   262-662-5911
Sara Trampf, prin.   Fax 662-5502

Muscoda, Grant, Pop. 1,425
Riverdale SD   900/PK-12
PO Box 66 53573   608-739-3832
Duane Bark, supt.   Fax 739-3751
www.riverdale.k12.wi.us/
Riverdale HS   300/9-12
PO Box 66 53573   608-739-3116
David McHenry, prin.   Fax 739-4486
Riverdale MS   200/6-8
800 N 6th St 53573   608-739-3101
Sharon Ennis, prin.   Fax 739-9118

Muskego, Waukesha, Pop. 22,314
Muskego-Norway SD   4,600/PK-12
S87W18763 Woods Rd 53150   262-679-5400
Richard Drury, supt.   Fax 679-5790
www.mnsd.k12.wi.us
Bay Lane MS   700/5-8
S75W16399 Hilltop Dr 53150   414-422-0430
Bonnie Murphy, prin.   Fax 422-2204
Lake Denoon MS   700/5-8
W216S10586 Crowbar Dr 53150   262-662-1454
Ryan Oertel, prin.   Fax 662-1588
Muskego HS   1,600/9-12
W183S8750 Racine Ave 53150   262-679-2300
Dennis Bussen, prin.   Fax 679-3534

Nashotah, Waukesha, Pop. 1,377

Nashotah House   Post-Sec.
2777 Mission Rd 53058   262-646-6500

Necedah, Juneau, Pop. 869
Necedah Area SD   800/K-12
1801 S Main St 54646   608-565-2256
Charles Krupa, supt.   Fax 565-3201
www.necedah.k12.wi.us
Necedah MSHS   300/7-12
1801 S Main St 54646   608-565-2256
Peggy Saylor, prin.   Fax 565-7044

Neenah, Winnebago, Pop. 24,629
Neenah SD   6,300/PK-12
410 S Commercial St 54956   920-751-6800
James Wiswall, supt.   Fax 751-6809
www.neenah.k12.wi.us
Mann MS   600/6-8
1021 Oak St 54956   920-751-6940
Jon Fleming, prin.   Fax 751-7099
Neenah HS   2,200/9-12
1275 Tullar Rd 54956   920-751-6900
Mark Duerwaechter, prin.   Fax 751-7011
Shattuck MS   900/6-8
600 Elm St 54956   920-751-6850
Jon Fleming, prin.   Fax 751-6899

St. Mary Central HS   300/9-12
1050 Zephyr Dr 54956   920-722-7796
Sr. Rochelle Kerkhof, prin.   Fax 722-5940
Theda Clark Regional Medical Center   Post-Sec.
130 2nd St 54956   920-729-2004

Neillsville, Clark, Pop. 2,693
Neillsville SD   1,200/PK-12
614 E 5th St 54456   715-743-3323
John Gaier, supt.   Fax 743-8718
www.neillsville.k12.wi.us
Neillsville HS   400/9-12
401 Center St 54456   715-743-8738
Allen Mohr, prin.   Fax 743-8714
Neillsville MS   300/6-8
504 E 5th St 54456   715-743-8710
Tim Rueth, prin.   Fax 743-8715

Nekoosa, Wood, Pop. 2,631
Nekoosa SD   1,500/K-12
600 S Section St 54457   715-886-8000
Wayne Johnson, supt.   Fax 886-8012
www.nekoosa.k12.wi.us
Alexander MS   600/4-8
540 Birch St 54457   715-886-8040
Dale Green, prin.   Fax 886-8097
Nekoosa HS   500/9-12
500 Cedar St 54457   715-886-8060
Robb Jensen, prin.   Fax 886-8087

Neopit, Menominee, Pop. 615
Menominee Indian SD
Supt. — See Keshena
Menominee Indian MS   200/6-8
PO Box 9 54150   715-756-2324
Lori LaTender, prin.   Fax 756-2496

Neosho, Dodge, Pop. 591

Lake Country Victory Christian HS   50/9-12
PO Box 46 53059   920-625-3995
Bruce Dickman, prin.   Fax 625-3995

New Auburn, Chippewa, Pop. 550
New Auburn SD   300/PK-12
PO Box 110 54757   715-237-2202
Howard Hanson, supt.   Fax 237-2350
www.newauburn.k12.wi.us
New Auburn HS   100/9-12
PO Box 110 54757   715-237-2505
Brian Henning, prin.   Fax 237-2350

New Berlin, Waukesha, Pop. 38,627
New Berlin SD   4,600/PK-12
4333 S Sunnyslope Rd 53151   262-789-6220
James Benfield, supt.   Fax 786-0512
www.nbps.k12.wi.us
Eisenhower MSHS   1,200/7-12
4333 S Sunnyslope Rd 53151   262-789-6300
Michael Fesenmaier, prin.   Fax 789-6330
New Berlin West MSHS   1,100/7-12
18695 W Cleveland Ave 53146   262-789-6400
David LaBorde, prin.   Fax 789-6442

New Glarus, Green, Pop. 2,054
New Glarus SD   800/PK-12
  PO Box 7   53574   608-527-2410
  Barbara W. Thompson, supt.   Fax 527-5101
  www.ngsd.k12.wi.us
New Glarus MSHS   400/6-12
  PO Box 7   53574   608-527-2410
  Duane Schober, prin.   Fax 527-5101

New Holstein, Calumet, Pop. 3,270
New Holstein SD   1,200/PK-12
  1715 Plymouth St   53061   920-898-5115
  Joseph Wieser, supt.   Fax 898-4112
  nhsd.k12.wi.us
New Holstein HS   500/9-12
  1715 Plymouth St   53061   920-898-4256
  Kathy Kops, prin.   Fax 898-4112
New Holstein MS   300/6-8
  2226 Park Ave   53061   920-898-4208
  Rick Amundson, prin.   Fax 898-9152

New Lisbon, Juneau, Pop. 1,417
New Lisbon SD   700/PK-12
  500 S Forest St   53950   608-562-3700
  Ed Dombrowski, supt.   Fax 562-5333
  www.newlisbon.k12.wi.us
New Lisbon JSHS   300/7-12
  500 S Forest St   53950   608-562-3700
  Linda Hanson, prin.   Fax 562-5333

New London, Waupaca, Pop. 7,063
New London SD   2,500/PK-12
  901 W Washington St   54961   920-982-8530
  Bill Fitzpatrick, supt.   Fax 982-8551
  www.newlondon.k12.wi.us
New London HS   900/9-12
  1700 Klatt Rd   54961   920-982-8420
  Joe Pomrening, prin.   Fax 982-8440
New London MS   600/6-8
  1000 W Washington St   54961   920-982-8532
  Andy Jones, prin.   Fax 982-8605

Starr Academy   100/7-12
  E7475 Rawhide Rd   54961   920-982-6100
  Daniel Birr, admin.   Fax 982-7283

New Richmond, Saint Croix, Pop. 7,058
New Richmond SD   2,500/K-12
  701 E 11th St   54017   715-243-7411
  Craig H. Hitchens, supt.   Fax 246-3638
  www.newrichmond.k12.wi.us
New Richmond HS   800/9-12
  701 E 11th St   54017   715-243-7451
  Jeffrey Moberg, prin.   Fax 243-7464
New Richmond MS   600/6-8
  701 E 11th St   54017   715-243-7471
  Michael Ballard, prin.   Fax 246-0580

Wisconsin Indianhead Technical College   Post-Sec.
  1019 S Knowles Ave   54017   715-246-6561

Niagara, Marinette, Pop. 1,813
Niagara SD   500/K-12
  700 Jefferson Ave   54151   715-251-1330
  Peter Kososki, supt.   Fax 251-4544
  www.niagara.k12.wi.us
Niagara S   500/K-12
  700 Jefferson Ave   54151   715-251-4541
  Peter Kososki, prin.   Fax 251-3715

North Fond du Lac, Fond du Lac, Pop. 4,870
North Fond Du Lac SD   1,200/PK-12
  225 McKinley St   54937   920-929-3750
  James Sebert, supt.   Fax 929-3696
  www.nfdl.k12.wi.us
Allen MS   300/6-8
  305 Mckinley St   54937   920-929-3754
  Aaron Sadoff, prin.   Fax 929-3747
Mann HS   400/9-12
  325 Mckinley St   54937   920-929-3740
  Samantha McGill, prin.   Fax 929-3664

Oak Creek, Milwaukee, Pop. 31,983
Oak Creek-Franklin SD   5,000/PK-12
  7630 S 10th St   53154   414-768-5886
  Sara Larsen, supt.   Fax 768-6172
  www.oakcreek.k12.wi.us
Oak Creek East MS   600/6-8
  9330 S Shepard Ave   53154   414-768-6260
  Paul Sigler, prin.   Fax 768-6293
Oak Creek HS   1,700/9-12
  340 E Puetz Rd   53154   414-768-6210
  Kathleen Jorgenson, prin.   Fax 768-6130
Oak Creek West MS   600/6-8
  8401 S 13th St   53154   414-768-6250
  Donald Kreuser, prin.   Fax 768-6296

Milwaukee Area Technical College   Post-Sec.
  6665 S Howell Ave   53154   414-762-2500
Parkway Christian Academy   200/K-12
  10940 S Nicholson Rd   53154   414-571-2684
  Theresa Tamel, admin.   Fax 571-2690

Oakfield, Fond du Lac, Pop. 1,009
Oakfield SD   600/PK-12
  PO Box 99   53065   920-583-3146
  Joseph Heinzelman, supt.   Fax 583-4033
  www.oakfield.k12.wi.us/
Oakfield HS   200/9-12
  PO Box 39   53065   920-583-3141
  Paul Dix, prin.   Fax 583-4673
Oakfield MS   200/6-8
  PO Box 69   53065   920-583-4117
  Pam Dix, prin.   Fax 583-3820

Oconomowoc, Waukesha, Pop. 13,189
Oconomowoc Area SD   4,000/PK-12
  W360N7077 Brown St   53066   262-560-1115
  Patricia Neudecker, supt.   Fax 474-7595
  www.oasd.k12.wi.us
Oconomowoc HS   1,400/9-12
  641 E Forest St   53066   262-560-3100
  Joseph C. Moylan, prin.   Fax 567-8960
Oconomowoc MS   700/7-8
  623 Summit Ave   53066   262-560-4300
  Christine Maas, prin.   Fax 567-1618

Lake Country Lutheran HS   200/9-12
  1101 S Silver Lake St   53066   262-569-6500
  Mark Bahr, prin.   Fax 567-4324

Oconto, Oconto, Pop. 4,656
Oconto SD   1,300/PK-12
  400 Michigan Ave   54153   920-834-7800
  Dr. Sara L. Croney, supt.   Fax 834-9884
  www.oconto.k12.wi.us
Oconto HS   500/9-12
  1717 Superior Ave   54153   920-834-7812
  Kathy Denor, prin.   Fax 834-7804
Oconto MS   400/5-8
  400 Michigan Ave   54153   920-834-7806
  Jeffrey Werner, prin.   Fax 834-7810

Oconto Falls, Oconto, Pop. 2,813
Oconto Falls SD   2,000/PK-12
  200 N Farm Rd   54154   920-848-4471
  David Polashek, supt.   Fax 848-4474
  www.ocontofalls.k12.wi.us
Oconto Falls HS   600/9-12
  PO Box 988   54154   920-848-4467
  Bruce Russell, prin.   Fax 846-4444
Washington MS   500/6-8
  102 S Washington St   54154   920-846-4463
  Tom Menor, prin.   Fax 846-4453

Omro, Winnebago, Pop. 3,270
Omro SD   1,300/PK-12
  455 Fox Trl   54963   920-685-5666
  Paul Amundson, admin.   Fax 685-5757
  www.omro.k12.wi.us/
Omro HS   400/9-12
  455 Fox Trl   54963   920-685-7405
  Bret Steffen, prin.   Fax 685-7040
Omro MS, 455 Fox Trl   54963   300/6-8
  Paul Williams, prin.   920-685-7403

Onalaska, LaCrosse, Pop. 15,474
Onalaska SD   2,700/K-12
  PO Box 429   54650   608-781-9700
  John Burnett, supt.   Fax 781-9712
  www.onalaska.k12.wi.us
Onalaska HS   900/9-12
  700 Hilltopper Pl   54650   608-783-4561
  Peter Woerpel, prin.   Fax 783-0102
Onalaska MS   600/6-8
  711 Quincy St   54650   608-783-5366
  Roger Fruit, prin.   Fax 781-8030

Luther HS   300/9-12
  PO Box 129   54650   608-783-5435
  Paul Wichmann, prin.   Fax 783-4758

Ontario, Vernon, Pop. 484
Norwalk-Ontario-Wilton SD   700/PK-12
  PO Box 130   54651   608-337-4403
  Kelly Burhop, supt.   Fax 337-4348
  www.now.k12.wi.us/
Brookwood JSHS   300/7-12
  PO Box 130   54651   608-337-4401
  Brad Pettit, prin.   Fax 337-4348

Oostburg, Sheboygan, Pop. 2,679
Oostburg SD   900/PK-12
  410 New York Ave   53070   920-564-2346
  Brian Hanes, supt.   Fax 564-6138
  oostburg.k12.wi.us
Oostburg HS   300/9-12
  410 New York Ave   53070   920-564-2346
  Scott Greupink, prin.   Fax 564-6138
Oostburg MS   200/6-8
  408 New York Ave   53070   920-564-2383
  Steve Harder, prin.

Oregon, Dane, Pop. 8,037
Oregon SD   3,400/K-12
  200 N Main St   53575   608-835-4091
  Brian Busler, supt.   Fax 835-9509
  www.oregon.k12.wi.us
Oregon HS   1,100/9-12
  456 N Perry Pkwy   53575   608-835-4301
  Chris Ligocki, prin.   Fax 835-7894
Oregon MS   600/7-8
  601 Pleasant Oak Dr   53575   608-835-4801
  Kyle Cherry, prin.   Fax 835-3849

Orfordville, Rock, Pop. 1,302
Parkview SD   1,200/PK-12
  PO Box 250   53576   608-879-2717
  Gary Reineck, supt.   Fax 879-2732
  www.parkview.k12.wi.us
Parkview HS   300/9-12
  PO Box 247   53576   608-879-2994
  Chris Nelson, prin.   Fax 879-2732
Parkview JHS   200/7-8
  PO Box 247   53576   608-879-2994
  John Abrahamson, prin.   Fax 879-2732

Osceola, Polk, Pop. 2,641
Osceola SD   1,800/PK-12
  PO Box 128   54020   715-294-4140
  Roger Kumlien, supt.   Fax 294-2428
  www.osceola.k12.wi.us
Osceola HS   600/9-12
  PO Box 128   54020   715-294-2127
  Michael McMartin, prin.   Fax 755-2068

Osceola MS, PO Box 128   54020   400/6-8
  Rebecca Styles, prin.   715-294-4180

Oshkosh, Winnebago, Pop. 63,237
Oshkosh Area SD   10,200/PK-12
  PO Box 3048   54903   920-424-0160
  Dr. Ronald Heilmann, supt.   Fax 424-0466
  www.oshkosh.k12.wi.us
Merrill MS   600/6-8
  108 W New York Ave   54901   920-424-0177
  Christine Fabian, prin.   Fax 424-7512
Oshkosh North HS   1,500/9-12
  1100 W Smith Ave   54901   920-424-7000
  James Hoffman, prin.   Fax 424-4054
Oshkosh West HS   2,000/9-12
  375 N Eagle St   54902   920-424-4090
  Thomas Parker, prin.   Fax 424-4950
South Park MS   500/6-8
  1551 Delaware St   54902   920-424-0431
  Lisa McLaughlin, prin.   Fax 424-7513
Stanley MS   400/6-8
  915 Hazel St   54901   920-424-0442
  Marceline Peters-Felice, prin.   Fax 424-7515
Tipler MS   400/6-8
  325 S Eagle St   54902   920-424-0320
  Ann Schultz, prin.   Fax 424-7514
Traeger MS   600/6-8
  3000 W 20th Ave   54904   920-424-0065
  Jeanne Koepke, prin.   Fax 424-7511

Fox Valley Technical College   Post-Sec.
  150 N Campbell Rd   54902   920-735-5600
Lourdes HS   200/9-12
  110 N Sawyer St   54902   920-235-5670
  Sr. Michelle Wronkowski, prin.   Fax 235-7453
Mercy Medical Center   Post-Sec.
  PO Box 3370   54903   920-233-5110
Oshkosh/Valley Christian S   300/K-12
  3450 Vinland Rd   54901   920-231-9704
  Todd Benson, admin.   Fax 231-9804
St. John Neumann S   100/6-8
  110 N Sawyer St   54902   920-426-6421
  Nancy Crowley, prin.   Fax 235-7453
University of Wisconsin   Post-Sec.
  800 Algoma Blvd   54901   920-424-0200

Osseo, Trempealeau, Pop. 1,655
Osseo-Fairchild SD   1,000/PK-12
  PO Box 130   54758   715-597-3141
  Kerry Jacobson, supt.   Fax 597-3606
  www.ofsd.k12.wi.us
Osseo-Fairchild HS   300/9-12
  PO Box 130   54758   715-597-3141
  Steve Glocke, prin.   Fax 597-3647
Osseo MS   200/6-8
  PO Box 130   54758   715-597-3141
  Steve Glocke, prin.   Fax 597-3647

Owen, Clark, Pop. 929
Owen-Withee SD   600/PK-12
  PO Box 417   54460   715-229-2151
  James Friesen, supt.   Fax 229-4322
  www.owen-withee.k12.wi.us
Owen-Withee HS   200/9-12
  PO Box 417   54460   715-229-2151
  Dan Taft, prin.   Fax 229-4322
Owen-Withee JHS   100/7-8
  PO Box 417   54460   715-229-2151
  Dan Taft, prin.   Fax 229-4322

Palmyra, Jefferson, Pop. 1,762
Palmyra-Eagle Area SD   1,200/PK-12
  PO Box 901   53156   262-495-7101
  Lowell Holtz, supt.   Fax 495-7151
  www.palmyra.k12.wi.us
Palmyra-Eagle HS   400/9-12
  PO Box 901   53156   262-495-7101
  Bruce Gunderson, prin.   Fax 495-7146
Palmyra-Eagle MS   200/6-8
  PO Box 901   53156   262-495-7101
  Tim Kooi, prin.   Fax 495-7146

Pardeeville, Columbia, Pop. 2,043
Pardeeville Area SD   1,000/PK-12
  120 Oak St   53954   608-429-3666
  Wayne Edwards, supt.   Fax 429-2277
  www.pardeeville.k12.wi.us
Pardeeville HS   300/9-12
  120 Oak St   53954   608-429-2153
  Paul Peterson, prin.   Fax 429-2277
Pardeeville MS   300/6-8
  120 Oak St   53954   608-429-2153
  Tonya Groyles-Brouillard, prin.   Fax 429-2277

Park Falls, Price, Pop. 2,579
Park Falls SD   800/PK-12
  420 2nd Ave N   54552   715-762-4343
  Dennis F. Dervetski, admin.   Fax 762-5469
  www.cardinalcountry.net
Park Falls HS   300/9-12
  400 9th St N   54552   715-762-2474
  Cindy Greenwood, prin.   Fax 762-5674
Park Falls MS   200/6-8
  420 2nd Ave N   54552   715-762-3815
  Michael Plemon, prin.   Fax 762-5469

Patch Grove, Grant, Pop. 168
River Ridge SD   600/PK-12
  PO Box 78   53817   608-994-2715
  Michael Murphy, supt.   Fax 994-2891
  www.rrsd.k12.wi.us
River Ridge HS   200/9-12
  PO Box 78   53817   608-994-3719
  Rod Lewis, prin.   Fax 994-2891
Other Schools – See Bloomington

Pembine, Marinette
Beecher-Dunbar-Pembine SD — 300/PK-12
PO Box 247 54156 — 715-324-5314
Robert R. Berndt, supt. — Fax 324-5282
www.pembine.k12.wi.us/
Pembine JSHS — 100/7-12
PO Box 247 54156 — 715-324-5314
Robert F. Berndt, prin. — Fax 324-5282

Pepin, Pepin, Pop. 930
Pepin Area SD — 300/PK-12
PO Box 128 54759 — 715-442-2391
Bruce A. Quinton, supt. — Fax 442-3607
Pepin HS — 100/9-12
PO Box 128 54759 — 715-442-2391
Bruce Quinton, prin. — Fax 442-3607

Peshtigo, Marinette, Pop. 3,375
Peshtigo SD — 1,200/PK-12
341 N Emery Ave 54157 — 715-582-3677
Kim Eparvier, supt. — Fax 582-3850
www.peshtigo.k12.wi.us
Peshtigo MSHS — 600/7-12
380 Green St 54157 — 715-582-3711
Stephen Motkowski, prin. — Fax 582-0740

Pewaukee, Waukesha, Pop. 21,388
Pewaukee SD — 2,200/PK-12
404 Lake St 53072 — 262-691-2100
JoAnn Sternke, supt. — Fax 691-1052
www.pewaukee.k12.wi.us
Clark MS — 600/6-8
472 Lake St 53072 — 262-691-2100
Randy Daul, prin. — Fax 695-5004
Pewaukee HS — 700/9-12
510 Lake St 53072 — 262-691-2100
Marty Van Hulle, prin. — Fax 695-5006

Trinity Academy — 200/K-12
W225N3131 Duplainville Rd 53072 — 262-695-2933
Robin Mitchell, admin. — Fax 695-2934
Waukesha County Technical College — Post-Sec.
800 Main St 53072 — 262-691-5566

Phelps, Vilas
Phelps SD — 200/K-12
4451 Old School Rd 54554 — 715-545-2724
Richard Parks, supt. — Fax 545-3728
www.phelps.k12.wi.us
Phelps HS — 100/9-12
4451 Old School Rd 54554 — 715-545-2724
Jason Pertile, prin. — Fax 545-3728

Phillips, Price, Pop. 1,573
Phillips SD — 1,100/PK-12
PO Box 70 54555 — 715-339-2141
Jerry Trochinski, supt. — Fax 339-2144
www.phillips.k12.wi.us/
Phillips HS — 400/9-12
PO Box 70 54555 — 715-339-2141
Joe Huftel, prin. — Fax 339-2144
Phillips MS — 200/6-8
PO Box 70 54555 — 715-339-3393
Dale Houdek, prin. — Fax 339-6783

Pittsville, Wood, Pop. 852
Pittsville SD — 800/PK-12
5459 Elementary Ave #2 54466 — 715-884-6694
Mary Peterson, supt. — Fax 884-5218
www.pittsville.k12.wi.us
Pittsville HS — 200/9-12
5407 1st Ave 54466 — 715-884-6412
John Olig, prin. — Fax 884-2870

Plainfield, Waushara, Pop. 902
Tri-County Area SD — 800/PK-12
PO Box 67 54966 — 715-335-6366
Tony Marinack, supt. — Fax 335-6365
www.penguin.tricounty.k12.wi.us
Tri-County HS — 400/7-12
PO Box 67 54966 — 715-335-6366
Larry Mancl, prin. — Fax 335-6322

Platteville, Grant, Pop. 9,846
Platteville SD — 1,600/PK-12
780 N 2nd St 53818 — 608-342-4000
Dean Isaacson, supt. — Fax 342-4412
www.platteville.k12.wi.us
Platteville HS — 600/9-12
710 E Madison St 53818 — 608-342-4020
Jeffrey Jacobson, prin. — Fax 342-4427
Platteville MS — 400/5-8
40 E Madison St 53818 — 608-342-4010
David Allen, prin. — Fax 342-4497

University of Wisconsin — Post-Sec.
1 University Plz 53818 — 608-342-1200

Plum City, Pierce, Pop. 579
Plum City SD — 400/K-12
907 Main St 54761 — 715-647-2591
Todd Leroy, supt. — Fax 647-3015
www.plumcity.k12.wi.us
Plum City JSHS — 200/6-12
907 Main St 54761 — 715-647-2591
Paul Churchill, prin. — Fax 647-3015

Plymouth, Sheboygan, Pop. 8,132
Plymouth SD — 2,400/PK-12
125 Highland Ave 53073 — 920-892-2661
Clark Reinke, supt. — Fax 892-6366
www.plymouth.k12.wi.us
Plymouth HS — 900/9-12
125 S Highland Ave 53073 — 920-893-6911
Dan Mella, prin. — Fax 892-6366
Riverview MS — 500/6-8
300 Riverside Cir 53073 — 920-892-4353
Tom Malmstadt, prin. — Fax 892-5072

Poplar, Douglas, Pop. 580
Maple SD
Supt. — See Maple
Northwestern MS — 400/6-8
PO Box 46 54864 — 715-364-2218
Ken Bartelt, prin. — Fax 364-2540

Portage, Columbia, Pop. 9,959
Portage Community SD — 2,500/PK-12
904 De Witt St 53901 — 608-742-4879
Daniel Pulsfus, supt. — Fax 742-4950
www.portage.k12.wi.us
Portage HS — 900/9-12
301 E Collins St 53901 — 608-742-8545
Karin Exo, prin. — Fax 742-0617
Portage JHS — 400/7-8
2505 New Pinery Rd 53901 — 608-742-2165
Wayne Bartels, prin. — Fax 742-6987

Port Edwards, Wood, Pop. 1,857
Port Edwards SD — 500/K-12
801 2nd St 54469 — 715-887-9000
Mike Alexander, supt. — Fax 887-9040
www.pesd.k12.wi.us
Edwards HS — 200/9-12
801 2nd St 54469 — 715-887-9000
Steve Lutzke, prin. — Fax 887-9040
Edwards JHS — 200/5-8
801 2nd St 54469 — 715-887-9000
Steve Lutzke, prin. — Fax 887-9040

Port Washington, Ozaukee, Pop. 10,730
Port Washington-Saukville SD — 2,600/PK-12
100 W Monroe St 53074 — 262-268-6000
Michael Weber Ph.D., supt. — Fax 268-6020
www.pwssd.k12.wi.us
Jefferson MS — 800/5-8
1403 N Holden St 53074 — 262-268-6100
Arlan Galarowicz, prin. — Fax 268-6120
Port Washington HS — 900/9-12
427 W Jackson St 53074 — 262-268-5500
Duane Woelfel, prin. — Fax 268-5520

Port Wing, Bayfield
South Shore SD — 200/PK-12
PO Box 40 54865 — 715-774-3500
Marc Christianson, supt. — Fax 774-3569
www.sshore.k12.wi.us
South Shore JSHS — 100/7-12
PO Box 40 54865 — 715-774-3361
Marc Christianson, prin. — Fax 774-3569

Potosi, Grant, Pop. 726
Potosi SD — 400/PK-12
128 US Highway 61 N 53820 — 608-763-2162
Dr. Steven Lozeau, supt. — Fax 763-2035
www.potosisd.k12.wi.us
Potosi S — 400/PK-12
128 US Highway 61 N 53820 — 608-763-2163
Terry Mengel, prin. — Fax 763-2035

Poynette, Columbia, Pop. 2,445
Poynette SD — 1,100/PK-12
PO Box 10 53955 — 608-635-4347
Barbara Wolfe, supt. — Fax 635-9200
www.poynette.k12.wi.us
Poynette HS — 400/9-12
PO Box 10 53955 — 608-635-4347
Craig McCallum, prin. — Fax 635-9201
Poynette MS — 300/6-8
PO Box 10 53955 — 608-635-4347
Brian Sutton, prin. — Fax 635-9233

Prairie du Chien, Crawford, Pop. 5,803
Prairie du Chien Area SD — 1,200/PK-12
420 S Wacouta Ave 53821 — 608-326-8451
James P. O'Meara, supt. — Fax 326-0000
www.pdc.k12.wi.us
Bluff View IS — 500/3-8
1901 E Wells St 53821 — 608-326-0503
Joan Wick, prin. — Fax 326-5364
Prairie du Chien HS — 500/9-12
800 E Crawford St 53821 — 608-326-8437
Andy Banasik, prin. — Fax 326-2333

St. John Nepomucene MS — 100/6-8
720 S Wacouta Ave 53821 — 608-326-4400
Mary Novey, prin. — Fax 326-4876

Prairie du Sac, Sauk, Pop. 3,390
Sauk Prairie SD
Supt. — See Sauk City
Sauk Prairie HS — 900/9-12
105 9th St 53578 — 608-643-5900
Brian Salzer, prin. — Fax 643-5419

Prairie Farm, Barron, Pop. 502
Prairie Farm SD — 300/K-12
630 River Ave S 54762 — 715-455-1683
Dr. Donald E. Hauck, supt. — Fax 455-1056
www.prairiefarm.k12.wi.us
Prairie Farm HS — 100/9-12
630 River Ave S 54762 — 715-455-1861
Donald E. Hauck, prin. — Fax 455-1056
Prairie Farm S — 100/6-8
630 River Ave S 54762 — 715-455-1841
Gary Husmann, prin. — Fax 455-1056

Prentice, Price, Pop. 590
Prentice SD — 600/PK-12
PO Box 110 54556 — 715-428-2811
Daniel J. Paul, supt. — Fax 428-2815
www.prentice.k12.wi.us
Prentice HS — 200/9-12
PO Box 110 54556 — 715-428-2811
Richard Meneau, prin. — Fax 428-2815

Prescott, Pierce, Pop. 3,783
Prescott SD — 1,100/PK-12
1220 Saint Croix St 54021 — 715-262-5782
Roger Hulne, supt. — Fax 262-5091
www.prescott.k12.wi.us
Prescott HS — 400/9-12
1220 Saint Croix St 54021 — 715-262-5010
Steven Shaw, prin. — Fax 262-5091
Prescott MS — 200/7-8
1220 Saint Croix St 54021 — 715-262-5389
Steven Shaw, prin. — Fax 262-5091

Princeton, Green Lake, Pop. 1,486
Princeton SD — 400/K-12
PO Box 147 54968 — 920-295-6571
Robert Beaver, supt. — Fax 295-4778
www.princeton.k12.wi.us/
Princeton S — 400/K-12
PO Box 147 54968 — 920-295-6571
Jean Rigden, prin. — Fax 295-4778

Pulaski, Brown, Pop. 3,430
Pulaski Community SD — 3,500/PK-12
PO Box 36 54162 — 920-822-6000
Dr. Kristine Martin, supt. — Fax 822-6005
www.pulaski.k12.wi.us/index.htm
Pulaski Community MS — 900/6-8
911 S Saint Augustine St 54162 — 920-822-6500
William Derricks, prin. — Fax 822-6505
Pulaski HS — 1,100/9-12
1040 S Saint Augustine St 54162 — 920-822-6700
Glenn Schlender, prin. — Fax 822-6707

Racine, Racine, Pop. 80,266
Racine USD — 19,300/PK-12
2220 Northwestern Ave 53404 — 262-635-5600
Thomas A. Hicks Ph.D., supt. — Fax 631-7121
www.racine.k12.wi.us
Case HS — 2,000/9-12
7345 Washington Ave 53406 — 262-619-4200
Tom Sager, prin. — Fax 619-4259
Gilmore MS — 900/6-8
2330 Northwestern Ave 53404 — 262-619-4260
Dan Thielen, prin. — Fax 619-4272
Horlick HS — 2,200/9-12
2119 Rapids Dr 53404 — 262-619-4300
Nola Starling-Ratliff, prin. — Fax 619-4390
Jerstad-Agerholm MS — 800/6-8
3601 Lasalle St 53402 — 262-664-6075
Alfredo Cintron, prin. — Fax 664-6120
Mitchell MS — 1,000/6-8
2701 Drexel Ave 53403 — 262-664-6400
Robert Wilhelmi, prin. — Fax 664-6444
Park HS — 2,200/9-12
1901 12th St 53403 — 262-619-4400
John Scott, prin. — Fax 619-4490
Starbuck MS — 800/6-8
1516 Ohio St 53405 — 262-664-6500
Sandy Johannsen Brand, prin. — Fax 664-6510
Walden III MSHS — 6-12
1012 Center St 53403 — 262-664-6250
Robert Holzem, prin. — Fax 664-6255

All Saints Healthcare System — Post-Sec.
1320 Wisconsin Ave 53403 — 262-636-2846
Gateway Technical College — Post-Sec.
1001 Main St 53403 — 262-619-6200
Lutheran HS — 200/9-12
251 Luedtke Ave 53405 — 262-637-6538
Randy Baganz, prin. — Fax 637-6601
Midwest College of Oriental Medicine — Post-Sec.
6232 Bankers Rd 53403 — 262-554-2010
Prairie S — 700/K-12
4050 Lighthouse Dr 53402 — 262-260-3845
Wm. Mark H. Murphy, hdmstr. — Fax 260-3790
St. Catherine HS — 500/9-12
1200 Park Ave 53403 — 262-632-2785
Jeffrey Johnson, prin. — Fax 632-5144

Randolph, Columbia, Pop. 1,839
Randolph SD — 500/PK-12
110 Meadowood Dr 53956 — 920-326-2427
Marvin Groskreutz, supt. — Fax 326-2439
www.randolph.k12.wi.us
Randolph HS — 200/9-12
110 Meadowood Dr 53956 — 920-326-2425
Thomas Erdman, prin. — Fax 326-2430

Random Lake, Sheboygan, Pop. 1,561
Random Lake SD — 1,000/PK-12
PO Box 500 53075 — 920-994-4342
Joseph Gassert, supt. — Fax 994-4820
www.randomlake.k12.wi.us
Random Lake HS — 400/9-12
PO Box 500 53075 — 920-994-9193
Keith Hilts, prin. — Fax 994-4820
Random Lake MS — 300/6-8
PO Box 500 53075 — 920-994-2498
David Farnham, prin. — Fax 994-4820

Reedsburg, Sauk, Pop. 8,227
Reedsburg SD — 2,500/PK-12
710 N Webb Ave 53959 — 608-524-2401
Thomas L. Benson, supt. — Fax 524-6818
www.rsd.k12.wi.us
Reedsburg Area HS — 900/9-12
1100 S Albert Ave 53959 — 608-524-4327
Rob Taylor, prin. — Fax 524-1373
Webb MS — 500/6-8
707 N Webb Ave 53959 — 608-524-2328
Casey Campbell, prin. — Fax 524-1161

Reedsville, Manitowoc, Pop. 1,170
Reedsville SD — 700/PK-12
PO Box 340 54230 — 920-754-4341
Robert Scrivner, supt. — Fax 754-4344
www.reedsville.k12.wi.us
Reedsville HS — 300/9-12
PO Box 340 54230 — 920-754-4341
Tony Butturini, prin. — Fax 754-4577

Rhinelander, Oneida, Pop. 7,813
Rhinelander SD 2,300/K-12
665 Coolidge Ave Ste B 54501 715-365-9700
Dr. Roger G. Erdahl, supt. Fax 365-9719
www.rhinelander.k12.wi.us
Rhinelander HS 1,200/9-12
665 Coolidge Ave 54501 715-365-9500
Michael Werbowsky, prin. Fax 365-9568
Williams MS 700/6-8
915 Acacia Ln 54501 715-365-9220
Paul Johnson, prin. Fax 369-7562

Nicolet Area Technical College Post-Sec.
PO Box 518 54501 715-365-4410

Rib Lake, Taylor, Pop. 857
Rib Lake SD 500/PK-12
PO Box 278 54470 715-427-3222
Dan Boxx, supt. Fax 427-3221
www.riblake.k12.wi.us
Rib Lake HS 200/9-12
PO Box 278 54470 715-427-3220
Rick Cardey, prin. Fax 427-5022
Rib Lake MS 100/6-8
PO Box 278 54470 715-427-5446
Rick Cardey, prin. Fax 427-3221

Rice Lake, Barron, Pop. 8,270
Rice Lake Area SD 2,500/PK-12
700 Augusta St 54868 715-234-9007
Paul Vine, supt. Fax 234-4552
www.ricelake.k12.wi.us
Rice Lake HS 900/9-12
30 S Wisconsin Ave 54868 715-234-2181
Larry Zeman, prin. Fax 234-6679
Rice Lake MS 600/6-8
204 Cameron Rd 54868 715-234-8156
Steve Sirek, prin. Fax 234-9439

Univ. of Wisconsin Center-Barron County Post-Sec.
1800 College Dr 54868 715-234-8176

Richfield, Washington
Richfield J1 SD 400/PK-8
3117 Holly Hill Rd 53076 262-628-1032
Craig Baker, supt. Fax 628-3013
www.richfield.k12.wi.us
Richfield ES 300/3-8
3117 Holly Hill Rd 53076 262-628-1032
Craig Baker, prin. Fax 628-3013

Richland Center, Richland, Pop. 5,173
Ithaca SD 400/K-12
24615 State Hwy 58 53581 608-585-2512
Kristine Blakeley, supt. Fax 585-2505
www.ithaca.k12.wi.us/
Ithaca HS 100/9-12
24615 State Hwy 58 53581 608-585-2311
Kristine Blakeley, prin. Fax 585-2505
Ithaca MS 100/6-8
24615 State Hwy 58 53581 608-585-2311
Kristine Blakeley, prin. Fax 585-2505

Richland SD 1,500/PK-12
26220 Executive Ln Ste A 53581 608-647-6106
Rachel Schultz, supt. Fax 647-8454
www.richland.k12.wi.us
Richland Center HS 600/9-12
23200 Hornet High Rd 53581 608-647-6131
John Cler, prin. Fax 647-8734
Richland MS 300/6-8
1801 US Highway 80 S 53581 608-647-6381
David Guy, prin. Fax 647-4735

Eagle S 100/PK-12
26700 Fellowship Ln 53581 608-647-7226
Erwin Holmes, admin. Fax 647-5669
University of Wisconsin Center Post-Sec.
1200 US Hwy 14 W 53581 608-647-6186

Rio, Columbia, Pop. 966
Rio Community SD 500/PK-12
411 Church St 53960 920-992-3141
Mark McGuire, supt. Fax 992-3157
www.rio.k12.wi.us
Rio MSHS 300/6-12
411 Church St 53960 920-992-3141
Mark McGuire, prin. Fax 992-3157

Ripon, Fond du Lac, Pop. 7,274
Ripon SD 1,700/PK-12
PO Box 991 54971 920-748-4600
Richard N. Zimman, supt. Fax 748-2715
www.ripon.k12.wi.us
Ripon HS 500/9-12
PO Box 991 54971 920-748-4616
Dan Tjernagel, prin. Fax 748-4622
Ripon MS 400/6-8
PO Box 991 54971 920-748-4638
Melanie Oppor, prin. Fax 748-4653

Ripon College Post-Sec.
PO Box 248 54971 920-748-8115

River Falls, Pierce, Pop. 12,967
River Falls SD 2,900/PK-12
852 E Division St 54022 715-425-1800
Boyd McLarty, supt. Fax 425-1804
www.rfsd.k12.wi.us
Meyer MS 700/6-8
230 N 9th St 54022 715-425-1820
Greg Danke, prin. Fax 425-1823
River Falls HS 1,000/9-12
818 Cemetery Rd 54022 715-425-1830
Dr. Elaine Baumann, prin. Fax 425-1827

Good Shepherd Christian Academy 50/K-12
896 State Road 65 54022 715-425-0211
Jennifer Beierman, admin. Fax 425-6309
University of Wisconsin Post-Sec.
410 S 3rd St 54022 715-425-3911

Rosendale, Fond du Lac, Pop. 959
Rosendale-Brandon SD 1,100/PK-12
300 W Wisconsin St 54974 920-872-2851
Gary Hansen, supt. Fax 872-2647
www.rbsd.k12.wi.us
Laconia HS 300/9-12
301 W Division St 54974 920-872-2161
Jeff Lange, prin. Fax 872-2777
Rosendale IS 200/4-8
200 S Main St 54974 920-872-2126
John Hokenson, prin. Fax 872-2061

Rosholt, Portage, Pop. 489
Rosholt SD 700/PK-12
PO Box 310 54473 715-677-4542
Kathleen Martinsen Ph.D., supt. Fax 677-3543
www.rosholt.k12.wi.us
Rosholt HS 300/9-12
PO Box 310 54473 715-677-4541
Ken Camlek, prin. Fax 677-6767
Rosholt MS 100/6-8
PO Box 310 54473 715-677-4541
Ken Camlek, prin. Fax 677-6767

Saint Croix Falls, Polk, Pop. 2,052
St. Croix Falls SD 1,100/PK-12
PO Box 130 54024 715-483-9823
Glenn Martin, supt. Fax 483-3695
www.scf.k12.wi.us
St. Croix Falls HS 400/9-12
PO Box 130 54024 715-483-9823
Kevin Whelihan, prin. Fax 483-3695
St. Croix Falls MS 400/5-8
PO Box 130 54024 715-483-9823
Kathleen Willow, prin. Fax 483-3695

Valley Christian S 50/PK-12
1263 State Road 35 54024 715-483-9126
Ron Brace, admin. Fax 483-5679

Saint Francis, Milwaukee, Pop. 8,809
St. Francis SD 1,000/PK-12
4225 S Lake Dr 53235 414-747-3900
Dr. Ronda Ewald, supt. Fax 482-7198
www.stfrancissd.org
Deer Creek IS 300/4-8
3680 S Kinnickinnic Ave 53235 414-482-8400
Blake Peuse, prin. Fax 482-8406
Saint Francis HS 600/9-12
4225 S Lake Dr 53235 414-747-3600
Dr. Gerald Luecht, prin. Fax 747-3605

Salem, Kenosha
Central-Westosha UNHSD 1,200/9-12
PO Box 38 53168 262-843-4211
Doug Potter, supt. Fax 843-4069
www.westosha.k12.wi.us
Central HS 1,200/9-12
PO Box 38 53168 262-843-1987
Barb Sonnenberg, prin. Fax 843-4069

Salem SD 700/K-8
PO Box 160 53168 262-843-2356
David Milz, supt. Fax 843-4138
www.salem.k12.wi.us
Salem MS, PO Box 160 53168 6-8
Eileen Bruton, prin. 262-843-2356

Sauk City, Sauk, Pop. 3,025
Sauk Prairie SD 2,800/PK-12
213 Maple St 53583 608-643-5990
Craig Bender, supt. Fax 643-6216
www.saukpr.k12.wi.us
Sauk Prairie MS 700/6-8
207 Maple St 53583 608-643-5500
Ellen Paul, prin. Fax 643-5503
Other Schools – See Prairie du Sac

Schofield, Marathon, Pop. 2,234
D.C. Everest Area SD 5,200/PK-12
6300 Alderson St 54476 715-359-4221
Kristine Gilmore, supt. Fax 359-2056
www.dce.k12.wi.us
D.C. Everest HS 1,300/10-12
6500 Alderson St 54476 715-359-6561
Thomas Johanson, prin. Fax 355-7220
D.C. Everest JHS 900/8-9
1000 Machmueller St 54476 715-359-0511
Steven Pophal, prin. Fax 359-9395

Seneca, Crawford
Seneca SD 300/PK-12
PO Box 34 54654 608-734-3411
Richard Burby, supt. Fax 734-3430
www.seneca.k12.wi.us
Seneca HS 100/9-12
PO Box 34 54654 608-734-3411
Richard Burby, prin. Fax 734-3430
Seneca JHS 100/5-8
PO Box 34 54654 608-734-3411
Richard Burby, prin. Fax 734-3430

Seymour, Outagamie, Pop. 3,294
Seymour Community SD 2,500/PK-12
10 Circle Dr 54165 920-833-2304
William Loasching, supt. Fax 833-6037
www.seymour.k12.wi.us/
Seymour HS 800/9-12
10 Circle Dr 54165 920-833-2306
Susan Shuler, prin. Fax 833-7608
Seymour MS 500/6-8
10 Circle Dr 54165 920-833-7199
Robert Battisti, prin. Fax 833-9376

Shawano, Shawano, Pop. 8,351
Shawano-Gresham SD 2,900/PK-12
218 County Road B 54166 715-526-3194
Richard Hess, supt. Fax 526-6072
www.sgsd.k12.wi.us
Shawano Community HS 1,000/9-12
220 County Road B 54166 715-526-2175
Todd Stiede, prin. Fax 524-8414
Shawano Community MS 700/5-8
1050 S Union St 54166 715-526-2192
Daniel Labby, prin. Fax 526-5037
Other Schools – See Gresham

East Central WI Lutheran HS 100/9-12
PO Box 542 54166 715-524-5301
Paul Weismantel, prin. Fax 524-4876

Sheboygan, Sheboygan, Pop. 49,263
Sheboygan Area SD 10,300/PK-12
830 Virginia Ave 53081 920-459-3511
Joseph Sheehan Ph.D., supt. Fax 459-6487
www.sheboygan.k12.wi.us
Farnsworth MS 800/6-8
1017 Union Ave 53081 920-459-3655
David Williams, prin. Fax 459-3660
Mann MS 700/6-8
2820 Union Ave 53081 920-459-3666
Russ Groblewski, prin. Fax 459-3669
North HS 1,700/9-12
1042 School Ave 53083 920-459-3600
Rick Schultz, prin. Fax 459-3601
South HS 1,600/9-12
3128 S 12th St 53081 920-459-3637
Lee Benish, prin. Fax 459-6733
Urban MS 800/6-8
1226 North Ave 53083 920-459-3680
Susan Nennig, prin. Fax 459-4065

Lakeland College Post-Sec.
PO Box 359 53082 920-565-2111
Sheboygan Area Lutheran HS 200/9-12
3323 University Dr 53081 920-452-3323
Allen Holzheimer, prin. Fax 452-1310
Sheboygan County Christian HS 200/9-12
929 Greenfield Ave 53081 920-458-9981
Wayne Dykstra, prin. Fax 458-9957
University of Wisconsin Center Post-Sec.
1 University Dr 53081 920-459-3733

Sheboygan Falls, Sheboygan, Pop. 6,995
Sheboygan Falls SD 1,700/PK-12
220 Amherst Ave 53085 920-467-7893
Dr. C. Lee Riter, supt. Fax 467-7899
www.sheboyganfalls.k12.wi.us
Sheboygan Falls HS 600/9-12
220 Amherst Ave 53085 920-467-7890
Scott Sabol, prin. Fax 467-7825
Sheboygan Falls MS 500/5-8
101 School St 53085 920-467-7880
Robert Flaherty, prin. Fax 467-7885

Shell Lake, Washburn, Pop. 1,346
Shell Lake SD 600/K-12
271 Highway 63 S 54871 715-468-7816
Gerald Gauderman, supt. Fax 468-7812
www.shelllake.k12.wi.us
Shell Lake JSHS 300/7-12
271 Highway 63 S 54871 715-468-7814
Terry Reynolds, prin.

Wisconsin Indianhead Technical College Post-Sec.
505 Pine Ridge Dr 54871 715-468-2815

Shiocton, Outagamie, Pop. 933
Shiocton SD 900/PK-12
PO Box 68 54170 920-986-3351
Dave Moscinski, supt. Fax 986-3291
www.shiocton.k12.wi.us
Shiocton HS 300/9-12
PO Box 68 54170 920-986-3351
Pat Van Alstine, prin. Fax 986-3291

Shorewood, Milwaukee, Pop. 13,424
Shorewood SD 2,200/PK-12
1701 E Capitol Dr 53211 414-963-6901
Blane K McCann, supt. Fax 963-6904
www.shorewoodschools.org
Shorewood HS 700/9-12
1701 E Capitol Dr 53211 414-963-6921
Rick Monroe, prin. Fax 961-2819
Shorewood IS 300/7-8
3830 N Morris Blvd 53211 414-963-6951
Roxanne Hanney, prin. Fax 963-6946

Shullsburg, Lafayette, Pop. 1,229
Shullsburg SD 400/PK-12
444 N Judgement St 53586 608-965-4427
Loras Kruser, admin. Fax 965-3794
www.shullsburg.k12.wi.us
Shullsburg HS 100/9-12
444 N Judgement St 53586 608-965-4427
Loras Kruser, prin. Fax 965-3794
Shullsburg JHS 100/6-8
444 N Judgement St 53586 608-965-4427
Loras Kruser, prin. Fax 965-3794

Siren, Burnett, Pop. 1,015
Siren SD 500/PK-12
PO Box 29 54872 715-349-2290
Scott Johnson, supt. Fax 349-7476
www.siren.k12.wi.us
Siren JSHS 200/7-12
PO Box 29 54872 715-349-2277
Joseph Zirngibl, prin. Fax 349-7476

Slinger, Washington, Pop. 4,142
Slinger SD — 2,800/PK-12
  207 Polk St 53086 — 262-644-9615
  Robert Reynolds, supt. — Fax 644-7514
  www.slinger.k12.wi.us
Slinger HS — 900/9-12
  209 Polk St 53086 — 262-644-5261
  Vic Erickson, prin. — Fax 644-0479
Slinger MS — 700/6-8
  521 Olympic Dr 53086 — 262-644-5226
  Patricia Schultz, prin. — Fax 644-7353

Soldiers Grove, Crawford, Pop. 629
North Crawford SD — 600/PK-12
  47050 County Road X 54655 — 608-735-4318
  Daniel Davies, supt. — Fax 735-4317
  www.northcrawford.com/
North Crawford HS — 200/9-12
  47050 County Road X 54655 — 608-735-4311
  Daniel Davies, prin. — Fax 624-6269

Solon Springs, Douglas, Pop. 575
Solon Springs SD — 400/PK-12
  8993 E Baldwin Ave 54873 — 715-378-2263
  Gary Frankiewicz, supt. — Fax 378-2073
  eyrie.solonk12.net/school/
Solon Springs S — 400/PK-12
  8993 E Baldwin Ave 54873 — 715-378-2263
  Gary Frankiewicz, prin. — Fax 378-2073

Somers, Kenosha

Shoreland Lutheran HS — 300/9-12
  PO Box 295 53171 — 262-859-2595
  Jeffery Wiechman, prin. — Fax 859-2783

Somerset, Saint Croix, Pop. 2,264
Somerset SD — 1,300/PK-12
  PO Box 100 54025 — 715-247-3313
  Randal Rosburg, supt. — Fax 247-5588
  www.somerset.k12.wi.us
Somerset HS — 400/9-12
  PO Box 100 54025 — 715-247-3355
  Lynn Rieck-Hudnall, prin. — Fax 247-3864
Somerset MS — 400/5-8
  PO Box 100 54025 — 715-247-4400
  Richard Lange, prin. — Fax 247-4437

South Milwaukee, Milwaukee, Pop. 21,258
South Milwaukee SD — 3,500/PK-12
  901 15th Ave 53172 — 414-766-5000
  David Ewald, supt. — Fax 766-5005
  www.sdsm.k12.wi.us/
South Milwaukee HS — 1,200/9-12
  801 15th Ave 53172 — 414-766-5100
  Dr. Gary Kiltz, prin. — Fax 766-5131
South Milwaukee MS — 800/6-8
  1001 15th Ave 53172 — 414-766-5800
  Mike Connor, prin. — Fax 766-5803

Calvary Academy — 50/5-12
  2200 9th Ave 53172 — 414-571-1522
  Carlton Weisheim, prin. — Fax 571-5242

South Wayne, Lafayette, Pop. 479
Black Hawk SD — 500/PK-12
  PO Box 303 53587 — 608-439-5400
  Kevin Shetler, supt. — Fax 439-1022
  www.blackhawk.k12.wi.us
Black Hawk HS — 200/9-12
  PO Box 303 53587 — 608-439-5371
  Jerry Mortimer, prin. — Fax 439-1022
Other Schools – See Gratiot

Sparta, Monroe, Pop. 8,708
Sparta Area SD — 3,200/PK-12
  506 N Black River St 54656 — 608-269-3151
  John Hendricks, supt. — Fax 269-6428
  www.spartan.org
Sparta HS — 900/9-12
  506 N Black River St 54656 — 608-269-2107
  William Tourdot, prin. — Fax 269-7165
Sparta Meadowview MS — 600/6-8
  506 N Black River St 54656 — 608-269-2185
  Cheri Kulland, prin. — Fax 366-3404

Sparta Area Christian S — 50/PK-12
  413 Osborne Dr 54656 — 608-269-0358
  Tom Lago, admin. — Fax 269-0358

Spencer, Marathon, Pop. 1,886
Spencer SD — 800/PK-12
  300 School St 54479 — 715-659-5347
  David Wessel, supt. — Fax 659-5470
  www.spencer.k12.wi.us
Spencer HS — 300/9-12
  300 School St 54479 — 715-659-4211
  Harry Toufar, prin. — Fax 659-5470

Spooner, Washburn, Pop. 2,700
Spooner SD — 1,500/PK-12
  500 College St 54801 — 715-635-2171
  Dr. Donald Haack, supt. — Fax 635-7174
  www.spooner.k12.wi.us
Spooner HS — 600/9-12
  500 College St 54801 — 715-635-2172
  Robert Kinderman, prin. — Fax 635-7074
Spooner MS — 500/5-8
  500 College St 54801 — 715-635-2173
  Lynnea Lake, prin. — Fax 635-7074

Spring Green, Sauk, Pop. 1,417
River Valley SD — 1,500/PK-12
  660 W Daley St 53588 — 608-588-2551
  Jamie Benson, supt. — Fax 588-2558
  www.rvschools.org
River Valley HS — 600/9-12
  660 Varsity Blvd 53588 — 608-588-2554
  Kim Kaukl, prin. — Fax 588-2827

River Valley MS — 400/6-8
  660 W Daley St 53588 — 608-588-2556
  Roger Hoffman, prin. — Fax 588-2026

Spring Valley, Pierce, Pop. 1,206
Spring Valley SD — 800/K-12
  PO Box 249 54767 — 715-778-5551
  David A. Wellington, supt. — Fax 778-4761
  www.springvalley.k12.wi.us
Spring Valley MSHS — 400/7-12
  PO Box 249 54767 — 715-778-5554
  Gretchen Cipriano, prin. — Fax 778-5556

Stanley, Chippewa, Pop. 1,857
Stanley-Boyd Area SD — 1,100/PK-12
  507 E 1st Ave 54768 — 715-644-5534
  James Jones, supt. — Fax 644-5584
  www.stanleyboyd.k12.wi.us
Stanley-Boyd HS — 400/9-12
  507 E 1st Ave 54768 — 715-644-5534
  Mark Carlson, prin. — Fax 644-6701
Stanley-Boyd MS — 200/6-8
  507 E 1st Ave 54768 — 715-644-5715
  Patrick Marion, prin. — Fax 644-5584

Stevens Point, Portage, Pop. 24,412
Stevens Point Area SD — 5,100/PK-12
  1900 Polk St 54481 — 715-345-5444
  Bette Lang Ed.D., supt. — Fax 345-7302
  www.wisp.k12.wi.us
Franklin JHS — 900/7-9
  2000 Polk St 54481 — 715-345-5413
  Connie Negaard, prin. — Fax 345-5696
Jacobs JHS — 900/7-9
  2400 Main St 54481 — 715-345-5422
  Jeb Steckbauer, prin. — Fax 345-7340
Stevens Point Area SHS — 1,800/10-12
  1201 Northpoint Dr 54481 — 715-345-5400
  Mike Devine, prin. — Fax 345-5408

Mid-State Technical College — Post-Sec.
  933 Michigan Ave 54481 — 715-344-3063
Pacelli HS — 200/9-12
  1301 Maria Dr 54481 — 715-341-2442
  Gregg Hansel, prin. — Fax 341-6779
St. Peter MS — 200/6-8
  708 1st St 54481 — 715-344-1890
  Ellen Lopas, prin. — Fax 342-2005
Stevens Point Christian Academy — 100/K-12
  801 US Highway 10 W 54481 — 715-341-3275
  Michael Fasula, prin. — Fax 341-3023
University of Wisconsin — Post-Sec.
  2100 Main St 54481 — 715-346-0123

Stockbridge, Calumet, Pop. 672
Stockbridge SD — 300/PK-12
  PO Box 188 53088 — 920-439-1159
  LeRoy Kopecky, supt. — Fax 439-1150
  www.stockbridge.k12.wi.us/
Stockbridge HS — 100/9-12
  PO Box 188 53088 — 920-439-1159
  Kenneth Kappell, prin. — Fax 439-1150

Stoughton, Dane, Pop. 12,611
Stoughton Area SD — 3,600/PK-12
  320 North St 53589 — 608-877-5001
  Myron Palomba, supt. — Fax 877-5008
  www.stoughton.k12.wi.us
River Bluff MS — 600/7-8
  235 N Forrest St 53589 — 608-877-5501
  Richard Pertzborn, prin. — Fax 877-5508
Stoughton HS — 1,200/9-12
  600 Lincoln Ave 53589 — 608-877-5601
  Jerry Movrich, prin. — Fax 877-5619

Stratford, Marathon, Pop. 1,552
Stratford SD — 800/PK-12
  PO Box 7 54484 — 715-687-3130
  Scott Winch, supt. — Fax 687-4074
  www.stratford.k12.wi.us
Stratford JSHS — 400/7-12
  PO Box 7 54484 — 715-687-4311
  Paul Rozak, prin. — Fax 687-4652

Strum, Trempealeau, Pop. 977
Eleva-Strum SD — 600/PK-12
  W23597 US Highway 10 54770 — 715-695-2696
  Kenneth Rogers Ph.D., admin. — Fax 695-3519
  www.esschools.org/
Eleva-Strum MSHS — 300/7-12
  W23597 US Highway 10 54770 — 715-695-2696
  Mark Gruen, prin. — Fax 695-3938

Sturgeon Bay, Door, Pop. 9,484
Sevastopol SD — 600/PK-12
  4550 State Highway 57 54235 — 920-743-6282
  Ann Smejkal, supt. — Fax 743-4009
  www.sevastopol.k12.wi.us
Sevastopol HS — 300/9-12
  4550 State Highway 57 54235 — 920-743-6282
  Bob Nickel, prin. — Fax 743-4009
Sevastopol JHS — 100/7-8
  4550 State Highway 57 54235 — 920-743-6282
  Ann Smejkal, prin. — Fax 743-4009

Sturgeon Bay SD — 1,300/PK-12
  1230 Michigan St 54235 — 920-746-2800
  Robert Grimmer, supt. — Fax 746-3888
  www.sturbay.k12.wi.us
Sturgeon Bay HS — 500/9-12
  1230 Michigan St 54235 — 920-746-2800
  Daniel Moore, prin. — Fax 746-3888
Walker MS — 300/6-8
  19 N 14th Ave 54235 — 920-746-2810
  Randy Watermolen, prin. — Fax 746-3885

Northeast Wisconsin Technical College — Post-Sec.
  229 N 14th Ave 54235 — 920-743-2207

Sun Prairie, Dane, Pop. 23,484
Sun Prairie Area SD — 5,300/PK-12
  501 S Bird St 53590 — 608-834-6500
  Tim Culver, supt. — Fax 837-9311
  www.spasd.k12.wi.us
Marsh MS — 600/6-8
  1351 Columbus St 53590 — 608-834-7600
  Clark Luessman, prin. — Fax 834-7692
Prairie View MS — 600/6-8
  400 N Thompson Rd 53590 — 608-834-7800
  Nancy Hery, prin. — Fax 834-7892
Sun Prairie HS — 1,600/9-12
  220 Kroncke Dr 53590 — 608-834-6700
  Paul Keats, prin. — Fax 834-6792

Diesel Truck Driver Training School — Post-Sec.
  7190 Elder Ln 53590 — 608-837-7800

Superior, Douglas, Pop. 27,742
Superior SD — 4,900/PK-12
  3025 Tower Ave 54880 — 715-394-8700
  Jay Mitchell, supt. — Fax 394-8708
  www.superior.k12.wi.us
Superior HS — 1,700/9-12
  2600 Catlin Ave 54880 — 715-394-8720
  Kent Bergum, prin. — Fax 394-8760
Superior MS — 1,200/6-8
  3626 Hammond Ave 54880 — 715-394-8740
  Richard Flaherty, prin. — Fax 395-8483

Maranatha Academy — 100/PK-12
  4916 S State Road 35 54880 — 715-399-8757
  Rosemary Niebauer, admin. — Fax 399-0496
University of Wisconsin — Post-Sec.
  PO Box 2000 54880 — 715-394-8101

Suring, Oconto, Pop. 591
Suring SD — 600/PK-12
  PO Box 158 54174 — 920-842-2178
  Todd J. Carlson, supt. — Fax 842-4570
  www.suring.k12.wi.us
Suring HS — 200/9-12
  PO Box 158 54174 — 920-842-2182
  Robert Ray, prin. — Fax 842-4570

Sussex, Waukesha, Pop. 9,561
Hamilton SD — 3,900/K-12
  W220N6151 Town Line Rd 53089 — 262-246-1973
  Dr. Kathleen Cooke, supt. — Fax 246-6552
  www.hamiltondist.k12.wi.us/
Hamilton HS — 1,200/9-12
  W220N6151 Town Line Rd 53089 — 262-246-6471
  David Furrer, prin. — Fax 246-1885
Templeton MS — 900/6-8
  N59W22490 Silver Spring Dr 53089 — 262-246-6477
  Patricia Polczynski, prin. — Fax 246-0465

Richmond SD — 200/PK-8
  N56W26530 Richmond Rd 53089 — 262-538-1360
  George Zimmer, supt. — Fax 538-1572
  www.richmond.k12.wi.us
Richmond MS — 5-8
  N56W26530 Richmond Rd 53089 — 262-538-1360
  George Zimmer, prin. — Fax 538-1572

Thorp, Clark, Pop. 1,571
Thorp SD — 600/PK-12
  PO Box 449 54771 — 715-669-5401
  Barkley Anderson, admin. — Fax 669-5403
  www.thorp.k12.wi.us
Thorp HS — 200/9-12
  PO Box 449 54771 — 715-669-5401
  James Montgomery, prin. — Fax 669-5403

Three Lakes, Oneida
Three Lakes SD — 600/PK-12
  6930 W School St 54562 — 715-546-3496
  George Karling, supt. — Fax 546-8125
  www.threelakessd.k12.wi.us
Three Lakes HS — 300/9-12
  6930 W School St 54562 — 715-546-3321
  William Greb, prin. — Fax 546-2828
Three Lakes JHS — 7-8
  6930 W School St 54562 — 715-546-3321
  William Greb, prin. — Fax 546-2828

Tigerton, Shawano, Pop. 749
Tigerton SD — 400/PK-12
  PO Box 10 54486 — 715-535-3220
  Gerald N. Gerard, supt. — Fax 535-3215
  www.tigerton.k12.wi.us
Tigerton MSHS — 200/6-12
  PO Box 40 54486 — 715-535-2185
  Donald Aanonsen, prin. — Fax 535-1355

Tomah, Monroe, Pop. 8,525
Tomah Area SD — 3,000/PK-12
  129 W Clifton St 54660 — 608-374-7004
  Robert T. Fasbender, supt. — Fax 372-5087
  www.tomah.k12.wi.us
Tomah HS — 1,000/9-12
  901 Lincoln Ave 54660 — 608-374-7358
  Marlon Mee, prin. — Fax 374-7290
Tomah MS — 700/6-8
  612 Hollister Ave 54660 — 608-374-7882
  Cindy Zahrte, prin. — Fax 374-7303

Tomahawk, Lincoln, Pop. 3,807
Tomahawk SD — 1,600/PK-12
  1048 E King Rd 54487 — 715-453-5551
  Allan Prosser, supt. — Fax 453-1855
  www.tomahawk.k12.wi.us
Tomahawk HS — 600/9-12
  1048 E King Rd 54487 — 715-453-2106
  Scott Swenty, prin. — Fax 453-1437
Tomahawk MS — 400/6-8
  1048 E King Rd 54487 — 715-453-5371
  Tom Freude, prin. — Fax 453-9630

Tony, Rusk, Pop. 98
Flambeau SD | 700/PK-12
PO Box 86 54563 | 715-532-3183
William Pfalzgraf, supt. | Fax 532-5405
www.flambeau.k12.wi.us
Flambeau S | 700/PK-12
PO Box 86 54563 | 715-532-3183
Linda Michek, prin. | Fax 532-5405

Trempealeau, Trempealeau, Pop. 1,435
Galesville-Ettrick-Trempealeau SD
Supt. — See Galesville
Gale-Ettrick-Tremp MS | 200/7-8
PO Box 277 54661 | 608-534-6391
Paul Uhren, prin. | Fax 534-6395

Turtle Lake, Barron, Pop. 1,016
Turtle Lake SD | 500/PK-12
205 Oak St 54889 | 715-986-2597
Charles Dunlop, supt. | Fax 986-2444
www.cesa11.k12.wi.us/turtle-lake
Turtle Lake HS | 200/9-12
205 Oak St 54889 | 715-986-4470
Wayne Olson, prin. | Fax 986-2444

Two Rivers, Manitowoc, Pop. 12,239
Two Rivers SD | 2,100/PK-12
4521 Lincoln Ave 54241 | 920-793-4560
Randy Fredrikson, supt. | Fax 793-4014
www.trschools.k12.wi.us
Clarke MS | 500/6-8
4608 Bellevue Pl 54241 | 920-794-1614
Stanley Phelps, prin. | Fax 793-1819
Two Rivers HS | 700/9-12
4519 Lincoln Ave 54241 | 920-793-2291
Ridge Schott, prin. | Fax 793-5068

Union Grove, Racine, Pop. 4,498
Union Grove UNHSD | 700/9-12
3433 S Colony Ave 53182 | 262-878-4427
David Magar, supt. | Fax 878-3291
www.ug.k12.wi.us
Union Grove HS | 700/9-12
3433 S Colony Ave 53182 | 262-878-2434
Alan Mollerskov, prin. | Fax 878-4056

Union Grove Christian S | 200/PK-12
PO Box 87 53182 | 262-878-1265
Lee Morey, prin. | Fax 878-2085

Valders, Manitowoc, Pop. 992
Valders Area SD | 1,100/PK-12
138 Wilson St 54245 | 920-775-9500
Thomas Hughes, supt. | Fax 775-9509
www.valders.k12.wi.us
Valders HS, 201 W Wilson St 54245 | 400/9-12
Richard Druschke, prin. | 920-775-9530
Valders MS, 138 Jefferson St 54245 | 400/5-8
Derrick Krey, prin. | 920-775-9520

Verona, Dane, Pop. 9,371
Verona Area SD | 4,000/PK-12
700 N Main St 53593 | 608-845-4300
Dean Gorrell, supt. | Fax 845-4321
www.verona.k12.wi.us
Badger Ridge MS | 500/6-8
740 N Main St 53593 | 608-845-4100
David Jennings, prin. | Fax 845-4120
Verona Area HS | 1,400/9-12
300 Richard St 53593 | 608-845-4400
Kelly Meyers, prin. | Fax 845-4420
Other Schools – See Fitchburg

Viola, Richland, Pop. 656
Kickapoo Area SD | 500/K-12
S6520 State Highway 131 54664 | 608-627-0102
Thomas Simonson, supt. | Fax 627-0118
www.kickapoo.k12.wi.us
Kickapoo MSHS | 300/6-12
S6520 State Highway 131 54664 | 608-627-0100
Keith Rocklewitz, prin. | Fax 627-0132

Viroqua, Vernon, Pop. 4,351
Viroqua Area SD | 1,200/PK-12
115 N Education Ave 54665 | 608-637-1186
David Johnston, supt. | Fax 637-8554
www.viroqua.k12.wi.us
Viroqua HS | 400/9-12
100 Blackhawk Dr 54665 | 608-637-3191
Katherine Klos, prin. | Fax 637-8034
Viroqua MS | 300/5-8
100 Blackhawk Dr 54665 | 608-637-3171
Katherine Klos, prin. | Fax 637-1589

Cornerstone Christian Academy | 100/PK-12
S 3656 US Highway 14 54665 | 608-634-4102
Craig Skrede, admin. | Fax 634-4162

Wabeno, Forest
Wabeno Area SD | 600/PK-12
PO Box 460 54566 | 715-473-2592
Richard Huisman, supt. | Fax 473-5201
www.wabeno.k12.wi.us
Wabeno JSHS | 300/7-12
PO Box 460 54566 | 715-473-5122
Timothy Brauer, prin. | Fax 473-3406

Wales, Waukesha, Pop. 2,604
Kettle Moraine SD | 4,400/PK-12
563 A J Allen Cir 53183 | 262-968-6300
Patricia Deklotz, supt. | Fax 968-6391
www.kmsd.edu/
Kettle Moraine HS | 1,500/9-12
349 N Oak Crest Dr 53183 | 262-968-6200
Tanya Kotlowski, prin. | Fax 968-6217
Other Schools – See Dousman

Walworth, Walworth, Pop. 2,511
Big Foot UNHSD | 600/9-12
PO Box 99 53184 | 262-275-2116
Daniel Burke, supt. | Fax 275-5117
www.bigfoot.k12.wi.us
Big Foot Union HS | 600/9-12
PO Box 99 53184 | 262-275-2116
Patrick Brynes, prin. | Fax 275-5117

Washburn, Bayfield, Pop. 2,299
Washburn SD | 700/PK-12
PO Box 730 54891 | 715-373-6187
Gerald Eichman, supt. | Fax 373-5877
www.washburn.k12.wi.us
Dupont MS | 100/7-8
PO Box 730 54891 | 715-373-6188
Marc Christianson, prin. | Fax 373-5877
Washburn HS | 300/9-12
PO Box 730 54891 | 715-373-6188
Mitchell Hahn, prin. | Fax 373-5877

Washington Island, Door
Washington SD | 100/K-12
888 Main Rd 54246 | 920-847-2507
Susan Churchill-Chastan, supt. | Fax 847-2865
www.island.k12.wi.us
Washington Island HS | 9-12
888 Main Rd 54246 | 920-847-2507
Susan Churchill-Chastan, prin. | Fax 847-2865

Waterford, Racine, Pop. 4,483
Waterford J1 SD | 1,500/K-8
819 W Main St 53185 | 262-514-8250
Gwen O'Cull, supt. | Fax 514-8251
www.waterford.k12.wi.us
Fox River MS | 400/7-8
921 W Main St 53185 | 262-514-8240
Darlene Markle, prin. | Fax 514-8241

Waterford UNHSD | 1,100/9-12
507 W Main St 53185 | 262-534-9059
Keith Brandstetter, supt. | Fax 534-6871
www.waterforduhs.k12.wi.us
Waterford Union HS | 1,100/9-12
100 Field Dr 53185 | 262-534-3189
Larry Berg, prin. | Fax 534-4971

Waterloo, Jefferson, Pop. 3,268
Waterloo SD | 900/PK-12
813 N Monroe St 53594 | 920-478-3633
Connie L. Schiestl, supt. | Fax 478-3821
waterloo.k12.wi.us
Waterloo HS | 300/9-12
865 N Monroe St 53594 | 920-478-2171
Brad Donner, prin. | Fax 478-9539
Waterloo MS | 300/5-8
865 N Monroe St 53594 | 920-478-2696
Ann Kox, prin. | Fax 478-3987

Watertown, Jefferson, Pop. 22,675
Watertown Unified SD | 3,700/PK-12
111 Dodge St 53094 | 920-262-1460
Douglas W. Keiser Ph.D., supt. | Fax 262-1469
www.watertown.k12.wi.us
Riverside MS | 800/6-8
131 Hall St 53094 | 920-262-1480
Kent Jacobson, prin. | Fax 262-1468
Watertown HS | 1,400/9-12
825 Endevour Dr 53098 | 920-262-7500
Scott Bostwick, prin. | Fax 262-7545

Luther Preparatory S | 400/9-12
1300 Western Ave 53094 | 920-261-4352
Rev. Mark Schroeder, prin. | Fax 262-8118
Madison Area Technical College | Post-Sec.
1300 W Main St 53098 | 920-261-3303
Maranatha Baptist Bible College | Post-Sec.
745 W Main St 53094 | 920-261-9300

Waukesha, Waukesha, Pop. 66,840
Waukesha SD | 12,700/PK-12
222 Maple Ave 53186 | 262-970-1000
David S. Schmidt, supt. | Fax 970-1021
www.waukesha.k12.wi.us
Butler MS | 700/7-8
310 N Hine Ave 53188 | 262-970-2900
Michael Bralick, prin. | Fax 970-2920
Central MS | 600/7-8
400 N Grand Ave 53186 | 262-970-3100
Jeff Copson, prin. | Fax 970-3120
Horning MS | 700/7-8
2000 Wolf Rd 53186 | 262-970-3300
Dana Monogue, prin. | Fax 970-3320
North HS | 1,300/9-12
2222 Michigan Ave 53188 | 262-970-3500
Ryan Champeau, prin. | Fax 970-3520
South HS | 1,400/9-12
401 E Roberta Ave 53186 | 262-970-3705
Mark Hansen, prin. | Fax 970-3720
West HS | 1,400/9-12
3301 Saylesville Rd 53189 | 262-970-3900
Doug Straus, prin. | Fax 970-3920

Carroll College | Post-Sec.
100 N East Ave 53186 | 262-547-1211
Catholic Memorial HS | 1,000/9-12
601 E College Ave 53186 | 262-542-7101
Dr. Kathleen Cepelka, prin. | Fax 542-1633
Keller Graduate School | Post-Sec.
20935 Swenson Dr Ste 450 53186 | 262-798-9889
St. Joseph MS | 300/6-8
822 N East Ave 53186 | 262-896-2930
Kathy Rempe, prin. | Fax 896-2935
University of Wisconsin Waukesha | Post-Sec.
1500 N University Dr 53186 | 262-521-5200
Waukesha Christian Academy | 100/K-12
PO Box 31 53187 | 262-542-7766
Rev. Glen Teasdale, admin. | Fax 542-4171

Waunakee, Dane, Pop. 9,803
Waunakee Community SD | 3,200/PK-12
101 School Dr 53597 | 608-849-2000
Chuck Pursell, supt. | Fax 849-9746
www.waunakee.k12.wi.us
Waunakee HS | 1,000/9-12
100 School Dr 53597 | 608-849-2100
Brian Kersten, prin. | Fax 849-2164
Waunakee MS | 500/7-8
1001 South St 53597 | 608-849-2060
Shelley Weiss, prin. | Fax 849-2088

Madison Country Day S | 300/PK-12
5606 River Rd 53597 | 608-850-6000
Adam de Pencier, admin. | Fax 850-6006

Waupaca, Waupaca, Pop. 5,812
Waupaca SD | 2,100/K-12
515 School St 54981 | 715-258-4121
David Poeschl, supt. | Fax 258-4125
wsd.waupaca.k12.wi.us
Waupaca HS | 900/9-12
E2325 King Rd 54981 | 715-258-4131
John Erspamer, prin. | Fax 258-4135
Waupaca MS | 600/6-8
1149 Shoemaker Rd 54981 | 715-258-4140
Joseph McClone, prin. | Fax 256-5681

Waupun, Dodge, Pop. 10,451
Waupun SD | 1,700/PK-12
950 Wilcox St 53963 | 920-324-9341
John Zegers, supt. | Fax 324-2630
www.waupun.k12.wi.us
Waupun HS | 200/9-12
801 E Lincoln St 53963 | 920-324-5591
Jeff Finstad, prin. | Fax 324-6980
Waupun MS | 600/6-8
451 E Spring St 53963 | 920-324-9322
Delnice Hill, prin. | Fax 324-2929

Central Wisconsin Christian HS | 200/6-12
301 Fox Lake Rd 53963 | 920-324-4233
Ron Halma, prin. | Fax 324-5036

Wausau, Marathon, Pop. 37,430
Wausau SD | 8,500/PK-12
PO Box 359 54402 | 715-261-0505
Stephen Murley, supt. | Fax 261-2503
www.wausau.k12.wi.us
Mann MS | 900/6-8
3101 N 13th St 54403 | 715-261-0725
Ty Becker, prin. | Fax 261-2035
Muir MS | 1,100/6-8
1400 Stewart Ave 54401 | 715-261-0100
Dean Hess, prin. | Fax 261-2461
Wausau East HS | 1,300/9-12
2607 N 18th St 54403 | 715-261-0650
Bradley Peck, prin. | Fax 261-3600
Wausau West HS | 1,700/9-12
1200 W Wausau Ave 54401 | 715-261-0850
Joy Trollop, prin. | Fax 261-3260

Faith Christian Academy | 100/K-12
E1045 County Road J 54403 | 715-842-0797
Dr. William Bensheimer, prin. | Fax 842-0797
Newman Catholic HS | 200/9-12
1130 W Bridge St 54401 | 715-845-8274
Lawrence Theiss, prin. | Fax 842-1302
Newman Catholic MS at St. Matthew | 200/6-8
225 S 28th Ave 54401 | 715-842-4857
Tina Meyer, prin. | Fax 845-2937
Northcentral Technical College | Post-Sec.
1000 W Campus Dr 54401 | 715-675-3331
State College of Beauty Culture | Post-Sec.
1930 Grand Ave 54403 | 715-849-5368
University of Wisconsin Marathon County | Post-Sec.
518 S 7th Ave 54401 | 715-845-9602
Wausau Hospital Center | Post-Sec.
333 Pine Ridge Blvd 54401 | 715-847-2117

Wausaukee, Marinette, Pop. 552
Wausaukee SD | 700/PK-12
PO Box 258 54177 | 715-856-5153
William J. LaChapell, supt. | Fax 856-6592
www.wausaukee.k12.wi.us
Wausaukee HS | 200/9-12
PO Box 258 54177 | 715-856-5151
Pamela Beach, prin. | Fax 856-6592
Wausaukee JHS | 100/7-8
PO Box 258 54177 | 715-856-5151
Pamela Beach, prin. | Fax 856-6592

Wautoma, Waushara, Pop. 2,134
Wautoma Area SD | 1,600/PK-12
PO Box 870 54982 | 920-787-7112
Jeff Kasuboski, supt. | Fax 787-1389
www.wautoma.k12.wi.us
Parkside MS | 600/4-8
PO Box 870 54982 | 920-787-4577
Tom Rheinheimer, prin. | Fax 787-7336
Wautoma HS | 500/9-12
PO Box 870 54982 | 920-787-3354
Scott Lustig, prin. | Fax 787-1513

Wauwatosa, Milwaukee, Pop. 46,260
Wauwatosa SD | 6,800/PK-12
12121 W North Ave 53226 | 414-773-1000
Phil Ertl, supt. | Fax 773-1019
www.wauwatosaschools.org
East HS | 1,200/9-12
7500 Milwaukee Ave 53213 | 414-773-2000
Nick Hughes, prin. | Fax 773-2020
Longfellow MS | 900/6-8
7600 N North Ave 53213 | 414-773-2400
Dennis Mahony, prin. | Fax 773-2420
West HS | 1,000/9-12
11400 W Center St 53222 | 414-773-3000
Kristin Bowers, prin. | Fax 773-3020

Whitman MS | 600/6-8
11100 W Center St 53222 | 414-773-2600
Jeff Keranen, prin. | Fax 773-2620

Wauzeka, Crawford, Pop. 759
Wauzeka-Steuben SD | 300/PK-12
301 E Main St 53826 | 608-875-5311
Bryce Bird, supt. | Fax 875-5100
www.wauzeka.k12.wi.us
Wauzeka-Steuben S | 300/PK-12
301 E Main St 53826 | 608-875-5311
Bryce Bird, prin. | Fax 875-5100

Webster, Burnett, Pop. 666
Webster SD | 700/PK-12
PO Box 9 54893 | 715-866-4391
Jim Erickson, supt. | Fax 866-4283
www.webster.k12.wi.us
Webster HS | 400/7-12
7564 Alder St W 54893 | 715-866-4281
Tim Widiker, prin. | Fax 866-4377

West Allis, Milwaukee, Pop. 60,192
West Allis SD | 8,700/PK-12
9333 W Lincoln Ave 53227 | 414-604-3000
Kurt Wachholz, supt. | Fax 546-5795
www.wawm.k12.wi.us
Central HS | 1,600/9-12
8516 W Lincoln Ave 53227 | 414-604-3110
Jack Padek, prin. | Fax 546-5536
Hale HS | 1,300/9-12
11601 W Lincoln Ave 53227 | 414-604-3210
Kathleen MacDonald, prin. | Fax 546-5734
Wright MS | 800/7-8
9501 W Cleveland Ave 53227 | 414-604-3410
Joan Delaney, prin. | Fax 546-5785
Other Schools – See West Milwaukee
—————
Grace Christian Academy | 200/PK-12
8420 W Beloit Rd 53227 | 414-327-4200
Cynthia Hummitzsch, admin. | Fax 327-4386
Milwaukee Area Technical College | Post-Sec.
1200 S 71st St 53214 | 414-476-3040

West Bend, Washington, Pop. 28,932
West Bend SD | 6,700/PK-12
735 S Main St 53095 | 262-335-5435
Dr. Patricia Herdrich, supt. | Fax 335-5470
www.west-bend.k12.wi.us
Badger MS | 800/6-8
710 S Main St 53095 | 262-335-5456
Ted Neitzke, prin. | Fax 335-6187
East HS | 1,200/9-12
1305 E Decorah Rd 53095 | 262-335-5532
Cassandra Schug, prin. | Fax 335-8242
Silverbrook MS | 600/6-8
120 N Silverbrook Dr 53095 | 262-335-5499
Jean Broadwater, prin. | Fax 335-5610
West HS | 1,200/9-12
1305 E Decorah Rd 53095 | 262-335-5587
Patrick Gardon, prin. | Fax 335-8251
—————
Moraine Park Technical College | Post-Sec.
2151 N Main St 53090 | 262-334-3413
University of Wisconsin Center | Post-Sec.
400 S University Dr 53095 | 262-335-5201

Westby, Vernon, Pop. 2,116
Westby Area SD | 1,200/PK-12
206 West Ave S 54667 | 608-634-0101
Roy Green, supt. | Fax 634-0118
westby.k12.wi.us
Westby HS | 400/9-12
206 West Ave S 54667 | 608-634-3101
Ken Manning, prin. | Fax 634-0123
Westby MS | 300/5-8
206 West Ave S 54667 | 608-634-0200
Clarice Nestingen, prin. | Fax 634-0218

Westfield, Marquette, Pop. 1,222
Westfield SD | 1,300/PK-12
N7046 County Road CH 53964 | 608-296-2107
Roger Schmidt, supt. | Fax 296-2938
www.westfield.k12.wi.us
Pioneer Westfield HS | 500/9-12
N7046 County Road CH 53964 | 608-296-2141
Julia Ferris, prin. | Fax 296-2293
Pioneer Westfield MS | 200/7-8
N7046 County Road CH 53964 | 608-296-4721
Susan Porfilio, prin. | Fax 296-4232

West Milwaukee, Milwaukee, Pop. 4,093
West Allis SD
Supt. — See West Allis
West Milwaukee MS | 600/7-8
5104 W Greenfield Ave 53214 | 414-604-3310
| Fax 389-3815

West Salem, LaCrosse, Pop. 4,810
West Salem SD | 1,600/PK-12
405 E Hamlin St 54669 | 608-786-0700
Eugene Ertz, supt. | Fax 786-2960
www.wsalem.k12.wi.us
West Salem HS | 500/9-12
405 E Hamlin St 54669 | 608-786-1220
Troy Gunderson, prin. | Fax 786-1273

West Salem MS | 400/6-8
450 N Mark St 54669 | 608-786-2090
Dean Buchanan, prin. | Fax 786-1081
—————
Coulee Region Christian S | 200/PK-12
230 W Garland St 54669 | 608-786-3004
Marliss Katsma, supt. | Fax 786-3005

Weyauwega, Waupaca, Pop. 1,821
Weyauwega-Fremont SD | 1,100/PK-12
PO Box 580 54983 | 920-867-2148
F. James Harlan, supt. | Fax 867-2510
www.wegafremont.k12.wi.us
Weyauwega HS | 400/9-12
PO Box 580 54983 | 920-867-3191
Todd Kadolph, prin. | Fax 867-2510
Weyauwega MS | 300/6-8
PO Box 580 54983 | 920-867-2148
Scott Bleck, prin. | Fax 867-2510

Weyerhaeuser, Rusk, Pop. 337
Weyerhaeuser Area SD | 200/K-12
402 N 2nd St 54895 | 715-353-2254
Barbara Lorkowski, supt. | Fax 353-2288
www.fwsd.k12.wi.us
Weyerhaeuser HS | 100/9-12
402 N 2nd St 54895 | 715-353-2254
Todd Solberg, prin. | Fax 353-2288

Whitefish Bay, Milwaukee, Pop. 13,848
Whitefish Bay SD | 2,900/PK-12
1200 E Fairmount Ave 53217 | 414-963-3921
James Rickabaugh, supt. | Fax 963-3959
www.wfbschools.com
Whitefish Bay HS | 900/9-12
1200 E Fairmount Ave 53217 | 414-963-3928
William Henkle, prin. | Fax 963-3870
Whitefish Bay MS | 700/6-8
1144 E Henry Clay St 53217 | 414-963-6800
Lisa Gies, prin. | Fax 963-6808
—————
Dominican HS | 400/9-12
120 E Silver Spring Dr 53217 | 414-332-1170
Eamonn O'Keeffe, prin. | Fax 332-4101

Whitehall, Trempealeau, Pop. 1,622
Whitehall SD | 700/PK-12
PO Box 37 54773 | 715-538-4374
Michael Beighley, supt. | Fax 538-4639
www.whitehallsd.k12.wi.us
Whitehall HS | 200/9-12
PO Box 37 54773 | 715-538-4364
Susan Speltz, prin. | Fax 538-4717
Whitehall MS | 200/6-8
PO Box 37 54773 | 715-538-4364
Susan Speltz, prin. | Fax 538-4717

White Lake, Langlade, Pop. 345
White Lake SD | 300/K-12
PO Box 67 54491 | 715-882-8421
Doug Druse, supt. | Fax 882-2914
www.whitelake.k12.wi.us
White Lake JSHS | 200/7-12
PO Box 67 54491 | 715-882-2361
Doug Druse, prin. | Fax 882-2914

Whitewater, Walworth, Pop. 14,120
Whitewater USD | 2,000/K-12
419 S Elizabeth St 53190 | 262-472-8700
Leslie Steinhaus, supt. | Fax 472-8710
www.wwusd.org
Whitewater HS | 700/9-12
534 S Elizabeth St 53190 | 262-472-8100
Vance Dalzin, prin. | Fax 472-8181
Whitewater MS | 400/6-8
401 S Elizabeth St 53190 | 262-472-8300
Eric Runez, prin. | Fax 472-8310
—————
University of Wisconsin | Post-Sec.
800 W Main St 53190 | 262-472-1234

Wild Rose, Waushara, Pop. 756
Wild Rose SD | 700/PK-12
PO Box 276 54984 | 920-622-4203
Claude Olson, supt. | Fax 622-4604
www.wildrose.k12.wi.us
Wild Rose MSHS | 400/6-12
PO Box 276 54984 | 920-622-4201
Charles Schuessler, prin. | Fax 622-4801

Williams Bay, Walworth, Pop. 2,572
Williams Bay SD | 500/K-12
PO Box 259 53191 | 262-245-1575
Frederic C. Vorlop, supt. | Fax 245-5877
www.williamsbay.k12.wi.us
Williams Bay HS | 200/9-12
PO Box 259 53191 | 262-245-6224
Dan Bice, prin. | Fax 245-5877
Williams Bay JHS | 100/7-8
PO Box 259 53191 | 262-245-6224
Dan Bice, prin. | Fax 245-5877
—————
Faith Christian S | 200/PK-12
PO Box 1230 53191 | 262-245-9404
Ted Caucutt, admin. | Fax 245-0128

Wilmot, Kenosha
Wilmot UNHSD | 1,000/9-12
PO Box 8 53192 | 262-862-2884
William W. Heitman, supt. | Fax 862-6413
www.wilmothighschool.com
Wilmot HS | 1,000/9-12
PO Box 8 53192 | 262-862-2351
Carl Breitlow, prin. | Fax 862-6929

Winneconne, Winnebago, Pop. 2,418
Winneconne Community SD | 1,500/PK-12
PO Box 5000 54986 | 920-582-5802
Robert Reinke, supt. | Fax 582-5816
www.winneconne.k12.wi.us
Winneconne HS | 500/9-12
PO Box 5000 54986 | 920-582-5810
James Smasal, prin. | Fax 582-5813
Winneconne MS | 400/6-8
PO Box 5000 54986 | 920-582-5800
Peggy Larson, prin. | Fax 582-5812

Winter, Sawyer, Pop. 359
Winter SD | 400/K-12
PO Box 310 54896 | 715-266-3301
Stu Waller, admin. | Fax 266-2216
www.winter.k12.wi.us/
Winter S | 400/K-12
PO Box 310 54896 | 715-266-3301
Timothy M. Kief, prin. | Fax 266-2216

Wisconsin Dells, Columbia, Pop. 2,444
Wisconsin Dells SD | 1,700/PK-12
811 County Road H 53965 | 608-254-7769
Charles Whitsell, supt. | Fax 254-8058
www.sdwd.k12.wi.us
Spring Hill MS | 400/6-8
300 Vine St 53965 | 608-253-2468
Dan Wenkman, prin. | Fax 254-6397
Wisconsin Dells HS | 600/9-12
520 Race St 53965 | 608-253-1461
Randy Kuhnau, prin. | Fax 254-6288

Wisconsin Rapids, Wood, Pop. 18,041
Wisconsin Rapids SD | 5,500/PK-12
510 Peach St 54494 | 715-422-6000
Dean Ryerson, supt. | Fax 422-6070
www.wrps.org
East JHS | 800/7-9
311 Lincoln St 54494 | 715-422-6114
Kathi Stebbins-Hintz, prin. | Fax 422-6270
Lincoln SHS | 1,500/10-12
1801 16th St S 54494 | 715-423-1520
Thomas Mancuso, prin. | Fax 422-6097
West JHS | 600/7-9
1921 27th Ave S 54495 | 715-422-6200
Tracy Ginter, prin. | Fax 422-6187
—————
Assumption HS | 200/9-12
445 Chestnut St 54494 | 715-422-0910
Thomas Reichenbacher, prin. | Fax 422-0912
Assumption MS | 100/7-8
440 Mead St 54494 | 715-422-0950
Joan Bond, prin. | Fax 422-0955
Community Christian Academy | 100/K-12
550 Center St 54494 | 715-423-0770
Cheryl Ver Hulst, admin. | Fax 423-0779
Mid-State Technical College | Post-Sec.
500 32nd St N 54494 | 715-422-5300

Wittenberg, Shawano, Pop. 1,148
Wittenberg-Birnamwood SD | 1,400/PK-12
400 W Grand Ave 54499 | 715-253-2213
David Bardo, supt. | Fax 253-3588
www.wittbirn.k12.wi.us/
Wittenberg-Birnamwood HS | 500/9-12
400 W Grand Ave 54499 | 715-253-2211
Craig Kaney, prin. | Fax 253-3588

Wonewoc, Juneau, Pop. 811
Wonewoc-Union Center SD | 400/PK-12
PO Box 368 53968 | 608-464-3165
Arthur F. Keenan, supt. | Fax 464-3325
www.theclasslist.com/wcschools
Wonewoc HS | 200/9-12
PO Box 368 53968 | 608-464-3165
Michelle Noll, prin. | Fax 464-3325
Wonewoc JHS | 100/7-8
PO Box 368 53968 | 608-464-3165
Michelle Noll, prin. | Fax 464-3325

Woodville, Saint Croix, Pop. 1,207
Baldwin-Woodville Area SD
Supt. — See Baldwin
Viking MS | 400/5-8
500 Southside Dr 54028 | 715-698-2456
Henry Dupuis, prin. | Fax 698-3315

Wrightstown, Brown, Pop. 2,105
Wrightstown Community SD | 1,100/K-12
PO Box 128 54180 | 920-532-5551
Carla Buboltz, supt. | Fax 532-4664
www.wrightstown.k12.wi.us
Wrightstown HS | 400/9-12
PO Box 128 54180 | 920-532-0525
Scott Thompson, prin. | Fax 532-0860
Wrightstown MS | 300/5-8
PO Box 128 54180 | 920-532-5553
Rich Schenkus, prin. | Fax 532-3869

WYOMING

WYOMING DEPARTMENT OF EDUCATION
2300 Capitol Ave, Cheyenne 82001-3644
Telephone 307-777-7673
Fax 307-777-6234
Website http://www.k12.wy.us

Superintendent of Public Instruction   Jim McBride

WYOMING BOARD OF EDUCATION
2300 Capitol Ave, Cheyenne 82001-3644

Chairperson   Brent Young

BOARDS OF COOPERATIVE EDUCATIONAL SERVICES (BOCES)

Carbon Co. Higher Education Center BOCES
Joan Evans, dir. — 307-328-9204
705 Rodeo St, Rawlins 82301 — Fax 324-3338
www.cchec.org
Central Wyoming BOCES — 307-268-2617
, PO Box 231, Casper 82602 — Fax 268-2224
Douglas BOCES
Connie Woehl, dir. — 307-358-5622
203 N 6th St, Douglas 82633 — Fax 358-5629
Fremont County BOCES
Sandy Barton, dir. — 307-856-2028
201 E Washington Ave — Fax 856-4058
Riverton 82501
www.fcboces.org

Mountain View & Lyman BOCES
Lana Hillstead, dir. — 307-782-6401
PO Box 130, Mountain View 82939 — Fax 782-7410
Northeast Wyoming BOCES
John Balow, dir. — 307-682-0231
410 N Miller Ave, Gillette 82716 — Fax 686-7628
www.new-boces.k12.wy.us/
Northwest Wyoming BOCES
Carolyn Connor, dir. — 307-864-2171
PO Box 112, Thermopolis 82443 — Fax 864-9463
server1.thermopwy.net/nwboces/boces1set.html

Oyster Ridge BOCES
Dr. Michael Clark, dir. — 307-877-6958
PO Box 423, Kemmerer 83101 — Fax 828-9040
www.kemmereroutreach.com
Region V BOCES
Dr. Dennis Donohue, dir. — 307-733-8210
PO Box 240, Wilson 83014 — Fax 733-8462
Sweetwater County BOCES
Bernadine Craft Ph.D., dir. — 307-382-1607
PO Box 428, Rock Springs 82902 — Fax 382-1875
www.wwcc.wy.edu/boces/
Uinta BOCES
Michael Williams, dir. — 307-789-5742
1013 W Cheyenne Dr Ste A — Fax 789-7975
Evanston 82930

PUBLIC, PRIVATE AND CATHOLIC SECONDARY SCHOOLS

Afton, Lincoln, Pop. 1,781
Lincoln County SD 2 — 2,500/K-12
PO Box 219 83110 — 307-885-3811
Jon Abrams, supt. — Fax 885-9562
www.lcsd2.org
Star Valley HS — 700/9-12
PO Box 8000 83110 — 307-885-7847
Shannon Harris, prin. — Fax 885-3299
Star Valley MS — 400/7-8
PO Box 8001 83110 — 307-885-5208
Kem Cazier, prin. — Fax 885-0472
Other Schools – See Cokeville

Baggs, Carbon, Pop. 358
Carbon County SD 1
Supt. — See Rawlins
Little Snake River Valley S — 200/K-12
PO Box 9 82321 — 307-383-2185
Rick Newton, prin. — Fax 383-2184

Basin, Big Horn, Pop. 1,203
Big Horn County SD 4 — 300/PK-12
PO Box 151 82410 — 307-568-2684
Ray Yoder, supt. — Fax 568-2654
www.bgh4.k12.wy.us/
Riverside HS — 100/9-12
PO Box 151 82410 — 307-568-2416
Tony Anson, prin. — Fax 568-2415
Other Schools – See Manderson

Big Horn, Sheridan
Sheridan County SD 1
Supt. — See Ranchester
Big Horn HS — 100/9-12
PO Box 490 82833 — 307-674-8190
George Mirich, prin. — Fax 672-5306
Big Horn MS — 100/6-8
PO Box 490 82833 — 307-674-8190
George Mirich, prin. — Fax 672-5306

Big Piney, Sublette, Pop. 436
Sublette County SD 9 — 600/K-12
PO Box 769 83113 — 307-276-3322
B. Shelley, supt. — Fax 276-3731
Big Piney HS — 200/9-12
916 Piney Dr 83113 — 307-276-3324
Terry Statton, prin. — Fax 276-3480
Big Piney MS, 210 Nichols St S 83113 — 100/6-8
Gerry Chase, prin. — 307-276-3315

Buffalo, Johnson, Pop. 4,220
Johnson County SD 1 — 1,300/K-12
601 W Lott St 82834 — 307-684-9571
Rod Kessler, supt. — Fax 684-5182
www.jcsd1.k12.wy.us
Buffalo HS — 400/9-12
326 S Burritt Ave 82834 — 307-684-2269
Kelly Hornby, prin. — Fax 684-9481
Clear Creek MS — 300/5-8
58 N Adams Ave 82834 — 307-684-5594
Troy Stone, prin. — Fax 684-9096
Other Schools – See Kaycee

Burlington, Big Horn, Pop. 250
Big Horn County SD 1
Supt. — See Cowley

Burlington HS — 100/9-12
PO Box 9 82411 — 307-762-3334
George Risberg, prin. — Fax 762-3604
Burlington JHS — 50/7-8
PO Box 9 82411 — 307-762-3334
George Risberg, prin. — Fax 762-3604

Burns, Laramie, Pop. 309
Laramie County SD 2
Supt. — See Pine Bluffs
Burns JSHS — 200/7-12
PO Box 160 82053 — 307-547-3511
Mike Brownawell, prin. — Fax 547-3583

Byron, Big Horn, Pop. 546
Big Horn County SD 1
Supt. — See Cowley
Rocky Mountain HS — 200/9-12
PO Box 176 82412 — 307-548-2723
Tim Winland, prin. — Fax 548-6452

Casper, Natrona, Pop. 50,632
Natrona County SD 1 — 11,800/PK-12
970 N Glenn Rd 82601 — 307-577-0200
Jim Lowham Ed.D., supt. — Fax 577-4422
www.natronaschools.org/
Casper Classical Academy — 100/6-9
970 1/2 N Glenn Rd 82601 — 307-261-6181
Marie Puryear, prin. — Fax 261-6184
Centennial MS — 800/6-9
1421 Waterford St 82609 — 307-577-4600
Valerie Braughton, prin. — Fax 233-2891
CY JHS — 700/6-9
2211 Essex Ave 82604 — 307-577-4474
Dean Braughton, prin. — Fax 233-2683
Frontier MS — 300/6-8
900 S Beverly St 82609 — 307-577-4400
Verba Echols, prin. — Fax 233-2274
Morgan JHS — 1,000/6-9
1440 S Elm St 82601 — 307-577-4440
Walter Wilcox, prin. — Fax 233-2411
Natrona County SHS — 1,400/10-12
930 S Elm St 82601 — 307-577-0330
Byron Moore, prin. — Fax 233-1507
Walsh HS — 1,300/9-12
3500 E 12th St 82609 — 307-233-2000
Brad Diller, prin. — Fax 233-2066
Other Schools – See Midwest

Casper College — Post-Sec.
125 College Dr 82601 — 307-268-2110
Paradise Valley Christian S — 100/PK-12
3041 Paradise Dr 82604 — 307-234-2450
C. Jeanne Boyd, admin. — Fax 577-0763
Sage Technical School — Post-Sec.
2368 Oil Dr 82604 — 307-234-0242
Wyoming School for the Deaf — Post-Sec.
539 Payne Ave 82609

Cheyenne, Laramie, Pop. 54,374
Laramie County SD 1 — 12,800/K-12
2810 House Ave 82001 — 307-771-2100
Dan Stephan, supt. — Fax 771-2383
www.laramie1.k12.wy.us

Carey JHS — 1,100/7-9
1780 E Pershing Blvd 82001 — 307-771-2580
Evelyn Abbott, prin. — Fax 771-2578
Central SHS — 1,200/10-12
5500 Education Dr 82009 — 307-771-2680
Rick Porter, prin. — Fax 771-2699
East SHS — 1,500/10-12
2800 E Pershing Blvd 82001 — 307-771-2663
Sam Mirich, prin. — Fax 771-2679
Johnson JHS — 1,000/7-9
1236 W Allison Rd 82007 — 307-771-2640
Alice Hunter, prin. — Fax 771-2660
McCormick JHS — 1,100/7-9
6000 Education Dr 82009 — 307-771-2650
Jeff Conine, prin. — Fax 771-2661

Cheeks Intl Academy of Beauty Culture — Post-Sec.
207 W 18th St 82001 — 307-637-8700
Laramie County Community College — Post-Sec.
1400 E College Dr 82007 — 307-778-5222
St. Mary S — 300/PK-12
112 E 24th St 82001 — 307-638-9268
Carol Ricken, prin. — Fax 635-2847
Webster Christian S — 100/K-12
PO Box 5246 82003 — 307-635-2175
Leona Barkell, admin. — Fax 773-8523

Chugwater, Platte, Pop. 237
Platte County SD 1
Supt. — See Wheatland
Chugwater HS — 50/9-12
PO Box 68 82210 — 307-422-3501
George Kopf, prin. — Fax 422-3433
Chugwater JHS — 50/7-8
PO Box 68 82210 — 307-422-3501
George Kopf, prin. — Fax 422-3433

Clearmont, Sheridan, Pop. 117
Sheridan County SD 3 — 100/K-12
PO Box 125 82835 — 307-758-4412
John Baule, supt. — Fax 758-4444
Arvada-Clearmont HS — 50/9-12
PO Box 125 82835 — 307-758-4412
John Hazaleus, prin. — Fax 758-4444
Arvada-Clearmont JHS — 50/7-8
PO Box 125 82835 — 307-758-4412
John Hazaleus, prin. — Fax 758-4444

Cody, Park, Pop. 8,973
Park County SD 6 — 2,400/K-12
919 Cody Ave 82414 — 307-587-4253
Bryan Monteith, supt. — Fax 527-5762
www.park6.org/
Cody HS — 800/9-12
919 Cody Ave 82414 — 307-587-4251
Dave Treick, prin. — Fax 587-9369
Cody MS — 500/6-8
919 Cody Ave 82414 — 307-587-4273
Larry Gerber, prin. — Fax 587-3547

West Park Hospital — Post-Sec.
707 Sheridan Ave 82414 — 307-527-7501

Cokeville, Lincoln, Pop. 492
Lincoln County SD 2
Supt. — See Afton
Cokeville JSHS 100/7-12
PO Box 220 83114 307-279-3273
Keith Harris, prin. Fax 279-3221

Cowley, Big Horn, Pop. 571
Big Horn County SD 1 600/PK-12
PO Box 688 82420 307-548-2254
Kevin Mitchell, supt. Fax 548-7610
bighorn1.bgh1.k12.wy.us/
Other Schools – See Burlington, Byron, Deaver

Dayton, Sheridan, Pop. 703
Sheridan County SD 1
Supt. — See Ranchester
Tongue River HS 200/9-12
PO Box 408 82836 307-655-2236
Don White, prin. Fax 655-9798

Deaver, Big Horn, Pop. 179
Big Horn County SD 1
Supt. — See Cowley
Rocky Mountain MS 100/6-8
PO Box 185 82421 307-664-2252
Teresa Staab, prin. Fax 664-2314

Diamondville, Lincoln, Pop. 702
Lincoln County SD 1 600/K-12
PO Box 335 83116 307-877-9095
Gene Carmody, supt. Fax 877-9638
www.lcsd1.k12.wy.us
Other Schools – See Kemmerer

Douglas, Converse, Pop. 5,398
Converse County SD 1 2,200/K-12
615 Hamilton St 82633 307-358-2942
Dan Espeland, supt. Fax 358-3934
www.ccsd1.k12.wy.us
Douglas HS 600/9-12
615 Hamilton St 82633 307-358-2940
John Weigel, prin. Fax 358-2737
Douglas MS 400/6-8
615 Hamilton St 82633 307-358-9771
Fred George, prin. Fax 358-5315

Dubois, Fremont, Pop. 975
Fremont County SD 2 200/K-12
PO Box 188 82513 307-455-2323
Lon Streib, supt. Fax 455-2178
rams.fremont2.k12.wy.us/
Dubois HS 100/9-12
PO Box 188 82513 307-455-2279
Cheryl Gettings, prin. Fax 455-2178

Encampment, Carbon, Pop. 462
Carbon County SD 2
Supt. — See Saratoga
Encampment S 100/K-12
PO Box 277 82325 307-327-5442
Mike Erickson, prin. Fax 327-5142

Ethete, Fremont, Pop. 1,059
Fremont County SD 14 600/PK-12
638 Blue Sky Hwy 82520 307-332-3904
Michelle Hoffman, supt. Fax 332-7567
www.fremont14.k12.wy.us
Wyoming Indian HS 200/9-12
636 Blue Sky Hwy 82520 307-332-9765
Virginia Dias, prin. Fax 335-7739
Wyoming Indian MS 200/6-8
535 Ethete Rd 82520 307-332-2992
Michelle Hoffman, prin. Fax 335-7318

Evanston, Uinta, Pop. 11,375
Uinta County SD 1 2,900/K-12
PO Box 6002 82931 307-789-7571
Dennis Wilson, supt. Fax 789-6225
www.uinta1.k12.wy.us
Davis MS 300/6-8
PO Box 6002 82931 307-789-8096
Jim Harrell, prin. Fax 789-3386
Evanston HS 900/9-12
PO Box 6002 82931 307-789-0757
Jeffrey Harrah, prin. Fax 789-7447
Evanston MS 300/6-8
PO Box 6002 82931 307-789-5499
Monique Flickinger, prin. Fax 789-7972

Farson, Sweetwater
Sweetwater County SD 1
Supt. — See Rock Springs
Farson-Eden S 700/K-12
PO Box 400 82932 307-273-9301
Richard Horsley, prin. Fax 273-9313

Fort Washakie, Fremont, Pop. 1,334
Fremont County SD 21 200/PK-8
90 Ethete Rd 82514 307-332-3648
Karl Berlin, supt. Fax 332-7267
www.fremont21.k12.wy.us/
Fort Washakie MS 7-8
90 Ethete Rd 82514 307-332-2380
Mike Helenbolt, prin. Fax 332-3597

Gillette, Campbell, Pop. 21,840
Campbell County SD 1 7,500/K-12
PO Box 3033 82717 307-682-5171
Dr. Richard Strahorn, supt. Fax 682-6619
www.ccsd.k12.wy.us
Campbell County HS 1,500/10-12
1000 Camel Dr 82716 307-682-7247
Larry Steiger, prin. Fax 687-0032
Sage Valley JHS 800/7-9
1000 W Lakeway Rd 82718 307-682-2225
Alex Ayers, prin. Fax 687-7614
Twin Spruce JHS 900/7-9
100 E 7th St 82716 307-682-3144
Dave Foreman, prin. Fax 686-1969
Other Schools – See Wright

Heritage Christian S 100/PK-12
510 Wall Street Ct 82718 307-686-1392
Brent Potthoff, admin. Fax 682-6515
Northern Wyoming Community College Post-Sec.
300 W Sinclair St 82718 307-686-0254

Glendo, Platte, Pop. 226
Platte County SD 1
Supt. — See Wheatland
Glendo HS 9-12
PO Box 68 82213 307-735-4471
Stanetta Twiford, prin. Fax 735-4220
Glendo JHS 7-8
PO Box 68 82213 307-735-4471
Stanetta Twiford, prin. Fax 735-4220

Glenrock, Converse, Pop. 2,274
Converse County SD 2 1,100/K-12
PO Box 1300 82637 307-436-5331
Kirk Hughes, supt. Fax 436-8235
www.cnv2.k12.wy.us/
Glenrock HS 200/9-12
PO Box 1300 82637 307-436-9201
Christopher Gray, prin. Fax 436-8517
Glenrock MS 200/5-8
PO Box 1300 82637 307-436-9258
Tobey Cass, prin. Fax 436-7507

Green River, Sweetwater, Pop. 11,541
Sweetwater County SD 2 3,400/K-12
320 Monroe Ave 82935 307-872-5500
Barbara VanMatre, supt. Fax 872-5518
www.sw2.k12.wy.us
Expedition Academy 300/9-12
351 Monroe Ave 82935 307-872-4800
Susan Kinneman, prin. Fax 872-4808
Green River HS 800/9-12
1615 Hitching Post Dr 82935 307-872-4747
Brad Madison, prin. Fax 872-4758
Lincoln MS 400/7-8
350 Monroe Ave 82935 307-872-4400
Greg McClure, prin. Fax 872-5677

Greybull, Big Horn, Pop. 1,749
Big Horn County SD 3 500/K-12
636 14th Ave N 82426 307-765-4756
Craig Sorensen, supt. Fax 765-4617
Greybull HS 200/9-12
600 N 6th St 82426 307-765-2537
Larry Regnier, prin. Fax 765-2870
Greybull MS 100/6-8
640 8th Ave N 82426 307-765-4492
Kris Cundall, prin. Fax 765-2833

Guernsey, Platte, Pop. 1,115
Platte County SD 2 300/K-12
PO Box 189 82214 307-836-2735
Bruce Heimbuck, supt. Fax 836-2450
www.plt2.k12.wy.us
Guernsey-Sunrise JSHS 100/7-12
PO Box 189 82214 307-836-2745
Ken Griffith, prin. Fax 836-2729

Hanna, Carbon, Pop. 874
Carbon County SD 2
Supt. — See Saratoga
Hanna-Elk Mountain-Medicine Bow JSHS 100/7-12
PO Box 810 82327 307-325-6545
Brad Barlow, prin. Fax 325-9223

Hulett, Crook, Pop. 410
Crook County SD 1
Supt. — See Sundance
Hulett S 300/K-12
PO Box 127 82720 307-467-5231
Fax 467-5280

Jackson, Teton, Pop. 8,825
Teton County SD 1 2,300/K-12
PO Box 568 83001 307-733-2704
Pam Shea, supt. Fax 733-6443
www.tcsd.org/
Jackson Hole HS 700/9-12
PO Box 568 83025 307-732-3700
Dr. Gary Elliott, prin. Fax 732-3720
Jackson Hole MS 500/6-8
PO Box 568 83025 307-733-4234
Jean Coldsmith, prin. Fax 733-4254
Summit HS 50/9-12
PO Box 568 83025 307-733-9116
Jim Rooks, prin. Fax 739-8922

Kaycee, Johnson, Pop. 266
Johnson County SD 1
Supt. — See Buffalo
Kaycee JSHS 200/7-12
PO Box 6 82639 307-738-2323
Lana Latta, prin. Fax 738-2496

Kemmerer, Lincoln, Pop. 2,554
Lincoln County SD 1
Supt. — See Diamondville
Kemmerer HS 200/9-12
1525 3rd West Ave 83101 307-877-6991
Scott O'Tremba, prin. Fax 877-4117
Kemmerer MS 200/5-8
1310 Antelope St 83101 307-877-2286
Gene Carmody, prin. Fax 877-3365

Lander, Fremont, Pop. 6,864
Fremont County SD 1 1,900/K-12
400 Baldwin Creek Rd 82520 307-332-4711
Paige Fenton-Hughes, supt. Fax 332-6671
www.fcsd1.com
Lander Valley HS 700/9-12
350 Baldwin Creek Rd 82520 307-332-4433
Mike Helenbolt, prin. Fax 332-2861
Starrett JHS 300/7-8
863 Sweetwater St 82520 307-332-4040
Brian Janish, prin. Fax 332-0435

Wyoming State Training School Post-Sec.
8204 Wyoming Highway 789 82520 307-332-5302

Laramie, Albany, Pop. 26,956
Albany County SD 1 4,300/PK-12
1948 E Grand Ave 82070 307-721-4400
Dr. Brian Recht, supt. Fax 721-4408
www.ac1.k12.wy.us
Laramie JHS 800/7-9
1355 N 22nd St 82072 307-721-4430
Steve Hoff, prin. Fax 721-4435
Laramie SHS 800/10-12
1275 N 11th St 82072 307-721-4420
Kim Sorenson, prin. Fax 721-4419
Other Schools – See Rock River

Laramie Christian S 50/PK-12
710 E Garfield St #105B 82070 307-745-7814
Dr. Paul Jackson, admin. Fax 755-4104
University of Wyoming Post-Sec.
PO Box 3435 82071 307-766-1121
Wyoming Technical Institute Post-Sec.
4373 N 3rd St 82072 307-742-3776

Lingle, Goshen, Pop. 491
Goshen County SD 1
Supt. — See Torrington
Lingle-Ft. Laramie HS 100/9-12
PO Box 379 82223 307-837-2296
Ty Flock, prin. Fax 837-3025
Lingle-Fort Laramie MS 100/6-8
PO Box 379 82223 307-837-2283
Ty Flock, prin. Fax 837-2057

Lovell, Big Horn, Pop. 2,283
Big Horn County SD 2 700/K-12
502 Hampshire Ave 82431 307-548-2259
Dan Coe, supt. Fax 548-7555
www.bgh2.k12.wy.us/
Lovell HS 200/9-12
502 Hampshire Ave 82431 307-548-2256
Bill Schwan, prin. Fax 548-9452
Lovell MS 200/6-8
325 W 9th St 82431 307-548-6553
Mark Gaines, prin. Fax 548-6136

Lusk, Niobrara, Pop. 1,320
Niobrara County SD 1 500/K-12
PO Box 629 82225 307-334-3793
Richard Luchsinger, supt. Fax 334-0126
www.lusk.k12.wy.us/
Niobrara County HS 100/9-12
PO Box 1050 82225 307-334-3320
Joe Tully, prin. Fax 334-2331

Lyman, Uinta, Pop. 1,924
Uinta County SD 6 700/K-12
PO Box 1090 82937 307-786-4100
Randy Hillstead, supt. Fax 787-3241
www.uinta6.k12.wy.us/
Lyman HS 200/9-12
PO Box 1090 82937 307-787-6197
Todd Limoges, prin. Fax 787-6193
Lyman MS, PO Box 1090 82937 100/6-8
Christy Campbell, prin. 307-786-4608

Manderson, Big Horn, Pop. 103
Big Horn County SD 4
Supt. — See Basin
Cloud Peak S 100/6-8
PO Box 97 82432 307-568-2846
Becky Allred, prin. Fax 568-3885

Meeteetse, Park, Pop. 351
Park County SD 16 100/K-12
PO Box 218 82433 307-868-2501
Robert Lewandowski, supt. Fax 868-9264
www.park16.k12.wy.us/
Meeteetse S 100/K-12
PO Box 218 82433 307-868-2501
Clay Cates, prin. Fax 868-9264

Midwest, Natrona, Pop. 412
Natrona County SD 1
Supt. — See Casper
Midwest S 200/PK-12
PO Box 368 82643 307-437-6545
Bruce Youngquist, prin. Fax 437-6820

Moorcroft, Crook, Pop. 819
Crook County SD 1
Supt. — See Sundance
Moorcroft JSHS 200/7-12
PO Box 129 82721 307-756-3446
John Cook, prin. Fax 756-3724

Mountain View, Uinta, Pop. 1,154
Uinta County SD 4 700/K-12
PO Box 130 82939 307-782-3377
Jack Cozort, supt. Fax 782-6879
www.uinta4.k12.wy.us/
Mountain View HS 200/9-12
PO Box 130 82939 307-782-6340
Jeffrey Newton, prin. Fax 782-6967
Mountain View MS 100/6-8
PO Box 130 82939 307-782-6338
Kim Dolezal, prin. Fax 782-6876

Newcastle, Weston, Pop. 3,234
Weston County SD 1 900/K-12
116 Casper Ave 82701 307-746-4451
Brad LaCroix, supt. Fax 746-3289
www.weston1.k12.wy.us
Newcastle HS 300/9-12
116 Casper Ave 82701 307-746-2713
Tracy Ragland, prin. Fax 746-2350
Newcastle MS 200/6-8
116 Casper Ave 82701 307-746-2746
Scott Shoop, prin. Fax 746-4983

Pavillion, Fremont, Pop. 166
Fremont County SD 6 — 400/K-12
PO Box 10 82523 — 307-856-7970
Diana Clapp, supt. — Fax 856-3385
www.fre6.k12.wy.us/
Wind River JSHS — 200/6-12
PO Box 10 82523 — 307-856-6327
Brad Moon, prin. — Fax 856-4248

Pine Bluffs, Laramie, Pop. 1,177
Laramie County SD 2 — 900/K-12
PO Box 489 82082 — 307-245-3738
Margie Simineo, supt. — Fax 245-3561
web.lrm2.k12.wy.us/
Pine Bluffs JSHS — 200/7-12
PO Box 520 82082 — 307-245-3682
John Binning, prin. — Fax 245-3144
Other Schools – See Burns

Pinedale, Sublette, Pop. 1,501
Sublette County SD 1 — 700/K-12
PO Box 549 82941 — 307-367-2139
Charles Grove, supt. — Fax 367-4626
www.pinedaleschools.org/
Pinedale HS — 200/9-12
PO Box 549 82941 — 307-367-2137
Richard Kennedy, prin. — Fax 367-2611
Pinedale MS — 200/6-8
PO Box 549 82941 — 307-367-2821
Mike Vassallo, prin. — Fax 367-4217

Powell, Park, Pop. 5,253
Park County SD 1 — 1,600/K-12
160 N Evarts St 82435 — 307-754-2215
Jerry Maurer, supt. — Fax 754-4273
www.park1.k12.wy.us/
Powell HS — 500/9-12
160 N Evarts St 82435 — 307-754-2287
Bill Schwan, prin. — Fax 754-5996
Powell MS — 400/6-8
160 N Evarts St 82435 — 307-754-5716
Jason Sleep, prin. — Fax 754-2507

Northwest College — Post-Sec.
231 W 6th St 82435 — 307-754-6000

Ranchester, Sheridan, Pop. 719
Sheridan County SD 1 — 900/K-12
PO Box 819 82839 — 307-655-9541
Sue Belish, supt. — Fax 655-9477
www.sheridan.k12.wy.us/
Tongue River MS — 100/6-8
PO Box 879 82839 — 307-655-9533
Terry Myers, prin. — Fax 655-9894
Other Schools – See Big Horn, Dayton

Rawlins, Carbon, Pop. 8,665
Carbon County SD 1 — 1,800/K-12
PO Box 160 82301 — 307-328-9200
Peggy J. Sanders, supt. — Fax 328-9258
www.rawlins.crb1.k12.wy.us/
Rawlins HS — 500/9-12
1401 Colorado St 82301 — 307-328-9280
Jeff Thielbar, prin. — Fax 328-9286
Rawlins MS — 400/6-8
1500 Harshman St 82301 — 307-328-9205
Daniel Bryne, prin. — Fax 328-9226
Other Schools – See Baggs

Riverton, Fremont, Pop. 9,314
Fremont County SD 25 — 2,400/K-12
121 N 5th St W 82501 — 307-856-9407
Craig Beck, supt. — Fax 856-3390
www.fremont25.k12.wy.us
Riverton HS — 800/9-12
121 N 5th St W 82501 — 307-856-9491
JoAnne Flanagan, prin. — Fax 856-2333
Riverton MS — 600/6-8
121 N 5th St W 82501 — 307-856-9443
Cheryl Mowry, prin. — Fax 857-1695

Central Wyoming College — Post-Sec.
2660 Peck Ave 82501 — 307-855-2000

Rock River, Albany, Pop. 229
Albany County SD 1
Supt. — See Laramie

Rock River S — 400/K-12
PO Box 128 82083 — 307-378-2271
Heather Moro, prin. — Fax 378-2505

Rock Springs, Sweetwater, Pop. 18,400
Sweetwater County SD 1 — 4,700/K-12
PO Box 1089 82902 — 307-352-3400
Paul Grube, supt. — Fax 352-3411
www.sw1.k12.wy.us
Rock Springs East JHS — 700/7-8
PO Box 1089 82902 — 307-352-3474
Lu Wana Sweet, prin. — Fax 352-3482
Rock Springs HS — 1,100/9-12
PO Box 1089 82902 — 307-352-3440
Randy Wendling, prin. — Fax 352-3446
Other Schools – See Farson, Wamsutter

Columbia Commonwealth University — Post-Sec.
327 N St 82901 — 800-552-5522
Western Wyoming Community College — Post-Sec.
2500 College Dr 82901 — 307-382-1600

Saratoga, Carbon, Pop. 1,714
Carbon County SD 2 — 700/K-12
PO Box 1530 82331 — 307-326-5271
Robert Gates, supt. — Fax 326-8089
www.crb2.k12.wy.us
Saratoga MSHS — 100/7-12
PO Box 1710 82331 — 307-326-5246
Larry Uhling, prin. — Fax 326-9607
Other Schools – See Encampment, Hanna

Sheridan, Sheridan, Pop. 16,016
Sheridan County SD 2 — 2,700/K-12
PO Box 919 82801 — 307-674-7405
Craig Dougherty, supt. — Fax 674-5041
www.scsd2.com/
Sheridan HS — 800/9-12
1056 Long Dr 82801 — 307-672-2495
Dirlene Wheeler, prin. — Fax 672-8071
Sheridan JHS — 500/6-8
500 Lewis St 82801 — 307-674-6545
Scott Stults, prin. — Fax 672-5311

Sheridan College — Post-Sec.
PO Box 1500 82801 — 307-674-6446

Shoshoni, Fremont, Pop. 661
Fremont County SD 24 — 300/PK-12
112 W 3rd St 82649 — 307-876-2583
Jerry Erdahl, supt. — Fax 876-2469
www.f24.k12.wy.us
Shoshoni HS — 100/9-12
112 W 3rd St 82649 — 307-876-2576
Aaron Carr, prin. — Fax 876-9325
Shoshoni JHS — 7-8
112 W 3rd St 82649 — 307-876-2576
Aaron Carr, prin. — Fax 876-9325

Sundance, Crook, Pop. 1,160
Crook County SD 1 — 1,100/K-12
PO Box 830 82729 — 307-283-2299
Lon Streib, supt. — Fax 283-1810
www.crooknet.k12.wy.us
Sundance JSHS — 200/7-12
PO Box 850 82729 — 307-283-1007
Fax 283-2300

Other Schools – See Hulett, Moorcroft

Ten Sleep, Washakie, Pop. 310
Washakie County SD 2 — 50/K-12
PO Box 105 82442 — 307-366-2223
Judy Morrison, supt. — Fax 366-2304
Ten Sleep HS — 9-12
PO Box 105 82442 — 307-366-2233
Mike Sharum, prin. — Fax 366-2304
Ten Sleep MS — 7-8
PO Box 105 82442 — 307-366-2223
Mike Sharum, prin. — Fax 366-2304

Thermopolis, Hot Springs, Pop. 3,030
Hot Springs County SD 1 — 700/K-12
415 Springview St 82443 — 307-864-6515
Ray Schulte, supt. — Fax 864-6615
www.hotsprings.k12.wy.us

Hot Springs County HS — 300/9-12
415 Springview St 82443 — 307-864-6511
Steve Sexton, prin. — Fax 864-6611
Thermopolis MS — 200/6-8
415 Springview St 82443 — 307-864-6551
Jodie Cameron, prin. — Fax 864-6508

Torrington, Goshen, Pop. 5,581
Goshen County SD 1 — 1,900/K-12
2602 W E St 82240 — 307-532-2171
Ray Schulte, supt. — Fax 532-7085
www.goshen.k12.wy.us
Torrington HS — 400/9-12
2400 W C St 82240 — 307-532-7101
Marty Wood, prin. — Fax 532-2696
Torrington MS — 300/6-8
626 W 25th Ave 82240 — 307-532-7014
Marvin Haiman, prin. — Fax 532-8402
Other Schools – See Lingle, Yoder

Eastern Wyoming College — Post-Sec.
3200 W C St 82240 — 307-532-8200
St. Joseph's S — 100/PK-12
PO Box 1117 82240 — 307-532-4197
Travis Lenz, prin. — Fax 532-8405

Upton, Weston, Pop. 871
Weston County SD 7 — 300/K-12
PO Box 470 82730 — 307-468-2461
Troy Claycomb, supt. — Fax 468-2797
bobcat.weston7.k12.wy.us/
Upton HS — 100/9-12
PO Box 470 82730 — 307-468-2361
Gary Glodt, prin. — Fax 468-2459
Upton MS — 100/6-8
PO Box 470 82730 — 307-468-9331
Janice Peterson, prin. — Fax 468-2832

Wamsutter, Sweetwater, Pop. 262
Sweetwater County SD 1
Supt. — See Rock Springs
Desert MS — 50/6-8
PO Box 10 82336 — 307-324-7811
Richard Freudenberg, prin. — Fax 324-4824

Wheatland, Platte, Pop. 3,476
Platte County SD 1 — 1,200/K-12
1350 Oak St 82201 — 307-322-5480
Stuart Nelson, supt. — Fax 322-2084
www.platte1.k12.wy.us/
Wheatland HS — 300/9-12
1350 Oak St 82201 — 307-322-2075
Maureen Ryff, prin. — Fax 322-9739
Wheatland JHS — 300/6-8
1350 Oak St 82201 — 307-322-1550
Steven Loyd, prin. — Fax 322-1560
Other Schools – See Chugwater, Glendo

Worland, Washakie, Pop. 4,944
Washakie County SD 1 — 1,300/K-12
1900 Howell Ave 82401 — 307-347-9286
Mike Hejtmanek, supt. — Fax 347-8116
whs.1wyo.net/
Worland HS — 400/9-12
801 S 17th St 82401 — 307-347-2412
Hal Johnson, prin. — Fax 347-8549
Worland MS — 300/6-8
2150 Howell Ave 82401 — 307-347-3233
Richard Schaal, prin. — Fax 347-3710

Wright, Campbell, Pop. 1,414
Campbell County SD 1
Supt. — See Gillette
Wright JSHS — 300/7-12
PO Box 490 82732 — 307-464-0140
Charles Auzqui, prin. — Fax 464-0154

Yoder, Goshen, Pop. 163
Goshen County SD 1
Supt. — See Torrington
Southeast S — 100/9-12
PO Box 160 82244 — 307-532-7176
Brian Grasmick, prin. — Fax 532-5771
Southeast JHS — 100/7-8
PO Box 160 82244 — 307-532-7176
Brian Grasmick, prin. — Fax 532-5771

CHARTER SCHOOLS

School	Address	City,State	Zip code	Telephone	Fax	Grade	Contact
Alaska							
Academy Charter S	801 E Artic	Palmer, AK	99645	907-746-2358	746-2368	K-8	Barbara Gerard
Anvil City Science Academy	PO Box 131	Nome, AK	99762-0131	907-443-6207	443-5144	5-8	Todd Hindman
Aquarian Charter S	1705 W 32nd Ave	Anchorage, AK	99517-2002	907-742-4900	742-4919	K-6	Susan Forbes
Aurora Borealis Charter S	705 Frontage Rd Ste A	Kenai, AK	99611-7740	907-283-0292	283-0293	K-8	Larry Nauta
Career Education Center	725 26th Ave Ste 202	Fairbanks, AK	99701-7000	907-479-4061	479-0230	11-12	Annie Keep-Barnes
Chinook Charter S	3002 International St	Fairbanks, AK	99701-7391	907-452-5020	452-5048	K-8	Barbara Smith
Delta Cyber S	PO Box 1672	Delta Junction, AK	99737-1672	907-895-1043	895-5198	K-12	Michael Opp
Eagle Academy Charter S	10901 Mausel St Ste 101	Eagle River, AK	99577-8065	907-742-3025	742-3035	K-6	Kelly Nichols
Family Partnership Charter S	401 E Fireweed Ln Ste 101	Anchorage, AK	99503-2100	907-742-3700	742-3710	K-12	Reed Whitmore
Fireweed Academy	PO Box 474	Homer, AK	99603-0474	907-235-9728	235-8163	3-7	Kiki Abrahamson
Frontier Charter S	400 W Northern Lights Blvd	Anchorage, AK	99503-3802	907-742-1180	742-1188	K-12	Tim Scott
Galena Interior Learning Academy	PO Box 359	Galena, AK	99741-0359	907-656-2053	656-2107	9-12	Harry White
Highland Tech Charter S	5530 E Northern Lights Blvd	Anchorage, AK	99504-3135	907-742-1700	742-1711	7-12	Mark Standley
Juneau Community Charter S	10014 Crazy Horse Dr	Juneau, AK	99801-8529	907-586-2526	586-3543	K-6	Carol Valentine
Kaleidoscope S	549 N Forest Dr	Kenai, AK	99611-7410	907-283-0804	283-3786	1-3	Jacquie Steckel
Ketchikan Charter S	410 Schoenbar Rd	Ketchikan, AK	99901-6218	907-225-8568		K-6	Meg Spink
Kokrine Charter S	601 Loftus Rd	Fairbanks, AK	99709-3430	907-474-0958	479-2104	7-12	Eleanor Laughlin
Midnight Sun Family Learning Center	7362 W Parks Hwy # 714	Wasilla, AK	99654-9132	907-357-6786	373-6786	K-12	Jeanne Troshynski
North Pole Academy	300 N Santa Claus Ln	North Pole, AK	99705-6053	907-490-9025	490-9021	7-12	Annie Keep-Barnes
Winterberry Charter S	508 W 2nd Ave	Anchorage, AK	99501-2208	907-301-1201		K-6	Shanna Mall
Arizona							
AAEC - Chandler/Gilbert	1350 S Longmore	Mesa, AZ	85202-9603	480-833-8899	833-1266	9-12	Linda LaFontain
AAEC - Mesa	1350 S Longmore	Mesa, AZ	85202-9603	480-833-8899	833-1266	9-12	Linda LaFontain
AAEC - Paradise Valley	17811 N 32nd St	Phoenix, AZ	85032-1201	602-569-1101	569-6372	9-12	Dennis Gray
AAEC - Red Mountain	2165 N Power Rd	Mesa, AZ	85215-2971	480-833-8899	833-1266	9-12	Linda LaFontain
AAEC - SMCC Campus	7050 S 24th St	Phoenix, AZ	85042-5806	602-243-8004	243-8001	9-12	Dr. William Torres Conley
Academic & Personal Excellence HS	2859 E Elvira Rd	Tucson, AZ	85706-7126	520-889-4246	889-5812	6-12	Jim Parks
Academy of Arizona - Main	2100 W Indian School Rd	Phoenix, AZ	85015-4907	602-274-0422	274-0543	K-8	Diana Likes
Academy of Arizona North Campus	13002 N 33rd Ave	Phoenix, AZ	85029-1208	602-843-0681	843-2092	K-6	Diana Likes
Academy of Building Industries	1547 E Lipan Blvd	Fort Mohave, AZ	86426-6031	928-788-2601	788-2610	9-12	Jean Thomas
Academy of Excellence	425 N 36th St	Phoenix, AZ	85008-6303	602-389-4271	389-4278	K-8	Eula Dean
Academy of Hope	PO Box 435	Ash Fork, AZ	86320-0435	928-637-2487	637-2499	K-12	Terra Chesnutt
Academy of Math & Science	1557 W Prince Rd	Tucson, AZ	85705-3023	520-293-2676	888-1732	1-12	Tatyana Chayka
Academy of Tucson ES	9209 E Wrightstown Rd	Tucson, AZ	85715-5514	520-886-6076	886-6575	K-5	Caroline Martin
Academy of Tucson HS	10720 E 22nd St	Tucson, AZ	85748-7029	520-733-0096	733-0097	9-12	Susan Pearson
Academy of Tucson MS	2300 N Tanque Verde Loop Rd	Tucson, AZ	85749-9786	520-749-1413	749-2824	6-8	Laurie Ocampo
Academy With Community Partners	433 N Hall	Mesa, AZ	85203-7407	480-833-0068	833-8966	9-12	Margaret Williamson
Accelerated Learning Center	4101 E Shea Blvd	Phoenix, AZ	85028-3525	602-485-0309	485-9356	9-12	Frank Canady
Accelerated Learning Center Laboratory	5245 N Camino De Oeste	Tucson, AZ	85745-8925	520-743-2256	743-2417	K-12	David Jones
Accelerated Learning Charter S	320 S Main St	Cottonwood, AZ	86326-3905	928-634-0650	634-0672	K-8	Susan Glendening
ACCLAIM Charter S	5350 W Indian School Rd	Phoenix, AZ	85031-2607	623-691-0919	691-6091	K-8	Melanie Powers
ACE Charter HS	1901 N Stone Ave	Tucson, AZ	85705-5642	520-623-5843	791-9893	9-12	Kathleen Bibby
Acorn Montessori Charter S	8556 E Loos Dr	Prescott Valley, AZ	86314-6455	928-772-5778	775-8654	K-6	Cynthia Puplaua
Adventure S	1950 E Placita Sin Nombre	Tucson, AZ	85718-2092	602-821-6900	721-4472	K-4	Maryann Penczar
Ahwatukee Foothills Prep S	10210 S 50th Pl	Phoenix, AZ	85044-5209	480-763-5101	763-5107	1-8	Katharine Bush
All Aboard Charter S	5827 N 35th Ave	Phoenix, AZ	85017-1915	602-433-0500	973-8208	K-2	Frederick Miller
Allsports Academy	8570 E 22nd St	Tucson, AZ	85710-6522	520-731-2150	731-2160	5-9	Moses Montoya
Alta Vista Charter HS	5040 S Campbell Ave	Tucson, AZ	85706-1510	520-294-4922	294-4933	9-12	Alicia Alvarez
American Heritage Academy	2030 E Cherry St	Cottonwood, AZ	86326-6963	928-634-2144	634-9053	K-12	Steve Anderson
Amerischools Academy	1333 W Camelback Rd	Phoenix, AZ	85013-2106	602-532-0100	532-9964	K-12	Dr. Reginald Barr
Amerischools Academy	1150 N Country Club Rd	Tucson, AZ	85716-3942	520-620-1100	624-4376	K-12	Greg Gaines
Amerischools Academy - Yuma	2098 S 3rd Ave	Yuma, AZ	85364-6425	928-329-1100	329-9177	K-8	Dea Bermudez
Amerischools College Prep Academy	7444 E Broadway Blvd	Tucson, AZ	85710-1411	520-722-1200	722-0052	K-12	Charlene Mendoza
Apache Trail HS	945 W Apache Trl	Apache Junction, AZ	85220-5409	480-288-0337	288-0340	9-12	Giles Glithero
Apex Academy	945 W Apache Trl	Apache Junction, AZ	85220-5409	480-288-0337	288-0340	K-8	
Arizona Academy of Science & Technology	PO Box 13606	Phoenix, AZ	85002-3606	602-253-1199	595-8693	K-12	Joan Miller
AZ Call-A-Teen Center of Excellence	649 N 6th Ave	Phoenix, AZ	85003-1659	602-252-6721	252-2952	9-12	Pam Smith
Arizona Charter Academy	PO Box 1929	Surprise, AZ	85378-1929	623-974-4959	974-4840	K-12	Tracy Irwin
AZ Conservatory for Arts & Academics	2820 W Kelton Ln	Phoenix, AZ	85053-3028	602-266-4278	266-7827	6-12	Mary Cargill
AZ Montessori Charter S	10620 N 43rd Ave	Glendale, AZ	85304-4150	602-978-0011	978-0194	PK-6	Sandra Houston
AZ Montessori Charter S	42302 N Vision Way	Phoenix, AZ	85086-1466	623-551-5083	551-5083	K-8	Debra Slagle
Arizona School for the Arts	1313 N 2nd St	Phoenix, AZ	85004-1750	602-257-1444	252-7795	6-12	Dr. Mark Francis
Arizona Upgrade Academy	327 S 15th St	Cottonwood, AZ	86326-3432	928-634-0271	634-3695	5-8	Allen Smithson
Arizona Virtual Academy	1840 E Benson Hwy	Tucson, AZ	85714-1770	520-623-1483	623-1803	K-9	Mary Gifford
A R S A P Charter S	6574 S Dateland Dr	Tempe, AZ	85283-3658	480-968-6529	968-6522	K-8	Kisha Spellman-White
Arts Academy at Estrella Mountain	2504 S 91st Ave	Tolleson, AZ	85353-8921	623-474-2120	936-5337	K-8	Sheri Kisselbach
Arts Academy at South Mountain	4039 E Raymond St	Phoenix, AZ	85040-1930	602-437-2947	426-1342	K-8	Kris Johnson
Avalon S at San Marcos	1045 S San Marcos Dr	Apache Junction, AZ	85220-6337	480-671-4584	671-4586	K-8	Mathew Reese
Az-Tec HS	2330 W 28th St	Yuma, AZ	85364-6954	928-314-1900	726-2826	9-12	Linda Munk
Aztlan Academy	3376 S 6th Ave	South Tucson, AZ	85713-6139	520-844-0650	844-1602	6-12	Sr. Judy Bisignano
BASIS S - Tucson	3825 E 2nd St	Tucson, AZ	85716-4368	520-326-6367	326-6359	5-12	Carolyn McGarvey
Basis Scottsdale	9128 E San Salvador Dr	Scottsdale, AZ	85258-5556	480-451-7500	451-4555	5-12	Diane Moser
Belle Affeld Beloved Humanities Academy	PO Box 5554	Lake Montezuma, AZ	86342-5554	928-567-4475	567-4636	4-12	J'Anne Affeld
Benchmark ES	4120 E Acoma Dr	Phoenix, AZ	85032-4753	602-765-3582	765-1932	K-6	Barbara Darroch
Bennett Academy	2940 W Bethany Home Rd	Phoenix, AZ	85017-1615	602-943-1317	943-0280	K-8	Fred Bennett
Berean Academy	4699 E Highway 90	Sierra Vista, AZ	85635-2437	520-459-4113	459-4121	K-10	Mark Bennett
Berean S	400 Arizona St	Bisbee, AZ	85603-1504	520-236-8032		1-5	Kathleen Pace
Bradley Academy of Excellence	200 N Dysart Rd	Avondale, AZ	85323-2418	623-932-9902	932-9904	K-3	Tanya Burston
Bright Beginnings S	400 N Andersen Blvd	Chandler, AZ	85224-8273	480-821-1404	821-1463	K-8	Sydelle Hoffman
Bright Ideas Charter S - Van Buren	2720 S Dorsey Ln	Tempe, AZ	85282-2708	602-275-3400	275-3558	K-8	Beth Brantley
Burke Basic S	131 E Southern Ave	Mesa, AZ	85210-5355	480-964-4602	964-6566	K-8	Glen Gaddie
Calli Ollin Academy	200 N Stone Ave Fl 3	Tucson, AZ	85701-1208	520-882-3029	882-3041	9-12	Magdalena Verdugo
Cambridge Academy East	9412 E Brown Rd	Mesa, AZ	85207-4338	480-641-2828	325-2365	K-6	Linda Gonzalez
Camelback Academy	7634 W Camelback Rd	Glendale, AZ	85303-5627	623-247-2204	247-1113	K-6	Karen Kordon
Canyon Pointe Preparatory	3300 W Camelback Rd	Phoenix, AZ	85017-3030	602-445-5000	445-5001	9-12	Jonathan Eddy
Canyon Rose Academy	3686 W Orange Grove Rd	Tucson, AZ	85741-2852	520-514-5112	797-8868	9-12	Lisa Cothrun
Carden of Tucson S	5260 N Royal Palm Dr	Tucson, AZ	85705-1148	520-293-6661	408-7366	K-8	Bette Jeppson
Carden Traditional S of Glendale	4744 W Grovers Ave	Glendale, AZ	85308-3453	602-439-5026	547-2841	K-8	Timothy Smith
Carden Traditional S of Surprise	15688 W Acoma Dr	Surprise, AZ	85379-5652	623-556-2179	547-2806	K-8	Hector Placencia
Career Success HS	3816 N 27th Ave	Phoenix, AZ	85017-4703	602-285-5525	285-0026	9-12	Sonia Gonzales
Career Success HS - Cave Creek	PO Box 7010	Cave Creek, AZ	85327-7010	480-575-0075	575-0061	9-12	Maureen Racz
Career Success HS - Copper Square	301 W Roosevelt St	Phoenix, AZ	85003-1324	602-393-4200	393-4205	9-12	Kathy Scott
Career Success S - Glendale	8632 W Northern Ave Bldg 3	Glendale, AZ	85305-1308	602-285-5525	285-0026	9-12	Sonia Gonzales
Career Success S - Sage Campus	3120 N 32nd St	Phoenix, AZ	85018-6202	602-955-0355	508-0682	K-12	Kathy Randall
Carmel Community Arts & Technology S	97 W Oakland St	Chandler, AZ	85225-4536	480-899-6600	899-4122	K-12	Lynn Monson
Carpe Diem Academy	PO Box 6502	Yuma, AZ	85366-6502	928-317-3113	317-0828	6-12	Rick Ogston
Casa Verde Charter HS	1362 N Casa Grande Ave	Casa Grande, AZ	85222-2648	520-876-0661	876-0667	9-12	Charie Wallace
CASY Chandler S	550 W Warner Rd	Chandler, AZ	85225-4364	480-786-3133	786-3134	K-6	Steve Mills
CASY Country Day S 1	7214 E Jenan Dr	Scottsdale, AZ	85260-5416	480-951-3190	998-4029	K-5	Bill Thompson
CASY Country Day S 2	9350 E Cactus Rd	Scottsdale, AZ	85260-5020	480-661-1930	314-7306	K-5	Bill Thompson
CASY South Valley Academy	2033 E Southern Ave	Phoenix, AZ	85040-3344	602-276-2818		K-8	Bill Thompson
Center for Academic Success #1	650 E Wilcox Dr	Sierra Vista, AZ	85635-2534	520-458-9309	417-9910	K-12	Phillip Hirales
Center for Academic Success #2	510 N G Ave	Douglas, AZ	85607-2822	520-364-2616	805-0973	9-12	Stephen Huff
Center for Academic Success #3	1415 F Ave	Douglas, AZ	85607-1655	520-805-1558	805-1549	K-4	Stephen Huff
Center for Creative Education Charter S	762 E Cinnabar Dr	Cottonwood, AZ	86326-5007	928-634-3288	634-9781	K-6	Mary Ann Green
Center for Educational Excellence	1700 E Elliot Rd Ste 9	Tempe, AZ	85284-1631	480-632-1940	632-1398	K-8	Stacey Cochran
Challenge Charter S	5801 W Greenbriar Dr	Glendale, AZ	85308-3847	602-938-5411	938-5393	K-6	Gregory Miller
Challenger Basic S	1315 N Greenfield Rd	Gilbert, AZ	85234-2813	480-830-1750	830-1763	K-6	Brad Tobin
Chandler Preparatory Academy	2020 N Arizona Ave	Chandler, AZ	85225-3462	480-855-5410	855-7789	7-8	Helen Hayes
Chavez MS	3376 S 6th Ave	Tucson, AZ	85713-6139	520-573-1500	573-1600	6-8	Sr. Judy Bisignano
Children Reaching for the Sky Prep	1844 S Alvernon Way	Tucson, AZ	85711-5607	520-790-8400	620-6570	K-6	Lee Griffin

School	Address	City,State	Zip code	Telephone	Fax	Grade	Contact
Childrens Success Academy	PO Box 11368	Tucson, AZ	85734-1368	520-799-8403	799-8427	K-8	Nanci Aiken
City HS	PO Box 2608	Tucson, AZ	85702-2608	520-623-7223	547-0680	9-12	Carolyn Brennan
Civano Charter S	10673 E Mira Ln	Tucson, AZ	85747-5983	520-731-3466	731-3477	K-6	Connie Erickson
Civano MS	16335 S Houghton Rd	Vail, AZ	85641-2141	520-762-8534	762-8539	6-8	
Classics and Four Arts Academy	7475 E McDowell Rd	Scottsdale, AZ	85257-3511	480-874-3332	874-3231	K-12	Paula Banda
Compass HS	8250 E 22nd St	Tucson, AZ	85710-8548	520-296-4070	296-4103	9-12	John Ferguson
Coolidge HS Success Center	8470 N Overfield Rd	Coolidge, AZ	85228-9030	520-251-2320		9-12	Susan Price
Copper Canyon Academy	7985 W Peoria Ave	Peoria, AZ	85345	623-930-1734	930-8709	K-6	Jinny Ludwig
Cornerstone Charter S	7107 N Black Canyon Hwy	Phoenix, AZ	85021-7619	602-595-2198	242-2398	9-12	George Smith
Cortez Park Charter S	3535 W Dunlap Ave	Phoenix, AZ	85051-5303	602-589-9840	589-9841	K-8	Freddie Villalon
Country Gardens Charter S	6301 W Alta Vista Rd	Laveen, AZ	85339-9612	602-237-3741	237-3892	K-12	Goldie Burge
Crittenton Youth Academy	715 W Mariposa	Phoenix, AZ	85013	602-274-7318	288-4118	6-12	Dan Johnston
Crown Charter S	PO Box 363	Litchfield Park, AZ	85340-0363	623-535-9300	535-5410	K-6	James Shade
Daisy Early Learning	2255 W Ina Rd	Tucson, AZ	85741-2650	520-219-6700			Nuray Tugrul
Davis Education Center	5660 S 12th Ave	Tucson, AZ	85706-3102	520-722-8130	722-7089	K-8	Gwen Nesbitt
Day Star Academy	2030 N 36th St	Phoenix, AZ	85008-3027	602-275-3852	275-5685	K-12	Stacey Boyd
Deer Valley Charter HS	20402 N 15th Ave	Phoenix, AZ	85027-3699	623-445-4915	445-4915	9-12	Barbara Daggett
Desert Heights Charter S	5821 W Beverly Ln	Glendale, AZ	85306-1801	602-896-2900	467-9540	K-8	Mark Giles
Desert Hills HS	1515 S Val Vista Dr	Gilbert, AZ	85296-3854	480-813-1151	813-1161	9-12	William Coats
Desert Marigold S	6210 S 28th St	Phoenix, AZ	85042-4715	602-243-6909	243-6933	K-8	Amy Bird
Desert Mosaic S	5757 W Ajo Hwy	Tucson, AZ	85735-9334	520-578-2022	578-0834	K-12	Lynn Spoon
Desert Pointe Academy	7785 W Peoria Ave	Peoria, AZ	85345-5922	623-930-1734	930-8709	7-12	Jinny Ludwig
Desert Rose Academy	20 W Fort Lowell Rd	Tucson, AZ	85705-3810	520-696-0819	797-8868	9-12	Eileen Geraghty
Desert Springs Academy	3833 E 2nd St	Tucson, AZ	85716-4368	520-321-1709	321-9316	K-8	Lydia Capara
Desert Springs Academy	10355 E 29th St	Tucson, AZ	85748-7725	520-546-9966	546-9848	K-8	Lydia Capara
Desert Technology HS	3155 Maricopa Ave	Lk Havasu Cty, AZ	86406-8635	928-453-3383	453-3886	9-12	Leon Buttler
Desert View Academy	2363 S Kennedy Ln	Yuma, AZ	85365-2416	928-314-1102	314-1086	K-5	Rick Ogston
Destiny Community S	PO Box 3320	Gilbert, AZ	85299-3320	480-325-8950	539-0147	K-8	Wendy Noble
DINE Southwest HS	HC 63 Box 303	Winslow, AZ	86047-9424	928-657-3272	657-3272	9-12	Charlene Starlight
Discovery Plus Academy	PO Box 1089	Pima, AZ	85543-1089	928-485-2498	485-2508	K-8	Donna Bolinger
Dobson Academy	PO Box 6070	Chandler, AZ	85246-6070	480-855-6325	855-6323	K-8	George Ellis
Doby MS	1951 W Camelback Rd	Phoenix, AZ	85015-3403	623-878-8059	878-8175	5-8	Sharon Foster
Dove Academy College Preparatory	4530 N Central Ave	Phoenix, AZ	85012-1817	602-234-2130	234-2133	K-9	Shaloma Gray
Downtown Arts Academy	210 E Broadway Blvd	Tucson, AZ	85701-2014	520-882-9144	792-0668	K-9	Frank Dipietro
Dragonfleye Charter S	10202 N 19th Ave	Phoenix, AZ	85021-1910	602-944-4322	944-1450	K-9	Gail Battistella
E.A.G.L.E. Academy	423 Colorado Rd	Golden Valley, AZ	86413	928-565-3400	565-3454	K-12	Mary Stuart
Eagle's Aerie S	17019 S Greenfield Rd	Gilbert, AZ	85297-6900	480-988-3212	988-3280	K-12	Tim Peak
East Mesa Charter S	9701 E Southern Ave	Mesa, AZ	85209-3769	480-355-6830	355-6840	K-6	Monte Lang
Eastpointe HS	8495 E Broadway Blvd	Tucson, AZ	85710-4009	520-731-8180	731-8179	9-12	Todd Brown
East Valley Academy	910 N 85th Pl	Scottsdale, AZ	85257-4561	480-610-1711	421-0183	K-6	Janet Stoeppelman
East Valley HS	7420 E Main St	Mesa, AZ	85207-8306	480-981-2008	641-4473	9-12	Kathy Tolman
E-cadamie	417 N 16th St	Phoenix, AZ	85006-3710	602-416-6400	416-6393	9-12	Arturo Ortiz
Ecotech Agricultural Charter S	12221 E Pecos Rd	Chandler, AZ	85225-2001	480-814-9007	814-7484	K-8	Jameela Pugh
Edge Charter S-Child & Family Resources	2555 E 1st St	Tucson, AZ	85716-4153	520-881-1389	881-0852	9-12	Reese Millen
Edge Charter S - Himmel Park	2555 E 1st St	Tucson, AZ	85716-4153	520-881-1389	881-0852	9-12	Reese Millen
Edge Charter S - Northwest	2555 E 1st St	Tucson, AZ	85716-4153	520-877-9179	877-9225	9-12	Cathy Sivilli
Edge Charter S - Sahuarita	2555 E 1st St	Tucson, AZ	85716-4153	520-393-1690	881-1689	9-12	Reese Millen
Educational Opportunity Center	3810 W 16th St	Yuma, AZ	85364-4107	928-329-0990	782-9558	9-12	Brian Grossenburg
EduPreneurship Student Center	1201 N 85th Pl	Scottsdale, AZ	85257-4196	480-990-2475	990-0378	K-8	Carol Ann Sammans
EduPreneurship Student Center	7310 N 27th Ave	Phoenix, AZ	85051-7505	602-973-8998	973-5510	K-8	Carol Ann Sammans
Edu-Prize S	580 W Melody Ave	Gilbert, AZ	85233-1418	480-813-9537	813-6742	K-8	Lynn Robershotte
E-Institute at Acoma	15688 W Acoma Dr	Surprise, AZ	85379-5652	623-556-2179	556-2806	9-12	Hector Placencia
E-Institute at Union Hills	3515 W Union Hills Dr	Glendale, AZ	85308-2429	602-843-3077	843-4375	9-12	John Cortez
El Dorado HS	2200 N Arizona Ave Ste 17	Chandler, AZ	85225-3452	480-726-9536	726-9543	9-12	Ramona Gonzales
Enterprise Academy	415 W Grant St	Phoenix, AZ	85003-2431	602-254-1844	254-1533	K-6	Shane Stuckey
Esperanza Community Collegial Academy	2507 E Bell Rd	Phoenix, AZ	85032-2413	602-996-4217		9-12	
Estrella HS	510 N Central Ave	Avondale, AZ	85323-1909	623-932-6561	932-1263	9-12	William Horton
Excalibur Charter S	10839 E Apache Trl Ste 113	Apache Junction, AZ	85220-3415	480-373-9575	373-9600	K-12	Jeffrey Parker
Excel Education Center	2229 E Spruce Ave	Flagstaff, AZ	86004-5011	928-214-7442	214-7256	9-12	Michael Gerdes
Excel Education Center - Chino Valley	1985 N Rd 1 W	Chino Valley, AZ	86323	928-636-1444	636-1414	9-12	Katie Reynolds
Excel Education Center - Cottonwood	1229 E Cherry St	Cottonwood, AZ	86326-3458	928-634-2065	639-2952	9-12	Sharon Ackerman
Excel Education Center - Fort Mohave	1385 E Gemini St	Fort Mohave, AZ	86426-8326	928-758-5472	758-2821	9-12	Don Coe
Excel Education Center - Prescott	1040 Whipple St Ste 401	Prescott, AZ	86305-3405	928-541-1701	778-5766	6-12	Brenda Clark
Excel Education Center - San Carlos	PO Box 729	Peridot, AZ	85542-0729	928-475-2292	475-2441	9-12	Larry Beaver
Excel Education Centers-Prescott Valley	7515 E Long Look Dr	Prescott Valley, AZ	86314-5507	928-775-6681	775-6691	9-12	Mark Gorman
Excel Education Center - Williams Campus	790 E Rodeo Rd	Williams, AZ	86046-9653	928-635-3998	635-3999	9-12	Michael Gerdes
Flagstaff Arts and Leadership Academy	3100 N Fort Vlly Rd Bldg 41	Flagstaff, AZ	86001	928-779-7223	779-7041	9-12	Kirk Quitter
Flagstaff Junior Academy - Charter	306 W Cedar Ave	Flagstaff, AZ	86001-1413	928-774-6007	774-7268	PK-8	Dulcie Ambrose
Foothills Academy	7191 E Ashler Hills Dr	Scottsdale, AZ	85262-9300	480-488-5583	488-6902	6-12	Donald Senneville
Fountain Hills Charter S	15055 N Fountain Hills Blvd	Fountain Hills, AZ	85268-2330	480-837-0046	837-0024	K-8	Michael Bashaw
4 Winds Academy	PO Box 1773	Eagar, AZ	85925-1773	928-333-1060	333-2926	K-8	Steve Chavez
Franklin Arts Academy	862 E Elliot Rd	Gilbert, AZ	85234-6912	480-325-6100	807-1630	K-6	Dana Rodgers
Franklin Arts Academy - Gold	2929 E McKellips	Mesa, AZ	85204	480-924-1500	924-0552	K-8	Mike Epperson
Franklin Charter S	13732 E Warner Rd	Gilbert, AZ	85296-2808	480-632-0722	632-8716	K-6	Terry Nicoll
Franklin Charter S	21151 S Crismon Rd	Queen Creek, AZ	85242-8957	480-987-0722	987-3517	K-8	Jack McLeod
Franklin Charter S	2345 N Horne	Mesa, AZ	85203-1823	480-649-0712	649-8716	K-5	Debra Stoddard
Franklin HS	5646 E Main St	Mesa, AZ	85205-8800	480-218-2249	218-4483	9-12	Byram Beckstead
Franklin Phonetic S	6116 E State Route 69	Prescott Valley, AZ	86314-2806	928-775-6747	775-6740	K-8	Cindy Franklin
Freedom Academy	15014 N 56th St Ste 1	Scottsdale, AZ	85254-2407	602-424-0771	424-0773	K-8	Linda Hoffman
Freire Freedom S	300 E University Blvd	Tucson, AZ	85705-7899	520-624-7552	624-7518	6-8	JoAnn Groh
Friendly House Academia Del Pueblo S	201 E Durango St	Phoenix, AZ	85004-2913	602-258-4353	416-7375	K-8	Desiree Castillo
Gan Yeladeem: The Looking Glass S	3916 E Paradise Ln	Phoenix, AZ	85032-3232	602-493-8301	493-1222	K-8	Susan Heller
GateWay Early College HS	108 N 40th St	Phoenix, AZ	85034-1795	602-286-8759	286-8752	9-12	Yvonne Watterson
GEM Charter S	1704 N Center St	Mesa, AZ	85201-2223	480-833-2622	833-2655	K-6	Nelleke van Savooyen
Genesis Academy	640 N 1st Ave	Phoenix, AZ	85003-1515	602-223-4200	223-4210	9-12	Karen Callahan
Gila Preparatory Academy	1976 W Thatcher Blvd	Safford, AZ	85546-3318	928-348-8688	348-8877	6-12	Kathy Maxwell
Glenn Academy	7544 W Indian School Rd	Phoenix, AZ	85033-3030	623-247-4100	247-4101	9-12	Jeffrey DeMatte
Grand Canyon College Prep Charter S	5801 S Rural Rd	Tempe, AZ	85283-2901	480-233-3622	807-3176	6-12	David Gordon
Great Expectations Academy	1466 W Camino Antigua	Sahuarita, AZ	85629-9720	520-399-2121	399-2123	K-8	Beth Phillips
Guerrero MS	2797 N Introspect Dr	Tucson, AZ	85745-9454	520-807-2836	623-9679	3-8	Carmen Campuzano
Ha:San Prep & Leadership Charter S	1333 E 10th St	Tucson, AZ	85719-5808	520-882-8826	882-8651	9-12	Michael Norris
Happy Valley S	7140 W Happy Valley Rd	Peoria, AZ	85383-3255	623-376-2900	655-7870	K-8	Glen Gaddie
Harvest Preparatory Academy	PO Box 6826	Yuma, AZ	85366-6826	928-783-6266	783-4543	K-11	Deborah Ybarra
Hayes Memorial Applied Learning Ctr	PO Box 10899	Bapchule, AZ	85221-0899	520-315-5100	315-5115	9-12	Richard Stoner
Hearn Academy	17606 N 7th Ave	Phoenix, AZ	85023-1567	602-896-9160	896-1997	K-8	Jane Vert
Heritage Academy	32 S Center St	Mesa, AZ	85210-1306	480-969-5641	969-6972	7-12	Earl Taylor
Heritage Montessori Charter S	3501 W Wescott Dr	Glendale, AZ	85308-2329	623-582-4700		K-K	Susan Vespoli
Hermosa Montessori Charter S	12051 E Fort Lowell Rd	Tucson, AZ	85749-9702	520-749-5518	749-6087	K-8	Sheila Stolov
Higgins Institute	1805 E Elliot Rd #112	Tempe, AZ	85284	480-413-0829	413-9365	K-8	Martha Wallace
Highland Free S	510 S Highland Ave	Tucson, AZ	85719-6427	520-623-0104	903-1318	K-5	Nicholas Sofka
Horizon Community Learning Center	16233 S 48th St	Phoenix, AZ	85048-0801	480-659-3000	659-3022	K-12	Lawrence Pieratt
Horizons Back-to-Basics S	749 E Baseline Rd	Phoenix, AZ	85042-6614	602-304-1763	323-9704	K-8	Jorge Vega
Humanities and Science HS	1105 E Broadway Rd	Tempe, AZ	85282-1505	480-317-5900	829-4999	9-12	Michael Curd
Humanities & Sciences Institute	5201 N 7th St	Phoenix, AZ	85014-2802	602-650-1333	650-1881	9-12	Sue Durkin
Imagine Charter S at Bell Canyon	18052 N Black Canyon Hwy	Phoenix, AZ	85053-1715	602-547-7920	547-7923	K-6	Susan Scorza
Imagine Charter S at Rosefield	12050 N Bullard Ave	Surprise, AZ	85379-6325	623-344-4300	344-4310	K-5	Thomas Shearer
Imagine Charter S at Sierra Vista	1000 E Wilcox Dr	Sierra Vista, AZ	85635-2622	520-459-7286	459-7218	K-8	Ken King
Imagine Charter S at West Gilbert	14919 S Gilbert Rd	Gilbert, AZ	85296-5204	480-855-2700	855-2701	K-5	Linda Horner
Integrity Education Centre	1290 N Scottsdale Rd #123	Tempe, AZ	85281	480-731-4829	394-0711	K-12	Holly Mullan
Intelli School - Glendale	13806 N 51st Ave	Glendale, AZ	85306-4834	602-564-7210	564-7211	9-12	Mabel Vigil
Intelli School - Main	4629 E Chandler Blvd	Phoenix, AZ	85048-0428	602-564-7230	564-7231	9-12	Jonathan Owen
Intelli School - Metro Center	3101 W Peoria Ave Ste B305	Phoenix, AZ	85029-5210	602-564-7240	564-7241	9-12	Jennifer Lowing
Intelli School - Paradise Valley	1107 E Bell Rd # 109A	Phoenix, AZ	85022-2691	602-564-7280	564-7281	9-12	Timothy Howard
International Commerce Institute	5201 N 7th St	Phoenix, AZ	85014-2802	602-650-1116	650-1777	11-12	Sue Durkin
International Commerce Institute - Tempe	1105 E Broadway Rd	Tempe, AZ	85282-1505	480-317-5900	829-4999	7-12	Michael Curd
International Commerce Institute-Tsaile	Dine College - Bldg AJ	Tsaile, AZ	86556	800-762-0010	762-1622	7-12	Arthur Ben
International Studies Academy	4744 W Grovers Ave	Glendale, AZ	85308-3453	602-547-8806	547-2841	7-12	Timothy Smith
Jefferson Academy of Advanced Learning	40 S 11th St	Show Low, AZ	85901-6001	928-537-5432	537-0440	K-12	Sandy Stewart
Jefferson HS	921 W Camelback Rd	Phoenix, AZ	85013-2208	602-285-3003	285-5560	9-12	Helen Fortune
JWJ Academy	367 N 21st Ave	Phoenix, AZ	85009-4525	602-258-6060	258-6195	K-12	Walter Tilford
JWJ Academy - Avondale	367 N 21st Ave	Phoenix, AZ	85009-4525	623-925-2780	925-2461	K-9	Walter Tilford
JWJ Academy - Primary Campus	367 N 21st Ave	Phoenix, AZ	85009-4525	602-305-8440	305-8443	K-K	Walter Tilford
Kachina Country Day S	6602 E Malcomb Dr	Paradise Valley, AZ	85253-5318	480-951-0745	951-1267	PK-6	Janece Kline
Kestrel HS	PO Box 11028	Prescott, AZ	86304-1028	928-541-1090	541-9939	9-12	Stephen Myers
Keystone Montessori Charter S	1025 E Liberty Ln	Phoenix, AZ	85048-8462	480-460-7312	283-8402	1-8	Sherri Sampson
Khalsa Montessori S	2536 N 3rd St	Phoenix, AZ	85004-1308	602-252-3759	252-5224	K-8	Satwant Khalsa
Khalsa Montessori S	3701 E River Rd	Tucson, AZ	85718-6633	520-529-3611	615-0625	K-8	Nirvair Khalsa

School	Address	City,State	Zip code	Telephone	Fax	Grade	Contact
Kids at Hope Online Academy	1717 W Northern Ave	Phoenix, AZ	85021-5469	602-674-5555	943-9700	9-12	Barbara Day
Kingman Academy of Learning HS	2299 Beverly Ave	Kingman, AZ	86401	928-681-2900	681-2922	9-12	Jeff Martin
Kingman Academy of Learning IS	2299 Beverly Ave	Kingman, AZ	86401	928-681-3200	681-3202	3-5	Debbie Padilla
Kingman Academy of Learning MS	2299 Beverly Ave	Kingman, AZ	86401	928-692-5265	692-3444	6-8	Dawn Day
Kingman Academy of Learning PS	2299 Beverly Ave	Kingman, AZ	86401	928-718-2500	718-2505	K-2	Trudi Bradley
Kino Academy	2224 W Southern Ave Ste 1	Tempe, AZ	85282-4345	520-281-5109	281-5132	9-12	Sandra Canchola
Lake Havasu Charter S	1055 Empire Dr	Lk Havasu Cty, AZ	86404-2400	928-505-5427	505-3533	K-12	Patty Hauchrog
La Paloma Academy	2050 N Wilmot Rd	Tucson, AZ	85712-3039	520-721-4205	721-4263	K-10	Jackie Trujillo
La Paloma Academy - Lakeside	8140 E Golflinks Rd	Tucson, AZ	85730-1229	520-733-7373	733-7392	K-8	Randy Musgrove
La Paloma Academy - Midtown	225 N Country Club Rd	Tucson, AZ	85716-5233	520-325-5566	325-6622	K-6	Austin Thies
La Puerta HS	1951 W Camelback Rd	Phoenix, AZ	85015-3403	623-878-8059	878-8175	9-12	Sharon Foster
Leading Edge Academy	459 N Gilbert Rd Ste A146	Gilbert, AZ	85234-4773	480-545-8011	632-7151	K-10	Victoria Hallam
Leading Edge Academy	326 E Guadalupe Rd	Gilbert, AZ	85234-4659	480-545-8011	632-7151	9-12	Ron Body
Leading Edge Academy	4815 W Hunt Hwy	Queen Creek, AZ	85242-3271	480-655-6787	632-7151	K-8	Jim Lee
Learning Crossroads Basic Academy	1130 W 23rd St	Tempe, AZ	85282-1810	480-446-9288	449-9565	K-12	Robin Cubley
Learning Foundation Performing Arts S	851 N Stapley Dr Bldg 6	Mesa, AZ	85203-5644	480-834-6202	834-6210	K-12	Lori Graham
Learning Institute	5312 N 12th St	Phoenix, AZ	85014-2926	602-241-7876	241-7886	7-12	Adele Ferrini
Legacy S	7464 E Main St	Mesa, AZ	85207-8306	480-981-1500	641-4473	K-10	Kathy Tolman
Liberty Academy	3015 S Power Rd	Mesa, AZ	85212-3000	480-830-3444	830-4335	K-8	Linda Stansbury
Liberty HS	PO Box 2343	Globe, AZ	85502-2343	928-402-8024	402-8358	9-12	Sara Macdonald Ph.D.
Liberty Traditional Charter S	4027 N 45th Ave	Phoenix, AZ	85031-2840	602-442-8791	353-9270	K-8	Bonnie Knauel
Liberty Traditional Heritage S	13419 W Ocotillo Rd	Glendale, AZ	85307-3220	623-935-1931	935-1614	K-8	Aaron Robinson
Lifelong Learning Academy	3295 W Orange Grove Rd	Tucson, AZ	85741-2937	520-219-4383	544-0220	K-6	Mary Lou Klem
Life Skills Center of Arizona	8123 N 35th Ave	Phoenix, AZ	85051-9403	602-242-6400	242-6823	9-12	Benjamin Valdez
Luz Academy of Tucson	2797 N Introspect Dr	Tucson, AZ	85745-9454	520-882-6216	623-9291	9-12	Alfred Montes
Madison Preparatory S	5815 S Mcclintock Dr	Tempe, AZ	85283-3227	480-345-2306	345-0059	7-12	David Batchelder
Masada Charter S	PO Box 2277	Colorado City, AZ	86021-2277	928-875-2525	875-2526	K-9	Le Anne Timpson
Maya HS	3660 W Glendale Ave	Phoenix, AZ	85051-8335	602-242-3442	242-5255	9-12	Ricardo Borunda
Mesa Arts Academy	221 W 6th Ave	Mesa, AZ	85210-2446	480-844-3965	844-0205	K-8	Susan Douglas
Meta Academy HS	222 E 5th St	Tucson, AZ	85705-8412	520-622-1885	884-4704	9-12	Alan Rumsey
Metropolitan Arts Institute	1700 N 7th Ave	Phoenix, AZ	85007-1704	602-258-9500	258-9504	9-12	Matthew Baker
Mexicayotl Charter S	850 N Morley Ave	Nogales, AZ	85621-2924	520-287-6790	287-0037	K-12	Baltizar Garcia
Midtown HS	7318 W Lynwood St	Phoenix, AZ	85035-4542	623-936-8682	936-8559	9-12	John White
Midtown PS	4735 N 19th Ave	Phoenix, AZ	85015-3725	602-265-5133	604-2337	K-3	Judy White
Milestones Charter S	4707 E Robert E Lee St	Phoenix, AZ	85032-9529	602-404-1009	404-5456	K-5	Tara Cabardo
Mingus Mountain Academy	10451 W Palmeras Dr Ste 239	Sun City, AZ	85373-2013	602-335-2072		6-12	Cynthia Hancock
Mingus Springs Charter S	PO Box 827	Chino Valley, AZ	86323-0827	928-636-4766	636-5149	K-8	Cathryn A. O'Connell
Mission Charter S	7000 N Central Ave	Phoenix, AZ	85020-4817	602-943-4986	943-5936	1-6	Jane Shaw
Mission Montessori Academy	12990 E Shea Blvd	Scottsdale, AZ	85259-5305	480-860-4330	657-3715	K-5	Betty Matthews
Mohave Accelerated Learning Center	PO Box 21288	Bullhead City, AZ	86439-1288	928-704-9345	704-4977	K-12	Vickie Christensen
Montage Academy	32619 N Scottsdale Rd	Scottsdale, AZ	85262-1521	480-990-8763	488-0241	K-3	Esperanza Vega
Montessori Academy	2928 N 67th Pl	Scottsdale, AZ	85251-6002	480-945-1121	874-2928	K-8	Julianne Lewis
Montessori Charter S of Flagstaff	850 N Locust St	Flagstaff, AZ	86001-3343	928-226-1212	774-0337	K-8	Marina Smith
Montessori Childrens House	2400 W Datsi St	Camp Verde, AZ	86322-8412	928-567-1878	567-2107	K-K	Janet Taylor
Montessori Day Charter S - Mountainside	9215 N 14th St	Phoenix, AZ	85020-2713	602-943-7672	395-0271	K-8	Pat Freeman
Montessori Day Charter S - Scottsdale	6239 E Bell Rd	Scottsdale, AZ	85254-6400	480-596-7922	596-8293	K-3	Peggy Kraus
Montessori Day Charter S - Tempe	1700 W Warner Rd	Chandler, AZ	85224-2676	480-730-8886	917-1981	K-8	Colleen Ortega
Montessori de Santa Cruz Charter S	PO Box 4706	Tubac, AZ	85646-4706	520-398-0536	398-0776	K-6	Lisa Harrison
Montessori Education Centre Charter S	2834 E Southern Ave	Mesa, AZ	85204-5517	480-926-8375	503-0515	K-9	Tamara Whiting
Montessori Education Ctr - Charter S N	815 N Gilbert Rd	Mesa, AZ	85203-5805	480-964-1381	668-5457	K-9	Lisa Wakefield
Montessori House Charter S	2415 N Terrace Cir	Mesa, AZ	85203-1220	480-464-2800	464-2836	K-6	Sheryl Richardson
Montessori Schoolhouse	1301 E Fort Lowell Rd	Tucson, AZ	85719-2239	520-622-8668	622-2067	K-K	Regine Ebner
Montessori Schoolhouse	1301 E Fort Lowell Rd	Tucson, AZ	85719-2239	520-319-8668	881-4096	1-5	Michael Ebner
Montezuma MS	5040 S Price Rd	Tempe, AZ	85282-7445	480-831-6057	831-6095	6-8	Abelardo Batista
Morningstar Academy	1150 W Superstition Blvd	Apache Junction, AZ	85220-4043	480-671-5673	671-5675	K-6	Carol Kennedy
Mountainaire Academy	PO Box 2009	Saint Johns, AZ	85936-2009	928-337-3593	337-3594	K-12	Tony Rhinehart
Mountain English Spanish Academy	2300 E 6th Ave	Flagstaff, AZ	86004-4247	928-773-4088	773-4086	6-8	Ana Archuleta
Mountain Oak Charter S	124 N Virginia St	Prescott, AZ	86301-3224	928-541-7700	445-1301	K-8	Merrill Badger
Mountain Rose Academy	3686 W Orange Grove Rd	Tucson, AZ	85741-2852	520-229-1777	797-8868	9-12	Catherine Kinghorn
Mountain S	311 W Cattle Drive Trl	Flagstaff, AZ	86001-7060	928-779-2392	773-3246	PK-5	Renee Fauset
New Horizon S for the Performing Arts	446 E Broadway Rd	Mesa, AZ	85204-2020	480-655-7444	655-8220	K-6	Jim Wyler
New Samaritan HS	1455 S Stapley Dr	Mesa, AZ	85204-5849	480-833-7470	833-7480	9-12	Brian Miller
New School for the Arts	1216 E Apache Blvd	Tempe, AZ	85281-6005	480-481-9235	970-6625	9-12	Katy Cardenas
New School for the Arts MS	1112 E Apache Blvd	Tempe, AZ	85281-5822	480-446-7177	446-7309	7-8	Katy Cardenas
Newton Montessori & Charter S	PO Box 2166	Camp Verde, AZ	86322-2166	928-567-2363	567-5374	PK-5	Dr. Betty Chester
New Visions Academy	PO Box 1539	Cottonwood, AZ	86326-1539	928-634-7320	634-7494	9-12	Ann Jenkins
New Visions Academy - St John's Campus	PO Box 791	Saint Johns, AZ	85936-0791	928-337-3268	337-3383	9-12	Joey Grant
New West S	98 N Oak Dr	Benson, AZ	85602-7732	520-586-1976	586-1655	K-4	Hank Payton
New West S	98 N Oak Dr	Benson, AZ	85602-7732	520-586-1976	586-1655	5-12	Hank Payton
New World Educational Center Charter S	1313 N 2nd St Ste 200	Phoenix, AZ	85004-1701	602-238-9577	238-9210	K-12	Frank Garcia
New World Education Center	4710 E Baseline Rd	Mesa, AZ	85206-4602	480-807-2800	807-2916	K-12	Frank Garcia
NFL YET Academy	4848 S 2nd St	Phoenix, AZ	85040-2122	602-305-7788	243-7788	K-12	Raul Ruiz
Northern AZ Academy for Career Dev.	PO Box 125	Taylor, AZ	85939-0125	928-536-4222	536-4441	9-12	Kathy Doucette-Edwards
Northern AZ Academy for Career Dev.	502 Airport Rd	Winslow, AZ	86047-5400	928-289-3329	289-4485	9-12	Tamara Pogue
Northland Preparatory Academy	3300 E Sparrow Ave	Flagstaff, AZ	86004-6703	928-214-8776	214-8778	7-12	Ted Briggs
North Pointe Academy	4941 W Union Hills Dr	Glendale, AZ	85308-1486	602-896-1166	896-1164	K-6	Kim Agnew
North Star Charter S	10720 W Indian School Rd	Phoenix, AZ	85037-5721	623-907-2661	907-2501	9-12	Aldine Dickens
Nosotros Academy	440 N Grande Ave	Tucson, AZ	85745-2703	520-624-1023	624-7999	6-12	Paul Felix
Oasis HS	8632 W Northern Ave	Glendale, AZ	85305-1308	623-878-8059	878-8175	9-12	Sharon Foster
Ocotillo HS	2616 E Greenway Rd	Phoenix, AZ	85032-4320	602-765-8470	765-8471	9-12	Gabriel Trujillo
Old Pueblo Children's Academy	450 N Pantano Rd	Tucson, AZ	85710-2309	520-296-1600	298-0558	K-8	Ronda McCarthy
Ombudsman Learning Center - East	3943 E Thomas Rd	Phoenix, AZ	85018-7511	602-840-2997	840-1402	7-12	Janice Zagorniak
Ombudsman Learning Center - Metro	4220 W Northern Ave	Phoenix, AZ	85051-5753	602-840-1402	842-6157	6-12	Janice Zagorniak
Ombudsman Learning Center - Northeast	3242 E Bell Rd	Phoenix, AZ	85032-2727	602-485-9872	367-0367	6-12	Janice Zagorniak
Ombudsman Learning Center - Northwest	9516 W Peoria Ave	Peoria, AZ	85345-6100	602-840-2997	840-1402	6-12	Janice Zagorniak
Ombudsman Learning Center - West	3618 E Bell Rd	Phoenix, AZ	85032-2126	602-840-2997	840-1402	6-12	Janice Zagorniak
Omega Academy	1951 W Camelback Rd	Phoenix, AZ	85015-3403	602-269-1007	269-1073	K-12	Carmen Gulley
Omega Alpha Academy S	35 E Wilcox Dr	Sierra Vista, AZ	85635-2521	520-452-7965		K-12	Steve Carvalho
Pace Preparatory Academy	12900 E Prescott Dells Rd	Humboldt, AZ	86329	928-567-1805	567-1836	9-12	Holly Stiles
PACE Preparatory Academy	474 S Main St	Camp Verde, AZ	86322-7256	928-567-9905		6-12	
PACE Preparatory Academy	6287 E Copper Hill Dr	Prescott Valley, AZ	86314-2906	928-775-9675	775-9673	6-12	Richard Thelander
Pan-American Charter ES	3001 W Indian School Rd	Phoenix, AZ	85017-4168	602-266-3989	266-3979	K-6	Marta Pasos
Paradise Education Center	15533 W Paradise Ln	Surprise, AZ	85374-5851	623-975-2646	975-2841	K-8	Jeffrey Sloggett
Paramount Academy	11039 W Olive Ave	Peoria, AZ	85345-9200	623-977-0614	977-0615	K-8	Douglas Williams
Park View MS	8300 E Dana Dr	Prescott Valley, AZ	86314-8183	928-775-5115	775-6253	6-8	Mary Bruhn
Patagonia Community Montessori S	PO Box 1008	Patagonia, AZ	85624-1008	520-394-9530	394-2864	PK-8	Paisley McGuire
Pathfinder Academy	2542 N 76th Pl	Mesa, AZ	85207-1252	480-986-7071	986-9858	K-12	Susan Stradling
Pathways Charter S	PO Box 609	Camp Verde, AZ	86322-0609	928-567-9213	567-9304	6-12	Kathleen McCabe
Patriot Academy	19011 E San Tan Blvd	Queen Creek, AZ	85242-7301	480-279-4780	807-1290	K-8	Jay Brown
Paulden ES	PO Box 172	Paulden, AZ	86334-0172	928-583-0455	636-4568	K-6	Kay Deliman
Payson Center for Success	PO Box 919	Payson, AZ	85547-0919	928-472-2011	472-2039	9-12	Kathe Ketchem
Peak S	2016 N 1st St Ste A	Flagstaff, AZ	86004-4201	928-779-0771	779-0774	K-8	Paula Drossman
Peoria Accelerated HS	8885 W Peoria Ave	Peoria, AZ	85345-6442	623-979-0031	979-0113	9-12	Kerry Clark
Peoria Horizons Charter S	11820 N 81st Ave	Peoria, AZ	85345-5736	623-979-3559		K-6	Beth Eliason
Phoenix Advantage Charter S	3738 N 16th St	Phoenix, AZ	85016-5915	602-263-8777	263-8822	K-8	Mary Haluska
Phoenix School of Academic Excellence	5312 N 12th St	Phoenix, AZ	85014-2926	602-553-1988	954-8016	7-12	Adele Ferrini
Pillar Academy of Business & Finance	1589 Plantation Rd	Mohave Valley, AZ	86440-8413	928-346-3925	346-3930	9-12	Marv Lamer
Pima Partnership S	1346 N Stone Ave	Tucson, AZ	85705-7338	520-326-2528	326-2527	9-12	John Powers
Pima Vocational HS	97 E Congress St	Tucson, AZ	85701-1723	520-903-0102	903-0753	9-12	Gloria Proo
Pine Forest Charter S	1120 W Kaibab Ln	Flagstaff, AZ	86001-6217	928-779-9880	779-9792	K-6	Michael Heffernan
Pinnacle HS - Casa Grande	409 W McMurray Blvd	Casa Grande, AZ	85222-2314	520-423-2380	423-2383	9-12	Jim Simmons
Pinnacle HS - Mesa	151 N Centennial Way	Mesa, AZ	85201-6782	480-668-5003	668-5005	9-12	Ric Borom
Pinnacle HS - Tempe	4700 S McClintock Dr	Tempe, AZ	85282-7386	602-414-0950	414-0927	9-12	Michael Matwick
Pinnacle Pointe Academy	6753 W Pinnacle Peak Rd	Glendale, AZ	85310-5301	623-537-3535	537-4433	K-4	Ian Hodor
PPEP TEC - Arnold Learning Center	4140 W Ina Rd Ste 118	Tucson, AZ	85741-2236	520-579-8560	579-8566	9-12	Rebecca Edmonds
PPEP TEC - Borjorquez Learning Center	203 Bisbee Rd	Bisbee, AZ	85603-1122	520-741-4370	741-4372	9-12	Rebecca Edmonds
PPEP TEC - Chavez Learning Center	1233 N Main St	San Luis, AZ	85349	928-627-8550	627-8980	9-12	Rebecca Edmonds
PPEP TEC - Coy Payne Learning Center	670 N Arizona Ave Ste 9	Chandler, AZ	85225-6742	480-857-1499	857-3183	9-12	Rebecca Edmonds
PPEP TEC - Eugene Lopez Learning Center	158 W Maley St	Willcox, AZ	85643-2130	520-741-4370	741-4372	9-12	Rebecca Edmonds
PPEP TEC - Fernandez Learning Center	1840 E Benson Hwy	Tucson, AZ	85714-1770	520-889-8276	294-7738	9-12	Rebecca Edmonds
PPEP TEC - Paul Learning Center	220 E Florence Blvd	Casa Grande, AZ	85222-4031	520-836-6549	836-0290	9-12	Rebecca Edmonds
PPEP TEC - Pena Learning Center	725 N Central Ave Ste 113	Avondale, AZ	85323-1660	623-925-2161	925-1035	9-12	Rebecca Edmonds
PPEP TEC - Powell Learning Center	4116 Avenida Cochise Ste F	Sierra Vista, AZ	85635-5843	520-741-4370	741-4372	9-12	Rebecca Edmonds
PPEP TEC - Raul H. Castro Learning Ctr	530 12th St	Douglas, AZ	85607	520-741-4370	741-4372	9-12	Rebecca Edmonds
PPEP TEC - Soltero Learning Center	8230 E 22nd St #100-105	Tucson, AZ	85710-8547	520-290-9167	290-9220	9-12	Rebecca Edmonds
PPEP TEC - Yepez Learning Center	115 N Columbia Ave	Somerton, AZ	85350	928-627-9648	627-9197	9-12	Rebecca Edmonds
Precision Academy	7318 W Lynwood St	Phoenix, AZ	85035-4542	623-936-8682	936-8559	10-12	Dr. Caroline White

School	Address	City,State	Zip code	Telephone	Fax	Grade	Contact
Precision Academy System Charter S	3906 E Broadway Rd	Phoenix, AZ	85040-2996	602-453-3661	453-3667	9-12	Daniel Martinez
Premier Charter HS	7544 W Indian School Rd	Phoenix, AZ	85033-3030	623-245-1500	245-1506	9-12	Elisha Madden
Prescott Valley S	9500 E Lorna Ln	Prescott Valley, AZ	86314-2324	928-772-8744	775-4457	K-12	Jennifer Mraz
Presidio S	1695 E Fort Lowell Rd	Tucson, AZ	85719-2319	520-881-5222	322-8128	K-12	Terry Garza
Primavera Technical Learning Center	3029 N Alma School Rd	Chandler, AZ	85224-1464	480-456-6678	820-2168	9-12	Damian Creamer
Progressive Leadership Academy	1529 W Mcdowell Rd	Phoenix, AZ	85007-1630	602-523-9090	523-9091	K-8	Roland Pierce
Rawlins ES	7905 N 71st Ave	Glendale, AZ	85303-1322	623-934-0298	595-8693	K-5	Sarah Rollins
RCB HS - Phoenix	6049 N 43rd Ave	Phoenix, AZ	85019-1638	602-973-6018	589-1349	9-12	Mark Hebert
Redwood Elementary Academy	9510 N 75th Ave	Peoria, AZ	85345-6621	623-878-0986	776-7956	K-8	Ronald Palmer
Renaissance Academy - Anasazi Campus	PO Box 2741	Pinetop, AZ	85935-2741	928-367-3074	367-5307	9-12	Brad Call
Renaissance Academy - Heber/Overgaard	PO Box 2741	Pinetop, AZ	85935-2741	928-587-2906		K-12	Steve Chavez
Renaissance Academy - John Reeder Campus	PO Box 2741	Pinetop, AZ	85935-2741	928-532-0195	532-0243	K-8	Steve Chavez
Renaissance Academy - Malpais Campus	PO Box 2741	Pinetop, AZ	85935-2741	928-333-1554	333-1555	K-12	Brian Struble
Renaissance Academy - St. Johns Campus	PO Box 2741	Pinetop, AZ	85935-2741	928-337-4508	337-3176	1-8	Daniel Mikeworth
Romero HS	3005 E Fillmore St	Phoenix, AZ	85008-6120	602-850-2600	850-2615	9-11	Dr. Jane Juliano
SABIS International	1903 E Roeser Rd	Phoenix, AZ	85040-3341	602-305-8865	323-5526	K-12	David Singer
Sandoval Preparatory HS	3830 N 67th Ave	Phoenix, AZ	85033-4036	623-845-0781	849-2840	9-12	Ben Dutton
San Pedro Valley HS	197 E 7th St	Benson, AZ	85602-6629	520-586-8901	586-6189	9-12	Shad Housley
Satori Charter S	3727 N 1st Ave	Tucson, AZ	85719-1609	520-293-7555	293-7020	K-8	Phyllis Gold
Scholars' Academy	PO Box 3475	Quartzsite, AZ	85359-3475	928-927-9420	927-9425	9-12	Steve McClenning
School for Integrated Academics & Tech	518 S 3rd St	Phoenix, AZ	85004-2506	602-258-3927	258-3985	9-12	Geraldine Baumann
School for Integrated Academics & Tech	901 S Campbell Ave	Tucson, AZ	85719-6519	520-791-3016	791-3582	9-12	David Gerber
Scottsdale Horizons Charter S	7425 E Culver St	Scottsdale, AZ	85257-3503	480-990-7223	990-0936	1-8	Marie Linder
Sedona Charter S	165 Kachina Dr	Sedona, AZ	86336-4303	928-204-6464	204-6486	K-8	Alice Madar
SEES Charter S	1290 N Scottsdale Rd	Tempe, AZ	85281-1702	480-481-5051	481-5047	9-12	Thea Yockus
Self Development Charter S	1709 N Greenfield Rd	Mesa, AZ	85205-3103	480-641-2640	641-2678	K-6	Anjum Majeed
Sequoia Charter S	1460 S Horne	Mesa, AZ	85204-5760	480-649-7737	649-0711	K-12	
Sequoia Choice S - AZ Distance Learning	1460 E Horne	Mesa, AZ	85204	480-655-7005	655-7911	K-12	Linda Harless
Sequoia Ranch S	PO Box 399	Mayer, AZ	86333-0399	928-632-9851	632-9852	K-12	Michael Pospisil
Sequoia S for Deaf & Hard of Hearing	1460 S Horne	Mesa, AZ	85204-5760	480-649-7737	649-0711	K-12	Curt Radford
Sequoia School - Sequoia Village S	982 Full House Ln	Show Low, AZ	85901-4042	928-537-1208	537-4275	K-12	Tony Rhineheart
Shelby S	PO Box 31570	Mesa, AZ	85275-1570	480-833-4090	833-9828	K-10	Nicole Kamp
Sierra Oaks S	650 W Linda Vista Rd	Oracle, AZ	85623-6039	520-896-3100	896-3101	1-8	Paula Jensen
Sierra Summit Achievement S	PO Box 1360	Hereford, AZ	85615-1360	520-803-0508	803-0877	8-12	Siamak Khadjenoury
Skyline JHS	17667 N 91st Ave	Peoria, AZ	85382-3019	623-875-3175	875-9261	6-8	Brian Shipman
Skyline Ranch S	1084 San Tan Hills Dr	Queen Creek, AZ	85243-3489	480-888-7520	868-2302	K-8	G. Meko
Skyline Technical HS	15220 S 50th St Ste 109	Phoenix, AZ	85044-9132	480-763-8425	763-8427	9-12	Ronda Owens
Skyline West HS	17667 N 91st Ave	Peoria, AZ	85382-3019	623-875-3175	875-9261	9-12	Brian Shipman
Skyview S	125 S Rush St	Prescott, AZ	86303-4432	928-776-1730	776-1742	K-8	John Hurley
Solon Academy	2716 N Dobson Rd	Chandler, AZ	85224-1806	480-782-1082	782-1089	K-6	Kevin Sieling
Solon Senior Academy Charter S	1375 N McClintock Dr	Chandler, AZ	85226-1304	480-899-7717	899-7793	4-12	James Bush
Sonoran Desert S	4448 E Main St Ste 7	Mesa, AZ	85205-7916	480-396-5463	396-4980	9-12	Patricia Dalman
Sonoran Science Academy	2255 W Ina Rd	Tucson, AZ	85741-2650	520-797-9836	572-0586	3-12	Adam Oksuz
Southern Arizona Community HS	2470 N Tucson Blvd	Tucson, AZ	85716-2469	520-319-6113	319-6115	9-12	Abelardo Cubillas
Southgate Academy	850 W Valencia Rd	Tucson, AZ	85706-7619	520-741-7900	741-7901	K-9	Sherry Matyjasik
South Pointe HS	8325 S Central Ave	Phoenix, AZ	85042-6576	602-243-0600	243-0800	9-12	Larry McGill
Southside Community S	2701 S Campbell Ave	Tucson, AZ	85713-5080	520-623-7102	623-7125	K-8	Cynthia Richards
STAR Charter S	145 Leupp Rd	Flagstaff, AZ	86004-8501	928-606-7419	606-9965	K-6	Mark Sorenson
Starshine Academy	2801 N 31st St	Phoenix, AZ	85008-1126	602-957-9557	956-0065	K-12	Patricia Adams
STARS Prep Academy - Scottsdale	5334 E Thunderbird Rd	Scottsdale, AZ	85254-3655	602-393-6500	393-6501	K-12	Jeff Maynard
Star Valley S	HC 4 Box 4N	Payson, AZ	85541-8712	928-468-1401	468-1402	9-12	Russell Koch
Stellar Prep	8632 W Northern Ave	Glendale, AZ	85305-1308	623-878-8059	878-8175	K-4	Sharon Foster
Stepping Stones Academy	35812 N 7th St	Phoenix, AZ	85086-7410	623-465-4910	587-8514	K-8	Ann Marie Short
Student Choice HS	1833 N Scottsdale Rd	Tempe, AZ	85281-1563	480-947-9511	947-9624	9-12	Peggy Lynam
Sturgeon MS	1951 W Camelback Rd	Phoenix, AZ	85015-3403	602-269-1007	269-1073	5-8	Carmen Gulley
Summit ES	1313 N 2nd St	Phoenix, AZ	85004-1750	602-252-7727	252-7729	K-6	Carolyn Sawyer
Summit HS	728 E Mcdowell Rd	Phoenix, AZ	85006-2592	602-258-8959	258-8953	9-12	Mike Little
Sunnyside Charter & Montessori S	PO Box 2166	Camp Verde, AZ	86322-2166	928-567-2363	567-5374	6-8	Dowling Campbell
Sun Valley HS	1143 S Lindsay Rd	Mesa, AZ	85204-6298	480-497-4800	497-1314	7-12	Joe Procopio
Superior S	PO Box 1989	Surprise, AZ	85378-1989	623-875-5975	875-5985	7-12	Tina Davis
TAG S	10129 E Speedway Blvd	Tucson, AZ	85748-1921	520-296-0006	296-0046	K-8	Ron Hom
Teacher Preparation Charter HS	640 N 1st Ave	Phoenix, AZ	85003-1515	602-223-4101	223-4110	9-12	Leticia Ruiz
Telesis Preparatory Academy	2598 Starlite Ln	Lk Havasu Cty, AZ	86403-4946	928-855-8661	855-9302	K-12	Sandra Breece
Tempe Academy of Arts & Technology	97 W Oakland St	Chandler, AZ	85225-4536	480-899-6600	899-4122	K-8	Lynn Monson
Tempe Accelerated HS	5040 S Price Rd	Tempe, AZ	85282-7445	480-831-6057	831-6095	9-12	Abelardo Batista
Tempe Preparatory Academy	1251 E Southern Ave	Tempe, AZ	85282-5605	480-839-3402	755-0546	7-12	Ronald Bergez
Terra Nova Academy	1118 W Glendale Ave	Phoenix, AZ	85021-8635	602-870-3907	870-0696	K-8	Jessica Wise
Tertulia: A Learning Community	812 S 6th Ave	Phoenix, AZ	85003-2528	602-262-2200	262-2570	K-4	Gabriella Ketcham
Tertulia: A Learning Community #2	812 S 6th Ave	Phoenix, AZ	85003-2528	602-262-2200	262-2570	5-8	Juan Sierra
Tolani Lake Academy	HC 61 Box 300	Winslow, AZ	86047-9337	928-686-6101	686-6102	K-7	Ron White
Toltecali Academy	200 N Stone Ave	Tucson, AZ	85701-1208	520-807-7923	807-7827	9-12	Shannon Dineley
Transformational Learning Centers	PO Box 5310	Tucson, AZ	85703-0310	520-628-1404	628-1394	K-12	Tina Giberti
Tri-City College Prep HS	5522 Side Rd	Prescott, AZ	86301-8483	928-777-0403	777-0402	9-12	Dr. Mary Ellen Halvorson
Tri-City Vo/Tech HS	2957 N Highway 89	Prescott, AZ	86301	928-442-9125	442-9761	9-12	Terrell Jackson
Triumphant Learning Center	201 E Main St	Safford, AZ	85546-2051	928-348-8422	348-8423	K-8	Robin Dutt
Tucson Accelerated HS	7820 E Wrightstown Rd	Tucson, AZ	85715-4339	520-722-4721	722-4785	9-12	Shannon Hughes
Tucson Country Day S	9239 E Wrightstown Rd	Tucson, AZ	85715-5514	520-296-0883	290-1521	K-8	Richard Cooper
Tucson International Academy	1625 W Valencia Rd Ste 109	Tucson, AZ	85746-6022	520-295-3944	295-3943	1-8	Dr. Jennifer Herrera
Tucson International Academy	1230 E Broadway Blvd	Tucson, AZ	85719-5821	520-792-3255	792-3245	K-8	Dr. Jennifer Herrera
Tucson Preparatory S	1525 N Oracle Rd	Tucson, AZ	85705-7265	520-622-4185	622-4755	9-12	Jody Sullivan
Tucson Urban League S	2305 S Park Ave	Tucson, AZ	85713-3644	520-622-3651	622-4767	6-12	Charles Monroe
Tutor Time Charter S - Brill	725 E Brill St	Phoenix, AZ	85006-2512	602-200-9800	241-1039	K-1	Jennifer Thornton
Tutor Time Charter S - Chandler	4970 W Ray Rd	Chandler, AZ	85226-6219	480-838-6700	838-6764	K-3	Jennifer Thornton
Tutor Time Charter S - Deer Valley	8348 W Deer Valley Rd	Peoria, AZ	85382-2461	623-825-9840		K-3	Jennifer Thornton
Tutor Time Charter S - Gilbert	690 W Warner Rd	Gilbert, AZ	85233-7238	480-782-9119		K-K	Jennifer Thornton
Tutor Time Charter S - Glendale	5550 W Bell Rd	Glendale, AZ	85308-3866	602-504-1510		K-3	Jennifer Thornton
Tutor Time Charter School - Lone Mtn	4720 E Lone Mountain Rd	Cave Creek, AZ	85331-5532	480-488-9091		K-3	Jennifer Thornton
Tutor Time Charter S - N.E. Mesa	1928 N Gilbert Rd	Mesa, AZ	85203-2807	480-733-6977		K-2	Jennifer Thornton
Tutor Time Charter S - N.E. Phoenix	245 E Bell Rd	Phoenix, AZ	85022-2353	602-938-7050	241-1039	K-3	Jennifer Thornton
Tutor Time Charter S - Ocotillo	1900 S Alma School Rd	Chandler, AZ	85248-1904	480-857-4084	857-4090	K-1	Jennifer Thornton
Tutor Time Charter S - Paradise Valley	2400 N Central Ave	Phoenix, AZ	85004-1341	602-200-9100	266-7682	K-K	Jennifer Thornton
Tutor Time Charter S - Peoria	10260 N 67th Ave	Peoria, AZ	85302-1002	602-200-9800		K-K	Jennifer Thornton
Vah-ki MS	PO Box 10885	Bapchule, AZ	85221-0885	480-403-8580	315-2017	5-8	Beverly Crawford
Vail HS	9040 S Rita Rd Ste 1270	Tucson, AZ	85747-9192	520-382-3200	382-3226	9-12	Dennis Barger
Valley Academy - Charter S	1520 W Rose Garden Ln	Phoenix, AZ	85027-3529	623-516-7747	516-2703	K-8	Sharon Malone
Ventana Academic S	PO Box 1589	Cave Creek, AZ	85327-1589	480-488-9362	488-2079	K-8	Shawn Rutan
Veritas Preparatory Academy	2131 E Lincoln Dr	Phoenix, AZ	85016-1122	602-263-1128	263-7997	7-12	Andrew Ellison
Victory HS West Campus	PO Box 8374	Phoenix, AZ	85066-8374	602-243-7583	243-7563	7-12	Shirley Branham
Villa Montessori - Phoenix	4535 N 28th St	Phoenix, AZ	85016-4998	602-955-2210	957-4017	K-8	Margo O'Neill
Vision Charter S	PO Box 23455	Tucson, AZ	85734-3455	520-444-0241	741-8123	9-12	Dr. Wilma Soroosh
Visions Unlimited Academy	1275 E Barney Ln	Benson, AZ	85602-7955	520-586-8691	586-3074	K-8	Yvonne Shay
Webster Basic S	7301 E Baseline Rd	Mesa, AZ	85209-4907	480-986-2335	354-3490	K-6	Kelly Wade
Westland S	4141 N 67th Ave	Phoenix, AZ	85033-3314	623-247-6456	247-6520	K-12	Kathryn Couch
WestMark HS	3002 N Arizona Ave Ste 16	Chandler, AZ	85225-7159	480-633-9222	633-8666	K-12	Ric Borom
West Phoenix HS	3835 W Thomas Rd	Phoenix, AZ	85019-4434	602-269-1110	269-1112	9-12	Robert Trujillo
Westwind Preparatory Academy	2045 W Northern Ave	Phoenix, AZ	85021-5157	602-864-7731	864-7720	7-12	Debra Slagle
Willow Creek Charter S	2100 Willow Creek Rd	Prescott, AZ	86301-5391	928-776-1212	776-0009	K-8	Terese Soto
Woods HS	3160 N 33rd Ave	Phoenix, AZ	85017-4817	602-385-4490	864-7720	9-12	Lee Dillenbeck
YCFA Achieve Academy	10401 Highway 89A	Prescott Valley, AZ	86314	928-775-8000	775-8064	4-12	James Wojcik
Young Scholars Academy	1501 Valencia Rd	Bullhead City, AZ	86426-5218	928-704-1100	704-1177	K-8	Tonnie Smith
Youngtown Charter S	13226 N 113th Ave	Youngtown, AZ	85363-1026	623-974-0355	815-8902	K-8	Jacob Duran

Arkansas

School	Address	City,State	Zip code	Telephone	Fax	Grade	Contact
Academic Center of Excellence	PO Box 528	Osceola, AR	72370-0528	870-563-2150	622-1025	4-8	Ellouise Tubbs
Academics Plus Charter S	PO Box 13622	Maumelle, AR	72113-0622	501-851-3333	851-2599	3-12	Nancy Acres
Academy of Technology	PO Box 160	Vilonia, AR	72173-0160	501-796-2018	796-4322	K-12	Sue Farris
Arise Charter S	PO Box 880	Monticello, AR	71657-0880	870-367-6600	367-6395	4-8	Lorenza Simmons
Benton County School of the Arts	2005 S 12th St	Rogers, AR	72758-6307	479-636-2272	636-5447	K-8	Gary Moore
Blytheville Charter S	1700 W McHaney Dr	Blytheville, AR	72315-4994	870-763-7191	762-0172	7-12	Ann Lewis
Cabot Academic Center for Excellence	602 N Lincoln St	Cabot, AR	72023-2601	501-843-3363		K-12	
Focus Learning Academy	707 Robins St Ste 100	Conway, AR	72034-6516	501-513-9352	513-9353	K-5	
Grace Hill ES	901 N Dixieland Rd	Rogers, AR	72756-2199	479-631-3670	631-3672	K-5	Jennie Rehl
Haas Hall Academy	13370 Rheas Mill Rd	Farmington, AR	72730-9625	479-267-4805	267-4862	10-12	Martin Schoppmeyer
Imboden Area Charter S	PO Box 297	Imboden, AR	72434-0297	870-869-3015	869-3016	K-6	Judy Warren
KIPP: Delta College Preparatory S	215 Cherry St	Helena, AR	72342-3503	870-753-9444	753-9450	5-8	Scott Shirey
Lisa Academy	21 Corporate Hill Dr	Little Rock, AR	72205-4568	501-227-4942	227-4952	6-12	Birol Furat

School	Address	City,State	Zip code	Telephone	Fax	Grade	Contact
Mountain Home HS Career Academies	500 Bomber Blvd	Mountain Home, AR	72653-4628	870-425-1215		10-12	Susan Bergman
Raider Open Door Academy	4109 Race St	Jonesboro, AR	72401-7650	870-910-7800	910-7852	5-8	Nicole Covey
Ridgeroad Charter MS	4601 Ridge Rd	No Little Rock, AR	72116-7264	501-771-8155	771-8159	7-8	Dana Chadwick
West Woods S	1600 N Bradford	El Dorado, AR	71730	870-864-5093	864-5142	1-4	Dennis Tucker
California							
Academia Avance	115 N Avenue 53	Los Angeles, CA	90042-4005	213-447-4561	652-0994	6-12	Ricardo Mireles
Academia Semillas del Pueblo	4736 Huntington Dr S	Los Angeles, CA	90032-1942	323-225-4549	987-1240	K-6	Marcos Aguilar
Academic/Vocational Charter Institute	294 Green Valley Rd	Watsonville, CA	95076-1300	831-786-2100	786-2318	11-12	Lee Takemoto
Academy for Academic Excellence	17500 Mana Rd	Apple Valley, CA	92307-2181	760-946-5414		K-12	Gordon Soholt
Academy for Career Education Charter S	801 Olive St	Wheatland, CA	95692-9787	530-633-3113	633-3106	9-12	Claudia O'Leary
Accelerated Achievement Academy	1059 N State St	Ukiah, CA	95482-3413	707-467-0500		6-12	Dr. Kimberly Logan
Accelerated Charter S	119 E 37th St	Los Angeles, CA	90011-2603	323-235-6343	235-6346	K-5	Kevin Sved
Accelerated S	4000 S Main St	Los Angeles, CA	90037-1022	323-235-6343	235-6346	K-8	Johnathan Williams
Acorns to Oaks Charter S	PO Box 992418	Redding, CA	96099-2418	530-365-1055	347-4996	K-8	Terri Womack
Alameda Community Learning Center	210 Central Ave	Alameda, CA	94501-3246	510-521-7123	521-7350	7-12	Lora Lewis
Alianza Charter S	115 Casserly Rd	Watsonville, CA	95076-9740	831-728-6333	728-6947	K-6	Michael Jones
All Tribes American Indian Charter S	34320 Valley Center Rd	Valley Center, CA	92082-6046	760-723-5305		6-9	Mary Ann Donohue
Alvarado Academy Charter S	26247 Ellis St	Madera, CA	93638-0813	559-675-2070	675-2074	K-6	Nicolas Retana
Alvina S	295 W Saginaw Ave	Caruthers, CA	93609-9710	559-864-9411	864-1808	K-8	Paul Cannon
American Indian Charter S	3637 Magee Ave	Oakland, CA	94619-1427	510-482-6000	482-6002	6-9	Dr. Ben Chavis
Americas Choice HS	9320 Tech Center Dr Ste 206	Sacramento, CA	95826-2558	916-228-5750	643-9489	9-12	Beate Martinez
Anderson New Technology HS	2098 North St	Anderson, CA	96007-3477	530-365-3100	365-2957	9-12	Pat Allison
Animo Inglewood Charter HS	304 E Spruce Ave	Inglewood, CA	90301-2711	310-216-3278	673-0510	9-9	Steve Barr
Animo Leadership Charter HS	10319 Firmona Ave	Lennox, CA	90304-1419	310-216-3277		9-11	Mara Simmons
Animo South L.A. HS	11100 S Western Ave	Los Angeles, CA	90047-4845	310-350-7481	392-8752	9-12	John Newsom
Animo Venice HS	1015 Lincoln Blvd	Venice, CA	90291-3506	310-392-8751	392-8752	9-12	Tommy Chang
Annenberg HS	4000 S Main St	Los Angeles, CA	90037-1022	323-235-6343	235-6346	9-12	Johnathan Williams
Antelope View Charter S	3243 Center Court Ln	Antelope, CA	95843-9111	916-339-4690	339-4693	K-12	Mary Navarro
Archway Academy Charter S	108 Campus Way	Modesto, CA	95350-5803	209-558-4407	558-4453	9-12	Bob Vizzolini
Arroyo Vista Charter S	2491 School House Rd	Chula Vista, CA	91915-2534	619-656-9676	656-1858	K-6	Patricia Roth
Arundel ES	200 Arundel Rd	San Carlos, CA	94070-1999	650-508-7311	508-7314	K-4	Allison Liner
Aspire LA ES	6410 Rita Ave	Huntington Park, CA	90255-4126	323-585-1153	585-1283	K-5	Maribel Galan
Audeo Charter S	10170 Huennekens St	San Diego, CA	92121-2964	858-678-2051	552-9394	6-12	Tim Tuter
Banks Charter S	PO Box 80	Pala, CA	92059-0080	760-742-3300	742-3102	K-5	Ron Nachbar
Bay Area S of Enterprise	2750 Todd St	Alameda, CA	94501-7250	510-748-4314	748-4326	9-12	Page Tompkins
Bay Area Technology S	1920 Telegraph Ave	Oakland, CA	94612-2202	510-645-9932	645-9934		Oscar Yildiz
Bellevue-Sante Fe Charter S	1401 San Luis Bay Dr	San Luis Obispo, CA	93405-8007	805-595-7169	595-9013	K-8	Brian Getz
Berkley Maynard Academy	6200 San Pablo Ave	Oakland, CA	94608-2228	510-658-2900	251-1670	K-5	Kristyn Klei
Bitney Springs Charter HS	12338 McCourtney Rd	Grass Valley, CA	95949-9756	530-477-1235	272-1091	9-12	Marshall Goldberg
Bowling Green Charter ES	4211 Turnbridge Dr	Sacramento, CA	95823-1999	916-433-5426	433-5429	K-6	
Brittan Acres S	2000 Belle Ave	San Carlos, CA	94070-3798	650-508-7307	508-7310	K-4	Kenneth Gallegos
Buckingham Magnet Charter S	188 Bella Vista Rd Ste B	Vacaville, CA	95687-3719	707-453-7300	453-7303	K-12	Bob Hampton
Cali Calmecac Charter S	9491 Starr Rd	Windsor, CA	95492-9460	707-837-7747	837-7752	K-8	Ginger Dale
California Academy for Liberal Studies	700 Wilshire Blvd	Los Angeles, CA	90017-3811	213-239-0063	239-9008	9-12	Lisa Tremain
California Academy for Liberal Studies	3838 Eagle Rock Blvd	Los Angeles, CA	90065-3638	323-254-4427	254-4099	6-8	Ref Rodriguez
California College Prep Academy	6200 San Pablo Ave	Oakland, CA	94608-2228	510-658-2900	251-1670	6-7	Michael Prada
California Military Institute	227 N D St Ste C	Perris, CA	92570-1946	951-443-2731	657-3109	7-12	Richard Wallis
California Montessori Project	4718 Engle Rd	Carmichael, CA	95608-2224	916-971-2430	971-2435	K-8	Gary Bowman
California Science Center ES	3737 S Figueroa St	Los Angeles, CA	90007-4366	213-744-7409		K-5	Connie Smith
California Virtual Academy	2360 Shasta Way	Simi Valley, CA	93065-1877	805-581-0202	581-0330	K-5	James L. Konantz
Camino Nuevo Charter Academy	635 S Harvard Blvd	Los Angeles, CA	90005-2511	213-736-5542	736-5664	PK-8	Kendra Kecker
Camino Nuevo Charter HS	2990 W 6th St	Los Angeles, CA	90020-1260	213-210-3028	736-5066	9-12	Steve Seaford
Camptonville Academy	848 Gold Flat Rd Ste 3	Nevada City, CA	95959-3201	530-478-9458	478-9629	K-12	Janis Jablecki
Canyon Charter ES	421 Entrada Dr	Santa Monica, CA	90402-1303	310-454-7510	454-7543	K-5	Carol Henderson
Capitol Heights Academy	2520 33rd St	Sacramento, CA	95817-1943	916-739-8520	739-8529	K-8	Robert Spencer
Castle Rock Charter S	212 E Washington Blvd	Crescent City, CA	95531	707-464-0390	464-9606	K-12	Dennis Burns
Center for Advanced Research Technology	2555 Clovis Ave	Clovis, CA	93612-3901	559-248-7400	248-7423	11-12	Susan Fisher
Central City Value S	5156 Whittier Blvd	Los Angeles, CA	90022-3932	323-981-7149	981-0162	9-12	David Doyle
Challenge Charter High S	PO Box 5007	Oroville, CA	95966-0007	530-538-2359	538-2374	9-12	Jay Marchant
Charter Alternative Academy	6832 Avenue 280	Visalia, CA	93277-9429	559-730-7491	730-7490	7-12	Rudy Soleno
Charter Community S and Extended Day	6767 Green Valley Rd	Placerville, CA	95667-8984	530-295-2259	642-0492	K-12	Jeremy Meyers
Charter HS of Arts Multimedia/Performing	5156 Whittier Blvd	Sherman Oaks, CA	91403	818-419-3829		9-9	Norman Isaacs
Charter Home School Academy	31411 Road 160	Visalia, CA	93292-9019	559-730-7916	735-8060	K-8	Christine Fischer
Charter S of Morgan Hill	9530 Monterey Rd	Morgan Hill, CA	95037-9356	408-463-0618		K-7	Paige Cisewski
Charter S of San Diego	10170 Huennekens St	San Diego, CA	92121-2964	858-678-2020	552-6666	7-12	Mary Bixby
Chavez Dual Language Immersion Charter S	1102 E Yanonali St	Santa Barbara, CA	93103-2704	805-966-7392	966-7243	K-3	Eva Neuer
Chico Country Day S	102 W 11th St	Chico, CA	95928-6006	530-895-2650	895-9159	K-8	Paul Weber
Childrens Community Charter S	6830 Pentz Rd	Paradise, CA	95969-2902	530-877-2227	872-1396	K-8	Bruce Crist
CHIME Charter MS	22280 Devonshire St	Chatsworth, CA	91311-2736	818-998-6794	998-0121	6-8	Renee Harvey
CHIME Charter S	19722 Collier St	Woodland Hills, CA	91364-3618	818-346-5100	346-5120	K-5	
Choice 2000 On-Line S	11 S D St	Perris, CA	92570-2126	951-940-5700	940-5706	7-12	Cynthia Cartwright
Chrysalis Charter S	1155 Mistletoe Ln	Redding, CA	96002-0749	530-224-4129	223-9407	K-8	Paul Krafel
Chula Vista Learning Community Charter S	590 K St	Chula Vista, CA	91911-1118	619-426-2885	426-3048	K-6	Dr. Jorge Ramirez
Circle of Independent Learning	4700 Calaveras Ave	Fremont, CA	94538-1124	510-797-0100	797-0118	K-12	Mary Musgrove
City Arts & Technology HS	301 De Montfort Ave	San Francisco, CA	94112-1733	415-841-2200	585-3009	9-12	Daniel McLaughlin
City Life Downtown Charter S	700 Wilshire Blvd	Los Angeles, CA	90017-3811	213-989-2267	989-6814	6-12	Jacki Breger
Classical Academy	1330 E Grand Ave	Escondido, CA	92027-3019	760-546-0101	739-8289	K-8	Robert Goode
Clear View Charter S	455 Windrose Way	Chula Vista, CA	91910-7400	619-498-3000	498-3007	K-6	Sherrie Stogsdill-Posey
Coastal Academy Charter	4183 Avenida de la Plata	Oceanside, CA	92056-6002	760-631-4020	631-4027	K-8	Robert Goode
Coastal Grove Charter S	PO Box 510	Arcata, CA	95518-0510	707-825-8804		K-3	Bettina Eipper
College Ready Academy	1729 Martin Luther King Blv	Los Angeles, CA	90062	323-293-9169	293-0427	9-12	Howard Lappin
College Ready Middle Academy	5753 Rodeo Rd	Los Angeles, CA	90016-5013	323-556-2280	556-2281	6-8	Judy Burton
Collins Charter S at Cherry Valley	1001 Cherry St	Petaluma, CA	94952-2065	707-778-4740	778-4839	K-8	Karen McGahey
Community Charter MS	919 8th St	San Fernando, CA	91340-1312	818-837-4420	837-1420	6-8	Courtney Deardorff
Community Charter S	16945 Sherman Way	Van Nuys, CA	91406-3614	818-774-9888	837-1420	9-10	Gina Newton
Community Harvest Charter S	3202 W Adams Blvd	Los Angeles, CA	90018-1832	323-373-2000	373-9922	6-12	Charletta Johnson
Connecting Waters Charter S	219 N Reinway Ave	Waterford, CA	95386-8906	209-874-9463	874-9531	K-12	Sherri Nelson
Connections Charter S	17555 Tuolumne Rd	Tuolumne, CA	95379-9701	209-928-4228	928-1422	7-9	Michael Gibson
Constellation Charter MS	PO Box 2130	Long Beach, CA	90801-2130	562-435-7181	435-3981	6-8	Daphne Ching-Jackson
Cornerstone Prep Charter MS	2232 Lincoln Blvd	Venice, CA	90291-3953	310-636-2774	636-2775	6-8	Peter Schoenfeld
Cornerstone Prep S	7651 S Central Ave	Los Angeles, CA	90001-2945	323-581-4495	777-0089	K-6	Cheryl O'Connell
Corona Charter S	12953 Branford St	Pacoima, CA	91331-4303	818-834-5805	834-8075	6-8	Dixon Slingerland
Cortez Hill Academy	201 A St	San Diego, CA	92101-4003	619-338-9206	338-0448	9-12	Linda Reed
Creative Arts Charter S	1601 Turk St	San Francisco, CA	94115-4527	415-749-3512	749-3509	K-8	Stephen Good
Creative Connections Arts Academy	7201 Arutas Dr	North Highlands, CA	95660-2809	916-566-1870		K-8	Joe Breault
Crenshaw Arts-Tech Charter HS	5125 Crenshaw Blvd	Los Angeles, CA	90043-1853	323-296-3050	293-3057	9-12	Dana Adams
Crescendo Charter ES	4900 S Western Ave	Los Angeles, CA	90062-2326	323-945-3906		K-5	John Allen
Cross Cultural Environmental Leadership	682 Schofield Rd	San Francisco, CA	94129-1198	415-642-5822		K-12	Cristina Valdez
Crossroads Charter S	PO Box 368	Armona, CA	93202-0368	559-585-7295	585-7298	K-12	Laurie Blue
Crosswalk Charter S	PO Box 401448	Hesperia, CA	92340-1448	760-949-8002	947-9648	5-10	Chala Salisbury
Culture & Language Academy of Success	434 S Grevillea Ave	Inglewood, CA	90301-2300	310-680-7100	680-7103	K-8	Janis Bucknor
Cypress Charter HS	2039 Merrill St	Santa Cruz, CA	95062-4176	831-477-0302	477-7659	9-12	Les Forster
Cypress Grove Charter HS	PO Box 1219	Seaside, CA	93955-1219	831-392-0200	392-0400	9-12	Walt Ferguson
Darnall E-Charter S	6020 Hughes St	San Diego, CA	92115-6520	619-582-1822	287-4732	K-6	Lisa Berlanga
Dehesa Charter S	264 Landis Ave Ste 103	Chula Vista, CA	91910-2651	877-300-8299	498-1488	K-12	Chris Geiss
De La Hoya Animo S	5156 Whittier Blvd	Los Angeles, CA	90022-3932	323-780-1952	780-1953	9-12	Kris Terry
Delta Charter HS	31400 S Koster Rd	Tracy, CA	95304-8824	209-830-6363	830-9324	9-12	Mary Vink
Delta Charter S	343 Soquel Ave	Santa Cruz, CA	95062-2305	831-477-5213	479-6173	9-12	Robert Guzley
Delta View District-wide Charter S	1201 Lacey Blvd	Hanford, CA	93230-9306	559-582-3122	582-3139	K-8	Nancy Ruble
Denair Charter Academy	3460 Lester Rd	Denair, CA	95316-9502	209-634-0917	669-9282	K-12	Alex Marshall
Desert Sands Charter HS	3030 E Palmdale Blvd Ste G	Palmdale, CA	93550-5046	661-272-0044	272-0541	8-12	Jeff Brown
Discovery Charter S	1100 Camino Biscay	Chula Vista, CA	91910-7737	619-656-0797	656-3899	K-6	Michael Cole
Discovery Charter S	12550 Van Nuys Blvd	Pacoima, CA	91331-1354	818-897-1187	897-1295	9-12	Matthew Macarah
Discovery Charter S	51 E Beverly Pl	Tracy, CA	95376-3191	209-831-5240	831-5094	5-8	Virginia Stewart
Downtown College Preparatory	PO Box 90307	San Jose, CA	95109-3307	408-271-1730	271-1734	9-12	Jennifer Andaluz
Downtown Value S	950 W Washington Blvd	Los Angeles, CA	90015-3312	213-748-8868	748-8062	K-6	Gerry Jacoby
Eagle Peak Montessori S	800 Hutchinson Rd	Walnut Creek, CA	94598-4505	925-946-0994	676-1971	K-4	Michelle Hammons
Eagles Peak Charter S	981 Vale Terrace Dr	Vista, CA	92084-5213	760-630-3200	630-5323	K-12	Kathleen Hermsmyer
East Bay Conservation Corps Charter S	1021 3rd St	Oakland, CA	94607-2507	510-992-7855	992-7950	9-12	Carolyn Gransdorff
East Bay Conservation Corps Charter S	1086 Alcatraz Ave	Oakland, CA	94608-1265	510-420-3701	420-3703	K-5	Carolyn Gramstorff
East Oakland Leadership Academy	2614 Seminary Ave	Oakland, CA	94605-1570	510-562-5238	562-5239	6-7	Laura Armstrong
East Palo Alto Charter S	1286 Runnymede St	East Palo Alto, CA	94303-1332	650-614-9100	614-9183	K-8	Allie Leslie
East Palo Alto HS	475 Pope St	Menlo Park, CA	94025-2800	650-329-2828	321-6628	9-12	Nicole Ramos-Beban
Eastside Campus Westside Prep Charter S	6469 Guthrie St	North Highlands, CA	95660-3944	916-566-1860	339-2033	7-8	Ziggy Robeson
Edison-Bethune Charter Academy	1616 S Fruit Ave	Fresno, CA	93706-2819	559-457-2530	498-0711	K-6	Felicia Quarles

School	Address	City,State	Zip code	Telephone	Fax	Grade	Contact
Edison Charter Academy	3531 22nd St	San Francisco, CA	94114-3405	415-970-3330	285-0527	K-5	Margaret Quillen
Edison McNair Academy	2033 Pulgas Ave	East Palo Alto, CA	94303-2025	650-329-2888	473-9247	4-8	Doug Harrell
Education for Change	9860 Sunnyside St	Oakland, CA	94603-2750	510-568-7936		K-5	Michael Scott
Education for Change	1700 28th Ave	Oakland, CA	94601-2455	510-568-7936		K-4	Susan Sperber
Eel River Charter S	PO Box 218	Covelo, CA	95428-0218	707-983-6946	983-6197	K-8	Betty Tuttle
Einstein Academy	6104 Adelaide Ave	San Diego, CA	92115-5519	619-795-1190		K-6	Luci Fowers
Elk Grove Charter S	5900 Bamford Dr	Sacramento, CA	95823-4607	916-714-1653	428-8307	1-12	
El Rancho Charter MS	181 S Del Giorgio Rd	Anaheim, CA	92808-1399	714-997-6238	281-8791	7-8	John Besta
El Sol Science & Arts Charter Academy	1010 N Broadway	Santa Ana, CA	92701-3408	714-543-0023	543-0026	K-8	Monique Davis
Emerson Parkside Academy	2625 Josie Ave	Long Beach, CA	90815-1511	562-420-2631	420-7642	K-5	Cynthia Young
Environmental Charter HS	4161 W 147th St	Lawndale, CA	90260-1709	310-676-3107	676-3981	9-12	Joanna Paul
e-Scholar Charter S	PO Box 130	Mineral, CA	96063-0130	530-527-0188	527-0273	K-12	Harold Vietti
Escondido Charter HS	1868 E Valley Pkwy	Escondido, CA	92027-2525	760-737-3154	738-8996	9-12	Denny Snyder
Escuela Popular	1600 Las Palmas	San Jose, CA	95116	408-275-7193	275-7192	K-3	Patricia Reguerin
Etna Academy of Arts	PO Box 490	Etna, CA	96027-0490	530-467-3320	467-3465	K-12	
Evergreen Charter S	PO Box 992418	Redding, CA	96099-2418	530-247-1800	247-1824	K-5	Lisa Whitehorn
Excelsior Education Center Charter S	7151 SVL Box	Victorville, CA	92395-5153	760-245-4448	245-4009	7-12	Charles Gehrke
Explorer ES	8660 Gilman Dr	La Jolla, CA	92037-2202	858-554-1001	554-1005	K-6	Jill Green
FAME Public Charter S	39899 Balentine Dr	Newark, CA	94560-5355	510-687-9111	438-6842	K-12	Maram Alaiwat
Farnham Charter ES	15711 Woodard Rd	San Jose, CA	95124-2668	408-377-3321	377-7237	K-5	Maureen Ricketts
Father Keith B. Kenny Charter S	3525 Martin Luther King Blv	Sacramento, CA	95817	916-277-6500	277-6513	K-5	David Ermshar
Feaster-Edison Charter S	670 Flower St	Chula Vista, CA	91910-1399	619-422-8397	422-4780	K-6	Erik Latoni
Fenton Avenue Charter S	11828 Gain St	Sylmar, CA	91342-7132	818-896-7482	890-9986	PK-5	Irene Sumida
Five Keys Charter S	70 Oak Grove St	San Francisco, CA	94107-1019	415-734-3310	734-3314	9-12	Sheryl Corke
Folsom Community Charter S	101 Dean Way	Folsom, CA	95630-2801	916-817-8499	987-1167	K-8	Wayne Edney
Forest Charter S	224 Church St	Nevada City, CA	95959-2505	530-265-4823	265-5037	K-12	Sandy McDivitt
4 Winds Charter S	2345 Fair St	Chico, CA	95928-6749	530-879-7411	879-7414	K-12	Terri Tozier
Fremont Charter S	1120 W 22nd St	Merced, CA	95340-3540	209-385-6627	385-6301	K-5	Dalinda Saich
Freshwater Charter S	75 Greenwood Heights Dr	Eureka, CA	95503-9441	707-442-2969	442-9527	K-8	Thom McMahon
Fresno Preparatory Academy	3355 E Shields Ave	Fresno, CA	93726-6906	559-222-3840	222-3540	9-12	Bill Realin
Frontier Charter S	6691 Silverthorne Cir	Sacramento, CA	95842-2654	916-566-1840	344-8932	7-8	Ziggy Robeson
Futures HS	3701 Stephen Dr	North Highlands, CA	95660-4532	916-286-1900	263-6059	7-12	Jim Griffis
Gabriela Charter S	631 S Commonwealth Ave	Los Angeles, CA	90005-4003	213-487-0839	487-0894	K-5	Susan Gurman
Garfield Charter S	3600 Middlefield Rd	Menlo Park, CA	94025-3010	650-369-3759	367-4358	K-8	Cynthia Garrison-Arce
Gates ES	23882 Landisview Ave	Lake Forest, CA	92630-5199	949-837-2260	837-5013	K-6	Yvonne Estling
Gateway HS	1430 Scott St	San Francisco, CA	94115-3510	415-749-3600	749-2716	9-12	Peter Thorp
Gateway to College	4800 Magnolia Ave	Riverside, CA	92506-1201	951-222-8931	222-8975	9-12	Jill Marks
Genesis S	5601 47th Ave	Sacramento, CA	95824-4031	916-433-5300	433-5372	7-12	Judy Billingsley
Giraffe Charter ES	436 S Alexandria Ave	Los Angeles, CA	90020-2703	213-614-1745	614-2046	K-K	Jill Wells
Glacier Charter HS	50200 Road 427	Oakhurst, CA	93644-9506	559-642-1422	642-1592	9-12	Michael Cox
Golden Valley Charter S	PO Box 4557	Citrus Heights, CA	95611-4557	916-962-3104	962-3107	K-8	Patrick Songbird
Gold Oak Arts Charter S	3171 Pleasant Valley Rd	Placerville, CA	95667-9299	530-626-3157	626-3159	4-8	Sylvia Shannon
Gold Rush Charter S	14673 Mono Way	Sonora, CA	95370-9220	209-533-8644	586-2736	K-12	Kathleen Hanson
Gorman Learning Center	1902 Orange Tree Ln	Redlands, CA	92374-2888	909-307-6312	793-5964	K-12	Waldo Burford
Granada Hills HS	10535 Zelzah Ave	Granada Hills, CA	91344-5999	818-360-2361	363-9504	9-12	Sue Lepisto
Grant Community Outreach Center	5800 Skvarla Ave	Mc Clellan AFB, CA	95652-2418	916-643-9891	643-9893	K-12	Randy Orzalli
Grass Valley Charter S	342 S School St	Grass Valley, CA	95945-6699	530-273-8723	274-9872	K-8	Linda Brown
Grayson Charter S	PO Box 7	Westley, CA	95387-0007	209-894-3762	894-3393	K-5	Arturo Duran
Greater San Diego Academy	13881 Campo Rd	Jamul, CA	91935-3208	619-669-3050	669-3066	K-12	Gail Levine
Grizzly ChalleNGe Charter S	PO Box 3209	San Luis Obispo, CA	93403-3209	805-782-6882	594-6296	10-12	Jeanne Dukes
Grove Charter HS	200 Nevada St	Redlands, CA	92373-5385	909-798-7831	307-6464	9-12	Gina Engelfried
Growing Children Charter S	8000 International Blvd	Oakland, CA	94621-2424	510-568-0500	568-0505	K-6	Susan Harman
Guajome Park Academy	1234 Arcadia Ave	Vista, CA	92084-3404	760-631-6077	631-3411	6-12	Penny Harrison
Guidance Charter S	38648 33rd St E	Palmdale, CA	93550-4232	661-272-1701	272-1728	K-8	Kamal Al-Khatib
Hallmark Charter S	2551 9th St	Sanger, CA	93657-2769	559-875-1372	875-3573	K-12	Alfred Sanchez
Hart-Ransom Academic Charter S	3920 Shoemake Ave	Modesto, CA	95358-8577	209-523-0401	523-1064	K-8	Sherry Smith
Hawthorne Math Science & Tech S	4467 W Broadway	Hawthorne, CA	90250-3819	310-973-8184		9-12	David Morrow
Hearns Charter S	PO Box 398	Littlerock, CA	93543-0398	661-944-9797	944-9798	K-8	Patricia Rhodes
Hearthstone Charter S	2120B Robinson St	Oroville, CA	95965-4937	530-532-5848	532-5847	K-12	Michael Ramos
Heather S	2757 Melendy Dr	San Carlos, CA	94070-3604	650-508-7303	508-7306	K-4	Pam Jasso
Helix HS	7323 University Ave	La Mesa, CA	91941-6200	619-644-8200	462-9257	8-12	Dr. Douglas Smith
Heritage Charter S	1855 E Valley Pkwy	Escondido, CA	92027-2517	760-737-3154	738-8996	K-8	Dennis Snyder
Heritage College Ready HS	12204 S San Pedro St	Los Angeles, CA	90061-2848	213-943-4930	943-4931	9-12	Doc Ervin
Heritage S	PO Box 296000	Phelan, CA	92329-6000	760-868-2422	868-0589	K-8	John Garner
Hickman Charter S	13306 4th St	Hickman, CA	95323-9634	209-874-9070	874-1457	K-8	Patricia Golding
Hickman ES	13306 4th St	Hickman, CA	95323-9634	209-874-1816	874-3721	K-5	Christine Linder
Hickman MS	13306 4th St	Hickman, CA	95323-9634	209-874-1816	874-3721	6-8	Robert Loretelli
High Tech HS	2861 Womble Rd	San Diego, CA	92106-6025	619-243-5000	243-5050	9-12	Larry Rosenstock
High Tech HS - LA	17111 Victory Blvd	Van Nuys, CA	91406-5455	818-881-2640		9-12	Marsha Rybin
High Tech International HS	2855 Farragut Rd	San Diego, CA	92106-6029	619-398-4900		9-12	Larry Rosenstock
High Tech MS	2291 Truxtun Rd	San Diego, CA	92106-6040	619-816-5060		6-8	Larry Rosenstock
Holly Drive Leadership Academy	4999 Holly Dr	San Diego, CA	92113-2046	619-266-7333	266-7330	K-8	Alysia Smith
HomeTech Charter S	6445 Skyway	Paradise, CA	95969-4538	530-872-1171	872-1172	K-12	Sue Gioia
Huerta Learning Academy	1936 Courtland Ave	Oakland, CA	94601-4614	510-533-9790	533-9794	K-8	Kenneth Reed
Huntington Park College Ready Academy	2071 Saturn Ave	Huntington Park, CA	90255-3635	213-943-4930	943-4931	9-12	Judy Burton
Imagine Academy Charter S	16551 Rinaldi St	Granada Hills, CA	91344-3762	818-368-1557	368-1935	6-12	Carol Ann Scott
Inglewood Preparatory Academy	830 N La Brea Ave	Inglewood, CA	90302-2206	310-671-5578	671-2424	K-8	Raymond D. Wilder
Institute of Business	6650 Inglewood Ave	Stockton, CA	95207-3861	209-933-7475		9-12	Ron Huebert
Integrity Charter S	125 Palm Ave	National City, CA	91950-1719	619-336-0808		K-4	Sandra Dominguez
International S of Monterey	PO Box 711	Monterey, CA	93942-0711	831-583-2165	899-7653	K-7	Chrissie Jahn
Island S	7799 21st Ave	Lemoore, CA	93245-9694	559-924-6424	924-0247	K-8	Tom Bates
Ivy Academia	6221 Fallbrook Ave	Woodland Hills, CA	91367-1602	818-348-8190	332-4136	K-12	Christina Gordan
Jacoby Creek S	1617 Old Arcata Rd	Bayside, CA	95524-9324	707-822-4896	822-4898	K-8	Eric Grantz
Jardin De la Infancia	307 E 7th St	Los Angeles, CA	90014-2209	213-614-1745	614-2046	K-1	Alice Callaghan
Johnson JHS	1300 Stroud Ave	Kingsburg, CA	93631-1000	559-897-1091	897-6867	7-8	Laurie Goodman
Jordan MS	20920 Knapp St	Chatsworth, CA	91311-5906	818-468-3637	709-3961	6-8	Myranda Marsh
Journey S	PO Box 1027	San Clemente, CA	92674-1027	949-361-7726	361-7745	K-5	Michelle Daggett
Julian Charter S	PO Box 1780	Julian, CA	92036-1780	866-853-0003	765-3849	K-12	Jennifer Cauzza
Kenter Canyon Charter S	645 N Kenter Ave	Los Angeles, CA	90049-1999	310-472-5918	472-9738	K-5	Kevin Mullery
Kern Workforce 2000 Academy Charter	5801 Sundale Ave	Bakersfield, CA	93309-2924	661-827-3156	827-3320	10-12	Fuchsia Ward
Keyes To Learning Charter S	PO Box 519	Keyes, CA	95328-0519	209-634-6467	669-7121	K-9	Lee Ann Stangl
Kid Street Learning Center	PO Box 6784	Santa Rosa, CA	95406-0784	707-525-9223	525-9432	K-6	Linda Conklin
King Chavez Academy of Excellence	735 Cesar E Chavez Pkwy	San Diego, CA	92113-1118	619-232-2825	232-2943	K-8	Toni Smith
Kings River-Hardwick S	10300 Excelsior Ave	Hanford, CA	93230-9794	559-584-4475	585-1422	K-8	Leslie Ford
KIPP Academy of Opportunity	7019 S Van Ness Ave	Los Angeles, CA	90047-1659	323-778-0125	778-0162	5-8	Mikelle Willis
KIPP Adelante Preparatory S	1475 6th Ave Fl 2	San Diego, CA	92101-3245	619-233-3242		5-8	Kelly Wright
KIPP Bayview Academy	1060 Key Ave	San Francisco, CA	94124-3563	415-467-2522	467-9522	5-8	Molly Wood
KIPP LA College Prep S	1855 N Main St	Los Angeles, CA	90031-3227	323-223-5477	223-5410	5-8	Carolyn Ruff
KIPP San Francisco Bay Academy	1430 Scott St	San Francisco, CA	94115-3510	415-440-4306	440-4308	5-8	Lydia Glassie
KIPP Summit Academy	2005 Via Barrett	San Lorenzo, CA	94580-1315	510-798-9434		5-12	Jason Singer
LA Educ Achievement Partnership HS	20920 Knapp St	Chatsworth, CA	91311-5906	818-709-4282	709-3961	9-12	Terrence Dunn
LA International Charter S	2109 Merton Ave	Los Angeles, CA	90041-1913	323-257-1499		9-12	Clint Taylor
Lakeview Charter S	1445 Celis St	San Fernando, CA	91340-3207	818-837-9190	837-0520	6-8	Edward Vandenberg
Lammersville Charter S	16555 Von Sosten Rd	Tracy, CA	95304-7220	209-836-7400	835-1113	K-8	Bill Lebo
Language Academy	4500 Roosevelt Ave	Sacramento, CA	95820-4546	916-277-7137			Martha Quadros
Larchmont Charter S	1265 N Fairfax Ave	Los Angeles, CA	90046-5205	323-656-1480	656-1467	K-6	Alice Horevitz
La Sierra Military Academy	1735 E Houston Ave	Visalia, CA	93292-2349	559-733-6963	733-6845	9-12	Dr. Lorene Valentino
Latino College Preparatory Academy	14271 Story Rd	San Jose, CA	95127-3823	408-729-2283		9-12	Jess Barajas
La Vida Charter S	PO Box 1461	Ukiah, CA	95482-1461	707-459-6344	459-6377	K-12	Ann Kelly
Leadership Academy	300 Seneca Ave	San Francisco, CA	94112-3248	415-841-8910	841-8925	9-12	Greg Peters
Leadership Public S Richmond	715 Chanslor Ave	Richmond, CA	94801-3533	510-235-4522	358-4513	9-12	Jolene Lane
Learner-Centered S	PO Box 1521	Antioch, CA	94509-0152	925-755-1252	755-7527	K-9	Debbie Hobin
Learning Choice Academy	PO Box 531588	San Diego, CA	92153-1588	858-536-8388		K-12	Kathy Bass
Learning for Life Charter S	330 Reservation Rd Ste F	Marina, CA	93933-3286	831-582-9820	582-9825	7-12	Michael Shaw
Lemoore University Charter S	100 Vine St	Lemoore, CA	93245-3418	559-924-6800		7-8	Crescenciano Camarena
Lennox Math Science & Tech Academy	10319 Firmona Ave	Lennox, CA	90304-1419	310-330-3494	330-3496	9-12	Armando Mena
Life Learning Academy	651 8th St Bldg 229	San Francisco, CA	94130-1901	415-397-8957	397-9274	9-12	Craig Miller
Lifeline Learning Charter S	357 E Palmer	Compton, CA	90221	310-605-2510	764-4890	7-12	Paula DeGroat
Lighthouse Community Charter S	345 12th St	Oakland, CA	94607-4217	510-271-8801	271-8803	K-6	Jenna Stauffer
Lincoln ES	1900 Mariposa St	Kingsburg, CA	93631-2044	559-897-5141	897-3537	2-4	Jennifer DuPras
Linscott Charter S	220 Elm St	Watsonville, CA	95076-5025	831-728-6301	761-5478	K-8	Robin Higbee
Live Oak Charter S	100 Gnoss Concourse	Petaluma, CA	94952-3395	707-762-9020	762-3861	K-4	Will Stapp
Long Valley Charter S	PO Box 7	Doyle, CA	96109-0007	530-827-2395	827-3562	K-12	J. D. Lietaker
Los Angeles Academy of Arts & Enterprise	1201 W 5th St Ste T210	Los Angeles, CA	90017-2081	213-487-0600	487-0500	6-12	Sabrina Bow
Los Angeles Leadership Academy	668 S Catalina St	Los Angeles, CA	90005-1708	213-381-8484	381-8489	6-12	Roger Lowenstein
MAAC Community Charter S	1385 3rd Ave	Chula Vista, CA	91911-4302	619-476-0749	476-0913	9-12	Joe Lara
MACSA Academica Calmecac	660 Sinclair Dr	San Jose, CA	95116-3464	408-929-1080	929-1025	9-10	Adolfo Reyes

School	Address	City,State	Zip code	Telephone	Fax	Grade	Contact
MACSA El Portal Leadership Academy	240 Swanston Ln	Gilroy, CA	95020-4548	408-846-1715	846-1815	9-12	Noemi Reyes
Magnolia Science Academy	18238 Sherman Way	Reseda, CA	91335-4550	818-609-0507	609-0534	6-12	Engin Eryilmaz
Mammoth Olympic Academy	PO Box 3509	Mammoth Lakes, CA	93546-3509	760-934-7636	934-7510	1-12	
Manzanita Charter MS	3200 Barrett Ave	Richmond, CA	94804-1718	510-232-3000	232-0009	6-8	Kristin Kirkman
Mare Island Technology Academy HS	2 Positive Pl	Vallejo, CA	94589-1825	707-552-6482	552-0288	9-12	Louise Santiago
Mare Island Technology Academy MS	2 Positive Pl	Vallejo, CA	94589-1825	707-552-6482	552-0288	6-8	Louise Santiago
Maria Montessori Charter Academy	3175 Sunset Blvd Ste 104	Rocklin, CA	95677-3091	916-630-1510	624-7305	K-8	Brent Boothby
Marin S of Arts & Technology	1850 Ignacio Blvd	Novato, CA	94949-4902	415-883-7390	561-2901	9-12	Stewart Fox
Marquez Charter S	16821 Marquez Ave	Pacific Plsds, CA	90272-3294	310-454-4019	573-1532	K-5	Lewin Dover
Marysville Charter Academy for the Arts	1917 B St	Marysville, CA	95901-3731	530-749-6157	741-7892	7-12	John Pimentel
Mattole Valley Charter S	PO Box 39	Honeydew, CA	95545-0039	707-629-3634	629-3649	K-12	Richard Graey
McGill School of Success	3025 Fir St	San Diego, CA	92102-1123	619-239-0632	239-1318	K-2	Deborah Huggins
Memorial Academy Charter S	2850 Logan Ave	San Diego, CA	92113-2412	619-525-7400	525-7498	6-9	Robert Gallardo
Metropolitan Arts & Tech HS	1550 Treat Ave	San Francisco, CA	94110-5234	415-550-5920	585-3009	9-12	Jessica Alfaro
Met Sacramento S	810 V St	Sacramento, CA	95818-1330	916-264-4700	264-4701	9-10	Beth Kay
Mid Valley Alternative Charter S	9895 7th Ave	Hanford, CA	93230-8802	559-583-1149	582-7565	K-8	Charlotte Meade
Milagro Charter ES	2635 Pasadena Ave	Los Angeles, CA	90031-2323	323-223-1786	223-8593	K-5	Sacsha Robinett
Millsmont Academy	3200 62nd Ave	Oakland, CA	94605-1614	510-638-9445	638-0744	K-8	Diana Adams
Modoc Charter S	1135 Pine St Ste A	Redding, CA	96001-0750	530-229-0948	229-9276	K-12	Jim McLaughlin
Monarch Academy	1445 101st Ave	Oakland, CA	94603-3207	510-568-3101	568-3521	K-5	Tatiana Epanchin-Troyan
Monarch Learning Center	PO Box 992418	Redding, CA	96099-2418	530-247-7307	243-4819	K-8	Steve Essig
Montague Street School	13000 Montague St	Pacoima, CA	91331-4193	818-899-0215	834-9782	PK-5	Diane Pritchard
Monterey County Home Charter S	PO Box 80851	Salinas, CA	93912-0851	831-755-0331	755-0837	K-12	Mary Sgheiza
Mountain Home Charter S	41267 Highway 41	Oakhurst, CA	93644-9403	559-642-1422	642-1592	K-8	Michael Cox
Mountain Oaks S	PO Box 1209	San Andreas, CA	95249-1209	209-754-0532	754-3556	K-12	Richard Anderson
Mountain View Montessori Charter S	15579 8th St	Victorville, CA	92395-3360	760-843-3303	843-1074	K-6	Geraldine Terranova
Mueller Charter S	715 I St	Chula Vista, CA	91910-5199	619-422-6192	422-0356	K-6	Dr. Kevin Riley
Muir Charter S	112 Nevada City Hwy	Nevada City, CA	95959-3117	530-478-6400	478-6410	12-12	Buzz Breedlove
Multicultural Learning Center	7510 DeSoto Ave	Canoga Park, CA	91303-1430	818-716-5783	716-1085	K-5	Toby Bornstein
Museum Charter S	211 Maple St	San Diego, CA	92103-6527	619-236-8712	236-8906	3-6	Phil Beaumont
Napa Valley Language Academy	2700 Kilburn Ave	Napa, CA	94558-5623	707-253-3678	259-8427	K-5	Deborah Wallace
Natomas Charter S	4600 Blackrock Dr	Sacramento, CA	95835-1250	916-928-5353	928-5333	K-12	Charlie Leo
Nevada City Charter	215 Washington St	Nevada City, CA	95959-2595	530-265-1885	265-1889	K-8	Mike McGarr
Nevada City S for the Arts	13032 Bitney Springs Rd # 8	Nevada City, CA	95959-9017	530-273-7736	273-1378	K-8	Mary Ross
Nevada County Academy of Learning	112 Nevada City Hwy	Nevada City, CA	95959-3117	530-478-6400	478-6410	9-12	Terry McAteer
NEW Academy of Science & Arts	379 S Loma Ave	Los Angeles, CA	90017	213-413-9183	413-9187	K-5	Andres Versage
N.E.W. Canoga Park ES	21425 Cohasset St	Canoga Park, CA	91303-1450	818-887-6945	483-7848	K-5	
New City S	1230 Pine Ave	Long Beach, CA	90813-3123	562-436-0689	436-7475	K-5	Ted Harmony
New Designs S	3756 Santa Rosalia Dr Ste 5	Los Angeles, CA	90008-3606	323-293-7009	293-7130	6-12	Yaw Audtwun
New Jerusalem Charter S	31400 S Koster Rd	Tracy, CA	95304-9543	209-830-6789	830-9707	K-8	Mary Vink
New Millennium Institute of Education	830 Fresno St #400	Fresno, CA	93706-3117	559-497-9331	497-9109	7-12	Lois Harris-Perkins
New Technology HS	1400 Dickson St	Sacramento, CA	95822-3437	916-752-3101	433-2840	9-12	Paula M. Hanzel
New West Charter MS	11625 W Pico Blvd	Los Angeles, CA	90064-2908	310-943-5444	231-3399	6-8	Dr. Donald B. Gill
Northcoast Charter S	470 Union St	Arcata, CA	95521-6429	707-822-4845		K-12	John Schmidt
North Oakland Community Charter S	410 Alcatraz Ave	Oakland, CA	94609-1106	510-655-0540	655-1222	K-5	Julia Kassissieh
North Woods Discovery S	14732 Bass Dr	Redding, CA	96003-7303	530-275-5480	275-5416	K-8	Linda Johnson
Novato Charter S	936 C St	Novato, CA	94949-5060	415-883-4254	883-1859	K-8	Rachel Bishop
Nubia Leadership Academy	6134 Benson Ave	San Diego, CA	92114-4204	619-262-0050	262-4215	K-6	Myrion Doakes
Nuview Bridge HS	30401 Reservoir Ave	Nuevo, CA	92567-9263	951-928-8498	928-0186	9-12	Rebecca Mashatt
Oakdale Charter S	1235 E D St	Oakdale, CA	95361-3223	209-848-4361	848-4363	9-12	Hector Sanchez
Oakland Charter Academy	3001 International Blvd	Oakland, CA	94601-2203	510-532-6751	532-6753	6-8	Jorge Lopez
Oakland Military Institute	2405 W 14th St	Oakland, CA	94607-5005	510-267-3900	286-3935	6-12	Bruce Holaday
Oakland S for the Arts	1800 San Pablo Ave	Oakland, CA	94612-1545	510-873-8800	873-8816	9-9	Loni Berry
Oakland Unity HS	6038 Brann St	Oakland, CA	94605-1544	510-635-7170	635-3830	9-12	Jane Searight
Oasis Charter Academy	11988 Hesperia Rd Ste B	Hesperia, CA	92345-1851	760-947-0006	947-0008	7-12	Cynthia Ferguson
Oasis Charter S	PO Box 720	Salinas, CA	93902-0720	831-424-9003	424-9005	K-6	Jane Roberts
Oasis Charter S	285 17th St	Oakland, CA	94612	510-251-8103		9-12	Martha Diepenbrock
Ocean Charter School	12606 Culver Blvd	Los Angeles, CA	90066-6506	310-827-5511	827-2019	K-8	Alex Metcalf
Oceanside S of Business and Technology	1831 Mission Ave	Oceanside, CA	92054-7104	760-795-8731	795-8732	11-12	Rocky Chavez
Odyssey Charter S	1555 E Colorado Blvd	Pasadena, CA	91106-2132	626-229-0993	229-0586	K-8	Franca Campopiano
O'Farrell Community S	6130 Skyline Dr	San Diego, CA	92114-5620	619-263-3009	263-4339	6-8	Byron King
Olive Crest - Nova Academy	2130 E 4th St Ste 200	Santa Ana, CA	92705-3818	714-543-5437	543-5463	7-12	Renee Lancaster
Olive Grove Charter S	PO Box 208	Los Olivos, CA	93441-0208	805-693-5933	686-4218	K-12	Jesse Leyva
Open Charter Magnet S	5540 W 77th St	Los Angeles, CA	90045-3214	310-568-0735	568-0904	K-5	Robert Burke
Oportunities Unlimited	8825 S Vermont Ave	Los Angeles, CA	90044-4831	323-565-4300	565-4310	9-12	Laura Icedo
Opportunities for Learning Charter S	18259 Soledad Canyon Rd	Santa Clarita, CA	91387-3532	661-424-1337	424-1129	K-12	Shannon Butler
Opportunities for Learning Charter S	1150 Foothill Blvd	La Canada Flt, CA	91011-3248	818-952-1790	952-1795	K-12	Traci Nobles
Options for Youth	2627 Alta Arden Expy	Sacramento, CA	95825-1306	916-971-3175	971-3186		Chris Timpson
Options for Youth	5720 Watt Ave	North Highlands, CA	95660-4752	916-338-2375	338-2417	7-12	Chris Timpson
Options for Youth	11088 Olson Dr	Rancho Cordova, CA	95670-5650	916-631-8113	631-8121		Chris Timpson
Options for Youth Charter S	1701 W Verdugo Ave	Burbank, CA	91506-2147			K-12	Ellen Harris
Options for Youth Charter S	6110 Fair Oaks Blvd #E	Carmichael, CA	95608-4819	916-485-5155	485-5484	9-12	Christopher Timpson
Options for Youth-San Gabriel Charter S	3115 Foothill Blvd Ste K	La Crescenta, CA	91214-4244	818-236-2060	236-2062	K-12	Mary Jensen
Options for Youth - Upland	310 N Mountain Ave	Upland, CA	91786-5115			K-12	Joan Hall
Options for Youth Victor Valley Charter	15048 Bear Valley Rd	Victorville, CA	92395-9235	626-685-9300	685-9316	K-12	Pamela Hall
Orange County Arts Academy	825 N Broadway	Santa Ana, CA	92701-3423	714-558-2787	569-1033	K-8	Monique Parmentier
Orange County HS of the Arts	1010 N Main St	Santa Ana, CA	92701-3602	714-560-0900	664-0463	7-12	Ralph Opacic
Orchard View Charter S	700 Watertrough Rd	Sebastopol, CA	95472-3917	707-823-4709	823-6187	K-12	Carol Rogers
Our Community S	16514 Nordhoff St	North Hills, CA	91343-3724	818-920-5285	920-5383	K-6	Brenda Buonora
Pacifica Community Charter S	3754 Dunn Dr	Los Angeles, CA	90034-5805	310-845-9405	845-9402	K-8	Janette Kiso
Pacific Coast Charter S	PO Box 50010	Watsonville, CA	95077-5010	831-786-2180	786-2192	K-12	Vicki Carr
Pacific Collegiate Charter S	PO Box 1701	Santa Cruz, CA	95061-1701	831-479-7785	427-5254	7-12	Andrew Goldenkrantz
Pacific Community Charter S	PO Box 984	Point Arena, CA	95468-0984	707-882-4131	882-4132	K-12	Sigrid Hillscan
Pacific View Charter S	3355 Mission Ave Ste 139	Oceanside, CA	92054-1333	760-757-0161	435-2666	K-12	Gina Campbell
Pacific View Charter S	2937 Moore Ave	Eureka, CA	95501-3316	707-269-9490	269-9491	K-12	Ron Flenner
Pacoima Charter S	11016 Norris Ave	Pacoima, CA	91331-2598	818-899-0201	890-3812	K-5	Irene Smerigan
Palisades Charter ES	800 Via De La Paz	Pacific Plsds, CA	90272-3617	310-454-3700	459-5627	K-5	Tami Weiser
Palisades Charter HS	15777 Bowdoin St	Pacific Plsds, CA	90272-3586	310-454-0611	454-6076	9-12	Dr. Gloria Martinez
Paradise Charter MS	6473 Clark Rd	Paradise, CA	95969-3501	530-872-7277	872-2924	6-8	Chris Reid
Paradise Charter Network	622 Pearson Rd	Paradise, CA	95969-5133	530-872-6440	872-9708	K-12	Carol Mooney
Para Los Ninos Charter S	1617 E 7th St	Los Angeles, CA	90021-1243	213-239-6605	239-9821	K-5	Norma Silva
Pathways Charter S	607 Bobelaine Dr	Santa Rosa, CA	95405-6604	707-573-6117	573-6122	K-12	Karri Smith
Peabody Charter S	3018 Calle Noguera	Santa Barbara, CA	93105-2899	805-563-1172	569-7042	K-6	Patricia Morales
Phillips-Edison Charter S	1210 Shetler Ave	Napa, CA	94559-4205	707-253-3481	259-8425	K-6	Debra Brown
Phoenix Academy	PO Box 4925	San Rafael, CA	94913-4925	415-499-0581	491-0981	9-12	Lisa Schwartz
Phoenix Academy	2086 Clarke Ave	East Palo Alto, CA	94303-1916	650-328-2596	329-2877	K-8	She'ren Champion
Pine Mountain Learning Center	PO Box 876	Lebec, CA	93243-0876	661-248-6247	248-6714	K-6	John Wight
Piner-Olivet Charter S	2707 Francisco Ave	Santa Rosa, CA	95403-1869	707-522-3310	522-3317	6-8	Diana Drew-Ingham
Pioneer MS	101 W Pioneer Way	Hanford, CA	93230-9489	559-584-0112	584-0118	6-8	Rich Callaghan
Pioneer Union ES	8810 14th Ave	Hanford, CA	93230-9680	559-584-8831	584-1422	K-5	Cheryl Taylor
Plumas Charter S	2288 E Main St	Quincy, CA	95971-9660	530-283-3851	283-3841	K-12	Kent Frid
Plumas Lake Charter S	2743 Plumas School Rd	Marysville, CA	95901-8827	530-743-4428	743-1408	K-12	Karen McLaughlin
Port of Los Angeles HS	250 W 5th St	San Pedro, CA	90731-3304	310-832-9201	514-1568	9-12	Mary Collins
Preuss S	9500 Gilman Dr	La Jolla, CA	92093-5004	858-658-7404	658-0988	6-12	Dr. Doris Alvarez
Price Charter MS	2650 New Jersey Ave	San Jose, CA	95124-1520	408-377-2532	377-7406	6-8	Debra Negrete
P.R.I.D.E. Charter S	3804 Ocean View Blvd	San Diego, CA	92113-1737	619-264-8764		9-11	Sharon Whitehurst-Payne
Progressive Education Charter S	2600 S LaBrea Ave	Los Angeles, CA	90016-2807	323-954-4337	954-4301	6-12	Dr. Doris J. Sims
Promise Charter S	611 S 35th St	San Diego, CA	92113-2717	619-696-1338		K-5	Olivia Flores
Provisional Accelerated Learning Academy	PO Box 7100	San Bernardino, CA	92411-0100	909-887-7002	887-8942	9-12	Dr. Mildred Henry
Puente Charter S	501 S Boyle Ave	Los Angeles, CA	90033-3816	323-780-2961	780-0359	K-K	Jerome Greening
Quail Lake Environmental Charter S	4087 N Quail Lake Dr	Clovis, CA	93619-4646	559-292-1273	292-1276	K-8	Jon Yost
Rainbow Advanced Institute for Learning	5253 5th St	Fallbrook, CA	92028-9795	760-728-4305	728-7712	6-10	Paul Cartas
Redding S of the Arts	2200 Eureka Way	Redding, CA	96001-0337	530-247-6933	245-2633	K-8	Margaret Johnson
Redwood Academy of Ukiah	PO Box 1383	Ukiah, CA	95482-1383	707-467-0500	462-4230	7-12	Dr. Kimberly Logan
Reems Academy of Technology & Art	8425 Macarthur Blvd	Oakland, CA	94605-3553	510-729-6635	562-9539	K-8	Lisa Blair
Rehoboth Charter Academy	9191 Colorado Ave	Riverside, CA	92503-2636	951-683-0553	687-2622	K-6	Toya Y. Flakes
Renaissance Academy HS	1901 S Bundy Dr	Los Angeles, CA	90025-5203	310-820-5060	820-5090	9-12	Paul McGlathlin
Renaissance Arts Academy	1800 Colorado Blvd	Los Angeles, CA	90041-1340	323-259-5700	259-5718	6-12	P. K. Candaux
Revere Charter MS	1450 Allenford Ave	Los Angeles, CA	90049-3614	310-451-5789	576-7957	6-8	Art Copper
Ridgecrest Charter S	325 S Downs St	Ridgecrest, CA	93555-4531	760-375-1010	375-7766	K-8	Michael Noga
River Oaks Charter S	555 Leslie St	Ukiah, CA	95482-5507	707-467-1855	467-1857	K-8	David Taxis
River S Charter	2447 Old Sonoma Rd	Napa, CA	94558-6006	707-259-8048	258-2800	6-8	Linda Inlay
River Valley Charter HS	9707 1/2 Marilla Dr	Lakeside, CA	92040-2807	619-390-2579	390-2581	7-12	William Wellhouse
Roosevelt Community Learning Center	31191 Road 180	Visalia, CA	93292-9585	559-592-9160	592-2927	K-10	Klara East
Roosevelt ES	1185 10th Ave	Kingsburg, CA	93631-2100	559-897-5193	897-6865	5-6	Melanie Sembritzki
Roseland Charter S	1777 West Ave	Santa Rosa, CA	95407-7449	707-546-7050	546-0434	7-8	Rima Meechan
Roseland University Preparatory S	100 Sebastopol Rd	Santa Rosa, CA	95407-6928	707-566-9990	566-9992	9-10	Amy Jones-Kerr

School	Address	City,State	Zip code	Telephone	Fax	Grade	Contact
Russian River Charter S	PO Box 139	Guerneville, CA	95446-0139	707-887-8790	887-8759	8-12	Carol Miller
Sacramento HS	2315 34th St	Sacramento, CA	95817-1299	916-277-6200	277-6370	9-12	Kevin Johnson
Sacramento River Discovery Center	PO Box 1298	Red Bluff, CA	96080-1298	530-529-1650		6-11	Cathy Klinesteker
St. Hope Public School 7	5201 Strawberry Ln	Sacramento, CA	95820-4815	916-732-4625		K-4	Herinder Pegany
San Carlos Charter Learning Center	750 Dartmouth Ave	San Carlos, CA	94070-1769	650-508-7343	508-7341	K-8	Paula Hunter
San Carlos HS	PO Box 7143	San Carlos, CA	94070-7143	650-591-5400	598-9980	9-12	Dan Lyttle
San Diego Cooperative Charter S	2850 6th Ave	San Diego, CA	92103-6308	619-574-0694		K-8	Dr. Wendy Rank-Buhr
Sanger Academy Charter S	2207 9th St	Sanger, CA	93657-2711	559-875-5562	875-8045	2-12	Ken Garcia
San Jacinto Valley Academy	480 N San Jacinto Ave	San Jacinto, CA	92583-2729	951-654-6113	654-5083	K-8	Donna Buck
San Jose Conservation Corps Charter S	2650 Senter Rd	San Jose, CA	95111-1121	408-283-7171	288-6521	10-12	Donna Howe
San Jose-Edison Charter S	1500 E Francisquito Ave	West Covina, CA	91791-3823	626-918-6575		K-8	Dr. Denise Patton
San Juan Choices Charter S	3425 Arden Way	Sacramento, CA	95825-2018	916-575-2830	575-1935	7-12	Marie Pflugrath
San Lorenzo Valley USD Charter S	325 Marion Ave	Ben Lomond, CA	95005-9403	831-336-1827	336-9657	K-12	Eric Schoffstall
Santa Ana Arts Academy	825 N Broadway	Santa Ana, CA	92701-3423	714-240-9636		K-6	Ralph Opacic
Santa Barbara Charter S	6100 Stow Canyon Rd	Goleta, CA	93117-1705	805-967-6522	967-6382	K-8	Bev Abrams
Santa Monica Blvd Community Charter S	1022 N Van Ness Ave	Los Angeles, CA	90038-3252	323-469-0971	462-4093	K-5	Vahe Markarlan
Santa Rosa Accelerated Charter	4650 Badger Rd	Santa Rosa, CA	95409-2633	707-528-5255	528-5644		
Santa Rosa Charter S	1835A W Steele Ln	Santa Rosa, CA	95403-2628	707-547-2480	547-2482	K-8	Kate Vander Sluis
Santa Ynez Valley Charter S	PO Box 59	Santa Ynez, CA	93460-0059	805-693-1755	693-1765	K-8	Mary Ann Cooley
Santiago Charter MS	515 N Rancho Santiago Blvd	Orange, CA	92869-2724	714-997-6366	532-4758	7-8	Mary Henry
Sartorette Charter ES	3850 Woodford Dr	San Jose, CA	95124-3799	408-264-4380	264-1758	K-5	Richard Wendell
S.C.A.A.S.	10513 S Vermont Ave	Los Angeles, CA	90044-3021	323-755-5566	751-0033	6-12	Kenyatta Stiger
School of Arts & Enterprise	300 W 2nd St	Pomona, CA	91766-1634	909-622-0699		9-12	Lucille Berger
School of Unlimited Learning	2336 Calaveras St	Fresno, CA	93721-1104	559-498-8543	642-1592	7-12	Perry Angle
Sebastopol Independent Charter S	PO Box 1170	Sebastopol, CA	95473-1170	707-824-9700		K-6	Greg Haynes
Sedona Charter Academy	16519 Victor St	Victorville, CA	92395-3965	760-245-3222	245-3774	K-12	Ken Larson
Sequoia Charter S	21445 Centre Pointe Pkwy	Santa Clarita, CA	91350-2684	661-259-0033	286-2120	9-12	Lori Andrews
Serna Charter S	339 E Oak St	Lodi, CA	95240-2917	209-331-7809	331-7997	K-6	Michael Gillespie
Shasta Secondary Home S	1401 Gold St	Redding, CA	96001-1937	530-245-2600	245-2611	6-12	Lynn Peebles
Shearer Charter S	1590 Elm St	Napa, CA	94559-3924	707-253-3508	253-3847	K-5	Lisa Miri
Shenandoah HS	6540 Koki Ln	El Dorado, CA	95623-4328	530-622-6212	622-1071	9-9	Valerie Lott
Sherman Oaks Community Charter S	1800 Fruitdale Ave Ste C	San Jose, CA	95128-4976	408-795-1140	341-7180	K-5	Julie Henderson
Sierra Charter S	1931 N Fine Ave	Fresno, CA	93727-1510	559-490-4290	490-4292	K-12	Lisa Marasco
Six Rivers Charter HS	1720 M St	Arcata, CA	95521-5741	707-825-2428	825-2034	9-12	Chris Hartley
Sixth Street Prep S	15579 8th St	Victorville, CA	92395-3399	760-241-0962	241-0967	K-6	Linda Mikels
Soledad Enrichment Action Charter S	3763 E 4th St	Los Angeles, CA	90063-3917	213-480-4200	261-1445	9-12	Gerald Wolfe
Somis Academy	950 Flynn Rd	Camarillo, CA	93012-8764	805-987-1188	987-1108	9-12	Carol Andersen
Sonoma Valley Charter S	17202 Sonoma Hwy	Sonoma, CA	95476-3667	707-935-4232	935-4207	K-8	Nora Flood
South Sutter Charter S	2452 El Centro Blvd	East Nicolaus, CA	95659-9748	530-656-2307			Michael Talerico
Stella Middle Charter Academy	2636 S Mansfield Ave	Los Angeles, CA	90016-3512	323-954-9957	954-6415	5-8	Jeff Hilger
Stellar Charter School	PO Box 992418	Redding, CA	96099-2418	530-245-7730	245-7731	K-12	Cindy Anderson
Summit Charter Academy	2036 E Hatch Rd	Modesto, CA	95351-5142	209-538-8082	538-1620	K-8	Coleen Dowd
Summit Charter S	PO Box 130	Mammoth Lakes, CA	93546-0130	760-934-0031	934-1443	K-9	Roseanne Higley
Summit Leadership Academy	PO Box 401606	Hesperia, CA	92340-1606	760-949-9202	949-9257	9-12	William K. Postmus
Summit Preparatory HS	201 Marshall St	Redwood City, CA	94063-1534	650-369-5851		9-12	Diane Tavenner
SunRidge Charter S	487 Watertrough Rd	Sebastopol, CA	95472-3911	707-824-2844		K-7	Mark Rice
Sunset Charter S	1755 S Crystal Ave	Fresno, CA	93706-2797	559-457-3310	495-1334	K-7	Alicia Estigoy
Sun Valley Charter S	2102 Main St	Ramona, CA	92065-2528	760-788-8008	788-8616	9-12	David Tarr
Synergy Charter S	1010 E 34th St	Los Angeles, CA	90011-2527	323-233-8559	931-3298	K-5	Randy Palisoc
Temecula Preparatory S	35777 Abelia St	Winchester, CA	92596-8450	951-926-6776	926-6797	K-12	Paul Stich
Temecula Valley Charter S	35755 Abelia St	Winchester, CA	92596-8450	951-926-9037	926-9768	K-8	Jo Ann Burnett
The New S	127 W Elder St	Fallbrook, CA	92028-2853	760-451-3639	451-3422	K-5	Sue Miller-Hurst
Thomas Charter S	101 W Adell St	Madera, CA	93638-0877	559-674-1192	675-6612	K-6	Roger Leach
Tierra Linda MS	750 Dartmouth Ave	San Carlos, CA	94070-1769	650-508-7370	508-7374	5-8	Lesley Martin
Tierra Pacifica Charter S	2008 17th Ave	Santa Cruz, CA	95062-1808	831-462-9404	475-2638	K-8	Linda Lambdin
Todays Fresh Start Charter S	4514 Crenshaw Blvd	Los Angeles, CA	90043-1221	323-293-9826	293-0266	K-3	Dr. Jeanette Parker
Topanga ES	141 N Topanga Canyon Blvd	Topanga, CA	90290-3831	310-455-3711	455-3517	K-6	Liam Joyce
Tree of Life Charter S	PO Box 966	Ukiah, CA	95482-0966	707-462-0913	462-0914	1-8	Celeste Beck
Trillium Charter S	1464 Spear Ave	Arcata, CA	95521-4882	707-822-4721	822-7054	K-5	Marianne Keller
Tubman Village S	6880 Mohawk St	San Diego, CA	92115-1728	619-668-8635	668-2480	K-8	Catherine Pope
Twin Ridges Home Study Charter S	PO Box 529	North San Juan, CA	95960-0529	530-292-3305	292-1918	K-8	Peter Sagebiel
Twin Rivers Charter S	840 Cooper Ave	Yuba City, CA	95991-3849	530-755-2872	673-1847	K-8	Theresa Johansen
Union Hill Charter S	11638 Colfax Hwy	Grass Valley, CA	95945-8899	530-273-8456	273-0152	1-8	Erick Fredrickson
University Charter S	3313 Coffee Rd	Modesto, CA	95355-1534	209-544-8722	544-8864	K-5	
University Preparatory Charter Academy	3030 75th Ave	Oakland, CA	94605-2906	510-569-7880	569-7905	9-10	Isaac Haqq
Urbani Institute for Language	640 N San Joaquin St	Stockton, CA	95202-2030	209-933-7370	933-7371	4-8	Olivia Castillo
Valley Business HS	108 Campus Way	Modesto, CA	95350-5803	209-558-4407	558-4453	9-12	Bob Vizzolini
Valley Oak Charter S	PO Box 878	Ojai, CA	93024-0878	805-640-4421	640-4321	K-9	Laura Fulmer
Valley Oaks Charter S	3501 Chester Ave	Bakersfield, CA	93301-1629	661-633-5288	322-6415	K-12	Shirley Oesch
Vantage Point Charter S	10862 Spenceville Rd	Penn Valley, CA	95946-9625	530-432-5312	432-8744	K-12	Shane Carnahan
Vaughn Next Century Learning Center	13330 Vaughn St	San Fernando, CA	91340-2216	818-896-7461	834-9036	K-12	Yvonne Chan
Venture Academy	2829 Transworld Dr	Stockton, CA	95206-3950	209-468-5940		K-12	Kathleen Focacci
View Park Accelerated MS	5701 Crenshaw Blvd	Los Angeles, CA	90043-2409	323-293-0448	931-5504	6-8	Brian Taylor
View Park Prep. Accelerated Charter S	3751 W 54th St	Los Angeles, CA	90043-2356	323-295-2684	295-2660	K-5	Michael Piscal
View Park Prep Accelerated HS	5749 Crenshaw Blvd	Los Angeles, CA	90043-2409	323-293-0448		9-12	Robert Schwartz
Village Charter S	1415 Fulton Rd Pmb A2	Santa Rosa, CA	95403-7619	707-591-9262	591-9275	K-6	Diane Bagetzi
Visalia Charter Independent Study	909 W Murray Ave	Visalia, CA	93291-4825	559-735-8055	730-7693	7-12	Missy Yavasile
Visions in Education Charter S	4800 Manzanita Ave	Carmichael, CA	95608-0825	916-971-7037	971-5590	K-12	Lynda Gantenbein
Visual and Performing Arts Charter S	20 Business Park Way	Sacramento, CA	95828-0912	916-382-6040	382-6041	7-12	Joanna de la Cuesta
Vocational Education Academy	2201 Blue Gum Ave	Modesto, CA	95358-1052	209-575-7842		9-12	Bob Vizzolini
Washington Charter S	45768 Portola Ave	Palm Desert, CA	92260-4861	760-862-4350	862-4356	K-5	Allan Lehmann
Washington ES	1501 Ellis St	Kingsburg, CA	93631-1896	559-897-2955	897-6863	K-1	Mel Manley
Watsonville Charter S of the Arts	115 Casserly Rd	Watsonville, CA	95076-8645	831-728-8123	728-6286	K-6	Sue Forson
Watts Learning Center	310 W 95th St	Los Angeles, CA	90003-4012	323-754-9900	754-0935	K-5	Sandra Fisher
WEB DuBois Charter S	302 Fresno St Ste 205	Fresno, CA	93706-3641	559-230-3073	442-5811	9-12	Linda Washington
West Charter S	5350 Faught Rd	Santa Rosa, CA	95403-1205	707-524-2741	524-2976	K-8	Pam Carpenter
West Fresno Performing Arts Academy	1901 E Shields Ave	Fresno, CA	93726-5313	559-229-7223	229-7234	8-10	Dr. Derrick Spiva
West Oakland Community S	955 12th St	Oakland, CA	94607-3233	510-465-9627	465-8071	6-6	Akiyu Hatano
West Park Charter Academy	2695 S Valentine Ave	Fresno, CA	93706-9042	559-485-0727	485-0682	K-12	Marta Escarcega
Westside Preparatory Charter S	6537 W 2nd St	Rio Linda, CA	95673-3231	916-566-1990	991-5842	7-8	Ziggy Robeson
Westwood Charter S	2050 Selby Ave	Los Angeles, CA	90025-6397	310-474-7788	475-1295	K-5	Judy Utvich
Westwood Charter S	PO Box 56	Westwood, CA	96137-0056	877-261-5959	256-2964	K-12	Henry Bietz
Wheatland Charter Academy	123 Beale Hwy	Beale Afb, CA	95903	530-788-2097	788-2631	K-12	Mike Reid
White Oaks ES	1901 White Oak Way	San Carlos, CA	94070-4799	650-508-7317	508-7320	K-4	Betty Casey
Whitmore Charter S	PO Box 307	Ceres, CA	95307-0307	209-556-1073	541-0947	K-8	Paula Smith
Wilder's Preparatory Academy Charter S	830 N La Brea Ave	Inglewood, CA	90302-2206	310-671-5578	671-2424	K-8	Raymond Wilder
Willits Charter S	7 S Marin St	Willits, CA	95490	707-459-5506	459-5576	6-12	Sally Rulison
Willow Creek Academy	PO Box 366	Sausalito, CA	94966-0366	415-331-7530	331-1622	K-8	Carol Cooper
Wilshire Center Charter HS	3600 Wilshire Blvd	Los Angeles, CA	90010-2603	213-487-7003	386-5853	9-12	Gary Russell
Wilson College Prep S	400 105th Ave	Oakland, CA	94603-2968	510-635-7737	635-7727	6-11	Troyvoi Hicks
Winona Adult Education	3222 Winona Way	North Highlands, CA	95660-5523	916-286-3809		10-12	Toby Richardson
Woodland Star Charter S	17811 Arnold Dr	Sonoma, CA	95476-4019	707-996-3849	996-4369	K-8	Chip Romer
Woodson Charter S	3333 N Bond Ave	Fresno, CA	93726-5712	559-230-3073	442-5811	7-12	Linda Washington
Youth Employment Partnership	2300 International Blvd	Oakland, CA	94601-1019	510-533-3447	533-3469	9-12	Michelle Clark
Yuba City Charter S	990 Klamath Ln Ste 15	Yuba City, CA	95993-8979	530-822-9031	674-1322	K-12	Sandi Lininger
Yuba County Career Prep Charter S	1104 E St	Marysville, CA	95901-4825	530-741-6025	741-6032	K-12	Carol Holtz
Yuba River Charter S	13026 Bitney Springs Rd # 3	Nevada City, CA	95959-9017	530-272-8078	272-1952	K-8	Caleb Buckley

Colorado

School	Address	City,State	Zip code	Telephone	Fax	Grade	Contact
Academy Charter S	1551 Prairie Hawk Dr	Castle Rock, CO	80109-7900	303-660-4881	660-6385	K-8	Kindra Nelson
Academy of Charter S	601 E 64th Ave	Denver, CO	80229-7030	303-289-8088	289-8087	K-12	Donna Davis
Academy of Urban Learning Charter S	1380 S Santa Fe Dr	Denver, CO	80223-3260	303-282-0900	282-0902	9-12	Mark Koester
Ace Community Challenge Charter S	948 Santa Fe Dr	Denver, CO	80204-3937	303-436-9588	436-0919	8-10	Eloy Chavez
Alta Vista Charter ES	8785 County Road LL	Lamar, CO	81052-9512	719-336-2154	336-0170	K-6	Talara Coen
American Academy	8600 Park Meadows Dr	Lonetree, CO	80124-2756	303-663-1543		K-6	Roberta Harrell
Aspen Community Charter S	PO Box 336	Woody Creek, CO	81656-0336	970-923-4080	923-7380	K-8	
Aurora Academy Charter S	10251 E 1st Ave	Aurora, CO	80010-4308	303-367-5983	367-5820	K-8	Stephen Garretson
Battle Rock Charter S	12247 Road G	Cortez, CO	81321-9571	970-565-3237	564-1140	K-8	Moqui Mustain-Fuey
Belle Creek Charter S	9290 E 107th Ave	Henderson, CO	80640-8964	303-468-0160	468-0164	K-12	Irene German
Blair Edison Charter S	4905 Cathay St	Denver, CO	80249-8376	303-371-9570	371-8348	K-8	Kathy Garvey
Boulder Prep Charter HS	PO Box 4249	Boulder, CO	80306-4249	303-545-6186	545-6187	9-12	Bruce Blodgett
Brighton Charter S	1931 E Bridge St	Brighton, CO	80601-1974	303-655-0773		7-12	Chris McCandless
Bromley East Charter S	356 Longspur Dr	Brighton, CO	80601-8700	303-685-3297		K-12	Bob Bair
Carbondale Community Charter S	PO Box 365	Carbondale, CO	81623-0365	970-923-4080	704-0501	K-8	Leslie Emerson
Carbon Valley Charter S	4040 Coriolis Way	Frederick, CO	80530	303-774-9555		PK-6	Chad Auer
Cardinal Community Academy	3101 Weld Co Rd 65	Keenesburg, CO	80643	303-732-9312	732-9314	K-6	Gary Wilson

School	Address	City,State	Zip code	Telephone	Fax	Grade	Contact
Challenges Choices & Images Charter S	1537 Alton St	Aurora, CO	80010-1712	303-341-7554	340-2404	K-12	Carolyn Jones
Challenge to Excellence Charter S	16995 E Carlson Dr	Parker, CO	80134	303-841-9816	840-3246	K-6	Nila Flippin
Chavez Academy	2500 W 18th St	Pueblo, CO	81003-1152	719-295-1623	295-1625	K-8	Dr. Lawrence Hernandez
Cherry Creek Charter Academy	6260 S Dayton St	Englewood, CO	80111-5203	303-779-8988	779-8817	K-8	Donna Fitzgerald
Cheyenne Mountain Charter Academy	1832 S Wahsatch Ave	Colorado Spgs, CO	80906-2341	719-471-1999	471-4949	K-8	
CIVA Charter S	225 S Union Blvd	Colorado Spgs, CO	80910-3184	719-633-1306	633-1691	9-11	Linda Page
Classical Academy Central	1655 Springcrest Rd	Colorado Spgs, CO	80920-1545	719-265-9766		K-5	Don Stump
Classical Academy East	8650 Scarborough Dr	Colorado Spgs, CO	80920-7532	719-282-1181		K-6	Mark Wertheimer
Classical Academy North	975 Stout Dr	Colorado Spgs, CO	80921	719-484-0081	484-0078	K-12	Peter Hilts
Cole College Prep Charter S	3240 Humboldt St	Denver, CO	80205-3934	303-293-2653	293-2666	7-8	Sidra Smith Wahaltere
Collegiate Academy of Colorado	8420 Sangre De Cristo Rd	Littleton, CO	80127-4201	303-972-7433	932-0695	K-12	William Eggers
Colorado Charter HS	1175 Osage St #100	Denver, CO	80204	303-892-8475	825-3011	10-12	Lori Deacon
Community Leadership Academy	6880 Holly St	Commerce City, CO	80022-2536	303-288-2711	288-2714	K-8	Ryan Stadler
Community Prep Charter S	332 E Willamette Ave	Colorado Spgs, CO	80903-1116	719-227-8836	227-8897	9-12	Vicki Leaf
Compass Montessori Charter S	10399 W 44th Ave	Wheat Ridge, CO	80033-2701	303-420-8288	420-0139	PK-6	Dirk Angevine
Compass Montessori Secondary S	4441 Salvia St	Golden, CO	80403-1698	303-271-1977	271-1984	7-12	Katie Myers
Connect Charter S	104 E 7th St	Pueblo, CO	81003-4109	719-542-0224	583-9799	6-8	Judy Mikulas
Core Knowledge Charter S	11661 N Pine Dr	Parker, CO	80138-8022	303-840-7070	840-9785	K-8	Teri Aplin
Crestone Charter S	PO Box 400	Crestone, CO	81131-0400	719-256-4907	256-4908	K-12	Reynold Bean
Crown Pointe Charter Academy	7281 Irving St	Westminster, CO	80030-4907	303-428-1882	428-1938	K-6	Barbara Ridenour
Da Vinci Academy	1335 Bridle Oaks Ln	Colorado Spgs, CO	80921-3621	719-234-5400	234-5499	K-5	Lew Davis
DCS Montessori Charter S	311 Castle Pines Pkwy	Castle Rock, CO	80108-8101	303-387-5625	387-5626	PK-6	Bill Zajic
Denver Arts & Technology Academy	3702 Tennyson St	Denver, CO	80212-1914	720-855-7504	855-7529	K-8	Christina Burton
Denver S of Science and Technology	2000 Valentia St	Denver, CO	80238-2785	303-320-5570	377-5101	9-10	Bill Kurtz
Eagle County Charter Academy	PO Box 169	Wolcott, CO	81655-0169	970-926-0656	926-0786	1-8	Jay Cerny
Elbert County Charter S	PO Box 1490	Elizabeth, CO	80107-1490	303-646-2636	646-2635	K-12	Merlin Holmes
Emerson-Edison Jr Academy	4220 E Pikes Peak Ave	Colorado Spgs, CO	80909-6728	719-570-7822	570-7824	6-8	Casey Tencick
EXCEL Academy	11500 W 84th Ave	Arvada, CO	80005-5272	303-467-2295	467-2291	K-8	Dr. Dennis Corash
EXCEL Charter S	215 E 12th St	Durango, CO	81301-5206	970-259-0203		6-12	Jule Scoglund
Flagstaff Charter S	1841 Left Hand Cir	Longmont, CO	80501-6795	303-651-7900		K-6	Kim Bloemen
Free Horizon Montessori S	1921 Youngfield St Ste 204	Golden, CO	80401-6302	303-231-9801	231-9983	PK-6	Dave Seitenbach
Frontier Academy Charter S	2560 W 29th St	Greeley, CO	80631-8507	970-330-1780	330-4334	K-6	Rebecca Dougherty
Frontier Academy Charter S	6530 W 16th St	Greeley, CO	80634-8675	970-339-9153		7-12	Harlan Ptomey
Frontier Charter Academy	PO Box 418	Calhan, CO	80808-0418	719-347-3156	347-3054	K-8	Bruce Delaney
GLOBE Charter S	2132 E Bijou St	Colorado Spgs, CO	80909-5904	719-630-0577	630-0395	K-12	Marty Caldwell
Guffey Community Charter S	PO Box 147	Guffey, CO	80820-0147	719-689-2093	689-3407	K-8	Pam Moore
Highline Academy	7808 Cherry Creek South Dr	Denver, CO	80231-3218	720-449-0317	449-0328	K-7	Alyssa Whitehead-Bust
Horizons Alternative S	4545 Sioux Dr	Boulder, CO	80303-3732	303-447-5580	499-9680	K-8	Ann Kane
Huerta Preparatory HS	2500 W 18th St	Pueblo, CO	81003-1152	719-583-1030	583-1031	9-12	Gloria Guerrero
Indian Peaks Charter S	PO Box 1819	Granby, CO	80446-1819	970-887-3805	887-3829	K-8	Polly Gallagher
Irwin Charter HS	5525 Astrozon Blvd	Colorado Spgs, CO	80916-4226	719-576-8055	576-8071	9-12	Kim Will
Irwin Charter MS	5525 Astrozon Blvd	Colorado Spgs, CO	80916-4226	719-591-2122	591-9993	6-8	Elizabeth Richard
Jefferson Academy	9955 Yarrow St	Broomfield, CO	80021-4048	303-887-1992		7-12	Tammy Stringari
Jefferson Academy	9955 Yarrow St	Broomfield, CO	80021-4048	303-438-1011	438-1046	K-6	Mike Munier
KIPP Sunshine Peak Academy	375 S Tejon St	Denver, CO	80223-1961	303-623-5772	623-0410	5-8	Richard Barrett
Knowledge Quest Academy	110 S Centennial Dr Ste B	Milliken, CO	80543	970-587-5742	587-5750	K-8	Brenda Jaynes
Lake George Charter S	PO Box 420	Lake George, CO	80827-0420	719-748-3911	748-8151	PK-6	Kay Lynn Waddell
Liberty Common S	1725 Sharp Point Dr	Fort Collins, CO	80525-4424	970-482-9800	482-8007	K-9	Russ Spicer
Life Skills Center	1810 Eastlake Blvd	Colorado Spgs, CO	80910-3422	719-471-0684	471-4392	K-12	Charles Holt
Life Skills Center of Denver	1000 Cherokee St	Denver, CO	80204-4039	720-889-2898	889-2897	9-12	Bob Arkfeld
Lincoln Charter Academy	6980 Pierce St	Arvada, CO	80003-3646	303-467-5363	467-5367	PK-6	Mary Ann Mahoney
Littleton Charter Academy	1200 W Mineral Ave	Littleton, CO	80120-4536	303-798-5252	798-0298	K-8	Jan Johnson-Pote
Littleton Prep Charter S	5151 S Federal Blvd	Littleton, CO	80123-2975	303-734-1995	734-3620	K-8	Susanne Johnson
Madison Charter Academy	660 Syracuse St	Colorado Spgs, CO	80911-2546	719-391-3977	391-5143	K-6	Sean Shields
Marble Charter S	412 W Main St	Marble, CO	81623-9396	970-963-9550	963-8435	K-10	Wendy Boland
Model Charter S	56729 Colorado Ave	Strasburg, CO	80136-7809	303-622-9211		1-6	Deborah Lemmer
Montessori Peaks Academy	9904 W Capri Ave	Littleton, CO	80123-3535	303-972-2627	933-4182	PK-6	Char Weaver
Monument Academy	1890 Willow Park Way	Monument, CO	80132-9041	719-481-1950	481-1948	K-12	Mike AuClaire
Mountain View Core Knowledge S	890 Field Ave	Canon City, CO	81212-9250	719-275-1980	275-1998	K-8	Manuel Calderson
New America S	550 Thornton Pkwy Unit 130	Thornton, CO	80229-2166	303-991-0130	991-0135	9-12	Paulette Schoeder
Northeast Academy	4895 Peoria St	Denver, CO	80239-2847	303-307-8837	307-8867	K-8	Naomi Bradford
North Routt Charter S	PO Box 1002	Steamboat Spr, CO	80428-1002	970-871-6062		K-7	Colleen Poole
Odyssey Charter S	8800 E 28th Ave	Denver, CO	80238-2627	303-316-3944	316-4016	K-8	Nelson Chase
Paradox Valley Charter S	PO Box 420	Paradox, CO	81429-0420	970-859-7236	859-7236	K-8	Renee Owen
Passage Charter S	703 S 9th St	Montrose, CO	81401-4409	970-249-8066	249-3497	7-12	
Peak to Peak Charter S	800 Merlin Dr	Lafayette, CO	80026-2146	303-453-4600	453-4613	K-12	Anthony Fontana
Pikes Peak S of Expeditionary Learning	5450 Meridian Rd	Peyton, CO	80831-7773	719-683-9544	683-3475	K-8	Don Knapp
Pinnacle Charter S	1001 W 84th Ave	Federal Heights, CO	80260-4717	303-450-3985	255-6305	K-12	Margaret Summers
Pioneer Charter S	3230 E 38th Ave	Denver, CO	80205-3726	720-424-4760	424-4785	PK-6	Dorothy Ward
Pioneer S for Expeditionary Learning	2745 Minnesota Dr	Fort Collins, CO	80525-4767	970-206-0714	206-0738	7-12	Celeste Di Lorio
Platte River Academy	4085 Lark Sparrow St	Highlands Ranch, CO	80126-5209	303-221-1070	221-1069	K-8	Gary Stueven
Prairie Creeks Charter S	PO Box 889	Strasburg, CO	80136-0889	303-622-6328	622-6327	9-12	Jeffrey Rasp
PS 1 Charter S	1062 Delaware St	Denver, CO	80204-4033	303-575-6690	575-6661	6-12	Liz Aybar
Pueblo S for the Arts & Sciences	1745 Acero Ave	Pueblo, CO	81004-2645	719-549-2737	549-2659	K-8	Cheryl Gomez
Renaissance Expeditionary S	16700 Keystone Blvd	Parker, CO	80134-3544	303-387-8000	387-8001	K-8	Leslie Chislett
Ridge View Academy	28101A E Quincy Ave	Watkins, CO	80137-9502	303-214-1139	766-2151	6-12	John Fry
Ridgeview Classical S	1800 S Lemay Ave	Fort Collins, CO	80525-1240	970-494-4620	494-4625	9-12	Dr. Terrence Moore
Rocky Mountain Deaf S	430 S Kipling St	Lakewood, CO	80226-2721	303-984-5741	984-7290	PK-5	Sharon Kellogg
Rocky Mtn. Academy of Evergreen	PO Box 3162	Evergreen, CO	80437-3162	303-670-1070	670-1253	K-8	Jere Pearcy
Roosevelt/Emerson Edison Charter S	205 Byron Dr	Colorado Spgs, CO	80910-2508	719-637-0311	380-0176	K-8	Precious Broadnax
Shivers Academy of Art - Science & Tech	2573 Airport Rd	Colorado Spgs, CO	80910-3119	719-473-6566	473-6601	9-12	Wanda Cousar
Skyland Community HS	3240 Humboldt St	Denver, CO	80205-3934	303-388-4759	388-2470	9-12	Allen Smith
Southwest Early College	3001 S Federal Blvd	Denver, CO	80236-2711	303-935-5473	935-5591	9-11	Chris Gerboth
Southwest Open Charter S	PO Box DD	Cortez, CO	81321-0870	970-565-1150	565-8770	9-12	Judy Hite
Stargate Charter S	3951 Cottonwood Lakes Blvd	Thornton, CO	80241-2187	303-450-3936	450-3941	K-8	Linda Ciccarelli
Summit MS	PO Box 3125	Boulder, CO	80307-3125	303-447-5529	499-0215	6-8	David Finelll
Swallows Charter Academy	278 S Mcculloch Blvd	Pueblo West, CO	81007-2844	719-547-1627	547-2509	K-8	Eva Chamberlin
21st Century Charter S	510 E Cimarron St	Colorado Spgs, CO	80903-4435	719-432-9255		K-8	Greg Cope
Twin Peaks Charter Academy	820 Main St	Longmont, CO	80501-8014	303-652-8201	774-9855	PK-8	Leslie Fluke
Union Colony Prep S	2000 Clubhouse Dr	Greeley, CO	80634-3643	970-348-2800	348-2830	8-12	Pat Gilliam
University Schools	6525 W 18th St	Greeley, CO	80634-8674	970-330-2221	506-7070	K-12	Greg Pierson
Ute Creek Secondary Academy	1198 Boston Ave	Longmont, CO	80501-5856	303-774-0066	774-8291	9-12	Jay Ritter
Vista Charter S	PO Box 10000	Montrose, CO	81402-9701	970-249-4470	249-1172	10-12	Coni Wilson
Wilson Academy	8300 W 94th Ave	Westminster, CO	80021-4590	303-431-3694	423-4388	K-8	Tim Matlick
Windsor Charter Academy	680 Academy Ct	Windsor, CO	80550-3101	970-674-5020	674-5017	K-8	Lyn Tausan
Wyatt-Edison Charter S	3620 Franklin St	Denver, CO	80205-3325	303-292-5515	292-5111	K-8	Kay Frunzi
Youth & Family Academy Charter S	1920 Valley Dr	Pueblo, CO	81008-1764	719-549-7653	549-7685	7-12	Darryl Vaughn

Connecticut

School	Address	City,State	Zip code	Telephone	Fax	Grade	Contact
Amistad Academy	407 James St	New Haven, CT	06513-3016	203-773-0390	773-0364	5-8	Matt Taylor
Breakthrough Charter S	121 Cornwall St	Hartford, CT	06112-1499	860-695-5700	722-6814	PK-8	Norma Neumann-Johnson
Bridge Academy	PO Box 2267	Bridgeport, CT	06608-0267	203-336-9999	336-9852	9-12	Timothy Dutton
Common Ground HS	358 Springside Ave	New Haven, CT	06515-1024	203-389-4333	389-7458	9-12	Oliver Barton
Elm City College Preparatory S	240 Greene St	New Haven, CT	06511-6934	203-498-0702	498-0712	K-6	Marc Michaelson
Explorations	71 Spencer St	Winsted, CT	06098-1134	860-738-9070	738-9092	10-12	Gail Srebnik
Highville Mustard Seed Charter S	130 Leeder Hill Dr	Hamden, CT	06517-2730	203-287-0528	287-0693	PK-8	Lyndon Pitter
Integrated Day Charter S	68 Thermos Ave	Norwich, CT	06360-6943	860-892-1900	892-1902	PK-8	Rosemarie Rose
Interdistrict S for Arts & Communication	190 Governor Winthrop Blvd	New London, CT	06320-6633	860-447-1003	447-0470	6-8	Ruth Cole-Chu
Jumoke Academy	250 Blue Hills Ave	Hartford, CT	06112-1836	860-527-0575	525-7758	K-6	Michael Sharpe
New Beginnings Family Academy	510 Barnum Ave	Bridgeport, CT	06608-2432	203-384-2897	384-2898	K-6	Tania Kelley
Odyssey Community S	579 W Middle Turnpike	Manchester, CT	06040	860-645-1234	533-0324	4-8	Elaine Stancliffe
Side by Side Community S	10 Chestnut St	Norwalk, CT	06854-2928	203-857-0306	838-2666	PK-8	Matthew Nittoly
Stamford Academy	229 North St	Stamford, CT	06901-1112	203-324-6300	324-6310	9-12	Michael McGuire
Trailblazers Academy	PO Box 359	Stamford, CT	06904-0359	203-977-5690	977-5688	6-8	Craig Baker

Delaware

School	Address	City,State	Zip code	Telephone	Fax	Grade	Contact
Academy of Dover Charter S	104 Saulsbury Rd	Dover, DE	19904-2705	302-674-0684	674-3894	K-6	Leonard Litzi
Campus Community HS	350 Pear St	Dover, DE	19904-3016	302-736-0403	736-5330	9-12	Allen Zipke
Campus Community S	21 N Bradford St	Dover, DE	19904-3101	302-736-3300	736-3390	1-8	Allen Zipke
Charter S of Wilmington	100 N DuPont Rd	Wilmington, DE	19807-3199	302-651-2727	652-1246	9-12	Ronald Russo
Delaware Military Academy	112 Middleboro Rd	Wilmington, DE	19804-1621	302-998-0745	998-3521	9-12	Charles Baldwin
East Side Charter S	3000 N Claymont St	Wilmington, DE	19802-2807	302-762-5834	762-3864	K-7	Will Robinson
Edison Charter S	2200 N Locust St	Wilmington, DE	19802-4429	302-778-1101	778-2232	K-8	Charles Hughes
Kuumba Academy Charter S	519 N Market St	Wilmington, DE	19801-3004	302-472-6450	472-6452	K-8	Catherine Sielski
Marion T. Academy Charter S	1121 Thatcher St	Wilmington, DE	19802-5135	302-575-1190	575-1425	K-8	John Taylor

School	Address	City,State	Zip code	Telephone	Fax	Grade	Contact
MOT Charter S	1156 Levels Rd	Middletown, DE	19709-9078	302-376-5125	376-5120	K-8	Linda Jennings
Newark Charter S	2001 Patriot Way	Newark, DE	19711-1809	302-369-2001	368-3460	5-8	Greg Meece
Positive Outcomes Charter S	193 S Dupont Hwy	Camden, DE	19934-1310	302-697-8805	697-8813	7-12	Edward Emmett
Providence Creek Academy Charter S	PO Box 265	Clayton, DE	19938-0265	302-653-6276	653-7850	K-8	Charles Taylor
Sussex Academy of Arts and Sciences	21777 Sussex Pines Rd	Georgetown, DE	19947-3901	302-856-3636	856-3376	6-8	Patricia Oliphant Ed.D.

District Of Columbia

School	Address	City,State	Zip code	Telephone	Fax	Grade	Contact
Angelou Charter S	1851 9th St NW	Washington, DC	20001-4133	202-939-9080	939-9084	9-12	Gail Williams
Arts & Technology Academy	5300 Blaine St NE	Washington, DC	20019-6665	202-398-6811	388-8467	K-6	Anthony D. Jackson
Associates for Renewal in Education	45 P St NW	Washington, DC	20001-1133	202-483-9424	667-5299	8-12	Patricia Barr
Business & Finance Academy	5500 Eads St NE	Washington, DC	20019-6720	202-724-4512		9-12	Virgil Smith
Capital City Public Charter S	3029 14th St NW	Washington, DC	20009-6820	202-387-0309	387-7074	K-8	Karen Dresden
Chavez Public Policy Charter HS	1346 Florida Ave NW	Washington, DC	20009-4838	202-387-6980	387-7808	9-12	Irasema Salcido
Childrens Studio Public Charter S	1301 V St NW	Washington, DC	20009-4413	202-387-5880			Franklin Wassmer
Community Academy Charter S	1300 Allison St NW	Washington, DC	20011-4441	202-723-4100		PK-9	Barbara Nophlin
DC Bilingual Public Charter S	1420 Columbia Rd NW	Washington, DC	20009-4779	202-332-4200		PK-5	Laurent Gosselin
DC Preparatory Academy	PO Box 11513	Washington, DC	20008-0713	202-882-2800	882-3800	4-5	Bill Kappenhagen
Eagle Academy Public Charter S	770 M St SE	Washington, DC	20003-3609	202-544-2646	544-0187	PK-K	Cassandra Pinkney
Edison-Friendship Charter S Blow-Pierce	725 19th St NE	Washington, DC	20002-4713	202-572-1070	399-6157	K-12	Glenda Washington
Friendship Charter S - Chamberlain	1345 Potomac Ave SE	Washington, DC	20003-4411	202-547-5800	547-4554	PK-5	John Panneli
Friendship-Edison Collegiate Academy	4095 Minnesota Ave NE	Washington, DC	20019-3541	202-396-5500	396-8229	9-12	Linette Adams
Friendship Public Charter S - Woodridge	2959 Carlton Ave NE	Washington, DC	20018-2615	202-635-6500	635-6481	PK-6	Tenina Fleming
Haynes Public Charter S	3029 14th St NW	Washington, DC	20009-6820	202-667-4446	667-8811	PK-2	Jennifer Niles
Health & Human Services Academy	1700 E Capitol St NE	Washington, DC	20003-1622	202-698-4571		9-12	Faye Dixon
Hyde Leadership Public Charter S	101 T St NE	Washington, DC	20002-1519	202-529-4400			Don MacMillan
IDEA Academy	1027 45th St NE	Washington, DC	20019-3802	202-399-4750			Norman Johnson
Ideal Academy Charter S	100 Peabody St NW	Washington, DC	20011-2212	202-726-0313		PK-6	Paulette Bell-Imani
Jordan Public Charter S	100 Peabody St NW	Washington, DC	20011-2212	202-554-0922			Richard Rogers
JOS-ARZ Academy Public Charter S	220 Taylor St NE	Washington, DC	20017-1009	202-269-6004	269-6005	9-12	Marlind Boxley
Kamit Institute Magnificent Achievers	5922 Georgia Ave NW	Washington, DC	20011-5120	202-723-7886			Adsimbo Myers
KIPP DC/KEY Academy	770 M St SE	Washington, DC	20003-3609	202-543-6595	543-6594	5-6	Susan Schaeffler
Marriott Public Hospitality S	410 8th St NW	Washington, DC	20004-2103	202-737-9122	737-7363	9-12	Lorraine Gibbs
Meridian Public Charter S	1328 Florida Ave NW	Washington, DC	20009-4824	202-387-9830	387-7605	PK-5	Robinette Breedlove
Milburn Public Charter Alt. HS	100 Peabody St NW	Washington, DC	20011-2212	202-829-7045		9-12	Richard Johnson
Milburn Public Charter Alt. HS	1027 45th St NE	Washington, DC	20019-3802	202-397-8010		9-12	Dr. Thomas Simpson
New S for Enterprise & Development	1920 Bladensburg Rd NE	Washington, DC	20002-1812	202-526-0161	526-8349	9-12	Vivian Carson
Next Step Public Charter S	1419 Columbia Rd NW	Washington, DC	20009-4705	202-319-2249		9-12	Linda Ohmans
Options Public Charter S	1375 E St NE	Washington, DC	20002-5436	202-547-1028			Glenn Swanson
Pre-Engineering SWSC	1301 New Jersey Ave NW	Washington, DC	20001-1227	202-673-7233		9-12	Gertrude Turner Wills
Roots Public Charter S	115 Kennedy St NW	Washington, DC	20011-5260	202-882-8073		K-8	Dr. Bernida Thompson
Rosario International Public Charter S	1724 Kalorama Rd NW Ste 300	Washington, DC	20009-2694	202-234-6522		10-12	Sonia Gutierrez
SABIS International Charter S	3022 Chestnut St NW	Washington, DC	20015-1408	202-363-1118		K-12	Louis Steadwell
Sasha Bruce Public Charter S	745 8th St SE	Washington, DC	20003-2802	202-675-9354	675-0225	6-12	Harold Thomas
School for Arts in Learning	1100 16th St NW	Washington, DC	20036-4802	202-261-0200		K-6	Kim Morton
SEED Public Charter S	4300 C St SE	Washington, DC	20019-4100	202-248-7773	248-3021	7-12	Dr. Richard Jung
Southeast Academy of Excellence	645 Milwaukee Pl SE	Washington, DC	20032-2606	202-562-1980	562-6380	K-8	Nadia Casseus
Stokes Community Freedom Charter S	1525 Newton St NW	Washington, DC	20010-3103	202-265-7293		K-5	Patricia Crain deGalarce
Techworld Public Charter S	401 M St SW #2718	Washington, DC	20024-2610	202-488-1845		9-9	Daanen Strachan
Tree of Life Community Charter S	800 3rd St NE	Washington, DC	20002-4314	202-543-3682	543-3754	PK-5	Cheryll James
Tri-Community Charter S	3700 W Capitol St NW	Washington, DC	20011	202-882-1930		K-12	Gladys Morgan
Two Rivers Public Charter S	1150 5th St SE	Washington, DC	20003-3485	202-546-4477		PK-3	Jessica Wodatch
Urban Family Institute	1300 Allison St NW	Washington, DC	20011-4441	202-234-5437		K-10	Kent Amos
Washington Charter S for Technical Arts	1346 Florida Ave NW	Washington, DC	20009-4838	202-232-6090		11-12	Kenneth Green
Washington MST Public Charter HS	770 M St SE	Washington, DC	20003-3609	202-488-1996	543-6068	9-12	Floyd Gilmore
Washington Very Special Arts Charter S	1100 16th St NW	Washington, DC	20036-4802	202-296-9100	261-0200	PK-2	Lawrence Ricco
World Charter S of Washington	595 1/2 3rd St NW	Washington, DC	20001-2703	202-269-4800		PK-K	Dorothy Goodman
WVSA Auto Arts Academy Public Charter S	1100 16th St NW	Washington, DC	20036-4802	202-296-9100		9-10	Curtiss Brazil

Florida

School	Address	City,State	Zip code	Telephone	Fax	Grade	Contact
Academy at the Farm	9500 Alex Lange Way	Dade City, FL	33525-8213	352-588-9737	588-0508	K-8	Dr. Michael Rom
Academy Da Vinci	1380 Pinehurst Rd	Dunedin, FL	34698-5407	727-298-2778	298-2780	K-5	Dawn Dolden
Academy for International Studies	757 Lighthouse Dr	No Palm Beach, FL	33408-4741	561-776-1130	776-0975	6-6	Kendall Artusi
Academy for Positive Learning Charter S	128 N C St	Lake Worth, FL	33460-3232	561-585-6104	585-7849	K-8	Renatta Adan-Espinoza
Academy of Arts & Minds	3138 Commodore Plz	Miami, FL	33133-5814	305-448-1100	448-9737	9-12	Alex Tamargo
Academy of Environmental Science	12695 W Fort Island Trl	Crystal River, FL	34429-5290	352-795-8793	794-0065	10-12	
ACE Charter S	710 E Bella Vista St	Lakeland, FL	33805-3009	863-686-3189	682-1348	PK-PK	Susan Snover
Achievement Academy - Bartow	695 E Summerlin St	Bartow, FL	33830-4848	863-533-0690	534-0798	PK-PK	Paula Sullivan
Achievement Academy - Lakeland	716 E Bella Vista St	Lakeland, FL	33805-3009	863-683-6504	688-9292	PK-PK	Paula Sullivan
Achievement Academy - Winter Haven	2221 28th St NW	Winter Haven, FL	33881-1807	863-965-7586	968-5016	PK-PK	Paula Sullivan
Advanced Technology Center	1770 Technology Blvd	Daytona Beach, FL	32117-7149	386-226-4100	226-4191	11-12	Dr. Michelle McCraney
Alachua Learning Center	PO Box 1389	Alachua, FL	32616-1389	386-418-2080	418-4116	1-8	Tom Allin
Alee Academy Charter S	755 S Central Ave	Umatilla, FL	32784-9504	352-669-1280	669-1282	9-12	Jennings Neeld
Anderson Academy	2708 N Central Ave	Tampa, FL	33602-1602	813-273-6767	225-1639	K-5	Jeanette Anderson
Apalachicola Bay Charter S	350 Fred Meyer St	Apalachicola, FL	32320-1631	850-653-1222	653-1857	K-7	Don Hungerford
APPLE S	3425 New Jersey Rd	Lakeland, FL	33803-4225	863-619-7170	644-5882	K-8	Beth Nave
Archimedean Academy	12425 SW 72nd St	Miami, FL	33183-2513	305-640-6278	993-1328	K-2	Pat Booth
Archimedean Middle Conservatory	12425 SW 72nd St	Miami, FL	33183-2513	305-640-6278	993-1328	6-8	Vasiliki Moysidis
ASPIRA De Hostos Charter S	1910 NE Miami Ct	Miami, FL	33132-1027	305-576-1512		6-8	Fernando Lopez
ASPIRA South Youth Leadership	14112 SW 288th St	Leisure City, FL	33033-1864	305-246-1111	246-1433	6-9	Kevin Moore
ASPIRA Youth Leadership	13300 Memorial Hwy	North Miami, FL	33161-3940	305-893-8050	891-6055	6-8	Iliana Pena
Athenian Academy	2817 Saint Marks Dr	Dunedin, FL	34698-1920	727-298-2718	298-2719	K-5	Lemonia Poumakis
Aventura Charter ES	3333 NE 188th St	Aventura, FL	33180-2933	305-466-1499	466-1339	K-5	Dr. Katherine Murphy
Balere Language Academy	10600 Caribbean Blvd	Miami, FL	33189-1361	305-232-9797	232-4535	K-8	Rocka Malik
Bay Haven Charter Academy	2501 Hawks Landing Blvd	Panama City, FL	32405-6658	850-248-3500	248-3514	K-8	Dr. Tim Kitts
Bellalago Charter Academy	3651 Pleasant Hill Rd	Kissimmee, FL	34746-2935	407-933-1690	933-2143	K-12	Cecile Diez
Berkley Accelerated MS	300 Main St	Auburndale, FL	33823-4102	863-968-0904		6-6	Jill Bolender
Beulah Academy	5805 Beulah Church Rd	Pensacola, FL	32526-4222	850-944-2822		6-8	Sherry Bailey
Big Pine Key Neighborhood S	PO Box 432131	Big Pine Key, FL	33043-2131	305-872-1266	872-1265	PK-3	
Boca Raton Charter S	1295 NE 4th Ct	Boca Raton, FL	33432-2811	561-394-9483	394-9366	K-3	Deborah Nash-Utterback
Bonita Springs Charter S	25380 Bernwood Dr	Bonita Springs, FL	34135-7850	239-992-6932	992-7359	K-8	Pam Franco
Bradenton Charter S	2615 26th St W	Holmes Beach, FL	34217	941-739-6100	752-3250	3-8	Richard Donnelly
Bright Futures International	757 Lighthouse Dr	No Palm Beach, FL	33408-4741	561-776-1130	776-0975	K-5	Nicole Bret-Grant
Broward Community Charter S	201 N University Dr	Coral Springs, FL	33071-7323	954-341-0082	341-0024	K-5	John Drag
Byrneville Charter S	1600 Byrneville Rd	Century, FL	32535-3640	850-256-6350	256-6357	K-5	Dee Wolfe-Sullivan
Campus Charter S	3805 Curtis Blvd	Cocoa, FL	32927-3942	321-633-8234	633-8234	K-4	Richard Dunkel
Canoe Creek Charter S	3600 Canoe Creek Rd	Saint Cloud, FL	34772-9132	407-891-7320	891-7730	PK-8	Barbara Hernandez
Cape Coral Charter S	6851 Lancer Ave	Fort Myers, FL	33912-4334	239-995-0904		K-8	Beth Hanlon
Capstone Academy	4901 W Fairfield Dr	Pensacola, FL	32506-4111	850-455-7754		K-5	Charles Thomas
Caring & Sharing Charter S	PO Box 5936	Gainesville, FL	32627-5936	352-372-1004	372-0894	K-5	Dr. Simon Johnson
Central Charter S	4525 N State Rd 7	Fort Lauderdale, FL	33319	954-735-6295	735-6232	K-6	Tracy Nessl
Central City Academy	3916 E Hillsborough Ave	Tampa, FL	33610-4542	813-239-9827	239-9268	K-5	Wayne Quin
Central FL Speech & Hearing Charter S	710 E Bella Vista St	Lakeland, FL	33805-3009	863-686-3189	682-1348	PK-PK	Sue Snover
Chancellor Charter S	1395 S State Rd 7	N Lauderdale, FL	33068-4023	954-973-8900	974-5588	K-8	LaMarr Moses
Chancellor Charter S at Lantana	600 S East Coast Ave	Lantana, FL	33462-4577	561-585-1189	585-1166	K-5	Laurie Plotnick
Chancellor Charter S / Imagine S	2500 Glades Cir	Weston, FL	33327-2253	954-659-3600	659-3620	K-5	Susan Messing
Charter S at National Deaf Academy	19650 US Highway 441	Mount Dora, FL	32757-6959	352-735-9500	735-4939	PK-12	Rebecca Hilding
Charter S at Waterstone	855 Waterstone Way	Homestead, FL	33033-5941	305-248-6206	248-6208	K-8	Cristina Cruz
Charter S Institute Annex	5420 N State Rd 7	Fort Lauderdale, FL	33319	954-486-1640	486-4549	K-6	Roberto Porrata Doria
Charter S Institute Training	520 NW 5th St	Hallandale, FL	33009-3314	954-454-5348	454-2463	K-6	Sheila Bassoff
Charter S of Boynton Beach	801 N Congress Ave Ste 483	Boynton Beach, FL	33426-3365	561-738-2380	738-2378	K-5	Pam Owens
Charter S of Excellence	1217 SE 3rd Ave	Fort Lauderdale, FL	33316-1905	954-522-2997	522-3159	K-6	Terri Schneiderman
Chautauqua Learn & Serve Charter S	2731 E 3rd St Ste 1	Springfield, FL	32401-5442	850-785-5056	785-5056		Cynthia McCauley
Chiles Academy	1250 Reed Canal Rd Ste A	Port Orange, FL	32129-9106	386-322-6102		6-12	Anne Ferguson
Choices in Learning Charter S	893 E State Road 434	Longwood, FL	32750-5306	407-331-8477	331-5075	K-6	Shannon McCutcheon
City of Pembroke Pines ES - Central	12350 Sheridan St	Pembroke Pines, FL	33026-3813	954-322-3330	322-3383	K-5	Kenneth Bass
City of Pembroke Pines MS - Central	12350 Sheridan St	Pembroke Pines, FL	33026-3813	954-322-3300	322-3383	6-8	Kenneth Bass
COAST Charter S	48 Shell Island Rd	Saint Marks, FL	32355	850-925-6344	925-6396	K-8	Susan Flournoy
Collegiate HS	100 College Blvd E	Niceville, FL	32578-1347	850-678-5111	729-4950	10-12	Charla Cotton
Community Learning Center West	336 E Highbanks Rd	De Bary, FL	32713-2604	386-775-5285			Jennifer Heneghan
Compass Middle Charter S	550 E Clower St	Bartow, FL	33830-6403	863-519-8701	519-8704	6-8	Harry Williams
Coral Reef Montessori Academy	10853 SW 216th St	Miami, FL	33170-3146	305-255-0064		K-7	Juliet King
Coral Springs Charter S	3205 N University Dr	Coral Springs, FL	33065-4115	954-340-4100	340-4111	6-12	Billie Miller
Corebridge Educational Academy	7887 N Federal Hwy	Boca Raton, FL	33487-1640	561-826-0008	826-0009	K-8	Dianne Tetreault
Countryside Montessori Academy	5906 Ehren Cutoff	Land O Lakes, FL	34639-3430	813-996-0991	996-0993	1-6	Jean Audino
Crossroad Academy Charter S	635 Strong Rd	Quincy, FL	32351-4257	850-875-9626	875-1403	K-8	Millie Forehand

School	Address	City,State	Zip code	Telephone	Fax	Grade	Contact
Dayspring Academy ES	8911 Timber Oaks Ave	Port Richey, FL	34668-2426	727-862-8600	868-5175	K-5	Suzanne Chase
Dayspring Academy MS	9509 Palm Ave	Port Richey, FL	34668-4647	727-847-9003	848-8774	6-8	Suzanne Chase
DayStar Academy of Excellence	970 N Seacrest Blvd	Boynton Beach, FL	33435-4702	561-369-2323	369-2642	K-5	Doris Bennett
Delray Beach Academy	PO Box 1388	Boynton Beach, FL	33425-1388	561-736-8828		6-8	Joe Green
Delray Youth Vocational Charter S	2401 N Federal Hwy	Delray Beach, FL	33483-6132	561-330-6882		9-12	Daniel Silvey
DeSoto HS	PO Box 358604	Gainesville, FL	32635-8604	352-745-6890		9-12	Mary Malo
Discovery Academy at Lake Alfred	1000 N Buena Vista Dr	Lake Alfred, FL	33850-2031	863-295-5955	295-5978	6-8	Carol Fulks
Doctors Charter S of Miami Shores	11301 NW 5th Ave	Miami Shores, FL	33168-3343	305-754-2381	754-9928	6-12	Maggie Manrara
Doral Academy	2450 NW 97th Ave	Miami, FL	33172-2308	305-597-9999	591-2669	K-5	Ileana Gomez
Doral Academy HS	11100 NW 27th St	Miami, FL	33172-5001	305-597-9950	477-6762	9-12	Frank Jimenez
Doral Academy MS	2601 NW 112th Ave	Miami, FL	33172-1804	305-591-0020	591-9251	6-8	Jose Baca
Doral Performing Arts Academy	2601 NW 112th Ave	Miami, FL	33172-1804	305-591-0020	591-9251	9-12	Ofelia Alvarez
Downtown Academy of Tech & Arts	101 SE 3rd Ave	Fort Lauderdale, FL	33301-1920	954-767-0403	767-1011	6-8	Jim DiSebastian
Downtown Miami Charter S	305 NW 3rd St	Miami, FL	33128-1601	305-579-2112	579-2115	K-5	Terry Maus
Eagle Academy	3020 NW 33rd Ave	Laud Lakes, FL	33311-1106	954-343-9960	343-9970	6-8	Dewanda Chambers
Eagles Nest ES	1840 NE 41st St	Pompano Beach, FL	33064-6071	954-942-3318	942-3179	K-5	John Grant
Eagles Nest MS	1840 NE 41st St	Pompano Beach, FL	33064-6071	954-942-3318	942-3179	6-8	John Grant
Early Beginnings Academy-Civic Center	1411 NW 14th Ave	Miami, FL	33125-1616	305-325-1080	325-1044	PK-K	Carol Byrd
Early Beginnings Academy-North Shore	985 NW 91st St	Miami, FL	33150-2350	305-835-9006	696-1688	PK-K	Carol Byrd
Early Beginnings West	7676 Davie Road Ext	Hollywood, FL	33024-2624	954-584-7178	315-4099	PK-K	Ana Pardo
Easter Seals Charter S	1219 Dunn Ave	Daytona Beach, FL	32114-2405	386-255-4568		PK-K	Ruthann Jacobson
Educational Horizons Charter S	1281 S Wickham Rd	West Melbourne, FL	32904-2450	321-729-0786	951-8005	1-5	Aileen Tapp
Ed Venture Charter S	117 E Coast Ave	Lantana, FL	33462-5316	561-582-1454	582-0692	10-12	Laura Levin Mardyks Ed.D.
Einstein Montessori Charter S	5650 King St	Cocoa, FL	32926-2351	321-631-9876	631-8009	3-8	Richard Murphy
Einstein Montessori S	5930 SW Archer Rd	Gainesville, FL	32608-4702	352-335-4321	335-1575	2-8	Zach Osbrach
Escambia Charter S	PO Box 1147	Gonzalez, FL	32560-1147	850-937-0500	968-5605	9-12	Stan Callender
Everglades Preparatory Academy	183 S Lake Ave	Pahokee, FL	33476-1803	561-924-3002	924-3013	9-12	Antoine Russell
Explorer S	475 S John Rodes Blvd	West Melbourne, FL	32904-1093	321-733-1917	733-0748	K-8	Ruben Rosario
Expressions Learning Arts Academy	5408 SW 13th St	Gainesville, FL	32608-5038	352-373-5223	373-6327	K-5	Cheryl Valantis
First Coast Technical Institute	2980 Collins Ave	Saint Augustine, FL	32084-1919	904-824-4401	824-6750		Chris Cothron
Florida Intercultural Academy	1704 Buchanan St	Hollywood, FL	33020-4030	954-924-8006		K-5	Dr. Gwendolyn Purcell
Florida International Academy	7630 Biscayne Blvd	Miami, FL	33138-5136	305-758-6912	758-6985	6-8	Sonia Mitchell
Florida SIA Tech at Gainesville	5301 NE 40th Ter	Gainesville, FL	32609-1670	352-371-4424	371-4426	9-12	Tina Bullock
Foundation Middle Academy	2426 Remington Blvd	Kissimmee, FL	34744-8467	407-697-1020	697-1021	6-8	Diane Beatty
Foundation S	1325 George Jenkins Blvd	Lakeland, FL	33815-1367	863-682-8111	687-8205	6-12	Emory Welch
Four Corners Charter S	9100 Teacher Ln	Davenport, FL	33897-6212	407-787-4300	787-4301	PK-8	Dr. Walter Thomas
Gainer S	4000 W Fairfield Dr	Pensacola, FL	32505-4733	850-439-3888	439-3898	9-12	Dr. Ulysees Hughes
Gallagher Neighborhood S	3300 Schoolhouse Rd	Saint Cloud, FL	34773-6009	407-957-3570	957-6023	K-8	
Gateway Charter HS	12770 Gateway Blvd	Fort Myers, FL	33913-8654	239-768-3350		9-12	Dr. Jennifer Cheal
Gateway Charter S	12850 Commonwealth Dr	Fort Myers, FL	33913-8039	239-768-5048	768-5710	K-8	Dr. Deborah Nauss
Genesis Preparatory S	207 NW 23rd Ave	Gainesville, FL	32609-3604	352-379-1188	379-1142	K-3	Charmaine Henry
Gibson Charter S	3634 Grand Ave	Miami, FL	33133-4953	305-648-3126	669-4390	PK-8	Charles Bethel
Glades Academy	1200 E Main St	Pahokee, FL	33476-1102	561-924-9402	924-9279	K-5	Terry Gitler
Good Schools for all Leadership Academy	40 NW 4th Ave	Delray Beach, FL	33444-2626	561-278-3533	278-3633	K-8	Valarie Thompson
G-STAR School of the Arts	2065 Prairie Rd	West Palm Beach, FL	33406-7718	561-967-2023	963-8975	9-10	Reno Boffice
Guided Path Academy	1199 Lantana Rd	Lantana, FL	33462-1514	561-588-2800	588-0870	K-5	Evelyn Francis
Gulfstream Goodwill Career Academy	269 NE 14th St	Boca Raton, FL	33432-1821	561-367-1067	367-1372	9-12	Bob Fishbein
Gulfstream Goodwill LIFE Academy	3800 S Congress Ave Ste 12	Boynton Beach, FL	33426-8424	561-259-1000	259-1004	9-12	June Cole
Gulfstream Goodwill Transition Academy	1715 E Tiffany Dr	West Palm Beach, FL	33407-3224	561-312-0072	848-0346	9-12	Gloria Zimmerman
Haines City Literacy Learning Academy	2800 Hornet Dr	Haines City, FL	33844-6003	863-421-3281		9-12	Deborah Elmore
Harris Pyramid S of Learning	PO Box 2881	Pensacola, FL	32513-2881	850-432-2273	432-4624	K-5	Celestine Lewis
Hartridge Academy	1400 US Highway 92	Winter Haven, FL	33881-8137	863-956-4434	956-3267	K-5	Debra Richards
Healthy Learning Academy	2101 NW 39th Ave	Gainesville, FL	32609	352-372-2573		K-2	Bettianne Ford
Hoggetowne MS	3930 NE 15th St	Gainesville, FL	32609-2007	352-367-4369	376-3345	6-8	Kristine Santos
Hollywood Academy of Arts & Science	1720 Harrison St	Hollywood, FL	33020-6829	954-925-6404	925-8123	K-5	Leslie Brown
Hope Charter S	1450 Daniels Rd	Winter Garden, FL	34787-4376	407-656-4673	656-6094	K-6	Crystal Yoakum
Hope Preparatory Academy	3916 E Hillsborough Ave	Tampa, FL	33610-4542	813-236-1755	232-9680	K-5	JoAnn Shaw
IMAGINE S	2580 Metrocentre Blvd	West Palm Beach, FL	33407-3100	561-683-6200	683-7783	K-5	Alphonso Milligan
Immokalee Charter S	402 W Main St	Immokalee, FL	34142-3933	239-658-3560		K-4	Maria Jimenez
Indian River Charter HS	6055 College Ln	Vero Beach, FL	32966-1093	772-567-6600	567-2288	9-12	Cynthia Aversa
International Studies Charter HS	450 SW 4th St	Miami, FL	33130-1410	305-326-7047	326-7041	9-12	Ana Alvarez-Arimon
Island S	PO Box 1090	Boca Grande, FL	33921-1090	941-964-8016	964-8017	K-5	Beverly Sutton
Island Village Montessori S	2001 Pinebrook Rd	Venice, FL	34292-1560	941-484-4999	484-2150	K-5	Kym Elder
Jackson Preparatory S	546 Mary Esther Cut Off NW	Ft Walton Bch, FL	32548-4021	850-833-3321	833-3292	PK-8	Dr. Samantha Dawson
JFK Charter S	6216 S Congress Ave	Lantana, FL	33462-2322	561-649-8195		K-5	Lois Biddix
Keys Gate Charter S	2000 SE 28th Ave	Homestead, FL	33035-2102	305-230-1616		K-8	Christine Valadez
Kids Community College	10544 Lake St Charles Blvd	Riverview, FL	33569	813-671-1440	671-1245	K-2	Inga Taylor
King Academy	4180 NE 15th St	Gainesville, FL	32609-2011	352-376-4014	376-3345	1-5	Naomi Williams
Kissimmee Charter Academy	2850 Bill Beck Blvd	Kissimmee, FL	34744-4073	407-847-1400	847-1401	PK-6	Jo Ann Kandrac
Lake Eola Charter S	135 N Magnolia Ave	Orlando, FL	32801-2301	407-246-0900	246-6334	K-8	Ronnie Denoia
Lakeland Montessori Schoolhouse	PO Box 7521	Lakeland, FL	33807-7521	863-413-0003	413-0006	PK-5	Josie Zinninger
Lakeside Academy	710 S Main St	Belle Glade, FL	33430-4202	561-993-5000	993-5001	K-5	Barbara Litinski
Language Academy	4125 US Highway 19	New Port Richey, FL	34652-5948	727-847-9300	847-9315	4-8	Joyce Nunn
Lawrence Academy	777 W Palm Dr	Florida City, FL	33034-3223	305-247-4800	247-4895	6-8	Dr. Samuel Stinson
Leadership Academy West	2030 S Congress Ave	West Palm Beach, FL	33406-7602	561-434-0996	434-0575	K-12	Lois Layman
Learning Academy	2312 N Stewart St	Milton, FL	32570	850-983-3495	983-8098	6-12	Chad White
Learning Gate Charter S	16215 Hanna Rd	Lutz, FL	33549-5701	813-948-4190	948-7587	K-7	Patricia Girard
Lee Charter Academy	2438 2nd St	Fort Myers, FL	33901-3044	239-332-1067		K-8	Dr. Shirley Chapman
Liberty City Charter S	8700 NW 5th Ave	Miami, FL	33150-2407	305-751-2700	751-1316	K-6	Katrina Wilson-Davis
LIFE Academy	940D Tarpon St	Fort Myers, FL	33916-1139	239-334-4434		9-12	Lynn Pottorf
Life Skills	6000 N Federal Hwy	Fort Lauderdale, FL	33308-2226	954-764-1665	764-1655	9-12	Laurel Moorehead
Life Skills Center	407 E Memorial Blvd	Lakeland, FL	33801-1768	863-224-5543		9-12	Viesta Skipper
Life Skills Center	4901 Central Ave	St Petersburg, FL	33710-8239	727-322-1758		9-12	Bonnie Solinsky
Life Skills Center Miami-Dade County	3535 NW 7th St	Miami, FL	33125-4015	305-643-9111	643-9141	9-12	Jose Filpo
Life Skills Center of Palm Beach County	7000 W Camino Real	Boca Raton, FL	33433-5532	561-447-8240	447-8244	9-12	Barbara Kiddle
Life Skills S	4010 N Nebraska Ave	Tampa, FL	33603-4324	813-314-2154		9-12	Nicole Williams
Literacy/Leadership Technology Academy	6771 Madison Ave	Tampa, FL	33619-6836	813-793-3035	793-3043	6-8	Curt Miller
Littles Charter S	5829 Corporate Way Flr 2	West Palm Beach, FL	33407-2017	561-689-9970	682-1342	K-8	Amefika Geuka
Love to Learn Education Center	125 NW 23rd Ave Ste 3	Gainesville, FL	32609-3681	352-381-1900	381-8080	1-5	Dr. Lavetta Palmer
Manatee County Juvenile Justice	14470 Harllee Rd	Bradenton, FL	34205	941-747-3011	714-7333	9-12	Harry Reif
Manatee S for the Arts	700 Haben Blvd	Palmetto, FL	34221-4173	941-721-6800	721-6805	6-12	Bill Jones
Manatee S of Arts/Science	3700 32nd St W	Bradenton, FL	34205-2708	941-755-5012	755-7934	PK-5	Miriam Jolly
Marco Island Charter MS	1401 Trinidad Ave	Marco Island, FL	34145-3949	239-389-4818	389-4921	6-8	George Abounder
Marion Charter S	39 Cedar Rd	Ocala, FL	34472-8331	352-687-2100	687-2700	K-5	Gina Evers
Mater Academy	7700 NW 98th St	Hialeah Gardens, FL	33016-2403	305-698-9900	698-3822	K-8	Kim Guilarte
Mater Academy Charter HS	7901 NW 103rd St	Hialeah Gardens, FL	33016-2419	305-828-1886	828-6175	9-10	Judith Marty
Mater Academy Charter MS	7901 NW 103rd St	Hialeah Gardens, FL	33016-2419	305-828-1886	828-6175	6-8	Rene Rovirosa
Mater Academy East Charter S	450 SW 4th St	Miami, FL	33130-1410	305-324-4667	324-6580	K-5	Ana Valdes
Mater Performing Arts Academy	7901 NW 103rd St	Hialeah Gardens, FL	33016-2419	305-828-1886	828-6175	9-12	Christine McGuinn
Mc Intosh Area Charter S	PO Box 769	Mc Intosh, FL	32664-0769	352-591-9797	591-9747	K-2	Shirley Lane
McKeel Academy of Applied Tech	1810 W Parker St	Lakeland, FL	33815-1243	863-499-2818	284-4383	6-12	Harold Maready
McKeel ES	411 N Florida Ave	Lakeland, FL	33801-4803	863-499-1287	688-1607	K-5	Judith Morris
MESTA Charter S	PO Box 580038	Orlando, FL	32858-0038	407-298-6378		6-8	Elaine Morris
Metropolitan Ministries Charter S	2002 N Florida Ave	Tampa, FL	33602-2204	813-209-1003	209-1234	K-5	Bonnie Guertin
Miami Childrens Museum Charter S	980 MacArthur Cswy	Miami, FL	33132-1604	305-329-3758	329-3767	K-5	Maria Greer
Miami Community Charter S	101 SW Redland Rd	Florida City, FL	33034	305-245-2552	245-2527	K-5	Jila Rezaie
Micanopy Area Cooperative S	PO Box 386	Micanopy, FL	32667-0386	352-466-0990	466-4090	K-5	Carl Landry
Micanopy MS	PO Box 109	Micanopy, FL	32667-0109	352-466-1090	466-1030	6-8	Dr. Edward Daleuski
Milburn Academy	2400 S Ridgewood Ave Ste 20	South Daytona, FL	32119-3073	386-304-0086		9-12	Sam Smith
Milburn Academy	7545 Little Rd	New Port Richey, FL	34654-5522	727-859-9323	859-0834	9-12	Ramon Suarez
Milburn Academy	1404 Tech Blvd	Tampa, FL	33619-7865	813-627-9887	627-9871	9-12	Krista Morton
Milburn Academy	2207 Industrial Blvd	Sarasota, FL	34234-3119	941-355-0835	953-9014	9-12	Melanie Dunham
Milburn Academy	3830 Evans Ave	Fort Myers, FL	33901-9363	239-278-4774	278-0470	9-12	Patricia Lightner
Milburn Academy	6210 17th Ave W	Bradenton, FL	34209-7838	941-761-4393	761-2992	9-12	Edna Bailey
Milestones Community S	31600 Camp Challenge Rd	Sorrento, FL	32776-9558	352-385-0390	383-0744	K-8	Karen Gray
Minneola ES	300 E Pearl St	Minneola, FL	34715-9001	352-394-2600	394-2079	PK-5	Sandra Reaves
Montessori Academy Northern Palm Beach	9482 MacArthur Blvd	Palm Bch Gdns, FL	33403-1102	561-906-0024	625-4836	K-5	Virginia Smith
Montessori Academy of Early Enrichment	2929 10th Ave N Ste 108	Lake Worth, FL	33461-3005	561-649-0004	649-0964	K-12	Jean Ranck
Montessori Charter ES	1127 United St	Key West, FL	33040-3330	305-294-4910	294-1404	1-5	Lynn Barras
Montessori Island Charter S	92295 Old State Rd	Tavernier, FL	33070	305-852-3482	852-2432	K-5	Kelly Astin
Mount Pleasant Standard Base MS	PO Box 4729	Tampa, FL	33677-4729	813-253-0053	253-0182	6-8	Pocahontas Davis
Nap Ford Community Charter S	648 W Livingston St	Orlando, FL	32801-1418	407-245-8711	245-8712	K-3	Jeraldine Perkins
New Dimensions HS	4900 Pleasant Hill Rd	Kissimmee, FL	34759	407-870-9949	870-8976	9-12	Jacqueline Dodge
New Hope Charter S	108 NW 3rd Ave	Chiefland, FL	32626-0841	352-490-6690	490-5288	9-10	Kim Martin
Noahs Ark International Charter S	21 W 22nd St	Riviera Beach, FL	33404-5509	561-848-7575	844-9563	K-5	Clifford Durden
North Broward Academy of Excellence	957 SW 71st Ave	N Lauderdale, FL	33068-2313	954-718-2211	718-2215	K-4	Michael Hoffman
North Broward Academy of Excellence MS	8200 SW 17th St	N Lauderdale, FL	33068-4101	954-718-2211	764-1655	6-8	Michael Hoffman

School	Address	City,State	Zip code	Telephone	Fax	Grade	Contact
North County Charter S	11 N Willow St	Fellsmere, FL	32948-5330	772-571-0153	571-8489	1-5	Dori Miller
North Dade Community Charter S	13850 NW 26th Ave	Opa Locka, FL	33054-4078	305-687-2325	687-0098	K-5	Valerie Goram-Kinnon
Northeast Academy	1750 NE 168th St	North Miami, FL	33162-3021	305-948-1247		K-5	Terry Maus
North Lauderdale Academy HS	7101 Kimberly Blvd	N Lauderdale, FL	33068-2388	954-720-0299	722-1508	9-12	Rosbin Ivery
NorthStar Charter HS	14681 Riviera Pointe Dr	Orlando, FL	32828-7404	407-273-1188	277-3340	9-10	Kelly Young
Oakwood Academy	7145 Babcock St SE	Palm Bay, FL	32909-5462	321-723-0150	723-0650	K-12	
Oasis ES	3415 Oasis Blvd	Cape Coral, FL	33914-4924	239-542-1577		K-5	Dr. Patrick Mark
Oasis Enrichment Academy	PO Box 602	Gainesville, FL	32602-0602	352-692-3773	692-3774	6-8	Sharla Head-Jones
Odyssey Charter S	1755 Eldron Blvd SE	Palm Bay, FL	32909-6832	321-733-0442	733-1178	K-6	Irving Rashkover
Okaloosa Academy	81 Roberts Blvd	Ft Walton Bch, FL	32547-5118	850-864-3133	864-4305	6-12	Jerry White
Okaloosa Academy	2053 S Ferdon Blvd	Crestview, FL	32536-8424	850-689-7688		6-12	Ron Panucci
One Room S House Project	4180 NE 15th St	Gainesville, FL	32609-2011	352-376-4014	376-3345	K-5	Neil Drake
Opportunity Charter S	202 13th Ave E	Bradenton, FL	34208-3246	941-714-7260	714-7333	9-12	Joe Kinnan
Origins Montessori Charter S	26 Willow Dr	Orlando, FL	32807-3220	321-235-3739	235-3509	K-8	Julie Sanborn
Osprey ES	716 Roy Wall Blvd	Rockledge, FL	32955-6212	877-258-0060		K-5	Chris Terrill
Oxford Academy of Miami	10870 SW 113th Pl	Miami, FL	33176-3227	305-598-4494	598-4475	K-5	Toby Hernandez
PAL Academy Charter S	202 13th Ave E	Bradenton, FL	34208-3246	941-714-7260	714-7333	1-8	Joe Kinnan
Palm Bay Academy	1465 Baytree Dr NE	Palm Bay, FL	32905-3950	321-984-2710	984-0799	K-6	Madhu Longani
Palm Beach Maritime Academy	7719 S Dixie Hwy	West Palm Beach, FL	33405-4817	561-547-3775	540-5177	K-8	Marie Turchiaro
Paragon Academy of Technology	2210 Pierce St	Hollywood, FL	33020-4414	954-925-0155	925-0209	6-8	Dr. Steven Montes
Paragon ES	3311 N Andrews Ave	Pompano Beach, FL	33064	954-943-0471	943-0473	K-5	Marc Jabion
Parks Charter S	713 W Palm Dr	Florida City, FL	33034-3223	305-246-3336	246-3340	K-8	Marva de Silva
Parks Community S	430 NW 9th St	Homestead, FL	33030-4110	305-379-4905		K-6	Michael Banks
Parkway Academy	7451 Riviera Blvd	Miramar, FL	33023-6568	954-961-2911	961-2451	9-12	Dr. Clarissa Scott
Passport S	401 Magnolia Ave	Orlando, FL	32801	407-841-4814		K-8	Thomas Herdtner
PCC Collegiate HS	3425 Winter Lake Rd	Lakeland, FL	33803-9765	863-669-2322	669-2330	11-12	John Small
Pembroke Pines Charter HS	17189 Sheridan St	Pembroke Pines, FL	33331-1934	954-538-3700	538-3714	9-12	Peter Bayer
Pembroke Pines Charter MS West	18500 Pembroke Rd	Pembroke Pines, FL	33029-6108	954-443-4847	447-1691	6-8	Devarn Flowers
Pembroke Pines Charter S East Campus	10801 Pembroke Rd	Pembroke Pines, FL	33025-1707	954-443-4800	443-4811	K-5	Sean S. Chance
Pembroke Pines Charter S / West	1680 SW 184th Ave	Pembroke Pines, FL	33029-6120	954-450-6990	443-4820	K-5	Devarn Flowers
Pensacola Beach ES	900 Via De Luna Dr	Pensacola Beach, FL	32561-2262	850-934-4020	934-4040	K-5	Jeff Castleberry
Pepin Academy	3916 E Hillsborough Ave	Tampa, FL	33610-4542	813-236-1755	236-1195	6-12	Joanne Shaw
Pinecrest Academy MS	14301 SW 42nd St	Miami, FL	33175-7832	305-207-1027	207-1897	6-8	Victoria Larrauri
Pinecrest Preparatory Academy	14301 SW 42nd St	Miami, FL	33175-7832	305-207-1027		K-5	Susie Dopico
Pinellas Preparatory Academy	403 1st Ave SW	Largo, FL	33770-3437	727-581-9550	581-9590	4-8	Curtis Fuller
Plato Academy	401 S Old Coachman Rd	Clearwater, FL	33765-4410	727-793-2400		K-5	Steve Christopoulos
Potentials Charter S	1201 Australian Ave	Riviera Beach, FL	33404-6635	561-842-3213	863-4352	PK-5	Rosie Portera-Vaughn
Potentials South Charter S	701 NW 35th St	Boca Raton, FL	33431-6473	561-395-2012	395-4607	PK-5	Rosie Portera
Prince Academy	1006 N 50th St	Tampa, FL	33619	813-741-3191	741-2424	K-6	Carolina Edjor
Princeton House Charter S	720 W Princeton St	Orlando, FL	32804-5214	407-523-7121	523-7187	K-6	Carol Tucker
Quest MS	3916 E Hillsborough Ave	Tampa, FL	33610-4542	813-236-1755	232-9680	6-8	JoAnn Shaw
Rays of Hope Charter S	1780 W Airport Blvd	Sanford, FL	32771-4091	407-322-5010	322-8003	6-8	Carolyn Flanagan
Reading Edge Academy	2975 Enterprise Rd	De Bary, FL	32713-2708	386-668-8911		K-5	Margaret Comardo
ReBirth Academy Charter S	1924 E Comanche Ave	Tampa, FL	33610-8226	813-239-1321	239-2702	K-5	K.C. Williams
Redlands Christian Migrant Association	PO Box 980	Wimauma, FL	33598-0980	813-672-5159	633-6119	K-8	Daniel Oceguera
Renaissance Elementary Charter S	8360 NW 33rd St	Miami, FL	33122-1938	305-591-2225	591-2984	K-5	Ana Cordal
Renaissance Learning Center	11980 Highway A1A Alt	Palm Bch Gdns, FL	33410-2301	561-776-0961	776-0971	K-5	Debra Johnson
Richardson Academy	6815 N Rome Ave	Tampa, FL	33604-5839	813-930-2988	930-2929	K-6	Tommie Lee Brumfield
Ridgeview Global Studies Academy	1000 Dunson Rd	Davenport, FL	33896-8383	863-419-3171	419-3172	PK-5	Ralph Frier
Rio Grande Charter S	2210 S Rio Grande Ave	Orlando, FL	32805-5262	407-649-9122	649-8151	K-5	Barbara McLean-Smith
River's Edge Charter S	4400 Dixie Hwy NE	Palm Bay, FL	32905-4334	321-729-0500	729-0744	K-12	Scott Infante
Riviera Beach Academy Charter S	PO Box 11137	West Palm Beach, FL	33419-1137	561-882-9493	882-0151	6-8	Oscar Lewis
Round Lake ES	31333 Round Lake Rd	Mount Dora, FL	32757-9599	352-385-4399	735-1860	K-5	Dale Moxley
Royal Palm Charter S	7145 Babcock St SE	Palm Bay, FL	32909-5462	321-723-0650	723-0650	K-2	Carolyn Thon
Sagan Academy	4610 E Hanna Ave	Tampa, FL	33610-2521	813-612-4433	862-0220	6-7	Kelly Browning
St. Mary's Pre S Children with Autism	5325 Greenwood Ave Ste 101	West Palm Beach, FL	33407-2452	561-840-6681		PK-PK	Nancy Frank
Saint Peter's Academy	4250 38th Ave	Vero Beach, FL	32967-1711	772-562-1963	562-8920	K-5	Ruth Jefferson
St. Petersburg Collegiate HS	PO Box 13489	St Petersburg, FL	33733-3489	727-341-4610		10-12	Linda Benware
Sarasota Community S for Excellence	1751 Dr Martin Luther King	Sarasota, FL	34234	941-373-9755		K-5	Pauline Hodges
Sarasota Military Academy	801 Orange Ave	Sarasota, FL	34236-4116	941-926-1700	926-1701	9-12	Dan Kennedy
Sarasota S of Arts/Sciences	645 Central Ave	Sarasota, FL	34236-4016	941-330-1855	330-1835	6-8	Pepar Anspaugh
Sawgrass MS	716 Roy Wall Blvd	Rockledge, FL	32955-6212	877-258-0060		6-8	Chris Terrill
School of Arts & Sciences	3208 Thomasville Rd	Tallahassee, FL	32308-7904	850-386-6566	386-8183	K-8	Deborah Powers
School of Integrated Academics and Tech	4811 Payne Stewart Dr	Jacksonville, FL	32209-9208	904-360-8200	768-8618	9-12	Maureen Mikels
School of Success Academy	6974 Wilson Blvd	Jacksonville, FL	32210-3663	904-573-0880	573-0889	6-12	Genell Mills
Sculptor Charter S	1301 Armstrong Dr	Titusville, FL	32780-7907	321-264-9991	264-9995	PK-8	Ronald Watford
Seagull Academy for Independent Living	1801 12th Ave S	Lake Worth, FL	33461-5771	561-540-8110	540-8331	9-Adu	Lois Layman
Seaside Neighborhood S	10 Smolian Cir	Seaside, FL	32459	850-231-0396	231-4725	6-8	Shirley Foster
Sebastian Charter JHS	782 Wave St	Sebastian, FL	32958-5049	772-388-8838	388-8815	6-8	Donna Dittman
SIATech	12350 SW 285th St	Homestead, FL	33033-1251	305-258-9477	258-9584	9-12	Marjorie Lopez
SIATech	3050 NW 183rd St	Miami Gardens, FL	33056-3536	305-624-1144	624-9172	9-12	Marjorie Lopez
Six Mile Charter Academy	6851 Lancer Ave	Fort Myers, FL	33912-4334	239-768-9375		K-8	Margaret Cruckshank
Smart S Charter HS	3020 NW 33rd Ave	Laud Lakes, FL	33311-1106	954-343-9965	343-9970	9-12	David Harvin
Smart School Charter MS	3698 NW 15th St	Lauderhill, FL	33311-4133	954-321-6777	321-7760	6-8	Dwight Bernard
Sojourner Truth HS	4951 Richard St # C	Jacksonville, FL	32207-7328	904-448-5151	448-5159	9-11	Leslie Harris
Somerset Academy	20801 Johnson St	Pembroke Pines, FL	33029-1916	954-442-0233	442-0813	K-12	Shannine Sadesky-Hunt
Somerset Academy	18491 SW 134th Ave	Miami, FL	33177-2923	305-969-6074	969-6077	K-5	Suzette Ruiz
Somerset Academy Charter HS	SW 117th Ave & 232nd St	Miami, FL	33170	305-597-9950	477-6762	9-12	Diana Morales
Somerset Academy Davie	3788 SW 64th Ave	Davie, FL	33314-2417	954-584-5528	584-5598	K-5	Dina Miller
Somerset Academy MS	SW 117th Ave & 232nd St	Miami, FL	33170	305-969-6074	969-6077	6-8	Sandra Grau
Somerset Academy MSHS	20803 Johnson St	Pembroke Pines, FL	33029-1916	954-442-0233	442-0813	7-12	Bernardo Montero
Somerset Neighborhood S	12425 SW 53rd St	Miramar, FL	33027-5493	305-829-2406	829-4477	K-5	Lazara Hernandez
Spanish Academy Charter S	447 NW Spanish River Blvd	Boca Raton, FL	33431-4613	561-338-5700	338-5704	K-4	Judith Smith
Spiral Tech Charter S	12400 SW 72nd St	Miami, FL	33183-2514	305-273-0474	273-0242	K-5	Gisela Batan
Spirit City Academy	3400 NW 135th St	Miami, FL	33054-4708	305-953-0003	953-0144	K-5	Cecilia Honeywood
Spring Creek ES	44440 Spring Creek Rd	Paisley, FL	32767-9063	352-669-3275	669-3762	PK-5	Robert Curry
STAR Charter S	225 Avenue B NW	Winter Haven, FL	33881-4529	863-299-0063	299-2343	9-12	Chantel Griffin
Steele/Collins Charter MS	428 W Tennessee St	Tallahassee, FL	32301-1026	850-681-1929	224-1663	6-8	Mary Henry
Stepping Stones Charter S	4400 Dixie Hwy NE	Palm Bay, FL	32905-4334	321-729-0500	729-0744	K-4	Scott Infante
Summit Charter S	1250 N Maitland Ave	Maitland, FL	32751-4305	407-599-4001	599-4004	K-6	Alan Smolowe
Suncoast S for Innovative Studies	1300 S Tuttle Ave	Sarasota, FL	34239-2603	941-952-5277	952-5087	K-8	Phil Blankenship
Sunshine Academy	14550 NE 6th Ave	North Miami, FL	33161-2357	305-947-3650	947-3609	K-8	Alcira Manzano
Survivors Charter S	1310 N Congress Ave	West Palm Beach, FL	33409-6314	561-712-1800	712-0360	10-12	Randy Stafford
Survivors Charter S of Boynton Beach	1325 Gateway Blvd	Boynton Beach, FL	33426-8304	561-731-1800	375-6242	9-12	Marc Flamer
Tampa Bay Academy	12012 Boyette Rd	Riverview, FL	33569-5631	813-677-6700	677-5467	K-12	Joann Nelson
Tampa Charter S	5429 Beaumont Center Blvd	Tampa, FL	33634-5247	813-887-3800	885-9626	3-8	Sheila Thomley
Tapestry Park Charter S	410 Lyndell Ln	Panama City, FL	32407-3224	850-249-2144	249-2149	K-5	Antonius Barnes
Terrace Community Charter S	PO Box 16325	Tampa, FL	33687-6325	813-987-6555	987-6565	5-8	Gary Hocevar
Touchdowns4Life Charter S	10044 W McNab Rd	Tamarac, FL	33321-1894	954-726-8785	726-9590	6-8	Lori Bitar
Toussaint L'Ouverture HS	95 NE 1st Ave	Delray Beach, FL	33444-3711	561-243-3136	243-4070	9-12	Dr. Joseph Bemadel
Transitional Learning Academy	1411 NW 14th Ave	Miami, FL	33125-1616	305-325-1080	325-1044	8-12	Pamela Miller
Trinity S for Children	2402 W Osborne Ave	Tampa, FL	33603-1434	813-874-2402	874-2412	K-8	Madeline O'Dea
Trinity Upper S	4807 N Armenia Ave	Tampa, FL	33603-1427	813-874-2402	874-2412	6-8	Madeline O'Dea
UCP Charter S	3305 S Orange Ave	Orlando, FL	32806-6125	407-852-3333	852-3301	PK-5	Ilene Wilkins
UCP Child Development Center	448 W Donegan Ave	Kissimmee, FL	34741-2335	407-932-3445	932-3480	PK-PK	Heather Miller
UCP Seminole Child Development	301 S Oak Ave	Sanford, FL	32771-1823	407-322-6222	322-5596	PK-K	Ilene Wilkins
USF Charter S at Mosi	11801 USF Bull Run Dr	Tampa, FL	33617-5103	813-974-3831	974-1280	K-5	L. Rylene Stein
Village of Excellence Academy	8718 N 46th St	Temple Terrace, FL	33617-6002	813-988-8632	983-0683	K-3	Cametra Edwards
Villages Charter ES	420 Village Campus Cir	Lady Lake, FL	32162-7169	352-259-7700	259-7707	K-2	Leanne Yerk
Villages Charter HS	251 Buffalo Trl	Lady Lake, FL	32162-7176	352-259-3777	259-6802	9-11	Michael Kelly
Villages Charter MS	450 Village Campus Cir	Lady Lake, FL	32162-7169	352-259-0044	753-1113	6-8	Pam Roberts
Villages Charter S	521 Old School Rd	Lady Lake, FL	32162-7170	352-259-2300	259-2056	3-5	Leanne Yerk
Walton Academy	389 Dorsey Ave	Defuniak Spgs, FL	32435-3013	850-892-3999	892-7854	6-12	Jerry White
Walton Academy	4817 N Florida Ave	Tampa, FL	33603-2117	813-231-9272	231-9271	K-5	Tanika Walton
Wayman Academy of the Arts	1176 Labelle St	Jacksonville, FL	32205-6487	904-695-9995	695-9992	K-5	Tracy McGeathey
Wells Charter S	2426 Remington Blvd	Kissimmee, FL	34744-8467	407-697-1020	697-1021	PK-5	Diane Beatty
Western Academy Charter S	500 Royal Plaza Rd Ste F	Ryl Palm Bch, FL	33411-7688	561-792-4123	792-9905	K-8	Linda Terranova
Westminister Academy	830 29th St	Orlando, FL	32805-6201	407-841-6560	841-7311	K-12	Elizabeth Addeo
West Orange Co. Charter ES	PO Box 949	Orlando, FL	32802-0949	407-654-2039	654-3039	K-5	Nina Kuhn
Whispering Winds Charter S	12390 NW Old Fannin Rd	Chiefland, FL	32626-8115	352-490-5799	490-7242	K-8	Dr. Suzanne Cornell
Wiener S of Opportunity	PO Box 173470	Hialeah, FL	33017-3470	305-623-9631	623-9621	K-2	Lissa Gonzalez
Wiener S of Opportunity	11025 SW 84th St	Miami, FL	33173-3804	305-279-3064		K-5	Lissa Gonzalez
WINGS Academy	PO Box 48367	Sarasota, FL	34230-5367	941-351-7267	358-6957	6-8	Anthon Francis
Youth Co-Op Charter S	12051 W Okeechobee Rd	Hialeah Gardens, FL	33018-2933	305-819-8855	819-8455	K-8	Maritza Aragon

Georgia

School	Address	City,State	Zip code	Telephone	Fax	Grade	Contact
Academy of Lithonia	3235 Evans Mill Rd	Lithonia, GA	30038-3012	678-526-9655		K-6	Denise Hentz
Adairsville ES	122 King St	Adairsville, GA	30103-2300	770-606-5840	773-7755	K-5	Melissa Zerafoss
Addison ES	3055 Ebenezer Rd	Marietta, GA	30066-4542	770-578-2700	578-2702	PK-5	Judy Lindsey
Amana Academy	1565 Holcomb Bridge Rd	Roswell, GA	30076-2517	678-795-1080	992-7270	K-8	Shereen Salam
Atlanta Charter MS	688A Grant St SE	Atlanta, GA	30315-1420	404-904-0051	904-0052	6-8	Dr. Jacqueline Rosswurm
Baconton Community Charter S	260 E Walton St	Baconton, GA	31716-7706	229-787-9999	787-0077	PK-12	Lynn Pinson
Bishop Hall Charter S	1815 E Clay St	Thomasville, GA	31792-4736	229-227-1397	225-1093	9-12	Rich Johnson
Central Educational Center	PO Box 280	Newnan, GA	30264-0280	678-423-2000	423-2008	9-12	Mark Whitlock
Chamblee Charter HS	3688 Chamblee Dunwoody Rd	Chamblee, GA	30341-2185	678-676-6902	676-6910	9-12	Rochelle Lowery
Charter Conservatory Liberal Arts/Tech.	149 Northside Dr E	Statesboro, GA	30458-1089	912-764-5888		3-12	Dr. Kathy Harwood
Chesnut Charter ES	4576 N Peachtree Rd	Dunwoody, GA	30338-5892	678-676-7102	676-7110	PK-5	Sonja Alexander
Cloverleaf ES	PO Box 564	Cartersville, GA	30120-0564	770-606-5847	606-3842	K-5	Susan Stephens
DeKalb PATH Academy	3007 Hermance Dr NE	Atlanta, GA	30319-2627	404-846-3242	846-3243	5-8	Suttiwan Cox
Drew Charter S	301 E Lake Blvd SE	Atlanta, GA	30317-3152	404-687-0001	687-0480	K-8	Dr. Nicholas Stapleton
Druid Hills HS	1798 Haygood Dr NE	Atlanta, GA	30307-1119	678-874-6302	874-6310	9-12	Everett Patrick
Eastvalley ES	2570 Lower Roswell Rd	Marietta, GA	30068-3698	770-578-7214	578-7216	K-5	Althea Singletary
Ellis S	220 E 49th St	Savannah, GA	31405-2299	912-201-5470	201-5473	PK-8	Charles Wooten
Emerson ES	54 7th St	Emerson, GA	30137-2219	770-606-5848	606-3847	K-5	Denise Welker
Fargo Charter S	PO Box 267	Fargo, GA	31631-0267	912-637-5466	637-5242	K-3	Danny Ellis
Fulton Science Academy	1675 Hembree Rd	Alpharetta, GA	30004-2083	770-753-4141	753-4948	6-8	Selim Ozdemir
Futral Road ES	180 Futral Rd	Griffin, GA	30224-7454	770-229-3735	233-6001	K-5	Larry Jones
Green Acres ES	2000 Gober Ave SE	Smyrna, GA	30080-1111	678-842-6905	842-6907	PK-5	David Pearce
Hapeville Charter MS	3535 S Fulton Ave	Hapeville, GA	30354-1701	404-767-7730	767-7706	6-8	Jannard Rainey
International Community Charter	3260 Covington Hwy	Decatur, GA	30032-1121	404-499-8969	499-8968	K-5	Bill Moon
Jenkins-White Charter ES	800 15th Ave	Augusta, GA	30901-4145	706-737-7320	731-7651	K-5	Marva Tutt Gibson
Kennesaw Charter S	1370 Lockhart Dr NW	Kennesaw, GA	30144-7047	678-290-9628		K-5	Janice Gordon
KidsPeace S of Georgia	101 Kidspeace Dr	Bowdon, GA	30108-3447	770-437-7200		7-12	Scott Merritt
Kingsley ES	2051 Brendon Dr	Dunwoody, GA	30338-4599	678-874-8902	874-8910	PK-5	Karen Graham
Kingston ES	240 Hardin Bridge Rd	Kingston, GA	30145-2668	770-606-5850	336-5591	K-5	LaDonna Turrentine
KIPP Achieve Academy	1757 Mary Dell Dr SE	Atlanta, GA	30316-3636	404-214-0501	214-0506	5-8	David Morgan
KIPP South Fulton	1286 Washington Ave	East Point, GA	30344-3537	678-278-0160	278-0165	5-8	Marina Volanakis
KIPP WAYS Academy	80 Joseph E Lowery Blvd	Atlanta, GA	30314	404-475-1941		5-8	David Jernigan
Lewis Academy of Excellence	6390 Church St	Riverdale, GA	30274-1624	770-909-6697	909-6699	9-12	Dr. Patricia Lewis
Mercer MS	201 Rommel Ave	Garden City, GA	31408-1636	912-965-6700	965-6719	7-9	Gloria Dukes
Mission Road ES	1100 Mission Rd SW	Cartersville, GA	30120-5779	770-606-5863	606-3862	K-5	Nancy Summey
Mt. Bethel ES	1210 Johnson Ferry Rd	Marietta, GA	30068-2719	770-578-7248	578-7250	PK-5	Robin Lattizori
Murphey Charter MS	2610 Milledgeville Rd	Augusta, GA	30904-5181	706-737-7350	737-7353	6-8	Tonethia Frails Beasley
Neighborhood Charter S	688 Grant St SE	Atlanta, GA	30315-1420	404-624-6226		K-5	Dr. Jackie Rosswurm
Odyssey Charter S	1485 Highway 34 E Ste B1	Newnan, GA	30265-2126	678-423-5155		K-5	Andy Geeter
Oglethorpe Academy	707 Stiles Ave	Savannah, GA	31415-5324	912-201-5075	201-5077	6-8	Jeff Cheney
Peachtree MS	4664 N Peachtree Rd	Atlanta, GA	30338-5898	678-676-7702	676-7710	6-8	Steve Donahue
Pine Log ES	3370 Highway 140	Rydal, GA	30171-1100	770-606-5864	606-3866	K-5	Cathy Strickland
Rainbow ES	2801 Kelley Chapel Rd	Decatur, GA	30034-2299	678-874-1702	874-1710	PK-5	Annette Sanders-Roberts
School for Integrated Academics & Tech.	239 West Lake Ave	Atlanta, GA	30314	404-799-9101	799-5388	9-12	
Sedalia Park ES	2230 Lower Roswell Rd	Marietta, GA	30068-3359	770-509-5162	509-5342	K-5	Patty Thomas
Spalding Drive ES	130 W Spalding Dr NE	Atlanta, GA	30328-1999	770-551-5880	673-4090	PK-5	Christine Young
Talbot Co. Charter Alternative Academy	PO Box 515	Talbotton, GA	31827-0515	706-665-3620	665-8099	9-12	Jerome Harris
Taliaferro County Charter S	557 Broad St	Crawfordville, GA	30631	706-456-2575	456-2689	K-12	Algie Arbee
Taylorsville ES	1502 Old Alabama Rd	Taylorsville, GA	30178-1505	770-606-5867	606-2056	K-5	Bernadette Dipetta
Tech HS	1043 Memorial Dr SE	Atlanta, GA	30316-1473	678-904-5091		9-12	Dr. Byron White
Technical Career Academy N.E. Georgia	PO Box 80571	Athens, GA	30608-0571	706-369-5871	425-3114	10-12	Reginald Woods
Unidos Dual Language Charter S	4475 Hendrix Dr	Forest Park, GA	30297-1244	404-361-3494		K-1	Dell Perry
University Community Academy	953 Ralph D Abernathy SW	Atlanta, GA	30310	404-753-4050	215-3481	K-8	Dr. James Harris
Walton HS	1590 Bill Murdock Rd	Marietta, GA	30062-5999	770-578-3225	578-3227	9-12	Tom Higgins
White ES	1395 Cass White Rd NE	White, GA	30184-2600	770-606-5869	606-3876	K-5	Avis King
Woodland ES	1130 Spalding Dr	Atlanta, GA	30350-5013	770-551-5890	673-4091	PK-5	Noris Price

Hawaii

School	Address	City,State	Zip code	Telephone	Fax	Grade	Contact
Connections New Century Charter S	174 Kamehameha Ave	Hilo, HI	96720-2834	808-961-3664	961-2665	K-10	John Thatcher
Education Laboratory	1776 University Ave	Honolulu, HI	96822-2463	808-956-7833	956-7260	K-12	Peter Estomago
Hakipuu Learning Center	PO Box 1159	Kaneohe, HI	96744-1159	808-235-9155	235-9160	7-12	Charlene Hoe
Halau Ku Mana Charter S	3737 Manoa Rd	Honolulu, HI	96822-1138	808-988-8995	988-8999	6-12	Keola Nakanishi
Halau Lokahi Charter S	401 Waiakamilo Rd Unit 1A	Honolulu, HI	96817-4955	808-832-3594	842-9800	K-12	Laara Allbrett
Hawaii Academy of Arts & Science	PO Box 1494	Pahoa, HI	96778-1494	808-965-3730	965-3733	K-12	Steve Hirakami
Hawaii E-Charter S	475 22nd Ave #211	Honolulu, HI	96816-4400	808-735-6257	733-4730	9-12	Ana Blake
Innovations Public Charter S	76-147A Royal Poinciana Dr	Kailua Kona, HI	96740	808-327-6205	327-6209	1-6	Barbara Woerner
Kanuikapono Charter S	PO Box 12	Anahola, HI	96703-0012	808-822-9032	822-8321	K-12	Ku'uipo Torio
Kanu O Ka 'Aina New Century Charter S	PO Box 398	Kamuela, HI	96743-0398	808-887-8144	887-8146	K-12	Dr. Ku Kahakalau
Ka 'Umeke Ka'eo Public Charter S	222 Desha Ave	Hilo, HI	96720-4815	808-933-3482	933-3488	K-6	Albert Nahale-A
Ka Waihona O Ka Na'auao Charter S	89-195 Farrington Hwy	Waianae, HI	96792-4102	808-620-9030	620-9036	K-6	Alvin Parker
Ke Ana La'ahana Public Charter S	1500 Kalanianaole Ave	Hilo, HI	96720-4914	808-961-6228	961-6229	7-12	Lehua Veincent
Ke Kula Ni'ihau Kekaha Public Charter S	PO Box 129	Kekaha, HI	96752-0129	808-337-0481	337-1289	PK-12	Haunani Seward
Ke Kula O Kamakau Lab S	45-037 Kaneohe Bay Dr	Kaneohe, HI	96744-2417	808-235-9175	235-9173	K-12	Christine Plunkett
Ke Kula 'O Nawahiokalani'opu'u Charter S	PO Box 506	Keaau, HI	96749-0506	808-982-4260	966-7821	K-6	Kauanoe Kamana
Kihei Charter S	300 Ohukai Rd Unit 214	Kihei, HI	96753-7040	808-875-0700	874-6745	K-12	Mark Christiano
Kualapu'u Charter ES	PO Box 260	Kualapuu, HI	96757-0260	808-567-6900	567-6906	K-6	Lydia Trinidad
Kua O Ka La Public Charter S	PO Box 1413	Pahoa, HI	96778-1413	808-965-5098	965-9618	6-11	Susan Osborne
Kula Aupuni Niihau A Kahelelani Aloha	PO Box 690390	Makaweli, HI	96769-0390	808-337-2022	337-2033	K-12	Hinaleimoana Wong
Lanikai ES	140 Alala Rd	Kailua, HI	96734-3199	808-266-7844	266-7848	PK-6	Frederick Birkett
Thompson Academy	629 Pohukaina St Ste 3	Honolulu, HI	96813-5021	808-586-3636	586-3640	K-12	Diana H. Oshiro
Volcano S of Arts & Sciences	PO Box 845	Volcano, HI	96785-0845	808-985-9800	985-9898	K-8	Dr. David Rizor
Voyager Charter S	670 Auahi St Ste A5	Honolulu, HI	96813-5166	808-521-9770	521-9772	K-8	Susan Lee Deuber
Wai'alae ES	1045 19th Ave	Honolulu, HI	96816-4699	808-733-4880	733-4886	K-5	Wendy W. Lagareta
Waimea Charter MS	67-1229 Mamalahoa Hwy	Kamuela, HI	96743-8429	808-887-6090	887-6087	6-8	Tom Pepe
Waters of Life Charter S	PO Box 1012	Kurtistown, HI	96760-1012	808-966-6175	982-7863	K-12	Katheryn Shay
West Hawaii Explorations Academy	73-4460 Queen Kaahumanu Hwy	Kailua Kona, HI	96740-2632	808-327-4751	327-4750	7-12	Heather Nakakura

Idaho

School	Address	City,State	Zip code	Telephone	Fax	Grade	Contact
ANSER Charter S	1187 W River St	Boise, ID	83702-7048	208-426-9840	426-9863	K-7	Dr. Suzanne Gregg
Coeur D'Alene Charter Academy	711 W Kathleen Ave	Coeur d Alene, ID	83815-9404	208-676-1667	676-8667	6-12	Nelson Pitotti
Compass Charter S	2870 S Gold Bar Ave	Meridian, ID	83642-6794	208-888-9544	846-5950	K-7	Kelly Trudeau
Falcon Ridge Charter S	PO Box 326	Kuna, ID	83634-0326	208-703-0044		K-8	Gerald Chouinard
Hidden Springs Charter S	5480 W Hidden Springs Dr	Boise, ID	83714-9402	208-229-4727	229-4747	K-9	Chuck Ward
Idaho Arts Charter S	PO Box 114	Nampa, ID	83653-0114	208-463-2883		K-12	Robert DeCloss
Idaho Distance Education Academy	PO Box 339	Bovill, ID	83806-0339	208-826-3029	877-3360	K-12	Shauna Kron
Idaho Leadership Academy	PO Box 59	Pingree, ID	83262-0059	208-684-9696	684-9404	9-12	Gary Larsen
Idaho Virtual Academy	PO Box 191099	Boise, ID	83719-1099	208-332-3559	322-3688	K-9	Cody Claver
Inspire Virtual Charter S	404 S 8th St Ste 310	Boise, ID	83702-7133	208-938-3290	385-9768	K-12	Dr. Dallas Taylor
Liberty Charter S	PO Box 1901	Nampa, ID	83653-1901	208-466-7952	466-7961	K-12	Becky Stallcop
McKenna Charter HS	1993 E 8th N Ste 105	Mountain Home, ID	83647-2333	208-580-2449	580-2450	9-12	Larry Slade
Meridian Charter HS	3800 N Locust Grove Rd	Meridian, ID	83642	208-288-2928	288-5685	9-12	Jana Nichols
Meridian Medical Arts Charter HS	1789 E Leighfield Dr	Meridian, ID	83646-2692	208-855-4075		9-12	Gary Messinger
Moscow Charter S	1723 E F St	Moscow, ID	83843-9571	208-883-3195	892-3855	K-6	Trish Bechtel
North Star Charter S	PO Box 877	Eagle, ID	83616-0877	208-939-9600	939-6090	K-8	Nancy Smith
Pocatello Community Charter S	615 W Maple St	Pocatello, ID	83201-5153	208-478-2522	478-2622	K-8	Dr. Martha Martin
Rolling Hills Charter S	12781 W Ashcreek St	Boise, ID	83713-2088	208-375-1176	377-3969	K-8	Dr. Caroline Mauer
Sandpoint Charter S	614 S Madison Ave	Sandpoint, ID	83864-8724	208-255-7771	263-9441	7-8	Alan Millar
Upper Carmen Charter S	508 Carmen Creek Rd	Carmen, ID	83462	208-756-4590		K-6	Sue Smith
Victory Charter S	PO Box 3454	Nampa, ID	83653-3454	208-442-9400	442-9401	K-7	Dr. Marianne Saunders
White Pine Charter S	2959 John Adams Pkwy	Ammon, ID	83406-4508	208-522-4432	522-4452	K-8	Peggy Sharp

Illinois

School	Address	City,State	Zip code	Telephone	Fax	Grade	Contact
ACE Technical Charter HS	5410 S State St	Chicago, IL	60609-6382	773-548-8705	548-8706	9-12	Geri Harston
ACT Charter S	4319 W Washington Blvd	Chicago, IL	60624-2232	773-626-4200	626-4268	6-12	Sarah Howard
Addams Alternative HS	1800 W Cuyler Ave	Chicago, IL	60613-2402	773-871-1151	871-1787	9-12	Frederick Robincon
Aspira - Antonia Pantoja Alternative HS	3121 N Pulaski Rd	Chicago, IL	60641-5447	773-427-0759	427-0872	9-12	Nelson Rivera
ASPIRA at Haugan MS	3729 W Leland Ave	Chicago, IL	60625-5706	773-267-3568		6-8	Mitzie Ravid
ASPIRA - Mirta Ramirez	2435 N Western Ave	Chicago, IL	60647-2028	773-252-0970	252-0994	9-12	Patricia Munoz
Association House - El Cuarto Ano HS	1116 N Kedzie Ave	Chicago, IL	60651-4152	773-772-7170	772-8671	9-12	Harriet Sadauskas
Austin Career Education Center	5352 W Chicago Ave	Chicago, IL	60651-2857	773-626-6988	626-2641	9-12	Judy Vojta
Bronzeville Blue Gargoyle S	220 W 45th Pl	Chicago, IL	60609-3903	773-538-0059	538-0164	9-12	LaShaun Jackson
Chicago Choir Academy	3737 S Paulina St	Chicago, IL	60609-2047	773-890-4720	890-4773	4-8	Ron Giles
Chicago International Charter S	6105 S Michigan Ave	Chicago, IL	60637-2119	773-324-3300	324-3302	K-8	Steven Taylor

School	Address	City,State	Zip code	Telephone	Fax	Grade	Contact
Chicago International Charter S	8130 S California Ave	Chicago, IL	60652-2716	773-434-4575	434-2026	K-5	Tarsa Stovall
Chicago International Charter S - Avalon	1501 E 83rd Pl	Chicago, IL	60619-6501	773-721-3076	731-0142	K-4	Anthony Chambers
Chicago International Charter S Basil	1816 W Garfield Blvd	Chicago, IL	60609-5606	773-778-9455	778-9456	PK-8	Gloria Hall
Chicago International Charter S Bucktown	2235 N Hamilton Ave	Chicago, IL	60647-3360	773-645-3321	645-3327	K-8	Turon Ivy
Chicago International Charter S Longwood	1309 W 95th St	Chicago, IL	60643-1496	773-238-5330	238-5350	K-12	
Chicago International Charter S Prairie	11530 S Prairie Ave	Chicago, IL	60628-5612	773-928-0480	928-6971	K-8	Aisha Strong
Chicago International Charter S W Belden	2245 N McVicker Ave	Chicago, IL	60639-2766	773-637-9430	637-9791	K-8	Margaret O'Brien
Chicago International S Northtown	3900 W Peterson Ave	Chicago, IL	60659-3162	773-478-3655	478-6029	9-12	Loren Stillwell
Chicago Math and Science Academy	1709 W Lunt Ave	Chicago, IL	60626-3212	773-761-8960	761-8961	6-12	Salim Ucan
Community Services West - ASA	4651 W Madison St	Chicago, IL	60644-3646	773-921-1315	921-8324	9-12	Gladys Simpson
Community Youth Development Institute	7836 S Union Ave	Chicago, IL	60620-2409	773-224-2273	224-2214		Elfreda Austin
Donoghue Charter S	707 E 37th St	Chicago, IL	60653-1406	773-729-5300	729-5290	PK-3	Nicole Woodward-Iliev
DuSable Leadership Academy	4934 S Wabash Ave	Chicago, IL	60615-2136	773-535-1170	535-1912	9-9	Carla Ellis
Erie ES	2510 W Cortez St	Chicago, IL	60622-3422	773-486-7161	486-7234	K-1	Linda Ponce de Leon
Fort Bowman Academy Charter S	2734 Calvin Blvd	Cahokia, IL	62206-2707	618-332-7404	332-7561	K-12	Beth Peeples
Galapagos Charter S	3814 W Iowa St	Chicago, IL	60651-3708	773-384-9500	384-4866	K-4	Michael Lane
Houston Alternative HS	9035 S Langley Ave	Chicago, IL	60619-7596	773-723-9631	723-9022	9-12	Lisa Williams
Howard Area Alternative HS	7647 N Paulina St	Chicago, IL	60626-1017	773-381-0366	338-7693	9-12	Benjamin Churchill
KIPP Ascend Charter S	715 S Kildare Ave	Chicago, IL	60624-3564	773-533-1770	533-1784	5-7	Jim O'Conner
KIPP Chicago Youth Village Academy	2710 S Dearborn St	Chicago, IL	60616-2684	773-534-9977	534-9972	4-5	Sara Abella
LEARN Charter S	1132 S Homan Ave	Chicago, IL	60624-4344	773-826-6330	826-0015	K-8	Courtney Francis
Legacy Charter S	4217 W 18th St	Chicago, IL	60623-2325	773-542-1640	542-1699	PK-2	Lisa Kenner
Lincoln Charter S	300 4th St	Venice, IL	62090-1015	618-874-7792		9-12	Robert Falast
Locke Charter Academy	3141 W Jackson Blvd	Chicago, IL	60612-2729	773-265-7230	265-7258	PK-7	Lennie Jones
Lozano Leadership Academy	2570 S Blue Island Ave	Chicago, IL	60608-4817	773-890-0055	890-1537	9-12	Juan Salgado
Mandela Alternative HS	7105 S Ridgeland Ave	Chicago, IL	60649-2320	773-643-3258	643-4011	9-12	Pa Joof
McKinley Lakeside Campus	2929 S Wabash Ave	Chicago, IL	60616-3243	773-949-5010	949-5015	9-12	George Jones
Namaste S	3540 S Hermitage Ave	Chicago, IL	60609-1217	773-715-9558	376-6495	K-2	Allison Slade
Noble Street Charter S	1010 N Noble St	Chicago, IL	60622-4011	773-862-1449	278-0421	9-12	William Olsen
North Kenwood/Oakland Charter S	1119 E 46th St	Chicago, IL	60653-4403	773-536-2399	536-2435	PK-8	Stacy Beardsley
North Lawndale College Prep Charter HS	1616 S Spaulding Ave	Chicago, IL	60623-2653	773-542-1490	542-1492	9-12	John Horan
Octavio Paz Charter S	954 W Washington Blvd Ste 3	Chicago, IL	60607-2224	312-432-1170	432-1180	4-8	Dan Goodwin
Octavio Paz Charter S - Washtenaw	2651 W 23rd St	Chicago, IL	60608-3609	773-890-1054		K-3	Dan Goodwin
Passages Charter S	1447 W Montrose Ave	Chicago, IL	60613-1348	773-549-1052	549-1210	PK-5	Dr. Sally Ewing
Perspectives Charter S	1930 S Archer Ave	Chicago, IL	60616-6505	312-225-7400	225-7411	6-12	Kim Day
Prairie Crossing Charter S	1571 Jones Point Rd	Grayslake, IL	60030-3536	847-543-9722	543-9744	K-8	Linda Brazdil
Prologue Alternative HS	640 W Irving Park Rd	Chicago, IL	60613-3106	773-935-9925	665-8357	9-12	Pa Joof
Robertson Charter S	1454 E North St	Decatur, IL	62521-2044	217-428-7072	428-9214	K-3	Cordell Ingram
Rufino Tamayo Charter S	5135 S California Ave	Chicago, IL	60632-2124	773-434-6355	434-5036	K-8	Javier Arriola-Lopez
Shabazz International Charter S	7823 S Ellis Ave	Chicago, IL	60619-3213	773-651-1221	651-0302	K-8	Dr. Elaine Mosley
Simon Academy	3348 S Kedzie Ave	Chicago, IL	60623-5114	773-890-3129	847-2855	9-12	Cecilia Arroyo
SIU Charter S of East St. Louis	601 James R. Thompson Blvd	E Saint Louis, IL	62201	618-482-8370	482-8372	9-12	Anthony W. Neal
Sizemore Academy of B Shabazz	1540 W 84th St	Chicago, IL	60620-3918	773-779-5666	779-5668	6-8	Soyini Walton
Springfield Ball Charter S	2530 E Ash St	Springfield, IL	62703-5600	217-525-3275	525-3316	PK-8	Julie A. Ruskey
Tomorrows Builders Charter S	PO Box 6126	E Saint Louis, IL	62202-6126	618-874-1671		9-12	Vickie Forby
Truman Middle College HS	1145 W Wilson Ave	Chicago, IL	60640-5691	773-907-4841	907-4844	9-12	Tom O'Hale
Westside Holistic Alternative HS	820 N Central Ave	Chicago, IL	60651-2719	773-626-9744	921-1045	9-12	Dr. Romana Smith
West Town Academy Alternative HS	2039 W Fulton St	Chicago, IL	60612-2301	312-563-9044	563-9672	9-12	Bob Meyer
Young Womens Leadership S	2641 S Calumet Ave	Chicago, IL	60616-2901	312-949-9400	949-9142	7-12	Margaret Small
Youth Connection Charter S	3424 S State St	Chicago, IL	60616-3893	312-225-4668		9-12	Phyllis Crowe
Youth Connection-Latino Youth Alt HS	2200 S Marshall Blvd	Chicago, IL	60623-3530	773-277-0400	277-0401	9-12	Guadalupe Martinez
Youth Connections Albizu Campos HS	2739 W Division St	Chicago, IL	60622-2854	773-342-8022	342-6609	9-12	Lourdes Lugo
Youth Connection-Sullivan House Alt HS	8164 S South Chicago Ave	Chicago, IL	60617-1041	773-978-8680	375-1482	9-12	Dr. Thomas Gattuso

Indiana

School	Address	City,State	Zip code	Telephone	Fax	Grade	Contact
Bowman Leadership Academy	975 W 6th Ave	Gary, IN	46402-1708	219-226-3355		K-8	Vito Bianco
Brown Charter Academy	3600 N German Church Rd	Indianapolis, IN	46235-8504	317-891-0730		K-6	Thelma Wyatt
Campagna Academy Charter S	7403 Cline Ave	Schererville, IN	46375-2645	219-322-8614	322-8436	9-12	Bruce Hillman
Charter School of the Dunes	860 N Lake St	Gary, IN	46403-1070	219-939-9690	939-9031	K-7	Gari Voss
Christel House Academy	2717 S East St	Indianapolis, IN	46225-2104	317-783-4690	783-4693	K-7	Michelle Thompson
Community Montessori S	851 Highlander Point Dr	Floyds Knobs, IN	47119-9470	812-923-2000	923-5896	PK-5	Barbara Burke-Fondren
Decatur Discovery Academy	5125 Decatur Blvd	Indianapolis, IN	46241-9570	317-856-0900		9-12	John Pietrzak
East Chicago Urban Enterprise Academy	1402 E Chicago Ave	East Chicago, IN	46312-3587	219-392-3650			Charlotte Jackson
Flanner House ES	2424 Dr Mrtn Lthr Kng Jr St	Indianapolis, IN	46208	317-925-4231	923-9632	K-7	Cynthia Diamond
Flanner House Higher Learning Inc.	2424 Dr Mrtn Lthr Kng Jr St	Indianapolis, IN	46208	317-925-4231		9-12	Cynthia Diamond
Galileo Charter S	855 N 12th St	Richmond, IN	47374-2477	765-983-3709		K-3	John Hayden
Gary Lighthouse Charter S	3201 Pierce St	Gary, IN	46408-1100	219-880-1762		K-12	Karen Poplawski
Goodwill Education Initiatives II S	1635 W Michigan St	Indianapolis, IN	46222-4389	317-524-4501		K-12	Carolyn McCutcheon
Indianapolis Lighthouse Charter S	1780 Sloan Ave	Indianapolis, IN	46203-3140	317-351-1534		K-12	Misty Dumas
Irvington Community S	6705 Julian Ave	Indianapolis, IN	46219-6642	317-357-9752	357-9752	K-7	Timothy Ehrgott
Johnson Academy	7908 S Anthony Blvd	Fort Wayne, IN	46816-2504	260-441-8727	441-9357	K-8	Steve Bottlier
Joshua Academy	867 Walnut St	Evansville, IN	47713-1848	812-424-9498	401-6300	K-5	Pam Decker
KIPP Charter S	3125 Concord Ct	Indianapolis, IN	46222-3549	317-637-9780		K-12	Omotayo Ola-Niyi
New Community S	620 Cumberland Ave	West Lafayette, IN	47906-1522	765-464-8999	464-1999	K-7	Daniel Beaver
Options Charter S	PO Box 3790	Carmel, IN	46082-3790	317-815-2098	846-3806	9-12	Kevin Davis
Rural Community S	PO Box 85	Graysville, IN	47852-0085	812-382-4500		K-6	Sharon Goss
Signature S	610 Main St	Evansville, IN	47708-1618	812-421-1820	421-9189	9-12	Vicki Snyder
Southeast Neighborhood S of Excellence	1601 Barth Ave	Indianapolis, IN	46203-2704	317-423-0204		K-12	Dr. J.C. Lasmanis
Tindley Accelerated S	3960 Meadows Dr	Indianapolis, IN	46205-3114	317-545-1745		7-12	Marcus Robinson
Tri State University Charter S	1 University Ave	Angola, IN	46703-1752	260-665-4113		9-12	Dr. Dolores Tichenor
21st Century Charter S	2540 N Capitol Ave Ste 101	Indianapolis, IN	46208-5682	317-524-3750	524-3773	K-10	Kevin Teasley
21st Century Charter S Fountain Square	1516 Barth Ave	Indianapolis, IN	46203-2740	317-524-3771		6-10	Kevin Teasley
Veritas Academy	814 E La Salle Ave	South Bend, IN	46617-2815	574-287-3230	287-2643	K-8	Rachel Robinson

Iowa

School	Address	City,State	Zip code	Telephone	Fax	Grade	Contact
Buffalo Ridge Charter S	4440 US Highway 71	Sioux Rapids, IA	50585-2030	712-283-2571	283-2285	1-6	Rick Roghair
Iowa Central Charter HS	PO Box 49	Burnside, IA	50521-0049	515-359-2235	359-2236	9-12	Launi Dane

Kansas

School	Address	City,State	Zip code	Telephone	Fax	Grade	Contact
Alternative Learning Ctr at Enterprise	108 N Factory	Enterprise, KS	67441-9104	785-263-8330	493-0770	9-12	Larry Patrick
Basehor-Linwood Virtual Charter S	2108 N 155th St	Basehor, KS	66007-9395	913-724-1727	724-4518	K-12	Brenda DeGroot
Chanute Charter ES	500 N Forest St	Chanute, KS	66720	620-432-2530	431-7498	1-5	Jim Goracke
Complete HS Maize	11411 W 49th St N	Maize, KS	67101	316-722-4790	729-0621	9-12	Teresa Ott
Cornerstone Alternative HS	720 E 7th St	Galena, KS	66739-1704	620-783-4499	783-1718	9-12	Tony Simmons
Delia Charter S	PO Box 99	Delia, KS	66418-0099	785-771-3470	771-3461	K-12	James McDaniel
Elkhart Cyber S	PO Box 999	Elkhart, KS	67950-0999	620-697-1166	697-2607	K-12	Sherri Hurn
Greeley County Charter S	400 W Lawrence St	Tribune, KS	67879-9636	620-376-4265	376-2465	K-12	Dale Herl
Haysville Charter S	130 Stewart Ave	Haysville, KS	67060-1602	316-554-2305		K-12	Mark Foster
Hope Street Academy Charter S	1900 SW Hope St	Topeka, KS	66604-3557	785-438-4280	271-3684	1-12	William Bagshaw
Hutchinson Cyber Charter S	100 W 27th Ave	Hutchinson, KS	67502-3424	620-665-4670		K-12	Rod Rathbun
Learning Center of Harper	1014 Central St	Harper, KS	67058-1309	620-896-2447	896-2479	9-12	Emily Ximinez
McPherson Alternative Center	1600 E Euclid St	Mc Pherson, KS	67460-3899	620-241-9507	241-9509	K-12	Karen Meats
New Beginnings Academy	411 S Central Ave	Chanute, KS	66720-2323	620-432-2503	432-2506	9-12	Kent Wire
Peoria Street Charter S	PO Box 1270	Louisburg, KS	66053-1270	913-837-3458	837-3458	9-12	John Brooks
Pleasantview Academy	5013 S Dean Rd	Hutchinson, KS	67501-9123	620-662-5516	662-5031	PK-12	Brian Boston
Productivity Academy	123 N Oak	Pratt, KS	67124	620-672-4555	672-4558	9-12	Bill Harris
Reno County Academies	1 E 9th Ave	Hutchinson, KS	67501-6200	620-665-4125	665-4143	1-12	Don Thomas
Smoky Valley Virtual Charter S	1/2 Viking Blvd	Lindsborg, KS	67456	785-227-4254	227-2909		Marla Elmquist
Spring Hill ES	300 S Webster St	Spring Hill, KS	66083-8566	913-592-7277	592-5483	PK-5	Dr. Pam Bevan
21st Century Learning Academy	PO Box 124	Mullinville, KS	67109-0124	620-548-2289	548-2389	K-12	John Jones
West Franklin Charter S	PO Box 409	Williamsburg, KS	66095-0409	785-746-5440	746-5748	K-12	Robert Allen
Yoder Charter S	PO Box 78	Yoder, KS	67585-0078	620-465-2605	465-2307	K-8	Deleon Martens

Louisiana

School	Address	City,State	Zip code	Telephone	Fax	Grade	Contact
Audubon Charter S	428 Broadway St	New Orleans, LA	70118-3514	504-862-5135	866-1691	PK-8	Janice Dupuy
Avoyelles Charter S	201 Longfellow Rd	Mansura, LA	71350-4292	318-240-8285	253-8452	K-9	Julie Durand
Behrman S	715 Opelousas Ave	New Orleans, LA	70114-2499	504-363-1001	309-8174	PK-8	Rene Carter
Capdau Charter S	3821 Franklin Ave	New Orleans, LA	70122	504-872-9257		PK-9	
Children's Charter S	900 McClung St	Baton Rouge, LA	70802-8129	225-387-9273	387-9272	PK-5	
Community S for Apprenticeship Learning	1555 Madison Ave	Baton Rouge, LA	70802-3460	225-336-1410	336-1414	6-8	Dujan Johnson
Easton HS	3019 Canal St	New Orleans, LA	70126	504-827-4615	827-4545	9-12	Alexina Medley
Einstein Charter S	5100 Cannes St	New Orleans, LA	70129-1203	504-243-5823	243-5825	K-8	
Eisenhower ES	3700 Tall Pines Dr	New Orleans, LA	70131-8499	504-398-7127	398-7129	PK-8	Cynthia Bernard
Fischer ES	1801 L B Landry Ave	New Orleans, LA	70114-6166	504-363-1009	363-1013	PK-8	Dahme Bolden

School	Address	City,State	Zip code	Telephone	Fax	Grade	Contact
Franklin HS	2001 Leon C Simon Dr	New Orleans, LA	70122-3525	504-286-2600	286-2642	9-12	Carol Christian
Glencoe Charter S	4491 LA Highway 83	Franklin, LA	70538	337-923-6900	923-0982	K-8	Michael Toney Parrie
Green Charter S	2319 Valence St	New Orleans, LA	70115-5959	504-896-4086	896-4147	K-8	Anthony Recasner
Harte ES	5300 Berkley Dr	New Orleans, LA	70131-7204	504-398-7101	398-7103	PK-6	Henry Shepard
Haynes Charter ES	356 East Blvd	Baton Rouge, LA	70802-5914	225-346-0067	346-0069	PK-5	Maurice Haynes
Jefferson Community Charter S	3528 Montford St	Jefferson, LA	70121-1824	504-836-0808	828-6888	6-8	Priscilla E. Bourgeois
Karr HS	3332 Huntlee Dr	New Orleans, LA	70131-7099	504-398-7115	398-7118	9-12	John Hiser
King Charter S for Science & Tech	2300 St Claude Ave	New Orleans, LA	70117	504-942-1788	942-7404	PK-8	Doris Hicks
KIPP Believe College Prep S	1607 S Carrollton Ave	New Orleans, LA	70118	504-312-2420		5-8	Adam Meinig
Lafayette Academy	2727 S Carrollton Ave	New Orleans, LA	70118-4387	504-862-5130	309-8173	PK-7	Eileen Williams
Lafayette Charter HS	516 E Pinhook Rd	Lafayette, LA	70501-8610	337-261-8981	237-0493	9-12	Lawrence Lilly
Lake Forest Charter ES	12000 Hayne Blvd	New Orleans, LA	70126	504-243-5743	309-4410	K-7	Mardele Early
Louisiana S for Agricultural Sciences	5303 H 115	Bunkie, LA	71322	318-346-8029	346-4479	8-11	Jude Pitre
Lusher Charter S	5624 Freret St	New Orleans, LA	70115	504-862-5110	309-4171	6-11	Kathy Reidlinger
McDonogh 15 S	721 Saint Philip St	New Orleans, LA	70116-2795	504-782-4279		PK-8	Gary Robichaux
McDonogh 32 S	800 De Armas St	New Orleans, LA	70114-4414	504-363-1057	363-1060	PK-8	
Moton ES	3000 Abundance St	New Orleans, LA	70126-5639	504-942-3615	942-3616	PK-6	Paulette Bruno
Nelson Charter S	1111 Milan St	New Orleans, LA	70119	504-942-3670	309-8072	PK-8	Jonathan Williams
New Orleans Charter MS	3801 Monroe St	New Orleans, LA	70118-3405	504-486-0804	486-0540	6-8	Dr. Anthony Recasner
New Orleans Free S	3601 Camp St	New Orleans, LA	70115-2537	504-656-6763		PK-8	
New Vision Learning Academy	507 Swayze St	Monroe, LA	71201-8130	318-338-9995	338-9987	PK-6	Rev. Andrew Mansfield
Northwood HS	202 Robin St	Amite, LA	70422-5712	985-748-3989	748-3990	7-12	Rhea Marrs
Priestley Charter S	1607 S Carrollton Ave	New Orleans, LA	70118-2892	504-862-5100	862-5199	9-12	
Singleton Charter MS	1924 Philip St	New Orleans, LA	70113-2506	504-581-2388	561-0640	6-8	Doug Evans
Singleton Charter S	2220 Oretha C Haley Blvd	New Orleans, LA	70113	504-568-3466		PK-8	Melrose Biagas
Tubman S	2013 General Meyer Ave	New Orleans, LA	70114-1533	504-363-1065	363-1067	K-8	
Tureaud ES	2021 Pauger St	New Orleans, LA	70116-1533	504-942-3472	309-8124	K-5	
Walker HS	2832 General Meyer Ave	New Orleans, LA	70114-3097	504-363-1072	363-1085	9-12	Mary Laurie
Wicker S	2011 Bienville St	New Orleans, LA	70112-3397	504-592-8547	592-8545	K-8	
Wright Charter S	1426 Napoleon Ave	New Orleans, LA	70115-3980	504-304-3915	896-4095	K-8	Sharon Clark

Maryland

School	Address	City,State	Zip code	Telephone	Fax	Grade	Contact
City Neighbors Charter S	4301 Raspe Ave	Baltimore, MD	21206-1913	410-325-2627		PK-8	Roberta Mantione
Inner Harbor East S	200 N Central Ave	Baltimore, MD	21202-5005	410-537-5890		K-12	Mark Harris
KIPP Ujima Village Academy	4701 Greenspring Ave	Baltimore, MD	21209-4704	410-545-3669	664-6865	K-5	Jason Botel
Monocacy Valley Montessori S	217 Dill Ave	Frederick, MD	21701-4905	301-668-5013	668-5015	K-6	Bettejane Weiss
Northwood Appold S	4417 Loch Raven Blvd	Baltimore, MD	21218-1554	410-323-6712		K-8	Virginia Richardson
Patterson Park S	27 N Lakewood Ave	Baltimore, MD	21224-1155	410-558-1230		PK-8	Jennifer Ciavirella
Southwest Charter S	31 S Schroeder St	Baltimore, MD	21223-2559	443-980-9016		PK-8	Turi Nelson

Massachusetts

School	Address	City,State	Zip code	Telephone	Fax	Grade	Contact
Academy of Pacific Rim Charter S	1 Westinghouse Plz	Hyde Park, MA	02136-2059	617-361-0050	361-0045	6-12	Spencer Blasdale
Academy of Strategic Learning	9 Water St	Amesbury, MA	01913-2936	978-388-8037	388-8073	7-12	Donna Georges
Advanced Math & Science Academy	201 Forest St	Marlborough, MA	01752-3012	508-597-2400	597-2499	6-7	Julia Sigalovsky
Atlantis Charter S	37 Park St	Fall River, MA	02721-1712	508-672-3537	672-2474	K-8	Fernando Goulart
Banneker Charter S	21 Notre Dame Ave	Cambridge, MA	02140-2505	617-497-7771	497-4223	K-8	Lenora Jennings
Barnstable Horace Mann Charter S	730 Osterville-W Barnstable	Marstons Mills, MA	02648	508-420-0185	420-0229	5-6	Kara Peterson
Berkshire Arts & Technology Charter S	PO Box 267	Adams, MA	01220-0267	413-743-7311	743-7327	6-10	Julia Bowen
Boston Collegiate Charter S	11 Mayhew St	Dorchester, MA	02125-1628	617-265-1172	265-1176	5-12	Kathleen Sullivan
Boston Day & Evening Academy	20 Kearsarge Ave	Roxbury, MA	02119-2318	617-635-6789	635-6380	9-12	Margaret Maccini
Boston Preparatory Charter S	1286 Hyde Park Ave	Hyde Park, MA	02136-2714	617-333-6688	333-6689	6-7	Howard Mccue
Boston Renaissance Charter S	250 Stuart St	Boston, MA	02116-5435	617-357-0900	338-2647	K-6	Roger F. Harris
Brooke Charter S	190 Cummins Hwy	Roslindale, MA	02131-3722	617-325-7977	325-2260	5-8	Jon C. Clark
Cape Cod Lighthouse Charter S	225 Route 6A	Orleans, MA	02653	508-240-2800	240-3583	6-8	Sean O'Neil
Champion HMCS S	37 Erie Ave	Brockton, MA	02302-3117	508-894-4377	894-4380	9-12	Virginia Warn
Charter S	206 Jackson St	Lowell, MA	01852-2106	978-323-0800	323-4600	K-5	Rida Eng
City on a Hill Charter S	320 Huntington Ave	Boston, MA	02115-5018	617-262-9838	262-9064	9-12	Michael Duffy
Codman Academy	637 Washington St	Dorchester, MA	02124-3510	617-287-0700	287-9064	9-12	Meg Campbell
Community Charter S of Cambridge	245 Bent St	Cambridge, MA	02141-2001	617-354-0047	354-3624	7-9	Paula Evans
Community Day Charter S	190 Hampshire St	Lawrence, MA	01840-1251	978-682-6628	682-1013	K-8	Sheila Balboni
Conservatory Lab Charter S	25 Arlington St	Brighton, MA	02135-2124	617-254-8904	254-8909	K-5	Jonathan Rappaport
Excel Academy Charter S	1150 Saratoga St	East Boston, MA	02128-1228	617-561-1371	561-1378	7-8	Yutaka Tamura
Foster Regional Charter S	10 New Bond St	Worcester, MA	01606-2699	508-854-8400	854-8484	K-12	Dr. Cameron Dewar
Four Rivers Charter S	248 Colrain Rd	Greenfield, MA	01301-9701	413-775-4577	775-4578	7-10	Edward Blatchford
Foxboro Regional Charter S	131 Central St	Foxboro, MA	02035-2458	508-543-2508	543-7982	K-12	Mark Logan
Franklin Classical Charter S	201 Main St	Franklin, MA	02038-1933	508-541-3434	541-5396	K-8	Robin Coyne
Health Careers Academy	100 Fenway	Boston, MA	02115-3782	617-373-8576	373-7850	9-12	Albert Holland
Health Careers Academy	360 Huntington Ave	Boston, MA	02115-5005	617-373-8576	373-7850	9-12	Albert Holland
Hilltown Cooperative Charter S	PO Box 147	Haydenville, MA	01039-0147	413-268-3421	268-3185	K-8	Amy Aaron
Hill View Montessori S	PO Box 1545	Haverhill, MA	01831-2145	978-521-2616	521-2656	K-4	Margaret Roberts
Holyoke Community Charter S	2200 Northampton St	Holyoke, MA	01040-3430	413-533-0111	552-3991	K-7	Sonia Pope
Hughes Academy	91 School St	Springfield, MA	01105-1316	413-747-5200	747-4528	K-8	Douglas Greer
King Charter S of Excellence	106 Wilbraham Rd	Springfield, MA	01109-3117	413-746-3655		K-2	Allan Katz
Kipp Academy Lynn Charter S	25 Bessom St	Lynn, MA	01902-1204	781-598-1609	623-5700	5-6	Joshua Zoia
Lawrence Family Development Charter S	34 West St	Lawrence, MA	01841-3426	978-689-9863	689-8133	K-8	Patricia Karl
Lowell Community Charter S	206 Jackson St	Lowell, MA	01852-2106	978-323-0800	970-0715	K-8	Elizabeth Torosian
Lowell Middlesex Academy Charter S	33 Kearney Sq	Lowell, MA	01852-1901	978-656-3165	459-0546	9-12	Margaret McDevitt
Mann Champion Charter S	39 Erie Ave	Brockton, MA	02302-3117	508-894-4377	894-4380	9-12	Virginia Warn
Marblehead Community Charter S	17 Lime St	Marblehead, MA	01945-2530	781-631-0777	631-0500	4-8	Thomas Commeret
Marstons Mills East Horace Mann Charter	760 Osterville-W Barnstable	Marstons Mills, MA	02648	508-420-1100	420-1486	K-4	Edward Deusser
Martha's Vineyard Charter S	PO Box 1150	West Tisbury, MA	02575-1150	508-693-9900	696-9008	K-12	Robert Moore
McAuliffe Regional Charter S	25 Clinton St	Framingham, MA	01702-6702	508-879-9000	879-1066	6-8	Robert Kaufman
Media & Technology Charter HS	1001 Commonwealth Ave	Boston, MA	02215-1308	617-232-0300	232-2838	9-12	Alan Safran
Middlesex Charter S	33 Kearney Sq	Lowell, MA	01852-1901	978-656-0170		9-12	Lisa Bryant
Murdoch Middle Charter S	40 Brick Kiln Rd	Chelmsford, MA	01824-3222	978-970-0100	970-3522	5-8	Walter Landberg
Mystic Valley Advantage Regional S	770 Salem St	Malden, MA	02148-4415	781-388-0222	321-5688	K-12	Anthony Biegler
Neighborhood House Charter S	21 Queen St	Dorchester, MA	02122-2509	617-825-0703	825-1829	K-8	Kevin Andrews
New Bedford Global Learning Charter S	455 County St	New Bedford, MA	02740-5194	508-991-7000	991-4127	5-12	Paul Fay
New Leadership Charter S	180 Ashland Ave	Springfield, MA	01119-2704	413-782-9111	782-9991	6-12	Bruce Shaw
North Central Essential Charter S	1 Oak Hill Rd	Fitchburg, MA	01420-3958	978-345-2701	345-9127	7-12	Pater Garbus
Parker Charter Essential S	49 Antietam St	Ayer, MA	01434-5230	978-772-3293	772-3295	7-12	Teriann Schrader
Phoenix Charter Academy	PO Box 505064	Chelsea, MA	02150-5064	617-276-4670		9-12	Beth Anderson
Pioneer Valley Performing Arts Charter S	15 Mulligan Dr	South Hadley, MA	01075-7511	413-552-1580	552-1594	7-12	Robert Brick
Prospect Hill Academy Charter S	15 Webster Ave	Somerville, MA	02143-3311	617-284-7800	284-7841	K-12	Jon Drescher
Rising Tide Charter S	6 Resnik Rd	Plymouth, MA	02360-4873	508-747-2620	830-9441	5-8	Jill Crafts
River Valley Charter S	2 Perry Way	Newburyport, MA	01950-4001	978-465-0065	465-0119	K-8	Dr. Dale Bishop
Roxbury Charter HS	18 Hulbert St	Roxbury, MA	02119-1940	617-442-3500	442-3552	9-11	Dr. Carlos Brossard
Roxbury Preparatory Charter S	120 Fisher Ave	Roxbury, MA	02120-3320	617-566-2361	566-2373	6-8	Joshua Phillips
SABIS International Charter S	160 Joan St	Springfield, MA	01129-1530	413-783-2600	783-2555	K-12	Maretta Thomsen
Salem Academy Charter S	PO Box 8014	Salem, MA	01971-8014	978-744-2105	744-7246	6-9	Dennis Wright
Seven Hills Charter S	51 Gage St	Worcester, MA	01605-3014	508-799-7500	753-7318	K-8	Krista Osbourn
Smith Leadership Academy Charter S	23 Leonard St	Boston, MA	02122-2718	617-474-7950	474-7957	6-8	Karmala Sherwood
South Shore Charter S	100 Longwater Cir	Norwell, MA	02061-1616	781-982-4202	982-4201	K-12	Michael Munhall
Sturgis Charter S	427 Main St	Hyannis, MA	02601-3905	508-778-1782	771-6785	9-12	Eric Hieser
Uphams Corner Charter S	7 Elkins St	Boston, MA	02127-1601	617-268-4695	268-5604	5-8	Edward Cook

Michigan

School	Address	City,State	Zip code	Telephone	Fax	Grade	Contact
Abney Academy	1435 Fulton St E	Grand Rapids, MI	49503-3853	616-454-5541	454-5598	K-5	Tamasha James
Academic Transitional Academy	1520 Michigan Rd	Port Huron, MI	48060-4750	810-364-3449	364-3347	9-10	Pete Spencer
Academy for Tech & Enterprise	2102 Weiss St	Saginaw, MI	48602-5049	989-399-6150	399-6165	11-12	Julie Walker
Academy of Business and Technology	19625 Wood St	Melvindale, MI	48122-2201	313-382-3422	382-3906	6-12	John Kirk
Academy of Business and Technology ES	5277 Calhoun St	Dearborn, MI	48126-3203	313-581-2223	581-2247	K-5	Paul Merritt
Academy of Detroit - West	16418 W Mcnichols Rd	Detroit, MI	48235-3354	313-272-5473	272-4823	K-1	Mae Alexander
Academy of Detroit West - Redford	23749 Elmira	Redford, MI	48239-1405	313-387-9238	387-9261	2-6	Delores Snorton
Academy of Flint	4100 W Coldwater Rd	Flint, MI	48504-1102	810-789-9484	789-9483	K-8	Verdell Duncan
Academy of Inkster	28612 Avondale St	Inkster, MI	48141-1642	734-641-1312	641-1317	9-12	Raymond J. Alvarado
Academy of Lathrup Village	27700 Southfield Rd	Southfield, MI	48076-7901	248-569-0089	569-4944	K-8	Joe Moody
Academy of Michigan	20820 Greenfield Rd	Oak Park, MI	48237-3051	248-968-0440	968-0622	9-12	LaGuardia Summers
Academy of Oak Park	21700 Marlow St	Oak Park, MI	48237-2604	248-547-2323	547-2515	K-5	Rashid Fai'Sal
Academy of Oak Park	21300 Mendota Ave	Ferndale, MI	48220-2164	248-586-9358	586-9362	6-12	Maurice Pope
Academy of Southfield	18330 George Washington Dr	Southfield, MI	48075-2785	248-557-6121	557-2915	K-8	Carolyn Mosley
Academy of Warren	13943 E 8 Mile Rd	Warren, MI	48089-3351	586-552-8010	552-8014	K-8	Jerry Parker
Academy of Waterford	3000 Sashabaw Rd	Waterford, MI	48329-4040	248-674-1649	674-3173	K-8	Bradley Gibbs
Academy of Westland	300 S Henry Ruff Rd	Westland, MI	48186-5087	734-722-1465	722-8025	K-8	Christopher Lindsay
Advanced Technology Academy	7265 Calhoun St	Dearborn, MI	48126-1492	313-582-4500	582-9407	K-12	Barry Hawthorne

School	Address	City,State	Zip code	Telephone	Fax	Grade	Contact
A.G.B.U. Alex & Marie Manoogian S	22001 Northwestern Hwy	Southfield, MI	48075-4001	248-569-2988	569-1346	K-12	H. Torossian
Aisha Shule/W.E.B. Dubois Prep S	20119 Wisconsin St	Detroit, MI	48221-1132	313-345-6050	345-1059	K-12	Imani Humphrey
Allen Academy	8666 Quincy St	Detroit, MI	48204-2306	313-898-6444	898-6555	K-12	Tim Green
American Montessori Academy	14800 Middlebelt Rd	Livonia, MI	48154-4031	734-525-7100	525-8952	K-4	Amy Pogorzelski
Ann Arbor Learning Community	3980 Research Park Dr	Ann Arbor, MI	48108-2220	734-477-0340	477-0341	K-8	Jennifer Taylor
Arbor Academy	55 Arbor St	Battle Creek, MI	49015-2903	269-963-5851	964-2643	K-6	Paul Doersam
Arts Academy in the Woods	12900 Frazho Rd	Warren, MI	48089-1300	586-427-4569	427-4570	9-12	Kay Dyer
Arts & Technology Academy of Pontiac	48980 Woodward Ave	Pontiac, MI	48342-5034	248-452-9309	452-9312	K-8	Sadie Mahone
Battle Creek Area Learning Center	711 Riverside Dr	Battle Creek, MI	49015-4665	269-565-4782	565-4784	10-12	Charles Crider
Bay-Arenac Community HS	1608 Hudson St	Essexville, MI	48732-1387	989-893-8811	895-7749	9-12	Ryan Donlan
Bay County Public School Academy	1110 State St	Bay City, MI	48706-3699	989-684-6484	684-6202	K-8	William Ignatowski
Benton Harbor Charter S	455 Riverview Dr	Benton Harbor, MI	49022-5015	269-927-3807	927-3673	K-8	Cynthia Jack
Black River Public S	491 Columbia Ave	Holland, MI	49423-4838	616-355-0055	355-0057	1-12	David Angerer
Blue Water Learning Academy	5202 Taft Rd	Algonac, MI	48001-4701	810-794-8067	794-8888	7-12	James Lenore
Bradford Academy	26555 Franklin Rd	Southfield, MI	48033-5340	248-351-0000	356-4770	K-7	Fred Borowski
Bridge Academy	9600 Buffalo St	Hamtramck, MI	48212-3323	313-887-8100	887-8101	K-8	Naji Jaber
Bruce Academy	5555 Conner St	Detroit, MI	48213-3448	313-656-2610	924-0095	7-12	Henry McQueen
Bruce Academy	3500 John R St	Detroit, MI	48201-2402	313-494-3259	831-8202	5-12	Edythe Friley
Bruce Academy	330 Glendale St	Highland Park, MI	48203-3277	313-852-7506	852-7566	5-12	Douglas Gabriel
Burton Glen Charter Academy	4171 E Atherton Rd	Burton, MI	48519-1435	810-744-2300	744-2400	K-8	Sandra L. Ritter
Business Entrepreneurship Sci & Tech S	200 Highland St	Highland Park, MI	48203-3405	313-869-1000	869-1002	K-6	Delria Crippen
Campus ECC	1326 Thomas St SE	Grand Rapids, MI	49506-2652	616-819-3522	819-3535	PK-K	Jeaune Allard
Canton Charter Academy	49100 Ford Rd	Canton, MI	48187-5415	734-453-9517	453-9551	K-8	Claudia Williamson
Capitol Area Academy	5525 S Pennsylvania Ave	Lansing, MI	48911-4091	517-882-1400	882-0400	K-8	Michael Haggen
Carleton Academy	2001 W Hallett Rd	Hillsdale, MI	49242-1959	517-437-2000	437-2919	K-12	Julie Duncan
Carson Academy	1326 Saint Antoine St	Detroit, MI	48226-2301	313-967-2001	967-2238	5-12	Nathanial King
Carver Academy	14510 2nd Ave	Highland Park, MI	48203-5715	313-865-6024	865-6658	K-8	Marcie Wade
Casa Richard Academy	2635 Howard St	Detroit, MI	48216-2058	313-963-7757	963-7768	9-12	Mary Ellen Walenta
CASMAN Alternative Academy	1710 Merkey Rd W	Manistee, MI	49660-9180	231-723-4981	723-1555	7-12	Cameron Clark
Center Academy	310 W Oakley St	Flint, MI	48503-3915	810-341-6944	341-6949	K-8	Elizabeth Jordan
Center for Literacy & Creativity	18401 W McNichols Rd	Detroit, MI	48219-4113	313-537-9400	537-9410	K-8	Deborah Holt-Foster
Central Academy	2459 S Industrial Hwy	Ann Arbor, MI	48104-6129	734-822-1110	822-1101	PK-12	Luay Shalabi
Chandler Park Academy - Kelly	20100 Kelly Rd	Harper Woods, MI	48225-1201	313-839-9886	839-3221	K-6	Vivian Jackson
Chandler Park Academy - Oak Park	13400 Oak Park Blvd	Oak Park, MI	48237-3629	248-545-1016	545-1857	K-3	Dr. Carrie Hollaway
Chandler Park - Greenfield Charter S	19370 Greenfield Rd	Detroit, MI	48235-2003	313-345-5651	345-6346	4-8	Vivian Jackson
Chandler Park - Haverhill	4901 Haverhill St	Detroit, MI	48224-3559	313-884-8830	884-9130	6-8	Rosa Jackson
Chandler Park - Philip	897 Philip St	Detroit, MI	48215-2935	313-821-2552	821-2491	7-7	Darah Griffin
Chandler Woods Charter Academy	6895 Samrick Ave NE	Belmont, MI	49306-8844	616-866-6000	866-6001	K-8	Fred Slade
Chatfield S	231 Lake Dr	Lapeer, MI	48446-1661	810-667-8970	667-8983	K-6	Betty McCauley
Chavez Academy	8126 W Vernor Hwy	Detroit, MI	48209-1524	313-843-9440	297-6948	K-5	Cheri Wasiel
Chavez HS	1761 Waterman St	Detroit, MI	48209-2021	313-551-0611	551-0552	9-12	Christopher Silva
Chavez MS	6782 Goldsmith St	Detroit, MI	48209-2089	313-842-0006	842-0167	6-8	Rick Guerra
Cherry Hill School of Performing Arts	28500 Avondale St	Inkster, MI	48141-3916	734-722-2811	641-9439	K-12	J. Perkins
Cole Academy	1915 W Mount Hope Ave	Lansing, MI	48910-2434	517-372-0038	372-1446	K-5	James Henderson
Commonwealth Cmmnty Development Acad.	13477 Eureka St	Detroit, MI	48212-1754	313-336-9470	366-9471	K-6	Cullian Hill
Concord Academy-Antrim	5055 Corey Rd	Mancelona, MI	49659-9467	231-584-2080	584-2082	K-12	E. Evans
Concord Academy - Boyne	401 E Dietz Rd	Boyne City, MI	49712-9653	231-582-0194	582-4214	K-12	Larry Kubovchick
Concord Academy-Petoskey	2468 Atkins Rd	Petoskey, MI	49770-9003	231-439-6800	439-6803	K-12	Benjamin Jankens
Conner Creek Academy	28111 Imperial Dr	Warren, MI	48093-4281	586-575-9500	575-9483	K-12	Ruth Bowers
Conner Creek Academy East	16911 Eastland St	Roseville, MI	48066-2078	586-779-8055	498-8734	K-12	Charles Meredith
Consortium College Preparatory HS	1250 Rosa Parks Blvd	Detroit, MI	48216-1950	313-964-2339	964-3922	7-12	Rod Atkins
Countryside Charter S	4800 Meadowbrook Rd	Benton Harbor, MI	49022-9629	269-944-3319	944-3724	K-12	Paul Marazita
Creative Learning Academy of Science	540 Lang Rd	Beaverton, MI	48612-8101	989-435-8252	435-4187	K-8	Paige Pope
Creative Montessori Academy	15100 Northline Rd	Southgate, MI	48195-2408	734-284-5600	281-2637	K-8	Rochelle Cochran
Creative Technologies Academy	350 Pine St	Cedar Springs, MI	49319-8680	616-696-4905	696-4920	K-12	Lexie Coxon
Crescent Academy	17570 W 12 Mile Rd	Southfield, MI	48076-1905	248-423-4581	423-1027	K-7	Rose Marie Trotter
Crockett Academy	4851 14th St	Detroit, MI	48208-2204	313-896-6078	896-1363	K-12	Mary Lou Van Antwerp
Cross Creek Charter Academy	7701 Kalamazoo Ave SE	Byron Center, MI	49315-9320	616-656-4000	656-4001	PK-8	Bruce Bradford
Crossroads Charter Academy	215 N State St	Big Rapids, MI	49307-1444	231-796-9041	796-9790	K-12	David Vander Goot
da Vinci Institute	559 Murphy Dr	Jackson, MI	49202-1622	517-780-9980	780-9747	K-8	Kimberly Norton
da Vinci Institute	2255 Emmons Rd	Jackson, MI	49201-8335	517-796-0031	796-0320	9-12	Sandy Maxson
Dearborn Academy	19310 Ford Rd	Dearborn, MI	48128-2403	313-982-1300	982-9087	K-8	Cynthia Leaman
Detroit Academy of Arts & Sciences	2985 E Jefferson Ave	Detroit, MI	48207-4288	313-259-1744	259-8393	K-5	Stan Bowman
Detroit Academy of Arts and Sciences	2260 Medbury St	Detroit, MI	48211-2718	313-923-0281	923-0437	6-12	Anthony Jackson
Detroit Community HS	12675 Burt Rd	Detroit, MI	48223-3314	313-537-3570	537-6904	9-12	Bart Eddy
Detroit Community S - Oak Park	13400 Oak Park Blvd	Oak Park, MI	48237-3629	248-545-1016	545-1857	K-5	Mary Loenhardi
Detroit Edison Academy	1903 Wilkins St	Detroit, MI	48207-2112	313-833-1100	833-8653	K-8	Ralph Bland
Detroit Enterprise Academy	11224 Kercheval St	Detroit, MI	48214-3323	313-823-5799	823-0342	K-6	Ashanti Bryant
Detroit Merit Academy	1091 Alter Rd	Detroit, MI	48215-2861	313-331-3328	331-3278	K-8	Heidi Benser
Detroit Premier Academy	7781 Asbury Park	Detroit, MI	48228-3685	313-945-1472	945-1744	K-6	Kecia Evans
Detroit School of Industrial Arts	11406 Morang Dr	Detroit, MI	48224-1719	313-839-1883	839-4194	9-12	Holly Davis-Webster
Discovery Arts & Technology Academy	27355 Woodfield Rd	Inkster, MI	48141	313-827-0762	827-0763	K-4	Rita Bowman
Discovery S	PO Box 1070	Fennville, MI	49408-1070	269-561-2191	561-2302	K-8	Bruce Foerch
Dove Academy of Detroit	8210 Rolyat St	Detroit, MI	48234-3358	313-366-9110	366-9130	K-6	Frank Nardelli
Drew Academy	50 W Josephine St	Ecorse, MI	48229-1748	313-383-7501	383-7502	K-5	Sabin Duncan
Eagle Crest Charter Academy	11950 Riley St	Holland, MI	49424-8553	616-786-2400	786-4692	K-8	Daniel Harris
Eastern Washtenaw Multicultural Academy	5550 Platt Rd	Ann Arbor, MI	48108-9762	734-677-0732	677-0740	K-9	Dan Henry
Edison-Oakland Academy	22111 Woodward Ave	Ferndale, MI	48220-1812	248-582-8191	582-8196	K-6	Gail Georgette Parks
El-Hajj Malik El-Shabazz Academy	1028 W Barnes Ave	Lansing, MI	48910-1377	517-267-8474	484-0095	PK-6	Dr. Eugene L. Cain
Ellis Academy	18977 Schaefer Hwy	Detroit, MI	48235-1762	313-927-5395	927-5376	K-8	Machion Morris
Endeavor Charter Academy	380 Helmer Rd N	Battle Creek, MI	49015-1476	269-962-9300	962-9393	K-8	Russ Ainslee
Excel Charter Academy	4201 Breton Rd SE	Grand Rapids, MI	49512-3857	616-281-9339	281-6707	K-8	William Knoester
Ford Academy	PO Box 1148	Dearborn, MI	48121-1148	313-982-6200	982-6195	9-12	Cora Christmas
Forten Academy	5690 Cecil St	Detroit, MI	48210-1964	313-897-2203	897-2206	6-12	Cameron Owens
Fortis Academy	3875 Golfside Dr	Ypsilanti, MI	48197-3726	734-572-3623	572-5792	K-6	Chris Thompson
Frontier International Academy	2619 Florian St	Hamtramck, MI	48212-3452	313-758-0940		6-12	Harun Rashid
Gateway Middle HS	311 State St SE	Grand Rapids, MI	49503-4312	616-458-9646	458-9647	7-12	Meg Hackett Carrier
Gaudior Academy	27100 Avondale St	Inkster, MI	48141-1816	313-792-9444	792-9445	K-9	Rosemarie Gonzales
Gist Academy	28955 Rosewood St	Inkster, MI	48141-1656	734-728-4813	722-5111	5-8	Celestine Sanders
Gist Academy	4825 Dancy St	Westland, MI	48186-5148	734-721-5515	721-9129	K-4	Tina Hatcher
Grand Blanc Academy	5135 E Hill Rd	Grand Blanc, MI	48439-7637	810-953-3140	953-3165	K-8	Zel Seidenberg
Grand Rapids Child Discovery Center	640 5th St NW	Grand Rapids, MI	49504-5107	616-459-0330	732-4437	K-5	Susan Lukaart
Grand Traverse Academy	1245 Hammond Rd E	Traverse City, MI	49686-9000	231-995-0665	995-0880	K-12	Kaye Mentley
Grattan Academy	12047 Old Belding Rd NE	Belding, MI	48809-9367	616-691-8999	691-9857	K-5	Elizabeth Witt-Kreiner
Grattan Academy HS	9481 Jordan Rd	Greenville, MI	48838-9437	616-754-9360	754-9363	6-12	Catherine Browers
Great Lakes Academy	46312 Woodward Ave	Pontiac, MI	48342-5006	248-334-6434	334-6457	K-6	Carrie Hollaway
Great Oaks Academy	1075 E Gardenia Ave	Madison Heights, MI	48071-3433	248-399-3740	399-3325	K-6	Elise Seitz
Hamtramck Academy	11420 Conant St	Hamtramck, MI	48212-3134	313-368-7312	368-7376	K-5	S. Glenn
Hanley International Academy	2609 Poland St	Hamtramck, MI	48212-3459	313-875-8888	875-8889	K-5	Carolyn Glover
Health Career Academy of St Clair	PO Box 1500	Marysville, MI	48040-8000	810-364-8990	364-8139	11-12	Tom Kennedy
HEART Academy	19800 Anita St	Harper Woods, MI	48225-1109	313-882-4631	882-4761	9-12	Angela Allen-Baker
Hillsdale Preparatory S	160 Mechanic Rd Ste 170	Hillsdale, MI	49242-1053	517-437-4625	437-3830	K-6	Kathy Burk
Holly Academy	820 Academy Rd	Holly, MI	48442-1546	248-634-5554	634-5564	K-8	Julie Kildee
Honey Creek Community S	PO Box 1406	Ann Arbor, MI	48106-1406	734-994-2636	994-2203	K-8	Sarena Conaway
Hope Academy	10100 Grand River Ave	Detroit, MI	48204-2042	313-934-0054	934-0074	K-6	Veneda Fox Sanders
Hope of Detroit Academy	4443 N Campbell St	Detroit, MI	48210-2520	313-897-8720	897-5142	K-8	Anthony Hubbard
Horizons Community HS	2550 Rogers Lane Ave SW	Wyoming, MI	49509-1972	616-530-7535	249-7661	9-12	Teriena Schwartz
Hospitality Academy of St Clair	PO Box 1500	Marysville, MI	48040-8000	810-364-8990	364-8139	11-12	Tom Kennedy
Huron Academy	11401 Metropolitan Pkwy	Sterling Hts, MI	48312-2937	586-446-9170	446-9173	K-8	Rhonda Filippi
Industrial Technology Academy	PO Box 1500	Marysville, MI	48040-8000	810-364-8990	364-8139	11-12	Tom Kennedy
Information Technology Academy	PO Box 1500	Marysville, MI	48040-8000	810-364-8990	364-8139	11-12	Tom Kennedy
International Academy of Flint	2820 S Saginaw St	Flint, MI	48503-5708	810-251-5151	251-5154	K-12	Traci Cormier
Island City Academy	6421 S Clinton Trl	Eaton Rapids, MI	48827-9698	517-663-0111	663-0167	K-8	Thomas Ackerson
Jackson Arts & Technology Academy	500 Griswold St	Jackson, MI	49203-4062	517-796-0080	796-0104	K-6	Lezlie Bowles
JKL Bahweting Charter S	1301 Marquette Ave	Sault S Marie, MI	49783-9533	906-635-5055	635-3805	K-8	Nick Oshelski
Joy Preparatory Academy	1129 Oakman Blvd	Detroit, MI	48238-2950	313-867-7828	867-7831	K-2	Michael Jackson
Joy Preparatory Academy	15055 Dexter Ave	Detroit, MI	48238-2124	313-340-0023	340-0678	3-8	Frances Gardulescu
Kalamazoo Advantage Academy	121 W South St	Kalamazoo, MI	49007-4865	269-345-7850	345-7851	K-8	Frank Sebastian
Kensington Woods HS	3700 Cleary Dr	Howell, MI	48843-6614	517-545-0828	545-7588	9-12	James Perry
Keystone Academy	47925 Bemis Rd	Belleville, MI	48111-9760	734-697-9470	697-9471	K-8	Phil Price
King Education Center	16827 Appoline St	Detroit, MI	48235-4205	313-341-4944	341-7014	K-6	Constance Price
Knapp Charter Academy	1759 Leffingwell Ave NE	Grand Rapids, MI	49525-4531	616-364-1100	364-9780	K-8	Dayna Traynor
Lakeshore Public Academy	PO Box 9	Hart, MI	49420-0009	231-873-8199	873-8196	K-12	Floyd Strandberg
Landmark Academy	4800 Lapeer Rd	Kimball, MI	48074-1517	810-982-7210	982-0679	K-8	Nancy Gardner
Laurus Academy	24590 Lahser Rd	Southfield, MI	48033-6040	248-799-8401	799-8404	K-6	Jaqueline Cassell
Learning Center Academy	9930 Burlingame Ave SW	Byron Center, MI	49315-8631	616-878-4852	878-7196	PK-12	Tom Kruzel
Life Skills Center	3100 E Jefferson Ave	Detroit, MI	48207-4221	313-567-3235	567-8554	9-12	Demetria Wesley

School	Address	City,State	Zip code	Telephone	Fax	Grade	Contact
Life Skills Center of Pontiac	142 Auburn Ave	Pontiac, MI	48342-3008	248-322-1163	322-1164	9-12	Jason Porter
Linden Charter Academy	3244 N Linden Rd	Flint, MI	48504-1753	810-720-0515	720-0626	K-8	Joe Pakalnis
Lundy Academy	950 Selden St	Detroit, MI	48201-2234	313-831-4961	831-4964	6-12	Carlitta Cabell
Macomb Academy	39092 Garfield Rd	Clinton Twp, MI	48038-4094	586-228-2201	228-2210	12-12	Bert Sterling
Madison Academy	1291 E Maple Ave	Burton, MI	48529-1503	810-744-9100	743-1796	K-6	Kenneth Maurey
Marshall Academy	18203 Homer Rd	Marshall, MI	49068-8718	269-781-6330	781-8749	K-8	Larry L. Longwell
Merritt Academy	59900 Havenridge Rd	New Haven, MI	48048-1915	586-749-6000	749-8582	K-8	Ruth Carlson
Metro Charter Academy	34800 Ecorse Rd	Romulus, MI	48174-1642	734-641-3200	641-6530	K-8	Andrew Cook
Michigan Automotive Academy	19780 Meyers Rd	Detroit, MI	48235-1229	313-864-0595	864-2271	6-8	LaToniya Jones
Michigan Automotive Academy HS	28675 Northline Rd	Romulus, MI	48174-2831	734-955-9755	955-9750	9-12	Roger Sisler
Michigan Health Academy	5845 Auburn	Detroit, MI	48228	313-982-9422	982-9415	9-12	Angelo Brown
Michigan Technical Academy	19940 Mansfield St	Detroit, MI	48235-2332	313-272-1649	272-1849	3-5	Dennis Yerke
Midland Academy	4653 E Bailey Bridge Rd	Midland, MI	48640-8542	989-496-2404	496-2466	K-12	Kathryn Shick
Mid-Michigan Leadership Academy	730 W Maple St	Lansing, MI	48906-5086	517-485-5379	485-5892	K-8	Mark Eitrem
Morey Charter S	380 W Blanchard Rd	Shepherd, MI	48883-9552	989-866-6739	866-6737	PK-12	Shelly Patton
Mt. Clemens Montessori Academy	1070 Hampton Rd	Mount Clemens, MI	48043-2955	586-465-5545	465-2283	PK-5	Genie P'Sachoulias
Muskegon Technical Academy	2900 E Apple Ave	Muskegon, MI	49442-4504	231-777-3682	767-8488	5-12	Barbara Stellard
Nataki Talibah S of Detroit	19176 Northrop St	Detroit, MI	48219-1857	313-531-3720	531-3779	K-8	Carmen N'Namdi
New Bedford Academy	6315 Secor Rd	Lambertville, MI	48144-9411	734-854-5437	854-1573	K-8	Greg Sauter
New Beginnings Academy	211 E Michigan Ave	Ypsilanti, MI	48198-5677	734-481-9001	544-2706	K-5	Kim Overton
New Branches S	256 Alger St SE	Grand Rapids, MI	49507-3409	616-243-4763	243-0305	K-6	Pamela Duffy
New City Academy	2130 W Holmes Rd # B	Lansing, MI	48910-0331	517-272-3000	272-3544	K-8	Duane Shepherd
Northpointe Academy	53 Candler St	Highland Park, MI	48203-2827	313-868-7502	868-0443	K-8	Sharon Taylor
Northridge Academy	5306 North St	Flint, MI	48505-2927	810-785-8811	785-9844	K-8	Nat Burtley
North Saginaw Charter Academy	2332 Trautner Dr	Saginaw, MI	48604-9593	989-249-5400	249-5800	K-8	Tonya Reed
North Star Academy	PO Box 577	Ishpeming, MI	49849-0577	906-226-0156	226-0167	9-12	Mary St. Clair
North Star Academy - Polaris MS	PO Box 577	Marquette, MI	49855-0577	906-226-0156	226-0167	7-8	Deborah White
Northwest Academy	115 W Hurlbut St	Charlevoix, MI	49720-1510	231-547-9000	547-9464	K-12	Cindy Romero
Nsoroma Institute Public S Academy	22180 Parklawn St	Oak Park, MI	48237-2674	248-541-2548	541-2594	K-8	Malik Yakini
Oakland Academy	6325 Oakland Dr	Portage, MI	49024-2589	269-324-8951	324-8974	K-5	Melissa Dahlinger
Oakland International Academy	28650 W 11 Mile Rd Ste 200	Farmingtn Hls, MI	48336-1503	248-427-1906	427-1913	6-12	Azra Ali
Oakland International Academy	4001 Miller St	Detroit, MI	48211-1554	313-923-0790	923-0927	K-6	James Honey
Ojibwe Charter S	11507 W Industrial Dr	Brimley, MI	49715-9087	906-248-2530	248-2532	K-10	Ralph Crosslin
Old Redford Academy	17195 Redford St	Detroit, MI	48219-3259	313-799-2780	799-2317	K-12	Cherida Gary
Outlook Academy	310 Thomas St	Allegan, MI	49010-9158	269-686-8227	686-7036	5-10	Mike Hagerty
Pansophia Academy	52 Abbott Ave	Coldwater, MI	49036-1430	517-279-4686	279-0089	K-12	Tom Dove
Paragon Charter Academy	3750 McCain Rd	Jackson, MI	49201-7675	517-750-9500	750-9501	K-8	Kathy J. Watson
Paramount Charter Academy	3624 S Westnedge Ave	Kalamazoo, MI	49008-2969	269-553-6400	553-6401	K-8	Sharon Lockett
Plymouth Educational Center S	1460 E Forest Ave	Detroit, MI	48207-1000	313-831-3280	831-5766	PK-8	Phyllis A. Ross
Pontiac Academy of Excellence	196 Cesar E Chavez Ave	Pontiac, MI	48342-1094	248-745-9420	745-9485	K-12	Todd Evans
Powell Academy	4800 Coplin St	Detroit, MI	48215-2109	313-823-5791	823-3410	K-8	H. Waters
Presque Isle Academy	PO Box 731	Onaway, MI	49765-0731	989-733-6708	733-6701	9-12	Rick Bongard
Prevail Academy	353 Cass Ave	Mount Clemens, MI	48043-2112	586-783-0173	783-0179	K-6	Catherine Witt
Public Safety Academy	PO Box 1500	Marysville, MI	48040-8000	810-364-8990	364-8139	11-12	Tom Kennedy
Reh Academy	2201 Owen St	Saginaw, MI	48601-3466	989-753-2349	753-1819	K-8	Diane Hofman
Renaissance Public S Academy	2797 S Isabella Rd	Mount Pleasant, MI	48858-2067	989-773-9889	772-4503	K-8	David Krause
Richfield Public School Academy	3807 N Center Rd	Flint, MI	48506-2642	810-736-1281	736-2326	K-8	Gareth Volz
Ridge Park Charter S	4120 Camelot Ridge Dr SE	Grand Rapids, MI	49546-2432	616-222-0093	222-0138	K-8	David King
Riverside Academy	7124 Miller Rd	Dearborn, MI	48126-1918	313-586-0200	586-0201	K-6	Charles Shamey
Ross Charter Academy	8525 Cole Dr	Warren, MI	48093-5239	586-575-9418	575-9876	K-8	Thomas Smith
Ross Hill Academy	3111 Elmwood St	Detroit, MI	48207-2418	313-922-8088	922-2015	K-10	Nellie Williams
Ross Hill Junior Academy	317 Harper Ave	Detroit, MI	48202-3500	313-876-2207	875-9462	7-10	Nellie Williams
Saginaw County Transitional Academy	919 Veterans Memorial Pkwy	Saginaw, MI	48601-1432	989-752-6176	752-3111	7-12	William Pagel
Saginaw Learn to Earn Academy	PO Box 5679	Saginaw, MI	48603-0679	989-399-7400	399-7476	10-12	Richard Beck
Saginaw Preparatory Academy	5173 Lodge St	Saginaw, MI	48601-6829	989-752-9600	752-9618	PK-6	Pamela Williams
St. Clair Academy of Style	499 Range Rd	Marysville, MI	48040	810-364-8990	364-8139	11-12	Tom Kennedy
St. Clair County Learning Academy	499 Range Rd	Marysville, MI	48040	810-364-8990	364-7474	6-12	Denice Lapish
Sankofa Shule Public S Academy	4817 Bristol St	Lansing, MI	48910-6125	517-394-4544	394-9903	K-8	Maxine Hankins Cain
Shoreline Career Education Center	772 E Parkdale Ave	Manistee, MI	49660-9110	231-398-2985	398-3036	10-12	Daniel C. Long
South Arbor Charter Academy	8200 Carpenter Rd	Ypsilanti, MI	48197-9800	734-528-2821	528-2829	K-8	Timothy DiLaura
Star International Academy	24425 Hass	Dearborn Hts, MI	48127	313-724-8990	724-8994	K-12	Anita Hassan
Stockwell Academy	9758 E Highland Rd	Howell, MI	48843-9098	810-632-2200	632-2201	K-8	Shelley Stockwell
Summit Academy	30100 Olmstead Rd	Flat Rock, MI	48134-9619	734-379-6810	379-6745	K-8	Ria Cole
Summit Academy HS	PO Box 190	Flat Rock, MI	48134-0190	734-955-1730	955-1737	9-12	Jason Hamstra
Summit Academy MS	PO Box 190	Flat Rock, MI	48134-0190	734-955-1712	955-1729	6-8	Sally Emerson
Summit Academy North	28697 Sibley Rd	Romulus, MI	48174-9736	734-789-1428	789-1431	K-5	Marie Maci
Summit Academy North MS	PO Box 190	Flat Rock, MI	48134-0190	734-955-1712	955-1729	6-8	Dennis Kemp
Sunrise Educational Center	PO Box 788	Tawas City, MI	48764-0788	989-362-2945	362-7968	K-8	Julie Bather
Three Oaks Public School Academy	1212 Kingsley St	Muskegon, MI	49442-4025	231-767-3365	777-9815	K-9	Ken Horn
Threshold Academy	PO Box 458	Greenville, MI	48838-0458	616-225-8217	225-8272	K-6	Mary Boots
Timberland Charter Academy	2574 McLaughlin Ave	Muskegon, MI	49442-4439	231-767-9700	767-9710	K-8	Juanita Preston
Timbuktu Academy of Science & Technology	8085 Doyle St	Detroit, MI	48234-3921	313-365-5601	365-5981	K-8	Daryl Turner
Toussaint Academy	2450 S Beatrice St	Detroit, MI	48217-1631	313-383-1485	383-6532	K-8	Cynthia Moore
Traverse Bay Community S	7224 Supply Rd	Traverse City, MI	49686-9400	231-947-7474	947-7667	K-8	Mark Child
Trillium Academy	15740 Rancho Rd	Taylor, MI	48180	734-374-8222	374-5025	K-9	Angela Romanowski
Triumph Academy	3000 Vivian Rd	Monroe, MI	48162-8600	734-240-2610	240-2785	K-6	Tim Lenahan
Tri-Valley Academy of Arts and Academics	2140 Valley St	Muskegon, MI	49444-1261	231-722-7118	727-0042	K-8	Jaronique Benjamin
Universal Academy	4612 Lonyo St	Detroit, MI	48210-2105	313-581-5006	581-5514	K-12	Nawal Hamadeh
Universal Learning Academy	22579 Ann Arbor Trl	Dearborn Hts, MI	48127-2507	313-724-8060	724-8082	K-2	Halim Ahmed
University Preparatory Academy	5310 Saint Antoine St	Detroit, MI	48202-4131	313-831-0100	831-4197	6-8	Doug Ross
University Preparatory Academy HS	600 Antoinette St	Detroit, MI	48202-3457	313-874-4340	874-4510	9-10	Doug Ross
Vanderbilt Charter Academy	301 W 16th St	Holland, MI	49423-3329	616-820-5050	820-5051	K-8	Ivan J. Kraker
Vanguard Charter Academy	1620 52nd St SW	Wyoming, MI	49519-9629	616-538-3630	538-3646	K-8	Kim Blaszak
Vista Charter Academy	711 32nd St SE	Grand Rapids, MI	49548-2307	616-246-6920	246-6930	K-8	Joe Gandy
Voyageur Academy	4321 Military St	Detroit, MI	48210-2451	313-361-4180	361-4770	K-6	Rod Adkins
Walden Green Montessori	17771 W Spring Lake Rd	Spring Lake, MI	49456-1447	616-842-4523	842-4522	K-8	Tom Hicks
Walker Charter Academy	1801 3 Mile Rd NW	Grand Rapids, MI	49544-1445	616-785-2700	785-0894	K-8	Gary Carlson
Walton Charter Academy	744 E Walton Blvd	Pontiac, MI	48340-1361	248-371-9300	371-1642	K-8	April Butler
Warrendale Charter Academy	19400 Sawyer St	Detroit, MI	48228-3330	313-240-4200	240-4203	K-8	Brigitte Brown
Washtenaw Technical Middle College	PO Box D-1	Ann Arbor, MI	48106-1610	734-973-3410	973-3464	10-12	Lee Schleicher
Wells Academy	281 S Fair Ave	Benton Harbor, MI	49022-7219	269-926-2885		K-5	James Rutter
West MI Acad. Environmental Science	4463 Leonard St NW	Grand Rapids, MI	49534-2138	616-791-7320	791-1446	K-12	Laura Otten
West Michigan Acad for Arts & Academics	17350 Hazel St	Spring Lake, MI	49456-1222	616-844-9961	844-9941	K-8	David Lewis
Weston Technical Academy	22930 Chippewa St	Detroit, MI	48219-1161	313-387-6038	387-6180	7-12	Fiona Hinds
West Village Academy	3530 Westwood St	Dearborn, MI	48124-3100	313-274-9200	274-0062	K-5	Amy Harris
West Village Academy - North Campus	3771 Grandville	Detroit, MI	48228	313-274-9200	274-0062	6-8	Ghassan Taha
White Pine Academy	PO Box 495	Leslie, MI	49251-0495	517-589-8961	589-9194	K-8	Anita Bouth
Winans Academy Performing Arts HS	7616 E Nevada St	Detroit, MI	48234-3284	313-365-5578	365-5684	9-12	R. Hayward
Winans Academy Performing Arts	7616 E Nevada St	Detroit, MI	48234-3284	313-365-5578	365-5684	K-8	R. Hayward
Windemere Park Charter Academy	3100 W Saginaw St	Lansing, MI	48917-2307	517-327-0700	327-0800	K-8	Jeffrey Whipple
Windover HS	32 S Homer Rd	Midland, MI	48640-8383	989-832-0852	839-7699	9-12	Terrie Kaiser
Woodland Park Academy	9127 S Saginaw Rd	Grand Blanc, MI	48439-9502	810-695-4710	695-1658	K-8	Fritz Esch
Woodmont Academy	25175 Code Rd	Southfield, MI	48033-5805	248-352-1805	352-1810	K-6	Donita White
Woodward Academy	951 E Lafayette St	Detroit, MI	48207-2999	313-961-2108	961-1625	K-8	Georgia Hubbard
YMCA Service Learning Academy	21605 W 7 Mile Rd	Detroit, MI	48219-1810	313-541-7619	541-7656	K-8	Eylastine Green-Roberts

Minnesota

School	Address	City,State	Zip code	Telephone	Fax	Grade	Contact
Abdulle Academy	PO Box 1052	Rochester, MN	55903-1052	507-252-5995		K-8	Farah Hussein
Academia Cesar Chavez	930 Geranium Ave E	Saint Paul, MN	55106-2610	651-778-2940	778-2942	K-12	Ramona A. deRosales
Academy of Biosciences	4056 Central Ave NE	Columbia Hts, MN	55421-2916	763-571-5039		5-12	Siyad Abdullahi
Achieve Language Academy	2169 Stillwater Ave E	Saint Paul, MN	55119-3552	651-738-4875	738-8268	K-5	Mary Apuli
Agricultural & Food Sciences Academy	70 County Road B2 W	Little Canada, MN	55117-1402	651-415-5374	415-5506	9-12	Becky Meyer
Artech Charter S	PO Box 349	Northfield, MN	55057-0349	507-663-8806	663-8802	6-12	Timothy Goodwin
Ascension Academy Charter S	1704 Dupont Ave N	Minneapolis, MN	55411-3219	612-465-8121	465-8125	9-12	Mary Taylor
Augsburg Academy for Health Careers	1326 Energy Park Dr	Saint Paul, MN	55108-5202	651-645-5698		9-12	Mark Youngstrom
Aurora Charter S	2520 Minnehaha Ave	Minneapolis, MN	55404-4118	612-870-3891	870-4287	K-3	Cheryl Avina
Avalon Charter S	1745 University Ave W	Saint Paul, MN	55104-3923	651-649-5495	649-3801	9-12	Andrea Martin
Beacon Academy	12325 Highway 55	Plymouth, MN	55441-4750	763-546-9999	593-9382	K-8	Jordan Ford
Birch Grove Community S	PO Box 2242	Tofte, MN	55615-2242	218-663-0170		K-5	Lisa Hoff
Bluesky Online Charter S	1821 University Ave W	Saint Paul, MN	55104-2801	651-642-0888	642-0435	7-12	Tom Ellis
Bluffview Montessori S	1321 Gilmore Ave	Winona, MN	55987-2459	507-452-2807	452-6869	K-8	Joan Leonard
Cedar Riverside Community Charter S	1610 S 6th St #100	Minneapolis, MN	55454-1102	612-339-5767	339-2951	K-8	Shelton Rucker
City Academy	958 Jessie St	Saint Paul, MN	55130-4058	651-298-4624	292-6511	9-12	Milo Cutter
Community of Peace Academy	471 Magnolia Ave E	Saint Paul, MN	55130-3849	651-776-5151	771-4841	K-12	Karen Rusthoven
Concordia Creative Learning Academy	1355 Pierce Butler Rte #100	Saint Paul, MN	55104	651-649-5795	649-5799	K-6	Mary Donaldson
Coon Rapids Learning Center Charter S	11288 Robinson Dr NW	Coon Rapids, MN	55433-3762	763-862-9223	862-9250	9-12	James Steckart

School	Address	City,State	Zip code	Telephone	Fax	Grade	Contact
Crosslake Community S	PO Box 1079	Crosslake, MN	56442-1079	218-692-5437	692-5437	K-6	David Skogen
Cyber Village Academy	1336 Energy Park Dr	Saint Paul, MN	55108-5271	651-523-7170	523-7113	4-8	Bob Bilyk
Dakota Area Community Charter S	960 Frontage Rd	Dakota, MN	55925-7140	507-643-6869	643-6953	K-5	Darin Shepardson
Discovery Public S	126 8th St NW	Faribault, MN	55021-4241	507-331-5423	331-2618	7-12	Steve Darkow
Dugsi Academy	1821 University Ave W	Saint Paul, MN	55104-2801	651-642-0667	642-0668	K-5	Mohamed Osman
Duluth Edison Charter S	1750 Kenwood Ave	Duluth, MN	55811-2224	218-728-9556	728-2075	K-12	Bonnie Jorgenson
Eagle Ridge Academy Charter S	7255 Flying Cloud Dr	Eden Prairie, MN	55344-3549	952-746-7760	746-7765	6-12	Judy Ingeson
E.C.H.O. Charter S	PO Box 158	Echo, MN	56237-0158	507-925-4143	925-4165	K-8	Larry Schueler
Eci' Nompa Woonspe' Charter S	PO Box 10	Morton, MN	56270-0010	507-697-9055	697-9065	K-12	Tim Blue
Edvisions Off Campus S	501 Main St	Henderson, MN	56044	507-248-3738		9-12	Keven Kroehler
El Colegio Charter S	4137 Bloomington Ave	Minneapolis, MN	55407-3332	612-728-5727	728-5790	9-12	David Greenberg
Emily Charter S	PO Box 40	Emily, MN	56447-0040	218-763-3401	763-4401	K-6	Virginia Brannan
Excell Academy for Higher Learning	6510 Zane Ave N	Brooklyn Park, MN	55429-1559	763-533-0500	533-0508	PK-3	Doug Seiler
Face to Face Academy	1165 Arcade St	Saint Paul, MN	55106-2615	651-772-5555	772-5566	8-12	Jim Gitar
Family Academy	400 10th St NW	New Brighton, MN	55112-6806	651-638-2160		K-8	Anne Hennessey
Four Directions Charter S	1113 W Broadway Ave	Minneapolis, MN	55411-2505	612-588-0183	588-1844	9-12	Ronald Buckanaga
Fraser Academy	1601 Laurel Ave	Minneapolis, MN	55403-1205	612-465-8600	465-8603	K-5	Chris Bentley
Friendship Acad of Fine Arts Charter S	310 E 38th St	Minneapolis, MN	55409-1300	612-879-6703	879-6707	K-4	Ethel Norwood
Great Expectations S	PO Box 310	Grand Marais, MN	55604-0310	218-387-9322	387-9344	K-8	Pete James
Great River Education Center	400 Great Oak Dr Ste 108	Waite Park, MN	56387-2512	320-258-3117	258-3118	7-12	Alonzo Symalla
Great River S	1326 Energy Park Dr	Saint Paul, MN	55108-5202	651-305-2780	305-2781	7-12	Ben Moudry
Green Isle Community S	PO Box 277	Green Isle, MN	55338-0277	507-326-7144	326-5434	K-6	Kristen Kinzler
Harbor City International S	332 W Michigan St Ste 300	Duluth, MN	55802-1644	218-722-7574	625-6068	9-12	Chris Hazleton
Harvest Prep S	1300 Olson Memorial Hwy	Minneapolis, MN	55411-3968	612-381-9743		K-6	Eric Mahmoud
Heart of the Earth S	1209 4th St SE	Minneapolis, MN	55414-2084	612-331-8862	331-1747	K-12	Joel Pourier
Higher Ground Academy	1381 Marshall Ave	Saint Paul, MN	55104-6353	651-645-1000	645-2100	K-12	Bill Wilson
High School for Recording Arts	550 Vandalia St	Saint Paul, MN	55114-1833	651-287-0890	287-0891	9-12	David Ellis
Hmong Academy	1300 Olson Memorial Hwy	Minneapolis, MN	55411-3968	612-377-0221		9-12	Christianna Hang
Hope Academy	720 Payne Ave	Saint Paul, MN	55130-4127	651-796-4500	796-4599	K-6	MayChy Vu
Jennings Experiential HS	1919 University Ave W	Saint Paul, MN	55104-3453	651-649-5403	649-5490	9-12	Jeff Holte
Kaleidoscope Charter S	21755 129th Ave N	Rogers, MN	55374-4639	763-428-1890	428-1691	K-8	Michelle Strait
La Crescent Montessori Academy	28 S Oak St	La Crescent, MN	55947-1332	507-895-4054	895-4064	K-7	Kerrie Hauser
Lafayette Public Charter S	PO Box 125	Lafayette, MN	56054-0125	507-228-8943	228-2509	K-8	Sheila Howk
Lakes Area Charter S	601 W Nokomis St	Osakis, MN	56360-8203	320-859-5302	859-5342	7-12	Dennis Johnson
Lakes International Language Academy	246 11th Ave SE	Forest Lake, MN	55025-1883	651-464-0771	464-4429	K-4	Cameron Hedlund
Lake Superior HS	5215 Rice Lake Rd	Duluth, MN	55803-8422	218-529-2468	279-3628	7-12	Mike Degen
Liberty HS	308 Northtown Dr NE	Blaine, MN	55434-1039	763-786-4799		9-12	Gary Knox
Lighthouse School of Nations	2600 E 26th St	Minneapolis, MN	55406-1201	612-721-8687		9-12	Phil Lederman
Loveworks Academy for Arts	2225 Zenith Ave N	Golden Valley, MN	55422-3852	952-522-6830	522-6840	K-8	Patrice Dorral
Main Street S of Performing Arts	1320 Mainstreet	Hopkins, MN	55343-7497	952-224-1340	224-2955	9-12	Karen Charles
Math & Science Academy	8430 Woodbury Crossing	Woodbury, MN	55125	651-353-2317	578-7532	6-12	Paul Simone
McEvoy Early Literacy Academy	3400 Dupont Ave S	Minneapolis, MN	55408-4059	612-699-4641		K-5	Sharon Bahe
Metro Deaf Charter S	265 W Lafayette Frontage Rd	Saint Paul, MN	55107-1628	651-224-3995	222-0939	K-8	Dyan Sherwood
Minneapolis Academy Charter S	5011 31st Ave S	Minneapolis, MN	55417-1405	612-455-1340	455-1345	5-8	Leon Cooper
Minnesota Business Academy	505 Wabasha St N	Saint Paul, MN	55102-1016	651-726-2100	726-2103	9-12	Jerry Neff
Minnesota International MS	277 12th Ave N	Minneapolis, MN	55401-1026	612-821-6470	821-6477	5-8	Abdirashid Warsame
Minnesota Internship Center	1313 5th St SE Ste 208C	Minneapolis, MN	55414-4515	612-379-3900	379-3914	9-12	Kevin Byrne
Minnesota New Country S	PO Box 488	Henderson, MN	56044-0488	507-248-3353	248-3604	7-12	Dee Thomas
Minnesota North Star Academy	1669 Arcade St	Saint Paul, MN	55106-1041	651-771-2000	771-2200	9-12	Mandy Frederickson
Minnesota Online HS	1313 5th St SE	Minneapolis, MN	55414-4504	612-227-8499		9-12	Julie Williams
Minnesota Transitions Charter S	3244 34th Ave S	Minneapolis, MN	55406-3492	612-729-9140		K-12	Patty Brostrom
Nerstrand ES	PO Box 156	Nerstrand, MN	55053-0156	507-333-6850	333-6870	K-5	Lauren Satrom
New Century Charter S	PO Box 484	Hutchinson, MN	55350-0484	320-234-3660	234-3668	7-12	Dave Conrad
New City S	229 13th Ave NE	Minneapolis, MN	55413-1117	612-623-3309	623-3319	K-6	Terrance Russ
New Heights Charter S	614 Mulberry St W	Stillwater, MN	55082-4858	651-439-1962	439-0716	K-12	Thomas Kearney
New Spirit S	260 Edmund Ave	Saint Paul, MN	55103-1783	651-225-9177	225-9722	K-8	Walter Stull
New Visions Charter S	1800 2nd St NE	Minneapolis, MN	55418-4306	612-706-5566	706-5555	K-8	Bob DeBoer
New Voyage Academy	1745 University Ave W	Saint Paul, MN	55104-3923	651-649-5402	649-5490	K-8	Tyronne Carter
Northern Lights Community S	PO Box 2829	Warba, MN	55793-2829	218-492-4400		6-12	David Hagman
North Lakes Academy Charter S	255b 7th Ave NW	Forest Lake, MN	55025-1157	651-982-2773	464-6409	6-9	Jackie Saunders
North Shore Community S	5926 Ryan Rd	Duluth, MN	55804-9672	218-525-0663	525-0024	K-6	Sheri Camper
Nova Classical Academy	1668 Montreal Ave	Saint Paul, MN	55116-2469	651-227-8622	699-5959	K-12	John Greving
Odyssey Charter S	6201 Noble Ave N	Brooklyn Park, MN	55429-2483	763-971-8200	549-2380	K-9	Judi Hinck
PACT Charter S	7250 E Ramsey Pkwy	Ramsey, MN	55303-6902	763-712-4200	712-4201	K-12	Daniel DeBruyn
Paideia Academy Charter S	7200 147th St W	Apple Valley, MN	55124-9008	952-807-3713		K-8	Laura Jones
Partnership Academy	1 Main St SE Ste 200	Minneapolis, MN	55414-1002	612-521-1281		K-7	Lisa Ladue
Pillager Area Charter S	PO Box 130	Pillager, MN	56473-0130	218-746-3875	746-3876	9-12	Mark Wolhart
Prairie Creek Community S	27695 Denmark Ave	Northfield, MN	55057-5333	507-645-9640	645-8234	K-5	Caroline Jones
Prairie Seeds Academy	2201 Girard Ave N	Minneapolis, MN	55411-2548	612-302-8555	302-9041	K-8	Ger Cha Yang
Ridgeway Community S	35564 Winona Co Rd 12	Houston, MN	55943	507-454-9566	454-9567	K-6	Jodi Dansingburg
RiverBend Academy	110 N 6th St	Mankato, MN	56001-4443	507-387-5524	387-5680	7-12	Greg Schmidt
River Heights Charter S	60 Marie Ave E	West Saint Paul, MN	55118-5910	651-457-7427	554-7611	9-12	Jill Wohlman
Riverway Learning Community Charter S	PO Box 43	Minnesota City, MN	55959-0043	507-689-2844	689-2834	PK-12	Laura Krause
Rochester Off Campus Charter HS	2364 Valleyhigh Dr NW	Rochester, MN	55901-7641	507-282-3325	282-0976	9-12	Jay Martini
Sage Academy Charter S	3900 85th Ave N	Brooklyn Park, MN	55443-1908	763-315-4020	315-4028	9-12	Diane Scholten
Saint Croix Preparatory Academy	216 Myrtle St W	Stillwater, MN	55082-4805	651-379-3160	379-3165	K-9	Jon Gutierrez
Saint Paul Conservatory Performing Art	75 5th St W	Saint Paul, MN	55102-1431	651-290-2225	290-9000	9-12	Terry Tofte
Schoolcraft Learning Community S	PO Box 1685	Bemidji, MN	56619-1685	218-586-3284	586-3285	K-8	Scott Anderson
Skills for Tomorrow	547 Wheeler St N	Saint Paul, MN	55104-3078	651-647-6000	645-2388	9-12	Claude Maddox
Sobriety HS	2233 University Ave	Saint Paul, MN	55109	651-773-8378	748-5290	9-12	Jim Czarniecki
Sojourner Truth Academy	3820 Emerson Ave N	Minneapolis, MN	55412-2039	612-588-3599		K-8	Julie Guy
Soul Academy Charter S	1812 Park Ave	Minneapolis, MN	55404-1942	612-872-0800	872-0814	K-4	Jim Redfield
Stride Academy	1025 18th St N	Saint Cloud, MN	56303-1205	320-230-5340	253-0006	K-6	Dale Beutel
Studio Academy	707 1st Ave NE	Rochester, MN	55906-3618	507-529-1662	529-1643	10-12	Eric Holsen
Swan River Montessori Charter S	500 Maple St	Paynesville, MN	56362-1424	763-271-7926		K-6	Sandra Morrow
Tarek Ibn Ziyad Academy	4100 66th St E	Inver Grove, MN	55076-2230	651-457-7072	457-7190	K-5	Asad Zaman
TEAM Academy	501 Elm Ave E	Waseca, MN	56093-3360	507-835-3000		K-6	Mark Schmitz
Treknorth HS	2518 Hannah Ave NW	Bemidji, MN	56601-2110	218-444-1888	444-1893	7-12	Mike Munson
Trio Wolf Creek Distance Learning	13750 Lake Blvd	Lindstrom, MN	55045-9361	651-213-2017	257-0576	4-12	Tracy Quarnstrom
Twin Cities Academy Charter S	426 Osceola Ave S	Saint Paul, MN	55102-3535	651-205-4797	205-4799	6-8	Liz Wynne
Twin Cities German Immersion S	1399 Eustis St	Saint Paul, MN	55108-1548	651-492-7106	789-0107	K-8	Mary Watkins
Twin Cities International ES	277 12th Ave N	Minneapolis, MN	55401-1026	612-821-6470	821-6477	K-4	Helen Fisk
Ubah Medical Academy Charter S	227 12th Ave N	Minneapolis, MN	55401	612-600-7833	821-6477	9-12	Scott Fleming
Urban Academy Charter S	133 7th St E	Saint Paul, MN	55101-3377	651-215-9419	215-9571	K-6	Mongsher Ly
Vessey Leadership S	1000 Wheelock Pkwy E	Saint Paul, MN	55106-1888	651-206-2980		9-12	Doug Trenda
Village School of Northfield	1100 Bollenbacher Ct	Northfield, MN	55057-3610	507-663-8990	663-0392	K-8	Rose Ann Steenhoek
Voyageurs Expeditionary HS	PO Box 727	Bemidji, MN	56619-0727	218-586-8347	586-8348	9-12	Karen Baldwin
Watershed HS	2344 Nicollet Ave Ste 200	Minneapolis, MN	55404-3373	612-871-4363	871-1004	9-12	Scott Cole
Woodson Institute for Excellence	2620 Russell Ave N	Minneapolis, MN	55411-1725	612-522-4022	522-4012	K-6	LaTanya Washington
World Learner Charter S	112050 Hundertmark Rd	Chaska, MN	55318-2817	952-368-7398	368-6094	K-6	Randi Shapiro
Worthington Area Language Academy	PO Box 185	Bigelow, MN	56117-0185	507-683-2004	683-2013	K-6	Randy Haley
Yankton Country S	PO Box 406	Balaton, MN	56115-0406	507-734-2677	734-2678	9-12	Cynthia Duus

Mississippi

Hayes Cooper Center	500 N Martin Luther King Jr	Merigold, MS	38759-9632	662-748-2734	748-2735	PK-6	Beverly Hardy

Missouri

Academie Lafayette S	6903 Oak St	Kansas City, MO	64113-2530	816-361-7735	361-5788	K-8	Gerry Lukaska
Academy of Kansas City	2015 E 72nd St	Kansas City, MO	64132-1756	816-523-4707	523-5449	K-8	Yvette Robinson
Allen Village S	706 W 42nd St	Kansas City, MO	64111-3120	816-931-0177	561-4640	K-8	Phyllis Washington
Alta Vista Charter S	1722 Holly St	Kansas City, MO	64108-2217	816-471-2582	471-2139	9-12	Cassandra Cole
Banneker Charter Academy Technology	8310 Holmes Rd	Kansas City, MO	64131-2254	816-926-9110	926-0115	K-7	Marion Brown
Bosco Education Center	531 Garfield Ave	Kansas City, MO	64124-1513	816-691-2915	691-2927	9-12	Bill Elliott
Brookside Charter Academy	5220 Troost Ave	Kansas City, MO	64110-2546	816-531-2192	756-3055	K-6	Millie Krna
Confluence Academies	3017 N 13th St	Saint Louis, MO	63107-3924	314-241-1110	241-1115	K-5	Sharon Traylor
Construction Careers Center	1224 Grattan St	Saint Louis, MO	63104-2922	314-588-9991	588-1982	9-12	Dr. Michael Musick
Genesis S	3800 E 44th St	Kansas City, MO	64130-2183	816-921-0775	921-4268	K-8	Pamela Pearson
Hedgeman Lyle Academy	1509 Washington Ave #800S	Saint Louis, MO	63103-1821	314-436-1345	436-3746	PK-9	D'Anne Tombs-Shelton
Hogan Preparatory Academy	1221 E Meyer Blvd	Kansas City, MO	64131-1207	816-444-3464	363-0473	9-12	Bernard Williams
Lamb ES	1000 Charlotte St	Kansas City, MO	64106-3051	816-221-0043	221-0937	K-5	
Lift for Life Academy	1731 S Broadway	Saint Louis, MO	63104-4050	314-231-2337	231-1299	6-8	Katrice Noble
Parks ES	3715 Wyoming St	Kansas City, MO	64111-3945	816-753-6700	753-3436	K-4	Kajuan E. Cummings
St. Louis Academies	5223 N 20th St	Saint Louis, MO	63107-1138	314-534-1085	531-0815	K-8	James Gant
St. Louis Charter S	5279 Fyler Ave	Saint Louis, MO	63139-1300	314-645-9600	645-9700	K-8	Dr. Douglas Thaman
Scuola Vita Nuova	544 Wabash Ave	Kansas City, MO	64124-1747	816-231-5788	231-5181	K-7	Nicole C. King

School	Address	City,State	Zip code	Telephone	Fax	Grade	Contact
Southwest Charter S	6512 Wornall Rd	Kansas City, MO	64113-1899	816-363-1694	363-6228	6-12	Vonnelle Middleton
Thomas Academy	201 E Armour Blvd	Kansas City, MO	64111-1205	816-531-7144	753-8856	K-7	Leah Martisko
Tolbert Community Academy	3400 Paseo Blvd	Kansas City, MO	64109-2429	816-561-0114	561-1015	K-8	Vivian Roper
University Leadership Academy	5605 Troost Ave	Kansas City, MO	64110-2823	816-235-5657	235-6556	6-12	Patricia Henley
Urban Community Leadership Academy	1524 Paseo Blvd	Kansas City, MO	64108-1622	816-483-8035	483-8998	5-9	Joyce McGautha

Nevada

School	Address	City,State	Zip code	Telephone	Fax	Grade	Contact
Academy for Career Education	1375 Greg St	Sparks, NV	89431-6076	775-324-3900	356-3955	9-12	Forrest Gorden
Agassi Academy	1201 W Lake Mead Blvd	Las Vegas, NV	89106-2411	702-948-6000	948-6002	K-12	Brian Thomas
Bailey Charter ES	1090 Bresson Ave	Reno, NV	89502-2625	775-323-6767	323-6799	K-6	Francey Dennis
Coral Academy of Science	1350 E 9th St	Reno, NV	89512-2904	775-323-2332	323-2366	6-10	Ben Karaduman
Explore Knowledge Academy	4801 S Sandhill Rd	Las Vegas, NV	89121-6020	702-730-2933	730-2934	K-12	Joan Sando
High Desert Montessori Charter S	PO Box 5908	Reno, NV	89513-5908	775-624-2800	624-2801	PK-8	Carol Andrew
I Can Do Anything Charter HS	1195 Corporate Blvd Ste C	Reno, NV	89502-2363	775-857-1544	857-6825	9-12	Jill Wells
Keystone Academy Charter HS	777 Quartz Ave #7750	Sandy Valley, NV	89019-8501	702-723-1966	723-1967	9-12	Colt Goodman
Mariposa Academy of Language & Learning	3875 Glen St	Reno, NV	89502-4803	775-826-4040	826-4030	K-6	Aida Tadeo
Odyssey Charter S	2251 S Jones Blvd	Las Vegas, NV	89146-3164	702-257-0578	312-3260	K-12	Craig Butz
Rainshadow Community Charter HS	434 Washington St	Reno, NV	89503-4323	775-322-5566	322-5509	9-12	Carol White
Rite of Passage Charter HS	100 Rosaschi Rd	Yerington, NV	89447-8722	775-463-5580	463-5366	9-12	Russ Colletta
Sierra Nevada Academy	13880 Stead Blvd	Reno, NV	89506-1579	775-677-4500	677-4441	K-8	Kim Regan-Goatley
Silver State HS	3719 N Carson St	Carson City, NV	89706-1934	775-883-7900	883-9130	9-12	Steve Knight

New Hampshire

School	Address	City,State	Zip code	Telephone	Fax	Grade	Contact
Academy for Science & Design	20 University Dr	Nashua, NH	03063-1323	603-577-6600		7-12	Michael Fishbein
Clerc Academy	PO Box 2635	Concord, NH	03302-2635	603-223-6770	223-2332	1-8	Susan Brule
Cocheco Arts and Technology Academy	47 4th St	Dover, NH	03820-2931	603-516-2282	740-9778	9-12	Maria Minickiello
Equestrian Academy Charter S	89 South St	Concord, NH	03301-2828	267-408-6732		9-12	Leslie Brian
Great Bay eLearning Charter S	56 Linden St	Exeter, NH	03833-4104	603-775-8638	775-8988	9-10	Cheryl McDonough
New Heights Charter Academy	27 Wallace Rd	Goffstown, NH	03045-1824	603-497-4841	497-5257	11-12	Ray Dumais
North Country Charter Academy	260 Cottage St Ste A	Littleton, NH	03561-4137	603-444-1535	444-9843	7-12	Lisa Lavoie
Seacoast Charter S	PO Box 892	Exeter, NH	03833-0892	603-772-5019	772-5019	3-6	Emily Hamilton

New Jersey

School	Address	City,State	Zip code	Telephone	Fax	Grade	Contact
Academy Charter HS	1725 Main St	South Belmar, NJ	07719-3051	732-681-8377	681-8375	9-12	Mary Jo Kapalko
Camden Academy Charter HS	879 Beideman Ave	Camden, NJ	08105-4227	856-365-1000	365-1005	9-9	Joseph Conway
Camden's Promise Charter S	879 Beideman Ave	Camden, NJ	08105-4227	856-365-1000	365-1005	6-8	Joe Conway
ChARTer-TECHnical HS	413 New Rd	Somers Point, NJ	08244-2143	609-926-7458	926-8472	9-12	Janice Strigh
Classical Academy Charter S of Clifton	20 Valley Rd	Clifton, NJ	07013-1030	973-278-7707	278-7720	6-8	Vincent DeRosa
CREATE Charter S	164 Lembeck Ave	Jersey City, NJ	07305-3803	201-413-1500	413-1800	9-12	Stephen S. Lipski
Discovery Charter S	303 Washington St	Newark, NJ	07102-2738	973-623-0222	623-0024	4-8	Irene Hall
D.U.E. Season Charter S	1000 Atlantic Ave Ste 524	Camden, NJ	08104-1132	856-225-0511		K-12	Doris Carpenter
East Orange Community Charter S	PO Box 2186	East Orange, NJ	07019-2186	973-676-1199	676-8003	K-4	Linda Muchell
Elysian Charter S	301 Garden St	Hoboken, NJ	07030-3873	201-876-0102	876-9576	K-6	
Englewood on the Palisades Charter S	65 W Demarest Ave	Englewood, NJ	07631-2316	201-569-9765	568-9576	K-5	Anthony Barckett
Environment Comm Opportunity Charter S	817 Carpenter St	Camden, NJ	08102-1132	856-963-2627		K-12	Antoinette Dendtler
Fisher S of Advanced Studies	31 Chancery Ln	Trenton, NJ	08618-4805	609-656-1444	656-1894	6-12	G. Dallas Dixson
Freedom Academy Charter S	1400 Collings Rd	Camden, NJ	08104-3113	856-962-0766		5-5	Alana L. Walls
Galloway Community Charter S	112 S New York Rd	Galloway, NJ	08205-9608	609-652-7118		K-6	Deborah Nataloni
Gateway Charter S	119 Newkirk St	Jersey City, NJ	07306-3016	201-653-0016	653-1119	6-8	Aimee Rodriguez
Golden Door Charter S	180 9th St	Jersey City, NJ	07302-1703	201-795-4400	795-3308	K-8	Brian Stiles
Gray Charter S	55 Liberty St	Newark, NJ	07102-4815	973-824-6661	824-2296	K-8	Verna Gray
Greater Brunswick Charter S	429B Joyce Kilmer Ave	New Brunswick, NJ	08901-3322	732-448-1052		K-9	Rick Pressler
Hoboken Charter S	4th & Garden St 3rd Floor	Hoboken, NJ	07030	201-963-0222	963-0880	PK-12	Donald DePascale
Hope Academy Charter S	700 Grand Ave	Asbury Park, NJ	07712-6629	732-988-4227	988-9218	K-8	Alexis C. Harris
International Charter S of Trenton	105 Grand St	Trenton, NJ	08611-2417	609-394-3111	394-3116	K-5	Melissa Benford
Jersey City Community Charter S	128 Danforth Ave	Jersey City, NJ	07305-2626	201-433-2288	433-5803	K-8	Carletta Martin-Goldston
Lady Liberty Academy Charter S	PO Box 180	Newark, NJ	07101-0180	973-623-9005	623-4088	K-8	Fiona Thomas
LEAP Academy University Charter S	549 Cooper St	Camden, NJ	08102-1210	856-614-0400	614-5601	K-9	Dr. Stephanie Branch
Learning Community Charter S	1 Canal St	Jersey City, NJ	07302-4330	201-332-0900	332-4981	K-5	Susan Grierson
Liberty Academy Charter S	817 Carpenter St	Jersey City, NJ	07302	201-217-6771		K-8	Frank McCree
Newark Charter S	1 Avon Ave	Newark, NJ	07108-2801	973-242-3543	242-5792	5-7	Peter Turnamian
New Horizons Community Charter S	45 Hayes St #59	Newark, NJ	07103-3019	973-848-0400	596-0984	K-5	Juanda Boxley
North Star Academy Charter S	10 Washington Pl	Newark, NJ	07102-3106	973-642-0101	642-5800	5-12	Paul Bamrick Santoyo
Oceanside Charter S	1750 Bacharach Blvd	Atlantic City, NJ	08401-4308	609-348-3485	348-5951	PK-8	Jeanine Middleton
PACE Charter School of Hamilton	1949 Hamilton Ave	Hamilton, NJ	08619-3736	609-587-2288	587-8483	K-3	Michael Mikitish
Paterson Charter S Science & Tech	69-75 Lehigh Ave	Paterson, NJ	07503-1728	973-247-0600	247-9924	6-9	Furkan Kosar
PleasanTech Academy Charter S	535 Mrtn Luther King Jr Ave	Pleasantville, NJ	08232	609-383-1717	484-1085	K-8	Bridgette White
Pleasantville Charter S for Excellence	700 Black Horse Pike	Pleasantville, NJ	08232-2361	609-407-2145	407-6614	K-8	Robert Pupchik
Princeton Charter S	575 Ewing St	Princeton, NJ	08540-2760	609-924-0575	924-7183	K-8	Charles Marsee
Queen City Academy Charter S	815 W 7th St	Plainfield, NJ	07063-1449	908-753-4700	753-4816	K-8	Cynthia Cone
Red Bank Charter S	58 Oakland St	Red Bank, NJ	07701-1104	732-450-9799	936-1923	K-8	Meredith Pennotti
Ridge & Valley Charter S	1234 State Route 94	Blairstown, NJ	07825-4115	908-362-1114	362-6680	K-8	David Wyllie
Schomburg Charter S	508 Grand St	Jersey City, NJ	07302-4103	201-451-7770	451-1770	K-5	Dr. James Gaines
Soaring Heights Charter S	1 Romar Ave	Jersey City, NJ	07305-1713	201-434-4800		K-8	Claudia Zorick
Sussex Co. Charter S for Technology	105 N Church Rd	Sparta, NJ	07871-3203	973-383-6700	383-2901	7-8	Jill Ekel
TEAM Academy Charter S	85 Custer Ave	Newark, NJ	07112-2511	973-705-8326	556-1238	5-8	Ryan E. Hill
Teaneck Community Charter S	1650 Palisade Ave	Teaneck, NJ	07666-3610	201-833-9600	833-9225	K-8	Dr. Rex Shaw
Thomas Charter S	17 Muhammad Ali Ave	Newark, NJ	07108-3006	973-621-0060	621-0061	K-7	Karen Thomas
Treat Academy Charter S	443 Clifton Ave	Newark, NJ	07104-1339	973-482-8811	482-7681	K-5	Michael Pallante
Trenton Community Charter S	349 W State St	Trenton, NJ	08618-5705	609-393-3220	695-0193	K-8	Jerri L. Morrison
Union County TEAMS Charter S	PO Box 2741	Plainfield, NJ	07062-0741	908-754-3353		K-12	Sheila Thorpe
Unity Charter S	340 Speedwell Ave	Morristown, NJ	07960-2938	973-292-1808	267-9288	K-8	Dr. Char Stanko
University Academy Charter HS	275 W Side Ave	Jersey City, NJ	07305-1130	201-200-3200	200-3262	9-12	Linda Green
University Heights Charter S	275 W Market St	Newark, NJ	07103-2717	973-623-1099		K-12	Brenda Brown
Varisco-Rogers Charter S	PO Box 180	Newark, NJ	07101-0180	973-242-5690		6-8	Teresa Segarra
Village Charter S	101 Sullivan Way	Trenton, NJ	08628-3425	609-695-0110	695-1880	K-4	Dr. Dorian Dorsey

New Mexico

School	Address	City,State	Zip code	Telephone	Fax	Grade	Contact
Academia De Lengua Y Cultura	PO Box 12039	Albuquerque, NM	87195-0039	505-563-4242	563-4260	6-7	Colleen Adolph
Academy for Tech & Classics	PO Box 8646	Santa Fe, NM	87504-8646	505-473-4282	473-4292	7-12	Ruth La Blanc
Alma D Arte Charter HS	PO Box 7027	Las Cruces, NM	88006-7027	505-541-0145	541-0146	9-12	Irene Oliver-Lewis
Amistad Charter S	PO Box 168	Amistad, NM	88410-0168	505-633-2283	633-3383	K-6	Ruth Shields
Anansi Charter S	PO Box 1709	El Prado, NM	87529-1709	505-776-2256	776-5561	K-2	Michele Hunt
Biehl Charter HS	8300 Phoenix Ave NE	Albuquerque, NM	87110-3700	505-299-9409	299-9493	9-12	Mike May
Bridge Academy	PO Box 1119	Las Vegas, NM	87701-1119	505-425-3302	425-3309	9-12	Carole Winkel
Charter Vocational HS	1011 Lamberton Pl NE	Albuquerque, NM	87107-1641	505-341-0888	341-0749	9-12	Bettina Elklund
Charter Vo-Tech Center	1506 Candelaria Rd NE	Albuquerque, NM	87107-2117	505-341-0888	341-0749	10-12	Bruce Smith
Chavez Community S	1511 Central Ave NE	Albuquerque, NM	87106-4408	505-877-0558	242-7444	9-12	Caryl Thomas
Cottonwood Valley Charter S	PO Box 1829	Socorro, NM	87801-1829	505-838-2026	838-2420	K-8	Mary Nutt
Creative Education Prep Institute #1	PO Box 50880	Albuquerque, NM	87181-0880	505-314-2374	314-2377	9-12	Tom Crespin
Creative Education Prep Institute #2	PO Box 50880	Albuquerque, NM	87181-0880	505-237-2374	237-2380	9-12	Anna Zamora
Duncan Charter S	3011 Barcelona Rd SW	Albuquerque, NM	87105-5547	505-463-6461		6-8	Mary Ann Spracher
East Mountain HS	PO Box 340	Sandia Park, NM	87047-0340	505-281-7400	281-4173	9-12	Danielle Johnston
Espanola Military Academy	PO Box 100	Espanola, NM	87532-0100	505-747-3317	747-6084	6-12	Michael Mendoza
Gutierrez MS	4 Challenger Rd	Roswell, NM	88201	505-347-9703	347-9707	6-8	Joe Andreis
High Tech HS Albuquerque	2500 Yale Blvd SE	Albuquerque, NM	87106-4274	505-314-7272		9-12	Robin Troup
Horizon Academy - Northwest	7939 4th St NW	Albuquerque, NM	87114-1008	505-998-0501	998-0505	K-8	Jerald Snider
Horizon Academy - South	3713 Isleta Blvd SW	Albuquerque, NM	87105-5990	505-873-4100	873-4200	K-8	Jennifer Joyce
Horizon Academy Technology & Arts HS	3713 Isleta Blvd SW	Albuquerque, NM	87105-5990	505-873-4100	873-4200	7-12	John Harris
Horizon Academy - West	1900 Atrisco Dr NW	Albuquerque, NM	87120-1146	505-988-0459	998-0463	K-8	Amie Duran
Jefferson Montessori Academy	PO Box 2184	Carlsbad, NM	88221-2184	505-887-9380	887-9391	K-12	Arlene Standiford
Kennedy HS	1511 Central Ave NE	Albuquerque, NM	87106-4408	505-923-3024	242-7444	9-12	Greta Roskom
La Academia de Esperanza	5200 Sequoia Rd NW	Albuquerque, NM	87120-1208	505-352-3030	836-7424	6-12	Steve Woods
La Academia de Idiomas Y Cultura	505 S Main St Ste 249	Las Cruces, NM	88001-1243	505-526-2984		6-8	Luis Quinones
La Luz del Monte Learning Center	10301 Candelaria Rd NE	Albuquerque, NM	87112-1504	505-296-7677	296-0510	7-8	Scott Glasrud
La Promesa Early Learning Center	1224 Pennsylvania St NE	Albuquerque, NM	87110-7410	505-268-3275		K-3	Ann Kleeberg
La Resolana Learning Academy	2 Hendrix Ln	Los Lunas, NM	87031-7856	505-319-4919	866-0487	7-8	Juan Aragon
Learning Community Charter S	4575 San Mateo Blvd NE	Albuquerque, NM	87109-2008	505-332-3200	332-8780	7-12	Viola Martinez
Life Skills Center of Albuquerque	202 Central Ave SE	Albuquerque, NM	87102-3460	505-261-3767	247-9222	9-12	Khadijah Bottom
Los Puentes Charter S	PO Box 6485	Albuquerque, NM	87197-6485	505-342-5959	342-5955	8-12	Shelly Cherrin
Middle College HS Academy	200 College Rd # 9	Gallup, NM	87301-5603	505-863-7709	863-7681	11-12	Charles Kaplan
Monte Del Sol	4157 Walking Rain Rd	Santa Fe, NM	87507-0825	505-982-5225		7-12	Tony Gerlicz
Montessori ES Charter	3821 Singer Blvd NE	Albuquerque, NM	87109-5804	505-796-0149	796-0147	K-6	Mary Jane Besante
Montessori of the Rio Grande Charter S	1650 Gabaldon Dr NW	Albuquerque, NM	87104-2761	505-842-5993	242-2907	K-5	Bonnie MacCallum-Dodge

School	Address	City,State	Zip code	Telephone	Fax	Grade	Contact
Moreno Valley Charter S	PO Box 1037	Angel Fire, NM	87710-1037	505-377-3100	377-7263	9-12	Kurt Kaufman
Mountain Mahogany Community S	5014 4th St NW	Albuquerque, NM	87107-3908	505-341-1424		K-3	Vicki Lester
North Albuquerque Coop Community ES	7109 Capitol Dr NE	Albuquerque, NM	87109-5016	505-822-5545		K-6	Bonnie Barsun
Nuestros Valores Charter S	1021 Isleta Blvd SW	Albuquerque, NM	87105-3934	505-873-7758	873-3567	9-12	Monica Sanchez
Public Academy for Performing Arts	4665 Indian School Rd NE	Albuquerque, NM	87110-3918	505-262-4888	262-4893	6-12	Katy Harvey
Red River Valley Charter S	PO Box 742	Red River, NM	87558-0742	505-754-6117	754-3258	K-8	Karen Phillips
Roots & Wings Community S	PO Box 1152	El Prado, NM	87529-1152	505-586-2076	586-2087	6-12	Margaret Bartlett
San Diego Riverside S	PO Box 99	Jemez Pueblo, NM	87024-0099	505-834-7419	834-9167	K-8	Eugene Johnson
School for Integrated Academics & Tech	1500 Indian School Rd NW	Albuquerque, NM	87104-2306	505-242-6640	242-6872	9-12	Kelly Callahan
South Valley Academy	3426 Blake Rd SW	Albuquerque, NM	87105-5009	505-452-3132	452-3133	9-12	Alan Marks
Southwest Primary Learning Center	10301 Candelaria Rd NE	Albuquerque, NM	87112-1504	505-296-7677	296-0510	K-6	Deborah Young
Southwest Secondary Learning Center	10301 Candelaria Rd NE	Albuquerque, NM	87112-1504	505-296-7677	296-0510	7-12	Dalene Juarez
Taos Charter S	PO Box 3009	Ranchos de Taos, NM	87557-3009	505-751-7222	751-7546	K-5	Nancy O'Bryan
Turqoise Trail ES	13a San Marcos Loop	Santa Fe, NM	87508-8627	505-471-7282	474-7862	K-6	Sandra Davis
21st Century Public Academy	3100 Menaul Blvd NE	Albuquerque, NM	87107-1835	505-254-0280	254-8507	6-8	Donna Eldredge
Walatowa Charter HS	PO Box 669	Jemez Pueblo, NM	87024-0669	505-834-0443	834-0449	9-12	Tony Archuleta
YouthBuild Trade & Technology HS	1718 Yale Blvd SE	Albuquerque, NM	87106-4136	505-765-5517	765-5925	9-12	Ruth Johnson

New York

School	Address	City,State	Zip code	Telephone	Fax	Grade	Contact
Achievement First Charter S	557 Pennsylvania Ave	Brooklyn, NY	11207-5727	718-485-4924	342-5194	K-12	Jada Best
Achievement First Crown Heights Charter	790 E NY Ave	Brooklyn, NY	11203	718-774-0762	774-0830	K-12	Orpheus Williams
Amber Charter S	220 E 106th St	New York, NY	10029-4007	212-534-9667	534-6225	K-5	Evelyn Marzan
Ark Community Charter S	762 River St	Troy, NY	12180-1231	518-274-6312		K-5	Mary Streck
Beginning With Children Charter S	11 Bartlett St	Brooklyn, NY	11206-5001	718-388-8847	388-8936	K-8	Cynthia Bailey
Brighter Choice Charter S	250 Central Ave	Albany, NY	12206-2639	518-383-2877		K-3	Todd McKee
Bronx Charter for Better Learning	3740 Baychester Ave	Bronx, NY	10466-5031	718-655-6660	655-5555	K-4	Shubert Jacobs
Bronx Charter S for Children	388 Willis Ave	Bronx, NY	10454-1303	718-402-3300	402-3258	K-5	Karen Drezner
Bronx Charter S for Excellence	1508 Webster Ave	Bronx, NY	10457-8015	718-294-7327	294-1497	K-8	Marc Etienne
Bronx Charter S for the Arts	950 Longfellow Ave	Bronx, NY	10474-4809	718-893-1042	893-7910	K-5	Xanthe Jory
Bronx Lighthouse Charter S	977 Fox St	Bronx, NY	10459-3320	718-860-4340	860-4125	K-4	Min Kim
Bronx Preparatory Charter S	3872 3rd Ave	Bronx, NY	10457-8222	718-294-0841	294-2381	5-12	Kristin Jordan
Brooklyn Charter S	545 Willoughby Ave	Brooklyn, NY	11206-6815	718-302-2085	302-2426	K-6	Omigbade Escayg
Brooklyn Excelsior Charter S	856 Quincy St	Brooklyn, NY	11221-3612	718-246-5681	246-5864	K-8	Debra Coker
Buffalo Academy of Science Charter S	15 Jewett Pkwy	Buffalo, NY	14214-2319	716-446-5681	446-5682	7-12	Metin Cetiner
Buffalo United Charter S	325 Manhattan Ave	Buffalo, NY	14214-1809	716-835-9862		K-8	Diane Rowe
Charter S for Applied Technologies	2303 Kenmore Ave	Buffalo, NY	14207-1311	716-876-7505		K-10	J. Efrain Martinez
Charter S of Educational Excellence	260 Warburton Ave	Yonkers, NY	10701-2226	914-476-5070		K-5	Migda Agosto
Charter S of Science & Technology	690 Saint Paul St	Rochester, NY	14605-1742	585-454-0100		K-9	Andrew Turner
Child Dev. Center / Hamptons Charter S	PO Box 404	Wainscott, NY	11975-0404	631-324-0207		K-5	Cindy Golden-Allentuck
Community Charter S	404 Edison Ave	Buffalo, NY	14215-2936	716-832-2551		K-8	Mary Carroll
Community Partnership Charter S	241 Emerson Pl	Brooklyn, NY	11205-3808	718-399-1495	399-2149	K-5	Melanie Bryon
East Harlem Village Academy	413 E 120th St	New York, NY	10035-3602	212-369-3319	369-6916	5-12	Jamie White
Enterprise Charter S	275 Oak St	Buffalo, NY	14203-1638			K-8	
Excellence Charter S	600 Lafayette Ave	Brooklyn, NY	11216-1020	718-638-1830	638-2548	K-5	Jabali Sawicki
Explore Charter S	15 Snyder Ave	Brooklyn, NY	11226-4020	718-703-4484	703-8550	K-8	Morton Ballen
Family Life Academy Charter S	14 W 170th St	Bronx, NY	10452-3227	718-410-8100	410-8800	K-5	Marilyn Calo
Future Leaders Institute	134 W 122nd St	New York, NY	10027-5501	212-678-2798	678-2868	K-8	Gianna Cassetta
Genesee Community Charter S	657 East Ave	Rochester, NY	14607-2101	585-271-4552		K-5	Lisa Wing
Girls Preparatory Charter S	333 E 4th St	New York, NY	10009-6912	212-388-0241		K-8	Nakia Haskins
Global Concepts Charter S	1001 Ridge Rd	Buffalo, NY	14218-1755	716-821-1903		K-5	Lawrence Jungberg
Grand Concourse Academy Charter S	116 E 169th St	Bronx, NY	10452-7704	718-590-1300	590-1065	K-4	Ira Victor
Harbor Science & Arts Charter S	1 E 104th St	New York, NY	10029-4418	212-427-2244	360-7429	1-8	Joanne Hunt
Harlem Childrens Zone Charter S	35 E 125th St	New York, NY	10035-1816	212-534-0700	234-2340	K-12	Doreen Land
Harlem Childrens Zone Charter S	220 W 121st St	New York, NY	10027-6217	212-534-0700	234-2340	K-12	Doreen Land
Harlem Day Charter S	240 E 123rd St	New York, NY	10035-2038	212-876-9953	876-9926	K-5	Keith Meecham
Harlem Link Charter S	134 W 122nd St	New York, NY	10027-5501	646-472-7998		K-8	Steven Evangelista
Hellenic Classical Charter S	646 5th Ave	Brooklyn, NY	11215-5401	718-499-0957		K-8	Joseph Martucci
Icahn Charter S	1525 Brook Ave	Bronx, NY	10457-8005	718-716-8105	716-6716	K-5	Jeffrey Litt
International Charter S of Schenectady	408 Eleanor St	Schenectady, NY	12306-3122	518-344-5105		K-12	Lillian Turner
King Center Charter S	938 Genesee St	Buffalo, NY	14211-3025	716-891-7912		K-4	Claity Massey
KIPP Academy Charter S	250 E 156th St	Bronx, NY	10451-4796	718-665-3555	585-7982	5-8	Quinton Vance
KIPP A.M.P. Charter S	1224 Park Pl	Brooklyn, NY	11213-2703	718-363-0876	774-0524	5-8	Ky Adderley
KIPP Infinity Charter S	625 W 133rd St	New York, NY	10027-7303	212-694-5786		5-8	Joseph Negron
KIPP Sankofa Charter S	140 Central Park Plz	Buffalo, NY	14214-2235	716-446-5708		5-8	
KIPP S.T.A.R College Prep Charter S	433 W 123rd St	New York, NY	10027-5002	212-769-7615	769-7601	5-8	Maggie Shefa
KIPP Tech Valley Charter S	1 Dudley Hts	Albany, NY	12210-2601	518-289-5115	694-9411	5-5	Dan Ceaser
Leadership Village Academy Charter S	315 E 119th St	New York, NY	10035-4225	212-369-3319		5-8	Deborah Kenny
Lindsay Wildcat Academy Charter S	17 Battery Pl	New York, NY	10004-1207	212-209-6036	635-3874	9-12	Ronald Tabano
Manhattan Charter S	100 Attorney St	New York, NY	10002-3405	212-533-2743	499-4281	K-5	Pedro Santana
Maria de Hostos Charter S	938 Clifford Ave	Rochester, NY	14621-4808	585-544-6170		K-6	Miriam Vazquez
Merrick Academy-Queens Public Charter S	20701 Jamaica Ave	Queens Village, NY	11428-1544	718-479-3753	479-8108	K-12	Alma Alston
New Covenant Charter S	50 Lark St	Albany, NY	12210-1518	518-463-3912	626-9916	PK-8	Eleanor Bartlett
NY Center for Autism Charter S	433 E 100th St	New York, NY	10029-6606	212-759-3775			Jamie Pagliaro
Opportunity Charter S	222 W 134th St	New York, NY	10030-3002	212-283-0670	283-1138		Betty Marsella
Oracle Charter S	888 Delaware Ave	Buffalo, NY	14209-2008	716-362-3188	362-3187	7-9	Julia Forsberg
Our World Neighborhood Charter S	3612 35th Ave	Astoria, NY	11106-1227	718-392-3405	392-2840	K-8	Brian Ferguson
Peninsula Prep Academy Charter S	1045 Nameoke St	Far Rockaway, NY	11691-4906	718-471-7220	471-7385	K-5	Judith Tyler
Pinnacle Charter S	115 Ash St	Buffalo, NY	14204-1452	716-633-8146		K-8	Judith Schiffert
Public S 68	24 Westminster Ave	Buffalo, NY	14215-1699	716-816-3450	838-7458	K-8	Dr. Yvonne Ragan
ReadNet Bronx Charter S	429 E 148th St	Bronx, NY	10455-4128	718-292-3474	292-2904	K-8	Linda Vergera
Renaissance Charter S	3559 81st St	Jackson Heights, NY	11372-5033	718-803-0060	803-3785	K-12	Monte Joffee
Riverhead Charter S	3685 Middle Country Rd	Calverton, NY	11933-1807	631-369-5800		K-5	Robert Pinckney
Roosevelt Childrens Academy Charter S	105 Pleasant Ave	Roosevelt, NY	11575-2126	516-867-6202	867-6206	K-4	Roxanne Ashley
Sisulu-Walker Childrens Academy	125 W 115th St	New York, NY	10026-2908	212-663-8216	866-5793	K-8	Karen Jones
South Bronx Charter S	383 E 139th St	Bronx, NY	10454-2603	212-786-7936		K-5	Evelyn Hey
South Buffalo Charter S	2219 S Park Ave	Buffalo, NY	14220-2202	716-826-7213		K-8	Gregory Speranza
Southside Academy Charter S	800 S Wilbur Ave	Syracuse, NY	13204-2732	315-476-3019		K-8	Jerome Watts
Stepping Stone Academy Charter S	907 E Ferry St	Buffalo, NY	14211-1423	716-895-5766		K-8	D'Angelo Alexander
Syracuse Academy of Science Charter S	1001 Park Ave	Syracuse, NY	13204-2125	315-428-8997	428-9109	7-12	Hakki Karaman
Tapestry Charter S	40 North St	Buffalo, NY	14202-1106	716-332-0754		K-6	Joy Pepper
Tubman Charter S	3565 3rd Ave	Bronx, NY	10456-3403	718-537-9912	537-9858	K-6	Gwen Stephens
UFT Elementary Charter S	300 Wyona St	Brooklyn, NY	11207-3522	718-922-0438		K-5	Rita Danis
Western NY Maritime Charter S	833 Michigan Ave	Buffalo, NY	14203-1207	716-842-6289		9-12	Richard Middaugh
Westminster Community Charter S	24 Westminster Ave	Buffalo, NY	14215-1614	716-816-3450	838-7458	K-8	Yvonne Regan
Williamsburg Charter S	424 Leonard St	Brooklyn, NY	11222-3908	718-782-9830	782-9834	9-12	Eddie Melendez
Williamsburg Collegiate Charter S	157 Wilson St	Brooklyn, NY	11211-7706	718-302-4018	302-4641	5-12	Julie Trott

North Carolina

School	Address	City,State	Zip code	Telephone	Fax	Grade	Contact
Academy of Moore County	105 Turner St	Southern Pines, NC	28387-7054	910-693-7924	693-7925	5-8	Gail Reilly
Alpha Academy	PO Box 35476	Fayetteville, NC	28303-0476	910-223-7711	678-9011	K-8	Eugene Slocum
American Renaissance Charter S	111 Cooper St	Statesville, NC	28677-5855	704-924-8870	873-1398	K-5	Sharon Love
American Renaissance MS	217 S Center St	Statesville, NC	28677-5806	704-878-6009	878-9350	6-8	Stephen Gay
Arapahoe Charter S	9005 NC Highway 306 S	Arapahoe, NC	28510-9699	252-249-2599	249-1316	K-8	Robert Tyson
Arts Based ES	1380 N Martin Luther King	Winston Salem, NC	27101	336-748-4116		K-5	Robin Hollis
ArtSpace Charter S	2030 US 70 Hwy	Swannanoa, NC	28778-8211	828-298-2787	298-6221	K-8	Dr. Tony Horning
Atwater Community S	8305 Roxboro Rd	Bahama, NC	27503-9057	919-471-8655	471-8712	4-10	Gayle Erdheim
Baker Charter HS	PO Box 2415	Raleigh, NC	27602-2415	919-856-5929	857-9297	9-12	Marti Wilson
Bethany Community MS	181 Bethany Rd	Reidsville, NC	27320-7464	336-951-2500	951-0087	6-8	Mark Richardson
Bethel Hill Charter S	401 Bethel Hill School Rd	Roxboro, NC	27574-7503	336-599-2823	599-9299	K-6	John Betterton
Brevard Academy	PO Box 2375	Brevard, NC	28712-2375	828-885-2665	862-3497	K-8	Dr. Thomas Mahan
Bridges Charter S	2587 Pleasant Ridge Rd	State Road, NC	28676-9318	336-874-2721	874-3804	K-8	Paul Welborn
Cape Fear Center for Inquiry	3131 Randall Pkwy Ste B	Wilmington, NC	28403-2560	910-362-0000	362-0048	K-8	Dr. Lisa Griffin
Cape Lookout Marine Science HS	1108 Bridges St	Morehead City, NC	28557-3799	252-726-1601	726-5245	9-12	Susan Smith
Carolina International S	PO Box 366	Harrisburg, NC	28075-0366	704-455-7247	455-4672	K-8	Dr. Richard Beall
Carter Community S	1305 W Club Blvd	Durham, NC	27705-3513	919-416-9025	416-9815	K-8	Gail Taylor
Casa Esperanza Montessori S	2600 Sumner Blvd Ste 130	Raleigh, NC	27616-5146	919-855-9811	855-9813	PK-6	Janice Bonham West
Central Park S for Children	724 Foster St	Durham, NC	27701-2111	919-682-1200	683-1261	K-5	Carolyn Kirkland
Charter Day S	7055 Bacons Way NE	Leland, NC	28451-7960	910-655-1214	655-1549	K-7	Mark Cramer
Chatham Charter	PO Box 245	Siler City, NC	27344-0245	919-742-4550	742-4694	K-8	Ronald Joyce
Children's Community S	PO Box 2059	Davidson, NC	28036-2059	704-896-6262	896-2025	K-4	Joy K. Warner
Childrens Village Academy	PO Box 2206	Kinston, NC	28502-2206	252-939-1958	939-1242	K-6	Gloria Carr-Battle
CIS Academy	PO Box 706	Lumberton, NC	28359-0706	910-521-1669	521-1670	6-8	Ronald Bryant
Clover Garden S	2454 Altmhaw Union Ridge Rd	Burlington, NC	27217	336-586-9440	586-9477	K-12	Faye McDaniel
Community Charter S	926 Elizabeth Ave	Charlotte, NC	28204-2204	704-377-3180	377-3182	K-5	Dr. Carlton Thornton
Community Partners Charter HS	PO Box 100	Holly Springs, NC	27540-0100	919-567-9955	567-9956	9-12	Dr. Lynanne Fowle

School	Address	City,State	Zip code	Telephone	Fax	Grade	Contact
Crosscreek Charter S	PO Box 1075	Louisburg, NC	27549-1075	919-497-3198	497-0232	K-8	S. McFarland
Crossnore Academy	PO Box 309	Crossnore, NC	28616-0309	828-733-5241	737-7915	K-12	Marion Krege
Crossroads Charter HS	5500 N Tryon St	Charlotte, NC	28213-7120	704-597-5100	597-3941	9-12	Charles Newton
Delany New S	PO Box 16161	Asheville, NC	28816-0161	828-236-9441	236-9442	K-8	Buffy Fowler
Dillard Academy	PO Box 1188	Goldsboro, NC	27533-1188	919-581-0128	581-0122	K-3	Hilda Hicks
Downtown MS	280 S Liberty St	Winston Salem, NC	27101-5211	336-748-3838	748-3359	5-8	Amanda Davis Gane
East Wake Academy	400 NMC Dr	Zebulon, NC	27597-2759	919-404-0444	404-2377	K-12	Brandon Smith
East Winston ES	1612 E 14th St	Winston Salem, NC	27105-6735	336-725-7507	725-7508	K-6	Sylvia Simmons
Evergreen Community Charter S	50 Bell Rd	Asheville, NC	28805-1538	828-298-2173	298-2269	K-8	Dr. Jackie Williams
Exploris MS	207 E Hargett St	Raleigh, NC	27601-1437	919-821-3168	836-9768	6-8	Anne Bryan
Forsyth Academy	5426 Shattalon Dr	Winston Salem, NC	27106-1919	336-922-1121	922-1033	K-8	Dorothy Heath
Franklin Academy I & II	604 Franklin St	Wake Forest, NC	27587	919-554-4911	554-2340	K-12	Denise Kent
Gaston College Preparatory S	PO Box 1292	Gaston, NC	27832-1292	252-308-6932	308-6936	5-8	Caleb Dolan
Grandfather Academy	PO Box 2260	Banner Elk, NC	28604-2260	828-898-3868	898-3849	K-12	Doug Herman
Gray Stone Day S	PO Box 960	Misenheimer, NC	28109-0960	704-463-0567	463-0569	9-12	Helen Nance
Greensboro Academy	4049 Battleground Ave	Greensboro, NC	27410-8410	336-286-8404	286-8403	K-8	Rudy Swofford
Guilford Preparatory Charter S	900 16th St	Greensboro, NC	27405-4810	336-954-1344	954-1341	K-9	Dr. John von Rohr
Haliwa-Saponi Tribal S	130 Haliwa Saponi Trl	Hollister, NC	27844-9390	252-257-5853	257-1093	K-12	Goode Walter
Healthy Start Academy	807 W Chapel Hill St	Durham, NC	27701-3112	919-956-5599	688-9027	K-8	Dietrich Danner
Highland Charter S	PO Box 1653	Gastonia, NC	28053-1653	704-861-2283	866-8725	K-2	Sherida Lewis Stevens
Hope Elementary Charter S	1116 N Blount St	Raleigh, NC	27604-1302	919-834-0941	834-9338	K-5	Robbie Graham
Howard S	1004 Herring Ave E	Wilson, NC	27893-3311	252-293-4150	293-4151	K-8	Dr. Jo Anne Woodard
Imani Institute Charter MS	201 N Church St	Greensboro, NC	27401-2941	336-333-9484	333-9454	6-8	Bethel Smith
Jefferson Classical Academy	2527 US 221A Hwy	Mooresboro, NC	28114-7698	828-657-9998	657-9012	6-12	Joseph Maimone
Joy Charter S	1955 W Cornwallis Rd	Durham, NC	27705-5707	919-493-6056	402-4263	K-7	Jim Polk
Kennedy Charter S	PO Box 472527	Charlotte, NC	28247-2527	704-688-2939	688-2962	6-12	Stacey Rose
Kestrel Heights S	2119 Chapel Hill Rd	Durham, NC	27707-1405	919-403-9194	490-8658	6-12	Tim Dugan
Kinston Charter Academy	2000 Martin L King Jr Blvd	Kinston, NC	28501	252-522-0210	527-6878	K-8	Walter Anderson
Lake Norman Charter S	12820 Church St	Huntersville, NC	28078-4223	704-948-8600	948-8778	5-8	Ben Putman
Lakeside S	PO Box 157	Elon, NC	27244-0157	336-584-0091	417-5810	6-12	Dr. Suni Schulze
Laurinburg Charter S	PO Box 1575	Laurinburg, NC	28353-1575	910-276-6635	610-4070	9-12	Cynthia McDuffie
Laurinburg Homework Center	PO Box 929	Laurinburg, NC	28353-0929	910-277-8010	277-8019	8-12	Annie Cureton
Learning Center	945 Connahetta St	Murphy, NC	28906-3524	828-835-7240	835-9471	K-5	Mary Jo Dyre
Lincoln Charter S	133 Eagle Nest Rd	Lincolnton, NC	28092-7383	704-736-9888	736-1166	K-12	Keith Hain
Magellan Charter S	9400 Forum Dr	Raleigh, NC	27615-2971	919-844-0277	844-3882	4-8	Mary Griffin
Metrolina Regional Scholars Academy	7000 Endhaven Ln	Charlotte, NC	28277-2370	704-503-1112	503-1183	K-8	Dr. Marie Peine
Millennium Charter Academy	500 Old Springs Rd	Mount Airy, NC	27030-3034	336-789-7570	789-8445	K-5	Kirby McCrary
Mountain Community S	613 Glover St	Hendersonville, NC	28792-5451	828-696-8480	696-8451	K-8	Chadwick Hamby
Mountain Discovery Charter S	PO Box 1879	Bryson City, NC	28713-1879	828-488-1222	488-0526	K-8	Chantelle Carroll
New Century HS	PO Box 10	Saxapahaw, NC	27340-0010	336-376-1122	376-6995	9-12	Dr. Marcia Hugh
New Dimensions S	PO Box 2248	Morganton, NC	28680-2248	828-437-5753	437-2980	K-5	Angela G. Deal
Omuteko Gwamaziima S	PO Box 52072	Durham, NC	27717-2072	919-687-0870	680-2573	K-8	Bernitha Jenkins
Orange County Charter	920 Corporate Dr	Hillsborough, NC	27278-8557	919-644-6272	644-6275	K-8	David Christenbury
PACE Academy	1713 Legion Rd	Chapel Hill, NC	27517-2359	919-933-7699	967-9905	9-12	Rhonda R. Franklin
Phoenix Academy	4020 Meeting Way St	High Point, NC	27265-8233	336-869-0079	869-3399	K-8	Kim Norcross
Piedmont Community S	PO Box 3706	Gastonia, NC	28054-0020	704-853-2428	861-9463	K-12	Courtney Madden
PreEminent Charter S	3815 Rock Quarry Rd	Raleigh, NC	27610-5123	919-235-0511	235-0514	K-8	Dr. Les Stein
Provisions Academy	PO Box 5437	Sanford, NC	27331-5437	919-775-7800	775-7722	6-12	Dr. Sadie Jordan
Quality Education Academy	5012D Lansing Dr	Winston Salem, NC	27105-3026	336-744-0804	744-2523	3-8	Simon Johnson
Queens Grant Community S	6400 Matthews Mint Hill Rd	Mint Hill, NC	28227-9323	704-573-6611	573-0995	K-8	Christy Morrin
Quest Academy	9650 Strickland Rd Ste 175	Raleigh, NC	27615-2082	919-841-0441	841-0443	K-8	Dr. Charles Watson
Raleigh Charter HS	1111 Haynes St	Raleigh, NC	27604-1454	919-715-1155	839-1766	9-12	Dr. Thomas Humble
Research Triangle Academy	2418 Ellis Rd	Durham, NC	27703-5543	919-957-7108	957-9698	K-8	Terri Gullick
River Mill Academy	PO Box 1450	Graham, NC	27253-1450	336-229-0909	229-9975	K-12	Linda Humble
Rocky Mount Prep S	3334 Bishop Rd	Battleboro, NC	27809-9039	252-443-9923	443-9932	K-12	Michael Pratt
Rowan Academy Charter S	1010 Airport Rd	Salisbury, NC	28147-8909	704-630-9200	630-6707	K-5	Eugene C. Perry
Sandhills Theatre Arts Renaissance S	140 Southern Dunes Dr	Vass, NC	28394-9218	910-695-1004	695-7322	K-5	David Jackson
Socrates Academy	8310 McAlpine Park Dr	Charlotte, NC	28211-6247	704-366-1115	366-1585	K-5	Janis Dellinger-Holt
SPARC Academy	PO Box 37518	Raleigh, NC	27627-7518	919-835-2000	835-2009	PK-8	Jackie Mburu
Sterling Montessori Academy	202 Treybrooke Dr	Morrisville, NC	27560-9300	919-462-8889	462-8890	K-8	Mike Jordan
Success Institute	1424 Rickert St	Statesville, NC	28677-6856	704-881-0441	881-0870	K-8	Tenna Williams
Sugar Creek Charter S	4101 N Tryon St	Charlotte, NC	28206-2066	704-509-5470	921-1004	K-8	Cheryl Ellis
Summit Charter S	PO Box 1339	Cashiers, NC	28717-1339	828-743-5755	743-9157	K-8	Dr. Patrici Ingraham
Tiller S	1950 US Highway 70 E	Beaufort, NC	28516-7836	252-728-1995	728-3711	K-8	Jean Kruft
Torchlight Academy	2801 S Wilmington St	Raleigh, NC	27603-3552	919-829-9500	829-0820	K-6	Dr. Cynthia McQueen
Two Rivers Community S	196 Windy Dr	Boone, NC	28608-0001	828-297-6188		K-12	Linda Rigell
Union Academy	675 N Martin Luther Jr Blvd	Monroe, NC	28110	704-283-8883	283-8823	K-8	Ken Templeton
Vance Charter S	1227 Dabney Dr	Henderson, NC	27536-3558	252-431-0440	436-0688	K-8	Carolyn Powell
Visions Charter S	2952 N Oxford St	Claremont, NC	28610-9661	828-459-2051	459-1115	K-6	Craig Willis
Washington Montessori S	500 Avon Ctr	Washington, NC	27889-3851	252-946-1977	946-5938	K-8	Stacey Shepherd
Woods Charter S	PO Box 5008	Chapel Hill, NC	27514-5001	919-960-8353	960-0133	K-12	Pamela Blizzard
Woodson S of Challenge	437 Goldfloss St	Winston Salem, NC	27127-3125	336-723-6838	723-6425	K-12	Ruth Hopkins
Ohio							
A+ Arts Academy	3330 Scottwood Rd	Columbus, OH	43227-3564	614-338-0767		6-8	Carolyn Berkley
Academy of Business & Technology	1462 Woodland Ave	Toledo, OH	43607-3977	419-243-5880		K-8	Althea McClelland
Academy of Cleveland	9114 Miles Park Ave	Cleveland, OH	44105-5106	216-271-0237	271-0361	K-9	Linda Harris
Academy of Dayton	4095 Little Richmond Rd	Dayton, OH	45427-3310	937-274-7491	567-1075	K-9	Daisy Edwards
Akron Community S	1585 Frederick Blvd	Akron, OH	44320-4053	330-836-6370		K-6	Jane Bechtel
Akron Digital Academy	335 S Main St	Akron, OH	44308-1203	330-237-2200	237-2214	K-12	William Romano
Allen Academy	700 Heck Ave	Dayton, OH	45408-2641	937-586-9815	586-0271	K-8	Kim Cockrell
Allen Downtown Campus	400 E 2nd St	Dayton, OH	45402-1724	937-586-9756		K-8	Michelle Ferrell
Allen Preparatory S	1034 Superior Ave	Dayton, OH	45402-5953	937-567-9121		K-12	Amy Bettendorf
Alliance Academy of Cincinnati	1712 Duck Creek Rd	Cincinnati, OH	45207-1644	513-751-5555		K-6	Mary Martin
Alliance Academy of Toledo	1501 Monroe St Ste 2	Toledo, OH	43624-1752	419-418-5150		7-12	Jerri A. Heer
Alternative Education Academy	121 S Main St Ste 102	Akron, OH	44308-1436	330-730-7452		K-12	Mardy Chaplin
Amanda-Clearcreek Community S	328 E Main St	Amanda, OH	43102-9330	740-969-7250	969-7620	K-K	James Dick
Apex Academy	16005 Terrace Rd	East Cleveland, OH	44112-2001	216-451-1725		K-5	Kevin James
Arise Academy	1320 E 5th St	Dayton, OH	45402-2223	937-853-0560		9-12	Shane Floyd
Arise Sports Management Academy	834 Randolph St	Dayton, OH	45408-1749	937-263-3937		9-12	William Peterson
Arts Academy	4125 Leavitt Rd	Lorain, OH	44053-2341	440-960-0470		K-5	Alexis Rainbo
Arts & College Preparatory Academy	2002 S Hamilton Rd	Columbus, OH	43232-4111	614-986-9974		9-12	William Soltis
Aurora Academy	541 Utah St	Toledo, OH	43605-2299	419-693-6841	693-4799	K-8	Cindy Wilson
Autism Academy of Learning	219 Page St	Toledo, OH	43620-1430	419-865-7487	865-8360	K-12	Chris Loehrke
Booth Academy	300 Lytle St	Cincinnati, OH	45202-4212	513-241-1121		K-5	Marie Hanna
BOSS	519 Broadway St	East Liverpool, OH	43920-3137	330-385-1987		K-12	Richard E. Wolfe
Canton Digital Academy	617 McKinley Ave SW	Canton, OH	44707-4727	330-438-2500		K-12	George W. Burwell
Canton Local Digital	4526 Ridge Ave SE	Canton, OH	44707-1118	330-484-8010	484-8032	K-12	Jay Moody
CASTLE	1729 Superior Ave E	Cleveland, OH	44114-2934	216-443-5044		9-12	Rolando Peterson
Chase Academy for Communication Arts	2283 Sunbury Rd	Columbus, OH	43219-3528	614-509-2432		K-3	Celia Jones
Cincinnati College Prep Academy	1425 Linn St	Cincinnati, OH	45214-2605	513-684-0777	684-8888	K-8	Lisa K. Hamm
Citizens' Academy	1827 Ansel Rd	Cleveland, OH	44106-4107	216-791-4195	791-3013	K-5	Monyka Price
City Day Community S Inc.	318 S Main St	Dayton, OH	45402-2716	937-223-8130	223-8136	K-6	Roseda Goff
Cleve Academy of Math Science & Tech	1881 E 71st St	Cleveland, OH	44103-4005	216-391-3752		K-10	Sandra Brown
Columbus Youth Entrepreneurship	PO Box 29645	Columbus, OH	43229-0645	614-509-2428		9-11	Patrick Brown
Cornerstone Academy Community	61 E Mound St	Columbus, OH	43215-5121	614-225-8924	462-7384	K-3	Christine Emmerich
Crittenton Community S	1515 Indianola Ave	Columbus, OH	43201-2118	614-294-2661		6-8	Suzanne Robinson
Crossroads Preparatory Academy	350 City Center Dr	Columbus, OH	43215-5181	614-586-1800	586-1804	6-12	Anita Nelam
Cupe Community S	1132 Windsor Ave	Columbus, OH	43211-2836	614-294-3020		K-6	Estella Stephens
Dayton Academy	4401 Dayton Liberty Rd	Dayton, OH	45418-1903	937-262-4080	262-4091	K-8	Patricia Love
Dayton View Academy	1416 W Riverview Ave	Dayton, OH	45402-6217	937-567-9426	567-9446	K-8	Derrick Thomas
Dohn Community HS	608 E McMillan St	Cincinnati, OH	45206-1926	513-281-6100	281-6103	8-12	Kathleen E. Bower
Dunbar Academy	331 14th St	Toledo, OH	43624-1402	419-244-4202		K-6	Thomas Williams
Eagle Academy	1501 Monroe St	Toledo, OH	43624-1760	419-245-9862		K-12	Tammy Wells
Eagle Heights Academy	1833 Market St	Youngstown, OH	44507-1137	330-742-9090	742-9095	K-8	Alex Murphy
East End Community Heritage S	PO Box 9889	Cincinnati, OH	45209-0889	513-281-3900	281-0818	K-12	Cammie Montgomery
East End Community S	111 Xenia Ave	Dayton, OH	45410-1523	937-222-7355		K-4	Lourdes Lambert
Edge Academy	92 N Union St	Akron, OH	44304-1347	330-535-4581	535-5074	K-8	Keri Dornack
Electronic Classroom of Tomorrow	3700 S High St Ste 95	Columbus, OH	43207-4083	614-492-8884		K-12	James Thomas
Elgin Digital Academy	4616 Larue Prospect Rd W	Marion, OH	43302-8859	740-382-1101		K-12	Chris Kimball
Elida Digital Academy	1920 Slabtown Rd	Lima, OH	45801-3309	419-227-9252		7-12	Don Diglia
Elyria Community S	300 N Abbe Rd	Elyria, OH	44035	440-366-5225	366-6280	K-6	Tom Fox
Englewood Peace Academy	1120 Horace St	Toledo, OH	43606-4737	419-243-7260		K-8	Lincoln Kynard
Euclid Community S	7667 Day Dr	Parma, OH	44129-5603			K-3	Don Distantis
Excel Institute	2952 Dover Rd	Columbus, OH	43209-3022	614-888-9394		7-12	Nganga Njoroge
Fairborn Digital Academy	700 Black Ln	Fairborn, OH	45324-5844	937-879-0511		K-12	Robert Grinshaw

School	Address	City,State	Zip code	Telephone	Fax	Grade	Contact
Franklin Local Digital Academy	360 Cedar St	Duncan Falls, OH	43734-9710	740-674-5203	674-5214	K-12	Dr. Diane Longstreth
Garvey Academy	13830 Euclid Ave #2	Cleveland, OH	44112-4204	216-451-7949		6-8	Arthur Baker
Goal Digital Academy	PO Box 216	Edison, OH	43320-0216	419-946-1903	947-9551	K-12	Laura Chervenak
Golden Eagle Digital Academy	901 44th St NW	Canton, OH	44709-1611	330-492-3500		K-12	Deb Nicodemo
Graham Digital Academy	370 E Main St	Saint Paris, OH	43072-9200	937-663-4123	663-4670	K-12	Marcia Ward
Graham S	3950 Indianola Ave	Columbus, OH	43214-3158	614-262-1111	262-5878	9-12	Eileen G. Meers
Greater Achievement Community S	3443 E 93rd St	Cleveland, OH	44104-5252	216-341-8138		K-8	Angela Ross
Greater Cincinnati Community Academy	4781 Hamilton Ave	Cincinnati, OH	45223-1550	513-541-9750	541-9754	K-9	Marie Congo
Great Western Academy	310 N Wilson Rd	Columbus, OH	43204-6221	614-276-1028		K-3	James Cowardin
Hamilton County Math & Science S	7601 Harrison Ave	Mount Healthy, OH	45231-3107	513-728-8620		K-3	Dwan Moore
Hamilton Local Digital Academy	1055 Rathmell Rd	Columbus, OH	43207-4742	614-554-5598	491-8323	K-12	William Morrison
Handy Community MS	3400 Kohr Blvd	Columbus, OH	43224-3051	614-428-6013		6-8	Patricia Brown
Harmony Community S	1580 Summit Rd	Cincinnati, OH	45237-1904	513-921-5260		6-12	Deland McCullough
Harte S	350 City Center Dr	Columbus, OH	43215-5181	614-586-1800	586-1804	6-12	Anita Nelam
Hope Academy Broadway Campus	3398 E 55th St	Cleveland, OH	44127-1691	216-271-7747	271-6438	K-12	Lydia Harris
Hope Academy-Brown Street Campus E	1035 Clay St	Akron, OH	44301-1517	330-785-0180	785-0681	K-12	Wendy Rydarowicz
Hope Academy Canton Campus	1379 Garfield Ave SW	Canton, OH	44706-5200	330-454-3128		K-8	Virginia Desharnais
Hope Academy Cathedral Campus	10615 Lamontier Ave	Cleveland, OH	44104-4847	216-721-6909	721-1565	K-12	Jennifer Morrison
Hope Academy Chapelside Campus	3845 E 131st St	Cleveland, OH	44120-4661	216-283-6589	283-3087	K-12	Muata Niamke
Hope Academy - Cuyahoga Campus	12913 Bennington Ave	Cleveland, OH	44135-3761	216-251-5450	251-6410	K-8	Sharon Durant
Hope Academy East Campus	15720 Kipling Ave	Cleveland, OH	44110-3105	216-383-1214		K-12	Lee Lazar
Hope Academy Lincoln Park	2421 W 11th St	Cleveland, OH	44113-4401	216-263-7008	263-7007	K-8	Ray Terry
Hope Academy Northcoast Campus	6916 Krakow Ave	Cleveland, OH	44105-5737	216-280-1293		K-8	Shirley Reed
Hope Academy University Campus	220 S Broadway St	Akron, OH	44308-1531	330-535-7728	535-7864	K-12	Angela Stanley
Horizon Science Academy	1329 Bethel Rd	Columbus, OH	43220-2611	614-457-2231	457-5064	5-12	Hizir Disli
Horizon Science Academy	6000 S Marginal Rd	Cleveland, OH	44103-1042	216-432-3660		6-12	Sedat Duman
Imani Leadership Institute	1140 Euclid Ave	Cleveland, OH	44115-1603	216-344-9934		K-10	Dr. Donna Johnson
Imani Learning Academy	728 Parkside Blvd	Toledo, OH	43607-3858	419-535-7078	535-5915	K-8	Randel Grieser
Intergenerational S	12200 Fairhill Rd	Cleveland, OH	44120-1058	216-721-0120		K-4	Dr. Cathy Whitehouse
International Academy of Columbus	1201 Schrock Rd	Columbus, OH	43229-1117	614-844-5539		K-8	Kathleen Seiter
International Preparatory S	10701 Shaker Blvd	Cleveland, OH	44104-3752	216-791-2602		K-12	Khadeeja Morse M.Ed.
ISUS Trade & Tech Prep S Cincinnati	425 Ezzard Charles Dr	Cincinnati, OH	45203-1428	513-723-1513		9-12	Learwinson Jackson
Kent Digital Academy	321 N Depeyster St	Kent, OH	44240-2514	330-676-7610	676-7686	K-12	Joe Giancola
Kessler S	118 E Wood St	Youngstown, OH	44503-1625	330-746-3095		K-8	Lydia Brown-Payton
Lake Erie Academy	2740 W Central Ave	Toledo, OH	43606-3452	419-475-3786		K-8	Barbara Baker
Lakewood Digital Academy	PO Box 70	Hebron, OH	43025-0070	740-928-5878	928-3152	K-12	Jay Gault
Lancaster Digital Academy	111 S Broad St	Lancaster, OH	43130-4398	740-687-7364	687-7303	K-12	Steven Clippinger
Legacy Academy for Leaders & Arts	1812 Oak Hill Ave	Youngstown, OH	44507-1053	330-747-1620		K-8	Joyce Baldwin
Life Skills Center of Akron	80 W Bowery St	Akron, OH	44308-1137	330-376-8700	535-5055	9-12	Joseph Cole
Life Skills Center of Canton	1100 Cleveland Ave NW	Canton, OH	44702-1816	330-309-9085		9-12	Albert Lewis
Life Skills Center of Cincinnati	2612 Gilbert Ave	Cincinnati, OH	45206-1205	513-319-3536	475-0444	9-12	Victor Gray
Life Skills Center of Cleveland	4600 Carnegie Ave	Cleveland, OH	44103-4371	216-431-7571	431-7652	9-12	Yolanda Eiland
Life Skills Center of Elyria	2015 W River Rd N	Elyria, OH	44035-2309	440-324-1755	324-1723	9-12	Mark Sutherland
Life Skills Center of Hamilton County	7710 Reading Rd	Cincinnati, OH	45237-6800	513-821-6695		9-12	Paul Jungkunz
Life Skills Center of Lake Erie	9200 Madison Ave	Cleveland, OH	44102-2719	216-631-1090		9-12	Joseph Czerwien
Life Skills Center of Northern Columbus	1900 E Dublin Granville Rd	Columbus, OH	43229-3553	614-891-9041		9-12	Kathy Williams
Life Skills Center of SE Columbus	2400 S Hamilton Rd	Columbus, OH	43232-4963	614-296-5026		9-12	Janice Hoffman
Life Skills Center of Springfield	1637 Selma Rd	Springfield, OH	45505-4245	937-322-2940	322-2944	9-12	
Life Skills Center of Summit County	2168 Romig Rd	Akron, OH	44320-3879	330-671-4529		9-12	Lashawn Terrel
Life Skills Center of SW Columbus	3088 Southwest Blvd	Grove City, OH	43123-2335	614-801-1366		9-12	Tami Augustine
Life Skills Center of Toledo	1830 Adams St	Toledo, OH	43624-1428	419-503-0244		9-12	Thomas Robey
Life Skills Center of Trumbull County	458 Franklin St SE	Warren, OH	44483-5715	330-647-3211	392-0253	9-12	Thomas Kempe
Life Skills Center of Youngstown	3405 Market St	Youngstown, OH	44507-2009	330-743-6698	743-6702	9-12	Jeremy Batchelor
Lighthouse Community S	6100 Desmond St	Cincinnati, OH	45227-1897	513-561-7888	561-7818	6-12	Kevin Jamison
Lighthouse Community S	1585 Frederick Blvd Ste 100	Akron, OH	44320-4053	330-836-6370	237-9235	K-8	Jane Bechtel
London Digital Academy	60 S Walnut St	London, OH	43140-1246	740-852-5700	852-3078	K-12	Bob Blackburn
Lorain Community S	201 W Erie Ave	Lorain, OH	44052-1641	440-204-2130	204-2134	K-6	Charles Ziemke
Lorain Digital S	346 Illinois Ave	Lorain, OH	44052-2106	440-288-1680		K-12	Frederick Dull
Main St Education Center	407 E Main St	Louisville, OH	44641-1419	330-875-9591	875-7674	PK-K	Sherry Unger
Mansfield Community S	455 Park Ave W	Mansfield, OH	44906-3117	419-522-4578		K-6	Loretta Jennings
Marion City Digital Academy	169 E Center St	Marion, OH	43302-3813	740-223-4417		K-12	Raymond Haines
Meadows Choice Community S	5955 Seaman St	Oregon, OH	43616-4219	419-691-3805		3-9	Caroline Renz
Middletown Fitness & Prep Academy	816 2nd Ave	Middletown, OH	45044-4201	513-424-6110		K-7	Dr. Myrrha Pammer
Millenium Community ES	1850 Bostwick Rd	Columbus, OH	43227-3301	614-255-5585	255-5580	K-6	James Cowardin
Miree Fundamental Academy	1660 Sternblock Ln	Cincinnati, OH	45237-3805	513-351-8034	366-3395	K-8	Pauline Olverson
MODEL Community S	1615 Holland Rd	Maumee, OH	43537-1622	419-897-4400	897-4403	K-12	Mary Walters
Montessori Renaissance Experience	1895 Summit St	Columbus, OH	43201-1539	614-299-1126		K-5	Cynthia D. Frazier
Moraine Community S	5656 Springboro Pike	Dayton, OH	45449-2806	937-294-4522		K-11	Barbara Speelman
Mound Street Health Careers Academy	354 Mound St	Dayton, OH	45402-8325	937-223-3041		9-12	Sue Garretson
Mound Street IT Careers Academy	354 Mound St	Dayton, OH	45402-8325	937-223-3041		9-12	Sue Garretson
Mound Street Military Careers Academy	354 Mound St	Dayton, OH	45402-8325	937-223-3041		9-12	Susan Garretson
New Choices Community S	601 S Keowee St	Dayton, OH	45410-1168	937-224-8201		7-8	Gary L. Hardman
North Dayton S of Science & Discovery	3901 Turner Rd	Dayton, OH	45415-3654	937-278-6671		K-8	Patricia Dungy
Oak Tree Montessori S	20 E Central Pkwy	Cincinnati, OH	45202-7239	513-241-0448	241-0350	K-6	Judy McConnell
Ohio Virtual Academy	1655 Holland Rd Ste F	Maumee, OH	43537-1656	419-482-0948		K-12	Susan Stagner
Old Brooklyn Montessori S	4430 State Rd	Cleveland, OH	44109-4705	216-661-7888		K-9	Cherie Kaiser
Omega S of Excellence	1821 Emerson Ave	Dayton, OH	45406-4802	937-278-2372	278-0267	5-8	Vanessa Ward
Parma Community S	7667 Day Dr Fl 1	Parma, OH	44129-5603	440-888-5490	888-5890	K-8	Milton Levy
Pathway S of Discovery	173 Avondale Dr	Dayton, OH	45404-2123	937-235-5498		K-6	Karen Spencer
Performing Arts S	425 Jefferson Ave	Toledo, OH	43604-1060	419-243-4752		6-12	Keri DiCiani
Perry Panther Digital Academy	4201 13th St SW	Massillon, OH	44646-3447	330-478-6184		K-12	John Richard
Perrysburg Digital Academy	140 E Indiana Ave	Perrysburg, OH	43551-2261	419-874-3181	872-8813	K-12	R. Falkenstein
Phoenix Academy Community S	2238 Jefferson Ave	Toledo, OH	43624-1120	419-720-4510		7-12	Earl Apgar
Phoenix Community Learning Center	7030 Reading Rd Ste 350	Cincinnati, OH	45237-3839	513-351-5801		K-8	Dr. Glenda D. Brown
Plain Local Academy of Tech	901 44th St NW	Canton, OH	44709-1699	330-492-3500		4-8	Deb Nicodemo
Powell Leadership Academy	834 Randolph St	Dayton, OH	45408-1749	937-203-3937		K-8	Lorraine Renee Clemons
Quaker Digital Academy	248 Front Ave SW	New Phila, OH	44663-2150	330-364-0600	364-9310	K-12	Steve Eckert
Quest Academy Community S	190 E 8th St	Lima, OH	45804-2302	419-227-7730	227-7515	K-5	Oscar Marshall
Rhea Academy	113 E 3rd St	Dayton, OH	45402-2129	937-461-7432	461-6865	K-10	Monica Rhea
Riverside Academy	3280 River Rd	Cincinnati, OH	45204-1214	513-921-7777	921-7704	K-8	Roger Conners
Sciotoville S	224 Marshall St	Sciotoville, OH	45662-5549	740-927-3941	776-6812	7-12	Dennis DeCamp
Springfield Academy of Excellence	623 S Center St	Springfield, OH	45506-2209	937-325-0962		K-6	Edna Chapman
Summit Academy - Canton	2400 Cleveland Ave NW	Canton, OH	44709-3613	330-453-8547	453-8924	2-8	Ken Baker
Summit Academy Creative Arts	864 E Market St	Akron, OH	44305-2424	330-434-2343	434-5295	6-8	Tarik West
Summit Academy Lorain Community S	1949 Broadway	Lorain, OH	44052-3626	440-245-2593	245-2545	2-8	Karen Combs
Summit Academy - Middletown	7 S Marshall Rd	Middletown, OH	45044-5375	513-420-9767		2-8	Edward Lemmert
Summit Academy of Alternative Learners	819 E Market St	Akron, OH	44305-2441	330-253-7441		2-8	Robin Muscato
Summit Academy - Parma City	7667 Day Dr	Parma, OH	44129-5603	440-888-5407	888-5410	2-8	Frank Cheraso
Summit Academy - Xenia	870 S Detroit St	Xenia, OH	45385-5510	937-372-5210	372-5250	2-8	Carol Andrews
Summit Academy - Youngstown	1400 Oak Hill Ave	Youngstown, OH	44507-1018	330-747-0950		2-8	Kathleen Mioni
T.C.P. World Academy	6000 Ridge Ave	Cincinnati, OH	45213-1624	513-531-9500	531-2406	K-8	Karen Y. French
Toledo Academy of Learning	301 Collingwood Blvd	Toledo, OH	43602-1624	419-255-0253		K-8	Margie Blackmon
Toledo Accelerated Academy	1501 Monroe St	Toledo, OH	43624-1760	419-242-6160		6-11	Benard Crawford
Toledo S for the Arts	333 14th St	Toledo, OH	43624-1459	419-246-8732		6-12	Martin Porter
Tomorrow Center	PO Box 216	Edison, OH	43320-0216	419-946-1903	947-9551	3-12	Lane Warner
TRECA Digital Academy	1713 Marion Mount Gilead Rd	Marion, OH	43302-7867	740-389-4798	389-4517	K-12	Mike Carder
Trotwood Fitness & Prep Academy	3100 Shiloh Springs Rd	Trotwood, OH	45426-2247	937-854-4100		K-7	Myrrha Pammer
Virtual Community S of Ohio	6100 Channingway Blvd	Columbus, OH	43232-2910	614-501-9473		K-12	Don Musick
Washington Park Community S	4000 Washington Park Blvd	Newburgh Hts, OH	44105-3248	216-271-6055	271-6099	K-7	Robert Horrocks
W.E.B. DuBois Community Academy	1812 Central Pkwy	Cincinnati, OH	45214-2304	513-702-3057		1-8	Wilson Willard
Wells Community Academy	1180 Slosson St	Akron, OH	44320-2730	330-867-1085		K-8	Angela Anderson
West Central Learning Academy	1920 Slabtown Rd	Lima, OH	45801-3309	419-227-9252	227-2511	K-12	Todd Hanes
Westpark Community S	16210 Lorain Ave	Cleveland, OH	44111-5521	216-688-0271	688-0273	K-6	Sharon Morgan
Wilson Military Academy	1729 Superior Ave E	Cleveland, OH	44114-2934	216-707-9780		9-9	Charles Britton
Woods Community S	PO Box 9843	Columbus, OH	43209-0843	614-252-3630		K-5	Carol Rivers
Youngstown Community ES	50 Essex St	Youngstown, OH	44502-1838	330-746-2240	746-7144	K-6	Sr. Mary Dunn
YouthBuild Columbus Comm S	1183 Essex Ave	Columbus, OH	43201-2925	614-291-0805	291-0890	9-12	Dr. Joyce E. Swayne

Oklahoma

School	Address	City,State	Zip code	Telephone	Fax	Grade	Contact
ASTEC Charter S	2401 NW 23rd St	Oklahoma City, OK	73107-2442	405-947-6274	947-0035	6-10	Dr. Freda Deskin
Dove Science Academy	919 NW 23rd St	Oklahoma City, OK	73106-5691	405-524-9762	524-9471	6-12	Mustafa Guvercin
DOVE Science Academy	280 S Memorial Dr	Tulsa, OK	74112-2202	918-834-3936		6-12	Zekeruya Yuksel
Garvey S	1537 NE 24th St	Oklahoma City, OK	73111-3212	405-427-7616	425-4632	K-5	Dr. Kevin McPherson
Harding Charter Preparatory HS	3333 N Shartel Ave	Oklahoma City, OK	73118-7277	405-528-0562	556-5063	9-10	Richard Caram
Independence Charter MS	3232 NW 65th St	Oklahoma City, OK	73116-3512	405-841-3132	841-3134	6-8	Vana Baker
KIPP Enterprise S	1432 NE 7th St	Oklahoma City, OK	73117-2414	405-231-2001	231-2003	K-8	Tracy McDaniel

School	Address	City,State	Zip code	Telephone	Fax	Grade	Contact
KIPP Tulsa Academy	2740 E 41st St N	Tulsa, OK	74110-1432	918-925-1363	925-1374	5-8	Millard House
Santa Fe South HS	301 SE 38th St	Oklahoma City, OK	73129-3099	405-632-3062	634-7077	9-12	Chris Brewster
SeeWorth Academy	1025 NE 15th St	Oklahoma City, OK	73117-1007	405-424-6300	424-6301	3-12	Janet Grigg
Tulsa S of Arts and Sciences	5155 E 51st St Ste 200	Tulsa, OK	74135-7458	918-828-7727	828-7747	9-12	Elizabeth Martin
Wesley Academy	2240 NE 19th St	Oklahoma City, OK	73111-1708	405-427-6800	425-4614	9-12	Dick Curtis
Western Village ES	1508 NW 106th St	Oklahoma City, OK	73114-5299	405-751-1774	752-6833	PK-5	Margaret Brinson

Oregon

School	Address	City,State	Zip code	Telephone	Fax	Grade	Contact
Armadillo Technical Institute	PO Box 1560	Phoenix, OR	97535-1560	541-535-3287		6-12	Mike Warner
Arthur Academy	13709 SE Division	Portland, OR	97233	503-252-3753		K-4	Charles Arthur
Arts & Technology Charter S	8633 SW Main St	Wilsonville, OR	97070-8650	503-673-7777	673-7001	9-10	Mike Tannenbaum
Baker Charter S	999 Locust St NE	Salem, OR	97301-0954	503-364-4042	566-6929	K-5	Anne Griffith
Bandon Opportunity Charter S	455 9th St SW	Bandon, OR	97411-9008	541-347-4411	347-3974	8-12	Gary Chrismon
Bethany Charter S	11824 Hazelgreen Rd NE	Silverton, OR	97381-9611	503-873-4300	873-0143	K-8	Kathy Frank
Blue Mountain Charter S	76132 Blue Mountain School	Cottage Grove, OR	97424	541-942-7764	942-7597	K-12	Lesley Stine
Childs Way Charter S	PO Box 42	Culp Creek, OR	97427-0042	541-946-1821	946-2007	6-12	Angela Kerns
Clackamas Middle College HS	19729 Highway 213	Oregon City, OR	97045-4190	503-518-5929	518-5928	11-12	Tim King
CM2 Opal S	4015 SW Canyon Rd	Portland, OR	97221-2759	503-471-9902		PK-2	Judy Graves
Days Creek Charter S	PO Box 10	Days Creek, OR	97429-0010	541-825-3296	825-3052	6-12	Laurie Newton
Destinations Public Charter S	PO Box 509	Coos Bay, OR	97420-0102	541-267-1485	266-7314	6-12	Linda Vickrey
Douglas Avenue Charter S	PO Box 100	Gervais, OR	97026-0100	503-792-3803	792-3809	7-12	Linda Warbert
Eddyville Charter S	PO Box 68	Eddyville, OR	97343-0068	541-875-2942	875-2491	K-12	Don McDonald
Gold Beach Technology Charter S	29516 Ellensburg Ave	Gold Beach, OR	97444-7775	541-247-6647	247-9717	9-12	Jennifer Dukek
Goodall Environmental MS	2805 Lansing Ave NE	Salem, OR	97301-8555	503-399-3215	399-4070	6-8	Joe LaFountaine
Howard Street Charter S	710 Howard St SE	Salem, OR	97302-3098	503-399-3408	375-7861	6-8	Kim Vogel
Kings Valley Charter S	38840 Kings Valley Hwy	Philomath, OR	97370-9750	541-929-2134	929-8179	K-5	Mark Hazelton
Lighthouse S	93670 Viking Ln	North Bend, OR	97459-8651	541-297-4735		K-6	Alane Jennings
Lincoln City Career Tech HS	801 SW Highway 101 Ste 104	Lincoln City, OR	97367-2711	541-996-5534	265-8507	9-12	Marie Jones
Lourdes Charter S	39059 Jordan Rd	Scio, OR	97374-9330	503-394-3340		K-8	Linda Duman
Luckiamute Valley Charter S	12975 Kings Valley Hwy	Monmouth, OR	97361-9525	503-838-1933		4-8	Chrisi Cantamessa
McCoy Academy	3802 NE M L King Blvd	Portland, OR	97212-1113	503-281-9597	281-8817	6-12	Vicky Black
Milwaukie Academy of the Arts	11300 SE 23rd Ave	Milwaukie, OR	97222-7753	503-353-5830	353-5845	9-12	Kelly Carlisle
MITCH Charter S	PO Box 230575	Tigard, OR	97281-0575	503-639-5757		K-8	Debi Lorence
Morrison Charter S	1251 Main St	Dallas, OR	97338-2516	503-623-8480		9-12	Don Wildfang
Mosier Community S	PO Box 307	Mosier, OR	97040-0307	541-478-3321	478-2536	K-6	Carole Schmidt
Multisensory Learning Academy	PO Box 301295	Portland, OR	97294-9295	503-261-0202		K-4	Leigh Evans
New Urban HS	1901 SE Oak Grove Blvd	Milwaukie, OR	97267-2621	503-353-5925	353-5928	9-12	Tim King
Opal S	4015 SW Canyon Rd	Portland, OR	97221-2759	503-223-6500		PK-1	
Optimum Learning Environments Charter S	7905 June Reid Pl NE	Keizer, OR	97303-2559	503-399-5548	399-2647	1-5	Gary Etchemendy
Paisley Charter S	PO Box 97	Paisley, OR	97636-0097	541-943-3111	943-3129	K-12	Mark Jeffery
Pioneer Youth Corps Military Academy	1666 W 12th Ave	Eugene, OR	97402-3716	541-988-0121		6-12	Bill Lay
Resource Link Charter S	PO Box 509	Coos Bay, OR	97420-0102	541-267-1499	266-7314	5-12	Linda Vickrey
Ridgeline Montessori	2855 Lincoln St	Eugene, OR	97405-2737	541-681-9662	681-4394	K-7	Paul Randall
Rimrock Academy	1501 NE Neff Rd	Bend, OR	97701-6149	541-322-5323	322-5473	6-8	Mary Bryant
Sheridan Japanese S	430 SW Monroe St	Sheridan, OR	97378-1739	503-843-3400	843-7438	4-12	Candace Pelt
Siletz Valley S	PO Box 247	Siletz, OR	97380-0247	541-444-1100	444-2368	K-8	Van Peters
Sojourner ES	1905 SE Oak Grove Blvd	Milwaukie, OR	97267-2621	503-513-4540	513-4060	K-6	Denis Hickey
South Columbia Family S	52181 SW EM Watts Rd	Scappoose, OR	97056-2602	503-543-7077	543-7087	1-12	Anita Ott
Technology Learning Center	299 Bridge St	Vernonia, OR	97064-1319	503-429-3521	429-7049	7-12	Curt Scholl
Three Rivers Charter S	4975 Willamette Falls Dr	West Linn, OR	97068-3348	503-723-6019	723-6407	4-8	Katherine Holtgraves
21st Century Community Schoolhouse	210 Liberty St SE	Salem, OR	97301-3491	503-763-8958	763-8743	9-12	Mary Jean Sandall
Village S	2855 Lincoln St	Eugene, OR	97405-2737	541-345-7285	242-6874	K-8	Sandy Ludeman
West Salem Language Academy	2112 Linwood St NW	Salem, OR	97304-2134	503-399-3457	399-2173	K-3	Bill Wittman

Pennsylvania

School	Address	City,State	Zip code	Telephone	Fax	Grade	Contact
Academy Charter S	900 Agnew Rd	Pittsburgh, PA	15227-3902	412-885-5200		K-12	William Styche
Achievement House Charter S	1021 W Lancaster Ave	Bryn Mawr, PA	19010-2635	610-581-7590		K-12	Wallace Wallace
Ad Prima Charter S	124 Bryn Mawr Ave	Bala Cynwyd, PA	19004-3013	610-617-9121		K-8	Dr. June Brown
Agora Cyber Charter S	124 Bryn Mawr Ave	Bala Cynwyd, PA	19004-3013	610-617-9121		K-12	Dr. June Brown
Allen Preparatory Charter S	5151 Warren St	Philadelphia, PA	19131-4441	215-878-1544	878-8171	5-8	Lawrence F. Jones
Alliance For Progress Charter S	1821 Cecil B Moore Ave	Philadelphia, PA	19121-3135	215-232-4892	232-4893	K-5	Stacey E. Hill
Architecture & Design Charter HS	675 Sansom St	Philadelphia, PA	19106-3300	215-351-2900	351-9458	9-12	Dr. Peter Kountz
Attucks Youth Build Charter S	605 S Duke St	York, PA	17401-3111	717-848-3610	843-3914	12-12	Floyd Goff
Avon Grove Charter S	110 State Rd	West Grove, PA	19390-8908	484-667-5000		K-6	Dr. Kevin Brady
Bear Creek Community Charter S	2000 Bear Creek Blvd	Wilkes Barre, PA	18702-9684	570-820-4070		K-6	Dr. Janice Solkov
Beaver Area Academic Charter S	855 2nd St	Beaver, PA	15009-2600	724-774-0250		9-12	Brian White
Belmont Charter S	4030 Brown St	Philadelphia, PA	19104-4899	215-790-1294		K-6	Alice Lunsford
Bracetti Academy Charter S	2501 Kensington Ave	Philadelphia, PA	19125-1321	215-291-4436	291-4985	6-10	Angela Villani
Brown Charter S	279 Boas St	Harrisburg, PA	17102-2940	717-232-7696	236-3829	K-8	Rae L. Talley
Bucks County Montessori Charter S	8931 New Falls Rd	Levittown, PA	19054-1707	215-547-5230	547-5032	K-6	John Funston
Byers Charter S	1911 Arch St	Philadelphia, PA	19103-1403	215-972-1700		K-3	Barbara Rosini
Career Connections Charter HS	4412 Butler St	Pittsburgh, PA	15201-3012	412-682-1816	682-6559	9-11	Dr. Theresa Henderson
Center for Student Learning Charter S	134 Yardley Ave	Fallsington, PA	19054-1119	215-428-4100		6-12	Michelle Hunter
Central Pennsylvania Digital Charter S	1500 4th Ave	Altoona, PA	16602-3616	814-940-6989		K-12	Dr. Janette Kelly
Centre Learning Community Charter S	2634 W College Ave	State College, PA	16801-2603	814-861-7980	861-8030	5-8	Kosta Dussias
Chester Community Charter S	214 E 5th St	Chester, PA	19013-4510	610-447-0400	876-5716	K-6	Dr. Peter Idstein
Chester Co. Family Academy	323 E Gay St Ste B7	West Chester, PA	19380-2755	610-696-5910	696-6324	K-2	Lorraine Anderson
City Charter HS	717 Liberty Ave	Pittsburgh, PA	15222-3511	412-690-2489		9-10	Maxine Klimasara
Clemente Charter S	136 S 4th St	Allentown, PA	18102-5410	610-439-5181	435-4731	6-12	Carlos Lopez
Collegium Charter S	103 N Everhart Ave	West Chester, PA	19380-2848	610-903-1300	903-1317	K-12	Bill Winters
Columbus Charter S	916 Christian St	Philadelphia, PA	19147-3808	215-925-7400	925-7491	K-4	Rosemary Dougherty
Commonwealth Connections Charter S	5010 E Trindle Rd	Mechanicsburg, PA	17050-3631	717-605-8900		K-8	Earl Grier
Community Academy of Philadelphia	1100 E Erie Ave	Philadelphia, PA	19124-5424	215-533-6700		K-12	Joe Proietta
DeHostos Charter S	4322 N 5th St	Philadelphia, PA	19140-2302	215-455-2300	455-6312	K-K,	Evelyn Lebron
Delaware Valley Charter HS	5201 Old York Road	Philadelphia, PA	19141	215-455-2550		9-12	Ava Greene Bedden
Discovery Charter S	5070 Parkside Ave Unit 6200	Philadelphia, PA	19131-4750	215-879-8182		K-6	Jacquelyn Kelley
Family Charter S	907 N 41st St	Philadelphia, PA	19104-1278	215-790-1294		K-4	Alice Lunsford
Fell Charter S	777 Main St	Simpson, PA	18407-1236	570-282-5199		K-6	Michael Uebalherr
First Philadelphia Charter S	4300 Tacony St	Philadelphia, PA	19124-4134	215-743-3100		K-3	Stacy Cruise-Clark
Folk Arts-Cultural Treasures Charter S	1118 Market St	Philadelphia, PA	19107-3601	215-569-2600		K-8	Debbie Wei
Forbes Charter S	PO Box 197	Lincoln Univ, PA	19352-0197	610-932-8998	932-8798	K-3	Dr. Lenetta Lee
Franklin Towne Charter HS	PO Box 310	Philadelphia, PA	19105-0310	215-289-5000	535-8910	9-12	Joseph Venditti
Freire Charter S	2027 Chestnut St	Philadelphia, PA	19103-3301	215-557-8555	557-9051	8-12	Dr. Kelly Davenport
GECAC Community Charter S	1446 E Lake Rd	Erie, PA	16507-1936	814-461-9600	461-0226	K-7	Gregory Myers
Germantown Settlement Charter S	4811 Germantown Ave	Philadelphia, PA	19144-3014	215-713-0855	713-0553	5-8	Aaronda Beauford
Graystone Academy Charter S	139 Modena Rd	Coatesville, PA	19320-4036	610-383-4311		K-6	Dr. Linda Portlock
Green Woods Charter S	8480 Hagys Mill Rd	Philadelphia, PA	19128-1938	215-482-6337	482-9135	K-6	Deborah Binder
Hope Charter S	2116 E Haines St	Philadelphia, PA	19138-2600	215-336-2730		9-12	Richard L. Chapman
Imani Education Circle Charter S	5612 Greene St Fl 2	Philadelphia, PA	19144-2808	215-713-9240		K-8	Dr. Francine Fulton
Imhotep Institute Charter HS	2101 W Godfrey Ave	Philadelphia, PA	19138-2597	215-438-4140	438-4160	9-12	M. Christine Wiggins
Independence Charter S	105 S 7th St	Philadelphia, PA	19106-3324	215-238-8000	238-1998	K-4	Jurate Krokys
Infinity Charter S	51 Banks St Ste 1	Penbrook, PA	17103-2067	717-238-1880		K-6	Nancy Hall
Keystone Education Center Charter S	425 S Good Hope Rd	Greenville, PA	16125-8629	724-588-2511	588-2545	6-12	Mike Gentile
Khepera Charter S	144 Carpenter Ln	Philadelphia, PA	19119-2563	215-843-3527		K-8	Linda Ralph-Kern
KIPP Academy Charter S	2709 N Broad St	Philadelphia, PA	19132-2722	215-227-1728		5-5	Marc Mannella
La Academia Charter S	30 N Ann St	Lancaster, PA	17602-3063	717-295-7763	399-6456	6-12	Dr. Maritza Robert
Laboratory Charter S	124 Bryn Mawr Ave	Bala Cynwyd, PA	19004-3013	610-617-9121	660-8416	K-8	Dr. June Hairston-Brown
Leadership Learning Partners Charter S	1425 N 2nd St	Philadelphia, PA	19122-3801	215-739-2007	739-2606	K-6	Dr. Ruthie Green-Brown
Lehigh Valley Academy	1560 Valley Center Pkwy	Bethlehem, PA	18017-2275	610-866-9660		K-12	Susan Mauser
Lehigh Valley Charter HS	675 E Broad St	Bethlehem, PA	18018-6332	610-868-2971		9-12	Dr. Thomas Lubben
Lincoln Charter S	559 W King St	York, PA	17401-3776	717-699-1573	846-4031	K-5	Erin Holman
Manchester Academic Charter S	1214 Liverpool St	Pittsburgh, PA	15233-1309	412-322-0585	322-2176	K-8	Vasilios A. Scoumis
Maritime Academy Charter S	3020 Market St	Philadelphia, PA	19104-2801	215-387-7066		5-8	Dr. Ann Gillis Waiters
MAST Community Charter S	1800 Byberry Rd	Philadelphia, PA	19116-3012	215-348-1100		K-12	Richard Trzaska
Mastery Charter HS	35 S 4th St	Philadelphia, PA	19106-2703	215-922-1902	922-1903	9-10	Scott H. Gordon
Math Civics & Sciences Charter S	447 N Broad St	Philadelphia, PA	19123-3643	215-923-4880	923-4859	1-12	Veronica Joyner
Midwestern Regional Virtual Charter S	453 Maple St	Grove City, PA	16127-2399	724-458-6700	458-5083	K-12	Angelo Pezzuolo
Montessori Regional Charter S	2910 Sterrettania Rd	Erie, PA	16506-2646	814-833-7771		K-6	Lydia Cerroni
Morris Charter S	2600 W Thompson St	Philadelphia, PA	19121-4699	215-684-5087	684-8881	K-8	Ruth E. King
Multi-Cultural Academy Charter S	4666 N 15th St	Philadelphia, PA	19140-1109	215-457-6666	457-2982	9-12	Dr. Vuong Thuy
New Foundations Charter S	8001 Torresdale Ave	Philadelphia, PA	19136-2917	215-624-8100		K-8	Paul Stadelberger
New Media Technology Charter S	7800 Ogontz Ave	Philadelphia, PA	19150-1408	267-286-6900		9-12	Dr. Ina Walker
Nittany Valley Charter S	1612 Norma St	State College, PA	16801-6228	814-867-3842	231-0795	1-8	Kelly Herrity
Northside Urban Pathways Charter S	914 Penn Ave	Pittsburgh, PA	15222-3713	412-392-4601	392-4602	6-12	Linda Clautti
Northwest Pennsylvania Collegiate Acad	2825 State St	Erie, PA	16508-1829	814-874-6300	874-6307	9-12	Lori Gornall

School	Address	City,State	Zip code	Telephone	Fax	Grade	Contact
Northwood Academy	4621 Castor Ave	Philadelphia, PA	19124-3097	215-289-5606	676-8340	K-6	Brien Gardiner
Nueva Esperanza Academy Charter HS	301 W Hunting Park Ave	Philadelphia, PA	19140-2625	215-457-3667	457-4381	9-12	David Rossi
Penn Charter S	3000 W School House Ln	Philadelphia, PA	19144-5412	215-844-3460	843-3939	K-12	Earl Ball
Pennsylvania Cyber Charter S	900 Midland Ave	Midland, PA	15059-1514	724-643-1180	643-1181	K-12	Dr. Nick Trombetta
Pennsylvania Distance Learning Charter S	23 N Front St	Harrisburg, PA	17101-1640	717-232-3220		K-12	Dr. Rod Niner
Pennsylvania Global Academy	3740 W 26th St	Erie, PA	16506-2039	814-835-5322		K-12	Edward Grzelak
Pennsylvania Leadership Charter S	17 Ravine Rd Ste 100	Malvern, PA	19355-1941	610-993-9390		K-12	Dr. James Hanak
PA Learners Online Regional S	475 Waterfront Dr E	Homestead, PA	15120-1144	412-394-5733		K-12	Dr. David Martin
Pennsylvania Virtual Charter S	1 W Main St Ste 400	Norristown, PA	19401-4766	610-275-8501	275-1719	K-5	Joanne Jones Barnett
People for People Charter S	800 N Broad St	Philadelphia, PA	19130-2202	215-763-7060	235-6435	K-5	James Watson
Perseus House Charter S of Excellence	2931 Harvard Rd	Erie, PA	16508-1220	814-459-3954		7-12	Dr. John Linden
Philadelphia Academy Charter S	11000 Roosevelt Blvd	Philadelphia, PA	19116-3961	215-676-8320	676-8340	K-8	Brien Gardner
Philadelphia Electrical & Tech Charter S	1420 Chestnut St	Philadelphia, PA	19102-2505	267-514-1823	514-1834	9-10	Michael Nemitz
Philadelphia Harambee Inst Charter S	640 N 66th St	Philadelphia, PA	19151-3606	215-472-8770	472-9611	K-8	John Skief
Philadelphia Montessori Charter S	2227 Island Rd	Philadelphia, PA	19142-1009	215-365-4011	365-4367	PK-3	Kathleen Dzura
Philadelphia Performing Arts Charter S	2600 S Broad St	Philadelphia, PA	19145-4616	215-551-4000	551-1113	K-7	Angela Corosanite
Pocono Mountain Charter S	16 Carriage Sq	Tobyhanna, PA	18466-8979	570-894-5108		K-12	Dennis Bloom
Preparatory Charter S	1928 Point Breeze Ave	Philadelphia, PA	19145-2612	215-334-6144	334-6147	9-12	John Badagliacco
Propel Charter S	24 S 18th St	Pittsburgh, PA	15203-1767	412-325-7305		K-4	Jeremy Resnick
Raising Horizons Quest Charter S	4960 Master St	Philadelphia, PA	19131-4521	215-477-6672	477-6674	K-6	Martha Russell
RAPAH-Edison Charter S	120 S Whitfield St	Pittsburgh, PA	15206-3806	412-362-8818		K-2	Alecia Gibbs
Renaissance Academy - Edison Charter S	40 Pine Crest Ave	Phoenixville, PA	19460-2955	610-983-4080	983-4096	K-12	Jenifer MacFarland
Renaissance Advantage Charter S	1712 S 56th St	Philadelphia, PA	19143-5308	215-724-2343	724-2374	K-8	Anton Witherspoon
Renaissance Charter S	7500 Germantown Ave	Philadelphia, PA	19119-1600	215-753-0390	753-0615	6-8	A. Donald Lepore
Ridgeview Academy Charter S	1133 Village Way	Latrobe, PA	15650	724-537-9110	537-9114	1-12	Sherri L. Holler
Sankofa Academy	501 E Miner St	West Chester, PA	19382-3431	610-994-4273		5-12	Dr. LaMont McKim
School Lane Charter S	2400 Bristol Pike	Bensalem, PA	19020-5293	215-245-6055	245-6058	K-8	George Richards
Souderton Charter S Collaborative	110 E Broad St	Souderton, PA	18964-1276	215-721-4560	721-4071	K-7	Jennifer Arevalo
Spectrum Charter S	4369 Northern Pike	Monroeville, PA	15146-2807	412-374-8130	374-9629	9-12	Michelle Johnson
Sugar Valley Rural Charter S	PO Box 104	Loganton, PA	17747-0104	570-725-7822	725-7825	K-12	Logan Coney
SUSQ-Cyber Charter S	90 Lawton Ln	Milton, PA	17847-9756	570-523-1155	523-0674	9-12	James Street
Sylvan Heights Science Charter S	915 S 13th St	Harrisburg, PA	17104-3402	717-232-9220	232-9221	K-4	Dr. Kevin Moran
Tidioute Community Charter S	224 Main St	Tidioute, PA	16351-1156	814-484-3550		K-12	David Craig
Tuscarora Blended Learning Charter S	2527 US Highway 522 S	Mc Veytown, PA	17051-9434	814-542-2501		K-12	Tony Payne
21st Century Cyber Charter S	455 Boot Rd	Downingtown, PA	19335-3043	484-237-5206		6-12	Jon Marsh
Universal Institute Charter S	801 S 15th St	Philadelphia, PA	19146-2215	215-732-7988	732-8066	K-8	John Walker
Urban League of Pittsburgh Charter S	327 N Negley Ave	Pittsburgh, PA	15206-2851	412-361-1008	361-1042	K-5	Dr. Gail Edwards
Village Charter S of Chester-Upland	200 Commerce Dr	Chester, PA	19014-3203	610-494-2100		PK-12	Harry Hill
Vitalistic Therapeutic Charter S	902 4th Ave	Bethlehem, PA	18018-3702	610-861-7570		K-3	Naomi H. Grossman
Wakisha Charter S	1209 Vine St	Philadelphia, PA	19107-1111	267-256-0950	256-0953	6-8	Denise Johnson
West Oak Lane Charter S	7115 Stenton Ave	Philadelphia, PA	19138-1136	215-927-7995	927-7980	K-5	Donnamaria Parker
West Philadelphia Achievement Charter S	111 N 49th St	Philadelphia, PA	19139-2718	215-476-6471	476-6470	K-5	Stacey Gill-Phillips
Wissahickon Charter S	4700 G Wissahickon Ave	Philadelphia, PA	19144	267-338-1020		K-5	Julie Carroll
Wonderland Charter S	2112 Sandy Dr	State College, PA	16803-2282	814-234-5886		K-K	Harold Ohnmeis
World Communications Charter S	512 S Broad St #20	Philadelphia, PA	19146-1613	215-735-3197	735-3824	6-12	Dr. Martin Ryder
Young Scholars Charter S	1415 N Broad St	Philadelphia, PA	19122-3323	215-232-9727	232-4542	6-8	C. Lars Beck
Young Scholars of Central PA Charter S	3020 Research Dr	State College, PA	16801-2782	814-237-9727		K-5	Bulent Tarman
Youth Build Charter S	1231 N Broad St	Philadelphia, PA	19122-4021	215-627-8671	763-5774	9-12	Simran Sidhu

Rhode Island

School	Address	City,State	Zip code	Telephone	Fax	Grade	Contact
BEACON Charter S	35 George St	Woonsocket, RI	02895-1319	401-671-6261	671-6264	9-12	Robert Pilkington
Blackstone Academy	334 Pleasant St	Pawtucket, RI	02860-5273	401-726-1750	726-1753	9-12	Carolyn Sheehan
Compass S	537 Old North Rd	Kingston, RI	02881-1220	401-783-8322	788-8326	K-8	Gay Sonn
Construction Career Academy	4 Sharpe Dr	Cranston, RI	02920-4410	401-270-8692	270-8697	9-12	Dr. Michael Silva
Cuffee S	459 Promenade St	Providence, RI	02908-5601	401-453-2626	453-4964	K-8	David Bourns
CVS Highlander Charter S	45 Greeley St	Providence, RI	02904-2214	401-277-2600	277-2603	K-8	Jim Donahue
International Charter S	334 Pleasant St	Pawtucket, RI	02860-5273	401-721-0824	721-0976	K-5	Julie Nora
Kingston Hill Academy	850 Stony Fort Rd	Saunderstown, RI	02874-1003	401-783-8282	783-5656	K-5	Daniel Parker
Learning Community S	21 Lincoln Ave	Central Falls, RI	02863-2012	401-722-9998	722-0990	K-2	Sarah Friedman
Textron/Chamber of Commerce Academy	130 Broadway	Providence, RI	02903-3003	401-456-1738	521-0653	9-12	Lawrence DeSalvatore
Times 2 Academy	50 Fillmore St	Providence, RI	02908-3105	401-272-5094	272-0555	6-12	Ralph Taylor
Times 2 Academy	30 Barton St	Providence, RI	02909-1804	401-272-8945	272-6014	K-4	Ralph Taylor

South Carolina

School	Address	City,State	Zip code	Telephone	Fax	Grade	Contact
Aiken Academy	10612 Augusta Rd	Belton, SC	29627-9246	864-243-3443	243-5743	1-8	Glynda Caddell
Aiken Performing Arts Academy	363 Laurens St	Aiken, SC	29802	803-644-4824	641-1155	9-12	Keisha Kennedy
Boykin Academy	4851 Rivers Ave	N Charleston, SC	29406-6502	843-744-8882		K-12	Dee Gathers
Bridgewater Academy	316 Bush Dr	Myrtle Beach, SC	29579-7314	843-236-3689	236-4921	K-8	Carol Merrill
Charleston Development Academy	PO Box 20518	Charleston, SC	29413-0518	843-722-2689	722-2694	K-3	Cecelia Gordon Rogers
Children's Attention Home	PO Box 2912	Rock Hill, SC	29732-4912	803-328-8871	324-0437	K-8	Dr. Carey Harper
Children's S at Sylvia Circle	929 Sylvia Cir	Rock Hill, SC	29730-5768	803-981-1380	981-1494	K-5	Kiersten Byrd
CHOiCES	1405 Poinsett Dr	Florence, SC	29505-2638	843-664-8993	664-8881	5-9	Ralph Porter
Discovery S of Lancaster	PO Box 130	Lancaster, SC	29721-0130	803-285-8430	416-8907	K-5	Tom McDuffie
East Cooper Montessori Charter S	188 Civitas St	Mount Pleasant, SC	29464-2669	843-216-2883	216-8880	1-3	Jody Swanigan
Fox Creek HS	PO Box 6430	North Augusta, SC	29861-6430	803-613-9435	613-1533	9-12	John A. Gratop
Greenville Technical Charter HS	PO Box 5616	Greenville, SC	29606-5616	864-250-8845	250-8846	9-12	W. Fred Crawford
Infinity S	215 Broad St	Bennettsville, SC	29512-4003	843-454-2034	454-0113	7-12	Lori Heslewood
James Island Charter HS	1000 Fort Johnson Rd	Charleston, SC	29412-8898	843-762-2754	762-5228	9-12	Robert Bohnstengel
Kennedy Charter S	PO Box 418	Aiken, SC	29802-0418	803-644-4824	641-1155	5-8	Keisha Lloyd-Kennedy
Langston Charter MS	10 Ryedale Ct	Greenville, SC	29615-6037	864-234-5495	752-2350	6-8	Lisa Stevens
Meyer Center for Special Children	1132 Rutherford Rd	Greenville, SC	29609-3927	864-250-0005	250-0028	PK-2	Louise Anthony
Midlands Math & Business Academy	PO Box 6792	Columbia, SC	29260-6792	803-609-1882	790-0387	4-8	Michelle Spradley
Midland Valley Preparatory S	2432 Jefferson Davis Hwy	Graniteville, SC	29829-3828	803-594-1028	594-0511	K-7	Lilian Knight Thomas
MLD Learning Academy	54 Joe Rd	Bishopville, SC	29010-7460	803-428-3350	428-2750	4-8	Benita Robinson
Nevin Center	600 Laurens Rd	Greenville, SC	29607-1836	864-751-8325	751-8336	K-5	Darlene Grimes
Palmetto Youth Academy	PO Box 15054	Florence, SC	29506-0054	843-667-9311	667-9313	4-6	Yvonne Burgess
Phoenix Charter HS	PO Box 170	Alcolu, SC	29001-0170	803-505-6800	505-6801	9-12	Anne Darby
Richland One Middle College S	3560 Lynhaven Dr	Columbia, SC	29204-4413	803-738-7114	738-7117	11-12	Audrey Breland
RMMBA	914 White Horse Rd	Greenville, SC	29605-3556	864-422-0812	422-0812	K-8	Martha Evans
Wohali Academy	PO Box 1005	Travelers Rest, SC	29690-1005	864-834-8013	834-6977	K-12	Laura Blackmore
Youth Academy Charter S	PO Box 174	Kingstree, SC	29556-0174	843-355-5424	355-5753	7-12	Anissa Capers
YouthBuild Charleston Charter S	7555 Spartan Blvd N	N Charleston, SC	29420-8820	843-552-1474	552-1684	9-12	Helen McKune

Tennessee

School	Address	City,State	Zip code	Telephone	Fax	Grade	Contact
Circles of Success	867 S Parkway E	Memphis, TN	38106-5605	901-322-7978	322-7993	K-4	Bertharene Young
City University S of Liberal Arts	4748 Winchester Rd	Memphis, TN	38118-5335	901-368-9890	368-9894	9-12	Loell Winston
Memphis Academy of Health Sciences	3925 Chelsea Avenue Ext	Memphis, TN	38108-2612	901-525-9091		6-8	Curtis Weathers
Memphis Academy of Science & Engineering	20 Dudley St	Memphis, TN	38103-4904	901-448-6273	448-8850	7-12	Tommie Henderson
Memphis Business Academy	204 N 2nd St	Memphis, TN	38105-3500	901-521-4355		6-8	Celia Roussea
Promise Academy	1635 Georgian Dr	Memphis, TN	38127-4312	901-358-7752		K-K	Blakely Wallace
Southern Avenue Charter S	3311 Kimball Ave	Memphis, TN	38111-3846	901-743-7335		K-1	Joyce Mathis
Star Academy Charter S	3240 James Rd	Memphis, TN	38128-5311	901-387-5050		K-3	Dr. Kia Young
Stax Music Academy	910 E McLemore Ave	Memphis, TN	38106-3338	901-942-7627		6-8	David Hill
Yo Academy Charter S	2140 S 3rd St	Memphis, TN	38109-7734	901-947-5353		9-12	Menthia Clark

Texas

School	Address	City,State	Zip code	Telephone	Fax	Grade	Contact
A+ Academy	10327 Rylie Rd	Dallas, TX	75217-8240	972-557-5578	557-5807	PK-12	Brenton White
Academy of Accelerated Learning	6025 Chimney Rock Rd	Houston, TX	77081-4011	713-773-4766	666-2532	PK-5	Joyce Bethany
Academy of Accelerated Learning	6025 Chimney Rock Rd	Houston, TX	77081-4011	713-645-0336	640-2435	PK-5	Joyce Bethany
Academy of Beaumont	1275 Cedar St	Beaumont, TX	77701-2718	409-832-8600	832-5909	K-8	Cynthia Solomon
Academy of Careers & Technologies	807 Roosevelt Ave	San Antonio, TX	78210-3878	210-226-7568	572-5321	9-12	Pamela Bradley White
Academy of Dallas	1030 Oak Park Dr	Dallas, TX	75232-1238	214-371-9600	371-1053	PK-8	Conrad Hargest
Accelerated Interdisciplinary Academy	PO Box 20589	Houston, TX	77225-0589	713-283-6298	283-6190	PK-5	Dr. David Fuller
Accelerated Interdisciplinary Academy	PO Box 20589	Houston, TX	77225-0589	903-758-5300	758-5307	PK-5	Connie Isabell
Accelerated Interdisciplinary Academy	PO Box 20589	Houston, TX	77225-0589	409-886-3200	886-3217	PK-5	Dr. David Fuller
Accelerated Interdisciplinary Academy	PO Box 20589	Houston, TX	77225-0589	903-526-1730	526-3334	PK-5	Connie Isabell
Accelerated Intermediate Academy	PO Box 20589	Houston, TX	77225-0589	713-283-6298	283-6190	PK-8	Dr. David Fuller
Accelerated Intermediate Academy	PO Box 20589	Houston, TX	77225-0589	903-758-5300	758-5307	6-8	Connie Isabell
Accelerated Intermediate Academy	PO Box 20589	Houston, TX	77225-0589	409-886-3200	886-3217	6-8	Dr. David Fuller
Accelerated Intermediate Academy	PO Box 20589	Houston, TX	77225-0589	903-526-1730	526-3334	6-8	Connie Isabell
Accelerated Learning Center	721 Omaha Dr	Corpus Christi, TX	78408-2839	361-887-7766	887-6035	PK-12	Maria Garza
Alief Montessori Community S	4215 H St	Houston, TX	77072-5380	281-530-9406	564-1795	PK-6	Nancy Chieu
Allen Charter	5220 Nomas St	Dallas, TX	75212-3229	972-794-5100	794-5101	PK-3	Connie Hovseth
Alpha Charter S	701 W State St	Garland, TX	75040-6310	972-272-2173	205-9050	K-12	

School	Address	City,State	Zip code	Telephone	Fax	Grade	Contact
ALTA Academy	8329 Lawndale St	Houston, TX	77012-3707	713-923-8801	923-8255	9-12	Larry Mercado
American Academy of Excellence Charter S	PO Box 52877	Houston, TX	77052-2877	713-283-9235	571-9726	9-12	Jean LaGrone
American Youth Works Charter S	216 E 4th St	Austin, TX	78701-3610	512-236-6100	472-1189	9-12	Dr. Carole Lewis
American Youth Works Charter S	1901 E Ben White Blvd	Austin, TX	78741-7840	512-744-1900	916-4708	9-12	Kim Bookman
Amigos Por Vida-Friends for Life Charter	5500 El Camino Del Rey St	Houston, TX	77081-1867	713-399-9945	521-3416	PK-5	Carlos Villagrana
Arlington Classics Academy	2111 Roosevelt Dr	Arlington, TX	76013-5920	817-274-2008	274-8768	K-8	Ken Simon
Austin Can Academy Charter S	2406 Rosewood Ave	Austin, TX	78702-2408	512-477-4226	931-8034	9-12	Mary Bashara
Austin Discovery S	PO Box 4356	Austin, TX	78765-4356	512-674-0700	407-8373	K-5	Kelly McRee
Azleway Charter S	15892 County Road 26	Tyler, TX	75707-2728	903-566-8444	566-2053	K-12	Tom Evans
Banneker-McNair Math/Science Academy	4924 Griggs Rd	Houston, TX	77021-3251	713-748-2262	440-6767	PK-3	Glenda Fonteneaux
Bay Area Charter MS	PO Box 2126	League City, TX	77574-2126	281-316-0001	316-0018	6-8	Dr. Rosalind Perez
Bay Area Charter S	2600 Humble Dr	El Lago, TX	77586-5900	281-326-4555	326-4888	PK-8	Kris Wessale
Benji's Special Education Academy	2903 Jensen Dr	Houston, TX	77026-6019	713-229-0560	224-6724	PK-12	
Bexar County Academy	1485 Hillcrest Dr	San Antonio, TX	78228-3900	210-432-8600	432-1195	PK-8	Dr. Keyshar Breedlove
Big Springs Charter S	PO Box 399	Leakey, TX	78873-0399	830-232-7101	232-4279	6-12	Amber Shandley
Brazos River Charter S	PO Box 949	Nemo, TX	76070-0949	254-898-9226	898-2297	8-12	Mike Thames
Brazos S for Inquiry & Creativity	8787 N Houston Rosslyn Rd	Houston, TX	77088-6430	713-983-6877	983-7036	PK-6	Shondra Grisafi
Brazos S for Inquiry & Creativity	2110 Old Hearne Rd	Bryan, TX	77803-1813	979-778-8882	778-8289	PK-8	Chris Osgood
Brazos S for Inquiry & Creativity	802 Autumn Cir	College Station, TX	77840-7816	979-268-8884	268-8882	PK-12	Dr. Robert Slater
Brazos S for Inquiry & Creativity	4637 Gano St	Houston, TX	77009-3457	713-222-8400	222-8409	PK-8	Barbara Rueban
Briarmeadow Charter S	3601 Dunvale Rd	Houston, TX	77063-5707	713-458-5500	458-5506	PK-8	Lynn Barnes
Bright Ideas Charter S	2507 Central Fwy E	Wichita Falls, TX	76302-5802	940-767-1561	767-1904	K-12	Lynda Plummer
Brown-Fellowship Charter School	6901 S Westmoreland Rd	Dallas, TX	75237-2431	972-709-4700	709-6605	PK-6	Laura Middleton
Burch Charter S	5703 Blanco Rd	San Antonio, TX	78216-6616	210-431-9881	432-8467	4-6	Valerie Walker
Burnham Wood Charter S	7310 Bishop Flores Dr	El Paso, TX	79912-1429	915-584-9499	585-8814	K-6	Debbie Crinzi
Career Plus Learning Academy	1122 S WW White Rd	San Antonio, TX	78220-3424	210-333-8389	225-2448	6-12	Charles R. Hayes
Cedar Crest Charter S	3500 S Interstate 35	Belton, TX	76513-9498	254-939-4094	939-4046	K-12	Dr. Susan Perez
Cedar Ridge Charter S	PO Box 214	Lometa, TX	76853-0214	512-752-3142	752-3239	PK-12	Robin Beauregard
Cedars International Academy	1320 E 51st St	Austin, TX	78723-3037	512-458-3693	451-9554	K-7	Sam Greer
Children First Academy of Dallas	1638 E Ann Arbor Ave	Dallas, TX	75216-6335	214-371-2545	371-4682	PK-7	;
Children First Academy of Houston	7803 E Little York St	Houston, TX	77016	713-491-9030	491-9032	PK-7	
Children of the Sun Charter S	PO Box 164	Mc Allen, TX	78505-0164	956-488-8883	488-0889	PK-12	Augie Pena
Children of the Sun Charter S	PO Box 164	Mc Allen, TX	78505-0164	956-689-3300	292-0371	PK-12	Alejandro Perez
Coastal Bend Youth City S	PO Box 268	Driscoll, TX	78351-0268	361-387-4513	387-0995	4-12	Sally Irvine
Comquest Academy	PO Box 490	Tomball, TX	77377-0490	281-516-0611	516-0993	9-12	
Cornerstone Academy	9026 Westview Dr	Houston, TX	77055-4602	713-365-5766	365-5787	6-8	Jill Wright
Corpus Christi Academy	800 Ayers St	Corpus Christi, TX	78404	361-225-4240	225-4021	9-12	Joe Martinez
Corpus Christi Montessori S	3530 Gollihar Rd	Corpus Christi, TX	78415-2759	361-883-9306		1-4	
Crossroad Community Education Center	5830 Van Fleet St	Houston, TX	77033-2036	713-645-9122	645-9121	9-12	Andrea Williams
Crosstimbers Academy	1408 Meadow Mountain Dr	Waco, TX	76712	817-648-2047	866-4307	9-12	Mike Thames
Cumberland Academy	8225 S Broadway Ave	Tyler, TX	75703-5494	903-581-2890	581-1476	K-8	Karen Flowers
Dallas Can! Academy	325 W 12th St Ste 175	Dallas, TX	75208-6502	214-943-2244	946-4427	9-12	Laura Rodriguez
Dallas Can! Academy Charter S	4621 Ross Ave	Dallas, TX	75204-4994	214-824-4226	824-7951	9-12	Keith Lott
Dallas Community Charter S	722 Tenison Memorial Dr	Dallas, TX	75223-1138	214-824-8950	827-7683	PK-3	Terrybeth Ford
Destiny Honors Academy	1001 E Veterans Mem # 301	Killeen, TX	76541	254-690-3962	690-8376	K-8	Elliott Alvarado
Dietrich Road Community Center	6903 S Sunbelt Dr	San Antonio, TX	78218-3336	210-804-1786	804-1469	9-12	Barbara Hawkins
Dominion Academy	1102 Pinemont Dr	Houston, TX	77018-1300	713-476-9800	476-9707	6-8	Shinell Terrance-Clark
Draw Academy	3920 Stoney Brook Dr	Houston, TX	77063	713-706-3729	706-3711	PK-8	Lisa Newton
Eagle Academy of Abilene	3161 S 23rd St Ste 4	Abilene, TX	79605-5861	325-698-8111	695-5620	6-12	Jerry Kiser
Eagle Academy of Austin	1701 W Ben White Blvd #100A	Austin, TX	78704	512-444-8442	444-1266	9-12	
Eagle Academy of Beaumont	209 N 11th St	Beaumont, TX	77702-2213	409-835-4303	835-2882	6-12	Brenda Lewis
Eagle Academy of Brownsville	955 Paredes Line Rd	Brownsville, TX	78521-2659	956-550-0084	554-0809	6-12	Norma Sorola
Eagle Academy of Del Rio	1306 E Gibbs St	Del Rio, TX	78840-4822	830-774-1559	775-0769	6-12	Kim Middleton
Eagle Academy of Fort Worth	6411 Camp Bowie Blvd Ste B	Fort Worth, TX	76116-5449	817-731-2028	731-2129	6-12	David Lee
Eagle Academy of Laredo	1720 E Hillside Rd	Laredo, TX	78041-3336	956-723-7788	753-6101	6-12	Joe Lambert
Eagle Academy of Lindale	17141 Highway 110 N	Lindale, TX	75771	903-881-9940	882-0183	9-12	
Eagle Academy of Lubbock	3501 50th St Ste 200	Lubbock, TX	79413-4043	806-763-1518	763-9310	6-12	Michael Griffin
Eagle Academy of Midland	2500 W Illinois Ave	Midland, TX	79701-6339	432-682-0384	682-0897	6-12	Charles Cook
Eagle Academy of Mission	1203 St Claire Blvd	Mission, TX	78572-6601	956-424-9290	424-7661	9-12	
Eagle Academy of Pharr	200 E Expressway 83 Ste C	Pharr, TX	78577-6506	956-781-8800	781-7464	6-12	Rosalinda Gonzalez
Eagle Academy of San Antonio	3622 Fredericksburg Rd	San Antonio, TX	78201-3841	210-434-6090	434-7578	6-12	Nery Vazquez
Eagle Academy of Trinity	219 Bette St	Trinity, TX	75862-7208	936-594-1427	594-1395	6-12	Mike Morrow
Eagle Academy of Tyler	2235 W Gentry Pkwy	Tyler, TX	75702-2809	903-592-5222	592-0324	6-12	Laqueta Timmons
Eagle Academy of Waco	1601 Washington Ave	Waco, TX	76701-1134	254-752-0441	752-0445	6-12	Terry Antoine
Eagle Advantage Charter S	4011 Joseph Hardin Dr	Dallas, TX	75236-1507	214-467-9101	467-9131	K-12	Martha Brown
East Fort Worth Montessori Academy	501 Oakland Blvd	Fort Worth, TX	76103-1014	817-496-3003	496-3004	PK-2	Joyce Brown
East Texas Charter HS	2402 Alpine Rd	Longview, TX	75601-3407	903-753-9400	753-0285	9-12	Terry Lapic
Eastwood Academy	1315 Dumble St	Houston, TX	77023-1902	713-924-1697	924-1715	9-12	Rogelio Lopez
Eden Park Academy	6215 Manchaca Rd Bldg D	Austin, TX	78745-4927	512-383-0613	383-0665	K-8	Lisa Robinson
Education and Training Center	6903 S Sunbelt Dr	San Antonio, TX	78218-3336	210-804-1786	804-1469	9-12	Barbara Hawkins
Education Center at Little Elm	9146 Lonesome Dove Dr	Little Elm, TX	75068-3270	972-292-3562	292-2373	K-12	Nickie Farley
Education Center at The Colony	5901 Crestwood Pl	Little Elm, TX	75068-3754	972-292-2405	292-2373	K-12	Nickie Farley
Education Center International Academy	2800 W Kingsley Rd	Garland, TX	75041-2400	972-271-3165	271-3253	K-12	Jonathan Fryer
Ehrhart S of Fine Arts & Athletics	PO Box 7733	Beaumont, TX	77726-7733	409-839-8200	839-8242	PK-8	T. Chris Comick
El Paso Academy	11000 Argal Ct	El Paso, TX	79935-3712	915-590-8589	590-0052	9-12	Charles Smith
El Paso Academy West	11000 Argal Ct	El Paso, TX	79935-3712	915-845-7997	845-7522	9-12	Dr. Margaret Gresham
El Paso S of Excellence	1599 George Dieter Dr	El Paso, TX	79936-7604	915-595-1599	595-3100	PK-5	Judy Jimenez
El Paso S of Excellence MS	1605 George Dieter Dr #301	El Paso, TX	79936	915-598-1755	598-8188	6-8	J. L. Lewis
Encino S	PO Box 106	Encino, TX	78353-0106	361-568-3375	568-3625	PK-8	Roberto Gonzalez
Energized for Excellence Academy	6201 Bissonnet St	Houston, TX	77081-6809	713-773-3600	773-3630	PK-8	Lois Bullock
Erath Excels! Academy	2900 W Washington St Ste 12	Stephenville, TX	76401-3710	254-965-8883	965-8654	9-12	
Evolution Academy Charter S	1100 Business Pkwy	Richardson, TX	75081-5025	972-907-3755	907-3765	9-12	Cynthia Jones Trigg
Faith Family Academy of Oak Cliff	1620 Falcon Dr	De Soto, TX	75115-2418	214-375-7682	375-7681	PK-12	Sonja Jackson
Focus Learning Academy	PO Box 210835	Dallas, TX	75211-0835	972-283-1414	709-1111	K-6	Linus Walton
Fort Worth Academy of Fine Arts	3901 S Hulen St	Fort Worth, TX	76109-3321	817-924-1482	926-9932	3-12	John Shreve
Fort Worth Can! Academy	4301 Campus Dr	Fort Worth, TX	76119-5535	817-431-4226	531-0443	9-12	Cynthia Miles
Fort Worth Can! Academy	5508 Black Oak Ln	River Oaks, TX	76114	817-735-1515	735-1465	9-12	Hoyt Mann
Fruit of Excellence	PO Box 431	Elgin, TX	78621-0431	512-281-3738	363-4063	1-12	Roslyn Martin
Galaviz Academy	5206 Airline Dr	Houston, TX	77022-1902	713-694-6027	694-0419	9-12	Luis Cano
Garza-Gonzales Charter S	4129 Greenwood Dr	Corpus Christi, TX	78416-1841	361-881-9988	881-9994	6-12	Adolfo Chapa
Gateway Academy	1230 Townlake Dr	Laredo, TX	78041-3796	956-722-0747	722-0767	9-12	Frances Johnson
Gateway Charter Academy	6103 Houston School Rd	Dallas, TX	75241-2516	214-375-2039	375-1842	K-6	Lester Singleton
GCCLR Institute of Technology	4129 Greenwood Dr	Corpus Christi, TX	78416	361-881-9988	881-9994	PK-12	Adolfo Chapa
Gervin Academy	6903 S Sunbelt Dr	San Antonio, TX	78218-3336	210-804-1786	804-1469	9-12	Barbara Hawkins
Girls & Boys Prep Academy	8415 W Bellfort St	Houston, TX	77071-2205	713-270-5994	270-1302	6-12	Kimya McKinney
Girls & Boys Prep Academy	8415 W Bellfort St	Houston, TX	77071-2205	713-270-2006	270-2046	K-5	Vonda Washington
Golden Rule Charter S	2602 W Illinois Ave	Dallas, TX	75233-1002	214-333-9171	330-8810	PK-12	Martha Delgado
Guardian Angel Performance Academy	2361 Austin Hwy #101	San Antonio, TX	78218-1982	210-737-9377		6-8	Jacquelyn Darby
Gulf Shores Academy	11300 S Post Oak Rd Ste 1	Houston, TX	77035-5739	713-723-3494	723-3513	9-12	Tiffany Taylor
Gulf Shores Academy	11300 S Post Oak Rd Ste 1	Houston, TX	77035	713-723-3494	723-3513	7-8	Linda Johnson
Harllee ES	1216 E 8th St	Dallas, TX	75203-2500	972-925-6500	925-6501	PK-6	Yolunda Wilson
Harmony ES	5435 S Braeswood Blvd	Houston, TX	77096	713-541-3030	541-3032	K-5	Ozgur Ozer
Harmony Science Academy	5435 S Braeswood Blvd	Houston, TX	77096-4001	713-729-4400	729-6600	6-12	Kadir Almus
Harmony Science Academy	5435 S Braeswood Blvd	Houston, TX	77096	972-234-9993	234-9994	6-12	Nihat Guvercin
Harmony Science Academy - Austin	930 E Rundberg Ln	Austin, TX	78753-4826	512-835-7900	835-7901	6-12	Kaan Camuz
Hawkins HS	1826 Basse Rd	San Antonio, TX	78213-4606	210-461-9881	253-2197	9-12	Ernesto Velazquez
Higgs Carter King Gifted & Talented S	PO Box 18854	San Antonio, TX	78218-0854	210-735-2341	733-6434	PK-12	Claudette Yarbrough
Highland Heights ES	865 Paul Quinn St	Houston, TX	77091-4154	713-696-2920		PK-5	Bernnell Peltier-Glaze
Hill Country Youth Ranch	PO Box 399	Leakey, TX	78873	830-367-2131	367-6108	1-5	Jeanie Williamson
Horizon Montessori S	116 W 5th St	Weslaco, TX	78596	956-380-1101	380-5110	PK-4	Irma Infante
Houston Alternative Prep Charter S	17300 El Camino Real	Houston, TX	77058-2715	713-524-6905	524-6344	PK-12	Dr. Lucille Abney
Houston Can! Academy - Hobby	9020 Gulf Fwy	Houston, TX	77017-7007	832-379-4226	944-6736	9-12	Ledy Garza
Houston Can! Academy - Main	2301 Main St	Houston, TX	77002-9101	713-659-4226	651-1493	9-12	Tiffany Abrams
Houston Gateway Academy	3400 Evergreen Dr	Houston, TX	77087-3715	713-649-3092	649-8165	K-10	Fransico Penning
Houston Heights HS	1125 Lawrence St	Houston, TX	77008-6651	713-868-9797	868-9750	8-12	Richard Mik
Houston Heights Learning Academy	902 W 8th St	Houston, TX	77007-1408	713-869-9453	869-0785	PK-5	Yvette East
I Am That I Am Academy	PO Box 41614	Dallas, TX	75241-0614	214-372-6838	372-6871	4-12	Walter Parker
IDEA Academy	401 S 1st St	Donna, TX	78537-3055	956-464-0203	464-4137	K-8	Tom Torkelson
IDEA College Prep S	401 S 1st St	Donna, TX	78537	956-464-0203	464-8532	9-12	Jeremy Beard
Inspired Vision Academy I	10327 Rylie Rd	Dallas, TX	75217-8240	214-391-7964	391-7954	PK-6	Lana Sprayberry-King
Inspired Vision II	10327 Rylie Rd	Dallas, TX	75217-8240	972-557-5578	557-5807	PK-8	Tony Rorie
Jackson Academy	5400 Griggs Rd	Houston, TX	77021-3757	713-845-2451	643-9850	9-12	A. Jackson
Jamie's House Charter S	PO Box 681183	Houston, TX	77268-1183	281-866-9777	880-9919	6-12	Jewel Teagle
Jubilee Academic Center	4434 Roland Rd	San Antonio, TX	78222-2830	210-333-6227	337-2357	PK-12	Daniel Amador
Kaleidoscope Charter S	5909 Glenmont Dr	Houston, TX	77081-1692	713-661-1670	660-9259	6-8	Marie Moreno
Kandy Stripe Academy	5310 Southlea St	Houston, TX	77033-1727	713-734-4909	731-7890	PK-8	Kaye Anderson
Kelley Charter S	802 Oblate Dr	San Antonio, TX	78216-7330	210-431-9881	432-8467	K-3	Alma Garza

School	Address	City,State	Zip code	Telephone	Fax	Grade	Contact
KIPP 3D Academy	4610 E Crosstimbers St	Houston, TX	77016-6337	713-636-6082	636-6084	5-8	Dan Caesar
KIPP Academy Charter	10711 Kipp Way Dr	Houston, TX	77099-2675	832-328-1051	328-0178	5-9	Elliott Witney
KIPP Aspire Academy	1401 West Ave # 3	San Antonio, TX	78201-3504	210-735-7300	735-7305	5-7	Mark Larson
KIPP Austin College Prep S	8509 FM 969	Austin, TX	78724	512-637-6870		5-8	Steven Epstein
KIPP Truth Academy	3200 S Lancaster Rd # 230A	Dallas, TX	75216	214-375-8326	375-2990	5-6	Steven Colmus
La Academia de Estrellas	908 Place Louie	De Soto, TX	75115-2120	972-283-4083		K-5	Lorraine Mantei
La Amistad Love & Learning Academy	6600 Sanford Rd	Houston, TX	77096-5548	713-981-1100	981-1171	PK-5	
Landmark S	101 Brushy Creek Rd	Palestine, TX	75803-8619	903-729-4208	729-1389	7-12	Mike Anderson
Lanier MS	2600 Woodhead St	Houston, TX	77098-1615	713-942-1900	942-1907	6-8	Julia Dimmitt
Lawson Institute	3810 Ruth St	Houston, TX	77004-6506	713-225-1551	225-1561	6-8	Lloyd Choice
Lee Academy	4327 E Lancaster Ave	Fort Worth, TX	76103-3224	817-534-5595	534-3813	9-12	Artie Jackson
Legacy HS	601 S Washington St	Kaufman, TX	75142-2407	972-962-0306	962-2265	8-12	Leo Mohan
Life S - Oak Cliff	4400 S R L Thornton Fwy	Dallas, TX	75224-5110	214-376-8208	376-8209	K-12	J. Wood
Life S - Red Oak	777 S Interstate 35 E	Red Oak, TX	75154	972-376-8200	617-5767	K-7	Joseph Mena
Lighthouse Charter S	8750 Fourwinds Dr	Windcrest, TX	78239-1917	210-798-1674	798-1679	K-7	Joyce Williams
Mainland Preparatory Academy	319 Newman Rd	La Marque, TX	77568-3440	409-934-9100	934-9130	PK-8	Wilma Green
Massieu Academy	823 N Center St	Arlington, TX	76011-5859	817-460-0396	460-4762	PK-12	Bobby Dunivan
Mayes Institute	5807 Calhoun Rd	Houston, TX	77021-3301	713-747-5629	747-5683	K-8	Beatrice Mayes
McCullough Academy of Excellence	1605 Kramer Ln	Austin, TX	78758-4284	512-977-9200	977-9206	K-5	Magnolia McCullough
Medical Center Charter S	1920 N Braeswood Blvd	Houston, TX	77030-3711	713-791-9980	791-9594	PK-6	James McKey
Medical Center Charter S Southwest	10420 Mullins Dr	Houston, TX	77096-4927	713-726-0223		PK-6	William Heard
Metro Charter Academy	500 Houston St	Arlington, TX	76011-7429	817-226-1261	226-1758	PK-12	Richard Hobart
Meyerpark Charter S	PO Box 35616	Houston, TX	77235	713-729-9712	729-9720	K-5	Julia Hutcherson
Midland Academy Charter S	500 N Baird St	Midland, TX	79701-4704	432-686-0003	686-0845	K-8	Wade Cherry
Mid-Valley Academy	200 N 17th St	Mc Allen, TX	78501	956-618-2308	618-2323	9-12	Martin Perez
Mid-Valley Academy	103 E 2nd St	Mercedes, TX	78570-2701	956-618-2303	618-2323	9-12	Martin Perez
Milburn Academy - Amarillo	4106 W 51st Ave	Amarillo, TX	79109-6132	806-463-2284	463-2331	9-12	Bill Flowers
Milburn Academy - Beaumont	1310 Pennsylvania St #C	Beaumont, TX	77701-5606	409-833-7757	833-7767	9-12	Luther J. Thompson
Milburn Academy-Corpus Christi	3875 S Staples St	Corpus Christi, TX	78411-2347	361-225-4424	225-4945	9-12	Su Cline
Milburn Academy - Ector County	2525 N Grandview Ave # 600	Odessa, TX	79761	432-550-7833	550-7884	9-12	David Cavitt
Milburn Academy - Fort Worth	6777 Camp Bowie Blvd St 300	Fort Worth, TX	76116	817-731-7627	731-7628	9-12	Calvin H. Lawrence
Milburn Academy - Houston	500 Century Plaza Dr St 140	Houston, TX	77073	281-443-3111	443-3116	9-12	Starlette Gill
Milburn Academy - Killeen	1001 E Veterans Mem # 301C	Killeen, TX	76541	254-634-4444	634-4044	9-12	Rose Thompson
Milburn Academy - Lubbock	4902 34th St	Lubbock, TX	79410-2339	806-740-0811	740-0804	9-12	Chantell Denson
Milburn Academy - Midland	3306 Andrews Hwy	Midland, TX	79703-5131	432-522-7200	522-5201	9-12	Camal Dakil
Nelms Charter HS	20625 Clay Rd	Katy, TX	77449-5593	281-398-8031	398-8032	9-12	Barbara Shrout
Nelms Charter MS	20625 Clay Rd	Katy, TX	77449-5593	281-398-8031	398-8032	6-8	Dr. Ron Nelms
Newcomer Charter HS	6529 Beverlyhill St	Houston, TX	77057-6406	713-787-1700	787-1723	9-12	Monico Rivas
New Directions Charter S	1201 Austin Hwy Ste 200	San Antonio, TX	78209-4858	210-828-2161	826-9962	9-12	Sue Eakle
New Frontiers Charter	4018 S Presa St	San Antonio, TX	78223-1005	210-533-3655	533-5077	K-8	Jesse Sandoz,
Ney Charter S	PO Box 311268	New Braunfels, TX	78131-1268	830-627-2682	627-2845	4-12	Gwendolyn Rehling
North Hills S	606 E Royal Ln	Irving, TX	75039-3503	972-501-0645	501-9439	K-12	Raymond Doerge
North Houston HS for Business	455 W Parker Rd	Houston, TX	77091-3202	713-691-3123	691-2511	9-12	
Northwest Preparatory S	4705 Lyons Ave	Houston, TX	77020-4306	713-674-2105	676-1940	PK-8	Erik Singleton
Northwest Preparatory S	4905 Kelley St	Houston, TX	77026	713-491-9220		1-8	Steve Roberts
Nova Charter S	PO Box 170127	Dallas, TX	75217-0127	214-381-3422	381-3499	PK-4	Antonio Williamson
Nova Charter S Southeast	PO Box 170127	Dallas, TX	75217-0127	214-398-6300	398-6363	PK-6	John Carson
Now College Prep Charter S	10711 Kipp Way Dr	Houston, TX	77099-2675	832-328-1051	328-0178	K-8	Gary Robichaux
NYOS Charter S	8007 Gessner Dr	Austin, TX	78753-6507	512-835-6601	835-6692	K-3	Linda Whatley
NYOS Charter S	12301 N Lamar Blvd	Austin, TX	78753-1320	512-836-7620	583-6973	K-12	Teresa Elliott
Odyssey Academy	901 13th St	Galveston, TX	77550-6109	409-750-9289	750-9356	PK-8	Henry James Amparan
Omega Academic Center	4434 Roland Rd	San Antonio, TX	78222-2830	210-922-0132	923-2788	6-12	Thomas Baldwin
One Stop Multiservice Charter S	PO Box 164	Mc Allen, TX	78505	956-380-6616	292-0371	PK-12	George Banda
One Stop Multiservice Charter S	PO Box 164	Mc Allen, TX	78505	956-969-2600	969-1191	PK-12	Anival Henrichson
One-Stop Multiservice Charter S	PO Box 164	Mc Allen, TX	78505-0164	956-519-2227	292-0371	PK-12	Martin Perez
Osborne ES	800 Ringold St	Houston, TX	77088-6337	281-405-2525	405-2529	PK-5	Jacqueline Parnell
Outreach Word Academy	PO Box 4873	Victoria, TX	77903	361-579-6922	573-5788	PK-12	Oliver Burbridge
Panola Charter S	PO Box 610	Carthage, TX	75633-0610	903-693-6355	693-6391	8-12	Mark Thornton
Paradigm Accelerated S	PO Box 160	Dublin, TX	76446-0160	254-445-4844	445-4907	7-12	Ronald Johnson
Paso Del Norte Academy Charter S	711 N Mesa St	El Paso, TX	79902-3925	915-532-7216	532-2251	9-12	Joe Curry
Peak Academy	4605 Live Oak St	Dallas, TX	75204-7015	214-821-7325	370-3972	K-12	Dawn Osborne
Pegasus Charter HS	604 N Akard St Ste 203	Dallas, TX	75201-3304	214-740-9991	740-9799	7-12	Ted Shobe
Phoenix Charter S	8501 Jack Finney Blvd	Greenville, TX	75402-3018	903-454-7153	454-7806	PK-7	Vickie Glasscock
Pineywoods Community Academy	2515 E Lufkin Ave	Lufkin, TX	75901-5133	936-634-5515	634-5518	K-9	John Malloy
Pinnacle S	6550 Camp Bowie Blvd	Fort Worth, TX	76116-4396	817-735-8527	735-1910	1-8	Lorrie Gann
Pleasant Hill Academy	1305 Benson St	Houston, TX	77020-4099	713-224-3232		PK-5	Helen Stout
Porter S	PO Box 2025	Wimberley, TX	78676-6925	512-847-6867	847-0737	9-12	Dr. Yana Bland
Por Vida Academy	1135 Mission Rd	San Antonio, TX	78210-4505	210-534-8816	534-0795	9-12	Steve Langseth
Positive Solutions Charter S	1325 N Flores St	San Antonio, TX	78212-4900	210-299-1025	299-1052	9-12	Pamela Solitarie
Positive Solutions Charter S	1325 N Flores St	San Antonio, TX	78212-4900	979-822-9988	822-9988	7-12	Pamela Solitarie
Project Chrysalis MS	4528 Leeland St	Houston, TX	77023-3047	713-924-1700	924-1704	6-8	Alicia Y. Moreno
Pro-Vision Charter S	4422 Balkin St	Houston, TX	77021-4104	713-748-0030	748-0037	5-8	Alphonso Fulton
Quest Academy	111 N Beckley Ave	Dallas, TX	75203-2243	214-946-5157	946-5150	6-9	Julie Gilmour
Radiance Academy of Learning	2845 Thousand Oaks Dr	San Antonio, TX	78232-4107	210-545-4415	545-4478	9-12	
Radiance Academy of Learning	2235 Thousand Oaks Dr #130	San Antonio, TX	78232	210-404-9650	404-1271	PK-12	Linda Britton
Radiance Academy of Learning West Lake	1305 SW Loop 410 Ste 210	San Antonio, TX	78227-1671	210-670-8800	670-0903	PK-12	Linda Britton
Ramirez Charter S	702 Avenue T	Lubbock, TX	79401-2303	806-766-1833	766-1825	K-6	Lisa Ramirez
Ranch Academy	3120 VZ County Road 2318	Canton, TX	75103-4671	903-479-3933	479-1161	6-12	Richard Boardman
Rapoport Academy	2000 J J Flewellen Rd	Waco, TX	76704-1642	254-799-4191	799-4525	PK-4	Bonnie Luft
Rapoport Academy - Quinn Campus	2000 J J Flewellen Rd	Waco, TX	76704	254-754-8000	754-8009	5-8	Dr. Nancy Grayson
Raven S	PO Box 515	New Waverly, TX	77358-0515	936-344-6677	344-7236	9-12	Sandi Belcher
Reach Charter S	520 Mercury Dr	Houston, TX	77013-5217	713-675-1118		K-12	Bertie Simmons
Ripley House Charter S	4410 Navigation Blvd	Houston, TX	77011-1036	713-669-5258	669-5236	K-2	Alejandro Morua
Rise Academy	PO Box 5171	Lubbock, TX	79408-5171	806-744-0438	208-9563	PK-6	Richard Baumgartner
Saenz Charter JHS	1830 Basse Rd	San Antonio, TX	78213-4606	210-431-9881	435-8096	7-8	Ernesto Velazquez
St. Anthony Academy	3732 Myrtle St	Dallas, TX	75215-3849	214-421-3645	421-7416	PK-8	David Ray
St. Johns Academy	2019 Crawford St	Houston, TX	77002-9002	713-659-3237		1-1	Shundra Cannon
St. Marys Academy Charter S	PO Box 279	Beeville, TX	78104-0279	361-358-5601	358-5704	K-8	Stan Simonson
San Antonio Can Academy	502 E Southcross Blvd	San Antonio, TX	78214-2044	210-923-1226	928-3366	9-12	Veronica Hernandez
San Antonio Preparatory Academy	8308 Fredericksburg Rd	San Antonio, TX	78229-3316	210-593-0111	614-7199	K-6	Raul Garcia
San Antonio S for Inquiry & Creativity	4618 San Pedro Ave	San Antonio, TX	78212-1411	210-738-0020	738-0033	K-12	Tony Espinar
San Antonio Technology Academy	122 Stribling St	San Antonio, TX	78204	210-527-9250	527-9251	9-9	Henry Egeolu
Sanchez HS	6001 Gulf Fwy	Houston, TX	77023-5423	713-926-1112	926-1346	9-12	Roberto Lopez
Sanchez HS	436 S Main Ave	San Antonio, TX	78204-1114	210-270-8567	223-2146	8-12	Wendell Beene
School of Liberal Arts & Science	PO Box 5129	Dallas, TX	75208-9129	214-946-9100	946-9194	PK-8	Linda Gromowsky
School of Science and Technology	1450 NE Loop 410	San Antonio, TX	78209-1543	210-804-0222	822-3422	6-8	Mark Namver
Seashore Learning Center	14493 S Padre Island Dr	Corpus Christi, TX	78418-5939	361-949-1222	949-6762	PK-7	Dr. Jan Loveless
Sentry Technology Prep S	PO Box 164	Mc Allen, TX	78505-0164	956-542-3363	292-0371	9-12	Elsa Haman
SER-Ninos Charter S	5815 Alder Dr	Houston, TX	77081-2708	713-667-6145	667-0645	PK-5	Charmaine Constantine
Shekinah Radiance Academy	5130 Casey St	La Marque, TX	77568-2707	409-935-8773	935-4426	K-12	
Shekinah Radiance Academy	6663 Walzem Rd	San Antonio, TX	78239-3612	210-967-6933	967-6280	PK-12	Ray Garcia
Shekinah Radiance Academy	13069 N IH 35	San Antonio, TX	78233-2615	210-590-0838	590-0856	PK-12	June Gillesphire
Shekinah Radiance Academy	5203 Pearsall Rd	San Antonio, TX	78242	210-623-3030	623-3046	K-5	Margaret Eckhoff
South Plains Academy	4008 Avenue R	Lubbock, TX	79412-1603	806-744-0330	741-1089	9-12	Linda Murray
Southwest Ctr for Success & Independence	3333 Bering Dr Ste 200	Houston, TX	77057	713-784-6345	974-3137	5-12	Ken Goeddeke
Southwest ES	3333 Bering Dr Ste 200	Houston, TX	77057	713-784-6345	974-3137	PK-3	Ken Goeddeke
Southwest HS	6400 Southwest Fwy	Houston, TX	77074-2213	713-954-9528	953-0119	9-12	Ken Goeddeke
Southwest HS - Incentives	6400 Southwest Fwy	Houston, TX	77074	713-954-9528	953-0119	K-12	Nancy Trunk
Southwest MS	3333 Bering Dr Ste 200	Houston, TX	77057	713-954-9528	953-0119	7-8	Ken Goeddeke
Southwest Preparatory S NE Campus	1258 Austin Hwy Ste 220	San Antonio, TX	78209-4820	210-829-8017	829-8514	9-12	James Hope
Southwest Preparatory S NW Campus	4550 NW Loop 410 Ste 111	San Antonio, TX	78229-5169	210-432-2634	432-5482	9-12	Tom McCloskey
Southwest Preparatory S SE Campus	735 S WW White Rd	San Antonio, TX	78220-2524	210-333-1403	333-3024	9-12	Cyndy Spivey
Star Charter S	1901 Fleischer Dr	Austin, TX	78728-5704	512-989-2672	989-3150	1-12	Rollie Ford
Stepping Stones Charter S	11250 S Wilcrest Dr	Houston, TX	77099	281-988-9855	988-9894	K-6	William Clark
Summit Academy	1220 W Presidio St	Fort Worth, TX	76102-4512	817-336-5134	336-2573	K-12	Vicki Sendejo
Tafolla Charter S	PO Box 1709	Uvalde, TX	78802-1709	830-278-1297	591-1465	PK-12	Jorge Botello
Technology Education Charter HS	116 W 5th St	Weslaco, TX	78596-6008	956-668-7761	969-8614	9-12	Alim Ansari
Tekoa Academy	326 Thomas Blvd	Port Arthur, TX	77640-5242	409-982-5400	982-8498	K-6	
Temple Education Center	1400 E Avenue B	Temple, TX	76501-4710	254-778-8682	778-8690	PK-12	Rick Haley
Texans Can! Academy at Paul Quinn	3837 Simpson Stuart Rd	Dallas, TX	75241-4331	214-371-6226	372-2294	9-12	Mene Khepera
Texans Can! S at Carrollton/Farmers	2720 Hollandale Ln	Farmers Branch, TX	75234-2035	972-243-2178	243-2669	9-12	Eric Brown
Texas Empowerment Academy	3613 Bluestein Dr	Austin, TX	78721-2900	512-494-0760	494-0199	5-12	David Nowlin
Texas Preparatory S	715 Valley St	San Marcos, TX	78666	512-805-7737	805-7739	PK-8	Mark Terry
Texas Serenity Academy	530 N Sam Houston Pkwy E	Houston, TX	77060-4038	936-334-8700	337-8700	7-12	Edward Watson
Texas Serenity Academy	530 N Sam Houston Pkwy E	Houston, TX	77060-4038	361-882-7831		6-12	Edward Watson
Texas Virtual Academy at Southwest	3333 Bering Dr Ste 200	Houston, TX	77057	713-784-6345	972-3137	3-6	Ken Goeddeke
Transformative Charter Academy	807 N 8th St	Killeen, TX	76541-4818	254-628-8985	628-8981	9-12	Claudette Morgan-Scott

School	Address	City,State	Zip code	Telephone	Fax	Grade	Contact
Treetops School International	12500 S Pipeline Rd	Euless, TX	76040-5853	817-283-1771	684-0892	K-12	Lou Blanchard
Trinity Basin Prep S	PO Box 5129	Dallas, TX	75208-9129	214-942-6501	942-8864	PK-8	Janice Chancelor
Trinity Charter S	5638 Medical Center Dr	Katy, TX	77494-6325	281-392-7505	392-7560	1-12	Amanda Broussard
Trinity Charter S	650 Scarbourough	Canyon Lake, TX	78133-4529	830-964-4390	964-4391	1-12	Debi Christensen
Trinity Charter S	4601 N Interstate 35	Denton, TX	76207-3419	940-484-8232	484-1385	1-12	Mary Littlepage
Trinity Charter S	PO Box 141125	Austin, TX	78714-1125	361-994-1214	994-0555	1-12	Brayde McClure
Two Dimensions Preparatory Academy	12121 Veterans Memorial # 9	Houston, TX	77067	281-440-8853	440-4233	PK-5	Daisy Simpson
Two Dimensions Preparatory Academy	12121 Veterans Memorial # 9	Houston, TX	77067	281-872-2988	872-2858	PK-8	Karen Williams
Two Dimensions Preparatory Academy	12121 Veterans Memorial # 9	Houston, TX	77067	281-987-7300	987-7306	PK-8	Sally Wickers
Universal Academy	2616 N MacArthur Blvd	Irving, TX	75062-5401	972-317-2624	255-6122	PK-12	Janice Blackmon
University Charter S	2200 E 6th St	Austin, TX	78702-3457	512-471-4363	499-4240	K-12	Dr. Edwin Sharpe
University of Houston Charter S of Tech	3855 Holman St	Houston, TX	77204-6015	713-743-9107	743-9121	K-5	Carolyn Black
University S	1404 W Walnut Hill Ln	Irving, TX	75038-3009	972-753-6165	550-1425	7-12	Tre John
Vanguard Academy	PO Box 730	Pharr, TX	78577-1614	956-283-1700	702-2180	PK-3	Dalila Garcia
Varnett Charter S	PO Box 1457	Houston, TX	77251-1457	713-723-4699	723-5853	PK-5	Kelvin Williamson
Varnett Charter S - East	PO Box 1457	Houston, TX	77251-1457	713-637-6574	637-8319	PK-5	Lennon Phillips
Varnett Charter S - Northeast	PO Box 1457	Houston, TX	77251-1457	713-631-4396	491-3597	PK-5	Dora Morrow
Waco Charter S	615 N 25th St	Waco, TX	76707-3443	254-754-8169	754-7389	K-5	Valerie Ovalle
Waxahachie Faith Family Academy	701 Ovilla Rd	Waxahachie, TX	75167-9430	972-938-3996	937-5806	PK-12	Mary Plasket Ozuna
Wesley ES	800 Dillard St	Houston, TX	77091-2301	713-696-2860	696-2866	PK-5	Dr. Kimberly Agnew
West Houston Charter S	5618 11th St	Katy, TX	77493-1971	281-391-5003	391-5010	K-12	Denise Jordan
Westlake Academy	2600 Ottinger Rd	Westlake, TX	76262-8012	817-490-5757	490-5758	K-7	Barbara Brizuela
White Memorial HS	PO Box 2126	League City, TX	77574-2126	281-316-0001	316-0018	9-12	Dr. Rosalind Perez
Williams Charter MS	6100 Knox St	Houston, TX	77091-4143	713-696-2600	696-2604	6-8	Delesa O'Dell-Thomas
Winfree Academy Charter S	6221 Riverside Dr Ste 110	Irving, TX	75039-3529	972-234-9855	234-9975	9-12	Demetrius Griffin
Winfree Academy Charter S	6221 Riverside Dr Ste 110	Irving, TX	75039-3529	817-481-5803	329-6307	9-12	Paulette Gillespie
Winfree Academy Charter S	6221 Riverside Dr Ste 110	Irving, TX	75039-3529	972-251-2010	251-4301	9-12	Brenda Cupps
Winfree Academy Charter S	6221 Riverside Dr Ste 110	Irving, TX	75039-3529	214-222-2200	222-0201	9-12	Lisa Ehrke
Winfree Academy Charter S	6221 Riverside Dr Ste 110	Irving, TX	75039-3529	817-590-2240	590-8724	9-12	Melody Chalkley
Wood Charter S at Afton Oaks	3201 Cherry Ridge Ste C315	San Antonio, TX	78230	210-499-0351	403-3058	5-12	Susie Mariano
Wood Charter S at Huebner Road	3201 Cherry Ridge Ste C315	San Antonio, TX	78230	210-798-0350	690-4139	6-12	Joe Inman
Wood Charter S at St. Francis	3201 Cherry Ridge Ste C315	San Antonio, TX	78230	210-923-1421	921-4948	5-12	George Pena
Yes College Preparatory S	353 Crenshaw Rd	Houston, TX	77034-1543	713-910-2510	910-2350	6-12	Chris Barbic
Yes College Preparatory S	2000 Preston St	Richmond, TX	77469	281-238-8000	238-8098	6-12	Robert Lundin
Yes College Preparatory S	3401 Hardy St	Houston, TX	77009	713-208-1519	910-2350	6-12	Bill Durbin
Young Learners Charter S	3333 Bering Dr	Houston, TX	77057-6703	713-784-1215		1-12	Sara Gallo
Young Scholars Academy of Excellence	1809 Louisiana St	Houston, TX	77002-8013	713-654-1400	654-1401	PK-K	Anella Coleman
Yzaguirre S for Success	2950 Broadway St	Houston, TX	77017-1706	713-644-2340	644-5397	PK-12	Adriana Tamez
Yzaguirre S for Success	355 W Elizabeth St	Brownsville, TX	78520-5550	956-542-2404	542-2667	PK-5	Janis Sotherden
Zoe Learning Academy	6701 Cullen Blvd	Houston, TX	77021-5005	817-535-5655	531-6310	PK-6	Charles Polk
Zoe Learning Academy	3505 Alice St	Houston, TX	77021	713-748-4228	748-7833	PK-6	Linda Ware

Utah

School	Address	City,State	Zip code	Telephone	Fax	Grade	Contact
Academy of Math Engineering & Science	5715 S 1300 E	Salt Lake City, UT	84121-1023	801-278-9460	277-3527	9-12	Al Church
American Leadership Academy	PO Box 301	Spanish Fork, UT	84660-0301	801-735-3585		K-12	Ruel Haymond
American Preparatory Academy	12892 Pony Express Rd	Draper, UT	84020-9273	801-553-8500	576-9300	K-9	Carolyn Sharette
Beehive Science & Tech Academy	3098 S Highland Dr Ste 100	Salt Lake City, UT	84106	801-322-2782	560-3393	7-8	Zack Kiyma
City Academy	2416 E 1700 S	Salt Lake City, UT	84108-2702	801-596-8489	521-4181	7-12	Sonja Woodbury
DaVinci Academy of Science and the Arts	2033 Grant Ave	Ogden, UT	84401-0409	801-409-0700	866-1311	9-12	Gary Nelson
East Hollywood HS	2185 S 3600 W	West Valley, UT	84119-1121	801-886-8181	972-9585	9-12	Eric Lindsay
Edison Charter S - North	180 E 2600 N	North Logan, UT	84341-1551	435-787-2820	787-0299	K-8	Scott Jackson
Edison Charter S - South	PO Box 231	Providence, UT	84332-0231	435-752-0123	752-0418	K-7	Eldon Budge
Fast Forward Charter S	875 W 1400 N	Logan, UT	84321-6804	435-713-4255	753-9615	9-12	Stephanie Sorenson
Freedom Academy	1958 S 950 E	Provo, UT	84606-6200	801-437-3100	437-3149	K-8	Lynne Herring
Hancock Charter S	125 N 100 E	Pleasant Grove, UT	84062-2355	801-796-5646	785-4934	K-8	Julie Adamic
Itineris Early College HS	9301 Wights Fort Rd	West Jordan, UT	84088-8850	801-256-5970	256-5992	9-12	Stephen Jolley
Lincoln Academy	PO Box 546	American Fork, UT	84003-0546	801-437-6108		K-8	Mark Dennison
Moab Community S	PO Box 1533	Moab, UT	84532-1533	435-259-2277		K-8	Rosie O'Connor
Navigator Pointe Academy	PO Box 1932	West Jordan, UT	84084-8932	801-553-8500	576-9300	K-8	Bryan Christiansen
North Davis Preparatory Academy	1765 W Hill Field Rd	Layton, UT	84041	801-547-1809	547-1649	K-6	Deborrah Gomberg
Northern Utah Academy	PO Box 248	Roy, UT	84067-0248	801-402-5920	402-5921	9-12	Gary Reed
North Star Academy	2920 W 14010 S	Bluffdale, UT	84065-5331	801-302-9579		K-8	Mark Johnson
Odyssey Charter S	PO Box 1532	American Fork, UT	84003-6532	801-492-8105		K-6	Paul Waldron
Ogden Preparatory Academy	2221 Grant Ave	Ogden, UT	84401-1405	801-627-2066	394-2267	K-8	Kathleen Thornburg
Pinnacle Canyon Academy	210 N 600 E	Price, UT	84501-2613	435-613-8102	613-8105	K-9	Roberta Hardy
Ranches Academy	7789 Tawny Owl Cir	Lehi, UT	84005-4308	801-789-4000	789-4001	K-6	Darren Beck
Reagan Academy	1143 W Center St	Springville, UT	84663-3028	801-489-7828		K-8	Brandi Belot
Salt Lake Arts Academy	275 E 200 S	Salt Lake City, UT	84111-2002	801-531-1173	531-7726	5-8	Amy Wadsworth
Soldier Hollow S	PO Box 779	Midway, UT	84049-0779	435-654-1347	654-1349	1-6	Richard Rasband
Success Academy	351 W Center St	Cedar City, UT	84720-2470	435-865-8790	865-8795	9-12	Vickie Wilson
Success S	4122 S 1785 W #2b	Taylorsville, UT	84119	801-964-4258	964-4259	7-12	Diane Austin
Summit Academy	PO Box 401	Sandy, UT	84091-0401	801-231-2523		K-6	Jill Neff
Timpanogos Academy	55 S 100 E	Lindon, UT	84042-2058	801-785-4979	785-9690	K-8	Errol Porter
Tuacahn HS for the Performing Arts	1100 Tuacahn	Ivins, UT	84738-6088	435-652-3201	652-3306	9-12	
Uintah River HS	PO Box 235	Fort Duchesne, UT	84026-0235	435-726-4088	722-0811	10-12	Marlies Burns
Utah County Academy of Sciences	940 W 800 S	Orem, UT	84058-5915	801-225-8227	225-2214	10-12	Clark Baron
Walden S of Liberal Arts	250 W 500 N	Provo, UT	84601-2819	801-623-1388	225-5732	6-8	Diana West
Wasatch Peak Academy	414 Cutler Dr	North Salt Lake, UT	84054-2951	801-936-3066	936-0887	K-6	Vivian Powell

Virginia

School	Address	City,State	Zip code	Telephone	Fax	Grade	Contact
Chesterfield Community HS	8610 Perrymont Rd	Richmond, VA	23237-2815	804-743-3701		9-12	Jamie Accashian
Hampton Harbour Academy	23 Semple Farm Rd	Hampton, VA	23666-1456	757-766-5313	766-5319	6-8	Andrea James
Murray Charter HS	1200 Forrest St	Charlottesville, VA	22903-5264	434-296-3090	979-6479	9-12	Dr. Vicki Crews-Miller
New Directions Academy	PO Box 1320	Stanardsville, VA	22973-1320	434-985-1403		6-12	Dr. Susan Burgess
York River Academy	9300 George Washington Mem	Yorktown, VA	23692	757-898-0516	890-1045	9-10	Walter Cross

Washington

School	Address	City,State	Zip code	Telephone	Fax	Grade	Contact
5/12 Learning Community	3230 85th St S	Lakewood, WA	98499-8814	253-583-5418	583-5348	5-12	Judy Springer

Wisconsin

School	Address	City,State	Zip code	Telephone	Fax	Grade	Contact
Academic Center HS	601 University Ave	Colfax, WI	54730-9773	715-962-3676	962-4024	9-12	Dennis Geissler
Academy of Learning & Leadership	1530 W Center St	Milwaukee, WI	53206-2101	414-372-3942	372-8260	K-8	M. Camille Mortimore
Accelerated Education Resource Options	15 S Brearly St	Madison, WI	53703-2918	608-204-4225	204-0543	7-12	Anne Fischer
A L A S	971 W Windlake Ave	Milwaukee, WI	53204-3822	414-481-6225		9-12	Linda Peters
A L B A	1515 W Lapham Blvd	Milwaukee, WI	53204-3236	414-908-8323	902-8424	K-5	Brenda Martinez
Alliance Charter S	215 E Forest Ave	Neenah, WI	54956-2765	920-751-6970	751-6861	K-5	Robert Lindner
Alliance S	234 W Galena St	Milwaukee, WI	53212-3955	414-227-2550		9-12	Tina Owen
ALPS Charter S	108 W New York Ave	Oshkosh, WI	54901-3760	920-424-0349	424-7596	3-7	Shelly Muza
Alternative Program 2	1700 Edgewood Ave E	Ladysmith, WI	54848-3003	715-532-5277	532-7445	9-12	James Schuchardt
Appleton Central Alternative HS	PO Box 2019	Appleton, WI	54912-2019	920-832-6136	993-7074	9-12	Nichole Schweitzer
Appleton Community Learning Center	PO Box 2019	Appleton, WI	54912-2019	920-997-1497	993-7074	7-8	Nichole Schweitzer
Appleton eSchool	2121 E Emmers Dr	Appleton, WI	54915-3802	920-997-1399	832-1741	9-12	Connie Radtke
Appleton Montessori Charter S	2725 E Forest St	Appleton, WI	54915	920-832-6265	832-6199	1-6	Dom Ferrito
Argyle Land Ethic Academy	PO Box 256	Argyle, WI	53504-0256	608-543-3318	543-3868	11-12	Gerry Benish
Ascend Academy	PO Box 40	Drummond, WI	54832-0040	715-739-6669	739-6345	9-12	Al Gillberg
Audubon Technology & Communication Ctr	3300 S 39th St	Milwaukee, WI	53215-4019	414-902-7800	902-7815	6-8	Katrice Cotton
Barron County Learning Center	1725 S Main St	Rice Lake, WI	54868-2915	715-736-3464	234-4552	9-12	Paul Vine
Beaver Dam Charter S	400 E Burnett St	Beaver Dam, WI	53916-1902	920-885-7423	885-7429	1-12	Martha Hyke
Brompton S	7951 36th Ave	Kenosha, WI	53142-2119	262-942-2191	942-2194	K-5	Patricia Jones
Bruce - Guadalupe Community S	1028 S 9th St	Milwaukee, WI	53204-1335	414-643-6441	649-9022	K-8	Pascual Rodriquez
Capitol West Academy	3939 N 88th St	Milwaukee, WI	53222-2748	414-465-1302	463-2770	PK-4	Donna Niccolai-Weber
C.A.R.E. Charter S	2000 Polk St	Stevens Point, WI	54481-5876	715-345-5620	345-5696	7-9	Connie Negaard
CASTLE Charter S	1700 Klatt Rd	New London, WI	54961-8603	920-982-8420	982-8440	9-12	Joe Pemrening
Central City Cyberschool	4301 N 44th St	Milwaukee, WI	53216-1473	414-444-2330	444-2435	1-8	Christine Faltz
Chippewa Valley Technology Charter S	400 Cameron St	Eau Claire, WI	54703-5101	715-852-3101	852-6304	9-12	Holly Hart
CITIES - Project Hi	700 W Michigan St	Milwaukee, WI	53233-2415	414-344-8480	347-0110	9-11	Daniel Grego
Clark County Alternative Charter S	1115 W 4th St Ste A	Neillsville, WI	54456-1605	715-743-7443		9-12	Kelly Timmons
Classical Charter S	3310 N Durkee St	Appleton, WI	54911-1215	920-832-4968	997-1390	K-8	Constance Ford
Community HS	1017 N 12th St	Milwaukee, WI	53233-1307	414-212-3122	212-3114	9-10	Roxane Mayeur
Community Trade & Business Center	2670 N 1st St	Milwaukee, WI	53212-2807	414-267-0012	267-0015	9-9	Robert Brown
Comprehensive Learning Center	678 S Park St	Richland Center, WI	53581-2748	608-647-9177		9-12	Rachel Schultz
Connects Learning Center	6201 S Barland Ave	Cudahy, WI	53110-2951	414-766-5000	766-5005	9-12	Dr. Gary Kiltz
Core Knowledge Charter S	740 N Main St	Verona, WI	53593-1153	608-845-4130	845-4961	K-8	Bob McNallie
Coulee Montessori Charter S	1307 Hayes St	La Crosse, WI	54603-1949	608-789-7760	789-7080	K-6	Harvey Witzenburg

School	Address	City,State	Zip code	Telephone	Fax	Grade	Contact
Crandon Alternative Resource S	9750 US Highway 8 W	Crandon, WI	54520-8499	715-478-3713	478-5570	6-12	John Gruber
Deerfield Charter HS	300 Simonson Blvd	Deerfield, WI	53531-9543	608-764-5431	764-5433	9-12	Barb Callahan
Denmark Empowerment Charter S	450 N Wall St	Denmark, WI	54208-9416	920-863-4031	863-5526	K-12	Steve Pasono
Dimensions of Learning Academy	6218 25th Ave	Kenosha, WI	53143-4370	262-605-6849	605-1234	K-8	Diana Pearson
DLH Academy	7151 N 86th St	Milwaukee, WI	53224-4861	414-358-3542	760-4364	K-12	Barbara Horton
Downtown Montessori Academy	2319 E Kenwood Blvd	Milwaukee, WI	53211-3315	414-332-8214	332-8215	K-K	Virginia Flynn
EAA Charter S	1225 N Oakwood Rd	Oshkosh, WI	54904-8456	920-424-0315	424-7591	3-3	Kirby Schultz
EAA Charter S	1050 W 18th Ave	Oshkosh, WI	54902-6602	920-424-0164	424-7594	3-3	Lynn Brown
Eagleville Charter S	S101W34511 Highway LO	Eagle, WI	53119	262-363-6258	594-5495	1-5	Bruce Sturm
Eastman Community Home	202 S Main St	Eastman, WI	54626-7101	608-874-4011	874-4411	PK-5	James P. O'Meara
Enterprise Charter S	8389 Liberty School Rd	Omro, WI	54963-9607	920-685-7410		6-12	Carol Zarske
Environmental Education Charter S	1225 N Oakwood Rd	Oshkosh, WI	54904-8456	920-424-0315	424-7591	4-5	Kirby Schultz
Fairview S	6500 W Knncknnic River Pkwy	Milwaukee, WI	53219	414-546-7700	546-7715	PK-8	Jacqueline Scudder
Fifth Dimension	PO Box 76	Marshall, WI	53559-0076	608-655-3466	655-4481	11-12	Stacy Graff
Flambeau Charter S	N4540 County Road I	Tony, WI	54563-9629	715-532-5559		1-12	Linda Michek
Foster ES	305 W Foster St	Appleton, WI	54915-1515	920-832-6288	832-4831	K-6	Judith Baseman
Fox River Academy	1000 S Mason St	Appleton, WI	54914	920-932-6260	993-7060	3-6	Tom Marquette
Fox River Academy	2020 S Carpenter St	Appleton, WI	54915	920-832-6276	832-6337	7-8	Chris VanderHeyden
Fritsche MS	2969 S Howell Ave	Milwaukee, WI	53207-2083	414-294-1000	294-1015	6-8	Robin Kitzrow
Genesis HS	1011 W Center St	Milwaukee, WI	53206-3299	414-267-5003	267-4915	9-10	Kathelyne Dye
Gilman Charter S	325 N 5th Ave	Gilman, WI	54433-9242	715-447-8216	447-8731	9-12	Dawn Randall
Grantsburg Virtual S	480 E James Ave	Grantsburg, WI	54840-7959	715-463-5165	463-5068	9-12	Stanley Marczak
HACIL	PO Box 860	Hayward, WI	54843-0860	715-865-3107	934-8080	K-12	Kathryn Hexum
Highland Community S	3030 W Highland Blvd	Milwaukee, WI	53208-3246	414-342-1412	342-1408	PK-3	Kathy Ronco
Hmong American Peace Academy	1418 S Layton Blvd	Milwaukee, WI	53215-1923	414-383-4944	383-4950	K-10	Chris Her-Xiong
Honey Creek Continuous Progess ES	6701 W Eden Pl	Milwaukee, WI	53220-1335	414-604-7900	604-7915	PK-5	Santa Consiglio
Humboldt Park ES	3230 S Adams Ave	Milwaukee, WI	53207-2700	414-294-1700	294-1715	PK-5	Kristi Cole
IDEAL Charter S	4965 S 20th St	Milwaukee, WI	53221-2860	414-304-6200	304-6215	K-8	Barbara Ernest
IQ Academy of Wisconsin	222 Maple Ave	Waukesha, WI	53186-4725	262-970-1096	970-1020		Kristine Diener
Janesville Academy for Intl Studies	31 W Milwaukee St	Janesville, WI	53548-2911	608-314-1180	314-1180	9-12	Donna Behn
Jefferson County Alternative S	700 W Milwaukee St	Jefferson, WI	53549-1436	920-675-1100	675-1120	9-12	Karen Craig
Jefferson S for the Arts	1800 East Ave	Stevens Point, WI	54481-3799	715-345-5418	345-7352	K-6	Dave Lockett
Journeys Charter S	405 Washington Ave	Oshkosh, WI	54901-5043	920-232-0673	232-0676	7-12	Jeff Walters
Juneau Business HS	6415 W Mount Vernon Ave	Milwaukee, WI	53213-4025	414-256-8200	256-8215	9-12	Myron Cain
Juneau County Charter S	N11003 17th Ave	Necedah, WI	54646-7618	608-565-7494	565-7559	9-12	Michele Yates-Wickus
Kiel eSchool	PO Box 201	Kiel, WI	53042-0201	920-894-2266	894-5100	7-12	Jerry Schutz
Kilbourn Academy	520 Race St	Wisconsin Dells, WI	53965-1824	608-254-8004	254-6288	9-12	Troy Couillard
La Causa S	PO Box 04188	Milwaukee, WI	53204-0188	414-902-1660	902-1676	K-5	Rose Guajardo
LaCrossroads Charter HS	1500 Ranger Dr	La Crosse, WI	54603-2713	608-789-7700	789-7711	9-12	Doug Leclair
Lafayette County Community Charter S	1300 Industrial Dr	Fennimore, WI	53809-9702	608-822-3276		9-12	Jeanetta Kirkpatrick
Lakeshore Alternative S	915 2nd St	Kewaunee, WI	54216-1619	920-388-4558	388-5174	10-12	Michael Holtz
Lalich Charter S	5503 W Rangeview Dr	Hurley, WI	54534-9000	715-561-4600	561-4157	6-12	Elizabeth Jorgensen
Laurel HS	100 Blackhawk Dr	Viroqua, WI	54665-1399	608-637-3191	637-8034	9-12	Katherine Klos
LEARN Charter S	PO Box 48	Lena, WI	54139-0048	920-829-5244		9-12	Robert Werley
LIFT Charter S	PO Box 70	Clinton, WI	53525-0070	608-676-2211	676-5717		Denise Wellnitz
Lodi Charter S	1100 Sauk St	Lodi, WI	53555-1446	608-592-3853	592-1045	8-12	Kim Amidon
Lucas Charter S	N5639 200th St	Menomonie, WI	54751-5256	715-232-1790	232-2026	9-12	Thomas Schmelzle
Maasai Institute	4744 N 39th St	Milwaukee, WI	53209-5862	414-286-2221			Janis McCollum
Magellan Charter S	225 N Badger Ave	Appleton, WI	54914-3832	920-832-6226	832-4857	7-8	Lisa Eastman
Malcolm X Academy	2760 N 1st St	Milwaukee, WI	53212-2402	414-267-8600	267-8615	6-8	Lonnie Anderson
Mauston Alternative Resource	508 Grayside Ave	Mauston, WI	53948-1921	608-847-6603	847-4925	6-8	Tom Reisenauer
McDill Academies	2516 School St	Stevens Point, WI	54481-6100	715-345-5420	345-7345	K-6	Dennis Raabe
McKinley Center	2926 Blaine St	Stevens Point, WI	54481-4799	715-345-5421	345-7350	PK-6	John Blader
McKinley Charter MS	2340 Mohr Ave	Racine, WI	53405-2645	262-664-6150	664-6196	6-8	Lori Sue Pelk
McKinley Charter S	400 Cameron St	Eau Claire, WI	54703-5101	715-852-6900	852-6904	6-12	Dr. Holly Hart
Meeme LEADS Charter S	12121 County Road XX	Newton, WI	53063-9732	920-693-8255	693-8730	K-4	Chad Ramminger
Milwaukee Academy of Aviation	3620 N 18th St	Milwaukee, WI	53206-2362	414-875-6400		9-12	Dura Hale
Milwaukee Academy of Science	2000 W Kilbourn Ave	Milwaukee, WI	53233-1625	414-933-0302	933-1914	K-7	Tracey Sparrow
Milwaukee College Prep S	2449 N 36th St	Milwaukee, WI	53210-3040	414-445-8020	445-8167	K-12	Robert Rauh
Milwaukee Leadership Training Center	2360 N 52nd St	Milwaukee, WI	53210-2701	414-874-8588	874-8515	K-12	Leslie Seib
Milwaukee Learning Lab	6506 W Warnimont Ave	Milwaukee, WI	53220-1344	414-604-7940		9-12	David Coyle
Monona Grove Alternative HS	4400 Monona Dr	Monona, WI	53716-1097	608-221-7666	221-7690	9-12	Paul Brost
Monroe Alternative Charter S	1220 16th Ave	Monroe, WI	53566-2047	608-328-7227	328-7826	9-12	Dan Bauer
Monroe Independent Virtual Charter S	1220 16th Ave	Monroe, WI	53566-2047	888-947-6437	328-7288	9-12	Dan Bauer
Montessori Charter S	400 Cameron St	Eau Claire, WI	54703-5101	715-852-6950	852-3504	K-5	Holly Hart
New Century Charter S	401 W Verona Ave	Verona, WI	53593	608-845-4900	845-4720	K-5	Tim Bubon
New Hope Institute	1501 S Layton Blvd Ste 118	Milwaukee, WI	53215-1924	414-263-2300	263-2799	9-10	Rosella Tucker
New Horizons Charter S	120 S 14th Ave	Wausau, WI	54401-4217	715-261-0150	261-2461	7-9	Julie Sprague
New Horizons for Learning	1701 E Capitol Dr	Shorewood, WI	53211-1911	414-963-6933	963-6933	9-12	Richard Monroe
Next Door Charter S	2545 N 29th St	Milwaukee, WI	53210-3155	414-562-2929	562-1979	K-5	Sharon Schulz
Northern Star S	5075 N Sherman Blvd	Milwaukee, WI	53209-5246	414-393-6183	393-6377	6-8	Valerie Benton-Davis
Northwoods Community Secondary S	511 S Pelham St	Rhinelander, WI	54501-3316	715-365-9663	365-9687	6-12	Dave Wall
Nuestro Mundo Community S	4201 Buckeye Rd	Madison, WI	53716-1648	608-204-1076	204-0364	K-1	Gary Zehrbach
Oconto Falls Alternative Learning Site	320 E Central Ave	Oconto Falls, WI	54154-1456	920-848-4455		9-12	Becky James
Odyssey Charter S	305 W Foster St	Appleton, WI	54915-1515	920-832-6288	832-4831	5-6	Judy Baseman
Odyssey Charter S	2037 N Elinor St	Appleton, WI	54914	920-832-6250	832-4389	3-6	Val Dreier
Oshkosh East HS	405 Washington Ave	Oshkosh, WI	54901-5043	920-232-0698	232-0676	9-12	Jeff Walters
Paideia Charter School Academy	5821 10th Ave	Kenosha, WI	53140-4008	262-658-4540	658-4583	6-8	Ellen Becker
Parkview Charter S	PO Box 247	Orfordville, WI	53576-0247	608-876-4184	876-4183	9-12	Chris Nelson
Passage Middle S	9501 W Watertown Plank Rd	Milwaukee, WI	53226-3552	414-476-2122			Christy Johnson
Philip Alternative Charter S	621 W College Ave	Waukesha, WI	53186-4505	262-970-4355	970-4380	6-12	James Haessly
Phoenix HS	3620 N 18th St	Milwaukee, WI	53206-2362	414-875-6438	875-6454	9-12	Phil Musickant
Portage Academy of Achievement	2600 Woodcrest Dr	Portage, WI	53901-1262	608-742-1409		9-12	Tonya Kotlowski
Preparatory School for Global Leadership	1916 N 4th St	Milwaukee, WI	53212-3612	414-264-3380	264-4450	6-7	Angela Dye
Professional Learning Institute	4965 S 20th St	Milwaukee, WI	53221-2860	414-304-6180	304-6188	9-10	Theresa Erbe
Project Change Alt Recovery Charter Schl	111 E Main St	Waukesha, WI	53186-5016	262-524-8677	524-8653	9-12	James Haessly
REAL Charter S	5915 Erie St	Racine, WI	53402-1925	262-664-8100	664-8110	6-12	Robert Holzem
Renaissance Charter Alternative Academy	211 N Fremont St	River Falls, WI	54022-2148	715-425-7645	425-7671	9-12	Donna Hill
Renaissance S for the Arts	610 N Badger Ave	Appleton, WI	54914-3405	920-832-5708	832-4198	9-12	Greg Hartjes
River Cities HS	680 W Grand Ave	Wisc Rapids, WI	54495-2708	715-422-6360	422-6370	9-12	Steve Smith
River Crossings Charter S	2600 Woodcrest Dr	Portage, WI	53901-1262	608-742-1409		7-8	Wayne Bartels
River Falls Public Montessori Academy	211 N Fremont St	River Falls, WI	54022-2148	715-425-7645	425-7671	K-5	Charles Eaton
Rock River Charter S	31 W Milwaukee St	Janesville, WI	53548-2911	608-752-8273	752-8430	9-12	Marge Hollenbeck
Roosevelt IDEA	2200 Wisconsin Ave	Plover, WI	54467-2981	715-345-5425	345-7347	K-6	Pam Bork
School for Early Develpmnt & Achievmnt	2020 W Wells St	Milwaukee, WI	53233-2720	414-937-2020	937-2021	K-12	Gena Stezela
School of Humanities	1011 W Center St	Milwaukee, WI	53206-3262	414-267-5001	267-4915	9-10	Reginald Lawrence
School of Technology & Arts	1111 7th St S	La Crosse, WI	54601-5474	608-789-7695	789-7030	K-5	Nancy Matchett
School of Technology & Arts II	1900 Denton St	La Crosse, WI	54601-5816	608-789-7695	789-7030	6-8	Penny Reedy
School on the Lake	1600 Midway Rd	Menasha, WI	54952-1228	920-967-1600	832-5837	6-9	Bev Sturke
Siefert ES	1547 N 14th St	Milwaukee, WI	53205-2109	414-935-1500	935-1515	PK-5	Janel Howard-Hawkins
Soset Charter S	PO Box 125	Blair, WI	54616-0125	608-989-9835	989-2451	3-6	Connie Biedron
Spalding Academy	PO Box 2019	Appleton, WI	54912-2019	920-832-6136	993-7074	7-12	Nichole Schweitzer
Sparta Area Independent Learning	506 N Black River St	Sparta, WI	54656-1548	608-366-3491	366-3455	K-12	Peggy Jadack
Sparta Charter Preschool	506 N Black River St	Sparta, WI	54656-1548	608-269-3151	366-3473		Tarry Hall
Sparta Charter Preschool	506 N Black River St	Sparta, WI	54656-1548	608-366-3459		PK-PK	Michael Roddick
Sparta High Point S	506 N Black River St	Sparta, WI	54656-1548	608-366-3456		9-12	Mathew Toetz
Synectics Charter S	1859 Northgate Dr	Beloit, WI	53511-2667	608-361-3605	361-3620	6-8	Margaret Thomas
Tenor High S	840 N Jackson St	Milwaukee, WI	53202-3807	414-431-4371	431-4376	9-12	Marcia Spector
Tesla Engineering Charter S	2121 E Emmers Dr	Appleton, WI	54915-3802	920-997-1399	832-4880	9-12	Becky Walker
Time 4 Learning Charter S	5900 S 51st St	Greendale, WI	53129-2634	414-423-2750	423-0592		Theresa A. West
Transitional Skills Center	PO Box 339	Glenwood City, WI	54013-0339	715-265-4266	265-7129	10-12	Timothy Johnson
Trevor Charter S	26325 Wilmot Rd	Trevor, WI	53179-9701	262-862-2356	862-9226	PK-K	Jayme Donaldson
Truth Institute	1011 W Center St	Milwaukee, WI	53206-3262	414-267-4978	267-4915	9-10	Sharnissa Dunlap-Parker
21st Century Prep S	1220 Mound Ave	Racine, WI	53404-3350	262-598-0026	598-0031	K-4	K. Michele Clarke
Urban League Academy	3814 W North Ave	Milwaukee, WI	53208-1351	414-615-3915	444-2291	PK-8	Barbara Fisher
Valley New S	10 E College Ave Ste 225	Appleton, WI	54911	920-993-7037	832-1725	7-12	Todd Gray
Veritas HS	3025 W Oklahoma Ave	Milwaukee, WI	53215-4347	414-389-5575	389-5576	9-12	Marcia Spector
Vernon County Area Better Futures HS	100 Blackhawk Dr	Viroqua, WI	54665-1399	608-637-3191	637-8034	9-12	Kathrine Klos
Waadookodaading S	PO Box 860	Hayward, WI	54843-0860	715-634-2619		K-4	Cathy Begay
Walker International MS	1712 S 32nd St	Milwaukee, WI	53215-2104	414-902-7500	902-7515	6-8	Hector Perez LaBoy
Walworth County Education Alternative HS	400 County Road H	Elkhorn, WI	53121-2035	262-741-8138	741-8131	11-12	Jerry Hawver
Washington Service Learning Center	3500 Prais St	Stevens Point, WI	54481-2298	715-345-5426	345-7353	K-6	William Carlson
Waukesha Academy of Health Professions	401 E Roberta Ave	Waukesha, WI	53186-6637	262-970-3100	970-3120	9-12	Mark Hansen
Waupaca County Charter S	PO Box 457	Weyauwega, WI	54983-0457	920-867-4744		9-12	Michele Wickus
Waupun Alternative HS	801 E Lincoln St	Waupun, WI	53963-1753	920-324-5591	324-6980	9-12	Jeff Finstad
Wausau Area Montessori Charter S	3101 N 13th St	Wausau, WI	54403-2317	715-261-0795	261-2035	1-5	Kurt Weyers
W.E.B. DuBois HS	4141 N 64th St	Milwaukee, WI	53216-1198	414-393-2580	393-2585	9-12	Larry Miller

School	Address	City,State	Zip code	Telephone	Fax	Grade	Contact
Westside Academy	1940 N 36th St	Milwaukee, WI	53208-1927	414-934-4400	934-4415	3-8	James Sonnenberg
Westside Academy I	1945 N 31st St	Milwaukee, WI	53208-1902	414-934-5000		PK-8	James Sonnenberg
Whittier ES	4382 S 3rd St	Milwaukee, WI	53207-4999	414-294-1400	294-1415	PK-5	Peggy Mystrow
Wildlands Research Charter S	E19320 Bartig Rd	Augusta, WI	54722-7501	715-877-2292		7-12	Paul Tweed
Wilmot Bright Horizons	PO Box 68	Wilmot, WI	53192-0068	262-862-6461	862-7301	K-8	Teresa Curley
Wings Academy	1501 S Layton Blvd	Milwaukee, WI	53215-1924	414-431-1356	431-1358	3-12	Dani LaPorte
Wisconsin Career Academy	4801 S 2nd St	Milwaukee, WI	53207-5919	414-483-2117	483-2152	6-12	Tarik Celik
Wisconsin Connections Academy	PO Box 2019	Appleton, WI	54912-2019	920-832-4800	832-6284	K-8	Nichole Schweitzer
Wisconsin Rivers Community Charter S	1201 Northpoint Dr	Stevens Point, WI	54481-1114	715-345-5504		10-12	Mike Devine
Wisconsin Virtual Academy	401 Highland Dr	Fredonia, WI	53021-9491	262-692-3988	692-3952	K-8	Daniel Hanrahan
Woodlands S	5510 W Bluemound Rd	Milwaukee, WI	53208-3012	414-475-1600	475-9575		Maureen Sullivan
Woodlands S	5510 W Bluemound Rd	Milwaukee, WI	53208-3012	414-475-1600	475-9575	K-6	Maureen Sullivan
Work & Learn Center	15 S Brearly St	Madison, WI	53703-2918	608-204-4340	204-0543	9-12	Anne Fisher
Work & Learn Center	1810 S Park St	Madison, WI	53713-1247	608-442-0941	442-0940	11-12	Trina Keith-Spaeni
Wright Charter MS	1717 Fish Hatchery Rd	Madison, WI	53713-1244	608-204-1340	204-0547	6-8	Nancy Evans
YMCA Young Leaders Academy	1350 W North Avenue St	Milwaukee, WI	53212	414-374-9400	374-9459	K-12	Ronn Johnson

· **Wyoming** ·

School	Address	City,State	Zip code	Telephone	Fax	Grade	Contact
Fort Washakie Charter HS	90 Ethete Rd	Fort Washakie, WY	82514	307-332-2380	332-7267	9-12	Shad Hamilton

BUREAU OF INDIAN AFFAIRS SCHOOLS

BUREAU OF INDIAN AFFAIRS
1849 C St NW, Washington, DC 20240-0001
Telephone 202-208-6123
Fax 208-3312
Website http://www.oiep.bia.edu/

Agency/School	Address	City,State	Zip code	Telephone	Fax	Grade	Enr	Superintendent/Principal
Billings Area Office · · · · · · · · ·	316 N 26th St · · · · · ·	Billings, MT · · · · · ·	59101-1377	406-247-7953	247-7965	K-12		
Blackfeet Dormitory	PO Box 880	Browning, MT	59417-0880	406-338-7441	338-5732	1-12		
Northern Cheyenne Tribal S of Busby	PO Box 150	Busby, MT	59016-0150	406-592-3733	592-3645	K-12		
St. Stephens Indian S	PO Box 345	Saint Stephens, WY	82524-0345	307-856-4147	856-3742	K-12		
Cheyenne River Agency · · · · · · ·	PO Box 2020 · · · · · ·	Eagle Butte, SD · · · ·	57625-2020	605-964-8722	964-1155	K-12		Dr. Cherie Farlee
Cheyenne-Eagle Butte S	PO Box 672	Eagle Butte, SD	57625-0672	605-964-8777	964-8776	K-12		
Pierre Indian Learning Center	3001 E Sully Ave	Pierre, SD	57501-4403	605-224-8661	224-8465	K-8		Darrell Jeanotte
Takini S	HC 77 Box 537	Howes, SD	57748-9511	605-538-4399	538-4315	K-12		Larry Mendoza
Tiospaye Topa S	PO Box 300	Ridgeview, SD	57652-0300	605-733-2290	733-2299	K-12		Don Farlee
Chinle Agency · · · · · · · · · · ·	PO Box 6003 · · · · · ·	Chinle, AZ · · · · · · ·	86503-6003	928-674-5131	674-5134	K-12		Dr. Rena Yazzie
Black Mesa Community S	PO Box 97	Pinon, AZ	86510-0097	928-674-3632	659-8187	K-8		Marie Rose
Chinle Boarding S	PO Box 70	Many Farms, AZ	86538-3070	928-781-6221	781-6376	K-8		Gregory Morring
Cottonwood Day S	Navajo Route 4	Chinle, AZ	86503	928-725-3256	725-3255	K-8		Esther Frejo
Jeehdeez'a Academy	PO Box 1073	Pinon, AZ	86510-1073	928-725-3308	725-3306	K-5		Jim Davis
Lukachukai Community S	Navajo Route 13	Lukachukai, AZ	86507	928-787-4400	787-2311	K-8		Herbert Harvey
Many Farms HS	PO Box 307	Many Farms, AZ	86538-3307	928-781-6226	781-6355	9-12		Brian Dillon
Nazlini Community S	HC 58 Box 35	Ganado, AZ	86505-9704	928-755-6125	755-3729	K-8		Ronald Arias
Pinon Community S	PO Box 159	Pinon, AZ	86510-0159	928-725-3234	725-3232	K-12		Phillip Belone
Rock Point Community S	Highway 191	Rock Point, AZ	86545	928-659-4221	659-4235	K-12		Peter Belleto
Rough Rock Community S	HC 61 Box 5050PTT	Chinle, AZ	86503-9801	928-728-3501	728-3564	K-12		Dr. Charles Monty Roessel
Crow Creek/Lower Brule/Agency · · ·	PO Box 139 · · · · · · ·	Fort Thompson, SD · · ·	57339-0139	605-473-5531	473-9217	K-12		Dan Shroyer
Crow Creek Reservation HS	PO Box 12	Stephan, SD	57346-0012	605-852-2455	852-2140	6-12		Joe Ashley
Crow Creek Sioux Tribal ES	PO Box 469	Fort Thompson, SD	57339-0469	605-245-2373	245-2310	K-5	100	Robyn Thompson
Enemy Swim S	13495 446th Ave	Waubay, SD	57273-5318	605-947-4605	947-4188	K-8		Sherry Johnson
Lower Brule Day S	PO Box 245	Lower Brule, SD	57548-0245	605-473-5382	473-0214	PK-6	100	Richard Baysinger
Lower Brule HS	PO Box 245	Lower Brule, SD	57548-0245	605-473-5510	473-5525	7-12		Neil Russell
Tiospa Zina Tribal S	PO Box 719	Agency Village, SD	57262-0719	605-698-3954	698-6556	K-12		Ron Campbell
Eastern Navajo Agency · · · · · · ·	PO Box 328 · · · · · · ·	Crownpoint, NM · · · · ·	87313-0328	505-786-6138	786-6112	K-12	4,500	
Alamo Navajo S	PO Box 907	Magdalena, NM	87825-0907	505-854-2543	854-2545	K-12		
Baca Community S	PO Box 509	Prewitt, NM	87045-0509	505-876-2769	876-2769	K-4		
Bread Springs Day S	PO Box 1117	Gallup, NM	87305-1117	505-778-5665	778-5692	K-3		
Chi-Chil Tah/Jones Ranch S	PO Box 278	Vanderwagen, NM	87326-0278	505-778-5574	778-5573	K-8		
Dibe Yazhi Habitiin Olta S	PO Box 679	Crownpoint, NM	87313-0679	505-786-5237	786-7078	K-8		
Dzilth-Na-O-Dith-Hle Comm. S	35 Rd 7585 #5003	Bloomfield, NM	87413-4936	505-632-1697	632-3674	K-12		
Huerfano Dormitory	PO Box 639	Bloomfield, NM	87413-0639	505-325-3411	327-3591	K-12		
Lake Valley Navajo S	PO Box 748	Crownpoint, NM	87313-0748	505-786-6151	786-5956	K-8		
Mariano Lake Community S	PO Box 498	Crownpoint, NM	87313-0498	505-786-5265	786-5203	K-6		
NaNeel Zhiin Ji'olta S	HC 79 Box 9	Cuba, NM	87013-9701	505-731-2272	731-2252	K-8		
Ojo Encino S	HC 79 Box 7	Cuba, NM	87013-9701	505-731-2333	731-2361	K-8		
Pueblo Pintado Community S	HC 79 Box 80	Cuba, NM	87013-9600	505-655-3341	655-3342	K-8		
T'iists'oozi Bi'olta S	PO Box 178	Crownpoint, NM	87313-0178	505-786-6159	786-6163	K-8	500	
To'Hajiilee Ji'Olta S	PO Box 438	Canoncito, NM	87026	505-831-6426	831-4914	K-12		
Tse'ii'ahi' Community S	PO Box 828	Crownpoint, NM	87313-0828	505-786-5389	786-5635	K-4		
Wingate HS	PO Box 2	Fort Wingate, NM	87316-0002	505-488-6400	488-6444	9-12		
Wingate S	PO Box 1	Fort Wingate, NM	87316-0001	505-488-6470	488-6470	K-8		
Fort Apache Agency · · · · · · · ·	PO Box 920 · · · · · · ·	Whiteriver, AZ · · · · ·	85941-0920	928-338-5442	338-1944	K-12		Kevin Skenandore
Cibecue Community S	PO Box 80068	Cibecue, AZ	85911-0068	928-332-2480	332-2341	K-12		Linda Roma
Kennedy S, John F.	PO Box 130	Whiteriver, AZ	85941-0130	928-338-4593	338-4592	K-8		Michael Bragiel
Roosevelt JHS, Theodore	PO Box 567	Fort Apache, AZ	85926-0567	928-338-4464	338-1009	6-8		Wil Numkena
Fort Defiance Agency · · · · · · ·	PO Box 110 · · · · · · ·	Fort Defiance, AZ · · · ·	86504-0110	928-729-7255	729-7286	K-12		Jacqueline Wade
Ch'ooshgai Community S	PO Box 321	Tohatchi, NM	87325-0321	505-733-2719	733-2703	K-8	700	Johanson Phillips
Crystal Boarding S		Navajo, NM	87328	505-777-2385	777-2648	K-6		
Dilcon Community S	HC 63 Box G	Winslow, AZ	86047-9414	928-657-3485	657-3213	K-8		
Greasewood Springs Community S	HC 58 Box 60	Ganado, AZ	86505-9706	928-654-3383	654-3384	K-8		Arlene Tuchawena
Hunters Point Boarding S	PO Box 99	Saint Michaels, AZ	86511-0099	928-871-4439	871-4435	K-5		Cindy G. Joe
Kin Dah Lichi'i Olta	PO Box 800	Ganado, AZ	86505-0800	928-755-3707	755-3448	K-6		Ora James
Pine Springs Day S	PO Box 4198	Houck, AZ	86506-4198	928-871-4311	871-4341	K-4		Lou Ann M. Jones
Seba Dalkai Boarding S	HC 63 Box H	Winslow, AZ	86047-9415	928-657-3208	657-3224	K-8		
Tiiyaatin Residential Hall	1100 W Buffalo St	Holbrook, AZ	86025-2330	928-524-6222	524-2231	9-12		Maye Bigboy
Wide Ruins Community S	PO Box 309	Chambers, AZ	86502-0309	928-652-3251	652-3252	K-6		James Byrnes
Winslow Residential Hall	600 N Alfred Ave	Winslow, AZ	86047-3130	928-289-4483	289-2821	7-12		Mike K. James
Hopi Agency · · · · · · · · · · ·	PO Box 568 · · · · · · ·	Keams Canyon, AZ · · ·	86034-0568	928-738-5139	738-5139	K-12		Jimmy Hastings
First Mesa ES	PO Box 750	Polacca, AZ	86042-0750	928-737-2581	738-5139	K-6		Bruce Steele
Havasupai S	PO Box 40	Supai, AZ	86435-0040	928-448-2901	448-2551	K-8		Virginia Velasquez
Hopi Day S	PO Box 42	Kykotsmovi, AZ	86039-0042	928-734-2468	734-2470	K-6		Dr. John Thomas
Hopi JSHS	PO Box 337	Keams Canyon, AZ	86034-0337	928-738-5111	738-5333	7-12		Dr. Paul Reynolds
Hotevilla-Bacavi Community S	PO Box 48	Hotevilla, AZ	86030-0048	928-734-2462	734-2225	K-6		Alma Sinquah
Keams Canyon ES	PO Box 397	Keams Canyon, AZ	86034-0397	928-738-2385	738-5519	K-6		Michael Krug
Moencopi Day S	PO Box 185	Tuba City, AZ	86045-0185	928-283-5361	283-4662	K-6		Joel Longie
Second Mesa Day S	PO Box 98	Second Mesa, AZ	86043-0098	928-737-2571	737-2565	K-6		Donald Harvey
Minneapolis Agency · · · · · · · ·	1 Federal Dr Rm 550 · ·	Fort Snelling, MN · · · ·	55111-4008	612-725-4591	713-4438	K-12		Bill Walters
Bug-O-Nay-Ge-Shig S	15353 Silver Eagle Dr	Bena, MN	56626	218-665-3000	665-3024	K-12		Michelle Johnson
Circle of Life S	PO Box 447	White Earth, MN	56591-0447	218-983-4180	983-3767	K-12		Mitch Vogt
Circle of Nations Indian Boarding S	832 8th St N	Wahpeton, ND	58075-3642	701-642-3796	642-5880	4-8		David Keehn
Flandreau Indian S	1005 S Mountain Chief Dr #1	Flandreau, SD	57028	605-997-3773	997-2601	9-12	300	Betty Belkham
Fond du Lac Ojibwe S	105 University Rd	Cloquet, MN	55720-8520	218-878-7571	878-7573	K-12		Rae Villebran
Hannahville Indian S	N14911 Hannahville B1 Rd	Wilson, MI	49896	906-466-2952	466-2556	K-12	200	William Boda

Agency/School	Address	City,State	Zip code	Telephone	Fax	Grade	Enr	Superintendent/Principal
Lac Courte Oreilles Ojibwa S	8875 N Round Lake School Rd	Hayward, WI	54843	715-634-8924	634-6058	K-12		Craig Euneau
Lumsden Bahweting Anishinabe S, J.K.	1301 Marquette Ave	Sault S Marie, MI	49783-9533	906-635-5055	635-3805	K-8		Nick Oshleski
Menominee Tribal S	PO Box 39	Neopit, WI	54150-0039	715-756-2354	756-2364	K-8		Alan Coldwell
Meskwaki Settlement S	1605 305th St	Tama, IA	52339-9698	641-484-4990	484-3264	K-12		Jerry Stephens
Nay Ah Shing S	43651 Oodena Dr	Onamia, MN	56359	320-532-4695	532-4675	K-12	50	Eric North
Oneida Nation ES	PO Box 365	Oneida, WI	54155-0365	920-869-1676	869-1684	K-12		Sharon Mousseau
Navajo Co. Special Services Consortium	**PO Box 668**	**Holbrook, AZ**	**86025-0668**	**928-524-2123**	**524-6367**	**K-12**		**Betty Walch**
Rainbow Accomodation	PO Box 668	Holbrook, AZ	86025-0668	928-524-1821	524-6367	K-12		Autumn Hanson
Northern Navajo Agency	**PO Box 3239**	**Shiprock, NM**	**87420-3239**	**505-368-3400**	**368-3409**	**K-12**		**Dr. Angelita Felix**
Aneth Community S	PO Box 600	Montezuma Creek, UT	84534-0600	435-651-3271	651-3272	K-6		Clayton Michael Aaron
Atsa'biya'a'zh Community S	PO Box 1809	Shiprock, NM	87420-1809	505-368-2084	368-2100	K-6	50	Melissa Culler
Aztec Dormitory	1600 Lydia Rippey Rd	Aztec, NM	87410-1662	505-334-6565	334-8630	9-12		John Nolan
Beclabito Day S	PO Box 1200	Shiprock, NM	87420-1200	928-656-3555		K-4		Daniel Sosnowski
Cove Day S	PO Box 2000	Red Valley, AZ	86544-2000	928-653-4457	653-4415	K-6		Perfilliea Charlie
Navajo Prep S	1220 W Apache St	Farmington, NM	87401-3886	505-326-6571	326-2155	9-12		Betty O'Jaye
Nenahnezad Community S	PO Box 337	Fruitland, NM	87416-0337	505-598-6922	598-0970	K-6		Sylvia Ashley
Red Rock Day S	PO Box 2007	Red Valley, AZ	86544-2007	928-653-4456	653-5711	K-8		Mike Luther
Sanostee Day S	PO Box 159	Sanostee, NM	87461-0159	505-723-2476	723-2425	K-3		Jeannie Haskie
Shiprock Alternative Dormitory Program	PO Box 1809	Shiprock, NM	87420-1809	505-368-2074	368-5102	9-12	50	Johnny Anderson
Shiprock Northwest HS	PO Box 1809	Shiprock, NM	87420-1809	505-368-2070	368-5102	9-12		Rick Hover
T'iisNazbas Community S	PO Box 102	Teec Nos Pos, AZ	86514-0102	928-656-3252	656-3486	K-8		Oelphina John
Tohaali' Community S	PO Box 9857	Newcomb, NM	87455-9857	505-789-3201	789-3202	K-8		Delores Bitsilly
Northern Pueblos Agency	**PO Box 4269**	**Espanola, NM**	**87533-4269**	**505-753-1465**	**753-1475**	**K-12**		
Jicarilla Dormitory	PO Box 1009	Dulce, NM	87528-1009	505-759-3101	759-3338	1-12		
Ohkay Owingeh Community S	PO Box 1077	San Juan Pueblo, NM	87566-1077	505-852-2154	852-4305	K-8		Alfred Garcia
San Ildefonso S	RR 5 Box 308	Santa Fe, NM	87506-2642	505-455-2366	455-7194	K-6		
Santa Clara S	PO Box 2183	Espanola, NM	87532-2183	505-753-4406	753-8866	K-6		
Santa Fe Indian S	PO Box 5340	Santa Fe, NM	87502-5340	505-989-6300	989-6317	7-12	500	
Taos S	PO Box X	Taos, NM	87571-1189	505-758-3652	758-1566	K-8	200	
Te Tsu Geh Oweenge S	RR 11 Box 2	Santa Fe, NM	87501	505-982-1516	982-2331	K-6		
Oklahoma Education Office	**4149 Highline Blvd Ste 380**	**Oklahoma City, OK**	**73108-2076**	**405-605-6051**	**605-6057**	**K-12**		**Joy Martin**
Carter Seminary	2400 Chickasaw Blvd	Ardmore, OK	73401-1347	580-223-8547	223-6325	1-12		Mike Abla
Eufaula Dormitory	Swadley Dr	Eufaula, OK	74432	918-689-2522	689-2438	1-12		Greg Anderson
Jones Academy	HC 74 Box 102-5	Hartshorne, OK	74547-9717	918-297-2518	297-2364	1-12		Brad Spears
Kickapoo Nation S	PO Box 106	Powhattan, KS	66527-0106	785-474-3550	474-3530	K-12		Pat McAfee
Riverside Indian S	RR 1	Anadarko, OK	73005-9801	405-247-6673	247-5529	4-12	300	Don Sims
Sequoyah HS	PO Box 948	Tahlequah, OK	74465-0948	918-456-0631	456-0634	9-12		Gina Stanley
Papago - Pima Agency	**HC 1 Box 8600**	**Sells, AZ**	**85634-9743**	**520-361-3510**	**361-3514**	**K-12**		**Lester Hudson**
Blackwater Community S	RR 1 Box 95	Coolidge, AZ	85228-9681	520-215-5859	215-5862	K-2		Jacquelyn Power
Casa Blanca S	PO Box 10940	Bapchule, AZ	85221-0940	520-315-3489	315-3504	K-4		Rachel Carroll
Gila Crossing S	PO Box 10	Laveen, AZ	85339-0010	520-550-4834	550-4252	PK-4		Ronald Shuler
Salt River HS	10005 E Osborn Rd	Scottsdale, AZ	85256-4019	480-362-2000	362-2090	7-12	200	Mike McCarthy
Salt River S	10000 E McDowell Rd	Scottsdale, AZ	85256-5201	480-850-2900	850-7600	K-6		Jacque Bradley
San Simon S	HC 1 Box 8292	Sells, AZ	85634-9711	520-362-2231	362-2405	K-8		Frank Rogers
Santa Rosa Boarding S	HC 01 Box 8400	Sells, AZ	85634	520-361-2276	361-2511	K-8		Keith Seaman
Santa Rosa Ranch S	HC 01 Box 7570	Sells, AZ	85634	520-383-2359	383-3960	K-8		Delbert Ortiz
Tohono O'Odham HS	HC 01 Box 8513	Sells, AZ	85634	520-362-2400	362-2256	9-12		William Reese
Pine Ridge Agency	**PO Box 333**	**Pine Ridge, SD**	**57770-0333**	**605-867-1306**	**867-5610**	**K-12**		**Norma Tibbitts**
American Horse S	PO Box 660	Allen, SD	57714-0660	605-455-6750	455-2249	K-8	100	Gloria Kitsopoulas
Crazy Horse S	PO Box 260	Wanblee, SD	57577-0260	605-455-6800	462-6510	K-12		Donald Standing Elk
Little Wound S	PO Box 500	Kyle, SD	57752-0500	605-455-6175	455-2703	K-12		Linda Hunter
Loneman S	PO Box 50	Oglala, SD	57764-0050	605-455-6882	867-5109	K-8		Deborah Bordeaux
Pine Ridge S	PO Box 1202	Pine Ridge, SD	57770-1202	605-455-6500	867-5482	K-12		Justin Conroy
Porcupine S	PO Box 180	Porcupine, SD	57772-0180	605-455-6450	867-5480	K-8		Thomas Raymond
Wounded Knee S	PO Box 350	Manderson, SD	57756-0350	605-455-6363	867-2051	K-8		Chris Bordeaux
Portland Area Office	**911 NE 11th Ave**	**Portland, OR**	**97232-4128**	**503-872-2743**	**231-6219**	**PK-12**		**John Reimer**
Chemawa Indian S	3700 Chemawa Rd NE	Salem, OR	97305-1199	503-399-5721	399-5870	9-12		
Chief Leschi S	5625 52nd St E	Puyallup, WA	98371-3610	253-445-3003	445-2350	K-12		
Couer D'Alene Tribal S	PO Box 338	Desmet, ID	83824-0338	208-686-5126	686-5080	K-8		
Lummi HS	2530 Kwina Rd	Bellingham, WA	98226-9278	360-384-2330	380-1464	9-12		
Lummi Tribal S	2530 Kwina Rd	Bellingham, WA	98226-9278	360-384-2293	384-2334	K-8		
Muckleshoot Tribal S	39015 172nd Ave SE	Auburn, WA	98092-9763	253-931-6709	939-2922	K-12		
Paschal Sherman Indian S	25 A Mission Rd	Omak, WA	98841	509-422-7590	422-7539	K-9		
Quileute Tribal S	PO Box 39	La Push, WA	98350-0039	360-374-5602	374-9608	K-12		
Shoshone Bannock S	PO Box 790	Fort Hall, ID	83203-0790	208-238-4200	238-2628	K-8	200	
Two Eagle River S	PO Box 160	Pablo, MT	59855-0160	406-675-0292	675-0294	K-8		
Wa He Lut Indian S	11110 Conine Ave SE	Olympia, WA	98513-9603	360-456-1311	456-1319	K-8		
Yakima Tribal S	PO Box 151	Toppenish, WA	98948-0151	509-865-5121	865-6092	7-12		
Rosebud Agency	**PO Box 669**	**Mission, SD**	**57555-0669**	**605-856-4478**	**856-4487**	**K-12**		**Neva Sherwood**
Marty Indian S	PO Box 187	Marty, SD	57361-0187	605-384-2212	384-5933	K-12		Terry Mayer
St. Francis Indian S	PO Box 379	Saint Francis, SD	57572-0379	605-747-2299	747-2379	K-12		Larry Parker
Sicangu Owaye Oti	PO Box 669	Mission, SD	57555-0669	605-856-4486	856-4490	1-12		Nancy Hernandez
Sacramento Area Office	**2800 Cottage Way**	**Sacramento, CA**	**95825-1846**	**916-978-6057**	**978-6056**	**K-12**		**Fayetta Babby**
Duckwater Shoshone S	PO Box 140038	Duckwater, NV	89314-0038	775-863-0180	863-0199	K-8		Keith Honnaker
Noli S	PO Box 487	San Jacinto, CA	92581-0487	951-654-5596	654-4198	6-12	200	Donovan Post
Pyramid Lake HS	PO Box 256	Nixon, NV	89424-0256	775-574-1016	574-1037	7-12		Randy Melendez
Sherman Indian HS	9010 Magnolia Ave	Riverside, CA	92503-3972	951-276-6332	276-6336	9-12		Pedro Vallejo
South & Eastern States Agency	**545 Marriott Dr Ste 700**	**Nashville, TN**	**37214-5081**	**615-564-6632**	**564-6631**	**PK-12**		
Ahafachkee S	HC 61 Box 40	Clewiston, FL	33440-9771	863-983-6348	983-6535	K-12		Lee Zepeda
Bogue Chitto S	13241 Highway 491 N	Philadelphia, MS	39350-5463	601-389-1000	389-1002	K-8	100	Ty Cobb
Cherokee Central JSHS	PO Box 134	Cherokee, NC	28719-0134	828-497-4472	497-4373	7-12		Arlen Middleton
Cherokee Central S	PO Box 134	Cherokee, NC	28719-0134	828-497-9130	497-4351	K-8		Charlee Easton
Chitimacha Day S	3613 Chitimacha Trl	Jeanerette, LA	70544-8317	337-923-9960	923-7346	K-8		Tanya Rosamond
Choctaw Central HS	150 Recreation Rd	Choctaw, MS	39350-7180	601-656-8870	656-7077	9-12	400	Sherry Tubby
Choctaw Central MS	RR 7 Box 72	Choctaw, MS	39350-9807	601-656-8938	656-7558	7-8	200	Roger McLeod
Conehatta S	851 Tushka Dr	Conehatta, MS	39057	601-775-8254	775-9229	K-8		Charles Hull
Indian Island S	1 River St	Old Town, ME	04468-1128	207-827-4285	827-3599	PK-8	100	Linda McLeod
Indian Township S	13 School Dr	Princeton, ME	04668-5000	207-796-2362	796-2726	PK-8	100	Ralph Shannon
Miccosukee Indian S	PO Box 440021	Miami, FL	33144-0021	305-894-2364	223-1011	K-12		Tom Albano
Pearl River ES	470 Industrial Rd	Choctaw, MS	39350-4256	601-656-9051	656-9054	K-6		Greg Carlyle
Rafferty S, Beatrice	RR 1 Box 338	Perry, ME	04667-9732	207-853-6085	853-6210	PK-8	100	Mike Chadwick
Red Water S	555 Red Water Rd	Carthage, MS	39051-9103	601-267-8500	267-5193	K-8		Bobbie Boone
Standing Pine ES	538 Highway 487 E	Carthage, MS	39051-6031	601-267-9225	267-9129	K-6		Jackie Harpole
Tucker S	126 E Tucker Cir	Philadelphia, MS	39350-8351	601-656-8775	656-9341	K-8		Joe Wood
Southern Pueblos Agency	**PO Box 26567**	**Albuquerque, NM**	**87125-6567**	**505-563-3690**	**563-3078**	**K-12**	**2,800**	**Dr. Benjamin Atencio**
Isleta ES	PO Box 550	Isleta, NM	87022-0550	505-869-2321	869-1625	K-6		Joe Robledo
Jemez Day S	PO Box 139	Jemez Pueblo, NM	87024-0139	505-834-7304	834-7081	K-6		Freddie Cardenas
Laguna ES	PO Box 191	Laguna, NM	87026-0191	505-552-9200	552-7294	K-5		Brenda Kofahl
Laguna MS	PO Box 268	Laguna, NM	87026-0268	505-552-9091	552-6466	6-8		Yolanda Batrez
Mescalero Apache S	PO Box 230	Mescalero, NM	88340-0230	505-464-4470	464-4822	K-12	500	Marcia Saenz
Pine Hill S	PO Box 220	Pinehill, NM	87357-0220	505-775-3243	775-3241	K-12		Sam Alonza
San Felipe Pueblo S	PO Box 4343	San Felipe Pb, NM	87001-4343	505-867-3364	867-6253	K-7		Greg Rockhold
Sky City Community S	PO Box 349	Pueblo of Acoma, NM	87034-0349	505-552-6671	552-6672	K-8		Richard Jaramillo
T'siya S, Zia	1000 Borrego Canyon Rd	Zia Pueblo, NM	87053-6104	505-867-3553	867-5079	K-8	100	Robert Lovato
Standing Rock Agency	**PO Box E**	**Fort Yates, ND**	**58538-0523**	**701-854-3497**	**854-7280**	**K-12**		
Jamerson S, Theodore	3315 University Dr	Bismarck, ND	58504-7565	701-255-3285	530-0601	K-8	200	
Little Eagle S	PO Box 26	Little Eagle, SD	57639-0026	605-823-4235	823-2292	K-8		
Rock Creek Grant S	PO Box 127	Bullhead, SD	57621-0127	605-823-4971	823-4350	K-8		
Tate Topa Tribal S	PO Box 199	Fort Totten, ND	58335-0199	701-766-1470	766-4766	K-8	400	
Turtle Mountain Education Line Office	**PO Box 30**	**Belcourt, ND**	**58316-0030**	**701-477-3463**	**477-9364**	**PK-12**		**Rose-Marie Davis**
Dunseith Day S	PO Box 759	Dunseith, ND	58329-0759	701-263-4636	263-4200	K-8		Yvonne St. Claire
Mandaree S	PO Box 488	Mandaree, ND	58757-0488	701-759-3311	759-3493	K-12	200	Anna Rubia
Ojibwa Indian S	PO Box 600	Belcourt, ND	58316-0600	701-477-3108	477-3760	K-8	300	Michael Blue
Trenton S	PO Box 239	Trenton, ND	58853-0239	701-774-8221	774-8040	PK-12		Michael O'Brien
Turtle Mountain ES	PO Box 440	Belcourt, ND	58316-0440	701-477-6471	477-6470	K-5	700	Dave Gourneau
Turtle Mountain HS	PO Box 440	Belcourt, ND	58316-0440	701-477-6471	477-8821	9-12	500	Rosemary Jaros
Turtle Mountain MS	PO Box 440	Belcourt, ND	58316-0440	701-477-6471	477-6470	6-8	300	Louis Dauphinais
Twin Buttes S	7997 7A St NW	Halliday, ND	58636-4004	701-938-4396	938-4398	K-8	100	Chad Dahlen
White Shield S	2 2nd Ave W	Roseglen, ND	58775-6009	701-743-4355	743-4501	K-12		Ioane Schmidt
Western Navajo Agency	**PO Box 746**	**Tuba City, AZ**	**86045-0746**	**928-283-2218**	**283-2286**	**K-12**		**Joe Frazier**
Chilchinbeto Community S	PO Box 740	Kayenta, AZ	86033-0740	928-697-3800	697-3448	K-8		Leonard Eltsosie
Dennehotso Boarding S	PO Box 2570	Dennehotso, AZ	86535-2570	928-658-3201	658-3221	K-8		James Brown
Greyhills Academy HS	PO Box 160	Tuba City, AZ	86045-0160	928-283-6271	283-6604	9-12		Andrew Tan

Agency/School	Address	City,State	Zip code	Telephone	Fax	Grade	Enr	Superintendent/Principal
Kaibito Boarding S	PO Box 1420	Kaibito, AZ	86053-1420	928-673-3480	673-3489	K-8		Richard Harjo
Kayenta Community S	PO Box 188	Kayenta, AZ	86033-0188	928-697-3439	697-3490	K-8		Velma Eisenberger
KinLani Bordertown Dormitory	901 N Kinlani Dr	Flagstaff, AZ	86001-1585	928-774-5270	774-5270	9-12		James Kimery
Leupp S	HC 61 Box D	Winslow, AZ	86047-9313	928-686-6211	686-6216	K-12		Emma Yazzie
Little Singer Community S	HC 61 Box 310	Winslow, AZ	86047-9801	928-526-6680	526-8894	K-6		Lucinda Godinez
Naa Tsis 'Aan Community S	PO Box 10010	Tonalea, AZ	86044-5010	928-672-2335	672-2609	K-8		Mary Rule
Richfield Residential Hall	PO Box 638	Richfield, UT	84701-0638	435-896-5101	896-6157	9-12		Boyd Kiesel
Rocky Ridge Boarding S	PO Box 299	Kykotsmovi, AZ	86039-0299	928-725-3650	725-3655	K-8		Bart Moore
Shonto Preparatory S	PO Box 7900	Shonto, AZ	86054-7900	928-672-2652	672-2849	K-12		Eugene Thomas
Tonalea Day S	PO Box 39	Tonalea, AZ	86044-0039	928-283-6325	283-6326	K-8		Gregory Mooring
Tuba City Boarding S	PO Box 187	Tuba City, AZ	86045-0187	928-283-2330	283-2348	K-8		Don Coffland

DEPARTMENT OF DEFENSE DEPENDENT SCHOOLS

DEPT. OF DEFENSE DEPENDENT SCHOOLS
4040 Fairfax Dr Fl 9, Arlington, VA 22203-1613
Telephone 703-696-4247
Website http://www.odedodea.edu

District/School	Address	City,State	Zip code	Telephone	Fax	Grade	Enr	Superintendent/Principal
Fort Campbell Dependent SD	77 Texas Ave	Fort Campbell, KY	42223-5127	270-439-1927	439-3179	PK-12	4,900	Martha Brown
Barkley ES	4720 Polk Rd	Fort Campbell, KY	42223-1900	270-439-3795	439-1901	PK-5	500	Madeline Haller
Fort Campbell HS	1101 Bastogne Ave	Fort Campbell, KY	42223-5133	931-431-5056	431-9386	9-12	500	Dr. Elaine Gallivan
Jackson ES	675 Mississippi Ave	Fort Campbell, KY	42223-5353	931-431-6211	431-4453	PK-5	600	Susan Ahart
Lincoln ES	4718 Polk Rd	Fort Campbell, KY	42223-1400	270-439-3794	439-2335	PK-5	400	Sandy Meacham
Lucas ES, Andre	2115 Airborne St	Fort Campbell, KY	42223-5382	931-431-7711	431-5842	PK-5	500	James Walker
Mahaffey MS	585 S Carolina Ave	Fort Campbell, KY	42223-5134	270-439-3792	439-3472	6-8	300	Dr. Floyd Hines
Marshall ES	75 Texas Ave	Fort Campbell, KY	42223-5135	270-439-3793	439-4382	PK-5	400	Dr. Suzanne Jones
Wassom MS	3066 Forrest Rd	Fort Campbell, KY	42223-5272	270-439-3791	439-0671	6-8	300	Peter Price
Fort Knox Community SD	4553 Fayette Ave	Fort Knox, KY	40121	502-624-2345	624-3969	PK-12	3,300	Todd Curkendall
Fort Knox HS	7501 Missouri St	Fort Knox, KY	40121-2293	502-624-3697	624-6171	9-12	500	Sarah Turner
Kingsolver ES	1488 3rd Ave	Fort Knox, KY	40121-2287	502-624-8650	624-3969	PK-3	200	William Lyon
Macdonald IS	7729 McCracken St	Fort Knox, KY	40121-2706	502-624-5650	624-3969	4-6	300	Youlanda Washington
Mudge ES	5373 Paquette St	Fort Knox, KY	40121-2573	502-624-8345	624-3969	PK-3	200	Anne Campbell
Pierce ES	7502 Dixie St	Fort Knox, KY	40121-2288	502-624-7449	624-3969	PK-3	300	Joe Medley
Scott MS	7474 Mississippi St	Fort Knox, KY	40121-2708	502-624-2236	624-5433	7-8	400	Gary Gibson
Van Voorhis ES	5550 Folger St	Fort Knox, KY	40121-6086	502-624-5854	624-7267	PK-3	500	Dr. Jo Blease
Walker IS	5549 Conroy Ave	Fort Knox, KY	40121-4002	502-624-7835	624-6759	4-6	400	David Reed
Fort Stewart/South Carolina SD	376 Davis Ave Bldg 5605	Fort Stewart, GA	31315-1033	912-369-6691	876-8417	PK-6	1,600	Dr. Joseph R. Guiendon
Bolden ES, Charles Frank	Laurel Bay Rd	Beaufort, SC	29906	843-846-6112	846-6316	4-6	200	Dr. Vinita Swinty
Brittin ES	2772 Hero Rd Bldg 7392	Fort Stewart, GA	31315-1713	912-368-3324	368-7515	K-6	100	Noel Tillman
Diamond ES	516 Davis Ave Bldg 5602	Fort Stewart, GA	31315-1044	912-876-5797	876-8350	PK-6	100	Dr. Ford Stone
Elliott ES	Larel Bay Blvd	Beaufort, SC	29906	843-846-6112	846-9283	1-3	100	Barbara Hazzard
Fort Stewart ES	324 Davis Ave Bldg 5606G	Fort Stewart, GA	31314-4437	912-369-1494	876-8417	PK-5	200	Carol Lee Kipp Caldwell
Galer ES, Robert Edward	1310 Cardinal Ln	Beaufort, SC	29906-3477	843-846-6100	846-1860	PK-3		Barbara MacDermant
Hood Street ES	5615 Hood St	Columbia, SC	29206-5360	803-787-8266	782-8863	2-3	50	Thelma Gibson
Pierce Terrace ES	5715 Adams Ct	Columbia, SC	29206-5379	803-782-1772	738-8895	PK-1	100	Mr. Jan Long
Pinckney ES, Charles C.	5900 Chesnut Rd	Columbia, SC	29206-5365	803-787-6815	787-7108	4-6	100	Carol Kress
Georgia / Alabama Dependent SD	7201 Custer Rd Bldg 2670	Fort Benning, GA	31905-9597	706-545-7276	545-8227	PK-8	2,600	Dr. Dell McMullen
Dexter ES, Herbert J.	99 Yeager Ave	Fort Benning, GA	31905-9699	706-545-3424	545-7775	PK-5		Vicki Rogers
Faith MS, Don C.	1375 Ingersoll St	Fort Benning, GA	31905-7200	706-545-5524		6-8		Dr. Julio Gonzalez
Fort Rucker ES	PO Box 620279	Fort Rucker, AL	36362-0279	334-598-4408	598-8622	2-6	500	Barbara Doherty
Fort Rucker PS	PO Box 620279	Fort Rucker, AL	36362-0279	334-598-4473		PK-2	400	Deborah Patton
Loyd ES, Frank R.	900 Santa Fe Rd	Fort Benning, GA	31905-7400	706-544-8964	544-8972	PK-5	300	Dr. Tom Dignan
Maxwell AFB ES	800 Magnolia Blvd	Maxwell AFB, AL	36113-6147	334-953-7804	953-4339	PK-5	400	Sharon Davis
McBride ES, Morris R.	700 Custer Rd	Fort Benning, GA	31905-7402	706-544-9411	544-9299	PK-3	400	Delbert Hicks
Robins AFB ES	895 11th St	Robins AFB, GA	31098	478-926-5003	926-5745	PK-6	400	Jeanne Roberts
Stowers ES, Freddie	7791 Stowers Dr	Fort Benning, GA	31905-3130	706-544-2312	544-2349	PK-5	500	Angie McPherson
White ES, Edward A.	300 1st Division Rd	Fort Benning, GA	31905-6627	706-545-4623	545-5469	PK-5		Dr. Tommy Lee
Wilson ES, Richard G.	112 Lavoie Ave	Fort Benning, GA	31905-7523	706-545-5723	545-9505	PK-5		Phyllis Parker
NY/VA Domestic Dependent School System	3308 John Quick Rd # 201	Quantico, VA	22134-1752	703-784-2319	784-3100	PK-12	1,200	Lawanna Mangleburg
Ashurst ES	4320 Dulaney Rd	Quantico, VA	22134-2248	703-221-4108	784-2694	PK-3		Janice Weiss
Burrows ES, W.W.	3308 John Quick Rd	Quantico, VA	22134-1702	703-640-6118	704-1353	4-5		Dr. William Ramos
Dahlgren S	193 Sampson Rd	Dahlgren, VA	22448	540-653-8822	653-4591	PK-8		Steve Hovanic
Quantico MSHS	3307 Purvis Rd	Quantico, VA	22134-2198	703-784-0303	784-4851	6-12		Charlie Winters
Russell ES, John H.	3301 Purvis Rd	Quantico, VA	22134-2199	703-221-4161	784-4870	PK-3		Randall Ekanger
West Point ES	705A Barry Rd	West Point, NY	10996-1196	845-938-2313	938-3352	PK-4	600	Ed Drozdowski
West Point MS	705 Barry Rd	West Point, NY	10996-1110	845-938-2923	938-2568	5-8	300	Michael Hollier
North Carolina Dependent SD	PO Box 70089	Fort Bragg, NC	28307-0089	910-907-0200	907-1405	PK-9		Thomas Hager
Albritton JHS	PO Box 70089	Fort Bragg, NC	28307-0089	910-907-0201	432-4072	7-9		Mike Thornburg
Bitz IS	PO Box 70089	Fort Bragg, NC	28307-0089	910-451-2575	451-1475	3-5		Dr. Rick Scroggs
Bowley ES	PO Box 70089	Fort Bragg, NC	28307-0089	910-907-0202	907-3513	PK-4		Dr. Susan Walters
Brewster MS	PO Box 70089	Fort Bragg, NC	28307-0089	910-451-2561	451-2600	6-8		Eric Steimel
Butner ES	PO Box 70089	Fort Bragg, NC	28307-0089	910-907-0203	432-8400	PK-4		Dr. Mary Brigham
Camp Lejeune HS	PO Box 70089	Fort Bragg, NC	28307-0089	910-451-2451	451-3130	9-12		Daniel Osgood
Delalio ES	PO Box 70089	Fort Bragg, NC	28307-0089	910-449-0601	449-0677	PK-5		Carol Perry
Devers ES	PO Box 70089	Fort Bragg, NC	28307-0089	910-907-0204	396-7374	PK-4		Ginny Breece
Holbrook ES	PO Box 70089	Fort Bragg, NC	28307-0089	910-907-0205	432-8385	PK-4		Priscilla Joiner
Irwin IS	PO Box 70089	Fort Bragg, NC	28307-0089	910-907-0206	907-1247	5-6		Rob Richardson
Johnson PS	PO Box 70089	Fort Bragg, NC	28307-0089	910-451-2431	451-2433	K-1		Dr. Janet Kinney
McNair ES	PO Box 70089	Fort Bragg, NC	28307-0089	910-907-0207	432-8386	PK-4		
Murray ES	PO Box 70089	Fort Bragg, NC	28307-0089	910-907-0208	907-0506	PK-4		Charles Council
Pope ES	PO Box 70089	Fort Bragg, NC	28307-0089	910-907-0209	907-0901	PK-4		Dr. Bob Kirkpatrick
Tarawa Terrace II ES	PO Box 70089	Fort Bragg, NC	28307-0089	910-450-1635	450-1637	PK-5		Elizabeth Thomas
Tarawa Terrace I PS	PO Box 70089	Fort Bragg, NC	28307-0089	910-450-1662	450-1661	K-1	100	Linda Hawes

CATHOLIC SCHOOL SUPERINTENDENTS

NATIONAL CATHOLIC EDUCATIONAL ASSOC.
1077 30th St NW Ste 100, Washington, DC 20007-3816
Telephone 202-337-6232
Fax 333-6706
Website ncea.org

CATHOLIC SCHOOL SUPERINTENDENTS

Archdiocese/Diocese	Address	City,State	Zip code	Telephone	Fax	Grade	Enr	Superintendent
Diocese of Albany	40 N Main Ave	Albany, NY	12203-1481	518-453-6666	453-6667	PK-12	12,900	Sr. Mary Jane Herb
Diocese of Alexandria	PO Box 7417	Alexandria, LA	71306-0417	318-445-2401	448-6121	PK-12	3,000	Sr. Marice Elvekrog
Diocese of Allentown	PO Box 20607	Lehigh Valley, PA	18002-0607	610-866-0581	867-8702	PK-12	18,900	Philip J. Fromuth
Diocese of Altoona-Johnstown	126A Logan Blvd	Hollidaysburg, PA	16648-2698	814-693-1401	695-8894	PK-12	6,200	Dr. Charles Koren
Diocese of Amarillo	1800 N Spring St	Amarillo, TX	79107-7252	806-383-2243	383-8452	PK-12	1,000	Bernice Noggler
Archdiocese of Anchorage	225 Cordova St	Anchorage, AK	99501-2409	907-297-7721	279-3885	PK-12	500	
Diocese of Arlington	200 N Glebe Rd	Arlington, VA	22203-3728	703-841-2519	524-8670	PK-12	17,800	Dr. Timothy McNiff
Archdiocese of Atlanta	680 W Peachtree St NW	Atlanta, GA	30308-1931	404-888-7833	885-7430	PK-12	9,800	Judith Mucheck
Diocese of Austin	1625 Rutherford Ln	Austin, TX	78754-5100	512-873-7771	873-8338	PK-12	4,800	Dr. Ned Vanders
Diocese of Baker	PO Box 5999	The Dalles, OR	97058	541-388-4004	388-2566	PK-8	700	Roger Richmond
Archdiocese of Baltimore	320 Cathedral St	Baltimore, MD	21201-4421	410-547-5515	547-5566	PK-12	38,400	Dr. Ronald Valenti
Diocese of Baton Rouge	PO Box 2028	Baton Rouge, LA	70821-2028	225-336-8735	336-8711	PK-12	16,600	Sr. Mary Michaeline
Diocese of Beaumont	PO Box 3948	Beaumont, TX	77704-3948	409-838-0451	838-4511	PK-12	2,300	George A. Pressey
Diocese of Belleville	2620 Lebanon Ave	Belleville, IL	62221-3233	618-235-9601	235-7115	PK-12	8,600	Thomas Posnanski
Diocese of Biloxi	1790 Popps Ferry Rd	Biloxi, MS	39532-2118	228-702-2130	702-2135	PK-12	5,000	Dr. Mike Ladner
Diocese of Birmingham	PO Box 12047	Birmingham, AL	35202-2047	205-838-8303	838-8330	PK-12	7,000	Sr. Leanne Welch
Diocese of Bismarck	PO Box 1137	Bismarck, ND	58502-1137	701-222-3035	222-0269	PK-12	2,900	Betty Greff
Diocese of Boise	303 S Federal Way	Boise, ID	83705-5925	208-342-1311	342-0224	PK-12	3,100	Dan Makley
Diocese of Boston	2200 Dorchester Ave	Boston, MA	02124-5607	617-298-6555	298-6622	PK-12	56,500	Sr. Kathleen Carr
Diocese of Bridgeport	238 Jewett Ave	Bridgeport, CT	06606-2892	203-372-4301	372-1961	PK-12	14,100	Dr. Margaret Dames
Diocese of Brooklyn	PO Box 159013	Brooklyn, NY	11215-9013	718-965-7300	965-7323	PK-12	71,400	Dr. Thomas Chadzutko
Diocese of Brownsville	700 N Virgen de San Juan	San Juan, TX	78589	956-787-8571	784-5081	PK-12	3,800	Sr. Marcella Ewers
Diocese of Buffalo	795 Main St	Buffalo, NY	14203-1250	716-847-5501	847-5593	PK-12	27,600	Diane Vigrass
Diocese of Burlington	PO Box 489	Burlington, VT	05402-0489	802-658-6110	860-0451	PK-12	3,700	Sr. Marie Kelly
Diocese of Camden	631 Market St	Camden, NJ	08102-1103	856-756-7900	756-0225	PK-12	21,700	Sr. Dawn Gear
Diocese of Charleston	1662 Ingram Rd	Charleston, SC	29407-4242	843-402-9115	402-7724	PK-12	8,000	Sr. Julia Hutchison
Diocese of Charlotte	1123 S Church St	Charlotte, NC	28203-4003	704-370-3270	370-3292	K-12	7,200	Linda L. Cherry
Diocese of Cheyenne	623 S Wolcott St	Casper, WY	82601-3157	307-237-2723	235-9157	PK-12	1,000	Ed McCarthy
Archdiocese of Chicago	PO Box 1979	Chicago, IL	60690-1979	312-751-5200	751-5295	PK-12	123,400	Dr. Nicholas Wolsonovich
Archdiocese of Cincinnati	100 E 8th St	Cincinnati, OH	45202-2129	513-421-3131	421-6271	PK-12	57,300	Br. Joseph Kamis
Diocese of Cleveland	1031 Superior Ave E	Cleveland, OH	44114-2513	216-696-6525	579-9655	PK-12	64,600	Margaret Lyons
Diocese of Colorado Springs	228 N Cascade Ave	Colorado Spgs, CO	80903-1324	719-636-2345	866-6453	PK-12	2,000	Michelle Maher
Diocese of Columbus	197 E Gay St	Columbus, OH	43215-3229	614-221-5829	241-2563	PK-12	19,900	Lucia McQuaide
Diocese of Corpus Christi	PO Box 2620	Corpus Christi, TX	78403-2620	361-882-6191	814-1831	PK-12	3,100	Rene Gonzalez
Diocese of Covington	PO Box 15550	Covington, KY	41015-0550	859-392-1530	392-1537	K-12	12,700	Dr. Lawrence Bowman
Diocese of Crookston	1200 Memorial Dr	Crookston, MN	56716-1134	218-281-4533	281-5991	PK-12	1,500	Sr. Pat Murphy
Diocese of Dallas	PO Box 190507	Dallas, TX	75219-0507	214-528-2360	522-1753	PK-12	15,000	Charles LeBlanc Ed.D.
Diocese of Davenport	2706 N Gaines St	Davenport, IA	52804-1998	563-324-1911	324-5811	PK-12	6,000	Mary Wieser
Archdiocese of Denver	1300 S Steele St	Denver, CO	80210-2599	303-715-3200	715-2042	PK-12	14,700	Richard Thompson
Diocese of Des Moines	601 Grand Ave	Des Moines, IA	50309-2501	515-237-5013	237-5070	PK-12	6,400	Luvern A. Gubbels Ed.D.
Archdiocese of Detroit	305 Michigan Ave	Detroit, MI	48226-2631	313-237-5775	237-5857	PK-12	53,200	Sr. Mary Gehringer
Diocese of Dodge City	910 Central Ave	Dodge City, KS	67801-4905	620-227-1500	227-1570	PK-8	1,500	Ann Depperschmidt
Archdiocese of Dubuque	1229 Mount Loretta Ave	Dubuque, IA	52003-8787	563-556-2580	556-5464	PK-12	15,800	Msgr. Thomas Toale Ph.D.
Diocese of Duluth	2830 E 4th St	Duluth, MN	55812-1501	218-724-9111	724-1056	PK-8	1,900	Cynthia Zook
Diocese of El Paso	499 Saint Matthews St	El Paso, TX	79907-4214	915-872-8426	872-8434	PK-12	4,800	Sr. Elizabeth Swartz
Diocese of Erie	PO Box 10397	Erie, PA	16514-0397	814-824-1241	824-1239	PK-12	13,700	Rev. John M. Schultz
Diocese of Evansville	PO Box 4169	Evansville, IN	47724-0169	812-424-5536	421-1334	PK-12	7,700	Phyllis Bussing Ph.D.
Diocese of Fairbanks	1316 Peger Rd	Fairbanks, AK	99709-5168	907-374-9500	374-9580	K-12	500	Rose Anne Sample
Diocese of Fall River	423 Highland Ave	Fall River, MA	02720-3718	508-678-2828	674-4218	PK-12	9,200	Dr. George A. Milot
Diocese of Fargo	5201 Bishops Blvd S Ste A	Fargo, ND	58104-7605	701-356-7900	356-7994	PK-12	2,200	Thomas Frei
Diocese of Fort Worth	800 W Loop 820 S	Fort Worth, TX	76108-2936	817-560-3300	244-8839	PK-12	7,100	Donald Miller
Diocese of Fresno	1510 N Fresno St	Fresno, CA	93703-3711	559-488-7420	488-7422	PK-12	7,000	Richard Sexton
Diocese of Ft. Wayne-South Bend	PO Box 390	Fort Wayne, IN	46801-0390	260-422-4611	426-3077	PK-12	15,100	Rev. Stephen Kempinger
Diocese of Gallup	PO Box 1338	Gallup, NM	87305-1338	505-863-4406	863-8150	PK-12	2,100	David Weimer
Diocese of Galveston-Houston	2403 Holcombe Blvd	Houston, TX	77021-2023	713-741-8704	741-7379	PK-12	17,900	Sally Landram
Diocese of Gary	9292 Broadway	Merrillville, IN	46410-7088	219-769-9292	738-9034	K-12	9,100	Kim Pryzbylski
Diocese of Gaylord	611 W North St	Gaylord, MI	49735-8349	989-732-5147	705-3589	PK-12	4,100	Michael Buell
Diocese of Grand Island	PO Box 996	Grand Island, NE	68802-0996	308-382-6565	382-6569	PK-12	1,800	Rev. Thomas Ryan
Diocese of Grand Rapids	600 Burton St SE	Grand Rapids, MI	49507-3202	616-243-0491	243-1442	PK-12	10,300	
Diocese of Great Falls-Billings	PO Box 31158	Billings, MT	59107-1158	406-252-9595	252-9875	PK-12	2,900	Sr. Jean Dawson
Diocese of Green Bay	PO Box 23825	Green Bay, WI	54305-3825	920-437-7531	437-0694	PK-12	15,500	Leland Nagel
Diocese of Greensburg	723 E Pittsburgh St	Greensburg, PA	15601-2697	724-836-1281	837-0857	PK-12	5,700	Sr. Gertrude Foley
Diocese of Harrisburg	PO Box 3553	Harrisburg, PA	17105-3553	717-657-4804	657-3790	PK-12	15,600	Sr. Sue Ann Steves
Archdiocese of Hartford	467 Bloomfield Ave	Bloomfield, CT	06002-2903	860-242-4362	242-8683	PK-12	22,900	Dr. Dale R. Hoyt
Diocese of Helena	PO Box 1729	Helena, MT	59624-1729	406-594-1461	327-8537	PK-12	1,100	Patrick Haggarty
Diocese of Honolulu	6301 Pali Hwy	Kaneohe, HI	96744-5224	808-263-8844	262-6126	PK-12	11,300	
Diocese of Houma-Thibodaux	PO Box 505	Schriever, LA	70395-0505	985-850-3113	850-3225	PK-12	6,000	Sr. Immaculata Paisant
Archdiocese of Indianapolis	PO Box 1410	Indianapolis, IN	46206-1410	317-236-1430	261-3364	PK-12	24,900	Annette Lentz
Diocese of Jackson	PO Box 2248	Jackson, MS	39225-2248	601-969-2742	960-8469	PK-12	5,100	Sr. Deborah Hughes
Diocese of Jefferson City	PO Box 104900	Jefferson City, MO	65110-4900	573-635-9127	635-2286	PK-12	7,300	Donald F. Novotney
Diocese of Joliet	402 S Independence Blvd	Romeoville, IL	60446-2264	815-838-2181	838-2182	PK-12	26,300	Sr. Helen Kormelink
Diocese of Juneau	415 6th St Ste 300	Juneau, AK	99801-1091	907-225-7400	247-0041	K-6	100	John Lepetit
Diocese of Kalamazoo	215 N Westnedge Ave	Kalamazoo, MI	49007-3718	269-349-8714	349-6440	PK-12	5,300	Dr. Frank Wippel
Archdiocese of Kansas City	12615 Parallel Ave	Kansas City, KS	66109-3748	913-721-1570	721-5598	PK-12	16,500	Dr. Kathleen O'Hara
Diocese of Kansas City-Saint Joseph	PO Box 419037	Kansas City, MO	64141-6037	816-756-1850	756-1571	PK-12	13,700	Dr. Judith Warren
Diocese of Knoxville	PO Box 11127	Knoxville, TN	37939-1127	865-584-3307	584-4319	PK-12	3,500	Dr. Sherry Morgan
Diocese of La Crosse	PO Box 4004	La Crosse, WI	54602-4004	608-788-7707	788-7709	PK-12	12,200	Diana Roberts
Diocese of Lafayette	2300 S 9th St	Lafayette, IN	47909-2400	765-474-6644	474-3403	PK-12	4,300	Dr. Lois Ann Meyer
Diocese of Lafayette	1408 Carmel Ave	Lafayette, LA	70501-5215	337-261-5529	261-5572	PK-12	14,900	Anna Larriviere
Diocese of Lake Charles	411 Iris St	Lake Charles, LA	70601-5234	337-439-7426	439-7428	PK-12	3,200	Michael Mathews
Diocese of Lansing	300 W Ottawa St	Lansing, MI	48933-1577	517-342-2482		PK-12	12,600	Sr. Dorita Wotiska
Diocese of Laredo	1901 Corpus Christi St	Laredo, TX	78043-3308	956-753-5208	753-5203	K-12	2,500	Dr. Rosa Maria Vida
Diocese of Las Cruces	1280 Med Park Dr	Las Cruces, NM	88005-3239	505-523-7577	524-3874	PK-8	700	Dr. David Garcia
Diocese of Las Vegas	PO Box 18316	Las Vegas, NV	89114-8316	702-697-5918	735-8941	K-12	3,600	Richard Facciolo Ed.D.
Diocese of Lexington	1310 W Main St	Lexington, KY	40508-2048	859-253-1993	254-6284	K-12	3,900	Sr. Bernadette McManigal
Diocese of Lincoln	PO Box 80328	Lincoln, NE	68501-0328	402-488-2040	488-6525	K-12	7,600	Rev. John Perkinton
Diocese of Little Rock	PO Box 7565	Little Rock, AR	72217-7565	501-664-0340	603-0518	K-12	8,700	Vernell Bowen M.Ed.
Archdiocese of Los Angeles	3424 Wilshire Blvd	Los Angeles, CA	90010-2241	213-637-7300	637-6140	PK-12	100,100	Nancy Coonis
Archdiocese of Louisville	1935 Lewiston Dr	Louisville, KY	40216-2523	502-448-8581	448-5518	PK-12	24,600	Leisa Speer
Diocese of Lubbock	4620 4th St	Lubbock, TX	79416-4726	806-792-3943	792-8109	PK-9	400	Roberta Meyer
Diocese of Madison	PO Box 44983	Madison, WI	53744-4983	608-821-3180	821-3181	PK-12	8,000	James Silver Ed.D.
Diocese of Manchester	PO Box 310	Manchester, NH	03105-0310	603-669-3100	669-0377	PK-12	10,600	Mary Moran
Diocese of Marquette	PO Box 1000	Marquette, MI	49855-1000	906-227-9127	225-0437	PK-8	1,600	Gloria Kalbfleisch
Diocese of Memphis	5825 Shelby Oaks Dr	Memphis, TN	38134-7316	901-373-1219	373-1223	PK-12	6,900	Dr. Mary McDonald
Diocese of Metuchen	PO Box 191	Metuchen, NJ	08840-0191	732-562-1990	562-1016	PK-12	17,200	Msgr. Michael J. Corona
Archdiocese of Miami	9401 Biscayne Blvd	Miami Shores, FL	33138-2970	305-762-1076	762-1115	PK-12	38,400	Br. Richard DeMaria

Archdiocese/Diocese	Address	City,State	Zip code	Telephone	Fax	Grade	Enr	Superintendent
Archdiocese of Milwaukee	PO Box 070912	Milwaukee, WI	53207-0912	414-769-3300	769-3408	PK-12	39,800	Br. Bob Smith
Diocese of Mobile	PO Box 129	Mobile, AL	36601-0129	251-438-4611	438-4612	PK-12	6,900	Gwen Byrd
Diocese of Monterey	485 Church St	Monterey, CA	93940-3207	831-373-1608	373-0173	PK-12	5,800	Jack Marchi Ph.D.
Diocese of Nashville	30 White Bridge Rd	Nashville, TN	37205-1401	615-352-7218	353-7972	PK-12	6,200	Dr. Therese Williams
Archdiocese of Newark	PO Box 9500	Newark, NJ	07104-0500	973-497-4260	497-4249	PK-12	59,100	Sr. Dominica Rocchio
Archdiocese of New Orleans	7887 Walmsley Ave	New Orleans, LA	70125-3496	504-866-7916	861-6260	PK-12	52,400	Rev. William Maestri
Diocese of New Ulm	1400 6th St N	New Ulm, MN	56073-2057	507-359-2966	354-3667	PK-12	3,400	Wayne Pelzel
Archdiocese of New York	1011 1st Ave	New York, NY	10022-4112	212-371-1000	317-9236	PK-12	111,000	Dr. Catherine Hickey
Diocese of Norwich	43 Perkins Ave	Norwich, CT	06360-3643	860-887-4086	887-9371	PK-12	7,000	Sr. Joan O'Connor
Diocese of Oakland	3014 Lakeshore Ave	Oakland, CA	94610-3615	510-628-2154	451-5331	PK-12	21,500	Mark DeMarco
Diocese of Ogdensburg	PO Box 369	Ogdensburg, NY	13669-0369	315-393-2920	393-8977	PK-12	3,800	Sr. Ellen Coughlin
Archdiocese of Oklahoma City	PO Box 32180	Oklahoma City, OK	73123-0380	405-721-5651	709-2811	PK-12	5,200	Sr. Catherine Powers
Archdiocese of Omaha	PO Box 4130	Omaha, NE	68104-0130	402-554-8493	827-3792	PK-12	22,300	Sr. Michelle Faltus
Diocese of Orange	PO Box 14195	Orange, CA	92863-1595	714-282-3055	282-5059	PK-12	20,800	Rev. Gerald Horan
Diocese of Orlando	PO Box 1800	Orlando, FL	32802-1800	407-246-4900	246-4940	PK-12	15,800	Dr. Harry Purpur
Diocese of Owensboro	600 Locust St	Owensboro, KY	42301-2130	270-683-1545	683-6883	K-12	5,300	Jim Mattingly
Diocese of Palm Beach	PO Box 109650	Palm Bch Gdns, FL	33410-9650	561-775-9547	775-9545	PK-12	8,500	Sr. Joan Dawson
Diocese of Paterson	777 Valley Rd	Clifton, NJ	07013-2297	973-777-8818	779-0083	PK-12	20,800	Dr. Frank Petrucelli
Diocese of Pensacola-Tallahassee	PO Box 17329	Pensacola, FL	32522-7329	850-435-3500	436-6424	PK-12	3,700	Susan Jones Mueller
Diocese of Peoria	412 NE Madison Ave	Peoria, IL	61603-3720	309-671-1579	671-1595	PK-12	15,500	Br. William Dygert
Archdiocese of Philadelphia	222 N 17th St	Philadelphia, PA	19103-1295	215-587-3700	587-5644	PK-12	120,300	Dr. Thomas F. O'Brien
Diocese of Phoenix	400 E Monroe St	Phoenix, AZ	85004-2336	602-354-2345	354-2436	PK-12	13,300	MaryBeth Mueller
Diocese of Pittsburgh	111 Blvd Of The Allies	Pittsburgh, PA	15222-1618	412-456-3090	456-3098	PK-12	32,700	Dr. Robert Paserba
Archdiocese of Portland	2838 E Burnside St	Portland, OR	97214-1895	503-233-8300	236-3683	PK-12	14,500	Robert Mizia
Diocese of Portland	PO Box 11559	Portland, ME	04104-7559	207-773-6471	773-0182	PK-12	5,300	Sr. Rosemary Donohue
Diocese of Providence	1 Cathedral Sq	Providence, RI	02903-3695	401-278-4550	278-4596	PK-12	19,100	Sheila Durante
Diocese of Pueblo	1001 N Grand Ave	Pueblo, CO	81003-2915	719-544-9861	544-5202	PK-12	1,300	Sr. Betty Werner
Diocese of Raleigh	715 Nazareth St	Raleigh, NC	27606-2187	919-821-9749	821-8140	PK-12	8,300	Michael Fedewa
Diocese of Rapid City	300 Fairmont Blvd	Rapid City, SD	57701-5423	605-343-3541	348-7985	K-12	1,400	
Diocese of Reno	290 S Arlington Ave Ste 200	Reno, NV	89501-1713	775-326-9430	348-8619	PK-12	1,900	Kitty Bergin
Diocese of Richmond	811 S Cathedral Pl #A	Richmond, VA	23220-4800	804-359-5661	358-9159	PK-12	11,200	John Elcesser
Diocese of Rochester	1150 Buffalo Rd	Rochester, NY	14624-1890	585-328-3228	328-3149	PK-12	16,900	Sr. Elizabeth Meegan Ph.D.
Diocese of Rockford	PO Box 7044	Rockford, IL	61125-7044	815-399-4300	399-6278	PK-12	16,300	Sr. Patricia Downey
Diocese of Rockville Center	PO Box 9023	Rockville Ctr, NY	11571-9023	516-678-5800	678-7362	PK-12	40,000	Sr. Joanne Callahan
Diocese of Sacramento	2110 Broadway	Sacramento, CA	95818-2518	916-733-0110	733-0120	PK-12	17,200	Domenic Puglisi
Diocese of Saginaw	5800 Weiss St	Saginaw, MI	48603-2799	989-799-7910	797-6645	PK-12	5,300	Barbara Geary
Diocese of St. Augustine	11625 Saint Augustine Rd	Jacksonville, FL	32258-2056	904-262-3200	596-1042	PK-12	9,700	Patricia Tierney
Diocese of St. Cloud	305 7th Ave N Ste 201	Saint Cloud, MN	56303-3633	320-251-0111	251-0259	PK-12	6,700	Linda Kaiser
Archdiocese of St. Louis	20 Archbishop May Dr	Saint Louis, MO	63119-5738	314-792-7300	792-7350	PK-12	57,800	George Henry
Archdiocese of St. Paul	328 Kellogg Blvd W	Saint Paul, MN	55102-1900	651-291-4498	290-1628	PK-12	36,700	Dr. Lori Glynn
Diocese of St. Petersburg	PO Box 40200	St Petersburg, FL	33743-0200	727-347-5539	374-0209	PK-12	15,400	Br. John L. Cummings
Diocese of Salina	PO Box 825	Salina, KS	67402-0825	785-827-8746	827-6133	PK-12	2,700	Dr. Nick Compagnone
Diocese of Salt Lake City	27 C St	Salt Lake City, UT	84103-2302	801-328-8641	328-9680	PK-12	5,400	Sr. Catherine Kamphaus
Diocese of San Angelo	PO Box 1829	San Angelo, TX	76902-1829	325-651-7500	651-6688	PK-8	800	Sr. Elizabeth Ann Swartz
Archdiocese of San Antonio	2718 W Woodlawn Ave	San Antonio, TX	78228-5195	210-734-2620	734-9112	PK-12	15,900	Sr. Carla Marie Lusch
Diocese of San Bernardino	1201 E Highland Ave	San Bernardino, CA	92404-4607	909-475-5437	475-5477	PK-12	9,300	Sr. Sara Kane
Diocese of San Diego	PO Box 85728	San Diego, CA	92186-5728	858-490-8240	490-8272	PK-12	17,800	Thomas Beecher
Archdiocese of San Francisco	1 Peter Yorke Way	San Francisco, CA	94109-6602	415-614-5660	614-5664	PK-12	29,400	Maureen Huntington
Diocese of San Jose	900 Lafayette St Ste 301	Santa Clara, CA	95050-4966	408-983-0185	983-0192	PK-12	16,600	Marian Stuckey
Archdiocese of Santa Fe	4000 Saint Josephs Pl NW	Albuquerque, NM	87120-1714	505-831-8173	831-8107	PK-12	5,800	Sr. Mary Klersey M.P.
Diocese of Santa Rosa	PO Box 6654	Santa Rosa, CA	95406-0654	707-566-3311	566-3382	PK-12	5,000	Dr. John Collins
Diocese of Savannah	601 E Liberty St	Savannah, GA	31401-5118	912-201-4121	201-4101	K-12	6,700	Sr. Rose Mary Collins
Diocese of Scranton	300 Wyoming Ave	Scranton, PA	18503-1243	570-207-2251	207-2261	PK-12	16,500	Joseph Casciano
Archdiocese of Seattle	910 Marion St	Seattle, WA	98104-1274	206-382-4861	654-4651	PK-12	22,300	Sr. Joyce M. Cox Ph.D.
Diocese of Shreveport	3500 Fairfield Ave	Shreveport, LA	71104-4108	318-219-7253	868-5057	PK-12	2,800	Sr. Carol Shively
Diocese of Sioux City	PO Box 3379	Sioux City, IA	51102-3379	712-255-7933	233-7598	PK-12	7,500	Kevin Vickery
Diocese of Sioux Falls	523 N Duluth Ave	Sioux Falls, SD	57104-2714	605-988-3766	988-3795	PK-12	5,400	Sr. Nathalie Meyer
Diocese of Spokane	PO Box 1453	Spokane, WA	99210-1453	509-358-7330	358-7302	PK-12	4,800	Duane Schafer Ph.D.
Diocese of Springfield-Cape Girardeau	601 S Jefferson Ave	Springfield, MO	65806-3107	417-866-0841	866-1140	PK-12	4,700	Leon Witt
Diocese of Springfield	PO Box 3187	Springfield, IL	62708-3187	217-698-8500	698-8620	PK-12	13,800	Rose Mersinger
Diocese of Springfield	PO Box 1730	Springfield, MA	01102-1730	413-452-0830	732-4297	PK-12	8,800	Sr. M. Andrea Ciszewski
Diocese of Steubenville	PO Box 969	Steubenville, OH	43952-5969	740-282-3631	282-3327	PK-12	3,400	Dr. Peter Chila
Diocese of Stockton	1105 N Lincoln St	Stockton, CA	95203-2410	209-466-0636	941-9722	PK-12	4,800	Sr. Marian Clare Valenteen
Diocese of Superior	PO Box 969	Superior, WI	54880-0017	715-392-1042	392-2015	PK-8	3,200	Phyllis Schlagel
Diocese of Syracuse	PO Box 511	Syracuse, NY	13201-0511	315-470-1450	470-1470	PK-12	11,900	John Cataldo
Diocese of Toledo	PO Box 985	Toledo, OH	43697-0985	419-244-6711	255-8269	PK-12	30,500	Jack Altenburger
Diocese of Trenton	PO Box 5147	Trenton, NJ	08638-0147	609-406-7400	406-7416	PK-12	26,500	Judith Caviston Ed.D.
Diocese of Tucson	PO Box 31	Tucson, AZ	85702-0031	520-792-3410	838-2589	PK-12	7,000	Sr. Rosa Maria Ruiz
Diocese of Tulsa	820 S Boulder Ave	Tulsa, OK	74119-1624	918-582-9177	582-1851	PK-12	4,700	Todd C. Goldsmith
Diocese of Tyler	1015 E Southeast Loop 323	Tyler, TX	75701-9656	903-534-1077	534-1370	PK-12	800	Dr. C. Charles LeBlanc
Diocese of Venice	1000 Pinebrook Rd	Venice, FL	34285-6426	941-484-9543	484-1121	PK-12	5,200	Rosemary Bratton
Diocese of Victoria	PO Box 4070	Victoria, TX	77903-4070	361-573-0828	573-5725	PK-12	3,500	Sr. Gloria Cain
Archdiocese of Washington DC	PO Box 29260	Washington, DC	20017-0260	301-853-4518	853-7670	PK-12	33,500	Patricia O'Neill Ph.D.
Diocese of Wheeling-Charleston	PO Box 230	Wheeling, WV	26003-0010	304-233-0444	233-8551	PK-12	6,700	John Yelenic
Diocese of Wichita	424 N Broadway St	Wichita, KS	67202-2310	316-269-3950	269-2486	PK-12	10,200	Bob Voboril
Diocese of Wilmington	1626 N Union St	Wilmington, DE	19806-2540	302-573-3133	573-3143	PK-12	16,000	Br. James Malone
Diocese of Winona	PO Box 588	Winona, MN	55987-0588	507-454-4643	454-8106	PK-12	6,700	P.J. Thompson
Diocese of Worcester	49 Elm St	Worcester, MA	01609-2514	508-929-4317	929-4386	PK-12	10,300	Stephen Perla
Diocese of Yakima	5301 Tieton Dr Ste B	Yakima, WA	98908-3479	509-965-7110	966-0596	PK-12	2,000	Cathy Colver
Diocese of Youngstown	144 W Wood St	Youngstown, OH	44503-1030	330-744-8451	744-5099	K-12	15,300	Dr. Michael Skube

LUTHERAN SCHOOL SUPERINTENDENTS

LUTHERAN CHURCH MISSOURI SYNOD
1333 S Kirkwood Rd, Saint Louis, MO 63122-7295
Telephone 314-965-9000
Fax 822-8307
Website http://www.lcms.org

LUTHERAN SCHOOL SUPERINTENDENTS

Region	Address	City,State	Zip code	Telephone	Fax	Superintendent
Atlantic	171 White Plains Rd	Bronxville, NY	10708-1923	914-337-5700	337-7471	
California-Nevada-Hawaii	2772 Constitution Dr Ste A	Livermore, CA	94551-7571	925-245-4000	245-1107	
Central Illinois	PO Box 7003	Springfield, IL	62791-7003	217-793-1802	793-1822	
Eastern	5111 Main St	Williamsville, NY	14221-5203	716-634-5111	634-5452	
English	33100 Freedom Rd	Farmington, MI	48336-4030	248-476-0039	476-0188	
Florida-Georgia	7207 Monetary Dr	Orlando, FL	32809-5753	407-857-5556	857-5665	
Indiana	1145 Barr St	Fort Wayne, IN	46802-3135	800-837-1145	423-1514	
Iowa East	1100 Blairs Ferry Rd	Marion, IA	52302-3093	319-373-2112	373-9827	
Iowa West	PO Box 1155	Fort Dodge, IA	50501-1155	515-576-7666	576-2323	
Kansas	1000 SW 10th Ave	Topeka, KS	66604-1104	785-357-4441	357-5071	
Michigan	3773 Geddes Rd	Ann Arbor, MI	48105-3028	734-665-3791	665-0255	
Mid-South	1675 Wynne Rd	Cordova, TN	38016-4905	901-373-1343	373-4826	
Minnesota North	PO Box 604	Brainerd, MN	56401-0604	218-829-1781	829-0037	
Minnesota South	14301 Grand Ave	Burnsville, MN	55306-5790	952-435-2550	435-2581	
Missouri	660 Msn Ridge Cntr Dr #100	Saint Louis, MO	63141	314-317-4550	317-4575	
Montana	30 Broadwater Ave	Billings, MT	59101-1826	406-259-2908	259-1305	
Nebraska	PO Box 407	Seward, NE	68434-0407	402-643-2961	643-2990	
New England	400 Wilbraham Rd	Springfield, MA	01109-2723	413-783-0131	783-0909	
New Jersey	1168 Springfield Ave	Mountainside, NJ	07092-2906	908-233-8111	233-3883	

Region	Address	City,State	Zip code	Telephone	Fax	Superintendent
North Dakota	PO Box 9029	Fargo, ND	58106-9029	701-293-9001	293-9022	
Northern Illinois	2301 S Wolf Rd	Hillside, IL	60162-2221	708-449-3020	449-3026	
Northwest	1700 NE Knott St	Portland, OR	97212-3301	503-288-8383	284-2785	
North Wisconsin	PO Box 8064	Wausau, WI	54402-8064	715-845-8241	845-3836	
Ohio	PO Box 38277	Olmsted Falls, OH	44138-0277	440-235-2297	235-1970	
Oklahoma	1032 NW 12th St	Moore, OK	73160-1604	405-912-5847	912-5829	
Pacific Southwest	1540 Concordia	Irvine, CA	92612-3203	949-854-3232	854-8140	
Rocky Mountain	14334 E Evans Ave	Aurora, CO	80014-1408	303-695-8001	695-4047	
SELC	4850 S Lake Dr	Cudahy, WI	53110-1743	414-481-8286	481-0736	
South Dakota	PO Box 89110	Sioux Falls, SD	57109-9110	605-361-1514	361-7959	
Southeastern	6315 Grovedale Dr	Alexandria, VA	22310-2501	703-971-9371	922-6047	
Southern	PO Box 8396	New Orleans, LA	70182-8396	504-282-2632	283-4885	
Southern Illinois	2408 Lebanon Ave	Belleville, IL	62221-2529	618-234-4767	234-4830	
South Wisconsin	8100 W Capitol Dr	Milwaukee, WI	53222-1981	414-464-8100	464-0602	
Texas	7900 E Highway 290	Austin, TX	78724-2402	512-926-4272	926-1006	
Wyoming	2400 S Hickory St	Casper, WY	82604-3471	307-265-9000	234-6629	

GENERAL CONFERENCE OF SEVENTH-DAY ADVENTISTS SUPERINTENDENTS

NORTH AMERICAN DIV. OFFICE OF EDUCATION
12501 Old Columbia Pike, Silver Spring, MD 20904-6601
Telephone 301-680-6440
Fax 680-6463
Website http://www.nadeducation.adventist.org

GENERAL CONFERENCE OF SEVENTH-DAY ADVENTISTS SUPERINTENDENTS

Conference	Address	City,State	Zip code	Telephone	Fax	Superintendent
Atlantic Union	PO Box 1189	South Lancaster, MA	01561-1189	978-368-8333	368-7948	Astrid Thomassian
Greater New York Conference	PO Box 5029	Manhasset, NY	11030-5029	516-627-9350	627-9272	Dioniso Olivo
New York Conference	4930 W Seneca Tpke	Syracuse, NY	13215-2225	315-469-6921	469-6924	Stan Rouse M.A.
Northeastern Conference	11550 Merrick Blvd	Jamaica, NY	11434-1852	718-291-8006	739-5133	Pollyanna Barnes Ph.D.
Northern New England Conference	91 Allen Ave	Portland, ME	04103-3710	207-797-3760	797-2851	Trudy Wright M.A.
Southern New England Conference	PO Box 1169	South Lancaster, MA	01561-1169	978-365-4551	365-3838	Gary Swinyar
Columbia Union Conference	5427 Twin Knolls Rd	Columbia, MD	21045-3200	410-997-3414	997-7420	Hamlet Canosa
Allegheny East Conference	PO Box 266	Pine Forge, PA	19548-0266	610-326-4610	326-3946	James P. Willis M.Ed.
Allegheny West Conference	1339 E Broad St	Columbus, OH	43205-1588	614-252-5271	252-3246	Jerome Hurst B.S.
Chesapeake Conference	6600 Martin Rd	Columbia, MD	21044-3999	410-995-1910	995-1434	Carole Smith Ed.D.
Mountain View Conference	1400 Liberty St	Parkersburg, WV	26101-4124	304-422-4581	422-4582	Kingsley Whitsett
New Jersey Conference	2160 US Highway 1	Trenton, NJ	08648-4489	609-392-7131	396-9273	David Cadavero M.A.
Ohio Conference	PO Box 1230	Mount Vernon, OH	43050-8230	740-397-4665	397-1648	E. Jay Colburn
Pennsylvania Conference	720 Museum Rd	Reading, PA	19611-1429	610-374-8331	374-9331	Vaughn Jennings
Potomac Conference	606 Greenville Ave	Staunton, VA	24401-4881	540-886-0771	886-5734	Larry D. Marsh M.Ed.
Lake Union Conference	PO Box C	Berrien Springs, MI	49103-0904	269-473-8200	473-8272	Gary Randolph
Illinois Conference	619 Plainfield Rd	Willowbrook, IL	60527-8437	630-734-0920	734-0929	James Martz
Indiana Conference	PO Box 1950	Carmel, IN	46082-1950	317-844-6201	571-9281	Archie Moore M.A.
Lake Region Conference	8517 S State St	Chicago, IL	60619-5697	773-846-2661	846-5309	Edward Woods
Michigan Conference	PO Box 19009	Lansing, MI	48901-9009	517-316-1500	316-1501	Duane Roush M.A.
Wisconsin Conference	PO Box 7310	Madison, WI	53707-7310	608-241-5236	837-9421	Kenneth Kirkham M.A.
Mid-America Union Conference	PO Box 6128	Lincoln, NE	68506-0128	402-484-3000	483-4453	Ronald Russell M.Ed.
Central States Conference	3301 Parallel Pkwy	Kansas City, KS	66104-4354	913-371-1071	371-1609	Desiree Bryant M.A.
Dakota Conference	PO Box 520	Pierre, SD	57501-0520	605-224-8868	224-7886	Janell Hurst
Iowa-Missouri Conference	PO Box 65665	West Des Moines, IA	50265-0665	515-223-3556	223-5692	Gary Rouse M.A.
Kansas-Nebraska Conference	3440 SW Urish Rd	Topeka, KS	66614-4601	785-478-4726	478-1000	Chuck Castle M.A.
Minnesota Conference	7384 Kirkwood Ct	Maple Grove, MN	55369-5200	763-424-8923	424-9576	Pamela Consuegra M.A.
Rocky Mountain Conference	2520 S Downing St	Denver, CO	80210-5818	303-282-3650	733-1843	Lonnie Hetterle B.A.
North Pacific Union Conference	PO Box 871150	Vancouver, WA	98687-1150	360-816-1400	816-1401	Alan Hurlbert M.Ed.
Alaska Conference	6100 OMalley Rd	Anchorage, AK	99507-6958	907-346-1004	346-3279	John Kriegelstein M.Ed.
Idaho Conference	7777 W Fairview Ave	Boise, ID	83704-8418	208-375-7524	375-7526	Arne Nielsen
Montana Conference	175 Canyon View Rd	Bozeman, MT	59715-0607	406-587-3101	587-1598	
Oregon Conference	13455 SE 97th Ave	Clackamas, OR	97015-8662	503-652-2225	794-4286	John Gatchet M.Ed.
Upper Columbia Conference	PO Box 19039	Spokane, WA	99219-9039	509-838-2761	838-4882	Keith Waters M.S.
Washington Conference	3450 S 344th Way Ste 200	Federal Way, WA	98001-9540	253-681-6008	681-6009	Lon Gruesbeck M.A.
Pacific Union Conference	PO Box 5005	Westlake Vlg, CA	91359-5005	805-413-7314	413-7319	Dr. Kelly Bock
Arizona Conference	PO Box 12340	Scottsdale, AZ	85267-2340	480-991-6777	991-4833	Ivan E. Weiss M.A.
Central California Conference	PO Box 770	Clovis, CA	93613-0770	559-347-3000	347-3054	DeVerne Biloff M.A.
Hawaii Conference	2728 Pali Hwy	Honolulu, HI	96817-1428	808-595-7591	595-2345	Deloris Trujillo M.Ed.
Nevada-Utah Conference	PO Box 10730	Reno, NV	89510-0730	775-322-6929	954-0005	Larry Unterseher
Northern California Conference	PO Box 23165	Pleasant Hill, CA	94523-0165	925-685-4300	685-2014	Berit VonPohle
Southeastern California Conference	PO Box 8050	Riverside, CA	92515-8050	951-509-2200	509-2392	Donald Dudley
Southern California Conference	PO Box 969	Glendale, CA	91209-0969	818-546-8400	546-8454	Richard Carey
Southern Union Conference	PO Box 849	Decatur, GA	30031-0849	404-299-1832	299-9726	Conrad Gill M.A.
Carolina Conference	PO Box 560339	Charlotte, NC	28256-0339	704-596-3200	596-5775	Robert Crux
Florida Conference	PO Box 2626	Winter Park, FL	32790-2626	407-644-5000	644-7550	Jim Epperson Ed.D.
Georgia-Cumberland Conference	PO Box 12000	Calhoun, GA	30703-7001	706-629-7951	526-3684	Cynthia Gettys Ph.D.
Gulf States Conference	PO Box 240249	Montgomery, AL	36124-0249	334-272-7493	272-7987	Leslie Louis M.A.
Kentucky-Tennessee Conference	PO Box 1088	Goodlettsville, TN	37070-1088	615-859-1391	859-2120	Larry Boughman Ph.D.
South Atlantic Conference	PO Box 92447	Atlanta, GA	30314-0447	404-792-0535	792-7817	Pennie Lister-Archie
South Central Conference	715 Youngs Ln	Nashville, TN	37207-4898	615-226-6500	262-9141	Auldwin Humphrey
Southeastern Conference	PO Box 160067	Altamonte Spg, FL	32716-0067	352-735-3142	735-4547	Elisa Young
Southwestern Union Conference	PO Box 4000	Burleson, TX	76097-1630	817-295-0476	447-2443	Doug Walker M.A.
Arkansas-Louisiana Conference	PO Box 31000	Shreveport, LA	71130-1000	318-631-6240	631-6247	Don Hevener M.A.
Oklahoma Conference	PO Box 32098	Oklahoma City, OK	73123-0298	405-721-6110	721-7594	Jack Francisco M.A.
Southwest Region Conference	PO Box 226289	Dallas, TX	75222-6289	214-943-4491	946-2528	Frank Jones
Texas Conference	PO Box 800	Alvarado, TX	76009-0800	817-783-2223	783-5266	Bonnie Eder Ed.D.
Texico Conference	PO Box 1366	Corrales, NM	87048-1366	505-244-1611	244-1811	Chuck Workman M.A.

Patterson's
SCHOOLS CLASSIFIED

Part II

POST-SECONDARY SCHOOLS

HOW TO USE PATTERSON'S SCHOOLS CLASSIFIED

Patterson's SCHOOLS CLASSIFIED contains the broadest assortment of post-secondary schools available in any single directory. More than 7,000 post-secondary schools, accredited by the organizations shown below, are classified by school type and academic discipline.

The basic listing for the School Classification contains the school name, mailing address, contact person and phone number needed for supplementary information or registration details. Many of the listings are in larger type or contain additional descriptive material supplied by the school. The student should interpret the added emphasis as an indication of the school's desire to attract qualified students. Listings are arranged alphabetically within each classification, first by state and then by school name.

In addition to our regular editorial work, each school has been contacted within the past twelve months to verify names, addresses, academic subjects covered and degrees offered. The contributions of the responding schools is sincerely appreciated.

11 Institutional Accrediting Organizations

Accrediting Association of Bible Colleges
Accrediting Commission of Career
  Schools/Colleges of Technology
Accrediting Council for Independent Colleges
  and Schools
Association of Advanced Rabbinical &
  Talmudic Schools
Association of Theological Schools in the
  USA & Canada
Middle States Association of
  Colleges & Schools
New England Association of Schools &
  Colleges
North Central Association of Colleges &
  Schools
Northwest Association of Schools & Colleges
Southern Association of Colleges & Schools
Western Association of Schools & Colleges

40 Professional and Specialized Accrediting Organizations

Accreditation Board for Engineering &
  Technology
Accrediting Bureau of Health Education
  Schools
Accrediting Commission on Education for
  Health Services Administration
Accrediting Council on Education in
  Journalism & Mass Communication
American Association of Family and
  Consumer Sciences
American Bar Association
American Board of Funeral Service Education
American Council for Construction Education
American Council on Pharmaceutical
  Education
American Dental Association
American Dietetic Association
American Institute of Certified Planners
American Library Association
American Optometric Association
American Osteopathic Association
American Physical Therapy Association
American Podiatric Medical Association
American Psychological Association
American Society of Landscape Architects
American Speech-Language-Hearing
  Association
American Veterinary Medical Association
Association of American Law Schools
Association to Advance Collegiate Schools of
  Business
Computer Science Accreditation Commission
Council for Accreditation of Counseling &
  Related Educational Programs
Council on Chiropractic Education
Council on Education for Public Health
Council on Occupational Education
Council on Rehabilitation Education
Council on Social Work Education
Foundation for Interior Design Education
  Research
Liaison Committee on Medical Education
National Architectural Accrediting Board
National Association of Schools of Art &
  Design
National Association of Schools of Music
National Association of Schools of Public
  Affairs & Administration
National Council for Accreditation of Teacher
  Education
National League for Nursing
National Recreation & Park Association
Society of American Foresters

SCHOOL CLASSIFICATIONS

If you are interested in a particular type of school, such as a **Career School** or a **Community** or **Junior College**, go directly to that classification and you will find a listing of accredited schools.

If you are looking for a particular school by name go to the index where you will find an alphabetical listing of the schools contained in this book along with the state abbreviation and classification code. Refer to page 953 for an explanation of how the index works.

ACADEMIC CLASSIFICATIONS

Academic Classifications cover the major areas of study selected by more than 90% of secondary students. Once the student has selected a major, reference to that classification will direct him to an appropriate selection of schools.

Academic Classifications offered by a relatively small number of schools, such as **Architecture** and **Engineering** are intended to be complete at the Baccalaureate level. However, to list every school under every possible classification would make the directory so large as to be a disservice to the student. **Music**, for example, is taught in one form or another by virtually every school.

Music listings include all schools approved by the National Association of Schools of Music. They do not, however, include all of the schools that offer degrees in music. The reader should recognize that the omission of a school from such disciplines as **Music**, **Liberal Arts and Sciences** or **Business and Management** is not a failure in editorial content but, an effort to reduce redundancy.

Inclusion in Academic Classifications of schools below the Baccalaureate Degree is progressively more selective. For a broader selection, the student may choose to contact schools from a School Classification.

COMMINGLED SCHOOLS IN ACADEMIC CLASSIFICATIONS

A special feature of this book is the commingling of colleges, community and junior colleges and career schools in Academic Classifications. The student considering further education is exposed to a wide range of educational opportunities without the need for multiple directories. In all cases listings for schools which offer less than a Baccalaureate Degree are identified by a symbol to the left of the school name to help the reader quickly identify the highest degree, diploma or certificate offered. See page 677.

GUIDE TO EDITORIAL STYLE

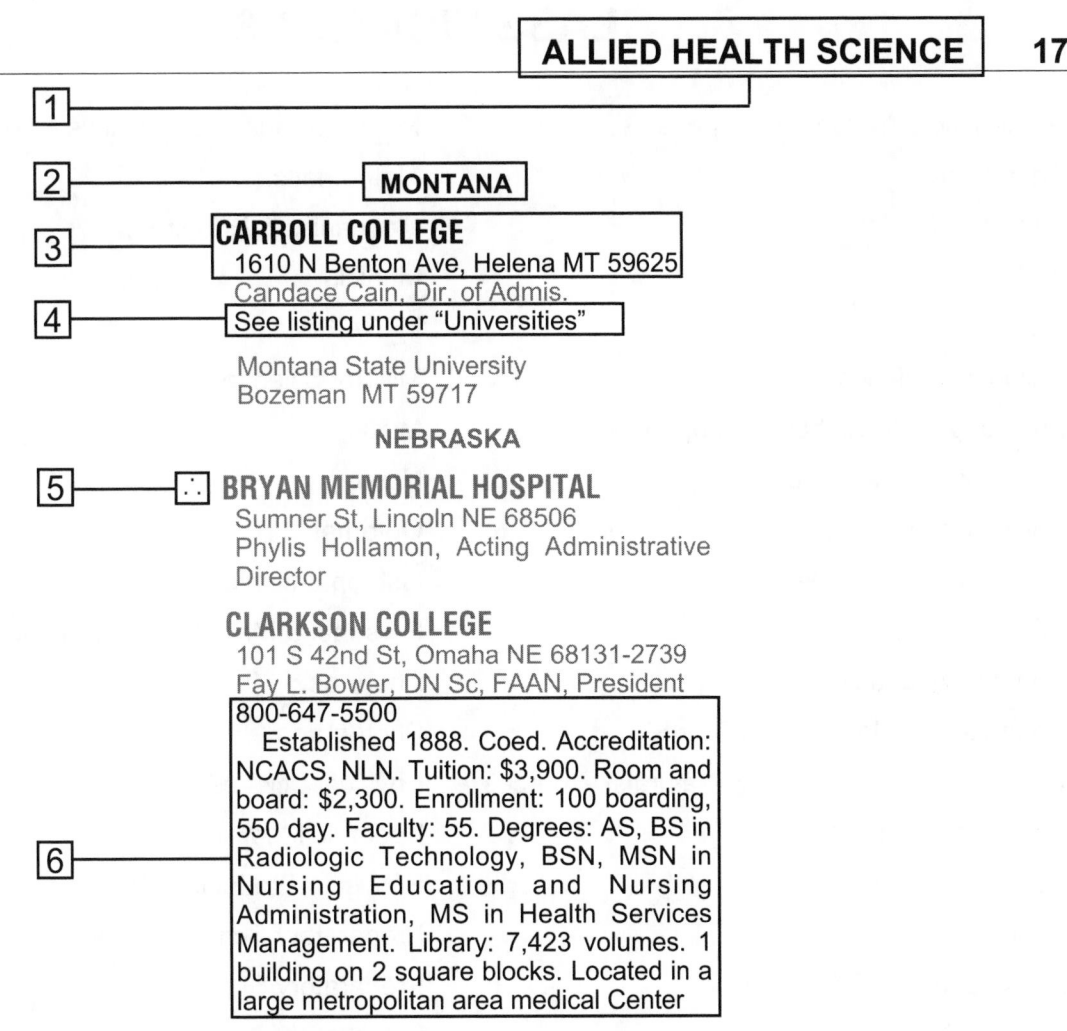

1. Classification and page number.
2. State (in alphabetical sequence within each classification).
3. School name and address (in alphabetical sequence within each state).
4. Cross reference line (to direct the reader's attention to a school's larger listing in a different classification).
5. School type code (identifies school type if below the baccalaureate degree in academic classifications).

· Community and Junior Colleges	: : Preparatory Schools
: Career Schools	∴: Handicapped Schools
∴· Teaching Hospitals	∷ Home Study Schools

6. Supplemental information provided by the school.

CLASSIFICATIONS

Aeronautics, Aviation and Space

Agriculture

Allied Health Science

Architecture

Art

Biological Science

Business - Administrative Support

Business and Management

Career Schools

Chiropractic Medicine

Communications

Community and Junior Colleges

Computer and Information Science

Conservation & Renewable Natural Resources

Construction Trades

Dentistry

Engineering

Engineering Technology

Ethnic Studies

Fashion Art

Graduate Schools

Handicapped, Schools for the

Home Economics

Home Study and Correspondence

Interior Design

Landscape Architecture

Law

Letters

Liberal Arts and Sciences

Library Science

Marketing and Distribution

Master of Business Administration

Mathematics

Mechanics & Repairers

Medicine

Men's Colleges

Military Science

Music

Nursing

Optometry

Osteopathic Medicine

Personal & Miscellaneous Services

Pharmacy

Photography

Physical Science

Podiatric Medicine

Precision Production Trades

Preparatory Schools for Boys

Preparatory Schools - Coeducational

Preparatory Schools for Girls

Protective Services

Psychology

Public Health

Social Science

Speech and Drama

Study Abroad

Summer Sessions

Teacher Education

Theological Studies & Religious Vocations

Universities and Colleges

Veterinary Medicine

Women's Colleges

Women's Studies

AERONAUTICS, AVIATION AND SPACE

ALABAMA

CALHOUN COMMUNITY COLLEGE
PO Box 2216, Decatur AL 35609-2216
M. Wayne Tosh, Registrar
256-306-2500 Fax: 256-306-2941
Website: www.calhoun.edu
E-mail: rls@calhoun.edu
See listing under "Community and Junior Colleges"

ALASKA

University of Alaska Anchorage
PO Box 141629, Anchorage AK 99514-1629
Cecile Mitchell, Director of Enrollment Services
907-786-1480 Fax: 907-786-4888
Website: www.uaa.alaska.edu/
E-mail: enroll@uaa.alaska.edu

ARIZONA

University of Arizona
Tucson AZ 85721-0040
Paul Kohn, Director of Admissions
520-621-3237 Fax: 520-621-9799
Website: www.admissions.arizona.edu or
www.arizona.edu

CALIFORNIA

Orange Coast College
PO Box 5005, Costa Mesa CA 92628-5005
Kristin Clark, Director of Admissions
714-432-5773 Fax: 714-432-5736
Website: www.orangecoastcollege.edu
E-mail: kclark@cccd.edu

San Diego Christian College
2100 Greenfield Dr, El Cajon CA 92019-1157
Jon Melone, Director of Admissions
800-676-2242 Fax: 619-590-1739
Website: www.sdcc.edu
E-mail: admissions@sdcc.edu

San Joaquin Valley College
Fresno Aviation Campus
4985 E Anderson Ave, Fresno CA 93727-1501
Joseph Holt, Director of Admissions
559-453-0123 Fax: 559-651-4864
Website: www.sjvc.edu
E-mail: josephh@sjvc.edu

FLORIDA

EVERGLADES UNIVERSITY (MAIN CAMPUS)
5002 T-Rex Ave Suite 100, Boca Raton FL 33431
Kristi Mollis, President
888-772-6077 Fax: 561-912-1191
Website: www.evergladesuniversity.edu
E-mail: admissions-boca@evergladesuniversity.edu
See listing under "Universities"

EVERGLADES UNIVERSITY
Orlando Campus (Branch Campus)
5600 Lake Underhill Rd Suite 200, Orlando FL 32807
Shirley Long, Vice President
866-289-1078 Fax: 407-482-9801
Website: www.evergladesuniversity.edu
E-mail: admissions-orl@evergladesuniversity.edu
See listing under "Universities"

EVERGLADES UNIVERSITY
Sarasota Campus (Branch Campus)
6001 Lake Osprey Dr, Sarasota FL 34240
Brad Brewer, Vice President
866-907-2262 Fax: 941-907-6634
Website: www.evergladesuniversity.edu
E-mail: admissions-sar@evergladesuniversity.edu
See listing under "Universities"

GEORGE T. BAKER AVIATION SCHOOL
3275 NW 42nd Ave, Miami FL 33142-5626
Sean E. Gallagan, Principal
305-871-3143 Fax: 305-871-5840
Website: www.bakeraviation.edu
E-mail: gtba@dadeschools.net

Lynn University
3601 N Military Trl, Boca Raton FL 33431-5598
Brett Ormandy, Director of Admissions
561-237-7900 Fax: 561-237-7100
Website: www.lynn.edu
E-mail: admission@lynn.edu

NATIONAL AVIATION ACADEMY
6225 Ulmerton Rd, Clearwater FL 33760
Karen Acker, Registrar
727-531-2080 or 800-659-2080 Fax: 727-535-8727
Website: www.naa.edu
E-mail: admissions@naa.edu

PELICAN FLIGHT TRAINING CENTER
1601 SW 75th Ave, Pembroke Pines FL 33023
Meg Fensome, Vice President
954-966-9750 Fax: 954-985-8271
Website: www.pelican-airways.com
E-mail: pelicanftc@pelican-airways.com

Phoenix East Aviation, Inc.
Daytona Beach
561 Pearl Harbor Dr, Daytona Beach FL 32114-3845
Andre Maye, Director of Admissions
386-258-0703 or 800-868-4359 Fax: 386-254-6842
Website: pea.com
E-mail: andrem@pea.com
See listing under "Career Schools"

GEORGIA

AVIATION INSTITUTE OF MAINTENANCE
500 Briscoe Blvd, Lawrenceville GA 30045-6707
Gene Love, School Director
770-377-5600 Fax: 770-377-5609
Website: www.aviationmaintenance.edu
E-mail: directorama@tidetech.com

GEORGIA AVIATION TECHNICAL COLLEGE
71 Airport Rd, Eastman GA 31023
Donna Rogers, Admissions Specialist
478-374-6402 Fax: 478-374-6809
Website: www.gavtc.org
E-mail: drogers@gaaviationtech.edu

IOWA

Iowa Lakes Community College
300 S 18th St, Estherville IA 51334-2721
Anne Stansbury, Asst. Director of Admissions
712-362-7945 Fax: 712-362-8363
Website: www.iowalakes.edu
E-mail: info@iowalakes.edu

KENTUCKY

Morehead State University
Morehead KY 40351-1689
Dayna Seelig, Enrollment Services
800-585-6781 Fax: 606-783-5038
Website: www.moreheadstate.edu
E-mail: admissions@moreheadstate.edu

LOUISIANA

VORTEX HELICOPTERS
PO Box 9789, New Iberia LA 70562-9789
Mary Sheeran, Vice President
228-864-7357 Fax: 228-864-5850
Website: www.vortex-helicopters.com
E-mail: vortexheli@earthlink.net

MASSACHUSETTS

Boston University
121 Bay State Rd, Boston MA 02215
Kelly Walter, Executive Director of Admissions
617-353-2300 Fax: 617-353-9695
Website: web.bu.edu
E-mail: admissions@bu.edu

Massachusetts Institute of Technology
77 Massachusetts Ave, Cambridge MA 02139-4307
Marilee Jones, Dean of Admission
617-253-1000 Fax: 617-253-4016
Website: my.mit.edu
E-mail: admissions@mit.edu

MICHIGAN

Andrews University
Berrien Springs MI 49104-0001
Randall Graves, Director of Recruitment Services
800-253-2874 Fax: 269-471-2670
Website: www.connect.andrews.edu
E-mail: gravesr@andrews.edu

Delta College
University Center MI 48710-0001
Duff Zube, Director of Admissions
989-686-9093 Fax: 989-667-2202
Website: www.delta.edu
E-mail: admit@delta.edu

Northwestern Michigan College
1701 E Front St, Traverse City MI 49686-3061
Jim Bensley, Admissions Coordinator
800-748-0566 Fax: 231-995-1339
Website: www.nmc.edu
E-mail: jbensley@nmc.edu

MINNESOTA

ACADEMY COLLEGE
1101 E 78th St, Bloomington MN 55420-1402
952-851-0066 Fax: 952-851-0094
Website: www.academycollege.edu
E-mail: info@academycollege.edu
See listing under "Career Schools"

Northland Community & Technical College
Highway 1 E, Thief River Falls MN 56701
Lynn McGlynn, Contact
800-959-6282 or 218-681-0829 Fax: 218-681-0826
Website: www.northlandcollege.edu

MONTANA

Rocky Mountain College
1511 Poly Dr, Billings MT 59102-1796
Bonnie Knapp, Director of Admissions
800-877-6259 Fax: 406-657-1189
Website: www.rocky.edu
E-mail: admissions@rocky.edu

NEW JERSEY

Teterboro School of Aeronautics
80 Moonachie Ave, Teterboro NJ 07608-1003
Richard Ciasulli, Director of Admissions
201-288-6300 Fax: 201-288-5609
Website: www.teterboroschool.com
E-mail: teterboroschool@nj.rr.com

NEW YORK

VAUGHN COLLEGE OF AERONAUTICS AND TECHNOLOGY
8601 23rd Ave, Flushing NY 11369-1037
Vincent Papandrea, Director of Admissions
800-776-2376 Fax: 718-429-0671
Website: www.vaughn.edu
E-mail: admitme@vaughn.edu
    Established 1932. Private. Coed. Accreditation: MSACS, ABET. Tuition: $13,400. Fees: $280. Enrollment: 842 full-time, 284 part-time. Faculty: 59. Student-faculty ratio: 11:1. Degrees: BS, AAS, AOS. Library: 62,000 vols. Offering bachelor and associate degrees in airport management, aviation maintenance, flight training, electronic technology, engineering, general management, mechatronic engineering, pre-engineering and computerized design/animated graphics. Hands-on training. Extensive career development services and financial aid available.

NORTH DAKOTA

Williston State College
PO Box 1326, Williston ND 58802-1326
Penny Powell, Director Enrollment Services
701-774-4200 Fax: 701-774-4544
Website: www.wsc.nodak.edu
E-mail: penny.soiseth@wsc.nodak.edu

OHIO

The Ohio State University
Department of Aerospace Engineering
328 Bolz Hall, 2036 Neil Avenue Mall
Columbus OH 43210
614-292-2691 Fax: 614-292-8290
Website: aerospace.eng.ohio-state.edu
E-mail: haritonidis.1@osu.edu

The Ohio State University, Department of Aviation
Aviation Building, 164 W 19th Ave
Columbus OH 43210
614-292-2405, Fax: 614-292-1014
Website: aviation.osu.edu/
E-mail: aviation@osu.edu

OKLAHOMA

Oklahoma State University
Stillwater OK 74078
Steven K. Marks, Department Head
405-744-6275
Website: www.okstate.edu
E-mail: steve.marks@okstate.edu

SPARTAN COLLEGE OF AERONAUTICS AND TECHNOLOGY
8820 E Pine St, Tulsa OK 74115-5802
Director of Admissions
800-331-1204 Fax: 918-831-8609
Website: www.spartan.edu
E-mail: spartan@mail.spartan.edu
    Established 1928. Coed. Accredited member school: ACCSCT. Providing Technical training and education in Avionics, Instruments, and Maintenance; Nondestructive Testing and Quality Control. Complete flight training program. Offering Diplomas, Associate of Applied Science and Bachelor of Science in Aviation Technology Management.

PENNSYLVANIA

PIA SCHOOL OF SPECIALIZED TECHNOLOGY
(Pittsburgh Institute of Aeronautics)
PO Box 10897, Pittsburgh PA 15236-0897
Vincent J. Mezza, Director of Admissions
800-444-1440 Fax: 412-466-0513
Website: www.pia.edu
E-mail: admissions@pia.edu
    Established in 1929. Coed. Accredited Member School: ACCSCT. Providing technical training in Aviation Maintenance, Aviation Electronics and Electronic Systems (Associate in Specialized Technology Degree). Financial aid to those who qualify. Scholarship match program. Ongoing placement assistance. Varsity sports in bowling and golf, member of WPCC and PCAA.

TENNESSEE

NORTH CENTRAL INSTITUTE
168 Jack Miller Blvd, Clarksville TN 37042-4810
Dr. John McCurdy, President
931-431-9700 Fax: 931-431-9771
Website: www.nci.edu
E-mail: admissions@nci.edu
    Established 1988. Private. Coed. Accreditation: Accrediting Commission of the Council on Occupational Education. Student-faculty ratio: 20:1. Degrees: AAS in Aviation Technology - concentrations in Flight, Maintenance, or Operations/Air Traffic Control. FAA part 147 Aviation Maintenance Technician Program enables students to become FAA Certified Airframe/Powerplant Technicians. Our Credit Inventory Evaluation Service turns military training into college credit. Financial Aid and Veterans benefits to those who qualify.

TEXAS

Angelo State University
ASU Station 11014, San Angelo TX 76909
Bonnie Stennett, Coordinator of Recruiting
800-946-8627 Fax: 325-942-2078
Website: www.angelo.edu
E-mail: admissions@angelo.edu

AVIATION INSTITUTE OF MAINTENANCE
7555 Lemmon Ave, Dallas TX 75209-3017
James Cooper, School Director
214-333-9711 Fax: 214-333-9185
Website: www.aviationmaintenance.edu
E-mail: directoramd@aviationmaintenance.edu

Hallmark Institute of Aeronautics
Aeronautics Campus-Aviation Technology
8901 Wetmore Rd, San Antonio TX 78216-4229
Joe Fisher, President
210-826-1000 Fax: 210-826-3707
Website: www.hallmarkinstitute.edu
E-mail: sross@hallmarkinstitute.edu

University of Texas at Arlington
Box 19111, Arlington TX 76019-0111
Hans Gatterdam, Director of Admission
817-272-6287 Fax: 817-272-3435
Website: www.uta.edu
E-mail: admissions@uta.edu

VIRGINIA

AVIATION INSTITUTE OF MAINTENANCE
1429 Miller Store Rd, Virginia Beach VA 23455-3324
Michael Huffman, Director
757-363-2121 Fax: 757-363-2044
Website: www.aviationmaintenance.edu
E-mail: directoramn@tidetech.com

WASHINGTON

Everett Community College
2000 Tower St, Everett WA 98201
Christine Kerlin, Associate Dean
425-388-9100 Fax: 425-388-9173
Website: www.everettcc.edu
E-mail: ckerlin@everettcc.edu

WEST VIRGINIA

Fairmont State University
1201 Locust Ave, Fairmont WV 26554-2470
Steve Leadman, Director of Admissions
304-367-4892 or 800-641-5678 Fax: 304-367-4789
Website: www.fairmontstate.edu
E-mail: admit@fairmontstate.edu

WISCONSIN

Blackhawk Technical College
PO Box 5009, Janesville WI 53547-5009
Gregg Bosak, Administration, Community Information
608-757-7769 Fax: 608-757-7740
Website: www.blackhawk.edu
E-mail: gbosak@blackhawk.edu

AGRICULTURE

ALABAMA

Alabama A & M University
PO Box 908, Normal AL 35762
Antonio Boyle, Director of Admissions
256-372-5245 Fax: 256-372-5249
Website: www.aamu.edu
E-mail: aboyle@aamu.edu

CALHOUN COMMUNITY COLLEGE
PO Box 2216, Decatur AL 35609-2216
M. Wayne Tosh, Registrar
256-306-2500 Fax: 256-306-2941
Website: www.calhoun.edu
E-mail: jmc@calhoun.edu

ARIZONA

University of Arizona
Tucson AZ 85721-0040
Paul Kohn, Director of Admissions
520-621-3237 Fax: 520-621-9799
Website: www.admissions.arizona.edu or
www.arizona.edu

COLORADO

NORTHEASTERN JUNIOR COLLEGE
100 College Ave, Sterling CO 80751-2399
Judy Giacomini, Interim Chief Administrative Officer
Tina Joyce, Director of Admissions
970-521-7000 or 970-521-6752 Fax: 970-521-6801
Website: www.njc.edu
E-mail: tina.joyce@njc.edu

San Juan Basin Technical College
PO Box 970, Cortez CO 81321-0970
Shannon South, Director of Student Services
970-565-8457 Fax: 970-565-8450
Website: www.sjbtc.edu
E-mail: ssouth@sjbtc.edu

GEORGIA

North Georgia Technical College
434 Meeks Ave, Blairsville GA 30512-2983
Admissions
706-781-2300 Fax: 706-781-2307
Website: www.northgatech.edu
E-mail: info@northgatech.edu

North Georgia Technical College
Clarkesville Campus
PO Box 65, Clarkesville GA 30523-0002
Admissions
706-754-7700 Fax: 706-754-7777
Website: www.northgatech.edu
E-mail: info@northgatech.edu

IDAHO

Brigham Young University - Idaho
120 Kimball Bldg, Rexburg ID 83460
Gordon Westenskow, Director of Admissions
208-496-1020 Fax: 208-496-1220
Website: www.byui.edu
E-mail: admissions@byui.edu

University of Idaho
Moscow ID 83844-4253
Lloyd Scott, Director of New Student Services
208-885-6163 Fax: 208-885-4477
Website: www.uidaho.edu
E-mail: nss@uidaho.edu

IOWA

Iowa Lakes Community College
3200 College Dr, Emmetsburg IA 50536-1055
Anne Stansbury, Asst. Director of Admissions
712-852-5212 Fax: 712-362-8363
Website: www.iowalakes.edu
E-mail: info@iowalakes.edu

KANSAS

COLBY COMMUNITY COLLEGE
1255 S Range Ave, Colby KS 67701-4099
Director of Admissions
888-634-9350 or 785-460-4690 Fax: 785-460-4691
Website: www.colbycc.edu
E-mail: bobbi@colbycc.edu

KENTUCKY

Morehead State University
Morehead KY 40351-1689
Dayna Seelig, Enrollment Services
800-585-6781 Fax: 606-783-5038
Website: www.moreheadstate.edu
E-mail: admissions@moreheadstate.edu

MICHIGAN

Andrews University
Berrien Springs MI 49104-0001
Randall Graves, Director of Recruitment Services
800-253-2874 Fax: 269-471-2670
Website: www.connect.andrews.edu
E-mail: gravesr@andrews.edu

MINNESOTA

Ridgewater College-Willmar Campus
PO Box 1097, Willmar MN 56201-1097
Sally Kerfeld, Director of Admissions
800-722-1151 Fax: 320-231-7677
Website: www.ridgewater.edu
E-mail: skerfeld@ridgewater.edu

MISSOURI

Truman State University
100 E Normal, Kirksville MO 63501
Office of Admission
660-785-4000 Fax: 660-785-4181
Website: admissions.truman.edu
E-mail: admissions@truman.edu

NEVADA

GREAT BASIN COLLEGE
1500 College Pkwy, Elko NV 89801-5032
Julie G. Byrnes, Director of Enrollment Management
775-753-2271 Fax: 775-753-2311
Website: www.gbcnv.edu
E-mail: bjulie@gbcnv.edu

NEW JERSEY

Bergen Community College
400 Paramus Rd, Paramus NJ 07652
Julian Gomez, Asst. Director of Admissions
201-447-7100 Fax: 201-444-7036
Website: www.bergen.edu
E-mail: jgomez@bergen.edu

NEW YORK

SUNY College of Technology
Alfred NY 14802
Deborah J. Goodrich, Director of Admissions
800-4AL-FRED Fax: 607-587-4299
Website: www.alfredstate.edu
E-mail: admissions@alfredstate.edu

SUNY College of Technology
2 Main St, Delhi NY 13753-1110
Robert W. Mazzei, Director of Admissions
800-96-DELHI Fax: 607-746-4104
Website: www.delhi.edu
E-mail: enroll@delhi.edu

NORTH CAROLINA

James Sprunt Community College
PO Box 398, Kenansville NC 28349-0398
Rita Brown, Registrar
910-296-2500 Fax: 910-296-1636
Website: www.sprunt.com

Mt. Olive College
634 Henderson St, Mount Olive NC 28365
Tim Woodard, Director of Admissions
919-658-2502 Fax: 919-658-9816
Website: www.moc.edu
E-mail: admissions@moc.edu
See listing under "Universities"

NORTH DAKOTA

Dickinson State University
Dickinson ND 58601-4896
Steve Glasser, Director of Student Recruitment
800-279-4295 Fax: 701-483-2409
Website: www.dickinsonstate.edu
E-mail: dsu.hawks@dickinsonstate.edu

Williston State College
PO Box 1326, Williston ND 58802-1326
Penny Powell, Director Enrollment Services
701-774-4200 Fax: 701-774-4544
Website: www.wsc.nodak.edu
E-mail: penny.soiseth@wsc.nodak.edu

OHIO

The Ohio State University
College of Food, Agriculture, and Environmental
Sciences
Agricultural Admin Bldg, 2120 Fyffe Rd
Columbus OH 43210
614-292-6891 Fax: 614-292-1218
Website: cfaes.osu.edu

Owens Community College
300 Davis St, Findlay OH 45840-3631
William J. Ivoska PhD., Vice President of Student
Services
567-429-3500 Fax: 567-423-0246
Website: www.owens.edu
E-mail: admissions@owens.edu

Owens Community College
PO Box 10000, Toledo OH 43699-1947
William J. Ivoska, Ph.D, Vice President of Student
Services
567-661-7000 Fax: 567-661-7607
Website: www.owens.edu
E-mail: admissions@owens.edu

OKLAHOMA

Oklahoma State University
Stillwater OK 74078
Edwin Miller, Assoc. Dean
405-744-5398
Website: www.okstate.edu
E-mail: ed.miller@okstate.edu

OREGON

Linn-Benton Community College
6500 Pacific Blvd SW, Albany OR 97321-3774
Christine Baker, Outreach Coordinator
541-917-4811 Fax: 541-917-4868
Website: www.linnbenton.edu
E-mail: admissions@linnbenton.edu

SOUTH DAKOTA

Western Dakota Technical Institute
800 Mickelson Dr, Rapid City SD 57703-4018
Janell Oberlander, Manager of Student Services
605-394-4034 or 800-544-8765 Fax: 605-394-1789
Website: www.westerndakotatech.org
E-mail: admissions@wdti.tec.sd.us
See listing under "Career Schools"

TEXAS

Angelo State University
ASU Station 11014, San Angelo TX 76909
Bonnie Stennett, Coordinator of Recruiting
800-946-8627 Fax: 325-942-2078
Website: www.angelo.edu
E-mail: admissions@angelo.edu

- Blinn College
  902 College Ave, Brenham TX 77833-4098
  Dennis K. Crowson, Registrar
  979-830-4000 Fax: 979-830-4110
  Website: www.blinn.edu
  E-mail: recruiting@blinn.edu

- North Central Texas College
  1525 W California St, Gainesville TX 76240-4636
  Michelle Winters, Registrar
  940-668-3315 Fax: 940-665-7075
  Website: www.nctc.edu
  E-mail: mwinters@nctc.edu

WASHINGTON

- Walla Walla Community College
  500 Tausick Way, Walla Walla WA 99362-9270
  Jerry Kjack, Director
  509-527-4283 or 877-992-9922 Fax: 509-527-4572
  Website: www.wwcc.edu
  E-mail: jerry.kjack@wwcc.edu
  See listing under "Community and Junior Colleges"

- Wenatchee Valley College
  1300 5th St, Wenatchee WA 98801-1799
  Marco Azurdia, Dean, Student Development
  509-682-6805 Fax: 509-682-6541
  Website: www.wvc.edu

WISCONSIN

Wisconsin Indianhead Technical College
505 Pine Ridge Dr, Shell Lake WI 54871
Walt Peters, Dean
800-243-9482 Fax: 715-468-2819
Website: www.witc.edu
E-mail: mcrandal@witc.edu

WYOMING

University of Wyoming
Admissions Office
Dept 3435, Laramie WY 82071-3435
Aaron Appelhans, Contact
800-342-5996 Fax: 307-766-4042
Website: www.uwyo.edu
E-mail: why-wyo@uwyo.edu

GUAM

University of Guam
UOG Station, Mangilao GU 96923
Deborah Leon Guerrero, Registrar
671-735-2201 or 671-735-2208 Fax: 671-735-2203
Website: www.uog.edu
E-mail: admitme@uog9.uog.edu

ALLIED HEALTH SCIENCE

ALABAMA

Alabama A & M University
PO Box 908, Normal AL 35762
Antonio Boyle, Director of Admissions
256-372-5245 Fax: 256-372-5249
Website: www.aamu.edu
E-mail: aboyle@aamu.edu

Auburn University
Auburn AL 36849
334-844-4000

Auburn University at Montgomery
PO Box 244023, Montgomery AL 36124
334-244-3000

∴ Baptist Health System
PO Box 830605, Birmingham AL 35283-0605
205-715-5319

∴ Baptist Medical Center
301 Brown Springs Rd, Montgomery AL 36117
334-273-4400

Bessemer State Technical College
PO Box 308, Bessemer AL 35021-0308
205-428-6391

CALHOUN COMMUNITY COLLEGE
PO Box 2216, Decatur AL 35609-2216
M. Wayne Tosh, Registrar
256-306-2500 Fax: 256-306-2941
Website: www.calhoun.edu
E-mail: aww@calhoun.edu

∴ Carraway Methodist Medical Center
1600 Carraway Blvd, Birmingham AL 35234-2804
205-226-6000

Faulkner University
5345 Atlanta Hwy, Montgomery AL 36109-3398
Keith Mock, Director of Admissions
800-879-9816 ext. 7200 or 334-386-7200
Fax: 334-386-7137
Website: www.faulkner.edu
E-mail: admissions@faulkner.edu

Gadsden State Community College
PO Box 227, Gadsden AL 35902-0227
256-549-8200

- George C. Wallace Community College - Dothan
  1141 Wallace Dr, Dothan AL 36303
  334-983-3521

Herzing College
280 W Valley Ave, Homewood AL 35209-4816
Kim Conway, Director of Admissions
205-916-2800 Fax: 205-916-2807
Website: www.herzing.edu/birmingham
E-mail: info@bhm.herzing.edu

Jacksonville State University
700 Pelham Rd N, Jacksonville AL 36265-1602
256-782-5000

- James H. Faulkner State Community College
  1900 S US Highway 31, Bay Minette AL 36507-2619
  334-580-2100

- Jefferson State Community College
  2601 Carson Rd, Birmingham AL 35215-3098
  205-853-1200

- Lurleen B. Wallace Community College
  PO Box 1418, Andalusia AL 36420-1418
  Judy Hall, Director of Student Services
  334-222-6591 ext. 2271

∴ The Robert B Adams/LabCorp CLS Program
543 S Hull St, Montgomery AL 36104-4609
334-263-5745

Samford University
800 Lakeshore Dr, Birmingham AL 35229-0002
205-726-3673

- Shelton State Community College
  9500 Old Greensboro Rd
  Tuscaloosa AL 35405-8522
  205-759-1541

∴ Southern Union State Community College
1701 Lafayette Pkwy, Opelika AL 36801-3113
334-745-6437

- South University
  5355 Vaughn Rd, Montgomery AL 36116-1120
  334-395-8800

- Trenholm State Technical College
  Trenholm Campus
  1225 Air Base Blvd, Montgomery AL 36108-3199
  Dr. Anthony Molina, President
  334-420-4200 Fax: 334-420-4206
  Website: www.trenholmtech.cc.al.us
  E-mail: amolina@trenholmtech.cc.al.us

Troy University
Troy AL 36082-0001
Jim Hutto, Dean of Enrollment Management
334-670-3175

Tuskegee University
Tuskegee Institute AL 36088
334-727-8011

University of Alabama
Box 870118, Tuscaloosa AL 35487
Dr. Lisa B. Harris, Director of Admissions
205-348-5666

University of Alabama at Birmingham
Univ Sta, Birmingham AL 35294-0001
205-934-4011

∴ University of Alabama Hospital
619 19th St S, Birmingham AL 35249-0001
205-934-5490

University of Alabama in Huntsville
PO Box 1247, Huntsville AL 35899-0001
Ann Lee, Assoc. Director for Recruiting Program and Events
1-800-UAH-CALL Fax: 256-824-6073
Website: www.uah.edu
E-mail: leev@uah.edu

University of Montevallo
Station 6030, Montevallo AL 35115
205-665-6030

University of South Alabama
307 University Blvd N, Mobile AL 36688-3053
Melissa Haab, Director of Admissions
251-460-6141 Fax: 251-460-7876
Website: www.southalabama.edu
E-mail: admiss@usouthal.edu

- Wallace State Community College - Hanceville
  PO Box 2000, Hanceville AL 35077-2000
  256-352-8000

ALASKA

University of Alaska Anchorage
PO Box 141629, Anchorage AK 99514-1629
Cecile Mitchell, Director of Enrollment Services
907-786-1480 Fax: 907-786-4888
Website: www.uaa.alaska.edu/
E-mail: enroll@uaa.alaska.edu

University of Alaska Southeast
11120 Glacier Hwy, Juneau AK 99801-8625
Paul Kraft, Dean of Students/Enrollment Management
907-796-6000 Fax: 907-796-6005
Website: www.uas.alaska.edu
E-mail: paul.kraft@uas.alaska.edu

ARIZONA

Apollo College
2701 W Bethany Home Rd, Phoenix AZ 85017-1705
602-433-1333

ARIZONA SCHOOL OF HEALTH SCIENCES A.T. STILL UNIVERSITY
5850 E Still Circle, Mesa AZ 85206
Admissions Counselor
866-626-2878 or 480-219-6000 Fax: 480-219-6100
Website: www.atsu.edu
E-mail: info@ashs.edu

Arizona State University
PO Box 870112, Tempe AZ 85287-0112
480-965-9011

- Bryman School
  2250 W Peoria Ave Ste A100, Phoenix AZ 85029
  602-274-4300

∴ Carondelet Saint Marys Hospital
1601 W Saint Marys Rd, Tucson AZ 85745-2623
520-622-5833

- GateWay Community College
  108 N 40th St, Phoenix AZ 85034-1795
  Cathy Gibson, Director of Admissions & Records
  602-286-8052

International Institute of the Americas
925 S Gilbert Rd Ste 201, Mesa AZ 85204-4440
Meredith Kiljan, Director
480-545-8755 Fax: 480-926-1371
Website: www.iia.edu
E-mail: mjensen@iia.edu

- International Institute of the Americas
  6049 N 43rd Ave, Phoenix AZ 85019-1600
  Lynn McConnell, Director
  602-242-6265 Fax: 602-589-1353
  Website: www.iia.edu
  E-mail: lmcconnell@iia.edu

International Institute of the Americas
4136 N 75th Ave Ste 211, Phoenix AZ 85033-3169
Dr. Lori Ebert, Director
623-849-8208 Fax: 623-849-0110
Website: www.iia.edu
E-mail: nsabino@iia.edu

International Institute of the Americas
5441 E 22nd St, Tucson AZ 85710
Leigh Anne Pechota, Director
520-748-9799 Fax: 520-748-9355
Website: www.iia.edu
E-mail: lpechota@iia.edu

LONG TECHNICAL COLLEGE
Phoenix Campus
13450 N Black Canyon Hwy Ste 104
Phoenix AZ 85029-6323
602-548-1955 Fax: 602-548-1956
Website: www.longtechnicalcollege.com
E-mail: mcrone@longtechnicalcollege.com

Northern Arizona University
PO Box 4084, Flagstaff AZ 86011-0001
520-523-9011

- Phoenix College
  1202 W Thomas Rd, Phoenix AZ 85013-4234
  602-264-2492

- Pima Community College
  4905 E Broadway Blvd, Tucson AZ 85709-1010
  Wendy Kilgore, Ph.D., Director of Admissions
  520-206-4500 Fax: 520-206-4790
  Website: www.pima.edu
  E-mail: infocenter@pima.edu

∷ PIMA MEDICAL INSTITUTE
957 S Dobson Rd, Mesa AZ 85202-2903
Christopher Luebke, Director
480-644-0267 Fax: 480-649-5249
Website: www.pmi.edu
E-mail: asc@pmi.edu

∷ Pima Medical Institute
3350 E Grant Rd, Tucson AZ 85716-2800
520-326-1600

∷ TUCSON COLLEGE
7310 E 22nd St, Tucson AZ 85710
Rebecca Montgomery, Director of Admissions
520-296-3261 Fax: 520-296-3484
Website: www.tucsoncollege.edu
E-mail: Rmontgomery@tucsoncollege.edu

University of Arizona
Tucson AZ 85721-0040
Paul Kohn, Director of Admissions
520-621-3237 Fax: 520-621-9799
Website: www.admissions.arizona.edu or
www.arizona.edu

University of Phoenix
4615 E Elwood St, Phoenix AZ 85040-1908
480-966-9577

∴ Walter Boswell Memorial Hospital
10401 W Thunderbird Blvd, Sun City AZ 85351-3004
623-977-7211

ARKANSAS

Arkansas State University
PO Box 1630, State University AR 72467-1630
870-972-2100

Arkansas State University - Beebe
PO Box 1000, Beebe AR 72012-1000
501-882-6452

Arkansas Tech University
215 W O St, Russellville AR 72801-2222
479-968-0389

Arkansas Valley Technical Institute
PO Box 506, Ozark AR 72949-0506
479-667-2117

Black River Technical College
PO Box 468, Pocahontas AR 72455-0468
870-892-4565

Central Arkansas Radiation Therapy Institute
PO Box 55050, Little Rock AR 72215-5050
501-664-8573

Cotton Boll Technical Institute
PO Box 36, Burdette AR 72321-0036
Brenda Morris, Supervisor of Instruction
870-763-1486

Harding University
900 E Center Ave, Searcy AR 72149
501-279-4000

National Park Community College
101 College Dr
Hot Springs National Park AR 71913-9173
501-760-4222

North Arkansas College
1515 Pioneer Ridge Dr, Harrison AR 72601
870-743-3000

Northwest Arkansas Community College
1 College Dr, Bentonville AR 72712-5091
479-636-9222

Northwest Technical Institute
709 S Old Missouri Rd, Springdale AR 72764
Charles L. Kelley, President
479-751-8824 Fax: 479-751-7780
Website: www.nti.tec.ar.us
E-mail: info@nit.tec.ar.us

Ouachita Baptist University
410 Ouachita St, Arkadelphia AR 71998-0001
David Goodman, Director of Admissions
870-245-5110 Fax: 870-245-5500
Website: www.obu.edu
E-mail: admissions@obu.edu

Phillips Community College of the University of Arkansas
PO Box 785, Helena AR 72342-0785
Dr. Steven Murray, Chancellor
Lynn Boone, Vice Chancellor for Student Services /
Registrar
870-338-6474 Fax: 870-338-7542
Website: www.pccua.edu
E-mail: lboone@pccua.edu

Pulaski Technical College
3000 W Scenic Dr, North Little Rock AR 72118-3347
501-771-1000

∴ St. Vincent Infirmary Medical Center
2 Saint Vincent Cir, Little Rock AR 72205-5402
501-660-3910

South Arkansas Community College
PO Box 7010, El Dorado AR 71731-7010
870-862-8131

University of Arkansas at Fayetteville
1 University of Arkansas, Fayetteville AR 72701-1201
479-575-2000

University of Arkansas at Fort Smith
PO Box 3649, Fort Smith AR 72913-3649
479-788-7000

University of Arkansas at Little Rock
2801 S University Ave, Little Rock AR 72204-1000
501-569-3000

University of Arkansas at Pine Bluff
1200 University Dr, Pine Bluff AR 71601-2799
870-543-8000

University of Arkansas Community College at Hope
PO Box 140, Hope AR 71802-0140
Laura Massey, Health Professions Division Chair
870-777-5722

University of Central Arkansas
201 Donaghey Ave, Conway AR 72035-5003
501-450-5000

CALIFORNIA

ACADEMY OF CHINESE CULTURE AND HEALTH SCIENCES
1601 Clay St, Oakland CA 94612-1531
Ruth Kierans, Director of Admission
510-763-7787 Fax: 510-834-8646
Website: www.acchs.edu
E-mail: info@acchs.edu

American Career College
4021 Rosewood Ave, Los Angeles CA 90004-6818
Rita Totten, Campus Director
323-383-2862

American College of Health Professions
700 E Redlands Blvd #U227
Redlands CA 92373-6109
Admissions
909-307-6022

AMERICAN COLLEGE OF MEDICAL TECHNOLOGY
555 W Redondo Beach Blvd #100
Gardena CA 90248
Scott Jacobus, Contact
310-324-1000 Fax: 310-515-3944
Website: www.acmt.ac
E-mail: info@acmt.ac

AMERICAN COLLEGE OF TRADITIONAL CHINESE MEDICINE
455 Arkansas St, San Francisco CA 94107-2813
JoAnn Vandenberg, Dean of Student Services
415-282-7600 Fax: 415-282-0856
Website: www.actcm.edu
E-mail: admissions@actcm.edu

American River College
4700 College Oak Dr, Sacramento CA 95841-4286
916-484-8011

Associated Technical College
1670 Wilshire Blvd, Los Angeles CA 90017-1690
Samuel Romano, Director of Admissions
213-353-1845 Fax: 213-413-4864
Website: www.associatedtechcollege.com
E-mail: decatc@earthlink.net

Bakersfield College
1801 Panorama Dr, Bakersfield CA 93305-1299
661-395-4301

Bryman College
2215 W Mission Rd, Alhambra CA 91803-1310
626-979-4970

Bryman College
511 N Brookhurst St Ste 300
Anaheim CA 92801-5229
714-953-6500

Bryman College
1045 W Redondo Beach Blvd #275
Gardena CA 90247
310-527-7105

BRYMAN COLLEGE
22336 Main St, Hayward CA 94541
H. Albizo, President
510-582-9500 Fax: 510-582-9645
Website: www.cci.edu
E-mail: halbizo@cci.edu

Bryman College
3460 Wilshire Blvd Ste 500
Los Angeles CA 90010-2223
Marie Guerrero, Director of Admissions
213-388-9950

Bryman College
18040 Sherman Way #400, Reseda CA 91335-4631
Lani Townsend, School President
818-774-0550

Bryman College
217 Club Center Dr Ste A, San Bernardino CA 92408
Mary Coutts, Director of Admissions
909-777-3300

Bryman College
814 Mission St Ste 500
San Francisco CA 94103-3038
415-777-2500

Bryman College
1245 S Winchester Blvd #102, San Jose CA 95128
408-246-0859

Butte College
3536 Butte Campus Dr, Oroville CA 95965-8399
530-895-2511

Cabrillo College
6500 Soquel Dr, Aptos CA 95003-3194
831-479-6100

CALIFORNIA COLLEGE SAN DIEGO
2820 Camino Del Rio S # 300, San Diego CA 92108
Denise Galvez-Kirk, Director of Admissions
619-295-5785 Fax: 619-295-5762
Website: www.cc-sd.edu
E-mail: dgalves-kirk@cc-sd.edu

California Polytechnic State University
San Luis Obispo CA 93407
805-756-1111

California State Polytechnic University
3801 W Temple Ave, Pomona CA 91768-2557
909-869-2000

California State University-Chico
Chico CA 95929-0001
530-898-6116

California State University-Dominguez Hills
1000 E Victoria St, Carson CA 90747-0001
310-243-3300

California State University-East Bay
25800 Carlos Bee Blvd, Hayward CA 94542-3001
510-885-3000

California State University-Fresno
Fresno CA 93740-0001
559-278-4240

California State University-Fullerton
PO Box 34080
Fullerton CA 92634
714-278-2011

California State University-Long Beach
1250 N Bellflower Blvd, Long Beach CA 90840-0006
562-985-4111

California State University-Los Angeles
5151 State University Dr, Los Angeles CA 90032
323-343-3000

California State University-Northridge
18111 Nordhoff St, Northridge CA 91330-0001
818-677-1200

California State University-Sacramento
6000 J St, Sacramento CA 95819-2605
916-278-6011

California State University-San Bernadino
5500 University Pkwy
San Bernardino CA 92407-2393
Olivia Rosas, Director of Admissions
909-880-5000 Fax: 909-880-7034
Website: enrollment.csusb.edu
E-mail: orosas@csusb.edu

Canada College
4200 Farm Hill Blvd, Redwood City CA 94061-1099
Marilyn McBride, Dean

CENTER OF EMPLOYMENT TRAINING
701 Vine St, San Jose CA 95110
Luis Aguilar, Contact
408-287-7924 Fax: 408-534-5238
Website: www.cetweb.org
E-mail: luis@cet2000.org

Cerritos College
11110 Alondra Blvd, Norwalk CA 90650-6296
562-860-2451

Chabot College
25555 Hesperian Blvd, Hayward CA 94545-2400
Judy Young, Director of Admissions
510-723-6600 Fax: 510-723-7510
Website: www.chabotcollege.edu
E-mail: ccarcom@clpccd.cc.ca.us

Chaffey College
5885 Haven Ave, Alta Loma CA 91737-9400
909-941-2358

Chapman University
One University Drive, Orange CA 92866-1099
Michael Drummy, Assistant Vice President for
Enrollment
Services and Chief Admission Officer
714-997-6411 or 888-CUAPPLY Fax: 714-997-6713
Website: www.chapman.edu
E-mail: admit@chapman.edu

Charles R. Drew University of Medicine & Science
1621 E 120th St, Los Angeles CA 90059
323-563-4800

Citrus College
1000 W Foothill Blvd, Glendora CA 91741-1885
626-963-0323

City College of San Francisco
50 Phelan Ave, San Francisco CA 94112-1821
415-239-3000

College of Alameda
555 Atlantic Ave, Alameda CA 94501-2109
510-522-7221

COLLEGE OF INFORMATION TECHNOLOGY
2701 E Chapman Ave Ste 101, Fullerton CA 92831
Mohammad Qamaruddin, Director
714-879-5100 Fax: 714-879-2272
Website: www.collegeofit.com
E-mail: mqamar@collegeofit.com

College of Marin
835 College Ave, Kentfield CA 94904-2590
415-457-8811

College of San Mateo
1700 W Hillsdale Blvd, San Mateo CA 94402-3784
650-574-6161

College of the Desert
43500 Monterey Ave, Palm Desert CA 92260-9399
760-346-8041

CONCORDE CAREER COLLEGE
12412 Victory Blvd, North Hollywood CA 91606-3134
Guy Lopatin, Director of Admissions
818-766-8151 Fax: 818-766-1587
Website: www.concorde.edu
E-mail: glopatin@concorde.edu

CONCORDE CAREER COLLEGE
201 E Airport Dr #A, San Bernardino CA 92408
Rosie Brownlee, Director of Admissions
909-884-8891 Fax: 909-384-1768
Website: www.concorde.edu
E-mail: rbrownlee@concorde.edu

CONCORDE CAREER INSTITUTE
12951 Euclid St Ste 101
Garden Grove CA 92840-9201
Craig McVey, Director of Admissions
714-703-1900 Fax: 714-530-4737
Website: www.concorde.edu
E-mail: cmcvey@concorde.edu

CONCORDE CAREER INSTITUTE
4393 Imperial Ave Suite 100, San Diego CA 92113
Denise Galvez, Director of Admissions
619-688-0800 Fax: 619-220-4177
Website: www.concorde.edu
E-mail: dgalvez@concorde.edu

Contra Costa College
2600 Mission Bell Dr, San Pablo CA 94806-3195
510-235-7800

Cosumnes River College
8401 Center Pkwy, Sacramento CA 95823-5799
916-691-7344

Crafton Hills College
11711 Sand Canyon Rd, Yucaipa CA 92399-1799
Dr. Luis S. Gomez, President
909-389-3200

Cypress College
9200 Valley View St, Cypress CA 90630-5897
714-484-7000

DeAnza College
21250 Stevens Creek Blvd
Cupertino CA 95014-5793
408-864-5678

Diablo Valley College
321 Golf Club Rd, Pleasant Hill CA 94523-1544
925-685-1230

East Los Angeles College
1301 Avenida Cesar Chavez
Monterey Park CA 91754-6001
323-265-8650

East Los Angeles Occupational Center
2100 Marengo St, Los Angeles CA 90033-1321
323-223-1283

Eisenhower Memorial Hospital
39000 Bob Hope Dr, Rancho Mirage CA 92270-3221
760-340-3911

El Camino College
16007 Crenshaw Blvd, Torrance CA 90506-0002
310-660-3670

EMPEROR'S COLLEGE OF TRADITIONAL ORIENTAL MEDICINE
1807 Wilshire Blvd Ste B
Santa Monica CA 90403-5678
Sun Han, Director of Admissions
310-453-8300 Fax: 310-829-3838
Website: www.emperors.edu
E-mail: sun@emperors.edu

FIVE BRANCHES INSTITUTE
3031 Tisch Way Ste 605, San Jose CA 95128
408-260-0208 Fax: 408-261-3166
Website: www.fivebrances.edu
E-mail: sicampus@fivebrances.edu

FIVE BRANCHES INSTITUTE
College of Traditional Chinese Medicine
200 7th Ave, Santa Cruz CA 95062-4668
Eleonor Mendelson, Admissions
831-476-9424 Fax: 831-476-8928
Website: www.fivebranches.edu
E-mail: tcm@fivebranches.edu

FRESNO CITY COLLEGE
1101 E University Ave, Fresno CA 93741-0002
Dayann Dietrich, Contact
559-442-8241 Fax: 559-237-4232
Website: www.fresnocitycollege.com
E-mail: fcc.admissions@scccd.com

Grossmont College
8800 Grossmont College Dr, El Cajon CA 92020-1798
619-644-7000

Haciende LaPuente Valley Adult Education
14101 Nelson Ave, La Puente CA 91746
626-934-2800

Health Staff Training Institute
1505 E 17th St Ste 122, Santa Ana CA 92705-8520
714-543-9828

Institute of Technology - Sacramento
3695 Bleckely St, Mather CA 95655
916-363-4300

Loma Linda University
Loma Linda CA 92350-0001
Richard Weismeyer, Director
800-422-4558

Los Angeles City College
855 N Vermont Ave, Los Angeles CA 90029-3588
323-953-4000

Los Angeles County College of
Nursing and Allied Health
1200 N State St, Los Angeles CA 90033-1029
323-226-4911

Los Angeles Valley College
5800 Fulton Ave, Van Nuys CA 91401-4062
818-947-2600

Loyola Marymount University
7900 Loyola Blvd, Los Angeles CA 90045-2699
310-338-2700

MARIC COLLEGE
5172 Kiernan Ct, Salida CA 95358-9083
Curtis Anderson, Director of Admissions
209-543-7000 Fax: 209-543-1755
Website: www.mariccollege.edu
E-mail: canderson@mariccollege.edu

Maric College
9055 Balboa Ave, San Diego CA 92123
Geraldine Rorrison, Director of Admissions
858-279-4500 Fax: 858-279-4885
Website: www.mariccollege.edu
E-mail: grorrison@mariccollege.edu

MARIC COLLEGE
722 W March Ln, Stockton CA 95207-6216
John Bermudez, Director of Admissions
209-462-8777 Fax: 209-462-3219
Website: www.mariccollege.edu
E-mail: jbermudez@mariccollege.edu

Merced College
3600 M St, Merced CA 95348-2898
209-384-6000

Merritt College
12500 Campus Dr, Oakland CA 94619-3196
510-531-4911

Modesto Junior College
435 College Ave, Modesto CA 95350-5800
209-575-6498

Monterey Peninsula College
980 Fremont Ave, Monterey CA 93940-4799
Rich Montori, Contact
831-645-1376

Moorpark College
7075 Campus Rd, Moorpark CA 93021-1695
805-378-1400

Mt. San Antonio College
1100 N Grand Ave, Walnut CA 91789-1399
909-594-5611

MTI BUSINESS COLLEGE OF STOCKTON
6006 N El Dorado St, Stockton CA 95207-4349
Steven Brenner, Director
888-302-2009 Fax: 209-474-8705
Website: www.mtistockton.com
E-mail: mtistockton@comcast.net
Established 1968. Accredited: ACCSCT. Family owned/operated 36 years.

MTI College
5221 Madison Ave, Sacramento CA 95841-3003
Marije Miller, Director of Admissions
916-339-1500 Fax: 916-339-0305
Website: www.mticollege.edu
E-mail: mmiller@mticollege.edu

MUELLER COLLEGE OF HOLISTIC MASSAGE
4607 Park Blvd, San Diego CA 92116
David Taylor, Registrar
619-291-9811 Fax: 619-543-1113
Website: www.muellercollege.com
E-mail: david@mueller.edu

Napa State Hospital
2100 Napa Vallejo Hwy, Napa CA 94558-6293
707-253-5428

Napa Valley College
2277 Napa Vallejo Hwy, Napa CA 94558-6236
707-253-3076

Notre Dame de Namur University
1500 Ralston Ave, Belmont CA 94002-1997
Martin Bednarek, Director of Admissions
800-263-0545

Ohlone College
PO Box 3909, Fremont CA 94539-0390
510-659-6000

Olive View/UCLA Medical Centers
14445 Olive View Dr, Sylmar CA 91342-1438
818-364-4224

Orange Coast College
PO Box 5005, Costa Mesa CA 92628-5005
Kristin Clark, Director of Admissions
714-432-5773 Fax: 714-432-5736
Website: www.orangecoastcollege.edu
E-mail: kclark@cccd.edu

Oxnard College
4000 S Rose Ave, Oxnard CA 93033-6699
805-986-5800

PACIFIC COLLEGE OF ORIENTAL MEDICINE
7445 Mission Valley Rd #105, San Diego CA 92108
619-574-6909 Fax: 619-574-6641
Website: www.pacificcollege.edu
E-mail: admissions-sd@pacificcollege.edu

Palomar College
1140 W Mission Rd, San Marcos CA 92069-1415
760-744-1150

Pasadena City College
1570 E Colorado Blvd, Pasadena CA 91106-2041
626-585-7123

Patton State Hospital
3102 E Highland Ave, Patton CA 92369
909-425-7297

Pepperdine University
24255 Pacific Coast Hwy, Malibu CA 90263-0002
310-456-4000

Redwoods Community College
7351 Tompkins Hill Rd, Eureka CA 95501-9300
707-476-4100

Sacramento City College
3835 Freeport Blvd, Sacramento CA 95822-1386
916-558-2111

Sacramento Medical Foundation Blood Bank
1625 Stockton Blvd, Sacramento CA 95816-7053
916-456-1500

St. Joseph Hospital
1100 Stewart Dr, Orange CA 92868
714-771-8111

SAMRA UNIVERSITY OF ORIENTAL MEDICINE
3000 S Robertson Blvd 4 Fl
Los Angeles CA 90034-3158
Simon Song, Director of Operations
310-202-6444 Fax: 310-202-6007
Website: www.samra.edu
E-mail: admissions@samra.edu

San Bernardino Valley College
701 S Mount Vernon Ave
San Bernardino CA 92410-2798
909-888-6511

San Diego Mesa College
7250 Mesa College Dr, San Diego CA 92111-4996
858-627-2600

San Diego State University
5500 Campanile Dr, San Diego CA 92182-0002
619-594-5200

San Francisco State University
1600 Holloway Ave, San Francisco CA 94132-1722
415-338-1111

San Joaquin Valley College
201 New Stine Rd, Bakersfield CA 93309-2659
Jaime Delgado, Enrollment Services Director
661-834-1026 Fax: 559-651-4864
Website: www.sjvc.edu
E-mail: jaime.delgado@sjvc.edu

San Joaquin Valley College
295 E Sierra Ave, Fresno CA 93710-3616
Nora Twarynski, Enrollment Services Director
559-448-8282 Fax: 559-651-4864
Website: www.sjvc.edu
E-mail: nora.twarynski@sjvc.edu

San Joaquin Valley College
1700 McHenry Village Way Suite 6
Modesto CA 95350
Joseph Holt, Director of Admissions
209-527-7822 Fax: 559-651-4864
Website: www.sjvc.edu
E-mail: josephh@sjvc.edu

San Joaquin Valley College
11050 Olson Dr, Rancho Cordova CA 95670
Joseph Holt, Director of Admissions
559-651-2500 Fax: 559-651-4864
Website: www.sjvc.edu
E-mail: joseph.holt@sjvc.edu

San Joaquin Valley College
8400 W Mineral King Ave, Visalia CA 93291-9283
Susie Topjian, Enrollment Services Director
559-651-2500 Fax: 559-651-4864
Website: www.sjvc.edu
E-mail: susiet@sjvc.edu

San Jose City College
2100 Moorpark Ave, San Jose CA 95128-2797
408-298-2181

San Jose State University
1 Washington Sq, San Jose CA 95192-0001
408-924-1000

Santa Ana College
1530 W 17th St, Santa Ana CA 92706-3398
714-564-6000

Santa Barbara City College
721 Cliff Dr, Santa Barbara CA 93109-2394
Patricia E. Canning, Coordinator, School Relations
805-965-0581 ext. 2201

Santa Monica College
1900 Pico Blvd, Santa Monica CA 90405-1644
310-434-4000

Santa Rosa Junior College
1501 Mendocino Ave, Santa Rosa CA 95401-4395
Renee LoPilato, Dean of Admissions
707-527-4011

Simi Valley Adult Education
3192 E Los Angeles Ave, Simi Valley CA 93065-3940
805-579-6200

Skyline College
3300 College Dr, San Bruno CA 94066-1698
650-738-4100

Sonoma State University
1801 E Cotati Ave, Rohnert Park CA 94928-3609
Louis T. Levy, Senior Director Enrollment Services
707-664-2880

SOUTH BAYLO UNIVERSITY
School of Acupuncture & Oriental Medicine
1126 N Brookhurst St, Anaheim CA 92801
Dr. Melvin L. Shirer, D.C., Director of Admissions
714-533-1495 Fax: 714-533-6040
Website: www.southbaylo.edu
E-mail: mshirer@southbaylo.edu

Southwestern College
900 Otay Lakes Rd, Chula Vista CA 91910-7297
619-421-6700

Stanford University
520 Lasuen Mall Union 232, Stanford CA 94305-3005
650-723-2300

Taft College
29 Emmons Park Dr, Taft CA 93268-2317
661-763-7700

Uni Health America/Glendale Memorial Hospital
1420 S Central Ave, Glendale CA 91204-2508
818-502-2334

University of California
110 Sproul Hall, Berkeley CA 94720-5804
510-642-6000

University of California
1 Shields Ave, Davis CA 95616
530-752-1011

University of California
Irvine CA 92697-0001
949-824-5011

University of California
Parnassus and 3rd Ave
San Francisco CA 94143-0001
415-476-9000

University of California Los Angeles
Center for the Health Sciences
10833 Le Conte Ave, Los Angeles CA 90095-3075
310-825-5654

University of California Medical Center
200 W Arbor Dr #H-910C, San Diego CA 92103-1911
619-543-6654

University of Redlands
PO Box 3080, Redlands CA 92373-0999
909-793-2121

University of Southern California
Univ Park, Los Angeles CA 90089-0001
213-740-2311

University of the Pacific
3601 Pacific Ave, Stockton CA 95211-0197
209-946-2011

∴ Veterans Affairs Medical Center
3350 La Jolla Village Dr, San Diego CA 92161-0002
858-552-8585

∙ Victor Valley Community College
18422 Bear Valley Rd, Victorville CA 92395-5849
760-245-4271

∙ Western Career College
2157 Country Hills Dr, Antioch CA 94509-7435
Tim Gienapp, Director of Admissions
925-522-7777
Website: www.westerncollege.edu

∙ Western Career College
7301 Greenback Ln Bldg A, Citrus Heights CA 95621
Jim Murphy, Contact
916-722-8200 Fax: 916-722-6883
Website: www.westerncollege.edu

∙ Western Career College
6001 Shellmound St 2nd Floor, Emeryville CA 94608
Elvie Engstrom, Director of Admissions
510-601-0133 Fax: 510-601-0793
Website: www.westerncollege.edu

∙ Western Career College
380 Civic Dr Ste 300, Pleasant Hill CA 94523-1984
LaShawn Wells, Contact
925-609-6650 Fax: 926-609-6666
Website: www.westerncollege.edu

∙ Western Career College
8909 Folsom Blvd, Sacramento CA 95826-3203
Sue Smith, Contact
916-361-1660 Fax: 916-361-6666
Website: www.westerncollege.edu

∙ Western Career College
6201 San Ignacio Ave, San Jose CA 95119
Steve Ashab, Director of Admissions
408-360-0840 Fax: 408-360-0848
Website: www.westerncollege.edu

∙ Western Career College
15555 E 14th St Ste 500, San Leandro CA 94578
Julie Elmquist, Contact
510-276-3888 Fax: 510-276-3653
Website: www.westerncollege.edu

∙ Western Career College
1313 W Robinhood Dr Ste B, Stockton CA 95207
Dave Semrau, Contact
209-956-1240 Fax: 209-956-1244
Website: www.westerncollege.edu

Western University of Health Sciences
College of Allied Health Professions
309 E 2nd St, Pomona CA 91766-1854
Kathryn Ford, Director
909-469-5335

∙ West Los Angeles College
4800 Freshman Dr, Culver City CA 90230-3519
310-287-4200

∴ West Los Angeles VA Medical Center
Wilshire & Sawtelle Blvds, Los Angeles CA 90073
310-824-3132

∙ West Valley College
14000 Fruitvale Ave, Saratoga CA 95070-5697
408-867-2200

Whittier College
PO Box 634, Whittier CA 90608-0634
Kieron Miller, Director of Admissions
562-907-4200 Fax: 562-907-4870
Website: www.whittier.edu
E-mail: kmiller@whittier.edu

∙ Yuba College
2088 N Beale Rd, Marysville CA 95901-7699
Connie Elder, Registrar
530-741-6989

COLORADO

Adams State College
Alamosa CO 81102
Matt Gallegos, Director of Admissions
800-824-6494

∙ Aims Community College
PO Box 69, Greeley CO 80632-0069
970-330-8008

∙ Arapahoe Community College
5900 S Sante Fe Dr, Littleton CO 80160
Howard Fukaye, Contact
303-797-4ACC (4222)

∙ Bel-Rea Institute of Animal Technology
1681 S Dayton St, Denver CO 80247-3048
Paulette Kaufman, Administrator
303-751-8700 Fax: 303-751-9969
Website: www.bel-rea.com
E-mail: admissions@bel-rea.com

∙ Blair College
1815 Jet Wing Dr, Colorado Springs CO 80916-2300
719-638-6580

THE COLORADO CENTER FOR MEDICAL LABORATORY SCIENCE
1719 E 19th Ave, Denver CO 80218
Karen Myers, Director
303-839-6485 Fax: 303-869-1720
Website: www.medlabed.org
E-mail: medlabed@coloradohealth.org

COLORADO SCHOOL OF TRADITIONAL CHINESE MEDICINE
1441 York St Ste 202, Denver CO 80206
David DiBrigida, Administrative Director
303-329-6355 Fax: 303-388-8165
Website: www.uchsc.edu
E-mail: admin@cstcm.edu

Colorado State University
102 Administration, Fort Collins CO 80523-0001
970-491-1101

∴ Columbia HealthOne
501 E Hampden, Englewood CO 80113
303-788-6484

∙ Community College of Denver
PO Box 173363, Denver CO 80217-3363
303-556-2600

CONCORDE CAREER COLLEGE
111 N Havana St, Aurora CO 80010-4314
Kevin McNeil, Director of Admissions
303-861-1151 Fax: 303-839-5478
Website: www.concorde.edu
E-mail: kmcneil@concorde.edu

∙ Denver Career College
500 E 84th Ave Suite W200
Thornton CO 80229-5316
JoAnn Navarro, Director of Admissions
800-848-0550 Fax: 303-295-0102
Website: www.denvercareercollege.com
E-mail: admissions-045@denvercareercollege.com

Denver Seminary
6399 S Santa Fe Dr, Littleton CO 80120
Robert Fomer, VP Student Services
303-762-6982 Fax: 303-783-3122
Website: denverseminary.edu
E-mail: bob.fomer@denverseminary.edu

∙ Emily Griffith Opportunity School
1250 Welton St, Denver CO 80204-2124
720-423-4700

∴ HealthONE North Suburban Medical Center
9191 Grant St, Thornton CO 80229-4361
303-451-7800

∶ Heritage College
12 Lakeside Ln, Denver CO 80212-7413
Jennifer Sprague, Director
303-477-7240 Fax: 303-477-7276
Website: www.heritage-education.com
E-mail: info@heritage-education.com
See listing under "Career Schools"

∙ IntelliTec College
772 Horizon Dr, Grand Junction CO 81506-3907
Rich Counts, Contact
970-245-8101 Fax: 970-243-8074
Website: www.intelliteccollege.edu
E-mail: admgj@intelliteccollege.edu

∙ IntelliTec College
3673 Parker Blvd Ste 250, Pueblo CO 81008
Crystal Barajas, Director of Admissions
719-542-3181 Fax: 719-242-0068
Website: www.intelliteccollege.edu
E-mail: admpbl@intelliteccollege.edu

∙ IntelliTec Medical Institute
2345 N Academy Blvd
Colorado Springs CO 80909-1570
Kiersten Murdoch, Contact
719-596-7400 Fax: 719-596-2464
Website: www.IntellitecCollege.edu
E-mail: kmurdoch@intellitec.edu

∙ Mesa State College
1100 North Ave, Grand Junction CO 81501
970-248-1020

∙ Morgan Community College
17800 County Road 20, Fort Morgan CO 80701
Judy Beckmann, Director of Student Support
800-622-0216

Naropa University
2130 Arapahoe Ave, Boulder CO 80302-6697
303-546-3572

Parks College
14280 E Jewell Ave, Aurora CO 80012-5692
Julie Rosenthal, Director of Admissions
303-367-2757 Fax: 303-745-6245
Website: www.cci.edu

∶ Pickens Technical Center
500 Airport Blvd, Aurora CO 80011-9307
303-344-4910

∶ Pikes Peak Community College
5675 S Academy Blvd
Colorado Springs CO 80906-5498
719-576-7711

∙ Pima Medical Institute
1701 W 72nd Ave Ste 130, Denver CO 80221-2727
Sue Anderson, Director
303-426-1800

∙ Pueblo Community College
900 W Orman Ave, Pueblo CO 81004-1499
719-549-3200

∙ Red Rocks Community College
13300 W 6th Ave, Lakewood CO 80228-1255
303-988-6160

Regis University
3333 Regis Blvd, Denver CO 80221-1099
303-458-4900

∴ Tri-County Health Nutrition Services
7000 E Bl_levue Ave #301
Englewood CO 80111-1628
303-220-9200

University of Colorado
Boulder CO 80309-0001
303-492-1411

University of Colorado at Denver and Health Sciences Center
Health Sciences Program
4200 E 9th Ave Box C245, Denver CO 80262
Phoebe Lindsey Barton, Ph.D., Director
Website: www.uchsc.edu

University of Northern Colorado
Greeley CO 80639
Vincent Scalia, Dean / Health & Human Sciences
970-351-2877

∙ Westwood College - Denver North
7350 Broadway, Denver CO 80221-3610
303-426-7000

CONNECTICUT

∙ Branford Hall Career Institute
1 Summit Pl, Branford CT 06405
800-959-7599

∙ Briarwood College
2279 Mount Vernon Rd, Southington CT 06489-1057
860-628-4751

∙ Capital Community College
950 Main St, Hartford CT 06103-1211
860-906-5000

∙ Connecticut Center for Massage Therapy
75 Kitts Ln, Newington CT 06111-3954
877-282-2268 Fax: 860-667-4566
Website: www.ccmt.com
E-mail: info@ccmt.com

∴ Connecticut Childrens Medical Center
282 Washington St, Hartford CT 06106
Rich Janis, Team Leader
860-545-8514

∴ Connecticut Childrens Medical Center
170 Ridge Rd, Wethersfield CT 06109-1044
860-545-8551

Fairfield University
1073 N Benson Rd, Fairfield CT 06824-5171
203-254-4000

∙ Fox Institute of Business
99 South St, West Hartford CT 06110-1922
860-947-2299

∙ Gateway Community College
60 Sargent Dr, New Haven CT 06511-5918
203-789-7071

Goodwin College
745 Burnside Ave, East Hartford CT 06108-2777
Daniel Noonan, Director of Enrollment and Student Services
860-528-4111

∙ Housatonic Community College
900 Lafayette Blvd, Bridgeport CT 06604
203-332-5000

∙ Manchester Community College
PO Box 1046, Manchester CT 06045-1046
860-647-6000

∙ Middlesex Community College
100 Training Hill Rd, Middletown CT 06457-4889
Mensimah Shabazz, Director of Admissions
860-343-5800 Fax: 860-344-3055
Website: www.mxcc.commnet.edu
E-mail: mshabazz@mxcc.commnet.edu

∙ Naugatuck Valley Community College
750 Chase Pkwy, Waterbury CT 06708-3089
203-575-8040

∙ Northwestern Connecticut Community-Technical College
2 Park Pl, Winsted CT 06098-1706
860-738-6300

∙ Porter and Chester Institute
138 Weymouth Rd, Enfield CT 06082
860-741-2561

∙ Porter and Chester Institute
670 Lordship Blvd, Stratford CT 06615-7158
Mark Breslin, Director of Admissions
203-375-4463 Fax: 203-375-5285
Website: www.porterchester.com

∙ Porter and Chester Institute
320 Sylvan Lake Rd, Watertown CT 06779-1459
Jack Burke, Executive Director
860-274-9294

∙ Porter and Chester Institute
125 Silas Deane Hwy, Wethersfield CT 06109-1255
860-529-2519

∙ Prince Regional Vocational Technical School
500 Brookfield St, Hartford CT 06106
860-246-8594

∙ Quinebaug Valley Community College
742 Upper Maple St, Danielson CT 06239-1440
860-774-1160

Quinnipiac University
275 Mount Carmel Ave, Hamden CT 06518-1905
Joan Isaac Mohr, VP & Dean of Admissions
203-582-8600

∙ Ridley-Lowell Business & Technical Inst
PO Box 652, New London CT 06320-0652
Kimberly L. Mayer, Director
860-443-7441

Sacred Heart University
5151 Park Ave, Fairfield CT 06825-1023
203-371-7999

St. Joseph College
1678 Asylum Ave, West Hartford CT 06117-2791
860-232-4571

∴ St. Mary's Hospital
56 Franklin St, Waterbury CT 06706-1281
203-574-6300

∙ St. Vincent's College
2800 Main St, Bridgeport CT 06606-4292
Director of Admissions
203-576-5513

Southern Connecticut State University
501 Crescent St, New Haven CT 06515-1355
203-392-5200

STAMFORD HOSPITAL
PO Box 9317, Stamford CT 06904-9317
Dorothy Saia, MA, RT, Program Director
203-276-7877 Fax: 203-276-7352
Website: www.stamhealth.org
E-mail: dsaia@stamhealth.org

STONE ACADEMY
1315 Dixwell Ave, Hamden CT 06514-4155
Jeanna LaBella, Director of Admissions
203-288-7474 Fax: 203-288-8869
Website: stoneacademy.com
E-mail: jlabella.stone@snet.net

Tunxis Community College
271 Scott Swamp Rd, Farmington CT 06032-3187
860-677-7701

University of Bridgeport
126 Park Ave, Bridgeport CT 06604-5620
Barbara L. Maryak, Dean of Admissions
203-576-4552

University of Connecticut
Storrs CT 06269-0001
860-486-2000

University of Hartford
200 Bloomfield Ave, West Hartford CT 06117-1599
860-768-4100

University of New Haven
300 Boston Post Rd, West Haven CT 06516
Director of Undergraduate Admissions
203-932-7319 Fax: 203-931-6093
Website: www.newhaven.edu
E-mail: adminfo@newhaven.edu

Western Connecticut State University
181 White St, Danbury CT 06810-6826
203-837-8200

Windham Regional Vocational Technical School
210 Birch St, Willimantic CT 06226-2108
860-456-3789

Yale-New Haven Hospital
20 York St, New Haven CT 06504
203-785-5074

Yale University
38 Hillhouse Ave, New Haven CT 06511
203-432-4771

DELAWARE

Bayhealth Medical Center
640 S State St, Dover DE 19901-3530
302-674-7001

Christiana Care Health Services
PO Box 1668, Wilmington DE 19899-1668
302-428-2571

DAWN TRAINING CENTRE
3700 Lancaster Pike, Wilmington DE 19805-1511
Hollis C. Anglin, President
302-633-9075 Fax: 302-633-9077
Website: www.dawntrainingcentre.edu
E-mail: hcanglin@dawntrainingcentre.edu

Delaware State University
1200 N DuPont Hwy, Dover DE 19901-2275
302-857-6060

Delaware Technical & Community College
PO Box 610, Georgetown DE 19947-0610
302-856-5400

Delaware Technical & Community College
333 N Shipley St, Wilmington DE 19801-2499
302-571-5474

University of Delaware
Newark DE 19711
302-831-2000

Wesley College
120 N State St, Dover DE 19901-3876
302-736-2300 Fax: 302-736-2301
Website: www.wesley.edu

Wilmington College
320 N DuPont Hwy, New Castle DE 19720-6491
302-328-9401

DISTRICT OF COLUMBIA

Gallaudet University
800 Florida Ave NE, Washington DC 20002-3695
Charity Reedy Hines, Director of Admissions
202-651-5750

Georgetown University
37th and O St NW, Washington DC 20057-0001
202-687-0100

George Washington University
2035 H St NW, Washington DC 20052-0002
202-994-1000

Howard University
2400 6th St NW, Washington DC 20059-0002
202-806-6100

University of the District of Columbia
4200 Connecticut Ave NW
Washington DC 20008-1174
LaVerne M. Hill-Flanagan, Director of Admissions
202-274-5100

FLORIDA

ACUPUNCTURE & MASSAGE COLLEGE
10506 N Kendall Dr, Miami FL 33176
Joe Calareso, Admissions Director
305-595-9500 Fax: 305-595-2622
Website: www.amcollege.edu
E-mail: admissions@amcollege.edu

ATLANTIC INSTITUTE OF ORIENTAL MEDICINE
100 E Broward Blvd Ste 100
Fort Lauderdale FL 33301-3510
Prof. Yan Cheng, Academic Dean
954-763-9840 Fax: 954-763-9844
Website: www.atom.edu
E-mail: dean@atom.edu

Barry University
11300 NE 2nd Ave, Miami Shores FL 33161-6695
800-695-2279

BAYFRONT MEDICAL CENTER
701 6th St S, Saint Petersburg FL 33701-4891
June Schurig, Education Coordinator
727-893-6604 Fax: 727-893-6977
Website: www.bayfront.org
E-mail: june.schurig@bayfront.org

Bay Medical Center
615 N Bonita Ave, Panama City FL 32401
Sherry Tindall, Director of Education, Training, &
Research
800-422-2418

Bethune-Cookman College
640 Dr Mary McLeod Bethune Blvd
Daytona Beach FL 32114-3099
Edwin Coffie, Director of Admissions
800-448-0228

Brevard Community College
1519 Clearlake Rd, Cocoa FL 32922-6597
321-632-1111

Broward Community College
225 E Las Olas Blvd, Fort Lauderdale FL 33301-2298
954-475-6500

Central Florida Community College
PO Box 1388, Ocala FL 34478-1388
352-854-2322

Central Florida Institute
30522 US Highway 19 N, Palm Harbor FL 34684
727-786-4707

Charlotte Technical Center
18300 Toledo Blade Blvd
Port Charlotte FL 33948-3399
Carolyn Gorton, Assistant Principal
941-255-7500

City College
2000 W Commercial Blvd, Fort Lauderdale FL 33309
Britt Carpenter, Director of Admissions
954-492-5353 Fax: 954-491-1965
Website: www.citycollege.edu
E-mail: bcarpenter@citycollege.edu

COMPU-MED VOCATIONAL CAREERS
9738 SW 24th St, Miami FL 33165-7513
Mayra Rodriguez, President
305-553-2898 Fax: 305-553-7423
Website: www.compumedschools.com
E-mail: compumed44@aol.com

CONCORDE CAREER INSTITUTE
7960 Arlington Expy, Jacksonville FL 32211-7429
Christine Knouff, Executive Campus Director
904-725-0525 Fax: 904-721-9944
Website: www.concorde.edu
E-mail: cknouff@concorde.edu

CONCORDE CAREER INSTITUTE
4000 N State Rd #7
Lauderdale Lakes FL 33319-4804
Claudette Simpson, Director of Admissions
954-731-8880 Fax: 954-485-2961
Website: www.concorde.edu
E-mail: csimpson@concorde.edu

CONCORDE CAREER INSTITUTE
4202 W Spruce St, Tampa FL 33607-4127
Steve Worrell, Executive Campus Director
813-874-0094 Fax: 813-872-6884
Website: www.concorde.edu
E-mail: sworrell@concorde.edu

Daytona Beach Community College
PO Box 2811, Daytona Beach FL 32120-2811
Tom LoBasso, Dean of Enrollment/Development
386-255-8131

D.G. Erwin Technical Center
2010 E Hillsborough Ave, Tampa FL 33610-8299
813-231-1800

Edison College
PO Box 60210, Fort Myers FL 33906-6210
Billee Silva, Director Student Development
239-489-9054

EVERGLADES UNIVERSITY (MAIN CAMPUS)
5002 T-Rex Ave Suite 100, Boca Raton FL 33431
Kristi Mollis, President
888-772-6077 Fax: 561-912-1191
Website: www.evergladesuniversity.edu
E-mail: admissions-boca@evergladesuniversity.edu
See listing under "Universities"

EVERGLADES UNIVERSITY
Orlando Campus (Branch Campus)
5600 Lake Underhill Rd Suite 200, Orlando FL 32807
Shirley Long, Vice President
866-289-1078 Fax: 407-482-9801
Website: www.evergladesuniversity.edu
E-mail: admissions-orl@evergladesuniversity.edu
See listing under "Universities"

EVERGLADES UNIVERSITY
Sarasota Campus (Branch Campus)
6001 Lake Osprey Dr, Sarasota FL 34240
Brad Brewer, Vice President
866-907-2262 Fax: 941-907-6634
Website: www.evergladesuniversity.edu
E-mail: admissions-sar@evergladesuniversity.edu
See listing under "Universities"

First Coast Technical Institute
2980 Collins Ave, Saint Augustine FL 32084-1919
904-829-1010

Florida A&M University
Tallahassee FL 32307
850-599-3000

Florida Atlantic University
PO Box 3091, Boca Raton FL 33431-0991
800-299-4328

FLORIDA CAREER INSTITUTE
5925 Imperial Pkwy Ste 200, Mulberry FL 33860
863-646-1400
Website: www.floridacareerinstitute.com
E-mail: sethridge@edaff.com

Florida Community College
North Campus
4501 Capper Rd, Jacksonville FL 32218-4436
904-766-6500

FLORIDA HOSPITAL COLLEGE OF HEALTH SCIENCES
800 Lake Estelle Dr, Orlando FL 32803-1237
Office of Admissions
800-500-7747 or 407-303-9798 Fax: 407-303-9408
Website: www.fhchs.edu
E-mail: gina.flenoy@fhchs.edu
Established in 1992. Private. Coed. Accreditation.
Commission on Colleges of the Southern Association of
Colleges and Schools, 1866 Southern Lane, Decatur, GA
30033-4097. 404-679-4500. Tuition: $240 per credit hour
(matriculation & program fees additional). Room and
Board: $6,900 (estimate). Enrollment: 1,034 full-time, 739
part-time. Faculty: 45. Degrees: BS, AS, and Certificates.
Professional Programs: Diagnostic Medical Sonography,
Health Sciences, Nuclear Medicine Technology, Nursing, Occupational Therapy Assistant, Pre-Professional
Studies, Radiography. Professional programs are accredited by their respective accrediting bodies. The College provides state-of-the-art learning labs where
students hone their skills before entering the clinical
arena. Small class sizes allow instructors to have students on an individual basis. Graduates continue to outscore the national averages on licensure and
credentialing examinations. Job outlook for careers in
healthcare is excellent. College housing and financial aid
available for qualified students.

FLORIDA INSTITUTE OF ULTRASOUND, INC.
8800 University Pkwy Ste A4
Pensacola FL 32514-4913
Polly Christensen, Administrative Assistant
850-478-7300 Fax: 850-478-3727
Website: www.fiuonline.net
E-mail: fiupcola@aol.com

Florida International University
Tamiami Trl, Miami FL 33199-0001
305-348-2000

Florida Metropolitan University-Brandon
3924 Coconut Palm Dr, Tampa FL 33619-1354
Marty Baca, Director of Admissions
877-338-0068 (Toll Free)

Florida Metropolitan University
Melbourne Campus
2401 N Harbor City Blvd, Melbourne FL 32935
321-253-2929

Florida Metropolitan University
Orlando College - North
5421 Diplomat Cir, Orlando FL 32810-5601
Charlene Donnelly, Director of Admissions
800-628-5870

Florida Metropolitan University
Orlando South
9200 Southpark Center Loop, Orlando FL 32819
Annette Cloin, Contact
407-851-2525 Fax: 407-851-1477
Website: www.fmu.edu
E-mail: acloin@cci.edu

FLORIDA METROPOLITAN UNIVERSITY
Pinellas Campus
2471 N McMullen Booth Rd
Clearwater FL 33759-1359
Sandra Williams, Director of Admissions
800-353-3687 or 727-725-2688 Fax: 727-725-3827
Website: www.fmu.edu
E-mail: sawilliams@cci.edu

Florida Metropolitan University
Tampa Campus
3319 W Hillsborough Ave, Tampa FL 33614-5801
Donnie Broughton, Director of Admissions
813-879-6000

Florida National College
Hialeah Campus
4425 W 20th Ave, Hialeah FL 33012
Jorge Afonso, Campus Dean
305-821-3333 ext. 1022 Fax: 305-362-0595
Website: www.fnc.edu
E-mail: omarsnc@fnc.edu

Florida National College
South Campus
11865 SW 26th St, Miami FL 33175
Jon Beisenherz, Campus Dean
305-266-9999
Website: www.fnc.edu
E-mail: omarsnc@fnc.edu

Florida Southern College
Athletic Training
111 Lake Hollingsworth Dr, Lakeland FL 33801-5607
Robert B. Palmer, V.P., Dean of Enrollment
Management
863-680-4131

Gulf Coast Community College
5230 W Highway 98, Panama City FL 32401-1058
850-769-1551

Heritage Institute
6811 Palisades Park Ct, Fort Myers FL 33912
Eva Hutson, Director
239-936-5822 Fax: 239-225-9117
Website: www.heritage-education.com
E-mail: info@heritage-education.com
See listing under "Career Schools"

Heritage Institute
4130 N Salisbury Rd Suite 1100
Jacksonville FL 32216
Sonnie Willingham, Director
904-332-0910 Fax: 904-332-0920
Website: www.heritage-education.com
E-mail: info@heritage-education.com
See listing under "Career Schools"

HERZING COLLEGE
1595 S Semoran Blvd #1501
Winter Park FL 32792-5509
Kathy Nagle, Director of Admissions
407-478-0500 Fax: 407-478-0501
Website: www.herzing.edu
E-mail: info@orl.herzing.edu

High-Tech Institute
3710 Maguire Blvd, Orlando FL 32803-3013
407-893-7400 Fax: 407-895-1804
Website: www.hightechinstitute.edu

Hillsborough Community College
1404 Tech Blvd, Tampa FL 33619-7865
813-253-7000

Indian River Community College
3209 Virginia Ave, Fort Pierce FL 34981-5596
772-462-4700

INTERNATIONAL COLLEGE
4501 Colonial Blvd, Fort Myers FL 33966
Rita Lampus, Vice President of Enrollment
Management
800-466-0019 or 239-482-0019 Fax: 239-938-7891
Website: www.internationalcollege.edu
E-mail: cmorrison@internationalcollege.edu

INTERNATIONAL COLLEGE
2655 Northbrooke Dr, Naples FL 34119
Rita Lampus, Vice President of Enrollment
Management
800-466-8017 or 239-513-1122 Fax: 239-598-6254
Website: www.internationalcollege.edu
E-mail: admit@internationalcollege.edu
See listing under "Universities"

James Haley Veteran's Hospital
13000 Bruce B Downs Blvd, Tampa FL 33612-4745
813-972-2000

Jones College
5353 Arlington Expy, Jacksonville FL 32211-5588
Dorothy D. Jones, Chief Executive Officer
904-743-1122 Fax: 904-744-4446
Website: www.jones.edu
E-mail: lwade@jones.edu

Keiser College
1800 Business Park Blvd, Daytona Beach FL 32114
Matt McEnany, Vice President
386-274-5060 Fax: 386-274-2725
Website: www.keisercollege.edu
E-mail: mmcenany@keisercollege.edu

Keiser College
1500 NW 49th St, Fort Lauderdale FL 33309-3700
Anne O'Connell, Director Community Relations
954-776-4456

Keiser College
900 S Babcock St, Melbourne FL 32901-1461
321-255-2255

Key College
225 E Dania Beach Blvd #130
Dania Beach FL 33004
Ronald Dooley, President
954-923-4440 Fax: 954-923-9226
Website: www.keycollege.edu
E-mail: admissions@keycollege.edu

Lake City Community College
149 SE College Pl, Lake City FL 32025
386-752-1822

Lake Technical Center
2001 Kurt St, Eustis FL 32726-6164
352-589-2250

Lindsey Hopkins Technical Education Center
750 NW 20th St, Miami FL 33127-4618
305-324-6070

Lively Area Vocational Technical School
500 Appleyard Dr, Tallahassee FL 32304-2810
850-487-7555

Lorenzo Walker Institute of Technology
3702 Estey Ave, Naples FL 34104-4405
239-430-6900

Manatee Technical Institute East Campus
5520 Lakewood Ranch Blvd, Bradenton FL 34211
Carla Brokaw, Director of Admissions
941-752-8100

Marion County School of Radiologic Technology
1014 SW 7th Rd, Ocala FL 34474-3172
352-671-7200

Medical Career Center
19 W Garden St, Pensacola FL 32502-5678
850-436-8444

Miami-Dade College
300 NE 2nd Ave, Miami FL 33132-2296
305-237-3316

National School of Technology
111 NW 183rd St Ste 200, Miami FL 33169-4538
305-949-9500

New England Institute of Technology
2410 Metrocentre Blvd
West Palm Beach FL 33407-3105
Michael Schwam, Director of Admissions
561-688-2001

North Technical Education Center
7071 Garden Rd, Riviera Beach FL 33404-4906
561-881-4600

Nova Southeastern University
3301 College Ave, Davie FL 33314-7796
954-262-7300

Nova Southeastern University Health Profession
3200 S University Dr, Davie FL 33328-2018
Marla Frohlinger, Director of Admissions
954-262-1101 Fax: 954-262-2282
Website: www.nova.edu
E-mail: marlaf@nsu.nova.edu

Orange Technical Education Center - Orlando Tech
301 W Amelia St, Orlando FL 32801-1122
407-246-7060

Orange Technical Education Centers-Winter Park Tech
901 W Webster Ave, Winter Park FL 32789-3049
Diane Culpepper, Director
407-622-2900

Pasco-Hernando Community College
10230 Ridge Rd, New Port Richey FL 34654-5129
727-847-2727

Pensacola Junior College
1000 College Blvd, Pensacola FL 32504-8998
850-484-1000

Pinellas Technical Education Center
901 34th St S, Saint Petersburg FL 33711-2209
727-893-2500

Polk Community College
999 Avenue H NE, Winter Haven FL 33881-4299
863-297-1000

PROFESSIONAL TRAINING CENTER
13926 SW 47th St, Miami FL 33175
Maria Rizo, Admission Director
305-220-4120 Fax: 305-220-2889
Website: www.ptcmatt.com
E-mail: emattia@ptcmatt.com

Radiation Therapy Services, Inc.
1419 SE 8th Terrace, Cape Coral FL 33990
Donald E. Moody, Program Director
239-772-3202

REMINGTON COLLEGE
7011 A C Skinner Pky Suite 140
Jacksonville FL 32256-6953
Bobby Johns, Director of Student Recruitment
904-296-3435 Fax: 904-296-9097
Website: www.remingtoncollege.edu
E-mail: bobby.johns@remingtoncollege.edu

Remington College, Tampa Campus
2410 E Busch Blvd, Tampa FL 33612-8410
Director of Recruitment
813-935-5700 Fax: 813-935-7415
Website: www.remingtoncollege.edu

Robert Morgan Educational Center
18180 SW 122nd Ave, Miami FL 33177-2407
Antonio Martinez, Principal
305-253-9920

Rollins College
1000 Holt Ave, Winter Park FL 32789
407-646-2000

Saint Leo University
PO Box 6665, Saint Leo FL 33574
Deborah Bandy, Director of Admissions
352-588-8200 or 800-334-5532 Fax: 352-588-8257
Website: www.saintleo.edu
E-mail: admission@saintleo.edu

St. Luke's Hospital/Mayo Clinic
4201 Belfort Rd, Jacksonville FL 32216-1431
904-296-3733

St. Petersburg College
PO Box 13489, Saint Petersburg FL 33733-3489
727-341-3600

SANFORD BROWN INSTITUTE
4780 N State Road 7 Suite 100
Lauderdale Lakes FL 33319-5860
Todd Oxendine, Director of Admissions
954-308-7400 Fax: 954-733-8994
Website: www.sbftlaud.com
E-mail: toxendine@sbftlaud.com

SANFORD BROWN INSTITUTE
5701 E Hillsborough Ave #1417, Tampa FL 33610
Patricia Meredith, President
813-621-0072 Fax: 813-626-0392
Website: www.sbtampa.com

Santa Fe Community College
3000 NW 83rd St, Gainesville FL 32606-6200
Jackson N. Sasser, President
352-395-5787 Fax: 352-395-4118
Website: www.sfcc.edu
E-mail: ouida.mcneil@sfcc.edu

Sarasota County Technical Institute
4748 Beneva Rd, Sarasota FL 34233-1798
Wm. A. Storms Jr., Director
941-924-1365 ext. 325

Sarasota Memorial Hospital
1700 S Tamiami Trl, Sarasota FL 34239-3555
941-917-1080

Seminole Community College
100 Weldon Blvd, Sanford FL 32773-6199
407-328-4722

Sheridan Vocational-Technical Center
5400 Sheridan St, Hollywood FL 33021-3399
Rosa Lee, Guidance Director
754-321-5400

South Florida Community College
600 W College Dr, Avon Park FL 33825-9356
863-453-6661

South University
1760 N Congress Ave
West Palm Beach FL 33409-5178
Steven A. Schwab, President
561-697-9200 Fax: 561-697-9944
Website: www.southuniversity.edu
E-mail: wpb@southuniversity.edu
SACS Accreditation.

SOUTHWEST FLORIDA COLLEGE
1685 Medical Ln, Fort Myers FL 33907-1157
866-SWFC-NOW or 239-939-4766 Fax: 239-936-4040
Website: www.swfc.edu
E-mail: studentinfo@swfc.edu

Stetson University
421 N Woodland Boulevard, De Land FL 32720-3761
386-822-7000

Tallahassee Community College
444 Appleyard Dr, Tallahassee FL 32304-2895
850-201-8595

Tampa General Hospital
School of Medical Technology
PO Box 1289, Tampa FL 33601-1289
Laura Ferguson, Education Coordinator
813-844-7985

Tom P. Haney Technical Center
3016 Highway 77, Panama City FL 32405-5004
850-747-5500

Traviss Technical Center
3225 Winter Lake Rd, Lakeland FL 33803-9709
863-499-2700

University of Central Florida
PO Box 160111, Orlando FL 32816
407-823-3000

University of Florida
PO Box 114000, Gainesville FL 32611-4000
352-392-3261

University of Miami
PO Box 248006, Coral Gables FL 33124-8006
305-284-2211

University of North Florida
4567 Saint Johns Bluff Rd S
Jacksonville FL 32224-2645
904-620-1000

University of South Florida
4202 E Fowler Ave, Tampa FL 33620-6900
J. Robert Spatig, Director of Admissions
813-974-3350 Fax: 813-974-9689
Website: www.usf.edu
E-mail: admissions@admin.usf.edu

University of West Florida
11000 University Pkwy, Pensacola FL 32514-5750
850-474-2000

Valencia Community College
PO Box 3028, Orlando FL 32802-3028
407-299-5000

West Boca Medical Center
21644 State Road 7, Boca Raton FL 33428-1899
561-488-8000

William T. McFatter Technical Center
6500 Nova Dr, Davie FL 33317-7405
954-370-8324

GEORGIA

Albany Technical College
1704 S Slappey Blvd, Albany GA 31701
229-430-3500

American Red Cross Blood Services
1925 Monroe Dr NE, Atlanta GA 30324-4828
404-881-9800

Armstrong Atlantic State University
11935 Abercorn St, Savannah GA 31419-1997
Kim West, Asst. Dean and Registrar Enrollment
Services
912-927-5277 Fax: 912-921-5462
Website: www.armstrong.edu
E-mail: admissions@mail.armstrong.edu

Athens Technical College
800 Highway 29 N, Athens GA 30601-1546
706-355-5000

ATLANTA SCHOOL OF MASSAGE
2 Dunwoody Park, Atlanta GA 30338-6704
Admissions Department
770-454-7167 ext. 120 Fax: 770-454-7367
Website: www.atlantaschoolofmassage.com
E-mail: admissions@atlantaschoolofmassage.com

Atlanta Technical College
1560 Metropolitan Pkwy SW, Atlanta GA 30310-4499
404-756-3700

Augusta Technical College
3116 Deans Bridge Rd, Augusta GA 30906-3399
706-771-4000

Brenau College
1 Centennial Cir, Gainesville GA 30501-3668
770-534-6299

Central Georgia Technical College
3300 Macon Tech Dr, Macon GA 31206-3628
478-757-3501

Chattahoochee Technical College
980 S Cobb Dr SE, Marietta GA 30060-3300
Nichole H. Kennedy, Director of Admissions
770-528-4465

Clark Atlanta University
223 James Brawley Dr SW, Atlanta GA 30314
404-880-8000

Clayton State University
5900 N Lee St, Morrow GA 30260
770-961-3500

Coastal Georgia Community College
3700 Altama Ave, Brunswick GA 31520-3632
912-264-7235

Columbus State University
4225 University Ave, Columbus GA 31907-5645
706-568-2001

Columbus Technical College
928 Manchester Expressway
Columbus GA 31904-6577
706-649-1837

Coosa Valley Technical Institute
1 Maurice Culberson Dr SW, Rome GA 30161
706-295-6927

Dalton State College
213 College Dr, Dalton GA 30720-3745
706-272-4436

Darton College
2400 Gillionville Rd, Albany GA 31707-3098
229-430-6000

DeKalb Technical College
495 N Indian Creek Dr, Clarkston GA 30021-2397
Terry Richardson, Director of Admissions
404-297-9522 Fax: 404-294-6496
Website: www.dekalbtech.edu
E-mail: richardt@dekalbtech.edu

Emory University
200B Jones Center, Atlanta GA 30322
404-727-6123

Fort Valley State University
1005 State University Dr, Fort Valley GA 31030-3298
478-825-6307

GEORGIA MEDICAL INSTITUTE
1706 Northeast Expy, Atlanta GA 30329
Director of Admissions
404-327-8787 Fax: 404-327-8980
Website: www.georgia-med.com

Georgia Southern University
PO Box 8024, Statesboro GA 30460
Admissions Office
912-681-5532

Georgia State University
PO Box 4009, Atlanta GA 30302-4009
404-651-2365

Grady Health System
PO Box 26189, Atlanta GA 30303-0001
404-616-4252

Griffin Technical College
501 Varsity Rd, Griffin GA 30223-2042
770-228-7366

Gupton-Jones College of Funeral Service
5141 Snapfinger Woods Dr, Decatur GA 30035-4022
Patty S. Hutcheson, President
770-593-2257 Fax: 770-593-1891
Website: www.gupton-jones.edu
E-mail: gjcfs@mindspring.com

Gwinnett Technical College
5150 Sugarloaf Pkwy, Lawrenceville GA 30043-5702
770-962-7580

Heart of Georgia Area Technical Institute
560 Pinehill Rd, Dublin GA 31021-1253
478-275-6590

Lanier Technical College
2990 Landrum Education Dr
Oakwood GA 30566-3405
Michael C. Marlowe, Director of Admissions
770-531-6328

Life University
1269 Barclay Cir SE, Marietta GA 30060-2903
Dr. Deborah E. Heairlston, Director of New Student
Development
770-426-2884 Fax: 770-426-2895
Website: www.life.edu
E-mail: admissions@life.edu

Macon State College
100 College Station Dr, Macon GA 31206-5145
478-471-2700

Medical College of Georgia
1120 15th St, Augusta GA 30912-0004
706-721-2725

Medix School
2108 Cobb Pkwy SE, Smyrna GA 30080-7630
Crystal Henry, Director of Admissions
770-980-0002

Middle Georgia College
1100 2nd St SE, Cochran GA 31014-1564
478-934-6221

Moultrie Technical College
800 Veterans Pkwy N, Moultrie GA 31788
229-891-7000

North Georgia College & State University
Dahlonega GA 30597-0001
706-864-1400

North Georgia Technical College
434 Meeks Ave, Blairsville GA 30512-2983
Admissions
706-781-2300 Fax: 706-781-2307
Website: www.northgatech.edu
E-mail: info@northgatech.edu

North Georgia Technical College
8989 Highway 17, Toccoa GA 30577
706-779-5591
Website: www.northgatech.edu
E-mail: info@northgatech.edu

North Georgia Technical College
Clarkesville Campus
PO Box 65, Clarkesville GA 30523-0002
Admissions
706-754-7700 Fax: 706-754-7777
Website: www.northgatech.edu
E-mail: info@northgatech.edu

North Metro Technical College
5198 Ross Rd SE, Acworth GA 30102-3129
Missy Cusack, Director of Admissions
770-975-4000 Fax: 770-975-4142
Website: www.northmetrotech.edu
E-mail: info@northmetrotech.edu

Northwestern Technical College
265 Bicentennial Trl, Rock Spring GA 30739-2306
Dr. Ray Brooks, President
Greg Cross, Vice President for Student Services
706-764-3518

Ogeechee Technical College
1 Joseph E Kennedy Blvd
Statesboro GA 30458-3199
912-681-5500

Oglethorpe University
4484 Peachtree Rd NE, Atlanta GA 30319-2797
Kelly Gosnell, Director of Admission
404-261-1441 Fax: 404-364-8491
Website: www.oglethorpe.edu
E-mail: admission@oglethorpe.edu

Okefenokee Technical College
1701 Carswell Ave, Waycross GA 31503-4016
912-287-6584

SAVANNAH RIVER COLLEGE
2528 Centerwest Pkwy Bldg A, Augusta GA 30909
Dawn McCraith, Director
706-738-5046 Fax: 706-736-3599
Website: www.savannahrivercollege.com
E-mail: info@savannahrivercollege.com

Savannah Technical College
5717 White Bluff Rd, Savannah GA 31405-5521
912-351-6362

Southern Regional Medical Center
11 Upper Riverdale Rd SW
Riverdale GA 30274-2615
770-991-8053

Southwest Georgia Technical College
15689 US Highway 19 N, Thomasville GA 31792
229-225-5096

Swainsboro Technical College
346 Kite Rd, Swainsboro GA 30401-5700
478-289-2200

Thomas University
1501 Millpond Rd, Thomasville GA 31792-7478
Darla M. Glass, Director of Student Affairs
229-226-1621

University Hospital Health System
1350 Walton Way, Augusta GA 30901-2629
706-722-9011

University of Georgia
Athens GA 30602-0001
706-542-3000

Valdosta State University
N Patterson St, Valdosta GA 31698-0001
229-333-5952

Valdosta Technical College
4089 Val Tech Rd, Valdosta GA 31602
James Bridges, President
229-333-2100

West Central Technical College
4600 Timber Ridge Dr, Douglasville GA 30135-1225
770-947-7200

West Georgia Technical College
303 Fort Dr, La Grange GA 30240-5901
706-845-4323

HAWAII

Heald College, Honolulu
1500 Kapiolani Blvd, Honolulu HI 96814-3732
Lon K. Ibaraki, Director of Admissions
808-955-1500 or 800-940-0530 Fax: 808-955-6964
Website: www.heald.edu
E-mail: lon_ibaraki@heald.edu

Kapiolani Community College
4303 Diamond Head Rd, Honolulu HI 96816-4496
808-734-9111

University of Hawaii at Manoa
2444 Dole St, Honolulu HI 96822-2302
808-956-5280

IDAHO

Apollo College Boise
1200 N Liberty St, Boise ID 83704-8742
208-377-8080

Boise State University
1910 University Dr, Boise ID 83725-0399
208-426-1011

Brigham Young University - Idaho
120 Kimball Bldg, Rexburg ID 83460
Gordon Westenskow, Director of Admissions
208-496-1020 Fax: 208-496-1220
Website: www.byui.edu
E-mail: admissions@byui.edu

College of Southern Idaho
PO Box 1238, Twin Falls ID 83303-1238
208-733-9554

Eastern Idaho Technical College
1600 S 25th E, Idaho Falls ID 83404
208-524-3000

Idaho State University
PO Box 8270, Pocatello ID 83209-0001
208-282-0211

St. Alphonsus Regional Medical Center
1055 N Curtis Rd, Boise ID 83706-1309
208-378-2000

ILLINOIS

ADVOCATE ILLINOIS MASONIC
School of Radiologic Technology
836 W Wellington Ave, Chicago IL 60657
Philis George, Director
773-296-8950 Fax: 773-296-8960
Website: www.advocatehealth.com
E-mail: IMMCSRT@advocatehealth.com

Aurora University
347 S Gladstone Ave, Aurora IL 60506-4892
Carol R. Dunn, Ed.D., Vice President for Enrollment
800-742-5281 Fax: 630-844-5535
Website: www.aurora.edu
E-mail: admission@aurora.edu

Benedictine University
5700 College Rd, Lisle IL 60532-0900
630-829-6300 or 888-829-6363 Fax: 630-829-6301
Website: www.ben.edu
E-mail: admissions@ben.edu
See listing under "Universities"

Black Hawk College
6600 34th Ave, Moline IL 61265-5899
309-796-5000

BLOOMINGTON-NORMAL SCHOOL OF RADIOGRAPHY
900 Franklin Ave, Normal IL 61761-4604
Beth Kuhfuss, MS, RT (R) ARRT, Program Director
309-452-2834 Fax: 309-392-2835
Website: www.bnradiography.com

Bradley University
1501 W Bradley Ave, Peoria IL 61625-0002
800-447-6460

Carl Sandburg College
2232 S Lake Storey Rd, Galesburg IL 61401-9576
309-344-2518

Central Medical Education
550 E Washington St, West Chicago IL 60185-2200
630-682-1600

Chicago State University
9501 S King Dr, Chicago IL 60628-1598
773-995-2000

College of DuPage
425 22nd St, Glen Ellyn IL 60137-6599
630-942-2800

College of Lake County
19351 W Washington St, Grayslake IL 60030-1148
847-223-6601

College of Office Technology
1514 W Division St # 2, Chicago IL 60622-3312
Greg Brown, Director of Admissions
773-278-0042 Fax: 773-278-0143
Website: www.cot.edu
E-mail: kgalva@cotedu.com

Dominican University
7900 Division St, River Forest IL 60305-1066
708-366-2490

Eastern Illinois University
600 Lincoln Ave, Charleston IL 61920-3099
217-581-5000

Elgin Community College
1700 Spartan Dr, Elgin IL 60123-7193
847-214-7385

Governors State University
1 University Pkwy, University Park IL 60466-0975
708-534-5000

Harry S. Truman College
1145 W Wilson Ave, Chicago IL 60640-5691
773-878-1700

Illinois Central College
1 College Dr, Peoria IL 61635-0002
309-694-5011

Illinois Institute of Technology
3300 S Federal St, Chicago IL 60616-3793
Brent Benner, Director of Admissions
312-567-3000

ILLINOIS SCHOOL OF HEALTH CAREERS
220 S State St Ste 600, Chicago IL 60604-2098
Jeffrey L. Jarmes, Executive Director
312-913-1230 Fax: 312-913-1113
Website: www.ishc.edu
E-mail: jjarmes@ishc.edu

Illinois State University
Normal IL 61790-0001
309-438-2111

Illinois Valley Community College
815 N Orlando Smith St, Oglesby IL 61348-9692
815-224-2720

Ingalls Memorial Hospital
1 Ingalls Dr, Harvey IL 60426-3558
708-333-2300

John A. Logan College
700 Logan College Rd, Carterville IL 62918
Terry Crain, Associate Dean Student Services
618-985-3741

Kankakee Community College
PO Box 888, Kankakee IL 60901-0888
815-933-0345

Kaskaskia College
27210 College Rd, Centralia IL 62801-7878
Tyra Taylor, Dean of Enrollment Management and
Retention Services
618-545-3000 Fax: 618-532-1990
Website: www.kaskaskia.edu
E-mail: ttaylor@kaskaskia.edu

Kennedy-King College
6800 S Wentworth Ave, Chicago IL 60621-3798
773-602-5000

Kishwaukee College
21193 Malta Rd, Malta IL 60150-9699
815-825-2086

Lake Land College
5001 Lake Land Blvd, Mattoon IL 61938-9366
217-234-5253

Lewis & Clark Community College
5800 Godfrey Rd, Godfrey IL 62035-2426
618-466-3411

Lincoln Land Community College
5250 Shepherd Rd, Springfield IL 62703-5408
217-786-2200

Loyola University of Chicago
820 N Michigan Ave, Chicago IL 60611-2103
312-915-6000

Malcolm X College
1900 W Van Buren St, Chicago IL 60612-3197
312-850-7031

Midstate College
411 W Northmoor Rd, Peoria IL 61614-3595
309-692-4092

MIDWEST COLLEGE OF ORIENTAL MEDICINE
4334 N Hazel St Ste 206, Chicago IL 60613-1429
Kelly Westerlund, Contact
800-593-2320 Fax: 262-554-7475
Website: www.acupuncture.edu
E-mail: mwcadmissions@yahoo.com

Midwestern University
555 31st St, Downers Grove IL 60515-1235
Raelene Brower, Director of Admissions
630-969-4400

Moraine Valley Community College
10900 S 88th Ave, Palos Hills IL 60465-0937
708-974-4300

Morton College
3801 S Central Ave, Cicero IL 60804-4398
708-656-8000

National-Louis University
2840 Sheridan Rd, Evanston IL 60201-1796

North Central College
30 N Brainard St, Naperville IL 60540-4690
Martha Stolze, Director of Admissions
630-637-5800 Fax: 630-637-5819
Website: www.northcentralcollege.edu
E-mail: admissions@noctrl.edu

Northern Illinois University
DeKalb IL 60115
815-753-1000

Northwestern Business College
7725 S Harlem Ave, Bridgeview IL 60455-1318
800-682-9113

Northwestern Business College
4829 N Lipps Ave, Chicago IL 60630-2298
Mark Sliz, Director of Admissions
773-777-4220

Northwestern University
1801 Hinman Ave, Evanston IL 60208-1260
847-491-3741

Oakton Community College
1600 E Golf Rd, Des Plaines IL 60016-1256
David Cole, Director of Enrollment Management
847-635-1600

Olivet Nazarene University
1 University Ave
Bourbonnais IL 60914
815-939-5011

Olney Central College
305 N West St, Olney IL 62450-1099
618-395-7777

Parkland College
2400 W Bradley Ave, Champaign IL 61821-1899
Mike Henry, Contact
217-351-2208

Prairie State College
202 S Halsted St, Chicago Heights IL 60411-8226
708-709-3500

Provena United Samaritans Medical Center
812 N Logan Ave, Danville IL 61832
217-443-5201

Robert Morris College
401 S State St, Chicago IL 60605-1229
312-935-6800

Rockford Business College
730 N Church St, Rockford IL 61103-6968
Tammy Rockett-Box, Director of Enrollment Services
815-965-8616

Rockford Memorial Hospital
2400 N Rockton Ave, Rockford IL 61103-3681
815-971-5000

Rock Valley College
3301 N Mulford Rd, Rockford IL 61114-5699
815-654-4250

Roosevelt University
430 S Michigan Ave, Chicago IL 60605
Gwen E. Kanelos, Asst. Vice President for Enrollment Services
877-APPLY-RU Fax: 312-341-4216
Website: www.roosevelt.edu
E-mail: applyru@roosevelt.edu

Rosalind Franklin University of Medicine and Science
3333 Green Bay Rd, North Chicago IL 60064-3037
847-578-3000

Rush University
College Admission Services
600 S Paulina St #440, Chicago IL 60612-3806
Hicela Castruita, Director
312-942-7100

St. Anthony Medical Center
5666 E State St, Rockford IL 61108-2472
815-226-2000

St. Augustine College
1333 W Argyle St, Chicago IL 60640-3593
773-878-8756

St. John's Hospital
800 E Carpenter St, Springfield IL 62769-0002
217-544-6464

St. Xavier University
3700 W 103rd St, Chicago IL 60655-3199
773-298-3000

Sauk Valley Community College
173 Illinois Route 2, Dixon IL 61021
815-288-5511

School of the Art Institute of Chicago
Art Therapy Program
37 S Wabash Ave, Chicago IL 60603-3002
800-232-7242

Southeastern Illinois College
3575 College Rd, Harrisburg IL 62946-4925
618-252-6376

Southern Illinois University
Carbondale IL 62901-4400
618-453-2121

Southern Illinois University Edwardsville
Edwardsville IL 62026-0001
618-650-3705

South Suburban College of Cook County
15800 State St, South Holland IL 60473
Jane Ellen Stocker, Dean of Enrollment Services
708-596-2000 Fax: 708-225-5806
Website: www.southsuburbancollege.edu
E-mail: jstocker@southsuburbancollege.edu

Southwestern Illinois College
2500 Carlyle Ave, Belleville IL 62221-5899
618-235-2700

Trinity College of Nursing & Health Sciences
2122 25th Ave, Rock Island IL 61201-5317
Joanne Cunningham, Director of Admissions
309-779-7700 Fax: 309-799-7748
Website: www.trinitycollegeqc.edu
E-mail: con@trinityqc.edu

Triton College
2000 5th Ave, River Grove IL 60171-1995
Mary-Rita Moore, Dean of Enrollment Services
708-456-0300 ext. 3130 Fax: 708-583-3147
Website: www.triton.edu
E-mail: triton@triton.edu
See listing under "Community and Junior Colleges"

University of Chicago Hospital/Roosevelt University
5841 S Maryland Ave, Chicago IL 60637-1463
773-702-6240

University of Illinois
901 W Illinois St, Urbana IL 61801
217-333-1000

University of Illinois at Chicago
PO Box 5220, Chicago IL 60680-5220
312-996-3000

University of Illinois at Springfield
One University Plaza, Springfield IL 62794
217-206-4847

Waubonsee Community College
Route 47 at Waubonsee Dr, Sugar Grove IL 60554
630-466-7900

Western Illinois University
1 University Cir, Macomb IL 61455-1390
309-295-1414

Wilbur Wright College North
4300 N Narragansett Ave, Chicago IL 60634-1591
773-777-7900

William Rainey Harper College
1200 W Algonquin Rd, Palatine IL 60067-7373
847-925-6000

INDIANA

Ancilla Domini College
Donaldson IN 46513
Erin Wittmeyer, Director of Admissions
574-936-8898 Fax: 574-935-1773
Website: www.ancilla.edu
E-mail: erin.wittmeyer@ancilla.edu

Anderson University
1100 E 5th St, Anderson IN 46012-3495
765-649-9071

Ball State University
2000 W University Ave, Muncie IN 47306-0002
765-285-5555

Bloomington Hospital
PO Box 1149, Bloomington IN 47402-1149
812-336-6821

Brown Mackie College - Fort Wayne
3000 E Coliseum Blvd, Fort Wayne IN 46805
Daniel Summer, Campus President
260-484-4400 Fax: 260-484-2678
Website: www.brownmackie.edu

Brown Mackie College - South Bend
1030 E Jefferson Blvd, South Bend IN 46617-3123
Connie Adelman, Campus President
574-237-0774 Fax: 574-237-3585
Website: www.brownmackie.edu

Butler University
4600 Sunset Ave, Indianapolis IN 46208-3443
317-940-8000

Columbus Regional Hospital
2400 17th St, Columbus IN 47201-5360
812-376-5439

Community College of Indiana - Valparaiso
2401 Valley Dr, Valparaiso IN 46383-2520
219-464-8514

Fort Wayne School of Radiography
700 Broadway, Fort Wayne IN 46802-1402
Ann Lewis, Program Director
260-425-3990

Franklin College
101 Branigin Blvd, Franklin IN 46131
Jacqueline S. Acosta, Director of Admissions
800-852-0232 Fax: 317-738-8274
Website: www.franklincollege.edu
E-mail: admissions@franklincollege.edu

Hancock Memorial Hospital
801 N State St, Greenfield IN 46140-1270
317-462-0457

Indiana Business College
550 E Washington St, Indianapolis IN 46204
317-264-5656

Indiana State University
Terre Haute IN 47809-0001
Richard Toomey, Director of Admissions
812-237-6311

Indiana University
300 N Jordan Ave, Bloomington IN 47405-1106
812-855-4848

Indiana University at South Bend
PO Box 7111, South Bend IN 46634-7111
574-237-4111

Indiana University Northwest
3400 Broadway, Gary IN 46408-1101
219-980-6500

Indiana University-Purdue University at Fort Wayne
2101 E Coliseum Blvd, Fort Wayne IN 46805-1445
260-481-6100

Indiana University-Purdue University at Indianapolis
355 Lansing St, Indianapolis IN 46202-2815
317-274-5555

Indiana University School of Allied Health Sciences
1140 W Michigan St, Indianapolis IN 46202-5119
317-274-4702

Indiana Vocational Technical College
PO Box 1763, Indianapolis IN 46206-1763
317-921-4882

Indiana Wesleyan University
4201 S Washington St, Marion IN 46953-4974
765-674-6901

International Business College
5699 Coventry Ln, Fort Wayne IN 46804
260-459-4500 Fax: 260-436-1896
Website: www.ibcfortwayne.edu
E-mail: skinzer@ibcfortwayne.edu

International Business College
7205 Shadeland Station Way
Indianapolis IN 46256-3954
317-841-6400

Ivy Tech Community College - North Central
220 Dean Johnson Blvd, South Bend IN 46601-3415
Pam Decker, Director of Admissions
574-289-7001 Fax: 574-236-7177
Website: www.ivytech.edu
E-mail: pdecker@ivytech.edu

Ivy Tech Community College of Indiana - Columbus
4475 Central Ave, Columbus IN 47203-1868
812-372-9925

Ivy Tech Community College of Indiana - East Central
4301 S Cowan Rd, Muncie IN 47302-9448
765-289-2291

Ivy Tech Community College of Indiana - Kokomo
PO Box 1373, Kokomo IN 46903-1373
765-459-0561

Ivy Tech Community College of Indiana - Lafayette
PO Box 6299, Lafayette IN 47903-6299
765-772-9100

Ivy Tech Community College of Indiana - Northeast
3800 N Anthony Blvd, Fort Wayne IN 46805-1430
260-482-9171

Ivy Tech Community College of Indiana - Northwest
1440 E 35th Ave, Gary IN 46409-1401
219-981-1111

Ivy Tech Community College of Indiana - Richmond
2325 Chester Blvd, Richmond IN 47374-1220
765-966-2656

Ivy Tech Community College of Indiana - Southeast
590 Ivy Tech Dr, Madison IN 47250
812-265-2580

Ivy Tech Community College of Indiana - Southern Indiana
8204 Highway 311, Sellersburg IN 47172-1829
812-246-3301

Ivy Tech Community College of Indiana - Southwest
3501 N 1st Ave, Evansville IN 47710-3319
812-426-2865

Ivy Tech Community College Wabash Valley
7999 S US Highway 41, Terre Haute IN 47802-4845
812-299-1121

Ivy Tech State College
104 W 53rd St, Anderson IN 46013
765-643-7133

King's Daughter's Hospital
PO Box 447, Madison IN 47250-0447
812-265-5211

Lakeshore Medical Laboratory Training Programs
402 Franklin St, Michigan City IN 46360-3327
Gina Watson, MT (ASCP), Program Director
219-872-7032

Marian College
3200 Cold Spring Rd, Indianapolis IN 46222-1997
317-955-6000

Methodist Hospital/Clarian Health Partners
PO Box 1367, Indianapolis IN 46206-1367
317-929-5900

Porter Memorial Hospital
814 LaPorte Ave, Valparaiso IN 46383-5898
Bridget Burge, B.S., R.T., Program Director
219-465-4883

Professional Careers Institute
7302 Woodland Dr, Indianapolis IN 46278-1736
317-299-6001

Purdue University
2200 169th St, Hammond IN 46323
219-989-2993

Purdue University
1401 S US Highway 421, Westville IN 46391-9542
219-785-5200

Reid Hospital & Health Care Services
1401 Chester Blvd, Richmond IN 47374-1908
765-983-3167

St. Francis Hospital Center
1600 Albany St, Beech Grove IN 46107-1593
317-783-8220

St. Joseph Hospital & Health Center
1907 W Sycamore St, Kokomo IN 46901-4197
765-452-5611

St. Margaret Hospital
5454 S Hohman Ave, Hammond IN 46320-1931
219-932-2300

University of Evansville
1800 Lincoln Ave, Evansville IN 47722-0001
Thomas E. Bear, V.P. of Enrollment Services
800-423-8633 Fax: 812-488-4076
Website: www.evansville.edu
E-mail: admission@evansville.edu

University of Indianapolis
1400 E Hanna Ave, Indianapolis IN 46227-3697
317-788-3368

University of St. Francis
2701 Spring St, Fort Wayne IN 46808-3994
Matthew P. Nettleton, Director of Admissions
260-434-3279

University of Southern Indiana
8600 University Blvd, Evansville IN 47712-3591
812-464-8600

Vincennes University
1002 N 1st St, Vincennes IN 47591-1504
Chris M. Crews, Director of Admission
812-888-4313

Welborn Baptist Hospital
401 SE 6th St, Evansville IN 47713-1299
812-426-8264

IOWA

Allen College
1825 Logan Ave, Waterloo IA 50703-1999
319-226-2000

Briar Cliff University
PO Box 2100, Sioux City IA 51104-0100
Sharisue Wilcoxon, VP for Enrollment Management
712-279-5200 Fax: 712-279-1632
Website: www.briarcliff.edu
E-mail: admissions@briarcliff.edu

Clarke College
1550 Clarke Dr, Dubuque IA 52001-3198
Andy Schroeder, Director of Admissions
800-383-2345 Fax: 563-584-8666
Website: www.clarke.edu
E-mail: andy.schroeder@clarke.edu

Covenant Medical Center
3421 W 9th St, Waterloo IA 50702-5401
319-272-7296

Des Moines Area Community College
Ankeny Campus
2006 S Ankeny Blvd, Ankeny IA 50023-8995
515-964-6200

Des Moines University - Osteopathic Medical Center
3200 Grand Ave, Des Moines IA 50312-4198
Dr. Gilbert Ramirez, P.H., Dean, College of Health
Sciences
515-271-1650
Website: www.dmu.edu
E-mail: dmuadmit@dmu.edu

Graceland University
1 University Place, Lamoni IA 50140
Brian Shantz, Vice President for Enrollment and Dean
of Admissions
641-784-5196 Fax: 641-784-5480
Website: www.admissions.graceland.edu
E-mail: admissions@graceland.edu

Hamilton College
7009 Nordic Dr, Cedar Falls IA 50613
Tim Cole, Campus President
319-277-0220 Fax: 319-363-3812
Website: www.hamiltonia.edu
E-mail: ticole@hamiltoncf.com

Hamilton College
3165 Edgewood Pkwy SW, Cedar Rapids IA 52404
Susan Spivey, Campus President
319-363-0481 Fax: 319-363-3812
Website: www.hamiltonia.edu
E-mail: spiveys@hamiltonia.edu

Hamilton College
2570 4th St SW, Mason City IA 50401-4665
Joe Albers, Executive Director
641-423-2530 Fax: 641-423-7512
Website: www.hamiltonia.edu
E-mail: jalbers@hamiltonia.edu

Hamilton College
4655 121st St, Urbandale IA 50323-2311
Ed Rogan, Campus President
515-727-2100 Fax: 515-727-2115
Website: www.hamiltonia.edu
E-mail: erogan_dm@hamiltonia.edu

Hamilton Technical College
1011 E 53rd St, Davenport IA 52807-2653
Mark Christy, Director
563-386-3570 Fax: 563-386-6756
Website: www.hamiltontechcollege.com
E-mail: mchristy@hamiltontechcollege.com
See listing under "Career Schools"

Hawkeye Community College
1501 E Orange Rd, Waterloo IA 50704
Molly Quinn, Director of Admissions
800-670-4769

Indian Hills Community College
525 Grandview Ave, Ottumwa IA 52501-1398
641-683-5111

Iowa Central Community College
330 Avenue M, Fort Dodge IA 50501-5798
515-576-7201

Iowa Lakes Community College
1900 Grand Ave, Suite 8, Spencer IA 51301
Anne Stansbury, Assistant Director of Admissions
712-262-7141 Fax: 712-262-4047
Website: www.iowalakes.edu
E-mail: info@iowalakes.edu

Iowa Methodist Medical Center
1200 Pleasant St, Des Moines IA 50309-1453
515-241-6201

Iowa State University
Ames IA 50011-0001
515-294-4111

Iowa Western Community College
2700 College Rd, Council Bluffs IA 51503-0567
800-432-5852

Jennie Edmundson Memorial Hospital
933 E Pierce St, Council Bluffs IA 51503-4652
712-328-6239

Kaplan University
1801 E Kimberly Rd #1, Davenport IA 52807-2095
563-355-3500

Kirkwood Community College
PO Box 2068, Cedar Rapids IA 52406-2068
319-398-5411

Marshalltown Community College
3700 S Center St, Marshalltown IA 50158-4760
641-752-7106

MERCY COLLEGE OF HEALTH SCIENCES
928 6th Ave, Des Moines IA 50309-1225
Susan Rhoades, Dean Enrollment & Student Services
515-643-3180 Fax: 515-643-6698
Website: www.mchs.edu
E-mail: srhoades@mercydesmoines.org

Mercy Medical Center - Sioux City
801 5th St, Sioux City IA 51101-1399
712-279-2018

Mercy-St. Luke's Hospital
1026 A Ave NE, Cedar Rapids IA 52402-5098
319-369-7204

Northeast Iowa Community College
PO Box 400, Calmar IA 52132-0400
563-562-3263

Northeast Iowa Community College
RR 1, Peosta IA 52068
563-556-5110

North Iowa Area Community College
500 College Dr, Mason City IA 50401-7213
641-423-1264

North Iowa Mercy Health Center
1000 4th St SW, Mason City IA 50401
641-422-7722

PALMER COLLEGE OF CHIROPRACTIC
1000 Brady St, Davenport IA 52803-5287
800-722-3648 or 563-884-5656 Fax: 563-884-5414
Website: admissions.palmer.edu
E-mail: pcadmit@palmer.edu

St. Ambrose University
518 W Locust St, Davenport IA 52803-2898
563-333-6000

St. Luke's College
2720 Stone Park Blvd, Sioux City IA 51104-3734
712-279-3149

Scott Community College
500 Belmont Rd, Riverdale IA 52722-6804
563-441-4000

Southeastern Community College
PO Box 180, West Burlington IA 52655
319-752-2731

University of Iowa
107 Calvin Hall, Iowa City IA 52242-1315
319-335-3500

University of Northern Iowa
Cedar Falls IA 50614-0001
319-273-2311

Wartburg College
PO Box 1003, Waverly IA 50677-0903
Brent Matthias, Interim Director of Admissions
319-352-8200 Fax: 319-352-8579
Website: www.wartburg.edu
E-mail: admissions@wartburg.edu

Western Iowa Tech Community College
PO Box 5199, Sioux City IA 51102-5199
Dr. Carolyn Rants, Dean of Students
712-274-6400

KANSAS

Allen County Community College
1801 N Cottonwood St, Iola KS 66749-1607
John Masterson, President
Randy Weber, Director of Admissions
620-365-5116 Fax: 620-365-3284
Website: www.allencc.net
E-mail: weber@allencc.edu

Barton County Community College
245 NE 30th Rd, Great Bend KS 67530-9107
Mary Anne Clark, Associate Dean
800-748-7594

COLBY COMMUNITY COLLEGE
1255 S Range Ave, Colby KS 67701-4099
Director of Admissions
888-634-9350 or 785-460-4690 Fax: 785-460-4691
Website: www.colbycc.edu
E-mail: bobbi@colbycc.edu

Emporia State University
1200 Commercial St, Emporia KS 66801-5087
620-343-1200

Flint Hills Technical College
3301 W 18th Ave, Emporia KS 66801-5957
Lisa Kirmer, Dean of Student Services
620-343-4600 Fax: 620-343-4610
Website: www.fhtc.net
E-mail: lkirmer@fhtc.net

Fort Hays State University
600 Park St, Hays KS 67601-4099
785-628-4000

Johnson County Community College
12345 College Blvd, Overland Park KS 66210-1299
913-469-3803

Kansas State University
Manhattan KS 66506
785-532-6250

Labette Community College
200 S 14th St, Parsons KS 67357-9966
620-421-6700

Newman University
3100 W McCormick St, Wichita KS 67213
Jann Reusser, Admissions Recruitment Coordinator
316-942-4291 ext. 2144 Fax: 316-942-4483
Website: www.newmanu.edu
E-mail: reusserj@newmanu.edu

Pittsburg State University
1701 S Broadway St, Pittsburg KS 66762-7500
620-231-7000

Salina Area Vocational Technical School
2562 Centennial Rd, Salina KS 67401
785-309-3100

Seward County Community College
PO Box 1137, Liberal KS 67905-1137
620-629-2710

Tabor College
400 S Jefferson St, Hillsboro KS 67063-1758
Rusty Allen, Dean of Enrollment Management
620-947-3121 Fax: 620-947-6276
Website: www.tabor.edu
E-mail: admissions@tabor.edu

University of Kansas
Lawrence KS 66045-0001
Alan Cerveny, Director of Admissions

University of Kansas Medical Center
3901 Rainbow Blvd, Kansas City KS 66160-0001
Lydia Wingate, Dean
913-588-5000

Washburn University
1700 SW College Ave, Topeka KS 66621-0001
785-231-1010

Wichita Area Technical College
324 N Emporia St, Wichita KS 67202-2512
316-833-4664

Wichita State University
1845 N Fairmount St, Wichita KS 67260-0124
Gina Crabtree, Director of Admissions
316-978-3085

KENTUCKY

Ashland Community and Technical College
1400 College Dr, Ashland KY 41101-3683
606-329-2999

Berea College
Berea KY 40404-0001
859-985-3000

Bluegrass Community and Technical College
Oswald Building
470 Cooper Drive, Lexington KY 40506-0235
Shelbie Hugle, Director of Admissions
859-246-6200 Fax: 859-246-4664
Website: www.bluegrass.kctcs.edu
E-mail: bctc_info@kctcs.edu

Bowling Green Technical College
1845 Loop Ave, Bowling Green KY 42101-3601
270-746-7461

Brown Cancer Center
529 S Jackson St, Louisville KY 40202-3229
502-588-6905

Brown Mackie College - Louisville
300 High Rise Dr, Louisville KY 40213-3263
Kathleen Belanger, Director of Admissions
502-968-7191 Fax: 502-357-9956
Website: www.brownmackie.edu
E-mail: kbelanger@brownmackie.edu

BROWN MACKIE COLLEGE
Northern Kentucky Campus
309 Buttermilk Pike, Fort Mitchell KY 41017-2191
Joanne Dellefield, Director of Admissions
859-341-5627 Fax: 859-341-6483
Website: www.brownmackie.edu
E-mail: jdellefield@brownmackie.edu

Central Kentucky Technical College
308 Vo Tech Rd, Lexington KY 40511
Dr. Michael Krause, Dean of Student Affairs
859-246-2400

Cumberland Technical College Rockcastle County
PO Box 275, Mount Vernon KY 40456-0275
606-256-4346

Daymar College
4400 Breckenridge Ln #415, Louisville KY 40218
Shawn McDaniel, Director of Admissions
502-495-1040 Fax: 502-495-1518
Website: www.daymarcollege.com

Daymar College
3361 Buckland Sq, Owensboro KY 42301-5830
Vickie McDougal Director of Admissions
800-960-4090 Fax: 270-685-4090
Website: www.daymarcollege.com

Eastern Kentucky University
521 Lancaster Ave, Richmond KY 40475-3102
859-622-1000

Elizabethtown Technical College
620 College Street Rd, Elizabethtown KY 42701
270-766-5133

Henderson Community College
2660 S Green St, Henderson KY 42420-4699
270-827-1867

Jefferson Community & Technical College
109 E Broadway, Louisville KY 40202-2000
502-584-0181

Jefferson Technical College
727 W Chestnut St, Louisville KY 40203-2036
502-213-4290

Lindsey Wilson College
210 Lindsey Wilson St, Columbia KY 42728-1223
270-384-8100

Madisonville Community College
2000 College Dr, Madisonville KY 42431-9199
270-821-2250

Mayo Technical College
513 3rd St, Paintsville KY 41240-1032
606-789-5321

Maysville Community College
1401 Dixie Hwy, Park Hills KY 41011-2816

Methodist Hospital of Kentucky
911 S Bypass Rd, Pikeville KY 41501-1595
606-437-3500

Midway College
512 E Stephens St, Midway KY 40347-1120
800-755-0031

Morehead State University
Morehead KY 40351-1689
Dayna Seelig, Enrollment Services
800-585-6781 Fax: 606-783-5038
Website: www.moreheadstate.edu
E-mail: admissions@moreheadstate.edu

Murray State University
Murray KY 42071
Phil Bryan, Director of Admissions
270-762-3011

National College of Business & Technology
115 E Lexington Ave, Danville KY 40422-1517
Larry Steele, Director of Admissions
859-236-6991

National College of Business & Technology
7627 Ewing Blvd, Florence KY 41042-1812
Larry Steele, Director of Admissions
859-525-6510

National College of Business & Technology
628 E Main St, Lexington KY 40508-2312
Larry Steele, Director of Admissions
859-253-0621

National College of Business & Technology
288 S Mayo Trl #2, Pikeville KY 41501-1518
Larry Steele, Director of Admissions
606-432-5477

Northern Kentucky University
Newport KY 41099-0001
859-572-5100

Owensboro Community & Technical College
1501 Frederica St, Owensboro KY 42301-4806
270-687-7255

Owensboro Community and Technical College
4800 New Hartford Rd, Owensboro KY 42303-1899
270-686-4400

Owensboro Mercy Health System
811 E Parrish Ave, Owensboro KY 42303-3258
270-688-2100

Pathology and Cytology Laboratories
290 Big Run Rd, Lexington KY 40503-2934
859-278-9513

Rowan Technical College
609 Viking Dr, Morehead KY 40351-8320
606-783-1538

ST. ELIZABETH MEDICAL CENTER
School of Medical Technology
1 Medical Village Dr, Edgewood KY 41017-3441
Beth Warning, MS, MT(ASCP), Program Director
859-344-2170 Fax: 859-344-5560
Website: www.stelizabeth.com
E-mail: bwarning@stelizabeth.com

St. Joseph's Hospital
1 Saint Joseph Dr, Lexington KY 40504-3754
859-278-3436

Somerset Community College
808 Monticello St, Somerset KY 42501-2936
606-679-8501

Southeast Kentucky Community and Technical College
300 College Rd, Cumberland KY 40823-1031
606-589-2145

Spalding University
851 S 4th St, Louisville KY 40203-2188
502-585-9911

Spencerian College
1575 Winchester Rd, Lexington KY 40505
Victor Lamoin Adcock II, Director of Admissions
800-456-3253

Spencerian College
4627 Dixie Hwy, Louisville KY 40216
Terri Thomas, Director of Admissions
502-447-1000

University of Kentucky
Lexington KY 40506-0001
Don Witt, Director of Admissions
859-257-9000

University of Kentucky Chandler Medical Center
103 Administration Plz A311
Lexington KY 40536-0001
859-323-5126

University of Louisville
2301 S 3rd St, Louisville KY 40292-2001
502-852-5555

Western Kentucky University
1 Big Red Way, Bowling Green KY 42101
270-745-0111

West Kentucky Community and Technical College
PO Box 7380, Paducah KY 42002-7380
270-554-9200

LOUISIANA

Baton Rouge General Medical Center
PO Box 2511, Baton Rouge LA 70821-2511
225-387-7767

Bossier Parish Community College
6220 E Texas St, Bossier City LA 71111
318-678-6000

Bryman College
824 Elmwood Park Blvd Ste 110
New Orleans LA 70123
504-733-7117

Delgado Community College
615 City Park Ave, New Orleans LA 70119
Gwen A. Boutte, Director of Admissions
504-483-4114

Delta School of Business and Technology
517 Broad St, Lake Charles LA 70601-4334
Gary Holt, President
337-439-5765 Fax: 337-436-5151
Website: www.deltatech.edu
E-mail: susan@deltatech.edu

Grambling State University
PO Box 864, Grambling LA 71245
318-274-3811

Lafayette General Medical Center
PO Box 52009, Lafayette LA 70505-2009
337-261-7381

Lake Charles Memorial Hospital
1701 Oak Park Blvd, Lake Charles LA 70601-8911
337-494-3200

Louisiana State University
1100 Florida Ave, New Orleans LA 70119-2714
504-948-8530

Louisiana State University
1 University Pl, Shreveport LA 71115-2301
318-797-5000

Louisiana State University and A & M College
Louisiana State Univ, Baton Rouge LA 70803-0001
225-578-3202

Louisiana State University at Eunice
PO Box 1129, Eunice LA 70535-1129
Ron Ryder, Registrar
337-457-7311 Fax: 337-550-1306
Website: www.lsue.edu
E-mail: rryder@lsue.edu

Louisiana State University Health Sciences Center
433 Bolivar St, New Orleans LA 70112-2223
504-568-4808

Louisiana Technical College
Lafayette Campus
1101 Bertrand Dr, Lafayette LA 70506-4909
Gen M. Bienvenu, Director of Admissions
337-262-5962

Louisiana Technical College
West Jefferson Campus
475 Manhattan Blvd, Harvey LA 70058-4441
504-361-6464

Louisiana Tech University
PO Box 3168, Ruston LA 71272-0001
318-257-0211

Loyola University New Orleans
6363 Saint Charles Ave, New Orleans LA 70118-6143
504-865-2011

McNeese State University
4100 Ryan St, Lake Charles LA 70605-4510
337-475-5000

Medical Center of Louisiana - Charity Campus
1532 Tulane Ave, New Orleans LA 70112-2802
504-568-2311

Nicholls State University
University Station, Thibodaux LA 70310-0001
985-446-8111

North Oaks Medical Center
15790 Medical Arts Dr, Hammond LA 70403-1436
985-543-6600

Northwestern State University
Natchitoches LA 71497-0001
Jana Lucky, Director of Enrollment Services
318-357-4503

Ochsner School of Allied Health Sciences
1516 Jefferson Hwy, New Orleans LA 70121-2429
504-842-3267

Our Lady of Holy Cross College
4123 Woodland Dr, New Orleans LA 70131-7399
Office of Enrollment Services
504-394-7744 Fax: 504-391-2421
Website: www.olhcc.edu

OUR LADY OF THE LAKE COLLEGE
7434 Perkins Rd, Baton Rouge LA 70808
Marvell Nesmith, Director of Admissions
225-768-1700 Fax: 225-768-1726
Website: www.ololcollege.edu
E-mail: mnesmith@ololcollege.edu

Overton Brooks VA Medical Center
510 E Stoner Ave, Shreveport LA 71101-4243
318-424-6037

Rapides Regional Medical Center
PO Box 30101, Alexandria LA 71301
318-473-3150

St. Francis Medical Center
PO Box 1901, Monroe LA 71210-1901
318-327-4141

St. Patrick's Hospital
524 S Ryan St, Lake Charles LA 70601-5799
337-491-7730

Southeastern Louisiana University
PO Box 784, Hammond LA 70404-0784
985-549-2000

Southern University A&M College
Southern University, Baton Rouge LA 70813-0001
225-771-4500

Southern University at Shreveport
3050 M L King Dr, Shreveport LA 71107
318-674-3300

Touro Infirmary
1401 Foucher St, New Orleans LA 70115-3593
504-897-8244

Tulane University
6823 Saint Charles Ave, New Orleans LA 70118-5698
504-865-4000

University Medical Center
2390 W Congress St, Lafayette LA 70506-4298
337-261-6004

University of Louisiana at Lafayette
PO Box 42210, Lafayette LA 70504
337-482-6278

University of Louisiana at Monroe
700 University Ave, Monroe LA 71209-9001
318-342-1000

University of New Orleans
New Orleans LA 70148-0001
504-280-6000

MAINE

Beal College
99 Farm Rd, Bangor ME 04401-6831
207-947-4591

Central Maine Community College
1250 Turner St, Auburn ME 04210-6498
Walter Clark, Director of Admissions
207-755-5100

Central Maine Medical Center
300 Main St, Lewiston ME 04240-7041
207-795-2840

Eastern Maine Community College
354 Hogan Rd, Bangor ME 04401-4206
207-974-4600

Eastern Maine Medical Center
489 State St, Bangor ME 04401-6674
207-973-7051

HUSSON COLLEGE
One College Cir, Bangor ME 04401-2999
800-477-4723 or 207-941-7100 Fax: 207-941-7935
Website: www.husson.edu
E-mail: admit@husson.edu
M.S. in Physical Therapy & Occupational Therapy.
See listing under "Universities"

Kennebec Valley Community College
92 Western Ave, Fairfield ME 04937-1337
Kathy Moore, Director of Admissions
207-453-5035

Maine Medical Center
School of Surgical Technology
SMTC Fort Rd, South Portland ME 04106
Maureen Bien, RN, Program Director
207-767-9589

Mercy Hospital
144 State St, Portland ME 04101-3795
207-879-3000

St. Joseph's College of Maine
278 Whites Bridge Rd, Standish ME 04084-5263
Vincent Kloskowski, Dean of Admissions
800-338-7057 Fax: 207-893-7862
Website: www.sjcme.edu
E-mail: admission@sjcme.edu

Southern Maine Community College
2 Fort Rd, South Portland ME 04106-1698
Dr. James Ortiz, President
Scott MacDonald, Director of Financial Aid
207-741-5500 Fax: 207-741-5671
Website: www.smccme.edu
E-mail: oharmon@maine.rr.com

University of Maine
46 University Dr, Augusta ME 04330
207-621-3000

University of Maine
Orono ME 04469-0001
207-581-1110

University of Maine at Presque Isle
181 Main St, Presque Isle ME 04769-2844
207-768-9532

University of New England
11 Hills Beach Rd, Biddeford ME 04005-9526
207-283-0171

University of Southern Maine
PO Box 9300, Portland ME 04104-9300
207-780-4141

MARYLAND

Allegany College of Maryland
12401 Willowbrook Rd, Cumberland MD 21502-2596
301-784-5000

Baltimore City Community College
2901 Liberty Heights Ave, Baltimore MD 21215
Scheherazade Foreman, Director of Admissions
410-462-8000

Carroll Community College
1601 Washington Rd, Westminster MD 21157-6913
410-386-8000

Cecil Community College
One Seahawk Dr, North East MD 21901
Sandra S. Rajaski, Registrar & Director of Admissions
410-287-1000 Fax: 410-287-1001
Website: www.cecilcc.edu
E-mail: srajaski@cecilcc.edu

Chesapeake College
PO Box 8, Wye Mills MD 21679-0008
410-822-5400

Columbia Union College
7600 Flower Ave, Takoma Park MD 20912-7794
301-891-4000

The Community College of Baltimore County
Catonsville Campus
800 S Rolling Rd, Catonsville MD 21228-5317
Diane Drake, Director of Admissions
410-455-4555

Community College of Baltimore County
Essex Campus
7201 Rossville Blvd, Baltimore MD 21237-3898
Marcia Amaimo, Director of Admissions
410-780-6363

Coppin State University
2500 W North Ave, Baltimore MD 21216-3698
410-951-3000

Frederick Community College
7932 Opossumtown Pike, Frederick MD 21702-2097
Welcome and Registration Center
301-846-2430

Greater Baltimore Medical Center
6701 N Charles St, Baltimore MD 21204-6881
410-828-2121

Hagerstown Business College
18618 Crestwood Dr, Hagerstown MD 21742-2797
W. Christopher Motz, President
Jim Klein, Director of Admissions
800-422-2670

Hagerstown Community College
11400 Robinwood Dr, Hagerstown MD 21742-6590
Dr. Daniel E. Bock, Assistant Director of Admissions
301-790-2800 Fax: 301-791-9165
Website: www.hagerstowncc.edu
E-mail: bockd@hagerstowncc.edu

Harford Community College
401 Thomas Run Rd, Bel Air MD 21015-1696
410-836-4000

Holy Cross Hospital
1500 Forest Glen Rd, Silver Spring MD 20910-1484
301-905-1216

Johns Hopkins University
600 N Wolfe St, Baltimore MD 21287-0005
410-955-3182

Johns Hopkins University
3400 N Charles St, Baltimore MD 21218-2680
410-516-8000

Loyola College
4501 N Charles St, Baltimore MD 21210-2694
410-617-2000

Maryland General Hospital
827 Linden Ave, Baltimore MD 21201-4606
410-995-8600

MEDIX SCHOOL

700 York Rd, Towson MD 21204-2503
Lisa Harper, Director of Admissions
410-337-5155 Fax: 410-337-5104
Website: www.medixschooltowson.edu
E-mail: admissions@medixsch.com

Mercy Hospital
301 Saint Paul St, Baltimore MD 21202-2147
410-332-9202

Montgomery College
51 Mannakee St, Rockville MD 20850-1199
301-279-5000

Morgan State University
1700 E Cold Spring Ln, Baltimore MD 21251-0002
443-885-3000

Salisbury University
1101 Camden Ave, Salisbury MD 21801-6837
410-543-6000

Sodexho Marriott Healthcare Mid-Atlantic
9801 Washingtonian Blvd
Gaithersburg MD 20878-5355
301-987-4127

Towson State University
8000 York Rd, Towson MD 21252-0002
410-830-2000

University of Maryland
520 W Lombard St, Baltimore MD 21201
410-706-3100

University of Maryland
1000 Hilltop Cir, Baltimore MD 21250-0001
410-455-1000

University of Maryland
College Park MD 20742-0001
301-405-1000

University of Maryland Eastern Shore
Princess Anne MD 21853
Edwina Morse, Director of Admissions
410-651-6410

Villa Julie College
1525 Greenspring Valley Rd
Stevenson MD 21153-0641
Mark Hergan, V.P. Enrollment Services
410-486-7001 Fax: 410-602-6600
Website: www.vjc.edu/admissions
E-mail: admissions@mail.vjc.edu

Washington Adventist Hospital
7600 Carroll Ave, Takoma Park MD 20912
301-891-7600

Wor-Wic Community College
32000 Campus Dr, Salisbury MD 21804-1485
410-334-2800

MASSACHUSETTS

Anna Maria College
50 Sunset Ln, Paxton MA 01612
Julie A. Mitchell, Director of Admissions
508-849-3360 Fax: 508-849-3362
Website: www.annamaria.edu
E-mail: admissions@annamaria.edu

Assumption College
500 Salisbury St, Worcester MA 01609-1294
Kathleen Murphy, Dean of Enrollment
508-767-7000 Fax: 508-799-4412
Website: www.assumption.edu
E-mail: admiss@assumption.edu

Bay Path College
588 Longmeadow St, Longmeadow MA 01106-2292
Lisa Casassa, Director of Admissions
413-565-1331 Fax: 413-565-1105
Website: www.baypath.edu
E-mail: lcasassa@baypath.edu

Bay State College
122 Commonwealth Ave, Boston MA 02116-2901
Craig Pfannenstiehl, President
617-217-9000 Fax: 617-536-1735

BAY STATE COLLEGE

71 E Grove St, Middleboro MA 02346-1825
Gina Cormier, Contact
508-946-5559 Fax: 508-946-8281
Website: www.baystate.edu
E-mail: rcormier@baystate.edu

Becker College
Campuses in Worcester and Leicester, MA
61 Sever St, Worcester MA 01609-2165
Karen H. Schedin, Director of Admissions
508-791-9241 Fax: 508-890-1500
Website: www.becker.edu
E-mail: admissions@becker.edu
See listing under "Universities"

Berklee College of Music
1140 Boylston St, Boston MA 02215-3693
Suzanne Hanser, Chair Music Therapy Dept.
617-266-1400 Fax: 617-262-6203
Website: www.berklee.edu
E-mail: musictherapy@berklee.edu

Berkshire Medical Center
725 North St, Pittsfield MA 01201-4124
413-447-2144

Beth Israel Healthcare
330 Brookline Ave, Boston MA 02215-5400
617-667-2539

Boston University
121 Bay State Rd, Boston MA 02215
Kelly Walter, Executive Director of Admissions
617-353-2300 Fax: 617-353-9695
Website: web.bu.edu
E-mail: admissions@bu.edu

Brandeis University
415 South St, Waltham MA 02453-2700
781-736-3500

Bridgewater State College
Bridgewater MA 02325-0001
508-697-1237

Brigham and Women's Hospital
75 Francis St, Boston MA 02115-6110
617-732-7493

Bristol Community College
777 Elsbree St, Fall River MA 02720-7395
Rodney S. Clark, Director of Admissions
508-678-2811 ext. 2516, 2179 Fax: 508-730-3265
Website: www.bristol.mass.edu
E-mail: admissions@bristol.mass.edu

Bunker Hill Community College
250 Rutherford Ave, Boston MA 02129-2925
617-228-2000

Cape Cod Community College
2240 Iyannough Rd, West Barnstable MA 02668
508-362-2131

Caritas Laboure College
2120 Dorchester Ave, Dorchester MA 02124-5698
617-296-8300

Children's Hospital
300 Longwood Ave, Boston MA 02115-5737
617-355-6433

C.H. McCann Technical School
70 Hodges Cross Road, North Adams MA 01247
Patricia E. Durkee, Admissions
413-663-5383

Endicott College
376 Hale St, Beverly MA 01915-2098
978-927-0585

Fisher College
118 Beacon St, Boston MA 02116-1501
Stephen Carter, Director of Admissions
800-446-1226

Fitchburg State College
160 Pearl St, Fitchburg MA 01420-2697
978-345-2151

Framingham State College
PO Box 9101, Framingham MA 01704-0101
508-620-1220

Greenfield Community College
1 College Dr, Greenfield MA 01301-9739
413-775-1000

Holyoke Community College
303 Homestead Ave, Holyoke MA 01040-1099
413-538-7000

Lasell College
1844 Commonwealth Ave, Newton MA 02466-2716
617-243-2225

Lesley University
29 Everett St, Cambridge MA 02138-2790
Jane Raley, Director of Admissions
617-349-8800

Massachusetts Bay Community College
50 Oakland St, Wellesley MA 02481-5307
781-239-3000

Massachusetts College of Pharmacy and Health Sciences
179 Longwood Ave, Boston MA 02115-5896
Kathleen B. Houghton, Director of Admissions
617-732-2850

Massachusetts Institute of Technology
77 Massachusetts Ave, Cambridge MA 02139-4307
Marilee Jones, Dean of Admission
617-253-1000 Fax: 617-253-4016
Website: my.mit.edu
E-mail: admissions@mit.edu

MGH Institute of Health Professions
36 1st Ave, Boston MA 02129-4557
Michael Bonanno, Manager of Admissions
617-726-3140

Middlesex Community College
Springs Rd, Bedford MA 01730-1114
Darcy Orellana, Director of Admissions
800-818-3434

Middlesex Community College
33 Kearney Sq, Lowell MA 01852-1987
Darcy Orellana, Director of Admissions
800-818-3434

Mt. Ida College
777 Dedham St, Newton Center MA 02459-3323
617-969-7000

Mt. Wachusett Community College
444 Green St, Gardner MA 01440
Karin Schedin, Director of Admissions
978-632-6600 ext. 110

Newbury College
129 Fisher Ave, Brookline MA 02445-5796
Salvadore Liberto, Vice President of Enrollment
617-730-7000 Fax: 617-731-9618
Website: www.newbury.edu

Northeastern University
360 Huntington Ave, Boston MA 02115-5000
617-373-2000

NORTHERN ESSEX COMMUNITY COLLEGE

100 Elliott St, Haverhill MA 01830
Nora B. Sheridan, Director of Admission
978-556-3700
Website: www.NECC.Mass.edu
E-mail: nsheridan@necc.mass.edu

North Shore Community College
1 Ferncroft Rd, Danvers MA 01923-4093
Joanne Light, Director of Enrollment & Student Records
978-762-4000

Quincy College
34 Coddington St, Quincy MA 02169-4501
617-984-1600

Quinsigamond Community College
670 W Boylston St, Worcester MA 01606-2092
508-853-2300

St. Luke's Hospital
101 Page St, New Bedford MA 02740-3464
508-997-1525

Salem State College
352 Lafayette St, Salem MA 01970-5353
978-741-6000

Salter School
155 Ararat St, Worcester MA 01606-3421
508-853-1074

Simmons College
300 Fenway, Boston MA 02115-5898
617-521-2000

∴ Sodexho Marriott Services
PO Box 9196, Lexington MA 02420
800-926-7429

: Southeastern Technical Institute
250 Foundry St, South Easton MA 02375-1780
Beverly A. Pusateri, Director
508-238-1860 Fax: 508-230-1558
Website: ti.sersd.org
E-mail: bpusateri@sersd.org

Springfield College
263 Alden St, Springfield MA 01109-3788
Mary DeAngelo, Director of Admissions
800-343-1257

· Springfield Technical Community College
1 Armory Sq, Springfield MA 01105-1296
Andrea Lucy-Allen, Director of Admissions
413-755-4202

Tufts University
520 Boston Ave, Medford MA 02155-5555
617-628-5000

University of Massachusetts
Amherst MA 01003
413-545-0111

University of Massachusetts at Worcester
55 Lake Ave N, Worcester MA 01655-0001
508-856-8989

University of Massachusetts Boston
100 William T Morrissey Blvd, Boston MA 02125-3393
Liliana Mickle, Director of Undergraduate Admissions
617-287-6000

University of Massachusetts Dartmouth
Old Westport Rd, North Dartmouth MA 02747-2300
Steven T. Briggs, Director of Admissions
508-999-8605 Fax: 508-999-8755
Website: explore.umassd.edu
E-mail: sbriggs@umassd.edu

University of Massachusetts Lowell
1 University Ave, Lowell MA 01854-2893
978-934-4000

∴ Veterans Administration Medical Center
150 S Huntington Ave, Boston MA 02130-4817
617-232-9500

Worcester State College
486 Chandler St, Worcester MA 01602-2597
508-929-8000

MICHIGAN

· Alpena Community College
666 Johnson St, Alpena MI 49707-1495
989-356-9021

Andrews University
Berrien Springs MI 49104-0001
Randall Graves, Director of Recruitment Services
800-253-2874 Fax: 269-471-2670
Website: www.connect.andrews.edu
E-mail: gravesr@andrews.edu

Baker College of Auburn Hills
1500 University Dr, Auburn Hills MI 48326-2642
248-340-0600

Baker College of Cadillac
9600 E 13th St, Cadillac MI 49601-9574
Mike Tisdale, Director of Admissions
231-876-3100

Baker College of Clinton Township
34950 Little Mack Ave
Clinton Township MI 48035-4701
586-791-6610

Baker College of Flint
1050 W Bristol Rd, Flint MI 48507-5508
810-767-4000

Baker College of Jackson
2800 Springport Rd, Jackson MI 49202-1230
Kelli Hoban, Director of Admissions
517-789-6123

Baker College of Muskegon
1903 Marquette Ave, Muskegon MI 49442-1453
231-726-4904

Baker College of Owosso
1020 S Washington St, Owosso MI 48867-4400
989-729-3300

Baker College of Port Huron
3403 Lapeer Rd, Port Huron MI 48060-2597
Dan Kenny, Director of Admissions
888-262-2442

CARNEGIE INSTITUTE
550 Stephenson Hwy Ste 100, Troy MI 48083-1159
Gloria J. McEachern, President
248-589-1078 Fax: 248-589-1631
Website: www.carnegie-institute.com
E-mail: carnegie47@aol.com

Central Michigan University
100 Warriner Hall, Mount Pleasant MI 48859-0001
989-774-4000

· Charles S. Mott Community College
1401 E Court St, Flint MI 48503-6208
810-762-0200

Charles Stewart Mott Community College
2100 W Thompson Rd, Fenton MI 48430
810-762-0200

Davenport University
4123 W Main St, Kalamazoo MI 49006-2748
Debra Burley, Director of Admissions
269-552-3308

Davenport University
5300 Bay Rd, Saginaw MI 48604
989-799-7800

Davenport University - Central Region
3555 E Patrick Rd, Midland MI 48642-5891
989-835-5588

· Delta College
University Center MI 48710-0001
Duff Zube, Director of Admissions
989-686-9093 Fax: 989-667-2202
Website: www.delta.edu
E-mail: admit@delta.edu

: Detroit Business Institute
23077 Greenfield Rd #LL28
Southfield MI 48075-3751
Greg Mitchell, Director of Admissions
248-552-6300 Fax: 248-552-7300
Website: www.dbisouthfield.com
E-mail: info@dbisouthfield.com

· Detroit Business Institute - Downriver
19100 Fort St, Riverview MI 48193
Theresa Hernandez, Director of Admissions
734-479-0660 Fax: 734-479-0738
Website: www.dbidownriver.com
E-mail: info@dbidownriver.com

· Detroit Health Department
1151 Taylor St, Detroit MI 48202
313-876-4090

· Detroit Institute of Ophthalmology
15415 E Jefferson Ave, Grosse Pointe MI 48230-1328
Deanna Presnell, BA, COMT, Program Director
313-824-4710 ext. 223

∴ DMC University Laboratories
4201 Saint Antoine St, Detroit MI 48201-2153
313-745-3053

Eastern Michigan University
Ypsilanti MI 48197
800-GO-TO-EMU

∴ Grace Hospital
6071 W Outer Dr, Detroit MI 48235-2679
313-966-3525

· Grand Rapids Community College
143 Bostwick Ave NE, Grand Rapids MI 49503-3201
616-234-4000

Grand Valley State University
1 Campus Dr, Allendale MI 49401-9403
Jodi Chycinski, Director of Admissions
616-331-6611 Fax: 616-331-2000
Website: www.gvsu.edu
E-mail: go2gvsu@gvsu.edu

· Great Lakes College
3930 Traxler Ct, Bay City MI 48706-9286
989-686-1572

· Great Lakes College
1231 Cleaver Rd, Caro MI 48723-9376
989-673-5857

∴ Harper Hospital
3990 John R St, Detroit MI 48201-2018
313-745-9375

· Henry Ford Community College
5101 Evergreen Rd, Dearborn MI 48128-2407
313-845-9615

∴ Henry Ford Hospital
2799 W Grand Blvd, Detroit MI 48202-2689
313-876-1257

Hope College
PO Box 9000, Holland MI 49422-9000
616-395-7000

∴ Hurley Medical Center
701 W 8th Ave, Flint MI 48503-1261
810-257-9237

· Jackson Community College
2111 Emmons Rd, Jackson MI 49201-8399
517-796-8425

· Kalamazoo Valley Community College
PO Box 4070, Kalamazoo MI 49003-4070
Marilyn Schlack, President
269-372-5000

· Kellogg Community College
450 North Ave, Battle Creek MI 49017-3397
269-965-3931

· Lake Michigan College
2755 E Napier Ave, Benton Harbor MI 49022-1899
269-927-8100

· Lansing Community College
419 N Capitol Ave, Lansing MI 48933-1293
517-483-1620

MACOMB COMMUNITY COLLEGE
44575 Garfield Rd, Clinton Township MI 48038-1139
Information Center
586-445-7999
Website: www.macomb.edu
E-mail: answer@macomb.edu

MACOMB COMMUNITY COLLEGE
14500 E 12 Mile Rd, Warren MI 48088-3896
Information Center
586-445-7999
Website: www.macomb.edu
E-mail: answer@macomb.edu

Madonna University
36600 Schoolcraft Rd, Livonia MI 48150-1173
734-432-5300

∴ Marquette General Hospital
420 W Magnetic St, Marquette MI 49855-2794
906-225-3434

Michigan State University
450 Administration Bldg, East Lansing MI 48824
517-355-1855

· Mid-Michigan Community College
1375 S Clare Ave, Harrison MI 48625-9447
989-386-6622

· Monroe County Community College
1555 S Raisinville Rd, Monroe MI 48161-9047
734-242-7300

∴ Munson Medical Center
1105 6th St, Traverse City MI 49684-2386
231-935-6501

· Muskegon Community College
221 S Quarterline Rd, Muskegon MI 49442-1493
231-773-9131

· National Institute of Technology
26111 Evergreen Rd Ste 201
Southfield MI 48076-4491
Marchelle Weaver, President
248-799-9933 Fax: 248-799-2912
Website: www.cci.edu
E-mail: mweaver@cci.edu

· Northern Michigan University
1401 Presque Isle Ave, Marquette MI 49855-5301
906-227-1000

· Northwestern Michigan College
1701 E Front St, Traverse City MI 49686-3061
Jim Bensley, Admissions Coordinator
800-748-0566 Fax: 231-995-1339
Website: www.nmc.edu
E-mail: jbensley@nmc.edu

· Oakland Community College
27055 Orchard Lake Rd, Farmington Hills MI 48334
248-522-3400

· Oakland Community College
7350 Cooley Lake Rd, Waterford MI 48327-4187
248-942-3100

· Oakland County Health Division
1200 N Telegraph Rd, Pontiac MI 48341
248-858-1832

Oakland University
2200 N Squirrel Rd, Rochester MI 48309
Eleanor L. Reynolds, Assistant Vice President &
Director of Admissions
248-370-2100
Website: www.oakland.edu
E-mail: ouinfo@oakland.edu

∴ Oakwood - Hospital Annapolis Center
33155 Annapolis St, Wayne MI 48184-2405
734-467-4000

OLYMPIA CAREER TRAINING INSTITUTE
1750 Woodworth St NE
Grand Rapids MI 49525-2301
Bobbi Blok, Director of Admissions
616-364-8464 Fax: 616-364-5454
Website: www.cci.edu
E-mail: rblok@cci.edu

· Olympia Career Training Institute
5177 W Main St, Kalamazoo MI 49009
Susan Smith, Director of Admission
269-381-9616 Fax: 269-381-2513
Website: www.olympia-institute.com
E-mail: susans@cci.edu

∴ Port Huron Hospital
1001 Kearney St, Port Huron MI 48060-3531
810-987-5000

∴ Providence Hospital
16001 W 9 Mile Rd, Southfield MI 48075-4854
248-424-3000

Saginaw Valley State University
7400 Bay Rd, University Center MI 48710-0001
989-790-4000

∴ St. John's Hospital
22101 Moross Rd, Detroit MI 48236-2172
313-343-7531

∴ St. Mary's Medical Center
830 S Jefferson Ave, Saginaw MI 48601-2594
989-776-8176

Schoolcraft College
18600 Haggerty Rd, Livonia MI 48152-2696
734-462-4400

∴ Spectrum Health
100 Michigan St NE, Grand Rapids MI 49503-2551
616-391-1605

University of Detroit-Mercy
PO Box 19900, Detroit MI 48219-0900
313-993-1000

University of Michigan-Ann Arbor
1220 Student Activities Bldg, Ann Arbor MI 48109
734-764-1817

University of Michigan-Flint
303 E Kearsley St, Flint MI 48502-1950
810-762-3000

· Washtenaw Community College
PO Box D-1, Ann Arbor MI 48106-1610
734-973-3300

· Wayne County Community College
801 W Fort St, Detroit MI 48226-3095
313-496-2500

Wayne State University
5980 Cass Ave, Detroit MI 48202-3489
313-577-2424

Western Michigan University
Kalamazoo MI 49008
269-387-1000

∴ William Beaumont Hospital
3601 W 13 Mile Rd, Royal Oak MI 48073-6769
248-551-0681

MINNESOTA

· Alexandria Technical College
1601 Jefferson St, Alexandria MN 56308-3707
320-762-0221

· Anoka Technical College
1355 Highway 10, Anoka MN 55303
763-576-4700

ARGOSY UNIVERSITY / TWIN CITIES
(formerly Medical Institute of Minnesota)
1515 Central Pkwy, Eagan MN 55121-1756
O. Jeanne Stoneking, Director of Admissions
651-846-2882 Fax: 651-994-7956
Website: www.argosyu.edu
E-mail: tcadmissions@argosyu.edu

Augsburg College
2211 Riverside Ave, Minneapolis MN 55454-1350
612-330-1000

Central Lakes College
501 W College Dr, Brainerd MN 56401-3900
218-855-8000

College of Saint Benedict
37 College Ave S, Saint Joseph MN 56374-2099
320-363-5011

College of St. Catherine
2004 Randolph Ave, Saint Paul MN 55105-1789
651-690-6000

College of Saint Scholastica
1200 Kenwood Ave, Duluth MN 55811-4199
Brian Dalton, V.P. of Enrollment Management
800-447-5444

Concordia College
901 8th St S, Moorhead MN 56562-0002
Scott Ellingson, Director of Admissions
218-299-3004

Dakota County Technical College
1300 145th St E, Rosemount MN 55068-2999
800-548-5502

Duluth Business University
4724 Mike Colalillo Dr, Duluth MN 55807-2723
Bonnie Kupczynski, Director
800-777-8406 Fax: 218-628-2127
Website: www.dbumn.edu
E-mail: info@dbumn.edu

Globe College
7166 10th St N, Oakdale MN 55128
Mike Hughes, Campus Director
651-730-5100 Fax: 651-730-5151
Website: www.globecollege.edu
E-mail: admissions@globecollege.edu

Gustavus Adolphus College
800 W College Ave, Saint Peter MN 56082-1485
Mark H. Anderson, Dean of Admission
800-GUSTAVUS Fax: 507-933-7474
Website: www.gustavus.edu
E-mail: admission@gustavus.edu

Health System Minnesota/Methodist Hospital
6500 Excelsior Blvd, Saint Louis Park MN 55426-4700
952-993-3601

Hennepin County Medical Center
701 Park Ave, Minneapolis MN 55415-1829
612-347-2352

Hennepin Technical College
9000 Brooklyn Blvd, Brooklyn Park MN 55445-2320
952-995-1300

Hibbing Community College
1515 E 25th St, Hibbing MN 55746-3300
Holly Bigelow, Director of Enrollment
800-224-4HCC or 218-262-7200 Fax: 218-262-6717
Website: www.hibbing.edu
E-mail: admissions@hibbing.edu

Lake Superior College
2101 Trinity Rd, Duluth MN 55811-3399
218-733-7600

Mayo School of Health Sciences
200 1st Ave SW, Rochester MN 55905-0001
507-284-3678

Minneapolis Business College
1711 County Road B W, Roseville MN 55113-4036
651-636-7406

Minneapolis Community and Technical College
1501 Hennepin Ave, Minneapolis MN 55403-1779
Dena Russell, Director of Admissions
612-659-6282 Fax: 612-659-6210
Website: www.minneapolis.edu
E-mail: admissions.office@minneapolis.edu

Minneapolis VA Medical Center
1 Veterans Dr, Minneapolis MN 55417-2300
612-725-2000

Minnesota School of Business
5910 Shingle Creek Pkwy #200
Brooklyn Center MN 55430-2319
763-566-7777

Minnesota School of Business
1401 W 76th St Ste 500, Richfield MN 55423-3846
612-861-2000

Minnesota State Community & Technical College
900 Highway 34 E, Detroit Lakes MN 56501-2698
Dale Westley, Director of Admissions
800-492-4836 Fax: 218-846-3710
Website: www.minnesota.edu
E-mail: dale.westley@minnesota.edu

Minnesota State Community & Technical College
PO Box 566, Wadena MN 56482-0566
Paul Drange, Director of Admissions
800-247-2007 Fax: 218-631-7901
Website: www.minnesota.edu
E-mail: paul.drange@minnesota.edu

Minnesota State Community and Technical College
1900 28th Ave S, Moorhead MN 56560-4899
Laurie McKeever, Director of Admissions
800-426-5603 Fax: 218-299-6584
Website: www.minnesota.edu
E-mail: laurie.mckeever@minnesota.edu

Minnesota State Community and Technical College
Fergus Falls
1414 College Way, Fergus Falls MN 56537-1009
218-739-7500

Minnesota State University Mankato
228 Wiecking Center, Mankato MN 56001
507-389-1866

Minnesota State University Moorhead
1104 7th Ave S, Moorhead MN 56563-0002
218-236-2011

Minnesota West Community and Technical College
Granite Falls Campus
1593 11th Ave, Granite Falls MN 56241-1061
Becky Weber, Contact
800-657-3247

National American University
1550 W Highway 36, Roseville MN 55113
Matthew Mottl, Director of Admissions
651-644-1265 Fax: 651-644-0690
Website: www.national.edu
E-mail: mmottl@national.edu

Normandale Community College
9700 France Ave S, Bloomington MN 55431-4399
Rick Smith, Director of Admissions
952-832-6000

North Hennepin Community College
7411 85th Ave N, Brooklyn Park MN 55445-2299
763-424-0702

Northland Community & Technical College
Highway 1 E, Thief River Falls MN 56701
Sue Field, Chairperson
800-959-6282 or 218-681-0841 Fax: 218-681-0774
Website: www.northlandcollege.edu

Northland Community and Technical College
2022 Central Ave NE
East Grand Forks MN 56721-2702
Elizabeth McMahon, Allied Health Division Chair
800-451-3441 Fax: 218-773-4502
Website: www.northlandcollege.edu
E-mail: admissions@northlandcollege.edu

North Memorial Medical Center
3300 Oakdale Ave N, Minneapolis MN 55422-2900
763-520-5200

Northwest Technical College
905 Grant Ave SE, Bemidji MN 56601
Richard Lehmann, Director of Admissions
800-942-8324

Rasmussen College
7905 Golden Triangle Dr Ste 100
Eden Prairie MN 55344-7220
952-545-2000

Rice Memorial Hospital
School of Radiologic Technology
301 Becker Ave SW, Willmar MN 56201-3395
Luther Linn RT, Program Director
320-231-4553

Ridgewater College-Hutchinson Campus
2 Century Ave SE, Hutchinson MN 55350-3100
Dawn Bjork, Counselor
800-222-4424 Fax: 320-231-7767
Website: www.ridgewater.edu
E-mail: dawn.bjork@ridgewater.edu

Ridgewater College-Willmar Campus
PO Box 1097, Willmar MN 56201-1097
Sally Kerfeld, Director of Admissions
800-722-1151 Fax: 320-231-7677
Website: www.ridgewater.edu
E-mail: skerfeld@ridgewater.edu

Riverland Community College
1900 8th Ave NW, Austin MN 55912-1400
Dani Heiny, Director of Admissions
800-247-5039

Riverland Community College
Albert Lea Campus
2200 Riverland Dr, Albert Lea MN 56007
Dani Heiny, Director of Admissions
800-333-2584

Riverland Technical College
1225 3rd St SW, Faribault MN 55021-5720
800-422-0391

Rochester Community & Technical College
851 30th Ave SE, Rochester MN 55904-4999
507-285-7210

St. Cloud Hospital
1406 6th Ave N, Saint Cloud MN 56303-1901
320-255-5666

St. Cloud State University
720 4th Ave S, Saint Cloud MN 56301-4442
877-654-7278

St. Cloud Technical College
1540 Northway Dr, Saint Cloud MN 56303-1240
Jodi Elness, Director of Enrollment Management
800-222-1009 Fax: 320-308-5981
Website: www.sctc.edu
E-mail: jelness@sctc.edu

St. Mary's Hospital/Mayo Medical Center
1216 2nd St NW, Rochester MN 55901-0322
507-255-5221

St. Mary's University of Minnesota
700 Terrace Hts Ste 2, Winona MN 55987-1321
507-452-4430

St. Paul College
A Community & Technical College
235 Marshall Ave, Saint Paul MN 55102-1800
651-221-1300

South Central College
1920 Lee Blvd, North Mankato MN 56003-2508
507-389-7200

Sr. Rosalind Gefre Schools of Massage
416 S Front St, Mankato MN 56001
Alyssa Beyer, Director of Admissions
507-344-0220 Fax: 507-344-0204
Website: www.sisterrosalind.org
E-mail: mankatocampus@sisterrosalind.org

Sr. Rosalind Gefre Schools of Massage
300 Elton Hills Dr NW, Rochester MN 55901
Jason Egginton, Director of Admissions
507-286-8608 Fax: 507-282-2893
Website: www.sisterrosalind.org
E-mail: rochestercampus@sisterrosalind.org

Sr. Rosalind Gefre Schools of Massage
1007 Industrial Dr S, Sauk Rapids MN 56379
Kelly Christopheron, Director of Admissions
320-259-6185 Fax: 320-259-6173
Website: www.sisterrosalind.org
E-mail: saukrapidscampus@sisterrosalind.org

Sr. Rosalind Gefre Schools of Massage
149 Thompson Ave Ste 150
West Saint Paul MN 55118
Jen Maudel, Director of Admissions
651-554-3010 Fax: 651-554-7608
Website: www.sisterrosalind.org
E-mail: stpaulcampus@sisterrosalind.org

University of Minnesota
2900 University Ave, Crookston MN 56716-5001
218-281-6510

University of Minnesota
10 University Dr, Duluth MN 55812-2496
Beth Esselstrom, Director of Admissions
218-726-7171

University of Minnesota
231 Pillsbury Dr SE, Minneapolis MN 55455-0230
612-625-2008

MISSISSIPPI

Alcorn State University
PO Box 359, Lorman MS 39096
601-877-6147

Copiah-Lincoln Community College
PO Box 457, Wesson MS 39191-0457
601-643-5101

Delta State University
Hwy 8 W, Cleveland MS 38733
662-846-3000

Forrest General Hospital
6051 U S Highway 49, Hattiesburg MS 39401-7225
601-288-4201

Hattiesburg Radiology Group
5000 W 4th St, Hattiesburg MS 39402-1077
601-288-4241

Hinds Community College
PO Box 1100, Raymond MS 39154
601-857-5261

Itawamba Community College
602 W Hill St, Fulton MS 38843
662-862-8000

Jackson State University
1440 J.R. Lynch St, Jackson MS 39217
Stephanie Chatman, Director of Admissions
601-979-2100

Jones County Junior College
900 S Court St, Ellisville MS 39437-3999
601-477-4000

Meridian Community College
910 Highway 19 N, Meridian MS 39307-5801
601-483-8241

Mississippi Baptist Medical Center
1225 N State St, Jackson MS 39202-2002
601-968-5130

Mississippi Delta Community College
PO Box 668, Moorhead MS 38761-0668
662-246-6322

Mississippi Gulf Coast Community College
PO Box 609, Perkinston MS 39573
601-928-5211

Mississippi State University
PO Box J, Mississippi State MS 39762-5509
662-325-2323

Mississippi University for Women
1100 College St Unit W1613, Columbus MS 39701
Terri Heath, Director of Admissions
877-GO-2-THEW

Northeast Mississippi Community College
101 Cunningham Blvd, Booneville MS 38829-1726
662-728-7751

North Mississippi Medical Center
830 S Gloster St, Tupelo MS 38801-4934
662-841-3136

Northwest Mississippi Community College
4975 Highway 51 N, Senatobia MS 38668
662-562-3200

Pearl River Community College
Station A, Poplarville MS 39470
601-795-6801

St. Dominic-Jackson Memorial Hospital
969 Lakeland Dr, Jackson MS 39216-4602
601-364-6935

Southwest Mississippi Regional Medical Center
PO Box 1307, Mc Comb MS 39649-1307
601-249-1807

University of Mississippi
University MS 38677
662-232-7226

University of Mississippi Medical Center
2500 N State St, Jackson MS 39216-4500
601-984-1010

University of Southern Mississippi
PO Box 5165, Hattiesburg MS 39406-1000
601-266-5000

William Carey College
498 Tuscan Ave, Hattiesburg MS 39401-5461
800-962-5991

MISSOURI

ALLIED COLLEGE - NORTH
13723 Riverport Dr Ste 103
Maryland Heights MO 63043
866-501-1291
Website: www.alliedcollege.edu

ARAMARK Healthcare Support Services SW
1000 Carondelet Dr, Kansas City MO 64114-4673
816-943-2146

Avila University
11901 Wornall Rd, Kansas City MO 64145-1698
816-942-8400

Cape Girardeau Career & Technology Center
1080 S Silver Springs Rd
Cape Girardeau MO 63703-7511
573-334-0826

Central Institute for the Deaf
818 S Euclid Ave, Saint Louis MO 63110-1594
314-652-3200

Central Missouri State University
Warrensburg MO 64093-8888
Charles Petentler, Associate Director of Admissions
800-956-0177

College of the Ozarks
Point Lookout MO 65726
417-334-6411

CONCORDE CAREER COLLEGE
3239 Broadway St, Kansas City MO 64111-2407
Steve Koberlein, Director of Admissions
816-531-5223 Fax: 816-756-3231
Website: www.concorde.edu
E-mail: skoberlein@concorde.edu

Cox College of Nursing & Health Sciences
1423 N Jefferson Ave, Springfield MO 65802-1917
417-269-3401

DVA Medical Center
1 Jefferson Barracks Rd, Saint Louis MO 63125-4181
314-894-6631

East Central College
1964 Prairie Dell Rd, Union MO 63084
Karen Wieda, Registrar
636-583-5195 ext. 2220 Fax: 636-583-1897
Website: www.eastcentral.edu
E-mail: wiedaks@eastcentral.edu

Fontbonne University
6800 Wydown Blvd, Saint Louis MO 63105-3098
314-889-1419

Hannibal Area Vocational Technical School
4550 McMasters Ave, Hannibal MO 63401-2242
Harold D. Ward, Director
573-221-4430

Heritage College
534 E 99th St, Kansas City MO 64131
Larry Cartmill, Director
816-942-5474 Fax: 816-942-5405
Website: www.heritage-education.com
E-mail: info@heritage-education.com
See listing under "Career Schools"

IHM Health Studies Center
3663 Lindell Blvd, Saint Louis MO 63108
314-768-1000

Lindenwood University
209 S Kingshighway St
Saint Charles MO 63301-1695
Sheryl Guffey, Director of Admissions
636-949-2000 Fax: 636-949-4989
Website: www.lindenwood.edu

Linn State Technical College
1 Technology Dr, Linn MO 65051-9606
Becky Dunn, Admissions
800-743-8324 Fax: 573-897-5026
Website: www.linnstate.edu
E-mail: admissions@linnstate.edu

Mineral Area Regional Medical Center
1212 Weber Rd, Farmington MO 63640-3309
573-756-4581

Missouri College
10121 Manchester Rd, Saint Louis MO 63122-1525
Erin Cunningham, Director of Admissions
314-821-7700

Missouri Southern State University - Joplin
3950 Newman Rd, Joplin MO 64801-1512
417-625-9300

Missouri State University
901 S National Ave, Springfield MO 65897
417-836-5000

Missouri Western State College
4525 Downs Dr, Saint Joseph MO 64507-2294
800-662-7041

Nichols Career Center
605 Union St, Jefferson City MO 65101-2814
573-659-3100

North Kansas City Hospital
2800 Clay Edwards Dr
North Kansas City MO 64116-3220
816-691-2000

Northwest Missouri State University
800 University Dr, Maryville MO 64468-6001
660-562-1212

Ozarks Technical Community College
PO Box 5958, Springfield MO 65801-5958
417-895-7000

Penn Valley Community College
3201 SW Traffic Way, Kansas City MO 64111
816-759-4000

Research Medical Center
2316 E Meyer Blvd, Kansas City MO 64132-1199
816-276-4101

Rockhurst University
1100 Rockhurst Rd, Kansas City MO 64110-2561
Mark Kopenski, VP of Enrollment Management
816-501-4000

St. Charles Community College
4601 Mid Rivers Mall Dr, Saint Peters MO 63376
Kathy Brockgreitens-Gober, Director of Admissions
636-922-8000 Fax: 636-922-8236
Website: www.stchas.edu
E-mail: adm-reg@stchas.edu

St. John's Mercy Medical Center
615 S New Ballas Rd, Saint Louis MO 63141-8277
314-569-6182

St. John's Regional Health Center
1235 E Cherokee St, Springfield MO 65804-2263
417-885-2845

St. John's Regional Medical Center
2727 Mc Clelland Blvd, Joplin MO 64804-1694
417-781-2727

St. Louis Community College
11333 Big Bend Rd, Kirkwood MO 63122-5799
314-984-7500

St. Louis Community College
5600 Oakland Ave, Saint Louis MO 63110-1316
314-644-9100

St. Louis Community College at Florissant Valley
3400 Pershall Rd, Saint Louis MO 63135-1408
Janice Evans, Chair, Enrollment Management
314-595-4368

St. Louis University
221 N Grand Blvd, Saint Louis MO 63103-2097
314-977-2222

Saint Luke's College
8320 Ward Parkway Suite 300
Kansas City MO 64114
Josh Richards Asst. Director of Admissions
816-932-2367 Fax: 816-932-9064
Website: www.saintlukescollege.edu
E-mail: slc-admissions@saint-lukes.org

Sanford-Brown College
1345 Smizer Mill Rd, Fenton MO 63026
Kevin Frank, Director of HS Admissions
636-349-4900

Southeast Missouri Hospital
College of Nursing and Health Sciences
2001 William St #2, Cape Girardeau MO 63703-5815
Don Pugh, Registrar
573-334-6825

Southeast Missouri State University
1 University Plz, Cape Girardeau MO 63701-4710
573-651-2000

SPRINGFIELD COLLEGE
1010 W Sunshine St, Springfield MO 65807-2446
Scott Lester, Contact
417-864-7220 or 800-475-2699 Fax: 417-866-3335
Website: www.springfield-college.com
E-mail: slester@cci.edu

Stephens College
PO Box 2121, Columbia MO 65215-0001
David Adams, Dean of Enrollment Management
573-442-2211 Fax: 573-876-7237
Website: www.stephens.edu
E-mail: dadams@stephens.edu

Three Rivers Community College
2080 Three Rivers Blvd, Poplar Bluff MO 63901
573-840-9605

Truman Medical Center
2301 Holmes St, Kansas City MO 64108-2677
816-556-3153

Truman State University
100 E Normal, Kirksville MO 63501
Office of Admission
660-785-4000 Fax: 660-785-4181
Website: admissions.truman.edu
E-mail: admissions@truman.edu

University of Missouri
228 Jesse Hall, Columbia MO 65211-0001
573-882-2121

University of Missouri
5100 Rockhill Rd, Kansas City MO 64110-2446
816-235-1000

Vatterott College
12970 Maurer Industrial Dr, Saint Louis MO 63127
Sherri Bremer, Director of Admissions
314-843-4200 Fax: 314-843-1709
Website: www.vatterott-college.edu
E-mail: sherri.bremer@vatterott-college.edu

Washington University in St. Louis
1 Brookings Dr, Saint Louis MO 63130-4899
314-935-5000

MONTANA

Benefits Health Care-West Campus
PO Box 5013, Great Falls MT 59403-5013
406-727-3333

Carroll College
1601 N Benton Ave, Helena MT 59625-0002
Cynthia Thornquist, Director of Admissions &
Enrollment Operations
406-447-4384

Flathead Valley Community College
777 Grandview Dr, Kalispell MT 59901-2622
406-756-3846

Montana State University - Billings
1500 University Dr, Billings MT 59101-0252
Karen Everett, Director
800-565-MSUB

Montana State University - Bozeman
103 Culbertson Hall, Bozeman MT 59715-5072
406-994-2452

Montana State University
Great Falls College of Technology
2100 16th Ave S, Great Falls MT 59405-4909
406-771-4300

Rocky Mountain College
1511 Poly Dr, Billings MT 59102-1796
Bonnie Knapp, Director of Admissions
800-877-6259 Fax: 406-657-1189
Website: www.rocky.edu
E-mail: admissions@rocky.edu

St. Patrick Hospital
PO Box 4587, Missoula MT 59806-4587
406-543-7271

St. Vincent's Hospital & Health Center
PO Box 35200, Billings MT 59107
406-657-7102

Salish Kootenai College
PO Box 70, Pablo MT 59855
Jackie Moran, Admissions/Transfers
406-275-4866

NEBRASKA

Bishop Clarkson Memorial Hospital
4350 Dewey Ave, Omaha NE 68105-1017
402-552-3203

Central Community College-Hastings Campus
PO Box 1024, Hastings NE 68902-1024
Bob Glenn, Contact
402-463-9811 Fax: 402-562-1201
Website: www.cccneb.edu
E-mail: rglenn@cccneb.edu

Clarkson College
101 S 42nd St, Omaha NE 68131-2715
Sara Bonney, Director of Admissions
402-552-3100 Fax: 402-552-6057
Website: www.clarksoncollege.edu
E-mail: admiss@clarksoncollege.edu

College of Saint Mary
7000 Mercy Rd, Omaha NE 68106
Lorin Werth, V.P. for Enrollment
800-926-5534 or 402-399-2407 Fax: 402-399-2412
Website: www.csm.edu
E-mail: lwerth@csm.edu

Creighton University
2500 California Plz, Omaha NE 68178-0001
402-280-2700

Hamilton College
3350 N 90th St, Omaha NE 68134-4710
402-572-8500

Immanuel Medical Center
6901 N 72nd St, Omaha NE 68122-1709
402-572-2270

Mary Lanning Memorial Hospital
715 N Saint Joseph Ave, Hastings NE 68901-4497
402-463-4521

Metropolitan Community College
PO Box 3777, Omaha NE 68103-0777
402-449-8400

Mid-Plains Community College
North Platte Community College - South Campus
601 W State Farm Rd, North Platte NE 69101
Kelly Rippen, Director of Recruitment
800-658-4308 ext. 8107 Fax: 308-535-3789
Website: www.mpcc.edu
E-mail: rippenk@mpcc.edu

Nebraska Methodist College
720 N 87th St, Omaha NE 68114
Deann Sterner, Director of Admissions
402-354-7200

Nebraska Wesleyan University
5000 Saint Paul Ave, Lincoln NE 68504-2794
Patricia Karthauser, V.P. for University Enrollment
402-466-2371 Fax: 402-465-2177
Website: www.nebrwesleyan.edu
E-mail: admissions@nebrwesleyan.edu

Northeast Community College
PO Box 469, Norfolk NE 68702-0469
402-371-2020

Regional West Medical Center
4021 Avenue B, Scottsbluff NE 69361-4695
308-635-3711

Southeast Community College
8800 O St, Lincoln NE 68520-1299
402-437-2500

Union College
3800 S 48th St, Lincoln NE 68506-4300
Buell Fogg, V.P. for Enrollment Services
800-228-4600

University of Nebraska
14th & R Sts, Lincoln NE 68588
402-472-7211

University of Nebraska at Kearney
905 W 25th St, Kearney NE 68849-0001
Dusty Newton, Director of Admissions
800-KEARNEY Fax: 308-865-8987
Website: www.unk.edu
E-mail: admissionsug@unk.edu

University of Nebraska at Omaha
60th and Dodge St, Omaha NE 68182-0001
402-554-2800

University of Nebraska Medical Center
985150 Nebraska Medical Center
Omaha NE 68198-5150
800-626-8431

NEVADA

Associated Pathologist Laboratories
4230 Burnham Ave, Las Vegas NV 89119-5408
702-733-7866

Career College of Northern Nevada
1195-A Corporate Blvd, Reno NV 89502-2331
Nathan Clark, Director
775-856-2266 Fax: 775-856-0935
Website: www.ccnn.edu
E-mail: lgoldhammer@ccnn4u.com
See listing under "Career Schools"

Community College of Southern Nevada
3200 E Cheyenne Ave
North Las Vegas NV 89030-4228
Arlie J. Stops, Assoc. VP Admissions / Records
702-651-4536

GREAT BASIN COLLEGE
1500 College Pkwy, Elko NV 89801-5032
Julie G. Byrnes, Director of Enrollment Management
775-753-2271 Fax: 775-753-2311
Website: www.gbcnv.edu
E-mail: bjulie@gbcnv.edu

Heritage College
3315 Spring Mountain Rd, Las Vegas NV 89102
Mimi Ritenour, Director of Admissions
702-368-2338

Truckee Meadows Community College
7000 Dandini Blvd, Reno NV 89512-3999
Rita Huneycutt, Interim President
775-673-7000

University of Nevada
Reno NV 89557-0001
775-784-1110

University of Nevada Las Vegas
4505 S Maryland Pkwy, Las Vegas NV 89154-9901
800-334-8658

NEW HAMPSHIRE

Keene State College
229 Main St, Keene NH 03435-0002
603-358-2276

New Hampshire Community Technical College
1 College Dr, Claremont NH 03743
Charles Kusselow, Admissions Counselor
603-542-7744

New Hampshire Community Technical College
1066 Front St, Manchester NH 03102-8528
603-668-6706

New Hampshire Technical Institute
11 Institute Dr, Concord NH 03301-7400
603-271-6484

Plymouth State University
17 High St, MSC #44, Bagley House
Plymouth NH 03264-1595
603-535-5000

University of New Hampshire
Durham NH 03824
603-862-1234

NEW JERSEY

Atlantic Cape Community College
5100 Black Horse Pike
Mays Landing NJ 08330-2699
Linda McLeod, Assistant Director of College Recruitment
609-343-5000 Fax: 609-343-4921
Website: www.atlantic.edu
E-mail: accadmit@atlantic.edu
See listing under "Community and Junior Colleges"

Atlantic County Vocational Technical School
5080 Atlantic Ave, Mays Landing NJ 08330-2022
609-625-2249

Bergen Community College
400 Paramus Rd, Paramus NJ 07652
Julian Gomez, Asst. Director of Admissions
201-447-7100 Fax: 201-444-7036
Website: www.bergen.edu
E-mail: jgomez@bergen.edu

BEST CARE TRAINING INSTITUTE
68 S Harrison St, East Orange NJ 07017
Florence Brown, RN, MSN, APNC, Contact
973-673-3900 Fax: 973-673-0597
Website: www.bestcarehealth.com
E-mail: fbrown3260@aol.com

Burdette Tomlin Memorial Hospital
2 Stone Harbor Blvd
Cape May Court House NJ 08210-2171
609-463-2180

Burlington County College
County Route 530, Pemberton NJ 08068
609-894-9311

Burlington County Institute of Technology - Adult Education
695 Woodlane Rd, Mount Holly NJ 08060-3813
Dr. Fred Laier, Contact
609-267-4226

Camden County College
PO Box 200, Blackwood NJ 08012-0200
856-227-7200

Camden County Technical School
343 Berlin Cross Keys Rd, Sicklerville NJ 08081-4000
Gayle Butler, Director of Admissions
856-767-7002

College of New Jersey
PO Box 7718, Ewing NJ 08628-0718
609-771-1855

College of Saint Elizabeth
2 Convent Rd, Morristown NJ 07960-6923
973-292-4000

Cooper Hospital/University Medical Center
1 Cooper Plz #217, Camden NJ 08103-1461
Joan D'Antonio, Director
856-342-2416

County College of Morris
214 Center Grove Rd, Randolph NJ 07869-2086
973-328-5000

Cumberland County College
PO Box 1500, Vineland NJ 08362-1500
856-691-8600

Cumberland County Technical Education Center
601 Bridgeton Ave, Bridgeton NJ 08302-4810
856-451-9000

Dover Business College
15 E Blackwell St, Dover NJ 07801-4643
973-285-8400

Dover Business College
East 81 Route 4 W, Paramus NJ 07652
201-843-8500

Elizabeth General Medical Center School
925 E Jersey St, Elizabeth NJ 07201-2789
908-965-7390

Englewood Hospital & Medical Center
350 Engle St, Englewood NJ 07631-1898
201-894-3002

Essex County College
303 University Ave, Newark NJ 07102-1798
973-877-3000

Fairleigh Dickinson University
1000 River Rd, Teaneck NJ 07666-1996
201-692-2000

Felician College
262 S Main St, Lodi NJ 07644-2198
973-559-6000

Gloucester County College
1400 Tanyard Rd, Sewell NJ 08080
856-468-5000

Hackensack Univ Medical Center
30 Prospect Ave, Hackensack NJ 07601-1991
201-996-2000

Helene Fuld Medical Center
750 Brunswick Ave, Trenton NJ 08638-4174
609-394-3174

Hohokus School - RETS Nutley
103 Park Ave, Nutley NJ 07110-3505
Thomas Eastwick, President
973-661-0600 Fax: 973-661-2954
Website: www.rets-institute.com
E-mail: admissions@rets-institute.com

HUDSON AREA SCHOOL OF RADIOLOGIC TECHNOLOGY
176 Palisade Ave, Jersey City NJ 07306
Kenneth Lee, D.H.S., R.T. (R)(M)
201-795-8246 Fax: 201-795-5818
Website: www.christhospital.org
E-mail: lleclaire@christhospital.com

Hudson County Community College
25 Journal Sq, Jersey City NJ 07306
201-656-2020

The Institute for Health Education
7 Spielman Rd, Fairfield NJ 07004-3403
973-808-1666

Jersey Shore Medical Center
1945 State Route 33, Neptune City NJ 07753-4889
732-776-4603

Kean University
1000 Morris Ave, Union NJ 07083-7133
908-527-2000

Mercer County Community College
West Windsor Campus
PO Box B, Trenton NJ 08690
Savita Bambhrolia, Director of Admissions
609-586-4800 Fax: 609-587-4666
Website: www.mccc.edu
E-mail: admiss@mccc.edu

Middlesex County College
2600 Woodbridge Ave, Edison NJ 08837-3675
732-548-6000

Monmouth Medical Center
300 2nd Ave, Long Branch NJ 07740-6395
John A. Mihok, MT Program Director
732-222-5200

Montclair State University
Montclair State University, Montclair NJ 07043-1624
973-655-4000

Morristown Memorial Hospital
100 Madison Ave, Morristown NJ 07960-6095
973-971-5177

Mountainside Hospital
1 Bay Ave, Montclair NJ 07042-4898
973-429-6850

MUHLENBERG REGIONAL MEDICAL CENTER
Schools of Nursing, Medical Imaging & Therapeutic Sciences
Plainfield NJ 07061
Jane Vatsky, Director of Admissions
908-668-2400 Fax: 908-226-4568
Website: www.muhlenbergschools.org
E-mail: ssonmits@solarishs.org
See listing under "Nursing"

New Jersey City University
2039 John F Kennedy Blvd
Jersey City NJ 07305-1588
Carmen Panlilio, Asst. V.P. for Admissions and Financial Aid
201-200-3234 Fax: 201-200-2044
Website: www.njcu.edu
E-mail: admissions@njcu.edu

Ocean County College
College Dr, Toms River NJ 08754
732-255-0400

Pascack Valley Hospital
250 Old Hook Rd, Westwood NJ 07675-3181
201-358-3010

Passaic Co. Community College
1 College Blvd, Paterson NJ 07505
973-684-6800

Raritan Valley Community College
PO Box 3300, Somerville NJ 08876-1265
908-526-1200

Richard Stockton College of New Jersey
PO Box 195, Pomona NJ 08240
609-652-1776

Rutgers-The State University of New Jersey
New Brunswick Campus
35 College Ave, New Brunswick NJ 08901
732-932-4636

St. Barnabas Medical Center
94 Old Short Hills Rd, Livingston NJ 07039-5668
973-533-5628

St. Francis Medical Center
601 Hamilton Ave, Trenton NJ 08629-1986
609-599-5000

Shore Memorial Hospital
Shore Rd, Somers Point NJ 08244
609-653-3545

STAR TECHNICAL INSTITUTE
3003 English Creek Ave Suite 212
Egg Harbor Township NJ 08234-4880
George Z. Negrete, Director
609-407-2999 Fax: 609-646-9472
Website: www.startechnicalinstitute.com
E-mail: info@stareggharbor.com

Sussex County Community College
1 College Hill, Newton NJ 07860
973-300-2100

UMDNJ-University of Medicine and Dentistry of New Jersey
65 Bergen St, Newark NJ 07107-3001
973-972-4300

Union County College
1033 Springfield Ave, Cranford NJ 07016-1528
908-709-7000

Valley Hospital
223 N Van Dien Ave, Ridgewood NJ 07450-2736
201-447-8002

Warren County Community College
475 State Route 57 W, Washington NJ 07882-4343
908-835-9222

West Jersey Health System
1000 Atlantic Ave, Camden NJ 08104-1595
856-342-4600

William Paterson University
300 Pompton Rd, Wayne NJ 07470-2103
973-720-2000

NEW MEXICO

Albuquerque TVI Community College
525 Buena Vista Dr SE, Albuquerque NM 87106-4096
Jane Campbell, Registrar
505-224-3061

Apollo College
5301 Central Ave NE Ste 101
Albuquerque NM 87108-1514
800-368-7246

Clovis Community College
417 Schepps Blvd, Clovis NM 88101-8381
505-769-2811

Eastern New Mexico University
Portales NM 88130
800-367-3668

Eastern New Mexico University-Roswell
PO Box 6000, Roswell NM 88202-6000
505-624-7000

International Institute of the Americas
4201 Central Ave NW Suite J
Albuquerque NM 87105-1649
Ed Sigman, Director
505-880-2877 Fax: 505-352-0199
Website: www.iia.edu
E-mail: syelton@iia.edu

New Mexico State University
2400 Scenic Dr, Alamogordo NM 88310-3722
505-439-3600

New Mexico State University
PO Box 30001, Las Cruces NM 88003-8001
505-646-0111

New Mexico State University
Dona Ana Branch Community College
PO Box 30001, Las Cruces NM 88003-8001
505-527-7500

Northern New Mexico College
921 Paseo de Onate, Espanola NM 87532
505-747-2100

Pima Medical Institute
2201 San Pedro Dr NE, Albuquerque NM 87110-4155
505-881-1234

San Juan College
4601 College Blvd, Farmington NM 87402-4699
505-326-3311

Southwestern Indian Polytechnic Institute
PO Box 10146, Albuquerque NM 87184-0146
505-346-2347

University of New Mexico
1 University Campus, Albuquerque NM 87131-0001
505-277-0111

University of New Mexico
200 College Rd, Gallup NM 87301-5603
505-863-7500

NEW YORK

Adelphi University
Garden City NY 11530
516-877-3100

Advanced Software Analysis Institute of Business and
Computer Technology
151 Lawrence St Ste 2, Brooklyn NY 11201-5208
718-522-9073

Albany College of Pharmacy
106 New Scotland Ave, Albany NY 12208
Jean Taylor, Program Director
518-445-7390

ARNOT-OGDEN MEDICAL CENTER
School of Radiologic Technology
600 Roe Ave, Elmira NY 14905-1629
Ellen Richards, BS RT (R) Director
607-737-4289 Fax: 607-737-4116
Website: www.aomc.org
E-mail: erichards@aomc.org

Bellevue Hospital Center
462 1st Ave, New York NY 10016-9198
212-561-4132

Bronx Lebanon Hospital Center
1650 Grand Concourse, Bronx NY 10457-7697
718-518-1800

Brooklyn Hospital
121 DeKalb Ave, Brooklyn NY 11201-5493
718-250-8005

Broome Community College
907 Upper Front St, Binghamton NY 13905
Anthony S. Fiorelli, Director of Admissions
607-778-5001 Fax: 607-778-5442
Website: www.sunybroome.edu
E-mail: fiorelli_a@sunybroome.edu

Bryant & Stratton College
1259 Central Ave, Albany NY 12205
518-437-1802

Bryant & Stratton College
465 Main St Ste 400, Buffalo NY 14203-1713
716-884-9120

Bryant & Stratton College
150 Bellwood Dr, Rochester NY 14606
585-720-0660

Bryant & Stratton College
1225 Jeffson Rd, Rochester NY 14623
585-292-5627

Bryant & Stratton College
953 James St, Syracuse NY 13203-2502
315-472-6603

CAREER INSTITUTE OF HEALTH & TECHNOLOGY
340 Flatbush Avenue Ext, Brooklyn NY 11201
Mary Miller, Contact
718-422-1212 Fax: 718-422-1222
Website: www.careerinstitute.edu
E-mail: admissions@careerinstitute.edu

CAREER INSTITUTE OF HEALTH & TECHNOLOGY
200 Garden City Plz, Garden City NY 11530
Mary Miller, Contact
516-877-1225 Fax: 516-877-1959
Website: www.careerinstitute.edu
E-mail: admissions@careerinstitute.edu

CAREER INSTITUTE OF HEALTH & TECHNOLOGY
9525 Queens Blvd Ste 600, Rego Park NY 11374
Mary Miller, Contact
718-897-4868 Fax: 718-897-4863
Website: www.careerinstitute.edu
E-mail: admissions@careerinstitute.edu

Central Suffolk Hospital
1300 Roanoke Ave, Riverhead NY 11901-2058
631-548-6000

Champlain Valley Physicians Hospital
75 Beekman St, Plattsburgh NY 12901
518-561-2000

THE CHUBB INSTITUTE
498 7th Ave, New York NY 10018
Joe Rodriguez, Director of Admissions
212-659-2116 Fax: 212-659-2175
Website: www.chubbinstitute.edu
E-mail: jrodriguez@chubbinstitute.edu

Clinton Community College
136 Clinton Point Dr, Plattsburgh NY 12901-6002
Robert C. Wood, Assoc. Dean for Enrollment
518-562-4200

College of New Rochelle
29 Castle Pl, New Rochelle NY 10805-2339
914-654-5000

College of Saint Rose
432 Western Ave, Albany NY 12203-1419
Maryelizabeth Amico, Asst V.P. for Undergraduate
Admissions
518-454-5150 Fax: 518-454-2013
Website: www.strose.edu
E-mail: admit@strose.edu

Columbia University
168th & Broadway, New York NY 10032
212-305-5756

Cornell University
410 Thurston Ave, Ithaca NY 14850-2432
607-255-2000

County University School of Dental & Oral Surgery
630 W 168th St, New York NY 10032

CUNY Borough of Manhattan Community College
199 Chambers St, New York NY 10007-1044
212-346-8800

CUNY Bronx Community College
W 181st and University Ave, Bronx NY 10453-2895
718-289-5100

CUNY Brooklyn College
2900 Bedford Ave, Brooklyn NY 11210-2814
718-951-5000

CUNY City College
Convent Ave at 138th St, New York NY 10031
Celia Lloyd, Interim Director of Admissions
212-650-6977

CUNY College of Staten Island
2800 Victory Blvd, Staten Island NY 10314-6600
718-982-2000

CUNY Hunter College
695 Park Ave, New York NY 10021
Aaron Gibbs, Assistant Director of Recruitment
212-772-4497 Fax: 212-650-3336
Website: www.hunter.cuny.edu
E-mail: aaron.gibbs@hunter.cuny.edu

CUNY Lehman College
250 Bedford Park Blvd W, Bronx NY 10468-1527
718-960-8000

CUNY Queens College
6530 Kissena Blvd, Flushing NY 11367-1575
718-997-5000

CUNY York College
9420 Guy R Brewer Blvd, Jamaica NY 11451-0001
718-262-2000

Daemen College
4380 Main St, Amherst NY 14226-3592
Donna Shaffner, Director of Admissions
800-462-7652 or 716-839-8225 Fax: 716-839-8229
Website: www.daemen.edu
E-mail: admissions@daemen.edu
See listing under "Universities"

Dutchess Community College
53 Pendell Rd, Poughkeepsie NY 12601-1512
845-431-8000

D'Youville College
320 Porter Ave, Buffalo NY 14201-1084
716-829-7600

Elmira Business Institute
303 N Main St, Elmira NY 14901
Lisa Roan, Admissions Director
607-733-7177 or 800-843-1812 Fax: 607-733-7178
Website: www.ebi-college.com
E-mail: lroan@ebi-college.com

Erie Community College
City Campus
121 Ellicott St, Buffalo NY 14203-2698
716-842-2770

Erie Community College North
6205 Main St, Williamsville NY 14221-8402
716-634-0800

Erie Community College South
4041 Southwestern Blvd
Orchard Park NY 14127-2199
716-648-5400

Farmingdale SUNY
2350 Broadhollow Rd, Farmingdale NY 11735
631-420-2200

FAXTON-ST. LUKE'S HEALTHCARE SCHOOL OF MEDICAL RADIOGRAPHY
PO Box 479, Utica NY 13503-0479
Rosemary Morin, MS, RTR, Director
315-624-6136 Fax: 315-624-4787
Website: mvnhealth.com
E-mail: xrayed@dreamscape.com

Genesee Community College
1 College Rd, Batavia NY 14020-9703
585-343-0055

Glens Falls Hospital
100 Park St, Glens Falls NY 12801-4447
518-792-3151

Gloden Hall Health Care Center
Golden Hill Dr, Kingston NY 12401
845-339-4540

Herkimer County Community College
100 Reservoir Rd, Herkimer NY 13350-1545
888-464-4222

Hochstim School of Radiography
PO Box 9007, Oceanside NY 11572-9007
516-763-2030

Hofstra University
100 Hofstra University, Hempstead NY 11549-1000
516-463-6600

Hostos Community College - CUNY
500 Grand Concourse, Bronx NY 10451-5323
Roland Velez, Director of Admissions
718-518-4406

Institute of Allied Medical Professions
405 Park Ave, New York NY 10022-4405
212-758-1410

Interboro Institute
450 W 56th St, New York NY 10019
212-399-0091

Ithaca College
953 Danby Rd, Ithaca NY 14850-7002
607-274-3011

Keuka College
PO Box 98, Keuka Park NY 14478-0098
315-536-4411

LaGuardia Community College / CUNY
31-10 Thompson Ave, Long Island City NY 11101
718-482-7200

Le Moyne College
1419 Salt Springs Rd, Syracuse NY 13214-1301
800-333-4733

Long Island College Hospital School of Nursing
397 Hicks St, Brooklyn NY 11201-5940
718-780-1953

Long Island University-Brooklyn Campus
1 University Plz, Brooklyn NY 11201-5372
718-488-1000

Long Island University-C. W. Post Campus
720 Northern Blvd, Brookville NY 11548-1300
Joanne Graziano, Executive Director of Admissions
516-299-2900 Fax: 516-299-2137
Website: www.liu.edu/cwpost
E-mail: enroll@cwpost.liu.edu

Manhattan College
4513 Manhattan College Pkwy
Riverdale NY 10471-4099
Dr. William Merriman, Dean of Education
718-862-7200

Maria College of Albany
700 New Scotland Ave, Albany NY 12208-1715
518-438-3111

Marymount College at Fordham University
100 Marymount Ave, Tarrytown NY 10591-3796
914-631-3200

Memorial Sloan Kettering Cancer Center
1275 York Ave, New York NY 10021-6007
212-639-6561

Mercy College
555 Broadway, Dobbs Ferry NY 10522-1189
Kathleen Jackson, Director of Admissions
800-MERCY-NY

Mercy Medical Center
PO Box 9024, Rockville Centre NY 11571-9024
516-705-2525

Mohawk Valley Community College
1101 Sherman Dr, Utica NY 13501-5394
315-792-5400

Molloy College
1000 Hempstead Ave
Rockville Centre NY 11570-1100
Marguerite Lane, Director of Admissions
516-678-5000 ext. 6291 Fax: 516-256-2247
Website: www.molloy.edu
E-mail: admissions@molloy.edu
See listing under "Universities"

Monroe Community College
1000 E Henrietta Rd, Rochester NY 14623-5701
585-292-2000

Montefiore Medical Center
111 E 210th St, Bronx NY 10467-2490
718-920-4001

Mount Sinai School of Medicine of New York University
Box 1022, 1 Gustave L Levy Place
New York NY 10029
212-241-6546

Nassau Community College
1 Education Dr, Garden City NY 11530-6719
516-572-7501

Nazareth College of Rochester
4245 East Ave, Rochester NY 14618-3790
585-389-2525

New York City College of Technology CUNY
300 Jay St, Brooklyn NY 11201-1909
Joe Lento, Director of Admissions
718-260-5000

NEW YORK COLLEGE OF HEALTH PROFESSIONS
6801 Jericho Tpke, Syosset NY 11791
Barbara Carver, Senior Vice President
800-9-CAREER Fax: 516-364-0989
Website: www.nycollege.edu
E-mail: bcarver@nycollege.edu

NEW YORK EYE & EAR INFIRMARY / ORTHOPTIC PROGRAM
310 E 14th St, New York NY 10003-4201
Sara Shippman, Chief Orthoptist
212-979-4375 Fax: 212-979-4564
Website: www.nyee.edu
E-mail: sshippman@nyee.edu

New York Institute of Technology
PO Box 8000, Old Westbury NY 11568-8000
516-686-7516

New York Medical College
Valhalla NY 10595
914-594-4000

NEW YORK METHODIST HOSPITAL
Clinical Laboratory Science/School of Medical
Technology
506 6th St, Brooklyn NY 11215-3609
Adrienne Arso-Paez, Program Director
718-780-3706 Fax: 718-780-3673
Website: www.nym.org
E-mail: ada9003@nyp.org

New York Presbyterian Hospital
525 E 68th St, New York NY 10021-4885
212-746-4000

NEW YORK SCHOOL FOR MEDICAL AND DENTAL ASSISTANTS
33-10 Queens Blvd, Long Island City NY 11101-2327
Donna Stirber-Gamelin, Executive Director of
Admissions
718-793-2330 Fax: 718-793-0619
Website: www.nysmda.com
E-mail: info@nysmda.com

New York University
70 Washington Sq S, New York NY 10012-1019
212-998-1212

New York University Medical Center
550 1st Ave, New York NY 10016-6481
212-263-5111

North Country Community College
School of Health Professions
23 Santanoni, Saranac Lake NY 12983-2046
Edwin Trathen, Assistant to the President for Enrollment
Services
1-888-TRY-NCCC ext. 686

Northport VA Medical Center
79 Middleville Rd, Northport NY 11768-2200
631-261-4400

Onondaga Community College
4941 Onondaga Rd, Syracuse NY 13215-2001
315-498-2622

Ridley-Lowell Business & Technical Institute
116 Front St, Binghamton NY 13905-3102
David Lounsbury, Executive Director
607-724-2941 Fax: 607-724-0799
Website: www.ridley.edu
E-mail: info@ridley.edu

Ridley-Lowell Business & Technical Institute
26 S Hamilton St, Poughkeepsie NY 12601-3328
E. Ann Bida, Director of Admissions
845-471-0330 Fax: 845-471-4990
Website: www.ridley.edu
E-mail: pcadmissions@ridley.edu

Rochester General Hospital
1425 Portland Ave, Rochester NY 14621-3095
585-338-4430

Rochester Institute of Technology
1 Lomb Memorial Dr, Rochester NY 14623-5603
585-475-2411

Russell Sage College
45 Ferry St, Troy NY 12180-4115
518-244-2000

Russell Sage Graduate School
45 Ferry St, Troy NY 12180-4115
518-244-2264

St. Elizabeth College of Nursing
2215 Genesee St, Utica NY 13501-5930
315-798-8125

St. James Mercy Hospital
411 Canisteo St, Hornell NY 14843-2197
607-324-3900

St. John's University
8000 Utopia Pkwy, Queens NY 11439
Office of Admission
718-990-2000 or 888-9-STJOHNS Fax: 718-990-2096
Website: www.stjohns.edu
E-mail: admissions@stjohns.edu
See listing under "Universities"

St. Joseph's College
245 Clinton Ave, Brooklyn NY 11205-3688
Theresa LaRocca Meyer, V.P. for Enrollment
Management
718-636-6800 Fax: 718-636-8303
Website: www.sjcny.edu
E-mail: tlaroccameyer@sjcny.edu

St. Vincent's Hospital & Medical Center
153 W 11th St, New York NY 10011-8397
212-604-7500

St. Vincent's Medical Center
355 Bard Ave, Staten Island NY 10310-1699

Samaritan Medical Center
830 Washington St, Watertown NY 13601-4034
315-785-4000

Sarah Lawrence College
1 Meadway, Bronxville NY 10708
914-337-0700

Sisters of Charity Medical Center - Bayley Seton Campus
75 Vanderbilt Ave, Staten Island NY 10304-3850
718-818-6470

SUNY Adirondack Community College
640 Bay Rd, Queensbury NY 12804
Sarah Jane Linehan, Director of Enrollment
Management
518-743-2264

SUNY at Albany
1400 Washington Ave, Albany NY 12222-1000
Thomas Flemming, Associate Director of Admissions
518-442-5435

SUNY at Stony Brook
Stony Brook NY 11794-0001
631-689-6000

SUNY Canton - College of Technology
34 Cornell Dr, Canton NY 13617-1037
315-386-7011

SUNY College at Brockport
350 New Campus Dr, Brockport NY 14420-2997
Bernard S. Valento, Director of Undergraduate
Admissions
585-395-2751 Fax: 585-395-5452
Website: www.brockport.edu
E-mail: admit@brockport.edu

SUNY College at Buffalo
1300 Elmwood Ave, Buffalo NY 14222-1004
716-878-4000

SUNY College at Cortland
PO Box 2000, Cortland NY 13045-0900
Mark Yacavone, Assistant Director
607-753-4711

SUNY College at Fredonia
Fredonia NY 14063
716-673-3111

SUNY College at Geneseo
1 College Cir, Geneseo NY 14454-1401
585-245-5211

SUNY College at New Paltz
75 S Manheim Blvd Ste 1, New Paltz NY 12561-2400
845-257-2121

SUNY College at Oneonta
Oneonta NY 13820
607-436-3500

SUNY College at Plattsburgh
Plattsburgh NY 12901
518-564-2000

SUNY College of Agriculture & Technology
107 Schenectady Ave, Cobleskill NY 12043
Clayton A. Smith, Director of Admissions
800-295-8988

SUNY College of Agriculture & Technology
Morrisville NY 13408
Thomas Ver Dow, Dean of Enrollment Management
800-258-0111

SUNY College of Technology
Alfred NY 14802
Deborah J. Goodrich, Director of Admissions
800-4AL-FRED Fax: 607-587-4299
Website: www.alfredstate.edu
E-mail: admissions@alfredstate.edu

SUNY Educational Opportunity Center
465 Washington St, Buffalo NY 14203-1707
716-849-6725

SUNY Health Science Center
450 Clarkson Ave, Brooklyn NY 11203-2056
718-270-1000

SUNY Hudson Valley Community College
80 Vandenburgh Ave, Troy NY 12180-6025
Jack Mahoney, Director of Admissions
518-629-HVCC (629-4822)

SUNY Institute of Technology Utica/Rome
PO Box 3050, Utica NY 13504-3050
315-792-7100

SUNY Niagara County Community College
3111 Saunders Settlement Rd
Sanborn NY 14132-9487
Kathleen Saunders, Director of Admissions
716-614-6200 Fax: 716-614-6820
Website: www.niagaracc.suny.edu
E-mail: saunders@niagaracc.suny.edu

SUNY Orange County Community College
115 South St, Middletown NY 10940-6437
Margot St. Lawrence, Director of Admissions
845-341-4030 Fax: 845-342-8662
Website: www.sunyorange.edu
E-mail: apply@sunyorange.edu
See listing under "Community and Junior Colleges"

SUNY Rockland Community College
145 College Rd, Suffern NY 10901-3611
Charles Connolly, Coordinator of Admissions &
Recruitment
845-574-4000

SUNY Suffolk County Community College
Crooked Hill Rd, Brentwood NY 11717-1017
Andrea Bhella, Contact
631-851-6276

SUNY Suffolk County Community College
533 College Rd, Selden NY 11784-2851
631-451-4110

SUNY Upstate Medical University
750 E Adams St, Syracuse NY 13210
315-464-5540

SWEDISH INSTITUTE

College of Health Sciences
226 W 26th St, New York NY 10001-6700
Leslie Kielson, Dean of Admissions
212-924-5900 ext. 125 Fax: 212-924-7600
Website: www.swedishinstitute.edu
E-mail: admissions@swedishinstitute.edu
Established 1916. Private. Coed. Degrees: Associate
in Occupational Studies in Massage Therapy. Master of
Science in Acupuncture. Focused program in massage
therapy features Western & Eastern approaches. Can be
completed in 16 months full-time. The Master of Science
in Acupuncture focuses on classical Chinese Acupuncture. Full time students can complete the degree in three
years.

Syracuse University
Syracuse NY 13244-0001
315-443-1870

Teachers College of Columbia University
525 W 120th St, New York NY 10027-6625
212-678-3000

Touro College
27 W 23rd St Ste 33, New York NY 10010-4202
212-463-0400

Trocaire College
360 Choate Ave, Buffalo NY 14220-2003
Paul B. Hurley, Ph.D., President
716-826-1200 Fax: 716-828-6107
Website: www.trocaire.edu
E-mail: info@trocaire.edu
See listing under "Community and Junior Colleges"

United Health Services Hospital
33-57 Harrison St, Johnson City NY 13790-2174
607-763-6000

University of Rochester
Meliora Hall, Rochester NY 14627
585-275-2121

Utica School of Commerce
201 Bleecker St, Utica NY 13501-2280
Cindy Delaney, Director of Admissions
315-733-2307 Fax: 315-733-9281
Website: www.uscny.edu
E-mail: admissions@uscny.edu

Veterans Affairs Medical Center
130 W Kingsbridge Rd, Bronx NY 10468-3992
718-579-1640

Wagner College
One Campus Rd, Staten Island NY 10301
Leigh Ann DePascale, Director of Admissions
718-390-3411

Weill Medical College of Cornell University
1300 York Ave, New York NY 10021-4896
212-746-5454

Westchester Community College
75 Grasslands Rd, Valhalla NY 10595-1693
914-785-6600

Westchester County Medical Center
Grasslands Rd, Valhalla NY 10595
914-285-7276

Winthrop University Hospital
259 1st St, Mineola NY 11501-3987
516-663-2201

Woman's Christian Association Hospital
207 Foote Ave, Jamestown NY 14701-7077
716-664-8110

Wood Tobe-Coburn School
8 E 40th St, New York NY 10016-0102
212-686-9040

NORTH CAROLINA

Alamance Community College
PO Box 8000, Graham NC 27253-8000
336-578-2002

Appalachian State University
ASU Station, Boone NC 28608-0001
828-262-2000

Asheville Buncombe Technical Community College
340 Victoria Rd, Asheville NC 28801-4897
828-254-1921

Beaufort County Community College
PO Box 1069, Washington NC 27889
252-946-6194

Bennett College
900 E Washington St, Greensboro NC 27401-3298
336-273-4431

Brunswick Community College
PO Box 30, Supply NC 28462-0030
910-755-7300

CABARRUS COLLEGE OF HEALTH SCIENCES

401 Medical Park Dr, Concord NC 28025
Mark Ellison, Director of Admissions
704-783-1556 Fax: 704-783-2077
Website: www.cabarruscollege.edu
E-mail: admissions@cabarruscollege.edu
See listing under "Universities"

Caldwell Community College and Technical Institute
2855 Hickory Blvd, Hudson NC 28638
828-726-2200

Cape Fear Community College
411 N Front St, Wilmington NC 28401-3910
910-251-5100

Carolinas College of Health Sciences
PO Box 32861, Charlotte NC 28232-2861
Elizabeth West, Admissions Officer
704-355-5043 Fax: 704-355-9336
Website: www.carolinascollege.edu
E-mail: elizabeth.west@carolinascollege.edu
See listing under "Nursing"

Carteret Community College
Dept. of Respiratory Care & Radiography
3505 Arendell St, Morehead City NC 28557-2989
Rick Hill, Beth Belcher, Counselors
252-247-4142 ext. 153

Catawba Valley Community College
2550 US Highway 70 SE, Hickory NC 28602-8302
828-327-7000

Central Carolina Community College
1105 Kelly Dr, Sanford NC 27330-9000
Preston Sellers, Dean
919-775-5401

Central Piedmont Community College
PO Box 35009, Charlotte NC 28235-5009
704-330-2722

Cleveland Community College
137 S Post Rd, Shelby NC 28152-6205
704-484-4000

Coastal Carolina Community College
444 Western Blvd, Jacksonville NC 28546-6899
910-455-1221

Davidson County Community College
PO Box 1287, Lexington NC 27293-1287
336-249-8186

Duke University
Durham NC 27706-8001
919-684-8111

Durham Technical Community College
1637 E Lawson St, Durham NC 27703-5023
919-686-3333

East Carolina University
Belk 302C, Greenville NC 27858
Dr. Harold P. Jones, Dean

Edgecombe Community College
2009 W Wilson St, Tarboro NC 27886-9361
Thomas B. Anderson, VP of Student Services
252-823-5166

Fayetteville Technical Community College
PO Box 35236, Fayetteville NC 28303-0236
910-678-8400

Forsyth Technical Community College
2100 Silas Creek Pkwy
Winston Salem NC 27103-5150
336-723-0371

Gaston College
201 Highway 321 S, Dallas NC 28034-1499
704-922-6200

Guilford Technical Community College
PO Box 309, Jamestown NC 27282-0309
336-334-4822

Haywood Community College
185 Freedlander Dr, Clyde NC 28721
Debbie Rowland, Coordinator of Admissions
828-627-4500 Fax: 828-627-4513
Website: www.haywood.edu
E-mail: drowland@haywood.edu

High Point University
933 Montlieu Ave, High Point NC 27262-3598
336-841-9000

James Sprunt Community College
PO Box 398, Kenansville NC 28349-0398
Rita Brown, Registrar
910-296-2500 Fax: 910-296-1636
Website: www.sprunt.com

Johnston Community College
PO Box 2350, Smithfield NC 27577-2350
919-934-3051

King's College
322 Lamar Ave, Charlotte NC 28204-2493
704-372-0266

Lenoir Community College
PO Box 188, Kinston NC 28502-0188
252-527-6223

Lenoir Memorial Hospital
100 Airport Rd, Kinston NC 28501-1604
252-522-7797

Lenoir-Rhyne College
7th Ave and 8th St, Hickory NC 28603
828-328-1741

Louisburg College
501 N Main St, Louisburg NC 27549-2399
800-775-0208 or 919-496-2521 Fax: 919-496-1788
Website: www.louisburg.edu
E-mail: admissions@louisburg.edu

Mars Hill College
Mars Hill NC 28754
Chad Holt, Dean of Enrollment
866-MHC-4-YOU Fax: 828-689-1473
Website: www.mhc.edu
E-mail: cholt@mhc.edu

Martin Community College
1161 Kehukee Park Rd, Williamston NC 27892-8307
252-792-1521

Meredith College
3800 Hillsborough St, Raleigh NC 27607-5298
Heidi L. Fletcher, Director of Admissions
919-760-8581 Fax: 919-760-2348
Website: www.meredith.edu
E-mail: admissions@meredith.edu
See listing under "Women's Colleges"

Methodist College
5400 Ramsey St, Fayetteville NC 28311-1498
910-630-7000

Miller-Motte Technical College
5000 Market St, Wilmington NC 28405-3430
800-784-2110

Mitchell Community College
500 W Broad St, Statesville NC 28677-5264
704-878-3200

Montgomery Community College
1011 Page St, Troy NC 27371-8387
910-576-6222

Moses H. Cone Memorial Hospital
1200 N Elm St, Greensboro NC 27401-1020
336-574-7881

Nash Community College
PO Box 7488, Rocky Mount NC 27804-0488
252-443-4011

New Hanover Regional Medical Center
2131 S 17th St, Wilmington NC 28401-7407
910-343-7074

North Carolina A&T State University
1601 E Market St, Greensboro NC 27411
Lee Young, AVC Enrollment
336-334-7500 Fax: 336-334-7478
Website: www.ncat.edu
E-mail: uadmit@ncat.edu

North Carolina Central University
PO Box 19617, Durham NC 27707-0022
919-560-6100

North Carolina State University
PO Box 7001, Raleigh NC 27695-0001
919-515-2011

Pitt Community College
PO Box 7007, Greenville NC 27835-7007
252-321-4200

Presbyterian Hospital
PO Box 33549, Charlotte NC 28233-3549
Michael P. Smith, Director of Admissions
704-384-4141

Queens University of Charlotte
1900 Selwyn Ave, Charlotte NC 28274-0002
704-337-2212

Robeson Community College
PO Box 1420, Lumberton NC 28359
Judith Revels, Director of Admissions
910-738-7101

Rockingham Community College
PO Box 38, Wentworth NC 27375-0038
336-342-4261

Rowan-Cabarrus Community College
PO Box 1595, Salisbury NC 28145-1595
704-637-0760

Salem College
Winston Salem NC 27108
Dana Evans, Dean of Admissions/Fin. Aid
800-32-SALEM Fax: 336-917-5572
Website: www.salem.edu
E-mail: admissions@salem.edu
See listing under "Women's Colleges"

Sandhills Community College
3395 Airport Rd, Pinehurst NC 28374
910-692-6185

South College
1567 Patton Ave, Asheville NC 28806-1748
Robert Davis, Dean of Academic Affairs
828-252-2486 Fax: 828-252-8558
Website: southcollegenc.com
E-mail: bdavis@southcollegenc.com

South Piedmont Community College
PO Box 126, Polkton NC 28135-0126
Joy Pope, Contact
704-272-5338
Website: www.spcc.edu
E-mail: jpope@spcc.edu

Southwestern Community College
447 College Dr, Sylva NC 28779-8581
828-586-4091

Stanly Community College
141 College Dr, Albemarle NC 28001-6418
704-982-0121

University of North Carolina
Chapel Hill NC 27599-0001
919-962-2211

University of North Carolina
9201 University City Blvd, Charlotte NC 28223
704-547-2000

University of North Carolina
601 S College Rd, Wilmington NC 28403-3201
910-962-3000

University of North Carolina at Greensboro
1000 Spring Garden St, Greensboro NC 27412-0001
336-334-5243

University of North Carolina Hospitals
101 Manning Dr, Chapel Hill NC 27514-4220
919-966-5111

Vance-Granville Community College
PO Box 917, Henderson NC 27536-0917
252-492-2061

Wake Forest University
Medical Center Blvd, Winston Salem NC 27157-0001
336-748-4424

Wake Technical Community College
9101 Fayetteville Rd, Raleigh NC 27603-5696
Dr. Robert E. Ireland, Director of Admissions
919-662-3357

Wayne Community College
PO Box 8002, Goldsboro NC 27533-8002
Kathy Garner, Public Information Officer
919-735-5151

Western Carolina University
University Dr, Cullowhee NC 28723-9646
828-227-7211

Western Piedmont Community College
1001 Burkemont Ave, Morganton NC 28655-4511
828-438-6000

WILKES REGIONAL MEDICAL CENTER
School of Radiologic Technology
PO Box 609, North Wilkesboro NC 28659-0609
336-651-8431 Fax: 336-651-8432
E-mail: bwinslow@wilkesregional.com

Winston-Salem State University
601 S Mrtn Lther King Jr Dr
Winston Salem NC 27110-0003
336-750-2000

NORTH DAKOTA

Bismarck State College
PO Box 5587, Bismarck ND 58506
701-224-5400

Dickinson State University
Dickinson ND 58601-4896
Steve Glasser, Director of Student Recruitment
800-279-4295 Fax: 701-483-2409
Website: www.dickinsonstate.edu
E-mail: dsu.hawks@dickinsonstate.edu

Medcenter One Health System
222 N 7th St, Bismarck ND 58501-4436
701-222-5413

Minot State University
500 University Ave W, Minot ND 58707-0002
Dennis Parisien, Enrollment Services Rep.
800-777-0750 ext. 3350

Minot State University-Bottineau Campus
105 Simrall Blvd, Bottineau ND 58318-1159
Paula Berg, Associate Dean of Student Affairs
800-542-6866 Fax: 701-228-5499
Website: www.misu-b.nodak.edu
E-mail: paula.berg@misu.nodak.edu

North Dakota State College of Science
800 6th Ave N, Wahpeton ND 58075-3602
701-671-1130

North Dakota State University
Fargo ND 58105
701-237-7211

St. Alexius Medical Center
PO Box 5510, Bismarck ND 58506-5510
701-224-7600

Sr. Rosalind Gefre Schools of Massage
3101 39th St SW Ste E, Fargo ND 58104
Annie Thorseth, Director of Admissions
701-297-5993 Fax: 701-297-5994
Website: www.sisterrosalind.org
E-mail: fargocampus@sisterrosalind.org

Trinity Medical Center
3 Burdick Expy, Minot ND 58701
701-857-5000

Turtle Mountain Community College
PO Box 340, Belcourt ND 58316-0340
701-477-7862

United Tribes Technical College
3315 University Dr, Bismarck ND 58504-7596
701-255-3285

University of Mary
7500 University Dr, Bismarck ND 58504-9652
701-255-7500

University of North Dakota
Box 8193 University Station, Grand Forks ND 58203
701-777-2011

Williston State College
PO Box 1326, Williston ND 58802-1326
Penny Powell, Director Enrollment Services
701-774-4200 Fax: 701-774-4544
Website: www.wsc.nodak.edu
E-mail: penny.soiseth@wsc.nodak.edu

OHIO

Akron General Medical Center
400 Wabash Ave, Akron OH 44307-2463
330-846-6548

Akron Institute
1600 S Arlington St Ste 100, Akron OH 44306
330-724-1600

Arthur James Cancer Hospital
300 W 10th Ave, Columbus OH 43210
614-293-5485

Aultman Hospital
2600 6th St SW, Canton OH 44710-1799
330-438-6241

Baldwin-Wallace College
275 Eastland Rd, Berea OH 44017-2088
440-826-2900

Belmont Technical College
120 Fox Shannon Pl, Saint Clairsville OH 43950-8751
740-695-9500

Bluffton University
1 University Dr, Bluffton OH 45817
419-358-3000

Bowling Green State University
110 McFall Center, Bowling Green OH 43403-0001
866-CHOOSE-BGSU

Bradford School
2469 Stelzer Rd, Columbus OH 43219-3129
Raeann Lee, Director of Admissions
614-416-6200

Brown Mackie College - Akron
2791 Mogadore Rd, Akron OH 44312-1596
330-733-8766

Brown Mackie College - Cincinnati
1011 Glendale Milford Rd, Cincinnati OH 45215-1107
Robin Krout, President
513-771-2424 Fax: 513-771-3413
Website: www.brownmackie.edu
E-mail: rkrout@brownmackie.edu

Capital University
2199 E Main St, Columbus OH 43209-2394
614-236-6011

Case Western Reserve University
10900 Euclid Ave, Cleveland OH 44106
216-368-2000

Central Ohio Technical College
1179 University Dr, Newark OH 43055-1767
740-366-9222

Children's Hospital & Medical Center
1 Perkins Sq, Akron OH 44308-1062
330-379-8293

Christ Hospital
2139 Auburn Ave, Cincinnati OH 45219-2989
513-369-2201

Cincinnati State Technical & Community College
3520 Central Pkwy, Cincinnati OH 45223-2612
513-569-1500

Clark State Community College
570 E Leffel Ln, Springfield OH 45505-4749
937-325-0691

CLEVELAND CLINIC FOUNDATION
9500 Euclid Ave, Cleveland OH 44195-0001
216-445-5719
E-mail: education@ccf.org

Cleveland State University
2121 Euclid Ave RW 204, Cleveland OH 44115
Dr. Richard Arndt, Dean of Undergraduate Recruitment
and College Partnerships
888-CSU-OHIO Fax: 216-687-9210
Website: www.csuohio.edu
E-mail: admissions@csuohio.edu

Cleveland Veterans Affairs Medical Center
10701 East Blvd, Cleveland OH 44106-1702
216-421-3028

Collins Career Center
11627 State Route 243, Chesapeake OH 45619-7962
740-867-6641 Fax: 740-867-9626
Website: www.collins-cc.k12.oh.us

Columbus State Community College
550 E Spring St, Columbus OH 43215-1786
Ken Conner, Director of Admissions
614-287-3669

COOPERATIVE MEDICAL TECHNOLOGY PROGRAM OF AKRON
1 Perkins Sq, Akron OH 44308-1062
Sharon K. Shriber, MBA, Program Director
330-543-8720 Fax: 330-543-6303
Website: www.akronchildrens.org
E-mail: sshriber@chmca.org

- Cuyahoga Community College
  25444 Harvard Rd, Highland Hills OH 44122-6202
  216-987-2019

Davis College
  4747 Monroe St, Toledo OH 43623-4389
  Dana Stern, Admissions Director
  419-473-2700 Fax: 419-473-2472
  Website: www.daviscollege.edu
  E-mail: learn@daviscollege.edu

Franciscan University of Steubenville
  University Blvd, Steubenville OH 43952
  Margaret J. Weber, Director of Admissions
  800-783-6220 or 740-283-6226 Fax: 740-284-5456
  Website: www.admissions.edu
  E-mail: mweber@franciscan.edu

- Good Samaritan Hospital
  375 Dixmyth Ave, Cincinnati OH 45220-2489
  513-872-1983

Hocking College
  3301 Hocking Pkwy, Nelsonville OH 45764-9704
  Diane K. Wolf, Assistant Director of Admissions
  Information
  800-282-4163

- James A. Rhodes State College
  4240 Campus Dr, Lima OH 45804-3597
  419-995-8000

Jefferson Community College
  4000 Sunset Blvd, Steubenville OH 43952-3598
  740-264-5591

Kent State University
  PO Box 5190, Kent OH 44242-0001
  Paul Deutsch, Director of Admissions
  330-672-2444

Kettering College of Medical Arts
  3737 Southern Blvd, Kettering OH 45429-1299
  David Lofthouse, Director of Enrollment Services
  800-433-5262

: Knox County Career Center
  306 Martinsburg Rd, Mount Vernon OH 43050-4225
  740-397-5820

Lakeland Community College
  7700 Clocktower Dr, Kirtland OH 44094-5198
  Tracey Cooper, Director of Admissions
  440-953-7100

Marietta College
  215 5th St, Marietta OH 45750-4047
  740-376-4600

- Marion General Hospital
  1000 McKinley Park Dr, Marion OH 43302
  740-383-8700

- Marion Technical College
  1467 Mount Vernon Ave, Marion OH 43302-5628
  Joel Liles, Director of Admissions
  740-389-4636

Medical University of Ohio
  3000 Arlington Ave, Toledo OH 43614
  419-383-4000 Fax: 419-383-2800
  Website: www.meduohio.edu

: Medina County Career Center
  1101 W Liberty St, Medina OH 44256-1346
  330-725-8461

- Memorial Hospital
  401 Matthew St, Marietta OH 45750-1635
  740-374-1412

- Meridia Health System
  17325 Euclid Ave, Cleveland OH 44112-1209
  440-446-8260

- MetroHealth Medical Center
  2500 Metrohealth Dr, Cleveland OH 44109-1900
  216-459-5700

Miami-Jacobs Career College
  110 N Patterson Blvd, Dayton OH 45402
  Sean Kuhn, Regional Director of Admissions
  937-222-7337

Miami University
  E High St, Oxford OH 45056
  513-529-2531

- Miami Valley Hospital
  1 Wyoming St, Dayton OH 45409-2722
  937-223-6192

- Middletown Regional Hospital
  105 McKnight Dr, Middletown OH 45044-4898
  513-420-5100

Mount Carmel College of Nursing
  127 S Davis Ave, Columbus OH 43222-1504
  800-556-6972

Mount Vernon Nazarene University
  800 Martinsburg Rd, Mount Vernon OH 43050-9509
  Timothy Eades, Director of Admissions
  866-462-6868 Fax: 740-393-0511
  Website: www.gotomvnu.edu
  E-mail: admissions@mvnu.edu
  See listing under "Universities"

- North Central State College
  PO Box 698, Mansfield OH 44901-0698
  Troy Shutler, Director of Admissions
  419-755-4800

Northwest State Community College
  22600 State Route 34, Archbold OH 43502-9542
  Mark Thompson, Director of Admissions
  419-267-5511 Fax: 419-267-5587
  Website: www.northweststate.edu
  E-mail: mthompson@northweststate.edu

Notre Dame College
  4545 College Rd, Cleveland OH 44121-4293
  216-381-1680

- Ohio Institute of Photography & Technology
  2029 Edgefield Rd, Dayton OH 45439-1917
  Robert A. Martin, Executive Director
  937-294-6155

The Ohio State University
  School of Allied Medical Professions
  Atwell Hall, 453 W 10th Ave, Columbus OH 43210
  614-292-1706 Fax: 614-292-0210
  Website: amp.osu.edu
  E-mail: studentaffairs@osu.edu

Ohio State University Hospitals
  450 W 10th Ave, Columbus OH 43210-1240
  614-293-5555

Ohio University
  Chillicothe Campus
  PO Box 629, Chillicothe OH 45601
  Student Services
  740-774-7200 Fax: 740-774-7295
  Website: www.ohiou.edu/chillicothe/

OHIO VALLEY COLLEGE OF TECHNOLOGY
16808 St. Clair Ave, PO Box 7000
East Liverpool OH 43920
Scott S. Rogers, Director
330-385-1070 Fax: 330-385-4606
Website: www.ovct.edu
E-mail: info@ovct.edu

- Owens Community College
  300 Davis St, Findlay OH 45840-3631
  William J. Ivoska PhD., Vice President of Student
  Services
  567-429-3500 Fax: 567-423-0246
  Website: www.owens.edu
  E-mail: admissions@owens.edu

- Owens Community College
  PO Box 10000, Toledo OH 43699-1947
  William J. Ivoska, Ph.D, Vice President of Student
  Services
  567-661-7000 Fax: 567-661-7607
  Website: www.owens.edu
  E-mail: admissions@owens.edu

- Parma Community General Hospital
  7007 Powers Blvd, Parma OH 44129-5495
  440-743-3000

PROFESSIONAL SKILLS INSTITUTE
20 Arco Dr, Toledo OH 43607-2901
Daniel A. Finch, Chairman/CEO
419-531-9610 Fax: 419-531-4732
Website: www.proskills.com
E-mail: admissions@proskills.com

- Riverside Hospital
  3404 W Sylvania Ave, Toledo OH 43623-4467
  419-729-6059

- St. Charles Hospital
  2600 Navarre Ave, Oregon OH 43616-3286
  419-698-7341

- St. Elizabeth Hospital
  PO Box 1790, Youngstown OH 44501-1790
  330-746-7211

- St. Luke's Medical Center
  2351 E 22nd St, Cleveland OH 44115-3111
  216-368-7000

Shawnee State University
  940 2nd St, Portsmouth OH 45662-4344
  740-354-3205

- Sinclair Community College
  444 W 3rd St, Dayton OH 45402-1460
  Sara P. Smith, Director of Outreach Services
  937-512-3000 Fax: 937-512-2393
  Website: www.sinclair.edu
  E-mail: admit@sinclair.edu

- Southern State Community College
  100 Hobart Rd, Hillsboro OH 45133-9488
  937-393-3431

- Southwest General Hospital
  18697 Bagley Rd, Cleveland OH 44130-3497
  440-816-6801

- Stark State College of Technology
  6200 Frank Ave NW, Canton OH 44720-7228
  330-494-6170

- Timken Mercy Medical Center
  1320 Mercy Dr NW, Canton OH 44708-2641
  330-489-1001

- University Hospital of Cleveland
  11100 Euclid Ave, Cleveland OH 44106-1736
  216-844-7565

University of Akron
  381 Buchtel Mall, Akron OH 44304-1584
  330-972-7111

University of Cincinnati
  2700 Clifton Ave, Cincinnati OH 45220-2873
  513-556-6000

University of Cincinnati
  College of Allied Health Sciences
  PO Box 670394, Cincinnati OH 45267-0394
  Gilbert Hageman, Associate Dean
  513-558-7495

University of Findlay
  1000 N Main St, Findlay OH 45840-3695
  419-422-8313

University of Rio Grande
  School for Medical Lab Technicians
  General Delivery, Rio Grande OH 45674-9999
  Ron Cheadle, Program Director
  740-245-5353 ext. 7301

University of Toledo
  2801 W Bancroft St, Toledo OH 43606-3390
  419-530-4636

Ursuline College
  2550 Lander Rd, Cleveland OH 44124-4398
  Sarah E. Sundermeier, Director of Admissions
  888-URSULINE Toll Free Fax: 440-684-6138
  Website: www.admission.ursuline.edu
  E-mail: admission@ursuline.edu

- Washington State Community College
  710 Colegate Dr, Marietta OH 45750-9225
  740-374-8716

- Western Reserve Care System
  345 Oak Hill Ave, Youngstown OH 44502-1894
  330-747-0777

Wright State University
  3640 Colonel Glenn Hwy, Dayton OH 45435-0002
  937-775-3333

Xavier University
  3800 Victory Pkwy, Cincinnati OH 45207-1092
  513-745-3000

Youngstown State University
  Sweeney Welcome Ctr, One University Plz
  Youngstown OH 44555-0002
  Sue Davis, Contact
  877-GO-TO-YSU

Zane State College
  1555 Newark Rd, Zanesville OH 43701-2694
  740-454-2501

OKLAHOMA
Bacone College
  2299 Old Bacone Rd, Muskogee OK 74403-1568
  Jerrett Phillips, Director of Admissions
  918-781-7340

- Comanche Co. Memorial Hospital
  PO Box 129, Lawton OK 73502-0129
  580-355-8620

East Central University
  1100 E 14th St
  Ada OK 74820-6999
  Pamla Armstrong, Director of Admissions
  580-332-8000

- Great Plains Area Vocational Technical School
  4500 SW Lee Blvd, Lawton OK 73505-8304
  580-355-6371

: Heritage College
  7100 S I-35 Service Rd Suite 7118
  Oklahoma City OK 73149
  Cheryl Morris, Director
  405-631-3399 Fax: 405-631-6711
  Website: www.heritage-education.com
  E-mail: info@heritage-education.com
  See listing under "Career Schools"

- Indian Meridian Vocational Technical School
  1312 S Sangre Rd, Stillwater OK 74074-1899
  405-377-3333

Langston University
  PO Box 907, Langston OK 73050-0907
  405-466-2231

- Muskogee General Hospital
  300 Rockefeller Dr, Muskogee OK 74401-5075
  918-682-5501

- Northeastern Oklahoma A & M College
  200 I St NE, Miami OK 74354-6434
  Linda Oldham Barns, Director of Admissions
  800-234-3409

Northeastern State University
  600 N Grand Ave, Tahlequah OK 74464-2301
  918-456-5511

- Oklahoma City Community College
  7777 S May Ave, Oklahoma City OK 73159-4419
  405-682-1611

Oklahoma State University
  Stillwater OK 74078
  Pamela Hathorn, Coordinator
  405-744-6243
  Website: www.okstate.edu
  E-mail: pamela.hathorn@okstate.edu

- Oklahoma State University-Okmulgee
  1801 E 4th St, Okmulgee OK 74447-3901
  Cary Fox, Director of Admissions
  800-722-4471

Oral Roberts University
  7777 S Lewis Ave, Tulsa OK 74171-0001
  Chris Belcher, Director of Undergraduate Admissions
  800-678-8876 Fax: 918-495-6222
  Website: www.oru.edu
  E-mail: admissions@oru.edu

- O. T. Autry Area Vocational Technical Center
  1201 W Willow Rd, Enid OK 73703-2506
  580-242-2750

- Platt College
  3801 S Sheridan Rd, Tulsa OK 74145-1111
  Angie Morelock, Director of Admissions
  918-663-9000 Fax: 918-622-1240
  Website: www.plattcollege.org
  E-mail: angiem@plattcollege.org

- Rose State College
  6420 SE 15th St, Midwest City OK 73110-2799
  405-733-7300

- St. Francis Hospital
  6161 S Yale Ave, Tulsa OK 74136-1992
  918-494-1370

∴ St. Mary's Hospital
305 S 5th St, Enid OK 73701-5899
580-233-6100

· Seminole State College
PO Box 351, Seminole OK 74818-0351
405-382-9950

· Southwestern Oklahoma State University
100 Campus Dr, Weatherford OK 73096-3098
580-772-6611

· Tulsa Community College
6111 E Skelly Dr Ste 200, Tulsa OK 74135-6198
918-595-7000

∶ Tulsa County Area Vocational Technical District 18
3420 S Memorial Dr, Tulsa OK 74145-1340
918-627-7200

∶ Tuttle Vocational Technical Center
12777 N Rockwell Ave
Oklahoma City OK 73142-2710
405-722-7799

∴ University Hospital of Oklahoma City
PO Box 26307, Oklahoma City OK 73126-0307
405-271-4000

· University of Central Oklahoma
100 N University Dr, Edmond OK 73034-5209
405-974-2000

· University of Oklahoma Health Sciences
1000 Stanton L Young Blvd
Oklahoma City OK 73190
405-271-4000

· University of Tulsa
600 S College Ave, Tulsa OK 74104-3126
Earl Johnson, Dean of Admission
918-631-2307 Fax: 918-631-5003
Website: www.utulsa.edu
E-mail: admission@utulsa.edu

∴ Valley View Regional Hospital
430 N Monte Vista St, Ada OK 74820-4657
580-332-2323

· Vatterott College - Tulsa
555 S Memorial Dr, Tulsa OK 74112
Kevin Wolfe, Director of Admissions
918-835-8288 Fax: 918-836-9698
Website: www.vatterott-college.com
E-mail: kevin.wolfe@vatterott-college.com

OREGON

· Blue Mountain Community College
PO Box 100, Pendleton OR 97801-1000
541-276-1260

· Central Oregon Community College
2600 NW College Way, Bend OR 97701-5933
Alicia Moore, Director of Admissions and Records
541-383-7500

· Chemeketa Community College
PO Box 14007, Salem OR 97309-7070
Kay Carnegie, Dean
503-399-5058

CONCORDE CAREER INSTITUTE
1827 NE 44th Ave, Portland OR 97213-1443
Rick Stillman, Director of Admissions
503-281-4181 Fax: 503-281-6739
Website: www.concorde.edu
E-mail: rstillman@concorde.edu

· Lane Community College
4000 E 30th Ave, Eugene OR 97405-0640
541-747-4501

· Linn-Benton Community College
6500 Pacific Blvd SW, Albany OR 97321-3774
Christine Baker, Outreach Coordinator
541-917-4811 Fax: 541-917-4868
Website: www.linnbenton.edu
E-mail: admissions@linnbenton.edu

· Mt. Hood Community College
26000 SE Stark St, Gresham OR 97030-3300
503-491-6422

OREGON COLLEGE OF ORIENTAL MEDICINE
10525 SE Cherry Blossom Dr, Portland OR 97216
Linda Powell, Admissions Coordinator
503-253-3443 Fax: 503-253-2701
Website: www.ocom.edu
E-mail: admissions@ocom.edu

· Oregon Health & Science University
3181 SW Sam Jackson Park Rd
Portland OR 97239-3079
503-494-7800

· Oregon Institute of Technology
3201 Campus Dr, Klamath Falls OR 97601-8801
541-885-1000

· Oregon State University
Corvallis OR 97333-9800
541-737-0123

· Pacific University
2043 College Way, Forest Grove OR 97116-1797
Karen M. Dunston, Executive Director of Admissions
800-635-0561 Fax: 503-352-2975
Website: www.pacificu.edu
E-mail: admissions@pacificu.edu

· Portland Community College
PO Box 19000, Portland OR 97280-0990
Dennis Bailey-Fougnier, Director of Admissions
503-977-4519

· Portland State University
PO Box 751, Portland OR 97207-0751
503-725-3000

· Rogue Community College
3345 Redwood Hwy, Grants Pass OR 97527-9298
Claudia Sullivan, Director of Enrollment Services
541-956-7500 Fax: 541-471-3585
Website: www.roguecc.edu
E-mail: csullivan@roguecc.edu
See listing under "Community and Junior Colleges"

∴ St. Vincent Hospital & Medical Center
9205 SW Barnes Rd, Portland OR 97225-6603
503-216-3031

· University of Oregon
1217 University of Oregon, Eugene OR 97403
541-346-1000

∴ Veterans Administration Medical Center
PO Box 1034, Portland OR 97207-1034
503-220-8262

· Western Oregon University
345 Monmouth Ave N, Monmouth OR 97361-1314
David McDonald, Dean, Admission, Retention &
Enrollment Management
877-877-1593 Fax: 503-838-8067
Website: www.wou.edu
E-mail: wolfgram@fsa.wou.edu

· Willamette University
900 State St, Salem OR 97301-3931
503-370-6300

PENNSYLVANIA

∴ Abington Memorial Hospital
1200 Old York Rd, Abington PA 19001-3788
215-576-2000

· Academy of Medical Arts and Business
2301 Academy Dr, Harrisburg PA 17112-1012
717-545-4747
Website: www.ACADcampus.com
E-mail: info@ACADcampus.com

∴ Albert Einstein Medical Center
5501 Old York Rd, Philadelphia PA 19141-3098
Christine Szymkowski, Interim Program Director
215-456-7010

∴ Allegheny Valley Hospital
1301 Carlisle St, Natrona Heights PA 15065-1152
724-226-7000

∴ Altoona Hospital
620 Howard Ave, Altoona PA 16601-4899
814-946-2223

∴ ARAMARK Healthcare Support Services
1101 Market St 12th Fl, Philadelphia PA 19107-2934
610-687-8600

· Arcadia University
450 S Easton Rd, Glenside PA 19038-3295
Dennis Nostrand, VP for Enrollment Management
877-ARCADIA (877-272-2342) Fax: 215-881-8767
Website: www.arcadia.edu
E-mail: admiss@arcadia.edu
See listing under "Universities"

∴ Armstrong County Memorial Hospital
1 Nolte Dr, Kittanning PA 16201-7199
724-543-8404

· Berks Technical Institute
2205 Ridgewood Rd, Wyomissing PA 19610-1168
Jean Vokes, Director of Admissions
610-372-1722

· Bloomsburg University of Pennsylvania
400 E 2nd St, Bloomsburg PA 17815-1399
570-389-4000

∴ Bradford Regional Medical Center
School of Radiography
116 Interstate Pkwy, Bradford PA 16701-1036
S. Gregoire, Program Director
814-362-8292

· Bradford School
125 W Station Square Dr, Pittsburgh PA 15219
Director of Admissions
412-391-6710 Fax: 412-471-6714
Website: www.bradfordpittsburgh.edu

∴ Brandywine Hospital
School of Nursing
201 Reeceville Rd, Coatesville PA 19320-1536

· Butler County Community College
PO Box 1203, Butler PA 16003-1203
724-287-8711

· California University of Pennsylvania
250 University Ave, California PA 15419-1394
724-938-4000

· Career Training Academy
4314 Old William Penn Highway Ste 103
Monroeville PA 15146
Gina Hudac, Admissions Representitive
412-372-3900 Fax: 412-373-4262
Website: www.careerta.edu
E-mail: admissions2@careerta.edu

· Career Training Academy
950 5th Ave, New Kensington PA 15068-6308
John Reddy, Director
Tyna Putignano, Director of Admissions
724-337-1000 Fax: 724-335-7140
Website: www.careerta.edu
E-mail: admissions@careerta.edu
See listing under "Career Schools"

· Career Training Academy
1500 Northway Mall, Pittsburgh PA 15237
Anna Bartolini, Director North Hills Branch Campus
412-367-4000 Fax: 412-369-7223
Website: www.careerta.edu
E-mail: admissions3@careerta.edu

· Cedar Crest College
100 College Dr, Allentown PA 18104-6196
Judith A. Neyhart, Vice President Enrollment
800-360-1222

CENTER FOR EMERGENCY MEDICINE
Western PA
230 McKee Pl #500, Pittsburgh PA 15213-4912
Thomas E. Platt, Program Director
412-647-4665 Fax: 412-647-4670
Website: www.centerem.com

· Central Pennsylvania College
College Hill & Valley Rds, Summerdale PA 17093
Katie Bogovic, Admissions Director
800-759-2727 Fax: 717-728-2505
Website: www.centralpenn.edu
E-mail: katie.bogovic@centralpenn.edu

· Chatham College
Woodland Rd, Pittsburgh PA 15232-2826
412-365-1100

· Clarion University of Pennsylvania
840 Wood St, Clarion PA 16214-1232
William Bailey, Dean of Enrollment Management
814-393-2306 Fax: 814-393-2030
Website: www.clarion.edu
E-mail: admissions@clarion.edu

∴ Clearfield Hospital
PO Box 992, Clearfield PA 16830-0992
814-768-2496

· College Misericordia
301 Lake St, Dallas PA 18612-1008
Admissions
570-674-6400

· Community College of Allegheny County
South Campus
1750 Clairton Rd, West Mifflin PA 15122-3029
412-469-1100

· Community College of Beaver County
1 Campus Dr, Monaca PA 15061-2566
724-775-8561

· Community College of Philadelphia
1700 Spring Garden St, Philadelphia PA 19130-3936
215-751-8010

CONEMAUGH VALLEY MEMORIAL HOSPITAL
1086 Franklin St, Johnstown PA 15905-4398
Louise Pugliese, Director
814-534-9844 Fax: 814-534-3354
Website: www.conemaugh.org
E-mail: lpuglie@conemaugh.org
Programs include: Program for Surgical Technology;
School of Radiologic Technology; School of Histotech-
nology; Program for Emergency Medicine Technician-
Paramedic; and Medical Technologist Program.

· Delaware County Community College
901 Media Line Rd, Media PA 19063-1094
610-359-5000

DELAWARE VALLEY ACADEMY OF MEDICAL &
DENTAL ASSISTANTS
3330 Grant Ave, Philadelphia PA 19114-2600
Glenn Goldsmith, Director
215-676-1200
Website: delawarevalleyacademy.com
E-mail: delvalacad@aol.com

· DeSales University
2755 Station Ave, Center Valley PA 18034-9565
610-282-1100 Fax: 610-282-2342
Website: www.desales.edu

∴ Divine Providence Hospital
1100 Grampian Blvd, Williamsport PA 17701-1995
570-326-8101

· Douglas Education Center
130 7th St, Monessen PA 15062-1097
Sherry Lee Walters, Director of Enrollment Services
800-413-6013 Fax: 724-684-7463
Website: www.douglas-school.com
E-mail: swalters@douglas-school.com

· Drexel University
3141 Chestnut St, Philadelphia PA 19104-2875
Dana R. Davies, Director of Undergraduate Enrollment
800-2-DREXEL

DUBOIS BUSINESS COLLEGE
1 Beaver Dr, Du Bois PA 15801-2490
Lisa J. Doty, Director of Admissions
814-371-6920 Fax: 814-371-3974
Website: www.dbcollege.com
E-mail: dotylj@dbcollege.com

DUBOIS BUSINESS COLLEGE
1001 Moore St, Huntingdon PA 16652-1846
Lisa J. Doty, Director of Admissions
814-641-0440 Fax: 814-641-0205
Website: www.dbcollege.com
E-mail: dotylj@dbcollege.com

DUBOIS BUSINESS COLLEGE
701 E 3rd St, Oil City PA 16301-2407
Lisa J. Doty, Director of Admissions
814-677-1322 Fax: 814-677-8237
Website: www.dbcollege.com
E-mail: dotylj@dbcollege.com

· Duffs Business Institute
100 Forbes Ave Ste 1200, Pittsburgh PA 15222-1320
412-261-4520

· Duquesne University
600 Forbes Ave, Pittsburgh PA 15282-0001
Paul-James Cukanna, Director of Admissions
412-396-5000

· East Stroudsburg University of PA
200 Prospect St
East Stroudsburg PA 18301
570-424-3211

· Edinboro University of Pennsylvania
Edinboro PA 16444-0001
814-732-2000

Elizabethtown College
1 Alpha Dr, Elizabethtown PA 17022-2298
717-361-1000

Episcopal Hospital
100 E Lehigh Ave, Philadelphia PA 19125-1098
Annmarie Weisman, Chair Admissions & Recruitment
215-427-7449

Gannon University
109 University Sq, Erie PA 16541-0001
Christopher Tremblay, Director of Admissions
800-GANNON-U Fax: 814-871-5803
Website: www.gannon.edu
E-mail: admissions@gannon.edu

Geisinger Medical Center
100 N Academy Ave, Danville PA 17822-9800
570-271-5200

Greater Johnstown Area Vocational Technical School
445 Schoolhouse Rd, Johnstown PA 15904-2927
814-266-6073

Gwynedd-Mercy College
1325 Sumneytown Pike, Gwynedd Valley PA 19437
Dennis Murphy, V.P. Enrollment Management
800-DIAL-GMC

Harcum College
750 Montgomery Ave, Bryn Mawr PA 19010-3476
610-525-4100

Harrisburg Area Community College
1 HACC Dr, Harrisburg PA 17110-2999
717-780-2300

Holy Family University
9801 Frankford Avenue, Philadelphia PA 19114
Lauren Campbell, Director of Admissions
215-637-3050 Fax: 215-281-1022
Website: www.holyfamily.edu
E-mail: admissions@holyfamily.edu

Holy Spirit Hospital
505 N 21st St, Camp Hill PA 17011-2288
717-763-2106

ICM School of Business and Medical Careers
10 Wood St, Pittsburgh PA 15222-1931
Maureen McBride, Assistant Director of Admissions
800-441-5222

Indiana University of Pennsylvania
Indiana PA 15705-0001
724-357-2100

INTERNATIONAL ACADEMY OF ADVANCED REFLEXOLOGY & MEDICAL REFLEXOLOGY CLINIC
1701 Snyder Rd, Green Lane PA 18054
Professor L.J. Telepo, President
215-234-0307 or 866-248-8420 Pin 2020
Fax: 215-234-4563
Website: www.reflexology.net
E-mail: postsecondary@reflexology.net
Established 1987. Private. Coed. Tuition: $1,600 for Program. Student-faculty ratio: 20:1. Diploma Offered. Access the Student Handbook table of contents page for all official government codes which gives you your permissions and restrictions, especially under "Medical Services". We are located in beautiful Green Lane Park, see Website for more information. This program falls under Medical Reflexology.

INTERNATIONAL ACADEMY OF ADVANCED REFLEXOLOGY & MEDICAL REFLEXOLOGY CLINIC
1177 6th St, Whitehall PA 18052
Professor L.J. Telepo, President
215-234-0307 or 866-248-8420 Pin 2020
Fax: 215-234-4563
Website: www.reflexology.net
E-mail: postsecondary@reflexology.net
See listing under "Allied Health Science"

Johnson College
3427 N Main Ave, Scranton PA 18508-1495
Dr. Ann L. Pipinski, President & CEO
Melissa Ide, Director of Enrollment Management
800-2WE-WORK or 570-342-6404 ext. 125
Fax: 570-348-2181
Website: www.johnson.edu
E-mail: admit@johnson.edu

Juniata College
1700 Moore St, Huntingdon PA 16652-2196
Michelle Bartol, Dean of Enrollment
877-JUNIATA Fax: 814-641-3100
Website: www.juniata.edu
E-mail: admissions@juniata.edu

King's College
133 N River St, Wilkes Barre PA 18711-0801
Michelle Lawrence-Schmude, Director of Admission
570-208-5900 Fax: 570-208-5971
Website: www.kings.edu
E-mail: admissions@kings.edu

Lancaster General College of Nursing and Health Sciences
410 N Lime St, Lancaster PA 17602-2337
Elma Hess, Director of Admissions
717-544-4902 Fax: 717-544-5970
Website: www.lancastergeneralcollege.org
E-mail: elhess@lancastergeneral.org

Lankenau Hospital
100 E Lancaster Ave, Wynnewood PA 19096-3498
610-526-3019

La Roche College
9000 Babcock Blvd, Pittsburgh PA 15237-5898
Thomas Hassett, Director of Freshman and International Admissions
412-536-1272 or 800-838-4LRC Fax: 412-536-1272
Website: www.laroche.edu
E-mail: admissions@laroche.edu

Latrobe Area Hospital
101 W 2nd Ave, Latrobe PA 15650-1068
724-537-1001

LAUREL BUSINESS INSTITUTE
11-15 Penn St, Uniontown PA 15401
Lisa Tressler, Supervisor of Enrollment
724-439-4900 Fax: 724-439-3607
Website: www.laurelbusiness.edu
E-mail: lbi@laurelbusiness.edu
Established 1985. Private. Coed. Accreditation: ACICS, Licensed by the Pennsylvania Department of Education. Enrollment: 310 full-time, 35 part-time. Student-faculty ratio: 12:1. Associate degrees: Accounting, Child Care Education, Cosmetology, I.T. - Computer Software Support, I.T. - Network Administration, Medical Assistant, Medical Insurance Management, Medical Secretary Transcription, Office Administration, Small Business Management, Therapeutic Massage. Diplomas: Legal Secretary, Massage Therapy, Medical Secretary, Word Processing Secretary. Independent Certifications, Authorized Prometric Testing Center, Authorized MOS Testing Center, Financial Aid Services, Job Placement Services.

Lebanon Valley College
101 N College Ave, Annville PA 17003-1400
William Brown, Dean of Admissions & Financial Aid
866-LVC-4ADM or 717-867-6181 Fax: 717-867-6026
Website: www.lvc.edu
E-mail: admission@lvc.edu

Lehigh Carbon Community College
4525 Education Park Dr
Schnecksville PA 18078-2502
610-799-1134

Lehigh Valley College
2809 E Saucon Valley Rd
Center Valley PA 18034-8447
Joshua Padron, Vice President of Marketing and Admissions
800-227-9109 Fax: 610-791-7810
Website: www.lehighvalley.edu
E-mail: joshua.padron@lehighvalley.edu

Lehigh Valley Hospital & Health Network
Center for Education
PO Box 7017, Allentown PA 18105-7017
610-402-2556

Lincoln University
Lincoln University PA 19352
Michael C. Taylor, Director of Admissions
800-790-0191 Fax: 610-932-1209
Website: www.lincoln.edu
E-mail: mtaylor@lu.lincoln.edu

Lock Haven University
Lock Haven PA 17745
James C. Reeser, Dean of Admissions
570-893-2027

Luzerne County Community College
1333 S Prospect St, Nanticoke PA 18634-3899
800-377-5222 ext. 337

Manor College
700 Fox Chase Rd, Jenkintown PA 19046-4118
215-885-2360

Mansfield University of Pennsylvania
Academy St, Mansfield PA 16933
570-662-4000

Marywood University
2300 Adams Ave, Scranton PA 18509-1598
570-348-6211

Medical Center of Beaver County
1000 Dutch Ridge Rd, Beaver PA 15009-9700
724-728-7000

Medical College Hospitals
60 Township Line Rd, Elkins Park PA 19027-2220
215-663-6150

Mercyhurst College
501 E 38th St, Erie PA 16546-0001
800-825-1926

Messiah College
1 S College Ave, Grantham PA 17027
717-766-2511

Millersville University of Pennsylvania
PO Box 1002, Millersville PA 17551-0302
717-872-3024

Milton S. Hershey Medical Center Hospital
PO Box 850, Hershey PA 17033-0850
717-531-8803

Monsour Medical Center
70 Lincoln Hwy E, Jeannette PA 15644-3185
724-527-0600

Montgomery County Community College
340 DeKalb Pike, Blue Bell PA 19422-1400
215-641-6300

MOUNT ALOYSIUS COLLEGE
7373 Admiral Peary Hwy, Cresson PA 16630-1999
Frank C. Crouse Jr., Vice President for Enrollment Management
814-886-6383 or 888-823-2220 Fax: 814-886-6441
Website: www.mtaloy.edu
E-mail: admissions@mtaloy.edu

Nazareth Hospital
2601 Holme Ave, Philadelphia PA 19152-2096
215-335-6000

Neumann College
1 Neumann Dr, Aston PA 19014-1298
Dennis Murphy, Director of Admissions
610-459-0905 Fax: 610-558-5652
Website: www.neumann.edu
E-mail: neumann@neumann.edu

Newport Business Institute
945 Greensburg Rd, Lower Burrell PA 15068-3929
Admissions Department
800-752-7695 Fax: 724-339-2950
Website: www.nbi.edu
E-mail: tjpomatto@nbi.edu

Northampton Co. Area Community College
3835 Green Pond Rd, Bethlehem PA 18020-7599
610-861-5300

Northwest Medical Center
100 Fairfield Dr, Seneca PA 16346
814-677-1711

Pennco Tech
3815 Otter St, Bristol PA 19007-3618
Glenn Slater, Director of Admissions
215-785-0111 Fax: 215-785-1945
Website: www.penncotech.com
E-mail: admissions@penncotech.com

Pennsylvania College of Technology
1 College Ave, Williamsport PA 17701-5778
570-326-3761

Pennsylvania Hospital
800 Spruce St, Philadelphia PA 19107-6192
215-829-3312

Pennsylvania Institute of Technology
800 Manchester Ave, Media PA 19063-4036
Angela Cassetta, Dean of Enrollment Management
800-422-0025 or 610-892-1500 Fax: 610-892-1510
Website: www.pit.edu
E-mail: info@pit.edu
See listing under "Community and Junior Colleges"

Pennsylvania State Milton S Hershey Medical Center College of Medicine
500 University Dr Box 850, Hershey PA 17033
717-534-8521

Pennsylvania State University
Hazelton Campus, Hazleton PA 18201
570-450-3000

Pennsylvania State University
3550 7th St Rd, New Kensington PA 15068-1765
Patricia K. Brady, Director of Admissions
724-334-5466

Pennsylvania State University
200 University Dr, Schuylkill Haven PA 17972-2202
570-385-6000

Pennsylvania State University
201 Shields Bldg PO Box 300
University Park PA 16802-3000
814-865-4700

Philadelphia University
4201 Henry Ave, Philadelphia PA 19144-5409
215-951-2700

Point Park University
St. Francis Medical Center
201 Wood St, Pittsburgh PA 15222-1912
412-392-3879

Reading Area Community College
PO Box 1706, Reading PA 19603-1706
David J. Adams, Director of Admissions
610-607-6224

Reading Hospital & Medical Center
PO Box 16052, Reading PA 19612-6052
610-378-6664

Robert Morris University
881 Narrows Run Rd, Coraopolis PA 15108-1169
412-262-8200

Robert Packer Hospital
1 Guthrie Sq, Sayre PA 18840-1698
570-888-6666

Sacred Heart Hospital
421 W Chew St, Allentown PA 18102-3490
610-776-4745

St. Francis University
PO Box 600, Loretto PA 15940-0600
814-472-3000

St. Joseph's Hospital
PO Box 316, Reading PA 19603-0316
610-378-2000

Seton Hill University
Greensburg PA 15601-1599
Mary Kay Cooper, Director of Admissions and Adult Student Services
800-826-6234

Sewickley Valley Hospital
700 Blackburn Rd, Sewickley PA 15143-1454
412-741-6600

Shadyside Hospital
5230 Centre Ave, Pittsburgh PA 15232-1381
412-622-2010

SHARON REGIONAL HEALTH SYSTEM
School of Radiography
740 E State St, Sharon PA 16146-3395
Sherry A. Masotto, Program Director
724-983-5603 Fax: 724-983-5614
Website: www.sharonregional.com
E-mail: smasotto@srhs-pa.org

Slippery Rock University
14 Maltby Dr, Slippery Rock PA 16057-1326
724-738-9000

Somerset Community Hospital
225 S Center Ave, Somerset PA 15501-2088
814-443-5221

South Hills School of Business & Technology
480 Waupelani Dr, State College PA 16801-4516
Maralyn Mazza, Director
888-282-7427

Temple University
Broad St & Montgomery Ave, Philadelphia PA 19122
215-204-7000

Temple University
3307 N Broad St, Philadelphia PA 19140-5101
215-787-7000

Thiel College
75 College Ave, Greenville PA 16125-2181
724-589-2000

Thomas Jefferson University
111 S 11th St, Philadelphia PA 19107-4824
215-955-6000

Thompson Institute
5650 Derry St, Harrisburg PA 17111-3571
Roy Hawkins, Director
717-564-4112

University Health Center
300 Halket St, Pittsburgh PA 15213-3108
412-641-4664

University of Pittsburgh
4200 5th Ave, Pittsburgh PA 15260-3583
412-624-4141

University of Pittsburgh at Johnstown
450 Schoolhouse Rd, Johnstown PA 15904-2990
814-269-7000

University of Scranton
800 Linden St, Scranton PA 18510-4501
570-941-7400

UPMC SCHOOL OF MEDICAL IMAGING
3434 Forbes Ave Murdoch Bldg Ste 206
Pittsburgh PA 15213-2582
Denise Csonka Lake, Program Director
412-647-3528 Fax: 412-647-3713
Website: www.schoolofmedicalimaging.upmc.com
E-mail: laked@upmc.edu

Washington & Jefferson College
60 S Lincoln St, Washington PA 15301-4801
Alton E. Newell, Vice President for Enrollment
724-223-6025 Fax: 724-223-6534
Website: www.washjeff.edu
E-mail: admission@washjeff.edu

West Chester University of Pennsylvania
S High St, West Chester PA 19383-0001
610-436-1000

Western School of Health & Business Careers
421 7th Ave, Pittsburgh PA 15219-1907
Michael Joyce, Director of Admissions
800-333-6607 Fax: 412-227-0419
Website: www.western-school.com
E-mail: mjoyce@western-school.com

Westmoreland County Community College
400 Armbrust Rd, Youngwood PA 15697-1898
724-925-4000

Wilkes Barre General Hospital
575 N River St, Wilkes Barre PA 18764-0001
570-829-8111

Williamsport Hospital
777 Rural Ave, Williamsport PA 17701-3191
570-326-8101

York College of Pennsylvania
PO Box 15199, York PA 17405-7199
717-846-7788

York Hospital
1001 S George St, York PA 17403-3645
717-851-2942

York Technical Institute
Lancaster Campus
3050 Hempland Rd, Lancaster PA 17601
Cathi Killingsworth Bost, Vice President
800-227-9675 or 717-295-1100 Fax: 717-295-1135
Website: www.yti.edu
E-mail: info@yti.edu
See listing under "Career Schools"

RHODE ISLAND

Community College of Rhode Island
Knight Campus
400 East Ave, Warwick RI 02886-1805
Elizabeth A. Mancini, Assistant Dean of Enrollment
Services
401-825-2003

New England Institute of Technology
2500 Post Rd, Warwick RI 02886-2244
Michael Kwiatkowski, Director of Admissions
401-739-5000 Fax: 401-738-5122
Website: www.neit.edu
E-mail: eflynn@neit.edu

Rhode Island Hospital
593 Eddy St, Providence RI 02903-4923
401-444-5123

St. Joseph's Hospital
200 High Service Ave
North Providence RI 02904-5199
401-456-3050

University of Rhode Island
Kingston RI 02881
401-874-1000

Women & Infants Hospital
101 Dudley St, Providence RI 02905-2499
401-274-1100

SOUTH CAROLINA

Aiken Technical College
PO Box 696, Aiken SC 29802-0796
803-593-9231

Anderson Memorial Hospital
800 N Fant St, Anderson SC 29621-5708
864-261-1109

Baptist Medical Center
1519 Marion St, Columbia SC 29201-2910
803-771-5042

Charleston Southern University
PO Box 118087, Charleston SC 29423-8087
Cheryl Burton, Director of Admissions
800-947-7474

Clemson University
105 Sikes Hall, Clemson SC 29634
864-656-2287

Erskine College & Seminary
PO Box 176, Due West SC 29639
Bart Walker, Director of Admissions
864-379-8838 Fax: 864-379-3048
Website: www.erskine.edu
E-mail: admissions@erskine.edu

Florence-Darlington Technical College
PO Box 100548, Florence SC 29501-0548
843-661-8324

Forrest Junior College
601 E River St, Anderson SC 29624-2405
Dr. Julia R. Barnes, President
864-225-7653 Fax: 864-261-7471
Website: www.forrestcollege.edu
E-mail: info@forrestcollege.edu
See listing under "Community and Junior Colleges"

Greenville Technical College
PO Box 5616, Greenville SC 29606-5616
Martha White, Director of Admissions
800-723-0673 (US) or 800-922-1183 (SC)
Website: www.greenvilletech.com

Horry-Georgetown Technical College
PO Box 261966, Conway SC 29528-6066
843-349-5277

McLeod Regional Medical Center
555 E Cheves St, Florence SC 29506-2606
843-667-2297

Medical University of South Carolina
PO Box 250402, Charleston SC 29425
843-792-2300

Midlands Technical College
PO Box 2408, Columbia SC 29202-2408
803-738-8324

Orangeburg-Calhoun Technical College
3250 Saint Matthews Rd NE
Orangeburg SC 29118-8299
803-536-0311

Piedmont Technical College
PO Box 1467, Greenwood SC 29648-1467
864-941-8324

South Carolina State University
PO Box 7127, Orangeburg SC 29117-0001
Lillian M. Adderson, Director of Admissions
803-536-7185

South University
9 Science Court, Columbia SC 29203
Trish Wade, Contact
803-799-9082 Fax: 803-799-9038
Website: www.southuniversity.edu
E-mail: twade@southuniversity.edu

Spartanburg Technical College
PO Box 4386, Spartanburg SC 29305-4386
Nancy Garmroth, Dean of Admissions & Financial Aid
864-592-4810 Fax: 864-592-4945
Website: stcsc.edu

Tri-County Tech College
PO Box 587, Pendleton SC 29670-0587
864-646-8361

Trident Technical College
PO Box 118067, Charleston SC 29423-8067
843-574-6111

University of South Carolina
Columbia SC 29208-0001
803-777-7700

Winthrop University
701 W Oakland Ave, Rock Hill SC 29733-0001
803-323-2211

York Technical College
452 Anderson Rd S, Rock Hill SC 29730-7318
803-327-8000

SOUTH DAKOTA

Colorado Technical University
3901 W 59th St, Sioux Falls SD 57108
605-361-0200

Dakota State University
820 N Washington Ave, Madison SD 57042-1799
605-256-5112

Lake Area Technical Institute
230 11th St NE, Watertown SD 57201
605-882-5284

McKennan Hospital
800 E 21st St, Sioux Falls SD 57105-1096
605-339-8113

Mitchell Technical Institute
821 N Capital St, Mitchell SD 57301-2002
Allen Dvorak, Director of Admissions
800-952-0042

Mt. Marty College
1105 W 8th St, Yankton SD 57078-3724
605-668-1514

Presentation College
1500 N Main St, Aberdeen SD 57401-1280
JoEllen Lindner, Dean of Admissions
605-229-8492 Fax: 605-229-8425
Website: www.presentation.edu
E-mail: admit@presentation.edu

Queen of Peace Hospital
5th & Foster, Mitchell SD 57301
605-995-2250

Rapid City Regional Hospital
353 Fairmont Blvd, Rapid City SD 57701-7375
605-341-8100

Sacred Heart Hospital
501 Summit St, Yankton SD 57078-3855
605-655-9371

St. Luke's Midland Regional Medical Center
305 S State St, Aberdeen SD 57401-4590
605-622-5230

Sioux Valley Hospital
PO Box 5039, Sioux Falls SD 57117-5039
605-333-6424

South Dakota State University
PO Box 2201, Brookings SD 57007-0001
605-688-4151

Southeast Technical Institute
2301 N Career Pl, Sioux Falls SD 57107-1301
Tracy Noldner, Supervisor Student/Instructional
Services
605-367-7624

University of South Dakota
414 E Clark St, Vermillion SD 57069-2307
605-677-5011

TENNESSEE

Austin Peay State University
601 College St, Clarksville TN 37044-0002
931-221-7011

Baptist Memorial College of Health Science
1003 Monroe Ave, Memphis TN 38104-3104
Office of Admissions
866-575-2247

Baptist Memorial Hospital
350 N Humphreys Blvd #EaglBld2
Memphis TN 38120-2177
901-227-5121

Carson-Newman College
1646 Russell Ave, Jefferson City TN 37760
865-471-4000

Chattanooga State Technical Community College
4501 Amnicola Hwy, Chattanooga TN 37406-1018
423-697-4400

Cleveland State Community College
PO Box 3570, Cleveland TN 37320-3570
423-472-7141

Columbia State Community College
PO Box 1315, Columbia TN 38402-1315
931-540-2722

CONCORDE CAREER COLLEGE
5100 Poplar Ave Ste 132, Memphis TN 38137-0132
Tommy Stewart, Executive Campus Director
901-761-9494 Fax: 901-761-3293
Website: www.concorde.edu
E-mail: tstewart@concorde.edu

East Tennessee State University
PO Box 70623, Johnson City TN 37614
Dr. Wilsie Bishop, Dean of Public & Allied Health
423-439-4243

Jackson State Community College
2046 N Parkway, Jackson TN 38301-3797
731-424-3520

Lincoln Memorial University
PO Box 2012, Harrogate TN 37752
423-869-3611

Lipscomb University
3901 Granny White Pike, Nashville TN 37204-3951
Ricky Holaway, Director of Admissions
800-333-4358 ext. 1776 Fax: 615-269-1804
Website: www.lipscomb.edu
E-mail: admissions@lipscomb.edu

MEDVANCE INSTITUTE
1025 Highway 111, Cookeville TN 38501-4305
Shirley Cole, Campus Director
866-86-GO-MED or 931-526-3660 Fax: 931-372-2603
Website: www.medvance.edu

Methodist Hospital
1265 Union Ave, Memphis TN 38104-3415
901-726-8274

MIDDLE TENNESSEE SCHOOL OF ANESTHESIA
PO Box 6414, Madison TN 37116-6414
Mary E. DeVasher, Dean
615-868-6503 Fax: 615-868-9885
Website: www.mtsa.edu
E-mail: ikey@mtsa.edu

Middle Tennessee State University
1301 E Main St, Murfreesboro TN 37132-0001
615-898-2300

Miller-Motte Technical College
1820 Business Park Dr, Clarksville TN 37040-6023
Lisa Teague, Director of Admissions
931-553-0071 Fax: 931-552-2916
Website: www.miller-motte.com
E-mail: lteague@miller-motte.com

MILLER-MOTTE TECHNICAL COLLEGE
801 Space Park N, Goodlettsville TN 37072
Kevin Suhr, Campus Administrator
615-859-8090 Fax: 615-859-9634
Website: www.miller-motte.com
E-mail: ksuhr@miller-motte.com

Nashville State Technical Community College
120 White Bridge Pike, Nashville TN 37209-4515
615-353-3333

Northeast State Technical Community College
PO Box 246, Blountville TN 37617-0246
423-323-3191

Roane State Community College
276 Patton Ln, Harriman TN 37748-8664
865-354-3000

St. Thomas Hospital
PO Box 380, Nashville TN 37202-0380
615-222-2111

Southwest Tennessee Community College
5983 Macon Cove, Memphis TN 38134
901-333-7822

Tennessee State University
3500 John A Merritt Blvd, Nashville TN 37209-1561
John Cade, Dean of Admissions & Records
615-963-5101 Fax: 615-963-2930
Website: www.tnstate.edu
E-mail: jcade@tnstate.edu

Tennessee Technological University
PO Box 5006, Cookeville TN 38505-0001
931-372-3101

Tennessee Technology Center at Knoxville
1100 Liberty St, Knoxville TN 37919-2327
Marilyn Canady, Coordinator of Student Services
865-546-5567

Tennessee Technology Center at Livingston
740 Hi Tech Dr, Livingston TN 38570
931-823-5525

Tennessee Technology Center at Memphis
550 Alabama Ave, Memphis TN 38105-3604
901-543-6100

Trevecca Nazarene University
333 Murfreesboro Rd, Nashville TN 37210-2834
615-248-1200

Tusculum College
PO Box 5051, Greeneville TN 37743
Melissa Ripley, Associate Director of Admissions
800-729-0256 Fax: 423-798-1622
Website: www.tusculum.edu
E-mail: mripley@tusculum.edu

University of Memphis
Memphis TN 38152-0001
901-678-2000

University of Tennessee
615 McCallie Ave, Chattanooga TN 37403-2504
Yancy Freeman, Director of Admissions
423-425-4111 Fax: 423-425-4157
Website: www.utc.edu
E-mail: Yancy-Freeman@utc.edu

University of Tennessee
527 Andy Holt Tower, Knoxville TN 37996-0001
865-974-1000

University of Tennessee
Martin TN 38238-0001
731-587-7000

University of Tennessee Health Science Center
800 Madison Ave, Memphis TN 38163-0002
901-448-5500

University of Tennessee Medical Center
1924 Alcoa Hwy, Knoxville TN 37920
865-544-6404

Vanderbilt University
W End Ave, Nashville TN 37240-0001
615-322-7311

Volunteer State Community College
1480 Nashville Pike, Gallatin TN 37066-3188
615-452-8600

Walters State Community College
500 S Davy Crockett Pkwy
Morristown TN 37813-6899
423-585-2600

TEXAS

Abilene Christian University
ACU Box 29000, Abilene TX 79699-0001
325-674-2000

ACADEMY OF ORIENTAL MEDICINE AT AUSTIN
2700 W Anderson Ln Ste 204, Austin TX 78757
Amy Scott, Admissions Director
512-454-1188 ext. 217 Fax: 512-454-7001
Website: www.aoma.edu
E-mail: info@aoma.edu

Alvin Community College
Pearland College Center
3110 Mustang Rd, Alvin TX 77511-4807
281-756-3526

Amarillo College
PO Box 447, Amarillo TX 79178-0001
806-371-5000

Angelina College
PO Box 1768, Lufkin TX 75902-1768
Judith M. Cutting, Director of Admissions/Registration
936-639-1301

Angelo State University
ASU Station 11014, San Angelo TX 76909
Bonnie Stennett, Coordinator of Recruiting
800-946-8627 Fax: 325-942-2078
Website: www.angelo.edu
E-mail: admissions@angelo.edu

ATI Health Education Center
701 Highlander Blvd Ste 200
Arlington TX 76015-4395
817-557-3337

Baptist Health System
215 E Quincy St, San Antonio TX 78215
210-297-1040

Baptist Hospital
608 Strickland Dr, Orange TX 77630-4717
409-883-9361

Baptist Hospital of Southeast Texas
PO Box 1591, Beaumont TX 77704-1591
409-654-5351

Baylor College of Medicine
1 Baylor Plz, Houston TX 77030-3498
713-798-4951

Baylor University
Po Box 97008, Waco TX 76798-7008
254-710-1011

Baylor University Medical Center
3500 Gaston Ave, Dallas TX 75246-2088
214-820-2731

Ben Taub Hospital
2525 Holly Hall St, Houston TX 77054-4124
713-746-6400

Blinn College
902 College Ave, Brenham TX 77833-4098
Dennis K. Crowson, Registrar
979-830-4000 Fax: 979-830-4110
Website: www.blinn.edu
E-mail: recruiting@blinn.edu

Bradford School of Business
4669 Southwest Freeway Ste 300, Houston TX 77027
713-629-1500

CANCER THERAPY AND RESEARCH CENTER
School of Medical Dosimetry
7979 Wurzbach Rd, San Antonio TX 78229-4427
Melissa Blough, Ph.D., DABR, School Director
210-616-5669 Fax: 210-616-5636
Website: www.ctrc.saci.org
E-mail: mblough@saci.org

Central Texas College
PO Box 1800, Killeen TX 76540-1800
Lillian Kroeger, Director of Admissions
254-526-1104

Cisco Junior College
RR 3 Box 3, Cisco TX 76437-9321
254-442-2567

Citizens Medical Center
2701 Hospital Dr, Victoria TX 77901-5748
361-573-9181

Coastal Bend College
3800 Charco Rd, Beeville TX 78102-2197
361-358-2838

College of the Mainland
1200 N Amburn Rd, Texas City TX 77591-2499
409-938-1211

Collin County Community College
4800 Preston Park Blvd, Plano TX 75093
972-881-5790

CONCORDE CAREER INSTITUTE
601 Ryan Plaza Dr Ste 200, Arlington TX 76011
Annette Latshaw, Director of Admissions
817-261-1594 Fax: 817-461-3443
Website: www.concorde.edu
E-mail: alatshaw@concorde.edu

COVENANT SCHOOL OF NURSING AND ALLIED HEALTH
2002 Miami Ave, Lubbock TX 79410-1096
Admissions
806-797-0955 Fax: 806-793-0720
Website: www.covenantson.com
E-mail: admissionscsn@covhs.org

Del Mar College
101 Baldwin Blvd, Corpus Christi TX 78404-3894
361-698-1200

El Centro College
801 Main St, Dallas TX 75202-3698
214-860-2037

El Paso Community College
PO Box 20500, El Paso TX 79998-0500
915-831-2000

Galveston College
4015 Avenue Q, Galveston TX 77550-7496
Brian Lowery, Registrar
409-763-6551 Fax: 409-944-1501
Website: www.gc.edu
E-mail: blowery@gc.edu

Grayson County College
6101 Grayson Dr, Denison TX 75020
903-465-6030

Gulf Coast Regional Blood Center
1400 La Concha Ln, Houston TX 77054-1887
713-790-1200

Hallmark Institute of Technology - Technology Campus
10401 W IH 10, San Antonio TX 78230-1736
Joe Fisher, President
210-690-9000 Fax: 210-697-8225
Website: www.hallmarkinstitute.com
E-mail: sross@hallmarkinstitute.com
Electronics Engineering Technology, Business Office
Administration, Computer Network Systems
Technology, & Medical Assistant.

Harris Hospital
1301 Pennsylvania Ave, Fort Worth TX 76104-2190
817-878-2106

Hendrick Medical Center
1242 N 19th St, Abilene TX 79601-2392
325-670-2201

Hillcrest Baptist Medical Center
3000 Herring Ave, Waco TX 76708-3299
254-756-8551

Houston Community College
PO Box 667517, Houston TX 77266-7517
713-718-2000

Howard College
3197 Executive Dr, San Angelo TX 76904-6801
LeAnne Byrd, Contact
325-944-9585

JPS Institute for Health Career Development
2400 Circle Dr, Fort Worth TX 76119
Byron D. Lancaster, Marketing Coordinator
817-920-7380

Kilgore College
1100 Broadway Blvd, Kilgore TX 75662-3299
Ray McLeod, Director, Marketing & Enrollment
903-984-8531

KINGWOOD COLLEGE
20000 Kingwood Dr, Kingwood TX 77339-3801
Isaac Williams, Director of Enrollment Management
281-312-1600 Fax: 281-312-1477
Website: wwwkc.nhmccd.edu
E-mail: ike.williams@nhmccd.edu

Lamar State College-Orange
410 W Front St, Orange TX 77630-5899
Rebecca Campbell, Registrar
409-883-7750 Fax: 409-882-3055
Website: www.lsco.edu
E-mail: becky.campbell@lsco.edu

Lamar University
PO Box 10009, Beaumont TX 77710-0009
409-880-8845

Laredo Community College
1 W End Washington St, Laredo TX 78040-4348
956-722-0521

Lee College
PO Box 818, Baytown TX 77522-0818
Dr. Dennis Dressler, Director of Admissions
281-427-5611

McLennan Community College
1400 College Dr, Waco TX 76708-1498
Dr. Bridget Moore, Director, Health Sciences
254-299-8000 Fax: 254-299-8854
Website: www.mclennan.edu
E-mail: bmoore@mclennan.edu

Memorial Hospital System
7737 SW Freeway, Houston TX 77074
713-776-5100

METHODIST HOSPITAL
6565 Fannin St, B154, Houston TX 77030-2707
Judy Jobe, MT (ASCP), Program Director
713-441-2599 Fax: 713-793-7408
E-mail: jjobe@tmh.tmc.edu

Methodist Hospital
3615 19th St, Lubbock TX 79410-1209
806-792-1011

Midland College
3600 N Garfield St, Midland TX 79705-6397
432-685-4500

Midwestern State University
3410 Taft Blvd, Wichita Falls TX 76308-2096
940-397-4000

Navarro College
3200 W 7th Ave, Corsicana TX 75110-4899
903-874-6501

North Central Texas College
1525 W California St, Gainesville TX 76240-4636
Michelle Winters, Registrar
940-668-3315 Fax: 940-665-7075
Website: www.nctc.edu
E-mail: mwinters@nctc.edu

Northwest Texas Healthcare System
PO Box 1110, Amarillo TX 79105
806-354-1110

Odessa College
201 W University Blvd, Odessa TX 79764-7127
432-335-6400

Our Lady of the Lake University
411 SW 24th St, San Antonio TX 78207-4666
Mary Kay Cooper, Dean of Enrollment
210-434-6711 Fax: 210-431-4013
Website: www.ollusa.edu
E-mail: admission@lakeollusa.edu

Prairie View A&M University
PO Box 188, Prairie View TX 77446
936-857-3311

Presbyterian Hospital
8200 Walnut Hill Ln, Dallas TX 75231-4402
214-345-7558

Remington College - Fort Worth Campus
300 E Loop 820, Fort Worth TX 76112-1280
Director of Recruitment
817-451-0017 Fax: 817-496-1257
Website: www.remingtoncollege.edu
E-mail: lynn.wey@remingtoncollege.edu

St. Elizabeth Hospital
2830 Calder St, Beaumont TX 77702-1892
409-892-7171

St. Phillip's College
1801 Martin Luther King Dr
San Antonio TX 78203-2098
210-531-3200

Sam Houston State University
PO Box 2026, Huntsville TX 77341
936-294-1111

San Antonio College
1300 San Pedro Ave, San Antonio TX 78212-4299
210-733-2000

San Antonio College Medical Dental Assistants
1500 S Jackson Rd, Mc Allen TX 78503-9902
Gabe Garcia, Director of Admissions
956-630-1499 Fax: 956-630-2746
Website: www.sacmda.com
E-mail: gagarcia@sac-mda.com

SAN ANTONIO COLLEGE MEDICAL DENTAL ASSISTANTS
7142 San Pedro Ave Ste 100, San Antonio TX 78216
Carig Czubati, Director of Admissions
210-733-0777 Fax: 210-735-2431
Website: www.sacmda.com
E-mail: cczubati@sac-mda.com

San Jacinto College
8060 Spencer Hwy, Pasadena TX 77505-5998
281-476-1501

∴ Scenic Mountain Medical Center
1601 W 11th Pl, Big Spring TX 79720-4198
432-263-1211

SCOTT & WHITE MEMORIAL HOSPITAL AND CLINIC
2401 S 31st St, Temple TX 76508-0002
Janet Duben-Engelkirk Ed.D., MT(ASCP), Program Director
254-724-5177 Fax: 254-724-0819
Website: www.sw.org/ed/clin_lab/clshp.htm
E-mail: jengelkirk@swmail.sw.org

∴ Shannon West Texas Memorial Hospital
120 E Harris Ave, San Angelo TX 76903-5904
325-653-6741

Southern Methodist University
PO Box 750181, Dallas TX 75275-0181
Ron Moss, Dean of Admission
214-768-2058

· South Plains College - Reese Campus
9730 Reese Blvd, Lubbock TX 79416
Kimbra Quinn, Director of New Student Relations
806-894-9611 ext. 2113

Stephen F. Austin State University
PO Box 6078, Nacogdoches TX 75962-0001
936-468-2011

Tarleton State University
PO Box T0030, Stephenville TX 76402
254-968-9000

· Tarrant County Junior College
Northeast Campus
828 W Harwood Rd, Hurst TX 76054-3299
Cathie J. Jackson, Director of Admissions and Records
817-515-6100

· Temple College
2600 S 1st St, Temple TX 76504-7435
Angela Balch, Director of Admissions & Records
254-298-8300 Fax: 254-298-8288
Website: www.templejc.edu
E-mail: ruth.bridges@templejc.edu

Texas A&M University
College Station TX 77843-0001
979-845-3211

Texas A&M University
700 University Blvd, Kingsville TX 78363
361-593-2111

Texas A&M University - Corpus Christi
6300 Ocean Dr, Corpus Christi TX 78412-5503
361-825-5700

TEXAS CAREERS
1015 Jackson-Keller Rd #102
San Antonio TX 78213-3752
Laura Bledsoe, Campus President
210-308-8584 Fax: 210-308-8985
Website: www.texascareers.com
E-mail: lbledsoe@texascareers.com

Texas Christian University
TCU Box 297013, Fort Worth TX 76129
817-257-7000

TEXAS COLLEGE OF TRADITIONAL CHINESE MEDICINE
4005 Manchaca Rd, Austin TX 78704
Admissions Coordinator
512-444-8082 Fax: 512-444-6345
Website: www.tctcm.edu
E-mail: info@texastcm.edu

∴ Texas Heart Institute
PO Box 20345, Houston TX 77225-0345
713-791-4026

Texas Southern University
3100 Cleburne St, Houston TX 77004-4583
713-313-7011

· Texas Southmost College
80 Fort Brown St, Brownsville TX 78520-4993
956-544-3879

· Texas State Technical College
1901 N Loop 499, Harlingen TX 78550
956-364-4001

Texas State University - San Marcos
601 University Dr, San Marcos TX 78666-4685
512-245-2111

Texas Tech University Health Science Center
Lubbock TX 79430
806-743-3111

Texas Woman's University
PO Box 425589, Denton TX 76204-5589
Erma Nieto, Director of Admissions
866-809-6130 Fax: 940-898-3081
Website: www.twu.edu
E-mail: admissions@twu.edu

Texas Woman's University
1130 John Freeman Ave, Houston TX 77030
Erma Nieto, Director of Admissions
866-809-6130 Fax: 940-898-3081
Website: www.twu.edu
E-mail: admissions@twu.edu

· Trinity Valley Community College
500 S Prairieville St, Athens TX 75751-2734
903-677-8822

· Tyler Junior College
PO Box 9020, Tyler TX 75711-9020
Joan Jones, Interim Dean
800-687-5680
Website: www.tjc.edu
E-mail: jjon@tjc.edu
See listing under "Community and Junior Colleges"

UNITED REGIONAL HEALTH CARE SYSTEM
Medical Technology Program
1600 11th St, Wichita Falls TX 76301
Gwen Morman, MS, MT(ASCP), Program Director
940-764-3187 Fax: 940-764-3328
Website: urhcs.org
E-mail: gmorman@urhcs.org

∴ University Hospital
4502 Medical Dr, San Antonio TX 78229-4492
210-616-2000

University of Houston
122 E Cullen Bldg, Houston TX 77204-2023
Office of Admission
713-743-9595
Website: www.uh.edu
E-mail: admissions@uh.edu

University of Houston-Clear Lake
2700 Bay Area Blvd, Houston TX 77058-1025
281-283-2500

University of North Texas
PO Box 305309, Denton TX 76203-5309
940-565-2000

University of St. Thomas
3800 Montrose Blvd, Houston TX 77006-4626
Eduardo Prieto, Director of Admissions
713-522-7911 Fax: 713-525-3558
Website: www.stthom.edu
E-mail: prietoe@stthom.edu

University of Texas at Arlington
Box 19111, Arlington TX 76019-0111
Hans Gatterdam, Director of Admission
817-272-6287 Fax: 817-272-3435
Website: www.uta.edu
E-mail: admissions@uta.edu

University of Texas at Austin
0 the Univ of Texas, Austin TX 78712
512-471-3434

University of Texas at Dallas
PO Box 830688, Richardson TX 75083-0688
972-690-2111

University of Texas at El Paso
500 W University Ave, El Paso TX 79968-8900
915-747-5000

University of Texas at Tyler
3900 University Blvd, Tyler TX 75701-6622
Jim Hutto, Dean Enrollment Management
800-888-9537

University of Texas Health Science Center
PO Box 20036, Houston TX 77225-0036
713-500-4472

University of Texas Health Science Center
7703 Floyd Curl Dr, San Antonio TX 78229
210-567-7000

UNIVERSITY OF TEXAS M.D. ANDERSON CANCER CENTER
1515 Holcombe Blvd, Houston TX 77030-4009
Anne Bettinger, Academic Recruiter
713-745-1205 Fax: 713-792-0800
Website: www.mdanderson.org/healthsciences
E-mail: ambettin@mdanderson.org

The University of Texas Medical Branch
301 University Blvd, Galveston TX 77555-0802
409-772-1215

University of Texas-Pan American
1201 W University Dr, Edinburg TX 78539-2909
956-381-2011

University of Texas Southwestern Medical Center
5323 Harry Hines Blvd, Dallas TX 75390-7208
214-648-3111

University of the Incarnate Word
4301 Broadway St, San Antonio TX 78209-6318
210-829-6000

∴ Veterans Affairs Medical Center
2002 Holcombe Blvd, Houston TX 77030-4211
713-794-7100

· Victoria College
2200 E Red River St, Victoria TX 77901-4494
361-573-3291

∴ Wadley Regional Medical Center
1000 Pine St, Texarkana TX 75501-5170
903-798-8000

· Western Technical College
9624 Plaza Cir, El Paso TX 79927-2105
Bill Terrell, Chief Administrative Officer
915-760-8123
Website: www.wtc-ep.edu
E-mail: bterrell@wtc-ep.edu

· Western Technical College
9451 Diana Dr, El Paso TX 79924-6936
Bill Terrell, Chief Administrative Officer
915-566-9621 Fax: 915-565-9903
Website: www.wtc-ep.edu
E-mail: bterrell@wtc-ep.edu

West Texas A & M University
WTAMU Box 907, Canyon TX 79016-0001
806-651-2000

· Wharton County Junior College
911 E Boling Hwy, Wharton TX 77488-3298
979-532-4560

UTAH

: American Institute of Medical-Dental Technology
1675 N Freedom Blvd, Provo UT 84604-2540
801-377-2900

Brigham Young University
Provo UT 84602-0001
801-378-5000

: California College for Health Sciences
5295 Commerce Dr, Salt Lake City UT 84107
800-221-7374

L.D.S. BUSINESS COLLEGE
95 North 300 West, Salt Lake City UT 84101-3500
Kathleen Howe, Assistant Director of Admissions
801-524-8145 Fax: 801-524-1900
Website: www.ldsbc.edu
E-mail: admissions@ldsbc.edu
See listing under "Career Schools"

· Provo College
1450 W 820 N, Provo UT 84601-1305
801-375-1861

· Salt Lake Community College
PO Box 30808, Salt Lake City UT 84130-0808
801-957-4111

· Stevens Henager College
755 Main St, Logan UT 84321
Sherman R. Conger, Director of Admissions
435-713-4777
Website: www.stevenshenager.edu

Stevens Henager College
PO Box 9428, Ogden UT 84409-0428
Cindy Williams, Director of Admissions
801-394-7791 Fax: 801-621-0866
Website: www.stevenshenager.edu
E-mail: shcogden@yahoo.com

University of Utah
1460 E 201 S, Salt Lake City UT 84112
801-581-7200

· Utah Career College
1902 W 7800 S, West Jordan UT 84088-4021
Denice Dunker, Director of Admissions
801-304-4224

Utah State University
Logan UT 84322-0001
435-797-1000

∴ Utah Valley Regional Medical Center
1034 N 500 W, Provo UT 84604-3380
801-373-7850

∴ Veterans Affairs Medical Center
500 Foothill Dr, Salt Lake City UT 84148-0001
801-582-1565

· Weber State University
1001 University Cir, Ogden UT 84408
801-626-6000

VERMONT

Champlain College
PO Box 670, Burlington VT 05402-0670
802-860-2727

FLETCHER ALLEN HEALTH CARE SCHOOL OF CYTOTECHNOLOGY
111 Colchester Ave, Burlington VT 05401-1473
Sandra Giroux, Program Director
802-847-5133 Fax: 802-847-3632
Website: www.fahc.org/cytoschool
E-mail: sandra.giroux@vtmednet.org

∴ Rutland Regional Medical Center
160 Allen St, Rutland VT 05701-4595
802-775-7111

University of Vermont
194 S Prospect St, Burlington VT 05401-3518
802-656-3131

VIRGINIA

∴ AUGUSTA MEDICAL CENTER
School of Clinical Laboratory Science
PO Box 1000, Fishersville VA 22939-1000
Bernadette Bekken, Program Director
540-332-4539 Fax: 540-332-4543
Website: www.augustamed.com/cls
E-mail: bbekken@augustamed.com

· Bryant & Stratton College
301 Centre Pointe Dr, Virginia Beach VA 23462-4417
Tracy Nannery, Director
757-499-7900

∴ Carilion Health Systems
PO Box 13727, Roanoke VA 24036-3727
540-981-7347

· Centra Health
1920 Atherholt Rd, Lynchburg VA 24501-1120
804-947-4705

· Central Virginia Community College
3506 Wards Rd, Lynchburg VA 24502-2498
804-832-7600

∴ De Paul Medical Center
150 Kingsley Ln, Norfolk VA 23505-4650
757-489-5120

∴ Fairfax Hospital
3300 Gallows Rd, Falls Church VA 22042-3300
703-698-3371

Hampton University
Hampton VA 23669
757-727-5000

: Heritage Institute
350 S Washington St, Falls Church VA 22046
Christine Knouff, Director
703-773-5050 Fax: 703-534-1142
Website: www.heritage-education.com
E-mail: info@heritage-education.com
See listing under "Career Schools"

: Heritage Institute
8255 Shoppers Square, Manassas VA 20111-2176
Tess Anderson, Director
703-361-7775 Fax: 703-335-9987
Website: www.heritage-education.com
E-mail: info@heritage-education.com
See listing under "Career Schools"

James Madison University
800 S Main St, Harrisonburg VA 22807-0002
540-568-6211

Jefferson College of Health Sciences
Formerly Community Hospital
PO Box 13186, Roanoke VA 24031-3186
Judith McKeon, Director of Admissions
540-985-8483

· J. Sargeant Reynolds Community College
PO Box 85622, Richmond VA 23285-5622
804-371-3000

: **KEE BUSINESS COLLEGE**
803 Diligence Dr, Newport News VA 23606-4203
Sandi Bell, Director of Education
757-873-1111 Fax: 757-873-0728
Website: www.cci.edu
E-mail: sbell@cci.edu

Longwood University
201 High St, Farmville VA 23909-1801
804-395-2000

Mary Baldwin College
Staunton VA 24401
Lisa A. Branson, Executive Director of Admissions and
Financial Aid
800-468-2262 Fax: 540-887-7292
Website: www.mbc.edu
E-mail: admit@mbc.edu

∴ Mary Washington Hospital
1001 Sam Perry Blvd, Fredericksburg VA 22401-3354
Marcia R. Floyd, Education Director
540-899-1565

· Mountain Empire Community College
3441 Mountain Empire Rd
Big Stone Gap VA 24219-0700
276-523-2400

Norfolk State University
700 Park Ave, Norfolk VA 23504
Michelle Marable, Director of Admissions
757-823-8600

Old Dominion University
1 Old Dominion University, Norfolk VA 23529-1000
757-683-3000

Radford University
PO Box 6903, Radford VA 24142
David W. Kraus, Director of Admissions
800-890-4265 Fax: 540-831-5038
Website: www.radford.edu
E-mail: ruadmiss@radford.edu

: Riverside School of Health Careers
316 Main St, Newport News VA 23601
Tracey Hiller, Recruitment Coordinator
757-240-2200 Fax: 757-240-2225
Website: www.riversideonline.com/rshc
E-mail: tracey.hiller@rivhs.com

∴ Rockingham Memorial Hospital
School of Medical Technology
235 Cantrell Ave, Harrisonburg VA 22801-3293
Randall Vandevander, Program Director
540-564-5407

∴ St. Mary's Hospital
5801 Bremo Rd, Richmond VA 23226-1900
804-285-2011

∴ Sentara School of Health Professions
1441 Crossways Blvd Suite 105
Chesapeake VA 23320
Shelly Vinson, Director
Phyllis Moran, Recruiter
757-388-2900 Fax: 757-388-2905
Website: www.sentara.com/healthprofessions
E-mail: healthprofessions@sentara.com

Shenandoah University
1460 University Dr, Winchester VA 22601-5195
Michael D. Carpenter, Director of Admissions
800-432-2266

∴ Southside Regional Medical Center
801 S Adams St, Petersburg VA 23803-5133
Tonia Little, Director of Admissions
804-862-5800 Fax: 804-862-5937
Website: www.srmcnursing.org
E-mail: tlittle@chs.net

· Southwest Virginia Community College
PO Box SVCC, Richlands VA 24641-1101
276-964-2555

· Thomas Nelson Community College
PO Box 9407, Hampton VA 23670-0407
757-825-2700

· Tidewater Community College
State Route 135, Portsmouth VA 23703
757-484-2121

: Tidewater Tech
7020 N Military Hwy, Norfolk VA 23518-4833
757-853-2121

University of Virginia
PO Box 400160, Charlottesville VA 22904
804-924-0311

Virginia Commonwealth University
901 W Franklin St, Richmond VA 23284
804-828-0100

Virginia Polytechnic Institute & State University
Blacksburg VA 24061
540-231-6000

Virginia State University
1 Hayden Dr, Petersburg VA 23806-0001
804-524-5000

· Virginia Western Community College
PO Box 14007, Roanoke VA 24038-4007
540-857-7311

∴ Winchester Memorial Hospital
PO Box 3340, Winchester VA 22604-2540
540-722-8000

· Wytheville Community College
1000 E Main St, Wytheville VA 24382-3308
276-223-4700

WASHINGTON

Bastyr University
14500 Juanita Dr NE, Bothell WA 98028-4966
425-823-1300

BATES TECHNICAL COLLEGE
1101 S Yakima Ave, Tacoma WA 98405-4895
David Borofsky, President
253-680-7000 Fax: 253-680-7101
Website: www.bates.ctc.edu
E-mail: info@bates.ctc.edu

· Bellevue Community College
3000 Landerholm Cir SE, Bellevue WA 98007-6484
425-564-1000

· Bellingham Technical College
3028 Lindbergh Ave, Bellingham WA 98225-1599
360-738-0221

BRYMAN COLLEGE
981 Powell Ave SW, Renton WA 98057
Amanda Gaugler, Director of Education
425-255-3281 Fax: 425-255-9327
Website: www.cci.edu
E-mail: agaugler@cci.edu

Central Washington University
400 E University Way, Ellensburg WA 98926
William Swain, Director of Admissions
509-963-3001

· Clark College
1800 E McLoughlin Blvd, Vancouver WA 98663-3598
360-992-2000

· Clover Park Technical College
4500 Steilacoom Blvd SW
Lakewood WA 98499-4098
Dr. Sharon McGavick, President
253-589-5678 Fax: 253-589-5601
Website: www.cptc.edu
E-mail: jim.griffith@cptc.edu

Eastern Washington University
Cheney WA 99004
509-359-6200

· Everett Community College
2000 Tower St, Everett WA 98201
Christine Kerlin, Associate Dean
425-388-9100 Fax: 425-388-9173
Website: www.everettcc.edu
E-mail: ckerlin@everettcc.edu

· Green River Community College
12401 SE 320th St, Auburn WA 98092-3622
253-833-9111

· Highline Community College
PO Box 98000, Des Moines WA 98198-9800
206-878-3710

∴ Holy Family Hospital
5633 N Lidgerwood St, Spokane WA 99208-1224
509-482-2450

· Lake Washington Technical College
11605 132nd Ave NE, Kirkland WA 98034-8505
425-739-8100

· North Seattle Community College
9600 College Way N, Seattle WA 98103-3599
206-527-3600

· Pierce College Fort Steilacoom
9401 Farwest Dr SW, Lakewood WA 98498-1999
Cherilyn Williams, Communications Coordinator
253-964-6435

: Pima Medical Institute
555 S Renton Village Pl Ste 400, Renton WA 98057
425-228-9600

PIMA MEDICAL INSTITUTE
9709 3rd Ave NE Ste 400, Seattle WA 98115
George Borchers, Campus Director
206-322-6100 Fax: 206-324-1985
Website: www.pmi.edu
E-mail: spima@pmi.edu

: Pima Medical Institute
9709 3rd Ave NE Ste 400, Seattle WA 98115
206-322-6100

RENTON TECHNICAL COLLEGE
3000 NE 4th St, Renton WA 98056-4195
Becky Riverman, Registrar
425-235-2352 or 425-235-5840 Fax: 425-235-7832
Website: www.RTC.edu
E-mail: dgrant@RTC.edu

∴ Sacred Heart Medical Center
101 W 8th Ave, Spokane WA 99204-2307
509-455-3040

Seattle Pacific University
3307 3rd Ave W, Seattle WA 98119-1997
206-281-2000

Seattle University
900 Broadway, Seattle WA 98122-4340
206-296-6000

· Shoreline Community College
16101 Greenwood Ave N, Shoreline WA 98133-5696
Robin Thompson, Director of Admissions
206-546-4101

· South Puget Sound Community College
2011 Mottman Rd SW, Tumwater WA 98512-6292
360-754-7711

· Spokane Community College
1810 N Greene St, Spokane WA 99217-5399
509-533-7000

· Tacoma Community College
6501 S 19th St, Tacoma WA 98466
253-566-5000

University of Puget Sound
1500 N Warner St, Tacoma WA 98416-0005
253-879-3100

University of Washington
Seattle WA 98195-0001
206-543-2100

· Walla Walla Community College
500 Tausick Way, Walla Walla WA 99362-9270
Marilyn Galusha, Director
509-527-4240 or 877-992-9922 Fax: 509-527-3667
Website: www.wwcc.edu
E-mail: marilyn.galusha@wwcc.edu
See listing under "Community and Junior Colleges"

Washington State University
1 SE Stadium Way, Pullman WA 99164-0001
509-335-3564

· Wenatchee Valley College
PO Box 2058, Omak WA 98841
Alex Roberts, Director
509-422-7805 Fax: 509-682-6541
Website: www.wvc.edu

· Wenatchee Valley College
1300 5th St, Wenatchee WA 98801-1799
Marco Azurdia, Dean, Student Development
509-682-6805 Fax: 509-682-6541
Website: www.wvc.edu

Western Washington University
516 High St, Bellingham WA 98225-5996
360-650-3000

· Yakima Valley Community College
PO Box 22520, Yakima WA 98907
509-574-4600

WEST VIRGINIA

∴ Bluefield Regional Medical Center
500 Cherry St, Bluefield WV 24701-3390
304-327-1701

Bluefield State College
219 Rock St, Bluefield WV 24701-2198
304-327-4000

∴ Cabell Huntington Hospital
1340 Hal Greer Blvd, Huntington WV 25701-0195
304-526-2111

∴ **CAMCARE HEALTH EDUCATION & RESEARCH INSTITUTE**
School of Cytotechnology
3200 MacCorkle Ave SE, Charleston WV 25304-1200
Carolyn Stevens, Director
304-348-5570 Fax: 304-348-4352
E-mail: carolyn.stevens@camcare.com

∴ Camden Clark Memorial Hospital
800 Garfield Ave, Parkersburg WV 26101-5378
304-424-2204

: Carver Career and Tech Education Center
4799 Midland Dr, Charleston WV 25306-6353
304-348-1965

Concord University
Athens WV 24712
Michael Curry, Vice President of Financial Aid &
Admissions
888-384-5249 Fax: 304-384-3218
Website: www.concord.edu
E-mail: admissions@concord.edu

Fairmont State University
1201 Locust Ave, Fairmont WV 26554-2470
Steve Leadman, Director of Admissions
304-367-4003 or 800-641-5678 Fax: 304-367-4789
Website: www.fairmontstate.edu
E-mail: admit@fairmontstate.edu

Marshall University
400 Hal Greer Blvd, Huntington WV 25755-0003
304-696-3170

· Mountain State College
1508 Spring St, Parkersburg WV 26101-3993
Judith Sutton, Director
304-485-5487 Fax: 304-485-3524
Website: www.mountainstate.org
E-mail: admin@mountainstate.org
See listing under "Career Schools"

Mountain State University
Box 9003, Beckley WV 25802-9003
866-FOR-MSU1 or 304-929-INFO Fax: 304-253-5072
Website: www.mountainstate.edu
E-mail: gomsu@mountainstate.edu
See listing under "Universities"

∴ Ohio Valley Medical Center
2000 Eoff St, Wheeling WV 26003-3870
304-234-8294

∴ **ST. MARY'S MEDICAL CENTER**
2900 1st Ave, Huntington WV 25702-1272
Dr. Sheila Kyle, VP Schools of Nursing & Health
Professions
304-526-1270 Fax: 304-526-1517
Website: www.st-marys.org
E-mail: skyle@st-marys.org

· Southern West Virginia Community & Technical College
PO Box 2900, Mount Gay WV 25637
304-792-7160

∴ United Hospital Center
PO Box 2308, Clarksburg WV 26302-2308
304-624-2332

∴ Veterans Administration Hospital
200 Veterans Ave, Beckley WV 25801-6444
304-255-2121

West Liberty State College
PO Box 295, West Liberty WV 26074
304-336-5000

· West Virginia Northern Community College
1704 Market St, Wheeling WV 26003-3643
304-233-5900

West Virginia State University
PO Box 1000, Institute WV 25112-1000
304-766-3000

West Virginia University
PO Box 6001, Morgantown WV 26506-6001
304-293-0111

∴ West Virginia University Hospital
PO Box 8150, Morgantown WV 26506-8150
304-598-4000

West Virginia University Institute of Technology
405 Fayette Pike, Montgomery WV 25136-2436
304-442-3071

West Virginia Wesleyan College
59 College Ave, Buckhannon WV 26201-2699
Robert N. Skinner II, Director of Admission
800-722-9933 Fax: 304-473-8108
Website: www.wvwc.edu
E-mail: admission@wvwc.edu

∴ Wheeling Hospital
1 Medical Park, Wheeling WV 26003-6300
304-243-3000

Wheeling Jesuit University
316 Washington Ave, Wheeling WV 26003-6295
304-243-2000

WISCONSIN

∴ All Saints Healthcare System
1320 Wisconsin Ave, Racine WI 53403-1978
262-636-2846

Alverno College
PO Box 343922, Milwaukee WI 53234-3922
Mary Kay Farrell, Director of Admissions
414-382-6100 Fax: 414-382-6354
Website: www.alverno.edu
E-mail: admissions@alverno.edu

∴ Aurora Health Care
3000 W Montana St, Milwaukee WI 53215-3686
414-647-3000

∴ **BELLIN HOSPITAL**
PO Box 23400, Green Bay WI 54305-3400
Randy Griswold, Program Director
920-433-3673
Website: www.bellin.org
E-mail: rcgris@bellin.org

Blackhawk Technical College
PO Box 5009, Janesville WI 53547-5009
Gregg Bosak, Administration, Community Information
608-757-7769 Fax: 608-757-7740
Website: www.blackhawk.edu
E-mail: gbosak@blackhawk.edu

∴ Blood Center of SE Wisconsin
1701 W Wisconsin Ave, Milwaukee WI 53233-2113
414-937-6338

∴ Bryant & Stratton College
310 W Wisconsin Ave Suite 500, Milwaukee WI 53203
Kathryn Cotey, Director of Admissions
414-276-5200

Chippewa Valley Technical College
620 W Clairemont Ave, Eau Claire WI 54701-6162
Admissions Office
715-833-6246

∴ Columbia Hospital
2025 E Newport Ave, Milwaukee WI 53211-2990
414-961-3800

Concordia University
12800 N Lake Shore Dr, Mequon WI 53097-2402
262-243-5700

Fox Valley Technical College
PO Box 2277, Appleton WI 54912-2277
Bob Burdick, Registrar
920-735-5600

∴ Froedtert Memorial Lutheran Hospital
PO Box 26099, Milwaukee WI 53226-0099
414-259-2606

∴ Gateway Technical College
3520 30th Ave, Kenosha WI 53144-1690
Zina Haywood, Director of Admissions
262-564-2200

∴ Gunderson Medical Foundation
1836 South Ave, La Crosse WI 54601-5429
608-782-7300

Lakeshore Technical College
1290 North Ave, Cleveland WI 53015-1414
Information Fulfillment Specialist
888-GOTOLTC Fax: 920-693-3561
Website: www.gotoltc.edu
E-mail: info@gotoltc.edu

Madison Area Technical College
3550 Anderson St, Madison WI 53704-2599
608-246-6282

Marquette University
PO Box 1881, Milwaukee WI 53201-1881
Robert Blust, Director of Admissions
414-288-7302 Fax: 414-288-3764
Website: www.mu.edu
E-mail: admissions@marquette.edu

∴ **MARSHFIELD CLINIC/ST. JOSEPH'S HOSPITAL**
611 Saint Joseph's Avenue
Marshfield WI 54449-5795
Julie J. Seehafer, MS, MT(ASCP)SH
Director, Laboratory Education
715-387-7440 Fax: 715-387-7121
Website: www.marshfieldlaboratories.org
E-mail: seehafer.julie@marshfieldclinic.org (Office)

· Mercy Medical Center
PO Box 3370, Oshkosh WI 54903-3370
920-233-5110

· Mid-State Technical College
500 32nd St N, Wisconsin Rapids WI 54494-5512
715-423-5300

MIDWEST COLLEGE OF ORIENTAL MEDICINE
6232 Bankers Rd, Racine WI 53403-9747
Kelly Westerlund, Contact
800-593-2320 Fax: 262-554-7475
Website: www.acupuncture.edu
E-mail: mwcadmissions@yahoo.com

· Milwaukee Area Technical College
700 W State St, Milwaukee WI 53233-1419
414-297-6600

Milwaukee School of Engineering
1025 N Broadway, Milwaukee WI 53202-3109
414-277-7300

Moraine Park Technical College
235 N National Ave, Fond du Lac WI 54935
920-922-8611

Mount Mary College
2900 N Menomonee River Pkwy
Milwaukee WI 53222-4597
414-256-1219

Northcentral Technical College
1000 W Campus Dr, Wausau WI 54401-1880
Carolyn Michalski, Director of Admissions
715-675-3331

Northeast Wisconsin Technical College
PO Box 19042, Green Bay WI 54307-9042
800-422-NWTC

∴ Sacred Heart Hospital
900 W Clairemont Ave, Eau Claire WI 54701-5105
715-839-4131

∴ St. Elizabeth Hospital
1506 S Oneida St, Appleton WI 54915-1396
920-738-2015

∴ St. Francis Hospital
3237 S 16th St, Milwaukee WI 53215-4592
414-647-5106

∴ St. Joseph Hospital/Marshfield Clinic
611 Saint Joseph Ave, Marshfield WI 54449-1898
715-387-1713

∴ St. Luke's Medical Center
2900 W Oklahoma Ave, Milwaukee WI 53215-4330
414-649-7500

St. Norbert College
100 Grant St, De Pere WI 54115
Brian Studebaker, Director of Admission
800-236-4878 Fax: 920-403-4072
Website: www.snc.edu
E-mail: admit@snc.edu

∴ St. Vincent Hospital
PO Box 13508, Green Bay WI 54307-3508
920-433-8155

State Laboratory of Hygiene
465 Henry Mall, Madison WI 53706-1578
Lynn Sterud, Ed. Coordinator
608-262-2802

∴ Theda Clark Regional Medical Center
130 2nd St, Neenah WI 54956-2883
920-729-2004

University of Wisconsin
PO Box 4004, Eau Claire WI 54702
715-836-2637

University of Wisconsin
716 Langdon St, Madison WI 53706-1481
608-262-1234

University of Wisconsin
PO Box 413, Milwaukee WI 53201-0413
414-229-1122

University of Wisconsin
410 S 3rd St, River Falls WI 54022
715-425-3911

University of Wisconsin
2100 Main St, Stevens Point WI 54481-3871
715-346-0123

University of Wisconsin
800 W Main St, Whitewater WI 53190-1705
262-472-1234

University of Wisconsin Green Bay
2420 Nicolet Dr, Green Bay WI 54311-7003
Pamela Harvey-Jacobs, Interim Director of Admissions
920-465-2111

University of Wisconsin in La Crosse
115 Graff Main Hall, La Crosse WI 54601
Tim Lewis, Director of Admissions
608-785-8939

University of Wisconsin - Oshkosh
800 Algoma Blvd, Oshkosh WI 54901-8602
920-424-0202

University of Wisconsin-Stout
124 Bowman Hall, Menomonie WI 54751-2662
715-232-1123

Viterbo University
815 9th St S, La Crosse WI 54601-8802
608-796-3000

· Waukesha County Technical College
800 Main St, Pewaukee WI 53072-4601
262-691-5566

∴ Wausau Hospital Center
333 Pine Ridge Blvd, Wausau WI 54401-4187
715-847-2117

· Western Wisconsin Technical College
PO Box 908, La Crosse WI 54602-0908
608-785-9200

· Wisconsin Indianhead Technical College
1019 S Knowles Ave, New Richmond WI 54017-1738
715-246-6561

∴ Zablocki VA Medical Center
5000 W National Ave, Milwaukee WI 53295-0001
414-384-2000

WYOMING

· Casper College
125 College Dr, Casper WY 82601-4699
307-268-2110

· Laramie County Community College
1400 E College Dr, Cheyenne WY 82007-3204
Jenny Hargett, Director of Admissions
307-778-5222 Fax: 307-778-1350
Website: www.lccc.wy.edu
E-mail: learnmore@lccc.wy.edu

· Sheridan College
PO Box 1500, Sheridan WY 82801-1500
307-674-6446

University of Wyoming
Admissions Office
Dept 3435, Laramie WY 82071-3435
Aaron Appelhans, Contact
800-342-5996 Fax: 307-766-4042
Website: www.uwyo.edu
E-mail: why-wyo@uwyo.edu

Western Wyoming Community College
2500 College Dr, Rock Springs WY 82901-5802
Laurie Watkins, Director of Admissions
307-382-1600

∴ West Park Hospital
707 Sheridan Ave, Cody WY 82414-3409
307-527-7501

GUAM

· Guam Community College
PO Box 23069, G.M.F. GU 96921-0307
Virginia Charfauros Tudela, Ph.D., Registrar
671-735-5531 Fax: 671-734-5238
Website: www.guamcc.edu
E-mail: Webmaster@guamcc.edu

PUERTO RICO

· Colegio Mayor de Technologia
PO Box 1490, Arroyo PR 00714
Julia Melendez, Director of Admissions
787-839-5266 Fax: 787-839-0033
Website: www.colegiomayortec.edu
E-mail: cmtarroy@coqui.net

· EDIC College
PO Box 9120, Caguas PR 00726-9120
Virginia Cartagena, Director of Admissions
787-744-8519 Fax: 787-743-0855
Website: www.ediccollege.com
E-mail: edic@coqui.net

· Huertas Junior College
PO Box 8429, Caguas PR 00726-8429
787-746-1400

· Humacao Community College
PO Box 9139, Humacao PR 00792
787-852-1430

Inter American University of Puerto Rico
PO Box 191293, Hato Rey PR 00919
787-250-1912

Inter American University of Puerto Rico
PO Box 5100, San German PR 00683
787-264-1912

PONCE PARAMEDICAL COLLEGE
1213 Calle Acacia Villa Flores, Ponce PR 00716-2901
Alberto Aristizabal, President
787-848-1589 Fax: 787-259-0169
E-mail: ppcadmin@popac.edu

Pontifical Catholic University of Puerto Rico
2250 Ave Las Americas, Ponce PR 00717-0777
787-841-2000

Universidad Adventista de las Antillas
PO Box 118, Mayaguez PR 00919-0118
Evelyn Del Valle Rivera, Director of Admissions
787-834-9595 Fax: 787-834-9597
Website: www.uaa.edu
E-mail: admissions@uaa.edu

Universidad Central Del Caribe
PO Box 60327, Bayamon PR 00960-6032
787-798-3001

· Universidad del Este
PO Box 2010, Carolina PR 00984
787-257-7373

Universidad Metropolitana
PO Box 21150, San Juan PR 00928-1150
787-766-1717

University of Puerto Rico
PO Box 365067, San Juan PR 00936-5067
787-758-2525

University of the Sacred Heart
PO Box 12383, Santurce PR 00914
787-728-1515

ARCHITECTURE

ALASKA

University of Alaska Anchorage
PO Box 141629, Anchorage AK 99514-1629
Cecile Mitchell, Director of Enrollment Services
907-786-1480 Fax: 907-786-4888
Website: www.uaa.alaska.edu/
E-mail: enroll@uaa.alaska.edu

ARIZONA

FRANK LLOYD WRIGHT SCHOOL OF ARCHITECTURE

Taliesin West, Scottsdale AZ 85261
Pamela S. Stefansson, Director of Admissions
480-860-2700 Fax: 480-391-4009
Website: www.taliesin.edu
E-mail: nikita@taliesin.edu

University of Arizona
Tucson AZ 85721-0040
Paul Kohn, Director of Admissions
520-621-3237 Fax: 520-621-9799
Website: www.admissions.arizona.edu or
www.arizona.edu

ARKANSAS

Northwest Technical Institute
709 S Old Missouri Rd, Springdale AR 72764
Charles L. Kelley, President
479-751-8824 Fax: 479-751-7780
Website: www.nti.tec.ar.us
E-mail: info@nit.tec.ar.us

CALIFORNIA

California College of the Arts
1111 Eighth St, San Francisco CA 94107
Robynne Royster, Director of Admission
800-447-1-ART or 415-703-9523 Fax: 415-703-9539
Website: www.cca.edu
E-mail: enroll@cca.edu

Chabot College
25555 Hesperian Blvd, Hayward CA 94545-2400
Judy Young, Director of Admissions
510-723-6600 Fax: 510-723-7510
Website: www.chabotcollege.edu
E-mail: ccarcom@clpccd.cc.ca.us

Orange Coast College
PO Box 5005, Costa Mesa CA 92628-5005
Kristin Clark, Director of Admissions
714-432-5773 Fax: 714-432-5736
Website: www.orangecoastcollege.edu
E-mail: kclark@cccd.edu

COLORADO

University of Colorado at Denver and Health Sciences
Center
Downtown Denver Campus
PO Box 173364, Denver CO 80217-3364
303-556-3382 Fax: 303-556-3687
Website:
www.cudenver.edu/academics/colleges/architecturepl
anning

CONNECTICUT

Porter and Chester Institute
670 Lordship Blvd, Stratford CT 06615-7158
Mark Breslin, Director of Admissions
203-375-4463 Fax: 203-375-5285
Website: www.porterchester.com

FLORIDA

University of South Florida
4202 E Fowler Ave, Tampa FL 33620-6900
J. Robert Spatig, Director of Admissions
813-974-3350 Fax: 813-974-9689
Website: www.usf.edu
E-mail: admissions@admin.usf.edu

GEORGIA

Savannah College of Art and Design

PO Box 2072, Savannah, GA 31402-2072
PO Box 77300, Atlanta, GA 30357
Phone: 800-869-7223 (Savannah) or 877-722-3285 (Atlanta)
E-mail: admission@scad.edu (Savannah) or sca-datl@scad.edu (Atlanta)
www.scad.edu
  SCAD is a private, nonprofit institution accredited by the Commission on Colleges of the Southern Association of Colleges and Schools to award bachelor's and master's degrees. The college offers B.F.A., M.Arch., M.A., M.F.A., and M.U.D. degrees. Enrollment is approximately 7,350; 6 percent are international. More than 30 areas of study. Online programs via SCAD e-Learning.

IDAHO

University of Idaho
Moscow ID 83844-4253
Lloyd Scott, Director of New Student Services
208-885-6163 Fax: 208-885-4477
Website: www.uidaho.edu
E-mail: nss@uidaho.edu

ILLINOIS

Columbia College Chicago
600 S Michigan Ave, Chicago IL 60605-1996
Murphy Monroe, Executive Director of Admissions
312-344-7130 Fax: 312-344-8024
Website: www.colum.edu
E-mail: admissions@colum.edu

IOWA

Iowa Lakes Community College
300 S 18th St, Estherville IA 51334-2721
Anne Stansbury, Asst. Director of Admissions
712-362-7945 Fax: 712-362-8363
Website: www.iowalakes.edu
E-mail: info@iowalakes.edu

KENTUCKY

Spencerian College
1575 Winchester Rd, Lexington KY 40505
Victor Lamoin Adcock II, Director of Admissions
800-456-3253

LOUISIANA

Delta School of Business and Technology
517 Broad St, Lake Charles LA 70601-4334
Gary Holt, President
337-439-5765 Fax: 337-436-5151
Website: www.deltatech.edu
E-mail: susan@deltatech.edu

MAINE

Northern Maine Community College
33 Edgemont Dr, Presque Isle ME 04769-2016
Bill Casavant, Director of Admissions
207-768-2700 Fax: 207-768-2831
Website: www.nmcc.edu
E-mail: admissions@nmcc.edu

Southern Maine Community College
2 Fort Rd, South Portland ME 04106-1698
Dr. James Ortiz, President
Scott MacDonald, Director of Financial Aid
207-741-5500 Fax: 207-741-5671
Website: www.smccme.edu
E-mail: oharmon@maine.rr.com

MASSACHUSETTS

Benjamin Franklin Institute of Technology
41 Berkeley St, Boston MA 02116-6307
Norman Kraft, Dean of Enrollment
617-423-4630 ext. 121 Fax: 617-482-3706
Website: www.bfit.edu
E-mail: admissions@bfit.edu

Massachusetts Institute of Technology
77 Massachusetts Ave, Cambridge MA 02139-4307
Marilee Jones, Dean of Admission
617-253-1000 Fax: 617-253-4016
Website: my.mit.edu
E-mail: admissions@mit.edu

Wentworth Institute of Technology
550 Huntington Ave, Boston MA 02115-5998
David C. Planchard, Director of Admissions
617-442-9010
Website: www.wit.edu/apply
E-mail: planchardd@wit.edu

MICHIGAN

Andrews University
Berrien Springs MI 49104-0001
Randall Graves, Director of Recruitment Services
800-253-2874 Fax: 269-471-2670
Website: www.connect.andrews.edu
E-mail: gravesr@andrews.edu

ITT TECHNICAL INSTITUTE

4020 Sparks Dr SE, Grand Rapids MI 49546-6192
Dennis Hormel, Director
616-956-1060 Fax: 616-956-5606
Website: www.itt-tech.edu
E-mail: dhormel@itt-tech.edu

Lawrence Technological University
21000 W 10 Mile Rd, Southfield MI 48075-1058
Jane Rohrback, Director of Admissions
800-225-5588 Fax: 248-204-2228
Website: www.ltu.edu
E-mail: admissions@ltu.edu
See listing under "Universities"

MACOMB COMMUNITY COLLEGE

14500 E 12 Mile Rd, Warren MI 48088-3896
Information Center
586-445-7999
Website: www.macomb.edu
E-mail: answer@macomb.edu

MINNESOTA

Dunwoody College of Technology
818 Dunwoody Blvd, Minneapolis MN 55403-1192
John Slama, Vice President Enrollment Management
800-292-4625 or 612-374-5800 Fax: 612-374-4128
Website: www.dunwoody.edu
E-mail: jslama@dunwoody.edu
See listing under "Career Schools"

Northland Community & Technical College
Highway 1 E, Thief River Falls MN 56701
Rod Lahren, Contact
800-959-6282 or 218-681-0813 Fax: 218-681-0774
Website: www.northlandcollege.edu

MISSOURI

Ranken Technical College
4431 Finney Ave, Saint Louis MO 63113-2898
Elizabeth M. Keserauskis, Director of Admissions
314-371-0233 Fax: 314-371-0241
Website: www.ranken.edu
E-mail: admissions@ranken.edu

NEW YORK

ISLAND DRAFTING & TECHNICAL INSTITUTE

128 Broadway (Route 110), Amityville NY 11701-2704
James G. DiLiberto, President
631-691-8733 Fax: 631-691-8738
Website: www.idti.edu
E-mail: info@idti.edu

Pratt Institute
200 Willoughby Ave, Brooklyn NY 11205-3899
Heidi Metcalf, Director of Admissions
718-636-3600 Fax: 718-636-3670
Website: www.pratt.edu
E-mail: hmetcalf@pratt.edu

SUNY College of Technology
Alfred NY 14802
Deborah J. Goodrich, Director of Admissions
800-4AL-FRED Fax: 607-587-4299
Website: www.alfredstate.edu
E-mail: admissions@alfredstate.edu

SUNY Orange County Community College
115 South St, Middletown NY 10940-6437
Margot St. Lawrence, Director of Admissions
845-341-4030 Fax: 845-342-8662
Website: www.sunyorange.edu
E-mail: apply@sunyorange.edu
See listing under "Community and Junior Colleges"

OHIO

The Ohio State University
Austin E. Knowlton School of Architecture
Knowlton Arch Bldg, 275 W Woodruff Ave
Columbus OH 43210
614-292-1012 Fax: 614-292-7106
Website: knowlton.osu.edu
E-mail: ugadvisor@knowlton.osu.edu

OKLAHOMA

Oklahoma State University
Stillwater OK 74078
J. Randall Seitsinger, Department Head
405-744-6043
Website: www.okstate.edu
E-mail: randy.seitsinger@okstate.edu

PENNSYLVANIA

Pennsylvania Institute of Technology
800 Manchester Ave, Media PA 19063-4036
Angela Cassetta, Dean of Enrollment Management
800-422-0025 or 610-892-1500 Fax: 610-892-1510
Website: www.pit.edu
E-mail: info@pit.edu
See listing under "Community and Junior Colleges"

TEXAS

ITT TECHNICAL INSTITUTE

2950 S Gessner Rd Ste 100, Houston TX 77063-3751
Jennifer Gomez, Director of Recruitment
713-952-2294 Fax: 713-952-2393
Website: www.itt-tech.edu
E-mail: jgomez@itt-tech.edu

University of Houston
122 E Cullen Bldg, Houston TX 77204-2023
Office of Admission
713-743-9595
Website: www.uh.edu
E-mail: admissions@uh.edu

University of Texas at Arlington
Box 19111, Arlington TX 76019-0111
Hans Gatterdam, Director of Admission
817-272-6287 Fax: 817-272-3435
Website: www.uta.edu
E-mail: admissions@uta.edu

VERMONT

Bennington College
One College Drive, Bennington VT 05201
Ken Himmelman, Dean of Admissions & Financial Aid
800-833-6845 Fax: 802-440-4320
Website: www.bennington.edu
E-mail: admissions@bennington.edu

NORWICH UNIVERSITY

158 Harmon Dr, Northfield VT 05663
Arthur Schaller, Division Head
800-468-6679 Fax: 802-485-2624
Website: www.norwich.edu
E-mail: schaller@norwich.edu

WISCONSIN

Herzing College
5218 E Terrace Dr, Madison WI 53718-8340
Donald Madelung, President
800-582-1227 Fax: 608-249-8593
Website: www.herzing.edu
E-mail: info@msn.herzing.edu
See listing under "Universities"

ART

ALABAMA

Alabama A & M University
PO Box 908, Normal AL 35762
Antonio Boyle, Director of Admissions
256-372-5245 Fax: 256-372-5249
Website: www.aamu.edu
E-mail: aboyle@aamu.edu

CALHOUN COMMUNITY COLLEGE
PO Box 2216, Decatur AL 35609-2216
M. Wayne Tosh, Registrar
256-306-2500 Fax: 256-306-2941
Website: www.calhoun.edu
E-mail: aprater@calhoun.edu

Judson College
302 Bibb St, Marion AL 36756
Michael Scotto, Director of Admissions
800-447-9472 Fax: 334-683-5147
Website: www.judson.edu
E-mail: admissions@judson.edu

University of Alabama in Huntsville
PO Box 1247, Huntsville AL 35899-0001
Ann Lee, Assoc. Director for Recruiting Program and Events
1-800-UAH-CALL Fax: 256-824-6073
Website: www.uah.edu
E-mail: leev@uah.edu

University of South Alabama
307 University Blvd N, Mobile AL 36688-3053
Melissa Haab, Director of Admissions
251-460-6141 Fax: 251-460-7876
Website: www.southalabama.edu
E-mail: admiss@usouthal.edu

ALASKA

University of Alaska Anchorage
PO Box 141629, Anchorage AK 99514-1629
Cecile Mitchell, Director of Enrollment Services
907-786-1480 Fax: 907-786-4888
Website: www.uaa.alaska.edu/
E-mail: enroll@uaa.alaska.edu

University of Alaska Southeast
11120 Glacier Hwy, Juneau AK 99801-8625
Paul Kraft, Dean of Students/Enrollment Management
907-796-6000 Fax: 907-796-6005
Website: www.uas.alaska.edu
E-mail: paul.kraft@uas.alaska.edu

ARIZONA

Collins College: A School of Design and Technology
(Formerly Al Collins Graphic Design School)
1140 S Priest Dr, Tempe AZ 85281-5240
Toby Craver, Director of National Admissions
800-876-7070 Fax: 480-829-0183
Website: www.collinscollege.edu
E-mail: nationaladmissions@collinscollege.edu

The Conservatory of Recording Arts & Sciences
2300 E Broadway Rd, Tempe AZ 85282-1707
Tonya Visconti, Director of Admissions
800-562-6383 or 480-858-9400 Fax: 480-829-1332
Website: cras.org
E-mail: info@cras.org
See listing under "Music"

University of Arizona
Tucson AZ 85721-0040
Paul Kohn, Director of Admissions
520-621-3237 Fax: 520-621-9799
Website: www.admissions.arizona.edu or www.arizona.edu

ARKANSAS

Ouachita Baptist University
410 Ouachita St, Arkadelphia AR 71998-0001
David Goodman, Director of Admissions
870-245-5110 Fax: 870-245-5500
Website: www.obu.edu
E-mail: admissions@obu.edu

CALIFORNIA

American Film Institute
AFI Conservatory
2021 N Western Ave, Los Angeles CA 90027
Scott Hardman, Admissions Counselor
323-856-7628 Fax: 323-856-7720
Website: www.afi.com
E-mail: shardman@afi.com

ART CENTER COLLEGE OF DESIGN
1700 Lida St, Pasadena CA 91103-1999
Kit Baron, V.P. Admissions
626-396-2373 Fax: 626-795-0578
Website: www.artcenter.edu
E-mail: admissions@artcenter.edu
    Established 1930. Private. Coed. Accreditation: WASC, NASAD. Tuition: $26,310. Enrollment: 1,400. Faculty: 425. Student-faculty ratio: 9:1. Degrees: BFA, BS, MFA, MA, MS. Library: 65,000 volumes. Specialized programs in advertising, illustration, industrial design, film, photography, graphic design, fine arts. Emphasis on preparation for professional specialty through both skill and concept development and intense exposure to professional projects.

THE ART INSTITUTE OF CALIFORNIA - ORANGE COUNTY
3601 W Sunflower Ave, Santa Ana CA 92704-9888
Vincent David, Director of Admissions
888-549-3055 Fax: 714-556-1923
Website: www.aicaoc.aii.edu
E-mail: aicaocadm@aii.edu
    Private. Coed. Accreditation: Accredited by the Accrediting Council for Independent Colleges and Schools (ACICS) and by the Bureau of Private Postsecondary and Vocational Education Bureau as a California private postsecondary degree-granting institution. The Art Institute of California-Orange County is one of The Art Institutes, with 32 education institutions located throughout North America. Tuition: $393 per credit hour. Fees: $315 per quarter (culinary only). Enrollment: 1,800. Student-faculty ratio: 20:1. Degrees: Advertising, Culinary Arts; Game Art & Design, Graphic Design, Industrial Design, Interior Design, Media Arts & Animation, Interactive Media Design.
    The Art Institute of California - Orange County is an educational institution for career preparation in culinary arts, design and media arts. The school's mission is to provide postsecondary education programs that will prepare students for entry-level positions in their chosen fields through market-driven curricula. The school involves employers in the development of curricula that respond to industry needs; creating an environment that encourages academic freedom, responsible decision making and critical thinking among students, faculty and staff; fostering a collaborative environment that encourages personal and professional growth; and continually improving operations by promoting teamwork and communications through the institutional effectiveness process.
    The Art Institute of California - Orange County is located in beautiful Southern California, within easy driving distance to local beaches and entertainment. The Art Institute affords students the opportunity to learn from top professionals in their industry. As part of their chosen program, students learn sought-after techniques, create professional portfolios and establish networks that will help lead them to their chosen career. The campus includes 11 open computer labs, four professional kitchens, a student gallery, a learning resource center, an interior design resource center, an industrial design workshop and constantly-updated industrial, technological and professional equipment. Students have access to student housing, public transportaion, part-time job opportunities and a wealth of leisure time activities.
    The Art Institute of California - Orange County offers financial planning assistance for students. Financial aid consisting of grants, loans and work-study programs is available for students who qualify. The Art Institute also offers scholarships to its new and continuing students based on merit, motivation and financial need. Students should contact the Admissions department for more information.

California College of the Arts
1111 Eighth St, San Francisco CA 94107
Robynne Royster, Director of Admission
800-447-1-ART or 415-703-9523 Fax: 415-703-9539
Website: www.cca.edu
E-mail: enroll@cca.edu

California State University-San Bernadino
5500 University Pkwy
San Bernardino CA 92407-2393
Olivia Rosas, Director of Admissions
909-880-5000 Fax: 909-880-7034
Website: enrollment.csusb.edu
E-mail: orosas@csusb.edu

Chabot College
25555 Hesperian Blvd, Hayward CA 94545-2400
Judy Young, Director of Admissions
510-723-6600 Fax: 510-723-7510
Website: www.chabotcollege.edu
E-mail: ccarcom@clpccd.cc.ca.us

Chapman University
One University Drive, Orange CA 92866-1099
Michael Drummy, Assistant Vice President for Enrollment
Services and Chief Admission Officer
714-997-6411 or 888-CUAPPLY Fax: 714-997-6713
Website: www.chapman.edu
E-mail: admit@chapman.edu

Cogswell College
1175 Bordeaux Dr, Sunnyvale CA 94089-1210
Dr. Valarie Brown, Dean of Enrollment Management
800-264-7955 or 408-541-0100 Fax: 408-747-0764
Website: www.cogswell.edu
E-mail: info@cogswell.edu
See listing under "Universities"

Concordia University
1530 Concordia, Irvine CA 92612-3203
Lori McDonald, Executive Director of Enrollment Services
800-229-1200 or 949-854-8002 Fax: 949-854-6894
Website: www.cui.edu
E-mail: admission@cui.edu

FIDM/THE FASHION INSTITUTE OF DESIGN & MERCHANDISING
919 S Grand Ave, Los Angeles CA 90015-1421
Director of Admissions
213-624-1201 or 800-624-1200 Fax: 213-624-4799
Website: www.fidm.edu
E-mail: info@fidm.com
See listing under "Community and Junior Colleges"

IDYLLWILD ARTS ACADEMY
PO Box 38, Idyllwild CA 92549-0038
Karen Porter, Dean of Admission
951-659-2171 ext. 2223 Fax: 951-659-5463
Website: www.idyllwildarts.org
E-mail: admission@idyllwildarts.org

Orange Coast College
PO Box 5005, Costa Mesa CA 92628-5005
Kristin Clark, Director of Admissions
714-432-5773 Fax: 714-432-5736
Website: www.orangecoastcollege.edu
E-mail: kclark@cccd.edu

PLATT COLLEGE
6250 El Cajon Blvd, San Diego CA 92115-3916
Carly Westerfield, Admissions Coordinator
619-265-0107 or 866-752-8826 Fax: 619-308-0570
Website: www.platt.edu
E-mail: info@platt.edu
    Established 1980. Private. Coed. Accreditation: ACCSCT. Tuition: Approximately $16,000. Fees: $100. Enrollment: 350. Faculty: 25. Student-faculty ratio: 14:1. Library: 1,700 volumes + online. 2 buildings. Design school offering BS, AAS and diploma programs. "Hands on" programs in Graphic Design, Multimedia Design, Animation, Digital Video Production, and Web page design. Full range of General Education courses required to complete AAS + BS degrees. Classes offered morning, afternoon and evening. Job placement and financial aid services available. Visit www.platt.edu.

SAN FRANCISCO ART INSTITUTE
800 Chestnut St, San Francisco CA 94133
Paula Farmer, Director of Admission
800-345-SFAI Fax: 415-749-4503
Website: www.sfai.edu
E-mail: admissions@sfai.edu
    Founded in 1871, SFAI offers one of the most innovative and interdisciplinary environments in higher education. Through its School of Studio Practice, SFAI offers accredited Bachelor of Fine Arts (BFA), Master of Fine Arts (MFA), Summer Master of Fine Arts (SMFA), and Post-Baccalaureate (PB) programs. SFAI's School of Studio Practice centers on the development of the artist's vision and consists of the departments of: Design+Technology, Film, New Genres, Painting, Photography, Printmaking, and Sculpture. At SFAI students become part of an educational environment that sees experimentation as necessary for independent and collaborative invention. The School of Interdisciplinary Studies is the complementary other half of SFAI, offering three areas of study: History and Theory of Contemporary Art (BA, MA); Urban Studies (BA, MA); and Exhibition and Museum Studies (MA). Together the two schools provide an inclusive model to address contemporary art and culture. The BFA, MFA, and PB programs are at their core interdisciplinary, and students can take courses in any department. The Summer MFA program has the same rigor as the Academic Year MFA program, yet is designed for those who choose an alternate academic schedule. The Post-Baccalaureate program is an excellent way to prepare for entrance into an MFA program or to enhance skills and knowledge. SFAI's faculty is comprised of active artists, scholars, writers, and curators. Dean of Academic Affairs is renowned curator and critic Okwui Enwezor. Dean of Graduate Studies is artist and filmmaker Renee Green. Director of Exhibitions and Public Programs is curator Hou Hanru. Visiting artists and scholars play a significant role in education at SFAI, with recent visitors including Matthew Barney, William Kentridge, Raqs Media Collective, and others. All students have 24-hour access to the SFAI campus, SFAI's main campus includes painting, photography, sculture, and printmaking studios, postproduction facilities, and the first high-definition video research lab in the Bay Area. The Diego Rivera Gallery, an open-air amphitheater, and a 250-seat theater are also available to students for exhibiting and screening work. SFAI's library collection includes more than 26,000 volumes with emphasis on modern and contemporary art, over 200 current periodicals, and an extensive image, video, and audio archive available only to SFAI students. The 62,000 square-foot Graduate Center includes a digital lab, film and sound studios, darkrooms, a woodshop, and a gallery for student work. SFAI has rolling application deadlines, and there are competitive and need-based scholarships available to undergraduates, a fellowship program for graduate students, and community college scholarships for transfer students. Visit the SFAI website for specific application requirements.

Western Career College
6001 Shellmound St 2nd Floor, Emeryville CA 94608
Elvie Engstrom, Director of Admissions
510-601-0133 Fax: 510-601-0793
Website: www.westerncollege.edu

Western Career College
380 Civic Dr Ste 300, Pleasant Hill CA 94523-1984
LaShawn Wells, Contact
925-609-6650 Fax: 926-609-6666
Website: www.westerncollege.edu

Western Career College
6201 San Ignacio Ave, San Jose CA 95119
Steve Ashab, Director of Admissions
408-360-0840 Fax: 408-360-0848
Website: www.westerncollege.edu

COLORADO

Whittier College
PO Box 634, Whittier CA 90608-0634
Kieron Miller, Director of Admissions
562-907-4200 Fax: 562-907-4870
Website: www.whittier.edu
E-mail: kmiller@whittier.edu

Art Institute of Colorado
1200 Lincoln St, Denver CO 80203-2172
David Zorn, President
Brian A. Parker, Director of Admissions
800-275-2420 Fax: 303-860-8520
Website: www.artinstitutes.edu
E-mail: baparker@aii.edu

ROCKY MOUNTAIN COLLEGE OF ART & DESIGN

1600 Pierce St, Lakewood CO 80214
Marianna Bagge, Director of Admissions
800-888-2787 Fax: 303-759-4970
Website: www.rmcad.edu
E-mail: admissions@rmcad.edu

CONNECTICUT

Albertus Magnus College
700 Prospect St, New Haven CT 06511-1189
Richard Lolatte, Dean of Admission
203-773-8501 or 800-578-9160 Fax: 203-773-5248
Website: www.albertus.edu
E-mail: admissions@albertus.edu

University of New Haven
300 Boston Post Rd, West Haven CT 06516
Director of Undergraduate Admissions
203-932-7319 Fax: 203-931-6093
Website: www.newhaven.edu
E-mail: adminfo@newhaven.edu

DISTRICT OF COLUMBIA

CORCORAN COLLEGE OF ART AND DESIGN

500 17th St NW, Washington DC 20006-4804
Elizabeth Paladino, Director of Admission
202-639-1814 or 888-CORCORAN Fax: 202-639-1830
Website: www.corcoran.edu
E-mail: admissions@corcoran.org

FLORIDA

Art Institute of Fort Lauderdale
1799 SE 17th St, Fort Lauderdale FL 33316-3013
Eileen Northrop, V.P./Director of Admissions
800-275-7603 Fax: 954-728-8637
Website: www.aifl.edu

Florida State University
600 W College Ave, Tallahassee FL 32306-1096
Janice V. Finney, Director of Admissions
850-644-2525 Fax: 850-644-0197
Website: admissions.fsu.edu
E-mail: admissions@admin.fsu.edu

International Academy of Design & Technology
5104 Eisenhower Blvd, Tampa FL 33634-6313
Richard Costa, V.P. of Admissions and Marketing
813-880-8092 Fax: 813-881-0008
Website: www.academy.edu
E-mail: admissions@academy.edu

INTERNATIONAL ACADEMY OF DESIGN AND TECHNOLOGY

5959 Lake Ellenor Dr, Orlando FL 32809-4633
Dr. John Dietrich, VP of Admissions
877-753-0007 Fax: 407-251-0465
Website: www.iadt.edu
E-mail: info@iadt.edu

Lynn University
3601 N Military Trl, Boca Raton FL 33431-5598
Brett Ormandy, Director of Admissions
561-237-7900 Fax: 561-237-7100
Website: www.lynn.edu
E-mail: admission@lynn.edu

University of South Florida
4202 E Fowler Ave, Tampa FL 33620-6900
J. Robert Spatig, Director of Admissions
813-974-3350 Fax: 813-974-9689
Website: www.usf.edu
E-mail: admissions@admin.usf.edu

GEORGIA

Kennesaw State University
1000 Chastain Rd NW, Kennesaw GA 30144-5591
Joseph Meeks, Dean of the School of the Arts
770-423-6742
Website: www.kennesaw.edu

Savannah College of Art and Design

PO Box 2072, Savannah, GA 31402-2072
PO Box 77300, Atlanta, GA 30357
Phone: 800-869-7223 (Savannah) or 877-722-3285 (Atlanta)
E-mail: admission@scad.edu (Savannah) or scadatl@scad.edu (Atlanta)
www.scad.edu
  SCAD is a private, nonprofit institution accredited by the Commission on Colleges of the Southern Association of Colleges and Schools to award bachelor's and master's degrees. The college offers B.F.A., M.Arch., M.A., M.F.A., and M.U.D. degrees. Enrollment is approximately 7,350; 6 percent are international. More than 30 areas of study. Online programs via SCAD e-Learning.

IDAHO

Brigham Young University - Idaho
120 Kimball Bldg, Rexburg ID 83460
Gordon Westenskow, Director of Admissions
208-496-1020 Fax: 208-496-1220
Website: www.byui.edu
E-mail: admissions@byui.edu

University of Idaho
Moscow ID 83844-4253
Lloyd Scott, Director of New Student Services
208-885-6163 Fax: 208-885-4477
Website: www.uidaho.edu
E-mail: nss@uidaho.edu

ILLINOIS

American Academy of Art
332 S Michigan Ave Fl 3, Chicago IL 60604-4302
Stuart Rosenbloom, Director of Admissions
312-461-0600 Fax: 312-294-9570
Website: www.aaart.edu
E-mail: info@aaart.edu

Columbia College Chicago
600 S Michigan Ave, Chicago IL 60605-1996
Murphy Monroe, Executive Director of Admissions
312-344-7130 Fax: 312-344-8024
Website: www.colum.edu
E-mail: admissions@colum.edu

CONCORDIA UNIVERSITY

7400 Augusta St, River Forest IL 60305-1402
708-209-3100 Fax: 708-209-3473
Website: www.curf.edu
E-mail: crfadmis.edu

HARRINGTON COLLEGE OF DESIGN

200 W Madison St, Chicago IL 60606-3433
Wendi Franczyk, VP of Admissions
877-939-4975 Fax: 312-697-8032
Website: www.harringtoncollege.com
E-mail: wfranczyk@interiordesign.edu
See listing under "Universities"

North Central College
30 N Brainard St, Naperville IL 60540-4690
Martha Stolze, Director of Admissions
630-637-5800 Fax: 630-637-5819
Website: www.northcentralcollege.edu
E-mail: admissions@noctrl.edu

South Suburban College of Cook County
15800 State St, South Holland IL 60473
Jane Ellen Stocker, Dean of Enrollment Services
708-596-2000 Fax: 708-225-5806
Website: www.southsuburbancollege.edu
E-mail: jstocker@southsuburbancollege.edu

INDIANA

Ancilla Domini College
Donaldson IN 46513
Erin Wittmeyer, Director of Admissions
574-936-8898 Fax: 574-935-1773
Website: www.ancilla.edu
E-mail: erin.wittmeyer@ancilla.edu

Hanover College
PO Box 108, Hanover IN 47243-0108
William D. Preble, Dean of Admission
800-213-2178 Fax: 812-866-7098
Website: www.hanover.edu
E-mail: admissions@hanover.edu

International Business College
5699 Coventry Ln, Fort Wayne IN 46804
260-459-4500 Fax: 260-436-1896
Website: www.ibcfortwayne.edu
E-mail: skinzer@ibcfortwayne.edu

Ivy Tech Community College - North Central
220 Dean Johnson Blvd, South Bend IN 46601-3415
Pam Decker, Director of Admissions
574-289-7001 Fax: 574-236-7177
Website: www.ivytech.edu
E-mail: pdecker@ivytech.edu

Oakland City University
138 N Lucretia St, Oakland City IN 47660
Brian J. Baker, Director of Admissions
800-737-5125 Fax: 812-749-1433
Website: www.oak.edu
E-mail: bbaker@oak.edu
See listing under "Universities"

St. Mary-of-the-Woods College
Saint Mary of the Woods IN 47876-1001
James P. Malley, Jr., Director of Admission
800-926-7692 Fax: 812-535-5010
Website: www.smwc.edu
E-mail: smwcadms@smwc.edu

University of Evansville
1800 Lincoln Ave, Evansville IN 47722-0001
Thomas E. Bear, V.P. of Enrollment Services
800-423-8633 Fax: 812-488-4076
Website: www.evansville.edu
E-mail: admission@evansville.edu

IOWA

Briar Cliff University
PO Box 2100, Sioux City IA 51104-0100
Sharisue Wilcoxon, VP for Enrollment Management
712-279-5200 Fax: 712-279-1632
Website: www.briarcliff.edu
E-mail: admissions@briarcliff.edu

Clarke College
1550 Clarke Dr, Dubuque IA 52001-3198
Andy Schroeder, Director of Admissions
800-383-2345 Fax: 563-584-8666
Website: www.clarke.edu
E-mail: andy.schroeder@clarke.edu

Graceland University
1 University Place, Lamoni IA 50140
Brian Shantz, Vice President for Enrollment and Dean of Admissions
641-784-5196 Fax: 641-784-5480
Website: www.admissions.graceland.edu
E-mail: admissions@graceland.edu

Iowa Lakes Community College
300 S 18th St, Estherville IA 51334-2721
Anne Stansbury, Asst. Director of Admissions
712-362-7945 Fax: 712-362-8363
Website: www.iowalakes.edu
E-mail: info@iowalakes.edu

Mount Mercy College
1330 Elmhurst Dr NE, Cedar Rapids IA 52402-4797
Jim Krystofiak, Dean of Admission
800-248-4504 Fax: 319-363-5270
Website: www.mtmercy.edu
E-mail: admission@mtmercy.edu

KANSAS

Flint Hills Technical College
3301 W 18th Ave, Emporia KS 66801-5957
Lisa Kirmer, Dean of Student Services
620-343-4600 Fax: 620-343-4610
Website: www.fhtc.net
E-mail: lkirmer@fhtc.net

Newman University
3100 W McCormick St, Wichita KS 67213
Jann Reusser, Admissions Recruitment Coordinator
316-942-4291 ext. 2144 Fax: 316-942-4483
Website: www.newmanu.edu
E-mail: reusserj@newmanu.edu

KENTUCKY

Morehead State University
Morehead KY 40351-1689
Dayna Seelig, Enrollment Services
800-585-6781 Fax: 606-783-5038
Website: www.moreheadstate.edu
E-mail: admissions@moreheadstate.edu

Spencerian College
1575 Winchester Rd, Lexington KY 40505
Victor Lamoin Adcock II, Director of Admissions
800-456-3253

LOUISIANA

Dillard University
2601 Gentilly Blvd, New Orleans LA 70122-3097
Linda G. Nash, Director of Admissions
Website: www.dillard.edu
E-mail: admissions@dillard.edu

MAINE

HEARTWOOD COLLEGE OF ART

123 York St, Kennebunk ME 04043
Berri Kramer, President
207-985-0985 Fax: 207-985-6333
Website: www.heartwoodcollegeofart.org
E-mail: hca@heartwoodcollegeofart.org
  Established 1992. Private. Coed. Tuition: $9,750. Enrollment: 30 full-time, 20 part-time. Faculty: 20. Student-faculty ratio: 6:1. Small art college on the coast of Maine, offering an Associate and a Bachelor's degree in Fine Arts; Design and Crafts; and Photography. Studio facilities include ceramics, jewelry, photography, painting & drawing, printmaking, book arts, lampworking, and weaving. Inspirational faculty, studios, and location.

MARYLAND

Cecil Community College
One Seahawk Dr, North East MD 21901
Sandra S. Rajaski, Registrar & Director of Admissions
410-287-1000 Fax: 410-287-1001
Website: www.cecilcc.edu
E-mail: srajaski@cecilcc.edu

Hagerstown Community College
11400 Robinwood Dr, Hagerstown MD 21742-6590
Dr. Daniel E. Bock, Assistant Director of Admissions
301-790-2800 Fax: 301-791-9165
Website: www.hagerstowncc.edu
E-mail: bockd@hagerstowncc.edu

MASSACHUSETTS

Anna Maria College
50 Sunset Ln, Paxton MA 01612
Julie A. Mitchell, Director of Admissions
508-849-3360 Fax: 508-849-3362
Website: www.annamaria.edu
E-mail: admissions@annamaria.edu

The Art Institute of Boston at Lesley University
700 Beacon St, Boston MA 02215-2598
Office of Admissions
617-585-6710 Fax: 617-585-6720
Website: www.aiboston.edu
E-mail: admissions@aiboston.edu

Assumption College
500 Salisbury St, Worcester MA 01609-1294
Kathleen Murphy, Dean of Enrollment
508-767-7000 Fax: 508-799-4412
Website: www.assumption.edu
E-mail: admiss@assumption.edu

Boston University
121 Bay State Rd, Boston MA 02215
Kelly Walter, Executive Director of Admissions
617-353-2300 Fax: 617-353-9695
Website: web.bu.edu
E-mail: admissions@bu.edu

Bristol Community College
777 Elsbree St, Fall River MA 02720-7395
Rodney S. Clark, Director of Admissions
508-678-2811 ext. 2516, 2179 Fax: 508-730-3265
Website: www.bristol.mass.edu
E-mail: admissions@bristol.mass.edu

Montserrat College of Art
PO Box 26, 23 Essex St, Beverly MA 01915-0026
Jessica Sarin-Perry, Dean of Admissions and Enrollment Management
800-836-0487 ext 1153 Fax: 978-921-4241
Website: www.montserrat.edu
E-mail: admiss@montserrat.edu

School of the Museum of Fine Arts, Boston
230 The Fenway, Boston MA 02115-5534
Office of Admissions
617-369-3626 or 800-643-6078 Fax: 617-369-4264
Website: www.smfa.edu
E-mail: admissions@smfa.edu
See listing under "Universities"

Smith College
Northampton MA 01063-0001
Debra Shaver, Director of Admissions
800-383-3232 Fax: 413-585-2527
Website: www.smith.edu
E-mail: admission@smith.edu

University of Massachusetts Dartmouth
Old Westport Rd, North Dartmouth MA 02747-2300
Steven T. Briggs, Director of Admissions
508-999-8605 Fax: 508-999-8755
Website: explore.umassd.edu
E-mail: sbriggs@umassd.edu

Westfield State College
PO Box 1630, Westfield MA 01086
Michelle Mattie, Associate Dean, Admission and
Enrollment Services
413-572-5300
Website: www.wsc.ma.edu
E-mail: admission@wsc.ma.edu

MICHIGAN

Alma College
614 W Superior St, Alma MI 48801-1599
Anne Monroe, Director of Admissions
800-321-ALMA Fax: 989-463-7057
Website: www.alma.edu
E-mail: admissions@alma.edu

Andrews University
Berrien Springs MI 49104-0001
Randall Graves, Director of Recruitment Services
800-253-2874 Fax: 269-471-2670
Website: www.connect.andrews.edu
E-mail: gravesr@andrews.edu

College for Creative Studies
201 E Kirby St, Detroit MI 48202-4048
Julie Hingelberg, Dean of Enrollment Services
313-664-7425
Website: www.ccscad.edu

Concordia University
4090 Geddes Rd, Ann Arbor MI 48105-2797
Gary Neumann, Director of Admissions
734-995-7300 Fax: 734-995-4610
Website: www.cuaa.edu
E-mail: admissions@cuaa.edu

CRANBROOK ACADEMY OF ART
PO Box 801, Bloomfield Hills MI 48303-0801
Katharine Willman, Dean of Admissions
248-645-3300 Fax: 248-646-0046
Website: www.cranbrookart.edu
E-mail: caaadmissions@cranbrook.edu
Graduate Only, Visual Arts and Architecture

Delta College
University Center MI 48710-0001
Duff Zube, Director of Admissions
989-686-9093 Fax: 989-667-2202
Website: www.delta.edu
E-mail: admit@delta.edu

Grand Valley State University
1 Campus Dr, Allendale MI 49401-9403
Jodi Chycinski, Director of Admissions
616-331-6611 Fax: 616-331-2000
Website: www.gvsu.edu
E-mail: go2gvsu@gvsu.edu

HILLSDALE COLLEGE
33 E College St, Hillsdale MI 49242-1298
Professor Sam Knecht, Director
517-607-2269 Fax: 517-607-2657
Website: www.hillsdale.edu
E-mail: sam.knecht@hillsdale.edu

Interlochen Arts Academy
PO Box 199, Interlochen MI 49643-0199
231-276-7472
Website: www.interlochen.org
E-mail: admissions@interlochen.org

Kendall College of Art & Design
17 Fountain St NW, Grand Rapids MI 49503-3002
Dr. Oliver H. Evans, President
800-676-2787 or 616-451-2787 Fax: 616-831-9689
Website: www.kcad.edu
E-mail: brittons@ferris.edu

Lawrence Technological University
21000 W 10 Mile Rd, Southfield MI 48075-1058
Jane Rohrback, Director of Admissions
800-225-5588 Fax: 248-204-2228
Website: www.ltu.edu
E-mail: admissions@ltu.edu
See listing under "Universities"

MACOMB COMMUNITY COLLEGE
44575 Garfield Rd, Clinton Township MI 48038-1139
Information Center
586-445-7999
Website: www.macomb.edu
E-mail: answer@macomb.edu

MACOMB COMMUNITY COLLEGE
14500 E 12 Mile Rd, Warren MI 48088-3896
Information Center
586-445-7999
Website: www.macomb.edu
E-mail: answer@macomb.edu

MINNESOTA

ACADEMY COLLEGE
1101 E 78th St, Bloomington MN 55420-1402
952-851-0066 Fax: 952-851-0094
Website: www.academycollege.edu
E-mail: info@academycollege.edu
See listing under "Career Schools"

Bethany Lutheran College
700 Luther Dr, Mankato MN 56001
Don Westphal, Dean of Admissions
507-344-7000 Fax: 507-344-7376
Website: www.blc.edu
E-mail: admiss@blc.edu

Carleton College
1 N College St, Northfield MN 55057-4044
800-995-2275 or 507-646-4190 Fax: 507-646-4526
Website: www.carleton.edu
E-mail: admissions@acs.carleton.edu

Minneapolis College of Art & Design
2501 Stevens Ave, Minneapolis MN 55404-4347
Admissions Office
800-874-6223 or 612-874-3760 Fax: 612-874-3701
Website: www.mcad.edu
E-mail: admissions@mcad.edu

Pillsbury Baptist Bible College
315 S Grove Ave, Owatonna MN 55060-3097
Stephen R. Seidler, Director of Admissions
507-451-2710 Fax: 507-451-0156
Website: www.pillsbury.edu
E-mail: steveseidler@pillsbury.edu

MISSISSIPPI

Tougaloo College
500 W County Line Rd, Tougaloo MS 39174-9799
Juno Leggette Jacobs, Director of Admissions
601-977-7768 Fax: 601-977-4501
Website: www.tougaloo.edu
E-mail: jjacobs@tougaloo.edu

MISSOURI

Columbia College
1001 Rogers St, Columbia MO 65216-0001
Regina Morin, Director of Admissions
573-875-7352 Fax: 573-875-7506
Website: www.ccis.edu
E-mail: admissions@ccis.edu

Hickey College
940 Westport Plz, Saint Louis MO 63146-3127
Christopher A. Gearin, President
800-777-1544 or 314-434-2212 Fax: 314-434-1974
Website: www.hickeycollege.edu
E-mail: admin@hickeycollege.edu

St. Charles Community College
4601 Mid Rivers Mall Dr, Saint Peters MO 63376
Kathy Brockgreitens-Gober, Director of Admissions
636-922-8000 Fax: 636-922-8236
Website: www.stchas.edu
E-mail: adm-reg@stchas.edu

Truman State University
100 E Normal, Kirksville MO 63501
Office of Admission
660-785-4000 Fax: 660-785-4181
Website: admissions.truman.edu
E-mail: admissions@truman.edu

University of Missouri
1 University Blvd, Saint Louis MO 63121-4499
Dr. Mark Burkholder, Dean-College of Arts & Sciences
314-516-5501 Fax: 314-516-5415
Website: www.umsl.edu
E-mail: admissions@umsl.edu

Webster University
470 E Lockwood Ave, Saint Louis MO 63119-3194
Peter Sargent, Dean, College of Fine Arts
314-968-7006 Fax: 314-968-7139
Website: www.webster.edu
E-mail: langtk@webster.edu
See listing under "Universities"

William Woods University
1 University Ave, Fulton MO 65251-1098
Jimmy Clay, Director of Admissions
573-642-2251 Fax: 573-592-1146
Website: www.williamwoods.edu
E-mail: admissions@williamwoods.edu
See listing under "Universities"

MONTANA

Rocky Mountain College
1511 Poly Dr, Billings MT 59102-1796
Bonnie Knapp, Director of Admissions
800-877-6259 Fax: 406-657-1189
Website: www.rocky.edu
E-mail: admissions@rocky.edu

NEBRASKA

Peru State College
PO Box 10, Peru NE 68421-0010
Office of Admissions
800-742-4412 Fax: 402-872-2296
Website: www.peru.edu
E-mail: admissions@oakmail.peru.edu

University of Nebraska at Kearney
905 W 25th St, Kearney NE 68849-0001
Dusty Newton, Director of Admissions
800-KEARNEY Fax: 308-865-8987
Website: www.unk.edu
E-mail: admissionsug@unk.edu

NEW JERSEY

Bergen Community College
400 Paramus Rd, Paramus NJ 07652
Julian Gomez, Asst. Director of Admissions
201-447-7100 Fax: 201-444-7036
Website: www.bergen.edu
E-mail: jgomez@bergen.edu

New Jersey City University
2039 John F Kennedy Blvd
Jersey City NJ 07305-1588
Carmen Panlilio, Asst. V.P. for Admissions and
Financial Aid
201-200-3234 Fax: 201-200-2044
Website: www.njcu.edu
E-mail: admissions@njcu.edu

Ramapo College of New Jersey
505 Ramapo Valley Rd, Mahwah NJ 07430-1623
Director of Admissions
201-684-7300 or 201-684-7301 Fax: 201-684-7964
Website: www.ramapo.edu
E-mail: admissions@ramapo.edu

NEW MEXICO

Institute of American Indian Arts
83 A Van Nu Po, Santa Fe NM 87508-1300
Myra Garro, Manager of Enrollment & Admissions
505-424-2328 Fax: 505-424-4500
Website: www.iaia.edu
E-mail: recruitment@iaia.edu

NEW YORK

College of Saint Rose
432 Western Ave, Albany NY 12203-1419
Maryelizabeth Amico, Asst V.P. for Undergraduate
Admissions
518-454-5150 Fax: 518-454-2013
Website: www.strose.edu
E-mail: admit@strose.edu

CUNY Hunter College
695 Park Ave, New York NY 10021
Aaron Gibbs, Assistant Director of Recruitment
212-772-4497 Fax: 212-650-3336
Website: www.hunter.cuny.edu
E-mail: aaron.gibbs@hunter.cuny.edu

Daemen College
4380 Main St, Amherst NY 14226-3592
Donna Shaffner, Director of Admissions
800-462-7652 or 716-839-8225 Fax: 716-839-8229
Website: www.daemen.edu
E-mail: admissions@daemen.edu
See listing under "Universities"

Long Island University-C. W. Post Campus
720 Northern Blvd, Brookville NY 11548-1300
Joanne Graziano, Executive Director of Admissions
516-299-2900 Fax: 516-299-2137
Website: www.liu.edu/cwpost
E-mail: enroll@cwpost.liu.edu

Molloy College
1000 Hempstead Ave
Rockville Centre NY 11570-1100
Marguerite Lane, Director of Admissions
516-678-5000 ext. 6291 Fax: 516-256-2247
Website: www.molloy.edu
E-mail: admissions@molloy.edu
See listing under "Universities"

MUNSON-WILLIAMS-PROCTOR INSTITUTE
310 Genesee St, Utica NY 13502-4799
Robert E. Baber, Dean
315-797-8260 Fax: 315-797-9349
Website: www.mwpai.edu
E-mail: rbaber@mwpai.edu

NEW YORK SCHOOL OF INTERIOR DESIGN
170 E 70th St, New York NY 10021-5110
David Sprouls, Director of Admissions
800-33-NYSID or 212-472-1500 Fax: 212-472-1867
Website: www.nysid.edu
E-mail: admissions@nysid.edu
Established 1916. Private. Coed. College devoted to
Interior Design education. Tuition: $20,460 per year.
Fees: $110. Enrollment: 750. Faculty: 95. Accreditation:
NASAD, FIDER. Four programs offered: Master of Fine
Arts, 4-year Bachelor degree, 2-year Associate degree,
1-year non-degree Basic Interior Design. Located in
Manhattan's historic Upper East Side near center of inte-
rior design industry. Faculty consists of Designers, Archi-
tects and Artists.

Pratt Institute
200 Willoughby Ave, Brooklyn NY 11205-3899
Heidi Metcalf, Director of Admissions
718-636-3600 Fax: 718-636-3670
Website: www.pratt.edu
E-mail: hmetcalf@pratt.edu

PURCHASE COLLEGE STATE UNIVERSITY OF
NEW YORK (SUNY)
735 Anderson Hill Rd, Purchase NY 10577-1400
Betsy Immergut, Director of Admissions
914-251-6300 Fax: 914-251-6314
Website: www.purchase.edu
See listing under "Universities"

Roberts Wesleyan College
2301 Westside Dr, Rochester NY 14624-1997
Office of Admissions
585-594-6400 Fax: 585-594-6371
Website: www.roberts.edu
E-mail: admissions@roberts.edu

SOTHEBY'S INSTITUTE OF ART
1334 York Ave, New York NY 10021-4806
212-894-1111 Fax: 212-894-1112
Website: www.sothebys.com
E-mail: americanartscourse@sothebys.com

SUNY College at Brockport
350 New Campus Dr, Brockport NY 14420-2997
Bernard S. Valento, Director of Undergraduate
Admissions
585-395-2751 Fax: 585-395-5452
Website: www.brockport.edu
E-mail: admit@brockport.edu

SUNY Orange County Community College
115 South St, Middletown NY 10940-6437
Margot St. Lawrence, Director of Admissions
845-341-4030 Fax: 845-342-8662
Website: www.sunyorange.edu
E-mail: apply@sunyorange.edu
See listing under "Community and Junior Colleges"

NORTH CAROLINA

Haywood Community College
185 Freedlander Dr, Clyde NC 28721
Debbie Rowland, Coordinator of Admissions
828-627-4500 Fax: 828-627-4513
Website: www.haywood.edu
E-mail: drowland@haywood.edu

Louisburg College
501 N Main St, Louisburg NC 27549-2399
800-775-0208 or 919-496-2521 Fax: 919-496-1788
Website: www.louisburg.edu
E-mail: admissions@louisburg.edu

Meredith College
3800 Hillsborough St, Raleigh NC 27607-5298
Heidi L. Fletcher, Director of Admissions
919-760-8581 Fax: 919-760-2348
Website: www.meredith.edu
E-mail: admissions@meredith.edu
See listing under "Women's Colleges"

Mt. Olive College
634 Henderson St, Mount Olive NC 28365
Tim Woodard, Director of Admissions
919-658-2502 Fax: 919-658-9816
Website: www.moc.edu
E-mail: admissions@moc.edu
See listing under "Universities"

Salem College
Winston Salem NC 27108
Dana Evans, Dean of Admissions/Fin. Aid
800-32-SALEM Fax: 336-917-5572
Website: www.salem.edu
E-mail: admissions@salem.edu
See listing under "Women's Colleges"

SCHOOL OF COMMUNICATION ARTS
3000 Wakefield Crossing Dr, Raleigh NC 27614-7076
Debra Ann Hooper, Director and VP
919-981-0972 Fax: 919-981-0946
Website: www.higherdigital.com
E-mail: school@higherdigital.com

NORTH DAKOTA

Dickinson State University
Dickinson ND 58601-4896
Steve Glasser, Director of Student Recruitment
800-279-4295 Fax: 701-483-2409
Website: www.dickinsonstate.edu
E-mail: dsu.hawks@dickinsonstate.edu

OHIO

ART ACADEMY OF CINCINNATI
1212 Jackson St, Cincinnati OH 45202
Gregory Allgire Smith, President
Mary Jane Zumwalde, Director of Admissions
513-562-6262 Fax: 513-562-8778
Website: www.artacademy.edu
E-mail: admissions@artacademy.edu
Established 1887. Private. Coed. Accreditation: NCACS, NASAD. Tuition: $19,250. Student Activities Fee: $350. Enrollment: 200. Faculty: 18. Student-Faculty ratio: 12-1. Degrees: BFA in Fine Arts, Communications Arts, Art History. AS in Graphic Design. MA in Art Education (summer program). Financial Aid and Scholarships available.

THE ART INSTITUTE OF CINCINNATI
1171 E Kemper Rd, Cincinnati OH 45246
Cyndi Mendell, Director of Admissions
513-751-1206 Fax: 513-751-1209
Website: www.theartinstituteofcincinnati.com
E-mail: aic@theartinstituteofcincinnati.com
Established 1976. Two year design college. Small classes, individual instruction. Faculty: 7 (professional designers). Limited enrollment of 75. Accreditation: ACCSCT. First year, art foundation; Second year, integrates illustration, design with computers - a computer on each table. Associate degree offered.

Cleveland State University
2121 Euclid Ave RW 204, Cleveland OH 44115
Dr. Richard Arndt, Dean of Undergraduate Recruitment and College Partnerships
888-CSU-OHIO Fax: 216-687-9210
Website: www.csuohio.edu
E-mail: admissions@csuohio.edu

Columbus College of Art & Design
107 N 9th St, Columbus OH 43215-1700
877-997-CCAD or 614-222-3261 Fax: 614-232-8344
Website: www.ccad.edu
E-mail: admissions@ccad.edu

Davis College
4747 Monroe St, Toledo OH 43623-4389
Dana Stern, Admissions Director
419-473-2700 Fax: 419-473-2472
Website: www.daviscollege.edu
E-mail: learn@daviscollege.edu

Mount Vernon Nazarene University
800 Martinsburg Rd, Mount Vernon OH 43050-9509
Timothy Eades, Director of Admissions
866-462-6868 Fax: 740-393-0511
Website: www.gotomvnu.edu
E-mail: admissions@mvnu.edu
See listing under "Universities"

The Ohio State University
Department of Art
Hopkins Hall, 128 N Oval Mall, Columbus OH 43210
Sergio Soave, Department Chair
614-292-5072 Fax: 614-292-1674
Website: art.osu.edu
E-mail: soave.1@osu.edu

Owens Community College
300 Davis St, Findlay OH 45840-3631
William J. Ivoska PhD., Vice President of Student Services
567-429-3500 Fax: 567-423-0246
Website: www.owens.edu
E-mail: admissions@owens.edu

Owens Community College
PO Box 10000, Toledo OH 43699-1947
William J. Ivoska, Ph.D, Vice President of Student Services
567-661-7000 Fax: 567-661-7607
Website: www.owens.edu
E-mail: admissions@owens.edu

THE SCHOOL OF ADVERTISING ART
1725 E David Rd, Kettering OH 45440-1612
Jayne Fahncke, Director of Admissions
877-300-9326 Fax: 937-294-5869
Website: www.saacollege.com
E-mail: jayne@saacollege.com

University of Dayton
300 College Park, Dayton OH 45469-1300
Robert F. Durkle, Director of Admissions
800-837-7433 Fax: 937-229-4729
Website: admission.udayton.edu
E-mail: admission@udayton.edu

Ursuline College
2550 Lander Rd, Cleveland OH 44124-4398
Sarah E. Sundermeier, Director of Admissions
888-URSULINE Toll Free Fax: 440-684-6138
Website: www.admission.ursuline.edu
E-mail: admission@ursuline.edu

OKLAHOMA

Oklahoma State University
Stillwater OK 74078
Nicholas Bormann, Department Head
405-744-6016
Website: www.okstate.edu
E-mail: nborman@okstate.edu

Oral Roberts University
7777 S Lewis Ave, Tulsa OK 74171-0001
Chris Belcher, Director of Undergraduate Admissions
800-678-8876 Fax: 918-495-6222
Website: www.oru.edu
E-mail: admissions@oru.edu

OREGON

Marylhurst University
17600 Pacific Hwy (Hwy 43)
Marylhurst OR 97036-0261
Director of Admissions
800-634-9982 ext. 6268 Fax: 503-635-6585
Website: www.marylhurst.edu
E-mail: studentinfo@marylhurst.edu

OREGON COLLEGE OF ART & CRAFT
8245 SW Barnes Rd, Portland OR 97225-6399
Barry Beach, Director of Admissions
503-297-5544 or 800-390-0632 Fax: 503-297-9651
Website: www.ocac.edu
E-mail: admissions@ocac.edu

Western Oregon University
345 Monmouth Ave N, Monmouth OR 97361-1314
David McDonald, Dean, Admission, Retention & Enrollment Management
877-877-1593 Fax: 503-838-8067
Website: www.wou.edu
E-mail: wolfgram@fsa.wou.edu

PENNSYLVANIA

Antonelli Institute - Art & Photography
300 Montgomery Ave, Erdenheim PA 19038-8242
Dr. Thomas Treacy, President
215-836-2222 or 800-722-7871 Fax: 215-836-2794
Website: www.antonelli.edu
E-mail: admissions@antonelli.edu

Arcadia University
450 S Easton Rd, Glenside PA 19038-3295
Dennis Nostrand, VP for Enrollment Management
877-ARCADIA (877-272-2342) Fax: 215-881-8767
Website: www.arcadia.edu
E-mail: admiss@arcadia.edu
See listing under "Universities"

Art Institute of Philadelphia
1622 Chestnut St, Philadelphia PA 19103-5119
Larry McHugh, Director of Admissions
800-275-2474 Fax: 215-405-6399
Website: www.aiph.aii.edu
E-mail: aiphinfo@aii.edu

ART INSTITUTE OF PITTSBURGH
420 Boulevard Of The Allies, Pittsburgh PA 15219
Newton I. Myvett, VP/Director of Admissions
800-275-2470 Fax: 412-263-6667
Website: www.aip.aii.edu
E-mail: pahughes@aii.edu
See listing under "Universities"

Douglas Education Center
130 7th St, Monessen PA 15062-1097
Sherry Lee Walters, Director of Enrollment Services
800-413-6013 Fax: 724-684-7463
Website: www.douglas-school.com
E-mail: swalters@douglas-school.com

DUBOIS BUSINESS COLLEGE
1 Beaver Dr, Du Bois PA 15801-2490
Lisa J. Doty, Director of Admissions
814-371-6920 Fax: 814-371-3974
Website: www.dbcollege.com
E-mail: dotylj@dbcollege.com

DUBOIS BUSINESS COLLEGE
1001 Moore St, Huntingdon PA 16652-1846
Lisa J. Doty, Director of Admissions
814-641-0440 Fax: 814-641-0205
Website: www.dbcollege.com
E-mail: dotylj@dbcollege.com

DUBOIS BUSINESS COLLEGE
701 E 3rd St, Oil City PA 16301-2407
Lisa J. Doty, Director of Admissions
814-677-1322 Fax: 814-677-8237
Website: www.dbcollege.com
E-mail: dotylj@dbcollege.com

Holy Family University
9801 Frankford Avenue, Philadelphia PA 19114
Lauren Campbell, Director of Admissions
215-637-3050 Fax: 215-281-1022
Website: www.holyfamily.edu
E-mail: admissions@holyfamily.edu

HUSSIAN SCHOOL OF ART
1118 Market St, Philadelphia PA 19107-3679
Lynne Wartman, Director of Admissions
215-981-0900 Fax: 215-864-9115
Website: www.hussianart.edu
E-mail: info@hussianart.edu

Juniata College
1700 Moore St, Huntingdon PA 16652-2196
Michelle Bartol, Dean of Enrollment
877-JUNIATA Fax: 814-641-3100
Website: www.juniata.edu
E-mail: admissions@juniata.edu

La Roche College
9000 Babcock Blvd, Pittsburgh PA 15237-5898
Thomas Hassett, Director of Freshman and International Admissions
412-536-1272 or 800-838-4LRC Fax: 412-536-1272
Website: www.laroche.edu
E-mail: admissions@laroche.edu

Lebanon Valley College
101 N College Ave, Annville PA 17003-1400
William Brown, Dean of Admissions & Financial Aid
866-LVC-4ADM or 717-867-6181 Fax: 717-867-6026
Website: www.lvc.edu
E-mail: admission@lvc.edu

Lehigh Valley College
2809 E Saucon Valley Rd
Center Valley PA 18034-8447
Joshua Padron, Vice President of Marketing and Admissions
800-227-9109 Fax: 610-791-7810
Website: www.lehighvalley.edu
E-mail: joshua.padron@lehighvalley.edu

Pennsylvania College of Art and Design
PO Box 59, Lancaster PA 17608-0059
Susan Matson, Director of Enrollment Management
717-396-7833 Fax: 717-396-1339
Website: www.pcad.edu
E-mail: admissions@pcad.edu

University of the Arts
320 S Broad St, Philadelphia PA 19102-4994
Susan Gandy, Director of Admissions
800-616-2787 Fax: 215-717-6045
Website: www.uarts.edu
E-mail: admissions@uarts.edu

Washington & Jefferson College
60 S Lincoln St, Washington PA 15301-4801
Alton E. Newell, Vice President for Enrollment
724-223-6025 Fax: 724-223-6534
Website: www.washjeff.edu
E-mail: admission@washjeff.edu

SOUTH CAROLINA

Erskine College & Seminary
PO Box 176, Due West SC 29639
Bart Walker, Director of Admissions
864-379-8838 Fax: 864-379-3048
Website: www.erskine.edu
E-mail: admissions@erskine.edu

North Greenville University
PO Box 1892, Tigerville SC 29688-1892
Jim Craft, Art Department
Website: www.ngc.edu
See listing under "Universities"

PRESBYTERIAN COLLEGE
503 S Broad St, Clinton SC 29325
Richard Dana Paul, Dean of Admissions
800-476-7272 Fax: 864-833-8481
Website: www.presby.edu
E-mail: admissions@presby.edu

TENNESSEE

Lipscomb University
3901 Granny White Pike, Nashville TN 37204-3951
Ricky Holaway, Director of Admissions
800-333-4358 ext. 1776 Fax: 615-269-1804
Website: www.lipscomb.edu
E-mail: admissions@lipscomb.edu

NOSSI COLLEGE OF ART
907 Rivergate Pkwy Ste E6, Goodlettsville TN 37072
Cyrus Vatandoost, Executive Director
615-851-1088 Fax: 615-851-1087
Website: www.nossi.com
E-mail: cyrus@nossi.com

O'More College of Design
    423 S Margin St, Franklin TN 37064-2816
    Dr. K. Mark Hilliard, President
    Chris Lee, Director of Enrollment Management
    615-794-4254 Fax: 615-790-1662
    Website: www.omorecollege.edu
    E-mail: clee@omorecollege.edu

Tennessee State University
    3500 John A Merritt Blvd, Nashville TN 37209-1561
    John Cade, Dean of Admissions & Records
    615-963-5101 Fax: 615-963-2930
    Website: www.tnstate.edu
    E-mail: jcade@tnstate.edu

University of Tennessee
    615 McCallie Ave, Chattanooga TN 37403-2504
    Yancy Freeman, Director of Admissions
    423-425-4111 Fax: 423-425-4157
    Website: www.utc.edu
    E-mail: Yancy-Freeman@utc.edu

TEXAS

Angelo State University
    ASU Station 11014, San Angelo TX 76909
    Bonnie Stennett, Coordinator of Recruiting
    800-946-8627 Fax: 325-942-2078
    Website: www.angelo.edu
    E-mail: admissions@angelo.edu

ART INSTITUTE OF HOUSTON
    1900 Yorktown St, Houston TX 77056
    Brian A. Shumaker, Director of Admissions
    800-275-4244 Fax: 713-966-2797
    Website: www.aih.artinstitutes.edu

North Central Texas College
    1525 W California St, Gainesville TX 76240-4636
    Michelle Winters, Registrar
    940-668-3315 Fax: 940-665-7075
    Website: www.nctc.edu
    E-mail: mwinters@nctc.edu

Remington College - Fort Worth Campus
    300 E Loop 820, Fort Worth TX 76112-1280
    Director of Recruitment
    817-451-0017 Fax: 817-496-1257
    Website: www.remingtoncollege.edu
    E-mail: lynn.wey@remingtoncollege.edu

Texas Woman's University
    PO Box 425589, Denton TX 76204-5589
    Erma Nieto, Director of Admissions
    866-809-6130 Fax: 940-898-3081
    Website: www.twu.edu
    E-mail: admissions@twu.edu

University of Houston
    122 E Cullen Bldg, Houston TX 77204-2023
    Office of Admission
    713-743-9595
    Website: www.uh.edu
    E-mail: admissions@uh.edu

University of Texas at Arlington
    Box 19111, Arlington TX 76019-0111
    Hans Gatterdam, Director of Admission
    817-272-6287 Fax: 817-272-3435
    Website: www.uta.edu
    E-mail: admissions@uta.edu

VERMONT

Bennington College
    One College Drive, Bennington VT 05201
    Ken Himmelman, Dean of Admissions & Financial Aid
    800-833-6845 Fax: 802-440-4320
    Website: www.bennington.edu
    E-mail: admissions@bennington.edu

VIRGINIA

Mary Baldwin College
    Staunton VA 24401
    Lisa A. Branson, Executive Director of Admissions and Financial Aid
    800-468-2262 Fax: 540-887-7292
    Website: www.mbc.edu
    E-mail: admit@mbc.edu

Radford University
    PO Box 6903, Radford VA 24142
    David W. Kraus, Director of Admissions
    800-890-4265 Fax: 540-831-5038
    Website: www.radford.edu
    E-mail: ruadmiss@radford.edu

Randolph-Macon Woman's College
    2500 Rivermont Ave, Lynchburg VA 24503
    Patricia LeDonne, Director of Admissions
    434-947-8100 Fax: 434-947-8996
    Website: www.rmwc.edu
    E-mail: admissions@rmwc.edu

WASHINGTON

Cornish College of the Arts
    1000 Lenora St, Seattle WA 98121
    Eric Pedersen, Director of Admission
    800-726-ARTS (2787) Fax: 206-720-1011
    Website: www.cornish.edu
    E-mail: admissions@cornish.edu

Gonzaga University
    502 E Boone Ave, Spokane WA 99258-0102
    Julie McCulloh, Dean of Admission
    800-322-2584 or 509-323-6572 Fax: 509-323-5780
    Website: www.gonzaga.edu
    E-mail: mcculloh@gu.gonzaga.edu

Henry Cogswell College
    3002 Colby Ave, Everett WA 98201-4012
    Jane Buckman, Director of Admissions
    866-411-4221 Fax: 425-257-0405
    Website: www.henrycogswell.edu
    E-mail: admissions@henrycogswell.edu

WEST VIRGINIA

Concord University
    Athens WV 24712
    Michael Curry, Vice President of Financial Aid & Admissions
    888-384-5249 Fax: 304-384-3218
    Website: www.concord.edu
    E-mail: admissions@concord.edu

Davis & Elkins College
    100 Campus Dr, Elkins WV 26241-3996
    Renee Heckel, Director of Enrollment Management
    800-624-3157 Fax: 304-637-1800
    Website: www.davisandelkins.edu
    E-mail: admiss@davisandelkins.edu

Fairmont State University
    1201 Locust Ave, Fairmont WV 26554-2470
    Steve Leadman, Director of Admissions
    304-367-4892 or 800-641-5678 Fax: 304-367-4789
    Website: www.fairmontstate.edu
    E-mail: admit@fairmontstate.edu

West Virginia Wesleyan College
    59 College Ave, Buckhannon WV 26201-2699
    Robert N. Skinner II, Director of Admission
    800-722-9933 Fax: 304-473-8108
    Website: www.wvwc.edu
    E-mail: admission@wvwc.edu

WISCONSIN

Alverno College
    PO Box 343922, Milwaukee WI 53234-3922
    Mary Kay Farrell, Director of Admissions
    414-382-6100 Fax: 414-382-6354
    Website: www.alverno.edu
    E-mail: admissions@alverno.edu

Herzing College
    5218 E Terrace Dr, Madison WI 53718-8340
    Donald Madelung, President
    800-582-1227 Fax: 608-249-8593
    Website: www.herzing.edu
    E-mail: info@msn.herzing.edu
    See listing under "Universities"

MADISON MEDIA INSTITUTE
    2702 Agriculture Dr, Madison WI 53718-6787
    Chris Hutchings, Director of Admissions
    800-236-4997 or 608-663-2000 Fax: 608-442-0141
    Website: www.madisonmedia.com
    E-mail: mmi@madisonmedia.com

St. Norbert College
    100 Grant St, De Pere WI 54115
    Brian Studebaker, Director of Admission
    800-236-4878 Fax: 920-403-4072
    Website: www.snc.edu
    E-mail: admit@snc.edu

WYOMING

University of Wyoming
    Admissions Office
    Dept 3435, Laramie WY 82071-3435
    Aaron Appelhans, Contact
    800-342-5996 Fax: 307-766-4042
    Website: www.uwyo.edu
    E-mail: why-wyo@uwyo.edu

GUAM

University of Guam
    UOG Station, Mangilao GU 96923
    Deborah Leon Guerrero, Registrar
    671-735-2201 or 671-735-2208 Fax: 671-735-2203
    Website: www.uog.edu
    E-mail: admitme@uog9.uog.edu

PUERTO RICO

Atlantic College
    PO Box 1774, Guaynabo PR 00970-1774
    Zaida Perez, Director of Admissions
    787-720-1022 Fax: 787-720-1092
    Website: www.atlanticcollege-pr.com
    E-mail: atlancol@coqui.net

BIOLOGICAL SCIENCE

ALABAMA

Alabama A & M University
    PO Box 908, Normal AL 35762
    Antonio Boyle, Director of Admissions
    256-372-5245 Fax: 256-372-5249
    Website: www.aamu.edu
    E-mail: aboyle@aamu.edu

CALHOUN COMMUNITY COLLEGE
    PO Box 2216, Decatur AL 35609-2216
    M. Wayne Tosh, Registrar
    256-306-2500 Fax: 256-306-2941
    Website: www.calhoun.edu
    E-mail: psl@calhoun.edu

Faulkner University
    5345 Atlanta Hwy, Montgomery AL 36109-3398
    Keith Mock, Director of Admissions
    800-879-9816 ext. 7200 or 334-386-7200
    Fax: 334-386-7137
    Website: www.faulkner.edu
    E-mail: admissions@faulkner.edu

Judson College
    302 Bibb St, Marion AL 36756
    Michael Scotto, Director of Admissions
    800-447-9472 Fax: 334-683-5147
    Website: www.judson.edu
    E-mail: admissions@judson.edu

University of Alabama in Huntsville
    PO Box 1247, Huntsville AL 35899-0001
    Ann Lee, Assoc. Director for Recruiting Program and Events
    1-800-UAH-CALL Fax: 256-824-6073
    Website: www.uah.edu
    E-mail: leev@uah.edu

University of South Alabama
    307 University Blvd N, Mobile AL 36688-3053
    Melissa Haab, Director of Admissions
    251-460-6141 Fax: 251-460-7876
    Website: www.southalabama.edu
    E-mail: admiss@usouthal.edu

ALASKA

University of Alaska Anchorage
    PO Box 141629, Anchorage AK 99514-1629
    Cecile Mitchell, Director of Enrollment Services
    907-786-1480 Fax: 907-786-4888
    Website: www.uaa.alaska.edu/
    E-mail: enroll@uaa.alaska.edu

University of Alaska Southeast
    11120 Glacier Hwy, Juneau AK 99801-8625
    Paul Kraft, Dean of Students/Enrollment Management
    907-796-6000 Fax: 907-796-6005
    Website: www.uas.alaska.edu
    E-mail: paul.kraft@uas.alaska.edu

ARIZONA

Pima Community College
    4905 E Broadway Blvd, Tucson AZ 85709-1010
    Wendy Kilgore, Ph.D., Director of Admissions
    520-206-4500 Fax: 520-206-4790
    Website: www.pima.edu
    E-mail: infocenter@pima.edu

University of Arizona
    Tucson AZ 85721-0040
    Paul Kohn, Director of Admissions
    520-621-3237 Fax: 520-621-9799
    Website: www.admissions.arizona.edu or www.arizona.edu

ARKANSAS

Ouachita Baptist University
    410 Ouachita St, Arkadelphia AR 71998-0001
    David Goodman, Director of Admissions
    870-245-5110 Fax: 870-245-5500
    Website: www.obu.edu
    E-mail: admissions@obu.edu

CALIFORNIA

California State University-San Bernadino
    5500 University Pkwy
    San Bernardino CA 92407-2393
    Olivia Rosas, Director of Admissions
    909-880-5000 Fax: 909-880-7034
    Website: enrollment.csusb.edu
    E-mail: orosas@csusb.edu

Chapman University
    One University Drive, Orange CA 92866-1099
    Michael Drummy, Assistant Vice President for Enrollment
    Services and Chief Admission Officer
    714-997-6411 or 888-CUAPPLY Fax: 714-997-6713
    Website: www.chapman.edu
    E-mail: admit@chapman.edu

Cleveland Chiropractic College - Los Angeles Campus
    590 N Vermont Ave, Los Angeles CA 90004-2196
    Melissa Denton, Multicampus Director of Admissions
    800-466-CCLA (2252) or 323-906-2031
    Fax: 323-906-2094
    Website: www.cleveland.edu
    E-mail: la.admissions@cleveland.edu

Concordia University
    1530 Concordia, Irvine CA 92612-3203
    Lori McDonald, Executive Director of Enrollment Services
    800-229-1200 or 949-854-8002 Fax: 949-854-6894
    Website: www.cui.edu
    E-mail: admission@cui.edu

FRESNO CITY COLLEGE
1101 E University Ave, Fresno CA 93741-0002
Dayann Dietrich, Contact
559-442-8241 Fax: 559-237-4232
Website: www.fresnocitycollege.com
E-mail: fcc.admissions@scccd.com

Harvey Mudd College
Claremont CA 91711-3104
Peter Osgood, Contact
909-621-8011 Fax: 909-607-7046
Website: www.hmc.edu
E-mail: admission@hmc.edu

Orange Coast College
PO Box 5005, Costa Mesa CA 92628-5005
Kristin Clark, Director of Admissions
714-432-5773 Fax: 714-432-5736
Website: www.orangecoastcollege.edu
E-mail: kclark@cccd.edu

San Diego Christian College
2100 Greenfield Dr, El Cajon CA 92019-1157
Jon Melone, Director of Admissions
800-676-2242 Fax: 619-590-1739
Website: www.sdcc.edu
E-mail: admissions@sdcc.edu

Whittier College
PO Box 634, Whittier CA 90608-0634
Kieron Miller, Director of Admissions
562-907-4200 Fax: 562-907-4870
Website: www.whittier.edu
E-mail: kmiller@whittier.edu

COLORADO

University of Colorado at Denver and Health Sciences
Center
Health Sciences Program
4200 E 9th Ave Box C245, Denver CO 80262
Phoebe Lindsey Barton, Ph.D., Director
Website: www.uchsc.edu

CONNECTICUT

Albertus Magnus College
700 Prospect St, New Haven CT 06511-1189
Richard Lolatte, Dean of Admission
203-773-8501 or 888-578-9160 Fax: 203-773-5248
Website: www.albertus.edu
E-mail: admissions@albertus.edu

University of New Haven
300 Boston Post Rd, West Haven CT 06516
Director of Undergraduate Admissions
203-932-7319 Fax: 203-931-6093
Website: www.newhaven.edu
E-mail: adminfo@newhaven.edu

DELAWARE

Wesley College
120 N State St, Dover DE 19901-3876
302-736-2300 Fax: 302-736-2301
Website: www.wesley.edu

FLORIDA

Florida State University
600 W College Ave, Tallahassee FL 32306-1096
Janice V. Finney, Director of Admissions
850-644-2525 Fax: 850-644-0197
Website: admissions.fsu.edu
E-mail: admissions@admin.fsu.edu

Lynn University
3601 N Military Trl, Boca Raton FL 33431-5598
Brett Ormandy, Director of Admissions
561-237-7900 Fax: 561-237-7100
Website: www.lynn.edu
E-mail: admission@lynn.edu

Nova Southeastern University Health Profession
3200 S University Dr, Davie FL 33328-2018
Marla Frohlinger, Director of Admissions
954-262-1101 Fax: 954-262-2282
Website: www.nova.edu
E-mail: marlaf@nsu.nova.edu

Saint Leo University
PO Box 6665, Saint Leo FL 33574
Deborah Bandy, Director of Admissions
352-588-8200 or 800-334-5532 Fax: 352-588-8257
Website: www.saintleo.edu
E-mail: admission@saintleo.edu

St. Thomas University
16401 NW 37th Ave, Miami Gardens FL 33054
Dr. Edward Ajhar, Contact
800-367-9010 or 305-628-6546 Fax: 305-628-6591
Website: www.stu.edu
E-mail: signup@stu.edu

University of South Florida
4202 E Fowler Ave, Tampa FL 33620-6900
J. Robert Spatig, Director of Admissions
813-974-3350 Fax: 813-974-9689
Website: www.usf.edu
E-mail: admissions@admin.usf.edu

GEORGIA

Armstrong Atlantic State University
11935 Abercorn St, Savannah GA 31419-1997
Kim West, Asst. Dean and Registrar Enrollment
Services
912-927-5277 Fax: 912-921-5462
Website: www.armstrong.edu
E-mail: admissions@mail.armstrong.edu

Kennesaw State University
1000 Chastain Rd NW, Kennesaw GA 30144-5591
Laurence Peterson, Dean of College of Science and
Mathematics
770-423-6160
Website: www.kennesaw.edu

Life University
1269 Barclay Cir SE, Marietta GA 30060-2903
Dr. Deborah E. Heairlston, Director of New Student
Development
770-426-2884 Fax: 770-426-2895
Website: www.life.edu
E-mail: admissions@life.edu

Oglethorpe University
4484 Peachtree Rd NE, Atlanta GA 30319-2797
Kelly Gosnell, Director of Admission
404-261-1441 Fax: 404-364-8491
Website: www.oglethorpe.edu
E-mail: admission@oglethorpe.edu

TOCCOA FALLS COLLEGE
PO Box 800899, Toccoa Falls GA 30598
Christy Meadows, Director of Admissions
888-785-5624 Fax: 706-282-6012
Website: www.tfc.edu
E-mail: admissions@tfc.edu

IDAHO

Brigham Young University - Idaho
120 Kimball Bldg, Rexburg ID 83460
Gordon Westenskow, Director of Admissions
208-496-1020 Fax: 208-496-1220
Website: www.byui.edu
E-mail: admissions@byui.edu

University of Idaho
Moscow ID 83844-4253
Lloyd Scott, Director of New Student Services
208-885-6163 Fax: 208-885-4477
Website: www.uidaho.edu
E-mail: nss@uidaho.edu

ILLINOIS

Aurora University
347 S Gladstone Ave, Aurora IL 60506-4892
Carol R. Dunn, Ed.D., Vice President for Enrollment
800-742-5281 Fax: 630-844-5535
Website: www.aurora.edu
E-mail: admission@aurora.edu

Benedictine University
5700 College Rd, Lisle IL 60532-0900
630-829-6300 or 888-829-6363 Fax: 630-829-6301
Website: www.ben.edu
E-mail: admissions@ben.edu
See listing under "Universities"

CONCORDIA UNIVERSITY
7400 Augusta St, River Forest IL 60305-1402
708-209-3100 Fax: 708-209-3473
Website: www.curf.edu
E-mail: crfadmis.edu

National University of Health Sciences
200 E Roosevelt Rd, Lombard IL 60148-4583
Dr. James Winterstein, President
800-826-6285 Fax: 630-889-6554
Website: www.nuhs.edu
E-mail: admissions@nuhs.edu

North Central College
30 N Brainard St, Naperville IL 60540-4690
Martha Stolze, Director of Admissions
630-637-5800 Fax: 630-637-5819
Website: www.northcentralcollege.edu
E-mail: admissions@noctrl.edu

Roosevelt University
430 S Michigan Ave, Chicago IL 60605
Gwen E. Kanelos, Asst. Vice President for Enrollment
Services
877-APPLY-RU Fax: 312-341-4216
Website: www.roosevelt.edu
E-mail: applyru@roosevelt.edu

INDIANA

Ancilla Domini College
Donaldson IN 46513
Erin Wittmeyer, Director of Admissions
574-936-8898 Fax: 574-935-1773
Website: www.ancilla.edu
E-mail: erin.wittmeyer@ancilla.edu

Franklin College
101 Branigin Blvd, Franklin IN 46131
Jacqueline S. Acosta, Director of Admissions
800-852-0232 Fax: 317-738-8274
Website: www.franklincollege.edu
E-mail: admissions@franklincollege.edu

Hanover College
PO Box 108, Hanover IN 47243-0108
William D. Preble, Dean of Admission
800-213-2178 Fax: 812-866-7098
Website: www.hanover.edu
E-mail: admissions@hanover.edu

Ivy Tech Community College - North Central
220 Dean Johnson Blvd, South Bend IN 46601-3415
Pam Decker, Director of Admissions
574-289-7001 Fax: 574-236-7177
Website: www.ivytech.edu
E-mail: pdecker@ivytech.edu

Oakland City University
138 N Lucretia St, Oakland City IN 47660
Brian J. Baker, Director of Admissions
800-737-5125 Fax: 812-749-1433
Website: www.oak.edu
E-mail: bbaker@oak.edu
See listing under "Universities"

Rose-Hulman Institute of Technology
5500 Wabash Ave, Terre Haute IN 47803-3920
James A. Goecker, Dean of Admissions
812-877-8213 Fax: 812-877-8941
Website: www.rose-hulman.edu
E-mail: admis.ofc@rose-hulman.edu

St. Mary-of-the-Woods College
Saint Mary of the Woods IN 47876-1001
James P. Malley, Jr., Director of Admission
800-926-7692 Fax: 812-535-5010
Website: www.smwc.edu
E-mail: smwcadms@smwc.edu

University of Evansville
1800 Lincoln Ave, Evansville IN 47722-0001
Thomas E. Bear, V.P. of Enrollment Services
800-423-8633 Fax: 812-488-4076
Website: www.evansville.edu
E-mail: admission@evansville.edu

IOWA

Briar Cliff University
PO Box 2100, Sioux City IA 51104-0100
Sharisue Wilcoxon, VP for Enrollment Management
712-279-5200 Fax: 712-279-1632
Website: www.briarcliff.edu
E-mail: admissions@briarcliff.edu

Clarke College
1550 Clarke Dr, Dubuque IA 52001-3198
Andy Schroeder, Director of Admissions
800-383-2345 Fax: 563-584-8666
Website: www.clarke.edu
E-mail: andy.schroeder@clarke.edu

Graceland University
1 University Place, Lamoni IA 50140
Brian Shantz, Vice President for Enrollment and Dean of
Admissions
641-784-5196 Fax: 641-784-5480
Website: www.admissions.graceland.edu
E-mail: admissions@graceland.edu

Iowa Lakes Community College
300 S 18th St, Estherville IA 51334-2721
Anne Stansbury, Asst. Director of Admissions
712-362-7945 Fax: 712-362-8363
Website: www.iowalakes.edu
E-mail: info@iowalakes.edu

Mount Mercy College
1330 Elmhurst Dr NE, Cedar Rapids IA 52402-4797
Jim Krystofiak, Dean of Admission
800-248-4504 Fax: 319-363-5270
Website: www.mtmercy.edu
E-mail: admission@mtmercy.edu

PALMER COLLEGE OF CHIROPRACTIC
1000 Brady St, Davenport IA 52803-5287
800-722-3648 or 563-884-5656 Fax: 563-884-5414
Website: admissions.palmer.edu
E-mail: pcadmit@palmer.edu

Waldorf College
106 S 6th St, Forest City IA 50436-1713
Steve Lovik, Vice President of Enrollment Management
800-292-1903 or 641-585-8112 Fax: 641-585-8125
Website: www.waldorf.edu
E-mail: loviks@waldorf.edu
See listing under "Universities"

Wartburg College
PO Box 1003, Waverly IA 50677-0903
Brent Matthias, Interim Director of Admissions
319-352-8200 Fax: 319-352-8579
Website: www.wartburg.edu
E-mail: admissions@wartburg.edu

KANSAS

Allen County Community College
1801 N Cottonwood St, Iola KS 66749-1607
John Masterson, President
Randy Weber, Director of Admissions
620-365-5116 Fax: 620-365-3284
Website: www.allencc.net
E-mail: weber@allencc.edu

COLBY COMMUNITY COLLEGE
1255 S Range Ave, Colby KS 67701-4099
Director of Admissions
888-634-9350 or 785-460-4690 Fax: 785-460-4691
Website: www.colbycc.edu
E-mail: bobbi@colbycc.edu

Independence Community College
PO Box 708, Independence KS 67301-0708
Dr. Terry Hetrick, President
800-842-6063 Fax: 620-331-5344
Website: www.indycc.edu
E-mail: admissions@indycc.edu

Newman University
3100 W McCormick St, Wichita KS 67213
Jann Reusser, Admissions Recruitment Coordinator
316-942-4291 ext. 2144 Fax: 316-942-4483
Website: www.newmanu.edu
E-mail: reusserj@newmanu.edu

Tabor College
400 S Jefferson St, Hillsboro KS 67063-1758
Rusty Allen, Dean of Enrollment Management
620-947-3121 Fax: 620-947-6276
Website: www.tabor.edu
E-mail: admissions@tabor.edu

KENTUCKY

Morehead State University
Morehead KY 40351-1689
Dayna Seelig, Enrollment Services
800-585-6781 Fax: 606-783-5038
Website: www.moreheadstate.edu
E-mail: admissions@moreheadstate.edu

Transylvania University
300 N Broadway, Lexington KY 40508-1776
859-233-8242 Fax: 859-233-8797
Website: www.transy.edu
E-mail: admissions@transy.edu

LOUISIANA

Dillard University
2601 Gentilly Blvd, New Orleans LA 70122-3097
Linda G. Nash, Director of Admissions
Website: www.dillard.edu
E-mail: admissions@dillard.edu

Our Lady of Holy Cross College
4123 Woodland Dr, New Orleans LA 70131-7399
Office of Enrollment Services
504-394-7744 Fax: 504-391-2421
Website: www.olhcc.edu

MAINE

HUSSON COLLEGE

One College Cir, Bangor ME 04401-2999
Jane Goodwin, Director of Admissions
800-4HU-SSON or 207-941-7100 Fax: 207-941-7935
Website: www.husson.edu
E-mail: admit@husson.edu
See listing under "Universities"

St. Joseph's College of Maine
278 Whites Bridge Rd, Standish ME 04084-5263
Vincent Kloskowski, Dean of Admissions
800-338-7057 Fax: 207-893-7862
Website: www.sjcme.edu
E-mail: admission@sjcme.edu

MARYLAND

Cecil Community College
One Seahawk Dr, North East MD 21901
Sandra S. Rajaski, Registrar & Director of Admissions
410-287-1000 Fax: 410-287-1001
Website: www.cecilcc.edu
E-mail: srajaski@cecilcc.edu

Hagerstown Community College
11400 Robinwood Dr, Hagerstown MD 21742-6590
Dr. Daniel E. Bock, Assistant Director of Admissions
301-790-2800 Fax: 301-791-9165
Website: www.hagerstowncc.edu
E-mail: bockd@hagerstowncc.edu

Villa Julie College
1525 Greenspring Valley Rd
Stevenson MD 21153-0641
Mark Hergan, V.P. Enrollment Services
410-486-7001 Fax: 410-602-6600
Website: www.vjc.edu/admissions
E-mail: admissions@mail.vjc.edu

MASSACHUSETTS

Assumption College
500 Salisbury St, Worcester MA 01609-1294
Kathleen Murphy, Dean of Enrollment
508-767-7000 Fax: 508-799-4412
Website: www.assumption.edu
E-mail: admiss@assumption.edu

Bay Path College
588 Longmeadow St, Longmeadow MA 01106-2292
Lisa Casassa, Director of Admissions
413-565-1331 Fax: 413-565-1105
Website: www.baypath.edu
E-mail: lcasassa@baypath.edu

Boston University
121 Bay State Rd, Boston MA 02215
Kelly Walter, Executive Director of Admissions
617-353-2300 Fax: 617-353-9695
Website: web.bu.edu
E-mail: admissions@bu.edu

Gordon College
255 Grapevine Rd, Wenham MA 01984-1899
Nancy Mering, Director of Admissions
866-464-6736 Fax: 978-867-4682
Website: www.gordon.edu
E-mail: admissions@gordon.edu

Massachusetts Institute of Technology
77 Massachusetts Ave, Cambridge MA 02139-4307
Marilee Jones, Dean of Admission
617-253-1000 Fax: 617-253-4016
Website: my.mit.edu
E-mail: admissions@mit.edu

Smith College
Northampton MA 01063-0001
Debra Shaver, Director of Admissions
800-383-3232 Fax: 413-585-2527
Website: www.smith.edu
E-mail: admission@smith.edu

University of Massachusetts Dartmouth
Old Westport Rd, North Dartmouth MA 02747-2300
Steven T. Briggs, Director of Admissions
508-999-8605 Fax: 508-999-8755
Website: explore.umassd.edu
E-mail: sbriggs@umassd.edu

Westfield State College
PO Box 1630, Westfield MA 01086
Michelle Mattie, Associate Dean, Admission and
Enrollment Services
413-572-5300
Website: www.wsc.ma.edu
E-mail: admission@wsc.ma.edu

Worcester Polytechnic Institute
100 Institute Rd, Worcester MA 01609-2280
Edward J. Connor, Director of Admissions
508-831-5286 Fax: 508-831-5875
Website: admissions.wpi.edu
E-mail: admissions@wpi.edu

MICHIGAN

Alma College
614 W Superior St, Alma MI 48801-1599
Anne Monroe, Director of Admissions
800-321-ALMA Fax: 989-463-7057
Website: www.alma.edu
E-mail: admissions@alma.edu

Andrews University
Berrien Springs MI 49104-0001
Randall Graves, Director of Recruitment Services
800-253-2874 Fax: 269-471-2670
Website: www.connect.andrews.edu
E-mail: gravesr@andrews.edu

Concordia University
4090 Geddes Rd, Ann Arbor MI 48105-2797
Gary Neumann, Director of Admissions
734-995-7300 Fax: 734-995-4610
Website: www.cuaa.edu
E-mail: admissions@cuaa.edu

Delta College
University Center MI 48710-0001
Duff Zube, Director of Admissions
989-686-9093 Fax: 989-667-2202
Website: www.delta.edu
E-mail: admit@delta.edu

Grand Valley State University
1 Campus Dr, Allendale MI 49401-9403
Jodi Chycinski, Director of Admissions
616-331-6611 Fax: 616-331-2000
Website: www.gvsu.edu
E-mail: go2gvsu@gvsu.edu

HILLSDALE COLLEGE

33 E College St, Hillsdale MI 49242-1298
Dr. Francis Steiner, Chairperson
517-607-2399 Fax: 517-607-2399
Website: www.hillsdale.edu
E-mail: fxs@hillsdale.edu

MACOMB COMMUNITY COLLEGE

44575 Garfield Rd, Clinton Township MI 48038-1139
Information Center
586-445-7999
Website: www.macomb.edu
E-mail: answer@macomb.edu

MACOMB COMMUNITY COLLEGE

14500 E 12 Mile Rd, Warren MI 48088-3896
Information Center
586-445-7999
Website: www.macomb.edu
E-mail: answer@macomb.edu

Northwestern Michigan College
1701 E Front St, Traverse City MI 49686-3061
Jim Bensley, Admissions Coordinator
800-748-0566 Fax: 231-995-1339
Website: www.nmc.edu
E-mail: jbensley@nmc.edu

Oakland University
2200 N Squirrel Rd, Rochester MI 48309
Eleanor L. Reynolds, Assistant Vice President &
Director of Admissions
248-370-2100
Website: www.oakland.edu
E-mail: ouinfo@oakland.edu

University of Michigan-Dearborn
4901 Evergreen Rd, Dearborn MI 48128-1491
The Office of Admissions & Orientation
313-593-5100 Fax: 313-436-9167
Website: www.umd.umich.edu
E-mail: admissions@umd.umich.edu

MINNESOTA

Bethany Lutheran College
700 Luther Dr, Mankato MN 56001
Don Westphal, Dean of Admissions
507-344-7000 Fax: 507-344-7376
Website: www.blc.edu
E-mail: admiss@blc.edu

Carleton College
1 N College St, Northfield MN 55057-4044
800-995-2275 or 507-646-4190 Fax: 507-646-4526
Website: www.carleton.edu
E-mail: admissions@acs.carleton.edu

Gustavus Adolphus College
800 W College Ave, Saint Peter MN 56082-1485
Mark H. Anderson, Dean of Admission
800-GUSTAVUS Fax: 507-933-7474
Website: www.gustavus.edu
E-mail: admission@gustavus.edu

Northland Community & Technical College
Highway 1 E, Thief River Falls MN 56701
Terry Wiseth, Chairperson
800-959-6282 Fax: 218-681-0774
Website: www.northlandcollege.edu

NORTHWESTERN HEALTH SCIENCES UNIVERSITY

2501 W 84th St, Bloomington MN 55431-1599
Bill Kuehl, Director of Admissions
952-888-4777 ext. 409 Fax: 952-888-6713
Website: www.nwhealth.edu
E-mail: admit@nwhealth.edu
See listing under "Chiropractic Medicine"

Pillsbury Baptist Bible College
315 S Grove Ave, Owatonna MN 55060-3097
Stephen R. Seidler, Director of Admissions
507-451-2710 Fax: 507-451-0156
Website: www.pillsbury.edu
E-mail: steveseidler@pillsbury.edu

MISSISSIPPI

Tougaloo College
500 W County Line Rd, Tougaloo MS 39174-9799
Juno Leggette Jacobs, Director of Admissions
601-977-7768 Fax: 601-977-4501
Website: www.tougaloo.edu
E-mail: jjacobs@tougaloo.edu

MISSOURI

Cleveland Chiropractic College - Kansas City Campus
6401 Rockhill Rd, Kansas City MO 64131-1122
Melissa Denton, Multicampus Director of Admissions
800-467-CCKC (2252) or 816-501-0100
Fax: 816-501-0205
Website: www.cleveland.edu
E-mail: kc.admissions@cleveland.edu

East Central College
1964 Prairie Dell Rd, Union MO 63084
Karen Wieda, Registrar
636-583-5195 ext. 2220 Fax: 636-583-1897
Website: www.eastcentral.edu
E-mail: wiedaks@eastcentral.edu

Lindenwood University
209 S Kingshighway St
Saint Charles MO 63301-1695
Sheryl Guffey, Director of Admissions
636-949-2000 Fax: 636-949-4989
Website: www.lindenwood.edu

Stephens College
PO Box 2121, Columbia MO 65215-0001
David Adams, Dean of Enrollment Management
573-442-2211 Fax: 573-876-7237
Website: www.stephens.edu
E-mail: dadams@stephens.edu

Truman State University
100 E Normal, Kirksville MO 63501
Office of Admission
660-785-4000 Fax: 660-785-4181
Website: admissions.truman.edu
E-mail: admissions@truman.edu

University of Missouri
1 University Blvd, Saint Louis MO 63121-4499
Dr. Mark Burkholder, Dean-College of Arts & Sciences
314-516-5458 Fax: 314-516-6759
Website: www.umsl.edu
E-mail: admissions@umsl.edu

Webster University
470 E Lockwood Ave, Saint Louis MO 63119-3194
Dr. Ron Gaddis, Chairman, Biological Sciences
314-968-7160 Fax: 314-968-7194
Website: www.webster.edu
E-mail: rgaddis@webster.edu
See listing under "Universities"

William Woods University
1 University Ave, Fulton MO 65251-1098
Jimmy Clay, Director of Admissions
573-642-2251 Fax: 573-592-1146
Website: www.williamwoods.edu
E-mail: admissions@williamwoods.edu
See listing under "Universities"

MONTANA

Rocky Mountain College
1511 Poly Dr, Billings MT 59102-1796
Bonnie Knapp, Director of Admissions
800-877-6259 Fax: 406-657-1189
Website: www.rocky.edu
E-mail: admissions@rocky.edu

NEBRASKA

College of Saint Mary
7000 Mercy Rd, Omaha NE 68106
Lorin Werth, V.P. for Enrollment
800-926-5534 or 402-399-2407 Fax: 402-399-2412
Website: www.csm.edu
E-mail: lwerth@csm.edu

Midland Lutheran College
900 N Clarkson St, Fremont NE 68025-4200
Todd Hansen, Associate Director of Admissions
402-941-6501 Fax: 402-941-6513
Website: www.mlc.edu
E-mail: admissions@mlc.edu

Nebraska Wesleyan University
5000 Saint Paul Ave, Lincoln NE 68504-2794
Patricia Karthauser, V.P. for University Enrollment
402-466-2371 Fax: 402-465-2177
Website: www.nebrwesleyan.edu
E-mail: admissions@nebrwesleyan.edu

Peru State College
PO Box 10, Peru NE 68421-0010
Office of Admissions
800-742-4412 Fax: 402-872-2296
Website: www.peru.edu
E-mail: admissions@oakmail.peru.edu

University of Nebraska at Kearney
905 W 25th St, Kearney NE 68849-0001
Dusty Newton, Director of Admissions
800-KEARNEY Fax: 308-865-8987
Website: www.unk.edu
E-mail: admissionsug@unk.edu

NEW JERSEY

Mercer County Community College
West Windsor Campus
PO Box B, Trenton NJ 08690
Savita Bambhrolia, Director of Admissions
609-586-4800 Fax: 609-587-4666
Website: www.mccc.edu
E-mail: admiss@mccc.edu

New Jersey City University
2039 John F Kennedy Blvd
Jersey City NJ 07305-1588
Carmen Panlilio, Asst. V.P. for Admissions and
Financial Aid
201-200-3234 Fax: 201-200-2044
Website: www.njcu.edu
E-mail: admissions@njcu.edu

Ramapo College of New Jersey
505 Ramapo Valley Rd, Mahwah NJ 07430-1623
Director of Admissions
201-684-7300 or 201-684-7301 Fax: 201-684-7964
Website: www.ramapo.edu
E-mail: admissions@ramapo.edu

NEW MEXICO

New Mexico Military Institute
101 W College Blvd, Roswell NM 88201-5173
LTC. Craig Collins, Director of Admissions
800-421-5376 or 505-624-8050 Fax: 505-624-8058
Website: www.nmmi.edu
E-mail: admissions@nmmi.edu
See listing under "Community and Junior Colleges"

NEW YORK

College of Saint Rose
432 Western Ave, Albany NY 12203-1419
Maryelizabeth Amico, Asst V.P. for Undergraduate
Admissions
518-454-5150 Fax: 518-454-2013
Website: www.strose.edu
E-mail: admit@strose.edu

CUNY Hunter College
695 Park Ave, New York NY 10021
Aaron Gibbs, Assistant Director of Recruitment
212-772-4497 Fax: 212-650-3336
Website: www.hunter.cuny.edu
E-mail: aaron.gibbs@hunter.cuny.edu

Daemen College
4380 Main St, Amherst NY 14226-3592
Donna Shaffner, Director of Admissions
800-462-7652 or 716-839-8225 Fax: 716-839-8229
Website: www.daemen.edu
E-mail: admissions@daemen.edu
See listing under "Universities"

Hobart & William Smith Colleges
Pulteney St, Geneva NY 14456
John Young, Director of Admissions
315-789-5500 Fax: 315-781-3654
Website: www.hws.edu
E-mail: young@hws.edu

Long Island University-C. W. Post Campus
720 Northern Blvd, Brookville NY 11548-1300
Joanne Graziano, Executive Director of Admissions
516-299-2900 Fax: 516-299-2137
Website: www.liu.edu/cwpost
E-mail: enroll@cwpost.liu.edu

Molloy College
1000 Hempstead Ave
Rockville Centre NY 11570-1100
Marguerite Lane, Director of Admissions
516-678-5000 ext. 6291 Fax: 516-256-2247
Website: www.molloy.edu
E-mail: admissions@molloy.edu
See listing under "Universities"

Paul Smith's College
Paul Smiths NY 12970
Amber DeBeer, Assistant Director of Admissions
800-421-2605 Fax: 518-327-6016
Website: www.paulsmiths.edu
E-mail: admiss@paulsmiths.edu

PURCHASE COLLEGE STATE UNIVERSITY OF NEW YORK (SUNY)

735 Anderson Hill Rd, Purchase NY 10577-1400
Betsy Immergut, Director of Admissions
914-251-6300 Fax: 914-251-6314
Website: www.purchase.edu
See listing under "Universities"

Roberts Wesleyan College
2301 Westside Dr, Rochester NY 14624-1997
Office of Admissions
585-594-6400 Fax: 585-594-6371
Website: www.roberts.edu
E-mail: admissions@roberts.edu

St. John's University
8000 Utopia Pkwy, Queens NY 11439
Office of Admission
718-990-2000 or 888-9-STJOHNS Fax: 718-990-2096
Website: www.stjohns.edu
E-mail: admissions@stjohns.edu
See listing under "Universities"

St. Joseph's College
245 Clinton Ave, Brooklyn NY 11205-3688
Theresa LaRocca Meyer, V.P. for Enrollment
Management
718-636-6800 Fax: 718-636-8303
Website: www.sjcny.edu
E-mail: tlaroccameyer@sjcny.edu

SUNY College at Brockport
350 New Campus Dr, Brockport NY 14420-2997
Bernard S. Valento, Director of Undergraduate
Admissions
585-395-2751 Fax: 585-395-5452
Website: www.brockport.edu
E-mail: admit@brockport.edu

SUNY College of Technology
Alfred NY 14802
Deborah J. Goodrich, Director of Admissions
800-4AL-FRED Fax: 607-587-4299
Website: www.alfredstate.edu
E-mail: admissions@alfredstate.edu

SUNY Orange County Community College
115 South St, Middletown NY 10940-6437
Margot St. Lawrence, Director of Admissions
845-341-4030 Fax: 845-342-8662
Website: www.sunyorange.edu
E-mail: apply@sunyorange.edu
See listing under "Community and Junior Colleges"

Wells College
PO Box 500, Aurora NY 13026
Susan Sloan, Director of Admissions
800-952-9355 Fax: 315-364-3227
Website: www.wells.edu
E-mail: ssloan@wells.edu

NORTH CAROLINA

Belmont Abbey College
100 Belmont Mount Holly Rd
Belmont NC 28012-1802
888-222-0110 Fax: 704-825-6670
Website: www.belmontabbeycollege.edu
E-mail: admissions@bac.edu

Lees-McRae College
PO Box 128, Banner Elk NC 28604-0128
Walt Crutchfield, Dean of Admissions
800-280-4562 Fax: 828-898-8707
Website: www.lmc.edu
E-mail: admissions@lmc.edu

Mars Hill College
Mars Hill NC 28754
Chad Holt, Dean of Enrollment
866-MHC-4-YOU Fax: 828-689-1473
Website: www.mhc.edu
E-mail: cholt@mhc.edu

Meredith College
3800 Hillsborough St, Raleigh NC 27607-5298
Heidi L. Fletcher, Director of Admissions
919-760-8581 Fax: 919-760-2348
Website: www.meredith.edu
E-mail: admissions@meredith.edu
See listing under "Women's Colleges"

Mt. Olive College
634 Henderson St, Mount Olive NC 28365
Tim Woodard, Director of Admissions
919-658-2502 Fax: 919-658-9816
Website: www.moc.edu
E-mail: admissions@moc.edu
See listing under "Universities"

Salem College
Winston Salem NC 27108
Dana Evans, Dean of Admissions/Fin. Aid
800-32-SALEM Fax: 336-917-5572
Website: www.salem.edu
E-mail: admissions@salem.edu
See listing under "Women's Colleges"

NORTH DAKOTA

Dickinson State University
Dickinson ND 58601-4896
Steve Glasser, Director of Student Recruitment
800-279-4295 Fax: 701-483-2409
Website: www.dickinsonstate.edu
E-mail: dsu.hawks@dickinsonstate.edu

Valley City State University
101 College St SW, Valley City ND 58072-4024
Dan Klein, Director of Enrollment Services
800-532-8641 ext. 7101 Fax: 701-845-7299
Website: www.vcsu.edu
E-mail: enrollment.services@vcsu.edu
See listing under "Universities"

OHIO

Cleveland State University
2121 Euclid Ave RW 204, Cleveland OH 44115
Dr. Richard Arndt, Dean of Undergraduate Recruitment
and College Partnerships
888-CSU-OHIO Fax: 216-687-9210
Website: www.csuohio.edu
E-mail: admissions@csuohio.edu

Franciscan University of Steubenville
University Blvd, Steubenville OH 43952
Margaret J. Weber, Director of Admissions
800-783-6220 or 740-283-6226 Fax: 740-284-5456
Website: www.admissions.edu
E-mail: mweber@franciscan.edu

Mount Vernon Nazarene University
800 Martinsburg Rd, Mount Vernon OH 43050-9509
Timothy Eades, Director of Admissions
866-462-6868 Fax: 740-393-0511
Website: www.gotomvnu.com
E-mail: admissions@mvnu.edu
See listing under "Universities"

OHIO NORTHERN UNIVERSITY

525 S Main St, Ada OH 45810-1555
Terry Keiser, Chair of Biological Sciences Dept.
419-772-2325
Website: www.onu.edu
E-mail: admissions-ug@onu.edu
See listing under "Universities"

The Ohio State University
College of Biological Sciences
Biological Sciences Bldg, 484 W 12th Ave
Columbus OH 43210
614-292-8772
Website: www.biosci.ohio-state.edu

OHIO WESLEYAN UNIVERSITY

61 S Sandusky St, Delaware OH 43015-2398
Director of Admission
740-368-3020 Fax: 740-368-3314
Website: www.owu.edu
E-mail: owuadmit@owu.edu

Owens Community College
300 Davis St, Findlay OH 45840-3631
William J. Ivoska PhD., Vice President of Student
Services
567-429-3500 Fax: 567-423-0246
Website: www.owens.edu
E-mail: admissions@owens.edu

Owens Community College
PO Box 10000, Toledo OH 43699-1947
William J. Ivoska, Ph.D, Vice President of Student
Services
567-661-7000 Fax: 567-661-7607
Website: www.owens.edu
E-mail: admissions@owens.edu

University of Dayton
300 College Park, Dayton OH 45469-1300
Robert F. Durkle, Director of Admissions
800-837-7433 Fax: 937-229-4729
Website: admission.udayton.edu
E-mail: admission@udayton.edu

Ursuline College
2550 Lander Rd, Cleveland OH 44124-4398
Sarah E. Sundermeier, Director of Admissions
888-URSULINE Toll Free Fax: 440-684-6138
Website: www.admission.ursuline.edu
E-mail: admission@ursuline.edu

OKLAHOMA

Oklahoma State University
Stillwater OK 74078
James Shaw, Department Head
405-744-5555
Website: www.okstate.edu
E-mail: shawjh@okstate.edu

Oral Roberts University
7777 S Lewis Ave, Tulsa OK 74171-0001
Chris Belcher, Director of Undergraduate Admissions
800-678-8876 Fax: 918-495-6222
Website: www.oru.edu
E-mail: admissions@oru.edu

University of Tulsa
600 S College Ave, Tulsa OK 74104-3126
Earl Johnson, Dean of Admission
918-631-2307 Fax: 918-631-5003
Website: www.utulsa.edu
E-mail: admission@utulsa.edu

OREGON

Cascade College
9101 E Burnside St, Portland OR 97216-1599
800-550-7678 Fax: 503-257-1222
Website: www.cascade.edu
E-mail: admissions@cascade.edu

Concordia University
2811 NE Holman St, Portland OR 97211-6099
Bobi Swan, Director of Admissions
503-288-9371 Fax: 503-280-8531
Website: www.cu-portland.edu
E-mail: cu-admissions@cu-portland.edu

Linn-Benton Community College
6500 Pacific Blvd SW, Albany OR 97321-3774
Christine Baker, Outreach Coordinator
541-917-4811 Fax: 541-917-4868
Website: www.linnbenton.edu
E-mail: admissions@linnbenton.edu

Warner Pacific College
2219 SE 68th Ave, Portland OR 97215-4026
Shannon Mackey, Director of Admissions
503-517-1000 Fax: 503-517-1352
Website: www.warnerpacific.edu
E-mail: admissions@warnerpacific.edu

Western Oregon University
345 Monmouth Ave N, Monmouth OR 97361-1314
David McDonald, Dean, Admission, Retention &
Enrollment Management
877-877-1593 Fax: 503-838-8067
Website: www.wou.edu
E-mail: wolfgram@fsa.wou.edu

PENNSYLVANIA

Arcadia University
450 S Easton Rd, Glenside PA 19038-3295
Dennis Nostrand, VP for Enrollment Management
877-ARCADIA (877-272-2342) Fax: 215-881-8767
Website: www.arcadia.edu
E-mail: admiss@arcadia.edu
See listing under "Universities"

Clarion University of Pennsylvania
840 Wood St, Clarion PA 16214-1232
William Bailey, Dean of Enrollment Management
814-393-2306 Fax: 814-393-2030
Website: www.clarion.edu
E-mail: admissions@clarion.edu

DeSales University
2755 Station Ave, Center Valley PA 18034-9565
610-282-1100 Fax: 610-282-2342
Website: www.desales.edu

Gannon University
109 University Sq, Erie PA 16541-0001
Christopher Tremblay, Director of Admissions
800-GANNON-U Fax: 814-871-5803
Website: www.gannon.edu
E-mail: admissions@gannon.edu

Holy Family University
9801 Frankford Avenue, Philadelphia PA 19114
Lauren Campbell, Director of Admissions
215-637-3050 Fax: 215-281-1022
Website: www.holyfamily.edu
E-mail: admissions@holyfamily.edu

Juniata College
1700 Moore St, Huntingdon PA 16652-2196
Michelle Bartol, Dean of Enrollment
877-JUNIATA Fax: 814-641-3100
Website: www.juniata.edu
E-mail: admissions@juniata.edu

King's College
133 N River St, Wilkes Barre PA 18711-0801
Michelle Lawrence-Schmude, Director of Admission
570-208-5900 Fax: 570-208-5971
Website: www.kings.edu
E-mail: admissions@kings.edu

La Roche College
9000 Babcock Blvd, Pittsburgh PA 15237-5898
Thomas Hassett, Director of Freshman and
International Admissions
412-536-1272 or 800-838-4LRC Fax: 412-536-1272
Website: www.laroche.edu
E-mail: admissions@laroche.edu

Lebanon Valley College
101 N College Ave, Annville PA 17003-1400
William Brown, Dean of Admissions & Financial Aid
866-LVC-4ADM or 717-867-6181 Fax: 717-867-6026
Website: www.lvc.edu
E-mail: admission@lvc.edu

Lincoln University
Lincoln University PA 19352
Michael C. Taylor, Director of Admissions
800-790-0191 Fax: 610-932-1209
Website: www.lincoln.edu
E-mail: mtaylor@lu.lincoln.edu

Neumann College
1 Neumann Dr, Aston PA 19014-1298
Dennis Murphy, Director of Admissions
610-459-0905 Fax: 610-558-5652
Website: www.neumann.edu
E-mail: neumann@neumann.edu

University of Pittsburgh
1150 Mount Pleasant Rd
Greensburg PA 15601-5860
Brandi S. Darr, Director of Admissions and Financial
Aid
724-836-9880 Fax: 724-836-7160
Website: www.upg.pitt.edu
E-mail: upgadmit@pitt.edu

Washington & Jefferson College
60 S Lincoln St, Washington PA 15301-4801
Alton E. Newell, Vice President for Enrollment
724-223-6025 Fax: 724-223-6534
Website: www.washjeff.edu
E-mail: admission@washjeff.edu

Westminster College
New Wilmington PA 16172-0001
Doug Swartz, Director of Admissions
724-946-7100 Fax: 724-946-6171
Website: www.westminster.edu
E-mail: swartzdl@westminster.edu

SOUTH CAROLINA

Bob Jones University
1700 Wade Hampton Blvd
Greenville SC 29614-0001
David Christ, Director of Admissions
800-BJ-AND-ME Fax: 800-2-FAX-BJU
Website: www.bju.edu
E-mail: admissions@bju.edu
See listing under "Universities"

Coastal Carolina University
PO Box 261954, Conway SC 29528-6054
Office of Admissions
800-277-7000 Fax: 843-349-2127
Website: www.coastal.edu
E-mail: admissions@coastal.edu

Erskine College & Seminary
PO Box 176, Due West SC 29639
Bart Walker, Director of Admissions
864-379-8838 Fax: 864-379-3048
Website: www.erskine.edu
E-mail: admissions@erskine.edu

Limestone College
1115 College Dr, Gaffney SC 29340-3799
Chris Phenicie, V.P. for Enrollment
864-489-7151 Fax: 864-488-8206
Website: www.limestone.edu
E-mail: cphenicie@limestone.edu

North Greenville University
PO Box 1892, Tigerville SC 29688-1892
Website: www.ngc.edu
See listing under "Universities"

PRESBYTERIAN COLLEGE
503 S Broad St, Clinton SC 29325
Richard Dana Paul, Dean of Admissions
800-476-7272 Fax: 864-833-8481
Website: www.presby.edu
E-mail: admissions@presby.edu

University of South Carolina - Upstate
800 University Way, Spartanburg SC 29303-4932
Donette Stewart, Assistant VC for Enrollment Services
864-503-5246 Fax: 864-503-5727
Website: www.uscupstate.edu
E-mail: dstewart@uscupstate.edu
See listing under "Universities"

SOUTH DAKOTA

Presentation College
1500 N Main St, Aberdeen SD 57401-1280
JoEllen Lindner, Dean of Admissions
605-229-8492 Fax: 605-229-8425
Website: www.presentation.edu
E-mail: admit@presentation.edu

TENNESSEE

Lipscomb University
3901 Granny White Pike, Nashville TN 37204-3951
Ricky Holaway, Director of Admissions
800-333-4358 ext. 1776 Fax: 615-269-1804
Website: www.lipscomb.edu
E-mail: admissions@lipscomb.edu

Tennessee State University
3500 John A Merritt Blvd, Nashville TN 37209-1561
John Cade, Dean of Admissions & Records
615-963-5101 Fax: 615-963-2930
Website: www.tnstate.edu
E-mail: jcade@tnstate.edu

Tusculum College
PO Box 5051, Greeneville TN 37743
Melissa Ripley, Associate Director of Admissions
800-729-0256 Fax: 423-798-1622
Website: www.tusculum.edu
E-mail: mripley@tusculum.edu

University of Tennessee
615 McCallie Ave, Chattanooga TN 37403-2504
Yancy Freeman, Director of Admissions
423-425-4111 Fax: 423-425-4157
E-mail: Yancy-Freeman@utc.edu

TEXAS

Angelo State University
ASU Station 11014, San Angelo TX 76909
Bonnie Stennett, Coordinator of Recruiting
800-946-8627 Fax: 325-942-2078
Website: www.angelo.edu
E-mail: admissions@angelo.edu

Blinn College
902 College Ave, Brenham TX 77833-4098
Dennis K. Crowson, Registrar
979-830-4000 Fax: 979-830-4110
Website: www.blinn.edu
E-mail: recruiting@blinn.edu

Blinn College
PO Box 6030, Bryan TX 77805-6030
Dennis K. Crowson, Registrar
979-209-7200 Fax: 979-209-7229
Website: www.blinn.edu
E-mail: recruiting@blinn.edu

Blinn College
100 Ranger Dr, Schulenburg TX 78956-2247
Dennis K. Crowson, Registrar
979-743-5003 Fax: 979-743-5225
Website: www.blinn.edu
E-mail: recruiting@blinn.edu

Blinn College
3701 Outlet Center Dr, Sealy TX 77474
Dennis K. Crowson, Registrar
979-627-7997 Fax: 979-627-0830
Website: www.blinn.edu
E-mail: recruiting@blinn.edu

Galveston College
4015 Avenue Q, Galveston TX 77550-7496
Brian Lowery, Registrar
409-763-6551 Fax: 409-944-1501
Website: www.gc.edu
E-mail: blowery@gc.edu

Our Lady of the Lake University
411 SW 24th St, San Antonio TX 78207-4666
Mary Kay Cooper, Dean of Enrollment
210-434-6711 Fax: 210-431-4013
Website: www.ollusa.edu
E-mail: admission@lakeollusa.edu

Parker College of Chiropractic
2500 Walnut Hill Ln, Dallas TX 75229-5609
Andrea Robles, Asst. Director of Admissions
972-438-6932 Fax: 214-902-2413
Website: www.parkercc.edu
E-mail: admissions@parkercc.edu

Temple College
2600 S 1st St, Temple TX 76504-7435
Angela Balch, Director of Admissions & Records
254-298-8300 Fax: 254-298-8288
Website: www.templejc.edu
E-mail: ruth.bridges@templejc.edu

Texas Woman's University
PO Box 425589, Denton TX 76204-5589
Erma Nieto, Director of Admissions
866-809-6130 Fax: 940-898-3081
Website: www.twu.edu
E-mail: admissions@twu.edu

Tyler Junior College
PO Box 9020, Tyler TX 75711-9020
Joan Jones, Interim Dean
800-687-5680
Website: www.tjc.edu
E-mail: jjon@tjc.edu
See listing under "Community and Junior Colleges"

University of Houston
122 E Cullen Bldg, Houston TX 77204-2023
Office of Admission
713-743-9595
Website: www.uh.edu
E-mail: admissions@uh.edu

University of St. Thomas
3800 Montrose Blvd, Houston TX 77006-4626
Eduardo Prieto, Director of Admissions
713-522-7911 Fax: 713-525-3558
Website: www.stthom.edu
E-mail: prietoe@stthom.edu

University of Texas at Arlington
Box 19111, Arlington TX 76019-0111
Hans Gatterdam, Director of Admission
817-272-6287 Fax: 817-272-3435
Website: www.uta.edu
E-mail: admissions@uta.edu

VERMONT

Bennington College
One College Drive, Bennington VT 05201
Ken Himmelman, Dean of Admissions & Financial Aid
800-833-6845 Fax: 802-440-4320
Website: www.bennington.edu
E-mail: admissions@bennington.edu

NORWICH UNIVERSITY
158 Harmon Dr, Northfield VT 05663
Dr. Lauren Howard, Department Head
800-468-6679 Fax: 802-485-2333
Website: www.norwich.edu
E-mail: howard@norwich.edu
See listing under "Universities"

VIRGINIA

Mary Baldwin College
Staunton VA 24401
Lisa A. Branson, Executive Director of Admissions and
Financial Aid
800-468-2262 Fax: 540-887-7292
Website: www.mbc.edu
E-mail: admit@mbc.edu

Radford University
PO Box 6903, Radford VA 24142
David W. Kraus, Director of Admissions
800-890-4265 Fax: 540-831-5038
Website: www.radford.edu
E-mail: ruadmiss@radford.edu

Randolph-Macon Woman's College
2500 Rivermont Ave, Lynchburg VA 24503
Patricia LeDonne, Director of Admissions
434-947-8100 Fax: 434-947-8996
Website: www.rmwc.edu
E-mail: admissions@rmwc.edu

University of Mary Washington
1301 College Ave, Fredericksburg VA 22401-5300
Dr. Martin A. Wilder, Jr., Director of Admissions
540-654-2000 Fax: 540-654-1857
Website: www.umw.edu
E-mail: admit@umw.edu

WASHINGTON

Gonzaga University
502 E Boone Ave, Spokane WA 99258-0102
Julie McCulloh, Dean of Admission
800-322-2584 or 509-323-6572 Fax: 509-323-5780
Website: www.gonzaga.edu
E-mail: mcculloh@gu.gonzaga.edu

WEST VIRGINIA

Concord University
Athens WV 24712
Michael Curry, Vice President of Financial Aid &
Admissions
888-384-5249 Fax: 304-384-3218
Website: www.concord.edu
E-mail: admissions@concord.edu

Davis & Elkins College
100 Campus Dr, Elkins WV 26241-3996
Renee Heckel, Director of Enrollment Management
800-624-3157 Fax: 304-637-1800
Website: www.davisandelkins.edu
E-mail: admiss@davisandelkins.edu

Fairmont State University
1201 Locust Ave, Fairmont WV 26554-2470
Steve Leadman, Director of Admissions
304-367-4642 or 800-641-5678 Fax: 304-367-4789
Website: www.fairmontstate.edu
E-mail: admit@fairmontstate.edu

Mountain State University
Box 9003, Beckley WV 25802-9003
866-FOR-MSU1 or 304-929-INFO Fax: 304-253-5072
Website: www.mountainstate.edu
E-mail: gomsu@mountainstate.edu
See listing under "Universities"

West Virginia Wesleyan College
59 College Ave, Buckhannon WV 26201-2699
Robert N. Skinner II, Director of Admission
800-722-9933 Fax: 304-473-8108
Website: www.wvwc.edu
E-mail: admission@wvwc.edu

WISCONSIN

Alverno College
PO Box 343922, Milwaukee WI 53234-3922
Mary Kay Farrell, Director of Admissions
414-382-6100 Fax: 414-382-6354
Website: www.alverno.edu
E-mail: admissions@alverno.edu

Lakeland College
PO Box 359, Sheboygan WI 53082-0359
Nathan Dehne, Director of Admission
920-565-1100 Fax: 920-565-1215
Website: www.lakeland.edu
E-mail: admissions@lakeland.edu

Marquette University
PO Box 1881, Milwaukee WI 53201-1881
Robert Blust, Director of Admissions
414-288-7302 Fax: 414-288-3764
Website: www.mu.edu
E-mail: admissions@marquette.edu

Medical College of Wisconsin
PO Box 26509, Milwaukee WI 53226-0509
Michael Istwan, Director of Admissions
414-456-8296 Fax: 414-456-6506
Website: www.mcw.edu
E-mail: mcwms@mcw.edu

St. Norbert College
100 Grant St, De Pere WI 54115
Brian Studebaker, Director of Admission
800-236-4878 Fax: 920-403-4072
Website: www.snc.edu
E-mail: admit@snc.edu

WYOMING

Laramie County Community College
1400 E College Dr, Cheyenne WY 82007-3204
Jenny Hargett, Director of Admissions
307-778-5222 Fax: 307-778-1350
Website: www.lccc.wy.edu
E-mail: learnmore@lccc.wy.edu

University of Wyoming
Admissions Office
Dept 3435, Laramie WY 82071-3435
Aaron Appelhans, Contact
800-342-5996 Fax: 307-766-4042
Website: www.uwyo.edu
E-mail: why-wyo@uwyo.edu

GUAM

University of Guam
UOG Station, Mangilao GU 96923
Deborah Leon Guerrero, Registrar
671-735-2201 or 671-735-2208 Fax: 671-735-2203
Website: www.uog.edu
E-mail: admitme@uog9.uog.edu

PUERTO RICO

Universidad Adventista de las Antillas
PO Box 118, Mayaguez PR 00919-0118
Evelyn Del Valle Rivera, Director of Admissions
787-834-9595 Fax: 787-834-9597
Website: www.uaa.edu
E-mail: admissions@uaa.edu

BUSINESS - ADMINISTRATIVE SUPPORT

ALABAMA

Alabama A & M University
PO Box 908, Normal AL 35762
Antonio Boyle, Director of Admissions
256-372-5245 Fax: 256-372-5249
Website: www.aamu.edu
E-mail: aboyle@aamu.edu

Faulkner University
5345 Atlanta Hwy, Montgomery AL 36109-3398
Keith Mock, Director of Admissions
800-879-9816 ext. 7200 or 334-386-7200
Fax: 334-386-7137
Website: www.faulkner.edu
E-mail: admissions@faulkner.edu

Herzing College
280 W Valley Ave, Homewood AL 35209-4816
Kim Conway, Director of Admissions
205-916-2800 Fax: 205-916-2807
Website: www.herzing.edu/birmingham
E-mail: info@bhm.herzing.edu

Trenholm State Technical College
Trenholm Campus
1225 Air Base Blvd, Montgomery AL 36108-3199
Dr. Anthony Molina, President
334-420-4200 Fax: 334-420-4206
Website: www.trenholmtech.cc.al.us
E-mail: amolina@trenholmtech.cc.al.us

ALASKA

University of Alaska Anchorage
PO Box 141629, Anchorage AK 99514-1629
Cecile Mitchell, Director of Enrollment Services
907-786-1480 Fax: 907-786-4888
Website: www.uaa.alaska.edu/
E-mail: enroll@uaa.alaska.edu

University of Alaska Southeast
11120 Glacier Hwy, Juneau AK 99801-8625
Paul Kraft, Dean of Students/Enrollment Management
907-796-6000 Fax: 907-796-6005
Website: www.uas.alaska.edu
E-mail: paul.kraft@uas.alaska.edu

ARIZONA

International Institute of the Americas
925 S Gilbert Rd Ste 201, Mesa AZ 85204-4440
Meredith Kiljan, Director
480-545-8755 Fax: 480-926-1371
Website: www.iia.edu
E-mail: mjensen@iia.edu

International Institute of the Americas
6049 N 43rd Ave, Phoenix AZ 85019-1600
Lynn McConnell, Director
602-242-6265 Fax: 602-589-1353
Website: www.iia.edu
E-mail: lmcconnell@iia.edu

International Institute of the Americas
4136 N 75th Ave Ste 211, Phoenix AZ 85033-3169
Dr. Lori Ebert, Director
623-849-8208 Fax: 623-849-0110
Website: www.iia.edu
E-mail: nsabino@iia.edu

International Institute of the Americas
5441 E 22nd St, Tucson AZ 85710
Leigh Anne Pechota, Director
520-748-9799 Fax: 520-748-9355
Website: www.iia.edu
E-mail: lpechota@iia.edu

Pima Community College
4905 E Broadway Blvd, Tucson AZ 85709-1010
Wendy Kilgore, Ph.D., Director of Admissions
520-206-4500 Fax: 520-206-4790
Website: www.pima.edu
E-mail: infocenter@pima.edu

TUCSON COLLEGE
7310 E 22nd St, Tucson AZ 85710
Rebecca Montgomery, Director of Admissions
520-296-3261 Fax: 520-296-3484
Website: www.tucsoncollege.edu
E-mail: Rmontgomery@tucsoncollege.edu

ARKANSAS

Northwest Technical Institute
709 S Old Missouri Rd, Springdale AR 72764
Charles L. Kelley, President
479-751-8824 Fax: 479-751-7780
Website: www.nti.tec.ar.us
E-mail: info@nit.tec.ar.us

Phillips Community College of the University of Arkansas
PO Box 785, Helena AR 72342-0785
Dr. Steven Murray, Chancellor
Lynn Boone, Vice Chancellor for Student Services /
Registrar
870-338-6474 Fax: 870-338-7542
Website: www.pccua.edu
E-mail: lboone@pccua.edu

CALIFORNIA

Chabot College
25555 Hesperian Blvd, Hayward CA 94545-2400
Judy Young, Director of Admissions
510-723-6600 Fax: 510-723-7510
Website: www.chabotcollege.edu
E-mail: ccarcom@clpccd.cc.ca.us

FRESNO CITY COLLEGE
1101 E University Ave, Fresno CA 93741-0002
Dayann Dietrich, Contact
559-442-8241 Fax: 559-237-4232
Website: www.fresnocitycollege.com
E-mail: fcc.admissions@scccd.com

HEALD COLLEGE, MILPITAS
341 Great Mall Pkwy, Milpitas CA 95035-8008
Sharon Kitko, Director's Assistant
408-934-4900 Fax: 408-934-7777
Website: www.heald.edu

HEALD COLLEGE RANCHO CORDOVA
2910 Prospect Park Dr
Rancho Cordova CA 95670-6005
Donald Ed Hardenbrook, Regional Director
916-638-1616 Fax: 916-638-1580
Website: www.heald.edu
E-mail: ed_hardenbrook@heald.edu

Institute of Technology - Sacramento
3695 Bleckely St, Mather CA 95655
916-363-4300

MARIC COLLEGE
14355 Roscoe Blvd, Panorama City CA 91402-4222
Kristine Schepps, Contact
818-672-8907 Fax: 818-672-8919
Website: www.mariccollege.edu
E-mail: kschepps@mariccollege.edu

MTI BUSINESS COLLEGE OF STOCKTON
6006 N El Dorado St, Stockton CA 95207-4349
Steven Brenner, Director
888-302-2009 Fax: 209-474-8705
Website: www.mtistockton.com
E-mail: mtistockton@comcast.net
   Established 1968. Accredited: ACCSCT. Family
owned/operated 36 years.

MTI College
5221 Madison Ave, Sacramento CA 95841-3003
Marije Miller, Director of Admissions
916-339-1500 Fax: 916-339-0305
Website: www.mticollege.edu
E-mail: mmiller@mticollege.edu

Orange Coast College
PO Box 5005, Costa Mesa CA 92628-5005
Kristin Clark, Director of Admissions
714-432-5773 Fax: 714-432-5736
Website: www.orangecoastcollege.edu
E-mail: kclark@cccd.edu

San Joaquin Valley College
201 New Stine Rd, Bakersfield CA 93309-2659
Jaime Delgado, Enrollment Services Director
661-834-1026 Fax: 559-651-4864
Website: www.sjvc.edu
E-mail: jaime.delgado@sjvc.edu

San Joaquin Valley College
295 E Sierra Ave, Fresno CA 93710-3616
Nora Twarynski, Enrollment Services Director
559-448-8282 Fax: 559-651-4864
Website: www.sjvc.edu
E-mail: nora.twarynski@sjvc.edu

San Joaquin Valley College
1700 McHenry Village Way Suite 6
Modesto CA 95350
Joseph Holt, Director of Admissions
209-527-7582 Fax: 559-651-4864
Website: www.sjvc.edu
E-mail: josephh@sjvc.edu

San Joaquin Valley College
11050 Olson Dr, Rancho Cordova CA 95670
Joseph Holt, Director of Admissions
559-651-2500 Fax: 559-651-4864
Website: www.sjvc.edu
E-mail: joseph.holt@sjvc.edu

San Joaquin Valley College
10641 Church St, Rancho Cucamonga CA 91730
Ramon Abreu, Enrollment Services Director
909-948-7582 Fax: 559-651-4864
Website: www.sjvc.edu
E-mail: ramon.abreu@sjvc.edu

San Joaquin Valley College
8400 W Mineral King Ave, Visalia CA 93291-9283
Susie Topjian, Enrollment Services Director
559-651-2500 Fax: 559-651-4864
Website: www.sjvc.edu
E-mail: susiet@sjvc.edu

COLORADO

IntelliTec College
772 Horizon Dr, Grand Junction CO 81506-3907
Rich Counts, Contact
970-245-8101 Fax: 970-243-8074
Website: www.intelliteccollege.edu
E-mail: admgj@intelliteccollege.edu

IntelliTec College
3673 Parker Blvd Ste 250, Pueblo CO 81008
Crystal Barajas, Director of Admissions
719-542-3181 Fax: 719-242-0068
Website: www.intelliteccollege.edu
E-mail: admpbl@intelliteccollege.edu

Parks College
14280 E Jewell Ave, Aurora CO 80012-5692
Julie Rosenthal, Director of Admissions
303-367-2757 Fax: 303-745-6245
Website: www.cci.edu

San Juan Basin Technical College
PO Box 970, Cortez CO 81321-0970
Shannon South, Director of Student Services
970-565-8457 Fax: 970-565-8450
Website: www.sjbtc.edu
E-mail: ssouth@sjbtc.edu

CONNECTICUT

Middlesex Community College
100 Training Hill Rd, Middletown CT 06457-4889
Mensimah Shabazz, Director of Admissions
860-343-5800 Fax: 860-344-3055
Website: www.mxcc.commnet.edu
E-mail: mshabazz@mxcc.commnet.edu

DELAWARE

Goldey-Beacom College
4701 Limestone Rd, Wilmington DE 19808-1993
Stacey Schwartz, Assistant Director of Admissions
302-998-8814 Fax: 302-996-5408
Website: www.gbc.edu
E-mail: admissions@gbc.edu

FLORIDA

City College
2000 W Commercial Blvd, Fort Lauderdale FL 33309
Britt Carpenter, Director of Admissions
954-492-5353 Fax: 954-491-1965
Website: www.citycollege.edu
E-mail: bcarpenter@citycollege.edu

Florida National College
Hialeah Campus
4425 W 20th Ave, Hialeah FL 33012
Jorge Afonso, Campus Dean
305-821-3333 ext. 1022 Fax: 305-362-0595
Website: www.fnc.edu
E-mail: omarsnc@fnc.edu

Florida National College
South Campus
11865 SW 26th St, Miami FL 33175
Jon Beisenherz, Campus Dean
305-266-9999
Website: www.fnc.edu
E-mail: omarsnc@fnc.edu

Florida State University
600 W College Ave, Tallahassee FL 32306-1096
Janice V. Finney, Director of Admissions
850-644-2525 Fax: 850-644-0197
Website: admissions.fsu.edu
E-mail: admissions@admin.fsu.edu

Jones College
5353 Arlington Expy, Jacksonville FL 32211-5588
Dorothy D. Jones, Chief Executive Officer
904-743-1122 Fax: 904-744-4446
Website: www.jones.edu
E-mail: lwade@jones.edu

Jones College
11430 N Kendall Dr Ste 200, Miami FL 33176
Barclay Charles, Contact
305-275-9996 Fax: 305-743-4446
Website: www.jones.edu
E-mail: pcarbone@jones.edu

SOUTHWEST FLORIDA COLLEGE
1685 Medical Ln, Fort Myers FL 33907-1157
866-SWFC-NOW or 239-939-4766 Fax: 239-936-4040
Website: www.swfc.edu
E-mail: studentinfo@swfc.edu

GEORGIA

**BROWN COLLEGE OF COURT REPORTING &
MEDICAL TRANSCRIPTION**
1740 Peachtree St NW, Atlanta GA 30309-2335
Lynette Eggers, President
404-876-1227 Fax: 404-876-4415
Website: browncollege.com
E-mail: lynette.eggers@browncollege.com

Kennesaw State University
    1000 Chastain Rd NW, Kennesaw GA 30144-5591
    Timothy Mescon, Dean of College of Business
    770-423-6425
    Website: www.kennesaw.edu

North Georgia Technical College
    434 Meeks Ave, Blairsville GA 30512-2983
    Admissions
    706-781-2300 Fax: 706-781-2307
    Website: www.northgatech.edu
    E-mail: info@northgatech.edu

North Georgia Technical College
    8989 Highway 17, Toccoa GA 30577
    706-779-5591
    Website: www.northgatech.edu
    E-mail: info@northgatech.edu

North Georgia Technical College
    Clarkesville Campus
    PO Box 65, Clarkesville GA 30523-0002
    Admissions
    706-754-7700 Fax: 706-754-7777
    Website: www.northgatech.edu
    E-mail: info@northgatech.edu

North Metro Technical College
    5198 Ross Rd SE, Acworth GA 30102-3129
    Missy Cusack, Director of Admissions
    770-975-4000 Fax: 770-975-4142
    Website: www.northmetrotech.edu
    E-mail: info@northmetrotech.edu

SAVANNAH RIVER COLLEGE
    2528 Centerwest Pkwy Bldg A, Augusta GA 30909
    Dawn McCraith, Director
    706-738-5046 Fax: 706-736-3599
    Website: www.savannahrivercollege.com
    E-mail: info@savannahrivercollege.com

TOCCOA FALLS COLLEGE
    PO Box 800899, Toccoa Falls GA 30598
    Christy Meadows, Director of Admissions
    888-785-5624 Fax: 706-282-6012
    Website: www.tfc.edu
    E-mail: admissions@tfc.edu

IDAHO

Brigham Young University - Idaho
    120 Kimball Bldg, Rexburg ID 83460
    Gordon Westenskow, Director of Admissions
    208-496-1020 Fax: 208-496-1220
    Website: www.byui.edu
    E-mail: admissions@byui.edu

ILLINOIS

Aurora University
    347 S Gladstone Ave, Aurora IL 60506-4892
    Carol R. Dunn, Ed.D., Vice President for Enrollment
    800-742-5281 Fax: 630-844-5535
    Website: www.aurora.edu
    E-mail: admission@aurora.edu

College of Office Technology
    1514 W Division St # 2, Chicago IL 60622-3312
    Greg Brown, Director of Admissions
    773-278-0042 Fax: 773-278-0143
    Website: www.cot.edu
    E-mail: kgalva@cotedu.com

Kaskaskia College
    27210 College Rd, Centralia IL 62801-7878
    Tyra Taylor, Dean of Enrollment Management and
    Retention Services
    618-545-3000 Fax: 618-532-1990
    Website: www.kaskaskia.edu
    E-mail: ttaylor@kaskaskia.edu

North Central College
    30 N Brainard St, Naperville IL 60540-4690
    Martha Stolze, Director of Admissions
    630-637-5800 Fax: 630-637-5819
    Website: www.northcentralcollege.edu
    E-mail: admissions@noctrl.edu

South Suburban College of Cook County
    15800 State St, South Holland IL 60473
    Jane Ellen Stocker, Dean of Enrollment Services
    708-596-2000 Fax: 708-225-5806
    Website: www.southsuburbancollege.edu
    E-mail: jstocker@southsuburbancollege.edu

INDIANA

Ancilla Domini College
    Donaldson IN 46513
    Erin Wittmeyer, Director of Admissions
    574-936-8898 Fax: 574-935-1773
    Website: www.ancilla.edu
    E-mail: erin.wittmeyer@ancilla.edu

Brown Mackie College - Fort Wayne
    3000 E Coliseum Blvd, Fort Wayne IN 46805
    Daniel Summer, Campus President
    260-484-4400 Fax: 260-484-2678
    Website: www.brownmackie.edu

Brown Mackie College - South Bend
    1030 E Jefferson Blvd, South Bend IN 46617-3123
    Connie Adelman, Campus President
    574-237-0774 Fax: 574-237-3585
    Website: www.brownmackie.edu

International Business College
    5699 Coventry Ln, Fort Wayne IN 46804
    260-459-4500 Fax: 260-436-1896
    Website: www.ibcfortwayne.edu
    E-mail: skinzer@ibcfortwayne.edu

Ivy Tech Community College - North Central
    220 Dean Johnson Blvd, South Bend IN 46601-3415
    Pam Decker, Director of Admissions
    574-289-7001 Fax: 574-236-7177
    Website: www.ivytech.edu
    E-mail: pdecker@ivytech.edu

Oakland City University
    138 N Lucretia St, Oakland City IN 47660
    Brian J. Baker, Director of Admissions
    800-737-5125 Fax: 812-749-1433
    Website: www.oak.edu
    E-mail: bbaker@oak.edu
    See listing under "Universities"

University of Evansville
    1800 Lincoln Ave, Evansville IN 47722-0001
    Thomas E. Bear, V.P. of Enrollment Services
    800-423-8633 Fax: 812-488-4076
    Website: www.evansville.edu
    E-mail: admission@evansville.edu

IOWA

AIB College of Business
    2500 Fleur Dr, Des Moines IA 50321-1799
    800-444-1921 Fax: 515-244-6773
    Website: www.aib.edu
    E-mail: admissions@aib.edu

Hamilton College
    7009 Nordic Dr, Cedar Falls IA 50613
    Tim Cole, Campus President
    319-277-0220 Fax: 319-363-3812
    Website: www.hamiltonia.edu
    E-mail: ticole@hamiltoncf.com

Hamilton College
    3165 Edgewood Pkwy SW, Cedar Rapids IA 52404
    Susan Spivey, Campus President
    319-363-0481 Fax: 319-363-3812
    Website: www.hamiltonia.edu
    E-mail: spiveys@hamiltonia.edu

Hamilton College
    2570 4th St SW, Mason City IA 50401-4665
    Joe Albers, Executive Director
    641-423-2530 Fax: 641-423-7512
    Website: www.hamiltonia.edu
    E-mail: jalbers@hamiltonia.edu

Hamilton College
    4655 121st St, Urbandale IA 50323-2311
    Ed Rogan, Campus President
    515-727-2100 Fax: 515-727-2115
    Website: www.hamiltonia.edu
    E-mail: erogan_dm@hamiltonia.edu

Iowa Lakes Community College
    3200 College Dr, Emmetsburg IA 50536-1055
    Anne Stansbury, Asst. Director of Admissions
    712-852-5212 Fax: 712-362-8363
    Website: www.iowalakes.edu
    E-mail: info@iowalakes.edu

Iowa Lakes Community College
    300 S 18th St, Estherville IA 51334-2721
    Anne Stansbury, Asst. Director of Admissions
    712-362-7945 Fax: 712-362-8363
    Website: www.iowalakes.edu
    E-mail: info@iowalakes.edu

Iowa Lakes Community College
    1900 Grand Ave, Suite 8, Spencer IA 51301
    Anne Stansbury, Assistant Director of Admissions
    712-262-7141 Fax: 712-262-4047
    Website: www.iowalakes.edu
    E-mail: info@iowalakes.edu

Northwest Iowa Community College
    603 W Park St, Sheldon IA 51201-1046
    Lisa Story, Director of Enrollment Management
    712-324-5061 Fax: 712-324-4136
    Website: www.nwicc.edu
    E-mail: lstory@nwicc.edu

Wartburg College
    PO Box 1003, Waverly IA 50677-0903
    Brent Matthias, Interim Director of Admissions
    319-352-8200 Fax: 319-352-8579
    Website: www.wartburg.edu
    E-mail: admissions@wartburg.edu

KANSAS

Allen County Community College
    1801 N Cottonwood St, Iola KS 66749-1607
    John Masterson, President
    Randy Weber, Director of Admissions
    620-365-5116 Fax: 620-365-3284
    Website: www.allencc.net
    E-mail: weber@allencc.edu

COLBY COMMUNITY COLLEGE
    1255 S Range Ave, Colby KS 67701-4099
    Director of Admissions
    888-634-9350 or 785-460-4690 Fax: 785-460-4691
    Website: www.colbycc.edu
    E-mail: bobbi@colbycc.edu

Flint Hills Technical College
    3301 W 18th Ave, Emporia KS 66801-5957
    Lisa Kirmer, Dean of Student Services
    620-343-4600 Fax: 620-343-4610
    Website: www.fhtc.net
    E-mail: lkirmer@fhtc.net

Independence Community College
    PO Box 708, Independence KS 67301-0708
    Dr. Terry Hetrick, President
    800-842-6063 Fax: 620-331-5344
    Website: www.indycc.edu
    E-mail: admissions@indycc.edu

PINNACLE CAREER INSTITUTE
    1601 W 23rd St Ste 200, Lawrence KS 66046-2703
    Lisa Allen, Admissions Representative
    785-841-9640 Fax: 785-841-4854
    Website: www.pinnaclecareerinstitute.edu
    E-mail: lallen@pcitraining.edu

Tabor College
    400 S Jefferson St, Hillsboro KS 67063-1758
    Rusty Allen, Dean of Enrollment Management
    620-947-3121 Fax: 620-947-6276
    Website: www.tabor.edu
    E-mail: admissions@tabor.edu

KENTUCKY

BECKFIELD COLLEGE
    16 Spiral Drive, Florence KY 41042
    Leah Boerger, Contact
    859-371-9393 Fax: 859-371-5096
    Website: www.beckfieldcollege.com
    E-mail: lboerger@beckfield.edu

Brown Mackie College - Louisville
    300 High Rise Dr, Louisville KY 40213-3263
    Kathleen Belanger, Director of Admissions
    502-968-7191 Fax: 502-357-9956
    Website: www.brownmackie.edu
    E-mail: kbelanger@brownmackie.edu

BROWN MACKIE COLLEGE
    Northern Kentucky Campus
    309 Buttermilk Pike, Fort Mitchell KY 41017-2191
    Joanne Dellefield, Director of Admissions
    859-341-5627 Fax: 859-341-6483
    Website: www.brownmackie.edu
    E-mail: jdellefield@brownmackie.edu

Daymar College
    3361 Buckland Sq, Owensboro KY 42301-5830
    Vickie McDougal Director of Admissions
    800-960-4090 Fax: 270-685-4090
    Website: www.daymarcollege.com

Morehead State University
    Morehead KY 40351-1689
    Dayna Seelig, Enrollment Services
    800-585-6781 Fax: 606-783-5038
    Website: www.moreheadstate.edu
    E-mail: admissions@moreheadstate.edu

LOUISIANA

Delta School of Business and Technology
    517 Broad St, Lake Charles LA 70601-4334
    Gary Holt, President
    337-439-5765 Fax: 337-436-5151
    Website: www.deltatech.edu
    E-mail: susan@deltatech.edu

HERZING COLLEGE
    2400 Veterans Memorial Blvd #410
    Kenner LA 70062-4715
    Genny Bordelon, Director of Admissions
    504-733-0074 Fax: 504-733-0020
    Website: www.herzing.edu
    E-mail: info@nor.herzing.edu

Louisiana State University at Eunice
    PO Box 1129, Eunice LA 70535-1129
    Ron Ryder, Registrar
    337-457-7311 Fax: 337-550-1306
    Website: www.lsue.edu
    E-mail: rryder@lsue.edu

MAINE

Northern Maine Community College
    33 Edgemont Dr, Presque Isle ME 04769-2016
    Bill Casavant, Director of Admissions
    207-768-2700 Fax: 207-768-2831
    Website: www.nmcc.edu
    E-mail: admissions@nmcc.edu

St. Joseph's College of Maine
    278 Whites Bridge Rd, Standish ME 04084-5263
    Vincent Kloskowski, Dean of Admissions
    800-338-7057 Fax: 207-893-7862
    Website: www.sjcme.edu
    E-mail: admission@sjcme.edu

Southern Maine Community College
    2 Fort Rd, South Portland ME 04106-1698
    Dr. James Ortiz, President
    Scott MacDonald, Director of Financial Aid
    207-741-5500 Fax: 207-741-5671
    Website: www.smccme.edu
    E-mail: oharmon@maine.rr.com

MARYLAND

Cecil Community College
    One Seahawk Dr, North East MD 21901
    Sandra S. Rajaski, Registrar & Director of Admissions
    410-287-1000 Fax: 410-287-1001
    Website: www.cecilcc.edu
    E-mail: srajaski@cecilcc.edu

Hagerstown Community College
    11400 Robinwood Dr, Hagerstown MD 21742-6590
    Dr. Daniel E. Bock, Assistant Director of Admissions
    301-790-2800 Fax: 301-791-9165
    Website: www.hagerstowncc.edu
    E-mail: bockd@hagerstowncc.edu

Villa Julie College
    1525 Greenspring Valley Rd
    Stevenson MD 21153-0641
    Mark Hergan, V.P. Enrollment Services
    410-486-7001 Fax: 410-602-6600
    Website: www.vjc.edu/admissions
    E-mail: admissions@mail.vjc.edu

MASSACHUSETTS

Bay State College
    122 Commonwealth Ave, Boston MA 02116-2901
    Craig Pfannenstiehl, President
    617-217-9000 Fax: 617-536-1735

Gibbs College of Boston
    a Private Two-Year College
    126 Newbury St, Boston MA 02116-2904
    Ida Zecco, Vice President of Admissions
    617-578-7100 Fax: 617-578-7163
    Website: www.gibbsboston.edu

Newbury College
    129 Fisher Ave, Brookline MA 02445-5796
    Salvadore Liberto, Vice President of Enrollment
    617-730-7000 Fax: 617-731-9618
    Website: www.newbury.edu

: Southeastern Technical Institute
250 Foundry St, South Easton MA 02375-1780
Beverly A. Pusateri, Director
508-238-1860 Fax: 508-230-1558
Website: ti.sersd.org
E-mail: bpusateri@sersd.org

MICHIGAN

Andrews University
Berrien Springs MI 49104-0001
Randall Graves, Director of Recruitment Services
800-253-2874 Fax: 269-471-2670
Website: www.connect.andrews.edu
E-mail: gravesr@andrews.edu

: **CARNEGIE INSTITUTE**
550 Stephenson Hwy Ste 100, Troy MI 48083-1159
Gloria J. McEachern, President
248-589-1078 Fax: 248-589-1631
Website: www.carnegie-institute.com
E-mail: carnegie47@aol.com

· Delta College
University Center MI 48710-0001
Duff Zube, Director of Admissions
989-686-9093 Fax: 989-667-2202
Website: www.delta.edu
E-mail: admit@delta.edu

: Detroit Business Institute
23077 Greenfield Rd #LL28
Southfield MI 48075-3751
Greg Mitchell, Director of Admissions
248-552-6300 Fax: 248-552-7300
Website: www.dbisouthfield.com
E-mail: info@dbisouthfield.com

· Detroit Business Institute - Downriver
19100 Fort St, Riverview MI 48193
Theresa Hernandez, Director of Admissions
734-479-0660 Fax: 734-479-0738
Website: www.dbidownriver.com
E-mail: info@dbidownriver.com

· **MACOMB COMMUNITY COLLEGE**
44575 Garfield Rd, Clinton Township MI 48038-1139
Information Center
586-445-7999
Website: www.macomb.edu
E-mail: answer@macomb.edu

· **MACOMB COMMUNITY COLLEGE**
14500 E 12 Mile Rd, Warren MI 48088-3896
Information Center
586-445-7999
Website: www.macomb.edu
E-mail: answer@macomb.edu

· Northwestern Michigan College
1701 E Front St, Traverse City MI 49686-3061
Jim Bensley, Admissions Coordinator
800-748-0566 Fax: 231-995-1339
Website: www.nmc.edu
E-mail: jbensley@nmc.edu

· Oakland Community College
2480 Opdyke Rd, Bloomfield Hills MI 48304
Dr. Maurice McCall, Director of Admissions
248-341-2000
Website: www.oaklandcc.edu
E-mail: mhmcall@oaklandcc.edu

: Olympia Career Training Institute
5177 W Main St, Kalamazoo MI 49009
Susan Smith, Director of Admission
269-381-9616 Fax: 269-381-2513
Website: www.olympia-institute.com
E-mail: susans@cci.edu

MINNESOTA

· **ACADEMY COLLEGE**
1101 E 78th St, Bloomington MN 55420-1402
952-851-0066 Fax: 952-851-0094
Website: www.academycollege.edu
E-mail: info@academycollege.edu
See listing under "Career Schools"

· Duluth Business University
4724 Mike Colalillo Dr, Duluth MN 55807-2723
Bonnie Kupczynski, Director
800-777-8406 Fax: 218-628-2127
Website: www.dbumn.edu
E-mail: info@dbumn.edu

· Globe College
7166 10th St N, Oakdale MN 55128
Mike Hughes, Campus Director
651-730-5100 Fax: 651-730-5151
Website: www.globecollege.edu
E-mail: admissions@globecollege.edu

· Hibbing Community College
1515 E 25th St, Hibbing MN 55746-3300
Holly Bigelow, Director of Enrollment
800-224-4HCC or 218-262-7200 Fax: 218-262-6717
Website: www.hibbing.edu
E-mail: admissions@hibbing.edu

· Minnesota State Community & Technical College
900 Highway 34 E, Detroit Lakes MN 56501-2698
Dale Westley, Director of Admissions
800-492-4836 Fax: 218-846-3710
Website: www.minnesota.edu
E-mail: dale.westley@minnesota.edu

: Minnesota State Community & Technical College
PO Box 566, Wadena MN 56482-0566
Paul Drange, Director of Admissions
800-247-2007 Fax: 218-631-7901
Website: www.minnesota.edu
E-mail: paul.drange@minnesota.edu

: Minnesota State Community and Technical College
1900 28th Ave S, Moorhead MN 56560-4899
Laurie McKeever, Director of Admissions
800-426-5603 Fax: 218-299-6584
Website: www.minnesota.edu
E-mail: laurie.mckeever@minnesota.edu

National American University
1550 W Highway 36, Roseville MN 55113
Matthew Mottl, Director of Admissions
651-644-1265 Fax: 651-644-0690
Website: www.national.edu
E-mail: mmottl@national.edu

· Northland Community & Technical College
Highway 1 E, Thief River Falls MN 56701
Kathy Olson, Chairperson
800-959-6282 or 218-681-0850 Fax: 218-681-0774
Website: www.northlandcollege.edu

· Northland Community and Technical College
2022 Central Ave NE
East Grand Forks MN 56721-2702
Deb Riely, Business Program Chair
800-451-3441 Fax: 218-773-4502
Website: www.northlandcollege.edu
E-mail: admissions@northlandcollege.edu

Pillsbury Baptist Bible College
315 S Grove Ave, Owatonna MN 55060-3097
Stephen R. Seidler, Director of Admissions
507-451-2710 Fax: 507-451-0156
Website: www.pillsbury.edu
E-mail: steveseidler@pillsbury.edu

: Ridgewater College-Hutchinson Campus
2 Century Ave SE, Hutchinson MN 55350-3100
Dawn Bjork, Counselor
800-222-4424 Fax: 320-231-7767
Website: www.ridgewater.edu
E-mail: dawn.bjork@ridgewater.edu

· Ridgewater College-Willmar Campus
PO Box 1097, Willmar MN 56201-1097
Sally Kerfeld, Director of Admissions
800-722-1151 Fax: 320-231-7677
Website: www.ridgewater.edu
E-mail: skerfeld@ridgewater.edu

· St. Cloud Technical College
1540 Northway Dr, Saint Cloud MN 56303-1240
Jodi Elness, Director of Enrollment Management
800-222-1009 Fax: 320-308-5981
Website: www.sctc.edu
E-mail: jelness@sctc.edu

MISSOURI

· East Central College
1964 Prairie Dell Rd, Union MO 63084
Karen Wieda, Registrar
636-583-5195 ext. 2220 Fax: 636-583-1897
Website: www.eastcentral.edu
E-mail: wiedaks@eastcentral.edu

· Hickey College
940 Westport Plz, Saint Louis MO 63146-3127
Christopher A. Gearin, President
800-777-1544 or 314-434-2212 Fax: 314-434-1974
Website: www.hickeycollege.edu
E-mail: admin@hickeycollege.edu

· St. Charles Community College
4601 Mid Rivers Mall Dr, Saint Peters MO 63376
Kathy Brockgreitens-Gober, Director of Admissions
636-922-8000 Fax: 636-922-8236
Website: www.stchas.edu
E-mail: adm-reg@stchas.edu

· **SPRINGFIELD COLLEGE**
1010 W Sunshine St, Springfield MO 65807-2446
Scott Lester, Contact
417-864-7220 or 800-475-2699 Fax: 417-866-3335
Website: www.springfield-college.com
E-mail: slester@cci.edu

· Vatterott College
12970 Maurer Industrial Dr, Saint Louis MO 63127
Sherri Bremer, Director of Admissions
314-843-4200 Fax: 314-843-1709
Website: www.vatterott.edu
E-mail: sherri.bremer@vatterott-college.edu

NEBRASKA

Midland Lutheran College
900 N Clarkson St, Fremont NE 68025-4200
Todd Hansen, Associate Director of Admissions
402-941-6501 Fax: 402-941-6513
Website: www.mlc.edu
E-mail: admissions@mlc.edu

· Mid-Plains Community College
McCook Community College Campus
1205 E 3rd St, Mc Cook NE 69001-2631
Kelly Rippen, Director of Recruitment
800-658-4348 Fax: 308-345-8180
Website: www.mpcc.edu
E-mail: rippenk@mpcc.edu

· Mid-Plains Community College
North Platte Community College - South Campus
601 W State Farm Rd, North Platte NE 69101
Kelly Rippen, Director of Recruitment
800-658-4308 ext. 8107 Fax: 308-535-3789
Website: www.mpcc.edu
E-mail: rippenk@mpcc.edu

University of Nebraska at Kearney
905 W 25th St, Kearney NE 68849-0001
Dusty Newton, Director of Admissions
800-KEARNEY Fax: 308-865-8987
Website: www.unk.edu
E-mail: admissionsug@unk.edu

NEVADA

· Career College of Northern Nevada
1195-A Corporate Blvd, Reno NV 89502-2331
Nathan Clark, Director
775-856-2266 Fax: 775-856-0935
Website: www.ccnn.edu
E-mail: lgoldhammer@ccnn4u.com
See listing under "Career Schools"

· **GREAT BASIN COLLEGE**
1500 College Pkwy, Elko NV 89801-5032
Julie G. Byrnes, Director of Enrollment Management
775-753-2271 Fax: 775-753-2311
Website: www.gbcnv.edu
E-mail: bjulie@gbcnv.edu

Morrison University
10315 Professional Circle Suite 201
Reno NV 89521-4826
Charles Timinsky, Director of Enrollment
775-850-0700 Fax: 775-850-0711
Website: www.morrisonuniversity.com

NEW JERSEY

· Atlantic Cape Community College
5100 Black Horse Pike
Mays Landing NJ 08330-2699
Linda McLeod, Assistant Director of College
Recruitment
609-343-5000 Fax: 609-343-4921
Website: www.atlantic.edu
E-mail: accadmit@atlantic.edu
See listing under "Community and Junior Colleges"

· Bergen Community College
400 Paramus Rd, Paramus NJ 07652
Julian Gomez, Asst. Director of Admissions
201-447-7100 Fax: 201-444-7036
Website: www.bergen.edu
E-mail: jgomez@bergen.edu

· Hohokus School - RETS Nutley
103 Park Ave, Nutley NJ 07110-3505
Thomas Eastwick, President
973-661-0600 Fax: 973-661-2954
Website: www.rets-institute.com
E-mail: admissions@rets-institute.com

· Mercer County Community College
West Windsor Campus
PO Box B, Trenton NJ 08690
Savita Bambhrolia, Director of Admissions
609-586-4800 Fax: 609-587-4666
Website: www.mccc.edu
E-mail: admiss@mccc.edu

NEW MEXICO

· International Institute of the Americas
4201 Central Ave NW Suite J
Albuquerque NM 87105-1649
Ed Sigman, Director
505-880-2877 Fax: 505-352-0199
Website: www.iia.edu
E-mail: syelton@iia.edu

· New Mexico State University
1500 N 3rd St, Grants NM 87020-2025
505-287-7981 Fax: 505-287-2329
Website: www.grants.nmsu.edu

NEW YORK

Briarcliffe College
1055 Stewart Ave, Bethpage NY 11714-3545
Theresa Donohue, Director of Admissions
516-918-3600 Fax: 516-470-6020
Website: www.briarcliffe.edu

· Broome Community College
907 Upper Front St, Binghamton NY 13905
Anthony S. Fiorelli, Director of Admissions
607-778-5001 Fax: 607-778-5442
Website: www.sunybroome.edu
E-mail: fiorelli_a@sunybroome.edu

: **CAREER INSTITUTE OF HEALTH & TECHNOLOGY**
340 Flatbush Avenue Ext, Brooklyn NY 11201
Mary Miller, Contact
718-422-1212 Fax: 718-422-1222
Website: www.careerinstitute.edu
E-mail: admissions@careerinstitute.edu

: **CAREER INSTITUTE OF HEALTH & TECHNOLOGY**
200 Garden City Plz, Garden City NY 11530
Mary Miller, Contact
516-877-1225 Fax: 516-877-1959
Website: www.careerinstitute.edu
E-mail: admissions@careerinstitute.edu

: **CAREER INSTITUTE OF HEALTH & TECHNOLOGY**
9525 Queens Blvd Ste 600, Rego Park NY 11374
Mary Miller, Contact
718-897-4868 Fax: 718-897-4863
Website: www.careerinstitute.edu
E-mail: admissions@careerinstitute.edu

· Elmira Business Institute
303 N Main St, Elmira NY 14901
Lisa Roan, Admissions Director
607-733-7177 or 800-843-1812 Fax: 607-733-7178
Website: www.ebi-college.com
E-mail: lroan@ebi-college.com

Hilbert College
5200 S Park Ave, Hamburg NY 14075-1597
Timothy Lee, Director of Admissions
716-649-7900 Fax: 716-649-0702
Website: www.hilbert.edu
E-mail: tlee@hilbert.edu

LONG ISLAND BUSINESS INSTITUTE
6500 Jericho Tpke, Commack NY 11725-2907
Dr. Philip Stander, President
631-499-7100 Fax: 631-499-7114
Website: www.libi.edu
E-mail: rnazar@libi.edu
    Private. Coed. Accreditation: ACICS. Approvals: National Court Reporting Association, NY State Board of Regents. Tuition: $275.00 per credit hour. Fees: $50.00 application fee. Enrollment: 250. Faculty: 25. Student-faculty ratio: 12:1. Associate of Occupational Studies degree offered in Court Reporting, Office Technology. Diploma programs in Medical Transcription, Legal Secretarial, Office Technology, Administrative Assistant.

LONG ISLAND BUSINESS INSTITUTE
37-12 Prince St, Flushing NY 11354-4429
Dr. Philip Stander, President
718-939-5100 Fax: 718-989-9235
Website: www.libi.edu
E-mail: dwang@libi.edu
    Private. Coed. Accreditation: ACICS. Approvals. National Court Reporting Association, NY State Board of Regents. Tuition: $275.00 per credit hour. Fees: $50.00 application fee. Enrollment: 250. Faculty: 25. Student-faculty ratio: 12:1. Associate of Occupational Studies degree offered in Computer Programmer, Administrative Assistant, Office Technology, Business Management, Accounting. Diploma programs in Legal Secretarial, Office Technology, Administrative Assistant.

Monroe College
2501 Jerome Ave, Bronx NY 10468-4305
Evan Jerome, Director of Admissions
718-933-6700 Fax: 718-364-3552
Website: www.monroecollege.edu
E-mail: ejerome@monroecollege.edu

Ridley-Lowell Business & Technical Institute
116 Front St, Binghamton NY 13905-3102
David Lounsbury, Executive Director
607-724-2941 Fax: 607-724-0799
Website: www.ridley.edu
E-mail: info@ridley.edu

Ridley-Lowell Business & Technical Institute
26 S Hamilton St, Poughkeepsie NY 12601-3328
E. Ann Bida, Director of Admissions
845-471-0330 Fax: 845-471-4990
Website: www.ridley.edu
E-mail: pcadmissions@ridley.edu

SUNY College of Technology
2 Main St, Delhi NY 13753-1110
Robert W. Mazzei, Director of Admissions
800-96-DELHI Fax: 607-746-4104
Website: www.delhi.edu
E-mail: enroll@delhi.edu

SUNY Niagara County Community College
3111 Saunders Settlement Rd
Sanborn NY 14132-9487
Kathleen Saunders, Director of Admissions
716-614-6200 Fax: 716-614-6820
Website: www.niagaracc.suny.edu
E-mail: saunders@niagaracc.suny.edu

SUNY Orange County Community College
115 South St, Middletown NY 10940-6437
Margot St. Lawrence, Director of Admissions
845-341-4030 Fax: 845-342-8662
Website: www.sunyorange.edu
E-mail: apply@sunyorange.edu
See listing under "Community and Junior Colleges"

Taylor Business Institute
23 W 17th St 7th Floor, New York NY 10011-5501
800-959-9999 Fax: 212-229-2187
Website: www.tbiglobal.com
E-mail: admissions@tbiglobal.com

Trocaire College
360 Choate Ave, Buffalo NY 14220-2003
Paul B. Hurley, Ph.D., President
716-826-1200 Fax: 716-828-6107
Website: www.trocaire.edu
E-mail: info@trocaire.edu
See listing under "Community and Junior Colleges"

Utica School of Commerce
17 Elm St, Oneonta NY 13820-1828
Misty Davis, Admissions
607-432-7003 Fax: 607-432-7004
Website: www.uscny.com
E-mail: mdavis@uscny.com

Utica School of Commerce
201 Bleecker St, Utica NY 13501-2280
Cindy Delaney, Director of Admissions
315-733-2307 Fax: 315-733-9281
Website: www.uscny.edu
E-mail: admissions@uscny.edu

NORTH CAROLINA

Haywood Community College
185 Freedlander Dr, Clyde NC 28721
Debbie Rowland, Coordinator of Admissions
828-627-4500 Fax: 828-627-4513
Website: www.haywood.edu
E-mail: drowland@haywood.edu

James Sprunt Community College
PO Box 398, Kenansville NC 28349-0398
Rita Brown, Registrar
910-296-2500 Fax: 910-296-1636
Website: www.sprunt.com

Mars Hill College
Mars Hill NC 28754
Chad Holt, Dean of Enrollment
866-MHC-4-YOU Fax: 828-689-1473
Website: www.mhc.edu
E-mail: cholt@mhc.edu

South Piedmont Community College
PO Box 126, Polkton NC 28135-0126
John Curtis, Contact
704-272-5324 Fax: 704-272-8904
Website: www.spcc.edu
E-mail: jcurtis@spcc.edu

NORTH DAKOTA

AAKERS COLLEGE
4012 19th Ave S, Fargo ND 58103-7196
Elizabeth Largent, Director
701-277-3889 Fax: 701-277-5604
Website: www.aakers.edu
E-mail: blargent@aakers.edu

Dickinson State University
Dickinson ND 58601-4896
Steve Glasser, Director of Student Recruitment
800-279-4295 Fax: 701-483-2409
Website: www.dickinsonstate.edu
E-mail: dsu.hawks@dickinsonstate.edu

Minot State University-Bottineau Campus
105 Simrall Blvd, Bottineau ND 58318-1159
Paula Berg, Associate Dean of Student Affairs
800-542-6866 Fax: 701-228-5499
Website: www.misu-b.nodak.edu
E-mail: paula.berg@misu.nodak.edu

Williston State College
PO Box 1326, Williston ND 58802-1326
Penny Powell, Director Enrollment Services
701-774-4200 Fax: 701-774-4544
Website: www.wsc.nodak.edu
E-mail: penny.soiseth@wsc.nodak.edu

OHIO

Brown Mackie College - Cincinnati
1011 Glendale Milford Rd, Cincinnati OH 45215-1107
Robin Krout, President
513-771-2424 Fax: 513-771-3413
Website: www.brownmackie.edu
E-mail: rkrout@brownmackie.edu

Davis College
4747 Monroe St, Toledo OH 43623-4389
Dana Stern, Admissions Director
419-473-2700 Fax: 419-473-2472
Website: www.daviscollege.edu
E-mail: learn@daviscollege.edu

Mount Vernon Nazarene University
800 Martinsburg Rd, Mount Vernon OH 43050-9509
Timothy Eades, Director of Admissions
866-462-6868 Fax: 740-393-0511
Website: www.gotomvnu.com
E-mail: admissions@mvnu.edu
See listing under "Universities"

Ohio University
Chillicothe Campus
PO Box 629, Chillicothe OH 45601
Student Services
740-774-7200 Fax: 740-774-7295
Website: www.ohiou.edu/chillicothe/

OHIO VALLEY COLLEGE OF TECHNOLOGY
16808 St. Clair Ave, PO Box 7000
East Liverpool OH 43920
Scott S. Rogers, Director
330-385-1070 Fax: 330-385-4606
Website: www.ovct.edu
E-mail: info@ovct.edu

Owens Community College
300 Davis St, Findlay OH 45840-3631
William J. Ivoska PhD., Vice President of Student Services
567-429-3500 Fax: 567-423-0246
Website: www.owens.edu
E-mail: admissions@owens.edu

Owens Community College
PO Box 10000, Toledo OH 43699-1947
William J. Ivoska, Ph.D, Vice President of Student Services
567-661-7000 Fax: 567-661-7607
Website: www.owens.edu
E-mail: admissions@owens.edu

Sinclair Community College
444 W 3rd St, Dayton OH 45402-1460
Sara P. Smith, Director of Outreach Services
937-512-3000 Fax: 937-512-2393
Website: www.sinclair.edu
E-mail: admit@sinclair.edu

OKLAHOMA

CAREER POINT INSTITUTE
3138 S Garnett Rd, Tulsa OK 74146-1933
Brad Oakley, Director of Admissions
918-627-8074 Fax: 918-627-4007
E-mail: tadmdir@career-point.org

OREGON

Linn-Benton Community College
6500 Pacific Blvd SW, Albany OR 97321-3774
Christine Baker, Outreach Coordinator
541-917-4811 Fax: 541-917-4868
Website: www.linnbenton.edu
E-mail: admissions@linnbenton.edu

Rogue Community College
3345 Redwood Hwy, Grants Pass OR 97527-9298
Claudia Sullivan, Director of Enrollment Services
541-956-7500 Fax: 541-471-3585
Website: www.roguecc.edu
E-mail: csullivan@roguecc.edu
See listing under "Community and Junior Colleges"

PENNSYLVANIA

Academy of Medical Arts and Business
2301 Academy Dr, Harrisburg PA 17112-1012
717-545-4747
Website: www.ACADcampus.com
E-mail: info@ACADcampus.com

Bradford School
125 W Station Square Dr, Pittsburgh PA 15219
Director of Admissions
412-391-6710 Fax: 412-471-6714
Website: www.bradfordpittsburgh.edu

Career Training Academy
4314 Old William Penn Highway Ste 103
Monroeville PA 15146
Gina Hudac, Admissions Representitive
412-372-3900 Fax: 412-373-4262
Website: www.careerta.edu
E-mail: admissions2@careerta.edu

Career Training Academy
950 5th Ave, New Kensington PA 15068-6308
John Reddy, Director
Tyna Putignano, Director of Admissions
724-337-1000 Fax: 724-335-7140
Website: www.careerta.edu
E-mail: admissions@careerta.edu
See listing under "Career Schools"

Career Training Academy
1500 Northway Mall, Pittsburgh PA 15237
Anna Bartolini, Director North Hills Branch Campus
412-367-4000 Fax: 412-369-7223
Website: www.careerta.edu
E-mail: admissions3@careerta.edu

Central Pennsylvania College
College Hill & Valley Rds, Summerdale PA 17093
Katie Bogovic, Admissions Director
800-759-2727 Fax: 717-728-2505
Website: www.centralpenn.edu
E-mail: katie.bogovic@centralpenn.edu

Computer Learning Network
401 E Winding Hill Rd Ste 101
Mechanicsburg PA 17055-4989
Marlene Macauley, Director of Admissions
717-761-1481 Fax: 717-761-0558
Website: www.clntraining.net
E-mail: mmacauley@clntraining.net

Consolidated School of Business
1605 Clugston Rd, York PA 17404-1779
Robert Safran Jr., Vice President
717-764-9550 Fax: 717-764-9469
Website: www.csb.edu
E-mail: bobjr@csb.edu

Douglas Education Center
130 7th St, Monessen PA 15062-1097
Sherry Lee Walters, Director of Enrollment Services
800-413-6013 Fax: 724-684-7463
Website: www.douglas-school.com
E-mail: swalters@douglas-school.com

DUBOIS BUSINESS COLLEGE
1 Beaver Dr, Du Bois PA 15801-2490
Lisa J. Doty, Director of Admissions
814-371-6920 Fax: 814-371-3974
Website: www.dbcollege.com
E-mail: dotylj@dbcollege.com

DUBOIS BUSINESS COLLEGE
1001 Moore St, Huntingdon PA 16652-1846
Lisa J. Doty, Director of Admissions
814-641-0440 Fax: 814-641-0205
Website: www.dbcollege.com
E-mail: dotylj@dbcollege.com

DUBOIS BUSINESS COLLEGE
701 E 3rd St, Oil City PA 16301-2407
Lisa J. Doty, Director of Admissions
814-677-1322 Fax: 814-677-8237
Website: www.dbcollege.com
E-mail: dotylj@dbcollege.com

Erie Business Center
246 W 9th St, Erie PA 16501-1392
Donna Perino, Director
814-456-7504 Fax: 814-456-6015
Website: www.eriebc.edu
E-mail: perinod@eriebc.edu

Lancaster Bible College
901 Eden Rd, Lancaster PA 17601-5036
Joanne M. Roper, Associate VP for Admissions
866-LBC-4YOU or 717-560-8271 Fax: 717-560-8213
Website: www.lbc.edu
E-mail: admissions@lbc.edu
See listing under "Theological Studies & Religious Vocations"

LAUREL BUSINESS INSTITUTE
11-15 Penn St, Uniontown PA 15401
Lisa Tressler, Supervisor of Enrollment
724-439-4900 Fax: 724-439-3607
Website: www.laurelbusiness.edu
E-mail: lbi@laurelbusiness.edu
    Established 1985. Private. Coed. Accreditation: ACICS, Licensed by the Pennsylvania Department of Education. Enrollment: 310 full-time, 35 part-time. Student-faculty ratio: 12:1. Associate degrees: Accounting, Child Care Education, Cosmetology, I.T. - Computer Software Support, I.T. - Network Administration, Medical Assistant, Medical Insurance Management, Medical Secretary Transcription, Office Administration, Small Business Management, Therapeutic Massage. Diplomas: Legal Secretary, Massage Therapy, Medical Secretary, Word Processing Secretary. Independent Certifications, Authorized Prometric Testing Center, Authorized MOS Testing Center, Financial Aid Services, Job Placement Services.

Lehigh Valley College
2809 E Saucon Valley Rd
Center Valley PA 18034-8447
Joshua Padron, Vice President of Marketing and
Admissions
800-227-9109 Fax: 610-791-7810
Website: www.lehighvalley.edu
E-mail: joshua.padron@lehighvalley.edu

McCann School of Business & Technology
1147 N 4th St, Sunbury PA 17801-1221
Lisa Davis, Director of Admissions
570-286-3058 Fax: 570-286-4723
Website: www.mccannschool.com
E-mail: ldavis@mccannschool.com

Newport Business Institute
945 Greensburg Rd, Lower Burrell PA 15068-3929
Admissions Department
800-752-7695 Fax: 724-339-2950
Website: www.nbi.edu
E-mail: tjpomatto@nbi.edu

Pennco Tech
3815 Otter St, Bristol PA 19007-3618
Glenn Slater, Director of Admissions
215-785-0111 Fax: 215-785-1945
Website: www.penncotech.com
E-mail: admissions@penncotech.com

Western School of Health & Business Careers
421 7th Ave, Pittsburgh PA 15219-1907
Michael Joyce, Director of Admissions
800-333-6607 Fax: 412-227-0419
Website: www.western-school.com
E-mail: mjoyce@western-school.com

York Technical Institute
1405 Williams Rd, York PA 17402
Cathi Killingsworth Bost, Vice President
800-227-9675 or 717-757-1100 Fax: 717-757-4964
Website: www.yti.edu
E-mail: info@yti.edu
See listing under "Career Schools"

RHODE ISLAND

New England Institute of Technology
2500 Post Rd, Warwick RI 02886-2244
Michael Kwiatkowski, Director of Admissions
401-739-5000 Fax: 401-738-5122
Website: www.neit.edu
E-mail: eflynn@neit.edu

SOUTH CAROLINA

Forrest Junior College
601 E River St, Anderson SC 29624-2405
Dr. Julia R. Barnes, President
864-225-7653 Fax: 864-261-7471
Website: www.forrestcollege.edu
E-mail: info@forrestcollege.edu
See listing under "Community and Junior Colleges"

Spartanburg Technical College
PO Box 4386, Spartanburg SC 29305-4386
Nancy Garmroth, Dean of Admissions & Financial Aid
864-592-4810 Fax: 864-592-4945
Website: stcsc.edu

SOUTH DAKOTA

NATIONAL AMERICAN UNIVERSITY
321 Kansas City St, Rapid City SD 57701-3692
Angela G. Beck, Director of Enrollment Management
605-394-4800 Fax: 605-394-4871
Website: www.national.edu/rc/index.html
E-mail: rcadmissions@national.edu

National American University
2801 S Kiwanis Ave Ste 100
Sioux Falls SD 57105-4293
605-334-5430 Fax: 605-334-1575
Website: www.national.edu

Presentation College
1500 N Main St, Aberdeen SD 57401-1280
JoEllen Lindner, Dean of Admissions
605-229-8492 Fax: 605-229-8425
Website: www.presentation.edu
E-mail: admit@presentation.edu

Western Dakota Technical Institute
800 Mickelson Dr, Rapid City SD 57703-4018
Janell Oberlander, Manager of Student Services
605-394-4034 or 800-544-8765 Fax: 605-394-1789
Website: www.westerndakotatech.org
E-mail: admissions@wdti.tec.sd.us
See listing under "Career Schools"

TENNESSEE

Draughons Junior College
PO Box 17386, Nashville TN 37217-0386
615-361-7555 Fax: 615-367-2736
Website: www.draughons.edu

Lipscomb University
3901 Granny White Pike, Nashville TN 37204-3951
Ricky Holaway, Director of Admissions
800-333-4358 ext. 1776 Fax: 615-269-1804
Website: www.lipscomb.edu
E-mail: admissions@lipscomb.edu

Miller-Motte Technical College
1820 Business Park Dr, Clarksville TN 37040-6023
Lisa Teague, Director of Admissions
931-553-0071 Fax: 931-552-2916
Website: www.miller-motte.com
E-mail: lteague@miller-motte.com

Pellissippi State Technical Community College
PO Box 22990, Knoxville TN 37933-0990
Donna Mack, Contact
865-694-6568 Fax: 865-539-7217
Website: www.pstcc.edu
E-mail: dmack@pstcc.edu

Tennessee State University
3500 John A Merritt Blvd, Nashville TN 37209-1561
John Cade, Dean of Admissions & Records
615-963-5101 Fax: 615-963-2930
Website: www.tnstate.edu
E-mail: jcade@tnstate.edu

University of Tennessee
615 McCallie Ave, Chattanooga TN 37403-2504
Yancy Freeman, Director of Admissions
423-425-4111 Fax: 423-425-4157
Website: www.utc.edu
E-mail: Yancy-Freeman@utc.edu

TEXAS

American Commercial College
2007 34th St, Lubbock TX 79411-1899
Michael Otto, Director
806-747-4339 Fax: 806-765-9838
Website: www.acc-careers.com
E-mail: mjotto@acc-careers.com

American Commercial College
5119 Twin Towers Blvd, Odessa TX 79762-5504
Donna Duree, Director
432-362-6768 Fax: 432-550-0556
Website: www.acc-careers.com
E-mail: americancc@acc-careers.com

Angelo State University
ASU Station 11014, San Angelo TX 76909
Bonnie Stennett, Coordinator of Recruiting
800-946-8627 Fax: 325-942-2078
Website: www.angelo.edu
E-mail: admissions@angelo.edu

Blinn College
902 College Ave, Brenham TX 77833-4098
Dennis K. Crowson, Registrar
979-830-4000 Fax: 979-830-4110
Website: www.blinn.edu
E-mail: recruiting@blinn.edu

Blinn College
PO Box 6030, Bryan TX 77805-6030
Dennis K. Crowson, Registrar
979-209-7200 Fax: 979-209-7229
Website: www.blinn.edu
E-mail: recruiting@blinn.edu

Blinn College
100 Ranger Dr, Schulenburg TX 78956-2247
Dennis K. Crowson, Registrar
979-743-5003 Fax: 979-743-5225
Website: www.blinn.edu
E-mail: recruiting@blinn.edu

Blinn College
3701 Outlet Center Dr, Sealy TX 77474
Dennis K. Crowson, Registrar
979-627-7997 Fax: 979-627-0830
Website: www.blinn.edu
E-mail: recruiting@blinn.edu

COURT REPORTING INSTITUTE OF DALLAS
1341 W Mockingbird Ln Ste 200 East
Dallas TX 75247
Eric Juhlin, Regional Director
214-350-9722 Fax: 214-631-0143
Website: www.crid.com
E-mail: ejuhlin@crid.com

COURT REPORTING INSTITUTE OF HOUSTON
13101 Northwest Fwy Ste 100, Houston TX 77040
Cindy Smith, Director
713-996-8300 Fax: 713-996-8360
Website: www.crid.com
E-mail: csmith@crid.com

Galveston College
4015 Avenue Q, Galveston TX 77550-7496
Brian Lowery, Registrar
409-763-6551 Fax: 409-944-1501
Website: www.gc.edu
E-mail: blowery@gc.edu

Hallmark Institute of Technology - Technology Campus
10401 W IH 10, San Antonio TX 78230-1736
Joe Fisher, President
210-690-9000 Fax: 210-697-8225
Website: www.hallmarkinstitute.com
E-mail: sross@hallmarkinstitute.com
Electronics Engineering Technology, Business Office
Administration, Computer Network Systems
Technology, & Medical Assistant.

McLennan Community College
1400 College Dr, Waco TX 76708-1498
Linda Stanford, Director, Business Programs
254-299-8000 Fax: 254-299-8854
Website: www.mclennan.edu
E-mail: lstanford@mclennan.edu

North Central Texas College
1525 W California St, Gainesville TX 76240-4636
Michelle Winters, Registrar
940-668-3315 Fax: 940-665-7075
Website: www.nctc.edu
E-mail: mwinters@nctc.edu

Remington College - Fort Worth Campus
300 E Loop 820, Fort Worth TX 76112-1280
Director of Recruitment
817-451-0017 Fax: 817-496-1257
Website: www.remingtoncollege.edu
E-mail: lynn.wey@remingtoncollege.edu

San Antonio College Medical Dental Assistants
1500 S Jackson Rd, Mc Allen TX 78503-9902
Gabe Garcia, Director of Admissions
956-630-1499 Fax: 956-630-2746
Website: www.sacmda.com
E-mail: gagarcia@sac-mda.com

Temple College
2600 S 1st St, Temple TX 76504-7435
Angela Balch, Director of Admissions & Records
254-298-8300 Fax: 254-298-8288
Website: www.templejc.edu
E-mail: ruth.bridges@templejc.edu

Tyler Junior College
PO Box 9020, Tyler TX 75711-9020
Joan Jones, Interim Dean
800-687-5680
Website: www.tjc.edu
E-mail: jjon@tjc.edu
See listing under "Community and Junior Colleges"

University of Houston
122 E Cullen Bldg, Houston TX 77204-2023
Office of Admission
713-743-9595
Website: www.uh.edu
E-mail: admissions@uh.edu

UTAH

L.D.S. BUSINESS COLLEGE
95 North 300 West, Salt Lake City UT 84101-3500
Kathleen Howe, Assistant Director of Admissions
801-524-8145 Fax: 801-524-1900
Website: www.ldsbc.edu
E-mail: admissions@ldsbc.edu
See listing under "Career Schools"

Stevens Henager College
PO Box 9428, Ogden UT 84409-0428
Cindy Williams, Director of Admissions
801-394-7791 Fax: 801-621-0866
Website: www.stevenshenager.edu
E-mail: shcogden@yahoo.com

VIRGINIA

Radford University
PO Box 6903, Radford VA 24142
David W. Kraus, Director of Admissions
800-890-4265 Fax: 540-831-5038
Website: www.radford.edu
E-mail: ruadmiss@radford.edu

Southside Virginia Community College
109 Campus Dr, Alberta VA 23821-2930
Ronald E. Mattox, Dean of Admissions
434-949-1014 Fax: 434-949-7863
Website: www.sv.vccs.edu
E-mail: ronald.mattox@sv.vccs.edu

Southside Virginia Community College
200 Daniel Rd, Keysville VA 23947
Ronald E. Mattox, Dean of Admissions
434-736-2018 Fax: 434-736-2082
Website: www.sv.vccs.edu
E-mail: ronald.mattox@sv.vccs.edu

WASHINGTON

Clover Park Technical College
4500 Steilacoom Blvd SW
Lakewood WA 98499-4098
Dr. Sharon McGavick, President
253-589-5678 Fax: 253-589-5601
Website: www.cptc.edu
E-mail: jim.griffith@cptc.edu

Everett Community College
2000 Tower St, Everett WA 98201
Christine Kerlin, Associate Dean
425-388-9100 Fax: 425-388-9173
Website: www.everettcc.edu
E-mail: ckerlin@everettcc.edu

Walla Walla Community College
500 Tausick Way, Walla Walla WA 99362-9270
Dan Biagi, Director
509-527-4283 or 877-992-9922 Fax: 509-527-4480
Website: www.wwcc.edu
E-mail: dan.biagi@wwcc.edu
See listing under "Community and Junior Colleges"

Wenatchee Valley College
PO Box 2058, Omak WA 98841
Alex Roberts, Director
509-422-7805 Fax: 509-682-6541
Website: www.wvc.edu

Wenatchee Valley College
1300 5th St, Wenatchee WA 98801-1799
Marco Azurdia, Dean, Student Development
509-682-6805 Fax: 509-682-6541
Website: www.wvc.edu

WEST VIRGINIA

Concord University
Athens WV 24712
Michael Curry, Vice President of Financial Aid &
Admissions
888-384-5249 Fax: 304-384-3218
Website: www.concord.edu
E-mail: admissions@concord.edu

Davis & Elkins College
100 Campus Dr, Elkins WV 26241-3996
Renee Heckel, Director of Enrollment Management
800-624-3157 Fax: 304-637-1800
Website: www.davisandelkins.edu
E-mail: admiss@davisandelkins.edu

Mountain State College
1508 Spring St, Parkersburg WV 26101-3993
Judith Sutton, Director
304-485-5487 Fax: 304-485-3524
Website: www.mountainstate.org
E-mail: admin@mountainstate.org
See listing under "Career Schools"

Mountain State University
Box 9003, Beckley WV 25802-9003
866-FOR-MSU1 or 304-929-INFO Fax: 304-253-5072
Website: www.mountainstate.edu
E-mail: gomsu@mountainstate.edu
See listing under "Universities"

WISCONSIN

Blackhawk Technical College
PO Box 5009, Janesville WI 53547-5009
Gregg Bosak, Administration, Community Information
608-757-7769 Fax: 608-757-7740
Website: www.blackhawk.edu
E-mail: gbosak@blackhawk.edu

Wisconsin Indianhead Technical College
505 Pine Ridge Dr, Shell Lake WI 54871
Laura Urban, Dean
800-243-9482 Fax: 715-468-2819
Website: www.witc.edu
E-mail: mcrandal@witc.edu

WYOMING

Laramie County Community College
1400 E College Dr, Cheyenne WY 82007-3204
Jenny Hargett, Director of Admissions
307-778-5222 Fax: 307-778-1350
Website: www.lccc.wy.edu
E-mail: learnmore@lccc.wy.edu

University of Wyoming
Admissions Office
Dept 3435, Laramie WY 82071-3435
Aaron Appelhans, Contact
800-342-5996 Fax: 307-766-4042
Website: www.uwyo.edu
E-mail: why-wyo@uwyo.edu

PUERTO RICO

Atlantic College
PO Box 1774, Guaynabo PR 00970-1774
Zaida Perez, Director of Admissions
787-720-1022 Fax: 787-720-1092
Website: www.atlanticcollege-pr.com
E-mail: atlancol@coqui.net

Colegio Mayor de Technologia
PO Box 1490, Arroyo PR 00714
Julia Melendez, Director of Admissions
787-839-5266 Fax: 787-839-0033
Website: www.colegiomayortec.com
E-mail: cmtarroy@coqui.net

EDIC College
PO Box 9120, Caguas PR 00726-9120
Virginia Cartagena, Director of Admissions
787-744-8519 Fax: 787-743-0855
Website: www.ediccollege.com
E-mail: edic@coqui.net

Instituto de Banca y Comercio
61 Ponce De Leon Ave, Hato Rey PR 00919
Rafael Jimenez, Vice President
787-754-7120 Fax: 787-754-7143
Website: www.ibanca.net
E-mail: rjimenez@ibancapr.com

MBTI Business Training Institute
1256 Ave Ponce de Leon, Santurce PR 00907-3965
Miguel A. Fernandez, Contact
787-723-9403 Fax: 787-723-9447
Website: www.mbti.com
E-mail: hdavila@mbti.com

PONCE PARAMEDICAL COLLEGE
1213 Calle Acacia Villa Flores, Ponce PR 00716-2901
Alberto Aristizabal, President
787-848-1589 Fax: 787-259-0169
E-mail: ppcadmin@popac.edu

Universidad Adventista de las Antillas
PO Box 118, Mayaguez PR 00919-0118
Evelyn Del Valle Rivera, Director of Admissions
787-834-9595 Fax: 787-834-9597
Website: www.uaa.edu
E-mail: admissions@uaa.edu

BUSINESS AND MANAGEMENT

ALABAMA

Alabama A & M University
PO Box 908, Normal AL 35762
Antonio Boyle, Director of Admissions
256-372-5245 Fax: 256-372-5249
Website: www.aamu.edu
E-mail: aboyle@aamu.edu

Auburn University
Auburn AL 36849
334-844-4000

Auburn University at Montgomery
PO Box 244023, Montgomery AL 36124
334-244-3000

Bishop State Community College - Four Campuses
351 N Broad St, Mobile AL 36603-5898
Dr. Terry Hazzard, Dean of Students
251-690-6801 Fax: 251-690-6446
Website: www.bishop.edu
E-mail: thazzard@bishop.edu

CALHOUN COMMUNITY COLLEGE
PO Box 2216, Decatur AL 35609-2216
M. Wayne Tosh, Registrar
256-306-2500 Fax: 256-306-2941
Website: www.calhoun.edu
E-mail: sla@calhoun.edu

Faulkner University
5345 Atlanta Hwy, Montgomery AL 36109-3398
Keith Mock, Director of Admissions
800-879-9816 ext. 7200 or 334-386-7200
Fax: 334-386-7137
Website: www.faulkner.edu
E-mail: admissions@faulkner.edu

Herzing College
280 W Valley Ave, Homewood AL 35209-4816
Kim Conway, Director of Admissions
205-916-2800 Fax: 205-916-2807
Website: www.herzing.edu/birmingham
E-mail: info@bhm.herzing.edu

Huntingdon College
1500 E Fairview Ave, Montgomery AL 36106-2148
334-833-4222

Judson College
302 Bibb St, Marion AL 36756
Michael Scotto, Director of Admissions
800-447-9472 Fax: 334-683-5147
Website: www.judson.edu
E-mail: admissions@judson.edu

Oakwood College
Oakwood Rd NW, Huntsville AL 35896-0001
256-726-7000

Samford University
800 Lakeshore Dr, Birmingham AL 35229-0002
205-726-3673

Spring Hill College
4000 Dauphin St, Mobile AL 36608-1791
334-460-4000

Stillman College
PO Box 1430, Tuscaloosa AL 35403-1430
205-349-4240

Talladega College
627 Battle St W, Talladega AL 35160-2354
256-362-0206

Troy University
Troy AL 36082-0001
Jim Hutto, Dean of Enrollment Management
334-670-3175

Troy University Dothan
PO Box 8368, Dothan AL 36304-0368
334-983-6556

University of Alabama
Box 870118, Tuscaloosa AL 35487
Dr. Lisa B. Harris, Director of Admissions
205-348-5666

University of Alabama at Birmingham
Univ Sta, Birmingham AL 35294-0001
205-934-4011

University of Alabama in Huntsville
PO Box 1247, Huntsville AL 35899-0001
Ann Lee, Assoc. Director for Recruiting Program and Events
1-800-UAH-CALL Fax: 256-824-6073
Website: www.uah.edu
E-mail: leev@uah.edu

University of Mobile
PO Box 13220, Mobile AL 36663-0220
251-675-5990

University of Montevallo
Station 6030, Montevallo AL 35115
205-665-6030

University of South Alabama
307 University Blvd N, Mobile AL 36688-3053
Melissa Haab, Director of Admissions
251-460-6141 Fax: 251-460-7876
Website: www.southalabama.edu
E-mail: admiss@usouthal.edu

University of West Alabama
Hwy 11, Livingston AL 35470
205-652-3400

ALASKA

Sheldon Jackson College
801 Lincoln St, Sitka AK 99835-7651
800-478-4556

University of Alaska Anchorage
PO Box 141629, Anchorage AK 99514-1629
Cecile Mitchell, Director of Enrollment Services
907-786-1480 Fax: 907-786-4888
Website: www.uaa.alaska.edu/
E-mail: enroll@uaa.alaska.edu

University of Alaska Fairbanks
PO Box 757480, Fairbanks AK 99775
907-474-7581

University of Alaska Southeast
11120 Glacier Hwy, Juneau AK 99801-8625
Paul Kraft, Dean of Students/Enrollment Management
907-796-6000 Fax: 907-796-6005
Website: www.uas.alaska.edu
E-mail: paul.kraft@uas.alaska.edu

ARIZONA

Arizona State University
PO Box 870112, Tempe AZ 85287-0112
480-965-9011

Arizona State University West
PO Box 37110, Phoenix AZ 85069-7110
602-543-5500

International Institute of the Americas
925 S Gilbert Rd Ste 201, Mesa AZ 85204-4440
Meredith Kiljan, Director
480-545-8755 Fax: 480-926-1371
Website: www.iia.edu
E-mail: mjensen@iia.edu

International Institute of the Americas
6049 N 43rd Ave, Phoenix AZ 85019-1600
Lynn McConnell, Director
602-242-6265 Fax: 602-589-1353
Website: www.iia.edu
E-mail: lmcconnell@iia.edu

International Institute of the Americas
4136 N 75th Ave Ste 211, Phoenix AZ 85033-3169
Dr. Lori Ebert, Director
623-849-8208 Fax: 623-849-0110
Website: www.iia.edu
E-mail: nsabino@iia.edu

International Institute of the Americas
5441 E 22nd St, Tucson AZ 85710
Leigh Anne Pechota, Director
520-748-9799 Fax: 520-748-9355
Website: www.iia.edu
E-mail: lpechota@iia.edu

Mundus Institute
2001 W Camelback Rd Ste 400
Phoenix AZ 85015-3466
Gene Lambert, Admissions
602-246-7111 Fax: 602-246-7222
Website: www.mundusinstitute.com
E-mail: admissions@mundusinstitute.com

Northern Arizona University
PO Box 4084, Flagstaff AZ 86011-0001
520-523-9011

Pima Community College
4905 E Broadway Blvd, Tucson AZ 85709-1010
Wendy Kilgore, Ph.D., Director of Admissions
520-206-4500 Fax: 520-206-4790
Website: www.pima.edu
E-mail: infocenter@pima.edu

Southwestern College
2625 E Cactus Rd, Phoenix AZ 85032-7097
Admissions/Financial Aid Office
800-247-2697 or 602-992-6101 Fax: 602-404-2159
Website: www.swcaz.edu
E-mail: admissions@swcaz.edu

Thunderbird, The Garvin School of International Management
15249 N 59th Ave, Glendale AZ 85306-3236
Judy Johnson, Associate VP of Admissions & Financial Aid
800-848-9084 or 602-978-7100 Fax: 602-439-5432
Website: www.thunderbird.edu
E-mail: johnsonj@thunderbird.edu

University of Arizona
Tucson AZ 85721-0040
Paul Kohn, Director of Admissions
520-621-3237 Fax: 520-621-9799
Website: www.admissions.arizona.edu or www.arizona.edu

University of Phoenix
4615 E Elwood St, Phoenix AZ 85040-1908
480-966-9577

ARKANSAS

Arkansas State University
PO Box 1630, State University AR 72467-1630
870-972-2100

Hendrix College
1600 Washington Ave, Conway AR 72032-3080
501-329-6811

John Brown University
2000 W University St, Siloam Springs AR 72761-2121
877-JBU-INFO

Lyon College
PO Box 2317, Batesville AR 72503-2317
Dan Rutledge, Director of Admissions
870-793-9813

Ouachita Baptist University
410 Ouachita St, Arkadelphia AR 71998-0001
David Goodman, Director of Admissions
870-245-5110 Fax: 870-245-5500
Website: www.obu.edu
E-mail: admissions@obu.edu

Phillips Community College of the University of Arkansas
PO Box 785, Helena AR 72342-0785
Dr. Steven Murray, Chancellor
Lynn Boone, Vice Chancellor for Student Services /
Registrar
870-338-6474 Fax: 870-338-7542
Website: www.pccua.edu
E-mail: lboone@pccua.edu

Southern Arkansas University
100 E University, Magnolia AR 71753
870-235-4000

University of Arkansas at Fayetteville
1 University of Arkansas, Fayetteville AR 72701-1201
479-575-2000

University of Arkansas at Little Rock
2801 S University Ave, Little Rock AR 72204-1000
501-569-3000

University of Arkansas at Monticello
PO Box 3600, Monticello AR 71656
870-367-6811

University of Arkansas at Pine Bluff
1200 University Dr, Pine Bluff AR 71601-2799
870-543-8000

University of Central Arkansas
201 Donaghey Ave, Conway AR 72035-5003
501-450-5000

University of the Ozarks
415 N College Ave, Clarksville AR 72830-2880
Jim Decker, Director of Admissions
479-979-1000

CALIFORNIA

Antioch University
801 Garden St Ste 101
Santa Barbara CA 93101-1581
Ankara McPherson, Director of Admissions
805-962-8179 Fax: 805-962-4786
Website: www.antiochsb.edu
E-mail: amcpherson@antiochsb.edu

Antioch University Southern California
400 Corporate Pointe, Culver City CA 90230-7615
Admissions Office
800-7-ANTIOCH Fax: 310-821-6032
E-mail: admissions@antiochla.edu
Master of Arts in Organizational Management.

Azusa Pacific University
901 E Alosta Ave, Azusa CA 91702
626-969-3434

Biola University
13800 Biola Ave, La Mirada CA 90639-0001
562-903-6000

California Baptist University
8432 Magnolia Ave, Riverside CA 92504-3297
951-689-5771

CALIFORNIA COAST UNIVERSITY
700 N Main St, Santa Ana CA 92701
Admissions Office: 888-CCU-UNIV or 714-547-9625
Fax: 714-547-5777
Dr. Thomas Neal, President
Dr. Cynthia Teeple, Academic Vice President
Website: www.calcoast.edu
E-mail: info@calcoast.edu
Established 1973. Proprietary. Coed. Accreditation: California Coast University holds accreditation through the Accrediting Commission of the Distance Education and Training Council (DETC). The DETC is an educational association located in Washington, D.C. Founded in 1926, it is the standard setting agency for distance education institutions. Approval: Bureau for Private Post-secondary and Vocational Education - State of California, charter member California Association of State Approved Colleges & Universities, member Association for Adult & Continuing Education, member The Alliance for Private Post Secondary Academic Institutions.
Tuition: $2,805-$12,070. California Coast University has selected the SLM Corporation, commonly known as Sallie Mae, to help the university provide financing for its students. Sallie Mae is the nation's leading provider of education funding. Sallie Mae also allows students to borrow additional loan amounts to cover additional expenses, such as textbooks, equipment, or living expenses.
Enrollment: 30,000. California Coast University is approved by the California State Approving Agency to enroll veterans or other eligible persons under Title 38, U.S. Code. California Coast University holds a Memorandum of Understanding with Defense Activity for Non-Traditional Education Support (DANTES) as an external degree provider.
A private college offering off-campus independent study programs in the traditional areas of business administration, management, psychology, education. Admissions: enroll year round, requires official transcripts, letters of recommendation, detailed curriculum vita or occupational history.
Process: evaluation of prior academic work followed by analysis of occupational history, including participation in workshops, seminars, training programs, specialized projects for credit. Credit is demonstrated by accelerated learning guides or study guides.
Residency: All course work may be completed off campus, utilizing correspondence methods. Interest free loans available to students.

California Polytechnic State University
San Luis Obispo CA 93407
805-756-1111

California State Polytechnic University
3801 W Temple Ave, Pomona CA 91768-2557
909-869-2000

California State University-Bakersfield
9001 Stockdale Hwy, Bakersfield CA 93311-1022
661-664-2011

California State University-Chico
Chico CA 95929-0001
530-898-6116

California State University-East Bay
25800 Carlos Bee Blvd, Hayward CA 94542-3001
510-885-3000

California State University-Fresno
Fresno CA 93740-0001
559-278-4240

California State University-Fullerton
PO Box 34080
Fullerton CA 92634
714-278-2011

California State University-Long Beach
1250 N Bellflower Blvd, Long Beach CA 90840-0006
562-985-4111

California State University-Los Angeles
5151 State University Dr, Los Angeles CA 90032
323-343-3000

California State University-Northridge
18111 Nordhoff St, Northridge CA 91330-0001
818-677-1200

California State University-Sacramento
6000 J St, Sacramento CA 95819-2605
916-278-6011

California State University-San Bernadino
5500 University Pkwy
San Bernardino CA 92407-2393
Olivia Rosas, Director of Admissions
909-880-5000 Fax: 909-880-7034
Website: enrollment.csusb.edu
E-mail: orosas@csusb.edu

California State University-Stanislaus
801 W Monte Vista Ave, Turlock CA 95382-0256
Lisa Bernardo, Director of Admissions
209-667-3507

Chapman University
One University Drive, Orange CA 92866-1099
Michael Drummy, Assistant Vice President for Enrollment
Services and Chief Admission Officer
714-997-6411 or 888-CUAPPLY Fax: 714-997-6713
Website: www.chapman.edu
E-mail: admit@chapman.edu

CONCORDIA UNIVERSITY
1530 Concordia, Irvine CA 92612-3203
Lori McDonald, Executive Director of Enrollment Services
800-229-1200 or 949-854-8002 Fax: 949-854-6894
Website: www.cui.edu
E-mail: admission@cui.edu

FASHION CAREERS COLLEGE
1923 Morena Blvd, San Diego CA 92110-3555
Tanya McAnear, Director of Admissions
619-275-4700 Fax: 619-275-0635
Website: www.fashioncareerscollege.com
E-mail: info@fashioncareerscollege.com
Established 1979. Private. Coed. Accreditation: ACICS. Tuition: $15,900 per year for Fashion Business & Technology. $15,900 per year for Fashion Design & Technology program, day or evening program (tuition includes required books & certain supplies). Registration Fee: $25. Enrollment: 120 full-time. Faculty: 15. Student-faculty ratio: 10:1. Degree & Certificate programs. Library: 850 volumes. Theoretical and practical training gives students a relevant and comprehensive education in Fashion Business & Technology and Fashion Design & Technology. Placement assistance and internships available.

FRESNO CITY COLLEGE
1101 E University Ave, Fresno CA 93741-0002
Dayann Dietrich, Contact
559-442-8241 Fax: 559-237-4232
Website: www.fresnocitycollege.com
E-mail: fcc.admissions@scccd.com

Fresno Pacific University
1717 S Chestnut Ave, Fresno CA 93702-4798
559-453-2000

GEMOLOGICAL INSTITUTE OF AMERICA
The Robert Mouawad Campus
5345 Armada Dr, Carlsbad CA 92008-4602
Jason Drake, Admissions Manager
800-421-7250 ext. 4001 or 760-603-4001
Fax: 760-603-4003
Website: www.gia.edu
E-mail: eduinfo@gia.edu
Established 1931. Nonprofit. Private. Coed. Accreditation: ACCSCT. Diplomas: Graduate Gemologist, Graduate Jeweler, Graduate Jeweler Gemologist, Jewelry Business Management, Applied Jewelry Arts. Programs and courses range from five days to 17 months. Financial aid. Classes begin year round.
See listing under "Home Study and Correspondence"

Holy Names University
3500 Mountain Blvd, Oakland CA 94619-1699
Dr. Hoffman-Marr, Director of Admissions
510-436-1010

Humboldt State University
1 Harpst St, Arcata CA 95521-8299
707-826-3011

ITT Technical Institute
12669 Encinitas Ave, Sylmar CA 91342-3664
Kelly Christensen, Director of Admissions
818-364-5151 Fax: 818-364-5150
Website: www.itt-tech.edu
E-mail: kchristensen@itt-tech.edu

John F. Kennedy University
100 Ellinwood Way, Pleasant Hill CA 94523-4817
Ellena Bloedorn, Director of Admissions
925-969-3300

La Sierra University
4700 Pierce St, Riverside CA 92515-8247
Bobby Brown, Director of Admissions
800-874-5587

Loyola Marymount University
7900 Loyola Blvd, Los Angeles CA 90045-2699
310-338-2700

Maric College
9055 Balboa Ave, San Diego CA 92123
Geraldine Rorrison, Director of Admissions
858-279-4500 Fax: 858-279-4885
Website: www.mariccollege.edu
E-mail: grorrison@mariccollege.edu

Menlo College
1000 El Camino Real, Atherton CA 94027-4300
650-688-3753

MTI College
5221 Madison Ave, Sacramento CA 95841-3003
Marije Miller, Director of Admissions
916-339-1500 Fax: 916-339-0305
Website: www.mticollege.edu
E-mail: mmiller@mticollege.edu

Mt. St. Mary's College
12001 Chalon Rd, Los Angeles CA 90049-1599
310-954-4000

National University
11255 N Torrey Pines Rd, La Jolla CA 92037-1011
858-642-8000

Northwestern Polytechnic University
47671 Westinghouse Dr, Fremont CA 94539
Paul Jensen, Contact
510-657-5913 Fax: 510-657-8975
Website: www.npu.edu
E-mail: npuadm@npu.edu

Notre Dame de Namur University
1500 Ralston Ave, Belmont CA 94002-1997
Martin Bednarek, Director of Admissions
800-263-0545

Orange Coast College
PO Box 5005, Costa Mesa CA 92628-5005
Kristin Clark, Director of Admissions
714-432-5773 Fax: 714-432-5736
Website: www.orangecoastcollege.edu
E-mail: kclark@cccd.edu

Pacific States University
1516 S Western Ave, Los Angeles CA 90006
Dr. Brandon Kim, Associate University Dean
323-731-2383 Fax: 323-731-7276
Website: www.psuca.edu
E-mail: admissions@psuca.edu
See listing under "Universities"

Pacific Union College
1 Angwin Ave, Angwin CA 94508-9797
707-965-6311

Point Loma Nazarene University
3900 Lomaland Dr, San Diego CA 92106-2810
Eric Groves, Director of Admissions
800-733-7770

San Diego Christian College
2100 Greenfield Dr, El Cajon CA 92019-1157
Jon Melone, Director of Admissions
800-676-2242 Fax: 619-590-1739
Website: www.sdcc.edu
E-mail: admissions@sdcc.edu

San Diego State University
5500 Campanile Dr, San Diego CA 92182-0002
619-594-5200

San Francisco State University
1600 Holloway Ave, San Francisco CA 94132-1722
415-338-1111

San Joaquin Valley College
201 New Stine Rd, Bakersfield CA 93309-2659
Jaime Delgado, Enrollment Services Director
661-834-1026 Fax: 559-651-4864
Website: www.sjvc.edu
E-mail: jaime.delgado@sjvc.edu

San Joaquin Valley College
295 E Sierra Ave, Fresno CA 93710-3616
Nora Twarynski, Enrollment Services Director
559-448-8282 Fax: 559-651-4864
Website: www.sjvc.edu
E-mail: nora.twarynski@sjvc.edu

San Joaquin Valley College
1700 McHenry Village Way Suite 6
Modesto CA 95350
Joseph Holt, Director of Admissions
209-527-7582 Fax: 559-651-4864
Website: www.sjvc.edu
E-mail: josephh@sjvc.edu

San Joaquin Valley College
11050 Olson Dr, Rancho Cordova CA 95670
Joseph Holt, Director of Admissions
559-651-2500 Fax: 559-651-4864
Website: www.sjvc.edu
E-mail: joseph.holt@sjvc.edu

San Joaquin Valley College
10641 Church St, Rancho Cucamonga CA 91730
Ramon Abreu, Enrollment Services Director
909-948-7582 Fax: 559-651-4864
Website: www.sjvc.edu
E-mail: ramon.abreu@sjvc.edu

San Joaquin Valley College
8400 W Mineral King Ave, Visalia CA 93291-9283
Susie Topjian, Enrollment Services Director
559-651-2500 Fax: 559-651-4864
Website: www.sjvc.edu
E-mail: susiet@sjvc.edu

San Jose State University
1 Washington Sq, San Jose CA 95192-0001
408-924-1000

Santa Clara University
500 El Camino Real, Santa Clara CA 95053-0001
408-554-4000

Simpson University
2211 College View Dr, Redding CA 96003-8606
Jim Herberger, Director of Admissions
888-9-SIMPSON Fax: 530-226-4861
Website: www.simpsonuniversity.edu
E-mail: admissions@simpsonuniversity.edu
See listing under "Liberal Arts and Sciences"

Sonoma State University
1801 E Cotati Ave, Rohnert Park CA 94928-3609
Louis T. Levy, Senior Director Enrollment Services
707-664-2880

Stanford University
520 Lasuen Mall Union 232, Stanford CA 94305-3005
650-723-2300

University of California
110 Sproul Hall, Berkeley CA 94720-5804
510-642-6000

University of California
1 Shields Ave, Davis CA 95616
530-752-1011

University of California
Irvine CA 92697-0001
949-824-5011

University of California
Los Angeles CA 90095-0001
310-825-4321

University of California
900 University Ave, Riverside CA 92521-0001
951-827-1012

University of California-Santa Cruz
Santa Cruz CA 95064
831-459-0111

University of Judaism
15600 Mulholland Dr, Los Angeles CA 90077-1599
Bryan Pisetsky, Director of Undergraduate Admissions
310-476-9777

University of La Verne
1950 3rd St, La Verne CA 91750-4443
800-876-4858

University of San Diego
5998 Alcala Park, San Diego CA 92110-2492
Admissions
619-260-4506

University of San Francisco
2130 Fulton St, San Francisco CA 94117-1050
415-422-5555

University of Southern California
Univ Park, Los Angeles CA 90089-0001
213-740-2311

University of the Pacific
3601 Pacific Ave, Stockton CA 95211-0197
209-946-2011

Vanguard University of Southern California
55 Fair Dr, Costa Mesa CA 92626-6597
714-556-3610

Whittier College
PO Box 634, Whittier CA 90608-0634
Kieron Miller, Director of Admissions
562-907-4200 Fax: 562-907-4870
Website: www.whittier.edu
E-mail: kmiller@whittier.edu

COLORADO

Adams State College
Alamosa CO 81102
Matt Gallegos, Director of Admissions
800-824-6494

Colorado State University
102 Administration, Fort Collins CO 80523-0001
970-491-1101

Colorado State University - Pueblo
2200 Bonforte Blvd, Pueblo CO 81001-4990
719-549-2461

Community College of Aurora
16000 E Centretech Pkwy, Aurora CO 80011-9036
303-360-4700 Fax: 303-361-7432
Website: www.ccaurora.edu
E-mail: admissions@ccaurora.edu

Denver Career College
500 E 84th Ave Suite W200
Thornton CO 80229-5316
JoAnn Navarro, Director of Admissions
800-848-0550 Fax: 303-295-0102
Website: www.denvercareercollege.com
E-mail: admissions-045@denvercareercollege.com

Fort Lewis College
1000 Rim Dr, Durango CO 81301-3999
970-247-7010

Mesa State College
1100 North Ave, Grand Junction CO 81501
970-248-1020

Metropolitan State College
PO Box 173362, Campus Box 13
Denver CO 80217-3362
303-556-3245

National American University
5125 N Academy Blvd
Colorado Springs CO 80918-4001
Jeanne Liepe, Campus Director
719-277-0588

National American University
1325 S Colorado Blvd #100, Denver CO 80222-3308
Nathan Larson, Regional President
303-758-6700

NORTHEASTERN JUNIOR COLLEGE

100 College Ave, Sterling CO 80751-2399
Judy Giacomini, Interim Chief Administrative Officer
Tina Joyce, Director of Admissions
970-521-7000 or 970-521-6752 Fax: 970-521-6801
Website: www.njc.edu
E-mail: tina.joyce@njc.edu

Parks College
14280 E Jewell Ave, Aurora CO 80012-5692
Julie Rosenthal, Director of Admissions
303-367-2757 Fax: 303-745-6245
Website: www.cci.edu

Regis University
3333 Regis Blvd, Denver CO 80221-1099
303-458-4900

San Juan Basin Technical College
PO Box 970, Cortez CO 81321-0970
Shannon South, Director of Student Services
970-565-8457 Fax: 970-565-8450
Website: www.sjbtc.edu
E-mail: ssouth@sjbtc.edu

University of Colorado
Boulder CO 80309-0001
303-492-1411

University of Colorado
1420 Austin Bluffs Pkwy
Colorado Springs CO 80918-3735
719-262-3000

University of Colorado at Denver and Health Sciences Center
Downtown Denver Campus
PO Box 173364, Denver CO 80217-3364
303-556-5800 Fax: 303-556-5904
Website:
www.cudenver.edu/academics/colleges/business

University of Denver
2199 S University Blvd, Denver CO 80208-0001
303-871-2000

UNIVERSITY OF DENVER UNIVERSITY COLLEGE

2211 S Josephine St, Denver CO 80208
Dr. Denise Pearson, Assistant Dean of Academics
303-871-3354 Fax: 303-871-4047
Website: www.universitycollege.du.edu
E-mail: ucolinfo@du.edu

University of Northern Colorado
Greeley CO 80639
Robert Lynch, Dean
970-351-2764

Western State College of Colorado
Gunnison CO 81231-0001
Director of Admissions
800-876-5309

CONNECTICUT

Albertus Magnus College
700 Prospect St, New Haven CT 06511-1189
Richard Lolatte, Dean of Admission
203-773-8501 or 800-578-9160 Fax: 203-773-5248
Website: www.albertus.edu
E-mail: admissions@albertus.edu

Eastern Connecticut State University
83 Windham St, Willimantic CT 06226-2295
860-456-5000

Fairfield University
1073 N Benson Rd, Fairfield CT 06824-5171
203-254-4000

INTERNATIONAL COLLEGE OF HOSPITALITY MANAGEMENT

1760 Mapleton Ave, Suffield CT 06078
Tina Merullo, Admissions
860-668-3515 Fax: 860-668-7369
Website: www.ichm.edu
E-mail: admissions@ichm.edu

Middlesex Community College
100 Training Hill Rd, Middletown CT 06457-4889
Mensimah Shabazz, Director of Admissions
860-343-5800 Fax: 860-344-3055
Website: www.mxcc.commnet.edu
E-mail: mshabazz@mxcc.commnet.edu

Post University
800 Country Club Rd, Waterbury CT 06708-3240
Sandra M. Fernandes, Associate Director of Admissions
Will Johnson, Associate Director of Admissions
203-596-4520

Quinnipiac University
275 Mount Carmel Ave, Hamden CT 06518-1905
Joan Isaac Mohr, VP & Dean of Admissions
203-582-8600

St. Joseph College
1678 Asylum Ave, West Hartford CT 06117-2791
860-232-4571

University of Bridgeport
126 Park Ave, Bridgeport CT 06604-5620
Barbara L. Maryak, Dean of Admissions
203-576-4552

University of Connecticut
Storrs CT 06269-0001
860-486-2000

University of Hartford
200 Bloomfield Ave, West Hartford CT 06117-1599
860-768-4100

University of New Haven
300 Boston Post Rd, West Haven CT 06516
Director of Undergraduate Admissions
203-932-7319 Fax: 203-931-6093
Website: www.newhaven.edu
E-mail: adminfo@newhaven.edu

Yale University
38 Hillhouse Ave, New Haven CT 06511
203-432-4771

DELAWARE

Goldey-Beacom College
4701 Limestone Rd, Wilmington DE 19808-1993
Stacey Schwartz, Assistant Director of Admissions
302-998-8814 Fax: 302-996-5408
Website: www.gbc.edu
E-mail: admissions@gbc.edu

University of Delaware
Newark DE 19711
302-831-2000

Wesley College
120 N State St, Dover DE 19901-3876
302-736-2300 Fax: 302-736-2301
Website: www.wesley.edu

DISTRICT OF COLUMBIA

American University
4400 Massachusetts Ave NW
Washington DC 20016-8200
202-885-1000

Gallaudet University
800 Florida Ave NE, Washington DC 20002-3695
Charity Reedy Hines, Director of Admissions
202-651-5750

Georgetown University
37th and O St NW, Washington DC 20057-0001
202-687-0100

George Washington University
2035 H St NW, Washington DC 20052-0002
202-994-1000

Howard University
2400 6th St NW, Washington DC 20059-0002
202-806-6100

Potomac College
4000 Chesapeake St NW, Washington DC 20016
Florence Tate, President
202-686-0876 Fax: 202-686-0818
Website: www.potomac.edu
E-mail: ftate@potomac.edu

SOUTHEASTERN UNIVERSITY

501 I St SW, Washington DC 20024-2788
Sean Jamieson, Director of Admissions
202-478-8210 Fax: 202-488-8093
Website: www.seu.edu
E-mail: admissions@admin.seu.edu

Trinity University
125 Michigan Ave NE, Washington DC 20017-1090
202-884-9000

University of the District of Columbia
4200 Connecticut Ave NW
Washington DC 20008-1174
LaVerne M. Hill-Flanagan, Director of Admissions
202-274-5100

FLORIDA

Barry University
11300 NE 2nd Ave, Miami Shores FL 33161-6695
800-695-2279

Bethune-Cookman College
640 Dr Mary McLeod Bethune Blvd
Daytona Beach FL 32114-3099
Edwin Coffie, Director of Admissions
800-448-0228

CARLOS ALBIZU UNIVERSITY

2173 NW 99th Ave, Miami FL 33172-2209
Gerardo Alvarado, MBA, Director of Admissions, Recruitment & Outreach
305-593-1223 ext. 137 Fax: 305-593-1854
Website: www.mia.albizu.edu
E-mail: admissions@albizu.edu

City College
2000 W Commercial Blvd, Fort Lauderdale FL 33309
Britt Carpenter, Director of Admissions
954-492-5353 Fax: 954-491-1965
Website: www.citycollege.edu
E-mail: bcarpenter@citycollege.edu

Clearwater Christian College
3400 Gulf To Bay Blvd, Clearwater FL 33759-4595
727-726-1153

Eckerd College
4200 54th Ave S, Saint Petersburg FL 33711
727-867-1166

EVERGLADES UNIVERSITY (MAIN CAMPUS)

5002 T-Rex Ave Suite 100, Boca Raton FL 33431
Kristi Mollis, President
888-772-6077 Fax: 561-912-1191
Website: www.evergladesuniversity.edu
E-mail: admissions-boca@evergladesuniversity.edu
See listing under "Universities"

EVERGLADES UNIVERSITY

Orlando Campus (Branch Campus)
5600 Lake Underhill Rd Suite 200, Orlando FL 32807
Shirley Long, Vice President
866-289-1078 Fax: 407-482-9801
Website: www.evergladesuniversity.edu
E-mail: admissions-orl@evergladesuniversity.edu
See listing under "Universities"

EVERGLADES UNIVERSITY

Sarasota Campus (Branch Campus)
6001 Lake Osprey Dr, Sarasota FL 34240
Brad Brewer, Vice President
866-907-2262 Fax: 941-907-6634
Website: www.evergladesuniversity.edu
E-mail: admissions-sar@evergladesuniversity.edu
See listing under "Universities"

Flagler College
PO Box 1027, Saint Augustine FL 32085-1027
904-829-6481

Florida A&M University
Tallahassee FL 32307
850-599-3000

Florida Atlantic University
PO Box 3091, Boca Raton FL 33431-0991
800-299-4328

Florida International University
Tamiami Trl, Miami FL 33199-0001
305-348-2000

Florida Metropolitan University
Orlando South
9200 Southpark Center Loop, Orlando FL 32819
Annette Cloin, Contact
407-851-2525 Fax: 407-851-1477
Website: www.fmu.edu
E-mail: acloin@cci.edu

FLORIDA METROPOLITAN UNIVERSITY
Pinellas Campus
2471 N McMullen Booth Rd
Clearwater FL 33759-1359
Sandra Williams, Director of Admissions
800-353-3687 or 727-725-2688 Fax: 727-725-3827
Website: www.fmu.edu
E-mail: sawilliams@cci.edu

Florida Southern College
111 Lake Hollingsworth Dr, Lakeland FL 33801-5607
Robert B. Palmer, V.P., Dean of Enrollment
Management
863-680-4131

Florida State University
600 W College Ave, Tallahassee FL 32306-1096
Janice V. Finney, Director of Admissions
850-644-2525 Fax: 850-644-0197
Website: admissions.fsu.edu
E-mail: admissions@admin.fsu.edu

HERZING COLLEGE
1595 S Semoran Blvd #1501
Winter Park FL 32792-5509
Kathy Nagle, Director of Admissions
407-478-0500 Fax: 407-478-0501
Website: www.herzing.edu
E-mail: info@orl.herzing.edu

International Academy of Design & Technology
5104 Eisenhower Blvd, Tampa FL 33634-6313
Richard Costa, V.P. of Admissions and Marketing
813-880-8092 Fax: 813-881-0008
Website: www.academy.edu
E-mail: admissions@academy.edu

INTERNATIONAL COLLEGE
4501 Colonial Blvd, Fort Myers FL 33966
Rita Lampus, Vice President of Enrollment
Management
800-466-0019 or 239-482-0019 Fax: 239-938-7891
Website: www.internationalcollege.edu
E-mail: cmorrison@internationalcollege.edu

INTERNATIONAL COLLEGE
2655 Northbrooke Dr, Naples FL 34119
Rita Lampus, Vice President of Enrollment
Management
800-466-8017 or 239-513-1122 Fax: 239-598-6254
Website: www.internationalcollege.edu
E-mail: admit@internationalcollege.edu
See listing under "Universities"

Jones College
5353 Arlington Expy, Jacksonville FL 32211-5588
Dorothy D. Jones, Chief Executive Officer
904-743-1122 Fax: 904-744-4446
Website: www.jones.edu
E-mail: lwade@jones.edu

Jones College
11430 N Kendall Dr Ste 200, Miami FL 33176
Barclay Charles, Contact
305-275-9996 Fax: 305-743-4446
Website: www.jones.edu
E-mail: pcarbone@jones.edu

Keiser College
1800 Business Park Blvd, Daytona Beach FL 32114
Matt McEnany, Vice President
386-274-5060 Fax: 386-274-2725
Website: www.keisercollege.edu
E-mail: mmcenany@keisercollege.edu

Lynn University
3601 N Military Trl, Boca Raton FL 33431-5598
Brett Ormandy, Director of Admissions
561-237-7900 Fax: 561-237-7100
Website: www.lynn.edu
E-mail: admission@lynn.edu

Northwood University
2600 N Military Trl, West Palm Beach FL 33409-2999
Jack Letvinchuk, Director of Admissions
800-458-8325 Fax: 561-640-3328
Website: www.northwood.edu
E-mail: fladmit@northwood.edu

Nova Southeastern University Health Profession
3200 S University Dr, Davie FL 33328-2018
Marla Frohlinger, Director of Admissions
954-262-1101 Fax: 954-262-2282
Website: www.nova.edu
E-mail: marlaf@nsu.nova.edu

Palm Beach Atlantic University
PO Box 24708, West Palm Beach FL 33416-4708
561-803-2000

Remington College, Tampa Campus
2410 E Busch Blvd, Tampa FL 33612-8410
Director of Recruitment
813-935-5700 Fax: 813-935-7415
Website: www.remingtoncollege.edu

Rollins College
1000 Holt Ave, Winter Park FL 32789
407-646-2000

Saint Leo University
PO Box 6665, Saint Leo FL 33574
Deborah Bandy, Director of Admissions
352-588-8200 or 800-334-5532 Fax: 352-588-8257
Website: www.saintleo.edu
E-mail: admission@saintleo.edu

St. Thomas University
16401 NW 37th Ave, Miami Gardens FL 33054
Dr. Ted Abernathy, Contact
800-367-9010 or 305-628-6546 Fax: 305-628-6591
Website: www.stu.edu
E-mail: signup@stu.edu

Santa Fe Community College
3000 NW 83rd St, Gainesville FL 32606-6200
Jackson N. Sasser, President
352-395-5787 Fax: 352-395-4118
Website: www.sfcc.edu
E-mail: ouida.mcneil@sfcc.edu

South University
1760 N Congress Ave
West Palm Beach FL 33409-5178
Steven A. Schwab, President
561-697-9200 Fax: 561-697-9944
Website: www.southuniversity.edu
E-mail: wpb@southuniversity.edu
SACS Accreditation.

SOUTHWEST FLORIDA COLLEGE
1685 Medical Ln, Fort Myers FL 33907-1157
866-SWFC-NOW or 239-939-4766 Fax: 239-936-4040
Website: www.swfc.edu
E-mail: studentinfo@swfc.edu

Stetson University
421 N Woodland Boulevard, De Land FL 32720-3761
386-822-7000

TRINITY COLLEGE OF FLORIDA
2430 Welbilt Blvd, Trinity FL 34655-4401
Dr. David Colburn, VP of Enrollment & Adult Education
727-376-6911 Fax: 727-376-0781
Website: www.trinitycollege.edu
E-mail: tquest2@trinitycollege.edu
See listing under "Universities"

University of Central Florida
PO Box 160111, Orlando FL 32816
407-823-3000

University of Florida
PO Box 114000, Gainesville FL 32611-4000
352-392-3261

University of Miami
PO Box 248006, Coral Gables FL 33124-8006
305-284-2211

University of North Florida
4567 Saint Johns Bluff Rd S
Jacksonville FL 32224-2645
904-620-1000

University of South Florida
4202 E Fowler Ave, Tampa FL 33620-6900
J. Robert Spatig, Director of Admissions
813-974-3350 Fax: 813-974-9689
Website: www.usf.edu
E-mail: admissions@admin.usf.edu

University of West Florida
11000 University Pkwy, Pensacola FL 32514-5750
850-474-2000

Warner Southern College
5301 US Highway 27 S, Lake Wales FL 33859-8725
863-638-1426

GEORGIA

American InterContinental University
3330 Peachtree Rd NE, Atlanta GA 30326-1016
404-965-5700

American InterContinental University
6600 Peachtree Dunwoody Rd
500 Embassy Row, Atlanta GA 30328
404-965-6500

Augusta State University
2500 Walton Way, Augusta GA 30904-4562
706-737-1400

Brewton-Parker College
Highway 280, Mount Vernon GA 30445
800-342-1087

Clark Atlanta University
223 James Brawley Dr SW, Atlanta GA 30314
404-880-8000

Clayton State University
5900 N Lee St, Morrow GA 30260
770-961-3500

Emory University
200B Jones Center, Atlanta GA 30322
404-727-6123

Georgia College and State University
231 W Hancock St, Milledgeville GA 31061-3371
478-445-5350

Georgia Institute of Technology
225 North Ave NW, Atlanta GA 30332-0002
404-894-2000

Georgia Southern University
PO Box 8024, Statesboro GA 30460
Admissions Office
912-681-5532

Georgia State University
PO Box 4009, Atlanta GA 30302-4009
404-651-2365

Kennesaw State University
1000 Chastain Rd NW, Kennesaw GA 30144-5591
Timothy Mescon, Dean of College of Business
770-423-6425
Website: www.kennesaw.edu

LaGrange College
601 Broad St, LaGrange GA 30240-2955
Andy Geeter, Director of Admission
800-593-2885

Life University
1269 Barclay Cir SE, Marietta GA 30060-2903
Dr. Deborah E. Heairlston, Director of New Student
Development
770-426-2884 Fax: 770-426-2895
Website: www.life.edu
E-mail: admissions@life.edu

Mercer University in Atlanta
3001 Mercer University Dr, Atlanta GA 30341-4155
678-547-6000

Mercer University in Macon
1400 Coleman Ave, Macon GA 31207-0003
John P. Cole, Sr. Assoc. V.P. for Admissions
478-301-2650

North Georgia College & State University
Dahlonega GA 30597-0001
706-864-1400

North Georgia Technical College
434 Meeks Ave, Blairsville GA 30512-2983
Admissions
706-781-2300 Fax: 706-781-2307
Website: www.northgatech.edu
E-mail: info@northgatech.edu

North Georgia Technical College
8989 Highway 17, Toccoa GA 30577
706-779-5591
Website: www.northgatech.edu
E-mail: info@northgatech.edu

North Georgia Technical College
Clarkesville Campus
PO Box 65, Clarkesville GA 30523-0002
Admissions
706-754-7700 Fax: 706-754-7777
Website: www.northgatech.edu
E-mail: info@northgatech.edu

North Metro Technical College
5198 Ross Rd SE, Acworth GA 30102-3129
Missy Cusack, Director of Admissions
770-975-4000 Fax: 770-975-4142
Website: www.northmetrotech.edu
E-mail: info@northmetrotech.edu

Oglethorpe University
4484 Peachtree Rd NE, Atlanta GA 30319-2797
Kelly Gosnell, Director of Admission
404-261-1441 Fax: 404-364-8491
Website: www.oglethorpe.edu
E-mail: admission@oglethorpe.edu

Paine College
1235 15th St, Augusta GA 30901-3182
800-476-7703

Piedmont College
PO Box 10, Demorest GA 30535-0010
800-277-7020

Savannah State University
3219 College St, Savannah GA 31404-5255
912-356-2187

Thomas University
1501 Millpond Rd, Thomasville GA 31792-7478
Darla M. Glass, Director of Student Affairs
229-226-1621

TOCCOA FALLS COLLEGE
PO Box 800899, Toccoa Falls GA 30598
Christy Meadows, Director of Admissions
888-785-5624 Fax: 706-282-6012
Website: www.tfc.edu
E-mail: admissions@tfc.edu

University of Georgia
Athens GA 30602-0001
706-542-3000

University of West Georgia
Carrollton GA 30118-0001
770-836-6500

Valdosta State University
N Patterson St, Valdosta GA 31698-0001
229-333-5952

HAWAII

Brigham Young University
55-220 Kulanui St, Laie HI 96762-1293
808-293-3211

Chaminade University of Honolulu
3140 Waialae Ave, Honolulu HI 96816-1510
Joy Bouey, Dean of Enrollment Management
808-739-4619

Hawaii Pacific University
45-045 Kamehameha Hwy, Kaneohe HI 96744-5297
808-235-3641

Heald College, Honolulu
1500 Kapiolani Blvd, Honolulu HI 96814-3732
Lon K. Ibaraki, Director of Admissions
808-955-1500 or 800-940-0530 Fax: 808-955-6964
Website: www.heald.edu
E-mail: lon_ibaraki@heald.edu

Kauai Community College
3-1901 Kaumualii Hwy, Lihue HI 96766-9500
808-245-8225 Fax: 808-245-8297
Website: kauai.hawaii.edu
E-mail: arkauai@hawaii.edu

University of Hawaii at Manoa
2444 Dole St, Honolulu HI 96822-2302
808-956-5280

IDAHO

Boise State University
1910 University Dr, Boise ID 83725-0399
208-426-1011

Brigham Young University - Idaho
120 Kimball Bldg, Rexburg ID 83460
Gordon Westenskow, Director of Admissions
208-496-1020 Fax: 208-496-1220
Website: www.byui.edu
E-mail: admissions@byui.edu

Idaho State University
PO Box 8270, Pocatello ID 83209-0001
208-282-0211

University of Idaho
Moscow ID 83844-4253
Lloyd Scott, Director of New Student Services
208-885-6163 Fax: 208-885-4477
Website: www.uidaho.edu
E-mail: nss@uidaho.edu

ILLINOIS

AMERICAN INTERCONTINENTAL UNIVERSITY ONLINE
5550 Prairie Stone Parkway Suite 400
Hoffman Estates IL 60192
Admissions Department
877-701-3800
Website: www.aiuonline.edu
E-mail: info@aiuonline.edu

ARGOSY UNIVERSITY/CHICAGO
350 N Orleans St, Merchandise Mart
Chicago IL 60654
Ashley Delaney, Director of Admissions
800-626-4123 Fax: 312-777-7750
Website: www.argosy.edu
E-mail: adelaney@argosyu.edu

Augustana College
639 38th St, Rock Island IL 61201-2296
309-794-7000

Aurora University
347 S Gladstone Ave, Aurora IL 60506-4892
Carol R. Dunn, Ed.D., Vice President for Enrollment
800-742-5281 Fax: 630-844-5535
Website: www.aurora.edu
E-mail: admission@aurora.edu

Benedictine University
5700 College Rd, Lisle IL 60532-0900
630-829-6300 or 888-829-6363 Fax: 630-829-6301
Website: www.ben.edu
E-mail: admissions@ben.edu
See listing under "Universities"

Bradley University
1501 W Bradley Ave, Peoria IL 61625-0002
800-447-6460

Columbia College Chicago
600 S Michigan Ave, Chicago IL 60605-1996
Murphy Monroe, Executive Director of Admissions
312-344-7130 Fax: 312-344-8024
Website: www.colum.edu
E-mail: admissions@colum.edu

CONCORDIA UNIVERSITY
7400 Augusta St, River Forest IL 60305-1402
708-209-3100 Fax: 708-209-3473
Website: www.curf.edu
E-mail: crfadmis.edu

De Paul University
1 E Jackson Blvd, Chicago IL 60604-2287
Carlene Klaas, Director of Admissions
312-362-8000

Eastern Illinois University
600 Lincoln Ave, Charleston IL 61920-3099
217-581-5000

Elmhurst College
190 S Prospect Ave, Elmhurst IL 60126-3296
630-279-4100

Eureka College
300 E College Ave, Eureka IL 61530-1500
309-467-3721

Greenville College
315 E College Ave, Greenville IL 62246-1199
618-664-1840

Illinois College
1101 W College Ave, Jacksonville IL 62650-2299
217-245-3000

Illinois State University
Normal IL 61790-0001
309-438-2111

Illinois Wesleyan University
PO Box 2900, Bloomington IL 61702-2900
Dr. David Marvin & Dr. David Willis, Co-Chairpersons
309-556-3171

Kaskaskia College
27210 College Rd, Centralia IL 62801-7878
Tyra Taylor, Dean of Enrollment Management and
Retention Services
618-545-3000 Fax: 618-532-1990
Website: www.kaskaskia.edu
E-mail: ttaylor@kaskaskia.edu

Lewis University
One University Parkway, Romeoville IL 60446
800-897-9000

Loyola University - Mundelein College
6525 N Sheridan Rd, Chicago IL 60626-5311
773-262-8100

Loyola University of Chicago
820 N Michigan Ave, Chicago IL 60611-2103
312-915-6000

MacCormac College
29 E Madison St, Chicago IL 60602-4405
David F. Grassi, Admissions Counselor
312-922-1884 ext. 101 Fax: 312-922-4328
Website: www.maccormac.edu
E-mail: dgrassi@maccormac.edu

MacMurray College
447 E College Ave, Jacksonville IL 62650-2590
217-479-7000

Millikin University
1184 W Main St, Decatur IL 62522-2084
Lin Stoner, Dean of Admission
800-373-7733

Monmouth College
700 E Broadway, Monmouth IL 61462-1963
Kristi Hippen, Director of Admission
309-457-2131

National-Louis University
2840 Sheridan Rd, Evanston IL 60201-1796

North Central College
30 N Brainard St, Naperville IL 60540-4690
Martha Stolze, Director of Admissions
630-637-5800 Fax: 630-637-5819
Website: www.northcentralcollege.edu
E-mail: admissions@noctrl.edu

NORTHEASTERN ILLINOIS UNIVERSITY
5500 N Saint Louis Ave, Chicago IL 60625-4699
Varkey Titus, Dean
773-442-4050 Fax: 773-442-4020
Website: www.neiu.edu
E-mail: v_titus@neiu.edu

Northern Illinois University
DeKalb IL 60115
815-753-1000

Northwestern University
1801 Hinman Ave, Evanston IL 60208-1260
847-491-3741

Olivet Nazarene University
1 University Ave
Bourbonnais IL 60914
815-939-5011

Principia College
Elsah IL 62028-9799
618-374-2131

Quincy University
1800 College Ave, Quincy IL 62301-2670
217-222-8020

Rockford College
5050 E State St, Rockford IL 61108-2393
William Laffey, Director of Admission
800-892-2984

Roosevelt University
430 S Michigan Ave, Chicago IL 60605
Gwen E. Kanelos, Asst. Vice President for Enrollment
Services
877-APPLY-RU Fax: 312-341-4216
Website: www.roosevelt.edu
E-mail: applyru@roosevelt.edu

Southern Illinois University
Carbondale IL 62901-4400
618-453-2121

Southern Illinois University Edwardsville
Edwardsville IL 62026-0001
618-650-3705

South Suburban College of Cook County
15800 State St, South Holland IL 60473
Jane Ellen Stocker, Dean of Enrollment Services
708-596-2000 Fax: 708-225-5806
Website: www.southsuburbancollege.edu
E-mail: jstocker@southsuburbancollege.edu

Trinity Christian College
6601 W College Dr, Palos Heights IL 60463-0929
Joshua Lenarz, Director of Admissions
708-597-3000

Trinity International University
2065 Half Day Rd, Deerfield IL 60015-1241
847-945-8800

Triton College
2000 5th Ave, River Grove IL 60171-1995
Mary-Rita Moore, Dean of Enrollment Services
708-456-0300 ext. 3130 Fax: 708-583-3147
Website: www.triton.edu
E-mail: triton@triton.edu
See listing under "Community and Junior Colleges"

University of Chicago
5801 S Ellis Ave, Chicago IL 60637-1476
773-702-1234

University of Illinois
901 W Illinois St, Urbana IL 61801
217-333-1000

University of Illinois at Chicago
PO Box 5220, Chicago IL 60680-5220
312-996-3000

University of Illinois at Springfield
One University Plaza, Springfield IL 62794
217-206-4847

University of St. Francis
500 Wilcox St, Joliet IL 60435
800-735-7500

Western Illinois University
1 University Cir, Macomb IL 61455-1390
309-295-1414

INDIANA

Ancilla Domini College
Donaldson IN 46513
Erin Wittmeyer, Director of Admissions
574-936-8898 Fax: 574-935-1773
Website: www.ancilla.edu
E-mail: erin.wittmeyer@ancilla.edu

Ball State University
2000 W University Ave, Muncie IN 47306-0002
765-285-5555

Bethel College
1001 W McKinley Ave, Mishawaka IN 46545-5591
Office of Admissions
574-257-3339

Brown Mackie College - Fort Wayne
3000 E Coliseum Blvd, Fort Wayne IN 46805
Daniel Summer, Campus President
260-484-4400 Fax: 260-484-2678
Website: www.brownmackie.edu

Brown Mackie College - South Bend
1030 E Jefferson Blvd, South Bend IN 46617-3123
Connie Adelman, Campus President
574-237-0774 Fax: 574-237-3585
Website: www.brownmackie.edu

Butler University
4600 Sunset Ave, Indianapolis IN 46208-3443
317-940-8000

Calumet College of St. Joseph
2400 New York Ave, Whiting IN 46394-2195
219-473-7770

Franklin College
101 Branigin Blvd, Franklin IN 46131
Jacqueline S. Acosta, Director of Admissions
800-852-0232 Fax: 317-738-8274
Website: www.franklincollege.edu
E-mail: admissions@franklincollege.edu

Goshen College
1700 S Main St, Goshen IN 46526-4794
574-535-7000

Grace College
200 Seminary Dr, Winona Lake IN 46590-1224
800-54-GRACE

Hanover College
PO Box 108, Hanover IN 47243-0108
William D. Preble, Dean of Admission
800-213-2178 Fax: 812-866-7098
Website: www.hanover.edu
E-mail: admissions@hanover.edu

Huntington College
2303 College Ave, Huntington IN 46750-1299
260-356-6000

Indiana State University
Terre Haute IN 47809-0001
Richard Toomey, Director of Admissions
812-237-6311

Indiana University
300 N Jordan Ave, Bloomington IN 47405-1106
812-855-4848

Indiana University at South Bend
PO Box 7111, South Bend IN 46634-7111
574-237-4111

Indiana University Northwest
3400 Broadway, Gary IN 46408-1101
219-980-6500

Indiana University-Purdue University at Fort Wayne
2101 E Coliseum Blvd, Fort Wayne IN 46805-1445
260-481-6100

Indiana University Southeast
4201 Grant Line Rd, New Albany IN 47150-2158
812-941-2000

Indiana Wesleyan University
4201 S Washington St, Marion IN 46953-4974
765-674-6901

International Business College
5699 Coventry Ln, Fort Wayne IN 46804
260-459-4500 Fax: 260-436-1896
Website: www.ibcfortwayne.edu
E-mail: skinzer@ibcfortwayne.edu

Ivy Tech Community College - North Central
220 Dean Johnson Blvd, South Bend IN 46601-3415
Pam Decker, Director of Admissions
574-289-7001 Fax: 574-236-7177
Website: www.ivytech.edu
E-mail: pdecker@ivytech.edu

Manchester College
604 E College Ave, North Manchester IN 46962-1276
260-982-5000

Marian College
3200 Cold Spring Rd, Indianapolis IN 46222-1997
317-955-6000

Oakland City University
138 N Lucretia St, Oakland City IN 47660
Brian J. Baker, Director of Admissions
800-737-5125 Fax: 812-749-1433
Website: www.oak.edu
E-mail: bbaker@oak.edu
See listing under "Universities"

Purdue University
2200 169th St, Hammond IN 46323
219-989-2993

Purdue University
1401 S US Highway 421, Westville IN 46391-9542
219-785-5200

St. Mary-of-the-Woods College
Saint Mary of the Woods IN 47876-1001
James P. Malley, Jr., Director of Admission
800-926-7692 Fax: 812-535-5010
Website: www.smwc.edu
E-mail: smwcadms@smwc.edu

St. Mary's College
46 Madeliva St, Notre Dame IN 46556
574-284-4000

Taylor University
500 W Reade Ave, Upland IN 46989-1002
765-998-2751

University of Evansville
1800 Lincoln Ave, Evansville IN 47722-0001
Thomas E. Bear, V.P. of Enrollment Services
800-423-8633 Fax: 812-488-4076
Website: www.evansville.edu
E-mail: admission@evansville.edu

University of Indianapolis
1400 E Hanna Ave, Indianapolis IN 46227-3697
317-788-3368

University of Notre Dame
220 Main Building, Notre Dame IN 46556
574-631-5000

University of Southern Indiana
8600 University Blvd, Evansville IN 47712-3591
812-464-8600

Valparaiso University
Valparaiso IN 46383
219-464-5000

IOWA

AIB College of Business
2500 Fleur Dr, Des Moines IA 50321-1799
800-444-1921 Fax: 515-244-6773
Website: www.aib.edu
E-mail: admissions@aib.edu

Briar Cliff University
PO Box 2100, Sioux City IA 51104-0100
Sharisue Wilcoxon, VP for Enrollment Management
712-279-5200 Fax: 712-279-1632
Website: www.briarcliff.edu
E-mail: admissions@briarcliff.edu

Buena Vista University
610 W 4th St, Storm Lake IA 50588-1798
712-749-2235

Clarke College
1550 Clarke Dr, Dubuque IA 52001-3198
Andy Schroeder, Director of Admissions
800-383-2345 Fax: 563-584-8666
Website: www.clarke.edu
E-mail: andy.schroeder@clarke.edu

Coe College
1220 1st Ave NE, Cedar Rapids IA 52402-5092
319-399-8000

Dordt College
498 4th Ave NE, Sioux Center IA 51250-1697
Quentin Van Essen, Executive Director of Admissions
800-343-6738

Drake University
2507 University Ave, Des Moines IA 50311-4505
Laura Linn, Director of Admissions
515-271-2011

Graceland University
1 University Place, Lamoni IA 50140
Brian Shantz, Vice President for Enrollment and Dean
of Admissions
641-784-5196 Fax: 641-784-5480
Website: www.admissions.graceland.edu
E-mail: admissions@graceland.edu

Grand View College
1200 Grandview Ave, Des Moines IA 50316-1599
515-263-2800

Hamilton College
3165 Edgewood Pkwy SW, Cedar Rapids IA 52404
Susan Spivey, Campus President
319-363-0481 Fax: 319-363-3812
Website: www.hamiltonia.edu
E-mail: spiveys@hamiltonia.edu

Hamilton College
4655 121st St, Urbandale IA 50323-2311
Ed Rogan, Campus President
515-727-2100 Fax: 515-727-2115
Website: www.hamiltonia.edu
E-mail: erogan_dm@hamiltonia.edu

Iowa Lakes Community College
3200 College Dr, Emmetsburg IA 50536-1055
Anne Stansbury, Asst. Director of Admissions
712-852-5212 Fax: 712-362-8363
Website: www.iowalakes.edu
E-mail: info@iowalakes.edu

Iowa Lakes Community College
300 S 18th St, Estherville IA 51334-2721
Anne Stansbury, Asst. Director of Admissions
712-362-7945 Fax: 712-362-8363
Website: www.iowalakes.edu
E-mail: info@iowalakes.edu

Iowa Lakes Community College
1900 Grand Ave, Suite 8, Spencer IA 51301
Anne Stansbury, Assistant Director of Admissions
712-262-7141 Fax: 712-262-4047
Website: www.iowalakes.edu
E-mail: info@iowalakes.edu

Iowa State University
Ames IA 50011-0001
515-294-4111

Loras College
1450 Alta Vista St, Dubuque IA 52001-4399
Tim Hauber, Director of Admissions
800-245-6727

Luther College
700 College Dr, Decorah IA 52101-1045
563-387-2000

Morningside College
1501 Morningside Ave, Sioux City IA 51106-1717
712-274-5000

Mount Mercy College
1330 Elmhurst Dr NE, Cedar Rapids IA 52402-4797
Jim Krystofiak, Dean of Admission
800-248-4504 Fax: 319-363-5270
Website: www.mtmercy.edu
E-mail: admission@mtmercy.edu

Northwestern College
101 7th St SW, Orange City IA 51041-1996
712-737-7000

Northwest Iowa Community College
603 W Park St, Sheldon IA 51201-1046
Lisa Story, Director of Enrollment Management
712-324-5061 Fax: 712-324-4136
Website: www.nwicc.edu
E-mail: lstory@nwicc.edu

University of Iowa
107 Calvin Hall, Iowa City IA 52242-1315
319-335-3500

University of Northern Iowa
Cedar Falls IA 50614-0001
319-273-2311

Upper Iowa University
PO Box 1857, Fayette IA 52142-1857
563-425-5200

Waldorf College
106 S 6th St, Forest City IA 50436-1713
Steve Lovik, Vice President of Enrollment Management
800-292-1903 or 641-585-8112 Fax: 641-585-8125
Website: www.waldorf.edu
E-mail: loviks@waldorf.edu
See listing under "Universities"

Wartburg College
PO Box 1003, Waverly IA 50677-0903
Brent Matthias, Interim Director of Admissions
319-352-8200 Fax: 319-352-8579
Website: www.wartburg.edu
E-mail: admissions@wartburg.edu

KANSAS

Allen County Community College
1801 N Cottonwood St, Iola KS 66749-1607
John Masterson, President
Randy Weber, Director of Admissions
620-365-5116 Fax: 620-365-3284
Website: www.allencc.net
E-mail: weber@allencc.edu

Barclay College
607 N Kingman, Haviland KS 67059
Herb Frazier, Director of Admissions
800-862-0226 Fax: 620-862-5242
Website: www.barclaycollege.edu
E-mail: admissions@barclaycollege.edu

Benedictine College
1020 N 2nd St, Atchison KS 66002-1499
913-367-5340

Bethany College
421 N 1st St, Lindsborg KS 67456-1897
785-227-3311

COLBY COMMUNITY COLLEGE

1255 S Range Ave, Colby KS 67701-4099
Director of Admissions
888-634-9350 or 785-460-4690 Fax: 785-460-4691
Website: www.colbycc.edu
E-mail: bobbi@colbycc.edu

Emporia State University
1200 Commercial St, Emporia KS 66801-5087
620-343-1200

Fort Hays State University
600 Park St, Hays KS 67601-4099
785-628-4000

Independence Community College
PO Box 708, Independence KS 67301-0708
Dr. Terry Hetrick, President
800-842-6063 Fax: 620-331-5344
Website: www.indycc.edu
E-mail: admissions@indycc.edu

Kansas State University
Manhattan KS 66506
785-532-6250

McPherson College
PO Box 1402, Mc Pherson KS 67460-1402
620-241-0731

Newman University
3100 W McCormick St, Wichita KS 67213
Jann Reusser, Admissions Recruitment Coordinator
316-942-4291 ext. 2144 Fax: 316-942-4483
Website: www.newmanu.edu
E-mail: reusserj@newmanu.edu

Ottawa University
1001 S Cedar St, Ottawa KS 66067-3399
785-242-5200

Pittsburg State University
1701 S Broadway St, Pittsburg KS 66762-7500
620-231-7000

Southwestern College
100 College St, Winfield KS 67156-2499
620-229-6000

Tabor College
400 S Jefferson St, Hillsboro KS 67063-1758
Rusty Allen, Dean of Enrollment Management
620-947-3121 Fax: 620-947-6276
Website: www.tabor.edu
E-mail: admissions@tabor.edu

University of Kansas
Lawrence KS 66045-0001
Tom, Sarowski, Dean

University of Saint Mary
4100 S 4th St, Leavenworth KS 66048-5023
913-682-5151

Wichita State University
1845 N Fairmount St, Wichita KS 67260-0124
Gina Crabtree, Director of Admissions
316-978-3085

KENTUCKY

Alice Lloyd College
100 Purpose Rd, Pippa Passes KY 41844-9005
John Mills, Director of Admissions
888-280-4252

Asbury College
1 Macklem Dr, Wilmore KY 40390-1198
859-858-3511

Bellarmine University
2001 Newburg Rd, Louisville KY 40205-1877
502-452-8000

Bluegrass Community and Technical College
Oswald Building
470 Cooper Drive, Lexington KY 40506-0235
Shelbie Hugle, Director of Admissions
859-246-6200 Fax: 859-246-4664
Website: www.bluegrass.kctcs.edu
E-mail: bctc_info@kctcs.edu

Brescia University
717 Frederica St, Owensboro KY 42301-3023
Sr. Mary Austin Blank, OSB, Director of Admissions
877-BRESCIA

Brown Mackie College - Louisville
300 High Rise Dr, Louisville KY 40213-3263
Kathleen Belanger, Director of Admissions
502-968-7191 Fax: 502-357-9956
Website: www.brownmackie.edu
E-mail: kbelanger@brownmackie.edu

BROWN MACKIE COLLEGE

Northern Kentucky Campus
309 Buttermilk Pike, Fort Mitchell KY 41017-2191
Joanne Dellefield, Director of Admissions
859-341-5627 Fax: 859-341-6483
Website: www.brownmackie.edu
E-mail: jdellefield@brownmackie.edu

Campbellsville University
1 University Dr, Campbellsville KY 42718-2799
Scott Necessary, Coordinator of Undergraduate
Admissions
270-789-5000

Daymar College
3361 Buckland Sq, Owensboro KY 42301-5830
Vickie McDougal Director of Admissions
800-960-4090 Fax: 270-685-4090
Website: www.daymarcollege.com

Kentucky Wesleyan College
3000 Frederica St, Owensboro KY 42301-6055
800-999-0592

Morehead State University
Morehead KY 40351-1689
Dayna Seelig, Enrollment Services
800-585-6781 Fax: 606-783-5038
Website: www.moreheadstate.edu
E-mail: admissions@moreheadstate.edu

Murray State University
Murray KY 42071
Phil Bryan, Director of Admissions
270-762-3011

Northern Kentucky University
Newport KY 41099-0001
859-572-5100

Pikeville College
147 Sycamore St, Pikeville KY 41501
606-218-5250

Spalding University
851 S 4th St, Louisville KY 40203-2188
502-585-9911

Transylvania University
300 N Broadway, Lexington KY 40508-1776
859-233-8242 Fax: 859-233-8797
Website: www.transy.edu
E-mail: admissions@transy.edu

Union College
310 College St, Barbourville KY 40906-1499
Joretta Nelson, Vice President for Enrollment
Management
800-489-8646

University of Kentucky
Lexington KY 40506-0001
Don Witt, Director of Admissions
859-257-9000

University of Louisville
2301 S 3rd St, Louisville KY 40292-2001
502-852-5555

Western Kentucky University
1 Big Red Way, Bowling Green KY 42101
270-745-0111

LOUISIANA

Centenary College of Louisiana
PO Box 41188, Shreveport LA 71134-1188
318-869-5011

Delta School of Business and Technology
517 Broad St, Lake Charles LA 70601-4334
Gary Holt, President
337-439-5765 Fax: 337-436-5151
Website: www.deltatech.edu
E-mail: susan@deltatech.edu

Dillard University
2601 Gentilly Blvd, New Orleans LA 70122-3097
Linda G. Nash, Director of Admissions
Website: www.dillard.edu
E-mail: admissions@dillard.edu

Grambling State University
PO Box 864, Grambling LA 71245
318-274-3811

Louisiana College
PO Box 560, Pineville LA 71359-0001
Mary Wagner, Director of Admissions
318-487-7259

Louisiana State University
1 University Pl, Shreveport LA 71115-2301
318-797-5000

Louisiana State University and A & M College
Louisiana State Univ, Baton Rouge LA 70803-0001
225-578-3202

Louisiana Tech University
PO Box 3168, Ruston LA 71272-0001
318-257-0211

Loyola University New Orleans
6363 Saint Charles Ave, New Orleans LA 70118-6143
504-865-2011

McNeese State University
4100 Ryan St, Lake Charles LA 70605-4510
337-475-5000

Nicholls State University
University Station, Thibodaux LA 70310-0001
985-446-8111

Northwestern State University
Natchitoches LA 71497-0001
Jana Lucky, Director of Enrollment Services
318-357-4503

Our Lady of Holy Cross College
4123 Woodland Dr, New Orleans LA 70131-7399
Office of Enrollment Services
504-394-7744 Fax: 504-391-2421
Website: www.olhcc.edu

Southeastern Louisiana University
PO Box 784, Hammond LA 70404-0784
985-549-2000

Tulane University
6823 Saint Charles Ave, New Orleans LA 70118-5698
504-865-4000

University of Louisiana at Lafayette
PO Box 43570, Lafayette LA 70504
337-482-6087

University of Louisiana at Monroe
700 University Ave, Monroe LA 71209-9001
318-342-1000

University of New Orleans
New Orleans LA 70148-0001
504-280-6000

MAINE

HUSSON COLLEGE
One College Cir, Bangor ME 04401-2999
Jane Goodwin, Director of Admissions
800-4HU-SSON or 207-941-7100 Fax: 207-941-7935
Website: www.husson.edu
E-mail: admit@husson.edu
See listing under "Universities"

Northern Maine Community College
33 Edgemont Dr, Presque Isle ME 04769-2016
Bill Casavant, Director of Admissions
207-768-2700 Fax: 207-768-2831
Website: www.nmcc.edu
E-mail: admissions@nmcc.edu

St. Joseph's College of Maine
278 Whites Bridge Rd, Standish ME 04084-5263
Vincent Kloskowski, Dean of Admissions
800-338-7057 Fax: 207-893-7862
Website: www.sjcme.edu
E-mail: admission@sjcme.edu

Southern Maine Community College
2 Fort Rd, South Portland ME 04106-1698
Dr. James Ortiz, President
Scott MacDonald, Director of Financial Aid
207-741-5500 Fax: 207-741-5671
Website: www.smccme.edu
E-mail: oharmon@maine.rr.com

Thomas College
180 W River Rd, Waterville ME 04901-5097
207-859-1111

University of Maine
246 Main St, Farmington ME 04938
Sharon M. Oliver, Director of Admissions
207-778-7000

University of Maine
Orono ME 04469-0001
207-581-1110

University of Maine at Fort Kent
23 University Dr, Fort Kent ME 04743
888-TRY-UMFK

University of Southern Maine
PO Box 9300, Portland ME 04104-9300
207-780-4141

Westbrook College
716 Stevens Ave, Portland ME 04103-2693
207-797-7261

MARYLAND

BALTIMORE INTERNATIONAL COLLEGE
17 Commerce St, Baltimore MD 21202-3230
Kristin Ciarlo, Director of Admissions
410-752-4710 ext. 120 Fax: 410-752-3730
Website: www.bic.edu
E-mail: admissions@bic.edu
See listing under "Universities"

Cecil Community College
One Seahawk Dr, North East MD 21901
Sandra S. Rajaski, Registrar & Director of Admissions
410-287-1000 Fax: 410-287-1001
Website: www.cecilcc.edu
E-mail: srajaski@cecilcc.edu

Frostburg State University
Frostburg MD 21532-1001
301-687-4000

Goucher College
1021 Dulaney Valley Rd, Baltimore MD 21204-2780
410-337-6000

Griggs University
PO Box 4437, Silver Spring MD 20914-4437
Anita L. Jacobs, Director of Admissions
301-680-6570 Fax: 301-680-6583
Website: www.griggs.edu
E-mail: registrar@griggs.edu

Hagerstown Community College
11400 Robinwood Dr, Hagerstown MD 21742-6590
Dr. Daniel E. Bock, Assistant Director of Admissions
301-790-2800 Fax: 301-791-9165
Website: www.hagerstowncc.edu
E-mail: bockd@hagerstowncc.edu

Loyola College
4501 N Charles St, Baltimore MD 21210-2694
410-617-2000

Morgan State University
1700 E Cold Spring Ln, Baltimore MD 21251-0002
443-885-3000

Mt. St. Mary's University
16300 Old Emmitsburg Rd
Emmitsburg MD 21727-7799
301-447-6122

Salisbury University
1101 Camden Ave, Salisbury MD 21801-6837
410-543-6000

Towson State University
8000 York Rd, Towson MD 21252-0002
410-830-2000

University of Baltimore
1420 N Charles St, Baltimore MD 21201-5779
410-837-4200

University of Maryland
College Park MD 20742-0001
301-405-1000

University of Maryland Eastern Shore
Princess Anne MD 21853
Edwina Morse, Director of Admissions
410-651-6410

Villa Julie College
1525 Greenspring Valley Rd
Stevenson MD 21153-0641
Mark Hergan, V.P. Enrollment Services
410-486-7001 Fax: 410-602-6600
Website: www.vjc.edu/admissions
E-mail: admissions@mail.vjc.edu

MASSACHUSETTS

American International College
1000 State St, Springfield MA 01109-3155
Peter Miller, Dean of Admissions
413-737-7000

Anna Maria College
50 Sunset Ln, Paxton MA 01612
Julie A. Mitchell, Director of Admissions
508-849-3360 Fax: 508-849-3362
Website: www.annamaria.edu
E-mail: admissions@annamaria.edu

Assumption College
500 Salisbury St, Worcester MA 01609-1294
Kathleen Murphy, Dean of Enrollment
508-767-7000 Fax: 508-799-4412
Website: www.assumption.edu
E-mail: admiss@assumption.edu

Atlantic Union College
PO Box 1000, South Lancaster MA 01561-1000
Office of Enrollment Services
800-282-2030

Babson College
PO Box 57310, Babson Park MA 02457-0310
781-235-1200

Bay Path College
588 Longmeadow St, Longmeadow MA 01106-2292
Lisa Casassa, Director of Admissions
413-565-1331 Fax: 413-565-1105
Website: www.baypath.edu
E-mail: lcasassa@baypath.edu

Bay State College
122 Commonwealth Ave, Boston MA 02116-2901
Craig Pfannenstiehl, President
617-217-9000 Fax: 617-536-1735

Becker College
Campuses in Worcester and Leicester, MA
61 Sever St, Worcester MA 01609-2165
Karen H. Schedin, Director of Admissions
508-791-9241 Fax: 508-890-1500
Website: www.becker.edu
E-mail: admissions@becker.edu
See listing under "Universities"

Bentley College
175 Forest St, Waltham MA 02452-4705
781-891-2000

Boston College
140 Commonwealth Ave
Chestnut Hill MA 02467-3800
617-552-8000

Boston University
121 Bay State Rd, Boston MA 02215
Kelly Walter, Executive Director of Admissions
617-353-2300 Fax: 617-353-9695
Website: web.bu.edu
E-mail: admissions@bu.edu

Bristol Community College
777 Elsbree St, Fall River MA 02720-7395
Rodney S. Clark, Director of Admissions
508-678-2811 ext. 2516, 2179 Fax: 508-730-3265
Website: www.bristol.mass.edu
E-mail: admissions@bristol.mass.edu

Clark University
950 Main St, Worcester MA 01610-1473
508-793-7711

Curry College
1071 Blue Hill Ave, Milton MA 02186-2395
Bruce Weckworth, Director of Admissions
617-333-2210

Elms College
291 Springfield St, Chicopee MA 01013-2839
800-255-3567

Fisher College
118 Beacon St, Boston MA 02116-1501
Stephen Carter, Director of Admissions
800-446-1226

Gibbs College of Boston
a Private Two-Year College
126 Newbury St, Boston MA 02116-2904
Ida Zecco, Vice President of Admissions
617-578-7100 Fax: 617-578-7163
Website: www.gibbsboston.edu

Gordon College
255 Grapevine Rd, Wenham MA 01984-1899
Nancy Mering, Director of Admissions
866-464-6736 Fax: 978-867-4682
Website: www.gordon.edu
E-mail: admissions@gordon.edu

Harvard University
8 Garden St, Cambridge MA 02138-3630
617-495-1000

Lasell College
1844 Commonwealth Ave, Newton MA 02466-2716
617-243-2225

Lesley University
29 Everett St, Cambridge MA 02138-2790
Jane Raley, Director of Admissions
617-349-8800

Massachusetts College of Liberal Arts
375 Church St, North Adams MA 01247-4100
413-662-5311

Massachusetts Institute of Technology
77 Massachusetts Ave, Cambridge MA 02139-4307
Marilee Jones, Dean of Admission
617-253-1000 Fax: 617-253-4016
Website: my.mit.edu
E-mail: admissions@mit.edu

Merrimack College
315 Turnpike St, North Andover MA 01845-5800
978-683-7111

Mt. Ida College
777 Dedham St, Newton Center MA 02459-3323
617-969-7000

THE NATIONAL GRADUATE SCHOOL OF QUALITY SYSTEMS MANAGEMENT
186 Jones Rd, Falmouth MA 02540-2908
Virginia C. Petisce, VP Enrollment Management
508-457-1313 Fax: 508-457-5347
Website: www.ngs.edu
E-mail: vpetisce@ngs.edu

Nichols College
Dudley MA 01571-5000
Kimberly A. Kossuth, Director of Admissions
508-943-1560

Northeastern University
360 Huntington Ave, Boston MA 02115-5000
617-373-2000

NORTHERN ESSEX COMMUNITY COLLEGE
100 Elliott St, Haverhill MA 01830
Nora B. Sheridan, Director of Admission
978-556-3700
Website: www.NECC.Mass.edu
E-mail: nsheridan@necc.mass.edu

Pine Manor College
400 Heath St, Chestnut Hill MA 02467-2332
Bill Nichols, Dean of Admission
617-731-7167

Regis College
235 Wellesley St, Weston MA 02493-1571
781-768-2000

Salem State College
352 Lafayette St, Salem MA 01970-5353
978-741-6000

Springfield College
263 Alden St, Springfield MA 01109-3788
Mary DeAngelo, Director of Admissions
800-343-1257

Stonehill College
320 Washington St, Easton MA 02357-5610
508-565-1373

Suffolk University
8 Ashburton Pl, Boston MA 02108-2770
617-573-8460

University of Massachusetts
Amherst MA 01003
413-545-0111

University of Massachusetts Boston
100 William T Morrissey Blvd, Boston MA 02125-3393
Liliana Mickle, Director of Undergraduate Admissions
617-287-6000

University of Massachusetts Dartmouth
Old Westport Rd, North Dartmouth MA 02747-2300
Steven T. Briggs, Director of Admissions
508-999-8605 Fax: 508-999-8755
Website: explore.umassd.edu
E-mail: sbriggs@umassd.edu

University of Massachusetts Lowell
1 University Ave, Lowell MA 01854-2893
978-934-4000

Western New England College
1215 Wilbraham Rd, Springfield MA 01119-2655
413-782-1321

Westfield State College
PO Box 1630, Westfield MA 01086
Michelle Mattie, Associate Dean, Admission and Enrollment Services
413-572-5300
Website: www.wsc.ma.edu
E-mail: admission@wsc.ma.edu

Worcester Polytechnic Institute
100 Institute Rd, Worcester MA 01609-2280
Edward J. Connor, Director of Admissions
508-831-5286 Fax: 508-831-5875
Website: admissions.wpi.edu
E-mail: admissions@wpi.edu

Worcester State College
486 Chandler St, Worcester MA 01602-2597
508-929-8000

MICHIGAN

Albion College
611 E Porter St, Albion MI 49224-1831
800-858-6770

Alma College
614 W Superior St, Alma MI 48801-1599
Anne Monroe, Director of Admissions
800-321-ALMA Fax: 989-463-7057
Website: www.alma.edu
E-mail: admissions@alma.edu

Andrews University
Berrien Springs MI 49104-0001
Randall Graves, Director of Recruitment Services
800-253-2874 Fax: 269-471-2670
Website: www.connect.andrews.edu
E-mail: gravesr@andrews.edu

Aquinas College
1607 Robinson Rd SE, Grand Rapids MI 49506-1799
Paula Meehan, Dean of Admissions
616-732-4460

Baker College of Cadillac
9600 E 13th St, Cadillac MI 49601-9574
Mike Tisdale, Director of Admissions
231-876-3100

Baker College of Clinton Township
34950 Little Mack Ave
Clinton Township MI 48035-4701
586-791-6610

Baker College of Flint
1050 W Bristol Rd, Flint MI 48507-5508
810-767-4000

Baker College of Jackson
2800 Springport Rd, Jackson MI 49202-1230
Kelli Hoban, Director of Admissions
517-789-6123

Baker College of Muskegon
1903 Marquette Ave, Muskegon MI 49442-1453
231-726-4904

Baker College of Owosso
1020 S Washington St, Owosso MI 48867-4400
989-729-3300

Baker College of Port Huron
3403 Lapeer Rd, Port Huron MI 48060-2597
Dan Kenny, Director of Admissions
888-262-2442

Calvin College
3201 Burton St SE, Grand Rapids MI 49546-4388
800-688-0122

Central Michigan University
100 Warriner Hall, Mount Pleasant MI 48859-0001
989-774-4000

Cleary University - Washtenaw Campus
3601 Plymouth Rd, Ann Arbor MI 48105-2659
734-332-4477

Concordia University
4090 Geddes Rd, Ann Arbor MI 48105-2797
Gary Neumann, Director of Admissions
734-995-7300 Fax: 734-995-4610
Website: www.cuaa.edu
E-mail: admissions@cuaa.edu

Delta College
University Center MI 48710-0001
Duff Zube, Director of Admissions
989-686-9093 Fax: 989-667-2202
Website: www.delta.edu
E-mail: admit@delta.edu

Eastern Michigan University
Ypsilanti MI 48197
800-GO-TO-EMU

Ferris State University
901 S State St, Big Rapids MI 49307-2295
231-591-2000

Grand Valley State University
1 Campus Dr, Allendale MI 49401-9403
Jodi Chycinski, Director of Admissions
616-331-6611 Fax: 616-331-2000
Website: www.gvsu.edu
E-mail: go2gvsu@gvsu.edu

HILLSDALE COLLEGE
33 E College St, Hillsdale MI 49242-1298
Dr. David Paas, Director
517-607-2547 Fax: 517-437-3923
Website: www.hillsdale.edu

ITT TECHNICAL INSTITUTE
4020 Sparks Dr SE, Grand Rapids MI 49546-6192
Dennis Hormel, Director
616-956-1060 Fax: 616-956-5606
Website: www.itt-tech.edu
E-mail: dhormel@itt-tech.edu

Lake Superior State University
1000 College Dr, Sault Sainte Marie MI 49783-1637
906-632-6841

Lawrence Technological University
21000 W 10 Mile Rd, Southfield MI 48075-1058
Jane Rohrback, Director of Admissions
800-225-5588 Fax: 248-204-2228
Website: www.ltu.edu
E-mail: admissions@ltu.edu
See listing under "Universities"

MACOMB COMMUNITY COLLEGE
44575 Garfield Rd, Clinton Township MI 48038-1139
Information Center
586-445-7999
Website: www.macomb.edu
E-mail: answer@macomb.edu

MACOMB COMMUNITY COLLEGE
14500 E 12 Mile Rd, Warren MI 48088-3896
Information Center
586-445-7999
Website: www.macomb.edu
E-mail: answer@macomb.edu

Michigan State University
450 Administration Bldg, East Lansing MI 48824
517-355-1855

Michigan Technological University
1400 Townsend Dr, Houghton MI 49931-1200
Nancy Rehling, Director of Admissions
906-487-2335

Northern Michigan University
1401 Presque Isle Ave, Marquette MI 49855-5301
906-227-1000

Northwestern Michigan College
1701 E Front St, Traverse City MI 49686-3061
Jim Bensley, Admissions Coordinator
800-748-0566 Fax: 231-995-1339
Website: www.nmc.edu
E-mail: jbensley@nmc.edu

Northwood University
4000 Whiting Dr, Midland MI 48640
Daniel F. Toland, Dean of Admissions
800-457-7878 Fax: 989-837-4490
Website: www.northwood.edu
E-mail: miadmit@northwood.edu

Oakland Community College
2480 Opdyke Rd, Bloomfield Hills MI 48304
Dr. Maurice McCall, Director of Admissions
248-341-2000
Website: www.oaklandcc.edu
E-mail: mhmcall@oaklandcc.edu

Oakland University
2200 N Squirrel Rd, Rochester MI 48309
Eleanor L. Reynolds, Assistant Vice President & Director of Admissions
248-370-2100
Website: www.oakland.edu
E-mail: ouinfo@oakland.edu

Olivet College
300 S Main St, Olivet MI 49076-9724
269-749-7000

Saginaw Valley State University
7400 Bay Rd, University Center MI 48710-0001
989-790-4000

University of Detroit-Mercy
PO Box 19900, Detroit MI 48219-0900
313-993-1000

University of Michigan-Ann Arbor
1220 Student Activities Bldg, Ann Arbor MI 48109
734-764-1817

University of Michigan-Dearborn
4901 Evergreen Rd, Dearborn MI 48128-1491
The Office of Admissions & Orientation
313-593-5100 Fax: 313-436-9167
Website: www.umd.umich.edu
E-mail: admissions@umd.umich.edu

University of Michigan-Flint
303 E Kearsley St, Flint MI 48502-1950
810-762-3000

Wayne State University
5980 Cass Ave, Detroit MI 48202-3489
313-577-2424

Western Michigan University
Kalamazoo MI 49008
269-387-1000

MINNESOTA

ACADEMY COLLEGE
1101 E 78th St, Bloomington MN 55420-1402
952-851-0066 Fax: 952-851-0094
Website: www.academycollege.edu
E-mail: info@academycollege.edu
See listing under "Career Schools"

ARGOSY UNIVERSITY / TWIN CITIES
1515 Central Pkwy, Eagan MN 55121-1756
O. Jeanne Stoneking, Director of Admissions
651-846-2882 Fax: 651-994-7956
Website: www.argosy.edu
E-mail: tcadmissions@argosy.edu

Augsburg College
2211 Riverside Ave, Minneapolis MN 55454-1350
612-330-1000

Bethany Lutheran College
700 Luther Dr, Mankato MN 56001
Don Westphal, Dean of Admissions
507-344-7000 Fax: 507-344-7376
Website: www.blc.edu
E-mail: admiss@blc.edu

Bethel College
3900 Bethel Dr, Saint Paul MN 55112-6999
651-638-6400

College of Saint Benedict
37 College Ave S, Saint Joseph MN 56374-2099
320-363-5011

College of St. Catherine
2004 Randolph Ave, Saint Paul MN 55105-1789
651-690-6000

College of Saint Scholastica
1200 Kenwood Ave, Duluth MN 55811-4199
Brian Dalton, V.P. of Enrollment Management
800-447-5444

Concordia College
901 8th St S, Moorhead MN 56562-0002
Scott Ellingson, Director of Admissions
218-299-3004

Concordia University-Saint Paul
275 Syndicate St N, Saint Paul MN 55104-5494
651-641-8278

Duluth Business University
4724 Mike Colalillo Dr, Duluth MN 55807-2723
Bonnie Kupczynski, Director
800-777-8406 Fax: 218-628-2127
Website: www.dbumn.edu
E-mail: info@dbumn.edu

Dunwoody College of Technology
818 Dunwoody Blvd, Minneapolis MN 55403-1192
John Slama, Vice President Enrollment Management
800-292-4625 or 612-374-5800 Fax: 612-374-4128
Website: www.dunwoody.edu
E-mail: jslama@dunwoody.edu
See listing under "Career Schools"

Globe College
7166 10th St N, Oakdale MN 55128
Mike Hughes, Campus Director
651-730-5100 Fax: 651-730-5151
Website: www.globecollege.edu
E-mail: admissions@globecollege.edu

Gustavus Adolphus College
800 W College Ave, Saint Peter MN 56082-1485
Mark H. Anderson, Dean of Admission
800-GUSTAVUS Fax: 507-933-7474
Website: www.gustavus.edu
E-mail: admission@gustavus.edu

Hamline University
1536 Hewitt Ave, Saint Paul MN 55104-1284
651-523-2800

Hibbing Community College
1515 E 25th St, Hibbing MN 55746-3300
Holly Bigelow, Director of Enrollment
800-224-4HCC or 218-262-7200 Fax: 218-262-6717
Website: www.hibbing.edu
E-mail: admissions@hibbing.edu

McNally Smith College of Music
19 Exchange St East, St. Paul MN 55101
Debbie Sandridge, Director of Admissions
800-594-9500 Fax: 651-291-0366
Website: www.mcnallysmith.edu
E-mail: dsandridge@mcnallysmith.edu
See listing under "Universities"

Minneapolis Community and Technical College
1501 Hennepin Ave, Minneapolis MN 55403-1779
Dena Russell, Director of Admissions
612-659-6282 Fax: 612-659-6210
Website: www.minneapolis.edu
E-mail: admissions.office@minneapolis.edu

Minnesota State Community & Technical College
900 Highway 34 E, Detroit Lakes MN 56501-2698
Dale Westley, Director of Admissions
800-492-4836 Fax: 218-846-3710
Website: www.minnesota.edu
E-mail: dale.westley@minnesota.edu

Minnesota State Community & Technical College
PO Box 566, Wadena MN 56482-0566
Paul Drange, Director of Admissions
800-247-2007 Fax: 218-631-7901
Website: www.minnesota.edu
E-mail: paul.drange@minnesota.edu

Minnesota State Community and Technical College
1900 28th Ave S, Moorhead MN 56560-4899
Laurie McKeever, Director of Admissions
800-426-5603 Fax: 218-299-6584
Website: www.minnesota.edu
E-mail: laurie.mckeever@minnesota.edu

Minnesota State University Mankato
228 Wiecking Center, Mankato MN 56001
507-389-1866

National American University
1550 W Highway 36, Roseville MN 55113
Matthew Mottl, Director of Admissions
651-644-1265 Fax: 651-644-0690
Website: www.national.edu
E-mail: mmottl@national.edu

Northland Community & Technical College
Highway 1 E, Thief River Falls MN 56701
Norma Konschak, Chairperson
800-959-6282 or 218-681-0766 Fax: 218-681-0774
Website: www.northlandcollege.edu

Northland Community and Technical College
2022 Central Ave NE
East Grand Forks MN 56721-2702
Deb Riely, Business Program Chair
800-451-3441 Fax: 218-773-4502
Website: www.northlandcollege.edu
E-mail: admissions@northlandcollege.edu

Pillsbury Baptist Bible College
315 S Grove Ave, Owatonna MN 55060-3097
Stephen R. Seidler, Director of Admissions
507-451-2710 Fax: 507-451-0156
Website: www.pillsbury.edu
E-mail: steveseidler@pillsbury.edu

Ridgewater College-Hutchinson Campus
2 Century Ave SE, Hutchinson MN 55350-3100
Dawn Bjork, Counselor
800-222-4424 Fax: 320-231-7767
Website: www.ridgewater.edu
E-mail: dawn.bjork@ridgewater.edu

Ridgewater College-Willmar Campus
PO Box 1097, Willmar MN 56201-1097
Sally Kerfeld, Director of Admissions
800-722-1151 Fax: 320-231-7677
Website: www.ridgewater.edu
E-mail: skerfeld@ridgewater.edu

St. Cloud State University
720 4th Ave S, Saint Cloud MN 56301-4442
877-654-7278

St. Mary's University of Minnesota
700 Terrace Hts Ste 2, Winona MN 55987-1321
507-452-4430

Southwest Minnesota State University
1501 State St, Marshall MN 56258-1598
507-537-7678

University of Minnesota
2900 University Ave, Crookston MN 56716-5001
218-281-6510

University of Minnesota
10 University Dr, Duluth MN 55812-2496
Beth Esselstrom, Director of Admissions
218-726-7171

University of Minnesota
231 Pillsbury Dr SE, Minneapolis MN 55455-0230
612-625-2008

University of Minnesota - Morris
600 E 4th St, Morris MN 56267-2132
Rodney Oto, Director
800-992-8863

Winona State University
PO Box 5838, Winona MN 55987-0838
507-457-5000

MISSISSIPPI

Belhaven College
1500 Peachtree St, Jackson MS 39202-1789
601-968-5927

Delta State University
Hwy 8 W, Cleveland MS 38733
662-846-3000

Jackson State University
1440 J.R. Lynch St, Jackson MS 39217
Stephanie Chatman, Director of Admissions
601-979-2100

Millsaps College
PO Box 15495, Jackson MS 39210
601-974-1000

Mississippi College
PO Box 4086, Clinton MS 39058-0001
601-925-3000

Mississippi State University
PO Box J, Mississippi State MS 39762-5509
662-325-2323

Mississippi University for Women
1100 College St Unit W1613, Columbus MS 39701
Terri Heath, Director of Admissions
877-GO-2-THEW

Mississippi Valley State University
14000 Highway 82 W Box 7222
Itta Bena MS 38941-1401
Office of Admissions
662-254-3347

Tougaloo College
500 W County Line Rd, Tougaloo MS 39174-9799
Juno Leggette Jacobs, Director of Admissions
601-977-7768 Fax: 601-977-4501
Website: www.tougaloo.edu
E-mail: jjacobs@tougaloo.edu

University of Mississippi
University MS 38677
662-232-7226

University of Southern Mississippi
PO Box 5165, Hattiesburg MS 39406-1000
601-266-5000

MISSOURI

Central Missouri State University
Warrensburg MO 64093-8888
Charles Petentler, Associate Director of Admissions
800-956-0177

College of the Ozarks
Point Lookout MO 65726
417-334-6411

Columbia College
1001 Rogers St, Columbia MO 65216-0001
Regina Morin, Director of Admissions
573-875-7352 Fax: 573-875-7506
Website: www.ccis.edu
E-mail: admissions@ccis.edu

Culver-Stockton College
1 College Hl, Canton MO 63435-1299
Betty Smith, Director of Enrollment Services
800-537-1883

Drury University
900 N Benton Ave, Springfield MO 65802-3791
417-873-7879

East Central College
1964 Prairie Dell Rd, Union MO 63084
Karen Wieda, Registrar
636-583-5195 ext. 2220 Fax: 636-583-1897
Website: www.eastcentral.edu
E-mail: wiedaks@eastcentral.edu

Harris-Stowe State University
3026 Laclede Ave, Saint Louis MO 63103-2199
LaShanda R. Boone, Director of Admissions
314-340-3300 Fax: 314-340-3555
Website: www.hssu.edu
E-mail: admissions@hssu.edu

Hickey College
940 Westport Plz, Saint Louis MO 63146-3127
Christopher A. Gearin, President
800-777-1544 or 314-434-2212 Fax: 314-434-1974
Website: www.hickeycollege.edu
E-mail: admin@hickeycollege.edu

Lindenwood University
209 S Kingshighway St
Saint Charles MO 63301-1695
Sheryl Guffey, Director of Admissions
636-949-2000 Fax: 636-949-4989
Website: www.lindenwood.edu

Missouri Southern State University - Joplin
3950 Newman Rd, Joplin MO 64801-1512
417-625-9300

Missouri State University
901 S National Ave, Springfield MO 65897
417-836-5000

Missouri Valley College
500 E College St, Marshall MO 65340-3197
John R. Campbell, Division Dean
660-831-4165

Missouri Western State College
4525 Downs Dr, Saint Joseph MO 64507-2294
800-662-7041

Park University
8700 NW River Park Dr, Parkville MO 64152-3795
816-741-2000

Rockhurst University
1100 Rockhurst Rd, Kansas City MO 64110-2561
Mark Kopenski, VP of Enrollment Management
816-501-4000

St. Charles Community College
4601 Mid Rivers Mall Dr, Saint Peters MO 63376
Kathy Brockgreitens-Gober, Director of Admissions
636-922-8000 Fax: 636-922-8236
Website: www.stchas.edu
E-mail: adm-reg@stchas.edu

St. Louis University
221 N Grand Blvd, Saint Louis MO 63103-2097
314-977-2222

Southeast Missouri State University
1 University Plz, Cape Girardeau MO 63701-4710
573-651-2000

Southwest Baptist University
1600 University Ave, Bolivar MO 65613-2597
417-328-5281

SPRINGFIELD COLLEGE
1010 W Sunshine St, Springfield MO 65807-2446
Scott Lester, Contact
417-864-7220 or 800-475-2699 Fax: 417-866-3335
Website: www.springfield-college.com
E-mail: slester@cci.edu

Stephens College
PO Box 2121, Columbia MO 65215-0001
David Adams, Dean of Enrollment Management
573-442-2211 Fax: 573-876-7237
Website: www.stephens.edu
E-mail: dadams@stephens.edu

Truman State University
100 E Normal, Kirksville MO 63501
Office of Admission
660-785-4000 Fax: 660-785-4181
Website: admissions.truman.edu
E-mail: admissions@truman.edu

University of Missouri
228 Jesse Hall, Columbia MO 65211-0001
573-882-2121

University of Missouri
5100 Rockhill Rd, Kansas City MO 64110-2446
816-235-1000

University of Missouri
102 Parker, Rolla MO 65409
Lynn Stichnote, Director of Admission
573-341-4164

University of Missouri
1 University Blvd, Saint Louis MO 63121-4499
Dr. Keith Womer, Dean-College of Business
314-516-5888 Fax: 314-516-6420
Website: www.umsl.edu
E-mail: admissions@umsl.edu

Washington University in St. Louis
1 Brookings Dr, Saint Louis MO 63130-4899
314-935-5000

Webster University
470 E Lockwood Ave, Saint Louis MO 63119-3194
Dr. Benjamin Akande, Dean School of Business and Management
314-961-2660 ext. 5950 Fax: 314-968-7077
Website: www.webster.edu
E-mail: mtaylor@webster.edu
See listing under "Universities"

Westminister College
501 Westminster Ave, Fulton MO 65251-1299
573-642-3361

William Jewell College
500 College Hill, Liberty MO 64068-1896
800-753-7009

William Woods University
1 University Ave, Fulton MO 65251-1098
Jimmy Clay, Director of Admissions
573-642-2251 Fax: 573-592-1146
Website: www.williamwoods.edu
E-mail: admissions@williamwoods.edu
See listing under "Universities"

MONTANA

Carroll College
1601 N Benton Ave, Helena MT 59625-0002
Cynthia Thornquist, Director of Admissions & Enrollment Operations
406-447-4384

Montana State University - Billings
1500 University Dr, Billings MT 59101-0252
Karen Everett, Director
800-565-MSUB

Montana State University - Bozeman
103 Culbertson Hall, Bozeman MT 59715-5072
406-994-2452

Montana Tech of the University of Montana
1300 W Park St, Butte MT 59701-8997
800-445-TECH

Rocky Mountain College
1511 Poly Dr, Billings MT 59102-1796
Bonnie Knapp, Director of Admissions
800-877-6259 Fax: 406-657-1189
Website: www.rocky.edu
E-mail: admissions@rocky.edu

University of Montana
Missoula MT 59812-0001
406-243-0211

NEBRASKA

Bellevue University
1000 Galvin Rd S, Bellevue NE 68005-3098
Doug Frost, Dean of College of Business

Chadron State College
1000 Main St, Chadron NE 69337-2690
308-432-6000

College of Saint Mary
7000 Mercy Rd, Omaha NE 68106
Lorin Werth,V.P. for Enrollment
800-926-5534 or 402-399-2407 Fax: 402-399-2412
Website: www.csm.edu
E-mail: lwerth@csm.edu

Creighton University
2500 California Plz, Omaha NE 68178-0001
402-280-2700

Dana College
2848 College Dr, Blair NE 68008-1099
James Lynes, Director of Admissions
800-444-3262

Midland Lutheran College
900 N Clarkson St, Fremont NE 68025-4200
Todd Hansen, Associate Director of Admissions
402-941-6501 Fax: 402-941-6513
Website: www.mlc.edu
E-mail: admissions@mlc.edu

Mid-Plains Community College
McCook Community College Campus
1205 E 3rd St, Mc Cook NE 69001-2631
Kelly Rippen, Director of Recruitment
800-658-4348 Fax: 308-345-8180
Website: www.mpcc.edu
E-mail: rippenk@mpcc.edu

Mid-Plains Community College
North Platte Community College - South Campus
601 W State Farm Rd, North Platte NE 69101
Kelly Rippen, Director of Recruitment
800-658-4308 ext. 8107 Fax: 308-535-3789
Website: www.mpcc.edu
E-mail: rippenk@mpcc.edu

Nebraska Wesleyan University
5000 Saint Paul Ave, Lincoln NE 68504-2794
Patricia Karthauser, V.P. for University Enrollment
402-466-2371 Fax: 402-465-2177
Website: www.nebrwesleyan.edu
E-mail: admissions@nebrwesleyan.edu

Peru State College
PO Box 10, Peru NE 68421-0010
Office of Admissions
800-742-4412 Fax: 402-872-2296
Website: www.peru.edu
E-mail: admissions@oakmail.peru.edu

Union College
3800 S 48th St, Lincoln NE 68506-4300
Buell Fogg, V.P. for Enrollment Services
800-228-4600

University of Nebraska
14th & R Sts, Lincoln NE 68588
402-472-7211

University of Nebraska at Kearney
905 W 25th St, Kearney NE 68849-0001
Dusty Newton, Director of Admissions
800-KEARNEY Fax: 308-865-8987
Website: www.unk.edu
E-mail: admissionsug@unk.edu

University of Nebraska at Omaha
60th and Dodge St, Omaha NE 68182-0001
402-554-2800

VATTEROTT COLLEGE
11818 I St, Omaha NE 68137
Todd S. Clark, Director
402-891-9411 Fax: 402-891-9413
Website: www.vatterott-college.edu
E-mail: tclark@vatterott-college.edu

NEVADA

Career College of Northern Nevada
1195-A Corporate Blvd, Reno NV 89502-2331
Nathan Clark, Director
775-856-2266 Fax: 775-856-0935
Website: www.ccnn.edu
E-mail: lgoldhammer@ccnn4u.com
See listing under "Career Schools"

GREAT BASIN COLLEGE
1500 College Pkwy, Elko NV 89801-5032
Julie G. Byrnes, Director of Enrollment Management
775-753-2271 Fax: 775-753-2311
Website: www.gbcnv.edu
E-mail: bjulie@gbcnv.edu

Morrison University
10315 Professional Circle Suite 201
Reno NV 89521-4826
Charles Timinsky, Director of Enrollment
775-850-0700 Fax: 775-850-0711
Website: www.morrisonuniversity.com

University of Nevada
Reno NV 89557-0001
775-784-1110

University of Nevada Las Vegas
4505 S Maryland Pkwy, Las Vegas NV 89154-9901
800-334-8658

NEW HAMPSHIRE

Antioch University New England
40 Avon St, Keene NH 03431-3516
David Caruso, President
Leatrice A. Johnson, Director of Admissions
603-357-6265 Fax: 603-357-0718
Website: www.antiochne.edu
E-mail: admissions@antiochne.edu

Daniel Webster College
20 University Dr, Nashua NH 03063-1323
Paul LaBarre, Director of Enrollment Services
603-577-6600

Dartmouth College
Hanover NH 03755
603-646-1110

Franklin Pierce College
20 College Rd, Rindge NH 03461
800-437-0048

New England College
26 Bridge St, Henniker NH 03242-3297
603-428-2211

Rivier College
420 S Main St, Nashua NH 03060-5086
David Boisvert, Director of Undergraduate Admissions
603-897-8507

St. Anselm College
100 Saint Anselms Dr, Manchester NH 03102-1310
603-641-7000

Southern New Hampshire University
2500 N River Rd, Hooksett NH 03106-1045
Steve Soba, Director of Admissions
603-645-9611 Fax: 603-645-9693
Website: www.snhu.edu
E-mail: s.soba@snhu.edu

University of New Hampshire
Durham NH 03824
603-862-1234

NEW JERSEY

Atlantic Cape Community College
5100 Black Horse Pike
Mays Landing NJ 08330-2699
Linda McLeod, Assistant Director of College Recruitment
609-343-5000 Fax: 609-343-4921
Website: www.atlantic.edu
E-mail: accadmit@atlantic.edu
See listing under "Community and Junior Colleges"

Bergen Community College
400 Paramus Rd, Paramus NJ 07652
Julian Gomez, Asst. Director of Admissions
201-447-7100 Fax: 201-444-7036
Website: www.bergen.edu
E-mail: jgomez@bergen.edu

Bloomfield College
467 Franklin St, Bloomfield NJ 07003
973-748-9000

Caldwell College
9 Ryerson Ave, Caldwell NJ 07006-6195
973-618-3000

Centenary College
400 Jefferson St, Hackettstown NJ 07840-2100
Glenna Warren, Director of Admissions
908-852-1400 Fax: 908-852-3454
Website: www.centenarycollege.edu
E-mail: warreng@centenarycollege.edu

College of New Jersey
PO Box 7718, Ewing NJ 08628-0718
609-771-1855

Fairleigh Dickinson University
285 Madison Ave, Madison NJ 07940-1099
800-338-8803

Felician College
262 S Main St, Lodi NJ 07644-2198
973-559-6000

Hohokus School - RETS Nutley
103 Park Ave, Nutley NJ 07110-3505
Thomas Eastwick, President
973-661-0600 Fax: 973-661-2954
Website: www.rets-institute.com
E-mail: admissions@rets-institute.com

Mercer County Community College
West Windsor Campus
PO Box B, Trenton NJ 08690
Savita Bambhrolia, Director of Admissions
609-586-4800 Fax: 609-587-4666
Website: www.mccc.edu
E-mail: admiss@mccc.edu

Monmouth University
400 Cedar Ave, West Long Branch NJ 07764-1890
732-571-3400

Montclair State University
Montclair State University, Montclair NJ 07043-1624
973-655-4000

New Jersey City University
2039 John F Kennedy Blvd
Jersey City NJ 07305-1588
Carmen Panlilio, Asst. V.P. for Admissions and Financial Aid
201-200-3234 Fax: 201-200-2044
Website: www.njcu.edu
E-mail: admissions@njcu.edu

New Jersey Institute of Technology
University Heights, Newark NJ 07102
973-596-3000

Ramapo College of New Jersey
505 Ramapo Valley Rd, Mahwah NJ 07430-1623
Director of Admissions
201-684-7300 or 201-684-7301 Fax: 201-684-7964
Website: www.ramapo.edu
E-mail: admissions@ramapo.edu

Richard Stockton College of New Jersey
PO Box 195, Pomona NJ 08240
609-652-1776

Rider University
2083 Lawrenceville Rd, Lawrenceville NJ 08648-3099
Susan Christian, Director of Admissions
609-896-5042

Rowan University
201 Mullica Hill Rd, Glassboro NJ 08028-1700
856-256-4000

Rutgers-The State University of New Jersey
Camden Campus
311 N 5th St, Camden NJ 08102-1405
856-225-6026

Rutgers-The State University of New Jersey
Newark Campus
Newark NJ 07102
973-353-5568

Rutgers-The State University of New Jersey
New Brunswick Campus
35 College Ave, New Brunswick NJ 08901
732-932-4636

St. Peter's College
Hudson Terrace, Englewood Cliffs NJ 07632
201-568-7730

St. Peter's College
2627 John F Kennedy Blvd, Jersey City NJ 07306
888-SPC-9933

Seton Hall University
400 S Orange Ave, South Orange NJ 07079-2697
973-761-9000

Thomas Edison State College
101 W State St, Trenton NJ 08608-1101
609-984-1100

NEW MEXICO

Eastern New Mexico University
Portales NM 88130
800-367-3668

International Institute of the Americas
4201 Central Ave NW Suite J
Albuquerque NM 87105-1649
Ed Sigman, Director
505-880-2877 Fax: 505-352-0199
Website: www.iia.edu
E-mail: syelton@iia.edu

National American University
4775 Indian Sch Rd NE #200
Albuquerque NM 87110-3976
505-265-7517

National American University
1601 Rio Rancho Dr SE #200
Rio Rancho NM 87124-1093
505-891-1111

New Mexico Highlands University
PO Box 9000, Las Vegas NM 87701
Margaret Young, Contact
505-454-3115

New Mexico State University
1500 N 3rd St, Grants NM 87020-2025
505-287-7981 Fax: 505-287-2329
Website: www.grants.nmsu.edu

New Mexico State University
PO Box 30001, Las Cruces NM 88003-8001
505-646-0111

University of New Mexico
1 University Campus, Albuquerque NM 87131-0001
505-277-0111

NEW YORK

Adelphi University
Garden City NY 11530
516-877-3100

Alfred University
1 Saxson Dr, Alfred NY 14802
607-871-2111

Briarcliffe College
1055 Stewart Ave, Bethpage NY 11714-3545
Theresa Donohue, Director of Admissions
516-918-3600 Fax: 516-470-6020
Website: www.briarcliffe.edu

Broome Community College
907 Upper Front St, Binghamton NY 13905
Anthony S. Fiorelli, Director of Admissions
607-778-5001 Fax: 607-778-5442
Website: www.sunybroome.edu
E-mail: fiorelli_a@sunybroome.edu

Canisius College
2001 Main St, Buffalo NY 14208-1098
716-883-7000

Cazenovia College
Cazenovia NY 13035-1084
Robert Croot, Dean of Admissions & Financial Aid
800-654-3210

Clarkson University
PO Box 5500, Potsdam NY 13699
315-268-6400

College of New Rochelle
29 Castle Pl, New Rochelle NY 10805-2339
914-654-5000

College of Saint Rose
432 Western Ave, Albany NY 12203-1419
Maryelizabeth Amico, Asst V.P. for Undergraduate Admissions
518-454-5150 Fax: 518-454-2013
Website: www.strose.edu
E-mail: admit@strose.edu

Columbia University
2960 Broadway, New York NY 10027-6900
212-854-1754

Cornell University
410 Thurston Ave, Ithaca NY 14850-2432
607-255-2000

CULINARY ACADEMY OF NEW YORK
154 W 14th St, New York NY 10011-7307
Harold Kaplan, Contact
212-675-6655 Fax: 212-463-9194
Website: www.culinaryacademy.edu
E-mail: hkaplan@culinaryacademy.edu

CUNY Bernard M. Baruch College
17 Lexington Ave, New York NY 10010-5518
212-802-2000

CUNY City College
Convent Ave at 138th St, New York NY 10031
Celia Lloyd, Interim Director of Admissions
212-650-6977

CUNY York College
9420 Guy R Brewer Blvd, Jamaica NY 11451-0001
718-262-2000

Daemen College
4380 Main St, Amherst NY 14226-3592
Donna Shaffner, Director of Admissions
800-462-7652 or 716-839-8225 Fax: 716-839-8229
Website: www.daemen.edu
E-mail: admissions@daemen.edu
See listing under "Universities"

Dominican College of Blauvelt
470 Western Hwy, Orangeburg NY 10962-1210
845-359-7800

D'Youville College
320 Porter Ave, Buffalo NY 14201-1084
716-829-7600

Elmira Business Institute
303 N Main St, Elmira NY 14901
Lisa Roan, Admissions Director
607-733-7177 or 800-843-1812 Fax: 607-733-7178
Website: www.ebi-college.com
E-mail: lroan@ebi-college.com

Elmira College
1 Park Pl, Elmira NY 14901-2099
Gary Fallis, Dean of Admissions
607-735-1724

Excelsior College
7 Columbia Cir, Albany NY 12203-5156
518-464-8500

Farmingdale SUNY
2350 Broadhollow Rd, Farmingdale NY 11735
631-420-2200

FIVE TOWNS COLLEGE
305 N Service Rd, Dix Hills NY 11746-5871
631-424-7000 ext. 2110 Fax: 631-656-2172
Website: www.fivetowns.edu
E-mail: admissions@ftc.edu
See listing under "Universities"

Fordham University
441 E Fordham Rd, Bronx NY 10458-9993
Sharon Smith, Dean
718-817-4000

Hilbert College
5200 S Park Ave, Hamburg NY 14075-1597
Timothy Lee, Director of Admissions
716-649-7900 Fax: 716-649-0702
Website: www.hilbert.edu
E-mail: tlee@hilbert.edu

Hofstra University
100 Hofstra University, Hempstead NY 11549-1000
516-463-6600

Houghton College
PO Box 128, Houghton NY 14744-0128
585-567-9200

Iona College
715 North Ave, New Rochelle NY 10801-1890
Tom Weede, Director of Admissions
914-633-2000

Ithaca College
953 Danby Rd, Ithaca NY 14850-7002
607-274-3011

Keuka College
PO Box 98, Keuka Park NY 14478-0098
315-536-4411

LABORATORY INSTITUTE OF MERCHANDISING
12 E 53rd St, New York NY 10022-5268
Kristina Gibson, Director of Admissions
800-677-1323 or 212-752-1530 Fax: 212-750-3432
Website: www.limcollege.edu
E-mail: admissions@limcollege.edu
See listing under "Universities"

Le Moyne College
1419 Salt Springs Rd, Syracuse NY 13214-1301
800-333-4733

Long Island University-C. W. Post Campus
720 Northern Blvd, Brookville NY 11548-1300
Joanne Graziano, Executive Director of Admissions
516-299-2900 Fax: 516-299-2137
Website: www.liu.edu/cwpost
E-mail: enroll@cwpost.liu.edu

Long Island University - Southampton College
239 Montauk Hwy, Southampton NY 11968
631-283-4000

Manhattan College
4513 Manhattan College Pkwy
Riverdale NY 10471-4099
Dr. James Suarez, Dean of Business
718-862-7200

Manhattanville College
2900 Purchase St, Purchase NY 10577-2132
914-694-2200

Marist College
3399 North Rd, Poughkeepsie NY 12601
Jay E. Murray, Director of Admissions
845-575-3000

Marymount College at Fordham University
100 Marymount Ave, Tarrytown NY 10591-3796
914-631-3200

Medaille College
18 Agassiz Cir, Buffalo NY 14214-2695
716-884-3281

Mercy College
555 Broadway, Dobbs Ferry NY 10522-1189
Kathleen Jackson, Director of Admissions
800-MERCY-NY

Molloy College
1000 Hempstead Ave
Rockville Centre NY 11570-1100
Marguerite Lane, Director of Admissions
516-678-5000 ext. 6291 Fax: 516-256-2247
Website: www.molloy.edu
E-mail: admissions@molloy.edu
See listing under "Universities"

Monroe College
2501 Jerome Ave, Bronx NY 10468-4305
Evan Jerome, Director of Admissions
718-933-6700 Fax: 718-364-3552
Website: www.monroecollege.edu
E-mail: ejerome@monroecollege.edu

Mt. St. Mary College
330 Powell Ave, Newburgh NY 12550-3494
845-561-0800

Nazareth College of Rochester
4245 East Ave, Rochester NY 14618-3790
585-389-2525

New York Institute of Technology
PO Box 8000, Old Westbury NY 11568-8000
516-686-7516

New York University
70 Washington Sq S, New York NY 10012-1019
212-998-1212

Niagara University
PO Box 2011, Niagara University NY 14109-2011
George Pachter, Dean of Admissions & Records
800-462-2111

Nyack College
1 South Boulevard
Nyack NY 10960-3698
845-358-1710

Pace University
1 Pace Plz, New York NY 10038-1502
212-346-1200

Paul Smith's College
Paul Smiths NY 12970
Amber DeBeer, Assistant Director of Admissions
800-421-2605 Fax: 518-327-6016
Website: www.paulsmiths.edu
E-mail: admiss@paulsmiths.edu

Polytechnic University
6 Metrotech Ctr, Brooklyn NY 11201-3840
718-260-3600

Rensselaer Polytechnic Institute
110 8th St, Troy NY 12180-3590
518-276-6000

Roberts Wesleyan College
2301 Westside Dr, Rochester NY 14624-1997
Office of Admissions
585-594-6400 Fax: 585-594-6371
Website: www.roberts.edu
E-mail: admissions@roberts.edu

Rochester Institute of Technology
1 Lomb Memorial Dr, Rochester NY 14623-5603
585-475-2411

Russell Sage College
45 Ferry St, Troy NY 12180-4115
518-244-2000

St. Bonaventure University
Saint Bonaventure NY 14778-9999
585-375-2000

St. John Fisher College
3690 East Ave, Rochester NY 14618-3597
585-385-8000

St. John's University
8000 Utopia Pkwy, Queens NY 11439
Office of Admission
718-990-2000 or 888-9-STJOHNS Fax: 718-990-2096
Website: www.stjohns.edu
E-mail: admissions@stjohns.edu
See listing under "Universities"

St. Joseph's College
245 Clinton Ave, Brooklyn NY 11205-3688
Theresa LaRocca Meyer, V.P. for Enrollment Management
718-636-6800 Fax: 718-636-8303
Website: www.sjcny.edu
E-mail: tlaroccameyer@sjcny.edu

St. Joseph's College
155 W Roe Blvd, Patchogue NY 11772
631-447-3200

Siena College
515 Loudonville Rd, Loudonville NY 12211-1462
Ned Jones, Director of Admissions
518-783-2300

Skidmore College
815 N Broadway, Saratoga Springs NY 12866-1698
518-580-5000

SUNY at Albany
1400 Washington Ave, Albany NY 12222-1000
Thomas Flemming, Associate Director of Admissions
518-442-5435

SUNY at Binghamton
PO Box 6001, Binghamton NY 13902-6001
607-777-2000

SUNY College at Brockport
350 New Campus Dr, Brockport NY 14420-2997
Bernard S. Valento, Director of Undergraduate Admissions
585-395-2751 Fax: 585-395-5452
Website: www.brockport.edu
E-mail: admit@brockport.edu

SUNY College at Old Westbury
PO Box 210, Old Westbury NY 11568-0210
516-876-3000

SUNY College of Agriculture & Technology
107 Schenectady Ave, Cobleskill NY 12043
Clayton A. Smith, Director of Admissions
800-295-8988

SUNY College of Technology
Alfred NY 14802
Deborah J. Goodrich, Director of Admissions
800-4AL-FRED Fax: 607-587-4299
Website: www.alfredstate.edu
E-mail: admissions@alfredstate.edu

SUNY College of Technology
2 Main St, Delhi NY 13753-1110
Robert W. Mazzei, Director of Admissions
800-96-DELHI Fax: 607-746-4104
Website: www.delhi.edu
E-mail: enroll@delhi.edu

SUNY Institute of Technology Utica/Rome
PO Box 3050, Utica NY 13504-3050
315-792-7100

SUNY Niagara County Community College
3111 Saunders Settlement Rd
Sanborn NY 14132-9487
Kathleen Saunders, Director of Admissions
716-614-6200 Fax: 716-614-6820
Website: www.niagaracc.suny.edu
E-mail: saunders@niagaracc.suny.edu

SUNY Orange County Community College
115 South St, Middletown NY 10940-6437
Margot St. Lawrence, Director of Admissions
845-341-4030 Fax: 845-342-8662
Website: www.sunyorange.edu
E-mail: apply@sunyorange.edu
See listing under "Community and Junior Colleges"

Syracuse University
Syracuse NY 13244-0001
315-443-1870

Taylor Business Institute
23 W 17th St 7th Floor, New York NY 10011-5501
800-959-9999 Fax: 212-229-2187
Website: www.tbiglobal.com
E-mail: admissions@tbiglobal.com

United States Military Academy West Point
646 Swift Rd, West Point NY 10996-1905
Colonel Michael L. Jones, Director of Admissions
845-938-4041 Fax: 845-938-8121
Website: admissions.usma.edu
E-mail: admissions@usma.edu

University at Buffalo, The State University of New York
15 Capen Hall, Buffalo NY 14260-1660
Patricia G. Armstrong, Director of Admissions
888-UB-ADMIT

University of Rochester
Meliora Hall, Rochester NY 14627
585-275-2121

Utica College
1600 Burrstone Rd, Utica NY 13502-4857
315-792-3111

Utica School of Commerce
17 Elm St, Oneonta NY 13820-1828
Misty Davis, Admissions
607-432-7003 Fax: 607-432-7004
Website: www.uscny.com
E-mail: mdavis@uscny.com

Utica School of Commerce
201 Bleecker St, Utica NY 13501-2280
Cindy Delaney, Director of Admissions
315-733-2307 Fax: 315-733-9281
Website: www.uscny.edu
E-mail: admissions@uscny.edu

VAUGHN COLLEGE OF AERONAUTICS AND TECHNOLOGY

8601 23rd Ave, Flushing NY 11369-1037
Vincent Papandrea, Director of Admissions
800-776-2376 Fax: 718-429-0671
Website: www.vaughn.edu
E-mail: admitme@vaughn.edu
Established 1932. Private. Coed. Accreditation: MSACS, ABET. Tuition: $13,400. Fees: $280. Enrollment: 842 full-time, 284 part-time. Faculty: 59. Student-faculty ratio: 11:1. Degrees: BS, AAS, AOS. Library: 62,000 vols. Offering bachelor and associate degrees in airport management, aviation maintenance, flight training, electronic technology, engineering, general management, mechatronic engineering, pre-engineering and computerized design/animated graphics. Hands-on training. Extensive career development services and financial aid available.

Wagner College
One Campus Rd, Staten Island NY 10301
Leigh Ann DePascale, Director of Admissions
718-390-3411

NORTH CAROLINA

Appalachian State University
ASU Station, Boone NC 28608-0001
828-262-2000

Barton College
PO Box 5000, Wilson NC 27893
252-399-6300

Belmont Abbey College
100 Belmont Mount Holly Rd
Belmont NC 28012-1802
888-222-0110 Fax: 704-825-6670
Website: www.belmontabbeycollege.edu
E-mail: admissions@bac.edu

Campbell University
PO Box 546, Buies Creek NC 27506-0546
Herbert V. Kerner, Jr., Director of Admissions
800-334-4111

Catawba College
2300 W Innes St, Salisbury NC 28144-2488
Gordon A. Kirkland, Associate Director of Admissions
704-637-4402

Duke University
Durham NC 27706-8001
919-684-8111

East Carolina University
General Classroom Bldg. 3119, Greenville NC 27858
Dr. Ernest B. Uhr, Dean

Gardner-Webb University
PO Box 817, Boiling Springs NC 28017
704-406-2361

Greensboro College
815 W Market St, Greensboro NC 27401-1875
336-272-7102

Guilford College
5800 W Friendly Ave, Greensboro NC 27410-4173
Randy Doss, Dean of Enrollment
336-316-2100

Haywood Community College
185 Freedlander Dr, Clyde NC 28721
Debbie Rowland, Coordinator of Admissions
828-627-4500 Fax: 828-627-4513
Website: www.haywood.edu
E-mail: drowland@haywood.edu

High Point University
933 Montlieu Ave, High Point NC 27262-3598
336-841-9000

James Sprunt Community College
PO Box 398, Kenansville NC 28349-0398
Rita Brown, Registrar
910-296-2500 Fax: 910-296-1636
Website: www.sprunt.com

JOHN WESLEY COLLEGE

2314 N Centennial St, High Point NC 27265-3197
Greg Workman, Admissions Officer
336-889-2262 ext. 127 Fax: 336-889-2261
Website: www.johnwesley.edu
E-mail: admissions@johnwesley.edu
See listing under "Theological Studies & Religious Vocations"

Lees-McRae College
PO Box 128, Banner Elk NC 28604-0128
Walt Crutchfield, Dean of Admissions
800-280-4562 Fax: 828-898-8707
Website: www.lmc.edu
E-mail: admissions@lmc.edu

Livingstone College
701 W Monroe St, Salisbury NC 28144-5298
704-797-1000

Louisburg College
501 N Main St, Louisburg NC 27549-2399
800-775-0208 or 919-496-2521 Fax: 919-496-1788
Website: www.louisburg.edu
E-mail: admissions@louisburg.edu

Mars Hill College
Mars Hill NC 28754
Chad Holt, Dean of Enrollment
866-MHC-4-YOU Fax: 828-689-1473
Website: www.mhc.edu
E-mail: cholt@mhc.edu

Meredith College
3800 Hillsborough St, Raleigh NC 27607-5298
Heidi L. Fletcher, Director of Admissions
919-760-8581 Fax: 919-760-2348
Website: www.meredith.edu
E-mail: admissions@meredith.edu
See listing under "Women's Colleges"

Methodist College
5400 Ramsey St, Fayetteville NC 28311-1498
910-630-7000

Montreat College
PO Box 1267, Montreat NC 28757-1267
800-622-6968

Mt. Olive College
634 Henderson St, Mount Olive NC 28365
Tim Woodard, Director of Admissions
919-658-2502 Fax: 919-658-9816
Website: www.moc.edu
E-mail: admissions@moc.edu
See listing under "Universities"

North Carolina A&T State University
1601 E Market St, Greensboro NC 27411
Lee Young, AVC Enrollment
336-334-7500 Fax: 336-334-7478
Website: www.ncat.edu
E-mail: uadmit@ncat.edu

North Carolina State University
PO Box 7001, Raleigh NC 27695-0001
919-515-2011

North Carolina Wesleyan College
3400 N Wesleyan Blvd, Rocky Mount NC 27804-8677
252-985-5100

Pfeiffer University
PO Box 960, Misenheimer NC 28109-0960
704-463-1360

Queens University of Charlotte
1900 Selwyn Ave, Charlotte NC 28274-0002
704-337-2212

St. Andrews Presbyterian College
1700 Dogwood Mile St, Laurinburg NC 28352-5521
Glenn Batten, Vice President for Enrollment
910-277-5554

Salem College
Winston Salem NC 27108
Dana Evans, Dean of Admissions/Fin. Aid
800-32-SALEM Fax: 336-917-5572
Website: www.salem.edu
E-mail: admissions@salem.edu
See listing under "Women's Colleges"

South College
1567 Patton Ave, Asheville NC 28806-1748
Robert Davis, Dean of Academic Affairs
828-252-2486 Fax: 828-252-8558
Website: southcollegenc.com
E-mail: bdavis@southcollegenc.com

South Piedmont Community College
PO Box 126, Polkton NC 28135-0126
John Curtis, Contact
704-272-5324 Fax: 704-272-8904
Website: www.spcc.edu
E-mail: jcurtis@spcc.edu

University of North Carolina
Chapel Hill NC 27599-0001
919-962-2211

University of North Carolina
9201 University City Blvd, Charlotte NC 28223
704-547-2000

University of North Carolina
601 S College Rd, Wilmington NC 28403-3201
910-962-3000

University of North Carolina at Greensboro
1000 Spring Garden St, Greensboro NC 27412-0001
336-334-5243

University of North Carolina at Pembroke
PO Box 1510, Pembroke NC 28372-1510
910-521-6000

Wake Forest University
PO Box 7305, Winston Salem NC 27109-7305
336-759-5000

Warren Wilson College
PO Box 9000, Asheville NC 28815-9000
Richard Blomgren, Dean of Admissions
828-298-3325

Western Carolina University
University Dr, Cullowhee NC 28723-9646
828-227-7211

Winston-Salem State University
601 S Mrtn Lther King Jr Dr
Winston Salem NC 27110-0003
336-750-2000

NORTH DAKOTA

Dickinson State University
Dickinson ND 58601-4896
Steve Glasser, Director of Student Recruitment
800-279-4295 Fax: 701-483-2409
Website: www.dickinsonstate.edu
E-mail: dsu.hawks@dickinsonstate.edu

Jamestown College
6000 College Ln, Jamestown ND 58405-0002
701-252-3467

Mayville State University
330 3rd St NE, Mayville ND 58257-1299
Brian Larson, Director of Enrollment Services
800-437-4104

Minot State University
500 University Ave W, Minot ND 58707-0002
Dennis Parisien, Enrollment Services Rep.
800-777-0750 ext. 3350

Minot State University-Bottineau Campus
105 Simrall Blvd, Bottineau ND 58318-1159
Paula Berg, Associate Dean of Student Affairs
800-542-6866 Fax: 701-228-5499
Website: www.misu-b.nodak.edu
E-mail: paula.berg@misu.nodak.edu

Sitting Bull College
1341 92nd St, Fort Yates ND 58538
Melody Azure, Director of Admissions / Registrar
701-854-3861 Fax: 701-854-3403
Website: www.sittingbull.edu
E-mail: melodya@sbci.edu

University of Mary
7500 University Dr, Bismarck ND 58504-9652
701-255-7500

University of North Dakota
Box 8193 University Station, Grand Forks ND 58203
701-777-2011

Valley City State University
101 College St SW, Valley City ND 58072-4024
Dan Klein, Director of Enrollment Services
800-532-8641 ext. 7101 Fax: 701-845-7299
Website: www.vcsu.edu
E-mail: enrollment.services@vcsu.edu
See listing under "Universities"

Williston State College
PO Box 1326, Williston ND 58802-1326
Penny Powell, Director Enrollment Services
701-774-4200 Fax: 701-774-4544
Website: www.wsc.nodak.edu
E-mail: penny.soiseth@wsc.nodak.edu

OHIO

Antioch College
795 Livermore St, Yellow Springs OH 45387-1697
937-754-5000

Baldwin-Wallace College
275 Eastland Rd, Berea OH 44017-2088
440-826-2900

Bowling Green State University
110 McFall Center, Bowling Green OH 43403-0001
866-CHOOSE-BGSU

Brown Mackie College - Cincinnati
1011 Glendale Milford Rd, Cincinnati OH 45215-1107
Robin Krout, President
513-771-2424 Fax: 513-771-3413
Website: www.brownmackie.edu
E-mail: rkrout@brownmackie.edu

Capital University
2199 E Main St, Columbus OH 43209-2394
614-236-6011

Case Western Reserve University
10900 Euclid Ave, Cleveland OH 44106
216-368-2000

Cleveland State University
2121 Euclid Ave RW 204, Cleveland OH 44115
Dr. Richard Arndt, Dean of Undergraduate Recruitment
and College Partnerships
888-CSU-OHIO Fax: 216-687-9210
Website: www.csuohio.edu
E-mail: admissions@csuohio.edu

College of Wooster
Wooster OH 44691-2363
Paul J. Deutsch, Dean of Admissions
800-877-9905

Davis College
4747 Monroe St, Toledo OH 43623-4389
Dana Stern, Admissions Director
419-473-2700 Fax: 419-473-2472
Website: www.daviscollege.edu
E-mail: learn@daviscollege.edu

Defiance College
701 N Clinton St, Defiance OH 43512-1695
419-784-4010

Franciscan University of Steubenville
University Blvd, Steubenville OH 43952
Margaret J. Weber, Director of Admissions
800-783-6220 or 740-283-6226 Fax: 740-284-5456
Website: www.admissions.edu
E-mail: mweber@franciscan.edu

Franklin University
201 S Grant Ave, Columbus OH 43215-5399
614-341-6300

Heidelberg College
310 E Market St, Tiffin OH 44883-2462
418-448-2000

Hiram College
PO Box 96, Hiram OH 44234-0096
800-362-5280

ITT Technical Institute
3325 Stop 8 Rd, Dayton OH 45414-3425
Joe Graham, Director of Admissions
937-454-2267 Fax: 937-454-2278
Website: www.itt-tech.edu
E-mail: jgraham@itt-tech.edu

John Carroll University
20700 N Park Blvd, Cleveland OH 44118-4581
216-397-1886

Kent State University
PO Box 5190, Kent OH 44242-0001
Paul Deutsch, Director of Admissions
330-672-2444

Lake Erie College
391 W Washington St, Painesville OH 44077-3389
440-352-3361

Malone College
515 25th St NW, Canton OH 44709-3897
John Chopka, Dean of Admissions
330-471-8100

Marietta College
215 5th St, Marietta OH 45750-4047
740-376-4600

Miami University
E High St, Oxford OH 45056
513-529-2531

Mt. Union College
1972 Clark Ave, Alliance OH 44601-3929
Vincent Heslop, Director of Admissions
800-334-6682

Mount Vernon Nazarene University
800 Martinsburg Rd, Mount Vernon OH 43050-9509
Timothy Eades, Director of Admissions
866-462-6868 Fax: 740-393-0511
Website: www.gotomvnu.com
E-mail: admissions@mvnu.edu
See listing under "Universities"

Myers University
3813 Euclid Ave, Cleveland OH 44115
Ronald G. Brown, Vice President for Enrollment
Management
216-432-8992
Website: www.myers.edu
E-mail: rgbrown@myers.edu

Notre Dame College
4545 College Rd, Cleveland OH 44121-4293
216-381-1680

Ohio Dominican University
1216 Sunbury Rd, Columbus OH 43219-2099
614-253-2741

OHIO NORTHERN UNIVERSITY
525 S Main St, Ada OH 45810-1555
James Fenton, Dean
419-772-2070
Website: www.onu.edu
See listing under "Universities"

The Ohio State University
Fisher College of Business
Schoenbaum Hall, 210 W Woodruff Ave
Columbus OH 43210
614-292-2715 Fax: 614-292-5735
Website: fisher.osu.edu
E-mail: fisherundergrad@cob.osu.edu

Ohio State University-Lima Campus
4240 Campus Dr, Lima OH 45804-3576
Garlene Smithson, Dir. Enrollment Services
419-995-8396

Ohio University
Chillicothe Campus
PO Box 629, Chillicothe OH 45601
Student Services
740-774-7200 Fax: 740-774-7295
Website: www.ohiou.edu/chillicothe/

Ohio University - Zanesville Branch
1425 Newark Rd, Zanesville OH 43701-2695
740-588-1439

OHIO WESLEYAN UNIVERSITY
61 S Sandusky St, Delaware OH 43015-2398
Director of Admission
740-368-3020 Fax: 740-368-3314
Website: www.owu.edu
E-mail: owuadmit@owu.edu

Owens Community College
300 Davis St, Findlay OH 45840-3631
William J. Ivoska PhD., Vice President of Student
Services
567-429-3500 Fax: 567-423-0246
Website: www.owens.edu
E-mail: admissions@owens.edu

Owens Community College
PO Box 10000, Toledo OH 43699-1947
William J. Ivoska, Ph.D, Vice President of Student
Services
567-661-7000 Fax: 567-661-7607
Website: www.owens.edu
E-mail: admissions@owens.edu

Shawnee State University
940 2nd St, Portsmouth OH 45662-4344
740-354-3205

Sinclair Community College
444 W 3rd St, Dayton OH 45402-1460
Sara P. Smith, Director of Outreach Services
937-512-3000 Fax: 937-512-2393
Website: www.sinclair.edu
E-mail: admit@sinclair.edu

University of Akron
381 Buchtel Mall, Akron OH 44304-1584
330-972-7111

University of Cincinnati
2700 Clifton Ave, Cincinnati OH 45220-2873
513-556-6000

University of Dayton
300 College Park, Dayton OH 45469-1300
Robert F. Durkle, Director of Admissions
800-837-7433 Fax: 937-229-4729
Website: admission.udayton.edu
E-mail: admission@udayton.edu

University of Findlay
1000 N Main St, Findlay OH 45840-3695
419-422-8313

University of Northwestern Ohio
1441 N Cable Rd, Lima OH 45805-1498
Rick Morrison, Director of Admissions
419-998-3120

University of Rio Grande
General Delivery, Rio Grande OH 45674-9999
Dr. George Ulrich, Dean
740-245-5353 ext. 7287

University of Toledo
2801 W Bancroft St, Toledo OH 43606-3390
419-530-4636

Urbana University
579 College Way, Urbana OH 43078
937-484-1301

Ursuline College
2550 Lander Rd, Cleveland OH 44124-4398
Sarah E. Sundermeier, Director of Admissions
888-URSULINE Toll Free Fax: 440-684-6138
Website: www.admission.ursuline.edu
E-mail: admission@ursuline.edu

Wilmington College
251 Ludovic St, Wilmington OH 45177
937-382-6661

Wittenberg University
PO Box 720, Springfield OH 45501-0720
937-327-6231

Wright State University
3640 Colonel Glenn Hwy, Dayton OH 45435-0002
937-775-3333

Xavier University
3800 Victory Pkwy, Cincinnati OH 45207-1092
513-745-3000

Youngstown State University
Sweeney Welcome Ctr, One University Plz
Youngstown OH 44555-0002
Sue Davis, Contact
877-GO-TO-YSU

OKLAHOMA

Bacone College
2299 Old Bacone Rd, Muskogee OK 74403-1568
Jerrett Phillips, Director of Admissions
918-781-7340

Cameron University
2800 W Gore Blvd, Lawton OK 73505-6377
580-581-2200

Mid-America Christian University
3500 SW 119th St, Oklahoma City OK 73170-4504
Haley Hope, Director of Admissions
405-691-3800 Fax: 405-692-3165
Website: www.macu.edu
E-mail: info@macu.edu

Oklahoma Christian University
PO Box 11000, Oklahoma City OK 73136-1100
405-425-5000

Oklahoma City University
2501 N Blackwelder Ave
Oklahoma City OK 73106-1493
Shery Boyles, Director of Admissions
405-521-5050

Oklahoma Panhandle State University
PO Box 430, Goodwell OK 73939-0430
580-349-2611

Oklahoma State University
Stillwater OK 74078
Ken Eastman, Department Head
405-744-5201
Website: www.okstate.edu
E-mail: ken.eastman@okstate.edu

Oklahoma Wesleyan University
2201 Silver Lake Rd, Bartlesville OK 74006-6299
918-333-6151

Oral Roberts University
7777 S Lewis Ave, Tulsa OK 74171-0001
Chris Belcher, Director of Undergraduate Admissions
800-678-8876 Fax: 918-495-6222
Website: www.oru.edu
E-mail: admissions@oru.edu

Rogers State University - Claremore Campus
1701 W Will Rogers Blvd, Claremore OK 74017-3259
Joe Wiley, President
918-343-7777

Southwestern Oklahoma State University
100 Campus Dr, Weatherford OK 73096-3098
580-772-6611

SPARTAN COLLEGE OF AERONAUTICS AND TECHNOLOGY

8820 E Pine St, Tulsa OK 74115-5802
Director of Admissions
800-331-1204 Fax: 918-831-8609
Website: www.spartan.edu
E-mail: spartan@mail.spartan.edu
Established 1928. Coed. Accredited member school: ACCSCT. Providing Technical training and education in Avionics, Instruments, and Maintenance; Nondestructive Testing and Quality Control. Complete flight training program. Offering Diplomas, Associate of Applied Science and Bachelor of Science in Aviation Technology Management.

University of Oklahoma at Norman
660 Parrington Oval, Norman OK 73019-3070
405-325-0311

University of Tulsa
600 S College Ave, Tulsa OK 74104-3126
Earl Johnson, Dean of Admission
918-631-2307 Fax: 918-631-5003
Website: www.utulsa.edu
E-mail: admission@utulsa.edu

OREGON

Cascade College
9101 E Burnside St, Portland OR 97216-1599
800-550-7678 Fax: 503-257-1222
Website: www.cascade.edu
E-mail: admissions@cascade.edu

Concordia University
2811 NE Holman St, Portland OR 97211-6099
Bobi Swan, Director of Admissions
503-288-9371 Fax: 503-280-8531
Website: www.cu-portland.edu
E-mail: cu-admissions@cu-portland.edu

Corban College
5000 Deer Park Dr SE, Salem OR 97317-9330
503-581-8600

Linn-Benton Community College
6500 Pacific Blvd SW, Albany OR 97321-3774
Christine Baker, Outreach Coordinator
541-917-4811 Fax: 541-917-4868
Website: www.linnbenton.edu
E-mail: admissions@linnbenton.edu

Marylhurst University
17600 Pacific Hwy (Hwy 43)
Marylhurst OR 97036-0261
Director of Admissions
800-634-9982 ext. 6268 Fax: 503-635-6585
Website: www.marylhurst.edu
E-mail: studentinfo@marylhurst.edu

Oregon Institute of Technology
3201 Campus Dr, Klamath Falls OR 97601-8801
541-885-1000

Oregon State University
Corvallis OR 97333-9800
541-737-0123

Pacific University
2043 College Way, Forest Grove OR 97116-1797
Karen M. Dunston, Executive Director of Admissions
800-635-0561 Fax: 503-352-2975
Website: www.pacificu.edu
E-mail: admissions@pacificu.edu

Portland State University
PO Box 751, Portland OR 97207-0751
503-725-3000

Southern Oregon University
1250 Siskiyou Blvd, Ashland OR 97520-5010
541-552-7672

University of Oregon
1217 University of Oregon, Eugene OR 97403
541-346-1000

University of Portland
5000 N Willamette Blvd, Portland OR 97203-5798
503-943-7911

Warner Pacific College
2219 SE 68th Ave, Portland OR 97215-4026
Shannon Mackey, Director of Admissions
503-517-1000 Fax: 503-517-1352
Website: www.warnerpacific.edu
E-mail: admissions@warnerpacific.edu

Western Oregon University
345 Monmouth Ave N, Monmouth OR 97361-1314
David McDonald, Dean, Admission, Retention & Enrollment Management
877-877-1593 Fax: 503-838-8067
Website: www.wou.edu
E-mail: wolfgram@fsa.wou.edu

Willamette University
900 State St, Salem OR 97301-3931
503-370-6300

PENNSYLVANIA

Albright College
PO Box 15234, Reading PA 19612-5234
610-921-2381

Alvernia University
400 Saint Bernardine St, Reading PA 19607
610-796-8200

Arcadia University
450 S Easton Rd, Glenside PA 19038-3295
Dennis Nostrand, VP for Enrollment Management
877-ARCADIA (877-272-2342) Fax: 215-881-8767
Website: www.arcadia.edu
E-mail: admiss@arcadia.edu
See listing under "Universities"

ART INSTITUTE OF PITTSBURGH

420 Boulevard Of The Allies, Pittsburgh PA 15219
Newton I. Myvett, VP/Director of Admissions
800-275-2470 Fax: 412-263-6667
Website: www.aip.aii.edu
E-mail: pahughes@aii.edu
See listing under "Universities"

Bloomsburg University of Pennsylvania
400 E 2nd St, Bloomsburg PA 17815-1399
570-389-4000

Bradford School
125 W Station Square Dr, Pittsburgh PA 15219
Director of Admissions
412-391-6710 Fax: 412-471-6714
Website: www.bradfordpittsburgh.edu

Cabrini College
610 King of Prussia Rd, Radnor PA 19087-3698
Mark T. Osborn, VP for Enrollment Management
610-902-8100

California University of Pennsylvania
250 University Ave, California PA 15419-1394
724-938-4000

Carlow University
3333 5th Ave, Pittsburgh PA 15213-3165
412-578-6000

Carnegie Mellon University
5000 Forbes Ave, Pittsburgh PA 15213-3890
412-268-2000

Cedar Crest College
100 College Dr, Allentown PA 18104-6196
Judith A. Neyhart, Vice President Enrollment
800-360-1222

Central Pennsylvania College
College Hill & Valley Rds, Summerdale PA 17093
Katie Bogovic, Admissions Director
800-759-2727 Fax: 717-728-2505
Website: www.centralpenn.edu
E-mail: katie.bogovic@centralpenn.edu

Chatham College
Woodland Rd, Pittsburgh PA 15232-2826
412-365-1100

Chestnut Hill College
9601 Germantown Ave, Philadelphia PA 19118-2693
Jodie King, Director of Admissions
215-248-7001

Clarion University of Pennsylvania
840 Wood St, Clarion PA 16214-1232
William Bailey, Dean of Enrollment Management
814-393-2306 Fax: 814-393-2030
Website: www.clarion.edu
E-mail: admissions@clarion.edu

College Misericordia
301 Lake St, Dallas PA 18612-1008
Admissions
570-674-6400

Consolidated School of Business
1605 Clugston Rd, York PA 17404-1779
Robert Safran Jr., Vice President
717-764-9550 Fax: 717-764-9469
Website: www.csb.edu
E-mail: bobjr@csb.edu

Delaware Valley College
700 E Butler Ave, Doylestown PA 18901-2697
Stephen W. Zenko, Director of Admissions
800-2DE-LVAL

DeSales University
2755 Station Ave, Center Valley PA 18034-9565
610-282-1100 Fax: 610-282-2342
Website: www.desales.edu

Douglas Education Center
130 7th St, Monessen PA 15062-1097
Sherry Lee Walters, Director of Enrollment Services
800-413-6013 Fax: 724-684-7463
Website: www.douglas-school.com
E-mail: swalters@douglas-school.com

Drexel University
3141 Chestnut St, Philadelphia PA 19104-2875
Dana R. Davies, Director of Undergraduate Enrollment
800-2-DREXEL

DUBOIS BUSINESS COLLEGE

1 Beaver Dr, Du Bois PA 15801-2490
Lisa J. Doty, Director of Admissions
814-371-6920 Fax: 814-371-3974
Website: www.dbcollege.com
E-mail: dotylj@dbcollege.com

DUBOIS BUSINESS COLLEGE

1001 Moore St, Huntingdon PA 16652-1846
Lisa J. Doty, Director of Admissions
814-641-0440 Fax: 814-641-0205
Website: www.dbcollege.com
E-mail: dotylj@dbcollege.com

DUBOIS BUSINESS COLLEGE

701 E 3rd St, Oil City PA 16301-2407
Lisa J. Doty, Director of Admissions
814-677-1322 Fax: 814-677-8237
Website: www.dbcollege.com
E-mail: dotylj@dbcollege.com

Duquesne University
600 Forbes Ave, Pittsburgh PA 15282-0001
Paul-James Cukanna, Director of Admissions
412-396-5000

Eastern University
1300 Eagle Rd, Saint Davids PA 19087-3696
610-341-5800

Edinboro University of Pennsylvania
Edinboro PA 16444-0001
814-732-2000

Elizabethtown College
1 Alpha Dr, Elizabethtown PA 17022-2298
717-361-1000

Erie Business Center
246 W 9th St, Erie PA 16501-1392
Donna Perino, Director
814-456-7504 Fax: 814-456-6015
Website: www.eriebc.edu
E-mail: perinod@eriebc.edu

Gannon University
109 University Sq, Erie PA 16541-0001
Christopher Tremblay, Director of Admissions
800-GANNON-U Fax: 814-871-5803
Website: www.gannon.edu
E-mail: admissions@gannon.edu

Geneva College
3200 College Ave, Beaver Falls PA 15010-3599
724-846-5100

Gettysburg College
300 N Washington St, Gettysburg PA 17325-1483
Gail Sweezey, Director of Admissions
717-337-6100

Gwynedd-Mercy College
1325 Sumneytown Pike, Gwynedd Valley PA 19437
Dennis Murphy, V.P. Enrollment Management
800-DIAL-GMC

Holy Family University
9801 Frankford Avenue, Philadelphia PA 19114
Lauren Campbell, Director of Admissions
215-637-3050 Fax: 215-281-1022
Website: www.holyfamily.edu
E-mail: admissions@holyfamily.edu

Immaculata University
Immaculata PA 19345
Women's College Office of Admissions
610-647-4400

Juniata College
1700 Moore St, Huntingdon PA 16652-2196
Michelle Bartol, Dean of Enrollment
877-JUNIATA Fax: 814-641-3100
Website: www.juniata.edu
E-mail: admissions@juniata.edu

King's College
133 N River St, Wilkes Barre PA 18711-0801
Michelle Lawrence-Schmude, Director of Admission
570-208-5900 Fax: 570-208-5971
Website: www.kings.edu
E-mail: admissions@kings.edu

La Roche College
9000 Babcock Blvd, Pittsburgh PA 15237-5898
Thomas Hassett, Director of Freshman and
International Admissions
412-536-1272 or 800-838-4LRC Fax: 412-536-1272
Website: www.laroche.edu
E-mail: admissions@laroche.edu

La Salle University
1900 W Olney Ave, Philadelphia PA 19141-1199
Robert Voss, Dean of Admissions
215-951-1500

LAUREL BUSINESS INSTITUTE
11-15 Penn St, Uniontown PA 15401
Lisa Tressler, Supervisor of Enrollment
724-439-4900 Fax: 724-439-3607
Website: www.laurelbusiness.edu
E-mail: lbi@laurelbusiness.edu
Established 1985. Private. Coed. Accreditation:
ACICS, Licensed by the Pennsylvania Department of
Education. Enrollment: 310 full-time, 35 part-time.
Student-faculty ratio: 12:1. Associate degrees: Account-
ing, Child Care Education, Cosmetology, I.T. - Computer
Software Support, I.T. - Network Administration, Medical
Assistant, Medical Insurance Management, Medical
Secretary Transcription, Office Administration, Small
Business Management, Therapeutic Massage. Diplo-
mas: Legal Secretary, Massage Therapy, Medical Secre-
tary, Word Processing Secretary. Independent
Certifications, Authorized Prometric Testing Center,
Authorized MOS Testing Center, Financial Aid Services,
Job Placement Services.

Lebanon Valley College
101 N College Ave, Annville PA 17003-1400
William Brown, Dean of Admissions & Financial Aid
866-LVC-4ADM or 717-867-6181 Fax: 717-867-6026
Website: www.lvc.edu
E-mail: admission@lvc.edu

Lehigh University
27 Memorial Dr West, Bethlehem PA 18015-3094
Eric Kaplan, Dean of Admissions
610-758-3100

Lehigh Valley College
2809 E Saucon Valley Rd
Center Valley PA 18034-8447
Joshua Padron, Vice President of Marketing and
Admissions
800-227-9109 Fax: 610-791-7810
Website: www.lehighvalley.edu
E-mail: joshua.padron@lehighvalley.edu

Lincoln University
Lincoln University PA 19352
Michael C. Taylor, Director of Admissions
800-790-0191 Fax: 610-932-1209
Website: www.lincoln.edu
E-mail: mtaylor@lu.lincoln.edu

Lock Haven University
Lock Haven PA 17745
James C. Reeser, Dean of Admissions
570-893-2027

Lycoming College
700 College Pl, Williamsport PA 17701-5192
570-321-4000

Marywood University
2300 Adams Ave, Scranton PA 18509-1598
570-348-6211

Mercyhurst College
501 E 38th St, Erie PA 16546-0001
800-825-1926

Messiah College
1 S College Ave, Grantham PA 17027
717-766-2511

Millersville University of Pennsylvania
PO Box 1002, Millersville PA 17551-0302
717-872-3024

MOUNT ALOYSIUS COLLEGE
7373 Admiral Peary Hwy, Cresson PA 16630-1999
Frank C. Crouse Jr., Vice President for Enrollment
Management
814-886-6383 or 888-823-2220 Fax: 814-886-6441
Website: www.mtaloy.edu
E-mail: admissions@mtaloy.edu

Muhlenberg College
2400 W Chew St, Allentown PA 18104-5586
610-821-3100

Neumann College
1 Neumann Dr, Aston PA 19014-1298
Dennis Murphy, Director of Admissions
610-459-0905 Fax: 610-558-5652
Website: www.neumann.edu
E-mail: neumann@neumann.edu

Pennsylvania College of Technology
1 College Ave, Williamsport PA 17701-5778
570-326-3761

Pennsylvania Institute of Technology
800 Manchester Ave, Media PA 19063-4036
Angela Cassetta, Dean of Enrollment Management
800-422-0025 or 610-892-1500 Fax: 610-892-1510
Website: www.pit.edu
E-mail: info@pit.edu
See listing under "Community and Junior Colleges"

Pennsylvania State University
Broadhead Rd, Monaca PA 15061
724-773-3500

Pennsylvania State University
3550 7th St Rd, New Kensington PA 15068-1765
Patricia K. Brady, Director of Admissions
724-334-5466

Pennsylvania State University
201 Shields Bldg PO Box 300
University Park PA 16802-3000
814-865-4700

Point Park University
201 Wood St, Pittsburgh PA 15222-1984
Philip Clarke, Associate Director of Admissions
412-392-3430

THE RESTAURANT SCHOOL AT WALNUT HILL COLLEGE
4207 Walnut St, Philadelphia PA 19104-5296
Karl D. Becker, Admissions Director
215-222-4200 ext. 3011 Fax: 215-222-4219
Website: www.walnuthillcollege.com
E-mail: info@walnuthillcollege.com

Robert Morris College
600 5th Ave, Pittsburgh PA 15219-3010
412-227-6800

Robert Morris University
881 Narrows Run Rd, Coraopolis PA 15108-1169
412-262-8200

Rosemont College
1400 Montgomery Ave, Rosemont PA 19010-1699
Ms. Rennie Andrews, Director of Admissions
610-526-2966

St. Vincent College
300 Fraser Purchase Rd, Latrobe PA 15650-2690
724-539-9761

Seton Hill University
Greensburg PA 15601-1599
Mary Kay Cooper, Director of Admissions and Adult
Student Services
800-826-6234

Shippensburg University
1871 Old Main Dr, Shippensburg PA 17257-2299
717-477-7447

Slippery Rock University
14 Maltby Dr, Slippery Rock PA 16057-1326
724-738-9000

Susquehanna University
514 University Ave, Selinsgrove PA 17870-1164
570-374-0101

Temple University
Broad St & Montgomery Ave, Philadelphia PA 19122
215-204-7000

Temple University Ambler
Ambler PA 19002
David Kaiser, Contact
215-283-1674

Thiel College
75 College Ave, Greenville PA 16125-2181
724-589-2000

University of Pennsylvania
3400 Spruce St, Philadelphia PA 19104-4274
215-898-5000

University of Pittsburgh
1150 Mount Pleasant Rd
Greensburg PA 15601-5860
Brandi S. Darr, Director of Admissions and Financial
Aid
724-836-9880 Fax: 724-836-7160
Website: www.upg.pitt.edu
E-mail: upgadmit@pitt.edu

University of Pittsburgh
4200 5th Ave, Pittsburgh PA 15260-3583
412-624-4141

University of Pittsburgh at Bradford
300 Campus Dr, Bradford PA 16701-2812
Alexander Nazemetz, Director of Admissions
814-362-7555

University of Scranton
800 Linden St, Scranton PA 18510-4501
570-941-7400

Villanova University
800 E Lancaster Ave, Villanova PA 19085
610-519-4500

Washington & Jefferson College
60 S Lincoln St, Washington PA 15301-4801
Alton E. Newell, Vice President for Enrollment
724-223-6025 Fax: 724-223-6534
Website: www.washjeff.edu
E-mail: admission@washjeff.edu

Waynesburg College
51 W College St, Waynesburg PA 15370-1222
Robin L. Moore, Dean of Admissions
800-225-7393

West Chester University of Pennsylvania
S High St, West Chester PA 19383-0001
610-436-1000

Westminster College
New Wilmington PA 16172-0001
Doug Swartz, Director of Admissions
724-946-7100 Fax: 724-946-6171
Website: www.westminster.edu
E-mail: swartzdl@westminster.edu

Widener University
1 University Pl, Chester PA 19013-5792
610-499-4000

Wilkes University
170 S Franklin St, Wilkes Barre PA 18766-0001
570-408-5000

York College of Pennsylvania
PO Box 15199, York PA 17405-7199
717-846-7788

York Technical Institute
1405 Williams Rd, York PA 17402
Cathi Killingsworth Bost, Vice President
800-227-9675 or 717-757-1100 Fax: 717-757-4964
Website: www.yti.edu
E-mail: info@yti.edu
See listing under "Career Schools"

RHODE ISLAND
Bryant University
1150 Douglas Pike, Smithfield RI 02917-1287
401-232-6000

New England Institute of Technology
2500 Post Rd, Warwick RI 02886-2244
Michael Kwiatkowski, Director of Admissions
401-739-5000 Fax: 401-738-5122
Website: www.neit.edu
E-mail: eflynn@neit.edu

Providence College
549 River Ave, Providence RI 02918-0002
401-865-1000

Rhode Island College
600 Mount Pleasant Ave, Providence RI 02908-1924
401-456-8000

Salve Regina University
100 Ochre Point Ave, Newport RI 02840-4192
401-847-6650

University of Rhode Island
Kingston RI 02881
401-874-1000

SOUTH CAROLINA
Benedict College
1600 Harden St, Columbia SC 29204-1086
Phyllis L. Thompson, Director of Admissions
803-253-5143

Charleston Southern University
PO Box 118087, Charleston SC 29423-8087
Cheryl Burton, Director of Admissions
800-947-7474

The Citadel
171 Moultrie St, Charleston SC 29409-0002
843-953-5000

Clemson University
105 Sikes Hall, Clemson SC 29634
864-656-2287

Coastal Carolina University
PO Box 261954, Conway SC 29528-6054
Office of Admissions
800-277-7000 Fax: 843-349-2127
Website: www.coastal.edu
E-mail: admissions@coastal.edu

College of Charleston
66 George St, Charleston SC 29424-1407
Suzette Stille, Admissions
843-953-5670

Columbia College
1301 Columbia College Dr, Columbia SC 29203-5998
Elizabeth G. Quackenbush, Director of Admissions
803-786-3871

Columbia International University
PO Box 3122, Columbia SC 29230-3122
John Basie, Director of University Admissions
800-777-2227 Fax: 803-786-4209
Website: www.ciu.edu
E-mail: yesciu@ciu.edu
See listing under "Theological Studies & Religious
Vocations"

Erskine College & Seminary
PO Box 176, Due West SC 29639
Bart Walker, Director of Admissions
864-379-8838 Fax: 864-379-3048
Website: www.erskine.edu
E-mail: admissions@erskine.edu

Forrest Junior College
601 E River St, Anderson SC 29624-2405
Dr. Julia R. Barnes, President
864-225-7653 Fax: 864-261-7471
Website: www.forrestcollege.edu
E-mail: info@forrestcollege.edu
See listing under "Community and Junior Colleges"

Francis Marion University
PO Box 100547, Florence SC 29501-0547
843-661-1362

Furman University
3300 Poinsett Hwy, Greenville SC 29613-0002
864-294-2000

Greenville Technical College
PO Box 5616, Greenville SC 29606-5616
Martha White, Director of Admissions
800-723-0673 (US) or 800-922-1183 (SC)
Website: www.greenvilletech.com

Lander University
320 Stanley Ave, Greenwood SC 29649-2099
Jonathan Reece, Director of Admissions
888-4-LANDER

Limestone College
1115 College Dr, Gaffney SC 29340-3799
Chris Phenicie, V.P. for Enrollment
864-489-7151 Fax: 864-488-8206
Website: www.limestone.edu
E-mail: cphenicie@limestone.edu

North Greenville University
PO Box 1892, Tigerville SC 29688-1892
Dr. Ralph Johnson, Dept. Chair
Website: www.ngc.edu
See listing under "Universities"

PRESBYTERIAN COLLEGE
503 S Broad St, Clinton SC 29325
Richard Dana Paul, Dean of Admissions
800-476-7272 Fax: 864-833-8481
Website: www.presby.edu
E-mail: admissions@presby.edu

South Carolina State University
PO Box 7127, Orangeburg SC 29117-0001
Lillian M. Adderson, Director of Admissions
803-536-7185

Southern Wesleyan University
PO Box 1020, Central SC 29630-1020
864-644-5000

South University
9 Science Court, Columbia SC 29203
Trish Wade, Contact
803-799-9082 Fax: 803-799-9038
Website: www.southuniversity.edu
E-mail: twade@southuniversity.edu

Spartanburg Technical College
PO Box 4386, Spartanburg SC 29305-4386
Nancy Garmroth, Dean of Admissions & Financial Aid
864-592-4810 Fax: 864-592-4945
Website: stcsc.edu

University of South Carolina
Columbia SC 29208-0001
803-777-7700

University of South Carolina - Upstate
800 University Way, Spartanburg SC 29303-4932
Donette Stewart, Assistant VC for Enrollment Services
864-503-5246 Fax: 864-503-5727
Website: www.uscupstate.edu
E-mail: dstewart@uscupstate.edu
See listing under "Universities"

Voorhees College
Voorhees Rd, Denmark SC 29042
803-793-3351

Winthrop University
701 W Oakland Ave, Rock Hill SC 29733-0001
803-323-2211

Wofford College
429 N Church St, Spartanburg SC 29303-3663
864-597-4000

SOUTH DAKOTA

Dakota State University
820 N Washington Ave, Madison SD 57042-1799
605-256-5112

Dakota Wesleyan University
1200 W University Ave, Mitchell SD 57301
605-995-2600

Mt. Marty College
1105 W 8th St, Yankton SD 57078-3724
605-668-1514

National American University
1270 Ryan St - 28 MSS/DPE, Ellsworth AFB SD 57706
605-923-5856

NATIONAL AMERICAN UNIVERSITY
321 Kansas City St, Rapid City SD 57701-3692
Angela G. Beck, Director of Enrollment Management
605-394-4800 Fax: 605-394-4871
Website: www.national.edu/rc/index.html
E-mail: rcadmissions@national.edu

National American University
2801 S Kiwanis Ave Ste 100
Sioux Falls SD 57105-4293
605-334-5430 Fax: 605-334-1575
Website: www.national.edu

Northern State University
1200 S Jay St, Aberdeen SD 57401-7198
605-626-3011

Presentation College
1500 N Main St, Aberdeen SD 57401-1280
JoEllen Lindner, Dean of Admissions
605-229-8492 Fax: 605-229-8425
Website: www.presentation.edu
E-mail: admit@presentation.edu

South Dakota State University
PO Box 2201, Brookings SD 57007-0001
605-688-4151

University of South Dakota
414 E Clark St, Vermillion SD 57069-2307
605-677-5011

Western Dakota Technical Institute
800 Mickelson Dr, Rapid City SD 57703-4018
Janell Oberlander, Manager of Student Services
605-394-4034 or 800-544-8765 Fax: 605-394-1789
Website: www.westerndakotatech.org
E-mail: admissions@wdti.tec.sd.us
See listing under "Career Schools"

TENNESSEE

Aquinas College
4210 Harding Pike, Nashville TN 37205-2086
Diane C. LeJeune, Director of Admissions
615-297-7545 ext. 460 Fax: 615-297-7970
Website: www.aquinas-tn.edu
E-mail: lejeuned@aquinas-tn.edu

Austin Peay State University
601 College St, Clarksville TN 37044-0002
931-221-7011

Belmont University
1900 Belmont Blvd, Nashville TN 37212-3757
615-460-6000

Bryan College
PO Box 7000, Dayton TN 37321-7000
423-775-2041

Carson-Newman College
1646 Russell Ave, Jefferson City TN 37760
865-471-4000

Christian Brothers University
650 E Parkway S, Memphis TN 38104-5568
901-321-3000

Draughons Junior College
PO Box 17386, Nashville TN 37217-0386
615-361-7555 Fax: 615-367-2736
Website: www.draughons.edu

East Tennessee State University
PO Box 70699, Johnson City TN 37614
Dr. Linda Garceau, Dean of Business
423-439-5489

Fisk University
1000 17th Ave N, Nashville TN 37208-3051
William Carter, Director of Admissions
615-329-8766

Freed-Hardeman University
158 E Main St, Henderson TN 38340-2398
731-989-6000

Free Will Baptist Bible College
3606 W End Ave, Nashville TN 37205
Ryan Lewis, Director of Recruitment
800-76-FWBBC Fax: 615-269-6028
Website: www.fwbbc.edu
E-mail: recruit@fwbbc.edu

Lee University
PO Box 3450, Cleveland TN 37320-3450
Evaline Echols, Chairperson - Department of Business
800-533-9930

Le Moyne-Owen College
807 Walker Ave, Memphis TN 38126-6595
901-774-9090

Lincoln Memorial University
PO Box 2012, Harrogate TN 37752
423-869-3611

Lipscomb University
3901 Granny White Pike, Nashville TN 37204-3951
Ricky Holaway, Director of Admissions
800-333-4358 ext. 1776 Fax: 615-269-1804
Website: www.lipscomb.edu
E-mail: admissions@lipscomb.edu

Maryville College
502 E Lamar Alexander Pkwy
Maryville TN 37804-5919
865-981-8000

Middle Tennessee State University
1301 E Main St, Murfreesboro TN 37132-0001
615-898-2300

Pellissippi State Technical Community College
PO Box 22990, Knoxville TN 37933-0990
Donna Mack, Contact
865-694-6568 Fax: 865-539-7217
Website: www.pstcc.edu
E-mail: dmack@pstcc.edu

Rhodes College
2000 N Parkway, Memphis TN 38112-1624
901-843-3000

Tennessee State University
3500 John A Merritt Blvd, Nashville TN 37209-1561
John Cade, Dean of Admissions & Records
615-963-5101 Fax: 615-963-2930
Website: www.tnstate.edu
E-mail: jcade@tnstate.edu

Tennessee Technological University
PO Box 5006, Cookeville TN 38505-0001
931-372-3101

Tennessee Temple University
1815 Union Ave, Chattanooga TN 37404-3587
423-493-4100

Trevecca Nazarene University
333 Murfreesboro Rd, Nashville TN 37210-2834
615-248-1200

Tusculum College
PO Box 5051, Greeneville TN 37743
Melissa Ripley, Associate Director of Admissions
800-729-0256 Fax: 423-798-1622
Website: www.tusculum.edu
E-mail: mripley@tusculum.edu

Union University
1050 Union University Dr, Jackson TN 38305
731-668-1818

University of Memphis
Memphis TN 38152-0001
901-678-2000

University of Tennessee
615 McCallie Ave, Chattanooga TN 37403-2504
Yancy Freeman, Director of Admissions
423-425-4111 Fax: 423-425-4157
Website: www.utc.edu
E-mail: Yancy-Freeman@utc.edu

University of Tennessee
527 Andy Holt Tower, Knoxville TN 37996-0001
865-974-1000

University of Tennessee
Martin TN 38238-0001
731-587-7000

Vanderbilt University
W End Ave, Nashville TN 37240-0001
615-322-7311

TEXAS

Angelo State University
ASU Station 11014, San Angelo TX 76909
Bonnie Stennett, Coordinator of Recruiting
800-946-8627 Fax: 325-942-2078
Website: www.angelo.edu
E-mail: admissions@angelo.edu

Austin College
900 N Grand Ave, Sherman TX 75090-4400
903-813-2000

Baylor University
Po Box 97008, Waco TX 76798-7008
254-710-1011

Blinn College
902 College Ave, Brenham TX 77833-4098
Dennis K. Crowson, Registrar
979-830-4000 Fax: 979-830-4110
Website: www.blinn.edu
E-mail: recruiting@blinn.edu

Blinn College
PO Box 6030, Bryan TX 77805-6030
Dennis K. Crowson, Registrar
979-209-7200 Fax: 979-209-7229
Website: www.blinn.edu
E-mail: recruiting@blinn.edu

Blinn College
100 Ranger Dr, Schulenburg TX 78956-2247
Dennis K. Crowson, Registrar
979-743-5003 Fax: 979-743-5225
Website: www.blinn.edu
E-mail: recruiting@blinn.edu

Blinn College
3701 Outlet Center Dr, Sealy TX 77474
Dennis K. Crowson, Registrar
979-627-7997 Fax: 979-627-0830
Website: www.blinn.edu
E-mail: recruiting@blinn.edu

Concordia University
3400 N I H 35, Austin TX 78705-2702
512-486-2000

East Texas Baptist University
1209 N Grove St, Marshall TX 75670-1498
903-935-7963

Galveston College
4015 Avenue Q, Galveston TX 77550-7496
Brian Lowery, Registrar
409-763-6551 Fax: 409-944-1501
Website: www.gc.edu
E-mail: blowery@gc.edu

Hallmark Institute of Technology - Technology Campus
10401 W IH 10, San Antonio TX 78230-1736
Joe Fisher, President
210-690-9000 Fax: 210-697-8225
Website: www.hallmarkinstitute.com
E-mail: sross@hallmarkinstitute.com
Electronics Engineering Technology, Business Office
Administration, Computer Network Systems
Technology, & Medical Assistant.

Lamar State College-Orange
410 W Front St, Orange TX 77630-5899
Rebecca Campbell, Registrar
409-883-7750 Fax: 409-882-3055
Website: www.lsco.edu
E-mail: becky.campbell@lsco.edu

Lamar University
PO Box 10009, Beaumont TX 77710-0009
409-880-8622

Le Tourneau University
PO Box 7001, Longview TX 75607-7001
903-233-3000

McLennan Community College
1400 College Dr, Waco TX 76708-1498
Annette Bigham, Program Director, Business Programs
254-299-8000 Fax: 254-299-8964
Website: www.mclennan.edu
E-mail: abigham@mclennan.edu

Midwestern State University
3410 Taft Blvd, Wichita Falls TX 76308-2096
940-397-4000

North Central Texas College
1525 W California St, Gainesville TX 76240-4636
Michelle Winters, Registrar
940-668-3315 Fax: 940-665-7075
Website: www.nctc.edu
E-mail: mwinters@nctc.edu

Northwood University
1114 W FM 1382, Cedar Hill TX 75104-1204
Sylvia Correa, Director of Admissions
800-927-WOOD Fax: 972-291-3824
Website: www.northwood.edu
E-mail: ray@northwood.edu

Our Lady of the Lake University
411 SW 24th St, San Antonio TX 78207-4666
Mary Kay Cooper, Dean of Enrollment
210-434-6711 Fax: 210-431-4013
Website: www.ollusa.edu
E-mail: admission@lakeollusa.edu

Prairie View A&M University
PO Box 188, Prairie View TX 77446
936-857-3311

Remington College - Fort Worth Campus
300 E Loop 820, Fort Worth TX 76112-1280
Director of Recruitment
817-451-0017 Fax: 817-496-1257
Website: www.remingtoncollege.edu
E-mail: lynn.wey@remingtoncollege.edu

St. Edward's University
3001 S Congress Ave, Austin TX 78704-6489
512-448-8400

St. Mary's University of San Antonio
1 Camino Santa Maria St
San Antonio TX 78228-8500
210-436-3011

Sam Houston State University
PO Box 2026, Huntsville TX 77341
936-294-1111

Schreiner University
2100 Memorial Blvd, Kerrville TX 78028-5697
Todd D. Brown, Director of Admissions
800-343-4919

Southern Methodist University
PO Box 750181, Dallas TX 75275-0181
Ron Moss, Dean of Admission
214-768-2058

Stephen F. Austin State University
PO Box 6078, Nacogdoches TX 75962-0001
936-468-2011

Temple College
2600 S 1st St, Temple TX 76504-7435
Angela Balch, Director of Admissions & Records
254-298-8300 Fax: 254-298-8288
Website: www.templejc.edu
E-mail: ruth.bridges@templejc.edu

Texas A&M University
College Station TX 77843-0001
979-845-3211

Texas A&M University
700 University Blvd, Kingsville TX 78363
361-593-2111

Texas A&M University - Commerce
PO Box 3011, Commerce TX 75429
903-886-5102

Texas A&M University - Corpus Christi
6300 Ocean Dr, Corpus Christi TX 78412-5503
361-825-5700

Texas Christian University
TCU Box 297013, Fort Worth TX 76129
817-257-7000

Texas Lutheran University
1000 W Court St, Seguin TX 78155-5978
830-372-8000

Texas Southern University
3100 Cleburne St, Houston TX 77004-4583
713-313-7011

Texas State University - San Marcos
601 University Dr, San Marcos TX 78666-4685
512-245-2111

Texas Tech University
1 Texas Tech University, Lubbock TX 79409-0001
806-742-2011

Texas Wesleyan University
1201 Wesleyan St, Fort Worth TX 76105-1536
Stephanie Boatner, Director of Freshman Admission
800-580-8980

Texas Woman's University
PO Box 425589, Denton TX 76204-5589
Erma Nieto, Director of Admissions
866-809-6130 Fax: 940-898-3081
Website: www.twu.edu
E-mail: admissions@twu.edu

Trinity University
715 Stadium Dr, San Antonio TX 78212-7200
210-999-7011

Tyler Junior College
PO Box 9020, Tyler TX 75711-9020
Joan Jones, Interim Dean
800-687-5680
Website: www.tjc.edu
E-mail: jjon@tjc.edu
See listing under "Community and Junior Colleges"

University of Dallas
1845 E Northgate Dr, Irving TX 75062-4736
972-721-5000

University of Houston
122 E Cullen Bldg, Houston TX 77204-2023
Office of Admission
713-743-9595
Website: www.uh.edu
E-mail: admissions@uh.edu

University of Houston-Clear Lake
2700 Bay Area Blvd, Houston TX 77058-1025
281-283-2500

University of Houston-Downtown
1 Main St, Houston TX 77002-1014
713-221-8000

University of North Texas
PO Box 305309, Denton TX 76203-5309
940-565-2000

University of St. Thomas
3800 Montrose Blvd, Houston TX 77006-4626
Eduardo Prieto, Director of Admissions
713-522-7911 Fax: 713-525-3558
Website: www.stthom.edu
E-mail: prietoe@stthom.edu

University of Texas at Arlington
Box 19111, Arlington TX 76019-0111
Hans Gatterdam, Director of Admission
817-272-6287 Fax: 817-272-3435
Website: www.uta.edu
E-mail: admissions@uta.edu

University of Texas at Austin
0 the Univ of Texas, Austin TX 78712
512-471-3434

University of Texas at Dallas
PO Box 830688, Richardson TX 75083-0688
972-690-2111

University of Texas at El Paso
500 W University Ave, El Paso TX 79968-8900
915-747-5000

University of Texas at San Antonio
6900 N Loop 1604 W, San Antonio TX 78249-1130
210-458-4011

University of Texas at Tyler
3900 University Blvd, Tyler TX 75701-6622
Jim Hutto, Dean Enrollment Management
800-888-9537

University of Texas-Pan American
1201 W University Dr, Edinburg TX 78539-2909
956-381-2011

University of the Incarnate Word
4301 Broadway St, San Antonio TX 78209-6318
210-829-6000

Wade College
Dallas Market Center
PO Box 421149, Dallas TX 75342
Harry Davros, President
800-624-4850 or 214-637-3530 Fax: 214-637-0827
Website: www.wadecollege.edu
E-mail: admissions@wadecollege.edu
See listing under "Community and Junior Colleges"

West Texas A & M University
WTAMU Box 907, Canyon TX 79016-0001
806-651-2000

UTAH

Brigham Young University
Provo UT 84602-0001
801-378-5000

ITT TECHNICAL INSTITUTE
920 Levoy Dr, Murray UT 84123-2500
Gary Wood, Director of Recruitment
801-263-3313 Fax: 801-263-3497
Website: www.itt-tech.edu
E-mail: gwood@itt-tech.edu

Southern Utah University
351 W Center St, Cedar City UT 84720-2470
Carl Templin, Dean
435-586-5401

Stevens Henager College
755 Main St, Logan UT 84321
Sherman R. Conger, Director of Admissions
435-713-4777
Website: www.stevenshenager.edu

Stevens Henager College
PO Box 9428, Ogden UT 84409-0428
Cindy Williams, Director of Admissions
801-394-7791 Fax: 801-621-0866
Website: www.stevenshenager.edu
E-mail: shcogden@yahoo.com

University of Utah
1460 E 201 S, Salt Lake City UT 84112
801-581-7200

Utah State University
Logan UT 84322-0001
435-797-1000

Weber State University
1001 University Cir, Ogden UT 84408
801-626-6000

Westminster College
1840 S 1300 E, Salt Lake City UT 84105-3617
801-832-2200

VERMONT

Castleton State College
Castleton VT 05735
William Allen Jr., Dean of Enrollment
800-639-8521

College of St. Joseph
71 Clement Rd, Rutland VT 05701-3899
802-773-5900

Goddard College
121 Pitkin Rd, Plainfield VT 05667
802-454-8311

NEW ENGLAND CULINARY INSTITUTE
250 Main St, Montpelier VT 05602
Dawn Hayward, Director of Admissions
877-223-6324 Fax: 802-225-3280
Website: www.neci.edu
E-mail: Admissions@neci.edu
Established in 1980. Private. Coed. Accreditation: ACCSCT. Located in Vermont. Tuition: $18,650. Room and board: $6,950. Low student:teacher ratio. Associate's and Bachelor's degrees in Food and Beverage Management. The Associate's degree is a 15-month program that utilizes a hands-on method of teaching to prepare students for management careers in the rapidly growing food service industry. The Bachelor's degree is an 18-month program (beyond the Associate's or other qualifying educational credits) designed to develop management and entreprenuerial skills of those seeking top-of-the house and hospitality management careers. Both programs include a 6-month, paid internship following the residency period. Both programs are offered in March and September.

NORWICH UNIVERSITY
158 Harmon Dr, Northfield VT 05663
Dr. Frank Vanecek, Division Head
800-468-6679 Fax: 802-485-2087
Website: www.norwich.edu
E-mail: vanecek@norwich.edu
See listing under "Universities"

Saint Michael's College
One Winooski Park, Colchester VT 05439-0001
Jacqueline Murphy, Director
802-654-3000

Southern Vermont College
982 Mansion Dr, Bennington VT 05201-6002
Kathleen James Ring, Director of Admissions
800-378-2782 Fax: 802-447-4695
Website: www.svc.edu
E-mail: admis@svc.edu

University of Vermont
194 S Prospect St, Burlington VT 05401-3518
802-656-3131

VIRGINIA

Averett University
420 W Main St, Danville VA 24541-3692
804-791-5600

Bluefield College
3000 College Dr, Bluefield VA 24605-1799
276-326-3682

Bridgewater College
402 E College St, Bridgewater VA 22812-1599
540-828-8000

Christopher Newport University
1 University Pl, Newport News VA 23606
757-594-7000

College of William and Mary
PO Box 8795, Williamsburg VA 23187-8795
757-221-4000

Eastern Mennonite University
1200 Park Rd, Harrisonburg VA 22802-2404
540-432-4000

Emory & Henry College
PO Box 947, Emory VA 24327-0947
276-944-4121

Ferrum College
PO Box 1000, Ferrum VA 24088-9001
Gilda Q. Woods, Director of Admissions
800-868-9797

George Mason University
4400 University Dr, Fairfax VA 22030-4444
Eddie Tallent, Director of Admissions
703-993-2400

James Madison University
800 S Main St, Harrisonburg VA 22807-0002
540-568-6211

Liberty University
PO Box 20000, Lynchburg VA 24506-8001
804-582-2000

Longwood University
201 High St, Farmville VA 23909-1801
804-395-2000

Lynchburg College
1501 Lakeside Dr, Lynchburg VA 24501-3199
804-544-8100

Mary Baldwin College
Staunton VA 24401
Lisa A. Branson, Executive Director of Admissions and Financial Aid
800-468-2262 Fax: 540-887-7292
Website: www.mbc.edu
E-mail: admit@mbc.edu

Marymount University
2807 N Glebe Rd, Arlington VA 22207-4299
703-522-5600

Norfolk State University
700 Park Ave, Norfolk VA 23504
Michelle Marable, Director of Admissions
757-823-8600

Old Dominion University
1 Old Dominion University, Norfolk VA 23529-1000
757-683-3000

Radford University
PO Box 6903, Radford VA 24142
David W. Kraus, Director of Admissions
800-890-4265 Fax: 540-831-5038
Website: www.radford.edu
E-mail: ruadmiss@radford.edu

Randolph-Macon College
PO Box 5005, Ashland VA 23005-5505
804-752-7200

Roanoke College
221 College Ln, Salem VA 24153-3794
540-375-2500

Shenandoah University
1460 University Dr, Winchester VA 22601-5195
Michael D. Carpenter, Director of Admissions
800-432-2266

Southside Virginia Community College
109 Campus Dr, Alberta VA 23821-2930
Ronald E. Mattox, Dean of Admissions
434-949-1014 Fax: 434-949-7863
Website: www.sv.vccs.edu
E-mail: ronald.mattox@sv.vccs.edu

Southside Virginia Community College
200 Daniel Rd, Keysville VA 23947
Ronald E. Mattox, Dean of Admissions
434-736-2018 Fax: 434-736-2082
Website: www.sv.vccs.edu
E-mail: ronald.mattox@sv.vccs.edu

Stratford University
7777 Leesburg Pike #100 South
Falls Church VA 22043
Keith Evans, Contact
703-821-8570 Fax: 703-734-5335
Website: www.stratford.edu
E-mail: admissions@stratford.edu

UNIVERSITY OF MANAGEMENT AND TECHNOLOGY
1901 Fort Myer Dr Ste 700, Arlington VA 22209
703-516-0035 Fax: 703-516-0985
Website: www.umtweb.edu
E-mail: info@umtweb.edu

University of Mary Washington
1301 College Ave, Fredericksburg VA 22401-5300
Dr. Martin A. Wilder, Jr., Director of Admissions
540-654-2000 Fax: 540-654-1857
Website: www.umw.edu
E-mail: admit@umw.edu

University of Richmond
Richmond VA 23173
804-289-8000

University of Virginia
PO Box 400160, Charlottesville VA 22904
804-924-0311

University of Virginia College at Wise
1 College Ave, Wise VA 24293
276-328-0100

Virginia Commonwealth University
901 W Franklin St, Richmond VA 23284
804-828-0100

Virginia Intermont College
1013 Moore St, Bristol VA 24201-4225
540-669-6101

Virginia Military Institute
Lexington VA 24450
540-464-7000

Virginia Polytechnic Institute & State University
Blacksburg VA 24061
540-231-6000

Virginia Wesleyan College
1584 Wesleyan Dr, Norfolk VA 23502-5599
757-455-3200

Washington & Lee University
Lexington VA 24450
540-463-8400

WASHINGTON

Antioch University
2326 6th Ave, Seattle WA 98121
Pam Smith Mentz, Director of Enrollment Services
888-268-4477

Central Washington University
400 E University Way, Ellensburg WA 98926
William Swain, Director of Admissions
509-963-3001

City University
11900 NE 1st St, Bellevue WA 98005-3030
800-426-5596

CROWN COLLEGE

8739 S Hosmer St, Tacoma WA 98444-1836
John Wabel, CEO
253-531-3123 Fax: 253-531-3521
Website: www.crowncollege.edu
E-mail: jwabel@crowncollege.edu

Eastern Washington University
Cheney WA 99004
509-359-6200

Everett Community College
2000 Tower St, Everett WA 98201
Christine Kerlin, Associate Dean
425-388-9100 Fax: 425-388-9173
Website: www.everettcc.edu
E-mail: ckerlin@everettcc.edu

Gonzaga University
502 E Boone Ave, Spokane WA 99258-0102
Julie McCulloh, Dean of Admission
800-322-2584 or 509-323-6572 Fax: 509-323-5780
Website: www.gonzaga.edu
E-mail: mcculloh@gu.gonzaga.edu

Heritage University
3240 Fort Rd, Toppenish WA 98948-9599
509-865-8500

Pacific Lutheran University
12180 Park Ave S, Tacoma WA 98447-0014
David E. Gunovich, Director of Admissions
253-535-7151

St. Martin's University
5300 Pacific Ave SE, Lacey WA 98503-1297
360-491-4700

Seattle Pacific University
3307 3rd Ave W, Seattle WA 98119-1997
206-281-2000

Seattle University
900 Broadway, Seattle WA 98122-4340
206-296-6000

University of Puget Sound
1500 N Warner St, Tacoma WA 98416-0005
253-879-3100

University of Washington
Seattle WA 98195-0001
206-543-2100

Walla Walla College
204 S College Ave, College Place WA 99324-1198
509-527-2615

Walla Walla Community College
500 Tausick Way, Walla Walla WA 99362-9270
Dan Biagi, Director
509-527-4283 or 877-471-9292 Fax: 509-527-4480
Website: www.wwcc.edu
E-mail: dan.biagi@wwcc.edu
See listing under "Community and Junior Colleges"

Washington State University
1 SE Stadium Way, Pullman WA 99164-0001
509-335-3564

Wenatchee Valley College
1300 5th St, Wenatchee WA 98801-1799
Marco Azurdia, Dean, Student Development
509-682-6805 Fax: 509-682-6541
Website: www.wvc.edu

Western Washington University
516 High St, Bellingham WA 98225-5996
360-650-3000

Whitworth College
300 W Hawthorne Rd, Spokane WA 99251-0001
Fred Pfursich, Dean of Admissions & Financial Aid
800-533-4668

WEST VIRGINIA

Alderson-Broaddus College
Philippi WV 26416
Eric A. Ruf, Director of Admissions
800-263-1549

Concord University
Athens WV 24712
Michael Curry, Vice President of Financial Aid &
Admissions
888-384-5249 Fax: 304-384-3218
Website: www.concord.edu
E-mail: admissions@concord.edu

Davis & Elkins College
100 Campus Dr, Elkins WV 26241-3996
Renee Heckel, Director of Enrollment Management
800-624-3157 Fax: 304-637-1800
Website: www.davisandelkins.edu
E-mail: admiss@davisandelkins.edu

Fairmont State University
1201 Locust Ave, Fairmont WV 26554-2470
Steve Leadman, Director of Admissions
304-367-4261 or 800-641-5678 Fax: 304-367-4789
Website: www.fairmontstate.edu
E-mail: admit@fairmontstate.edu

Glenville State College
200 High St, Glenville WV 26351-1200
304-462-4128

Marshall University
400 Hal Greer Blvd, Huntington WV 25755-0003
304-696-3170

Mountain State University
Box 9003, Beckley WV 25802-9003
866-FOR-MSU1 or 304-929-INFO Fax: 304-253-5072
Website: www.mountainstate.edu
E-mail: gomsu@mountainstate.edu
See listing under "Universities"

Shepherd University
PO Box 3210
Shepherdstown WV 25443
304-876-5000

University of Charleston
2300 MacCorkle Ave SE, Charleston WV 25304-1099
304-357-4800

West Virginia State University
PO Box 1000, Institute WV 25112-1000
304-766-3000

West Virginia University
PO Box 6001, Morgantown WV 26506-6001
304-293-0111

West Virginia Wesleyan College
59 College Ave, Buckhannon WV 26201-2699
Robert N. Skinner II, Director of Admission
800-722-9933 Fax: 304-473-8108
Website: www.wvwc.edu
E-mail: admission@wvwc.edu

Wheeling Jesuit University
316 Washington Ave, Wheeling WV 26003-6295
304-243-2000

WISCONSIN

Alverno College
PO Box 343922, Milwaukee WI 53234-3922
Mary Kay Farrell, Director of Admissions
414-382-6100 Fax: 414-382-6354
Website: www.alverno.edu
E-mail: admissions@alverno.edu

Beloit College
700 College St, Beloit WI 53511-5596
Jeffrey L. Adams, Professor and Chair
608-363-2327

Blackhawk Technical College
PO Box 5009, Janesville WI 53547-5009
Gregg Bosak, Administration, Community Information
608-757-7769 Fax: 608-757-7740
Website: www.blackhawk.edu
E-mail: gbosak@blackhawk.edu

Cardinal Stritch University
6801 N Yates Rd, Milwaukee WI 53217-3985
414-410-4000

Carroll College
100 N East Ave, Waukesha WI 53186-5593
James Wiseman, Dean of Admissions
800-CARROLL

Carthage College
2001 Alford Park Dr, Kenosha WI 53140-1994
262-551-6000

COLLEGE OF MENOMINEE NATION

PO Box 1179, Keshena WI 54135-1179
Cynthia Norton, Admissions Representative
715-799-5600 Fax: 715-799-4392
Website: www.menominee.edu
E-mail: cnorton@menominee.edu

Concordia University
12800 N Lake Shore Dr, Mequon WI 53097-2402
262-243-5700

Edgewood College
1000 Edgewood College Dr, Madison WI 53711
608-663-4861

Herzing College
5218 E Terrace Dr, Madison WI 53718-8340
Donald Madelung, President
800-582-1227 Fax: 608-249-8593
Website: www.herzing.edu
E-mail: info@msn.herzing.edu
See listing under "Universities"

Lakeland College
PO Box 359, Sheboygan WI 53082-0359
Nathan Dehne, Director of Admissions
920-565-1100 Fax: 920-565-1215
Website: www.lakeland.edu
E-mail: admissions@lakeland.edu

Marquette University
PO Box 1881, Milwaukee WI 53201-1881
Robert Blust, Director of Admissions
414-288-7302 Fax: 414-288-3764
Website: www.mu.edu
E-mail: admissions@marquette.edu

Mount Mary College
2900 N Menomonee River Pkwy
Milwaukee WI 53222-4597
414-256-1219

Ripon College
PO Box 248, Ripon WI 54971-0248
920-748-8115

St. Norbert College
100 Grant St, De Pere WI 54115
Brian Studebaker, Director of Admission
800-236-4878 Fax: 920-403-4072
Website: www.snc.edu
E-mail: admit@snc.edu

Silver Lake College
2406 S Alverno Rd, Manitowoc WI 54220-9319
920-684-6691

University of Wisconsin
PO Box 4004, Eau Claire WI 54702
715-836-2637

University of Wisconsin
PO Box 2000, Kenosha WI 53141-2000
262-595-2345

University of Wisconsin
716 Langdon St, Madison WI 53706-1481
608-262-1234

University of Wisconsin
PO Box 413, Milwaukee WI 53201-0413
414-229-1122

University of Wisconsin
1 University Plz, Platteville WI 53818-3001
Angela Udelhofen, Recruitment Manager
608-342-1200

University of Wisconsin
410 S 3rd St, River Falls WI 54022
715-425-3911

University of Wisconsin
PO Box 2000, Superior WI 54880
715-394-8101

University of Wisconsin
800 W Main St, Whitewater WI 53190-1705
262-472-1234

University of Wisconsin Green Bay
2420 Nicolet Dr, Green Bay WI 54311-7003
Pamela Harvey-Jacobs, Interim Director of Admissions
920-465-2111

University of Wisconsin in La Crosse
115 Graff Main Hall, La Crosse WI 54601
Tim Lewis, Director of Admissions
608-785-8939

University of Wisconsin - Oshkosh
800 Algoma Blvd, Oshkosh WI 54901-8602
920-424-0202

University of Wisconsin-Stout
124 Bowman Hall, Menomonie WI 54751-2662
715-232-1123

Viterbo University
815 9th St S, La Crosse WI 54601-8802
608-796-3000

Wisconsin Indianhead Technical College
505 Pine Ridge Dr, Shell Lake WI 54871
Miriam Crandall, Dean of Student Services
800-243-9482 Fax: 715-468-2819
Website: www.witc.edu
E-mail: mcrandal@witc.edu
Campuses in Ashland, New Richmond, Rice Lake,
Superior.

WYOMING

Laramie County Community College
1400 E College Dr, Cheyenne WY 82007-3204
Jenny Hargett, Director of Admissions
307-778-5222 Fax: 307-778-1350
Website: www.lccc.wy.edu
E-mail: learnmore@lccc.wy.edu

University of Wyoming
Admissions Office
Dept 3435, Laramie WY 82071-3435
Aaron Appelhans, Contact
800-342-5996 Fax: 307-766-4042
Website: www.uwyo.edu
E-mail: why-wyo@uwyo.edu

GUAM

Guam Community College
PO Box 23069, G.M.F. GU 96921-0307
Virginia Charfauros Tudela, Ph.D., Registrar
671-735-5531 Fax: 671-734-5238
Website: www.guamcc.edu
E-mail: Webmaster@guamcc.edu

University of Guam
UOG Station, Mangilao GU 96923
Deborah Leon Guerrero, Registrar
671-735-2201 or 671-735-2208 Fax: 671-735-2203
Website: www.uog.edu
E-mail: admitme@uog9.uog.edu

PUERTO RICO

Atlantic College
PO Box 1774, Guaynabo PR 00970-1774
Zaida Perez, Director of Admissions
787-720-1022 Fax: 787-720-1092
Website: www.atlanticcollege-pr.com
E-mail: atlancol@coqui.net

: MBTI Business Training Institute
1256 Ave Ponce de Leon, Santurce PR 00907-3965
Miguel A. Fernandez, Contact
787-723-9403 Fax: 787-723-9447
Website: www.mbti.com
E-mail: hdavila@mbti.com

Pontifical Catholic University of Puerto Rico
2250 Ave Las Americas, Ponce PR 00717-0777
787-841-2000

Universidad Adventista de las Antillas
PO Box 118, Mayaguez PR 00919-0118
Evelyn Del Valle Rivera, Director of Admissions
787-834-9595 Fax: 787-834-9597
Website: www.uaa.edu
E-mail: admissions@uaa.edu

University of Puerto Rico
R Ave Antonio R Barcelo, Cayey PR 00736-5534
787-738-2161

University of Puerto Rico
CUH Station Rd 908 Bo Tejas, Humacao PR 00791
787-850-0000

University of Puerto Rico
PO Box 9020, Mayaguez PR 00681
787-832-4040

University of Puerto Rico
PO Box 23303, Rio Piedras PR 00931-3303
787-764-0000

University of Puerto Rico at Arecibo
PO Box 4010, Arecibo PR 00614
787-815-0000

University of Puerto Rico at Ponce
PO Box 7186, Ponce PR 00732-7186
787-844-8181

University of Puerto Rico
Bayamn University College
Carretera 174, Km 2.8, Bayamn PR 00959
787-786-2885

:CAREER SCHOOLS

ALABAMA

Alabama State College of Barber Styling
9480 Parkway E, Birmingham AL 35215
205-836-2404

.∵. Baptist Health System
PO Box 830605, Birmingham AL 35283-0605
205-715-5319

.∵. Baptist Medical Center
301 Brown Springs Rd, Montgomery AL 36117
334-273-4400

· Bishop State Community College-Carver
414 Stanton Rd, Mobile AL 36617-2313
Mrs. M.O. Taylor, Contact
251-473-8692

· Bishop State Community College-Southwest Campus
925 Dauphin Island Pkwy, Mobile AL 36605-3299
334-479-0003

Blue Cliff School of Therapeutic Massage
2970 Cottage Hill Rd Ste 175, Mobile AL 36606-4749
251-665-9900

CAPPS College
3590 Pleasant Valley Rd, Mobile AL 36609
334-473-1393

.∵. Carraway Methodist Medical Center
1600 Carraway Blvd, Birmingham AL 35234-2804
205-226-6000

DCH Regional Medical Center
809 University Blvd E, Tuscaloosa AL 35401-2071
205-759-7177

Flowers Hospital
School of Surgical Technology
PO Box 6907, Dothan AL 36302
334-793-5000

Gadsden Business College
PO Box 8365, Gadsden AL 35902-8365
Dennis Kerr, President
256-546-2863

Gadsden Business College of Anniston
1809 Hillyer Robinson Pkwy Ste B
Anniston AL 36207
Randy Kerr, President
256-831-3838

Gaither Beauty College
414 E Willow St, Scottsboro AL 35768
256-259-1001

Huntsville Hospital
101 Sivley Rd SW, Huntsville AL 35801-4470
256-533-8123

Jefferson Davis Community College
PO Box 1119, Atmore AL 36504-1119
334-368-8118

Montgomery Job Corps Center
1145 Air Base Blvd, Montgomery AL 36108
334-262-8883

Pivot Point the Masters
8215 Stephanie Dr SW, Huntsville AL 35802
256-881-8587

· Remington College
828 Downtowner Loop W, Mobile AL 36609-5519
334-343-8200

Southeast Alabama Medical Center
PO Box 6987, Dothan AL 36302
334-793-8100

Southeastern School of Cosmetology
26B Phillips Dr, Midfield AL 35228
205-925-0011

· Trenholm State Technical College
Trenholm Campus
1225 Air Base Blvd, Montgomery AL 36108-3199
Dr. Anthony Molina, President
334-420-4200 Fax: 334-420-4206
Website: www.trenholmtech.cc.al.us
E-mail: amolina@trenholmtech.cc.al.us

· Virginia College
2800 Bob Wallace Ave SW #A
Huntsville AL 35805-4164
256-533-7387

ALASKA

Alaska Vocational Technical School
PO Box 889, Seward AK 99664
907-224-4159

Career Academy
1415 E Tudor Rd, Anchorage AK 99507-1033
907-563-7575

University of Alaska Anchorage
PO Box 141629, Anchorage AK 99514-1629
Cecile Mitchell, Director of Enrollment Services
907-786-1480 Fax: 907-786-4888
Website: www.uaa.alaska.edu/
E-mail: enroll@uaa.alaska.edu

ARIZONA

American Institute of Technology
440 S 54th Ave, Phoenix AZ 85043-4729
602-233-2222

Apollo College
630 W Southern Ave, Mesa AZ 85210-5005
480-831-6585

Apollo College
8503 N 27th Ave, Phoenix AZ 85051-4063
602-864-1571

Apollo College
2701 W Bethany Home Rd, Phoenix AZ 85017-1705
602-433-1333

Apollo College
3550 N Oracle Rd, Tucson AZ 85705
520-888-5885

Arizona Academy of Beauty
5631 E Speedway Blvd, Tucson AZ 85712
520-885-4120

Arizona Academy of Beauty - North
4066 N Oracle Rd, Tucson AZ 85705
520-888-0170

· Arizona Automotive Institute
6829 N 46th Ave, Glendale AZ 85301-3597
623-934-7273

· Arizona College of Allied Health
4425 W Olive Ave Ste 300, Glendale AZ 85302-3843
602-222-9300

ART INSTITUTE OF PHOENIX
2233 W Dunlap Ave, Phoenix AZ 85021-2859
Jerry Driskill, Director of Admissions
602-331-7500 or 800-474-2479 Fax: 602-331-5301
Website: www.aipx.edu
E-mail: aipxadm@aii.edu

Artistic Beauty College
2978 N Alma School Rd Ste 3, Chandler AZ 85224
480-855-7901

Artistic Beauty College
1790 E Route 66, Flagstaff AZ 86004
928-774-7146

Artistic Beauty College
10820 N 43rd Ave, Glendale AZ 85304
623-937-2749

Artistic Beauty College
2727 W Glendale Ave Ste 200
Phoenix AZ 85051-8412
623-939-8364

Artistic Beauty College
410 W Goodwin St, Prescott AZ 86303
928-778-5064

Artistic Beauty College
7730 E McDowell Rd, Scottsdale AZ 85257
480-949-7557

Artistic Beauty College
3210 E Speedway Blvd, Tucson AZ 85716
520-327-6544

Bryman School
2250 W Peoria Ave Ste A100, Phoenix AZ 85029
602-274-4300

Carsten Institute of Hair and Beauty
3345 S Rural Rd, Tempe AZ 85282
480-491-0449

Chaparral College
4585 E Speedway Blvd #204, Tucson AZ 85712-5311
Scott Rhude, President
520-327-6866

Charles of Italy Beauty College
1987 McCulloch Blvd #205
Lake Havasu City AZ 86403
928-453-6666

CollegeAmerica
1800 S Milton Rd, Flagstaff AZ 86001
Joshua Swayne, Executive Director
928-526-0763

CollegeAmerica
6533 N Black Canyon Hwy, Phoenix AZ 85015
Daryl Goldberg, Executive Director
602-246-3041

Collins College: A School of Design and Technology
(Formerly Al Collins Graphic Design School)
1140 S Priest Dr, Tempe AZ 85281-5240
Toby Craver, Director of National Admissions
800-876-7070 Fax: 480-829-0183
Website: www.collinscollege.edu
E-mail: nationaladmissions@collinscollege.edu

Conservatory of Recording Arts & Sciences
1205 N Fiesta Blvd, Gilbert AZ 85233
Tonya Visconti, Director of Admissions
480-858-9400 Fax: 480-829-1332
Website: www.audiorecordingschool.com
E-mail: info@cras.org

The Conservatory of Recording Arts & Sciences
2300 E Broadway Rd, Tempe AZ 85282-1707
Tonya Visconti, Director of Admissions
800-562-6383 or 480-858-9400 Fax: 480-829-1332
Website: cras.org
E-mail: info@cras.org
See listing under "Music"

Desert Institute of the Healing Arts
639 N 6th Ave, Tucson AZ 85705-8330
David Shahan, Director of Admissions
520-733-8098

DeVoe College of Beauty
750 Bartow Dr, Sierra Vista AZ 85635
520-458-8660

Earl's Academy of Beauty
2111 S Alma School Rd #21, Mesa AZ 85210
480-897-1688

· Everest College
10400 N 25th Ave Suite 190, Phoenix AZ 85021-1610
Melissa Agee, Director of Admissions
602-942-4141

· Golf Academy of Arizona
670 N Arizona Ave Ste 13, Chandler AZ 85225-6742
Dona K. Powell, President
800-342-7342

HDS TRUCK DRIVING INSTITUTE
PO Box 17600, Tucson AZ 85731
Robert Knapp, School Director
520-721-5825 Fax: 520-798-3247
Website: www.hdsdrivers.com
E-mail: bob_knapp@hdsdrivers.com

INTERNATIONAL ACADEMY OF BEAUTY
42 N Stapley Dr, Mesa AZ 85203-8841
480-964-8675

INTERNATIONAL ACADEMY OF HAIR DESIGN
3350 N Arizona Ave Ste 4, Chandler AZ 85225
480-820-9422 Fax: 480-820-9348

· ITT Technical Institute
5005 S Wendler Dr, Tempe AZ 85282
602-437-7500

· ITT Technical Institute
1455 W River Rd, Tucson AZ 85704-5829
520-408-7488

LAMSON COLLEGE
1126 N Scottsdale Rd Ste 17, Tempe AZ 85281
Al Frazier, Director of Admissions
480-898-7000 Fax: 480-967-6645
Website: www.lamsoncollege.com
E-mail: afrazier@lamsoncollege.com

· Long Technical College
4646 E Van Buren St Ste 350
Phoenix AZ 85008-6952
Michael Meckstroth, Director of Admissions
602-252-2171

LONG TECHNICAL COLLEGE
Phoenix Campus
13450 N Black Canyon Hwy Ste 104
Phoenix AZ 85029-6323
602-548-1955 Fax: 602-548-1956
Website: www.longtechnicalcollege.com
E-mail: mcrone@longtechnicalcollege.com

Maricopa Beauty College
515 W Western Ave, Avondale AZ 85323
623-932-4414

MOTORCYCLE MECHANICS INSTITUTE
A division of Clinton Technical Institute
2844 W Deer Valley Rd, Phoenix AZ 85027-2399
Bruce Trexler, Director of Admissions
800-528-7995 Fax: 623-581-2871
Website: www.uticorp.com
E-mail: mmi@crl.com
   Established 1971. Comprehensive technical training in all aspects of motorcycle and personal watercraft repair. Endorsed and equipped by Harley-Davidson, Honda, Yamaha, Suzuki, and Kawasaki. Classes are scheduled 5-hours per day in the morning, afternoon, or evening. Accredited member school: ACCSCT. A graduate placement department is available to assist students in finding full-time employment in the motorcycle industry. Manufacturers' assist with placement through promotional campaigns to their dealership network. Housing coordinator works with local apartment complexes to find housing while in school. Job advisor will assist with local employment while in school. Financial aid available to those who qualify. VA and Agency assistance where applicable.

Mundus Institute
2001 W Camelback Rd Ste 400
Phoenix AZ 85015-3466
Gene Lambert, Admissions
602-246-7111 Fax: 602-246-7222
Website: www.mundusinstitute.com
E-mail: admissions@mundusinstitute.com

PIMA MEDICAL INSTITUTE
957 S Dobson Rd, Mesa AZ 85202-2903
Christopher Luebke, Director
480-644-0267 Fax: 480-649-5249
Website: www.pmi.edu
E-mail: asc@pmi.edu

Pima Medical Institute
3350 E Grant Rd, Tucson AZ 85716-2800
520-326-1600

Quantum Helicopters
2370 S Airport Blvd, Chandler AZ 85249
480-814-8118

RainStar University
8370 E Via de Ventura, Scottsdale AZ 85258
Ranay Yarian, Director of Community & Student Relations
480-423-0375 ext 1

Refrigeration School
4210 E Washington St, Phoenix AZ 85034-1894
Mary Simmons, Director of Admissions
602-275-7133

Roberto-Venn Guitar Making School
4011 S 16th St, Phoenix AZ 85040-1314
Ann Fountain, Admissions Director
602-243-1179

Safford College of Beauty Culture
1550 W Thatcher Blvd, Safford AZ 85546
928-428-0331

Scott Cole Academy
7201 E Camelback Rd Ste 100, Scottsdale AZ 85251
480-994-4222

Scottsdale Culinary Institute
8100 E Camelback Rd, Scottsdale AZ 85251-2729
Admissions Department
480-990-3773

SOUTHWEST INSTITUTE OF HEALING ARTS
1100 E Apache Blvd, Tempe AZ 85281
Admissions
480-994-9244 Fax: 480-994-3228
Website: www.swiha.org
E-mail: doyourdream@swiha.org

TUCSON COLLEGE
7310 E 22nd St, Tucson AZ 85710
Rebecca Montgomery, Director of Admissions
520-296-3261 Fax: 520-296-3484
Website: www.tucsoncollege.edu
E-mail: Rmontgomery@tucsoncollege.edu

Universal Technical Institute
10695 W Pierce St, Avondale AZ 85323-7946
John Palumbo, Director of Admissions
623-245-4600 Fax: 623-245-4603
Website: www.uticorp.com

University of Advancing Technology
2625 W Baseline Rd, Tempe AZ 85283
Lary Dougherty, Director of Admissions
800-658-5744

ARKANSAS

American Professional Institute
103 S Avalon St, West Memphis AR 72301

Arkadelphia Beauty College
2708 Pine St, Arkadelphia AR 71923
870-246-6726

Arkansas Aviation Technologies Center
4248 S School Ave, Fayetteville AR 72701
479-443-2283

Arkansas Beauty School
5108 Baseline Rd, Little Rock AR 72209
501-562-5673

Arkansas Beauty School - Conway
1061 Markham St, Conway AR 72032-4309
501-329-8303

Arkansas Career Training Institute
105 Reserve St, Hot Springs National Park AR 71901
501-624-4411

Arkansas College of Barbering and Hair Design
200 Washington Ave, North Little Rock AR 72114
501-376-9696

Arkansas State University
Searcy Campus
PO Box 909, Searcy AR 72145-0909
501-207-4000

Arkansas Valley Technical Institute
PO Box 506, Ozark AR 72949-0506
479-667-2117

Arthur's Beauty College
2600 John Harden Dr, Jacksonville AR 72076
501-982-8987

Baptist Schools of Allied Health
11900 Colonel Glenn Rd, Little Rock AR 72210-2820
501-202-7415

Bee-Jay's Hairstyling Academy
130 W Main St, Batesville AR 72501
870-793-3898

Bee-Jay's Hairstyling Academy
1907 Hinson Loop Rd, Little Rock AR 72212
501-224-2442

Black River Technical College
PO Box 468, Pocahontas AR 72455-0468
870-892-4565

Blytheville Academy of Cosmetology
100 E Main St, Blytheville AR 72315
870-763-6326

Cass Civilian Conservation Job Corps Center
21424 N Highway 23, Ozark AR 72949
479-667-3686

Central Arkansas Radiation Therapy Institute
PO Box 55050, Little Rock AR 72215-5050
501-664-8573

Cotton Boll Technical Institute
PO Box 36, Burdette AR 72321-0036
Brenda Morris, Supervisor of Instruction
870-763-1486

Crowley's Ridge Technical Institute
1620 Newcastle Rd, Forrest City AR 72335
870-633-5411

Delta Technical Institute
PO Box 280, Marked Tree AR 72365-0280
Keith Steele, President
870-358-2117

Eastern College of Health Vocations
6423 Forbing Rd, Little Rock AR 72209-3535
501-568-0211

Eaton Beauty Stylist College
814 W 7th St, Little Rock AR 72201
501-375-0211

Fayetteville Beauty College
2167 W 6th St, Fayetteville AR 72701
479-442-5181

Forest Echoes Technical Institute
1326 Highway 82W, Crossett AR 71635
870-364-6414

Hot Springs Beauty College
100 Cones Rd, Hot Springs AR 71901
501-624-0203

ITT Technical Institute
4520 S University Ave, Little Rock AR 72204-7739
501-565-5550

Jefferson Regional Medical Center
1515 W 42nd Ave, Pine Bluff AR 71603-7055
870-541-7269

Lee's School of Cosmetology
2700 W Pershing Blvd
North Little Rock AR 72114-3800
501-758-2800

Leon's Hair Training Academy
200 Holcomb St, Springdale AR 72764-4403
479-756-6060

Marsha Kay Beauty College
408 Highway 201 N, Mountain Home AR 72653
870-425-7575

Mellie's Beauty College
311 S 16th St, Fort Smith AR 72901
479-782-5059

New Tyler Barber College
1221 E 7th St, North Little Rock AR 72114
501-375-0377

Northwest Technical Institute
709 S Old Missouri Rd, Springdale AR 72764
Charles L. Kelley, President
479-751-8824 Fax: 479-751-7780
Website: www.nti.tec.ar.us
E-mail: info@nit.tec.ar.us

Ozarka College
PO Box 10, Melbourne AR 72556-0010
870-368-7371

Phillips Community College of the University of Arkansas
PO Box 785, Helena AR 72342-0785
Dr. Steven Murray, Chancellor
Lynn Boone, Vice Chancellor for Student Services / Registrar
870-338-6474 Fax: 870-338-7542
Website: www.pccua.edu
E-mail: lboone@pccua.edu

Professional Cosmetology Education Center
PO Box 429, Camden AR 71701
870-836-5481

Pulaski Technical College
3000 W Scenic Dr, North Little Rock AR 72118-3347
501-771-1000

Remington College
19 Remington Rd, Little Rock AR 72204
501-312-0007

Searcy Beauty College
1004 S Main St, Searcy AR 72143
501-268-6300

Southeast Arkansas College
1900 S Hazel St, Pine Bluff AR 71603-3900
870-543-5900

Southern Institute of Cosmetology
103 S Avalon St, West Memphis AR 72301
870-735-2800

University of Arkansas Community College at Morrilton
1 Bruce St, Morrilton AR 72110-9601
Susan Dewey, Admissions Counselor
800-264-1094

University of Arkansas - Monticello
College of Technology - Crossett
1326 Highway 52 W, Crossett AR 71635-4853
870-364-6414

Velvatex College of Beauty Culture
1520 Dr Martin Luther King, Little Rock AR 72202
501-372-9678

CALIFORNIA

Academy Education Services
3151 W 5th St Ste E101, Oxnard CA 93030
805-984-2511

Academy Pacific Travel College
1777 Vine St #30, Hollywood CA 90028-5218
323-462-3211

Adcon Technical Institute
12440 Firestone Blvd Ste 2001, Norwalk CA 90650
562-864-0506

Adcon Technical Institute
17821 17th St Ste 120, Tustin CA 92780
714-730-7080

Adrian's Beauty College of Turlock
2253 Geer Rd, Turlock CA 95382
209-632-2233

Advanced College
13180 Paramount Blvd, South Gate CA 90280
562-408-6969

ADVANCED TRAINING ASSOCIATES
1810 Gillespie Way Ste 4, El Cajon CA 92020-0918
Joann Ferrera-Zakarin, President
800-720-2125 Fax: 619-596-4526
Website: www.advancedtraining.edu
E-mail: joann@advancedtraining.edu

Alameda Beauty College
2318 Central Ave, Alameda CA 94501
510-523-1050

Alhambra Beauty College
PO Box 7494, Alhambra CA 91802
626-282-6433

American Academy of Dramatic Arts - Hollywood
1336 N LaBrea Ave, Hollywood CA 90028
Dan Justin, Director of Admissions
800-222-2867 Fax: 323-464-1250
Website: www.aada.org
E-mail: admissions-ca@aada.org

American Beauty College
16512 Bellflower Blvd, Bellflower CA 90706
562-866-0728

American Career College
1200 N Magnolia Ave, Anaheim CA 92801
714-952-9066

American Career College
4021 Rosewood Ave, Los Angeles CA 90004-6818
Rita Totten, Campus Director
323-383-2862

American College of California
760 Market St Ste 1009
San Francisco CA 94102-2305
Sherris Goodwin, Director
415-677-9717 Fax: 415-677-9810
Website: www.acca.edu
E-mail: info@acca.edu

American College of Health Professions
700 E Redlands Blvd #U227
Redlands CA 92373-6109
Admissions
909-307-6022

AMERICAN COLLEGE OF MEDICAL TECHNOLOGY
555 W Redondo Beach Blvd #100
Gardena CA 90248
Scott Jacobus, Contact
310-324-1000 Fax: 310-515-3944
Website: www.acmt.ac
E-mail: info@acmt.ac

Arrowhead Regional Medical Center
400 N Pepper Ave, Colton CA 92324
909-580-1000

The Art Institute of California
2900 31st St, Santa Monica CA 90405
310-752-4700

The Art Institute of California - San Diego
7650 Mission Valley Rd, San Diego CA 92108
Jo-Ann White, Director of Admissions
858-598-1200 Fax: 619-291-3206
Website: www.aicasd.artinstitutes.edu

Asian American International Beauty College
7871 Westminster Blvd, Westminster CA 92683-4043
Le Nguyen, General Manager
714-891-0508

Associated Technical College
1670 Wilshire Blvd, Los Angeles CA 90017-1690
Samuel Romano, Director of Admissions
213-353-1845 Fax: 213-413-4864
Website: www.associatedtechcollege.com
E-mail: decato@earthlink.net

Associated Technical College
1445 6th Ave, San Diego CA 92101-3204
619-234-2181

Avalon Beauty College
504 N Milpas St, Santa Barbara CA 93103
805-966-1931

Avance Beauty College
750 Beyer Way Ste B, San Diego CA 92154
619-575-1511

Aviation & Electronic School of America
PO Box 1810, Colfax CA 95713
800-345-2742

Bay Vista College of Beauty
1520 E Plaza Blvd, National City CA 91950
619-474-6607

Brooks Institute of Photography
801 Alston Rd, Santa Barbara CA 93108-2399
Inge B. Kautzmann, Director of Admissions
805-966-3888 ext. 217 or 218

BROWNSON TECHNICAL SCHOOL
1110 S Technology Cir Ste D
Anaheim CA 92805-6316
William D. Brown, Director
714-774-9443 Fax: 714-774-5025
Website: www.brownsontechnicalschool.com
E-mail: brownson98@earthlink.net

Bryan College
2333 Beverly Blvd, Los Angeles CA 90057-2209
213-484-8850

Bryman College
2215 W Mission Rd, Alhambra CA 91803-1310
626-979-4970

Bryman College
511 N Brookhurst St Ste 300
Anaheim CA 92801-5229
714-953-6500

Bryman College
12801 Crossroads Pkwy S
city of Industry CA 91746-3412
562-908-2500

Bryman College
1045 W Redondo Beach Blvd #275
Gardena CA 90247
310-527-7105

BRYMAN COLLEGE
22336 Main St, Hayward CA 94541
H. Albizo, President
510-582-9500 Fax: 510-582-9645
Website: www.cci.edu
E-mail: halbizo@cci.edu

Bryman College
3460 Wilshire Blvd Ste 500
Los Angeles CA 90010-2223
Marie Guerrero, Director of Admissions
213-388-9950

Bryman College
3000 S Robertson Blvd, Los Angeles CA 90034-3158
Daniel Santillan, Director of Admissions
310-840-5777

Bryman College
1460 S Milliken Ave, Ontario CA 91761-2338
909-984-5027

Bryman College
18040 Sherman Way #400, Reseda CA 91335-4631
Lani Townsend, School President
818-774-0550

Bryman College
217 Club Center Dr Ste A, San Bernardino CA 92408
Mary Coutts, Director of Admissions
909-777-3300

Bryman College
814 Mission St Ste 500
San Francisco CA 94103-3038
415-777-2500

Bryman College
1245 S Winchester Blvd #102, San Jose CA 95128
408-246-0859

California Beauty College
1115 15th St, Modesto CA 95354
209-524-5184

California Career School
1100 Technology Cir, Anaheim CA 92805-6329
A. Charles Emanuele, Director
714-635-6585

California College of Communication
700 W Hamilton Ave Ste 210, Campbell CA 95008
408-374-5066

CALIFORNIA COLLEGE SAN DIEGO
2820 Camino Del Rio S # 300, San Diego CA 92108
Denise Galvez-Kirk, Director of Admissions
619-295-5785 Fax: 619-295-5762
Website: www.cc-sd.edu
E-mail: dgalves-kirk@cc-sd.edu

California Cosmetology College
955 Monroe St, Santa Clara CA 95050-4808
408-247-2200

California Culinary Academy
625 Polk St, San Francisco CA 94102
Barry Gordon, President
Nancy Seyfert, V.P. of Admissions
800-BAY-CHEF

California Design College
3440 Wilshire Blvd Ste 700
Los Angeles CA 90010-2102
Sabrina Kay, Executive Director
213-251-3636

California Hair Design Academy
8011 University Ave #A-2, La Mesa CA 91941
619-461-8600

California Healing Arts College
12217 Santa Monica Blvd, Los Angeles CA 90025
310-826-7622

CALIFORNIA INSTITUTE OF LOCKSMITHING
(Friedman College)
14719 1/2 Oxnard St, Van Nuys CA 91411-3122
J. Corey Friedman, President
877-LOCK-411 or 818-994-7425 Fax: 818-994-7427
Website: www.lock411.com
E-mail: friedmancollege@usa.com

California Learning Center
6812 Pacific Blvd, Huntington Park CA 90255-4197
323-581-0600

California Maritime Academy
PO Box 1392, Vallejo CA 94590-0644
707-654-1000

California School of Culinary Arts
521 E Green St, Pasadena CA 91101
Sandra Stevens, Director of Admissions
626-403-8490

Career Academy of Beauty
663 N Euclid St, Anaheim CA 92801
Dayna Pattison, Director
714-776-8400

Career Academy of Beauty
12471 Valley View St, Garden Grove CA 92845
714-897-3010

CAREER COLLEGE OF AMERICA
5612 Imperial Hwy, South Gate CA 90280
Avi Nemazee, Director of Operations
562-861-8702 Fax: 562-869-7013
Website: www.careercolleges.org
E-mail: avin@careercolleges.org

CEI
20700 Avalon Blvd Ste 210, Carson CA 90746-3734
310-532-6328

CEI
4900 Rivergrade Rd Ste E210
Irwindale CA 91706-1438
626-338-8886

CEI
25361 Commercentre Dr #100
Lake Forest CA 92630-8858
949-472-4192

CEI
3699 Wilshire Blvd Fl 4, Los Angeles CA 90010-2719
213-351-2000

CEI
980 Corporate Center Dr, Pomona CA 91768-2643
909-865-9008

CEI
1635 Spruce St, Riverside CA 92507-2494
951-276-1704

CEI
1050 Los Vallecitos Blvd
San Marcos CA 92069-1469
760-471-9300

CENTER OF EMPLOYMENT TRAINING
701 Vine St, San Jose CA 95110
Luis Aguilar, Contact
408-287-7924 Fax: 408-534-5238
Website: www.cetweb.org
E-mail: luis@cet2000.org

Central California School of Continuing Education
271 Ott St Ste 23, Corona CA 92882-7104
951-549-0693

Central California School of Continuing Education
3195 McMillan Ave Ste F
San Luis Obispo CA 93401-6739
805-543-9123

Chase College
3580 Wilshire Blvd 4th Flr, Los Angeles CA 90010
213-365-1999

Children's Hospital of Los Angeles
4650 W Sunset Blvd, Los Angeles CA 90027-6062
323-669-2301

City College of San Francisco
50 Phelan Ave, San Francisco CA 94112-1821
415-239-3000

City of Hope Medical Center
1500 Duarte Rd, Duarte CA 91010-3000
626-359-8111

Clarita Career College
27125 Sierra Hwy Ste 329
Canyon Country CA 91351-5488
Julie Ha, Director
661-252-1864

Coachella Valley Technical Skills Center
35325 Date Palm Dr Ste 101
Cathedral City CA 92234
760-328-5554

COLBURN SCHOOL
200 S Grand Ave, Los Angeles CA 90012-3007
Kathleen Tesar, Director of Admissions and Student Affairs
213-621-2200 Fax: 213-621-2110
Website: www.colburnschool.edu
E-mail: ktesar@colburnschool.edu

Colleen O'Hara's Beauty Academy
102 N Glassell St, Orange CA 92866
714-633-5950

Colleen O'Hara's Beauty Academy
109 W 4th St Floor 2, Santa Ana CA 92701
714-568-5399

College of Automotive Management
3000 W MacArthur Blvd Fl 3
Santa Ana CA 92704-6916
Eric Andersen, President
714-755-6894

COLLEGE OF CAREER TRAINING
7220 Fair Oaks Blvd Ste A, Carmichael CA 95608
916-481-9001 Fax: 916-481-9002
E-mail: sima84344@aol.com

COLLEGE OF INFORMATION TECHNOLOGY
2701 E Chapman Ave Ste 101, Fullerton CA 92831
Mohammad Qamaruddin, Director
714-879-5100 Fax: 714-879-2272
Website: www.collegeofit.com
E-mail: mqamar@collegeofit.com

Columbia College Hollywood
18618 Oxnard St, Tarzana CA 91356-1411
Carmen Munoz & Nicole Anderson, Admissions Coordinators
800-785-0585 Fax: 818-345-9053
Website: www.columbiacollege.edu
E-mail: admissions@columbiacollege.edu

Community Business College
3800 McHenry Ave, Modesto CA 95356
209-529-3648

Computer Tutor Business & Technical Institute
4306 Sisk Rd, Modesto CA 95356
209-545-5200

CONCORDE CAREER INSTITUTE
4393 Imperial Ave Suite 100, San Diego CA 92113
Denise Galvez, Director of Admissions
619-688-0800 Fax: 619-220-4177
Website: www.concorde.edu
E-mail: dgalvez@concorde.edu

Court Reporting Institute
8665 Gibbs Dr Ste 204, San Diego CA 92123-1754
619-294-5700

CULINARY INSTITUTE OF AMERICA AT GREYSTONE
2555 Main St, Saint Helena CA 94574-9504
800-888-7850 Fax: 845-451-1078
Website: www.ciaprochef.com
E-mail: ciaprochef@culinary.edu

Cynthia's Beauty Academy
4130 Gage Ave, Bell CA 90201
323-560-2207

Daniel Freeman Memorial Hospital
333 N Prairie Ave, Inglewood CA 90301-4514
310-674-7050

Desert Career College
490 S Farrell Dr Ste C200
Palm Springs CA 92262-7992
Ron Oden, Executive Director
760-864-1356

Design School of Cosemetology
715 24th St Ste E, El Paso de Robles CA 93446
805-237-8575

East Los Angeles Occupational Center
2100 Marengo St, Los Angeles CA 90033-1321
323-223-1283

Edgewood College of California
4930 Earle Ave, Rosemead CA 91770
626-291-5000

Elegance International
1622 Highland Ave, Hollywood CA 90028
323-871-8318

Elegante Beauty College
200 N San Fernando Blvd, Burbank CA 91502
818-954-8894

Elegante Beauty College
1600 S Azusa Ave Unit 244
City of Industry CA 91748-1674
626-965-2532

Elegante Beauty College
23635 El Toro Rd Ste K, Lake Forest CA 92630
949-586-4900

Elegante Beauty College
24741 Alessandro Blvd
Moreno Valley CA 92553-3941
Rita Calafatello, Office Manager
951-247-2047

Elite Progressive School of Cosmetology
5522 Garfield Ave, Sacramento CA 95841
916-338-1885

Emergency Medical Sciences Training Institute
343 E Main St Ste 906, Stockton CA 95202
209-461-5550

Empire College School of Business & Law
3035 Cleveland Ave, Santa Rosa CA 95403
Roy O. Hurd, President
707-546-4000

Escuelas Leicester
1940 S Figueroa St, Los Angeles CA 90007
213-746-7666

Estes Institute Cosmetology Arts & Sciences
324 E Main St, Visalia CA 93291
559-733-3617

Executive 2000
2041 Business Center Dr Ste 107, Irvine CA 92612
949-794-9090

FASHION CAREERS COLLEGE
1923 Morena Blvd, San Diego CA 92110-3555
Tanya McAnear, Director of Admissions
619-275-4700 Fax: 619-275-0635
Website: www.fashioncareerscollege.com
E-mail: info@fashioncareerscollege.com
    Established 1979. Private. Coed. Accreditation: ACICS. Tuition: $15,900 per year for Fashion Business & Technology. $15,900 per year for Fashion Design & Technology program, day or evening program (tuition includes required books & certain supplies). Registration Fee: $25. Enrollment: 120 full-time. Faculty: 15. Student-faculty ratio: 10:1. Degree & Certificate programs. Library: 850 volumes. Theoretical and practical training

gives students a relevant and comprehensive education in Fashion Business & Technology and Fashion Design & Technology. Placement assistance and internships available.

Federico College of Hairstyling
1515 Sports Dr, Sacramento CA 95834-1905
916-929-4242

· FIDM/The Fashion Institute of Design & Merchandising
17590 Gillette Ave, Irvine CA 92614
Director of Admissions
949-851-6200 or 888-974-3436 Fax: 949-851-6808
Website: www.fidm.edu
E-mail: info@fidm.edu
See listing under "Community and Junior Colleges"

· FIDM/The Fashion Institute of Design & Merchandising
919 S Grand Ave, Los Angeles CA 90015-1421
Director of Admissions
213-624-1201 or 800-624-1200 Fax: 213-624-4799
Website: www.fidm.edu
E-mail: info@fidm.edu
See listing under "Community and Junior Colleges"

· FIDM/The Fashion Institute of Design & Merchandising
1010 2nd Ave, San Diego CA 92101-4903
Director of Admissions
619-235-2049 or 800-243-3436 Fax: 619-232-4322
Website: www.fidm.edu
E-mail: info@fidm.com
See listing under "Community and Junior Colleges"

· FIDM/The Fashion Institute of Design & Merchandising
55 Stockton St, San Francisco CA 94108-5829
Director of Admissions
415-675-5200 or 800-422-3436 Fax: 415-296-7299
Website: www.fidm.edu
E-mail: info@fidm.com
See listing under "Community and Junior Colleges"

Four-D College
1020 E Washington St, Colton CA 92324-4187
909-783-9331

Franklin Career College
1274 Slater Cir, Ontario CA 91761-1522
909-937-9007

Frederick and Charles Beauty College
831 F St, Eureka CA 95501
707-443-2733

Galen College Medical & Dental Assts.
1325 N Wishon Ave, Fresno CA 93728-2348
559-264-9726

Galen College of Medical & Dental Assistants
1604 Ford Ave Ste 10, Modesto CA 95350-4655
209-527-5084

Gates College
4450 182nd St, Redondo Beach CA 90278
310-542-4411

Gemological Institute of America
600 Corporate Pointe Ste 100, Culver City CA 90230
310-670-2100

GEMOLOGICAL INSTITUTE OF AMERICA
The Robert Mouawad Campus
5345 Armada Dr, Carlsbad CA 92008-4602
Jason Drake, Admissions Manager
800-421-7250 ext. 4001 or 760-603-4001
Fax: 760-603-4003
Website: www.gia.edu
E-mail: eduinfo@gia.edu
    Established 1931. Nonprofit. Private. Coed. Accreditation: ACCSCT. Diplomas: Graduate Gemologist, Graduate Jeweler, Graduate Jeweler Gemologist, Jewelry Business Management, Applied Jewelry Arts. Programs and courses range from five days to 17 months. Financial aid. Classes begin year round.
    See listing under "Home Study and Correspondence"

Glendale Career College
1015 Grandview Ave, Glendale CA 91201
818-243-1131

· Golf Academy of San Diego
1910 Shadowridge Dr Ste 111, Vista CA 92083-9007
Dona K. Powell, President
800-342-7342

Haciende LaPuente Valley Adult Education
14101 Nelson Ave, La Puente CA 91746
626-934-2800

Hair Masters University of Beauty
208 W Highland Ave, San Bernardino CA 92405
909-882-2987

· Heald College, Concord
5130 Commercial Cir, Concord CA 94520
925-827-1300

· Heald College, Fresno
255 W Bullard Ave, Fresno CA 93704-1706
Chris Souza, Director of Admissions
559-438-4222

· Heald College, Hayward
25500 Industrial Blvd., Hayward CA 94545-1552
Ken Gardner, Director of Admissions
510-783-2100

HEALD COLLEGE RANCHO CORDOVA
2910 Prospect Park Dr
Rancho Cordova CA 95670-6005
Donald Ed Hardenbrook, Regional Director
916-638-1616 Fax: 916-638-1580
Website: www.heald.edu
E-mail: ed_hardenbrook@heald.edu

HEALD COLLEGE, ROSEVILLE
7 Sierra Gate Plz, Roseville CA 95678-6602
Cindi Stevens, Director of Admissions
916-789-8600 Fax: 916-789-8616
Website: www.heald.edu
E-mail: cindi_stevens@heald.edu

· Heald College, Salinas
1450 N Main St, Salinas CA 93906-5100
831-443-1700

· Heald College, San Francisco
350 Mission St, San Francisco CA 94105-2206
415-808-3000

Heald College, Stockton
1605 E March Ln, Stockton CA 95210-6632
209-477-1114

Health Staff Training Institute
1505 E 17th St Ste 122, Santa Ana CA 92705-8520
714-543-9828

· High-Tech Institute
9738 Lincoln Village Dr, Sacramento CA 95827-3302
866-502-2627

Hilltop Beauty School
6317 Mission St, Daly City CA 94014
650-756-2720

HOSPITALITY MANAGEMENT TRAINING INSTITUTE, INC.
A Division of American College of California
760 Market St Ste 1009
San Francisco CA 94102-2305
Sherris Goodwin, Director
415-677-9717 Fax: 415-677-9810
Website: www.acca.edu
E-mail: info@acca.edu

Huntington College of Dental Technology
14848 Monroe St, Midway City CA 92655
Patrick Vu, President

Huntington Memorial Hospital
100 W California Blvd, Pasadena CA 91105-3097
626-397-5000

ICDC College
6330 Pacific Blvd Ste 200, Huntington Park CA 90255
323-655-9100

ICDC College
5422 W Sunset Blvd, Los Angeles CA 90027-5614
323-468-0404

ICDC College
14434 Sherman Way, Van Nuys CA 91405
818-787-0007

Image School of Cosmetology
13070 Palm Dr, Desert Hot Springs CA 92240
760-251-5373

Image School of Cosmetology
2627 W Florida Ave, Hemet CA 92545
951-766-5759

· Inland Technical Skills Center
101 E Redlands Blvd Ste 247, Redlands CA 92373

Institute for Business and Technology
2400 Walsh Ave, Santa Clara CA 95051-1303
408-727-1060

Institute of Computer Technology
3200 Wilshire Blvd, Los Angeles CA 90010-1308
Director of Admissions
213-381-3333

Institute of Network Technology
2525 Cherry Ave Ste 110, Signal Hill CA 90755-2054
562-424-9200

Institute of Technology - Clovis Campus
564 W Herndon Ave, Clovis CA 93612
Joseph Haydock, Director of Admissions
559-297-4500

Institute of Technology - Modesto Campus
5737 Stoddard Rd, Modesto CA 95356
Richard Dyer, Director of Admissions
209-545-3100

Institute of Technology - Sacramento
3695 Bleckely St, Mather CA 95655
916-363-4300

Institute of Technology - Sacramento Campus
3695 Bleckely St, Mather CA 95655
Gib Linzman, Director of Admissions
916-363-4300

Integrated Digital Technologies
2555 E Colorado Blvd Ste 200, Pasadena CA 91107
Juan Rodriguez, CEO
626-585-6300

Intercoast Colleges
401 S Glenoaks Blvd Ste 211, Burbank CA 91502
818-500-8400

INTERNATIONAL CHRISTIAN EDUCATION COLLEGE
Early Childhood Education
3807 Wilshire Blvd Ste 730
Los Angeles CA 90010-3108
Dr. Charles Chong Y. Lee, President
213-368-0316 Fax: 213-368-0318
E-mail: icec@sbcglobal.net

International Professional School of Body Work
1366 Hornblend St, San Diego CA 92109-4227
858-272-4142

INTERNATIONAL SCHOOL OF COSMETOLOGY
13613 Hawthorne Blvd, Hawthorne CA 90250-5809
Mary Costello, President
310-973-7774 Fax: 310-355-1158
Website: www.isoc.edu
E-mail: isoc@socal.rr.com

· ITT Technical Institute
16916 S Harlan Rd, Lathrop CA 95330-8737
Donald Fraser, Director
209-858-0077

· ITT Technical Institute
12669 Encinitas Ave, Sylmar CA 91342-3664
Kelly Christensen, Director of Admissions
818-364-5151 Fax: 818-364-5150
Website: www.itt-tech.edu
E-mail: kchristensen@itt-tech.edu

· ITT Technical Institute
20050 S Vermont Ave, Torrance CA 90502
310-380-1555

· ITT Technical Institute
1530 W Cameron Ave, West Covina CA 91790-2711
626-960-8681

Ivory Dental Technology College
16600 Harbor Blvd Ste I
Fountain Valley CA 92708-1363
714-899-8382

James Albert School of Cosmetology
281 E 17th St, Costa Mesa CA 92627
949-642-0606

Je Boutique College of Beauty
1073 E Main St, El Cajon CA 92021
619-442-3407

John Wesley International Barber and Beauty College
717 Pine Ave, Long Beach CA 90813
562-435-7060

Kaiser Permanente Medical Center
901 Nevin Ave, Richmond CA 94801
510-307-2412

Kensington College
2428 N Grand Ave Ste D, Santa Ana CA 92705
714-542-8086

Kim Anh Academy of Beauty
12141 Brookhurst St Ste 101
Garden Grove CA 92840-2816
714-896-9847

Lake College
2655 Bechelli Ln, Redding CA 96002
530-224-7227

Lake Forest Beauty College
23600 Rockfield Blvd Ste 3C, Lake Forest CA 92630
949-951-8883

Lancaster Beauty School
44646 10th St W, Lancaster CA 93534
661-948-1672

Learning Tree University
20916 Knapp St, Chatsworth CA 91311-5906
818-882-5685

Liberty Training Institute
2706 Wilshire Blvd, Los Angeles CA 90057
213-383-9545

Lola Beauty College
11883 Valley View St, Garden Grove CA 92845
714-894-3366

Los Amigos Research & Education Institute
PO Box 3500, Downey CA 90242
562-401-8111

· Los Angeles County College of Nursing and Allied Health
1200 N State St, Los Angeles CA 90033-1029
323-226-4911

Los Angeles County Harbor-UCLA Medical Center
1000 W Carson St, Torrance CA 90502-2004
310-533-2101

Lyle's Bakersfield College of Beauty
2935 F St, Bakersfield CA 93301
661-327-9784

Lyle's College of Beauty
6735 N 1st St Ste 112, Fresno CA 93710
559-431-6060

Lyle's Fresno College of Beauty
3125 W Shaw Ave, Fresno CA 93711
559-222-6060

Lytle's Redwood Empire Beauty College
186 Wikiup Dr, Santa Rosa CA 95403
707-545-8490

Madera Beauty College
325 N Gateway Dr, Madera CA 93637
559-673-9201

MAKE-UP DESIGNORY
129 S San Fernando Blvd, Burbank CA 91502
Tate Holland, School Director
818-729-9420 Fax: 818-729-9971
Website: www.mud.edu
E-mail: tate@mud.edu

Manchester Beauty College
3756 N Blackstone Ave, Fresno CA 93726
559-224-4242

· Maric College
1360 S Anaheim Blvd, Anaheim CA 92805-6205
714-758-1500

· Maric College
1914 Wible Rd, Bakersfield CA 93304
866-574-5550

· Maric College
6180 Laurel Canyon Blvd Ste 101
North Hollywood CA 91606-3249
818-763-2563

MARIC COLLEGE
14355 Roscoe Blvd, Panorama City CA 91402-4222
Kristine Schepps, Contact
818-672-8907 Fax: 818-672-8919
Website: www.mariccollege.edu
E-mail: kschepps@mariccollege.edu

MARIC COLLEGE
5172 Kiernan Ct, Salida CA 95358-9083
Curtis Anderson, Director of Admissions
209-543-7000 Fax: 209-543-1755
Website: www.mariccollege.edu
E-mail: canderson@mariccollege.edu

Maric College
9055 Balboa Ave, San Diego CA 92123
Geraldine Rorrison, Director of Admissions
858-279-4500 Fax: 858-279-4885
Website: www.mariccollege.edu
E-mail: grorrison@mariccollege.edu

MARIC COLLEGE
722 W March Ln, Stockton CA 95207-6216
John Bermudez, Director of Admissions
209-462-8777 Fax: 209-462-3219
Website: www.mariccollege.edu
E-mail: jbermudez@mariccollege.edu

Maric College
2022 University Dr, Vista CA 92083-7736
Jann Underwood, Executive Director
760-630-1555

Maric College East County
6160 Mission Gorge Rd #108
San Diego CA 92120-3425
619-282-9000

Maric College - Sacramento Campus
4330 Watt Ave Ste 400, Sacramento CA 95821-5512
Charlie Reese, Director of Admissions
916-649-8168

Marinello School of Beauty
240 S Market St, Inglewood CA 90301
310-674-8100

Marinello School of Beauty
716 S Broadway 2nd Floor, Los Angeles CA 90014
213-627-5561

Marinello School of Beauty
6111 Wilshire Blvd, Los Angeles CA 90048
323-938-2005

Marinello School of Beauty
2700 Colorado Blvd Ste 266, Los Angeles CA 90041
323-254-6226

Marinello School of Beauty
6219 Laurel Canyon Blvd, North Hollywood CA 91606
818-980-1300

Marinello School of Beauty
940 N Mountain Ave, Ontario CA 91762
909-984-5884

Marinello School of Beauty
18442 Sherman Way, Reseda CA 91335
818-881-2521

Marinello School of Beauty
721 W 2nd St Ste E, San Bernardino CA 92410
909-884-8747

Marinello School of Beauty
1226 University Ave, San Diego CA 92103
619-298-7187

Marinello School of Beauty
118 Plaza Dr, West Covina CA 91790
626-962-1021

Marinello School of Beauty
6538 Greenleaf Ave, Whittier CA 90601
562-698-0068

Martinez Adult Education
600 F St, Martinez CA 94553
925-228-3276

MCed Career College
School of Business & Technology
2002 N Gateway Blvd, Fresno CA 93727-1620
559-456-0623

Medical Institute
5170 Santa Monica Blvd #300
Los Angeles CA 90029
323-663-2700

Mills - Peninsula Health Services
1783 El Camino Real, Burlingame CA 94010-3282
650-696-5678

Miss Marty's School of Beauty & Hairstyling
1087 Mission St, San Francisco CA 94103
415-227-4240

Modern Beauty Academy
699 S C St, Oxnard CA 93030
805-483-4994

Modern Technology School
16560 Harbor Blvd, Fountain Valley CA 92708-1362
714-418-9100

Moler Barber College
3815 Telegraph Ave, Oakland CA 94609-2419
510-652-4177

Montebello Beauty College
2201 W Whittier Blvd, Montebello CA 90640
323-727-7851

Moro Beauty College
124 N Brand Blvd, Glendale CA 91203
818-246-7376

Mount Sierra College
101 E Huntington Dr, Monrovia CA 91016
Vaughn Hartunian, President & CEO
626-873-2100

MTI BUSINESS COLLEGE OF STOCKTON
6006 N El Dorado St, Stockton CA 95207-4349
Steven Brenner, Director
888-302-2009 Fax: 209-474-8705
Website: www.mtistockton.com
E-mail: mtistockton@comcast.net
    Established 1968. Accredited: ACCSCT. Family
owned/operated 36 years.

MUELLER COLLEGE OF HOLISTIC MASSAGE
4607 Park Blvd, San Diego CA 92116
David Taylor, Registrar
619-291-9811 Fax: 619-543-1113
Website: www.muellercollege.com
E-mail: david@mueller.edu

MUSICIANS INSTITUTE
1655 N McCadden Pl, Hollywood CA 90028
Steve Lunn, Director of Admissions
323-462-1384 Fax: 323-462-6978
Website: www.mi.edu
E-mail: admissions@mi.edu

My-Le's Beauty College
5972 Stockton Blvd, Sacramento CA 95824
916-422-0223

National Career Education
6060 Sunrise Vista Dr #3000
Citrus Heights CA 95610

National Institute of Technology
2161 Technology Pl, Long Beach CA 90810-3800
Therese El Khoury, Director of Admissions
562-437-0501

National Polytechnic College
2465 W Whittier Blvd # 201, Montebello CA 90640
323-728-9636

National Polytechnic College of Engineering &
Oceaneering
272 S Fries Ave, Wilmington CA 90744-6399
Jim Sparks, Director of Admissions
800-432-DIVE (3483)

Newberry School of Beauty
16860 Devonshire St, Granada Hills CA 91344
Deanna L. Jacobsen, CEO
818-366-3211

Newbridge College
1840 E 17th St Ste 140, Santa Ana CA 92705-8605
714-550-8000

Newbridge College - Monterey Park
583 Monterey Pass Rd
Monterey Park CA 91754-2416
626-576-2444

Newbridge College - Stanton
12362 Beach Blvd Ste 100, Stanton CA 90680
714-901-9447

Newschool of Architecture and Design
1249 F St, San Diego CA 92101-6634
Gilbert D. Cooke, AIA, Dean
Barbara Wingate, Director of Admissions
619-235-4100 ext. 123

NICK HARRIS DETECTIVE ACADEMY
(Friedman College)
14721 Oxnard St, Van Nuys CA 91411
J. Corey Friedman, President
800-245-9007 or 818-343-6611 Fax: 818-994-7427
Website: www.nickharrisdetectives.com
E-mail: nickharrisdetectives@usa.com

North Adrian's Beauty College
124 Floyd Ave, Modesto CA 95350
209-526-2040

North American Computer Consultants
570 W Stocker St Unit 311, Glendale CA 91202-2237
818-500-7227

Northwest College of Medical & Dental Assistants
221 N Brand Blvd, Glendale CA 91203-2609
818-242-0205

Northwest College of Medical & Dental Assistants
530 E Union St, Pasadena CA 91101-1744
626-796-5815

Northwest College of Medical & Dental Assistants
134 W Holt Ave, Pomona CA 91768-3101
909-623-1552

Northwest College of Medical & Dental Assistants
2121 W Garvey Ave N, West Covina CA 91790-2051
626-960-5046

Northwestern College
2317 Gold Meadow Way, Gold River CA 95670
866-649-2400

NTMA Training Center of Southern California
14926 Bloomfield Ave, Norwalk CA 90650-6099
Gina Marinello, Campus Director
562-404-4295

NTMA Training Center of Southern California
1717 S Grove Ave, Ontario CA 91761
909-947-9363

NTMA Training Center of Southern California
13230 Firestone Blvd Ste A
Santa Fe Springs CA 90670
562-404-4295

Occupational Training Services
8799 Balboa Ave Ste 100, San Diego CA 92123
858-560-0411

Oceanside College of Beauty
1575 S Coast Hwy, Oceanside CA 92054
760-757-6161

Oxman College
375 3rd Ave, San Francisco CA 94118
415-751-6461

Pacific College
3160 Redhill Ave, Costa Mesa CA 92626
714-662-4402

Palladium Technical Academy
10507 Valley Blvd Ste 806, El Monte CA 91731
626-444-0880

Palomar Institute of Cosmetology
355 Via Vera Cruz Ste 3, San Marcos CA 92078
760-744-7900

Paramount School of Beauty
8527 Alondra Blvd Ste 129, Paramount CA 90723
714-998-7461

Paris Beauty College
1950 Market St, Concord CA 94520
925-685-7600

Paul Mitchell The School
1534 Adams Ave, Costa Mesa CA 92626
714-546-8786

Pima Medical Institute - Chula Vista
780 Bay Blvd Ste 101, Chula Vista CA 91910
619-425-3200

Platt College
7755 Center Ave Ste 400
Huntington Beach CA 92647-9114
714-373-3240

PLATT COLLEGE
6250 El Cajon Blvd, San Diego CA 92115-3916
Carly Westerfield, Admissions Coordinator
619-265-0107 or 866-752-8826 Fax: 619-308-0570
Website: www.platt.edu
E-mail: info@platt.edu
    Established 1980. Private. Coed. Accreditation:
ACCSCT. Tuition: Approximately $16,000. Fees: $100.
Enrollment: 350. Faculty: 25. Student-faculty ratio: 14:1.
Library: 1,700 volumes + online. 2 buildings. Design
school offering BS, AAS and diploma programs. "Hands
on" programs in Graphic Design, Multimedia Design,
Animation, Digital Video Production, and Web page design. Full range of General Education courses required to
complete AAS + BS degrees. Classes offered morning,
afternoon and evening. Job placement and financial aid
services available. Visit www.platt.edu.

Platt College Los Angeles
1000 S Fremont Ave Building A-9 West
Alhambra CA 91803
Pamela Ramirez, Director of Admissions
626-300-5444

Platt College Ontario
3700 Inland Empire Blvd #400
Ontario CA 91764-4907
Joe Blackman, Campus President
909-941-9410

Porterville Development Center
PO Box 2000, Porterville CA 93258
559-782-2753

Poway Academy of Hair Design
13266 Poway Rd, Poway CA 92064
858-748-1490

Precision Technical Institute
9342 Tech Center Suite 600
Sacramento CA 95826-2558
916-366-3431

Premiere Career College
12901 Ramona Blvd Ste D, Irwindale CA 91706-3746
626-814-2080

Professional Career Institute
17215 Studebaker Rd Ste 310, Cerritos CA 90703
562-916-5055

PROFESSIONAL GOLFERS CAREER COLLEGE
26109 Ynez Rd, Temecula CA 92591-6013
Dr. Tim Somerville, President
800-877-4380 Fax: 951-719-1643
Website: www.golfcollege.edu
E-mail: admin@golfcollege.edu

Professional Institute of Beauty
10801 Valley Mall, El Monte CA 91731
626-443-9401

Public Health Foundation Enterprises
12781 Schabarum Ave, Irwindale CA 91706
626-856-6376

Richard's Beauty College
200 N Euclid Ave, Ontario CA 91762-3513
909-988-7584

Rosemead Beauty School
8531 Valley Blvd, Rosemead CA 91770
626-286-2147

ROYALE COLLEGE OF BEAUTY
27485 Commerce Center Dr
Temecula CA 92590-2525
951-676-0833 Fax: 951-676-0653
Website: www.beautyschools.com
E-mail: roylcoll@aol.com

Sage College
12125 Day St Ste L, Moreno Valley CA 92557-6720
951-781-2727

St. Francis Career College
3630 E Imperial Hwy, Lynwood CA 90262
310-603-1830

St. John's Regional Medical Center
1600 N Rose Ave, Oxnard CA 93030-3723
805-988-2500

SAN FERNANDO BEAUTY ACADEMY
8700 Van Nuys Blvd, Panorama City CA 91402
Jorge Luna, Admissions
818-894-9550 Fax: 818-894-9551
Website: www.sfba.edu
E-mail: contact@sfba.edu

San Joaquin General Hospital
PO Box 1020, Stockton CA 95201-3120
209-468-6600

San Joaquin Valley College
201 New Stine Rd, Bakersfield CA 93309-2659
Jaime Delgado, Enrollment Services Director
661-834-1026 Fax: 559-651-4864
Website: www.sjvc.edu
E-mail: jaime.delgado@sjvc.edu

San Joaquin Valley College
295 E Sierra Ave, Fresno CA 93710-3616
Nora Twarynski, Enrollment Services Director
559-448-8282 Fax: 559-651-4864
Website: www.sjvc.edu
E-mail: nora.twarynski@sjvc.edu

San Joaquin Valley College
1700 McHenry Village Way Suite 6
Modesto CA 95350
Joseph Holt, Director of Admissions
209-527-7582 Fax: 559-651-4864
Website: www.sjvc.edu
E-mail: josephh@sjvc.edu

San Joaquin Valley College
11050 Olson Dr, Rancho Cordova CA 95670
Joseph Holt, Director of Admissions
559-651-2500 Fax: 559-651-4864
Website: www.sjvc.edu
E-mail: joseph.holt@sjvc.edu

San Joaquin Valley College
10641 Church St, Rancho Cucamonga CA 91730
Ramon Abreu, Enrollment Services Director
909-948-7582 Fax: 559-651-4864
Website: www.sjvc.edu
E-mail: ramon.abreu@sjvc.edu

San Joaquin Valley College
8400 W Mineral King Ave, Visalia CA 93291-9283
Susie Topjian, Enrollment Services Director
559-651-2500 Fax: 559-651-4864
Website: www.sjvc.edu
E-mail: susiet@sjvc.edu

San Joaquin Valley College
Fresno Aviation Campus
4985 E Anderson Ave, Fresno CA 93727-1501
Joseph Holt, Director of Admissions
559-453-0123 Fax: 559-651-4864
Website: www.sjvc.edu
E-mail: josephh@sjvc.edu

Santa Barbara Business College
211 S Real Rd, Bakersfield CA 93309-2139
661-835-1100

Santa Barbara Business College
5266 Hollister Ave, Santa Barbara CA 93111-4026
805-967-9677

Santa Barbara Business College
303 Plaza Dr, Santa Maria CA 93454-6943
805-922-8256

Santa Barbara Cottage & General Hospital
PO Box 689, Santa Barbara CA 93102-0689
805-569-7290

Scripps Memorial Hospital
9888 Genesee Ave, La Jolla CA 92037-1200
858-457-6100

Sequoia Institute
200 Whitney Pl, Fremont CA 94539-7655
510-490-6900

Sierra Academy of Aeronautics
Oakland International Airport, Oakland CA 94614
Joe File, Director of Admissions
800-243-6300

Sierra College of Beauty
1340 W 18th St, Merced CA 95340
209-723-2989

Sierra Valley Business College
4747 N 1st St # D, Fresno CA 93726-0563
559-222-0947

Simi Valley Adult Education
3192 E Los Angeles Ave, Simi Valley CA 93065-3940
805-579-6200

Sonoma College
1304 Southpoint Blvd Ste 280, Petaluma CA 94954
800-437-9474

Sonoma College - San Francisco
301 Howard St Ste 510, San Francisco CA 94105
888-649-7801

South Coast College
2011 W Chapman Ave, Orange CA 92868-2616
Kevin J. Magner, Director of Admissions
800-33-STENO

Southern California Institute of Technology
1900 W Crescent Ave, Anaheim CA 92801-3801
714-520-5552

Southern California Regional Occupational Center
2300 Crenshaw Blvd, Torrance CA 90501
310-224-4220

SUTECH School of Voc/Tech Training
PO Box 23098, Los Angeles CA 90023-0098
Oswaldo Forero, Director
323-262-3210

Thanh Le College School of Cosmetology
12875 Chapman Ave, Garden Grove CA 92840-4100
714-971-5844

TRAVEL UNIVERSITY INTERNATIONAL
3870 Murphy Canyon Rd Suite #310
San Diego CA 92123-4403
Nancy Chappie, President
858-292-9755 Fax: 858-292-8008
Website: www.traveluniversity.edu
E-mail: travel@traveluniversity.edu

Truck Driving Academy
5711 Florin Perkins Rd, Sacramento CA 95828-1034
916-381-2285

Tulare Beauty College
1400 W Inyo Ave, Tulare CA 93274
559-688-2901

United Beauty College
9324 Garvey Ave Ste D, South El Monte CA 91733
626-433-1371

United Truck & Car Driving School
2425 Camino Del Rio S, San Diego CA 92108
619-296-2020

Universal College of Beauty
718 W Compton Blvd, Compton CA 90220
310-635-6969

Universal College of Beauty
8619 S Vermont Ave, Los Angeles CA 90044
323-750-5750

Universal College of Beauty
3419 W 43rd Pl, Los Angeles CA 90008
323-298-0045

Universal Technical Institute
9494 Haven Ave
Rancho Cucamonga CA 91730-5843
909-484-1929

Universal Technical Institute
4400 E Commerce Way, Sacramento CA 95834

Universal Training Center
3875 Atlantic Ave, Highland CA 92346
909-864-1918

VICTOR VALLEY BEAUTY COLLEGE
16515 Mojave Dr, Victorville CA 92395-3821
Irma Silva, Director
760-245-2522 Fax: 760-245-5681
Website: www.victorvalleybeautycollege.com

Virginia School Center
1033 S Broadway, Los Angeles CA 90015
Sara Cristi, Director
213-747-8292

West Coast Ultrasound Institute
291 S La Cienega Blvd # 500, Beverly Hills CA 90211
310-289-5123

Westech College
3491 Concours, Ontario CA 91764-4988
909-980-4474

Western Career College
2157 Country Hills Dr, Antioch CA 94509-7435
Tim Gienapp, Director of Admissions
925-522-7777
Website: www.westerncollege.edu

Western Career College
7301 Greenback Ln Bldg A, Citrus Heights CA 95621
Jim Murphy, Contact
916-722-8200 Fax: 916-722-6883
Website: www.westerncollege.edu

Western Career College
6001 Shellmound St 2nd Floor, Emeryville CA 94608
Elvie Engstrom, Director of Admissions
510-601-0133 Fax: 510-601-0793
Website: www.westerncollege.edu

Western Career College
380 Civic Dr Ste 300, Pleasant Hill CA 94523-1984
LaShawn Wells, Contact
925-609-6650 Fax: 926-609-6666
Website: www.westerncollege.edu

Western Career College
8909 Folsom Blvd, Sacramento CA 95826-3203
Sue Smith, Contact
916-361-1660 Fax: 916-361-6666
Website: www.westerncollege.edu

Western Career College
6201 San Ignacio Ave, San Jose CA 95119
Steve Ashab, Director of Admissions
408-360-0840 Fax: 408-360-0848
Website: www.westerncollege.edu

Western Career College
15555 E 14th St Ste 500, San Leandro CA 94578
Julie Elmquist, Contact
510-276-3888 Fax: 510-276-3653
Website: www.westerncollege.edu

Western Career College
1313 W Robinhood Dr Ste B, Stockton CA 95207
Dave Semrau, Contact
209-956-1240 Fax: 209-956-1244
Website: www.westerncollege.edu

Western College of Southern California
10900 183rd St Ste 290, Cerritos CA 90703-5347
Robert Cios, Executive Director
562-809-5100

WESTERN PACIFIC TRUCK SCHOOL
2316 Nickerson Dr, Modesto CA 95358-9483
Ruben Ramirez, Campus Manager
800-333-1233 Fax: 209-538-6773
Website: www.wptruckschool.com
E-mail: gnord@wptruckschool.net

WESTERN PACIFIC TRUCK SCHOOL
8720 Fruitridge Rd, Sacramento CA 95826-9740
Sean Day, Campus Manager
800-333-1233 Fax: 916-388-2183
Website: www.wptruckschool.com
E-mail: gnord@wptruckschool.net

WESTERN PACIFIC TRUCK SCHOOL
1002 N Broadway Ave, Stockton CA 95205-3928
Ray VerSteeg, Campus Manager
800-333-1233 Fax: 209-465-1723
Website: www.wptruckschool.com
E-mail: gnord@wptruckschool.net

Westwood College
1551 S Douglass Rd, Anaheim CA 92806
714-704-2727

Westwood College - Inland Empire
20 W 7th St, Upland CA 91786
909-931-7500

Westwood College of Aviation Technology
8911 Aviation Blvd, Inglewood CA 90301-2904
800-597-8690

Westwood College
South Bay Campus
19700 S Vermont Ave Ste 100
Torrance CA 90502-1148
310-965-0888

WYOTECH
980 Riverside Pkwy, West Sacramento CA 95605
Steve Coffee, Director of Admissions
916-376-8888 Fax: 916-617-2069
Website: www.wyotech.com
E-mail: scoffee@wyotech.edu

COLORADO

Academy of Beauty Culture
2992 North Ave, Grand Junction CO 81504
970-245-5570

Americana Beauty College II
3650 Austin Bluff Pky #174
Colorado Springs CO 80918
719-598-4188

Art Institute of Colorado
1200 Lincoln St, Denver CO 80203-2172
David Zorn, President
Brian A. Parker, Director of Admissions
800-275-2420 Fax: 303-860-8520
Website: www.artinstitutes.edu
E-mail: baparker@aii.edu

Artistic Beauty College
1225 Wadsworth Blvd, Lakewood CO 80214-4207
303-238-7501

Artistic Beauty College
3811 E 120th Ave, Thornton CO 80233-1659
303-451-5808

Artistic Beauty College
3049 W 74th Ave Ste A, Westminster CO 80030
303-428-5100

Bel-Rea Institute of Animal Technology
1681 S Dayton St, Denver CO 80247-3048
Paulette Kaufman, Administrator
303-751-8700 Fax: 303-751-9969
Website: www.bel-rea.com
E-mail: admissions@bel-rea.com

BOULDER COLLEGE OF MASSAGE THERAPY
6255 Longbow Dr, Boulder CO 80301-3295
Admissions Department
303-530-2100 Fax: 303-530-2204
Website: www.bcmt.org
E-mail: admissions@bcmt.org

Cambridge College
350 Blackhawk St, Aurora CO 80011-8754
Sandi Parks, Campus President
303-338-9700

Centura-St. Anthony Hospital
4231 W 16th Ave, Denver CO 80204-1335
303-629-4350

Cheeks International Academy of Beauty Culture
4025 S Mason St #5, Fort Collins CO 80525
970-226-1416

Cheeks International Academy of Beauty Culture
2547 11th Ave Ste B, Greeley CO 80631
970-352-4500

CollegeAmerica - Colorado
Main Campus
1385 S Colorado Blvd 5th Floor
Denver CO 80222-3304
Barbara Thomas, President
303-691-9756

THE COLORADO CENTER FOR MEDICAL LABORATORY SCIENCE
1719 E 19th Ave, Denver CO 80218
Karen Myers, Director
303-839-6485 Fax: 303-869-1720
Website: www.medlabed.org
E-mail: medlabed@coloradohealth.org

Colorado Institute of Taxidermy
708 Royal Gorge Blvd, Canon City CO 81212
719-276-2883

Colorado School of Healing Arts
7655 W Mississippi #100, Lakewood CO 80226-4332
Victoria Steere, Director
303-986-2320

Colorado School of Trades
1575 Hoyt St, Lakewood CO 80215-2996
Patti O'Shea, Contact
303-233-4697

Cortiva Institute - Colorado
390 Interlocken Crescent Ste 450
Broomfield CO 80021-8039
303-996-5050

Denver Academy of Court Reporting
9051 Harlan St Ste 20, Westminster CO 80031-2943
Charles W. Jarstfer, President
800-574-2087

Denver Automotive & Diesel College
PO Box 9366, Denver CO 80209
Joseph R. Chalupa, College Director
800-347-3232

Denver Career College
500 E 84th Ave Suite W200
Thornton CO 80229-5316
JoAnn Navarro, Director of Admissions
800-848-0550 Fax: 303-295-0102
Website: www.denvercareercollege.com
E-mail: admissions-045@denvercareercollege.com

Denver Health Medical Center
660 Bannock St, Denver CO 80204
303-436-6611

Durango Air Service
1340 Airport Rd, Durango CO 81303-6791
Don Watkins, Contact
970-247-5535

Emily Griffith Opportunity School
1250 Welton St, Denver CO 80204-2124
720-423-4700

Glenwood Beauty Academy
51241 Highway 6 Ste 1, Glenwood Springs CO 81601
970-945-0485

Hair Dynamics Education Center
6464 S College Ave, Fort Collins CO 80525
970-223-9943

HERITAGE COLLEGE
12 Lakeside Ln, Denver CO 80212-7413
Jennifer Sprague, Director
303-477-7240 Fax: 303-477-7276
Website: www.heritage-education.com
E-mail: info@heritage-education.com
Accredited Member School: ACCSCT. Providing quality education in Esthetician, Massage Therapy, Personal Trainer, Pharmacy Technician and X-Ray Medical Technician. Financial aid available to those who qualify.

Institute of Business & Medical Careers
1609 Oakridge Dr Ste 102
Fort Collins CO 80525-5563
Steve Steele, Director of Operations
970-223-2669

IntelliTec College
2315 E Pikes Peak Ave
Colorado Springs CO 80909-6096
Michael Castellano, Contact
719-632-7626 Fax: 719-632-7451
Website: www.intelliteccollege.edu
E-mail: admcs@intelliteccollege.edu

IntelliTec College
772 Horizon Dr, Grand Junction CO 81506-3907
Rich Counts, Contact
970-245-8101 Fax: 970-243-8074
Website: www.intelliteccollege.edu
E-mail: admgj@intelliteccollege.edu

IntelliTec College
3673 Parker Blvd Ste 250, Pueblo CO 81008
Crystal Barajas, Director of Admissions
719-542-3181 Fax: 719-242-0068
Website: www.intelliteccollege.edu
E-mail: admpbl@intelliteccollege.edu

IntelliTec Medical Institute
2345 N Academy Blvd
Colorado Springs CO 80909-1570
Kiersten Murdoch, Contact
719-596-7400 Fax: 719-596-2464
Website: www.IntelliTecCollege.edu
E-mail: kmurdoch@intelliteccollege.edu

International Beauty Academy
1360 N Academy Blvd, Colorado Springs CO 80909
719-598-4188

JOHNSON & WALES UNIVERSITY
7150 Montview Blvd, Denver CO 80220-1866
Kim Ostrowski, Director of Admissions
303-256-9300 Fax: 303-256-9333
Website: www.jwu.edu
E-mail: admissions@jwu.edu

Memorial Hospital
1400 E Boulder St, Colorado Springs CO 80909-5599
719-365-6819

Misers Inspection and Training
1825 W Baker Ave, Englewood CO 80110
Eric Peters, Training Coordinator
303-922-8821

Misers Inspection and Training Inc
2401 S Raritan St, Englewood CO 80110
Eric Peters, Training Coordinator
303-761-8860

MJM Institute of Cosmetology
1048 Independent Ave #A113
Grand Junction CO 81505
970-241-9060

Ohio Center for Broadcasting - Colorado
1310 Wadsworth Blvd Ste 100, Lakewood CO 80214
303-937-7070

Parks College
14280 E Jewell Ave, Aurora CO 80012-5692
Julie Rosenthal, Director of Admissions
303-367-2757 Fax: 303-745-6245
Website: www.cci.edu

Parks College
9065 Grant St, Denver CO 80229-4339
303-457-2757

Parkview Medical Center
400 W 16th St, Pueblo CO 81003-2745
719-584-4573

Penrose-St. Francis Health System
2215 N Cascade Ave
Colorado Springs CO 80907-6736
719-776-5111

PHLEBOTOMY LEARNING CENTER
1780 S Bellaire St Ste 780, Denver CO 80222
Amira Stillwater, Contact
303-584-0575 Fax: 303-756-0066
Website: www.plcofdenver.com
E-mail: astillwater@plcofdenver.com

Pickens Technical Center
500 Airport Blvd, Aurora CO 80011-9307
303-344-4910

Pima Medical Institute
1701 W 72nd Ave Ste 130, Denver CO 80221-2727
Sue Anderson, Director
303-426-1800

Platt College
3100 S Parker Rd, Aurora CO 80014-3141
Jerald B. Sirbu, President
303-369-5151

Remington College
6050 Erin Park Dr #250
Colorado Springs CO 80918-3401
719-532-1234

Remington College - Denver Campus
11011 W 6th Ave, Lakewood CO 80215-5501
Robert Dillman, Director of Recruitment
303-445-0500

ROLF INSTITUTE OF STRUCTURAL INTEGRATION
5055 Chaparral Ct Ste 103, Boulder CO 80301
Jim Jones, Director of Education
303-449-5903 Fax: 303-449-5978
Website: www.rolf.org
E-mail: jjones@rolf.org

San Juan Basin Technical College
PO Box 970, Cortez CO 81321-0970
Shannon South, Director of Student Services
970-565-8457 Fax: 970-565-8450
Website: www.sjbtc.edu
E-mail: ssouth@sjbtc.edu

TONY@GUY Hairdressing Academy
332 Main St, Colorado Springs CO 80911
719-390-9898

Westwood College - Denver North
7350 Broadway, Denver CO 80221-3610
303-426-7000

Westwood College - Denver South
Health Careers Division
3150 S Sheridan Blvd, Denver CO 80227
303-934-2790

Westwood College of Aviation Technology
10851 W 120th Ave, Broomfield CO 80021-3465
Mike Foss, President / Director
Laura Goldhammer, Regional Director of Admissions
800-888-3995

XENON INTERNATIONAL SCHOOL OF HAIR DESIGN III
2231 S Peoria St, Aurora CO 80014
Connie Voss, Director
303-752-1560 Fax: 303-752-0218
Website: www.xenonintl.com
E-mail: cvoss@xenonintl.com

CONNECTICUT

ALLEN INSTITUTE CENTER FOR INNOVATIVE LEARNING
PO Box 100, Hebron CT 06248
866-666-6910
Website: www.alleninstitute.info
E-mail: info@alleninstitute.info

AMERICAN ACADEMY OF COSMETOLOGY
109 South St, Danbury CT 06810-8039
Melissa Diacri, Director of Admissions
203-744-0900 Fax: 203-790-7382
Website: www.americanacademyofcosmetology.com
E-mail: mdiacri@hotmail.com

BARAN INSTITUTE OF TECHNOLOGY
97 Newberry Rd, East Windsor CT 06088
800-688-3353
Website: www.baraninstitute.com
E-mail: info@baraninstitute.com

Baran Institute of Technology
225 Ella Grasso Tpke, Windsor Locks CT 06096
860-688-3353

Branford Hall Career Institute
1 Summit Pl, Branford CT 06405
800-959-7599

Branford Hall Career Institute
35 N Main St, Southington CT 06489-2577
860-276-0600

Branford Hall Career Institute
995 Day Hill Rd, Windsor CT 06095-1722
860-683-4900

Bridgeport Hospital
267 Grant St, Bridgeport CT 06610-2870
203-384-3464

Bridgeport Hospital School of Nursing
200 Mill Hill Ave, Bridgeport CT 06610
Yolanda Torres, Contact
203-384-3022

Brio Academy of Cosmetology
1231 E Main St, Meriden CT 06450
203-237-6683

Butler Business School
2710 North Ave, Bridgeport CT 06604-2383
203-333-3601

Connecticut Center for Massage Therapy
1154 Poquonnock Rd, Groton CT 06340
Susan Scoboria, Contact
877-295-2268 Fax: 860-446-9410
Website: www.ccmt.com
E-mail: info@ccmt.com

Connecticut Center for Massage Therapy
75 Kitts Ln, Newington CT 06111-3954
877-282-2268 Fax: 860-667-4566
Website: www.ccmt.com
E-mail: info@ccmt.com

Connecticut Center for Massage Therapy
25 Sylvan Rd S, Westport CT 06880-4619
Jocelyn Keith, Contact
877-292-2268 Fax: 203-221-0144
Website: www.ccmt.com
E-mail: info@ccmt.com

Connecticut Childrens Medical Center
282 Washington St, Hartford CT 06106
Rich Janis, Team Leader
860-545-8514

CONNECTICUT CULINARY INSTITUTE
85 Sigourney St, Hartford CT 06105
Tina Merullo, Director of Admissions
860-677-7869 or 800-76-CHEFS (762-4337)
Fax: 860-676-0679
Website: www.ctculinary.edu
E-mail: tmerullo@ctculinary.edu
Established 1987. Private. Coed. Accreditation: ACCSCT. Tuition: $15,000 - $24,000. Fees vary. Federal Financial Aid, private payment plans, and scholarships available (for qualified applicants).
Enrollment: 500 full time, 150 part time. Faculty: 30 (includes full & part time). Student-Professional Chef/Instructor ratio 15:1, allowing for extensive individualized attention. Classes are predominantly "hands-on".
Two programs offered year round. Advanced Culinary Arts Program: 60 weeks/full-time days and 90 weeks/part-time evenings; 60.5 credit hours including 660-hour paid externship. Pastry & Baking Program: 35 weeks/full-time days and 47 weeks/part-time evenings; 36 credit hours.
Advanced Culinary Arts Program includes International Cuisines and American Regional Cuisine, Foundation Skills, Business and Nutrition, Pastry & Baking, Special Diets, Garde Manger, Facilities and Career Planning.
Admissions requirements: A minimum of High School Diploma or GED, plus $100 registration/application fee. No prior culinary experience required.
Student housing available. Located in the "Hub" of scenic and Historic New England; close to NYC, Boston, Cape Cod, Newport, New Hampshire & Vermont. Enjoy the "bonus" pleasures of: hiking, biking, camping, boating, fishing, skiing, and sports, historical tours, and some of the best restaurants in the country!
Outstanding employment placement (state and national): restaurants, hotels, country clubs, private clubs, private estates, caterers, pastry shops, bed & breakfasts, country inns, resorts, cruise ships, casinos, schools and universities, retirement communities, industrial cafeterias, hospital dining services. Some students start their own businesses.

Connecticut Culinary Institute
1760 Mapleton Ave, Suffield CT 06078-1433
860-668-3518

Connecticut Institute of Hair Design
1000 Main St, East Hartford CT 06108-2220
Ms. Peters, President
860-528-5032

Connecticut Institute of Hair Design
1681 Meriden Rd, Wolcott CT 06716
203-879-4247

Connecticut School of Electronics
221 W Main St, Branford CT 06405-4022
203-315-1060

Danbury Hospital
24 Hospital Ave, Danbury CT 06810-6099
203-797-7210

Eli Whitney Regional Vocational Technical School
71 Jones Rd, Hamden CT 06514
203-397-4037

Fox Institute of Business
99 South St, West Hartford CT 06110-1922
860-947-2299

Gal Mar Academy of Hairdressing, Skin & Nails, LLC
97 Washington Ave Ste 8, North Haven CT 06473
203-281-4477

Gibbs College
10 Norden Pl, Norwalk CT 06855-1436
Eddie Prosper, Director of Admissions
800-845-5333

Goodwin Institute
1315 Dixwell Ave, Hamden CT 06514-4125
800-889-3282

Goodwin Institute Business School
101 Pierpont Rd, Waterbury CT 06705-3823
203-756-5500

Hartford Conservatory
834 Asylum Ave, Hartford CT 06105-2807
Lynn Tracey, Director of Admissions
860-246-2588

Hartford Hospital
PO Box 5037, Hartford CT 06102-5037
860-545-2100

Industrial Management and Training
233 Mill St, Waterbury CT 06706-1211
203-753-7910

INTERNATIONAL COLLEGE OF HOSPITALITY MANAGEMENT
1760 Mapleton Ave, Suffield CT 06078
Tina Merullo, Admissions
860-668-3515 Fax: 860-668-7369
Website: www.ichm.edu
E-mail: admissions@ichm.edu

Leon Institute of Hair Design
111 Wall St, Bridgeport CT 06604
203-333-1465

New England Technical Institute
109 Sanford St, Hamden CT 06514
203-287-7300

New England Technical Institute
200 John Downey Dr, New Britain CT 06051-2904
Robert Dockendorff, Director of Education
860-225-8641

New England Technical Institute
8 Progress Dr, Shelton CT 06484
203-929-0592

New England Tractor Trailer Training
PO Box 326, Somers CT 06071-0326
860-749-0711

Norwalk Hospital
24 Stevens St, Norwalk CT 06850-3852
203-852-2211

Porter and Chester Institute
138 Weymouth Rd, Enfield CT 06082
860-741-2561

Porter and Chester Institute
670 Lordship Blvd, Stratford CT 06615-7158
Mark Breslin, Director of Admissions
203-375-4463 Fax: 203-375-5285
Website: www.porterchester.com

Porter and Chester Institute
320 Sylvan Lake Rd, Watertown CT 06779-1459
Jack Burke, Executive Director
860-274-9294

Porter and Chester Institute
125 Silas Deane Hwy, Wethersfield CT 06109-1255
860-529-2519

Prince Regional Vocational Technical School
500 Brookfield St, Hartford CT 06106
860-246-8594

Ridley-Lowell Business & Technical Inst
PO Box 652, New London CT 06320-0652
Kimberly L. Mayer, Director
860-443-7441

Sawyer School
1125 Dixwell Ave, Hamden CT 06514-4735
203-865-2900

Sawyer School
141 Washington St, Hartford CT 06106
860-568-1554

STAMFORD HOSPITAL
PO Box 9317, Stamford CT 06904-9317
Dorothy Saia, MA, RT, Program Director
203-276-7877 Fax: 203-276-7352
Website: www.stamhealth.org
E-mail: dsaia@stamhealth.org

STONE ACADEMY
1315 Dixwell Ave, Hamden CT 06514-4155
Jeanna LaBella, Director of Admissions
203-288-7474 Fax: 203-288-8869
Website: stoneacademy.com
E-mail: jlabella.stone@snet.net

Windham Community Memorial Hospital
112 Mansfield Ave, Willimantic CT 06226-2041
860-456-6800

Windham Regional Vocational Technical School
210 Birch St, Willimantic CT 06226-2108
860-456-3789

DELAWARE

Beebe Medical Center School of Nursing
424 Savannah Rd, Lewes DE 19958-1462
Connie E. Bushey, Director
302-645-3251

DAWN TRAINING CENTRE
3700 Lancaster Pike, Wilmington DE 19805-1511
Hollis C. Anglin, President
302-633-9075 Fax: 302-633-9077
Website: www.dawntrainingcentre.edu
E-mail: hcanglin@dawntrainingcentre.edu

Deep Muscle Therapy School
5341 Limestone Rd, Wilmington DE 19808
Patricia Draper, LMT, Director
302-234-8525

Harrison Career Institute
631 W Newport Pike, Wilmington DE 19804-3259
302-999-7827

National Massage Therapy Institute
Route 113 Box 144D, Dagsboro DE 19939
800-264-9835

Schilling-Douglas School of Hair Design
70 Amstel Ave, Newark DE 19711
302-737-5100

Star Technical Institute
655 S Bay Rd Ste 562, Dover DE 19901
302-736-6111

DISTRICT OF COLUMBIA

Bennett Beauty Institute
700 Monroe St NE, Washington DC 20017
202-526-1400

Dudley Beauty College
2031 Rhode Island Ave NE, Washington DC 20018
202-269-3666

Levine School of Music
2801 Upton St NW, Washington DC 20008-3829
202-686-8000

NATIONAL CONSERVATORY OF DRAMATIC ARTS
1556 Wisconsin Ave NW
Washington DC 20007-2758
Nan Kyle Ficca, Vice President
202-333-2202 Fax: 202-333-1753
Website: theconservatory.org
E-mail: ncdadrama@aol.com

Walter Reed Medical Center
6825 16th St NW, Washington DC 20307-0002
202-782-6104

Washington Conservatory of Music
PO Box 5758, Washington DC 20016-1358
202-320-2770

Washington Hospital Center
110 Irving St NW, Washington DC 20010-2975
202-877-6101

FLORIDA

Academy for Practical Nursing & Health Occupations
5154 Okeechobee Blvd #201
West Palm Beach FL 33417
561-683-1400

Academy of Healing Arts Massage & Facial Skin Care
3141 S Military Trl, Lake Worth FL 33463
561-965-4686

Advanced/Basic Hair Design Training Center
85 Richland Ave, Merritt Island FL 32953
321-452-8490

Advance Science Institute
3750 W 12th Ave, Hialeah FL 33012
305-827-5452

Americare School of Nursing
7275 Estapona Circle, Fern Park FL 32730
407-673-7406

Ari Ben Aviator
3800 Saint Lucie Blvd, Fort Pierce FL 34946-9022
772-466-4822

Art Institute of Fort Lauderdale
1799 SE 17th St, Fort Lauderdale FL 33316-3013
Eileen Northrop, V.P./Director of Admissions
800-275-7603 Fax: 954-728-8637
Website: www.aifl.edu

ASM BEAUTY WORLD ACADEMY
6423 Stirling Rd, Davie FL 33314
Leticia Milazzo, Assistant School Director
877-678-9532 or 954-321-8411 Fax: 954-321-8683
E-mail: asm60@bellsouth.net

ATI Career Training Center
2890 W Cypress Creek Rd, Fort Lauderdale FL 33309
954-973-4760

ATI Career Training Center
7265 NW 25th St, Miami FL 33122
305-573-1600

ATI CAREER TRAINING CENTER
3501 Powerline Rd, Oakland Park FL 33309-5916
Michael Ackerman, Executive Director
954-563-5899 Fax: 954-568-0874
Website: www.aticareertraining.com
E-mail: pcampbell@atienterprises.edu

Atlantic Technical Center
4700 Coconut Creek Pkwy, Margate FL 33063-3999
954-977-2000

Audio Recording Technology Institute
4525 Vineland Rd Ste 201B, Orlando FL 32811
407-423-2784

Baptist/St. Vincent's Health System
1800 Barrs St, Jacksonville FL 32204-4799
904-387-7300

Baptist Medical Centers
800 Prudential Dr, Jacksonville FL 32207-8203
904-393-2001

BAYFRONT MEDICAL CENTER
701 6th St S, Saint Petersburg FL 33701-4891
June Schurig, Education Coordinator
727-893-6604 Fax: 727-893-6977
Website: www.bayfront.org
E-mail: june.schurig@bayfront.org

Beauty and Barber Academy
5505 Manatee Ave W, Bradenton FL 34209
941-761-4400

Beauty Schools of America
1060 W 49th St, Hialeah FL 33012
305-362-9003

Beauty Schools of America
1176 SW 67th Ave, Miami FL 33144

BENE'S INTERNATIONAL SCHOOL OF BEAUTY, INC.
7127 US Highway 19
New Port Richey FL 34652-1638
Patricia Martin, Contact
727-848-8415 Fax: 727-846-0269
Website: www.isbschool.com
E-mail: isbschool@aol.com

Bethesda Memorial Hospital
2815 S Seacrest Blvd
Boynton Beach FL 33435-7995
561-737-7733

BRADFORD-UNION AREA VO-TECH CENTER
609 N Orange St, Starke FL 32091
904-966-6760 Fax: 904-966-6786
Website: www.daccess.net/votech1

Cape Coral Beauty School
1214 SE 47th St, Cape Coral FL 33904
239-549-1819

Career Training Institute
3318 Edgewater Dr, Orlando FL 32804
407-884-1816

Central Florida Blood Bank
8669 Commodity Cir, Orlando FL 32819-9054
407-849-6100

Central Florida College
1573 W Fairbanks Ave #100
Winter Park FL 32789-4679
407-843-9828

Central Florida Institute
30522 US Highway 19 N, Palm Harbor FL 34684
727-786-4707

CHAPMAN SCHOOL OF SEAMANSHIP
4343 SE Saint Lucie Blvd, Stuart FL 34997-6898
Bruce Robertson, Registrar
800-225-2841 Fax: 772-283-2019
Website: www.chapman.org
E-mail: info@chapman.org

Charlotte Technical Center
18300 Toledo Blade Blvd
Port Charlotte FL 33948-3399
Carolyn Gorton, Assistant Principal
941-255-7500

CITY COLLEGE
853 Semoran Blvd Ste 200, Casselberry FL 32707
Dr. Diane Owens, Executive Director
407-831-9816 Fax: 407-831-1147
Website: www.citycollegeorlando.edu
E-mail: dowens@citycollege.edu

COLLEGE OF BUSINESS & TECHNOLOGY
8991 SW 107th Ave #200, Miami FL 33176-1412
Luis Llerena, Executive Director
305-273-4499 Fax: 305-596-3835
Website: www.cbt.edu
E-mail: admissions@cbt.edu

Compu-Med Vocational Careers
2900 W 12th Ave Ste 3, Hialeah FL 33012-4861
305-888-9200

COMPU-MED VOCATIONAL CAREERS
9738 SW 24th St, Miami FL 33165-7513
Mayra Rodriguez, President
305-553-2898 Fax: 305-553-7423
Website: www.compumedschools.com
E-mail: compumed44@aol.com

Coral Ridge Nurse's Assistant Training School
2740 E Oakland Park Blvd
Fort Lauderdale FL 33306-1626
E. Mais, Director
954-561-2022

Core Institute
223 W Carolina St, Tallahassee FL 32301
866-830-0108

Darlyne McGee's Academy of Cosmetology
4711 Babcock St NE Ste 26, Palm Bay FL 32905
321-951-0595

Delta Connection Academy
2700 Flightline Ave, Sanford FL 32773-9683
Tracy Thomason, Director of Admissions
407-430-4112

D.G. Erwin Technical Center
2010 E Hillsborough Ave, Tampa FL 33610-8299
813-231-1800

Educating Hands School of Massage
120 SW 8th St, Miami FL 33130
305-285-6991

EDUTECH CENTERS
2262 S Falkenburg Rd, Riverview FL 33569
Nannette Worlinsky, Admissions Director
800-485-0717 Fax: 813-621-5150
Website: www.edutechctr.com
E-mail: nworlinsky@edutechctr.com

EDUTECH CENTERS INC.
410 Park Place Blvd, Clearwater FL 33759-3924
Nancy O'Donnell-Kenny, Executive Director
727-724-1037 Fax: 727-723-7630
Website: www.edutechctr.com
E-mail: director@edutechctr.com

The English Center
3501 SW 28th St, Miami FL 33133
305-445-7731

Euro Hair Design Institute
5995 University Blvd W #3
Jacksonville FL 32216-4933
904-731-4766

FAA Center for Management Development
4500 Palm Coast Pkwy SE
Palm Coast FL 32137-8011
386-446-7136

Fashion Focus Hair Academy
2184 Gulf Gate Dr, Sarasota FL 34231-4813
941-921-4877

First Coast Technical Institute
2980 Collins Ave, Saint Augustine FL 32084-1919
904-829-1010

FlightSafety International
PO Box 2708, Vero Beach FL 32961-2708
772-564-7600

Florida Barber Academy
3269 N Federal Hwy, Pompano Beach FL 33064
954-781-6066

Florida Blood Services
10100 Dr Mrtn Lthr King St
Saint Petersburg FL 33716
727-568-5433

Florida Career College
1321 SW 107th Ave Ste 201B, Miami FL 33174-2521
305-553-6065

FLORIDA CAREER COLLEGE
7891 Pines Blvd, Pembroke Pines FL 33024-6916
Michael Schwam, Executive Director
954-965-7272 Fax: 954-983-2707
Website: www.careercollege.edu
E-mail: mschwam@careercollege.edu

FLORIDA CAREER INSTITUTE
5925 Imperial Pkwy Ste 200, Mulberry FL 33860
863-646-1400
Website: www.floridacareerinstitute.com
E-mail: sethridge@edaff.com

Florida College of Natural Health
616 67th Street Circle East, Bradenton FL 34208
Wayne Dawson, Campus Director
941-954-8999

Florida College of Natural Health
2600 Lake Lucien Dr Suite 140, Maitland FL 32751
Steve Richards, Campus Director
800-393-7337

Florida College of Natural Health
7925 NW 12th St Ste 201, Miami FL 33126-1821
800-599-9599

Florida College of Natural Health
2001 W Sample Rd Ste 100
Pompano Beach FL 33064-1342
954-975-6400

Florida Education Institute
5818 SW 8th St, West Miami FL 33144
305-444-1515

FLORIDA INSTITUTE OF ANIMAL ARTS
3776 Howell Branch Rd, Winter Park FL 32792
407-657-8088 Fax: 407-359-8829
Website: www.fifi-inc.com
E-mail: info@fifi-inc.com

FLORIDA INSTITUTE OF ULTRASOUND, INC.
8800 University Pkwy Ste A4
Pensacola FL 32514-4913
Polly Christensen, Administrative Assistant
850-478-7300 Fax: 850-478-3727
Website: www.fiuonline.net
E-mail: fiupcola@aol.com

Florida Keys Community College
5901 College Rd, Key West FL 33040-4397
Cheryl Malsheimer, Director of Admissions & Records
305-296-9081 ext. 495

Florida Metropolitan University-Brandon
3924 Coconut Palm Dr, Tampa FL 33619-1354
Marty Baca, Director of Admissions
877-338-0068 (Toll Free)

FLORIDA METROPOLITAN UNIVERSITY
Pinellas Campus
2471 N McMullen Booth Rd
Clearwater FL 33759-1359
Sandra Williams, Director of Admissions
800-353-3687 or 727-725-2688 Fax: 727-725-3827
Website: www.fmu.edu
E-mail: sawilliams@cci.edu

Florida School of Massage
6421 SW 13th St, Gainesville FL 32608
352-378-7891

Florida Technical College
298 Havendale Blvd, Auburndale FL 33823-4508
Sandra Herndon, Dean
863-967-8822

Florida Technical College
8711 Lone Star Rd, Jacksonville FL 32211-5123
Joseph Rogalski, Director of Admissions
904-724-2229

Fort Pierce Beauty Academy
3028 S US 1, Fort Pierce FL 34982
772-464-4885

Full Sail - Real World Education
3300 University Blvd, Winter Park FL 32792
407-679-0100

George Stone Vocational Technical Center
2400 Longleaf Dr, Pensacola FL 32526-8901
850-941-6200

GEORGE T. BAKER AVIATION SCHOOL
3275 NW 42nd Ave, Miami FL 33142-5626
Sean E. Gallagan, Principal
305-871-3143 Fax: 305-871-5840
Website: www.bakeraviation.edu
E-mail: gtba@dadeschools.net

Golf Academy of the South
1200 E Altamonte Dr #1010
Altamonte Springs FL 32701-5050
Dona K. Powell, President
800-342-SDGA

Guadalupe Vocational Institute
2500 SW 107th Ave Ste 29, Miami FL 33165
305-559-7728

Gulf Coast College
3910 N US Highway 301 Ste 200
Tampa FL 33619-1283
813-620-1446

Halifax Medical Center
PO Box 2830, Daytona Beach FL 32120-2830
386-254-4065

HARRY WENDELSTEDT UMPIRE SCHOOL
88 S Saint Andrews Dr
Ormond Beach FL 32174-3857
Harry Wendelstedt, President
386-672-4879 Fax: 386-672-3212
Website: www.umpireschool.com
E-mail: umpsch@aol.com

Helicopter Adventures
365 Golden Knights Blvd, Titusville FL 32780
321-385-2919

HENRY W. BREWSTER TECHNICAL CENTER
2222 N Tampa St, Tampa FL 33602-2196
William Cade, Department Head/Counselor
813-276-5464 Fax: 813-276-5756
Website: www.brewstertech.org

HERITAGE INSTITUTE
6811 Palisades Park Ct, Fort Myers FL 33912
Eva Hutson, Director
239-936-5822 Fax: 239-225-9117
Website: www.heritage-education.com
E-mail: info@heritage-education.com
    Accredited Member School: ACCSCT. Providing quality education in Esthetician, Massage Therapy, Personal Trainer and X-Ray Medical Technician. Financial aid available to those who qualify.

HERITAGE INSTITUTE
4130 N Salisbury Rd Suite 1100
Jacksonville FL 32216
Sonnie Willingham, Director
904-332-0910 Fax: 904-332-0920
Website: www.heritage-education.com
E-mail: info@heritage-education.com
    Accredited Member School: ACCSCT. Providing quality education in Esthetician, Massage Therapy and X-Ray Medical Technician. Financial aid available to those who qualify.

HERZING COLLEGE
1595 S Semoran Blvd #1501
Winter Park FL 32792-5509
Kathy Nagle, Director of Admissions
407-478-0500 Fax: 407-478-0501
Website: www.herzing.edu
E-mail: info@orl.herzing.edu

High-Tech Institute
3710 Maguire Blvd, Orlando FL 32803-3013
407-893-7400 Fax: 407-895-1804
Website: www.hightechinstitute.edu

Hope Career Institute
3714 W Oakland Park Blvd
Lauderdale Lakes FL 33311
954-741-0088

Hope Career Institute
3101 Forest Hill Blvd, West Palm Beach FL 33406

Humanities Center Institute of Allied Health
4045 Park Blvd, Pinellas Park FL 33781-3634
727-541-5200

INTERNATIONAL ACADEMY
2550 S Ridgewood Ave
South Daytona FL 32119-3536
Tracy Franchina, Contact
386-767-4600 Fax: 386-271-0009
Website: www.intl-academy.com
E-mail: tracy@intl-academy.com

International Academy of Design & Technology
5104 Eisenhower Blvd, Tampa FL 33634-6313
Richard Costa, V.P. of Admissions and Marketing
813-880-8092 Fax: 813-881-0008
Website: www.academy.edu
E-mail: admissions@academy.edu

INTERNATIONAL ACADEMY OF DESIGN AND TECHNOLOGY
5959 Lake Ellenor Dr, Orlando FL 32809-4633
Dr. John Dietrich, VP of Admissions
877-753-0007 Fax: 407-251-0465
Website: www.iadt.edu
E-mail: info@iadt.edu

International Training Careers
7360 Coral Way, Miami FL 33155
305-263-9696

ITT Technical Institute
4809 Memorial Hwy, Tampa FL 33634-7515
813-885-2244

Jackson Memorial Medical Center
1611 NW 12th Ave, Miami FL 33136-1096
305-585-6754

Keiser Career College
6812 Forest Hill Blvd Ste D1, Greenacres FL 33413
561-433-2330

Keiser Career College
17395 NW 59th Ave, Hialeah FL 33015
305-820-5003

Keiser Career College
9468 S US 1, Port Saint Lucie FL 34652
727-398-9990

Key College
225 E Dania Beach Blvd #130
Dania Beach FL 33004
Ronald Dooley, President
954-923-4440 Fax: 954-923-9226
Website: www.keycollege.edu
E-mail: admissions@keycollege.edu

La Belle Beauty Academy
2960 SW 8th St, Miami FL 33135
305-649-4899

La Belle Beauty School
775 W 49th St Ste 5, Hialeah FL 33012
305-558-0562

Lakeland Regional Medical Center
1324 Lakeland Hills Blvd, Lakeland FL 33805-4500
863-687-1100

Lake Technical Center
2001 Kurt St, Eustis FL 32726-6164
352-589-2250

Le Cordon Bleu College of Culinary Arts
3221 Enterprise Way, Miramar FL 33025
954-438-8882

Lee County High Tech Center North
360 Santa Barbara Blvd N, Cape Coral FL 33993
239-574-4440

Lee County High Technical Center Central
3800 Michigan Ave, Fort Myers FL 33916-2299
239-334-4544

Lindsey Hopkins Technical Education Center
750 NW 20th St, Miami FL 33127-4618
305-324-6070

Lively Area Vocational Technical Center
3290 Capital Cir SW, Tallahassee FL 32310
850-488-2460

Lively Area Vocational Technical School
500 Appleyard Dr, Tallahassee FL 32304-2810
850-487-7555

Loraine's Academy
1012 58th St N, Saint Petersburg FL 33710-6391
Nancy Fordham, Administrator
727-347-4247

Lorenzo Walker Institute of Technology
614 S 5th St, Immokalee FL 34142

Lorenzo Walker Institute of Technology
3702 Estey Ave, Naples FL 34104-4405
239-430-6900

Manatee Technical Institute
5603 34th St W, Bradenton FL 34210-3509
Aurea Martinez, Director of Admissions
941-751-7900

Manatee Technical Institute East Campus
5520 Lakewood Ranch Blvd, Bradenton FL 34211
Carla Brokaw, Director of Admissions
941-752-8100

Manhattan Beauty School
2317 E Fletcher Ave, Tampa FL 33612-9405
813-264-3535

Manhattan Hairstyling Academy
1906 W Platt St, Tampa FL 33606-1709
813-837-2525

Manhattan Hairstyling Academy
3244 Lithia Pinecrest #103, Valrico FL 33594
813-655-4545

Margate School of Beauty
5281 Coconut Creek Pkwy, Margate FL 33063
954-972-9630

Marion County School of Radiologic Technology
1014 SW 7th Rd, Ocala FL 34474-3172
352-671-7200

Medical Career Center
19 W Garden St, Pensacola FL 32502-5678
850-436-8444

Medical Career Institute of South Florida
802 S Dixie Hwy, Lake Worth FL 33460
561-493-5022

Melbourne Beauty School
686 N Wickham Rd, Melbourne FL 32935
321-259-0001

Miami Ad School
955 Alton Rd, Miami Beach FL 33139-5203
Pippa Seichrist, President
305-538-3193

Miami Job Corps Center
3050 NW 183rd St, Miami Gardens FL 33056-3536
Janet Perales, Business Community Liaison
305-626-7800

Miami Lakes Educational Center
5780 NW 158th St, Hialeah FL 33014-6785
305-557-1100

MOTORCYCLE MECHANICS & MARINE MECHANICS INSTITUTES
Divisions of Clinton Technical Institute
9751 Delegates Dr, Orlando FL 32837-8351
Karen Duncan, Director of Admissions
800-528-7995 Fax: 407-240-1318
Website: www.uticorp.com
E-mail: mmi@crl.com
    Established 1971. Comprehensive technical training in all aspects of motorcycle and personal watercraft repair. Endorsed and equipped by Harley-Davidson, Honda, Mercury Marine, Yamaha, Suzuki, and Kawasaki. Classes are scheduled 5-hours per day in the morning, afternoon, or evening. Accredited member school: ACCSCT. A graduate placement department is available to assist students in finding full-time employment in the motorcycle industry. Manufacturers' assist with placement through promotional campaigns to their dealership network. Housing coordinator works with local apartment complexes to find housing while in school. Job advisor will assist with local employment while in school. Financial aid available to those who qualify. VA and Agency assistance where applicable.

Mt. Sinai Medical Center
4300 Alton Rd, Miami Beach FL 33140-2800
305-674-2222

NATIONAL AVIATION ACADEMY
6225 Ulmerton Rd, Clearwater FL 33760
Karen Acker, Registrar
727-531-2080 or 800-659-2080 Fax: 727-535-8727
Website: www.naa.edu
E-mail: admissions@naa.edu

NATIONAL HEAVY EQUIPMENT OPERATOR SCHOOL
PO Box 65789, Orange Park FL 32065
Larry Lark, Director
904-272-4000 Fax: 904-272-6702
Website: www.earthmoverschool.com
E-mail: heinforequests@nationaltrainingschools.com

National School of Technology
4410 W 16th Ave Ste 52, Hialeah FL 33012-7193
305-558-9500

National School of Technology
111 NW 183rd St Ste 200, Miami FL 33169-4538
305-949-9500

National School of Technology
9020 SW 137th Ave, Miami FL 33186
305-386-9900

New Concept Massage & Beauty School
2022 SW 1st St, Miami FL 33135
305-642-3020

New Professions Technical Institute
4000 W Flagler St, Coral Gables FL 33134
Maria Z. Faughaner, Contact
305-461-2223

Normandy Beauty School of Jacksonville
5373 Lenox Ave, Jacksonville FL 32205
904-786-6250

North Florida Cosmetology Institute
2424 Allen Rd, Tallahassee FL 32312
850-878-5269

North Florida Institute
560 Wells Rd, Orange Park FL 32073-2999
904-269-7086

North Technical Education Center
7071 Garden Rd, Riviera Beach FL 33404-4906
561-881-4600

Nouvelle Institute
500 W 49th St 2nd Floor, Hialeah FL 33012
305-557-3017

Nouvelle Institute
3271 NW 7th St Ste 106, Miami FL 33125
305-643-3360

Okaloosa Applied Technical Center
1976 Lewis Turner Blvd
Fort Walton Beach FL 32547-1217
850-833-3500

Orange Technical Education Center
Mid-Florida Technical Institute
2900 W Oak Ridge Rd, Orlando FL 32809-3701
407-855-5880

Orange Technical Education Center - Orlando Tech
301 W Amelia St, Orlando FL 32801-1122
407-246-7060

Orange Technical Education Centers-Winter Park Tech
901 W Webster Ave, Winter Park FL 32789-3049
Diane Culpepper, Director
407-622-2900

Orange Technical Education Center
Westside Technical Center
955 E Story Rd, Winter Garden FL 34787-3798
407-905-2001

PC Professor
7056 Beracasa Way, Boca Raton FL 33433
561-750-7879

PC PROFESSOR
600 N Hiatus Rd Ste 105, Pembroke Pines FL 33026
954-704-4444 Fax: 954-704-2222
Website: www.pcprofessor.edu
E-mail: train@pcprofessor.com

PC Professor
6080 Okeechobee Blvd, West Palm Beach FL 33417
561-684-3333

PELICAN FLIGHT TRAINING CENTER
1601 SW 75th Ave, Pembroke Pines FL 33023
Meg Fensome, Vice President
954-966-9750 Fax: 954-985-8271
Website: www.pelican-airways.com
E-mail: pelicanftc@pelican-airways.com

PHOENIX EAST AVIATION, INC.
Daytona Beach
561 Pearl Harbor Dr
Daytona Beach FL 32114
386-258-0703 or 800-868-4359, Fax: 386-258-8609
Website: pea.com
E-mail: andrem@pea.com
Spence Edwards, President
Accredited by ACCET
   Established 1972. Private. Coed. Accreditation: FAA approved, FAR Part 141 and FAR Part 61. Tuition, Room and board vary. Enrollment fee: $50. Enrollment: 250 full-time, 50 part-time. Faculty: 55 Flight Instructors. Student-faculty ratio: 5:1. Degrees: FAA Pilot Certificates - Private, Commercial, Instrument, Multi CFI, CFII, MEI, ATP, King Air. Phoenix East Aviation offers a wide variety of teaching programs from professional pilot courses to airline transport pilot. In addition, Phoenix East Aviation has developed advanced programs to enhance the training of the student and meet the needs of the industry. The reputation for quality is enhanced by its Florida location, which provides an excellent environment for the training of career pilots. Students are exposed to every facet of professional training with year-round flying conditions.

Pinellas Technical Education Center
6100 154th Ave N, Clearwater FL 33760-2140
727-538-7167

Pinellas Technical Education Center
901 34th St S, Saint Petersburg FL 33711-2209
727-893-2500

Port St. Lucie Beauty Academy
7644 S US 1, Port Saint Lucie FL 34983
772-340-3540

Poynter Institute for Media Studies
801 3rd St S, Saint Petersburg FL 33701-4920
727-821-9494

THE PRAXIS INSTITUTE
4162 W 12th Ave, Hialeah FL 33012
Rebecca Alfie, Executive Director
305-556-1424 Fax: 305-556-1422
Website: www.the-praxisinstitute.com
E-mail: ads2000@bellsouth.net

THE PRAXIS INSTITUTE
1850 SW 8th St, Miami FL 33135
Rebecca Alfie, Executive Director
305-642-4104 Fax: 305-642-6063
Website: www.the-praxisinstitute.com
E-mail: ads2000@bellsouth.net

PROFESSIONAL TRAINING CENTER
13926 SW 47th St, Miami FL 33175
Maria Rizo, Admission Director
305-220-4120 Fax: 305-220-2889
Website: www.ptcmatt.com
E-mail: emattia@ptcmatt.com

Radford M. Locklin Technical Center
5330 Berryhill Rd, Milton FL 32570-8015
850-983-5700

Radiation Therapy Services, Inc.
1419 SE 8th Terrace, Cape Coral FL 33990
Donald E. Moody, Program Director
239-772-3202

REMINGTON COLLEGE
7011 A C Skinner Pky Suite 140
Jacksonville FL 32256-6953
Bobby Johns, Director of Student Recruitment
904-296-3435 Fax: 904-296-9097
Website: www.remingtoncollege.edu
E-mail: bobby.johns@remingtoncollege.edu

Remington College
8550 Ulmerton Rd Ste 100, Largo FL 33771
727-532-1999

Remington College, Tampa Campus
2410 E Busch Blvd, Tampa FL 33612-8410
Director of Recruitment
813-935-5700 Fax: 813-935-7415
Website: www.remingtoncollege.edu

Ridge Vocational-Technical Center
7700 State Rd 544, Winter Haven FL 33881-9518
863-419-3060

Riverside Hairstyling Academy
3530 Beach Blvd, Jacksonville FL 32207
904-398-0502

Robert Morgan Educational Center
18180 SW 122nd Ave, Miami FL 33177-2407
Antonio Martinez, Principal
305-253-9920

Ross Medical Education Center
6847 Taft St, Hollywood FL 33024
954-963-0043

Ross Medical Education Center
2601 S Military Trl Ste 29
West Palm Beach FL 33415-7512
561-433-1288

Sanford-Brown Inst
10255 Fortune Pkwy Ste 501
Jacksonville FL 32256-3520
904-363-6221

SANFORD BROWN INSTITUTE
4780 N State Road 7 Suite 100
Lauderdale Lakes FL 33319-5860
Todd Oxendine, Director of Admissions
954-308-7400 Fax: 954-733-8994
Website: www.sbftlaud.com
E-mail: toxendine@sbftlaud.com

SANFORD BROWN INSTITUTE
5701 E Hillsborough Ave #1417, Tampa FL 33610
Patricia Meredith, President
813-621-0072 Fax: 813-626-0392
Website: www.sbtampa.com

Sarasota County Technical Institute
4748 Beneva Rd, Sarasota FL 34233-1798
Wm. A. Storms Jr., Director
941-924-1365 ext. 325

Sarasota School of Massage Therapy
1932 Ringling Blvd, Sarasota FL 34236-5919
941-957-0577

The School of Health Careers
3190 N State Road 7, Lauderdale Lakes FL 33319
954-777-0083

Shands Jacksonville Medical Center
655 W 8th St, Jacksonville FL 32209-6511
904-244-0411

Sheridan Vocational-Technical Center
5400 Sheridan St, Hollywood FL 33021-3399
Rosa Lee, Guidance Director
754-321-5400

Southeastern School of Neuromuscular and Massage Therapy
9424 Baymeadows Rd Suite 200
Jacksonville FL 32256
904-448-9499

South Florida Institute of Technology
2141 SW 1st St Ste 104, Miami FL 33135
305-649-2050

Space Coast Health Institute
1070 S Wickham Rd, West Melbourne FL 32904
321-729-9000

Star Academy for Pet Stylists
2201 SE Indian St Unit C6, Stuart FL 34997
Curtis, Chief Administrative Officer
772-221-9330

Stenotype Institute Court Reporting School
3986 Boulevard Center Dr Bldg. 1200 #200
Jacksonville FL 32207-2819
904-246-7466

Suncoast II - The Tampa Bay School of Health
2005 Pan Am Cir Ste 100, Tampa FL 33607-2380
813-287-1099

SUNSTATE ACADEMY OF HAIR DESIGN
18453 US Highway 19 N, Clearwater FL 33764-2702
Linda Kennedy, Campus Director
727-538-3827 Fax: 727-539-6118
Website: www.sunstate.edu
E-mail: lkennedy@sunstate.edu

SUNSTATE ACADEMY OF HAIR DESIGN
2418 Colonial Blvd, Fort Myers FL 33907-1415
Debbie Rodriguez, Campus Director
239-278-1311 Fax: 239-278-1432
Website: www.sunstate.edu
E-mail: drodriguez@sunstate.edu

SUNSTATE ACADEMY OF HAIR DESIGN
4424 Bee Ridge Rd, Sarasota FL 34233-2502
Kelly King, Interim Campus Director
941-377-4880 Fax: 941-378-2842
Website: www.sunstate.edu
E-mail: kking@sunstate.edu

Suwannee-Hamilton Technical Center
415 Pinewood Dr SW, Live Oak FL 32064-4099
Dianne Westcott, Principal
386-364-2750

Tallahassee Memorial Hospital
1300 Miccosukee Rd, Tallahassee FL 32308-5037
850-681-5385

Tampa General Hospital
School of Medical Technology
PO Box 1289, Tampa FL 33601-1289
Laura Ferguson, Education Coordinator
813-844-7985

Taylor Technical Institute
3233 Highway 19 S, Perry FL 32347
850-838-2545

Technical Career Institute
7757 W Flagler St Ste 23, Miami FL 33144
305-863-1818

Technical Education Center - Osceola
501 Simpson Rd, Kissimmee FL 34744-4459
407-344-5080

Tom P. Haney Technical Center
3016 Highway 77, Panama City FL 32405-5004
850-747-5500

Traviss Technical Center
3225 Winter Lake Rd, Lakeland FL 33803-9709
863-499-2700

TULSA WELDING SCHOOL
3500 Southside Blvd, Jacksonville FL 32216-4634
Roger Hess, President
877-935-3529 Fax: 904-646-9956
Website: www.weldingschool.com
E-mail: tws@ionet.net

Washington Holmes Technical Center
757 Hoyt St, Chipley FL 32428-1618
850-638-1180

William T. McFatter Technical Center
6500 Nova Dr, Davie FL 33317-7405
954-370-8324

Withlacoochee Technical Institute
1201 W Main St, Inverness FL 34450-4696
352-726-2430

Youth Co-op Training Institute
12051 W Okeechobee Rd
Hialeah Gardens FL 33018
305-819-8855

GEORGIA

Albany Technical College
1704 S Slappey Blvd, Albany GA 31701
229-430-3500

Albany Technical College
40 Harold Regan Blvd, Blakely GA 39823
229-724-2100

Altamaha Technical College
1777 W Cherry St, Jesup GA 31545-0612
Karla Eubanks, Associate VP of Student Services
912-427-5800

AMERICAN PROFESSIONAL INSTITUTE
1990 Riverside Dr, Macon GA 31201-1370
Richard M. Covington, Jr., School Director
478-746-3243 Fax: 478-746-1255
Website: www.americanprofessionalinstitute.com
E-mail: rcovington@api.edu

Appalachian Technical College
100 Campus Dr, Jasper GA 30143
706-253-4500

Arnold/Padrick's University of Cosmetology
4971 Courtney Dr, Forest Park GA 30297
404-361-5641

Atlanta Job Corps Center
239 W Lake Ave NW, Atlanta GA 30314-1894
404-794-9512

Atlanta Medical Center
303 Parkway Dr NE, Atlanta GA 30312
404-265-4203

ATLANTA SCHOOL OF MASSAGE
2 Dunwoody Park, Atlanta GA 30338-6704
Admissions Department
770-454-7167 ext. 120 Fax: 770-454-7367
Website: www.atlantaschoolofmassage.com
E-mail: admissions@atlantaschoolofmassage.com

Atlanta Technical College
1560 Metropolitan Pkwy SW, Atlanta GA 30310-4499
404-756-3700

AVIATION INSTITUTE OF MAINTENANCE
500 Briscoe Blvd, Lawrenceville GA 30045-6707
Gene Love, School Director
770-377-5600 Fax: 770-377-5609
Website: www.aviationmaintenance.edu
E-mail: directorama@tidetech.com

Beauty College of America
1171 Main St, Forest Park GA 30297
404-361-4098

BROWN COLLEGE OF COURT REPORTING & MEDICAL TRANSCRIPTION
1740 Peachtree St NW, Atlanta GA 30309-2335
Lynette Eggers, President
404-876-1227 Fax: 404-876-4415
Website: browncollege.com
E-mail: lynette.eggers@browncollege.com

CAREER EDUCATION INSTITUTE
5675 Jimmy Carter Blvd #100, Norcross GA 30071
Myra Hadley, Executive Director
678-966-9411 Fax: 678-966-9687
Website: www.ceitraining.com
E-mail: mhadley@ceitraining.com

Central Georgia Technical College
3300 Macon Tech Dr, Macon GA 31206-3628
478-757-3501

Central Georgia Technical College
54 GA Highway 22 W, Milledgeville GA 31061

Cobb Beauty College
3096 Cherokee St, Kennesaw GA 30144
770-424-6915

Coosa Valley Technical College
1151 Highway 53 Spur SW, Calhoun GA 30701

Coosa Valley Technical College
466 Brock Rd, Rockmart GA 30153

Coosa Valley Technical Institute
1 Maurice Culberson Dr SW, Rome GA 30161
706-295-6927

The Creative Circus
812 Lambert Dr, Atlanta GA 30324
Benita Van Winkle, Director of Admission
800-728-1590 ext. 111 or 103

DeKalb Medical Center
2701 N Decatur Rd, Decatur GA 30033-5918
404-501-5206

East Central Technical College
667 Perry House Rd, Fitzgerald GA 31750-8806
229-468-2000

Empire Beauty College
1455 Pleasant Hill Rd #105, Lawrenceville GA 30044
800-575-5983

Empire Beauty School
4719 Ashford-Dunwoody Rd #205
Dunwoody GA 30338
800-575-5983

Empire Beauty School
425 Ernest Barrett Pkwy Suite H-2
Kennesaw GA 30144
800-575-5983

ETI Career Institute
9500 S Main St, Jonesboro GA 30236
770-477-2799

Fayette Beauty Academy
386 Glynn St N, Fayetteville GA 30214
770-461-4669

Flint River Technical College
1533 Highway 19 S, Thomaston GA 30286-4752
706-646-6144

GEORGIA AVIATION TECHNICAL COLLEGE
71 Airport Rd, Eastman GA 31023
Donna Rogers, Admissions Specialist
478-374-6402 Fax: 478-374-6809
Website: www.gavtc.org
E-mail: drogers@gaaviationtech.edu

Georgia Career Institute
1820 Highway 20 Ste 200, Conyers GA 30013
770-922-7653

GEORGIA DRIVING ACADEMY
1449 V F W Dr SW, Conyers GA 30012-5237
Brad Barber, President
770-918-8501 Fax: 770-918-8770
Website: www.gadrivingacademy.com
E-mail: bbarber651@aol.com

Georgia Institute of Cosmetology
3531 Atlanta Hwy, Athens GA 30606-3152
706-549-6003

Georgia Institute of Cosmetology
2803 Wrightsboro Rd, Augusta GA 30909

Georgia Medical Institute
101 Marietta St NW Suite 600, Atlanta GA 30303
Sonya Jabriel, Director of Admissions
404-525-1111

GEORGIA MEDICAL INSTITUTE
1706 Northeast Expy, Atlanta GA 30329
Director of Admissions
404-327-8787 Fax: 404-327-8980
Website: www.georgia-med.com

Georgia Medical Institute
6431 Tara Blvd, Jonesboro GA 30236-1214
770-603-0000

Georgia Medical Institute
1600 Terrell Rd Suite G, Marietta GA 30067
770-428-6303

Georgia Medical Institute
1750 Beaver Ruin Rd Ste 500, Norcross GA 30093
770-921-1085

Griffin Technical College
501 Varsity Rd, Griffin GA 30223-2042
770-228-7366

Gwinnett College of Business
4230 Lwrncvll Hwy NW #11, Lilburn GA 30047
770-381-7200

Heart of Georgia Area Technical Institute
560 Pinehill Rd, Dublin GA 31021-1253
478-275-6590

Herzing College
3355 Lenox Rd NE Ste 100, Atlanta GA 30326-1332
Richard Hinton, Director of Admissions
404-816-4533

High-Tech Institute
1090 Northchase Pky Ste 150, Marietta GA 30067
770-988-9877

Interactive College of Technology
5303 New Peachtree Rd, Chamblee GA 30341-2818
Troy Maloveri, Contact
770-216-2960

Interactive College of Technology
2323 Browns Bridge Rd, Gainesville GA 30504
678-450-0550

Interactive College of Technology
1078 Citizens Pkwy Ste A, Morrow GA 30260
770-960-1298

International City Beauty College
1859 Watson Blvd, Warner Robins GA 31093
478-923-0915

INTERNATIONAL SCHOOL OF SKIN AND NAILCARE
5600 Roswell Rd NE, Atlanta GA 30342-1150
Alan R. Shinall, Operations Manager
404-843-1005 Fax: 404-843-1007
Website: www.skin-nails.com
E-mail: issn@skin-nails.com

Iverson Business School
500 Pinnacle Ct, Norcross GA 30071
770-446-1333

Javelin Technical Training Center
4501 Circle 75 Ste C-3180, Atlanta GA 30339
770-859-9779

Javelin Technical Training Center
1396 Southlake Plaza Dr, Morrow GA 30260
770-968-9155

Lanier Technical College
7745 Majors Rd, Cumming GA 30041-7050
Gary Bush, Director of Student Services / Placement
770-781-6770

Le Cordon Bleu College of Culinary Arts
1957 Lakeside Pkwy Ste 515, Tucker GA 30084
770-938-4711

Medical Center
PO Box 951, Columbus GA 31902
706-571-1200

Medical Center of Central Georgia
777 Hemlock St, Macon GA 31201-2155
478-633-1234

Medix School
2108 Cobb Pkwy SE, Smyrna GA 30080-7630
Crystal Henry, Director of Admissions
770-980-0002

MIDDLE GEORGIA TECHNICAL COLLEGE
80 Cohen Walker Dr, Warner Robins GA 31088-2729
Dr. Ivan Allen, President
478-988-6800 Fax: 478-988-6835
Website: www.middlegatech.edu

Moultrie Technical College
222 Rock House Rd, Ashburn GA 31714

Moultrie Technical College
800 Veterans Pkwy N, Moultrie GA 31788
229-891-7000

Moultrie Technical College
52 Tech Dr, Tifton GA 31794
229-391-2600

North Fulton Beauty College
408 S Atlanta St Ste 180, Roswell GA 30075
770-552-9570

North Georgia Technical College
434 Meeks Ave, Blairsville GA 30512-2983
Admissions
706-781-2300 Fax: 706-781-2307
Website: www.northgatech.edu
E-mail: info@northgatech.edu

North Georgia Technical College
8989 Highway 17, Toccoa GA 30577
706-779-5591
Website: www.northgatech.edu
E-mail: info@northgatech.edu

North Georgia Technical College
Clarkesville Campus
PO Box 65, Clarkesville GA 30523-0002
Admissions
706-754-7700 Fax: 706-754-7777
Website: www.northgatech.edu
E-mail: info@northgatech.edu

North Metro Technical College
5198 Ross Rd SE, Acworth GA 30102-3129
Missy Cusack, Director of Admissions
770-975-4000 Fax: 770-975-4142
Website: www.northmetrotech.edu
E-mail: info@northmetrotech.edu

Ogeechee Technical College
1 Joseph E Kennedy Blvd
Statesboro GA 30458-3199
912-681-5500

Okefenokee Technical College
1701 Carswell Ave, Waycross GA 31503-4016
912-287-6584

Omnitech Institute
4319 Covington Hwy Ste 202, Decatur GA 30035
404-284-8121

Portfolio Center
125 Bennett St NW, Atlanta GA 30309-1268
Fernando Guerrero, Admissions Department
404-351-5055 ext. 12

Powder Springs Beauty College
4114 Austell Powder Springs Rd
Powder Springs GA 30127
770-439-9432

Pro Way Hair School
5684 Memorial Dr, Stone Mountain GA 30083
770-879-6673

Rising Spirit Institute of Natural Health Excellence
4536 Chamblee Dunwoody Rd Ste 250
Atlanta GA 30338-6239
770-457-2021

Rivertown School of Beauty
4747 Hamilton Rd Ste B, Columbus GA 31904-6360
706-653-9223

Roffler Moler Hairstyling College
1311 Roswell Rd, Marietta GA 30062
770-565-3285

St. Joseph's Hospital
5665 Pchtree Dunwoody Rd NE
Atlanta GA 30342-1764
404-851-7120

Sandersville Technical College
1189 Deepstep Rd, Sandersville GA 31082
478-553-2060

SAVANNAH RIVER COLLEGE
2528 Centerwest Pkwy Bldg A, Augusta GA 30909
Dawn McCraith, Director
706-738-5046 Fax: 706-736-3599
Website: www.savannahrivercollege.com
E-mail: info@savannahrivercollege.com

Savannah Technical College
5717 White Bluff Rd, Savannah GA 31405-5521
912-351-6362

Southeastern Beauty School
PO Box 12483, Columbus GA 31917-2483
706-687-1054

Southeastern Beauty School
PO Box 12483, Columbus GA 31917-2483
706-687-1054

Southeastern Technical College
3001 E 1st St, Vidalia GA 30474-8817
912-538-3100

South Georgia Technical College
900 S Georgia Tech Pkwy, Americus GA 31709
229-931-2004

South Georgia Technical College
402 N Midway Rd, Cordele GA 31015
229-271-4040

Southwest Georgia Technical College
15689 US Highway 19 N, Thomasville GA 31792
229-225-5096

Swainsboro Technical College
346 Kite Rd, Swainsboro GA 30401-5700
478-289-2200

Turner Job Corps Center
2000 Schilling Ave, Albany GA 31705-1524
229-883-8500

Ultrasound Diagnostic School
1140 Hammond Dr NE #8-1150
Atlanta GA 30328-5338
Dr. Richard C. Farmer, Executive Director
404-248-9070

Valdosta Technical College
1001 S Elm St, Sparks GA 31647
229-549-7368

Valdosta Technical College
4089 Val Tech Rd, Valdosta GA 31602
James Bridges, President
229-333-2100

West Central Technical College
997 Newnan Rd, Carrollton GA 30116-6476
770-836-6800

West Central Technical College
4600 Timber Ridge Dr, Douglasville GA 30135-1225
770-947-7200

West Central Technical College
160 Martin Luther King Dr, Newnan GA 30263
678-423-2000

West Central Technical College
176 Murphy Campus Blvd, Waco GA 30182
770-537-6000

West Georgia Technical College
303 Fort Dr, La Grange GA 30240-5901
706-845-4323

Westwood College
1100 Spring St NW Ste 102, Atlanta GA 30309
404-745-9096

Westwood College
2220 Parklake Dr NE, Atlanta GA 30345
404-962-2999

HAWAII

Golf Academy of Hawaii
45-550 Kionaole Rd, Kaneohe HI 96744
Dona K. Powell, President
800-342-7342

Hawaii Business College
33 S King St 4th Floor, Honolulu HI 96813-4316
Roger Ramos, Director of Admissions
808-524-4014

Hawaii Institute of Hair Design
71 S Hotel St, Honolulu HI 96813
808-533-6596

Hawaii Technology Institute
629 Pohukaina St, Honolulu HI 96813-5021
808-522-2700

Heald College, Honolulu
1500 Kapiolani Blvd, Honolulu HI 96814-3732
Lon K. Ibaraki, Director of Admissions
808-955-1500 or 800-940-0530 Fax: 808-955-6964
Website: www.heald.edu
E-mail: lon_ibaraki@heald.edu

Hollywood Beauty College
99-084 Kauhale St Bldg A, Aiea HI 96701
808-486-7255

Medical Assisting School of Hawaii
33 S King St Ste 223, Honolulu HI 96813-4322
808-524-3363

NEW YORK TECHNICAL INSTITUTE OF HAWAII
1375 Dillingham Blvd, Honolulu HI 96817-4438
Brian Hamilton, Principal
808-841-5827 Fax: 808-841-5829
E-mail: nytihhawaii@verizon.net

Remington College
1111 Bishop St Ste 400, Honolulu HI 96813-2811
Del McCormick, Director of Admissions
808-942-1000

Travel Institute of the Pacific
1314 S King St Ste 1164, Honolulu HI 96814-1946
808-591-2708

IDAHO

Apollo College Boise
1200 N Liberty St, Boise ID 83704-8742
208-377-8080

Boise Court Reporting Institute
1951 S Saturn Way Ste 120, Boise ID 83709-2900
208-322-8517

Career Beauty College
57 College Ave, Rexburg ID 83440
208-356-0222

The Headmasters School of Hair Design
317 Coeur D Alene Lake Dr, Coeur d Alene ID 83814
208-664-0541

The Headmasters School of Hair Design
602 Main St, Lewiston ID 83501
208-743-1512

Mr. Juan's College of Hair Design
586 Blue Lakes Blvd N, Twin Falls ID 83301-4033
208-733-7777

Mr. Leon's School of Hair Design
205 10th St, Lewiston ID 83501-1910
Lisa Salisbury, Owner
208-743-6822

Mr. Leon's School of Hair Design
618 S Main St, Moscow ID 83843
Lisa Salisbury, Owner
208-882-2923

New Images Academy of Beauty
317 E Brookhollow Dr, Boise ID 83706
Dodi Warner, CEO
208-375-0190

NORTHWEST LINEMAN COLLEGE
7600 S Meridian Rd, Meridian ID 83642
Leann Day, Manager of Administration
208-888-4817 Fax: 208-888-4275
Website: www.lineman.com
E-mail: nlc@lineman.com

RAZZLE DAZZLE COLLEGE OF HAIR DESIGN
120 Holly St, Nampa ID 83686-5102
Christina Brown, President
208-465-7660 Fax: 208-463-0643
Website: www.razzledazzlecollege.com
E-mail: razzledazzle@cableone.net

Sage Technical Services
2845 W Seltice Way, Coeur D Alene ID 83814-8901
208-765-6346

THE SCHOOL OF HAIRSTYLING
141 E Chubbuck Rd, Chubbuck ID 83202
Linda K. Mottishaw, Director of Education
208-232-9170 Fax: 208-232-9486
E-mail: lindamottishaw@msn.com

ILLINOIS

ADVOCATE ILLINOIS MASONIC
School of Radiologic Technology
836 W Wellington Ave, Chicago IL 60657
Philis George, Director
773-296-8950 Fax: 773-296-8960
Website: www.advocatehealth.com
E-mail: IMMCSRT@advocatehealth.com

Advocate Trinity Hospital
2320 E 93rd St, Chicago IL 60617-3982
773-978-2000

Alvareita's College of Cosmetology
5400 W Main St, Belleville IL 62226
618-257-9193

Alvareita's College of Cosmetology
333 S Kansas St, Edwardsville IL 62025
618-656-2593

Alvareita's College of Cosmetology
3048 Godfrey Rd, Godfrey IL 62035
618-466-8952

AMERICAN FLORAL ART SCHOOL
634 S Wabash Ave #210, Chicago IL 60605-1808
James Moretz, Owner
312-922-9328 Fax: 312-922-9329

Blessing Hospital
PO Box 7005, Quincy IL 62305-7005
217-223-8400

Brown Mackie College - Moline
1527 47th Ave, Moline IL 61265-7062
309-762-2100

Cain's Barber College
365 E 51st St, Chicago IL 60615
773-536-4441

CALC Institute of Technology
235A E Center Dr, Alton IL 62002
618-474-0616

Cameo Beauty Academy
9714 S Cicero Ave, Oak Lawn IL 60453
708-636-4660

Cannella School of Hair Design
12840 Western Ave, Blue Island IL 60406
708-388-4949

Cannella School of Hair Design
9012 S Commercial Ave, Chicago IL 60617
773-221-4700

Cannella School of Hair Design
5912 W Roosevelt Rd, Chicago IL 60644-1471
773-287-3400

Cannella School of Hair Design
4269 S Archer Ave, Chicago IL 60632
773-890-0412

Cannella School of Hair Design
4217 W North Ave, Chicago IL 60639
773-278-4477

Cannella School of Hair Design
113 W Chicago St, Elgin IL 60123-5401
847-742-6611

Cannella School of Hair Design
191 N York St, Elmhurst IL 60126
630-833-6118

Capri Garfield Ridge School of Beauty College
2653 W 63rd St, Chicago IL 60629
773-778-8161

Capri Oak Forest College of Beauty Culture
15815 Rob Roy Dr, Oak Forest IL 60452
708-687-3020

Chicago School of Massage Therapy
17 N State St Fl 5, Chicago IL 60602-3047
312-753-7900

Chubb Institute
25 E Washington St, Chicago IL 60602
800-248-2237

College of Office Technology
1514 W Division St # 2, Chicago IL 60622-3312
Greg Brown, Director of Admissions
773-278-0042 Fax: 773-278-0143
Website: www.cot.edu
E-mail: kgalva@cotedu.com

Computer Systems Institute
318 W Adams, 10th Floor, Chicago IL 60606
Charles Woods, Director of Admissions
312-346-6774

Computer Systems Institute
8930 Gross Point Rd, Skokie IL 60077-1854
Tony Jacobs, Career Advisor
847-967-5030

Concept College of Cosmetology
2500 Georgetown Rd, Danville IL 61832
217-442-9329

Concept College of Cosmetology
129 N Race St, Urbana IL 61801
217-344-7550

Cook County Hospital
1825 W Harrison St, Chicago IL 60612-3701
312-633-8533

Cooking & Hospitality Institute of Chicago
361 W Chestnut St, Chicago IL 60610-3050
Catherine Brokenshire, Contact
312-944-0884

Cosmetology & Spa Institute
700 E Terra Cotta Ave, Crystal Lake IL 60014
815-385-9663

Coyne American Institute
330 N Green St, Chicago IL 60607
800-999-5220

DuQuoin Beauty College
202 S Washington St, Du Quoin IL 62832
Carol Porterfield, Administrative Assistant
618-542-9777

Educators of Beauty
122 Wright St, La Salle IL 61301
800-610-2300

Educators of Beauty
128 S 5th St, Rockford IL 61104
815-969-7030

Educators of Beauty
211 E 3rd St, Sterling IL 61081
815-625-0247

Edward Hines Veterans Admin. Hospital
PO Box 5000, Hines IL 60141-1489
708-216-2153

Environmental Technical Institute
13010 Division St, Blue Island IL 60406-2607
708-385-0707

Environmental Technical Institute
1101 W Thorndale Ave, Itasca IL 60143-1334
630-285-9100

Fox College
4201 W 93rd St, Oak Lawn IL 60453-1999
Edward Kapelinski Jr., Director of Admissions
708-636-7700

GRAHAM HOSPITAL
210 W Walnut St, Canton IL 61520-2497
Mary Kepple, Coordinator of Admissions, Recruitment
309-647-5240 ext. 2347 or 309-647-4086
Fax: 309-649-5127
Website: www.grahamschoolofnursing.org
E-mail: mkepple@grahamhospital.org

Greater West Town Woodworking & Shipping & Receiving School
2021 W Fulton St #204, Chicago IL 60612
Bob Fittin, Director of Training
312-563-9570

Hairmasters Institute of Cosmetology
506 S McClun St, Bloomington IL 61701
309-828-1884

Hair Professionals Academy of Cosmetology
825B Village Quarter Rd, West Dundee IL 60118
847-622-7871

Hair Professionals Academy of Cosmetology
1145 Butterfield Rd, Wheaton IL 60187
630-653-6630

HAIR PROFESSIONALS CAREER COLLEGE
10321 S Roberts Rd, Palos Hills IL 60465-1929
Linda Grant or Stephanie Marsala, Contacts
708-430-1755 Fax: 708-430-2282
Website: www.hairpros.edu
E-mail: paloshills@hairpros.edu

HAIR PROFESSIONALS CAREER COLLEGE
2245 Gateway Dr, Sycamore IL 60178-3164
Linda Grant, Admissions
815-756-3596 Fax: 815-756-8983
Website: www.hairpros.edu
E-mail: sycamorehairpros@aol.com

HAIR PROFESSIONALS SCHOOL OF COSMETOLOGY
PO Box 40, Oswego IL 60543
Rosalie Clark, Contact
630-554-2266 Fax: 630-554-9574
Website: www.hairpros.edu
E-mail: oswego@hairpros.edu

Hanover Park College of Beauty Culture
1166 E Lake St, Hanover Park IL 60133
630-830-6560

Illinois Center for Broadcasting
55 W 22nd St Ste 240, Lombard IL 60148-4888
Patrick Johnsen, Director
630-916-1700

Illinois Institute of Art, The
350 N Orleans St Lbby 136, Chicago IL 60654-1510
312-280-3500

ILLINOIS SCHOOL OF HEALTH CAREERS
220 S State St Ste 600, Chicago IL 60604-2098
Jeffrey L. Jarmes, Executive Director
312-913-1230 Fax: 312-913-1113
Website: www.ishc.edu
E-mail: jjarmes@ishc.edu

Illinois Welding School
5901 Washington St, Bartonville IL 61607
309-633-0379

ITT Technical Institute
7040 High Grove Blvd, Burr Ridge IL 60527-7595
Leo Rodriguez, Director of Recruitment
630-455-6470

ITT TECHNICAL INSTITUTE
600 Holiday Plaza Dr, Matteson IL 60443-2241
Lillian McClain, Director
708-747-2571 Fax: 708-747-0023
Website: www.itt-tech.edu
E-mail: lcclain@itt-tech.edu

John Amico's School of Hair Design
15301 Cicero Ave, Oak Forest IL 60452
708-687-7800

La' James College of Hairstyling
485 Avenue of the Cities, East Moline IL 61244
309-755-1313

LaMonts International School of Cosmetology
60 E Elm St, Canton IL 61520
309-647-4224

Lincoln Land Community College
5250 Shepherd Rd, Springfield IL 62703-5408
217-786-2200

Lincoln Technical Institute
8317 W North Ave, Melrose Park IL 60160-1605
708-344-4700

Loyola University Medical Center
2160 S 1st Ave, Maywood IL 60153-5590
708-216-9000

Mac Daniels Beauty School
5228 N Clark St, Chicago IL 60640
773-561-2376

McDonough District Hospital
525 E Grant St, Macomb IL 61455-3318
309-833-4101

Medical Careers Institute
116 S Michigan Ave, Chicago IL 60603-6001
312-782-9804

METHODIST COLLEGE OF NURSING
415 St Mark Ct, Peoria IL 61603
Mary Jane Dowling, Recruitment Coordinator
309-672-5566 Fax: 309-671-2752
Website: www.methodistcollegeofnursing.com
E-mail: mjdowling@mmci.org

Midwest Technical Institute
405 N Limit St, Lincoln IL 62656
217-735-3105

Moraine Valley Community College
10900 S 88th Ave, Palos Hills IL 60465-0937
708-974-4300

MORRISON INSTITUTE OF TECHNOLOGY
701 Portland Ave, Morrison IL 61270-2959
Richard C. Parkinson, Interim Director
815-772-7584 Fax: 815-772-7218
Website: www.morrison.tec.il.us
E-mail: admissions@morrison.tec.il.us
Private. Coed. Accreditation: ABET. Enrollment: 140. Student-faculty ratio: 13:1. Engineering Technology Associate of Applied Science degree in Architectural, Construction, Civil, Mechanical, Drafting & Design, and Surveying Technology. AAS degree in Systems & Network Administration.

Mr. John's School of Cosmetology
1745 E Eldorado St, Decatur IL 62521
217-423-8173

Mr. John's School of Cosmetology
300 S Broadway Ave Suite 111
Urbana IL 61801-3302
217-355-1466

Mr. John's School of Cosmetology & Nails
1429 S Main St, Jacksonville IL 62650
217-243-1744

Ms. Robert's Academy of Beauty Culture
17 E Park Blvd, Villa Park IL 60181
630-941-3880

Music Center of the North Shore
300 Green Bay Rd, Winnetka IL 60093-4088
847-446-3822

Niles School of Beauty Culture
8057 N Milwaukee Ave, Niles IL 60714
847-965-8061

Northwest Community Hospital
800 W Central Rd, Arlington Heights IL 60005-2392
847-618-1000

Northwestern Memorial Hospital
251 E Huron St, Chicago IL 60611
312-926-2000

Oehrlein School of Cosmetology
100 Meadow Ave, East Peoria IL 61611
309-699-1561

Olympia College
6880 N Frontage Rd, Burr Ridge IL 60527
630-920-1102

Olympia College
247 S State St Ste 400, Chicago IL 60604
312-913-1616

Olympia College
9811 Woods Dr #200, Skokie IL 60077
847-470-0277

ORT TECHNICAL INSTITUTE
5440 Fargo Ave, Skokie IL 60077
Arthur Eldar, Director
847-324-5588 Fax: 847-324-5580
Website: www.zg-ort.org
E-mail: aeldar@zg-ort.org

Pivot Point Cosmetology Research Center
144 E Lake St Ste C, Bloomingdale IL 60108
847-985-5900

PIVOT POINT INTERNATIONAL
1560 Sherman Ave Ste 700, Evanston IL 60201-4813
Lars Juhl, Manager of Admissions
847-866-0500 Ext. 7422 Fax: 847-866-7184
Website: www.pivot-point.com
E-mail: admissions@pivot-point.com

Professional Choice Hair Design Academy
2719 W Jefferson St, Joliet IL 60435
815-741-8224

Provena United Samaritans Medical Center
812 N Logan Ave, Danville IL 61832
217-443-5201

Pyramid Career Institute
3057 N Lincoln Ave, Chicago IL 60657-4207
773-975-9898

Rockford Business College
730 N Church St, Rockford IL 61103-6968
Tammy Rockett-Box, Director of Enrollment Services
815-965-8616

Rosel School of Cosmetology
2444 W Devon Ave, Chicago IL 60659
773-508-5600

ST. ANTHONY COLLEGE OF NURSING
5658 E State St, Rockford IL 61108-2468
Cheryl Delgado, Admission Representative
815-227-2141 Fax: 815-395-2275
Website: sacn.edu
E-mail: cheryldelgado@sacn.edu

St. Elizabeth Hospital
211 S 3rd St, Belleville IL 62220-1998
618-234-2120

St. Francis Hospital
355 Ridge Ave, Evanston IL 60202-3399
847-492-4000

St. Francis Medical Center
530 NE Glen Oak Ave, Peoria IL 61603-3117
309-655-2020

SAINT FRANCIS MEDICAL CENTER COLLEGE OF NURSING
511 NE Greenleaf St, Peoria IL 61603-3744
Janice Farquharson, Director of Admissions/Registrar
309-655-2596 Fax: 309-624-8973
Website: www.sfmccon.edu
E-mail: janice.farquharson@osfhealthcare.org

Sanford-Brown College
1101 Eastport Plaza Dr, Collinsville IL 62234-6108
618-344-5600

SER Business and Technical Institute
3948 W 26th St Ste 213, Chicago IL 60623-3705
773-227-3377

Spanish Coalition for Jobs
2011 W Pershing Rd, Chicago IL 60609
773-247-0707

Sparks College
131 S Morgan St, Shelbyville IL 62565-2241
217-774-5112

Swedish-American Hospital
1401 E State St, Rockford IL 61104-2298
815-968-4400

Taylor Business Institute
200 N Michigan Ave Ste 301, Chicago IL 60601-5908
312-658-5100

Trend Setters College of Cosmetology
665 W Jefferson St, Bradley IL 60915
815-932-5049

Trend Setters College of Cosmetology
19031 Old LaGrange Rd, Mokena IL 60448
708-478-6907

Tri-County Beauty Academy
219 N State St, Litchfield IL 62056
217-324-9062

Triton College
2000 5th Ave, River Grove IL 60171-1995
Mary-Rita Moore, Dean of Enrollment Services
708-456-0300 ext. 3130 Fax: 708-583-3147
Website: www.triton.edu
E-mail: triton@triton.edu
See listing under "Community and Junior Colleges"

Undergraduate School of Cosmetology
PO Box 195, Springfield IL 62705
217-753-8990

UNIVERSAL TECHNICAL INSTITUTE
601 Regency Dr, Glendale Heights IL 60139-2208
Karl Lewandowski, School Director
630-529-2662 Fax: 630-529-7567
Website: www.uticorp.com
E-mail: karllewandowski@uticorp.com

Vatterott College
501 N 3rd St, Quincy IL 62301-2599
217-224-0600

Vee's School of Beauty Culture
2701 State St, East Saint Louis IL 62205
618-274-1751

Westwood College
80 River Oaks Dr Ste D-49, Calumet City IL 60409
708-832-1988

Westwood College
17 N State St 3rd Floor, Chicago IL 60602
312-739-0850

Westwood College
7155 Janes Ave, Woodridge IL 60517
630-434-8244

Westwood College of Technology
8501 W Higgins Rd Ste 500, Chicago IL 60631
847-928-0200

Worsham College of Mortuary Science
495 Northgate Pkwy, Wheeling IL 60090-2646
Dede L. Frank, Director of Admissions
Stephanie J. Kann, Program Director
847-808-8444

INDIANA

A Cut Above Beauty College
3810 E Southport Rd, Indianapolis IN 46237
317-781-0959

Apex School of Beauty Culture
333 Jackson St, Anderson IN 46016
765-642-7560

Aviation Institute of Maintenance
7251 W McCarty St, Indianapolis IN 46241
317-243-4519

Ball Memorial Hospital
2401 W University Ave, Muncie IN 47303-3499
765-747-3393

Brown Mackie College - Fort Wayne
3000 E Coliseum Blvd, Fort Wayne IN 46805
Daniel Summer, Campus President
260-484-4400 Fax: 260-484-2678
Website: www.brownmackie.edu

Brown Mackie College - Merrillville
1000 E 80th Pl Ste 101N, Merrillville IN 46410-5644
219-769-3321

Brown Mackie College - Michigan City
325 E US Highway 20, Michigan City IN 46360-7362
219-877-3100

Brown Mackie College - South Bend
1030 E Jefferson Blvd, South Bend IN 46617-3123
Connie Adelman, Campus President
574-237-0774 Fax: 574-237-3585
Website: www.brownmackie.edu

College of Court Reporting
111 W 10th St Ste 111, Hobart IN 46342-5969
219-942-1459

Community Hospital of Indianapolis
1500 N Ritter Ave, Indianapolis IN 46219-3027
317-355-5529

Creative Hair Styling Academy
2549 Highway Ave, Highland IN 46322
219-838-2004

David Demuth Institute of Cosmetology
2 SW 5th St, Richmond IN 47374
765-935-7964

Don Roberts Beauty Academy
152 E US Highway 30, Schererville IN 46375
219-864-1600

Don Roberts Beauty School
1354 Lincoln Way, Valparaiso IN 46383
219-462-5189

Evansville Tri-State Beauty College
4920 Tippecanoe Dr, Evansville IN 47715
812-479-6989

Good Samaritan Hospital
520 S 7th St, Vincennes IN 47591-1098
812-885-3195

Hair Arts Academy
933 N Walnut St, Bloomington IN 47404
812-339-1117

Indiana Business College
140 E 53rd St, Anderson IN 46013-1717
765-644-7514

Indiana Business College
2222 Poshard Rd, Columbus IN 47203-1843
812-379-9000

Indiana Business College
4601 Theatre Dr, Evansville IN 47715-3901
812-476-6000

Indiana Business College
6413 N Clinton St, Fort Wayne IN 46825
260-471-7667

Indiana Business College
550 E Washington St, Indianapolis IN 46204
317-264-5656

Indiana Business College
5460 Victory Dr Ste 100, Indianapolis IN 46203-5970
317-783-5100

Indiana Business College
2 Executive Dr, Lafayette IN 47905-4859
765-447-9550

Indiana Business College
830 N Miller Ave, Marion IN 46952-2338
765-662-7497

Indiana Business College
411 W Riggin Rd, Muncie IN 47303-6413
765-288-8681

Indiana Business College
3175 S 3rd Pl, Terre Haute IN 47802-3785
812-232-4458

Indiana University School of Allied Health Sciences
1140 W Michigan St, Indianapolis IN 46202-5119
317-274-4702

Indiana Vocational Technical College
PO Box 1763, Indianapolis IN 46206-1763
317-921-4882

International Business College
7205 Shadeland Station Way
Indianapolis IN 46256-3954
317-841-6400

ITT Technical Institute
9511 Angola Ct, Indianapolis IN 46268-1119
317-875-8640

IVY TECH COMMUNITY COLLEGE - BLOOMINGTON
200 Daniels Way, Bloomington IN 47404-1511
Neil Frederick, Contact
812-332-1559 Fax: 812-330-6106
Website: www.ivytech.edu
E-mail: nfrederi@ivytech.edu

Ivy Tech Community College - North Central
220 Dean Johnson Blvd, South Bend IN 46601-3415
Pam Decker, Director of Admissions
574-289-7001 Fax: 574-236-7177
Website: www.ivytech.edu
E-mail: pdecker@ivytech.edu

Ivy Tech Community College of Indiana - East Central
4301 S Cowan Rd, Muncie IN 47302-9448
765-289-2291

Ivy Tech Community College of Indiana - Kokomo
PO Box 1373, Kokomo IN 46903-1373
765-459-0561

Ivy Tech Community College of Indiana - Lafayette
PO Box 6299, Lafayette IN 47903-6299
765-772-9100

Ivy Tech Community College of Indiana - Northeast
3800 N Anthony Blvd, Fort Wayne IN 46805-1430
260-482-9171

Ivy Tech Community College of Indiana - Northwest
1440 E 35th Ave, Gary IN 46409-1401
219-981-1111

Ivy Tech Community College of Indiana - Richmond
2325 Chester Blvd, Richmond IN 47374-1220
765-966-2656

Ivy Tech Community College of Indiana - Southeast
590 Ivy Tech Dr, Madison IN 47250
812-265-2580

Ivy Tech Community College of Indiana - Southwest
3501 N 1st Ave, Evansville IN 47710-3319
812-426-2865

Ivy Tech Community College Wabash Valley
7999 S US Highway 41, Terre Haute IN 47802-4845
812-299-1121

Kaye Beauty College
6346 E 82nd St, Indianapolis IN 46250
317-576-5000

Kaye Beauty College
1111 S 10th St, Noblesville IN 46060
317-773-6189

LAFAYETTE BEAUTY ACADEMY
833 Ferry St, Lafayette IN 47901-1149
Anita Harbolt-Keim, Financial Aid Officer
765-742-0068 Fax: 765-420-0875
Website: www.lafayettebeautyacademy.com
E-mail: anitaharboltkeim@lafayettebeautyacademy.com

Lakeshore Medical Laboratory Training Programs
402 Franklin St, Michigan City IN 46360-3327
Gina Watson, MT (ASCP), Program Director
219-872-7032

Lincoln Technical Institute
7225 Winton Dr Bldg 128
Indianapolis IN 46268-4198
Tony Rios, Executive Director
800-554-4465

The Masters of Cosmetology College
1732 Bluffton Rd, Fort Wayne IN 46809
260-747-6667

MedTech College
6612 E 75th St Ste 300, Indianapolis IN 46250
317-845-0100

Merrillville Beauty College
48 W 67th Pl, Merrillville IN 46410
219-769-2232

OLYMPIA COLLEGE
707 E 80th Pl Ste 200, Merrillville IN 46410
James Powell, President
219-756-6811 Fax: 219-756-6812
Website: www.cci.edu
E-mail: jpowell@cci.edu

PJ's College of Cosmetology
1414 Blackiston Mill Rd, Clarksville IN 47129
812-282-0459

PJ's College of Cosmetology
1400 W Main St, Greenfield IN 46140

PJ's College of Cosmetology
5539 Madison Ave, Indianapolis IN 46227

PJ's College of Cosmetology
2006 N Walnut St, Muncie IN 47303

PJ's College of Cosmetology
2026 Stafford Rd, Plainfield IN 46168

PJ's College of Cosmetology
115 N 9th St, Richmond IN 47374
765-962-3005

Professional Careers Institute
7302 Woodland Dr, Indianapolis IN 46278-1736
317-299-6001

Ravenscroft Beauty College
6110 Stellhorn Rd, Fort Wayne IN 46815
260-486-8868

Reppert School of Auctioneering
PO Box 190, Auburn IN 46706-0190
Dennis Kruse, President
800-968-4444

Roger's Academy of Hair Design
2903 Mount Vernon Ave, Evansville IN 47712
812-428-4027

Rudae's School of Beauty Culture
5317 Coldwater Rd, Fort Wayne IN 46825
260-483-2466

Rudae's School of Beauty Culture
208 W Jefferson St, Kokomo IN 46901
765-459-4197

ST. ELIZABETH SCHOOL OF NURSING
1508 Tippecanoe St, Lafayette IN 47904-2198
Anita K. Reed, Admissions Coordinator
765-423-6400 Fax: 765-423-6383
Website: www.ste.org/newson
E-mail: schoolinfo@steson.org

St. Francis Hospital Center
1600 Albany St, Beech Grove IN 46107-1593
317-783-8220

Sawyer College
7833 Indianapolis Blvd, Hammond IN 46324
Chris Artim, Director
219-844-0100

Sawyer College
3803 E Lincoln Hwy, Merrillville IN 46410-5809
Linda Yednak, Interim Director
219-947-4555

Vincennes Beauty College
12 S 2nd St, Vincennes IN 47591
812-882-1086

IOWA

Allen College
1825 Logan Ave, Waterloo IA 50703-1999
319-226-2000

American College of Hairstyling
1531 1st Ave SE, Cedar Rapids IA 52402
319-362-1488

American College of Hairstyling
603 E 6th St, Des Moines IA 50309
515-244-0971

Bill Hill's College of Cosmetology
910 Avenue G, Fort Madison IA 52627
319-372-6248

Capri College
2945 Williams Pkwy SW
Cedar Rapids IA 52404-1475
319-364-1541

Capri College
425 E 59th St, Davenport IA 52807
563-388-6642

Capri College
PO Box 873, Dubuque IA 52004
563-588-2379

College of Hair Design
722 Water St Ste 201, Waterloo IA 50703
319-232-9995

Davenport Barber-Styling College
730 E Kimberly Rd, Davenport IA 52807
563-391-9950

Dayton's School of Hair Design
315 N Main St, Burlington IA 52601
319-752-3193

Dayton's School of Hair Design
23 S 2nd St, Keokuk IA 52632
319-524-6445

EQ School of Hair Design
536 W Broadway, Council Bluffs IA 51503
712-328-2613

The Faust Institute of Cosmetology
1543 18th St Ste 15, Spirit Lake IA 51360
712-336-3518

The Faust Institute of Cosmetology
PO Box 29, Storm Lake IA 50588
712-732-6571

HAMILTON TECHNICAL COLLEGE
1011 E 53rd St, Davenport IA 52807-2653
Maryanne Hamilton, President
Mark Christy, Director
563-386-3570 Fax: 563-386-6756
Website: www.hamiltontechcollege.com
E-mail: mchristy@hamiltontechcollege.com
Established 1969. Coed. Accreditation: ACCSCT. Tuition: $6,300 per year. Enrollment: 350. Staff and faculty: 35. Degrees: Diploma, Associate and Bachelor areas of study include biomedical electronics, communication electronics, computer technology, industrial electronics, computer aided drafting and medical assisting technology. Suburban campus. Student services: employment service for undergraduates, placement service for graduates and facilities for handicapped.

Hawkeye Community College
1501 E Orange Rd, Waterloo IA 50704
Molly Quinn, Director of Admissions
800-670-4769

Iowa School of Beauty
3305 70th St, Des Moines IA 50322
515-278-9939

Iowa School of Beauty
112 Nicholas Dr, Marshalltown IA 50158
641-752-4223

Iowa School of Beauty
609 W 2nd St, Ottumwa IA 52501
641-684-6504

Iowa School of Beauty
2524 Glenn Ave, Sioux City IA 51106
712-274-9733

Iowa Western Community College
2700 College Rd, Council Bluffs IA 51503-0567
800-432-5852

La' James College of Hairstyling
6322 University Ave, Cedar Falls IA 50613
319-277-2150

La' James College of Hairstyling
3802 E 53rd St, Davenport IA 52807
563-441-7900

La' James College of Hairstyling
2604 1st Ave S, Fort Dodge IA 50501
515-576-3119

La' James College of Hairstyling
227 E Market St, Iowa City IA 52245-2164
319-337-2109

La' James College of Hairstyling
24 2nd St NE, Mason City IA 50401
641-424-2161

La' James International College
8805 Chambery Blvd, Johnston IA 50131
515-278-2208

Professional Cosmetology Institute
627 Main St, Ames IA 50010
515-232-7250

Total Look School of Cosmetology & Massage Therapy
806 3rd St W, Cresco IA 52136
563-547-3624

Vatterott College
6100 Thornton Ave Ste 290
Des Moines IA 50321-2405
515-309-9000

WORLD WIDE COLLEGE OF AUCTIONEERING
(formerly Reisch)
PO Box 949, Mason City IA 50402-0949
Paul C. Behr, President
800-423-5242 Fax: 641-423-3067
Website: www.worldwidecollegeofauctioneering.com
E-mail: wwca@netconx.net

KANSAS

Academy of Hair Design
115 S 5th St, Salina KS 67401
785-825-8155

American Academy of Hair Design
901 SW 37th St, Topeka KS 66611
785-267-5800

AMERICAN INSTITUTE OF BAKING
PO Box 3999, Manhattan KS 66505-3999
Ken Embers, Admissions
800-633-5137 or 785-537-4750 Fax: 785-537-1493
Website: www.aibonline.org
E-mail: kembers@aibonline.org
Established 1919. Accredited by North Central Association of Colleges & Schools. Provides training for professional bakers for all industrial and retail levels and product types and for food plant maintenance engineers. Publishes specialized distance learning courses and training materials in several formats and languages, including print, video, on-line, and CD-ROMs in English, Spanish, French, and Chinese. Several types of certification awarded. Federal financial aid and scholarships available. Some dormitory housing by arrangement.

Bryan Career College
1527 SW Fairlawn Rd, Topeka KS 66604-2411
785-272-0889

Classic College of Hair Design
1675 S Rock Rd Ste 101, Wichita KS 67207
316-681-2288

College of Hair Design
10324 Mastin St, Overland Park KS 66212
913-492-4114

Community College of Cosmetology
3602 SW Topeka Blvd, Topeka KS 66611
785-267-7701

Crum's Beauty College
512 Poyntz Ave, Manhattan KS 66502
785-776-4794

Cutting Edge Hairstyling Academy
4327 State Ave, Kansas City KS 66102
913-321-0214

Cutting Edge Hairstyling Academy
12148 Shawnee Mission Pkwy, Shawnee KS 66216
913-962-0076

Hays Academy of Hair Design
119 W 10th St, Hays KS 67601
785-628-3981

KAW Area Technical School
5724 Huntoon St, Topeka KS 66604
785-273-7140

LaBaron Hairdressing Academy
8119 Robinson St, Overland Park KS 66204
913-642-0077

North Central Kansas Technical College
PO Box 507, Beloit KS 67420-0507
785-738-2276

Northeast Kansas Technical College
1501 W Riley St, Atchison KS 66002
913-367-6204

Northwest Kansas Technical College
1209 Harrison St, Goodland KS 67735
785-899-3641

Old Town Barber & Beauty College
1207 E Douglas Ave, Wichita KS 67211
316-264-4891

PINNACLE CAREER INSTITUTE
1601 W 23rd St Ste 200, Lawrence KS 66046-2703
Lisa Allen, Admissions Representative
785-841-9640 Fax: 785-841-4854
Website: www.pinnaclecareerinstitute.edu
E-mail: lallen@pcitraining.edu

Salina Area Vocational Technical School
2562 Centennial Rd, Salina KS 67401
785-309-3100

Sidney's Hairdressing College
916 E 4th Ave, Hutchinson KS 67501
620-662-5481

SOUTHWEST KANSAS TECHNICAL SCHOOL
PO Box 1599, Liberal KS 67905-1599
Ed Poley, Assistant Director
620-604-2900 or 800-818-3819 Fax: 620-624-0108
Website: www.swkts.com
E-mail: epoley@usd480.net

SUPERIOR SCHOOL OF HAIRDRESSING
1215 E Santa Fe St, Olathe KS 66061
Joe Hancock, Owner
913-782-4004 Fax: 913-782-0449
Website: www.superiorbeautyschool.com
E-mail: jhancock1@sbcglobal.net

Vatterott College
3639 N Comotara St, Wichita KS 67226
Diana Otis, Co-Director
316-634-0066

Vernon's Kansas School of Cosmetology
2531 S Seneca St, Wichita KS 67217-2803
316-265-2629

Wichita Area Technical College
324 N Emporia St, Wichita KS 67202-2512
316-833-4664

Wichita Area Technical College
301 S Grove St, Wichita KS 67211
316-677-9282

Wichita Technical Institute
2051 S Meridian Ave, Wichita KS 67213-1927
316-943-2241

Wright Business School
8951 Metcalf Ave, Overland Park KS 66212-1402
913-385-7700

WTI Topeka Campus
3712 SW Burlingame Cir, Topeka KS 66609
785-354-4568

XENON INTERNATIONAL SCHOOL OF HAIR DESIGN
3804 W Douglas Ave, Wichita KS 67203
Kim McIntosh, Executive Director
316-943-5516 Fax: 316-943-7244
Website: www.xenonintl.com
E-mail: kmcintosh@xenonschool.com

KENTUCKY

Barrett & Company School of Hair Design
973 Kimberly Sq, Nicholasville KY 40356
859-885-9136

BECKFIELD COLLEGE
16 Spiral Drive, Florence KY 41042
Leah Boerger, Contact
859-371-9393 Fax: 859-371-5096
Website: www.beckfieldcollege.com
E-mail: lboerger@beckfield.edu

Bowling Green Technical College
1845 Loop Ave, Bowling Green KY 42101-3601
270-746-7461

Bowling Green Technical College
1127 Morgantown Rd, Bowling Green KY 42101-9202
270-746-7807

Bowling Green Technical College
129 State Ave, Glasgow KY 42141
270-651-5373

Brighton Center
601 Washington Ave, Newport KY 41071
859-491-8303

Brown Mackie College - Hopkinsville
4001 Fort Campbell Blvd
Hopkinsville KY 42240-4948
270-886-1302

Brown Mackie College - Louisville
300 High Rise Dr, Louisville KY 40213-3263
Kathleen Belanger, Director of Admissions
502-968-7191 Fax: 502-357-9956
Website: www.brownmackie.edu
E-mail: kbelanger@brownmackie.edu

BROWN MACKIE COLLEGE
Northern Kentucky Campus
309 Buttermilk Pike, Fort Mitchell KY 41017-2191
Joanne Dellefield, Director of Admissions
859-341-5627 Fax: 859-341-6483
Website: www.brownmackie.edu
E-mail: jdellefield@brownmackie.edu

Carl D. Perkins Job Corps Center
478 Meadows Br, Prestonsburg KY 41653-1519
Billie S. Gipson, Deputy Director Education & Training
606-886-1037

Central Kentucky Technical College
59 Corporate Dr, Danville KY 40422
859-239-7030

Central Kentucky Technical College
1500 Bypass N, Lawrenceburg KY 40342
502-839-8488

Central Kentucky Technical College
308 Vo Tech Rd, Lexington KY 40511-2626
Dr. Michael Krause, Dean of Student Affairs
859-246-2400

Collins School of Cosmetology
111 W Chester Ave, Middlesboro KY 40965-2809
606-248-3602

Cumberland Technical College Rockcastle County
PO Box 275, Mount Vernon KY 40456-0275
606-256-4346

Daymar College
4400 Breckenridge Ln #415, Louisville KY 40218
Shawn McDaniel, Director of Admissions
502-495-1040 Fax: 502-495-1518
Website: www.daymarcollege.com

Daymar College
3361 Buckland Sq, Owensboro KY 42301-5830
Vickie McDougal Director of Admissions
800-960-4090 Fax: 270-685-4090
Website: www.daymarcollege.com

Decker College
10830 Penion Dr, Louisville KY 40299
502-266-6676

Donta School of Beauty Culture
515 W Oak St, Louisville KY 40203
502-583-1018

Draughons Junior College
2421 Industrial Dr, Bowling Green KY 42101-4071
270-843-6750

Earle C. Clements Job Corps Center
2302 US Highway 60 E, Morganfield KY 42437-6608
270-389-5310

East Kentucky Beauty College
5333 N Mayo Trl, Pikeville KY 41501
606-432-3627

Elizabethtown Beauty School
308 N Miles St, Elizabethtown KY 42701
270-765-2118

Elizabethtown Technical College
620 College Street Rd, Elizabethtown KY 42701
270-766-5133

Ezell's Cosmetology School
PO Box 1431, Murray KY 42071
270-753-4723

Gateway Community & Technical College
790 Thomas More Pkwy, Edgewood KY 41017
859-442-4150

Gateway Community & Technical College
90 Campbell Dr, Highland Heights KY 41076
859-442-4108

Gateway Community & Technical College
1025 Amsterdam Rd, Park Hills KY 41011-2031
859-292-3930

Hair Design School
7285 Turfway Rd, Florence KY 41042
859-283-2690

The Hair Design School
151 Chenoweth Ln, Louisville KY 40207
502-897-9401

Hair Design School
1049 Bardstown Rd, Louisville KY 40204
502-459-8150

Hair Design School
4160 Bardstown Rd, Louisville KY 40218
502-491-0077

Hair Design School
640 Knox Blvd, Radcliff KY 40160
270-351-4473

Hazard Community and Technical College
One Community College Dr, Hazard KY 41701-2402
Germaine Shaffer, Director of Enrollment and Diversity Services
800-246-7521 ext. 73409

Interactive College of Technology
11 Spiral Dr Ste 8, Florence KY 41042
859-282-8989

ITT Technical Institute
10509 Timberwood Cir, Louisville KY 40223-5392
Alan S. Crews, Director
502-327-7424

J & M Academy of Cosmetology
110A Brighton Park Blvd, Frankfort KY 40601
502-695-8001

Jefferson Technical College
727 W Chestnut St, Louisville KY 40203-2036
502-213-4290

Jenny Lea Academy of Cosmetology
114 N Cumberland Ave, Harlan KY 40831
606-573-4276

Jenny Lea Academy of Cosmetology
74 Parkway Plaza Loop, Whitesburg KY 41858
606-573-4276

Kaufman Beauty School
701 E High St, Lexington KY 40502
859-266-2024

Lexington Beauty College
90 Southport Dr, Lexington KY 40503
859-278-7483

Louisville Technical Institute
3901 Atkinson Square Dr, Louisville KY 40218
George Wright, Director of Admissions
800-844-6528

Mayo Technical College
513 3rd St, Paintsville KY 41240-1032
606-789-5321

Motif Beauty Academy
23 W Lexington Ave, Winchester KY 40391
859-745-5886

Mr. Jim's Beauty College
1240 Carter Rd, Owensboro KY 42301
270-684-3505

Muhlenberg Job Corps Center
3875 Highway 181 N, Greenville KY 42345
270-338-5460

National College of Business & Technology
115 E Lexington Ave, Danville KY 40422-1517
Larry Steele, Director of Admissions
859-236-6991

National College of Business & Technology
7627 Ewing Blvd, Florence KY 41042-1812
Larry Steele, Director of Admissions
859-525-6510

National College of Business & Technology
628 E Main St, Lexington KY 40508-2312
Larry Steele, Director of Admissions
859-253-0621

National College of Business & Technology
4205 Dixie Hwy, Louisville KY 40216
Larry Steele, Director of Admissions
502-447-7634

National College of Business & Technology
288 S Mayo Trl #2, Pikeville KY 41501-1518
Larry Steele, Director of Admissions
606-432-5477

National College of Business & Technology
139 S Killarney Ln, Richmond KY 40475
Larry Steele, Director of Admissions
859-623-8956

Nu-Tek Academy of Beauty
153 Evans Dr, Mount Sterling KY 40353
859-498-4460

Owensboro Community & Technical College
1501 Frederica St, Owensboro KY 42301-4806
270-687-7255

Paducah Technical College
509 S 30th St, Paducah KY 42001-4181
Arnold Harris, School Relations
800-995-4438

Pathology and Cytology Laboratories
290 Big Run Rd, Lexington KY 40503-2934
859-278-9513

Pat Wilson Beauty College
326 N Main St, Henderson KY 42420
270-826-5195

PJ's College of Cosmetology
1901 Russellville Rd Ste 10, Bowling Green KY 42101
270-846-6444

PJ's College of Cosmetology
124 S Public Sq, Glasgow KY 42141
270-651-6553

Rowan Technical College
609 Viking Dr, Morehead KY 40351-8320
606-783-1538

ST. ELIZABETH MEDICAL CENTER
School of Medical Technology
1 Medical Village Dr, Edgewood KY 41017-3441
Beth Warning, MS, MT(ASCP), Program Director
859-344-2170 Fax: 859-344-5560
Website: www.stelizabeth.com
E-mail: bwarning@stelizabeth.com

School of Hair Design
3968 Park Dr, Louisville KY 40216
502-447-0111

Southeast School of Cosmetology
PO Box 493, Manchester KY 40962
606-598-7901

Southwestern College of Business
8095 Connector Dr, Florence KY 41042
859-282-9999

Spencerian College
1575 Winchester Rd, Lexington KY 40505
Victor Lamoin Adcock II, Director of Admissions
800-456-3253

Spencerian College
4627 Dixie Hwy, Louisville KY 40216
Terri Thomas, Director of Admissions
502-447-1000

TREND SETTER'S ACADEMY OF BEAUTY CULTURE
6539 W Highway 22, Crestwood KY 40014
E-mail: mbinghamtsa@aol.com

TREND SETTER'S ACADEMY OF BEAUTY CULTURE
622B Westport Rd, Elizabethtown KY 42701-2848
270-765-5243
E-mail: mbinghamtsa@aol.com

TREND SETTER'S ACADEMY OF BEAUTY CULTURE
7283 Dixie Hwy, Louisville KY 40258
502-937-6816
E-mail: mbinghamtsa@aol.com

LOUISIANA
Academy of Creative Hair Design
3805 Pontchartrain Dr #16, Slidell LA 70458
985-643-2614

Alexandria Academy of Beauty
2305 Rapides Ave, Alexandria LA 71301
318-442-7715

American School of Business
702 Professional Dr N, Shreveport LA 71105-5646
318-798-3333

ASCENSION COLLEGE
320 E Ascension St, Gonzales LA 70737-2912
Dennis Kerr, President
225-647-6609 Fax: 225-647-4849
Website: www.ascensioncollege.org
E-mail: dkerrascen@etel.net

Aveda Institute
1355 Polders Ln, Covington LA 70433-5638
985-892-9953

Ayers Institute
3010 Knight St Ste 300, Shreveport LA 71105-2577
318-868-3000

Bastrop Beauty School #1
117 S Vine St, Bastrop LA 71220
318-281-8652

Baton Rouge School of Computers
10425 Plaza Americana Dr
Baton Rouge LA 70816-8188
225-923-2525

Blue Cliff College
100 Asma Blvd Ste 350, Lafayette LA 70508
337-269-0620

Blue Cliff College
3501 Severn Ave Ste 20, Metairie LA 70002
504-456-3141

Blue Cliff College
200 N Thomas Dr #A, Shreveport LA 71107
318-425-7941

Bryman College
824 Elmwood Park Blvd Ste 110
New Orleans LA 70123
504-733-7117

Camelot College
2618 Wooddale Blvd #A
Baton Rouge LA 70805-7539
225-928-3005

CAMERON COLLEGE
PO Box 19288, New Orleans LA 70119-0288
Eleanor Cameron Skov, President
504-821-5881 or 800-878-5881 Fax: 504-822-3467
Website: www.cameron.com
E-mail: cameroncollege@mindspring.com

CAREER TECHNICAL COLLEGE
2319 Louisville Ave, Monroe LA 71201
Rick Nail, Director
318-323-2889 Fax: 318-324-9883
Website: www.careertc.com
E-mail: rnail@careertc.com

Cloyd's Beauty School #1
603 Natchitoches St, West Monroe LA 71291
318-322-5314

Cloyd's Beauty School #2
1311 Winnsboro Rd, Monroe LA 71202
318-322-5314

CLOYD'S BEAUTY SCHOOL #3
2514 Ferrand St, Monroe LA 71201
Tina Mathieu, Contact
318-322-5314 Fax: 318-322-5465
E-mail: tmath@bayou.com

Cosmetology Training Center
2516 Johnston St, Lafayette LA 70503
337-237-6868

Court Reporting Institute of Louisiana
12090 S Harrells Ferry Rd Ste A
Baton Rouge LA 70816
225-292-1950

Culinary Institute of New Orleans
2100 Saint Charles Ave, New Orleans LA 70130-7100
Robert Koehl, Director
504-525-2433

DELTA COLLEGE
19231 N 6th St, Covington LA 70433
Linda DeoGracias, Director
985-892-6651 Fax: 985-892-5332
E-mail: annhebert@bellsouth.net

Delta College of Arts & Technology
7380 Exchange Pl, Baton Rouge LA 70806-1529
225-928-7770

Delta School of Business and Technology
517 Broad St, Lake Charles LA 70601-4334
Gary Holt, President
337-439-5765 Fax: 337-436-5151
Website: www.deltatech.edu
E-mail: susan@deltatech.edu

Demmon School of Beauty
1222 Ryan St, Lake Charles LA 70601
337-439-9265

Denham Springs Beauty College
923 Florida Ave SE, Denham Springs LA 70726
225-665-6188

Diesel Driving Academy
8067 Airline Hwy, Baton Rouge LA 70815-8108
225-929-9990

Diesel Driving Academy
PO Box 36949, Shreveport LA 71133-6949
318-636-6300

D-Jay's School of Beauty Arts & Sciences
5131 Government St, Baton Rouge LA 70806
225-926-2530

Domestic Health Care Institute
4826 Jamestown Ave, Baton Rouge LA 70808-3224
225-925-5312

Eastern College of Health Vocations
201 Evans Rd Ste 400, New Orleans LA 70123
504-885-3353

Gretna Career College Training Institute
1415 Whitney Ave, Gretna LA 70053-2436
Ava Himes, Director of Admissions
504-366-5409 Fax: 504-366-1294

Guy's Shreveport Academy of Cosmetology
1141 Shreveport Barksdale Hwy
Shreveport LA 71105
318-865-5591

HERZING COLLEGE
2400 Veterans Memorial Blvd #410
Kenner LA 70062-4715
Genny Bordelon, Director of Admissions
504-733-0074 Fax: 504-733-0020
Website: www.herzing.edu
E-mail: info@nor.herzing.edu

ITI Technical College
13944 Airline Hwy, Baton Rouge LA 70817-5927
225-752-4230

ITT Technical Institute
140 James Dr E, Saint Rose LA 70087-4005
Heidi J. Munoz, Director of Recruitment
504-463-0338

John Jay Beauty College
540 Robert E Lee Blvd, New Orleans LA 70124
504-282-8128

John Jay Kenner Academy
2844 Tennessee Ave, Kenner LA 70062
504-467-2951

John Jay Slidell Beauty College
3144 Pontchartrain Dr, Slidell LA 70458
985-643-0677

L.E. Fletcher Technical Community College
PO Box 5033, Houma LA 70361-5033
985-857-3655

Lockworks Academie of Hairdressing
2834 S Sherwood Forest Blvd
Baton Rouge LA 70816
225-295-1435

Lockworks Academie of Hairdressing
2922 Johnston St, Lafayette LA 70503
337-233-0511

Louisiana Academy of Beauty
550 E Laurel Ave, Eunice LA 70535
337-457-7627

Louisiana Technical College
Acadian Campus
1933 W Hutchinson Ave, Crowley LA 70526-3215
337-788-7521

Louisiana Technical College
Alexandria Campus
PO Box 5698, Alexandria LA 71307-5698
318-487-5439

Louisiana Technical College
Ascension Campus
9697 Airline Hwy, Sorrento LA 70778-3007
225-675-5398

Louisiana Technical College
Avoyelles Campus
508 Choupique Ln, Cottonport LA 71327
318-876-2401

Louisiana Technical College
Bastrop Campus
PO Box 1120, Bastrop LA 71221-1120
Vettye Garrett, Asst. Dean
318-283-0836

Louisiana Technical College
Baton Rouge Campus
3250 N Acadian Thruway E
Baton Rouge LA 70805-6699
225-359-9204

Louisiana Technical College
Charles B. Coreil Campus
1124 Vocational Dr, Ville Platte LA 70586-2425
337-363-2197

Louisiana Technical College
Delta-Ouachita Technical Institute
609 Vocational Pkwy, West Monroe LA 71292-0127
318-397-6100

Louisiana Technical College
Evangeline Campus
PO Box 68, Saint Martinville LA 70582
337-394-6466

Louisiana Technical College
Florida Parishes Campus
PO Box 1300, Greensburg LA 70441
225-222-4251

Louisiana Technical College
Folkes Campus
3337 Highway 10, Jackson LA 70748-6240
225-634-2636

Louisiana Technical College
Gulf Area Campus
PO Box 878, Abbeville LA 70511-0878
Ray E. Lavergne, Director
337-893-4984

Louisiana Technical College
Hammond Area Campus
PO Box 489, Hammond LA 70404-0489
Dr Eddy Anne Ouder, Director of Admissions

Louisiana Technical College
Huey P. Long Campus
303 S Jones St, Winnfield LA 71483-3562
318-628-3815

Louisiana Technical College
Jefferson Campus
5200 Blair Rd, Metairie LA 70001-5605
Shannon Chaisson, Director of Admissions
504-736-7072

Louisiana Technical College
Jumonville Memorial Campus
605 Hospital Rd, New Roads LA 70760-2628
Clayton Chenevert, FAO
225-342-3768

Louisiana Technical College
Lafourche Campus
1425 Tiger Dr, Thibodaux LA 70301-4336
985-447-0924

Louisiana Technical College
Lamar Salter Campus
15014 Lake Charles Hwy, Leesville LA 71446-6511
Alan P. Dunbar, Coordinator Student Services
337-537-3135

Louisiana Technical College
Mansfield Campus
PO Box 1236, Mansfield LA 71052-1236
318-872-2243

Louisiana Technical College
Morgan Smith Campus
1230 N Main St, Jennings LA 70546-4110
337-824-4811

Louisiana Technical College
Natchitoches Campus
PO Box 657, Natchitoches LA 71458-0657
318-357-3162

Louisiana Technical College
North Central Campus
PO Box 548, Farmerville LA 71241-0548
318-368-3179

Louisiana Technical College
Northeast Louisiana Campus
1710 Warren St, Winnsboro LA 71295-2940
318-435-2163

Louisiana Technical College
Northwest Louisiana Campus
PO Box 835, Minden LA 71058-0835
Charles T. Strong, Director
318-371-3035

Louisiana Technical College
Oakdale Campus
PO Box EM, Oakdale LA 71463-1708
J. Darrell Rodriguez, Dean
318-335-3944

Louisiana Technical College
River Parishes Campus
PO Box AQ, Reserve LA 70084-0555
985-536-4418

Louisiana Technical College
Ruston Campus
PO Box 1070, Ruston LA 71273
318-251-4145

Louisiana Technical College
Sabine Valley Campus
PO Box 790, Many LA 71449-3839
318-256-4101

Louisiana Technical College
Shelby M. Jackson Campus
PO Box 1465, Ferriday LA 71334
318-757-6501

Louisiana Technical College
Shreveport-Bossier Campus
PO Box 78527, Shreveport LA 71137-8527
318-676-7811

Louisiana Technical College
Sullivan Campus
1710 Sullivan Dr, Bogalusa LA 70427-5866
Brenda Simon, Contact
985-732-6640

LOUISIANA TECHNICAL COLLEGE
Tallulah Campus
132 Old Highway 65, Tallulah LA 71284
Patrick T. Murphy, Dean
318-574-4820 Fax: 318-574-1868
Website: www.ltctallulah.com
E-mail: sccox@theltc.net

Louisiana Technical College
Tallulah Campus - Margaret Surles Extension
PO Box 368, Lake Providence LA 71254
318-559-0239

Louisiana Technical College
Teche Area Campus
PO Box 11057, New Iberia LA 70562-1057
337-373-0011

Louisiana Technical College
T. H. Harris Campus
332 E South St, Opelousas LA 70570-6113
Henrietta Brown, Student Personnel Services Officer
337-948-0239

Louisiana Technical College
West Jefferson Campus
475 Manhattan Blvd, Harvey LA 70058-4441
504-361-6464

Louisiana Technical College
Westside Campus
59125 Bayou Rd, Plaquemine LA 70764-2957
225-687-6392

Louisiana Technical College
Young Memorial Campus
PO Box 2148, Morgan City LA 70381-2148
985-380-2436

Medical Training College
10525 Plaza Americana Dr
Baton Rouge LA 70816-8190
225-926-5820

Moler Beauty College
59 Westbank Expy, Gretna LA 70053
504-362-1999

Moler Beauty College
1919 Veterans Blvd #100, Kenner LA 70062
504-467-1888

Moler Beauty College
3968 Old Gentilly Rd, New Orleans LA 70126-4859
504-282-2539

Moler Beauty College
2940 Canal St, New Orleans LA 70119
504-821-8842

Neill Institute
1301A W Saint Peter St, New Iberia LA 70560
337-365-6570

New Orleans Job Corps Center
3801 Hollygrove St, New Orleans LA 70118-2529
504-486-0641

Ochsner School of Allied Health Sciences
1516 Jefferson Hwy, New Orleans LA 70121-2429
504-842-3267

OMEGA INSTITUTE OF COSMETOLOGY
229 S Hollywood Rd, Houma LA 70360-2716
985-876-9334 Fax: 985-876-3612
Website: www.omegainstitutes.com
E-mail: pricilla@omegainstitutes.com

Opelousas School of Cosmetology
529 E Vine St, Opelousas LA 70570
337-942-6147

Our Lady of the Lake Medical Center
5000 Hennessy Blvd, Baton Rouge LA 70808-4350
225-769-7799

Pat Goins Beauty School
3138 Louisville Ave, Monroe LA 71201
318-322-0796

Pat Goins Benton Road Beauty School
1701 Old Minden Rd Ste 36, Bossier City LA 71111
318-746-7674

Pat Goins Ruston Beauty School
213 W Alabama Ave, Ruston LA 71270
318-255-2717

Pat Goins Shreveport Beauty School
6363 Hearne Ave Ste 106, Shreveport LA 71108
318-631-1833

Pineville Beauty School
1008 Main St, Pineville LA 71360
318-445-1040

Remington College
10551 Coursey Blvd, Baton Rouge LA 70816
225-922-3990

Remington College
303 Rue Louis XIV #8, Lafayette LA 70508-5760
337-981-4010

Remington College
321 Veterans Blvd, Metairie LA 70005
504-831-8889

Ronnie & Dorman's School of Hair Design
2002 Johnston St, Lafayette LA 70503
337-232-1806

Shreveport Job Corps Center
2815 Lillian St, Shreveport LA 71109-2899
318-227-9331

South Louisiana Beauty College
300 Howard Ave, Houma LA 70363
985-873-8978

Sowela Technical Community College
PO Box 16950, Lake Charles LA 70616
Susan Simmons, Dept. Head Student Services
337-491-2688

Stage One - The Hair School
209 W College St, Lake Charles LA 70605
337-474-0533

Stevenson's Academy of Hair Design
2039 Lapeyrouse St, New Orleans LA 70116
504-945-2312

Stevenson's Academy of Hair Design
401 Opelousas Ave, New Orleans LA 70114
504-368-6377

Unitech Training Academy
3605 Ambassador Caffery Pkwy, Lafayette LA 70503
337-988-6764

Vidalia Beauty School
208 Westside Dr, Vidalia LA 71373
318-336-2377

VORTEX HELICOPTERS
PO Box 9789, New Iberia LA 70562-9789
Mary Sheeran, Vice President
228-864-7357 Fax: 228-864-5850
Website: www.vortex-helicopters.com
E-mail: vortexheli@earthlink.net

MAINE

Headhunter Institute
1041 Brighton Ave, Portland ME 04102
207-772-2591

Kennebec Valley Community College
92 Western Ave, Fairfield ME 04937-1337
Kathy Moore, Director of Admissions
207-453-5035

Landing School of Boatbuilding & Design
PO Box 1490, Kennebunkport ME 04046-1490
Dennis Collins, Director of Admissions
207-985-7976 Fax: 207-985-7942
Website: www.landingschool.edu
E-mail: denniscollins@landingschool.edu

Maine Medical Center
School of Surgical Technology
SMTC Fort Rd, South Portland ME 04106
Maureen Bien, RN, Program Director
207-767-9589

Mr. Bernard's School of Hair Fashion
PO Box 1163, Lewiston ME 04243
207-783-7765

New England School of Communications
One College Cir, Bangor ME 04401-2929
Nelson Jewell, Director of Admissions
888-877-1876

Northern Maine Community College
33 Edgemont Dr, Presque Isle ME 04769-2016
Bill Casavant, Director of Admissions
207-768-2700 Fax: 207-768-2831
Website: www.nmcc.edu
E-mail: admissions@nmcc.edu

Pierre's School of Cosmetology
635 Broadway, Bangor ME 04401-3363
207-942-0039

Pierre's School of Cosmetology
30 Skyway Dr, Caribou ME 04736
207-498-6067

Pierre's School of Cosmetology
319 Marginal Way, Portland ME 04101
207-774-9413

Pierre's School of Cosmetology
913 Main St, Sanford ME 04073
207-490-1274

Pierre's School of Cosmetology
251 Kennedy Memorial Dr, Waterville ME 04901
207-873-0682

Southern Maine Community College
2 Fort Rd, South Portland ME 04106-1698
Dr. James Ortiz, President
Scott MacDonald, Director of Financial Aid
207-741-5500 Fax: 207-741-5671
Website: www.smccme.edu
E-mail: oharmon@maine.rr.com

MARYLAND

Aaron's Academy of Beauty
340 Post Office Rd, Waldorf MD 20602
301-645-3681

ABI - AccuTech Business Institute
5310 Spectrum Dr # A, Frederick MD 21703-7337
301-694-0211

Adventist HealthCare Health Careers Training Center
501 Sligo Ave, Silver Spring MD 20910
Kimbery Arbuthnot, RN, BSN
301-585-7006

Aesthetics Institutes of Cosmetology
15958C Shady Grove Rd, Gaithersburg MD 20877
301-330-9252

ALL-STATE CAREER SCHOOL
2200 Broening Hwy Ste 160
Baltimore MD 21224-6628
John McCullough, School Director/Director of Extension

Campuses
410-631-1818 Fax: 410-631-6180
Website: www.allstatecareer.com
E-mail: johnm@marcogrp.com

American Beauty Academy
2518 University Blvd W, Wheaton MD 20902
301-949-3000

Award Beauty School
26 E Antietam St, Hagerstown MD 21740
301-733-4520

Baltimore School of Massage
6401 Dogwood Rd, Baltimore MD 21207-5225
Angela DenHerder, Campus Director
410-944-8855

BALTIMORE STUDIO OF HAIR DESIGN
318 N Howard St, Baltimore MD 21201
Maxine Sisserman, Administrator
410-539-1935 Fax: 410-539-2840
Website: www.baltimorestudio.net
E-mail: baltimorestudio@netscape.net

Blades School of Hair Design
PO Box 226, California MD 20619
301-862-9797

Broadcasting Institute of Maryland
7200 Harford Rd, Baltimore MD 21234-7765
410-254-2770

Del-Mar-Va Beauty Academy
111 Milford St, Salisbury MD 21804-6952
410-742-7929

Empire Beauty School
5633 Reisterstown Rd, Baltimore MD 21215
800-575-5983

Empire Beauty School
9616 Reistertown Rd Ste 105
Owings Mills MD 21117
800-575-5983

Everest Institute
8757 Georgia Ave Ste 650, Silver Spring MD 20910
301-495-4400

Hair Academy
8435 Annapolis Rd, New Carrollton MD 20784
301-459-2509

Harrison Career Institute
1040 Park Ave, Baltimore MD 21201
410-962-0303

International Beauty School
227 Archer St, Bel Air MD 21014
410-838-0845

International Beauty School
214 Paca St, Cumberland MD 21502
301-777-3020

Lincoln Technical Institute
9325 Snowden River Pkwy
Columbia MD 21046-1544
Paul McGuirk, Executive Director
410-290-7100

MARYLAND BEAUTY ACADEMY
152 Chartley Dr, Reisterstown MD 21136
Jaime Davidov, Director
410-517-0442 Fax: 410-517-2513
Website: www.baltimorestudio.net
E-mail: mdbeautyacademy@netscape.net

MARYLAND BEAUTY ACADEMY OF ESSEX
505 Eastern Blvd, Baltimore MD 21221
Justin Sisserman, Administrator
410-686-4477 Fax: 410-686-0786
Website: www.baltimorestudio.net
E-mail: mdbeautyacademy@netscape.net

MEDIX SCHOOL
700 York Rd, Towson MD 21204-2503
Lisa Harper, Director of Admissions
410-337-5155 Fax: 410-337-5104
Website: www.medixschooltowson.edu
E-mail: admissions@medixsch.com

Montgomery Beauty School
8736 Arliss St, Silver Spring MD 20901
301-459-2509

New Creation Academy of Hair Design
3930 Bexley Pl, Suitland MD 20746
Carla Robinson, President
Brandi Smith, Contact
301-899-9100

North American Trade Schools
6901 Security Blvd Ste 16, Baltimore MD 21244
Jerry Daly, Director
410-298-4844

Robert Paul Academy of Cosmetology Arts & Sciences
1811B York Rd Ste B, Timonium MD 21093
410-252-4481

TESST College of Technology
1520 S Caton Ave, Baltimore MD 21227-1063
H. V. Leslie, President
410-644-6400

TESST College of Technology
803 Glen Eagles Ct, Towson MD 21286-2201
Dianne McRae, President
410-296-5350

TESST Technology Institute
4600 Powder Mill Rd Ste 500
Beltsville MD 20705-2675
Tina Turk, Director of Admissions
301-937-8448

Ultrasound Diagnostic School
8401 Corporate Dr Ste 500
Landover MD 20785-2287
301-588-0786

MASSACHUSETTS

Ailano School of Aesthetics
553 Forest Ave, Brockton MA 02301
Kera Arnone, Contact
508-587-3883 Fax: 508-588-7227
Website: www.ailanoschool.com
E-mail: ailanoki@conversent.net

AILANO SCHOOL OF COSMETOLOGY
PO Box 4740, Brockton MA 02303-4740
Karen Iolli, Owner/Adm
508-583-5433 Fax: 508-588-7227
Website: www.ailanoschool.com
E-mail: ailanoki@conversent.net

BANCROFT SCHOOL OF MASSAGE THERAPY
333 Shrewsbury St, Worcester MA 01604-4614
Judie Morin, Admissions
508-757-7923 Fax: 508-791-5930
Website: bancroftsmt.com
E-mail: jmorin@bancroftsmt.com

Bay State School of Technology
225 Turnpike St, Canton MA 02021-2358
781-828-3434

Benjamin Franklin Institute of Technology
41 Berkeley St, Boston MA 02116-6307
Norman Kraft, Dean of Enrollment
617-423-4630 ext. 121 Fax: 617-482-3706
Website: www.bfit.edu
E-mail: admissions@bfit.edu

Blaine, The Beauty Career School
Boston Campus
30 West St, Boston MA 02111-1204
Wayne Fortes, Education Director
617-266-2661

Blaine, The Beauty Career School
Corporate Office
624 Worcester Rd, Framingham MA 01702
Teresa Ferent, Scholarship Director
580-370-7447

Blaine, The Beauty Career School
Framingham Campus
624 Worcester Rd, Framingham MA 01702
Gloria Weekes, Education Director
508-370-3700

Blaine, The Beauty Career School
Hyannis Campus
18 Center St, Hyannis MA 02601-5536
Ruthann Foss, Education Director
508-771-1680

Blaine, The Beauty Career School
Lowell Campus
231 Central St, Lowell MA 01852-2214
Annette Voss, Education Director
978-459-9959

Blaine, The Beauty Career School
Malden Campus
347 Pleasant St, Malden MA 02148-8121
David Maietta, Education Director
781-397-7400

Blaine, The Beauty Career School
Waltham Campus
314 Moody St, Waltham MA 02453-5202
Maryanne Crane, Education Director
781-899-1500

Bryman Institute
1505 Commonwealth Ave, Brighton MA 02135-3605
Kathleen Devine, Director of Admissions
617-783-9955

Butera School of Art
111 Beacon St, Boston MA 02116-1597
617-536-4623

Cambridge School of Culinary Arts
2020 Massachusetts Ave
Cambridge MA 02140-2104
Lillian Ascenzo, Contact
617-354-2020

Catherine E. Hinds Institute of Esthetics
300 Wildwood Ave, Woburn MA 01801-6815
Kim St. Cyr, Director of Admissions
781-935-3344

Center for Digital Imaging Arts at Boston University
282 Moody St, Waltham MA 02453
800-808-2342

C.H. McCann Technical School
70 Hodges Cross Road, North Adams MA 01247
Patricia E. Durkee, Admissions
413-663-5383

Computer-Ed Business Institute
375 Westgate Dr, Brockton MA 02301-1818
508-941-0730

Computer-Ed Business Institute
5 Middlesex Ave, Somerville MA 02145
781-933-7681

East Coast Aero Tech School
150 Hanscom Dr, Bedford MA 01730-2630
Marty Goguen, Director of Admissions
781-274-8448

E.I.N.E. Inc. Electrology Institute of N.E.Sm
Esthetics Institute of N.E.sm
1501 Main St Suite 50, Tewksbury MA 01876
Mary Evangelista, Director
800-548-6339

The Elizabeth Grady School of Esthetics
222 Boston Ave, Medford MA 02155
781-391-9380

FINE MORTUARY COLLEGE
A Private Two Year College
150 Kerry Pl, Norwood MA 02062-4766
Lyn Prendergast, Ph.D., Executive Vice President
781-762-1211 Fax: 781-762-7177
Website: www.fine-ne.com
E-mail: fine@fine-ne.com

Gibbs College of Boston
a Private Two-Year College
126 Newbury St, Boston MA 02116-2904
Ida Zecco, Vice President of Admissions
617-578-7100 Fax: 617-578-7163
Website: www.gibbsboston.edu

Hair in Motion Beauty Academy
73 Hamilton St, Worcester MA 01604
508-756-6060

HALLMARK INSTITUTE OF PHOTOGRAPHY
PO Box 308, Turners Falls MA 01376-0308
Shelley Nicholson, Director of Enrollment Services
413-863-2478 Fax: 413-863-4118
Website: hallmark.edu
E-mail: info@hallmark.edu

Henri's School of Hair Design
PO Box 2244, Fitchburg MA 01420
978-342-6061

ITT TECHNICAL INSTITUTE
333 Boston Providence Tpke
Norwood MA 02062-3932
Tom Ryan, Director of Recruiting
800-879-TECH (8324) Fax: 781-278-0766
Website: www.itt-tech.edu
E-mail: tryan@itt-tech.edu
Established 1990. Private. Coed. Accreditation: ACICS. Enrollment: 300. Student-faculty ratio: 11:1. Associate Degrees offered: Computer Drafting & Design, Computer Electronics Technology, Computer Network Systems, Multimedia.

ITT TECHNICAL INSTITUTE
10 Forbes Rd, Woburn MA 01801
Marilyn Lamont, Contact
781-937-8324 Fax: 781-937-3402
Website: www.itt-tech.edu
E-mail: mlamont@itt-tech.edu

Jolie Hair and Beauty Academy
44 Sewall St, Ludlow MA 01056
413-589-0747

Kay Harvey Hairdressing Academy
11 Central St, West Springfield MA 01089
413-732-7117

LaBaron Hairdressing Academy
240 Liberty St, Brockton MA 02301-5570
508-583-1700

LaBaron Hairdressing Academy
281 Union St, New Bedford MA 02740
508-996-6611

LAWRENCE MEMORIAL/REGIS COLLEGE NURSING AND RADIOGRAPHY PROGRAMS
170 Governors Ave, Medford MA 02155-1643
Admissions Coordinator
781-306-6600 Fax: 781-306-6142
Website: www.lmregis.org
E-mail: admissions@lmregis.org

Learning Institute for Beauty Sciences
867 Boylston St, Boston MA 02116
617-424-6565

Learning Institute for Beauty Sciences
384 Main St, Malden MA 02148
781-324-3400

Lowell Academy Hairstyling Institute
136 Central St, Lowell MA 01852
978-453-3235

Mansfield Beauty School
200 Parkingway St, Quincy MA 02169
617-479-1090

Mansfield Beauty School
266 Bridge St, Springfield MA 01103
413-788-7575

Massachusetts School of Barbering & Mens Hairstyling
1585 Hancock St, Quincy MA 02169
617-770-4444

Mildred Elley Business School
505 East St, Pittsfield MA 01201
413-499-8618

New England Hair Academy
110 Florence St Suite 203, Malden MA 02148-3967
781-324-6799

New England Institute of Art
10 Brookline Place, Brookline MA 02445
Deborah Brent, Director of Admissions
800-903-4425

New England School of Art & Design at Suffolk University
75 Arlington St, Boston MA 02116
John Harnel, Director of Admissions
617-573-8785

NEW ENGLAND SCHOOL OF PHOTOGRAPHY
537 Commonwealth Ave, Boston MA 02215-2005
Arthur Levi Rainville, Academic Director
800-676-3767 Fax: 617-437-0261
Website: www.nesop.com
E-mail: admissions@nesop.com

North Bennet Street School
39 N Bennet St, Boston MA 02113-1914
Cynthia Stone, Executive Director
617-227-0155

Porter and Chester Institute
134 Dulong Cir, Chicopee MA 01022-1153
413-593-3339

RETS Electronic School
570 Rutherford Ave, Charlestown MA 02129
800-739-8700

Rob Roy Academy
1872 Acushnet Ave, New Bedford MA 02746
508-995-8711

Rob Roy Academy
150 Pleasant St, Worcester MA 01609
508-799-2111

Rob Roy Academy Fall River Campus
260 S Main St, Fall River MA 02721
508-672-4751

Rob Roy Academy Taunton Campus
1 School St, Taunton MA 02780
508-822-1405

Salter School
155 Ararat St, Worcester MA 01606-3421
508-853-1074

Southeastern Technical Institute
250 Foundry St, South Easton MA 02375-1780
Beverly A. Pusateri, Director
508-238-1860 Fax: 508-230-1558
Website: ti.sersd.org
E-mail: bpusateri@sersd.org

Ultrasound Diagnostic School
365 Cadwell Dr, Springfield MA 01104-1739
413-739-4700

Universal Technical Institute
1 Upland Rd, Norwood MA 02062
781-948-2030

MICHIGAN

Academy of Court Reporting
1330 W 14 Mile Rd, Clawson MI 48017-1495
248-353-4880

BAYSHIRE BEAUTY ACADEMY
917 Saginaw St, Bay City MI 48708-5614
Jim Goodrow, CEO
989-894-2431 Fax: 989-894-6033
Website: www.bayshire.com
E-mail: bayshire@speednetllc.com

Career Quest Learning Center
5000 Northwind Dr Ste 120, East Lansing MI 48823
517-318-3330

CARNEGIE INSTITUTE
550 Stephenson Hwy Ste 100, Troy MI 48083-1159
Gloria J. McEachern, President
248-589-1078 Fax: 248-589-1631
Website: www.carnegie-institute.com
E-mail: carnegie47@aol.com

Chic University of Cosmetology
1735 4 Mile Rd NE, Grand Rapids MI 49525
616-363-9853

Chic University of Cosmetology
455 Standale Plaza NW, Grand Rapids MI 49534
616-735-9680

Chic University of Cosmetology
6091 Constitution Blvd, Portage MI 49024
269-329-3333

Davenport College of Business
200 Van Buren St W, Battle Creek MI 49017-3007
269-968-6105

Davenport College of Business
220 E Kalamazoo St, Lansing MI 48933-2110
517-484-2600

David Pressley School of Cosmetology
1127 S Washington Ave, Royal Oak MI 48067
Sally Pressley, Vice President
248-548-5090

Detroit Business Institute
23077 Greenfield Rd #LL28
Southfield MI 48075-3751
Greg Mitchell, Director of Admissions
248-552-6300 Fax: 248-552-7300
Website: www.dbisouthfield.com
E-mail: info@dbisouthfield.com

Detroit Business Institute - Downriver
19100 Fort St, Riverview MI 48193
Theresa Hernandez, Director of Admissions
734-479-0660 Fax: 734-479-0738
Website: www.dbidownriver.com
E-mail: info@dbidownriver.com

Detroit Institute of Ophthalmology
15415 E Jefferson Ave, Grosse Pointe MI 48230-1328
Deanna Presnell, BA, COMT, Program Director
313-824-4710 ext. 223

Dorsey Business School
30821 Barrington St, Madison Heights MI 48071-1871
248-588-9660

Dorsey Business School
31542 Gratiot Ave, Roseville MI 48066-4555
586-296-3225

Dorsey Business School
15755 Northline Rd, Southgate MI 48195-2334
734-285-5400

Dorsey Business School
34841 Veterans Plz, Wayne MI 48184-1733
734-595-1540

Douglas J Educational Center
333 Albert Ave Ste 110, East Lansing MI 48823
517-333-9656

Educational Institute of the American Hotel & Lodging Association
2113 N High St, Lansing MI 48906
800-344-4381 ext. PSC

FISER'S COLLEGE OF COSMETOLOGY
329 1/2 E Maumee St, Adrian MI 49221-2907
Pam Fiser, Owner
517-264-2199 Fax: 517-263-2754
E-mail: adrianbeauty@tc3net.com

Flint Institute of Barbering
3214 Flushing Rd, Flint MI 48504
810-232-4711

HEALTH ENRICHMENT CENTER, INC.
204 E Nepessing St, Lapeer MI 48446
Roxanne Sears, Business Manager
810-667-9453 Fax: 810-667-4095
Website: www.healthenrichment.com
E-mail: hec@tir.com

Hillsdale Beauty College
64 Waldron St, Hillsdale MI 49242
517-437-4670

Houghton Lake Institute of Cosmetology
PO Box 669, Houghton Lake MI 48629

Howell College of Cosmetology
1800 Dorr Rd, Howell MI 48843-8801
517-546-4155

Kent Career/Technical Center
1655 E Beltline Ave NE
Grand Rapids MI 49525-4509
616-364-8421

Lawton School
20755 Greenfield Rd Ste 300
Southfield MI 48075-5406
248-569-7787

MACOMB COMMUNITY COLLEGE
44575 Garfield Rd, Clinton Township MI 48038-1139
Information Center
586-445-7999
Website: www.macomb.edu
E-mail: answer@macomb.edu

MACOMB COMMUNITY COLLEGE
14500 E 12 Mile Rd, Warren MI 48088-3896
Information Center
586-445-7999
Website: www.macomb.edu
E-mail: answer@macomb.edu

Michigan Barber School
8988-90 Grand River, Detroit MI 48204
313-894-2300

Michigan College of Beauty
15232 1/2 S Dixie Hwy, Monroe MI 48161
734-241-8877

Michigan College of Beauty
3498 Rochester Rd, Troy MI 48083
248-528-0303

MICHIGAN COLLEGE OF BEAUTY
5620 Dixie Hwy, Waterford MI 48329
Susan Pantello, CEO
Allison Murphy, Director of Admissions
248-623-9494 Fax: 248-623-6505
Website: www.michigancollegeofbeauty.com
E-mail: mcb1@myexcel.com

Michigan Institute of Aeronautics
47884 D St, Belleville MI 48111-1181
734-483-3758

M.J. Murphy Beauty College
201 W Broadway, Mount Pleasant MI 48858
989-772-2339

Mr. Bela's School of Cosmetology
29475 John R Rd, Madison Heights MI 48071
248-543-4333

Mr. David's School of Cosmetolgy
3600 S Dort Hwy, Flint MI 48507
810-742-9010

National Institute of Technology
23400 Michigan Ave Ste 200, Dearborn MI 48124
888-463-0494

National Institute of Technology
300 River Place Dr Ste 1000, Detroit MI 48207
313-567-5350

National Institute of Technology
26111 Evergreen Rd Ste 201
Southfield MI 48076-4491
Marchelle Weaver, President
248-799-9933 Fax: 248-799-2912
Website: www.cci.edu
E-mail: mweaver@cci.edu

Northwestern Technological Institute
24567 Northwestern Hwy #200
Southfield MI 48075-2412
248-358-4006

OLYMPIA CAREER TRAINING INSTITUTE
1750 Woodworth St NE
Grand Rapids MI 49525-2301
Bobbi Blok, Director of Admissions
616-364-8464 Fax: 616-364-5454
Website: www.cci.edu
E-mail: rblok@cci.edu

Olympia Career Training Institute
5177 W Main St, Kalamazoo MI 49009
Susan Smith, Director of Admission
269-381-9616 Fax: 269-381-2513
Website: www.olympia-institute.com
E-mail: susans@cci.edu

Ross Medical Education Center
4741 Washtenaw Ave, Ann Arbor MI 48108
734-434-7320

Ross Medical Education Center
5757 Whitmore Lake Rd #800
Brighton MI 48116-1962
810-227-0160

Ross Medical Education Center
1036 Gilbert St, Flint MI 48532-3527
810-230-1100

Ross Medical Education Center
2035 28th St SE Ste O, Grand Rapids MI 49508-1539
616-243-3070

Ross Medical Education Center
913 W Holmes Rd Ste 260, Lansing MI 48910-4490
517-887-0180

Ross Medical Education Center
950 W Norton Ave, Muskegon MI 49441-4169
231-730-9531

Ross Medical Education Center
3568 Pine Grove Ave, Port Huron MI 48060-1958
810-982-0454

Ross Medical Education Center
9327 Telegraph Rd, Redford MI 48239-1260
313-794-6448

Ross Medical Education Center
4054 Bay Rd, Saginaw MI 48603-1201
989-793-9800

Ross Medical Education Center
27120 Dequindre Rd, Warren MI 48092-3537
586-574-0830

School of Creative Hair Design
470 Marshall St, Coldwater MI 49036-1139
517-279-2355

SER Business and Technical Institute
9301 Michigan Ave, Detroit MI 48210-2038
313-846-2240

Sharps Academy of Hairstyling
115 Main St, Flushing MI 48433
810-659-3348

Sharps Academy of Hairstyling
8166 Holly Rd, Grand Blanc MI 48439
810-695-6742

Specs Howard School of Broadcast Arts
19900 W 9 Mile Rd, Southfield MI 48075-3953
Nancy Shiner, Admissions Director
248-358-9000 Fax: 248-746-9772
Website: www.specshoward.edu
E-mail: info@specshoward.edu

Taratuta School of Truck Driving
2215 Oak Industrial Dr NE
Grand Rapids MI 49505-6037
John Taratuta, President
616-742-9000

TAYLORTOWN SCHOOL OF BEAUTY
23129 Ecorse Rd, Taylor MI 48180
Cynthia Stramecky, President
313-291-2177 Fax: 313-292-9754
Website: www.1800cutclass.com
E-mail: cabtylady@aol.com

Twin City Beauty College
2600 Lincoln Ave, Saint Joseph MI 49085
269-428-2900

U.P. Academy of Hair Design
1619 Ludington St, Escanaba MI 49829
906-786-5750

Virginia Farrell Beauty School
22925 Woodward Ave, Ferndale MI 48220
248-398-4647

Virginia Farrell Beauty School
33425 5 Mile Rd, Livonia MI 48154
734-427-3970

Virginia Farrell Beauty School
23620 Harper Ave, Saint Clair Shores MI 48080-1448
586-775-6640

Virginia Farrell Beauty School
34580 Ford Rd, Westland MI 48185
734-729-9220

West Michigan College of Barbering & Beauty
3026 Lovers Ln, Kalamazoo MI 49001
269-381-4424

Wright Beauty Academy
492 Capital Ave SW, Battle Creek MI 49015
269-964-4016

Wright Beauty Academy
6666 Lovers Ln, Portage MI 49002
269-321-8708

MINNESOTA
ACADEMY COLLEGE
1101 E 78th St, Bloomington MN 55420-1402
Marvin Kimble, Director of Admissions
952-851-0066 Fax: 952-851-0094
Website: www.academycollege.edu
E-mail: info@academycollege.edu
Established 1936. Private. Accreditation: ACICS. Offering BS degrees in Business Administration, Accounting, Digital Arts & Design, and Computer Science, and AAS degrees and certificates in: web design, e-business, web developer, web administrator, networking, programming, tech support, computer animation, graphic design, medical administrative assistant, legal office assistant, project management, office management, professional pilot, aviation business, and accounting. Day and evening classes. Financial aid for those who qualify. Employment placement assistance.

Alexandria Technical College
1601 Jefferson St, Alexandria MN 56308-3707
320-762-0221

American Academy of Acupuncture & Oriental Medicine
1925 County Road B2 W, Roseville MN 55113
651-631-0204

Art Institutes International Minnesota
15 S 9th St, Minneapolis MN 55402-3137
612-332-3361

Aveda Institute
400 Central Ave SE, Minneapolis MN 55414
612-378-7404

Brown College
6860 Shingle Creek Pkwy, Brooklyn Center MN 55430
763-566-2279

Brown College
1440 Northland Dr, Mendota Heights MN 55120-1004
Dawn Bravo, VP Marketing
800-6-BROWN-6

Cosmetology Careers Unlimited - Duluth
121 W Superior St, Duluth MN 55802
218-722-7484

Cosmetology Careers Unlimited - Hibbing
110 E Howard St, Hibbing MN 55746
218-263-8354

Dakota County Technical College
1300 145th St E, Rosemount MN 55068-2999
800-548-5502

Duluth Business University
4724 Mike Colalillo Dr, Duluth MN 55807-2723
Bonnie Kupczynski, Director
800-777-8406 Fax: 218-628-2127
Website: www.dbumn.edu
E-mail: info@dbumn.edu

DUNWOODY COLLEGE OF TECHNOLOGY
818 Dunwoody Blvd, Minneapolis MN 55403-1192
Dr. C. Ben Wright, President
John Slama, Vice President Enrollment Management
612-374-5800 or 800-292-4625 Fax: 612-374-4128
Website: www.dunwoody.edu
Founded in 1914. Dunwoody is a private, non-profit, technical school offering AAS degrees or diplomas in 22 programs which can be completed in two years or less. Dunwoody College of Technology is accredited by the Commission on Institutions of Higher Education of the North Central Association of Colleges and Schools (NCA). Tuition: Approx. $3,100/Qtr. Enrollment: 1,300 full-time, 1,000 part-time. Faculty: 75. Student-faculty ratio: 12:1. Two buildings on a 12 acre campus. Programs include Architectural Drafting and Estimating, Automated Systems and Robotics, Automotive Collision and Refinishing, Automotive Collision Apprenticeship Cooperative, Automotive Service Technology, Automotive Technician Apprenticeship Cooperative, Computer Networking Systems, Construction Accounting, Electrical Construction Design & Management, Electrical Construction & Maintenance, Electronics Engineering Technology, Engineering Drafting and Design Technology, Food Technology, Graphic Design, Graphics & Printing

Technologies, Heating & Cooling (HVAC), Home Appliance Technician, HVAC Systems Servicing, Interior Design, Land Surveying Educational Cooperative, Machining Technology, Mechanical/Architectural Design: Heating, Ventilation & Air Conditioning, Sound, Data and Alarms Systems Design, Welding, Information Professional.
Dunwoody offers scholarships for outstanding students, women, students in selected courses, plus comprehensive financial aid. For further information, call the Admissions Office at Dunwoody.

East Metro Opportunities Industrialization Center
1919 University Ave Ste 500, Saint Paul MN 55104
Norma Fuglie, Director of Training
651-291-5088

Globe College
7166 10th St N, Oakdale MN 55128
Mike Hughes, Campus Director
651-730-5100 Fax: 651-730-5151
Website: www.globecollege.edu
E-mail: admissions@globecollege.edu

Hennepin Technical College
9000 Brooklyn Blvd, Brooklyn Park MN 55445-2320
952-995-1300

Herzing College
5700 W Broadway Ave, Minneapolis MN 55428-3597
763-535-3000

Hibbing Community College
1515 E 25th St, Hibbing MN 55746-3300
Holly Bigelow, Director of Enrollment
800-224-4HCC or 218-262-7200 Fax: 218-262-6717
Website: www.hibbing.edu
E-mail: admissions@hibbing.edu

High-Tech Institute
5100 Gamble Dr Ste 200
Saint Louis Park MN 55416-1521
763-560-9700

Minneapolis Business College
1711 County Road B W, Roseville MN 55113-4036
651-636-7406

Minneapolis Community and Technical College
1501 Hennepin Ave, Minneapolis MN 55403-1779
Dena Russell, Director of Admissions
612-659-6282 Fax: 612-659-6210
Website: www.minneapolis.edu
E-mail: admissions.office@minneapolis.edu

Minneapolis School of Massage & Bodywork
81 Lowry Ave NE, Minneapolis MN 55418-3343
612-788-8907

Minnesota School of Business
5910 Shingle Creek Pkwy #200
Brooklyn Center MN 55430-2319
763-566-7777

Minnesota School of Business
1401 W 76th St Ste 500, Richfield MN 55423-3846
612-861-2000

Minnesota State College - Southeast Technical
308 Pioneer Rd, Red Wing MN 55066-3964
Al Ducett, Director of Admissions
800-657-4849 Fax: 507-453-2715
Website: www.southeastmn.edu
E-mail: aducett@southeastmn.edu

Minnesota State College - Southeast Technical
Airport Campus
110 Galewski Dr, Winona MN 55987
Al Ducett, Director of Admissions
507-453-2630 Fax: 507-453-2715
Website: www.southeastmn.edu
E-mail: aducett@southeastmn.edu

Minnesota State College - Southeast Technical
Winona Campus
1250 Homer Rd PO Box 409, Winona MN 55987-0409
Al Ducett, Director of Admissions
800-372-8164 Fax: 507-453-2715
Website: www.southeastmn.edu
E-mail: aducett@southeastmn.edu

Minnesota State Community & Technical College
900 Highway 34 E, Detroit Lakes MN 56501-2698
Dale Westley, Director of Admissions
800-492-4836 Fax: 218-846-3710
Website: www.minnesota.edu
E-mail: dale.westley@minnesota.edu

Minnesota State Community & Technical College
PO Box 566, Wadena MN 56482-0566
Paul Drange, Director of Admissions
800-247-2007 Fax: 218-631-7901
Website: www.minnesota.edu
E-mail: paul.drange@minnesota.edu

Minnesota State Community and Technical College
1900 28th Ave S, Moorhead MN 56560-4899
Laurie McKeever, Director of Admissions
800-426-5603 Fax: 218-299-6584
Website: www.minnesota.edu
E-mail: laurie.mckeever@minnesota.edu

Minnesota West Community and Technical College
Canby Campus
1011 1st St W, Canby MN 56220-9494
Jodi Weber, Contact
800-658-2535

Minnesota West Community and Technical College
Granite Falls Campus
1593 11th Ave, Granite Falls MN 56241-1061
Becky Weber, Contact
800-657-3247

Minnesota West Community and Technical College
Jackson Campus
PO Box 269, Jackson MN 56143-0269
Lynne Liepold, Contact
800-658-2522

Minnesota West Community and Technical College
Pipestone Campus
1314 N Hiawatha Ave, Pipestone MN 56164-2282
Laurel Berg, Contact
800-658-2330

Minnesota West Community and Technical College
Worthington Campus
1450 Collegeway, Worthington MN 56187-3024
Mitz Diemer, Contact
800-657-3966

Model College of Hair Design
201 8th Ave S, Saint Cloud MN 56301
320-253-4222

Northwest Technical College
905 Grant Ave SE, Bemidji MN 56601
Richard Lehmann, Director of Admissions
800-942-8324

NTI-School of CAD Technology
11995 Singletree Ln, Eden Prairie MN 55344-5351
800-443-4223

Oliver Thein Beauty College
150 Cobblestone Ln, Burnsville MN 55337
612-435-3882

Rasmussen College
3500 Federal Dr, Eagan MN 55122-1346
651-687-9000

Rasmussen College
7905 Golden Triangle Dr Ste 100
Eden Prairie MN 55344-7220
952-545-2000

Rasmussen College
501 Holly Ln, Mankato MN 56001-6803
507-625-6556

RASMUSSEN COLLEGE - ST. CLOUD
226 Park Ave S, Saint Cloud MN 56301-3713
Admissions
320-251-5600 or 800-852-0460 Fax: 320-251-3702
Website: www.rasmussen.edu
E-mail: stcloud@rasmussen.edu

Regency Beauty Academy
40 County Road 10 NE, Blaine MN 55434
763-784-9102

Ridgewater College-Hutchinson Campus
2 Century Ave SE, Hutchinson MN 55350-3100
Dawn Bjork, Counselor
800-222-4424 Fax: 320-231-7767
Website: www.ridgewater.edu
E-mail: dawn.bjork@ridgewater.edu

Ridgewater College-Willmar Campus
PO Box 1097, Willmar MN 56201-1097
Sally Kerfeld, Director of Admissions
800-722-1151 Fax: 320-231-7677
Website: www.ridgewater.edu
E-mail: skerfeld@ridgewater.edu

Rita's Moorhead Beauty College
17 4th St S, Moorhead MN 56560
218-236-7201

Riverland Community College
1900 8th Ave NW, Austin MN 55912-1400
Dani Heiny, Director of Admissions
800-247-5039

Riverland Community College
Albert Lea Campus
2200 Riverland Dr, Albert Lea MN 56007
Dani Heiny, Director of Admissions
800-333-2584

Riverland Technical College
1225 3rd St SW, Faribault MN 55021-5720
800-422-0391

Rochester Community & Technical College
1926 Collegeview Rd E, Rochester MN 55904-8201
800-247-1296

St. Cloud Regency Beauty Academy
110 2nd St S, Waite Park MN 56387
320-251-0500

St. Cloud Technical College
1540 Northway Dr, Saint Cloud MN 56303-1240
Jodi Elness, Director of Enrollment Management
800-222-1009 Fax: 320-308-5981
Website: www.sctc.edu
E-mail: jelness@sctc.edu

Scot Lewis Beauty School
4124 Lancaster Ln N, Plymouth MN 55441
763-551-0562

Scot Lewis School
1905 Suburban Ave, Saint Paul MN 55119
651-209-6930

Scot Lewis School of Cosmetology
9749 Lyndale Ave S, Bloomington MN 55420
Carol Olinger, Director of Admissions
952-881-8662

Sr. Rosalind Gefre Schools of Massage
416 S Front St, Mankato MN 56001
Alyssa Beyer, Director of Admissions
507-344-0220 Fax: 507-344-0204
Website: www.sisterrosalind.org
E-mail: mankatocampus@sisterrosalind.org

Sr. Rosalind Gefre Schools of Massage
300 Elton Hills Dr NW, Rochester MN 55901
Jason Egginton, Director of Admissions
507-286-8608 Fax: 507-282-2893
Website: www.sisterrosalind.org
E-mail: rochestercampus@sisterrosalind.org

Sr. Rosalind Gefre Schools of Massage
1007 Industrial Dr S, Sauk Rapids MN 56379
Kelly Christopheron, Director of Admissions
320-259-6185 Fax: 320-259-6173
Website: www.sisterrosalind.org
E-mail: saukrapidscampus@sisterrosalind.org

Sr. Rosalind Gefre Schools of Massage
149 Thompson Ave Ste 150
West Saint Paul MN 55118
Jen Maudel, Director of Admissions
651-554-3010 Fax: 651-554-7608
Website: www.sisterrosalind.org
E-mail: stpaulcampus@sisterrosalind.org

Summit Academy OIC
935 Olson Memorial Hwy
Minneapolis MN 55405-1359
612-377-0150

MISSISSIPPI

Academy of Hair Design #1
2003B Commerce St, Grenada MS 38901
662-226-2462

Academy of Hair Design #3
1815 Terry Rd, Jackson MS 39204
601-372-9800

Academy of Hair Design #4
3167 Highway 80 E, Pearl MS 39208-3503
601-939-4441

Academy of Hair Design #6
5912 US Highway 49, Hattiesburg MS 39401
601-583-1290

Academy of Hair Design #7
215 Highway 35 N, Carthage MS 39051
601-267-8031

Antonelli College
1500 N 31st Ave, Hattiesburg MS 39401-3056
601-583-4100

Antonelli College
2323 Lakeland Dr, Jackson MS 39232-9514
601-362-9991

Batesville Job Corps Center
821 Highway 51 S, Batesville MS 38606-2545
Fletcher Harris, Center Director
662-563-4656

Blue Cliff College
2200 25th Ave, Gulfport MS 39501
228-896-9727

Chris' Beauty College
1265 Pass Rd, Gulfport MS 39501
228-864-2920

Creations College of Cosmetology
PO Box 2635, Tupelo MS 38803-2635
662-844-9264

Day Spa Career College
3900 Bienville Blvd, Ocean Springs MS 39564
228-875-4809

Delta Beauty College
697 Delta Pl, Greenville MS 38701
662-332-0587

Final Touch Beauty School
5700 N Hills St, Meridian MS 39307
601-485-7733

Foster's Cosmetology College
PO Box 66, Ripley MS 38663
662-837-9334

Gibson's Barber & Beauty College
PO Box 990, West Point MS 39773
662-494-5444

GULFPORT JOB CORPS CENTER
3300 20th St, Gulfport MS 39501-4311
Samuel Kolapo, Center Director
228-864-9691 Fax: 228-865-0154
Website: jobcorpsregion3.com
E-mail: cd.gulfport@jobcorps.org

ICS the Wright Beauty College
2077 Highway 72 E Annex, Corinth MS 38834
662-287-0944

J & J Hair Design College
116 E Franklin St, Carthage MS 39051-3716
601-267-3678

J & J Hair Design College
562 W Main St Ste B, Senatobia MS 38668
662-562-8010

Magnolia College of Cosmetology
4725 I-55 N, Jackson MS 39206
601-362-6940

Mississippi College of Beauty Culture
732 Sawmill Rd, Laurel MS 39440
601-428-7127

Mississippi Job Corps Center
PO Box 817, Crystal Springs MS 39059-0817
Rowan Torrey, Center Director
601-892-3348

Traxler School of Hair
2845 Suncrest Dr, Jackson MS 39212
601-371-3253

VIRGINIA COLLEGE
5360 I 55 N, Jackson MS 39211
601-977-0960 Fax: 601-956-4325

MISSOURI

Abbott Academy of Cosmetology Arts & Sciences
2101 Parkway Dr, Saint Peters MO 63376
636-447-0100

ALLIED COLLEGE - NORTH
13723 Riverport Dr Ste 103
Maryland Heights MO 63043
866-501-1291
Website: www.alliedcollege.edu

Allied College - South
645 Gravois Bluffs Blvd, Fenton MO 63026
866-502-2627

American College of Hair Design
125 Duke Rd, Sedalia MO 65301
660-827-3295

Aviation Institute of Maintenance
3130 Terrace St, Kansas City MO 64111
816-753-9920

Bryan College
237 S Florence Ave, Springfield MO 65806
Brian Stewart, President
417-862-5700

Cape Girardeau Career & Technology Center
1080 S Silver Springs Rd
Cape Girardeau MO 63703-7511
573-334-0826

Central College of Cosmetology
PO Box 463, Waynesville MO 65583
573-336-3888

CHILLICOTHE BEAUTY ACADEMY
505 Elm St, Chillicothe MO 64601
Yvonne Good, Financial Aid Advisor
660-646-4198 Fax: 660-646-9983
Website: www.chillicothecosmetology.com
E-mail: cbainc@greenhills.net

Class Act I School of Cosmetology
512 Main St, Joplin MO 64801
417-781-7070

Columbia Beauty Academy
1729 W Broadway Ste 5, Columbia MO 65203
573-445-6611

Elaine Steven Beauty College
10420 W Florissant Ave, Saint Louis MO 63136
314-868-8196

FRANKLIN TECHNOLOGY - MSSU
3950 Newman Rd, Joplin MO 64801
Dr. Richard Saporito, Director of Postsecondary
Education
417-659-4400 Fax: 414-659-4408
Website: www.ftcjoplin.com
E-mail: saporito-r@mssu.edu

Grabber School of Hair Design
14557 Manchester Rd, Ballwin MO 63011-3960
636-227-4440

Hannibal Area Vocational Technical School
4550 McMasters Ave, Hannibal MO 63401-2285
Dr. Harold D. Ward, Director
573-221-4430

HERITAGE COLLEGE
534 E 99th St, Kansas City MO 64131
Larry Cartmill, Director
816-942-5474 Fax: 816-942-5405
Website: www.heritage-education.com
E-mail: info@heritage-education.com
Accredited Member School: ACCSCT. Providing quality education in Massage Therapy, Personal Trainer, X-Ray Medical Technician and Pharmacy Technician. Financial aid available to those who qualify.

Hickey College
940 Westport Plz, Saint Louis MO 63146-3127
Christopher A. Gearin, President
800-777-1544 or 314-434-2212 Fax: 314-434-1974
Website: www.hickeycollege.edu
E-mail: admin@hickeycollege.edu

High-Tech Institute - Kansas City
9001 State Line Rd, Kansas City MO 64114
816-444-4300

House of Heavilin Beauty College
2000 SW State Route 7, Blue Springs MO 64014
816-229-9000

HOUSE OF HEAVILIN BEAUTY COLLEGE
12020 Blue Ridge Ext, Grandview MO 64030
Amber Reed, Contact
816-767-8000 Fax: 816-767-8604
Website: www.kc-hair.com
E-mail: sheavilin@kc-hair.com

House of Heavilin Beauty College
5720 Troost Ave, Kansas City MO 64110-2826
Jerry Heavilin, President
816-523-2471

IHM Health Studies Center
2500 Abbott Pl, Saint Louis MO 63143-2636
Taz A. Meyer, Director
314-768-1234

Independence College of Cosmetology
815 W 23rd St S, Independence MO 64055
816-252-4247

Jerry's School of Hairstyling
1001 Royal Birkdale Dr, Columbia MO 65203
573-449-7527

LEWIS & CLARK CAREER CENTER
2400 Zumbehl Rd, Saint Charles MO 63301-1131
Midge Haas, Counselor
636-443-4950 Fax: 636-443-4951
Website: www.stcharles.k12.mo.us/lewis&clark
E-mail: mhaas@mail.stcharles.k12.mo.us

Linn State Technical College
1 Technology Dr, Linn MO 65051-9606
Becky Dunn, Admissions
800-743-8324 Fax: 573-897-5026
Website: www.linnstate.edu
E-mail: admissions@linnstate.edu

LUTHERAN SCHOOL OF NURSING
3547 S Jefferson Ave, Saint Louis MO 63118-3909
Mary Debatin-Merod, Admissions Assistant
314-577-5850 Fax: 314-268-6160
Website: www.nursingschoollmc.com
E-mail: mary.merod@sonstl.edu

Martinez School of Cosmetology
248 1/2 E Broadway St, Excelsior Springs MO 64024
816-630-3900

Merrell University of Beauty Arts & Science
1101R Southwest Boulevard
Jefferson City MO 65109
573-635-4433

Metro Business College
1732 N Kingshighway St
Cape Girardeau MO 63701-2122
573-334-9181

Metro Business College
1407 Southwest Blvd, Jefferson City MO 65109-5508
573-635-6600

Metro Business College
1202 E State Route 72, Rolla MO 65401-3938
573-364-8464

Midwest Institute for Medical Assistants
10910 Manchester Rd, Saint Louis MO 63122-1242
314-965-8363

Missouri Beauty Academy
222 E Columbia St, Farmington MO 63640
573-756-2730

Missouri College
10121 Manchester Rd, Saint Louis MO 63122-1525
Erin Cunningham, Director of Admissions
314-821-7700

Missouri College of Cosmetology North
2555 W Kearney St, Springfield MO 65803
417-866-2786

Missouri School of Barbering & Hairstyling
1125 N US Highway 67, Florissant MO 63031
314-839-0310

Missouri Tech
1167 Corporate Lake Dr, Saint Louis MO 63132
314-569-3600

NATIONAL ACADEMY OF BEAUTY ARTS
157 Concord Plz, Saint Louis MO 63128
Kathy, Contact
314-842-3616 Fax: 314-842-9396
Website: www.nationalacademyofbeautyarts.com
E-mail: nationalacademy@sbcglobal.net

Neosho Beauty College
116 N Wood St, Neosho MO 64850
417-451-7216

New Dimensions School of Hair Design
705 Illinois Ave Ste 12, Joplin MO 64801
417-782-2875

Nichols Career Center
605 Union St, Jefferson City MO 65101-2814
573-659-3100

Paris II Educational Center
6840 N Oak Trafficway, Gladstone MO 64118
816-468-6666

Parks College of Engineering and Aviation
of Saint Louis University
221 N Grand Blvd #119, Saint Louis MO 63103-2006
Edwin Harris, Ph.D., Dean of Admission
314-977-2500

Patricia Stevens College
330 N 4th St Ste 306, Saint Louis MO 63102-2008
Cynthia Musterman, J.D., President
800-871-0949

Patsy & Rob's Academy of Beauty
18 Northwest Plz, Saint Ann MO 63074
314-298-8808

Pinnacle Career Institute
1001 101st Ter Ste 325, Kansas City MO 64131-3367
800-614-0900

Professional Massage Training Center
229 E Commercial, Springfield MO 65803
417-863-7682

Ranken Technical College
4431 Finney Ave, Saint Louis MO 63113-2898
Elizabeth M. Keserauskis, Director of Admissions
314-371-0233 Fax: 314-371-0241
Website: www.ranken.edu
E-mail: admissions@ranken.edu

St. Louis College of Health Careers
1297 N Highway Dr, Fenton MO 63026-1909
636-529-0000

St. Louis College of Health Careers
909 S Taylor Ave, Saint Louis MO 63110-1511
314-652-0300

St. Louis Hair Academy
3701 Kossuth Ave, Saint Louis MO 63107
314-533-3125

Salem College of Hairstyling
1051 Kingshighway St Ste 1, Rolla MO 65401
573-368-3136

Sanford-Brown College
1345 Smizer Mill Rd, Fenton MO 63026
Kevin Frank, Director of HS Admissions
636-349-4900

Sanford-Brown College
75 Village Square Shop Ctr, Hazelwood MO 63042
314-731-1101

Sanford-Brown College
100 Richmond Center Blvd
Saint Peters MO 63376-5950
888-793-2433

Southeast Missouri Hospital
College of Nursing and Health Sciences
2001 William St #2, Cape Girardeau MO 63703-5815
Don Pugh, Registrar
573-334-6825

Stage One, The Hair Academy
547 County Highway, Benton MO 63736
573-335-5078

Vatterott College
809 Illinois Ave, Joplin MO 64801
417-781-5633

Vatterott College
8955 E 38th Terr, Kansas City MO 64129-1692
816-861-1000

Vatterott College
3925 Industrial Dr, Saint Ann MO 63074-1807
Jennifer Commuso, Director of Admissions
800-345-6018 Fax: 314-428-5956
Website: www.vatterott-college.edu
E-mail: jennifer.commuso@vatterott-college.edu

Vatterott College
3131 Frederick Ave, Saint Joseph MO 64506-2911
Sandra Wisdom, Director of Admissions
816-364-5399

Vatterott College
12970 Maurer Industrial Dr, Saint Louis MO 63127
Sherri Bremer, Director of Admissions
314-843-4200 Fax: 314-843-1709
Website: www.vatterott-college.edu
E-mail: sherri.bremer@vatterott-college.edu

Vatterott College
3850 S Campbell Ave, Springfield MO 65807-5340
417-831-8116

Wichita Technical Institute
1531 E 32nd St, Joplin MO 64804
417-206-9115

MONTANA

ACADEMY OF COSMETOLOGY, INC.
133 W Mendenhall St, Bozeman MT 59715
406-587-1265 Fax: 406-585-7357
Website: www.academycosmetology.com

Butte Academy of Beauty Culture
303 W Park St, Butte MT 59701
406-723-8565

College of Coiffure Art
1423 Wyoming Ave, Billings MT 59102
406-656-9114

Dahl's College of Beauty
718 Central Ave, Great Falls MT 59401
406-454-3453

Modern Beauty School
2700 Paxson St Ste G, Missoula MT 59801
406-721-1800

Montana State University
Billings College of Technology
3803 Central Ave, Billings MT 59102-4307
R. J. Carr, Dean
406-656-4445

Montana Tech College of Technology
25 Basin Creek Rd, Butte MT 59701-9704
406-496-3701

SAGE TECHNICAL COMMERICAL DRIVING SCHOOL
3044 Hesper Rd, Billings MT 59102-6732
Carmella or Lisa, Contacts
800-545-4546 Fax: 406-652-3129
Website: www.sageschools.com
E-mail: sage01cc@aol.com

NEBRASKA

Bahner College of Hairstyling
1660 N Grant St, Fremont NE 68025
402-721-6500

Bryan LGH College of Health Science School of Nursing
5035 Everett St, Lincoln NE 68506
Verla Youngquist, Recruiter
402-481-8697

Capitol School of Hairstyling - West
2819 S 125th Ave Ste 268, Omaha NE 68144
402-333-3329

College of Hair Design
304 S 11th St, Lincoln NE 68508
402-477-4040

The Creative Center
10850 Emmet St, Omaha NE 68164-2911
Kim Guyer, Executive Director
402-898-1000

Hamilton College - Lincoln Campus
PO Box 82826, Lincoln NE 68501-2826
Todd Lardenoit, Executive Director
402-474-5315

Joseph's College of Beauty
618 Court St, Beatrice NE 68310
402-223-3588

Joseph's College of Beauty
305 W 3rd St, Grand Island NE 68801
308-381-8848

Joseph's College of Beauty
828 W 2nd St, Hastings NE 68901
402-463-1357

Joseph's College of Beauty
2637 O St, Lincoln NE 68510
402-435-2333

Joseph's College of Beauty
202 Madison Ave, Norfolk NE 68701
402-371-3358

Joseph's of Kearney School of Hair Design
2213 Central Ave, Kearney NE 68847
308-234-6594

Myotherapy Institute
6020 S 58th St, Lincoln NE 68516
402-421-7410

North Platte Beauty Academy
107 W 6th St, North Platte NE 69101
308-532-4664

OMAHA SCHOOL OF MASSAGE THERAPY
9748 Park Dr, Omaha NE 68127-5002
Kym Kessler, Admission Advisor
402-331-3694 Fax: 402-331-0280
Website: www.osmt.com
E-mail: info@osmtomaha.org

VATTEROTT COLLEGE
11818 I St, Omaha NE 68137
Todd S. Clark, Director
402-891-9411 Fax: 402-891-9413
Website: www.vatterott-college.edu
E-mail: tclark@vatterott-college.edu

Xenon International School of Hair Design
8516 Park Dr, Omaha NE 68127
402-393-2933

NEVADA

ACADEMY OF HAIR DESIGN
4445 W Charleston Blvd, Las Vegas NV 89102
Sandy Dunham, Director
702-878-1185 Fax: 702-878-7289
Website: ahdvegas.com
E-mail: sdunham@ahd.lvcoxmail.com

ACES-FULL ACADEMY FOR CASINO DEALERS
557 E Sahara Ave Ste 220
Las Vegas NV 89104-2733
Douglas Mitchell, General Manager
702-369-1194 Fax: 702-369-2165
E-mail: acesfullacademy@aol.com

American Institute of Technology
4610 Vandenberg Dr Ste A
North Las Vegas NV 89081
702-644-1234

CAREER COLLEGE OF NORTHERN NEVADA
1195-A Corporate Blvd, Reno NV 89502-2331
Nathan Clark, Director
775-856-2266 Fax: 775-856-0935
Website: www.ccnn.edu
E-mail: lgoldhammer@ccnn4u.com
    Established 1984. Private. Coed. Accreditation: Accrediting Commission of Career Schools and Colleges of Technology. Degrees offered: Electronic Engineering Technology, Computerized Business Management, Medical Assisting, Paralegal. Diploma programs available in Legal Office Administrator, Medical Assisting, Medical Insurance, Coding and Billing, Data Processing. Morning, afternoon, evening and weekend classes available. High school Diploma or GED required for admission.

Carson City Beauty Academy
2531 N Carson St, Carson City NV 89706
775-885-9853

Dahan Institute of Massage Studies
10381 Starthistle Ln, Las Vegas NV 89135-2826
702-434-1338

Heritage College
3315 Spring Mountain Rd, Las Vegas NV 89102
Mimi Ritenour, Director of Admissions
702-368-2338

High-Tech Institute
2320 S Rancho Dr, Las Vegas NV 89102
702-385-6700

ITT Technical Institute
168 Gibson Rd, Henderson NV 89014
702-558-5404

Las Vegas College
170 N Stephanie St Ste 145
Henderson NV 89074-8811
888-741-4270

LE CORDON BLEU COLLEGE OF CULINARY ARTS
1451 Center Crossing Rd, Las Vegas NV 89144
Admission Dept.
866-450-2433 or 702-365-7690 Fax: 702-365-7911
Website: www.vegasculinary.com

Marinello School of Beauty
5001 E Bonanza Rd Ste 110, Las Vegas NV 89110
702-796-6200

Morrison University
10315 Professional Circle Suite 201
Reno NV 89521-4826
Charles Timinsky, Director of Enrollment
775-850-0700 Fax: 775-850-0711
Website: www.morrisonuniversity.com

PCI Dealers School
920 S Valley View Blvd, Las Vegas NV 89107-4416
Joel Lauer, Owner
702-877-4724

Pima Medical Institute
3333 E Flamingo Rd, Las Vegas NV 89121
702-458-7650

RENO TAHOE JOB TRAINING ACADEMY
130B E Plumb Ln, Reno NV 89502
Kathleen Shupp, President/Director
775-329-5665 Fax: 775-324-1969
Website: www.renodealingschool.com

Southern Nevada University of Cosmetology
3430 E Tropicana Ave, Las Vegas NV 89121
702-458-6333

NEW HAMPSHIRE

Concord Academy of Hair Design
20 S Main St, Concord NH 03301
603-224-2211

CONTINENTAL ACADEMIE OF HAIR DESIGN
PO Box 370, Hudson NH 03051-0370
603-889-1614 Fax: 603-883-9546
Website: www.continentalacademie.net
E-mail: conacad1@aol.com

CONTINENTAL ACADEMIE OF HAIR DESIGN
228 Maple St, Manchester NH 03103
Sylvia Donah, Business Manager
603-622-5851 Fax: 603-883-9546
Website: www.continentalacademie.net
E-mail: conacad2@aol.com

Empire Beauty School
556 Main St, Laconia NH 03246
603-524-8777

Empire Beauty School #3
362 Route 108, Somersworth NH 03878
603-692-1515

KEENE BEAUTY ACADEMY
800 Park Ave, Keene NH 03431-1513
Heather Hammond, Admissions
603-357-3736 Fax: 603-355-8916
Website: www.keenebeautyacademy.com

McIntosh College
23 Cataract Ave, Dover NH 03820-3990
Karen Arnold, Director of Admissions
888-876-3000

Michael's School of Hair Design
73 S River Rd Ste 26, Bedford NH 03110
603-668-4300

New England EMS Institute
1 Elliot Way, Manchester NH 03103-3502
603-628-2220

New Hampshire Community Technical College
505 Amherst St, Nashua NH 03063
Patricia Goodman, Director of Student Services
603-882-7022

New Hampshire Community Technical College
277 Portsmouth Ave, Stratham NH 03885-2231
Laurilee A. Shennett, Admissions Recruiter
603-772-1194 ext. 317

PORTSMOUTH BEAUTY SCHOOL OF HAIR DESIGN
140 Congress St, Portsmouth NH 03801
Mr. Fran Nardello, Administrator
603-436-7775 Fax: 603-436-5456
Website: www.portsmouthbeautyschool.com
E-mail: admissions@portsmouthbeautyschool.com

Upper Valley Teacher Institute
1 Court St Ste 210, Lebanon NH 03766
603-448-6507

NEW JERSEY

Academy of Massage Therapy
321 Main St, Hackensack NJ 07601
888-AMT-7898

American Business Academy
66 Moore St, Hackensack NJ 07601-7104
Kim Staudt, Director
201-488-9400

Artistic Academy of Hair Design
21 Broadway, Fair Lawn NJ 07410
201-794-3502

Berdan Institute
201 Willowbrook Blvd, Wayne NJ 07470-7041
973-837-1818

BEST CARE TRAINING INSTITUTE
68 S Harrison St, East Orange NJ 07017
Florence Brown, RN, MSN, APNC, Contact
973-673-3900 Fax: 973-673-0597
Website: www.bestcarehealth.com
E-mail: fbrown3260@aol.com

Burlington County Institute of Technology - Adult Education
695 Woodlane Rd, Mount Holly NJ 08060-3813
Dr. Fred Laier, Contact
609-267-4226

Camden County Technical School
343 Berlin Cross Keys Rd, Sicklerville NJ 08081-4000
Gayle Butler, Director of Admissions
856-767-7002

Cape May County Technical Institute
188 Crest Haven Rd
Cape May Court House NJ 08210
609-465-2161

Capri Institute of Hair Design
268 Brick Blvd, Brick NJ 08723
732-920-3600

Capri Institute of Hair Design
1595 Main Ave, Clifton NJ 07011
973-772-4610

Capri Institute of Hair Design
660 N Michigan Ave, Kenilworth NJ 07033
908-964-1330

Capri Institute of Hair Design
615 Winters Ave, Paramus NJ 07652
201-599-0880

Capri Institute of Hair Design
Roxbury Mall Route 10 E, Succasunna NJ 07876
973-584-9030

Central Career School
126 Corporate Blvd, South Plainfield NJ 07080-2408
908-412-8600

Christ Hospital School of Nursing
176 Palisade Ave, Jersey City NJ 07306-1196
Lisa Cieckiewicz, Coordinator of Student Services
201-795-8360

Chubb Institute
2100 Route 38, Cherry Hill NJ 08002-2043
856-988-9880

THE CHUBB INSTITUTE
40 Journal Sq, Jersey City NJ 07306-4097
Valerie Yancey, Campus President
201-876-3800 Fax: 201-656-2091
Website: www.chubbinstitute.edu
E-mail: gduchnowski@chubbinstitute.edu

Chubb Institute
651 US Highway 1, North Brunswick NJ 08902
732-448-2600

Chubb Institute
8 Sylvan Way, Parsippany NJ 07054
973-682-4900

Cittone Institute
1697 Oak Tree Rd, Edison NJ 08820-2896
John Willie, Executive Director
732-548-8798

Cittone Institute
1000 Howard Blvd # 2, Mount Laurel NJ 08054-2355
Vivian Wagner, Executive Director
856-722-9333

Cittone Institute
160 E State Route 4, Paramus NJ 07652-5002
Laurie Brown, Executive Director
201-828-5911

Concorde School of Hair Design
9 Ward St, Bloomfield NJ 07003
973-680-0099

Concorde School of Hair Design
Route 35 & Sunset Ave, Ocean NJ 07712
732-918-0505

Cooper Hospital/University Medical Center
1 Cooper Plz #217, Camden NJ 08103-1461
Joan D'Antonio, Director
856-342-2416

Cumberland County Technical Education Center
601 Bridgeton Ave, Bridgeton NJ 08302-4810
856-451-9000

DIVERS ACADEMY INTERNATIONAL
1500 Liberty Pl, Erial NJ 08081
Tamara M. Brown, Director
800-238-3483 Fax: 856-404-6104
Website: www.diversacademy.com
E-mail: cdiver@worldnet.att.net

Dover Business College
15 E Blackwell St, Dover NJ 07801-4643
973-285-8400

Dover Business College
East 81 Route 4 W, Paramus NJ 07652
201-843-8500

Drake College of Business
125 Broad St, Elizabeth NJ 07201-2334
908-352-5509

Du Cret School of the Arts
1030 Central Ave, Plainfield NJ 07060-2898
908-757-7171

Eastern School of Acupuncture & Traditional Medicine
427 Bloomfield Ave Ste 301, Montclair NJ 07042
973-746-8717

Empire Beauty School
2100 State Highway #38, Cherry Hill NJ 08002
800-575-5983

Empire Beauty School
1305 Blackwood Clementon Rd
Laurel Springs NJ 08021
800-575-5983

Empire Beauty School
1719 Brunswick Ave, Lawrenceville NJ 08648
800-575-5983

Engine City Technical Institute
DIESEL MECHANIC SCHOOL AND TRAINING
CENTER
901 Hadley Rd, South Plainfield NJ 07080-2424
800-305-3487

European Academy of Cosmetology
1126 Morris Ave, Union NJ 07083
908-686-4422

Harrison Career Institute
4000 Route 130 N, Delran NJ 08075
856-764-8933

Harrison Career Institute
1450 Clements Bridge Rd, Deptford NJ 08096
856-384-2888

Harrison Career Institute
1001 Spruce St Ste 7, Ewing NJ 08638
609-656-4303

Harrison Career Institute
600 Pavonia Ave, Jersey City NJ 07306
201-222-1700

Harrison Career Institute
2105 State Route 35, Oakhurst NJ 07755
732-493-1660

Harrison Career Institute
1386 S Delsea Dr, Vineland NJ 08360-6210
856-696-0500

Harris School of Business
One Mall Dr Suite 700, Cherry Hill NJ 08002
Barbara Harris Miles, Contact
856-662-5300

Healthcare Training Institute
1969 Morris Ave, Union NJ 07083
908-851-7711

Helma Institute Massage Therapy
190 Midland Ave, Saddle Brook NJ 07663
201-226-0056

Ho Ho Kus School of Business & Medical Sciences
10 S Franklin Tpke, Ramsey NJ 07446-2546
Thomas Eastwick, Director
201-327-8877

HOHOKUS SCHOOL OF TRADE AND TECHNICAL SCIENCES
634-638 Market St, Paterson NJ 07513-1402
Alan E. Concha, Vice President/Director
800-646-9353 Fax: 908-486-9321
Website: www.hohokustrades.com
E-mail: aconcha21@aol.com

Hohokus School - RETS Nutley
103 Park Ave, Nutley NJ 07110-3505
Thomas Eastwick, President
973-661-0600 Fax: 973-661-2954
Website: www.rets-institute.com
E-mail: admissions@rets-institute.com

HOLY NAME HOSPITAL SCHOOL OF NURSING
690 Teaneck Rd, Teaneck NJ 07666-4254
Maureen Schmude, Registrar
201-833-3005 Fax: 201-833-7209
Website: www.schoolofnursing.info
E-mail: sr-tynan@mail.holyname.org

HUDSON AREA SCHOOL OF RADIOLOGIC TECHNOLOGY
176 Palisade Ave, Jersey City NJ 07306
Kenneth Lee, D.H.S., R.T. (R)(M)
201-795-8246 Fax: 201-795-5818
Website: www.christhospital.org
E-mail: lleclaire@christhospital.org

The Institute for Health Education
7 Spielman Rd, Fairfield NJ 07004-3403
973-808-1666

Institute for Therapeutic Massage
125 Wanaque Ave, Pompton Lakes NJ 07442
973-839-6131

Joe Kubert School of Cartoon & Graphic Arts
37 Myrtle Ave, Dover NJ 07801-4028
973-361-1327

Joy's School of Hair Design
44 Glenwood Ave, East Orange NJ 07017
973-673-4141

Katharine Gibbs School
180 Centennial Ave, Piscataway NJ 08854-3908
L. Terry Nighan, President
732-885-1580

KeySkills Learning
50 Mount Prospect Ave, Clifton NJ 07013
973-778-8136

Lincoln Technical Institute
70 McKee Dr, Mahwah NJ 07430-2106
Al Dobbs, Executive Director
201-529-1414

Lincoln Technical Institute
2299 Vauxhall Rd, Union NJ 07083-5032
Mark Dugan, Executive Director
908-964-7800

McEllis Training Institute
800 Broad St, Newark NJ 07102
973-643-6917

Mercer County Vocational-Technical School
1085 Old Trenton Rd, Trenton NJ 08690
609-586-2129

Micropower Computer Institute
1203 W Saint Georges Ave, Linden NJ 07036
908-587-9070

Micro Tech Training Center
3000 Kennedy Blvd, Jersey City NJ 07306
201-216-9901

Monmouth Medical Center
300 2nd Ave, Long Branch NJ 07740-6395
John A. Mihok, MT Program Director
732-222-5200

Natural Motion Institute of Hair Design
2800 John F Kennedy Blvd, Jersey City NJ 07306
201-659-0303

New Community Workforce Development Center
201 Bergen St, Newark NJ 07103
Karen Harrison-Bowers, Director
973-824-6484

New Horizons Beauty School
5518 Bergenline Ave, West New York NJ 07093
201-866-4000

New Jersey School of Locksmithing
392 Summit Ave, Jersey City NJ 07306
201-963-9688

Omega Institute
7050 Kaighns Ave, Pennsauken NJ 08109-4417
856-663-4299

Parisian Academy
Paul Mitchell Partner School
362 State St, Hackensack NJ 07601
201-487-2203

P.B. Cosmetology Education Centre
110 Monmouth St, Gloucester City NJ 08030
856-456-4927

Pennco Tech
PO Box 1427, Blackwood NJ 08012-7127
856-232-0310

Performance Training
1012 Cox Cro Rd, Toms River NJ 08755-1344
732-505-9119

Raritan Valley Flying School
Route 206, Princeton NJ 08540
609-921-3100

Reignbow Beauty Academy
312 State St, Perth Amboy NJ 08861
732-442-6007

Reignbow Hair Fashion Institute
121 Watchung Ave, North Plainfield NJ 07060
908-754-4247

Rizzieri Aveda School for Beauty & Wellness
6001 W Lincoln Dr, Marlton NJ 08053
Meg Stezzi, Director of Recruiting
856-988-8600

Roman Academy of Beauty Culture
431 Lafayette Ave, Hawthorne NJ 07506
973-423-2223

Shore Beauty School
103 W Washington Ave, Pleasantville NJ 08232
609-645-3635

STAR TECHNICAL INSTITUTE
3003 English Creek Ave Suite 212
Egg Harbor Township NJ 08234-4880
George Z. Negrete, Director
609-407-2999 Fax: 609-646-9472
Website: www.startechnicalinstitute.com
E-mail: info@stareggharbor.com

Star Technical Institute
1255 Highway 70 Ste 12N, Lakewood NJ 08701-5900
732-901-9710

Star Technical Institute
43 S White Horse Pike, Stratford NJ 08084-1520
856-435-7827

StenoTech Career Institute
20 Just Rd, Fairfield NJ 07004-3490
Jean Melone, Director
973-882-4875

Stuart School of Business Administration
2400 Belmar Blvd, Wall NJ 07719-3970
732-681-7200

Teterboro School of Aeronautics
80 Moonachie Ave, Teterboro NJ 07608-1003
Richard Ciasulli, Director of Admissions
201-288-6300 Fax: 201-288-5609
Website: www.teterboroschool.com
E-mail: teterboroschool@nj.rr.com

Ultrasound Diagnostic School
675 US Highway 1 S 2nd Flr, Iselin NJ 08830
732-634-1131

NEW MEXICO

ALADDIN BEAUTY COLLEGE #22
108 S Union Ave, Roswell NM 88203
Peggy Richburg, Contact
505-623-6331 Fax: 505-622-2072
E-mail: abcinc2@qwest.net

Albuquerque Barber College
601 San Pedro Dr Ste 104, Albuquerque NM 87108
505-266-4900

Albuquerque TVI Community College
525 Buena Vista Dr SE, Albuquerque NM 87106-4096
Michael J. Glennon, President
Jane Campbell, Registrar
505-224-3061

Apollo College
5301 Central Ave NE Ste 101
Albuquerque NM 87108-1514
800-368-7246

Business Skills Institute
Las Cruces Campus
1400 El Paseo St, Las Cruces NM 88001-6022
505-526-5579

DeWolff College of Hairstyling & Cosmetology
1500 Eubank Blvd NE, Albuquerque NM 87112
505-296-4100

Eddy County Beauty College
1115 W Mermod St, Carlsbad NM 88220
505-885-4545

International School
141 Quinella Rd, Sunland Park NM 88063
505-589-1414

New Mexico Aveda Institute de Bellas Artes
2614 Pennsylvania St NE, Albuquerque NM 87110
505-294-5333

Olympian University of Cosmetology
1810 10th St, Alamogordo NM 88310
505-437-2221

Olympian University of Cosmetology
800 Juan Tabo NE #1-J, Albuquerque NM 87123
Angela Lopez, Contact
505-765-1044

Olympian University of Cosmetology
1460 Missouri Ave # 5, Las Cruces NM 88001-5330
505-523-7181

Pima Medical Institute
2201 San Pedro Dr NE, Albuquerque NM 87110-4155
505-881-1234

UNIVERSAL THERAPEUTIC MASSAGE INSTITUTE
3410 Aztec Rd NE, Albuquerque NM 87107-4403
Pamela Berben, School Director
505-888-0020 Fax: 505-837-1828
Website: www.utmi.com
E-mail: info@utmi.com

NEW YORK

Adirondack Beauty School
108 Dix Ave, Glens Falls NY 12801
518-745-1646

Advanced Software Analysis Institute of Business and Computer Technology
151 Lawrence St Ste 2, Brooklyn NY 11201-5208
718-522-9073

Albany College of Pharmacy
106 New Scotland Ave, Albany NY 12208-3412
Jean Taylor, Program Director
518-445-7390

Allen School
16318 Jamaica Ave, Jamaica NY 11432
718-291-2200

American Academy of Dramatic Arts - New York
120 Madison Ave, New York NY 10016-7089
Karen Higginbotham, Director of Admissions
800-463-8990 Fax: 212-685-8093
Website: www.aada.org
E-mail: admissions-ny@aada.org

American Barber Institute
252 W 29th St, New York NY 10001
212-290-2289

APEX TECHNICAL SCHOOL
635 Avenue of the Americas
New York NY 10011-2008
William Ott, Admissions Director
212-645-3300 Fax: 212-645-6984
Website: www.apextechnical.com

An Apex Tech education provides you with a foundation for achieving some of the things you want most in life: a challenging career opportunity and a promising future.

Licensed by the State of New York and accredited by The Accrediting Commission of Career Schools and Colleges of Technology, Apex Tech is a recognized leader in its field. We have provided companies in the New York metropolitan area with more than 15,000 skilled graduates since our founding in 1961.

We offer a choice of five certificate programs - which may be completed in as few as 5 to 7 months - in Automotive Mechanics (which is the only ASE (Automotive Service Excellence) certified program in NYC), Refrigeration & Air Conditioning, Welding Technology, Auto Body Repair and Automotive Service & Repair with ESL Spanish.

All of our programs have been evaluated by the New York Regents National Program on Non-collegiate Sponsored Instruction (PONSI) for college credit hour recommendations. As a result, you may be able to advance toward a degree through your studies at Apex.

Each are part of a focused hands-on training program designed to get you an entree in your field of choice in a minimum of time.

ARNOT OGDEN MEDICAL CENTER SCHOOL OF NURSING
600 Roe Ave, Elmira NY 14905-1676
Linda MacAuslan, Director
607-737-4153 Fax: 607-737-4116
Website: www.arnothealth.org
E-mail: lmacauslan@aomc.org

ARNOT-OGDEN MEDICAL CENTER
School of Radiologic Technology
600 Roe Ave, Elmira NY 14905-1629
Ellen Richards, BS RT (R) Director
607-737-4289 Fax: 607-737-4116
Website: www.aomc.org
E-mail: erichards@aomc.org

The Art Institute of New York City
75 Varick St Fl 16, New York NY 10013-1917
Alfred W. Parcells, Jr., Director of Admissions
212-226-5500

Austin Beauty School
527 Central Ave, Albany NY 12206
518-438-7879

Beauty School of Middletown
RR 9, Hyde Park NY 12538
845-229-6541

Beauty School of Middletown
225 Dolson Ave Ste 100, Middletown NY 10940
845-343-2171

Berk Trade School
383 Pearl St, Brooklyn NY 11201
718-625-6037

BRAMSON O R T COLLEGE
6930 Austin St, Forest Hills NY 11375-4222
Rita Baskin, Admissions Coordinator
718-261-5800 Fax: 718-575-5119
Website: www.bramsonort.edu
E-mail: rbaskin@bramsonort.edu

Bryant & Stratton College
1259 Central Ave, Albany NY 12205
518-437-1802

Bryant & Stratton College
40 Hazelwood Dr, Amherst NY 14228-2230
716-691-0012

Bryant & Stratton College
8687 Carling Rd, Liverpool NY 13090
315-472-6603

Bryant & Stratton College
200 Red Tail, Orchard Park NY 14127
716-677-9500

Bryant & Stratton College
150 Bellwood Dr, Rochester NY 14606
585-720-0660

Bryant & Stratton College
1225 Jefferson Rd, Rochester NY 14623
585-292-5627

Bryant & Stratton College
953 James St, Syracuse NY 13203-2502
315-472-6603

Caliber Training Institute
500 Fashion Ave 2nd Floor, New York NY 10018
212-564-0500

Capri Cosmetology Learning Center
251 W Route 59, Nanuet NY 10954
845-623-6339

Career & Educational Consultants
270 Flatbush Ave Ext, Brooklyn NY 11201
718-858-8500

CAREER INSTITUTE OF HEALTH & TECHNOLOGY
340 Flatbush Avenue Ext, Brooklyn NY 11201
Mary Miller, Contact
718-422-1212 Fax: 718-422-1222
Website: www.careerinstitute.edu
E-mail: admissions@careerinstitute.edu

CAREER INSTITUTE OF HEALTH & TECHNOLOGY
200 Garden City Plz, Garden City NY 11530
Mary Miller, Contact
516-877-1225 Fax: 516-877-1959
Website: www.careerinstitute.edu
E-mail: admissions@careerinstitute.edu

CAREER INSTITUTE OF HEALTH & TECHNOLOGY
9525 Queens Blvd Ste 600, Rego Park NY 11374
Mary Miller, Contact
718-897-4868 Fax: 718-897-4863
Website: www.careerinstitute.edu
E-mail: admissions@careerinstitute.edu

Center for Natural Wellness School
3 Cerone Commercial Dr, Albany NY 12205
518-449-2737

Centurion Professional Training
2619 E 16th St, Brooklyn NY 11235
718-646-4507

Charles Stuart School of Locksmithing
1420 Kings Hwy, Brooklyn NY 11229-2004
Charles Wechsler, CEO
718-339-2640

Cheryl Fell's School of Business
2541 Military Rd, Niagara Falls NY 14304-1505
716-297-2750

THE CHUBB INSTITUTE
498 7th Ave, New York NY 10018
Joe Rodriguez, Director of Admissions
212-659-2116 Fax: 212-659-2175
Website: www.chubbinstitute.edu
E-mail: jrodriguez@chubbinstitute.edu

Cochran School of Nursing
967 N Broadway, Yonkers NY 10701-1301
Sandra Sclafani, Admissions/Registrar
914-964-4283

Columbia-Greene Beauty School
342 Main St, Catskill NY 12414
518-943-2224

Commercial Driver Training School
600 Patton Ave, West Babylon NY 11704-1421
631-249-1330

Continental School
633 Jefferson Rd, Rochester NY 14623-3231
585-272-8060

Continental School of Beauty Culture
215 Main St, Batavia NY 14020
585-344-0886

Continental School of Beauty Culture
326 Kenmore Ave, Buffalo NY 14223
716-833-5016

Continental School of Beauty Culture
515 N Union St, Olean NY 14760-2618
Rosemary Swick, Director
716-372-5095

Continental School of Beauty Culture
1050 Union Rd, West Seneca NY 14224
716-675-8205

Cope Institute
225 Broadway Fl 2, New York NY 10007
212-809-5935

CULINARY ACADEMY OF LONG ISLAND
125 Michael Dr, Syosset NY 11791
Harold Kaplan, Director of Admissions
516-364-4344 Fax: 516-364-1894
Website: www.culinaryacademy.edu
E-mail: admissions@culinaryacademy.edu

CULINARY ACADEMY OF NEW YORK
154 W 14th St, New York NY 10011-7307
Harold Kaplan, Contact
212-675-6655 Fax: 212-463-9194
Website: www.culinaryacademy.edu
E-mail: hkaplan@culinaryacademy.edu

David Hochstein Memorial Music School
50 Plymouth Ave N, Rochester NY 14614-1221
585-454-4596

Ellis Hospital School of Nursing
1101 Nott St, Schenectady NY 12308-2425
518-243-4471

Elmira Business Institute
303 N Main St, Elmira NY 14901
Lisa Roan, Admissions Director
607-733-7177 or 800-843-1812 Fax: 607-733-7178
Website: www.ebi-college.com
E-mail: lroan@ebi-college.com

FAXTON-ST. LUKE'S HEALTHCARE SCHOOL OF MEDICAL RADIOGRAPHY
PO Box 479, Utica NY 13503-0479
Rosemary Morin, MS, RTR, Director
315-624-6136 Fax: 315-624-4787
Website: mvnhealth.com
E-mail: xrayed@dreamscape.com

FEGS Trades & Business School
80 Vandam St, New York NY 10013
212-366-8466

Folk Art Institute
45 W 53rd St, New York NY 10022
212-977-7170

FRANKLIN CAREER INSTITUTE
5323 5th Ave, Brooklyn NY 11220
Richard C. Crance, Executive Director
718-535-3333 Fax: 718-535-3345
Website: www.franklincareer.edu
E-mail: rcrance@franklincareer.edu

FRANKLIN CAREER INSTITUTE
91 N Franklin St, Hempstead NY 11550
Richard C. Crance, Executive Director
516-481-4444 Fax: 516-481-8694
Website: www.franklincareer.edu
E-mail: rcrance@franklincareer.edu

THE FRENCH CULINARY INSTITUTE
462 Broadway, New York NY 10013-2618
Judy Currie-Hellmann, Director of Admission
212-219-8890 Fax: 212-431-3054
Website: www.frenchculinary.com
E-mail: jcurrie-hellmann@frenchculinary.com

Gemological Institute of America
580 5th Ave, New York NY 10036
212-944-5900

Global Business Institute
1931 Mott Ave, Far Rockaway NY 11691-4103
718-327-2220

Global Business Institute
209 W 125th St, New York NY 10027-4410
212-663-1500

Hair Design Institute at Fifth Avenue
6711 5th Ave, Brooklyn NY 11220
718-745-1000

Harlem School of Technology
215 W 125th St, New York NY 10027
212-932-2849

Helene Fuld College of Nursing
1879 Madison Ave, New York NY 10035-2709
212-423-2700

Hunter Business School
3601 Hempstead Tpke, Levittown NY 11756-1375
516-796-1000

Institute of Allied Medical Professions
405 Park Ave, New York NY 10022-4405
212-758-1410

INSTITUTE OF AUDIO RESEARCH
64 University Pl, New York NY 10003-4595
Mark L. Kahn, Director of Admissions
800-544-2501 Fax: 212-677-6549
Website: www.audioschool.com
E-mail: contact@audioschool.com

Established 1969. Private. Coed. Accreditation: Accrediting Commission of Career Schools and Colleges of Technology (ACCSCT). Tuition: $13,575. Fees: $100. Faculty: 26. Student-faculty ratio: 15:1. Degrees: Diploma in Audio Recording and Production. 20,000 sq. ft. facility featuring a state-of-the-art all-digital recording studio and individual digital audio workstations for students. IAR offers 9-12 month career training in audio and recording arts. Program includes analog and digital audio technology with heavy emphasis on digital music production and audio post-production for film and video. Uniquely situated in the heart of NYC, the recording capital of the world and home of all major TV networks, IAR graduates find employment in recording studios, television stations, live concert sound, audio and video production houses, theater sound, radio, satellite and cable companies, jingle houses, post-production for film and television and more. In addition, IAR grads receive transfer credit towards a bachelors degree at various colleges nationwide. Financial aid available for eligible students.

The Institute of Culinary Education
50 W 23rd St, New York NY 10010
Tae Ellin, Contact
212-847-0711

Institute of Design and Construction
141 Willoughby St, Brooklyn NY 11201
718-855-3661

Interboro Institute
450 W 56th St, New York NY 10019
212-399-0091

ISLAND DRAFTING & TECHNICAL INSTITUTE
128 Broadway (Route 110), Amityville NY 11701-2704
James G. DiLiberto, President
631-691-8733 Fax: 631-691-8738
Website: www.idti.edu
E-mail: info@idti.edu

ITT Technical Institute
PO Box 327, Getzville NY 14068
716-689-2200

Jamestown Business College
PO Box 429, Jamestown NY 14702
716-664-5100

Jon Louis School of Beauty
9114 Merrick Blvd, Jamaica NY 11432
718-658-6240

Katharine Gibbs School
320 S Service Rd, Melville NY 11747-3201
Phil Cincotta, Director of Admissions
631-370-3300

Katharine Gibbs School
50 W 40th St, New York NY 10018-2602
212-867-9300

Learning Institute for Beauty Sciences
3815 Broadway, Astoria NY 11103
718-726-8383

Learning Institute for Beauty Sciences
2384 86th St, Brooklyn NY 11214
718-373-2400

Learning Institute for Beauty Sciences
544 Route 111, Hauppauge NY 11788
631-724-0440

Learning Institute for Beauty Sciences
173A Fulton Ave, Hempstead NY 11550
516-483-6259

Learning Institute for Beauty Sciences
2981 Hempstead Tpke, Levittown NY 11756-1330
516-731-8300

Learning Institute for Beauty Sciences
22 W 34th St, New York NY 10001
212-695-4555

Leon Studio One School of Hair Design
5221 Main St, Williamsville NY 14221
716-631-3878

Lia Schorr Inst of Cosmetic Skin Care
686 Lexington Ave, New York NY 10022-2614
Lia Schorr, President
212-486-9541

Long Island College Hospital School of Nursing
397 Hicks St, Brooklyn NY 11201-5940
718-780-1953

Mandl, The College of Allied Health
254 W 54th St, New York NY 10019-5516
Melvyn Weiner, President
212-247-3434

Manhattan School of Computer Technology
42 Broadway Fl 22, New York NY 10004-1638
212-349-9768

MarJon School of Beauty Culture
1154 Niagara Falls Blvd, Tonawanda NY 14150-9329
716-836-6240

Memorial Sloan Kettering Cancer Center
1275 York Ave, New York NY 10021-6007
212-639-6561

Merkaz Bnos - Business School
2115 Benson Ave, Brooklyn NY 11214
718-234-4000

METROPOLITAN LEARNING INSTITUTE
9745 Queens Blvd Ste 401, Rego Park NY 11374
Boris Davydov, President
718-897-0482 Fax: 718-897-5667
Website: www.gettraining.org
E-mail: mli@gettraining.org

Midway Paris Beauty School
5440 Myrtle Ave, Ridgewood NY 11385
718-418-2790

Mildred Elley the College for Careers
800 New Loudon Rd Ste 5120
Latham NY 12110-3902
Jill Herrick, Enrollment Manager
800-622-6327

Modern Welding School
1842 State St, Schenectady NY 12304-2033
Pat Aucompaugh, Administrator
518-374-1216

MUNSON-WILLIAMS-PROCTOR INSTITUTE
310 Genesee St, Utica NY 13502-4799
Robert E. Baber, Dean
315-797-8260 Fax: 315-797-9349
Website: www.mwpai.edu
E-mail: rbaber@mwpai.edu

Music Conservatory of Westchester
216 Central Ave, White Plains NY 10606-1102
914-761-3715

The Nail Academy
16204 Jamaica Ave, Jamaica NY 11432
718-297-6330

National Tractor Trailer School
175 Katherine St, Buffalo NY 14210-2007
716-849-6887

NATIONAL TRACTOR TRAILER SCHOOL
PO Box 208, Liverpool NY 13088-0208
Kimberley Sather, Contact
315-451-2430 Fax: 315-453-7336
Website: www.ntts.edu

New York Automotive & Diesel Institute
17818 Liberty Ave, Jamaica NY 11433-1433
Mr. Dante Cicchetti, Director of Admissions
718-361-1300

NEW YORK CAREER INSTITUTE
11 Park Pl 4th Floor, New York NY 10007-2833
Cindy McMahon, Director of Admissions
212-962-0002 Fax: 212-385-7574
Website: www.nyci.com
E-mail: info@nyci.com

NEW YORK EYE & EAR INFIRMARY / ORTHOPTIC PROGRAM
310 E 14th St, New York NY 10003-4201
Sara Shippman, Chief Orthoptist
212-979-4375 Fax: 212-979-4564
Website: www.nyee.edu
E-mail: sshippman@nyee.edu

New York Institute of Business Technology
248 W 35th St, New York NY 10001-2505
Leith E. Yetman, Director of Admissions
212-725-9400

New York Institute of Massage
PO Box 645, Buffalo NY 14231
716-633-0355

New York International Beauty School
500 8th Ave Room 803, New York NY 10018-4133
212-868-7171

NEW YORK METHODIST HOSPITAL
Clinical Laboratory Science/School of Medical Technology
506 6th St, Brooklyn NY 11215-3609
Adrienne Arso-Paez, Program Director
718-780-3706 Fax: 718-780-3673
Website: www.nym.org
E-mail: ada9003@nyp.org

New York Paralegal School
299 Broadway Ste 200, New York NY 10007-1901
212-349-8800

NEW YORK SCHOOL FOR MEDICAL AND DENTAL ASSISTANTS
33-10 Queens Blvd, Long Island City NY 11101-2327
Donna Stirber-Gamelin, Executive Director of Admissions
718-793-2330 Fax: 718-793-0619
Website: www.nysmda.com
E-mail: info@nysmda.com

Northern Westchester School of Hairdressing
19 Bank St, Peekskill NY 10566
914-739-8400

Olean Business Institute
301 N Union St, Olean NY 14760-2691
Lori Kincaid, Director of Admissions
716-372-7978

The Orlo School of Hair Design and Cosmetology
232 N Allen St, Albany NY 12206
518-459-7832

Phillips Beth Israel School of Nursing
776 Avenue of the Americas 4th Flr
New York NY 10001-6354
212-614-6110

Phillips Hairstyling Institute
709 E Genesee St, Syracuse NY 13210
315-422-9656

Plaza College
74-09 37th Ave, Jackson Heights NY 11372
Rose Ann Black, Dean of Administration
718-779-1430

Professional Business College
125 Canal St, New York NY 10002-5049
William Chong, Admissions Director
212-226-7300

Ridley-Lowell Business & Technical Institute
116 Front St, Binghamton NY 13905-3102
David Lounsbury, Executive Director
607-724-2941 Fax: 607-724-0799
Website: www.ridley.edu
E-mail: info@ridley.edu

Ridley-Lowell Business & Technical Institute
26 S Hamilton St, Poughkeepsie NY 12601-3328
E. Ann Bida, Director of Admissions
845-471-0330 Fax: 845-471-4990
Website: www.ridley.edu
E-mail: pcadmissions@ridley.edu

Rochester Business Institute
1630 Portland Ave, Rochester NY 14621-3007
585-266-0430

St. Elizabeth College of Nursing
2215 Genesee St, Utica NY 13501-5930
315-798-8125

ST. JOSEPH'S COLLEGE OF NURSING AT SJHHC
206 Prospect Ave, Syracuse NY 13203-1806
Rhonda Reader, Assistant Dean for Admissions
315-448-5040 Fax: 315-448-5745
Website: www.sjhsyr.org/nursing
E-mail: collegeofnursing@sjhsyr.org

St. Vincent Catholic Medical Centers of New York
175-05 Horace Harding Expy
Flushing NY 11365-1535
718-357-0500

Samaritan Hospital
School of Nursing AD & LPN
2215 Burdett Ave, Troy NY 12180-2475
Mary Harknett-Martin, Director
518-271-3285

Sanford-Brown Institute
333 Westchester Ave, White Plains NY 10604
Director of Admissions
914-347-6817

SHEAR EGO INTERNATIONAL SCHOOL OF HAIR DESIGN
525 Titus Ave, Rochester NY 14617
Sharon Roemer, Director of Admissions
585-342-0070 Fax: 585-342-0863
Website: www.shearego.com
E-mail: sei@shearego.com

SIMMONS INSTITUTE OF FUNERAL SERVICE
1828 South Ave, Syracuse NY 13207-2005
Maurice C. Wightman, CEO
315-475-5142 Fax: 315-475-3817
Website: www.simmonsinstitute.com
E-mail: mcwightman20@aol.com

SOTHEBY'S INSTITUTE OF ART
1334 York Ave, New York NY 10021-4806
212-894-1111 Fax: 212-894-1112
Website: www.sothebys.com
E-mail: americanartscourse@sothebys.com

Spanish-American Institute
215 W 43rd St, New York NY 10036-3967
212-840-7111

Spencer Business & Technical Institute
795 Pattersonville Rd, Pattersonville NY 12137-4329
518-374-7619

Studio Jewelers
32 E 31st St, New York NY 10016
212-686-1944

Suburban Technical School
175 Fulton Ave, Hempstead NY 11550-3771
516-481-6660

SUNY College of Agriculture & Technology
Morrisville NY 13408
Thomas Ver Dow, Dean of Enrollment Management
800-258-0111

SUNY College of Technology
Alfred NY 14802
Deborah J. Goodrich, Director of Admissions
800-4AL-FRED Fax: 607-587-4299
Website: www.alfredstate.edu
E-mail: admissions@alfredstate.edu

SUNY Schenectady County Community College
78 Washington Ave, Schenectady NY 12305-2215
Robert Dinello, Director of Admissions
518-381-1366

SUNY Sullivan County Community College
112 College Rd, Loch Sheldrake NY 12759-5151
Dan Baldo, Director of Admissions
845-434-5750

Taylor Business Institute
23 W 17th St 7th Floor, New York NY 10011-5501
800-959-9999 Fax: 212-229-2187
Website: www.tbiglobal.com
E-mail: admissions@tbiglobal.com

Triple Cities School of Beauty Culture
5 Court St, Binghamton NY 13901
607-722-1279

Troy School of Beauty Culture
86 Congress St, Troy NY 12180
518-273-7741

Ultrasound Diagnostic School
711 Stewart Ave Suite 200
Garden City NY 11530-4734
516-248-6060

Ultrasound Diagnostic School
120 E 16th St Fl 2, New York NY 10003-2103
212-645-9116

Utica School of Commerce
PO Box 462, Canastota NY 13032-0462
315-697-8200

VAUGHN COLLEGE OF AERONAUTICS AND TECHNOLOGY
8601 23rd Ave, Flushing NY 11369-1037
Vincent Papandrea, Director of Admissions
800-776-2376 Fax: 718-429-0671
Website: www.vaughn.edu
E-mail: admitme@vaughn.edu
    Established 1932. Private. Coed. Accreditation: MSACS, ABET. Tuition: $13,400. Fees: $280. Enrollment: 842 full-time, 284 part-time. Faculty: 59. Student-faculty ratio: 11:1. Degrees: BS, AAS, AOS. Library: 62,000 vols. Offering bachelor and associate degrees in airport management, aviation maintenance, flight training, electronic technology, engineering, general management, mechatronic engineering, pre-engineering and computerized design/animated graphics. Hands-on training. Extensive career development services and financial aid available.

Westchester School of Beauty Culture
6 Gramatan Ave, Mount Vernon NY 10550
914-699-2344

NORTH CAROLINA

Anson College of Cosmetology
1217 E Caswell St, Wadesboro NC 28170
704-694-6677

Art Institute of Charlotte
2110 Water Ridge Pkwy, Charlotte NC 28217-4536
800-872-4417

Brookstone College of Business
10125 Berkeley Place Dr, Charlotte NC 28262
704-547-8600

Brookstone College of Business
7815 National Service Rd
Greensboro NC 27409-9423
336-668-2627

Carolina Beauty College
5430 N Tryon St Ste O, Charlotte NC 28213
704-597-5503

Carolina Beauty College
5106 N Roxboro St, Durham NC 27704
919-477-1444

Carolina Beauty College
1917 E Wendover Ave, Greensboro NC 27405
336-886-4712

Carolina Beauty College
2001 E Wendover Ave, Greensboro NC 27405
336-272-2966

Carolina Beauty College
7736 N Point Blvd Ste C, Winston Salem NC 27106
336-759-7969

Carteret Community College
3505 Arendell St, Morehead City NC 28557-2989
Don Thompson, Director of Student Support
252-247-4142 ext. 149

Cheveux School Hair Design and Hairport
4781 Gum Branch Rd #1, Jacksonville NC 28540
910-455-5767

Cosmetology Institute of Beauty Arts & Science
807 Silas Creek Pkwy, Winston Salem NC 27127
336-773-1472

Dudley Beauty College
1950 John McDonald Ave, Charlotte NC 28216
704-392-2564

DUDLEY COSMETOLOGY UNIVERSITY
900 E Mountain St, Kernersville NC 27284
Eunice M. Dudley, President
336-996-2030 Fax: 336-996-9752
Website: www.dudleyq.com
E-mail: emdudley@dudleyq.com

ECPI College of Technology
4800 Airport Center Pkwy, Charlotte NC 28208-5886
704-399-1010

ECPI College of Technology
7802 Airport Center Dr, Greensboro NC 27409-9048
336-665-1400

ECPI College of Technology
4101 Doie Cope Rd, Raleigh NC 27613-7387
919-571-0057

Empire Beauty School
11032 E Independence Blvd, Matthews NC 28105
800-575-5983

Empire Beauty School
Shoppes at Kings Grant
10075 Weddington Road Ext, Concord NC 28027
800-575-5983

EnVisionary I-Care
133 Highway 70 W, Garner NC 27529
919-661-7773

Fayetteville Beauty College
3442 Bragg Blvd, Fayetteville NC 28303
910-487-0227

Hairstyling Institute of Charlotte
209B S Kings Dr, Charlotte NC 28204
704-334-5511

Hairstylist Academy
113 Water St, Statesville NC 28677
704-873-8805

Haywood Community College
185 Freedlander Dr, Clyde NC 28721
Debbie Rowland, Coordinator of Admissions
828-627-4500 Fax: 828-627-4513
Website: www.haywood.edu
E-mail: drowland@haywood.edu

King's College
322 Lamar Ave, Charlotte NC 28204-2493
704-372-0266

Leon's Beauty School
1410 W Lee St, Greensboro NC 27403
336-274-4601

Mercy School of Nursing
1921 Vail Ave, Charlotte NC 28207-1142
Pamela Hatley, RN, MSN, Student Services
704-379-5841

MILLER-MOTTE TECHNICAL COLLEGE
2205 Walnut St, Cary NC 27518
919-532-7171
Website: www.miller-motte.com

Miller-Motte Technical College
5000 Market St, Wilmington NC 28405-3430
800-784-2110

Mitchell's Hairstyling Academy
222 Tallywood Shopping Ctr, Fayetteville NC 28303
910-485-6310

Mitchell's Hairstyling Academy
1021 N Spence Ave, Goldsboro NC 27534
919-778-8200

Mitchell's Hairstyling Academy
426 E Arlington Blvd, Greenville NC 27858
252-756-3050

Mitchell's Hairstyling Academy
2620 Forest Hills Rd #A, Wilson NC 27893
252-243-3158

Mr. David's School of Hair Design
4348 Market St #N-17, Wilmington NC 28403
910-763-4418

NASCAR Technical Institute
220 Byers Creek Rd, Mooresville NC 28117
704-658-1950

Oconaluftee Job Corps Center
502 Oconaluftee Job Corps Rd
Cherokee NC 28719-9203
Danny Muse, Education Supervisor
828-497-5411

Schenck Civilian Conservation Center
98 Schenck Dr, Pisgah Forest NC 28768-9718
828-862-6100

SCHOOL OF COMMUNICATION ARTS
3000 Wakefield Crossing Dr, Raleigh NC 27614-7076
Debra Ann Hooper, Director and VP
919-981-0972 Fax: 919-981-0946
Website: www.higherdigital.com
E-mail: school@higherdigital.com

Southeastern School of Neuromuscular
4 Woodlawn Green #200, Charlotte NC 28217
704-527-4979

Universal College of Beauty
1701 W Trade St, Charlotte NC 28216
704-333-6969

WILKES REGIONAL MEDICAL CENTER
School of Radiologic Technology
PO Box 609, North Wilkesboro NC 28659-0609
336-651-8431 Fax: 336-651-8432
E-mail: bwinslow@wilkesregional.com

Winston-Salem Barber School
1531 Silas Creek Pkwy, Winston Salem NC 27127
336-724-1459

NORTH DAKOTA

AAKERS COLLEGE
4012 19th Ave S, Fargo ND 58103-7196
Elizabeth Largent, Director
701-277-3889 Fax: 701-277-5604
Website: www.aakers.edu
E-mail: blargent@aakers.edu

Headquarters Academy of Hair Design
108 Main St S, Minot ND 58701
701-852-8329

Josef's School of Hair Design
627 NP Ave N, Fargo ND 58102
701-235-0011

Josef's School of Hair Design
2011 S Washington St, Grand Forks ND 58201
701-772-2728

Moler Barber College of HairStyling
16 S 8th St, Fargo ND 58103
701-232-6773

R.D. Hairstyling College
124 N 4th St, Bismarck ND 58501
701-223-8804

Sr. Rosalind Gefre Schools of Massage
3101 39th St SW Ste E, Fargo ND 58104
Annie Thorseth, Director of Admissions
701-297-5993 Fax: 701-297-5994
Website: www.sisterrosalind.org
E-mail: fargocampus@sisterrosalind.org

OHIO

Academy of Court Reporting
2044 Euclid Ave, Cleveland OH 44115-2282
216-861-3222

Academy of Court Reporting
630 E Broad St, Columbus OH 43215-3902
614-221-7770

Academy of Court Reporting
2930 W Market St, Fairlawn OH 44333-3607
330-867-4030

Akron Institute
1600 S Arlington St Ste 100, Akron OH 44306
330-724-1600

Akron Machining Institute
2959 Barber Rd, Norton OH 44203-1005
330-745-1111

AMERICAN INSTITUTE OF ALTERNATIVE MEDICINE
formerly Massage Away School of Therapy
6685 Doubletree Ave, Columbus OH 43229-1113
Nerissa Pancake, Business Development Manager
614-825-6278 Fax: 614-825-6279
Website: www.aiam.edu
E-mail: info@aiam.edu

American School of Technology
2100 Morse Rd #4599, Columbus OH 43229-6665
614-436-4820

Antonelli College
124 E 7th St, Cincinnati OH 45202-2528
513-241-4338

The Art Institute of Cincinnati
1171 E Kemper Rd, Cincinnati OH 45246
Marion Allman, President
513-751-1206 Fax: 513-751-1209
Website: www.theartinstituteofcincinnati.com
E-mail: aic@theartinstituteofcincinnati.com
See listing under "Art"

Ashland County - West Holmes Career Center
1783 State Route 60, Ashland OH 44805-9287
419-289-3313

ATS INSTITUTE OF TECHNOLOGY
230 Alpha Park, Highland Heights OH 44143-2216
Helen Bykov, Director of Education
440-449-1700 Fax: 440-449-1389
Website: www.atsinstitute.com
E-mail: info@atsinstitute.com

Beatrice Academy of Beauty
10500 Cedar Ave, Cleveland OH 44106
216-421-2313

Bohecker College
653 Enterprise Pkwy, Ravenna OH 44266
800-794-2856

Bradford School
2469 Stelzer Rd, Columbus OH 43219-3129
Raeann Lee, Director of Admissions
614-416-6200

Brown Aveda Institute
8816 Mentor Ave, Mentor OH 44060-6212
Susan Partin, Contact
440-255-9494

Brown Mackie College - Cincinnati
1011 Glendale Milford Rd, Cincinnati OH 45215-1107
Robin Krout, President
513-771-2424 Fax: 513-771-3413
Website: www.brownmackie.edu
E-mail: rkrout@brownmackie.edu

Brown Mackie College - Findlay
1700 Fostoria Ave Ste 100, Findlay OH 45840-6220
888-296-5059

Bryant & Stratton College
1700 E 13th St, Cleveland OH 44114-3238
Shawn T. Kampa, Market Director of Admissions
216-771-1700 Fax: 216-771-7787
Website: www.bryantstratton.edu
E-mail: stkampa@bryantstratton.edu

Bryant & Stratton College
27557 Chardon Rd, Willoughby Hills OH 44092-2794
Shawn Kampa, Director of Admissions
440-944-6800

Carousel Beauty College
125 E 2nd St, Dayton OH 45402
937-223-3572

Carousel Beauty College
3120 Woodman Dr, Kettering OH 45420
937-298-5752

Carousel Beauty College
633 S Breiel Blvd, Middletown OH 45044
513-422-2962

Carousel Beauty College
1475 Upper Valley Pike #956, Springfield OH 45504
937-323-0277

Carousel of Miami Valley Beauty College
7809 Waynetowne Blvd, Huber Heights OH 45424
937-233-8818

Century School of Cosmetology
434 Market St, Steubenville OH 43952
740-282-3312

CLEVELAND CLINIC FOUNDATION
9500 Euclid Ave, Cleveland OH 44195-0001
216-445-5719
E-mail: education@ccf.org

Cleveland Institute of Dental and Medical Assistants
2450 Prospect Ave, Cleveland OH 44115
James N. Gallagher, General Manager
216-241-2930

Cleveland Institute of Dental and Medical Assistants
5564 Mayfield Rd, Lyndhurst OH 44124-2928
James N. Gallagher, General Manager
440-473-6273

Cleveland Institute of Dental and Medical Assistants
5733 Hopkins Rd, Mentor OH 44060-2035
James N. Gallagher, General Manager
440-946-9530

Cleveland Institute of Electronics
1776 E 17th St, Cleveland OH 44114-3679
Scott Katzenmeyer, Director of Admissions
800-243-6446 Fax: 216-781-0331
Website: www.cie-wc.edu
E-mail: instruct@cie-wc.edu

College of Art Advertising
4343 Bridgetown Rd, Cincinnati OH 45211-4441
513-574-1010

Collins Career Center
11627 State Route 243, Chesapeake OH 45619-7962
740-867-6641 Fax: 740-867-9626
Website: www.collins-cc.k12.oh.us

Columbus State Community College
550 E Spring St, Columbus OH 43215-1786
Ken Conner, Director of Admissions
614-287-3669

COMMUNITY HOSPITAL SCHOOL OF NURSING
2615 E High St, Springfield OH 45505-1494
Jamie Schoening, Recruiter
937-328-8905 Fax: 937-328-8668
Website: www.chsn.com
E-mail: jamie.schoening@health-partners.org

COOPERATIVE MEDICAL TECHNOLOGY PROGRAM OF AKRON
1 Perkins Sq, Akron OH 44308-1062
Sharon K. Shriber, MBA, Program Director
330-543-8720 Fax: 330-543-6303
Website: www.akronchildrens.org
E-mail: sshriber@chmca.org

Creative Images - A Certified Matrix Design Academy
1076 Kauffman Ave, Fairborn OH 45324
937-878-9555

Dayton Barber College
28 W 5th St, Dayton OH 45402
937-222-9101

ENGLISH NANNY AND GOVERNESS SCHOOL
30 S Franklin St, Chagrin Falls OH 44022-3213
Sheilagh Roth, Executive Director
800-733-1984 Fax: 440-247-0602
Website: www.nanny-governess.com
E-mail: admissions@nanny-governess.com

ETI Technical College
2076 Youngstown Warren Rd, Niles OH 44446-4398
330-652-9919

Fairfield Career Center
4465 S Hamilton Rd, Groveport OH 43125-9333
614-836-5725

Fairview Academy
22610 Lorain Rd, Fairview Park OH 44126
440-734-5555

FIRELANDS REGIONAL MEDICAL CENTER SCHOOL OF NURSING
1912 Hayes Ave, Sandusky OH 44870-4788
Holly J. Price, RN, Director
419-557-7111 Fax: 419-557-7116
Website: www.firelands.com
E-mail: priceh@firelands.com

Gallipolis Career College
1176 Jackson Pike #312, Gallipolis OH 45631
740-446-4367

Gerber Akron Beauty School
33 Shiawassee Ave, Fairlawn OH 44333
330-867-6200

Hair Academy
6000 Mahoning Ave, Austintown OH 44515
330-792-6504

Hamrick Truck Driving School
1156 Medina Rd, Medina OH 44256-8121
330-239-2229

Hobart Institute of Welding Technology
400 Trade Sq E, Troy OH 45373-2463
Ron L. Scott, Vice President and General Manager
800-332-9448

Hocking College
3301 Hocking Pkwy, Nelsonville OH 45764-9704
Diane K. Wolf, Assistant Director of Admissions Information
800-282-4163

Hondros College
7410 South Ave, Boardman OH 44512-5719
Site Director
888-HONDROS

Hondros College
4675 Cornell Rd Suite 175
Cincinnati OH 45241-2495
Site Director
888-HONDROS

Hondros College
1810 Successful Dr, Fairborn OH 45324
Site Director
888-HONDROS

Hondros College
4100 Rockside Rd 2nd Floor
Independence OH 44131
Site Director
888-HONDROS

Hondros College
7350 Industrial Park Blvd, Mentor OH 44060
Site Director
888-HONDROS

Hondros College
1505 Corporate Woods Parkway #100
Uniontown OH 44685
Site Director
888-HONDROS

Hondros College
4140 Executive Pkwy, Westerville OH 43081-3855
Andrea Nameche, V.P. Degree Division
888-HONDROS

Hondros College
The Trust Company Building
6135 Trust Dr Suite 110, Holland OH 43528-9358
Site Director
888-HONDROS

HURON SCHOOL OF NURSING
Cleveland Clinic Health System
13951 Terrace Rd, East Cleveland OH 44112-4308
Barbara Szigeti, MA, Coordinator of Student Services
216-761-7996 Fax: 216-761-7541
Website: www.cchseast.org/schools
E-mail: bszigeti@cchseast.org

Inner State Beauty School
5150 Mayfield Rd, Lyndhurst OH 44124
440-442-4500

Institute of Medical & Dental Technology
375 Glensprings Dr Ste 201
Cincinnati OH 45246-2396
513-851-8500

International Academy of Hair Design
8419 Colerain Ave, Cincinnati OH 45239
513-741-4777

International College of Broadcasting
6 S Smithville Rd, Dayton OH 45431-1833
J. Michael LeMaster, President
937-258-8251 Fax: 937-258-8714
Website: www.icbcollege.com
E-mail: admissions@icbcollege.com

ITT Technical Institute
4750 Wesley Ave, Cincinnati OH 45212-2244
Michael Thompson, Director
513-531-8300

ITT Technical Institute
14955 W Sprague Rd, Strongsville OH 44136-1758
440-234-9091

Kent State University
PO Box 5190, Kent OH 44242-0001
Paul Deutsch, Director of Admissions
330-672-2444

Kent State University-Ashtabula Campus
3325 W 13th St, Ashtabula OH 44004-2299
Kelly Sanford, Contact
440-964-3322

Kent State University-East Liverpool Campus
400 E 4th St, East Liverpool OH 43920-3497
Jamie Kenneally, Contact
330-385-3805

Kent State University-Geauga Campus
14111 Claridon Troy Rd, Burton OH 44021-9581
Dave Chappell, Contact
440-834-4187

Kent State University-Salem Campus
2491 State Route 45 S, Salem OH 44460-9412
Dennis Giacomino, Contact
330-332-0361

Kent State University-Stark Campus
6000 Frank Ave NW, North Canton OH 44720-7548
Jim Barrett, Contact
330-499-9600

Kent State University-Trumbull Campus
4314 Mahoning Ave NW, Warren OH 44483-1998
Linda Petrilla, Contact
330-678-4281

Kent State University - Tuscarawas Campus
330 University Dr NE, New Philadelphia OH 44663
Denise Testa, Contact
330-339-3391

Knox County Career Center
306 Martinsburg Rd, Mount Vernon OH 43050-4225
740-397-5820

Marinello-Eastern Hills Academy of Hair Design
7681 Beechmont Ave, Cincinnati OH 45255
513-231-8621

Marion Technical College
1467 Mount Vernon Ave, Marion OH 43302-5628
Joel Liles, Director of Admissions
740-389-4636

Medina County Career Center
1101 W Liberty St, Medina OH 44256-1346
330-725-8461

Moler-Hollywood Beauty College
130 E 6th St 2nd Floor, Cincinnati OH 45202-3210
513-621-5262

Moler-Pickens Beauty College
5951 Boymel Dr Ste S, Fairfield OH 45014-5548
513-874-5116

NATIONAL BEAUTY COLLEGE
4642 Cleveland Ave NW, Canton OH 44709-1837
Lori Campbell, Contact
330-499-9444 Fax: 330-499-2090
Website: www.nationalbc.com
E-mail: nationalbeauty@neo.rr.com

National Institute of Technology
2545 Bailey Rd, Cuyahoga Falls OH 44221-2949
330-923-9959

Nationwide Beauty Academy
5300 WestPointe Plaza Dr, Columbus OH 43228
614-921-9109

New England School of Hair Design
12 Interchange Dr, West Lebanon OH 03784-2003
603-298-5199

Northern Institute of Cosmetology
667 Broadway, Lorain OH 44052
440-244-4282

Ohio Business College
1907 N Ridge Rd E, Lorain OH 44055-3344
440-277-0021

Ohio Business College
4020 Milan Rd, Sandusky OH 44870-5871
419-627-8345

Ohio Center for Broadcasting
6703 Madison Rd, Cincinnati OH 45227-2029
513-271-6060

OHIO CENTER FOR BROADCASTING
9000 Sweet Valley Dr, Valley View OH 44125-4220
Kathy Wenner, Admissions Director
216-447-9117 Fax: 216-642-9232
Website: www.beonair.com
E-mail: ocb@beonair.com

OHIO COLLEGE OF MASSOTHERAPY
225 Heritage Woods Dr, Copley OH 44321-1363
John T. Adkins Sr., Admissions
330-665-1084 Fax: 330-665-5021
Website: www.ocm.edu
E-mail: johna@ocm.edu

Ohio Institute of Health Careers
1880 E Dublin Granville Rd, Columbus OH 43229
614-891-5030

Ohio Institute of Health Careers
631 Griswold Rd, Elyria OH 44035
800-725-0882

Ohio Institute of Photography & Technology
2029 Edgefield Rd, Dayton OH 45439-1917
Robert A. Martin, Executive Director
937-294-6155

Ohio State Beauty Academy
57 Town Sq, Lima OH 45801
419-229-7896

Ohio State College of Barber Styling
4614 E Broad St, Columbus OH 43213
614-868-1015

Ohio State Cosmetology School
5970 Westerville Rd, Westerville OH 43081
614-890-3535

Ohio State Sch of Cosmetology Northland
4390 Karl Rd, Columbus OH 43224
614-263-1661

Ohio State School of Cosmetology
3717 S High St, Columbus OH 43207
614-491-0492

Ohio State School of Cosmetology East
6320 E Livingston Ave, Reynoldsburg OH 43068
614-868-1601

OHIO TECHNICAL COLLEGE
1374 E 51st St, Cleveland OH 44103-1228
Marc Brenner, President
216-881-1700 Fax: 216-881-9145
Website: www.ohiotechnicalcollege.com
E-mail: info@ohiotechnicalcollege.com

OHIO VALLEY COLLEGE OF TECHNOLOGY
16808 St. Clair Ave, PO Box 7000
East Liverpool OH 43920
Scott S. Rogers, Director
330-385-1070 Fax: 330-385-4606
Website: www.ovct.edu
E-mail: info@ovct.edu

Paramount Beauty Academy
1745 11th St, Portsmouth OH 45662
740-353-2436

PROFESSIONAL SKILLS INSTITUTE
20 Arco Dr, Toledo OH 43607-2901
Daniel A. Finch, Chairman/CEO
419-531-9610 Fax: 419-531-4732
Website: www.proskills.com
E-mail: admissions@proskills.com

Raphael's School of Beauty Culture
1324 Youngstown Warren Rd, Niles OH 44446
330-652-1559

Recording Workshop
455 Massieville Rd, Chillicothe OH 45601
740-663-1000

Remington College
14445 Broadway Ave, Cleveland OH 44125-1957
216-475-7520

REMINGTON COLLEGE - CLEVELAND WEST CAMPUS
26350 Brookpark Rd, North Olmsted OH 44070
Gary A. Azotea, Campus President
440-777-2560 Fax: 440-777-3238
Website: www.remingtoncollege.edu
E-mail: gary.azotea@remingtoncollege.edu

RETS Technical Center
555 E Alex Bell Rd, Centerville OH 45459-2712
Ken Miller, Director of Admissions
937-433-3410

Riggs Le Mar Beauty College
3464 Hudson Dr, Cuyahoga Falls OH 44221
330-945-4045

Sanford-Brown College
17535 Rosbough Blvd, Cleveland OH 44130-8362
Christine Smith, Executive Director
440-239-9640

THE SCHOOL OF ADVERTISING ART
1725 E David Rd, Kettering OH 45440-1612
Jayne Fahncke, Director of Admissions
877-300-9326 Fax: 937-294-5869
Website: www.saacollege.com
E-mail: jayne@saacollege.com

Southeastern Business College
1855 Western Ave, Chillicothe OH 45601-1038
Clark Derexson, Director
740-774-6300

Southeastern Business College
504 McCarty Ln, Jackson OH 45640
Connie Blackburn, Director
740-286-1554

Southeastern Business College
1522 Sheridan Dr, Lancaster OH 43130-1368
Katrina Sims, Director
740-687-6126

Southeastern Business College
3879 Rhodes Ave Ste A, New Boston OH 45662-4900
Janet Travis, Director
740-456-4124

Southwestern College of Business
111 W 1st St Ste 1140, Dayton OH 45402-1113
937-224-0061

Spa School
5050 N High St, Columbus OH 43214
614-888-1092

Stark State College of Technology
6200 Frank Ave NW, Canton OH 44720-7228
330-494-6170

Stautzenberger College
5355 Southwyck Blvd, Toledo OH 43614-1561
George Simon, President
800-552-5099

TDDS TECHNICAL INSTITUTE
1688 N Pricetown Rd - S.R. 534
Lake Milton OH 44429
Michael Rouzzo, Director of Admissions
330-538-2216 Fax: 330-538-0609
Website: www.tdds.edu
E-mail: info@tdds.edu

Technology Education College
2745 Winchester Pike, Columbus OH 43232-4827
Thomas Greenhouse, Director
614-759-7700

Tiffin Academy of Hair Design
104 E Market St, Tiffin OH 44883
419-447-3117

Toledo Academy of Beauty Culture - East
2592 Woodville Rd, Northwood OH 43619
419-693-7257

Toledo Academy of Beauty Culture - North
5020 Lewis Ave, Toledo OH 43612
419-478-5325

Toledo Academy of Beauty Culture - South
1554 S Byrne Rd, Toledo OH 43614
419-381-7218

Total Technical Institute
8720 Brookpark Rd, Cleveland OH 44129-6810
Dave Bryant, Director of Admissions
216-485-0900 Fax: 216-661-6842
Website: www.ttinst.com
E-mail: dbryant@ttinst.com

Tri County Beauty College
111 Kemper Rd, Cincinnati OH 45246
513-671-8340

Tri-State College of Massotherapy
9159 Market St #26, North Lima OH 44452
330-629-9998

Trumbull Business College
3200 Ridge Ave SE, Warren OH 44484-3200
330-369-3200

Valley Beauty School
1315 Cisler Dr, Marietta OH 45750-9452
740-373-3617

Valley Beauty School
627 Main St, Zanesville OH 43701
740-452-6821

Vatterott College - Cleveland
5025 E Royalton Rd, Broadview Heights OH 44147
440-526-1660

Virginia Marti College of Art & Design
11724 Detroit Ave, Lakewood OH 44107
Quinn Marti, Director of Admissions
216-221-8584 Fax: 216-221-2311
Website: www.vmcad.edu
E-mail: qmarti@vmcad.edu

Western Hills School of Beauty & Hair Design
6490 Glenway Ave, Cincinnati OH 45211
513-574-3818

YOUNGSTOWN COLLEGE OF MASSOTHERAPY
14 Highland Ave, Struthers OH 44471-2321
Angela Shodd, Student Relations
330-755-1406 Fax: 330-755-1605
Website: www.ycm.edu
E-mail: ycm@ycm.edu

OKLAHOMA

Academy of Cosmetology
607 W Grand Ave, Chickasha OK 73018
405-222-2323

Beauty Technical College
PO Box 1506, Tahlequah OK 74465
918-456-6360

Broken Arrow Beauty College
400 S Elm Pl, Broken Arrow OK 74012
918-251-9660

Canadian Valley Area Voc-Tech School
6505 E US Highway 66, El Reno OK 73036-9117
405-262-2629

CAREER POINT INSTITUTE
3138 S Garnett Rd, Tulsa OK 74146-1933
Brad Oakley, Director of Admissions
918-627-8074 Fax: 918-627-4007
E-mail: tadmdir@career-point.org

CC's Cosmetology College
4439 NW 50th St, Oklahoma City OK 73112
405-943-2300

CC's Cosmetology College
11630 E 21st St, Tulsa OK 74129
918-234-9444

Central State Beauty Academy
8494 NW Expressway St, Oklahoma City OK 73162
405-722-4499

Claremore Beauty College
200 N Cherokee Ave, Claremore OK 74017
918-341-4370

Enid Beauty College
1601 E Broadway Ave, Enid OK 73701
580-237-6677

Eve's College of Hairstyling
912 SW C Ave, Lawton OK 73501
580-355-6620

Great Plains Area Vocational Technical School
4500 SW Lee Blvd, Lawton OK 73505-8304
580-355-6371

HERITAGE COLLEGE
7100 S I-35 Service Rd Suite 7118
Oklahoma City OK 73149
Cheryl Morris, Director
405-631-3399 Fax: 405-631-6711
Website: www.heritage-education.com
E-mail: info@heritage-education.com
Accredited Member School: ACCSCT. Providing quality education in Esthetician, Massage Therapy, Personal Trainer, X-Ray Medical Technician and Surgical Technician. Financial aid available to those who qualify.

Hollywood Cosmetology Center
PO Box 890488, Oklahoma City OK 73189-0488
Janet Goble, Contact
405-364-3375

Indian Meridian Vocational Technical School
1312 S Sangre Rd, Stillwater OK 74074-1899
405-377-3333

Jenks Beauty College
535 W Main St, Jenks OK 74037
918-299-0901

Metro Area Vocational Technical School
1900 Springlake Dr, Oklahoma City OK 73111-5238
405-424-8324

Oklahoma Farriers College
PO Box 788, Sperry OK 74073-0788
Kathie R. Beaston, Director of Administration
918-288-7221

Oklahoma Health Academy
1939 N Moore Ave, Moore OK 73160
405-912-2777

Oklahoma Health Academy
2865 E Skelly Dr Ste 224, Tulsa OK 74105
918-748-9900

Oklahoma State Horseshoeing School
4802 Dogwood Rd, Ardmore OK 73401
Marcella Kester, Owner
800-634-2811

O. T. Autry Area Vocational Technical Center
1201 W Willow Rd, Enid OK 73703-2506
580-242-2750

Platt College
112 SW 11th St, Lawton OK 73501
580-355-4416

Platt College
309 S Ann Arbor Ave, Oklahoma City OK 73128-1112
405-946-7799

Platt College
2727 W Memorial Rd, Oklahoma City OK 73134
405-749-2433

Platt College
3801 S Sheridan Rd, Tulsa OK 74145-1111
Angie Morelock, Director of Admissions
918-663-9000 Fax: 918-622-1240
Website: www.plattcollege.org
E-mail: angiem@plattcollege.org

Ponca City Beauty College
122 N 1st St, Ponca City OK 74601
888-557-6709

Poteau Beauty College
301 Turman St, Poteau OK 74953-2343
918-647-4119

Pryor Beauty College
330 W Graham Ave, Pryor OK 74361
918-825-2795

Sand Springs Beauty College
28 E 2nd St, Sand Springs OK 74063
918-245-6627

School of Hair Design
116 W Jackson St, Hugo OK 74743
580-326-7338

School of Hair Design
1437 SE Washington St, Idabel OK 74745
580-286-7840

Shawnee Beauty College
410 E Main St, Shawnee OK 74801
405-275-3182

Southern School of Beauty
140 W Main St, Durant OK 74701
580-924-1049

SPARTAN COLLEGE OF AERONAUTICS AND TECHNOLOGY
8820 E Pine St, Tulsa OK 74115-5802
Director of Admissions
800-331-1204 Fax: 918-831-8609
Website: www.spartan.edu
E-mail: spartan@mail.spartan.edu
Established 1928. Coed. Accredited member school: ACCSCT. Providing Technical training and education in Avionics, Instruments, and Maintenance; Nondestructive Testing and Quality Control. Complete flight training program. Offering Diplomas, Associate of Applied Science and Bachelor of Science in Aviation Technology Management.

State Barber and Hair Design College
2514 S Agnew, Oklahoma City OK 73108
405-631-8621

Stillwater Beauty Academy
1684 Cimarron Plz, Stillwater OK 74075
405-377-4100

Technical Institute of Cosmetology Arts & Sciences
822 E 6th St, Tulsa OK 74120-3610
918-660-8828

Tulsa County Area Vocational Technical District 18
3420 S Memorial Dr, Tulsa OK 74145-1340
918-627-7200

TULSA WELDING SCHOOL
2545 E 11th St, Tulsa OK 74104-3909
Mike Thurber, Director of Admissions
800-WELD-USA Fax: 918-587-8170
Website: www.weldingschool.edu
E-mail: tws@ionet.net

Tuttle Vocational Technical Center
12777 N Rockwell Ave
Oklahoma City OK 73142-2710
405-722-7799

Vatterott College
4621 NW 23rd St, Oklahoma City OK 73127
405-945-0088

Vatterott College - Tulsa
555 S Memorial Dr, Tulsa OK 74112
Kevin Wolfe, Director of Admissions
918-835-8288 Fax: 918-836-9698
Website: www.vatterott-college.com
E-mail: kevin.wolfe@vatterott-college.com

Virgil's Beauty College
111 N 9th St, Muskogee OK 74401
918-682-9429

Woodward Beauty College
502 Texas St, Woodward OK 73801
580-256-7520

Wright Business School
2219 SW 74th St Ste 122
Oklahoma City OK 73159-3931
800-645-9364

Yukon Beauty College
1231 Garth Brooks Blvd, Yukon OK 73099
405-354-3172

OREGON

Abdill Career College
843 E Main St Ste 203, Medford OR 97504
541-779-8384

Academy of Hair Design
305 Court St NE, Salem OR 97301
503-585-8122

Airman Proficiency Center
3565 NE Cornell Rd, Hillsboro OR 97124-6374
503-648-2831

Apollo College
2004 Lloyd Ctr Fl 3, Portland OR 97232-1309
503-761-6100

Astoria Beauty College
1180 Commercial St, Astoria OR 97103
503-325-3163

BEAU MONDE COLLEGE ACADEMY OF COSMETOLOGY
11131 NE Halsey St, Portland OR 97220
Dianna Peterson, Owner
503-252-7444 Fax: 503-252-7555
Website: www.beaumondecollege.com
E-mail: diannapeterson@cs.com

BEAU MONDE COLLEGE OF HAIR DESIGN
1221 SW 12th Ave, Portland OR 97205
Dianna Peterson, Owner
503-226-7355 Fax: 503-226-6512
Website: www.beaumondecollege.com
E-mail: diannapeterson@cs.com

Chemeketa Community College
PO Box 14007, Salem OR 97309-7070
Mike Morgan, Dean
503-399-5172

College of Cosmetology
357 E Main St, Klamath Falls OR 97601
541-882-6644

College of Hair Design Careers
1684 Clay St NE, Salem OR 97301-1952
503-588-5888

College of Legal Arts
8909 SW Barbur Blvd, Portland OR 97219
800-342-3465

Heald College, Portland
625 SW Broadway 4th Floor, Portland OR 97205-3408
Joan Hayward, Campus Director
503-229-0492

Magee Brothers Beaverton School of Beauty
18295A SW Tualatin Valley, Aloha OR 97007
503-649-1388

Northwest College of Hair Design
210 SE 4th Ave, Hillsboro OR 97123
503-844-7320

Northwest College of Hair Design
6128 SE King Rd, Milwaukie OR 97222
503-659-2834

Phagans' Beauty College
142 SW 2nd St, Corvallis OR 97333
541-753-6466

Phagans' Central Oregon Beauty College
355 NE 2nd St, Bend OR 97701
541-382-6171

Phagans' Grants Pass College of Beauty
304 NE Agness Ave Ste F, Grants Pass OR 97526
541-479-6678

Phagans' Medford Beauty School
2320 Poplar Dr, Medford OR 97504-5273
541-772-6155

Phagans' Newport Academy of Cosmetology Careers
333 SW 7th St, Newport OR 97365
541-265-3083

Phagans' School of Beauty
622 Lancaster Dr NE, Salem OR 97301
503-363-6800

Phagans' School of Hair Design
16550 SE McLoughlin Blvd, Milwaukie OR 97267
503-652-2668

Phagans' School of Hair Design
1542 NE Weidler St, Portland OR 97232-1411
503-239-0838

Phagans' Tigard Beauty School
8820 SW Center St, Tigard OR 97223
503-639-6107

PIONEER PACIFIC COLLEGE
27501 SW Parkway Ave, Wilsonville OR 97070-9296
503-682-3903 Fax: 503-682-1514
Website: www.pioneerpacific.edu
E-mail: inquiries@pioneerpacific.edu

Pioneer Pacific College
Clackamas Learning Site
8800 SE Sunnyside Rd, Clackamas OR 97015
Sandey Church, Executive Director
503-654-8000
Website: www.pioneerpacific.edu
E-mail: inquiries@pioneerpacific.edu

Pioneer Pacific College
Health Career Education Center
27375 SW Parkway Ave, Wilsonville OR 97070
Joanna Russell, Executive Director
503-682-1862 Fax: 503-682-6801
Website: www.hcioregon.com
E-mail: inquiries@pioneerpacific.edu

Pioneer Pacific College
Springfield Branch Campus
3800 Sports Way, Springfield OR 97477
Debra Marcus, Executive Director
541-684-4664 Fax: 541-684-0665
Website: www.pioneerpacific.edu
E-mail: inquiries@pioneerpacific.edu

Roseburg Beauty College
700 SE Stephens St, Roseburg OR 97470
541-673-5533

Springfield College of Beauty
307 Q St, Springfield OR 97477
541-746-4473

Western Business College
425 SW Washington St, Portland OR 97204-2296
503-222-3225

WESTERN CULINARY INSTITUTE
921 SW Morrison St Suite 400, Portland OR 97205
Joanne Lazo, Director of Marketing
503-223-2245 or 888-848-3202 Fax: 503-223-5554
Website: www.wci.edu
E-mail: info@wci.edu

PENNSYLVANIA

Academy of Creative Hair Design
252 W Side Mall Ste 1, Kingston PA 18704
570-288-4574

Academy of Hair Design
1057 N Church St Suite A, Hazleton PA 18202-1465
570-784-1020

Academy of Medical Arts and Business
2301 Academy Dr, Harrisburg PA 17112-1012
717-545-4747
Website: www.ACADcampus.com
E-mail: info@ACADcampus.com

Allentown School of Cosmetology
1921 Union Blvd, Allentown PA 18109-1629
610-437-4626

Allied Medical & Technical Careers
517 Ash St, Scranton PA 18509-2903
Heather Petrochko, Director of Admissions
570-558-1818

All-State Career School
501 Seminole St, Lester PA 19029-1827
610-521-1818

All-State Career School
97 2nd St, N Versailles PA 15137
412-823-1818

Altoona Beauty School
1528 Valley View Blvd, Altoona PA 16602
814-942-3141

Ambler Beauty Academy
50 E Butler Ave, Ambler PA 19002
215-643-5994

American Beauty Academy
6912 Frankford Ave, Philadelphia PA 19135
215-331-1515

Antonelli Medical & Professional Institute
1700 Industrial Hwy, Pottstown PA 19464-9244
Randall Wampole, Director of Admissions
610-323-7270

THE ART INSTITUTE OF PITTSBURGH
The College for Creative Minds
420 Boulevard Of The Allies, Pittsburgh PA 15219
Newton I. Myvett, VP/Director of Admissions
800-275-2470 or 412-263-6600 Fax: 412-263-6667
Website: www.aip.aii.edu
E-mail: pahughes@aii.edu
Established in 1921. Known as a leader in creative education. College is located in the heart of downtown, surrounded by limitless cultural, educational, and recreational opportunities. Licensed by the State of PA and accredited by Accrediting Council for Independent Colleges and Schools to confer Associate of Science and Bachelor of Science degrees. Approved for training of veterans and eligible veteran's dependents. Authorized by federal law to enroll non-immigrant alien students.
Enrollment: 2700+ students; Co-ed.
Financial Aid available to qualified students through various federal and state programs. Awards based on individual need and availability of funds. Other Institute scholarship programs are available. Information regarding eligibility can be obtained by contacting an admissions representative at 1-800-275-2470.
Student Housing: School sponsored housing available in the form of furnished apartments.
Bachelor degrees available in: Advertising, Culinary Management, Game Art and Design, Digital Media Production, Graphic Design, Industrial Design, Interactive Media Design, Interior Design, Media Arts and Animation, Photography, Visual Effects and Motion Graphics.
Associate Degrees available in: Culinary Arts, Graphic Design, Industrial Design, Interactive Media Design, Photography, Video Production.
Diploma programs include: The Art of Cooking, Digital Design, Residential Planning, Web Design. Some classes available evenings, Saturdays, and online.
Admissions: Prospective students must be a high school graduate or hold a General Educational Development (GED) Certificate. High school students who have not yet graduated should submit a partial transcript that indicates their expected graduation date, SAT and ACT testing not required for admission, however, may be used to determine the student's preparedness for college-level course work in English and/or mathematics.
Faculty: 98 full-time and 47 part-time instructors.
Facilities: 10 floors of fully networked computer labs and specialty facilities such as editing suites, digital photography labs, a television production studio, an industrial design machine shop, fully equipped culinary kitchens and more.

AUTOMOTIVE TRAINING CENTER
114 Pickering Way, Exton PA 19341-1310
Don VanDemark, Vice President/Chief Operating Officer
610-363-6716 Fax: 610-363-8524
Website: www.autotraining.edu
E-mail: atc@autotraining.edu
Established 1917. Private. Coed. Accreditation: Accrediting Commission of Career Schools and Colleges of Technology. Fees: $150. Enrollment: 414 full-time, 34 part-time. Faculty: 65. Student-faculty ratio: 22:1. Diplomas in Automotive Technology, Collision Repair Technology, Diesel Technology. Library: 2,000 volumes. 2 buildings on 5 acres. Small, specialized classes in each aspect of Automotive, Diesel and Collision Repair Technology. High performance engine dynamometer. ASE/NATEF MASTER certified programs. Extensive hands-on training. Financial aid to those who qualify. No unrelated general academic course requirement. Experienced ASE certified instructors.

Automotive Training Center
900 Johnsville Blvd, Warminster PA 18974
Kimberly Ewing, Executive Director of Admissions
877-411-8041 Fax: 215-442-1030
Website: www.autotraining.edu
E-mail: kewing@autotraining.edu
See listing under "Career Schools"

Aviation Institute of Maintenance
3001 Grant Ave, Philadelphia PA 19114-1018
John Norton, School Director
215-676-7700

Baltimore School of Massage - York Campus
170 Red Rock Rd, York PA 17406-6046
Anita Perry-Strong, Campus Director
717-268-1881

Beaver Falls Beauty Academy
720 13th St, Beaver Falls PA 15010
724-843-7700

Berean Institute
1901 W Girard Ave, Philadelphia PA 19130
215-763-4833

Berks Technical Institute
2205 Ridgewood Rd, Wyomissing PA 19610-1168
Jean Vokes, Director of Admissions
610-372-1722

Bidwell Training Center
1815 Metropolitan St, Pittsburgh PA 15233-2233
412-323-4000

Bradford Regional Medical Center
School of Radiography
116 Interstate Pkwy, Bradford PA 16701-1036
S. Gregoire, Program Director
814-362-8292

Bradford School
125 W Station Square Dr, Pittsburgh PA 15219
Director of Admissions
412-391-6710 Fax: 412-471-6714
Website: www.bradfordpittsburgh.edu

Bradley Academy for the Visual Arts
1409 Williams Rd, York PA 17402-9012
James T. Hannigan, Jr., Director of Admissions
800-864-7725

Bucks County School of Beauty Culture
1761 Bustleton Pike, Feasterville Trevose PA 19053
215-322-0666

BUSINESS INSTITUTE OF PENNSYLVANIA
632 Arch St, Meadville PA 16335-2720
800-289-2069 Fax: 814-724-2777
Website: www.biop.edu
E-mail: info@biop.edu

BUSINESS INSTITUTE OF PENNSYLVANIA
335 Boyd Dr, Sharon PA 16146-3843
800-289-2069 Fax: 724-983-8355
Website: www.biop.edu
E-mail: info@biop.edu

Butler Beauty School
233 S Main St, Butler PA 16001
724-287-0708

Cambria-Rowe Business College
422 S 13th St, Indiana PA 15701-2804
724-463-0222

Career Training Academy
4314 Old William Penn Highway Ste 103
Monroeville PA 15146
Gina Hudac, Admissions Representitive
412-372-3900 Fax: 412-373-4262
Website: www.careerta.edu
E-mail: admissions2@careerta.edu

CAREER TRAINING ACADEMY
950 5th Ave, New Kensington PA 15068-6308
John Reddy, Director
Tyna Putignano, Director of Admissions
724-337-1000 Fax: 724-335-7140
Website: www.careerta.edu
E-mail: admissions@careerta.edu
Branch campus in Monroeville, PA and in North Hills, PA. Accreditation: ACCSCT. Federal and state financial aid available for those who qualify.
Associate in Specialized Technology degrees available (15 to 19 months) for Advanced Bodyworker and Medical Assistant Comprehensive. Associate in Specialized Business degree available (17.5 months) for Advanced Medical Coder/Biller. Programs ranging from 3 to 9 months offer diplomas in Dental Assisting, Medical Assisting, Health Insurance Claims Examiner/Medical Biller, Swedish Massage Practitioner, Therapeutic Massage Technician, Comprehensive Massage Therapist, Basic Shiatsu Technician, Advanced Shiatsu Technician, Administrative Assistant, Executive Administrative Assistant and Receptionist. Day & evening classes available for many of our programs. Distance Learning available for Paralegal/Legal Assistant. New class sessions begin often.
Student Massage Clinic available to the public most Saturdays throughout the year, which provides unique learning opportunity for students in any of our massage programs.
Admission requirements include application and $30.00 fee, high school transcripts and applicant must be a high school graduate or possess a GED diploma prior to beginning classes at Career Training Academy.
All locations offer free parking and small classes. Wide range of student participation in community service projects spearheaded by school.

Career Training Academy
1500 Northway Mall, Pittsburgh PA 15237
Anna Bartolini, Director North Hills Branch Campus
412-367-4000 Fax: 412-369-7223
Website: www.careerta.edu
E-mail: admissions3@careerta.edu

Center for Innovative Training & Education
714 Market St Ste 433, Philadelphia PA 19106
215-922-6555

Center for Innovative Training & Education
135 Franklin Ave, Scranton PA 18503-1935
570-922-6555

CHI Institute
520 Street Rd, Southampton PA 18966-3747
Mike Herbert, Director of Admissions
215-357-5100

CHI Institute/RETS Campus
1991 Sproul Rd Ste 42, Broomall PA 19008-3516
610-359-7630

Chubb Institute-Keystone School
400 S State Rd, Springfield PA 19064-1243
610-543-1747

CITTONE INSTITUTE
3600 Market St, Philadelphia PA 19104-2641
James Beatty, Director of Admissions
215-382-1553 Fax: 215-382-3875
Website: www.cittone.com
E-mail: jbeatty@cittone.com

Clearfield Beauty Academy
22 N 3rd St, Clearfield PA 16830
814-765-2022

Computer Learning Network
2900 Fairway Dr, Altoona PA 16602-4457
814-944-5643

Computer Learning Network
401 E Winding Hill Rd Ste 101
Mechanicsburg PA 17055-4989
Marlene Macauley, Director of Admissions
717-761-1481 Fax: 717-761-0558
Website: www.clntraining.net
E-mail: mmacauley@clntraining.net

Consolidated School of Business
2124 Ambassador Cir, Lancaster PA 17603-2389
Millie Liberatore, Director of Admissions
717-394-6211

Consolidated School of Business
1605 Clugston Rd, York PA 17404-1779
Robert Safran Jr., Vice President
717-764-9550 Fax: 717-764-9469
Website: www.csb.edu
E-mail: bobjr@csb.edu

Dean Institute of Technology
1501 W Liberty Ave, Pittsburgh PA 15226-1103
412-531-4433

DELAWARE VALLEY ACADEMY OF MEDICAL & DENTAL ASSISTANTS
3330 Grant Ave, Philadelphia PA 19114-2600
Glenn Goldsmith, Director
215-676-1200
Website: delawarevalleyacademy.com
E-mail: delvalacad@aol.com

Douglas Education Center
130 7th St, Monessen PA 15062-1097
Sherry Lee Walters, Director of Enrollment Services
800-413-6013 Fax: 724-684-7463
Website: www.douglas-school.com
E-mail: swalters@douglas-school.com

DUBOIS BUSINESS COLLEGE
1 Beaver Dr, Du Bois PA 15801-2490
Lisa J. Doty, Director of Admissions
814-371-6920 Fax: 814-371-3974
Website: www.dbcollege.com
E-mail: dotylj@dbcollege.com

DUBOIS BUSINESS COLLEGE
1001 Moore St, Huntingdon PA 16652-1846
Lisa J. Doty, Director of Admissions
814-641-0440 Fax: 814-641-0205
Website: www.dbcollege.com
E-mail: dotylj@dbcollege.com

DUBOIS BUSINESS COLLEGE
701 E 3rd St, Oil City PA 16301-2407
Lisa J. Doty, Director of Admissions
814-677-1322 Fax: 814-677-8237
Website: www.dbcollege.com
E-mail: dotylj@dbcollege.com

Duffs Business Institute
100 Forbes Ave Ste 1200, Pittsburgh PA 15222-1320
412-261-4520

Empire Beauty School
1000 Carlisle St, Hanover PA 17331
800-575-5983

Empire Beauty School
3941 Jonestown Rd, Harrisburg PA 17109
800-575-5983

Empire Beauty School
1801 Columbia Ave, Lancaster PA 17603-4335
800-575-5983

Empire Beauty School
1776 Quentin Rd, Lebanon PA 17042
800-575-5983

Empire Beauty School
320 Mall Blvd The Plaza, Monroeville PA 15146
800-575-5983

Empire Beauty School
3370 S Birney Ave, Moosic PA 18507-1500
800-575-5893

Empire Beauty School
2632 S Broad St, Philadelphia PA 19145
800-575-5983

Empire Beauty School
4026 Woodhaven Rd, Philadelphia PA 19154
800-575-5983

Empire Beauty School
1522 Chestnut St, Philadelphia PA 19102
800-575-5983

Empire Beauty School
1000 McKnight Park Dr Ste 1006A
Pittsburgh PA 15237
800-575-5983

Empire Beauty School
141 High St, Pottstown PA 19464
800-575-5983

Empire Beauty School
324 N Centre St, Pottsville PA 17901
800-575-5983

Empire Beauty School
2302 N 5th Street Hwy, Reading PA 19605
800-575-5983

Empire Beauty School
PO Box 397, Shamokin Dam PA 17876
800-575-5983

Empire Beauty School
206 W Hamilton Ave, State College PA 16801
800-575-5983

Empire Beauty School
435 York Rd, Warminster PA 18974
800-575-5983

Empire Beauty School
313 W Market St, West Chester PA 19382
800-575-5983

Empire Beauty School
2393 Mountain View Dr, West Mifflin PA 15122
800-575-5983

Empire Beauty School
1634 MacArthur Rd, Whitehall PA 18052
800-575-5983

Empire Beauty School
1808 E 3rd St, Williamsport PA 17701
800-575-5983

Empire Beauty School
2592 Eastern Blvd, York PA 17402
800-575-5983

Erie Business Center
246 W 9th St, Erie PA 16501-1392
Donna Perino, Director
814-456-7504 Fax: 814-456-6015
Website: www.eriebc.edu
E-mail: perinod@eriebc.edu

GECAC Training Institute
1006 W 10th St, Erie PA 16502
814-451-5610

Greater Johnstown Area Vocational Technical School
445 Schoolhouse Rd, Johnstown PA 15904-2927
814-266-6073

Great Lakes Institute of Technology
5100 Peach St, Erie PA 16509-2482
Barbara Bolt, Director of Admissions
800-394-4548

Harrisburg Institute of Trade & Technology
3000 Pineford Dr, Middletown PA 17057
717-944-2731

Harrison Career Institute
2102 Union Blvd, Allentown PA 18109-1670
610-434-9963

Harrison Career Institute
1619 Walnut St 3rd Floor, Philadelphia PA 19103
215-640-0177

Harrison Career Institute
645 Penn St, Reading PA 19601
610-374-2469

HUSSIAN SCHOOL OF ART
1118 Market St, Philadelphia PA 19107-3679
Lynne Wartman, Director of Admissions
215-981-0900 Fax: 215-864-9115
Website: www.hussianart.edu
E-mail: info@hussianart.edu

ICM School of Business and Medical Careers
10 Wood St, Pittsburgh PA 15222-1931
Maureen McBride, Assistant Director of Admissions
800-441-5222

ICT School of Welding
358 Market St, Sunbury PA 17801-3404
Miki Borich, Director of Admissions
570-988-3960

INTERNATIONAL ACADEMY OF ADVANCED REFLEXOLOGY & MEDICAL REFLEXOLOGY CLINIC
1701 Snyder Rd, Green Lane PA 18054
Professor L.J. Telepo, President
215-234-0307 or 866-248-8420 Pin 2020
Fax: 215-234-4563
Website: www.reflexology.net
E-mail: postsecondary@reflexology.net
See listing under "Allied Health Science"

INTERNATIONAL ACADEMY OF ADVANCED REFLEXOLOGY & MEDICAL REFLEXOLOGY CLINIC
1177 6th St, Whitehall PA 18052
Professor L.J. Telepo, President
215-234-0307 or 866-248-8420 Pin 2020
Fax: 215-234-4563
Website: www.reflexology.net
E-mail: postsecondary@reflexology.net
See listing under "Allied Health Science"

International Academy of Design and Technology
555 Grant St, Pittsburgh PA 15219
Deborah L. Love, Director of Admissions
800-447-8324

ITT Technical Institute
3330 Tillman Dr, Bensalem PA 19020
215-244-8871

ITT Technical Institute
5020 Louise Dr, Mechanicsburg PA 17055-4899
Glen Feist, Director of Admissions
717-691-9263

ITT Technical Institute
105 Mall Blvd #200, Monroeville PA 15146-2230
412-856-5920

ITT TECHNICAL INSTITUTE
10 Parkway Ctr, Pittsburgh PA 15220-3805
Rebekah Sabo, Director of Recruitment
800-353-8324 Fax: 412-937-9425
Website: www.itt-tech.edu
E-mail: rsabo@itt-tech.edu

Jean Madeline Education Center for Cosmetology
315A Bainbridge St, Philadelphia PA 19147
215-238-9998

JNA INSTITUTE OF CULINARY ARTS
1212 S Broad St, Philadelphia PA 19146-3119
Admissions Office
215-468-8800 Fax: 215-468-8838
Website: www.culinaryarts.com
E-mail: admissions@culinaryarts.com

Johnson College
3427 N Main Ave, Scranton PA 18508-1495
Dr. Ann L. Pipinski, President & CEO
Melissa Ide, Director of Enrollment Management
800-2WE-WORK or 570-342-6404 ext. 125
Fax: 570-348-2181
Website: www.johnson.edu
E-mail: admit@johnson.edu

Kittanning Beauty School
120 Market St, Kittanning PA 16201
800-833-4247

Lancaster School of Cosmetology
50 Ranck Ave, Lancaster PA 17602-3222
Deborah A. Dunn, CEO
717-299-0200

Lansdale School of Cosmetology
215 W Main St, Lansdale PA 19446
215-362-2322

LAUREL BUSINESS INSTITUTE
11-15 Penn St, Uniontown PA 15401
Lisa Tressler, Supervisor of Enrollment
724-439-4900 Fax: 724-439-3607
Website: www.laurelbusiness.edu
E-mail: lbi@laurelbusiness.edu
Established 1985. Private. Coed. Accreditation: ACICS, Licensed by the Pennsylvania Department of Education. Enrollment: 310 full-time, 35 part-time. Student-faculty ratio: 12:1. Associate degrees: Accounting, Child Care Education, Cosmetology, I.T. - Computer Software Support, I.T. - Network Administration, Medical Assistant, Medical Insurance Management, Medical Secretary Transcription, Office Administration, Small Business Management, Therapeutic Massage. Diplomas: Legal Secretary, Massage Therapy, Medical Secretary, Word Processing Secretary. Independent Certifications, Authorized Prometric Testing Center, Authorized MOS Testing Center, Financial Aid Services, Job Placement Services.

Lebanon County Career School
18 E Weidman St, Lebanon PA 17046
800-694-8804

Lehigh Valley College
2809 E Saucon Valley Rd
Center Valley PA 18034-8447
Joshua Padron, Vice President of Marketing and Admissions
800-227-9109 Fax: 610-791-7810
Website: www.lehighvalley.edu
E-mail: joshua.padron@lehighvalley.edu

Lehigh Valley Hospital & Health Network
Center for Education
PO Box 7017, Allentown PA 18105-7017
610-402-2556

LEVITTOWN BEAUTY ACADEMY LLC
Vermillion Square
8919 New Falls Rd, Levittown PA 19054
Cecelia Pine, Contact
866-820-0322 or 215-943-0298 Fax: 215-943-0966
Website: www.levittownbeautyacademy.com
E-mail: info@levittownbeautyacademy.com

Lincoln Technical Institute
5151 W Tilghman St, Allentown PA 18104-3212
Lisa Kuntz, Executive Director
610-398-5300

Lincoln Technical Institute
9191 Torresdale Ave, Philadelphia PA 19136-1595
Jim Kuntz, Executive Director
215-335-0800

L.T. International Beauty School
1238 Spring Garden St, Philadelphia PA 19123
215-922-4478

MBF Center
25 E Marshall St, Norristown PA 19401-4818
610-292-0710

McCann School of Business & Technology
1147 N 4th St, Sunbury PA 17801-1221
Lisa Davis, Director of Admissions
570-286-3058 Fax: 570-286-4723
Website: www.mccannschool.com
E-mail: ldavis@mccannschool.com

MERCY HOSPITAL SCHOOL OF NURSING
1401 Boulevard of the Allies
Pittsburgh PA 15219-5107
Joanne Sperry, RN, MN Director
412-232-7940 Fax: 412-232-7951
Website: www.pmhs.org/son
E-mail: jsperry@mercy.pmhs.org

Metropolitan Career Center
162 W Chelten Ave, Philadelphia PA 19144-3359
215-843-7023

Metropolitan Career Center
Computer Technology Institute
100 S Broad St 8th Floor, Philadelphia PA 19110
215-568-9975

Mifflin-Juniata Career & Technology Center
700 Pitt St, Lewistown PA 17044
717-248-3933

NAWCC School of Horology
514 Poplar St, Columbia PA 17512
717-684-8261

New Castle School of Beauty Culture
314 E Washington St, New Castle PA 16101
724-654-6611

New Castle School of Trades
New Castle Youngstown Rd, Pulaski PA 16143
724-964-8811

North Central Industrial Technical Education Center
651 Montmorenci Rd, Ridgway PA 15853
814-772-1012

Northeastern Hospital School of Nursing
2301 E Allegheny Ave, Philadelphia PA 19134-4497
Pat Fleetwood, Recruiter
215-291-3145

North Hills Beauty Academy
434 Perry Hwy, Pittsburgh PA 15229
412-931-8563

Oakbridge Academy of Arts
1250 Greensburg Rd, Lower Burrell PA 15068
Admissions Department
724-335-5336
Website: www.oaa.edu
E-mail: tjpomatto@nbi.edu

Orleans Technical Institute
1330 Rhawn St, Philadelphia PA 19111-2802
215-728-4450

Orleans Technical Institute
Center City Campus
1845 Walnut St 7th Fl, Philadelphia PA 19103-4709
215-854-1853

Pace Institute
606 Court St, Reading PA 19601-3542
610-375-7223

Penn Commercial Business/Technical School
242 Oak Spring Rd, Washington PA 15301-2871
Office of Admissions
888-309-784

Pennco Tech
3815 Otter St, Bristol PA 19007-3618
Glenn Slater, Director of Admissions
215-785-0111 Fax: 215-785-1945
Website: www.penncotech.com
E-mail: admissions@penncotech.com

Penn State Cosmetology Academy
2200 E State St, Hermitage PA 16148
724-347-4503

Pennsylvania Academy of Cosmetic Arts & Sciences
19 N Brady St, Du Bois PA 15801
814-371-4151

Pennsylvania Academy of Cosmetic Arts & Sciences
2445 Bedford St, Johnstown PA 15904
814-269-3444

Pennsylvania Academy of the Fine Arts
118 N Broad St, Philadelphia PA 19102-1598
Angela Smith, Director of Admissions
215-972-7625

PENNSYLVANIA GUNSMITH SCHOOL
812 Ohio River Blvd, Pittsburgh PA 15202-2699
George Thacker, Director
412-766-1812 Fax: 412-766-0855
Website: www.pagunsmith.com
E-mail: pgs@pagunsmith.edu

PENNSYLVANIA INSTITUTE OF TAXIDERMY
118 Industrial Park Rd, Ebensburg PA 15931
Ruthann Pinos, Director
814-472-4510 Fax: 814-472-4545
Website: www.studytaxidermy.com
E-mail: info@studytaxidermy.com

PENNSYLVANIA INSTITUTE OF TECHNOLOGY
800 Manchester Ave, Media PA 19063-4036
Dr. Paul N. Smith, President
Angela Cassetta, Dean of Enrollment Management
800-422-0025 or 610-892-1500 Fax: 610-892-1510
Website: www.pit.edu
E-mail: info@pit.edu
A TWO YEAR COLLEGE
Established 1953. Private. Coed. Full-time, part-time, continuing education programs. Accreditation: Commission on Higher Education, Middle States Association of Colleges and Schools. Enrollment: 369. Student/Faculty ratio: 15:1. Associates Degrees: AAS in Architectural/Civil, Computer Drafting and Design, Electronic, Mechanical Engineering and Web Design Technologies; AS in Business Administration, Medical Office Management and Office Technologies. Microsoft and Cisco certification is also available. Emphasizes "hands-on" (applied) academics and cooperative education programs. Master and peer tutoring offered in all programs, together with pre-technology instruction. Computerized instruction and learning utilized in all courses. Tech Prep/School to Career program with local school districts. 94% job placement of available graduates since 1974.

PITTSBURGH INSTITUTE OF MORTUARY SCIENCE
5808 Baum Blvd, Pittsburgh PA 15206-3706
Karen Rocco, Registrar
412-362-8500 Fax: 412-362-1684
Website: www.pims.edu
E-mail: pims5808@aol.com

Pittsburgh Technical Institute
Cranberry Center at the Regional Learning Alliance
850 Cranberry Woods Dr
Cranberry Township PA 16066
866-233-5556

Pittsburgh Technical Institute
Downtown Campus
635 Smithfield St, Pittsburgh PA 15222-2560
800-784-9675

Pittsburgh Technical Institute
North Fayette Campus
1111 McKee Rd, Oakdale PA 15071
800-784-9675

PJA School
7900 W Chester Pike, Upper Darby PA 19082-1917
610-789-6700

POTTSVILLE HOSPITAL SCHOOL OF NURSING
420 S Jackson St, Pottsville PA 17901-3625
Angela Pasco, RN, MSN, Director
570-621-5028 Fax: 570-621-5113
Website: www.pottsvillehospitalschoolofnursing.com
E-mail: phson@pothosp.com

Princeton Information Technology Center
137 S Easton Rd, Glenside PA 19038
215-576-7377

Pruonto's Hair Design Institute
705 12th St, Altoona PA 16602
814-944-4494

Punxy Beauty School of Cosmetology Arts & Science
222 N Findley St, Punxsutawney PA 15767
814-938-8811

THE RESTAURANT SCHOOL AT WALNUT HILL COLLEGE
4207 Walnut St, Philadelphia PA 19104-5296
Karl D. Becker, Admissions Director
215-222-4200 ext. 3011 Fax: 215-222-4219
Website: www.walnuthillcollege.com
E-mail: info@walnuthillcollege.com

ROSEDALE TECHNICAL INSTITUTE
215 Beecham Dr Ste 2, Pittsburgh PA 15205
Kevin Auld, Contact
412-521-6200 Fax: 412-521-2520
Website: www.rosedaletech.org
E-mail: admissions@rosedaletech.org

Roxborough Memorial Hospital
5800 Ridge Ave, Philadelphia PA 19128-1737
Patricia E. Burke, R.N., Manager, Admissions & Recruitment
215-487-4459

ST. MARGARET HOSPITAL SCHOOL OF NURSING
221 Seventh St Suite 100, Pittsburgh PA 15238
Ann D. Ciak, Director
412-784-4980 Fax: 412-784-4994
Website: www.upmc.edu/StMargaret/SchofNursing
E-mail: smhsonrninfo@upmc.edu

Schuylkill Institute of Business & Technology
118 S Centre St Ste 2, Pottsville PA 17901
570-622-4835

South Hills Beauty Academy
3269 W Liberty Ave, Pittsburgh PA 15216
412-561-3381

South Hills School of Business & Technology
508 58th St, Altoona PA 16602-1188
814-944-6134

South Hills School of Business & Technology
124 E Market St, Lewistown PA 17044-2125
Gloria Runk, Learning Site Director
717-248-8140

South Hills School of Business & Technology
200 Shady Lane, Philipsburg PA 16866-1900
Kris Matson, Learning Site Director
814-342-7427

South Hills School of Business & Technology
480 Waupelani Dr, State College PA 16801-4516
Maralyn Mazza, Director
888-282-7427

Star Technical Institute
9121 Roosevelt Blvd, Philadelphia PA 19114
215-969-5877

Star Technical Institute
1570 Garrett Rd, Upper Darby PA 19082-4500
Angela M. Toney, BS, CMA, EMT, Director
610-626-2700

Stroudsburg School of Cosmetology
100 N 8th St, Stroudsburg PA 18360
570-421-3387

Talent Academy
1345 W Chester Pike, Havertown PA 19083
610-352-1401

Thompson Institute
5650 Derry St, Harrisburg PA 17111-3571
Roy Hawkins, Director
717-564-4112

Thompson Institute
3010 Market St, Philadelphia PA 19104
Scott Dams, Director of Admissions
215-594-4000

Toni & Guy Hairdressing Academy
930 Peach St, Erie PA 16501
Barbara Bolt, Director of Admissions
800-775-4187

Triangle Tech
PO Box 551, Du Bois PA 15801-0551
Jason Vallozzi, Director of Admissions
814-371-2090

Triangle Tech
2000 Liberty St, Erie PA 16502-2594
814-453-6016

Triangle Tech
222 E Pittsburgh St #A, Greensburg PA 15601-3328
724-832-1050

Triangle Tech
1940 Perrysville Ave, Pittsburgh PA 15214-3897
412-359-1000

Triangle Tech
RR 1 Box 51, Sunbury PA 17801
570-988-0700

Tri-State Business Institute
5757 W Ridge Rd, Erie PA 16506-1013
814-838-7673

Ultrasound Diagnostic School
3600 Horizon Blvd, Trevose PA 19053-4900
215-244-4906

UNIVERSAL TECHNICAL INSTITUTE
750 Pennsylvania Dr, Exton PA 19341
Karen Hannigan-Robinson, Campus Admissions Director
877-884-3986 Fax: 610-646-8549
Website: www.uti-auto-tech.com
E-mail: khannigan@uticorp.com

UPMC SCHOOL OF MEDICAL IMAGING
3434 Forbes Ave Murdoch Bldg Ste 206
Pittsburgh PA 15213-2582
Denise Csonka Lake, Program Director
412-647-3528 Fax: 412-647-3713
Website: www.schoolofmedicalimaging.upmc.com
E-mail: laked@upmc.edu

Venus Beauty Academy
1033 Chester Pike, Sharon Hill PA 19079
610-586-2500

VET TECH INSTITUTE
125 7th St, Pittsburgh PA 15222-3410
Cheri Yaworski, Director of Admissions
800-570-0693 Fax: 412-232-4348
Website: www.vettechinstitute.com
E-mail: cyaworski@vettechinstitute.com

Welder Training & Testing Institute
729 E Highland St, Allentown PA 18109-3253
610-437-9720

WESTERN PENNSYLVANIA HOSPITAL SCHOOL OF NURSING
4900 Friendship Ave, Pittsburgh PA 15224-1724
Joan Brooks, Recruiter
412-578-5538 Fax: 412-578-1837
Website: www.wpahs.org/education
E-mail: sonadmissions@wpahs.org

Western School of Health & Business Careers
1 Monroeville Center, Monroeville PA 15146
412-373-6400

Western School of Health & Business Careers
421 7th Ave, Pittsburgh PA 15219-1907
Michael Joyce, Director of Admissions
800-333-6607 Fax: 412-227-0419
Website: www.western-school.com
E-mail: mjoyce@western-school.com

West Virginia Career Institute
PO Box 278, Mount Braddock PA 15465-0278
Sharron K. Stephens, Executive Director
724-437-4600

Williamson Free School of Mechanical Trades
106 S New Middletown Rd, Media PA 19063-5202
Ed Bailey, Director of Enrollment
610-566-1776

Winner Institute of Arts & Sciences
1 Winner Pl, Transfer PA 16154
724-646-2433

Wrightco Technologies Technical Training Institute
HC 1 Box 22, Alexandria PA 16611
814-669-4241

Wrightco Technologies Technical Training Institute
225 Sollenberger Rd, Chambersburg PA 17201
717-263-8142

Wrightco Technologies Technical Training Institute
728 Ben Franklin Hwy, Ebensburg PA 15931
814-472-5211

Wrightco Technologies Technical Training Institute
Route 422 W, Shelocta PA 15774
724-354-5162

Wrightco Technologies Technical Training Institute
2 W Main St Ste 200, Uniontown PA 15401
724-439-2000

WyoTech - Blairsville
500 Innovation Dr, Blairsville PA 15717
724-459-9500

YORK TECHNICAL INSTITUTE
1405 Williams Rd, York PA 17402
Cathi Killingsworth Bost, Vice President
800-227-9675 or 717-757-1100 Fax: 717-757-4964
Website: www.yti.edu
E-mail: info@yti.edu
    Established 1967. Private. Coed. Accreditation: ACCSCT. Tuition: $17,000+. Enrollment: 1,600. Faculty: 200. Student-faculty ratio: 25:1. Degrees: Associates in Specialized Business + Technology. 2 campuses. On line Internet access - all students.

YORK TECHNICAL INSTITUTE
Lancaster Campus
3050 Hempland Rd, Lancaster PA 17601
Cathi Killingsworth Bost, Vice President
800-227-9675 or 717-295-1100 Fax: 717-295-1135
Website: www.yti.edu
E-mail: info@yti.edu
See listing under "Career Schools"

Yorktowne Business Institute
W 7th Ave, York PA 17404-2099
Bonnie Gillespie, Admissions Director
800-840-1004

RHODE ISLAND

Arthur Angelo School of Cosmetology Hair Design
151 Broadway, Providence RI 02903
401-272-4300

Computer-Ed Business Institute
622 George Washington Hwy, Lincoln RI 02865
401-334-2430

International Yacht Restoration School
449 Thames St, Newport RI 02840
401-848-5777

Katharine Gibbs School
85 Garfield Ave, Cranston RI 02920-7807
Director of Admissions
401-861-1420

MTTI - MOTORING TECHNICAL TRAINING INSTITUTE
54 Water St, East Providence RI 02914-5022
Nick Azzarone, Director of Admissions
401-434-4840 or 866-454-6884 Fax: 401-434-9540
Website: www.mtti.edu
E-mail: mtti2@aol.com

NEW ENGLAND TRACTOR TRAILER TRAINING
600 Moshassuck Valley Industrial Hwy
Pawtucket RI 02860-1752
Frederick Hazard, Director
401-725-1220 Fax: 401-724-1340
Website: www.nettts.com
E-mail: fhazard@nettts.com

Newport School of Hairdressing
226 Main St, Pawtucket RI 02860
401-725-6882

Sawyer School
101 Main St, Pawtucket RI 02860-4117
401-272-8400

Sawyer School
550 Hartford Ave, Providence RI 02909-5800
401-272-3280

Warwick Academy of Beauty Culture
1276 Bald Hill Rd Unit 100, Warwick RI 02886
401-737-4946

SOUTH CAROLINA

Academy of Cosmetology
5117 Dorchester Rd, Charleston SC 29418
843-552-3241

Academy of Hair Technology
3715 E North St Ste F, Greenville SC 29615
864-322-0300

BAMBERG JOB CORPS CENTER
PO Box 967, Bamberg SC 29003
Sam Kolapo, Center Director
803-245-5101 Fax: 803-245-5915
E-mail: kolapo.samuel@jobcorps.org

BETA TECH
7500 Two Notch Rd, Columbia SC 29223
803-754-7544 Fax: 803-714-6797
Website: www.betatech.edu

BETA TECH
8088 Rivers Ave, North Charleston SC 29406-9235
Katrina Varner, Director
843-569-0889 Fax: 843-569-0471
Website: www.tidetech.com
E-mail: directorbtc@tidetech.com

CHARLESTON COSMETOLOGY INSTITUTE
8484 Dorchester Rd, Charleston SC 29420-7319
Jerry R. Poer, Owner
843-552-3670 Fax: 843-760-0976
Website: www.charlestoncosmetology.com
E-mail: ccisc@aol.com

Columbia Beauty School
1824 Airport Blvd, Cayce SC 29033-1821
Gloria Smith, Assistant Director
803-796-5252

ECPI College of Technology
250 Berryhill Rd Ste 300, Columbia SC 29210
803-772-3333

ECPI College of Technology
1001 Keys Dr #100, Greenville SC 29615
864-288-2828

ECPI College of Technology
7410 Northside Dr Ste G101
North Charleston SC 29420
843-414-0350

Golf Academy of the Carolinas
3268 Waccamaw Blvd, Myrtle Beach SC 29579
Dona K. Powell, President
800-342-7342

ITT Technical Institute
6 Independence Pointe, Greenville SC 29615-4506
David Murray, Director
864-288-0777

Kenneth Shuler's School of Cosmetology
736 Martintown Rd, North Augusta SC 29841
803-278-1200

Kenneth Shuler's School of Cosmetology/Nail Design
449 Saint Andrews Rd, Columbia SC 29210
803-772-6042

Lacy Cosmetology School
3084 Whiskey Rd, Aiken SC 29803
803-648-6181

MILLER-MOTTE TECHNICAL COLLEGE
8085 Rivers Ave, North Charleston SC 29406-9239
James Weaver, Director
843-574-0101 Fax: 843-266-3424
Website: www.miller-motte.net

Plaza School of Beauty Culture
946 Oakland Ave, Rock Hill SC 29730
803-328-5166

South Carolina Criminal Justice Academy
PO Box 1993, Blythewood SC 29016
William R. Neill, Deputy Director
803-896-7779

Southeastern School of Neuromuscular & Massage Therapy
1420 Colonial Life Blvd W Ste 80
Columbia SC 29210
803-798-8800

Southeastern School of Neuromuscular Massage Therapy
4600 Goer Dr Ste 105, North Charleston SC 29406
Ronda Villa, Director
843-747-1279

Strand College of Hair Design
423 79th Ave W, Myrtle Beach SC 29572
843-449-1017

Sumter Beauty College
921 Carolina Ave, Sumter SC 29150
803-773-7311

Trident Technical College
1001 S Live Oak Dr, Moncks Corner SC 29461
843-899-8033

SOUTH DAKOTA

Black Hills Beauty College
623 Saint Joseph St, Rapid City SD 57701
605-342-0697

Lake Area Technical Institute
230 11th St NE, Watertown SD 57201
605-882-5284

Mitchell Technical Institute
821 N Capital St, Mitchell SD 57301-2002
Allen Dvorak, Director of Admissions
800-952-0042

Si Tanka University
PO Box 220, Eagle Butte SD 57625
605-964-6045

Southeast Technical Institute
2301 N Career Pl, Sioux Falls SD 57107-1301
Tracy Noldner, Supervisor Student/Instructional
Services
605-367-7624

WESTERN DAKOTA TECHNICAL INSTITUTE
800 Mickelson Dr, Rapid City SD 57703-4018
Janell Oberlander, Manager of Student Services
605-394-4034 or 800-544-8765 Fax: 605-394-2204
Website: www.westerndakotatech.org
E-mail: admissions@wdti.tec.sd.us
Established 1969. Public. Coed. Accreditation: NCACS. Est. Tuition: $2,304. Fees: $1,688. Enrollment: 800 full-time, 100 part-time. Faculty: 75. Student-faculty ratio: 15:1. Degree: AAS in 13 areas. Library: 4,000 volumes. 3 buildings. Skill training in 26 areas including business, mechanics, construction trades, electronics, agriculture, health and human services, nursing, law enforcement, paralegal, and office technology. Internship options available. Excellent job placement entry-level salary history.

TENNESSEE

Academy of Beauty Arts
633 Mimosa Dr NW, Cleveland TN 37312
423-476-3742

Arnold's Beauty School
1179 S 2nd St, Milan TN 38358
731-686-7351

The Beauty Institute
568 Colonial Rd, Memphis TN 38117
901-761-1888

CONCORDE CAREER COLLEGE
5100 Poplar Ave Ste 132, Memphis TN 38137-0132
Tommy Stewart, Executive Campus Director
901-761-9494 Fax: 901-761-3293
Website: www.concorde.edu
E-mail: tstewart@concorde.edu

Electronic Computer Programming College
3805 Brainerd Rd, Chattanooga TN 37411-3701
423-624-0077

Fayetteville Beauty School
201 Main Ave S, Fayetteville TN 37334
931-433-1305

Georgia Career Institute
755 N Chancery St, Mc Minnville TN 37110

High-Tech Institute
560 Royal Pkwy, Nashville TN 37214-3645
866-502-2627

HIGH-TECH INSTITUTE - MEMPHIS
5865 Shelby Oaks Cir, Memphis TN 38134
Gwen Brown, Director of Admissions
901-387-4555 Fax: 901-387-1181
Website: www.hightechinstitute.edu
E-mail: ebrown@hightechinstitute.edu

ITT Technical Institute
7260 Goodlett Farms Pkwy, Cordova TN 38016-4908
901-381-0200

Jacobs Creek Job Corps Civilian Conservation Center
984 Denton Valley Rd, Bristol TN 37620
Thomas J. Scott, Principal
423-878-4021

Jon Nave University of Cosmetology
5128 Charlotte Pike, Nashville TN 37209
615-383-2255

McCollum & Ross, The Hair School
1433 Hollywood Dr, Jackson TN 38301
731-427-6642

Middle Tennessee School of Cosmetology
880A E 10th St, Cookeville TN 38501
931-526-8735

Miller-Motte Technical College
6020 Shallowford Rd, Chattanooga TN 37421
423-510-9675

Miller-Motte Technical College
1820 Business Park Dr, Clarksville TN 37040-6023
Lisa Teague, Director of Admissions
931-553-0071 Fax: 931-552-2916
Website: www.miller-motte.com
E-mail: lteague@miller-motte.com

MILLER-MOTTE TECHNICAL COLLEGE
801 Space Park N, Goodlettsville TN 37072
Kevin Suhr, Campus Administrator
615-859-8090 Fax: 615-859-9634
Website: www.miller-motte.com
E-mail: ksuhr@miller-motte.com

Mister Wayne's School of Unisex Hair Design
170 S Willow Ave, Cookeville TN 38501
931-526-1478

NASHVILLE AUTO-DIESEL COLLEGE
1524 Gallatin Ave, Nashville TN 37206-3298
Peggie Werrbach, Director of Admissions
800-228-6232 Fax: 615-262-8466
Website: www.nadcedu.com
E-mail: admissions@nadcedu.com
Established 1919. Private. Coed. Accreditation: ACCSCT. Enrollment: 2000+. Faculty: 71. Student-faculty ratio: 25:1. Diploma and academic associate degrees in auto-diesel, auto body repair, high performance and performance fabrication offered. 16 acre campus with on campus dormitories and cafeteria. Text books in technical courses included in tuition. Associate Degree general education classes may be taken on-line. Tools provided for students while in school.

Nashville College
1556 Crestview Dr, Madison TN 37115-2120
615-868-2963

National College of Business & Technology
3748 Nolensville Pike, Nashville TN 37211-3322
Larry Steele, Director of Admissions
615-333-3344

New Directions Hair Academy
3744 Annex Ave #A-2, Nashville TN 37209
615-353-8333

New Wave Hair Academy
3250 Coleman Rd, Memphis TN 38128
901-323-6100

New Wave Hair Academy
804 S Highland St, Memphis TN 38111
901-320-9283

NORTH CENTRAL INSTITUTE
168 Jack Miller Blvd, Clarksville TN 37042-4810
Dr. John McCurdy, President
931-431-9700 Fax: 931-431-9771
Website: www.nci.edu
E-mail: admissions@nci.edu
Established 1988. Private. Coed. Accreditation: Accrediting Commission of the Council on Occupational Education. Student-faculty ratio: 20:1. Degrees: AAS in Aviation Technology - concentrations in Flight, Maintenance, or Operations/Air Traffic Control. FAA part 147 Aviation Maintenance Technician Program enables students to become FAA Certified Airframe/Powerplant Technicians. Our Credit Inventory Evaluation Service turns military training into college credit. Financial Aid and Veterans benefits to those who qualify.

Pellissippi State Technical Community College
PO Box 22990, Knoxville TN 37933-0990
Donna Mack, Contact
865-694-6568 Fax: 865-539-7217
Website: www.pstcc.edu
E-mail: dmack@pstcc.edu

Plaza Beauty School
4682 Spottswood Ave, Memphis TN 38117
901-761-4445

QUEEN CITY COLLEGE
1594 Fort Campbell Blvd, Clarksville TN 37042-3545
Laura Payne, Chief Administrator
931-645-2361 Fax: 931-551-4955
Website: www.queencitycollege.com
E-mail: qcc1594@aol.com

Remington College
Nashville Campus
441 Donelson Pike Ste 150, Nashville TN 37214
615-889-5520

Reuben Allen College
120 Center Park Dr, Knoxville TN 37922
865-966-0400

SAE Institute Nashville
7 Music Circle North, Nashville TN 37203
Mark Martin, Director
Cindy Cyrus, Admissions Manager
877-27-AUDIO

Southeastern Career College
2416 21st Ave S Ste 300, Nashville TN 37212-5318
Janice Miller, Director
800-336-4457

Southern Institute of Cosmetology
3099 S Perkins Rd, Memphis TN 38118
901-363-3553

Stylemasters Beauty Academy
223 N Cumberland St, Lebanon TN 37087
615-444-4908

Styles & Profiles Beauty College
119 S 2nd St, Selmer TN 38375
731-645-9728

Tennessee Academy of Cosmetology
7041 Stage Rd Ste 101, Memphis TN 38133
901-382-9085

Tennessee Academy of Cosmetology
7020 E Shelby Dr Ste 104, Memphis TN 38125
901-757-4166

Tennessee School of Beauty
4704 Western Ave, Knoxville TN 37921
865-588-7878

Tennessee Technology Center at Athens
PO Box 848, Athens TN 37371-0848
423-744-2814

Tennessee Technology Center at Covington
1600 Highway 51 S, Covington TN 38019
901-475-2526

Tennessee Technology Center at Crossville
PO Box 2959, Crossville TN 38557
931-484-7502

Tennessee Technology Center at Crump
PO Box 89, Crump TN 38327
731-632-3393

Tennessee Technology Center at Dickson
740 Highway 46 S, Dickson TN 37055-2556
615-441-6220

Tennessee Technology Center at Elizabethton
PO Box 789, Elizabethton TN 37644-0789
423-543-0070

Tennessee Technology Center at Harriman
PO Box 1109, Harriman TN 37748-1109
Amy Keeling, Coordinator Student Services
865-882-6703

Tennessee Technology Center at Hartsville
716 McMurry Blvd, Hartsville TN 37074-2028
615-374-2147

Tennessee Technology Center at Hohenwald
813 W Main St, Hohenwald TN 38462-2206
931-796-5351

Tennessee Technology Center at Jacksboro
PO Box 419, Jacksboro TN 37757
423-566-9629

Tennessee Technology Center at Jackson
2468 Technology Center Dr, Jackson TN 38301
Jane Wicker, Coordinator of Student Services
731-424-0691

Tennessee Technology Center at Knoxville
1100 Liberty St, Knoxville TN 37919-2327
Marilyn Canady, Coordinator of Student Services
865-546-5567

Tennessee Technology Center at Livingston
740 Hi Tech Dr, Livingston TN 38570
931-823-5525

Tennessee Technology Center at McKenzie
PO Box 427, Mc Kenzie TN 38201-0427
Willie Huffman, Student Services
Carol Lynch, Student Services
731-352-5364

Tennessee Technology Center at Mc Minnville
241 Vo Tech Dr, Mc Minnville TN 37110-1322
931-473-5587

Tennessee Technology Center at Memphis
550 Alabama Ave, Memphis TN 38105-3604
901-543-6100

Tennessee Technology Center at Morristown
821 W Louise Ave, Morristown TN 37813-2094
423-586-5771

Tennessee Technology Center at Morristown
323 Phipps Bend Rd, Surgoinsville TN 37873
423-345-4130

Tennessee Technology Center at Murfreesboro
1303 Old Fort Pkwy, Murfreesboro TN 37129-3311
615-898-8010

Tennessee Technology Center at Nashville
100 White Bridge Rd, Nashville TN 37209-4515
615-741-1241

Tennessee Technology Center at Newbern
340 Washington St, Newbern TN 38059-1138
731-627-2511

Tennessee Technology Center at Oneida/Huntsville
355 Scott High Dr, Huntsville TN 37756-4149
423-663-4900

Tennessee Technology Center at Paris
312 S Wilson St, Paris TN 38242-5023
731-644-7365

Tennessee Technology Center at Pulaski
PO Box 614, Pulaski TN 38478-0614
931-424-4014

Tennessee Technology Center at Ripley
127 Industrial Dr, Ripley TN 38063-7360
731-635-3368

Tennessee Technology Center at Shelbyville
1405 Madison St, Shelbyville TN 37160-3629
931-685-5013

Tennessee Technology Center at Whiteville
PO Box 489, Whiteville TN 38075-0489
731-254-8521

University of Tennessee Medical Center
1924 Alcoa Hwy, Knoxville TN 37920
865-544-6404

Vatterott College - Memphis Campus
2655 Dividend Dr, Memphis TN 38132
Joe Lockwood, Director of Admissions
901-761-5730 Fax: 901-763-2897
Website: www.vatterott-college.edu
E-mail: joe.lockwood@vatterott-college.edu

Volunteer Beauty Academy
1791 Gallatin Pike N, Madison TN 37115
615-860-4200

Volunteer Beauty Academy
5666 Nolensville Pike, Nashville TN 37211
615-331-9111

West Tennessee Business College
1186 Highway 45 Bypass, Jackson TN 38301-3256
800-737-9822

William R. Moore College of Technology
1200 Poplar Ave, Memphis TN 38104-7240
Susan Smith, Admissions
901-726-1977

TEXAS

Academy of Hair Design
744 FM 1960 Rd W Ste G, Houston TX 77090
281-893-0980

Academy of Hair Design
512 S Chestnut St, Lufkin TX 75901
936-634-8440

Academy of Hair Design
3141 College St #A10, Port Arthur TX 77642
409-813-3100

Advanced Barber College and Hair Design
2818 S International, Weslaco TX 78596
956-969-0341

AIMS Academy
1106 N Highway 360 #305
Grand Prairie TX 75050-2511
972-988-3202

Alfred G. Glassell Jr. School of Art
PO Box 6826, Houston TX 77265-6826
713-639-7500

Allied Health Careers
5424 W Highway 290 Ste 105, Austin TX 78735-8828
Rebecca Serwatt, Director
512-892-5210

Amarillo College of Hairdressing
2400 E 27th Ave, Amarillo TX 79103
806-371-7600

American Commercial College
402 Butternut St, Abilene TX 79602-1399
Tony Delgado, Director
325-672-8495

American Commercial College
2007 34th St, Lubbock TX 79411-1899
Michael Otto, Director
806-747-4339 Fax: 806-765-9838
Website: www.acc-careers.com
E-mail: mjotto@acc-careers.com

American Commercial College
5119 Twin Towers Blvd, Odessa TX 79762-5504
Donna Duree, Director
432-362-6768 Fax: 432-550-0556
Website: www.acc-careers.com
E-mail: americancc@acc-careers.com

American Commercial College
3177 Executive Dr, San Angelo TX 76904-6801
Nikki Lambert, Director of Admissions
325-942-6797

AMERICAN COMMERCIAL COLLEGE
4317 Barnett Rd, Wichita Falls TX 76310-2303
Don Dobbins, Director
940-691-0454 Fax: 940-691-0470
Website: www.acc-careers.com
E-mail: ddobbins@acc-careers.com

Anderson County Beauty College
217 W Oak St, Palestine TX 75801
903-729-0801

A New Beginning School of Massage
2525 Wallingwood Dr Ste 1501, Austin TX 78746
512-306-0975

Arlington Career Institute
901 E Avenue K, Grand Prairie TX 75050-2636
972-647-1607

Arlington Medical Institute
2301 N Collins St Ste 100, Arlington TX 76011-2645
817-265-0706

Art Institute of Dallas
8080 Park Ln Ste 100, Dallas TX 75231-5900
214-692-8080

ART INSTITUTE OF HOUSTON
1900 Yorktown St, Houston TX 77056
Brian A. Shumaker, Director of Admissions
800-275-4244 Fax: 713-966-2797
Website: www.aih.artinstitutes.edu

THE ART INSTITUTE OF HOUSTON - CULINARY
1900 Yorktown St, Houston TX 77056-4113
Director of Admissions
800-275-4244 Fax: 713-966-2797
Website: www.aih.aii.edu
E-mail: aihadm@www.aih.aii.edu

ASTRODOME DENTAL CAREER CENTER
2646 South Loop W Ste 415, Houston TX 77054-2678
Martina Torres, Contact
713-664-5300 Fax: 713-644-7951
Website: www.astrodomeresource.com
E-mail: astrodome.careercenter@gte.net

ATI Career Training Center
10003 Technology Blvd W, Dallas TX 75220-4316
Debra Chapman, Director of Admissions
214-902-8191

ATI Career Training Center
6351 Boulevard 26 Ste 100
North Richland Hills TX 76180
817-284-1141
Website: www.aticareertraining.edu

ATI Technical Training Center
6627 Maple Ave, Dallas TX 75235-4690
Rod Cass, Director of Admissions
214-352-2222

Austin Business College
2101 S IH-35 Ste 300, Austin TX 78741-3854
Lisa Ruszczuk, Contact
512-447-9415

Aveda Institute
1212D S Frazier St, Conroe TX 77301
936-539-6770

AVIATION INSTITUTE OF MAINTENANCE
7555 Lemmon Ave, Dallas TX 75209-3017
James Cooper, School Director
214-333-9711 Fax: 214-333-9185
Website: www.aviationmaintenance.edu
E-mail: directoramd@aviationmaintenance.edu

Baldwin Beauty School #5
3005 S Lamar Blvd Ste 103, Austin TX 78704
512-441-6898

Baldwin Beauty School - North
8440 Burnet Rd, Austin TX 78758
512-458-4127

Behold! Beauty Academy
9937 Homestead Rd, Houston TX 77016
713-635-5252

Bill J. Priest Institute for Economic Development
1402 Corinth St, Dallas TX 75215
214-860-5900

Border Institute of Technology
9611 Acer Ave, El Paso TX 79925-6709
Miguel A. Gamino, Director of Admissions
915-593-7328

Bradford School of Business
4669 Southwest Freeway Ste 300, Houston TX 77027
713-629-1500

Business Skills Institute
El Paso Campus
7850 Paseo Del Norte #216, El Paso TX 79912-8001
915-845-7772

CANCER THERAPY AND RESEARCH CENTER
School of Medical Dosimetry
7979 Wurzbach Rd, San Antonio TX 78229-4427
Melissa Blough, Ph.D., DABR, School Director
210-616-5669 Fax: 210-616-5636
Website: www.ctrc.saci.org
E-mail: mblough@saci.org

Capitol City Careers
5424 W Highway 290 Ste 200, Austin TX 78735-8800
Richard S. Anthens, Director
512-892-2640

Capitol City Trade and Technical School
205 E Riverside Dr, Austin TX 78704-1281
Ray Perrilloux, Director
512-444-3257

Career Academy
32 Oaklawn Vlg, Texarkana TX 75501-4128
903-832-1021

Career Advancement & Applied Technology
9350 S Presa St, San Antonio TX 78223-4733
210-633-1000

Career Centers of Texas
1900 N Expressway, Brownsville TX 78521
956-547-8200

Career Centers of Texas
1620 S Padre Island Dr, Corpus Christi TX 78416
361-852-2900

Career Centers of Texas
8360 Burnham Rd Ste 100, El Paso TX 79907-1526
Aldo Melucci, Director of Admissions
915-595-1935

Career Centers of Texas
2001 Beach St, Fort Worth TX 76103
817-688-1132

Career Point Institute
485 Spencer Ln, San Antonio TX 78201-2027
David Murguia III, VP of Marketing
Adrienne Divin, Director
210-732-3000

CAREER QUEST
5430 Fredericksburg Rd #310, San Antonio TX 78229
Mike Maloto, Director of Admissions
210-366-2701 Fax: 210-366-0738
Website: www.careerquestusa.com
E-mail: mmaloto@careerquest-usa.com

Careers Unlimited
10058 Long Point, Houston TX 77055
713-464-0770

Careers Unlimited
335 S Bonner St, Tyler TX 75702
903-593-4424

Center for Advanced Legal Studies
3910 Kirby Dr Ste 200, Houston TX 77098-4151
Debra Garcia, Director of Admissions
713-529-2778

Central Texas Beauty College
2010 S 57th St, Temple TX 76504-6948
254-773-9911

Central Texas Beauty College #2
1350 E Palm Valley Rd #A, Round Rock TX 78664
512-244-2235

Central Texas Commercial College
PO Box 1324, Brownwood TX 76804-1324
325-646-0521

Central Texas Commercial College
9400 N Central Expy Ste 200, Dallas TX 75231-5034
214-368-3680

Charlie & Sue's School of Hair Design
1711 Briarcrest Dr, Bryan TX 77802
979-776-4375

Circle J Beauty School
1611 Spencer Hwy Ste E, South Houston TX 77587
713-946-5055

Compu Tech Consultants School
811 S Central Expy Ste 500, Richardson TX 75080
214-570-0404

COMPUTER CAREER CENTER
6101 Montana Ave, El Paso TX 79925-2021
Amber Borrego, Director
915-779-8031 Fax: 915-779-8097
Website: www.computercareercenter.com
E-mail: ccctrain@aol.com

Conlee's College of Cosmetology
402 Quinlan St, Kerrville TX 78028
830-896-2380

Coryell Cosmetology College
608 Leon, Gatesville TX 76528
254-248-1716

COURT REPORTING INSTITUTE OF DALLAS
1341 W Mockingbird Ln Ste 200 East
Dallas TX 75247
Eric Juhlin, Regional Director
214-350-9722 Fax: 214-631-0143
Website: www.crid.com
E-mail: ejuhlin@crid.com

COURT REPORTING INSTITUTE OF HOUSTON
13101 Northwest Fwy Ste 100, Houston TX 77040
Cindy Smith, Director
713-996-8300 Fax: 713-996-8360
Website: www.crid.com
E-mail: csmith@crid.com

CULINARY ACADEMY OF AUSTIN
6020 Dillard Cir Ste B, Austin TX 78752
Steve Mannion, Director
512-451-5743 Fax: 512-467-9120
Website: www.culinaryacademyofaustin.com
E-mail: smannion@culinaryacademyofaustin.com

CULINARY INSTITUTE
7070 Allensby St, Houston TX 77022-4322
Henry Cittone, Director of Admissions
713-692-0077 Fax: 713-692-7399

Dallas Barber and Stylist College
9357 Forest Ln, Dallas TX 75243-4205
214-360-9570

David L. Carrasco Job Corps Center
11155 Gateway Blvd W, El Paso TX 79935-5401
915-594-0022

Dolphin Technical Institute
4835 Concord Rd, Beaumont TX 77703
409-892-0677

Everest College
6060 N Central Expy Ste 101, Dallas TX 75206
214-234-4850

Exposito School of Hair Design
3710 Mockingbird Ln, Amarillo TX 79109
806-355-9111

Faris Computer School
1119 Kent Ave, Nederland TX 77627-3818
409-722-4072

Fort Worth Beauty School
6785 Camp Bowie Blvd Ste 100, Fort Worth TX 76116
817-924-4289

FRANKLIN BEAUTY SCHOOL #2
4965 Martin Luther King, Houston TX 77021
Ron Jemison, Vice President
713-645-9060 Fax: 713-645-6859
Website: www.thefranklinbeautyschool.com
E-mail: rjem6969@aol.com

Gary Job Corps Center
PO Box 967, San Marcos TX 78667-0967
Lonnie Hall, Center Director
512-396-6561

Gulf Coast Trades Center
PO Box 515, New Waverly TX 77358-0515
936-344-6677

Hallmark Institute of Aeronautics
Aeronautics Campus-Aviation Technology
8901 Wetmore Rd, San Antonio TX 78216-4229
Joe Fisher, President
210-826-1000 Fax: 210-826-3707
Website: www.hallmarkinstitute.edu
E-mail: sross@hallmarkinstitute.com

Hallmark Institute of Technology - Technology Campus
10401 W IH 10, San Antonio TX 78230-1736
Joe Fisher, President
210-690-9000 Fax: 210-697-8225
Website: www.hallmarkinstitute.com
E-mail: sross@hallmarkinstitute.com
Electronics Engineering Technology, Business Office
Administration, Computer Network Systems
Technology, & Medical Assistant.

High-Tech Institute
4250 N Belt Line Rd, Irving TX 75038-4201
Tara Meredith, Office Manager
972-871-2824

Houstons Training and Education Center
7457 Harwin Dr Ste 190, Houston TX 77036
713-783-2221

Houston Training School
709 Shotwell St, Houston TX 77020-4801
713-675-4300

Houston Training School
6630 Gulf Freeway, Houston TX 77087

ICC Technical Institute
3333 Fannin St Ste 203, Houston TX 77004-2930
713-522-7799

Institute of Cosmetic Arts and Science
Massage Therapy
1105 Airline Rd, Corpus Christi TX 78412
Denise Miller, Director
361-991-8868

Institute of Cosmetology
7011 Harwin Dr Ste 100, Houston TX 77036
713-783-9988

Interactive Learning Systems
8585 N Stemmons Fwy Ste C15
Dallas TX 75247-3805
214-637-3377

Interactive Learning Systems
6200 Hillcroft St Ste 200, Houston TX 77081-3007
713-771-5336

Interactive Learning Systems
256 N Sam Houston Pkwy E, Houston TX 77060
281-931-7717

Interactive Learning Systems
1001 Southmore Ave, Pasadena TX 77502
713-920-1120

International Beauty College #3
1225 Belt Line Rd Ste 7, Garland TX 75040
972-530-1103

International Beauty College #4
2716 W Irving Blvd, Irving TX 75061
972-513-1176

International Business College
2006 W University Dr, Denton TX 76201-0644
940-380-0024

International Business College
5700 Cromo Dr, El Paso TX 79912-5538
915-842-0422

International Business College
1155 N Zaragoza Rd, El Paso TX 79907
915-859-3986

International Business College
5020 50th St Unit 108, Lubbock TX 79414-3422
806-797-1933

International Business School
1434 N Central Expressway Ste 116
Mc Kinney TX 75070
972-548-0774

International Business School
3305 Andrews Hwy, Midland TX 79703-5130
432-694-7584

International Business School
4107 N Texoma Parkway, Sherman TX 75090
903-893-6604

ITT Technical Institute
15621 Blue Ash Dr Ste 160, Houston TX 77090-5819
281-873-0512 Fax: 281-873-0518
Website: www.itt-tech.edu

ITT TECHNICAL INSTITUTE
2950 S Gessner Rd Ste 100, Houston TX 77063-3751
Jennifer Gomez, Director of Recruitment
713-952-2294 Fax: 713-952-2393
Website: www.itt-tech.edu
E-mail: jgomez@itt-tech.edu

Jay's Technical Institute
10754 S Gessner, Houston TX 77071
713-772-2410

Jones Beauty College
10909 Webbs Chapel Rd # 129, Dallas TX 75229
214-956-0088

Jones Beauty College #2
311A W Pioneer Pkwy, Grand Prairie TX 75051
214-956-0088

KD STUDIO - ACTORS CONSERVATORY
2600 N Stemmons Fwy Ste 117
Dallas TX 75207-2168
T. A. Taylor, Director of Education
877-278-2283 Fax: 214-630-5140
Website: www.kdstudio.com
E-mail: admissions@kdstudio.com
Established 1979. Private. Coed. Accreditation: TEA, NAST, Texas Higher Education Coordinating Board. Tuition: $11,000. Enrollment: 100 full-time. Faculty: 26. Student-faculty ratio: 18:1. Degrees: Applied Associates Degree. Private library Resource Center. This program is aimed at developing camera acting skills as well as stage acting. Faculty are involved as industry professionals. A showcase is performed upon graduation where agents, casting directors and local producers and directors attend. FA available. VA approved.

KINGS WAY MISSIONARY INSTITUTE
401 S 35th St, Mc Allen TX 78501
Don Russell, President - BOD
956-682-6187 Fax: 956-682-9030
Website: www.kingswaymissionary.com
E-mail: kingswaymissionary@aol.com

KINGWOOD COLLEGE
20000 Kingwood Dr, Kingwood TX 77339-3801
Isaac Williams, Director of Enrollment Management
281-312-1600 Fax: 281-312-1477
Website: wwwkc.nhmccd.edu
E-mail: ike.williams@nhmccd.edu

Laredo Beauty College
3020 Meadow Ave, Laredo TX 78040-2226
956-723-2059

Lincoln Technical Institute
2501 Arkansas Ln, Grand Prairie TX 75052-7206
Mike Ackerman, Executive Director
972-660-5701

Lubbock Hair Academy
2844 34th St, Lubbock TX 79410
806-795-0806

Metroplex Beauty School
519 N Galloway Ave, Mesquite TX 75149
972-288-5485

MID CITIES BARBER COLLEGE
2345 SW 3rd St Ste 101, Grand Prairie TX 75051
Nachita Cano, Director
972-642-1892 Fax: 972-642-8198
Website: www.midcitiesbarbercollege.com
E-mail: midcitiesbarber@earthlink.net

Mims Classic Beauty College
5121 Blanco Rd, San Antonio TX 78216
210-344-2041

MJ's Beauty Academy
3939 S Polk St Ste 505, Dallas TX 75224
214-374-7500

MTI College of Business & Technology
7277 Regency Square Blvd, Houston TX 77036
713-974-7181

MTI College of Business & Technology
11420 East Fwy, Houston TX 77029
713-979-1800

National Beauty College
149 W Kingsley Rd Ste 230, Garland TX 75041
972-278-2020

National Institute of Technology
9100 US Highway 290 E Ste 100, Austin TX 78754
512-928-1933

National Institute of Technology
4150 Westheimer Rd Ste 200
Houston TX 77027-4417
713-629-1637

National Institute of Technology
255 Northpoint Dr #100, Houston TX 77060-3203
Jeff Brown, Director of Admissions
281-447-7037

National Institute of Technology
7151 Office City Dr, Houston TX 77087
713-645-7404

National Institute of Technology
6550 First Park Ten Blvd Ste 210
San Antonio TX 78213-4302
James W. Alexander, Director of Admissions
210-732-7800

Neilson Beauty College
416 W Jefferson Blvd, Dallas TX 75208
214-941-8756

North Central Texas College
1525 W California St, Gainesville TX 76240-4636
Michelle Winters, Registrar
940-668-3315 Fax: 940-665-7075
Website: www.nctc.edu
E-mail: mwinters@nctc.edu

Northwest Educational Center
2910 Antoine Dr Ste B100, Houston TX 77092-7063
713-680-2929

Northwest Texas Healthcare System
PO Box 1110, Amarillo TX 79105
806-354-1110

THE OCEAN CORPORATION
10840 Rockley Rd, Houston TX 77099-3416
John Wood, President
281-530-0202 or 800-321-0298 Fax: 281-530-9143
Website: www.oceancorp.com
E-mail: admissions@oceancorp.com

Ogle School of Hair Design
6333 E Mockingbird Ln #201, Dallas TX 75214
214-821-0819

Ogle School of Hair Design
5063 Granbury Rd, Fort Worth TX 76133
817-294-2950

Ogle School of Hair Design
720 Arcadia St Apt B, Hurst TX 76053
817-284-9231

Ogle School of Hair Design
2200 W Park Row Dr Ste 106, Pantego TX 76013
817-277-6341

Page Parkes Center of Modeling and Acting
1535 West Loop S Ste 100, Houston TX 77027
Shannon Fergason, Director
713-807-8200

Pasadena Academy
2155 Red Bluff Rd, Pasadena TX 77506
713-473-1777

PCI Health Training Center
8101 John W Carpenter Fwy, Dallas TX 75247-4720
Mr. Kelly Drake, Director of Admissions
214-630-0568

PCI Health Training Center
1300 International Pkwy, Richardson TX 75081
214-630-0568

Pipo Academy of Hair Design
3000 Pershing Dr, El Paso TX 79903
915-565-3491

Polytechnic Institute
5206 Airline Dr, Houston TX 77022-1902
713-694-6027

Remington College
1800 Eastgate Dr, Garland TX 75041-5513
972-686-7878

Remington College
3110 Hayes Rd, Houston TX 77082
281-899-1240

Royal Beauty Careers
5020 FM 1960 W Ste A12, Houston TX 77069
281-580-2554

San Antonio Beauty College #3
4130 Naco Perrin Blvd, San Antonio TX 78217-2508
210-654-9734

San Antonio Beauty College #4
2423 Jamar St # 2, San Antonio TX 78226
210-433-7222

San Antonio College Medical Dental Assistants
1500 S Jackson Rd, Mc Allen TX 78503-9902
Gabe Garcia, Director of Admissions
956-630-1499 Fax: 956-630-2746
Website: www.sacmda.com
E-mail: gagarcia@sac-mda.com

SAN ANTONIO COLLEGE MEDICAL DENTAL ASSISTANTS
7142 San Pedro Ave Ste 100, San Antonio TX 78216
Carig Czubati, Director of Admissions
210-733-0777 Fax: 210-735-2431
Website: www.sacmda.com
E-mail: cczubati@sac-mda.com

SCHOOL OF AUTOMOTIVE MACHINISTS
1911 Antoine Dr, Houston TX 77055-1803
Admissions
713-683-3817 Fax: 713-683-7077
Website: www.samracing.com
E-mail: admissions@samracing.com

SCOTT & WHITE MEMORIAL HOSPITAL AND CLINIC
2401 S 31st St, Temple TX 76508-0002
Janet Duben-Engelkirk Ed.D., MT(ASCP), Program Director
254-724-5177 Fax: 254-724-0819
Website: www.sw.org/ed/clin_lab/clshp.htm
E-mail: jengelkirk@swmail.sw.org

Sebring Career School
7060 Bissonnet St, Houston TX 77074
713-772-0702

Seguin Beauty College
102 E Court St, Seguin TX 78155
830-372-0935

SOUTHEASTERN CAREER INSTITUTE
12005 Ford Rd Suite 100, Dallas TX 75234-7288
972-385-1446 or 800-524-8800 Fax: 972-385-0641
Website: www.southeasterncareerinstitute.com

Southern Careers Institute
2301 S Congress Ave Ste 24A, Austin TX 78704-5298
512-448-4795

Southern Careers Institute
2422 Airline Rd, Corpus Christi TX 78414-2904
361-857-5700

Southern Careers Institute
4805 Maher Ave, Laredo TX 78041
956-723-2345

Southern Careers Institute
1414 N Jackson Rd, Pharr TX 78577
956-687-1415

Southern Careers Institute
1405 N Main Ste 100, San Antonio TX 78212
210-271-0096

SOUTH TEXAS BARBER COLLEGE
3917 Ayers St, Corpus Christi TX 78415
Juan A. Garcia, President
361-855-2297 Fax: 361-855-7212
E-mail: southtexasbarber@sbcglobal.net

South Texas Vocational-Technical Institute
2144 Central Blvd, Brownsville TX 78520
956-554-3515

South Texas Vocational - Technical Institute
2400 Daffodil Ave, Mc Allen TX 78501-6148
956-631-1107

South Texas Vocational-Technical Institute
2419 E Hagger Ave, Weslaco TX 78596
Mark S. Hudson, School Director
956-969-1564

Southwestern Professional Institute
3033 Chimney Rock #200, Houston TX 77056
713-781-5908

Southwest Institute of Technology
5424 W Highway 290 Ste 200, Austin TX 78735-8800
Howard Roose, Director
512-892-2640

Southwest School of Business & Technical Careers
272 Commercial St, Eagle Pass TX 78852-4859
830-773-1373

Southwest School of Business & Technical Careers
602 W Southcross Blvd, San Antonio TX 78221-1038
210-921-0951

Southwest School of Business & Technical Careers
2402 San Pedro Ave, San Antonio TX 78212-2840
210-731-8449

Southwest School of Business & Technical Careers
122 W North St, Uvalde TX 78801

Star College of Cosmetology
700 E Whaley St, Longview TX 75601
903-758-8611

Star College of Cosmetology
705 N University Dr, Nacogdoches TX 75961
936-462-7232

Star College of Cosmetology
520 E Front St, Tyler TX 75702
903-596-7860

State Beauty Academy
663 Oriole Blvd, Duncanville TX 75116
972-298-0100

Stephenville Beauty College
951 S Lillian St, Stephenville TX 76401
254-968-2111

Sterling Health Center
15070 E Beltwood Pkwy, Addison TX 75001
Sterling Mansoori, Ph.D., Director
972-992-9293

Success Institute of Business
16120 Stuebner Airline Rd #104
Spring TX 77379-7321
713-682-2262

Sylvia's International School of Beauty
434 W Parker Rd, Houston TX 77091
713-697-1200

Texas Barber Colleges & Hairstyling School
5148 S Lancaster Rd Ste A, Dallas TX 75241
214-943-7255

Texas Barber Colleges & Hairstyling Schools
9275 Richmond Ave Ste 180, Houston TX 77063
713-953-0262

Texas Beauty College
6151 NW Loop 410 Ste 201, San Antonio TX 78238
210-647-5100

Texas Careers
194 Gateway St, Beaumont TX 77701
409-833-2722

Texas Careers
6410 McPherson Rd, Laredo TX 78041
956-717-5909

TEXAS CAREERS
1421 9th St, Lubbock TX 79401
Debra Sawyer, President
806-765-7051 Fax: 806-765-6980
Website: www.texascareers.com
E-mail: dsawyer@texascareers.com

TEXAS CAREERS
1015 Jackson-Keller Rd #102
San Antonio TX 78213-3752
Laura Bledsoe, Campus President
210-308-8584 Fax: 210-308-8985
Website: www.texascareers.com
E-mail: lbledsoe@texascareers.com

Texas College of Cosmetology
117 Sayles Blvd, Abilene TX 79605
325-677-0532

Texas College of Cosmetology
918 N Chadbourne St, San Angelo TX 76903
325-677-0532

Texas School of Business
3208 W Parkwood Ave, Friendswood TX 77546
281-648-0880

Texas School of Business
711 E Airtex Dr, Houston TX 77073-6032
281-443-8900

Texas School of Business Southwest
6363 Richmond Ave Ste 300
Houston TX 77057-5914
Diane Nguyen, Director of Admissions
713-975-7527

Texas Vocational School
1921 E Red River St, Victoria TX 77901-5625
361-575-4768

Toni & Guy Hairdressing Academy
2810 E Trinity Mills Rd, Carrollton TX 75006
972-416-8396

Trend Barber College
7725 W Bellfort St, Houston TX 77071-2104
Obinna Mbachu, President
713-721-0000

Tri-State Cosmetology Institute
3910 Doniphan Dr Ste C, El Paso TX 79922
915-585-8777

Tri-State Cosmetology Institute
6800 Gateway Blvd E Ste 4A, El Paso TX 79915
915-778-1741

Ultrasound Diagnostic School
2998 N Stemmons Fwy #B, Dallas TX 75247-6103
214-638-6400

Ultrasound Diagnostic School
10500 Forum Place Dr #200, Houston TX 77036-8507
713-664-9632

UNITED REGIONAL HEALTH CARE SYSTEM
Medical Technology Program
1600 11th St, Wichita Falls TX 76301
Gwen Morman, MS, MT(ASCP), Program Director
940-764-3187 Fax: 940-764-3328
Website: urhcs.org
E-mail: gmorman@urhcs.org

Universal Technical Institute
721 Lockhaven Dr, Houston TX 77073-5598
281-443-6262

University of Cosmetology Arts & Science
913 N 13th St, Harlingen TX 78550-5034
Lorena Salinas, Corp. Dir.
956-412-1212

University of Cosmetology Arts & Sciences
PO Box 720391, Mc Allen TX 78504-0391
956-687-9444

UNIVERSITY OF TEXAS M.D. ANDERSON CANCER CENTER
1515 Holcombe Blvd, Houston TX 77030-4009
Anne Bettinger, Academic Recruiter
713-745-1205 Fax: 713-792-0800
Website: www.mdanderson.org/healthsciences
E-mail: ambettin@mdanderson.org

Vanguard Institute of Technology
3107 N Sugar Rd, Pharr TX 78577-9656
956-787-4388

Velma B's Beauty Academy
1511 S Ewing Ave, Dallas TX 75216
214-942-1541

Victoria Beauty College
1508 N Laurent St, Victoria TX 77901
361-575-4526

Western Technical College
9624 Plaza Cir, El Paso TX 79927-2105
Bill Terrell, Chief Administrative Officer
915-760-8123
Website: www.wtc-ep.edu
E-mail: bterrell@wtc-ep.edu

Western Technical College
9451 Diana Dr, El Paso TX 79924-6936
Bill Terrell, Chief Administrative Officer
915-566-9621 Fax: 915-565-9903
Website: www.wtc-ep.edu
E-mail: bterrell@wtc-ep.edu

Westwood Aviation Institute
8880 Telephone Rd, Houston TX 77061-5114
Glen Feist, Director of Admissions
800-776-7423

Westwood College
4232 North Fwy, Fort Worth TX 76137-5021
817-685-9994

Westwood College - Houston South
7322 Southwest Fwy Ste 1900, Houston TX 77074
713-777-4433

Westwood College of Technology
8390 Lyndon B Johnson Fwy, Dallas TX 75243
214-570-0100

UTAH

American Institute of Medical-Dental Technology
1675 N Freedom Blvd, Provo UT 84604-2540
801-377-2900

Ameritech College
12257 Business Park Dr Ste 108, Draper UT 84020
800-652-0907

Beau La Reine College of Beauty Culture
PO Box 6504, Logan UT 84341
435-752-8688

Bridgerland Applied Technology Center
1301 N 600 W, Logan UT 84321
435-753-6780

Cameo College of Essential Beauty
1600 S State St, Salt Lake City UT 84115
801-484-6173

Careers Unlimited
University Mall #I-163, Orem UT 84097
801-687-1271

Certified Careers Institute
775 S 2000 E, Clearfield UT 84015
801-774-9900

Certified Careers Institute
1385 W 2200 S Ste 100
Salt Lake City UT 84119-7205
801-973-7008

Dallas Roberts Academy of Hair Design
1700 N State St Ste 18, Provo UT 84604
801-375-1501

David Applied Technology College
550 E 300 S, Kaysville UT 84037
801-593-2500

Eagle Gate College
5588 S Green St, Murray UT 84123
801-268-9201

Evan's Hairstyling College
798 W 400 N, Orem UT 84057
801-224-6034

Evan's Hairstyling College
955 E Tabernacle St, Saint George UT 84770
435-673-6128

Fran Brown College of Beauty
521 W 600 N, Layton UT 84041
801-546-6166

Francois D. Hair Design Academy
111 W 9000 S, Sandy UT 84070
801-561-2244

Hairitage College of Beauty
5414 S 900 E, Salt Lake City UT 84117
801-266-4693

Hairitage Hair Academy
900 S Bluff St Ste 9, Saint George UT 84770
435-673-5233

ITT TECHNICAL INSTITUTE
920 Levoy Dr, Murray UT 84123-2500
Gary Wood, Director of Recruitment
801-263-3313 Fax: 801-263-3497
Website: www.itt-tech.edu
E-mail: gwood@itt-tech.edu

Kendall's Academy of Beauty Arts & Science
7353 S 900 E, Midvale UT 84047
801-561-5610

Kendall's Academy of Beauty Arts & Science
2230 S 700 E, Salt Lake City UT 84106
801-486-0101

L.D.S. BUSINESS COLLEGE
95 North 300 West, Salt Lake City UT 84101-3500
Kathleen Howe, Assistant Director of Admissions
801-524-8145 Fax: 801-524-1900
Website: www.ldsbc.edu
E-mail: admissions@ldsbc.edu
Established 1886. Owned by The Church of Jesus Christ of Latter-day Saints. Accredited by the Commission on Colleges and Universities of the Northwest Association of Schools, Colleges and Universities; Health programs accredited by Commission on Accreditation of Allied Health Programs.
Coed. Approximately 1,300 enrolled. 96% LDS. Students from every state and 40 foreign countries; 73% full time; average age 22.5 years.
2006-2007 Tuition: $1,270 for full-time, members of the LDS Church; $2,540 for others. Financial aid available: Federal Pell Grants; Federal Stafford Student Loans, Federal Subsidized and Unsubsidized Stafford Loans; Federal Parent Loans for Undergraduate Students; other campus loans. Application: complete financial aid information form, complete the Free Application for Federal Student Aid form; request that financial aid transcript be sent to the college.
On-campus residence halls for men and women. $4,160 to $4,580 per academic year including meal plans.
Two-year degrees in financial/managerial accounting; business; business information systems; interior design; executive medical assistant; medical administrative assistant; office technology with emphasis in executive assistant and legal administrative assistant; associate of science in business; and general studies. One-year certificates in accounting; professional sales; IT support specialist; windows administration certificate; interior de-

sign sales associate; medical assistant; medical office assistant; transcription; coding; and office technology support. All students take courses offered by the College's LDS Institute of Religion.
Enrollment open to persons of any race, creed, gender, religion or national origin. Admission requirements include application (parts 1 through 7), $30 fee, and high school transcript or evidence of high school graduation. TOEFL and declaration of finances for international students.
Faculty: 15 full-time; 81 part-time. Student/faculty ratio: 20/1; Most faculty are practicing professionals with strong career-related skills.
Located in downtown Salt Lake City, close to world-class skiing, mountain sports, water sports. Wide range of on- and off-campus student activities. Two LDS wards. Devotional lectures featuring LDS general authorities; 90%+ placement rate; Career Services Center; Learning Assistance Lab. Library: 6,000 volumes, CD-ROM holdings.

MOUNTAINLAND APPLIED TECHNOLOGY COLLEGE
987 S Geneva Rd, Orem UT 84058
Mark Middlebrook, Director of Marketing/Development
801-863-7662 Fax: 801-863-7531
Website: www.uvsc.edu/matc
E-mail: mark.middlebrook@mountainlandatc.org

Mountain West College
3280 W 3500 S, West Valley City UT 84119
John Rios, Director of Admissions
801-840-4800

MYOTHERAPY COLLEGE OF UTAH
2120 South 1300 East Suite 102
Salt Lake City UT 84106
Vaughn L. Belnap, President/Director
801-484-7624 Fax: 801-484-1928
Website: myotherapycollege.com
E-mail: vbelnap@myotherapycollege.com

New Horizons Beauty College
550 N Main St Ste 115, Logan UT 84321
435-753-9779

OGDEN-WEBER APPLIED TECHNOLOGY COLLEGE
200 N Washington Blvd, Ogden UT 84404
Elsa Zweifel, Student Recruitment
801-627-8300 Fax: 801-395-3727
Website: www.owatc.com

Premier Hair Academy
4062 S 4000 W, West Valley UT 84120-4040
801-966-8414

Provo College
1450 W 820 N, Provo UT 84601-1305
801-375-1861

Skin Works School of Advanced Skin Care
2121 S 230 E, Salt Lake City UT 84115
801-530-0001

Southeast Applied Technology College
375 S Carbon Ave, Price UT 84501
435-613-1438

Southwest Applied Technology College
510 W 800 S, Cedar City UT 84720
435-586-2899

Stacey's Hands of Champions Beauty College
3721 S 250 W, Ogden UT 84405
801-394-5718

Stevens Henager College
755 Main St, Logan UT 84321
Sherman R. Conger, Director of Admissions
435-713-4777
Website: www.stevenshenager.edu

Tooele Applied Technology College
1655 E 3300 S, Salt Lake City UT 84106
801-493-8700

Uintah Basin Applied Technology College
1100 E Lagoon St, Roosevelt UT 84066
435-722-4523

Utah Career College
1902 W 7800 S, West Jordan UT 84088-4021
Denice Dunker, Director of Admissions
801-304-4224

Von Curtis Academy of Hair Design
480 N 900 E, Provo UT 84606
801-374-5111

VERMONT

Essex Technical Center
3 Educational Dr, Essex Junction VT 05452-3172

FLETCHER ALLEN HEALTH CARE SCHOOL OF CYTOTECHNOLOGY
111 Colchester Ave, Burlington VT 05401-1473
Sandra Giroux, Program Director
802-847-5133 Fax: 802-847-3632
Website: www.fahc.org/cytoschool
E-mail: sandra.giroux@vtmednet.org

NEW ENGLAND CULINARY INSTITUTE
250 Main St, Montpelier VT 05602
Dawn Hayward, Director of Admissions
877-223-6324 Fax: 802-225-3280
Website: www.neci.edu
E-mail: Admissions@neci.edu
Established in 1980. Private. Coed. Accreditation: ACCSCT, State of Vermont. Tuition: $8,875 - $21,505, depending on program - 2005. Room and board: $3,705 - $6,950, depending on program - 2005. Enrollment: 551. Faculty: 65. Programs have one of the lowest student-to-teacher ratios in culinary education, averaging 7 students with a maximum of 10 to each instructor in production classes. Degrees: Associate of Occupational Studies in Culinary Arts; Associate of Occupational Studies in Baking & Pastry Arts; Associate of Occupational Studies in

Hospitality and Restaurant Management; Bachelor of Arts in Hospitality and Restaurant Management; Certificate program in Basic Cooking; Certificate program in Baking; Certificate program in Pastry. Paid internships. Intense, hands-on training in a variety of real foodservice operations on 2 campuses in scenic, safe Vermont. Advanced placement program for experienced students.

O'Briens Training Center
1475 Shelburne Rd, South Burlington VT 05403
802-658-9591

Vermont College of Cosmetology
400 Cornerstone Dr Ste 220, Williston VT 05495
802-863-4666

Woodbury College
660 Elm St, Montpelier VT 05602-4017
Kathleen Moore, Director of Admissions
800-639-6039 Fax: 802-229-2141
Website: www.woodbury-college.edu
E-mail: admiss@woodbury-college.edu

VIRGINIA

ACT COLLEGE
1100 Wilson Blvd Suite M780, Arlington VA 22209
Robert Boderman, EVP of Operations
703-527-6660 Fax: 703-527-6688
Website: www.actcollege.edu
E-mail: bboderman@actcollege.edu

Advanced Technology Institute
5700 Southern Blvd #100
Virginia Beach VA 23462-2409
757-490-1241

AKS Massage School
462 Herndon Pkwy Ste 208, Herndon VA 20170
703-464-0333

APPRENTICE SCHOOL - NORTHROP GRUMMAN NEWPORT NEWS
4101 Washington Ave
Newport News VA 23607-2704
Paul Hoffmann, Admissions Administrator
757-880-3717 Fax: 757-688-0305
Website: www.apprenticeschool.com
E-mail: paul.hoffmann@ngc.com

The Art Institute of Washington
1820 N Fort Myer Dr, Arlington VA 22209
Larry McHugh, Director of Admissions
703-358-9550

AUGUSTA MEDICAL CENTER
School of Clinical Laboratory Science
PO Box 1000, Fishersville VA 22939-1000
Bernadette Bekken, Program Director
540-332-4539 Fax: 540-332-4543
Website: www.augustamed.com/cls
E-mail: bbekken@augustamed.com

AVIATION INSTITUTE OF MAINTENANCE
1429 Miller Store Rd, Virginia Beach VA 23455-3324
Michael Huffman, Director
757-363-2121 Fax: 757-363-2044
Website: www.aviationmaintenance.edu
E-mail: directoramn@tidetech.com

BarPalma Beauty Careers Academy
3535 Franklin Rd SW Ste D, Roanoke VA 24014
540-343-0153

Beta Tech
7914 Midlothian Tpke, Richmond VA 23235-5230
Melissa Schick, Director
804-330-0111

Beta Tech West
7001 W Broad St, Richmond VA 23294-3701
804-672-2300

Blue Ridge Job Corps Center
245 W Main St, Marion VA 24354
276-783-7221

Braxton School
3600 W Broad St Ste 190, Richmond VA 23230-4939
804-353-4458

CAREER TRAINING SOLUTIONS
100 Riverside Pkwy Suite 123
Fredericksburg VA 22406
Christine Carroll, President
540-373-2200 Fax: 540-373-4465
Website: www.careertrainingsolutions.com
E-mail: christine.carroll@careertrainingsolutions.com

Carilion Health Systems
PO Box 13727, Roanoke VA 24036-3727
540-981-7347

Crescent Cosmetology University
34 Holloway Dr, Hampton VA 23666
757-826-4609

Danville Regional Medical Center
142 S Main St, Danville VA 24541-2987
Janet Nicol, Coordinator of Admissions
434-799-4510

ECPI College of Technology
10021 Balls Ford Rd #100, Manassas VA 20109-2666
703-330-5300

ECPI College of Technology
1001 Omni Blvd Ste 100
Newport News VA 23606-4215
757-838-9191

ECPI College of Technology
5555 Greenwich Rd Ste 300
Virginia Beach VA 23462-6542
757-671-7171

ECPI Technical College
4305 Cox Rd, Glen Allen VA 23060-3359
804-934-0100

ECPI Technical College
800 Moorefield Park Dr, Richmond VA 23236-3686
804-330-5533

ECPI Technical College
5234 Airport Rd NW, Roanoke VA 24012-1603
540-563-8080

Empire Beauty School
10807 Hull Street Rd, Midlothian VA 23112
800-575-5983

Flatwoods Civilian Conservation Center
2803 Dungannon Rd, Coeburn VA 24230-5914
276-395-3384

Ghent Beauty Academy
2811 Lafayette Blvd, Norfolk VA 23509
757-855-2103

Gibbs College - Northern Virginia
1980 Gallows Rd, Vienna VA 22182-3913
877-660-EARN (3276)

Graham Webb International Academy of Hair
1621 N Kent St #1617LL, Arlington VA 22209
703-243-9322

HERITAGE INSTITUTE
350 S Washington St, Falls Church VA 22046
Christine Knouff, Director
703-773-5050 Fax: 703-534-1142
Website: www.heritage-education.com
E-mail: info@heritage-education.com
Accredited Member School: ACCSCT. Providing quality education in Massage Therapy, Cosmetology, Personal Trainer and X-Ray Technician. Financial aid available to those who qualify.

HERITAGE INSTITUTE
8255 Shoppers Square, Manassas VA 20111-2176
Tess Anderson, Director
703-361-7775 Fax: 703-335-9987
Website: www.heritage-education.com
E-mail: info@heritage-education.com
Accredited Member School: ACCSCT. Providing quality education in Massage Therapy, Cosmetology, Personal Trainer and X-Ray Medical Technician. Financial aid available to those who qualify.

Hicks Academy of Beauty Culture
904 Loudoun Ave, Portsmouth VA 23707
757-399-2400

International Beauty School
2024 Holiday Dr, Charlottesville VA 22901
434-296-0159

Jefferson College of Health Sciences
Formerly Community Hospital
PO Box 13186, Roanoke VA 24031-3186
Judith McKeon, Director of Admissions
540-985-8483

KEE BUSINESS COLLEGE
803 Diligence Dr, Newport News VA 23606-4203
Sandi Bell, Director of Education
757-873-1111 Fax: 757-873-0728
Website: www.cci.edu
E-mail: sbell@cci.edu

Medical Careers Institute
1001 Omni Blvd Ste 200
Newport News VA 23606-4215
757-873-2423

Medical Careers Institute
800 Moorefield Park Dr #302, Richmond VA 23236
804-521-0400

Medical Careers Institute
5501 Greenwich Rd, Virginia Beach VA 23462-6540
757-497-8400

Miller-Motte Technical College
1011 Creekside Ln, Lynchburg VA 24502-4353
877-333-6622

National College of Business & Tech.
PO Box 6400, Roanoke VA 24017-0400
540-986-1800

National College of Business & Technology
100 Logan St, Bluefield VA 24605
Larry Steele, Director of Admissions
276-326-3621

National College of Business & Technology
300A Piedmont Ave, Bristol VA 24201-4022
Larry Steele, Director of Admissions
276-669-5333

National College of Business & Technology
1819 Emmet St N, Charlottesville VA 22901-2812
Larry Steele, Director of Admissions
434-295-0136

National College of Business & Technology
734 Main St, Danville VA 24541-1819
Larry Steele, Director of Admissions
434-793-6822

National College of Business & Technology
51B Burgess Rd, Harrisonburg VA 22801-9709
Larry Steele, Director of Admissions
540-432-0943

National College of Business & Technology
104 Candlewood Ct, Lynchburg VA 24502-2653
Larry Steele, Director of Admissions
434-239-3500

National College of Business & Technology
10 Church St, Martinsville VA 24114
Larry Steele, Director of Admissions
276-632-5621

National College of Business & Technology
1813 E Main St, Salem VA 24153-4598
Larry Steele, Director of Admissions
540-986-1800

Norfolk Skills Center
922 W 21st St, Norfolk VA 23517-1516
757-628-3300

Old Dominion Job Corps Center
1073 Father Judge Rd, Monroe VA 24574
804-929-4081

Potomac Academy of Hair Design
350 S Washington St, Falls Church VA 22046
703-532-5050

Ralph's Virginia School of Cosmetology
3225 Old Forest Rd Ste 5, Lynchburg VA 24501
434-385-7722

Riverside School of Health Careers
316 Main St, Newport News VA 23601
Tracey Hiller, Recruitment Coordinator
757-240-2200 Fax: 757-240-2225
Website: www.riversideonline.com/rshc
E-mail: tracey.hiller@rivhs.com

Rockingham Memorial Hospital
School of Medical Technology
235 Cantrell Ave, Harrisonburg VA 22801-3293
Randall Vandevander, Program Director
540-564-5407

RSHT Training Center
702 Charlton Ave Ste A, Charlottesville VA 22903
434-245-0400

RSHT Training Center
1601 Willow Lawn Dr Ste 320, Richmond VA 23230
804-288-1500

Rudy & Kelly Academy of Hair & Nails
5606 Princess Anne Rd, Virginia Beach VA 23462
757-473-0994

Southside Virginia Community College
109 Campus Dr, Alberta VA 23821-2930
Ronald E. Mattox, Dean of Admissions
434-949-1014 Fax: 434-949-7863
Website: www.sv.vccs.edu
E-mail: ronald.mattox@sv.vccs.edu

Southside Virginia Community College
200 Daniel Rd, Keysville VA 23947
Ronald E. Mattox, Dean of Admissions
434-736-2018 Fax: 434-736-2082
Website: www.sv.vccs.edu
E-mail: ronald.mattox@sv.vccs.edu

Springfield Beauty Academy
4223 Annandale Rd, Annandale VA 22003
703-256-5662

Staunton School of Cosmetology
PO Box 2385, Staunton VA 24402-2385
540-885-0808

Stratford University
7777 Leesburg Pike #100 South
Falls Church VA 22043
Keith Evans, Contact
703-821-8570 Fax: 703-734-5335
Website: www.stratford.edu
E-mail: admissions@stratford.edu

Suffolk Beauty Academy
860 Portsmouth Blvd, Suffolk VA 23434
757-934-0656

TAP Center for Employment Training
108 N Jefferson St Suite 303, Roanoke VA 24016
Dr. Tom Bryant, Program Manager
540-767-6222

TESST Electronic School
6315 Bren Mar Dr, Alexandria VA 22312-3403
703-354-1005

Tidewater Tech
932 Ventures Way, Chesapeake VA 23320-2882
757-549-2121

Tidewater Tech
616 Denbigh Blvd, Newport News VA 23608-4416
757-874-2121

Tidewater Tech
7020 N Military Hwy, Norfolk VA 23518-4833
757-853-2121

Tidewater Tech
2697 Dean Dr Ste 100
Virginia Beach VA 23452-7431
757-340-2121

Virginia Career Institute
100 Constitution Dr Ste 101
Virginia Beach VA 23462-6758
Andy Tysinger, School Director
757-499-5447

Virginia School of Hair Design
101 W Queens Way, Hampton VA 23669
757-722-0211

Virginia School of Massage
2008 Morton Dr, Charlottesville VA 22903-6803
Admissions Department
434-293-4031

Virginia School of Technology
9210 Arboretum Pkwy Suite 100
Richmond VA 23236-3472
804-323-1020

Wards Corner Beauty Academy
7525 Tidewater Dr Ste 45, Norfolk VA 23505
757-583-3300

Washington County Adult Skill Center
848 Thompson Dr, Abingdon VA 24210-2346
276-676-1948

Woodrow Wilson Rehabilitation Center
PO Box 1500, Fishersville VA 22939
540-332-7265

WASHINGTON

The Academy of Hair Design
208 S Wenatchee Ave, Wenatchee WA 98801-3062
509-662-9082

Apollo College
10102 E Knox Ave, Spokane WA 99206-4146
509-532-8888

The Art Institute of Seattle
2323 Elliott Ave, Seattle WA 98121-1642
206-448-0900

BATES TECHNICAL COLLEGE
1101 S Yakima Ave, Tacoma WA 98405-4895
David Borofsky, President
253-680-7000 Fax: 253-680-7101
Website: www.bates.ctc.edu
E-mail: info@bates.ctc.edu

Bellingham Beauty School
4192 Meridian St, Bellingham WA 98226
360-734-1090

Bellingham Technical College
3028 Lindbergh Ave, Bellingham WA 98225-1599
360-738-0221

Bellvue Beauty School
14045 NE 20th St, Bellevue WA 98007
425-643-0270

BJ's Beauty & Barber College
12020 Meridian E #K, Puyallup WA 98373
253-848-1595

BJ's Beauty & Barber College
5239 S Tacoma Way, Tacoma WA 98409
253-473-4320

Bryman College
906 SE Everett Mall Way #600, Everett WA 98208
Rob Daniel, Director of Admissions
425-789-7960

Bryman College
19020 33rd Ave W Ste 250, Lynnwood WA 98036
425-778-9894

Bryman College
3649 W Frontage Rd, Port Orchard WA 98367-9131
Rob Daniel, Director of Admissions
360-473-1120

BRYMAN COLLEGE
981 Powell Ave SW, Renton WA 98057
Amanda Gaugler, Director of Education
425-255-3281 Fax: 425-255-9327
Website: www.cci.edu
E-mail: agaugler@cci.edu

Clare's Beauty College
104 N 4th Ave, Pasco WA 99301
509-547-8871

Clover Park Technical College
4500 Steilacoom Blvd SW
Lakewood WA 98499-4098
Dr. Sharon McGavick, President
253-589-5678 Fax: 253-589-5601
Website: www.cptc.edu
E-mail: jim.griffith@cptc.edu

Columbia Basin College
2600 N 20th Ave, Pasco WA 99301-3379
Patricia Campbell, Director Admissions/Registration
509-547-0511

Court Reporting Institute
929 N 130th St Ste 2, Seattle WA 98133-7500
Thomas Fielding, Director of Admissions
206-363-8300

Divers Institute of Technology
PO Box 70667, Seattle WA 98107-0667
800-634-8377

Emil Fries School of Piano Tuning & Technology
2510 E Evergreen Blvd, Vancouver WA 98661-4323
Dr. Judy K. Dresser, President
360-693-1511

Everett Beauty Academy
607 SE Everett Mall Way #5, Everett WA 98208
425-353-8193

Gene Juarez Academy of Beauty
2222 S 314th St, Federal Way WA 98003
253-839-6483

Gene Juarez Academy of Beauty
10715 8th Ave NE, Seattle WA 98125
206-365-6900

Glen Dow Academy of Hair Design
309 W Riverside Ave, Spokane WA 99201
Laura Manson, Enrollments
509-624-3244

Greenwood Academy of Hair Design
8501 Greenwood Ave N, Seattle WA 98103
206-782-0220

Inland Northwest HVAC Training Center
811 E Sprague Ave Ste 6, Spokane WA 99202-2105
Tena Risley, Coordinator
509-747-8810

International Air and Hospitality Academy
2901 E Mill Plain Blvd, Vancouver WA 98661-4899
Lynn Rullman, School Director
800-868-1816

ITT Technical Institute
1615 75th St SW Ste 220, Everett WA 98203-6261
800-272-3791

ITT Technical Institute
13518 Indiana Ave, Spokane Valley WA 99216
Greg Alexander, Director of Admissions
509-926-2900

Kirkland Beauty School
17311 140th Ave NE, Woodinville WA 98072
425-487-0437

Lake Washington Technical College
11605 132nd Ave NE, Kirkland WA 98034-8505
425-739-8100

Mount Vernon Beauty School
615 S 1st St, Mount Vernon WA 98273
360-336-6553

Northwest Aviation College
506 23rd St NE, Auburn WA 98002-1609
Jamelle R. Garcia, President
253-854-4960

NORTHWEST SCHOOL OF WOODEN BOATBUILDING
42 N Water St, Port Hadlock WA 98339
Kendra Seaman, Contact Person
360-385-4948 Fax: 360-385-5089
Website: www.nwboatschool.org
E-mail: info@nwboatschool.org

Perry Technical Institute
2011 W Washington Ave, Yakima WA 98903-1296
509-453-0374 Fax: 509-453-0375
Website: www.perrytech.edu
E-mail: frankj@perrytech.edu

Phagans' Orchards Beauty School
10411 NE 4th Plain Blvd 109, Vancouver WA 98662
360-254-9519

Photographic Center Northwest
900 12th Ave, Seattle WA 98122-4412
206-720-7222

Pima Medical Institute
555 S Renton Village Pl Ste 400, Renton WA 98057
425-228-9600

PIMA MEDICAL INSTITUTE
9709 3rd Ave NE Ste 400, Seattle WA 98115
George Borchers, Campus Director
206-322-6100 Fax: 206-324-1985
Website: www.pmi.edu
E-mail: spima@pmi.edu

Pima Medical Institute
9709 3rd Ave NE Ste 400, Seattle WA 98115
206-322-6100

Professional Beauty School
214 S 6th St, Sunnyside WA 98944
509-837-4040

Professional Beauty School
PO Box 9243, Yakima WA 98909-0243
509-877-6443

Skagit Valley College
2405 E College Way, Mount Vernon WA 98273-5899
360-416-7600

SkillSource Office & Technology Center
234 N Mission St, Wenatchee WA 98801
509-665-0313

Stylemasters College of Hair Design
1224 Commerce Ave, Longview WA 98632
360-636-2720

WEST COAST TRAINING INC.
PO Box 970, Woodland WA 98674-1000
Eileen Kelgard, President
Adonica Simpson, Director
800-755-5477 Fax: 360-225-6760
Website: www.heavyequipmenttraining.com
E-mail: wct@heavyequipmenttraining.com

WCT is a privately owned, co-ed institution established in 1959. Licensed with Oregon and Washington Dept. of Vocational Education. We are eligible to participate with the State of Alaska Student Loan Program, US Veterans Affairs Dept. and to provide training for various state Vocational Rehabilitation Departments, the Bureau of Indian Affairs, Native Tribal Corporations and other agencies such as Workmen's Compensation, Dept. of Labor and Industries, W.I.N., W.I.A. and T.R.A., T.R.B., T.A.A and Dislocated Worker's Programs. This institution is an associate member of the Associated General Contractors and an honorary member of the Better Business Bureau.

HEAVY EQUIPMENT OPERATOR: Learn 6 pcs. of equipment: dozers, backhoes, trackhoes, graders, scrapers and loaders. Specialize on any 2 of your choice. Also learn basic surveying, grade checking, site preparation, and be a certified flagger. Classes start every month, year round. $5,230 tuition (includes registration fee, books and tools) plus $13.88 Wash. sales tax; 8 week training program. Includes job placement assistance.

CRANE & RIGGER'S COURSE: Learn track mounted, truck mounted and self-propelled cranes; lattice and hydraulic booms; practice with hook block, dragline and clamshell. Be certified up to 50 tons. 4 week program offered every month. $4,395 tuition (includes reg. fee, books and tools) plus $11.25 Wash. sales tax. Woodland, WA is located 30 miles north of Portland, Oregon. Housing referrals provided upon request. Includes Job Placement Assistance.

Western Business College
120 NE 136th Ave Ste 130
Vancouver WA 98684-6950
360-254-3282

WESTERN PACIFIC TRUCK SCHOOL
9901 Evergreen Way, Everett WA 98204-3831
Eric Wiltse, Campus Manager
800-333-1233 Fax: 425-438-1443
Website: www.wptruckschool.com
E-mail: gnord@wptruckschool.net

WESTERN PACIFIC TRUCK SCHOOL
11020 S Tacoma Way, Tacoma WA 98499-4687
Al Auge, Campus Manager
800-333-1233 Fax: 253-581-1617
Website: www.wptruckschool.com
E-mail: gnord@wptruckschool.net

WEST VIRGINIA

Beckley Beauty Academy
109 S Fayette St, Beckley WV 25801
304-253-8326

Boone County Career Center
HC 81 Box 50B, Danville WV 25053-9613
304-369-4585

CAMCARE HEALTH EDUCATION & RESEARCH INSTITUTE
School of Cytotechnology
3200 MacCorkle Ave SE, Charleston WV 25304-1200
Carolyn Stevens, Director
304-348-5570 Fax: 304-348-4352
E-mail: carolyn.stevens@camcare.com

Carver Career and Tech Education Center
4799 Midland Dr, Charleston WV 25306-6353
304-348-1965

Charleston School of Beauty Culture
210 Capitol St, Charleston WV 25301
304-346-9603

Clarksburg Beauty Academy
120 S 3rd St, Clarksburg WV 26301
304-624-6475

Garnet Career Center
422 Dickinson St, Charleston WV 25301-1787
304-348-6195

Harpers Ferry Job Corps Civilian Conservation Center
146 Buffalo Dr, Harpers Ferry WV 25425
304-728-5772

Huntington School of Beauty Culture
5185 US Route 60 Ste 115, Huntington WV 25705
304-736-6289

International Beauty School
201 W King St, Martinsburg WV 25401-3211
304-263-4929

Monongalia County Tech Education Center
1000 Mississippi St, Morgantown WV 26501-6841
304-291-9240

Morgantown Beauty College
276 Walnut St, Morgantown WV 26505
304-292-8475

Mountaineer Beauty College
PO Box 547, Saint Albans WV 25177
304-727-9999

MOUNTAIN STATE COLLEGE
1508 Spring St, Parkersburg WV 26101-3993
A. Michael McPeek, President
Judith Sutton, Director
304-485-5487 Fax: 304-485-3524
Website: www.mountainstate.org
E-mail: admin@mountainstate.org

Founded in 1888, devoted exclusively to training men and women for career employment and advancement. Accredited by the Accrediting Council for Independent Colleges and Schools (ACICS). The college operates on a quarter term calendar year. New students may begin the first week of each quarter or at the mid point of any quarter allowing for eight starting dates per year. Tuition is payable on a per term basis and books may be purchased from the book store located at the college. Federal Financial Aid programs are available to qualified students. Approved for Veterans Training, Vocational Rehabilitation Act, Trade Retraining Allowance. Associate Degrees: Medical Assistant, Medical Transcriptionist, Administrative Assistant, Computer Information Technology, Computer Information Technology with Diagnostic, Higher Accounting Management, Legal Office Technology, Dependency Disorders Technology. Diploma programs: Medical Secretarial, Legal Office. Small college, small classes, day & evening sessions. Free lifetime Career Services and Lifetime Refresher Privileges for graduates. "Friday Plus" non-instructional day allowing faculty to tutor students desiring additional assistance. Student Organizations & Academic recognitions include: Student Government, Golden Girl Honor Society, President's List, and Honor List. Admissions requirements include personal interview, application, High School Diploma or GED, attend the "Your Key to Success" seminar and satisfactory completion of the CPAt (Career Programs Assessment) developed by ACT. Friendly and caring faculty and staff dedicated to assisting student in achieving skills for employment requirements of industry, government, business, medical and legal offices, and community service agencies with promotable competence.

ST. MARY'S MEDICAL CENTER
2900 1st Ave, Huntington WV 25702-1272
Dr. Sheila Kyle, VP Schools of Nursing & Health Professions
304-526-1270 Fax: 304-526-1517
Website: www.st-marys.org
E-mail: skyle@st-marys.org

Scott College of Cosmetology
1502 Market St, Wheeling WV 26003-3532
304-232-7798

Valley Beauty School
707 Market St, Parkersburg WV 26101
304-422-2226

Valley College of Technology
713 S Oakwood Ave, Beckley WV 25801-5968
304-252-9547

Valley College of Technology
287 Aikens Ctr, Martinsburg WV 25404
304-263-0979

West Virginia Business College
116 Pennsylvania Ave
Nutter Fort Stonewood WV 26301-4516
304-624-7695

West Virginia Business College
1052 Main St, Wheeling WV 26003-2702
304-232-0361

West Virginia Junior College
1000 Virginia St E, Charleston WV 25301-2817
Thomas A. Crouse, President
304-345-2820

West Virginia Junior College
148 Willey St, Morgantown WV 26505-5521
304-296-8282

WISCONSIN

Aurora Health Care
3000 W Montana St, Milwaukee WI 53215-3686
414-647-3000

BELLIN HOSPITAL
PO Box 23400, Green Bay WI 54305-3400
Randy Griswold, Program Director
920-433-3673
Website: www.bellin.org
E-mail: rcgris@bellin.org

Blackhawk Technical College
PO Box 5009, Janesville WI 53547-5009
Gregg Bosak, Administration, Community Information
608-757-7769 Fax: 608-757-7740
Website: www.blackhawk.edu
E-mail: gbosak@blackhawk.edu

Bryant & Stratton College
310 W Wisconsin Ave Suite 500, Milwaukee WI 53203
Kathryn Cotey, Director of Admissions
414-276-5200

Diesel Truck Driver Training School
7190 Elder Ln, Sun Prairie WI 53590
608-837-7800

Four Seasons Salon and Day Spa School
128 W 8th St Ste 8, Monroe WI 53566
608-325-4007

GILL-TECH ACADEMY OF HAIR DESIGN
423 W College Ave, Appleton WI 54911-5830
Ann Everson, Director
920-739-8684 Fax: 920-739-0145
Website: www.gill-tech.com
E-mail: kay@gill-tech.com

HERZING COLLEGE
5218 E Terrace Dr, Madison WI 53718-8340
Donald Madelung, President
Rebecca Abrams, Director of Admissions
800-582-1227 or 608-249-6611 Fax: 608-249-8593
Website: www.herzing.edu
E-mail: info@msn.herzing.edu
    Established 1948. Private. Coed. Accreditation: NCA. Tuition: $7,600 - $8,600 (2 semesters). Fees: $75 - $600. Enrollment: 590 full-time, 87 part-time. Faculty: 29. Student-Faculty ratio: 23:1. Degrees offered: AS, BS in Computer Information Systems; AS, BS in Computer Network & Security Technology; CAD Drafting; Computers, Electronics and Telecommunications Technology; BS in Technology Management & Information Technology; AS, BS in Business Administration; BS in Homeland Security & Public Safety; AS in Interactive & Graphic Arts; Diploma & AAS in Medical Billing & Insurance Coding. Minors in Business Management, Accounting, Legal Studies & Healthcare.
    Founded in 1948 as one of the nation's first electronics schools. Certification preparation inbedded in curriculum: A+, Net+, MCSE, CCNA, Certified Electronics Technician and Associate. Three-year bachelor degree. Bachelor-completion program available online.
    No dorms, but housing and job assistance to new and existing students.

Lakeshore Technical College
1290 North Ave, Cleveland WI 53015-1414
Information Fulfillment Specialist
888-GOTOLTC Fax: 920-693-3561
Website: www.gotoltc.edu
E-mail: info@gotoltc.edu

Lakeside School of Massage Therapy
1726 N 1st St, Milwaukee WI 53212
414-372-4345

Madison Cosmetology College
310 Westgate Mall, Madison WI 53711
608-271-4206

MADISON MEDIA INSTITUTE
2702 Agriculture Dr, Madison WI 53718-6787
Chris Hutchings, Director of Admissions
800-236-4997 or 608-663-2000 Fax: 608-442-0141
Website: www.madisonmedia.com
E-mail: mmi@madisonmedia.com

MARSHFIELD CLINIC/ST. JOSEPH'S HOSPITAL
611 Saint Joseph's Avenue
Marshfield WI 54449-5795
Julie J. Seehafer, MS, MT(ASCP)SH
Director, Laboratory Education
715-387-7440 Fax: 715-387-7121
Website: www.marshfieldlaboratories.org
E-mail: seehafer.julie@marshfieldclinic.org (Office)

Martin's College of Cosmetology
2575 W Mason St, Green Bay WI 54303
920-494-1430

Martin's College of Cosmetology
6414 Odana Rd, Madison WI 53719-1111
608-270-0188

Martin's College of Cosmetology
1034 S 18th St, Manitowoc WI 54220
920-684-3028

Professional Hair Design Academy
3408 Mall Dr, Eau Claire WI 54701
715-835-2345

Scientific College of Beauty/Barbering
326 Pearl St, La Crosse WI 54601
608-784-4702

Southwest Wisconsin Technical College
1800 Bronson Blvd, Fennimore WI 53809-9778
Student Services/Admissions
800-362-3322 ext. 2354

STATE COLLEGE OF BEAUTY CULTURE
1930 Grand Ave, Wausau WI 54403-6870
715-845-2888 Fax: 715-848-2121
Website: www.statecollegeofbeauty.com
E-mail: info@statecollegeofbeauty.com

Vici Beauty School
11010 W Hampton Ave, Milwaukee WI 53225-3859
Kyle Davis, Administrator
414-464-5002

Wisconsin College of Cosmetology
2960 Allied St, Green Bay WI 54304
920-336-8888

WISCONSIN CONSERVATORY OF MUSIC
1584 N Prospect Ave, Milwaukee WI 53202-6501
Sarah Wright, VP Business
414-276-5760 Fax: 414-276-6076
Website: www.wcmusic.org
E-mail: sarahwright@wcmusic.org

WYOMING

Cheeks Intl Academy of Beauty Culture
207 W 18th St, Cheyenne WY 82001
307-637-8700

Eastern Wyoming College
3200 W C St, Torrington WY 82240-1699
Dr. Jack Bottenfield, President
Tanya Howery, High School & College Relations
800-658-3195

Sage Technical School
2368 Oil Dr, Casper WY 82604-1505
Donald Washburn, Director
307-234-0242

Western Wyoming Community College
2500 College Dr, Rock Springs WY 82901-5802
Laurie Watkins, Director of Admissions
307-382-1600

PUERTO RICO

Academia Maison D'Esthetique
904 Ave Ponce de Leon, Santurce PR 00907
787-723-4672

ACADEMIA SERRANT
8180 Calle Concordia, Ponce PR 00717-1568
Yanira Pachecho Serrant, Financial Aid Director
787-259-4900 Fax: 787-842-4646
Website: www.serrant.com
E-mail: aserrant@tld.net

Academia Vocacional Del Turabo
41 Calle Campio Alonso, Caguas PR 00725-3657
Sr. Jaime Cruz, Contact
787-746-6634

Advance Tech College
PO Box 6602, Bayamn PR 00960
787-785-6841

Aguadilla Technical College
PO Box 988, Manat PR 00674
787-891-6966

American Business College
19 Calle Marti, Bayamn PR 00961
787-780-4000

American Business College of Puerto Rico
2449 Ave Militar # 2 Road Km 113.9
Isabela PR 00662
787-830-4617

American Educational College
PO Box 62, Bayamon PR 00960-0062
787-798-1199

American Technological College
7310 Edif Embajador #3 Calle Ramon Powe
Ponce PR 00717
787-259-1341

American Technological College
Arzauga 112 Mendino Center 1105
Ro Piedras PR 00928
787-753-9118

Antilles School of Technical Careers
1851 Ave Fernandez Juncos
Santurce PR 00909-3006
787-764-7576

Bayamon Community College
PO Box 055176, Bayamon PR 00960
787-780-4370

Centro de Capacitacion y Asesoramiento
PO Box 295, Aguadilla PR 00605
787-818-3115

Centro de Capacitacion y Asesoramiento
Calle de Diego #159, Arecibo PR 00612
787-880-0146

Centro de Capacitacion y Asesoramiento
PMB Dept 484 HC 1 Box 29030, Caguas PR 00725
787-880-0146

Centro de Estudios Multidisciplinarios
6 Dr Vidal St, Humacao PR 00791
787-850-8333

Centro de Estudios Multidisciplinarios
1206 Calle 13, San Juan PR 00926
787-765-4210

Century College
Calle Progresso #125, Aguadilla PR 00603
787-882-5086

Colegio Educativo Tecnologico Industrial
Calle Eugenio Maria De Host, Arecibo PR 00613
Nilsa Lopez Rivera, Directora Ejecutiva
787-879-3300

Colegio Mayor de Technologia
PO Box 1490, Arroyo PR 00714
Julia Melendez, Director of Admissions
787-839-5266 Fax: 787-839-0033
Website: www.colegiomayortec.com
E-mail: cmtarroy@coqui.net

Colegio Tecnico de Electricidad Galloza
HC 3 Box 32562, Aguada PR 00602
787-868-2974

Colegio Tecnico Metropolitano
1251 Franklin D Roosevelt Ave
Puerto Nuevo PR 00920
787-781-5140

Colegio Tecnologico y Comercial
165 Calle La Paz, Aguada PR 00602
Roberto Davila, Director
787-868-2688

Columbia Centro Universitario
PO Box 3062, Yauco PR 00698
787-856-0845

D'Mart Institute
Centro Comercial San Cristobal #215
Barranquitas PR 00794
787-857-6929

D'Mart Institute
Carreterra 159 KM 1.5 Desivo de Corozal
Corozal PR 00783
787-859-5391

EDIC College
PO Box 9120, Caguas PR 00726-9120
Virginia Cartagena, Director of Admissions
787-744-8519 Fax: 787-743-0855
Website: www.ediccollege.com
E-mail: edic@coqui.net

Educational Technical College
5 Calle Ramon Powell, Coamo PR 00769
787-825-0379

Educational Technical College
Segundo Nivel Ste 12
Carretera Num 2 Esquina #167, Bayamn PR 00959
787-780-8234

EMMAS BEAUTY ACADEMY
Carr 417 Bo Guanabano, Aguada PR 00602
Carlos Ramos Camara, CEO
787-868-4711 Fax: 787-252-0775
Website: www.emmasbeautyacademy.com
E-mail: emmasbeautyacademy@yahoo.com

Emmas Beauty Academy
Carr 149 Barrio Amuelas, Juana Daz PR 00795
787-837-0303

EMMAS BEAUTY ACADEMY
9 Calle Munoz Rivera W, Mayaguez PR 00680
Carlos Ramos Camara, CEO
787-833-0980 Fax: 787-833-0613
Website: www.emmasbeautyacademy.com
E-mail: emmasbeautyacademy@yahoo.com

Escuela de Peritos Electricitas de Isabela, Inc.
PO Box 457, Isabela PR 00662-0457
Maria M. Santiago, Director
787-872-1747

Escuela Hotelera de San Juan
229 Calle Guayama, San Juan PR 00917
787-766-0606

Ferrer Zoraida Hispanic American College
52 Calle Ruiz Belvis #54, Caguas PR 00725-3586
787-734-4311

Globelle Technical Institute
114 Calle Marginal, Urb. Monte Carlo
Vega Baja PR 00693-4218
Gloria E. Cruz Lugo, President
787-858-0236

Guaynabo Technical College
71st Carazo St, Guaynabo PR 00969
787-644-0146

Humacao Community College
PO Box 9139, Humacao PR 00792
787-852-1430

Industrial Technical College
PO Box 8480, Humacao PR 00792
787-852-8806

Institucion Chaviano de Mayaguez
116 Calle Ramos Antonini E
Mayagez PR 00680-5045
787-833-2474

Institute of Beauty Careers
1119 Ave Llorens Torres, Arecibo PR 00612
787-878-2880

Institute of Beauty Occupation
500 Calle Concepcion Vera, Moca PR 00676
787-818-4230

Instituto de Banca y Comercio
164 Jose de Diego, Cayey PR 00737
787-738-5555

Instituto de Banca y Comercio
250 Munoz Rivera, Fajardo PR 00738
787-860-6262

Instituto de Banca y Comercio
PO Box 6092, Guayama PR 00784
787-864-3220

Instituto de Banca y Comercio
61 Ponce De Leon Ave, Hato Rey PR 00919
Rafael Jimenez, Vice President
787-754-7120 Fax: 787-754-7143
Website: www.ibanca.net
E-mail: rjimenez@ibancapr.com

Instituto de Banca y Comercio
56 Carr 2, Manati PR 00674
787-854-6709

Instituto de Banca y Comercio
155 E Mendez Vigo St, Mayaguez PR 00680
787-833-4647

Instituto de Educacion Tecnica Ocupacional La Reine
9 Calle Mercedes Moreno, Aguadilla PR 00603
787-819-0222

Instituto de Educacion Tecnica Ocupacional La Reine
A8 Avenida Colon, Manat PR 00674
787-854-1119

Instituto de Educacion Vocacional
HC 3 Box 17272, Corozal PR 00783
787-859-6823

Instituto de Educacion Vocacional
Calle Comercio, Morovis PR 06578
787-862-1100

Instituto Irma Valentin
18 Calle Betances, Manat PR 00674
787-854-2316

Instituto Irma Valentin
2018 Ave Borinquen, Santurce PR 00915
787-982-1716

Instituto Irma Valentin
137 Calle Dr Cueto, Utuado PR 00641
787-894-1395

Instituto Merlix
20 Calle Betances, Bayamon PR 00961
787-786-7035

Instituto Tecnico Del Futuro
PO Box 55016, Bayamon PR 00960
787-740-5030

Instituto Vocacional Aurea E Mendez
PO Box 8655, Caguas PR 00726
787-743-5327

International Junior College
57 Calle Estrella, Ponce PR 00730-3829
787-844-5325

International Junior College
1254 Ave Ponce de Leon, San Juan PR 00907-3917
787-723-3333

International Technical College
104 Loaiza Cordero St, San Juan PR 00918
787-767-8389

John Dewey College
RD 2 Corujo Industrial Park, Bayamn PR 00959
787-648-4353

John Dewey College
Carr 3 KM 11 lote 7, Carolina PR 00986
787-769-1515

John Dewey College
PO Box 19538, San Juan PR 00910
787-753-0039

Leston College
Calle Dr Veve #52, Bayamn PR 00961
787-787-9661

Liceo de Arte Y Disenos
PO Box 1889, Caguas PR 00726-1889
Angel L. Garcia Viera, Presidente
787-743-7447

Liceo de Arte Y Tecnologia
PO Box 192346, San Juan PR 00919
787-754-8250

MBTI Business Training Institute
1256 Ave Ponce de Leon, Santurce PR 00907-3965
Miguel A. Fernandez, Contact
787-723-9403 Fax: 787-723-9447
Website: www.mbti.com
E-mail: hdavila@mbti.com

Modern Hairstyling Institute
Carr 2 Km 30 O Marginal, Arecibo PR 00612
787-816-2991

Modern Hairstyling Institute
57 Calle Dr Veve, Bayamn PR 00961
787-778-0300

Modern Hairstyling Institute
60 Calle Fernandez Juncos N, Carolina PR 00985
787-752-8383

Modern Hairstyling Institute
Celis Aguilera 51, Fajardo PR 00648
787-863-9922

Montecarlo: Escuela de Hoteleria y Artes Servicios de
Hospitalidad Monteclaro
PO Box 447, Palmer PR 00721
787-888-1135

National College of Business & Technology
PO Box 2036, Bayamon PR 00960-2036
787-780-5134

National College of Business and Technology
PO Box 4035, Arecibo PR 00614
787-879-5044

Politec Institute
78 Calle Guadalupe # 335577, Ponce PR 00730
787-843-0204

Ponce Paramedical College
PO Box 800106, Coto Laurel PR 00780
787-848-1589

PONCE PARAMEDICAL COLLEGE
1213 Calle Acacia Villa Flores, Ponce PR 00716-2901
Alberto Aristizabal, President
787-848-1589 Fax: 787-259-0169
E-mail: ppcadmin@popac.edu

PROFESSIONAL ELECTRICAL SCHOOL
PO Box 1797, Manati PR 00674
Paulino Delgado, Director
787-854-4776 Fax: 787-854-4776
E-mail: pes@atenas.com

Professional Technical Institute
PO Box 607061, Bayamon PR 00960
787-740-6810

Puerto Rico Technical Jr College
703 Ave Ponce De Leon, Hato Rey PR 00917-5013
787-751-0133

Puerto Rico Technical Jr College
Calle Santiago R Palmer #15, Mayagez PR 00680
787-832-2762

Ramirez College of Business Technology
PO Box 195460, San Juan PR 00919-5460
787-763-3120

Rogie's School of Beauty Culture
26 Res Gautier Benitez, Caguas PR 00725
787-746-3777

Rogie's School of Beauty Culture
PO Box 19828, San Juan PR 00910
787-722-2293

Serbia's Technical College
Calle Hostos 27 Esquina Vicente Pales
Guayama PR 00785
Merags Santos Arrida, Director
787-864-7254

Star Career College
19 Degerau St, Bayamn PR 00961
787-740-7490

TRINITY COLLEGE OF PUERTO RICO
PO Box 34360, Ponce PR 00734-4360
Ms. Maria I. Colon, Executive Director
787-842-0000 Fax: 787-284-2537
Website: www.csifpr.org/trinitycollege
E-mail: micolon@csifpr.org

Universal Career Counseling
113 Paseo De La Atenas, Manat PR 00674
787-728-7211

Universal Career Counseling Center
6 Antonio Lopez St, Humacao PR 00791
787-728-7211

Universal Career Counseling Center
1902 Ave Fernandez Juncos, Santurce PR 00909
787-728-7268

Universal Technology College of Puerto Rico
Apartado 1955 Victoria Sta, Aguadilla PR 00605
787-882-2065

Universal Technology College of Puerto Rico
167 Ave Munoz Rivera Oeste Ste 2
Camuy PR 00627-2334
787-262-5786

Universidad del Este
PO Box 2010, Carolina PR 00984
787-257-7373

CHIROPRACTIC MEDICINE

CALIFORNIA

Cleveland Chiropractic College - Los Angeles Campus
590 N Vermont Ave, Los Angeles CA 90004-2196
Melissa Denton, Multicampus Director of Admissions
800-466-CCLA (2252) or 323-906-2031
Fax: 323-906-2094
Website: www.cleveland.edu
E-mail: la.admissions@cleveland.edu

LIFE CHIROPRACTIC COLLEGE WEST
25001 Industrial Blvd, Hayward CA 94545-2801
Stephen D. Eckstone, Director of Admissions
800-788-4476 Fax: 510-780-4525
Website: www.lifewest.edu
E-mail: admissions@lifewest.edu

PALMER COLLEGE OF CHIROPRACTIC WEST
90 E Tasman Dr, San Jose CA 95134-1617
Director of Admissions
866-303-7939 Fax: 408-944-6032
Website: www.palmer.edu
E-mail: pccw_admiss@palmer.edu

FLORIDA

**PALMER COLLEGE OF CHIROPRACTIC
FLORIDA**
4777 City Center Pkwy, Port Orange FL 32129-4153
Director of Admissions
866-585-9677 or 386-763-2709 Fax: 386-763-2620
Website: www.palmer.edu
E-mail: pccf_admiss@palmer.edu

GEORGIA

Life University
1269 Barclay Cir SE, Marietta GA 30060-2903
Dr. Deborah E. Heairlston, Director of New Student
Development
770-426-2884 Fax: 770-426-2895
Website: www.life.edu
E-mail: admissions@life.edu

ILLINOIS

National University of Health Sciences
200 E Roosevelt Rd, Lombard IL 60148-4583
Dr. James Winterstein, President
800-826-6285 Fax: 630-889-6554
Website: www.nuhs.edu
E-mail: admissions@nuhs.edu

IOWA

Iowa Lakes Community College
300 S 18th St, Estherville IA 51334-2721
Anne Stansbury, Asst. Director of Admissions
712-362-7945 Fax: 712-362-8363
Website: www.iowalakes.edu
E-mail: info@iowalakes.edu

PALMER COLLEGE OF CHIROPRACTIC
1000 Brady St, Davenport IA 52803-5287
800-722-3648 or 563-884-5656 Fax: 563-884-5414
Website: admissions.palmer.edu
E-mail: pcadmit@palmer.edu

MINNESOTA

**NORTHWESTERN HEALTH SCIENCES
UNIVERSITY**
Northwestern College of Chiropractic Admissions
Office
2501 W 84th St, Minneapolis MN 55431-1599
Dr. Alfred Traina, President
Bill Kuehl, Director of Admissions
800-888-4777 ext. 409 or 952-888-4777
Fax: 952-888-6713
Website: www.nwhealth.edu
E-mail: admit@nwhealth.edu

Established 1941. Private. Coed. Accredited by the Council on Chiropractic Education (CCE) and the North Central Association of Colleges and Schools (NCA). Tuition for the 2004-05 school year is approximately $6,265 per trimester excluding books, activity fees and lab fees. Northwestern Health Sciences University admits about 205 students each year distributed over two entering classes in September & January. The college maintains a total enrollment of about 750 students. Approximately 35 percent are women.

NWHSU offers a ten-trimester (three terms per year) program leading to the Doctor of Chiropractic (DC) degree. A Bachelor of Science degree in Human Biology is available for students interested in pursuing both degrees concurrently. The chiropractic curriculum is divided into the following three parts: basic sciences, chiropractic methods, and clinical (intern) experience at one of the College's six University clinics in the Twin Cities area. NWHSU prepares students to be skilled diagnosticians who serve as primary-care physicians. The Chiropractic Physicians Associate Program provides further in-depth clinical experience by allowing students to spend their last academic term as associates in private practices of participating doctors of chiropractic

throughout the United States. More than 94 percent of all Northwestern graduates are successfully practicing chiropractic throughout the United States, Canada, Europe, Australia and Asia. At the College's research facility, the Wolfe-Harris Center for Clinical Studies, primary research is conducted in the area of outcomes of chiropractic versus non-chiropractic care. Students are strongly encouraged to become involved in research.

Financial aid is available through programs that include Federal Pell Grants, Federal Supplemental Educational Opportunity Grants, Minnesota State Grants, Federal Perkins Loans, Stafford Student Loans, as well as Federal Work-Study and institutional work programs, including teaching assistantships. Many state and private scholarships are awarded to the college's students each year on a competitive basis.

The campus consists of 25 acres. The building complex is complete with laboratories, lecture halls, classrooms, a library, auditorium, cafeteria, gymnasium, indoor swimming pool, and fitness center.

The Minneapolis/St. Paul metropolitan area is a progressive community with a population of 3 million, combines the advantages of a big city with those of a small community. The Twin Cities provide more public parks than any other large city in the nation. The area is noted for its many lakes and rivers. Many cultural and recreational facilities are located within or near the metropolitan area, including the Guthrie Theater, the Minneapolis Institute of Art, two zoos, and four professional sports teams. Educational facilities are also quite diverse; they include the University of Minnesota, eleven private colleges, and eight junior and community colleges, all located within the Twin Cities. The climate presents four distinct seasons.

The college maintains no on-campus housing, but the admissions department offers information about housing for both new and continuing students. Adequate accommodations are readily available near the campus and throughout the Twin Cities area. Generally single, independent students can expect costs of $550 per month for an apartment. APPLYING: Applicants should write to the Director of Admissions for application materials. Applicants must have a minimum grade point average of 2.5 and 90 semester credits (or 135 quarter credits) of undergraduate studies, including courses in biology, general and organic chemistry, physics, psychology, and English or communication skills. Students should write to the college for a preadmissions requirements brochure. Applications are accepted for two starting dates: September and January.

MISSOURI

Cleveland Chiropractic College - Kansas City Campus
6401 Rockhill Rd, Kansas City MO 64131-1122
Melissa Denton, Multicampus Director of Admissions
800-467-CCKC (2252) or 816-501-0100
Fax: 816-501-0205
Website: www.cleveland.edu
E-mail: kc.admissions@cleveland.edu

NEW YORK
NEW YORK CHIROPRACTIC COLLEGE
PO Box 800, Seneca Falls NY 13148-0800
Michael P. Lynch, Director of Admissions
800-234-6922 (NYCC) Fax: 315-568-3087
Website: www.nycc.edu
E-mail: enrolnow@nycc.edu

PENNSYLVANIA

Juniata College
1700 Moore St, Huntingdon PA 16652-2196
Michelle Bartol, Dean of Enrollment
877-JUNIATA Fax: 814-641-3100
Website: www.juniata.edu
E-mail: admissions@juniata.edu

SOUTH CAROLINA
SHERMAN COLLEGE OF STRAIGHT CHIROPRACTIC
PO Box 1452, Spartanburg SC 29304-1452
Lisa Hildebrand, Director of Admission
800-849-8771 or 864-578-8770 Fax: 864-599-4860
Website: www.sherman.edu
E-mail: admissions@sherman.edu

TEXAS

Parker College of Chiropractic
2500 Walnut Hill Ln, Dallas TX 75229-5609
Andrea Robles, Asst. Director of Admissions
972-438-6932 Fax: 214-902-2413
Website: www.parkercc.edu
E-mail: admissions@parkercc.edu

TEXAS CHIROPRACTIC COLLEGE
5912 Spencer Hwy, Pasadena TX 77505-1699
Sandra Hughes, D.C.; Director of Admission
281-487-1170 Fax: 281-991-4871
Website: www.txchiro.edu
E-mail: shughes@txchiro.edu

COMMUNICATIONS

ALABAMA

Judson College
302 Bibb St, Marion AL 36756
Michael Scotto, Director of Admissions
800-447-9472 Fax: 334-683-5147
Website: www.judson.edu
E-mail: admissions@judson.edu

University of Alabama in Huntsville
PO Box 1247, Huntsville AL 35899-0001
Ann Lee, Assoc. Director for Recruiting Program and Events
1-800-UAH-CALL Fax: 256-824-6073
Website: www.uah.edu
E-mail: leev@uah.edu

University of South Alabama
307 University Blvd N, Mobile AL 36688-3053
Melissa Haab, Director of Admissions
251-460-6141 Fax: 251-460-7876
Website: www.southalabama.edu
E-mail: admiss@usouthal.edu

ALASKA

University of Alaska Anchorage
PO Box 141629, Anchorage AK 99514-1629
Cecile Mitchell, Director of Enrollment Services
907-786-1480 Fax: 907-786-4888
Website: www.uaa.alaska.edu/
E-mail: enroll@uaa.alaska.edu

University of Alaska Southeast
11120 Glacier Hwy, Juneau AK 99801-8625
Paul Kraft, Dean of Students/Enrollment Management
907-796-6000 Fax: 907-796-6005
Website: www.uas.alaska.edu
E-mail: paul.kraft@uas.alaska.edu

ARIZONA

Pima Community College
4905 E Broadway Blvd, Tucson AZ 85709-1010
Wendy Kilgore, Ph.D., Director of Admissions
520-206-4500 Fax: 520-206-4790
Website: www.pima.edu
E-mail: infocenter@pima.edu

University of Arizona
Tucson AZ 85721-0040
Paul Kohn, Director of Admissions
520-621-3237 Fax: 520-621-9799
Website: www.admissions.arizona.edu or www.arizona.edu

ARKANSAS

Ouachita Baptist University
410 Ouachita St, Arkadelphia AR 71998-0001
David Goodman, Director of Admissions
870-245-5110 Fax: 870-245-5500
Website: www.obu.edu
E-mail: admissions@obu.edu

CALIFORNIA

American Film Institute
AFI Conservatory
2021 N Western Ave, Los Angeles CA 90027
Scott Hardman, Admissions Counselor
323-856-7628 Fax: 323-856-7720
Website: www.afi.com
E-mail: shardman@afi.com

Antioch University
801 Garden St Ste 101
Santa Barbara CA 93101-1581
Ankara McPherson, Director of Admissions
805-962-8179 Fax: 805-962-4786
Website: www.antiochsb.edu
E-mail: amcpherson@antiochsb.edu

Associated Technical College
1670 Wilshire Blvd, Los Angeles CA 90017-1690
Samuel Romano, Director of Admissions
213-353-1845 Fax: 213-413-4864
Website: www.associatedtechcollege.com
E-mail: decatc@earthlink.net

California State University-San Bernadino
5500 University Pkwy
San Bernardino CA 92407-2393
Olivia Rosas, Director of Admissions
909-880-5000 Fax: 909-880-7034
Website: enrollment.csusb.edu
E-mail: orosas@csusb.edu

Chapman University
One University Drive, Orange CA 92866-1099
Michael Drummy, Assistant Vice President for Enrollment
Services and Chief Admission Officer
714-997-6411 or 888-CUAPPLY Fax: 714-997-6713
Website: www.chapman.edu
E-mail: admit@chapman.edu

Columbia College Hollywood
18618 Oxnard St, Tarzana CA 91356-1411
Carmen Munoz & Nicole Anderson, Admissions Coordinators
800-785-0585 Fax: 818-345-9053
Website: www.columbiacollege.edu
E-mail: admissions@columbiacollege.edu

Concordia University
1530 Concordia, Irvine CA 92612-3203
Lori McDonald, Executive Director of Enrollment Services
800-229-1200 or 949-854-8002 Fax: 949-854-6894
Website: www.cui.edu
E-mail: admission@cui.edu

FRESNO CITY COLLEGE
1101 E University Ave, Fresno CA 93741-0002
Dayann Dietrich, Contact
559-442-8241 Fax: 559-237-4232
Website: www.fresnocitycollege.com
E-mail: fcc.admissions@scccd.com

Orange Coast College
PO Box 5005, Costa Mesa CA 92628-5005
Kristin Clark, Director of Admissions
714-432-5773 Fax: 714-432-5736
Website: www.orangecoastcollege.edu
E-mail: kclark@cccd.edu

PLATT COLLEGE
6250 El Cajon Blvd, San Diego CA 92115-3916
Carly Westerfield, Admissions Coordinator
619-265-0107 or 866-752-8826 Fax: 619-308-0570
Website: www.platt.edu
E-mail: info@platt.edu
Established 1980. Private. Coed. Accreditation: ACCSCT. Tuition: Approximately $16,000. Fees: $100. Enrollment: 350. Faculty: 25. Student-faculty ratio: 14:1. Library: 1,700 volumes + online. 2 buildings. Design school offering BS, AAS and diploma programs. "Hands on" programs in Graphic Design, Multimedia Design, Animation, Digital Video Production, and Web page design. Full range of General Education courses required to complete AAS + BS degrees. Classes offered morning, afternoon and evening. Job placement and financial aid services available. Visit www.platt.edu.

San Diego Christian College
2100 Greenfield Dr, El Cajon CA 92019-1157
Jon Melone, Director of Admissions
800-676-2242 Fax: 619-590-1739
Website: www.sdcc.edu
E-mail: admissions@sdcc.edu

Simpson University
2211 College View Dr, Redding CA 96003-8606
Jim Herberger, Director of Admissions
888-9-SIMPSON Fax: 530-226-4861
Website: www.simpsonuniversity.edu
E-mail: admissions@simpsonuniversity.edu
See listing under "Liberal Arts and Sciences"

COLORADO

San Juan Basin Technical College
PO Box 970, Cortez CO 81321-0970
Shannon South, Director of Student Services
970-565-8457 Fax: 970-565-8450
Website: www.sjbtc.edu
E-mail: ssouth@sjbtc.edu

UNIVERSITY OF DENVER UNIVERSITY COLLEGE
2211 S Josephine St, Denver CO 80208
Dr. Denise Pearson, Assistant Dean of Academics
303-871-3354 Fax: 303-871-4047
Website: www.universitycollege.du.edu
E-mail: ucolinfo@du.edu

CONNECTICUT

Albertus Magnus College
700 Prospect St, New Haven CT 06511-1189
Richard Lolatte, Dean of Admission
203-773-8501 or 800-578-9160 Fax: 203-773-5248
Website: www.albertus.edu
E-mail: admissions@albertus.edu

Middlesex Community College
100 Training Hill Rd, Middletown CT 06457-4889
Mensimah Shabazz, Director of Admissions
860-343-5800 Fax: 860-344-3055
Website: www.mxcc.commnet.edu
E-mail: mshabazz@mxcc.commnet.edu

University of New Haven
300 Boston Post Rd, West Haven CT 06516
Director of Undergraduate Admissions
203-932-7319 Fax: 203-931-6093
Website: www.newhaven.edu
E-mail: adminfo@newhaven.edu

DELAWARE

Wesley College
120 N State St, Dover DE 19901-3876
302-736-2300 Fax: 302-736-2301
Website: www.wesley.edu

FLORIDA

City College
2000 W Commercial Blvd, Fort Lauderdale FL 33309
Britt Carpenter, Director of Admissions
954-492-5353 Fax: 954-491-1965
Website: www.citycollege.edu
E-mail: bcarpenter@citycollege.edu

Florida State University
600 W College Ave, Tallahassee FL 32306-1096
Janice V. Finney, Director of Admissions
850-644-2525 Fax: 850-644-0197
Website: admissions.fsu.edu
E-mail: admissions@admin.fsu.edu

Keiser College
1800 Business Park Blvd, Daytona Beach FL 32114
Matt McEnany, Vice President
386-274-5060 Fax: 386-274-2725
Website: www.keisercollege.edu
E-mail: mmcenany@keisercollege.edu

Lynn University
3601 N Military Trl, Boca Raton FL 33431-5598
Brett Ormandy, Director of Admissions
561-237-7900 Fax: 561-237-7100
Website: www.lynn.edu
E-mail: admission@lynn.edu

Northwood University
2600 N Military Trl, West Palm Beach FL 33409-2999
Jack Letvinchuk, Director of Admissions
800-458-8325 Fax: 561-640-3328
Website: www.northwood.edu
E-mail: fladmit@northwood.edu

St. Thomas University
16401 NW 37th Ave, Miami Gardens FL 33054
Dr. Gloria Ruiz, Contact
800-367-9010 or 305-628-6546 Fax: 305-628-6591
Website: www.stu.edu
E-mail: signup@stu.edu

University of South Florida
4202 E Fowler Ave, Tampa FL 33620-6900
J. Robert Spatig, Director of Admissions
813-974-3350 Fax: 813-974-9689
Website: www.usf.edu
E-mail: admissions@admin.usf.edu

GEORGIA

DeKalb Technical College
495 N Indian Creek Dr, Clarkston GA 30021-2397
Terry Richardson, Director of Admissions
404-297-9522 Fax: 404-294-6496
Website: www.dekalbtech.edu
E-mail: richardt@dekalbtech.edu

Kennesaw State University
1000 Chastain Rd NW, Kennesaw GA 30144-5591
Dr. Helen Ridley, Dean of Humanities and Social
Science
770-423-6124
Website: www.kennesaw.edu

Oglethorpe University
4484 Peachtree Rd NE, Atlanta GA 30319-2797
Kelly Gosnell, Director of Admission
404-261-1441 Fax: 404-364-8491
Website: www.oglethorpe.edu
E-mail: admission@oglethorpe.edu

TOCCOA FALLS COLLEGE
PO Box 800899, Toccoa Falls GA 30598
Christy Meadows, Director of Admissions
888-785-5624 Fax: 706-282-6012
Website: www.tfc.edu
E-mail: admissions@tfc.edu

IDAHO

Brigham Young University - Idaho
120 Kimball Bldg, Rexburg ID 83460
Gordon Westenskow, Director of Admissions
208-496-1020 Fax: 208-496-1220
Website: www.byui.edu
E-mail: admissions@byui.edu

University of Idaho
Moscow ID 83844-4253
Lloyd Scott, Director of New Student Services
208-885-6163 Fax: 208-885-4477
Website: www.uidaho.edu
E-mail: nss@uidaho.edu

ILLINOIS

Aurora University
347 S Gladstone Ave, Aurora IL 60506-4892
Carol R. Dunn, Ed.D., Vice President for Enrollment
800-742-5281 Fax: 630-844-5535
Website: www.aurora.edu
E-mail: admission@aurora.edu

Benedictine University
5700 College Rd, Lisle IL 60532-0900
630-829-6300 or 888-829-6363 Fax: 630-829-6301
Website: www.ben.edu
E-mail: admissions@ben.edu
See listing under "Universities"

Columbia College Chicago
600 S Michigan Ave, Chicago IL 60605-1996
Murphy Monroe, Executive Director of Admissions
312-344-7130 Fax: 312-344-8024
Website: www.colum.edu
E-mail: admissions@colum.edu

CONCORDIA UNIVERSITY
7400 Augusta St, River Forest IL 60305-1402
708-209-3100 Fax: 708-209-3473
Website: www.curf.edu
E-mail: crfadmis.edu

North Central College
30 N Brainard St, Naperville IL 60540-4690
Martha Stolze, Director of Admissions
630-637-5800 Fax: 630-637-5819
Website: www.northcentralcollege.edu
E-mail: admissions@noctrl.edu

Roosevelt University
430 S Michigan Ave, Chicago IL 60605
Gwen E. Kanelos, Asst. Vice President for Enrollment
Services
877-APPLY-RU Fax: 312-341-4216
Website: www.roosevelt.edu
E-mail: applyru@roosevelt.edu

South Suburban College of Cook County
15800 State St, South Holland IL 60473
Jane Ellen Stocker, Dean of Enrollment Services
708-596-2000 Fax: 708-225-5806
Website: www.southsuburbancollege.edu
E-mail: jstocker@southsuburbancollege.edu

INDIANA

Franklin College
101 Branigin Blvd, Franklin IN 46131
Jacqueline S. Acosta, Director of Admissions
800-852-0232 Fax: 317-738-8274
Website: www.franklincollege.edu
E-mail: admissions@franklincollege.edu

Hanover College
PO Box 108, Hanover IN 47243-0108
William D. Preble, Dean of Admission
800-213-2178 Fax: 812-866-7098
Website: www.hanover.edu
E-mail: admissions@hanover.edu

St. Mary-of-the-Woods College
Saint Mary of the Woods IN 47876-1001
James P. Malley, Jr., Director of Admission
800-926-7692 Fax: 812-535-5010
Website: www.smwc.edu
E-mail: smwcadms@smwc.edu

University of Evansville
1800 Lincoln Ave, Evansville IN 47722-0001
Thomas E. Bear, V.P. of Enrollment Services
800-423-8633 Fax: 812-488-4076
Website: www.evansville.edu
E-mail: admission@evansville.edu

IOWA

Briar Cliff University
PO Box 2100, Sioux City IA 51104-0100
Sharisue Wilcoxon, VP for Enrollment Management
712-279-5200 Fax: 712-279-1632
Website: www.briarcliff.edu
E-mail: admissions@briarcliff.edu

Clarke College
1550 Clarke Dr, Dubuque IA 52001-3198
Andy Schroeder, Director of Admissions
800-383-2345 Fax: 563-584-8666
Website: www.clarke.edu
E-mail: andy.schroeder@clarke.edu

Graceland University
1 University Place, Lamoni IA 50140
Brian Shantz, Vice President for Enrollment and Dean
of Admissions
641-784-5196 Fax: 641-784-5480
Website: www.admissions.graceland.edu
E-mail: admissions@graceland.edu

Iowa Lakes Community College
300 S 18th St, Estherville IA 51334-2721
Anne Stansbury, Asst. Director of Admissions
712-362-7945 Fax: 712-362-8363
Website: www.iowalakes.edu
E-mail: info@iowalakes.edu

Mount Mercy College
1330 Elmhurst Dr NE, Cedar Rapids IA 52402-4797
Jim Krystofiak, Dean of Admission
800-248-4504 Fax: 319-363-5270
Website: www.mtmercy.edu
E-mail: admission@mtmercy.edu

Waldorf College
106 S 6th St, Forest City IA 50436-1713
Steve Lovik, Vice President of Enrollment Management
800-292-1903 or 641-585-8112 Fax: 641-585-8125
Website: www.waldorf.edu
E-mail: loviks@waldorf.edu
See listing under "Universities"

Wartburg College
PO Box 1003, Waverly IA 50677-0903
Brent Matthias, Interim Director of Admissions
319-352-8200 Fax: 319-352-8579
Website: www.wartburg.edu
E-mail: admissions@wartburg.edu

KANSAS

Allen County Community College
1801 N Cottonwood St, Iola KS 66749-1607
John Masterson, President
Randy Weber, Director of Admissions
620-365-5116 Fax: 620-365-3284
Website: www.allencc.net
E-mail: weber@allencc.net

COLBY COMMUNITY COLLEGE
1255 S Range Ave, Colby KS 67701-4099
Director of Admissions
888-634-9350 or 785-460-4690 Fax: 785-460-4691
Website: www.colbycc.edu
E-mail: bobbi@colbycc.edu

Independence Community College
PO Box 708, Independence KS 67301-0708
Dr. Terry Hetrick, President
800-842-6063 Fax: 620-331-5344
Website: www.indycc.edu
E-mail: admissions@indycc.edu

Newman University
3100 W McCormick St, Wichita KS 67213
Jann Reusser, Admissions Recruitment Coordinator
316-942-4291 ext. 2144 Fax: 316-942-4483
Website: www.newmanu.edu
E-mail: reusserj@newmanu.edu

Tabor College
400 S Jefferson St, Hillsboro KS 67063-1758
Rusty Allen, Dean of Enrollment Management
620-947-3121 Fax: 620-947-6276
Website: www.tabor.edu
E-mail: admissions@tabor.edu

KENTUCKY

Morehead State University
Morehead KY 40351-1689
Dayna Seelig, Enrollment Services
800-585-6781 Fax: 606-783-5038
Website: www.moreheadstate.edu
E-mail: admissions@moreheadstate.edu

LOUISIANA

Dillard University
2601 Gentilly Blvd, New Orleans LA 70122-3097
Linda G. Nash, Director of Admissions
Website: www.dillard.edu
E-mail: admissions@dillard.edu

MAINE

HUSSON COLLEGE
One College Cir, Bangor ME 04401-2999
Jane Goodwin, Director of Admissions
800-4HU-SSON or 207-941-7100 Fax: 207-941-7935
Website: www.husson.edu
E-mail: admit@husson.edu
See listing under "Universities"

St. Joseph's College of Maine
278 Whites Bridge Rd, Standish ME 04084-5263
Vincent Kloskowski, Dean of Admissions
800-338-7057 Fax: 207-893-7862
Website: www.sjcme.edu
E-mail: admission@sjcme.edu

MARYLAND

Cecil Community College
One Seahawk Dr, North East MD 21901
Sandra S. Rajaski, Registrar & Director of Admissions
410-287-1000 Fax: 410-287-1001
Website: www.cecilcc.edu
E-mail: srajaski@cecilcc.edu

Villa Julie College
1525 Greenspring Valley Rd
Stevenson MD 21153-0641
Mark Hergan, V.P. Enrollment Services
410-486-7001 Fax: 410-602-6600
Website: www.vjc.edu/admissions
E-mail: admissions@mail.vjc.edu

MASSACHUSETTS

Assumption College
500 Salisbury St, Worcester MA 01609-1294
Kathleen Murphy, Dean of Enrollment
508-767-7000 Fax: 508-799-4412
Website: www.assumption.edu
E-mail: admiss@assumption.edu

Boston University
121 Bay State Rd, Boston MA 02215
Kelly Walter, Executive Director of Admissions
617-353-2300 Fax: 617-353-9695
Website: web.bu.edu
E-mail: admissions@bu.edu

Bristol Community College
777 Elsbree St, Fall River MA 02720-7395
Rodney S. Clark, Director of Admissions
508-678-2811 ext. 2516, 2179 Fax: 508-730-3265
Website: www.bristol.mass.edu
E-mail: admissions@bristol.mass.edu

Emerson College
120 Boylston St, Boston MA 02116-4624
Sara S. Ramirez, Director of Undergraduate Admission
617-824-8600 Fax: 617-824-8609
Website: www.emerson.edu
E-mail: admission@emerson.edu

Massachusetts Institute of Technology
77 Massachusetts Ave, Cambridge MA 02139-4307
Marilee Jones, Dean of Admission
617-253-1000 Fax: 617-253-4016
Website: my.mit.edu
E-mail: admissions@mit.edu

Newbury College
129 Fisher Ave, Brookline MA 02445-5796
Salvadore Liberto, Vice President of Enrollment
617-730-7000 Fax: 617-731-9618
Website: www.newbury.edu

University of Massachusetts Dartmouth
Old Westport Rd, North Dartmouth MA 02747-2300
Steven T. Briggs, Director of Admissions
508-999-8605 Fax: 508-999-8755
Website: explore.umassd.edu
E-mail: sbriggs@umassd.edu

Westfield State College
PO Box 1630, Westfield MA 01086
Michelle Mattie, Associate Dean, Admission and
Enrollment Services
413-572-5300
Website: www.wsc.ma.edu
E-mail: admission@wsc.ma.edu

MICHIGAN

Alma College
614 W Superior St, Alma MI 48801-1599
Anne Monroe, Director of Admissions
800-321-ALMA Fax: 989-463-7057
Website: www.alma.edu
E-mail: admissions@alma.edu

Andrews University
Berrien Springs MI 49104-0001
Randall Graves, Director of Recruitment Services
800-253-2874 Fax: 269-471-2670
Website: www.connect.andrews.edu
E-mail: gravesr@andrews.edu

Concordia University
4090 Geddes Rd, Ann Arbor MI 48105-2797
Gary Neumann, Director of Admissions
734-995-7300 Fax: 734-995-4610
Website: www.cuaa.edu
E-mail: admissions@cuaa.edu

Delta College
University Center MI 48710-0001
Duff Zube, Director of Admissions
989-686-9093 Fax: 989-667-2202
Website: www.delta.edu
E-mail: admit@delta.edu

Grand Valley State University
1 Campus Dr, Allendale MI 49401-9403
Jodi Chycinski, Director of Admissions
616-331-6611 Fax: 616-331-2000
Website: www.gvsu.edu
E-mail: go2gvsu@gvsu.edu

HILLSDALE COLLEGE
33 E College St, Hillsdale MI 49242-1298
Dr. Kirstin Kiledal, Director
517-607-2327 Fax: 517-607-2223
Website: www.hillsdale.edu
E-mail: kirstin.kiledal@hillsdale.edu

Lawrence Technological University
21000 W 10 Mile Rd, Southfield MI 48075-1058
Jane Rohrback, Director of Admissions
800-225-5588 Fax: 248-204-2228
Website: www.ltu.edu
E-mail: admissions@ltu.edu
See listing under "Universities"

MACOMB COMMUNITY COLLEGE
14500 E 12 Mile Rd, Warren MI 48088-3896
Information Center
586-445-7999
Website: www.macomb.edu
E-mail: answer@macomb.edu

Northwood University
4000 Whiting Dr, Midland MI 48640
Daniel F. Toland, Dean of Admissions
800-457-7878 Fax: 989-837-4490
Website: www.northwood.edu
E-mail: miadmit@northwood.edu

Oakland University
2200 N Squirrel Rd, Rochester MI 48309
Eleanor L. Reynolds, Assistant Vice President &
Director of Admissions
248-370-2100
Website: www.oakland.edu
E-mail: ouinfo@oakland.edu

Specs Howard School of Broadcast Arts
19900 W 9 Mile Rd, Southfield MI 48075-3953
Nancy Shiner, Admissions Director
248-358-9000 Fax: 248-746-9772
Website: www.specshoward.edu
E-mail: info@specshoward.edu

University of Michigan-Dearborn
4901 Evergreen Rd, Dearborn MI 48128-1491
The Office of Admissions & Orientation
313-593-5100 Fax: 313-436-9167
Website: www.umd.umich.edu
E-mail: admissions@umd.umich.edu

MINNESOTA

Bethany Lutheran College
700 Luther Dr, Mankato MN 56001
Don Westphal, Dean of Admissions
507-344-7000 Fax: 507-344-7376
Website: www.blc.edu
E-mail: admiss@blc.edu

Gustavus Adolphus College
800 W College Ave, Saint Peter MN 56082-1485
Mark H. Anderson, Dean of Admission
800-GUSTAVUS Fax: 507-933-7474
Website: www.gustavus.edu
E-mail: admission@gustavus.edu

Minneapolis College of Art & Design
2501 Stevens Ave, Minneapolis MN 55404-4347
Admissions Office
800-874-6223 or 612-874-3760 Fax: 612-874-3701
Website: www.mcad.edu
E-mail: admissions@mcad.edu

Minneapolis Community and Technical College
1501 Hennepin Ave, Minneapolis MN 55403-1779
Dena Russell, Director of Admissions
612-659-6282 Fax: 612-659-6210
Website: www.minneapolis.edu
E-mail: admissions.office@minneapolis.edu

Minnesota State Community & Technical College
PO Box 566, Wadena MN 56482-0566
Paul Drange, Director of Admissions
800-247-2007 Fax: 218-631-7901
Website: www.minnesota.edu
E-mail: paul.drange@minnesota.edu

Pillsbury Baptist Bible College
315 S Grove Ave, Owatonna MN 55060-3097
Stephen R. Seidler, Director of Admissions
507-451-2710 Fax: 507-451-0156
Website: www.pillsbury.edu
E-mail: steveseidler@pillsbury.edu

Ridgewater College-Hutchinson Campus
2 Century Ave SE, Hutchinson MN 55350-3100
Dawn Bjork, Counselor
800-222-4424 Fax: 320-231-7767
Website: www.ridgewater.edu
E-mail: dawn.bjork@ridgewater.edu

St. Cloud Technical College
1540 Northway Dr, Saint Cloud MN 56303-1240
Jodi Elness, Director of Enrollment Management
800-222-1009 Fax: 320-308-5981
Website: www.sctc.edu
E-mail: jelness@sctc.edu

MISSISSIPPI

Tougaloo College
500 W County Line Rd, Tougaloo MS 39174-9799
Juno Leggette Jacobs, Director of Admissions
601-977-7768 Fax: 601-977-4501
Website: www.tougaloo.edu
E-mail: jjacobs@tougaloo.edu

MISSOURI

East Central College
1964 Prairie Dell Rd, Union MO 63084
Karen Wieda, Registrar
636-583-5195 ext. 2220 Fax: 636-583-1897
Website: www.eastcentral.edu
E-mail: wiedaks@eastcentral.edu

Lindenwood University
209 S Kingshighway St
Saint Charles MO 63301-1695
Sheryl Guffey, Director of Admissions
636-949-2000 Fax: 636-949-4989
Website: www.lindenwood.edu

Stephens College
PO Box 2121, Columbia MO 65215-0001
David Adams, Dean of Enrollment Management
573-442-2211 Fax: 573-876-7237
Website: www.stephens.edu
E-mail: dadams@stephens.edu

Truman State University
100 E Normal, Kirksville MO 63501
Office of Admission
660-785-4000 Fax: 660-785-4181
Website: admissions.truman.edu
E-mail: admissions@truman.edu

University of Missouri
1 University Blvd, Saint Louis MO 63121-4499
Dr. John Hylton, Dean, Fine Arts & Communication
314-516-5458 Fax: 314-516-6759
Website: www.umsl.edu
E-mail: admissions@umsl.edu

WEBSTER UNIVERSITY
470 E Lockwood Ave, Saint Louis MO 63119-3194
Dr. Debra Carpenter, Dean, School of Communications
Website: www.webster.edu
E-mail: carpenda@webster.edu
800-753-6765 ext. 6924
314-968-7100 Fax: 314-968-7116 (graduate)
314-968-6991 Fax: 314-968-7115 (undergraduate)
   Established 1915. Private. Coed. Accreditation:
NCACS. Tuition: $18,240. Room and board: $7,500. Enrollment: 2,460 full-time, 1,153 part-time. Faculty: 160,
Student-faculty ratio: 15:1. Degrees: BA, BFA, BM,
BMEd, BS, BSN, MA, MBA, MAT, MSN, DMGT. Library:
400,000 volumes. 36 buildings on 45 acres. Nationally
recognized program in communications including film,
video and audio production as well as advertising and
journalism. Students from 40 states and 30 countries.
Beautiful suburban campus in a wooded community of
20,000. Average class size of 15. New 30,000 Sq. ft. library with 24 hour cyber cafe open in 2003. New Residence Halls for 320 additional students open in 2006.
Campuses in four European countries, China and Thailand.

William Woods University
1 University Ave, Fulton MO 65251-1098
Jimmy Clay, Director of Admissions
573-642-2251 Fax: 573-592-1146
Website: www.williamwoods.edu
E-mail: admissions@williamwoods.edu
See listing under "Universities"

NEBRASKA

College of Saint Mary
7000 Mercy Rd, Omaha NE 68106
Lorin Werth,V.P. for Enrollment
800-926-5534 or 402-399-2407 Fax: 402-399-2412
Website: www.csm.edu
E-mail: lwerth@csm.edu

Midland Lutheran College
900 N Clarkson St, Fremont NE 68025-4200
Todd Hansen, Associate Director of Admissions
402-941-6501 Fax: 402-941-6513
Website: www.mlc.edu
E-mail: admissions@mlc.edu

Nebraska Wesleyan University
5000 Saint Paul Ave, Lincoln NE 68504-2794
Patricia Karthauser, V.P. for University Enrollment
402-466-2371 Fax: 402-465-2177
Website: www.nebrwesleyan.edu
E-mail: admissions@nebrwesleyan.edu

University of Nebraska at Kearney
905 W 25th St, Kearney NE 68849-0001
Dusty Newton, Director of Admissions
800-KEARNEY Fax: 308-865-8987
Website: www.unk.edu
E-mail: admissionsug@unk.edu

NEW HAMPSHIRE

Southern New Hampshire University
2500 N River Rd, Hooksett NH 03106-1045
Steve Soba, Director of Admissions
603-645-9611 Fax: 603-645-9693
Website: www.snhu.edu
E-mail: s.soba@snhu.edu

NEW JERSEY

Atlantic Cape Community College
5100 Black Horse Pike
Mays Landing NJ 08330-2699
Linda McLeod, Assistant Director of College
Recruitment
609-343-5000 Fax: 609-343-4921
Website: www.atlantic.edu
E-mail: accadmit@atlantic.edu
See listing under "Community and Junior Colleges"

Bergen Community College
400 Paramus Rd, Paramus NJ 07652
Julian Gomez, Asst. Director of Admissions
201-447-7100 Fax: 201-444-7036
Website: www.bergen.edu
E-mail: jgomez@bergen.edu

Centenary College
400 Jefferson St, Hackettstown NJ 07840-2100
Glenna Warren, Director of Admissions
908-852-1400 Fax: 908-852-3454
Website: www.centenarycollege.edu
E-mail: warreng@centenarycollege.edu

Mercer County Community College
West Windsor Campus
PO Box B, Trenton NJ 08690
Savita Bambhrolia, Director of Admissions
609-586-4800 Fax: 609-587-4666
Website: www.mccc.edu
E-mail: admiss@mccc.edu

New Jersey City University
2039 John F Kennedy Blvd
Jersey City NJ 07305-1588
Carmen Panlilio, Asst. V.P. for Admissions and
Financial Aid
201-200-3234 Fax: 201-200-2044
Website: www.njcu.edu
E-mail: admissions@njcu.edu

Ramapo College of New Jersey
505 Ramapo Valley Rd, Mahwah NJ 07430-1623
Director of Admissions
201-684-7300 or 201-684-7301 Fax: 201-684-7964
Website: www.ramapo.edu
E-mail: admissions@ramapo.edu

NEW YORK

Broome Community College
907 Upper Front St, Binghamton NY 13905
Anthony S. Fiorelli, Director of Admissions
607-778-5001 Fax: 607-778-5442
Website: www.sunybroome.edu
E-mail: fiorelli_a@sunybroome.edu

College of Saint Rose
432 Western Ave, Albany NY 12203-1419
Maryelizabeth Amico, Asst V.P. for Undergraduate
Admissions
518-454-5150 Fax: 518-454-2013
Website: www.strose.edu
E-mail: admit@strose.edu

CUNY Hunter College
695 Park Ave, New York NY 10021
Aaron Gibbs, Assistant Director of Recruitment
212-772-4497 Fax: 212-650-3336
Website: www.hunter.cuny.edu
E-mail: aaron.gibbs@hunter.cuny.edu

FIVE TOWNS COLLEGE
305 N Service Rd, Dix Hills NY 11746-5871
631-424-7000 ext. 2110 Fax: 631-656-2172
Website: www.fivetowns.edu
E-mail: admissions@ftc.edu
See listing under "Universities"

Hilbert College
5200 S Park Ave, Hamburg NY 14075-1597
Timothy Lee, Director of Admissions
716-649-7900 Fax: 716-649-0702
Website: www.hilbert.edu
E-mail: tlee@hilbert.edu

Institute of Audio Research
64 University Pl, New York NY 10003-4595
Mark L. Kahn, Director of Admissions
800-544-2501 or 212-777-8550 (NY, NJ, CT)
Fax: 212-677-6549
Website: www.audioschool.com
E-mail: contact@audioschool.com
See listing under "Career Schools"

Long Island University-C. W. Post Campus
720 Northern Blvd, Brookville NY 11548-1300
Joanne Graziano, Executive Director of Admissions
516-299-2900 Fax: 516-299-2137
Website: www.liu.edu/cwpost
E-mail: enroll@cwpost.liu.edu

Molloy College
1000 Hempstead Ave
Rockville Centre NY 11570-1100
Marguerite Lane, Director of Admissions
516-678-5000 ext. 6291 Fax: 516-256-2247
Website: www.molloy.edu
E-mail: admissions@molloy.edu
See listing under "Universities"

Pratt Institute
200 Willoughby Ave, Brooklyn NY 11205-3899
Heidi Metcalf, Director of Admissions
718-636-3600 Fax: 718-636-3670
Website: www.pratt.edu
E-mail: hmetcalf@pratt.edu

Roberts Wesleyan College
2301 Westside Dr, Rochester NY 14624-1997
Office of Admissions
585-594-6400 Fax: 585-594-6371
Website: www.roberts.edu
E-mail: admissions@roberts.edu

St. John's University
8000 Utopia Pkwy, Queens NY 11439
Office of Admission
718-990-2000 or 888-9-STJOHNS Fax: 718-990-2096
Website: www.stjohns.edu
E-mail: admissions@stjohns.edu
See listing under "Universities"

SUNY College at Brockport
350 New Campus Dr, Brockport NY 14420-2997
Bernard S. Valento, Director of Undergraduate
Admissions
585-395-2751 Fax: 585-395-5452
Website: www.brockport.edu
E-mail: admit@brockport.edu

SUNY Niagara County Community College
3111 Saunders Settlement Rd
Sanborn NY 14132-9487
Kathleen Saunders, Director of Admissions
716-614-6200 Fax: 716-614-6820
Website: www.niagaracc.suny.edu
E-mail: saunders@niagaracc.suny.edu

SUNY Orange County Community College
115 South St, Middletown NY 10940-6437
Margot St. Lawrence, Director of Admissions
845-341-4030 Fax: 845-342-8662
Website: www.sunyorange.edu
E-mail: apply@sunyorange.edu
See listing under "Community and Junior Colleges"

NORTH CAROLINA

Haywood Community College
185 Freedlander Dr, Clyde NC 28721
Debbie Rowland, Coordinator of Admissions
828-627-4500 Fax: 828-627-4513
Website: www.haywood.edu
E-mail: drowland@haywood.edu

Lees-McRae College
PO Box 128, Banner Elk NC 28604-0128
Walt Crutchfield, Dean of Admissions
800-280-4562 Fax: 828-898-8707
Website: www.lmc.edu
E-mail: admissions@lmc.edu

Louisburg College
501 N Main St, Louisburg NC 27549-2399
800-775-0208 or 919-496-2521 Fax: 919-496-1788
Website: www.louisburg.edu
E-mail: admissions@louisburg.edu

Mars Hill College
Mars Hill NC 28754
Chad Holt, Dean of Enrollment
866-MHC-4-YOU Fax: 828-689-1473
Website: www.mhc.edu
E-mail: cholt@mhc.edu

Meredith College
3800 Hillsborough St, Raleigh NC 27607-5298
Heidi L. Fletcher, Director of Admissions
919-760-8581 Fax: 919-760-2348
Website: www.meredith.edu
E-mail: admissions@meredith.edu
See listing under "Women's Colleges"

North Carolina A&T State University
1601 E Market St, Greensboro NC 27411
Lee Young, AVC Enrollment
336-334-7500 Fax: 336-334-7478
Website: www.ncat.edu
E-mail: uadmit@ncat.edu

Salem College
Winston Salem NC 27108
Dana Evans, Dean of Admissions/Fin. Aid
800-32-SALEM Fax: 336-917-5572
Website: www.salem.edu
E-mail: admissions@salem.edu
See listing under "Women's Colleges"

NORTH DAKOTA

Dickinson State University
Dickinson ND 58601-4896
Steve Glasser, Director of Student Recruitment
800-279-4295 Fax: 701-483-2409
Website: www.dickinsonstate.edu
E-mail: dsu.hawks@dickinsonstate.edu

OHIO

Brown Mackie College - Cincinnati
1011 Glendale Milford Rd, Cincinnati OH 45215-1107
Robin Krout, President
513-771-2424 Fax: 513-771-3413
Website: www.brownmackie.edu
E-mail: rkrout@brownmackie.edu

Cleveland State University
2121 Euclid Ave RW 204, Cleveland OH 44115
Dr. Richard Arndt, Dean of Undergraduate Recruitment and College Partnerships
888-CSU-OHIO Fax: 216-687-9210
Website: www.csuohio.edu
E-mail: admissions@csuohio.edu

Franciscan University of Steubenville
University Blvd, Steubenville OH 43952
Margaret J. Weber, Director of Admissions
800-783-6220 or 740-283-6226 Fax: 740-284-5456
Website: www.admissions.edu
E-mail: mweber@franciscan.edu

International College of Broadcasting
6 S Smithville Rd, Dayton OH 45431-1833
J. Michael LeMaster, President
937-258-8251 Fax: 937-258-8714
Website: www.icbcollege.com
E-mail: admissions@icbcollege.com

Mount Vernon Nazarene University
800 Martinsburg Rd, Mount Vernon OH 43050-9509
Timothy Eades, Director of Admissions
866-462-6868 Fax: 740-393-0511
Website: www.gotomvnu.com
E-mail: admissions@mvnu.edu
See listing under "Universities"

OHIO CENTER FOR BROADCASTING
9000 Sweet Valley Dr, Valley View OH 44125-4220
Kathy Wenner, Admissions Director
216-447-9117 Fax: 216-642-9232
Website: www.beonair.com
E-mail: ocb@beonair.com

OHIO NORTHERN UNIVERSITY
525 S Main St, Ada OH 45810-1555
Nils Riess, Chair of the Communication Arts Dept.
419-772-2049
Website: www.onu.edu
E-mail: admissions-ug@onu.edu
See listing under "Universities"

The Ohio State University
School of Journalism and Communication
Derby Hall, 154 N Oval Mall, Columbus OH 43210
614-292-3400 Fax: 614-292-2055
Website: www.comm.ohio-state.edu
E-mail: krichbaum.19@osu.edu

Sinclair Community College
444 W 3rd St, Dayton OH 45402-1460
Sara P. Smith, Director of Outreach Services
937-512-3000 Fax: 937-512-2393
Website: www.sinclair.edu
E-mail: admit@sinclair.edu

United Theological Seminary
4501 Denlinger Rd, Trotwood OH 45426
Betty J. Stutler, Director of Admissions
800-322-5817 Fax: 937-529-2292
Website: www.united.edu
E-mail: admissions@united.edu

University of Dayton
300 College Park, Dayton OH 45469-1300
Robert F. Durkle, Director of Admissions
800-837-7433 Fax: 937-229-4729
Website: admission.udayton.edu
E-mail: admission@udayton.edu

OKLAHOMA

Oklahoma State University
Stillwater OK 74078
Paul Smeyak, Department Head
405-744-6150
Website: www.okstate.edu
E-mail: paul.smeyak@okstate.edu

Oral Roberts University
7777 S Lewis Ave, Tulsa OK 74171-0001
Chris Belcher, Director of Undergraduate Admissions
800-678-8876 Fax: 918-495-6222
Website: www.oru.edu
E-mail: admissions@oru.edu

University of Tulsa
600 S College Ave, Tulsa OK 74104-3126
Earl Johnson, Dean of Admission
918-631-2307 Fax: 918-631-5003
Website: www.utulsa.edu
E-mail: admission@utulsa.edu

OREGON

Cascade College
9101 E Burnside St, Portland OR 97216-1599
800-550-7678 Fax: 503-257-1222
Website: www.cascade.edu
E-mail: admissions@cascade.edu

Linn-Benton Community College
6500 Pacific Blvd SW, Albany OR 97321-3774
Christine Baker, Outreach Coordinator
541-917-4811 Fax: 541-917-4868
Website: www.linnbenton.edu
E-mail: admissions@linnbenton.edu

Marylhurst University
17600 Pacific Hwy (Hwy 43)
Marylhurst OR 97036-0261
Director of Admissions
800-634-9982 ext. 6268 Fax: 503-635-6585
Website: www.marylhurst.edu
E-mail: studentinfo@marylhurst.edu

Pacific University
2043 College Way, Forest Grove OR 97116-1797
Karen M. Dunston, Executive Director of Admissions
800-635-0561 Fax: 503-352-2975
Website: www.pacificu.edu
E-mail: admissions@pacificu.edu

Warner Pacific College
2219 SE 68th Ave, Portland OR 97215-4026
Shannon Mackey, Director of Admissions
503-517-1000 Fax: 503-517-1352
Website: www.warnerpacific.edu
E-mail: admissions@warnerpacific.edu

PENNSYLVANIA

Arcadia University
450 S Easton Rd, Glenside PA 19038-3295
Dennis Nostrand, VP for Enrollment Management
877-ARCADIA (877-272-2342) Fax: 215-881-8767
Website: www.arcadia.edu
E-mail: admiss@arcadia.edu
See listing under "Universities"

ART INSTITUTE OF PITTSBURGH
420 Boulevard Of The Allies, Pittsburgh PA 15219
Newton I. Myvett, VP/Director of Admissions
800-275-2470 Fax: 412-263-6667
Website: www.aip.aii.edu
E-mail: pahughes@aii.edu
See listing under "Universities"

Central Pennsylvania College
College Hill & Valley Rds, Summerdale PA 17093
Katie Bogovic, Admissions Director
800-759-2727 Fax: 717-728-2505
Website: www.centralpenn.edu
E-mail: katie.bogovic@centralpenn.edu

Clarion University of Pennsylvania
840 Wood St, Clarion PA 16214-1232
William Bailey, Dean of Enrollment Management
814-393-2306 Fax: 814-393-2030
Website: www.clarion.edu
E-mail: admissions@clarion.edu

DeSales University
2755 Station Ave, Center Valley PA 18034-9565
610-282-1100 Fax: 610-282-2342
Website: www.desales.edu

Gannon University
109 University Sq, Erie PA 16541-0001
Christopher Tremblay, Director of Admissions
800-GANNON-U Fax: 814-871-5803
Website: www.gannon.edu
E-mail: admissions@gannon.edu

Holy Family University
9801 Frankford Avenue, Philadelphia PA 19114
Lauren Campbell, Director of Admissions
215-637-3050 Fax: 215-281-1022
Website: www.holyfamily.edu
E-mail: admissions@holyfamily.edu

Juniata College
1700 Moore St, Huntingdon PA 16652-2196
Michelle Bartol, Dean of Enrollment
877-JUNIATA Fax: 814-641-3100
Website: www.juniata.edu
E-mail: admissions@juniata.edu

King's College
133 N River St, Wilkes Barre PA 18711-0801
Michelle Lawrence-Schmude, Director of Admission
570-208-5900 Fax: 570-208-5971
Website: www.kings.edu
E-mail: admissions@kings.edu

La Roche College
9000 Babcock Blvd, Pittsburgh PA 15237-5898
Thomas Hassett, Director of Freshman and International Admissions
412-536-1272 or 800-838-4LRC Fax: 412-536-1272
Website: www.laroche.edu
E-mail: admissions@laroche.edu

Lebanon Valley College
101 N College Ave, Annville PA 17003-1400
William Brown, Dean of Admissions & Financial Aid
866-LVC-4ADM or 717-867-6181 Fax: 717-867-6026
Website: www.lvc.edu
E-mail: admission@lvc.edu

Lincoln University
Lincoln University PA 19352
Michael C. Taylor, Director of Admissions
800-790-0191 Fax: 610-932-1209
Website: www.lincoln.edu
E-mail: mtaylor@lu.lincoln.edu

Neumann College
1 Neumann Dr, Aston PA 19014-1298
Dennis Murphy, Director of Admissions
610-459-0905 Fax: 610-558-5652
Website: www.neumann.edu
E-mail: neumann@neumann.edu

University of Pittsburgh
1150 Mount Pleasant Rd
Greensburg PA 15601-5860
Brandi S. Darr, Director of Admissions and Financial Aid
724-836-9880 Fax: 724-836-7160
Website: www.upg.pitt.edu
E-mail: upgadmit@pitt.edu

University of the Arts
320 S Broad St, Philadelphia PA 19102-4994
Susan Gandy, Director of Admissions
800-616-2787 Fax: 215-717-6045
Website: www.uarts.edu
E-mail: admissions@uarts.edu

Westminster College
New Wilmington PA 16172-0001
Doug Swartz, Director of Admissions
724-946-7100 Fax: 724-946-6171
Website: www.westminster.edu
E-mail: swartzdl@westminster.edu

RHODE ISLAND

New England Institute of Technology
2500 Post Rd, Warwick RI 02886-2244
Michael Kwiatkowski, Director of Admissions
401-739-5000 Fax: 401-738-5122
Website: www.neit.edu
E-mail: eflynn@neit.edu

SOUTH CAROLINA

Bob Jones University
1700 Wade Hampton Blvd
Greenville SC 29614-0001
David Christ, Director of Admissions
800-BJ-AND-ME Fax: 800-2-FAX-BJU
Website: www.bju.edu
E-mail: admissions@bju.edu
See listing under "Universities"

Columbia International University
PO Box 3122, Columbia SC 29230-3122
John Basie, Director of University Admissions
800-777-2227 Fax: 803-786-4209
Website: www.ciu.edu
E-mail: yesciu@ciu.edu
See listing under "Theological Studies & Religious Vocations"

North Greenville University
PO Box 1892, Tigerville SC 29688-1892
Dr. Linwood Hagin, Dept. Chair
Website: www.ngc.edu
See listing under "Universities"

University of South Carolina - Upstate
800 University Way, Spartanburg SC 29303-4932
Donette Stewart, Assistant VC for Enrollment Services
864-503-5246 Fax: 864-503-5727
Website: www.uscupstate.edu
E-mail: dstewart@uscupstate.edu
See listing under "Universities"

SOUTH DAKOTA

Presentation College
1500 N Main St, Aberdeen SD 57401-1280
JoEllen Lindner, Dean of Admissions
605-229-8492 Fax: 605-229-8425
Website: www.presentation.edu
E-mail: admit@presentation.edu

TENNESSEE

Draughons Junior College
PO Box 17386, Nashville TN 37217-0386
615-361-7555 Fax: 615-367-2736
Website: www.draughons.edu

Lipscomb University
3901 Granny White Pike, Nashville TN 37204-3951
Ricky Holaway, Director of Admissions
800-333-4358 ext. 1776 Fax: 615-269-1804
Website: www.lipscomb.edu
E-mail: admissions@lipscomb.edu

Tennessee State University
3500 John A Merritt Blvd, Nashville TN 37209-1561
John Cade, Dean of Admissions & Records
615-963-5101 Fax: 615-963-2930
Website: www.tnstate.edu
E-mail: jcade@tnstate.edu

Tusculum College
PO Box 5051, Greeneville TN 37743
Melissa Ripley, Associate Director of Admissions
800-729-0256 Fax: 423-798-1622
Website: www.tusculum.edu
E-mail: mripley@tusculum.edu

University of Tennessee
615 McCallie Ave, Chattanooga TN 37403-2504
Yancy Freeman, Director of Admissions
423-425-4111 Fax: 423-425-4157
Website: www.utc.edu
E-mail: Yancy-Freeman@utc.edu

TEXAS

Angelo State University
ASU Station 11014, San Angelo TX 76909
Bonnie Stennett, Coordinator of Recruiting
800-946-8627 Fax: 325-942-2078
Website: www.angelo.edu
E-mail: admissions@angelo.edu

Galveston College
4015 Avenue Q, Galveston TX 77550-7496
Brian Lowery, Registrar
409-763-6551 Fax: 409-944-1501
Website: www.gc.edu
E-mail: blowery@gc.edu

Northwood University
1114 W FM 1382, Cedar Hill TX 75104-1204
Sylvia Correa, Director of Admissions
800-927-WOOD Fax: 972-291-3824
Website: www.northwood.edu
E-mail: ray@northwood.edu

Our Lady of the Lake University
411 SW 24th St, San Antonio TX 78207-4666
Mary Kay Cooper, Dean of Enrollment
210-434-6711 Fax: 210-431-4013
Website: www.ollusa.edu
E-mail: admission@lakeollusa.edu

Tyler Junior College
PO Box 9020, Tyler TX 75711-9020
Richard Minter, Dean
800-687-5680
Website: www.tjc.edu
E-mail: rmin@tjc.edu
See listing under "Community and Junior Colleges"

University of Houston
122 E Cullen Bldg, Houston TX 77204-2023
Office of Admission
713-743-9595
Website: www.uh.edu
E-mail: admissions@uh.edu

University of St. Thomas
3800 Montrose Blvd, Houston TX 77006-4626
Eduardo Prieto, Director of Admissions
713-522-7911 Fax: 713-525-3558
Website: www.stthom.edu
E-mail: prietoe@stthom.edu

University of Texas at Arlington
Box 19111, Arlington TX 76019-0111
Hans Gatterdam, Director of Admission
817-272-6287 Fax: 817-272-3435
Website: www.uta.edu
E-mail: admissions@uta.edu

VERMONT

NORWICH UNIVERSITY

158 Harmon Dr, Northfield VT 05663
Dr. Bill Estill, Department Head
800-468-6679 Fax: 802-485-2565
Website: www.norwich.edu
E-mail: westill@norwich.edu
See listing under "Universities"

Southern Vermont College
982 Mansion Dr, Bennington VT 05201-6002
Kathleen James Ring, Director of Admissions
800-378-2782 Fax: 802-447-4695
Website: www.svc.edu
E-mail: admis@svc.edu

VIRGINIA

Radford University
PO Box 6903, Radford VA 24142
David W. Kraus, Director of Admissions
800-890-4265 Fax: 540-831-5038
Website: www.radford.edu
E-mail: ruadmiss@radford.edu

Randolph-Macon Woman's College
2500 Rivermont Ave, Lynchburg VA 24503
Patricia LeDonne, Director of Admissions
434-947-8100 Fax: 434-947-8996
Website: www.rmwc.edu
E-mail: admissions@rmwc.edu

WASHINGTON

Gonzaga University
502 E Boone Ave, Spokane WA 99258-0102
Julie McCulloh, Dean of Admission
800-322-2584 or 509-323-6572 Fax: 509-323-5780
Website: www.gonzaga.edu
E-mail: mcculloh@gu.gonzaga.edu

WEST VIRGINIA

Concord University
Athens WV 24712
Michael Curry, Vice President of Financial Aid &
Admissions
888-384-5249 Fax: 304-384-3218
Website: www.concord.edu
E-mail: admissions@concord.edu

Davis & Elkins College
100 Campus Dr, Elkins WV 26241-3996
Renee Heckel, Director of Enrollment Management
800-624-3157 Fax: 304-637-1800
Website: www.davisandelkins.edu
E-mail: admiss@davisandelkins.edu

Fairmont State University
1201 Locust Ave, Fairmont WV 26554-2470
Steve Leadman, Director of Admissions
304-367-4219 or 800-641-5678 Fax: 304-367-4789
Website: www.fairmontstate.edu
E-mail: admit@fairmontstate.edu

West Virginia Wesleyan College
59 College Ave, Buckhannon WV 26201-2699
Robert N. Skinner II, Director of Admission
800-722-9933 Fax: 304-473-8108
Website: www.wvwc.edu
E-mail: admission@wvwc.edu

WISCONSIN

Alverno College
PO Box 343922, Milwaukee WI 53234-3922
Mary Kay Farrell, Director of Admissions
414-382-6100 Fax: 414-382-6354
Website: www.alverno.edu
E-mail: admissions@alverno.edu

Lakeland College
PO Box 359, Sheboygan WI 53082-0359
Nathan Dehne, Director of Admission
920-565-1100 Fax: 920-565-1215
Website: www.lakeland.edu
E-mail: admissions@lakeland.edu

MADISON MEDIA INSTITUTE

2702 Agriculture Dr, Madison WI 53718-6787
Chris Hutchings, Director of Admissions
800-236-4997 or 608-663-2000 Fax: 608-442-0141
Website: www.madisonmedia.com
E-mail: mmi@madisonmedia.com

Marquette University
PO Box 1881, Milwaukee WI 53201-1881
Robert Blust, Director of Admissions
414-288-7302 Fax: 414-288-3764
Website: www.mu.edu
E-mail: admissions@marquette.edu

St. Norbert College
100 Grant St, De Pere WI 54115
Brian Studebaker, Director of Admission
800-236-4878 Fax: 920-403-4072
Website: www.snc.edu
E-mail: admit@snc.edu

WYOMING

Laramie County Community College
1400 E College Dr, Cheyenne WY 82007-3204
Jenny Hargett, Director of Admissions
307-778-5222 Fax: 307-778-1350
Website: www.lccc.wy.edu
E-mail: learnmore@lccc.wy.edu

University of Wyoming
Admissions Office
Dept 3435, Laramie WY 82071-3435
Aaron Appelhans, Contact
800-342-5996 Fax: 307-766-4042
Website: www.uwyo.edu
E-mail: why-wyo@uwyo.edu

GUAM

University of Guam
UOG Station, Mangilao GU 96923
Deborah Leon Guerrero, Registrar
671-735-2201 or 671-735-2208 Fax: 671-735-2203
Website: www.uog.edu
E-mail: admitme@uog9.uog.edu

·COMMUNITY AND JUNIOR COLLEGES

And Career Schools offering an Associate Degree

ALABAMA

Alabama Southern Community College
PO Box 2000, Monroeville AL 36461-2000
334-575-3156

Alabama Southern Community College
PO Box 2000, Thomasville AL 36784
334-636-4429

Bessemer State Technical College
PO Box 308, Bessemer AL 35021-0308
205-428-6391

Bevill State Community College
2631 Temple Ave N, Fayette AL 35555-1198
800-526-5755

Bevill State Community College
PO Box 9, Hamilton AL 35570-0009
205-921-3177

Bevill State Community College
1411 Indiana Ave, Jasper AL 35501-4962
800-777-0372

Bevill State Community College
PO Box 800, Sumiton AL 35148-0800
205-648-3271

Bishop State Community College
1365 Martin Luther King Ave, Mobile AL 36603
334-405-4400

BISHOP STATE COMMUNITY COLLEGE-MAIN

351 N Broad St, Mobile AL 36603-5898
Dr. Terry Hazzard, Dean of Students
251-690-6419 Fax: 251-690-6446
Website: www.bishop.edu
E-mail: thazzard@bishop.edu
Established 1927. Public. Coed. Accreditation: Commission on Colleges of the Southern Association of Colleges and Schools as well as program specific accrediting agencies. Tuition: $1,728. Fees: $432. Enrollment: 2,869 full-time, 2,353 part-time. Faculty: 208. Student-faculty ratio: 25:1. Degrees: Associate in Arts,

Associate in Science, Associate in Applied Science, Associate in Occupational Technologies. Library: 63,304 volumes. 30 buildings. Four convenient locations; flexible class schedules; career opportunities; quality instructors; state-of-the-art facilities; small classes; online courses; off-campus locations; and adult education courses. Financial Aid and Scholarships are available.

CALHOUN COMMUNITY COLLEGE

PO Box 2216, Decatur AL 35609-2216
M. Wayne Tosh, Registrar
256-306-2500 Fax: 256-306-2941
Website: www.calhoun.edu
E-mail: pml@calhoun.edu
Established 1947. Coed. Accredited Member: SACS:CC. Offering AS and AAS degrees. As the largest of the 32 two-year institutions comprising The Alabama College System, Calhoun Community College is an open-admission, community based, state-supported, comprehensive community college dedicated to providing affordable, high-quality and accessible education to individuals in its service area.

Central Alabama Community College
PO Box 699, Alexander City AL 35011-0699
256-234-6346

Chattahoochee Valley Community College
2602 College Dr, Phenix City AL 36869-7960
334-291-4900

Community College of the Air Force
130 W Maxwell Blvd, Montgomery AL 36112
334-953-5033

Enterprise - Ozark Community College
PO Box 1300, Enterprise AL 36331-1300
334-347-2623

Gadsden State Community College
PO Box 227, Gadsden AL 35902-0227
256-549-8200

Gadsden State Community College
Harry M Ayers Campus
1801 Coleman Rd, Anniston AL 36207
256-835-5400

George C. Wallace Community College - Dothan
1141 Wallace Dr, Dothan AL 36303
334-983-3521

George C. Wallace State Community College
PO Box 2530, Selma AL 36702-9985
Dr. Lisa D. Hammons, Director of Admissions
334-876-9227

ITT Technical Institute
6270 Park South Dr, Bessmer AL 35022
205-497-5700

James H. Faulkner State Community College
1900 S US Highway 31, Bay Minette AL 36507-2619
334-580-2100

Jefferson Davis Community College
PO Box 958, Brewton AL 36427-0958
334-867-4832

Jefferson State Community College
2601 Carson Rd, Birmingham AL 35215-3098
205-853-1200

J. F. Drake State Technical College
3421 Meridian St N, Huntsville AL 35811
256-539-8161

J. F. Ingram State Technical College
PO Box 220350, Deatsville AL 36022-0350
334-285-7870

Lawson State Community College
3060 Wilson Rd SW, Birmingham AL 35221-1717
205-925-2515

LBW Community College
MacArthur Campus
PO Box 910, Opp AL 36467
334-493-3573

Lurleen B. Wallace Community College
PO Box 1418, Andalusia AL 36420-1418
Judy Hall, Director of Student Services
334-222-6591 ext. 2271

Marion Military Institute
1101 Washington St, Marion AL 36756
800-MMI-1842

Northeast Alabama Community College
PO Box 159, Rainsville AL 35986-0159
256-638-4418

Northwest-Shoals Community College
PO Box 2545, Muscle Shoals AL 35662-2545
256-331-5200

Prince Institute of Professional Studies
7735 Atlanta Hwy, Montgomery AL 36117-4231
334-271-1670

Reid State Technical College
PO Box 588, Evergreen AL 36401-0588
334-578-1313

Shelton State Community College
9500 Old Greensboro Rd
Tuscaloosa AL 35405-8522
205-759-1541

Snead State Community College
Walnut Rd, Boaz AL 35957
256-593-5120

Southern Community College
PO Box 830688, Tuskegee AL 36083-0688
334-727-5220

Southern Union State Community College
PO Box 1000, Wadley AL 36276-1000
256-395-2211

South University
5355 Vaughn Rd, Montgomery AL 36116-1120
334-395-8800

Trenholm State Technical College
Trenholm Campus
1225 Air Base Blvd, Montgomery AL 36108-3199
Dr. Anthony Molina, President
334-420-4200 Fax: 334-420-4206
Website: www.trenholmtech.cc.al.us
E-mail: amolina@trenholmtech.cc.al.us

Wallace Community College Sparks Campus
PO Drawer 580, Eufaula AL 36072-0580
Jane Boyette, Coordinator Student Affairs
334-687-3543 ext. 4270

Wallace State Community College - Hanceville
PO Box 2000, Hanceville AL 35077-2000
256-352-8000

ALASKA

Ilisagvik College
PO Box 749, Barrow AK 99723
907-852-3333

Kenai Peninsula College
34820 College Dr, Soldotna AK 99669-9732
907-262-0300

Kodiak College
117 Benny Benson Dr, Kodiak AK 99615-6643
907-486-1235

Prince William Sound Community College
PO Box 97, Valdez AK 99686-0097
907-834-1600

University of Alaska Kuskokwim Campus
PO Box 368, Bethel AK 99559-0368
907-543-4500

University of Alaska Matanuska-Susitna
PO Box 2889, Palmer AK 99645-2889
907-745-9712

University of Alaska Northwest Campus
PO Box 400, Nome AK 99762-0400
907-443-2201

University of Alaska Sitka Campus
1332 Seward Ave, Sitka AK 99835-9418
907-747-6653

University of Alaska Southeast-Ketchikan
2600 7th Ave, Ketchikan AK 99901-5728
907-225-6177

ARIZONA

Apollo College
630 W Southern Ave, Mesa AZ 85210-5005
480-831-6585

Apollo College
8503 N 27th Ave, Phoenix AZ 85051-4063
602-864-1571

Apollo College
2701 W Bethany Home Rd, Phoenix AZ 85017-1705
602-433-1333

Apollo College
3550 N Oracle Rd, Tucson AZ 85705
520-888-5885

Arizona Western College
PO Box 929, Yuma AZ 85366-0929
Bryan Doak, Associate Dean for Enrollment Services
928-317-6000

Central Arizona College
273 E US Highway 60, Apache Junction AZ 85219
480-982-7261

Central Arizona College
8470 N Overfield Rd, Coolidge AZ 85228-9779
520-426-4444

Chandler-Gilbert Community College
2626 E Pecos Rd, Chandler AZ 85225-2499
480-732-7000

Cochise College
901 N Colombo Ave, Sierra Vista AZ 85635
Debbie Quick, Director of Admissions
520-515-5412

Coconino Community College
2800 S Lone Tree Rd, Flagstaff AZ 86001-2701
Steve Miller, Director of Admissions
520-527-1222 ext. 302

The Conservatory of Recording Arts & Sciences
2300 E Broadway Rd, Tempe AZ 85282-1707
Tonya Visconti, Director of Admissions
800-562-6383 or 480-858-9400 Fax: 480-829-1332
Website: cras.org
E-mail: info@cras.org
See listing under "Music"

Din College
Tsaile AZ 86556
520-724-3311

Eastern Arizona College
3714 W Church St, Thatcher AZ 85552
928-428-8233

Estrella Mountain Community College
3000 N Dysart Rd, Avondale AZ 85323
623-935-8015

Everest College
10400 N 25th Ave Suite 190, Phoenix AZ 85021-1610
Melissa Agee, Director of Admissions
602-942-4141

GateWay Community College
108 N 40th St, Phoenix AZ 85034-1795
Cathy Gibson, Director of Admissions & Records
602-286-8052

Glendale Community College
6000 W Olive Ave, Glendale AZ 85302-3090
Mary Lou Massal, Sr. Associate Dean, Enrollment Services
623-845-3000

High-Tech Institute
1515 E Indian School Rd, Phoenix AZ 85014-4973
602-279-9700

International Institute of the Americas
925 S Gilbert Rd Ste 201, Mesa AZ 85204-4440
Meredith Kiljan, Director
480-545-8755 Fax: 480-926-1371
Website: www.iia.edu
E-mail: mjensen@iia.edu

International Institute of the Americas
6049 N 43rd Ave, Phoenix AZ 85019-1600
Lynn McConnell, Director
602-242-6265 Fax: 602-589-1353
Website: www.iia.edu
E-mail: lmcconnell@iia.edu

International Institute of the Americas
4136 N 75th Ave Ste 211, Phoenix AZ 85033-3169
Dr. Lori Ebert, Director
623-849-8208 Fax: 623-849-0110
Website: www.iia.edu
E-mail: nsabino@iia.edu

International Institute of the Americas
5441 E 22nd St, Tucson AZ 85710
Leigh Anne Pechota, Director
520-748-9799 Fax: 520-748-9355
Website: www.iia.edu
E-mail: lpechota@iia.edu

Mesa Community College
1833 W Southern Ave, Mesa AZ 85202-4822
480-461-7000

Mohave Community College
1971 E Jagerson Ave, Kingman AZ 86409-1299
520-757-0879

Northland Pioneer College
PO Box 610, Holbrook AZ 86025-0610
520-524-7606

Paradise Valley Community College
18401 N 32nd St, Phoenix AZ 85032-1200
Dr. Shirley Green, Dean, Student Affairs
602-787-7020

Phoenix College
1202 W Thomas Rd, Phoenix AZ 85013-4234
602-264-2492

Pima Community College
4905 E Broadway Blvd, Tucson AZ 85709-1010
Wendy Kilgore, Ph.D., Director of Admissions
520-206-4500 Fax: 520-206-4790
Website: www.pima.edu
E-mail: infocenter@pima.edu

Rio Salado Community College
2323 W 14th St, Tempe AZ 85281-6950
480-517-8000

Scottsdale Community College
9000 E Chaparral Rd, Scottsdale AZ 85250-2699
480-423-6000

South Mountain Community College
7050 S 24th St, Phoenix AZ 85042-5898
602-243-8000

Tohono O'odham Community College
PO Box 3129, Sells AZ 85634
520-383-8401

Yavapai College
1100 E Sheldon St, Prescott AZ 86301-3297
928-445-7300

ARKANSAS

Arkansas Northeastern College
2501 S Division St, Blytheville AR 72315-5111
870-762-1020

Arkansas State University - Beebe
PO Box 1000, Beebe AR 72012-1000
501-882-6452

Arkansas State University - Newport
7648 Victory Blvd, Newport AR 72112
870-512-7800

Cossatot Community College of the University of Arkansas
PO Box 960, De Queen AR 71832-0960
Brenda Morris, Director of Admissions
870-584-4471

Crowley's Ridge College
100 College Dr, Paragould AR 72450-9775
Larry Bills, President
Nancy Joneshill, Director of Admissions
800-264-1096

East Arkansas Community College
1700 Newcastle Rd
Forrest City AR 72335
870-633-4480

Mid-South Community College
2000 W Broadway St, West Memphis AR 72301-3829
870-733-6722

National Park Community College
101 College Dr
Hot Springs National Park AR 71913-9173
501-760-4222

North Arkansas College
1515 Pioneer Ridge Dr, Harrison AR 72601
870-743-3000

Northwest Arkansas Community College
1 College Dr, Bentonville AR 72712-5091
479-636-9222

OUACHITA TECHNICAL COLLEGE
One College Cir, Malvern AR 72104
Linda Johnson, V.P. Student Affairs & Registrar
501-337-5000 ext. 1118 Fax: 501-337-9382
Website: www.otcweb.edu
E-mail: ljohnson@otcweb.edu

Phillips Community College of the University of Arkansas
PO Box 785, Helena AR 72342-0785
Dr. Steven Murray, Chancellor
Lynn Boone, Vice Chancellor for Student Services / Registrar
870-338-6474 Fax: 870-338-7542
Website: www.pccua.edu
E-mail: lboone@pccua.edu

Rich Mountain Community College
1100 College Dr, Mena AR 71953-2500
479-394-7622

South Arkansas Community College
PO Box 7010, El Dorado AR 71731-7010
870-862-8131

Southern Arkansas University Tech
100 Carr Rd, Camden AR 71701
870-574-4500

University of Arkansas at Fort Smith
PO Box 3649, Fort Smith AR 72913-3649
479-788-7000

University of Arkansas Community College at Batesville
PO Box 3350, Batesville AR 72503-3350
Andy Thomas, Director of Admissions
870-793-7581

University of Arkansas Community College at Hope
PO Box 140, Hope AR 71802-0140
Danita Ormand, Director of Enrollment Services
870-777-5722

University of Arkansas Community College at Morrilton
1 Bruce St, Morrilton AR 72110-9601
Susan Dewey, Admissions Counselor
800-264-1094

CALIFORNIA

Allan Hancock College
800 S College Dr, Santa Maria CA 93454-6399
805-922-6966

American River College
4700 College Oak Dr, Sacramento CA 95841-4286
916-484-8011

Antelope Valley College
3041 W Avenue K, Lancaster CA 93536-5426
661-722-6300

Bakersfield College
1801 Panorama Dr, Bakersfield CA 93305-1299
661-395-4301

Bakersfield College
1942 Randolph St, Delano CA 93215-1527
661-725-8020

Barstow Community College
2700 Barstow Rd, Barstow CA 92311-6608
760-252-2411

Berkeley City College
2020 Milvia St, Berkeley CA 94704-1111
510-981-2805

Brooks College
4825 E Pacific Coast Hwy
Long Beach CA 90804-3291
Chelena Adkins, Director of Admissions
562-597-6611

Brooks College
1120 Kifer Rd, Sunnyvale CA 94086-5303
408-328-5700

Butte College
3536 Butte Campus Dr, Oroville CA 95965-8399
530-895-2511

Cabrillo College
6500 Soquel Dr, Aptos CA 95003-3194
831-479-6100

California Culinary Academy
625 Polk St, San Francisco CA 94102-3336
Nancy Seyfert, V.P. of Admissions
800-BAY-CHEF

Canada College
4200 Farm Hill Blvd, Redwood City CA 94061-1099
Michael McPartlin, Dean of Enrollment Services
650-306-3170

Cerritos College
11110 Alondra Blvd, Norwalk CA 90650-6296
562-860-2451

Cerro Coso Community College
3000 College Heights Blvd
Ridgecrest CA 93555-9571
Dr. Mitjl Capet, V.P. of Student Learning
760-384-6100

CHABOT COLLEGE

25555 Hesperian Blvd, Hayward CA 94545-2400
Judy Young, Director of Admissions
510-723-6600 Fax: 510-723-7510
Website: www.chabotcollege.edu
E-mail: ccarcom@clpccd.cc.ca.us

Chaffey College
5885 Haven Ave, Alta Loma CA 91737-9400
909-987-1737

Citrus College
1000 W Foothill Blvd, Glendora CA 91741-1885
626-963-0323

City college of San Francisco
50 Phelan Ave, San Francisco CA 94112-1821
415-239-3000

Coastline Community College
11460 Warner Ave, Fountain Valley CA 92708-2597
714-546-7600

College of Alameda
555 Atlantic Ave, Alameda CA 94501-2109
510-522-7221

College of Marin
835 College Ave, Kentfield CA 94904-2590
415-457-8811

College of Marin
1800 Ignacio Blvd, Novato CA 94949-4900
415-883-2211

College of San Mateo
1700 W Hillsdale Blvd, San Mateo CA 94402-3784
650-574-6161

College of the Canyons
26455 Rockwell Canyon Rd
Santa Clarita CA 91355-1899
661-259-7800

College of the Desert
43500 Monterey Ave, Palm Desert CA 92260-9399
760-346-8041

College of the Sequoias
915 S Mooney Blvd, Visalia CA 93277-2234
559-730-3700

College of the Siskiyous
800 College Ave, Weed CA 96094-2899
530-938-4461

Columbia College
11600 Columbia College Dr, Sonora CA 95370-8580
209-588-5100

Compton Community College
1111 E Artesia Blvd, Compton CA 90221-5393
310-900-1600

Consumnes River College-Eldorado Center
6699 Campus Dr, Placerville CA 95667-7744
530-642-5621

Contra Costa College
2600 Mission Bell Dr, San Pablo CA 94806-3195
510-235-7800

Copper Mountain College
PO Box 1398, Joshua Tree CA 92252-0879
760-366-3791

Cosumnes River College
8401 Center Pkwy, Sacramento CA 95823-5799
916-691-7344

Crafton Hills College
11711 Sand Canyon Rd, Yucaipa CA 92399-1799
Dr. Luis S. Gomez, President
909-389-3200

Cuesta College
PO Box 8106, San Luis Obispo CA 93403-8106
805-546-3100

Cuyamaca College
900 Rancho San Diego Pkwy
El Cajon CA 92019-4369
619-660-4000

Cypress College
9200 Valley View St, Cypress CA 90630-5897
714-484-7000

DeAnza College
21250 Stevens Creek Blvd
Cupertino CA 95014-5793
408-864-5678

Diablo Valley College
321 Golf Club Rd, Pleasant Hill CA 94523-1544
925-685-1230

D-Q University
PO Box 409, Davis CA 95617-0409
530-758-0470

East Los Angeles College
1301 Avenida Cesar Chavez
Monterey Park CA 91754-6001
323-265-8650

El Camino College
16007 Crenshaw Blvd, Torrance CA 90506-0002
310-660-3670

Evergreen Valley College
3095 Yerba Buena Rd, San Jose CA 95135-1598
Archie Sherman, Interim Director of Admissions &
Records
408-274-7900 ext. 6423

Feather River Community College
570 Golden Eagle Ave, Quincy CA 95971-9124
530-283-0202

FIDM/The Fashion Institute of Design & Merchandising
17590 Gillette Ave, Irvine CA 92614
Director of Admissions
949-851-6200 or 888-974-3436 Fax: 949-851-6808
Website: www.fidm.edu
E-mail: info@fidm.com
See listing under "Community and Junior Colleges"

FIDM/THE FASHION INSTITUTE OF DESIGN & MERCHANDISING

919 S Grand Ave, Los Angeles CA 90015-1421
Tonian Hohberg, President
Website: www.fidm.edu
E-mail: info@fidm.com
Three other locations in California (see below)
Established 1969. Private. Coed. Admission open to
high school graduates, GED, and some Ability-to-Benefit
students. Accreditation: WASC and NASAD. Total enrollment 5,500 at four modern campuses located in cosmopolitan West Coast cities. Day, evening and weekend
classes. Some courses are available online. State, Federal and institutional financial aid available. Scholarships.
The college offers Associate Degrees and AA Professional Designation programs in Fashion Design,
Merchandise Marketing, Interior Design, Visual Communications, Graphic Design, Digital Media, Film & TV Costume Design, Merchandise Product Development,
Footwear Design, Beauty Industry Merchandising & Marketing, Textile Design, Theatre Costume Design, International Manufacturing and Product Development, and
Apparel Manufacturing Management. Collegiate level
general studies and ESL access programs available.
Courses are taught by a faculty of over 200 industry
professionals complemented by an active advisory
board of internationally known executives. Unique features of the Institute include specialized libraries and
workrooms, large costume and textile collections, tutoring centers and job placement assistance for part-time
and graduate positions. Internships and complimentary
portfolio evaluation are available.
The Student Housing Office provides resources and
referrals for housing needs, roommate assistance, trans-
portation and community resources. Student activities include clubs for each major, International Student Club
and special parties, dances and social events.
New programs begin every 12 weeks. A Foreign Student Advisor is available. Admissions Advisors assist
with required personal interviews (out-of-state by telephone) and requesting high school transcripts, college
records (if applicable), entrance requirement project and
references.
Tours/interviews:
Los Angeles:
213-624-1201 or 800-624-1200 Fax: 213-624-4799
San Francisco:
415-675-5200 or 800-422-3436 Fax: 415-296-7299
Irvine:
949-851-6200 or 888-974-3436 Fax: 949-851-6808
San Diego:
619-235-2049 or 800-243-3436 Fax: 619-232-4322

FIDM/The Fashion Institute of Design & Merchandising
1010 2nd Ave, San Diego CA 92101-4903
Director of Admissions
619-235-2049 or 800-243-3436 Fax: 619-232-4322
Website: www.fidm.edu
E-mail: info@fidm.com
See listing under "Community and Junior Colleges"

FIDM/The Fashion Institute of Design & Merchandising
55 Stockton St, San Francisco CA 94108-5829
Director of Admissions
415-675-5200 or 800-422-3436 Fax: 415-296-7299
Website: www.fidm.edu
E-mail: info@fidm.com
See listing under "Community and Junior Colleges"

Folsom Lake College
100 Scholar Way, Folsom CA 95630
916-608-6500

Foothill College
12345 S El Monte Rd, Los Altos Hills CA 94022-4597
650-949-7777

FRESNO CITY COLLEGE

1101 E University Ave, Fresno CA 93741-0002
Dayann Dietrich, Contact
559-442-8241 Fax: 559-237-4232
Website: www.fresnocitycollege.com
E-mail: fcc.admissions@scccd.com

Fullerton College
321 E Chapman Ave, Fullerton CA 92832-2011
714-992-7000

Gavilan Community College
5055 Santa Teresa Blvd, Gilroy CA 95020-9599
408-847-1400

Glendale Community College
1500 N Verdugo Rd, Glendale CA 91208-2894
818-240-1000

Golden West College
15744 Goldenwest St
Huntington Beach CA 92647-3197
714-892-7711

Grossmont College
8800 Grossmont College Dr, El Cajon CA 92020-1798
619-644-7000

Hartnell College
156 Homestead Ave, Salinas CA 93901-1697
831-755-6700

HEALD COLLEGE, MILPITAS

341 Great Mall Pkwy, Milpitas CA 95035-8008
Sharon Kitko, Director's Assistant
408-934-4900 Fax: 408-934-7777
Website: www.heald.edu

Imperial Valley College
PO Box 158, Imperial CA 92251-0158
760-352-8320

Irvine Valley College
5500 Irvine Center Dr, Irvine CA 92618-0300
949-451-5100

ITT Technical Institute
525 N Muller St, Anaheim CA 92801-5454
714-535-3700

ITT Technical Institute
2051 Solar Dr Ste 150, Oxnard CA 93030-0641
Claudia Wilroy, Director of Career Services
805-988-0143

ITT Technical Institute
10863 Gold Center Dr
Rancho Cordova CA 95670-6047
916-851-3900

ITT Technical Institute
670 Carnegie Dr, San Bernardino CA 92408-3519
909-889-4600

Lake Tahoe Community College
1 College Dr, South Lake Tahoe CA 96150-4500
530-541-4660

Laney College
900 Fallon St, Oakland CA 94607-4893
510-834-5740

Las Positas College
3033 Collier Canyon Rd, Livermore CA 94551-9797
925-373-5800

Lassen Community College
PO Box 3000, Susanville CA 96130-3000
530-257-6181

Long Beach City College
4901 E Carson St, Long Beach CA 90808-1780
562-938-4111

Los Angeles City College
855 N Vermont Ave, Los Angeles CA 90029-3588
323-953-4000

Los Angeles Harbor College
1111 Figueroa Pl, Wilmington CA 90744-2311
310-522-8200

Los Angeles Mission College
13356 Eldridge Ave, Sylmar CA 91342-3200
818-364-7600

Los Angeles Pierce College
6201 Winnetka Ave, Woodland Hills CA 91371-0001
818-347-0551

Los Angeles Southwest College
1600 W Imperial Hwy, Los Angeles CA 90047-4810
323-241-5225

Los Angeles Trade-Technical College
400 W Washington Blvd
Los Angeles CA 90015-4108
213-744-9058

Los Angeles Valley College
5800 Fulton Ave, Van Nuys CA 91401-4062
818-947-2600

Los Medanos College
2700 E Leland Rd, Pittsburg CA 94565-5197
925-439-2181

Marymount College
30800 Palos Verdes Dr E
Rancho Palos Verdes CA 90275-6299
310-377-5501

Mendocino College
PO Box 3000, Ukiah CA 95482-3000
707-468-3000

Merced College
3600 M St, Merced CA 95348-2898
209-384-6000

Merced College-Los Banos Campus
16570 S Mercey Springs Rd
Los Banos CA 93635-9558

Merritt College
12500 Campus Dr, Oakland CA 94619-3196
510-531-4911

Mira Costa College
1 Barnard Dr, Oceanside CA 92056-3899
760-757-2121

Mission College
3000 Mission College Blvd
Santa Clara CA 95054-1897
408-988-2200

Modesto Junior College
435 College Ave, Modesto CA 95350-5800
209-575-6498

Monterey Peninsula College
980 Fremont Ave, Monterey CA 93940-4799
Rich Montori, Contact
831-645-1376

Moorpark College
7075 Campus Rd, Moorpark CA 93021-1695
805-378-1400

Mt. San Antonio College
1100 N Grand Ave, Walnut CA 91789-1399
909-594-5611

Mt. San Jacinto College
1499 N State St, San Jacinto CA 92583-2399
951-487-6752

MTI College
5221 Madison Ave, Sacramento CA 95841-3003
Marije Miller, Director of Admissions
916-339-1500 Fax: 916-339-0305
Website: www.mticollege.edu
E-mail: mmiller@mticollege.edu

Napa Valley College
2277 Napa Vallejo Hwy, Napa CA 94558-6236
707-253-3076

Ohlone College
PO Box 3909, Fremont CA 94539-0390
510-659-6000

Orange Coast College
PO Box 5005, Costa Mesa CA 92628-5005
Kristin Clark, Director of Admissions
714-432-5773 Fax: 714-432-5736
Website: www.orangecoastcollege.edu
E-mail: kclark@cccd.edu

Oxnard College
4000 S Rose Ave, Oxnard CA 93033-6699
805-986-5800

Palomar College
1140 W Mission Rd, San Marcos CA 92069-1415
760-744-1150

Palo Verde College
1 College Dr, Blythe CA 92225-9561
760-921-5500

Pasadena City College
1570 E Colorado Blvd, Pasadena CA 91106-2041
626-585-7123

Porterville College
100 E College Ave, Porterville CA 93257-6058
559-791-2200

Queen of the Holy Rosary College
43326 Mission Blvd, Fremont CA 94539
510-657-2468

Redwoods Community College
7351 Tompkins Hill Rd, Eureka CA 95501-9300
707-476-4100

Reedley College
995 N Reed Ave, Reedley CA 93654-2099
Leticia Alvarez, Director of Admissions
559-638-3641

Rio Hondo College
3600 Workman Mill Rd, Whittier CA 90601-1699
562-692-0921

Riverside Community College
16130 Lasselle St, Moreno Valley CA 92551
951-571-6100

Riverside Community College
4800 Magnolia Ave, Riverside CA 92506-1293
951-222-8000

Sacramento City College
3835 Freeport Blvd, Sacramento CA 95822-1386
916-558-2111

Saddleback College
28000 Marguerite Pkwy
Mission Viejo CA 92692-3635
949-582-4500

San Bernardino Valley College
701 S Mount Vernon Ave
San Bernardino CA 92410-2798
909-888-6511

San Diego City College
1313 Park Blvd, San Diego CA 92101-4787
619-230-2400

San Diego Mesa College
7250 Mesa College Dr, San Diego CA 92111-4996
858-627-2600

San Diego Miramar College
10440 Black Mountain Rd, San Diego CA 92126-2999
619-388-7800

San Joaquin Delta College
5151 Pacific Ave, Stockton CA 95207-6370
209-954-5151

San Joaquin Valley College
201 New Stine Rd, Bakersfield CA 93309-2659
Jaime Delgado, Enrollment Services Director
661-834-1026 Fax: 559-651-4864
Website: www.sjvc.edu
E-mail: jaime.delgado@sjvc.edu

San Joaquin Valley College
295 E Sierra Ave, Fresno CA 93710-3616
Nora Twarynski, Enrollment Services Director
559-448-8282 Fax: 559-651-4864
Website: www.sjvc.edu
E-mail: nora.twarynski@sjvc.edu

San Joaquin Valley College
1700 McHenry Village Way Suite 6
Modesto CA 95350
Joseph Holt, Director of Admissions
209-527-7582 Fax: 559-651-4864
Website: www.sjvc.edu
E-mail: josephh@sjvc.edu

San Joaquin Valley College
11050 Olson Dr, Rancho Cordova CA 95670
Joseph Holt, Director of Admissions
559-651-2500 Fax: 559-651-4864
Website: www.sjvc.edu
E-mail: joseph.holt@sjvc.edu

San Joaquin Valley College
10641 Church St, Rancho Cucamonga CA 91730
Ramon Abreu, Enrollment Services Director
909-948-7582 Fax: 559-651-4864
Website: www.sjvc.edu
E-mail: ramon.abreu@sjvc.edu

San Joaquin Valley College
8400 W Mineral King Ave, Visalia CA 93291-9283
Susie Topjian, Enrollment Services Director
559-651-2500 Fax: 559-651-4864
Website: www.sjvc.edu
E-mail: susiet@sjvc.edu

San Joaquin Valley College
Fresno Aviation Campus
4985 E Anderson Ave, Fresno CA 93727-1501
Joseph Holt, Director of Admissions
559-453-0123 Fax: 559-651-4864
Website: www.sjvc.edu
E-mail: josephh@sjvc.edu

San Jose City College
2100 Moorpark Ave, San Jose CA 95128-2797
408-298-2181

Santa Ana College
1530 W 17th St, Santa Ana CA 92706-3398
714-564-6000

Santa Barbara Business College
211 S Real Rd, Bakersfield CA 93309-2139
661-835-1100

Santa Barbara City College
721 Cliff Dr, Santa Barbara CA 93109-2394
Patricia E. Canning, Coordinator, School Relations
805-965-0581 ext. 2201

Santa Monica College
1900 Pico Blvd, Santa Monica CA 90405-1644
310-434-4000

Santa Rosa Junior College
680 Sonoma Mountain Pkwy
Petaluma CA 94954-8553
707-778-2415

Santa Rosa Junior College
1501 Mendocino Ave, Santa Rosa CA 95401-4395
Renee LoPilato, Dean of Admissions
707-527-4011

Santiago Canyon College
8045 E Chapman Ave, Orange CA 92869
714-564-4000

Shasta College
PO Box 496006, Redding CA 96049-6006
530-225-4600

Sierra College
5000 Rocklin Rd, Rocklin CA 95677-3397
916-624-3333

Skyline College
3300 College Dr, San Bruno CA 94066-1698
650-738-4100

Solano Community College
4000 Suisun Valley Rd, Fairfield CA 94534-3197
707-864-7000

Southwestern College
900 Otay Lakes Rd, Chula Vista CA 91910-7297
619-421-6700

Taft College
29 Emmons Park Dr, Taft CA 93268-2317
661-763-7700

Ventura College
4667 Telegraph Rd, Ventura CA 93003-3899
805-654-6400

Victor Valley Community College
18422 Bear Valley Rd, Victorville CA 92395-5849
760-245-4271

West Hills Community College
300 W Cherry Ln, Coalinga CA 93210-1399
559-935-0801

West Los Angeles College
4800 Freshman Dr, Culver City CA 90230-3519
310-287-4200

West Valley College
14000 Fruitvale Ave, Saratoga CA 95070-5697
408-867-2200

Wyotech
980 Riverside Pkwy, West Sacramento CA 95605
916-376-8888

Yuba College
2088 N Beale Rd, Marysville CA 95901-7699
Connie Elder, Registrar
530-741-6989

COLORADO

Aims Community College
PO Box 69, Greeley CO 80632-0069
970-330-8008

Arapahoe Community College
5900 S Sante Fe Dr, Littleton CO 80160
Howard Fukaye, Contact
303-797-4ACC (4222)

Blair College
1815 Jet Wing Dr, Colorado Springs CO 80916-2300
719-638-6580

Colorado Mountain College
PO Box 10001, Glenwood Springs CO 81602
800-621-8559

Colorado Mountain College
901 US Highway 24, Leadville CO 80461-9725
800-621-8559

Colorado Mountain College
PO Box 775288, Steamboat Springs CO 80477-5288
800-621-8559

Colorado Northwestern Community College
500 Kennedy Dr, Rangely CO 81648-3502
800-562-1105

Community College of Aurora
16000 E Centretech Pkwy, Aurora CO 80011-9036
303-360-4700 Fax: 303-361-7432
Website: www.ccaurora.edu
E-mail: admissions@ccaurora.edu

Community College of Denver
PO Box 173363, Denver CO 80217-3363
303-556-2600

Denver Automotive & Diesel College
PO Box 9366, Denver CO 80209
Joseph R. Chalupa, College Director
800-347-3232

Front Range Community College
4616 S Shields St, Fort Collins CO 80526-3812
970-226-2500

Front Range Community College
3645 W 112th Ave, Westminster CO 80031-2105
303-466-8811

ITT Technical Institute
500 E 84th Ave, Thornton CO 80229-5328
Veronica Donahue, Director of Admissions
303-288-4488

Lamar Community College
2401 S Main St, Lamar CO 81052-3999
Bette Matkowski, President
719-336-2248

Morgan Community College
17800 County Road 20, Fort Morgan CO 80701
Judy Beckmann, Director of Student Support
800-622-0216

NORTHEASTERN JUNIOR COLLEGE
100 College Ave, Sterling CO 80751-2399
Judy Giacomini, Interim Chief Administrative Officer
Tina Joyce, Director of Admissions
970-521-7000 or 970-521-6752 Fax: 970-521-6801
Website: www.njc.edu
E-mail: tina.joyce@njc.edu

Otero Junior College
1802 Colorado Ave, La Junta CO 81050-3346
719-384-6831

Pikes Peak Community College
5675 S Academy Blvd
Colorado Springs CO 80906-5498
719-576-7711

Platt College
3100 S Parker Rd, Aurora CO 80014-3141
Jerald B. Sirbu, President
303-369-5151

Pueblo Community College
900 W Orman Ave, Pueblo CO 81004-1499
719-549-3200

Red Rocks Community College
13300 W 6th Ave, Lakewood CO 80228-1255
303-988-6160

Trinidad State Junior College
600 Prospect St, Trinidad CO 81082-2396
719-846-5621

CONNECTICUT

Asnuntuck Community College
170 Elm St, Enfield CT 06082-3873
Donna Shaw, Director of Admissions / Marketing
860-253-3010

Briarwood College
2279 Mount Vernon Rd, Southington CT 06489-1057
860-628-4751

Capital Community College
950 Main St, Hartford CT 06103-1211
860-906-5000

Gateway Community College
60 Sargent Dr, New Haven CT 06511-5918
203-789-7071

Gibbs College
10 Norden Pl, Norwalk CT 06855-1436
Eddie Prosper, Director of Admissions
800-845-5333

Hartford College for Women
1265 Asylum Ave, Hartford CT 06105-2299
860-236-1215

Housatonic Community College
900 Lafayette Blvd, Bridgeport CT 06604
203-332-5000

Manchester Community College
PO Box 1046, Manchester CT 06045-1046
860-647-6000

Middlesex Community College
100 Training Hill Rd, Middletown CT 06457-4889
Mensimah Shabazz, Director of Admissions
860-343-5800 Fax: 860-344-3055
Website: www.mxcc.commnet.edu
E-mail: mshabazz@mxcc.commnet.edu

Mitchell College
437 Pequot Ave, New London CT 06320-4498
860-701-5000

Naugatuck Valley Community College
750 Chase Pkwy, Waterbury CT 06708-3089
203-575-8040

Northwestern Connecticut Community-Technical College
2 Park Pl, Winsted CT 06098-1706
860-738-6300

Norwalk Community College
188 Richards Ave, Norwalk CT 06854-1634
203-857-7000

Quinebaug Valley Community College
742 Upper Maple St, Danielson CT 06239-1440
860-774-1160

St. Vincent's College
2800 Main St, Bridgeport CT 06606-4292
Director of Admissions
203-576-5513

Three Rivers Community Technical College
574 New London Tpke, Norwich CT 06360-6500
860-823-2845

Three Rivers Community Technical College
Mahan Dr, Norwich CT 06360
860-886-0177

Tunxis Community College
271 Scott Swamp Rd, Farmington CT 06032-3187
860-677-7701

DELAWARE

Delaware Technical & Community College
100 Campus Dr, Dover DE 19904-1383
302-857-1000

Delaware Technical & Community College
PO Box 610, Georgetown DE 19947-0610
302-856-5400

Delaware Technical & Community College
400 Stanton Christiana Rd, Newark DE 19713-2197
302-454-3900

Delaware Technical & Community College
333 N Shipley St, Wilmington DE 19801-2499
302-571-5474

FLORIDA

ATI College of Health
1395 NW 167th St Ste 200, Miami FL 33169-5742
305-628-1000

Brevard Community College
1519 Clearlake Rd, Cocoa FL 32922-6597
321-632-1111

Broward Community College
225 E Las Olas Blvd, Fort Lauderdale FL 33301-2298
954-475-6500

Broward Community College-North Campus
1000 Coconut Creek Blvd
Coconut Creek FL 33066-1697
954-972-9100

Broward Community College-South Campus
7200 Pines Blvd, Pembroke Pines FL 33024-7299
954-963-8835

Central Florida Community College
PO Box 1388, Ocala FL 34478-1388
352-854-2322

Chipola College
3094 Indian Cir, Marianna FL 32446-3065
850-526-2761

City College
2400 SW 13th St, Gainesville FL 32608-2000
352-335-4000

City College
9300 S Dadeland Blvd Suite PH, Miami FL 33156
305-666-9242

Daytona Beach Community College
PO Box 2811, Daytona Beach FL 32120-2811
Tom LoBasso, Dean of Enrollment/Development
386-255-8131

Florida College
119 N Glen Arven Ave
Temple Terrace FL 33617-5578
813-988-5131

Florida Community College
Downtown Campus
101 W State St, Jacksonville FL 32202-3099
904-633-8100

Florida Community College
Kent Campus
3939 Roosevelt Blvd, Jacksonville FL 32205-8997
904-381-3400

Florida Community College
North Campus
4501 Capper Rd, Jacksonville FL 32218-4436
904-766-6500

Florida Community College
South Campus
11901 Beach Blvd, Jacksonville FL 32246-6624
904-646-2111

Florida Keys Community College
5901 College Rd, Key West FL 33040-4397
Cheryl Malsheimer, Director of Admissions & Records
305-296-9081 ext. 495

Florida Metropolitan University-Lakeland Campus
995 E Memorial Blvd Ste 110
Lakeland FL 33801-1973
Jodi De La Garza, Director of Admissions
863-686-1444

Florida National College
Hialeah Campus
4425 W 20th Ave, Hialeah FL 33012
Jorge Afonso, Campus Dean
305-821-3333 ext. 1022 Fax: 305-362-0595
Website: www.fnc.edu
E-mail: omarsnc@fnc.edu

Florida National College
South Campus
11865 SW 26th St, Miami FL 33175
Jon Beisenherz, Campus Dean
305-266-9999
Website: www.fnc.edu
E-mail: omarsnc@fnc.edu

Florida Technical College
1199 S Woodland Blvd, De Land FL 32720-7767
386-734-3303

Florida Technical College
12689 Challenger Pkwy # 130
Orlando FL 32826-2707
Timothy Vogeley, Dean
407-678-5600

Full Sail - Real World Education
3300 University Blvd, Winter Park FL 32792
Chuck Weiss, Contact
407-679-6333

Gulf Coast Community College
5230 W Highway 98, Panama City FL 32401-1058
850-769-1551

Hillsborough Community College
1206 N Park Rd, Plant City FL 33563-1540
813-757-2100

Hillsborough Community College
1404 Tech Blvd, Tampa FL 33619-7865
813-253-7000

Hillsborough Community College
PO Box 30030, Tampa FL 33630-3030
813-253-7000

Hillsborough Community College
Ybor City Campus
PO Box 5096, Tampa FL 33675-5096
813-253-7601

Indian River Community College
3209 Virginia Ave, Fort Pierce FL 34981-5596
772-462-4700

ITT Technical Institute
3401 S University Dr, Davie FL 33328-2021
Darren Frost, Director of Recruitment
954-476-9300

ITT Technical Institute
7955 NW 12th St, Doral FL 33126-1823
305-477-3080

ITT Technical Institute
6600 Youngerman Cir Ste 10
Jacksonville FL 32244-6630
904-573-9100

ITT Technical Institute
1400 S International Pkwy, Lake Mary FL 32746-1607
407-660-2900

Keiser College
1800 Business Park Blvd, Daytona Beach FL 32114
Matt McEnany, Vice President
386-274-5060 Fax: 386-274-2725
Website: www.keisercollege.edu
E-mail: mmcenany@keisercollege.edu

Keiser College
1500 NW 49th St, Fort Lauderdale FL 33309-3700
Anne O'Connell, Director Community Relations
954-776-4456

Keiser College
3515 Aviation Dr, Lakeland FL 33811
John Mathias, Campus Director
863-701-7789

Keiser College
900 S Babcock St, Melbourne FL 32901-1461
321-255-2255

KEISER COLLEGE

5600 Lake Underhill Rd, Orlando FL 32807
Vicki Maurer, Director of Admissions
407-273-5800 Fax: 407-381-1233
Website: www.keisercollege.edu
E-mail: vmaurer@keisercollege.edu

Keiser College
6151 Lake Osprey Dr, Sarasota FL 34240-8441
Richard A. Rodman, Director of Admissions
941-907-3900

Keiser College
1700 Halstead Blvd, Tallahassee FL 32309-3489
James Wallis, Director of Admissions
850-906-9494

Lake City Community College
149 SE College Pl, Lake City FL 32025
386-752-1822

Lake-Sumter Community College
9501 US Highway 441, Leesburg FL 34788-8751
352-787-3747

Manatee Community College
5840 26th St W, Bradenton FL 34207-3596
941-752-5000

MedVance Institute
1630 S Congress Ave, Palm Springs FL 33461
561-304-3466

Miami-Dade College
300 NE 2nd Ave, Miami FL 33132-2296
305-237-3316

Miami-Dade Community College
11380 NW 27th Ave, Miami FL 33167-3495
305-237-1245

Miami-Dade Community College
11011 SW 104th St, Miami FL 33176-3393
305-237-2000

Miami-Dade Community College
Medical Center Campus
950 NW 20th St, Miami FL 33127-4693
305-347-4101

New England Institute of Technology
2410 Metrocentre Blvd
West Palm Beach FL 33407-3105
Michael Schwam, Director of Admissions
561-688-2001

North Florida Community College
1000 Turner Davis Dr, Madison FL 32340-1602
850-973-2288

Okaloosa-Walton College
100 College Blvd E, Niceville FL 32578-1347
850-678-5111

Palm Beach Community College
4200 S Congress Ave, Lake Worth FL 33461-4796
561-439-8000

Pasco-Hernando Community College
11415 Ponce De Leon Blvd
Brooksville FL 34601-8698
352-796-6726

Pasco-Hernando Community College
34727 Blanton Rd, Dade City FL 33523-6283
352-567-6701

Pasco-Hernando Community College
10230 Ridge Rd, New Port Richey FL 34654-5129
727-847-2727

Pensacola Junior College
1000 College Blvd, Pensacola FL 32504-8998
850-484-1000

Polk Community College
999 Avenue H NE, Winter Haven FL 33881-4299
863-297-1000

St. John's River Community College
5001 Saint Johns Ave, Palatka FL 32177-3807
386-312-4200

St. Petersburg College
PO Box 13489, Saint Petersburg FL 33733-3489
727-341-3600

St. Petersburg College
600 Klosterman Rd, Tarpon Springs FL 34689-1299
727-791-2400

Santa Fe Community College
3000 NW 83rd St, Gainesville FL 32606-6200
Jackson N. Sasser, President
352-395-5787 Fax: 352-395-4118
Website: www.sfcc.edu
E-mail: ouida.mcneil@sfcc.edu

Seminole Community College
100 Weldon Blvd, Sanford FL 32773-6199
407-328-4722

South Florida Community College
600 W College Dr, Avon Park FL 33825-9356
863-453-6661

SOUTHWEST FLORIDA COLLEGE

1685 Medical Ln, Fort Myers FL 33907-1157
866-SWFC-NOW or 239-939-4766 Fax: 239-936-4040
Website: www.swfc.edu
E-mail: studentinfo@swfc.edu

Tallahassee Community College
444 Appleyard Dr, Tallahassee FL 32304-2895
850-201-8595

Valencia Community College
PO Box 3028, Orlando FL 32802-3028
407-299-5000

Valencia Community College East Campus
701 N Econlockhatchee Trl, Orlando FL 32825-6404
407-299-5000

Webster College
2127 Grand Blvd, Holiday FL 34690-4554
727-942-0069

Webster College
2221 SW 19th Avenue Rd, Ocala FL 34474-4073
Todd A. Matthews, Sr., Executive Director
352-629-1941

GEORGIA

Abraham Baldwin Agriculture College
2802 Moore Highway, Tifton GA 31793
229-391-5000

Andrew College
413 College St, Cuthbert GA 39840
E. Dean Sims, Director of Admissions
229-732-2171

Athens Technical College
800 Highway 29 N, Athens GA 30601-1546
706-355-5000

Atlanta Institute of Music
5985 Financial Dr #200, Norcross GA 30071-2950
770-242-7717

Atlanta Metro College
1630 Metropolitan Pkwy SW, Atlanta GA 30310-4498
404-756-4000

Augusta Technical College
3116 Deans Bridge Rd, Augusta GA 30906-3399
706-771-4000

Bainbridge College
2500 E Shotwell St, Bainbridge GA 39819-8409
229-248-2500

Bauder College
384 Northyards Blvd NW Ste 190
Atlanta GA 30313-2439
Terri A. Holte, Director of Admissions
404-237-7573

Brown Mackie College - Atlanta
6600 Peachtree Dunwoody NE, Atlanta GA 30328
770-638-0121

Chattahoochee Technical College
980 S Cobb Dr SE, Marietta GA 30060-3300
Nichole H. Kennedy, Director of Admissions
770-528-4465

Coastal Georgia Community College
3700 Altama Ave, Brunswick GA 31520-3632
912-264-7235

Columbus Technical College
928 Manchester Expressway
Columbus GA 31904-6577
706-649-1837

Dalton State College
213 College Dr, Dalton GA 30720-3745
706-272-4436

Darton College
2400 Gillionville Rd, Albany GA 31707-3098
229-430-6000

DeKalb Technical College
495 N Indian Creek Dr, Clarkston GA 30021-2397
Terry Richardson, Director of Admissions
404-297-9522 Fax: 404-294-6496
Website: www.dekalbtech.edu
E-mail: richardt@dekalbtech.edu

East Georgia College
131 College Cir, Swainsboro GA 30401
478-289-2000

Gainesville College
PO Box 1358, Gainesville GA 30503-1358
770-718-3639

Georgia Highlands College
PO Box 1864, Rome GA 30162-1864
706-802-5000

Georgia Military College
201 E Greene St, Milledgeville GA 31061-3398
478-445-2700

Georgia Perimeter College
555 N Indian Creek Dr, Clarkston GA 30021-2396
404-299-4561

Georgia Perimeter College
3251 Panthersville Rd, Decatur GA 30034
404-244-5090

Gordon College
419 College Dr, Barnesville GA 30204-1762
Dr. Katrina Tobin, Director of Enrollment Services
770-358-5021

Gupton-Jones College of Funeral Service
5141 Snapfinger Woods Dr, Decatur GA 30035-4022
Patty S. Hutcheson, President
770-593-2257 Fax: 770-593-1891
Website: www.gupton-jones.edu
E-mail: gjcfs@mindspring.com

Gwinnett Technical College
5150 Sugarloaf Pkwy, Lawrenceville GA 30043-5702
770-962-7580

Lanier Technical College
2990 Landrum Education Dr
Oakwood GA 30566-3405
Michael C. Marlowe, Director of Admissions
770-531-6328

Macon State College
100 College Station Dr, Macon GA 31206-5145
478-471-2700

Middle Georgia College
1100 2nd St SE, Cochran GA 31014-1564
478-934-6221

Northwestern Technical College
265 Bicentennial Trl, Rock Spring GA 30739-2306
Dr. Ray Brooks, President
Greg Cross, Vice President for Student Services
706-764-3518

South Georgia College
100 College Park Dr W, Douglas GA 31533-5020
912-389-4231

Truett McConnell College
100 Alumni Dr, Cleveland GA 30528-1264
706-865-2134

Waycross College
2100 S Georgia Pkwy W, Waycross GA 31503-0154
912-285-6133

Young Harris College
PO Box 98, Young Harris GA 30582-0098
706-379-3111

HAWAII

Hawaii Community College
200 W Kawili St, Hilo HI 96720-4075
808-974-7311

HAWAII TOKAI INTERNATIONAL COLLEGE

2241 Kapiolani Blvd, Honolulu HI 96826-4310
Derrick Kerr, Director of Student Services
808-983-4154 Fax: 808-983-4107
Website: www.tokai.edu/htic
E-mail: htic@tokai.edu

Heald College, Honolulu
1500 Kapiolani Blvd, Honolulu HI 96814-3732
Lon K. Ibaraki, Director of Admissions
808-955-1500 or 800-940-0530 Fax: 808-955-6964
Website: www.heald.edu
E-mail: lon_ibaraki@heald.edu

Honolulu Community College
874 Dillingham Blvd, Honolulu HI 96817-4598
808-845-9211

Kapiolani Community College
4303 Diamond Head Rd, Honolulu HI 96816-4496
808-734-9111

Kauai Community College
3-1901 Kaumualii Hwy, Lihue HI 96766-9500
808-245-8225 Fax: 808-245-8297
Website: kauai.hawaii.edu
E-mail: arkauai@hawaii.edu

Leeward Community College
96-045 Ala Ike St, Pearl City HI 96782-3393
808-455-0011

Maui Community College
310 W Kaahumanu Ave, Kahului HI 96732-1617
808-244-9181

TransPacific Hawaii College
5257 Kalanianaole Hwy, Honolulu HI 96821
John Norris, President
808-377-5402

Windward Community College
45-720 Keaahala Rd, Kaneohe HI 96744-3598
808-235-7400

IDAHO

College of Southern Idaho
PO Box 1238, Twin Falls ID 83303-1238
208-733-9554

Eastern Idaho Technical College
1600 S 25th E, Idaho Falls ID 83404
208-524-3000

ITT Technical Institute
12302 W Explorer Dr, Boise ID 83713-1569
208-322-8844

North Idaho College
1000 W Garden Ave, Coeur d Alene ID 83814-2199
208-769-3300

ILLINOIS

Black Hawk College
1501 State Highway 78, Kewanee IL 61443-8630
309-852-5671

Black Hawk College
6600 34th Ave, Moline IL 61265-5899
309-796-5000

Career College of Chicago
11 E Adams St, Chicago IL 60603-6301
312-895-6300

Carl Sandburg College
2232 S Lake Storey Rd, Galesburg IL 61401-9576
309-344-2518

College of DuPage
425 22nd St, Glen Ellyn IL 60137-6599
630-942-2800

College of Lake County
19351 W Washington St, Grayslake IL 60030-1148
847-223-6601

Danville Area Community College
2000 E Main St, Danville IL 61832-5118
217-443-3222

Elgin Community College
1700 Spartan Dr, Elgin IL 60123-7193
847-214-7385

Frontier Community College
RR 1, Fairfield IL 62837-9801
618-842-3711

Gem City College
700 State St, Quincy IL 62301
217-222-0391

Harold S. Washington College
30 E Lake St, Chicago IL 60601-2403
312-553-5600

Harry S. Truman College
1145 W Wilson Ave, Chicago IL 60640-5691
773-878-1700

Heartland Community College
1500 W Raab Rd, Normal IL 61761-9446
309-827-0500

Highland Community College
2998 W Pearl City Rd, Freeport IL 61032-9341
815-235-6121

Illinois Central College
1 College Dr, Peoria IL 61635-0002
309-694-5011

Illinois Valley Community College
815 N Orlando Smith St, Oglesby IL 61348-9692
815-224-2720

ITT Technical Institute
1401 Feehanville Dr, Mount Prospect IL 60056-6005
847-375-8800

John A. Logan College
700 Logan College Rd, Carterville IL 62918
Terry Crain, Associate Dean Student Services
618-985-3741

John Wood Community College
150 S 48th St, Quincy IL 62305-0400
217-224-6500

Joliet Junior College
1216 Houbolt Rd, Joliet IL 60431-8311
815-729-9020

Kankakee Community College
PO Box 888, Kankakee IL 60901-0888
815-933-0345

Kaskaskia College
27210 College Rd, Centralia IL 62801-7878
Tyra Taylor, Dean of Enrollment Management and
Retention Services
618-545-3000 Fax: 618-532-1990
Website: www.kaskaskia.edu
E-mail: ttaylor@kaskaskia.edu

Kennedy-King College
6800 S Wentworth Ave, Chicago IL 60621-3798
773-602-5000

Kishwaukee College
21193 Malta Rd, Malta IL 60150-9699
815-825-2086

Lake Land College
5001 Lake Land Blvd, Mattoon IL 61938-9366
217-234-5253

Lewis & Clark Community College
5800 Godfrey Rd, Godfrey IL 62035-2426
618-466-3411

Lincoln College
300 Keokuk St, Lincoln IL 62656-1699
Stacy Rachel, Director of Enrollment Management
800-569-0556

Lincoln Land Community College
5250 Shepherd Rd, Springfield IL 62703-5408
217-786-2200

Lincoln Trail College
11220 State Highway 1, Robinson IL 62454
618-544-8657

MACCORMAC COLLEGE

29 E Madison St, Chicago IL 60602-4405
David F. Grassi, Associate Dean, Admissions
312-922-1884 ext. 101 Fax: 312-922-4328
Website: www.maccormac.edu
E-mail: dgrassi@maccormac.edu

Malcolm X College
1900 W Van Buren St, Chicago IL 60612-3197
312-850-7031

McHenry County College
8900 US Highway 14, Crystal Lake IL 60012-2761
815-455-3700

Moraine Valley Community College
10900 S 88th Ave, Palos Hills IL 60465-0937
708-974-4300

MORRISON INSTITUTE OF TECHNOLOGY

701 Portland Ave, Morrison IL 61270-2959
Richard C. Parkinson, Interim Director
815-772-7584 Fax: 815-772-7218
Website: www.morrison.tec.il.us
E-mail: admissions@morrison.tec.il.us
    Private. Coed. Accreditation: ABET. Enrollment: 140. Student-faculty ratio: 13:1. Engineering Technology Associate of Applied Science degree in Architectural, Construction, Civil, Mechanical, Drafting & Design, and Surveying Technology. AAS degree in Systems & Network Administration.

Morton College
3801 S Central Ave, Cicero IL 60804-4398
708-656-8000

Northwestern Business College
7725 S Harlem Ave, Bridgeview IL 60455-1318
800-682-9113

Northwestern Business College
4829 N Lipps Ave, Chicago IL 60630-2298
Mark Sliz, Director of Admissions
773-777-4220

Oakton Community College
1600 E Golf Rd, Des Plaines IL 60016-1256
David Cole, Director of Enrollment Management
847-635-1600

Olive-Harvey College
10001 S Woodlawn Ave, Chicago IL 60628-1696
773-291-6100

Olney Central College
305 N West St, Olney IL 62450-1099
618-395-7777

Parkland College
2400 W Bradley Ave, Champaign IL 61821-1899
Mike Henry, Contact
217-351-2208

Prairie State College
202 S Halsted St, Chicago Heights IL 60411-8226
708-709-3500

Rend Lake College
RR 1, Ina IL 62846-9801
618-437-5321

Richard J. Daley College
7500 S Pulaski Rd, Chicago IL 60652-1299
773-838-7500

Richland Community College
1 College Park, Decatur IL 62521-8513
217-875-7200

Rock Valley College
3301 N Mulford Rd, Rockford IL 61114-5699
815-654-4250

St. Augustine College
1333 W Argyle St, Chicago IL 60640-3593
773-878-8756

Sauk Valley Community College
173 Illinois Route 2, Dixon IL 61021
815-288-5511

Shawnee Community College
8364 Shawnee College Rd, Ullin IL 62992
618-634-2242

Southeastern Illinois College
3575 College Rd, Harrisburg IL 62946-4925
618-252-6376

South Suburban College of Cook County
15800 State St, South Holland IL 60473
Jane Ellen Stocker, Dean of Enrollment Services
708-596-2000 Fax: 708-225-5806
Website: www.southsuburbancollege.edu
E-mail: jstocker@southsuburbancollege.edu

Southwestern Illinois College
2500 Carlyle Ave, Belleville IL 62221-5899
618-235-2700

Spoon River College
23235 N County Road 22, Canton IL 61520
309-647-4645

Springfield College in Illinois
1500 N 5th St, Springfield IL 62702-2643
217-525-1420

TRITON COLLEGE

2000 5th Ave, River Grove IL 60171-1995
Mary-Rita Moore, Dean of Enrollment Services
708-456-0300 ext. 3130 Fax: 708-583-3147
Website: www.triton.edu
E-mail: triton@triton.edu
    Established 1964. Coed. Tuition: $56.00 per semester hour. Est. total yearly exp.: $1,600 for in district students. Enrollment: 19,000. Faculty: 600. Degrees: AA, AAS, AES, AS, AFA. Library: 81,000 volumes. 18 buildings on 100+ acres. Training offered in over 84 career fields. University transfer program, pre-professional, liberal arts courses offered day, evening, and online. State and federal financial programs available. Strong athletic program with excellent facilities. Rolling admissions.

Wabash Valley College
2200 College Dr, Mount Carmel IL 62863-2657
618-262-8641

Waubonsee Community College
Route 47 at Waubonsee Dr, Sugar Grove IL 60554
630-466-7900

Wilbur Wright College North
4300 N Narragansett Ave, Chicago IL 60634-1591
773-777-7900

William Rainey Harper College
1200 W Algonquin Rd, Palatine IL 60067-7373
847-925-6000

INDIANA

Ancilla Domini College
Donaldson IN 46513
Erin Wittmeyer, Director of Admissions
574-936-8898 Fax: 574-935-1773
Website: www.ancilla.edu
E-mail: erin.wittmeyer@ancilla.edu

Brown Mackie College - Fort Wayne
3000 E Coliseum Blvd, Fort Wayne IN 46805
Daniel Summer, Campus President
260-484-4400 Fax: 260-484-2678
Website: www.brownmackie.edu

Brown Mackie College - Merrillville
1000 E 80th Pl Ste 101N, Merrillville IN 46410-5644
219-769-3321

Brown Mackie College - Michigan City
325 E US Highway 20, Michigan City IN 46360-7362
219-877-3100

Brown Mackie College - South Bend
1030 E Jefferson Blvd, South Bend IN 46617-3123
Connie Adelman, Campus President
574-237-0774 Fax: 574-237-3585
Website: www.brownmackie.edu

Community College of Indiana - Valparaiso
2401 Valley Dr, Valparaiso IN 46383-2520
219-464-8514

Davenport College of Business
7121 Grape Rd, Granger IN 46530-9069
574-277-8447

Indiana Business College Northwest
6300 Technology Dr, Indianapolis IN 46278
317-873-6500

International Business College
7205 Shadeland Station Way
Indianapolis IN 46256-3954
317-841-6400

ITT Technical Institute
2810 Dupont Commerce Ct, Fort Wayne IN 46825
260-497-6200

ITT Technical Institute
10999 Stahl Rd, Newburgh IN 47630-7430
Thomas G. Campbell Jr., Director of Admissions
812-858-1600

Ivy Tech Community College-Central Indiana
1 W 26th St, Indianapolis IN 46208-4777
317-921-4882

Ivy Tech Community College - North Central
220 Dean Johnson Blvd, South Bend IN 46601-3415
Pam Decker, Director of Admissions
574-289-7001 Fax: 574-236-7177
Website: www.ivytech.edu
E-mail: pdecker@ivytech.edu

Ivy Tech Community College of Indiana - Columbus
4475 Central Ave, Columbus IN 47203-1868
812-372-9925

Ivy Tech Community College of Indiana - Southern
Indiana
8204 Highway 311, Sellersburg IN 47172-1829
812-246-3301

Ivy Tech State College
104 W 53rd St, Anderson IN 46013
765-643-7133

Mid-America College of Funeral Service
3111 Hamburg Pike, Jeffersonville IN 47130-9630
812-288-8878

Vincennes University
1002 N 1st St, Vincennes IN 47591-1504
Chris M. Crews, Director of Admission
812-888-4313

IOWA

AIB College of Business
2500 Fleur Dr, Des Moines IA 50321-1799
800-444-1921 Fax: 515-244-6773
Website: www.aib.edu
E-mail: admissions@aib.edu

Clinton Community College
1000 Lincoln Blvd, Clinton IA 52732-6299
563-244-7000

Des Moines Area Community College
600 N 2nd Ave W, Newton IA 50208-3049
641-791-3622

Des Moines Area Community College
Ankeny Campus
2006 S Ankeny Blvd, Ankeny IA 50023-8995
515-964-6200

Des Moines Area Community College
Boone Campus
1125 Hancock Dr, Boone IA 50036-5326
515-432-7203

Des Moines Area Community College
Carroll Campus
906 N Grant Rd, Carroll IA 51401-2525
712-792-1755

Des Moines Area Community College
Urban Campus
1100 7th St, Des Moines IA 50314-2503
515-244-4226

Ellsworth Community College
1100 College Ave, Iowa Falls IA 50126-1199
Annie Stelow, Admissions
800-322-9235

Hawkeye Community College
1501 E Orange Rd, Waterloo IA 50704
Molly Quinn, Director of Admissions
800-670-4769

Indian Hills Community College
721 N 1st St, Centerville IA 52544-1200
641-856-2143

Indian Hills Community College
525 Grandview Ave, Ottumwa IA 52501-1398
641-683-5111

Iowa Central Community College
316 NW 3rd St, Eagle Grove IA 50533-1399
515-448-4723

Iowa Central Community College
330 Avenue M, Fort Dodge IA 50501-5798
515-576-7201

Iowa Central Community College
916 Russell St, Storm Lake IA 50588-2018
712-732-2991

Iowa Central Community College
1725 Beach St, Webster City IA 50595-2699
515-832-1632

Iowa Lakes Community College
3200 College Dr, Emmetsburg IA 50536-1055
Anne Stansbury, Asst. Director of Admissions
712-852-5212 Fax: 712-362-8363
Website: www.iowalakes.edu
E-mail: info@iowalakes.edu

Iowa Lakes Community College
300 S 18th St, Estherville IA 51334-2721
Anne Stansbury, Asst. Director of Admissions
712-362-7945 Fax: 712-362-8363
Website: www.iowalakes.edu
E-mail: info@iowalakes.edu

Iowa Lakes Community College
1900 Grand Ave, Suite 8, Spencer IA 51301
Anne Stansbury, Assistant Director of Admissions
712-262-7141 Fax: 712-262-4047
Website: www.iowalakes.edu
E-mail: info@iowalakes.edu

Iowa Western Community College
923 E Washington St, Clarinda IA 51632-1958
712-542-5117

Iowa Western Community College
2700 College Rd, Council Bluffs IA 51503-0567
800-432-5852

Kirkwood Community College
PO Box 2068, Cedar Rapids IA 52406-2068
319-398-5411

Marshalltown Community College
3700 S Center St, Marshalltown IA 50158-4760
641-752-7106

Muscatine Community College
152 Colorado St, Muscatine IA 52761-5396
563-288-6001

Northeast Iowa Community College
PO Box 400, Calmar IA 52132-0400
563-562-3263

Northeast Iowa Community College
RR 1, Peosta IA 52068
563-556-5110

North Iowa Area Community College
500 College Dr, Mason City IA 50401-7213
641-423-1264

Northwest Iowa Community College
603 W Park St, Sheldon IA 51201-1046
Lisa Story, Director of Enrollment Management
712-324-5061 Fax: 712-324-4136
Website: www.nwicc.edu
E-mail: lstory@nwicc.edu

St. Luke's College
2720 Stone Park Blvd, Sioux City IA 51104-3734
712-279-3149

Scott Community College
500 Belmont Rd, Riverdale IA 52722-6804
563-441-4000

Southeastern Community College
PO Box 6007, Keokuk IA 52632
Kari Bevans, Director of Admissions
319-524-3221

Southeastern Community College
PO Box 180, West Burlington IA 52655
319-752-2731

SOUTHWESTERN COMMUNITY COLLEGE

1501 W Townline St, Creston IA 50801-1042
Lisa Carstens, Director of Admissions
641-782-7081 Fax: 641-782-3312
Website: www.swcciowa.edu
E-mail: carstens@swcciowa.edu

Western Iowa Tech Community College
200 Victory Dr, Cherokee IA 51012-2237
712-225-0238

Western Iowa Tech Community College
PO Box 5199, Sioux City IA 51102-5199
Dr. Carolyn Rants, Dean of Students
712-274-6400

KANSAS

Allen County Community College
1801 N Cottonwood St, Iola KS 66749-1607
John Masterson, President
Randy Weber, Director of Admissions
620-365-5116 Fax: 620-365-3284
Website: www.allencc.net
E-mail: weber@allencc.edu

Barton County Community College
245 NE 30th Rd, Great Bend KS 67530-9107
Dr. Veldon Law, President
800-748-7594

Barton County Community College
540 Grant Ave, Junction City KS 66441
785-238-8550

Brown Mackie College - Kansas City
9705 Lenexa Dr, Lenexa KS 66215
913-768-1900

Brown Mackie College - Salina
2106 S 9th St, Salina KS 67401-7307
785-825-5422

Butler Community College
901 S Haverhill Rd, El Dorado KS 67042-3225
316-321-2222

Cloud County Community College
PO Box 1002, Concordia KS 66901-1002
Heath Martin, Director of Admission
785-243-1435

Coffeyville Community College / Area Technical School
400 W 11th St, Coffeyville KS 67337-5065
620-251-7700

COLBY COMMUNITY COLLEGE

1255 S Range Ave, Colby KS 67701-4099
Director of Admissions
888-634-9350 or 785-460-4690 Fax: 785-460-4691
Website: www.colbycc.edu
E-mail: bobbi@colbycc.edu

Cowley County Community College
PO Box 1147, Arkansas City KS 67005-1147
620-442-0430

Dodge City Community College
2501 N 14th Ave, Dodge City KS 67801-2399
620-225-1321

Donnelly College
608 N 18th St, Kansas City KS 66102-4298
Sr. Mary Agnes Patterson, Vice President
913-621-8724

Fort Scott Community College
2108 Horton St, Fort Scott KS 66701-3199
Mert Barrows, Director of Admissions
620-223-2700

Garden City Community College
801 N Campus Dr, Garden City KS 67846-6333
Nikki Geier, Director of Admissions
620-276-7611

Haskell Indian Nations University
155 Indian Ave Rm 1305, Lawrence KS 66046-4817
785-749-8404

Hesston College
PO Box 3000, Hesston KS 67062-2093
620-327-4221

Highland Community College
PO Box 68, Highland KS 66035-0068
785-442-6000

Hutchinson Community College
1300 N Plum St, Hutchinson KS 67501-5831
620-665-3500

Independence Community College
PO Box 708, Independence KS 67301-0708
Dr. Terry Hetrick, President
800-842-6063 Fax: 620-331-5344
Website: www.indycc.edu
E-mail: admissions@indycc.edu

Johnson County Community College
12345 College Blvd, Overland Park KS 66210-1299
913-469-3803

Kansas City Kansas Community College
7250 State Ave, Kansas City KS 66112-3003
913-596-9600

Labette Community College
200 S 14th St, Parsons KS 67357-9966
620-421-6700

Neosho County Community College
800 W 14th St, Chanute KS 66720-2639
620-431-2820

Pratt Community College
Hwy 61, Pratt KS 67124
620-672-5641

Seward County Community College
PO Box 1137, Liberal KS 67905-1137
620-629-2710

KENTUCKY

Ashland Community and Technical College
1400 College Dr, Ashland KY 41101-3683
606-329-2999

Bluegrass Community and Technical College
Oswald Building
470 Cooper Drive, Lexington KY 40506-0235
Shelbie Hugle, Director of Admissions
859-246-6200 Fax: 859-246-4664
Website: www.bluegrass.kctcs.edu
E-mail: bctc_info@kctcs.edu

Daymar College
4400 Breckenridge Ln #415, Louisville KY 40218
Shawn McDaniel, Director of Admissions
502-495-1040 Fax: 502-495-1518
Website: www.daymarcollege.com

Daymar College
3361 Buckland Sq, Owensboro KY 42301-5830
Vickie McDougal Director of Admissions
800-960-4090 Fax: 270-685-4090
Website: www.daymarcollege.com

Daymar College - Northern Kentucky
76 Carothers Rd, Newport KY 41071
859-291-0800

Elizabethtown Community College
600 College St Rd, Elizabethtown KY 42701-3053
800-260-2ECC

Hazard Community and Technical College
One Community College Dr, Hazard KY 41701-2402
Germaine Shaffer, Director of Enrollment and Diversity
Services
800-246-7521 ext. 73409

Henderson Community College
2660 S Green St, Henderson KY 42420-4699
270-827-1867

Hopkinsville Community College
PO Box 2100, Hopkinsville KY 42241-2100
270-886-3921

Jefferson Community & Technical College
109 E Broadway, Louisville KY 40202-2000
502-584-0181

Madisonville Community College
2000 College Dr, Madisonville KY 42431-9199
270-821-2250

Maysville Community & Technical College
1755 US Highway 68, Maysville KY 41056-8910
606-759-7141

Maysville Community College
1401 Dixie Hwy, Park Hills KY 41011-2816

National College of Business & Technology
115 E Lexington Ave, Danville KY 40422-1517
Larry Steele, Director of Admissions
859-236-6991

National College of Business & Technology
7627 Ewing Blvd, Florence KY 41042-1812
Larry Steele, Director of Admissions
859-525-6510

National College of Business & Technology
628 E Main St, Lexington KY 40508-2312
Larry Steele, Director of Admissions
859-253-0621

National College of Business & Technology
4205 Dixie Hwy, Louisville KY 40216
Larry Steele, Director of Admissions
502-447-7634

National College of Business & Technology
288 S Mayo Trl #2, Pikeville KY 41501-1518
Larry Steele, Director of Admissions
606-432-5477

National College of Business & Technology
139 S Killarney Ln, Richmond KY 40475
Larry Steele, Director of Admissions
859-623-8956

Owensboro Community and Technical College
4800 New Hartford Rd, Owensboro KY 42303-1899
270-686-4400

Paducah Technical College
509 S 30th St, Paducah KY 42001-4181
Arnold Harris, School Relations
800-995-4438

Prestonsburg Community College
110 Bert T Combs Dr, Prestonsburg KY 41653-1815
606-886-3863

St. Catharine College
2375 Bardstown Rd, Saint Catharine KY 40061
800-599-2000

Somerset Community College
808 Monticello St, Somerset KY 42501-2936
606-679-8501

Southeast Kentucky Community and Technical College
300 College Rd, Cumberland KY 40823-1031
606-589-2145

West Kentucky Community and Technical College
PO Box 7380, Paducah KY 42002-7380
270-554-9200

LOUISIANA

Baton Rouge Community College
5310 Florida Blvd, Baton Rouge LA 70806
225-216-8040

Bossier Parish Community College
6220 E Texas St, Bossier City LA 71111
318-678-6000

Delgado Community College
615 City Park Ave, New Orleans LA 70119
Gwen A. Boutte, Director of Admissions
504-483-4114

Louisiana State University
1100 Florida Ave, New Orleans LA 70119-2714
504-948-8530

Louisiana State University at Eunice
PO Box 1129, Eunice LA 70535-1129
Ron Ryder, Registrar
337-457-7311 Fax: 337-550-1306
Website: www.lsue.edu
E-mail: rryder@lsue.edu

Louisiana Technical College
Lafayette Campus
1101 Bertrand St, Lafayette LA 70506-4909
Gen M. Bienvenu, Director of Admissions
337-262-5962

MedVance Institute
9255 Interline Ave, Baton Rouge LA 70809
225-248-1015

New Orleans School of Urban Missions
PO Box 53344, New Orleans LA 70153
800-385-6364

Nunez Community College
3700 LaFontaine St, Chalmette LA 70043
504-680-2240

River Parishes Community College
PO Box 310, Sorrento LA 70778
225-675-8270

School of Urban Missions
511 Westbank Expy, Gretna LA 70053
504-362-3634

Southern University at Shreveport
3050 M L King Dr, Shreveport LA 71107
318-674-3300

South Louisiana Community College
320 Devalcourt St, Lafayette LA 70506
337-521-8896

MAINE

Andover College
475 Lisbon St, Lewiston ME 04240
Wendy Burbank, Associate Director of Admissions
800-639-3110

Andover College
901 Washington Ave, Portland ME 04103-2791
Woody Burbank, Associate Director of Admissions
207-774-6126

Beal College
99 Farm Rd, Bangor ME 04401-6831
207-947-4591

Central Maine Community College
1250 Turner St, Auburn ME 04210-6498
Walter Clark, Director of Admissions
207-755-5100

Central Maine Medical Center
300 Main St, Lewiston ME 04240-7041
207-795-2840

Eastern Maine Community College
354 Hogan Rd, Bangor ME 04401-4206
207-974-4600

Kennebec Valley Community College
92 Western Ave, Fairfield ME 04937-1337
Kathy Moore, Director of Admissions
207-453-5035

Northern Maine Community College
33 Edgemont Dr, Presque Isle ME 04769-2016
Bill Casavant, Director of Admissions
207-768-2700 Fax: 207-768-2831
Website: www.nmcc.edu
E-mail: admissions@nmcc.edu

Southern Maine Community College
2 Fort Rd, South Portland ME 04106-1698
Dr. James Ortiz, President
Scott MacDonald, Director of Financial Aid
207-741-5500 Fax: 207-741-5671
Website: www.smccme.edu
E-mail: oharmon@maine.rr.com

Washington County Community College
RR 1 Box 22C, River Rd, Calais ME 04619
David R. Sousa, Dean of Students
207-454-1000

York County Community College
PO Box 529, Wells ME 04090-0529
207-646-9282

MARYLAND

Allegany College of Maryland
12401 Willowbrook Rd, Cumberland MD 21502-2596
301-784-5000

Anne Arundel Community College
101 College Pkwy, Arnold MD 21012-1857
410-647-7100

Baltimore City Community College
2901 Liberty Heights Ave, Baltimore MD 21215
Scheherazade Foreman, Director of Admissions
410-462-8000

BALTIMORE INTERNATIONAL COLLEGE

17 Commerce St, Baltimore MD 21202-3230
Kristin Ciarlo, Director of Admissions
410-752-4710 ext. 120 Fax: 410-752-3730
Website: www.bic.edu
E-mail: admissions@bic.edu
    Founded in 1972, Baltimore International College is an independent college regionally accredited by the Commission on Higher Education, Middle States Association of Colleges and Schools. The college offers specialized masters, baccalaureate and associate's degrees, and a certificate program through its School of Culinary Arts, School of Hotel Restaurant and Catering Management, and School of Graduate Studies. The college's programs include a master of science in Hospitality Management degree, bachelor's degrees in Culinary Management, Hospitality Management, Hospitality Management with Marketing Concentration; associate's degrees in Professional Cooking, Professional Cooking and Baking and Professional Baking and Pastry; and certificates in Professional Culinary Arts.
    The college has a campus in Baltimore, MD., just two blocks from Baltimore's famous Inner Harbor and within easy walking distance of many of the city's major attractions. The college also has Virginia Park, a sprawling 100-acre preserve along the shore of Lough Ramor in Virginia, County Cavan, Ireland. The Virginia Park campus is home to the Park Hotel and a golf course, pleasure gardens, and 15 miles of walking paths. Students may take courses at the Virginia Park campus studying under European-educated chefs and hoteliers.
    The mission of Baltimore International College is to provide qualified students with the education and experience they need to pursue progressive careers within the international foodservice and lodging industry.

Carroll Community College
1601 Washington Rd, Westminster MD 21157-6913
410-386-8000

Cecil Community College
One Seahawk Dr, North East MD 21901
Sandra S. Rajaski, Registrar & Director of Admissions
410-287-1000 Fax: 410-287-1001
Website: www.cecilcc.edu
E-mail: srajaski@cecilcc.edu

Chesapeake College
PO Box 8, Wye Mills MD 21679-0008
410-822-5400

College of Southern Maryland
PO Box 910, La Plata MD 20646-0910
301-934-2251

The Community College of Baltimore County
Catonsville Campus
800 S Rolling Rd, Catonsville MD 21228-5317
Diane Drake, Director of Admissions
410-455-4555

Community College of Baltimore County
Dundalk Campus
7200 Sollers Point Rd, Baltimore MD 21222-4692
Theresa Carr, Director of Admissions
410-285-9801

Community College of Baltimore County
Essex Campus
7201 Rossville Blvd, Baltimore MD 21237-3898
Marcia Amaimo, Director of Admissions
410-780-6363

Frederick Community College
7932 Opossumtown Pike, Frederick MD 21702-2097
Welcome and Registration Center
301-846-2430

Garrett College
PO Box 151, Mc Henry MD 21541
301-387-3000

Hagerstown Business College
18618 Crestwood Dr, Hagerstown MD 21742-2797
W. Christopher Motz, President
Jim Klein, Director of Admissions
800-422-2670

Hagerstown Community College
11400 Robinwood Dr, Hagerstown MD 21742-6590
Dr. Daniel E. Bock, Assistant Director of Admissions
301-790-2800 Fax: 301-791-9165
Website: www.hagerstowncc.edu
E-mail: bockd@hagerstowncc.edu

Harford Community College
401 Thomas Run Rd, Bel Air MD 21015-1696
410-836-4000

Howard Community College
10901 Little Patuxent Pkwy
Columbia MD 21044-3197
Mary Ellen Duncan, President
410-772-4800

Montgomery College
20200 Observation Dr, Germantown MD 20876-4098
Sherman Helberg, Contact
301-279-5036

Montgomery College
51 Mannakee St, Rockville MD 20850-1199
301-279-5000

Montgomery College
7600 Takoma Ave, Takoma Park MD 20912-4197
Sherman Helberg, Contact
301-279-5036

Prince George's Community College
301 Largo Rd, Largo MD 20774-2199
Vera L. Bagley, Director of Admissions & Records
301-322-0801

School of Art & Design at Montgomery College
10500 Georgia Ave, Silver Spring MD 20902-4111
301-649-4454

Wor-Wic Community College
10452 Old Ocean City Blvd #7, Berlin MD 21811
410-641-4134

Wor-Wic Community College
32000 Campus Dr, Salisbury MD 21804-1485
410-334-2800

MASSACHUSETTS

Benjamin Franklin Institute of Technology
41 Berkeley St, Boston MA 02116-6307
Norman Kraft, Dean of Enrollment
617-423-4630 ext. 121 Fax: 617-482-3706
Website: www.bfit.edu
E-mail: admissions@bfit.edu

Berkshire Community College
1350 West St, Pittsfield MA 01201-5786
413-499-4660

BRISTOL COMMUNITY COLLEGE

777 Elsbree St, Fall River MA 02720
Rodney S. Clark, Director of Admissions
508-678-2811 ext. 2516, 2179 Fax: 508-730-3265
Website: www.bristol.mass.edu
E-mail: admissions@bristol.mass.edu
    Established 1965. Public. Coed. Accreditation: New England Association of Schools and Colleges. Enrollment: 3,098 full-time, 3,775 part-time. Faculty: 345. Student-faculty ratio: 18:1. Degrees offered: Liberal Arts, Business Administration, Computer Information Systems, Engineering Technology, Health Sciences, Human Services & Public Safety, Office Administration. Library: 65,000 volumes. 9 buildings.

Bunker Hill Community College
250 Rutherford Ave, Boston MA 02129-2925
617-228-2000

Cape Cod Community College
2240 Iyannough Rd, West Barnstable MA 02668
508-362-2131

Caritas Laboure College
2120 Dorchester Ave, Dorchester MA 02124-5698
617-296-8300

Dean College
99 Main St, Franklin MA 02038-1994
508-541-1900

Endicott College
376 Hale St, Beverly MA 01915-2098
978-927-0585

Fisher College
118 Beacon St, Boston MA 02116-1501
Stephen Carter, Director of Admissions
800-446-1226

Greenfield Community College
1 College Dr, Greenfield MA 01301-9739
413-775-1000

Holyoke Community College
303 Homestead Ave, Holyoke MA 01040-1099
413-538-7000

Marian Court College
35 Littles Point Rd, Swampscott MA 01907-2840
781-595-6768

Massachusetts Bay Community College
50 Oakland St, Wellesley MA 02481-5307
781-239-3000

Massasoit Community College
1 Massasoit Blvd, Brockton MA 02302-3996
508-588-9100

Middlesex Community College
Springs Rd, Bedford MA 01730-1114
Darcy Orellana, Director of Admissions
800-818-3434

Middlesex Community College
33 Kearney Sq, Lowell MA 01852-1987
Darcy Orellana, Director of Admissions
800-818-3434

Mt. Wachusett Community College
444 Green St, Gardner MA 01440
Karin Schedin, Director of Admissions
978-632-6600 ext. 110

New England College of Finance
10 High St Ste 204, Boston MA 02110
617-951-2350

NORTHERN ESSEX COMMUNITY COLLEGE
100 Elliott St, Haverhill MA 01830
Nora B. Sheridan, Director of Admission
978-556-3700
Website: www.NECC.Mass.edu
E-mail: nsheridan@necc.mass.edu

North Shore Community College
1 Ferncroft Rd, Danvers MA 01923-4093
Joanne Light, Director of Enrollment & Student Records
978-762-4000

Quincy College
34 Coddington St, Quincy MA 02169-4501
617-984-1600

Quinsigamond Community College
670 W Boylston St, Worcester MA 01606-2092
508-853-2300

Roxbury Community College
1234 Columbus Ave, Boston MA 02120-3400
Dr. Rudolph Jones, Director of Admissions
617-541-5310

Springfield Technical Community College
1 Armory Sq, Springfield MA 01105-1296
Andrea Lucy-Allen, Director of Admissions
413-755-4202

URBAN COLLEGE OF BOSTON
178 Tremont St, Boston MA 02111-1006
Dr. Henry J. Johnson, Dean of Enrollment Services/Registrar
617-292-4723 ext. 6357 Fax: 617-423-4758
Website: www.urbancollege.edu
E-mail: johnson@urbancollege.edu
Chartered 1993. Private. Coed. Accreditation: Accredited by NEASC. Tuition: $125.00 per credit. Mission: To increase college access, retention, and degree completion among nontraditional students and adult learners from Boston's urban neighborhoods. Enrollment: 700 multicultural, and ethnically diverse students. The college provides a highly supportive environment that integrates a college education with career preparation, skill development and access to supportive services. Degrees: AA, Programs: Early Childhood Education, Human Services Administration, General Studies. Certificates: Early Childhood Education, Human Services Administration, General Studies, Direct Service Worker (Youth - Age 6-18) Family Services, Management, Personal Computer Applications, Youth Program Administration, Early Childhood Education in Spanish.

MICHIGAN
Alpena Community College
666 Johnson St, Alpena MI 49707-1495
989-356-9021

Bay de Noc Community College
2001 N Lincoln Rd, Escanaba MI 49829-2524
906-786-5802

Bay Mills Community College
12214 W Lakeshore Dr, Brimley MI 49715
906-248-3354

Charles S. Mott Community College
1401 E Court St, Flint MI 48503-6208
810-762-0200

Charles Stewart Mott Community College
2100 W Thompson Rd, Fenton MI 48430
810-762-0200

Delta College
University Center MI 48710-0001
Duff Zube, Director of Admissions
989-686-9093 Fax: 989-667-2202
Website: www.delta.edu
E-mail: admit@delta.edu

Finlandia University
601 Quincy St, Hancock MI 49930-1882
906-482-5300

Glen Oaks Community College
62249 Shimmel Rd, Centreville MI 49032-9784
269-467-9945

Gogebic Community College
E4946 Jackson Rd, Ironwood MI 49938-1366
906-932-4231

Grand Rapids Community College
143 Bostwick Ave NE, Grand Rapids MI 49503-3201
616-234-4000

Great Lakes College
150 Nugent Rd, Bad Axe MI 48413-8705
989-755-3444

Great Lakes College
3930 Traxler Ct, Bay City MI 48706-9286
989-686-1572

Great Lakes College
1231 Cleaver Rd, Caro MI 48723-9376
989-673-5857

Henry Ford Community College
5101 Evergreen Rd, Dearborn MI 48128-2407
313-845-9615

ITT TECHNICAL INSTITUTE
4020 Sparks Dr SE, Grand Rapids MI 49546-6192
Dennis Hormel, Director
616-956-1060 Fax: 616-956-5606
Website: www.itt-tech.edu
E-mail: dhormel@itt-tech.edu

ITT TECHNICAL INSTITUTE
1522 E Big Beaver Rd, Troy MI 48083-2008
Patricia Hyman, Director of Recruitment
248-524-1800 Fax: 248-528-2218
Website: www.itt-tech.edu

Jackson Community College
2111 Emmons Rd, Jackson MI 49201-8399
517-796-8425

Jackson Community College
at Lenawee Vo-Tech
1376 N Main St, Adrian MI 49221
517-265-5515

Jackson Community College
Hillsdale LeTarte Center
3120 W Carleton Rd PO Box 712, Hillsdale MI 49242
517-437-3343

Jackson Community College
JCC Flight Center Reynolds Municipal Airport
3610 Wildwood Ave, Jackson MI 49202
517-787-7012

Jackson Community College
JCC Lenawee Flight Center Lenawee County Airport
2651 Cadmus Rd, Adrian MI 49221
517-263-1351

Kalamazoo Valley Community College
PO Box 4070, Kalamazoo MI 49003-4070
Marilyn Schlack, President
269-372-5000

Kellogg Community College
450 North Ave, Battle Creek MI 49017-3397
269-965-3931

Kirtland Community College
10775 N Saint Helen Rd, Roscommon MI 48653-9699
989-275-5000

Lake Michigan College
2755 E Napier Ave, Benton Harbor MI 49022-1899
269-927-8100

Lansing Community College
419 N Capitol Ave, Lansing MI 48933-1293
517-483-1620

Lewis College of Business
17370 Meyers Rd, Detroit MI 48235-1423
313-862-6300

MACOMB COMMUNITY COLLEGE
44575 Garfield Rd, Clinton Township MI 48038-1139
Information Center
586-445-7999
Website: www.macomb.edu
E-mail: answer@macomb.edu

MACOMB COMMUNITY COLLEGE
14500 E 12 Mile Rd, Warren MI 48088-3896
Information Center
586-445-7999
Website: www.macomb.edu
E-mail: answer@macomb.edu

Mid-Michigan Community College
1375 S Clare Ave, Harrison MI 48625-9447
989-386-6622

Monroe County Community College
1555 S Raisinville Rd, Monroe MI 48161-9047
734-242-7300

Montcalm Community College
2800 College Dr, Sidney MI 48885-9723
989-328-2111

Muskegon Community College
221 S Quarterline Rd, Muskegon MI 49442-1493
231-773-9131

North Central Michigan College
1515 Howard St, Petoskey MI 49770-8740
Naomi DeWinter, Director Enrollment Management
888-298-6605

Northwestern Michigan College
1701 E Front St, Traverse City MI 49686-3061
Jim Bensley, Admissions Coordinator
800-748-0566 Fax: 231-995-1339
Website: www.nmc.edu
E-mail: jbensley@nmc.edu

Oakland Community College
2480 Opdyke Rd, Bloomfield Hills MI 48304
Dr. Maurice McCall, Director of Admissions
248-341-2000
Website: www.oaklandcc.edu
E-mail: mhmcall@oaklandcc.edu

Oakland Community College
27055 Orchard Lake Rd, Farmington Hills MI 48334
248-522-3400

Oakland Community College
739 S Washington, Royal Oak MI 48067
248-246-2400

Oakland Community College
22322 Rutland Dr, Southfield MI 48075
248-233-2700

Oakland Community College
7350 Cooley Lake Rd, Waterford MI 48327-4187
248-942-3100

Saginaw Chippewa Tribal College
2274 Enterprise Dr, Mount Pleasant MI 48858
989-775-4123

St. Clair County Community College
323 Erie St, Port Huron MI 48060-3812
810-984-3881

Schoolcraft College
18600 Haggerty Rd, Livonia MI 48152-2696
734-462-4400

Southwestern Michigan College
58900 Cherry Grove Rd, Dowagiac MI 49047-9726
Admissions Office
269-782-1000

Washtenaw Community College
PO Box D-1, Ann Arbor MI 48106-1610
734-973-3300

Wayne County Community College
801 W Fort St, Detroit MI 48226-3095
313-496-2500

West Shore Community College
PO Box 277, Scottville MI 49454-0277
231-845-6211

MINNESOTA

ACADEMY COLLEGE
1101 E 78th St, Bloomington MN 55420-1402
952-851-0066 Fax: 952-851-0094
Website: www.academycollege.edu
E-mail: info@academycollege.edu
See listing under "Career Schools"

Alexandria Technical College
1601 Jefferson St, Alexandria MN 56308-3707
320-762-0221

Anoka-Ramsey Community College
Cambridge Campus
300 Polk Street South, Cambridge MN 55008
Charlotte Lindahl, Director of Admissions
763-689-7000

Anoka-Ramsey Community College
Coon Rapids Campus
11200 Mississippi Blvd NW
Coon Rapids MN 55433-3470
763-427-2600

Anoka Technical College
1355 Highway 10, Anoka MN 55303
763-576-4700

Art Institutes International Minnesota
15 S 9th St, Minneapolis MN 55402-3137
612-332-3361

Brown College
1440 Northland Dr, Mendota Heights MN 55120-1004
Dawn Bravo, VP Marketing
800-6-BROWN-6

Central Lakes College
501 W College Dr, Brainerd MN 56401-3900
218-855-8000

Central Lakes College
1830 Airport Rd, Staples MN 56479-3252
218-894-5100

Century College
3300 Century Ave N
White Bear Lake MN 55110-1842
651-779-3200

Dunwoody College of Technology
818 Dunwoody Blvd, Minneapolis MN 55403-1192
John Slama, Vice President Enrollment Management
800-292-4625 or 612-374-5800 Fax: 612-374-4128
Website: www.dunwoody.edu
E-mail: jslama@dunwoody.edu
See listing under "Career Schools"

Fond du Lac Tribal Community College
2101 14th St, Cloquet MN 55720
218-879-0800

HIBBING COMMUNITY COLLEGE
1515 E 25th St, Hibbing MN 55746-3300
Holly Bigelow, Director of Enrollment
800-224-4HCC or 218-262-7200 Fax: 218-262-6717
Website: www.hibbing.edu
E-mail: admissions@hibbing.edu

Inver Hills Community College
2500 80th St E, Inver Grove Heights MN 55076
651-450-8500

ITASCA COMMUNITY COLLEGE
1851 E US Highway 169
Grand Rapids MN 55744-3397
Candace Perry, Director of Enrollment Services
218-327-4464 or 800-996-6422 Fax: 218-327-4350
Website: www.itascacc.edu
E-mail: iccinfo@itascacc.edu
Established 1922. Public. Coed. Accreditation: NCACS. Enrollment: 890 full-time, 250 part-time. Degrees: AA, AS, AAS, (start towards a bachelor's degree in any field) or a 2 year AAS degrees in Natural Res/Forestry or Accounting. Itasca offers specialty and transfer programs in American Indian Studies, Psychology, Engineering, Business, Education and Geography. Ten bldgs. on 25 acres. Located in scenic northern Minnesota. Itasca is the best place to start.

Lake Superior College
2101 Trinity Rd, Duluth MN 55811-3399
218-733-7600

Le Cordon Bleu College of Culinary Arts
1408 Northland Dr Ste 102
Mendota Heights MN 55120
651-675-4700

Mesabi Range Community & Technical College
1100 Industrial Park, Eveleth MN 55734-8628
218-744-3302

Mesabi Range Community & Technical College
1001 Chestnut St W, Virginia MN 55792-3401
218-749-7700

Minneapolis Community and Technical College
1501 Hennepin Ave, Minneapolis MN 55403-1779
Dena Russell, Director of Admissions
612-659-6282 Fax: 612-659-6210
Website: www.minneapolis.edu
E-mail: admissions.office@minneapolis.edu

Minnesota State Community and Technical College
Fergus Falls
1414 College Way, Fergus Falls MN 56537-1009
218-739-7500

Minnesota West Community and Technical College
Canby Campus
1011 1st St W, Canby MN 56220-9494
Jodi Weber, Contact
800-658-2535

Minnesota West Community and Technical College
Granite Falls Campus
1593 11th Ave, Granite Falls MN 56241-1061
Becky Weber, Contact
800-657-3247

Minnesota West Community and Technical College
Jackson Campus
PO Box 269, Jackson MN 56143-0269
Lynne Liepold, Contact
800-658-2522

Minnesota West Community and Technical College
Pipestone Campus
1314 N Hiawatha Ave, Pipestone MN 56164-2282
Laurel Berg, Contact
800-658-2330

Minnesota West Community and Technical College
Worthington Campus
1450 Collegeway, Worthington MN 56187-3024
Mitz Diemer, Contact
800-657-3966

Normandale Community College
9700 France Ave S, Bloomington MN 55431-4399
Rick Smith, Director of Admissions
952-832-6000

North Hennepin Community College
7411 85th Ave N, Brooklyn Park MN 55445-2299
763-424-0702

Northland Community & Technical College
Highway 1 E, Thief River Falls MN 56701
Eugene Klinke, Director of Enrollment Management
800-959-6282 or 218-681-0862 Fax: 218-681-0774
Website: www.northlandcollege.edu
E-mail: eugene.klinke@northlandcollege.edu

Northland Community and Technical College
2022 Central Ave NE
East Grand Forks MN 56721-2702
Mary Fontes, Dean of Students
800-451-3441 Fax: 218-773-4502
Website: www.northlandcollege.edu
E-mail: admissions@northlandcollege.edu

Pine Technical College
900 4th St SE, Pine City MN 55063-2198
320-629-5100

Rainy River Community College
1501 Highway 71, International Falls MN 56649-2187
Berta Hagen, Registrar
218-285-2207

Ridgewater College-Hutchinson Campus
2 Century Ave SE, Hutchinson MN 55350-3100
Dawn Bjork, Counselor
800-222-4424 Fax: 320-231-7767
Website: www.ridgewater.edu
E-mail: dawn.bjork@ridgewater.edu

Ridgewater College-Willmar Campus
PO Box 1097, Willmar MN 56201-1097
Sally Kerfeld, Director of Admissions
800-722-1151 Fax: 320-231-7677
Website: www.ridgewater.edu
E-mail: skerfeld@ridgewater.edu

Riverland Community College
1900 8th Ave NW, Austin MN 55912-1400
Dani Heiny, Director of Admissions
800-247-5039

Rochester Community & Technical College
851 30th Ave SE, Rochester MN 55904-4999
507-285-7210

St. Cloud Technical College
1540 Northway Dr, Saint Cloud MN 56303-1240
Jodi Elness, Director of Enrollment Management
800-222-1009 Fax: 320-308-5981
Website: www.sctc.edu
E-mail: jelness@sctc.edu

St. Mary's Campus of the College of St. Catherine
2500 S 6th St, Minneapolis MN 55454-1401
612-332-5521

St. Paul College
A Community & Technical College
235 Marshall Ave, Saint Paul MN 55102-1800
651-221-1300

South Central College
1920 Lee Blvd, North Mankato MN 56003-2508
507-389-7200

Vermillion Community College
1900 E Camp St, Ely MN 55731-1996
800-475-6666

MISSISSIPPI

Coahoma Community College
3240 Friars Point Rd, Clarksdale MS 38614-9700
662-627-2571

Copiah-Lincoln Community College
11 Copiah Lincoln Circle, Natchez MS 39120
601-442-9111

Copiah-Lincoln Community College
PO Box 457, Wesson MS 39191-0457
601-643-5101

East Central Community College
PO Box 129, Decatur MS 39327-0129
601-635-2111

East Mississippi Community College
PO Box 158, Scooba MS 39358-0158
662-476-8442

Hinds Community College
1750 Chadwick Dr, Jackson MS 39204-3402
601-372-6507

Hinds Community College
PO Box 1100, Raymond MS 39154
601-857-5261

Hinds Community College
755 Highway 27, Vicksburg MS 39180-8699
601-638-0600

Holmes Community College
PO Box 369, Goodman MS 39079-0369
662-472-2312

Itawamba Community College
602 W Hill St, Fulton MS 38843
662-862-8000

Jones County Junior College
900 S Court St, Ellisville MS 39437-3999
601-477-4000

Mary Holmes College
PO Box 1257, West Point MS 39773-1257
662-494-6820

Meridian Community College
910 Highway 19 N, Meridian MS 39307-5801
601-483-8241

Mississippi Delta Community College
PO Box 668, Moorhead MS 38761-0668
662-246-6322

Mississippi Gulf Coast Community College
Gautier MS 39553
228-497-9602

Mississippi Gulf Coast Community College
Gulfport MS 39507
228-896-3355

Mississippi Gulf Coast Community College
PO Box 609, Perkinston MS 39573
601-928-5211

Northeast Mississippi Community College
101 Cunningham Blvd, Booneville MS 38829-1726
662-728-7751

Northwest Mississippi Community College
4975 Highway 51 N, Senatobia MS 38668
662-562-3200

Northwest Mississippi Community College
5197 W E Ross Pkwy, Southaven MS 38671
662-342-1570

Pearl River Community College
Station A, Poplarville MS 39470
601-795-6801

Southwest Mississippi Community College
Summit MS 39666
601-276-2001

MISSOURI

Blur River Community College
20301 E State Route 78
Independence MO 64057-2053
816-220-6550

Crowder College
601 Laclede Ave, Neosho MO 64850-9165
Dr. Kent Farnsworth, President
Sonya Pearson, Dean of Students
1-866-238-7788

East Central College
1964 Prairie Dell Rd, Union MO 63084
Karen Wieda, Registrar
636-583-5195 ext. 2220 Fax: 636-583-1897
Website: www.eastcentral.edu
E-mail: wiedaks@eastcentral.edu

ITT Technical Institute
1930 Meyer Drury Dr, Arnold MO 63010
636-464-6600

ITT Technical Institute
9150 E 41st Ter, Kansas City MO 64133
816-276-1400

Jefferson College
1000 Viking Dr, Hillsboro MO 63050-2441
Amy Martin-Small, Director of Admissions and Financial Aid
636-797-3000

Longview Community College
500 SW Longview Rd, Lees Summit MO 64081-2105
Dr. Fred Grogan, President
816-672-2000

Maple Woods Community College
2601 NE Barry Rd, Kansas City MO 64156-1299
816-437-3000

Messenger College
300 E 50th St, Joplin MO 64804-4909
417-624-7070

Midwest Institute - Earth City
4260 Shoreline Dr, Earth City MO 63045
314-344-3334

Mineral Area College
PO Box 1000, Desloge MO 63601
573-431-4593

Moberly Area Community College
101 College Ave, Moberly MO 65270-1304
Dr. James Grant, Dean of Student Services
800-MACC-070

North Central Missouri College
1301 Main St, Trenton MO 64683-1824
Blaire Birdsong, Director of Admissions
660-359-3948

Ozarks Technical Community College
PO Box 5958, Springfield MO 65801-5958
417-895-7000

Penn Valley Community College
3201 SW Traffic Way, Kansas City MO 64111
816-759-4000

Ranken Technical College
4431 Finney Ave, Saint Louis MO 63113-2898
Elizabeth M. Keserauskis, Director of Admissions
314-371-0233 Fax: 314-371-0241
Website: www.ranken.edu
E-mail: admissions@ranken.edu

St. Charles Community College
4601 Mid Rivers Mall Dr, Saint Peters MO 63376
Kathy Brockgreitens-Gober, Director of Admissions
636-922-8000 Fax: 636-922-8236
Website: www.stchas.edu
E-mail: adm-reg@stchas.edu

St. Louis Community College
11333 Big Bend Rd, Kirkwood MO 63122-5799
314-984-7500

St. Louis Community College
5600 Oakland Ave, Saint Louis MO 63110-1316
314-644-9100

St. Louis Community College at Florissant Valley
3400 Pershall Rd, Saint Louis MO 63135-1408
Janice Evans, Chair, Enrollment Management
314-595-4368

SPRINGFIELD COLLEGE
1010 W Sunshine St, Springfield MO 65807-2446
Scott Lester, Contact
417-864-7220 or 800-475-2699 Fax: 417-866-3335
Website: www.springfield-college.com
E-mail: slester@cci.edu

State Fair Community College
3201 W 16th St, Sedalia MO 65301-2199
Matthew Heck, Director of Admissions
660-530-5800

Three Rivers Community College
2080 Three Rivers Blvd, Poplar Bluff MO 63901
573-840-9605

WENTWORTH MILITARY ACADEMY & JUNIOR COLLEGE
1880 Washington Ave, Lexington MO 64067
MAJ Mike Herman, Director of Admissions
800-962-7682 or 660-259-2221 Fax: 660-259-2677
Website: www.wma.edu, wjc.wma.edu
E-mail: admissions@wma1880.org

Junior College established 1923. Accreditation: The Higher Learning Commission of the NCA. Enrollment: 80+ boarding students. 300 FTE non-boarding students. Junior college has both military junior college (MJC) and community JC (CJC) divisions. MJC offers AA and AS degrees. Early Commissioning Program allows eligible ROTC cadets to earn Army commission in 2 years. Four-year ROTC scholarship also offered, with follow-on at an approved 4-year college or university. CJC offers AA and AS degrees at Lexington campus and three satellites: Sheldon, Hermitage and Cameron. The JC prides itself on offering an affordable, quality education with small class sizes, individualized attention and outstanding faculty.

MONTANA

Blackfeet Community College
PO Box 819, Browning MT 59417
406-338-5441

Chief Dull Knife College
PO Box 98, Lame Deer MT 59043-0098
406-477-6215

Dawson Community College
PO Box 421, Glendive MT 59330-0421
Katherine Lee, Marketing Director
800-821-8320

Flathead Valley Community College
777 Grandview Dr, Kalispell MT 59901-2622
406-756-3846

Fort Belknap College
PO Box 159, Harlem MT 59526-0159
406-353-2607

Fort Peck Community College
PO Box 398, Poplar MT 59255
406-768-5551

Helena College of Technology of the Univ of Montana
1115 N Roberts St, Helena MT 59601-3054
406-444-6800

Little Big Horn College
Crow Agency MT 59022
406-638-3104

Miles Community College
2715 Dickinson St, Miles City MT 59301-4799
800-541-9281

Montana State University
Great Falls College of Technology
2100 16th Ave S, Great Falls MT 59405-4909
406-771-4300

Salish Kootenai College
PO Box 70, Pablo MT 59855
Jackie Moran, Admissions/Transfers
406-275-4866

Stone Child College
PO Box 1082, Box Elder MT 59521
406-395-4313

University of Montana
Missoula College of Technology
909 South Ave W, Missoula MT 59801-7910
406-243-7882

NEBRASKA

Central Community College-Columbus Campus
PO Box 1027, Columbus NE 68602-1027
Mary Young, Contact
402-564-7132 Fax: 402-562-1201
Website: www.cccneb.edu
E-mail: myoung@cccneb.edu

Central Community College-Grand Island Campus
PO Box 4903, Grand Island NE 68802-4903
Angie Pacheco, Contact
308-398-4222 Fax: 308-398-7398
Website: www.cccneb.edu
E-mail: apacheco@cccneb.edu

Central Community College-Hastings Campus
PO Box 1024, Hastings NE 68902-1024
Bob Glenn, Contact
402-463-9811 Fax: 402-562-1201
Website: www.cccneb.edu
E-mail: rglenn@cccneb.edu

Hamilton College
3350 N 90th St, Omaha NE 68134-4710
402-572-8500

ITT TECHNICAL INSTITUTE

9814 M St, Omaha NE 68127-2056
Frank de Monteur, Director
800-677-9260 Fax: 402-331-9495
Website: www.itt-tech.edu
E-mail: snielsen@itt-tech.edu

Little Priest Tribal College
PO Box 720, Winnebago NE 68071
402-878-2380

Metropolitan Community College
PO Box 3777, Omaha NE 68103-0777
402-449-8400

Metropolitan Community College
30th & Fort Sts, Omaha NE 68111
402-449-8300

Metropolitan Community College
204th & Dodge St, Omaha NE 68103
402-457-2000

Mid-Plains Community College
McCook Community College Campus
1205 E 3rd St, Mc Cook NE 69001-2631
Kelly Rippen, Director of Recruitment
800-658-4348 Fax: 308-345-8180
Website: www.mpcc.edu
E-mail: rippenk@mpcc.edu

Mid-Plains Community College
North Platte Community College - North Campus
1101 Halligan Dr, North Platte NE 69101-7659
Kelly Rippen, Director of Recruitment
800-658-4308 ext. 8107 Fax: 308-534-5770
Website: www.mpcc.edu
E-mail: rippenk@mpcc.edu

Mid-Plains Community College
North Platte Community College - South Campus
601 W State Farm Rd, North Platte NE 69101
Kelly Rippen, Director of Recruitment
800-658-4308 ext. 8107 Fax: 308-535-3789
Website: www.mpcc.edu
E-mail: rippenk@mpcc.edu

Nebraska College of Technical Agriculture
RR 3 Box 23A, Curtis NE 69025-9525
308-367-4124

Nebraska Indian Community College
PO Box 428, Macy NE 68039-0428
402-837-5078

Northeast Community College
PO Box 469, Norfolk NE 68702-0469
402-371-2020

Southeast Community College
4771 W Scott Rd, Beatrice NE 68310-7042
402-228-3468

Southeast Community College
8800 O St, Lincoln NE 68520-1299
402-437-2500

Southeast Community College
600 State St, Milford NE 68405
Larry Meyer, Director of Admissions
800-933-7223

Western Nebraska Community College
1601 E 27th St, Scottsbluff NE 69361-1815
308-635-3606

Western Nebraska Community College
Sidney NE 69162
800-221-9682

NEVADA

Career College of Northern Nevada
1195-A Corporate Blvd, Reno NV 89502-2331
Nathan Clark, Director
775-856-2266 Fax: 775-856-0935
Website: www.ccnn.edu
E-mail: lgoldhammer@ccnn4u.com
See listing under "Career Schools"

Community College of Southern Nevada
3200 E Cheyenne Ave
North Las Vegas NV 89030-4228
Arlie J. Stops, Assoc. VP Admissions / Records
702-651-4536

Deep Springs College
Deep Springs, CA
HC 72 Box 45001, Dyer NV 89010-9712
760-872-2000

GREAT BASIN COLLEGE

1500 College Pkwy, Elko NV 89801-9930
Julie G. Byrnes, Director of Enrollment Management
775-753-2271 Fax: 775-753-2311
Website: www.gbcnv.edu
E-mail: bjulie@gbcnv.edu
    Public. Coed. Accreditation: Northwest Association of
Schools & Colleges. Tuition: $51-$75 per credit plus
non-resident tuition of $2,457.50 per semester if applica-
ble. Enrollment: 861 full-time, 1,759 part-time. Faculty: 64
full time and adjunct 120. Student-faculty ratio: 18:1. Degrees: Associate and some Baccalaureate. 12 buildings
plus residence halls on 44 acres. GBC is the major provider of post-secondary education in central and northeastern Nevada and has been from its first days as an
upstart college thirty-eight years ago.

Truckee Meadows Community College
7000 Dandini Blvd, Reno NV 89512-3999
Rita Huneycutt, Interim President
775-673-7000

Western Nevada Community College
2201 W College Pkwy, Carson City NV 89703-7316
775-445-3000

NEW HAMPSHIRE

Chester College of New England
40 Chester St, Chester NH 03036-4331
603-887-4401

New Hampshire Community Technical College
2020 Riverside Dr, Berlin NH 03570-3717
603-752-1113

New Hampshire Community Tech College
1 College Dr, Claremont NH 03743-9707
Charles Kusselow, Admissions Counselor
603-542-7744

New Hampshire Community Technical College
1066 Front St, Manchester NH 03102-8528
603-668-6706

New Hampshire Community Technical College
505 Amherst St, Nashua NH 03063
Patricia Goodman, Director of Student Services
603-882-7022

New Hampshire Community Technical College
277 Portsmouth Ave, Stratham NH 03885-2231
Laurilee A. Shennett, Admissions Recruiter
603-772-1194 ext. 317

New Hampshire Technical College
379 Belmont Rd, Laconia NH 03246
603-524-3207

New Hampshire Technical Institute
11 Institute Dr, Concord NH 03301-7400
603-271-6484

NEW JERSEY

Assumption College for Sisters
350 Bernardsville Rd, Mendham NJ 07945-2923
Sr. Mary Joseph Schultz, S.C.C., President
973-543-6528

ATLANTIC CAPE COMMUNITY COLLEGE

5100 Black Horse Pike
Mays Landing NJ 08330-2699
Linda McLeod, Assistant Director of College
Recruitment
609-343-5000 Fax: 609-343-4921
Website: www.atlantic.edu
E-mail: accadmit@atlantic.edu
    Established 1964. Public. Coed. Accreditation: Middle
States Association of Colleges and Secondary Schools.
Tuition: $79.00 per credit. Fees: $17.00 per credit. Enroll-
ment: 2,524 full-time, 3,339 part-time. Faculty: 70 full-
time, 200 part-time. Degrees: AS, AA, AAS. Library:
78,000. 15 buildings on 537 acres. Home of New Jersey
largest cooking school. Leader in technology. Casino
Career Training. On-line degrees.

Bergen Community College
400 Paramus Rd, Paramus NJ 07652
Julian Gomez, Asst. Director of Admissions
201-447-7100 Fax: 201-444-7036
Website: www.bergen.edu
E-mail: jgomez@bergen.edu

Berkeley College
64 E Midland Ave, Paramus NJ 07652
800-446-5400

Berkeley College
430 Rahway Ave, Woodbridge NJ 07095-3305
800-446-5400

Brookdale Community College
765 Newman Springs Rd, Lincroft NJ 07738-1597
732-842-1900

Burlington County College
County Route 530, Pemberton NJ 08068
609-894-9311

Camden County College
PO Box 200, Blackwood NJ 08012-0200
856-227-7200

County College of Morris
214 Center Grove Rd, Randolph NJ 07869-2086
973-328-5000

Cumberland County College
PO Box 1500, Vineland NJ 08362-1500
856-691-8600

Essex County College
303 University Ave, Newark NJ 07102-1798
973-877-3000

Essex County College
West Essex Campus
730 Bloomfield Ave, West Caldwell NJ 07006-6783
Cheryl Newton-Banks, Assistant Director Enrollment
Services
973-403-2560

Fairleigh Dickinson University
150 Kotte Pl, Hackensack NJ 07601-6112
201-692-2675

Gibbs College
630 W Mount Pleasant Ave
Livingston NJ 07039-1611
973-744-2010

Gloucester County College
1400 Tanyard Rd, Sewell NJ 08080
856-468-5000

Hudson County Community College
25 Journal Sq, Jersey City NJ 07306
201-656-2020

Mercer County Community College
James Kerney Campus
N Broad & Academy Sts, Trenton NJ 08608
609-586-0505

Mercer County Community College
West Windsor Campus
PO Box B, Trenton NJ 08690
Savita Bambhrolia, Director of Admissions
609-586-4800 Fax: 609-587-4666
Website: www.mccc.edu
E-mail: admiss@mccc.edu

Middlesex County College
2600 Woodbridge Ave, Edison NJ 08837-3675
732-548-6000

Ocean County College
College Dr, Toms River NJ 08754
732-255-0400

Passaic Co. Community College
1 College Blvd, Paterson NJ 07505
973-684-6800

Raritan Valley Community College
PO Box 3300, Somerville NJ 08876-1265
908-526-1200

Salem Community College
460 Hollywood Ave, Carneys Point NJ 08069-2799
856-299-2100

Sussex County Community College
1 College Hill, Newton NJ 07860
973-300-2100

Union County College
1033 Springfield Ave, Cranford NJ 07016-1528
908-709-7000

Union County College
12 W Jersey St, Elizabeth NJ 07201-2314
908-965-6000

Union County College
232 E 2nd St, Plainfield NJ 07060-1308
908-412-3559

Warren County Community College
475 State Route 57 W, Washington NJ 07882-4343
908-835-9222

NEW MEXICO

Albuquerque TVI Community College
525 Buena Vista Dr SE, Albuquerque NM 87106-4096
Jane Campbell, Registrar
505-224-3061

Apollo
5301 Central Ave NE Ste 101
Albuquerque NM 87108-1514
800-368-7246

Clovis Community College
417 Schepps Blvd, Clovis NM 88101-8381
505-769-2811

Eastern New Mexico University-Roswell
PO Box 6000, Roswell NM 88202-6000
505-624-7000

International Institute of the Americas
4201 Central Ave NW Suite J
Albuquerque NM 87105-1649
Ed Sigman, Director
505-880-2877 Fax: 505-352-0199
Website: www.iia.edu
E-mail: syelton@iia.edu

ITT Technical Institute
5100 Masthead St NE, Albuquerque NM 87109-4366
505-828-1114

Luna Community College
366 Luna Dr, Las Vegas NM 87701
Louella Marr-Montoya, Director of Admissions
505-454-2500

Mesalands Community College
911 S 10th St, Tucumcari NM 88401
505-461-4413

New Mexico Junior College
5317 N Lovington Hwy, Hobbs NM 88240-9123
505-392-4510

NEW MEXICO MILITARY INSTITUTE

101 W College Blvd, Roswell NM 88201-5173
Rear Admiral David R. Ellison, USN (Ret.),
Superintendent
LTC. Craig Collins Director of Admissions
800-421-5376 or 505-624-8050 Fax: 505-624-8058
Website: www.nmmi.edu
E-mail: admissions@nmmi.edu
    Established 1891. State Supported. Coed. Accredita-
tion: NCACS, New Mexico Department of Education. Esti-
mated costs for 2004-2005 school year, out-of-state

student: $10,166, in-state student: $7,670. Enrollment: 950. Faculty: 68. Student-faculty ratio: 18:1. Degree: AA. Library: 68,000 volumes. 19 buildings on 40 acre main campus. Additional acreage includes an 18-hole championship golf course. ROTC - offering an ARMY two year commissioning program. Prep school for all service academies. 90% of high school graduates receive their 4 year college degrees. 90% of junior college graduates receive their baccalaureate degrees. Quality education at a fair price.

New Mexico State University
2400 Scenic Dr, Alamogordo NM 88310-3722
505-439-3600

New Mexico State University
1500 University Dr, Carlsbad NM 88220-3509
505-234-9200

New Mexico State University
1500 N 3rd St, Grants NM 87020-2025
505-287-7981 Fax: 505-287-2329
Website: www.grants.nmsu.edu

New Mexico State University
Dona Ana Branch Community College
PO Box 30001, Las Cruces NM 88003-8001
505-527-7500

Northern New Mexico College
921 Paseo de Onate, Espanola NM 87532
505-747-2100

Northern New Mexico Community College
El Rito NM 87530
505-581-4501

San Juan College
4601 College Blvd, Farmington NM 87402-4699
505-326-3311

Santa Fe Community College
6401 S Richards Ave, Santa Fe NM 87508-4887
505-428-1000

Southwestern Indian Polytechnic Institute
PO Box 10146, Albuquerque NM 87184-0146
505-346-2347

University of New Mexico
200 College Rd, Gallup NM 87301-5603
505-863-7500

University of New Mexico
4000 University Dr, Los Alamos NM 87544-2233
505-662-5919

University of New Mexico
280 La Entrada Rd, Los Lunas NM 87031-7633
505-925-8500

UNIVERSITY OF NEW MEXICO
115 Civic Plaza Dr, Taos NM 87571-6401
Henry Trujillo, Senior Student Enrollment Associate
505-737-6200 Fax: 505-737-9317
Website: taos.unm.edu
E-mail: htrujil1@unm.edu

NEW YORK

AMERICAN ACADEMY MCALLISTER INSTITUTE OF FUNERAL SERVICE
619 W 54th St 6th Floor, New York NY 10019
Meg Dunn, President
212-757-1190 Fax: 212-765-5923
Website: www.funeraleducation.org
E-mail: info@funeraleducation.org

Briarcliffe College
1055 Stewart Ave, Bethpage NY 11714-3545
Theresa Donohue, Director of Admissions
516-918-3600 Fax: 516-470-6020
Website: www.briarcliffe.edu

Briarcliffe College
225 W Main St, Patchogue NY 11772-3019
888-756-9900

Broome Community College
907 Upper Front St, Binghamton NY 13905
Anthony S. Fiorelli, Director of Admissions
607-778-5001 Fax: 607-778-5442
Website: www.sunybroome.edu
E-mail: fiorelli_a@sunybroome.edu

Bryant & Stratton College
465 Main St Ste 400, Buffalo NY 14203-1713
716-884-9120

Business Informatics Center
134 S Central Ave, Valley Stream NY 11580-5431
516-561-0050

Clinton Community College
136 Clinton Point Dr, Plattsburgh NY 12901-6002
Robert C. Wood, Assoc. Dean for Enrollment
518-562-4200

The College of Westchester
PO Box 710, White Plains NY 10602
914-948-4442

Columbia-Greene Community College
4400 State Route 23, Hudson NY 12534-9543
518-828-4181

Corning Community College
1 Academic Dr, Corning NY 14830-3299
607-962-9011

Culinary Institute of America
1946 Campus Dr, Hyde Park NY 12538-1499
Dennis Craig, Director of Admissions
800-CULINARY (285-4627)

CUNY Borough of Manhattan Community College
199 Chambers St, New York NY 10007-1044
212-346-8800

CUNY Bronx Community College
W 181st and University Ave, Bronx NY 10453-2895
718-289-5100

CUNY Kingsborough Community College
2001 Oriental Blvd, Brooklyn NY 11235-2398
718-368-5000

CUNY Queensborough Community College
22205 56th Ave, Bayside NY 11364-1432
Winston Yarde, Director of Admissions
718-631-6262

Dutchess Community College
53 Pendell Rd, Poughkeepsie NY 12601-1512
845-431-8000

Erie Community College
City Campus
121 Ellicott St, Buffalo NY 14203-2698
716-842-2770

Erie Community College North
6205 Main St, Williamsville NY 14221-8402
716-634-0800

Erie Community College South
4041 Southwestern Blvd
Orchard Park NY 14127-2199
716-648-5400

Finger Lakes Community College
4355 Lakeshore Dr, Canandaigua NY 14424-8347
585-394-3500

Fulton-Montgomery Community College
2805 State Highway 67, Johnstown NY 12095
518-762-4651

Gamla College
1213 Elm Ave, Brooklyn NY 11230
718-339-4747

Genesee Community College
1 College Rd, Batavia NY 14020-9703
585-343-0055

Herkimer County Community College
100 Reservoir Rd, Herkimer NY 13350-1545
888-464-4222

Hostos Community College - CUNY
500 Grand Concourse, Bronx NY 10451-5323
Roland Velez, Director of Admissions
718-518-4406

ISLAND DRAFTING & TECHNICAL INSTITUTE
128 Broadway (Route 110), Amityville NY 11701-2704
James G. DiLiberto, President
631-691-8733 Fax: 631-691-8738
Website: www.idti.edu
E-mail: info@idti.edu

Jamestown Community College
PO Box 20, Jamestown NY 14702-0020
Nelson J. Garifi, Jr., Director of Marketing
800-388-8557

Jamestown Community College
Olean NY 14760
585-372-1661

Jefferson Community College
1220 Coffeen St, Watertown NY 13601-1897
315-786-2200

LaGuardia Community College / CUNY
31-10 Thompson Ave, Long Island City NY 11101
718-482-7200

LONG ISLAND BUSINESS INSTITUTE
6500 Jericho Tpke, Commack NY 11725-2907
Dr. Philip Stander, President
631-499-7100 Fax: 631-499-7114
Website: www.libi.edu
E-mail: rnazar@libi.edu
Private. Coed. Accreditation: ACICS. Approvals: National Court Reporting Association, NY State Board of Regents. Tuition: $275.00 per credit hour. Fees: $50.00 application fee. Enrollment: 250. Faculty: 25. Student-faculty ratio: 12:1. Associate of Occupational Studies degree offered in Court Reporting, Office Technology. Diploma programs in Medical Transcription, Legal Secretarial, Office Technology, Administrative Assistant.

LONG ISLAND BUSINESS INSTITUTE
37-12 Prince St, Flushing NY 11354-4429
Dr. Philip Stander, President
718-939-5100 Fax: 718-989-9235
Website: www.libi.edu
E-mail: dwang@libi.edu
Private. Coed. Accreditation: ACICS. Approvals. National Court Reporting Association, NY State Board of Regents. Tuition: $275.00 per credit hour. Fees: $50.00 application fee. Enrollment: 250. Faculty: 25. Student-faculty ratio: 12:1. Associate of Occupational Studies degree offered in Computer Programmer, Administrative Assistant, Office Technology, Business Management, Accounting. Diploma programs in Legal Secretarial, Office Technology, Administrative Assistant.

Maria College of Albany
700 New Scotland Ave, Albany NY 12208-1715
518-438-3111

Mohawk Valley Community College
1101 Sherman Dr, Utica NY 13501-5394
315-792-5400

Monroe College
434 Main St, New Rochelle NY 10801-6410
914-632-5400

Monroe Community College
1000 E Henrietta Rd, Rochester NY 14623-5701
585-292-2000

Nassau Community College
1 Education Dr, Garden City NY 11530-6719
516-572-7501

North Country Community College
23 Santanoni, Saranac Lake NY 12983
Edwin Trathen, Assistant to the President for Enrollment Services
1-888-TRY-NCCC ext. 686

Onondaga Community College
4941 Onondaga Rd, Syracuse NY 13215-2001
315-498-2622

ROCHESTER INSTITUTE OF TECHNOLOGY NATIONAL TECHNICAL INSTITUTE FOR THE DEAF (NTID)
52 Lomb Memorial Dr, Rochester NY 14623-5604
Robert Borden, Director of NTID Admissions
585-475-6700 (v/TTY) Fax: 585-475-2696
Website: www.rit.edu/ntid/getinfo
E-mail: NTIDAdmissions@rit.edu
Established 1965. Private. Coed. Tuition $8,559 (NTID or NTID supported students only). Room & Board: $8,748. Fees: $642. Enrollment: 1,100. Faculty: 210. Degrees offered: MS, BS, AS, AAS, AOS. Library: 800,000 volumes. 237 buildings on 1,300 acres. Qualified deaf and hard-of-hearing students can earn bachelor's or master's degrees in more than 200 programs offered by RIT's seven other colleges - Applied Science and Technology, Business, Computing and Information Sciences, Engineering, Imaging Arts and Sciences, Liberal Arts, and Science. They also can earn associate degrees in more than 30 accredited NTID programs including: Accounting Technology, Administrative Support Technology, Applied Computer Technology, Applied Optical Technology, Art and Business Technology, Automation Technologies - Robotics, Computer Design, Computer Aided Drafting Technology, Computer Integrated Machining Technology, Digital Imaging & Publishing Technology, and Laboratory Science Technology. Additionally NTID offers degrees in American Sign Language-English Interpretation and a Master's of Science in Secondary Education of Students who are Deaf or Hard of Hearing.

Sage College of Albany
140 New Scotland Ave, Albany NY 12208-3425
518-292-1717

SUNY Adirondack Community College
640 Bay Rd, Queensbury NY 12804
Sarah Jane Linehan, Director of Enrollment Management
518-743-2264

SUNY Canton - College of Technology
34 Cornell Dr, Canton NY 13617-1037
315-386-7011

SUNY Cayuga County Community College
197 Franklin St, Auburn NY 13021-3011
Richard F. Landers, Director of Admissions
315-255-1743

SUNY College of Agriculture & Technology
Morrisville NY 13408
Thomas Ver Dow, Dean of Enrollment Management
800-258-0111

SUNY College of Technology
Alfred NY 14802
Deborah J. Goodrich, Director of Admissions
800-4AL-FRED Fax: 607-587-4299
Website: www.alfredstate.edu
E-mail: admissions@alfredstate.edu

SUNY College of Technology
2 Main St, Delhi NY 13753-1110
Robert W. Mazzei, Director of Admissions
800-96-DELHI Fax: 607-746-4104
Website: www.delhi.edu
E-mail: enroll@delhi.edu

SUNY Hudson Valley Community College
80 Vandenburgh Ave, Troy NY 12180-6025
Jack Mahoney, Director of Admissions
518-629-HVCC (629-4822)

SUNY Niagara County Community College
3111 Saunders Settlement Rd
Sanborn NY 14132-9487
Kathleen Saunders, Director of Admissions
716-614-6200 Fax: 716-614-6820
Website: www.niagaracc.suny.edu
E-mail: saunders@niagaracc.suny.edu

SUNY North Country Community College
PO Box 311, Ticonderoga NY 12883-0311
518-585-4454

SUNY ORANGE COUNTY COMMUNITY COLLEGE
115 South St, Middletown NY 10940-6437
Margot St. Lawrence, Director of Admissions
845-341-4030 Fax: 845-342-8662
Website: www.sunyorange.edu
E-mail: apply@sunyorange.edu
Established 1950. Public. Coed. Accreditation: Middle States Association of Colleges & Schools. Tuition: $2,900. Fees: $100 student activity/athletic fee, $200 technology fee, $18 insurance. Enrollment: 2,933 full-time, 3,118 part-time. Faculty: 175. Student-faculty ratio: 15:1. Library: 95,000 volumes, 33,000 microforms, 500 periodicals. 16 buildings on 32 acres. Also has an Extension Center in Newburgh servicing 1,000 students.

SUNY Rockland Community College
766 N Main St, Spring Valley NY 10977-1985
845-352-5535

SUNY Rockland Community College
185 N Main St, Spring Valley NY 10977-4105
845-352-5535

SUNY Rockland Community College
145 College Rd, Suffern NY 10901-3611
Charles Connolly, Coordinator of Admissions & Recruitment
845-574-4000

SUNY Schenectady County Community College
78 Washington Ave, Schenectady NY 12305-2215
Robert Dinello, Director of Admissions
518-381-1366

SUNY Suffolk County Community College
Crooked Hill Rd, Brentwood NY 11717-1017
631-851-6700

SUNY Suffolk County Community College
2 Speonk Riverhead Rd, Riverhead NY 11901-3433
631-548-2500

SUNY Suffolk County Community College
533 College Rd, Selden NY 11784-2851
631-451-4110

SUNY Sullivan County Community College
112 College Rd, Loch Sheldrake NY 12759-5151
Dan Baldo, Director of Admissions
845-434-5750

T.C.I. Institute, The College of Technology
320 W 31st St, New York NY 10001-2789
Thomas Coleman, President
212-594-4001

Tompkins Cortland Community College
PO Box 139, Dryden NY 13053-0139
607-844-8211

TROCAIRE COLLEGE

360 Choate Ave, Buffalo NY 14220-2094
Paul B. Hurley, Ph.D., President
Claudia M. Lesinski, Enrollment Management Officer
716-826-1200 Fax: 716-828-6107
Website: www.trocaire.edu
E-mail: info@trocaire.edu
   Established 1958. Private. Coed. Accreditation: Middle States Association of Colleges and Schools. Tuition: $9,850. Enrollment: 691 full-time, 324 part-time. Student-faculty ratio: 18:1. Degrees offered: A.A., A.S., A.A.S. Strong on health related careers, business, computer network technology, young child education.

Ulster County Community College
Stone Ridge NY 12484
845-687-5000

Utica School of Commerce
17 Elm St, Oneonta NY 13820-1828
Misty Davis, Admissions
607-432-7003 Fax: 607-432-7004
Website: www.uscny.com
E-mail: mdavis@uscny.com

Villa Maria College of Buffalo
240 Pine Ridge Rd, Buffalo NY 14225-3913
Kevin Donovan, Director of Enrollment
Management/Marketing
716-896-0700

Westchester Community College
75 Grasslands Rd, Valhalla NY 10595-1693
914-785-6600

Wood Tobe-Coburn School
8 E 40th St, New York NY 10016-0102
212-686-9040

NORTH CAROLINA

Alamance Community College
PO Box 8000, Graham NC 27253-8000
336-578-2002

Asheville Buncombe Technical Community College
340 Victoria Rd, Asheville NC 28801-4897
828-254-1921

Beaufort County Community College
PO Box 1069, Washington NC 27889
252-946-6194

Bladen Community College
PO Box 266, Dublin NC 28332-0266
910-862-2164

Blue Ridge Community College
College Dr, Flat Rock NC 28731
828-694-1700

Brunswick Community College
PO Box 30, Supply NC 28462-0030
910-755-7300

Caldwell Community College and Technical Institute
2855 Hickory Blvd, Hudson NC 28638
828-726-2200

Cape Fear Community College
411 N Front St, Wilmington NC 28401-3910
910-251-5100

Carolinas College of Health Sciences
PO Box 32861, Charlotte NC 28232-2861
Elizabeth West, Admissions Officer
704-355-5043 Fax: 704-355-9336
Website: www.carolinascollege.edu
E-mail: elizabeth.west@carolinascollege.edu
See listing under "Nursing"

Carteret Community College
3505 Arendell St, Morehead City NC 28557-2989
Pamela Hilbert, V.P. for Instruction & Student Support
252-247-3058 ext. 144

Catawba Valley Community College
2550 US Highway 70 SE, Hickory NC 28602-8302
828-327-7000

Central Carolina Community College
1105 Kelly Dr, Sanford NC 27330-9000
Ron Miriello, Director of Admissions
919-775-5401

Central Piedmont Community College
PO Box 35009, Charlotte NC 28235-5009
704-330-2722

Cleveland Community College
137 S Post Rd, Shelby NC 28152-6205
704-484-4000

Coastal Carolina Community College
444 Western Blvd, Jacksonville NC 28546-6899
910-455-1221

College of the Albemarle
PO Box 2327, Elizabeth City NC 27906-2327
252-335-0821

Craven Community College
PO Box 885, New Bern NC 28563-0885
252-638-4131

Davidson County Community College
PO Box 1287, Lexington NC 27293-1287
336-249-8186

Durham Technical Community College
1637 E Lawson St, Durham NC 27703-5023
919-686-3333

ECPI College of Technology
4101 Doie Cope Rd, Raleigh NC 27613-7387
919-571-0057

Edgecombe Community College
2009 W Wilson St, Tarboro NC 27886-9361
Thomas B. Anderson, VP of Student Services
252-823-5166

Fayetteville Technical Community College
PO Box 35236, Fayetteville NC 28303-0236
910-678-8400

Forsyth Technical Community College
2100 Silas Creek Pkwy
Winston Salem NC 27103-5150
336-723-0371

Gaston College
201 Highway 321 S, Dallas NC 28034-1499
704-922-6200

Guilford Technical Community College
PO Box 309, Jamestown NC 27282-0309
336-334-4822

Halifax Community College
PO Box 809, Weldon NC 27890-0809
252-536-2551

Haywood Community College
185 Freedlander Dr, Clyde NC 28721
Debbie Rowland, Coordinator of Admissions
828-627-4500 Fax: 828-627-4513
Website: www.haywood.edu
E-mail: drowland@haywood.edu

Heritage Bible College
PO Box 1628, Dunn NC 28335
910-892-3178 Fax: 910-892-1809
Website: www.heritagebiblecollege.org
E-mail: generalinfo@heritagebiblecollege.org

Isothermal Community College
PO Box 804, Spindale NC 28160-0804
828-286-3636

James Sprunt Community College
PO Box 398, Kenansville NC 28349-0398
Rita Brown, Registrar
910-296-2500 Fax: 910-296-1636
Website: www.sprunt.com

Johnston Community College
PO Box 2350, Smithfield NC 27577-2350
919-934-3051

King's College
322 Lamar Ave, Charlotte NC 28204-2493
704-372-0266

Lenoir Community College
PO Box 188, Kinston NC 28502-0188
252-527-6223

Louisburg College
501 N Main St, Louisburg NC 27549-2399
800-775-0208 or 919-496-2521 Fax: 919-496-1788
Website: www.louisburg.edu
E-mail: admissions@louisburg.edu

Martin Community College
1161 Kehukee Park Rd, Williamston NC 27892-8307
252-792-1521

Mayland Community College
PO Box 547, Spruce Pine NC 28777-0547
828-765-7351

McDowell Technical Community College
54 College Dr, Marion NC 28752
828-652-6021

Mitchell Community College
500 W Broad St, Statesville NC 28677-5264
704-878-3200

Montgomery Community College
1011 Page St, Troy NC 27371-8387
910-576-6222

Nash Community College
PO Box 7488, Rocky Mount NC 27804-0488
252-443-4011

Pamlico Community College
PO Box 185, Grantsboro NC 28529-0185
252-249-1851

Piedmont Community College
PO Box 1197, Roxboro NC 27573-1197
336-599-1181

Pitt Community College
PO Box 7007, Greenville NC 27835-7007
252-321-4200

Randolph Community College
PO Box 1009, Asheboro NC 27204-1009
336-633-0200

Richmond Community College
PO Box 1189, Hamlet NC 28345-1189
910-582-7000

Roanoke-Chowan Community College
109 Community College Rd, Ahoskie NC 27910
252-862-1200

Robeson Community College
PO Box 1420, Lumberton NC 28359
Judith Revels, Director of Admissions
910-738-7101

Rockingham Community College
PO Box 38, Wentworth NC 27375-0038
336-342-4261

Rowan-Cabarrus Community College
PO Box 1595, Salisbury NC 28145-1595
704-637-0760

Sampson Community College
PO Box 318, Clinton NC 28329-0318
910-592-8081

Sandhills Community College
3395 Airport Rd, Pinehurst NC 28374
910-692-6185

South College
1567 Patton Ave, Asheville NC 28806-1748
Robert Davis, Dean of Academic Affairs
828-252-2486 Fax: 828-252-8558
Website: southcollegenc.com
E-mail: bdavis@southcollegenc.com

Southeastern Community College
PO Box 151, Whiteville NC 28472-0151
910-642-7141

South Piedmont Community College
PO Box 126, Polkton NC 28135-0126
John Curtis, Contact
704-272-5324 Fax: 704-272-8904
Website: www.spcc.edu
E-mail: jcurtis@spcc.edu

Southwestern Community College
447 College Dr, Sylva NC 28779-8581
828-586-4091

Stanly Community College
141 College Dr, Albemarle NC 28001-6418
704-982-0121

Surry Community College
630 S Main St, Dobson NC 27017-8432
336-386-8121

Tri-County Community College
2300 US Highway 64 E, Murphy NC 28906-7919
828-837-6810

Vance-Granville Community College
PO Box 917, Henderson NC 27536-0917
252-492-2061

Wake Technical Community College
9101 Fayetteville Rd, Raleigh NC 27603-5696
Dr. Robert E. Ireland, Director of Admissions
919-662-3357

Wayne Community College
PO Box 8002, Goldsboro NC 27533-8002
Kathy Garner, Public Information Officer
919-735-5151

Western Piedmont Community College
1001 Burkemont Ave, Morganton NC 28655-4511
828-438-6000

Wilkes Community College
PO Box 120, Wilkesboro NC 28697-0120
336-838-6100

Wilson Technical Community College
PO Box 4305, Wilson NC 27893-0305
252-291-1195

NORTH DAKOTA

Bismarck State College
PO Box 5587, Bismarck ND 58506
701-224-5400

Cankdeska Cikana Community College
PO Box 269, Fort Totten ND 58335-0269
701-766-4415

Fort Berthold Community College
PO Box 490, New Town ND 58763-0490
701-627-4738

Lake Region State College
1801 College Dr N, Devils Lake ND 58301
701-662-1600

Minot State University-Bottineau Campus
105 Simrall Blvd, Bottineau ND 58318-1159
Paula Berg, Associate Dean of Student Affairs
800-542-6866 Fax: 701-228-5499
Website: www.misu-b.nodak.edu
E-mail: paula.berg@misu.nodak.edu

North Dakota State College of Science
800 6th Ave N, Wahpeton ND 58075-3602
701-671-1130

Sitting Bull College
1341 92nd St, Fort Yates ND 58538
Melody Azure, Director of Admissions / Registrar
701-854-3861 Fax: 701-854-3403
Website: www.sittingbull.edu
E-mail: melodya@sbci.edu

Turtle Mountain Community College
PO Box 340, Belcourt ND 58316-0340
701-477-7862

United Tribes Technical College
3315 University Dr, Bismarck ND 58504-7596
701-255-3285

Williston State College
PO Box 1326, Williston ND 58802-1326
Penny Powell, Director Enrollment Services
701-774-4200 Fax: 701-774-4544
Website: www.wsc.nodak.edu
E-mail: penny.soiseth@wsc.nodak.edu

OHIO

The Art Institute of Cincinnati
1171 E Kemper Rd, Cincinnati OH 45246
Marion Allman, President
513-751-1206 Fax: 513-751-1209
Website: www.theartinstituteofcincinnati.com
E-mail: aic@theartinstituteofcincinnati.com
See listing under "Art"

Belmont Technical College
120 Fox Shannon Pl, Saint Clairsville OH 43950-8751
740-695-9500

Bowling Green State University - Firelands Campus
1 University Dr, Huron OH 44839
419-433-5560

Bradford School
2469 Stelzer Rd, Columbus OH 43219-3129
Raeann Lee, Director of Admissions
614-416-6200

Brown Mackie College - Akron
2791 Mogadore Rd, Akron OH 44312-1596
330-733-8766

Brown Mackie College - Cincinnati
1011 Glendale Milford Rd, Cincinnati OH 45215-1107
Robin Krout, President
513-771-2424 Fax: 513-771-3413
Website: www.brownmackie.edu
E-mail: rkrout@brownmackie.edu

Brown Mackie College - North Canton
1320 W Maple St, North Canton OH 44720
330-494-1214

Bryant & Stratton College
12955 Snow Rd, Cleveland OH 44130-1013
Thomas M. Hartman, Director
216-265-3151

Central Ohio Technical College
1179 University Dr, Newark OH 43055-1767
740-366-9222

Chatfield College
20918 State Route 251, Saint Martin OH 45118-9059
513-875-3344

Cincinnati State Technical & Community College
3520 Central Pkwy, Cincinnati OH 45223-2612
513-569-1500

Clark State Community College
570 E Leffel Ln, Springfield OH 45505-4749
937-325-0691

Cleveland Institute of Electronics
1776 E 17th St, Cleveland OH 44114-3679
Scott Katzenmeyer, Director of Admissions
800-243-6446 Fax: 216-781-0331
Website: www.cie-wc.edu
E-mail: instruct@cie-wc.edu

Columbus State Community College
550 E Spring St, Columbus OH 43215-1786
Ken Conner, Director of Admissions
614-287-3669

Cuyahoga Community College
2900 Community College Ave
Cleveland OH 44115-3196
216-987-4000

Cuyahoga Community College
25444 Harvard Rd, Highland Hills OH 44122-6202
216-987-2019

Cuyahoga Community College
11000 W Pleasant Valley Rd
Parma Heights OH 44130-5199
440-842-7773

Edison State Community College
1973 Edison Dr, Piqua OH 45356-9239
937-778-8600

Hocking College
3301 Hocking Pkwy, Nelsonville OH 45764-9704
Diane K. Wolf, Assistant Director of Admissions
Information
800-282-4163

ITT Technical Institute
3325 Stop 8 Rd, Dayton OH 45414-3425
Joe Graham, Director of Admissions
937-454-2267 Fax: 937-454-2278
Website: www.itt-tech.edu
E-mail: jgraham@itt-tech.edu

ITT Technical Institute
4700 Richmond Rd, Warrensville Heights OH 44128
216-896-6500

ITT Technical Institute
1030 N Meridian Rd, Youngstown OH 44509-4098
Tom Flynn, Director of Admissions
800-832-5001

James A. Rhodes State College
4240 Campus Dr, Lima OH 45804-3597
419-995-8000

Jefferson Community College
4000 Sunset Blvd, Steubenville OH 43952-3598
740-264-5591

Kent State University-Ashtabula Campus
3325 W 13th St, Ashtabula OH 44004-2299
Kelly Sanford, Contact
440-964-3322

Kent State University-East Liverpool Campus
400 E 4th St, East Liverpool OH 43920-3497
Jamie Kenneally, Contact
330-385-3805

Kent State University-Geauga Campus
14111 Claridon Troy Rd, Burton OH 44021-9581
Dave Chappell, Contact
440-834-4187

Kent State University-Salem Campus
2491 State Route 45 S, Salem OH 44460-9412
Dennis Giacomino, Contact
330-332-0361

Kent State University-Stark Campus
6000 Frank Ave NW, North Canton OH 44720-7548
Jim Barrett, Contact
330-499-9600

Kent State University-Trumbull Campus
4314 Mahoning Ave NW, Warren OH 44483-1998
Linda Petrilla, Contact
330-678-4281

Kent State University - Tuscarawas Campus
330 University Dr NE, New Philadelphia OH 44663
Denise Testa, Contact
330-339-3391

Lakeland Community College
7700 Clocktower Dr, Kirtland OH 44094-5198
Tracey Cooper, Director of Admissions
440-953-7100

Lorain County Community College
1005 Abbe Rd N, Elyria OH 44035
Dione Somerville, Director of Admissions
440-365-5222

Marion Technical College
1467 Mount Vernon Ave, Marion OH 43302-5628
Joel Liles, Director of Admissions
740-389-4636

Mercy College of Northwest Ohio
2221 Madison Ave, Toledo OH 43624
419-251-1279

Miami-Jacobs Career College
110 N Patterson Blvd, Dayton OH 45402
Sean Kuhn, Regional Director of Admissions
937-222-7337

Miami University-Hamilton Campus
1601 University Blvd, Hamilton OH 45011-3399
513-785-3000

Miami University-Middletown Campus
4200 E University Blvd, Middletown OH 45042
513-727-3200

North Central State College
PO Box 698, Mansfield OH 44901-0698
Troy Shutler, Director of Admissions
419-755-4800

Northwest State Community College
22600 State Route 34, Archbold OH 43502-9542
Mark Thompson, Director of Admissions
419-267-5511 Fax: 419-267-5587
Website: www.northweststate.edu
E-mail: mthompson@northweststate.edu

Ohio Institute of Photography & Technology
2029 Edgefield Rd, Dayton OH 45439-1917
Robert A. Martin, Executive Director
937-294-6155

Ohio State University-A & T Institute
1328 Dover Rd, Wooster OH 44691-8905
330-264-3911

Owens Community College
300 Davis St, Findlay OH 45840-3631
William J. Ivoska PhD., Vice President of Student
Services
567-429-3500 Fax: 567-423-0246
Website: www.owens.edu
E-mail: admissions@owens.edu

Owens Community College
PO Box 10000, Toledo OH 43699-1947
William J. Ivoska, Ph.D, Vice President of Student
Services
567-661-7000 Fax: 567-661-7607
Website: www.owens.edu
E-mail: admissions@owens.edu

Sinclair Community College
444 W 3rd St, Dayton OH 45402-1460
Sara P. Smith, Director of Outreach Services
937-512-3000 Fax: 937-512-2393
Website: www.sinclair.edu
E-mail: admit@sinclair.edu

Southern State Community College
100 Hobart Rd, Hillsboro OH 45133-9488
937-393-3431

Southern State Community College
12681 US Route 62, Sardinia OH 45171
937-695-0307

Southern State Community College
1850 Davids Dr, Wilmington OH 45177
937-382-6645

Southwestern College
201 E 2nd St, Franklin OH 45005-2267
937-746-6633

Southwestern College of Business
149 Northland Blvd, Cincinnati OH 45246
513-874-0432

Southwestern College of Business
630 Vine St Ste 200, Cincinnati OH 45202-2421
513-421-3212

Terra State Community College
2830 Napoleon Rd, Fremont OH 43420-9670
419-334-8400

University of Akron-Wayne College
1901 Smucker Rd, Orrville OH 44667-9192
330-683-2010

University of Cincinnati
Clermont College
4200 Clermont College Dr, Batavia OH 45103-1748
513-732-5200

University of Cincinnati
College of Allied Health Sciences
PO Box 670394, Cincinnati OH 45267-0394
Gilbert Hageman, Associate Dean
513-558-7495

University of Cincinnati
Raymond Walters College
9555 Plainfield Rd, Cincinnati OH 45236-1007
513-745-5700

Washington State Community College
710 Colegate Dr, Marietta OH 45750-9225
740-374-8716

Wright State University
7600 State Route 703, Celina OH 45822-2921
419-586-0300

Zane State College
1555 Newark Rd, Zanesville OH 43701-2694
740-454-2501

OKLAHOMA

Carl Albert State College
1507 S McKenna St, Poteau OK 74953-5207
918-647-1200

Connors State College
RR 1 Box 1000, Warner OK 74469-9700
918-463-2931

Eastern Oklahoma State College
1301 W Main St, Wilburton OK 74578-4901
918-465-2361

Murray State College
1 Murray Campus St, Tishomingo OK 73460-3137
580-371-2371

Northeastern Oklahoma A & M College
200 I St NE, Miami OK 74354-6434
Linda Oldham Barns, Director of Admissions
800-234-3409

Northern Oklahoma College
PO Box 310, Tonkawa OK 74653-0310
580-628-6200

Oklahoma City Community College
7777 S May Ave, Oklahoma City OK 73159-4419
405-682-1611

Oklahoma State University-Oklahoma City
900 N Portland Ave, Oklahoma City OK 73107-6120
405-947-4421

Oklahoma State University-Okmulgee
1801 E 4th St, Okmulgee OK 74447-3901
Cary Fox, Director of Admissions
800-722-4471

Redlands Community College
1300 S Country Club Rd, El Reno OK 73036-5300
Trish Hobson, Director of Admissions
405-262-2552

Rose State College
6420 SE 15th St, Midwest City OK 73110-2799
405-733-7300

Seminole State College
PO Box 351, Seminole OK 74818-0351
405-382-9950

Southwestern Oklahoma State University
409 E Mississippi Ave, Sayre OK 73662-1200
580-928-5533

SPARTAN COLLEGE OF AERONAUTICS AND TECHNOLOGY
8820 E Pine St, Tulsa OK 74115-5802
Director of Admissions
800-331-1204 Fax: 918-831-8609
Website: www.spartan.edu
E-mail: spartan@mail.spartan.edu
Established 1928. Coed. Accredited member school:
ACCSCT. Providing Technical training and education in
Avionics, Instruments, and Maintenance; Nondestructive
Testing and Quality Control. Complete flight training pro-
gram. Offering Diplomas, Associate of Applied Science
and Bachelor of Science in Aviation Technology Man-
agement.

Tulsa Community College
6111 E Skelly Dr Ste 200, Tulsa OK 74135-6198
918-595-7000

Tulsa Community College
3727 E Apache St, Tulsa OK 74115
918-595-7000

Western Oklahoma State College
2801 N Main St, Altus OK 73521-1397
580-477-2000

OREGON

Apollo College
2004 Lloyd Ctr Fl 3, Portland OR 97232-1309
503-761-6100

Blue Mountain Community College
PO Box 100, Pendleton OR 97801-1000
541-276-1260

Central Oregon Community College
2600 NW College Way, Bend OR 97701-5933
Alicia Moore, Director of Admissions and Records
541-383-7500

Chemeketa Community College
PO Box 14007, Salem OR 97309-7070
Jeri Hunter, Director of Admissions
503-399-5106

Clackamas Community College
19600 S Molalla Ave, Oregon City OR 97045-7998
Cheryl Hollatz-Wisely, Director of Student Outreach
503-657-6958 ext. 2455

Clatsop Community College
1653 Jerome Ave, Astoria OR 97103-3698
503-325-0910

Klamath Community College
7390 S 6th St, Klamath Falls OR 97603
541-882-3521

Lane Community College
4000 E 30th Ave, Eugene OR 97405-0640
541-747-4501

Linn-Benton Community College
6500 Pacific Blvd SW, Albany OR 97321-3774
Christine Baker, Outreach Coordinator
541-917-4811 Fax: 541-917-4868
Website: www.linnbenton.edu
E-mail: admissions@linnbenton.edu

Mt. Hood Community College
26000 SE Stark St, Gresham OR 97030-3300
503-491-6422

Portland Community College
PO Box 19000, Portland OR 97280-0990
Dennis Bailey-Fougnier, Director of Admissions
503-977-4519

ROGUE COMMUNITY COLLEGE
3345 Redwood Hwy, Grants Pass OR 97527-9298
Peter Angstadt, President
Claudia Sullivan, Director of Enrollment Services
541-956-7500 Fax: 541-471-3585
Website: www.roguecc.edu
E-mail: csullivan@roguecc.edu
Established 1970. Public. Coed. Accreditation:
NWASC. Tuition: $2,418. Enrollment: 10,000 full-time,
7,000 part-time. Faculty: 106 full-time, 372 part-time. Degrees offered: AA, AAS, AGS, AS. Programs in: Business
technology, nursing, respiratory therapy, electronics,
human services, fire science, automotive/diesel, computer science, criminal justice, construction technology,
humanities, social science, and science/math.

Southwestern Oregon Community College
1988 Newmark Ave, Coos Bay OR 97420-2911
541-888-2525

Treasure Valley Community College
650 College Blvd, Ontario OR 97914-3423
541-889-6493

Umpqua Community College
PO Box 967, Roseburg OR 97470-0226
541-440-4600

PENNSYLVANIA

Allied Medical & Technical Institute
166 Slocum St, Forty Fort PA 18704-2936
570-288-8400

Antonelli Institute - Art & Photography
300 Montgomery Ave, Erdenheim PA 19038-8242
Dr. Thomas Treacy, President
215-836-2222 or 800-722-7871 Fax: 215-836-2794
Website: www.antonelli.edu
E-mail: admissions@antonelli.edu

Bradley Academy for the Visual Arts
1409 Williams Rd, York PA 17402-9012
James T. Hannigan, Jr., Director of Admissions
800-864-7725

Bucks County Community College
Swamp Rd, Newtown PA 18940
215-968-8000

Butler County Community College
PO Box 1203, Butler PA 16003-1203
724-287-8711

Cambria-Rowe Business College
221 Central Ave, Johnstown PA 15902-2406
814-536-5168

Commonwealth Technical Institute
Hiram G. Andrews Center
727 Goucher St, Johnstown PA 15905-3025
Joseph R. Rizzo, Sr., Contact
814-255-8200

Community College of Allegheny County
8701 Perry Hwy, Pittsburgh PA 15237-5353
412-366-7000

Community College of Allegheny County
Allegheny Campus
808 Ridge Ave, Pittsburgh PA 15212-6003
412-237-2525

Community College of Allegheny County
Boyce Campus
595 Beatty Rd, Monroeville PA 15146-1348
724-325-1327

Community College of Allegheny County
South Campus
1750 Clairton Rd, West Mifflin PA 15122-3029
412-469-1100

Community College of Beaver County
1 Campus Dr, Monaca PA 15061-2566
724-775-8561

Community College of Philadelphia
1700 Spring Garden St, Philadelphia PA 19130-3936
215-751-8010

Delaware County Community College
901 Media Line Rd, Media PA 19063-1094
610-359-5000

Erie Business Center South
170 Cascade Galleria, New Castle PA 16101
724-658-9066

Erie Institute of Technology
5539 Peach St, Erie PA 16509-2603
Barbara Bolt, Director of Admissions
814-868-9900

Harcum College
750 Montgomery Ave, Bryn Mawr PA 19010-3476
610-525-4100

Harrisburg Area Community College
1 HACC Dr, Harrisburg PA 17110-2999
717-780-2300

Johnson College
3427 N Main Ave, Scranton PA 18508-1495
Dr. Ann L. Pipinski, President & CEO
Melissa Ide, Director of Enrollment Management
800-2WE-WORK or 570-342-6404 ext. 125
Fax: 570-348-2181
Website: www.johnson.edu
E-mail: admit@johnson.edu

Keystone College
PO Box 50, La Plume PA 18440-0200
570-945-5141

Lackawanna College
501 Vine St, Scranton PA 18509-3251
570-961-7810

Lansdale School of Business
201 Church Rd, North Wales PA 19454-4148
215-699-5700

Lehigh Carbon Community College
4525 Education Park Dr
Schnecksville PA 18078-2502
610-799-1134

Lehigh Valley College
2809 E Saucon Valley Rd
Center Valley PA 18034-8447
Joshua Padron, Vice President of Marketing and
Admissions
800-227-9109 Fax: 610-791-7810
Website: www.lehighvalley.edu
E-mail: joshua.padron@lehighvalley.edu

Lock Haven University-Clearfield Campus
PO Box 1410, Clearfield PA 16830-5410
James C. Reeser, Dean of Admissions
814-765-0559

Luzerne County Community College
1333 S Prospect St, Nanticoke PA 18634-3899
800-377-5222 ext. 337

Manor College
700 Fox Chase Rd, Jenkintown PA 19046-4118
215-885-2360

McCann School of Business & Technology
47 S Main St, Mahanoy City PA 17948-2698
570-773-1820

McCann School of Business & Technology
2650 Woodglen Rd, Pottsville PA 17901-1335
570-622-7622

Montgomery County Community College
340 DeKalb Pike, Blue Bell PA 19422-1400
215-641-6300

Newport Business Institute
945 Greensburg Rd, Lower Burrell PA 15068-3929
Admissions Department
800-752-7695 Fax: 724-339-2950
Website: www.nbi.edu
E-mail: tjpomatto@nbi.edu

Newport Business Institute
941 W 3rd St, Williamsport PA 17701-5855
570-326-2869

Northampton Co. Area Community College
3835 Green Pond Rd, Bethlehem PA 18020-7599
610-861-5300

Peirce College
1420 Pine St, Philadelphia PA 19102-4603
215-545-6400

Penn State Fayette
The Eberly Campus
PO Box 519, Uniontown PA 15401-0519
724-430-4100

Pennsylvania College of Technology
Mansfield Rd, Wellsboro PA 16901
570-724-7703

Pennsylvania Culinary Institute
717 Liberty Ave, Pittsburgh PA 15222-3500
Jason Remaley, V.P. of Enrollment Management Office
800-432-2433

Pennsylvania Highlands Community College
PO Box 68, Johnstown PA 15907-0068
814-532-5300

PENNSYLVANIA INSTITUTE OF TECHNOLOGY
800 Manchester Ave, Media PA 19063-4036
Dr. Paul N. Smith, President
Angela Cassetta, Dean of Enrollment Management
800-422-0025 or 610-892-1500 Fax: 610-892-1510
Website: www.pit.edu
E-mail: info@pit.edu
A TWO YEAR COLLEGE
Established 1953. Private. Coed. Full-time, part-time,
continuing education programs. Accreditation: Commission on Higher Education, Middle States Association of
Colleges and Schools. Enrollment: 369. Student/Faculty
ratio: 15:1. Associates Degrees: AAS in Architec-
tural/Civil, Computer Drafting and Design, Electronic,
Mechanical Engineering and Web Design Technologies;
AS in Business Administration, Medical Office Management and Office Technologies. Microsoft and Cisco certification is also available. Emphasizes "hands-on"
(applied) academics and cooperative education programs. Master and peer tutoring offered in all programs,
together with pre-technology instruction. Computerized
instruction and learning utilized in all courses. Tech
Prep/School to Career program with local school districts. 94% job placement of available graduates since
1974.

Pennsylvania School of Business
406 W Hamilton St, Allentown PA 18101-1604
610-264-8029

Pennsylvania State University
1600 Woodland Rd, Abington PA 19001-3918
215-881-7300

Pennsylvania State University
3000 Ivyside Park, Altoona PA 16601-3760
814-949-5000

Pennsylvania State University
College Place, Du Bois PA 15801
814-375-4700

Pennsylvania State University
120 Ridgeview Dr, Dunmore PA 18512-1602
570-963-4757

Pennsylvania State University
8380 Mohr Ln, Fogelsville PA 18051-1918
610-285-5000

Pennsylvania State University
Hazelton Campus, Hazleton PA 18201
570-450-3000

Pennsylvania State University
0 University Dr, Mc Keesport PA 15132-7647
412-675-9000

Pennsylvania State University
25 Yearsley Mill Rd, Media PA 19063-5522
610-892-1350

Pennsylvania State University
Mont Alto Campus, Mont Alto PA 17237
717-749-6000

Pennsylvania State University
PO Box 7009, Reading PA 19610-6009
610-320-4800

Pennsylvania State University
200 University Dr, Schuylkill Haven PA 17972-2202
570-385-6000

Pennsylvania State University
147 Shenango Ave, Sharon PA 16146-1537
724-983-5800

Pennsylvania State University
1031 Edgecomb Ave, York PA 17403-3326
717-771-4000

Pennsylvania State University - Wilkes Barre
PO Box PSU, Lehman PA 18627-0217
John S. Barnes, Admissions Officer
800-966-6613

PIA School of Specialized Technology
PO Box 10897, Pittsburgh PA 15236-0897
Vincent J. Mezza, Director of Admissions
800-444-1440 Fax: 412-466-0513
Website: www.pia.edu
E-mail: admissions@pia.edu
See listing under "Aeronautics, Aviation and Space"

PITTSBURGH INSTITUTE OF MORTUARY SCIENCE
5808 Baum Blvd, Pittsburgh PA 15206-3706
Karen Rocco, Registrar
412-362-8500 Fax: 412-362-1684
Website: www.pims.edu
E-mail: pims5808@aol.com

Reading Area Community College
PO Box 1706, Reading PA 19603-1706
David J. Adams, Director of Admissions
610-607-6224

Thaddeus Stevens College of Technology
750 E King St, Lancaster PA 17602-3113
717-299-7730

Westmoreland County Community College
400 Armbrust Rd, Youngwood PA 15697-1898
724-925-4000

RHODE ISLAND
Community College of Rhode Island
Flanagan Campus
1762 Louisquisset Pike, Lincoln RI 02865-4513
Elizabeth A. Mancini, Assistant Dean of Enrollment
Services
401-825-2003

Community College of Rhode Island
Knight Campus
400 East Ave, Warwick RI 02886-1805
Elizabeth A. Mancini, Assistant Dean of Enrollment
Services
401-825-2003

Community College of Rhode Island
Providence Campus
1 Hilton St, Providence RI 02905-2313
Elizabeth A. Mancini, Assistant Dean of Enrollment
Services
401-828-8146

SOUTH CAROLINA
Aiken Technical College
PO Box 696, Aiken SC 29802-0796
803-593-9231

Central Carolina Technical College
506 N Guignard Dr, Sumter SC 29150-2499
803-778-1961

Clinton Junior College
1029 Crawford Rd, Rock Hill SC 29730
803-327-7402

Denmark Technical College
PO Box 327, Denmark SC 29042-0327
803-793-5149

ECPI College of Technology
1001 Keys Dr #100, Greenville SC 29615
864-288-2828

Florence-Darlington Technical College
PO Box 100548, Florence SC 29501-0548
843-661-8324

FORREST JUNIOR COLLEGE
601 E River St, Anderson SC 29624-2405
Dr. Julia R. Barnes, President
864-225-7653 Fax: 864-261-7471
Website: www.forrestcollege.edu
E-mail: info@forrestcollege.edu
Established 1946. Private. Coed. Accreditation:
ACICS. Tuition: $110 per quarter hour. Fees: $250. Enrollment: 230 full-time, 10 part-time. Faculty: 18. Student-
faculty ratio: 18:1. Degrees: Associate in Applied Science. Library: 6,500 volumes. 2 buildings on 3.5 acres.
Small, personalized instruction. Career, Entrepreneurship oriented. Caters to working adults with children.

Greenville Technical College
PO Box 5616, Greenville SC 29606-5616
Martha White, Director of Admissions
800-723-0673 (US) or 800-922-1183 (SC)
Website: www.greenvilletech.com

Horry-Georgetown Technical College
PO Box 261966, Conway SC 29528-6066
843-349-5277

Horry-Georgetown Technical College
743 Hemlock Ave, Myrtle Beach SC 29577-5044
843-477-0808

Midlands Technical College
PO Box 2408, Columbia SC 29202-2408
803-738-8324

Northeastern Technical College
PO Box 1007, Cheraw SC 29520-1007
843-537-5286

Orangeburg-Calhoun Technical College
3250 Saint Matthews Rd NE
Orangeburg SC 29118-8299
803-536-0311

Piedmont Technical College
PO Box 1467, Greenwood SC 29648-1467
864-941-8324

Spartanburg Methodist College
1200 Textile Rd, Spartanburg SC 29301-0009
800-772-7286

Spartanburg Technical College
PO Box 4386, Spartanburg SC 29305-4386
Nancy Garmroth, Dean of Admissions & Financial Aid
864-592-4810 Fax: 864-592-4945
Website: stcsc.edu

Technical College of the Lowcountry
PO Box 1288, Beaufort SC 29901
843-525-8324

Tri-County Tech College
PO Box 587, Pendleton SC 29670-0587
864-646-8361

Trident Technical College
PO Box 118067, Charleston SC 29423-8067
843-574-6111

University of South Carolina
PO Box 617, Allendale SC 29810-0617
Jane T. Brewer, Associate Dean for Student Services
803-584-6314

University of South Carolina
PO Box 889, Lancaster SC 29721-0889
803-285-7471

University of South Carolina
200 Miller Rd, Sumter SC 29150-2478
803-775-6341

University of South Carolina
PO Box 729, Union SC 29379-0729
864-429-8728

Williamsburg Technical College
601 Martin Luther King Ave
Kingstree SC 29556-4197
843-354-2021

York Technical College
452 Anderson Rd S, Rock Hill SC 29730-7318
803-327-8000

SOUTH DAKOTA

Colorado Technical University
3901 W 59th St, Sioux Falls SD 57108
605-361-0200

Kilian Community College
300 E 6th St, Sioux Falls SD 57103
Jacque Danielson, Director of Admissions
605-221-3100

Oglala Lakota Community College
PO Box 861, Pine Ridge SD 57770-0861
605-867-5857

Sisseton Wahpeton Community College
PO Box 689, Sisseton SD 57262-0689
605-698-3966

TENNESSEE

Chattanooga State Technical Community College
4501 Amnicola Hwy, Chattanooga TN 37406-1018
423-697-4400

Cleveland State Community College
PO Box 3570, Cleveland TN 37320-3570
423-472-7141

Columbia State Community College
PO Box 1315, Columbia TN 38402-1315
931-540-2722

Draughons Junior College
1860 Wilma Rudolph Blvd, Clarksville TN 37040-6718
Christi Nolder, Director of Admissions
931-552-7600

Draughons Junior College
PO Box 17386, Nashville TN 37217-0386
615-361-7555 Fax: 615-367-2736
Website: www.draughons.edu

Draughons Junior College - Murfreesboro
415 Golden Bear Ct, Murfreesboro TN 37128
615-217-9347

Dyersburg State Community College
1516 Lake Rd, Dyersburg TN 38024-2411
731-286-3200

Hiwassee College
225 Hiwassee College Dr, Madisonville TN 37354
Jamie Williamson, Director of Admissions
423-442-2001

ITT Technical Institute
10208 Technology Dr, Knoxville TN 37932-3343
865-671-2800

Jackson State Community College
2046 N Parkway, Jackson TN 38301-3797
731-424-3520

John A. Gupton College
1616 Church St, Nashville TN 37203-2934
615-327-3927

Martin Methodist College
433 W Madison St, Pulaski TN 38478-2716
800-727-1273

MEDVANCE INSTITUTE
1025 Highway 111, Cookeville TN 38501-4305
Shirley Cole, Campus Director
866-86-GO-MED or 931-526-3660 Fax: 931-372-2603
Website: www.medvance.edu

Motlow State Community College
PO Box 8500, Lynchburg TN 37352-8500
931-393-1500

Nashville State Technical Community College
120 White Bridge Pike, Nashville TN 37209-4515
615-353-3333

National College of Business & Technology
3748 Nolensville Pike, Nashville TN 37211-3322
Larry Steele, Director of Admissions
615-333-3344

Northeast State Technical Community College
PO Box 246, Blountville TN 37617-0246
423-323-3191

NOSSI COLLEGE OF ART
907 Rivergate Pkwy Ste E6, Goodlettsville TN 37072
Cyrus Vatandoost, Executive Director
615-851-1088 Fax: 615-851-1087
Website: www.nossi.com
E-mail: cyrus@nossi.com

Pellissippi State Technical Community College
PO Box 22990, Knoxville TN 37933-0990
Donna Mack, Contact
865-694-6568 Fax: 865-539-7217
Website: www.pstcc.edu
E-mail: dmack@pstcc.edu

Remington College
2731 Nonconnah Blvd #160
Memphis TN 38132-2131
901-345-1000

Roane State Community College
276 Patton Ln, Harriman TN 37748-8664
865-354-3000

Southwest Tennessee Community College
5983 Macon Cove, Memphis TN 38134
901-333-7822

State Technical Institute
5983 Macon Cv, Memphis TN 38134-7642
901-377-4111

Volunteer State Community College
1480 Nashville Pike, Gallatin TN 37066-3188
615-452-8600

Walters State Community College
500 S Davy Crockett Pkwy
Morristown TN 37813-6899
423-585-2600

TEXAS

Alvin Community College
Pearland College Center
3110 Mustang Rd, Alvin TX 77511-4807
281-756-3526

Amarillo College
PO Box 447, Amarillo TX 79178-0001
806-371-5000

Angelina College
PO Box 1768, Lufkin TX 75902-1768
Dr. Larry M. Phillips, President
Judith M. Cutting, Director of Admissions/Registration
936-639-1301

ART INSTITUTE OF HOUSTON
1900 Yorktown St, Houston TX 77056
Brian A. Shumaker, Director of Admissions
800-275-4244 Fax: 713-966-2797
Website: www.aih.artinstitutes.edu

Austin Community College
5930 Middle Fiskville Rd, Austin TX 78752-4390
512-223-7598

Blinn College
902 College Ave, Brenham TX 77833-4098
Dennis K. Crowson, Registrar
979-830-4000 Fax: 979-830-4110
Website: www.blinn.edu
E-mail: recruiting@blinn.edu

Blinn College
PO Box 6030, Bryan TX 77805-6030
Dennis K. Crowson, Registrar
979-209-7200 Fax: 979-209-7229
Website: www.blinn.edu
E-mail: recruiting@blinn.edu

Blinn College
100 Ranger Dr, Schulenburg TX 78956-2247
Dennis K. Crowson, Registrar
979-743-5003 Fax: 979-743-5225
Website: www.blinn.edu
E-mail: recruiting@blinn.edu

Blinn College
3701 Outlet Center Dr, Sealy TX 77474
Dennis K. Crowson, Registrar
979-627-7997 Fax: 979-627-0830
Website: www.blinn.edu
E-mail: recruiting@blinn.edu

Brookhaven College
3939 Valley View Ln, Farmers Branch TX 75244-4997
972-860-4700

Brown Mackie College
8080 Park Ln Ste 315, Dallas TX 75231
972-279-4446

Brown Mackie College - Fort Worth
301 NE Loop 820, Hurst TX 76053
817-589-0505

Cedar Valley College
3030 N Dallas Ave, Lancaster TX 75134-3799
972-860-8200

Central Texas College
PO Box 1800, Killeen TX 76540-1800
Lillian Kroeger, Director of Admissions
254-526-1104

Cisco Junior College
RR 3 Box 3, Cisco TX 76437-9321
254-442-2567

Clarendon College
PO Box 968, Clarendon TX 79226-0968
806-874-3571

Coastal Bend College
3800 Charco Rd, Beeville TX 78102-2197
361-358-2838

College of Biblical Studies
7000 Regency Square Blvd Ste 110
Houston TX 77036-3211
713-785-5995

College of the Mainland
1200 N Amburn Rd, Texas City TX 77591-2499
409-938-1211

Collin County Community College
4800 Preston Park Blvd, Plano TX 75093
972-881-5790

Commonwealth Institute of Funeral Service
415 Barren Springs Dr, Houston TX 77090-5918
281-873-0262

COVENANT SCHOOL OF NURSING AND ALLIED HEALTH
2002 Miami Ave, Lubbock TX 79410-1096
Admissions
806-797-0955 Fax: 806-793-0720
Website: www.covenantson.com
E-mail: admissionscsn@covhs.org

Del Mar College
101 Baldwin Blvd, Corpus Christi TX 78404-3894
361-698-1200

Eastfield College
3737 Motley Dr, Mesquite TX 75150-2099
214-860-7002

El Centro College
801 Main St, Dallas TX 75202-3698
214-860-2037

El Paso Community College
PO Box 20500, El Paso TX 79998-0500
915-831-2000

Frank Phillips College
PO Box 5118, Borger TX 79008-5118
806-274-5311

Galveston College
4015 Avenue Q, Galveston TX 77550-7496
Brian Lowery, Registrar
409-763-6551 Fax: 409-944-1501
Website: www.gc.edu
E-mail: blowery@gc.edu

Grayson County College
6101 Grayson Dr, Denison TX 75020
903-465-6030

Hill College - Hill County Campus
PO Box 619, Hillsboro TX 76645-0619
W. R. Auvenshine, President
254-582-2555

Hill College - Johnson County Campus
PO Box 1899, Cleburne TX 76033-1899
Pam Boehm, V.P. Student Services
817-641-9887

Houston Community College
PO Box 667517, Houston TX 77266-7517
713-718-2000

Howard College
1001 N Birdwell Ln, Big Spring TX 79720-0213
915-264-5022

Howard College
3200 Avenue C, Big Spring TX 79720
Brooke Everett, Contact
432-264-3700

Howard College
3197 Executive Dr, San Angelo TX 76904-6801
LeAnne Byrd, Contact
325-944-9585

ITT Technical Institute
551 Ryan Plaza Dr, Arlington TX 76011
817-794-5100 Fax: 817-275-8446
Website: www.itt-tech.edu

ITT Technical Institute
6330 E Highway 290 Ste 150, Austin TX 78723-1035
James Branham, Director of Admissions
512-467-6800

ITT TECHNICAL INSTITUTE
2222 Bay Area Blvd, Houston TX 77058-2070
Linda Womack, Registrar
281-486-2630 Fax: 281-486-6099
Website: itt.tech.edu
E-mail: lwomack@itt-tech.edu

ITT Technical Institute
2101 Waterview Pkwy, Richardson TX 75080-2208
972-279-0500

ITT Technical Institute
5700 Northwest Pkwy, San Antonio TX 78249-3303
Doug Howard, Director of Recruitment
210-694-4612

JACKSONVILLE COLLEGE
105 B J Albritton Dr, Jacksonville TX 75766-4759
Tam Clark, Academic Dean
903-586-2518 Fax: 903-586-0743
Website: www.jacksonville-college.edu
E-mail: acadean@jacksonville-college.edu
   Established 1899. Private. Coed. Accreditation: SACS.
Tuition: $5,280. Room and board: $2,496. Fees: $520.
Enrollment: 200 full-time, 50 part-time. Faculty: 18.

Student-faculty ratio: 15:1. Degrees: AA, AS, Junior College Diploma. Library: 23,000 volumes. 12 buildings on 18 acres. Quality education in a Christian environment. Outstanding music department with traveling choir, vocal and wind ensembles. International student office. NJCAA men's and women's basketball.

KD Studio - Actors Conservatory
2600 N Stemmons Fwy Ste 117
Dallas TX 75207-2168
T. A. Taylor, Director of Education
877-278-2283 Fax: 214-630-5140
Website: www.kdstudio.com
E-mail: admissions@kdstudio.com
See listing under "Career Schools"

Kilgore College
1100 Broadway Blvd, Kilgore TX 75662-3299
Ray McLeod, Director, Marketing & Enrollment
903-984-8531

LAMAR INSTITUTE OF TECHNOLOGY
855 E Lavaca St, Beaumont TX 77705
409-880-8321
Website: www.lit.edu
E-mail: comments@lit.edu

Lamar State College-Orange
410 W Front St, Orange TX 77630-5899
Rebecca Campbell, Registrar
409-883-7750 Fax: 409-882-3055
Website: www.lsco.edu
E-mail: becky.campbell@lsco.edu

Lamar State College-Port Arthur
PO Box 310, Port Arthur TX 77641-0310
409-983-4921

Laredo Community College
1 W End Washington St, Laredo TX 78040-4348
956-722-0521

Lee College
PO Box 818, Baytown TX 77522-0818
Dr. Dennis Dressler, Director of Admissions
281-427-5611

Lon Morris College
800 College Ave, Jacksonville TX 75766
903-589-4000

McLennan Community College
1400 College Dr, Waco TX 76708-1498
Karen Clark, Coordinator, Student Admissions
254-299-8000 Fax: 254-299-8964
Website: www.mclennan.edu
E-mail: kclark@mclennan.edu

MedVance Institute
6220 W Park #180, Houston TX 77057
713-266-6594

Midland College
3600 N Garfield St, Midland TX 79705-6397
432-685-4500

Mountain View College
4849 W Illinois Ave, Dallas TX 75211-6599
214-860-8680

Navarro College
3200 W 7th Ave, Corsicana TX 75110-4899
903-874-6501

North Central Texas College
1525 W California St, Gainesville TX 76240-4636
Michelle Winters, Registrar
940-668-3315 Fax: 940-665-7075
Website: www.nctc.edu
E-mail: mwinters@nctc.edu

Northeast Texas Community College
PO Box 1307, Mount Pleasant TX 75456-9991
903-572-1911

North Harris Montgomery Community College
250 N Sam Houston Parkway East, Houston TX 77060
281-260-3500

North Lake College
5001 N MacArthur Blvd, Irving TX 75038-3899
972-273-3000

Northwest Vista College
3535 N Ellison Dr, San Antonio TX 78251
210-348-2001

Odessa College
201 W University Blvd, Odessa TX 79764-7127
432-335-6400

Palo Alto College
1400 W Villaret Blvd, San Antonio TX 78224-2499
210-921-5000

Panola College
1109 W Panola St, Carthage TX 75633-2397
800-776-8153

Paris Junior College
2400 Clarksville St, Paris TX 75460-6298
903-785-7661

Ranger College
1100 College Cir, Ranger TX 76470-3298
254-647-3234

Remington College - Fort Worth Campus
300 E Loop 820, Fort Worth TX 76112-1280
Director of Recruitment
817-451-0017 Fax: 817-496-1257
Website: www.remingtoncollege.edu
E-mail: lynn.wey@remingtoncollege.edu

Richland College
12800 Abrams Rd, Dallas TX 75243-2199
972-238-6100

St. Phillip's College
1801 Martin Luther King Dr
San Antonio TX 78203-2098
210-531-3200

San Antonio College
1300 San Pedro Ave, San Antonio TX 78212-4299
210-733-2000

Sanford-Brown Institute Houston
10500 Forum Place Dr, Houston TX 77036
713-779-1110

San Jacinto College
5800 Uvalde Rd, Houston TX 77049-4513
281-458-4050

San Jacinto College
13735 Beamer Rd, Houston TX 77089-6099
281-484-1900

San Jacinto College
8060 Spencer Hwy, Pasadena TX 77505-5998
281-476-1501

SOUTH PLAINS COLLEGE
1401 College Ave, Levelland TX 79336-6595
Kimbra Quinn, Director of Enrollment Management
806-894-9611 ext. 2113 Fax: 806-897-3167
Website: www.southplainscollege.com
E-mail: kquinn@spc.cc.tx.us

South Plains College - Reese Campus
9730 Reese Blvd, Lubbock TX 79416
Kimbra Quinn, Director of New Student Relations
806-894-9611 ext. 2113

South Texas College
3201 Pecan Blvd, Mc Allen TX 78501-6661
956-631-4922

Southwest Texas Junior College
2401 Garner Field Rd, Uvalde TX 78801-6221
Joe C. Barker, Dean of Admissions
830-278-4401

Tarrant County Junior College
Northeast Campus
828 W Harwood Rd, Hurst TX 76054-3299
Cathie J. Jackson, Director of Admissions and Records
817-515-6100

Tarrant County Junior College
Northwest Campus
4801 Marine Creek Pkwy, Fort Worth TX 76179-3599
Cathie J. Jackson, Director of Admissions and Records
817-515-7100

Tarrant County Junior College
South Campus
5301 Campus Dr, Fort Worth TX 76119-5998
Cathie J. Jackson, Director of Admissions and Records
817-515-4100

Tarrant County Junior College
Southeast Campus
2100 Southeast Parkway, Arlington TX 76018
Cathie L. Jackson, Director of Admissions and Records
817-515-3100

Temple College
2600 S 1st St, Temple TX 76504-7435
Angela Balch, Director of Admissions & Records
254-298-8300 Fax: 254-298-8288
Website: www.templejc.edu
E-mail: ruth.bridges@templejc.edu

Texarkana Community College
2500 N Robison Rd, Texarkana TX 75501-3078
903-838-4541

Texas Culinary Academy
11400 Burnet Rd #2100, Austin TX 78758-3403
Paula M. Paulette, Vice President of Marketing & Admissions
512-837-2665

Texas Southmost College
80 Fort Brown St, Brownsville TX 78520-4993
956-544-3879

Texas State Technical College
1901 N Loop 499, Harlingen TX 78550
956-364-4001

Texas State Technical College Marshall
2400 E End Blvd S, Marshall TX 75672
903-935-1010

Texas State Technical College - Waco
3801 Campus Dr, Waco TX 76705-1696
Dawn Khoury, Director of Admissions
254-799-3611

Texas State Technical College
West Texas
300 Homer K Taylor Dr, Sweetwater TX 79556-4108
325-235-7300

Trinity Valley Community College
500 S Prairieville St, Athens TX 75751-2734
903-677-8822

Trinity Valley Community College
800 W Highway 243, Kaufman TX 75142-1899
972-932-4309

TYLER JUNIOR COLLEGE
PO Box 9020, Tyler TX 75711-9020
Joel Renaud, Director of Enrollment Management
903-510-2398 or 800-687-5680 ext. 2399
Fax: 903-510-2161
Website: www.tjc.edu
E-mail: jren@tjc.edu
Established 1926. Public. Coed. Accreditation: SACS. Tuition: $1,760. Room and board: $3,700. Enrollment: 9,000 full-time, 4,200 part-time. Faculty: 300. Student-faculty ratio: 20-25:1. Degrees offered: AA, AAS, Certificate. 30 buildings on 73 acres. Strong Liberal Arts - College Transfer. 35 Vocational Technical Programs. Strong Allied Health program. Outstanding Music-Drama department. Excellent Science, Mathematics program. Athletic programs: football, baseball, men's & women's basketball, men's & women's golf, women's volleyball, tennis, and soccer. Residential Life: 600 spaces available and Support Services available.

Vernon College
4400 College Dr, Vernon TX 76384-4092
940-552-6291

Victoria College
2200 E Red River St, Victoria TX 77901-4494
361-573-3291

WADE COLLEGE
Dallas Market Center, Suite 158
PO Box 421149, Dallas TX 75342
800-624-4850 or 214-637-3530 Fax: 214-637-0827
Harry Davros, President
Suzun Wade, Executive Director
Theresa Fleury, Director of Education
Website: www.wadecollege.edu
E-mail: admissions@wadecollege.edu
Established 1962. Coed. Private. Accreditation: SACS Commission on Colleges. Tuition: $9,050. Room: $3,360. Fees: $125. Enrollment: 250. Faculty: 20. Student-faculty ratio: 15:1. Degrees: AA in Merchandising and Design. Library: 5,000 volumes. Part of the world's largest wholesale merchandising complex - the Dallas Market Center.

Weatherford College
225 College Park Dr, Weatherford TX 76086
Dr. Don Huff, President
800-287-5471

Western Texas College
6200 College Ave, Snyder TX 79549-6189
Deborah Baremore, Director of College Relations
888-GO-TO-WTC (468-6982)

Wharton County Junior College
911 E Boling Hwy, Wharton TX 77488-3298
979-532-4560

UTAH

College of Eastern Utah
451 E 400 N, Price UT 84501-2699
435-637-2120

Dixie State College of Utah
225 S 700 E, Saint George UT 84770-3876
435-652-7500

ITT TECHNICAL INSTITUTE
920 Levoy Dr, Murray UT 84123-2500
Gary Wood, Director of Recruitment
801-263-3313 Fax: 801-263-3497
Website: www.itt-tech.edu
E-mail: gwood@itt-tech.edu

L.D.S. BUSINESS COLLEGE
95 North 300 West, Salt Lake City UT 84101-3500
Kathleen Howe, Assistant Director of Admissions
801-524-8145 Fax: 801-524-1900
Website: www.ldsbc.edu
E-mail: admissions@ldsbc.edu
See listing under "Career Schools"

Mountain West College
3280 W 3500 S, West Valley City UT 84119
John Rios, Director of Admissions
801-840-4800

Salt Lake Community College
PO Box 30808, Salt Lake City UT 84130-0808
801-957-4111

Snow College
150 College Ave, Ephraim UT 84627-1299
435-283-7000

Stevens Henager College
755 Main St, Logan UT 84321
Sherman R. Conger, Director of Admissions
435-713-4777
Website: www.stevenshenager.edu

Stevens Henager College
1476 Sandhill Rd, Orem UT 84058-7310
801-375-5455

Stevens Henager College
383 W Vine St, Salt Lake City UT 84123
801-261-7600

Utah Valley State College
800 W University Pkwy, Orem UT 84058-0001
801-222-8000

VERMONT

Community College of Vermont
PO Box 120, Waterbury VT 05676-0120
802-241-3535

Landmark College
PO Box 820, River Rd S, Putney VT 05346-0820
Dale Herold, Dean of Admissions
802-387-6718

Sterling College
PO Box 72, Craftsbury Common VT 05827
802-586-7711

Vermont Technical College
PO Box 500, Randolph Center VT 05061
802-728-1000

VIRGINIA

Blue Ridge Community College
PO Box 80, Weyers Cave VA 24486-0080
540-234-9261

Bryant & Stratton College
8141 Hull St Rd, Richmond VA 23235-6411
804-745-2444

Bryant & Stratton College
301 Centre Pointe Dr, Virginia Beach VA 23462-4417
Tracy Nannery, Director
757-499-7900

Central Virginia Community College
3506 Wards Rd, Lynchburg VA 24502-2498
804-832-7600

Dabney S. Lancaster Community College
PO Box 1000, Clifton Forge VA 24422-1000
540-863-2800

Danville Community College
1008 S Main St, Danville VA 24541-4088
804-797-2222

Eastern Shore Community College
29300 Lankford Hwy, Melfa VA 23410-3000
757-787-5900

ECPI College of Technology
10021 Balls Ford Rd #100, Manassas VA 20109-2666
703-330-5300

ECPI College of Technology
1001 Omni Blvd Ste 100
Newport News VA 23606-4215
757-838-9191

ECPI College of Technology
5555 Greenwich Rd Ste 300
Virginia Beach VA 23462-6542
757-671-7171

ECPI Technical College
800 Moorefield Park Dr, Richmond VA 23236-3686
804-330-5533

ECPI Technical College
5234 Airport Rd NW, Roanoke VA 24012-1603
540-563-8080

Germanna Community College
2130 Germanna Hwy, Locust Grove VA 22508
540-727-3000

ITT Technical Institute
863 Glenrock Rd Ste 100, Norfolk VA 23502-3701
757-466-1260

ITT Technical Institute
300 Gateway Center Pkwy, Richmond VA 23235
804-330-4992

Jefferson College of Health Sciences
Formerly Community Hospital
PO Box 13186, Roanoke VA 24031-3186
Judith McKeon, Director of Admissions
540-985-8483

John Tyler Community College
13101 Jefferson Davis Hwy, Chester VA 23831-5316
800-522-3490

J. Sargeant Reynolds Community College
PO Box 85622, Richmond VA 23285-5622
804-371-3000

Lord Fairfax Community College
173 Skirmisher Ln, Middletown VA 22645-1745
800-906-5322

Mountain Empire Community College
3441 Mountain Empire Rd
Big Stone Gap VA 24219-0700
276-523-2400

National College of Business & Technology
100 Logan St, Bluefield VA 24605
Larry Steele, Director of Admissions
276-326-3621

National College of Business & Technology
300A Piedmont Ave, Bristol VA 24201-4022
Larry Steele, Director of Admissions
276-669-5333

National College of Business & Technology
1819 Emmet St N, Charlottesville VA 22901-2812
Larry Steele, Director of Admissions
434-295-0136

National College of Business & Technology
734 Main St, Danville VA 24541-1819
Larry Steele, Director of Admissions
434-793-6822

National College of Business & Technology
51B Burgess Rd, Harrisonburg VA 22801-9709
Larry Steele, Director of Admissions
540-432-0943

National College of Business & Technology
104 Candlewood Ct, Lynchburg VA 24502-2653
Larry Steele, Director of Admissions
434-239-3500

National College of Business & Technology
10 Church St, Martinsville VA 24114
Larry Steele, Director of Admissions
276-632-5621

New River Community College
PO Box 1127, Dublin VA 24084-1127
540-674-3600

Northern Virginia Community College
3001 N Beauregard St, Alexandria VA 22311-5065
703-845-6200

Northern Virginia Community College
4001 Wakefield Chapel Rd, Annandale VA 22003
703-323-3000

Northern Virginia Community College
6901 Sudley Rd, Manassas VA 20109-2305
703-368-0184

Northern Virginia Community College
1000 Harry Flood Byrd Hwy, Sterling VA 20164-8699
703-323-3000

Northern Virginia Community College
15200 Neabsco Mills Rd
Woodbridge VA 22191-4006
703-670-2191

Patrick Henry Community College
PO Box 5311, Martinsville VA 24115-5311
276-638-8777

Paul D. Camp Community College
100 N College Dr, Franklin VA 23851-2422
757-569-6700

Piedmont Virginia Community College
501 College Dr, Charlottesville VA 22902
804-977-3900

Rappahannock Community College
12745 College Dr, Saluda VA 23149
804-758-6700

Rappahannock Community College
52 Campus Dr, Warsaw VA 22572-4272
804-333-6700

Richard Bland College
11301 Johnson Rd, Petersburg VA 23805-7100
804-862-6100

Southside Virginia Community College
109 Campus Dr, Alberta VA 23821-2930
Ronald E. Mattox, Dean of Admissions
434-949-1014 Fax: 434-949-7863
Website: www.sv.vccs.edu
E-mail: ronald.mattox@sv.vccs.edu

Southside Virginia Community College
200 Daniel Rd, Keysville VA 23947
Ronald E. Mattox, Dean of Admissions
434-736-2018 Fax: 434-736-2082
Website: www.sv.vccs.edu
E-mail: ronald.mattox@sv.vccs.edu

Southwest Virginia Community College
PO Box SVCC, Richlands VA 24641-1101
276-964-2555

Thomas Nelson Community College
PO Box 9407, Hampton VA 23670-0407
757-825-2700

Tidewater Community College
1428 Cedar Rd, Chesapeake VA 23322-7199
757-547-9271

Tidewater Community College
121 College Pl, Norfolk VA 23510
757-822-1030

Tidewater Community College
State Route 135, Portsmouth VA 23703
757-484-2121

Tidewater Community College
1700 College Cres, Virginia Beach VA 23453-1999
757-468-6348

Virginia Highlands Community College
PO Box 828, Abingdon VA 24212-0828
276-676-5484

Virginia Western Community College
PO Box 14007, Roanoke VA 24038-4007
540-857-7311

Wytheville Community College
1000 E Main St, Wytheville VA 24382-3308
276-223-4700

WASHINGTON

Apollo College
10102 E Knox Ave, Spokane WA 99206-4146
509-532-8888

Bellevue Community College
3000 Landerholm Cir SE, Bellevue WA 98007-6484
425-564-1000

Big Bend Community College
7662 Chanute St NE, Moses Lake WA 98837-3299
509-762-5351

Bryman College
2156 Pacific Ave, Tacoma WA 98402
Rob Daniel, Director of Admissions
253-207-4000

Centralia College
600 W Locust St, Centralia WA 98531-4035
360-736-9391

Clark College
1800 E McLoughlin Blvd, Vancouver WA 98663-3598
360-992-2000

Columbia Basin College
2600 N 20th Ave, Pasco WA 99301-3379
Patricia Campbell, Director Admissions/Registration
509-547-0511

Edmonds Community College
20000 68th Ave W, Lynnwood WA 98036-5999
425-640-1500

Everett Community College
2000 Tower St, Everett WA 98201
Christine Kerlin, Associate Dean
425-388-9100 Fax: 425-388-9173
Website: www.everettcc.edu
E-mail: ckerlin@everettcc.edu

Grays Harbor College
1620 Edward P Smith Dr, Aberdeen WA 98520-7599
360-532-9020

Green River Community College
12401 SE 320th St, Auburn WA 98092-3622
253-833-9111

Highline Community College
PO Box 98000, Des Moines WA 98198-9800
206-878-3710

ITT Technical Institute
12720 Gateway Dr Ste 100, Seattle WA 98168-3334
Donna L. Green, Director
206-244-3300

ITT Technical Institute
13518 E Indiana Ave, Spokane Valley WA 99216
Greg Alexander, Director of Admissions
509-926-2900

Lower Columbia College
PO Box 3010, Longview WA 98632-0310
360-577-2300

North Seattle Community College
9600 College Way N, Seattle WA 98103-3599
206-527-3600

NORTHWEST INDIAN COLLEGE

2522 Kwina Rd, Bellingham WA 98226-9278
Leilani Ignacio, Director of Admissions
360-676-2772 Fax: 360-392-4333
Website: www.nwic.edu/
E-mail: lignacio@nwic.edu

Olympic College
1600 Chester Ave, Bremerton WA 98337-1699
360-792-7479

Peninsula College
1502 E Lauridsen Blvd, Port Angeles WA 98362-6698
360-452-9277

Pierce College Fort Steilacoom
9401 Farwest Dr SW, Lakewood WA 98498-1999
Cherilyn Williams, Communications Coordinator
253-964-6435

Pierce College Puyallup
1601 39th Ave SE, Puyallup WA 98374-2210
Ruth Schindler, Admissions Coordinator
253-840-8470

RENTON TECHNICAL COLLEGE

3000 NE 4th St, Renton WA 98056-4195
Don Bressler, President
Becky Riverman, Registrar
425-235-2352 or 425-235-5840 Fax: 425-235-7832
Website: www.RTC.edu
E-mail: dgrant@RTC.edu
    Established 1942. Coed. Accreditation: NASC. Enrollment: 3,356 (day). Faculty: 95. Degree: Associate's, Certificates of completion. 13 buildings on 30 acre main campus with many satellite locations. Day, evening and night training, retraining and upgrading in cooperation with industry for 16,000 total registrants.

Seattle Central Community College
1701 Broadway, Seattle WA 98122-2400
206-587-3800

Shoreline Community College
16101 Greenwood Ave N, Shoreline WA 98133-5696
Robin Thompson, Director of Admissions
206-546-4101

Skagit Valley College
2405 E College Way, Mount Vernon WA 98273-5899
360-416-7600

South Puget Sound Community College
2011 Mottman Rd SW, Tumwater WA 98512-6292
360-754-7711

South Seattle Community College
6000 16th Ave SW, Seattle WA 98106-1499
206-764-5300

Spokane Community College
1810 N Greene St, Spokane WA 99217-5399
509-533-7000

Spokane Falls Community College
3410 W Fort George Wright Dr
Spokane WA 99224-5288
509-533-3500

Tacoma Community College
6501 S 19th St, Tacoma WA 98466
253-566-5000

WALLA WALLA COMMUNITY COLLEGE

500 Tausick Way, Walla Walla WA 99362-9270
Dr. Steven VanAusdle, President
509-527-4282 or 877-471-9292 Fax: 509-527-3661
Website: www.wwcc.edu
    Established 1967. Public. State. Accreditation: NASC, SBCTC. Tuition: $2,048 resident, $2,407 non-resident. Faculty: 105. Library: over 36,000 volumes. Degree: AA or AS; Associate's degree for transfer & certified vocational programs such as enology & viticulture, farrier, cosmetology, business & commerce, culinary arts, mechanical & technical, and health science.

Wenatchee Valley College
PO Box 2058, Omak WA 98841
Alex Roberts, Director
509-422-7805 Fax: 509-682-6541
Website: www.wvc.edu

Wenatchee Valley College
1300 5th St, Wenatchee WA 98801-1799
Marco Azurdia, Dean, Student Development
509-682-6805 Fax: 509-682-6541
Website: www.wvc.edu

Whatcom Community College
237 W Kellogg Rd, Bellingham WA 98226-8003
360-676-2170

Yakima Valley Community College
PO Box 22520, Yakima WA 98907
509-574-4600

WEST VIRGINIA

CTC of Shepherd
400 W Stephen St, Martinsburg WV 25401
304-260-4380

Huntington Junior College
900 5th Ave, Huntington WV 25701-2004
304-697-7550

National Institute of Technology
5514 Big Tyler Rd, Cross Lanes WV 25313-1304
304-776-6290

New River Community & Technical College
167 Dye Dr, Beckley WV 25801
304-255-5812

Potomac State College of West Virginia University
101 Fort Ave Bldg 1, Keyser WV 26726-2694
304-788-6800

Southern West Virginia Community & Technical College
PO Box 2900, Mount Gay WV 25637
304-792-7160

Southern West Virginia Community & Technical College
Williamson WV 25661
304-235-2800

Valley College of Technology
616 Harrison St, Princeton WV 24740-3141
304-425-2323

Webster College
176 Thompson Dr, Bridgeport WV 26330-1644
304-363-8824

West Virginia Northern Community College
150 Park Ave, Weirton WV 26062-3797
Frank Targoss, Counselor
304-723-2210

West Virginia Northern Community College
1704 Market St, Wheeling WV 26003-3643
304-233-5900

WV State Community & Technical College
PO Box 1000, Institute WV 25112
304-766-3118

WISCONSIN

Blackhawk Technical College
PO Box 5009, Janesville WI 53547-5009
Gregg Bosak, Administration, Community Information
608-757-7769 Fax: 608-757-7740
Website: www.blackhawk.edu
E-mail: gbosak@blackhawk.edu

Bryant & Stratton College
310 W Wisconsin Ave Suite 500, Milwaukee WI 53203
Kathryn Cotey, Director of Admissions
414-276-5200

Chippewa Valley Technical College
620 W Clairemont Ave, Eau Claire WI 54701-6162
Admissions Office
715-833-6246

COLLEGE OF MENOMINEE NATION
PO Box 1179, Keshena WI 54135-1179
Cynthia Norton, Admissions Representative
715-799-5600 Fax: 715-799-4392
Website: www.menominee.edu
E-mail: cnorton@menominee.edu

Fox Valley Technical College
PO Box 2277, Appleton WI 54912-2277
Bob Burdick, Registrar
920-735-5600

Fox Valley Technical College
150 N Campbell Rd, Oshkosh WI 54902-3498
920-735-5600

Gateway Technical College
400 County Road H, Elkhorn WI 53121-2046
Zina Haywood, Director of Admissions
262-741-8200

Gateway Technical College
3520 30th Ave, Kenosha WI 53144-1690
Zina Haywood, Director of Admissions
262-564-2200

Gateway Technical College
1001 S Main St, Racine WI 53403-1582
Zina Haywood, Director of Admissions
262-619-6200

Herzing College
5218 E Terrace Dr, Madison WI 53718-8340
Donald Madelung, President
800-582-1227 Fax: 608-249-8593
Website: www.herzing.edu
E-mail: info@msn.herzing.edu
See listing under "Universities"

ITT Technical Institute
6300 W Layton Ave, Milwaukee WI 53220-4612
414-282-9494

Lac Courte Oreilles Ojibwa Community College
13466 W Trepania Rd, Hayward WI 54843
715-634-4790

Madison Area Technical College
3550 Anderson St, Madison WI 53704-2599
608-246-6282

Madison Area Technical College
1300 W Main St, Watertown WI 53098-3526
920-261-3303

Mid-State Technical College
2600 W 5th St, Marshfield WI 54449-3209
715-387-2538

Mid-State Technical College
933 Michigan Ave, Stevens Point WI 54481-3195
715-344-3063

Mid-State Technical College
500 32nd St N, Wisconsin Rapids WI 54494-5512
715-423-5300

Milwaukee Area Technical College
5555 W Highland Rd, Mequon WI 53092-1143
262-238-2200

Milwaukee Area Technical College
700 W State St, Milwaukee WI 53233-1419
414-297-6600

Milwaukee Area Technical College
6665 S Howell Ave, Oak Creek WI 53154-1107
414-762-2500

Milwaukee Area Technical College
1200 S 71st St, West Allis WI 53214-3110
414-476-3040

Moraine Park Technical College
700 Gould St, Beaver Dam WI 53916-1994
920-887-1101

Moraine Park Technical College
235 N National Ave, Fond du Lac WI 54935
920-922-8611

Moraine Park Technical College
2151 N Main St, West Bend WI 53090-1598
262-334-3413

Nicolet Area Technical College
PO Box 518, Rhinelander WI 54501-0518
715-365-4410

Northcentral Technical College
1000 W Campus Dr, Wausau WI 54401-1880
Carolyn Michalski, Director of Admissions
715-675-3331

Northeast Wisconsin Technical College
PO Box 19042, Green Bay WI 54307-9042
800-422-NWTC

Northeast Wisconsin Technical College
1601 University Dr, Marinette WI 54143-4132
800-422-NWTC

Northeast Wisconsin Technical College
229 N 14th Ave, Sturgeon Bay WI 54235-1317
800-422-NWTC

Southwest Wisconsin Technical College
1800 Bronson Blvd, Fennimore WI 53809-9778
Student Services/Admissions
800-362-3322 ext. 2354

University of Wisconsin Barron County
1800 College Dr, Rice Lake WI 54868-2414
Dale Fenton, Director of Student Services
715-234-8024

University of Wisconsin Center
2909 Kellogg Ave, Janesville WI 53546-5606
608-755-2823

University of Wisconsin Center
705 Viebahn St, Manitowoc WI 54220-6601
920-683-4707

University of Wisconsin Center
1478 Midway Rd, Menasha WI 54952-1224
920-832-2620

University of Wisconsin Center
1200 US Hwy 14 W, Richland Center WI 53581-1316
608-647-6186

University of Wisconsin Center
1 University Dr, Sheboygan WI 53081-4760
920-459-3733

University of Wisconsin Center
400 S University Dr, West Bend WI 53095-3699
262-335-5201

University of Wisconsin Center-Fond du Lac
400 University Dr, Fond du Lac WI 54935
920-929-3606

University of Wisconsin Marathon County
518 S 7th Ave, Wausau WI 54401-5362
Nolan Beck, Director of Student Services
715-261-6239

University of Wisconsin-Marinette
750 W Bay Shore St, Marinette WI 54143-4253
Cynthia M. Bailey, Director Student Services
715-735-4301

University of Wisconsin - Marshfield/Wood County
2000 W 5th St, Marshfield WI 54449-3310
715-389-6530

University of Wisconsin Waukesha
1500 N University Dr, Waukesha WI 53188-2720
262-521-5200

Waukesha County Technical College
800 Main St, Pewaukee WI 53072-4601
262-691-5566

Western Wisconsin Technical College
PO Box 908, La Crosse WI 54602-0908
608-785-9200

Wisconsin Indianhead Technical College
1019 S Knowles Ave, New Richmond WI 54017-1738
715-246-6561

Wisconsin Indianhead Technical College
505 Pine Ridge Dr, Shell Lake WI 54871
Miriam Crandall, Dean of Student Services
800-243-9482 Fax: 715-468-2819
Website: www.witc.edu
E-mail: mcrandal@witc.edu
Campuses in Ashland, New Richmond, Rice Lake,
Superior.

WYOMING

Casper College
125 College Dr, Casper WY 82601-4699
307-268-2110

Central Wyoming College
2660 Peck Ave, Riverton WY 82501-2273
Tami Shultz, Director of Admissions
307-855-2231

Eastern Wyoming College
3200 W C St, Torrington WY 82240-1699
Dr. Jack Bottenfield, President
Tanya Howery, High School & College Relations
800-658-3195

Laramie County Community College
1400 E College Dr, Cheyenne WY 82007-3204
Jenny Hargett, Director of Admissions
307-778-5222 Fax: 307-778-1350
Website: www.lccc.wy.edu
E-mail: learnmore@lccc.wy.edu

Northern Wyoming Community College
300 W Sinclair St, Gillette WY 82718-7834
307-686-0254

Northwest College
231 W 6th St, Powell WY 82435-1895
307-754-6000

Sheridan College
PO Box 1500, Sheridan WY 82801-1500
307-674-6446

Western Wyoming Community College
2500 College Dr, Rock Springs WY 82901-5802
307-382-1600

WYOMING TECHNICAL INSTITUTE
4373 N 3rd St, Laramie WY 82072-9519
Glenn R. Halsey, Director of Admissions
307-742-3776 Fax: 307-721-4854
Website: www.wyotech.com
E-mail: admissions@wyotech.com

AMERICAN SAMOA

American Samoa Community College
PO Box 2609, Pago Pago AS 96799-2609
684-699-9155

GUAM

Guam Community College
PO Box 23069, G.M.F. GU 96921-0307
Virginia Charfauros Tudela, Ph.D., Registrar
671-735-5531 Fax: 671-734-5238
Website: www.guamcc.edu
E-mail: Webmaster@guamcc.edu

MARIANA ISLANDS

Northern Marianas College
PO Box 1250, Saipan MP 96950
670-234-5499

MARSHALL ISLANDS

College of the Marshall Islands
PO Box 1258, Majuro MH 96960-1258
692-625-5427

MICRONESIA

College of Micronesia
PO Box 159, Pohnpei FM 96941-0159
691-320-2480

PALAU

Palau Community College
PO Box 9, Palau PW 96940-0009
680-488-2470

PUERTO RICO

Columbia Centro Universitario
PO Box 8517, Caguas PR 00726-8517
787-743-4041

Electronic Data Processing College
PO Box 1674, San Sebastian PR 00685-1674
787-896-2137

Huertas Junior College
PO Box 8429, Caguas PR 00726-8429
787-746-1400

ICPR Junior College
558 Ave Munoz Rivera, San Juan PR 00918-3610
787-753-6335

Instituto de Banca y Comercio
61 Ponce De Leon Ave, Hato Rey PR 00919
Rafael Jimenez, Vice President
787-754-7120 Fax: 787-754-7143
Website: www.ibanca.net
E-mail: rjimenez@ibancapr.com

University College of San Juan
180 Jose R. Oliver St, San Juan PR 00918
787-250-7111

University of Puerto Rico - Aguadilla
PO Box 160, Aguadilla PR 00604-0160
787-890-2681

University of Puerto Rico at Utuado
PO Box 2500, Utuado PR 00641-0500
787-894-2828

COMPUTER AND INFORMATION SCIENCE

ALABAMA

Alabama A & M University
PO Box 908, Normal AL 35762
Antonio Boyle, Director of Admissions
256-372-5245 Fax: 256-372-5249
Website: www.aamu.edu
E-mail: aboyle@aamu.edu

Bishop State Community College - Four Campuses
351 N Broad St, Mobile AL 36603-5898
Dr. Terry Hazzard, Dean of Students
251-690-6801 Fax: 251-690-6446
Website: www.bishop.edu
E-mail: thazzard@bishop.edu

CALHOUN COMMUNITY COLLEGE
PO Box 2216, Decatur AL 35609-2216
M. Wayne Tosh, Registrar
256-306-2500 Fax: 256-306-2941
Website: www.calhoun.edu
E-mail: sla@calhoun.edu

Faulkner University
5345 Atlanta Hwy, Montgomery AL 36109-3398
Keith Mock, Director of Admissions
800-879-9816 ext. 7200 or 334-386-7200
Fax: 334-386-7137
Website: www.faulkner.edu
E-mail: admissions@faulkner.edu

Herzing College
280 W Valley Ave, Homewood AL 35209-4816
Kim Conway, Director of Admissions
205-916-2800 Fax: 205-916-2807
Website: www.herzing.edu/birmingham
E-mail: info@bhm.herzing.edu

Trenholm State Technical College
Patterson Campus
3920 Troy Hwy, Montgomery AL 36116
Dr. Anthony Molina, President
334-420-4200 Fax: 334-420-4206
Website: www.trenholmtech.cc.al.us
E-mail: amolina@trenholmtech.cc.al.us

University of Alabama in Huntsville
PO Box 1247, Huntsville AL 35899-0001
Ann Lee, Assoc. Director for Recruiting Program and Events
1-800-UAH-CALL Fax: 256-824-6073
Website: www.uah.edu
E-mail: leev@uah.edu

University of South Alabama
307 University Blvd N, Mobile AL 36688-3053
Melissa Haab, Director of Admissions
251-460-6141 Fax: 251-460-7876
Website: www.southalabama.edu
E-mail: admiss@usouthal.edu

ALASKA

University of Alaska Anchorage
PO Box 141629, Anchorage AK 99514-1629
Cecile Mitchell, Director of Enrollment Services
907-786-1480 Fax: 907-786-4888
Website: www.uaa.alaska.edu/
E-mail: enroll@uaa.alaska.edu

University of Alaska Southeast
11120 Glacier Hwy, Juneau AK 99801-8625
Paul Kraft, Dean of Students/Enrollment Management
907-796-6000 Fax: 907-796-6005
Website: www.uas.alaska.edu
E-mail: paul.kraft@uas.alaska.edu

ARIZONA

Collins College: A School of Design and Technology
(Formerly Al Collins Graphic Design School)
1140 S Priest Dr, Tempe AZ 85281-5240
Toby Craver, Director of National Admissions
800-876-7070 Fax: 480-829-0183
Website: www.collinscollege.edu
E-mail: nationaladmissions@collinscollege.edu

International Institute of the Americas
925 S Gilbert Rd Ste 201, Mesa AZ 85204-4440
Meredith Kiljan, Director
480-545-8755 Fax: 480-926-1371
Website: www.iia.edu
E-mail: mjensen@iia.edu

International Institute of the Americas
6049 N 43rd Ave, Phoenix AZ 85019-1600
Lynn McConnell, Director
602-242-6265 Fax: 602-589-1353
Website: www.iia.edu
E-mail: lmcconnell@iia.edu

International Institute of the Americas
4136 N 75th Ave Ste 211, Phoenix AZ 85033-3169
Dr. Lori Ebert, Director
623-849-8208 Fax: 623-849-0110
Website: www.iia.edu
E-mail: nsabino@iia.edu

International Institute of the Americas
5441 E 22nd St, Tucson AZ 85710
Leigh Anne Pechota, Director
520-748-9799 Fax: 520-748-9355
Website: www.iia.edu
E-mail: lpechota@iia.edu

Pima Community College
4905 E Broadway Blvd, Tucson AZ 85709-1010
Wendy Kilgore, Ph.D., Director of Admissions
520-206-4500 Fax: 520-206-4790
Website: www.pima.edu
E-mail: infocenter@pima.edu

University of Arizona
Tucson AZ 85721-0040
Paul Kohn, Director of Admissions
520-621-3237 Fax: 520-621-9799
Website: www.admissions.arizona.edu or
www.arizona.edu

ARKANSAS

Northwest Technical Institute
709 S Old Missouri Rd, Springdale AR 72764
Charles L. Kelley, President
479-751-8824 Fax: 479-751-7780
Website: www.nti.tec.ar.us
E-mail: info@nit.tec.ar.us

Ouachita Baptist University
410 Ouachita St, Arkadelphia AR 71998-0001
David Goodman, Director of Admissions
870-245-5110 Fax: 870-245-5500
Website: www.obu.edu
E-mail: admissions@obu.edu

Phillips Community College of the University of Arkansas
PO Box 785, Helena AR 72342-0785
Dr. Steven Murray, Chancellor
Lynn Boone, Vice Chancellor for Student Services /
Registrar
870-338-6474 Fax: 870-338-7542
Website: www.pccua.edu
E-mail: lboone@pccua.edu

CALIFORNIA

California State University-San Bernadino
5500 University Pkwy
San Bernardino CA 92407-2393
Olivia Rosas, Director of Admissions
909-880-5000 Fax: 909-880-7034
Website: enrollment.csusb.edu
E-mail: orosas@csusb.edu

Chabot College
25555 Hesperian Blvd, Hayward CA 94545-2400
Judy Young, Director of Admissions
510-723-6600 Fax: 510-723-7510
Website: www.chabotcollege.edu
E-mail: ccarcom@clpccd.cc.ca.us

Chapman University
One University Drive, Orange CA 92866-1099
Michael Drummy, Assistant Vice President for Enrollment
Services and Chief Admission Officer
714-997-6411 or 888-CUAPPLY Fax: 714-997-6713
Website: www.chapman.edu
E-mail: admit@chapman.edu

COLEMAN COLLEGE
8888 Balboa Ave, San Diego CA 92123-1506
Sheryl L. Ridens, Dean of Academics
858-499-0202 Fax: 858-499-0233
Website: www.coleman.edu
E-mail: admissions@coleman.edu

COLLEGE OF INFORMATION TECHNOLOGY
2701 E Chapman Ave Ste 101, Fullerton CA 92831
Mohammad Qamaruddin, Director
714-879-5000 Fax: 714-879-2272
Website: www.collegeofit.com
E-mail: mqamar@collegeofit.com

FRESNO CITY COLLEGE
1101 E University Ave, Fresno CA 93741-0002
Dayann Dietrich, Contact
559-442-8241 Fax: 559-237-4232
Website: www.fresnocitycollege.com
E-mail: fcc.admissions@scccd.com

Harvey Mudd College
Claremont CA 91711-3104
Peter Osgood, Contact
909-621-8011 Fax: 909-607-7046
Website: www.hmc.edu
E-mail: admission@hmc.edu

Institute of Technology - Sacramento
3695 Bleckely St, Mather CA 95655
916-363-4300

ITT Technical Institute
12669 Encinitas Ave, Sylmar CA 91342-3664
Kelly Christensen, Director of Admissions
818-364-5151 Fax: 818-364-5150
Website: www.itt-tech.edu
E-mail: kchristensen@itt-tech.edu

MTI BUSINESS COLLEGE OF STOCKTON
6006 N El Dorado St, Stockton CA 95207-4349
Steven Brenner, Director
888-302-2009 Fax: 209-474-8705
Website: www.mtistockton.com
E-mail: mtistockton@comcast.net
Established 1968. Accredited: ACCSCT. Family owned/operated 36 years.

MTI College
5221 Madison Ave, Sacramento CA 95841-3003
Marije Miller, Director of Admissions
916-339-1500 Fax: 916-339-0305
Website: www.mticollege.edu
E-mail: mmiller@mticollege.edu

Northwestern Polytechnic University
47671 Westinghouse Dr, Fremont CA 94539
Dr. P. Hsu, Contact
510-657-5913 Fax: 510-657-8975
Website: www.npu.edu
E-mail: npuadm@npu.edu

Orange Coast College
PO Box 5005, Costa Mesa CA 92628-5005
Kristin Clark, Director of Admissions
714-432-5773 Fax: 714-432-5736
Website: www.orangecoastcollege.edu
E-mail: kclark@cccd.edu

Pacific States University
1516 S Western Ave, Los Angeles CA 90006
Dr. Brandon Kim, Associate University Dean
323-731-2383 Fax: 323-731-7276
Website: www.psuca.edu
E-mail: admissions@psuca.edu
See listing under "Universities"

San Joaquin Valley College
8400 W Mineral King Ave, Visalia CA 93291-9283
Susie Topjian, Enrollment Services Director
559-651-2500 Fax: 559-651-4864
Website: www.sjvc.edu
E-mail: susiet@sjvc.edu

Western Career College
6001 Shellmound St 2nd Floor, Emeryville CA 94608
Elvie Engstrom, Director of Admissions
510-601-0133 Fax: 510-601-0793
Website: www.westerncollege.edu

Western Career College
380 Civic Dr Ste 300, Pleasant Hill CA 94523-1984
LaShawn Wells, Contact
925-609-6650 Fax: 926-609-6666
Website: www.westerncollege.edu

Western Career College
6201 San Ignacio Ave, San Jose CA 95119
Steve Ashab, Director of Admissions
408-360-0840 Fax: 408-360-0848
Website: www.westerncollege.edu

COLORADO

Community College of Aurora
16000 E Centretech Pkwy, Aurora CO 80011-9036
303-360-4700 Fax: 303-361-7432
Website: www.ccaurora.edu
E-mail: admissions@ccaurora.edu

IntelliTec College
2315 E Pikes Peak Ave
Colorado Springs CO 80909-6096
Michael Castellano, Contact
719-632-7626 Fax: 719-632-7451
Website: www.intelliteccollege.edu
E-mail: admcs@intelliteccollege.edu

IntelliTec College
772 Horizon Dr, Grand Junction CO 81506-3907
Rich Counts, Contact
970-245-8101 Fax: 970-243-8074
Website: www.intelliteccollege.edu
E-mail: admgj@intelliteccollege.edu

NORTHEASTERN JUNIOR COLLEGE
100 College Ave, Sterling CO 80751-2399
Judy Giacomini, Interim Chief Administrative Officer
Tina Joyce, Director of Admissions
970-521-7000 or 970-521-6752 Fax: 970-521-6801
Website: www.njc.edu
E-mail: tina.joyce@njc.edu

San Juan Basin Technical College
PO Box 970, Cortez CO 81321-0970
Shannon South, Director of Student Services
970-565-8457 Fax: 970-565-8450
Website: www.sjbtc.edu
E-mail: ssouth@sjbtc.edu

UNIVERSITY OF DENVER UNIVERSITY COLLEGE
2211 S Josephine St, Denver CO 80208
Dr. Ernest Eugster, Academic Director
303-871-3354 Fax: 303-871-4047
Website: www.universitycollege.du.edu
E-mail: ucolinfo@du.edu

CONNECTICUT

Albertus Magnus College
700 Prospect St, New Haven CT 06511-1189
Richard Lolatte, Dean of Admission
203-773-8501 or 800-578-9160 Fax: 203-773-5248
Website: www.albertus.edu
E-mail: admissions@albertus.edu

Porter and Chester Institute
670 Lordship Blvd, Stratford CT 06615-7158
Mark Breslin, Director of Admissions
203-375-4463 Fax: 203-375-5285
Website: www.porterchester.com

University of New Haven
300 Boston Post Rd, West Haven CT 06516
Director of Undergraduate Admissions
203-932-7319 Fax: 203-931-6093
Website: www.newhaven.edu
E-mail: adminfo@newhaven.edu

DELAWARE

Goldey-Beacom College
4701 Limestone Rd, Wilmington DE 19808-1993
Stacey Schwartz, Assistant Director of Admissions
302-998-8814 Fax: 302-996-5408
Website: www.gbc.edu
E-mail: admissions@gbc.edu

DISTRICT OF COLUMBIA

Potomac College
4000 Chesapeake St NW, Washington DC 20016
Florence Tate, President
202-686-0876 Fax: 202-686-0818
Website: www.potomac.edu
E-mail: ftate@potomac.edu

FLORIDA

City College
2000 W Commercial Blvd, Fort Lauderdale FL 33309
Britt Carpenter, Director of Admissions
954-492-5353 Fax: 954-491-1965
Website: www.citycollege.edu
E-mail: bcarpenter@citycollege.edu

COLLEGE OF BUSINESS & TECHNOLOGY
8991 SW 107th Ave #200, Miami FL 33176-1412
Luis Llerena, Executive Director
305-273-4499 Fax: 305-596-3835
Website: www.cbt.edu
E-mail: admissions@cbt.edu

EVERGLADES UNIVERSITY (MAIN CAMPUS)
5002 T-Rex Ave Suite 100, Boca Raton FL 33431
Kristi Mollis, President
888-772-6077 Fax: 561-912-1191
Website: www.evergladesuniversity.edu
E-mail: admissions-boca@evergladesuniversity.edu
See listing under "Universities"

EVERGLADES UNIVERSITY
Orlando Campus (Branch Campus)
5600 Lake Underhill Rd Suite 200, Orlando FL 32807
Shirley Long, Vice President
866-289-1078 Fax: 407-482-9801
Website: www.evergladesuniversity.edu
E-mail: admissions-orl@evergladesuniversity.edu
See listing under "Universities"

EVERGLADES UNIVERSITY
Sarasota Campus (Branch Campus)
6001 Lake Osprey Dr, Sarasota FL 34240
Brad Brewer, Vice President
866-907-2262 Fax: 941-907-6634
Website: www.evergladesuniversity.edu
E-mail: admissions-sar@evergladesuniversity.edu
See listing under "Universities"

Florida Metropolitan University
Orlando South
9200 Southpark Center Loop, Orlando FL 32819
Annette Cloin, Contact
407-851-2525 Fax: 407-851-1477
Website: www.fmu.edu
E-mail: acloin@cci.edu

FLORIDA METROPOLITAN UNIVERSITY
Pinellas Campus
2471 N McMullen Booth Rd
Clearwater FL 33759-1359
Sandra Williams, Director of Admissions
800-353-3687 or 727-725-2688 Fax: 727-725-3827
Website: www.fmu.edu
E-mail: sawilliams@cci.edu

Florida National College
Hialeah Campus
4425 W 20th Ave, Hialeah FL 33012
Jorge Afonso, Campus Dean
305-821-3333 ext. 1022 Fax: 305-362-0595
Website: www.fnc.edu
E-mail: omarsnc@fnc.edu

Florida National College
South Campus
11865 SW 26th St, Miami FL 33175
Jon Beisenherz, Campus Dean
305-266-9999
Website: www.fnc.edu
E-mail: omarsnc@fnc.edu

Florida State University
600 W College Ave, Tallahassee FL 32306-1096
Janice V. Finney, Director of Admissions
850-644-2525 Fax: 850-644-0197
Website: admissions.fsu.edu
E-mail: admissions@admin.fsu.edu

HERZING COLLEGE
1595 S Semoran Blvd #1501
Winter Park FL 32792-5509
Kathy Nagle, Director of Admissions
407-478-0500 Fax: 407-478-0501
Website: www.herzing.edu
E-mail: info@orl.herzing.edu

High-Tech Institute
3710 Maguire Blvd, Orlando FL 32803-3013
407-893-7400 Fax: 407-895-1804
Website: www.hightechinstitute.com

International Academy of Design & Technology
5104 Eisenhower Blvd, Tampa FL 33634-6313
Richard Costa, V.P. of Admissions and Marketing
813-880-8092 Fax: 813-881-0008
Website: www.academy.edu
E-mail: admissions@academy.edu

INTERNATIONAL ACADEMY OF DESIGN AND TECHNOLOGY
5959 Lake Ellenor Dr, Orlando FL 32809-4633
Dr. John Dietrich, VP of Admissions
877-753-0007 Fax: 407-251-0465
Website: www.iadt.edu
E-mail: info@iadt.edu

INTERNATIONAL COLLEGE
4501 Colonial Blvd, Fort Myers FL 33966
Rita Lampus, Vice President of Enrollment
Management
800-466-0019 or 239-482-0019 Fax: 239-938-7891
Website: www.internationalcollege.edu
E-mail: cmorrison@internationalcollege.edu

INTERNATIONAL COLLEGE
2655 Northbrooke Dr, Naples FL 34119
Rita Lampus, Vice President of Enrollment
Management
800-466-8017 or 239-513-1122 Fax: 239-598-6254
Website: www.internationalcollege.edu
E-mail: admit@internationalcollege.edu
See listing under "Universities"

Jones College
5353 Arlington Expy, Jacksonville FL 32211-5588
Dorothy D. Jones, Chief Executive Officer
904-743-1122 Fax: 904-744-4446
Website: www.jones.edu
E-mail: lwade@jones.edu

Jones College
11430 N Kendall Dr Ste 200, Miami FL 33176
Barclay Charles, Contact
305-275-9996 Fax: 305-743-4446
Website: www.jones.edu
E-mail: pcarbone@jones.edu

Keiser College
1800 Business Park Blvd, Daytona Beach FL 32114
Matt McEnany, Vice President
386-274-5060 Fax: 386-274-2725
Website: www.keisercollege.edu
E-mail: mmcenany@keisercollege.edu

Key College
225 E Dania Beach Blvd #130
Dania Beach FL 33004
Ronald Dooley, President
954-923-4440 Fax: 954-923-9226
Website: www.keycollege.edu
E-mail: admissions@keycollege.edu

Northwood University
2600 N Military Trl, West Palm Beach FL 33409-2999
Jack Letvinchuk, Director of Admissions
800-458-8325 Fax: 561-640-3328
Website: www.northwood.edu
E-mail: fladmit@northwood.edu

Nova Southeastern University Health Profession
3200 S University Dr, Davie FL 33328-2018
Marla Frohlinger, Director of Admissions
954-262-1101 Fax: 954-262-2282
Website: www.nova.edu
E-mail: marlaf@nsu.nova.edu

PC PROFESSOR
600 N Hiatus Rd Ste 105, Pembroke Pines FL 33026
954-704-4444 Fax: 954-704-2222
Website: www.pcprofessor.edu
E-mail: train@pcprofessor.com

REMINGTON COLLEGE
7011 A C Skinner Pky Suite 140
Jacksonville FL 32256-6953
Bobby Johns, Director of Student Recruitment
904-296-3435 Fax: 904-296-9097
Website: www.remingtoncollege.edu
E-mail: bobby.johns@remingtoncollege.edu

Remington College, Tampa Campus
2410 E Busch Blvd, Tampa FL 33612-8410
Director of Recruitment
813-935-5700 Fax: 813-935-7415
Website: www.remingtoncollege.edu

St. Thomas University
16401 NW 37th Ave, Miami Gardens FL 33054
Dr. Edward Ajhar, Contact
800-367-9010 or 305-628-6546 Fax: 305-628-6591
Website: www.stu.edu
E-mail: signup@stu.edu

Santa Fe Community College
3000 NW 83rd St, Gainesville FL 32606-6200
Jackson N. Sasser, President
352-395-5787 Fax: 352-395-4118
Website: www.sfcc.edu
E-mail: ouida.mcneil@sfcc.edu

South University
1760 N Congress Ave
West Palm Beach FL 33409-5178
Steven A. Schwab, President
561-697-9200 Fax: 561-697-9944
Website: www.southuniversity.edu
E-mail: wpb@southuniversity.edu
SACS Accreditation.

SOUTHWEST FLORIDA COLLEGE
1685 Medical Ln, Fort Myers FL 33907-1157
866-SWFC-NOW or 239-939-4766 Fax: 239-936-4040
Website: www.swfc.edu
E-mail: studentinfo@swfc.edu

University of South Florida
4202 E Fowler Ave, Tampa FL 33620-6900
J. Robert Spatig, Director of Admissions
813-974-3350 Fax: 813-974-9689
Website: www.usf.edu
E-mail: admissions@admin.usf.edu

GEORGIA

Armstrong Atlantic State University
11935 Abercorn St, Savannah GA 31419-1997
Kim West, Asst. Dean and Registrar Enrollment
Services
912-927-5277 Fax: 912-921-5462
Website: www.armstrong.edu
E-mail: admissions@mail.armstrong.edu

DeKalb Technical College
495 N Indian Creek Dr, Clarkston GA 30021-2397
Terry Richardson, Director of Admissions
404-297-9522 Fax: 404-294-6496
Website: www.dekalbtech.edu
E-mail: richardt@dekalbtech.edu

Kennesaw State University
1000 Chastain Rd NW, Kennesaw GA 30144-5591
Laurence Peterson, Dean of College of Science and
Mathematics
770-423-6160
Website: www.kennesaw.edu

MIDDLE GEORGIA TECHNICAL COLLEGE
80 Cohen Walker Dr, Warner Robins GA 31088-2729
Dr. Ivan Allen, President
478-988-6800 Fax: 478-988-6835
Website: www.middlegatech.edu

North Georgia Technical College
434 Meeks Ave, Blairsville GA 30512-2983
Admissions
706-781-2300 Fax: 706-781-2307
Website: www.northgatech.edu
E-mail: info@northgatech.edu

North Georgia Technical College
8989 Highway 17, Toccoa GA 30577
706-779-5591
Website: www.northgatech.edu
E-mail: info@northgatech.edu

North Georgia Technical College
Clarkesville Campus
PO Box 65, Clarkesville GA 30523-0002
Admissions
706-754-7700 Fax: 706-754-7777
Website: www.northgatech.edu
E-mail: info@northgatech.edu

North Metro Technical College
5198 Ross Rd SE, Acworth GA 30102-3129
Missy Cusack, Director of Admissions
770-975-4000 Fax: 770-975-4142
Website: www.northmetrotech.edu
E-mail: info@northmetrotech.edu

Oglethorpe University
4484 Peachtree Rd NE, Atlanta GA 30319-2797
Kelly Gosnell, Director of Admission
404-261-1441 Fax: 404-364-8491
Website: www.oglethorpe.edu
E-mail: admission@oglethorpe.edu

SAVANNAH RIVER COLLEGE
2528 Centerwest Pkwy Bldg A, Augusta GA 30909
Dawn McCraith, Director
706-738-5046 Fax: 706-736-3599
Website: www.savannahrivercollege.com
E-mail: info@savannahrivercollege.com

HAWAII

Heald College, Honolulu
1500 Kapiolani Blvd, Honolulu HI 96814-3732
Lon K. Ibaraki, Director of Admissions
808-955-1500 or 800-940-0530 Fax: 808-955-6964
Website: www.heald.edu
E-mail: lon_ibaraki@heald.edu

IDAHO

Brigham Young University - Idaho
120 Kimball Bldg, Rexburg ID 83460
Gordon Westenskow, Director of Admissions
208-496-1020 Fax: 208-496-1220
Website: www.byui.edu
E-mail: admissions@byui.edu

University of Idaho
Moscow ID 83844-4253
Lloyd Scott, Director of New Student Services
208-885-6163 Fax: 208-885-4477
Website: www.uidaho.edu
E-mail: nss@uidaho.edu

ILLINOIS

AMERICAN INTERCONTINENTAL UNIVERSITY ONLINE
5550 Prairie Stone Parkway Suite 400
Hoffman Estates IL 60192
Admissions Department
877-701-3800
Website: www.aiuonline.edu
E-mail: info@aiuonline.edu

Aurora University
347 S Gladstone Ave, Aurora IL 60506-4892
Carol R. Dunn, Ed.D., Vice President for Enrollment
800-742-5281 Fax: 630-844-5535
Website: www.aurora.edu
E-mail: admission@aurora.edu

Benedictine University
5700 College Rd, Lisle IL 60532-0900
630-829-6300 or 888-829-6363 Fax: 630-829-6301
Website: www.ben.edu
E-mail: admissions@ben.edu
See listing under "Universities"

College of Office Technology
1514 W Division St # 2, Chicago IL 60622-3312
Greg Brown, Director of Admissions
773-278-0042 Fax: 773-278-0143
Website: www.cot.edu
E-mail: kgalva@cotedu.com

Columbia College Chicago
600 S Michigan Ave, Chicago IL 60605-1996
Murphy Monroe, Executive Director of Admissions
312-344-7130 Fax: 312-344-8024
Website: www.colum.edu
E-mail: admissions@colum.edu

CONCORDIA UNIVERSITY
7400 Augusta St, River Forest IL 60305-1402
708-209-3100 Fax: 708-209-3473
Website: www.curf.edu
E-mail: crfadmis.edu

Kaskaskia College
27210 College Rd, Centralia IL 62801-7878
Tyra Taylor, Dean of Enrollment Management and
Retention Services
618-545-3000 Fax: 618-532-1990
Website: www.kaskaskia.edu
E-mail: ttaylor@kaskaskia.edu

MacCormac College
29 E Madison St, Chicago IL 60602-4405
David F. Grassi, Admissions Counselor
312-922-1884 ext. 101 Fax: 312-922-4328
Website: www.maccormac.edu
E-mail: dgrassi@maccormac.edu

MORRISON INSTITUTE OF TECHNOLOGY
701 Portland Ave, Morrison IL 61270-2959
Richard C. Parkinson, Interim Director
815-772-7584 Fax: 815-772-7218
Website: www.morrison.tec.il.us
E-mail: admissions@morrison.tec.il.us
Private. Coed. Accreditation: ABET. Enrollment: 140.
Student-faculty ratio: 13:1. Engineering Technology Associate of Applied Science degree in Architectural, Construction, Civil, Mechanical, Drafting & Design, and Surveying Technology. AAS degree in Systems & Network Administration.

North Central College
30 N Brainard St, Naperville IL 60540-4690
Martha Stolze, Director of Admissions
630-637-5800 Fax: 630-637-5819
Website: www.northcentralcollege.edu
E-mail: admissions@noctrl.edu

Roosevelt University
430 S Michigan Ave, Chicago IL 60605
Gwen E. Kanelos, Asst. Vice President for Enrollment Services
877-APPLY-RU Fax: 312-341-4216
Website: www.roosevelt.edu
E-mail: applyru@roosevelt.edu

South Suburban College of Cook County
15800 State St, South Holland IL 60473
Jane Ellen Stocker, Dean of Enrollment Services
708-596-2000 Fax: 708-225-5806
Website: www.southsuburbancollege.edu
E-mail: jstocker@southsuburbancollege.edu

Triton College
2000 5th Ave, River Grove IL 60171-1995
Mary-Rita Moore, Dean of Enrollment Services
708-456-0300 ext. 3130 Fax: 708-583-3147
Website: www.triton.edu
E-mail: triton@triton.edu
See listing under "Community and Junior Colleges"

INDIANA

Brown Mackie College - Fort Wayne
3000 E Coliseum Blvd, Fort Wayne IN 46805
Daniel Summer, Campus President
260-484-4400 Fax: 260-484-2678
Website: www.brownmackie.edu

Brown Mackie College - South Bend
1030 E Jefferson Blvd, South Bend IN 46617-3123
Connie Adelman, Campus President
574-237-0774 Fax: 574-237-3585
Website: www.brownmackie.edu

Franklin College
101 Branigin Blvd, Franklin IN 46131
Jacqueline S. Acosta, Director of Admissions
800-852-0232 Fax: 317-738-8274
Website: www.franklincollege.edu
E-mail: admissions@franklincollege.edu

International Business College
5699 Coventry Ln, Fort Wayne IN 46804
260-459-4500 Fax: 260-436-1896
Website: www.ibcfortwayne.edu
E-mail: skinzer@ibcfortwayne.edu

Ivy Tech Community College - North Central
220 Dean Johnson Blvd, South Bend IN 46601-3415
Pam Decker, Director of Admissions
574-289-7001 Fax: 574-236-7177
Website: www.ivytech.edu
E-mail: pdecker@ivytech.edu

Oakland City University
138 N Lucretia St, Oakland City IN 47660
Brian J. Baker, Director of Admissions
800-737-5125 Fax: 812-749-1433
Website: www.oak.edu
E-mail: bbaker@oak.edu
See listing under "Universities"

Rose-Hulman Institute of Technology
5500 Wabash Ave, Terre Haute IN 47803-3920
James A. Goecker, Dean of Admissions
812-877-8213 Fax: 812-877-8941
Website: www.rose-hulman.edu
E-mail: admis.ofc@rose-hulman.edu

St. Mary-of-the-Woods College
Saint Mary of the Woods IN 47876-1001
James P. Malley, Jr., Director of Admission
800-926-7692 Fax: 812-535-5010
Website: www.smwc.edu
E-mail: smwcadms@smwc.edu

University of Evansville
1800 Lincoln Ave, Evansville IN 47722-0001
Thomas E. Bear, V.P. of Enrollment Services
800-423-8633 Fax: 812-488-4076
Website: www.evansville.edu
E-mail: admission@evansville.edu

IOWA

AIB College of Business
2500 Fleur Dr, Des Moines IA 50321-1799
800-444-1921 Fax: 515-244-6773
Website: www.aib.edu
E-mail: admissions@aib.edu

Briar Cliff University
PO Box 2100, Sioux City IA 51104-0100
Sharisue Wilcoxon, VP for Enrollment Management
712-279-5200 Fax: 712-279-1632
Website: www.briarcliff.edu
E-mail: admissions@briarcliff.edu

Clarke College
1550 Clarke Dr, Dubuque IA 52001-3198
Andy Schroeder, Director of Admissions
800-383-2345 Fax: 563-584-8666
Website: www.clarke.edu
E-mail: andy.schroeder@clarke.edu

Graceland University
1 University Place, Lamoni IA 50140
Brian Shantz, Vice President for Enrollment and Dean of Admissions
641-784-5196 Fax: 641-784-5480
Website: www.admissions.graceland.edu
E-mail: admissions@graceland.edu

Hamilton College
7009 Nordic Dr, Cedar Falls IA 50613
Tim Cole, Campus President
319-277-0220 Fax: 319-363-3812
Website: www.hamiltonia.edu
E-mail: ticole@hamiltoncf.com

Hamilton College
3165 Edgewood Pkwy SW, Cedar Rapids IA 52404
Susan Spivey, Campus President
319-363-0481 Fax: 319-363-3812
Website: www.hamiltonia.edu
E-mail: spiveys@hamiltonia.edu

Hamilton College
2570 4th St SW, Mason City IA 50401-4665
Joe Albers, Executive Director
641-423-2530 Fax: 641-423-7512
Website: www.hamiltonia.edu
E-mail: jalbers@hamiltonia.edu

Hamilton College
4655 121st St, Urbandale IA 50323-2311
Ed Rogan, Campus President
515-727-2100 Fax: 515-727-2115
Website: www.hamiltonia.edu
E-mail: erogan_dm@hamiltonia.edu

Iowa Lakes Community College
3200 College Dr, Emmetsburg IA 50536-1055
Anne Stansbury, Asst. Director of Admissions
712-852-5212 Fax: 712-362-8363
Website: www.iowalakes.edu
E-mail: info@iowalakes.edu

Iowa Lakes Community College
300 S 18th St, Estherville IA 51334-2721
Anne Stansbury, Asst. Director of Admissions
712-362-7945 Fax: 712-362-8363
Website: www.iowalakes.edu
E-mail: info@iowalakes.edu

Mount Mercy College
1330 Elmhurst Dr NE, Cedar Rapids IA 52402-4797
Jim Krystofiak, Dean of Admission
800-248-4504 Fax: 319-363-5270
Website: www.mtmercy.edu
E-mail: admission@mtmercy.edu

Northwest Iowa Community College
603 W Park St, Sheldon IA 51201-1046
Lisa Story, Director of Enrollment Management
712-324-5061 Fax: 712-324-4136
Website: www.nwicc.edu
E-mail: lstory@nwicc.edu

Waldorf College
106 S 6th St, Forest City IA 50436-1713
Steve Lovik, Vice President of Enrollment Management
800-292-1903 or 641-585-8112 Fax: 641-585-8125
Website: www.waldorf.edu
E-mail: loviks@waldorf.edu
See listing under "Universities"

Wartburg College
PO Box 1003, Waverly IA 50677-0903
Brent Matthias, Interim Director of Admissions
319-352-8200 Fax: 319-352-8579
Website: www.wartburg.edu
E-mail: admissions@wartburg.edu

KANSAS

Allen County Community College
1801 N Cottonwood St, Iola KS 66749-1607
John Masterson, President
Randy Weber, Director of Admissions
620-365-5116 Fax: 620-365-3284
Website: www.allencc.net
E-mail: weber@allencc.net

COLBY COMMUNITY COLLEGE
1255 S Range Ave, Colby KS 67701-4099
Director of Admissions
888-634-9350 or 785-460-4690 Fax: 785-460-4691
Website: www.colbycc.edu
E-mail: bobbi@colbycc.edu

Flint Hills Technical College
3301 W 18th Ave, Emporia KS 66801-5957
Lisa Kirmer, Dean of Student Services
620-343-4600 Fax: 620-343-4610
Website: www.fhtc.net
E-mail: lkirmer@fhtc.net

Independence Community College
PO Box 708, Independence KS 67301-0708
Dr. Terry Hetrick, President
800-842-6063 Fax: 620-331-5344
Website: www.indycc.edu
E-mail: admissions@indycc.edu

Newman University
3100 W McCormick St, Wichita KS 67213
Jann Reusser, Admissions Recruitment Coordinator
316-942-4291 ext. 2144 Fax: 316-942-4483
Website: www.newmanu.edu
E-mail: reusserj@newmanu.edu

Tabor College
400 S Jefferson St, Hillsboro KS 67063-1758
Rusty Allen, Dean of Enrollment Management
620-947-3121 Fax: 620-947-6276
Website: www.tabor.edu
E-mail: admissions@tabor.edu

KENTUCKY

Bluegrass Community and Technical College
Oswald Building
470 Cooper Drive, Lexington KY 40506-0235
Shelbie Hugle, Director of Admissions
859-246-6200 Fax: 859-246-4664
Website: www.bluegrass.kctcs.edu
E-mail: bctc_info@kctcs.edu

Brown Mackie College - Louisville
300 High Rise Dr, Louisville KY 40213-3263
Kathleen Belanger, Director of Admissions
502-968-7191 Fax: 502-357-9956
Website: www.brownmackie.edu
E-mail: kbelanger@brownmackie.edu

BROWN MACKIE COLLEGE
Northern Kentucky Campus
309 Buttermilk Pike, Fort Mitchell KY 41017-2191
Joanne Dellefield, Director of Admissions
859-341-5627 Fax: 859-341-6483
Website: www.brownmackie.edu
E-mail: jdellefield@brownmackie.edu

Daymar College
4400 Breckenridge Ln #415, Louisville KY 40218
Shawn McDaniel, Director of Admissions
502-495-1040 Fax: 502-495-1518
Website: www.daymarcollege.com

Daymar College
3361 Buckland Sq, Owensboro KY 42301-5830
Vickie McDougal Director of Admissions
800-960-4090 Fax: 270-685-4090
Website: www.daymarcollege.com

Morehead State University
Morehead KY 40351-1689
Dayna Seelig, Enrollment Services
800-585-6781 Fax: 606-783-5038
Website: www.moreheadstate.edu
E-mail: admissions@moreheadstate.edu

Spencerian College
1575 Winchester Rd, Lexington KY 40505
Victor Lamoin Adcock II, Director of Admissions
800-456-3253

Transylvania University
300 N Broadway, Lexington KY 40508-1776
859-233-8242 Fax: 859-233-8797
Website: www.transy.edu
E-mail: admissions@transy.edu

LOUISIANA

ASCENSION COLLEGE
320 E Ascension St, Gonzales LA 70737-2912
Dennis Kerr, President
225-647-6609 Fax: 225-647-4849
Website: www.ascensioncollege.org
E-mail: dkerrascen@etel.net

CAMERON COLLEGE
PO Box 19288, New Orleans LA 70119-0288
Eleanor Cameron Skov, President
504-821-5881 or 800-878-5881 Fax: 504-822-3467
Website: www.cameron.com
E-mail: cameroncollege@mindspring.com

CAREER TECHNICAL COLLEGE
2319 Louisville Ave, Monroe LA 71201
Rick Nail, Director
318-323-2889 Fax: 318-324-9883
Website: www.careertc.com
E-mail: rnail@careertc.com

Delta School of Business and Technology
517 Broad St, Lake Charles LA 70601-4334
Gary Holt, President
337-439-5765 Fax: 337-436-5151
Website: www.deltatech.edu
E-mail: susan@deltatech.edu

Dillard University
2601 Gentilly Blvd, New Orleans LA 70122-3097
Linda G. Nash, Director of Admissions
Website: www.dillard.edu
E-mail: admissions@dillard.edu

Louisiana State University at Eunice
PO Box 1129, Eunice LA 70535-1129
Ron Ryder, Registrar
337-457-7311 Fax: 337-550-1306
Website: www.lsue.edu
E-mail: rryder@lsue.edu

MAINE

HUSSON COLLEGE
One College Cir, Bangor ME 04401-2999
Jane Goodwin, Director of Admissions
800-4HU-SSON or 207-941-7100 Fax: 207-941-7935
Website: www.husson.edu
E-mail: admit@husson.edu
See listing under "Universities"

Northern Maine Community College
33 Edgemont Dr, Presque Isle ME 04769-2016
Bill Casavant, Director of Admissions
207-768-2700 Fax: 207-768-2831
Website: www.nmcc.edu
E-mail: admissions@nmcc.edu

St. Joseph's College of Maine
278 Whites Bridge Rd, Standish ME 04084-5263
Vincent Kloskowski, Dean of Admissions
800-338-7057 Fax: 207-893-7862
Website: www.sjcme.edu
E-mail: admission@sjcme.edu

Southern Maine Community College
2 Fort Rd, South Portland ME 04106-1698
Dr. James Ortiz, President
Scott MacDonald, Director of Financial Aid
207-741-5500 Fax: 207-741-5671
Website: www.smccme.edu
E-mail: oharmon@maine.rr.com

MARYLAND

Cecil Community College
One Seahawk Dr, North East MD 21901
Sandra S. Rajaski, Registrar & Director of Admissions
410-287-1000 Fax: 410-287-1001
Website: www.cecilcc.edu
E-mail: srajaski@cecilcc.edu

Hagerstown Community College
11400 Robinwood Dr, Hagerstown MD 21742-6590
Dr. Daniel E. Bock, Assistant Director of Admissions
301-790-2800 Fax: 301-791-9165
Website: www.hagerstowncc.edu
E-mail: bockd@hagerstowncc.edu

Villa Julie College
1525 Greenspring Valley Rd
Stevenson MD 21153-0641
Mark Hergan, V.P. Enrollment Services
410-486-7001 Fax: 410-602-6600
Website: www.vjc.edu/admissions
E-mail: admissions@mail.vjc.edu

MASSACHUSETTS

Anna Maria College
50 Sunset Ln, Paxton MA 01612
Julie A. Mitchell, Director of Admissions
508-849-3360 Fax: 508-849-3362
Website: www.annamaria.edu
E-mail: admissions@annamaria.edu

Assumption College
500 Salisbury St, Worcester MA 01609-1294
Kathleen Murphy, Dean of Enrollment
508-767-7000 Fax: 508-799-4412
Website: www.assumption.edu
E-mail: admiss@assumption.edu

Becker College
Campuses in Worcester and Leicester, MA
61 Sever St, Worcester MA 01609-2165
Karen H. Schedin, Director of Admissions
508-791-9241 Fax: 508-890-1500
Website: www.becker.edu
E-mail: admissions@becker.edu
See listing under "Universities"

Benjamin Franklin Institute of Technology
41 Berkeley St, Boston MA 02116-6307
Norman Kraft, Dean of Enrollment
617-423-4630 ext. 119 Fax: 617-482-3706
Website: www.bfit.edu
E-mail: admissions@bfit.edu

Boston University
121 Bay State Rd, Boston MA 02215
Kelly Walter, Executive Director of Admissions
617-353-2300 Fax: 617-353-9695
Website: web.bu.edu
E-mail: admissions@bu.edu

Bristol Community College
777 Elsbree St, Fall River MA 02720-7395
Rodney S. Clark, Director of Admissions
508-678-2811 ext. 2516, 2179 Fax: 508-730-3265
Website: www.bristol.mass.edu
E-mail: admissions@bristol.mass.edu

Gibbs College of Boston
a Private Two-Year College
126 Newbury St, Boston MA 02116-2904
Ida Zecco, Vice President of Admissions
617-578-7100 Fax: 617-578-7163
Website: www.gibbsboston.edu

Gordon College
255 Grapevine Rd, Wenham MA 01984-1899
Nancy Mering, Director of Admissions
866-464-6736 Fax: 978-867-4682
Website: www.gordon.edu
E-mail: admissions@gordon.edu

ITT TECHNICAL INSTITUTE
333 Boston Providence Tpke
Norwood MA 02062-3932
Tom Ryan, Director of Recruiting
800-879-TECH (8324) Fax: 781-278-0766
Website: www.itt-tech.edu
E-mail: tryan@itt-tech.edu
Established 1990. Private. Coed. Accreditation: ACICS. Enrollment: 300. Student-faculty ratio: 11:1. Associate Degrees offered: Computer Drafting & Design, Computer Electronics Technology, Computer Network Systems, Multimedia.

Massachusetts Institute of Technology
77 Massachusetts Ave, Cambridge MA 02139-4307
Marilee Jones, Dean of Admission
617-253-1000 Fax: 617-253-4016
Website: my.mit.edu
E-mail: admissions@mit.edu

Newbury College
129 Fisher Ave, Brookline MA 02445-5796
Salvadore Liberto, Vice President of Enrollment
617-730-7000 Fax: 617-731-9618
Website: www.newbury.edu

University of Massachusetts Dartmouth
Old Westport Rd, North Dartmouth MA 02747-2300
Steven T. Briggs, Director of Admissions
508-999-8605 Fax: 508-999-8755
Website: explore.umassd.edu
E-mail: sbriggs@umassd.edu

Wentworth Institute of Technology
550 Huntington Ave, Boston MA 02115-5998
David C. Planchard, Director of Admissions
617-442-9010
Website: www.wit.edu/apply
E-mail: planchardd@wit.edu

Westfield State College
PO Box 1630, Westfield MA 01086
Michelle Mattie, Associate Dean, Admission and Enrollment Services
413-572-5300
Website: www.wsc.ma.edu
E-mail: admission@wsc.ma.edu

Worcester Polytechnic Institute
100 Institute Rd, Worcester MA 01609-2280
Edward J. Connor, Director of Admissions
508-831-5286 Fax: 508-831-5875
Website: admissions.wpi.edu
E-mail: admissions@wpi.edu

MICHIGAN

Alma College
614 W Superior St, Alma MI 48801-1599
Anne Monroe, Director of Admissions
800-321-ALMA Fax: 989-463-7057
Website: www.alma.edu
E-mail: admissions@alma.edu

Andrews University
Berrien Springs MI 49104-0001
Randall Graves, Director of Recruitment Services
800-253-2874 Fax: 269-471-2670
Website: www.connect.andrews.edu
E-mail: gravesr@andrews.edu

CARNEGIE INSTITUTE
550 Stephenson Hwy Ste 100, Troy MI 48083-1159
Gloria J. McEachern, President
248-589-1078 Fax: 248-589-1631
Website: www.carnegie-institute.com
E-mail: carnegie47@aol.com

Delta College
University Center MI 48710-0001
Duff Zube, Director of Admissions
989-686-9093 Fax: 989-667-2202
Website: www.delta.edu
E-mail: admit@delta.edu

Grand Valley State University
1 Campus Dr, Allendale MI 49401-9403
Jodi Chycinski, Director of Admissions
616-331-6611 Fax: 616-331-2000
Website: www.gvsu.edu
E-mail: go2gvsu@gvsu.edu

ITT TECHNICAL INSTITUTE
4020 Sparks Dr SE, Grand Rapids MI 49546-6192
Dennis Hormel, Director
616-956-1060 Fax: 616-956-5606
Website: www.itt-tech.edu
E-mail: dhormel@itt-tech.edu

Lawrence Technological University
21000 W 10 Mile Rd, Southfield MI 48075-1058
Jane Rohrback, Director of Admissions
800-225-5588 Fax: 248-204-2228
Website: www.ltu.edu
E-mail: admissions@ltu.edu
See listing under "Universities"

MACOMB COMMUNITY COLLEGE
44575 Garfield Rd, Clinton Township MI 48038-1139
Information Center
586-445-7999
Website: www.macomb.edu
E-mail: answer@macomb.edu

MACOMB COMMUNITY COLLEGE
14500 E 12 Mile Rd, Warren MI 48088-3896
Information Center
586-445-7999
Website: www.macomb.edu
E-mail: answer@macomb.edu

National Institute of Technology
26111 Evergreen Rd Ste 201
Southfield MI 48076-4491
Marchelle Weaver, President
248-799-9933 Fax: 248-799-2912
Website: www.cci.edu
E-mail: mweaver@cci.edu

Northwestern Michigan College
1701 E Front St, Traverse City MI 49686-3061
Jim Bensley, Admissions Coordinator
800-748-0566 Fax: 231-995-1339
Website: www.nmc.edu
E-mail: jbensley@nmc.edu

Northwood University
4000 Whiting Dr, Midland MI 48640
Daniel F. Toland, Dean of Admissions
800-457-7878 Fax: 989-837-4490
Website: www.northwood.edu
E-mail: miadmit@northwood.edu

Oakland Community College
2480 Opdyke Rd, Bloomfield Hills MI 48304
Dr. Maurice McCall, Director of Admissions
248-341-2000
Website: www.oaklandcc.edu
E-mail: mhmccall@oaklandcc.edu

Oakland University
2200 N Squirrel Rd, Rochester MI 48309
Eleanor L. Reynolds, Assistant Vice President & Director of Admissions
248-370-2100
Website: www.oakland.edu
E-mail: ouinfo@oakland.edu

University of Michigan-Dearborn
4901 Evergreen Rd, Dearborn MI 48128-1491
The Office of Admissions & Orientation
313-593-5100 Fax: 313-436-9167
Website: www.umd.umich.edu
E-mail: admissions@umd.umich.edu

MINNESOTA

ACADEMY COLLEGE
1101 E 78th St, Bloomington MN 55420-1402
952-851-0066 Fax: 952-851-0094
Website: www.academycollege.edu
E-mail: info@academycollege.edu
See listing under "Career Schools"

Carleton College
1 N College St, Northfield MN 55057-4044
800-995-2275 or 507-646-4190 Fax: 507-646-4526
Website: www.carleton.edu
E-mail: admissions@acs.carleton.edu

Duluth Business University
4724 Mike Colalillo Dr, Duluth MN 55807-2723
Bonnie Kupczynski, Director
800-777-8406 Fax: 218-628-2127
Website: www.dbumn.edu
E-mail: info@dbumn.edu

Dunwoody College of Technology
818 Dunwoody Blvd, Minneapolis MN 55403-1192
John Slama, Vice President Enrollment Management
800-292-4625 or 612-374-5800 Fax: 612-374-4128
Website: www.dunwoody.edu
E-mail: jslama@dunwoody.edu
See listing under "Career Schools"

Globe College
7166 10th St N, Oakdale MN 55128
Mike Hughes, Campus Director
651-730-5100 Fax: 651-730-5151
Website: www.globecollege.edu
E-mail: admissions@globecollege.edu

Gustavus Adolphus College
800 W College Ave, Saint Peter MN 56082-1485
Mark H. Anderson, Dean of Admission
800-GUSTAVUS Fax: 507-933-7474
Website: www.gustavus.edu
E-mail: admission@gustavus.edu

Hibbing Community College
1515 E 25th St, Hibbing MN 55746-3300
Holly Bigelow, Director of Enrollment
800-224-4HCC or 218-262-7200 Fax: 218-262-6717
Website: www.hibbing.edu
E-mail: admissions@hibbing.edu

Minneapolis Community and Technical College
1501 Hennepin Ave, Minneapolis MN 55403-1779
Dena Russell, Director of Admissions
612-659-6282 Fax: 612-659-6210
Website: www.minneapolis.edu
E-mail: admissions.office@minneapolis.edu

Minnesota State Community & Technical College
900 Highway 34 E, Detroit Lakes MN 56501-2698
Dale Westley, Director of Admissions
800-492-4836 Fax: 218-846-3710
Website: www.minnesota.edu
E-mail: dale.westley@minnesota.edu

Minnesota State Community & Technical College
PO Box 566, Wadena MN 56482-0566
Paul Drange, Director of Admissions
800-247-2007 Fax: 218-631-7901
Website: www.minnesota.edu
E-mail: paul.drange@minnesota.edu

Minnesota State Community and Technical College
1900 28th Ave S, Moorhead MN 56560-4899
Laurie McKeever, Director of Admissions
800-426-5603 Fax: 218-299-6584
Website: www.minnesota.edu
E-mail: laurie.mckeever@minnesota.edu

National American University
1550 W Highway 36, Roseville MN 55113
Matthew Mottl, Director of Admissions
651-644-1265 Fax: 651-644-0690
Website: www.national.edu
E-mail: mmottl@national.edu

Northland Community & Technical College
Highway 1 E, Thief River Falls MN 56701
Roger Peterson, Chairperson
800-959-6282 or 218-681-0749 Fax: 218-681-0774
Website: www.northlandcollege.edu

Northland Community and Technical College
2022 Central Ave NE
East Grand Forks MN 56721-2702
Deb Riely, Business Program Chair
800-451-3441 Fax: 218-773-4502
Website: www.northlandcollege.edu
E-mail: admissions@northlandcollege.edu

Pillsbury Baptist Bible College
315 S Grove Ave, Owatonna MN 55060-3097
Stephen R. Seidler, Director of Admissions
507-451-2710 Fax: 507-451-0156
Website: www.pillsbury.edu
E-mail: steveseidler@pillsbury.edu

Ridgewater College-Hutchinson Campus
2 Century Ave SE, Hutchinson MN 55350-3100
Dawn Bjork, Counselor
800-222-4424 Fax: 320-231-7767
Website: www.ridgewater.edu
E-mail: dawn.bjork@ridgewater.edu

St. Cloud Technical College
1540 Northway Dr, Saint Cloud MN 56303-1240
Jodi Elness, Director of Enrollment Management
800-222-1009 Fax: 320-308-5981
Website: www.sctc.edu
E-mail: jelness@sctc.edu

MISSOURI

Columbia College
1001 Rogers St, Columbia MO 65216-0001
Regina Morin, Director of Admissions
573-875-7352 Fax: 573-875-7506
Website: www.ccis.edu
E-mail: admissions@ccis.edu

East Central College
1964 Prairie Dell Rd, Union MO 63084
Karen Wieda, Registrar
636-583-5195 ext. 2220 Fax: 636-583-1897
Website: www.eastcentral.edu
E-mail: wiedaks@eastcentral.edu

Harris-Stowe State University
3026 Laclede Ave, Saint Louis MO 63103-2199
LaShanda R. Boone, Director of Admissions
314-340-3300 Fax: 314-340-3555
Website: www.hssu.edu
E-mail: admissions@hssu.edu

Hickey College
940 Westport Plz, Saint Louis MO 63146-3127
Christopher A. Gearin, President
800-777-1544 or 314-434-2212 Fax: 314-434-1974
Website: www.hickeycollege.edu
E-mail: admin@hickeycollege.edu

Lindenwood University
209 S Kingshighway St
Saint Charles MO 63301-1695
Sheryl Guffey, Director of Admissions
636-949-2000 Fax: 636-949-4989
Website: www.lindenwood.edu

Ranken Technical College
4431 Finney Ave, Saint Louis MO 63113-2898
Elizabeth M. Keserauskis, Director of Admissions
314-371-0233 Fax: 314-371-0241
Website: www.ranken.edu
E-mail: admissions@ranken.edu

St. Charles Community College
4601 Mid Rivers Mall Dr, Saint Peters MO 63376
Kathy Brockgreitens-Gober, Director of Admissions
636-922-8000 Fax: 636-922-8236
Website: www.stchas.edu
E-mail: adm-reg@stchas.edu

SPRINGFIELD COLLEGE
1010 W Sunshine St, Springfield MO 65807-2446
Scott Lester, Contact
417-864-7220 or 800-475-2699 Fax: 417-866-3335
Website: www.springfield-college.com
E-mail: slester@cci.edu

Truman State University
100 E Normal, Kirksville MO 63501
Office of Admission
660-785-4000 Fax: 660-785-4181
Website: admissions.truman.edu
E-mail: admissions@truman.edu

University of Missouri
1 University Blvd, Saint Louis MO 63121-4499
Dr. Mark Burkholder, Dean-College of Arts & Sciences
314-516-5501 Fax: 314-516-5415
Website: www.umsl.edu
E-mail: admissions@umsl.edu

Vatterott College
3925 Industrial Dr, Saint Ann MO 63074-1807
Jennifer Commuso, Director of Admissions
800-345-6018 Fax: 314-428-5956
Website: www.vatterott-college.edu
E-mail: jennifer.commuso@vatterott-college.edu

Vatterott College
12970 Maurer Industrial Dr, Saint Louis MO 63127
Sherri Bremer, Director of Admissions
314-843-4200 Fax: 314-843-1709
Website: www.vatterott-college.edu
E-mail: sherri.bremer@vatterott-college.edu

Webster University
470 E Lockwood Ave, Saint Louis MO 63119-3194
Al Cawns, Chairman, Math & Computer Science
314-968-7023 Fax: 314-963-6050
Website: www.webster.edu
See listing under "Universities"

William Woods University
1 University Ave, Fulton MO 65251-1098
Jimmy Clay, Director of Admissions
573-642-2251 Fax: 573-592-1146
Website: www.williamwoods.edu
E-mail: admissions@williamwoods.edu
See listing under "Universities"

MONTANA

Rocky Mountain College
1511 Poly Dr, Billings MT 59102-1796
Bonnie Knapp, Director of Admissions
800-877-6259 Fax: 406-657-1189
Website: www.rocky.edu
E-mail: admissions@rocky.edu

NEBRASKA

College of Saint Mary
7000 Mercy Rd, Omaha NE 68106
Lorin Werth,V.P. for Enrollment
800-926-5534 or 402-399-2407 Fax: 402-399-2412
Website: www.csm.edu
E-mail: lwerth@csm.edu

Midland Lutheran College
900 N Clarkson St, Fremont NE 68025-4200
Todd Hansen, Associate Director of Admissions
402-941-6501 Fax: 402-941-6513
Website: www.mlc.edu
E-mail: admissions@mlc.edu

Mid-Plains Community College
McCook Community College Campus
1205 E 3rd St, Mc Cook NE 69001-2631
Kelly Rippen, Director of Recruitment
800-658-4348 Fax: 308-345-8180
Website: www.mpcc.edu
E-mail: rippenk@mpcc.edu

Mid-Plains Community College
North Platte Community College - South Campus
601 W State Farm Rd, North Platte NE 69101
Kelly Rippen, Director of Recruitment
800-658-4308 ext. 8107 Fax: 308-535-3789
Website: www.mpcc.edu
E-mail: rippenk@mpcc.edu

Nebraska Wesleyan University
5000 Saint Paul Ave, Lincoln NE 68504-2794
Patricia Karthauser, V.P. for University Enrollment
402-466-2371 Fax: 402-465-2177
Website: www.nebrwesleyan.edu
E-mail: admissions@nebrwesleyan.edu

Peru State College
PO Box 10, Peru NE 68421-0010
Office of Admissions
800-742-4412 Fax: 402-872-2296
Website: www.peru.edu
E-mail: admissions@oakmail.peru.edu

University of Nebraska at Kearney
905 W 25th St, Kearney NE 68849-0001
Dusty Newton, Director of Admissions
800-KEARNEY Fax: 308-865-8987
Website: www.unk.edu
E-mail: admissionsug@unk.edu

VATTEROTT COLLEGE
11818 I St, Omaha NE 68137
Todd S. Clark, Director
402-891-9411 Fax: 402-891-9413
Website: www.vatterott-college.edu
E-mail: tclark@vatterott-college.edu

NEVADA

Career College of Northern Nevada
1195-A Corporate Blvd, Reno NV 89502-2331
Nathan Clark, Director
775-856-2266 Fax: 775-856-0935
Website: www.ccnn.edu
E-mail: lgoldhammer@ccnn4u.com
See listing under "Career Schools"

GREAT BASIN COLLEGE
1500 College Pkwy, Elko NV 89801-5032
Julie G. Byrnes, Director of Enrollment Management
775-753-2271 Fax: 775-753-2311
Website: www.gbcnv.edu
E-mail: bjulie@gbcnv.edu

Morrison University
10315 Professional Circle Suite 201
Reno NV 89521-4826
Charles Timinsky, Director of Enrollment
775-850-0700 Fax: 775-850-0711
Website: www.morrisonuniversity.com

NEW HAMPSHIRE

Southern New Hampshire University
2500 N River Rd, Hooksett NH 03106-1045
Steve Soba, Director of Admissions
603-645-9611 Fax: 603-645-9693
Website: www.snhu.edu
E-mail: s.soba@snhu.edu

NEW JERSEY

Atlantic Cape Community College
5100 Black Horse Pike
Mays Landing NJ 08330-2699
Linda McLeod, Assistant Director of College Recruitment
609-343-5000 Fax: 609-343-4921
Website: www.atlantic.edu
E-mail: accadmit@atlantic.edu
See listing under "Community and Junior Colleges"

Bergen Community College
400 Paramus Rd, Paramus NJ 07652
Julian Gomez, Asst. Director of Admissions
201-447-7100 Fax: 201-444-7036
Website: www.bergen.edu
E-mail: jgomez@bergen.edu

Centenary College
400 Jefferson St, Hackettstown NJ 07840-2100
Glenna Warren, Director of Admissions
908-852-1400 Fax: 908-852-3454
Website: www.centenarycollege.edu
E-mail: warreng@centenarycollege.edu

THE CHUBB INSTITUTE
40 Journal Sq, Jersey City NJ 07306-4097
Valerie Yancey, Campus President
201-876-3800 Fax: 201-656-2091
Website: www.chubbinstitute.edu
E-mail: gduchnowski@chubbinstitute.edu

Mercer County Community College
West Windsor Campus
PO Box B, Trenton NJ 08690
Savita Bambhrolia, Director of Admissions
609-586-4800 Fax: 609-587-4666
Website: www.mccc.edu
E-mail: admiss@mccc.edu

New Jersey City University
2039 John F Kennedy Blvd
Jersey City NJ 07305-1588
Carmen Panlilio, Asst. V.P. for Admissions and Financial Aid
201-200-3234 Fax: 201-200-2044
Website: www.njcu.edu
E-mail: admissions@njcu.edu

Ramapo College of New Jersey
505 Ramapo Valley Rd, Mahwah NJ 07430-1623
Director of Admissions
201-684-7300 or 201-684-7301 Fax: 201-684-7964
Website: www.ramapo.edu
E-mail: admissions@ramapo.edu

STAR TECHNICAL INSTITUTE
3003 English Creek Ave Suite 212
Egg Harbor Township NJ 08234-4880
George Z. Negrete, Director
609-407-2999 Fax: 609-646-9472
Website: www.startechnicalinstitute.com
E-mail: info@stareggharbor.com

NEW MEXICO

International Institute of the Americas
4201 Central Ave NW Suite J
Albuquerque NM 87105-1649
Ed Sigman, Director
505-880-2877 Fax: 505-352-0199
Website: www.iia.edu
E-mail: syelton@iia.edu

New Mexico State University
1500 N 3rd St, Grants NM 87020-2025
505-287-7981 Fax: 505-287-2329
Website: www.grants.nmsu.edu

NEW YORK

Briarcliffe College
1055 Stewart Ave, Bethpage NY 11714-3545
Theresa Donohue, Director of Admissions
516-918-3600 Fax: 516-470-6020
Website: www.briarcliffe.edu

Broome Community College
907 Upper Front St, Binghamton NY 13905
Anthony S. Fiorelli, Director of Admissions
607-778-5001 Fax: 607-778-5442
Website: www.sunybroome.edu
E-mail: fiorelli_a@sunybroome.edu

CAREER INSTITUTE OF HEALTH & TECHNOLOGY
340 Flatbush Avenue Ext, Brooklyn NY 11201
Mary Miller, Contact
718-422-1212 Fax: 718-422-1222
Website: www.careerinstitute.edu
E-mail: admissions@careerinstitute.edu

CAREER INSTITUTE OF HEALTH & TECHNOLOGY
200 Garden City Plz, Garden City NY 11530
Mary Miller, Contact
516-877-1225 Fax: 516-877-1959
Website: www.careerinstitute.edu
E-mail: admissions@careerinstitute.edu

CAREER INSTITUTE OF HEALTH & TECHNOLOGY
9525 Queens Blvd Ste 600, Rego Park NY 11374
Mary Miller, Contact
718-897-4868 Fax: 718-897-4863
Website: www.careerinstitute.edu
E-mail: admissions@careerinstitute.edu

THE CHUBB INSTITUTE
498 7th Ave, New York NY 10018
Joe Rodriguez, Director of Admissions
212-659-2116 Fax: 212-659-2175
Website: www.chubbinstitute.edu
E-mail: jrodriguez@chubbinstitute.edu

College of Saint Rose
432 Western Ave, Albany NY 12203-1419
Maryelizabeth Amico, Asst V.P. for Undergraduate Admissions
518-454-5150 Fax: 518-454-2013
Website: www.strose.edu
E-mail: admit@strose.edu

CUNY Hunter College
695 Park Ave, New York NY 10021
Aaron Gibbs, Assistant Director of Recruitment
212-772-4497 Fax: 212-650-3336
Website: www.hunter.cuny.edu
E-mail: aaron.gibbs@hunter.cuny.edu

Elmira Business Institute
303 N Main St, Elmira NY 14901
Lisa Roan, Admissions Director
607-733-7177 or 800-843-1812 Fax: 607-733-7178
Website: www.ebi-college.com
E-mail: lroan@ebi-college.com

Hilbert College
5200 S Park Ave, Hamburg NY 14075-1597
Timothy Lee, Director of Admissions
716-649-7900 Fax: 716-649-0702
Website: www.hilbert.edu
E-mail: tlee@hilbert.edu

Hobart & William Smith Colleges
Pulteney St, Geneva NY 14456
John Young, Director of Admissions
315-789-5500 Fax: 315-781-3654
Website: www.hws.edu
E-mail: young@hws.edu

ISLAND DRAFTING & TECHNICAL INSTITUTE
128 Broadway (Route 110), Amityville NY 11701-2704
James G. DiLiberto, President
631-691-8733 Fax: 631-691-8738
Website: www.idti.edu
E-mail: info@idti.edu

LONG ISLAND BUSINESS INSTITUTE
6500 Jericho Tpke, Commack NY 11725-2907
Dr. Philip Stander, President
631-499-7100 Fax: 631-499-7114
Website: www.libi.edu
E-mail: rnazar@libi.edu
    Private. Coed. Accreditation: ACICS. Approvals: National Court Reporting Association, NY State Board of Re-

gents. Tuition: $275.00 per credit hour. Fees: $50.00 application fee. Enrollment: 250. Faculty: 25. Student-faculty ratio: 12:1. Associate of Occupational Studies degree offered in Court Reporting, Office Technology. Diploma programs in Medical Transcription, Legal Secretarial, Office Technology, Administrative Assistant.

LONG ISLAND BUSINESS INSTITUTE
37-12 Prince St, Flushing NY 11354-4429
Dr. Philip Stander, President
718-939-5100 Fax: 718-989-9235
Website: www.libi.edu
E-mail: dwang@libi.edu
Private. Coed. Accreditation: ACICS. Approvals. National Court Reporting Association, NY State Board of Regents. Tuition: $275.00 per credit hour. Fees: $50.00 application fee. Enrollment: 250. Faculty: 25. Student-faculty ratio: 12:1. Associate of Occupational Studies degree offered in Computer Programmer, Administrative Assistant, Office Technology, Business Management, Accounting. Diploma programs in Legal Secretarial, Office Technology, Administrative Assistant.

Long Island University-C. W. Post Campus
720 Northern Blvd, Brookville NY 11548-1300
Joanne Graziano, Executive Director of Admissions
516-299-2900 Fax: 516-299-2137
Website: www.liu.edu/cwpost
E-mail: enroll@cwpost.liu.edu

Molloy College
1000 Hempstead Ave
Rockville Centre NY 11570-1100
Marguerite Lane, Director of Admissions
516-678-5000 ext. 6291 Fax: 516-256-2247
Website: www.molloy.edu
E-mail: admissions@molloy.edu
See listing under "Universities"

Monroe College
2501 Jerome Ave, Bronx NY 10468-4305
Evan Jerome, Director of Admissions
718-933-6700 Fax: 718-364-3552
Website: www.monroecollege.edu
E-mail: ejerome@monroecollege.edu

Ridley-Lowell Business & Technical Institute
116 Front St, Binghamton NY 13905-3102
David Lounsbury, Executive Director
607-724-2941 Fax: 607-724-0799
Website: www.ridley.edu
E-mail: info@ridley.edu

Ridley-Lowell Business & Technical Institute
26 S Hamilton St, Poughkeepsie NY 12601-3328
E. Ann Bida, Director of Admissions
845-471-0330 Fax: 845-471-4990
Website: www.ridley.edu
E-mail: pcadmissions@ridley.edu

Roberts Wesleyan College
2301 Westside Dr, Rochester NY 14624-1997
Office of Admissions
585-594-6400 Fax: 585-594-6371
Website: www.roberts.edu
E-mail: admissions@roberts.edu

St. John's University
8000 Utopia Pkwy, Queens NY 11439
Office of Admission
718-990-2000 or 888-9-STJOHNS Fax: 718-990-2096
Website: www.stjohns.edu
E-mail: admissions@stjohns.edu
See listing under "Universities"

St. Joseph's College
245 Clinton Ave, Brooklyn NY 11205-3688
Theresa LaRocca Meyer, V.P. for Enrollment Management
718-636-6800 Fax: 718-636-8303
Website: www.sjcny.edu
E-mail: tlaroccameyer@sjcny.edu

SUNY College at Brockport
350 New Campus Dr, Brockport NY 14420-2997
Bernard S. Valento, Director of Undergraduate Admissions
585-395-2751 Fax: 585-395-5452
Website: www.brockport.edu
E-mail: admit@brockport.edu

SUNY College of Technology
Alfred NY 14802
Deborah J. Goodrich, Director of Admissions
800-4AL-FRED Fax: 607-587-4299
Website: www.alfredstate.edu
E-mail: admissions@alfredstate.edu

SUNY College of Technology
2 Main St, Delhi NY 13753-1110
Robert W. Mazzei, Director of Admissions
800-96-DELHI Fax: 607-746-4104
Website: www.delhi.edu
E-mail: enroll@delhi.edu

SUNY Niagara County Community College
3111 Saunders Settlement Rd
Sanborn NY 14132-9487
Kathleen Saunders, Director of Admissions
716-614-6200 Fax: 716-614-6820
Website: www.niagaracc.suny.edu
E-mail: saunders@niagaracc.suny.edu

SUNY Orange County Community College
115 South St, Middletown NY 10940-6437
Margot St. Lawrence, Director of Admissions
845-341-4030 Fax: 845-342-8662
Website: www.sunyorange.edu
E-mail: apply@sunyorange.edu
See listing under "Community and Junior Colleges"

Trocaire College
360 Choate Ave, Buffalo NY 14220-2003
Paul B. Hurley, Ph.D., President
716-826-1200 Fax: 716-828-6107
Website: www.trocaire.edu
E-mail: info@trocaire.edu
See listing under "Community and Junior Colleges"

United States Military Academy West Point
646 Swift Rd, West Point NY 10996-1905
Colonel Michael L. Jones, Director of Admissions
845-938-4041 Fax: 845-938-8121
Website: admissions.usma.edu
E-mail: admissions@usma.edu

Utica School of Commerce
17 Elm St, Oneonta NY 13820-1828
Misty Davis, Admissions
607-432-7003 Fax: 607-432-7004
Website: www.uscny.com
E-mail: mdavis@uscny.edu

Utica School of Commerce
201 Bleecker St, Utica NY 13501-2280
Cindy Delaney, Director of Admissions
315-733-2307 Fax: 315-733-9281
Website: www.uscny.edu
E-mail: admissions@uscny.edu

Wells College
PO Box 500, Aurora NY 13026
Susan Sloan, Director of Admissions
800-952-9355 Fax: 315-364-3227
Website: www.wells.edu
E-mail: ssloan@wells.edu

NORTH CAROLINA
Belmont Abbey College
100 Belmont Mount Holly Rd
Belmont NC 28012-1802
888-222-0110 Fax: 704-825-6670
Website: www.belmontabbeycollege.edu
E-mail: admissions@bac.edu

Haywood Community College
185 Freedlander Dr, Clyde NC 28721
Debbie Rowland, Coordinator of Admissions
828-627-4500 Fax: 828-627-4513
Website: www.haywood.edu
E-mail: drowland@haywood.edu

Lees-McRae College
PO Box 128, Banner Elk NC 28604-0128
Walt Crutchfield, Dean of Admissions
800-280-4562 Fax: 828-898-8707
Website: www.lmc.edu
E-mail: admissions@lmc.edu

Louisburg College
501 N Main St, Louisburg NC 27549-2399
800-775-0208 or 919-496-2521 Fax: 919-496-1788
Website: www.louisburg.edu
E-mail: admissions@louisburg.edu

Mars Hill College
Mars Hill NC 28754
Chad Holt, Dean of Enrollment
866-MHC-4-YOU Fax: 828-689-1473
Website: www.mhc.edu
E-mail: cholt@mhc.edu

Meredith College
3800 Hillsborough St, Raleigh NC 27607-5298
Heidi L. Fletcher, Director of Admissions
919-760-8581 Fax: 919-760-2348
Website: www.meredith.edu
E-mail: admissions@meredith.edu
See listing under "Women's Colleges"

Mt. Olive College
634 Henderson St, Mount Olive NC 28365
Tim Woodard, Director of Admissions
919-658-2502 Fax: 919-658-9816
Website: www.moc.edu
E-mail: admissions@moc.edu
See listing under "Universities"

North Carolina A&T State University
1601 E Market St, Greensboro NC 27411
Lee Young, AVC Enrollment
336-334-7500 Fax: 336-334-7478
Website: www.ncat.edu
E-mail: uadmit@ncat.edu

South College
1567 Patton Ave, Asheville NC 28806-1748
Robert Davis, Dean of Academic Affairs
828-252-2486 Fax: 828-252-8558
Website: southcollegenc.com
E-mail: bdavis@southcollegenc.com

South Piedmont Community College
PO Box 126, Polkton NC 28135-0126
John Curtis, Contact
704-272-5324 Fax: 704-272-8904
Website: www.spcc.edu
E-mail: jcurtis@spcc.edu

NORTH DAKOTA
Dickinson State University
Dickinson ND 58601-4896
Steve Glasser, Director of Student Recruitment
800-279-4295 Fax: 701-483-2409
Website: www.dickinsonstate.edu
E-mail: dsu.hawks@dickinsonstate.edu

Minot State University-Bottineau Campus
105 Simrall Blvd, Bottineau ND 58318-1159
Paula Berg, Associate Dean of Student Affairs
800-542-6866 Fax: 701-228-5499
Website: www.misu-b.nodak.edu
E-mail: paula.berg@misu.nodak.edu

Valley City State University
101 College St SW, Valley City ND 58072-4024
Dan Klein, Director of Enrollment Services
800-532-8641 ext. 7101 Fax: 701-845-7299
Website: www.vcsu.edu
E-mail: enrollment.services@vcsu.edu
See listing under "Universities"

Williston State College
PO Box 1326, Williston ND 58802-1326
Penny Powell, Director Enrollment Services
701-774-4200 Fax: 701-774-4544
Website: www.wsc.nodak.edu
E-mail: penny.soiseth@wsc.nodak.edu

OHIO
Brown Mackie College - Cincinnati
1011 Glendale Milford Rd, Cincinnati OH 45215-1107
Robin Krout, President
513-771-2424 Fax: 513-771-3413
Website: www.brownmackie.edu
E-mail: rkrout@brownmackie.edu

Bryant & Stratton College
1700 E 13th St, Cleveland OH 44114-3238
Shawn T. Kampa, Market Director of Admissions
216-771-1700 Fax: 216-771-7787
Website: www.bryantstratton.edu
E-mail: stkampa@bryantstratton.edu

Cleveland Institute of Electronics
1776 E 17th St, Cleveland OH 44114-3679
Scott Katzenmeyer, Director of Admissions
800-243-6446 Fax: 216-781-0331
Website: www.cie-wc.edu
E-mail: instruct@cie-wc.edu

Cleveland State University
2121 Euclid Ave RW 204, Cleveland OH 44115
Dr. Richard Arndt, Dean of Undergraduate Recruitment and College Partnerships
888-CSU-OHIO Fax: 216-687-9210
Website: www.csuohio.edu
E-mail: admissions@csuohio.edu

Collins Career Center
11627 State Route 243, Chesapeake OH 45619-7962
740-867-6641 Fax: 740-867-9626
Website: www.collins-cc.k12.oh.us

Davis College
4747 Monroe St, Toledo OH 43623-4389
Dana Stern, Admissions Director
419-473-2700 Fax: 419-473-2472
Website: www.daviscollege.edu
E-mail: learn@daviscollege.edu

Franciscan University of Steubenville
University Blvd, Steubenville OH 43952
Margaret J. Weber, Director of Admissions
800-783-6220 or 740-283-6226 Fax: 740-284-5456
Website: www.admissions.edu
E-mail: mweber@franciscan.edu

Mount Vernon Nazarene University
800 Martinsburg Rd, Mount Vernon OH 43050-9509
Timothy Eades, Director of Admissions
866-462-6868 Fax: 740-393-0511
Website: www.gotomvnu.com
E-mail: admissions@mvnu.edu
See listing under "Universities"

Northwest State Community College
22600 State Route 34, Archbold OH 43502-9542
Mark Thompson, Director of Admissions
419-267-5511 Fax: 419-267-5587
Website: www.northweststate.edu
E-mail: mthompson@northweststate.edu

OHIO NORTHERN UNIVERSITY
525 S Main St, Ada OH 45810-1555
Robert A. Manzer, Dean
419-772-2130
Website: www.onu.edu
E-mail: admissions-ug@onu.edu
See listing under "Universities"

The Ohio State University
Department of Computer Science and Engineering
Dreese Laboratories, 2015 Neil Ave
Columbus OH 43210
614-292-5813 Fax: 614-292-2911
Website: cse.osu.edu
E-mail: webmaster@cse.ohio-state.edu

OHIO VALLEY COLLEGE OF TECHNOLOGY
16808 St. Clair Ave, PO Box 7000
East Liverpool OH 43920
Scott S. Rogers, Director
330-385-1070 Fax: 330-385-4606
Website: www.ovct.edu
E-mail: info@ovct.edu

Owens Community College
300 Davis St, Findlay OH 45840-3631
William J. Ivoska PhD., Vice President of Student Services
567-429-3500 Fax: 567-423-0246
Website: www.owens.edu
E-mail: admissions@owens.edu

Owens Community College
PO Box 10000, Toledo OH 43699-1947
William J. Ivoska, Ph.D, Vice President of Student Services
567-661-7000 Fax: 567-661-7607
Website: www.owens.edu
E-mail: admissions@owens.edu

REMINGTON COLLEGE - CLEVELAND WEST CAMPUS
26350 Brookpark Rd, North Olmsted OH 44070
Gary A. Azotea, Campus President
440-777-2560 Fax: 440-777-3238
Website: www.remingtoncollege.edu
E-mail: gary.azotea@remingtoncollege.edu

Sinclair Community College
444 W 3rd St, Dayton OH 45402-1460
Sara P. Smith, Director of Outreach Services
937-512-3000 Fax: 937-512-2393
Website: www.sinclair.edu
E-mail: admit@sinclair.edu

University of Dayton
300 College Park, Dayton OH 45469-1300
Robert F. Durkle, Director of Admissions
800-837-7433 Fax: 937-229-4729
Website: admission.udayton.edu
E-mail: admission@udayton.edu

Ursuline College
2550 Lander Rd, Cleveland OH 44124-4398
Sarah E. Sundermeier, Director of Admissions
888-URSULINE Toll Free Fax: 440-684-6138
Website: www.admission.ursuline.edu
E-mail: admission@ursuline.edu

OKLAHOMA

Oklahoma State University
Stillwater OK 74078
G.E. Hedrick, Department Head
405-744-5668
Website: www.okstate.edu
E-mail: geh@a.cs.okstate.edu

Oral Roberts University
7777 S Lewis Ave, Tulsa OK 74171-0001
Chris Belcher, Director of Undergraduate Admissions
800-678-8876 Fax: 918-495-6222
Website: www.oru.edu
E-mail: admissions@oru.edu

University of Tulsa
600 S College Ave, Tulsa OK 74104-3126
Earl Johnson, Dean of Admission
918-631-2307 Fax: 918-631-5003
Website: www.utulsa.edu
E-mail: admission@utulsa.edu

Vatterott College - Tulsa
555 S Memorial Dr, Tulsa OK 74112
Kevin Wolfe, Director of Admissions
918-835-8288 Fax: 918-836-9698
Website: www.vatterott-college.com
E-mail: kevin.wolfe@vatterott-college.com

OREGON

Linn-Benton Community College
6500 Pacific Blvd SW, Albany OR 97321-3774
Christine Baker, Outreach Coordinator
541-917-4811 Fax: 541-917-4868
Website: www.linnbenton.edu
E-mail: admissions@linnbenton.edu

Pacific University
2043 College Way, Forest Grove OR 97116-1797
Karen A. Dunston, Executive Director of Admissions
800-635-0561 Fax: 503-352-2975
Website: www.pacificu.edu
E-mail: admissions@pacificu.edu

Rogue Community College
3345 Redwood Hwy, Grants Pass OR 97527-9298
Claudia Sullivan, Director of Enrollment Services
541-956-7500 Fax: 541-471-3585
Website: www.roguecc.edu
E-mail: csullivan@roguecc.edu
See listing under "Community and Junior Colleges"

Western Oregon University
345 Monmouth Ave N, Monmouth OR 97361-1314
David McDonald, Dean, Admission, Retention &
Enrollment Management
877-877-1593 Fax: 503-838-8067
Website: www.wou.edu
E-mail: wolfgram@fsa.wou.edu

PENNSYLVANIA

Academy of Medical Arts and Business
2301 Academy Dr, Harrisburg PA 17112-1012
717-545-4747
Website: www.ACADcampus.com
E-mail: info@ACADcampus.com

Arcadia University
450 S Easton Rd, Glenside PA 19038-3295
Dennis Nostrand, VP for Enrollment Management
877-ARCADIA (877-272-2342) Fax: 215-881-8767
Website: www.arcadia.edu
E-mail: admiss@arcadia.edu
See listing under "Universities"

Bradford School
125 W Station Square Dr, Pittsburgh PA 15219
Director of Admissions
412-391-6710 Fax: 412-471-6714
Website: www.bradfordpittsburgh.edu

Central Pennsylvania College
College Hill & Valley Rds, Summerdale PA 17093
Katie Bogovic, Admissions Director
800-759-2727 Fax: 717-728-2505
Website: www.centralpenn.edu
E-mail: katie.bogovic@centralpenn.edu

Clarion University of Pennsylvania
840 Wood St, Clarion PA 16214-1232
William Bailey, Dean of Enrollment Management
814-393-2306 Fax: 814-393-2030
Website: www.clarion.edu
E-mail: admissions@clarion.edu

Computer Learning Network
401 E Winding Hill Rd Ste 101
Mechanicsburg PA 17055-4989
Marlene Macauley, Director of Admissions
717-761-1481 Fax: 717-761-0558
Website: www.clntraining.net
E-mail: mmacauley@clntraining.net

Consolidated School of Business
1605 Clugston Rd, York PA 17404-1779
Robert Safran Jr., Vice President
717-764-9550 Fax: 717-764-9469
Website: www.csb.edu
E-mail: bobjr@csb.edu

DeSales University
2755 Station Ave, Center Valley PA 18034-9565
610-282-1100 Fax: 610-282-2342
Website: www.desales.edu

DUBOIS BUSINESS COLLEGE
1 Beaver Dr, Du Bois PA 15801-2490
Lisa J. Doty, Director of Admissions
814-371-6920 Fax: 814-371-3974
Website: www.dbcollege.com
E-mail: dotylj@dbcollege.com

DUBOIS BUSINESS COLLEGE
1001 Moore St, Huntingdon PA 16652-1846
Lisa J. Doty, Director of Admissions
814-641-0440 Fax: 814-641-0205
Website: www.dbcollege.com
E-mail: dotylj@dbcollege.com

DUBOIS BUSINESS COLLEGE
701 E 3rd St, Oil City PA 16301-2407
Lisa J. Doty, Director of Admissions
814-677-1322 Fax: 814-677-8237
Website: www.dbcollege.com
E-mail: dotylj@dbcollege.com

Erie Business Center
246 W 9th St, Erie PA 16501-1392
Donna Perino, Director
814-456-7504 Fax: 814-456-6015
Website: www.eriebc.edu
E-mail: perinod@eriebc.edu

Gannon University
109 University Sq, Erie PA 16541-0001
Christopher Tremblay, Director of Admissions
800-GANNON-U Fax: 814-871-5803
Website: www.gannon.edu
E-mail: admissions@gannon.edu

Haverford College
370 Lancaster Ave, Haverford PA 19041-1392
Jess Lord, Dean of Admission
610-896-1000 Fax: 610-896-1338
Website: www.haverford.edu
E-mail: admission@haverford.edu

Holy Family University
9801 Frankford Avenue, Philadelphia PA 19114
Lauren Campbell, Director of Admissions
215-637-3050 Fax: 215-281-1022
Website: www.holyfamily.edu
E-mail: admissions@holyfamily.edu

Johnson College
3427 N Main Ave, Scranton PA 18508-1495
Dr. Ann L. Pipinski, President & CEO
Melissa Ide, Director of Enrollment Management
800-2WE-WORK or 570-342-6404 ext. 125
Fax: 570-348-2181
Website: www.johnson.edu
E-mail: admit@johnson.edu

Juniata College
1700 Moore St, Huntingdon PA 16652-2196
Michelle Bartol, Dean of Enrollment
877-JUNIATA Fax: 814-641-3100
Website: www.juniata.edu
E-mail: admissions@juniata.edu

King's College
133 N River St, Wilkes Barre PA 18711-0801
Michelle Lawrence-Schmude, Director of Admission
570-208-5900 Fax: 570-208-5971
Website: www.kings.edu
E-mail: admissions@kings.edu

La Roche College
9000 Babcock Blvd, Pittsburgh PA 15237-5898
Thomas Hassett, Director of Freshman and
International Admissions
412-536-1272 or 800-838-4LRC Fax: 412-536-1272
Website: www.laroche.edu
E-mail: admissions@laroche.edu

LAUREL BUSINESS INSTITUTE
11-15 Penn St, Uniontown PA 15401
Lisa Tressler, Supervisor of Enrollment
724-439-4900 Fax: 724-439-3607
Website: www.laurelbusiness.edu
E-mail: lbi@laurelbusiness.edu
Established 1985. Private. Coed. Accreditation:
ACICS, Licensed by the Pennsylvania Department of
Education. Enrollment: 310 full-time, 35 part-time.
Student-faculty ratio: 12:1. Associate degrees: Account-
ing, Child Care Education, Cosmetology, I.T. - Computer
Software Support, I.T. - Network Administration, Medical
Assistant, Medical Insurance Management, Medical
Secretary Transcription, Office Administration, Small
Business Management, Therapeutic Massage. Diplo-
mas: Legal Secretary, Massage Therapy, Medical Secre-
tary, Word Processing Secretary. Independent
Certifications, Authorized Prometric Testing Center,
Authorized MOS Testing Center, Financial Aid Services,
Job Placement Services.

Lebanon Valley College
101 N College Ave, Annville PA 17003-1400
William Brown, Dean of Admissions & Financial Aid
866-LVC-4ADM or 717-867-6181 Fax: 717-867-6026
Website: www.lvc.edu
E-mail: admission@lvc.edu

Lehigh Valley College
2809 E Saucon Valley Rd
Center Valley PA 18034-8447
Joshua Padron, Vice President of Marketing and
Admissions
800-227-9109 Fax: 610-791-7810
Website: www.lehighvalley.edu
E-mail: joshua.padron@lehighvalley.edu

Lincoln University
Lincoln University PA 19352
Michael C. Taylor, Director of Admissions
800-790-0191 Fax: 610-932-1209
Website: www.lincoln.edu
E-mail: mtaylor@lu.lincoln.edu

McCann School of Business & Technology
1147 N 4th St, Sunbury PA 17801-1221
Lisa Davis, Director of Admissions
570-286-3058 Fax: 570-286-4723
Website: www.mccannschool.com
E-mail: ldavis@mccannschool.com

Mount Aloysius College
7373 Admiral Peary Hwy, Cresson PA 16630-1999
Frank C. Crouse Jr., Vice President for Enrollment
Management
814-886-6383 or 888-823-2220 Fax: 814-886-6441
Website: www.mtaloy.edu
E-mail: admissions@mtaloy.edu

Neumann College
1 Neumann Dr, Aston PA 19014-1298
Dennis Murphy, Director of Admissions
610-459-0905 Fax: 610-558-5652
Website: www.neumann.edu
E-mail: neumann@neumann.edu

Newport Business Institute
945 Greensburg Rd, Lower Burrell PA 15068-3929
Admissions Department
800-752-7695 Fax: 724-339-2950
Website: www.nbi.edu
E-mail: tjpomatto@nbi.edu

Pennco Tech
3815 Otter St, Bristol PA 19007-3618
Glenn Slater, Director of Admissions
215-785-0111 Fax: 215-785-1945
Website: www.penncotech.com
E-mail: admissions@penncotech.com

Pennsylvania Institute of Technology
800 Manchester Ave, Media PA 19063-4036
Angela Cassetta, Dean of Enrollment Management
800-422-0025 or 610-892-1500 Fax: 610-892-1510
Website: www.pit.edu
E-mail: info@pit.edu
See listing under "Community and Junior Colleges"

University of Pittsburgh
1150 Mount Pleasant Rd
Greensburg PA 15601-5860
Brandi S. Darr, Director of Admissions and Financial
Aid
724-836-9880 Fax: 724-836-7160
Website: www.upg.pitt.edu
E-mail: upgadmit@pitt.edu

Washington & Jefferson College
60 S Lincoln St, Washington PA 15301-4801
Alton E. Newell, Vice President for Enrollment
724-223-6025 Fax: 724-223-6534
Website: www.washjeff.edu
E-mail: admission@washjeff.edu

Westminster College
New Wilmington PA 16172-0001
Doug Swartz, Director of Admissions
724-946-7100 Fax: 724-946-6171
Website: www.westminster.edu
E-mail: swartzdl@westminster.edu

York Technical Institute
1405 Williams Rd, York PA 17402
Cathi Killingsworth Bost, Vice President
800-227-9675 or 717-757-1100 Fax: 717-757-4964
Website: www.yti.edu
E-mail: info@yti.edu
See listing under "Career Schools"

RHODE ISLAND

New England Institute of Technology
2500 Post Rd, Warwick RI 02886-2244
Michael Kwiatkowski, Director of Admissions
401-739-5000 Fax: 401-738-5122
Website: www.neit.edu
E-mail: eflynn@neit.edu

SOUTH CAROLINA

BETA TECH
8088 Rivers Ave, North Charleston SC 29406-9235
Katrina Varner, Director
843-569-0889 Fax: 843-569-0471
Website: www.tidetech.com
E-mail: directorbtc@tidetech.com

Bob Jones University
1700 Wade Hampton Blvd
Greenville SC 29614-0001
David Christ, Director of Admissions
800-BJ-AND-ME Fax: 800-2-FAX-BJU
Website: www.bju.edu
E-mail: admissions@bju.edu
See listing under "Universities"

Forrest Junior College
601 E River St, Anderson SC 29624-2405
Dr. Julia Barnes, President
864-225-7653 Fax: 864-261-7471
Website: www.forrestcollege.edu
E-mail: info@forrestcollege.edu
PC Repair, Networking, A+ Certification, N+
Certification.

Greenville Technical College
PO Box 5616, Greenville SC 29606-5616
Martha White, Director of Admissions
800-723-0673 (US) or 800-922-1183 (SC)
Website: www.greenvilletech.com

Limestone College
1115 College Dr, Gaffney SC 29340-3799
Chris Phenicie, V.P. for Enrollment
864-489-7151 Fax: 864-488-8206
Website: www.limestone.edu
E-mail: cphenicie@limestone.edu

PRESBYTERIAN COLLEGE
503 S Broad St, Clinton SC 29325
Richard Dana Paul, Dean of Admissions
800-476-7272 Fax: 864-833-8481
Website: www.presby.edu
E-mail: admissions@presby.edu

South University
9 Science Court, Columbia SC 29203
Trish Wade, Contact
803-799-9082 Fax: 803-799-9038
Website: www.southuniversity.edu
E-mail: twade@southuniversity.edu

Spartanburg Technical College
PO Box 4386, Spartanburg SC 29305-4386
Nancy Garmroth, Dean of Admissions & Financial Aid
864-592-4810 Fax: 864-592-4945
Website: stcsc.edu

University of South Carolina - Upstate
800 University Way, Spartanburg SC 29303-4932
Donette Stewart, Assistant VC for Enrollment Services
864-503-5246 Fax: 864-503-5727
Website: www.uscupstate.edu
E-mail: dstewart@uscupstate.edu
See listing under "Universities"

SOUTH DAKOTA
NATIONAL AMERICAN UNIVERSITY
321 Kansas City St, Rapid City SD 57701-3692
Angela G. Beck, Director of Enrollment Management
605-394-4800 Fax: 605-394-4871
Website: www.national.edu/rc/index.html
E-mail: rcadmissions@national.edu

National American University
2801 S Kiwanis Ave Ste 100
Sioux Falls SD 57105-4293
605-334-5430 Fax: 605-334-1575
Website: www.national.edu

Western Dakota Technical Institute
800 Mickelson Dr, Rapid City SD 57703-4018
Janell Oberlander, Manager of Student Services
605-394-4034 or 800-544-8765 Fax: 605-394-1789
Website: www.westerndakotatech.org
E-mail: admissions@wdti.tec.sd.us
See listing under "Career Schools"

TENNESSEE
Draughons Junior College
PO Box 17386, Nashville TN 37217-0386
615-361-7555 Fax: 615-367-2736
Website: www.draughons.edu

Lipscomb University
3901 Granny White Pike, Nashville TN 37204-3951
Ricky Holaway, Director of Admissions
800-333-4358 ext. 1776 Fax: 615-269-1804
Website: www.lipscomb.edu
E-mail: admissions@lipscomb.edu

Miller-Motte Technical College
1820 Business Park Dr, Clarksville TN 37040-6023
Lisa Teague, Director of Admissions
931-553-0071 Fax: 931-552-2916
Website: www.miller-motte.com
E-mail: lteague@miller-motte.com

Pellissippi State Technical Community College
PO Box 22990, Knoxville TN 37933-0990
Donna Mack, Contact
865-694-6568 Fax: 865-539-7217
Website: www.pstcc.edu
E-mail: dmack@pstcc.edu

Tennessee State University
3500 John A Merritt Blvd, Nashville TN 37209-1561
John Cade, Dean of Admissions & Records
615-963-5101 Fax: 615-963-2930
Website: www.tnstate.edu
E-mail: jcade@tnstate.edu

Tusculum College
PO Box 5051, Greeneville TN 37743
Melissa Ripley, Associate Director of Admissions
800-729-0256 Fax: 423-798-1622
Website: www.tusculum.edu
E-mail: mripley@tusculum.edu

University of Tennessee
615 McCallie Ave, Chattanooga TN 37403-2504
Yancy Freeman, Director of Admissions
423-425-4111 Fax: 423-425-4157
Website: www.utc.edu
E-mail: Yancy-Freeman@utc.edu

Vatterott College - Memphis Campus
2655 Dividend Dr, Memphis TN 38132
Joe Lockwood, Director of Admissions
901-761-5730 Fax: 901-763-2897
Website: www.vatterott-college.edu
E-mail: joe.lockwood@vatterott-college.edu

TEXAS
American Commercial College
2007 34th St, Lubbock TX 79411-1899
Michael Otto, Director
806-747-4339 Fax: 806-765-9838
Website: www.acc-careers.com
E-mail: mjotto@acc-careers.com

American Commercial College
5119 Twin Towers Blvd, Odessa TX 79762-5504
Donna Duree, Director
432-362-6768 Fax: 432-550-0556
Website: www.acc-careers.com
E-mail: americancc@acc-careers.com

Angelo State University
ASU Station 11014, San Angelo TX 76909
Bonnie Stennett, Coordinator of Recruiting
800-946-8627 Fax: 325-942-2078
Website: www.angelo.edu
E-mail: admissions@angelo.edu

Blinn College
902 College Ave, Brenham TX 77833-4098
Dennis K. Crowson, Registrar
979-830-4000 Fax: 979-830-4110
Website: www.blinn.edu
E-mail: recruiting@blinn.edu

Blinn College
PO Box 6030, Bryan TX 77805-6030
Dennis K. Crowson, Registrar
979-209-7200 Fax: 979-209-7229
Website: www.blinn.edu
E-mail: recruiting@blinn.edu

Blinn College
100 Ranger Dr, Schulenburg TX 78956-2247
Dennis K. Crowson, Registrar
979-743-5003 Fax: 979-743-5225
Website: www.blinn.edu
E-mail: recruiting@blinn.edu

Blinn College
3701 Outlet Center Dr, Sealy TX 77474
Dennis K. Crowson, Registrar
979-627-7997 Fax: 979-627-0830
Website: www.blinn.edu
E-mail: recruiting@blinn.edu

COMPUTER CAREER CENTER
6101 Montana Ave, El Paso TX 79925-2021
Amber Borrego, Director
915-779-8031 Fax: 915-779-8097
Website: www.computercareercenter.com
E-mail: ccctrain@aol.com

Galveston College
4015 Avenue Q, Galveston TX 77550-7496
Brian Lowery, Registrar
409-763-6551 Fax: 409-944-1501
Website: www.gc.edu
E-mail: blowery@gc.edu

Hallmark Institute of Technology - Technology Campus
10401 W IH 10, San Antonio TX 78230-1736
Joe Fisher, President
210-690-9000 Fax: 210-697-8225
Website: www.hallmarkinstitute.com
E-mail: sross@hallmarkinstitute.com
Electronics Engineering Technology, Business Office
Administration, Computer Network Systems
Technology, & Medical Assistant.

ITT TECHNICAL INSTITUTE
2950 S Gessner Rd Ste 100, Houston TX 77063-3751
Jennifer Gomez, Director of Recruitment
713-952-2294 Fax: 713-952-2393
Website: www.itt-tech.edu
E-mail: jgomez@itt-tech.edu

Lamar State College-Orange
410 W Front St, Orange TX 77630-5899
Rebecca Campbell, Registrar
409-883-7750 Fax: 409-882-3055
Website: www.lsco.edu
E-mail: becky.campbell@lsco.edu

McLennan Community College
1400 College Dr, Waco TX 76708-1498
Fred Hills, Program Director, Computer Information
Systems
254-299-8000 Fax: 254-299-8854
Website: www.mclennan.edu
E-mail: fhills@mclennan.edu

North Central Texas College
1525 W California St, Gainesville TX 76240-4636
Michelle Winters, Registrar
940-668-3315 Fax: 940-665-7075
Website: www.nctc.edu
E-mail: mwinters@nctc.edu

Northwood University
1114 W FM 1382, Cedar Hill TX 75104-1204
Sylvia Correa, Director of Admissions
800-927-WOOD Fax: 972-291-3824
Website: www.northwood.edu
E-mail: ray@northwood.edu

Our Lady of the Lake University
411 SW 24th St, San Antonio TX 78207-4666
Mary Kay Cooper, Dean of Enrollment
210-434-6711 Fax: 210-431-4013
Website: www.ollusa.edu
E-mail: admission@lakeollusa.edu

Remington College - Fort Worth Campus
300 E Loop 820, Fort Worth TX 76112-1280
Director of Recruitment
817-451-0017 Fax: 817-496-1257
Website: www.remingtoncollege.edu
E-mail: lynn.wey@remingtoncollege.edu

San Antonio College Medical Dental Assistants
1500 S Jackson Rd, Mc Allen TX 78503-9902
Gabe Garcia, Director of Admissions
956-630-1499 Fax: 956-630-2746
Website: www.sacmda.com
E-mail: gagarcia@sac-mda.com

Temple College
2600 S 1st St, Temple TX 76504-7435
Angela Balch, Director of Admissions & Records
254-298-8300 Fax: 254-298-8288
Website: www.templejc.edu
E-mail: ruth.bridges@templejc.edu

Texas Woman's University
PO Box 425589, Denton TX 76204-5589
Erma Nieto, Director of Admissions
866-809-6130 Fax: 940-898-3081
Website: www.twu.edu
E-mail: admissions@twu.edu

Tyler Junior College
PO Box 9020, Tyler TX 75711-9020
Joan Jones, Interim Dean
800-687-5680
Website: www.tjc.edu
E-mail: jjon@tjc.edu
See listing under "Community and Junior Colleges"

University of Houston
122 E Cullen Bldg, Houston TX 77204-2023
Office of Admission
713-743-9595
Website: www.uh.edu
E-mail: admissions@uh.edu

University of St. Thomas
3800 Montrose Blvd, Houston TX 77006-4626
Eduardo Prieto, Director of Admissions
713-522-7911 Fax: 713-525-3558
Website: www.stthom.edu
E-mail: prietoe@stthom.edu

University of Texas at Arlington
Box 19111, Arlington TX 76019-0111
Hans Gatterdam, Director of Admission
817-272-6287 Fax: 817-272-3435
Website: www.uta.edu
E-mail: admissions@uta.edu

UTAH
L.D.S. BUSINESS COLLEGE
95 North 300 West, Salt Lake City UT 84101-3500
Kathleen Howe, Assistant Director of Admissions
801-524-8145 Fax: 801-524-1900
Website: www.ldsbc.edu
E-mail: admissions@ldsbc.edu
See listing under "Career Schools"

Stevens Henager College
755 Main St, Logan UT 84321
Sherman R. Conger, Director of Admissions
435-713-4777
Website: www.stevenshenager.edu

Stevens Henager College
PO Box 9428, Ogden UT 84409-0428
Cindy Williams, Director of Admissions
801-394-7791 Fax: 801-621-0866
Website: www.stevenshenager.edu
E-mail: shcogden@yahoo.com

VERMONT
NORWICH UNIVERSITY
158 Harmon Dr, Northfield VT 05663
Dr. Frank Vanecek, Division Head
800-468-6679 Fax: 802-485-2087
Website: www.norwich.edu
E-mail: vanecek@norwich.edu
See listing under "Universities"

VIRGINIA
Radford University
PO Box 6903, Radford VA 24142
David W. Kraus, Director of Admissions
800-890-4265 Fax: 540-831-5038
Website: www.radford.edu
E-mail: ruadmiss@radford.edu

Southside Virginia Community College
109 Campus Dr, Alberta VA 23821-2930
Ronald E. Mattox, Dean of Admissions
434-949-1014 Fax: 434-949-7863
Website: www.sv.vccs.edu
E-mail: ronald.mattox@sv.vccs.edu

Southside Virginia Community College
200 Daniel Rd, Keysville VA 23947
Ronald E. Mattox, Dean of Admissions
434-736-2018 Fax: 434-736-2082
Website: www.sv.vccs.edu
E-mail: ronald.mattox@sv.vccs.edu

UNIVERSITY OF MANAGEMENT AND TECHNOLOGY
1901 Fort Myer Dr Ste 700, Arlington VA 22209
703-516-0035 Fax: 703-516-0985
Website: www.umtweb.edu
E-mail: info@umtweb.edu

University of Mary Washington
1301 College Ave, Fredericksburg VA 22401-5300
Dr. Martin A. Wilder, Jr., Director of Admissions
540-654-2000 Fax: 540-654-1857
Website: www.umw.edu
E-mail: admit@umw.edu

WASHINGTON
BATES TECHNICAL COLLEGE
1101 S Yakima Ave, Tacoma WA 98405-4895
David Borofsky, President
253-680-7000 Fax: 253-680-7101
Website: www.bates.ctc.edu
E-mail: info@bates.ctc.edu

Clover Park Technical College
4500 Steilacoom Blvd SW
Lakewood WA 98499-4098
Dr. Sharon McGavick, President
253-589-5678 Fax: 253-589-5601
Website: www.cptc.edu
E-mail: jim.griffith@cptc.edu

Everett Community College
2000 Tower St, Everett WA 98201
Christine Kerlin, Associate Dean
425-388-9100 Fax: 425-388-9173
Website: www.everettcc.edu
E-mail: ckerlin@everettcc.edu

Gonzaga University
502 E Boone Ave, Spokane WA 99258-0102
Julie McCulloh, Dean of Admission
800-322-2584 or 509-323-6572 Fax: 509-323-5780
Website: www.gonzaga.edu
E-mail: mcculloh@gu.gonzaga.edu

Henry Cogswell College
3002 Colby Ave, Everett WA 98201-4012
Jane Buckman, Director of Admissions
866-411-4221 Fax: 425-257-0405
Website: www.henrycogswell.edu
E-mail: admissions@henrycogswell.edu

RENTON TECHNICAL COLLEGE
3000 NE 4th St, Renton WA 98056-4195
Becky Riverman, Registrar
425-235-2352 or 425-235-5840 Fax: 425-235-7832
Website: www.RTC.edu
E-mail: dgrant@RTC.edu

Walla Walla Community College
500 Tausick Way, Walla Walla WA 99362-9270
Susan Quinn, Director
509-527-4232 or 877-992-9922 Fax: 509-527-4232
Website: www.wwcc.edu
E-mail: susan.quinn@wwcc.edu
See listing under "Community and Junior Colleges"

Wenatchee Valley College
PO Box 2058, Omak WA 98841
Alex Roberts, Director
509-422-7805 Fax: 509-682-6541
Website: www.wvc.edu

Wenatchee Valley College
1300 5th St, Wenatchee WA 98801-1799
Marco Azurdia, Dean, Student Development
509-682-6805 Fax: 509-682-6541
Website: www.wvc.edu

WEST VIRGINIA

Concord University
Athens WV 24712
Michael Curry, Vice President of Financial Aid &
Admissions
888-384-5249 Fax: 304-384-3218
Website: www.concord.edu
E-mail: admissions@concord.edu

Davis & Elkins College
100 Campus Dr, Elkins WV 26241-3996
Renee Heckel, Director of Enrollment Management
800-624-3157 Fax: 304-637-1800
Website: www.davisandelkins.edu
E-mail: admiss@davisandelkins.edu

Fairmont State University
1201 Locust Ave, Fairmont WV 26554-2470
Steve Leadman, Director of Admissions
304-367-4892 or 800-641-5678 Fax: 304-367-4789
Website: www.fairmontstate.edu
E-mail: admit@fairmontstate.edu

Mountain State College
1508 Spring St, Parkersburg WV 26101-3993
Judith Sutton, Director
304-485-5487 Fax: 304-485-3524
Website: www.mountainstate.org
E-mail: admin@mountainstate.org
See listing under "Career Schools"

Mountain State University
Box 9003, Beckley WV 25802-9003
866-FOR-MSU1 or 304-929-INFO Fax: 304-253-5072
Website: www.mountainstate.edu
E-mail: gomsu@mountainstate.edu
See listing under "Universities"

West Virginia Wesleyan College
59 College Ave, Buckhannon WV 26201-2699
Robert N. Skinner II, Director of Admission
800-722-9933 Fax: 304-473-8108
Website: www.wvwc.edu
E-mail: admission@wvwc.edu

WISCONSIN

Alverno College
PO Box 343922, Milwaukee WI 53234-3922
Mary Kay Farrell, Director of Admissions
414-382-6100 Fax: 414-382-6354
Website: www.alverno.edu
E-mail: admissions@alverno.edu

Blackhawk Technical College
PO Box 5009, Janesville WI 53547-5009
Gregg Bosak, Administration, Community Information
608-757-7769 Fax: 608-757-7740
Website: www.blackhawk.edu
E-mail: gbosak@blackhawk.edu

COLLEGE OF MENOMINEE NATION
PO Box 1179, Keshena WI 54135-1179
Cynthia Norton, Admissions Representative
715-799-5600 Fax: 715-799-4392
Website: www.menominee.edu
E-mail: cnorton@menominee.edu

Herzing College
5218 E Terrace Dr, Madison WI 53718-8340
Donald Madelung, President
800-582-1227 Fax: 608-249-8593
Website: www.herzing.edu
E-mail: info@msn.herzing.edu
See listing under "Universities"

Lakeland College
PO Box 359, Sheboygan WI 53082-0359
Nathan Dehne, Director of Admission
920-565-1100 Fax: 920-565-1215
Website: www.lakeland.edu
E-mail: admissions@lakeland.edu

Marquette University
PO Box 1881, Milwaukee WI 53201-1881
Robert Blust, Director of Admissions
414-288-7302 Fax: 414-288-3764
Website: www.mu.edu
E-mail: admissions@marquette.edu

St. Norbert College
100 Grant St, De Pere WI 54115
Brian Studebaker, Director of Admission
800-236-4878 Fax: 920-403-4072
Website: www.snc.edu
E-mail: admit@snc.edu

Wisconsin Indianhead Technical College
505 Pine Ridge Dr, Shell Lake WI 54871
Laura Urban, Dean
800-243-9482 Fax: 715-468-2819
Website: www.witc.edu
E-mail: mcrandal@witc.edu

WYOMING

Laramie County Community College
1400 E College Dr, Cheyenne WY 82007-3204
Jenny Hargett, Director of Admissions
307-778-5222 Fax: 307-778-1350
Website: www.lccc.wy.edu
E-mail: learnmore@lccc.wy.edu

University of Wyoming
Admissions Office
Dept 3435, Laramie WY 82071-3435
Aaron Appelhans, Contact
800-342-5996 Fax: 307-766-4042
Website: www.uwyo.edu
E-mail: why-wyo@uwyo.edu

GUAM

Guam Community College
PO Box 23069, G.M.F. GU 96921-0307
Virginia Charfauros Tudela, Ph.D., Registrar
671-735-5531 Fax: 671-734-5238
Website: www.guamcc.edu
E-mail: Webmaster@guamcc.edu

University of Guam
UOG Station, Mangilao GU 96923
Deborah Leon Guerrero, Registrar
671-735-2201 or 671-735-2208 Fax: 671-735-2203
Website: www.uog.edu
E-mail: admitme@uog9.uog.edu

PUERTO RICO

Atlantic College
PO Box 1774, Guaynabo PR 00970-1774
Zaida Perez, Director of Admissions
787-720-1022 Fax: 787-720-1092
Website: www.atlanticcollege-pr.com
E-mail: atlancol@coqui.net

Colegio Mayor de Technologia
PO Box 1490, Arroyo PR 00714
Julia Melendez, Director of Admissions
787-839-5266 Fax: 787-839-0033
Website: www.colegiomayortec.com
E-mail: cmtarroy@coqui.net

Instituto de Banca y Comercio
61 Ponce De Leon Ave, Hato Rey PR 00919
Rafael Jimenez, Vice President
787-754-7120 Fax: 787-754-7143
Website: www.ibanca.net
E-mail: rjimenez@ibancapr.com

TRINITY COLLEGE OF PUERTO RICO
PO Box 34360, Ponce PR 00734-4360
Ms. Maria I. Colon, Executive Director
787-842-0000 Fax: 787-284-2537
Website: www.csifpr.org/trinitycollege
E-mail: micolon@csifpr.org

Universidad Adventista de las Antillas
PO Box 118, Mayaguez PR 00919-0118
Evelyn Del Valle Rivera, Director of Admissions
787-834-9595 Fax: 787-834-9597
Website: www.uaa.edu
E-mail: admissions@uaa.edu

CONSERVATION/RENEWABLE NATURAL RESOURCES

ALABAMA

Alabama A & M University
PO Box 908, Normal AL 35762
Antonio Boyle, Director of Admissions
256-372-5245 Fax: 256-372-5249
Website: www.aamu.edu
E-mail: aboyle@aamu.edu

ALASKA

University of Alaska Anchorage
PO Box 141629, Anchorage AK 99514-1629
Cecile Mitchell, Director of Enrollment Services
907-786-1480 Fax: 907-786-4888
Website: www.uaa.alaska.edu/
E-mail: enroll@uaa.alaska.edu

COLORADO

UNIVERSITY OF DENVER UNIVERSITY COLLEGE
2211 S Josephine St, Denver CO 80208
Dr. John Hill, Academic Director
303-871-3354 Fax: 303-871-4047
Website: www.universitycollege.du.edu
E-mail: ucolinfo@du.edu

FLORIDA

University of South Florida
4202 E Fowler Ave, Tampa FL 33620-6900
J. Robert Spatig, Director of Admissions
813-974-3350 Fax: 813-974-9689
Website: www.usf.edu
E-mail: admissions@admin.usf.edu

GEORGIA

North Georgia Technical College
Clarkesville Campus
PO Box 65, Clarkesville GA 30523-0002
Admissions
706-754-7700 Fax: 706-754-7777
Website: www.northgatech.edu
E-mail: info@northgatech.edu

IDAHO

University of Idaho
Moscow ID 83844-4253
Lloyd Scott, Director of New Student Services
208-885-6163 Fax: 208-885-4477
Website: www.uidaho.edu
E-mail: nss@uidaho.edu

ILLINOIS

Roosevelt University
430 S Michigan Ave, Chicago IL 60605
Gwen E. Kanelos, Asst. Vice President for Enrollment Services
877-APPLY-RU Fax: 312-341-4216
Website: www.roosevelt.edu
E-mail: applyru@roosevelt.edu

INDIANA

University of Evansville
1800 Lincoln Ave, Evansville IN 47722-0001
Thomas E. Bear, V.P. of Enrollment Services
800-423-8633 Fax: 812-488-4076
Website: www.evansville.edu
E-mail: admission@evansville.edu

IOWA

Iowa Lakes Community College
300 S 18th St, Estherville IA 51334-2721
Anne Stansbury, Asst. Director of Admissions
712-362-7945 Fax: 712-362-8363
Website: www.iowalakes.edu
E-mail: info@iowalakes.edu

MICHIGAN

Grand Valley State University
1 Campus Dr, Allendale MI 49401-9403
Jodi Chycinski, Director of Admissions
616-331-6611 Fax: 616-331-2000
Website: www.gvsu.edu
E-mail: go2gvsu@gvsu.edu

University of Michigan-Dearborn
4901 Evergreen Rd, Dearborn MI 48128-1491
The Office of Admissions & Orientation
313-593-5100 Fax: 313-436-9167
Website: www.umd.umich.edu
E-mail: admissions@umd.umich.edu

NEVADA

GREAT BASIN COLLEGE
1500 College Pkwy, Elko NV 89801-5032
Julie G. Byrnes, Director of Enrollment Management
775-753-2271 Fax: 775-753-2311
Website: www.gbcnv.edu
E-mail: bjulie@gbcnv.edu

NEW HAMPSHIRE

Antioch University New England
40 Avon St, Keene NH 03431-3516
David Caruso, President
Leatrice A. Johnson, Director of Admissions
603-357-6265 Fax: 603-357-0718
Website: www.antiochne.edu
E-mail: admissions@antiochne.edu

NEW YORK

Paul Smith's College
Paul Smiths NY 12970
Amber DeBeer, Assistant Director of Admissions
800-421-2605 Fax: 518-327-6016
Website: www.paulsmiths.edu
E-mail: admiss@paulsmiths.edu

NORTH CAROLINA

Haywood Community College
185 Freedlander Dr, Clyde NC 28721
Debbie Rowland, Coordinator of Admissions
828-627-4500 Fax: 828-627-4513
Website: www.haywood.edu
E-mail: drowland@haywood.edu

Lees-McRae College
PO Box 128, Banner Elk NC 28604-0128
Walt Crutchfield, Dean of Admissions
800-280-4562 Fax: 828-898-8707
Website: www.lmc.edu
E-mail: admissions@lmc.edu

NORTH DAKOTA

Minot State University-Bottineau Campus
105 Simrall Blvd, Bottineau ND 58318-1159
Paula Berg, Associate Dean of Student Affairs
800-542-6866 Fax: 701-228-5499
Website: www.misu-b.nodak.edu
E-mail: paula.berg@misu.nodak.edu

OHIO

Cleveland State University
2121 Euclid Ave RW 204, Cleveland OH 44115
Dr. Richard Arndt, Dean of Undergraduate Recruitment
and College Partnerships
888-CSU-OHIO Fax: 216-687-9210
Website: www.csuohio.edu
E-mail: admissions@csuohio.edu

The Ohio State University
School of Natural Resources
Kottman Hall, 2021 Coffey Rd, Columbus OH 43210
614-292-2265 Fax: 614-292-7432
Website: snr.osu.edu
E-mail: burks.39@osu.edu

OKLAHOMA

Oklahoma State University
Stillwater OK 74078
Craig McKinley, Department Head
405-744-5438
Website: www.okstate.edu
E-mail: craig.mckinley@okstate.edu

PENNSYLVANIA

Juniata College
1700 Moore St, Huntingdon PA 16652-2196
Michelle Bartol, Dean of Enrollment
877-JUNIATA Fax: 814-641-3100
Website: www.juniata.edu
E-mail: admissions@juniata.edu

SOUTH DAKOTA

Western Dakota Technical Institute
800 Mickelson Dr, Rapid City SD 57703-4018
Janell Oberlander, Manager of Student Services
605-394-4034 or 800-544-8765 Fax: 605-394-1789
Website: www.westerndakotatech.org
E-mail: admissions@wdti.tec.sd.us
See listing under "Career Schools"

WASHINGTON

NORTHWEST INDIAN COLLEGE
2522 Kwina Rd, Bellingham WA 98226-9278
Leilani Ignacio, Director of Admissions
360-676-2772 Fax: 360-392-4333
Website: www.nwic.edu/
E-mail: lignacio@nwic.edu

WEST VIRGINIA

West Virginia Wesleyan College
59 College Ave, Buckhannon WV 26201-2699
Robert N. Skinner II, Director of Admission
800-722-9933 Fax: 304-473-8108
Website: www.wvwc.edu
E-mail: admission@wvwc.edu

WISCONSIN

COLLEGE OF MENOMINEE NATION
PO Box 1179, Keshena WI 54135-1179
Cynthia Norton, Admissions Representative
715-799-5600 Fax: 715-799-4392
Website: www.menominee.edu
E-mail: cnorton@menominee.edu

WYOMING

University of Wyoming
Admissions Office
Dept 3435, Laramie WY 82071-3435
Aaron Appelhans, Contact
800-342-5996 Fax: 307-766-4042
Website: www.uwyo.edu
E-mail: why-wyo@uwyo.edu

CONSTRUCTION TRADES

ALABAMA

Trenholm State Technical College
Patterson Campus
3920 Troy Hwy, Montgomery AL 36116
Dr. Anthony Molina, President
334-420-4200 Fax: 334-420-4206
Website: www.trenholmtech.cc.al.us
E-mail: amolina@trenholmtech.cc.al.us

ALASKA

University of Alaska Southeast
11120 Glacier Hwy, Juneau AK 99801-8625
Paul Kraft, Dean of Students/Enrollment Management
907-796-6000 Fax: 907-796-6005
Website: www.uas.alaska.edu
E-mail: paul.kraft@uas.alaska.edu

ARIZONA

Pima Community College
4905 E Broadway Blvd, Tucson AZ 85709-1010
Wendy Kilgore, Ph.D., Director of Admissions
520-206-4500 Fax: 520-206-4790
Website: www.pima.edu
E-mail: infocenter@pima.edu

ARKANSAS

Northwest Technical Institute
709 S Old Missouri Rd, Springdale AR 72764
Charles L. Kelley, President
479-751-8824 Fax: 479-751-7780
Website: www.nit.tec.ar.us
E-mail: info@nit.tec.ar.us

CALIFORNIA

FRESNO CITY COLLEGE
1101 E University Ave, Fresno CA 93741-0002
Dayann Dietrich, Contact
559-442-8241 Fax: 559-237-4232
Website: www.fresnocitycollege.com
E-mail: fcc.admissions@scccd.com

Orange Coast College
PO Box 5005, Costa Mesa CA 92628-5005
Kristin Clark, Director of Admissions
714-432-5773 Fax: 714-432-5736
Website: www.orangecoastcollege.edu
E-mail: kclark@cccd.edu

San Joaquin Valley College
201 New Stine Rd, Bakersfield CA 93309-2659
Jaime Delgado, Enrollment Services Director
661-834-1026 Fax: 559-651-4864
Website: www.sjvc.edu
E-mail: jaime.delgado@sjvc.edu

San Joaquin Valley College
295 E Sierra Ave, Fresno CA 93710-3616
Nora Twarynski, Enrollment Services Director
559-448-8282 Fax: 559-651-4864
Website: www.sjvc.edu
E-mail: nora.twarynski@sjvc.edu

San Joaquin Valley College
10641 Church St, Rancho Cucamonga CA 91730
Ramon Abreu, Enrollment Services Director
909-948-7582 Fax: 559-651-4864
Website: www.sjvc.edu
E-mail: ramon.abreu@sjvc.edu

COLORADO

San Juan Basin Technical College
PO Box 970, Cortez CO 81321-0970
Shannon South, Director of Student Services
970-565-8457 Fax: 970-565-8450
Website: www.sjbtc.edu
E-mail: ssouth@sjbtc.edu

FLORIDA

EVERGLADES UNIVERSITY (MAIN CAMPUS)
5002 T-Rex Ave Suite 100, Boca Raton FL 33431
Kristi Mollis, President
888-772-6077 Fax: 561-912-1191
Website: www.evergladesuniversity.edu
E-mail: admissions-boca@evergladesuniversity.edu
See listing under "Universities"

EVERGLADES UNIVERSITY
Orlando Campus (Branch Campus)
5600 Lake Underhill Rd Suite 200, Orlando FL 32807
Shirley Long, Vice President
866-289-1078 Fax: 407-482-9801
Website: www.evergladesuniversity.edu
E-mail: admissions-orl@evergladesuniversity.edu
See listing under "Universities"

EVERGLADES UNIVERSITY
Sarasota Campus (Branch Campus)
6001 Lake Osprey Dr, Sarasota FL 34240
Brad Brewer, Vice President
866-907-2262 Fax: 941-907-6634
Website: www.evergladesuniversity.edu
E-mail: admissions-sar@evergladesuniversity.edu
See listing under "Universities"

Santa Fe Community College
3000 NW 83rd St, Gainesville FL 32606-6200
Jackson N. Sasser, President
352-395-5787 Fax: 352-395-4118
Website: www.sfcc.edu
E-mail: ouida.mcneil@sfcc.edu

GEORGIA

North Georgia Technical College
434 Meeks Ave, Blairsville GA 30512-2983
Admissions
706-781-2300 Fax: 706-781-2307
Website: www.northgatech.edu
E-mail: info@northgatech.edu

North Georgia Technical College
8989 Highway 17, Toccoa GA 30577
706-779-5591
Website: www.northgatech.edu
E-mail: info@northgatech.edu

North Georgia Technical College
Clarkesville Campus
PO Box 65, Clarkesville GA 30523-0002
Admissions
706-754-7700 Fax: 706-754-7777
Website: www.northgatech.edu
E-mail: info@northgatech.edu

IDAHO

Brigham Young University - Idaho
120 Kimball Bldg, Rexburg ID 83460
Gordon Westenskow, Director of Admissions
208-496-1020 Fax: 208-496-1220
Website: www.byui.edu
E-mail: admissions@byui.edu

ILLINOIS

Kaskaskia College
27210 College Rd, Centralia IL 62801-7878
Tyra Taylor, Dean of Enrollment Management and
Retention Services
618-545-3000 Fax: 618-532-1990
Website: www.kaskaskia.edu
E-mail: ttaylor@kaskaskia.edu

South Suburban College of Cook County
15800 State St, South Holland IL 60473
Jane Ellen Stocker, Dean of Enrollment Services
708-596-2000 Fax: 708-225-5806
Website: www.southsuburbancollege.edu
E-mail: jstocker@southsuburbancollege.edu

Triton College
2000 5th Ave, River Grove IL 60171-1995
Mary-Rita Moore, Dean of Enrollment Services
708-456-0300 ext. 3130 Fax: 708-583-3147
Website: www.triton.edu
E-mail: triton@triton.edu
See listing under "Community and Junior Colleges"

INDIANA

Ivy Tech Community College - North Central
220 Dean Johnson Blvd, South Bend IN 46601-3415
Pam Decker, Director of Admissions
574-289-7001 Fax: 574-236-7177
Website: www.ivytech.edu
E-mail: pdecker@ivytech.edu

IOWA

Iowa Lakes Community College
3200 College Dr, Emmetsburg IA 50536-1055
Anne Stansbury, Asst. Director of Admissions
712-852-5212 Fax: 712-362-8363
Website: www.iowalakes.edu
E-mail: info@iowalakes.edu

Northwest Iowa Community College
603 W Park St, Sheldon IA 51201-1046
Lisa Story, Director of Enrollment Management
712-324-5061 Fax: 712-324-4136
Website: www.nwicc.edu
E-mail: lstory@nwicc.edu

KANSAS

Flint Hills Technical College
3301 W 18th Ave, Emporia KS 66801-5957
Lisa Kirmer, Dean of Student Services
620-343-4600 Fax: 620-343-4610
Website: www.fhtc.net
E-mail: lkirmer@fhtc.net

SOUTHWEST KANSAS TECHNICAL SCHOOL
PO Box 1599, Liberal KS 67905-1599
Ed Poley, Assistant Director
620-604-2900 or 800-818-3819 Fax: 620-624-0108
Website: www.swkts.com
E-mail: epoley@usd480.net

KENTUCKY

Bluegrass Community and Technical College
Oswald Building
470 Cooper Drive, Lexington KY 40506-0235
Shelbie Hugle, Director of Admissions
859-246-6200 Fax: 859-246-4664
Website: www.bluegrass.kctcs.edu
E-mail: bctc_info@kctcs.edu

MAINE

Northern Maine Community College
33 Edgemont Dr, Presque Isle ME 04769-2016
Bill Casavant, Director of Admissions
207-768-2700 Fax: 207-768-2831
Website: www.nmcc.edu
E-mail: admissions@nmcc.edu

Southern Maine Community College
2 Fort Rd, South Portland ME 04106-1698
Dr. James Ortiz, President
Scott MacDonald, Director of Financial Aid
207-741-5500 Fax: 207-741-5671
Website: www.smccme.edu
E-mail: oharmon@maine.rr.com

MASSACHUSETTS

Benjamin Franklin Institute of Technology
41 Berkeley St, Boston MA 02116-6307
Norman Kraft, Dean of Enrollment
617-423-4630 ext. 121 Fax: 617-482-3706
Website: www.bfit.edu
E-mail: admissions@bfit.edu

Wentworth Institute of Technology
550 Huntington Ave, Boston MA 02115-5998
David C. Planchard, Director of Admissions
617-442-9010
Website: www.wit.edu/apply
E-mail: planchardd@wit.edu

MICHIGAN

Delta College
University Center MI 48710-0001
Duff Zube, Director of Admissions
989-686-9093 Fax: 989-667-2202
Website: www.delta.edu
E-mail: admit@delta.edu

MACOMB COMMUNITY COLLEGE

14500 E 12 Mile Rd, Warren MI 48088-3896
Information Center
586-445-7999
Website: www.macomb.edu
E-mail: answer@macomb.edu

MINNESOTA

Dunwoody College of Technology
818 Dunwoody Blvd, Minneapolis MN 55403-1192
John Slama, Vice President Enrollment Management
800-292-4625 or 612-374-5800 Fax: 612-374-4128
Website: www.dunwoody.edu
E-mail: jslama@dunwoody.edu
See listing under "Career Schools"

Hibbing Community College
1515 E 25th St, Hibbing MN 55746-3300
Holly Bigelow, Director of Enrollment
800-224-4HCC or 218-262-7200 Fax: 218-262-6717
Website: www.hibbing.edu
E-mail: admissions@hibbing.edu

Minneapolis Community and Technical College
1501 Hennepin Ave, Minneapolis MN 55403-1779
Dena Russell, Director of Admissions
612-659-6282 Fax: 612-659-6210
Website: www.minneapolis.edu
E-mail: admissions.office@minneapolis.edu

Minnesota State College - Southeast Technical
308 Pioneer Rd, Red Wing MN 55066-3964
Al Ducett, Director of Admissions
800-657-4849 Fax: 507-453-2715
Website: www.southeastmn.edu
E-mail: aducett@southeastmn.edu

Northland Community & Technical College
Highway 1 E, Thief River Falls MN 56701
Eugene Klinke, Director of Enrollment Management
800-959-6282 or 218-681-0862 Fax: 218-681-0774
Website: www.northlandcollege.edu
E-mail: eugene.klinke@northlandcollege.edu

Northland Community and Technical College
2022 Central Ave NE
East Grand Forks MN 56721-2702
Loren Abel, Carpentry Instructor
800-451-3441 Fax: 218-773-4502
Website: www.northlandcollege.edu
E-mail: admissions@northlandcollege.edu

Ridgewater College-Willmar Campus
PO Box 1097, Willmar MN 56201-1097
Sally Kerfeld, Director of Admissions
800-722-1151 Fax: 320-231-7677
Website: www.ridgewater.edu
E-mail: skerfeld@ridgewater.edu

St. Cloud Technical College
1540 Northway Dr, Saint Cloud MN 56303-1240
Jodi Elness, Director of Enrollment Management
800-222-1009 Fax: 320-308-5981
Website: www.sctc.edu
E-mail: jelness@sctc.edu

MISSOURI

Linn State Technical College
1 Technology Dr, Linn MO 65051-9606
Becky Dunn, Admissions
800-743-8324 Fax: 573-897-5026
Website: www.linnstate.edu
E-mail: admissions@linnstate.edu

Ranken Technical College
4431 Finney Ave, Saint Louis MO 63113-2898
Elizabeth M. Keserauskis, Director of Admissions
314-371-0233 Fax: 314-371-0241
Website: www.ranken.edu
E-mail: admissions@ranken.edu

Vatterott College
3925 Industrial Dr, Saint Ann MO 63074-1807
Jennifer Commuso, Director of Admissions
800-345-6018 Fax: 314-428-5956
Website: www.vatterott-college.edu
E-mail: jennifer.commuso@vatterott-college.edu

NEBRASKA

VATTEROTT COLLEGE

11818 I St, Omaha NE 68137
Todd S. Clark, Director
402-891-9411 Fax: 402-891-9413
Website: www.vatterott-college.edu
E-mail: tclark@vatterott-college.edu

NEW MEXICO

New Mexico State University
1500 N 3rd St, Grants NM 87020-2025
505-287-7981 Fax: 505-287-2329
Website: www.grants.nmsu.edu

NEW YORK

CAREER INSTITUTE OF HEALTH & TECHNOLOGY

340 Flatbush Avenue Ext, Brooklyn NY 11201
Mary Miller, Contact
718-422-1212 Fax: 718-422-1222
Website: www.careerinstitute.edu
E-mail: admissions@careerinstitute.edu

CAREER INSTITUTE OF HEALTH & TECHNOLOGY

200 Garden City Plz, Garden City NY 11530
Mary Miller, Contact
516-877-1225 Fax: 516-877-1959
Website: www.careerinstitute.edu
E-mail: admissions@careerinstitute.edu

CAREER INSTITUTE OF HEALTH & TECHNOLOGY

9525 Queens Blvd Ste 600, Rego Park NY 11374
Mary Miller, Contact
718-897-4868 Fax: 718-897-4863
Website: www.careerinstitute.edu
E-mail: admissions@careerinstitute.edu

ISLAND DRAFTING & TECHNICAL INSTITUTE

128 Broadway (Route 110), Amityville NY 11701-2704
James G. DiLiberto, President
631-691-8733 Fax: 631-691-8738
Website: www.idti.edu
E-mail: info@idti.edu

Pratt Institute
200 Willoughby Ave, Brooklyn NY 11205-3899
Heidi Metcalf, Director of Admissions
718-636-3600 Fax: 718-636-3670
Website: www.pratt.edu
E-mail: hmetcalf@pratt.edu

SUNY College of Technology
Alfred NY 14802
Deborah J. Goodrich, Director of Admissions
800-4AL-FRED Fax: 607-587-4299
Website: www.alfredstate.edu
E-mail: admissions@alfredstate.edu

SUNY College of Technology
2 Main St, Delhi NY 13753-1110
Robert W. Mazzei, Director of Admissions
800-96-DELHI Fax: 607-746-4104
Website: www.delhi.edu
E-mail: enroll@delhi.edu

SUNY Orange County Community College
115 South St, Middletown NY 10940-6437
Margot St. Lawrence, Director of Admissions
845-341-4030 Fax: 845-342-8662
Website: www.sunyorange.edu
E-mail: apply@sunyorange.edu
See listing under "Community and Junior Colleges"

NORTH CAROLINA

Haywood Community College
185 Freedlander Dr, Clyde NC 28721
Debbie Rowland, Coordinator of Admissions
828-627-4500 Fax: 828-627-4513
Website: www.haywood.edu
E-mail: drowland@haywood.edu

James Sprunt Community College
PO Box 398, Kenansville NC 28349-0398
Rita Brown, Registrar
910-296-2500 Fax: 910-296-1636
Website: www.sprunt.com

South Piedmont Community College
PO Box 126, Polkton NC 28135-0126
John Curtis, Contact
704-272-5324 Fax: 704-272-8904
Website: www.spcc.edu
E-mail: jcurtis@spcc.edu

NORTH DAKOTA

Sitting Bull College
1341 92nd St, Fort Yates ND 58538
Melody Azure, Director of Admissions / Registrar
701-854-3861 Fax: 701-854-3403
Website: www.sittingbull.edu
E-mail: melodya@sbci.edu

OHIO

Collins Career Center
11627 State Route 243, Chesapeake OH 45619-7962
740-867-6641 Fax: 740-867-9626
Website: www.collins-cc.k12.oh.us

Owens Community College
PO Box 10000, Toledo OH 43699-1947
William J. Ivoska, Ph.D, Vice President of Student Services
567-661-7000 Fax: 567-661-7607
Website: www.owens.edu
E-mail: admissions@owens.edu

Total Technical Institute
8720 Brookpark Rd, Cleveland OH 44129-6810
Dave Bryant, Director of Admissions
216-485-0900 Fax: 216-661-6842
Website: www.ttinst.com
E-mail: dbryant@ttinst.com

OREGON

Rogue Community College
3345 Redwood Hwy, Grants Pass OR 97527-9298
Claudia Sullivan, Director of Enrollment Services
541-956-7500 Fax: 541-471-3585
Website: www.roguecc.edu
E-mail: csullivan@roguecc.edu
See listing under "Community and Junior Colleges"

PENNSYLVANIA

Johnson College
3427 N Main Ave, Scranton PA 18508-1495
Dr. Ann L. Pipinski, President & CEO
Melissa Ide, Director of Enrollment Management
800-2WE-WORK or 570-342-6404 ext. 125
Fax: 570-348-2181
Website: www.johnson.edu
E-mail: admit@johnson.edu

RHODE ISLAND

MTTI - MOTORING TECHNICAL TRAINING INSTITUTE

54 Water St, East Providence RI 02914-5022
Nick Azzarone, Director of Admissions
401-434-4840 or 866-454-6884 Fax: 401-434-9540
Website: www.mtti.edu
E-mail: mtti2@aol.com

New England Institute of Technology
2500 Post Rd, Warwick RI 02886-2244
Michael Kwiatkowski, Director of Admissions
401-739-5000 Fax: 401-738-5122
Website: www.neit.edu
E-mail: eflynn@neit.edu

SOUTH CAROLINA

Bob Jones University
1700 Wade Hampton Blvd
Greenville SC 29614-0001
David Christ, Director of Admissions
800-BJ-AND-ME Fax: 800-2-FAX-BJU
Website: www.bju.edu
E-mail: admissions@bju.edu
See listing under "Universities"

SOUTH DAKOTA

Western Dakota Technical Institute
800 Mickelson Dr, Rapid City SD 57703-4018
Janell Oberlander, Manager of Student Services
605-394-4034 or 800-544-8765 Fax: 605-394-1789
Website: www.westerndakotatech.org
E-mail: admissions@wdti.tec.sd.us
See listing under "Career Schools"

TEXAS

McLennan Community College
1400 College Dr, Waco TX 76708-1498
Fred Quick, Coordinator, Building Construction Trade
254-753-6212 Fax: 254-299-8854
Website: www.mclennan.edu
E-mail: fquick@mclennan.edu

SAN ANTONIO COLLEGE MEDICAL DENTAL ASSISTANTS

7142 San Pedro Ave Ste 100, San Antonio TX 78216
Carig Czubati, Director of Admissions
210-733-0777 Fax: 210-735-2431
Website: www.sacmda.com
E-mail: cczubati@sac-mda.com

WASHINGTON

BATES TECHNICAL COLLEGE

1101 S Yakima Ave, Tacoma WA 98405-4895
David Borofsky, President
253-680-7000 Fax: 253-680-7101
Website: www.bates.ctc.edu
E-mail: info@bates.ctc.edu

Perry Technical Institute
2011 W Washington Ave, Yakima WA 98903-1296
509-453-0374 Fax: 509-453-0375
Website: www.perrytech.edu
E-mail: frankj@perrytech.edu

RENTON TECHNICAL COLLEGE

3000 NE 4th St, Renton WA 98056-4195
Becky Riverman, Registrar
425-235-2352 or 425-235-5840 Fax: 425-235-7832
Website: www.RTC.edu
E-mail: dgrant@RTC.edu

Walla Walla Community College
500 Tausick Way, Walla Walla WA 99362-9270
Jerry Kjack, Director
509-527-4283 or 877-992-9922 Fax: 509-527-4572
Website: www.wwcc.edu
E-mail: jerry.kjack@wwcc.edu
See listing under "Community and Junior Colleges"

WEST COAST TRAINING INC.

PO Box 970, Woodland WA 98674-1000
Eileen Kelgard, President
Adonica Simpson, Director
800-755-5477 Fax: 360-225-6760
Website: www.heavyequipmenttraining.com
E-mail: wct@heavyequipmenttraining.com
See listing under "Career Schools"

WISCONSIN

Wisconsin Indianhead Technical College
505 Pine Ridge Dr, Shell Lake WI 54871
Walt Peters, Dean
800-243-9482 Fax: 715-468-2819
Website: www.witc.edu
E-mail: mcrandal@witc.edu

WYOMING

· Laramie County Community College
1400 E College Dr, Cheyenne WY 82007-3204
Jenny Hargett, Director of Admissions
307-778-5222 Fax: 307-778-1350
Website: www.lccc.wy.edu
E-mail: learnmore@lccc.wy.edu

PUERTO RICO

: Instituto de Banca y Comercio
61 Ponce De Leon Ave, Hato Rey PR 00919
Rafael Jimenez, Vice President
787-754-7120 Fax: 787-754-7143
Website: www.ibanca.net
E-mail: rjimenez@ibancapr.com

DENTISTRY

ALABAMA

Judson College
302 Bibb St, Marion AL 36756
Michael Scotto, Director of Admissions
800-447-9472 Fax: 334-683-5147
Website: www.judson.edu
E-mail: admissions@judson.edu

ALASKA

University of Alaska Anchorage
PO Box 141629, Anchorage AK 99514-1629
Cecile Mitchell, Director of Enrollment Services
907-786-1480 Fax: 907-786-4888
Website: www.uaa.alaska.edu/
E-mail: enroll@uaa.alaska.edu

ARIZONA

: **ARIZONA SCHOOL OF DENTISTRY AND ORAL HEALTH**
A.T. STILL UNIVERSITY
5850 E Still Cir, Mesa AZ 85206
Admissions Counselor
866-626-2878 or 480-219-6000 Fax: 480-219-6100
Website: www.atsu.edu
E-mail: info@ashs.edu

ARKANSAS

Ouachita Baptist University
410 Ouachita St, Arkadelphia AR 71998-0001
David Goodman, Director of Admissions
870-245-5110 Fax: 870-245-5500
Website: www.obu.edu
E-mail: admissions@obu.edu

CALIFORNIA

Chapman University
One University Drive, Orange CA 92866-1099
Michael Drummy, Assistant Vice President for Enrollment
Services and Chief Admission Officer
714-997-6411 or 888-CUAPPLY Fax: 714-997-6713
Website: www.chapman.edu
E-mail: admit@chapman.edu

UNIVERSITY OF THE PACIFIC
Arthur A. Dugoni School of Dentistry
2155 Webster St, San Francisco CA 94115-2333
Kathy Candito, Director of Admissions
415-929-6491 Fax: 415-749-3363
Website: www.dental.pacific.edu

· Western Career College
2157 Country Hills Dr, Antioch CA 94509-7435
Tim Gienapp, Director of Admissions
925-522-7777
Website: www.westerncollege.edu

· Western Career College
7301 Greenback Ln Bldg A, Citrus Heights CA 95621
Jim Murphy, Contact
916-722-8200 Fax: 916-722-6883
Website: www.westerncollege.edu

· Western Career College
380 Civic Dr Ste 300, Pleasant Hill CA 94523-1984
LaShawn Wells, Contact
925-609-6650 Fax: 926-609-6666
Website: www.westerncollege.edu

· Western Career College
8909 Folsom Blvd, Sacramento CA 95826-3203
Sue Smith, Contact
916-361-1660 Fax: 916-361-6666
Website: www.westerncollege.edu

· Western Career College
6201 San Ignacio Ave, San Jose CA 95119
Steve Ashab, Director of Admissions
408-360-0840 Fax: 408-360-0848
Website: www.westerncollege.edu

· Western Career College
15555 E 14th St Ste 500, San Leandro CA 94578
Julie Elmquist, Contact
510-276-3888 Fax: 510-276-3653
Website: www.westerncollege.edu

COLORADO

· IntelliTec College
772 Horizon Dr, Grand Junction CO 81506-3907
Rich Counts, Contact
970-245-8101 Fax: 970-243-8074
Website: www.intelliteccollege.edu
E-mail: admgj@intelliteccollege.edu

: IntelliTec Medical Institute
2345 N Academy Blvd
Colorado Springs CO 80909-1570
Kiersten Murdoch, Contact
719-596-7400 Fax: 719-596-2464
Website: www.IntellitecCollege.edu
E-mail: kmurdoch@intelliteccollege.edu

University of Colorado at Denver and Health Sciences Center
Health Sciences Program
4200 E 9th Ave Box C245, Denver CO 80262
Phoebe Lindsey Barton, Ph.D., Director
Website: www.uchsc.edu

FLORIDA

Nova Southeastern University Health Profession
3200 S University Dr, Davie FL 33328-2018
Marla Frohlinger, Director of Admissions
954-262-1101 Fax: 954-262-2282
Website: www.nova.edu
E-mail: marlaf@nsu.nova.edu

· Santa Fe Community College
3000 NW 83rd St, Gainesville FL 32606-6200
Jackson N. Sasser, President
352-395-5787 Fax: 352-395-4118
Website: www.sfcc.edu
E-mail: ouida.mcneil@sfcc.edu

ILLINOIS

Roosevelt University
430 S Michigan Ave, Chicago IL 60605
Gwen E. Kanelos, Asst. Vice President for Enrollment Services
877-APPLY-RU Fax: 312-341-4216
Website: www.roosevelt.edu
E-mail: applyru@roosevelt.edu

IOWA

Briar Cliff University
PO Box 2100, Sioux City IA 51104-0100
Sharisue Wilcoxon, VP for Enrollment Management
712-279-5200 Fax: 712-279-1632
Website: www.briarcliff.edu
E-mail: admissions@briarcliff.edu

· Iowa Lakes Community College
300 S 18th St, Estherville IA 51334-2721
Anne Stansbury, Asst. Director of Admissions
712-362-7945 Fax: 712-362-8363
Website: www.iowalakes.edu
E-mail: info@iowalakes.edu

KANSAS

COLBY COMMUNITY COLLEGE
1255 S Range Ave, Colby KS 67701-4099
Director of Admissions
888-634-9350 or 785-460-4690 Fax: 785-460-4691
Website: www.colbycc.edu
E-mail: bobbi@colbycc.edu

: Flint Hills Technical College
3301 W 18th Ave, Emporia KS 66801-5957
Lisa Kirmer, Dean of Student Services
620-343-4600 Fax: 620-343-4610
Website: www.fhtc.net
E-mail: lkirmer@fhtc.net

Newman University
3100 W McCormick St, Wichita KS 67213
Jann Reusser, Admissions Recruitment Coordinator
316-942-4291 ext. 2144 Fax: 316-942-4483
Website: www.newmanu.edu
E-mail: reusserj@newmanu.edu

NEW JERSEY

· Bergen Community College
400 Paramus Rd, Paramus NJ 07652
Julian Gomez, Asst. Director of Admissions
201-447-7100 Fax: 201-444-7036
Website: www.bergen.edu
E-mail: jgomez@bergen.edu

NEW YORK

Roberts Wesleyan College
2301 Westside Dr, Rochester NY 14624-1997
Office of Admissions
585-594-6400 Fax: 585-594-6371
Website: www.roberts.edu
E-mail: admissions@roberts.edu

NORTH CAROLINA

Lees-McRae College
PO Box 128, Banner Elk NC 28604-0128
Walt Crutchfield, Dean of Admissions
800-280-4562 Fax: 828-898-8707
Website: www.lmc.edu
E-mail: admissions@lmc.edu

OHIO

The Ohio State University
College of Dentistry
Postle Hall 305 W 12th Ave PO Box 182357
Columbus OH 43219
614-292-3361 Fax: 614-292-0813
Website: dent.osu.edu
E-mail: admissions@dentistry.dent.ohio-state.edu

PENNSYLVANIA

· Academy of Medical Arts and Business
2301 Academy Dr, Harrisburg PA 17112-1012
717-545-4747
Website: www.ACADcampus.com
E-mail: info@ACADcampus.com

Juniata College
1700 Moore St, Huntingdon PA 16652-2196
Michelle Bartol, Dean of Enrollment
877-JUNIATA Fax: 814-641-3100
Website: www.juniata.edu
E-mail: admissions@juniata.edu

TEXAS

: **SAN ANTONIO COLLEGE MEDICAL DENTAL ASSISTANTS**
7142 San Pedro Ave Ste 100, San Antonio TX 78216
Carig Czubati, Director of Admissions
210-733-0777 Fax: 210-735-2431
Website: www.sacmda.com
E-mail: cczubati@sac-mda.com

WASHINGTON

Gonzaga University
502 E Boone Ave, Spokane WA 99258-0102
Julie McCulloh, Dean of Admission
800-322-2584 or 509-323-6572 Fax: 509-323-5780
Website: www.gonzaga.edu
E-mail: mcculloh@gu.gonzaga.edu

WEST VIRGINIA

West Virginia Wesleyan College
59 College Ave, Buckhannon WV 26201-2699
Robert N. Skinner II, Director of Admission
800-722-9933 Fax: 304-473-8108
Website: www.wvwc.edu
E-mail: admission@wvwc.edu

WISCONSIN

Marquette University
PO Box 1881, Milwaukee WI 53201-1881
Robert Blust, Director of Admissions
414-288-7302 Fax: 414-288-3764
Website: www.mu.edu
E-mail: admissions@marquette.edu

St. Norbert College
100 Grant St, De Pere WI 54115
Brian Studebaker, Director of Admission
800-236-4878 Fax: 920-403-4072
Website: www.snc.edu
E-mail: admit@snc.edu

WYOMING

University of Wyoming
Admissions Office
Dept 3435, Laramie WY 82071-3435
Aaron Appelhans, Contact
800-342-5996 Fax: 307-766-4042
Website: www.uwyo.edu
E-mail: why-wyo@uwyo.edu

PUERTO RICO

: Colegio Mayor de Technologia
PO Box 1490, Arroyo PR 00714
Julia Melendez, Director of Admissions
787-839-5266 Fax: 787-839-0033
Website: www.colegiomayortec.com
E-mail: cmtarroy@coqui.net

ENGINEERING

ALABAMA

Alabama A & M University
PO Box 908, Normal AL 35762
Antonio Boyle, Director of Admissions
256-372-5245 Fax: 256-372-5249
Website: www.aamu.edu
E-mail: aboyle@aamu.edu

University of Alabama in Huntsville
PO Box 1247, Huntsville AL 35899-0001
Ann Lee, Assoc. Director for Recruiting Program and Events
1-800-UAH-CALL Fax: 256-824-6073
Website: www.uah.edu
E-mail: leev@uah.edu

University of South Alabama
307 University Blvd N, Mobile AL 36688-3053
Melissa Haab, Director of Admissions
251-460-6141 Fax: 251-460-7876
Website: www.southalabama.edu
E-mail: admiss@usouthal.edu

ALASKA

University of Alaska Anchorage
PO Box 141629, Anchorage AK 99514-1629
Cecile Mitchell, Director of Enrollment Services
907-786-1480 Fax: 907-786-4888
Website: www.uaa.alaska.edu/
E-mail: enroll@uaa.alaska.edu

ARIZONA

Pima Community College
4905 E Broadway Blvd, Tucson AZ 85709-1010
Wendy Kilgore, Ph.D., Director of Admissions
520-206-4500 Fax: 520-206-4790
Website: www.pima.edu
E-mail: infocenter@pima.edu

University of Arizona
Tucson AZ 85721-0040
Paul Kohn, Director of Admissions
520-621-3237 Fax: 520-621-9799
Website: www.admissions.arizona.edu or www.arizona.edu

CALIFORNIA

Chapman University
One University Drive, Orange CA 92866-1099
Michael Drummy, Assistant Vice President for Enrollment
Services and Chief Admission Officer
714-997-6411 or 888-CUAPPLY Fax: 714-997-6713
Website: www.chapman.edu
E-mail: admit@chapman.edu

Cogswell College
1175 Bordeaux Dr, Sunnyvale CA 94089-1210
Dr. Vinh Phat, Engineering Contact
800-264-7955 or 408-541-0100 Fax: 408-747-0764
Website: www.cogswell.edu
E-mail: info@cogswell.edu

FRESNO CITY COLLEGE
1101 E University Ave, Fresno CA 93741-0002
Dayann Dietrich, Contact
559-442-8241 Fax: 559-237-4232
Website: www.fresnocitycollege.com
E-mail: fcc.admissions@scccd.com

Harvey Mudd College
Claremont CA 91711-3104
Peter Osgood, Contact
909-621-8011 Fax: 909-607-7046
Website: www.hmc.edu
E-mail: admission@hmc.edu

Northwestern Polytechnic University
47671 Westinghouse Dr, Fremont CA 94539
Dr. P. Hsu, Contact
510-657-5913 Fax: 510-657-8975
Website: www.npu.edu
E-mail: npuadm@npu.edu

Orange Coast College
PO Box 5005, Costa Mesa CA 92628-5005
Kristin Clark, Director of Admissions
714-432-5773 Fax: 714-432-5736
Website: www.orangecoastcollege.edu
E-mail: kclark@cccd.edu

Whittier College
PO Box 634, Whittier CA 90608-0634
Kieron Miller, Director of Admissions
562-907-4200 Fax: 562-907-4870
Website: www.whittier.edu
E-mail: kmiller@whittier.edu

COLORADO

University of Colorado at Denver and Health Sciences Center
Downtown Denver Campus
PO Box 173364, Denver CO 80217-3364
303-556-2870 Fax: 303-556-2511
Website: www.cudenver.edu/academics/colleges/college+of+engineering+applied+scie nce

CONNECTICUT

University of New Haven
300 Boston Post Rd, West Haven CT 06516
Director of Undergraduate Admissions
203-932-7319 Fax: 203-931-6093
Website: www.newhaven.edu
E-mail: adminfo@newhaven.edu

FLORIDA

Florida State University
600 W College Ave, Tallahassee FL 32306-1096
Janice V. Finney, Director of Admissions
850-644-2525 Fax: 850-644-0197
Website: admissions.fsu.edu
E-mail: admissions@admin.fsu.edu

St. Thomas University
16401 NW 37th Ave, Miami Gardens FL 33054
Dr. Edward Ajhar, Contact
800-367-9010 or 305-628-6546 Fax: 305-628-6591
Website: www.stu.edu
E-mail: signup@stu.edu

Santa Fe Community College
3000 NW 83rd St, Gainesville FL 32606-6200
Jackson N. Sasser, President
352-395-5787 Fax: 352-395-4118
Website: www.sfcc.edu
E-mail: ouida.mcneil@sfcc.edu

University of South Florida
4202 E Fowler Ave, Tampa FL 33620-6900
J. Robert Spatig, Director of Admissions
813-974-3350 Fax: 813-974-9689
Website: www.usf.edu
E-mail: admissions@admin.usf.edu

GEORGIA

Oglethorpe University
4484 Peachtree Rd NE, Atlanta GA 30319-2797
Kelly Gosnell, Director of Admission
404-261-1441 Fax: 404-364-8491
Website: www.oglethorpe.edu
E-mail: admission@oglethorpe.edu

IDAHO

Brigham Young University - Idaho
120 Kimball Bldg, Rexburg ID 83460
Gordon Westenskow, Director of Admissions
208-496-1020 Fax: 208-496-1220
Website: www.byui.edu
E-mail: admissions@byui.edu

University of Idaho
Moscow ID 83844-4253
Lloyd Scott, Director of New Student Services
208-885-6163 Fax: 208-885-4477
Website: www.uidaho.edu
E-mail: nss@uidaho.edu

ILLINOIS

Benedictine University
5700 College Rd, Lisle IL 60532-0900
630-829-6300 or 888-829-6363 Fax: 630-829-6301
Website: www.ben.edu
E-mail: admissions@ben.edu
See listing under "Universities"

Kaskaskia College
27210 College Rd, Centralia IL 62801-7878
Tyra Taylor, Dean of Enrollment Management and Retention Services
618-545-3000 Fax: 618-532-1990
Website: www.kaskaskia.edu
E-mail: ttaylor@kaskaskia.edu

North Central College
30 N Brainard St, Naperville IL 60540-4690
Martha Stolze, Director of Admissions
630-637-5800 Fax: 630-637-5819
Website: www.northcentralcollege.edu
E-mail: admissions@noctrl.edu

South Suburban College of Cook County
15800 State St, South Holland IL 60473
Jane Ellen Stocker, Dean of Enrollment Services
708-596-2000 Fax: 708-225-5806
Website: www.southsuburbancollege.edu
E-mail: jstocker@southsuburbancollege.edu

INDIANA

Rose-Hulman Institute of Technology
5500 Wabash Ave, Terre Haute IN 47803-3920
James A. Goecker, Dean of Admissions
812-877-8213 Fax: 812-877-8941
Website: www.rose-hulman.edu
E-mail: admis.ofc@rose-hulman.edu

University of Evansville
1800 Lincoln Ave, Evansville IN 47722-0001
Thomas E. Bear, V.P. of Enrollment Services
800-423-8633 Fax: 812-488-4076
Website: www.evansville.edu
E-mail: admission@evansville.edu

IOWA

Briar Cliff University
PO Box 2100, Sioux City IA 51104-0100
Sharisue Wilcoxon, VP for Enrollment Management
712-279-5200 Fax: 712-279-1632
Website: www.briarcliff.edu
E-mail: admissions@briarcliff.edu

Hamilton College
4655 121st St, Urbandale IA 50323-2311
Ed Rogan, Campus President
515-727-2100 Fax: 515-727-2115
Website: www.hamiltonia.edu
E-mail: erogan_dm@hamiltonia.edu

Iowa Lakes Community College
300 S 18th St, Estherville IA 51334-2721
Anne Stansbury, Asst. Director of Admissions
712-362-7945 Fax: 712-362-8363
Website: www.iowalakes.edu
E-mail: info@iowalakes.edu

Northwest Iowa Community College
603 W Park St, Sheldon IA 51201-1046
Lisa Story, Director of Enrollment Management
712-324-5061 Fax: 712-324-4136
Website: www.nwicc.edu
E-mail: lstory@nwicc.edu

Wartburg College
PO Box 1003, Waverly IA 50677-0903
Brent Matthias, Interim Director of Admissions
319-352-8200 Fax: 319-352-8579
Website: www.wartburg.edu
E-mail: admissions@wartburg.edu

KANSAS

Allen County Community College
1801 N Cottonwood St, Iola KS 66749-1607
John Masterson, President
Randy Weber, Director of Admissions
620-365-5116 Fax: 620-365-3284
Website: www.allencc.net
E-mail: weber@allencc.edu

COLBY COMMUNITY COLLEGE
1255 S Range Ave, Colby KS 67701-4099
Director of Admissions
888-634-9350 or 785-460-4690 Fax: 785-460-4691
Website: www.colbycc.edu
E-mail: bobbi@colbycc.edu

Independence Community College
PO Box 708, Independence KS 67301-0708
Dr. Terry Hetrick, President
800-842-6063 Fax: 620-331-5344
Website: www.indycc.edu
E-mail: admissions@indycc.edu

KENTUCKY

Transylvania University
300 N Broadway, Lexington KY 40508-1776
859-233-8242 Fax: 859-233-8797
Website: www.transy.edu
E-mail: admissions@transy.edu

LOUISIANA

Dillard University
2601 Gentilly Blvd, New Orleans LA 70122-3097
Linda G. Nash, Director of Admissions
Website: www.dillard.edu
E-mail: admissions@dillard.edu

MAINE

Landing School of Boatbuilding & Design
PO Box 1490, Kennebunkport ME 04046-1490
Dennis Collins, Director of Admissions
207-985-7976 Fax: 207-985-7942
Website: www.landingschool.edu
E-mail: denniscollins@landingschool.edu

Southern Maine Community College
2 Fort Rd, South Portland ME 04106-1698
Dr. James Ortiz, President
Scott MacDonald, Director of Financial Aid
207-741-5500 Fax: 207-741-5671
Website: www.smccme.edu
E-mail: oharmon@maine.rr.com

MARYLAND

Hagerstown Community College
11400 Robinwood Dr, Hagerstown MD 21742-6590
Dr. Daniel E. Bock, Assistant Director of Admissions
301-790-2800 Fax: 301-791-9165
Website: www.hagerstowncc.edu
E-mail: bockd@hagerstowncc.edu

MASSACHUSETTS

Boston University
121 Bay State Rd, Boston MA 02215
Kelly Walter, Executive Director of Admissions
617-353-2300 Fax: 617-353-9695
Website: web.bu.edu
E-mail: admissions@bu.edu

Massachusetts Institute of Technology
77 Massachusetts Ave, Cambridge MA 02139-4307
Marilee Jones, Dean of Admission
617-253-1000 Fax: 617-253-4016
Website: my.mit.edu
E-mail: admissions@mit.edu

NORTHERN ESSEX COMMUNITY COLLEGE
100 Elliott St, Haverhill MA 01830
Nora B. Sheridan, Director of Admission
978-556-3700
Website: www.NECC.Mass.edu
E-mail: nsheridan@necc.mass.edu

Smith College
Northampton MA 01063-0001
Debra Shaver, Director of Admissions
800-383-3232 Fax: 413-585-2527
Website: www.smith.edu
E-mail: admission@smith.edu

University of Massachusetts Dartmouth
Old Westport Rd, North Dartmouth MA 02747-2300
Steven T. Briggs, Director of Admissions
508-999-8605 Fax: 508-999-8755
Website: explore.umassd.edu
E-mail: sbriggs@umassd.edu

Wentworth Institute of Technology
550 Huntington Ave, Boston MA 02115-5998
David C. Planchard, Director of Admissions
617-442-9010
Website: www.wit.edu/apply
E-mail: planchardd@wit.edu

Worcester Polytechnic Institute
100 Institute Rd, Worcester MA 01609-2280
Edward J. Connor, Director of Admissions
508-831-5286 Fax: 508-831-5875
Website: admissions.wpi.edu
E-mail: admissions@wpi.edu

MICHIGAN

Andrews University
Berrien Springs MI 49104-0001
Randall Graves, Director of Recruitment Services
800-253-2874 Fax: 269-471-2670
Website: www.connect.andrews.edu
E-mail: gravesr@andrews.edu

Delta College
University Center MI 48710-0001
Duff Zube, Director of Admissions
989-686-9093 Fax: 989-667-2202
Website: www.delta.edu
E-mail: admit@delta.edu

Grand Valley State University
1 Campus Dr, Allendale MI 49401-9403
Jodi Chycinski, Director of Admissions
616-331-6611 Fax: 616-331-2000
Website: www.gvsu.edu
E-mail: go2gvsu@gvsu.edu

Lawrence Technological University
21000 W 10 Mile Rd, Southfield MI 48075-1058
Jane Rohrback, Director of Admissions
800-225-5588 Fax: 248-204-2228
Website: www.ltu.edu
E-mail: admissions@ltu.edu
See listing under "Universities"

MACOMB COMMUNITY COLLEGE

44575 Garfield Rd, Clinton Township MI 48038-1139
Information Center
586-445-7999
Website: www.macomb.edu
E-mail: answer@macomb.edu

MACOMB COMMUNITY COLLEGE

14500 E 12 Mile Rd, Warren MI 48088-3896
Information Center
586-445-7999
Website: www.macomb.edu
E-mail: answer@macomb.edu

Northwestern Michigan College
1701 E Front St, Traverse City MI 49686-3061
Jim Bensley, Admissions Coordinator
800-748-0566 Fax: 231-995-1339
Website: www.nmc.edu
E-mail: jbensley@nmc.edu

Oakland Community College
2480 Opdyke Rd, Bloomfield Hills MI 48304
Dr. Maurice McCall, Director of Admissions
248-341-2000
Website: www.oaklandcc.edu
E-mail: mhmcall@oaklandcc.edu

Oakland University
2200 N Squirrel Rd, Rochester MI 48309
Eleanor L. Reynolds, Assistant Vice President &
Director of Admissions
248-370-2100
Website: www.oakland.edu
E-mail: ouinfo@oakland.edu

University of Michigan-Dearborn
4901 Evergreen Rd, Dearborn MI 48128-1491
The Office of Admissions & Orientation
313-593-5100 Fax: 313-436-9167
Website: www.umd.umich.edu
E-mail: admissions@umd.umich.edu

MINNESOTA

Bethany Lutheran College
700 Luther Dr, Mankato MN 56001
Don Westphal, Dean of Admissions
507-344-7000 Fax: 507-344-7376
Website: www.blc.edu
E-mail: admiss@blc.edu

Dunwoody College of Technology
818 Dunwoody Blvd, Minneapolis MN 55403-1192
John Slama, Vice President Enrollment Management
800-292-4625 or 612-374-5800 Fax: 612-374-4128
Website: www.dunwoody.edu
E-mail: jslama@dunwoody.edu
See listing under "Career Schools"

Hibbing Community College
1515 E 25th St, Hibbing MN 55746-3300
Holly Bigelow, Director of Enrollment
800-224-4HCC or 218-262-7200 Fax: 218-262-6717
Website: www.hibbing.edu
E-mail: admissions@hibbing.edu

MISSOURI

East Central College
1964 Prairie Dell Rd, Union MO 63084
Karen Wieda, Registrar
636-583-5195 ext. 2220 Fax: 636-583-1897
Website: www.eastcentral.edu
E-mail: wiedaks@eastcentral.edu

University of Missouri
1 University Blvd, Saint Louis MO 63121-4499
Dr. Bill Darby, Dean
314-516-6800 Fax: 314-516-6801
Website: www.umsl.edu
E-mail: admissions@umsl.edu

NEBRASKA

College of Saint Mary
7000 Mercy Rd, Omaha NE 68106
Lorin Werth, V.P. for Enrollment
800-926-5534 or 402-399-2407 Fax: 402-399-2412
Website: www.csm.edu
E-mail: lwerth@csm.edu

NEW JERSEY

Bergen Community College
400 Paramus Rd, Paramus NJ 07652
Julian Gomez, Asst. Director of Admissions
201-447-7100 Fax: 201-444-7036
Website: www.bergen.edu
E-mail: jgomez@bergen.edu

NEW MEXICO

New Mexico Military Institute
101 W College Blvd, Roswell NM 88201-5173
LTC. Craig Collins, Director of Admissions
800-421-5376 or 505-624-8050 Fax: 505-624-8058
Website: www.nmmi.edu
E-mail: admissions@nmmi.edu
See listing under "Community and Junior Colleges"

NEW YORK

Broome Community College
907 Upper Front St, Binghamton NY 13905
Anthony S. Fiorelli, Director of Admissions
607-778-5001 Fax: 607-778-5442
Website: www.sunybroome.edu
E-mail: fiorelli_a@sunybroome.edu

College of Saint Rose
432 Western Ave, Albany NY 12203-1419
Maryelizabeth Amico, Asst V.P. for Undergraduate
Admissions
518-454-5150 Fax: 518-454-2013
Website: www.strose.edu
E-mail: admit@strose.edu

Institute of Audio Research
64 University Pl, New York NY 10003-4595
Mark L. Kahn, Director of Admissions
800-544-2501 or 212-777-8550 (NY, NJ, CT)
Fax: 212-677-6549
Website: www.audioschool.com
E-mail: contact@audioschool.com
See listing under "Career Schools"

Roberts Wesleyan College
2301 Westside Dr, Rochester NY 14624-1997
Office of Admissions
585-594-6400 Fax: 585-594-6371
Website: www.roberts.edu
E-mail: admissions@roberts.edu

SUNY College of Technology
Alfred NY 14802
Deborah J. Goodrich, Director of Admissions
800-4AL-FRED Fax: 607-587-4299
Website: www.alfredstate.edu
E-mail: admissions@alfredstate.edu

SUNY College of Technology
2 Main St, Delhi NY 13753-1110
Robert W. Mazzei, Director of Admissions
800-96-DELHI Fax: 607-746-4104
Website: www.delhi.edu
E-mail: enroll@delhi.edu

SUNY Orange County Community College
115 South St, Middletown NY 10940-6437
Margot St. Lawrence, Director of Admissions
845-341-4030 Fax: 845-342-8662
Website: www.sunyorange.edu
E-mail: apply@sunyorange.edu
See listing under "Community and Junior Colleges"

United States Military Academy West Point
646 Swift Rd, West Point NY 10996-1905
Colonel Michael L. Jones, Director of Admissions
845-938-4041 Fax: 845-938-8121
Website: admissions.usma.edu
E-mail: admissions@usma.edu

VAUGHN COLLEGE OF AERONAUTICS AND TECHNOLOGY

8601 23rd Ave, Flushing NY 11369-1037
Vincent Papandrea, Director of Admissions
800-776-2376 Fax: 718-429-0671
Website: www.vaughn.edu
E-mail: admitme@vaughn.edu
Established 1932. Private. Coed. Accreditation: MSACS, ABET. Tuition: $13,400. Fees: $280. Enrollment: 842 full-time, 284 part-time. Faculty: 59. Student-faculty ratio: 11:1. Degrees: BS, AAS, AOS. Library: 62,000 vols. Offering bachelor and associate degrees in airport management, aviation maintenance, flight training, electronic technology, engineering, general management, mechatronic engineering, pre-engineering and computerized design/animated graphics. Hands-on training. Extensive career development services and financial aid available.

NORTH CAROLINA

Haywood Community College
185 Freedlander Dr, Clyde NC 28721
Debbie Rowland, Coordinator of Admissions
828-627-4500 Fax: 828-627-4513
Website: www.haywood.edu
E-mail: drowland@haywood.edu

Louisburg College
501 N Main St, Louisburg NC 27549-2399
800-775-0208 or 919-496-2521 Fax: 919-496-1788
Website: www.louisburg.edu
E-mail: admissions@louisburg.edu

Meredith College
3800 Hillsborough St, Raleigh NC 27607-5298
Heidi L. Fletcher, Director of Admissions
919-760-8581 Fax: 919-760-2348
Website: www.meredith.edu
E-mail: admissions@meredith.edu
See listing under "Women's Colleges"

North Carolina A&T State University
1601 E Market St, Greensboro NC 27411
Lee Young, AVC Enrollment
336-334-7500 Fax: 336-334-7478
Website: www.ncat.edu
E-mail: uadmit@ncat.edu

OHIO

Cleveland Institute of Electronics
1776 E 17th St, Cleveland OH 44114-3679
Scott Katzenmeyer, Director of Admissions
800-243-6446 Fax: 216-781-0331
Website: www.cie-wc.edu
E-mail: instruct@cie-wc.edu

Cleveland State University
2121 Euclid Ave RW 204, Cleveland OH 44115
Dr. Richard Arndt, Dean of Undergraduate Recruitment
and College Partnerships
888-CSU-OHIO Fax: 216-687-9210
Website: www.csuohio.edu
E-mail: admissions@csuohio.edu

ITT Technical Institute
3325 Stop 8 Rd, Dayton OH 45414-3425
Joe Graham, Director of Admissions
937-454-2267 Fax: 937-454-2278
Website: www.itt-tech.edu
E-mail: jgraham@itt-tech.edu

OHIO NORTHERN UNIVERSITY

525 S Main St, Ada OH 45810-1555
419-772-2371
Website: www.onu.edu
E-mail: admissions-ug@onu.edu
See listing under "Universities"

The Ohio State University
College of Engineering
Hitchcock Hall, 2070 Neil Ave, Columbus OH 43210
614-292-2651 Fax: 614-688-3805
Website: engineering.osu.edu
E-mail: engosu@osu.edu

OHIO WESLEYAN UNIVERSITY

61 S Sandusky St, Delaware OH 43015-2398
Director of Admission
740-368-3020 Fax: 740-368-3314
Website: www.owu.edu
E-mail: owuadmit@owu.edu

Sinclair Community College
444 W 3rd St, Dayton OH 45402-1460
Sara P. Smith, Director of Outreach Services
937-512-3000 Fax: 937-512-2393
Website: www.sinclair.edu
E-mail: admit@sinclair.edu

University of Dayton
300 College Park, Dayton OH 45469-1300
Robert F. Durkle, Director of Admissions
800-837-7433 Fax: 937-229-4729
Website: admission.udayton.edu
E-mail: admission@udayton.edu

OKLAHOMA

Oklahoma State University
Stillwater OK 74078
David Thompson, Assoc. Dean
405-744-5140
Website: www.okstate.edu
E-mail: david.r.thompson@okstate.edu

Oral Roberts University
7777 S Lewis Ave, Tulsa OK 74171-0001
Chris Belcher, Director of Undergraduate Admissions
800-678-8876 Fax: 918-495-6222
Website: www.oru.edu
E-mail: admissions@oru.edu

University of Tulsa
600 S College Ave, Tulsa OK 74104-3126
Earl Johnson, Dean of Admission
918-631-2307 Fax: 918-631-5003
Website: www.utulsa.edu
E-mail: admission@utulsa.edu

OREGON

Linn-Benton Community College
6500 Pacific Blvd SW, Albany OR 97321-3774
Christine Baker, Outreach Coordinator
541-917-4811 Fax: 541-917-4868
Website: www.linnbenton.edu
E-mail: admissions@linnbenton.edu

PENNSYLVANIA

Arcadia University
450 S Easton Rd, Glenside PA 19038-3295
Dennis Nostrand, VP for Enrollment Management
877-ARCADIA (877-272-2342) Fax: 215-881-8767
Website: www.arcadia.edu
E-mail: admiss@arcadia.edu
See listing under "Universities"

Gannon University
109 University Sq, Erie PA 16541-0001
Christopher Tremblay, Director of Admissions
800-GANNON-U Fax: 814-871-5803
Website: www.gannon.edu
E-mail: admissions@gannon.edu

Juniata College
1700 Moore St, Huntingdon PA 16652-2196
Michelle Bartol, Dean of Enrollment
877-JUNIATA Fax: 814-641-3100
Website: www.juniata.edu
E-mail: admissions@juniata.edu

La Roche College
9000 Babcock Blvd, Pittsburgh PA 15237-5898
Thomas Hassett, Director of Freshman and
International Admissions
412-536-1272 or 800-838-4LRC Fax: 412-536-1272
Website: www.laroche.edu
E-mail: admissions@laroche.edu

Lebanon Valley College
101 N College Ave, Annville PA 17003-1400
William Brown, Dean of Admissions & Financial Aid
866-LVC-4ADM or 717-867-6181 Fax: 717-867-6026
Website: www.lvc.edu
E-mail: admission@lvc.edu

Lincoln University
Lincoln University PA 19352
Michael C. Taylor, Director of Admissions
800-790-0191 Fax: 610-932-1209
Website: www.lincoln.edu
E-mail: mtaylor@lu.lincoln.edu

University of Pittsburgh
1150 Mount Pleasant Rd
Greensburg PA 15601-5860
Brandi S. Darr, Director of Admissions and Financial
Aid
724-836-9880 Fax: 724-836-7160
Website: www.upg.pitt.edu
E-mail: upgadmit@pitt.edu

Washington & Jefferson College
60 S Lincoln St, Washington PA 15301-4801
Alton E. Newell, Vice President for Enrollment
724-223-6025 Fax: 724-223-6534
Website: www.washjeff.edu
E-mail: admission@washjeff.edu

Westminster College
New Wilmington PA 16172-0001
Doug Swartz, Director of Admissions
724-946-7100 Fax: 724-946-6171
Website: www.westminster.edu
E-mail: swartzdl@westminster.edu

SOUTH CAROLINA

Bob Jones University
1700 Wade Hampton Blvd
Greenville SC 29614-0001
David Christ, Director of Admissions
800-BJ-AND-ME Fax: 800-2-FAX-BJU
Website: www.bju.edu
E-mail: admissions@bju.edu
See listing under "Universities"

PRESBYTERIAN COLLEGE
503 S Broad St, Clinton SC 29325
Richard Dana Paul, Dean of Admissions
800-476-7272 Fax: 864-833-8481
Website: www.presby.edu
E-mail: admissions@presby.edu

TENNESSEE

Lipscomb University
3901 Granny White Pike, Nashville TN 37204-3951
Ricky Holaway, Director of Admissions
800-333-4358 ext. 1776 Fax: 615-269-1804
Website: www.lipscomb.edu
E-mail: admissions@lipscomb.edu

University of Tennessee
615 McCallie Ave, Chattanooga TN 37403-2504
Yancy Freeman, Director of Admissions
423-425-4111 Fax: 423-425-4157
Website: www.utc.edu
E-mail: Yancy-Freeman@utc.edu

TEXAS

North Central Texas College
1525 W California St, Gainesville TX 76240-4636
Michelle Winters, Registrar
940-668-3315 Fax: 940-665-7075
Website: www.nctc.edu
E-mail: mwinters@nctc.edu

Tyler Junior College
PO Box 9020, Tyler TX 75711-9020
Richard Minter, Dean
800-687-5680
Website: www.tjc.edu
E-mail: rmin@tjc.edu
See listing under "Community and Junior Colleges"

University of Houston
122 E Cullen Bldg, Houston TX 77204-2023
Office of Admission
713-743-9595
Website: www.uh.edu
E-mail: admissions@uh.edu

University of Texas at Arlington
Box 19111, Arlington TX 76019-0111
Hans Gatterdam, Director of Admission
817-272-6287 Fax: 817-272-3435
Website: www.uta.edu
E-mail: admissions@uta.edu

VERMONT
NORWICH UNIVERSITY
158 Harmon Dr, Northfield VT 05663
Dr. Dennis Tyner, Division Head
800-468-6679 Fax: 802-485-2260
Website: www.norwich.edu
E-mail: dtyner@norwich.edu
See listing under "Universities"

WASHINGTON

Everett Community College
2000 Tower St, Everett WA 98201
Christine Kerlin, Associate Dean
425-388-9100 Fax: 425-388-9173
Website: www.everettcc.edu
E-mail: ckerlin@everettcc.edu

Gonzaga University
502 E Boone Ave, Spokane WA 99258-0102
Julie McCulloh, Dean of Admission
800-322-2584 or 509-323-6572 Fax: 509-323-5780
Website: www.gonzaga.edu
E-mail: mcculloh@gu.gonzaga.edu

Henry Cogswell College
3002 Colby Ave, Everett WA 98201-4012
Jane Buckman, Director of Admissions
866-411-4221 Fax: 425-257-0405
Website: www.henrycogswell.edu
E-mail: admissions@henrycogswell.edu

WEST VIRGINIA

West Virginia Wesleyan College
59 College Ave, Buckhannon WV 26201-2699
Robert N. Skinner II, Director of Admission
800-722-9933 Fax: 304-473-8108
Website: www.wvwc.edu
E-mail: admission@wvwc.edu

WISCONSIN

Blackhawk Technical College
PO Box 5009, Janesville WI 53547-5009
Gregg Bosak, Administration, Community Information
608-757-7769 Fax: 608-757-7740
Website: www.blackhawk.edu
E-mail: gbosak@blackhawk.edu

Marquette University
PO Box 1881, Milwaukee WI 53201-1881
Robert Blust, Director of Admissions
414-288-7302 Fax: 414-288-3764
Website: www.mu.edu
E-mail: admissions@marquette.edu

WYOMING

Laramie County Community College
1400 E College Dr, Cheyenne WY 82007-3204
Jenny Hargett, Director of Admissions
307-778-5222 Fax: 307-778-1350
Website: www.lccc.wy.edu
E-mail: learnmore@lccc.wy.edu

University of Wyoming
Admissions Office
Dept 3435, Laramie WY 82071-3435
Aaron Appelhans, Contact
800-342-5996 Fax: 307-766-4042
Website: www.uwyo.edu
E-mail: why-wyo@uwyo.edu

ENGINEERING TECHNOLOGY

ALABAMA

Alabama A & M University
PO Box 908, Normal AL 35762
Antonio Boyle, Director of Admissions
256-372-5245 Fax: 256-372-5249
Website: www.aamu.edu
E-mail: aboyle@aamu.edu

Herzing College
280 W Valley Ave, Homewood AL 35209-4816
Kim Conway, Director of Admissions
205-916-2800 Fax: 205-916-2807
Website: www.herzing.edu/birmingham
E-mail: info@bhm.herzing.edu

ALASKA

University of Alaska Anchorage
PO Box 141629, Anchorage AK 99514-1629
Cecile Mitchell, Director of Enrollment Services
907-786-1480 Fax: 907-786-4888
Website: www.uaa.alaska.edu/
E-mail: enroll@uaa.alaska.edu

ARIZONA

Pima Community College
4905 E Broadway Blvd, Tucson AZ 85709-1010
Wendy Kilgore, Ph.D., Director of Admissions
520-206-4500 Fax: 520-206-4790
Website: www.pima.edu
E-mail: infocenter@pima.edu

CALIFORNIA

California State University-San Bernadino
5500 University Pkwy
San Bernardino CA 92407-2393
Olivia Rosas, Director of Admissions
909-880-5000 Fax: 909-880-7034
Website: enrollment.csusb.edu
E-mail: orosas@csusb.edu

Chabot College
25555 Hesperian Blvd, Hayward CA 94545-2400
Judy Young, Director of Admissions
510-723-6600 Fax: 510-723-7510
Website: www.chabotcollege.edu
E-mail: ccarcom@clpccd.cc.ca.us

FRESNO CITY COLLEGE
1101 E University Ave, Fresno CA 93741-0002
Dayann Dietrich, Contact
559-442-8241 Fax: 559-237-4232
Website: www.fresnocitycollege.com
E-mail: fcc.admissions@scccd.com

HEALD COLLEGE, ROSEVILLE
7 Sierra Gate Plz, Roseville CA 95678-6602
Cindi Stevens, Director of Admissions
916-789-8600 Fax: 916-789-8616
Website: www.heald.edu
E-mail: cindi_stevens@heald.edu

ITT Technical Institute
12669 Encinitas Ave, Sylmar CA 91342-3664
Kelly Christensen, Director of Admissions
818-364-5151 Fax: 818-364-5150
Website: www.itt-tech.edu
E-mail: kchristensen@itt-tech.edu

CONNECTICUT

Middlesex Community College
100 Training Hill Rd, Middletown CT 06457-4889
Mensimah Shabazz, Director of Admissions
860-343-5800 Fax: 860-344-3055
Website: www.mxcc.commnet.edu
E-mail: mshabazz@mxcc.commnet.edu

University of New Haven
300 Boston Post Rd, West Haven CT 06516
Director of Undergraduate Admissions
203-932-7319 Fax: 203-931-6093
Website: www.newhaven.edu
E-mail: adminfo@newhaven.edu

FLORIDA

Remington College, Tampa Campus
2410 E Busch Blvd, Tampa FL 33612-8410
Director of Recruitment
813-935-5700 Fax: 813-935-7415
Website: www.remingtoncollege.edu

University of South Florida
4202 E Fowler Ave, Tampa FL 33620-6900
J. Robert Spatig, Director of Admissions
813-974-3350 Fax: 813-974-9689
Website: www.usf.edu
E-mail: admissions@admin.usf.edu

GEORGIA

DeKalb Technical College
495 N Indian Creek Dr, Clarkston GA 30021-2397
Terry Richardson, Director of Admissions
404-297-9522 Fax: 404-294-6496
Website: www.dekalbtech.edu
E-mail: richardt@dekalbtech.edu

HAWAII

Heald College, Honolulu
1500 Kapiolani Blvd, Honolulu HI 96814-3732
Lon K. Ibaraki, Director of Admissions
808-955-1500 or 800-940-0530 Fax: 808-955-6964
Website: www.heald.edu
E-mail: lon_ibaraki@heald.edu

IDAHO

Brigham Young University - Idaho
120 Kimball Bldg, Rexburg ID 83460
Gordon Westenskow, Director of Admissions
208-496-1020 Fax: 208-496-1220
Website: www.byui.edu
E-mail: admissions@byui.edu

ILLINOIS

Kaskaskia College
27210 College Rd, Centralia IL 62801-7878
Tyra Taylor, Dean of Enrollment Management and Retention Services
618-545-3000 Fax: 618-532-1990
Website: www.kaskaskia.edu
E-mail: ttaylor@kaskaskia.edu

MORRISON INSTITUTE OF TECHNOLOGY

701 Portland Ave, Morrison IL 61270-2959
Richard C. Parkinson, Interim Director
815-772-7584 Fax: 815-772-7218
Website: www.morrison.tec.il.us
E-mail: admissions@morrison.tec.il.us
    Private. Coed. Accreditation: ABET. Enrollment: 140. Student-faculty ratio: 13:1. Engineering Technology Associate of Applied Science degree in Architectural, Construction, Civil, Mechanical, Drafting & Design, and Surveying Technology. AAS degree in Systems & Network Administration.

Roosevelt University
430 S Michigan Ave, Chicago IL 60605
Gwen E. Kanelos, Asst. Vice President for Enrollment Services
877-APPLY-RU Fax: 312-341-4216
Website: www.roosevelt.edu
E-mail: applyru@roosevelt.edu

South Suburban College of Cook County
15800 State St, South Holland IL 60473
Jane Ellen Stocker, Dean of Enrollment Services
708-596-2000 Fax: 708-225-5806
Website: www.southsuburbancollege.edu
E-mail: jstocker@southsuburbancollege.edu

Triton College
2000 5th Ave, River Grove IL 60171-1995
Mary-Rita Moore, Dean of Enrollment Services
708-456-0300 ext. 3130 Fax: 708-583-3147
Website: www.triton.edu
E-mail: triton@triton.edu
See listing under "Community and Junior Colleges"

INDIANA

Ivy Tech Community College - North Central
220 Dean Johnson Blvd, South Bend IN 46601-3415
Pam Decker, Director of Admissions
574-289-7001 Fax: 574-236-7177
Website: www.ivytech.edu
E-mail: pdecker@ivytech.edu

IOWA

Hamilton Technical College
1011 E 53rd St, Davenport IA 52807-2653
Mark Christy, Director
563-386-3570 Fax: 563-386-6756
Website: www.hamiltontechcollege.com
E-mail: mchristy@hamiltontechcollege.com
See listing under "Career Schools"

Northwest Iowa Community College
603 W Park St, Sheldon IA 51201-1046
Lisa Story, Director of Enrollment Management
712-324-5061 Fax: 712-324-4136
Website: www.nwicc.edu
E-mail: lstory@nwicc.edu

KANSAS

Allen County Community College
1801 N Cottonwood St, Iola KS 66749-1607
John Masterson, President
Randy Weber, Director of Admissions
620-365-5116 Fax: 620-365-3284
Website: www.allencc.net
E-mail: weber@allencc.edu

AIB International
1213 Bakers Way, Manhattan KS 66502-4576
Ken Embers, Admissions
800-633-5137 or 785-537-4750 Fax: 785-537-1493
Website: www.aibonline.org
E-mail: kembers@aibonline.org
See listing under "Career Schools"

KENTUCKY

Bluegrass Community and Technical College
Oswald Building
470 Cooper Drive, Lexington KY 40506-0235
Shelbie Hugle, Director of Admissions
859-246-6200 Fax: 859-246-4664
Website: www.bluegrass.kctcs.edu
E-mail: bctc_info@kctcs.edu

Morehead State University
Morehead KY 40351-1689
Dayna Seelig, Enrollment Services
800-585-6781 Fax: 606-783-5038
Website: www.moreheadstate.edu
E-mail: admissions@moreheadstate.edu

Spencerian College
1575 Winchester Rd, Lexington KY 40505
Victor Lamoin Adcock II, Director of Admissions
800-456-3253

MAINE

Northern Maine Community College
33 Edgemont Dr, Presque Isle ME 04769-2016
Bill Casavant, Director of Admissions
207-768-2700 Fax: 207-768-2831
Website: www.nmcc.edu
E-mail: admissions@nmcc.edu

Southern Maine Community College
2 Fort Rd, South Portland ME 04106-1698
Dr. James Ortiz, President
Scott MacDonald, Director of Financial Aid
207-741-5500 Fax: 207-741-5671
Website: www.smccme.edu
E-mail: oharmon@maine.rr.com

MARYLAND

Hagerstown Community College
11400 Robinwood Dr, Hagerstown MD 21742-6590
Dr. Daniel E. Bock, Assistant Director of Admissions
301-790-2800 Fax: 301-791-9165
Website: www.hagerstowncc.edu
E-mail: bockd@hagerstowncc.edu

MASSACHUSETTS

Benjamin Franklin Institute of Technology
41 Berkeley St, Boston MA 02116-6307
Norman Kraft, Dean of Enrollment
617-423-4630 ext. 121 Fax: 617-482-3706
Website: www.bfit.edu
E-mail: admissions@bfit.edu

Bristol Community College
777 Elsbree St, Fall River MA 02720-7395
Rodney S. Clark, Director of Admissions
508-678-2811 ext. 2516, 2179 Fax: 508-730-3265
Website: www.bristol.mass.edu
E-mail: admissions@bristol.mass.edu

ITT TECHNICAL INSTITUTE

333 Boston Providence Tpke
Norwood MA 02062-3932
Tom Ryan, Director of Recruiting
800-879-TECH (8324) Fax: 781-278-0766
Website: www.itt-tech.edu
E-mail: tryan@itt-tech.edu
    Established 1990. Private. Coed. Accreditation: ACICS. Enrollment: 300. Student-faculty ratio: 11:1. Associate Degrees offered: Computer Drafting & Design, Computer Electronics Technology, Computer Network Systems, Multimedia.

Massachusetts Institute of Technology
77 Massachusetts Ave, Cambridge MA 02139-4307
Marilee Jones, Dean of Admission
617-253-1000 Fax: 617-253-4016
Website: my.mit.edu
E-mail: admissions@mit.edu

Wentworth Institute of Technology
550 Huntington Ave, Boston MA 02115-5998
David C. Planchard, Director of Admissions
617-442-9010
Website: www.wit.edu/apply
E-mail: planchardd@wit.edu

MICHIGAN

Andrews University
Berrien Springs MI 49104-0001
Randall Graves, Director of Recruitment Services
800-253-2874 Fax: 269-471-2670
Website: www.connect.andrews.edu
E-mail: gravesr@andrews.edu

Delta College
University Center MI 48710-0001
Duff Zube, Director of Admissions
989-686-9093 Fax: 989-667-2202
Website: www.delta.edu
E-mail: admit@delta.edu

ITT TECHNICAL INSTITUTE

4020 Sparks Dr SE, Grand Rapids MI 49546-6192
Dennis Hormel, Director
616-956-1060 Fax: 616-956-5606
Website: www.itt-tech.edu
E-mail: dhormel@itt-tech.edu

Lawrence Technological University
21000 W 10 Mile Rd, Southfield MI 48075-1058
Jane Rohrback, Director of Admissions
800-225-5588 Fax: 248-204-2228
Website: www.ltu.edu
E-mail: admissions@ltu.edu
See listing under "Universities"

MACOMB COMMUNITY COLLEGE

14500 E 12 Mile Rd, Warren MI 48088-3896
Information Center
586-445-7999
Website: www.macomb.edu
E-mail: answer@macomb.edu

Oakland Community College
2480 Opdyke Rd, Bloomfield Hills MI 48304
Dr. Maurice McCall, Director of Admissions
248-341-2000
Website: www.oaklandcc.edu
E-mail: mhmcall@oaklandcc.edu

MINNESOTA

Dunwoody College of Technology
818 Dunwoody Blvd, Minneapolis MN 55403-1192
John Slama, Vice President Enrollment Management
800-292-4625 or 612-374-5800 Fax: 612-374-4128
Website: www.dunwoody.edu
E-mail: jslama@dunwoody.edu
See listing under "Career Schools"

McNally Smith College of Music
19 Exchange St East, St. Paul MN 55101
Debbie Sandridge, Director of Admissions
800-594-9500 Fax: 651-291-0366
Website: www.mcnallysmith.edu
E-mail: dsandridge@mcnallysmith.edu
See listing under "Universities"

Minnesota State College - Southeast Technical
308 Pioneer Rd, Red Wing MN 55066-3964
Al Ducett, Director of Admissions
800-657-4849 Fax: 507-453-2715
Website: www.southeastmn.edu
E-mail: aducett@southeastmn.edu

Ridgewater College-Willmar Campus
PO Box 1097, Willmar MN 56201-1097
Sally Kerfeld, Director of Admissions
800-722-1151 Fax: 320-231-7677
Website: www.ridgewater.edu
E-mail: skerfeld@ridgewater.edu

St. Cloud Technical College
1540 Northway Dr, Saint Cloud MN 56303-1240
Jodi Elness, Director of Enrollment Management
800-222-1009 Fax: 320-308-5981
Website: www.sctc.edu
E-mail: jelness@sctc.edu

MISSOURI

East Central College
1964 Prairie Dell Rd, Union MO 63084
Karen Wieda, Registrar
636-583-5195 ext. 2220 Fax: 636-583-1897
Website: www.eastcentral.edu
E-mail: wiedaks@eastcentral.edu

Vatterott College
3925 Industrial Dr, Saint Ann MO 63074-1807
Jennifer Commuso, Director of Admissions
800-345-6018 Fax: 314-428-5956
Website: www.vatterott-college.edu
E-mail: jennifer.commuso@vatterott-college.edu

NEVADA

Career College of Northern Nevada
1195-A Corporate Blvd, Reno NV 89502-2331
Nathan Clark, Director
775-856-2266 Fax: 775-856-0935
Website: www.ccnn.edu
E-mail: lgoldhammer@ccnn4u.com
See listing under "Career Schools"

NEW JERSEY

Bergen Community College
400 Paramus Rd, Paramus NJ 07652
Julian Gomez, Asst. Director of Admissions
201-447-7100 Fax: 201-444-7036
Website: www.bergen.edu
E-mail: jgomez@bergen.edu

Hohokus School - RETS Nutley
103 Park Ave, Nutley NJ 07110-3505
Thomas Eastwick, President
973-661-0600 Fax: 973-661-2954
Website: www.rets-institute.com
E-mail: admissions@rets-institute.com

Mercer County Community College
West Windsor Campus
PO Box B, Trenton NJ 08690
Savita Bambhrolia, Director of Admissions
609-586-4800 Fax: 609-587-4666
Website: www.mccc.edu
E-mail: admiss@mccc.edu

NEW MEXICO

New Mexico State University
1500 N 3rd St, Grants NM 87020-2025
505-287-7981 Fax: 505-287-2329
Website: www.grants.nmsu.edu

NEW YORK

Broome Community College
907 Upper Front St, Binghamton NY 13905
Anthony S. Fiorelli, Director of Admissions
607-778-5001 Fax: 607-778-5442
Website: www.sunybroome.edu
E-mail: fiorelli_a@sunybroome.edu

Institute of Audio Research
64 University Pl, New York NY 10003-4595
Mark L. Kahn, Director of Admissions
800-544-2501 or 212-777-8550 (NY, NJ, CT)
Fax: 212-677-6549
Website: www.audioschool.com
E-mail: contact@audioschool.com
See listing under "Career Schools"

ISLAND DRAFTING & TECHNICAL INSTITUTE

128 Broadway (Route 110), Amityville NY 11701-2704
James G. DiLiberto, President
631-691-8733 Fax: 631-691-8738
Website: www.idti.edu
E-mail: info@idti.edu

SUNY College of Technology
Alfred NY 14802
Deborah J. Goodrich, Director of Admissions
800-4AL-FRED Fax: 607-587-4299
Website: www.alfredstate.edu
E-mail: admissions@alfredstate.edu

SUNY College of Technology
2 Main St, Delhi NY 13753-1110
Robert W. Mazzei, Director of Admissions
800-96-DELHI Fax: 607-746-4104
Website: www.delhi.edu
E-mail: enroll@delhi.edu

SUNY Orange County Community College
115 South St, Middletown NY 10940-6437
Margot St. Lawrence, Director of Admissions
845-341-4030 Fax: 845-342-8662
Website: www.sunyorange.edu
E-mail: apply@sunyorange.edu
See listing under "Community and Junior Colleges"

VAUGHN COLLEGE OF AERONAUTICS AND TECHNOLOGY

8601 23rd Ave, Flushing NY 11369-1037
Vincent Papandrea, Director of Admissions
800-776-2376 Fax: 718-429-0671
Website: www.vaughn.edu
E-mail: admitme@vaughn.edu
    Established 1932. Private. Coed. Accreditation: MSACS, ABET. Tuition: $13,400. Fees: $280. Enrollment: 842 full-time, 284 part-time. Faculty: 59. Student-faculty ratio: 11:1. Degrees: BS, AAS, AOS. Library: 62,000 vols.

Offering bachelor and associate degrees in airport management, aviation maintenance, flight training, electronic technology, engineering, general management, mechatronic engineering, pre-engineering and computerized design/animated graphics. Hands-on training. Extensive career development services and financial aid available.

NORTH CAROLINA

· Haywood Community College
185 Freedlander Dr, Clyde NC 28721
Debbie Rowland, Coordinator of Admissions
828-627-4500 Fax: 828-627-4513
Website: www.haywood.edu
E-mail: drowland@haywood.edu

North Carolina A&T State University
1601 E Market St, Greensboro NC 27411
Lee Young, AVC Enrollment
336-334-7500 Fax: 336-334-7478
Website: www.ncat.edu
E-mail: uadmit@ncat.edu

· South Piedmont Community College
PO Box 126, Polkton NC 28135-0126
John Curtis, Contact
704-272-5324 Fax: 704-272-8904
Website: www.spcc.edu
E-mail: jcurtis@spcc.edu

OHIO

· Bryant & Stratton College
1700 E 13th St, Cleveland OH 44114-3238
Shawn T. Kampa, Market Director of Admissions
216-771-1700 Fax: 216-771-7787
Website: www.bryantstratton.edu
E-mail: stkampa@bryantstratton.edu

· Cleveland Institute of Electronics
1776 E 17th St, Cleveland OH 44114-3679
Scott Katzenmeyer, Director of Admissions
800-243-6446 Fax: 216-781-0331
Website: www.cie-wc.edu
E-mail: instruct@cie-wc.edu

Cleveland State University
2121 Euclid Ave RW 204, Cleveland OH 44115
Dr. Richard Arndt, Dean of Undergraduate Recruitment and College Partnerships
888-CSU-OHIO Fax: 216-687-9210
Website: www.csuohio.edu
E-mail: admissions@csuohio.edu

· ITT Technical Institute
3325 Stop 8 Rd, Dayton OH 45414-3425
Joe Graham, Director of Admissions
937-454-2267 Fax: 937-454-2278
Website: www.itt-tech.edu
E-mail: jgraham@itt-tech.edu

· Northwest State Community College
22600 State Route 34, Archbold OH 43502-9542
Mark Thompson, Director of Admissions
419-267-5511 Fax: 419-267-5587
Website: www.northweststate.edu
E-mail: mthompson@northweststate.edu

OHIO NORTHERN UNIVERSITY
525 S Main St, Ada OH 45810-1555
Dave Rouch, Chair of Technology Dept.
419-772-2168
Website: www.onu.edu
E-mail: admissions-ug@onu.edu
See listing under "Universities"

· Owens Community College
300 Davis St, Findlay OH 45840-3631
William J. Ivoska PhD., Vice President of Student Services
567-429-3500 Fax: 567-423-0246
Website: www.owens.edu
E-mail: admissions@owens.edu

· Owens Community College
PO Box 10000, Toledo OH 43699-1947
William J. Ivoska, Ph.D, Vice President of Student Services
567-661-7000 Fax: 567-661-7607
Website: www.owens.edu
E-mail: admissions@owens.edu

· Sinclair Community College
444 W 3rd St, Dayton OH 45402-1460
Sara P. Smith, Director of Outreach Services
937-512-3000 Fax: 937-512-2393
Website: www.sinclair.edu
E-mail: admit@sinclair.edu

University of Dayton
300 College Park, Dayton OH 45469-1300
Robert F. Durkle, Director of Admissions
800-837-7433 Fax: 937-229-4729
Website: admission.udayton.edu
E-mail: admission@udayton.edu

OKLAHOMA

Oklahoma State University
Stillwater OK 74078
James Bose, Director
405-744-5638
Website: www.okstate.edu
E-mail: jim.bose@master.ceat.okstate.edu

OREGON

· Linn-Benton Community College
6500 Pacific Blvd SW, Albany OR 97321-3774
Christine Baker, Outreach Coordinator
541-917-4811 Fax: 541-917-4868
Website: www.linnbenton.edu
E-mail: admissions@linnbenton.edu

Rogue Community College
3345 Redwood Hwy, Grants Pass OR 97527-9298
Claudia Sullivan, Director of Enrollment Services
541-956-7500 Fax: 541-471-3585
Website: www.roguecc.edu
E-mail: csullivan@roguecc.edu
See listing under "Community and Junior Colleges"

PENNSYLVANIA

· Johnson College
3427 N Main Ave, Scranton PA 18508-1495
Dr. Ann L. Pipinski, President & CEO
Melissa Ide, Director of Enrollment Management
800-2WE-WORK or 570-342-6404 ext. 125
Fax: 570-348-2181
Website: www.johnson.edu
E-mail: admit@johnson.edu

La Roche College
9000 Babcock Blvd, Pittsburgh PA 15237-5898
Thomas Hassett, Director of Freshman and International Admissions
412-536-1272 or 800-838-4LRC Fax: 412-536-1272
Website: www.laroche.edu
E-mail: admissions@laroche.edu

· Pennsylvania Institute of Technology
800 Manchester Ave, Media PA 19063-4036
Angela Cassetta, Dean of Enrollment Management
800-422-0025 or 610-892-1500 Fax: 610-892-1510
Website: www.pit.edu
E-mail: info@pit.edu
See listing under "Community and Junior Colleges"

· PIA School of Specialized Technology
PO Box 10897, Pittsburgh PA 15236-0897
Vincent J. Mezza, Director of Admissions
800-444-1440 Fax: 412-466-0513
Website: www.pia.edu
E-mail: admissions@pia.edu
See listing under "Aeronautics, Aviation and Space"

· York Technical Institute
1405 Williams Rd, York PA 17402
Cathi Killingsworth Bost, Vice President
800-227-9675 or 717-757-1100 Fax: 717-757-4964
Website: www.yti.edu
E-mail: info@yti.edu
See listing under "Career Schools"

RHODE ISLAND

New England Institute of Technology
2500 Post Rd, Warwick RI 02886-2244
Michael Kwiatkowski, Director of Admissions
401-739-5000 Fax: 401-738-5122
Website: www.neit.edu
E-mail: eflynn@neit.edu

SOUTH CAROLINA

· Greenville Technical College
PO Box 5616, Greenville SC 29606-5616
Martha White, Director of Admissions
800-723-0673 (US) or 800-922-1183 (SC)
Website: www.greenvilletech.com

· Spartanburg Technical College
PO Box 4386, Spartanburg SC 29305-4386
Nancy Garmroth, Dean of Admissions & Financial Aid
864-592-4810 Fax: 864-592-4945
Website: stcsc.edu

TENNESSEE

ITT TECHNICAL INSTITUTE
2845 Elm Hill Pike, Nashville TN 37214-3717
James Royster, Director of Recruitment
615-889-8700 Fax: 615-872-7209
Website: www.itt-tech.edu
E-mail: jroyster@itt-tech.edu

· Pellissippi State Technical Community College
PO Box 22990, Knoxville TN 37933-0990
Donna Mack, Contact
865-694-6568 Fax: 865-539-7217
Website: www.pstcc.edu
E-mail: dmack@pstcc.edu

Tennessee State University
3500 John A Merritt Blvd, Nashville TN 37209-1561
John Cade, Dean of Admissions & Records
615-963-5101 Fax: 615-963-2930
Website: www.tnstate.edu
E-mail: jcade@tnstate.edu

TEXAS

· Hallmark Institute of Technology - Technology Campus
10401 W IH 10, San Antonio TX 78230-1736
Joe Fisher, President
210-690-9000 Fax: 210-697-8225
Website: www.hallmarkinstitute.com
E-mail: sross@hallmarkinstitute.com
Electronics Engineering Technology, Business Office Administration, Computer Network Systems Technology, & Medical Assistant.

· ITT Technical Institute
551 Ryan Plaza Dr, Arlington TX 76011
817-794-5100 Fax: 817-275-8446
Website: www.itt-tech.edu

· ITT Technical Institute
15621 Blue Ash Dr Ste 160, Houston TX 77090-5819
281-873-0512 Fax: 281-873-0518
Website: www.itt-tech.edu

ITT TECHNICAL INSTITUTE
2950 S Gessner Rd Ste 100, Houston TX 77063-3751
Jennifer Gomez, Director of Recruitment
713-952-2294 Fax: 713-952-2393
Website: www.itt-tech.edu
E-mail: jgomez@itt-tech.edu

North Central Texas College
1525 W California St, Gainesville TX 76240-4636
Michelle Winters, Registrar
940-668-3315 Fax: 940-665-7075
Website: www.nctc.edu
E-mail: mwinters@nctc.edu

· Temple College
2600 S 1st St, Temple TX 76504-7435
Angela Balch, Director of Admissions & Records
254-298-8300 Fax: 254-298-8288
Website: www.templejc.edu
E-mail: ruth.bridges@templejc.edu

· Tyler Junior College
PO Box 9020, Tyler TX 75711-9020
Joan Jones, Interim Dean
800-687-5680
Website: www.tjc.edu
E-mail: jjon@tjc.edu
See listing under "Community and Junior Colleges"

University of Houston
122 E Cullen Bldg, Houston TX 77204-2023
Office of Admission
713-743-9595
Website: www.uh.edu
E-mail: admissions@uh.edu

Western Technical College
9451 Diana Dr, El Paso TX 79924-6936
Bill Terrell, Chief Administrative Officer
915-566-9621 Fax: 915-565-9903
Website: www.wtc-ep.edu
E-mail: bterrell@wtc-ep.edu

UTAH

ITT TECHNICAL INSTITUTE
920 Levoy Dr, Murray UT 84123-2500
Gary Wood, Director of Recruitment
801-263-3313 Fax: 801-263-3497
Website: www.itt-tech.edu
E-mail: gwood@itt-tech.edu

VIRGINIA

· Southside Virginia Community College
109 Campus Dr, Alberta VA 23821-2930
Ronald E. Mattox, Dean of Admissions
434-949-1014 Fax: 434-949-7863
Website: www.sv.vccs.edu
E-mail: ronald.mattox@sv.vccs.edu

· Southside Virginia Community College
200 Daniel Rd, Keysville VA 23947
Ronald E. Mattox, Dean of Admissions
434-736-2018 Fax: 434-736-2082
Website: www.sv.vccs.edu
E-mail: ronald.mattox@sv.vccs.edu

WASHINGTON

BATES TECHNICAL COLLEGE
1101 S Yakima Ave, Tacoma WA 98405-4895
David Borofsky, President
253-680-7000 Fax: 253-680-7101
Website: www.bates.ctc.edu
E-mail: info@bates.ctc.edu

· Clover Park Technical College
4500 Steilacoom Blvd SW
Lakewood WA 98499-4098
Dr. Sharon McGavick, President
253-589-5678 Fax: 253-589-5601
Website: www.cptc.edu
E-mail: jim.griffith@cptc.edu

Everett Community College
2000 Tower St, Everett WA 98201
Christine Kerlin, Associate Dean
425-388-9100 Fax: 425-388-9173
Website: www.everettcc.edu
E-mail: ckerlin@everettcc.edu

Gonzaga University
502 E Boone Ave, Spokane WA 99258-0102
Julie McCulloh, Dean of Admission
800-322-2584 or 509-323-6572 Fax: 509-323-5780
Website: www.gonzaga.edu
E-mail: mcculloh@gu.gonzaga.edu

Perry Technical Institute
2011 W Washington Ave, Yakima WA 98903-1296
509-453-0374 Fax: 509-453-0375
Website: www.perrytech.edu
E-mail: frankj@perrytech.edu

Walla Walla Community College
500 Tausick Way, Walla Walla WA 99362-9270
Greg Farrens, Director
509-527-4684 or 877-992-9922 Fax: 509-527-4480
Website: www.wwcc.edu
E-mail: greg.farrens@wwcc.edu
See listing under "Community and Junior Colleges"

WEST VIRGINIA

Fairmont State University
1201 Locust Ave, Fairmont WV 26554-2470
Steve Leadman, Director of Admissions
304-367-4156 or 800-641-5678 Fax: 304-367-4789
Website: www.fairmontstate.edu
E-mail: admit@fairmontstate.edu

Mountain State University
Box 9003, Beckley WV 25802-9003
866-FOR-MSU1 or 304-929-INFO Fax: 304-253-5072
Website: www.mountainstate.edu
E-mail: gomsu@mountainstate.edu
See listing under "Universities"

WISCONSIN

Herzing College
5218 E Terrace Dr, Madison WI 53718-8340
Donald Madelung, President
800-582-1227 Fax: 608-249-8593
Website: www.herzing.edu
E-mail: info@msn.herzing.edu
See listing under "Universities"

WYOMING

Laramie County Community College
1400 E College Dr, Cheyenne WY 82007-3204
Jenny Hargett, Director of Admissions
307-778-5222 Fax: 307-778-1350
Website: www.lccc.wy.edu
E-mail: learnmore@lccc.wy.edu

University of Wyoming
Admissions Office
Dept 3435, Laramie WY 82071-3435
Aaron Appelhans, Contact
800-342-5996 Fax: 307-766-4042
Website: www.uwyo.edu
E-mail: why-wyo@uwyo.edu

GUAM

Guam Community College
PO Box 23069, G.M.F. GU 96921-0307
Virginia Charfauros Tudela, Ph.D., Registrar
671-735-5531 Fax: 671-734-5238
Website: www.guamcc.edu
E-mail: Webmaster@guamcc.edu

PUERTO RICO

Instituto de Banca y Comercio
61 Ponce De Leon Ave, Hato Rey PR 00919
Rafael Jimenez, Vice President
787-754-7120 Fax: 787-754-7143
Website: www.ibanca.net
E-mail: rjimenez@ibancapr.com

ETHNIC STUDIES

ALASKA

University of Alaska Anchorage
PO Box 141629, Anchorage AK 99514-1629
Cecile Mitchell, Director of Enrollment Services
907-786-1480 Fax: 907-786-4888
Website: www.uaa.alaska.edu/
E-mail: enroll@uaa.alaska.edu

CALIFORNIA

California State University-San Bernadino
5500 University Pkwy
San Bernardino CA 92407-2393
Olivia Rosas, Director of Admissions
909-880-5000 Fax: 909-880-7034
Website: enrollment.csusb.edu
E-mail: orosas@csusb.edu

FLORIDA

University of South Florida
4202 E Fowler Ave, Tampa FL 33620-6900
J. Robert Spatig, Director of Admissions
813-974-3350 Fax: 813-974-9689
Website: www.usf.edu
E-mail: admissions@admin.usf.edu

GEORGIA

Kennesaw State University
1000 Chastain Rd NW Box 115
Kennesaw GA 30144-5591
Website: www.kennesaw.edu

ILLINOIS

Columbia College Chicago
600 S Michigan Ave, Chicago IL 60605-1996
Murphy Monroe, Executive Director of Admissions
312-344-7130 Fax: 312-344-8024
Website: www.colum.edu
E-mail: admissions@colum.edu

Roosevelt University
430 S Michigan Ave, Chicago IL 60605
Gwen E. Kanelos, Asst. Vice President for Enrollment Services
877-APPLY-RU Fax: 312-341-4216
Website: www.roosevelt.edu
E-mail: applyru@roosevelt.edu

MASSACHUSETTS

Smith College
Northampton MA 01063-0001
Debra Shaver, Director of Admissions
800-383-3232 Fax: 413-585-2527
Website: www.smith.edu
E-mail: admission@smith.edu

MICHIGAN

University of Michigan-Dearborn
4901 Evergreen Rd, Dearborn MI 48128-1491
The Office of Admissions & Orientation
313-593-5100 Fax: 313-436-9167
Website: www.umd.umich.edu
E-mail: admissions@umd.umich.edu

MINNESOTA

Carleton College
1 N College St, Northfield MN 55057-4044
800-995-2275 or 507-646-4190 Fax: 507-646-4526
Website: www.carleton.edu
E-mail: admissions@acs.carleton.edu

MISSISSIPPI

Tougaloo College
500 W County Line Rd, Tougaloo MS 39174-9799
Juno Leggette Jacobs, Director of Admissions
601-977-7768 Fax: 601-977-4501
Website: www.tougaloo.edu
E-mail: jjacobs@tougaloo.edu

NEW JERSEY

New Jersey City University
2039 John F Kennedy Blvd
Jersey City NJ 07305-1588
Carmen Panlilio, Asst. V.P. for Admissions and Financial Aid
201-200-3234 Fax: 201-200-2044
Website: www.njcu.edu
E-mail: admissions@njcu.edu

NEW MEXICO

Institute of American Indian Arts
83 A Van Nu Po, Santa Fe NM 87508-1300
Myra Garro, Manager of Enrollment & Admissions
505-424-2328 Fax: 505-424-4500
Website: www.iaia.edu
E-mail: recruitment@iaia.edu

NEW YORK

College of Saint Rose
432 Western Ave, Albany NY 12203-1419
Maryelizabeth Amico, Asst V.P. for Undergraduate Admissions
518-454-5150 Fax: 518-454-2013
Website: www.strose.edu
E-mail: admit@strose.edu

CUNY Hunter College
695 Park Ave, New York NY 10021
Aaron Gibbs, Assistant Director of Recruitment
212-772-4497 Fax: 212-650-3336
Website: www.hunter.cuny.edu
E-mail: aaron.gibbs@hunter.cuny.edu

TEXAS

University of Houston
122 E Cullen Bldg, Houston TX 77204-2023
Office of Admission
713-743-9595
Website: www.uh.edu
E-mail: admissions@uh.edu

WEST VIRGINIA

Concord University
Athens WV 24712
Michael Curry, Vice President of Financial Aid & Admissions
888-384-5249 Fax: 304-384-3218
Website: www.concord.edu
E-mail: admissions@concord.edu

WYOMING

University of Wyoming
Admissions Office
Dept 3435, Laramie WY 82071-3435
Aaron Appelhans, Contact
800-342-5996 Fax: 307-766-4042
Website: www.uwyo.edu
E-mail: why-wyo@uwyo.edu

GUAM

University of Guam
UOG Station, Mangilao GU 96923
Deborah Leon Guerrero, Registrar
671-735-2201 or 671-735-2208 Fax: 671-735-2203
Website: www.uog.edu
E-mail: admitme@uog9.uog.edu

FASHION ART

CALIFORNIA

California College of the Arts
1111 Eighth St, San Francisco CA 94107
Robynne Royster, Director of Admission
800-447-1-ART or 415-703-9523 Fax: 415-703-9539
Website: www.cca.edu
E-mail: enroll@cca.edu

FASHION CAREERS COLLEGE
1923 Morena Blvd, San Diego CA 92110-3555
Tanya McAnear, Director of Admissions
619-275-4700 Fax: 619-275-0635
Website: www.fashioncareerscollege.com
E-mail: info@fashioncareerscollege.com
Established 1979. Private. Coed. Accreditation: ACICS. Tuition: $15,900 per year for Fashion Business & Technology. $15,900 per year for Fashion Design & Technology program, day or evening program (tuition includes required books & certain supplies). Registration Fee: $25. Enrollment: 120 full-time. Faculty: 15. Student-faculty ratio: 10:1. Degree & Certificate programs. Library: 850 volumes. Theoretical and practical training gives students a relevant and comprehensive education in Fashion Business & Technology and Fashion Design & Technology. Placement assistance and internships available.

FIDM/The Fashion Institute of Design & Merchandising
17590 Gillette Ave, Irvine CA 92614
Director of Admissions
949-851-6200 or 888-974-3436 Fax: 949-851-6808
Website: www.fidm.edu
E-mail: info@fidm.com
See listing under "Community and Junior Colleges"

FIDM/THE FASHION INSTITUTE OF DESIGN & MERCHANDISING
919 S Grand Ave, Los Angeles CA 90015-1421
Director of Admissions
213-624-1201 or 800-624-1200 Fax: 213-624-4799
Website: www.fidm.edu
E-mail: info@fidm.com
See listing under "Community and Junior Colleges"

FIDM/The Fashion Institute of Design & Merchandising
1010 2nd Ave, San Diego CA 92101-4903
Director of Admissions
619-235-2049 or 800-243-3436 Fax: 619-232-4322
Website: www.fidm.edu
E-mail: info@fidm.com
See listing under "Community and Junior Colleges"

FIDM/The Fashion Institute of Design & Merchandising
55 Stockton St, San Francisco CA 94108-5829
Director of Admissions
415-675-5200 or 800-422-3436 Fax: 415-296-7299
Website: www.fidm.edu
E-mail: info@fidm.com
See listing under "Community and Junior Colleges"

GEMOLOGICAL INSTITUTE OF AMERICA
The Robert Mouawad Campus
5345 Armada Dr, Carlsbad CA 92008-4602
Jason Drake, Admissions Manager
800-421-7250 ext. 4001 or 760-603-4001
Fax: 760-603-4003
Website: www.gia.edu
E-mail: eduinfo@gia.edu
Established 1931. Nonprofit. Private. Coed. Accreditation: ACCSCT. Diplomas: Graduate Gemologist, Graduate Jeweler, Graduate Jeweler Gemologist, Jewelry Business Management, Applied Jewelry Arts. Programs and courses range from five days to 17 months. Financial aid. Classes begin year round.
See listing under "Home Study and Correspondence"

FLORIDA
Art Institute of Fort Lauderdale
1799 SE 17th St, Fort Lauderdale FL 33316-3013
Eileen Northrop, V.P./Director of Admissions
800-275-7603 Fax: 954-728-8637
Website: www.aifl.edu

International Academy of Design & Technology
5104 Eisenhower Blvd, Tampa FL 33634-6313
Richard Costa, V.P. of Admissions and Marketing
813-880-8092 Fax: 813-881-0008
Website: www.academy.edu
E-mail: admissions@academy.edu

INTERNATIONAL ACADEMY OF DESIGN AND TECHNOLOGY
5959 Lake Ellenor Dr, Orlando FL 32809-4633
Dr. John Dietrich, VP of Admissions
877-753-0007 Fax: 407-251-0465
Website: www.iadt.edu
E-mail: info@iadt.edu

Lynn University
3601 N Military Trl, Boca Raton FL 33431-5598
Brett Ormandy, Director of Admissions
561-237-7900 Fax: 561-237-7100
Website: www.lynn.edu
E-mail: admission@lynn.edu

GEORGIA
Savannah College of Art and Design
PO Box 2072, Savannah, GA 31402-2072
PO Box 77300, Atlanta, GA 30357
Phone: 800-869-7223 (Savannah) or 877-722-3285 (Atlanta)
E-mail: admission@scad.edu (Savannah) or sca-datl@scad.edu (Atlanta)
www.scad.edu
SCAD is a private, nonprofit institution accredited by the Commission on Colleges of the Southern Association of Colleges and Schools to award bachelor's and master's degrees. The college offers B.F.A., M.Arch., M.A., M.F.A., and M.U.D. degrees. Enrollment is appoximately 7,350; 6 percent are international. More than 30 areas of study. Online programs via SCAD e-Learning.

ILLINOIS
Columbia College Chicago
600 S Michigan Ave, Chicago IL 60605-1996
Murphy Monroe, Executive Director of Admissions
312-344-7130 Fax: 312-344-8024
Website: www.colum.edu
E-mail: admissions@colum.edu

MASSACHUSETTS
Bay State College
122 Commonwealth Ave, Boston MA 02116-2901
Craig Pfannenstiehl, President
617-217-9000 Fax: 617-536-1735

NEW JERSEY
New Jersey City University
2039 John F Kennedy Blvd
Jersey City NJ 07305-1588
Carmen Panlilio, Asst. V.P. for Admissions and Financial Aid
201-200-3234 Fax: 201-200-2044
Website: www.njcu.edu
E-mail: admissions@njcu.edu

NEW YORK
LABORATORY INSTITUTE OF MERCHANDISING
12 E 53rd St, New York NY 10022-5268
Kristina Gibson, Director of Admissions
800-677-1323 or 212-752-1530 Fax: 212-750-3432
Website: www.limcollege.edu
E-mail: admissions@limcollege.edu
See listing under "Universities"

Pratt Institute
200 Willoughby Ave, Brooklyn NY 11205-3899
Heidi Metcalf, Director of Admissions
718-636-3600 Fax: 718-636-3670
Website: www.pratt.edu
E-mail: hmetcalf@pratt.edu

NORTH CAROLINA
Meredith College
3800 Hillsborough St, Raleigh NC 27607-5298
Heidi L. Fletcher, Director of Admissions
919-760-8581 Fax: 919-760-2348
Website: www.meredith.edu
E-mail: admissions@meredith.edu
See listing under "Women's Colleges"

OHIO
Columbus College of Art & Design
107 N 9th St, Columbus OH 43215-1700
877-997-CCAD or 614-222-3261 Fax: 614-232-8344
Website: www.ccad.edu
E-mail: admissions@ccad.edu

Davis College
4747 Monroe St, Toledo OH 43623-4389
Dana Stern, Admissions Director
419-473-2700 Fax: 419-473-2472
Website: www.daviscollege.edu
E-mail: learn@daviscollege.edu

The Ohio State University
Coll of Human Ecology, Dept of Consumer Sciences, Textiles
Campbell Hall, 1787 Neil Ave, Columbus OH 43210
614-292-6612 Fax: 614-688-3019
Website: hec.osu.edu/cs/programs/tc/undergraduate.php
E-mail: mawhirter.1@osu.edu

Ursuline College
2550 Lander Rd, Cleveland OH 44124-4398
Sarah E. Sundermeier, Director of Admissions
888-URSULINE Toll Free Fax: 440-684-6138
Website: www.admission.ursuline.edu
E-mail: admission@ursuline.edu

PENNSYLVANIA
Art Institute of Philadelphia
1622 Chestnut St, Philadelphia PA 19103-5119
Larry McHugh, Director of Admissions
800-275-2474 Fax: 215-405-6399
Website: www.aiph.aii.edu
E-mail: aiphinfo@aii.edu

ART INSTITUTE OF PITTSBURGH
420 Boulevard Of The Allies, Pittsburgh PA 15219
Newton I. Myvett, VP/Director of Admissions
800-275-2470 Fax: 412-263-6667
Website: www.aip.aii.edu
E-mail: pahughes@aii.edu
See listing under "Universities"

Lehigh Valley College
2809 E Saucon Valley Rd
Center Valley PA 18034-8447
Joshua Padron, Vice President of Marketing and Admissions
800-227-9109 Fax: 610-791-7810
Website: www.lehighvalley.edu
E-mail: joshua.padron@lehighvalley.edu

TENNESSEE
O'More College of Design
423 S Margin St, Franklin TN 37064-2816
Dr. K. Mark Hilliard, President
Chris Lee, Director of Enrollment Management
615-794-4254 Fax: 615-790-1662
Website: www.omorecollege.edu
E-mail: clee@omorecollege.edu

TEXAS
Texas Woman's University
PO Box 425589, Denton TX 76204-5589
Erma Nieto, Director of Admissions
866-809-6130 Fax: 940-898-3081
Website: www.twu.edu
E-mail: admissions@twu.edu

Wade College
Dallas Market Center
PO Box 421149, Dallas TX 75342
Harry Davros, President
800-624-4850 or 214-637-3530 Fax: 214-637-0827
Website: www.wadecollege.edu
E-mail: admissions@wadecollege.edu
See listing under "Community and Junior Colleges"

VIRGINIA
Radford University
PO Box 6903, Radford VA 24142
David W. Kraus, Director of Admissions
800-890-4265 Fax: 540-831-5038
Website: www.radford.edu
E-mail: ruadmiss@radford.edu

GRADUATE SCHOOLS

ALABAMA
Faulkner University
5345 Atlanta Hwy, Montgomery AL 36109-3390
Mark Hunt, Director of Adult Enrollment
800-879-9816 ext. 7140 or 334-386-7140
Fax: 334-386-7137
Website: www.faulkner.edu
E-mail: mhunt@faulkner.edu

Samford University
800 Lakeshore Dr, Birmingham AL 35229-0002
205-726-3673

Troy University
Troy AL 36082-0001
Jim Hutto, Dean of Enrollment Management
334-670-3175

Troy University Dothan
PO Box 8368, Dothan AL 36304-0368
334-983-6556

United States Sports Academy
1 Academy Dr, Daphne AL 36526-7055
Charles Cornwall, Dean of Student Services
251-626-3303

University of Alabama
Box 870118, Tuscaloosa AL 35487
Dr. Lisa B. Harris, Director of Admissions
205-348-5666

University of Alabama in Huntsville
PO Box 1247, Huntsville AL 35899-0001
256-824-6199 Fax: 256-824-6405
Website: www.uah.edu
E-mail: admitme@email.uah.edu

ALASKA
University of Alaska Anchorage
PO Box 141629, Anchorage AK 99514-1629
Cecile Mitchell, Director of Enrollment Services
907-786-1480 Fax: 907-786-4888
Website: www.uaa.alaska.edu/
E-mail: enroll@uaa.alaska.edu

ARIZONA
Argosy University/Phoenix
2233 W Dunlap Ave, Phoenix AZ 85021-2859
Andy Hughes, Director of Admissions
866-216-2777 (toll Free)

ARIZONA SCHOOL OF HEALTH SCIENCES A.T. STILL UNIVERSITY
5850 E Still Circle, Mesa AZ 85206
Admissions Counselor
866-626-2878 or 480-219-6000 Fax: 480-219-6100
Website: www.atsu.edu
E-mail: info@ashs.edu

Asian Institute of Medical Studies
3131 N Country Club Rd #100, Tucson AZ 85716
520-322-6330

AZ School of Acupuncture & Oriental Medicine
4646 E Ft Lowell Rd Ste 105, Tucson AZ 85712
520-795-0787

FRANK LLOYD WRIGHT SCHOOL OF ARCHITECTURE
Taliesin West, Scottsdale AZ 85261
Pamela S. Stefansson, Director of Admissions
480-860-2700 Fax: 480-391-4009
Website: www.taliesin.edu
E-mail: nikita@taliesin.edu

Phoenix Institute of Herbal Medicine & Acupuncture
301 E Bethany Home Rd #A100, Phoenix AZ 85012
602-274-1885

Southwest Coll of Naturopathic Medicine & Health Sciences
2140 E Broadway Rd, Tempe AZ 85282
480-858-9100

Thunderbird, The Garvin School of International Management
15249 N 59th Ave, Glendale AZ 85306-3236
Judy Johnson, Associate VP of Admissions & Financial Aid
800-848-9084 or 602-978-7100 Fax: 602-439-5432
Website: www.thunderbird.edu
E-mail: johnsonj@thunderbird.edu

University of Advancing Technology
2625 W Baseline Rd, Tempe AZ 85283
Lary Dougherty, Director of Admissions
800-658-5744

CALIFORNIA

ACADEMY OF CHINESE CULTURE AND HEALTH SCIENCES
1601 Clay St, Oakland CA 94612-1531
Ruth Kierans, Director of Admission
510-763-7787 Fax: 510-834-8646
Website: www.acchs.edu
E-mail: info@acchs.edu

Acupuncture and Integrative Medicine College - Berkeley
2550 Shattuck Ave, Berkeley CA 94704
510-666-8248

Alliant International University
1000 S Fremont Ave, Alhambra CA 91803-4737
Stephanie Byers-Bell, Director of Admissions
626-284-2777

Alliant International University
5130 E Clinton Way, Fresno CA 93727-2014
Gregory Timberlake, Director of Admissions
559-456-2777

Alliant International University
2500 Michelson Dr Ste 250, Irvine CA 92612
949-833-2651

Alliant International University
425 University Ave Ste 211, Sacramento CA 95825
Gregory Timberlake, Director of Admissions
916-565-2955

Alliant International University - San Diego
10455 Pomerado Rd, San Diego CA 92131-1799
858-635-4772

AMERICAN BAPTIST SEMINARY OF THE WEST
2606 Dwight Way, Berkeley CA 94704-3029
510-841-1905 Fax: 510-841-2446
Website: www.absw.edu
E-mail: admissions@absw.edu

AMERICAN COLLEGE OF TRADITIONAL CHINESE MEDICINE
455 Arkansas St, San Francisco CA 94107-2813
JoAnn Vandenberg, Dean of Student Services
415-282-7600 Fax: 415-282-0856
Website: www.actcm.edu
E-mail: admissions@actcm.edu

AMERICAN CONSERVATORY THEATER
30 Grant Ave, San Francisco CA 94108-5800
Melissa Smith, Conservatory Director
415-439-2350
Website: www.act-sf.org

American Graduate University
733 N Dodsworth Ave, Covina CA 91724-2408
Marie Sirney, V.P. Administration
626-966-4576

Antioch University
801 Garden St Ste 101
Santa Barbara CA 93101-1581
Ankara McPherson, Director of Admissions
805-962-8179 Fax: 805-962-4786
Website: www.antiochsb.edu
E-mail: amcpherson@antiochsb.edu

Argosy University / Orange County
3501 W Sunflower Ave, Santa Ana CA 92704
714-338-6200

Argosy University
San Francisco Bay Area Campus
999A Canal Blvd, Point Richmond CA 94804-3547
Cynthia Sirkin, Associate Director of Admissions
510-215-0277

Brooks Institute of Photography
801 Alston Rd, Santa Barbara CA 93108-2399
Inge B. Kautzmann, Director of Admissions
805-966-3888 ext. 217 or 218

California Baptist University
8432 Magnolia Ave, Riverside CA 92504-3297
951-689-5771

CALIFORNIA COAST UNIVERSITY
700 N Main St, Santa Ana CA 92701
Admissions Office: 888-CCU-UNIV or 714-547-9625
Fax: 714-547-5777
Dr. Thomas Neal, President
Dr. Cynthia Teeple, Academic Vice President
Website: www.calcoast.edu
E-mail: info@calcoast.edu
Established 1973. Proprietary. Coed. Accreditation: California Coast University holds accreditation through the Accrediting Commission of the Distance Education and Training Council (DETC). The DETC is an educational association located in Washington, D.C. Founded in 1926, it is the standard setting agency for distance education institutions. Approval: Bureau for Private Postsecondary and Vocational Education - State of California, charter member California Association of State Approved Colleges & Universities, member Association for Adult & Continuing Education, member The Alliance for Private Post Secondary Academic Institutions.
Tuition: $2,805-$12,070. California Coast University has selected the SLM Corporation, commonly known as Sallie Mae, to help the university provide financing for its students. Sallie Mae is the nation's leading provider of education funding. Sallie Mae also allows students to borrow additional loan amounts to cover additional expenses, such as textbooks, equipment, or living expenses.
Enrollment: 30,000. California Coast University is approved by the California State Approving Agency to enroll veterans or other eligible persons under Title 38, U.S. Code. California Coast University holds a Memorandum of Understanding with Defense Activity for Non-Traditional Education Support (DANTES) as an external degree provider.
A private college offering off-campus independent study programs in the traditional areas of business administration, management, psychology, education. Ad-

missions: enroll year round, requires official transcripts, letters of recommendation, detailed curriculum vita or occupational history.
Process: evaluation of prior academic work followed by analysis of occupational history, including participation in workshops, seminars, training programs, specialized projects for credit. Credit is demonstrated by accelerated learning guides or study guides.
Residency: All course work may be completed off campus, utilizing correspondence methods. Interest free loans available to students.

California Institute of Integral Studies
1453 Mission St, San Francisco CA 94103
415-575-6150

California Institute of Technology
1200 E California Blvd, Pasadena CA 91106
626-395-6341

California Institute of the Arts
24700 McBean Pkwy, Valencia CA 91355-2397
Carol Kim, Director of Enrollment Services
800-545-ARTS

California National University for Advanced Studies
8550 Balboa Blvd Ste 210
Northridge CA 91325-3576
800-782-2422

California School of Podiatric Medicine
Samuel Merritt College
370 Hawthorne Ave, Oakland CA 94609
510-869-8727

California State University-Stanislaus
801 W Monte Vista Ave, Turlock CA 95382-0256
Lisa Bernardo, Director of Admissions
209-667-3129

California Western School of Law
225 Cedar St, San Diego CA 92101-3090
619-239-0391

Chapman University
One University Drive, Orange CA 92866-1099
Michael Drummy, Assistant Vice President for Enrollment
Services and Chief Admission Officer
714-997-6411 or 888-CUAPPLY Fax: 714-997-6713
Website: www.chapman.edu
E-mail: admit@chapman.edu

CHURCH DIVINITY SCHOOL OF THE PACIFIC
2451 Ridge Rd, Berkeley CA 94709-1217
Kathleen Crisp, Director of Admissions and Recruitment
510-204-0715 Fax: 510-204-0749
Website: www.cdsp.edu
E-mail: admissions@cdsp.edu

Claremont Graduate University
170 E 10th St, Claremont CA 91711-5909
Diane J. Guido, Associate Dean of Student Affairs
909-621-8069

Claremont School of Theology
1325 N College Ave, Claremont CA 91711-3154
Rev. Janet Cromwell, Director of Admissions
866-274-6500

Concordia University
1530 Concordia, Irvine CA 92612-3203
Lori McDonald, Executive Director of Enrollment Services
800-229-1200 or 949-854-8002 Fax: 949-854-6894
Website: www.cui.edu
E-mail: admission@cui.edu

DOMINICAN SCHOOL OF PHILOSOPHY & THEOLOGY
2301 Vine St, Berkeley CA 94708
John Knutsen, Director of Admissions
888-450-DSPT or 510-883-2073 Fax: 510-849-1372
Website: www.dspt.edu
E-mail: admissions@dspt.edu

Dongguk Royal University
440 Shatto Pl, Los Angeles CA 90020
213-487-0110

EMPEROR'S COLLEGE OF TRADITIONAL ORIENTAL MEDICINE
1807 Wilshire Blvd Ste B
Santa Monica CA 90403-5678
Sun Han, Director of Admissions
310-453-8300 Fax: 310-829-3838
Website: www.emperors.edu
E-mail: sun@emperors.edu

Fielding Graduate University
2112 Santa Barbara St
Santa Barbara CA 93105-3538
805-687-1099

FIVE BRANCHES INSTITUTE
3031 Tisch Way Ste 605, San Jose CA 95128
408-260-0208 Fax: 408-261-3166
Website: www.fivebranches.edu
E-mail: sjcampus@fivebrances.edu

FIVE BRANCHES INSTITUTE
College of Traditional Chinese Medicine
200 7th Ave, Santa Cruz CA 95062-4668
Eleonor Mendelson, Admissions
831-476-9424 Fax: 831-476-8928
Website: www.fivebranches.edu
E-mail: tcm@fivebranches.edu

Franciscan School of Theology
1712 Euclid Ave, Berkeley CA 94709-1294
Registrar
510-848-5232

Fuller Theological Seminary
135 N Oakland Ave, Pasadena CA 91182
David Dufault-Hunter, Director of Admissions & Financial Aid
626-584-5200

Golden Gate Baptist Theological Seminary
201 Seminary Dr, Mill Valley CA 94941-3197
415-380-1300

GRADUATE THEOLOGICAL UNION
2400 Ridge Rd, Berkeley CA 94709-1212
Kathleen Kook, Assistant Dean for Admissions
800-826-4488 Fax: 510-649-1730
Website: www.gtu.edu
E-mail: gtuadm@gtu.edu

HEBREW UNION COLLEGE - JEWISH INSTITUTE OF RELIGION
3077 University Ave, Los Angeles CA 90007-3796
Dr. Matt Albert, Regional Director of Admissions and Recruitment
213-749-3424 Fax: 213-747-6128
Website: www.huc.edu
E-mail: malbert@huc.edu

Institute for Creation Research Graduate School
10946 Woodside Ave N, Santee CA 92071
619-448-0900

Institute of Transpersonal Psychology
1069 E Meadow Cir, Palo Alto CA 94303-4231
John Hofmann, Director of Admissions
650-493-4430

JESUIT SCHOOL OF THEOLOGY AT BERKELEY
1735 LeRoy Ave, Berkeley CA 94709-1193
Patricia Abracia, Director of Admissions
800-824-0122 or 510-549-5000 Fax: 510-841-8536
Website: www.jstb.edu
E-mail: admissions@jstb.edu
Established 1934. Private. Coed. Accreditation: ATS, WASC. Tuition: $11,750 - $14,000, MA tuition: $12,080. Fees: included in tuition. Enrollment: 197. Faculty: 25. Student-faculty ratio: 10:1. Degrees: MDiv, MTS, MA, ThM, STL, STD, PhD through GTU, New Directions, Sabbatical Program, Special Student. status, Certificate of Theological Studies, Certificate of Ministry Studies, Summer Hispanic Institute. The Jesuit School of Theology is a member school of the Graduate Theological Union. Cross-registration with UC Berkeley. Lay students welcome. Scholarships available. High quality Jesuit education.

Keck Graduate Institute
535 Watson Dr, Claremont CA 91711
909-607-7855

La Sierra University
4700 Pierce St, Riverside CA 92515-8247
Bobby Brown, Director of Admissions
800-874-5587

LIFE CHIROPRACTIC COLLEGE WEST
25001 Industrial Blvd, Hayward CA 94545-2801
Stephen D. Eckstone, Director of Admissions
800-788-4476 Fax: 510-780-4525
Website: www.lifewest.edu
E-mail: admissions@lifewest.edu

Logos Evangelical Seminary
9358 Telstar Ave, El Monte CA 91731-2816
626-571-5110

Loyola Marymount University
PO Box 15019, Los Angeles CA 90015-0019
213-736-1180

Mennonite Brethren Biblical Seminary
4824 E Butler Ave, Fresno CA 93727-5097
Chris Patton, Director of Admissions
559-251-8628

Monterey Institute of International Studies
460 Pierce St, Monterey CA 93940
Admissions Office
831-647-4100 Fax: 831-647-6405
Website: www.miis.edu
E-mail: admit@miis.edu

National University School of Law
3580 Aero Ct, San Diego CA 92123-1711
619-563-7300

Newschool of Architecture and Design
1249 F St, San Diego CA 92101-6634
Gilbert D. Cooke, AIA, Dean
Barbara Wingate, Director of Admissions
619-235-4100 ext. 123

Northwestern Polytechnic University
47671 Westinghouse Dr, Fremont CA 94539
Dr. P. Hsu, Contact
510-657-5913 Fax: 510-657-8975
Website: www.npu.edu
E-mail: npuadm@npu.edu

Notre Dame de Namur University
1500 Ralston Ave, Belmont CA 94002-1997
Elaine Cohen, Graduate Dean
650-508-3527

Pacifica Graduate Institute
249 Lambert Rd, Carpinteria CA 93013-3019
Diane Huerta, Director of Admissions
805-969-3626 ext. 128

PACIFIC COLLEGE OF ORIENTAL MEDICINE
7445 Mission Valley Rd #105, San Diego CA 92108
619-574-6909 Fax: 619-574-6641
Website: www.pacificcollege.edu
E-mail: admissions-sd@pacificcollege.edu

Pacific Graduate School of Psychology
940 E Meadow Dr, Palo Alto CA 94303-4232
L. Barbara Bell, Director of Admissions
800-818-6136

Pacific Lutheran Theological Seminary
2770 Marin Ave, Berkeley CA 94708-1597
510-524-5264

Pacific Oaks College
5 Westmoreland Pl, Pasadena CA 91103-3592
800-684-0900

Pacific School of Religion
1798 Scenic Ave, Berkeley CA 94709-1323
Debra J. Mumford, Director of Recruitment and Admissions
800-999-0528

PALMER COLLEGE OF CHIROPRACTIC WEST
90 E Tasman Dr, San Jose CA 95134-1617
Director of Admissions
866-303-7939 Fax: 408-944-6032
Website: www.palmer.edu
E-mail: pccw_admiss@palmer.edu

Pardee RAND Graduate School of Policy Studies
PO Box 2138, Santa Monica CA 90407-2138
310-393-0411

Phillips Graduate Institute
5445 Balboa Blvd, Encino CA 91316-1509
Steven Weir, Director of Admissions
818-386-5600 Fax: 818-386-5636
Website: www.pgi.edu
E-mail: sweir@pgi.edu

Point Loma Nazarene University
3900 Lomaland Dr, San Diego CA 92106-2810
Eric Groves, Director of Admissions
800-733-7770

Remington College
123 Camino De La Reina #100N
San Diego CA 92108-3002
Christopher Tilley, Campus President
619-686-8600

St. Patrick's Seminary & University
320 Middlefield Rd, Menlo Park CA 94025-3563
Dr. Charles James, Contact
650-325-5621

SAMRA UNIVERSITY OF ORIENTAL MEDICINE
3000 S Robertson Blvd 4 Fl
Los Angeles CA 90034-3158
Simon Song, Director of Operations
310-202-6444 Fax: 310-202-6007
Website: www.samra.edu
E-mail: admissions@samra.edu

SAN FRANCISCO ART INSTITUTE
800 Chestnut St, San Francisco CA 94133
Paula Farmer, Director of Admission
800-345-SFAI Fax: 415-749-4503
Website: www.sfai.edu
E-mail: admissions@sfai.edu
  Founded in 1871, SFAI offers one of the most innovative and interdisciplinary environments in higher education. Offering accredited Master of Fine Arts, Summer Master of Fine Arts (MFA, SMFA), Post-Baccalaureate (PB), and Master of Arts (MA) programs, SFAI is committed to furthering the relationship between the practices and theories of contemporary art. SFAI's School of Studio Practice centers on the development of the artist's vision and MFA students work with faculty from each of the school's studio departments: Design+Technology, Film, New Genres, Painting, Photography, Printmaking, and Sculpture. SFAI's School of Interdisciplinary Studies is based on the premise that imagination combined with critical intelligence is essential for engaging and understanding contemporary art and global society, and offers three MA programs: History and Theory of Contemporary Art, Urban Studies, and Exhibition and Museum Studies. Together the two schools provide an inclusive model to address contemporary art and culture. The Summer MFA program has the same rigor as the Academic Year MFA program yet is designed for those who choose an alternate academic schedule. The Post-Baccalaureate program is an excellent way to prepare for entrance into an MFA program or to enhance skills and knowledge. SFAI's faculty is comprised of active artists, curators, writers, and scholars. Dean of Academic Affairs is renowned curator and critic Okwui Enwezor. Dean of Graduate Studies is artist and filmmaker Renee Green. Director of Exhibitions and Public Programs is curator Hou Hanru. Visiting artists and scholars play a significant role in education at SFAI, with recent visitors including Matthew Barney, William Kentridge, Raqs Media Collective, and others. SFAI's Graduate Center provides individual and group studios with 24-hour access. The 62,000 square-foot Graduate Center also includes a digital lab, film and sound studios, darkrooms, a woodshop, and a gallery for student work. Graduate students also take advantage of the resources at SFAI's main campus, which includes postproduction facilities and the first high-definition video research lab in the Bay Area. The Diego Rivera Gallery, and open-air amphitheater, and a 250-seat theater are also available to students for exhibiting and screening work. SFAI's Library collection includes more than 26,000 volumes with emphasis on modern and contemporary art, and over 200 current periodicals and an extensive image, video, and audio archive available only to students. SFAI has rolling application deadlines, and there is a fellowship program for students admitted into the graduate programs. Visit the SFAI website for application requirements.

San Francisco Theological Seminary
105 Seminary Rd, San Anselmo CA 94960-2925
The Rev. Gloria M. Pulido, Assoc. Dean for Admissions
415-451-2800

SAN JOAQUIN COLLEGE OF LAW
901 5th St, Clovis CA 93612-1312
Joyce Morodomi, Director of Student Services
559-323-2100 Fax: 559-323-5566
Website: www.sjcl.edu
E-mail: studylaw@sjcl.edu

Santa Barbara College of Oriental Medicine
1919 State St, Santa Barbara CA 93101
Laura Schlieske, Contact
800-549-6299

Saybrook Graduate School
747 Front St, 3rd Floor
San Francisco CA 94111-1920
Diana Hernandez, Dean of Admissions
800-825-4480

Scripps Research Institute
10550 N Torrey Pines Rd, La Jolla CA 92037
858-784-8469

Simpson University
2211 College View Dr, Redding CA 96003-8606
Jim Herberger, Director of Admissions
888-9-SIMPSON Fax: 530-226-4861
Website: www.simpsonuniversity.edu
E-mail: admissions@simpsonuniversity.edu
See listing under "Liberal Arts and Sciences"

SOUTH BAYLO UNIVERSITY
School of Acupuncture & Oriental Medicine
1126 N Brookhurst St, Anaheim CA 92801
Dr. Melvin L. Shirer, D.C., Director of Admissions
714-533-1495 Fax: 714-533-6040
Website: www.southbaylo.edu
E-mail: mshirer@southbaylo.edu

Southern California College of Optometry
2575 Yorba Linda Blvd, Fullerton CA 92831-1615
714-449-7450

Southern California Institute of Architecture
960 E 3rd St, Los Angeles CA 90013-1822
Wenona Colinco, Director of Admissions
213-613-2200

Southern California University of Health Science
16200 Amber Valley Dr, Whittier CA 90604
Jan Price, Interim Admissions Director
877-434-7757

Southwestern University School of Law
675 S Westmoreland Ave
Los Angeles CA 90005-3905
213-738-6700

Starr King School for the Ministry
2441 Le Conte Ave, Berkeley CA 94709-1209
510-845-6232

Thomas Jefferson School of Law
2121 San Diego Ave, San Diego CA 92110-2928
Kenneth Vandevelde, Dean
619-297-9700 ext. 1600

TOURO UNIVERSITY COLLEGE OF OSTEOPATHIC MEDICINE - MARE ISLAND
1310 Johnson Ln, Vallejo CA 94592
Dr. Donald Haight, Director of Admissions
707-638-5270 Fax: 707-638-5250
Website: www.tu.edu
E-mail: haight@touro.edu

University of California
Parnassus and 3rd Ave
San Francisco CA 94143-0001
415-476-9000

University of California Hastings College of Law
200 McAllister St, San Francisco CA 94102
415-565-4600

University of East-West Medicine
970 W El Camino Real, Sunnyvale CA 94087
408-733-1878

University of Judaism
15600 Mulholland Dr, Los Angeles CA 90077-1519
Saul Korin, Director of Graduate Admissions
310-476-9777

University of La Verne
1950 3rd St, La Verne CA 91750-4443
800-876-4858

University of San Diego
5998 Alcala Park, San Diego CA 92110-2492
Admissions
619-260-4506

University of Southern California
Health Science Campus, Los Angeles CA 90033
323-226-6501

UNIVERSITY OF THE PACIFIC
Arthur A. Dugoni School of Dentistry
2155 Webster St, San Francisco CA 94115-2333
Kathy Candito, Director of Admissions
415-929-6491 Fax: 415-749-3363
Website: www.dental.pacific.edu

University of the Pacific McGeorge School of Law
3200 5th Ave, Sacramento CA 95817-2799
Adam Barrett, Asst. Dean and Director of Admissions
916-739-7105

University of West Los Angeles
School of Law, School of Paralegal Studies
9920 S La Cienega Blvd, Inglewood CA 90301-4423
Lynda Freeman, Admissions Counselor
310-342-5254

University of West Los Angeles
School of Law, School of Paralegal Studies
6400 Canoga Ave Ste 271, Woodland Hills CA 91367
Lynda Freeman, Admissions Counselor
818-883-0529

WESTERN STATE UNIVERSITY COLLEGE OF LAW
1111 N State College Blvd, Fullerton CA 92831-3014
Phyllis Hauptfeld, Assistant Dean of Admission
800-WSU-4LAW or 714-459-1107 Fax: 714-441-1748
Website: www.wsulaw.edu
E-mail: adm@wsulaw.edu

Westminster Theological Seminary
1725 Bear Valley Pkwy, Escondido CA 92027-4128
760-480-8474

Whittier College
School of Law
3333 Harbor Blvd, Costa Mesa CA 92626-1501
Betty Vu, Director of Admissions
714-444-4141

Wright Institute
2728 Durant Ave, Berkeley CA 94704-1796
510-841-9230

Yo San University of Traditional Chinese Medicine
13315 Washington Blvd, Los Angeles CA 90066
310-577-3000

COLORADO

Adams State College
Alamosa CO 81102
Matt Gallegos, Director of Admissions
800-824-6494

Colorado School of Professional Psychology
555 E Pikes Peak Ave Ste 108
Colorado Springs CO 80903-3612
877-442-0505

Colorado State University - Pueblo
2200 Bonforte Blvd, Pueblo CO 81001-4990
719-549-2461

Colorado Technical University
4435 N Chestnut St
Colorado Springs CO 80907-3895
719-598-0200

Denver Seminary
6399 S Santa Fe Dr, Littleton CO 80120
Robert Fomer, VP Student Services
303-762-6982 Fax: 303-783-3122
Website: denverseminary.edu
E-mail: bob.fomer@denverseminary.edu

ILIFF SCHOOL OF THEOLOGY
2201 S University Blvd, Denver CO 80210-4798
Peggy Blocker, Director of Admissions
800-678-3360 or 303-765-3112 Fax: 303-777-0164
Website: www.iliff.edu
E-mail: admissions@iliff.edu

Naropa University
2130 Arapahoe Ave, Boulder CO 80302-6697
303-546-3572

National Theatre Conservatory
1050 13th St, Denver CO 80204-2157
Daniel Renner, Director of Education
303-446-4855

University of Colorado at Denver and Health Sciences Center
Downtown Denver Campus
PO Box 173364, Denver CO 80217-3364
303-556-2550 Fax: 303-556-5855
Website:
www.cudenver.edu/academics/colleges/gradschool

University of Colorado at Denver and Health Sciences Center
Health Sciences Program
4200 E 9th Ave Box C245, Denver CO 80262
Phoebe Lindsey Barton, Ph.D., Director
Website: www.uchsc.edu

UNIVERSITY OF DENVER UNIVERSITY COLLEGE
2211 S Josephine St, Denver CO 80208
Dr. James R. Davis, Dean
303-871-3354 Fax: 303-871-4047
Website: www.universitycollege.du.edu
E-mail: ucolinfo@du.edu

University of Northern Colorado
Greeley CO 80639
Richard King, Interim Dean, Graduate School
970-351-2831

CONNECTICUT

Berkeley Divinity School at Yale
363 Saint Ronan St, New Haven CT 06511-2285
William Franklin, Dean
203-764-9300

HARTFORD SEMINARY
77 Sherman St, Hartford CT 06105-2260
Kelton Cobb, Seminary Academic Advisor
860-509-9513 Fax: 860-509-9509
Website: www.hartsem.edu
E-mail: info@hartsem.edu

Rensselaer at Hartford
275 Windsor St, Hartford CT 06120-2910
860-548-2400

St. Joseph College
1678 Asylum Ave, West Hartford CT 06117-2791
860-232-4571

University of Bridgeport
126 Park Ave, Bridgeport CT 06604-5620
Barbara L. Maryak, Dean of Admissions
203-576-4552

University of New Haven
300 Boston Post Rd, West Haven CT 06516
Director of Graduate Admissions
203-932-7133 Fax: 203-932-7137
Website: www.newhaven.edu
E-mail: gradinfo@newhaven.edu

DELAWARE

Widener University School of Law
PO Box 7474, Wilmington DE 19803-0474
Barbara Ayars, Assistant Dean of Admissions
302-477-2162

DISTRICT OF COLUMBIA

The Institute of World Politics
1521 16th St NW, Washington DC 20036
202-462-2101

Johns Hopkins University
1740 Massachusetts Ave NW
Washington DC 20036-1903
202-663-5600

University of the District of Columbia David A. Clarke
School of Law
4200 Connecticut Ave NW, Washington DC 20008
Vivian W. Canty, Director of Admission
202-274-7341

Washington Theological Union
6896 Laurel St NW, Washington DC 20012-2016
202-726-8800

Wesley Theological Seminary
4500 Massachusetts Ave NW
Washington DC 20016-5690
The Rev. Chip Aldridge, Director of Admissions
800-882-4987

FLORIDA

Academy for Five Element Acupuncture
1170A E Hallendale Beach, Hallandale FL 33009
954-456-6336

ACUPUNCTURE & MASSAGE COLLEGE
10506 N Kendall Dr, Miami FL 33176
Joe Calareso, Admissions Director
305-595-9500 Fax: 305-595-2622
Website: www.amcollege.edu
E-mail: admissions@amcollege.edu

Argosy University / Tampa
4401 N Himes Ave Ste 150, Tampa FL 33614-7001
813-740-1108

ATLANTIC INSTITUTE OF ORIENTAL MEDICINE
100 E Broward Blvd Ste 100
Fort Lauderdale FL 33301-3510
Prof. Yan Cheng, Academic Dean
954-763-9840 Fax: 954-763-9844
Website: www.atom.edu
E-mail: dean@atom.edu

Barry University
11300 NE 2nd Ave, Miami Shores FL 33161-6695
800-695-2279

Bay Medical Center
615 N Bonita Ave, Panama City FL 32401
Sherry Tindall, Director of Education, Training, &
Research
800-422-2418

CARLOS ALBIZU UNIVERSITY
2173 NW 99th Ave, Miami FL 33172-2209
Gerardo Alvarado, MBA, Director of Admissions,
Recruitment & Outreach
305-593-1223 ext. 137 Fax: 305-593-1854
Website: www.mia.albizu.edu
E-mail: admissions@albizu.edu

Dragon Rises College Oriental Medicine
901 NW 8th Ave Ste B5, Gainesville FL 32601
352-371-2833

East West College of Natural Medicine
3808 N Tamiami Trail, Sarasota FL 34234
Meredith McKay, Chief Administrative Officer
941-355-9080

EVERGLADES UNIVERSITY (MAIN CAMPUS)
5002 T-Rex Ave Suite 100, Boca Raton FL 33431
Kristi Mollis, President
888-772-6077 Fax: 561-912-1191
Website: www.evergladesuniversity.edu
E-mail: admissions-boca@evergladesuniversity.edu
See listing under "Universities"

EVERGLADES UNIVERSITY
Orlando Campus (Branch Campus)
5600 Lake Underhill Rd Suite 200, Orlando FL 32807
Shirley Long, Vice President
866-289-1078 Fax: 407-482-9801
Website: www.evergladesuniversity.edu
E-mail: admissions-orl@evergladesuniversity.edu
See listing under "Universities"

EVERGLADES UNIVERSITY
Sarasota Campus (Branch Campus)
6001 Lake Osprey Dr, Sarasota FL 34240
Brad Brewer, Vice President
866-907-2262 Fax: 941-907-6634
Website: www.evergladesuniversity.edu
E-mail: admissions-sar@evergladesuniversity.edu
See listing under "Universities"

Florida Atlantic University
PO Box 3091, Boca Raton FL 33431-0991
800-299-4328

Florida Coastal School of Law
7555 Beach Blvd, Jacksonville FL 32216
904-680-7700

Florida College of Integrative Medicine
7100 Lake Ellenor Dr, Orlando FL 32809
407-888-8689

Florida Metropolitan University
225 N Federal Hwy, Pompano Beach FL 33062
Fran Heaston, Director of Admissions
800-468-0168

Florida Metropolitan University-Brandon
3924 Coconut Palm Dr, Tampa FL 33619-1354
Marty Baca, Director of Admissions
877-338-0068

FLORIDA METROPOLITAN UNIVERSITY
Pinellas Campus
2471 N McMullen Booth Rd
Clearwater FL 33759-1359
Sandra Williams, Director of Admissions
800-353-3687 or 727-725-2688 Fax: 727-725-3827
Website: www.fmu.edu
E-mail: sawilliams@cci.edu

Knox Theological Seminary
5554 N Federal Hwy, Fort Lauderdale FL 33308
954-771-0376

Lynn University
3601 N Military Trl, Boca Raton FL 33431-5598
Brett Ormandy, Director of Admissions
561-237-7900 Fax: 561-237-7100
Website: www.lynn.edu
E-mail: admission@lynn.edu

PALMER COLLEGE OF CHIROPRACTIC FLORIDA
4777 City Center Pkwy, Port Orange FL 32129-4153
Director of Admissions
866-585-9677 or 386-763-2709 Fax: 386-763-2620
Website: www.palmer.edu
E-mail: pccf_admiss@palmer.edu

Reformed Theological Seminary
1231 Reformation Dr, Oviedo FL 32765
407-366-9493

St. Petersburg Theological Seminary
10830 Navajo Dr, Saint Petersburg FL 33708
727-399-0276

St. Thomas University
16401 NW 37th Ave, Miami Gardens FL 33054
Elizabeth Scheel/Cristen Scolastico, Graduate
Admissions
800-367-9010 or 305-628-6546 Fax: 305-628-6591
Website: www.stu.edu
E-mail: signup@stu.edu

Stetson University
1401 61st St S, Gulfport FL 33707-3299
727-345-1121

Trinity Baptist College
800-200 Hammond Blvd, Jacksonville FL 32221
R. Larry Appleby, Director of Admissions
904-596-2400 Fax: 904-596-2531
Website: www.tbc.edu
E-mail: emailtrinity@tbc.edu

Trinity International University
South Florida Campus
111 NW 183rd St Ste 500, Miami FL 33169-4541
305-577-4600

University of South Florida
3702 Spectrum Blvd Ste 180, Tampa FL 33612-9421
813-974-4031

GEORGIA

Argosy University/Atlanta
980 Hammond Dr NE Ste 100, Atlanta GA 30328
770-671-1200

Columbia Theological Seminary
701 S Columbia Dr, Decatur GA 30030-4118
Ann Clay Adams, Director of Admissions
404-378-8821

Emory University Hospital
1364 Clifton Rd NE, Atlanta GA 30322-1061
404-712-4881

Georgia State University
PO Box 4009, Atlanta GA 30302-4009
404-651-2365

INTERDENOMINATIONAL THEOLOGICAL CENTER
700 Martin Luther King Jr Dr SW
Atlanta GA 30314-4143
Walter Cabassa, Recruitment Coordinator
404-527-7792 Fax: 404-527-0901
Website: www.itc.edu
E-mail: wcabassa@itc.edu

Kennesaw State University
1000 Chastain Rd NW Box 0132
Kennesaw GA 30144-5591
David Baugher, Director of Graduate Admissions
770-420-4377 Fax: 770-423-6885
Website: www.kennesaw.edu

LaGrange College
601 Broad St, LaGrange GA 30240-2955
Andy Geeter, Director of Admission
800-593-2885

Mercer University in Macon
1400 Coleman Ave, Macon GA 31207-0003
John P. Cole, Sr. Assoc. V.P. for Admissions
478-301-2650

THE PSYCHOLOGICAL STUDIES INSTITUTE
2055 Mount Paran Rd NW McCarty Building
Atlanta GA 30327
Robin Lay, Director of Recruiting
888-924-6774 or 404-233-3949 Fax: 404-239-9460
Website: www.psy.edu
E-mail: rlay@psy.edu

University of Georgia
Athens GA 30602-0001
706-542-3000

HAWAII

Argosy University/Hawaii
1001 Bishop St Ste 400, Honolulu HI 96813-3403
808-536-5555

Chaminade University of Honolulu
3140 Waialae Ave, Honolulu HI 96816-1510
Joy Bouey, Dean of Enrollment Management
808-739-4619

Institute of Clinical Acupuncture and Oriental Medicine
1270 Queen Emma St Ste 107, Honolulu HI 96813
808-521-2288

Traditional Chinese Medical College of Hawaii
65-1206 Mamalahoa Hwy, Kamuela HI 96743
808-885-9226

World Medicine Institute
1110 University Ave Ste 308, Honolulu HI 96826-1508
808-949-1050

ILLINOIS

ADLER SCHOOL OF PROFESSIONAL PSYCHOLOGY
65 E Wacker Pl, Chicago IL 60601-7296
Craig Hines, Director of Admissions
312-201-5900 Fax: 312-201-5917
Website: www.adler.edu
E-mail: admissions@adler.edu

AMERICAN INTERCONTINENTAL UNIVERSITY ONLINE
5550 Prairie Stone Parkway Suite 400
Hoffman Estates IL 60192
Admissions Department
877-701-3800
Website: www.aiuonline.edu
E-mail: info@aiuonline.edu

ARGOSY UNIVERSITY/CHICAGO
350 N Orleans St, Merchandise Mart
Chicago IL 60654
Ashley Delaney, Director of Admissions
800-626-4123 Fax: 312-777-7750
Website: www.argosyu.edu
E-mail: adelaney@argosyu.edu

Argosy University/Chicago Northwest
1000 N Plaza Dr Ste 100, Schaumburg IL 60173-4990
847-290-7400

Aurora University
347 S Gladstone Ave, Aurora IL 60506-4892
Carol R. Dunn, Ed.D., Vice President for Enrollment
800-742-5281 Fax: 630-844-5535
Website: www.aurora.edu
E-mail: admission@aurora.edu

Catholic Theological Union
5401 S Cornell Ave, Chicago IL 60615-5698
Kathy Van Duser, Director of Recruitment and
Admissions
773-324-8000

Chicago School of Professional Psychology
325 N Wells St, Chicago IL 60610-4705
Office of Admission
312-329-6600

Chicago Theological Seminary
5757 S University Ave, Chicago IL 60637-1579
773-752-5757

De Paul University
2323 N Seminary Ave, Chicago IL 60614-3298
312-362-8000

Erikson Institute
420 N Wabash Ave, Chicago IL 60611
312-755-2250

Garrett Evangelical Theological Seminary
2121 Sheridan Rd, Evanston IL 60201-2926
847-866-3900

Illinois College of Optometry
3241 S Michigan Ave, Chicago IL 60616-3878
Lynn Petrica, Director of Recruitment
312-225-1700

INSTITUTE FOR CLINICAL SOCIAL WORK
200 N Michigan Ave Ste 407, Chicago IL 60601
Barbara Berger, Ph.D., Dean of Admissions
312-726-8480 Fax: 312-726-7216
Website: www.icsw.edu
E-mail: icsw@icsw.edu

John Marshall Law School
315 S Plymouth Ct, Chicago IL 60604-3907
William Powers, Assoc. Dean Admissions / Student
Services
312-987-1406

Knowledge Systems Institute Graduate School
3420 Main St, Skokie IL 60076-2453
Judy Pan, Director of Admissions
847-679-3135

Lake Forest Graduate School of Management
230 S LaSalle St Ste 100, Chicago IL 60604
312-435-5330

Lake Forest Graduate School of Management
1905 W Field Ct, Lake Forest IL 60045
847-234-5080

Lake Forest Graduate School of Management
1295 E Algonquin Rd, Schaumburg IL 60196-4040
847-576-1212

LUTHERAN SCHOOL OF THEOLOGY AT CHICAGO
1100 E 55th St, Chicago IL 60615-5199
Rev. Brian Halverson, Director of Admission
800-635-1116 ext. 726 or 773-256-0726
Fax: 773-256-0782
Website: www.lstc.edu
E-mail: admissions@lstc.edu

MCCORMICK THEOLOGICAL SEMINARY
5460 S University Ave, Chicago IL 60615
Rev. Craig Howard, Director of Recruitment and
Admissions
800-228-4687 Fax: 773-288-2612
Website: www.mccormick.edu
E-mail: admit@mccormick.edu

Meadville/Lombard Theological School
5701 S Woodlawn Ave, Chicago IL 60637-1602
773-753-3195

MIDWEST COLLEGE OF ORIENTAL MEDICINE
4334 N Hazel St Ste 206, Chicago IL 60613-1429
Kelly Westerlund, Contact
800-593-2320 Fax: 262-554-7475
Website: www.acupuncture.edu
E-mail: mwcadmissions@yahoo.com

National-Louis University
2840 Sheridan Rd, Evanston IL 60201-1796

National University of Health Sciences
200 E Roosevelt Rd, Lombard IL 60148-4583
Dr. James Winterstein, President
800-826-6285 Fax: 630-889-6554
Website: www.nuhs.edu
E-mail: admissions@nuhs.edu

NORTHEASTERN ILLINOIS UNIVERSITY
5500 N Saint Louis Ave, Chicago IL 60625-4699
Janet Fredericks, Dean of Graduate College
773-442-6000 Fax: 773-442-6020
Website: www.neiu.edu
E-mail: j-fredericks@neiu.edu

NORTHERN BAPTIST THEOLOGICAL SEMINARY
660 E Butterfield Rd, Lombard IL 60148-5698
Charles Dresser, Executive Director of Enrollment
Management
630-620-2180 Fax: 630-620-2190
Website: www.seminary.edu
E-mail: admissions@seminary.edu

Rockford College
5050 E State St, Rockford IL 61108-2393
William Laffey, Director of Admission
800-892-2984

Rosalind Franklin University of Medicine and Science
3333 Green Bay Rd, North Chicago IL 60064-3037
847-578-3000

School of the Art Institute of Chicago
37 S Wabash Ave, Chicago IL 60603-3002
Director of Admissions
800-232-7242

Seabury-Western Theological Seminary
2122 Sheridan Rd, Evanston IL 60201-2976
847-328-9300

Spertus College
618 S Michigan Ave, Chicago IL 60605-1901
312-922-9012 Fax: 312-922-6406
Website: www.spertus.edu
E-mail: college@spertus.edu

Trinity Evangelical Divinity School
2065 Half Day Rd, Deerfield IL 60015-1241
800-345-8337

University of Illinois
PO Box 1649, Peoria IL 61656-1649
309-438-2181

University of Illinois at Springfield
One University Plaza, Springfield IL 62794
217-206-4847

University of St. Mary of the Lake
1000 E Maple Ave, Mundelein IL 60060-1967
847-566-6401

VANDERCOOK COLLEGE OF MUSIC
3140 S Federal St, Chicago IL 60616-3704
Tamara V. Trutwin, Student Recruiter
Kelly Westergaard, Admissions Coordinator
800-448-2655 ext. 230 Fax: 312-225-5211
Website: www.vandercook.edu
E-mail: admissions@vandercook.edu
Established 1928. Private. Coed. Accreditation: NCA;
NASM; Illinois State Board of Higher Learning. Tuition:
$7,945 undergrad, $3,960 graduate. Room & Board:
$6,500 undergrad, $1,950 graduate. Enrollment: 85 undergraduate. Faculty: 35. Student-faculty ratio: 6:1. Degrees: Bachelor of Music Education, Master of Music
Education. The only College in the U.S. solely devoted to
the preparation of music educators. There is a 100%
placement rate for those seeking a career in music education after graduation.

Wheaton College
501 College Ave, Wheaton IL 60187-5571
630-752-5000

INDIANA

ASSOCIATED MENNONITE BIBLICAL SEMINARIES
3003 Benham Ave, Elkhart IN 46517-1947
Randall C. Miller, Director of Admissions
800-964-2627 Fax: 574-295-0092
Website: www.ambs.edu
E-mail: admissions@ambs.edu

BETHANY THEOLOGICAL SEMINARY
615 National Rd W, Richmond IN 47374-4019
Dr. Eugene F. Roop, President
800-287-8822 Fax: 765-983-1840
Website: www.brethren.org/bethany
E-mail: bethanysem@aol.com

Christian Theological Seminary
1000 W 42nd St, Indianapolis IN 46208-3301
Mary L. Harris, Associate Dean for Student Services
800-585-0508 or 317-931-2300 Fax: 317-923-1961
Website: www.cts.edu
E-mail: admissions@cts.edu
See listing under "Theological Studies & Religious
Vocations"

Concordia Theological Seminary
6600 N Clinton St, Fort Wayne IN 46825-4996
Dr. Dean O. Wenthe, President
260-452-2100

Grace College and Theological Seminary
200 Seminary Dr, Winona Lake IN 46590-1224
800-54-GRACE

Indiana Wesleyan University
4201 S Washington St, Marion IN 46953-4974
765-674-6901

Oakland City University
138 N Lucretia St, Oakland City IN 47660
Brian J. Baker, Director of Admissions
800-737-5125 Fax: 812-749-1433
Website: www.oak.edu
E-mail: bbaker@oak.edu
See listing under "Universities"

Saint Meinrad School of Theology
200 Hill Dr, St Meinrad IN 47577
Rev. Jonathan Fassero, OSB, Director of Enrollment
800-634-6723

IOWA

Graceland University
1 University Place, Lamoni IA 50140
Brian Shantz, Vice President for Enrollment and Dean
of Admissions
641-784-5196 Fax: 641-784-5480
Website: www.admissions.graceland.edu
E-mail: admissions@graceland.edu

Loras College
1450 Alta Vista St, Dubuque IA 52001-4399
Tim Hauber, Director of Admissions
800-245-6727

PALMER COLLEGE OF CHIROPRACTIC
1000 Brady St, Davenport IA 52803-5287
800-722-3648 or 563-884-5656 Fax: 563-884-5414
Website: admissions.palmer.edu
E-mail: pcadmit@palmer.edu

UNIVERSITY OF DUBUQUE THEOLOGICAL SEMINARY
2000 University Ave, Dubuque IA 52001-5050
800-369-8387 Fax: 563-589-3110
Website: udtseminary.net
E-mail: udtsadms@dbq.edu

WARTBURG THEOLOGICAL SEMINARY
PO Box 5004, Dubuque IA 52004-5004
Heather Devine, Director of Admissions
563-589-0200 Fax: 563-589-0333
Website: www.wartburgseminary.edu
E-mail: admissions@wartburgseminary.edu

KANSAS

Central Baptist Theological Seminary
741 N 31st St, Kansas City KS 66102-3964
800-677-CBTS (2287)

Fort Hays State University
600 Park St, Hays KS 67601-4099
785-628-4000

Southwestern College
100 College St, Winfield KS 67156-2499
620-229-6000

University of Kansas
Lawrence KS 66045-0001
Alan Cerveny, Director of Admissions

University of Kansas Medical Center
3901 Rainbow Blvd, Kansas City KS 66160-0001
913-588-5000

KENTUCKY

Asbury Theological Seminary
204 N Lexington Ave, Wilmore KY 40390-1199
Janelle Vernon, Director of Admissions
800-2-ASBURY

Brescia University
717 Frederica St, Owensboro KY 42301-3023
Sr. Mary Austin Blank, OSB, Director of Admissions
877-BRESCIA

LEXINGTON THEOLOGICAL SEMINARY
631 S Limestone, Lexington KY 40508-3288
Erika Smith, Director of Admissions
859-252-0361 Fax: 859-281-6042
Website: www.lextheo.edu
E-mail: esmith@lextheo.edu

Louisville Presbyterian Seminary
1044 Alta Vista Rd, Louisville KY 40205-1798
Kerry Rice, Director of Admissions
502-895-3411 or 800-264-1839 Fax: 502-992-9399
Website: www.lpts.edu
E-mail: admissions@lpts.edu
Degrees offered MDiv, MA, DMin, ThM

Southern Baptist Theological Seminary
2825 Lexington Rd, Louisville KY 40280-0004
502-897-4011

LOUISIANA

New Orleans Baptist Theological Seminary
3939 Gentilly Blvd, New Orleans LA 70126-4858
504-282-4455

MAINE

Bangor Theological Seminary
PO Box 411, Bangor ME 04402-0411
Michael K. Huddy Director of Admissions
800-287-6781

HUSSON COLLEGE
One College Cir, Bangor ME 04401-2999
800-477-4723 or 207-941-7100 Fax: 207-941-7935
Website: www.husson.edu
E-mail: springs@husson.edu
See listing under "Universities"

MARYLAND

Capital Bible Seminary
6511 Princess Garden Pkwy
Lanham Seabrook MD 20706-3538
301-552-1400

National Technological University
1001 Fleet St, Baltimore MD 21202-4346
410-843-6401

Peabody Institute of the Johns Hopkins University
1 E Mount Vernon Pl, Baltimore MD 21202-2397
410-659-8150

St. Mary's Seminary & University
5400 Roland Ave, Baltimore MD 21210-1929
410-864-4000

Tai Sophia Insitute
7750 Montpelier Rd, Laurel MD 20723-6010
800-735-2968

MASSACHUSETTS

Andover Newton Theological School
210 Herrick Rd, Newton Center MA 02459-2243
800-964-2687 ext. 272

Blessed John XXIII National Seminary
558 South Ave, Weston MA 02493-2618
781-899-5500

Boston College
885 Centre St, Newton MA 02459-1100
617-552-4350

Boston Graduate School for Psychoanalysis
1583 Beacon St, Brookline MA 02446-4602
617-277-3915

Cambridge College
1000 Massachusetts Ave
Cambridge MA 02138-5304
Joy King, Associate Director of Enrollment Services
800-877-GRAD

Conway School of Landscape Design
PO Box 179, Conway MA 01341
413-369-4044

Curry College
1071 Blue Hill Ave, Milton MA 02186-2395
Bruce Weckworth, Director of Admissions
617-333-2210

Elms College
291 Springfield St, Chicopee MA 01013-2839
800-255-3567

Episcopal Divinity School
99 Brattle St, Cambridge MA 02138-3494
Christopher J. Medeiros, Director of Admissions,
Recruitment & Financial Aid
617-868-3450

Gordon-Conwell Theological Seminary
130 Essex St, South Hamilton MA 01982-2395
William B. Levin, Director of Admissions
978-468-7111

Hellenic College/Holy Cross Greek Orthodox School of
Theology
50 Goddard Ave, Brookline MA 02445-7415
Sonia Belcher, Director
617-731-3500

Hult International Business School
1 Education St, Cambridge MA 02141
617-746-1990

Massachusetts College of Liberal Arts
375 Church St, North Adams MA 01247-4124
Monica Joslin, Dean of Academic Studies
413-662-5207

MASSACHUSETTS SCHOOL OF LAW AT ANDOVER
500 Federal St, Andover MA 01810
Paula Colby-Clements, Esq, Director of Admissions
978-681-0800 Fax: 978-681-6330
Website: www.mslaw.edu
E-mail: pcolby@mslaw.edu

MASSACHUSETTS SCHOOL PROFESSIONAL PSYCHOLOGY
221 Rivermoor St, Boston MA 02132-4935
Mario Murga, Director of Admissions
617-327-6777 or 888-664-MSPP Fax: 617-327-4447
Website: www.mspp.edu
E-mail: admissions@mspp.edu
See listing under "Psychology"

MGH Institute of Health Professions
36 1st Ave, Boston MA 02129-4557
Michael Bonanno, Manager of Admissions
617-726-3140

THE NATIONAL GRADUATE SCHOOL OF QUALITY SYSTEMS MANAGEMENT
186 Jones Rd, Falmouth MA 02540-2908
Virginia C. Petisce, VP Enrollment Management
508-457-1313 Fax: 508-457-5347
Website: www.ngs.edu
E-mail: vpetisce@ngs.edu

New England College of Optometry
424 Beacon St, Boston MA 02115-1129
Larry Shattuck, Director of Admissions
800-824-5526

New England School of Acupuncture
40 Belmont St, Watertown MA 02472
617-926-1788

Regis College
235 Wellesley St, Weston MA 02493-1571
781-768-2000

School of the Museum of Fine Arts, Boston
230 The Fenway, Boston MA 02115-5534
Office of Admissions
617-369-3626 or 800-643-6078 Fax: 617-369-4264
Website: www.smfa.edu
E-mail: admissions@smfa.edu
See listing under "Universities"

Simmons College
300 Fenway, Boston MA 02115-5898
617-521-2000

Southern New England School of Law
333 Faunce Corner Rd
North Dartmouth MA 02747-1252
508-998-9600

Springfield College
263 Alden St, Springfield MA 01109-3788
Donald Shaw, Director of Graduate Admissions
413-748-3684

Tufts University
136 Harrison Ave, Boston MA 02111-1800
617-636-7000

University of Massachusetts Boston
100 William T Morrissey Blvd, Boston MA 02125-3393
Liliana Mickle, Director of Undergraduate Admissions
617-287-6000

Western New England College
1215 Wilbraham Rd, Springfield MA 01119-2655
413-782-1321

Woods Hole Oceanographic Institution
86 Water St, Woods Hole MA 02543
508-289-2219

MICHIGAN

Andrews University
Berrien Springs MI 49104-0001
Randall Graves, Director of Recruitment Services
800-253-2874 Fax: 269-471-2670
Website: www.connect.andrews.edu
E-mail: gravesr@andrews.edu

CALVIN THEOLOGICAL SEMINARY
3233 Burton St SE, Grand Rapids MI 49546-4301
Greg Janke, Director of Admissions
616-957-6036 Fax: 616-957-8621
Website: www.calvinseminary.edu
E-mail: admissions@calvinseminary.edu

Center for Humanistic Studies
26811 Orchard Lake Rd
Farmington Hills MI 48334-4512
248-476-1122

Davenport University
415 Fulton St E, Grand Rapids MI 49503-4407
Lynnae Selberg, Director of Enrollment
616-451-3511

Kendall College of Art & Design
17 Fountain St NW, Grand Rapids MI 49503-3002
Dr. Oliver H. Evans, President
800-676-2787 or 616-451-2787 Fax: 616-831-9689
Website: www.kcad.edu
E-mail: brittons@ferris.edu

Kettering University
(formerly GMI Engineering & Management Institute)
1700 W 3rd Ave, Flint MI 48504-4898
Tony Hain, V.P., Graduate & Corporate Connections Program
800-955-4464

Michigan State University College of Law
316 Law College Bldg, East Lansing MI 48824-1300
LoRae A. Hamilton, Assistant Director of Admissions
517-432-0222

Michigan Technological University
1400 Townsend Dr, Houghton MI 49931-1200
Dr. Sung M. Lee, Dean
906-487-2327

Michigan Theological Seminary
41550 E Ann Arbor Trl, Plymouth MI 48170
734-207-9581

SAINTS CYRIL AND METHODIUS SEMINARY
3535 Indian Trl, Orchard Lake MI 48324-1623
Karen Shirilla, Academic Dean
248-683-0312 Fax: 248-738-6735
Website: www.orchardlakeseminary.org
E-mail: sscms.dean@comcast.net

Cooley Law School, Thomas M.
PO Box 13038, Lansing MI 48901-3038
517-371-5140

Western Michigan University
Kalamazoo MI 49008
269-387-1000

Western Theological Seminary
101 E 13th St, Holland MI 49423-3622
616-392-8555

MINNESOTA

ADLER GRADUATE SCHOOL
1001 Highway 7 #311, Hopkins MN 55305-4723
Evelyn Haas, Director of Admissions
952-988-4327 Fax: 952-988-4171
Website: www.alfredadler.edu
E-mail: ev@alfredadler.edu

Bethel Seminary
3949 Bethel Dr, Saint Paul MN 55112-6940
Joseph Dworak, Director of Admissions
651-638-6288

Capella University
225 S 6th St Fl 9, Minneapolis MN 55402-4652
Enrollment Services
888-CAPELLA (227-3552)

College of Saint Scholastica
1200 Kenwood Ave, Duluth MN 55811-4199
Brian Dalton, V.P. of Enrollment Management
800-447-5444

Crown College
8700 College View Dr, Saint Bonifacius MN 55375
Nancy Hyndman, Director of Crown Adult Programs
952-446-4300

Hazelden Graduate School
PO Box 11, Center City MN 55012
651-213-4175

LUTHER SEMINARY
2481 Como Ave, Saint Paul MN 55108-1496
Rev. Ronald Olson, Contact
800-588-4373 Fax: 651-641-3521
Website: www.luthersem.edu
E-mail: admissions@luthersem.edu

Mayo School of Health Sciences
200 1st Ave SW, Rochester MN 55905-0001
507-284-3678

Metropolitan State University
700 7th St E, Saint Paul MN 55106-5000
Rosa Rodriguez, Admissions Director
651-793-1300 Fax: 651-793-1546
Website: www.metrostate.edu
E-mail: rosa.rodriguez@metrostate.edu

NORTHWESTERN HEALTH SCIENCES UNIVERSITY
2501 W 84th St, Bloomington MN 55431-1599
Bill Kuehl, Director of Admissions
952-888-4777 ext. 409 Fax: 952-888-6713
Website: www.nwhealth.edu
E-mail: admit@nwhealth.edu
See listing under "Chiropractic Medicine"

St. Mary's University of Minnesota
2500 Park Ave, Minneapolis MN 55404-4403
866-437-2788

UNITED THEOLOGICAL SEMINARY OF THE TWIN CITIES
3000 5th St NW, New Brighton MN 55112-2598
Sandra H. Casmey, Director of Admissions
651-255-6107 or 800-937-1316 Fax: 651-633-4315
Website: www.unitedseminary-mn.org
E-mail: admissions@unitedseminary-mn.org

Walden University
155 5th Ave S Ste 100, Minneapolis MN 55401-2511
Office of Student Enrollment
800-444-6795

William Mitchell College of Law
875 Summit Ave, Saint Paul MN 55105-3030
651-227-9171

MISSISSIPPI

Mississippi College
151 E Griffith St, Jackson MS 39201-1302
601-353-3907

Mississippi University for Women
Box W-280, Columbus MS 39701
Dr. Barbara Moore, Coordinator
877-GO-2-THEW

Reformed Theological Seminary
5422 Clinton Blvd, Jackson MS 39209-3099
601-923-1600

Wesley Biblical Seminary
PO Box 9938, Jackson MS 39286-0938
John Wilson, Vice President of Student Affairs & Admissions
601-957-1314

MISSOURI

Aquinas Institute of Theology
3642 Lindell Blvd, Saint Louis MO 63108-3302
Ron Knapp, M.Div., Director of Admissions
800-977-3869

ASSEMBLIES OF GOD THEOLOGICAL SEMINARY
1435 N Glenstone Ave, Springfield MO 65802-2131
Dr. Mario Guerreiro, Director of Enrollment Management
800-467-AGTS Fax: 417-268-1001
Website: www.agts.edu
E-mail: agts@agseminary.edu

Calvary Bible College & Theological Seminary
15800 Calvary Rd, Kansas City MO 64147-1341
Robert M. Reinsch, Director of Admissions
800-326-3960 Fax: 816-331-4474
Website: www.calvary.edu
E-mail: admissions@calvary.edu

Central Missouri State University
Warrensburg MO 64093-8888
Steve Wilson, Dean of Graduate Studies
800-956-0177

Columbia College
1001 Rogers St, Columbia MO 65216-0001
Regina Morin, Director of Admissions
573-875-7352 Fax: 573-875-7506
Website: www.ccis.edu
E-mail: gradadmissions@ccis.edu

Concordia Seminary
801 De Mun Ave, Saint Louis MO 63105-3199
314-721-5934

COVENANT THEOLOGICAL SEMINARY
12330 Conway Rd, Saint Louis MO 63141-8697
Dr. Bryan Chapell, President
800-264-8064 Fax: 314-434-4819
Website: www.covenantseminary.edu
E-mail: admissions@covenantseminary.edu

Eden Theological Seminary
475 E Lockwood Ave
Webster Groves MO 63119-3192
Diane Windler, Director of Admissions
800-969-3627

Forest Institute of Professional Psychology
1322 S Campbell Ave, Springfield MO 65807-1445
417-831-7902

KANSAS CITY UNIVERSITY OF MEDICINE AND BIOSCIENCES
College of Osteopathic Medicine
1750 Independence Ave
Kansas City MO 64106-1453
Phil Byrne, Director of Recruitment
800-234-4847 Fax: 816-283-2484
Website: www.kcumb.edu
E-mail: admissions@kcumb.edu

KENRICK SCHOOL OF THEOLOGY
5200 Glennon Dr, Saint Louis MO 63119-4330
Msgr. Ted L. Wojcicki, President-Rector
314-792-6100 Fax: 314-792-6500
Website: www.kenrick.edu
E-mail: registrar@kenrick.edu

KIRKSVILLE COLLEGE OF OSTEOPATHIC MEDICINE
A.T. STILL UNIVERSITY
800 W Jefferson St, Kirksville MO 63501-1443
Admissions Counselor
866-626-2878 or 660-626-2237 Fax: 660-626-2969
Website: www.atsu.edu
E-mail: admissions@atsu.edu

Logan College of Chiropractic
1851 Schoettler Rd, Chesterfield MO 63017-5529
Patrick Browne, VP of Enrollment Services
800-533-9210

Midwestern Baptist Theological Seminary
5001 N Oak Trfy, Kansas City MO 64118-4697
816-414-3700

MIDWEST THEOLOGICAL SEMINARY
851 Parr Rd, PO Box 365, Wentzville MO 63385-0365
Dr. James Song, President
636-327-4645 Fax: 636-327-4715
Website: www.midwest.edu
E-mail: inf@midwest.edu

NAZARENE THEOLOGICAL SEMINARY
1700 E Meyer Blvd, Kansas City MO 64131-1263
Roger L. Hahn, Dean of the Faculty
816-333-6254 Fax: 816-333-6271
Website: www.nts.edu
E-mail: rlhahn@nts.edu

Rockhurst University
1100 Rockhurst Rd, Kansas City MO 64110-2561
Mark Kopenski, VP of Enrollment Management
816-501-4000

Saint Paul School of Theology
5123 Truman Rd, Kansas City MO 64127
Alan D. Herndon, Director of Admissions
816-483-9600

SCHOOL OF HEALTH MANAGEMENT - ONLINE
A.T. STILL UNIVERSITY
800 W Jefferson St, Kirksville MO 63501-1443
Admissions Counselor
866-626-2878 or 660-626-2237 Fax: 660-626-2969
Website: www.atsu.edu
E-mail: admissions@atsu.edu

Truman State University
100 E Normal, Kirksville MO 63501
Office of Admission
660-785-4000 Fax: 660-785-4181
Website: admissions.truman.edu
E-mail: admissions@truman.edu

University of Missouri
102 Parker, Rolla MO 65409
Lynn Stichnote, Director of Admission
573-341-4164

University of Missouri
1 University Blvd, Saint Louis MO 63121-4499
Dr. Judith Walker de Felix, Dean of Graduate School
314-516-5458 Fax: 314-516-6759
Website: www.umsl.edu
E-mail: gradadm@umsl.edu

Webster University
470 E Lockwood Ave, Saint Louis MO 63119-3194
Matt Noland, Director
314-968-7100 Fax: 314-968-7116
Website: www.webster.edu
E-mail: nolan@webster.edu
See listing under "Universities"

MONTANA

Montana State University - Billings
1500 University Dr, Billings MT 59101-0252
Karen Everett, Director
800-565-MSUB

Montana Tech of the University of Montana
1300 W Park St, Butte MT 59701-8997
800-445-TECH

NEBRASKA

Chadron State College
1000 Main St, Chadron NE 69337-2690
308-432-6000

Clarkson College
101 S 42nd St, Omaha NE 68131-2715
Sara Bonney, Director of Admissions
402-552-3100 Fax: 402-552-6057
Website: www.clarksoncollege.edu
E-mail: admiss@clarksoncollege.edu

Peru State College
PO Box 10, Peru NE 68421-0010
402-872-2241 Fax: 402-872-2375
E-mail: admissions@pscvax.peru.edu

University of Nebraska Medical Center
987810 Nebraska Medical Center
Omaha NE 68198-7810
800-626-8431

NEVADA

Touro University College of Osteopathic Medicine
874 American Pacific Dr, Henderson NV 89014
702-856-3262

University of Nevada Las Vegas
4505 S Maryland Pkwy, Las Vegas NV 89154-9901
800-334-8658

NEW HAMPSHIRE

Antioch University New England
40 Avon St, Keene NH 03431-3516
David Caruso, President
Leatrice A. Johnson, Director of Admissions
603-357-6265 Fax: 603-357-0718
Website: www.antiochne.edu
E-mail: admissions@antiochne.edu

Franklin Pierce Law Center
2 White St, Concord NH 03301-4176
603-228-9217

Rivier College
420 S Main St, Nashua NH 03060-5086
Ann McCormick, Director of Graduate Admissions
603-888-1311

NEW JERSEY

Immaculate Conception Seminary of Seton Hall University
400 S Orange Ave, South Orange NJ 07079-2646
973-761-9575

New Brunswick Theological Seminary
17 Seminary Pl, New Brunswick NJ 08901-1196
732-247-5241

New Jersey City University
2039 John F Kennedy Blvd, Jersey City NJ 07305
Carmen Panlilio, Asst. V.P. for Admissions and
Financial Aid
201-200-3409 Fax: 201-200-3411
Website: www.njcu.edu
E-mail: admissions@njcu.edu

Princeton Theological Seminary
PO Box 821, Princeton NJ 08542-0803
609-921-8300

Rider University
2083 Lawrenceville Rd, Lawrenceville NJ 08648-3099
Dr. John Carpenter, Dean Graduate Studies
609-896-5033

Seton Hall University School of Law
1 Newark Center, Newark NJ 07102
973-642-8747

UMDNJ Graduate School of Biomedical Sciences
185 S Orange Ave, Newark NJ 07103
973-972-4511

UMDNJ-New Jersey Dental School
110 Bergen St, Newark NJ 07103-2400
973-972-4633

UMDNJ-New Jersey Medical School
185 S Orange Ave, Newark NJ 07103-2757
973-972-4539

UMDNJ-Robert Wood Johnson Medical School
671 Hoes Ln, Piscataway NJ 08854-5627
732-235-5600

UMDNJ School of Public Health
170 Frelinghuysen Rd Rm 236, Piscataway NJ 08854
732-445-0199

UNIVERSITY OF MEDICINE AND DENTISTRY OF NEW JERSEY

School of Osteopathic Medicine
One Medical Center Dr Suite 210, Stratford NJ 08084
Paula F. Slade, M.A.S., Director of Enrollment Services
856-566-7050 Fax: 856-566-6895
Website: som.umdnj.edu
E-mail: fennerpa@umdnj.edu

Westminster Choir College of Rider University
101 Walnut Ln, Princeton NJ 08540-3819
Matthew T. Kadlubowski, Director of Admissions
609-921-7144

NEW MEXICO

Southwest Acupuncture College
1622 Galisteo St, Santa Fe NM 87505-4747
505-438-8884

NEW YORK

Adelphi University
Garden City NY 11530
516-877-3100

ALBANY LAW SCHOOL OF UNION UNIVERSITY

80 New Scotland Ave, Albany NY 12208-3494
Gail Bensen, Director of Admissions
518-445-2311 Fax: 518-445-2315
Website: www.albanylaw.edu
E-mail: admissions@albanylaw.edu

Bank Street College of Education
610 W 112th St, New York NY 10025-1898
212-875-4404

Bexley Hall Seminary
26 Broadway, Rochester NY 14607
585-546-2160

Brooklyn Law School
250 Joralemon St, Brooklyn NY 11201-3798
Henry W. Haverstick, III, Dean of Admissions &
Financial Aid
718-780-7906

Christ the King Seminary
PO Box 607, East Aurora NY 14052-0607
585-652-8900

COLGATE ROCHESTER CROZER DIVINITY SCHOOL

1100 S Goodman St, Rochester NY 14620-2589
Robert Jones, V.P. of Enrollment Services
585-271-1320 or 888-937-3732 Fax: 585-271-8013
Website: www.crcds.edu
E-mail: admissions@crcds.edu

CUNY City College
Convent Ave at 138th St, New York NY 10031
Celia Lloyd, Interim Director of Admissions
212-650-6977

CUNY Graduate Center
365 5th Ave, New York NY 10016-4309
212-817-7000

FIVE TOWNS COLLEGE

305 N Service Rd, Dix Hills NY 11746-5871
631-424-7000 ext. 2110 Fax: 631-656-2172
Website: www.fivetowns.edu
E-mail: admissions@ftc.edu
See listing under "Universities"

Fordham University - Lincoln Center
113 W 60th St, New York NY 10023-7484
212-636-6000

General Theological Seminary
175 9th Ave, New York NY 10011-4983
212-243-5150

Hebrew Union College
Jewish Institute of Religion
1 W 4th St, New York NY 10012-1186
212-674-5300

Iona College
715 North Ave, New Rochelle NY 10801-1890
Tom Weede, Director of Admissions
914-633-2000

LAMONT-DOHERTY EARTH OBSERVATORY

of Columbia University
Palisades NY 10964
Mia Leo, Department Administrator
845-365-8550 Fax: 845-365-8163
Website: eesc.columbia.edu
E-mail: ess@columbia.edu

Long Island University-C. W. Post Campus
720 Northern Blvd, Brookville NY 11548-1300
Beth Carson, Director of Graduate Admissions
516-299-2900 Fax: 516-299-2137
Website: www.liu.edu/cwpost
E-mail: enroll@cwpost.liu.edu

Long Island University
Rockland Graduate Campus
70 Route 340, Orangeburg NY 10962-2219
Kelly J. McCafferty, M.S., Director of Admissions
845-359-7200

Long Island University
Westchester Graduate Campus of Long Island
University
735 Anderson Hill Rd, Purchase NY 10577
Ellen Brief, Admissions, Marketing and Student
Services
800-472-3548

Manhattan College
4513 Manhattan College Pkwy
Riverdale NY 10471-4099
William J. Bisset Jr., Asst. V.P. for Enrollment
Management
718-862-7200

Manhattan School of Music
120 Claremont Ave, New York NY 10027-4698
Amy A. Anderson, Director of Admission & Financial
Aid
212-749-2802 ext. 2

MANNES COLLEGE OF MUSIC

150 W 85th St, New York NY 10024-4499
Office of Admissions
800-292-3040 or 212-580-0210 Fax: 212-580-1738
Website: www.mannes.edu
E-mail: mannesadmissions@newschool.edu

Mercy College
555 Broadway, Dobbs Ferry NY 10522-1189
Kathleen Jackson, Director of Admissions
800-MERCY-NY

Mid-America Baptist Theological Seminary
2810 Curry Rd, Schenectady NY 12303-3463
518-355-4000

Mount Sinai School of Medicine of New York University
Box 1022, 1 Gustave L Levy Place
New York NY 10029
212-241-6546

New York Academy of Art
111 Franklin St, New York NY 10013
212-966-0300

NEW YORK CHIROPRACTIC COLLEGE

PO Box 800, Seneca Falls NY 13148-0800
Michael P. Lynch, Director of Admissions
800-234-6922 (NYCC) Fax: 315-568-3087
Website: www.nycc.edu
E-mail: enrolnow@nycc.edu

NEW YORK COLLEGE OF PODIATRIC MEDICINE

1800 Park Ave, New York NY 10035-1940
Carlene Colston, Director of Admissions and Enrollment
Management
800-526-6966 Fax: 212-722-4918
Website: www.nycpm.edu
E-mail: ccolston@nycpm.edu

New York Law School
57 Worth St, New York NY 10013-2960
Tom Matos, Assistant Dean for Admissions
212-431-2888

New York Medical College
Valhalla NY 10595
914-594-4000

NEW YORK THEOLOGICAL SEMINARY

475 Riverside Suite Ste 500, New York NY 10115
Yon Su Kang, Contact
212-870-1211 Fax: 212-870-1236
Website: www.nyts.edu
E-mail: online@nyts.edu

Niagara University
PO Box 2011, Niagara University NY 14109-2011
George Pachter, Dean of Admissions & Records
800-462-2111

NY College of Traditional Chinese Medicine
155 1st St, Mineola NY 11501
516-739-1545

Ohr Somayach Tanenbaum Educational Center
PO Box 334, Monsey NY 10952-0334
845-425-1370

Pace University
1 Martine Ave, White Plains NY 10606
914-442-2000

Pacific College of Oriental Medicine - New York
915 Broadway 3rd Floor, New York NY 10010
212-982-3456

POLYTECHNIC UNIVERSITY

40 Saw Mill River Rd, Hawthorne NY 10532-1507
LaVerne Clark, Director of Campus Operations
914-323-2000 Fax: 914-323-2010
Website: www.poly.edu/west
E-mail: westinfo@west.poly.edu

PURCHASE COLLEGE STATE UNIVERSITY OF NEW YORK (SUNY)

735 Anderson Hill Rd, Purchase NY 10577-1400
Betsy Immergut, Director of Admissions
914-251-6300 Fax: 914-251-6314
Website: www.purchase.edu
See listing under "Universities"

Rabbi Isaac Elchanan Theological Seminary
2495 Amsterdam Ave, New York NY 10033
212-960-5344

Roberts Wesleyan College
2301 Westside Dr, Rochester NY 14624-1997
Office of Admissions
585-594-6400 Fax: 585-594-6371
Website: www.roberts.edu
E-mail: admissions@roberts.edu

Rockefeller University
1230 York Ave, New York NY 10021
212-327-8000

Russell Sage Graduate School
45 Ferry St, Troy NY 12180-4115
518-244-2264

St. Bernard's School of Theology and Ministry
120 French Rd, Rochester NY 14618
585-271-3657

St. Joseph's Seminary
201 Seminary Ave, Yonkers NY 10704-1896
914-968-6200

St. Vladimir's Orthodox Theological Seminary
575 Scarsdale Rd, Tuckahoe NY 10707-1659
914-961-8313

Seminary of the Immaculate Conception
440 W Neck Rd, Huntington NY 11743-1626
631-423-0483

Sunbridge College
285 Hungry Hollow Rd, Spring Valley NY 10977
845-425-0055

SUNY at Albany
1400 Washington Ave, Albany NY 12222-1000
Jonathan Bartow, Director of Graduate Studies
518-442-3980

SUNY Health Science Center
450 Clarkson Ave, Brooklyn NY 11203-2056
718-270-1000

Teachers College of Columbia University
525 W 120th St, New York NY 10027-6625
212-678-3000

Touro College
300 Nassau Rd, Huntington NY 11743-4342
631-421-2244

Tri-State College of Acupuncture
80 8th Ave #400, New York NY 10011-5126
212-242-2255

Unification Theological Seminary
30 Seminary Dr, Barrytown NY 12507-5021
Tessa Thonett, Director of Admissions
845-752-3015

UNION THEOLOGICAL SEMINARY

3041 Broadway, New York NY 10027-5792
Joseph C. Hough, Jr., President
212-662-7100 Fax: 212-280-1416
Website: www.uts.columbia.edu
E-mail: admissns@uts.columbia.edu

University at Buffalo SUNY
408 Capen Hall, Amherst NY 14260
716-645-2000

Weill Medical College of Cornell University
1300 York Ave, New York NY 10021-4896
212-746-5454

Yeshiva University
Benjamin N. Cardozo School of Law
55 5th Ave, New York NY 10003-4301
Robert Schwartz, Assistant Dean for Admissions
212-790-0274

Yeshiva Zichron Aryeh
100 Cedarhurst Ave, Cedarhurst NY 11516
516-295-5700

NORTH CAROLINA

Atlantic University of Chinese Medicine
64 Westgate Pkwy, Asheville NC 28806
828-225-8550

East Carolina University
Ragsdale 113, Greenville NC 27858
Dr. Thomas Feldbush, Dean

HOOD THEOLOGICAL SEMINARY
1810 Lutheran Synod Dr, Salisbury NC 28144
Albert J. D. Aymer, President
704-636-6823 Fax: 704-636-7699
Website: www.hoodseminary.edu
E-mail: dstewart@hoodseminary.com

Jung Tao School of Classical Chinese Medicine
207 Dale Adams Rd, Sugar Grove NC 28679
828-297-4181

NEW LIFE THEOLOGICAL SEMINARY
PO Box 790106, Charlotte NC 28206
Judith Mann, Registrar
704-334-6882 Fax: 704-334-6885
Website: www.nlts.org

Queens University of Charlotte
1900 Selwyn Ave, Charlotte NC 28274-0002
704-337-2212

Reformed Theological Seminary
2101 Carmel Rd, Charlotte NC 28226
704-366-5066

SOUTHEASTERN BAPTIST THEOLOGICAL SEMINARY
Southeastern College at Wake Forest
PO Box 1889, Wake Forest NC 27588-1889
Jerry L. Yandell, Director of Admissions
919-761-2280 or 800-284-6317 Fax: 919-556-0998
Website: www.sebts.edu
E-mail: admissions@sebts.edu

Southern Evangelical Seminary
3000 Tilley Morris Rd, Matthews NC 28105-8635
704-847-5600

University of North Carolina at Pembroke
PO Box 1510, Pembroke NC 28372-1510
910-521-6000

Wake Forest University
Medical Center Blvd, Winston Salem NC 27157-0001
336-748-4424

NORTH DAKOTA
Minot State University
500 University Ave W, Minot ND 58707-0002
Phyllis Butler, Contact
800-777-0750 ext. 3250

Tri-College University
Fargo ND 58105
701-231-8170

Valley City State University
101 College St SW, Valley City ND 58072-4024
School of Education - Graduate Studies
800-532-8641
Website: www.vcsu.edu/graduate
E-mail: graduate@vcsu.edu

OHIO
Ashland Theological Seminary
910 Center St, Ashland OH 44805-4007
Mario Guerreiro, Director of Admissions
419-289-5161

BEXLEY HALL SEMINARY
583 Sheridan Ave, Columbus OH 43209-2325
John Kevern, Dean & President
614-231-3095 Fax: 614-231-3236
Website: www.bexley.edu
E-mail: columbus@bexley.edu or
rochester@bexley.edu

Capital University Law School
303 E Broad St, Columbus OH 43215-3200
Linda J. Mihely, Asst. Dean of Admission & Financial Aid
614-236-6310

Cleveland State University
2121 Euclid Ave RW 204, Cleveland OH 44115
Dr. William Bailey, Director of Graduate Admissions
888-CSU-OHIO Fax: 216-687-9210
Website: www.csuohio.edu
E-mail: admissions@csuohio.edu

Hebrew Union College - Jewish Institute of Religion
3101 Clifton Ave, Cincinnati OH 45220-2488
513-221-1875

Kent State University
PO Box 5190, Kent OH 44242-0001
330-672-2661

Medical University of Ohio
3000 Arlington Ave, Toledo OH 43614
419-383-4000 Fax: 419-383-2800
Website: www.meduohio.edu

Methodist Theological School in Ohio
3081 Columbus Pike, Delaware OH 43015-3211
John W. Brown, Interim Director of Enrollment Management
800-333-6876

Miami University
E High St, Oxford OH 45056
513-529-2531

Northeastern Ohio Univ Coll of Medicine
PO Box 95, Rootstown OH 44272-0095
330-325-2511

OHIO COLLEGE OF PODIATRIC MEDICINE
10515 Carnegie Ave, Cleveland OH 44106
Lois Lott, Dean of Student Affairs
216-231-3300 Fax: 216-231-0453
Website: www.ocpm.edu
E-mail: llott@ocpm.edu

Trinity Lutheran Seminary
2199 E Main St, Columbus OH 43209-2334
Karen S. White, Diaconal Minister, Director of Admissions
614-235-4136

United Theological Seminary
4501 Denlinger Rd, Trotwood OH 45426
Betty J. Stutler, Director of Admissions
800-322-5817 Fax: 937-529-2292
Website: www.united.edu
E-mail: admissions@united.edu

Winebrenner Theological Seminary
950 N Main St, Findlay OH 45840
Dr. David Draper, President
800-992-4987

OKLAHOMA
Oklahoma City University
2501 N Blackwelder Ave
Oklahoma City OK 73106-1493
Shery Boyles, Director of Admissions
405-521-5050

Oklahoma State University
Stillwater OK 74078
Gordon Emslie, Dean
405-744-6368 Fax: 405-744-0355
Website: www.okstate.edu

Oklahoma State University Center of Health Sciences
College of Osteopathic Medicine
1111 W 17th St, Tulsa OK 74107-1898
918-582-1972

Oral Roberts University
Adult Learning Service Center
7777 S Lewis Ave, Tulsa OK 74171-0001
800-678-8876 Fax: 918-495-7965
Website: www.oru.edu
E-mail: alsc@oru.edu

Phillips Theological Seminary
901 N Mingo Rd, Tulsa OK 74116-5612
918-610-8303

OREGON
George Fox University
12753 SW 68th Ave, Portland OR 97223-8355
503-639-0559

Marylhurst University
17600 Pacific Hwy (Hwy 43)
Marylhurst OR 97036-0261
Director of Admissions
800-634-9982 ext. 6268 Fax: 503-635-6585
Website: www.marylhurst.edu
E-mail: studentinfo@marylhurst.edu

Mt. Angel Seminary
1 Abbey Dr, Saint Benedict OR 97373
503-845-3951

Multnomah Bible College and Biblical Seminary
8435 NE Glisan St, Portland OR 97220-5898
Daniel R. Lockwood, President
800-275-4672

National College of Naturopathic Medicine
049 SW Porter St, Portland OR 97201
503-499-4343

OREGON COLLEGE OF ORIENTAL MEDICINE
10525 SE Cherry Blossom Dr, Portland OR 97216
Linda Powell, Admissions Coordinator
503-253-3443 Fax: 503-253-2701
Website: www.ocom.edu
E-mail: admissions@ocom.edu

Oregon Graduate Institute of Science & Technology
20000 NW Walker Rd, Beaverton OR 97006-8921
503-748-1121

Western Seminary
5511 SE Hawthorne Blvd, Portland OR 97215-3367
503-517-1800

Western States Chiropractic College
2900 NE 132nd Ave, Portland OR 97230-3014
Lee Smith, Director of Admissions
800-641-5641

PENNSYLVANIA
American College
270 S Bryn Mawr Ave, Bryn Mawr PA 19010-2105
610-526-1000

Arcadia University
450 S Easton Rd, Glenside PA 19038-3295
Dennis Nostrand, VP for Enrollment Management
877-ARCADIA (877-272-2342) Fax: 215-881-8767
Website: www.arcadia.edu
E-mail: admiss@arcadia.edu
See listing under "Universities"

Bethel Seminary of the East
1605 Limekiln Pike, Dresher PA 19025-1007
215-641-4801

BIBLICAL THEOLOGICAL SEMINARY
200 N Main St, Hatfield PA 19440-2421
Pamela J. Smith, VP for Student Advancement
800-235-4021 Fax: 215-368-7002
Website: www.biblical.edu
E-mail: admissions@biblical.edu

Bryn Mawr College
101 N Merion Ave, Bryn Mawr PA 19010-2899
610-526-5000

Calvary Baptist Theological Seminary
1380 S Valley Forge Rd, Lansdale PA 19446
215-368-7538

Clarion University of Pennsylvania
840 Wood St, Clarion PA 16214-1232
William Bailey, Dean of Enrollment Management
814-393-2306 Fax: 814-393-2030
Website: www.clarion.edu
E-mail: admissions@clarion.edu

Duquesne University
600 Forbes Ave, Pittsburgh PA 15282-0001
Paul-James Cukanna, Director of Admissions
412-396-5000

Edinboro University of Pennsylvania
Edinboro PA 16444-0001
814-732-2000

EVANGELICAL SCHOOL OF THEOLOGY
121 S College St, Myerstown PA 17067-1299
Tom Maiello, Dean of Admissions
800-532-5775 Fax: 717-866-4667
Website: www.evangelical.edu
E-mail: admissions@evangelical.edu

Gannon University
109 University Sq, Erie PA 16541-0002
Debbie Meszaros, Director of Graduate Admissions
800-GANNON-U Fax: 814-871-5803
Website: www.gannon.edu
E-mail: admissions@gannon.edu

Gwynedd-Mercy College
1325 Sumneytown Pike, Gwynedd Valley PA 19437
Dennis Murphy, V.P. Enrollment Management
800-DIAL-GMC

Holy Family University
9801 Frankford Avenue, Philadelphia PA 19114
Margaret Wendling, Director of Graduate Admissions
215-637-7203 Fax: 215-637-1478
Website: www.holyfamily.edu

Lancaster Theological Seminary of the United Church of Christ
555 W James St, Lancaster PA 17603-2830
Patricia Huffman Matz, Director of Admissions
800-393-0654 ext. 141

Lock Haven University
Lock Haven PA 17745
Enrollment Services
570-893-2006

LUTHERAN THEOLOGICAL SEMINARY
7301 Germantown Ave, Philadelphia PA 19119-1794
Rick Summy, Director of Admissions
800-286-4616 Fax: 215-248-4577
Website: www.ltsp.edu
E-mail: admissions@ltsp.edu

LUTHERAN THEOLOGICAL SEMINARY AT GETTYSBURG
61 Seminary Ridge, Gettysburg PA 17325-1795
Nancy E. Gable (Diaconal Minister), Assoc. Dean of Church Vocations
800-MLU-THER Fax: 717-334-3469
Website: www.ltsg.edu
E-mail: admissions@ltsg.edu

MOUNT ALOYSIUS COLLEGE
7373 Admiral Peary Hwy, Cresson PA 16630-1999
Frank C. Crouse Jr., Vice President for Enrollment Management
814-886-6383 or 888-823-2220 Fax: 814-886-6441
Website: www.mtaloy.edu
E-mail: admissions@mtaloy.edu

Palmer Theological Seminary
6 E Lancaster Ave, Wynnewood PA 19096-3495
610-896-5000

Penn State Dickinson School of Law
150 S College St, Carlisle PA 17013-2861
717-240-5000

Penn State Great Valley School
of Graduate Professional Studies
30 E Swedesford Rd, Malvern PA 19355-1488
610-648-3200

Pennsylvania Academy of the Fine Arts
118 N Broad St, Philadelphia PA 19102-1598
Angela Smith, Director of Admissions
215-972-7625

Pennsylvania College of Optometry
8360 Old York Rd, Elkins Park PA 19027-1598
Dr. James Caldwell, Director of Admissions
800-824-6262

Pennsylvania State Milton S Hershey Medical Center
College of Medicine
500 University Dr Box 850, Hershey PA 17033
717-534-8521

Philadelphia College of Osteopathic Medicine
4170 City Ave, Philadelphia PA 19131-1610
Carol Fox, Associate Dean of Admissions
215-871-6700

Pittsburgh Theological Seminary
616 N Highland Ave, Pittsburgh PA 15206-2525
Sherry Sparks, Director of Admissions
800-451-4194 or 412-362-5610 ext. 2115
Fax: 412-363-3260
Website: www.pts.edu
E-mail: sparks@pts.edu
See listing under "Theological Studies & Religious Vocations"

Reformed Episcopal Seminary
826 2nd Ave, Blue Bell PA 19422-1257
Danae L. Smith, Contact
610-292-9852

Reformed Presbyterian Theological Seminary
7418 Penn Ave, Pittsburgh PA 15208-2594
Dr. Jerry O'Neill, President
412-731-8690

Robert Morris College
600 5th Ave, Pittsburgh PA 15219-3010
412-227-6800

Rosemont College
1400 Montgomery Ave, Rosemont PA 19010-1699
Richard Donagher, Director of Graduate Studies

ST. TIKHON'S ORTHODOX THEOLOGICAL SEMINARY
PO Box 130, South Canaan PA 18459-0130
Metropolitan Herman, President
Bishop Tikhon, Rector
Very Rev. Michael G. Dahulich, Ph.D., Dean

570-937-4411 Fax: 570-937-3100
Website: www.stots.edu
E-mail: stots@stots.edu

Seton Hill University
Greensburg PA 15601-1599
Jenell Krymowski, Program Advisor
800-826-6234

Temple University
3307 N Broad St, Philadelphia PA 19140-5101
215-787-7000

Temple University School of Podiatric Medicine
8th & Race St, Philadelphia PA 19107
215-629-0300

Temple University Tyler School of Art
Beech and Penrose Aves, Elkins Park PA 19027
215-782-2875

Trinity Episcopal School for Ministry
311 11th St, Ambridge PA 15003-2397
Shirley A. Bruce, Registrar/Financial Aid Director
724-266-3838

Westminster Theological Seminary
PO Box 27009, Philadelphia PA 19118-0009
Daniel A. Cason, Director of Admissions
800-373-0119

Widener University School of Law
PO Box 69380, Harrisburg PA 17106-9380
Eric Kniskern, Assistant Director of Admissions
717-541-3900

Won Institute of Graduate Studies
137 S Easton Rd, Glenside PA 19038
Director of Admissions
215-884-8942

SOUTH CAROLINA

Bob Jones University
1700 Wade Hampton Blvd
Greenville SC 29614-0001
David Christ, Director of Admissions
800-BJ-AND-ME Fax: 800-2-FAX-BJU
Website: www.bju.edu
E-mail: admissions@bju.edu
See listing under "Universities"

CIU Graduate School
PO Box 3122, Columbia SC 29230-3122
Michelle MacGregor, Director of University Admissions
800-777-2227 Fax: 803-333-0607
Website: www.ciu.edu
E-mail: yesgrad@ciu.edu
See listing under "Theological Studies & Religious Vocations"

Lutheran Theological Southern Seminary
4201 Main St, Columbia SC 29203-5863
803-786-5150

Medical University of South Carolina
PO Box 250402, Charleston SC 29425
843-792-2300

SHERMAN COLLEGE OF STRAIGHT CHIROPRACTIC
PO Box 1452, Spartanburg SC 29304-1452
Lisa Hildebrand, Director of Admission
800-849-8771 or 864-578-8770 Fax: 864-599-4860
Website: www.sherman.edu
E-mail: admissions@sherman.edu

South Carolina State University
PO Box 7127, Orangeburg SC 29117-0001
Lillian M. Adderson, Director of Admissions
803-536-7185

SOUTH DAKOTA

North American Baptist Seminary
1525 S Grange Ave, Sioux Falls SD 57105-1526
Melissa Hiatt, Director of Admissions
800-440-NABS (6227)

TENNESSEE

Church of God Theological Seminary
PO Box 3330, Cleveland TN 37320-3330
Dr. John T. Ramos, Registrar
423-478-1131

EMMANUEL SCHOOL OF RELIGION
One Walker Dr, Johnson City TN 37601-9438
David Fulks, Director of Admissions
423-461-1535 or 800-933-3771 Fax: 423-926-6198
Website: www.esr.edu
E-mail: admissions@esr.edu

Harding University Graduate School of Religion
1000 Cherry Rd, Memphis TN 38117-5424
Mark Parker, Director of Admissions
800-680-0809

Johnson Bible College
7900 Johnson Dr, Knoxville TN 37998-0001
Dr. John Ketchen, Director of Distance Learning
800-669-7889

Lipscomb University
3901 Granny White Pike, Nashville TN 37204-3951
Ricky Holaway, Director of Admissions
800-333-4358 ext. 1776 Fax: 615-269-1804
Website: www.lipscomb.edu
E-mail: admissions@lipscomb.edu

Meharry Medical College
1005 Dr DB Todd Jr Blvd, Nashville TN 37208-3599
615-327-6111

Memphis Theological Seminary
168 E Parkway S, Memphis TN 38104-4340
Barry Anderson, Director of Admissions
901-458-8232

Mid-America Baptist Theological Seminary
PO Box 381528, Germantown TN 38183-1528
Duffy Guyton, Director of Admissions
901-751-8453

MIDDLE TENNESSEE SCHOOL OF ANESTHESIA
PO Box 6414, Madison TN 37116-6414
Mary E. DeVasher, Dean
615-868-6503 Fax: 615-868-9885
Website: www.mtsa.edu
E-mail: ikey@mtsa.edu

Oxford Graduate School
500 Oxford Dr, Dayton TN 37321
423-775-6596

Peabody College of Vanderbilt University
Box 327, Nashville TN 37203
615-322-8410

Southern College of Optometry
1245 Madison Ave, Memphis TN 38104-2222
800-238-0180

Temple Baptist Seminary
1815 Union Ave, Chattanooga TN 37404
423-493-4221

TEXAS

ACADEMY OF ORIENTAL MEDICINE AT AUSTIN
2700 W Anderson Ln Ste 204, Austin TX 78757
Amy Scott, Admissions Director
512-454-1188 ext. 217 Fax: 512-454-7001
Website: www.aoma.edu
E-mail: info@aoma.edu

American College of Acupuncture
9100 Park West Dr, Houston TX 77063
John Paul Liang, Director
713-780-9777

Angelo State University
ASU Station 11025, San Angelo TX 76909
Dr. Carol Diminnie, Dean of Graduate School
325-942-2169 Fax: 325-942-2194
Website: www.angelo.edu
E-mail: graduate.school@angelo.edu

Austin Presbyterian Theological Seminary
100 E 27th St, Austin TX 78705-5711
Sam Riccobene, Director of Vocation & Admissions
512-472-6736

BAPTIST MISSIONARY ASSOCIATION THEOLOGICAL SEMINARY
1530 E Pine St, Jacksonville TX 75766-5407
Charley Holmes, President
903-586-2501 Fax: 903-586-0378
Website: www.bmats.edu
E-mail: bmatsem@bmats.edu

Baylor College of Medicine
1 Baylor Plz, Houston TX 77030-3498
713-798-4951

Baylor University Medical Center
3500 Gaston Ave, Dallas TX 75246-2088
214-820-2731

DALLAS THEOLOGICAL SEMINARY
3909 Swiss Ave, Dallas TX 75204-6411
Greg Hatteberg, Director of Admissions
214-841-3661 or 866-DTS-WORD Fax: 214-841-3664
Website: www.dts.edu
E-mail: admissions@dts.edu

Episcopal Theological Seminary of the Southwest
PO Box 2247, Austin TX 78768-2247
512-472-4133

Graduate Institute of Applied Linguistics
7500 W Camp Wisdom Rd, Dallas TX 75236
972-708-7340

Lamar University
PO Box 10009, Beaumont TX 77710-0009
409-880-8356

Oblate School of Theology
285 Oblate Dr, San Antonio TX 78216-6693
Dr. Marcella Hoesl, MM, Academic Dean
210-341-1366

South Texas College of Law
1303 San Jacinto St, Houston TX 77002-7000
Alicia Cramer, Director of Admissions
713-646-1510

Southwestern Assemblies of God University
1200 Sycamore St, Waxahachie TX 75165-2397
Pat Thompson, Admissions Counselor
972-937-4010

Texas A & M University System Health Science
Baylor College of Dentistry
3302 Gaston Ave, Dallas TX 75246-2013
214-828-8100

TEXAS COLLEGE OF TRADITIONAL CHINESE MEDICINE
4005 Manchaca Rd, Austin TX 78704
Admissions Coordinator
512-444-8082 Fax: 512-444-6345
Website: www.tctcm.edu
E-mail: info@texastcm.edu

TEXAS WOMAN'S UNIVERSITY
PO Box 425589, Denton TX 76204-5589
Erma Nieto, Director of Admissions
866-809-6130 Fax: 940-898-3081
Website: www.twu.edu
E-mail: admissions@twu.edu

University of Houston
122 E Cullen Bldg, Houston TX 77204-2023
Office of Admission
713-743-9595
Website: www.uh.edu
E-mail: admissions@uh.edu

University of North Texas Health Science Center
3500 Camp Bowie Blvd, Fort Worth TX 76107-2690
Lynn Scott, Contact
817-735-2204

The University of Texas Medical Branch
301 University Blvd, Galveston TX 77555-0802
409-772-1215

UTAH

Southern Utah University
351 W Center St, Cedar City UT 84720-2470
Lou Workman, Dean, School of Continuing & Professional Studies
435-586-7850

University of Utah
1460 E 201 S, Salt Lake City UT 84112
801-581-7200

VERMONT

Bennington College
One College Drive, Bennington VT 05201
Ken Himmelman, Dean of Admissions & Financial Aid
800-833-6845 Fax: 802-440-4320
Website: www.bennington.edu
E-mail: admissions@bennington.edu

Saint Michael's College
Graduate Programs
One Winooski Park, Colchester VT 05439-0001
Dee Goodrich, Director
802-654-2100

School for International Training
World Learning
PO Box 676, Brattleboro VT 05302-0676
Meredith McDill, Contact
800-336-1616

Union Institute & University
Montpelier Campus
College St, Montpelier VT 05602
Dr. Brian Webb, Head
800-336-6794

Vermont Law School
PO Box 96, South Royalton VT 05068
802-763-8303

Woodbury College
660 Elm St, Montpelier VT 05602-4017
Kathleen Moore, Director of Admissions
800-639-6039 Fax: 802-229-2141
Website: www.woodbury-college.edu
E-mail: admiss@woodbury-college.edu

VIRGINIA

ARGOSY UNIVERSITY/WASHINGTON DC
1550 Wilson Blvd Ste 600, Arlington VA 22209
Emily Peck, Director of Admissions
703-526-5800 Fax: 703-243-8973
Website: www.argosyu.edu
E-mail: epeck@argosyu.edu

Atlantic University
215 67th St, Virginia Beach VA 23451-2061
Gregory Deming, Director of Admissions
800-428-1512

Baptist Theological Seminary at Richmond
3400 Brook Rd, Richmond VA 23227-4536
Rob Fox, Director of Admissions
888-345-BTSR

Catholic Distance University
120 E Colonial Hwy, Hamilton VA 20158-9012
Marianne Evans Mount, Executive VP
888-254-4CDU Fax: 540-338-4788
Website: www.cdu.edu
E-mail: tcashen@cdu.edu

Eastern Virginia Medical School
PO Box 1980, Norfolk VA 23501-1980
757-446-5600

Notre Dame Graduate School of Christendom College
134 Christendom Dr, Front Royal VA 22630
800-877-5456

Protestant Episcopal Theological Seminary
3737 Seminary Rd, Alexandria VA 22304-5202
Janice Sienkiewicz, Coordinator for Admissions and Community Life
703-370-6600

Radford University
PO Box 6928, Radford VA 24142
Dr. Carole Seyfrit, Director of Graduate Admissions
540-831-5431 Fax: 540-831-6061
Website: www.radford.edu
E-mail: gradcoll@radford.edu

Reformed Theological Seminary
12500 Fair Lakes Cir Ste 325, Fairfax VA 22033
703-222-7077

Regent University
1000 Regent University Dr
Virginia Beach VA 23464-9800
757-226-4000

UNION THEOLOGICAL SEMINARY AND PRESBYTERIAN SCHOOL OF CHRISTIAN EDUCATION
3401 Brook Rd, Richmond VA 23227-4597
Pat Morgan, Associate Director of Admissions
800-229-2990 Fax: 804-355-3919
Website: www.union-psce.edu
E-mail: admissn@union-psce.edu

University of Northern Virginia
10021 Balls Ford Rd, Manassas VA 20109
703-392-0771

Virginia College of Osteopathic Medicine
2265 Kraft Dr, Blacksburg VA 24060
540-231-4000

WASHINGTON

Argosy University/Seattle
2601-A Elliott Ave, Seattle WA 98121-1318
206-283-4500

BAKKE GRADUATE UNIVERSITY OF MINISTRY
1013 8th Ave, Seattle WA 98104-1222
Judi Melton, Registrar
206-264-9100 Fax: 206-264-0613
Website: www.bgu.edu
E-mail: bgu@bgu.edu

Bastyr University
14500 Juanita Dr NE, Bothell WA 98028-4966
425-823-1300

Central Washington University
400 E University Way, Ellensburg WA 98926
Duncan Perry, Dean of Graduate Studies/Research

City University
11900 NE 1st St, Bellevue WA 98005-3030
800-426-5596

Faith Evangelical Lutheran Seminary
3504 N Pearl St, Tacoma WA 98407
253-752-2020

Gonzaga University
Spokane WA 99258-0029
Julie McCulloh, Dean of Admission
509-323-6572 Fax: 509-323-5700
Website: www.gonzaga.edu
E-mail: mcculloh@gu.gonzaga.edu

Heritage University
3240 Fort Rd, Toppenish WA 98948-9599
509-865-8500

Mars Hill Graduate School
2525 220th St SE Ste 100, Bothell WA 98021
425-415-0505

Pacific Lutheran University
12180 Park Ave S, Tacoma WA 98447-0014
David E. Gunovich, Director of Admissions
253-535-7151

Seattle Institute of Oriental Medicine
916 NE 65th St #B, Seattle WA 98115
206-517-4541

Seattle University School of Law
900 Broadway, Seattle WA 98122-4340
Carol Cochran, Director of Admission
206-398-4200

WEST VIRGINIA

Alderson-Broaddus College
Philippi WV 26416
Eric A. Ruf, Director of Admissions
800-263-1549

Fairmont State University
1201 Locust Ave, Fairmont WV 26554-2470
Steve Leadman, Director of Admissions
304-367-4892 or 800-641-5678 Fax: 304-367-4789
Website: www.fairmontstate.edu
E-mail: admit@fairmontstate.edu

MOUNTAIN STATE UNIVERSITY
Box 9003, Beckley WV 25802-9003
866-FOR-MSU1 or 304-929-INFO Fax: 304-253-0789
Website: www.mountainstate.edu
E-mail: gomsu@mountainstate.edu
  Master of Science in Nursing, Master of Health Science, Master of Arts or Master of Science in Interdisciplinary Studies, Master of Criminal Justice Administration, Master of Science in Physician Assistant, Master of Science in Strategic Leadership.
  See listing under "Universities"

West Virginia School of Osteopathic Medicine
400 N Lee St, Lewisburg WV 24901-1196
304-645-6270

West Virginia Wesleyan College
59 College Ave, Buckhannon WV 26201-2699
Robert N. Skinner II, Director of Admission
800-722-9933 Fax: 304-473-8108
Website: www.wvwc.edu
E-mail: admission@wvwc.edu

WISCONSIN

Medical College of Wisconsin
PO Box 26509, Milwaukee WI 53226-0509
Michael Istwan, Director of Admissions
414-456-8296 Fax: 414-456-6506
Website: www.mcw.edu
E-mail: mcwms@mcw.edu

MIDWEST COLLEGE OF ORIENTAL MEDICINE
6232 Bankers Rd, Racine WI 53403-9747
Kelly Westerlund, Contact
800-593-2320 Fax: 262-554-7475
Website: www.acupuncture.edu
E-mail: mwcadmissions@yahoo.com

NASHOTAH HOUSE
2777 Mission Rd, Nashotah WI 53058-9793
The Very Rev. Robert S. Munday, Ph.D., Dean and President
262-646-6500 Fax: 262-646-6504
Website: www.nashotah.edu
E-mail: nashotah@nashotah.edu

Sacred Heart School of Theology
PO Box 429, Hales Corners WI 53130-0429
414-425-8300

Saint Francis Seminary
3257 S Lake Dr, Milwaukee WI 53235-3795
Registrar
414-747-6400

University of Wisconsin in La Crosse
115 Graff Main Hall, La Crosse WI 54601
Tim Lewis, Director of Admissions
608-785-8939

University of Wisconsin - Oshkosh
800 Algoma Blvd, Oshkosh WI 54901-8602
920-424-1223

WISCONSIN SCHOOL OF PROFESSIONAL PSYCHOLOGY
9120 W Hampton Ave Ste 212
Milwaukee WI 53225-4960
Howard Haven, Ph.D., Dean
414-464-9777 Fax: 414-358-5590
Website: www.wspp.edu
E-mail: admissions@wspp.edu

WYOMING

::: Columbia Commonwealth University
327 N St, Rock Springs WY 82901-5332
800-552-5522

GUAM

University of Guam
UOG Station, Mangilao GU 96923
Graduate Studies Office
671-735-2170
Website: www.uog.edu
E-mail: admitme@uog9.uog.edu

PUERTO RICO

CARLOS ALBIZU UNIVERSITY - SAN JUAN CAMPUS
PO Box 9023711, San Juan PR 00902-3711
Carlos Rodriguez, Director of Admissions
787-725-6500 Fax: 787-721-7187
Website: albizu.edu
E-mail: crodriguez@albizu.edu

Center for Advanced Studies on Puerto Rico and the Caribbean
PO Box 9023970, San Juan PR 00902-3970
787-723-4481

Evangelical Seminary of Puerto Rico
776 Ave Ponce de Leon, San Juan PR 00925-2207
Wilmarie Leduc Jorge, Registrar
787-763-6700 ext. 238

Inter American University of Puerto Rico
PO Box 70351, San Juan PR 00936
787-751-1912

Inter American University of Puerto Rico
School of Optometry
118 Calle Eleonor Roosevelt
San Juan PR 00918-3105
787-765-1915

Ponce School of Medicine
PO Box 7004, Ponce PR 00732
787-840-2575

∴HANDICAPPED, SCHOOLS FOR THE

ARIZONA

DEVEREUX-ARIZONA TREATMENT NETWORK
6436 E Sweetwater Ave, Scottsdale AZ 85254-4581
Admissions Office
480-998-2920 Fax: 480-443-1531
Website: www.devereuxaz.org

CALIFORNIA

DEVEREUX CALIFORNIA
PO Box 6784, Santa Barbara CA 93160
805-968-2525 Fax: 805-968-3247
Website: www.devereuxca.org

CONNECTICUT

DEVEREUX CENTER IN CONNECTICUT
81 Sabbaday Ln, Washington Depot CT 06793-1318
Admissions Office
860-868-7377 Fax: 860-868-7413
Website: www.devereuxct.org

Lake Grove School at Durham CT
459R Wallingford Rd, Durham CT 06422-1116
Referral Development
888-585-9007 Fax: 631-716-2136
Website: www.lgstc.org
E-mail: admissions@lgadmissions.org

FLORIDA

DEVEREUX-FLORIDA TREATMENT NETWORK
5850 T G Lee Blvd Ste 400, Orlando FL 32822
Linda Brooks, Director of Admissions
800-338-3738 or 407-812-4555 Fax: 407-816-6481
Website: www.devereuxfl.org
Locations throughout Florida

HOPE CENTER
PO Box 10789, Miami FL 33101-0789
Social Service Department
305-545-7572 Fax: 305-325-0382
Website: www.hopecenterhc.org

GEORGIA

ATLANTA AREA SCHOOL FOR THE DEAF
890 N Indian Creek Dr, Clarkston GA 30021-2228
Gail Allen, Outreach Coordinator
404-296-7101 (V,TTY) Fax: 404-299-4485
Website: www.aasdweb.com
E-mail: gallen@doe.k12.ga.us

DEVEREUX-GEORGIA TREATMENT NETWORK
1291 Stanley Rd NW, Kennesaw GA 30152-4359
Admissions Office
800-342-3357 or 770-427-0147 Fax: 770-424-9408
Website: www.devereuxga.org

GEORGIA SCHOOL FOR THE DEAF
232 Perry Farm Rd SW, Cave Spring GA 30124-3018
Dr. Leah Shiver, School Director
800-497-3371 Fax: 706-777-2204
Website: www.gsdweb.org
E-mail: lshiver@doe.k12.ga.us

INDIANA

INDIANA STATE SCHOOL FOR THE BLIND AND VISUALLY IMPAIRED
7725 N College Ave, Indianapolis IN 46240-2504
James Durst, Superintendent
317-253-1481 ext. 141 Fax: 317-251-6511
Website: www.isbrockets.org
E-mail: jdurst@isb.state.in.us

MAINE

GOVERNOR BAXTER SCHOOL FOR THE DEAF
Maine Educational Center for the Deaf and Hard of Hearing
Mackworth Island, Falmouth ME 04105
Larry S. Taub, Ed.D., Superintendent
207-781-3165 Fax: 207-781-6319
Website: www.baxter.pvt.k12.me.us
E-mail: larry.taub@gbsd.org

MASSACHUSETTS

DEVEREUX CENTER IN MASSACHUSETTS
60 Miles Rd, Rutland MA 01543-0197
Admissions Office
508-886-4746 Fax: 508-886-4773
Website: www.devereuxma.org

Lake Grove School
PO Box 767, Wendell MA 01379-0767
Referral Development
888-585-9007 Fax: 631-716-2136
Website: www.lgstc.org
E-mail: admissions@lgadmissions.org

PERKINS SCHOOL FOR THE BLIND
175 N Beacon St, Watertown MA 02472
Christopher Underwood, Supervisor
617-924-3434 Fax: 617-972-7715
Website: www.perkins.org
E-mail: info@perkins.org

NEW YORK

DEVEREUX CENTER IN NEW YORK
40 Devereux Way, Red Hook NY 12571
Admissions Office
845-758-1899 Fax: 845-758-1817
Website: www.devereuxny.org

Lake Grove School
PO Box 712, Lake Grove NY 11755-0712
Referral Development
888-585-9007 Fax: 631-716-2136
Website: www.lgstc.org
E-mail: admissions@lgadmissions.org

Mountain Lake Children's Residence
50 Riverside Dr, Lake Placid NY 12946
Referral Development
888-585-9007 Fax: 631-716-2136
Website: www.lgstc.org
E-mail: admissions@lgadmissions.org

ROCHESTER INSTITUTE OF TECHNOLOGY NATIONAL TECHNICAL INSTITUTE FOR THE DEAF (NTID)
52 Lomb Memorial Dr, Rochester NY 14623-5604
Robert Borden, Director of NTID Admissions
585-475-6700 (v/TTY) Fax: 585-475-2696
Website: www.rit.edu/ntid/getinfo
E-mail: NTIDAdmissions@rit.edu
Established 1965. Private. Coed. Tution $8,559 (NTID or NTID supported students only). Room & Board: $8,748. Fees: $642. Enrollment: 1,100. Faculty: 210. Degrees offered: MS, BS, AS, AAS, AOS. Library: 800,000 volumes. 237 buildings on 1,300 acres. Qualified deaf and hard-of-hearing students can earn bachelor's or master's degrees in more than 200 programs offered by RIT's seven other colleges - Applied Science and Technology, Business, Computing and Information Sciences, Engineering, Imaging Arts and Sciences, Liberal Arts, and Science. They also can earn associate degrees in more than 30 accredited NTID programs including: Accounting Technology, Administrative Support Technology, Applied Computer Technology, Applied Optical Technology, Art and Business Technology, Automation Technologies - Robotics, Computer Design, Computer Aided Drafting Technology, Computer Integrated Machining Technology, Digital Imaging & Publishing Technology, and Laboratory Science Technology. Additionally NTID offers degrees in American Sign Language-English Interpretation and a Master's of Science in Secondary Education of Students who are Deaf or Hard of Hearing.

ROCHESTER SCHOOL FOR THE DEAF
1545 Saint Paul St, Rochester NY 14621-3197
Harold Mowl Jr., Ph.D., Superintendent
585-544-1240 Fax: 585-544-0383
Website: www.rsdeaf.org
E-mail: gboorum@rsdeaf.org

OHIO
ST. RITA SCHOOL FOR THE DEAF
1720 Glendale Milford Rd, Cincinnati OH 45215-1258
Gregory Ernst, Executive Director
513-771-7600 Fax: 513-326-8264
Website: www.srsdeaf.org
E-mail: gernst@srsdeaf.org

PENNSYLVANIA
DEVEREUX BENETO CENTER
655 Sugartown Rd Box 297, Malvern PA 19355
Admissions Office
800-935-6789 or 610-251-2407 Fax: 610-251-2415
Website: www.devereuxbeneto.org
LOCATIONS THROUGHOUT SOUTHEASTERN PENNSYLVANIA

THE DEVEREUX FOUNDATION
National Referral Office
444 Devereux Dr, Villanova PA 19085
Kimberleigh A. Nash
800-345-1292 or 610-542-3030 Fax: 610-542-3141
Website: www.devereux.org

DEVEREUX KANNER CENTER
390 E Boot Rd, West Chester PA 19380
Admissions Office
866-532-2212 Fax: 610-431-8191
Website: www.devereuxkanner.org

OVERBROOK SCHOOL FOR THE BLIND
6333 Malvern Ave, Philadelphia PA 19151
Bernadette M. Kappen, Director
215-877-0313 Fax: 215-877-2466
Website: www.obs.org
E-mail: bmk@obs.org

PATHWAY SCHOOL
162 Egypt Rd, Norristown PA 19403-3090
Louise Robertson, Director of Admissions
610-277-0660 Fax: 610-539-1493
Website: www.pathwayschool.org
E-mail: louiser@pathwayschool.org

WOODS SERVICES
PO Box 36, Langhorne PA 19047
Dan Shine, Director, Referral Development
800-782-3646 Fax: 215-750-4591
Website: www.woods.org
E-mail: dshine@woods.org

SOUTH CAROLINA
SOUTH CAROLINA SCHOOL FOR DEAF AND BLIND
355 Cedar Springs Rd, Spartanburg SC 29302
Lin Mackechnie, Special Education Director
864-577-7521 Fax: 864-585-3555
Website: www.scsdb.k12.sc.us
E-mail: lmackechnie@scsdb.k12.sc.us

TEXAS
DEVEREUX-TEXAS TREATMENT NETWORK-HOUSTON PROGRAM
1150 Devereux Dr, League City TX 77573-2043
Admissions Office
800-373-0011 or 281-335-1000 Fax: 281-332-2301
Website: www.devereuxtx.org

DEVEREUX-TEXAS TREATMENT NETWORK-VICTORIA PROGRAM
120 David Wade Dr, Victoria TX 77902-2666
Admissions Office
800-383-5000 or 361-575-8271 Fax: 361-575-6520
Website: www.devereuxtx.org

UTAH
UTAH SCHOOLS FOR THE DEAF AND THE BLIND
742 Harrison Blvd, Ogden UT 84404-5231
Linda Rutledge, Superintendent
801-629-4700 Fax: 801-629-4896
Website: www.usdb.org
E-mail: lindar@usdb.org

VERMONT
AUSTINE SCHOOL FOR THE DEAF
60 Austine Dr, Brattleboro VT 05301
Cyndy Ward, Director of Related Services
802-258-9522 Voice/tty Fax: 802-258-9541
Website: www.state.vt.us/schools/aus/
E-mail: cynthia@austine.pvt.k12.vt.us

VIRGINIA
VIRGINIA SCHOOL FOR THE DEAF AND BLIND
700 Shell Rd, Hampton VA 23661-2218
Donna Y. Lawson, Director of Instruction
757-247-2058 Fax: 757-247-2122
E-mail: donna.lawson@vsdbmh.virginia.gov

HOME ECONOMICS

ALABAMA

Alabama A & M University
PO Box 908, Normal AL 35762
Antonio Boyle, Director of Admissions
256-372-5245 Fax: 256-372-5249
Website: www.aamu.edu
E-mail: aboyle@aamu.edu

ARIZONA

University of Arizona
Tucson AZ 85721-0040
Paul Kohn, Director of Admissions
520-621-3237 Fax: 520-621-9799
Website: www.admissions.arizona.edu or www.arizona.edu

CALIFORNIA

California State University-San Bernadino
5500 University Pkwy
San Bernardino CA 92407-2393
Olivia Rosas, Director of Admissions
909-880-5000 Fax: 909-880-7034
Website: enrollment.csusb.edu
E-mail: orosas@csusb.edu

Orange Coast College
PO Box 5005, Costa Mesa CA 92628-5005
Kristin Clark, Director of Admissions
714-432-5773 Fax: 714-432-5736
Website: www.orangecoastcollege.edu
E-mail: kclark@cccd.edu

CONNECTICUT

University of New Haven
300 Boston Post Rd, West Haven CT 06516
Director of Undergraduate Admissions
203-932-7319 Fax: 203-931-6093
Website: www.newhaven.edu
E-mail: adminfo@newhaven.edu

FLORIDA

Florida State University
600 W College Ave, Tallahassee FL 32306-1096
Janice V. Finney, Director of Admissions
850-644-2525 Fax: 850-644-0197
Website: admissions.fsu.edu
E-mail: admissions@admin.fsu.edu

IDAHO

Brigham Young University - Idaho
120 Kimball Bldg, Rexburg ID 83460
Gordon Westenskow, Director of Admissions
208-496-1020 Fax: 208-496-1220
Website: www.byui.edu
E-mail: admissions@byui.edu

University of Idaho
Moscow ID 83844-4253
Lloyd Scott, Director of New Student Services
208-885-6163 Fax: 208-885-4477
Website: www.uidaho.edu
E-mail: nss@uidaho.edu

IOWA

Iowa Lakes Community College
300 S 18th St, Estherville IA 51334-2721
Anne Stansbury, Asst. Director of Admissions
712-362-7945 Fax: 712-362-8363
Website: www.iowalakes.edu
E-mail: info@iowalakes.edu

MAINE

Southern Maine Community College
2 Fort Rd, South Portland ME 04106-1698
Dr. James Ortiz, President
Scott MacDonald, Director of Financial Aid
207-741-5500 Fax: 207-741-5671
Website: www.smccme.edu
E-mail: oharmon@maine.rr.com

MASSACHUSETTS

Boston University
121 Bay State Rd, Boston MA 02215
Kelly Walter, Executive Director of Admissions
617-353-2300 Fax: 617-353-9695
Website: web.bu.edu
E-mail: admissions@bu.edu

NORTH CAROLINA

Meredith College
3800 Hillsborough St, Raleigh NC 27607-5298
Heidi L. Fletcher, Director of Admissions
919-760-8581 Fax: 919-760-2348
Website: www.meredith.edu
E-mail: admissions@meredith.edu
See listing under "Women's Colleges"

North Carolina A&T State University
1601 E Market St, Greensboro NC 27411
Lee Young, AVC Enrollment
336-334-7500 Fax: 336-334-7478
Website: www.ncat.edu
E-mail: uadmit@ncat.edu

OHIO

Mount Vernon Nazarene University
800 Martinsburg Rd, Mount Vernon OH 43050-9509
Timothy Eades, Director of Admissions
866-462-6868 Fax: 740-393-0511
Website: www.gotomvnu.com
E-mail: admissions@mvnu.edu
See listing under "Universities"

OKLAHOMA

Oklahoma State University
Stillwater OK 74078
Lona Robertson, Asst. Dean
405-744-5053
Website: www.okstate.edu
E-mail: lona.robertson@okstate.edu

OREGON

Linn-Benton Community College
6500 Pacific Blvd SW, Albany OR 97321-3774
Christine Baker, Outreach Coordinator
541-917-4811 Fax: 541-917-4868
Website: www.linnbenton.edu
E-mail: admissions@linnbenton.edu

PENNSYLVANIA

Academy of Medical Arts and Business
2301 Academy Dr, Harrisburg PA 17112-1012
717-545-4747
Website: www.ACADcampus.com
E-mail: info@ACADcampus.com

TENNESSEE

Lipscomb University
3901 Granny White Pike, Nashville TN 37204-3951
Ricky Holaway, Director of Admissions
800-333-4358 ext. 1776 Fax: 615-269-1804
Website: www.lipscomb.edu
E-mail: admissions@lipscomb.edu

Tennessee State University
3500 John A Merritt Blvd, Nashville TN 37209-1561
John Cade, Dean of Admissions & Records
615-963-5101 Fax: 615-963-2930
Website: www.tnstate.edu
E-mail: jcade@tnstate.edu

University of Tennessee
615 McCallie Ave, Chattanooga TN 37403-2504
Yancy Freeman, Director of Admissions
423-425-4111 Fax: 423-425-4157
Website: www.utc.edu
E-mail: Yancy-Freeman@utc.edu

TEXAS

Texas Woman's University
PO Box 425589, Denton TX 76204-5589
Erma Nieto, Director of Admissions
866-809-6130 Fax: 940-898-3081
Website: www.twu.edu
E-mail: admissions@twu.edu

University of Houston
122 E Cullen Bldg, Houston TX 77204-2023
Office of Admission
713-743-9595
Website: www.uh.edu
E-mail: admissions@uh.edu

VIRGINIA

Radford University
PO Box 6903, Radford VA 24142
David W. Kraus, Director of Admissions
800-890-4265 Fax: 540-831-5038
Website: www.radford.edu
E-mail: ruadmiss@radford.edu

WYOMING

University of Wyoming
Admissions Office
Dept 3435, Laramie WY 82071-3435
Aaron Appelhans, Contact
800-342-5996 Fax: 307-766-4042
Website: www.uwyo.edu
E-mail: why-wyo@uwyo.edu

GUAM

University of Guam
UOG Station, Mangilao GU 96923
Deborah Leon Guerrero, Registrar
671-735-2201 or 671-735-2208 Fax: 671-735-2203
Website: www.uog.edu
E-mail: admitme@uog9.uog.edu

PUERTO RICO

Colegio Mayor de Technologia
PO Box 1490, Arroyo PR 00714
Julia Melendez, Director of Admissions
787-839-5266 Fax: 787-839-0033
Website: www.colegiomayortec.com
E-mail: cmtarroy@coqui.net

: : :HOME STUDY AND CORRESPONDENCE

ALABAMA

American Sentinel University
2101 Magnolia Ave Ste 207, Birmingham AL 35205
205-323-6191

Andrew Jackson University
10 Old Montgomery Hwy, Birmingham AL 35209
205-871-9288

COLUMBIA SOUTHERN UNIVERSITY

25326 Canal Rd, Orange Beach AL 36561
251-981-3771 Fax: 251-981-3815
Website: www.columbiasouthern.edu
E-mail: admissions@columbiasouthern.edu

ARIZONA

COLLEGE OF THE HUMANITIES AND SCIENCES HARRISON MIDDLETON UNIVERSITY

1105 E Broadway Rd, Tempe AZ 85282
Kathleen Mirabile, Vice President
480-317-5955 Fax: 480-829-4999
Website: www.chumsci.edu
E-mail: kmirabile@chumsci.edu

International Import-Export Institute
11225 N 28th Dr Ste B201, Phoenix AZ 85029
602-648-5750

The Paralegal Institute
PO Box 11408, Phoenix AZ 85061-1408
602-212-0501 Fax: 602-212-0502
Website: www.theparalegalinstitute.edu
E-mail: paralegalinst@mindspring.com

SONORAN DESERT INSTITUTE

10245 E Via Linda Ste 102, Scottsdale AZ 85258
Ms. Toni Pino, Assistant Director
480-314-2102 Fax: 480-314-2138
Website: www.sonoranlearning.com
E-mail: info@sonoranlearning.com

CALIFORNIA

ALLIED BUSINESS SCHOOL

22952 Alcalde Dr, Laguna Hills CA 92653
949-598-0875 Fax: 949-461-9556
Website: www.alliedschools.com
E-mail: chislop@alliedschools.com

Applied Professional Training
PO Box 131717, Carlsbad CA 92013
800-431-8488

CALIFORNIA COAST UNIVERSITY

700 N Main St, Santa Ana CA 92701
Admissions Office: 888-CCU-UNIV or 714-547-9625
Fax: 714-547-5777
Dr. Thomas Neal, President
Dr. Cynthia Teeple, Academic Vice President
Website: www.calcoast.edu
E-mail: info@calcoast.edu
Established 1973. Proprietary. Coed. Accreditation: California Coast University holds accreditation through the Accrediting Commission of the Distance Education and Training Council (DETC). The DETC is an educational association located in Washington, D.C. Founded in 1926, it is the standard setting agency for distance education institutions. Approval: Bureau for Private Postsecondary and Vocational Education - State of California, charter member California Association of State Approved Colleges & Universities, member Association for Adult & Continuing Education, member The Alliance for Private Post Secondary Academic Institutions.
Tuition: $2,805-$12,070. California Coast University has selected the SLM Corporation, commonly known as Sallie Mae, to help the university provide financing for its students. Sallie Mae is the nation's leading provider of education funding. Sallie Mae also allows students to borrow additional loan amounts to cover additional expenses, such as textbooks, equipment, or living expenses.
Enrollment: 30,000. California Coast University is approved by the California State Approving Agency to enroll veterans or other eligible persons under Title 38, U.S. Code. California Coast University holds a Memoran-

dum of Understanding with Defense Activity for Non-Traditional Education Support (DANTES) as an external degree provider.
A private college offering off-campus independent study programs in the traditional areas of business administration, management, psychology, education. Admissions: enroll year round, requires official transcripts, letters of recommendation, detailed curriculum vita or occupational history.
Process: evaluation of prior academic work followed by analysis of occupational history, including participation in workshops, seminars, training programs, specialized projects for credit. Credit is demonstrated by accelerated learning guides or study guides.
Residency: All course work may be completed off campus, utilizing correspondence methods. Interest free loans available to students.

Futures International High School
2204 El Camino Real #312, Oceanside CA 92054
760-721-0121

GEMOLOGICAL INSTITUTE OF AMERICA

The Robert Mouawad Campus
5345 Armada Dr, Carlsbad CA 92008-4602
Jason Drake, Admissions Manager
800-421-7250 ext. 4001 or 760-603-4001
Fax: 760-603-4003
Website: www.gia.edu
E-mail: eduinfo@gia.edu
Established 1931. Nonprofit. Private. Accreditation: Distance Education Training Council. Diploma: Gemologist, Graduate Gemologist, Accredited Jewelry Professional. Courses: Diamond Essentials, Diamonds & Diamond Grading, Colored Stone Essentials, Colored Stones, Gem Identification, Jewelry Essentials, Pearls, Pearl and Bead Stringing, Jewelry Business Management. Degree: BBA (Bachelor of Business Administration).
See listing under "Career Schools"

Holmes Institute
School of Consciousness Studies
2600 W Magnolia Blvd, Burbank CA 91505
818-556-7757

HUNTINGTON COLLEGE OF HEALTH SCIENCES AMERICAN ACADEMY OF NUTRITION

7339 Lakeside Dr, Riverside CA 92509
800-290-4226 Fax: 949-760-1788
Website: www.hchs.edu

Hypnosis Motivation Institute
Extension School
18607 Ventura Blvd Ste 310, Tarzana CA 91356
800-479-9464

John Tracy Clinic
806 W Adams Blvd, Los Angeles CA 90007-2599
Gisele Ragusa, Ph.D., Program Director
Professional Distance Education
800-522-4582

Truck Marketing Institute
1090 Eugenia Pl Ste 101, Carpinteria CA 93013-2011
805-684-4558

William Howard Taft University
3700 S Susan St, Santa Ana CA 92704
714-850-4800

COLORADO

AMERICAN HEALTH SCIENCE UNIVERSITY

1010 S Joliet St #107, Aurora CO 80012-3150
Ann Peterson, Academic Dean
303-340-2054 Fax: 303-367-2577
Website: www.ahsu.edu
E-mail: cn@ahsu.edu

Aspen University
501 S Cherry St Ste 350, Denver CO 80246
800-441-4746

Remington College Online
11011 W 6th Ave, Lakewood CO 80215-5501
Rob Dillman, Director of Recruitment
800-829-5488

WESTON DISTANCE LEARNING

At-Home Professions - U.S. Career Institute
2001 Lowe St, Fort Collins CO 80525
Joyce Lindquist, Director of Student Services
800-347-7899 Fax: 970-223-1678
Website: www.uscareerinstitute.com
E-mail: enroll@uscareerinstitute.com

CONNECTICUT

Charter Oak State College
55 Paul Manafort Dr, New Britain CT 06053-2142
860-832-3800

Hanger Orthopedic Group
181 Patricia M Genova Dr, Newington CT 06111
860-667-5304

Westlawn Institute of Marine Technology
PO Box 6000, Mystic CT 06355
860-572-7900

FLORIDA

Citizen's High School
PO Box 66089, Orange Park FL 32065
904-276-1700

IMPAC University
900 W Marion Ave, Punta Gorda FL 33950
941-639-7512

National Training
PO Box 65789, Orange Park FL 32065
904-272-4000

Stenotype Institute Court Reporting School
3986 Boulevard Center Dr Bldg. 1200 #200
Jacksonville FL 32207-2819
904-246-7466

Universidad FLET
14540 SW 136th St Ste 202, Miami FL 33186
305-378-8700

University of St. Augustine for Health Sciences
1 University Blvd, Saint Augustine FL 32086
904-826-0084

GEORGIA

Ashworth College
430 Technology Pkwy, Norcross GA 30092
770-729-8400

James Madison High School
430 Technology Pkwy, Norcross GA 30092
770-729-8400

Professional Career Development Institute
430 Technology Pkwy, Norcross GA 30092
770-729-8400

HAWAII

Babel University Professional School of Translation
1720 Ala Moana Blvd Tradewinds Ste A5
Honolulu HI 96815
808-946-3773

ILLINOIS

American Health Information Management
233 N Michigan Ave Ste 2150, Chicago IL 60601
312-233-1184

AMERICAN INTERCONTINENTAL UNIVERSITY ONLINE

5550 Prairie Stone Parkway Suite 400
Hoffman Estates IL 60192
Admissions Department
877-701-3800
Website: www.aiuonline.edu
E-mail: info@aiuonline.edu

AMERICAN SCHOOL

2200 E 170th St, Lansing IL 60438-1002
William H. Hunding, President
708-418-2800
Website: www.americanschoolofcorr.org

Cardean University
111 N Canal St Ste 455, Chicago IL 60606
866-948-1289

KANSAS

Barclay College
607 N Kingman, Haviland KS 67059
Herb Frazier, Director of Admissions
800-862-0226 Fax: 620-862-5242
Website: www.barclaycollege.edu
E-mail: admissions@barclaycollege.edu

LOUISIANA

SOUTHWEST UNIVERSITY

2200 Veterans Blvd, Kenner LA 70062
Dr. Grayce Lee, Director of Education
504-468-2900 Fax: 504-468-3213
Website: www.southwest.edu
E-mail: southwest@southwest.edu
Degree Granting Distance Education.

MARYLAND

GRIGGS INTERNATIONAL ACADEMY

PO Box 4437, Silver Spring MD 20914
Anita L. Jacobs, Director of Admissions/Registrar
301-680-6570 Fax: 301-680-5157
Website: www.griggs.edu
E-mail: contact@griggs.edu

Griggs University
PO Box 4437, Silver Spring MD 20914-4437
Anita L. Jacobs, Director of Admissions
301-680-6570 Fax: 301-680-6583
Website: www.griggs.edu
E-mail: registrar@griggs.edu

MASSACHUSETTS

RHODEC INTERNATIONAL

59 Coddington St Ste 104, Quincy MA 02169
Maureen Randall, Contact
617-472-4942 Fax: 617-472-3400
Website: www.rhodec.edu/us
E-mail: uscontact@rhodec.edu

MICHIGAN

Educational Institute of the American Hotel & Lodging Association
2113 N High St, Lansing MI 48906
800-344-4381 ext. PSC

MINNESOTA

ART INSTRUCTION SCHOOLS

3400 Technology Dr, Minneapolis MN 55418
612-362-5000 Fax: 612-362-5260
Website: www.artists-ais.edu

MISSOURI

Global University
1211 S Glenstone Ave, Springfield MO 65804-0315
417-862-9533

Grantham University
7200 NW 86th St Ste M, Kansas City MO 64153
800-955-2527

NEVADA

American Career Institute
2340 Paseo Del Prado Ste D-208
Las Vegas NV 89102
702-222-3522

NEW JERSEY

INSTITUTE OF LOGISTICAL MANAGEMENT

PO Box 427, Burlington NJ 08016
Frank R. Breslin, Dean
609-747-1515 Fax: 609-747-1517
Website: www.logistics-edu.com
E-mail: info@logistics-edu.com

National Tax Training School
PO Box 767, Mahwah NJ 07430-0767
800-914-8138

NEW YORK

SESSIONS.EDU ONLINE SCHOOL OF DESIGN

350 7th Ave Rm 1203, New York NY 10001-5013
Bob Timm, Director of Student Services & Office Infrastructure
212-239-3080 Fax: 212-239-3084
Website: www.sessions.edu
E-mail: admissions@sessions.edu

NORTH CAROLINA

AMERICAN INSTITUTE OF APPLIED SCIENCE

Criminal Investigation and Forensic Science
100 Hunter Pl, Youngsville NC 27596-9447
Marvin Joy, Director of Education
919-554-2500 Fax: 919-556-6784
Website: www.aiasinc.com
E-mail: aias@mindspring.com

OHIO

BRIGHTON COLLEGE

85 S Main St Ste G, Hudson OH 44236-3038
800-231-3803 Fax: 330-342-8502
Website: www.brightoncollege.edu
E-mail: info@brightoncollege.edu

Cleveland Institute of Electronics
1776 E 17th St, Cleveland OH 44114-3679
Scott Katzenmeyer, Director of Admissions
800-243-6446 Fax: 216-781-0331
Website: www.cie-wc.edu
E-mail: instruct@cie-wc.edu

HARDI Home Study Institute
1389 Dublin Rd, Columbus OH 43215-1084
614-488-1835

OKLAHOMA

Oral Roberts University
Adult Learning Service Center
7777 S Lewis Ave, Tulsa OK 74171-0001
888-900-4678 Fax: 918-495-7965
Website: www.oru.edu
E-mail: alsc@oru.edu

OREGON

Australasian College of Health Sciences
5940 SW Hood Ave, Portland OR 97239
503-244-0726

PENNSYLVANIA

Education Direct
925 Oak St, Scranton PA 18515-0999
570-342-7701

KEYSTONE NATIONAL HIGH SCHOOL

420 W 5th St, Bloomsburg PA 17815-1564
William Belcher, Contact
570-784-5220 Fax: 570-784-2129
Website: www.keystonehighschool.com
E-mail: info@keystonehighschool.com

TENNESSEE

Diamond Council of America
3212 W End Ave Ste 202, Nashville TN 37203-5835
615-385-5301

Huntington College of Health Sciences
1204 Kenesaw Ave, Knoxville TN 37919
800-290-4226

Seminary Extension Independent Study Institute
901 Commerce St Ste 500, Nashville TN 37203-3631
Dr. Bill Vinson, Director
800-229-4612

UTAH

California College for Health Sciences
5295 Commerce Dr, Salt Lake City UT 84107
800-221-7374

Western Governors University
4001 S 700 E Suite 700, Salt Lake City UT 84107
801-274-3280

VERMONT

DLI Distance Learning International
PO Box 846, Saint Albans VT 05478-0846
Teresa Moore, Registrar
800-493-4114

VIRGINIA

Atlantic University
215 67th St, Virginia Beach VA 23451-2061
Gregory Deming, Director of Admissions
800-428-1512

Catholic Distance University
120 E Colonial Hwy, Hamilton VA 20158-9012
Marianne Evans Mount, Executive VP
888-254-4CDU Fax: 540-338-4788
Website: www.cdu.edu
E-mail: tcashen@cdu.edu

Richard Milburn High School
3421 Commission Ct Ste 201, Woodbridge VA 22192
703-494-0147

WORLD COLLEGE

5193 Shore Dr Ste 105, Virginia Beach VA 23455
John R. Drinko, Contact
757-464-4600 Fax: 757-464-3687
Website: www.worldcollege.edu
E-mail: instruct@cie-wc.edu

WASHINGTON

Skagit Valley College
2405 E College Way, Mount Vernon WA 98273-5899
Distance Education Officer
360-416-7600

WEST VIRGINIA

American Public University
111 W Congress St, Charles Town WV 25414
877-468-6268

WYOMING

Columbia Commonwealth University
327 N St, Rock Springs WY 82901-5332
800-552-5522

INTERIOR DESIGN

ALABAMA

Judson College
302 Bibb St, Marion AL 36756
Michael Scotto, Director of Admissions
800-447-9472 Fax: 334-683-5147
Website: www.judson.edu
E-mail: admissions@judson.edu

Trenholm State Technical College
Patterson Campus
3920 Troy Hwy, Montgomery AL 36116
Dr. Anthony Molina, President
334-420-4200 Fax: 334-420-4206
Website: www.trenholmtech.cc.al.us
E-mail: amolina@trenholmtech.cc.al.us

ARIZONA

Collins College: A School of Design and Technology
(Formerly Al Collins Graphic Design School)
1140 S Priest Dr, Tempe AZ 85281-5240
Toby Craver, Director of National Admissions
800-876-7070 Fax: 480-829-0183
Website: www.collinscollege.edu
E-mail: nationaladmissions@collinscollege.edu

CALIFORNIA

California College of the Arts
1111 Eighth St, San Francisco CA 94107
Robynne Royster, Director of Admission
800-447-1-ART or 415-703-9523 Fax: 415-703-9539
Website: www.cca.edu
E-mail: enroll@cca.edu

FIDM/THE FASHION INSTITUTE OF DESIGN & MERCHANDISING

919 S Grand Ave, Los Angeles CA 90015-1421
Director of Admissions
213-624-1201 or 800-624-1200 Fax: 213-624-4799
Website: www.fidm.edu
E-mail: info@fidm.edu
See listing under "Community and Junior Colleges"

FIDM/The Fashion Institute of Design & Merchandising
55 Stockton St, San Francisco CA 94108-5829
Director of Admissions
415-675-5200 or 800-422-3436 Fax: 415-296-7299
Website: www.fidm.edu
E-mail: info@fidm.edu
See listing under "Community and Junior Colleges"

Orange Coast College
PO Box 5005, Costa Mesa CA 92628-5005
Kristin Clark, Director of Admissions
714-432-5773 Fax: 714-432-5736
Website: www.orangecoastcollege.edu
E-mail: kclark@cccd.edu

COLORADO

Art Institute of Colorado
1200 Lincoln St, Denver CO 80203-2172
David Zorn, President
Brian A. Parker, Director of Admissions
800-275-2420 Fax: 303-860-8520
Website: www.artinstitutes.edu
E-mail: baparker@aii.edu

ROCKY MOUNTAIN COLLEGE OF ART & DESIGN

1600 Pierce St, Lakewood CO 80214
Marianna Bagge, Director of Admissions
800-888-2787 Fax: 303-759-4970
Website: www.rmcad.edu
E-mail: admissions@rmcad.edu

CONNECTICUT

University of New Haven
300 Boston Post Rd, West Haven CT 06516
Director of Undergraduate Admissions
203-932-7319 Fax: 203-931-6093
Website: www.newhaven.edu
E-mail: adminfo@newhaven.edu

FLORIDA

Art Institute of Fort Lauderdale
1799 SE 17th St, Fort Lauderdale FL 33316-3013
Eileen Northrop, V.P./Director of Admissions
800-275-7603 Fax: 954-728-8637
Website: www.aifl.edu

Florida State University
600 W College Ave, Tallahassee FL 32306-1096
Janice V. Finney, Director of Admissions
850-644-2525 Fax: 850-644-0197
Website: admissions.fsu.edu
E-mail: admissions@admin.fsu.edu

International Academy of Design & Technology
5104 Eisenhower Blvd, Tampa FL 33634-6313
Richard Costa, V.P. of Admissions and Marketing
813-880-8092 Fax: 813-881-0008
Website: www.academy.edu
E-mail: admissions@academy.edu

INTERNATIONAL ACADEMY OF DESIGN AND TECHNOLOGY
5959 Lake Ellenor Dr, Orlando FL 32809-4633
Dr. John Dietrich, VP of Admissions
877-753-0007 Fax: 407-251-0465
Website: www.iadt.edu
E-mail: info@iadt.edu

GEORGIA

Savannah College of Art and Design
PO Box 2072, Savannah, GA 31402-2072
PO Box 77300, Atlanta, GA 30357
Phone: 800-869-7223 (Savannah) or 877-722-3285 (Atlanta)
E-mail: admission@scad.edu (Savannah) or scadatl@scad.edu (Atlanta)
www.scad.edu
    SCAD is a private, nonprofit institution accredited by the Commission on Colleges of the Southern Association of Colleges and Schools to award bachelor's and master's degrees. The college offers B.F.A., M.Arch., M.A., M.F.A., and M.U.D. degrees. Enrollment is appoximately 7,350; 6 percent are international. More than 30 areas of study. Online programs via SCAD e-Learning.

IDAHO
Brigham Young University - Idaho
120 Kimball Bldg, Rexburg ID 83460
Gordon Westenskow, Director of Admissions
208-496-1020 Fax: 208-496-1220
Website: www.byui.edu
E-mail: admissions@byui.edu

ILLINOIS
Columbia College Chicago
600 S Michigan Ave, Chicago IL 60605-1996
Murphy Monroe, Executive Director of Admissions
312-344-7130 Fax: 312-344-8024
Website: www.colum.edu
E-mail: admissions@colum.edu

HARRINGTON COLLEGE OF DESIGN
200 W Madison St, Chicago IL 60606-3433
Wendi Franczyk, VP of Admissions
877-939-4975 Fax: 312-697-8032
Website: www.harringtoncollege.com
E-mail: wfranczyk@interiordesign.edu
See listing under "Universities"

Roosevelt University
430 S Michigan Ave, Chicago IL 60605
Gwen E. Kanelos, Asst. Vice President for Enrollment Services
877-APPLY-RU Fax: 312-341-4216
Website: www.roosevelt.edu
E-mail: applyru@roosevelt.edu

INDIANA
Ivy Tech Community College - North Central
220 Dean Johnson Blvd, South Bend IN 46601-3415
Pam Decker, Director of Admissions
574-289-7001 Fax: 574-236-7177
Website: www.ivytech.edu
E-mail: pdecker@ivytech.edu

MASSACHUSETTS
Bay Path College
588 Longmeadow St, Longmeadow MA 01106-2292
Lisa Casassa, Director of Admissions
413-565-1331 Fax: 413-565-1105
Website: www.baypath.edu
E-mail: lcasassa@baypath.edu

Becker College
Campuses in Worcester and Leicester, MA
61 Sever St, Worcester MA 01609-2165
Karen H. Schedin, Director of Admissions
508-791-9241 Fax: 508-890-1500
Website: www.becker.edu
E-mail: admissions@becker.edu
See listing under "Universities"

Newbury College
129 Fisher Ave, Brookline MA 02445-5796
Salvadore Liberto, Vice President of Enrollment
617-730-7000 Fax: 617-731-9618
Website: www.newbury.edu

Wentworth Institute of Technology
550 Huntington Ave, Boston MA 02115-5998
David C. Planchard, Director of Admissions
617-442-9010
Website: www.wit.edu/apply
E-mail: planchardd@wit.edu

MICHIGAN
College for Creative Studies
201 E Kirby St, Detroit MI 48202-4048
Julie Hingelberg, Dean of Enrollment Services
313-664-7425
Website: www.ccscad.edu

Delta College
University Center MI 48710-0001
Duff Zube, Director of Admissions
989-686-9093 Fax: 989-667-2202
Website: www.delta.edu
E-mail: admit@delta.edu

Kendall College of Art & Design
17 Fountain St NW, Grand Rapids MI 49503-3002
Dr. Oliver H. Evans, President
800-676-2787 or 616-451-2787 Fax: 616-831-9689
Website: www.kcad.edu
E-mail: brittons@ferris.edu

Lawrence Technological University
21000 W 10 Mile Rd, Southfield MI 48075-1058
Jane Rohrback, Director of Admissions
800-225-5588 Fax: 248-204-2228
Website: www.ltu.edu
E-mail: admissions@ltu.edu
See listing under "Universities"

MINNESOTA
Dunwoody College of Technology
818 Dunwoody Blvd, Minneapolis MN 55403-1192
John Slama, Vice President Enrollment Management
800-292-4625 or 612-374-5800 Fax: 612-374-4128
Website: www.dunwoody.edu
E-mail: jslama@dunwoody.edu
See listing under "Career Schools"

MISSOURI
Stephens College
PO Box 2121, Columbia MO 65215-0001
David Adams, Dean of Enrollment Management
573-442-2211 Fax: 573-876-7237
Website: www.stephens.edu
E-mail: dadams@stephens.edu

NEW YORK

NEW YORK SCHOOL OF INTERIOR DESIGN
170 E 70th St, New York NY 10021-5110
David Sprouls, Director of Admissions
800-33-NYSID or 212-472-1500 Fax: 212-472-1867
Website: www.nysid.edu
E-mail: admissions@nysid.edu
    Established 1916. Private. Coed. College devoted to Interior Design education. Tuition: $20,460 per year. Fees: $110. Enrollment: 750. Faculty: 95. Accreditation: NASAD, FIDER. Four programs offered: Master of Fine Arts, 4-year Bachelor degree, 2-year Associate degree, 1-year non-degree Basic Interior Design. Located in Manhattan's historic Upper East Side near center of interior design industry. Faculty consists of Designers, Architects and Artists.

Pratt Institute
200 Willoughby Ave, Brooklyn NY 11205-3899
Heidi Metcalf, Director of Admissions
718-636-3600 Fax: 718-636-3670
Website: www.pratt.edu
E-mail: hmetcalf@pratt.edu

SUNY College of Technology
Alfred NY 14802
Deborah J. Goodrich, Director of Admissions
800-4AL-FRED Fax: 607-587-4299
Website: www.alfredstate.edu
E-mail: admissions@alfredstate.edu

NORTH CAROLINA
Meredith College
3800 Hillsborough St, Raleigh NC 27607-5298
Heidi L. Fletcher, Director of Admissions
919-760-8581 Fax: 919-760-2348
Website: www.meredith.edu
E-mail: admissions@meredith.edu
See listing under "Women's Colleges"

Salem College
Winston Salem NC 27108
Dana Evans, Dean of Admissions/Fin. Aid
800-32-SALEM Fax: 336-917-5572
Website: www.salem.edu
E-mail: admissions@salem.edu
See listing under "Women's Colleges"

OHIO
Columbus College of Art & Design
107 N 9th St, Columbus OH 43215-1700
877-997-CCAD or 614-222-3261 Fax: 614-232-8344
Website: www.ccad.edu
E-mail: admissions@ccad.edu

Davis College
4747 Monroe St, Toledo OH 43623-4389
Dana Stern, Admissions Director
419-473-2700 Fax: 419-473-2472
Website: www.daviscollege.edu
E-mail: learn@daviscollege.edu

The Ohio State University
Dept of Industrial, Interior, & Visual Communication Design
380 Hopkins Hall, 128 N Oval Mall
Columbus OH 43210
614-292-6746 Fax: 614-292-0217
Website: design.osu.edu
E-mail: design@osu.edu

Owens Community College
PO Box 10000, Toledo OH 43699-1947
William J. Ivoska, Ph.D, Vice President of Student Services
567-661-7000 Fax: 567-661-7607
Website: www.owens.edu
E-mail: admissions@owens.edu

OKLAHOMA
Oklahoma State University
Stillwater OK 74078
Donna Branson, Department Head
405-744-5049
Website: www.okstate.edu
E-mail: donna.branson@okstate.edu

OREGON
Marylhurst University
17600 Pacific Hwy (Hwy 43)
Marylhurst OR 97036-0261
Director of Admissions
800-634-9982 ext. 6268 Fax: 503-635-6585
Website: www.marylhurst.edu
E-mail: studentinfo@marylhurst.edu

PENNSYLVANIA
Arcadia University
450 S Easton Rd, Glenside PA 19038-3295
Dennis Nostrand, VP for Enrollment Management
877-ARCADIA (877-272-2342) Fax: 215-881-8767
Website: www.arcadia.edu
E-mail: admiss@arcadia.edu
See listing under "Universities"

Art Institute of Philadelphia
1622 Chestnut St, Philadelphia PA 19103-5119
Larry McHugh, Director of Admissions
800-275-2474 Fax: 215-405-6399
Website: www.aiph.aii.edu
E-mail: aiphinfo@aii.edu

ART INSTITUTE OF PITTSBURGH
420 Boulevard Of The Allies, Pittsburgh PA 15219
Newton I. Myvett, VP/Director of Admissions
800-275-2470 Fax: 412-263-6667
Website: www.aip.aii.edu
E-mail: pahughes@aii.edu
See listing under "Universities"

La Roche College
9000 Babcock Blvd, Pittsburgh PA 15237-5898
Thomas Hassett, Director of Freshman and International Admissions
412-536-1272 or 800-838-4LRC Fax: 412-536-1272
Website: www.laroche.edu
E-mail: admissions@laroche.edu

RHODE ISLAND
New England Institute of Technology
2500 Post Rd, Warwick RI 02886-2244
Michael Kwiatkowski, Director of Admissions
401-739-5000 Fax: 401-738-5122
Website: www.neit.edu
E-mail: eflynn@neit.edu

TENNESSEE
O'More College of Design
423 S Margin St, Franklin TN 37064-2816
Dr. K. Mark Hilliard, President
Chris Lee, Director of Enrollment Management
615-794-4254 Fax: 615-790-1662
Website: www.omorecollege.edu
E-mail: clee@omorecollege.edu

TEXAS

ART INSTITUTE OF HOUSTON
1900 Yorktown St, Houston TX 77056
Brian A. Shumaker, Director of Admissions
800-275-4244 Fax: 713-966-2797
Website: www.aih.artinstitutes.edu

University of Texas at Arlington
Box 19111, Arlington TX 76019-0111
Hans Gatterdam, Director of Admission
817-272-6287 Fax: 817-272-3435
Website: www.uta.edu
E-mail: admissions@uta.edu

Wade College
Dallas Market Center
PO Box 421149, Dallas TX 75342
Harry Davros, President
800-624-4850 or 214-637-3530 Fax: 214-637-0827
Website: www.wadecollege.edu
E-mail: admissions@wadecollege.edu
See listing under "Community and Junior Colleges"

UTAH

L.D.S. BUSINESS COLLEGE
95 North 300 West, Salt Lake City UT 84101-3500
Kathleen Howe, Assistant Director of Admissions
801-524-8145 Fax: 801-524-1900
Website: www.ldsbc.edu
E-mail: admissions@ldsbc.edu
See listing under "Career Schools"

VIRGINIA
Radford University
PO Box 6903, Radford VA 24142
David W. Kraus, Director of Admissions
800-890-4265 Fax: 540-831-5038
Website: www.radford.edu
E-mail: ruadmiss@radford.edu

WASHINGTON
Cornish College of the Arts
1000 Lenora St, Seattle WA 98121
Eric Pedersen, Director of Admission
800-726-ARTS (2787) Fax: 206-720-1011
Website: www.cornish.edu
E-mail: admissions@cornish.edu

LANDSCAPE ARCHITECTURE

ARIZONA

University of Arizona
  Tucson AZ 85721-0040
  Paul Kohn, Director of Admissions
  520-621-3237 Fax: 520-621-9799
  Website: www.admissions.arizona.edu or
  www.arizona.edu

IDAHO

Brigham Young University - Idaho
  120 Kimball Bldg, Rexburg ID 83460
  Gordon Westenskow, Director of Admissions
  208-496-1020 Fax: 208-496-1220
  Website: www.byui.edu
  E-mail: admissions@byui.edu

University of Idaho
  Moscow ID 83844-4253
  Lloyd Scott, Director of New Student Services
  208-885-6163 Fax: 208-885-4477
  Website: www.uidaho.edu
  E-mail: nss@uidaho.edu

MAINE

· Southern Maine Community College
  2 Fort Rd, South Portland ME 04106-1698
  Dr. James Ortiz, President
  Scott MacDonald, Director of Financial Aid
  207-741-5500 Fax: 207-741-5671
  Website: www.smccme.edu
  E-mail: oharmon@maine.rr.com

MICHIGAN

Andrews University
  Berrien Springs MI 49104-0001
  Randall Graves, Director of Recruitment Services
  800-253-2874 Fax: 269-471-2670
  Website: www.connect.andrews.edu
  E-mail: gravesr@andrews.edu

NEW YORK

Paul Smith's College
  Paul Smiths NY 12970
  Amber DeBeer, Assistant Director of Admissions
  800-421-2605 Fax: 518-327-6016
  Website: www.paulsmiths.edu
  E-mail: admiss@paulsmiths.edu

· SUNY College of Technology
  2 Main St, Delhi NY 13753-1110
  Robert W. Mazzei, Director of Admissions
  800-96-DELHI Fax: 607-746-4104
  Website: www.delhi.edu
  E-mail: enroll@delhi.edu

NORTH CAROLINA

· Haywood Community College
  185 Freedlander Dr, Clyde NC 28721
  Debbie Rowland, Coordinator of Admissions
  828-627-4500 Fax: 828-627-4513
  Website: www.haywood.edu
  E-mail: drowland@haywood.edu

North Carolina A&T State University
  1601 E Market St, Greensboro NC 27411
  Lee Young, AVC Enrollment
  336-334-7500 Fax: 336-334-7478
  Website: www.ncat.edu
  E-mail: uadmit@ncat.edu

OHIO

The Ohio State University
  Austin E. Knowlton School of Architecture
  Knowlton Arch Bldg, 275 W Woodruff Ave
  Columbus OH 43210
  614-292-1012 Fax: 614-292-7106
  Website: knowlton.osu.edu
  E-mail: ugadvisor@knowlton.osu.edu

· Owens Community College
  PO Box 10000, Toledo OH 43699-1947
  William J. Ivoska, Ph.D, Vice President of Student
  Services
  567-661-7000 Fax: 567-661-7607
  Website: www.owens.edu
  E-mail: admissions@owens.edu

OKLAHOMA

Oklahoma State University
  Stillwater OK 74078
  Dale Maronek, Department Head
  405-744-5414
  Website: www.okstate.edu
  E-mail: dale.maronek@okstate.edu

TEXAS

University of Houston
  122 E Cullen Bldg, Houston TX 77204-2023
  Office of Admission
  713-743-9595
  Website: www.uh.edu
  E-mail: admissions@uh.edu

University of Texas at Arlington
  Box 19111, Arlington TX 76019-0111
  Hans Gatterdam, Director of Admission
  817-272-6287 Fax: 817-272-3435
  Website: www.uta.edu
  E-mail: admissions@uta.edu

LAW

ALABAMA

Faulkner University
  5345 Atlanta Hwy, Montgomery AL 36109-3398
  Paul Smith, Director of Jones School of Law
  800-879-9816 ext. 7200 or 334-386-7200
  Fax: 334-386-7137

Judson College
  302 Bibb St, Marion AL 36756
  Michael Scotto, Director of Admissions
  800-447-9472 Fax: 334-683-5147
  Website: www.judson.edu
  E-mail: admissions@judson.edu

ARIZONA

University of Arizona
  Tucson AZ 85721-0040
  Paul Kohn, Director of Admissions
  520-621-3237 Fax: 520-621-9799
  Website: www.admissions.arizona.edu or
  www.arizona.edu

CALIFORNIA

Chapman University
  One University Drive, Orange CA 92866-1099
  Michael Drummy, Assistant Vice President for
  Enrollment
  Services and Chief Admission Officer
  714-997-6411 or 888-CUAPPLY Fax: 714-997-6713
  Website: www.chapman.edu
  E-mail: admit@chapman.edu

SAN JOAQUIN COLLEGE OF LAW
  901 5th St, Clovis CA 93612-1312
  Joyce Morodomi, Director of Student Services
  559-323-2100 Fax: 559-323-5566
  Website: www.sjcl.edu
  E-mail: studylaw@sjcl.edu

WESTERN STATE UNIVERSITY COLLEGE OF LAW
  1111 N State College Blvd, Fullerton CA 92831-3014
  Phyllis Hauptfeld, Assistant Dean of Admission
  800-WSU-4LAW or 714-459-1107 Fax: 714-441-1748
  Website: www.wsulaw.edu
  E-mail: adm@wsulaw.edu

COLORADO

: Denver Career College
  500 E 84th Ave Suite W200
  Thornton CO 80229-5316
  JoAnn Navarro, Director of Admissions
  800-848-0550 Fax: 303-295-0102
  Website: www.denvercareercollege.com
  E-mail: admissions-045@denvercareercollege.com

DELAWARE

Wesley College
  120 N State St, Dover DE 19901-3876
  302-736-2300 Fax: 302-736-2301
  Website: www.wesley.edu

FLORIDA

City College
  2000 W Commercial Blvd, Fort Lauderdale FL 33309
  Britt Carpenter, Director of Admissions
  954-492-5353 Fax: 954-491-1965
  Website: www.citycollege.edu
  E-mail: bcarpenter@citycollege.edu

FLORIDA METROPOLITAN UNIVERSITY
  Pinellas Campus
  2471 N McMullen Booth Rd
  Clearwater FL 33759-1359
  Sandra Williams, Director of Admissions
  800-353-3687 or 727-725-2688 Fax: 727-725-3827
  Website: www.fmu.edu
  E-mail: sawilliams@cci.edu

Florida State University
  600 W College Ave, Tallahassee FL 32306-1096
  Janice V. Finney, Director of Admissions
  850-644-2525 Fax: 850-644-0197
  Website: admissions.fsu.edu
  E-mail: admissions@admin.fsu.edu

Key College
  225 E Dania Beach Blvd #130
  Dania Beach FL 33004
  Ronald Dooley, President
  954-923-4440 Fax: 954-923-9226
  Website: www.keycollege.edu
  E-mail: admissions@keycollege.edu

St. Thomas University
  16401 NW 37th Ave, Miami Gardens FL 33054
  Dr Gary Feinberg, Contact
  800-367-9010 or 305-628-6546 Fax: 305-628-6591
  Website: www.stu.edu
  E-mail: signup@stu.edu

South University
  1760 N Congress Ave
  West Palm Beach FL 33409-5178
  Steven A. Schwab, President
  561-697-9200 Fax: 561-697-9944
  Website: www.southuniversity.edu
  E-mail: wpb@southuniversity.edu
  SACS Accreditation.

SOUTHWEST FLORIDA COLLEGE
  1685 Medical Ln, Fort Myers FL 33907-1157
  866-SWFC-NOW or 239-939-4766 Fax: 239-936-4040
  Website: www.swfc.edu
  E-mail: studentinfo@swfc.edu

IDAHO

University of Idaho
  Moscow ID 83844-4253
  Lloyd Scott, Director of New Student Services
  208-885-6163 Fax: 208-885-4477
  Website: www.uidaho.edu
  E-mail: nss@uidaho.edu

ILLINOIS

Roosevelt University
  430 S Michigan Ave, Chicago IL 60605
  Gwen E. Kanelos, Asst. Vice President for Enrollment
  Services
  877-APPLY-RU Fax: 312-341-4216
  Website: www.roosevelt.edu
  E-mail: applyru@roosevelt.edu

IOWA

Briar Cliff University
  PO Box 2100, Sioux City IA 51104-0100
  Sharisue Wilcoxon, VP for Enrollment Management
  712-279-5200 Fax: 712-279-1632
  Website: www.briarcliff.edu
  E-mail: admissions@briarcliff.edu

· Iowa Lakes Community College
  300 S 18th St, Estherville IA 51334-2721
  Anne Stansbury, Asst. Director of Admissions
  712-362-7945 Fax: 712-362-8363
  Website: www.iowalakes.edu
  E-mail: info@iowalakes.edu

KANSAS

Newman University
  3100 W McCormick St, Wichita KS 67213
  Jann Reusser, Admissions Recruitment Coordinator
  316-942-4291 ext. 2144 Fax: 316-942-4483
  Website: www.newmanu.edu
  E-mail: reusserj@newmanu.edu

KENTUCKY

BROWN MACKIE COLLEGE
  Northern Kentucky Campus
  309 Buttermilk Pike, Fort Mitchell KY 41017-2191
  Joanne Dellefield, Director of Admissions
  859-341-5627 Fax: 859-341-6483
  Website: www.brownmackie.edu
  E-mail: jdellefield@brownmackie.edu

Daymar College
4400 Breckenridge Ln #415, Louisville KY 40218
Shawn McDaniel, Director of Admissions
502-495-1040 Fax: 502-495-1518
Website: www.daymarcollege.com

Daymar College
3361 Buckland Sq, Owensboro KY 42301-5830
Vickie McDougal Director of Admissions
800-960-4090 Fax: 270-685-4090
Website: www.daymarcollege.com

MASSACHUSETTS

Bay Path College
588 Longmeadow St, Longmeadow MA 01106-2292
Lisa Casassa, Director of Admissions
413-565-1331 Fax: 413-565-1105
Website: www.baypath.edu
E-mail: lcasassa@baypath.edu

Becker College
Campuses in Worcester and Leicester, MA
61 Sever St, Worcester MA 01609-2165
Karen H. Schedin, Director of Admissions
508-791-9241 Fax: 508-890-1500
Website: www.becker.edu
E-mail: admissions@becker.edu
See listing under "Universities"

Boston University
121 Bay State Rd, Boston MA 02215
Kelly Walter, Executive Director of Admissions
617-353-2300 Fax: 617-353-9695
Website: web.bu.edu
E-mail: admissions@bu.edu

MASSACHUSETTS SCHOOL OF LAW AT ANDOVER
500 Federal St, Andover MA 01810
Paula Colby-Clements, Esq, Director of Admissions
978-681-0800 Fax: 978-681-6330
Website: www.mslaw.edu
E-mail: pcolby@mslaw.edu

NEW ENGLAND SCHOOL OF LAW
154 Stuart St, Boston MA 02116-5616
Michelle C. L'Etoile, Director of Admissions
617-422-7210 Fax: 617-457-3033
Website: www.nesl.edu
E-mail: admit@admin.nesl.edu

MICHIGAN

MACOMB COMMUNITY COLLEGE
44575 Garfield Rd, Clinton Township MI 48038-1139
Information Center
586-445-7999
Website: www.macomb.edu
E-mail: answer@macomb.edu

MISSOURI

Stephens College
PO Box 2121, Columbia MO 65215-0001
David Adams, Dean of Enrollment Management
573-442-2211 Fax: 573-876-7237
Website: www.stephens.edu
E-mail: dadams@stephens.edu

Truman State University
100 E Normal, Kirksville MO 63501
Office of Admission
660-785-4000 Fax: 660-785-4181
Website: admissions.truman.edu
E-mail: admissions@truman.edu

William Woods University
1 University Ave, Fulton MO 65251-1098
Jimmy Clay, Director of Admissions
573-642-2251 Fax: 573-592-1146
Website: www.williamwoods.edu
E-mail: admissions@williamwoods.edu
See listing under "Universities"

NEVADA

Career College of Northern Nevada
1195-A Corporate Blvd, Reno NV 89502-2331
Nathan Clark, Director
775-856-2266 Fax: 775-856-0935
Website: www.ccnn.edu
E-mail: lgoldhammer@ccnn4u.com
See listing under "Career Schools"

NEW JERSEY

New Jersey City University
2039 John F Kennedy Blvd
Jersey City NJ 07305-1588
Carmen Panlilio, Asst. V.P. for Admissions and Financial Aid
201-200-3234 Fax: 201-200-2044
Website: www.njcu.edu
E-mail: admissions@njcu.edu

NEW YORK

ALBANY LAW SCHOOL OF UNION UNIVERSITY
80 New Scotland Ave, Albany NY 12208-3494
Gail Bensen, Director of Admissions
518-445-2311 Fax: 518-445-2315
Website: www.albanylaw.edu
E-mail: admissions@albanylaw.edu

College of Saint Rose
432 Western Ave, Albany NY 12203-1419
Maryelizabeth Amico, Asst V.P. for Undergraduate Admissions
518-454-5150 Fax: 518-454-2013
Website: www.strose.edu
E-mail: admit@strose.edu

Hilbert College
5200 S Park Ave, Hamburg NY 14075-1597
Timothy Lee, Director of Admissions
716-649-7900 Fax: 716-649-0702
Website: www.hilbert.edu
E-mail: tlee@hilbert.edu

Ridley-Lowell Business & Technical Institute
116 Front St, Binghamton NY 13905-3102
David Lounsbury, Executive Director
607-724-2941 Fax: 607-724-0799
Website: www.ridley.edu
E-mail: info@ridley.edu

Roberts Wesleyan College
2301 Westside Dr, Rochester NY 14624-1997
Office of Admissions
585-594-6400 Fax: 585-594-6371
Website: www.roberts.edu
E-mail: admissions@roberts.edu

St. John's University
8000 Utopia Pkwy, Queens NY 11439
Office of Admission
718-990-2000 or 888-9-STJOHNS Fax: 718-990-2096
Website: www.stjohns.edu
E-mail: admissions@stjohns.edu
See listing under "Universities"

NORTH CAROLINA

Louisburg College
501 N Main St, Louisburg NC 27549-2399
800-775-0208 or 919-496-2521 Fax: 919-496-1788
Website: www.louisburg.edu
E-mail: admissions@louisburg.edu

Salem College
Winston Salem NC 27108
Dana Evans, Dean of Admissions/Fin. Aid
800-32-SALEM Fax: 336-917-5572
Website: www.salem.edu
E-mail: admissions@salem.edu
See listing under "Women's Colleges"

OHIO

Brown Mackie College - Cincinnati
1011 Glendale Milford Rd, Cincinnati OH 45215-1107
Robin Krout, President
513-771-2424 Fax: 513-771-3413
Website: www.brownmackie.edu
E-mail: rkrout@brownmackie.edu

Cleveland State University
2121 Euclid Ave RW 204, Cleveland OH 44115
Dr. Richard Arndt, Dean of Undergraduate Recruitment and College Partnerships
888-CSU-OHIO Fax: 216-687-9210
Website: www.csuohio.edu
E-mail: admissions@csuohio.edu

OHIO NORTHERN UNIVERSITY
525 S Main St, Ada OH 45810-1555
Dr. David Crago, Dean
419-772-2205
Website: www.onu.edu
See listing under "Universities"

The Ohio State University
Moritz College of Law
Drinko Hall, 55 W 12th Ave, Columbus OH 43210
614-292-8810 Fax: 614-292-1492
Website: moritzlaw.osu.edu
E-mail: lawadmit@osu.edu

University of Dayton
300 College Park, Dayton OH 45469-1300
Robert F. Durkle, Director of Admissions
800-837-7433 Fax: 937-229-4729
Website: admission.udayton.edu
E-mail: admission@udayton.edu

Ursuline College
2550 Lander Rd, Cleveland OH 44124-4398
Sarah E. Sundermeier, Director of Admissions
888-URSULINE Toll Free Fax: 440-684-6138
Website: www.admission.ursuline.edu
E-mail: admission@ursuline.edu

OKLAHOMA

University of Tulsa
600 S College Ave, Tulsa OK 74104-3126
Earl Johnson, Dean of Admission
918-631-2307 Fax: 918-631-5003
Website: www.utulsa.edu
E-mail: admission@utulsa.edu

PENNSYLVANIA

Academy of Medical Arts and Business
2301 Academy Dr, Harrisburg PA 17112-1012
717-545-4747
Website: www.ACADcampus.com
E-mail: info@ACADcampus.com

Arcadia University
450 S Easton Rd, Glenside PA 19038-3295
Dennis Nostrand, VP for Enrollment Management
877-ARCADIA (877-272-2342) Fax: 215-881-8767
Website: www.arcadia.edu
E-mail: admiss@arcadia.edu
See listing under "Universities"

Juniata College
1700 Moore St, Huntingdon PA 16652-2196
Michelle Bartol, Dean of Enrollment
877-JUNIATA Fax: 814-641-3100
Website: www.juniata.edu
E-mail: admissions@juniata.edu

MOUNT ALOYSIUS COLLEGE
7373 Admiral Peary Hwy, Cresson PA 16630-1999
Frank C. Crouse Jr., Vice President for Enrollment Management
814-886-6383 or 888-823-2220 Fax: 814-886-6441
Website: www.mtaloy.edu
E-mail: admissions@mtaloy.edu

Neumann College
1 Neumann Dr, Aston PA 19014-1298
Dennis Murphy, Director of Admissions
610-459-0905 Fax: 610-558-5652
Website: www.neumann.edu
E-mail: neumann@neumann.edu

SOUTH CAROLINA

Forrest Junior College
601 E River St, Anderson SC 29624-2405
Dr. Julia R. Barnes, President
864-225-7653 Fax: 864-261-7471
Website: www.forrestcollege.edu
E-mail: info@forrestcollege.edu
See listing under "Community and Junior Colleges"

South University
9 Science Court, Columbia SC 29203
Trish Wade, Contact
803-799-9082 Fax: 803-799-9038
Website: www.southuniversity.edu
E-mail: twade@southuniversity.edu

SOUTH DAKOTA

NATIONAL AMERICAN UNIVERSITY
321 Kansas City St, Rapid City SD 57701-3692
Angela G. Beck, Director of Enrollment Management
605-394-4800 Fax: 605-394-4871
Website: www.national.edu/rc/index.html
E-mail: rcadmissions@national.edu

National American University
2801 S Kiwanis Ave Ste 100
Sioux Falls SD 57105-4293
605-334-5430 Fax: 605-334-1575
Website: www.national.edu

Western Dakota Technical Institute
800 Mickelson Dr, Rapid City SD 57703-4018
Janell Oberlander, Manager of Student Services
605-394-4034 or 800-544-8765 Fax: 605-394-1789
Website: www.westerndakotatech.org
E-mail: admissions@wdti.tec.sd.us
See listing under "Career Schools"

TENNESSEE

Miller-Motte Technical College
1820 Business Park Dr, Clarksville TN 37040-6023
Lisa Teague, Director of Admissions
931-553-0071 Fax: 931-552-2916
Website: www.miller-motte.com
E-mail: lteague@miller-motte.com

TEXAS

SOUTHEASTERN CAREER INSTITUTE
12005 Ford Rd Suite 100, Dallas TX 75234-7288
972-385-1446 or 800-524-8800 Fax: 972-385-0641
Website: www.southeasterncareerinstitute.com

University of Houston
122 E Cullen Bldg, Houston TX 77204-2023
Office of Admission
713-743-9595
Website: www.uh.edu
E-mail: admissions@uh.edu

University of St. Thomas
3800 Montrose Blvd, Houston TX 77006-4626
Eduardo Prieto, Director of Admissions
713-522-7911 Fax: 713-525-3558
Website: www.stthom.edu
E-mail: prietoe@stthom.edu

UTAH

ITT TECHNICAL INSTITUTE
920 Levoy Dr, Murray UT 84123-2500
Gary Wood, Director of Recruitment
801-263-3313 Fax: 801-263-3497
Website: www.itt-tech.edu
E-mail: gwood@itt-tech.edu

VERMONT

Woodbury College
660 Elm St, Montpelier VT 05602-4017
Kathleen Moore, Director of Admissions
800-639-6039 Fax: 802-229-2141
Website: www.woodbury-college.edu
E-mail: admiss@woodbury-college.edu

VIRGINIA

APPALACHIAN SCHOOL OF LAW
PO Box 2825, Grundy VA 24614-1825
Nancy Pruitt, Director of Student Services
800-895-7411 Fax: 276-935-8261
Website: www.asl.edu
E-mail: npruitt@asl.edu

WASHINGTON

CROWN COLLEGE
8739 S Hosmer St, Tacoma WA 98444-1836
John Wabel, CEO
253-531-3123 Fax: 253-531-3521
Website: www.crowncollege.edu
E-mail: jwabel@crowncollege.edu

Gonzaga University
Spokane WA 99258-0029
Daniel Morrissey, Dean
509-323-5546 Fax: 509-323-5744
Website: www.gonzaga.edu
E-mail: dmorrisey@lawschool.gonzaga.edu

WEST VIRGINIA

Mountain State College
1508 Spring St, Parkersburg WV 26101-3993
Judith Sutton, Director
304-485-5487 Fax: 304-485-3524
Website: www.mountainstate.org
E-mail: admin@mountainstate.org
See listing under "Career Schools"

West Virginia Wesleyan College
59 College Ave, Buckhannon WV 26201-2699
Robert N. Skinner II, Director of Admission
800-722-9933 Fax: 304-473-8108
Website: www.wvwc.edu
E-mail: admission@wvwc.edu

WISCONSIN

Marquette University
PO Box 1881, Milwaukee WI 53201-1881
Robert Blust, Director of Admissions
414-288-7302 Fax: 414-288-3764
Website: www.mu.edu
E-mail: admissions@marquette.edu

St. Norbert College
100 Grant St, De Pere WI 54115
Brian Studebaker, Director of Admission
800-236-4878 Fax: 920-403-4072
Website: www.snc.edu
E-mail: admit@snc.edu

WYOMING

University of Wyoming
Admissions Office
Dept 3435, Laramie WY 82071-3435
Aaron Appelhans, Contact
800-342-5996 Fax: 307-766-4042
Website: www.uwyo.edu
E-mail: why-wyo@uwyo.edu

LETTERS

ALABAMA

Bishop State Community College - Four Campuses
351 N Broad St, Mobile AL 36603-5898
Dr. Terry Hazzard, Dean of Students
251-690-6801 Fax: 251-690-6446
Website: www.bishop.edu
E-mail: thazzard@bishop.edu

Faulkner University
5345 Atlanta Hwy, Montgomery AL 36109-3398
Keith Mock, Director of Admissions
800-879-9816 ext. 7200 or 334-386-7200
Fax: 334-386-7137
Website: www.faulkner.edu
E-mail: admissions@faulkner.edu

University of South Alabama
307 University Blvd N, Mobile AL 36688-3053
Melissa Haab, Director of Admissions
251-460-6141 Fax: 251-460-7876
Website: www.southalabama.edu
E-mail: admiss@usouthal.edu

ARIZONA

Pima Community College
4905 E Broadway Blvd, Tucson AZ 85709-1010
Wendy Kilgore, Ph.D., Director of Admissions
520-206-4500 Fax: 520-206-4790
Website: www.pima.edu
E-mail: infocenter@pima.edu

University of Arizona
Tucson AZ 85721-0040
Paul Kohn, Director of Admissions
520-621-3237 Fax: 520-621-9799
Website: www.admissions.arizona.edu or
www.arizona.edu

CALIFORNIA

Antioch University Southern California
400 Corporate Pointe, Culver City CA 90230-7615
Admissions Office
800-7-ANTIOCH Fax: 310-821-6032
E-mail: admissions@antiochla.edu
Master of Fine Arts in Creative Writing.

California State University-San Bernadino
5500 University Pkwy
San Bernardino CA 92407-2393
Olivia Rosas, Director of Admissions
909-880-5000 Fax: 909-880-7034
Website: enrollment.csusb.edu
E-mail: orosas@csusb.edu

Chapman University
One University Drive, Orange CA 92866-1099
Michael Drummy, Assistant Vice President for
Enrollment
Services and Chief Admission Officer
714-997-6411 or 888-CUAPPLY Fax: 714-997-6713
Website: www.chapman.edu
E-mail: admit@chapman.edu

FRESNO CITY COLLEGE
1101 E University Ave, Fresno CA 93741-0002
Dayann Dietrich, Contact
559-442-8241 Fax: 559-237-4232
Website: www.fresnocitycollege.com
E-mail: fcc.admissions@scccd.com

San Diego Christian College
2100 Greenfield Dr, El Cajon CA 92019-1157
Jon Melone, Director of Admissions
800-676-2242 Fax: 619-590-1739
Website: www.sdcc.edu
E-mail: admissions@sdcc.edu

Simpson University
2211 College View Dr, Redding CA 96003-8606
Jim Herberger, Director of Admissions
888-9-SIMPSON Fax: 530-226-4861
Website: www.simpsonuniversity.edu
E-mail: admissions@simpsonuniversity.edu
See listing under "Liberal Arts and Sciences"

Whittier College
PO Box 634, Whittier CA 90608-0634
Kieron Miller, Director of Admissions
562-907-4200 Fax: 562-907-4870
Website: www.whittier.edu
E-mail: kmiller@whittier.edu

DELAWARE

Wesley College
120 N State St, Dover DE 19901-3876
302-736-2300 Fax: 302-736-2301
Website: www.wesley.edu

FLORIDA

Florida State University
600 W College Ave, Tallahassee FL 32306-1096
Janice V. Finney, Director of Admissions
850-644-2525 Fax: 850-644-0197
Website: admissions.fsu.edu
E-mail: admissions@admin.fsu.edu

Saint Leo University
PO Box 6665, Saint Leo FL 33574
Deborah Bandy, Director of Admissions
352-588-8200 or 800-334-5532 Fax: 352-588-8257
Website: www.saintleo.edu
E-mail: admission@saintleo.edu

St. Thomas University
16401 NW 37th Ave, Miami Gardens FL 33054
Andre Lightbourn, Director of Admissions
800-367-9010 or 305-628-6546 Fax: 305-628-6591
Website: www.stu.edu
E-mail: signup@stu.edu

Santa Fe Community College
3000 NW 83rd St, Gainesville FL 32606-6200
Jackson N. Sasser, President
352-395-5787 Fax: 352-395-4118
Website: www.sfcc.edu
E-mail: ouida.mcneil@sfcc.edu

University of South Florida
4202 E Fowler Ave, Tampa FL 33620-6900
J. Robert Spatig, Director of Admissions
813-974-3350 Fax: 813-974-9689
Website: www.usf.edu
E-mail: admissions@admin.usf.edu

GEORGIA

Armstrong Atlantic State University
11935 Abercorn St, Savannah GA 31419-1997
Kim West, Asst. Dean and Registrar Enrollment
Services
912-927-5277 Fax: 912-921-5462
Website: www.armstrong.edu
E-mail: admissions@mail.armstrong.edu

Oglethorpe University
4484 Peachtree Rd NE, Atlanta GA 30319-2797
Kelly Gosnell, Director of Admission
404-261-1441 Fax: 404-364-8491
Website: www.oglethorpe.edu
E-mail: admission@oglethorpe.edu

ILLINOIS

Columbia College Chicago
600 S Michigan Ave, Chicago IL 60605-1996
Murphy Monroe, Executive Director of Admissions
312-344-7130 Fax: 312-344-8024
Website: www.colum.edu
E-mail: admissions@colum.edu

North Central College
30 N Brainard St, Naperville IL 60540-4690
Martha Stolze, Director of Admissions
630-637-5800 Fax: 630-637-5819
Website: www.northcentralcollege.edu
E-mail: admissions@noctrl.edu

Roosevelt University
430 S Michigan Ave, Chicago IL 60605
Gwen E. Kanelos, Asst. Vice President for Enrollment
Services
877-APPLY-RU Fax: 312-341-4216
Website: www.roosevelt.edu
E-mail: applyru@roosevelt.edu

INDIANA

Franklin College
101 Branigin Blvd, Franklin IN 46131
Jacqueline S. Acosta, Director of Admissions
800-852-0232 Fax: 317-738-8274
Website: www.franklincollege.edu
E-mail: admissions@franklincollege.edu

Hanover College
PO Box 108, Hanover IN 47243-0108
William D. Preble, Dean of Admission
800-213-2178 Fax: 812-866-7098
Website: www.hanover.edu
E-mail: admissions@hanover.edu

Oakland City University
138 N Lucretia St, Oakland City IN 47660
Brian J. Baker, Director of Admissions
800-737-5125 Fax: 812-749-1433
Website: www.oak.edu
E-mail: bbaker@oak.edu
See listing under "Universities"

St. Mary-of-the-Woods College
Saint Mary of the Woods IN 47876-1001
James P. Malley, Jr., Director of Admission
800-926-7692 Fax: 812-535-5010
Website: www.smwc.edu
E-mail: smwcadms@smwc.edu

IOWA

Clarke College
1550 Clarke Dr, Dubuque IA 52001-3198
Andy Schroeder, Director of Admissions
800-383-2345 Fax: 563-584-8666
Website: www.clarke.edu
E-mail: andy.schroeder@clarke.edu

Wartburg College
PO Box 1003, Waverly IA 50677-0903
Brent Matthias, Interim Director of Admissions
319-352-8200 Fax: 319-352-8579
Website: www.wartburg.edu
E-mail: admissions@wartburg.edu

KANSAS

Allen County Community College
1801 N Cottonwood St, Iola KS 66749-1607
John Masterson, President
Randy Weber, Director of Admissions
620-365-5116 Fax: 620-365-3284
Website: www.allencc.net
E-mail: weber@allencc.edu

COLBY COMMUNITY COLLEGE
1255 S Range Ave, Colby KS 67701-4099
Director of Admissions
888-634-9350 or 785-460-4690 Fax: 785-460-4691
Website: www.colbycc.edu
E-mail: bobbi@colbycc.edu

Newman University
3100 W McCormick St, Wichita KS 67213
Jann Reusser, Admissions Recruitment Coordinator
316-942-4291 ext. 2144 Fax: 316-942-4483
Website: www.newmanu.edu
E-mail: reusserj@newmanu.edu

Tabor College
400 S Jefferson St, Hillsboro KS 67063-1758
Rusty Allen, Dean of Enrollment Management
620-947-3121 Fax: 620-947-6276
Website: www.tabor.edu
E-mail: admissions@tabor.edu

KENTUCKY

Morehead State University
Morehead KY 40351-1689
Dayna Seelig, Enrollment Services
800-585-6781 Fax: 606-783-5038
Website: www.moreheadstate.edu
E-mail: admissions@moreheadstate.edu

Transylvania University
300 N Broadway, Lexington KY 40508-1776
859-233-8242 Fax: 859-233-8797
Website: www.transy.edu
E-mail: admissions@transy.edu

LOUISIANA

Dillard University
2601 Gentilly Blvd, New Orleans LA 70122-3097
Linda G. Nash, Director of Admissions
Website: www.dillard.edu
E-mail: admissions@dillard.edu

Our Lady of Holy Cross College
4123 Woodland Dr, New Orleans LA 70131-7399
Office of Enrollment Services
504-394-7744 Fax: 504-391-2421
Website: www.olhcc.edu

MASSACHUSETTS

Assumption College
500 Salisbury St, Worcester MA 01609-1294
Kathleen Murphy, Dean of Enrollment
508-767-7000 Fax: 508-799-4412
Website: www.assumption.edu
E-mail: admiss@assumption.edu

Boston University
121 Bay State Rd, Boston MA 02215
Kelly Walter, Executive Director of Admissions
617-353-2300 Fax: 617-353-9695
Website: web.bu.edu
E-mail: admissions@bu.edu

Emerson College
120 Boylston St, Boston MA 02116-4624
Sara S. Ramirez, Director of Undergraduate Admission
617-824-8600 Fax: 617-824-8609
Website: www.emerson.edu
E-mail: admission@emerson.edu

Gordon College
255 Grapevine Rd, Wenham MA 01984-1899
Nancy Mering, Director of Admissions
866-464-6736 Fax: 978-867-4682
Website: www.gordon.edu
E-mail: admissions@gordon.edu

University of Massachusetts Dartmouth
Old Westport Rd, North Dartmouth MA 02747-2300
Steven T. Briggs, Director of Admissions
508-999-8605 Fax: 508-999-8755
Website: explore.umassd.edu
E-mail: sbriggs@umassd.edu

Westfield State College
PO Box 1630, Westfield MA 01086
Michelle Mattie, Associate Dean, Admission and
Enrollment Services
413-572-5300
Website: www.wsc.ma.edu
E-mail: admission@wsc.ma.edu

MICHIGAN

Alma College
614 W Superior St, Alma MI 48801-1599
Anne Monroe, Director of Admissions
800-321-ALMA Fax: 989-463-7057
Website: www.alma.edu
E-mail: admissions@alma.edu

Andrews University
Berrien Springs MI 49104-0001
Randall Graves, Director of Recruitment Services
800-253-2874 Fax: 269-471-2670
Website: www.connect.andrews.edu
E-mail: gravesr@andrews.edu

HILLSDALE COLLEGE
33 E College St, Hillsdale MI 49242-1298
Dr. Michael Jordan, Director
517-607-2445 Fax: 517-607-2208
Website: www.hillsdale.edu
E-mail: michael.jordan@hillsdale.edu

Oakland University
2200 N Squirrel Rd, Rochester MI 48309
Eleanor L. Reynolds, Assistant Vice President &
Director of Admissions
248-370-2100
Website: www.oakland.edu
E-mail: ouinfo@oakland.edu

University of Michigan-Dearborn
4901 Evergreen Rd, Dearborn MI 48128-1491
The Office of Admissions & Orientation
313-593-5100 Fax: 313-436-9167
Website: www.umd.umich.edu
E-mail: admissions@umd.umich.edu

MINNESOTA

Bethany Lutheran College
700 Luther Dr, Mankato MN 56001
Don Westphal, Dean of Admissions
507-344-7000 Fax: 507-344-7376
Website: www.blc.edu
E-mail: admiss@blc.edu

Carleton College
1 N College St, Northfield MN 55057-4044
800-995-2275 or 507-646-4190 Fax: 507-646-4526
Website: www.carleton.edu
E-mail: admissions@acs.carleton.edu

Gustavus Adolphus College
800 W College Ave, Saint Peter MN 56082-1485
Mark H. Anderson, Dean of Admission
800-GUSTAVUS Fax: 507-933-7474
Website: www.gustavus.edu
E-mail: admission@gustavus.edu

Pillsbury Baptist Bible College
315 S Grove Ave, Owatonna MN 55060-3097
Stephen R. Seidler, Director of Admissions
507-451-2710 Fax: 507-451-0156
Website: www.pillsbury.edu
E-mail: steveseidler@pillsbury.edu

MISSISSIPPI

Tougaloo College
500 W County Line Rd, Tougaloo MS 39174-9799
Juno Leggette Jacobs, Director of Admissions
601-977-7768 Fax: 601-977-4501
Website: www.tougaloo.edu
E-mail: jjacobs@tougaloo.edu

MISSOURI

East Central College
1964 Prairie Dell Rd, Union MO 63084
Karen Wieda, Registrar
636-583-5195 ext. 2220 Fax: 636-583-1897
Website: www.eastcentral.edu
E-mail: wiedaks@eastcentral.edu

Lindenwood University
209 S Kingshighway St
Saint Charles MO 63301-1695
Sheryl Guffey, Director of Admissions
636-949-2000 Fax: 636-949-4989
Website: www.lindenwood.edu

Stephens College
PO Box 2121, Columbia MO 65215-0001
David Adams, Dean of Enrollment Management
573-442-2211 Fax: 573-876-7237
Website: www.stephens.edu
E-mail: dadams@stephens.edu

Truman State University
100 E Normal, Kirksville MO 63501
Office of Admission
660-785-4000 Fax: 660-785-4181
Website: admissions.truman.edu
E-mail: admissions@truman.edu

Webster University
470 E Lockwood Ave, Saint Louis MO 63119-3194
Dr. David Wilson, Dean, College of Arts and Sciences
314-968-7160 Fax: 314-968-7173
Website: www.webster.edu
E-mail: clewelow@webster.edu
See listing under "Universities"

William Woods University
1 University Ave, Fulton MO 65251-1098
Jimmy Clay, Director of Admissions
573-642-2251 Fax: 573-592-1146
Website: www.williamwoods.edu
E-mail: admissions@williamwoods.edu
See listing under "Universities"

MONTANA

Rocky Mountain College
1511 Poly Dr, Billings MT 59102-1796
Bonnie Knapp, Director of Admissions
800-877-6259 Fax: 406-657-1189
Website: www.rocky.edu
E-mail: admissions@rocky.edu

NEBRASKA

Midland Lutheran College
900 N Clarkson St, Fremont NE 68025-4200
Todd Hansen, Associate Director of Admissions
402-941-6501 Fax: 402-941-6513
Website: www.mlc.edu
E-mail: admissions@mlc.edu

Mid-Plains Community College
McCook Community College Campus
1205 E 3rd St, Mc Cook NE 69001-2631
Kelly Rippen, Director of Recruitment
800-658-4348 Fax: 308-345-8180
Website: www.mpcc.edu
E-mail: rippenk@mpcc.edu

Mid-Plains Community College
North Platte Community College - South Campus
601 W State Farm Rd, North Platte NE 69101
Kelly Rippen, Director of Recruitment
800-658-4308 ext. 8107 Fax: 308-535-3789
Website: www.mpcc.edu
E-mail: rippenk@mpcc.edu

Nebraska Wesleyan University
5000 Saint Paul Ave, Lincoln NE 68504-2794
Patricia Karthauser, V.P. for University Enrollment
402-466-2371 Fax: 402-465-2177
Website: www.nebrwesleyan.edu
E-mail: admissions@nebrwesleyan.edu

NEW JERSEY

Bergen Community College
400 Paramus Rd, Paramus NJ 07652
Julian Gomez, Asst. Director of Admissions
201-447-7100 Fax: 201-444-7036
Website: www.bergen.edu
E-mail: jgomez@bergen.edu

New Jersey City University
2039 John F Kennedy Blvd
Jersey City NJ 07305-1588
Carmen Panlilio, Asst. V.P. for Admissions and
Financial Aid
201-200-3234 Fax: 201-200-2044
Website: www.njcu.edu
E-mail: admissions@njcu.edu

Ramapo College of New Jersey
505 Ramapo Valley Rd, Mahwah NJ 07430-1623
Director of Admissions
201-684-7300 or 201-684-7301 Fax: 201-684-7964
Website: www.ramapo.edu
E-mail: admissions@ramapo.edu

NEW YORK

College of Saint Rose
432 Western Ave, Albany NY 12203-1419
Maryelizabeth Amico, Asst V.P. for Undergraduate
Admissions
518-454-5150 Fax: 518-454-2013
Website: www.strose.edu
E-mail: admit@strose.edu

Hilbert College
5200 S Park Ave, Hamburg NY 14075-1597
Timothy Lee, Director of Admissions
716-649-7900 Fax: 716-649-0702
Website: www.hilbert.edu
E-mail: tlee@hilbert.edu

Hobart & William Smith Colleges
Pulteney St, Geneva NY 14456
John Young, Director of Admissions
315-789-5500 Fax: 315-781-3654
Website: www.hws.edu
E-mail: young@hws.edu

Molloy College
1000 Hempstead Ave
Rockville Centre NY 11570-1100
Marguerite Lane, Director of Admissions
516-678-5000 ext. 6291 Fax: 516-256-2247
Website: www.molloy.edu
E-mail: admissions@molloy.edu
See listing under "Universities"

PURCHASE COLLEGE STATE UNIVERSITY OF NEW YORK (SUNY)
735 Anderson Hill Rd, Purchase NY 10577-1400
Betsy Immergut, Director of Admissions
914-251-6300 Fax: 914-251-6314
Website: www.purchase.edu
See listing under "Universities"

Roberts Wesleyan College
2301 Westside Dr, Rochester NY 14624-1997
Office of Admissions
585-594-6400 Fax: 585-594-6371
Website: www.roberts.edu
E-mail: admissions@roberts.edu

St. Joseph's College
245 Clinton Ave, Brooklyn NY 11205-3688
Theresa LaRocca Meyer, V.P. for Enrollment
Management
718-636-6800 Fax: 718-636-8303
Website: www.sjcny.edu
E-mail: tlaroccameyer@sjcny.edu

SUNY College at Brockport
350 New Campus Dr, Brockport NY 14420-2997
Bernard S. Valento, Director of Undergraduate
Admissions
585-395-2751 Fax: 585-395-5452
Website: www.brockport.edu
E-mail: admit@brockport.edu

United States Military Academy West Point
646 Swift Rd, West Point NY 10996-1905
Colonel Michael L. Jones, Director of Admissions
845-938-4041 Fax: 845-938-8121
Website: admissions.usma.edu
E-mail: admissions@usma.edu

NORTH CAROLINA

Belmont Abbey College
100 Belmont Mount Holly Rd
Belmont NC 28012-1802
888-222-0110 Fax: 704-825-6670
Website: www.belmontabbeycollege.edu
E-mail: admissions@bac.edu

Mars Hill College
Mars Hill NC 28754
Chad Holt, Dean of Enrollment
866-MHC-4-YOU Fax: 828-689-1473
Website: www.mhc.edu
E-mail: cholt@mhc.edu

Meredith College
3800 Hillsborough St, Raleigh NC 27607-5298
Heidi L. Fletcher, Director of Admissions
919-760-8581 Fax: 919-760-2348
Website: www.meredith.edu
E-mail: admissions@meredith.edu
See listing under "Women's Colleges"

Mt. Olive College
634 Henderson St, Mount Olive NC 28365
Tim Woodard, Director of Admissions
919-658-2502 Fax: 919-658-9816
Website: www.moc.edu
E-mail: admissions@moc.edu
See listing under "Universities"

North Carolina A&T State University
1601 E Market St, Greensboro NC 27411
Lee Young, AVC Enrollment
336-334-7500 Fax: 336-334-7478
Website: www.ncat.edu
E-mail: uadmit@ncat.edu

NORTH DAKOTA

Minot State University-Bottineau Campus
105 Simrall Blvd, Bottineau ND 58318-1159
Paula Berg, Associate Dean of Student Affairs
800-542-6866 Fax: 701-228-5499
Website: www.misu-b.nodak.edu
E-mail: paula.berg@misu.nodak.edu

OHIO

Cleveland State University
2121 Euclid Ave RW 204, Cleveland OH 44115
Dr. Richard Arndt, Dean of Undergraduate Recruitment
and College Partnerships
888-CSU-OHIO Fax: 216-687-9210
Website: www.csuohio.edu
E-mail: admissions@csuohio.edu

Mount Vernon Nazarene University
800 Martinsburg Rd, Mount Vernon OH 43050-9509
Timothy Eades, Director of Admissions
866-462-6868 Fax: 740-393-0511
Website: www.gotomvnu.com
E-mail: admissions@mvnu.edu
See listing under "Universities"

OKLAHOMA

Oral Roberts University
7777 S Lewis Ave, Tulsa OK 74171-0001
Chris Belcher, Director of Undergraduate Admissions
800-678-8876 Fax: 918-495-6222
Website: www.oru.edu
E-mail: admissions@oru.edu

University of Tulsa
600 S College Ave, Tulsa OK 74104-3126
Earl Johnson, Dean of Admission
918-631-2307 Fax: 918-631-5003
Website: www.utulsa.edu
E-mail: admission@utulsa.edu

OREGON

Pacific University
2043 College Way, Forest Grove OR 97116-1797
Karen M. Dunston, Executive Director of Admissions
800-635-0561 Fax: 503-352-2975
Website: www.pacificu.edu
E-mail: admissions@pacificu.edu

Warner Pacific College
2219 SE 68th Ave, Portland OR 97215-4026
Shannon Mackey, Director of Admissions
503-517-1000 Fax: 503-517-1352
Website: www.warnerpacific.edu
E-mail: admissions@warnerpacific.edu

PENNSYLVANIA

DeSales University
2755 Station Ave, Center Valley PA 18034-9565
610-282-1100 Fax: 610-282-2342
Website: www.desales.edu

Haverford College
370 Lancaster Ave, Haverford PA 19041-1392
Jess Lord, Dean of Admission
610-896-1000 Fax: 610-896-1338
Website: www.haverford.edu
E-mail: admission@haverford.edu

Juniata College
1700 Moore St, Huntingdon PA 16652-2196
Michelle Bartol, Dean of Enrollment
877-JUNIATA Fax: 814-641-3100
Website: www.juniata.edu
E-mail: admissions@juniata.edu

King's College
133 N River St, Wilkes Barre PA 18711-0801
Michelle Lawrence-Schmude, Director of Admission
570-208-5900 Fax: 570-208-5971
Website: www.kings.edu
E-mail: admissions@kings.edu

Lebanon Valley College
101 N College Ave, Annville PA 17003-1400
William Brown, Dean of Admissions & Financial Aid
866-LVC-4ADM or 717-867-6181 Fax: 717-867-6026
Website: www.lvc.edu
E-mail: admission@lvc.edu

Lincoln University
Lincoln University PA 19352
Michael C. Taylor, Director of Admissions
800-790-0191 Fax: 610-932-1209
Website: www.lincoln.edu
E-mail: mtaylor@lu.lincoln.edu

MOUNT ALOYSIUS COLLEGE
7373 Admiral Peary Hwy, Cresson PA 16630-1999
Frank C. Crouse Jr., Vice President for Enrollment Management
814-886-6383 or 888-823-2220 Fax: 814-886-6441
Website: www.mtaloy.edu
E-mail: admissions@mtaloy.edu

Neumann College
1 Neumann Dr, Aston PA 19014-1298
Dennis Murphy, Director of Admissions
610-459-0905 Fax: 610-558-5652
Website: www.neumann.edu
E-mail: neumann@neumann.edu

Westminster College
New Wilmington PA 16172-0001
Doug Swartz, Director of Admissions
724-946-7100 Fax: 724-946-6171
Website: www.westminster.edu
E-mail: swartzdl@westminster.edu

SOUTH CAROLINA

PRESBYTERIAN COLLEGE
503 S Broad St, Clinton SC 29325
Richard Dana Paul, Dean of Admissions
800-476-7272 Fax: 864-833-8481
Website: www.presby.edu
E-mail: admissions@presby.edu

University of South Carolina - Upstate
800 University Way, Spartanburg SC 29303-4932
Donette Stewart, Assistant VC for Enrollment Services
864-503-5246 Fax: 864-503-5727
Website: www.uscupstate.edu
E-mail: dstewart@uscupstate.edu
See listing under "Universities"

TENNESSEE

Lipscomb University
3901 Granny White Pike, Nashville TN 37204-3951
Ricky Holaway, Director of Admissions
800-333-4358 ext. 1776 Fax: 615-269-1804
Website: www.lipscomb.edu
E-mail: admissions@lipscomb.edu

Pellissippi State Technical Community College
PO Box 22990, Knoxville TN 37933-0990
Donna Mack, Contact
865-694-6568 Fax: 865-539-7217
Website: www.pstcc.edu
E-mail: dmack@pstcc.edu

Tusculum College
PO Box 5051, Greeneville TN 37743
Melissa Ripley, Associate Director of Admissions
800-729-0256 Fax: 423-798-1622
Website: www.tusculum.edu
E-mail: mripley@tusculum.edu

University of Tennessee
615 McCallie Ave, Chattanooga TN 37403-2504
Yancy Freeman, Director of Admissions
423-425-4111 Fax: 423-425-4157
Website: www.utc.edu
E-mail: Yancy-Freeman@utc.edu

TEXAS

Galveston College
4015 Avenue Q, Galveston TX 77550-7496
Brian Lowery, Registrar
409-763-6551 Fax: 409-944-1501
Website: www.gc.edu
E-mail: blowery@gc.edu

Our Lady of the Lake University
411 SW 24th St, San Antonio TX 78207-4666
Mary Kay Cooper, Dean of Enrollment
210-434-6711 Fax: 210-431-4013
Website: www.ollusa.edu
E-mail: admission@lakeollusa.edu

Temple College
2600 S 1st St, Temple TX 76504-7435
Angela Balch, Director of Admissions & Records
254-298-8300 Fax: 254-298-8288
Website: www.templejc.edu
E-mail: ruth.bridges@templejc.edu

Tyler Junior College
PO Box 9020, Tyler TX 75711-9020
Joel Renaud, Director of Enrollment Management
800-687-5680
Website: www.tjc.edu
E-mail: jren@tjc.edu
See listing under "Community and Junior Colleges"

University of St. Thomas
3800 Montrose Blvd, Houston TX 77006-4626
Eduardo Prieto, Director of Admissions
713-522-7911 Fax: 713-525-3558
Website: www.stthom.edu
E-mail: prietoe@stthom.edu

VERMONT

Bennington College
One College Drive, Bennington VT 05201
Ken Himmelman, Dean of Admissions & Financial Aid
800-833-6845 Fax: 802-440-4320
Website: www.bennington.edu
E-mail: admissions@bennington.edu

VIRGINIA

Radford University
PO Box 6903, Radford VA 24142
David W. Kraus, Director of Admissions
800-890-4265 Fax: 540-831-5038
Website: www.radford.edu
E-mail: ruadmiss@radford.edu

Randolph-Macon Woman's College
2500 Rivermont Ave, Lynchburg VA 24503
Patricia LeDonne, Director of Admissions
434-947-8100 Fax: 434-947-8996
Website: www.rmwc.edu
E-mail: admissions@rmwc.edu

WASHINGTON

Gonzaga University
502 E Boone Ave, Spokane WA 99258-0102
Julie McCulloh, Dean of Admission
800-322-2584 or 509-323-6572 Fax: 509-323-5780
Website: www.gonzaga.edu
E-mail: mcculloh@gu.gonzaga.edu

WEST VIRGINIA

Concord University
Athens WV 24712
Michael Curry, Vice President of Financial Aid & Admissions
888-384-5249 Fax: 304-384-3218
Website: www.concord.edu
E-mail: admissions@concord.edu

WISCONSIN

Alverno College
PO Box 343922, Milwaukee WI 53234-3922
Mary Kay Farrell, Director of Admissions
414-382-6100 Fax: 414-382-6354
Website: www.alverno.edu
E-mail: admissions@alverno.edu

Lakeland College
PO Box 359, Sheboygan WI 53082-0359
Nathan Dehne, Director of Admission
920-565-1100 Fax: 920-565-1215
Website: www.lakeland.edu
E-mail: admissions@lakeland.edu

Marquette University
PO Box 1881, Milwaukee WI 53201-1881
Robert Blust, Director of Admissions
414-288-7302 Fax: 414-288-3764
Website: www.mu.edu
E-mail: admissions@marquette.edu

St. Norbert College
100 Grant St, De Pere WI 54115
Brian Studebaker, Director of Admission
800-236-4878 Fax: 920-403-4072
Website: www.snc.edu
E-mail: admit@snc.edu

WYOMING

Laramie County Community College
1400 E College Dr, Cheyenne WY 82007-3204
Jenny Hargett, Director of Admissions
307-778-5222 Fax: 307-778-1350
Website: www.lccc.wy.edu
E-mail: learnmore@lccc.wy.edu

LIBERAL ARTS AND SCIENCES

ALABAMA

Alabama A & M University
PO Box 908, Normal AL 35762
Antonio Boyle, Director of Admissions
256-372-5245 Fax: 256-372-5249
Website: www.aamu.edu
E-mail: aboyle@aamu.edu

Bishop State Community College - Four Campuses
351 N Broad St, Mobile AL 36603-5898
Dr. Terry Hazzard, Dean of Students
251-690-6801 Fax: 251-690-6446
Website: www.bishop.edu
E-mail: thazzard@bishop.edu

CALHOUN COMMUNITY COLLEGE
PO Box 2216, Decatur AL 35609-2216
M. Wayne Tosh, Registrar
256-306-2500 Fax: 256-306-2941
Website: www.calhoun.edu
E-mail: psl@calhoun.edu

Concordia College
1804 Green St, Selma AL 36703
Evelyn Pickens, Director of Enrollment Management
and Placement
334-874-5700

Faulkner University
5345 Atlanta Hwy, Montgomery AL 36109-3398
Keith Mock, Director of Admissions
800-879-9816 ext. 7200 or 334-386-7200
Fax: 334-386-7137
Website: www.faulkner.edu
E-mail: admissions@faulkner.edu

Huntingdon College
1500 E Fairview Ave, Montgomery AL 36106-2148
334-833-4222

Judson College
302 Bibb St, Marion AL 36756
Michael Scotto, Director of Admissions
800-447-9472 Fax: 334-683-5147
Website: www.judson.edu
E-mail: admissions@judson.edu

Samford University
800 Lakeshore Dr, Birmingham AL 35229-0002
205-726-3673

Stillman College
PO Box 1430, Tuscaloosa AL 35403-1430
205-349-4240

Troy University
Troy AL 36082-0001
Jim Hutto, Dean of Enrollment Management
334-670-3175

Troy University Dothan
PO Box 8368, Dothan AL 36304-0368
334-983-6556

Troy University Montgomery
PO Box 4419, Montgomery AL 36103-4419
334-834-1400

University of Alabama
Box 870118, Tuscaloosa AL 35487
Dr. Lisa B. Harris, Director of Admissions
205-348-5666

University of Alabama in Huntsville
PO Box 1247, Huntsville AL 35899-0001
Ann Lee, Assoc. Director for Recruiting Program and
Events
1-800-UAH-CALL Fax: 256-824-6073
Website: www.uah.edu
E-mail: leev@uah.edu

University of Mobile
PO Box 13220, Mobile AL 36663-0220
251-675-5990

University of South Alabama
307 University Blvd N, Mobile AL 36688-3053
Melissa Haab, Director of Admissions
251-460-6141 Fax: 251-460-7876
Website: www.southalabama.edu
E-mail: admiss@usouthal.edu

University of West Alabama
Hwy 11, Livingston AL 35470
205-652-3400

ALASKA

Sheldon Jackson College
801 Lincoln St, Sitka AK 99835-7651
800-478-4556

University of Alaska Anchorage
PO Box 141629, Anchorage AK 99514-1629
Cecile Mitchell, Director of Enrollment Services
907-786-1480 Fax: 907-786-4888
Website: www.uaa.alaska.edu/
E-mail: enroll@uaa.alaska.edu

University of Alaska Southeast
11120 Glacier Hwy, Juneau AK 99801-8625
Paul Kraft, Dean of Students/Enrollment Management
907-796-6000 Fax: 907-796-6005
Website: www.uas.alaska.edu
E-mail: paul.kraft@uas.alaska.edu

ARIZONA

Pima Community College
4905 E Broadway Blvd, Tucson AZ 85709-1010
Wendy Kilgore, Ph.D., Director of Admissions
520-206-4500 Fax: 520-206-4790
Website: www.pima.edu
E-mail: infocenter@pima.edu

Prescott College
220 Grove Ave, Prescott AZ 86301-2912
928-778-2090

University of Arizona
Tucson AZ 85721-0040
Paul Kohn, Director of Admissions
520-621-3237 Fax: 520-621-9799
Website: www.admissions.arizona.edu or
www.arizona.edu

ARKANSAS

ARKANSAS BAPTIST COLLEGE
1600 Bishop St, Little Rock AR 72202-6067
501-372-6883 Fax: 501-372-0321

Arkansas State University
PO Box 1630, State University AR 72467-1630
870-972-2100

Hendrix College
1600 Washington Ave, Conway AR 72032-3080
501-329-6811

John Brown University
2000 W University St, Siloam Springs AR 72761-2121
877-JBU-INFO

Lyon College
PO Box 2317, Batesville AR 72503-2317
Dan Rutledge, Director of Admissions
870-793-9813

Phillips Community College of the University of Arkansas
PO Box 785, Helena AR 72342-0785
Dr. Steven Murray, Chancellor
Lynn Boone, Vice Chancellor for Student Services /
Registrar
870-338-6474 Fax: 870-338-7542
Website: www.pccua.edu
E-mail: lboone@pccua.edu

University of the Ozarks
415 N College Ave, Clarksville AR 72830-2880
Jim Decker, Director of Admissions
479-979-1000

CALIFORNIA

Antioch University
801 Garden St Ste 101
Santa Barbara CA 93101-1581
Ankara McPherson, Director of Admissions
805-962-8179 Fax: 805-962-4786
Website: www.antiochsb.edu
E-mail: amcpherson@antiochsb.edu

Antioch University Southern California
400 Corporate Pointe, Culver City CA 90230
Admissions Office
800-7-ANTIOCH Fax: 310-821-6032
Website: www.admissions@antiochla.edu
E-mail: admissions@antiochla.edu
Bachelor of Arts in Liberal Studies.

Biola University
13800 Biola Ave, La Mirada CA 90639-0001
562-903-6000

California Baptist University
8432 Magnolia Ave, Riverside CA 92504-3297
951-689-5771

California State University-Chico
Chico CA 95929-0001
530-898-6116

California State University-San Bernadino
5500 University Pkwy
San Bernardino CA 92407-2393
Olivia Rosas, Director of Admissions
909-880-5000 Fax: 909-880-7034
Website: enrollment.csusb.edu
E-mail: orosas@csusb.edu

California State University-Stanislaus
801 W Monte Vista Ave, Turlock CA 95382-0256
Lisa Bernardo, Director of Admissions
209-667-3749

Chapman University
One University Drive, Orange CA 92866-1099
Michael Drummy, Assistant Vice President for
Enrollment
Services and Chief Admission Officer
714-997-6411 or 888-CUAPPLY Fax: 714-997-6713
Website: www.chapman.edu
E-mail: admit@chapman.edu

Claremont McKenna College
500 E 9th St, Claremont CA 91711-5903
909-621-8000

Concordia University
1530 Concordia, Irvine CA 92612-3203
Lori McDonald, Executive Director of Enrollment
Services
800-229-1200 or 949-854-8002 Fax: 949-854-6894
Website: www.cui.edu
E-mail: admission@cui.edu

FRESNO CITY COLLEGE
1101 E University Ave, Fresno CA 93741-0002
Dayann Dietrich, Contact
559-442-8241 Fax: 559-237-4232
Website: www.fresnocitycollege.com
E-mail: fcc.admissions@scccd.com

Fresno Pacific University
1717 S Chestnut Ave, Fresno CA 93702-4798
559-453-2000

Holy Names University
3500 Mountain Blvd, Oakland CA 94619-1699
Dr. Hoffman-Marr, Director of Admissions
510-436-1010

John F. Kennedy University
100 Ellinwood Way, Pleasant Hill CA 94523-4817
Ellena Bloedorn, Director of Admissions
925-969-3300

La Sierra University
4700 Pierce St, Riverside CA 92515-8247
Bobby Brown, Director of Admissions
800-874-5587

Mills College
5000 MacArthur Blvd, Oakland CA 94613-1000
510-430-2255

Notre Dame de Namur University
1500 Ralston Ave, Belmont CA 94002-1997
Martin Bednarek, Director of Admissions
800-263-0545

Orange Coast College
PO Box 5005, Costa Mesa CA 92628-5005
Kristin Clark, Director of Admissions
714-432-5773 Fax: 714-432-5736
Website: www.orangecoastcollege.edu
E-mail: kclark@cccd.edu

Point Loma Nazarene University
3900 Lomaland Dr, San Diego CA 92106-2810
Eric Groves, Director of Admissions
800-733-7770

Pomona College
333 N College Way, Claremont CA 91711-4429
Peter W. Stanley, President

SAN FRANCISCO ART INSTITUTE
800 Chestnut St, San Francisco CA 94133
Paula Farmer, Director of Admission
800-345-SFAI Fax: 415-749-4503
Website: www.sfai.edu
E-mail: admissions@sfai.edu
Founded in 1871, SFAI offers one of the most innovative and interdisciplinary environments in higher education. Through its School of Interdisciplinary Studies, SFAI offers accredited Bachelor of Arts (BA) and Master of Arts (MA) programs. The School of Interdisciplinary Studies is based on the premise that imagination combined with critical intelligence is essential for engaging and understanding contemporary art and global society. The School of Interdisciplinary Studies offers three areas of study: History and Theory of Contemporary Art (BA, MA); Urban Studies (BA, MA); and Exhibition and Museum Studies (MA). The School for Interdisciplinary Studies also holds under its aegis SFAI's four centers for interdisciplinary study: Art+Science; Public Practice; Word, Text, and Image; and Media Culture. Each center sponsors symposia, seminars, research fellowships, and residencies. The School of Studio Practice is the complementary other half of SFAI, offering BFA, MFA, and Post-Baccalaureate programs, and consisting of the departments of: Design+Technology, Film, New Genres, Painting, Photography, Printmaking, and Sculpture. Together the two schools are committed to furthering the relationship between the practices and theories of contemporary art. The BA and MA programs are at their core interdisciplinary, and students can take courses in any department. SFAI's faculty is comprised of active writers, scholars, artists, and curators. Dean of Academic Affairs is renowned curator and critic Okwui Enwezor. Dean of Graduate Studies is artist and filmmaker Renee Green. Director of Exhibitions and Public Programs is curator Hou Hanru. Visiting artists and scholars play a significant role in education at SFAI, with recent visitors including Matthew Barney, William Kentridge, Raqs Media Collective, and others. All students have 24-hour access to the SFAI campus. SFAI's main campus includes studios, postproduction facilities, and the first high definition video research lab in the Bay Area. The Diego Rivera Gallery, an open-air amphitheater, and a 250-seat theater are also available to students for exhibiting and screening work. SFAI's library collection includes more than 26,000 volumes with emphasis on modern and contemporary art, over 200 current periodicals, and an extensive image, video, and audio archive available only to SFAI students. The 62,000 square-foot Graduate Center includes a digital lab, film and sound studios, darkrooms, a woodshop, and a gallery for student work. SFAI has rolling application deadlines, and there are competitive and need-based scholarships available to undergraduates, a fellowship program for graduate students, and community college scholarships for transfer students. Visit the SFAI website for specific application requirements.

Scripps College
1030 Columbia Ave, Claremont CA 91711-3948
909-621-8000

SIMPSON UNIVERSITY
2211 College View Dr, Redding CA 96003-8606
Jim Herberger, Director of Admissions
888-9-SIMPSON Fax: 530-226-4861
Website: www.simpsonuniversity.edu
E-mail: admissions@simpsonuniversity.edu
Established 1921. Private. Coeducational. Accreditation: WASC. Tuition: $17,800. Room and board: $6,200. Fees: Internet: $72; Parking: $80; Deposit: $10; Application fee: $25; Music Lessons: $250 per credit. Enrollment: 1,000 full-time, 100 part-time. Faculty: 60. Student-faculty ratio: 18:1.
Degrees offered: Bible and Theology, Business Administration, Communication, Cross-Cultural Studies, Discipleship and Education Ministries, Elementary Edu-

cation, English, English for Teachers, General Ministries, History, Liberal Studies, Management Information Systems (MIS), Mathematics, Math for Teachers, Music Education, Music With Emphasis in Applied Piano, Music With Emphasis in Applied Voice, Music With Emphasis in Applied Instruments, Worship Ministries, Music Composition, Music with Liberal Arts Emphasis, Pastoral Studies, Psychology, Social Science, Social Science for teachers, World Missions, Youth Ministries.

Library: 100,000 volumes. 15 buildings on 85 acres. First school to have a Vice President for Spiritual Formation, Student led chapel, Professor translated the book of Obadiah for the NKJV of the Bible, Hebrew Professor is third most sought after Hebrew Scholar in the world, 85% of undergrads live on campus, fifty countries represented by our student body and faculty past and present.

Sonoma State University
1801 E Cotati Ave, Rohnert Park CA 94928-3609
Louis T. Levy, Senior Director Enrollment Services
707-664-2880

University of California-Santa Cruz
Santa Cruz CA 95064
831-459-0111

University of Judaism
15600 Mulholland Dr, Los Angeles CA 90077-1599
Bryan Pisetsky, Director of Undergraduate Admissions
310-476-9777

University of La Verne
1950 3rd St, La Verne CA 91750-4443
800-876-4858

University of San Diego
5998 Alcala Park, San Diego CA 92110-2492
Admissions
619-260-4506

Whittier College
PO Box 634, Whittier CA 90608-0634
Kieron Miller, Director of Admissions
562-907-4200 Fax: 562-907-4870
Website: www.whittier.edu
E-mail: kmiller@whittier.edu

COLORADO

Adams State College
Alamosa CO 81102
Matt Gallegos, Director of Admissions
800-824-6494

Colorado College
14 E Cache La Poudre St
Colorado Springs CO 80903-3243
719-389-6344

Colorado State University - Pueblo
2200 Bonforte Blvd, Pueblo CO 81001-4990
719-549-2461

Fort Lewis College
1000 Rim Dr, Durango CO 81301-3999
970-247-7010

Metropolitan State College
PO Box 173362, Campus Box 37
Denver CO 80217-3362
303-556-3215

NORTHEASTERN JUNIOR COLLEGE
100 College Ave, Sterling CO 80751-2399
Judy Giacomini, Interim Chief Administrative Officer
Tina Joyce, Director of Admissions
970-521-7000 or 970-521-6752 Fax: 970-521-6801
Website: www.njc.edu
E-mail: tina.joyce@njc.edu

Regis University
3333 Regis Blvd, Denver CO 80221-1099
303-458-4900

University of Colorado at Denver and Health Sciences Center
Downtown Denver Campus
PO Box 173364, Denver CO 80217-3364
303-556-2557 Fax: 303-556-4861
Website: www.cudenver.edu/academics/colleges/clas

UNIVERSITY OF DENVER UNIVERSITY COLLEGE
2211 S Josephine St, Denver CO 80208
Tripp Baltz, Academic Director
303-871-3354 Fax: 303-871-4047
Website: www.universitycollege.du.edu
E-mail: ucolinfo@du.edu

University of Northern Colorado
Greeley CO 80639
Sandra Flake, Dean of Arts and Sciences
970-351-2707

Western State College of Colorado
Gunnison CO 81231-0001
Director of Admissions
800-876-5309

CONNECTICUT

Albertus Magnus College
700 Prospect St, New Haven CT 06511-1189
Richard Lolatte, Dean of Admission
203-773-8501 or 800-578-9160 Fax: 203-773-5248
Website: www.albertus.edu
E-mail: admissions@albertus.edu

Charter Oak State College
55 Paul Manafort Dr, New Britain CT 06053-2142
860-832-3800

Middlesex Community College
100 Training Hill Rd, Middletown CT 06457-4889
Mensimah Shabazz, Director of Admissions
860-343-5800 Fax: 860-344-3055
Website: www.mxcc.commnet.edu
E-mail: mshabazz@mxcc.commnet.edu

Post University
800 Country Club Rd, Waterbury CT 06708-3240
Sandra M. Fernandes, Associate Director of Admissions
Will Johnson, Associate Director of Admissions
203-596-4520

Quinnipiac University
275 Mount Carmel Ave, Hamden CT 06518-1905
Joan Isaac Mohr, VP & Dean of Admissions
203-582-8600

Trinity College
300 Summit St, Hartford CT 06106-3186
Larry Dow, Dean of Admissions & Financial Aid
860-297-2180

University of Bridgeport
126 Park Ave, Bridgeport CT 06604-5620
Barbara L. Maryak, Dean of Admissions
203-576-4552

University of Hartford
200 Bloomfield Ave, West Hartford CT 06117-1599
860-768-4100

University of New Haven
300 Boston Post Rd, West Haven CT 06516
Director of Undergraduate Admissions
203-932-7319 Fax: 203-931-6093
Website: www.newhaven.edu
E-mail: adminfo@newhaven.edu

DELAWARE

Wesley College
120 N State St, Dover DE 19901-3876
302-736-2300 Fax: 302-736-2301
Website: www.wesley.edu

DISTRICT OF COLUMBIA

American University
4400 Massachusetts Ave NW
Washington DC 20016-8200
202-885-1000

Gallaudet University
800 Florida Ave NE, Washington DC 20002-3695
Charity Reedy Hines, Director of Admissions
202-651-5750

Trinity University
125 Michigan Ave NE, Washington DC 20017-1090
202-884-9000

University of the District of Columbia
4200 Connecticut Ave NW
Washington DC 20008-1174
LaVerne M. Hill-Flanagan, Director of Admissions
202-274-5100

FLORIDA

Barry University
11300 NE 2nd Ave, Miami Shores FL 33161-6695
800-695-2279

Bethune-Cookman College
640 Dr Mary McLeod Bethune Blvd
Daytona Beach FL 32114-3099
Edwin Coffie, Director of Admissions
800-448-0228

Clearwater Christian College
3400 Gulf To Bay Blvd, Clearwater FL 33759-4595
727-726-1153

Florida Atlantic University
PO Box 3091, Boca Raton FL 33431-0991
800-299-4328

Florida Southern College
111 Lake Hollingsworth Dr, Lakeland FL 33801-5607
Robert B. Palmer, V.P., Dean of Enrollment Management
863-680-4131

Florida State University
600 W College Ave, Tallahassee FL 32306-1096
Janice V. Finney, Director of Admissions
850-644-2525 Fax: 850-644-0197
Website: admissions.fsu.edu
E-mail: admissions@admin.fsu.edu

Lynn University
3601 N Military Trl, Boca Raton FL 33431-5598
Brett Ormandy, Director of Admissions
561-237-7900 Fax: 561-237-7100
Website: www.lynn.edu
E-mail: admission@lynn.edu

Palm Beach Atlantic University
PO Box 24708, West Palm Beach FL 33416-4708
561-803-2000

Saint Leo University
PO Box 6665, Saint Leo FL 33574
Deborah Bandy, Director of Admissions
352-588-8200 or 800-334-5532 Fax: 352-588-8257
Website: www.saintleo.edu
E-mail: admission@saintleo.edu

St. Thomas University
16401 NW 37th Ave, Miami Gardens FL 33054
Dr. Gloria Ruiz, Contact
800-367-9010 or 305-628-6546 Fax: 305-628-6591
Website: www.stu.edu
E-mail: signup@stu.edu

Santa Fe Community College
3000 NW 83rd St, Gainesville FL 32606-6200
Jackson N. Sasser, President
352-395-5787 Fax: 352-395-4118
Website: www.sfcc.edu
E-mail: ouida.mcneil@sfcc.edu

University of Central Florida
PO Box 160111, Orlando FL 32816
407-823-3000

University of South Florida
4202 E Fowler Ave, Tampa FL 33620-6900
J. Robert Spatig, Director of Admissions
813-974-3350 Fax: 813-974-9689
Website: www.usf.edu
E-mail: admissions@admin.usf.edu

University of Tampa
401 W Kennedy Blvd, Tampa FL 33606-1490
813-253-3333

Warner Southern College
5301 US Highway 27 S, Lake Wales FL 33859-8725
863-638-1426

GEORGIA

Armstrong Atlantic State University
11935 Abercorn St, Savannah GA 31419-1997
Kim West, Asst. Dean and Registrar Enrollment Services
912-927-5277 Fax: 912-921-5462
Website: www.armstrong.edu
E-mail: admissions@mail.armstrong.edu

BEACON UNIVERSITY
6003 Veterans Pkwy, Columbus GA 31909
Admissions Department
706-323-5364 Fax: 706-323-3236
Website: www.beacon.edu
E-mail: beacon@beacon.edu

Brewton-Parker College
Highway 280, Mount Vernon GA 30445
800-342-1087

Clayton State University
5900 N Lee St, Morrow GA 30260
770-961-3500

DeKalb Technical College
495 N Indian Creek Dr, Clarkston GA 30021-2397
Terry Richardson, Director of Admissions
404-297-9522 Fax: 404-294-6496
Website: www.dekalbtech.edu
E-mail: richardt@dekalbtech.edu

Fort Valley State University
1005 State University Dr, Fort Valley GA 31030-3298
478-825-6307

Georgia Southern University
PO Box 8024, Statesboro GA 30460
Admissions Office
912-681-5532

Georgia Southwestern State University
800 Wheatley St, Americus GA 31709-4635
229-928-1279

Georgia State University
PO Box 4009, Atlanta GA 30302-4009
404-651-2365

Kennesaw State University
1000 Chastain Rd NW, Kennesaw GA 30144-5591
Dr. Helen Ridley, Dean of Humanities and Social Science
770-423-6124
Website: www.kennesaw.edu

LaGrange College
601 Broad St, LaGrange GA 30240-2955
Andy Geeter, Director of Admission
800-593-2885

Luther Rice University
3038 Evans Mill Rd, Lithonia GA 30038
Russ Sorrow, Director of Enrollment Management
770-484-1204 Fax: 770-484-1155
Website: www.lru.edu
E-mail: admissions@lru.edu

Mercer University in Macon
1400 Coleman Ave, Macon GA 31207-0003
John P. Cole, Sr. Assoc. V.P. for Admissions
478-301-2650

North Georgia College & State University
Dahlonega GA 30597-0001
706-864-1400

Oglethorpe University
4484 Peachtree Rd NE, Atlanta GA 30319-2797
Kelly Gosnell, Director of Admission
404-261-1441 Fax: 404-364-8491
Website: www.oglethorpe.edu
E-mail: admission@oglethorpe.edu

Piedmont College
PO Box 10, Demorest GA 30535-0010
800-277-7020

Thomas University
1501 Millpond Rd, Thomasville GA 31792-7478
Darla M. Glass, Director of Student Affairs
229-226-1621

University of Georgia
Athens GA 30602-0001
706-542-3000

Valdosta State University
N Patterson St, Valdosta GA 31698-0001
229-333-5952

HAWAII

Brigham Young University
55-220 Kulanui St, Laie HI 96762-1293
808-293-3211

Kauai Community College
3-1901 Kaumualii Hwy, Lihue HI 96766-9500
808-245-8225 Fax: 808-245-8297
Website: kauai.hawaii.edu
E-mail: arkauai@hawaii.edu

IDAHO

University of Idaho
Moscow ID 83844-4253
Lloyd Scott, Director of New Student Services
208-885-6163 Fax: 208-885-4477
Website: www.uidaho.edu
E-mail: nss@uidaho.edu

ILLINOIS

Augustana College
639 38th St, Rock Island IL 61201-2296
309-794-7000

Aurora University
347 S Gladstone Ave, Aurora IL 60506-4892
Carol R. Dunn, Ed.D., Vice President for Enrollment
800-742-5281 Fax: 630-844-5535
Website: www.aurora.edu
E-mail: admission@aurora.edu

Benedictine University
5700 College Rd, Lisle IL 60532-0900
630-829-6300 or 888-829-6363 Fax: 630-829-6301
Website: www.ben.edu
E-mail: admissions@ben.edu
See listing under "Universities"

Columbia College Chicago
600 S Michigan Ave, Chicago IL 60605-1996
Murphy Monroe, Executive Director of Admissions
312-344-7130 Fax: 312-344-8024
Website: www.colum.edu
E-mail: admissions@colum.edu

CONCORDIA UNIVERSITY
7400 Augusta St, River Forest IL 60305-1402
708-209-3100 Fax: 708-209-3473
Website: www.curf.edu
E-mail: crfadmis@curf.edu

De Paul University
2323 N Seminary Ave, Chicago IL 60614-3298
312-362-8000

Illinois Wesleyan University
PO Box 2900, Bloomington IL 61702-2900
James R. Ruoti, Dean of Admissions
309-556-3031

Kaskaskia College
27210 College Rd, Centralia IL 62801-7878
Tyra Taylor, Dean of Enrollment Management and
Retention Services
618-545-3000 Fax: 618-532-1990
Website: www.kaskaskia.edu
E-mail: ttaylor@kaskaskia.edu

Knox College
Galesburg IL 61401
309-341-7100

Lewis University
One University Parkway, Romeoville IL 60446
800-897-9000

MacMurray College
447 E College Ave, Jacksonville IL 62650-2590
217-479-7000

Millikin University
1184 W Main St, Decatur IL 62522-2084
Lin Stoner, Dean of Admission
800-373-7733

Monmouth College
700 E Broadway, Monmouth IL 61462-1963
Kristi Hippen, Director of Admission
309-457-2131

National-Louis University
2840 Sheridan Rd, Evanston IL 60201-1796

North Central College
30 N Brainard St, Naperville IL 60540-4690
Martha Stolze, Director of Admissions
630-637-5800 Fax: 630-637-5819
Website: www.northcentralcollege.edu
E-mail: admissions@noctrl.edu

NORTHEASTERN ILLINOIS UNIVERSITY
5500 N Saint Louis Ave, Chicago IL 60625-4699
Kate Forhan, Dean
773-442-4050 Fax: 773-442-4020
Website: www.neiu.edu
E-mail: k-forhan@neiu.edu

Olivet Nazarene University
1 University Ave
Bourbonnais IL 60914
815-939-5011

Principia College
Elsah IL 62028-9799
618-374-2131

Quincy University
1800 College Ave, Quincy IL 62301-2670
217-222-8020

Rockford College
5050 E State St, Rockford IL 61108-2393
William Laffey, Director of Admission
800-892-2984

Roosevelt University
430 S Michigan Ave, Chicago IL 60605
Gwen E. Kanelos, Asst. Vice President for Enrollment
Services
877-APPLY-RU Fax: 312-341-4216
Website: www.roosevelt.edu
E-mail: applyru@roosevelt.edu

South Suburban College of Cook County
15800 State St, South Holland IL 60473
Jane Ellen Stocker, Dean of Enrollment Services
708-596-2000 Fax: 708-225-5806
Website: www.southsuburbancollege.edu
E-mail: jstocker@southsuburbancollege.edu

Spertus College
618 S Michigan Ave, Chicago IL 60605-1901
312-922-9012 Fax: 312-922-6406
Website: www.spertus.edu
E-mail: college@spertus.edu

Trinity Christian College
6601 W College Dr, Palos Heights IL 60463-0929
Joshua Lenarz, Director of Admissions
708-597-3000

Triton College
2000 5th Ave, River Grove IL 60171-1995
Mary-Rita Moore, Dean of Enrollment Services
708-456-0300 ext. 3130 Fax: 708-583-3147
Website: www.triton.edu
E-mail: triton@triton.edu
See listing under "Community and Junior Colleges"

University of Illinois at Springfield
One University Plaza, Springfield IL 62794
217-206-4847

University of St. Francis
500 Wilcox St, Joliet IL 60435
800-735-7500

Wheaton College
501 College Ave, Wheaton IL 60187-5571
630-752-5000

INDIANA

Ancilla Domini College
Donaldson IN 46513
Erin Wittmeyer, Director of Admissions
574-936-8898 Fax: 574-935-1773
Website: www.ancilla.edu
E-mail: erin.wittmeyer@ancilla.edu

Ball State University
2000 W University Ave, Muncie IN 47306-0002
765-285-5555

Bethel College
1001 W McKinley Ave, Mishawaka IN 46545-5591
Office of Admissions
574-257-3339

Franklin College
101 Branigin Blvd, Franklin IN 46131
Jacqueline S. Acosta, Director of Admissions
800-852-0232 Fax: 317-738-8274
Website: www.franklincollege.edu
E-mail: admissions@franklincollege.edu

Goshen College
1700 S Main St, Goshen IN 46526-4794
574-535-7000

Grace College
200 Seminary Dr, Winona Lake IN 46590-1224
800-54-GRACE

Hanover College
PO Box 108, Hanover IN 47243-0108
William D. Preble, Dean of Admission
800-213-2178 Fax: 812-866-7098
Website: www.hanover.edu
E-mail: admissions@hanover.edu

HOLY CROSS COLLEGE
PO Box 308, Notre Dame IN 46556-0308
Vincent M. Duke, Director of Admissions
574-239-8400 Fax: 574-239-8323
Website: www.hcc-nd.edu
E-mail: admissions@hcc-nd.edu

Indiana Wesleyan University
4201 S Washington St, Marion IN 46953-4974
765-674-6901

Ivy Tech Community College - North Central
220 Dean Johnson Blvd, South Bend IN 46601-3415
Pam Decker, Director of Admissions
574-289-7001 Fax: 574-236-7177
Website: www.ivytech.edu
E-mail: pdecker@ivytech.edu

Oakland City University
138 N Lucretia St, Oakland City IN 47660
Brian J. Baker, Director of Admissions
800-737-5125 Fax: 812-749-1433
Website: www.oak.edu
E-mail: bbaker@oak.edu
See listing under "Universities"

St. Mary-of-the-Woods College
Saint Mary of the Woods IN 47876-1001
James P. Malley, Jr., Director of Admission
800-926-7692 Fax: 812-535-5010
Website: www.smwc.edu
E-mail: smwcadms@smwc.edu

University of Evansville
1800 Lincoln Ave, Evansville IN 47722-0001
Thomas E. Bear, V.P. of Enrollment Services
800-423-8633 Fax: 812-488-4076
Website: www.evansville.edu
E-mail: admission@evansville.edu

Wabash College
301 W Wabash Ave, Crawfordsville IN 47933
David Collins, Sr. Assoc. Director of Admissions
800-345-5385

IOWA

Briar Cliff University
PO Box 2100, Sioux City IA 51104-0100
Sharisue Wilcoxon, VP for Enrollment Management
712-279-5200 Fax: 712-279-1632
Website: www.briarcliff.edu
E-mail: admissions@briarcliff.edu

Buena Vista University
610 W 4th St, Storm Lake IA 50588-1798
712-749-2235

Central College
812 University St, Pella IA 50219-1999
641-628-9000

DIVINE WORD COLLEGE SEMINARY
102 Jacoby Dr SW, Epworth IA 52045
Len Uhal, Director of Admissions
563-876-3332 Fax: 563-876-5515
Website: www.svdvocations.org
E-mail: dwm@mwci.net

Dordt College
498 4th Ave NE, Sioux Center IA 51250-1697
Quentin Van Essen, Executive Director of Admissions
800-343-6738

Graceland University
1 University Place, Lamoni IA 50140
Brian Shantz, Vice President for Enrollment and Dean of
Admissions
641-784-5196 Fax: 641-784-5480
Website: www.admissions.graceland.edu
E-mail: admissions@graceland.edu

Grand View College
1200 Grandview Ave, Des Moines IA 50316-1599
515-263-2800

Grinnell College
PO Box 805, Grinnell IA 50112-0805
641-269-4000

Iowa Lakes Community College
3200 College Dr, Emmetsburg IA 50536-1055
Anne Stansbury, Asst. Director of Admissions
712-852-5212 Fax: 712-362-8363
Website: www.iowalakes.edu
E-mail: info@iowalakes.edu

Iowa Lakes Community College
300 S 18th St, Estherville IA 51334-2721
Anne Stansbury, Asst. Director of Admissions
712-362-7945 Fax: 712-362-8363
Website: www.iowalakes.edu
E-mail: info@iowalakes.edu

Iowa Lakes Community College
1900 Grand Ave, Suite 8, Spencer IA 51301
Anne Stansbury, Assistant Director of Admissions
712-262-7141 Fax: 712-262-4047
Website: www.iowalakes.edu
E-mail: info@iowalakes.edu

Loras College
1450 Alta Vista St, Dubuque IA 52001-4399
Tim Hauber, Director of Admissions
800-245-6727

Mount Mercy College
1330 Elmhurst Dr NE, Cedar Rapids IA 52402-4797
Jim Krystofiak, Dean of Admission
800-248-4504 Fax: 319-363-5270
Website: www.mtmercy.edu
E-mail: admission@mtmercy.edu

Northwestern College
101 7th St SW, Orange City IA 51041-1996
712-737-7000

Northwest Iowa Community College
603 W Park St, Sheldon IA 51201-1046
Lisa Story, Director of Enrollment Management
712-324-5061 Fax: 712-324-4136
Website: www.nwicc.edu
E-mail: lstory@nwicc.edu

Wartburg College
PO Box 1003, Waverly IA 50677-0903
Brent Matthias, Interim Director of Admissions
319-352-8200 Fax: 319-352-8579
Website: www.wartburg.edu
E-mail: admissions@wartburg.edu

KANSAS

Baker University
PO Box 65, Baldwin City KS 66006-0065
785-594-6451

Bethel College
300 E 27th St, North Newton KS 67117-8061
316-283-2500

COLBY COMMUNITY COLLEGE
1255 S Range Ave, Colby KS 67701-4099
Director of Admissions
888-634-9350 or 785-460-4690 Fax: 785-460-4691
Website: www.colbycc.edu
E-mail: bobbi@colbycc.edu

Fort Hays State University
600 Park St, Hays KS 67601-4099
785-628-4000

Friends University
2100 W University Ave, Wichita KS 67213-3397
316-261-5800

Independence Community College
PO Box 708, Independence KS 67301-0708
Dr. Terry Hetrick, President
800-842-6063 Fax: 620-331-5344
Website: www.indycc.edu
E-mail: admissions@indycc.edu

Mid-America Nazarene University
2030 E College Way, Olathe KS 66062-1851
913-782-3750

Newman University
3100 W McCormick St, Wichita KS 67213
Jann Reusser, Admissions Recruitment Coordinator
316-942-4291 ext. 2144 Fax: 316-942-4483
Website: www.newmanu.edu
E-mail: reusserj@newmanu.edu

Ottawa University
1001 S Cedar St, Ottawa KS 66067-3399
785-242-5200

Southwestern College
100 College St, Winfield KS 67156-2499
620-229-6000

Tabor College
400 S Jefferson St, Hillsboro KS 67063-1758
Rusty Allen, Dean of Enrollment Management
620-947-3121 Fax: 620-947-6276
Website: www.tabor.edu
E-mail: admissions@tabor.edu

University of Kansas
Lawrence KS 66045-0001
Sally Frost-Mason, Dean

KENTUCKY

Alice Lloyd College
100 Purpose Rd, Pippa Passes KY 41844-9005
John Mills, Director of Admissions
888-280-4252

Bluegrass Community and Technical College
Oswald Building
470 Cooper Drive, Lexington KY 40506-0235
Shelbie Hugle, Director of Admissions
859-246-6200 Fax: 859-246-4664
Website: www.bluegrass.kctcs.edu
E-mail: bctc_info@kctcs.edu

Brescia University
717 Frederica St, Owensboro KY 42301-3023
Sr. Mary Austin Blank, OSB, Director of Admissions
877-BRESCIA

Campbellsville University
1 University Dr, Campbellsville KY 42718-2799
Scott Necessary, Coordinator of Undergraduate
Admissions
270-789-5000

Morehead State University
Morehead KY 40351-1689
Dayna Seelig, Enrollment Services
800-585-6781 Fax: 606-783-5038
Website: www.moreheadstate.edu
E-mail: admissions@moreheadstate.edu

Murray State University
Murray KY 42071
Phil Bryan, Director of Admissions
270-762-3011

Spalding University
851 S 4th St, Louisville KY 40203-2188
502-585-9911

Transylvania University
300 N Broadway, Lexington KY 40508-1776
859-233-8242 Fax: 859-233-8797
Website: www.transy.edu
E-mail: admissions@transy.edu

University of Kentucky
Lexington KY 40506-0001
Don Witt, Director of Admissions
859-257-9000

University of Louisville
2301 S 3rd St, Louisville KY 40292-2001
502-852-5555

LOUISIANA

Dillard University
2601 Gentilly Blvd, New Orleans LA 70122-3097
Linda G. Nash, Director of Admissions
Website: www.dillard.edu
E-mail: admissions@dillard.edu

Grambling State University
PO Box 864, Grambling LA 71245
318-274-3811

Louisiana College
PO Box 560, Pineville LA 71359-0001
Mary Wagner, Director of Admissions
318-487-7259

Louisiana State University at Eunice
PO Box 1129, Eunice LA 70535-1129
Ron Ryder, Registrar
337-457-7311 Fax: 337-550-1306
Website: www.lsue.edu
E-mail: rryder@lsue.edu

Northwestern State University
Natchitoches LA 71497-0001
Jana Lucky, Director of Enrollment Services
318-357-4503

Our Lady of Holy Cross College
4123 Woodland Dr, New Orleans LA 70131-7399
Office of Enrollment Services
504-394-7744 Fax: 504-391-2421
Website: www.olhcc.edu

MAINE

Bowdoin College
Brunswick ME 04011
207-725-3000

Colby College
150 Mayflower Hill Dr, Waterville ME 04901-4799
207-872-3000

St. Joseph's College of Maine
278 Whites Bridge Rd, Standish ME 04084-5263
Vincent Kloskowski, Dean of Admissions
800-338-7057 Fax: 207-893-7862
Website: www.sjcme.edu
E-mail: admission@sjcme.edu

Southern Maine Community College
2 Fort Rd, South Portland ME 04106-1698
Dr. James Ortiz, President
Scott MacDonald, Director of Financial Aid
207-741-5500 Fax: 207-741-5671
Website: www.smccme.edu
E-mail: oharmon@maine.rr.com

University of Maine
246 Main St, Farmington ME 04938
Sharon M. Oliver, Director of Admissions
207-778-7000

University of Maine
Orono ME 04469-0001
207-581-1110

University of Maine at Fort Kent
23 University Dr, Fort Kent ME 04743
888-TRY-UMFK

University of Southern Maine
PO Box 9300, Portland ME 04104-9300
207-780-4141

MARYLAND

Cecil Community College
One Seahawk Dr, North East MD 21901
Sandra S. Rajaski, Registrar & Director of Admissions
410-287-1000 Fax: 410-287-1001
Website: www.cecilcc.edu
E-mail: srajaski@cecilcc.edu

Goucher College
1021 Dulaney Valley Rd, Baltimore MD 21204-2780
410-337-6000

Griggs University
PO Box 4437, Silver Spring MD 20914-4437
Anita L. Jacobs, Director of Admissions
301-680-6570 Fax: 301-680-6583
Website: www.griggs.edu
E-mail: registrar@griggs.edu

Hagerstown Community College
11400 Robinwood Dr, Hagerstown MD 21742-6590
Dr. Daniel E. Bock, Assistant Director of Admissions
301-790-2800 Fax: 301-791-9165
Website: www.hagerstowncc.edu
E-mail: bockd@hagerstowncc.edu

Johns Hopkins University
3400 N Charles St, Baltimore MD 21218-2680
410-516-8000

Morgan State University
1700 E Cold Spring Ln, Baltimore MD 21251-0002
443-885-3000

ST. JOHN'S COLLEGE

PO Box 2800, Annapolis MD 21404-2800
John Christensen, Director of Admissions
800-727-9238 Fax: 410-269-7916
Website: www.stjohnscollege.edu
E-mail: admissions@sjca.edu

University of Baltimore
1420 N Charles St, Baltimore MD 21201-5779
410-837-4200

University of Maryland Eastern Shore
Princess Anne MD 21853
Edwina Morse, Director of Admissions
410-651-6410

Villa Julie College
1525 Greenspring Valley Rd
Stevenson MD 21153-0641
Mark Hergan, V.P. Enrollment Services
410-486-7001 Fax: 410-602-6600
Website: www.vjc.edu/admissions
E-mail: admissions@mail.vjc.edu

Washington College
300 Washington Ave, Chestertown MD 21620-1197
410-778-2800

MASSACHUSETTS

American International College
1000 State St, Springfield MA 01109-3155
Peter Miller, Dean of Admissions
413-737-7000

Anna Maria College
50 Sunset Ln, Paxton MA 01612
Julie A. Mitchell, Director of Admissions
508-849-3360 Fax: 508-849-3362
Website: www.annamaria.edu
E-mail: admissions@annamaria.edu

Assumption College
500 Salisbury St, Worcester MA 01609-1294
Kathleen Murphy, Dean of Enrollment
508-767-7000 Fax: 508-799-4412
Website: www.assumption.edu
E-mail: admiss@assumption.edu

Bay Path College
588 Longmeadow St, Longmeadow MA 01106-2292
Lisa Casassa, Director of Admissions
413-565-1331 Fax: 413-565-1105
Website: www.baypath.edu
E-mail: lcasassa@baypath.edu

Bay State College
122 Commonwealth Ave, Boston MA 02116-2901
Craig Pfannenstiehl, President
617-217-9000 Fax: 617-536-1735

Becker College
Campuses in Worcester and Leicester, MA
61 Sever St, Worcester MA 01609-2165
Karen H. Schedin, Director of Admissions
508-791-9241 Fax: 508-890-1500
Website: www.becker.edu
E-mail: admissions@becker.edu
See listing under "Universities"

Boston University
121 Bay State Rd, Boston MA 02215
Kelly Walter, Executive Director of Admissions
617-353-2300 Fax: 617-353-9695
Website: web.bu.edu
E-mail: admissions@bu.edu

Bristol Community College
777 Elsbree St, Fall River MA 02720-7395
Rodney S. Clark, Director of Admissions
508-678-2811 ext. 2516, 2179 Fax: 508-730-3265
Website: www.bristol.mass.edu
E-mail: admissions@bristol.mass.edu

College of the Holy Cross
1 College St, Worcester MA 01610-2322
508-793-2011

Curry College
1071 Blue Hill Ave, Milton MA 02186-2395
Bruce Weckworth, Director of Admissions
617-333-2210

Elms College
291 Springfield St, Chicopee MA 01013-2839
800-255-3567

Emerson College
120 Boylston St, Boston MA 02116-4624
Sara S. Ramirez, Director of Undergraduate Admission
617-824-8600 Fax: 617-824-8609
Website: www.emerson.edu
E-mail: admission@emerson.edu

Fisher College
118 Beacon St, Boston MA 02116-1501
Stephen Carter, Director of Admissions
800-446-1226

Gordon College
255 Grapevine Rd, Wenham MA 01984-1899
Nancy Mering, Director of Admissions
866-464-6736 Fax: 978-867-4682
Website: www.gordon.edu
E-mail: admissions@gordon.edu

Hampshire College
Amherst MA 01002
Karen S. Parker, Director of Admissions
413-559-5471

Hellenic College/Holy Cross Greek Orthodox School of
Theology
50 Goddard Ave, Brookline MA 02445-7415
Sonia Belcher, Director
617-731-3500

Lasell College
1844 Commonwealth Ave, Newton MA 02466-2716
617-243-2225

Lesley University
29 Everett St, Cambridge MA 02138-2790
Jane Raley, Director of Admissions
617-349-8800

Massachusetts College of Liberal Arts
375 Church St, North Adams MA 01247-4100
413-662-5000

Massachusetts Institute of Technology
77 Massachusetts Ave, Cambridge MA 02139-4307
Marilee Jones, Dean of Admission
617-253-1000 Fax: 617-253-4016
Website: my.mit.edu
E-mail: admissions@mit.edu

Mt. Ida College
777 Dedham St, Newton Center MA 02459-3323
617-969-7000

Nichols College
Dudley MA 01571-5000
Kimberly A. Kossuth, Director of Admissions
508-943-1560

NORTHERN ESSEX COMMUNITY COLLEGE

100 Elliott St, Haverhill MA 01830
Nora B. Sheridan, Director of Admission
978-556-3700
Website: www.NECC.Mass.edu
E-mail: nsheridan@necc.mass.edu

Pine Manor College
400 Heath St, Chestnut Hill MA 02467-2332
Bill Nichols, Dean of Admission
617-731-7167

Regis College
235 Wellesley St, Weston MA 02493-1571
781-768-2000

Smith College
Northampton MA 01063-0001
Debra Shaver, Director of Admissions
800-383-3232 Fax: 413-585-2527
Website: www.smith.edu
E-mail: admission@smith.edu

Springfield College
263 Alden St, Springfield MA 01109-3788
Mary DeAngelo, Director of Admissions
800-343-1257

Suffolk University
8 Ashburton Pl, Boston MA 02108-2770
617-573-8460

University of Massachusetts Boston
100 William T Morrissey Blvd, Boston MA 02125-3393
Liliana Mickle, Director of Undergraduate Admissions
617-287-6000

University of Massachusetts Dartmouth
Old Westport Rd, North Dartmouth MA 02747-2300
Steven T. Briggs, Director of Admissions
508-999-8605 Fax: 508-999-8755
Website: explore.umassd.edu
E-mail: sbriggs@umassd.edu

Wellesley College
106 Central St, Wellesley MA 02481-8203
Board of Admission
781-283-2270

Western New England College
1215 Wilbraham Rd, Springfield MA 01119-2655
413-782-1321

Westfield State College
PO Box 1630, Westfield MA 01086
Michelle Mattie, Associate Dean, Admission and
Enrollment Services
413-572-5300
Website: www.wsc.ma.edu
E-mail: admission@wsc.ma.edu

Wheaton College
26 E Main St, Norton MA 02766-2322
Gail Berson, Dean of Admissions & Student Aid
800-394-6003

Worcester Polytechnic Institute
100 Institute Rd, Worcester MA 01609-2280
Edward J. Connor, Director of Admissions
508-831-5286 Fax: 508-831-5875
Website: admissions.wpi.edu
E-mail: admissions@wpi.edu

MICHIGAN

Albion College
611 E Porter St, Albion MI 49224-1831
800-858-6770

Alma College
614 W Superior St, Alma MI 48801-1599
Anne Monroe, Director of Admissions
800-321-ALMA Fax: 989-463-7057
Website: www.alma.edu
E-mail: admissions@alma.edu

Andrews University
Berrien Springs MI 49104-0001
Randall Graves, Director of Recruitment Services
800-253-2874 Fax: 269-471-2670
Website: www.connect.andrews.edu
E-mail: gravesr@andrews.edu

Aquinas College
1607 Robinson Rd SE, Grand Rapids MI 49506-1799
Harry Knopke PhD, President
Paula Meehan, Dean of Admissions
800-678-9593

Ave Maria College
300 W Forest Ave, Ypsilanti MI 48197
Joshua McCallen, Director of Admissions
866-866-3030

Concordia University
4090 Geddes Rd, Ann Arbor MI 48105-2797
Gary Neumann, Director of Admissions
734-995-7300 Fax: 734-995-4610
Website: www.cuaa.edu
E-mail: admissions@cuaa.edu

Delta College
University Center MI 48710-0001
Duff Zube, Director of Admissions
989-686-9093 Fax: 989-667-2202
Website: www.delta.edu
E-mail: admit@delta.edu

Eastern Michigan University
Ypsilanti MI 48197
800-GO-TO-EMU

Grand Valley State University
1 Campus Dr, Allendale MI 49401-9403
Jodi Chycinski, Director of Admissions
616-331-6611 Fax: 616-331-2000
Website: www.gvsu.edu
E-mail: go2gvsu@gvsu.edu

HILLSDALE COLLEGE

33 E College St, Hillsdale MI 49242-1298
Dr. Thomas Burke, Chairperson
517-607-2368 Fax: 517-607-2208
Website: www.hillsdale.edu
E-mail: tom.burke@hillsdale.edu

Hope College
PO Box 9000, Holland MI 49422-9000
616-395-7000

Lake Superior State University
1000 College Dr, Sault Sainte Marie MI 49783-1637
906-632-6841

Lawrence Technological University
21000 W 10 Mile Rd, Southfield MI 48075-1058
Jane Rohrback, Director of Admissions
800-225-5588 Fax: 248-204-2228
Website: www.ltu.edu
E-mail: admissions@ltu.edu
See listing under "Universities"

MACOMB COMMUNITY COLLEGE

44575 Garfield Rd, Clinton Township MI 48038-1139
Information Center
586-445-7999
Website: www.macomb.edu
E-mail: answer@macomb.edu

MACOMB COMMUNITY COLLEGE

14500 E 12 Mile Rd, Warren MI 48088-3896
Information Center
586-445-7999
Website: www.macomb.edu
E-mail: answer@macomb.edu

Madonna University
36600 Schoolcraft Rd, Livonia MI 48150-1173
734-432-5300

Michigan Technological University
1400 Townsend Dr, Houghton MI 49931-1200
Nancy Rehling, Director of Admissions
906-487-2335

Northwestern Michigan College
1701 E Front St, Traverse City MI 49686-3061
Jim Bensley, Admissions Coordinator
800-748-0566 Fax: 231-995-1339
Website: www.nmc.edu
E-mail: jbensley@nmc.edu

Oakland Community College
2480 Opdyke Rd, Bloomfield Hills MI 48304
Dr. Maurice McCall, Director of Admissions
248-341-2000
Website: www.oaklandcc.edu
E-mail: mhmcall@oaklandcc.edu

Oakland University
2200 N Squirrel Rd, Rochester MI 48309
Eleanor L. Reynolds, Assistant Vice President &
Director of Admissions
248-370-2100
Website: www.oakland.edu
E-mail: ouinfo@oakland.edu

Olivet College
300 S Main St, Olivet MI 49076-9724
269-749-7000

Siena Heights University
1247 E Siena Heights Dr, Adrian MI 49221-1796
517-263-0731

University of Detroit-Mercy
PO Box 19900, Detroit MI 48219-0900
313-993-1000

University of Michigan-Dearborn
4901 Evergreen Rd, Dearborn MI 48128-1491
The Office of Admissions & Orientation
313-593-5100 Fax: 313-436-9167
Website: www.umd.umich.edu
E-mail: admissions@umd.umich.edu

Western Michigan University
Kalamazoo MI 49008
269-387-1000

MINNESOTA

Augsburg College
2211 Riverside Ave, Minneapolis MN 55454-1350
612-330-1000

Bethany Lutheran College
700 Luther Dr, Mankato MN 56001
Don Westphal, Dean of Admissions
507-344-7000 Fax: 507-344-7376
Website: www.blc.edu
E-mail: admiss@blc.edu

Carleton College
1 N College St, Northfield MN 55057-4044
800-995-2275 or 507-646-4190 Fax: 507-646-4526
Website: www.carleton.edu
E-mail: admissions@acs.carleton.edu

College of Saint Scholastica
1200 Kenwood Ave, Duluth MN 55811-4199
Brian Dalton, V.P. of Enrollment Management
800-447-5444

Gustavus Adolphus College
800 W College Ave, Saint Peter MN 56082-1485
Mark H. Anderson, Dean of Admission
800-GUSTAVUS Fax: 507-933-7474
Website: www.gustavus.edu
E-mail: admission@gustavus.edu

Hibbing Community College
1515 E 25th St, Hibbing MN 55746-3300
Holly Bigelow, Director of Enrollment
800-224-4HCC or 218-262-7200 Fax: 218-262-6717
Website: www.hibbing.edu
E-mail: admissions@hibbing.edu

Macalester College
1600 Grand Ave, Saint Paul MN 55105-1899
651-696-6000

Minneapolis Community and Technical College
1501 Hennepin Ave, Minneapolis MN 55403-1779
Dena Russell, Director of Admissions
612-659-6282 Fax: 612-659-6210
Website: www.minneapolis.edu
E-mail: admissions.office@minneapolis.edu

Northland Community & Technical College
Highway 1 E, Thief River Falls MN 56701
Rocky Ammerman, Contact
800-959-6282 Fax: 218-681-0774
Website: www.northlandcollege.edu

Northland Community and Technical College
2022 Central Ave NE
East Grand Forks MN 56721-2702
Brian Huschle, Liberal Arts Chair
800-451-3441 Fax: 218-773-4502
Website: www.northlandcollege.edu
E-mail: admissions@northlandcollege.edu

Ridgewater College-Hutchinson Campus
2 Century Ave SE, Hutchinson MN 55350-3100
Dawn Bjork, Counselor
800-222-4424 Fax: 320-231-7767
Website: www.ridgewater.edu
E-mail: dawn.bjork@ridgewater.edu

Ridgewater College-Willmar Campus
PO Box 1097, Willmar MN 56201-1097
Sally Kerfeld, Director of Admissions
800-722-1151 Fax: 320-231-7677
Website: www.ridgewater.edu
E-mail: skerfeld@ridgewater.edu

St. Cloud State University
720 4th Ave S, Saint Cloud MN 56301-4442
877-654-7278

St. Mary's University of Minnesota
700 Terrace Hts Ste 2, Winona MN 55987-1321
507-452-4430

University of Minnesota
10 University Dr, Duluth MN 55812-2496
Beth Esselstrom, Director of Admissions
218-726-7171

University of Minnesota - Morris
600 E 4th St, Morris MN 56267-2132
Rodney Oto, Director
800-992-8863

MISSISSIPPI

Millsaps College
PO Box 15495, Jackson MS 39210
601-974-1000

Mississippi University for Women
1100 College St Unit W1613, Columbus MS 39701
Terri Heath, Director of Admissions
877-GO-2-THEW

Mississippi Valley State University
14000 Highway 82 W Box 7222
Itta Bena MS 38941-1401
Office of Admissions
662-254-3347

MISSOURI

Central Missouri State University
Warrensburg MO 64093-8888
Charles Petentler, Associate Director of Admissions
800-956-0177

Columbia College
1001 Rogers St, Columbia MO 65216-0001
Regina Morin, Director of Admissions
573-875-7352 Fax: 573-875-7506
Website: www.ccis.edu
E-mail: admissions@ccis.edu

Culver-Stockton College
1 College Hl, Canton MO 63435-1299
Betty Smith, Director of Enrollment Services
800-537-1883

Drury University
900 N Benton Ave, Springfield MO 65802-3791
417-873-7879

East Central College
1964 Prairie Dell Rd, Union MO 63084
Karen Wieda, Registrar
636-583-5195 ext. 2220 Fax: 636-583-1897
Website: www.eastcentral.edu
E-mail: wiedaks@eastcentral.edu

Lindenwood University
209 S Kingshighway St
Saint Charles MO 63301-1695
Sheryl Guffey, Director of Admissions
636-949-2000 Fax: 636-949-4989
Website: www.lindenwood.edu

Missouri Southern State University - Joplin
3950 Newman Rd, Joplin MO 64801-1512
417-625-9300

Missouri Valley College
500 E College St, Marshall MO 65340-3197
Dr. Lori Gates, Division Dean
660-831-4166

Rockhurst University
1100 Rockhurst Rd, Kansas City MO 64110-2561
Mark Kopenski, VP of Enrollment Management
816-501-4000

St. Charles Community College
4601 Mid Rivers Mall Dr, Saint Peters MO 63376
Kathy Brockgreitens-Gober, Director of Admissions
636-922-8000 Fax: 636-922-8236
Website: www.stchas.edu
E-mail: adm-reg@stchas.edu

St. Louis University
221 N Grand Blvd, Saint Louis MO 63103-2097
314-977-2222

Southwest Baptist University
1600 University Ave, Bolivar MO 65613-2597
417-328-5281

Stephens College
PO Box 2121, Columbia MO 65215-0001
David Adams, Dean of Enrollment Management
573-442-2211 Fax: 573-876-7237
Website: www.stephens.edu
E-mail: dadams@stephens.edu

Truman State University
100 E Normal, Kirksville MO 63501
Office of Admission
660-785-4000 Fax: 660-785-4181
Website: admissions.truman.edu
E-mail: admissions@truman.edu

University of Missouri
102 Parker, Rolla MO 65409
Lynn Stichnote, Director of Admission
573-341-4164

University of Missouri
1 University Blvd, Saint Louis MO 63121-4499
Dr. Mark Burkholder, Dean-College of Arts & Sciences
314-516-5501 Fax: 314-516-5415
Website: www.umsl.edu
E-mail: admissions@umsl.edu

Webster University
470 E Lockwood Ave, Saint Louis MO 63119-3194
Dr. David Wilson, Dean, College of Arts and Sciences
314-968-7160 Fax: 314-968-7173
Website: www.webster.edu
E-mail: wilson@webster.edu
See listing under "Universities"

WENTWORTH MILITARY ACADEMY & JUNIOR COLLEGE

1880 Washington Ave, Lexington MO 64067
MAJ Mike Herman, Director of Admissions
800-962-7682 or 660-259-2221 Fax: 660-259-2677
Website: www.wma.edu, wjc.wma.edu
E-mail: admissions@wma1880.org

William Jewell College
500 College Hill, Liberty MO 64068-1896
800-753-7009

William Woods University
1 University Ave, Fulton MO 65251-1098
Jimmy Clay, Director of Admissions
573-642-2251 Fax: 573-592-1146
Website: www.williamwoods.edu
E-mail: admissions@williamwoods.edu
See listing under "Universities"

MONTANA

Carroll College
1601 N Benton Ave, Helena MT 59625-0002
Cynthia Thornquist, Director of Admissions &
Enrollment Operations
406-447-4384

Montana State University - Billings
1500 University Dr, Billings MT 59101-0252
Karen Everett, Director
800-565-MSUB

Montana Tech of the University of Montana
1300 W Park St, Butte MT 59701-8997
800-445-TECH

Rocky Mountain College
1511 Poly Dr, Billings MT 59102-1796
Bonnie Knapp, Director of Admissions
800-877-6259 Fax: 406-657-1189
Website: www.rocky.edu
E-mail: admissions@rocky.edu

University of Montana - Western
710 S Atlantic St, Dillon MT 59725-3598
406-683-7011

NEBRASKA

Bellevue University
1000 Galvin Rd S, Bellevue NE 68005-3098
Joseph Wydeven, Dean, College of Arts & Sciences

Chadron State College
1000 Main St, Chadron NE 69337-2690
308-432-6000

College of Saint Mary
7000 Mercy Rd, Omaha NE 68106
Lorin Werth,V.P. for Enrollment
800-926-5534 or 402-399-2407 Fax: 402-399-2412
Website: www.csm.edu
E-mail: lwerth@csm.edu

Dana College
2848 College Dr, Blair NE 68008-1099
James Lynes, Director of Admissions
800-444-3262

Doane College
1014 Boswell Ave, Crete NE 68333-2421
402-826-2161

Hastings College
PO Box 269, Hastings NE 68902-0269
402-463-2402

Midland Lutheran College
900 N Clarkson St, Fremont NE 68025-4200
Todd Hansen, Associate Director of Admissions
402-941-6501 Fax: 402-941-6513
Website: www.mlc.edu
E-mail: admissions@mlc.edu

Mid-Plains Community College
McCook Community College Campus
1205 E 3rd St, Mc Cook NE 69001-2631
Kelly Rippen, Director of Recruitment
800-658-4348 Fax: 308-345-8180
Website: www.mpcc.edu
E-mail: rippenk@mpcc.edu

Mid-Plains Community College
North Platte Community College - South Campus
601 W State Farm Rd, North Platte NE 69101
Kelly Rippen, Director of Recruitment
800-658-4308 ext. 8107 Fax: 308-535-3789
Website: www.mpcc.edu
E-mail: rippenk@mpcc.edu

Nebraska Wesleyan University
5000 Saint Paul Ave, Lincoln NE 68504-2794
Patricia Karthauser, V.P. for University Enrollment
402-466-2371 Fax: 402-465-2177
Website: www.nebrwesleyan.edu
E-mail: admissions@nebrwesleyan.edu

Peru State College
PO Box 10, Peru NE 68421-0010
Office of Admissions
800-742-4412 Fax: 402-872-2296
Website: www.peru.edu
E-mail: admissions@oakmail.peru.edu

Union College
3800 S 48th St, Lincoln NE 68506-4300
Buell Fogg, V.P. for Enrollment Services
800-228-4600

NEVADA

GREAT BASIN COLLEGE
1500 College Pkwy, Elko NV 89801-5032
Julie G. Byrnes, Director of Enrollment Management
775-753-2271 Fax: 775-753-2311
Website: www.gbcnv.edu
E-mail: bjulie@gbcnv.edu

University of Nevada Las Vegas
4505 S Maryland Pkwy, Las Vegas NV 89154-9901
800-334-8658

NEW HAMPSHIRE

Colby-Sawyer College
100 Main St, New London NH 03257-4648
603-526-3000

Rivier College
420 S Main St, Nashua NH 03060-5086
David Boisvert, Director of Undergraduate Admissions
603-897-8507

St. Anselm College
100 Saint Anselms Dr, Manchester NH 03102-1310
603-641-7000

Southern New Hampshire University
2500 N River Rd, Hooksett NH 03106-1045
Steve Soba, Director of Admissions
603-645-9611 Fax: 603-645-9693
Website: www.snhu.edu
E-mail: s.soba@snhu.edu

NEW JERSEY

Atlantic Cape Community College
5100 Black Horse Pike
Mays Landing NJ 08330-2699
Linda McLeod, Assistant Director of College Recruitment
609-343-5000 Fax: 609-343-4921
Website: www.atlantic.edu
E-mail: accadmit@atlantic.edu
See listing under "Community and Junior Colleges"

Bergen Community College
400 Paramus Rd, Paramus NJ 07652
Julian Gomez, Asst. Director of Admissions
201-447-7100 Fax: 201-444-7036
Website: www.bergen.edu
E-mail: jgomez@bergen.edu

Bloomfield College
467 Franklin St, Bloomfield NJ 07003
973-748-9000

Caldwell College
9 Ryerson Ave, Caldwell NJ 07006-6195
973-618-3000

Centenary College
400 Jefferson St, Hackettstown NJ 07840-2100
Glenna Warren, Director of Admissions
908-852-1400 Fax: 908-852-3454
Website: www.centenarycollege.edu
E-mail: warreng@centenarycollege.edu

College of Saint Elizabeth
2 Convent Rd, Morristown NJ 07960-6923
973-292-4000

Fairleigh Dickinson University
285 Madison Ave, Madison NJ 07940-1099
800-338-8803

Felician College
262 S Main St, Lodi NJ 07644-2198
973-559-6000

Mercer County Community College
West Windsor Campus
PO Box B, Trenton NJ 08690
Savita Bambhrolia, Director of Admissions
609-586-4800 Fax: 609-587-4666
Website: www.mccc.edu
E-mail: admiss@mccc.edu

Monmouth University
400 Cedar Ave, West Long Branch NJ 07764-1890
732-571-3400

New Jersey City University
2039 John F Kennedy Blvd
Jersey City NJ 07305-1588
Carmen Panlilio, Asst. V.P. for Admissions and Financial Aid
201-200-3234 Fax: 201-200-2044
Website: www.njcu.edu
E-mail: admissions@njcu.edu

Ramapo College of New Jersey
505 Ramapo Valley Rd, Mahwah NJ 07430-1623
Director of Admissions
201-684-7300 or 201-684-7301 Fax: 201-684-7964
Website: www.ramapo.edu
E-mail: admissions@ramapo.edu

Rider University
2083 Lawrenceville Rd, Lawrenceville NJ 08648-3099
Susan Christian, Director of Admissions
609-896-5042

St. Peter's College
2627 John F Kennedy Blvd, Jersey City NJ 07306
888-SPC-9933

NEW MEXICO

Eastern New Mexico University
Portales NM 88130
800-367-3668

New Mexico Highlands University
PO Box 9000, Las Vegas NM 87701
Sara Harris, Contact
505-454-3388

New Mexico Military Institute
101 W College Blvd, Roswell NM 88201-5173
LTC. Craig Collins, Director of Admissions
800-421-5376 or 505-624-8050 Fax: 505-624-8058
Website: www.nmmi.edu
E-mail: admissions@nmmi.edu
See listing under "Community and Junior Colleges"

New Mexico State University
1500 N 3rd St, Grants NM 87020-2025
505-287-7981 Fax: 505-287-2329
Website: www.grants.nmsu.edu

St. John's College
1160 Camino Cruz Blanca, Santa Fe NM 87505-4599
L. Clendenin, Director of Admissions
800-331-5232 Fax: 505-984-6162
Website: www.stjohnscollege.edu
E-mail: admissions@sjcsf.edu

UNIVERSITY OF NEW MEXICO
115 Civic Plaza Dr, Taos NM 87571-6401
Henry Trujillo, Senior Student Enrollment Associate
505-737-6200 Fax: 505-737-9317
Website: taos.unm.edu
E-mail: htrujil1@unm.edu

NEW YORK

Adelphi University
Garden City NY 11530
516-877-3100

Alfred University
1 Saxson Dr, Alfred NY 14802
607-871-2111

Broome Community College
907 Upper Front St, Binghamton NY 13905
Anthony S. Fiorelli, Director of Admissions
607-778-5001 Fax: 607-778-5442
Website: www.sunybroome.edu
E-mail: fiorelli_a@sunybroome.edu

Cazenovia College
Cazenovia NY 13035-1084
Robert Croot, Dean of Admissions & Financial Aid
800-654-3210

Colgate University
13 Oak Dr, Hamilton NY 13346-1386
Gary Ross, Director of Admissions
315-228-7401

College of New Rochelle
29 Castle Pl, New Rochelle NY 10805-2339
914-654-5000

College of Saint Rose
432 Western Ave, Albany NY 12203-1419
Maryelizabeth Amico, Asst V.P. for Undergraduate Admissions
518-454-5150 Fax: 518-454-2013
Website: www.strose.edu
E-mail: admit@strose.edu

CUNY City College
Convent Ave at 138th St, New York NY 10031
Celia Lloyd, Interim Director of Admissions
212-650-6977

CUNY Hunter College
695 Park Ave, New York NY 10021
Aaron Gibbs, Assistant Director of Recruitment
212-772-4497 Fax: 212-650-3336
Website: www.hunter.cuny.edu
E-mail: aaron.gibbs@hunter.cuny.edu

Daemen College
4380 Main St, Amherst NY 14226-3592
Donna Shaffner, Director of Admissions
800-462-7652 or 716-839-8225 Fax: 716-839-8229
Website: www.daemen.edu
E-mail: admissions@daemen.edu
See listing under "Universities"

D'Youville College
320 Porter Ave, Buffalo NY 14201-1084
716-829-7600

Elmira College
One Park Pl, Elmira NY 14901-2099
Dr. Thomas Meier, President
Gary Fallis, Dean of Admissions
800-935-6472

Excelsior College
7 Columbia Cir, Albany NY 12203-5156
518-464-8500

Farmingdale SUNY
2350 Broadhollow Rd, Farmingdale NY 11735
631-420-2200

FIVE TOWNS COLLEGE
305 N Service Rd, Dix Hills NY 11746-5871
631-424-7000 ext. 2110 Fax: 631-656-2172
Website: www.fivetowns.edu
E-mail: admissions@ftc.edu
See listing under "Universities"

Fordham University
441 E Fordham Rd, Bronx NY 10458-9993
John W. Buckley, Dean of Admissions
718-817-4000

Fordham University - Lincoln Center
113 W 60th St, New York NY 10023-7484
212-636-6710

Hamilton College
198 College Hill Rd, Clinton NY 13323-1295
Richard Fuller, Dean of Admissions
315-859-4421

Hilbert College
5200 S Park Ave, Hamburg NY 14075-1597
Timothy Lee, Director of Admissions
716-649-7900 Fax: 716-649-0702
Website: www.hilbert.edu
E-mail: tlee@hilbert.edu

Hobart & William Smith Colleges
Pulteney St, Geneva NY 14456
John Young, Director of Admissions
315-789-5500 Fax: 315-781-3654
Website: www.hws.edu
E-mail: young@hws.edu

Houghton College
PO Box 128, Houghton NY 14744-0128
585-567-9200

Iona College
715 North Ave, New Rochelle NY 10801-1890
Tom Weede, Director of Admissions
914-633-2000

Jewish Theological Seminary of America
3080 Broadway, New York NY 10027-4650
Jan Michael Skidds, Associate Director of Admissions
212-678-8000 Fax: 212-280-6022
Website: www.jtsa.edu
E-mail: lcadmissions@jtsa.edu

Juilliard School
60 Lincoln Center Plz, New York NY 10023-6588
Lee Cioppa, Associate Dean for Admissions
212-799-5000 Fax: 212-769-6420
Website: www.juilliard.edu
E-mail: admissions@juilliard.edu

Le Moyne College
1419 Salt Springs Rd, Syracuse NY 13214-1301
800-333-4733

Long Island University-C. W. Post Campus
720 Northern Blvd, Brookville NY 11548-1300
Joanne Graziano, Executive Director of Admissions
516-299-2900 Fax: 516-299-2137
Website: www.liu.edu/cwpost
E-mail: enroll@cwpost.liu.edu

Long Island University - Southampton College
239 Montauk Hwy, Southampton NY 11968
631-283-4000

Manhattan College
4513 Manhattan College Pkwy
Riverdale NY 10471-4099
Dr. Mary Ann O'Donnell, Dean of Arts
718-862-7200

Marist College
3399 North Rd, Poughkeepsie NY 12601
Jay E. Murray, Director of Admissions
845-575-3000

Marymount College at Fordham University
100 Marymount Ave, Tarrytown NY 10591-3796
914-631-3200

Mercy College
555 Broadway, Dobbs Ferry NY 10522-1189
Kathleen Jackson, Director of Admissions
800-MERCY-NY

Molloy College
1000 Hempstead Ave
Rockville Centre NY 11570-1100
Marguerite Lane, Director of Admissions
516-678-5000 ext. 6291 Fax: 516-256-2247
Website: www.molloy.edu
E-mail: admissions@molloy.edu
See listing under "Universities"

Mt. St. Mary College
330 Powell Ave, Newburgh NY 12550-3494
845-561-0800

Nazareth College of Rochester
4245 East Ave, Rochester NY 14618-3790
585-389-2525

New York City College of Technology CUNY
300 Jay St, Brooklyn NY 11201-1909
Joe Lento, Director of Admissions
718-260-5000

New York Institute of Technology
PO Box 8000, Old Westbury NY 11568-8000
516-686-7516

Niagara University
PO Box 2011, Niagara University NY 14109-2011
George Pachter, Dean of Admissions & Records
800-462-2111

Nyack College
1 South Boulevard
Nyack NY 10960-3698
845-358-1710

Paul Smith's College
Paul Smiths NY 12970
Amber DeBeer, Assistant Director of Admissions
800-421-2605 Fax: 518-327-6016
Website: www.paulsmiths.edu
E-mail: admiss@paulsmiths.edu

PURCHASE COLLEGE STATE UNIVERSITY OF NEW YORK (SUNY)
735 Anderson Hill Rd, Purchase NY 10577-1400
Betsy Immergut, Director of Admissions
914-251-6300 Fax: 914-251-6314
Website: www.purchase.edu
See listing under "Universities"

Roberts Wesleyan College
2301 Westside Dr, Rochester NY 14624-1997
Office of Admissions
585-594-6400 Fax: 585-594-6371
Website: www.roberts.edu
E-mail: admissions@roberts.edu

Rochester Institute of Technology
1 Lomb Memorial Dr, Rochester NY 14623-5603
585-475-2411

St. John's University
8000 Utopia Pkwy, Queens NY 11439
Office of Admission
718-990-2000 or 888-9-STJOHNS Fax: 718-990-2096
Website: www.stjohns.edu
E-mail: admissions@stjohns.edu
See listing under "Universities"

St. John's University
300 Howard Ave, Staten Island NY 10301-4496
718-447-4343

St. Joseph's College
245 Clinton Ave, Brooklyn NY 11205-3688
Theresa LaRocca Meyer, V.P. for Enrollment Management
718-636-6800 Fax: 718-636-8303
Website: www.sjcny.edu
E-mail: tlaroccameyer@sjcny.edu

St. Joseph's College
155 W Roe Blvd, Patchogue NY 11772
631-447-3200

St. Lawrence University
2501 Saint Lawrence Univ, Canton NY 13617-1475
315-229-5011

Sarah Lawrence College
1 Meadway, Bronxville NY 10708
914-337-0700

SUNY at Albany
1400 Washington Ave, Albany NY 12222-1000
Thomas Flemming, Associate Director of Admissions
518-442-5435

SUNY at Stony Brook
Stony Brook NY 11794-0001
631-689-6000

SUNY College at Brockport
350 New Campus Dr, Brockport NY 14420-2997
Bernard S. Valento, Director of Undergraduate Admissions
585-395-2751 Fax: 585-395-5452
Website: www.brockport.edu
E-mail: admit@brockport.edu

SUNY College at Old Westbury
PO Box 210, Old Westbury NY 11568-0210
516-876-3000

SUNY College at Potsdam
Potsdam NY 13676
Thomas W. Nesbitt, Director of Admissions
315-267-2000

SUNY College of Agriculture & Technology
107 Schenectady Ave, Cobleskill NY 12043
Clayton A. Smith, Director of Admissions
800-295-8988

SUNY College of Technology
Alfred NY 14802
Deborah J. Goodrich, Director of Admissions
800-4AL-FRED Fax: 607-587-4299
Website: www.alfredstate.edu
E-mail: admissions@alfredstate.edu

SUNY College of Technology
2 Main St, Delhi NY 13753-1110
Robert W. Mazzei, Director of Admissions
800-96-DELHI Fax: 607-746-4104
Website: www.delhi.edu
E-mail: enroll@delhi.edu

SUNY Empire State College
1 Union Ave, Saratoga Springs NY 12866-4309
518-587-2100

SUNY Institute of Technology Utica/Rome
PO Box 3050, Utica NY 13504-3050
315-792-7100

SUNY Niagara County Community College
3111 Saunders Settlement Rd
Sanborn NY 14132-9487
Kathleen Saunders, Director of Admissions
716-614-6200 Fax: 716-614-6820
Website: www.niagaracc.suny.edu
E-mail: saunders@niagaracc.suny.edu

SUNY Orange County Community College
115 South St, Middletown NY 10940-6437
Margot St. Lawrence, Director of Admissions
845-341-4030 Fax: 845-342-8662
Website: www.sunyorange.edu
E-mail: apply@sunyorange.edu
See listing under "Community and Junior Colleges"

Trocaire College
360 Choate Ave, Buffalo NY 14220-2003
Paul B. Hurley, Ph.D., President
716-826-1200 Fax: 716-828-6107
Website: www.trocaire.edu
E-mail: info@trocaire.edu
See listing under "Community and Junior Colleges"

University at Buffalo, The State University of New York
15 Capen Hall, Buffalo NY 14260-1660
Patricia G. Armstrong, Director of Admissions
888-UB-ADMIT

University of Rochester
Meliora Hall, Rochester NY 14627
585-275-2121

Utica College
1600 Burrstone Rd, Utica NY 13502-4857
315-792-3111

Wagner College
One Campus Rd, Staten Island NY 10301
Leigh Ann DePascale, Director of Admissions
718-390-3411

Wells College
PO Box 500, Aurora NY 13026
Susan Sloan, Director of Admissions
800-952-9355 Fax: 315-364-3227
Website: www.wells.edu
E-mail: ssloan@wells.edu

NORTH CAROLINA

Barton College
PO Box 5000, Wilson NC 27893
252-399-6300

Belmont Abbey College
100 Belmont Mount Holly Rd
Belmont NC 28012-1802
888-222-0110 Fax: 704-825-6670
Website: www.belmontabbeycollege.edu
E-mail: admissions@bac.edu

Catawba College
2300 W Innes St, Salisbury NC 28144-2488
Gordon A. Kirkland, Associate Director of Admissions
704-637-4402

Davidson College
PO Box 7156, Davidson NC 28035-7156
Chris Gruber, Acting Dean of Admission
800-768-0380

Greensboro College
815 W Market St, Greensboro NC 27401-1875
336-272-7102

Guilford College
5800 W Friendly Ave, Greensboro NC 27410-4173
Randy Doss, Dean of Enrollment
336-316-2100

Haywood Community College
185 Freedlander Dr, Clyde NC 28721
Debbie Rowland, Coordinator of Admissions
828-627-4500 Fax: 828-627-4513
Website: www.haywood.edu
E-mail: drowland@haywood.edu

Heritage Bible College
PO Box 1628, Dunn NC 28335
910-892-3178 Fax: 910-892-1809
Website: www.heritagebiblecollege.org
E-mail: generalinfo@heritagebiblecollege.org

James Sprunt Community College
PO Box 398, Kenansville NC 28349-0398
Rita Brown, Registrar
910-296-2500 Fax: 910-296-1636
Website: www.sprunt.com

Lees-McRae College
PO Box 128, Banner Elk NC 28604-0128
Walt Crutchfield, Dean of Admissions
800-280-4562 Fax: 828-898-8707
Website: www.lmc.edu
E-mail: admissions@lmc.edu

Louisburg College
501 N Main St, Louisburg NC 27549-2399
800-775-0208 or 919-496-2521 Fax: 919-496-1788
Website: www.louisburg.edu
E-mail: admissions@louisburg.edu

Mars Hill College
Mars Hill NC 28754
Chad Holt, Dean of Enrollment
866-MHC-4-YOU Fax: 828-689-1473
Website: www.mhc.edu
E-mail: cholt@mhc.edu

Meredith College
3800 Hillsborough St, Raleigh NC 27607-5298
Heidi L. Fletcher, Director of Admissions
919-760-8581 Fax: 919-760-2348
Website: www.meredith.edu
E-mail: admissions@meredith.edu
See listing under "Women's Colleges"

Montreat College
PO Box 1267, Montreat NC 28757-1267
800-622-6968

Mt. Olive College
634 Henderson St, Mount Olive NC 28365
Tim Woodard, Director of Admissions
919-658-2502 Fax: 919-658-9816
Website: www.moc.edu
E-mail: admissions@moc.edu
See listing under "Universities"

North Carolina State University
PO Box 7001, Raleigh NC 27695-0001
919-515-2011

Pfeiffer University
PO Box 960, Misenheimer NC 28109-0960
704-463-1360

Queens University of Charlotte
1900 Selwyn Ave, Charlotte NC 28274-0002
704-337-2212

St. Andrews Presbyterian College
1700 Dogwood Mile St, Laurinburg NC 28352-5521
Glenn Batten, Vice President for Enrollment
910-277-5554

Salem College
Winston Salem NC 27108
Dana Evans, Dean of Admissions/Fin. Aid
800-32-SALEM Fax: 336-917-5572
Website: www.salem.edu
E-mail: admissions@salem.edu
See listing under "Women's Colleges"

University of North Carolina at Greensboro
1000 Spring Garden St, Greensboro NC 27412-0001
336-334-5243

Warren Wilson College
PO Box 9000, Asheville NC 28815-9000
Richard Blomgren, Dean of Admissions
828-298-3325

Western Carolina University
University Dr, Cullowhee NC 28723-9646
828-227-7211

Wingate University
201 E Wilson St, Wingate NC 28174-9600
704-233-8000

Winston-Salem State University
601 S Mrtn Lther King Jr Dr
Winston Salem NC 27110-0003
336-750-2000

NORTH DAKOTA

Dickinson State University
Dickinson ND 58601-4896
Steve Glasser, Director of Student Recruitment
800-279-4295 Fax: 701-483-2409
Website: www.dickinsonstate.edu
E-mail: dsu.hawks@dickinsonstate.edu

Jamestown College
6000 College Ln, Jamestown ND 58405-0002
701-252-3467

Minot State University
500 University Ave W, Minot ND 58707-0002
Dennis Parisien, Enrollment Services Rep.
800-777-0750 ext. 3350

Minot State University-Bottineau Campus
105 Simrall Blvd, Bottineau ND 58318-1159
Paula Berg, Associate Dean of Student Affairs
800-542-6866 Fax: 701-228-5499
Website: www.misu-b.nodak.edu
E-mail: paula.berg@misu.nodak.edu

Sitting Bull College
1341 92nd St, Fort Yates ND 58538
Melody Azure, Director of Admissions / Registrar
701-854-3861 Fax: 701-854-3403
Website: www.sittingbull.edu
E-mail: melodya@sbci.edu

Valley City State University
101 College St SW, Valley City ND 58072-4024
Dan Klein, Director of Enrollment Services
800-532-8641 ext. 7101 Fax: 701-845-7299
Website: www.vcsu.edu
E-mail: enrollment.services@vcsu.edu
See listing under "Universities"

Williston State College
PO Box 1326, Williston ND 58802-1326
Penny Powell, Director Enrollment Services
701-774-4200 Fax: 701-774-4544
Website: www.wsc.nodak.edu
E-mail: penny.soiseth@wsc.nodak.edu

OHIO

Antioch College
795 Livermore St, Yellow Springs OH 45387-1697
937-754-5000

Baldwin-Wallace College
275 Eastland Rd, Berea OH 44017-2088
440-826-2900

Bowling Green State University
110 McFall Center, Bowling Green OH 43403-0001
866-CHOOSE-BGSU

Capital University
2199 E Main St, Columbus OH 43209-2394
614-236-6011

Cleveland State University
2121 Euclid Ave RW 204, Cleveland OH 44115
Dr. Richard Arndt, Dean of Undergraduate Recruitment
and College Partnerships
888-CSU-OHIO Fax: 216-687-9210
Website: www.csuohio.edu
E-mail: admissions@csuohio.edu

College of Wooster
Wooster OH 44691-2363
Paul J. Deutsch, Dean of Admissions
800-877-9905

Defiance College
701 N Clinton St, Defiance OH 43512-1695
419-784-4010

Franciscan University of Steubenville
University Blvd, Steubenville OH 43952
Margaret J. Weber, Director of Admissions
800-783-6220 or 740-283-6226 Fax: 740-284-5456
Website: www.admissions.edu
E-mail: mweber@franciscan.edu

Heidelberg College
310 E Market St, Tiffin OH 44883-2462
418-448-2000

Kent State University
PO Box 5190, Kent OH 44242-0001
Paul Deutsch, Director of Admissions
330-672-2444

Lake Erie College
391 W Washington St, Painesville OH 44077-3389
440-352-3361

Malone College
515 25th St NW, Canton OH 44709-3897
John Chopka, Dean of Admissions
330-471-8100

Marietta College
215 5th St, Marietta OH 45750-4047
740-376-4600

Miami University
E High St, Oxford OH 45056
513-529-2531

Mt. Union College
1972 Clark Ave, Alliance OH 44601-3929
Vincent Heslop, Director of Admissions
800-334-6682

Mount Vernon Nazarene University
800 Martinsburg Rd, Mount Vernon OH 43050-9509
Timothy Eades, Director of Admissions
866-462-6868 Fax: 740-393-0511
Website: www.gotomvnu.com
E-mail: admissions@mvnu.edu
See listing under "Universities"

Northwest State Community College
22600 State Route 34, Archbold OH 43502-9542
Mark Thompson, Director of Admissions
419-267-5511 Fax: 419-267-5587
Website: www.northweststate.edu
E-mail: mthompson@northwestate.edu

Notre Dame College
4545 College Rd, Cleveland OH 44121-4293
216-381-1680

Oberlin College
Carnegie Bldg, Oberlin OH 44074
Debra Chermonte, Dean of Admissions & Financial Aid

Ohio Dominican University
1216 Sunbury Rd, Columbus OH 43219-2099
614-253-2741

OHIO NORTHERN UNIVERSITY
525 S Main St, Ada OH 45810-1555
Robert A. Manzer, Dean
419-772-2130
Website: www.onu.edu
E-mail: admissions-ug@onu.edu
See listing under "Universities"

The Ohio State University
Colleges of Arts and Sciences
Denny Hall, 164 W 17th Ave, Columbus OH 43210
614-292-6961 Fax: 614-292-6303
Website: artsandsciences.osu.edu

Ohio State University-Lima Campus
4240 Campus Dr, Lima OH 45804-3576
Garlene Smithson, Dir. Enrollment Services
419-995-8396

Ohio University
Chillicothe Campus
PO Box 629, Chillicothe OH 45601
Student Services
740-774-7200 Fax: 740-774-7295
Website: www.ohiou.edu/chillicothe/

Ohio University - Zanesville Branch
1425 Newark Rd, Zanesville OH 43701-2695
740-588-1439

OHIO WESLEYAN UNIVERSITY
61 S Sandusky St, Delaware OH 43015-2398
Director of Admission
740-368-3020 Fax: 740-368-3314
Website: www.owu.edu
E-mail: owuadmit@owu.edu

Owens Community College
300 Davis St, Findlay OH 45840-3631
William J. Ivoska PhD., Vice President of Student
Services
567-429-3500 Fax: 567-423-0246
Website: www.owens.edu
E-mail: admissions@owens.edu

Owens Community College
PO Box 10000, Toledo OH 43699-1947
William J. Ivoska, Ph.D, Vice President of Student
Services
567-661-7000 Fax: 567-661-7607
Website: www.owens.edu
E-mail: admissions@owens.edu

Sinclair Community College
444 W 3rd St, Dayton OH 45402-1460
Sara P. Smith, Director of Outreach Services
937-512-3000 Fax: 937-512-2393
Website: www.sinclair.edu
E-mail: admit@sinclair.edu

University of Dayton
300 College Park, Dayton OH 45469-1300
Robert F. Durkle, Director of Admissions
800-837-7433 Fax: 937-229-4729
Website: admission.udayton.edu
E-mail: admission@udayton.edu

University of Rio Grande
General Delivery, Rio Grande OH 45674-9999
Dr. Barry Thompson, Dean
740-245-5353 ext. 7254

Ursuline College
2550 Lander Rd, Cleveland OH 44124-4398
Sarah E. Sundermeier, Director of Admissions
888-URSULINE Toll Free Fax: 440-684-6138
Website: www.admission.ursuline.edu
E-mail: admission@ursuline.edu

Walsh University
2020 E Maple St, North Canton OH 44720
800-362-9846

Wilmington College
251 Ludovic St, Wilmington OH 45177
937-382-6661

Youngstown State University
Sweeney Welcome Ctr, One University Plz
Youngstown OH 44555-0002
Sue Davis, Contact
877-GO-TO-YSU

OKLAHOMA

Bacone College
2299 Old Bacone Rd, Muskogee OK 74403-1568
Jerrett Phillips, Director of Admissions
918-781-7340

Oklahoma City University
2501 N Blackwelder Ave
Oklahoma City OK 73106-1493
Shery Boyles, Director of Admissions
405-521-5050

Oklahoma State University
Stillwater OK 74078
Bruce Crauder, Associate Dean
405-744-5663
Website: www.okstate.edu
E-mail: bruce.crauder@okstate.edu

Oklahoma Wesleyan University
2201 Silver Lake Rd, Bartlesville OK 74006-6299
918-333-6151

Oral Roberts University
7777 S Lewis Ave, Tulsa OK 74171-0001
Chris Belcher, Director of Undergraduate Admissions
800-678-8876 Fax: 918-495-6222
Website: www.oru.edu
E-mail: admissions@oru.edu

Rogers State University - Claremore Campus
1701 W Will Rogers Blvd, Claremore OK 74017-3259
Joe Wiley, President
918-343-7777

Southwestern Christian University
PO Box 340, Bethany OK 73008-0340
Megan Miles, Director of Admissions
405-789-7661 Fax: 405-495-0078
Website: www.swcu.edu
E-mail: jean@swcu.edu

University of Tulsa
600 S College Ave, Tulsa OK 74104-3126
Earl Johnson, Dean of Admission
918-631-2307 Fax: 918-631-5003
Website: www.utulsa.edu
E-mail: admission@utulsa.edu

OREGON

Cascade College
9101 E Burnside St, Portland OR 97216-1599
800-550-7678 Fax: 503-257-1222
Website: www.cascade.edu
E-mail: admissions@cascade.edu

Linfield College
900 SE Baker St, Mc Minnville OR 97128-6894
503-472-2200

Marylhurst University
17600 Pacific Hwy (Hwy 43)
Marylhurst OR 97036-0261
Director of Admissions
800-634-9982 ext. 6268 Fax: 503-635-6585
Website: www.marylhurst.edu
E-mail: studentinfo@marylhurst.edu

Oregon Institute of Technology
3201 Campus Dr, Klamath Falls OR 97601-8801
541-885-1000

Pacific University
2043 College Way, Forest Grove OR 97116-1797
Karen M. Dunston, Executive Director of Admissions
800-635-0561 Fax: 503-352-2975
Website: www.pacificu.edu
E-mail: admissions@pacificu.edu

Reed College
3202 SE Woodstock Blvd, Portland OR 97202-8139
503-771-1112

Rogue Community College
3345 Redwood Hwy, Grants Pass OR 97527-9298
Claudia Sullivan, Director of Enrollment Services
541-956-7500 Fax: 541-471-3585
Website: www.roguecc.edu
E-mail: csullivan@roguecc.edu
See listing under "Community and Junior Colleges"

Warner Pacific College
2219 SE 68th Ave, Portland OR 97215-4026
Shannon Mackey, Director of Admissions
503-517-1000 Fax: 503-517-1352
Website: www.warnerpacific.edu
E-mail: admissions@warnerpacific.edu

Western Oregon University
345 Monmouth Ave N, Monmouth OR 97361-1314
David McDonald, Dean, Admission, Retention &
Enrollment Management
877-877-1593 Fax: 503-838-8067
Website: www.wou.edu
E-mail: wolfgram@fsa.wou.edu

PENNSYLVANIA

Albright College
PO Box 15234, Reading PA 19612-5234
610-921-2381

Arcadia University
450 S Easton Rd, Glenside PA 19038-3295
Dennis Nostrand, VP for Enrollment Management
877-ARCADIA (877-272-2342) Fax: 215-881-8767
Website: www.arcadia.edu
E-mail: admiss@arcadia.edu
See listing under "Universities"

Cabrini College
610 King of Prussia Rd, Radnor PA 19087-3698
Mark T. Osborn, VP for Enrollment Management
610-902-8100

California University of Pennsylvania
250 University Ave, California PA 15419-1394
724-938-4000

Carnegie Mellon University
5000 Forbes Ave, Pittsburgh PA 15213-3890
412-268-2000

Cedar Crest College
100 College Dr, Allentown PA 18104-6196
Judith A. Neyhart, Vice President Enrollment
800-360-1222

Chatham College
Woodland Rd, Pittsburgh PA 15232-2826
412-365-1100

Chestnut Hill College
9601 Germantown Ave, Philadelphia PA 19118-2693
Jodie King, Director of Admissions
215-248-7001

Clarion University of Pennsylvania
840 Wood St, Clarion PA 16214-1232
William Bailey, Dean of Enrollment Management
814-393-2306 Fax: 814-393-2030
Website: www.clarion.edu
E-mail: admissions@clarion.edu

College Misericordia
301 Lake St, Dallas PA 18612-1008
Admissions
570-674-6400

DeSales University
2755 Station Ave, Center Valley PA 18034-9565
610-282-1100 Fax: 610-282-2342
Website: www.desales.edu

Duquesne University
600 Forbes Ave, Pittsburgh PA 15282-0001
Paul-James Cukanna, Director of Admissions
412-396-5000

Edinboro University of Pennsylvania
Edinboro PA 16444-0001
814-732-2000

Gannon University
109 University Sq, Erie PA 16541-0001
Christopher Tremblay, Director of Admissions
800-GANNON-U Fax: 814-871-5803
Website: www.gannon.edu
E-mail: admissions@gannon.edu

Gettysburg College
300 N Washington St, Gettysburg PA 17325-1483
Gail Sweezey, Director of Admissions
717-337-6100

Gratz College
7605 Old York Rd, Melrose Park PA 19027
Jill Sigman, Director of Admissions
215-635-7300 Fax: 215-635-7320
Website: www.gratzcollege.edu
E-mail: admissions@gratz.edu

Gwynedd-Mercy College
1325 Sumneytown Pike, Gwynedd Valley PA 19437
Dennis Murphy, V.P. Enrollment Management
800-DIAL-GMC

Haverford College
370 Lancaster Ave, Haverford PA 19041-1392
Jess Lord, Dean of Admission
610-896-1000 Fax: 610-896-1338
Website: www.haverford.edu
E-mail: admission@haverford.edu

Holy Family University
9801 Frankford Avenue, Philadelphia PA 19114
Lauren Campbell, Director of Admissions
215-637-3050 Fax: 215-281-1022
Website: www.holyfamily.edu
E-mail: admissions@holyfamily.edu

Immaculata University
Immaculata PA 19345
Women's College Office of Admissions
610-647-4400

Juniata College
1700 Moore St, Huntingdon PA 16652-2196
Michelle Bartol, Dean of Enrollment
877-JUNIATA Fax: 814-641-3100
Website: www.juniata.edu
E-mail: admissions@juniata.edu

King's College
133 N River St, Wilkes Barre PA 18711-0801
Michelle Lawrence-Schmude, Director of Admission
570-208-5900 Fax: 570-208-5971
Website: www.kings.edu
E-mail: admissions@kings.edu

Lafayette College
High St, Easton PA 18042
610-330-5000

La Roche College
9000 Babcock Blvd, Pittsburgh PA 15237-5898
Thomas Hassett, Director of Freshman and
International Admissions
412-536-1272 or 800-838-4LRC Fax: 412-536-1272
Website: www.laroche.edu
E-mail: admissions@laroche.edu

La Salle University
1900 W Olney Ave, Philadelphia PA 19141-1199
Robert Voss, Dean of Admissions
215-951-1500

Lebanon Valley College
101 N College Ave, Annville PA 17003-1400
William Brown, Dean of Admissions & Financial Aid
866-LVC-4ADM or 717-867-6181 Fax: 717-867-6026
Website: www.lvc.edu
E-mail: admission@lvc.edu

Lehigh University
27 Memorial Dr West, Bethlehem PA 18015-3094
Eric Kaplan, Dean of Admissions
610-758-3100

Lincoln University
Lincoln University PA 19352
Michael C. Taylor, Director of Admissions
800-790-0191 Fax: 610-932-1209
Website: www.lincoln.edu
E-mail: mtaylor@lu.lincoln.edu

Lock Haven University
Lock Haven PA 17745
James C. Reeser, Dean of Admissions
570-893-2027

Mansfield University of Pennsylvania
Academy St, Mansfield PA 16933
570-662-4000

Mercyhurst College
501 E 38th St, Erie PA 16546-0001
800-825-1926

Messiah College
1 S College Ave, Grantham PA 17027
717-766-2511

MOUNT ALOYSIUS COLLEGE
7373 Admiral Peary Hwy, Cresson PA 16630-1999
Frank C. Crouse Jr., Vice President for Enrollment
Management
814-886-6383 or 888-823-2220 Fax: 814-886-6441
Website: www.mtaloy.edu
E-mail: admissions@mtaloy.edu

Neumann College
1 Neumann Dr, Aston PA 19014-1298
Dennis Murphy, Director of Admissions
610-459-0905 Fax: 610-558-5652
Website: www.neumann.edu
E-mail: neumann@neumann.edu

Pennsylvania College of Technology
1 College Ave, Williamsport PA 17701-5778
570-326-3761

Pennsylvania State University
Broadhead Rd, Monaca PA 15061
724-773-3500

Pennsylvania State University
3550 7th St Rd, New Kensington PA 15068-1765
Patricia K. Brady, Director of Admissions
724-334-5466

Point Park University
201 Wood St, Pittsburgh PA 15222-1984
Philip Clarke, Associate Director of Admissions
412-392-3430

Robert Morris College
600 5th Ave, Pittsburgh PA 15219-3010
412-227-6800

Robert Morris University
881 Narrows Run Rd, Coraopolis PA 15108-1169
412-262-8200

Rosemont College
1400 Montgomery Ave, Rosemont PA 19010-1699
Ms. Rennie Andrews, Director of Admissions
610-526-2966

Seton Hill University
Greensburg PA 15601-1599
Mary Kay Cooper, Director of Admissions and Adult
Student Services
800-826-6234

Slippery Rock University
14 Maltby Dr, Slippery Rock PA 16057-1326
724-738-9000

Susquehanna University
514 University Ave, Selinsgrove PA 17870-1164
570-374-0101

Temple University
Broad St & Montgomery Ave, Philadelphia PA 19122
215-204-7000

Temple University Ambler
Ambler PA 19002
Michael Schlotterbeck, Contact
215-283-1252

Thiel College
75 College Ave, Greenville PA 16125-2181
724-589-2000

University of Pittsburgh
1150 Mount Pleasant Rd
Greensburg PA 15601-5860
Brandi S. Darr, Director of Admissions and Financial
Aid
724-836-9880 Fax: 724-836-7160
Website: www.upg.pitt.edu
E-mail: upgadmit@pitt.edu

University of Pittsburgh at Bradford
300 Campus Dr, Bradford PA 16701-2812
Alexander Nazemetz, Director of Admissions
814-362-7555

Washington & Jefferson College
60 S Lincoln St, Washington PA 15301-4801
Alton E. Newell, Vice President for Enrollment
724-223-6025 Fax: 724-223-6534
Website: www.washjeff.edu
E-mail: admission@washjeff.edu

Waynesburg College
51 W College St, Waynesburg PA 15370-1222
Robin L. Moore, Dean of Admissions
800-225-7393

Westminster College
New Wilmington PA 16172-0001
Doug Swartz, Director of Admissions
724-946-7100 Fax: 724-946-6171
Website: www.westminster.edu
E-mail: swartzdl@westminster.edu

Widener University
1 University Pl, Chester PA 19013-5792
610-499-4000

Wilkes University
170 S Franklin St, Wilkes Barre PA 18766-0001
570-408-5000

RHODE ISLAND

Providence College
549 River Ave, Providence RI 02918-0002
401-865-1000

University of Rhode Island
Kingston RI 02881
401-874-1000

SOUTH CAROLINA

Benedict College
1600 Harden St, Columbia SC 29204-1086
Phyllis L. Thompson, Director of Admissions
803-253-5143

Charleston Southern University
PO Box 118087, Charleston SC 29423-8087
Cheryl Burton, Director of Admissions
800-947-7474

Clemson University
105 Sikes Hall, Clemson SC 29634
864-656-2287

College of Charleston
66 George St, Charleston SC 29424-1407
Suzette Stille, Admissions
843-953-5670

Columbia College
1301 Columbia College Dr, Columbia SC 29203-5998
Elizabeth G. Quackenbush, Director of Admissions
803-786-3871

Erskine College & Seminary
PO Box 176, Due West SC 29639
Bart Walker, Director of Admissions
864-379-8838 Fax: 864-379-3048
Website: www.erskine.edu
E-mail: admissions@erskine.edu

Greenville Technical College
PO Box 5616, Greenville SC 29606-5616
Martha White, Director of Admissions
800-723-0673 (US) or 800-922-1183 (SC)
Website: www.greenvilletech.com

Lander University
320 Stanley Ave, Greenwood SC 29649-2099
Jonathan Reece, Director of Admissions
888-4-LANDER

Limestone College
1115 College Dr, Gaffney SC 29340-3799
Chris Phenicie, V.P. for Enrollment
864-489-7151 Fax: 864-488-8206
Website: www.limestone.edu
E-mail: cphenicie@limestone.edu

North Greenville University
PO Box 1892, Tigerville SC 29688-1892
Dr. Tom Allen, Dept. Chair
Website: www.ngc.edu
See listing under "Universities"

South Carolina State University
PO Box 7127, Orangeburg SC 29117-0001
Lillian M. Adderson, Director of Admissions
803-536-7185

Spartanburg Technical College
PO Box 4386, Spartanburg SC 29305-4386
Nancy Garmroth, Dean of Admissions & Financial Aid
864-592-4810 Fax: 864-592-4945
Website: stcsc.edu

University of South Carolina
Columbia SC 29208-0001
803-777-7700

University of South Carolina Beaufort
801 Carteret St, Beaufort SC 29902-4601
Anita M. Folsom, Director of Admissions
843-521-4101

University of South Carolina - Upstate
800 University Way, Spartanburg SC 29303-4932
Donette Stewart, Assistant VC for Enrollment Services
864-503-5246 Fax: 864-503-5727
Website: www.uscupstate.edu
E-mail: dstewart@uscupstate.edu
See listing under "Universities"

Winthrop University
701 W Oakland Ave, Rock Hill SC 29733-0001
803-323-2211

SOUTH DAKOTA

Black Hills State University
1200 University St, Spearfish SD 57799-0002
605-642-6011

Dakota State University
820 N Washington Ave, Madison SD 57042-1799
605-256-5112

TENNESSEE

Aquinas College
4210 Harding Pike, Nashville TN 37205-2086
Diane C. LeJeune, Director of Admissions
615-297-7545 ext. 460 Fax: 615-297-7970
Website: www.aquinas-tn.edu
E-mail: lejeuned@aquinas-tn.edu

Belmont University
1900 Belmont Blvd, Nashville TN 37212-3757
615-460-6000

Bryan College
PO Box 7000, Dayton TN 37321-7000
423-775-2041

Carson-Newman College
1646 Russell Ave, Jefferson City TN 37760
865-471-4000

Draughons Junior College
PO Box 17386, Nashville TN 37217-0386
615-361-7555 Fax: 615-367-2736
Website: www.draughons.edu

East Tennessee State University
PO Box 70730, Johnson City TN 37614
Dr. Don Johnson, Dean of Arts & Sciences
423-439-5671

Freed-Hardeman University
158 E Main St, Henderson TN 38340-2398
731-989-6000

King College
1350 King College Rd, Bristol TN 37620-2635
423-968-1187

Lee University
PO Box 3450, Cleveland TN 37320-3450
Dewayne Thompson, Dean of the College of Arts &
Sciences
800-533-9930

Lipscomb University
3901 Granny White Pike, Nashville TN 37204-3951
Ricky Holaway, Director of Admissions
800-333-4358 ext. 1776 Fax: 615-269-1804
Website: www.lipscomb.edu
E-mail: admissions@lipscomb.edu

Pellissippi State Technical Community College
PO Box 22990, Knoxville TN 37933-0990
Donna Mack, Contact
865-694-6568 Fax: 865-539-7217
Website: www.pstcc.edu
E-mail: dmack@pstcc.edu

Tennessee State University
3500 John A Merritt Blvd, Nashville TN 37209-1561
John Cade, Dean of Admissions & Records
615-963-5101 Fax: 615-963-2930
Website: www.tnstate.edu
E-mail: jcade@tnstate.edu

Tusculum College
PO Box 5051, Greeneville TN 37743
Melissa Ripley, Associate Director of Admissions
800-729-0256 Fax: 423-798-1622
Website: www.tusculum.edu
E-mail: mripley@tusculum.edu

Union University
1050 Union University Dr, Jackson TN 38305
731-668-1818

University of Memphis
Memphis TN 38152-0001
901-678-2000

University of Tennessee
615 McCallie Ave, Chattanooga TN 37403-2504
Yancy Freeman, Director of Admissions
423-425-4111 Fax: 423-425-4157
Website: www.utc.edu
E-mail: Yancy-Freeman@utc.edu

University of Tennessee
527 Andy Holt Tower, Knoxville TN 37996-0001
865-974-1000

University of Tennessee
Martin TN 38238-0001
731-587-7000

University of the South
735 University Ave, Sewanee TN 37383-1000
931-598-1000

TEXAS

:: **ALLEN ACADEMY**
3201 Boonville Rd, Bryan TX 77802
Camilla Viator, Director of Admissions
979-776-0731 Fax: 979-774-7769
Website: www.allenacademy.org
E-mail: cviator@allenacademy.org

Angelo State University
ASU Station 11014, San Angelo TX 76909
Bonnie Stennett, Coordinator of Recruiting
800-946-8627 Fax: 325-942-2078
Website: www.angelo.edu
E-mail: admissions@angelo.edu

Austin College
900 N Grand Ave, Sherman TX 75090-4400
903-813-2000

Blinn College
902 College Ave, Brenham TX 77833-4098
Dennis K. Crowson, Registrar
979-830-4000 Fax: 979-830-4110
Website: www.blinn.edu
E-mail: recruiting@blinn.edu

Blinn College
PO Box 6030, Bryan TX 77805-6030
Dennis K. Crowson, Registrar
979-209-7200 Fax: 979-209-7229
Website: www.blinn.edu
E-mail: recruiting@blinn.edu

Blinn College
100 Ranger Dr, Schulenburg TX 78956-2247
Dennis K. Crowson, Registrar
979-743-5003 Fax: 979-743-5225
Website: www.blinn.edu
E-mail: recruiting@blinn.edu

Blinn College
3701 Outlet Center Dr, Sealy TX 77474
Dennis K. Crowson, Registrar
979-627-7997 Fax: 979-627-0830
Website: www.blinn.edu
E-mail: recruiting@blinn.edu

Galveston College
4015 Avenue Q, Galveston TX 77550-7496
Brian Lowery, Registrar
409-763-6551 Fax: 409-944-1501
Website: www.gc.edu
E-mail: blowery@gc.edu

Jacksonville College
105 B J Albritton Dr, Jacksonville TX 75766-4759
903-586-2518 Fax: 903-586-0743
Website: www.jacksonville-college.edu
E-mail: acadean@jacksonville-college.edu
See listing under "Community and Junior Colleges"

Lamar University
PO Box 10009, Beaumont TX 77710-0009
409-880-8508

McLennan Community College
1400 College Dr, Waco TX 76708-1498
Dr. Harry "Buddy" Powell, Dean, Arts and Sciences
254-299-8000 Fax: 254-299-8854
Website: www.mclennan.edu
E-mail: bpowell@mclennan.edu

North Central Texas College
1525 W California St, Gainesville TX 76240-4636
Michelle Winters, Registrar
940-668-3315 Fax: 940-665-7075
Website: www.nctc.edu
E-mail: mwinters@nctc.edu

Our Lady of the Lake University
411 SW 24th St, San Antonio TX 78207-4666
Mary Kay Cooper, Dean of Enrollment
210-434-6711 Fax: 210-431-4013
Website: www.ollusa.edu
E-mail: admission@lakeollusa.edu

Prairie View A&M University
PO Box 188, Prairie View TX 77446
936-857-3311

Schreiner University
2100 Memorial Blvd, Kerrville TX 78028-5697
Todd D. Brown, Director of Admissions
800-343-4919

Southern Methodist University
PO Box 750181, Dallas TX 75275-0181
Ron Moss, Dean of Admission
214-768-2058

Temple College
2600 S 1st St, Temple TX 76504-7435
Angela Balch, Director of Admissions & Records
254-298-8300 Fax: 254-298-8288
Website: www.templejc.edu
E-mail: ruth.bridges@templejc.edu

Texas A&M International University
5201 University Blvd, Laredo TX 78041
956-326-2000

Texas A&M University
700 University Blvd, Kingsville TX 78363
361-593-2111

Texas Christian University
TCU Box 297013, Fort Worth TX 76129
817-257-7000

Texas Wesleyan University
1201 Wesleyan St, Fort Worth TX 76105-1536
Stephanie Boatner, Director of Freshman Admission
800-580-8980

Texas Woman's University
PO Box 425589, Denton TX 76204-5589
Erma Nieto, Director of Admissions
866-809-6130 Fax: 940-898-3081
Website: www.twu.edu
E-mail: admissions@twu.edu

Tyler Junior College
PO Box 9020, Tyler TX 75711-9020
Richard Minter, Dean
800-687-5680
Website: www.tjc.edu
E-mail: rmin@tjc.edu
See listing under "Community and Junior Colleges"

University of Houston
122 E Cullen Bldg, Houston TX 77204-2023
Office of Admission
713-743-9595
Website: www.uh.edu
E-mail: admissions@uh.edu

University of Houston-Clear Lake
2700 Bay Area Blvd, Houston TX 77058-1025
281-283-2500

University of Mary Hardin-Baylor
UMHB Station Box 8001, Belton TX 76513
254-295-8642

University of St. Thomas
3800 Montrose Blvd, Houston TX 77006-4626
Eduardo Prieto, Director of Admissions
713-522-7911 Fax: 713-525-3558
Website: www.stthom.edu
E-mail: prietoe@stthom.edu

University of Texas at Arlington
Box 19111, Arlington TX 76019-0111
Hans Gatterdam, Director of Admission
817-272-6287 Fax: 817-272-3435
Website: www.uta.edu
E-mail: admissions@uta.edu

University of Texas at Tyler
3900 University Blvd, Tyler TX 75701-6622
Jim Hutto, Dean Enrollment Management
800-888-9537

University of the Incarnate Word
4301 Broadway St, San Antonio TX 78209-6318
210-829-6000

UTAH

Brigham Young University
Provo UT 84602-0001
801-378-5000

L.D.S. BUSINESS COLLEGE
95 North 300 West, Salt Lake City UT 84101-3500
Kathleen Howe, Assistant Director of Admissions
801-524-8145 Fax: 801-524-1900
Website: www.ldsbc.edu
E-mail: admissions@ldsbc.edu
See listing under "Career Schools"

Westminster College
1840 S 1300 E, Salt Lake City UT 84105-3617
801-832-2200

VERMONT

Bennington College
One College Drive, Bennington VT 05201
Ken Himmelman, Dean of Admissions & Financial Aid
800-833-6845 Fax: 802-440-4320
Website: www.bennington.edu
E-mail: admissions@bennington.edu

Castleton State College
Castleton VT 05735
William Allen Jr., Dean of Enrollment
800-639-8521

Goddard College
121 Pitkin Rd, Plainfield VT 05667
802-454-8311

Johnson State College
337 College Hill, Johnson VT 05656
802-635-2356

Lyndon State College
PO Box 919, Lyndonville VT 05851
802-626-6200

Saint Michael's College
One Winooski Park, Colchester VT 05439-0001
Dr. Marc vanderHeyden, President
Jerry Flanagan, VP Admission & Enrollment
Management
802-654-3000

Southern Vermont College
982 Mansion Dr, Bennington VT 05201-6002
Kathleen James Ring, Director of Admissions
800-378-2782 Fax: 802-447-4695
Website: www.svc.edu
E-mail: admis@svc.edu

VIRGINIA

College of William and Mary
PO Box 8795, Williamsburg VA 23187-8795
757-221-4000

Ferrum College
PO Box 1000, Ferrum VA 24088-9001
Gilda Q. Woods, Director of Admissions
800-868-9797

George Mason University
4400 University Dr, Fairfax VA 22030-4444
Eddie Tallent, Director of Admissions
703-993-2400

Hampden-Sydney College
PO Box 128, Hampden Sydney VA 23943-0128
804-223-6000

James Madison University
800 S Main St, Harrisonburg VA 22807-0002
540-568-6211

Liberty University
PO Box 20000, Lynchburg VA 24506-8001
804-582-2000

Lynchburg College
1501 Lakeside Dr, Lynchburg VA 24501-3199
804-544-8100

Mary Baldwin College
Staunton VA 24401
Lisa A. Branson, Executive Director of Admissions and
Financial Aid
800-468-2262 Fax: 540-887-7292
Website: www.mbc.edu
E-mail: admit@mbc.edu

Marymount University
2807 N Glebe Rd, Arlington VA 22207-4299
703-522-5600

Norfolk State University
700 Park Ave, Norfolk VA 23504
Michelle Marable, Director of Admissions
757-823-8600

PATRICK HENRY COLLEGE
1 Patrick Henry Cir, Purcellville VA 20132
540-338-1776 Fax: 540-338-8707
Website: www.phc.edu
E-mail: admissions@phc.edu

Radford University
PO Box 6903, Radford VA 24142
David W. Kraus, Director of Admissions
800-890-4265 Fax: 540-831-5038
Website: www.radford.edu
E-mail: ruadmiss@radford.edu

Randolph-Macon College
PO Box 5005, Ashland VA 23005-5505
804-752-7200

Randolph-Macon Woman's College
2500 Rivermont Ave, Lynchburg VA 24503
Patricia LeDonne, Director of Admissions
434-947-8100 Fax: 434-947-8996
Website: www.rmwc.edu
E-mail: admissions@rmwc.edu

St. Paul's College
406 Windsor Ave, Lawrenceville VA 23868-1202
804-848-3111

Shenandoah University
1460 University Dr, Winchester VA 22601-5195
Michael D. Carpenter, Director of Admissions
800-432-2266

Southside Virginia Community College
109 Campus Dr, Alberta VA 23821-2930
Ronald E. Mattox, Dean of Admissions
434-949-1014 Fax: 434-949-7863
Website: www.sv.vccs.edu
E-mail: ronald.mattox@sv.vccs.edu

Southside Virginia Community College
200 Daniel Rd, Keysville VA 23947
Ronald E. Mattox, Dean of Admissions
434-736-2018 Fax: 434-736-2082
Website: www.sv.vccs.edu
E-mail: ronald.mattox@sv.vccs.edu

University of Mary Washington
1301 College Ave, Fredericksburg VA 22401-5300
Dr. Martin A. Wilder, Jr., Director of Admissions
540-654-2000 Fax: 540-654-1857
Website: www.umw.edu
E-mail: admit@umw.edu

Virginia Polytechnic Institute & State University
Blacksburg VA 24061
540-231-6000

WASHINGTON

Antioch University
2326 6th Ave, Seattle WA 98121
Pam Smith Mentz, Director of Enrollment Services
888-268-4477

Central Washington University
400 E University Way, Ellensburg WA 98926
William Swain, Director of Admissions
509-963-3001

Eastern Washington University
Cheney WA 99004
509-359-6200

Everett Community College
2000 Tower St, Everett WA 98201
Christine Kerlin, Associate Dean
425-388-9100 Fax: 425-388-9173
Website: www.everettcc.edu
E-mail: ckerlin@everettcc.edu

Gonzaga University
502 E Boone Ave, Spokane WA 99258-0102
Julie McCulloh, Dean of Admission
800-322-2584 or 509-323-6572 Fax: 509-323-5780
Website: www.gonzaga.edu
E-mail: mcculloh@gu.gonzaga.edu

Heritage University
3240 Fort Rd, Toppenish WA 98948-9599
509-865-8500

Pacific Lutheran University
12180 Park Ave S, Tacoma WA 98447-0014
David E. Gunovich, Director of Admissions
253-535-7151

Seattle Pacific University
3307 3rd Ave W, Seattle WA 98119-1997
206-281-2000

Walla Walla Community College
500 Tausick Way, Walla Walla WA 99362-9270
Dr. Sandra Blackaby, Vice President
509-527-4289 or 877-992-9922 Fax: 509-527-3661
Website: www.wwcc.edu
See listing under "Community and Junior Colleges"

Washington State University
1 SE Stadium Way, Pullman WA 99164-0001
509-335-3564

Wenatchee Valley College
PO Box 2058, Omak WA 98841
Alex Roberts, Director
509-422-7805 Fax: 509-682-6541
Website: www.wvc.edu

Wenatchee Valley College
1300 5th St, Wenatchee WA 98801-1799
Marco Azurdia, Dean, Student Development
509-682-6805 Fax: 509-682-6541
Website: www.wvc.edu

Whitworth College
300 W Hawthorne Rd, Spokane WA 99251-0001
Fred Pfursich, Dean of Admissions & Financial Aid
800-533-4668

WEST VIRGINIA

Alderson-Broaddus College
Philippi WV 26416
Eric A. Ruf, Director of Admissions
800-263-1549

Davis & Elkins College
100 Campus Dr, Elkins WV 26241-3996
Renee Heckel, Director of Enrollment Management
800-624-3157 Fax: 304-637-1800
Website: www.davisandelkins.edu
E-mail: admiss@davisandelkins.edu

Fairmont State University
1201 Locust Ave, Fairmont WV 26554-2470
Steve Leadman, Director of Admissions
304-367-4717 or 800-641-5678 Fax: 304-367-4789
Website: www.fairmontstate.edu
E-mail: admit@fairmontstate.edu

Glenville State College
200 High St, Glenville WV 26351-1200
304-462-4128

Mountain State University
Box 9003, Beckley WV 25802-9003
866-FOR-MSU1 or 304-929-INFO Fax: 304-253-5072
Website: www.mountainstate.edu
E-mail: gomsu@mountainstate.edu
See listing under "Universities"

Shepherd University
PO Box 3210
Shepherdstown WV 25443
304-876-5000

West Virginia State University
PO Box 1000, Institute WV 25112-1000
304-766-3000

West Virginia Wesleyan College
59 College Ave, Buckhannon WV 26201-2699
Robert N. Skinner II, Director of Admission
800-722-9933 Fax: 304-473-8108
Website: www.wvwc.edu
E-mail: admission@wvwc.edu

WISCONSIN

Alverno College
PO Box 343922, Milwaukee WI 53234-3922
Mary Kay Farrell, Director of Admissions
414-382-6100 Fax: 414-382-6354
Website: www.alverno.edu
E-mail: admissions@alverno.edu

Beloit College
700 College St, Beloit WI 53511-5596
David Burrows, Dean
608-363-2668

Carroll College
100 N East Ave, Waukesha WI 53186-5593
James Wiseman, Dean of Admissions
800-CARROLL

Carthage College
2001 Alford Park Dr, Kenosha WI 53140-1994
262-551-6000

COLLEGE OF MENOMINEE NATION
PO Box 1179, Keshena WI 54135-1179
Cynthia Norton, Admissions Representative
715-799-5600 Fax: 715-799-4392
Website: www.menominee.edu
E-mail: cnorton@menominee.edu

Concordia University
12800 N Lake Shore Dr, Mequon WI 53097-2402
262-243-5700

Lakeland College
PO Box 359, Sheboygan WI 53082-0359
Nathan Dehne, Director of Admission
920-565-1100 Fax: 920-565-1215
Website: www.lakeland.edu
E-mail: admissions@lakeland.edu

Lawrence University
PO Box 599, Appleton WI 54912-0599
920-832-7000

Marquette University
PO Box 1881, Milwaukee WI 53201-1881
Robert Blust, Director of Admissions
414-288-7302 Fax: 414-288-3764
Website: www.mu.edu
E-mail: admissions@marquette.edu

Mount Mary College
2900 N Menomonee River Pkwy
Milwaukee WI 53222-4597
414-256-1219

Northland College
1411 Ellis Ave, Ashland WI 54806-3999
800-753-1840

St. Norbert College
100 Grant St, De Pere WI 54115
Brian Studebaker, Director of Admission
800-236-4878 Fax: 920-403-4072
Website: www.snc.edu
E-mail: admit@snc.edu

University of Wisconsin
1 University Plz, Platteville WI 53818-3001
Angela Udelhofen, Recruitment Manager
608-342-1200

University of Wisconsin
800 W Main St, Whitewater WI 53190-1705
262-472-1234

University of Wisconsin Green Bay
2420 Nicolet Dr, Green Bay WI 54311-7003
Pamela Harvey-Jacobs, Interim Director of Admissions
920-465-2111

University of Wisconsin in La Crosse
115 Graff Main Hall, La Crosse WI 54601
Tim Lewis, Director of Admissions
608-785-8939

University of Wisconsin - Oshkosh
800 Algoma Blvd, Oshkosh WI 54901-8602
920-424-0202

Viterbo University
815 9th St S, La Crosse WI 54601-8802
608-796-3000

WYOMING

Laramie County Community College
1400 E College Dr, Cheyenne WY 82007-3204
Jenny Hargett, Director of Admissions
307-778-5222 Fax: 307-778-1350
Website: www.lccc.wy.edu
E-mail: learnmore@lccc.wy.edu

University of Wyoming
Admissions Office
Dept 3435, Laramie WY 82071-3435
Aaron Appelhans, Contact
800-342-5996 Fax: 307-766-4042
Website: www.uwyo.edu
E-mail: why-wyo@uwyo.edu

GUAM

Guam Community College
PO Box 23069, G.M.F. GU 96921-0307
Virginia Charfauros Tudela, Ph.D., Registrar
671-735-5531 Fax: 671-734-5238
Website: www.guamcc.edu
E-mail: Webmaster@guamcc.edu

University of Guam
UOG Station, Mangilao GU 96923
Deborah Leon Guerrero, Registrar
671-735-2201 or 671-735-2208 Fax: 671-735-2203
Website: www.uog.edu
E-mail: admitme@uog9.uog.edu

PUERTO RICO

Bayamon Central University
PO Box 1725, Bayamon PR 00960-1725
787-786-3030

Universidad Adventista de las Antillas
PO Box 118, Mayaguez PR 00919-0118
Evelyn Del Valle Rivera, Director of Admissions
787-834-9595 Fax: 787-834-9597
Website: www.uaa.edu
E-mail: admissions@uaa.edu

University of Puerto Rico
R Ave Antonio R Barcelo, Cayey PR 00736-5534
787-738-2161

University of Puerto Rico
PO Box 9020, Mayaguez PR 00681
787-832-4040

University of Puerto Rico
PO Box 23303, Rio Piedras PR 00931-3303
787-764-0000

VIRGIN ISLANDS

University of the Virgin Islands
2 John Brewers Bay, Saint Thomas VI 00802
340-776-9200

LIBRARY SCIENCE

ARIZONA

University of Arizona
Tucson AZ 85721-0040
Paul Kohn, Director of Admissions
520-621-3237 Fax: 520-621-9799
Website: www.admissions.arizona.edu or
www.arizona.edu

FLORIDA

Florida State University
600 W College Ave, Tallahassee FL 32306-1096
Janice V. Finney, Director of Admissions
850-644-2525 Fax: 850-644-0197
Website: admissions.fsu.edu
E-mail: admissions@admin.fsu.edu

University of South Florida
4202 E Fowler Ave, Tampa FL 33620-6900
J. Robert Spatig, Director of Admissions
813-974-3350 Fax: 813-974-9689
Website: www.usf.edu
E-mail: admissions@admin.usf.edu

IOWA

Iowa Lakes Community College
3200 College Dr, Emmetsburg IA 50536-1055
Anne Stansbury, Asst. Director of Admissions
712-852-5212 Fax: 712-362-8363
Website: www.iowalakes.edu
E-mail: info@iowalakes.edu

Iowa Lakes Community College
300 S 18th St, Estherville IA 51334-2721
Anne Stansbury, Asst. Director of Admissions
712-362-7945 Fax: 712-362-8363
Website: www.iowalakes.edu
E-mail: info@iowalakes.edu

MISSOURI

William Woods University
1 University Ave, Fulton MO 65251-1098
Jimmy Clay, Director of Admissions
573-642-2251 Fax: 573-592-1146
Website: www.williamwoods.edu
E-mail: admissions@williamwoods.edu
See listing under "Universities"

NEW YORK

Long Island University-C. W. Post Campus
720 Northern Blvd, Brookville NY 11548-1300
Beth Carson, Director of Graduate Admissions
516-299-2900 Fax: 516-299-2137
Website: www.liu.edu/cwpost
E-mail: enroll@cwpost.liu.edu

Pratt Institute
200 Willoughby Ave, Brooklyn NY 11205-3899
Heidi Metcalf, Director of Admissions
718-636-3600 Fax: 718-636-3670
Website: www.pratt.edu
E-mail: hmetcalf@pratt.edu

St. John's University
8000 Utopia Pkwy, Queens NY 11439
Office of Admission
718-990-2000 or 888-9-STJOHNS Fax: 718-990-2096
Website: www.stjohns.edu
E-mail: admissions@stjohns.edu
See listing under "Universities"

PENNSYLVANIA

Clarion University of Pennsylvania
840 Wood St, Clarion PA 16214-1232
William Bailey, Dean of Enrollment Management
814-393-2306 Fax: 814-393-2030
Website: www.clarion.edu
E-mail: admissions@clarion.edu

TEXAS

Our Lady of the Lake University
411 SW 24th St, San Antonio TX 78207-4666
Mary Kay Cooper, Dean of Enrollment
210-434-6711 Fax: 210-431-4013
Website: www.ollusa.edu
E-mail: admission@lakeollusa.edu

Texas Woman's University
PO Box 425589, Denton TX 76204-5589
Erma Nieto, Director of Admissions
866-809-6130 Fax: 940-898-3081
Website: www.twu.edu
E-mail: admissions@twu.edu

WEST VIRGINIA

Concord University
Athens WV 24712
Michael Curry, Vice President of Financial Aid &
Admissions
888-384-5249 Fax: 304-384-3218
Website: www.concord.edu
E-mail: admissions@concord.edu

MARKETING AND DISTRIBUTION

ALABAMA

Alabama A & M University
PO Box 908, Normal AL 35762
Antonio Boyle, Director of Admissions
256-372-5245 Fax: 256-372-5249
Website: www.aamu.edu
E-mail: aboyle@aamu.edu

Bishop State Community College - Four Campuses
351 N Broad St, Mobile AL 36603-5898
Dr. Terry Hazzard, Dean of Students
251-690-6801 Fax: 251-690-6446
Website: www.bishop.edu
E-mail: thazzard@bishop.edu

ALASKA

University of Alaska Anchorage
PO Box 141629, Anchorage AK 99514-1629
Cecile Mitchell, Director of Enrollment Services
907-786-1480 Fax: 907-786-4888
Website: www.uaa.alaska.edu/
E-mail: enroll@uaa.alaska.edu

University of Alaska Southeast
11120 Glacier Hwy, Juneau AK 99801-8625
Paul Kraft, Dean of Students/Enrollment Management
907-796-6000 Fax: 907-796-6005
Website: www.uas.alaska.edu
E-mail: paul.kraft@uas.alaska.edu

ARIZONA

Pima Community College
4905 E Broadway Blvd, Tucson AZ 85709-1010
Wendy Kilgore, Ph.D., Director of Admissions
520-206-4500 Fax: 520-206-4790
Website: www.pima.edu
E-mail: infocenter@pima.edu

University of Arizona
Tucson AZ 85721-0040
Paul Kohn, Director of Admissions
520-621-3237 Fax: 520-621-9799
Website: www.admissions.arizona.edu or
www.arizona.edu

ARKANSAS

Ouachita Baptist University
410 Ouachita St, Arkadelphia AR 71998-0001
David Goodman, Director of Admissions
870-245-5110 Fax: 870-245-5500
Website: www.obu.edu
E-mail: admissions@obu.edu

Phillips Community College of the University of Arkansas
PO Box 785, Helena AR 72342-0785
Dr. Steven Murray, Chancellor
Lynn Boone, Vice Chancellor for Student Services /
Registrar
870-338-6474 Fax: 870-338-7542
Website: www.pccua.edu
E-mail: lboone@pccua.edu

CALIFORNIA

The Art Institute of California - San Diego
7650 Mission Valley Rd, San Diego CA 92108
Jo-Ann White, Director of Admissions
858-598-1200 Fax: 619-291-3206
Website: www.aicasd.artinstitutes.edu

Concordia University
1530 Concordia, Irvine CA 92612-3203
Lori McDonald, Executive Director of Enrollment
Services
800-229-1200 or 949-854-8002 Fax: 949-854-6894
Website: www.cui.edu
E-mail: admission@cui.edu

Fashion Careers College
1923 Morena Blvd, San Diego CA 92110-3555
Tanya McAnear, Director of Admissions
619-275-4700 Fax: 619-275-0635
Website: www.fashioncareerscollege.com
E-mail: info@fashioncareerscollege.com
See listing under "Fashion Art"

FIDM/The Fashion Institute of Design & Merchandising
17590 Gillette Ave, Irvine CA 92614
Director of Admissions
949-851-6200 or 888-974-3436 Fax: 949-851-6808
Website: www.fidm.edu
E-mail: info@fidm.com
See listing under "Community and Junior Colleges"

FIDM/THE FASHION INSTITUTE OF DESIGN & MERCHANDISING

919 S Grand Ave, Los Angeles CA 90015-1421
Director of Admissions
213-624-1201 or 800-624-1200 Fax: 213-624-4799
Website: www.fidm.edu
E-mail: info@fidm.com
See listing under "Community and Junior Colleges"

FIDM/The Fashion Institute of Design & Merchandising
1010 2nd Ave, San Diego CA 92101-4903
Director of Admissions
619-235-2049 or 800-243-3436 Fax: 619-232-4322
Website: www.fidm.edu
E-mail: info@fidm.com
See listing under "Community and Junior Colleges"

FIDM/The Fashion Institute of Design & Merchandising
55 Stockton St, San Francisco CA 94108-5829
Director of Admissions
415-675-5200 or 800-422-3436 Fax: 415-296-7299
Website: www.fidm.edu
E-mail: info@fidm.com
See listing under "Community and Junior Colleges"

FRESNO CITY COLLEGE

1101 E University Ave, Fresno CA 93741-0002
Dayann Dietrich, Contact
559-442-8241 Fax: 559-237-4232
Website: www.fresnocitycollege.com
E-mail: fcc.admissions@scccd.com

Orange Coast College
PO Box 5005, Costa Mesa CA 92628-5005
Kristin Clark, Director of Admissions
714-432-5773 Fax: 714-432-5736
Website: www.orangecoastcollege.edu
E-mail: kclark@cccd.edu

TRAVEL UNIVERSITY INTERNATIONAL

3870 Murphy Canyon Rd Suite #310
San Diego CA 92123-4403
Nancy Chappie, President
858-292-9755 Fax: 858-292-8008
Website: www.traveluniversity.edu
E-mail: travel@traveluniversity.edu

CONNECTICUT

Middlesex Community College
100 Training Hill Rd, Middletown CT 06457-4889
Mensimah Shabazz, Director of Admissions
860-343-5800 Fax: 860-344-3055
Website: www.mxcc.commnet.edu
E-mail: mshabazz@mxcc.commnet.edu

University of New Haven
300 Boston Post Rd, West Haven CT 06516
Director of Undergraduate Admissions
203-932-7319 Fax: 203-931-6093
Website: www.newhaven.edu
E-mail: adminfo@newhaven.edu

DELAWARE

Goldey-Beacom College
4701 Limestone Rd, Wilmington DE 19808-1993
Stacey Schwartz, Assistant Director of Admissions
302-998-8814 Fax: 302-996-5408
Website: www.gbc.edu
E-mail: admissions@gbc.edu

Wesley College
120 N State St, Dover DE 19901-3876
302-736-2300 Fax: 302-736-2301
Website: www.wesley.edu

DISTRICT OF COLUMBIA

Southeastern University
501 I St SW, Washington DC 20024-2788
Sean Jamieson, Director of Admissions
202-478-8210 Fax: 202-488-8093
Website: www.seu.edu
E-mail: admissions@admin.seu.edu

FLORIDA

City College
2000 W Commercial Blvd, Fort Lauderdale FL 33309
Britt Carpenter, Director of Admissions
954-492-5353 Fax: 954-491-1965
Website: www.citycollege.edu
E-mail: bcarpenter@citycollege.edu

International Academy of Design & Technology
5104 Eisenhower Blvd, Tampa FL 33634-6313
Richard Costa, V.P. of Admissions and Marketing
813-880-8092 Fax: 813-881-0008
Website: www.academy.edu
E-mail: admissions@academy.edu

INTERNATIONAL ACADEMY OF DESIGN AND TECHNOLOGY

5959 Lake Ellenor Dr, Orlando FL 32809-4633
Dr. John Dietrich, VP of Admissions
877-753-0007 Fax: 407-251-0465
Website: www.iadt.edu
E-mail: info@iadt.edu

Northwood University
2600 N Military Trl, West Palm Beach FL 33409-2999
Jack Letvinchuk, Director of Admissions
800-458-8325 Fax: 561-640-3328
Website: www.northwood.edu
E-mail: fladmit@northwood.edu

Santa Fe Community College
3000 NW 83rd St, Gainesville FL 32606-6200
Jackson N. Sasser, President
352-395-5787 Fax: 352-395-4118
Website: www.sfcc.edu
E-mail: ouida.mcneil@sfcc.edu

SOUTHWEST FLORIDA COLLEGE

1685 Medical Ln, Fort Myers FL 33907-1157
866-SWFC-NOW or 239-939-4766 Fax: 239-936-4040
Website: www.swfc.edu
E-mail: studentinfo@swfc.edu

University of South Florida
4202 E Fowler Ave, Tampa FL 33620-6900
J. Robert Spatig, Director of Admissions
813-974-3350 Fax: 813-974-9689
Website: www.usf.edu
E-mail: admissions@admin.usf.edu

GEORGIA

DeKalb Technical College
495 N Indian Creek Dr, Clarkston GA 30021-2397
Terry Richardson, Director of Admissions
404-297-9522 Fax: 404-294-6496
Website: www.dekalbtech.edu
E-mail: richardt@dekalbtech.edu

Kennesaw State University
1000 Chastain Rd NW, Kennesaw GA 30144-5591
Timothy Mescon, Dean of College of Business
770-423-6425
Website: www.kennesaw.edu

IDAHO

University of Idaho
Moscow ID 83844-4253
Lloyd Scott, Director of New Student Services
208-885-6163 Fax: 208-885-4477
Website: www.uidaho.edu
E-mail: nss@uidaho.edu

ILLINOIS

AMERICAN INTERCONTINENTAL UNIVERSITY ONLINE

5550 Prairie Stone Parkway Suite 400
Hoffman Estates IL 60192
Admissions Department
877-701-3800
Website: www.aiuonline.edu
E-mail: info@aiuonline.edu

Aurora University
347 S Gladstone Ave, Aurora IL 60506-4892
Carol R. Dunn, Ed.D., Vice President for Enrollment
800-742-5281 Fax: 630-844-5535
Website: www.aurora.edu
E-mail: admission@aurora.edu

Columbia College Chicago
600 S Michigan Ave, Chicago IL 60605-1996
Murphy Monroe, Executive Director of Admissions
312-344-7130 Fax: 312-344-8024
Website: www.colum.edu
E-mail: admissions@colum.edu

Kaskaskia College
27210 College Rd, Centralia IL 62801-7878
Tyra Taylor, Dean of Enrollment Management and
Retention Services
618-545-3000 Fax: 618-532-1990
Website: www.kaskaskia.edu
E-mail: ttaylor@kaskaskia.edu

MacCormac College
29 E Madison St, Chicago IL 60602-4405
David F. Grassi, Admissions Counselor
312-922-1884 ext. 101 Fax: 312-922-4328
Website: www.maccormac.edu
E-mail: dgrassi@maccormac.edu

North Central College
30 N Brainard St, Naperville IL 60540-4690
Martha Stolze, Director of Admissions
630-637-5800 Fax: 630-637-5819
Website: www.northcentralcollege.edu
E-mail: admissions@noctrl.edu

Roosevelt University
430 S Michigan Ave, Chicago IL 60605
Gwen E. Kanelos, Asst. Vice President for Enrollment
Services
877-APPLY-RU Fax: 312-341-4216
Website: www.roosevelt.edu
E-mail: applyru@roosevelt.edu

INDIANA

St. Mary-of-the-Woods College
Saint Mary of the Woods IN 47876-1001
James P. Malley, Jr., Director of Admission
800-926-7692 Fax: 812-535-5010
Website: www.smwc.edu
E-mail: smwcadms@smwc.edu

University of Evansville
1800 Lincoln Ave, Evansville IN 47722-0001
Thomas E. Bear, V.P. of Enrollment Services
800-423-8633 Fax: 812-488-4076
Website: www.evansville.edu
E-mail: admission@evansville.edu

IOWA

AIB College of Business
2500 Fleur Dr, Des Moines IA 50321-1799
800-444-1921 Fax: 515-244-6773
Website: www.aib.edu
E-mail: admissions@aib.edu

Briar Cliff University
PO Box 2100, Sioux City IA 51104-0100
Sharisue Wilcoxon, VP for Enrollment Management
712-279-5200 Fax: 712-279-1632
Website: www.briarcliff.edu
E-mail: admissions@briarcliff.edu

Clarke College
1550 Clarke Dr, Dubuque IA 52001-3198
Andy Schroeder, Director of Admissions
800-383-2345 Fax: 563-584-8666
Website: www.clarke.edu
E-mail: andy.schroeder@clarke.edu

Graceland University
1 University Place, Lamoni IA 50140
Brian Shantz, Vice President for Enrollment and Dean of
Admissions
641-784-5196 Fax: 641-784-5480
Website: www.admissions.graceland.edu
E-mail: admissions@graceland.edu

Hamilton College
7009 Nordic Dr, Cedar Falls IA 50613
Tim Cole, Campus President
319-277-0220 Fax: 319-363-3812
Website: www.hamiltonia.edu
E-mail: ticole@hamiltoncf.com

Hamilton College
3165 Edgewood Pkwy SW, Cedar Rapids IA 52404
Susan Spivey, Campus President
319-363-0481 Fax: 319-363-3812
Website: www.hamiltonia.edu
E-mail: spiveys@hamiltonia.edu

Hamilton College
2570 4th St SW, Mason City IA 50401-4665
Joe Albers, Executive Director
641-423-2530 Fax: 641-423-7512
Website: www.hamiltonia.edu
E-mail: jalbers@hamiltonia.edu

Hamilton College
4655 121st St, Urbandale IA 50323-2311
Ed Rogan, Campus President
515-727-2100 Fax: 515-727-2115
Website: www.hamiltonia.edu
E-mail: erogan_dm@hamiltonia.edu

Mount Mercy College
1330 Elmhurst Dr NE, Cedar Rapids IA 52402-4797
Jim Krystofiak, Dean of Admission
800-248-4504 Fax: 319-363-5270
Website: www.mtmercy.edu
E-mail: admission@mtmercy.edu

Northwest Iowa Community College
603 W Park St, Sheldon IA 51201-1046
Lisa Story, Director of Enrollment Management
712-324-5061 Fax: 712-324-4136
Website: www.nwicc.edu
E-mail: lstory@nwicc.edu

KANSAS

COLBY COMMUNITY COLLEGE
1255 S Range Ave, Colby KS 67701-4099
Director of Admissions
888-634-9350 or 785-460-4690 Fax: 785-460-4691
Website: www.colbycc.edu
E-mail: bobbi@colbycc.edu

Independence Community College
PO Box 708, Independence KS 67301-0708
Dr. Terry Hetrick, President
800-842-6063 Fax: 620-331-5344
Website: www.indycc.edu
E-mail: admissions@indycc.edu

Newman University
3100 W McCormick St, Wichita KS 67213
Jann Reusser, Admissions Recruitment Coordinator
316-942-4291 ext. 2144 Fax: 316-942-4483
Website: www.newmanu.edu
E-mail: reusserj@newmanu.edu

KENTUCKY

Bluegrass Community and Technical College
Oswald Building
470 Cooper Drive, Lexington KY 40506-0235
Shelbie Hugle, Director of Admissions
859-246-6200 Fax: 859-246-4664
Website: www.bluegrass.kctcs.edu
E-mail: bctc_info@kctcs.edu

Morehead State University
Morehead KY 40351-1689
Dayna Seelig, Enrollment Services
800-585-6781 Fax: 606-783-5038
Website: www.moreheadstate.edu
E-mail: admissions@moreheadstate.edu

LOUISIANA

Our Lady of Holy Cross College
4123 Woodland Dr, New Orleans LA 70131-7399
Office of Enrollment Services
504-394-7744 Fax: 504-391-2421
Website: www.olhcc.edu

MAINE

HUSSON COLLEGE
One College Cir, Bangor ME 04401-2999
Jane Goodwin, Director of Admissions
800-4HU-SSON or 207-941-7100 Fax: 207-941-7935
Website: www.husson.edu
E-mail: admit@husson.edu
See listing under "Universities"

St. Joseph's College of Maine
278 Whites Bridge Rd, Standish ME 04084-5263
Vincent Kloskowski, Dean of Admissions
800-338-7057 Fax: 207-893-7862
Website: www.sjcme.edu
E-mail: admission@sjcme.edu

MARYLAND

Villa Julie College
1525 Greenspring Valley Rd
Stevenson MD 21153-0641
Mark Hergan, V.P. Enrollment Services
410-486-7001 Fax: 410-602-6600
Website: www.vjc.edu/admissions
E-mail: admissions@mail.vjc.edu

MASSACHUSETTS

Assumption College
500 Salisbury St, Worcester MA 01609-1294
Kathleen Murphy, Dean of Enrollment
508-767-7000 Fax: 508-799-4412
Website: www.assumption.edu
E-mail: admiss@assumption.edu

Bay Path College
588 Longmeadow St, Longmeadow MA 01106-2292
Lisa Casassa, Director of Admissions
413-565-1331 Fax: 413-565-1105
Website: www.baypath.edu
E-mail: lcasassa@baypath.edu

Bay State College
122 Commonwealth Ave, Boston MA 02116-2901
Craig Pfannenstiehl, President
617-217-9000 Fax: 617-536-1735

Becker College
Campuses in Worcester and Leicester, MA
61 Sever St, Worcester MA 01609-2165
Karen H. Schedin, Director of Admissions
508-791-9241 Fax: 508-890-1500
Website: www.becker.edu
E-mail: admissions@becker.edu
See listing under "Universities"

Boston University
121 Bay State Rd, Boston MA 02215
Kelly Walter, Executive Director of Admissions
617-353-2300 Fax: 617-353-9695
Website: web.bu.edu
E-mail: admissions@bu.edu

Emerson College
120 Boylston St, Boston MA 02116-4624
Sara S. Ramirez, Director of Undergraduate Admission
617-824-8600 Fax: 617-824-8609
Website: www.emerson.edu
E-mail: admission@emerson.edu

Newbury College
129 Fisher Ave, Brookline MA 02445-5796
Salvadore Liberto, Vice President of Enrollment
617-730-7000 Fax: 617-731-9618
Website: www.newbury.edu

University of Massachusetts Dartmouth
Old Westport Rd, North Dartmouth MA 02747-2300
Steven T. Briggs, Director of Admissions
508-999-8605 Fax: 508-999-8755
Website: explore.umassd.edu
E-mail: sbriggs@umassd.edu

MICHIGAN

Andrews University
Berrien Springs MI 49104-0001
Randall Graves, Director of Recruitment Services
800-253-2874 Fax: 269-471-2670
Website: www.connect.andrews.edu
E-mail: gravesr@andrews.edu

Delta College
University Center MI 48710-0001
Duff Zube, Director of Admissions
989-686-9093 Fax: 989-667-2202
Website: www.delta.edu
E-mail: admit@delta.edu

HILLSDALE COLLEGE
33 E College St, Hillsdale MI 49242-1298
Dr. Charles Davies, Director
517-607-2388 Fax: 517-607-2657
Website: www.hillsdale.edu
E-mail: charles.davies@hillsdale.edu

MACOMB COMMUNITY COLLEGE
44575 Garfield Rd, Clinton Township MI 48038-1139
Information Center
586-445-7999
Website: www.macomb.edu
E-mail: answer@macomb.edu

MACOMB COMMUNITY COLLEGE
14500 E 12 Mile Rd, Warren MI 48088-3896
Information Center
586-445-7999
Website: www.macomb.edu
E-mail: answer@macomb.edu

Northwood University
4000 Whiting Dr, Midland MI 48640
Daniel F. Toland, Dean of Admissions
800-457-7878 Fax: 989-837-4490
Website: www.northwood.edu
E-mail: miadmit@northwood.edu

University of Michigan-Dearborn
4901 Evergreen Rd, Dearborn MI 48128-1491
The Office of Admissions & Orientation
313-593-5100 Fax: 313-436-9167
Website: www.umd.umich.edu
E-mail: admissions@umd.umich.edu

MINNESOTA

Minnesota State Community & Technical College
900 Highway 34 E, Detroit Lakes MN 56501-2698
Dale Westley, Director of Admissions
800-492-4836 Fax: 218-846-3710
Website: www.minnesota.edu
E-mail: dale.westley@minnesota.edu

Minnesota State Community & Technical College
PO Box 566, Wadena MN 56482-0566
Paul Drange, Director of Admissions
800-247-2007 Fax: 218-631-7901
Website: www.minnesota.edu
E-mail: paul.drange@minnesota.edu

Minnesota State Community and Technical College
1900 28th Ave S, Moorhead MN 56560-4899
Laurie McKeever, Director of Admissions
800-426-5603 Fax: 218-299-6584
Website: www.minnesota.edu
E-mail: laurie.mckeever@minnesota.edu

National American University
1550 W Highway 36, Roseville MN 55113
Matthew Mottl, Director of Admissions
651-644-1265 Fax: 651-644-0690
Website: www.national.edu
E-mail: mmottl@national.edu

Northland Community & Technical College
Highway 1 E, Thief River Falls MN 56701
Eugene Klinke, Director of Enrollment Management
800-959-6282 or 218-681-0862 Fax: 218-681-0774
Website: www.northlandcollege.edu
E-mail: eugene.klinke@northlandcollege.edu

Northland Community and Technical College
2022 Central Ave NE
East Grand Forks MN 56721-2702
Kit Brenan, Sales & Marketing Instructor
800-451-3441 Fax: 218-773-4502
Website: www.northlandcollege.edu
E-mail: admissions@northlandcollege.edu

Ridgewater College-Willmar Campus
PO Box 1097, Willmar MN 56201-1097
Sally Kerfeld, Director of Admissions
800-722-1151 Fax: 320-231-7677
Website: www.ridgewater.edu
E-mail: skerfeld@ridgewater.edu

St. Cloud Technical College
1540 Northway Dr, Saint Cloud MN 56303-1240
Jodi Elness, Director of Enrollment Management
800-222-1009 Fax: 320-308-5981
Website: www.sctc.edu
E-mail: jelness@sctc.edu

MISSOURI

East Central College
1964 Prairie Dell Rd, Union MO 63084
Karen Wieda, Registrar
636-583-5195 ext. 2220 Fax: 636-583-1897
Website: www.eastcentral.edu
E-mail: wiedaks@eastcentral.edu

Lindenwood University
209 S Kingshighway St
Saint Charles MO 63301-1695
Sheryl Guffey, Director of Admissions
636-949-2000 Fax: 636-949-4989
Website: www.lindenwood.edu

Stephens College
PO Box 2121, Columbia MO 65215-0001
David Adams, Dean of Enrollment Management
573-442-2211 Fax: 573-876-7237
Website: www.stephens.edu
E-mail: dadams@stephens.edu

Truman State University
100 E Normal, Kirksville MO 63501
Office of Admission
660-785-4000 Fax: 660-785-4181
Website: admissions.truman.edu
E-mail: admissions@truman.edu

Webster University
470 E Lockwood Ave, Saint Louis MO 63119-3194
Dr. Benjamin Akande, Dean School of Business and
Management
314-961-2660 ext. 5950 Fax: 314-968-7077
Website: www.webster.edu
E-mail: mtaylor@webster.edu
See listing under "Universities"

William Woods University
1 University Ave, Fulton MO 65251-1098
Jimmy Clay, Director of Admissions
573-642-2251 Fax: 573-592-1146
Website: www.williamwoods.edu
E-mail: admissions@williamwoods.edu
See listing under "Universities"

NEBRASKA

Peru State College
PO Box 10, Peru NE 68421-0010
Office of Admissions
800-742-4412 Fax: 402-872-2296
Website: www.peru.edu
E-mail: admissions@oakmail.peru.edu

University of Nebraska at Kearney
905 W 25th St, Kearney NE 68849-0001
Dusty Newton, Director of Admissions
800-KEARNEY Fax: 308-865-8987
Website: www.unk.edu
E-mail: admissionsug@unk.edu

NEVADA

Career College of Northern Nevada
1195-A Corporate Blvd, Reno NV 89502-2331
Nathan Clark, Director
775-856-2266 Fax: 775-856-0935
Website: www.ccnn.edu
E-mail: lgoldhammer@ccnn4u.com
See listing under "Career Schools"

NEW HAMPSHIRE

Southern New Hampshire University
2500 N River Rd, Hooksett NH 03106-1045
Steve Soba, Director of Admissions
603-645-9611 Fax: 603-645-9693
Website: www.snhu.edu
E-mail: s.soba@snhu.edu

NEW JERSEY

Bergen Community College
400 Paramus Rd, Paramus NJ 07652
Julian Gomez, Asst. Director of Admissions
201-447-7100 Fax: 201-444-7036
Website: www.bergen.edu
E-mail: jgomez@bergen.edu

New Jersey City University
2039 John F Kennedy Blvd
Jersey City NJ 07305-1588
Carmen Panlilio, Asst. V.P. for Admissions and
Financial Aid
201-200-3234 Fax: 201-200-2044
Website: www.njcu.edu
E-mail: admissions@njcu.edu

Ramapo College of New Jersey
505 Ramapo Valley Rd, Mahwah NJ 07430-1623
Director of Admissions
201-684-7300 or 201-684-7301 Fax: 201-684-7964
Website: www.ramapo.edu
E-mail: admissions@ramapo.edu

NEW YORK

Broome Community College
907 Upper Front St, Binghamton NY 13905
Anthony S. Fiorelli, Director of Admissions
607-778-5001 Fax: 607-778-5442
Website: www.sunybroome.edu
E-mail: fiorelli_a@sunybroome.edu

LABORATORY INSTITUTE OF MERCHANDISING

12 E 53rd St, New York NY 10022-5268
Kristina Gibson, Director of Admissions
800-677-1323 or 212-752-1530 Fax: 212-750-3432
Website: www.limcollege.edu
E-mail: admissions@limcollege.edu
See listing under "Universities"

Long Island University-C. W. Post Campus
720 Northern Blvd, Brookville NY 11548-1300
Joanne Graziano, Executive Director of Admissions
516-299-2900 Fax: 516-299-2137
Website: www.liu.edu/cwpost
E-mail: enroll@cwpost.liu.edu

Monroe College
2501 Jerome Ave, Bronx NY 10468-4305
Evan Jerome, Director of Admissions
718-933-6700 Fax: 718-364-3552
Website: www.monroecollege.edu
E-mail: ejerome@monroecollege.edu

Roberts Wesleyan College
2301 Westside Dr, Rochester NY 14624-1997
Office of Admissions
585-594-6400 Fax: 585-594-6371
Website: www.roberts.edu
E-mail: admissions@roberts.edu

SUNY College of Technology
Alfred NY 14802
Deborah J. Goodrich, Director of Admissions
800-4AL-FRED Fax: 607-587-4299
Website: www.alfredstate.edu
E-mail: admissions@alfredstate.edu

SUNY College of Technology
2 Main St, Delhi NY 13753-1110
Robert W. Mazzei, Director of Admissions
800-96-DELHI Fax: 607-746-4104
Website: www.delhi.edu
E-mail: enroll@delhi.edu

SUNY Orange County Community College
115 South St, Middletown NY 10940-6437
Margot St. Lawrence, Director of Admissions
845-341-4030 Fax: 845-342-8662
Website: www.sunyorange.edu
E-mail: apply@sunyorange.edu
See listing under "Community and Junior Colleges"

Taylor Business Institute
23 W 17th St 7th Floor, New York NY 10011-5501
800-959-9999 Fax: 212-229-2187
Website: www.tbiglobal.com
E-mail: admissions@tbiglobal.com

Utica School of Commerce
201 Bleecker St, Utica NY 13501-2280
Cindy Delaney, Director of Admissions
315-733-2307 Fax: 315-733-9281
Website: www.uscny.edu
E-mail: admissions@uscny.edu

NORTH CAROLINA

Mars Hill College
Mars Hill NC 28754
Chad Holt, Dean of Enrollment
866-MHC-4-YOU Fax: 828-689-1473
Website: www.mhc.edu
E-mail: cholt@mhc.edu

Meredith College
3800 Hillsborough St, Raleigh NC 27607-5298
Heidi L. Fletcher, Director of Admissions
919-760-8581 Fax: 919-760-2348
Website: www.meredith.edu
E-mail: admissions@meredith.edu
See listing under "Women's Colleges"

North Carolina A&T State University
1601 E Market St, Greensboro NC 27411
Lee Young, AVC Enrollment
336-334-7500 Fax: 336-334-7478
Website: www.ncat.edu
E-mail: uadmit@ncat.edu

NORTH DAKOTA

Dickinson State University
Dickinson ND 58601-4896
Steve Glasser, Director of Student Recruitment
800-279-4295 Fax: 701-483-2409
Website: www.dickinsonstate.edu
E-mail: dsu.hawks@dickinsonstate.edu

Williston State College
PO Box 1326, Williston ND 58802-1326
Penny Powell, Director Enrollment Services
701-774-4200 Fax: 701-774-4544
Website: www.wsc.nodak.edu
E-mail: penny.soiseth@wsc.nodak.edu

OHIO

Brown Mackie College - Cincinnati
1011 Glendale Milford Rd, Cincinnati OH 45215-1107
Robin Krout, President
513-771-2424 Fax: 513-771-3413
Website: www.brownmackie.edu
E-mail: rkrout@brownmackie.edu

Davis College
4747 Monroe St, Toledo OH 43623-4389
Dana Stern, Admissions Director
419-473-2700 Fax: 419-473-2472
Website: www.daviscollege.edu
E-mail: learn@daviscollege.edu

Mount Vernon Nazarene University
800 Martinsburg Rd, Mount Vernon OH 43050-9509
Timothy Eades, Director of Admissions
866-462-6868 Fax: 740-393-0511
Website: www.gotomvnu.com
E-mail: admissions@mvnu.edu
See listing under "Universities"

The Ohio State University
Fisher College of Business, Marketing & Logistics
Schoenbaum Hall, 210 W Woodruff Ave
Columbus OH 43210
614-292-2715 Fax: 614-292-5735
Website: fisher.osu.edu
E-mail: fisherundergrad@cob.osu.edu

Ohio University
Chillicothe Campus
PO Box 629, Chillicothe OH 45601
Student Services
740-774-7200 Fax: 740-774-7295
Website: www.ohiou.edu/chillicothe/

Owens Community College
300 Davis St, Findlay OH 45840-3631
William J. Ivoska PhD., Vice President of Student Services
567-429-3500 Fax: 567-423-0246
Website: www.owens.edu
E-mail: admissions@owens.edu

Owens Community College
PO Box 10000, Toledo OH 43699-1947
William J. Ivoska, Ph.D, Vice President of Student Services
567-661-7000 Fax: 567-661-7607
Website: www.owens.edu
E-mail: admissions@owens.edu

University of Dayton
300 College Park, Dayton OH 45469-1300
Robert F. Durkle, Director of Admissions
800-837-7433 Fax: 937-229-4729
Website: admission.udayton.edu
E-mail: admission@udayton.edu

Ursuline College
2550 Lander Rd, Cleveland OH 44124-4398
Sarah E. Sundermeier, Director of Admissions
888-URSULINE Toll Free Fax: 440-684-6138
Website: www.admission.ursuline.edu
E-mail: admission@ursuline.edu

OKLAHOMA

Oklahoma State University
Stillwater OK 74078
Joshua Wiener, Department Head
405-744-5192
Website: www.okstate.edu
E-mail: josh.wiener@okstate.edu

OREGON

Cascade College
9101 E Burnside St, Portland OR 97216-1599
800-550-7678 Fax: 503-257-1222
Website: www.cascade.edu
E-mail: admissions@cascade.edu

Concordia University
2811 NE Holman St, Portland OR 97211-6099
Bobi Swan, Director of Admissions
503-288-9371 Fax: 503-280-8531
Website: www.cu-portland.edu
E-mail: cu-admissions@cu-portland.edu

PENNSYLVANIA

ART INSTITUTE OF PITTSBURGH

420 Boulevard Of The Allies, Pittsburgh PA 15219
Newton I. Myvett, VP/Director of Admissions
800-275-2470 Fax: 412-263-6667
Website: www.aip.aii.edu
E-mail: pahughes@aii.edu
See listing under "Universities"

Bradford School
125 W Station Square Dr, Pittsburgh PA 15219
Director of Admissions
412-391-6710 Fax: 412-471-6714
Website: www.bradfordpittsburgh.edu

Central Pennsylvania College
College Hill & Valley Rds, Summerdale PA 17093
Katie Bogovic, Admissions Director
800-759-2727 Fax: 717-728-2505
Website: www.centralpenn.edu
E-mail: katie.bogovic@centralpenn.edu

DeSales University
2755 Station Ave, Center Valley PA 18034-9565
610-282-1100 Fax: 610-282-2342
Website: www.desales.edu

Erie Business Center
246 W 9th St, Erie PA 16501-1392
Donna Perino, Director
814-456-7504 Fax: 814-456-6015
Website: www.eriebc.edu
E-mail: perinod@eriebc.edu

Gannon University
109 University Sq, Erie PA 16541-0001
Christopher Tremblay, Director of Admissions
800-GANNON-U Fax: 814-871-5803
Website: www.gannon.edu
E-mail: admissions@gannon.edu

Juniata College
1700 Moore St, Huntingdon PA 16652-2196
Michelle Bartol, Dean of Enrollment
877-JUNIATA Fax: 814-641-3100
Website: www.juniata.edu
E-mail: admissions@juniata.edu

King's College
133 N River St, Wilkes Barre PA 18711-0801
Michelle Lawrence-Schmude, Director of Admission
570-208-5900 Fax: 570-208-5971
Website: www.kings.edu
E-mail: admissions@kings.edu

Lehigh Valley College
2809 E Saucon Valley Rd
Center Valley PA 18034-8447
Joshua Padron, Vice President of Marketing and Admissions
800-227-9109 Fax: 610-791-7810
Website: www.lehighvalley.edu
E-mail: joshua.padron@lehighvalley.edu

MOUNT ALOYSIUS COLLEGE

7373 Admiral Peary Hwy, Cresson PA 16630-1999
Frank C. Crouse Jr., Vice President for Enrollment Management
814-886-6383 or 888-823-2220 Fax: 814-886-6441
Website: www.mtaloy.edu
E-mail: admissions@mtaloy.edu

Oakbridge Academy of Arts
1250 Greensburg Rd, Lower Burrell PA 15068
Admissions Department
724-335-5336
Website: www.oaa.edu
E-mail: tjpomatto@nbi.edu

York Technical Institute
1405 Williams Rd, York PA 17402
Cathi Killingsworth Bost, Vice President
800-227-9675 or 717-757-1100 Fax: 717-757-4964
Website: www.yti.edu
E-mail: info@yti.edu
See listing under "Career Schools"

SOUTH CAROLINA

Forrest Junior College
601 E River St, Anderson SC 29624-2405
Dr. Julia R. Barnes, President
864-225-7653 Fax: 864-261-7471
Website: www.forrestcollege.edu
E-mail: info@forrestcollege.edu
See listing under "Community and Junior Colleges"

North Greenville University
PO Box 1892, Tigerville SC 29688-1892
Website: www.ngc.edu
See listing under "Universities"

University of South Carolina - Upstate
800 University Way, Spartanburg SC 29303-4932
Donette Stewart, Assistant VC for Enrollment Services
864-503-5246 Fax: 864-503-5727
Website: www.uscupstate.edu
E-mail: dstewart@uscupstate.edu
See listing under "Universities"

SOUTH DAKOTA

NATIONAL AMERICAN UNIVERSITY

321 Kansas City St, Rapid City SD 57701-3692
Angela G. Beck, Director of Enrollment Management
605-394-4800 Fax: 605-394-4871
Website: www.national.edu/rc/index.html
E-mail: rcadmissions@national.edu

National American University
2801 S Kiwanis Ave Ste 100
Sioux Falls SD 57105-4293
605-334-5430 Fax: 605-334-1575
Website: www.national.edu

Western Dakota Technical Institute
800 Mickelson Dr, Rapid City SD 57703-4018
Janell Oberlander, Manager of Student Services
605-394-4034 or 800-544-8765 Fax: 605-394-1789
Website: www.westerndakotatech.org
E-mail: admissions@wdti.tec.sd.us
See listing under "Career Schools"

TENNESSEE

Draughons Junior College
PO Box 17386, Nashville TN 37217-0386
615-361-7555 Fax: 615-367-2736
Website: www.draughons.edu

Lipscomb University
3901 Granny White Pike, Nashville TN 37204-3951
Ricky Holaway, Director of Admissions
800-333-4358 ext. 1776 Fax: 615-269-1804
Website: www.lipscomb.edu
E-mail: admissions@lipscomb.edu

TEXAS

Angelo State University
ASU Station 11014, San Angelo TX 76909
Bonnie Stennett, Coordinator of Recruiting
800-946-8627 Fax: 325-942-2078
Website: www.angelo.edu
E-mail: admissions@angelo.edu

Galveston College
4015 Avenue Q, Galveston TX 77550-7496
Brian Lowery, Registrar
409-763-6551 Fax: 409-944-1501
Website: www.gc.edu
E-mail: blowery@gc.edu

North Central Texas College
1525 W California St, Gainesville TX 76240-4636
Michelle Winters, Registrar
940-668-3315 Fax: 940-665-7075
Website: www.nctc.edu
E-mail: mwinters@nctc.edu

Northwood University
1114 W FM 1382, Cedar Hill TX 75104-1204
Sylvia Correa, Director of Admissions
800-927-WOOD Fax: 972-291-3824
Website: www.northwood.edu
E-mail: ray@northwood.edu

Temple College
2600 S 1st St, Temple TX 76504-7435
Angela Balch, Director of Admissions & Records
254-298-8300 Fax: 254-298-8288
Website: www.templejc.edu
E-mail: ruth.bridges@templejc.edu

University of Houston
122 E Cullen Bldg, Houston TX 77204-2023
Office of Admission
713-743-9595
Website: www.uh.edu
E-mail: admissions@uh.edu

University of St. Thomas
3800 Montrose Blvd, Houston TX 77006-4626
Eduardo Prieto, Director of Admissions
713-522-7911 Fax: 713-525-3558
Website: www.stthom.edu
E-mail: prietoe@stthom.edu

University of Texas at Arlington
Box 19111, Arlington TX 76019-0111
Hans Gatterdam, Director of Admission
817-272-6287 Fax: 817-272-3435
Website: www.uta.edu
E-mail: admissions@uta.edu

UTAH

Stevens Henager College
PO Box 9428, Ogden UT 84409-0428
Cindy Williams, Director of Admissions
801-394-7791 Fax: 801-621-0866
Website: www.stevenshenager.edu
E-mail: shcogden@yahoo.com

VIRGINIA

Radford University
PO Box 6903, Radford VA 24142
David W. Kraus, Director of Admissions
800-890-4265 Fax: 540-831-5038
Website: www.radford.edu
E-mail: ruadmiss@radford.edu

WASHINGTON

Everett Community College
2000 Tower St, Everett WA 98201
Christine Kerlin, Associate Dean
425-388-9100 Fax: 425-388-9173
Website: www.everettcc.edu
E-mail: ckerlin@everettcc.edu

Gonzaga University
502 E Boone Ave, Spokane WA 99258-0102
Julie McCulloh, Dean of Admission
800-322-2584 or 509-323-6572 Fax: 509-323-5780
Website: www.gonzaga.edu
E-mail: mcculloh@gu.gonzaga.edu

Walla Walla Community College
500 Tausick Way, Walla Walla WA 99362-9270
Dan Biagi, Director
509-527-4283 or 877-992-9922 Fax: 509-527-4480
Website: www.wwcc.edu
E-mail: dan.biagi@wwcc.edu
See listing under "Community and Junior Colleges"

WEST VIRGINIA

Concord University
Athens WV 24712
Michael Curry, Vice President of Financial Aid &
Admissions
888-384-5249 Fax: 304-384-3218
Website: www.concord.edu
E-mail: admissions@concord.edu

Davis & Elkins College
100 Campus Dr, Elkins WV 26241-3996
Renee Heckel, Director of Enrollment Management
800-624-3157 Fax: 304-637-1800
Website: www.davisandelkins.edu
E-mail: admiss@davisandelkins.edu

Fairmont State University
1201 Locust Ave, Fairmont WV 26554-2470
Steve Leadman, Director of Admissions
304-367-4892 or 800-641-5678 Fax: 304-367-4789
Website: www.fairmontstate.edu
E-mail: admit@fairmontstate.edu

West Virginia Wesleyan College
59 College Ave, Buckhannon WV 26201-2699
Hobert N. Skinner II, Director of Admission
800-722-9933 Fax: 304-473-8108
Website: www.wvwc.edu
E-mail: admission@wvwc.edu

WISCONSIN

Blackhawk Technical College
PO Box 5009, Janesville WI 53547-5009
Gregg Bosak, Administration, Community Information
608-757-7769 Fax: 608-757-7740
Website: www.blackhawk.edu
E-mail: gbosak@blackhawk.edu

Wisconsin Indianhead Technical College
505 Pine Ridge Dr, Shell Lake WI 54871
Laura Urban, Dean
800-243-9482 Fax: 715-468-2819
Website: www.witc.edu
E-mail: mcrandal@witc.edu

WYOMING

Laramie County Community College
1400 E College Dr, Cheyenne WY 82007-3204
Jenny Hargett, Director of Admissions
307-778-5222 Fax: 307-778-1350
Website: www.lccc.wy.edu
E-mail: learnmore@lccc.wy.edu

University of Wyoming
Admissions Office
Dept 3435, Laramie WY 82071-3435
Aaron Appelhans, Contact
800-342-5996 Fax: 307-766-4042
Website: www.uwyo.edu
E-mail: why-wyo@uwyo.edu

GUAM

Guam Community College
PO Box 23069, G.M.F. GU 96921-0307
Virginia Charfauros Tudela, Ph.D., Registrar
671-735-5531 Fax: 671-734-5238
Website: www.guamcc.edu
E-mail: Webmaster@guamcc.edu

PUERTO RICO

MBTI Business Training Institute
1256 Ave Ponce de Leon, Santurce PR 00907-3965
Miguel A. Fernandez, Contact
787-723-9403 Fax: 787-723-9447
Website: www.mbti.com
E-mail: hdavila@mbti.com

MASTER OF BUSINESS ADMINISTRATION

ALABAMA

Alabama A & M University
PO Box 908, Normal AL 35762
Antonio Boyle, Director of Admissions
256-372-5245 Fax: 256-372-5249
Website: www.aamu.edu
E-mail: aboyle@aamu.edu

ALASKA

University of Alaska Anchorage
PO Box 141629, Anchorage AK 99514-1629
Cecile Mitchell, Director of Enrollment Services
907-786-1480 Fax: 907-786-4888
Website: www.uaa.alaska.edu/
E-mail: enroll@uaa.alaska.edu

University of Alaska Southeast
11120 Glacier Hwy, Juneau AK 99801-8625
Paul Kraft, Dean of Students/Enrollment Management
907-796-6000 Fax: 907-796-6005
Website: www.uas.alaska.edu
E-mail: paul.kraft@uas.alaska.edu

ARIZONA

Thunderbird, The Garvin School of International
Management
15249 N 59th Ave, Glendale AZ 85306-3236
Judy Johnson, Associate VP of Admissions & Financial
Aid
800-848-9084 or 602-978-7100 Fax: 602-439-5432
Website: www.thunderbird.edu
E-mail: johnsonj@thunderbird.edu

University of Arizona
Tucson AZ 85721-0040
Paul Kohn, Director of Admissions
520-621-3237 Fax: 520-621-9799
Website: www.admissions.arizona.edu or
www.arizona.edu

CALIFORNIA

CALIFORNIA COAST UNIVERSITY
700 N Main St, Santa Ana CA 92701
Admissions Office: 888-CCU-UNIV or 714-547-9625
Fax: 714-547-5777
Dr. Thomas Neal, President
Dr. Cynthia Teeple, Academic Vice President
Website: www.calcoast.edu
E-mail: info@calcoast.edu
Established 1973. Proprietary. Coed. Accreditation:
California Coast University holds accreditation through
the Accrediting Commission of the Distance Education
and Training Council (DETC). The DETC is an educa-
tional association located in Washington, D.C. Founded
in 1926, it is the standard setting agency for distance

education institutions. Approval: Bureau for Private Post-
secondary and Vocational Education - State of California,
charter member California Association of State Approved
Colleges & Universities, member Association for Adult &
Continuing Education, member The Alliance for Private
Post Secondary Academic Institutions.
Tuition: $2,805-$12,070. California Coast University
has selected the SLM Corporation, commonly known as
Sallie Mae, to help the university provide financing for its
students. Sallie Mae is the nation's leading provider of
education funding. Sallie Mae also allows students to
borrow additional loan amounts to cover additional expenses, such as textbooks, equipment, or living expenses.
Enrollment: 30,000. California Coast University is
approved by the California State Approving Agency to
enroll veterans or other eligible persons under Title 38,
U.S. Code. California Coast University holds a Memorandum of Understanding with Defense Activity for Non-
Traditional Education Support (DANTES) as an external
degree provider.
A private college offering off-campus independent
study programs in the traditional areas of business administration, management, psychology, education. Admissions: enroll year round, requires official transcripts,
letters of recommendation, detailed curriculum vita or occupational history.
Process: evaluation of prior academic work followed
by analysis of occupational history, including participation in workshops, seminars, training programs, specialized projects for credit. Credit is demonstrated by
accelerated learning guides or study guides.
Residency: All course work may be completed off
campus, utilizing correspondence methods. Interest free
loans available to students.

Chapman University
One University Drive, Orange CA 92866-1099
Michael Drummy, Assistant Vice President for
Enrollment
Services and Chief Admission Officer
714-997-6411 or 888-CUAPPLY Fax: 714-997-6713
Website: www.chapman.edu
E-mail: admit@chapman.edu

Concordia University
1530 Concordia, Irvine CA 92612-3203
Lori McDonald, Executive Director of Enrollment
Services
800-229-1200 or 949-854-8002 Fax: 949-854-6894
Website: www.cui.edu
E-mail: admission@cui.edu

ITT Technical Institute
12669 Encinitas Ave, Sylmar CA 91342-3664
Kelly Christensen, Director of Admissions
818-364-5151 Fax: 818-364-5150
Website: www.itt-tech.edu
E-mail: kchristensen@itt-tech.edu

Monterey Institute of International Studies
460 Pierce St, Monterey CA 93940
Admissions Office
831-647-4100 Fax: 831-647-6405
Website: www.miis.edu
E-mail: admit@miis.edu

CONNECTICUT

University of New Haven
300 Boston Post Rd, West Haven CT 06516
Director of Graduate Admissions
203-932-7133 Fax: 203-932-7137
Website: www.newhaven.edu
E-mail: gradinfo@newhaven.edu

DELAWARE

Goldey-Beacom College
4701 Limestone Rd, Wilmington DE 19808-1993
Stacey Schwartz, Assistant Director of Admissions
302-998-8814 Fax: 302-996-5408
Website: www.gbc.edu
E-mail: admissions@gbc.edu

Wesley College
120 N State St, Dover DE 19901-3876
302-736-2300 Fax: 302-736-2301
Website: www.wesley.edu

FLORIDA

EVERGLADES UNIVERSITY (MAIN CAMPUS)
5002 T-Rex Ave Suite 100, Boca Raton FL 33431
Kristi Mollis, President
888-772-6077 Fax: 561-912-1191
Website: www.evergladesuniversity.edu
E-mail: admissions-boca@evergladesuniversity.edu
See listing under "Universities"

EVERGLADES UNIVERSITY
Orlando Campus (Branch Campus)
5600 Lake Underhill Rd Suite 200, Orlando FL 32807
Shirley Long, Vice President
866-289-1078 Fax: 407-482-9801
Website: www.evergladesuniversity.edu
E-mail: admissions-orl@evergladesuniversity.edu
See listing under "Universities"

EVERGLADES UNIVERSITY
Sarasota Campus (Branch Campus)
6001 Lake Osprey Dr, Sarasota FL 34240
Brad Brewer, Vice President
866-907-2262 Fax: 941-907-6634
Website: www.evergladesuniversity.edu
E-mail: admissions-sar@evergladesuniversity.edu
See listing under "Universities"

Florida Metropolitan University
Orlando South
9200 Southpark Center Loop, Orlando FL 32819
Annette Cloin, Contact
407-851-2525 Fax: 407-851-1477
Website: www.fmu.edu
E-mail: acloin@cci.edu

FLORIDA METROPOLITAN UNIVERSITY
Pinellas Campus
2471 N McMullen Booth Rd
Clearwater FL 33759-1359
Sandra Williams, Director of Admissions
800-353-3687 or 727-725-2688 Fax: 727-725-3827
Website: www.fmu.edu
E-mail: sawilliams@cci.edu

INTERNATIONAL COLLEGE
4501 Colonial Blvd, Fort Myers FL 33966
Rita Lampus, Vice President of Enrollment
Management
800-466-0019 or 239-482-0019 Fax: 239-938-7891
Website: www.internationalcollege.edu
E-mail: cmorrison@internationalcollege.edu

INTERNATIONAL COLLEGE
2655 Northbrooke Dr, Naples FL 34119
Rita Lampus, Vice President of Enrollment
Management
800-466-8017 or 239-513-1122 Fax: 239-598-6254
Website: www.internationalcollege.edu
E-mail: admit@internationalcollege.edu
See listing under "Universities"

Lynn University
3601 N Military Trl, Boca Raton FL 33431-5598
Brett Ormandy, Director of Admissions
561-237-7900 Fax: 561-237-7100
Website: www.lynn.edu
E-mail: admission@lynn.edu

St. Thomas University
16401 NW 37th Ave, Miami Gardens FL 33054
Maria Espino, Graduate Admissions
800-367-9010 or 305-628-6546 Fax: 305-628-6591
Website: www.stu.edu
E-mail: signup@stu.edu

University of South Florida
4202 E Fowler Ave, Tampa FL 33620-6900
J. Robert Spatig, Director of Admissions
813-974-3350 Fax: 813-974-9689
Website: www.usf.edu
E-mail: admissions@admin.usf.edu

GEORGIA

Kennesaw State University
1000 Chastain Rd NW, Kennesaw GA 30144-5591
Timothy Mescon, Dean of College of Business
770-423-6425
Website: www.kennesaw.edu

ILLINOIS

AMERICAN INTERCONTINENTAL UNIVERSITY ONLINE
5550 Prairie Stone Parkway Suite 400
Hoffman Estates IL 60192
Admissions Department
877-701-3800
Website: www.aiuonline.edu
E-mail: info@aiuonline.edu

Aurora University
347 S Gladstone Ave, Aurora IL 60506-4892
Carol R. Dunn, Ed.D., Vice President for Enrollment
800-742-5281 Fax: 630-844-5535
Website: www.aurora.edu
E-mail: admission@aurora.edu

Benedictine University
5700 College Rd, Lisle IL 60532-0900
630-829-6300 or 888-829-6363 Fax: 630-829-6301
Website: www.ben.edu
E-mail: admissions@ben.edu
See listing under "Universities"

North Central College
30 N Brainard St, Naperville IL 60540-4690
Martha Stolze, Director of Admissions
630-637-5800 Fax: 630-637-5819
Website: www.northcentralcollege.edu
E-mail: admissions@noctrl.edu

Roosevelt University
430 S Michigan Ave, Chicago IL 60605
Gwen E. Kanelos, Asst. Vice President for Enrollment
Services
877-APPLY-RU Fax: 312-341-4216
Website: www.roosevelt.edu
E-mail: applyru@roosevelt.edu

IOWA

Clarke College
1550 Clarke Dr, Dubuque IA 52001-3198
Andy Schroeder, Director of Admissions
800-383-2345 Fax: 563-584-8666
Website: www.clarke.edu
E-mail: andy.schroeder@clarke.edu

KANSAS

Newman University
3100 W McCormick St, Wichita KS 67213
Jann Reusser, Admissions Recruitment Coordinator
316-942-4291 ext. 2144 Fax: 316-942-4483
Website: www.newmanu.edu
E-mail: reusserj@newmanu.edu

MASSACHUSETTS

Anna Maria College
50 Sunset Ln, Paxton MA 01612
Julie A. Mitchell, Director of Admissions
508-849-3360 Fax: 508-849-3362
Website: www.annamaria.edu
E-mail: admissions@annamaria.edu

University of Massachusetts Dartmouth
Old Westport Rd, North Dartmouth MA 02747-2300
Steven T. Briggs, Director of Admissions
508-999-8605 Fax: 508-999-8755
Website: explore.umassd.edu
E-mail: sbriggs@umassd.edu

MICHIGAN

Andrews University
Berrien Springs MI 49104-0001
Randall Graves, Director of Recruitment Services
800-253-2874 Fax: 269-471-2670
Website: www.connect.andrews.edu
E-mail: gravesr@andrews.edu

Grand Valley State University
1 Campus Dr, Allendale MI 49401-9403
Jodi Chycinski, Director of Admissions
616-331-6611 Fax: 616-331-2000
Website: www.gvsu.edu
E-mail: go2gvsu@gvsu.edu

Lawrence Technological University
21000 W 10 Mile Rd, Southfield MI 48075-1058
Jane Rohrback, Director of Admissions
800-225-5588 Fax: 248-204-2228
Website: www.ltu.edu
E-mail: admissions@ltu.edu
See listing under "Universities"

University of Michigan-Dearborn
4901 Evergreen Rd, Dearborn MI 48128-1491
The Office of Admissions & Orientation
313-593-5100 Fax: 313-436-9167
Website: www.umd.umich.edu
E-mail: admissions@umd.umich.edu

MINNESOTA

Globe College
7166 10th St N, Oakdale MN 55128
Mike Hughes, Campus Director
651-730-5100 Fax: 651-730-5151
Website: www.globecollege.edu
E-mail: admissions@globecollege.edu

MISSOURI

Columbia College
1001 Rogers St, Columbia MO 65216-0001
Regina Morin, Director of Admissions
573-875-7352 Fax: 573-875-7506
Website: www.ccis.edu
E-mail: admissions@ccis.edu

Stephens College
PO Box 2121, Columbia MO 65215-0001
David Adams, Dean of Enrollment Management
573-442-2211 Fax: 573-876-7237
Website: www.stephens.edu
E-mail: dadams@stephens.edu

University of Missouri
1 University Blvd, Saint Louis MO 63121-4499
Dr. Thomas Eyssell, Director-Graduate Studies
314-516-5885 Fax: 314-516-6420
Website: www.umsl.edu
E-mail: gradadm@umsl.edu

Webster University
470 E Lockwood Ave, Saint Louis MO 63119-3194
Dr. Benjamin Akande, Dean School of Business and
Management
314-961-2660 ext. 5950 Fax: 314-968-7077
Website: www.webster.edu
E-mail: mtaylor@webster.edu
See listing under "Universities"

William Woods University
1 University Ave, Fulton MO 65251-1098
Jimmy Clay, Director of Admissions
573-642-2251 Fax: 573-592-1146
Website: www.williamwoods.edu
E-mail: admissions@williamwoods.edu
See listing under "Universities"

NEW HAMPSHIRE

Southern New Hampshire University
2500 N River Rd, Hooksett NH 03106-1045
Steve Soba, Director of Admissions
603-645-9611 Fax: 603-645-9693
Website: www.snhu.edu
E-mail: s.soba@snhu.edu

NEW YORK

College of Saint Rose
432 Western Ave, Albany NY 12203-1419
Maryelizabeth Amico, Asst V.P. for Undergraduate
Admissions
518-454-5150 Fax: 518-454-2013
Website: www.strose.edu
E-mail: admit@strose.edu

Long Island University-C. W. Post Campus
720 Northern Blvd, Brookville NY 11548-1300
Beth Carson, Director of Graduate Admissions
516-299-2900 Fax: 516-299-2137
Website: www.liu.edu/cwpost
E-mail: enroll@cwpost.liu.edu

Monroe College
2501 Jerome Ave, Bronx NY 10468-4305
Evan Jerome, Director of Admissions
718-933-6700 Fax: 718-364-3552
Website: www.monroecollege.edu
E-mail: ejerome@monroecollege.edu

St. John's University
Peter J. Tobin College of Business
8000 Utopia Pkwy, Queens NY 11439
Sheila Russell, Director of Graduate Admission
718-990-1345 Fax: 718-990-5242
Website: www.stjohns.edu
E-mail: admissions@stjohns.edu
See listing under "Universities"

OHIO

Cleveland State University
2121 Euclid Ave RW 204, Cleveland OH 44115
Dr. Richard Arndt, Dean of Undergraduate Recruitment
and College Partnerships
888-CSU-OHIO Fax: 216-687-9210
Website: www.csuohio.edu
E-mail: admissions@csuohio.edu

OKLAHOMA

Oklahoma State University
Stillwater OK 74078
Ken Eastman, Program Director
405-744-2951
Website: www.okstate.edu
E-mail: ken.eastman@okstate.edu

Oral Roberts University
Adult Learning Service Center
7777 S Lewis Ave, Tulsa OK 74171-0001
888-900-4678 Fax: 918-495-7965
Website: www.oru.edu
E-mail: alsc@oru.edu

OREGON

Marylhurst University
17600 Pacific Hwy (Hwy 43)
Marylhurst OR 97036-0261
Director of Admissions
800-634-9982 ext. 6268 Fax: 503-635-6585
Website: www.marylhurst.edu
E-mail: studentinfo@marylhurst.edu

PENNSYLVANIA

Gannon University
109 University Sq, Erie PA 16541-0001
Christopher Tremblay, Director of Admissions
800-GANNON-U Fax: 814-871-5803
Website: www.gannon.edu
E-mail: admissions@gannon.edu

Holy Family University - Woodhaven
1311 Bristol Pike, Bensalem PA 19020
Honour Moore, Associate VP for Extended Learning
215-637-7700 ext. 5008 Fax: 215-633-0558
Website: www.holyfamily.edu
E-mail: hmoore@holyfamily.edu

Lebanon Valley College
101 N College Ave, Annville PA 17003-1400
William Brown, Dean of Admissions & Financial Aid
866-LVC-4ADM or 717-867-6181 Fax: 717-867-6026
Website: www.lvc.edu
E-mail: admission@lvc.edu

MOUNT ALOYSIUS COLLEGE
7373 Admiral Peary Hwy, Cresson PA 16630-1999
Frank C. Crouse Jr., Vice President for Enrollment
Management
814-886-6383 or 888-823-2220 Fax: 814-886-6441
Website: www.mtaloy.edu
E-mail: admissions@mtaloy.edu

SOUTH CAROLINA

North Greenville University
PO Box 1892, Tigerville SC 29688-1892
Dr. Sam Isgett, Exec. Director of Graduate School
Website: www.ngc.edu
See listing under "Universities"

SOUTH DAKOTA

NATIONAL AMERICAN UNIVERSITY
321 Kansas City St, Rapid City SD 57701-3692
Angela G. Beck, Director of Enrollment Management
605-394-4800 Fax: 605-394-4871
Website: www.national.edu/rc/index.html
E-mail: rcadmissions@national.edu

TENNESSEE

Lipscomb University
3901 Granny White Pike, Nashville TN 37204-3951
Ricky Holaway, Director of Admissions
800-333-4358 ext. 1776 Fax: 615-269-1804
Website: www.lipscomb.edu
E-mail: admissions@lipscomb.edu

TEXAS

Angelo State University
ASU Station 11025, San Angelo TX 76909
Dr. Carol Diminnie, Dean of Graduate School
325-942-2169 Fax: 325-942-2194
Website: www.angelo.edu
E-mail: graduate.school@angelo.edu

Texas Woman's University
PO Box 425589, Denton TX 76204-5589
Erma Nieto, Director of Admissions
866-809-6130 Fax: 940-898-3081
Website: www.twu.edu
E-mail: admissions@twu.edu

University of Houston
122 E Cullen Bldg, Houston TX 77204-2023
Office of Admission
713-743-9595
Website: www.uh.edu
E-mail: admissions@uh.edu

UTAH

ITT TECHNICAL INSTITUTE
920 Levoy Dr, Murray UT 84123-2500
Gary Wood, Director of Recruitment
801-263-3313 Fax: 801-263-3497
Website: www.itt-tech.edu
E-mail: gwood@itt-tech.edu

VERMONT

NORWICH UNIVERSITY
158 Harmon Dr, Northfield VT 05663
Dr. William Jolley, Program Director
800-686-6546
Website: www3.norwich.edu/mba
E-mail: mbainfo@norwich.edu
See listing under "Universities"

VIRGINIA

Radford University
PO Box 6903, Radford VA 24142
David W. Kraus, Director of Admissions
800-890-4265 Fax: 540-831-5038
Website: www.radford.edu
E-mail: ruadmiss@radford.edu

UNIVERSITY OF MANAGEMENT AND TECHNOLOGY
1901 Fort Myer Dr Ste 700, Arlington VA 22209
703-516-0035 Fax: 703-516-0985
Website: www.umtweb.edu
E-mail: info@umtweb.edu

University of Mary Washington
1301 College Ave, Fredericksburg VA 22401-5300
Dr. Martin A. Wilder, Jr., Director of Admissions
540-654-2000 Fax: 540-654-1857
Website: www.umw.edu
E-mail: admit@umw.edu

WASHINGTON

Gonzaga University
502 E Boone Ave, Spokane WA 99258-0102
Julie McCulloh, Dean of Admission
800-322-2584 or 509-323-6572 Fax: 509-323-5780
Website: www.gonzaga.edu
E-mail: mcculloh@gu.gonzaga.edu

WEST VIRGINIA

West Virginia Wesleyan College
59 College Ave, Buckhannon WV 26201-2699
Robert N. Skinner II, Director of Admission
800-722-9933 Fax: 304-473-8108
Website: www.wvwc.edu
E-mail: admission@wvwc.edu

WYOMING

University of Wyoming
Admissions Office
Dept 3435, Laramie WY 82071-3435
Aaron Appelhans, Contact
800-342-5996 Fax: 307-766-4042
Website: www.uwyo.edu
E-mail: why-wyo@uwyo.edu

GUAM

University of Guam
UOG Station, Mangilao GU 96923
Deborah Leon Guerrero, Registrar
671-735-2201 or 671-735-2208 Fax: 671-735-2203
Website: www.uog.edu
E-mail: admitme@uog9.uog.edu

MATHEMATICS

ALABAMA

Alabama A & M University
PO Box 908, Normal AL 35762
Antonio Boyle, Director of Admissions
256-372-5245 Fax: 256-372-5249
Website: www.aamu.edu
E-mail: aboyle@aamu.edu

CALHOUN COMMUNITY COLLEGE
PO Box 2216, Decatur AL 35609-2216
M. Wayne Tosh, Registrar
256-306-2500 Fax: 256-306-2941
Website: www.calhoun.edu
E-mail: bsm@calhoun.edu

Faulkner University
5345 Atlanta Hwy, Montgomery AL 36109-3398
Keith Mock, Director of Admissions
800-879-9816 ext. 7200 or 334-386-7200
Fax: 334-386-7137
Website: www.faulkner.edu
E-mail: admissions@faulkner.edu

Judson College
302 Bibb St, Marion AL 36756
Michael Scotto, Director of Admissions
800-447-9472 Fax: 334-683-5147
Website: www.judson.edu
E-mail: admissions@judson.edu

University of Alabama in Huntsville
PO Box 1247, Huntsville AL 35899-0001
Ann Lee, Assoc. Director for Recruiting Program and Events
1-800-UAH-CALL Fax: 256-824-6073
Website: www.uah.edu
E-mail: leev@uah.edu

University of South Alabama
307 University Blvd N, Mobile AL 36688-3053
Melissa Haab, Director of Admissions
251-460-6141 Fax: 251-460-7876
Website: www.southalabama.edu
E-mail: admiss@usouthal.edu

ALASKA

University of Alaska Anchorage
PO Box 141629, Anchorage AK 99514-1629
Cecile Mitchell, Director of Enrollment Services
907-786-1480 Fax: 907-786-4888
Website: www.uaa.alaska.edu/
E-mail: enroll@uaa.alaska.edu

University of Alaska Southeast
11120 Glacier Hwy, Juneau AK 99801-8625
Paul Kraft, Dean of Students/Enrollment Management
907-796-6000 Fax: 907-796-6005
Website: www.uas.alaska.edu
E-mail: paul.kraft@uas.alaska.edu

ARIZONA

University of Arizona
Tucson AZ 85721-0040
Paul Kohn, Director of Admissions
520-621-3237 Fax: 520-621-9799
Website: www.admissions.arizona.edu or www.arizona.edu

ARKANSAS

Ouachita Baptist University
410 Ouachita St, Arkadelphia AR 71998-0001
David Goodman, Director of Admissions
870-245-5110 Fax: 870-245-5500
Website: www.obu.edu
E-mail: admissions@obu.edu

CALIFORNIA

California State University-San Bernadino
5500 University Pkwy
San Bernardino CA 92407-2393
Olivia Rosas, Director of Admissions
909-880-5000 Fax: 909-880-7034
Website: enrollment.csusb.edu
E-mail: orosas@csusb.edu

Chapman University
One University Drive, Orange CA 92866-1099
Michael Drummy, Assistant Vice President for Enrollment
Services and Chief Admission Officer
714-997-6411 or 888-CUAPPLY Fax: 714-997-6713
Website: www.chapman.edu
E-mail: admit@chapman.edu

Concordia University
1530 Concordia, Irvine CA 92612-3203
Lori McDonald, Executive Director of Enrollment Services
800-229-1200 or 949-854-8002 Fax: 949-854-6894
Website: www.cui.edu
E-mail: admission@cui.edu

FRESNO CITY COLLEGE
1101 E University Ave, Fresno CA 93741-0002
Dayann Dietrich, Contact
559-442-8241 Fax: 559-237-4232
Website: www.fresnocitycollege.com
E-mail: fcc.admissions@scccd.com

Harvey Mudd College
Claremont CA 91711-3104
Peter Osgood, Contact
909-621-8011 Fax: 909-607-7046
Website: www.hmc.edu
E-mail: admission@hmc.edu

Orange Coast College
PO Box 5005, Costa Mesa CA 92628-5005
Kristin Clark, Director of Admissions
714-432-5773 Fax: 714-432-5736
Website: www.orangecoastcollege.edu
E-mail: kclark@cccd.edu

San Diego Christian College
2100 Greenfield Dr, El Cajon CA 92019-1157
Jon Melone, Director of Admissions
800-676-2242 Fax: 619-590-1739
Website: www.sdcc.edu
E-mail: admissions@sdcc.edu

Simpson University
2211 College View Dr, Redding CA 96003-8606
Jim Herberger, Director of Admissions
888-9-SIMPSON Fax: 530-226-4861
Website: www.simpsonuniversity.edu
E-mail: admissions@simpsonuniversity.edu
See listing under "Liberal Arts and Sciences"

Whittier College
PO Box 634, Whittier CA 90608-0634
Kieron Miller, Director of Admissions
562-907-4200 Fax: 562-907-4870
Website: www.whittier.edu
E-mail: kmiller@whittier.edu

CONNECTICUT

Albertus Magnus College
700 Prospect St, New Haven CT 06511-1189
Richard Lolatte, Dean of Admission
203-773-8501 or 800-578-9160 Fax: 203-773-5248
Website: www.albertus.edu
E-mail: admissions@albertus.edu

University of New Haven
300 Boston Post Rd, West Haven CT 06516
Director of Undergraduate Admissions
203-932-7319 Fax: 203-931-6093
Website: www.newhaven.edu
E-mail: adminfo@newhaven.edu

FLORIDA

Florida State University
600 W College Ave, Tallahassee FL 32306-1096
Janice V. Finney, Director of Admissions
850-644-2525 Fax: 850-644-0197
Website: admissions.fsu.edu
E-mail: admissions@admin.fsu.edu

University of South Florida
4202 E Fowler Ave, Tampa FL 33620-6900
J. Robert Spatig, Director of Admissions
813-974-3350 Fax: 813-974-9689
Website: www.usf.edu
E-mail: admissions@admin.usf.edu

GEORGIA

Armstrong Atlantic State University
11935 Abercorn St, Savannah GA 31419-1997
Kim West, Asst. Dean and Registrar Enrollment Services
912-927-5277 Fax: 912-921-5462
Website: www.armstrong.edu
E-mail: admissions@mail.armstrong.edu

Kennesaw State University
1000 Chastain Rd NW, Kennesaw GA 30144-5591
Laurence Peterson, Dean of College of Science and Mathematics
770-423-6160
Website: www.kennesaw.edu

Oglethorpe University
4484 Peachtree Rd NE, Atlanta GA 30319-2797
Kelly Gosnell, Director of Admission
404-261-1441 Fax: 404-364-8491
Website: www.oglethorpe.edu
E-mail: admission@oglethorpe.edu

IDAHO

Brigham Young University - Idaho
120 Kimball Bldg, Rexburg ID 83460
Gordon Westenskow, Director of Admissions
208-496-1020 Fax: 208-496-1220
Website: www.byui.edu
E-mail: admissions@byui.edu

University of Idaho
Moscow ID 83844-4253
Lloyd Scott, Director of New Student Services
208-885-6163 Fax: 208-885-4477
Website: www.uidaho.edu
E-mail: nss@uidaho.edu

ILLINOIS

Aurora University
347 S Gladstone Ave, Aurora IL 60506-4892
Carol R. Dunn, Ed.D., Vice President for Enrollment
800-742-5281 Fax: 630-844-5535
Website: www.aurora.edu
E-mail: admission@aurora.edu

Benedictine University
5700 College Rd, Lisle IL 60532-0900
630-829-6300 or 888-829-6363 Fax: 630-829-6301
Website: www.ben.edu
E-mail: admissions@ben.edu
See listing under "Universities"

CONCORDIA UNIVERSITY
7400 Augusta St, River Forest IL 60305-1402
708-209-3100 Fax: 708-209-3473
Website: www.curf.edu
E-mail: crfadmis.edu

North Central College
30 N Brainard St, Naperville IL 60540-4690
Martha Stolze, Director of Admissions
630-637-5800 Fax: 630-637-5819
Website: www.northcentralcollege.edu
E-mail: admissions@noctrl.edu

Roosevelt University
430 S Michigan Ave, Chicago IL 60605
Gwen E. Kanelos, Asst. Vice President for Enrollment
Services
877-APPLY-RU Fax: 312-341-4216
Website: www.roosevelt.edu
E-mail: applyru@roosevelt.edu

South Suburban College of Cook County
15800 State St, South Holland IL 60473
Jane Ellen Stocker, Dean of Enrollment Services
708-596-2000 Fax: 708-225-5806
Website: www.southsuburbancollege.edu
E-mail: jstocker@southsuburbancollege.edu

INDIANA

Ancilla Domini College
Donaldson IN 46513
Erin Wittmeyer, Director of Admissions
574-936-8898 Fax: 574-935-1773
Website: www.ancilla.edu
E-mail: erin.wittmeyer@ancilla.edu

Franklin College
101 Branigin Blvd, Franklin IN 46131
Jacqueline S. Acosta, Director of Admissions
800-852-0232 Fax: 317-738-8274
Website: www.franklincollege.edu
E-mail: admissions@franklincollege.edu

Hanover College
PO Box 108, Hanover IN 47243-0108
William D. Preble, Dean of Admission
800-213-2178 Fax: 812-866-7098
Website: www.hanover.edu
E-mail: admissions@hanover.edu

Oakland City University
138 N Lucretia St, Oakland City IN 47660
Brian J. Baker, Director of Admissions
800-737-5125 Fax: 812-749-1433
Website: www.oak.edu
E-mail: bbaker@oak.edu
See listing under "Universities"

Rose-Hulman Institute of Technology
5500 Wabash Ave, Terre Haute IN 47803-3920
James A. Goecker, Dean of Admissions
812-877-8213 Fax: 812-877-8941
Website: www.rose-hulman.edu
E-mail: admis.ofc@rose-hulman.edu

St. Mary-of-the-Woods College
Saint Mary of the Woods IN 47876-1001
James P. Malley, Jr., Director of Admission
800-926-7692 Fax: 812-535-5010
Website: www.smwc.edu
E-mail: smwcadms@smwc.edu

University of Evansville
1800 Lincoln Ave, Evansville IN 47722-0001
Thomas E. Bear, V.P. of Enrollment Services
800-423-8633 Fax: 812-488-4076
Website: www.evansville.edu
E-mail: admission@evansville.edu

IOWA

Briar Cliff University
PO Box 2100, Sioux City IA 51104-0100
Sharisue Wilcoxon, VP for Enrollment Management
712-279-5200 Fax: 712-279-1632
Website: www.briarcliff.edu
E-mail: admissions@briarcliff.edu

Clarke College
1550 Clarke Dr, Dubuque IA 52001-3198
Andy Schroeder, Director of Admissions
800-383-2345 Fax: 563-584-8666
Website: www.clarke.edu
E-mail: andy.schroeder@clarke.edu

Graceland University
1 University Place, Lamoni IA 50140
Brian Shantz, Vice President for Enrollment and Dean
of Admissions
641-784-5196 Fax: 641-784-5480
Website: www.admissions.graceland.edu
E-mail: admissions@graceland.edu

Iowa Lakes Community College
300 S 18th St, Estherville IA 51334-2721
Anne Stansbury, Asst. Director of Admissions
712-362-7945 Fax: 712-362-8363
Website: www.iowalakes.edu
E-mail: info@iowalakes.edu

Mount Mercy College
1330 Elmhurst Dr NE, Cedar Rapids IA 52402-4797
Jim Krystofiak, Dean of Admission
800-248-4504 Fax: 319-363-5270
Website: www.mtmercy.edu
E-mail: admission@mtmercy.edu

Wartburg College
PO Box 1003, Waverly IA 50677-0903
Brent Matthias, Interim Director of Admissions
319-352-8200 Fax: 319-352-8579
Website: www.wartburg.edu
E-mail: admissions@wartburg.edu

KANSAS

Independence Community College
PO Box 708, Independence KS 67301-0708
Dr. Terry Hetrick, President
800-842-6063 Fax: 620-331-5344
Website: www.indycc.edu
E-mail: admissions@indycc.edu

Newman University
3100 W McCormick St, Wichita KS 67213
Jann Reusser, Admissions Recruitment Coordinator
316-942-4291 ext. 2144 Fax: 316-942-4483
Website: www.newmanu.edu
E-mail: reusserj@newmanu.edu

Tabor College
400 S Jefferson St, Hillsboro KS 67063-1758
Rusty Allen, Dean of Enrollment Management
620-947-3121 Fax: 620-947-6276
Website: www.tabor.edu
E-mail: admissions@tabor.edu

KENTUCKY

Morehead State University
Morehead KY 40351-1689
Dayna Seelig, Enrollment Services
800-585-6781 Fax: 606-783-5038
Website: www.moreheadstate.edu
E-mail: admissions@moreheadstate.edu

LOUISIANA

Dillard University
2601 Gentilly Blvd, New Orleans LA 70122-3097
Linda G. Nash, Director of Admissions
Website: www.dillard.edu
E-mail: admissions@dillard.edu

Our Lady of Holy Cross College
4123 Woodland Dr, New Orleans LA 70131-7399
Office of Enrollment Services
504-394-7744 Fax: 504-391-2421
Website: www.olhcc.edu

MAINE

St. Joseph's College of Maine
278 Whites Bridge Rd, Standish ME 04084-5263
Vincent Kloskowski, Dean of Admissions
800-338-7057 Fax: 207-893-7862
Website: www.sjcme.edu
E-mail: admission@sjcme.edu

MARYLAND

Cecil Community College
One Seahawk Dr, North East MD 21901
Sandra S. Rajaski, Registrar & Director of Admissions
410-287-1000 Fax: 410-287-1001
Website: www.cecilcc.edu
E-mail: srajaski@cecilcc.edu

Hagerstown Community College
11400 Robinwood Dr, Hagerstown MD 21742-6590
Dr. Daniel E. Bock, Assistant Director of Admissions
301-790-2800 Fax: 301-791-9165
Website: www.hagerstowncc.edu
E-mail: bockd@hagerstowncc.edu

MASSACHUSETTS

Assumption College
500 Salisbury St, Worcester MA 01609-1294
Kathleen Murphy, Dean of Enrollment
508-767-7000 Fax: 508-799-4412
Website: www.assumption.edu
E-mail: admiss@assumption.edu

Boston University
121 Bay State Rd, Boston MA 02215
Kelly Walter, Executive Director of Admissions
617-353-2300 Fax: 617-353-9695
Website: web.bu.edu
E-mail: admissions@bu.edu

Massachusetts Institute of Technology
77 Massachusetts Ave, Cambridge MA 02139-4307
Marilee Jones, Dean of Admission
617-253-1000 Fax: 617-253-4016
Website: my.mit.edu
E-mail: admissions@mit.edu

Smith College
Northampton MA 01063-0001
Debra Shaver, Director of Admissions
800-383-3232 Fax: 413-585-2527
Website: www.smith.edu
E-mail: admission@smith.edu

University of Massachusetts Dartmouth
Old Westport Rd, North Dartmouth MA 02747-2300
Steven T. Briggs, Director of Admissions
508-999-8605 Fax: 508-999-8755
Website: explore.umassd.edu
E-mail: sbriggs@umassd.edu

Westfield State College
PO Box 1630, Westfield MA 01086
Michelle Mattie, Associate Dean, Admission and
Enrollment Services
413-572-5300
Website: www.wsc.ma.edu
E-mail: admission@wsc.ma.edu

Worcester Polytechnic Institute
100 Institute Rd, Worcester MA 01609-2280
Edward J. Connor, Director of Admissions
508-831-5286 Fax: 508-831-5875
Website: admissions.wpi.edu
E-mail: admissions@wpi.edu

MICHIGAN

Alma College
614 W Superior St, Alma MI 48801-1599
Anne Monroe, Director of Admissions
800-321-ALMA Fax: 989-463-7057
Website: www.alma.edu
E-mail: admissions@alma.edu

Andrews University
Berrien Springs MI 49104-0001
Randall Graves, Director of Recruitment Services
800-253-2874 Fax: 269-471-2670
Website: www.connect.andrews.edu
E-mail: gravesr@andrews.edu

Delta College
University Center MI 48710-0001
Duff Zube, Director of Admissions
989-686-9093 Fax: 989-667-2202
Website: www.delta.edu
E-mail: admit@delta.edu

Grand Valley State University
1 Campus Dr, Allendale MI 49401-9403
Jodi Chycinski, Director of Admissions
616-331-6611 Fax: 616-331-2000
Website: www.gvsu.edu
E-mail: go2gvsu@gvsu.edu

HILLSDALE COLLEGE
33 E College St, Hillsdale MI 49242-1298
Professor Mark Watson, Director
517-607-2384 Fax: 517-607-2252
Website: www.hillsdale.edu
E-mail: mark.watson@hillsdale.edu

Lawrence Technological University
21000 W 10 Mile Rd, Southfield MI 48075-1058
Jane Rohrback, Director of Admissions
800-225-5588 Fax: 248-204-2228
Website: www.ltu.edu
E-mail: admissions@ltu.edu
See listing under "Universities"

MACOMB COMMUNITY COLLEGE
44575 Garfield Rd, Clinton Township MI 48038-1139
Information Center
586-445-7999
Website: www.macomb.edu
E-mail: answer@macomb.edu

MACOMB COMMUNITY COLLEGE
14500 E 12 Mile Rd, Warren MI 48088-3896
Information Center
586-445-7999
Website: www.macomb.edu
E-mail: answer@macomb.edu

Oakland University
2200 N Squirrel Rd, Rochester MI 48309
Eleanor L. Reynolds, Assistant Vice President &
Director of Admissions
248-370-2100
Website: www.oakland.edu
E-mail: ouinfo@oakland.edu

University of Michigan-Dearborn
4901 Evergreen Rd, Dearborn MI 48128-1491
The Office of Admissions & Orientation
313-593-5100 Fax: 313-436-9167
Website: www.umd.umich.edu
E-mail: admissions@umd.umich.edu

MINNESOTA

Carleton College
1 N College St, Northfield MN 55057-4044
800-995-2275 or 507-646-4190 Fax: 507-646-4526
Website: www.carleton.edu
E-mail: admissions@acs.carleton.edu

Gustavus Adolphus College
800 W College Ave, Saint Peter MN 56082-1485
Mark H. Anderson, Dean of Admission
800-GUSTAVUS Fax: 507-933-7474
Website: www.gustavus.edu
E-mail: admission@gustavus.edu

Metropolitan State University
700 7th St E, Saint Paul MN 55106-5000
Rosa Rodriguez, Admissions Director
651-793-1300 Fax: 651-793-1546
Website: www.metrostate.edu
E-mail: rosa.rodriguez@metrostate.edu

Pillsbury Baptist Bible College
315 S Grove Ave, Owatonna MN 55060-3097
Stephen R. Seidler, Director of Admissions
507-451-2710 Fax: 507-451-0156
Website: www.pillsbury.edu
E-mail: steveseidler@pillsbury.edu

MISSISSIPPI

Tougaloo College
500 W County Line Rd, Tougaloo MS 39174-9799
Juno Leggette Jacobs, Director of Admissions
601-977-7768 Fax: 601-977-4501
Website: www.tougaloo.edu
E-mail: jjacobs@tougaloo.edu

MISSOURI

Columbia College
1001 Rogers St, Columbia MO 65216-0001
Regina Morin, Director of Admissions
573-875-7352 Fax: 573-875-7506
Website: www.ccis.edu
E-mail: admissions@ccis.edu

Lindenwood University
209 S Kingshighway St
Saint Charles MO 63301-1695
Sheryl Guffey, Director of Admissions
636-949-2000 Fax: 636-949-4989
Website: www.lindenwood.edu

Stephens College
PO Box 2121, Columbia MO 65215-0001
David Adams, Dean of Enrollment Management
573-442-2211 Fax: 573-876-7237
Website: www.stephens.edu
E-mail: dadams@stephens.edu

Truman State University
100 E Normal, Kirksville MO 63501
Office of Admission
660-785-4000 Fax: 660-785-4181
Website: admissions.truman.edu
E-mail: admissions@truman.edu

University of Missouri
1 University Blvd, Saint Louis MO 63121-4499
Dr. Mark Burkholder, Dean-College of Arts & Sciences
314-516-5501 Fax: 314-516-5415
Website: www.umsl.edu
E-mail: admissions@umsl.edu

Webster University
470 E Lockwood Ave, Saint Louis MO 63119-3194
Dr. Ed Sakurai, Chairman, Math and Computer Science
314-968-7023 Fax: 314-963-6050
Website: www.webster.edu
E-mail: sakuraab@webster.edu
See listing under "Universities"

William Woods University
1 University Ave, Fulton MO 65251-1098
Jimmy Clay, Director of Admissions
573-642-2251 Fax: 573-592-1146
Website: www.williamwoods.edu
E-mail: admissions@williamwoods.edu
See listing under "Universities"

MONTANA

Rocky Mountain College
1511 Poly Dr, Billings MT 59102-1796
Bonnie Knapp, Director of Admissions
800-877-6259 Fax: 406-657-1189
Website: www.rocky.edu
E-mail: admissions@rocky.edu

NEBRASKA

Midland Lutheran College
900 N Clarkson St, Fremont NE 68025-4200
Todd Hansen, Associate Director of Admissions
402-941-6501 Fax: 402-941-6513
Website: www.mlc.edu
E-mail: admissions@mlc.edu

Nebraska Wesleyan University
5000 Saint Paul Ave, Lincoln NE 68504-2794
Patricia Karthauser, V.P. for University Enrollment
402-466-2371 Fax: 402-465-2177
Website: www.nebrwesleyan.edu
E-mail: admissions@nebrwesleyan.edu

Peru State College
PO Box 10, Peru NE 68421-0010
Office of Admissions
800-742-4412 Fax: 402-872-2296
Website: www.peru.edu
E-mail: admissions@oakmail.peru.edu

University of Nebraska at Kearney
905 W 25th St, Kearney NE 68849-0001
Dusty Newton, Director of Admissions
800-KEARNEY Fax: 308-865-8987
Website: www.unk.edu
E-mail: admissionsug@unk.edu

NEW JERSEY

New Jersey City University
2039 John F Kennedy Blvd
Jersey City NJ 07305-1588
Carmen Panlilio, Asst. V.P. for Admissions and
Financial Aid
201-200-3234 Fax: 201-200-2044
Website: www.njcu.edu
E-mail: admissions@njcu.edu

Ramapo College of New Jersey
505 Ramapo Valley Rd, Mahwah NJ 07430-1623
Director of Admissions
201-684-7300 or 201-684-7301 Fax: 201-684-7964
Website: www.ramapo.edu
E-mail: admissions@ramapo.edu

NEW YORK

College of Saint Rose
432 Western Ave, Albany NY 12203-1419
Maryelizabeth Amico, Asst V.P. for Undergraduate
Admissions
518-454-5150 Fax: 518-454-2013
Website: www.strose.edu
E-mail: admit@strose.edu

CUNY Hunter College
695 Park Ave, New York NY 10021
Aaron Gibbs, Assistant Director of Recruitment
212-772-4497 Fax: 212-650-3336
Website: www.hunter.cuny.edu
E-mail: aaron.gibbs@hunter.cuny.edu

Daemen College
4380 Main St, Amherst NY 14226-3592
Donna Shaffner, Director of Admissions
800-462-7652 or 716-839-8225 Fax: 716-839-8229
Website: www.daemen.edu
E-mail: admissions@daemen.edu
See listing under "Universities"

Hobart & William Smith Colleges
Pulteney St, Geneva NY 14456
John Young, Director of Admissions
315-789-5500 Fax: 315-781-3654
Website: www.hws.edu
E-mail: young@hws.edu

Long Island University-C. W. Post Campus
720 Northern Blvd, Brookville NY 11548-1300
Joanne Graziano, Executive Director of Admissions
516-299-2900 Fax: 516-299-2137
Website: www.liu.edu/cwpost
E-mail: enroll@cwpost.liu.edu

Molloy College
1000 Hempstead Ave
Rockville Centre NY 11570-1100
Marguerite Lane, Director of Admissions
516-678-5000 ext. 6291 Fax: 516-256-2247
Website: www.molloy.edu
E-mail: admissions@molloy.edu
See listing under "Universities"

PURCHASE COLLEGE STATE UNIVERSITY OF NEW YORK (SUNY)
735 Anderson Hill Rd, Purchase NY 10577-1400
Betsy Immergut, Director of Admissions
914-251-6300 Fax: 914-251-6314
Website: www.purchase.edu
See listing under "Universities"

Roberts Wesleyan College
2301 Westside Dr, Rochester NY 14624-1997
Office of Admissions
585-594-6400 Fax: 585-594-6371
Website: www.roberts.edu
E-mail: admissions@roberts.edu

St. John's University
8000 Utopia Pkwy, Queens NY 11439
Office of Admission
718-990-2000 or 888-9-STJOHNS Fax: 718-990-2096
Website: www.stjohns.edu
E-mail: admissions@stjohns.edu
See listing under "Universities"

St. Joseph's College
245 Clinton Ave, Brooklyn NY 11205-3688
Theresa LaRocca Meyer, V.P. for Enrollment
Management
718-636-6800 Fax: 718-636-8303
Website: www.sjcny.edu
E-mail: tlaroccameyer@sjcny.edu

SUNY College at Brockport
350 New Campus Dr, Brockport NY 14420-2997
Bernard S. Valento, Director of Undergraduate
Admissions
585-395-2751 Fax: 585-395-5452
Website: www.brockport.edu
E-mail: admit@brockport.edu

SUNY College of Technology
Alfred NY 14802
Deborah J. Goodrich, Director of Admissions
800-4AL-FRED Fax: 607-587-4299
Website: www.alfredstate.edu
E-mail: admissions@alfredstate.edu

SUNY College of Technology
2 Main St, Delhi NY 13753-1110
Robert W. Mazzei, Director of Admissions
800-96-DELHI Fax: 607-746-4104
Website: www.delhi.edu
E-mail: enroll@delhi.edu

SUNY Orange County Community College
115 South St, Middletown NY 10940-6437
Margot St. Lawrence, Director of Admissions
845-341-4030 Fax: 845-342-8662
Website: www.sunyorange.edu
E-mail: apply@sunyorange.edu
See listing under "Community and Junior Colleges"

United States Military Academy West Point
646 Swift Rd, West Point NY 10996-1905
Colonel Michael L. Jones, Director of Admissions
845-938-4041 Fax: 845-938-8121
Website: admissions.usma.edu
E-mail: admissions@usma.edu

Wells College
PO Box 500, Aurora NY 13026
Susan Sloan, Director of Admissions
800-952-9355 Fax: 315-364-3227
Website: www.wells.edu
E-mail: ssloan@wells.edu

NORTH CAROLINA

Belmont Abbey College
100 Belmont Mount Holly Rd
Belmont NC 28012-1802
888-222-0110 Fax: 704-825-6670
Website: www.belmontabbeycollege.edu
E-mail: admissions@bac.edu

Lees-McRae College
PO Box 128, Banner Elk NC 28604-0128
Walt Crutchfield, Dean of Admissions
800-280-4562 Fax: 828-898-8707
Website: www.lmc.edu
E-mail: admissions@lmc.edu

Mars Hill College
Mars Hill NC 28754
Chad Holt, Dean of Enrollment
866-MHC-4-YOU Fax: 828-689-1473
Website: www.mhc.edu
E-mail: cholt@mhc.edu

Meredith College
3800 Hillsborough St, Raleigh NC 27607-5298
Heidi L. Fletcher, Director of Admissions
919-760-8581 Fax: 919-760-2348
Website: www.meredith.edu
E-mail: admissions@meredith.edu
See listing under "Women's Colleges"

Mt. Olive College
634 Henderson St, Mount Olive NC 28365
Tim Woodard, Director of Admissions
919-658-2502 Fax: 919-658-9816
Website: www.moc.edu
E-mail: admissions@moc.edu
See listing under "Universities"

Salem College
Winston Salem NC 27108
Dana Evans, Dean of Admissions/Fin. Aid
800-32-SALEM Fax: 336-917-5572
Website: www.salem.edu
E-mail: admissions@salem.edu
See listing under "Women's Colleges"

NORTH DAKOTA

Dickinson State University
Dickinson ND 58601-4896
Steve Glasser, Director of Student Recruitment
800-279-4295 Fax: 701-483-2409
Website: www.dickinsonstate.edu
E-mail: dsu.hawks@dickinsonstate.edu

OHIO

Cleveland State University
2121 Euclid Ave RW 204, Cleveland OH 44115
Dr. Richard Arndt, Dean of Undergraduate Recruitment
and College Partnerships
888-CSU-OHIO Fax: 216-687-9210
Website: www.csuohio.edu
E-mail: admissions@csuohio.edu

Franciscan University of Steubenville
University Blvd, Steubenville OH 43952
Margaret J. Weber, Director of Admissions
800-783-6220 or 740-283-6226 Fax: 740-284-5456
Website: www.admissions.edu
E-mail: mweber@franciscan.edu

Mount Vernon Nazarene University
800 Martinsburg Rd, Mount Vernon OH 43050-9509
Timothy Eades, Director of Admissions
866-462-6868 Fax: 740-393-0511
Website: www.gotomvnu.com
E-mail: admissions@mvnu.edu
See listing under "Universities"

OHIO NORTHERN UNIVERSITY
525 S Main St, Ada OH 45810-1555
William Fuller, Chair of Mathematics & Statistics Dept.
419-772-2346
Website: www.onu.edu
E-mail: admissions-ug@onu.edu

The Ohio State University
College of Mathematical and Physical Sciences
Stillman Hall, 1947 College Rd, Columbus OH 43210
614-292-2874 Fax: 614-292-3639
Website: www.mps.ohio-state.edu
E-mail: handon.1@osu.edu

OHIO WESLEYAN UNIVERSITY
61 S Sandusky St, Delaware OH 43015-2398
Director of Admission
740-368-3020 Fax: 740-368-3314
Website: www.owu.edu
E-mail: owuadmit@owu.edu

University of Dayton
300 College Park, Dayton OH 45469-1300
Robert F. Durkle, Director of Admissions
800-837-7433 Fax: 937-229-4729
Website: admission.udayton.edu
E-mail: admission@udayton.edu

Ursuline College
2550 Lander Rd, Cleveland OH 44124-4398
Sarah E. Sundermeier, Director of Admissions
888-URSULINE Toll Free Fax: 440-684-6138
Website: www.admission.ursuline.edu
E-mail: admission@ursuline.edu

OKLAHOMA

Oklahoma State University
Stillwater OK 74078
Alan Adolphson, Department Head
405-744-5688
Website: www.okstate.edu
E-mail: adolphs@okstate.edu

Oral Roberts University
7777 S Lewis Ave, Tulsa OK 74171-0001
Chris Belcher, Director of Undergraduate Admissions
800-678-8876 Fax: 918-495-6222
Website: www.oru.edu
E-mail: admissions@oru.edu

University of Tulsa
600 S College Ave, Tulsa OK 74104-3126
Earl Johnson, Dean of Admission
918-631-2307 Fax: 918-631-5003
Website: www.utulsa.edu
E-mail: admission@utulsa.edu

OREGON

Linn-Benton Community College
6500 Pacific Blvd SW, Albany OR 97321-3774
Christine Baker, Outreach Coordinator
541-917-4811 Fax: 541-917-4868
Website: www.linnbenton.edu
E-mail: admissions@linnbenton.edu

Warner Pacific College
2219 SE 68th Ave, Portland OR 97215-4026
Shannon Mackey, Director of Admissions
503-517-1000 Fax: 503-517-1352
Website: www.warnerpacific.edu
E-mail: admissions@warnerpacific.edu

PENNSYLVANIA

Arcadia University
450 S Easton Rd, Glenside PA 19038-3295
Dennis Nostrand, VP for Enrollment Management
877-ARCADIA (877-272-2342) Fax: 215-881-8767
Website: www.arcadia.edu
E-mail: admiss@arcadia.edu
See listing under "Universities"

Clarion University of Pennsylvania
840 Wood St, Clarion PA 16214-1232
William Bailey, Dean of Enrollment Management
814-393-2306 Fax: 814-393-2030
Website: www.clarion.edu
E-mail: admissions@clarion.edu

DeSales University
2755 Station Ave, Center Valley PA 18034-9565
610-282-1100 Fax: 610-282-2342
Website: www.desales.edu

Gannon University
109 University Sq, Erie PA 16541-0001
Christopher Tremblay, Director of Admissions
800-GANNON-U Fax: 814-871-5803
Website: www.gannon.edu
E-mail: admissions@gannon.edu

Holy Family University
9801 Frankford Avenue, Philadelphia PA 19114
Lauren Campbell, Director of Admissions
215-637-3050 Fax: 215-281-1022
Website: www.holyfamily.edu
E-mail: admissions@holyfamily.edu

Juniata College
1700 Moore St, Huntingdon PA 16652-2196
Michelle Bartol, Dean of Enrollment
877-JUNIATA Fax: 814-641-3100
Website: www.juniata.edu
E-mail: admissions@juniata.edu

King's College
133 N River St, Wilkes Barre PA 18711-0801
Michelle Lawrence-Schmude, Director of Admission
570-208-5900 Fax: 570-208-5971
Website: www.kings.edu
E-mail: admissions@kings.edu

La Roche College
9000 Babcock Blvd, Pittsburgh PA 15237-5898
Thomas Hassett, Director of Freshman and
International Admissions
412-536-1272 or 800-838-4LRC Fax: 412-536-1272
Website: www.laroche.edu
E-mail: admissions@laroche.edu

Lebanon Valley College
101 N College Ave, Annville PA 17003-1400
William Brown, Dean of Admissions & Financial Aid
866-LVC-4ADM or 717-867-6181 Fax: 717-867-6026
Website: www.lvc.edu
E-mail: admission@lvc.edu

Lincoln University
Lincoln University PA 19352
Michael C. Taylor, Director of Admissions
800-790-0191 Fax: 610-932-1209
Website: www.lincoln.edu
E-mail: mtaylor@lu.lincoln.edu

MOUNT ALOYSIUS COLLEGE
7373 Admiral Peary Hwy, Cresson PA 16630-1999
Frank C. Crouse Jr., Vice President for Enrollment
Management
814-886-6383 or 888-823-2220 Fax: 814-886-6441
Website: www.mtaloy.edu
E-mail: admissions@mtaloy.edu

University of Pittsburgh
1150 Mount Pleasant Rd
Greensburg PA 15601-5860
Brandi S. Darr, Director of Admissions and Financial
Aid
724-836-9880 Fax: 724-836-7160
Website: www.upg.pitt.edu
E-mail: upgadmit@pitt.edu

Washington & Jefferson College
60 S Lincoln St, Washington PA 15301-4801
Alton E. Newell, Vice President for Enrollment
724-223-6025 Fax: 724-223-6534
Website: www.washjeff.edu
E-mail: admission@washjeff.edu

Westminster College
New Wilmington PA 16172-0001
Doug Swartz, Director of Admissions
724-946-7100 Fax: 724-946-6171
Website: www.westminster.edu
E-mail: swartzdl@westminster.edu

SOUTH CAROLINA
Erskine College & Seminary
PO Box 176, Due West SC 29639
Bart Walker, Director of Admissions
864-379-8838 Fax: 864-379-3048
Website: www.erskine.edu
E-mail: admissions@erskine.edu

Limestone College
1115 College Dr, Gaffney SC 29340-3799
Chris Phenicie, V.P. for Enrollment
864-489-7151 Fax: 864-488-8206
Website: www.limestone.edu
E-mail: cphenicie@limestone.edu

PRESBYTERIAN COLLEGE
503 S Broad St, Clinton SC 29325
Richard Dana Paul, Dean of Admissions
800-476-7272 Fax: 864-833-8481
Website: www.presby.edu
E-mail: admissions@presby.edu

University of South Carolina - Upstate
800 University Way, Spartanburg SC 29303-4932
Donette Stewart, Assistant VC for Enrollment Services
864-503-5246 Fax: 864-503-5727
Website: www.uscupstate.edu
E-mail: dstewart@uscupstate.edu
See listing under "Universities"

TENNESSEE
Lipscomb University
3901 Granny White Pike, Nashville TN 37204-3951
Ricky Holaway, Director of Admissions
800-333-4358 ext. 1776 Fax: 615-269-1804
Website: www.lipscomb.edu
E-mail: admissions@lipscomb.edu

Pellissippi State Technical Community College
PO Box 22990, Knoxville TN 37933-0990
Donna Mack, Contact
865-694-6568 Fax: 865-539-7217
Website: www.pstcc.edu
E-mail: dmack@pstcc.edu

Tennessee State University
3500 John A Merritt Blvd, Nashville TN 37209-1561
John Cade, Dean of Admissions & Records
615-963-5101 Fax: 615-963-2930
Website: www.tnstate.edu
E-mail: jcade@tnstate.edu

Tusculum College
PO Box 5051, Greeneville TN 37743
Melissa Ripley, Associate Director of Admissions
800-729-0256 Fax: 423-798-1622
Website: www.tusculum.edu
E-mail: mripley@tusculum.edu

University of Tennessee
615 McCallie Ave, Chattanooga TN 37403-2504
Yancy Freeman, Director of Admissions
423-425-4111 Fax: 423-425-4157
Website: www.utc.edu
E-mail: Yancy-Freeman@utc.edu

TEXAS
Angelo State University
ASU Station 11014, San Angelo TX 76909
Bonnie Stennett, Coordinator of Recruiting
800-946-8627 Fax: 325-942-2078
Website: www.angelo.edu
E-mail: admissions@angelo.edu

Blinn College
902 College Ave, Brenham TX 77833-4098
Dennis K. Crowson, Registrar
979-830-4000 Fax: 979-830-4110
Website: www.blinn.edu
E-mail: recruiting@blinn.edu

Blinn College
PO Box 6030, Bryan TX 77805-6030
Dennis K. Crowson, Registrar
979-209-7200 Fax: 979-209-7229
Website: www.blinn.edu
E-mail: recruiting@blinn.edu

Blinn College
100 Ranger Dr, Schulenburg TX 78956-2247
Dennis K. Crowson, Registrar
979-743-5003 Fax: 979-743-5225
Website: www.blinn.edu
E-mail: recruiting@blinn.edu

Blinn College
3701 Outlet Center Dr, Sealy TX 77474
Dennis K. Crowson, Registrar
979-627-7997 Fax: 979-627-0830
Website: www.blinn.edu
E-mail: recruiting@blinn.edu

Our Lady of the Lake University
411 SW 24th St, San Antonio TX 78207-4666
Mary Kay Cooper, Dean of Enrollment
210-434-6711 Fax: 210-431-4013
Website: www.ollusa.edu
E-mail: admission@lakeollusa.edu

Texas Woman's University
PO Box 425589, Denton TX 76204-5589
Erma Nieto, Director of Admissions
866-809-6130 Fax: 940-898-3081
Website: www.twu.edu
E-mail: admissions@twu.edu

Tyler Junior College
PO Box 9020, Tyler TX 75711-9020
Richard Minter, Dean
800-687-5680
Website: www.tjc.edu
E-mail: rmin@tjc.edu
See listing under "Community and Junior Colleges"

University of Houston
122 E Cullen Bldg, Houston TX 77204-2023
Office of Admission
713-743-9595
Website: www.uh.edu
E-mail: admissions@uh.edu

University of St. Thomas
3800 Montrose Blvd, Houston TX 77006-4626
Eduardo Prieto, Director of Admissions
713-522-7911 Fax: 713-525-3558
Website: www.stthom.edu
E-mail: prietoe@stthom.edu

University of Texas at Arlington
Box 19111, Arlington TX 76019-0111
Hans Gatterdam, Director of Admission
817-272-6287 Fax: 817-272-3435
Website: www.uta.edu
E-mail: admissions@uta.edu

VERMONT
Bennington College
One College Drive, Bennington VT 05201
Ken Himmelman, Dean of Admissions & Financial Aid
800-833-6845 Fax: 802-440-4320
Website: www.bennington.edu
E-mail: admissions@bennington.edu

NORWICH UNIVERSITY
158 Harmon Dr, Northfield VT 05663
Dr. Cathy Frey, Department Head
800-468-6679 Fax: 802-485-2333
Website: www.norwich.edu
E-mail: frey@norwich.edu
See listing under "Universities"

VIRGINIA
Radford University
PO Box 6903, Radford VA 24142
David W. Kraus, Director of Admissions
800-890-4265 Fax: 540-831-5038
Website: www.radford.edu
E-mail: ruadmiss@radford.edu

Randolph-Macon Woman's College
2500 Rivermont Ave, Lynchburg VA 24503
Patricia LeDonne, Director of Admissions
434-947-8100 Fax: 434-947-8996
Website: www.rmwc.edu
E-mail: admissions@rmwc.edu

University of Mary Washington
1301 College Ave, Fredericksburg VA 22401-5300
Dr. Martin A. Wilder, Jr., Director of Admissions
540-654-2000 Fax: 540-654-1857
Website: www.umw.edu
E-mail: admit@umw.edu

WASHINGTON
Gonzaga University
502 E Boone Ave, Spokane WA 99258-0102
Julie McCulloh, Dean of Admission
800-322-2584 or 509-323-6572 Fax: 509-323-5780
Website: www.gonzaga.edu
E-mail: mcculloh@gu.gonzaga.edu

WEST VIRGINIA
Concord University
Athens WV 24712
Michael Curry, Vice President of Financial Aid &
Admissions
888-384-5249 Fax: 304-384-3218
Website: www.concord.edu
E-mail: admissions@concord.edu

Davis & Elkins College
100 Campus Dr, Elkins WV 26241-3996
Renee Heckel, Director of Enrollment Management
800-624-3157 Fax: 304-637-1800
Website: www.davisandelkins.edu
E-mail: admiss@davisandelkins.edu

Fairmont State University
1201 Locust Ave, Fairmont WV 26554-2470
Steve Leadman, Director of Admissions
304-367-4642 or 800-641-5678 Fax: 304-367-4789
Website: www.fairmontstate.edu
E-mail: admit@fairmontstate.edu

West Virginia Wesleyan College
59 College Ave, Buckhannon WV 26201-2699
Robert N. Skinner II, Director of Admission
800-722-9933 Fax: 304-473-8108
Website: www.wvwc.edu
E-mail: admission@wvwc.edu

WISCONSIN
Alverno College
PO Box 343922, Milwaukee WI 53234-3922
Mary Kay Farrell, Director of Admissions
414-382-6100 Fax: 414-382-6354
Website: www.alverno.edu
E-mail: admissions@alverno.edu

Lakeland College
PO Box 359, Sheboygan WI 53082-0359
Nathan Dehne, Director of Admission
920-565-1100 Fax: 920-565-1215
Website: www.lakeland.edu
E-mail: admissions@lakeland.edu

Marquette University
PO Box 1881, Milwaukee WI 53201-1881
Robert Blust, Director of Admissions
414-288-7302 Fax: 414-288-3764
Website: www.mu.edu
E-mail: admissions@marquette.edu

St. Norbert College
100 Grant St, De Pere WI 54115
Brian Studebaker, Director of Admission
800-236-4878 Fax: 920-403-4072
Website: www.snc.edu
E-mail: admit@snc.edu

WYOMING
University of Wyoming
Admissions Office
Dept 3435, Laramie WY 82071-3435
Aaron Appelhans, Contact
800-342-5996 Fax: 307-766-4042
Website: www.uwyo.edu
E-mail: why-wyo@uwyo.edu

GUAM
University of Guam
UOG Station, Mangilao GU 96923
Deborah Leon Guerrero, Registrar
671-735-2201 or 671-735-2208 Fax: 671-735-2203
Website: www.uog.edu
E-mail: admitme@uog9.uog.edu

MECHANICS AND REPAIRERS

ALABAMA

- Bishop State Community College - Four Campuses
  351 N Broad St, Mobile AL 36603-5898
  Dr. Terry Hazzard, Dean of Students
  251-690-6801 Fax: 251-690-6446
  Website: www.bishop.edu
  E-mail: thazzard@bishop.edu

- Trenholm State Technical College
  Patterson Campus
  3920 Troy Hwy, Montgomery AL 36116
  Dr. Anthony Molina, President
  334-420-4200 Fax: 334-420-4206
  Website: www.trenholmtech.cc.al.us
  E-mail: amolina@trenholmtech.cc.al.us

ALASKA

University of Alaska Anchorage
  PO Box 141629, Anchorage AK 99514-1629
  Cecile Mitchell, Director of Enrollment Services
  907-786-1480 Fax: 907-786-4888
  Website: www.uaa.alaska.edu/
  E-mail: enroll@uaa.alaska.edu

University of Alaska Southeast
  11120 Glacier Hwy, Juneau AK 99801-8625
  Paul Kraft, Dean of Students/Enrollment Management
  907-796-6000 Fax: 907-796-6005
  Website: www.uas.alaska.edu
  E-mail: paul.kraft@uas.alaska.edu

ARIZONA

- Pima Community College
  4905 E Broadway Blvd, Tucson AZ 85709-1010
  Wendy Kilgore, Ph.D., Director of Admissions
  520-206-4500 Fax: 520-206-4790
  Website: www.pima.edu
  E-mail: infocenter@pima.edu

- Universal Technical Institute
  10695 W Pierce St, Avondale AZ 85323-7946
  John Palumbo, Director of Admissions
  623-245-4600 Fax: 623-245-4603
  Website: www.uticorp.com

ARKANSAS

: Northwest Technical Institute
  709 S Old Missouri Rd, Springdale AR 72764
  Charles L. Kelley, President
  479-751-8824 Fax: 479-751-7780
  Website: www.nti.tec.ar.us
  E-mail: info@nti.tec.ar.us

OUACHITA TECHNICAL COLLEGE
  One College Cir, Malvern AR 72104
  Jerry Little, Division Chair Applied Science
  501-337-5000 ext. 1165 Fax: 501-337-9382
  Website: www.otcweb.edu
  E-mail: jlittle@otcweb.edu

CALIFORNIA

: **BROWNSON TECHNICAL SCHOOL**
  1110 S Technology Cir Ste D
  Anaheim CA 92805-6316
  William D. Brown, Director
  714-774-9443 Fax: 714-774-5025
  Website: www.brownsontechnicalschool.com
  E-mail: brownson98@earthlink.net

- Chabot College
  25555 Hesperian Blvd, Hayward CA 94545-2400
  Judy Young, Director of Admissions
  510-723-6600 Fax: 510-723-7510
  Website: www.chabotcollege.edu
  E-mail: ccarcom@clpccd.cc.ca.us

FRESNO CITY COLLEGE
  1101 E University Ave, Fresno CA 93741-0002
  Dayann Dietrich, Contact
  559-442-8241 Fax: 559-237-4232
  Website: www.fresnocitycollege.com
  E-mail: fcc.admissions@scccd.com

: Institute of Technology - Sacramento
  3695 Bleckely St, Mather CA 95655
  916-363-4300

- Orange Coast College
  PO Box 5005, Costa Mesa CA 92628-5005
  Kristin Clark, Director of Admissions
  714-432-5773 Fax: 714-432-5736
  Website: www.orangecoastcollege.edu
  E-mail: kclark@cccd.edu

WYOTECH
  980 Riverside Pkwy, West Sacramento CA 95605
  Steve Coffee, Director of Admissions
  916-376-8888 Fax: 916-617-2069
  Website: www.wyotech.com
  E-mail: scoffee@wyotech.edu

COLORADO

- IntelliTec College
  2315 E Pikes Peak Ave
  Colorado Springs CO 80909-6096
  Michael Castellano, Contact
  719-632-7626 Fax: 719-632-7451
  Website: www.intelliteccollege.edu
  E-mail: admcs@intelliteccollege.edu

- IntelliTec College
  772 Horizon Dr, Grand Junction CO 81506-3907
  Rich Counts, Contact
  970-245-8101 Fax: 970-243-8074
  Website: www.intelliteccollege.edu
  E-mail: admgj@intelliteccollege.edu

NORTHEASTERN JUNIOR COLLEGE
  100 College Ave, Sterling CO 80751-2399
  Judy Giacomini, Interim Chief Administrative Officer
  Tina Joyce, Director of Admissions
  970-521-7000 or 970-521-6752 Fax: 970-521-6801
  Website: www.njc.edu
  E-mail: tina.joyce@njc.edu

: San Juan Basin Technical College
  PO Box 970, Cortez CO 81321-0970
  Shannon South, Director of Student Services
  970-565-8457 Fax: 970-565-8450
  Website: www.sjbtc.edu
  E-mail: ssouth@sjbtc.edu

CONNECTICUT

: Porter and Chester Institute
  670 Lordship Blvd, Stratford CT 06615-7158
  Mark Breslin, Director of Admissions
  203-375-4463 Fax: 203-375-5285
  Website: www.porterchester.com

FLORIDA

ATI CAREER TRAINING CENTER
  3501 Powerline Rd, Oakland Park FL 33309-5916
  Michael Ackerman, Executive Director
  954-563-5899 Fax: 954-568-0874
  Website: www.aticareertraining.com
  E-mail: pcampbell@atienterprises.edu

HENRY W. BREWSTER TECHNICAL CENTER
  2222 N Tampa St, Tampa FL 33602-2196
  William Cade, Department Head/Counselor
  813-276-5464 Fax: 813-276-5756
  Website: www.brewstertech.org

NATIONAL AVIATION ACADEMY
  6225 Ulmerton Rd, Clearwater FL 33760
  Karen Acker, Registrar
  727-531-2080 or 800-659-2080 Fax: 727-535-8727
  Website: www.naa.edu
  E-mail: admissions@naa.edu

- Santa Fe Community College
  3000 NW 83rd St, Gainesville FL 32606-6200
  Jackson N. Sasser, President
  352-395-5787 Fax: 352-395-4118
  Website: www.sfcc.edu
  E-mail: ouida.mcneill@sfcc.edu

GEORGIA

- DeKalb Technical College
  495 N Indian Creek Dr, Clarkston GA 30021-2397
  Terry Richardson, Director of Admissions
  404-297-9522 Fax: 404-294-6496
  Website: www.dekalbtech.edu
  E-mail: richardt@dekalbtech.edu

- North Georgia Technical College
  Clarkesville Campus
  PO Box 65, Clarkesville GA 30523-0002
  Admissions
  706-754-7700 Fax: 706-754-7777
  Website: www.northgatech.edu
  E-mail: info@northgatech.edu

- North Metro Technical College
  5198 Ross Rd SE, Acworth GA 30102-3129
  Missy Cusack, Director of Admissions
  770-975-4000 Fax: 770-975-4142
  Website: www.northmetrotech.edu
  E-mail: info@northmetrotech.edu

HAWAII

- Kauai Community College
  3-1901 Kaumualii Hwy, Lihue HI 96766-9500
  808-245-8225 Fax: 808-245-8297
  Website: kauai.hawaii.edu
  E-mail: arkauai@hawaii.edu

NEW YORK TECHNICAL INSTITUTE OF HAWAII
  1375 Dillingham Blvd, Honolulu HI 96817-4438
  Brian Hamilton, Principal
  808-841-5827 Fax: 808-841-5829
  E-mail: nytihhawaii@verizon.net

IDAHO

Brigham Young University - Idaho
  120 Kimball Bldg, Rexburg ID 83460
  Gordon Westenskow, Director of Admissions
  208-496-1020 Fax: 208-496-1220
  Website: www.byui.edu
  E-mail: admissions@byui.edu

ILLINOIS

- Kaskaskia College
  27210 College Rd, Centralia IL 62801-7878
  Tyra Taylor, Dean of Enrollment Management and
  Retention Services
  618-545-3000 Fax: 618-532-1990
  Website: www.kaskaskia.edu
  E-mail: ttaylor@kaskaskia.edu

- Triton College
  2000 5th Ave, River Grove IL 60171-1995
  Mary-Rita Moore, Dean of Enrollment Services
  708-456-0300 ext. 3130 Fax: 708-583-3147
  Website: www.triton.edu
  E-mail: triton@triton.edu
  See listing under "Community and Junior Colleges"

UNIVERSAL TECHNICAL INSTITUTE
  601 Regency Dr, Glendale Heights IL 60139-2208
  Karl Lewandowski, School Director
  630-529-2662 Fax: 630-529-7567
  Website: www.uticorp.com
  E-mail: karllewandowski@uticorp.com

INDIANA

- Ivy Tech Community College - North Central
  220 Dean Johnson Blvd, South Bend IN 46601-3415
  Pam Decker, Director of Admissions
  574-289-7001 Fax: 574-236-7177
  Website: www.ivytech.edu
  E-mail: pdecker@ivytech.edu

IOWA

- Iowa Lakes Community College
  3200 College Dr, Emmetsburg IA 50536-1055
  Anne Stansbury, Asst. Director of Admissions
  712-852-5212 Fax: 712-362-8363
  Website: www.iowalakes.edu
  E-mail: info@iowalakes.edu

- Northwest Iowa Community College
  603 W Park St, Sheldon IA 51201-1046
  Lisa Story, Director of Enrollment Management
  712-324-5061 Fax: 712-324-4136
  Website: www.nwicc.edu
  E-mail: lstory@nwicc.edu

KANSAS

: Flint Hills Technical College
  3301 W 18th Ave, Emporia KS 66801-5957
  Lisa Kirmer, Dean of Student Services
  620-343-4600 Fax: 620-343-4610
  Website: www.fhtc.net
  E-mail: lkirmer@fhtc.net

KENTUCKY

- Bluegrass Community and Technical College
  Oswald Building
  470 Cooper Drive, Lexington KY 40506-0235
  Shelbie Hugle, Director of Admissions
  859-246-6200 Fax: 859-246-4664
  Website: www.bluegrass.kctcs.edu
  E-mail: bctc_info@kctcs.edu

LOUISIANA

LOUISIANA TECHNICAL COLLEGE
  Tallulah Campus
  132 Old Highway 65, Tallulah LA 71284
  Patrick T. Murphy, Dean
  318-574-4820 Fax: 318-574-1868
  Website: www.ltctallulah.com
  E-mail: sccox@theltc.net

MAINE

- Northern Maine Community College
  33 Edgemont Dr, Presque Isle ME 04769-2016
  Bill Casavant, Director of Admissions
  207-768-2700 Fax: 207-768-2831
  Website: www.nmcc.edu
  E-mail: admissions@nmcc.edu

- Southern Maine Community College
  2 Fort Rd, South Portland ME 04106-1698
  Dr. James Ortiz, President
  Scott MacDonald, Director of Financial Aid
  207-741-5500 Fax: 207-741-5671
  Website: www.smccme.edu
  E-mail: oharmon@maine.rr.com

MASSACHUSETTS

- Benjamin Franklin Institute of Technology
  41 Berkeley St, Boston MA 02116-6307
  Norman Kraft, Dean of Enrollment
  617-423-4630 ext. 121 Fax: 617-482-3706
  Website: www.bfit.edu
  E-mail: admissions@bfit.edu

MICHIGAN

- Delta College
  University Center MI 48710-0001
  Duff Zube, Director of Admissions
  989-686-9093 Fax: 989-667-2202
  Website: www.delta.edu
  E-mail: admit@delta.edu

MACOMB COMMUNITY COLLEGE
  14500 E 12 Mile Rd, Warren MI 48088-3896
  Information Center
  586-445-7999
  Website: www.macomb.edu
  E-mail: answer@macomb.edu

MINNESOTA

- Dunwoody College of Technology
  818 Dunwoody Blvd, Minneapolis MN 55403-1192
  John Slama, Vice President Enrollment Management
  800-292-4625 or 612-374-5800 Fax: 612-374-4128
  Website: www.dunwoody.edu
  E-mail: jslama@dunwoody.edu
  See listing under "Career Schools"

- Hibbing Community College
  1515 E 25th St, Hibbing MN 55746-3300
  Holly Bigelow, Director of Enrollment
  800-224-4HCC or 218-262-7200 Fax: 218-262-6717
  Website: www.hibbing.edu
  E-mail: admissions@hibbing.edu

Minneapolis Community and Technical College
1501 Hennepin Ave, Minneapolis MN 55403-1779
Dena Russell, Director of Admissions
612-659-6282 Fax: 612-659-6210
Website: www.minneapolis.edu
E-mail: admissions.office@minneapolis.edu

Minnesota State College - Southeast Technical
308 Pioneer Rd, Red Wing MN 55066-3964
Al Ducett, Director of Admissions
800-657-4849 Fax: 507-453-2715
Website: www.southeastmn.edu
E-mail: aducett@southeastmn.edu

Northland Community & Technical College
Highway 1 E, Thief River Falls MN 56701
Norm Halsa, Contact
800-959-6282 or 218-681-0862 Fax: 218-681-0774
Website: www.northlandcollege.edu

Northland Community and Technical College
2022 Central Ave NE
East Grand Forks MN 56721-2702
Dennis Wierma, Trades Division Chair
800-451-3441 Fax: 218-773-4502
Website: www.northlandcollege.edu
E-mail: admissions@northlandcollege.edu

Ridgewater College-Willmar Campus
PO Box 1097, Willmar MN 56201-1097
Sally Kerfeld, Director of Admissions
800-722-1151 Fax: 320-231-7677
Website: www.ridgewater.edu
E-mail: skerfeld@ridgewater.edu

St. Cloud Technical College
1540 Northway Dr, Saint Cloud MN 56303-1240
Jodi Elness, Director of Enrollment Management
800-222-1009 Fax: 320-308-5981
Website: www.sctc.edu
E-mail: jelness@sctc.edu

MISSOURI

Linn State Technical College
1 Technology Dr, Linn MO 65051-9606
Becky Dunn, Admissions
800-743-8324 Fax: 573-897-5026
Website: www.linnstate.edu
E-mail: admissions@linnstate.edu

Ranken Technical College
4431 Finney Ave, Saint Louis MO 63113-2898
Elizabeth M. Keserauskis, Director of Admissions
314-371-0233 Fax: 314-371-0241
Website: www.ranken.edu
E-mail: admissions@ranken.edu

Vatterott College
3925 Industrial Dr, Saint Ann MO 63074-1807
Jennifer Commuso, Director of Admissions
800-345-6018 Fax: 314-428-5956
Website: www.vatterott-college.edu
E-mail: jennifer.commuso@vatterott-college.edu

Vatterott College
12970 Maurer Industrial Dr, Saint Louis MO 63127
Sherri Bremer, Director of Admissions
314-843-4200 Fax: 314-843-1709
Website: www.vatterott-college.edu
E-mail: sherri.bremer@vatterott-college.edu

NEBRASKA

Mid-Plains Community College
North Platte Community College - North Campus
1101 Halligan Dr, North Platte NE 69101-7659
Kelly Rippen, Director of Recruitment
800-658-4308 ext. 8107 Fax: 308-534-5770
Website: www.mpcc.edu
E-mail: rippenk@mpcc.edu

NEVADA

Career College of Northern Nevada
1195-A Corporate Blvd, Reno NV 89502-2331
Nathan Clark, Director
775-856-2266 Fax: 775-856-0935
Website: www.ccnn.edu
E-mail: lgoldhammer@ccnn4u.com
See listing under "Career Schools"

GREAT BASIN COLLEGE

1500 College Pkwy, Elko NV 89801-5032
Julie G. Byrnes, Director of Enrollment Management
775-753-2271 Fax: 775-753-2311
Website: www.gbcnv.edu
E-mail: bjulie@gbcnv.edu

NEW JERSEY

Teterboro School of Aeronautics
80 Moonachie Ave, Teterboro NJ 07608-1003
Richard Ciasulli, Director of Admissions
201-288-6300 Fax: 201-288-5609
Website: www.teterboroschool.com
E-mail: teterboroschool@nj.rr.com

NEW MEXICO

New Mexico State University
1500 N 3rd St, Grants NM 87020-2025
505-287-7981 Fax: 505-287-2329
Website: www.grants.nmsu.edu

NEW YORK

APEX TECHNICAL SCHOOL

635 Avenue of the Americas
New York NY 10011-2008
William Ott, Admissions Director
212-645-3300 Fax: 212-645-6984
Website: www.apextechnical.com
See listing under "Career Schools"

CAREER INSTITUTE OF HEALTH & TECHNOLOGY

340 Flatbush Avenue Ext, Brooklyn NY 11201
Mary Miller, Contact
718-422-1212 Fax: 718-422-1222
Website: www.careerinstitute.edu
E-mail: admissions@careerinstitute.edu

CAREER INSTITUTE OF HEALTH & TECHNOLOGY

200 Garden City Plz, Garden City NY 11530
Mary Miller, Contact
516-877-1225 Fax: 516-877-1959
Website: www.careerinstitute.edu
E-mail: admissions@careerinstitute.edu

CAREER INSTITUTE OF HEALTH & TECHNOLOGY

9525 Queens Blvd Ste 600, Rego Park NY 11374
Mary Miller, Contact
718-897-4868 Fax: 718-897-4863
Website: www.careerinstitute.edu
E-mail: admissions@careerinstitute.edu

SUNY College of Technology
Alfred NY 14802
Deborah J. Goodrich, Director of Admissions
800-4AL-FRED Fax: 607-587-4299
Website: www.alfredstate.edu
E-mail: admissions@alfredstate.edu

SUNY College of Technology
2 Main St, Delhi NY 13753-1110
Robert W. Mazzei, Director of Admissions
800-96-DELHI Fax: 607-746-4104
Website: www.delhi.edu
E-mail: enroll@delhi.edu

NORTH CAROLINA

Haywood Community College
185 Freedlander Dr, Clyde NC 28721
Debbie Rowland, Coordinator of Admissions
828-627-4500 Fax: 828-627-4513
Website: www.haywood.edu
E-mail: drowland@haywood.edu

James Sprunt Community College
PO Box 398, Kenansville NC 28349-0398
Rita Brown, Registrar
910-296-2500 Fax: 910-296-1636
Website: www.sprunt.com

NORTH DAKOTA

Williston State College
PO Box 1326, Williston ND 58802-1326
Penny Powell, Director Enrollment Services
701-774-4200 Fax: 701-774-4544
Website: www.wsc.nodak.edu
E-mail: penny.soiseth@wsc.nodak.edu

OHIO

Collins Career Center
11627 State Route 243, Chesapeake OH 45619-7962
740-867-6641 Fax: 740-867-9626
Website: www.collins-cc.k12.oh.us

OHIO TECHNICAL COLLEGE

1374 E 51st St, Cleveland OH 44103-1228
Marc Brenner, President
216-881-1700 Fax: 216-881-9145
Website: www.ohiotechnicalcollege.com
E-mail: info@ohiotechnicalcollege.com

Owens Community College
300 Davis St, Findlay OH 45840-3631
William J. Ivoska PhD., Vice President of Student Services
567-429-3500 Fax: 567-423-0246
Website: www.owens.edu
E-mail: admissions@owens.edu

Owens Community College
PO Box 10000, Toledo OH 43699-1947
William J. Ivoska, Ph.D, Vice President of Student Services
567-661-7000 Fax: 567-661-7607
Website: www.owens.edu
E-mail: admissions@owens.edu

Total Technical Institute
8720 Brookpark Rd, Cleveland OH 44129-6810
Dave Bryant, Director of Admissions
216-485-0900 Fax: 216-661-6842
Website: www.ttinst.com
E-mail: dbryant@ttinst.com

OKLAHOMA

SPARTAN COLLEGE OF AERONAUTICS AND TECHNOLOGY

8820 E Pine St, Tulsa OK 74115-5802
Director of Admissions
800-331-1204 Fax: 918-831-8609
Website: www.spartan.edu
E-mail: spartan@mail.spartan.edu
    Established 1928. Coed. Accredited member school: ACCSCT. Providing Technical training and education in Avionics, Instruments, and Maintenance; Nondestructive Testing and Quality Control. Complete flight training program. Offering Diplomas, Associate of Applied Science and Bachelor of Science in Aviation Technology Management.

Vatterott College - Tulsa
555 S Memorial Dr, Tulsa OK 74112
Kevin Wolfe, Director of Admissions
918-835-8288 Fax: 918-836-9698
Website: www.vatterott-college.edu
E-mail: kevin.wolfe@vatterott-college.com

OREGON

Linn-Benton Community College
6500 Pacific Blvd SW, Albany OR 97321-3774
Christine Baker, Outreach Coordinator
541-917-4811 Fax: 541-917-4868
Website: www.linnbenton.edu
E-mail: admissions@linnbenton.edu

Rogue Community College
3345 Redwood Hwy, Grants Pass OR 97527-9298
Claudia Sullivan, Director of Enrollment Services
541-956-7500 Fax: 541-471-3585
Website: www.roguecc.edu
E-mail: csullivan@roguecc.edu
See listing under "Community and Junior Colleges"

PENNSYLVANIA

AUTOMOTIVE TRAINING CENTER

114 Pickering Way, Exton PA 19341-1310
Don VanDemark, Vice President/Chief Operating Officer
610-363-6716 Fax: 610-363-8524
Website: www.autotraining.edu
E-mail: atc@autotraining.edu
See listing under "Career Schools"

Automotive Training Center
900 Johnsville Blvd, Warminster PA 18974
Kimberly Ewing, Executive Director of Admissions
877-411-8041 Fax: 215-442-1030
Website: www.autotraining.edu
E-mail: kewing@autotraining.edu
See listing under "Career Schools"

Johnson College
3427 N Main Ave, Scranton PA 18508-1495
Dr. Ann L. Pipinski, President & CEO
Melissa Ide, Director of Enrollment Management
800-2WE-WORK or 570-342-6404 ext. 125
Fax: 570-348-2181
Website: www.johnson.edu
E-mail: admit@johnson.edu

Pennco Tech
3815 Otter St, Bristol PA 19007-3618
Glenn Slater, Director of Admissions
215-785-0111 Fax: 215-785-1945
Website: www.penncotech.com
E-mail: admissions@penncotech.com

PENNSYLVANIA GUNSMITH SCHOOL

812 Ohio River Blvd, Pittsburgh PA 15202-2699
George Thacker, Director
412-766-1812 Fax: 412-766-0855
Website: www.pagunsmith.com
E-mail: pgs@pagunsmith.edu

PIA School of Specialized Technology
PO Box 10897, Pittsburgh PA 15236-0897
Vincent J. Mezza, Director of Admissions
800-444-1440 Fax: 412-466-0513
Website: www.pia.edu
E-mail: admissions@pia.edu
See listing under "Aeronautics, Aviation and Space"

ROSEDALE TECHNICAL INSTITUTE

215 Beecham Dr Ste 2, Pittsburgh PA 15205
Kevin Auld, Contact
412-521-6200 Fax: 412-521-2520
Website: www.rosedaletech.org
E-mail: admissions@rosedaletech.org

UNIVERSAL TECHNICAL INSTITUTE

750 Pennsylvania Dr, Exton PA 19341
Karen Hannigan-Robinson, Campus Admissions Director
877-884-3986 Fax: 610-646-8549
Website: www.uti-auto-tech.com
E-mail: khannigan@uticorp.com

RHODE ISLAND

MTTI - MOTORING TECHNICAL TRAINING INSTITUTE

54 Water St, East Providence RI 02914-5022
Nick Azzarone, Director of Admissions
401-434-4840 or 866-454-6884 Fax: 401-434-9540
Website: www.mtti.edu
E-mail: mtti2@aol.com

New England Institute of Technology
2500 Post Rd, Warwick RI 02886-2244
Michael Kwiatkowski, Director of Admissions
401-739-5000 Fax: 401-738-5122
Website: www.neit.edu
E-mail: eflynn@neit.edu

NEW ENGLAND TRACTOR TRAILER TRAINING

600 Moshassuck Valley Industrial Hwy
Pawtucket RI 02860-1752
Frederick Hazard, Director
401-725-1220 Fax: 401-724-1340
Website: www.nettts.com
E-mail: fhazard@nettts.com

SOUTH CAROLINA

Spartanburg Technical College
PO Box 4386, Spartanburg SC 29305-4386
Nancy Garmroth, Dean of Admissions & Financial Aid
864-592-4810 Fax: 864-592-4945
Website: stcsc.edu

SOUTH DAKOTA

Western Dakota Technical Institute
800 Mickelson Dr, Rapid City SD 57703-4018
Janell Oberlander, Manager of Student Services
605-394-4034 or 800-544-8765 Fax: 605-394-1789
Website: www.westerndakotatech.org
E-mail: admissions@wdti.tec.sd.us
See listing under "Career Schools"

TENNESSEE

NASHVILLE AUTO-DIESEL COLLEGE
1524 Gallatin Ave, Nashville TN 37206-3298
Peggie Werrbach, Director of Admissions
800-228-6232 Fax: 615-262-8466
Website: www.nadcedu.com
E-mail: admissions@nadcedu.com
See listing under "Career Schools"

Vatterott College - Memphis Campus
2655 Dividend Dr, Memphis TN 38132
Joe Lockwood, Director of Admissions
901-761-5730 Fax: 901-763-2897
Website: www.vatterott-college.edu
E-mail: joe.lockwood@vatterott-college.edu

TEXAS

Hallmark Institute of Aeronautics
Aeronautics Campus-Aviation Technology
8901 Wetmore Rd, San Antonio TX 78216-4229
Joe Fisher, President
210-826-1000 Fax: 210-826-3707
Website: www.hallmarkinstitute.edu
E-mail: sross@hallmarkinstitute.edu

Temple College
2600 S 1st St, Temple TX 76504-7435
Angela Balch, Director of Admissions & Records
254-298-8300 Fax: 254-298-8288
Website: www.templejc.edu
E-mail: ruth.bridges@templejc.edu

Tyler Junior College
PO Box 9020, Tyler TX 75711-9020
Joan Jones, Interim Dean
800-687-5680
Website: www.tjc.edu
E-mail: jjon@tjc.edu
See listing under "Community and Junior Colleges"

Western Technical College
9624 Plaza Cir, El Paso TX 79927-2105
Bill Terrell, Chief Administrative Officer
915-760-8123
Website: www.wtc-ep.edu
E-mail: bterrell@wtc-ep.edu

Western Technical College
9451 Diana Dr, El Paso TX 79924-6936
Bill Terrell, Chief Administrative Officer
915-566-9621 Fax: 915-565-9903
Website: www.wtc-ep.edu
E-mail: bterrell@wtc-ep.edu

VIRGINIA

Southside Virginia Community College
109 Campus Dr, Alberta VA 23821-2930
Ronald E. Mattox, Dean of Admissions
434-949-1014 Fax: 434-949-7863
Website: www.sv.vccs.edu
E-mail: ronald.mattox@sv.vccs.edu

Southside Virginia Community College
200 Daniel Rd, Keysville VA 23947
Ronald E. Mattox, Dean of Admissions
434-736-2018 Fax: 434-736-2082
Website: www.sv.vccs.edu
E-mail: ronald.mattox@sv.vccs.edu

WASHINGTON

BATES TECHNICAL COLLEGE
1101 S Yakima Ave, Tacoma WA 98405-4895
David Borofsky, President
253-680-7000 Fax: 253-680-7101
Website: www.bates.ctc.edu
E-mail: info@bates.ctc.edu

Clover Park Technical College
4500 Steilacoom Blvd SW
Lakewood WA 98499-4098
Dr. Sharon McGavick, President
253-589-5678 Fax: 253-589-5601
Website: www.cptc.edu
E-mail: jim.griffith@cptc.edu

Everett Community College
2000 Tower St, Everett WA 98201
Christine Kerlin, Associate Dean
425-388-9100 Fax: 425-388-9173
Website: www.everettcc.edu
E-mail: ckerlin@everettcc.edu

Perry Technical Institute
2011 W Washington Ave, Yakima WA 98903-1296
509-453-0374 Fax: 509-453-0375
Website: www.perrytech.edu
E-mail: frankj@perrytech.edu

Walla Walla Community College
500 Tausick Way, Walla Walla WA 99362-9270
Del Wilde, Director
509-527-4283 or 877-992-9922 Fax: 509-527-4572
Website: www.wwcc.edu
E-mail: del.wilde@wwcc.edu

Wenatchee Valley College
1300 5th St, Wenatchee WA 98801-1799
Marco Azurdia, Dean, Student Development
509-682-6805 Fax: 509-682-6541
Website: www.wvc.edu

WISCONSIN

Blackhawk Technical College
PO Box 5009, Janesville WI 53547-5009
Gregg Bosak, Administration, Community Information
608-757-7769 Fax: 608-757-7740
Website: www.blackhawk.edu
E-mail: gbosak@blackhawk.edu

Wisconsin Indianhead Technical College
505 Pine Ridge Dr, Shell Lake WI 54871
Miriam Crandall, Dean of Student Services
800-243-9482 Fax: 715-468-2819
Website: www.witc.edu
E-mail: mcrandal@witc.edu
Campuses in Ashland, New Richmond, Rice Lake, Superior.

WYOMING

Laramie County Community College
1400 E College Dr, Cheyenne WY 82007-3204
Jenny Hargett, Director of Admissions
307-778-5222 Fax: 307-778-1350
Website: www.lccc.wy.edu
E-mail: learnmore@lccc.wy.edu

WYOMING TECHNICAL INSTITUTE
4373 N 3rd St, Laramie WY 82072-9519
Glenn R. Halsey, Director of Admissions
307-742-3776 Fax: 307-721-4854
Website: www.wyotech.com
E-mail: admissions@wyotech.com

GUAM

Guam Community College
PO Box 23069, G.M.F. GU 96921-0307
Virginia Charfauros Tudela, Ph.D., Registrar
671-735-5531 Fax: 671-734-5238
Website: www.guamcc.edu
E-mail: Webmaster@guamcc.edu

PUERTO RICO

Colegio Mayor de Technologia
PO Box 1490, Arroyo PR 00714
Julia Melendez, Director of Admissions
787-839-5266 Fax: 787-839-0033
Website: www.colegiomayortec.com
E-mail: cmtarroy@coqui.net

Instituto de Banca y Comercio
61 Ponce De Leon Ave, Hato Rey PR 00919
Rafael Jimenez, Vice President
787-754-7120 Fax: 787-754-7143
Website: www.ibanca.net
E-mail: rjimenez@ibancapr.com

PROFESSIONAL ELECTRICAL SCHOOL
PO Box 1797, Manati PR 00674
Paulino Delgado, Director
787-854-4776 Fax: 787-854-4776
E-mail: pes@atenas.com

MEDICINE

ALABAMA

Judson College
302 Bibb St, Marion AL 36756
Michael Scotto, Director of Admissions
800-447-9472 Fax: 334-683-5147
Website: www.judson.edu
E-mail: admissions@judson.edu

University of South Alabama
307 University Blvd N, Mobile AL 36688-3053
Melissa Haab, Director of Admissions
251-460-6141 Fax: 251-460-7876
Website: www.southalabama.edu
E-mail: admiss@usouthal.edu

ARIZONA

University of Arizona Medical Center
1501 N Campbell Ave, Tucson AZ 85724-5091
520-694-0111 or 520-694-9409
Website: www.umcarizona.org

ARKANSAS

Ouachita Baptist University
410 Ouachita St, Arkadelphia AR 71998-0001
David Goodman, Director of Admissions
870-245-5110 Fax: 870-245-5500
Website: www.obu.edu
E-mail: admissions@obu.edu

CALIFORNIA

Chapman University
One University Drive, Orange CA 92866-1099
Michael Drummy, Assistant Vice President for Enrollment
Services and Chief Admission Officer
714-997-6411 or 888-CUAPPLY Fax: 714-997-6713
Website: www.chapman.edu
E-mail: admit@chapman.edu

COLORADO

University of Colorado at Denver and Health Sciences
Center
Health Sciences Program
4200 E 9th Ave Box C245, Denver CO 80262
Phoebe Lindsey Barton, Ph.D., Director
Website: www.uchsc.edu

FLORIDA

Florida National College
Hialeah Campus
4425 W 20th Ave, Hialeah FL 33012
Jorge Afonso, Campus Dean
305-821-3333 ext. 1022 Fax: 305-362-0595
Website: www.fnc.edu
E-mail: omarsnc@fnc.edu

Florida National College
South Campus
11865 SW 26th St, Miami FL 33175
Jon Beisenherz, Campus Dean
305-266-9999
Website: www.fnc.edu
E-mail: omarsnc@fnc.edu

Florida State University
600 W College Ave, Tallahassee FL 32306-1096
Janice V. Finney, Director of Admissions
850-644-2525 Fax: 850-644-0197
Website: admissions.fsu.edu
E-mail: admissions@admin.fsu.edu

University of South Florida
4202 E Fowler Ave, Tampa FL 33620-6900
J. Robert Spatig, Director of Admissions
813-974-3350 Fax: 813-974-9689
Website: www.usf.edu
E-mail: admissions@admin.usf.edu

ILLINOIS

Roosevelt University
430 S Michigan Ave, Chicago IL 60605
Gwen E. Kanelos, Asst. Vice President for Enrollment
Services
877-APPLY-RU Fax: 312-341-4216
Website: www.roosevelt.edu
E-mail: applyru@roosevelt.edu

IOWA

Briar Cliff University
PO Box 2100, Sioux City IA 51104-0100
Sharisue Wilcoxon, VP for Enrollment Management
712-279-5200 Fax: 712-279-1632
Website: www.briarcliff.edu
E-mail: admissions@briarcliff.edu

Iowa Lakes Community College
300 S 18th St, Estherville IA 51334-2721
Anne Stansbury, Asst. Director of Admissions
712-362-7945 Fax: 712-362-8363
Website: www.iowalakes.edu
E-mail: info@iowalakes.edu

KANSAS

Newman University
3100 W McCormick St, Wichita KS 67213
Jann Reusser, Admissions Recruitment Coordinator
316-942-4291 ext. 2144 Fax: 316-942-4483
Website: www.newmanu.edu
E-mail: reusserj@newmanu.edu

MISSOURI

Truman State University
100 E Normal, Kirksville MO 63501
Office of Admission
660-785-4000 Fax: 660-785-4181
Website: admissions.truman.edu
E-mail: admissions@truman.edu

William Woods University
1 University Ave, Fulton MO 65251-1098
Jimmy Clay, Director of Admissions
573-642-2251 Fax: 573-592-1146
Website: www.williamwoods.edu
E-mail: admissions@williamwoods.edu
See listing under "Universities"

MONTANA

Rocky Mountain College
1511 Poly Dr, Billings MT 59102-1796
Bonnie Knapp, Director of Admissions
800-877-6259 Fax: 406-657-1189
Website: www.rocky.edu
E-mail: admissions@rocky.edu

NEBRASKA

College of Saint Mary
7000 Mercy Rd, Omaha NE 68106
Lorin Werth, V.P. for Enrollment
800-926-5534 or 402-399-2407 Fax: 402-399-2412
Website: www.csm.edu
E-mail: lwerth@csm.edu

NEW JERSEY

Bergen Community College
400 Paramus Rd, Paramus NJ 07652
Julian Gomez, Asst. Director of Admissions
201-447-7100 Fax: 201-444-7036
Website: www.bergen.edu
E-mail: jgomez@bergen.edu

New Jersey City University
2039 John F Kennedy Blvd
Jersey City NJ 07305-1588
Carmen Panlilio, Asst. V.P. for Admissions and
Financial Aid
201-200-3234 Fax: 201-200-2044
Website: www.njcu.edu
E-mail: admissions@njcu.edu

NEW YORK

Roberts Wesleyan College
2301 Westside Dr, Rochester NY 14624-1997
Office of Admissions
585-594-6400 Fax: 585-594-6371
Website: www.roberts.edu
E-mail: admissions@roberts.edu

Trocaire College
360 Choate Ave, Buffalo NY 14220-2003
Paul B. Hurley, Ph.D., President
716-826-1200 Fax: 716-828-6107
Website: www.trocaire.edu
E-mail: info@trocaire.edu
See listing under "Community and Junior Colleges"

NORTH CAROLINA

Lees-McRae College
PO Box 128, Banner Elk NC 28604-0128
Walt Crutchfield, Dean of Admissions
800-280-4562 Fax: 828-898-8707
Website: www.lmc.edu
E-mail: admissions@lmc.edu

Louisburg College
501 N Main St, Louisburg NC 27549-2399
800-775-0208 or 919-496-2521 Fax: 919-496-1788
Website: www.louisburg.edu
E-mail: admissions@louisburg.edu

OHIO

Brown Mackie College - Cincinnati
1011 Glendale Milford Rd, Cincinnati OH 45215-1107
Robin Krout, President
513-771-2424 Fax: 513-771-3413
Website: www.brownmackie.edu
E-mail: rkrout@brownmackie.edu

Medical University of Ohio
3000 Arlington Ave, Toledo OH 43614
419-383-4000 Fax: 419-383-2800
Website: www.meduohio.edu

The Ohio State University
College of Medicine and Public Health
Meiling Hall, 370 W 9th Ave, Columbus OH 43210
Fred Sanfilippo, M.D., Ph.D., Dean
614-292-2220 Fax: 614-247-7959
Website: medicine.osu.edu
E-mail: medicine@osu.edu

OHIO WESLEYAN UNIVERSITY

61 S Sandusky St, Delaware OH 43015-2398
Director of Admission
740-368-3020 Fax: 740-368-3314
Website: www.owu.edu
E-mail: owuadmit@owu.edu

Ursuline College
2550 Lander Rd, Cleveland OH 44124-4398
Sarah E. Sundermeier, Director of Admissions
888-URSULINE Toll Free Fax: 440-684-6138
Website: www.admission.ursuline.edu
E-mail: admission@ursuline.edu

PENNSYLVANIA

Computer Learning Network
401 E Winding Hill Rd Ste 101
Mechanicsburg PA 17055-4989
Marlene Macauley, Director of Admissions
717-761-1481 Fax: 717-761-0558
Website: www.clntraining.net
E-mail: mmacauley@clntraining.net

Juniata College
1700 Moore St, Huntingdon PA 16652-2196
Michelle Bartol, Dean of Enrollment
877-JUNIATA Fax: 814-641-3100
Website: www.juniata.edu
E-mail: admissions@juniata.edu

TENNESSEE

Vatterott College - Memphis Campus
2655 Dividend Dr, Memphis TN 38132
Joe Lockwood, Director of Admissions
901-761-5730 Fax: 901-763-2897
Website: www.vatterott-college.edu
E-mail: joe.lockwood@vatterott-college.edu

TEXAS

University of St. Thomas
3800 Montrose Blvd, Houston TX 77006-4626
Eduardo Prieto, Director of Admissions
713-522-7911 Fax: 713-525-3558
Website: www.stthom.edu
E-mail: prietoe@stthom.edu

WASHINGTON

Gonzaga University
502 E Boone Ave, Spokane WA 99258-0102
Julie McCulloh, Dean of Admission
800-322-2584 or 509-323-6572 Fax: 509-323-5780
Website: www.gonzaga.edu
E-mail: mcculloh@gu.gonzaga.edu

WEST VIRGINIA

West Virginia Wesleyan College
59 College Ave, Buckhannon WV 26201-2699
Robert N. Skinner II, Director of Admission
800-722-9933 Fax: 304-473-8108
Website: www.wvwc.edu
E-mail: admission@wvwc.edu

WISCONSIN

Medical College of Wisconsin
PO Box 26509, Milwaukee WI 53226-0509
Michael Istwan, Director of Admissions
414-456-8296 Fax: 414-456-6506
Website: www.mcw.edu
E-mail: mcwms@mcw.edu

St. Norbert College
100 Grant St, De Pere WI 54115
Brian Studebaker, Director of Admission
800-236-4878 Fax: 920-403-4072
Website: www.snc.edu
E-mail: admit@snc.edu

PUERTO RICO

SAN JUAN BAUTISTA SCHOOL OF MEDICINE

PO Box 4968, Caguas PR 00726-4968
Lissette Torres, Registrar
787-743-3038 Fax: 787-746-3093
Website: www.sanjuanbautista.edu
E-mail: ltorres@sanjuanbautista.edu

MEN'S COLLEGES

CALIFORNIA

Don Bosco Technical Institute
1151 San Gabriel Blvd, Rosemead CA 91770-4251
626-307-6500

Yeshiva Ohr Elchonon Chabad
West Coast Talmudical Seminary
7215 Waring Ave, Los Angeles CA 90046
323-937-3763

DISTRICT OF COLUMBIA

Dominican House of Studies
487 Michigan Ave NE, Washington DC 20017-1585
202-529-5300

FLORIDA

St. John Vianney College Seminary
2900 SW 87th Ave, Miami FL 33165-3244
305-223-4561

St. Vincent DePaul Regional Seminary
10701 S Military Trl, Boynton Beach FL 33436-4899
Rev. Steven O'Hala, Academic Dean
561-732-4424 ext. 151 Fax: 561-732-8808
Website: www.svdp.edu
E-mail: sohala@svdp.edu
M.Div and M.A.

Talmudic College of Florida
1910 Alton Rd, Miami Beach FL 33139-1507
305-534-7050

GEORGIA

Morehouse College
830 Westview Dr SW, Atlanta GA 30314-3773
404-681-2800

ILLINOIS

Telshe Yeshiva-Chicago
3535 W Foster Ave, Chicago IL 60625-5526
773-463-7738

INDIANA

Wabash College
301 W Wabash Ave, Crawfordsville IN 47933
David Collins, Sr. Assoc. Director of Admissions
800-345-5385

LOUISIANA

Notre Dame Seminary
2901 S Carrollton Ave, New Orleans LA 70118-4391
504-866-7426

MARYLAND

Ner Israel Rabbinical College
400 Mount Wilson Ln, Baltimore MD 21208-1198
410-484-7200

Yeshiva College of the Nation's Capital
1216 Arcola Ave, Silver Spring MD 20902
301-593-2534

MICHIGAN

Sacred Heart Major Seminary
2701 W Chicago, Detroit MI 48206-1704
313-883-8500

MINNESOTA

St. John's University
PO Box 7155, Collegeville MN 56321-7155
320-363-2011

MISSOURI

Conception Seminary College
Conception MO 64433
Vincent Casper, Director of Admissions
660-944-2886

NEW JERSEY

Beth Medrash Govoha
617 6th St, Lakewood NJ 08701-2797
732-367-1060

Rabbinical College of America
226 Sussex Ave, Morristown NJ 07960-3632
973-267-9404

Talmudical Academy of New Jersey
Route 524, Adelphia NJ 07710
732-431-1600

NEW YORK

Beis Medrash Heichal Dovid
275 Beach 17th St, Far Rockaway NY 11691
718-868-2300

Beth HaMedrash Shaarei Yosher
4102 16th Ave #10, Brooklyn NY 11204-1052
718-854-2290

Beth HaTalmud Rabbinical College
2127 82nd St, Brooklyn NY 11214-2509
718-259-2525

Darkei Noam Rabbinical College
2822 Avenue J, Brooklyn NY 11210-3736
718-338-6464

Holy Trinity Orthodox Seminary
PO Box 36, Jordanville NY 13361
315-858-0945

Kehilath Yakov Rabbinical Seminary
206 Wilson St, Brooklyn NY 11211-7207
718-963-1212

Kol Yaakov Torah Center
29 W Maple Ave, Monsey NY 10952-2954
845-425-3863

Machzikei Hadath Rabbinical College
5407 16th Ave, Brooklyn NY 11204-1805
718-854-8777

Mesivta of Eastern Parkway Rabbinical Seminary
510 Dahill Rd, Brooklyn NY 11218-5559
718-438-1002

Mesivta Tifereth Jerusalem of America
145 E Broadway, New York NY 10002-6382
212-964-2830

Mesivta Torah Vodaath Seminary
425 E 9th St, Brooklyn NY 11218-5209
718-941-8000

Mirrer Yeshiva Central Institute
1795 Ocean Pkwy, Brooklyn NY 11223-2010
718-645-0536

Ohr HaMeir Theological Seminary
PO Box 2130, Peekskill NY 10566-0990
914-736-1500

Rabbinical Academy Mesivta Rabbi Chaim
1605 Coney Island Ave, Brooklyn NY 11230-4715
718-377-0777

Rabbinical College Beth Shraga
28 Saddle River Rd, Airmont NY 10952-3035
845-356-1980

Rabbinical College Bobover Yeshiva B'nei Zion
1577 48th St, Brooklyn NY 11219-3250
718-438-2018

Rabbinical College Ch' San Sofer of New York
1876 50th St, Brooklyn NY 11204-1252
718-236-1171

Rabbinical College of Long Island
205 N Beech St, Long Beach NY 11561-3244
516-255-4700

Rabbinical College of Ohr Shimon Yisroel
215 Hewes St, Brooklyn NY 11211-8102
718-855-4092

Rabbinical Seminary Adas Yereim
185 Wilson St, Brooklyn NY 11211-7206
718-388-1751

Rabbinical Seminary M'Kor Chaim
1571 55th St, Brooklyn NY 11219-4314
718-851-0183

Rabbinical Seminary of America
9215 69th Ave, Forest Hills NY 11375-5817
718-268-4700

Shor Yoshuv Institute
1 Cedarlawn Dr, Lawrence NY 11559-1714
516-239-9002

Talmudical Institute of Upstate New York
769 Park Ave, Rochester NY 14607-3046
585-473-2810

Talmudical Seminary Oholei Torah
667 Eastern Pkwy, Brooklyn NY 11213-3310
718-774-5050

Torah Temimah Talmudical Seminary
507 Ocean Pkwy, Brooklyn NY 11218-5913
718-853-8500

United Talmudical Seminary
82 Lee Ave, Brooklyn NY 11211-7900
718-963-9770

UTA Mesivta of Kiryas Joel
33 Forest Ave Ste 101, Monroe NY 10950
845-783-9901

Yeshiva and Kollel Harbotzas Torah
1049 E 15th St, Brooklyn NY 11230-4462
718-692-0208

Yeshiva D'Monsey Rabbinical College
2 Roman Blvd, Monsey NY 10952
845-426-3276

Yeshiva Karlin Stolin
1818 54th St, Brooklyn NY 11204-1545
718-232-7800

Yeshiva of Nitra Rabbinical College
194 Division Ave, Brooklyn NY 11211-7108
718-387-0422

Yeshiva of the Telshe Alumni
4904 Independence Ave, Bronx NY 10471
718-601-3523

Yeshiva Shaarei Torah of Rockland
91 W Carlton Rd, Suffern NY 10901
845-352-3431

Yeshiva Shaar HaTorah - Grodno
8396 117th St, Richmond Hill NY 11418-1469
718-846-1940

Yeshivath Viznitz
PO Box 446, Monsey NY 10952-0446
845-356-1010

Yeshivath Zichron Moshe
Laurel Park Rd, South Fallsburg NY 12779
845-434-5240

Yeshivat Mikdash Melech
1326 Ocean Pkwy, Brooklyn NY 11230-5601
718-339-1090

OHIO

Pontifical College Josephinum
7625 N High St, Columbus OH 43235-1499
614-885-5585

Rabbinical College of Telshe
28400 Euclid Ave, Wickliffe OH 44092-2523
440-943-5300

PENNSYLVANIA

St. Charles Borromeo Seminary
100 E Wynnewood Rd, Wynnewood PA 19096
610-667-3394

Talmudical Yeshiva of Philadelphia
6063 Drexel Rd, Philadelphia PA 19131-1296
Rabbi Uri Mandelbaum, Director of Admissions
215-477-1000 Fax: 215-477-5065
E-mail: typ@attglobal.net

Valley Forge Military College
1001 Eagle Rd, Wayne PA 19087-3613
800-234-8362

Yeshiva Beth Moshe
930 Hickory St, Scranton PA 18505-2196
570-346-1747

SOUTH CAROLINA

The Citadel
171 Moultrie St, Charleston SC 29409-0002
843-953-5000

VIRGINIA

Hampden-Sydney College
PO Box 128, Hampden Sydney VA 23943-0128
804-223-6000

Virginia Military Institute
Lexington VA 24450
540-464-7000

MILITARY SCIENCE

ALABAMA

CALHOUN COMMUNITY COLLEGE
PO Box 2216, Decatur AL 35609-2216
M. Wayne Tosh, Registrar
256-306-2500 Fax: 256-306-2941
Website: www.calhoun.edu
E-mail: jtl@calhoun.edu

ARIZONA

University of Arizona
Tucson AZ 85721-0040
Paul Kohn, Director of Admissions
520-621-3237 Fax: 520-621-9799
Website: www.admissions.arizona.edu or
www.arizona.edu

CALIFORNIA

:: ARMY AND NAVY ACADEMY
PO Box 3000, Carlsbad CA 92018-3000
Elizabeth Kalivas, Director of Admissions
760-729-2385 ext. 400 Fax: 760-434-5948
Website: www.armyandnavyacademy.org
E-mail: admissions@armyandnavyacademy.org

FLORIDA

:: ADMIRAL FARRAGUT ACADEMY
501 Park St N, Saint Petersburg FL 33710
David Graham, Director of Admissions
727-384-5500 Fax: 727-347-5160
Website: www.farragut.org
E-mail: admissions@farragut.org

IDAHO

Brigham Young University - Idaho
120 Kimball Bldg, Rexburg ID 83460
Gordon Westenskow, Director of Admissions
208-496-1020 Fax: 208-496-1220
Website: www.byui.edu
E-mail: admissions@byui.edu

KENTUCKY

Morehead State University
Morehead KY 40351-1689
Dayna Seelig, Enrollment Services
800-585-6781 Fax: 606-783-5038
Website: www.moreheadstate.edu
E-mail: admissions@moreheadstate.edu

MISSOURI

Calvary Bible College & Theological Seminary
15800 Calvary Rd, Kansas City MO 64147-1341
Robert M. Reinsch, Director of Admissions
800-326-3960 Fax: 816-331-4474
Website: www.calvary.edu
E-mail: admissions@calvary.edu

:: MISSOURI MILITARY ACADEMY
800 Grand Ave, Mexico MO 65265
Maj. Dennis Diederich, Director of Admissions
888-564-6662 Fax: 573-581-0081
Website: www.mma-cadet.org
E-mail: info@mma.mexico.mo.us

:: WENTWORTH MILITARY ACADEMY & JUNIOR COLLEGE
1880 Washington Ave, Lexington MO 64067
MAJ Mike Herman, Director of Admissions
800-962-7682 or 660-259-2221 Fax: 660-259-2677
Website: www.wma.edu, wjc.wma.edu
E-mail: admissions@wma1880.org

NEW MEXICO

:: NEW MEXICO MILITARY INSTITUTE
101 W College Blvd, Roswell NM 88201-5173
Rear Admiral David R. Ellison, USN (Ret.),
Superintendent
LTC. Craig Collins Director of Admissions
800-421-5376 or 505-624-8050 Fax: 505-624-8058
Website: www.nmmi.edu
E-mail: admissions@nmmi.edu
Established 1891. State Supported. Coed. Accreditation: NCACS, New Mexico Department of Education. Estimated costs for 2004-2005 school year, out-of-state student: $10,166, in-state student: $7,670. Enrollment: 950. Faculty: 68. Student-faculty ratio: 18:1. Degree: AA. Library: 68,000 volumes. 19 buildings on 40 acre main campus. Additional acreage includes an 18-hole championship golf course. ROTC - offering an ARMY two year commissioning program. Prep school for all service academies. 90% of high school graduates receive their 4 year college degrees. 90% of junior college graduates receive their baccalaureate degrees. Quality education at a fair price.

NEW YORK

SUNY College at Brockport
350 New Campus Dr, Brockport NY 14420-2997
Bernard S. Valento, Director of Undergraduate
Admissions
585-395-2751 Fax: 585-395-5452
Website: www.brockport.edu
E-mail: admit@brockport.edu

OKLAHOMA

Oklahoma State University
Stillwater OK 74078
Jeffrey Hensley, Department Head
405-744-1775
Website: www.okstate.edu
E-mail: mnlinch@okstate.edu

PENNSYLVANIA

:: CARSON LONG MILITARY INSTITUTE
PO Box 98, New Bloomfield PA 17068-0098
Lieutenant Colonel David M. Comolli, Academic Dean
717-582-2121 Fax: 717-582-8763
Website: www.carsonlong.org
E-mail: carson6@pa.net

Gannon University
109 University Sq, Erie PA 16541-0001
Christopher Tremblay, Director of Admissions
800-GANNON-U Fax: 814-871-5803
Website: www.gannon.edu
E-mail: admissions@gannon.edu

SOUTH CAROLINA

PRESBYTERIAN COLLEGE
503 S Broad St, Clinton SC 29325
Richard Dana Paul, Dean of Admissions
800-476-7272 Fax: 864-833-8481
Website: www.presby.edu
E-mail: admissions@presby.edu

VERMONT

NORWICH UNIVERSITY
158 Harmon Dr, Northfield VT 05663
Col. William S. Knoebel, Professor of Military Science
800-468-6679
Website: www.norwich.edu/nationalservices
E-mail: nuadm@norwich.edu
See listing under "Universities"

VIRGINIA

:: Fishburne Military School
PO Box 988, Waynesboro VA 22980-0722
Colonel William Alexander, Superintendent
Captain Christopher A. Richmond, Director of
Admissions
800-946-7773 Fax: 540-946-7738
Website: www.fishburne.org
E-mail: crichmond@fishburne.org

:: FORK UNION MILITARY ACADEMY
PO Box 278, Fork Union VA 23055-0278
Lt. Gen. John E. Jackson Jr., USAF (Ret.), President
Lt. Col. Steve Macek, Director of Admissions
800-462-3862 or 434-842-4205 Fax: 434-842-4300
Website: www.forkunion.com
E-mail: maceks@fuma.org
Private. Men only. Accreditation: VAIS, SACS, NAIS, AMCS, SAIS. Tuition: $21,190. Fees: $3,080. Enrollment: 550. Faculty: 47. Student-faculty ratio: 12:1. Degrees: college-prep high school diploma and advanced college prep. Library: 19,000+ volumes. 19 buildings on 1,000 acres. One subject plan; technology center with over 300 networked multi-media computers; nationally-recognized athletic teams; 99% of our students go on to college.

:: Hargrave Military Academy
200 Military Dr, Chatham VA 24531-4683
Frank Martin, Director of Admissions
800-432-2480 Fax: 434-432-3129
Website: www.hargrave.edu
E-mail: admissions@hargrave.edu
See listing under "Preparatory Schools for Boys"

:: MASSANUTTEN MILITARY ACADEMY
614 S Main St, Woodstock VA 22664-1205
Murali Sinnathamby, Director of Admissions
877-466-6222 or 540-459-2167 Fax: 540-459-5421
Website: www.militaryschool.com
E-mail: admissions@militaryschool.com

Radford University
PO Box 6903, Radford VA 24142
David W. Kraus, Director of Admissions
800-890-4265 Fax: 540-831-5038
Website: www.radford.edu
E-mail: ruadmiss@radford.edu

WASHINGTON

Gonzaga University
　502 E Boone Ave, Spokane WA 99258-0102
　Julie McCulloh, Dean of Admission
　800-322-2584 or 509-323-6572 Fax: 509-323-5780
　Website: www.gonzaga.edu
　E-mail: mcculloh@gu.gonzaga.edu

WISCONSIN

:: **ST. JOHN'S NORTHWESTERN MILITARY ACADEMY**
　1101 N Genesee St, Delafield WI 53018-1498
　Mr. Jack H. Albert, Jr., President
　Cpt. Duane Rutherford, Director of Enrollment Services
　Lt. Kathleen McCormick, Enrollment Counselor

800-752-2338 or 262-646-7199 Fax: 262-646-7128
Website: www.sjnma.org
E-mail: admissions@sjnma.org
　Established in 1884. Private. Boys grades 7-12. Accreditation: ISACS, NAIS, AMCSUS. Tuition, room & board: $27,250. Enrollment: 325 boarding; 5 day. Faculty: 39. Student-faculty ratio: 12:1. 10 buildings on 150 acres. Gym, pool, tennis courts, golf course. College preparatory boy's boarding school. Day program for grades 7-8 only. 30 minutes from Milwaukee and 90 minutes from Chicago. Extensive athletic and extracurricular offerings. JROTC honor school with distinction.

St. Norbert College
　100 Grant St, De Pere WI 54115
　Brian Studebaker, Director of Admission
　800-236-4878 Fax: 920-403-4072
　Website: www.snc.edu
　E-mail: admit@snc.edu

GUAM

University of Guam
　UOG Station, Mangilao GU 96923
　Deborah Leon Guerrero, Registrar
　671-735-2201 or 671-735-2208 Fax: 671-735-2203
　Website: www.uog.edu
　E-mail: admitme@uog9.uog.edu

PUERTO RICO

:: **AMERICAN MILITARY ACADEMY**
　PO Box 7884, Guaynabo PR 00970-7884
　Vivian Simonet, Superintendent
　787-720-6801 Fax: 787-720-6841
　Website: www.amapr.org
　E-mail: vsimonet@amapr.org

MUSIC

ALABAMA

Alabama A & M University
　PO Box 908, Normal AL 35762
　Antonio Boyle, Director of Admissions
　256-372-5245 Fax: 256-372-5249
　Website: www.aamu.edu
　E-mail: aboyle@aamu.edu

CALHOUN COMMUNITY COLLEGE
　PO Box 2216, Decatur AL 35609-2216
　M. Wayne Tosh, Registrar
　256-306-2500 Fax: 256-306-2941
　Website: www.calhoun.edu
　E-mail: aprater@calhoun.edu

Faulkner University
　5345 Atlanta Hwy, Montgomery AL 36109-3398
　Keith Mock, Director of Admissions
　800-879-9816 ext. 7200 or 334-386-7200
　Fax: 334-386-7137
　Website: www.faulkner.edu
　E-mail: admissions@faulkner.edu

Judson College
　302 Bibb St, Marion AL 36756
　Michael Scotto, Director of Admissions
　800-447-9472 Fax: 334-683-5147
　Website: www.judson.edu
　E-mail: admissions@judson.edu

University of Alabama in Huntsville
　PO Box 1247, Huntsville AL 35899-0001
　Ann Lee, Assoc. Director for Recruiting Program and Events
　1-800-UAH-CALL Fax: 256-824-6073
　Website: www.uah.edu
　E-mail: leev@uah.edu

University of South Alabama
　307 University Blvd N, Mobile AL 36688-3053
　Melissa Haab, Director of Admissions
　251-460-6141 Fax: 251-460-7876
　Website: www.southalabama.edu
　E-mail: admiss@usouthal.edu

ALASKA

University of Alaska Anchorage
　PO Box 141629, Anchorage AK 99514-1629
　Cecile Mitchell, Director of Enrollment Services
　907-786-1480 Fax: 907-786-4888
　Website: www.uaa.alaska.edu/
　E-mail: enroll@uaa.alaska.edu

ARIZONA

:: **THE CONSERVATORY OF RECORDING ARTS & SCIENCES**
　2300 E Broadway Rd, Tempe AZ 85282-1707
　Tonya Visconti, Director of Admissions
　800-562-6383 or 480-858-9400 Fax: 480-829-1332
　Website: cras.org
　E-mail: info@cras.org
　Established 1987. Private. Coed. Accreditation: ACCSCT. Enrollment: 480. Faculty: 30. Student-faculty ratio: 12:1. Diploma: Master recording program. Certificate: Audio recording & production, music business, MIDI/computer/electronic music recording, sound reinforcement, concert sound, trouble shooting maintenance. Purpose is to train highly motivated students for entry level positions in the audio recording and music industries. Through extensive hands-on training with industry standard equipment and practice with current production techniques, students gain the confidence and expertise to enter the working world as Recording Engineers.

Southwestern College
　2625 E Cactus Rd, Phoenix AZ 85032-7097
　Admissions/Financial Aid Office
　800-247-2697 or 602-992-6101 Fax: 602-404-2159
　Website: www.swcaz.edu
　E-mail: admissions@swcaz.edu

University of Arizona
　Tucson AZ 85721-0040
　Paul Kohn, Director of Admissions
　520-621-3237 Fax: 520-621-9799
　Website: www.admissions.arizona.edu or www.arizona.edu

ARKANSAS

Ouachita Baptist University
　410 Ouachita St, Arkadelphia AR 71998-0001
　David Goodman, Director of Admissions
　870-245-5110 Fax: 870-245-5500
　Website: www.obu.edu
　E-mail: admissions@obu.edu

CALIFORNIA

Chapman University
　One University Drive, Orange CA 92866-1099
　Michael Drummy, Assistant Vice President for Enrollment
　Services and Chief Admission Officer
　714-997-6411 or 888-CUAPPLY Fax: 714-997-6713
　Website: www.chapman.edu
　E-mail: admit@chapman.edu

Cogswell College
　1175 Bordeaux Dr, Sunnyvale CA 94089-1210
　Dr. Tim Duncan, Dean of the College
　800-264-7955 or 408-541-0100 Fax: 408-747-0764
　Website: www.cogswell.edu
　E-mail: info@cogswell.edu

: **COLBURN SCHOOL**
　200 S Grand Ave, Los Angeles CA 90012-3007
　Kathleen Tesar, Director of Admissions and Student Affairs
　213-621-2200 Fax: 213-621-2110
　Website: www.colburnschool.edu
　E-mail: ktesar@colburnschool.edu

Concordia University
　1530 Concordia, Irvine CA 92612-3203
　Lori McDonald, Executive Director of Enrollment Services
　800-229-1200 or 949-854-8002 Fax: 949-854-6894
　Website: www.cui.edu
　E-mail: admission@cui.edu

MUSICIANS INSTITUTE
　1655 N McCadden Pl, Hollywood CA 90028
　Steve Lunn, Director of Admissions
　323-462-1384 Fax: 323-462-6978
　Website: www.mi.edu
　E-mail: admissions@mi.edu

Orange Coast College
　PO Box 5005, Costa Mesa CA 92628-5005
　Kristin Clark, Director of Admissions
　714-432-5773 Fax: 714-432-5736
　Website: www.orangecoastcollege.edu
　E-mail: kclark@cccd.edu

San Diego Christian College
　2100 Greenfield Dr, El Cajon CA 92019-1157
　Jon Melone, Director of Admissions
　800-676-2242 Fax: 619-590-1739
　Website: www.sdcc.edu
　E-mail: admissions@sdcc.edu

SAN FRANCISCO CONSERVATORY OF MUSIC
　50 Oak St, San Francisco CA 94102
　Alexander Brose, Director of Admission
　800-899-7326 Fax: 415-503-6299
　Website: www.sfcm.edu
　E-mail: admit@sfcm.edu

Whittier College
　PO Box 634, Whittier CA 90608-0634
　Kieron Miller, Director of Admissions
　562-907-4200 Fax: 562-907-4870
　Website: www.whittier.edu
　E-mail: kmiller@whittier.edu

COLORADO

Nazarene Bible College
　1111 Academy Park Loop
　Colorado Springs CO 80910-3717
　Dr. Laurel Matson, VP for Enrollment & Student Development
　719-596-5110 Fax: 719-884-5199
　Website: www.nbc.edu
　E-mail: admissions@nbc.edu

CONNECTICUT

University of New Haven
　300 Boston Post Rd, West Haven CT 06516
　Director of Undergraduate Admissions
　203-932-7319 Fax: 203-931-6093
　Website: www.newhaven.edu
　E-mail: adminfo@newhaven.edu

FLORIDA

THE BAPTIST COLLEGE OF FLORIDA
　5400 College Dr, Graceville FL 32440-1831
　Christopher M. Bishop, Director of Admissions
　800-328-2660 Fax: 850-263-9026
　Website: www.baptistcollege.edu
　E-mail: admissions@baptistcollege.edu

Florida State University
　600 W College Ave, Tallahassee FL 32306-1096
　Janice V. Finney, Director of Admissions
　850-644-2525 Fax: 850-644-0197
　Website: admissions.fsu.edu
　E-mail: admissions@admin.fsu.edu

HERZING COLLEGE
　1595 S Semoran Blvd #1501
　Winter Park FL 32792-5509
　Kathy Nagle, Director of Admissions
　407-478-0500 Fax: 407-478-0501
　Website: www.herzing.edu
　E-mail: info@orl.herzing.edu

Lynn University
　3601 N Military Trl, Boca Raton FL 33431-5598
　Brett Ormandy, Director of Admissions
　561-237-7900 Fax: 561-237-7100
　Website: www.lynn.edu
　E-mail: admission@lynn.edu

Trinity Baptist College
　800-200 Hammond Blvd, Jacksonville FL 32221
　R. Larry Appleby, Director of Admissions
　904-596-2400 Fax: 904-596-2531
　Website: www.tbc.edu
　E-mail: emailtrinity@tbc.edu

University of South Florida
　4202 E Fowler Ave, Tampa FL 33620-6900
　J. Robert Spatig, Director of Admissions
　813-974-3350 Fax: 813-974-9689
　Website: www.usf.edu
　E-mail: admissions@admin.usf.edu

GEORGIA

Armstrong Atlantic State University
　11935 Abercorn St, Savannah GA 31419-1997
　Kim West, Asst. Dean and Registrar Enrollment Services
　912-927-5277 Fax: 912-921-5462
　Website: www.armstrong.edu
　E-mail: admissions@mail.armstrong.edu

Kennesaw State University
　1000 Chastain Rd NW, Kennesaw GA 30144-5591
　Joseph Meeks, Dean of the School of the Arts
　770-423-6742
　Website: www.kennesaw.edu

Savannah College of Art and Design
　PO Box 2072, Savannah, GA 31402-2072
　PO Box 77300, Atlanta, GA 30357
　Phone: 800-869-7223 (Savannah) or 877-722-3285 (Atlanta)
　E-mail: admission@scad.edu (Savannah) or sca-datl@scad.edu (Atlanta)
　www.scad.edu
　SCAD is a private, nonprofit institution accredited by the Commission on Colleges of the Southern Association

of Colleges and Schools to award bachelor's and master's degrees. The college offers B.F.A., M.Arch., M.A., M.F.A., and M.U.D. degrees. Enrollment is approximately 7,350; 6 percent are international. More than 30 areas of study. Online programs via SCAD e-Learning.

TOCCOA FALLS COLLEGE
PO Box 800899, Toccoa Falls GA 30598
Christy Meadows, Director of Admissions
888-785-5624 Fax: 706-282-6012
Website: www.tfc.edu
E-mail: admissions@tfc.edu

IDAHO

Brigham Young University - Idaho
120 Kimball Bldg, Rexburg ID 83460
Gordon Westenskow, Director of Admissions
208-496-1020 Fax: 208-496-1220
Website: www.byui.edu
E-mail: admissions@byui.edu

University of Idaho
Moscow ID 83844-4253
Lloyd Scott, Director of New Student Services
208-885-6163 Fax: 208-885-4477
Website: www.uidaho.edu
E-mail: nss@uidaho.edu

ILLINOIS

Benedictine University
5700 College Rd, Lisle IL 60532-0900
630-829-6300 or 888-829-6363 Fax: 630-829-6301
Website: www.ben.edu
E-mail: admissions@ben.edu
See listing under "Universities"

Columbia College Chicago
600 S Michigan Ave, Chicago IL 60605-1996
Murphy Monroe, Executive Director of Admissions
312-344-7130 Fax: 312-344-8024
Website: www.colum.edu
E-mail: admissions@colum.edu

CONCORDIA UNIVERSITY
7400 Augusta St, River Forest IL 60305-1402
708-209-3100 Fax: 708-209-3473
Website: www.curf.edu
E-mail: crfadmis.edu

North Central College
30 N Brainard St, Naperville IL 60540-4690
Martha Stolze, Director of Admissions
630-637-5800 Fax: 630-637-5819
Website: www.northcentralcollege.edu
E-mail: admissions@noctrl.edu

Roosevelt University
430 S Michigan Ave, Chicago IL 60605
Gwen E. Kanelos, Asst. Vice President for Enrollment Services
877-APPLY-RU Fax: 312-341-4216
Website: www.roosevelt.edu
E-mail: applyru@roosevelt.edu

South Suburban College of Cook County
15800 State St, South Holland IL 60473
Jane Ellen Stocker, Dean of Enrollment Services
708-596-2000 Fax: 708-225-5806
Website: www.southsuburbancollege.edu
E-mail: jstocker@southsuburbancollege.edu

VANDERCOOK COLLEGE OF MUSIC
3140 S Federal St, Chicago IL 60616-3704
Tamara V. Trutwin, Student Recruiter
Kelly Westergaard, Admissions Coordinator
800-448-2655 ext. 230 Fax: 312-225-5211
Website: www.vandercook.edu
E-mail: admissions@vandercook.edu
    Established 1928. Private. Coed. Accreditation: NCA; NASM; Illinois State Board of Higher Learning. Tuition: $7,945 undergrad, $3,960 graduate. Room & Board: $6,500 undergrad, $1,650 graduate. Enrollment: 85 undergraduate. Faculty: 35. Student-faculty ratio: 6:1. Degrees: Bachelor of Music Education, Master of Music Education. The only College in the U.S. solely devoted to the preparation of music educators. There is a 100% placement rate for those seeking a career in music education after graduation.

INDIANA

Oakland City University
138 N Lucretia St, Oakland City IN 47660
Brian J. Baker, Director of Admissions
800-737-5125 Fax: 812-749-1433
Website: www.oak.edu
E-mail: bbaker@oak.edu
See listing under "Universities"

St. Mary-of-the-Woods College
Saint Mary of the Woods IN 47876-1001
James P. Malley, Jr., Director of Admission
800-926-7692 Fax: 812-535-5010
Website: www.smwc.edu
E-mail: smwcadms@smwc.edu

University of Evansville
1800 Lincoln Ave, Evansville IN 47722-0001
Thomas E. Bear, V.P. of Enrollment Services
800-423-8633 Fax: 812-488-4076
Website: www.evansville.edu
E-mail: admission@evansville.edu

IOWA

Briar Cliff University
PO Box 2100, Sioux City IA 51104-0100
Sharisue Wilcoxon, VP for Enrollment Management
712-279-5200 Fax: 712-279-1632
Website: www.briarcliff.edu
E-mail: admissions@briarcliff.edu

Clarke College
1550 Clarke Dr, Dubuque IA 52001-3198
Andy Schroeder, Director of Admissions
800-383-2345 Fax: 563-584-8666
Website: www.clarke.edu
E-mail: andy.schroeder@clarke.edu

Graceland University
1 University Place, Lamoni IA 50140
Brian Shantz, Vice President for Enrollment and Dean of Admissions
641-784-5196 Fax: 641-784-5480
Website: www.admissions.graceland.edu
E-mail: admissions@graceland.edu

Iowa Lakes Community College
300 S 18th St, Estherville IA 51334-2721
Anne Stansbury, Asst. Director of Admissions
712-362-7945 Fax: 712-362-8363
Website: www.iowalakes.edu
E-mail: info@iowalakes.edu

Waldorf College
106 S 6th St, Forest City IA 50436-1713
Steve Lovik, Vice President of Enrollment Management
800-292-1903 or 641-585-8112 Fax: 641-585-8125
Website: www.waldorf.edu
E-mail: loviks@waldorf.edu
See listing under "Universities"

Wartburg College
PO Box 1003, Waverly IA 50677-0903
Brent Matthias, Interim Director of Admissions
319-352-8200 Fax: 319-352-8579
Website: www.wartburg.edu
E-mail: admissions@wartburg.edu

KANSAS

Barclay College
607 N Kingman, Haviland KS 67059
Herb Frazier, Director of Admissions
800-862-0226 Fax: 620-862-5242
Website: www.barclaycollege.edu
E-mail: admissions@barclaycollege.edu

Independence Community College
PO Box 708, Independence KS 67301-0708
Dr. Terry Hetrick, President
800-842-6063 Fax: 620-331-5344
Website: www.indycc.edu
E-mail: admissions@indycc.edu

Newman University
3100 W McCormick St, Wichita KS 67213
Jann Reusser, Admissions Recruitment Coordinator
316-942-4291 ext. 2144 Fax: 316-942-4483
Website: www.newmanu.edu
E-mail: reusserj@newmanu.edu

Tabor College
400 S Jefferson St, Hillsboro KS 67063-1758
Rusty Allen, Dean of Enrollment Management
620-947-3121 Fax: 620-947-6276
Website: www.tabor.edu
E-mail: admissions@tabor.edu

KENTUCKY

Morehead State University
Morehead KY 40351-1689
Dayna Seelig, Enrollment Services
800-585-6781 Fax: 606-783-5038
Website: www.moreheadstate.edu
E-mail: admissions@moreheadstate.edu

LOUISIANA

Dillard University
2601 Gentilly Blvd, New Orleans LA 70122-3097
Linda G. Nash, Director of Admissions
Website: www.dillard.edu
E-mail: admissions@dillard.edu

MARYLAND

Cecil Community College
One Seahawk Dr, North East MD 21901
Sandra S. Rajaski, Registrar & Director of Admissions
410-287-1000 Fax: 410-287-1001
Website: www.cecilcc.edu
E-mail: srajaski@cecilcc.edu

Hagerstown Community College
11400 Robinwood Dr, Hagerstown MD 21742-6590
Dr. Daniel E. Bock, Assistant Director of Admissions
301-790-2800 Fax: 301-791-9165
Website: www.hagerstowncc.edu
E-mail: bockd@hagerstowncc.edu

MASSACHUSETTS

Anna Maria College
50 Sunset Ln, Paxton MA 01612
Julie A. Mitchell, Director of Admissions
508-849-3360 Fax: 508-849-3362
Website: www.annamaria.edu
E-mail: admissions@annamaria.edu

Berklee College of Music
1140 Boylston St, Boston MA 02215-3693
Damien S. Bracken, Director of Admissions
800-BERKLEE or 617-747-2222 Fax: 617-747-2047
Website: www.berklee.edu
E-mail: admissions@berklee.edu

Boston University
121 Bay State Rd, Boston MA 02215
Kelly Walter, Executive Director of Admissions
617-353-2300 Fax: 617-353-9695
Website: web.bu.edu
E-mail: admissions@bu.edu

Gordon College
255 Grapevine Rd, Wenham MA 01984-1899
Nancy Mering, Director of Admissions
866-464-6736 Fax: 978-867-4682
Website: www.gordon.edu
E-mail: admissions@gordon.edu

LONGY SCHOOL OF MUSIC
1 Follen St, Cambridge MA 02138-3599
Admissions Office
617-876-0956 ext. 521 Fax: 617-876-9326
Website: www.longy.edu
E-mail: music@longy.edu
    Established 1915. Private. Coed. Tuition: $14,600-$22,750. Enrollment (full-time & part-time): 50 undergraduate, 150 graduate, 300 non-degree. Faculty: 150, including members of the Boston Symphony Orchestra, Handel and Haydn Society, and international performers and teachers. Degrees: Undergraduate Diploma, Bachelor of Music (with Emerson College), Graduate Performance Diploma, Artist Diploma, Master of Music, Dalcroze Eurhythmics license and certificate. Two buildings in Harvard Square; acclaimed 300-seat concert hall is site of over 250 concerts yearly. Music Library. Degree or diploma programs in the following areas: chamber music, collaborative piano, composition, Dalcroze Eurhythmics, early music, modern American music, opera, organ, piano, strings, voice, woodwinds and brass.

Smith College
Northampton MA 01063-0001
Debra Shaver, Director of Admissions
800-383-3232 Fax: 413-585-2527
Website: www.smith.edu
E-mail: admission@smith.edu

University of Massachusetts Dartmouth
Old Westport Rd, North Dartmouth MA 02747-2300
Steven T. Briggs, Director of Admissions
508-999-8605 Fax: 508-999-8755
Website: explore.umassd.edu
E-mail: sbriggs@umassd.edu

Westfield State College
PO Box 1630, Westfield MA 01086
Michelle Mattie, Associate Dean, Admission and Enrollment Services
413-572-5300
Website: www.wsc.ma.edu
E-mail: admission@wsc.ma.edu

MICHIGAN

Alma College
614 W Superior St, Alma MI 48801-1599
Anne Monroe, Director of Admissions
800-321-ALMA Fax: 989-463-7057
Website: www.alma.edu
E-mail: admissions@alma.edu

Andrews University
Berrien Springs MI 49104-0001
Randall Graves, Director of Recruitment Services
800-253-2874 Fax: 269-471-2670
Website: www.connect.andrews.edu
E-mail: gravesr@andrews.edu

Concordia University
4090 Geddes Rd, Ann Arbor MI 48105-2797
Gary Neumann, Director of Admissions
734-995-7300 Fax: 734-995-4610
Website: www.cuaa.edu
E-mail: admissions@cuaa.edu

Delta College
University Center MI 48710-0001
Duff Zube, Director of Admissions
989-686-9093 Fax: 989-667-2202
Website: www.delta.edu
E-mail: admit@delta.edu

Grand Valley State University
1 Campus Dr, Allendale MI 49401-9403
Jodi Chycinski, Director of Admissions
616-331-6611 Fax: 616-331-2000
Website: www.gvsu.edu
E-mail: go2gvsu@gvsu.edu

HILLSDALE COLLEGE
33 E College St, Hillsdale MI 49242-1298
Professor James Holleman, Director
517-607-2363 Fax: 517-607-2665
Website: www.hillsdale.edu
E-mail: james.holleman@hillsdale.edu

Interlochen Arts Academy
PO Box 199, Interlochen MI 49643-0199
231-276-7472
Website: www.interlochen.org
E-mail: admissions@interlochen.org

MACOMB COMMUNITY COLLEGE
44575 Garfield Rd, Clinton Township MI 48038-1139
Information Center
586-445-7999
Website: www.macomb.edu
E-mail: answer@macomb.edu

MINNESOTA

Bethany Lutheran College
700 Luther Dr, Mankato MN 56001
Don Westphal, Dean of Admissions
507-344-7000 Fax: 507-344-7376
Website: www.blc.edu
E-mail: admiss@blc.edu

Gustavus Adolphus College
800 W College Ave, Saint Peter MN 56082-1485
Mark H. Anderson, Dean of Admission
800-GUSTAVUS Fax: 507-933-7474
Website: www.gustavus.edu
E-mail: admission@gustavus.edu

McNally Smith College of Music
19 Exchange St East, St. Paul MN 55101
Debbie Sandridge, Director of Admissions
800-594-9500 Fax: 651-291-0366
Website: www.mcnallysmith.edu
E-mail: dsandridge@mcnallysmith.edu
See listing under "Universities"

Pillsbury Baptist Bible College
315 S Grove Ave, Owatonna MN 55060-3097
Stephen R. Seidler, Director of Admissions
507-451-2710 Fax: 507-451-0156
Website: www.pillsbury.edu
E-mail: steveseidler@pillsbury.edu

:: **SHATTUCK-ST. MARY'S SCHOOL**
PO Box 218, Faribault MN 55021-0218
Amy D. Wolf, Director of Admissions
507-333-1618 Fax: 507-333-1661
Website: www.s-sm.org
E-mail: admissions@s-sm.org
See listing under "Preparatory Schools - Coed"

MISSISSIPPI

Tougaloo College
500 W County Line Rd, Tougaloo MS 39174-9799
Juno Leggette Jacobs, Director of Admissions
601-977-7768 Fax: 601-977-4501
Website: www.tougaloo.edu
E-mail: jjacobs@tougaloo.edu

MISSOURI

Calvary Bible College & Theological Seminary
15800 Calvary Rd, Kansas City MO 64147-1341
Robert M. Reinsch, Director of Admissions
800-326-3960 Fax: 816-331-4474
Website: www.calvary.edu
E-mail: admissions@calvary.edu

Stephens College
PO Box 2121, Columbia MO 65215-0001
David Adams, Dean of Enrollment Management
573-442-2211 Fax: 573-876-7237
Website: www.stephens.edu
E-mail: dadams@stephens.edu

Truman State University
100 E Normal, Kirksville MO 63501
Office of Admission
660-785-4000 Fax: 660-785-4181
Website: admissions.truman.edu
E-mail: admissions@truman.edu

University of Missouri
1 University Blvd, Saint Louis MO 63121-4499
Dr. James E. Richards, Jr., Department Chairperson
314-516-5980 Fax: 314-516-6593
Website: www.umsl.edu
E-mail: admissions@umsl.edu

WEBSTER UNIVERSITY
470 E Lockwood Ave, Saint Louis MO 63119-3194
Michael Parkinson, Department Chairman
800-752-6765 ext. 7032 Fax: 314-963-6048
Website: www.webster.edu
E-mail: parkinmi@webster.edu
Established 1915. Private. Coed. Accreditation: NCACS. Tuition: $18,240. Room and board: $7,300. Enrollment: 2,460 full-time, 1,153 part-time. Faculty: 160. Student-faculty ratio: 15:1. Degrees: BA, BFA, BM, BMEd, BS, BSN, MA, MBA, MAT, MSN, DMGT. Library: 400,000 volumes. 36 buildings on 45 acres. Nationally recognized programs in the performing arts and music including composition, jazz studies, vocal and instrumental performance, and music education. Students from 40 states and 30 countries. Beautiful suburban campus in a wooded community of 20,000. Average class size of 15. New Residence Halls for 320 additional students open in 2006. Campuses in four European countries, China and Thailand.

William Woods University
1 University Ave, Fulton MO 65251-1098
Jimmy Clay, Director of Admissions
573-642-2251 Fax: 573-592-1146
Website: www.williamwoods.edu
E-mail: admissions@williamwoods.edu
See listing under "Universities"

MONTANA

Rocky Mountain College
1511 Poly Dr, Billings MT 59102-1796
Bonnie Knapp, Director of Admissions
800-877-6259 Fax: 406-657-1189
Website: www.rocky.edu
E-mail: admissions@rocky.edu

NEBRASKA

Nebraska Wesleyan University
5000 Saint Paul Ave, Lincoln NE 68504-2794
Patricia Karthauser, V.P. for University Enrollment
402-466-2371 Fax: 402-465-2177
Website: www.nebrwesleyan.edu
E-mail: admissions@nebrwesleyan.edu

Peru State College
PO Box 10, Peru NE 68421-0010
Office of Admissions
800-742-4412 Fax: 402-872-2296
Website: www.peru.edu
E-mail: admissions@oakmail.peru.edu

University of Nebraska at Kearney
905 W 25th St, Kearney NE 68849-0001
Dusty Newton, Director of Admissions
800-KEARNEY Fax: 308-865-8987
Website: www.unk.edu
E-mail: admissionsug@unk.edu

NEW JERSEY

Bergen Community College
400 Paramus Rd, Paramus NJ 07652
Julian Gomez, Asst. Director of Admissions
201-447-7100 Fax: 201-444-7036
Website: www.bergen.edu
E-mail: jgomez@bergen.edu

New Jersey City University
2039 John F Kennedy Blvd
Jersey City NJ 07305-1588
Carmen Panlilio, Asst. V.P. for Admissions and Financial Aid
201-200-3234 Fax: 201-200-2044
Website: www.njcu.edu
E-mail: admissions@njcu.edu

Ramapo College of New Jersey
505 Ramapo Valley Rd, Mahwah NJ 07430-1623
Director of Admissions
201-684-7300 or 201-684-7301 Fax: 201-684-7964
Website: www.ramapo.edu
E-mail: admissions@ramapo.edu

NEW YORK

College of Saint Rose
432 Western Ave, Albany NY 12203-1419
Maryelizabeth Amico, Asst V.P. for Undergraduate Admissions
518-454-5150 Fax: 518-454-2013
Website: www.strose.edu
E-mail: admit@strose.edu

CUNY Hunter College
695 Park Ave, New York NY 10021
Aaron Gibbs, Assistant Director of Recruitment
212-772-4497 Fax: 212-650-3336
Website: www.hunter.cuny.edu
E-mail: aaron.gibbs@hunter.cuny.edu

**EASTMAN SCHOOL OF MUSIC
OF THE UNIVERSITY OF ROCHESTER**
26 Gibbs St, Rochester NY 14604-2599
Dr. Adrian Daly, Associate Dean for Admissions and Retention
585-274-1060 Fax: 585-232-8601
Website: www.esm.rochester.edu
E-mail: admissions@esm.rochester.edu

FIVE TOWNS COLLEGE
305 N Service Rd, Dix Hills NY 11746-5871
631-424-7000 ext. 2110 Fax: 631-656-2172
Website: www.fivetowns.edu
E-mail: admissions@ftc.edu
See listing under "Universities"

: Institute of Audio Research
64 University Pl, New York NY 10003-4595
Mark L. Kahn, Director of Admissions
800-544-2501 or 212-777-8550 (NY, NJ, CT)
Fax: 212-677-6549
Website: www.audioschool.com
E-mail: contact@audioschool.com
See listing under "Career Schools"

Long Island University-C. W. Post Campus
720 Northern Blvd, Brookville NY 11548-1300
Joanne Graziano, Executive Director of Admissions
516-299-2900 Fax: 516-299-2137
Website: www.liu.edu/cwpost
E-mail: enroll@cwpost.liu.edu

MANNES COLLEGE OF MUSIC
150 W 85th St, New York NY 10024-4499
Office of Admissions
800-292-3040 or 212-580-0210 Fax: 212-580-1738
Website: www.mannes.edu
E-mail: mannesadmissions@newschool.edu

Molloy College
1000 Hempstead Ave
Rockville Centre NY 11570-1100
Marguerite Lane, Director of Admissions
516-678-5000 ext. 6291 Fax: 516-256-2247
Website: www.molloy.edu
E-mail: admissions@molloy.edu
See listing under "Universities"

**PURCHASE COLLEGE STATE UNIVERSITY OF
NEW YORK (SUNY)**
735 Anderson Hill Rd, Purchase NY 10577-1400
Betsy Immergut, Director of Admissions
914-251-6300 Fax: 914-251-6314
Website: www.purchase.edu
See listing under "Universities"

Roberts Wesleyan College
2301 Westside Dr, Rochester NY 14624-1997
Office of Admissions
585-594-6400 Fax: 585-594-6371
Website: www.roberts.edu
E-mail: admissions@roberts.edu

SUNY Niagara County Community College
3111 Saunders Settlement Rd
Sanborn NY 14132-9487
Kathleen Saunders, Director of Admissions
716-614-6200 Fax: 716-614-6820
Website: www.niagaracc.suny.edu
E-mail: saunders@niagaracc.suny.edu

SUNY Orange County Community College
115 South St, Middletown NY 10940-6437
Margot St. Lawrence, Director of Admissions
845-341-4030 Fax: 845-342-8662
Website: www.sunyorange.edu
E-mail: apply@sunyorange.edu
See listing under "Community and Junior Colleges"

NORTH CAROLINA

Mars Hill College
Mars Hill NC 28754
Chad Holt, Dean of Enrollment
866-MHC-4-YOU Fax: 828-689-1473
Website: www.mhc.edu
E-mail: cholt@mhc.edu

Meredith College
3800 Hillsborough St, Raleigh NC 27607-5298
Heidi L. Fletcher, Director of Admissions
919-760-8581 Fax: 919-760-2348
Website: www.meredith.edu
E-mail: admissions@meredith.edu
See listing under "Women's Colleges"

Mt. Olive College
634 Henderson St, Mount Olive NC 28365
Tim Woodard, Director of Admissions
919-658-2502 Fax: 919-658-9816
Website: www.moc.edu
E-mail: admissions@moc.edu
See listing under "Universities"

North Carolina A&T State University
1601 E Market St, Greensboro NC 27411
Lee Young, AVC Enrollment
336-334-7500 Fax: 336-334-7478
Website: www.ncat.edu
E-mail: uadmit@ncat.edu

Salem College
Winston Salem NC 27108
Dana Evans, Dean of Admissions/Fin. Aid
800-32-SALEM Fax: 336-917-5572
Website: www.salem.edu
E-mail: admissions@salem.edu
See listing under "Women's Colleges"

NORTH DAKOTA

Dickinson State University
Dickinson ND 58601-4896
Steve Glasser, Director of Student Recruitment
800-279-4295 Fax: 701-483-2409
Website: www.dickinsonstate.edu
E-mail: dsu.hawks@dickinsonstate.edu

:: Oak Grove Lutheran School
124 N Terrace N, Fargo ND 58102-3899
Rachel Mathson, Director of Admissions
701-237-0212 Fax: 701-237-4217
Website: www.oakgrovelutheran.com
E-mail: oakgrove.lutheranschool@sendit.nodak.edu

Valley City State University
101 College St SW, Valley City ND 58072-4024
Dan Klein, Director of Enrollment Services
800-532-8641 ext. 7101 Fax: 701-845-7299
Website: www.vcsu.edu
E-mail: enrollment.services@vcsu.edu
See listing under "Universities"

OHIO

CLEVELAND INSTITUTE OF MUSIC
11021 East Blvd, Cleveland OH 44106-1705
William Fay, Director of Admission
216-795-3107
Website: www.cim.edu

Cleveland State University
2121 Euclid Ave RW 204, Cleveland OH 44115
Dr. Richard Arndt, Dean of Undergraduate Recruitment and College Partnerships
888-CSU-OHIO Fax: 216-687-9210
Website: www.csuohio.edu
E-mail: admissions@csuohio.edu

Mount Vernon Nazarene University
800 Martinsburg Rd, Mount Vernon OH 43050-9509
Timothy Eades, Director of Admissions
866-462-6868 Fax: 740-393-0511
Website: www.gotomvnu.com
E-mail: admissions@mvnu.edu
See listing under "Universities"

OHIO NORTHERN UNIVERSITY
525 S Main St, Ada OH 45810-1555
Nils Riess, Chair of Music Dept.
419-772-2150
Website: www.onu.edu
E-mail: admissions-ug@onu.edu
See listing under "Universities"

The Ohio State University
School of Music
Weigel Hall, 1866 College Rd, Columbus OH 43210
614-292-2870 Fax: 614-292-1102
Website: music.osu.edu
E-mail: music-ug@osu.edu

OHIO WESLEYAN UNIVERSITY
61 S Sandusky St, Delaware OH 43015-2398
Director of Admission
740-368-3020 Fax: 740-368-3314
Website: www.owu.edu
E-mail: owuadmit@owu.edu

Owens Community College
PO Box 10000, Toledo OH 43699-1947
William J. Ivoska, Ph.D, Vice President of Student Services
567-661-7000 Fax: 567-661-7607
Website: www.owens.edu
E-mail: admissions@owens.edu

University of Dayton
300 College Park, Dayton OH 45469-1300
Robert F. Durkle, Director of Admissions
800-837-7433 Fax: 937-229-4729
Website: admission.udayton.edu
E-mail: admission@udayton.edu

OKLAHOMA

Mid-America Christian University
3500 SW 119th St, Oklahoma City OK 73170-4504
Haley Hope, Director of Admissions
405-691-3800 Fax: 405-692-3165
Website: www.macu.edu
E-mail: info@macu.edu

Oklahoma State University
    Stillwater OK 74078
    Brant Adams, Interim Department Head
    405-744-6133
    Website: www.okstate.edu
    E-mail: brant.adams@okstate.edu

Oral Roberts University
    7777 S Lewis Ave, Tulsa OK 74171-0001
    Chris Belcher, Director of Undergraduate Admissions
    800-678-8876 Fax: 918-495-6222
    Website: www.oru.edu
    E-mail: admissions@oru.edu

University of Tulsa
    600 S College Ave, Tulsa OK 74104-3126
    Earl Johnson, Dean of Admission
    918-631-2307 Fax: 918-631-5003
    Website: www.utulsa.edu
    E-mail: admission@utulsa.edu

OREGON

Marylhurst University
    17600 Pacific Hwy (Hwy 43)
    Marylhurst OR 97036-0261
    Director of Admissions
    800-634-9982 ext. 6268 Fax: 503-635-6585
    Website: www.marylhurst.edu
    E-mail: studentinfo@marylhurst.edu

Pacific University
    2043 College Way, Forest Grove OR 97116-1797
    Karen M. Dunston, Executive Director of Admissions
    800-635-0561 Fax: 503-352-2975
    Website: www.pacificu.edu
    E-mail: admissions@pacificu.edu

Warner Pacific College
    2219 SE 68th Ave, Portland OR 97215-4026
    Shannon Mackey, Director of Admissions
    503-517-1000 Fax: 503-517-1352
    Website: www.warnerpacific.edu
    E-mail: admissions@warnerpacific.edu

Western Oregon University
    345 Monmouth Ave N, Monmouth OR 97361-1314
    David McDonald, Dean, Admission, Retention &
    Enrollment Management
    877-877-1593 Fax: 503-838-8067
    Website: www.wou.edu
    E-mail: wolfgram@fsa.wou.edu

PENNSYLVANIA

Lebanon Valley College
    101 N College Ave, Annville PA 17003-1400
    William Brown, Dean of Admissions & Financial Aid
    866-LVC-4ADM or 717-867-6181 Fax: 717-867-6026
    Website: www.lvc.edu
    E-mail: admission@lvc.edu

University of the Arts
    320 S Broad St, Philadelphia PA 19102-4994
    Susan Gandy, Director of Admissions
    800-616-2787 Fax: 215-717-6045
    Website: www.uarts.edu
    E-mail: admissions@uarts.edu

Washington & Jefferson College
    60 S Lincoln St, Washington PA 15301-4801
    Alton E. Newell, Vice President for Enrollment
    724-223-6025 Fax: 724-223-6534
    Website: www.washjeff.edu
    E-mail: admission@washjeff.edu

Westminster College
    New Wilmington PA 16172-0001
    Doug Swartz, Director of Admissions
    724-946-7100 Fax: 724-946-6171
    Website: www.westminster.edu
    E-mail: swartzdl@westminster.edu

SOUTH CAROLINA

Columbia International University
    PO Box 3122, Columbia SC 29230-3122
    John Basie, Director of University Admissions
    800-777-2227 Fax: 803-786-4209
    Website: www.ciu.edu
    E-mail: yesciu@ciu.edu
    See listing under "Theological Studies & Religious
    Vocations"

Erskine College & Seminary
    PO Box 176, Due West SC 29639
    Bart Walker, Director of Admissions
    864-379-8838 Fax: 864-379-3048
    Website: www.erskine.edu
    E-mail: admissions@erskine.edu

Limestone College
    1115 College Dr, Gaffney SC 29340-3799
    Chris Phenicie, V.P. for Enrollment
    864-489-7151 Fax: 864-488-8206
    Website: www.limestone.edu
    E-mail: cphenicie@limestone.edu

North Greenville University
    PO Box 1892, Tigerville SC 29688-1892
    Dr. Jacquelyn H. Griffin, Dept. Chair
    Website: www.ngc.edu
    See listing under "Universities"

PRESBYTERIAN COLLEGE
    503 S Broad St, Clinton SC 29325
    Richard Dana Paul, Dean of Admissions
    800-476-7272 Fax: 864-833-8481
    Website: www.presby.edu
    E-mail: admissions@presby.edu

TENNESSEE

BLAIR SCHOOL OF MUSIC OF VANDERBILT UNIVERSITY
    2400 Blakemore Ave, Nashville TN 37212-3406
    Dwayne Sagen, Assistant Dean for Admissions
    615-322-7679 Fax: 615-343-0324
    Website: www.vanderbilt.edu
    E-mail: dwayne.p.sagen@vanderbilt.edu

Lipscomb University
    3901 Granny White Pike, Nashville TN 37204-3951
    Ricky Holaway, Director of Admissions
    800-333-4358 ext. 1776 Fax: 615-269-1804
    Website: www.lipscomb.edu
    E-mail: admissions@lipscomb.edu

Tennessee State University
    3500 John A Merritt Blvd, Nashville TN 37209-1561
    John Cade, Dean of Admissions & Records
    615-963-5101 Fax: 615-963-2930
    Website: www.tnstate.edu
    E-mail: jcade@tnstate.edu

University of Tennessee
    615 McCallie Ave, Chattanooga TN 37403-2504
    Yancy Freeman, Director of Admissions
    423-425-4111 Fax: 423-425-4157
    Website: www.utc.edu
    E-mail: Yancy-Freeman@utc.edu

TEXAS

Angelo State University
    ASU Station 11014, San Angelo TX 76909
    Bonnie Stennett, Coordinator of Recruiting
    800-946-8627 Fax: 325-942-2078
    Website: www.angelo.edu
    E-mail: admissions@angelo.edu

Blinn College
    902 College Ave, Brenham TX 77833-4098
    Dennis K. Crowson, Registrar
    979-830-4000 Fax: 979-830-4110
    Website: www.blinn.edu
    E-mail: recruiting@blinn.edu

Texas Woman's University
    PO Box 425589, Denton TX 76204-5589
    Erma Nieto, Director of Admissions
    866-809-6130 Fax: 940-898-3081
    Website: www.twu.edu
    E-mail: admissions@twu.edu

University of Houston
    122 E Cullen Bldg, Houston TX 77204-2023
    Office of Admission
    713-743-9595
    Website: www.uh.edu
    E-mail: admissions@uh.edu

University of Texas at Arlington
    Box 19111, Arlington TX 76019-0111
    Hans Gatterdam, Director of Admission
    817-272-6287 Fax: 817-272-3435
    Website: www.uta.edu
    E-mail: admissions@uta.edu

VERMONT

Bennington College
    One College Drive, Bennington VT 05201
    Ken Himmelman, Dean of Admissions & Financial Aid
    800-833-6845 Fax: 802-440-4320
    Website: www.bennington.edu
    E-mail: admissions@bennington.edu

VIRGINIA

Mary Baldwin College
    Staunton VA 24401
    Lisa A. Branson, Executive Director of Admissions and
    Financial Aid
    800-468-2262 Fax: 540-887-7292
    Website: www.mbc.edu
    E-mail: admit@mbc.edu

Radford University
    PO Box 6903, Radford VA 24142
    David W. Kraus, Director of Admissions
    800-890-4265 Fax: 540-831-5038
    Website: www.radford.edu
    E-mail: ruadmiss@radford.edu

Randolph-Macon Woman's College
    2500 Rivermont Ave, Lynchburg VA 24503
    Patricia LeDonne, Director of Admissions
    434-947-8100 Fax: 434-947-8996
    Website: www.rmwc.edu
    E-mail: admissions@rmwc.edu

University of Mary Washington
    1301 College Ave, Fredericksburg VA 22401-5300
    Dr. Martin A. Wilder, Jr., Director of Admissions
    540-654-2000 Fax: 540-654-1857
    Website: www.umw.edu
    E-mail: admit@umw.edu

WASHINGTON

Cornish College of the Arts
    1000 Lenora St, Seattle WA 98121
    Eric Pedersen, Director of Admission
    800-726-ARTS (2787) Fax: 206-720-1011
    Website: www.cornish.edu
    E-mail: admissions@cornish.edu

Gonzaga University
    502 E Boone Ave, Spokane WA 99258-0102
    Julie McCulloh, Dean of Admission
    800-322-2584 or 509-323-6572 Fax: 509-323-5780
    Website: www.gonzaga.edu
    E-mail: mcculloh@gu.gonzaga.edu

WEST VIRGINIA

Concord University
    Athens WV 24712
    Michael Curry, Vice President of Financial Aid &
    Admissions
    888-384-5249 Fax: 304-384-3218
    Website: www.concord.edu
    E-mail: admissions@concord.edu

Davis & Elkins College
    100 Campus Dr, Elkins WV 26241-3996
    Renee Heckel, Director of Enrollment Management
    800-624-3157 Fax: 304-637-1800
    Website: www.davisandelkins.edu
    E-mail: admiss@davisandelkins.edu

West Virginia Wesleyan College
    59 College Ave, Buckhannon WV 26201-2699
    Robert N. Skinner II, Director of Admission
    800-722-9933 Fax: 304-473-8108
    Website: www.wvwc.edu
    E-mail: admission@wvwc.edu

WISCONSIN

MADISON MEDIA INSTITUTE
    2702 Agriculture Dr, Madison WI 53718-6787
    Chris Hutchings, Director of Admissions
    800-236-4997 or 608-663-2000 Fax: 608-442-0141
    Website: www.madisonmedia.com
    E-mail: mmi@madisonmedia.com

St. Norbert College
    100 Grant St, De Pere WI 54115
    Brian Studebaker, Director of Admission
    800-236-4878 Fax: 920-403-4072
    Website: www.snc.edu
    E-mail: admit@snc.edu

WISCONSIN CONSERVATORY OF MUSIC
    1584 N Prospect Ave, Milwaukee WI 53202-6501
    Sarah Wright, VP Business
    414-276-5760 Fax: 414-276-6076
    Website: www.wcmusic.org
    E-mail: sarahwright@wcmusic.org

WYOMING

University of Wyoming
    Admissions Office
    Dept 3435, Laramie WY 82071-3435
    Aaron Appelhans, Contact
    800-342-5996 Fax: 307-766-4042
    Website: www.uwyo.edu
    E-mail: why-wyo@uwyo.edu

PUERTO RICO

CONSERVATORY OF MUSIC
    350 Calle Rafael Lamar, San Juan PR 00918
    Eutimia Santiago, Director of Admissions
    787-751-0160 ext. 275 Fax: 787-758-8268
    Website: www.cmpr.edu
    E-mail: admisiones@cmpr.edu

NURSING

ALABAMA

CALHOUN COMMUNITY COLLEGE
PO Box 2216, Decatur AL 35609-2216
M. Wayne Tosh, Registrar
256-306-2500 Fax: 256-306-2941
Website: www.calhoun.edu
E-mail: jog@calhoun.edu

Herzing College
280 W Valley Ave, Homewood AL 35209-4816
Kim Conway, Director of Admissions
205-916-2800 Fax: 205-916-2807
Website: www.herzing.edu/birmingham
E-mail: info@bhm.herzing.edu

Trenholm State Technical College
Trenholm Campus
1225 Air Base Blvd, Montgomery AL 36108-3199
Dr. Anthony Molina, President
334-420-4200 Fax: 334-420-4206
Website: www.trenholmtech.cc.al.us
E-mail: amolina@trenholmtech.cc.al.us

University of Alabama in Huntsville
PO Box 1247, Huntsville AL 35899-0001
Ann Lee, Assoc. Director for Recruiting Program and Events
1-800-UAH-CALL Fax: 256-824-6073
Website: www.uah.edu
E-mail: leev@uah.edu

University of South Alabama
307 University Blvd N, Mobile AL 36688-3053
Melissa Haab, Director of Admissions
251-460-6141 Fax: 251-460-7876
Website: www.southalabama.edu
E-mail: admiss@usouthal.edu

ALASKA

University of Alaska Anchorage
PO Box 141629, Anchorage AK 99514-1629
Cecile Mitchell, Director of Enrollment Services
907-786-1480 Fax: 907-786-4888
Website: www.uaa.alaska.edu/
E-mail: enroll@uaa.alaska.edu

ARIZONA

Pima Community College
4905 E Broadway Blvd, Tucson AZ 85709-1010
Wendy Kilgore, Ph.D., Director of Admissions
520-206-4500 Fax: 520-206-4790
Website: www.pima.edu
E-mail: infocenter@pima.edu

University of Arizona
Tucson AZ 85721-0040
Paul Kohn, Director of Admissions
520-621-3237 Fax: 520-621-9799
Website: www.admissions.arizona.edu or
www.arizona.edu

ARKANSAS

Northwest Technical Institute
709 S Old Missouri Rd, Springdale AR 72764
Charles L. Kelley, President
479-751-8824 Fax: 479-751-7780
Website: www.nti.tec.ar.us
E-mail: info@nit.tec.ar.us

Phillips Community College of the University of Arkansas
PO Box 785, Helena AR 72342-0785
Dr. Steven Murray, Chancellor
Lynn Boone, Vice Chancellor for Student Services / Registrar
870-338-6474 Fax: 870-338-7542
Website: www.pccua.edu
E-mail: lboone@pccua.edu

CALIFORNIA

California State University-San Bernadino
5500 University Pkwy
San Bernardino CA 92407-2393
Olivia Rosas, Director of Admissions
909-880-5000 Fax: 909-880-7034
Website: enrollment.csusb.edu
E-mail: orosas@csusb.edu

Chabot College
25555 Hesperian Blvd, Hayward CA 94545-2400
Judy Young, Director of Admissions
510-723-6600 Fax: 510-723-7510
Website: www.chabotcollege.edu
E-mail: ccarcom@clpccd.cc.ca.us

Maric College
9055 Balboa Ave, San Diego CA 92123
Geraldine Rorrison, Director of Admissions
858-279-4500 Fax: 858-279-4885
Website: www.mariccollege.edu
E-mail: grorrison@mariccollege.edu

Orange Coast College
PO Box 5005, Costa Mesa CA 92628-5005
Kristin Clark, Director of Admissions
714-432-5773 Fax: 714-432-5736
Website: www.orangecoastcollege.edu
E-mail: kclark@cccd.edu

San Joaquin Valley College
8400 W Mineral King Ave, Visalia CA 93291-9283
Susie Topjian, Enrollment Services Director
559-651-2500 Fax: 559-651-4864
Website: www.sjvc.edu
E-mail: susiet@sjvc.edu

Western Career College
2157 Country Hills Dr, Antioch CA 94509-7435
Tim Gienapp, Director of Admissions
925-522-7777
Website: www.westerncollege.edu

Western Career College
8909 Folsom Blvd, Sacramento CA 95826-3203
Sue Smith, Contact
916-361-1660 Fax: 916-361-6666
Website: www.westerncollege.edu

Western Career College
6201 San Ignacio Ave, San Jose CA 95119
Steve Ashab, Director of Admissions
408-360-0840 Fax: 408-360-0848
Website: www.westerncollege.edu

Western Career College
15555 E 14th St Ste 500, San Leandro CA 94578
Julie Elmquist, Contact
510-276-3888 Fax: 510-276-3653
Website: www.westerncollege.edu

COLORADO

San Juan Basin Technical College
PO Box 970, Cortez CO 81321-0970
Shannon South, Director of Student Services
970-565-8457 Fax: 970-565-8450
Website: www.sjbtc.edu
E-mail: ssouth@sjbtc.edu

University of Colorado at Denver and Health Sciences Center
Health Sciences Program
4200 E 9th Ave Box C245, Denver CO 80262
Phoebe Lindsey Barton, Ph.D., Director
Website: www.uchsc.edu

DELAWARE

Wesley College
120 N State St, Dover DE 19901-3876
302-736-2300 Fax: 302-736-2301
Website: www.wesley.edu

FLORIDA

City College
2000 W Commercial Blvd, Fort Lauderdale FL 33309
Britt Carpenter, Director of Admissions
954-492-5353 Fax: 954-491-1965
Website: www.citycollege.edu
E-mail: bcarpenter@citycollege.edu

FLORIDA HOSPITAL COLLEGE OF HEALTH SCIENCES
800 Lake Estelle Dr, Orlando FL 32803-1237
Office of Admissions
800-500-7747 or 407-303-9798 Fax: 407-303-9408
Website: www.fhchs.edu
E-mail: gina.flenoy@fhchs.edu
  Established in 1992. Private. Coed. Accreditation. Commission on Colleges of the Southern Association of Colleges and Schools, 1866 Southern Lane, Decatur, GA 30033-4097. 404-679-4500. Tuition: $240 per credit hour (matriculation & program fees additional). Room and Board: $6,900 (estimate). Enrollment: 1,034 full-time, 739 part-time. Faculty: 45. Degrees: BS, AS, and Certificates. Professional Programs: Diagnostic Medical Sonography, Health Sciences, Nuclear Medicine Technology, Nursing, Occupational Therapy Assistant, Pre-Professional Studies, Radiography. Professional programs are accredited by their respective accrediting bodies. The College provides state-of-the-art learning labs where students hone their skills before entering the clinical arena. Small class sizes allow instructors to know students on an individual basis. Graduates continue to outscore the national averages on licensure and credentialing examinations. Job outlook for careers in healthcare is excellent. College housing and financial aid available for qualified students.

Florida State University
600 W College Ave, Tallahassee FL 32306-1096
Janice V. Finney, Director of Admissions
850-644-2525 Fax: 850-644-0197
Website: admissions.fsu.edu
E-mail: admissions@admin.fsu.edu

GALEN HEALTH INSTITUTES - SCHOOL OF NURSING
9549 Koger Boulevard North Suite 100
Saint Petersburg FL 33702-4372
727-577-1497 Fax: 727-576-4372
Website: www.galened.com
E-mail: wpotter@galened.com
  Galen Health Institute offers a full-time, two-year RN Program (one-year for licensed LPNs), a full-time, 12-month daytime LPN Program, and a part-time 18-month evening LPN Program. Programs are designed to prepare students to become registered nurses or licensed practical nurses who provide direct care to patients in a variety of settings. Programs include classroom lectures and activities, skills laboratory practice, and direct patient care experience in hospitals and other facilities (clinical rotations). For further information contact the Admissions Representative.

Nova Southeastern University Health Profession
3200 S University Dr, Davie FL 33328-2018
Marla Frohlinger, Director of Admissions
954-262-1101 Fax: 954-262-2282
Website: www.nova.edu
E-mail: marlaf@nsu.nova.edu

St. Thomas University
16401 NW 37th Ave, Miami Gardens FL 33054
Dr. John Abdirkin, Contact
800-367-9010 or 305-628-6546 Fax: 305-628-6591
Website: www.stu.edu
E-mail: signup@stu.edu

Santa Fe Community College
3000 NW 83rd St, Gainesville FL 32606-6200
Jackson N. Sasser, President
352-395-5787 Fax: 352-395-4118
Website: www.sfcc.edu
E-mail: ouida.mcneil@sfcc.edu

South University
1760 N Congress Ave
West Palm Beach FL 33409-5178
Steven A. Schwab, President
561-697-9200 Fax: 561-697-9944
Website: www.southuniversity.edu
E-mail: wpb@southuniversity.edu
SACS Accreditation.

University of South Florida
4202 E Fowler Ave, Tampa FL 33620-6900
J. Robert Spatig, Director of Admissions
813-974-3350 Fax: 813-974-9689
Website: www.usf.edu
E-mail: admissions@admin.usf.edu

GEORGIA

Armstrong Atlantic State University
11935 Abercorn St, Savannah GA 31419-1997
Kim West, Asst. Dean and Registrar Enrollment Services
912-927-5277 Fax: 912-921-5462
Website: www.armstrong.edu
E-mail: admissions@mail.armstrong.edu

Kennesaw State University
1000 Chastain Rd NW, Kennesaw GA 30144-5591
Richard Sowell, Dean of College of Health and Human Services
770-423-6565
Website: www.kennesaw.edu

North Georgia Technical College
434 Meeks Ave, Blairsville GA 30512-2983
Admissions
706-781-2300 Fax: 706-781-2307
Website: www.northgatech.edu
E-mail: info@northgatech.edu

North Georgia Technical College
Clarkesville Campus
PO Box 65, Clarkesville GA 30523-0002
Admissions
706-754-7700 Fax: 706-754-7777
Website: www.northgatech.edu
E-mail: info@northgatech.edu

North Metro Technical College
5198 Ross Rd SE, Acworth GA 30102-3129
Missy Cusack, Director of Admissions
770-975-4000 Fax: 770-975-4142
Website: www.northmetrotech.edu
E-mail: info@northmetrotech.edu

HAWAII

Kauai Community College
3-1901 Kaumualii Hwy, Lihue HI 96766-9500
808-245-8225 Fax: 808-245-8297
Website: kauai.hawaii.edu
E-mail: arkauai@hawaii.edu

IDAHO

Brigham Young University - Idaho
120 Kimball Bldg, Rexburg ID 83460
Gordon Westenskow, Director of Admissions
208-496-1020 Fax: 208-496-1220
Website: www.byui.edu
E-mail: admissions@byui.edu

ILLINOIS

Aurora University
347 S Gladstone Ave, Aurora IL 60506-4892
Carol R. Dunn, Ed.D., Vice President for Enrollment
800-742-5281 Fax: 630-844-5535
Website: www.aurora.edu
E-mail: admission@aurora.edu

Benedictine University
5700 College Rd, Lisle IL 60532-0900
630-829-6300 or 888-829-6363 Fax: 630-829-6301
Website: www.ben.edu
E-mail: admissions@ben.edu
See listing under "Universities"

BLESSING-RIEMAN COLLEGE OF NURSING
PO Box 7005, Quincy IL 62305-7005
Erin Flesner, Admission Counselor
Heather Mutter, Admission Counselor
217-228-5520 Fax: 217-223-4661
Website: www.brcn.edu
E-mail: admissions@brcn.edu

GRAHAM HOSPITAL
210 W Walnut St, Canton IL 61520-2497
Mary Kepple, Coordinator of Admissions, Recruitment
309-647-5240 ext. 2347 or 309-647-4086
Fax: 309-649-5127
Website: www.grahamschoolofnursing.org
E-mail: mkepple@grahamhospital.org

Kaskaskia College
27210 College Rd, Centralia IL 62801-7878
Tyra Taylor, Dean of Enrollment Management and Retention Services
618-545-3000 Fax: 618-532-1990
Website: www.kaskaskia.edu
E-mail: ttaylor@kaskaskia.edu

MENNONITE COLLEGE OF NURSING AT ILLINOIS STATE UNIVERSITY
PO Box 5810, Normal IL 61790-5810
Nancy Ridenour, Dean and Professor
309-438-7400 Fax: 309-438-2620
Website: www.mcn.ilstu.edu
E-mail: mcninfo@ilstu.edu

METHODIST COLLEGE OF NURSING
415 St Mark Ct, Peoria IL 61603
Mary Jane Dowling, Recruitment Coordinator
309-672-5566 Fax: 309-671-2752
Website: www.methodistcollegeofnursing.com
E-mail: mjdowling@mmci.org

ST. ANTHONY COLLEGE OF NURSING
5658 E State St, Rockford IL 61108-2468
Cheryl Delgado, Admission Representative
815-227-2141 Fax: 815-395-2275
Website: sacn.edu
E-mail: cheryldelgado@sacn.edu

SAINT FRANCIS MEDICAL CENTER COLLEGE OF NURSING
511 NE Greenleaf St, Peoria IL 61603-3744
Janice Farquharson, Director of Admissions/Registrar
309-655-2596 Fax: 309-624-8973
Website: www.sfmccon.edu
E-mail: janice.farquharson@osfhealthcare.org

South Suburban College of Cook County
15800 State St, South Holland IL 60473
Jane Ellen Stocker, Dean of Enrollment Services
708-596-2000 Fax: 708-225-5806
Website: www.southsuburbancollege.edu
E-mail: jstocker@southsuburbancollege.edu

Trinity College of Nursing & Health Sciences
2122 25th Ave, Rock Island IL 61201-5317
Joanne Cunningham, Director of Admissions
309-779-7700 Fax: 309-799-7748
Website: www.trinitycollegeqc.edu
E-mail: con@trinityqc.com

Triton College
2000 5th Ave, River Grove IL 60171-1995
Mary-Rita Moore, Dean of Enrollment Services
708-456-0300 ext. 3130 Fax: 708-583-3147
Website: www.triton.edu
E-mail: triton@triton.edu
See listing under "Community and Junior Colleges"

INDIANA
Ancilla Domini College
Donaldson IN 46513
Erin Wittmeyer, Director of Admissions
574-936-8898 Fax: 574-935-1773
Website: www.ancilla.edu
E-mail: erin.wittmeyer@ancilla.edu

Brown Mackie College - Fort Wayne
3000 E Coliseum Blvd, Fort Wayne IN 46805
Daniel Summer, Campus President
260-484-4400 Fax: 260-484-2678
Website: www.brownmackie.edu

Brown Mackie College - South Bend
1030 E Jefferson Blvd, South Bend IN 46617-3123
Connie Adelman, Campus President
574-237-0774 Fax: 574-237-3585
Website: www.brownmackie.edu

Ivy Tech Community College - North Central
220 Dean Johnson Blvd, South Bend IN 46601-3415
Pam Decker, Director of Admissions
574-289-7001 Fax: 574-236-7177
Website: www.ivytech.edu
E-mail: pdecker@ivytech.edu

ST. ELIZABETH SCHOOL OF NURSING
1508 Tippecanoe St, Lafayette IN 47904-2198
Anita K. Reed, Admissions Coordinator
765-423-6400 Fax: 765-423-6383
Website: www.ste.org/newson
E-mail: schoolinfo@steson.org

University of Evansville
1800 Lincoln Ave, Evansville IN 47722-0001
Thomas E. Bear, V.P. of Enrollment Services
800-423-8633 Fax: 812-488-4076
Website: www.evansville.edu
E-mail: admission@evansville.edu

IOWA
Briar Cliff University
PO Box 2100, Sioux City IA 51104-0100
Sharisue Wilcoxon, VP for Enrollment Management
712-279-5200 Fax: 712-279-1632
Website: www.briarcliff.edu
E-mail: admissions@briarcliff.edu

Clarke College
1550 Clarke Dr, Dubuque IA 52001-3198
Andy Schroeder, Director of Admissions
800-383-2345 Fax: 563-584-8666
Website: www.clarke.edu
E-mail: andy.schroeder@clarke.edu

Graceland University
1 University Place, Lamoni IA 50140
Brian Shantz, Vice President for Enrollment and Dean of Admissions
641-784-5196 Fax: 641-784-5480
Website: www.admissions.graceland.edu
E-mail: admissions@graceland.edu

Hamilton College
7009 Nordic Dr, Cedar Falls IA 50613
Tim Cole, Campus President
319-277-0220 Fax: 319-363-3812
Website: www.hamiltonia.edu
E-mail: ticole@hamiltoncf.com

Hamilton College
3165 Edgewood Pkwy SW, Cedar Rapids IA 52404
Susan Spivey, Campus President
319-363-0481 Fax: 319-363-3812
Website: www.hamiltonia.edu
E-mail: spiveys@hamiltonia.edu

Hamilton College
2570 4th St SW, Mason City IA 50401-4665
Joe Albers, Executive Director
641-423-2530 Fax: 641-423-7512
Website: www.hamiltonia.edu
E-mail: jalbers@hamiltonia.edu

Hamilton College
4655 121st St, Urbandale IA 50323-2311
Ed Rogan, Campus President
515-727-2100 Fax: 515-727-2115
Website: www.hamiltonia.edu
E-mail: erogan_dm@hamiltonia.edu

Iowa Lakes Community College
3200 College Dr, Emmetsburg IA 50536-1055
Anne Stansbury, Asst. Director of Admissions
712-852-5212 Fax: 712-362-8363
Website: www.iowalakes.edu
E-mail: info@iowalakes.edu

Iowa Lakes Community College
1900 Grand Ave, Suite 8, Spencer IA 51301
Anne Stansbury, Assistant Director of Admissions
712-262-7141 Fax: 712-262-4047
Website: www.iowalakes.edu
E-mail: info@iowalakes.edu

Mount Mercy College
1330 Elmhurst Dr NE, Cedar Rapids IA 52402-4797
Jim Krystofiak, Dean of Admission
800-248-4504 Fax: 319-363-5270
Website: www.mtmercy.edu
E-mail: admission@mtmercy.edu

Northwest Iowa Community College
603 W Park St, Sheldon IA 51201-1046
Lisa Story, Director of Enrollment Management
712-324-5061 Fax: 712-324-4136
Website: www.nwicc.edu
E-mail: lstory@nwicc.edu

KANSAS

COLBY COMMUNITY COLLEGE
1255 S Range Ave, Colby KS 67701-4099
Director of Admissions
888-634-9350 or 785-460-4690 Fax: 785-460-4691
Website: www.colbycc.edu
E-mail: bobbi@colbycc.edu

Flint Hills Technical College
3301 W 18th Ave, Emporia KS 66801-5957
Lisa Kirmer, Dean of Student Services
620-343-4600 Fax: 620-343-4610
Website: www.fhtc.net
E-mail: lkirmer@fhtc.net

Newman University
3100 W McCormick St, Wichita KS 67213
Jann Reusser, Admissions Recruitment Coordinator
316-942-4291 ext. 2144 Fax: 316-942-4483
Website: www.newmanu.edu
E-mail: reusserj@newmanu.edu

KENTUCKY
Bluegrass Community and Technical College
Oswald Building
470 Cooper Drive, Lexington KY 40506-0235
Shelbie Hugle, Director of Admissions
859-246-6200 Fax: 859-246-4664
Website: www.bluegrass.kctcs.edu
E-mail: bctc_info@kctcs.edu

BROWN MACKIE COLLEGE
Northern Kentucky Campus
309 Buttermilk Pike, Fort Mitchell KY 41017-2191
Joanne Dellefield, Director of Admissions
859-341-5627 Fax: 859-341-6483
Website: www.brownmackie.edu
E-mail: jdellefield@brownmackie.edu

GALEN COLLEGE OF NURSING
1031 Zorn Ave Ste 400, Louisville KY 40207
502-582-2305 Fax: 502-581-0425
Website: www.galencollege.edu
E-mail: mclaypoole@galened.com
    Galen College of Nursing offers a full-time, two-year RN Program (one-year for licensed LPN's), a full-time, 12-month daytime LPN Program, and a part-time 18-month evening LPN Program. Programs are designed to prepare students to become registered nurses or licensed practical nurses who provide direct care to patients in a variety of settings. Programs include classroom lectures and activities, skills laboratory practice, and direct patient care experience in hospitals and other facilities (clinical rotations). For further information contact the Admissions Representative.

Morehead State University
Morehead KY 40351-1689
Dayna Seelig, Enrollment Services
800-585-6781 Fax: 606-783-5038
Website: www.moreheadstate.edu
E-mail: admissions@moreheadstate.edu

LOUISIANA
Dillard University
2601 Gentilly Blvd, New Orleans LA 70122-3097
Linda G. Nash, Director of Admissions
Website: www.dillard.edu
E-mail: admissions@dillard.edu

Louisiana State University at Eunice
PO Box 1129, Eunice LA 70535-1129
Ron Ryder, Registrar
337-457-7311 Fax: 337-550-1306
Website: www.lsue.edu
E-mail: rryder@lsue.edu

Our Lady of Holy Cross College
4123 Woodland Dr, New Orleans LA 70131-7399
Office of Enrollment Services
504-394-7744 Fax: 504-391-2421
Website: www.olhcc.edu

MAINE

HUSSON COLLEGE
Eastern Maine Medical Center
One College Cir, Bangor ME 04401-2999
Jane Goodwin, Director of Admissions
800-4HU-SSON or 207-941-7100 Fax: 207-941-7935
Website: www.husson.edu
E-mail: admit@husson.edu
See listing under "Universities"

Northern Maine Community College
33 Edgemont Dr, Presque Isle ME 04769-2016
Bill Casavant, Director of Admissions
207-768-2700 Fax: 207-768-2831
Website: www.nmcc.edu
E-mail: admissions@nmcc.edu

St. Joseph's College of Maine
278 Whites Bridge Rd, Standish ME 04084-5263
Vincent Kloskowski, Dean of Admissions
800-338-7057 Fax: 207-893-7862
Website: www.sjcme.edu
E-mail: admission@sjcme.edu

Southern Maine Community College
2 Fort Rd, South Portland ME 04106-1698
Dr. James Ortiz, President
Scott MacDonald, Director of Financial Aid
207-741-5500 Fax: 207-741-5671
Website: www.smccme.edu
E-mail: oharmon@maine.rr.com

MARYLAND
Cecil Community College
One Seahawk Dr, North East MD 21901
Sandra S. Rajaski, Registrar & Director of Admissions
410-287-1000 Fax: 410-287-1001
Website: www.cecilcc.edu
E-mail: srajaski@cecilcc.edu

Villa Julie College
1525 Greenspring Valley Rd
Stevenson MD 21153-0641
Mark Hergan, V.P. Enrollment Services
410-486-7001 Fax: 410-602-6600
Website: www.vjc.edu/admissions
E-mail: admissions@mail.vjc.edu

MASSACHUSETTS
Becker College
Campuses in Worcester and Leicester, MA
61 Sever St, Worcester MA 01609-2165
Karen H. Schedin, Director of Admissions
508-791-9241 Fax: 508-890-1500
Website: www.becker.edu
E-mail: admissions@becker.edu
See listing under "Universities"

Bristol Community College
777 Elsbree St, Fall River MA 02720-7395
Rodney S. Clark, Director of Admissions
508-678-2811 ext. 2516, 2179 Fax: 508-730-3265
Website: www.bristol.mass.edu
E-mail: admissions@bristol.mass.edu

LAWRENCE MEMORIAL/REGIS COLLEGE NURSING AND RADIOGRAPHY PROGRAMS
170 Governors Ave, Medford MA 02155-1643
Admissions Coordinator
781-306-6600 Fax: 781-306-6142
Website: www.lmregis.org
E-mail: admissions@lmregis.org

Southeastern Technical Institute
250 Foundry St, South Easton MA 02375-1780
Beverly A. Pusateri, Director
508-238-1860 Fax: 508-230-1558
Website: ti.sersd.org
E-mail: bpusateri@sersd.org

University of Massachusetts Dartmouth
Old Westport Rd, North Dartmouth MA 02747-2300
Steven T. Briggs, Director of Admissions
508-999-8605 Fax: 508-999-8755
Website: explore.umassd.edu
E-mail: sbriggs@umassd.edu

MICHIGAN
Andrews University
Berrien Springs MI 49104-0001
Randall Graves, Director of Recruitment Services
800-253-2874 Fax: 269-471-2670
Website: www.connect.andrews.edu
E-mail: gravesr@andrews.edu

Delta College
University Center MI 48710-0001
Duff Zube, Director of Admissions
989-686-9093 Fax: 989-667-2202
Website: www.delta.edu
E-mail: admit@delta.edu

Grand Valley State University
1 Campus Dr, Allendale MI 49401-9403
Jodi Chycinski, Director of Admissions
616-331-6611 Fax: 616-331-2000
Website: www.gvsu.edu
E-mail: go2gvsu@gvsu.edu

MACOMB COMMUNITY COLLEGE
44575 Garfield Rd, Clinton Township MI 48038-1139
Information Center
586-445-7999
Website: www.macomb.edu
E-mail: answer@macomb.edu

Northwestern Michigan College
1701 E Front St, Traverse City MI 49686-3061
Jim Bensley, Admissions Coordinator
800-748-0566 Fax: 231-995-1339
Website: www.nmc.edu
E-mail: jbensley@nmc.edu

Oakland University
2200 N Squirrel Rd, Rochester MI 48309
Eleanor L. Reynolds, Assistant Vice President &
Director of Admissions
248-370-2100
Website: www.oakland.edu
E-mail: ouinfo@oakland.edu

MINNESOTA

Hibbing Community College
1515 E 25th St, Hibbing MN 55746-3300
Holly Bigelow, Director of Enrollment
800-224-4HCC or 218-262-7200 Fax: 218-262-6717
Website: www.hibbing.edu
E-mail: admissions@hibbing.edu

Metropolitan State University
700 7th St E, Saint Paul MN 55106-5000
Rosa Rodriguez, Admissions Director
651-793-1300 Fax: 651-793-1546
Website: www.metrostate.edu
E-mail: rosa.rodriguez@metrostate.edu

Minneapolis Community and Technical College
1501 Hennepin Ave, Minneapolis MN 55403-1779
Dena Russell, Director of Admissions
612-659-6282 Fax: 612-659-6210
Website: www.minneapolis.edu
E-mail: admissions.office@minneapolis.edu

Northland Community and Technical College
2022 Central Ave NE
East Grand Forks MN 56721-2702
Barb Forrest, Nursing Program Director
800-451-3441 Fax: 218-773-4502
Website: www.northlandcollege.edu
E-mail: admissions@northlandcollege.edu

Ridgewater College-Hutchinson Campus
2 Century Ave SE, Hutchinson MN 55350-3100
Dawn Bjork, Counselor
800-222-4424 Fax: 320-231-7767
Website: www.ridgewater.edu
E-mail: dawn.bjork@ridgewater.edu

Ridgewater College-Willmar Campus
PO Box 1097, Willmar MN 56201-1097
Sally Kerfeld, Director of Admissions
800-722-1151 Fax: 320-231-7677
Website: www.ridgewater.edu
E-mail: skerfeld@ridgewater.edu

St. Cloud Technical College
1540 Northway Dr, Saint Cloud MN 56303-1240
Jodi Elness, Director of Enrollment Management
800-222-1009 Fax: 320-308-5981
Website: www.sctc.edu
E-mail: jelness@sctc.edu

MISSOURI

Barnes-Jewish College of Nursing
306 S Kingshighway Blvd
Saint Louis MO 63110-1091
Christie Schneider, Director of Admissions
800-832-9009 Fax: 314-454-5239
Website: www.barnesjewishcollege.edu
E-mail: cns5347@bjc.org

DEACONESS COLLEGE OF NURSING
6150 Oakland Ave, Saint Louis MO 63139-3215
Michelle McGrail, Dean of Enrollment and Student
Affairs
314-768-3044 Fax: 314-768-5673
Website: www.deaconess.edu
E-mail: michelle.mcgrail@deaconess.edu

GRACELAND UNIVERSITY
1401 W Truman Rd, Independence MO 64050
Patricia K. Trachsel, Dean of Independence Campus
816-833-0524 Fax: 816-833-2990
Website: www.graceland.edu
E-mail: trachsel@graceland.edu

LUTHERAN SCHOOL OF NURSING
3547 S Jefferson Ave, Saint Louis MO 63118-3909
Mary Debatin-Merod, Admissions Assistant
314-577-5850 Fax: 314-268-6160
Website: www.nursingschoollmc.com
E-mail: mary.merod@sonstl.com

St. Charles Community College
4601 Mid Rivers Mall Dr, Saint Peters MO 63376
Kathy Brockgreitens-Gober, Director of Admissions
636-922-8000 Fax: 636-922-8236
Website: www.stchas.edu
E-mail: adm-reg@stchas.edu

Saint Luke's College
8320 Ward Parkway Suite 300
Kansas City MO 64114
Josh Richards Asst. Director of Admissions
816-932-2367 Fax: 816-932-9064
Website: www.saintlukescollege.edu
E-mail: slc-admissions@saint-lukes.org

Truman State University
100 E Normal, Kirksville MO 63501
Office of Admission
660-785-4000 Fax: 660-785-4181
Website: admissions.truman.edu
E-mail: admissions@truman.edu

University of Missouri
1 University Blvd, Saint Louis MO 63121-4499
314-516-6066 Fax: 314-516-6730
Website: www.umsl.edu
E-mail: admissions@umsl.edu

Webster University
470 E Lockwood Ave, Saint Louis MO 63119-3194
Anne Schappe, Chairperson
314-968-7488 Fax: 314-963-6101
Website: www.webster.edu
E-mail: schappan@webster.edu
See listing under "Universities"

NEBRASKA

Central Community College-Grand Island Campus
PO Box 4903, Grand Island NE 68802-4903
Angie Pacheco, Contact
308-398-4222 Fax: 308-398-7398
Website: www.cccneb.edu
E-mail: apacheco@cccneb.edu

Clarkson College
101 S 42nd St, Omaha NE 68131-2715
Sara Bonney, Director of Admissions
402-552-3100 Fax: 402-552-6057
Website: www.clarksoncollege.edu
E-mail: admiss@clarksoncollege.edu

College of Saint Mary
7000 Mercy Rd, Omaha NE 68106
Lorin Werth,V.P. for Enrollment
800-926-5534 or 402-399-2407 Fax: 402-399-2412
Website: www.csm.edu
E-mail: lwerth@csm.edu

Mid-Plains Community College
North Platte Community College - North Campus
1101 Halligan Dr, North Platte NE 69101-7659
Kelly Rippen, Director of Recruitment
800-658-4308 ext. 8107 Fax: 308-534-5770
Website: www.mpcc.edu
E-mail: rippenk@mpcc.edu

Nebraska Wesleyan University
5000 Saint Paul Ave, Lincoln NE 68504-2794
Patricia Karthauser, V.P. for University Enrollment
402-466-2371 Fax: 402-465-2177
Website: www.nebrwesleyan.edu
E-mail: admissions@nebrwesleyan.edu

University of Nebraska at Kearney
905 W 25th St, Kearney NE 68849-0001
Dusty Newton, Director of Admissions
800-KEARNEY Fax: 308-865-8987
Website: www.unk.edu
E-mail: admissionsug@unk.edu

NEVADA

Career College of Northern Nevada
1195-A Corporate Blvd, Reno NV 89502-2331
Nathan Clark, Director
775-856-2266 Fax: 775-856-0935
Website: www.ccnn.edu
E-mail: lgoldhammer@ccnn4u.com
See listing under "Career Schools"

GREAT BASIN COLLEGE
1500 College Pkwy, Elko NV 89801-5032
Julie G. Byrnes, Director of Enrollment Management
775-753-2271 Fax: 775-753-2311
Website: www.gbcnv.edu
E-mail: bjulie@gbcnv.edu

NEW JERSEY

Atlantic Cape Community College
5100 Black Horse Pike
Mays Landing NJ 08330-2699
Linda McLeod, Assistant Director of College
Recruitment
609-343-5000 Fax: 609-343-4921
Website: www.atlantic.edu
E-mail: accadmit@atlantic.edu
See listing under "Community and Junior Colleges"

Bergen Community College
400 Paramus Rd, Paramus NJ 07652
Julian Gomez, Asst. Director of Admissions
201-447-7100 Fax: 201-444-7036
Website: www.bergen.edu
E-mail: jgomez@bergen.edu

HELENE FULD SCHOOL OF NURSING
PO Box 1669, Blackwood NJ 08012-7369
Kim Packer, Assistant Dean for Admissions
856-374-0100 Fax: 856-374-0713
Website: www.helenefuld.virtua.org
E-mail: kpacker@virtua.org

HOLY NAME HOSPITAL SCHOOL OF NURSING
690 Teaneck Rd, Teaneck NJ 07666-4254
Maureen Schmude, Registrar
201-833-3005 Fax: 201-833-7209
Website: www.schoolofnursing.info
E-mail: sr-tynan@mail.holyname.org

Mercer County Community College
West Windsor Campus
PO Box B, Trenton NJ 08690
Savita Bambhrolia, Director of Admissions
609-586-4800 Fax: 609-587-4666
Website: www.mccc.edu
E-mail: admiss@mccc.edu

MUHLENBERG REGIONAL MEDICAL CENTER
Schools of Nursing, Medical Imaging & Therapeutic
Sciences
Plainfield NJ 07061
Jane Vatsky, Director of Admissions
908-668-2400 Fax: 908-226-4568
Website: www.muhlenbergschools.org
E-mail: ssonmits@solarishs.org
Established 1894. Private. Coed. Accreditation: SON -
N.J. Board of Nursing, NLN; SOR - JRCRT, NJDEP;
SONMT - JRCNMT, NJDEP. Total cost of entire program

(average by school) SON - $26,004; SOR - $27,997;
SONMT - $13,442; SORT - $12,308; SODMS - $18,929.
Federal, state and institutional financial aid available.
Residence $955/semester. Enrollment: 500. Student-
faculty ratio: 10:1. Degrees: AS and Diploma. Cooperative program with Union County College, Cranford, N.J.
Associate in Science degree awarded from UCC and diploma from Muhlenberg Schools of Nursing, Medical Imaging and Therapeutic Sciences. Professional programs
offered: Registered Nursing, Radiography, Nuclear
Medicine Technology, Radiation Therapy, and Diagnostic Medical Sonography. Articulated with four year colleges and universities for baccalaureate degree.
Advanced RN Residency program for professional RN's.

New Jersey City University
2039 John F Kennedy Blvd
Jersey City NJ 07305-1588
Carmen Panlilio, Asst. V.P. for Admissions and
Financial Aid
201-200-3234 Fax: 201-200-2044
Website: www.njcu.edu
E-mail: admissions@njcu.edu

OUR LADY OF LOURDES SCHOOL OF NURSING
1600 Haddon Ave, Camden NJ 08103
Dorothy M. Letizia, Ed.D., RN, Dean
856-757-3729 Fax: 856-757-3767
Website: www.ololnursing.com
E-mail: letiziad@lourdesnet.org

Ramapo College of New Jersey
505 Ramapo Valley Rd, Mahwah NJ 07430-1623
Director of Admissions
201-684-7300 or 201-684-7301 Fax: 201-684-7964
Website: www.ramapo.edu
E-mail: admissions@ramapo.edu

NEW YORK

ARNOT OGDEN MEDICAL CENTER SCHOOL OF NURSING
600 Roe Ave, Elmira NY 14905-1676
Linda MacAuslan, Director
607-737-4153 Fax: 607-737-4116
Website: www.arnothealth.org
E-mail: lmacauslan@aomc.org

Broome Community College
907 Upper Front St, Binghamton NY 13905
Anthony S. Fiorelli, Director of Admissions
607-778-5001 Fax: 607-778-5442
Website: www.sunybroome.edu
E-mail: fiorelli_a@sunybroome.edu

CROUSE HOSPITAL SCHOOL OF NURSING
736 Irving Ave, Syracuse NY 13210-1687
Amy Graham, Contact
315-470-7858 Fax: 315-470-5774
Website: www.crouse.org/nursing
E-mail: amygraham@crouse.org
Established 1913. Private, nonprofit. Coed. Accreditation (registration): NYS Board of Regents. Tuition: $7,352
per year. Room: $3,500. Enrollment: 290. Faculty: 28 full
and part-time. Degrees: Approved Associate degree
program. Close to Syracuse University and SUNY Upstate Medical University. Students use facilities at SUNY
Upstate Medical University for gym, pool, tennis &
squash courts. Within walking distance to downtown,
Carrier Dome, Everson Museum, Civic Center. Scholarships, loans and college work-study positions available
for eligible students.

CUNY Hunter College
695 Park Ave, New York NY 10021
Aaron Gibbs, Assistant Director of Recruitment
212-772-4497 Fax: 212-650-3336
Website: www.hunter.cuny.edu
E-mail: aaron.gibbs@hunter.cuny.edu

Daemen College
4380 Main St, Amherst NY 14226-3592
Donna Shaffner, Director of Admissions
800-462-7652 or 716-839-8225 Fax: 716-839-8229
Website: www.daemen.edu
E-mail: admissions@daemen.edu
See listing under "Universities"

Long Island University-C. W. Post Campus
720 Northern Blvd, Brookville NY 11548-1300
Joanne Graziano, Executive Director of Admissions
516-299-2900 Fax: 516-299-2137
Website: www.liu.edu/cwpost
E-mail: enroll@cwpost.liu.edu

Molloy College
1000 Hempstead Ave
Rockville Centre NY 11570-1100
Marguerite Lane, Director of Admissions
516-678-5000 ext. 6291 Fax: 516-256-2247
Website: www.molloy.edu
E-mail: admissions@molloy.edu
See listing under "Universities"

Roberts Wesleyan College
2301 Westside Dr, Rochester NY 14624-1997
Office of Admissions
585-594-6400 Fax: 585-594-6371
Website: www.roberts.edu
E-mail: admissions@roberts.edu

St. Joseph's College
245 Clinton Ave, Brooklyn NY 11205-3688
Theresa LaRocca Meyer, V.P. for Enrollment
Management
718-636-6800 Fax: 718-636-8303
Website: www.sjcny.edu
E-mail: tlaroccameyer@sjcny.edu

ST. JOSEPH'S COLLEGE OF NURSING AT SJHHC

206 Prospect Ave, Syracuse NY 13203-1806
Rhonda Reader, Assistant Dean for Admissions
315-448-5040 Fax: 315-448-5745
Website: www.sjhsyr.org/nursing
E-mail: collegeofnursing@sjhsyr.org

SUNY College at Brockport
350 New Campus Dr, Brockport NY 14420-2997
Bernard S. Valento, Director of Undergraduate
Admissions
585-395-2751 Fax: 585-395-5452
Website: www.brockport.edu
E-mail: admit@brockport.edu

SUNY College of Technology
Alfred NY 14802
Deborah J. Goodrich, Director of Admissions
800-4AL-FRED Fax: 607-587-4299
Website: www.alfredstate.edu
E-mail: admissions@alfredstate.edu

SUNY Niagara County Community College
3111 Saunders Settlement Rd
Sanborn NY 14132-9487
Kathleen Saunders, Director of Admissions
716-614-6200 Fax: 716-614-6820
Website: www.niagaracc.suny.edu
E-mail: saunders@niagaracc.suny.edu

SUNY Orange County Community College
115 South St, Middletown NY 10940-6437
Margot St. Lawrence, Director of Admissions
845-341-4030 Fax: 845-342-8662
Website: www.sunyorange.edu
E-mail: apply@sunyorange.edu
See listing under "Community and Junior Colleges"

Trocaire College
360 Choate Ave, Buffalo NY 14220-2003
Paul B. Hurley, Ph.D., President
716-826-1200 Fax: 716-828-6107
Website: www.trocaire.edu
E-mail: info@trocaire.edu
See listing under "Community and Junior Colleges"

NORTH CAROLINA

CABARRUS COLLEGE OF HEALTH SCIENCES

401 Medical Park Dr, Concord NC 28025
Mark Ellison, Director of Admissions
704-783-1556 Fax: 704-783-2077
Website: www.cabarruscollege.edu
E-mail: admissions@cabarruscollege.edu
See listing under "Universities"

CAROLINAS COLLEGE OF HEALTH SCIENCES

PO Box 32861, Charlotte NC 28232-2861
Elizabeth West, Admissions Officer
704-355-5043 Fax: 704-355-9336
Website: www.carolinascollege.edu
E-mail: elizabeth.west@carolinascollege.edu
Established 1990. Private. Coed. Accreditation: SACS, CAAHEP, JCERT, NAACLS, NLNAC, NCEMS. Tuition: $175 per credit hour. Fees: $280. Enrollment: 465 full-time, 98 part-time. Faculty: 66. Student-faculty ratio: 14:1. AAS degree offered. Library: 20,000 volumes. Carolinas College of Health Sciences offers several exciting programs in healthcare education featuring nursing and allied health related fields. The College is a subsidiary of Carolinas HealthCare System which is the nation's third largest non-profit healthcare system. Located next to Carolinas Medical Center, the area's only level 1 trauma center, Carolinas College offers a host of hands-on clinical experiences that make our students the best prepared new graduates entering healthcare today.

Haywood Community College
185 Freedlander Dr, Clyde NC 28721
Debbie Rowland, Coordinator of Admissions
828-627-4500 Fax: 828-627-4513
Website: www.haywood.edu
E-mail: drowland@haywood.edu

James Sprunt Community College
PO Box 398, Kenansville NC 28349-0398
Rita Brown, Registrar
910-296-2500 Fax: 910-296-1636
Website: www.sprunt.com

Louisburg College
501 N Main St, Louisburg NC 27549-2399
800-775-0208 or 919-496-2521 Fax: 919-496-1788
Website: www.louisburg.edu
E-mail: admissions@louisburg.edu

North Carolina A&T State University
1601 E Market St, Greensboro NC 27411
Lee Young, AVC Enrollment
336-334-7500 Fax: 336-334-7478
Website: www.ncat.edu
E-mail: uadmit@ncat.edu

South Piedmont Community College
PO Box 126, Polkton NC 28135-0126
Joy Pope, Contact
704-272-5338
Website: www.spcc.edu
E-mail: jpope@spcc.edu

NORTH DAKOTA

Dickinson State University
Dickinson ND 58601-4896
Steve Glasser, Director of Student Recruitment
800-279-4295 Fax: 701-483-2409
Website: www.dickinsonstate.edu
E-mail: dsu.hawks@dickinsonstate.edu

Sitting Bull College
1341 92nd St, Fort Yates ND 58538
Melody Azure, Director of Admissions / Registrar
701-854-3861 Fax: 701-854-3403
Website: www.sittingbull.edu
E-mail: melodya@sbci.edu

Williston State College
PO Box 1326, Williston ND 58802-1326
Penny Powell, Director Enrollment Services
701-774-4200 Fax: 701-774-4544
Website: www.wsc.nodak.edu
E-mail: penny.soiseth@wsc.nodak.edu

OHIO

Brown Mackie College - Cincinnati
1011 Glendale Milford Rd, Cincinnati OH 45215-1107
Robin Krout, President
513-771-2424 Fax: 513-771-3413
Website: www.brownmackie.edu
E-mail: rkrout@brownmackie.edu

Cleveland State University
2121 Euclid Ave RW 204, Cleveland OH 44115
Dr. Richard Arndt, Dean of Undergraduate Recruitment
and College Partnerships
888-CSU-OHIO Fax: 216-687-9210
Website: www.csuohio.edu
E-mail: admissions@csuohio.edu

COMMUNITY HOSPITAL SCHOOL OF NURSING

2615 E High St, Springfield OH 45505-1494
Jamie Schoening, Recruiter
937-328-8905 Fax: 937-328-8668
Website: www.chsn.com
E-mail: jamie.schoening@health-partners.org

FIRELANDS REGIONAL MEDICAL CENTER SCHOOL OF NURSING

1912 Hayes Ave, Sandusky OH 44870-4788
Holly J. Price, RN, Director
419-557-7111 Fax: 419-557-7116
Website: www.firelands.com
E-mail: priceh@firelands.com

Franciscan University of Steubenville
University Blvd, Steubenville OH 43952
Margaret J. Weber, Director of Admissions
800-783-6220 or 740-283-6226 Fax: 740-284-5456
Website: www.admissions.edu
E-mail: mweber@franciscan.edu

HURON SCHOOL OF NURSING

Cleveland Clinic Health System
13951 Terrace Rd, East Cleveland OH 44112-4308
Barbara Szigeti, MA, Coordinator of Student Services
216-761-7996 Fax: 216-761-7541
Website: www.cchseast.org/schools
E-mail: bszigeti@cchseast.org

MEDCENTRAL COLLEGE OF NURSING

335 Glessner Ave, Mansfield OH 44903-2265
Christopher M. Harris, Director for Enrollment
Management
419-520-2600 Fax: 419-520-2610
Website: www.medcentral.edu
E-mail: charris@medcentral.edu

Medical University of Ohio
3000 Arlington Ave, Toledo OH 43614
419-383-4000 Fax: 419-383-2800
Website: www.meduohio.edu

Northwest State Community College
22600 State Route 34, Archbold OH 43502-9542
Mark Thompson, Director of Admissions
419-267-5511 Fax: 419-267-5587
Website: www.northweststate.edu
E-mail: mthompson@northweststate.edu

The Ohio State University
College of Nursing
Newton Hall, 1585 Neil Ave, Columbus OH 43210
614-292-4041 Fax: 614-292-9399
Website: nursing.osu.edu
E-mail: nursing@osu.edu

Owens Community College
300 Davis St, Findlay OH 45840-3631
William J. Ivoska PhD., Vice President of Student
Services
567-429-3500 Fax: 567-423-0246
Website: www.owens.edu
E-mail: admissions@owens.edu

Owens Community College
PO Box 10000, Toledo OH 43699-1947
William J. Ivoska, Ph.D, Vice President of Student
Services
567-661-7000 Fax: 567-661-7607
Website: www.owens.edu
E-mail: admissions@owens.edu

Sinclair Community College
444 W 3rd St, Dayton OH 45402-1460
Sara P. Smith, Director of Outreach Services
937-512-3000 Fax: 937-512-2393
Website: www.sinclair.edu
E-mail: admit@sinclair.edu

Ursuline College
2550 Lander Rd, Cleveland OH 44124-4398
Sarah E. Sundermeier, Director of Admissions
888-URSULINE Toll Free Fax: 440-684-6138
Website: www.admission.ursuline.edu
E-mail: admission@ursuline.edu

OKLAHOMA

Oral Roberts University
7777 S Lewis Ave, Tulsa OK 74171-0001
Chris Belcher, Director of Undergraduate Admissions
800-678-8876 Fax: 918-495-6222
Website: www.oru.edu
E-mail: admissions@oru.edu

University of Tulsa
600 S College Ave, Tulsa OK 74104-3126
Earl Johnson, Dean of Admissions
918-631-2307 Fax: 918-631-5003
Website: www.utulsa.edu
E-mail: admission@utulsa.edu

OREGON

Concordia University
2811 NE Holman St, Portland OR 97211-6099
Bobi Swan, Director of Admissions
503-288-9371 Fax: 503-280-8531
Website: www.cu-portland.edu
E-mail: cu-admissions@cu-portland.edu

Rogue Community College
3345 Redwood Hwy, Grants Pass OR 97527-9298
Claudia Sullivan, Director of Enrollment Services
541-956-7500 Fax: 541-471-3585
Website: www.roguecc.edu
E-mail: csullivan@roguecc.edu
See listing under "Community and Junior Colleges"

PENNSYLVANIA

CONEMAUGH VALLEY MEMORIAL HOSPITAL

School of Nursing
1086 Franklin St, Johnstown PA 15905-4398
Louise Pugliese, Director
814-534-9844 Fax: 814-534-3354
Website: www.conemaugh.org
E-mail: lpuglie@conemaugh.org
Two year program. Fully accredited. Excellent success of first time candidates taking licensure exam. Over 1,000 hours of clinical experience in a trauma medical center and community outreach services. Articulation agreement with University of Pittsburgh and Mount Aloysius College. BSN degree can be completed in 1-1/2 - 2 years. Approximately one-quarter of enrollment are men. Scholarship and financial aid available.

DeSales University
2755 Station Ave, Center Valley PA 18034-9565
610-282-1100 Fax: 610-282-2342
Website: www.desales.edu

Gannon University
109 University Sq, Erie PA 16541-0001
Christopher Tremblay, Director of Admissions
800-GANNON-U Fax: 814-871-5803
Website: www.gannon.edu
E-mail: admissions@gannon.edu

Holy Family University
9801 Frankford Avenue, Philadelphia PA 19114
Lauren Campbell, Director of Admissions
215-637-3050 Fax: 215-281-1022
Website: www.holyfamily.edu
E-mail: admissions@holyfamily.edu

JAMESON MEMORIAL HOSPITAL SCHOOL OF NURSING

1211 Wilmington Ave, New Castle PA 16105-2595
Jayne Sheehan, RN, MSN, CRNP, Director of
Professional and Allied Health Education
724-656-4052 Fax: 724-656-4179
Website: www.jamesonhealthsystem.com
E-mail: lsoukovich@jamesonhealthsystem.com
Private. Coed. Accreditation: National League for Nursing Accrediting Commission, PA State Board of Nursing. Average tuition/year: $10,094. Average fees/year: $849 (PSU & JMH). Student-faculty ratio: 10-8:1. Diploma offered. Two year program with summers off. Clinical experience early in the program. Highly-skilled professional and caring faculty. Affiliated with Penn State University with college credits transferable to all colleges and universities. Most clinical experiences within Lawrence County. Approved for Veteran's Education.

Juniata College
1700 Moore St, Huntingdon PA 16652-2196
Michelle Bartol, Dean of Enrollment
877-JUNIATA Fax: 814-641-3100
Website: www.juniata.edu
E-mail: admissions@juniata.edu

Lancaster General College of Nursing and Health
Sciences
410 N Lime St, Lancaster PA 17602-2337
Elma Hess, Director of Admissions
717-544-4902 Fax: 717-544-5970
Website: www.lancastergeneralcollege.org
E-mail: elhess@lancastergeneral.org

La Roche College
9000 Babcock Blvd, Pittsburgh PA 15237-5898
Thomas Hassett, Director of Freshman and
International Admissions
412-536-1272 or 800-838-4LRC Fax: 412-536-1272
Website: www.laroche.edu
E-mail: admissions@laroche.edu

MERCY HOSPITAL SCHOOL OF NURSING

1401 Boulevard of the Allies
Pittsburgh PA 15219-5107
Joanne Sperry, RN, MN Director
412-232-7940 Fax: 412-232-7951
Website: www.pmhs.org/son
E-mail: jsperry@mercy.pmhs.org

MOUNT ALOYSIUS COLLEGE

7373 Admiral Peary Hwy, Cresson PA 16630-1999
Frank C. Crouse Jr., Vice President for Enrollment
Management
814-886-6383 or 888-823-2220 Fax: 814-886-6441
Website: www.mtaloy.edu
E-mail: admissions@mtaloy.edu

Neumann College
1 Neumann Dr, Aston PA 19014-1298
Dennis Murphy, Director of Admissions
610-459-0905 Fax: 610-558-5652
Website: www.neumann.edu
E-mail: admiss@neumann.edu

POTTSVILLE HOSPITAL SCHOOL OF NURSING

420 S Jackson St, Pottsville PA 17901-3625
Angela Pasco, RN, MSN, Director
570-621-5028 Fax: 570-621-5113
Website: www.pottsvillehospitalschoolofnursing.com
E-mail: phson@pothosp.com

ST. MARGARET HOSPITAL SCHOOL OF NURSING
221 Seventh St Suite 100, Pittsburgh PA 15238
Ann D. Ciak, Director
412-784-4980 Fax: 412-784-4994
Website: www.upmc.edu/StMargaret/SchofNursing
E-mail: smhsonrninfo@upmc.edu

SHARON REGIONAL HEALTH SYSTEM
740 E State St, Sharon PA 16146-3395
Nora Bennett, Director
724-983-3865 Fax: 724-983-5524
Website: www.sharonregional.com
E-mail: nbennett@srhs-pa.org

WESTERN PENNSYLVANIA HOSPITAL SCHOOL OF NURSING
4900 Friendship Ave, Pittsburgh PA 15224-1724
Joan Brooks, Recruiter
412-578-5538 Fax: 412-578-1837
Website: www.wpahs.org/education
E-mail: sonadmissions@wpahs.org

SOUTH CAROLINA

Bob Jones University
1700 Wade Hampton Blvd
Greenville SC 29614-0001
Kathleen Crispin, Director
800-BJ-AND-ME
Website: www.bju.edu
E-mail: admissions@bju.edu
See listing under "Universities"

Columbia International University
PO Box 3122, Columbia SC 29230-3122
John Basie, Director of University Admissions
800-777-2227 Fax: 803-786-4209
Website: www.ciu.edu
E-mail: yesciu@ciu.edu
See listing under "Theological Studies & Religious Vocations"

Greenville Technical College
PO Box 5616, Greenville SC 29606-5616
Martha White, Director of Admissions
800-723-0673 (US) or 800-922-1183 (SC)
Website: www.greenvilletech.com

University of South Carolina - Upstate
800 University Way, Spartanburg SC 29303-4932
Donette Stewart, Assistant VC for Enrollment Services
864-503-5246 Fax: 864-503-5727
Website: www.uscupstate.edu
E-mail: dstewart@uscupstate.edu
See listing under "Universities"

SOUTH DAKOTA

Presentation College
1500 N Main St, Aberdeen SD 57401-1280
JoEllen Lindner, Dean of Admissions
605-229-8492 Fax: 605-229-8425
Website: www.presentation.edu
E-mail: admit@presentation.edu

Western Dakota Technical Institute
800 Mickelson Dr, Rapid City SD 57703-4018
Janell Oberlander, Manager of Student Services
605-394-4034 or 800-544-8765 Fax: 605-394-1789
Website: www.westerndakotatech.org
E-mail: admissions@wdti.tec.sd.us
See listing under "Career Schools"

TENNESSEE

Aquinas College
4210 Harding Pike, Nashville TN 37205-2086
Diane C. LeJeune, Director of Admissions
615-297-7545 ext. 460 Fax: 615-297-7970
Website: www.aquinas-tn.edu
E-mail: lejeuned@aquinas-tn.edu

Lipscomb University
3901 Granny White Pike, Nashville TN 37204-3951
Ricky Holaway, Director of Admissions
800-333-4358 ext. 1776 Fax: 615-269-1804
Website: www.lipscomb.edu
E-mail: admissions@lipscomb.edu

Tennessee State University
3500 John A Merritt Blvd, Nashville TN 37209-1561
John Cade, Dean of Admissions & Records
615-963-5101 Fax: 615-963-2930
Website: www.tnstate.edu
E-mail: jcade@tnstate.edu

University of Tennessee
615 McCallie Ave, Chattanooga TN 37403-2504
Yancy Freeman, Director of Admissions
423-425-4111 Fax: 423-425-4157
Website: www.utc.edu
E-mail: Yancy-Freeman@utc.edu

TEXAS

American Commercial College
2007 34th St, Lubbock TX 79411-1899
Michael Otto, Director
806-747-4339 Fax: 806-765-9838
Website: www.acc-careers.com
E-mail: mjotto@acc-careers.com

Angelo State University
ASU Station 11014, San Angelo TX 76909
Bonnie Stennett, Coordinator of Recruiting
800-946-8627 Fax: 325-942-2078
Website: www.angelo.edu
E-mail: admissions@angelo.edu

Blinn College
902 College Ave, Brenham TX 77833-4098
Dennis K. Crowson, Registrar
979-830-4000 Fax: 979-830-4110
Website: www.blinn.edu
E-mail: recruiting@blinn.edu

Blinn College
PO Box 6030, Bryan TX 77805-6030
Dennis K. Crowson, Registrar
979-209-7200 Fax: 979-209-7229
Website: www.blinn.edu
E-mail: recruiting@blinn.edu

GALEN HEALTH INSTITUTE SCHOOL OF NURSING
4440 S Piedras Dr Suite 200, San Antonio TX 78228
210-733-3056 Fax: 210-733-5223
Website: www.galened.com
E-mail: emayo@galened.com
Galen Health Institute offers a full-time 12 month LVN Program. The program is designed to prepare students to become licensed vocational nurses who provide direct care to patients in a variety of settings. Programs include classroom lectures and activities, skills laboratory practice, and direct patient care experience in hospitals and other facilities (clinical rotations). For futher information contact the Admissions Representative.

Galveston College
4015 Avenue Q, Galveston TX 77550-7496
Brian Lowery, Registrar
409-763-6551 Fax: 409-944-1501
Website: www.gc.edu
E-mail: blowery@gc.edu

Lamar State College-Orange
410 W Front St, Orange TX 77630-5899
Rebecca Campbell, Registrar
409-883-7750 Fax: 409-882-3055
Website: www.lsco.edu
E-mail: becky.campbell@lsco.edu

McLennan Community College
1400 College Dr, Waco TX 76708-1498
Dr. Cherry Beckworth, Program Director, Nursing
254-299-8000 Fax: 254-299-8854
Website: www.mclennan.edu
E-mail: cbeckworth@mclennan.edu

North Central Texas College
1525 W California St, Gainesville TX 76240-4636
Michelle Winters, Registrar
940-668-3315 Fax: 940-665-7075
Website: www.nctc.edu
E-mail: mwinters@nctc.edu

Temple College
2600 S 1st St, Temple TX 76504-7435
Angela Balch, Director of Admissions & Records
254-298-8300 Fax: 254-298-8288
Website: www.templejc.edu
E-mail: ruth.bridges@templejc.edu

Texas Woman's University
PO Box 425589, Denton TX 76204-5589
Erma Nieto, Director of Admissions
866-809-6130 Fax: 940-898-3081
Website: www.twu.edu
E-mail: admissions@twu.edu

University of Texas at Arlington
Box 19111, Arlington TX 76019-0111
Hans Gatterdam, Director of Admission
817-272-6287 Fax: 817-272-3435
Website: www.uta.edu
E-mail: admissions@uta.edu

UNIVERSITY OF TEXAS-HOUSTON
6901 Bertner Ave, Houston TX 77030-3901
William D. Stewart, Coordinator of Admissions
713-500-2104 Fax: 713-500-2107
Website: http://son.uth.tmc.edu
E-mail: william.stewart@uth.tmc.edu

VERMONT

NORWICH UNIVERSITY
158 Harmon Dr, Northfield VT 05663
Marilyn Rinker, Department Head
800-468-6679 Fax: 802-485-2607
Website: www.norwich.edu
E-mail: mrinker@norwich.edu

Southern Vermont College
982 Mansion Dr, Bennington VT 05201-6002
Kathleen James Ring, Director of Admissions
800-378-2782 Fax: 802-447-4695
Website: www.svc.edu
E-mail: admis@svc.edu

VIRGINIA

Radford University
PO Box 6903, Radford VA 24142
David W. Kraus, Director of Admissions
800-890-4265 Fax: 540-831-5038
Website: www.radford.edu
E-mail: ruadmiss@radford.edu

Riverside School of Health Careers
316 Main St, Newport News VA 23601
Tracey Hiller, Recruitment Coordinator
757-240-2200 Fax: 757-240-2225
Website: www.riversideonline.com/rshc
E-mail: tracey.hiller@rivhs.com

Sentara School of Health Professions
1441 Crossways Blvd Suite 105
Chesapeake VA 23320
Shelly Vinson, Director
Phyllis Moran, Recruiter
757-388-2900 Fax: 757-388-2905
Website: www.sentara.com/healthprofessions
E-mail: healthprofessions@sentara.com

Southside Regional Medical Center
801 S Adams St, Petersburg VA 23803-5133
Tonia Little, Director of Admissions
804-862-5800 Fax: 804-862-5937
Website: www.srmcnursing.org
E-mail: tlittle@chs.net

Southside Virginia Community College
109 Campus Dr, Alberta VA 23821-2930
Ronald E. Mattox, Dean of Admissions
434-949-1014 Fax: 434-949-7863
Website: www.sv.vccs.edu
E-mail: ronald.mattox@sv.vccs.edu

Southside Virginia Community College
200 Daniel Rd, Keysville VA 23947
Ronald E. Mattox, Dean of Admissions
434-736-2018 Fax: 434-736-2082
Website: www.sv.vccs.edu
E-mail: ronald.mattox@sv.vccs.edu

WASHINGTON

Everett Community College
2000 Tower St, Everett WA 98201
Christine Kerlin, Associate Dean
425-388-9100 Fax: 425-388-9173
Website: www.everettcc.edu
E-mail: ckerlin@everettcc.edu

Gonzaga University
502 E Boone Ave, Spokane WA 99258-0102
Julie McCulloh, Dean of Admission
800-322-2584 or 509-323-6572 Fax: 509-323-5780
Website: www.gonzaga.edu
E-mail: mcculloh@gu.gonzaga.edu

Walla Walla Community College
500 Tausick Way, Walla Walla WA 99362-9270
Marilyn Galusha, Director of Nursing
509-527-4240 or 877-992-9922 Fax: 509-527-3667
Website: www.wwcc.edu
E-mail: marilyn.galusha@wwcc.edu
See listing under "Community and Junior Colleges"

Wenatchee Valley College
1300 5th St, Wenatchee WA 98801-1799
Marco Azurdia, Dean, Student Development
509-682-6805 Fax: 509-682-6541
Website: www.wvc.edu

WEST VIRGINIA

Davis & Elkins College
100 Campus Dr, Elkins WV 26241-3996
Renee Heckel, Director of Enrollment Management
800-624-3157 Fax: 304-637-1800
Website: www.davisandelkins.edu
E-mail: admiss@davisandelkins.edu

Fairmont State University
1201 Locust Ave, Fairmont WV 26554-2470
Steve Leadman, Director of Admissions
304-367-4003 or 800-641-5678 Fax: 304-367-4789
Website: www.fairmontstate.edu
E-mail: admit@fairmontstate.edu

Mountain State University
Box 9003, Beckley WV 25802-9003
866-FOR-MSU1 or 304-929-INFO Fax: 304-253-5072
Website: www.mountainstate.edu
E-mail: gomsu@mountainstate.edu
See listing under "Universities"

ST. MARY'S MEDICAL CENTER
2900 1st Ave, Huntington WV 25702-1272
Dr. Sheila Kyle, VP Schools of Nursing & Health Professions
304-526-1270 Fax: 304-526-1517
Website: www.st-marys.org
E-mail: skyle@st-marys.org

WISCONSIN

Alverno College
PO Box 343922, Milwaukee WI 53234-3922
Mary Kay Farrell, Director of Admissions
414-382-6100 Fax: 414-382-6354
Website: www.alverno.edu
E-mail: admissions@alverno.edu

BELLIN COLLEGE OF NURSING
PO Box 23400, Green Bay WI 54305-3400
Penny Croghan, Director of Admissions
920-433-5803 Fax: 920-433-7416
Website: www.bcon.edu
E-mail: admissio@bcon.edu

Blackhawk Technical College
PO Box 5009, Janesville WI 53547-5009
Gregg Bosak, Administration, Community Information
608-757-7769 Fax: 608-757-7740
Website: www.blackhawk.edu
E-mail: gbosak@blackhawk.edu

Lakeshore Technical College
1290 North Ave, Cleveland WI 53015-1414
Information Fulfillment Specialist
888-GOTOLTC Fax: 920-693-3561
Website: www.gotoltc.edu
E-mail: info@gotoltc.edu

Marquette University
PO Box 1881, Milwaukee WI 53201-1881
Robert Blust, Director of Admissions
414-288-7302 Fax: 414-288-3764
Website: www.mu.edu
E-mail: admissions@marquette.edu

Wisconsin Indianhead Technical College
505 Pine Ridge Dr, Shell Lake WI 54871
Piper Larson, Dean
800-243-9482 Fax: 715-468-2819
Website: www.witc.edu
E-mail: plarson@witc.edu

WYOMING

Laramie County Community College
1400 E College Dr, Cheyenne WY 82007-3204
Jenny Hargett, Director of Admissions
307-778-5222 Fax: 307-778-1350
Website: www.lccc.wy.edu
E-mail: learnmore@lccc.wy.edu

University of Wyoming
Admissions Office
Dept 3435, Laramie WY 82071-3435
Aaron Appelhans, Contact
800-342-5996 Fax: 307-766-4042
Website: www.uwyo.edu
E-mail: why-wyo@uwyo.edu

GUAM

University of Guam
UOG Station, Mangilao GU 96923
Deborah Leon Guerrero, Registrar
671-735-2201 or 671-735-2208 Fax: 671-735-2203
Website: www.uog.edu
E-mail: admitme@uog9.uog.edu

PUERTO RICO

Colegio Mayor de Technologia
PO Box 1490, Arroyo PR 00714
Julia Melendez, Director of Admissions
787-839-5266 Fax: 787-839-0033
Website: www.colegiomayortec.com
E-mail: cmtarroy@coqui.net

Instituto de Banca y Comercio
61 Ponce De Leon Ave, Hato Rey PR 00919
Rafael Jimenez, Vice President
787-754-7120 Fax: 787-754-7143
Website: www.ibanca.net
E-mail: rjimenez@ibancapr.com

Universidad Adventista de las Antillas
PO Box 118, Mayaguez PR 00919-0118
Evelyn Del Valle Rivera, Director of Admissions
787-834-9595 Fax: 787-834-9597
Website: www.uaa.edu
E-mail: admissions@uaa.edu

OPTOMETRY

ALABAMA

Judson College
302 Bibb St, Marion AL 36756
Michael Scotto, Director of Admissions
800-447-9472 Fax: 334-683-5147
Website: www.judson.edu
E-mail: admissions@judson.edu

FLORIDA

Nova Southeastern University Health Profession
3200 S University Dr, Davie FL 33328-2018
Marla Frohlinger, Director of Admissions
954-262-1101 Fax: 954-262-2282
Website: www.nova.edu
E-mail: marlaf@nsu.nova.edu

IOWA

Iowa Lakes Community College
300 S 18th St, Estherville IA 51334-2721
Anne Stansbury, Asst. Director of Admissions
712-362-7945 Fax: 712-362-8363
Website: www.iowalakes.edu
E-mail: info@iowalakes.edu

KANSAS

Newman University
3100 W McCormick St, Wichita KS 67213
Jann Reusser, Admissions Recruitment Coordinator
316-942-4291 ext. 2144 Fax: 316-942-4483
Website: www.newmanu.edu
E-mail: reusserj@newmanu.edu

MASSACHUSETTS

Benjamin Franklin Institute of Technology
41 Berkeley St, Boston MA 02116-6307
Norman Kraft, Dean of Enrollment
617-423-4630 ext. 121 Fax: 617-482-3706
Website: www.bfit.edu
E-mail: admissions@bfit.edu

MISSOURI

University of Missouri
1 University Blvd, Saint Louis MO 63121-4499
Dr. Larry J. Davis, Dean
314-516-5606 Fax: 314-516-6708
Website: www.umsl.edu
E-mail: admissions@umsl.edu

NEW YORK

SUNY COLLEGE OF OPTOMETRY

33 W 42nd St, New York NY 10036-8003
Dr. Edward R. Johnston, VP Student Affairs
212-938-5500 or 800-291-3937 Fax: 212-938-5504
Website: www.sunyopt.edu
E-mail: admissions@sunyopt.edu
  Established 1971. Public. Coed. Accreditation: Middle States Association of Colleges & Schools, Council on Optometric Education. Tuition: $13,620/$26,150. Enrollment: 285. Faculty: 134. Student-faculty ratio: 4:1. Degrees: O.D.; MS & PhD in Vision, Science. Library: 34,000 volumes.

OHIO

The Ohio State University
College of Optometry
Starling-Loving Hall, 320 W 10th Ave
Columbus OH 43210
614-292-2647 Fax: 614-292-7493
Website: optometry.osu.edu
E-mail: admissions@optometry.ohio-state.edu

Ursuline College
2550 Lander Rd, Cleveland OH 44124-4398
Sarah E. Sundermeier, Director of Admissions
888-URSULINE Toll Free Fax: 440-684-6138
Website: www.admission.ursuline.edu
E-mail: admission@ursuline.edu

OREGON

Pacific University
2043 College Way, Forest Grove OR 97116-1797
Karen M. Dunston, Executive Director of Admissions
800-635-0561 Fax: 503-352-2975
Website: www.pacificu.edu
E-mail: admissions@pacificu.edu

PENNSYLVANIA

Arcadia University
450 S Easton Rd, Glenside PA 19038-3295
Dennis Nostrand, VP for Enrollment Management
877-ARCADIA (877-272-2342) Fax: 215-881-8767
Website: www.arcadia.edu
E-mail: admiss@arcadia.edu
See listing under "Universities"

Juniata College
1700 Moore St, Huntingdon PA 16652-2196
Michelle Bartol, Dean of Enrollment
877-JUNIATA Fax: 814-641-3100
Website: www.juniata.edu
E-mail: admissions@juniata.edu

TEXAS

University of Houston
122 E Cullen Bldg, Houston TX 77204-2023
Office of Admission
713-743-9595
Website: www.uh.edu
E-mail: admissions@uh.edu

University of St. Thomas
3800 Montrose Blvd, Houston TX 77006-4626
Eduardo Prieto, Director of Admissions
713-522-7911 Fax: 713-525-3558
Website: www.stthom.edu
E-mail: prietoe@stthom.edu

WEST VIRGINIA

West Virginia Wesleyan College
59 College Ave, Buckhannon WV 26201-2699
Robert N. Skinner II, Director of Admission
800-722-9933 Fax: 304-473-8108
Website: www.wvwc.edu
E-mail: admission@wvwc.edu

OSTEOPATHIC MEDICINE

CALIFORNIA

TOURO UNIVERSITY COLLEGE OF OSTEOPATHIC MEDICINE - MARE ISLAND

1310 Johnson Ln, Vallejo CA 94592
Dr. Donald Haight, Director of Admissions
707-638-5270 Fax: 707-638-5250
Website: www.tu.edu
E-mail: haight@touro.edu

FLORIDA

Nova Southeastern University Health Profession
3200 S University Dr, Davie FL 33328-2018
Marla Frohlinger, Director of Admissions
954-262-1101 Fax: 954-262-2282
Website: www.nova.edu
E-mail: marlaf@nsu.nova.edu

University of South Florida
4202 E Fowler Ave, Tampa FL 33620-6900
J. Robert Spatig, Director of Admissions
813-974-3350 Fax: 813-974-9689
Website: www.usf.edu
E-mail: admissions@admin.usf.edu

IOWA

Des Moines University - Osteopathic Medical Center
3200 Grand Ave, Des Moines IA 50312-4198
Kendall Reed, D.O., F.A.C.O.S., Dean Osteopathic Medicine
515-271-1513 Fax: 515-271-7053
Website: www.dmu.edu
E-mail: dmuadmit@dmu.edu

KANSAS

Newman University
3100 W McCormick St, Wichita KS 67213
Jann Reusser, Admissions Recruitment Coordinator
316-942-4291 ext. 2144 Fax: 316-942-4483
Website: www.newmanu.edu
E-mail: reusserj@newmanu.edu

MISSOURI

KANSAS CITY UNIVERSITY OF MEDICINE AND BIOSCIENCES

College of Osteopathic Medicine
1750 Independence Ave
Kansas City MO 64106-1453
Phil Byrne, Director of Recruitment
800-234-4847 Fax: 816-283-2484
Website: www.kcumb.edu
E-mail: admissions@kcumb.edu

KIRKSVILLE COLLEGE OF OSTEOPATHIC MEDICINE
A.T. STILL UNIVERSITY
800 W Jefferson St, Kirksville MO 63501-1443
Admissions Counselor
866-626-2878 or 660-626-2237 Fax: 660-626-2969
Website: www.atsu.edu
E-mail: admissions@atsu.edu

NEW JERSEY
UNIVERSITY OF MEDICINE AND DENTISTRY OF NEW JERSEY
School of Osteopathic Medicine
One Medical Center Dr Suite 210, Stratford NJ 08084
Paula F. Slade, M.A.S., Director of Enrollment Services
856-566-7050 Fax: 856-566-6895
Website: som.umdnj.edu
E-mail: fennerpa@umdnj.edu

PENNSYLVANIA
Gannon University
109 University Sq, Erie PA 16541-0001
Christopher Tremblay, Director of Admissions
800-GANNON-U Fax: 814-871-5803
Website: www.gannon.edu
E-mail: admissions@gannon.edu

Juniata College
1700 Moore St, Huntingdon PA 16652-2196
Michelle Bartol, Dean of Enrollment
877-JUNIATA Fax: 814-641-3100
Website: www.juniata.edu
E-mail: admissions@juniata.edu

PERSONAL AND MISCELLANEOUS SERVICES

ARIZONA
INTERNATIONAL ACADEMY OF BEAUTY
42 N Stapley Dr, Mesa AZ 85203-8841
480-964-8675

INTERNATIONAL ACADEMY OF HAIR DESIGN
3350 N Arizona Ave Ste 4, Chandler AZ 85225
480-820-9422 Fax: 480-820-9348

SOUTHWEST INSTITUTE OF HEALING ARTS
1100 E Apache Blvd, Tempe AZ 85281
Admissions
480-994-9244 Fax: 480-994-3228
Website: www.swiha.org
E-mail: doyourdream@swiha.org

ARKANSAS
ARKANSAS STATE UNIVERSITY MOUNTAIN HOME
1600 S College St, Mountain Home AR 72653
Tonya Sexton, Director of Marketing & Public Relations
870-508-6109 Fax: 870-508-6287
Website: www.asumh.edu
E-mail: tsexton@asumh.edu

CALIFORNIA
CULINARY INSTITUTE OF AMERICA AT GREYSTONE
2555 Main St, Saint Helena CA 94574-9504
800-888-7850 Fax: 845-451-1078
Website: www.ciaprochef.com
E-mail: ciaprochef@culinary.edu

INTERNATIONAL SCHOOL OF COSMETOLOGY
13613 Hawthorne Blvd, Hawthorne CA 90250-5809
Mary Costello, President
310-973-7774 Fax: 310-355-1158
Website: www.isoc.edu
E-mail: isoc@socal.rr.com

MAKE-UP DESIGNORY
129 S San Fernando Blvd, Burbank CA 91502
Tate Holland, School Director
818-729-9420 Fax: 818-729-9971
Website: www.mud.edu
E-mail: tate@mud.edu

ROYALE COLLEGE OF BEAUTY
27485 Commerce Center Dr
Temecula CA 92590-2525
951-676-0833 Fax: 951-676-0653
Website: www.beautyschools.com
E-mail: roylcoll@aol.com

VICTOR VALLEY BEAUTY COLLEGE
16515 Mojave Dr, Victorville CA 92395-3821
Irma Silva, Director
760-245-2522 Fax: 760-245-5681
Website: www.victorvalleybeautycollege.com

CONNECTICUT
AMERICAN ACADEMY OF COSMETOLOGY
109 South St, Danbury CT 06810-8039
Melissa Diacri, Director of Admissions
203-744-0900 Fax: 203-790-7382
Website: www.americanacademyofcosmetology.com
E-mail: mdiacri@hotmail.com

FLORIDA
ASM BEAUTY WORLD ACADEMY
6423 Stirling Rd, Davie FL 33314
Leticia Milazzo, Assistant School Director
877-678-9532 or 954-321-8411 Fax: 954-321-8683
E-mail: asm60@bellsouth.net

BENE'S INTERNATIONAL SCHOOL OF BEAUTY, INC.
7127 US Highway 19
New Port Richey FL 34652-1638
Patricia Martin, Contact
727-848-8415 Fax: 727-846-0269
Website: www.isbschool.com
E-mail: isbschool@aol.com

INTERNATIONAL ACADEMY
2550 S Ridgewood Ave
South Daytona FL 32119-3536
Tracy Franchina, Contact
386-767-4600 Fax: 386-271-0009
Website: www.intl-academy.com
E-mail: tracy@intl-academy.com

SUNSTATE ACADEMY OF HAIR DESIGN
18453 US Highway 19 N, Clearwater FL 33764-2702
Linda Kennedy, Campus Director
727-538-3827 Fax: 727-539-6118
Website: www.sunstate.edu
E-mail: lkennedy@sunstate.edu

SUNSTATE ACADEMY OF HAIR DESIGN
2418 Colonial Blvd, Fort Myers FL 33907-1415
Debbie Rodriguez, Campus Director
239-278-1311 Fax: 239-278-1432
Website: www.sunstate.edu
E-mail: drodriguez@sunstate.edu

SUNSTATE ACADEMY OF HAIR DESIGN
4424 Bee Ridge Rd, Sarasota FL 34233-2502
Kelly King, Interim Campus Director
941-377-4880 Fax: 941-378-2842
Website: www.sunstate.edu
E-mail: kking@sunstate.edu

GEORGIA
GUPTON-JONES COLLEGE OF FUNERAL SERVICE
5141 Snapfinger Woods Dr, Decatur GA 30035-4022
Patty S. Hutcheson, President
770-593-2257 Fax: 770-593-1891
Website: www.gupton-jones.edu
E-mail: gjcfs@mindspring.com

INTERNATIONAL SCHOOL OF SKIN AND NAILCARE
5600 Roswell Rd NE, Atlanta GA 30342-1150
Alan R. Shinall, Operations Manager
404-843-1005 Fax: 404-843-1007
Website: www.skin-nails.com
E-mail: issn@skin-nails.com

IDAHO
RAZZLE DAZZLE COLLEGE OF HAIR DESIGN
120 Holly St, Nampa ID 83686-5102
Christina Brown, President
208-465-7660 Fax: 208-463-0643
Website: www.razzledazzlecollege.com
E-mail: razzledazzle@cableone.net

THE SCHOOL OF HAIRSTYLING
141 E Chubbuck Rd, Chubbuck ID 83202
Linda K. Mottishaw, Director of Education
208-232-9170 Fax: 208-232-9486
E-mail: lindamottishaw@msn.com

ILLINOIS
HAIR PROFESSIONALS CAREER COLLEGE
10321 S Roberts Rd, Palos Hills IL 60465-1929
Linda Grant or Stephanie Marsala, Contacts
708-430-1755 Fax: 708-430-2282
Website: www.hairpros.edu
E-mail: paloshills@hairpros.edu

HAIR PROFESSIONALS CAREER COLLEGE
2245 Gateway Rd, Sycamore IL 60178-3164
Linda Grant, Admissions
815-756-3596 Fax: 815-756-8983
Website: www.hairpros.edu
E-mail: sycamorehairpros@aol.com

HAIR PROFESSIONALS SCHOOL OF COSMETOLOGY
PO Box 40, Oswego IL 60543
Rosalie Clark, Contact
630-554-2266 Fax: 630-554-9574
Website: www.hairpros.edu
E-mail: oswego@hairpros.edu

PIVOT POINT INTERNATIONAL
1560 Sherman Ave Ste 700, Evanston IL 60201-4813
Lars Juhl, Manager of Admissions
847-866-0500 Ext. 7422 Fax: 847-866-7184
Website: www.pivot-point.com
E-mail: admissions@pivot-point.com

INDIANA
LAFAYETTE BEAUTY ACADEMY
833 Ferry St, Lafayette IN 47901-1149
Anita Harbolt-Keim, Financial Aid Officer
765-742-0068 Fax: 765-420-0875
Website: www.lafayettebeautyacademy.com
E-mail: anitaharboltkeim@lafayettebeautyacademy.com

OLYMPIA COLLEGE
707 E 80th Pl Ste 200, Merrillville IN 46410
James Powell, President
219-756-6811 Fax: 219-756-6812
Website: www.cci.edu
E-mail: jpowell@cci.edu

KANSAS
SUPERIOR SCHOOL OF HAIRDRESSING
1215 E Santa Fe St, Olathe KS 66061
Joe Hancock, Owner
913-782-4004 Fax: 913-782-0449
Website: www.superiorbeautyschool.com
E-mail: jhancock1@sbcglobal.net

XENON INTERNATIONAL SCHOOL OF HAIR DESIGN
3804 W Douglas Ave, Wichita KS 67203
Kim McIntosh, Executive Director
316-943-5516 Fax: 316-943-7244
Website: www.xenonintl.com
E-mail: kmcintosh@xenonschool.com

KENTUCKY
TREND SETTER'S ACADEMY OF BEAUTY CULTURE
6539 W Highway 22, Crestwood KY 40014
E-mail: mbinghamtsa@aol.com

TREND SETTER'S ACADEMY OF BEAUTY CULTURE
622B Westport Rd, Elizabethtown KY 42701-2848
270-765-5243
E-mail: mbinghamtsa@aol.com

TREND SETTER'S ACADEMY OF BEAUTY CULTURE
7283 Dixie Hwy, Louisville KY 40258
502-937-6816
E-mail: mbinghamtsa@aol.com

LOUISIANA
CLOYD'S BEAUTY SCHOOL #3
2514 Ferrand St, Monroe LA 71201
Tina Mathieu, Contact
318-322-5314 Fax: 318-322-5465
E-mail: tmath@bayou.com

OMEGA INSTITUTE OF COSMETOLOGY
229 S Hollywood Rd, Houma LA 70360-2716
985-876-9334 Fax: 985-876-3612
Website: www.omegainstitutes.com
E-mail: pricilla@omegainstitutes.com

MARYLAND
BALTIMORE STUDIO OF HAIR DESIGN
318 N Howard St, Baltimore MD 21201
Maxine Sisserman, Administrator
410-539-1935 Fax: 410-539-2840
Website: www.baltimorestudio.net
E-mail: baltimorestudio@netscape.net

MARYLAND BEAUTY ACADEMY
152 Chartley Dr, Reisterstown MD 21136
Jaime Davidov, Director
410-517-0442 Fax: 410-517-2513
Website: www.baltimorestudio.net
E-mail: mdbeautyacademy@netscape.net

MARYLAND BEAUTY ACADEMY OF ESSEX
505 Eastern Blvd, Baltimore MD 21221
Justin Sisserman, Administrator
410-686-4477 Fax: 410-686-0786
Website: www.baltimorestudio.net
E-mail: mdbeautyacademy@netscape.net

MASSACHUSETTS

Ailano School of Aesthetics
553 Forest Ave, Brockton MA 02301
Kera Arnone, Contact
508-587-3883 Fax: 508-588-7227
Website: www.ailanoschool.com
E-mail: ailanoki@conversent.net

AILANO SCHOOL OF COSMETOLOGY
PO Box 4740, Brockton MA 02303-4740
Karen Iolli, Owner/Adm
508-583-5433 Fax: 508-588-7227
Website: www.ailanoschool.com
E-mail: ailanoki@conversent.net

FINE MORTUARY COLLEGE
A Private Two Year College
150 Kerry Pl, Norwood MA 02062-4766
Lyn Prendergast, Ph.D., Executive Vice President
781-762-1211 Fax: 781-762-7177
Website: www.fine-ne.com
E-mail: fine@fine-ne.com

MICHIGAN

BAYSHIRE BEAUTY ACADEMY
917 Saginaw St, Bay City MI 48708-5614
Jim Goodrow, CEO
989-894-2431 Fax: 989-894-6033
Website: www.bayshire.com
E-mail: bayshire@speednetllc.com

FISER'S COLLEGE OF COSMETOLOGY
329 1/2 E Maumee St, Adrian MI 49221-2907
Pam Fiser, Owner
517-264-2199 Fax: 517-263-2754
E-mail: adrianbeauty@tc3net.com

MICHIGAN COLLEGE OF BEAUTY
5620 Dixie Hwy, Waterford MI 48329
Susan Pantello, CEO
Allison Murphy, Director of Admissions
248-623-9494 Fax: 248-623-6505
Website: www.michigancollegeofbeauty.com
E-mail: mcb1@myexcel.com

TAYLORTOWN SCHOOL OF BEAUTY
23129 Ecorse Rd, Taylor MI 48180
Cynthia Stramecky, President
313-291-2177 Fax: 313-292-9754
Website: www.1800cutclass.com
E-mail: cabtylady@aol.com

MISSOURI

CHILLICOTHE BEAUTY ACADEMY
505 Elm St, Chillicothe MO 64601
Yvonne Good, Financial Aid Advisor
660-646-4198 Fax: 660-646-9983
Website: www.chillicothecosmetology.com
E-mail: cbainc@greenhills.net

HOUSE OF HEAVILIN BEAUTY COLLEGE
12020 Blue Ridge Ext, Grandview MO 64030
Amber Reed, Contact
816-767-8000 Fax: 816-767-8604
Website: www.kc-hair.com
E-mail: sheavilin@kc-hair.com

NATIONAL ACADEMY OF BEAUTY ARTS
157 Concord Plz, Saint Louis MO 63128
Kathy, Contact
314-842-3616 Fax: 314-842-9396
Website: www.nationalacademyofbeautyarts.com
E-mail: nationalacademy@sbcglobal.net

MONTANA

ACADEMY OF COSMETOLOGY, INC.
133 W Mendenhall St, Bozeman MT 59715
406-587-1265 Fax: 406-585-7357
Website: www.academycosmetology.com

NEVADA

ACADEMY OF HAIR DESIGN
4445 W Charleston Blvd, Las Vegas NV 89102
Sandy Dunham, Director
702-878-1185 Fax: 702-878-7289
Website: ahdvegas.com
E-mail: sdunham@ahd.lvcoxmail.com

LE CORDON BLEU COLLEGE OF CULINARY ARTS
1451 Center Crossing Rd, Las Vegas NV 89144
Admission Dept.
866-450-2433 or 702-365-7690 Fax: 702-365-7911
Website: www.vegasculinary.com

NEW HAMPSHIRE

CONTINENTAL ACADEMIE OF HAIR DESIGN
PO Box 370, Hudson NH 03051-0370
603-889-1614 Fax: 603-883-9546
Website: www.continentalacademie.net
E-mail: conacad1@aol.com

CONTINENTAL ACADEMIE OF HAIR DESIGN
228 Maple St, Manchester NH 03103
Sylvia Donah, Business Manager
603-622-5851 Fax: 603-883-9546
Website: www.continentalacademie.net
E-mail: conacad2@aol.com

KEENE BEAUTY ACADEMY
800 Park Ave, Keene NH 03431-1513
Heather Hammond, Administrator
603-357-3736 Fax: 603-355-8916
Website: www.keenebeautyacademy.com

PORTSMOUTH BEAUTY SCHOOL OF HAIR DESIGN
140 Congress St, Portsmouth NH 03801
Mr. Fran Nardello, Administrator
603-436-7775 Fax: 603-436-5456
Website: www.portsmouthbeautyschool.com
E-mail: admissions@portsmouthbeautyschool.com

NEW JERSEY

Mercer County Community College
West Windsor Campus
PO Box B, Trenton NJ 08690
Savita Bambhrolia, Director of Admissions
609-586-4800 Fax: 609-587-4666
Website: www.mccc.edu
E-mail: admiss@mccc.edu

NEW MEXICO

ALADDIN BEAUTY COLLEGE #22
108 S Union Ave, Roswell NM 88203
Peggy Richburg, Contact
505-623-6331 Fax: 505-622-2072
E-mail: abcinc2@qwest.net

NEW YORK

AMERICAN ACADEMY MCALLISTER INSTITUTE OF FUNERAL SERVICE
619 W 54th St 6th Floor, New York NY 10019
Meg Dunn, President
212-757-1190 Fax: 212-765-5923
Website: www.funeraleducation.org
E-mail: info@funeraleducation.org

CULINARY ACADEMY OF LONG ISLAND
125 Michael Dr, Syosset NY 11791
Harold Kaplan, Director of Admissions
516-364-4344 Fax: 516-364-1894
Website: www.culinaryacademy.edu
E-mail: admissions@culinaryacademy.edu

Hilbert College
5200 S Park Ave, Hamburg NY 14075-1597
Timothy Lee, Director of Admissions
716-649-7900 Fax: 716-649-0702
Website: www.hilbert.edu
E-mail: tlee@hilbert.edu

SHEAR EGO INTERNATIONAL SCHOOL OF HAIR DESIGN
525 Titus Ave, Rochester NY 14617
Sharon Roemer, Director of Admissions
585-342-0070 Fax: 585-342-0863
Website: www.shearego.com
E-mail: sei@shearego.com

SIMMONS INSTITUTE OF FUNERAL SERVICE
1828 South Ave, Syracuse NY 13207-2005
Maurice C. Wightman, CEO
315-475-5142 Fax: 315-475-3817
Website: www.simmonsinstitute.com
E-mail: mcwightman20@aol.com

NORTH CAROLINA

DUDLEY COSMETOLOGY UNIVERSITY
900 E Mountain St, Kernersville NC 27284
Eunice M. Dudley, President
336-996-2030 Fax: 336-996-9752
Website: www.dudleyq.com
E-mail: emdudley@dudleyq.com

OHIO

AMERICAN INSTITUTE OF ALTERNATIVE MEDICINE
formerly Massage Away School of Therapy
6685 Doubletree Ave, Columbus OH 43229-1113
Nerissa Pancake, Business Development Manager
614-825-6278 Fax: 614-825-6279
Website: www.aiam.edu
E-mail: info@aiam.edu

Collins Career Center
11627 State Route 243, Chesapeake OH 45619-7962
740-867-6641 Fax: 740-867-9626
Website: www.collins-cc.k12.oh.us

YOUNGSTOWN COLLEGE OF MASSOTHERAPY
14 Highland Ave, Struthers OH 44471-2321
Angela Shodd, Student Relations
330-755-1406 Fax: 330-755-1605
Website: www.ycm.edu
E-mail: ycm@ycm.edu

OREGON

BEAU MONDE COLLEGE ACADEMY OF COSMETOLOGY
11131 NE Halsey St, Portland OR 97220
Dianna Peterson, Owner
503-252-7444 Fax: 503-252-7555
Website: www.beaumondecollege.com
E-mail: diannapeterson@cs.com

BEAU MONDE COLLEGE OF HAIR DESIGN
1221 SW 12th Ave, Portland OR 97205
Dianna Peterson, Owner
503-226-7355 Fax: 503-226-6512
Website: www.beaumondecollege.com
E-mail: diannapeterson@cs.com

WESTERN CULINARY INSTITUTE
921 SW Morrison St Suite 400, Portland OR 97205
Joanne Lazo, Director of Marketing
503-223-2245 or 888-848-3202 Fax: 503-223-5554
Website: www.wci.edu
E-mail: info@wci.edu

PENNSYLVANIA

Academy of Medical Arts and Business
2301 Academy Dr, Harrisburg PA 17112-1012
717-545-4747
Website: www.ACADcampus.com
E-mail: info@ACADcampus.com

Career Training Academy
4314 Old William Penn Highway Ste 103
Monroeville PA 15146
Gina Hudac, Admissions Representitive
412-372-3900 Fax: 412-373-4262
Website: www.careerta.edu
E-mail: admissions2@careerta.edu

Career Training Academy
950 5th Ave, New Kensington PA 15068-6308
John Reddy, Director
Tyna Putignano, Director of Admissions
724-337-1000 Fax: 724-335-7140
Website: www.careerta.edu
E-mail: admissions@careerta.edu
See listing under "Career Schools"

Career Training Academy
1500 Northway Mall, Pittsburgh PA 15237
Anna Bartolini, Director North Hills Branch Campus
412-367-4000 Fax: 412-369-7223
Website: www.careerta.edu
E-mail: admissions3@careerta.edu

LEVITTOWN BEAUTY ACADEMY LLC
Vermillion Square
8919 New Falls Rd, Levittown PA 19054
Cecelia Pine, Contact
866-820-0322 or 215-943-0298 Fax: 215-943-0966
Website: www.levittownbeautyacademy.com
E-mail: info@levittownbeautyacademy.com

PITTSBURGH INSTITUTE OF MORTUARY SCIENCE
5808 Baum Blvd, Pittsburgh PA 15206-3706
Karen Rocco, Registrar
412-362-8500 Fax: 412-362-1684
Website: www.pims.edu
E-mail: pims5808@aol.com

SOUTH CAROLINA

CHARLESTON COSMETOLOGY INSTITUTE
8484 Dorchester Rd, Charleston SC 29420-7319
Jerry R. Poer, Owner
843-552-3670 Fax: 843-760-0976
Website: www.charlestoncosmetology.com
E-mail: ccisc@aol.com

SOUTH DAKOTA

Western Dakota Technical Institute
800 Mickelson Dr, Rapid City SD 57703-4018
Janell Oberlander, Manager of Student Services
605-394-4034 or 800-544-8765 Fax: 605-394-1789
Website: www.westerndakotatech.org
E-mail: admissions@wdti.tec.sd.us
See listing under "Career Schools"

TEXAS

CULINARY INSTITUTE
7070 Allensby St, Houston TX 77022-4322
Henry Cittone, Director of Admissions
713-692-0077 Fax: 713-692-7399

DALLAS INSTITUTE OF FUNERAL SERVICE
3909 S Buckner Blvd, Dallas TX 75227-4314
Terry Parrish, Registrar/Admissions
800-235-5444 Fax: 214-388-0316
Website: dallasinstitute.edu
E-mail: difs@dallasinstitute.edu

FRANKLIN BEAUTY SCHOOL #2
4965 Martin Luther King, Houston TX 77021
Ron Jemison, Vice President
713-645-9060 Fax: 713-645-6859
Website: www.thefranklinbeautyschool.com
E-mail: rjem6969@aol.com

MID CITIES BARBER COLLEGE
2345 SW 3rd St Ste 101, Grand Prairie TX 75051
Nachita Cano, Director
972-642-1892 Fax: 972-642-8198
Website: www.midcitiesbarbercollege.com
E-mail: midcitiesbarber@earthlink.net

SOUTH TEXAS BARBER COLLEGE
3917 Ayers St, Corpus Christi TX 78415
Juan A. Garcia, President
361-855-2297 Fax: 361-855-7212
E-mail: southtexasbarber@sbcglobal.net

WASHINGTON

BATES TECHNICAL COLLEGE
1101 S Yakima Ave, Tacoma WA 98405-4895
David Borofsky, President
253-680-7000 Fax: 253-680-7101
Website: www.bates.ctc.edu
E-mail: info@bates.ctc.edu

WISCONSIN

GILL-TECH ACADEMY OF HAIR DESIGN
423 W College Ave, Appleton WI 54911-5830
Ann Everson, Director
920-739-8684 Fax: 920-739-0145
Website: www.gill-tech.com
E-mail: kay@gill-tech.com

STATE COLLEGE OF BEAUTY CULTURE
1930 Grand Ave, Wausau WI 54403-6870
715-845-2888 Fax: 715-848-2121
Website: www.statecollegeofbeauty.com
E-mail: info@statecollegeofbeauty.com

Wisconsin Indianhead Technical College
505 Pine Ridge Dr, Shell Lake WI 54871
Miriam Crandall, Dean of Student Services
800-243-9482 Fax: 715-468-2819
Website: www.witc.edu
E-mail: mcrandal@witc.edu
Campuses in Ashland, New Richmond, Rice Lake,
Superior.

PUERTO RICO
EMMAS BEAUTY ACADEMY
Carr 417 Bo Guanabano, Aguada PR 00602
Carlos Ramos Camara, CEO
787-868-4711 Fax: 787-252-0775
Website: www.emmasbeautyacademy.com
E-mail: emmasbeautyacademy@yahoo.com

EMMAS BEAUTY ACADEMY
9 Calle Munoz Rivera W, Mayaguez PR 00680
Carlos Ramos Camara, CEO
787-833-0980 Fax: 787-833-0613
Website: www.emmasbeautyacademy.com
E-mail: emmasbeautyacademy@yahoo.com

PHARMACY

ALABAMA

Judson College
302 Bibb St, Marion AL 36756
Michael Scotto, Director of Admissions
800-447-9472 Fax: 334-683-5147
Website: www.judson.edu
E-mail: admissions@judson.edu

ARIZONA

University of Arizona
Tucson AZ 85721-0040
Paul Kohn, Director of Admissions
520-621-3237 Fax: 520-621-9799
Website: www.admissions.arizona.edu or
www.arizona.edu

ARKANSAS

Ouachita Baptist University
410 Ouachita St, Arkadelphia AR 71998-0001
David Goodman, Director of Admissions
870-245-5110 Fax: 870-245-5500
Website: www.obu.edu
E-mail: admissions@obu.edu

CALIFORNIA

San Joaquin Valley College
201 New Stine Rd, Bakersfield CA 93309-2659
Jaime Delgado, Enrollment Services Director
661-834-1026 Fax: 559-651-4864
Website: www.sjvc.edu
E-mail: jaime.delgado@sjvc.edu

San Joaquin Valley College
295 E Sierra Ave, Fresno CA 93710-3616
Nora Twarynski, Enrollment Services Director
559-448-8282 Fax: 559-651-4864
Website: www.sjvc.edu
E-mail: nora.twarynski@sjvc.edu

San Joaquin Valley College
1700 McHenry Village Way Suite 6
Modesto CA 95350
Joseph Holt, Director of Admissions
209-527-7582 Fax: 559-651-4864
Website: www.sjvc.edu
E-mail: josephh@sjvc.edu

San Joaquin Valley College
11050 Olson Dr, Rancho Cordova CA 95670
Joseph Holt, Director of Admissions
559-651-2500 Fax: 559-651-4864
Website: www.sjvc.edu
E-mail: joseph.holt@sjvc.edu

San Joaquin Valley College
10641 Church St, Rancho Cucamonga CA 91730
Ramon Abreu, Enrollment Services Director
909-948-7582 Fax: 559-651-4864
Website: www.sjvc.edu
E-mail: ramon.abreu@sjvc.edu

San Joaquin Valley College
8400 W Mineral King Ave, Visalia CA 93291-9283
Susie Topjian, Enrollment Services Director
559-651-2500 Fax: 559-651-4864
Website: www.sjvc.edu
E-mail: susiet@sjvc.edu

COLORADO

University of Colorado at Denver and Health Sciences
Center
Health Sciences Program
4200 E 9th Ave Box C245, Denver CO 80262
Phoebe Lindsey Barton, Ph.D., Director
Website: www.uchsc.edu

FLORIDA

Nova Southeastern University Health Profession
3200 S University Dr, Davie FL 33328-2018
Marla Frohlinger, Director of Admissions
954-262-1101 Fax: 954-262-2282
Website: www.nova.edu
E-mail: marlaf@nsu.nova.edu

SOUTHWEST FLORIDA COLLEGE
1685 Medical Ln, Fort Myers FL 33907-1157
866-SWFC-NOW or 239-939-4766 Fax: 239-936-4040
Website: www.swfc.edu
E-mail: studentinfo@swfc.edu

ILLINOIS

Roosevelt University
430 S Michigan Ave, Chicago IL 60605
Gwen E. Kanelos, Asst. Vice President for Enrollment
Services
877-APPLY-RU Fax: 312-341-4216
Website: www.roosevelt.edu
E-mail: applyru@roosevelt.edu

South Suburban College of Cook County
15800 State St, South Holland IL 60473
Jane Ellen Stocker, Dean of Enrollment Services
708-596-2000 Fax: 708-225-5806
Website: www.southsuburbancollege.edu
E-mail: jstocker@southsuburbancollege.edu

IOWA

Briar Cliff University
PO Box 2100, Sioux City IA 51104-0100
Sharisue Wilcoxon, VP for Enrollment Management
712-279-5200 Fax: 712-279-1632
Website: www.briarcliff.edu
E-mail: admissions@briarcliff.edu

Iowa Lakes Community College
300 S 18th St, Estherville IA 51334-2721
Anne Stansbury, Asst. Director of Admissions
712-362-7945 Fax: 712-362-8363
Website: www.iowalakes.edu
E-mail: info@iowalakes.edu

KANSAS

Newman University
3100 W McCormick St, Wichita KS 67213
Jann Reusser, Admissions Recruitment Coordinator
316-942-4291 ext. 2144 Fax: 316-942-4483
Website: www.newmanu.edu
E-mail: reusserj@newmanu.edu

KENTUCKY

Brown Mackie College - Louisville
300 High Rise Dr, Louisville KY 40213-3263
Kathleen Belanger, Director of Admissions
502-968-7191 Fax: 502-357-9956
Website: www.brownmackie.edu
E-mail: kbelanger@brownmackie.edu

MAINE

Southern Maine Community College
2 Fort Rd, South Portland ME 04106-1698
Dr. James Ortiz, President
Scott MacDonald, Director of Financial Aid
207-741-5500 Fax: 207-741-5671
Website: www.smccme.edu
E-mail: oharmon@maine.rr.com

MASSACHUSETTS

Benjamin Franklin Institute of Technology
41 Berkeley St, Boston MA 02116-6307
Norman Kraft, Dean of Enrollment
617-423-4630 ext. 121 Fax: 617-482-3706
Website: www.bfit.edu
E-mail: admissions@bfit.edu

MINNESOTA

National American University
1550 W Highway 36, Roseville MN 55113
Matthew Mottl, Director of Admissions
651-644-1265 Fax: 651-644-0690
Website: www.national.edu
E-mail: mmottl@national.edu

MISSOURI

ST. LOUIS COLLEGE OF PHARMACY
4588 Parkview Pl, Saint Louis MO 63110-1088
Penny Bryant, Director of Admissions/Registrar
314-367-8700 Fax: 314-446-8310
Website: www.stlcop.edu

Truman State University
100 E Normal, Kirksville MO 63501
Office of Admission
660-785-4000 Fax: 660-785-4181
Website: admissions.truman.edu
E-mail: admissions@truman.edu

NEBRASKA

VATTEROTT COLLEGE
11818 I St, Omaha NE 68137
Todd S. Clark, Director
402-891-9411 Fax: 402-891-9413
Website: www.vatterott-college.edu
E-mail: tclark@vatterott-college.edu

NEW YORK

Roberts Wesleyan College
2301 Westside Dr, Rochester NY 14624-1997
Office of Admissions
585-594-6400 Fax: 585-594-6371
Website: www.roberts.edu
E-mail: admissions@roberts.edu

St. John's University
8000 Utopia Pkwy, Queens NY 11439
Office of Admission
718-990-2000 or 888-9-STJOHNS Fax: 718-990-2096
Website: www.stjohns.edu
E-mail: admissions@stjohns.edu
See listing under "Universities"

NORTH CAROLINA

Louisburg College
501 N Main St, Louisburg NC 27549-2399
800-775-0208 or 919-496-2521 Fax: 919-496-1788
Website: www.louisburg.edu
E-mail: admissions@louisburg.edu

OHIO

Brown Mackie College - Cincinnati
1011 Glendale Milford Rd, Cincinnati OH 45215-1107
Robin Krout, President
513-771-2424 Fax: 513-771-3413
Website: www.brownmackie.edu
E-mail: rkrout@brownmackie.edu

OHIO NORTHERN UNIVERSITY
525 S Main St, Ada OH 45810-1555
Bobby Bryant, Dean
419-772-2275
Website: www.onu.edu
E-mail: admissions-ug@onu.edu
See listing under "Universities"

Ohio State University
College of Pharmacy
150 Parks Hall, 500 W 12th Ave, Columbus OH 43210
614-292-5001 Fax: 614-292-6396
Website: www.pharmacy.ohio-state.edu
E-mail: agresta.6@osu.edu

Total Technical Institute
8720 Brookpark Rd, Cleveland OH 44129-6810
Dave Bryant, Director of Admissions
216-485-0900 Fax: 216-661-6842
Website: www.ttinst.com
E-mail: dbryant@ttinst.com

PENNSYLVANIA

Computer Learning Network
401 E Winding Hill Rd Ste 101
Mechanicsburg PA 17055-4989
Marlene Macauley, Director of Admissions
717-761-1481 Fax: 717-761-0558
Website: www.clntraining.net
E-mail: mmacauley@clntraining.net

Gannon University
109 University Sq, Erie PA 16541-0001
Christopher Tremblay, Director of Admissions
800-GANNON-U Fax: 814-871-5803
Website: www.gannon.edu
E-mail: admissions@gannon.edu

Juniata College
1700 Moore St, Huntingdon PA 16652-2196
Michelle Bartol, Dean of Enrollment
877-JUNIATA Fax: 814-641-3100
Website: www.juniata.edu
E-mail: admissions@juniata.edu

Pennco Tech
3815 Otter St, Bristol PA 19007-3618
Glenn Slater, Director of Admissions
215-785-0111 Fax: 215-785-1945
Website: www.penncotech.com
E-mail: admissions@penncotech.com

SOUTH DAKOTA

Western Dakota Technical Institute
800 Mickelson Dr, Rapid City SD 57703-4018
Janell Oberlander, Manager of Student Services
605-394-4034 or 800-544-8765 Fax: 605-394-1789
Website: www.westerndakotatech.org
E-mail: admissions@wdti.tec.sd.us
See listing under "Career Schools"

TEXAS

Remington College - Fort Worth Campus
300 E Loop 820, Fort Worth TX 76112-1280
Director of Recruitment
817-451-0017 Fax: 817-496-1257
Website: www.remingtoncollege.edu
E-mail: lynn.wey@remingtoncollege.edu

San Antonio College Medical Dental Assistants
1500 S Jackson Rd, Mc Allen TX 78503-9902
Gabe Garcia, Director of Admissions
956-630-1499 Fax: 956-630-2746
Website: www.sacmda.com
E-mail: gagarcia@sac-mda.com

SAN ANTONIO COLLEGE MEDICAL DENTAL ASSISTANTS

7142 San Pedro Ave Ste 100, San Antonio TX 78216
Carig Czubati, Director of Admissions
210-733-0777 Fax: 210-735-2431
Website: www.sacmda.com
E-mail: cczubati@sac-mda.com

University of Houston
122 E Cullen Bldg, Houston TX 77204-2023
Office of Admission
713-743-9595
Website: www.uh.edu
E-mail: admissions@uh.edu

University of St. Thomas
3800 Montrose Blvd, Houston TX 77006-4626
Eduardo Prieto, Director of Admissions
713-522-7911 Fax: 713-525-3558
Website: www.stthom.edu
E-mail: prietoe@stthom.edu

UTAH

Stevens Henager College
PO Box 9428, Ogden UT 84409-0428
Cindy Williams, Director of Admissions
801-394-7791 Fax: 801-621-0866
Website: www.stevenshenager.edu
E-mail: shcogden@yahoo.com

WEST VIRGINIA

West Virginia Wesleyan College
59 College Ave, Buckhannon WV 26201-2699
Robert N. Skinner II, Director of Admission
800-722-9933 Fax: 304-473-8108
Website: www.wvwc.edu
E-mail: admission@wvwc.edu

WYOMING

University of Wyoming
Admissions Office
Dept 3435, Laramie WY 82071-3435
Aaron Appelhans, Contact
800-342-5996 Fax: 307-766-4042
Website: www.uwyo.edu
E-mail: why-wyo@uwyo.edu

PHOTOGRAPHY

ALABAMA

CALHOUN COMMUNITY COLLEGE

PO Box 2216, Decatur AL 35609-2216
M. Wayne Tosh, Registrar
256-306-2500 Fax: 256-306-2941
Website: www.calhoun.edu
E-mail: aprater@calhoun.edu

ARIZONA

University of Arizona
Tucson AZ 85721-0040
Paul Kohn, Director of Admissions
520-621-3237 Fax: 520-621-9799
Website: www.admissions.arizona.edu or www.arizona.edu

CALIFORNIA

California College of the Arts
1111 Eighth St, San Francisco CA 94107
Robynne Royster, Director of Admission
800-447-1-ART or 415-703-9523 Fax: 415-703-9539
Website: www.cca.edu
E-mail: enroll@cca.edu

Orange Coast College
PO Box 5005, Costa Mesa CA 92628-5005
Kristin Clark, Director of Admissions
714-432-5773 Fax: 714-432-5736
Website: www.orangecoastcollege.edu
E-mail: kclark@cccd.edu

SAN FRANCISCO ART INSTITUTE

800 Chestnut St, San Francisco CA 94133
Paula Farmer, Director of Admission
800-345-SFAI Fax: 415-749-4503
Website: www.sfai.edu
E-mail: admissions@sfai.edu
Founded in 1871, SFAI offers one of the most innovative and interdisciplinary environments in higher education. Through its School of Studio Practice, SFAI offers accredited Bachelor of Fine Arts (BFA), Master of Fine Arts (MFA), Summer Master of Fine Arts (SMFA), and Post-Baccalaureate (PB) programs. SFAI's School of Studio Practice centers on the development of the artist's vision and consists of the departments of: Design+Technology, Film, New Genres, Painting, Photography, Printmaking, and Sculpture. At SFAI students become part of an educational environment that sees experimentation as necessary for independent and collaborative invention. Founded in 1945 by Ansel Adams, SFAI's Photography Department was the first fine art photography program established in the United States, and faculty members have included Minor White, Imogen Cunningham, Lisette Model, Edward Weston, and Dorothea Lange. Today, the department functions as a fulcrum, balancing a legacy of import with a spirit of inquiry into the medium's future. Whether using a pinhole or pixels, students are challenged to experiment, take risks, and develop a unique visual voice. SFAI's faculty is comprised of active artists, scholars, writers, and curators. Dean of Academic Affairs is renowned curator and critic Okwui Enwezor. Dean of Graduate Studies is artist and filmmaker Renee Green. Director of Exhibitions and Public Programs is curator Hou Hanru. Visiting artists and scholars play a significant role in education at SFAI, with recent visitors including Matthew Barney, William Kentridge, Raqs Media Collective, and others. All students have 24-hour access to the SFAI campus. SFAI's main campus includes painting, photography, sculpture, and printmaking studios, postproduction facilities, and the first high-definition video research lab in the Bay Area. The Diego Rivera Gallery, an open-air amphitheater, and a 250-seat theater are also available to students for exhibiting and screening work. SFAI's library collection includes more than 26,000 volumes with emphasis on modern and contemporary art, over 200 current periodicals, and an extensive image, video, and audio archive available only to SFAI students. The 62,000 square-foot Graduate Center includes a digital lab, film and sound studios, darkrooms, a woodshop, and a gallery for student work. SFAI has rolling application deadlines, and there are competitive and need-based scholarships available to undergraduates, a fellowship program for graduate students, and community college scholarships for transfer students. Visit the SFAI website for specific application requirements.

COLORADO

Art Institute of Colorado
1200 Lincoln St, Denver CO 80203-2172
David Zorn, President
Brian A. Parker, Director of Admissions
800-275-2420 Fax: 303-860-8520
Website: www.artinstitutes.edu
E-mail: baparker@aii.edu

CONNECTICUT

Albertus Magnus College
700 Prospect St, New Haven CT 06511-1189
Richard Lolatte, Dean of Admission
203-773-8501 or 800-578-9160 Fax: 203-773-5248
Website: www.albertus.edu
E-mail: admissions@albertus.edu

FLORIDA

Art Institute of Fort Lauderdale
1799 SE 17th St, Fort Lauderdale FL 33316-3013
Eileen Northrop, V.P./Director of Admissions
800-275-7603 Fax: 954-728-8637
Website: www.aifl.edu

International Academy of Design & Technology
5104 Eisenhower Blvd, Tampa FL 33634-6313
Richard Costa, V.P. of Admissions and Marketing
813-880-8092 Fax: 813-881-0008
Website: www.academy.edu
E-mail: admissions@academy.edu

GEORGIA

North Georgia Technical College
Clarkesville Campus
PO Box 65, Clarkesville GA 30523-0002
Admissions
706-754-7700 Fax: 706-754-7777
Website: www.northgatech.edu
E-mail: info@northgatech.edu

IDAHO

Brigham Young University - Idaho
120 Kimball Bldg, Rexburg ID 83460
Gordon Westenskow, Director of Admissions
208-496-1020 Fax: 208-496-1220
Website: www.byui.edu
E-mail: admissions@byui.edu

ILLINOIS

Columbia College Chicago
600 S Michigan Ave, Chicago IL 60605-1996
Murphy Monroe, Executive Director of Admissions
312-344-7130 Fax: 312-344-8024
Website: www.colum.edu
E-mail: admissions@colum.edu

HARRINGTON COLLEGE OF DESIGN

200 W Madison St, Chicago IL 60606-3433
Wendi Franczyk, VP of Admissions
877-939-4975 Fax: 312-697-8032
Website: www.harringtoncollege.com
E-mail: wfranczyk@interiordesign.edu
See listing under "Universities"

INDIANA

Ivy Tech Community College - North Central
220 Dean Johnson Blvd, South Bend IN 46601-3415
Pam Decker, Director of Admissions
574-289-7001 Fax: 574-236-7177
Website: www.ivytech.edu
E-mail: pdecker@ivytech.edu

IOWA

Iowa Lakes Community College
300 S 18th St, Estherville IA 51334-2721
Anne Stansbury, Asst. Director of Admissions
712-362-7945 Fax: 712-362-8363
Website: www.iowalakes.edu
E-mail: info@iowalakes.edu

KENTUCKY

Morehead State University
Morehead KY 40351-1689
Dayna Seelig, Enrollment Services
800-585-6781 Fax: 606-783-5038
Website: www.moreheadstate.edu
E-mail: admissions@moreheadstate.edu

MASSACHUSETTS

The Art Institute of Boston at Lesley University
700 Beacon St, Boston MA 02215-2598
Office of Admissions
617-585-6710 Fax: 617-585-6720
Website: www.aiboston.edu
E-mail: admissions@aiboston.edu

HALLMARK INSTITUTE OF PHOTOGRAPHY

PO Box 308, Turners Falls MA 01376-0308
Shelley Nicholson, Director of Enrollment Services
413-863-2478 Fax: 413-863-4118
Website: hallmark.edu
E-mail: info@hallmark.edu

NEW ENGLAND SCHOOL OF PHOTOGRAPHY

537 Commonwealth Ave, Boston MA 02215-2005
Arthur Levi Rainville, Academic Director
800-676-3767 Fax: 617-437-0261
Website: www.nesop.com
E-mail: admissions@nesop.com

School of the Museum of Fine Arts, Boston
230 The Fenway, Boston MA 02115-5534
Office of Admissions
617-369-3626 or 800-643-6078 Fax: 617-369-4264
Website: www.smfa.edu
E-mail: admissions@smfa.edu
See listing under "Universities"

University of Massachusetts Dartmouth
Old Westport Rd, North Dartmouth MA 02747-2300
Steven T. Briggs, Director of Admissions
508-999-8605 Fax: 508-999-8755
Website: explore.umassd.edu
E-mail: sbriggs@umassd.edu

MICHIGAN

Andrews University
Berrien Springs MI 49104-0001
Randall Graves, Director of Recruitment Services
800-253-2874 Fax: 269-471-2670
Website: www.connect.andrews.edu
E-mail: gravesr@andrews.edu

College for Creative Studies
201 E Kirby St, Detroit MI 48202-4048
Julie Hingelberg, Dean of Enrollment Services
313-664-7425
Website: www.ccscad.edu

Delta College
University Center MI 48710-0001
Duff Zube, Director of Admissions
989-686-9093 Fax: 989-667-2202
Website: www.delta.edu
E-mail: admit@delta.edu

Grand Valley State University
1 Campus Dr, Allendale MI 49401-9403
Jodi Chycinski, Director of Admissions
616-331-6611 Fax: 616-331-2000
Website: www.gvsu.edu
E-mail: go2gvsu@gvsu.edu

Kendall College of Art & Design
17 Fountain St NW, Grand Rapids MI 49503-3002
Dr. Oliver H. Evans, President
800-676-2787 or 616-451-2787 Fax: 616-831-9689
Website: www.kcad.edu
E-mail: brittons@ferris.edu

MINNESOTA

Minneapolis College of Art & Design
2501 Stevens Ave, Minneapolis MN 55404-4347
Admissions Office
800-874-6223 or 612-874-3760 Fax: 612-874-3701
Website: www.mcad.edu
E-mail: admissions@mcad.edu

Pillsbury Baptist Bible College
315 S Grove Ave, Owatonna MN 55060-3097
Stephen R. Seidler, Director of Admissions
507-451-2710 Fax: 507-451-0156
Website: www.pillsbury.edu
E-mail: steveseidler@pillsbury.edu

Ridgewater College-Willmar Campus
PO Box 1097, Willmar MN 56201-1097
Sally Kerfeld, Director of Admissions
800-722-1151 Fax: 320-231-7677
Website: www.ridgewater.edu
E-mail: skerfeld@ridgewater.edu

MISSOURI

Columbia College
1001 Rogers St, Columbia MO 65216-0001
Regina Morin, Director of Admissions
573-875-7352 Fax: 573-875-7506
Website: www.ccis.edu
E-mail: admissions@ccis.edu

Webster University
470 E Lockwood Ave, Saint Louis MO 63119-3194
Debra Carpenter, Dean, School of Communications
314-968-6924 Fax: 314-963-6106
Website: www.webster.edu
E-mail: carpenda@webster.edu
See listing under "Universities"

NEW JERSEY

New Jersey City University
2039 John F Kennedy Blvd
Jersey City NJ 07305-1588
Carmen Panlilio, Asst. V.P. for Admissions and
Financial Aid
201-200-3234 Fax: 201-200-2044
Website: www.njcu.edu
E-mail: admissions@njcu.edu

NEW MEXICO

Institute of American Indian Arts
83 A Van Nu Po, Santa Fe NM 87508-1300
Myra Garro, Manager of Enrollment & Admissions
505-424-2328 Fax: 505-424-4500
Website: www.iaia.edu
E-mail: recruitment@iaia.edu

NEW YORK

College of Saint Rose
432 Western Ave, Albany NY 12203-1419
Maryelizabeth Amico, Asst V.P. for Undergraduate
Admissions
518-454-5150 Fax: 518-454-2013
Website: www.strose.edu
E-mail: admit@strose.edu

Long Island University-C. W. Post Campus
720 Northern Blvd, Brookville NY 11548-1300
Joanne Graziano, Executive Director of Admissions
516-299-2900 Fax: 516-299-2137
Website: www.liu.edu/cwpost
E-mail: enroll@cwpost.liu.edu

Pratt Institute
200 Willoughby Ave, Brooklyn NY 11205-3899
Heidi Metcalf, Director of Admissions
718-636-3600 Fax: 718-636-3670
Website: www.pratt.edu
E-mail: hmetcalf@pratt.edu

PURCHASE COLLEGE STATE UNIVERSITY OF NEW YORK (SUNY)

735 Anderson Hill Rd, Purchase NY 10577-1400
Betsy Immergut, Director of Admissions
914-251-6300 Fax: 914-251-6314
Website: www.purchase.edu
See listing under "Universities"

NORTH CAROLINA

James Sprunt Community College
PO Box 398, Kenansville NC 28349-0398
Rita Brown, Registrar
910-296-2500 Fax: 910-296-1636
Website: www.sprunt.com

OHIO

Columbus College of Art & Design
107 N 9th St, Columbus OH 43215-1700
877-997-CCAD or 614-222-3261 Fax: 614-232-8344
Website: www.ccad.edu
E-mail: admissions@ccad.edu

Owens Community College
PO Box 10000, Toledo OH 43699-1947
William J. Ivoska, Ph.D, Vice President of Student
Services
567-661-7000 Fax: 567-661-7607
Website: www.owens.edu
E-mail: admissions@owens.edu

University of Dayton
300 College Park, Dayton OH 45469-1300
Robert F. Durkle, Director of Admissions
800-837-7433 Fax: 937-229-4729
Website: admission.udayton.edu
E-mail: admission@udayton.edu

OREGON

Marylhurst University
17600 Pacific Hwy (Hwy 43)
Marylhurst OR 97036-0261
Director of Admissions
800-634-9982 ext. 6268 Fax: 503-635-6585
Website: www.marylhurst.edu
E-mail: studentinfo@marylhurst.edu

PENNSYLVANIA

Antonelli Institute - Art & Photography
300 Montgomery Ave, Erdenheim PA 19038-8242
Dr. Thomas Treacy, President
215-836-2222 or 800-722-7871 Fax: 215-836-2794
Website: www.antonelli.edu
E-mail: admissions@antonelli.edu

Arcadia University
450 S Easton Rd, Glenside PA 19038-3295
Dennis Nostrand, VP for Enrollment Management
877-ARCADIA (877-272-2342) Fax: 215-881-8767
Website: www.arcadia.edu
E-mail: admiss@arcadia.edu
See listing under "Universities"

Art Institute of Philadelphia
1622 Chestnut St, Philadelphia PA 19103-5119
Larry McHugh, Director of Admissions
800-275-2474 Fax: 215-405-6399
Website: www.aiph.aii.edu
E-mail: aiphinfo@aii.edu

ART INSTITUTE OF PITTSBURGH

420 Boulevard Of The Allies, Pittsburgh PA 15219
Newton I. Myvett, VP/Director of Admissions
800-275-2470 Fax: 412-263-6667
Website: www.aip.aii.edu
E-mail: pahughes@aii.edu
See listing under "Universities"

University of the Arts
320 S Broad St, Philadelphia PA 19102-4994
Susan Gandy, Director of Admissions
800-616-2787 Fax: 215-717-6045
Website: www.uarts.edu
E-mail: admissions@uarts.edu

TEXAS

University of Houston
122 E Cullen Bldg, Houston TX 77204-2023
Office of Admission
713-743-9595
Website: www.uh.edu
E-mail: admissions@uh.edu

VERMONT

Bennington College
One College Drive, Bennington VT 05201
Ken Himmelman, Dean of Admissions & Financial Aid
800-833-6845 Fax: 802-440-4320
Website: www.bennington.edu
E-mail: admissions@bennington.edu

PHYSICAL SCIENCE

ALABAMA

Faulkner University
5345 Atlanta Hwy, Montgomery AL 36109-3398
Keith Mock, Director of Admissions
800-879-9816 ext. 7200 or 334-386-7200
Fax: 334-386-7137
Website: www.faulkner.edu
E-mail: admissions@faulkner.edu

University of Alabama in Huntsville
PO Box 1247, Huntsville AL 35899-0001
Ann Lee, Assoc. Director for Recruiting Program and
Events
1-800-UAH-CALL Fax: 256-824-6073
Website: www.uah.edu
E-mail: leev@uah.edu

ALASKA

University of Alaska Anchorage
PO Box 141629, Anchorage AK 99514-1629
Cecile Mitchell, Director of Enrollment Services
907-786-1480 Fax: 907-786-4888
Website: www.uaa.alaska.edu/
E-mail: enroll@uaa.alaska.edu

ARIZONA

University of Arizona
Tucson AZ 85721-0040
Paul Kohn, Director of Admissions
520-621-3237 Fax: 520-621-9799
Website: www.admissions.arizona.edu or
www.arizona.edu

ARKANSAS

Ouachita Baptist University
410 Ouachita St, Arkadelphia AR 71998-0001
David Goodman, Director of Admissions
870-245-5110 Fax: 870-245-5500
Website: www.obu.edu
E-mail: admissions@obu.edu

CALIFORNIA

Chapman University
One University Drive, Orange CA 92866-1099
Michael Drummy, Assistant Vice President for
Enrollment
Services and Chief Admission Officer
714-997-6411 or 888-CUAPPLY Fax: 714-997-6713
Website: www.chapman.edu
E-mail: admit@chapman.edu

Concordia University
1530 Concordia, Irvine CA 92612-3203
Lori McDonald, Executive Director of Enrollment
Services
800-229-1200 or 949-854-8002 Fax: 949-854-6894
Website: www.cui.edu
E-mail: admission@cui.edu

Harvey Mudd College
Claremont CA 91711-3104
Peter Osgood, Contact
909-621-8011 Fax: 909-607-7046
Website: www.hmc.edu
E-mail: admission@hmc.edu

DELAWARE

Wesley College
120 N State St, Dover DE 19901-3876
302-736-2300 Fax: 302-736-2301
Website: www.wesley.edu

FLORIDA

Florida State University
600 W College Ave, Tallahassee FL 32306-1096
Janice V. Finney, Director of Admissions
850-644-2525 Fax: 850-644-0197
Website: admissions.fsu.edu
E-mail: admissions@admin.fsu.edu

IDAHO

University of Idaho
Moscow ID 83844-4253
Lloyd Scott, Director of New Student Services
208-885-6163 Fax: 208-885-4477
Website: www.uidaho.edu
E-mail: nss@uidaho.edu

ILLINOIS

Benedictine University
5700 College Rd, Lisle IL 60532-0900
630-829-6300 or 888-829-6363 Fax: 630-829-6301
Website: www.ben.edu
E-mail: admissions@ben.edu
See listing under "Universities"

CONCORDIA UNIVERSITY
7400 Augusta St, River Forest IL 60305-1402
708-209-3100 Fax: 708-209-3473
Website: www.curf.edu
E-mail: crfadmis.edu

Roosevelt University
430 S Michigan Ave, Chicago IL 60605
Gwen E. Kanelos, Asst. Vice President for Enrollment
Services
877-APPLY-RU Fax: 312-341-4216
Website: www.roosevelt.edu
E-mail: applyru@roosevelt.edu

INDIANA

University of Evansville
1800 Lincoln Ave, Evansville IN 47722-0001
Thomas E. Bear, V.P. of Enrollment Services
800-423-8633 Fax: 812-488-4076
Website: www.evansville.edu
E-mail: admission@evansville.edu

IOWA

Clarke College
1550 Clarke Dr, Dubuque IA 52001-3198
Andy Schroeder, Director of Admissions
800-383-2345 Fax: 563-584-8666
Website: www.clarke.edu
E-mail: andy.schroeder@clarke.edu

Graceland University
1 University Place, Lamoni IA 50140
Brian Shantz, Vice President for Enrollment and Dean
of Admissions
641-784-5196 Fax: 641-784-5480
Website: www.admissions.graceland.edu
E-mail: admissions@graceland.edu

Iowa Lakes Community College
300 S 18th St, Estherville IA 51334-2721
Anne Stansbury, Asst. Director of Admissions
712-362-7945 Fax: 712-362-8363
Website: www.iowalakes.edu
E-mail: info@iowalakes.edu

KANSAS

Independence Community College
PO Box 708, Independence KS 67301-0708
Dr. Terry Hetrick, President
800-842-6063 Fax: 620-331-5344
Website: www.indycc.edu
E-mail: admissions@indycc.edu

Newman University
3100 W McCormick St, Wichita KS 67213
Jann Reusser, Admissions Recruitment Coordinator
316-942-4291 ext. 2144 Fax: 316-942-4483
Website: www.newmanu.edu
E-mail: reusserj@newmanu.edu

KENTUCKY

Bluegrass Community and Technical College
Oswald Building
470 Cooper Drive, Lexington KY 40506-0235
Shelbie Hugle, Director of Admissions
859-246-6200 Fax: 859-246-4664
Website: www.bluegrass.kctcs.edu
E-mail: bctc_info@kctcs.edu

Morehead State University
Morehead KY 40351-1689
Dayna Seelig, Enrollment Services
800-585-6781 Fax: 606-783-5038
Website: www.moreheadstate.edu
E-mail: admissions@moreheadstate.edu

MASSACHUSETTS

Boston University
121 Bay State Rd, Boston MA 02215
Kelly Walter, Executive Director of Admissions
617-353-2300 Fax: 617-353-9695
Website: web.bu.edu
E-mail: admissions@bu.edu

Massachusetts Institute of Technology
77 Massachusetts Ave, Cambridge MA 02139-4307
Marilee Jones, Dean of Admission
617-253-1000 Fax: 617-253-4016
Website: my.mit.edu
E-mail: admissions@mit.edu

Westfield State College
PO Box 1630, Westfield MA 01086
Michelle Mattie, Associate Dean, Admission and
Enrollment Services
413-572-5300
Website: www.wsc.ma.edu
E-mail: admission@wsc.ma.edu

Worcester Polytechnic Institute
100 Institute Rd, Worcester MA 01609-2280
Edward J. Connor, Director of Admissions
508-831-5286 Fax: 508-831-5875
Website: admissions.wpi.edu
E-mail: admissions@wpi.edu

MICHIGAN

Alma College
614 W Superior St, Alma MI 48801-1599
Anne Monroe, Director of Admissions
800-321-ALMA Fax: 989-463-7057
Website: www.alma.edu
E-mail: admissions@alma.edu

HILLSDALE COLLEGE
33 E College St, Hillsdale MI 49242-1298
Dr. James Peters, Director
517-607-2388 Fax: 517-607-2657
Website: www.hillsdale.edu
E-mail: jim.peters@hillsdale.edu

University of Michigan-Dearborn
4901 Evergreen Rd, Dearborn MI 48128-1491
The Office of Admissions & Orientation
313-593-5100 Fax: 313-436-9167
Website: www.umd.umich.edu
E-mail: admissions@umd.umich.edu

MISSOURI

Truman State University
100 E Normal, Kirksville MO 63501
Office of Admission
660-785-4000 Fax: 660-785-4181
Website: admissions.truman.edu
E-mail: admissions@truman.edu

University of Missouri
1 University Blvd, Saint Louis MO 63121-4499
Dr. Mark Burkholder, Dean-College of Arts & Sciences
314-516-5501 Fax: 314-516-5415
Website: www.umsl.edu
E-mail: admissions@umsl.edu

NEBRASKA

Peru State College
PO Box 10, Peru NE 68421-0010
Office of Admissions
800-742-4412 Fax: 402-872-2296
Website: www.peru.edu
E-mail: admissions@oakmail.peru.edu

NEW YORK

College of Saint Rose
432 Western Ave, Albany NY 12203-1419
Maryelizabeth Amico, Asst V.P. for Undergraduate
Admissions
518-454-5150 Fax: 518-454-2013
Website: www.strose.edu
E-mail: admit@strose.edu

Long Island University-C. W. Post Campus
720 Northern Blvd, Brookville NY 11548-1300
Joanne Graziano, Executive Director of Admissions
516-299-2900 Fax: 516-299-2137
Website: www.liu.edu/cwpost
E-mail: enroll@cwpost.liu.edu

Molloy College
1000 Hempstead Ave
Rockville Centre NY 11570-1100
Marguerite Lane, Director of Admissions
516-678-5000 ext. 6291 Fax: 516-256-2247
Website: www.molloy.edu
E-mail: admissions@molloy.edu
See listing under "Universities"

St. Joseph's College
245 Clinton Ave, Brooklyn NY 11205-3688
Theresa LaRocca Meyer, V.P. for Enrollment
Management
718-636-6800 Fax: 718-636-8303
Website: www.sjcny.edu
E-mail: tlaroccameyer@sjcny.edu

SUNY College of Technology
Alfred NY 14802
Deborah J. Goodrich, Director of Admissions
800-4AL-FRED Fax: 607-587-4299
Website: www.alfredstate.edu
E-mail: admissions@alfredstate.edu

SUNY Orange County Community College
115 South St, Middletown NY 10940-6437
Margot St. Lawrence, Director of Admissions
845-341-4030 Fax: 845-342-8662
Website: www.sunyorange.edu
E-mail: apply@sunyorange.edu
See listing under "Community and Junior Colleges"

NORTH CAROLINA

Meredith College
3800 Hillsborough St, Raleigh NC 27607-5298
Heidi L. Fletcher, Director of Admissions
919-760-8581 Fax: 919-760-2348
Website: www.meredith.edu
E-mail: admissions@meredith.edu
See listing under "Women's Colleges"

Mt. Olive College
634 Henderson St, Mount Olive NC 28365
Tim Woodard, Director of Admissions
919-658-2502 Fax: 919-658-9816
Website: www.moc.edu
E-mail: admissions@moc.edu
See listing under "Universities"

NORTH DAKOTA

Dickinson State University
Dickinson ND 58601-4896
Steve Glasser, Director of Student Recruitment
800-279-4295 Fax: 701-483-2524
Website: www.dickinsonstate.edu
E-mail: dsu.hawks@dickinsonstate.edu

OHIO

Mount Vernon Nazarene University
800 Martinsburg Rd, Mount Vernon OH 43050-9509
Timothy Eades, Director of Admissions
866-462-6868 Fax: 740-393-0511
Website: www.gotomvnu.com
E-mail: admissions@mvnu.edu
See listing under "Universities"

The Ohio State University
College of Mathematical and Physical Sciences
Stillman Hall, 1947 College Rd, Columbus OH 43210
614-292-2874 Fax: 614-292-3639
Website: www.mps.ohio-state.edu
E-mail: handon.1@osu.edu

OKLAHOMA

Oklahoma State University
Stillwater OK 74078
John Mintmire, Department Head
405-744-5796
Website: www.okstate.edu
E-mail: john.mintmire@okstate.edu

Oral Roberts University
7777 S Lewis Ave, Tulsa OK 74171-0001
Chris Belcher, Director of Undergraduate Admissions
800-678-8876 Fax: 918-495-6222
Website: www.oru.edu
E-mail: admissions@oru.edu

OREGON

Cascade College
9101 E Burnside St, Portland OR 97216-1599
800-550-7678 Fax: 503-257-1222
Website: www.cascade.edu
E-mail: admissions@cascade.edu

PENNSYLVANIA

Arcadia University
450 S Easton Rd, Glenside PA 19038-3295
Dennis Nostrand, VP for Enrollment Management
877-ARCADIA (877-272-2342) Fax: 215-881-8767
Website: www.arcadia.edu
E-mail: admiss@arcadia.edu
See listing under "Universities"

Juniata College
1700 Moore St, Huntingdon PA 16652-2196
Michelle Bartol, Dean of Enrollment
877-JUNIATA Fax: 814-641-3100
Website: www.juniata.edu
E-mail: admissions@juniata.edu

Washington & Jefferson College
60 S Lincoln St, Washington PA 15301-4801
Alton E. Newell, Vice President for Enrollment
724-223-6025 Fax: 724-223-6534
Website: www.washjeff.edu
E-mail: admission@washjeff.edu

TENNESSEE

Tennessee State University
3500 John A Merritt Blvd, Nashville TN 37209-1561
John Cade, Dean of Admissions & Records
615-963-5052 Fax: 615-963-2930
Website: www.tnstate.edu
E-mail: jcade@tnstate.edu

TEXAS

Angelo State University
ASU Station 11014, San Angelo TX 76909
Bonnie Stennett, Coordinator of Recruiting
800-946-8627 Fax: 325-942-2078
Website: www.angelo.edu
E-mail: admissions@angelo.edu

Texas Woman's University
PO Box 425589, Denton TX 76204-5589
Erma Nieto, Director of Admissions
866-809-6130 Fax: 940-898-3081
Website: www.twu.edu
E-mail: admissions@twu.edu

University of Houston
122 E Cullen Bldg, Houston TX 77204-2023
Office of Admission
713-743-9595
Website: www.uh.edu
E-mail: admissions@uh.edu

University of Texas at Arlington
Box 19111, Arlington TX 76019-0111
Hans Gatterdam, Director of Admission
817-272-6287 Fax: 817-272-3435
Website: www.uta.edu
E-mail: admissions@uta.edu

VERMONT

Bennington College
One College Drive, Bennington VT 05201
Ken Himmelman, Dean of Admissions & Financial Aid
800-833-6845 Fax: 802-440-4320
Website: www.bennington.edu
E-mail: admissions@bennington.edu

VIRGINIA

Radford University
PO Box 6903, Radford VA 24142
David W. Kraus, Director of Admissions
800-890-4265 Fax: 540-831-5038
Website: www.radford.edu
E-mail: ruadmiss@radford.edu

WASHINGTON

Gonzaga University
502 E Boone Ave, Spokane WA 99258-0102
Julie McCulloh, Dean of Admission
800-322-2584 or 509-323-6572 Fax: 509-323-5780
Website: www.gonzaga.edu
E-mail: mcculloh@gu.gonzaga.edu

WEST VIRGINIA

West Virginia Wesleyan College
  59 College Ave, Buckhannon WV 26201-2699
  Robert N. Skinner II, Director of Admission
  800-722-9933 Fax: 304-473-8108
  Website: www.wvwc.edu
  E-mail: admission@wvwc.edu

WYOMING

University of Wyoming
  Admissions Office
  Dept 3435, Laramie WY 82071-3435
  Aaron Appelhans, Contact
  800-342-5996 Fax: 307-766-4042
  Website: www.uwyo.edu
  E-mail: why-wyo@uwyo.edu

GUAM

University of Guam
  UOG Station, Mangilao GU 96923
  Deborah Leon Guerrero, Registrar
  671-735-2201 or 671-735-2208 Fax: 671-735-2203
  Website: www.uog.edu
  E-mail: admitme@uog9.uog.edu

PODIATRIC MEDICINE

IOWA

Des Moines University - Osteopathic Medical Center
  3200 Grand Ave, Des Moines IA 50312-4198
  Robert M. Yoho, D.P.M., M.S., Dean, College of
  Podiatric Medicine & Surgery, Interim V.P. for
  Academic Administration
  515-271-1464 Fax: 515-271-7017
  Website: www.dmu.edu
  E-mail: robert.yoho@dmu.edu

KANSAS

Newman University
  3100 W McCormick St, Wichita KS 67213
  Jann Reusser, Admissions Recruitment Coordinator
  316-942-4291 ext. 2144 Fax: 316-942-4483
  Website: www.newmanu.edu
  E-mail: reusserj@newmanu.edu

NEW JERSEY

New Jersey City University
  2039 John F Kennedy Blvd
  Jersey City NJ 07305-1588
  Carmen Panlilio, Asst. V.P. for Admissions and
  Financial Aid
  201-200-3234 Fax: 201-200-2044
  Website: www.njcu.edu
  E-mail: admissions@njcu.edu

NEW YORK
NEW YORK COLLEGE OF PODIATRIC MEDICINE

  1800 Park Ave, New York NY 10035-1940
  Carlene Colston, Director of Admissions and Enrollment
  Management
  800-526-6966 Fax: 212-722-4918
  Website: www.nycpm.edu
  E-mail: ccolston@nycpm.edu

OHIO
OHIO COLLEGE OF PODIATRIC MEDICINE

  10515 Carnegie Ave, Cleveland OH 44106
  Lois Lott, Dean of Student Affairs
  216-231-3300 Fax: 216-231-0453
  Website: www.ocpm.edu
  E-mail: llott@ocpm.edu

PENNSYLVANIA

Juniata College
  1700 Moore St, Huntingdon PA 16652-2196
  Michelle Bartol, Dean of Enrollment
  877-JUNIATA Fax: 814-641-3100
  Website: www.juniata.edu
  E-mail: admissions@juniata.edu

PRECISION PRODUCTION TRADES

ALABAMA

· Bishop State Community College - Four Campuses
  351 N Broad St, Mobile AL 36603-5898
  Dr. Terry Hazzard, Dean of Students
  251-690-6801 Fax: 251-690-6446
  Website: www.bishop.edu
  E-mail: thazzard@bishop.edu

· **CALHOUN COMMUNITY COLLEGE**
  PO Box 2216, Decatur AL 35609-2216
  M. Wayne Tosh, Registrar
  256-306-2500 Fax: 256-306-2941
  Website: www.calhoun.edu
  E-mail: rls@calhoun.edu
  See listing under "Community and Junior Colleges"

· Trenholm State Technical College
  Patterson Campus
  3920 Troy Hwy, Montgomery AL 36116
  Dr. Anthony Molina, President
  334-420-4200 Fax: 334-420-4206
  Website: www.trenholmtech.cc.al.us
  E-mail: amolina@trenholmtech.cc.al.us

ARIZONA

· Pima Community College
  4905 E Broadway Blvd, Tucson AZ 85709-1010
  Wendy Kilgore, Ph.D., Director of Admissions
  520-206-4500 Fax: 520-206-4790
  Website: www.pima.edu
  E-mail: infocenter@pima.edu

· Universal Technical Institute
  10695 W Pierce St, Avondale AZ 85323-7946
  John Palumbo, Director of Admissions
  623-245-4600 Fax: 623-245-4603
  Website: www.uticorp.com

ARKANSAS

⋮ Northwest Technical Institute
  709 S Old Missouri Rd, Springdale AR 72764
  Charles L. Kelley, President
  479-751-8824 Fax: 479-751-7780
  Website: www.nti.tec.ar.us
  E-mail: info@nit.tec.ar.us

· **OUACHITA TECHNICAL COLLEGE**
  One College Cir, Malvern AR 72104
  Jerry Little, Division Chair Applied Science
  501-337-5000 ext. 1165 Fax: 501-337-9382
  Website: www.otcweb.edu
  E-mail: jlittle@otcweb.edu

· Phillips Community College of the University of Arkansas
  PO Box 785, Helena AR 72342-0785
  Dr. Steven Murray, Chancellor
  Lynn Boone, Vice Chancellor for Student Services /
  Registrar
  870-338-6474 Fax: 870-338-7542
  Website: www.pccua.edu
  E-mail: lboone@pccua.edu

CALIFORNIA

· Chabot College
  25555 Hesperian Blvd, Hayward CA 94545-2400
  Judy Young, Director of Admissions
  510-723-6600 Fax: 510-723-7510
  Website: www.chabotcollege.edu
  E-mail: ccarcom@clpccd.cc.ca.us

· **FRESNO CITY COLLEGE**
  1101 E University Ave, Fresno CA 93741-0002
  Dayann Dietrich, Contact
  559-442-8241 Fax: 559-237-4232
  Website: www.fresnocitycollege.com
  E-mail: fcc.admissions@scccd.com

· Orange Coast College
  PO Box 5005, Costa Mesa CA 92628-5005
  Kristin Clark, Director of Admissions
  714-432-5773 Fax: 714-432-5736
  Website: www.orangecoastcollege.edu
  E-mail: kclark@cccd.edu

COLORADO

· IntelliTec College
  2315 E Pikes Peak Ave
  Colorado Springs CO 80909-6096
  Michael Castellano, Contact
  719-632-7626 Fax: 719-632-7451
  Website: www.intelliteccollege.edu
  E-mail: admcs@intelliteccollege.edu

· IntelliTec College
  772 Horizon Dr, Grand Junction CO 81506-3907
  Rich Counts, Contact
  970-245-8101 Fax: 970-243-8074
  Website: www.intelliteccollege.edu
  E-mail: admgj@intelliteccollege.edu

⋮ San Juan Basin Technical College
  PO Box 970, Cortez CO 81321-0970
  Shannon South, Director of Student Services
  970-565-8457 Fax: 970-565-8450
  Website: www.sjbtc.edu
  E-mail: ssouth@sjbtc.edu

CONNECTICUT

⋮ Porter and Chester Institute
  670 Lordship Blvd, Stratford CT 06615-7158
  Mark Breslin, Director of Admissions
  203-375-4463 Fax: 203-375-5285
  Website: www.porterchester.com

FLORIDA

· High-Tech Institute
  3710 Maguire Blvd, Orlando FL 32803-3013
  407-893-7400 Fax: 407-895-1804
  Website: www.hightechinstitute.edu

· **TULSA WELDING SCHOOL**
  3500 Southside Blvd, Jacksonville FL 32216-4634
  Roger Hess, President
  877-935-3529 Fax: 904-646-9956
  Website: www.weldingschool.com
  E-mail: tws@ionet.net

GEORGIA

· DeKalb Technical College
  495 N Indian Creek Dr, Clarkston GA 30021-2397
  Terry Richardson, Director of Admissions
  404-297-9522 Fax: 404-294-6496
  Website: www.dekalbtech.edu
  E-mail: richardt@dekalbtech.edu

· North Georgia Technical College
  Clarkesville Campus
  PO Box 65, Clarkesville GA 30523-0002
  Admissions
  706-754-7700 Fax: 706-754-7777
  Website: www.northgatech.edu
  E-mail: info@northgatech.edu

· North Metro Technical College
  5198 Ross Rd SE, Acworth GA 30102-3129
  Missy Cusack, Director of Admissions
  770-975-4000 Fax: 770-975-4142
  Website: www.northmetrotech.edu
  E-mail: info@northmetrotech.edu

ILLINOIS

· Kaskaskia College
  27210 College Rd, Centralia IL 62801-7878
  Tyra Taylor, Dean of Enrollment Management and
  Retention Services
  618-545-3000 Fax: 618-532-1990
  Website: www.kaskaskia.edu
  E-mail: ttaylor@kaskaskia.edu

Triton College
2000 5th Ave, River Grove IL 60171-1995
Mary-Rita Moore. Dean of Enrollment Services
708-456-0300 ext. 3130 Fax: 708-583-3147
Website: www.triton.edu
E-mail: triton@triton.edu
See listing under "Community and Junior Colleges"

INDIANA

Ivy Tech Community College - North Central
220 Dean Johnson Blvd, South Bend IN 46601-3415
Pam Decker, Director of Admissions
574-289-7001 Fax: 574-236-7177
Website: www.ivytech.edu
E-mail: pdecker@ivytech.edu

IOWA

Northwest Iowa Community College
603 W Park St, Sheldon IA 51201-1046
Lisa Story, Director of Enrollment Management
712-324-5061 Fax: 712-324-4136
Website: www.nwicc.edu
E-mail: lstory@nwicc.edu

KANSAS

Flint Hills Technical College
3301 W 18th Ave, Emporia KS 66801-5957
Lisa Kirmer, Dean of Student Services
620-343-4600 Fax: 620-343-4610
Website: www.fhtc.net
E-mail: lkirmer@fhtc.net

Independence Community College
PO Box 708, Independence KS 67301-0708
Dr. Terry Hetrick, President
800-842-6063 Fax: 620-331-5344
Website: www.indycc.edu
E-mail: admissions@indycc.edu

LOUISIANA

Gretna Career College Training Institute
1415 Whitney Ave, Gretna LA 70053-2436
Ava Himes, Director of Admissions
504-366-5409 Fax: 504-366-1294

LOUISIANA TECHNICAL COLLEGE
Tallulah Campus
132 Old Highway 65, Tallulah LA 71284
Patrick T. Murphy, Dean
318-574-4820 Fax: 318-574-1868
Website: www.ltctallulah.com
E-mail: sccox@theltc.net

MAINE

Landing School of Boatbuilding & Design
PO Box 1490, Kennebunkport ME 04046-1490
Dennis Collins, Director of Admissions
207-985-7976 Fax: 207-985-7942
Website: www.landingschool.edu
E-mail: denniscollins@landingschool.edu

Northern Maine Community College
33 Edgemont Dr, Presque Isle ME 04769-2016
Bill Casavant, Director of Admissions
207-768-2700 Fax: 207-768-2831
Website: www.nmcc.edu
E-mail: admissions@nmcc.edu

Southern Maine Community College
2 Fort Rd, South Portland ME 04106-1698
Dr. James Ortiz, President
Scott MacDonald, Director of Financial Aid
207-741-5500 Fax: 207-741-5671
Website: www.smccme.edu
E-mail: oharmon@maine.rr.com

MICHIGAN

Delta College
University Center MI 48710-0001
Duff Zube, Director of Admissions
989-686-9093 Fax: 989-667-2202
Website: www.delta.edu
E-mail: admit@delta.edu

ITT TECHNICAL INSTITUTE
1522 E Big Beaver Rd, Troy MI 48083-2008
Patricia Hyman, Director of Recruitment
248-524-1800 Fax: 248-528-2218
Website: www.itt-tech.edu

MACOMB COMMUNITY COLLEGE
14500 E 12 Mile Rd, Warren MI 48088-3896
Information Center
586-445-7999
Website: www.macomb.edu
E-mail: answer@macomb.edu

MINNESOTA

Dunwoody College of Technology
818 Dunwoody Blvd, Minneapolis MN 55403-1192
John Slama, Vice President Enrollment Management
800-292-4625 or 612-374-5800 Fax: 612-374-4128
Website: www.dunwoody.edu
E-mail: jslama@dunwoody.edu
See listing under "Career Schools"

Minneapolis Community and Technical College
1501 Hennepin Ave, Minneapolis MN 55403-1779
Dena Russell, Director of Admissions
612-659-6282 Fax: 612-659-6210
Website: www.minneapolis.edu
E-mail: admissions.office@minneapolis.edu

Minnesota State College - Southeast Technical
308 Pioneer Rd, Red Wing MN 55066-3964
Al Ducett, Director of Admissions
800-657-4849 Fax: 507-453-2715
Website: www.southeastmn.edu
E-mail: aducett@southeastmn.edu

Northland Community & Technical College
Highway 1 E, Thief River Falls MN 56701
Eugene Klinke, Director of Enrollment Management
800-959-6282 or 218-681-0862 Fax: 218-681-0774
Website: www.northlandcollege.edu
E-mail: eugene.klinke@northlandcollege.edu

Ridgewater College-Hutchinson Campus
2 Century Ave SE, Hutchinson MN 55350-3100
Dawn Bjork, Counselor
800-222-4424 Fax: 320-231-7767
Website: www.ridgewater.edu
E-mail: dawn.bjork@ridgewater.edu

St. Cloud Technical College
1540 Northway Dr, Saint Cloud MN 56303-1240
Jodi Elness, Director of Enrollment Management
800-222-1009 Fax: 320-308-5981
Website: www.sctc.edu
E-mail: jelness@sctc.edu

MISSOURI

East Central College
1964 Prairie Dell Rd, Union MO 63084
Karen Wieda, Registrar
636-583-5195 ext. 2220 Fax: 636-583-1897
Website: www.eastcentral.edu
E-mail: wiedaks@eastcentral.edu

Linn State Technical College
1 Technology Dr, Linn MO 65051-9606
Becky Dunn, Admissions
800-743-8324 Fax: 573-897-5026
Website: www.linnstate.edu
E-mail: admissions@linnstate.edu

Ranken Technical College
4431 Finney Ave, Saint Louis MO 63113-2898
Elizabeth M. Keserauskis, Director of Admissions
314-371-0233 Fax: 314-371-0241
Website: www.ranken.edu
E-mail: admissions@ranken.edu

Vatterott College
3925 Industrial Dr, Saint Ann MO 63074-1807
Jennifer Commuso, Director of Admissions
800-345-6018 Fax: 314-428-5956
Website: www.vatterott-college.edu
E-mail: jennifer.commuso@vatterott-college.edu

NEBRASKA

ITT TECHNICAL INSTITUTE
9814 M St, Omaha NE 68127-2056
Frank de Monteur, Director
800-677-9260 Fax: 402-331-9495
Website: www.itt-tech.edu
E-mail: snielsen@itt-tech.edu

Mid-Plains Community College
North Platte Community College - North Campus
1101 Halligan Dr, North Platte NE 69101-7659
Kelly Rippen, Director of Recruitment
800-658-4308 ext. 8107 Fax: 308-534-5770
Website: www.mpcc.edu
E-mail: rippenk@mpcc.edu

NEVADA

GREAT BASIN COLLEGE
1500 College Pkwy, Elko NV 89801-5032
Julie G. Byrnes, Director of Enrollment Management
775-753-2271 Fax: 775-753-2311
Website: www.gbcnv.edu
E-mail: bjulie@gbcnv.edu

NEW JERSEY

Bergen Community College
400 Paramus Rd, Paramus NJ 07652
Julian Gomez, Asst. Director of Admissions
201-447-7100 Fax: 201-444-7036
Website: www.bergen.edu
E-mail: jgomez@bergen.edu

HOHOKUS SCHOOL OF TRADE AND TECHNICAL SCIENCES
634-638 Market St, Paterson NJ 07513-1402
Alan E. Concha, Vice President/Director
800-646-9353 Fax: 908-486-9321
Website: www.hohokustrades.com
E-mail: aconcha21@aol.com

Mercer County Community College
West Windsor Campus
PO Box B, Trenton NJ 08690
Savita Bambhrolia, Director of Admissions
609-586-4800 Fax: 609-587-4666
Website: www.mccc.edu
E-mail: admiss@mccc.edu

NEW YORK

APEX TECHNICAL SCHOOL
635 Avenue of the Americas
New York NY 10011-2008
William Ott, Admissions Director
212-645-3300 Fax: 212-645-6984
Website: www.apextechnical.com
See listing under "Career Schools"

ISLAND DRAFTING & TECHNICAL INSTITUTE
128 Broadway (Route 110), Amityville NY 11701-2704
James G. DiLiberto, President
631-691-8733 Fax: 631-691-8738
Website: www.idti.edu
E-mail: info@idti.edu

SUNY College of Technology
Alfred NY 14802
Deborah J. Goodrich, Director of Admissions
800-4AL-FRED Fax: 607-587-4299
Website: www.alfredstate.edu
E-mail: admissions@alfredstate.edu

SUNY College of Technology
2 Main St. Delhi NY 13753-1110
Robert W. Mazzei, Director of Admissions
800-96-DELHI Fax: 607-746-4104
Website: www.delhi.edu
E-mail: enroll@delhi.edu

NORTH CAROLINA

AMERICAN INSTITUTE OF APPLIED SCIENCE
Criminal Investigation and Forensic Science
100 Hunter Pl, Youngsville NC 27596-9447
Marvin Joy, Director of Education
919-554-2500 Fax: 919-556-6784
Website: www.aiasinc.com
E-mail: aias@mindspring.com

Haywood Community College
185 Freedlander Dr, Clyde NC 28721
Debbie Rowland, Coordinator of Admissions
828-627-4500 Fax: 828-627-4513
Website: www.haywood.edu
E-mail: drowland@haywood.edu

James Sprunt Community College
PO Box 398, Kenansville NC 28349-0398
Rita Brown, Registrar
910-296-2500 Fax: 910-296-1636
Website: www.sprunt.com

OHIO

ITT Technical Institute
3325 Stop 8 Rd, Dayton OH 45414-3425
Joe Graham, Director of Admissions
937-454-2267 Fax: 937-454-2278
Website: www.itt-tech.edu
E-mail: jgraham@itt-tech.edu

Owens Community College
300 Davis St, Findlay OH 45840-3631
William J. Ivoska PhD., Vice President of Student Services
567-429-3500 Fax: 567-423-0246
Website: www.owens.edu
E-mail: admissions@owens.edu

Owens Community College
PO Box 10000, Toledo OH 43699-1947
William J. Ivoska, Ph.D, Vice President of Student Services
567-661-7000 Fax: 567-661-7607
Website: www.owens.edu
E-mail: admissions@owens.edu

Total Technical Institute
8720 Brookpark Rd, Cleveland OH 44129-6810
Dave Bryant, Director of Admissions
216-485-0900 Fax: 216-661-6842
Website: www.ttinst.com
E-mail: dbryant@ttinst.com

OKLAHOMA

TULSA WELDING SCHOOL
2545 E 11th St, Tulsa OK 74104-3909
Mike Thurber, Director of Admissions
800-WELD-USA Fax: 918-587-8170
Website: www.weldingschool.com
E-mail: tws@ionet.net

OREGON

Linn-Benton Community College
6500 Pacific Blvd SW, Albany OR 97321-3774
Christine Baker, Outreach Coordinator
541-917-4811 Fax: 541-917-4868
Website: www.linnbenton.edu
E-mail: admissions@linnbenton.edu

Rogue Community College
3345 Redwood Hwy, Grants Pass OR 97527-9298
Claudia Sullivan, Director of Enrollment Services
541-956-7500 Fax: 541-471-3585
Website: www.roguecc.edu
E-mail: csullivan@roguecc.edu
See listing under "Community and Junior Colleges"

PENNSYLVANIA

Johnson College
3427 N Main Ave, Scranton PA 18508-1495
Dr. Ann L. Pipinski, President & CEO
Melissa Ide, Director of Enrollment Management
800-2WE-WORK or 570-342-6404 ext. 125
Fax: 570-348-2181
Website: www.johnson.edu
E-mail: admit@johnson.edu

Pennco Tech
3815 Otter St, Bristol PA 19007-3618
Glenn Slater, Director of Admissions
215-785-0111 Fax: 215-785-1945
Website: www.penncotech.com
E-mail: admissions@penncotech.com

York Technical Institute
1405 Williams Rd, York PA 17402
Cathi Killingsworth Bost, Vice President
800-227-9675 or 717-757-1100 Fax: 717-757-4964
Website: www.yti.edu
E-mail: info@yti.edu
See listing under "Career Schools"

SOUTH CAROLINA

Spartanburg Technical College
PO Box 4386, Spartanburg SC 29305-4386
Nancy Garmroth, Dean of Admissions & Financial Aid
864-592-4810 Fax: 864-592-4945
Website: stcsc.edu

SOUTH DAKOTA

· Western Dakota Technical Institute
  800 Mickelson Dr, Rapid City SD 57703-4018
  Janell Oberlander, Manager of Student Services
  605-394-4034 or 800-544-8765 Fax: 605-394-1789
  Website: www.westerndakotatech.org
  E-mail: admissions@wdti.tec.sd.us
  See listing under "Career Schools"

TENNESSEE

· Pellissippi State Technical Community College
  PO Box 22990, Knoxville TN 37933-0990
  Donna Mack, Contact
  865-694-6568 Fax: 865-539-7217
  Website: www.pstcc.edu
  E-mail: dmack@pstcc.edu

TEXAS

· ITT Technical Institute
  551 Ryan Plaza Dr, Arlington TX 76011
  817-794-5100 Fax: 817-275-8446
  Website: www.itt-tech.edu

· ITT Technical Institute
  15621 Blue Ash Dr Ste 160, Houston TX 77090-5819
  281-873-0512 Fax: 281-873-0518
  Website: www.itt-tech.edu

· **ITT TECHNICAL INSTITUTE**
  2222 Bay Area Blvd, Houston TX 77058-2070
  Linda Womack, Registrar
  281-486-2630 Fax: 281-486-6099
  Website: itt.tech.edu
  E-mail: lwomack@itt-tech.edu

· North Central Texas College
  1525 W California St, Gainesville TX 76240-4636
  Michelle Winters, Registrar
  940-668-3315 Fax: 940-665-7075
  Website: www.nctc.edu
  E-mail: mwinters@nctc.edu

SCHOOL OF AUTOMOTIVE MACHINISTS

  1911 Antoine Dr, Houston TX 77055-1803
  Admissions
  713-683-3817 Fax: 713-683-7077
  Website: www.samracing.com
  E-mail: admissions@samracing.com

· Temple College
  2600 S 1st St, Temple TX 76504-7435
  Angela Balch, Director of Admissions & Records
  254-298-8300 Fax: 254-298-8288
  Website: www.templejc.edu
  E-mail: ruth.bridges@templejc.edu

· Tyler Junior College
  PO Box 9020, Tyler TX 75711-9020
  Joan Jones, Interim Dean
  800-687-5680
  Website: www.tjc.edu
  E-mail: jjon@tjc.edu
  See listing under "Community and Junior Colleges"

· Western Technical College
  9624 Plaza Cir, El Paso TX 79927-2105
  Bill Terrell, Chief Administrative Officer
  915-760-8123
  Website: www.wtc-ep.edu
  E-mail: bterrell@wtc-ep.edu

UTAH

ITT TECHNICAL INSTITUTE
  920 Levoy Dr, Murray UT 84123-2500
  Gary Wood, Director of Recruitment
  801-263-3313 Fax: 801-263-3497
  Website: www.itt-tech.edu
  E-mail: gwood@itt-tech.edu

WASHINGTON

· **BATES TECHNICAL COLLEGE**
  1101 S Yakima Ave, Tacoma WA 98405-4895
  David Borofsky, President
  253-680-7000 Fax: 253-680-7101
  Website: www.bates.ctc.edu
  E-mail: info@bates.ctc.edu

· Clover Park Technical College
  4500 Steilacoom Blvd SW
  Lakewood WA 98499-4098
  Dr. Sharon McGavick, President
  253-589-5678 Fax: 253-589-5601
  Website: www.cptc.edu
  E-mail: jim.griffith@cptc.edu

· Everett Community College
  2000 Tower St, Everett WA 98201
  Christine Kerlin, Associate Dean
  425-388-9100 Fax: 425-388-9173
  Website: www.everettcc.edu
  E-mail: ckerlin@everettcc.edu

· Perry Technical Institute
  2011 W Washington Ave, Yakima WA 98903-1296
  509-453-0374 Fax: 509-453-0375
  Website: www.perrytech.edu
  E-mail: frankj@perrytech.edu

· Walla Walla Community College
  500 Tausick Way, Walla Walla WA 99362-9270
  Greg Farrens, Director
  509-527-4684 or 877-992-9922 Fax: 509-527-4480
  Website: www.wwcc.edu
  E-mail: greg.farrens@wwcc.edu
  See listing under "Community and Junior Colleges"

WISCONSIN

Wisconsin Indianhead Technical College
  505 Pine Ridge Dr, Shell Lake WI 54871
  Walt Peters, Dean
  800-243-9482 Fax: 715-468-2819
  Website: www.witc.edu
  E-mail: mcrandal@witc.edu

GUAM

· Guam Community College
  PO Box 23069, G.M.F. GU 96921-0307
  Virginia Charfauros Tudela, Ph.D., Registrar
  671-735-5531 Fax: 671-734-5238
  Website: www.guamcc.edu
  E-mail: Webmaster@guamcc.edu

: :PREPARATORY SCHOOLS FOR BOYS

Primarily Boarding

ALABAMA

Lyman Ward Military Academy
  PO Box 550, Camp Hill AL 36850-0550
  Maj. Charles Livings, Director of Admissions
  256-896-4127

ARKANSAS

Subiaco Academy
  405 N Subiaco Ave, Subiaco AR 72865-9798
  Fr. Aaron Pirrera, O.S.B., Headmaster
  800-364-7824

CALIFORNIA

ARMY AND NAVY ACADEMY
  PO Box 3000, Carlsbad CA 92018-3000
  Elizabeth Kalivas, Director of Admissions
  760-729-2385 ext. 400 Fax: 760-434-5948
  Website: www.armyandnavyacademy.org
  E-mail: admissions@armyandnavyacademy.org

ST. CATHERINES MILITARY SCHOOL
  215 N Harbor Blvd, Anaheim CA 92805-2596
  Angelique M. Norton, Director of Admissions
  714-772-1363 Fax: 714-772-3004
  Website: www.stcatherinesmilitary.com
  E-mail: admissions@stcatherinesmilitary.com

St. Michael's Preparatory School
  19292 El Toro Rd, Silverado CA 92676-9710
  949-858-0222

CONNECTICUT

Avon Old Farms School
  500 Old Farms Rd, Avon CT 06001-2799
  Kenneth H. LaRocque, Headmaster
  800-464-2866

Oxford Academy
  1393 Boston Post Rd, Westbrook CT 06498-1953
  860-399-6247

The Rectory School
  PO Box 68, Pomfret CT 06258
  860-928-7759

ST. THOMAS MORE SCHOOL
  45 Cottage Rd, Oakdale CT 06370-1051
  Timothy Riordan, Director of Admissions
  860-823-3861 Fax: 860-823-3863
  Website: www.stthomasmoreschool.com
  E-mail: stmadmit@stthomasmoreschool.com

SALISBURY SCHOOL
  251 Canaan Rd, Salisbury CT 06068-1602
  Peter B. Gilbert, Director of Admissions & Financial Aid
  860-435-5700 Fax: 860-435-5750
  Website: www.salisburyschool.org
  E-mail: pgilbert@salisburyschool.org

SOUTH KENT SCHOOL
  40 Bulls Bridge Rd, South Kent CT 06785-1199
  Richard A. Brande, Director of Admissions & Financial Aid
  860-927-3539 Fax: 860-927-0024
  Website: www.southkentschool.net
  E-mail: admissions@southkentschool.net

Woodhall School
  PO Box 550, Bethlehem CT 06751-0550
  203-266-7788

DISTRICT OF COLUMBIA

ST. ALBANS SCHOOL
  Mount Saint Alban, Washington DC 20016
  Mason Lecky, Director of Admissions and Financial Aid
  202-537-6440 Fax: 202-537-2225
  Website: www.stalbansschool.org
  E-mail: sta_admission@cathedral.org

FLORIDA

Florida Air Academy
  1950 S Academy Dr, Melbourne FL 32901-4396
  Colonel James Dwight, President
  321-723-3211 ext. 30041

GEORGIA

Riverside Military Academy
  2001 Riverside Dr, Gainesville GA 30501-1227
  Jad Davis, Director of Admissions
  800-GO-CADET (462-2338)

ILLINOIS

Marmion Academy
  1000 Butterfield Rd, Aurora IL 60502
  630-897-6936

INDIANA

Howe Military School
  5755 N State Road 9, Howe IN 46746
  260-562-2131 ext. 221

KANSAS

Maur Hill - Mount Academy
  1000 Green St, Atchison KS 66002-3078
  913-367-5482

St. John's Military School
  PO Box 5020, Salina KS 67402
  Duane Rutherford, Director of Admissions
  785-823-7231

MAINE

Bridgton Academy
  PO Box 292, North Bridgton ME 04057-0292
  Randall M. Greason, Headmaster
  Lisa M. Antell, Director of Admissions
  207-647-3322

MARYLAND

Georgetown Preparatory School
  10900 Rockville Pike
  North Bethesda MD 20852-3299
  301-493-5000

MASSACHUSETTS

BELMONT HILL SCHOOL
  350 Prospect St, Belmont MA 02478-2662
  Michael R. Grant, Director of Admission
  617-484-4410 Fax: 617-484-4829
  Website: www.belmont-hill.org
  E-mail: grant@belmont-hill.org
  Day and 5-Day Boarding.

Eaglebrook School
  Pine Nook Rd, Deerfield MA 01342
  413-774-7411

THE FESSENDEN SCHOOL
  250 Waltham St, West Newton MA 02465-1750
  Caleb W. Thomson '79, Director of Admissions
  617-630-2300 Fax: 617-630-2303
  Website: www.fessenden.org
  E-mail: admissions@fessenden.org

HILLSIDE SCHOOL
  404 Robin Hill St, Marlborough MA 01752
  David Beecher, Headmaster
  508-485-2824 Fax: 508-485-4420
  Website: www.hillsideschool.net
  E-mail: admissions@hillsideschool.net

ST. JOHN'S PREPARATORY SCHOOL
  DAY SCHOOL ONLY
  72 Spring St, Danvers MA 01923-1545
  John A. Driscoll, Dean of Admissions and Freshman Academic Programs
  978-774-1050 Fax: 978-774-5069
  Website: www.stjohnsprep.org
  E-mail: jdriscoll@stjohnsprep.org

MICHIGAN
ST. MARY'S PREPARATORY HIGH SCHOOL
3535 Indian Trl, Orchard Lake MI 48324-1601
Kevin Kosco, Dean of Admission
248-683-0531 Fax: 248-683-1740
Website: www.stmarysprep.com
E-mail: info@stmarysprep.com

MINNESOTA
Saint Thomas Academy
949 Mendota Heights Rd
Mendota Heights MN 55120-1496
John Kenney, Director of Admissions
651-454-4570

MISSISSIPPI
ST. STANISLAUS COLLEGE PREP
304 S Beach Blvd, Bay Saint Louis MS 39520-4301
Dolores Richmond, Director of Admissions
228-467-9057 Fax: 228-466-2972
Website: www.ststan.com
E-mail: admissions@ststan.com

MISSOURI
Chaminade College Preparatory School
425 S Lindbergh Blvd, Saint Louis MO 63131-2799
Matthew J. Saxer, Admissions Director
314-993-4400

MISSOURI MILITARY ACADEMY
800 Grand Ave, Mexico MO 65265
Maj. Dennis Diederich, Director of Admissions
888-564-6662 Fax: 573-581-0081
Website: www.mma-cadet.org
E-mail: info@mma.mexico.mo.us

NEBRASKA
Mount Michael Benedictine School
22520 Mount Michael Rd, Elkhorn NE 68022-3401
Director of Admissions
402-289-2541

NEW HAMPSHIRE
CARDIGAN MOUNTAIN SCHOOL
62 Alumni Dr, Canaan NH 03741-7210
Rich Ryerson, Director of Admissions
603-523-3548 Fax: 603-523-3565
Website: www.cardigan.org
E-mail: rryerson@cardigan.org

Hampshire Country School
122 Hampshire Rd, Rindge NH 03461-3913
603-899-3325

NEW JERSEY
THE AMERICAN BOYCHOIR SCHOOL
19 Lambert Dr, Princeton NJ 08540-2304
Scott Smith, Director of Admissions
609-924-5858 Fax: 609-924-5812
Website: www.americanboychoir.org
E-mail: admissions@americanboychoir.org

NEW YORK
Gow School
PO Box 85, South Wales NY 14139
Robert Garcia, Director of Admissions
585-652-3450

MILFORD ACADEMY
PO Box 878, New Berlin NY 13411
Andrew Ruffino, Dean of Students
607-847-9280 Fax: 607-847-9250
Website: www.milfordacademy.org
E-mail: bc55@milfordacademy.org

SAINT THOMAS CHOIR SCHOOL
202 W 58th St, New York NY 10019-1406
Fr. Charles Wallace, Headmaster
Ruth Cobb, Director of Admissions
212-247-3311 Fax: 212-247-3393
Website: www.choirschool.org
E-mail: rcobb@choirschool.org

Trinity-Pawling School
700 State Route 22, Pawling NY 12564
845-855-3100

NORTH CAROLINA
CHRIST SCHOOL
500 Christ School Rd, Arden NC 28704-8405
Denis Stokes, Director of Admission
800-422-3212 or 828-684-6232 Fax: 828-684-4869
Website: www.christschool.org
E-mail: admission@christschool.org

Oak Ridge Military Academy
PO Box 498, Oak Ridge NC 27310-0498
Lieutenant Colonel Ray Wilson, Vice President for Admissions
336-643-4131 ext. 132

OHIO
Grand River Academy
PO Box 222, Austinburg OH 44010-0222
Sam Corabi, Director of Admission
440-275-2811

PENNSYLVANIA
Academy of the New Church Boys School
PO Box 707, Bryn Athyn PA 19009
215-947-4200

CARSON LONG MILITARY INSTITUTE
PO Box 98, New Bloomfield PA 17068-0098
Lieutenant Colonel David M. Comolli, Academic Dean
717-582-2121 Fax: 717-582-8763
Website: www.carsonlong.org
E-mail: carson6@pa.net

CFS The School at Church Farm
PO Box 2000, Paoli PA 19301-0319
Richard Lunardi, Director of Admissions
610-363-5347

The Kiski School
1888 Brett Ln, Saltsburg PA 15681-8951
Lawrence J. Jensen, Director of Admissions
877-KISKI-4-U

THE PHELPS SCHOOL
583 Sugartown Rd, Malvern PA 19355-2800
F. Christopher Chirieleison, Director of Admissions
610-644-1754 Fax: 610-644-6679
Website: www.thephelpsschool.org
E-mail: admis@thephelpsschool.org

Saint Gregory's Academy
RR 8 Box 8214, Moscow PA 18444
Alan J. Hicks, Headmaster
570-842-8112

Valley Forge Military Academy
1001 Eagle Rd, Wayne PA 19087-3695
610-989-1200

SOUTH CAROLINA
Camden Military Academy
520 Highway 1 N, Camden SC 29020-2599
803-432-6001

TENNESSEE
McCallie School
500 Dodds Ave, Chattanooga TN 37404-3991
David Hughes, Director of Boarding Admission
423-624-8300

TEXAS
CENTRAL CATHOLIC HIGH SCHOOL
1403 N Saint Marys St, San Antonio TX 78215-1785
Belia Gonzalez McDonald, Admissions Coordinator
210-225-6794 ext. 209 Fax: 210-227-9353
Website: www.cchs-satx.org
E-mail: admissions@cchs-satx.org

MARINE MILITARY ACADEMY
320 Iwo Jima Blvd, Harlingen TX 78550-3698
Admissions Department
956-423-6006 Fax: 956-421-9273
Website: www.marinemilitaryacademy.com
E-mail: admissions@mma-tx.org

VIRGINIA
Blue Ridge School
Bacon Hollow Rd, Saint George VA 22935
804-985-2811

CHRISTCHURCH SCHOOL
49 Seahorse Ln, Christchurch VA 23031
Nancy M. Nolan, Director of Admission
804-758-2306 or 800-296-2306 Fax: 804-758-0721
Website: www.christchurchschool.org
E-mail: admission@christchurchschool.org
Boys boarding grades 8-12 and post graduate. Co-ed day.

Fishburne Military School
PO Box 988, Waynesboro VA 22980-0722
Colonel William Alexander, Superintendent
Captain Christopher A. Richmond, Director of Admissions
800-946-7773 Fax: 540-946-7738
Website: www.fishburne.org
E-mail: crichmond@fishburne.org

FORK UNION MILITARY ACADEMY
PO Box 278, Fork Union VA 23055-0278
Lt. Gen. John E. Jackson Jr., USAF (Ret.), President
Lt. Col. Steve Macek, Director of Admissions
800-462-3862 or 434-842-4205 Fax: 434-842-4300
Website: www.forkunion.com
E-mail: maceks@fuma.org
Private. Men only. Accreditation: VAIS, SACS, NAIS, AMCS, SAIS. Tuition: $21,190. Fees: $3,080. Enrollment: 550. Faculty: 47. Student-faculty ratio: 12:1. Degrees: college-prep high school diploma and advanced college prep. Library: 19,000+ volumes. 19 buildings on 1,000 acres. One subject plan; technology center with over 300 networked multi-media computers; nationally-recognized athletic teams; 99% of our students go on to college.

HARGRAVE MILITARY ACADEMY
200 Military Dr, Chatham VA 24531-4683
Frank Martin, Director of Admissions
800-432-2480 Fax: 434-432-3129
Website: www.hargrave.edu
E-mail: admissions@hargrave.edu
Established 1909. Private. College Prep. Male Boarding 7th grade - post graduate. Accreditation: SACS, VAIS. Tuition: $22,625. Enrollment: 405. Faculty: 46. Student-faculty ratio: 11:1. Degrees: High School Diploma. Library: 6,000 volumes. 12 buildings on 214 acres. 8 computer labs, how to study course, indoor 50-meter pool, summer school, Judeo-Christian values, full athletic program.

Woodberry Forest School
Woodberry Forest VA 22989
Dennis M. Campbell, Headmaster
Joseph G. Coleman, Director of Admissions
540-672-3900

WISCONSIN
ST. JOHN'S NORTHWESTERN MILITARY ACADEMY
1101 N Genesee St, Delafield WI 53018-1498
Mr. Jack H. Albert, Jr., President
Cpt. Duane Rutherford, Director of Enrollment Services
Lt. Kathleen McCormick, Enrollment Counselor
800-752-2338 or 262-646-7199 Fax: 262-646-7128
Website: www.sjnma.org
E-mail: admissions@sjnma.org
Established in 1884. Private. Boys grades 7-12. Accreditation: ISACS, NAIS, AMCSUS. Tuition, room & board: $27,250. Enrollment: 325 boarding; 5 day. Faculty: 39. Student-faculty ratio: 12:1. 10 buildings on 150 acres. Gym, pool, tennis courts, golf course. College preparatory boy's boarding school. Day program for grades 7-8 only. 30 minutes from Milwaukee and 90 minutes from Chicago. Extensive athletic and extracurricular offerings. JROTC honor school with distinction.

St. Lawrence Seminary High School
301 Church St, Mount Calvary WI 53057-9699
920-753-3911

::PREPARATORY SCHOOLS - COEDUCATIONAL

Primarily Boarding

ALABAMA

INDIAN SPRINGS SCHOOL
190 Woodward Dr, Indian Springs AL 35124-3272
E.T. Brown III, Director of Admission
888-843-9493 Fax: 205-988-3797
Website: www.indiansprings.org
E-mail: ebrown@indiansprings.org

Marion Military Institute
1101 Washington St, Marion AL 36756
800-MMI-1842

RANDOLPH SCHOOL
1005 Drake Ave SE, Huntsville AL 35802-1099
Nancy Hodges, Admissions Director
256-881-1701 Fax: 256-881-1784
Website: www.randolphschool.net
E-mail: admissions@randolphschool.net

ARIZONA

Fenster School of Southern Arizona
8500 E Ocotillo Dr, Tucson AZ 85750-9670
Michael Lyles, Director of Admissions
520-749-3340

HOLBROOK SDA INDIAN SCHOOL
PO Box 910, Holbrook AZ 86025
Mary June Bragg, Vice Principal
928-524-6845 Fax: 928-524-3190
Website: www.hissda.org
E-mail: hischool@cybertrails.com

OAK CREEK RANCH SCHOOL
PO Box 4329, Sedona AZ 86340-4329
David Wick Jr., Headmaster
928-634-5571 Fax: 928-634-4915
Website: www.ocrs.com
E-mail: admissions@ocrs.com

Orme School
HC 63 Box 3040, Mayer AZ 86333-9799
520-632-7601

THUNDERBIRD ADVENTIST ACADEMY
7410 E Sutton Dr, Scottsdale AZ 85260-3915
480-948-3300
Website: www.thunderbirdacademy.org
E-mail: info@thunderbirdacademy.org

Verde Valley School
3511 Verde Valley School Rd
Sedona AZ 86351-9541
Donald W. Smith, Director of Admissions
928-284-2272

ARKANSAS

Harding Academy
PO Box 10775, Searcy AR 72149-0001
501-279-7200

CALIFORNIA

Athenian School
2100 Mount Diablo Scenic Blvd
Danville CA 94506-2002
925-837-5375

The Bishop's School
7607 La Jolla Blvd, La Jolla CA 92037-4703
Josie Alvarez, Director of Admissions
858-459-4021

Cate School
PO Box 5005, Carpinteria CA 93014-5005
Peter J. Mack, Director of Admission
805-684-4127

DUNN SCHOOL
PO Box 98, Los Olivos CA 93441-0098
Ann Greenough-Coats, Director of Admissions
805-688-6471 Fax: 805-686-2078
Website: www.dunnschool.org
E-mail: admissions@dunnschool.org

Happy Valley School
PO Box 850, Ojai CA 93024-0850
805-646-4343

HARKER SCHOOL
500 Saratoga Ave, San Jose CA 95129-1387
Nan Nielsen, Director of Admissions & Financial Aid
408-249-2510 Fax: 408-984-2325
Website: www.harker.org
E-mail: admissions@harker.org

IDYLLWILD ARTS ACADEMY
PO Box 38, Idyllwild CA 92549-0038
Karen Porter, Dean of Admission
951-659-2171 ext. 2223 Fax: 951-659-5463
Website: www.idyllwildarts.org
E-mail: admission@idyllwildarts.org

Linfield Christian School
31950 Pauba Rd, Temecula CA 92592-3523
Jeff Nichols, Director of Admissions
951-676-8111

LYCEE INTERNATIONAL DE LOS ANGELES
4155 Russell Ave, Los Angeles CA 90027-4509
Valerie Lesure, Director of Admissions
323-665-4526 Fax: 323-665-2607
Website: www.lilaschool.com
E-mail: valerie.lesure@lilaschool.com

Midland School
PO Box 8, Los Olivos CA 93441-0008
805-688-5114

MONTCLAIR COLLEGE PREPARATORY SCHOOL
8071 Sepulveda Blvd, Van Nuys CA 91402-4400
Dr. V.E. Simpson, Director
818-787-5290 Fax: 818-786-3382
Website: www.montclairprep.org

Monterey Bay Academy
783 San Andreas Rd
La Selva Beach CA 95076-1911
831-728-1481

Monte Vista Christian School
2 School Way, Watsonville CA 95076-9715
831-722-8178

OAK GROVE SCHOOL
220 W Lomita Ave, Ojai CA 93023-2298
Joy Maguire-Parsons, Admissions Director
805-646-8236 ext. 109 Fax: 805-646-6509
Website: www.oakgroveschool.com
E-mail: enroll@oakgroveschool.com

Ojai Valley School
723 El Paseo Rd, Ojai CA 93023-2498
805-646-1423

Robert Louis Stevenson High School
3152 Forest Lake Rd, Pebble Beach CA 93953-3200
831-626-5300

Sacred Heart Preparatory School
150 Valparaiso Ave, Atherton CA 94027-4402
Rick Diaz, Director of Admissions
650-322-1866

Southwestern Academy
2800 Monterey Rd, San Marino CA 91108-1798
626-799-5010

Squaw Valley Academy
PO Box 2667, Olympic Valley CA 96146-2667
Paul A. Jette, Head of School
530-583-1558

Thacher School
5025 Thacher Rd, Ojai CA 93023-9001
William P. McMahon, Director of Admission
805-646-4377

Villanova Prep School
12096 N Ventura Ave, Ojai CA 93023-3999
805-646-1464

The Webb Schools
1175 W Baseline Rd, Claremont CA 91711-2199
Leo G. Marshall, Director of Admission and Financial Aid
909-482-5214

WOODSIDE PRIORY SCHOOL
302 Portola Rd, Portola Valley CA 94028-7897
Al D. Zappelli, Director of Admissions
650-851-8221 Fax: 650-851-2839
Website: www.woodsidepriory.com
E-mail: azappelli@woodsidepriory.com

Located within 40 minutes of San Francisco, the Priory combines its rural 60-acre campus with a talented faculty, a 10:1 student/teacher ratio, a strong college and university preparatory curriculum, and a competitive athletic program. It seeks to embody the values at the heart of Benedictine education — belief in order and discipline in one's life, respect for learning, and an appreciation for the shared experience of community life. Priory students are challenged to develop their fullest potential in the classrooms, on the athletic fields and in their relationships with one another. The Boarding Program embodies a family model with professional residential advisors mentoring small groups of ten boarders each. International in scope, the program attracts students from all parts of the world and throughout the western United States. The goal of the Boarding Program is to develop individuals personally but to also be essential members of a community. Seemless interaction with the Priory's three hundred day students in the classrooms, sports, performing and visual arts, club and community service activities, as well as at Chapel and meals, provides for diversity and achievement of common goals. Come visit the Priory and see why it is the "Right Place at the Right Time" for you!

COLORADO

Accelerated Schools Foundation
2160 S Cook St, Denver CO 80210-4914
303-758-2003

Colorado Academy
3800 S Pierce St, Denver CO 80235-2404
Catherine Laskey, Director of Admissions
303-914-2513

COLORADO ROCKY MOUNTAIN SCHOOL
1493 County Road 106, Carbondale CO 81623
Molly Hall, Director of Admission
970-963-2562 Fax: 970-963-9865
Website: www.crms.org
E-mail: mhall@crms.org

The Colorado Springs School
21 Broadmoor Ave
Colorado Springs CO 80906-3699
Amie Hilles, Director of Admissions
719-475-9747

Colorado Timberline Academy
35554 Highway 550, Durango CO 81301-8653
970-247-5898

Crested Butte Academy
PO Box 1180, Crested Butte CO 81224
888-633-0222

Denver Academy
4400 E Iliff Ave, Denver CO 80222
Dan Loan, Director of Admissions
303-777-5870

FOUNTAIN VALLEY SCHOOL OF COLORADO
6155 Fountain Valley School Rd
Colorado Springs CO 80911-2299
Randy Roach, Director of Admission and Financial Aid
719-390-7035 Fax: 719-390-7762
Website: www.fvs.edu
E-mail: admissions@fvs.edu

The Lowell Whiteman School
42605 County Road 36
Steamboat Springs CO 80487-9215
Deb Smith, Director of Admissions
970-879-1350

CONNECTICUT

CANTERBURY SCHOOL
101 Aspetuck Ave, New Milford CT 06776-1739
Thomas J. Sheehy III, Headmaster
Keith R. Holton, Director of Admission
860-210-3832 Fax: 860-350-1120
Website: www.cbury.org
E-mail: admissions@cbury.org

Founded in 1915 and still guided by lay Roman Catholics, Canterbury is a college preparatory coeducational boarding and day school for students in grades 9-12.
Our School
150-acre hilltop campus in New Milford, CT. Complete wireless campus network with internet access for all. Average class size: 11. Traditional two-semester school year. Numerous clubs and community service organizations. Library with 18,000 books, 36 computers, and access to major daily and weekly periodicals as well as 3,500 videos and DVDs.
Our Students
360 students (225 boarders, 135 day). 60% male, 40% female. Students from 19 states and 15 countries. SAT: the middle 50% of the class of 2004 scored in the 540-640 range (verbal) and 500-600 (math). Tuition: $34,650 (boarding), $25,850 (day). 39% receive financial aid.
The Faculty
76 members. 58% male, 42% female. 45 have advanced degrees. More than 50% of the faculty has been at Canterbury 5 years or more.
Academics
Canterbury offers a complete range of courses, including 19 A.P. courses. The fields of study include English, Mathematics, the Sciences, Languages, History, Computer Science, Fine Arts, Music, Theology, and Independent Study.
Arts
In the visual arts, Canterbury offers 15 courses from drawing to ceramics. For the music minded student, we have 5 instrumental offerings and 2 vocal groups.
Athletics
All 360 students participate in interscholastic sports each season. 52 teams participate in 19 sports, including water polo, cross country, soccer, field hockey, football, crew, basketball, hockey, wrestling, swimming, squash, volleyball, baseball, lacrosse, softball, golf, and tennis.
College
Our college placement office works with students during their entire time at Canterbury as they proceed through the selection, application, and acceptance processes. Here is a sample list of colleges and universities our students have attended in the past five years: Bates, Yale, Cornell, USMA (West Point), WPI, Bowdoin, Dartmouth, Brown, Bucknell, Colgate, Fairfield, Holy Cross, Lehigh, Notre Dame, Northwestern, Providence, RPI, Tulane, Vanderbilt,.

Cheshire Academy
10 Main St, Cheshire CT 06410-2496
203-272-5396

Choate Rosemary Hall School
333 Christian St, Wallingford CT 06492-3818
203-697-2000

FORMAN SCHOOL
12 Norfolk Rd, Litchfield CT 06759-0080
Beth Rainey, Director of Admissions
860-567-1802 Fax: 860-567-3501
Website: www.formanschool.org
E-mail: admissions@formanschool.org

THE GUNNERY
99 Green Hill Rd, Washington CT 06793-1200
Thomas W. Adams, Director of Admissions
860-868-7334 Fax: 860-868-1614
Website: www.gunnery.org
E-mail: admissions@gunnery.org

THE HOTCHKISS SCHOOL
Lakeville CT 06039
Dr. Robert H. Mattoon Jr., Head of School
William D. Leahy, Dean of Admission
860-435-3102 Fax: 860-435-0042
Website: www.hotchkiss.org
E-mail: admission@hotchkiss.org

HYDE SCHOOL
PO Box 237, Woodstock CT 06281-0237
Holly E. Thompson, Director of Admissions
860-963-9096 Fax: 860-928-0612
Website: www.hyde.edu

INDIAN MOUNTAIN SCHOOL
211 Indian Mountain Rd, Lakeville CT 06039-2029
Christopher C. Wilkes, Director Admission and
Financial Aid
860-435-0871 Fax: 860-435-1380
Website: www.indianmountain.org
E-mail: admissions@indianmountain.org

Kent School
PO Box 2006, Kent CT 06757-0640
860-927-6000

LOOMIS CHAFFEE SCHOOL
4 Batchelder Rd, Windsor CT 06095-3031
Thomas D. Southworth, Director of Admissions
860-687-6000 Fax: 860-687-1100
Website: www.loomis.org
E-mail: admission@loomis.org

Marianapolis Preparatory School
PO Box 304, Thompson CT 06277
Daniel Harrop, Director of Admissions
& Immigration Officer
860-923-9565

Marvelwood School
PO Box 3001, Kent CT 06757-3001
860-927-0047

POMFRET SCHOOL
398 Pomfret St, PO Box 128, Pomfret CT 06258
Erik Bertelsen, Assistant Head for Enrollment
860-963-6100 Fax: 860-963-2042
Website: www.pomfretschool.org
E-mail: admission@pomfretschool.org

RUMSEY HALL SCHOOL
201 Romford Rd, Washington Depot CT 06794-1399
Matthew S. Hoeniger, Assistant Headmaster
860-868-0535 Fax: 860-868-7907
Website: www.rumseyhall.org
E-mail: admiss@rumseyhall.org

Suffield Academy
PO Box 999, Suffield CT 06078-0999
Charles Cahn III, Assistant Headmaster
800-668-7315

THE TAFT SCHOOL
110 Woodbury Rd, Watertown CT 06795-2100
Frederick Wandelt, Director of Admissions
860-945-7777 Fax: 860-945-7808
Website: www.taftschool.org
E-mail: admissions@taftschool.org

WATKINSON SCHOOL
180 Bloomfield Ave, Hartford CT 06105-1096
John Crosson, Director of Admissions
860-236-5618 Fax: 860-233-8295
Website: www.watkinson.org
E-mail: john_crosson@watkinson.org

WESTMINSTER SCHOOL
995 Hopmeadow St, Simsbury CT 06070
Jon C. Deveaux, Director of Admissions
860-408-3000 Fax: 860-408-3001
Website: www.westminster-school.org
E-mail: admit@westminster-school.org

WOOSTER SCHOOL
91 Miry Brook Rd, Danbury CT 06810-7417
George N. King, Jr., Headmaster
Samuel Gaudet, Director of Admissions
203-830-3916 Fax: 203-790-7147
Website: www.woosterschool.org
E-mail: samuel.gaudet@woostersch.org

DELAWARE

ARCHMERE ACADEMY
3600 Philadelphia Pike, Claymont DE 19703-3108
Daniel E. Hickey, Director of Admissions
302-798-6632 or 610-485-0373 Fax: 302-798-7290
Website: www.archmereacademy.com
E-mail: dhickey@archmereacademy.com
    Established 1932. Private. Coed. Accreditation:
MSACS. Tuition: $16,500. Enrollment: 500. Faculty: 53.
Student-faculty ratio: 9:1. Library: 13,900 volumes. 7
buildings on 38 acres, including Justin Diny Science
Center and Performing Arts Center. Strong visual and
performing arts programs. 18 Advanced Placement
classes offered. Quiet, scenic, college-like campus in
suburban setting. Multi-Media Center, Writing Center,
Campus ministry, computerized library and science
laboratories, extensive community service clubs, student
publications, 26 sports teams.

ST. ANDREW'S SCHOOL
350 Noxontown Rd, Middletown DE 19709-1605
Daniel T. Roach, Headmaster
Louisa H. Zendt, Director of Admission
302-285-4231 Fax: 302-378-7120
Website: www.standrews-de.org
E-mail: admissions@standrews-de.org

FLORIDA

ADMIRAL FARRAGUT ACADEMY
501 Park St N, Saint Petersburg FL 33710
David Graham, Director of Admissions
727-384-5500 Fax: 727-347-5160
Website: www.farragut.org
E-mail: admissions@farragut.org

Bolles School
7400 San Jose Blvd, Jacksonville FL 32217-3499
904-733-9292

FOREST LAKE ACADEMY
3909 E Semoran Blvd, Apopka FL 32703-6199
John Wheaton, Principal
407-862-8411 Fax: 407-862-7050
Website: www.forestlakeacademy.org
E-mail: beckerg@forestlake.org

Hobe Sound Christian Academy
PO Box 1065, Hobe Sound FL 33475-1065
800-881-5534

MONTVERDE ACADEMY
17235 7th St, Montverde FL 34756
Robin Revis-Pyke, Dean of Admission
407-469-2561 Fax: 407-469-3711
Website: www.montverde.org
E-mail: admissions@montverde.org

Pine Crest School
1501 NE 62nd St, Fort Lauderdale FL 33334-5199
954-492-4100

SADDLEBROOK PREPARATORY SCHOOL
5700 Saddlebrook Way
Wesley Chapel FL 33543-4499
Michelle Axthelm, Admissions Coordinator
813-907-4300 Fax: 813-991-4713
Website: www.saddlebrookprep.com
E-mail: maxthelm@saddlebrookresort.com

SAINT ANDREW'S SCHOOL
3900 Jog Rd, Boca Raton FL 33434-4498
George E. Andrews II, Headmaster
561-210-2000 Fax: 561-210-2027
Website: www.saintandrewsschool.net
E-mail: admission@saintandrewsschool.net

GEORGIA

DARLINGTON SCHOOL
1014 Cave Spring Rd SW, Rome GA 30161-4700
Casey Zimmer, Director of Admission & Financial Aid
706-235-6051 or 800-36-TIGER Fax: 706-232-3600
Website: www.darlingtonschool.org
E-mail: admission@darlingtonschool.org

HORIZONS SCHOOL
1900 Dekalb Ave NE, Atlanta GA 30307-2300
Les Garber, Administrator
404-378-2219 Fax: 404-378-8946
Website: www.horizonsschool.com
E-mail: horizonsschool@horizonsschool.com

RABUN GAP-NACOOCHEE SCHOOL
339 Nacoochee Dr, Rabun Gap GA 30568-2200
Adele Yermack, Director of Admission
706-746-7467 Fax: 706-746-2594
Website: www.rabungap.org
E-mail: admission@rabungap.org

St. Andrew's School
PO Box 30639, Savannah GA 31410-0639
Larry C. Berry, Headmaster
912-897-4941

TALLULAH FALLS SCHOOL
PO Box 249, Tallulah Falls GA 30573-0249
Susan M. Waldorf, Director of Admissions
706-754-0400 Fax: 706-754-3595
Website: tallulahfalls.org
E-mail: admissions@tallulahfalls.org

Woodward Academy
1662 Rugby Ave, College Park GA 30337
R.L. Slider, Vice-President\Dean of Admissions
404-765-4001

HAWAII

Hawaii Preparatory Academy
PO Box 428, Kamuela HI 96743-0428
808-885-7321

Mid-Pacific Institute
2445 Kaala St, Honolulu HI 96822-2299
808-973-5000

SEABURY HALL
480 Olinda Rd, Makawao HI 96768-7352
Elaine Nelson, Director of Admissions
808-572-0807 Fax: 808-572-0807
Website: www.seaburyhall.org
E-mail: enelson@seaburyhall.org

IDAHO

Gem State Academy
16115 S Montana Ave, Caldwell ID 83607-8365
208-459-1627

ILLINOIS

Elgin Academy
350 Park St, Elgin IL 60120-4471
Dr. John W. Cooper, Head of School
Erik C. Calhoun, Director of Admission
847-695-0303

The Governor French Academy
219 W Main St, Belleville IL 62220-1537
Carol Wilson, Director of Admissions
618-233-7542

LAKE FOREST ACADEMY
1500 W Kennedy Rd, Lake Forest IL 60045-1099
Karen Cegelski, Dean of Admission
847-615-3267
Website: www.lfanet.org
E-mail: kcegelski@lfanet.org

The Latin School of Chicago
59 W North Blvd, Chicago IL 60610
Frank Hogan, Headmaster
312-582-6000

Morgan Park Academy
2153 W 111th St, Chicago IL 60643-3917
J. William Adams, Headmaster
773-881-6700

INDIANA

Brebeuf Jesuit Preparatory School
2801 W 86th St, Indianapolis IN 46268-1925
317-876-4726

The Culver Academies and Summer Camps
1300 Academy Rd #157, Culver IN 46511-1234
Mike Turnbull, Director of Admissions
574-842-7100 Fax: 574-842-8066
Website: www.culver.org
E-mail: admissions@culver.org

Howe Military School
5755 N State Road 9, Howe IN 46746
260-562-2131 ext. 221

La Lumiere School
PO Box 5005, La Porte IN 46352-5005
219-326-7450

IOWA

Scattergood Friends School
1951 Delta Ave, West Branch IA 52358-8507
Kenneth Hinshaw, Director
Sarah French, Admissions Director
319-643-7628

KANSAS

Thomas More Preparatory-Marian
1701 Hall St, Hays KS 67601-3145
785-625-6577

KENTUCKY

The June Buchanan School
100 Purpose Rd, Pippa Passes KY 41844-9701
Jeemes Akers, Director
606-368-6108

Millersburg Military Academy
PO Box 278, Millersburg KY 40348
Brigadier General James Vicars, President
859-484-3352

ONEIDA BAPTIST INSTITUTE
PO Box 67, Oneida KY 40972
606-847-4111 Fax: 606-847-4496
Website: www.oneidaschool.org
E-mail: admissions4obi@yahoo.com

MAINE

Carrabassett Valley Academy
3197 Carrabassett Dr
Carrabassett Valley ME 04947-5705
207-237-2250

FRYEBURG ACADEMY
745 Main St, Fryeburg ME 04037-1329
Stephanie S. Morin, Director of Admission
877-935-2013 or 207-935-2013 Fax: 207-935-4292
Website: www.fryeburgacademy.org
E-mail: admissions@fryeburgacademy.org

Gould Academy
PO Box 860, Bethel ME 04217-0860
John A. Kerney, Director of Admissions & External
Affairs
207-824-7777

Hebron Academy
PO Box 309, Hebron ME 04238-0309
Office of Admission
888-432-7664

HYDE SCHOOL
616 High St, Bath ME 04530-5002
Melissa Burroughs, Director of Admissions
207-443-7101 Fax: 207-442-9346
Website: www.hyde.edu
E-mail: bath.admission@hyde.edu

Kents Hill School
PO Box 257, Kents Hill ME 04349-0257
Loren B. Mitchell, Director of Admissions
207-685-4914

MAINE CENTRAL INSTITUTE
125 S Main St, Pittsfield ME 04967
Clint Williams, Director of Admissions
207-487-2282 Fax: 207-487-3512
Website: www.mci-school.org
E-mail: cwilliams@mci-school.org

MARYLAND

Gunston Day School
PO Box 200, Centreville MD 21617-0200
Marc S. Buckley, Director of Admission
410-758-0620

McDonogh School
PO Box 380, Owings Mills MD 21117-0380
410-363-0600

Saint James School
College Rd, Saint James MD 21781-9999
Win Sherman, Director of Admissions
301-733-9330

SANDY SPRING FRIENDS SCHOOL
16923 Norwood Rd, Sandy Spring MD 20860-1199
Mecha Inman, Director of Admissions
301-774-7455 Fax: 301-924-1115
Website: www.ssfs.org
E-mail: admissions@ssfs.org

West Nottingham Academy
1079 Firetower Rd, Colora MD 21917-1599
Heidi K.L. Sprinkle, Director of Admission
410-658-5556

MASSACHUSETTS

Academy at Charlemont
Mohawk Trl, Charlemont MA 01339
413-339-4912

The Bement School
94 Main St, Deerfield MA 01342
Matthew Evans, Director of Admission
413-774-7061

BERKSHIRE SCHOOL
245 N Undermountain Rd, Sheffield MA 01257-9672
Andrew Bogardus, Director of Admission
413-229-1003 Fax: 413-229-1016
Website: www.berkshireschool.org
E-mail: admission@berkshireschool.org

Brooks School
1160 Great Pond Rd, North Andover MA 01845-1298
Judith Beams, Director of Admission
978-686-6101

Buxton School
291 South St, Williamstown MA 01267
413-458-3919

THE CAMBRIDGE SCHOOL OF WESTON
Georgian Rd, Weston MA 02493-2198
781-642-8600 Fax: 781-899-3870
Website: www.csw.org
E-mail: admissions@csw.org

CHAPEL HILL-CHAUNCY HALL SCHOOL
785 Beaver St, Waltham MA 02452-5606
Director of Admission
781-894-2644 Fax: 781-894-5205
Website: www.chch.org
E-mail: admissions@chch.org

CONCORD ACADEMY
166 Main St, Concord MA 01742-2454
Pamela J. Safford, Associate Head for Enrollment and Planning
978-402-2250 Fax: 978-402-2345
Website: www.concordacademy.org
E-mail: admissions@concordacademy.org

CUSHING ACADEMY
PO Box 8000, Ashburnham MA 01430-8000
Melanie J. Connors, Director of Admission
978-827-7300 Fax: 978-827-6253
Website: www.cushing.org
E-mail: admission@cushing.org

DEERFIELD ACADEMY
Deerfield MA 01342
Patricia L. Gimbel, Dean of Admission & Financial Aid
413-774-1400 Fax: 413-772-1100
Website: www.deerfield.edu
E-mail: admission@deerfield.edu

Desisto School
PO Box 369, Stockbridge MA 01262-0369
Ann Schulman, Director of Admissions
413-298-3776

Dewey Academy
389 Main St, Great Barrington MA 01230-1813
413-528-9800

Fay School
48 Main St, Southborough MA 01772-1595
508-485-0100

Governor Dummer Academy
1 Elm St, Byfield MA 01922-2799
John Martin Doggett, Jr., Headmaster
978-499-3120

Groton School
PO Box 991, Groton MA 01450-0991
John M. Niles, Director of Admission
978-448-7510

LANDMARK SCHOOL
PO Box 227, Prides Crossing MA 01965-0227
Director of Admission
978-236-3000 Fax: 978-927-7268
Website: www.landmarkschool.org
E-mail: admission@landmarkschool.org
Established 1971. Private. Coed. Accreditation: NEASC, NAIS, AISNE, MAAPS. Tuition: $38,900. Room & Board: $13,600. Enrollment: 447. Faculty: 214. Student-faculty ratio: 3:1. Library: 16,300 volumes. Landmark's Preparatory Program accepts emotionally healthy students in grades 9-12 and offers a full secondary curriculum for those diagnosed with a language-based learning disability. The curriculum is parallel at each grade level to that of other public and private schools. The goal of the program is to help students develop and integrate language, organizational, study, and advocacy skills which are essential for success in traditional secondary school classrooms and higher education.

LAWRENCE ACADEMY
PO Box 992, Groton MA 01450-0992
Scott Wiggins, Head of School
Andi O'Hearn, Director of Admission
978-448-6535 Fax: 978-448-1519
Website: www.lacademy.edu
E-mail: admiss@lacademy.edu
Coeducational boarding and day school for grades 9-12. Enrollment: 394. Faculty 65. Tuition: $39,200 boarding, $29,900 day. Accreditation: NEASC.

Established in 1793, Lawrence Academy has occupied a small hill in rural New England for over 200 years. Boston, with its rich cultural and historical resources, active student life and a major international airport, is only one hour away. The school's setting, blends safe and quiet living with the advantages of a major cosmopolitan city. The warm community environment provides an ideal place to study and live.

Lawrence Academy offers a progressive student-centered curriculum. Traditional teaching is enhanced with seminars, group projects and independent study to train students' intellectual skills actively. More than seventy-five computers are distributed throughout the school to integrate technology into classes on a daily basis. A brand new academic center opened in 2005.

Two special programs complement classroom study: Winterim, a two week mini-term of special projects and trips, and the Independent Immersion Program (IIP), a program which qualifies students to design their own one or two year course of study.

A brand new Arts Center contains spacious studios for drawing, painting, ceramics, dance, music and computerized music. The recording studio allows students to mix and record their own CD's. The drama department produces three main stage productions per year and smaller productions in the black box theatre.

Athletic training is provided for all skill levels. Basic instruction is offered with some players progressing to division one, Olympic, and professional competition. A new sports complex, ice rink and 14 acres of playing fields support the schools athletic program.

THE MACDUFFIE SCHOOL
One Ames Hill Drive, Springfield MA 01105-1400
Linda Keating, Director of Admissions
413-734-4971 Fax: 413-734-6693
Website: www.macduffie.com
E-mail: admissions@macduffie.com
Established 1890. Private. Coed. College Preparatory, Grades 6 - 12. Accreditation: NEASC. Tuition: $16,795 - $17,775. Room and board: $12,250. Cultural Activities Fee: $850. Enrollment: 225. Faculty: 36. Student-Faculty Ratio: 6:1. Library: 8,000 volumes. Outstanding academic preparation, full arts program, competitive athletics. Ames Hill Boarding Program: small boarding component for grades 9-12. Students live with faculty families in stately homes on a 20-acre residential campus.

Middlesex School
PO Box 9122, Concord MA 01742-9122
978-369-2550

Milton Academy
170 Centre St, Milton MA 02186-3397
Paul Rebuck, Dean of Admission
617-898-2227

NOBLE AND GREENOUGH SCHOOL
10 Campus Dr, Dedham MA 02026-4099
Jennifer Hines, Dean of Enrollment Management
781-326-3700 Fax: 781-320-1329
Website: www.nobles.edu
E-mail: admission@nobles.edu

Northfield Mt. Hermon School
206 Main St, Northfield MA 01360-1089
Richard Mueller, Head
Pamela Safford, Director of Admissions
413-498-3227

PHILLIPS ACADEMY
180 Main St, Andover MA 01810-4161
Jane F. Fried, Dean of Admission
978-749-4050 Fax: 978-749-4068
Website: www.andover.edu
E-mail: admissions@andover.edu

ST. MARK'S SCHOOL
PO Box 9105, Southborough MA 01772-9105
Anne Behnke, Director of Admission
508-786-6000 Fax: 508-786-6120
Website: www.stmarksschool.org
E-mail: admission@stmarksschool.org

Tabor Academy
66 Spring St, Marion MA 02738-1581
508-748-2000

Walnut Hill School
12 Highland St, Natick MA 01760-2199
508-653-4312

WILBRAHAM & MONSON ACADEMY
423 Main St, Wilbraham MA 01095-1715
Christopher Moore, Director of Admission
John Boozang, Associate Director
413-596-6811 Fax: 413-596-2448
Website: www.wmacademy.org
E-mail: cmoore@wmanet.org

Williston Northampton School
19 Payson Ave, Easthampton MA 01027-2246
Brian Wright, Headmaster
413-529-3241 Fax: 413-527-9494
Website: www.williston.com
E-mail: admission@williston.com

WINCHENDON SCHOOL
172 Ash St, Winchendon MA 01475-1700
J. William LaBelle, Headmaster
800-622-1119 Fax: 978-297-0911
Website: www.winchendon.org
E-mail: admissions@winchendon.org

WORCESTER ACADEMY
81 Providence St, Worcester MA 01604-4299
Jonathan G. Baker, Director of Admission & Financial Aid
508-754-5302 Fax: 508-752-2382
Website: www.worcesteracademy.org
E-mail: admission@worcesteracademy.org

MICHIGAN

Cranbrook Schools
PO Box 801, Bloomfield Hills MI 48303-0801
D. Scott Looney, Director of Admissions
248-645-3300

Detroit Country Day School
22305 W 13 Mile Rd, Beverly Hills MI 48025-4435
Jorge Prosperi, Director of Admissions
248-646-7717

Interlochen Arts Academy
PO Box 199, Interlochen MI 49643-0199
231-276-7472
Website: www.interlochen.org
E-mail: admissions@interlochen.org

The Leelanau School
1 Old Homestead Rd, Glen Arbor MI 49636-9720
Heather M. Sack, Director of Admission
231-334-5800

MINNESOTA

St. Croix Lutheran High School
1200 Oakdale Ave, West Saint Paul MN 55118-2699
651-455-1521

St. John's Preparatory School
PO Box 4000, Collegeville MN 56321-4000
320-363-3315

SHATTUCK-ST. MARY'S SCHOOL
PO Box 218, Faribault MN 55021-0218
Amy D. Wolf, Director of Admissions
507-333-1618 Fax: 507-333-1661
Website: www.s-sm.org
E-mail: admissions@s-sm.org
Established 1858. Private. Coed. Accreditation: ISACS. Boarding tuition: $29,900, Day tuition: $19,600. Enrollment: 335. Faculty: 52. Average class size: 12 students. Degrees: High School Diploma. 250 acre campus, located 45 minutes south of Minneapolis/St. Paul. Grades 6-12. Students from 27 states and 15 countries. Advanced Placement courses in every discipline. Award winning choir, orchestra, dance, and drama programs. Campus facilities include 18 hole golf course, 2 ice arenas, indoor domed soccer field.

MISSISSIPPI

All Saints' Episcopal School
2717 Confederate Ave, Vicksburg MS 39180-5173
The Rev. William V. Martin, Rector and Head
601-636-5266

Bass Memorial Academy
6433 U S Highway 11, Lumberton MS 39455-7504
601-794-8561

Piney Woods School
5096 Highway 49 S, Piney Woods MS 39148
Dexter D. Whitley, Director of Student Support Services
601-845-2214

MISSOURI

Principia School
13201 Clayton Rd, Saint Louis MO 63131-1002
314-434-2100

Saint Paul Lutheran High School
PO Box 719, Concordia MO 64020-0719
Gloria Burrow, Director of Recruitment
660-463-2238

Thomas Jefferson School
4100 S Lindbergh Blvd, Saint Louis MO 63127-1698
Marie DeJesus, Director of Admissions
314-843-4151

WENTWORTH MILITARY ACADEMY & JUNIOR COLLEGE
1880 Washington Ave, Lexington MO 64067
MAJ Mike Herman, Director of Admissions
800-962-7682 or 660-259-2221 Fax: 660-259-2677
Website: www.wma.edu, wjc.wma.edu
E-mail: admissions@wma1880.org
Established 1880. Non-denominational. Accreditation: NCA, the Higher Learning Commission of the NCA and the State of Missouri. Enrollment: 200-250 boarding students, 300 FTE non-boarding students. Currently accepts young men grades 9-14, young women grades 9-14. Dorms are single gender by floor. Tuition, room, board and fees for boarding students for the 2005/2006 are $25,990. Financial assistance is available. ROTC scholarships available for eligible junior college students.

Wentworth has three academic divisions: High School, military junior college (MJC) and community JC (CJC). HS provides a college preparatory diploma requiring 26 credits in language arts, math, science, social studies and electives. The co-location of the JC allows HS Students to dual enroll in college classes and receive joint credit for HS and College. Community service is a graduation requirement. MJC offers an AA degree. Early Commissioning Program allows eligible ROTC cadets to earn Army commission in 2 years. Four-year ROTC scholarship also offered, with follow-on at an approved 4-year college or university. CJC offers AA and AS degrees at Lexington campus and three satellites: Sheldon, Hermitage and Cameron.

Please see website for admissions requirements. Open enrollment in the HS allows students to enroll throughout most of the academic year. The HS operates on a two-semester calendar, with grades reported every three weeks. A five-week summer academic session with college dual enrollment courses is also offered. The JC operates on the semester system. Students may choose to enroll in either eight or sixteen-week classes during each semester.

The Academy prides itself on offering a quality education in a safe, structured small-town environment, with small class sizes and individualized attention. It challenges its students academically, physically and morally-spiritually and emphasizes leadership and service. Students must abide by an Honor Code. The historic 137-acre campus is 40 miles from Kansas City, allowing students access to big-city cultural and entertainment amenities.

MONTANA

Headwaters Academy
418 W Garfield St, Bozeman MT 59715-5545
406-585-9997

LUSTRE CHRISTIAN HIGH SCHOOL
HC 66 Box 57, Lustre MT 59225-9705
Al Leland, Supervising Teacher
406-392-5735 Fax: 406-392-5765
Website: www.lustrechristian.com
E-mail: 2lchs@nemontel.net
Established 1928. Private. Coed. Accreditation: ACSI, Montana Office of Public Instruction. Tuition: $1,000. Room & board: $2,535. Fees: $107. Enrollment: 26. Faculty: 6. Student-faculty ratio: 5:1. High school diploma offered. 5 buildings on 37 acres. Specializing in college prep yet sucessfully works with struggling students. A

modern dormitory houses out of state students. Offers a variety of extra curricular activities. Located in N.E. Montana in a rural setting. Evangelical Fundamental spiritual basis.

NEBRASKA

Platte Valley Academy
19338 W Campus Dr, Shelton NE 68876-9617
308-647-5151

NEW HAMPSHIRE

Brewster Academy
80 Academy Dr, Wolfeboro NH 03894-4128
603-569-1600

Dublin Christian Academy
PO Box 521, Dublin NH 03444-0521
603-563-8505

DUBLIN SCHOOL
PO Box 522, Dublin NH 03444-0522
Marylou T. Marcus, Director of Admission
603-563-8584 Fax: 603-563-7121
Website: www.dublinschool.org
E-mail: admission@dublinschool.org

HIGH MOWING SCHOOL-A WALDORF HIGH SCHOOL
222 Isaac Frye Hwy, Wilton NH 03086
Sam Rosario, Director of Admissions
603-654-2391 Fax: 603-654-6588
Website: www.highmowing.org
E-mail: admissions@highmowing.org

HOLDERNESS SCHOOL
PO Box 1879, Plymouth NH 03264-1879
Nancy Dalley, Admissions Administrator
603-536-1257 Fax: 603-536-1267
Website: www.holderness.org
E-mail: admissions@holderness.org

KIMBALL UNION ACADEMY
PO Box 188, Meriden NH 03770-0188
Rachel G. Tilney, Director of Admissions
603-469-2100 Fax: 603-469-2041
Website: www.kua.org
E-mail: admissions@kua.org

MEETING SCHOOL
120 Thomas Rd, Rindge NH 03461
Jacqueline Stillwell, Head of School
603-899-3366 Fax: 603-899-6216
Website: www.meetingschool.org
E-mail: office@meetingschool.org

NEW HAMPTON SCHOOL
PO Box 579, New Hampton NH 03256-0579
Dean of Admission
603-677-3401 Fax: 603-677-3481
Website: www.newhampton.org
E-mail: admissions@newhampton.org

Educating young people differently. Following a nationally acclaimed model for experience-based education, our students and adults work alongside each other to create a dynamic learning community marked by non-hierarchical relationships, mutual respect, and intentional responsibility. Our beautiful and well-equipped campus "village" is home to comprehensive, integrated- and life-changing-programs in academics, arts, athletics, adventure education, and community service/action. We care about college prep and campus life, a code of behavior rather than a code of dress. Come visit!

PHILLIPS EXETER ACADEMY
20 Main St, Exeter NH 03833-2460
Dr. Tyler C. Tingley, Principal
Michael Gary, Director of Admissions
603-777-3437 Fax: 603-777-4399
Website: www.exeter.edu
E-mail: admit@exeter.edu

Founded in 1781, Phillips Exeter Academy is well known for originating the Harkness teaching method whereby students and a teacher join in seminar style classes around an oval Harkness Table. Small classes and over 350 courses are offered to students who hail from 43 states and 28 foreign countries. Over $10 million in financial aid supports 39% of Exeter's students. A $757 million endowment supports Exeter's commitment to rigorous academics, an exceptional faculty, a diverse student body, a wide variety of co-curricular opportunities, and state-of-the-art resources.

Proctor Academy
PO Box 500, Andover NH 03216-0500
Michele E. Koenig, Director of Admission
603-735-6000

ST. PAUL'S SCHOOL
325 Pleasant St, Concord NH 03301-2591
Michael Hirschfeld, Director of Admissions
603-229-4700 Fax: 603-229-4771
Website: www.sps.edu
E-mail: admissions@sps.edu

TILTON SCHOOL
30 School St, Tilton NH 03276-5771
Katherine E. Saunders, Director of Admission
603-286-1733 Fax: 603-286-1705
Website: www.tiltonschool.org
E-mail: admissions@tiltonschool.org

Tilton School is an independent, coeducational, boarding and day school in Tilton, NH serving students in grades 9 through 12 and post-graduates. The school's curricular model stresses the acquisition of skills such as analytical thinking, problem solving, time management, collaboration, creativity, leadership, communication and adaptability. Tilton School challenges students to embrace and navigate a world marked by diversity and change. Through the quality of human relationships, Tilton School's faculty cultivates in its students the curiosity, the skills, the knowledge and understanding, the character and the integrity requisite for the passionate pursuit of lifelong personal success and service.

WHITE MOUNTAIN SCHOOL
371 W Farm Rd, Bethlehem NH 03574-5851
Amy Broberg, Director of Admission
603-444-2928 Fax: 603-444-5568
Website: www.whitemountain.org
E-mail: admissions@whitemountain.org

NEW JERSEY

BLAIR ACADEMY
PO Box 600, Blairstown NJ 07825-0600
T. Chandler Hardwick III, Headmaster
Barbara H. Haase, Dean of Admissions
800-462-5247 or 908-362-2024 Fax: 908-362-7975
Website: www.blair.edu
E-mail: admissions@blair.edu

Established 1848. Private. Coed. Accreditation: MSACS. Tuition, room & board: $35,000 (boarding)/$26,000 (day). Enrollment: 434. Faculty: 78. Student-faculty ratio: 6:1. Library: 22,000 volumes. 54 buildings on 315 acres. Blair's strong academic program offers Advanced Placement, Honors, and Independent Study courses. Other offerings of note: college level lecture series; dual student advisor system; SAT preparation. Blair has a competitive sports program and offers an extensive range of extracurricular activities.

HUN SCHOOL OF PRINCETON
176 Edgerstoune Rd, Princeton NJ 08540-6778
James M. Byer, Headmaster
609-921-7600 Fax: 609-279-9398
Website: www.hunschool.org
E-mail: admiss@hunschool.org

THE LAWRENCEVILLE SCHOOL
PO Box 6008, Lawrenceville NJ 08648-0008
Elizabeth A. Duffy, Head Master
Gregg Maloberti, Dean of Admissions
800-735-2030 or 609-895-2030 Fax: 609-895-2217
Website: www.lawrenceville.org
E-mail: admissions@lawrenceville.org

Established 1810. Coed. Accreditation: NAIS, NJAIS. Tuition: $37,660 boarding, $30,010 day. Est. extra expenses: $500. Enrollment: 541 boarding, 266 day. Faculty: 135. Degree: high school diploma. Library: 100,000 volumes. 31 major buildings on 500 acres. Gym. Pool. Hockey rink. Golf course. Rigorous academic. "English Plan" house system. Harkness Plan round-table teaching. Advanced placement. Near Princeton.

PEDDIE SCHOOL
PO Box A, Hightstown NJ 08520-1010
John F. Green, Head
Raymond H. Cabot, Director of Admission
609-490-7501 Fax: 609-944-7901
Website: www.peddie.org
E-mail: admission@peddie.org

Established 1864. Coed. Accreditation: MSACS, NAIS, NJAIS. Tuition: $35,500 (boarding), $26,900 (day). Enrollment: 341 boarding, 198 day. Faculty: 91. 22 buildings on 230 acres surrounding Peddie Lake. Small classes. Laptop computers provided to all students. Outstanding faculty and diverse student body. Over $4.7 million in financial aid supports 41% of student body. Campus-wide computer network/internet. Art center. Theatre. Athletic center. Pool. 18 hole golf course. Rigorous academics. College counseling. Advanced placement. Near Princeton, NYC, and Philadelphia.

PENNINGTON SCHOOL
112 W Delaware Ave, Pennington NJ 08534-1616
Diane P. Monteleone, Director of Admission
609-737-6128 Fax: 609-730-1405
Website: www.pennington.org
E-mail: admiss@pennington.org

Founded in 1838, Co-ed, day and boarding, grades 6-12, boarding starts in 7th. Enrollment: 465. Tuition 2006-2007: $35,800 boarding, $24,000 day. The school intentionally seeks a diverse student population and proves a range of academic and extracurricular offerings to develop the gifts of each of its students. AP and Honors courses as well as academic support classes are available. A comprehensive ESL program is offered for international students, as is a Center for Learning for bright students with diagnosed language-based learning disabilities.

NEW MEXICO

Hammer United World College
PO Box 248, Montezuma NM 87731-0248
Tim Smith, Director of Admission
505-454-4200

The Menaul School
301 Menaul Blvd NE, Albuquerque NM 87107-1527
505-345-7727

NEW MEXICO MILITARY INSTITUTE
101 W College Ave, Roswell NM 88201-5173
Rear Admiral David R. Ellison, USN (Ret.), Superintendent
LTC. Craig Collins, Director of Admissions
800-421-5376 or 505-624-8050 Fax: 505-624-8058
Website: www.nmmi.edu
E-mail: admissions@nmmi.edu

Established 1891. Public. Coed. Accreditation: NCACS, New Mexico Department of Education. Estimated costs for 2004-2005 school year, out-of-state student: $10,166, in-state student: $7,670. Enrollment: 950. Faculty: 68. Student-faculty ratio: 18:1. Degree: AA. Library: 68,000 volumes. 19 buildings on 40 acre main campus. Additional acreage includes an 18-hole championship golf course. Challenging college preparatory high curriculum with 98% of our graduates continuing on to four-year colleges and universities. Modern campus with state of the art computer and athletic facilities. Modern rooms equipped with Internet, phones, and television. NMMI offers the best value in military boarding education in the country.

NEW YORK

Cascadilla Prep School
116 Summit Ave, Ithaca NY 14850-4734
John Kendall, Headmaster
607-272-3110

Darrow School
110 Darrow Rd, New Lebanon NY 12125-2608
518-794-6000

Hackley School
293 Benedict Ave, Tarrytown NY 10591-4395
914-631-0128

Harvey School
260 Jay St, Katonah NY 10536-3707
Ronald Romanowicz, Director of Admissions
914-232-3161

The Hewlett School of East Islip
52 Suffolk Ln, East Islip NY 11730
631-581-1035

HOOSAC SCHOOL
PO Box 9, Hoosick NY 12089-0009
Dean S. Foster, Assistant Headmaster
800-822-0159 Fax: 518-686-3370
Website: www.hoosac.com
E-mail: info@hoosac.com

Houghton Academy
9790 Thayer St, Houghton NY 14744-8712
585-567-8115

Keio Academy of New York
3 College Rd, Purchase NY 10577-2108
914-694-4825

Kildonan School
425 Morse Hill Rd, Amenia NY 12501
845-373-8111

KNOX SCHOOL
541 Long Beach Rd, Saint James NY 11780-9735
Meredith Stanley, Director of Admissions
631-686-1600 Fax: 631-686-1650
Website: www.knoxschool.org
E-mail: mstanley@knoxschool.org

THE MASTERS SCHOOL
49 Clinton Ave, Dobbs Ferry NY 10522-2201
Lindsay C. Murphy, Director of Admission
914-479-6420 Fax: 914-693-7295
Website: www.themastersschool.com
E-mail: admission@themastersschool.com

Millbrook School
School Rd, Millbrook NY 12545
Cynthia S. McWilliams, Director of Admissions
845-677-6873

National Sports Academy
821 Mirror Lake Dr, Lake Placid NY 12946
518-523-3460

NEW YORK MILITARY ACADEMY
78 Academy Ave
Cornwall on Hudson NY 12520-1325
CAPT Robert D. Watts, USN (Ret.), Superintendent
Maureen T. Kelly, Director of Admissions
888-ASK-NYMA (275-6962) Fax: 845-534-7699
Website: www.nyma.org
E-mail: admissions@nyma.ouboces.org

Day & Boarding grades: 7-12. Enrollment: 270 Boarding, 20 Day. Accredited MSACS. Expenses $28,900 (includes Tuition, Room, Board & Uniforms). Founded in 1889, the Academy is an independent, coeducational boarding and day school. A challenging college preparatory education in a structured environment is complemented by small classes, an accessible and caring faculty, daily tutorials, supervised study periods, interscholastic sports and leadership development through our Junior Army ROTC program. Each provides an opportunity for young men and women to realize their potential. English as a Second Language, SAT prep, college counseling/placement, mentoring program, marching band, drill team, honor guard and equitation. The campus-wide computer network provides cadets with individual dormitory room connections for Internet, e-mail and telephones with voicemail. Summer programs available.

NORTH COUNTRY SCHOOL
PO Box 187, Lake Placid NY 12946-0187
Christine LeFevre, Admissions Director
518-523-9329 Fax: 518-523-4858
Website: www.nct.org
E-mail: admissions@nct.org

NORTHWOOD SCHOOL
PO Box 1070, Lake Placid NY 12946-5070
Timothy Weaver, Director of Admissions
518-523-3382 Fax: 518-523-3405
Website: www.northwoodschool.com
E-mail: admissions@northwoodschool.com

Oakwood Friends School
22 Spackenkill Rd, Poughkeepsie NY 12603
845-462-4200

Redemption Christian Academy
Boarding and Post Graduate School
192 9th St, Troy NY 12180
Ms. Frances Grimes, Director of Admissions
518-272-6679

Stony Brook School
1 Chapman Pkwy, Stony Brook NY 11790-1704
631-751-1800

THE STORM KING SCHOOL
314 Mountain Rd
Cornwall on Hudson NY 12520-1899
845-534-9860 Fax: 845-534-4128
Website: www.sks.org
E-mail: admissions@sks.org

Union Springs Academy
PO Box 524, Union Springs NY 13160-0524
Robert Raney, Admissions Director
315-889-7314

NORTH CAROLINA

Asheville School
360 Asheville School Rd, Asheville NC 28806-1571
William S. Peebles, Headmaster
Charles D. Buldecchi, Director of Admission
828-254-6345

Oak Ridge Military Academy
PO Box 498, Oak Ridge NC 27310-0498
Lieutenant Colonel Ray Wilson, Vice President for Admissions
336-643-4131 ext. 132

THE PATTERSON SCHOOL

PO Box 500, Patterson NC 28661-0500
Colin Stevens, Headmaster
828-758-2374 Fax: 828-758-9179
Website: www.pattersonschool.org
E-mail: admissions@pattersonschool.org

NORTH DAKOTA

Oak Grove Lutheran School
124 N Terrace N, Fargo ND 58102-3899
Rachel Mathson, Director of Admissions
701-237-0212 Fax: 701-237-4217
Website: www.oakgrovelutheran.com
E-mail: oakgrove.lutheranschool@sendit.nodak.edu

OHIO

Central Christian School
PO Box 9, Kidron OH 44636-0009
Barbara Reinford, Director of Development
330-857-7311

Gilmour Academy
34001 Cedar Rd, Gates Mills OH 44040-9356
440-473-8090

Notre Dame-Cathedral Latin School
13000 Auburn Rd, Chardon OH 44024-9330
440-286-6226

OLNEY FRIENDS SCHOOL

61830 Sandy Ridge Rd, Barnesville OH 43713-9404
Meg Short, Director of Admissions
740-425-3655 Fax: 740-425-3202
Website: www.olneyfriends.org
E-mail: admissions@olneyfriends.org

WESTERN RESERVE ACADEMY

115 College St, Hudson OH 44236-2999
Barbara A. Flanagan, Dean of Admission
330-650-9717 Fax: 330-650-5858
Website: www.wra.net
E-mail: admission@wra.net

OREGON

The Delphian School
20950 SW Rock Creek Rd, Sheridan OR 97378-9740
Donetta Phelps, Director of Admissions
800-626-6610

Milo Adventist Academy
PO Box 278, Days Creek OR 97429-0278
Steve Rae, Admissions & Marketing
541-825-3200

Oregon Episcopal School
6300 SW Nicol Rd, Portland OR 97223-7599
Dr. Dulany O. Bennett, Head of School
503-246-7771

PENNSYLVANIA

GEORGE SCHOOL

PO Box 4460, Newtown PA 18940
Karen S. Hallowell, Contact
215-579-6547 Fax: 215-579-6549
Website: www.georgeschool.org
E-mail: admissions@georgeschool.org

Girard College School
2101 S College Ave, Philadelphia PA 19121
215-787-2600

THE HILL SCHOOL

717 E High St, Pottstown PA 19464-5791
Sally Keidel, Director of Admission & Enrollment Management
610-326-1000 Fax: 610-705-1753
Website: www.thehill.org
E-mail: admission@thehill.org
　　Established 1851. Boys & girls, boarding and day. Enrollment: 485, grades 9-12/PG. Tuition: $34,300 boarding, $23,300 day. College prep. for 154 years, the Hill School has provided an education that addresses the whole person. We're proud of our reputation for inspiring growth on three levels: the mind, the body, and the spirit. Hill students get a solid liberal arts education, fully integrated with lessons in honesty, discipline, and compassion. Our boarding environment teaches tolerance and respect for others, breeding friendships that last a lifetime. Our form system fosters leadership. Our athletic fields and art center encourage students to push themselves beyond their limits. Parents or alumni will tell you the same thing: The Hill prepares students to master the challenges of life.

MERCERSBURG ACADEMY

300 E Seminary St, Mercersburg PA 17236
Douglas Hale, Head of School
Christopher R. Tompkins, Dir. of Admission & Financial Aid
717-328-6173 Fax: 717-328-6319
Website: www.mercersburg.edu
E-mail: admission@mercersburg.edu

Milton Hershey School
PO Box 830, Hershey PA 17033-0830
Dr. William L. Lepley, President & CEO
Dan Warner, Senior Officer, Admissions
800-322-3248

MMI PREPARATORY SCHOOL

154 Centre St, Freeland PA 18224
William A. Shergalis, Ph.D., President
570-636-1108 Fax: 570-636-0742
Website: www.mmiprep.org
E-mail: mmi@mmiprep.org

Moravian Academy
4313 Green Pond Rd, Bethlehem PA 18020-9770
610-691-1600

Perkiomen School
PO Box 130, Pennsburg PA 18073-0130
215-679-9511

Pine Forge Academy
PO Box 338, Pine Forge PA 19548-0338
610-326-5800

SHADY SIDE ACADEMY

423 Fox Chapel Rd, Pittsburgh PA 15238-2296
Katherine H. Mihm, Director of Admission
412-968-3180 Fax: 412-968-3213
Website: www.shadysideacademy.org
E-mail: kmihm@shadysideacademy.org

Solebury School
6832 Phillips Mill Rd, New Hope PA 18938
215-862-5261

WESTTOWN SCHOOL

PO Box 1799, Westtown PA 19395-1799
Kate Holz, Director of Admissions
610-399-7900 Fax: 610-399-7909
Website: www.westtown.edu
E-mail: admissions@westtown.edu

WYOMING SEMINARY

201 N Sprague Ave, Kingston PA 18704-3593
Randolph I. Granger, Director of Admission
570-270-2160 Fax: 570-270-2191
Website: www.wyomingseminary.org
E-mail: admission@wyomingseminary.org

RHODE ISLAND

MOSES BROWN SCHOOL

250 Lloyd Ave, Providence RI 02906-2398
Evelyn Ranone, Dean of Upper & Middle School Admissions
401-831-7373 Fax: 401-455-0084
Website: www.mosesbrown.org
E-mail: admissions@mosesbrown.org

Portsmouth Abbey School
285 Corys Ln, Portsmouth RI 02871-1362
401-683-2005

ST. ANDREW'S SCHOOL

63 Federal Rd, Barrington RI 02806-2425
John D. Martin, Head Master
R. Scott Telford, Director of Admissions
401-246-1230 Fax: 401-246-0510
Website: www.standrews-ri.org
E-mail: admissions@standrews-ri.org
　　Established 1893. Independent. Coed. Accreditation: NEASC, NAIS, State of Rhode Island. Day students: $21,075. boarding students: $33,600. Enrollment 204. Faculty: 41. Student-faculty ratio: 5:1. High School diploma offered. Library: 10,000 volumes. 31 buildings on 85 acres. St. Andrew's School college prep program offers small classes (usually 8-12), a great deal of individual attention from teachers and advisors, and a structured environment for students with average to high average ability. In 2002, St. Andrew's was named an "Exemplary School" by learning expert Dr. Mel Levine, whose 25+ years research on learning and groundbreaking program, Schools Attuned, are the backbone of our faculty's classroom methodology. Additionally, our programs for students with mild language-based learning disabilities and/or attentional issues are well regarded and successful. We search for students of good character who need academic attention, structure, and skill building.

St. George's School
372 Purgatory Rd, Middletown RI 02842
401-847-7565

SOUTH CAROLINA

Aiken Preparatory School
619 Barnwell Ave NW, Aiken SC 29801-6901
803-648-3223

Ben Lippen Schools
PO Box 3999, Columbia SC 29230-3999
Kay Perricelli, Admissions
803-786-7200

Bob Jones Academy
1700 Wade Hampton Blvd
Greenville SC 29614-1000
Stephen Jones III, President
David Christ, Director of Admissions
800-BJ-AND-ME Fax: 800-2FAX-BJU
Website: www.bju.edu
E-mail: admissions@bju.edu

SOUTH DAKOTA

Sunshine Bible Academy
400 Sunshine Dr, Miller SD 57362-6821
Gordon R. Werkema, Superintendent
605-853-3071

TENNESSEE

Baylor School
171 Baylor School Rd, Chattanooga TN 37405
423-267-8505

THE KING'S ACADEMY

202 Smothers Rd, Seymour TN 37865-5056
Janice Mink, Director of Admissions
865-573-8321 Fax: 865-573-8323
Website: www.thekingsacademy.net
E-mail: jmink@thekingsacademy.net

LAUSANNE COLLEGIATE SCHOOL

1381 W Massey Rd, Memphis TN 38120-3206
Molly B. Cook, Director of Admissions
901-474-1000 Fax: 901-474-1010
Website: www.lausanneschool.com
E-mail: mcook@lausanneschool.com

St. Andrew's-Sewanee School
290 Quintard Rd, Sewanee TN 37375-3000
931-598-5651

THE WEBB SCHOOL

PO Box 488, Bell Buckle TN 37020-0488
Matt Anderson, Director of Operations in Admissions
931-389-6003 Fax: 931-389-6657
Website: www.thewebbschool.com
E-mail: admissions@webbschool.com

TEXAS

ALLEN ACADEMY

3201 Boonville Rd, Bryan TX 77802
Camilla Viator, Director of Admissions
979-776-0731 Fax: 979-774-7769
Website: www.allenacademy.org
E-mail: cviator@allenacademy.org

Incarnate Word High School
727 E Hildebrand Ave, San Antonio TX 78212-2598
210-829-3100

MEMORIAL HALL SCHOOL

3721 Dacoma St, Houston TX 77092-8905
Rev. George Aurich, Headmaster
713-688-5566 Fax: 713-956-9751
Website: www.memorialhall.org
E-mail: memhallsch@aol.com

Presbyterian Pan American School
PO Box 1578, Kingsville TX 78364-1578
Barbara A. Chamness, Development Director
361-592-4307

SAINT MARY'S HALL

9401 Starcrest Dr, San Antonio TX 78217-4199
Elena D. Hicks, Director of Admission
210-483-9234 Fax: 210-655-5211
Website: www.smhall.org
E-mail: admissions@smhall.org

ST. STEPHEN'S EPISCOPAL SCHOOL

2900 Bunny Run, Austin TX 78746
Lawrence Sampleton, Director of Admission
512-327-1213 Fax: 512-327-6771
Website: www.sstx.org
E-mail: admission@sstx.org

San Marcos Baptist Academy
2801 Ranch Road 12, San Marcos TX 78666-9406
Jeffrey D. Baergen, Director of Admissions
800-428-5120

TMI - THE EPISCOPAL SCHOOL OF TEXAS

20955 W Tejas Trl, San Antonio TX 78257-1604
Cindy Schneid, Director of Admission
210-698-7171 Fax: 210-698-0715
Website: www.tmi-sa.org
E-mail: admission@tmi-sa.org

UTAH

WASATCH ACADEMY

120 S 100 W, Mount Pleasant UT 84647-1509
Kim Stephens, Director of Admissions
800-634-4690 Fax: 435-462-1450
Website: www.wacad.org
E-mail: admissions@wacad.org

VERMONT

Burke Mountain Academy
PO Box 78, East Burke VT 05832-0078
802-626-1516 ext. 1503

Burr and Burton Academy
PO Box 498, Manchester VT 05254-0498
802-362-1775

Green Mountain Valley School
271 Moulton Rd, Waitsfield VT 05673
802-496-2150

LONG TRAIL SCHOOL

1045 Kirby Hollow Rd, Dorset VT 05251-9776
Courtney M. Callo, Director of Admissions & Outreach
802-867-5717 Fax: 802-867-4525
Website: www.longtrailschool.org
E-mail: applylts@longtrailschool.org

LYNDON INSTITUTE

PO Box 127, Lyndon Center VT 05850-0127
Mary Thomas, Assistant Head for Admissions
802-626-5232 Fax: 802-626-6138
Website: www.lyndoninstitute.org
E-mail: admissions@lyndoninstitute.org

Pine Ridge School
9505 Williston Rd, Williston VT 05495-9598
Joshua Doyle, Director of Admissions
802-434-2161

Putney School
418 Houghton Brook Rd, Putney VT 05346
802-387-5566

Rock Point School
1 Rock Point Rd, Burlington VT 05408-2736
802-863-1104

St. Johnsbury Academy
PO Box 906, Saint Johnsbury VT 05819
John J. Cummings, Director of Admissions
802-748-8171

Stratton Mountain School
7 World Cup Circle, Stratton Mountain VT 05155
802-297-1886

VERMONT ACADEMY
PO Box 500, Saxtons River VT 05154-0500
William Newman, Dean of Admissions
802-869-6229 Fax: 802-869-6242
Website: www.vermontacademy.org
E-mail: admissions@vermontacademy.org

VIRGINIA
Eastern Mennonite High School
801 Parkwood Dr, Harrisonburg VA 22802-2416
Jean S. Fisher, Admissions
540-432-4521

Episcopal High School
1200 N Quaker Ln, Alexandria VA 22302-3000
Douglas C. Price, Director of Admissions
703-933-4062 Fax: 703-933-3016
Website: www.episcopalhighschool.org
E-mail: admissions@episcopalhighschool.org

MASSANUTTEN MILITARY ACADEMY
614 S Main St, Woodstock VA 22664-1205
Murali Sinnathamby, Director of Admissions
877-466-6222 or 540-459-2167 Fax: 540-459-5421
Website: www.militaryschool.com
E-mail: admissions@militaryschool.com

Miller School of Albemarle
1000 Samuel Miller Loop
Charlottesville VA 22903-7527
Jay Reeves, Director of Admissions
434-823-4805

NOTRE DAME ACADEMY
35321 Notre Dame Ln, Middleburg VA 20117-3621
Mrs. Cathy Struder, Director of Admission
540-687-5581 Fax: 540-687-3552
Website: www.notredameva.org
E-mail: cstruder@notredameva.org

OAK HILL ACADEMY
2635 Oak Hill Rd, Mouth of Wilson VA 24363-3004
Dr. Michael D. Groves, President
276-579-2619 Fax: 276-579-4722
Website: www.oak-hill.net
E-mail: info@oak-hill.net
    Established 1878. Private. College Preparatory. Boarding for grades 8-12. Accreditation: VAIS. Tuition, room, board, and spending money: $21,350. Enrollment: 130. Faculty: 17. Student-teacher ratio: 10:1. Library: 6,000 volumes. Regular and advanced diplomas. Dual-credit courses. 12 buildings on over 400 acres. Athletics and arts. 95% of our graduates go on to college. Beautiful mountain setting.

Randolph-Macon Academy
200 Academy Dr, Front Royal VA 22630-2692
Pia G. Crandell, Ph.D., Director of Admissions
800-272-1172

ST. ANNE'S-BELFIELD SCHOOL
2132 Ivy Rd, Charlottesville VA 22903-1785
Jean Craig, Director of Admissions
434-296-5106 Fax: 434-979-1486
Website: www.stab.org
E-mail: adm@stab.org

SHENANDOAH VALLEY ACADEMY
234 W Lee Hwy, New Market VA 22844-9558
Brian or Joi Becker, Enrollment Management
540-740-2210 Fax: 540-740-3336
Website: www.youracademy.org
E-mail: beckerb@sva-va.org

Stuart Hall
235 W Frederick St, Staunton VA 24401-3327
Stephanie Shafer, Dean of Admissions
888-306-8926

Tandem Friends School
279 Tandem Ln, Charlottesville VA 22902-7128
Tom O'Connor, Director of Admissions
434-296-1303

Virginia Episcopal School
PO Box 408, Lynchburg VA 24505-0408
Pamela Barile, Director of Admission
434-385-3607

WASHINGTON
AUBURN ADVENTIST ACADEMY
5000 Auburn Way S, Auburn WA 98092-7297
Steve Davis, Admissions Director
888-271-0808 or 253-939-5000 Fax: 253-351-9806
Website: www.auburn.org
E-mail: info@auburn.org

John F. Kennedy Memorial High School
140 S 140th St, Burien WA 98168
206-246-0500

NORTHWEST SCHOOL
1415 Summit Ave, Seattle WA 98122-3619
Anne Smith, Director of Admissions
206-682-7309 Fax: 206-467-7353
Website: www.northwestschool.org
E-mail: admission@northwestschool.org

Upper Columbia Academy
3025 E Spangle Waverly Rd
Spangle WA 99031-9799
509-245-3600

WEST VIRGINIA
Linsly School
60 Knox Ln, Wheeling WV 26003-6489
304-233-3260

WISCONSIN
Wayland Academy
101 N University Ave, Beaver Dam WI 53916-2253
Eric Peters, Dean of Admission and College Counseling
800-860-7725

GUAM
GUAM ADVENTIST ACADEMY
1200 Aguilar Rd, Yona GU 96915
John Youngberg, Principal
671-789-1515 Fax: 671-789-3547
Website: www.gaasda.org
E-mail: office@gaasda.org

PUERTO RICO
AMERICAN MILITARY ACADEMY
PO Box 7884, Guaynabo PR 00970-7884
Vivian Simonet, Superintendent
787-720-6801 Fax: 787-720-6841
Website: www.amapr.org
E-mail: vsimonet@amapr.org

: :PREPARATORY SCHOOLS FOR GIRLS

Primarily Boarding

ARKANSAS
MOUNT ST. MARY ACADEMY
3224 Kavanaugh Blvd, Little Rock AR 72205-1899
Rebecca Henle, Principal
501-664-8006 Fax: 501-666-4382
Website: www.mtstmary.edu
E-mail: bhenle@mtstmary.edu

CALIFORNIA
Flintridge Sacred Heart Academy
440 Saint Katherine Dr
La Canada Flintridge CA 91011-4198
Jan Price, Director of Admissions
626-685-8333

SAN DOMENICO SCHOOL
1500 Butterfield Rd, San Anselmo CA 94960-1099
Risa Oganesoff Heersche, Director of Upper School Admissions
415-258-1905 Fax: 415-258-1906
Website: www.sandomenico.org
E-mail: rheersche@sandomenico.org

SANTA CATALINA SCHOOL
1500 Mark Thomas Dr, Monterey CA 93940-5291
Louise B. Douglas, Director of Admission
831-655-9356 Fax: 831-655-7535
Website: www.santacatalina.org
E-mail: admissions@santacatalina.org

CONNECTICUT
ACADEMY OF THE HOLY FAMILY
PO Box 691, Baltic CT 06330-0691
Sister Mary Patrick, SCMC, Principal
860-822-9272 Fax: 860-822-1318
Website: www.academyoftheholyfamily.com
E-mail: academy.holy.family@snet.net

CONVENT OF THE SACRED HEART
1177 King St, Greenwich CT 06831-2998
Pamela McKenna, Director of Admissions
203-532-3534 Fax: 203-532-3301
Website: www.cshgreenwich.org
E-mail: admission@cshgreenwich.org

THE ETHEL WALKER SCHOOL
230 Bushy Hill Rd, Simsbury CT 06070-2698
Barbara Lundberg, Dean of Enrollment Management
860-408-4200 Fax: 860-408-4201
Website: www.ethelwalker.org
E-mail: admission_office@ethelwalker.org

Miss Porter's School
60 Main St, Farmington CT 06032-2288
860-409-3500

Westover School
PO Box 847, Middlebury CT 06762-0847
Ann S. Pollina, Head of School
203-758-2423

GEORGIA
Brenau Academy
One Centennial Cir, Gainesville GA 30501-3668
Dr. Frank M. Booth, Headmaster
770-534-6140

HAWAII
St. Francis High School
2707 Pamoa Rd, Honolulu HI 96822-1886
808-988-4111

ILLINOIS
Woodlands Academy of the Sacred Heart
760 E Westleigh Rd, Lake Forest IL 60045-3263
Kathleen Creed, Director of Admissions
847-234-4300

INDIANA
Howe Military School
5755 N State Road 9, Howe IN 46746
260-562-2131 ext. 221

IOWA
Ideal Girls School
1661 Highway 1, Fairfield IA 52556
641-472-7224

KANSAS
Mt. St. Scholastica Academy
1000 Green St, Atchison KS 66002-3079
Amy DuLac, Director of Admissions
913-367-1334

LOUISIANA
ACADEMY OF THE SACRED HEART
PO Box 310, Grand Coteau LA 70541-0310
D'Lane Wimberley, Director of Admission
337-662-5275 Fax: 337-662-3011
Website: www.ashcoteau.org
E-mail: admission@ashcoteau.org

MARYLAND
BRYN MAWR SCHOOL
109 W Melrose Ave, Baltimore MD 21210-1397
Maureen Walsh, Headmistress
410-323-8800 ext. 248 Fax: 410-435-4678
Website: www.brynmawrschool.org
E-mail: admissions@brynmawrschool.org

Garrison Forest School
300 Garrison Forest Rd
Owings Mills MD 21117-4064
410-363-1500

OLDFIELDS SCHOOL
1500 Glencoe Rd, Glencoe MD 21152
Kimberly C. Loughlin, Director of Admission
410-472-4800 Fax: 410-472-6839
Website: www.oldfieldsschool.org
E-mail: admissions@oldfieldsschool.org

ST. TIMOTHY'S SCHOOL
8400 Greenspring Ave, Stevenson MD 21153-0644
Randy Stevens, Head of School
410-486-7401 Fax: 410-486-1167
Website: www.sttims-school.org
E-mail: admis@sttims-school.org

MASSACHUSETTS
DANA HALL SCHOOL
45 Dana Rd
PO Box 9010, Wellesley MA 02482-9010
Heather Cameron, Director of Admissions/Financial Aid
781-235-3010 Fax: 781-235-0577
Website: www.danahall.org
E-mail: admission@danahall.org

MISS HALL'S SCHOOL
492 Holmes Rd, Pittsfield MA 01201-7196
Kimberly Boland, Director of Admission
413-499-1300 Fax: 413-448-2994
Website: www.misshalls.org
E-mail: info@misshalls.org

STONELEIGH-BURNHAM SCHOOL
574 Bernardston Rd, Greenfield MA 01301-1100
Sharon L. Pleasant, Director of Admissions
413-774-2711 Fax: 413-772-2602
Website: www.sbschool.org
E-mail: admissions@sbschool.org

NEW JERSEY
MOUNT SAINT MARY ACADEMY
1645 US Highway 22, Watchung NJ 07069-6587
Donna Venezia Toryak, Director of Admissions
908-757-0108 ext. 4506 Fax: 908-756-8085
Website: www.mountsaintmary.org
E-mail: dtoryak@mountsaintmary.org

PURNELL SCHOOL
PO Box 500 - 51 Pottersville Rd, Pottersville NJ 07979
Darlene Snell, Director of Admission
908-439-2154 Fax: 908-439-4088
Website: www.purnell.org
E-mail: info@purnell.org

NEW YORK
EMMA WILLARD SCHOOL
285 Pawling Ave, Troy NY 12180-5294
Kent H. Jones, Director of Enrollment
518-833-1320 Fax: 518-833-1805
Website: www.emmawillard.org
E-mail: admissions@emmawillard.org

NORTH CAROLINA
Oak Ridge Military Academy
PO Box 498, Oak Ridge NC 27310-0498
Lieutenant Colonel Ray Wilson, Vice President for Admissions
336-643-4131 ext. 132

SAINT MARY'S SCHOOL
900 Hillsborough St, Raleigh NC 27603-1689
Matthew R. Crane, Director of Admissions & Financial Aid
919-424-4100 or 800-948-2557 Fax: 919-424-4122
Website: www.saint-marys.edu
E-mail: admissions@saint-marys.edu

SALEM ACADEMY
500 E Salem Ave, Winston Salem NC 27101
Wayne Burkette, Head of School
336-721-2646 Fax: 336-917-5340
Website: www.salemacademy.com
E-mail: academy@salem.edu

OHIO
THE ANDREWS SCHOOL
38588 Mentor Ave, Willoughby OH 44094-7788
Kristina Dooley, Admission Director
440-942-3600 Fax: 440-954-5020
Website: www.andrews-school.org
E-mail: admissions@andrews-school.org

PENNSYLVANIA
Academy of the New Church Girls School
PO Box 707, Bryn Athyn PA 19009-0707
215-938-2595

Grier School
PO Box 308, Tyrone PA 16686-0308
Andrew Wilson, Director of Admissions
814-684-3000

LINDEN HALL
212 E Main St, Lititz PA 17543-2029
Kate R. Rill, Assistant Director of Admission
717-626-8512 Fax: 717-627-1384
Website: www.lindenhall.org
E-mail: admissions@lindenhall.org

TEXAS
Hockaday School
11600 Welch Rd, Dallas TX 75229-2999
214-363-6311

VIRGINIA
Chatham Hall
800 Chatham Hall Cir, Chatham VA 24531-3084
804-432-2941

FOXCROFT SCHOOL
PO Box 5555, Middleburg VA 20118-5555
Nicole Focareto, Director of Admission
540-687-4340 or 800-858-2364 Fax: 540-687-3627
Website: www.foxcroft.org
E-mail: admissions@foxcroft.org

Madeira School
8328 Georgetown Pike, Mc Lean VA 22102-1200
Meredith M. Cole, Director of Admissions
703-556-8200

St. Catherine's School
6001 Grove Ave, Richmond VA 23226-2600
Katherine S. Wallmeyer, Director of Admission
800-648-4982

St. Margaret's School
PO Box 158, Tappahannock VA 22560-0158
804-443-3357

WASHINGTON
Annie Wright School
827 Tacoma Ave N, Tacoma WA 98403-2899
Melinda Kinney, Director of Admission
253-272-2216

GUAM
Academy of Our Lady of Guam
233 Archbishop Felixberto C Flores St
Hagatna GU 96910-5102
Sister Francis Jerome Cruz, RSM, Principal
671-477-8203

PROTECTIVE SERVICES

ALABAMA
Bishop State Community College - Four Campuses
351 N Broad St, Mobile AL 36603-5898
Dr. Terry Hazzard, Dean of Students
251-690-6801 Fax: 251-690-6446
Website: www.bishop.edu
E-mail: thazzard@bishop.edu

Faulkner University
5345 Atlanta Hwy, Montgomery AL 36109-3398
Keith Mock, Director of Admissions
800-879-9816 ext. 7200 or 334-386-7200
Fax: 334-386-7137
Website: www.faulkner.edu
E-mail: admissions@faulkner.edu

University of South Alabama
307 University Blvd N, Mobile AL 36688-3053
Melissa Haab, Director of Admissions
251-460-6141 Fax: 251-460-7876
Website: www.southalabama.edu
E-mail: admiss@usouthal.edu

ALASKA
University of Alaska Southeast
11120 Glacier Hwy, Juneau AK 99801-8625
Paul Kraft, Dean of Students/Enrollment Management
907-796-6000 Fax: 907-796-6005
Website: www.uas.alaska.edu
E-mail: paul.kraft@uas.alaska.edu

ARIZONA
Pima Community College
4905 E Broadway Blvd, Tucson AZ 85709-1010
Wendy Kilgore, Ph.D., Director of Admissions
520-206-4500 Fax: 520-206-4790
Website: www.pima.edu
E-mail: infocenter@pima.edu

University of Arizona
Tucson AZ 85721-0040
Paul Kohn, Director of Admissions
520-621-3237 Fax: 520-621-9799
Website: www.admissions.arizona.edu or
www.arizona.edu

CALIFORNIA
California State University-San Bernadino
5500 University Pkwy
San Bernardino CA 92407-2393
Olivia Rosas, Director of Admissions
909-880-5000 Fax: 909-880-7034
Website: enrollment.csusb.edu
E-mail: orosas@csusb.edu

Chabot College
25555 Hesperian Blvd, Hayward CA 94545-2400
Judy Young, Director of Admissions
510-723-6600 Fax: 510-723-7510
Website: www.chabotcollege.edu
E-mail: ccarcom@clpccd.cc.ca.us

MARIC COLLEGE
5172 Kiernan Ct, Salida CA 95358-9083
Curtis Anderson, Director of Admissions
209-543-7000 Fax: 209-543-1755
Website: www.mariccollege.edu
E-mail: canderson@mariccollege.edu

San Joaquin Valley College
201 New Stine Rd, Bakersfield CA 93309-2659
Jaime Delgado, Enrollment Services Director
661-834-1026 Fax: 559-651-4864
Website: www.sjvc.edu
E-mail: jaime.delgado@sjvc.edu

San Joaquin Valley College
295 E Sierra Ave, Fresno CA 93710-3616
Nora Twarynski, Enrollment Services Director
559-448-8282 Fax: 559-651-4864
Website: www.sjvc.edu
E-mail: nora.twarynski@sjvc.edu

San Joaquin Valley College
1700 McHenry Village Way Suite 6
Modesto CA 95350
Joseph Holt, Director of Admissions
209-527-7582 Fax: 559-651-4864
Website: www.sjvc.edu
E-mail: josephh@sjvc.edu

San Joaquin Valley College
11050 Olson Dr, Rancho Cordova CA 95670
Joseph Holt, Director of Admissions
559-651-2500 Fax: 559-651-4864
Website: www.sjvc.edu
E-mail: joseph.holt@sjvc.edu

San Joaquin Valley College
10641 Church St, Rancho Cucamonga CA 91730
Ramon Abreu, Enrollment Services Director
909-948-7582 Fax: 559-651-4864
Website: www.sjvc.edu
E-mail: ramon.abreu@sjvc.edu

San Joaquin Valley College
8400 W Mineral King Ave, Visalia CA 93291-9283
Susie Topjian, Enrollment Services Director
559-651-2500 Fax: 559-651-4864
Website: www.sjvc.edu
E-mail: susiet@sjvc.edu

COLORADO
Parks College
14280 E Jewell Ave, Aurora CO 80012-5692
Julie Rosenthal, Director of Admissions
303-367-2757 Fax: 303-745-6245
Website: www.cci.edu

CONNECTICUT
University of New Haven
300 Boston Post Rd, West Haven CT 06516
Director of Undergraduate Admissions
203-932-7319 Fax: 203-931-6093
Website: www.newhaven.edu
E-mail: adminfo@newhaven.edu

FLORIDA
City College
2000 W Commercial Blvd, Fort Lauderdale FL 33309
Britt Carpenter, Director of Admissions
954-492-5353 Fax: 954-491-1965
Website: www.citycollege.edu
E-mail: bcarpenter@citycollege.edu

FLORIDA METROPOLITAN UNIVERSITY
Pinellas Campus
2471 N McMullen Booth Rd
Clearwater FL 33759-1359
Sandra Williams, Director of Admissions
800-353-3687 or 727-725-2688 Fax: 727-725-3827
Website: www.fmu.edu
E-mail: sawilliams@cci.edu
Master of Science in Criminal Justice.

Remington College, Tampa Campus
2410 E Busch Blvd, Tampa FL 33612-8410
Director of Recruitment
813-935-5700 Fax: 813-935-7415
Website: www.remingtoncollege.edu

Saint Leo University
PO Box 6665, Saint Leo FL 33574
Deborah Bandy, Director of Admissions
352-588-8200 or 800-334-5532 Fax: 352-588-8257
Website: www.saintleo.edu
E-mail: admission@saintleo.edu

Santa Fe Community College
3000 NW 83rd St, Gainesville FL 32606-6200
Jackson N. Sasser, President
352-395-5787 Fax: 352-395-4118
Website: www.sfcc.edu
E-mail: ouida.mcneil@sfcc.edu

GEORGIA
Armstrong Atlantic State University
11935 Abercorn St, Savannah GA 31419-1997
Ed Lyons, Director of Public Safety
Website: www.armstrong.edu

Kennesaw State University
1000 Chastain Rd NW Box 1402
Kennesaw GA 30144-5591
Ted Cochran, Director
770-423-6666
Website: www.kennesaw.edu

ILLINOIS
Kaskaskia College
27210 College Rd, Centralia IL 62801-7878
Tyra Taylor, Dean of Enrollment Management and Retention Services
618-545-3000 Fax: 618-532-1990
Website: www.kaskaskia.edu
E-mail: ttaylor@kaskaskia.edu

South Suburban College of Cook County
15800 State St, South Holland IL 60473
Jane Ellen Stocker, Dean of Enrollment Services
708-596-2000 Fax: 708-225-5806
Website: www.southsuburbancollege.edu
E-mail: jstocker@southsuburbancollege.edu

INDIANA
Ivy Tech Community College - North Central
220 Dean Johnson Blvd, South Bend IN 46601-3415
Pam Decker, Director of Admissions
574-289-7001 Fax: 574-236-7177
Website: www.ivytech.edu
E-mail: pdecker@ivytech.edu

University of Evansville
1800 Lincoln Ave, Evansville IN 47722-0001
Thomas E. Bear, V.P. of Enrollment Services
800-423-8633 Fax: 812-488-4076
Website: www.evansville.edu
E-mail: admission@evansville.edu

IOWA

Briar Cliff University
PO Box 2100, Sioux City IA 51104-0100
Sharisue Wilcoxon, VP for Enrollment Management
712-279-5200 Fax: 712-279-1632
Website: www.briarcliff.edu
E-mail: admissions@briarcliff.edu

Iowa Lakes Community College
300 S 18th St, Estherville IA 51334-2721
Anne Stansbury, Asst. Director of Admissions
712-362-7945 Fax: 712-362-8363
Website: www.iowalakes.edu
E-mail: info@iowalakes.edu

Wartburg College
PO Box 1003, Waverly IA 50677-0903
Brent Matthias, Interim Director of Admissions
319-352-8200 Fax: 319-352-8579
Website: www.wartburg.edu
E-mail: admissions@wartburg.edu

KANSAS

Allen County Community College
1801 N Cottonwood St, Iola KS 66749-1607
John Masterson, President
Randy Weber, Director of Admissions
620-365-5116 Fax: 620-365-3284
Website: www.allencc.net
E-mail: weber@allencc.edu

COLBY COMMUNITY COLLEGE

1255 S Range Ave, Colby KS 67701-4099
Director of Admissions
888-634-9350 or 785-460-4690 Fax: 785-460-4691
Website: www.colbycc.edu
E-mail: bobbi@colbycc.edu

LOUISIANA

Louisiana State University at Eunice
PO Box 1129, Eunice LA 70535-1129
Ron Ryder, Registrar
337-457-7311 Fax: 337-550-1306
Website: www.lsue.edu
E-mail: rryder@lsue.edu

MAINE

HUSSON COLLEGE

One College Cir, Bangor ME 04401-2999
Jane Goodwin, Director of Admissions
800-4HU-SSON or 207-941-7100 Fax: 207-941-7935
Website: www.husson.edu
E-mail: admit@husson.edu
See listing under "Universities"

Southern Maine Community College
2 Fort Rd, South Portland ME 04106-1698
Dr. James Ortiz, President
Scott MacDonald, Director of Financial Aid
207-741-5500 Fax: 207-741-5671
Website: www.smccme.edu
E-mail: oharmon@maine.rr.com

MARYLAND

Cecil Community College
One Seahawk Dr, North East MD 21901
Sandra S. Rajaski, Registrar & Director of Admissions
410-287-1000 Fax: 410-287-1001
Website: www.cecilcc.edu
E-mail: srajaski@cecilcc.edu

Hagerstown Community College
11400 Robinwood Dr, Hagerstown MD 21742-6590
Dr. Daniel E. Bock, Assistant Director of Admissions
301-790-2800 Fax: 301-791-9165
Website: www.hagerstowncc.edu
E-mail: bockd@hagerstowncc.edu

MASSACHUSETTS

Anna Maria College
50 Sunset Ln, Paxton MA 01612
Julie A. Mitchell, Director of Admissions
508-849-3360 Fax: 508-849-3362
Website: www.annamaria.edu
E-mail: admissions@annamaria.edu

Bay Path College
588 Longmeadow St, Longmeadow MA 01106-2292
Lisa Casassa, Director of Admissions
413-565-1331 Fax: 413-565-1105
Website: www.baypath.edu
E-mail: lcasassa@baypath.edu

Becker College
Campuses in Worcester and Leicester, MA
61 Sever St, Worcester MA 01609-2165
Karen H. Schedin, Director of Admissions
508-791-9241 Fax: 508-890-1500
Website: www.becker.edu
E-mail: admissions@becker.edu
See listing under "Universities"

Newbury College
129 Fisher Ave, Brookline MA 02445-5796
Salvadore Liberto, Vice President of Enrollment
617-730-7000 Fax: 617-731-9618
Website: www.newbury.edu

Westfield State College
PO Box 1630, Westfield MA 01086
Michelle Mattie, Associate Dean, Admission and Enrollment Services
413-572-5300
Website: www.wsc.ma.edu
E-mail: admission@wsc.ma.edu

MICHIGAN

Concordia University
4090 Geddes Rd, Ann Arbor MI 48105-2797
Gary Neumann, Director of Admissions
734-995-7300 Fax: 734-995-4610
Website: www.cuaa.edu
E-mail: admissions@cuaa.edu

Delta College
University Center MI 48710-0001
Duff Zube, Director of Admissions
989-686-9093 Fax: 989-667-2202
Website: www.delta.edu
E-mail: admit@delta.edu

MACOMB COMMUNITY COLLEGE

44575 Garfield Rd, Clinton Township MI 48038-1139
Information Center
586-445-7999
Website: www.macomb.edu
E-mail: answer@macomb.edu

Northwestern Michigan College
1701 E Front St, Traverse City MI 49686-3061
Jim Bensley, Admissions Coordinator
800-748-0566 Fax: 231-995-1339
Website: www.nmc.edu
E-mail: jbensley@nmc.edu

University of Michigan-Dearborn
4901 Evergreen Rd, Dearborn MI 48128-1491
The Office of Admissions & Orientation
313-593-5100 Fax: 313-436-9167
Website: www.umd.umich.edu
E-mail: admissions@umd.umich.edu
Criminal Justice Studies

MINNESOTA

Gustavus Adolphus College
800 W College Ave, Saint Peter MN 56082-1485
Mark H. Anderson, Dean of Admission
800-GUSTAVUS Fax: 507-933-7474
Website: www.gustavus.edu
E-mail: admission@gustavus.edu

Hibbing Community College
1515 E 25th St, Hibbing MN 55746-3300
Holly Bigelow, Director of Enrollment
800-224-4HCC or 218-262-7200 Fax: 218-262-6717
Website: www.hibbing.edu
E-mail: admissions@hibbing.edu

Minneapolis Community and Technical College
1501 Hennepin Ave, Minneapolis MN 55403-1779
Dena Russell, Director of Admissions
612-659-6282 Fax: 612-659-6210
Website: www.minneapolis.edu
E-mail: admissions.office@minneapolis.edu

Northland Community & Technical College
Highway 1 E, Thief River Falls MN 56701
Kevin Stuckey, Chairperson
800-959-6282 or 218-681-0727 Fax: 218-681-0774
Website: www.northlandcollege.edu

Ridgewater College-Willmar Campus
PO Box 1097, Willmar MN 56201-1097
Sally Kerfeld, Director of Admissions
800-722-1151 Fax: 320-231-7677
Website: www.ridgewater.edu
E-mail: skerfeld@ridgewater.edu

MISSOURI

East Central College
1964 Prairie Dell Rd, Union MO 63084
Karen Wieda, Registrar
636-583-5195 ext. 2220 Fax: 636-583-1897
Website: www.eastcentral.edu
E-mail: wiedaks@eastcentral.edu

Lindenwood University
209 S Kingshighway St
Saint Charles MO 63301-1695
Sheryl Guffey, Director of Admissions
636-949-2000 Fax: 636-949-4989
Website: www.lindenwood.edu

Truman State University
100 E Normal, Kirksville MO 63501
Office of Admission
660-785-4000 Fax: 660-785-4181
Website: www.truman.edu
E-mail: admissions@truman.edu

University of Missouri
1 University Blvd, Saint Louis MO 63121-4499
Dr. Mark Burkholder, Dean-College of Arts & Sciences
314-516-5501 Fax: 314-516-5415
Website: www.umsl.edu
E-mail: admissions@umsl.edu

NEBRASKA

Midland Lutheran College
900 N Clarkson St, Fremont NE 68025-4200
Todd Hansen, Associate Director of Admissions
402-941-6501 Fax: 402-941-6513
Website: www.mlc.edu
E-mail: admissions@mlc.edu

University of Nebraska at Kearney
905 W 25th St, Kearney NE 68849-0001
Dusty Newton, Director of Admissions
800-KEARNEY Fax: 308-865-8987
Website: www.unk.edu
E-mail: admissionsug@unk.edu

NEVADA

GREAT BASIN COLLEGE

1500 College Pkwy, Elko NV 89801-5032
Julie G. Byrnes, Director of Enrollment Management
775-753-2271 Fax: 775-753-2311
Website: www.gbcnv.edu
E-mail: bjulie@gbcnv.edu

NEW JERSEY

Bergen Community College
400 Paramus Rd, Paramus NJ 07652
Julian Gomez, Asst. Director of Admissions
201-447-7100 Fax: 201-444-7036
Website: www.bergen.edu
E-mail: jgomez@bergen.edu

Mercer County Community College
West Windsor Campus
PO Box B, Trenton NJ 08690
Savita Bambhrolia, Director of Admissions
609-586-4800 Fax: 609-587-4666
Website: www.mccc.edu
E-mail: admiss@mccc.edu

New Jersey City University
2039 John F Kennedy Blvd
Jersey City NJ 07305-1588
Carmen Panlilio, Asst. V.P. for Admissions and Financial Aid
201-200-3234 Fax: 201-200-2044
Website: www.njcu.edu
E-mail: admissions@njcu.edu

NEW MEXICO

New Mexico State University
1500 N 3rd St, Grants NM 87020-2025
505-287-7981 Fax: 505-287-2329
Website: www.grants.nmsu.edu

NEW YORK

Broome Community College
907 Upper Front St, Binghamton NY 13905
Anthony S. Fiorelli, Director of Admissions
607-778-5001 Fax: 607-778-5442
Website: www.sunybroome.edu
E-mail: fiorelli_a@sunybroome.edu

Hilbert College
5200 S Park Ave, Hamburg NY 14075-1597
Timothy Lee, Director of Admissions
716-649-7900 Fax: 716-649-0702
Website: www.hilbert.edu
E-mail: tlee@hilbert.edu

Molloy College
1000 Hempstead Ave
Rockville Centre NY 11570-1100
Marguerite Lane, Director of Admissions
516-678-5000 ext. 6291 Fax: 516-256-2247
Website: www.molloy.edu
E-mail: admissions@molloy.edu
See listing under "Universities"

SUNY College at Brockport
350 New Campus Dr, Brockport NY 14420-2997
Bernard S. Valento, Director of Undergraduate Admissions
585-395-2751 Fax: 585-395-5452
Website: www.brockport.edu
E-mail: admit@brockport.edu

NORTH CAROLINA

Haywood Community College
185 Freedlander Dr, Clyde NC 28721
Debbie Rowland, Coordinator of Admissions
828-627-4500 Fax: 828-627-4513
Website: www.haywood.edu
E-mail: drowland@haywood.edu

James Sprunt Community College
PO Box 398, Kenansville NC 28349-0398
Rita Brown, Registrar
910-296-2500 Fax: 910-296-1636
Website: www.sprunt.com

OHIO

Cleveland State University
2121 Euclid Ave RW 204, Cleveland OH 44115
Dr. Richard Arndt, Dean of Undergraduate Recruitment and College Partnerships
888-CSU-OHIO Fax: 216-687-9210
Website: www.csuohio.edu
E-mail: admissions@csuohio.edu

Collins Career Center
11627 State Route 243, Chesapeake OH 45619-7962
740-867-6641 Fax: 740-867-9626
Website: www.collins-cc.k12.oh.us

Mount Vernon Nazarene University
800 Martinsburg Rd, Mount Vernon OH 43050-9509
Timothy Eades, Director of Admissions
866-462-6868 Fax: 740-393-0511
Website: www.gotomvnu.com
E-mail: admissions@mvnu.edu
See listing under "Universities"

Ohio University
Chillicothe Campus
PO Box 629, Chillicothe OH 45601
Student Services
740-774-7200 Fax: 740-774-7295
Website: www.ohiou.edu/chillicothe/

Owens Community College
300 Davis St, Findlay OH 45840-3631
William J. Ivoska PhD., Vice President of Student Services
567-429-3500 Fax: 567-423-0246
Website: www.owens.edu
E-mail: admissions@owens.edu

Owens Community College
PO Box 10000, Toledo OH 43699-1947
William J. Ivoska, Ph.D, Vice President of Student Services
567-661-7000 Fax: 567-661-7607
Website: www.owens.edu
E-mail: admissions@owens.edu

OKLAHOMA

University of Tulsa
600 S College Ave, Tulsa OK 74104-3126
Earl Johnson, Dean of Admission
918-631-2307 Fax: 918-631-5003
Website: www.utulsa.edu
E-mail: admission@utulsa.edu

OREGON

· Linn-Benton Community College
6500 Pacific Blvd SW, Albany OR 97321-3774
Christine Baker, Outreach Coordinator
541-917-4811 Fax: 541-917-4868
Website: www.linnbenton.edu
E-mail: admissions@linnbenton.edu

· Rogue Community College
3345 Redwood Hwy, Grants Pass OR 97527-9298
Claudia Sullivan, Director of Enrollment Services
541-956-7500 Fax: 541-471-3585
Website: www.roguecc.edu
E-mail: csullivan@roguecc.edu
See listing under "Community and Junior Colleges"

Western Oregon University
345 Monmouth Ave N, Monmouth OR 97361-1314
David McDonald, Dean, Admission, Retention &
Enrollment Management
877-877-1593 Fax: 503-838-8067
Website: www.wou.edu
E-mail: wolfgram@fsa.wou.edu

PENNSYLVANIA

· Computer Learning Network
401 E Winding Hill Rd Ste 101
Mechanicsburg PA 17055-4989
Marlene Macauley, Director of Admissions
717-761-1481 Fax: 717-761-0558
Website: www.clntraining.net
E-mail: mmacauley@clntraining.net

DeSales University
2755 Station Ave, Center Valley PA 18034-9565
610-282-1100 Fax: 610-282-2342
Website: www.desales.edu

Juniata College
1700 Moore St, Huntingdon PA 16652-2196
Michelle Bartol, Dean of Enrollment
877-JUNIATA Fax: 814-641-3100
Website: www.juniata.edu
E-mail: admissions@juniata.edu

King's College
133 N River St, Wilkes Barre PA 18711-0801
Michelle Lawrence-Schmude, Director of Admission
570-208-5900 Fax: 570-208-5971
Website: www.kings.edu
E-mail: admissions@kings.edu

· Lehigh Valley College
2809 E Saucon Valley Rd
Center Valley PA 18034-8447
Joshua Padron, Vice President of Marketing and
Admissions
800-227-9109 Fax: 610-791-7810
Website: www.lehighvalley.edu
E-mail: joshua.padron@lehighvalley.edu

University of Pittsburgh
1150 Mount Pleasant Rd
Greensburg PA 15601-5860
Brandi S. Darr, Director of Admissions and Financial
Aid
724-836-9880 Fax: 724-836-7160
Website: www.upg.pitt.edu
E-mail: upgadmit@pitt.edu

· York Technical Institute
Lancaster Campus
3050 Hempland Rd, Lancaster PA 17601
Cathi Killingsworth Bost, Vice President
800-227-9675 or 717-295-1100 Fax: 717-295-1135
Website: www.yti.edu
E-mail: info@yti.edu
See listing under "Career Schools"

SOUTH DAKOTA

· Western Dakota Technical Institute
800 Mickelson Dr, Rapid City SD 57703-4018
Janell Oberlander, Manager of Student Services
605-394-4034 or 800-544-8765 Fax: 605-394-1789
Website: www.westerndakotatech.org
E-mail: admissions@wdti.tec.sd.us
See listing under "Career Schools"

TENNESSEE

Tennessee State University
3500 John A Merritt Blvd, Nashville TN 37209-1561
John Cade, Dean of Admissions & Records
615-963-5101 Fax: 615-963-2930
Website: www.tnstate.edu
E-mail: jcade@tnstate.edu

University of Tennessee
615 McCallie Ave, Chattanooga TN 37403-2504
Yancy Freeman, Director of Admissions
423-425-4111 Fax: 423-425-4157
Website: www.utc.edu
E-mail: Yancy-Freeman@utc.edu

TEXAS

· Blinn College
902 College Ave, Brenham TX 77833-4098
Dennis K. Crowson, Registrar
979-830-4000 Fax: 979-830-4110
Website: www.blinn.edu
E-mail: recruiting@blinn.edu

· Blinn College
PO Box 6030, Bryan TX 77805-6030
Dennis K. Crowson, Registrar
979-209-7200 Fax: 979-209-7229
Website: www.blinn.edu
E-mail: recruiting@blinn.edu

· Blinn College
100 Ranger Dr, Schulenburg TX 78956-2247
Dennis K. Crowson, Registrar
979-743-5003 Fax: 979-743-5225
Website: www.blinn.edu
E-mail: recruiting@blinn.edu

· Galveston College
4015 Avenue Q, Galveston TX 77550-7496
Brian Lowery, Registrar
409-763-6551 Fax: 409-944-1501
Website: www.gc.edu
E-mail: blowery@gc.edu

· McLennan Community College
1400 College Dr, Waco TX 76708-1498
Stephen Cook, Coordinator, Fire Fighters Academy
254-299-8000 Fax: 254-299-8854
Website: www.mclennan.edu
E-mail: scook@mclennan.edu

· North Central Texas College
1525 W California St, Gainesville TX 76240-4636
Michelle Winters, Registrar
940-668-3315 Fax: 940-665-7075
Website: www.nctc.edu
E-mail: mwinters@nctc.edu

· Our Lady of the Lake University
411 SW 24th St, San Antonio TX 78207-4666
Mary Kay Cooper, Dean of Enrollment
210-434-6711 Fax: 210-431-4013
Website: www.ollusa.edu
E-mail: admission@lakeollusa.edu

· Temple College
2600 S 1st St, Temple TX 76504-7435
Angela Balch, Director of Admissions & Records
254-298-8300 Fax: 254-298-8288
Website: www.templejc.edu
E-mail: ruth.bridges@templejc.edu

· Tyler Junior College
PO Box 9020, Tyler TX 75711-9020
Joan Jones, Interim Dean
800-687-5680
Website: www.tjc.edu
E-mail: jjon@tjc.edu
See listing under "Community and Junior Colleges"

VIRGINIA

Radford University
PO Box 6903, Radford VA 24142
David W. Kraus, Director of Admissions
800-890-4265 Fax: 540-831-5038
Website: www.radford.edu
E-mail: ruadmiss@radford.edu

· Southside Virginia Community College
109 Campus Dr, Alberta VA 23821-2930
Ronald E. Mattox, Dean of Admissions
434-949-1014 Fax: 434-949-7863
Website: www.sv.vccs.edu
E-mail: ronald.mattox@sv.vccs.edu

· Southside Virginia Community College
200 Daniel Rd, Keysville VA 23947
Ronald E. Mattox, Dean of Admissions
434-736-2018 Fax: 434-736-2082
Website: www.sv.vccs.edu
E-mail: ronald.mattox@sv.vccs.edu

WASHINGTON

CROWN COLLEGE

8739 S Hosmer St, Tacoma WA 98444-1836
John Wabel, CEO
253-531-3123 Fax: 253-531-3521
Website: www.crowncollege.edu
E-mail: jwabel@crowncollege.edu

· Everett Community College
2000 Tower St, Everett WA 98201
Christine Kerlin, Associate Dean
425-388-9100 Fax: 425-388-9173
Website: www.everettcc.edu
E-mail: ckerlin@everettcc.edu

WEST VIRGINIA

Fairmont State University
1201 Locust Ave, Fairmont WV 26554-2470
Steve Leadman, Director of Admissions
304-367-4161 or 800-641-5678 Fax: 304-367-4789
Website: www.fairmontstate.edu
E-mail: admit@fairmontstate.edu

Mountain State University
Box 9003, Beckley WV 25802-9003
866-FOR-MSU1 or 304-929-INFO Fax: 304-253-5072
Website: www.mountainstate.edu
E-mail: gomsu@mountainstate.edu
See listing under "Universities"

WISCONSIN

· Blackhawk Technical College
PO Box 5009, Janesville WI 53547-5009
Gregg Bosak, Administration, Community Information
608-757-7769 Fax: 608-757-7740
Website: www.blackhawk.edu
E-mail: gbosak@blackhawk.edu

Herzing College
5218 E Terrace Dr, Madison WI 53718-8340
Donald Madelung, President
800-582-1227 Fax: 608-249-8593
Website: www.herzing.edu
E-mail: info@msn.herzing.edu
See listing under "Universities"

Wisconsin Indianhead Technical College
505 Pine Ridge Dr, Shell Lake WI 54871
Jeff Dodge, Dean
800-243-9482 Fax: 715-468-2819
Website: www.witc.edu
E-mail: jdodge@witc.edu

WYOMING

· Laramie County Community College
1400 E College Dr, Cheyenne WY 82007-3204
Jenny Hargett, Director of Admissions
307-778-5222 Fax: 307-778-1350
Website: www.lccc.wy.edu
E-mail: learnmore@lccc.wy.edu

GUAM

University of Guam
UOG Station, Mangilao GU 96923
Deborah Leon Guerrero, Registrar
671-735-2201 or 671-735-2208 Fax: 671-735-2203
Website: www.uog.edu
E-mail: admitme@uog9.uog.edu

PUERTO RICO

· Colegio Mayor de Technologia
PO Box 1490, Arroyo PR 00714
Julia Melendez, Director of Admissions
787-839-5266 Fax: 787-839-0033
Website: www.colegiomayortec.com
E-mail: cmtarroy@coqui.net

PSYCHOLOGY

ALABAMA

Alabama A & M University
PO Box 908, Normal AL 35762
Antonio Boyle, Director of Admissions
256-372-5245 Fax: 256-372-5249
Website: www.aamu.edu
E-mail: aboyle@aamu.edu

Faulkner University
5345 Atlanta Hwy, Montgomery AL 36109-3398
Keith Mock, Director of Admissions
800-879-9816 ext. 7200 or 334-386-7200
Fax: 334-386-7137
Website: www.faulkner.edu
E-mail: admissions@faulkner.edu

University of Alabama in Huntsville
PO Box 1247, Huntsville AL 35899-0001
Ann Lee, Assoc. Director for Recruiting Program and Events
1-800-UAH-CALL Fax: 256-824-6073
Website: www.uah.edu
E-mail: leev@uah.edu

ALASKA

University of Alaska Anchorage
PO Box 141629, Anchorage AK 99514-1629
Cecile Mitchell, Director of Enrollment Services
907-786-1480 Fax: 907-786-4888
Website: www.uaa.alaska.edu/
E-mail: enroll@uaa.alaska.edu

ARIZONA

Southwestern College
2625 E Cactus Rd, Phoenix AZ 85032-7097
Admissions/Financial Aid Office
800-247-2697 or 602-992-6101 Fax: 602-404-2159
Website: www.swcaz.edu
E-mail: admissions@swcaz.edu

University of Arizona
Tucson AZ 85721-0040
Paul Kohn, Director of Admissions
520-621-3237 Fax: 520-621-9799
Website: www.admissions.arizona.edu or www.arizona.edu

ARKANSAS

Ouachita Baptist University
410 Ouachita St, Arkadelphia AR 71998-0001
David Goodman, Director of Admissions
870-245-5110 Fax: 870-245-5500
Website: www.obu.edu
E-mail: admissions@obu.edu

CALIFORNIA

Antioch University
801 Garden St Ste 101
Santa Barbara CA 93101-1581
Ankara McPherson, Director of Admissions
805-962-8179 Fax: 805-962-4786
Website: www.antiochsb.edu
E-mail: amcpherson@antiochsb.edu

Antioch University Southern California
400 Corporate Pointe, Culver City CA 90230-7615
Admissions Office
800-7-ANTIOCH Fax: 310-821-6032
E-mail: admissions@antiochla.edu
Master of Arts in Psychology.

CALIFORNIA COAST UNIVERSITY

700 N Main St, Santa Ana CA 92701
Admissions Office: 888-CCU-UNIV or 714-547-9625
Fax: 714-547-5777
Dr. Thomas Neal, President
Dr. Cynthia Teeple, Academic Vice President
Website: www.calcoast.edu
E-mail: info@calcoast.edu
Established 1973. Proprietary. Coed. Accreditation: California Coast University holds accreditation through the Accrediting Commission of the Distance Education and Training Council (DETC). The DETC is an educational association located in Washington, D.C. Founded in 1926, it is the standard setting agency for distance education institutions. Approval: Bureau for Private Post-secondary and Vocational Education - State of California, charter member California Association of State Approved Colleges & Universities, member Association for Adult & Continuing Education, member The Alliance for Private Post Secondary Academic Institutions.
Tuition: $2,805-$12,070. California Coast University has selected the SLM Corporation, commonly known as Sallie Mae, to help the university provide financing for its students. Sallie Mae is the nation's leading provider of education funding. Sallie Mae also allows students to borrow additional loan amounts to cover additional expenses, such as textbooks, equipment, or living expenses.
Enrollment: 30,000. California Coast University is approved by the California State Approving Agency to enroll veterans or other eligible persons under Title 38, U.S. Code. California Coast University holds a Memorandum of Understanding with Defense Activity for Non-Traditional Education Support (DANTES) as an external degree provider.
A private college offering off-campus independent study programs in the traditional areas of business administration, management, psychology, education. Admissions: enroll year round, requires official transcripts, letters of recommendation, detailed curriculum vita or occupational history.
Process: evaluation of prior academic work followed by analysis of occupational history, including participation in workshops, seminars, training programs, specialized projects for credit. Credit is demonstrated by accelerated learning guides or study guides.
Residency: All course work may be completed off campus, utilizing correspondence methods. Interest free loans available to students.

Chapman University
One University Drive, Orange CA 92866-1099
Michael Drummy, Assistant Vice President for Enrollment
Services and Chief Admission Officer
714-997-6411 or 888-CUAPPLY Fax: 714-997-6713
Website: www.chapman.edu
E-mail: admit@chapman.edu

Concordia University
1530 Concordia, Irvine CA 92612-3203
Lori McDonald, Executive Director of Enrollment Services
800-229-1200 or 949-854-8002 Fax: 949-854-6894
Website: www.cui.edu
E-mail: admission@cui.edu

Orange Coast College
PO Box 5005, Costa Mesa CA 92628-5005
Kristin Clark, Director of Admissions
714-432-5773 Fax: 714-432-5736
Website: www.orangecoastcollege.edu
E-mail: kclark@cccd.edu

PEPPERDINE UNIVERSITY

Graduate School of Education and Pschology
6100 Center Dr, Los Angeles CA 90045
Fionnbarr Kelly, Director of Admissions
310-568-5744 Fax: 310-568-5755
Website: www.gsep.pepperdine.edu
E-mail: gsep@pepperdine.edu
The Graduate School of Education and Psychology of Pepperdine University offers two different master's degree programs and one doctoral degree program in psychology:
*Master of Arts in Psychology
*Master of Arts on Clinical Psychology with an emphasis in Marriage and Family Therapy
*Doctor of Psychology in Clinical Psychology
For more info visit: www.gsep.pepperdine.edu/psychology.

Phillips Graduate Institute
5445 Balboa Blvd, Encino CA 91316-1509
Steven Weir, Director of Admissions
818-386-5600 Fax: 818-386-5636
Website: www.pgi.edu
E-mail: sweir@pgi.edu

San Diego Christian College
2100 Greenfield Dr, El Cajon CA 92019-1157
Jon Melone, Director of Admissions
800-676-2242 Fax: 619-590-1739
Website: www.sdcc.edu
E-mail: admissions@sdcc.edu

Whittier College
PO Box 634, Whittier CA 90608-0634
Kieron Miller, Director of Admissions
562-907-4200 Fax: 562-907-4870
Website: www.whittier.edu
E-mail: kmiller@whittier.edu

COLORADO

Denver Seminary
6399 S Santa Fe Dr, Littleton CO 80120
Robert Fomer, VP Student Services
303-762-6982 Fax: 303-783-3122
Website: denverseminary.edu
E-mail: bob.fomer@denverseminary.edu

CONNECTICUT

Albertus Magnus College
700 Prospect St, New Haven CT 06511-1189
Richard Lolatte, Dean of Admission
203-773-8501 or 800-578-9160 Fax: 203-773-5248
Website: www.albertus.edu
E-mail: admissions@albertus.edu

University of New Haven
300 Boston Post Rd, West Haven CT 06516
Director of Undergraduate Admissions
203-932-7319 Fax: 203-931-6093
Website: www.newhaven.edu
E-mail: adminfo@newhaven.edu

FLORIDA

CARLOS ALBIZU UNIVERSITY

2173 NW 99th Ave, Miami FL 33172-2209
Gerardo Alvarado, MBA, Director of Admissions, Recruitment & Outreach
305-593-1223 ext. 137 Fax: 305-593-1854
Website: www.mia.albizu.edu
E-mail: admissions@albizu.edu

Florida State University
600 W College Ave, Tallahassee FL 32306-1096
Janice V. Finney, Director of Admissions
850-644-2525 Fax: 850-644-0197
Website: admissions.fsu.edu
E-mail: admissions@admin.fsu.edu

Lynn University
3601 N Military Trl, Boca Raton FL 33431-5598
Brett Ormandy, Director of Admissions
561-237-7900 Fax: 561-237-7100
Website: www.lynn.edu
E-mail: admission@lynn.edu

St. Thomas University
16401 NW 37th Ave, Miami Gardens FL 33054
Dr. Gary Feinberg, Chair, Social Sciences
800-367-9010 or 305-628-6546 Fax: 305-628-6591
Website: www.stu.edu
E-mail: signup@stu.edu

University of South Florida
4202 E Fowler Ave, Tampa FL 33620-6900
J. Robert Spatig, Director of Admissions
813-974-3350 Fax: 813-974-9689
Website: www.usf.edu
E-mail: admissions@admin.usf.edu

GEORGIA

Kennesaw State University
1000 Chastain Rd NW, Kennesaw GA 30144-5591
Dr. Helen Ridley, Dean of Humanities and Social Science
770-423-6124
Website: www.kennesaw.edu

THE PSYCHOLOGICAL STUDIES INSTITUTE

2055 Mount Paran Rd NW McCarty Building
Atlanta GA 30327
Robin Lay, Director of Recruiting
888-924-6774 or 404-233-3949 Fax: 404-239-9460
Website: www.psy.edu
E-mail: rlay@psy.edu

TOCCOA FALLS COLLEGE

PO Box 800899, Toccoa Falls GA 30598
Christy Meadows, Director of Admissions
888-785-5624 Fax: 706-282-6012
Website: www.tfc.edu
E-mail: admissions@tfc.edu

IDAHO

Brigham Young University - Idaho
120 Kimball Bldg, Rexburg ID 83460
Gordon Westenskow, Director of Admissions
208-496-1020 Fax: 208-496-1220
Website: www.byui.edu
E-mail: admissions@byui.edu

University of Idaho
Moscow ID 83844-4253
Lloyd Scott, Director of New Student Services
208-885-6163 Fax: 208-885-4477
Website: www.uidaho.edu
E-mail: nss@uidaho.edu

ILLINOIS

ADLER SCHOOL OF PROFESSIONAL PSYCHOLOGY

65 E Wacker Pl, Chicago IL 60601-7296
Craig Hines, Director of Admissions
312-201-5900 Fax: 312-201-5917
Website: www.adler.edu
E-mail: admissions@adler.edu

AMERICAN INTERCONTINENTAL UNIVERSITY ONLINE

5550 Prairie Stone Parkway Suite 400
Hoffman Estates IL 60192
Admissions Department
877-701-3800
Website: www.aiuonline.edu
E-mail: info@aiuonline.edu

ARGOSY UNIVERSITY/CHICAGO

350 N Orleans St, Merchandise Mart
Chicago IL 60654
Ashley Delaney, Director of Admissions
800-626-4123 Fax: 312-777-7750
Website: www.argosyu.edu
E-mail: adelaney@argosyu.edu

Aurora University
347 S Gladstone Ave, Aurora IL 60506-4892
Carol R. Dunn, Ed.D., Vice President for Enrollment
800-742-5281 Fax: 630-844-5535
Website: www.aurora.edu
E-mail: admission@aurora.edu

Benedictine University
5700 College Rd, Lisle IL 60532-0900
630-829-6300 or 888-829-6363 Fax: 630-829-6301
Website: www.ben.edu
E-mail: admissions@ben.edu

CONCORDIA UNIVERSITY

7400 Augusta St, River Forest IL 60305-1402
708-209-3100 Fax: 708-209-3473
Website: www.curf.edu
E-mail: crfadmis.edu

North Central College
30 N Brainard St, Naperville IL 60540-4690
Martha Stolze, Director of Admissions
630-637-5800 Fax: 630-637-5819
Website: www.northcentralcollege.edu
E-mail: admissions@noctrl.edu

Roosevelt University
430 S Michigan Ave, Chicago IL 60605
Gwen E. Kanelos, Asst. Vice President for Enrollment Services
877-APPLY-RU Fax: 312-341-4216
Website: www.roosevelt.edu
E-mail: applyru@roosevelt.edu

South Suburban College of Cook County
15800 State St, South Holland IL 60473
Jane Ellen Stocker, Dean of Enrollment Services
708-596-2000 Fax: 708-225-5806
Website: www.southsuburbancollege.edu
E-mail: jstocker@southsuburbancollege.edu

INDIANA

St. Mary-of-the-Woods College
Saint Mary of the Woods IN 47876-1001
James P. Malley, Jr., Director of Admission
800-926-7692 Fax: 812-535-5010
Website: www.smwc.edu
E-mail: smwcadms@smwc.edu

University of Evansville
1800 Lincoln Ave, Evansville IN 47722-0001
Thomas E. Bear, V.P. of Enrollment Services
800-423-8633 Fax: 812-488-4076
Website: www.evansville.edu
E-mail: admission@evansville.edu

IOWA

Briar Cliff University
PO Box 2100, Sioux City IA 51104-0100
Sharisue Wilcoxon, VP for Enrollment Management
712-279-5200 Fax: 712-279-1632
Website: www.briarcliff.edu
E-mail: admissions@briarcliff.edu

Clarke College
1550 Clarke Dr, Dubuque IA 52001-3198
Andy Schroeder, Director of Admissions
800-383-2345 Fax: 563-584-8666
Website: www.clarke.edu
E-mail: andy.schroeder@clarke.edu

Graceland University
1 University Place, Lamoni IA 50140
Brian Shantz, Vice President for Enrollment and Dean
of Admissions
641-784-5196 Fax: 641-784-5480
Website: www.admissions.graceland.edu
E-mail: admissions@graceland.edu

Iowa Lakes Community College
300 S 18th St, Estherville IA 51334-2721
Anne Stansbury, Asst. Director of Admissions
712-362-7945 Fax: 712-362-8363
Website: www.iowalakes.edu
E-mail: info@iowalakes.edu

Mount Mercy College
1330 Elmhurst Dr NE, Cedar Rapids IA 52402-4797
Jim Krystofiak, Dean of Admission
800-248-4504 Fax: 319-363-5270
Website: www.mtmercy.edu
E-mail: admission@mtmercy.edu

Waldorf College
106 S 6th St, Forest City IA 50436-1713
Steve Lovik, Vice President of Enrollment Management
800-292-1903 or 641-585-8112 Fax: 641-585-8125
Website: www.waldorf.edu
E-mail: loviks@waldorf.edu
See listing under "Universities"

KANSAS

Barclay College
607 N Kingman, Haviland KS 67059
Herb Frazier, Director of Admissions
800-862-0226 Fax: 620-862-5242
Website: www.barclaycollege.edu
E-mail: admissions@barclaycollege.edu

Independence Community College
PO Box 708, Independence KS 67301-0708
Dr. Terry Hetrick, President
800-842-6063 Fax: 620-331-5344
Website: www.indycc.edu
E-mail: admissions@indycc.edu

Newman University
3100 W McCormick St, Wichita KS 67213
Jann Reusser, Admissions Recruitment Coordinator
316-942-4291 ext. 2144 Fax: 316-942-4483
Website: www.newmanu.edu
E-mail: reusserj@newmanu.edu

Tabor College
400 S Jefferson St, Hillsboro KS 67063-1758
Rusty Allen, Dean of Enrollment Management
620-947-3121 Fax: 620-947-6276
Website: www.tabor.edu
E-mail: admissions@tabor.edu

KENTUCKY

Louisville Presbyterian Seminary
1044 Alta Vista Rd, Louisville KY 40205-1798
Kerry Rice, Director of Admissions
502-895-3411 or 800-264-1839 Fax: 502-992-9399
Website: www.lpts.edu
E-mail: admissions@lpts.edu
Degrees offered MDiv, MA, DMin, ThM
M. A. Marriage & Family Therapy (COAMFTE/AAMFT &
AAPC Accred.)

Morehead State University
Morehead KY 40351-1689
Dayna Seelig, Enrollment Services
800-585-6781 Fax: 606-783-5038
Website: www.moreheadstate.edu
E-mail: admissions@moreheadstate.edu

LOUISIANA

Dillard University
2601 Gentilly Blvd, New Orleans LA 70122-3097
Linda G. Nash, Director of Admissions
Website: www.dillard.edu
E-mail: admissions@dillard.edu

MAINE

HUSSON COLLEGE
One College Cir, Bangor ME 04401-2999
Jane Goodwin, Director of Admissions
800-4HU-SSON or 207-941-7100 Fax: 207-941-7935
Website: www.husson.edu
E-mail: admit@husson.edu
See listing under "Universities"

MARYLAND

::: Griggs University
PO Box 4437, Silver Spring MD 20914-4437
Anita L. Jacobs, Director of Admissions
301-680-6570 Fax: 301-680-6583
Website: www.griggs.edu
E-mail: registrar@griggs.edu

Hagerstown Community College
11400 Robinwood Dr, Hagerstown MD 21742-6590
Dr. Daniel E. Bock, Assistant Director of Admissions
301-790-2800 Fax: 301-791-9165
Website: www.hagerstowncc.edu
E-mail: bockd@hagerstowncc.edu

MASSACHUSETTS

Anna Maria College
50 Sunset Ln, Paxton MA 01612
Julie A. Mitchell, Director of Admissions
508-849-3360 Fax: 508-849-3362
Website: www.annamaria.edu
E-mail: admissions@annamaria.edu

Bay Path College
588 Longmeadow St, Longmeadow MA 01106-2292
Lisa Casassa, Director of Admissions
413-565-1331 Fax: 413-565-1105
Website: www.baypath.edu
E-mail: lcasassa@baypath.edu

Becker College
Campuses in Worcester and Leicester, MA
61 Sever St, Worcester MA 01609-2165
Karen H. Schedin, Director of Admissions
508-791-9241 Fax: 508-890-1500
Website: www.becker.edu
E-mail: admissions@becker.edu
See listing under "Universities"

Boston University
121 Bay State Rd, Boston MA 02215
Kelly Walter, Executive Director of Admissions
617-353-2300 Fax: 617-353-9695
Website: web.bu.edu
E-mail: admissions@bu.edu

MASSACHUSETTS SCHOOL PROFESSIONAL PSYCHOLOGY
221 Rivermoor St, Boston MA 02132-4935
Mario Murga, Director of Admissions
617-327-6777 or 888-664-MSPP Fax: 617-327-4447
Website: www.mspp.edu
E-mail: admissions@mspp.edu
   Private. Accreditation: American Psychological Association (APA), National Register of Health Service Provid-
ers in Psychology, New England Association of Schools
and Colleges (NEASC). Tuition: $23,450. Enrollment:
220. Faculty: 33. Student-faculty ratio: 13:1. Degrees offered: Doctor of Psychology Psy.D., School Psychology
Specialist MA/CAGS, Clinical Psychopharmacology M.S.
Certificates offered: Respecialization in Clinical Pyschol-
ogy, Professional Executive Coaching. Library: 7,000 volumes. MSPP seeks a diverse group of students who
demonstrate academic and clinical aptitude with personal qualities to work with a variety of human problems.
Concurrent Theory and practice throughout the Psy.D.
and MA/CAGS Programs. Specialty Tracks available in
the Psy.D. program in: Forensic and Health Psychology.

University of Massachusetts Dartmouth
Old Westport Rd, North Dartmouth MA 02747-2300
Steven T. Briggs, Director of Admissions
508-999-8605 Fax: 508-999-8755
Website: explore.umassd.edu
E-mail: sbriggs@umassd.edu

Westfield State College
PO Box 1630, Westfield MA 01086
Michelle Mattie, Associate Dean, Admission and
Enrollment Services
413-572-5300
Website: www.wsc.ma.edu
E-mail: admission@wsc.ma.edu

MICHIGAN

Andrews University
Berrien Springs MI 49104-0001
Randall Graves, Director of Recruitment Services
800-253-2874 Fax: 269-471-2670
Website: www.connect.andrews.edu
E-mail: gravesr@andrews.edu

Delta College
University Center MI 48710-0001
Duff Zube, Director of Admissions
989-686-9093 Fax: 989-667-2202
Website: www.delta.edu
E-mail: admit@delta.edu

Grand Valley State University
1 Campus Dr, Allendale MI 49401-9403
616-331-2025 Fax: 616-331-2000
Website: www.gvsu.edu
E-mail: go2gvsu@gvsu.edu

HILLSDALE COLLEGE
33 E College St, Hillsdale MI 49242-1298
Dr. Fritz Tsao, Director
517-607-2473 Fax: 517-607-2208
Website: www.hillsdale.edu

MACOMB COMMUNITY COLLEGE
44575 Garfield Rd, Clinton Township MI 48038-1139
Information Center
586-445-7999
Website: www.macomb.edu
E-mail: answer@macomb.edu

MACOMB COMMUNITY COLLEGE
14500 E 12 Mile Rd, Warren MI 48088-3896
Information Center
586-445-7999
Website: www.macomb.edu
E-mail: answer@macomb.edu

University of Michigan-Dearborn
4901 Evergreen Rd, Dearborn MI 48128-1491
The Office of Admissions & Orientation
313-593-5100 Fax: 313-436-9167
Website: www.umd.umich.edu
E-mail: admissions@umd.umich.edu

MINNESOTA

ARGOSY UNIVERSITY / TWIN CITIES
(formerly Minnesota School of Professional Psychology)
1515 Central Pkwy, Eagan MN 55121-1756
O. Jeanne Stoneking, Director of Admissions
651-846-2882 Fax: 651-994-7956
Website: www.argosyu.edu
E-mail: tcadmissions@argosyu.edu

Bethany Lutheran College
700 Luther Dr, Mankato MN 56001
Don Westphal, Dean of Admissions
507-344-7000 Fax: 507-344-7376
Website: www.blc.edu
E-mail: admiss@blc.edu

Carleton College
1 N College St, Northfield MN 55057-4044
800-995-2275 or 507-646-4190 Fax: 507-646-4526
Website: www.carleton.edu
E-mail: admissions@acs.carleton.edu

MISSISSIPPI

Tougaloo College
500 W County Line Rd, Tougaloo MS 39174-9799
Juno Leggette Jacobs, Director of Admissions
601-977-7768 Fax: 601-977-4501
Website: www.tougaloo.edu
E-mail: jjacobs@tougaloo.edu

MISSOURI

Columbia College
1001 Rogers St, Columbia MO 65216-0001
Regina Morin, Director of Admissions
573-875-7352 Fax: 573-875-7506
Website: www.ccis.edu
E-mail: admissions@ccis.edu

Stephens College
PO Box 2121, Columbia MO 65215-0001
David Adams, Dean of Enrollment Management
573-442-2211 Fax: 573-876-7237
Website: www.stephens.edu
E-mail: dadams@stephens.edu

Truman State University
100 E Normal, Kirksville MO 63501
Office of Admission
660-785-4000 Fax: 660-785-4181
Website: admissions.truman.edu
E-mail: admissions@truman.edu

University of Missouri
1 University Blvd, Saint Louis MO 63121-4499
Dr. Mark Burkholder, Dean-College of Arts & Sciences
314-516-5501 Fax: 314-516-5415
Website: www.umsl.edu
E-mail: admissions@umsl.edu

Webster University
470 E Lockwood Ave, Saint Louis MO 63119-3194
Bill Huddleston-Berry, Chairman, Behavioral Sciences
314-968-7160 Fax: 314-963-6094
Website: www.webster.edu
E-mail: huddlews@webster.edu
See listing under "Universities"

William Woods University
1 University Ave, Fulton MO 65251-1098
Jimmy Clay, Director of Admissions
573-642-2251 Fax: 573-592-1146
Website: www.williamwoods.edu
E-mail: admissions@williamwoods.edu
See listing under "Universities"

MONTANA

Rocky Mountain College
1511 Poly Dr, Billings MT 59102-1796
Bonnie Knapp, Director of Admissions
800-877-6259 Fax: 406-657-1189
Website: www.rocky.edu
E-mail: admissions@rocky.edu

NEBRASKA

Peru State College
PO Box 10, Peru NE 68421-0010
Office of Admissions
800-742-4412 Fax: 402-872-2296
Website: www.peru.edu
E-mail: admissions@oakmail.peru.edu

NEW HAMPSHIRE

Antioch University New England
40 Avon St, Keene NH 03431-3516
David Caruso, President
Leatrice A. Johnson, Director of Admissions
603-357-6265 Fax: 603-357-0718
Website: www.antiochne.edu
E-mail: admissions@antiochne.edu

Southern New Hampshire University
2500 N River Rd, Hooksett NH 03106-1045
Steve Soba, Director of Admissions
603-645-9611 Fax: 603-645-9693
Website: www.snhu.edu
E-mail: s.soba@snhu.edu

NEW JERSEY

Bergen Community College
400 Paramus Rd, Paramus NJ 07652
Julian Gomez, Asst. Director of Admissions
201-447-7100 Fax: 201-444-7036
Website: www.bergen.edu
E-mail: jgomez@bergen.edu

New Jersey City University
2039 John F Kennedy Blvd
Jersey City NJ 07305-1588
Carmen Panlilio, Asst. V.P. for Admissions and
Financial Aid
201-200-3234 Fax: 201-200-2044
Website: www.njcu.edu
E-mail: admissions@njcu.edu

Ramapo College of New Jersey
505 Ramapo Valley Rd, Mahwah NJ 07430-1623
Director of Admissions
201-684-7300 or 201-684-7301 Fax: 201-684-7964
Website: www.ramapo.edu
E-mail: admissions@ramapo.edu

NEW YORK

College of Saint Rose
432 Western Ave, Albany NY 12203-1419
Maryelizabeth Amico, Asst V.P. for Undergraduate
Admissions
518-454-5150 Fax: 518-454-2013
Website: www.strose.edu
E-mail: admit@strose.edu

CUNY Hunter College
695 Park Ave, New York NY 10021
Aaron Gibbs, Assistant Director of Recruitment
212-772-4497 Fax: 212-650-3336
Website: www.hunter.cuny.edu
E-mail: aaron.gibbs@hunter.cuny.edu

Daemen College
4380 Main St, Amherst NY 14226-3592
Donna Shaffner, Director of Admissions
800-462-7652 or 716-839-8225 Fax: 716-839-8229
Website: www.daemen.edu
E-mail: admissions@daemen.edu
See listing under "Universities"

Hilbert College
5200 S Park Ave, Hamburg NY 14075-1597
Timothy Lee, Director of Admissions
716-649-7900 Fax: 716-649-0702
Website: www.hilbert.edu
E-mail: tlee@hilbert.edu

Long Island University-C. W. Post Campus
720 Northern Blvd, Brookville NY 11548-1300
Joanne Graziano, Executive Director of Admissions
516-299-2900 Fax: 516-299-2137
Website: www.liu.edu/cwpost
E-mail: enroll@cwpost.liu.edu

Molloy College
1000 Hempstead Ave
Rockville Centre NY 11570-1100
Marguerite Lane, Director of Admissions
516-678-5000 ext. 6291 Fax: 516-256-2247
Website: www.molloy.edu
E-mail: admissions@molloy.edu
See listing under "Universities"

PURCHASE COLLEGE STATE UNIVERSITY OF NEW YORK (SUNY)
735 Anderson Hill Rd, Purchase NY 10577-1400
Betsy Immergut, Director of Admissions
914-251-6300 Fax: 914-251-6314
Website: www.purchase.edu
See listing under "Universities"

Roberts Wesleyan College
2301 Westside Dr, Rochester NY 14624-1997
Office of Admissions
585-594-6400 Fax: 585-594-6371
Website: www.roberts.edu
E-mail: admissions@roberts.edu

St. John's University
8000 Utopia Pkwy, Queens NY 11439
Office of Admission
718-990-2000 or 888-9-STJOHNS Fax: 718-990-2096
Website: www.stjohns.edu
E-mail: admissions@stjohns.edu
See listing under "Universities"

St. Joseph's College
245 Clinton Ave, Brooklyn NY 11205-3688
Theresa LaRocca Meyer, V.P. for Enrollment
Management
718-636-6800 Fax: 718-636-8303
Website: www.sjcny.edu
E-mail: tlaroccameyer@sjcny.edu

SUNY College at Brockport
350 New Campus Dr, Brockport NY 14420-2997
Bernard S. Valento, Director of Undergraduate
Admissions
585-395-2751 Fax: 585-395-5452
Website: www.brockport.edu
E-mail: admit@brockport.edu

SUNY College of Technology
Alfred NY 14802
Deborah J. Goodrich, Director of Admissions
800-4AL-FRED Fax: 607-587-4299
Website: www.alfredstate.edu
E-mail: admissions@alfredstate.edu

SUNY Orange County Community College
115 South St, Middletown NY 10940-6437
Margot St. Lawrence, Director of Admissions
845-341-4030 Fax: 845-342-8662
Website: www.sunyorange.edu
E-mail: apply@sunyorange.edu
See listing under "Community and Junior Colleges"

Wells College
PO Box 500, Aurora NY 13026
Susan Sloan, Director of Admissions
800-952-9355 Fax: 315-364-3227
Website: www.wells.edu
E-mail: ssloan@wells.edu

NORTH CAROLINA

Belmont Abbey College
100 Belmont Mount Holly Rd
Belmont NC 28012-1802
888-222-0110 Fax: 704-825-6670
Website: www.belmontabbeycollege.edu
E-mail: admissions@bac.edu

Lees-McRae College
PO Box 128, Banner Elk NC 28604-0128
Walt Crutchfield, Dean of Admissions
800-280-4562 Fax: 828-898-8707
Website: www.lmc.edu
E-mail: admissions@lmc.edu

Louisburg College
501 N Main St, Louisburg NC 27549-2399
800-775-0208 or 919-496-2521 Fax: 919-496-1788
Website: www.louisburg.edu
E-mail: admissions@louisburg.edu

Meredith College
3800 Hillsborough St, Raleigh NC 27607-5298
Heidi L. Fletcher, Director of Admissions
919-760-8581 Fax: 919-760-2348
Website: www.meredith.edu
E-mail: admissions@meredith.edu
See listing under "Women's Colleges"

Mt. Olive College
634 Henderson St, Mount Olive NC 28365
Tim Woodard, Director of Admissions
919-658-2502 Fax: 919-658-9816
Website: www.moc.edu
E-mail: admissions@moc.edu
See listing under "Universities"

Salem College
Winston Salem NC 27108
Dana Evans, Dean of Admissions/Fin. Aid
800-32-SALEM Fax: 336-917-5572
Website: www.salem.edu
E-mail: admissions@salem.edu
See listing under "Women's Colleges"

NORTH DAKOTA

Dickinson State University
Dickinson ND 58601-4896
Steve Glasser, Director of Student Recruitment
800-279-4295 Fax: 701-483-2409
Website: www.dickinsonstate.edu
E-mail: dsu.hawks@dickinsonstate.edu

Valley City State University
101 College St SW, Valley City ND 58072-4024
Dan Klein, Director of Enrollment Services
800-532-8641 ext. 7101 Fax: 701-845-7299
Website: www.vcsu.edu
E-mail: enrollment.services@vcsu.edu
See listing under "Universities"

OHIO

Cleveland State University
2121 Euclid Ave RW 204, Cleveland OH 44115
Dr. Richard Arndt, Dean of Undergraduate Recruitment
and College Partnerships
888-CSU-OHIO Fax: 216-687-9210
Website: www.csuohio.edu
E-mail: admissions@csuohio.edu

Franciscan University of Steubenville
University Blvd, Steubenville OH 43952
Margaret J. Weber, Director of Admissions
800-783-6220 or 740-283-6226 Fax: 740-284-5456
Website: www.admissions.edu
E-mail: mweber@franciscan.edu

Mount Vernon Nazarene University
800 Martinsburg Rd, Mount Vernon OH 43050-9509
Timothy Eades, Director of Admissions
866-462-6868 Fax: 740-393-0511
Website: www.gotomvnu.edu
E-mail: admissions@mvnu.edu
See listing under "Universities"

The Ohio State University
Department of Psychology
Townshend Hall, 1885 Neil Avenue Mall
Columbus OH 43210
614-292-8185 Fax: 614-292-4537
Website: www.psy.ohio-state.edu

University of Dayton
300 College Park, Dayton OH 45469-1300
Robert F. Durkle, Director of Admissions
800-837-7433 Fax: 937-229-4729
Website: admission.udayton.edu
E-mail: admission@udayton.edu

Ursuline College
2550 Lander Rd, Cleveland OH 44124-4398
Sarah E. Sundermeier, Director of Admissions
888-URSULINE Toll Free Fax: 440-684-6138
Website: www.admission.ursuline.edu
E-mail: admission@ursuline.edu

OKLAHOMA

Mid-America Christian University
3500 SW 119th St, Oklahoma City OK 73170-4504
Haley Hope, Director of Admissions
405-691-3800 Fax: 405-692-3165
Website: www.macu.edu
E-mail: info@macu.edu

Oklahoma State University
Stillwater OK 74078
Maureen Sullivan, Department Head
405-744-7054
Website: www.okstate.edu
E-mail: maureen@okstate.edu

Oral Roberts University
7777 S Lewis Ave, Tulsa OK 74171-0001
Chris Belcher, Director of Undergraduate Admissions
800-678-8876 Fax: 918-495-6222
Website: www.oru.edu
E-mail: admissions@oru.edu

University of Tulsa
600 S College Ave, Tulsa OK 74104-3126
Earl Johnson, Dean of Admission
918-631-2307 Fax: 918-631-5003
Website: www.utulsa.edu
E-mail: admission@utulsa.edu

OREGON

Cascade College
9101 E Burnside St, Portland OR 97216-1599
800-550-7678 Fax: 503-257-1222
Website: www.cascade.edu
E-mail: admissions@cascade.edu

Marylhurst University
17600 Pacific Hwy (Hwy 43)
Marylhurst OR 97036-0261
Director of Admissions
800-634-9982 ext. 6268 Fax: 503-635-6585
Website: www.marylhurst.edu
E-mail: studentinfo@marylhurst.edu

Pacific University
2043 College Way, Forest Grove OR 97116-1797
Karen M. Dunston, Executive Director of Admissions
800-635-0561 Fax: 503-352-2975
Website: www.pacificu.edu
E-mail: admissions@pacificu.edu

Warner Pacific College
2219 SE 68th Ave, Portland OR 97215-4026
Shannon Mackey, Director of Admissions
503-517-1000 Fax: 503-517-1352
Website: www.warnerpacific.edu
E-mail: admissions@warnerpacific.edu

Western Oregon University
345 Monmouth Ave N, Monmouth OR 97361-1314
David McDonald, Dean, Admission, Retention &
Enrollment Management
877-877-1593 Fax: 503-838-8067
Website: www.wou.edu
E-mail: wolfgram@fsa.wou.edu

PENNSYLVANIA

Arcadia University
450 S Easton Rd, Glenside PA 19038-3295
Dennis Nostrand, VP for Enrollment Management
877-ARCADIA (877-272-2342) Fax: 215-881-8767
Website: www.arcadia.edu
E-mail: admiss@arcadia.edu
See listing under "Universities"

Clarion University of Pennsylvania
840 Wood St, Clarion PA 16214-1232
William Bailey, Dean of Enrollment Management
814-393-2306 Fax: 814-393-2030
Website: www.clarion.edu
E-mail: admissions@clarion.edu

Gannon University
109 University Sq, Erie PA 16541-0001
Christopher Tremblay, Director of Admissions
800-GANNON-U Fax: 814-871-5803
Website: www.gannon.edu
E-mail: admissions@gannon.edu

Holy Family University
9801 Frankford Avenue, Philadelphia PA 19114
Lauren Campbell, Director of Admissions
215-637-3050 Fax: 215-281-1022
Website: www.holyfamily.edu
E-mail: admissions@holyfamily.edu

Juniata College
1700 Moore St, Huntingdon PA 16652-2196
Michelle Bartol, Dean of Enrollment
877-JUNIATA Fax: 814-641-3100
Website: www.juniata.edu
E-mail: admissions@juniata.edu

La Roche College
9000 Babcock Blvd, Pittsburgh PA 15237-5898
Thomas Hassett, Director of Freshman and
International Admissions
412-536-1272 or 800-838-4LRC Fax: 412-536-1272
Website: www.laroche.edu
E-mail: admissions@laroche.edu

Lebanon Valley College
101 N College Ave, Annville PA 17003-1400
William Brown, Dean of Admissions & Financial Aid
866-LVC-4ADM or 717-867-6181 Fax: 717-867-6026
Website: www.lvc.edu
E-mail: admission@lvc.edu

MOUNT ALOYSIUS COLLEGE
7373 Admiral Peary Hwy, Cresson PA 16630-1999
Frank C. Crouse Jr., Vice President for Enrollment
Management
814-886-6383 or 888-823-2220 Fax: 814-886-6441
Website: www.mtaloy.edu
E-mail: admissions@mtaloy.edu

University of Pittsburgh
1150 Mount Pleasant Rd
Greensburg PA 15601-5860
Brandi S. Darr, Director of Admissions and Financial
Aid
724-836-9880 Fax: 724-836-7160
Website: www.upg.pitt.edu
E-mail: upgadmit@pitt.edu

Washington & Jefferson College
60 S Lincoln St, Washington PA 15301-4801
Alton E. Newell, Vice President for Enrollment
724-223-6025 Fax: 724-223-6534
Website: www.washjeff.edu
E-mail: admission@washjeff.edu

SOUTH CAROLINA

Columbia International University
PO Box 3122, Columbia SC 29230-3122
John Basie, Director of University Admissions
800-777-2227 Fax: 803-786-4209
Website: www.ciu.edu
E-mail: yesciu@ciu.edu
See listing under "Theological Studies & Religious
Vocations"

Erskine College & Seminary
PO Box 176, Due West SC 29639
Bart Walker, Director of Admissions
864-379-8838 Fax: 864-379-3048
Website: www.erskine.edu
E-mail: admissions@erskine.edu

North Greenville University
PO Box 1892, Tigerville SC 29688-1892
Website: www.ngc.edu
See listing under "Universities"

PRESBYTERIAN COLLEGE

503 S Broad St, Clinton SC 29325
Richard Dana Paul, Dean of Admissions
800-476-7272 Fax: 864-833-8481
Website: www.presby.edu
E-mail: admissions@presby.edu

South University
9 Science Court, Columbia SC 29203
Trish Wade, Contact
803-799-9082 Fax: 803-799-9038
Website: www.southuniversity.edu
E-mail: twade@southuniversity.edu

University of South Carolina - Upstate
800 University Way, Spartanburg SC 29303-4932
Donette Stewart, Assistant VC for Enrollment Services
864-503-5246 Fax: 864-503-5727
Website: www.uscupstate.edu
E-mail: dstewart@uscupstate.edu
See listing under "Universities"

TENNESSEE

Lipscomb University
3901 Granny White Pike, Nashville TN 37204-3951
Ricky Holaway, Director of Admissions
800-333-4358 ext. 1776 Fax: 615-269-1804
Website: www.lipscomb.edu
E-mail: admissions@lipscomb.edu

Tusculum College
PO Box 5051, Greeneville TN 37743
Melissa Ripley, Associate Director of Admissions
800-729-0256 Fax: 423-798-1622
Website: www.tusculum.edu
E-mail: mripley@tusculum.edu

TEXAS

Angelo State University
ASU Station 11014, San Angelo TX 76909
Bonnie Stennett, Coordinator of Recruiting
800-946-8627 Fax: 325-942-2078
Website: www.angelo.edu
E-mail: admissions@angelo.edu

Our Lady of the Lake University
411 SW 24th St, San Antonio TX 78207-4666
Mary Kay Cooper, Dean of Enrollment
210-434-6711 Fax: 210-431-4013
Website: www.ollusa.edu
E-mail: admission@lakeollusa.edu

Texas Woman's University
PO Box 425589, Denton TX 76204-5589
Erma Nieto, Director of Admissions
866-809-6130 Fax: 940-898-3081
Website: www.twu.edu
E-mail: admissions@twu.edu

University of Houston
122 E Cullen Bldg, Houston TX 77204-2023
Office of Admission
713-743-9595
Website: www.uh.edu
E-mail: admissions@uh.edu

University of Texas at Arlington
Box 19111, Arlington TX 76019-0111
Hans Gatterdam, Director of Admission
817-272-6287 Fax: 817-272-3435
Website: www.uta.edu
E-mail: admissions@uta.edu

VERMONT

Bennington College
One College Drive, Bennington VT 05201
Ken Himmelman, Dean of Admissions & Financial Aid
800-833-6845 Fax: 802-440-4320
Website: www.bennington.edu
E-mail: admissions@bennington.edu

NORWICH UNIVERSITY

158 Harmon Dr, Northfield VT 05663
Dr. Johnnie Stones, Department Head
800-468-6679 Fax: 802-485-2252
Website: www.norwich.edu
E-mail: stones@norwich.edu
See listing under "Universities"

Southern Vermont College
982 Mansion Dr, Bennington VT 05201-6002
Kathleen James Ring, Director of Admissions
800-378-2782 Fax: 802-447-4695
Website: www.svc.edu
E-mail: admis@svc.edu

VIRGINIA

ARGOSY UNIVERSITY/WASHINGTON DC

1550 Wilson Blvd Ste 600, Arlington VA 22209
Emily Peck, Director of Admissions
703-526-5800 Fax: 703-243-8973
Website: www.argosyu.edu
E-mail: epeck@argosyu.edu

Mary Baldwin College
Staunton VA 24401
Lisa A. Branson, Executive Director of Admissions and
Financial Aid
800-468-2262 Fax: 540-887-7292
Website: www.mbc.edu
E-mail: admit@mbc.edu

Radford University
PO Box 6903, Radford VA 24142
David W. Kraus, Director of Admissions
800-890-4265 Fax: 540-831-5038
Website: www.radford.edu
E-mail: ruadmiss@radford.edu

Randolph-Macon Woman's College
2500 Rivermont Ave, Lynchburg VA 24503
Patricia LeDonne, Director of Admissions
434-947-8100 Fax: 434-947-8996
Website: www.rmwc.edu
E-mail: admissions@rmwc.edu

WASHINGTON

Gonzaga University
502 E Boone Ave, Spokane WA 99258-0102
Julie McCulloh, Dean of Admission
800-322-2584 or 509-323-6572 Fax: 509-323-5780
Website: www.gonzaga.edu
E-mail: mcculloh@gu.gonzaga.edu

WEST VIRGINIA

Concord University
Athens WV 24712
Michael Curry, Vice President of Financial Aid &
Admissions
888-384-5249 Fax: 304-384-3218
Website: www.concord.edu
E-mail: admissions@concord.edu

Davis & Elkins College
100 Campus Dr, Elkins WV 26241-3996
Renee Heckel, Director of Enrollment Management
800-624-3157 Fax: 304-637-1800
Website: www.davisandelkins.edu
E-mail: admiss@davisandelkins.edu

Fairmont State University
1201 Locust Ave, Fairmont WV 26554-2470
Steve Leadman, Director of Admissions
304-367-4892 or 800-641-5678 Fax: 304-367-4789
Website: www.fairmontstate.edu
E-mail: admit@fairmontstate.edu

Mountain State College
1508 Spring St, Parkersburg WV 26101-3993
Judith Sutton, Director
304-485-5487 Fax: 304-485-3524
Website: www.mountainstate.org
E-mail: admin@mountainstate.org
See listing under "Career Schools"

West Virginia Wesleyan College
59 College Ave, Buckhannon WV 26201-2699
Robert N. Skinner II, Director of Admission
800-722-9933 Fax: 304-473-8108
Website: www.wvwc.edu
E-mail: admission@wvwc.edu

WISCONSIN

Alverno College
PO Box 343922, Milwaukee WI 53234-3922
Mary Kay Farrell, Director of Admissions
414-382-6100 Fax: 414-382-6354
Website: www.alverno.edu
E-mail: admissions@alverno.edu

St. Norbert College
100 Grant St, De Pere WI 54115
Brian Studebaker, Director of Admission
800-236-4878 Fax: 920-403-4072
Website: www.snc.edu
E-mail: admit@snc.edu

WISCONSIN SCHOOL OF PROFESSIONAL PSYCHOLOGY

9120 W Hampton Ave Ste 212
Milwaukee WI 53225-4960
Howard Haven, Ph.D., Dean
414-464-9777 Fax: 414-358-5590
Website: www.wspp.edu
E-mail: admissions@wspp.edu

WYOMING

University of Wyoming
Admissions Office
Dept 3435, Laramie WY 82071-3435
Aaron Appelhans, Contact
800-342-5996 Fax: 307-766-4042
Website: www.uwyo.edu
E-mail: why-wyo@uwyo.edu

GUAM

University of Guam
UOG Station, Mangilao GU 96923
Deborah Leon Guerrero, Registrar
671-735-2201 or 671-735-2208 Fax: 671-735-2203
Website: www.uog.edu
E-mail: admitme@uog9.uog.edu

PUERTO RICO

CARLOS ALBIZU UNIVERSITY - SAN JUAN CAMPUS

PO Box 9023711, San Juan PR 00902-3711
Carlos Rodriguez, Director of Admissions
787-725-6500 Fax: 787-721-7187
Website: albizu.edu
E-mail: crodriguez@albizu.edu

PUBLIC HEALTH

ALASKA

University of Alaska Anchorage
PO Box 141629, Anchorage AK 99514-1629
Cecile Mitchell, Director of Enrollment Services
907-786-1480 Fax: 907-786-4888
Website: www.uaa.alaska.edu/
E-mail: enroll@uaa.alaska.edu

University of Alaska Southeast
11120 Glacier Hwy, Juneau AK 99801-8625
Paul Kraft, Dean of Students/Enrollment Management
907-796-6000 Fax: 907-796-6005
Website: www.uas.alaska.edu
E-mail: paul.kraft@uas.alaska.edu

ARIZONA

University of Arizona
Tucson AZ 85721-0040
Paul Kohn, Director of Admissions
520-621-3237 Fax: 520-621-9799
Website: www.admissions.arizona.edu or
www.arizona.edu

COLORADO

University of Colorado at Denver and Health Sciences
Center
Health Sciences Program
4200 E 9th Ave Box C245, Denver CO 80262
Phoebe Lindsey Barton, Ph.D., Director
Website: www.uchsc.edu

FLORIDA

Nova Southeastern University Health Profession
3200 S University Dr, Davie FL 33328-2018
Marla Frohlinger, Director of Admissions
954-262-1101 Fax: 954-262-2282
Website: www.nova.edu
E-mail: marlaf@nsu.nova.edu

University of South Florida
4202 E Fowler Ave, Tampa FL 33620-6900
J. Robert Spatig, Director of Admissions
813-974-3350 Fax: 813-974-9689
Website: www.usf.edu
E-mail: admissions@admin.usf.edu

GEORGIA

North Georgia Technical College
434 Meeks Ave, Blairsville GA 30512-2983
Admissions
706-781-2300 Fax: 706-781-2307
Website: www.northgatech.edu
E-mail: info@northgatech.edu

North Georgia Technical College
Clarkesville Campus
PO Box 65, Clarkesville GA 30523-0002
Admissions
706-754-7700 Fax: 706-754-7777
Website: www.northgatech.edu
E-mail: info@northgatech.edu

ILLINOIS

Benedictine University
5700 College Rd, Lisle IL 60532-0900
630-829-6300 or 888-829-6363 Fax: 630-829-6301
Website: www.ben.edu
E-mail: admissions@ben.edu
See listing under "Universities"

LOUISIANA

Delta School of Business and Technology
517 Broad St, Lake Charles LA 70601-4334
Gary Holt, President
337-439-5765 Fax: 337-436-5151
Website: www.deltatech.edu
E-mail: susan@deltatech.edu

Dillard University
2601 Gentilly Blvd, New Orleans LA 70122-3097
Linda G. Nash, Director of Admissions
Website: www.dillard.edu
E-mail: admissions@dillard.edu

NEW YORK

CUNY Hunter College
695 Park Ave, New York NY 10021
Aaron Gibbs, Assistant Director of Recruitment
212-772-4497 Fax: 212-650-3336
Website: www.hunter.cuny.edu
E-mail: aaron.gibbs@hunter.cuny.edu

Long Island University-C. W. Post Campus
720 Northern Blvd, Brookville NY 11548-1300
Joanne Graziano, Executive Director of Admissions
516-299-2900 Fax: 516-299-2137
Website: www.liu.edu/cwpost
E-mail: enroll@cwpost.liu.edu

OHIO

The Ohio State University
School of Public Health
Starling-Loving Hall, 320 W 10th Ave
Columbus OH 43210
614-293-3907 Fax: 614-293-5412
Website: sph.osu.edu
E-mail: sph@osu.edu

TEXAS

Texas Woman's University
PO Box 425589, Denton TX 76204-5589
Erma Nieto, Director of Admissions
866-809-6130 Fax: 940-898-3081
Website: www.twu.edu
E-mail: admissions@twu.edu

VERMONT

Woodbury College
660 Elm St, Montpelier VT 05602-4017
Kathleen Moore, Director of Admissions
800-639-6039 Fax: 802-229-2141
Website: www.woodbury-college.edu
E-mail: admiss@woodbury-college.edu

WISCONSIN

Medical College of Wisconsin
PO Box 26509, Milwaukee WI 53226-0509
Michael Istwan, Director of Admissions
414-456-8296 Fax: 414-456-6506
Website: www.mcw.edu
E-mail: mcwms@mcw.edu

SOCIAL SCIENCE

ALABAMA

Alabama A & M University
PO Box 908, Normal AL 35762
Antonio Boyle, Director of Admissions
256-372-5245 Fax: 256-372-5249
Website: www.aamu.edu
E-mail: aboyle@aamu.edu

Faulkner University
5345 Atlanta Hwy, Montgomery AL 36109-3398
Keith Mock, Director of Admissions
800-879-9816 ext. 7200 or 334-386-7200
Fax: 334-386-7137
Website: www.faulkner.edu
E-mail: admissions@faulkner.edu

Judson College
302 Bibb St, Marion AL 36756
Michael Scotto, Director of Admissions
800-447-9472 Fax: 334-683-5147
Website: www.judson.edu
E-mail: admissions@judson.edu

University of Alabama in Huntsville
PO Box 1247, Huntsville AL 35899-0001
Ann Lee, Assoc. Director for Recruiting Program and
Events
1-800-UAH-CALL Fax: 256-824-6073
Website: www.uah.edu
E-mail: leev@uah.edu

University of South Alabama
307 University Blvd N, Mobile AL 36688-3053
Melissa Haab, Director of Admissions
251-460-6141 Fax: 251-460-7876
Website: www.southalabama.edu
E-mail: admiss@usouthal.edu

ALASKA

University of Alaska Anchorage
PO Box 141629, Anchorage AK 99514-1629
Cecile Mitchell, Director of Enrollment Services
907-786-1480 Fax: 907-786-4888
Website: www.uaa.alaska.edu/
E-mail: enroll@uaa.alaska.edu

University of Alaska Southeast
11120 Glacier Hwy, Juneau AK 99801-8625
Paul Kraft, Dean of Students/Enrollment Management
907-796-6000 Fax: 907-796-6005
Website: www.uas.alaska.edu
E-mail: paul.kraft@uas.alaska.edu

ARIZONA

University of Arizona
Tucson AZ 85721-0040
Paul Kohn, Director of Admissions
520-621-3237 Fax: 520-621-9799
Website: www.admissions.arizona.edu or
www.arizona.edu

ARKANSAS

Ouachita Baptist University
410 Ouachita St, Arkadelphia AR 71998-0001
David Goodman, Director of Admissions
870-245-5110 Fax: 870-245-5500
Website: www.obu.edu
E-mail: admissions@obu.edu

CALIFORNIA

Antioch University
801 Garden St Ste 101
Santa Barbara CA 93101-1581
Ankara McPherson, Director of Admissions
805-962-8179 Fax: 805-962-4786
Website: www.antiochsb.edu
E-mail: amcpherson@antiochsb.edu

California State University-San Bernadino
5500 University Pkwy
San Bernardino CA 92407-2393
Olivia Rosas, Director of Admissions
909-880-5000 Fax: 909-880-7034
Website: enrollment.csusb.edu
E-mail: orosas@csusb.edu

Chapman University
One University Drive, Orange CA 92866-1099
Michael Drummy, Assistant Vice President for
Enrollment
Services and Chief Admission Officer
714-997-6411 or 888-CUAPPLY Fax: 714-997-6713
Website: www.chapman.edu
E-mail: admit@chapman.edu

Concordia University
1530 Concordia, Irvine CA 92612-3203
Lori McDonald, Executive Director of Enrollment
Services
800-229-1200 or 949-854-8002 Fax: 949-854-6894
Website: www.cui.edu
E-mail: admission@cui.edu

FRESNO CITY COLLEGE
1101 E University Ave, Fresno CA 93741-0002
Dayann Dietrich, Contact
559-442-8241 Fax: 559-237-4232
Website: www.fresnocitycollege.com
E-mail: fcc.admissions@scccd.com

Monterey Institute of International Studies
460 Pierce St, Monterey CA 93940
Admissions Office
831-647-4100 Fax: 831-647-6405
Website: www.miis.edu
E-mail: admit@miis.edu

Orange Coast College
PO Box 5005, Costa Mesa CA 92628-5005
Kristin Clark, Director of Admissions
714-432-5773 Fax: 714-432-5736
Website: www.orangecoastcollege.edu
E-mail: kclark@cccd.edu

San Diego Christian College
2100 Greenfield Dr, El Cajon CA 92019-1157
Jon Melone, Director of Admissions
800-676-2242 Fax: 619-590-1739
Website: www.sdcc.edu
E-mail: admissions@sdcc.edu

Whittier College
PO Box 634, Whittier CA 90608-0634
Kieron Miller, Director of Admissions
562-907-4200 Fax: 562-907-4870
Website: www.whittier.edu
E-mail: kmiller@whittier.edu

CONNECTICUT

Albertus Magnus College
700 Prospect St, New Haven CT 06511-1189
Richard Lolatte, Dean of Admission
203-773-8501 or 800-578-9160 Fax: 203-773-5248
Website: www.albertus.edu
E-mail: admissions@albertus.edu

University of New Haven
300 Boston Post Rd, West Haven CT 06516
Director of Undergraduate Admissions
203-932-7319 Fax: 203-931-6093
Website: www.newhaven.edu
E-mail: adminfo@newhaven.edu

DELAWARE

Wesley College
120 N State St, Dover DE 19901-3876
302-736-2300 Fax: 302-736-2301
Website: www.wesley.edu

FLORIDA

Florida State University
600 W College Ave, Tallahassee FL 32306-1096
Janice V. Finney, Director of Admissions
850-644-2525 Fax: 850-644-0197
Website: admissions.fsu.edu
E-mail: admissions@admin.fsu.edu

Lynn University
3601 N Military Trl, Boca Raton FL 33431-5598
Brett Ormandy, Director of Admissions
561-237-7900 Fax: 561-237-7100
Website: www.lynn.edu
E-mail: admission@lynn.edu

Saint Leo University
PO Box 6665, Saint Leo FL 33574
Deborah Bandy, Director of Admissions
352-588-8200 or 800-334-5532 Fax: 352-588-8257
Website: www.saintleo.edu
E-mail: admission@saintleo.edu

St. Thomas University
16401 NW 37th Ave, Miami Gardens FL 33054
Dr. Gary Feinberg, Chair, Social Sciences
800-367-9010 or 305-628-6546 Fax: 305-628-6591
Website: www.stu.edu
E-mail: signup@stu.edu

University of South Florida
4202 E Fowler Ave, Tampa FL 33620-6900
J. Robert Spatig, Director of Admissions
813-974-3350 Fax: 813-974-9689
Website: www.usf.edu
E-mail: admissions@admin.usf.edu

GEORGIA

Armstrong Atlantic State University
11935 Abercorn St, Savannah GA 31419-1997
Kim West, Asst. Dean and Registrar Enrollment
Services
912-927-5277 Fax: 912-921-5462
Website: www.armstrong.edu
E-mail: admissions@mail.armstrong.edu

Kennesaw State University
1000 Chastain Rd NW, Kennesaw GA 30144-5591
Dr. Helen Ridley, Dean of Humanities and Social
Science
770-423-6124
Website: www.kennesaw.edu

Oglethorpe University
4484 Peachtree Rd NE, Atlanta GA 30319-2797
Kelly Gosnell, Director of Admission
404-261-1441 Fax: 404-364-8491
Website: www.oglethorpe.edu
E-mail: admission@oglethorpe.edu

IDAHO

Brigham Young University - Idaho
120 Kimball Bldg, Rexburg ID 83460
Gordon Westenskow, Director of Admissions
208-496-1020 Fax: 208-496-1220
Website: www.byui.edu
E-mail: admissions@byui.edu

University of Idaho
Moscow ID 83844-4253
Lloyd Scott, Director of New Student Services
208-885-6163 Fax: 208-885-4477
Website: www.uidaho.edu
E-mail: nss@uidaho.edu

ILLINOIS

Aurora University
347 S Gladstone Ave, Aurora IL 60506-4892
Carol R. Dunn, Ed.D., Vice President for Enrollment
800-742-5281 Fax: 630-844-5535
Website: www.aurora.edu
E-mail: admission@aurora.edu

Benedictine University
5700 College Rd, Lisle IL 60532-0900
630-829-6300 or 888-829-6363 Fax: 630-829-6301
Website: www.ben.edu
E-mail: admissions@ben.edu
See listing under "Universities"

CONCORDIA UNIVERSITY

7400 Augusta St, River Forest IL 60305-1402
708-209-3100 Fax: 708-209-3473
Website: www.curf.edu
E-mail: crfadmis.edu

INSTITUTE FOR CLINICAL SOCIAL WORK

200 N Michigan Ave Ste 407, Chicago IL 60601
Barbara Berger, Ph.D., Dean of Admissions
312-726-8480 Fax: 312-726-7216
Website: www.icsw.edu
E-mail: icsw@icsw.edu

North Central College
30 N Brainard St, Naperville IL 60540-4690
Martha Stolze, Director of Admissions
630-637-5800 Fax: 630-637-5819
Website: www.northcentralcollege.edu
E-mail: admissions@noctrl.edu

Roosevelt University
430 S Michigan Ave, Chicago IL 60605
Gwen E. Kanelos, Asst. Vice President for Enrollment
Services
877-APPLY-RU Fax: 312-341-4216
Website: www.roosevelt.edu
E-mail: applyru@roosevelt.edu

South Suburban College of Cook County
15800 State Rd, South Holland IL 60473
Jane Ellen Stocker, Dean of Enrollment Services
708-596-2000 Fax: 708-225-5806
Website: www.southsuburbancollege.edu
E-mail: jstocker@southsuburbancollege.edu

INDIANA

Ancilla Domini College
Donaldson IN 46513
Erin Wittmeyer, Director of Admissions
574-936-8898 Fax: 574-935-1773
Website: www.ancilla.edu
E-mail: erin.wittmeyer@ancilla.edu

Franklin College
101 Branigin Blvd, Franklin IN 46131
Jacqueline S. Acosta, Director of Admissions
800-852-0232 Fax: 317-738-8274
Website: www.franklincollege.edu
E-mail: admissions@franklincollege.edu

Hanover College
PO Box 108, Hanover IN 47243-0108
William D. Preble, Dean of Admission
800-213-2178 Fax: 812-866-7098
Website: www.hanover.edu
E-mail: admissions@hanover.edu

Oakland City University
138 N Lucretia St, Oakland City IN 47660
Brian J. Baker, Director of Admissions
800-737-5125 Fax: 812-749-1433
Website: www.oak.edu
E-mail: bbaker@oak.edu
See listing under "Universities"

St. Mary-of-the-Woods College
Saint Mary of the Woods IN 47876-1001
James P. Malley, Jr., Director of Admission
800-926-7692 Fax: 812-535-5010
Website: www.smwc.edu
E-mail: smwcadms@smwc.edu

University of Evansville
1800 Lincoln Ave, Evansville IN 47722-0001
Thomas E. Bear, V.P. of Enrollment Services
800-423-8633 Fax: 812-488-4076
Website: www.evansville.edu
E-mail: admission@evansville.edu

IOWA

Briar Cliff University
PO Box 2100, Sioux City IA 51104-0100
Sharisue Wilcoxon, VP for Enrollment Management
712-279-5200 Fax: 712-279-1632
Website: www.briarcliff.edu
E-mail: admissions@briarcliff.edu

Clarke College
1550 Clarke Dr, Dubuque IA 52001-3198
Andy Schroeder, Director of Admissions
800-383-2345 Fax: 563-584-8666
Website: www.clarke.edu
E-mail: andy.schroeder@clarke.edu

Graceland University
1 University Place, Lamoni IA 50140
Brian Shantz, Vice President for Enrollment and Dean
of Admissions
641-784-5196 Fax: 641-784-5480
Website: www.admissions.graceland.edu
E-mail: admissions@graceland.edu

Iowa Lakes Community College
300 S 18th St, Estherville IA 51334-2721
Anne Stansbury, Asst. Director of Admissions
712-362-7945 Fax: 712-362-8363
Website: www.iowalakes.edu
E-mail: info@iowalakes.edu

Mount Mercy College
1330 Elmhurst Dr NE, Cedar Rapids IA 52402-4797
Jim Krystofiak, Dean of Admission
800-248-4504 Fax: 319-363-5270
Website: www.mtmercy.edu
E-mail: admission@mtmercy.edu

Waldorf College
106 S 6th St, Forest City IA 50436-1713
Steve Lovik, Vice President of Enrollment Management
800-292-1903 or 641-585-8112 Fax: 641-585-8125
Website: www.waldorf.edu
E-mail: lovik@waldorf.edu
See listing under "Universities"

Wartburg College
PO Box 1003, Waverly IA 50677-0903
Brent Matthias, Interim Director of Admissions
319-352-8200 Fax: 319-352-8579
Website: www.wartburg.edu
E-mail: admissions@wartburg.edu

KANSAS

COLBY COMMUNITY COLLEGE

1255 S Range Ave, Colby KS 67701-4099
Director of Admissions
888-634-9350 or 785-460-4690 Fax: 785-460-4691
Website: www.colbycc.edu
E-mail: bobbi@colbycc.edu

Independence Community College
PO Box 708, Independence KS 67301-0708
Dr. Terry Hetrick, President
800-842-6063 Fax: 620-331-5344
Website: www.indycc.edu
E-mail: admissions@indycc.edu

Newman University
3100 W McCormick St, Wichita KS 67213
Jann Reusser, Admissions Recruitment Coordinator
316-942-4291 ext. 2144 Fax: 316-942-4483
Website: www.newmanu.edu
E-mail: reusserj@newmanu.edu

Tabor College
400 S Jefferson St, Hillsboro KS 67063-1758
Rusty Allen, Dean of Enrollment Management
620-947-3121 Fax: 620-947-6276
Website: www.tabor.edu
E-mail: admissions@tabor.edu

KENTUCKY

Bluegrass Community and Technical College
Oswald Building
470 Cooper Drive, Lexington KY 40506-0235
Shelbie Hugle, Director of Admissions
859-246-6200 Fax: 859-246-4664
Website: www.bluegrass.kctcs.edu
E-mail: bctc_info@kctcs.edu

Morehead State University
Morehead KY 40351-1689
Dayna Seelig, Enrollment Services
800-585-6781 Fax: 606-783-5038
Website: www.moreheadstate.edu
E-mail: admissions@moreheadstate.edu

Transylvania University
300 N Broadway, Lexington KY 40508-1776
859-233-8242 Fax: 859-233-8797
Website: www.transy.edu
E-mail: admissions@transy.edu

LOUISIANA

Dillard University
2601 Gentilly Blvd, New Orleans LA 70122-3097
Linda G. Nash, Director of Admissions
Website: www.dillard.edu
E-mail: admissions@dillard.edu

Our Lady of Holy Cross College
4123 Woodland Dr, New Orleans LA 70131-7399
Office of Enrollment Services
504-394-7744 Fax: 504-391-2421
Website: www.olhcc.edu

MARYLAND

Hagerstown Community College
11400 Robinwood Dr, Hagerstown MD 21742-6590
Dr. Daniel E. Bock, Assistant Director of Admissions
301-790-2800 Fax: 301-791-9165
Website: www.hagerstowncc.edu
E-mail: bockd@hagerstowncc.edu

Villa Julie College
1525 Greenspring Valley Rd
Stevenson MD 21153-0641
Mark Hergan, V.P. Enrollment Services
410-486-7001 Fax: 410-602-6600
Website: www.vjc.edu/admissions
E-mail: admissions@mail.vjc.edu

MASSACHUSETTS

Anna Maria College
50 Sunset Ln, Paxton MA 01612
Julie A. Mitchell, Director of Admissions
508-849-3360 Fax: 508-849-3362
Website: www.annamaria.edu
E-mail: admissions@annamaria.edu

Assumption College
500 Salisbury St, Worcester MA 01609-1294
Kathleen Murphy, Dean of Enrollment
508-767-7000 Fax: 508-799-4412
Website: www.assumption.edu
E-mail: admiss@assumption.edu

Bay State College
122 Commonwealth Ave, Boston MA 02116-2901
Craig Pfannenstiehl, President
617-217-9000 Fax: 617-536-1735

Boston University
121 Bay State Rd, Boston MA 02215
Kelly Walter, Executive Director of Admissions
617-353-2300 Fax: 617-353-9695
Website: web.bu.edu
E-mail: admissions@bu.edu

Gordon College
255 Grapevine Rd, Wenham MA 01984-1899
Nancy Mering, Director of Admissions
866-464-6736 Fax: 978-867-4682
Website: www.gordon.edu
E-mail: admissions@gordon.edu

Massachusetts Institute of Technology
77 Massachusetts Ave, Cambridge MA 02139-4307
Marilee Jones, Dean of Admission
617-253-1000 Fax: 617-253-4016
Website: my.mit.edu
E-mail: admissions@mit.edu

Smith College
Northampton MA 01063-0001
Debra Shaver, Director of Admissions
800-383-3232 Fax: 413-585-2527
Website: www.smith.edu
E-mail: admission@smith.edu

University of Massachusetts Dartmouth
Old Westport Rd, North Dartmouth MA 02747-2300
Steven T. Briggs, Director of Admissions
508-999-8605 Fax: 508-999-8755
Website: explore.umassd.edu
E-mail: sbriggs@umassd.edu

Westfield State College
PO Box 1630, Westfield MA 01086
Michelle Mattie, Associate Dean, Admission and
Enrollment Services
413-572-5300
Website: www.wsc.ma.edu
E-mail: admission@wsc.ma.edu

Worcester Polytechnic Institute
100 Institute Rd, Worcester MA 01609-2280
Edward J. Connor, Director of Admissions
508-831-5286 Fax: 508-831-5875
Website: admissions.wpi.edu
E-mail: admissions@wpi.edu

MICHIGAN

Alma College
614 W Superior St, Alma MI 48801-1599
Anne Monroe, Director of Admissions
800-321-ALMA Fax: 989-463-7057
Website: www.alma.edu
E-mail: admissions@alma.edu

Andrews University
Berrien Springs MI 49104-0001
Randall Graves, Director of Recruitment Services
800-253-2874 Fax: 269-471-2670
Website: www.connect.andrews.edu
E-mail: gravesr@andrews.edu

Concordia University
4090 Geddes Rd, Ann Arbor MI 48105-2797
Gary Neumann, Director of Admissions
734-995-7300 Fax: 734-995-4610
Website: www.cuaa.edu
E-mail: admissions@cuaa.edu

Grand Valley State University
1 Campus Dr, Allendale MI 49401-9403
616-331-2025 Fax: 616-331-2000
Website: www.gvsu.edu
E-mail: go2gvsu@gvsu.edu

HILLSDALE COLLEGE

33 E College St, Hillsdale MI 49242-1298
Dr. Mickey Craig, Director
517-607-2473 Fax: 517-607-2208
Website: www.hillsdale.edu
E-mail: mickey.craig@hillsdale.edu

MACOMB COMMUNITY COLLEGE

44575 Garfield Rd, Clinton Township MI 48038-1139
Information Center
586-445-7999
Website: www.macomb.edu
E-mail: answer@macomb.edu

MACOMB COMMUNITY COLLEGE

14500 E 12 Mile Rd, Warren MI 48088-3896
Information Center
586-445-7999
Website: www.macomb.edu
E-mail: answer@macomb.edu

Oakland University
2200 N Squirrel Rd, Rochester MI 48309
Eleanor L. Reynolds, Assistant Vice President &
Director of Admissions
248-370-2100
Website: www.oakland.edu
E-mail: ouinfo@oakland.edu

University of Michigan-Dearborn
4901 Evergreen Rd, Dearborn MI 48128-1491
The Office of Admissions & Orientation
313-593-5100 Fax: 313-436-9167
Website: www.umd.umich.edu
E-mail: admissions@umd.umich.edu

MINNESOTA

Bethany Lutheran College
700 Luther Dr, Mankato MN 56001
Don Westphal, Dean of Admissions
507-344-7000 Fax: 507-344-7376
Website: www.blc.edu
E-mail: admiss@blc.edu

Carleton College
1 N College St, Northfield MN 55057-4044
800-995-2275 or 507-646-4190 Fax: 507-646-4526
Website: www.carleton.edu
E-mail: admissions@acs.carleton.edu

Gustavus Adolphus College
800 W College Ave, Saint Peter MN 56082-1485
Mark H. Anderson, Dean of Admission
800-GUSTAVUS Fax: 507-933-7474
Website: www.gustavus.edu
E-mail: admission@gustavus.edu

Pillsbury Baptist Bible College
315 S Grove Ave, Owatonna MN 55060-3097
Stephen R. Seidler, Director of Admissions
507-451-2710 Fax: 507-451-0156
Website: www.pillsbury.edu
E-mail: steveseidler@pillsbury.edu

MISSISSIPPI

Tougaloo College
500 W County Line Rd, Tougaloo MS 39174-9799
Juno Leggette Jacobs, Director of Admissions
601-977-7768 Fax: 601-977-4501
Website: www.tougaloo.edu
E-mail: jjacobs@tougaloo.edu

MISSOURI

Columbia College
1001 Rogers St, Columbia MO 65216-0001
Regina Morin, Director of Admissions
573-875-7352 Fax: 573-875-7506
Website: www.ccis.edu
E-mail: admissions@ccis.edu

Lindenwood University
209 S Kingshighway St
Saint Charles MO 63301-1695
Sheryl Guffey, Director of Admissions
636-949-2000 Fax: 636-949-4989
Website: www.lindenwood.edu

Stephens College
PO Box 2121, Columbia MO 65215-0001
David Adams, Dean of Enrollment Management
573-442-2211 Fax: 573-876-7237
Website: www.stephens.edu
E-mail: dadams@stephens.edu

Truman State University
100 E Normal, Kirksville MO 63501
Office of Admission
660-785-4000 Fax: 660-785-4181
Website: admissions.truman.edu
E-mail: admissions@truman.edu

University of Missouri
1 University Blvd, Saint Louis MO 63121-4499
Dr. Mark Burkholder, Dean-College of Arts & Sciences
314-516-5501 Fax: 314-516-5415
Website: www.umsl.edu
E-mail: admissions@umsl.edu

Webster University
470 E Lockwood Ave, Saint Louis MO 63119-3194
Bill Huddleston-Berry, Chairman, Behavioral Sciences
314-968-7160 Fax: 314-963-6094
Website: www.webster.edu
E-mail: huddlews@webster.edu
See listing under "Universities"

William Woods University
1 University Ave, Fulton MO 65251-1098
Jimmy Clay, Director of Admissions
573-642-2251 Fax: 573-592-1146
Website: www.williamwoods.edu
E-mail: admissions@williamwoods.edu
See listing under "Universities"

MONTANA

Rocky Mountain College
1511 Poly Dr, Billings MT 59102-1796
Bonnie Knapp, Director of Admissions
800-877-6259 Fax: 406-657-1189
Website: www.rocky.edu
E-mail: admissions@rocky.edu

NEBRASKA

Midland Lutheran College
900 N Clarkson St, Fremont NE 68025-4200
Todd Hansen, Associate Director of Admissions
402-941-6501 Fax: 402-941-6513
Website: www.mlc.edu
E-mail: admissions@mlc.edu

Nebraska Wesleyan University
5000 Saint Paul Ave, Lincoln NE 68504-2794
Patricia Karthauser, V.P. for University Enrollment
402-466-2371 Fax: 402-465-2177
Website: www.nebrwesleyan.edu
E-mail: admissions@nebrwesleyan.edu

Peru State College
PO Box 10, Peru NE 68421-0010
Office of Admissions
800-742-4412 Fax: 402-872-2296
Website: www.peru.edu
E-mail: admissions@oakmail.peru.edu

University of Nebraska at Kearney
905 W 25th St, Kearney NE 68849-0001
Dusty Newton, Director of Admissions
800-KEARNEY Fax: 308-865-8987
Website: www.unk.edu
E-mail: admissionsug@unk.edu

NEVADA

GREAT BASIN COLLEGE

1500 College Pkwy, Elko NV 89801-5032
Julie G. Byrnes, Director of Enrollment Management
775-753-2271 Fax: 775-753-2311
Website: www.gbcnv.edu
E-mail: bjulie@gbcnv.edu

NEW HAMPSHIRE

Antioch University New England
40 Avon St, Keene NH 03431-3516
David Caruso, President
Leatrice A. Johnson, Director of Admissions
603-357-6265 Fax: 603-357-0718
Website: www.antiochne.edu
E-mail: admissions@antiochne.edu

Southern New Hampshire University
2500 N River Rd, Hooksett NH 03106-1045
Steve Soba, Director of Admissions
603-645-9611 Fax: 603-645-9693
Website: www.snhu.edu
E-mail: s.soba@snhu.edu

NEW JERSEY

Atlantic Cape Community College
5100 Black Horse Pike
Mays Landing NJ 08330-2699
Linda McLeod, Assistant Director of College Recruitment
609-343-5000 Fax: 609-343-4921
Website: www.atlantic.edu
E-mail: accadmit@atlantic.edu
See listing under "Community and Junior Colleges"

Bergen Community College
400 Paramus Rd, Paramus NJ 07652
Julian Gomez, Asst. Director of Admissions
201-447-7100 Fax: 201-444-7036
Website: www.bergen.edu
E-mail: jgomez@bergen.edu

Centenary College
400 Jefferson St, Hackettstown NJ 07840-2100
Glenna Warren, Director of Admissions
908-852-1400 Fax: 908-852-3454
Website: www.centenarycollege.edu
E-mail: warreng@centenarycollege.edu

New Jersey City University
2039 John F Kennedy Blvd
Jersey City NJ 07305-1588
Carmen Panlilio, Asst. V.P. for Admissions and Financial Aid
201-200-3234 Fax: 201-200-2044
Website: www.njcu.edu
E-mail: admissions@njcu.edu

Ramapo College of New Jersey
505 Ramapo Valley Rd, Mahwah NJ 07430-1623
Director of Admissions
201-684-7300 or 201-684-7301 Fax: 201-684-7964
Website: www.ramapo.edu
E-mail: admissions@ramapo.edu

NEW MEXICO

New Mexico State University
1500 N 3rd St, Grants NM 87020-2025
505-287-7981 Fax: 505-287-2329
Website: www.grants.nmsu.edu

NEW YORK

College of Saint Rose
432 Western Ave, Albany NY 12203-1419
Maryelizabeth Amico, Asst V.P. for Undergraduate Admissions
518-454-5191 Fax: 518-454-2013
Website: www.strose.edu
E-mail: admit@strose.edu

CUNY Hunter College
695 Park Ave, New York NY 10021
Aaron Gibbs, Assistant Director of Recruitment
212-772-4497 Fax: 212-650-3336
Website: www.hunter.cuny.edu
E-mail: aaron.gibbs@hunter.cuny.edu

Daemen College
4380 Main St, Amherst NY 14226-3592
Donna Shaffner, Director of Admissions
800-462-7652 or 716-839-8225 Fax: 716-839-8229
Website: www.daemen.edu
E-mail: admissions@daemen.edu
See listing under "Universities"

Hobart & William Smith Colleges
Pulteney St, Geneva NY 14456
John Young, Director of Admissions
315-789-5500 Fax: 315-781-3654
Website: www.hws.edu
E-mail: young@hws.edu

Long Island University-C. W. Post Campus
720 Northern Blvd, Brookville NY 11548-1300
Joanne Graziano, Executive Director of Admissions
516-299-2900 Fax: 516-299-2137
Website: www.liu.edu/cwpost
E-mail: enroll@cwpost.liu.edu

Molloy College
1000 Hempstead Ave
Rockville Centre NY 11570-1100
Marguerite Lane, Director of Admissions
516-678-5000 ext. 6291 Fax: 516-256-2247
Website: www.molloy.edu
E-mail: admissions@molloy.edu
See listing under "Universities"

Paul Smith's College
Paul Smiths NY 12970
Amber DeBeer, Assistant Director of Admissions
800-421-2605 Fax: 518-327-6016
Website: www.paulsmiths.edu
E-mail: admiss@paulsmiths.edu

PURCHASE COLLEGE STATE UNIVERSITY OF NEW YORK (SUNY)

735 Anderson Hill Rd, Purchase NY 10577-1400
Betsy Immergut, Director of Admissions
914-251-6300 Fax: 914-251-6314
Website: www.purchase.edu
See listing under "Universities"

Roberts Wesleyan College
2301 Westside Dr, Rochester NY 14624-1997
Office of Admissions
585-594-6400 Fax: 585-594-6371
Website: www.roberts.edu
E-mail: admissions@roberts.edu

St. John's University
8000 Utopia Pkwy, Queens NY 11439
Office of Admission
718-990-2000 or 888-9-STJOHNS Fax: 718-990-2096
Website: www.stjohns.edu
E-mail: admissions@stjohns.edu
See listing under "Universities"

St. Joseph's College
245 Clinton Ave, Brooklyn NY 11205-3688
Theresa LaRocca Meyer, V.P. for Enrollment Management
718-636-6800 Fax: 718-636-8303
Website: www.sjcny.edu
E-mail: tlaroccameyer@sjcny.edu

SUNY College at Brockport
350 New Campus Dr, Brockport NY 14420-2997
Bernard S. Valento, Director of Undergraduate Admissions
585-395-2751 Fax: 585-395-5452
Website: www.brockport.edu
E-mail: admit@brockport.edu

SUNY College of Technology
Alfred NY 14802
Deborah J. Goodrich, Director of Admissions
800-4AL-FRED Fax: 607-587-4299
Website: www.alfredstate.edu
E-mail: admissions@alfredstate.edu

SUNY College of Technology
2 Main St, Delhi NY 13753-1110
Robert W. Mazzei, Director of Admissions
800-96-DELHI Fax: 607-746-4104
Website: www.delhi.edu
E-mail: enroll@delhi.edu

SUNY Orange County Community College
115 South St, Middletown NY 10940-6437
Margot St. Lawrence, Director of Admissions
845-341-4030 Fax: 845-342-8662
Website: www.sunyorange.edu
E-mail: apply@sunyorange.edu
See listing under "Community and Junior Colleges"

United States Military Academy West Point
646 Swift Rd, West Point NY 10996-1905
Colonel Michael L. Jones, Director of Admissions
845-938-4041 Fax: 845-938-8121
Website: admissions.usma.edu
E-mail: admissions@usma.edu

Wells College
PO Box 500, Aurora NY 13026
Susan Sloan, Director of Admissions
800-952-9355 Fax: 315-364-3227
Website: www.wells.edu
E-mail: ssloan@wells.edu

NORTH CAROLINA

Belmont Abbey College
100 Belmont Mount Holly Rd
Belmont NC 28012-1802
888-222-0110 Fax: 704-825-6670
Website: www.belmontabbeycollege.edu
E-mail: admissions@bac.edu

Lees-McRae College
PO Box 128, Banner Elk NC 28604-0128
Walt Crutchfield, Dean of Admissions
800-280-4562 Fax: 828-898-8707
Website: www.lmc.edu
E-mail: admissions@lmc.edu

Mars Hill College
Mars Hill NC 28754
Chad Holt, Dean of Enrollment
866-MHC-4-YOU Fax: 828-689-1473
Website: www.mhc.edu
E-mail: cholt@mhc.edu

Meredith College
3800 Hillsborough St, Raleigh NC 27607-5298
Heidi L. Fletcher, Director of Admissions
919-760-8581 Fax: 919-760-2348
Website: www.meredith.edu
E-mail: admissions@meredith.edu
See listing under "Women's Colleges"

North Carolina A&T State University
1601 E Market St, Greensboro NC 27411
Lee Young, AVC Enrollment
336-334-7500 Fax: 336-334-7478
Website: www.ncat.edu
E-mail: uadmit@ncat.edu

Salem College
Winston Salem NC 27108
Dana Evans, Dean of Admissions/Fin. Aid
800-32-SALEM Fax: 336-917-5572
Website: www.salem.edu
E-mail: admissions@salem.edu
See listing under "Women's Colleges"

NORTH DAKOTA

Dickinson State University
Dickinson ND 58601-4896
Steve Glasser, Director of Student Recruitment
800-279-4295 Fax: 701-483-2409
Website: www.dickinsonstate.edu
E-mail: dsu.hawks@dickinsonstate.edu

Valley City State University
101 College St SW, Valley City ND 58072-4024
Dan Klein, Director of Enrollment Services
800-532-8641 ext. 7101 Fax: 701-845-7299
Website: www.vcsu.edu
E-mail: enrollment.services@vcsu.edu
See listing under "Universities"

OHIO

Cleveland State University
2121 Euclid Ave RW 204, Cleveland OH 44115
Dr. Richard Arndt, Dean of Undergraduate Recruitment
and College Partnerships
888-CSU-OHIO Fax: 216-687-9210
Website: www.csuohio.edu
E-mail: admissions@csuohio.edu

Franciscan University of Steubenville
University Blvd, Steubenville OH 43952
Margaret J. Weber, Director of Admissions
800-783-6220 or 740-283-6226 Fax: 740-284-5456
Website: www.admissions.edu
E-mail: mweber@franciscan.edu

Mount Vernon Nazarene University
800 Martinsburg Rd, Mount Vernon OH 43050-9509
Timothy Eades, Director of Admissions
866-462-6868 Fax: 740-393-0511
Website: www.gotomvnu.com
E-mail: admissions@mvnu.edu
See listing under "Universities"

OHIO NORTHERN UNIVERSITY
525 S Main St, Ada OH 45810-1555
Ellen Wilson, Chair of the Psychology & Sociology
Dept.
419-772-2135
Website: www.onu.edu
E-mail: admissions-ug@onu.edu
See listing under "Universities"

The Ohio State University
School of Social and Behavioral Sciences
Derby Hall, 154 N Oval Mall, Columbus OH 43210
614-292-8448 Fax: 614-292-9530
Website: sbs.osu.edu

University of Dayton
300 College Park, Dayton OH 45469-1300
Robert F. Durkle, Director of Admissions
800-837-7433 Fax: 937-229-4729
Website: admission.udayton.edu
E-mail: admission@udayton.edu

Ursuline College
2550 Lander Rd, Cleveland OH 44124-4398
Sarah E. Sundermeier, Director of Admissions
888-URSULINE Toll Free Fax: 440-684-6138
Website: www.admission.ursuline.edu
E-mail: admission@ursuline.edu

OKLAHOMA

Oklahoma State University
Stillwater OK 74078
Patricia Bell, Department Head
405-744-6104
Website: www.okstate.edu
E-mail: patricia.bell@okstate.edu

Oral Roberts University
7777 S Lewis Ave, Tulsa OK 74171-0001
Chris Belcher, Director of Undergraduate Admissions
800-678-8876 Fax: 918-495-6222
Website: www.oru.edu
E-mail: admissions@oru.edu

University of Tulsa
600 S College Ave, Tulsa OK 74104-3126
Earl Johnson, Dean of Admission
918-631-2307 Fax: 918-631-5003
Website: www.utulsa.edu
E-mail: admission@utulsa.edu

OREGON

Concordia University
2811 NE Holman St, Portland OR 97211-6099
Bobi Swan, Director of Admissions
503-288-9371 Fax: 503-280-8531
Website: www.cu-portland.edu
E-mail: cu-admissions@cu-portland.edu

Linn-Benton Community College
6500 Pacific Blvd SW, Albany OR 97321-3774
Christine Baker, Outreach Coordinator
541-917-4811 Fax: 541-917-4868
Website: www.linnbenton.edu
E-mail: admissions@linnbenton.edu

Marylhurst University
17600 Pacific Hwy (Hwy 43)
Marylhurst OR 97036-0261
Director of Admissions
800-634-9982 ext. 6268 Fax: 503-635-6585
Website: www.marylhurst.edu
E-mail: studentinfo@marylhurst.edu

Pacific University
2043 College Way, Forest Grove OR 97116-1797
Karen M. Dunston, Executive Director of Admissions
800-635-0561 Fax: 503-352-2975
Website: www.pacificu.edu
E-mail: admissions@pacificu.edu

Rogue Community College
3345 Redwood Hwy, Grants Pass OR 97527-9298
Claudia Sullivan, Director of Enrollment Services
541-956-7500 Fax: 541-471-3585
Website: www.roguecc.edu
E-mail: csullivan@roguecc.edu
See listing under "Community and Junior Colleges"

Warner Pacific College
2219 SE 68th Ave, Portland OR 97215-4026
Shannon Mackey, Director of Admissions
503-517-1000 Fax: 503-517-1352
Website: www.warnerpacific.edu
E-mail: admissions@warnerpacific.edu

Western Oregon University
345 Monmouth Ave N, Monmouth OR 97361-1314
David McDonald, Dean, Admission, Retention &
Enrollment Management
877-877-1593 Fax: 503-838-8067
Website: www.wou.edu
E-mail: wolfgram@fsa.wou.edu

PENNSYLVANIA

Clarion University of Pennsylvania
840 Wood St, Clarion PA 16214-1232
William Bailey, Dean of Enrollment Management
814-393-2306 Fax: 814-393-2030
Website: www.clarion.edu
E-mail: admissions@clarion.edu

DeSales University
2755 Station Ave, Center Valley PA 18034-9565
610-282-1100 Fax: 610-282-2342
Website: www.desales.edu

Gannon University
109 University Sq, Erie PA 16541-0001
Christopher Tremblay, Director of Admissions
800-GANNON-U Fax: 814-871-5803
Website: www.gannon.edu
E-mail: admissions@gannon.edu

Haverford College
370 Lancaster Ave, Haverford PA 19041-1392
Jess Lord, Dean of Admission
610-896-1000 Fax: 610-896-1338
Website: www.haverford.edu
E-mail: admission@haverford.edu

Holy Family University
9801 Frankford Avenue, Philadelphia PA 19114
Lauren Campbell, Director of Admissions
215-637-3050 Fax: 215-281-1022
Website: www.holyfamily.edu
E-mail: admissions@holyfamily.edu

Juniata College
1700 Moore St, Huntingdon PA 16652-2196
Michelle Bartol, Dean of Enrollment
877-JUNIATA Fax: 814-641-3100
Website: www.juniata.edu
E-mail: admissions@juniata.edu

King's College
133 N River St, Wilkes Barre PA 18711-0801
Michelle Lawrence-Schmude, Director of Admission
570-208-5900 Fax: 570-208-5971
Website: www.kings.edu
E-mail: admissions@kings.edu

La Roche College
9000 Babcock Blvd, Pittsburgh PA 15237-5898
Thomas Hassett, Director of Freshman and
International Admissions
412-536-1272 or 800-838-4LRC Fax: 412-536-1272
Website: www.laroche.edu
E-mail: admissions@laroche.edu

Lebanon Valley College
101 N College Ave, Annville PA 17003-1400
William Brown, Dean of Admissions & Financial Aid
866-LVC-4ADM or 717-867-6181 Fax: 717-867-6026
Website: www.lvc.edu
E-mail: admission@lvc.edu

Lincoln University
Lincoln University PA 19352
Michael C. Taylor, Director of Admissions
800-790-0191 Fax: 610-932-1209
Website: www.lincoln.edu
E-mail: mtaylor@lu.lincoln.edu

MOUNT ALOYSIUS COLLEGE
7373 Admiral Peary Hwy, Cresson PA 16630-1999
Frank C. Crouse Jr., Vice President for Enrollment
Management
814-886-6383 or 888-823-2220 Fax: 814-886-6441
Website: www.mtaloy.edu
E-mail: admissions@mtaloy.edu

University of Pittsburgh
1150 Mount Pleasant Rd
Greensburg PA 15601-5860
Brandi S. Darr, Director of Admissions and Financial
Aid
724-836-9880 Fax: 724-836-7160
Website: www.upg.pitt.edu
E-mail: upgadmit@pitt.edu

Washington & Jefferson College
60 S Lincoln St, Washington PA 15301-4801
Alton E. Newell, Vice President for Enrollment
724-223-6025 Fax: 724-223-6534
Website: www.washjeff.edu
E-mail: admission@washjeff.edu

Westminster College
New Wilmington PA 16172-0001
Doug Swartz, Director of Admissions
724-946-7100 Fax: 724-946-6171
Website: www.westminster.edu
E-mail: swartzdl@westminster.edu

SOUTH CAROLINA

Erskine College & Seminary
PO Box 176, Due West SC 29639
Bart Walker, Director of Admissions
864-379-8838 Fax: 864-379-3048
Website: www.erskine.edu
E-mail: admissions@erskine.edu

Limestone College
1115 College Dr, Gaffney SC 29340-3799
Chris Phenicie, V.P. for Enrollment
864-489-7151 Fax: 864-488-8206
Website: www.limestone.edu
E-mail: cphenicie@limestone.edu

PRESBYTERIAN COLLEGE
503 S Broad St, Clinton SC 29325
Richard Dana Paul, Dean of Admissions
800-476-7272 Fax: 864-833-8481
Website: www.presby.edu
E-mail: admissions@presby.edu

University of South Carolina - Upstate
800 University Way, Spartanburg SC 29303-4932
Donette Stewart, Assistant VC for Enrollment Services
864-503-5246 Fax: 864-503-5727
Website: www.uscupstate.edu
E-mail: dstewart@uscupstate.edu
See listing under "Universities"

SOUTH DAKOTA

Presentation College
1500 N Main St, Aberdeen SD 57401-1280
JoEllen Lindner, Dean of Admissions
605-229-8492 Fax: 605-229-8425
Website: www.presentation.edu
E-mail: admit@presentation.edu

TENNESSEE

Lipscomb University
3901 Granny White Pike, Nashville TN 37204-3951
Ricky Holaway, Director of Admissions
800-333-4358 ext. 1776 Fax: 615-269-1804
Website: www.lipscomb.edu
E-mail: admissions@lipscomb.edu

Tennessee State University
3500 John A Merritt Blvd, Nashville TN 37209-1561
John Cade, Dean of Admissions & Records
615-963-5101 Fax: 615-963-2930
Website: www.tnstate.edu
E-mail: jcade@tnstate.edu

Tusculum College
PO Box 5051, Greeneville TN 37743
Melissa Ripley, Associate Director of Admissions
800-729-0256 Fax: 423-798-1622
Website: www.tusculum.edu
E-mail: mripley@tusculum.edu

University of Tennessee
615 McCallie Ave, Chattanooga TN 37403-2504
Yancy Freeman, Director of Admissions
423-425-4111 Fax: 423-425-4157
Website: www.utc.edu
E-mail: Yancy-Freeman@utc.edu

TEXAS

Angelo State University
ASU Station 11014, San Angelo TX 76909
Bonnie Stennett, Coordinator of Recruiting
800-946-8627 Fax: 325-942-2078
Website: www.angelo.edu
E-mail: admissions@angelo.edu

Blinn College
902 College Ave, Brenham TX 77833-4098
Dennis K. Crowson, Registrar
979-830-4000 Fax: 979-830-4110
Website: www.blinn.edu
E-mail: recruiting@blinn.edu

Blinn College
PO Box 6030, Bryan TX 77805-6030
Dennis K. Crowson, Registrar
979-209-7200 Fax: 979-209-7229
Website: www.blinn.edu
E-mail: recruiting@blinn.edu

Blinn College
100 Ranger Dr, Schulenburg TX 78956-2247
Dennis K. Crowson, Registrar
979-743-5003 Fax: 979-743-5225
Website: www.blinn.edu
E-mail: recruiting@blinn.edu

Blinn College
3701 Outlet Center Dr, Sealy TX 77474
Dennis K. Crowson, Registrar
979-627-7997 Fax: 979-627-0830
Website: www.blinn.edu
E-mail: recruiting@blinn.edu

Our Lady of the Lake University
411 SW 24th St, San Antonio TX 78207-4666
Mary Kay Cooper, Dean of Enrollment
210-434-6711 Fax: 210-431-4013
Website: www.ollusa.edu
E-mail: admission@lakeollusa.edu

Texas Woman's University
PO Box 425589, Denton TX 76204-5589
Erma Nieto, Director of Admissions
866-809-6130 Fax: 940-898-3081
Website: www.twu.edu
E-mail: admissions@twu.edu

Tyler Junior College
PO Box 9020, Tyler TX 75711-9020
Richard Minter, Dean
800-687-5680
Website: www.tjc.edu
E-mail: rmin@tjc.edu
See listing under "Community and Junior Colleges"

University of Houston
122 E Cullen Bldg, Houston TX 77204-2023
Office of Admission
713-743-9595
Website: www.uh.edu
E-mail: admissions@uh.edu

University of St. Thomas
3800 Montrose Blvd, Houston TX 77006-4626
Eduardo Prieto, Director of Admissions
713-522-7911 Fax: 713-525-3558
Website: www.stthom.edu
E-mail: prietoe@stthom.edu

VERMONT

Bennington College
One College Drive, Bennington VT 05201
Ken Himmelman, Dean of Admissions & Financial Aid
800-833-6845 Fax: 802-440-4320
Website: www.bennington.edu
E-mail: admissions@bennington.edu

NORWICH UNIVERSITY
158 Harmon Dr, Northfield VT 05663
Dr. Thomas Taylor, Division Head
800-468-6679 Fax: 802-485-2252
Website: www.norwich.edu
E-mail: ttaylor@norwich.edu

Southern Vermont College
982 Mansion Dr, Bennington VT 05201-6002
Kathleen James Ring, Director of Admissions
800-378-2782 Fax: 802-447-4695
Website: www.svc.edu
E-mail: admis@svc.edu

Woodbury College
660 Elm St, Montpelier VT 05602-4017
Kathleen Moore, Director of Admissions
800-639-6039 Fax: 802-229-2141
Website: www.woodbury-college.edu
E-mail: admiss@woodbury-college.edu

VIRGINIA

Radford University
PO Box 6903, Radford VA 24142
David W. Kraus, Director of Admissions
800-890-4265 Fax: 540-831-5038
Website: www.radford.edu
E-mail: ruadmiss@radford.edu

Randolph-Macon Woman's College
2500 Rivermont Ave, Lynchburg VA 24503
Patricia LeDonne, Director of Admissions
434-947-8100 Fax: 434-947-8996
Website: www.rmwc.edu
E-mail: admissions@rmwc.edu

University of Mary Washington
1301 College Ave, Fredericksburg VA 22401-5300
Dr. Martin A. Wilder, Jr., Director of Admissions
540-654-2000 Fax: 540-654-1857
Website: www.umw.edu
E-mail: admit@umw.edu

WASHINGTON

Gonzaga University
502 E Boone Ave, Spokane WA 99258-0102
Julie McCulloh, Dean of Admission
800-322-2584 or 509-323-6572 Fax: 509-323-5780
Website: www.gonzaga.edu
E-mail: mcculloh@gu.gonzaga.edu

WEST VIRGINIA

Concord University
Athens WV 24712
Michael Curry, Vice President of Financial Aid & Admissions
888-384-5249 Fax: 304-384-3218
Website: www.concord.edu
E-mail: admissions@concord.edu

Davis & Elkins College
100 Campus Dr, Elkins WV 26241-3996
Renee Heckel, Director of Enrollment Management
800-624-3157 Fax: 304-637-1800
Website: www.davisandelkins.edu
E-mail: admiss@davisandelkins.edu

Fairmont State University
1201 Locust Ave, Fairmont WV 26554-2470
Steve Leadman, Director of Admissions
304-367-4161 or 800-641-5678 Fax: 304-367-4789
Website: www.fairmontstate.edu
E-mail: admit@fairmontstate.edu

West Virginia Wesleyan College
59 College Ave, Buckhannon WV 26201-2699
Robert N. Skinner II, Director of Admission
800-722-9933 Fax: 304-473-8108
Website: www.wvwc.edu
E-mail: admission@wvwc.edu

WISCONSIN

Alverno College
PO Box 343922, Milwaukee WI 53234-3922
Mary Kay Farrell, Director of Admissions
414-382-6100 Fax: 414-382-6354
Website: www.alverno.edu
E-mail: admissions@alverno.edu

Lakeland College
PO Box 359, Sheboygan WI 53082-0359
Nathan Dehne, Director of Admission
920-565-1100 Fax: 920-565-1215
Website: www.lakeland.edu
E-mail: admissions@lakeland.edu

Marquette University
PO Box 1881, Milwaukee WI 53201-1881
Robert Blust, Director of Admissions
414-288-7302 Fax: 414-288-3764
Website: www.mu.edu
E-mail: admissions@marquette.edu

St. Norbert College
100 Grant St, De Pere WI 54115
Brian Studebaker, Director of Admission
800-236-4878 Fax: 920-403-4072
Website: www.snc.edu
E-mail: admit@snc.edu

WYOMING

University of Wyoming
Admissions Office
Dept 3435, Laramie WY 82071-3435
Aaron Appelhans, Contact
800-342-5996 Fax: 307-766-4042
Website: www.uwyo.edu
E-mail: why-wyo@uwyo.edu

GUAM

University of Guam
UOG Station, Mangilao GU 96923
Deborah Leon Guerrero, Registrar
671-735-2201 or 671-735-2208 Fax: 671-735-2203
Website: www.uog.edu
E-mail: admitme@uog9.uog.edu

SPEECH AND DRAMA

ALABAMA

CALHOUN COMMUNITY COLLEGE
PO Box 2216, Decatur AL 35609-2216
M. Wayne Tosh, Registrar
256-306-2500 Fax: 256-306-2941
Website: www.calhoun.edu
E-mail: rds@calhoun.edu

Faulkner University
5345 Atlanta Hwy, Montgomery AL 36109-3398
Keith Mock, Director of Admissions
800-879-9816 ext. 7200 or 334-386-7200
Fax: 334-386-7137
Website: www.faulkner.edu
E-mail: admissions@faulkner.edu

ALASKA

University of Alaska Anchorage
PO Box 141629, Anchorage AK 99514-1629
Cecile Mitchell, Director of Enrollment Services
907-786-1480 Fax: 907-786-4888
Website: www.uaa.alaska.edu/
E-mail: enroll@uaa.alaska.edu

ARIZONA

University of Arizona
Tucson AZ 85721-0040
Paul Kohn, Director of Admissions
520-621-3237 Fax: 520-621-9799
Website: www.admissions.arizona.edu or www.arizona.edu

ARKANSAS

Ouachita Baptist University
410 Ouachita St, Arkadelphia AR 71998-0001
David Goodman, Director of Admissions
870-245-5110 Fax: 870-245-5500
Website: www.obu.edu
E-mail: admissions@obu.edu

CALIFORNIA

American Academy of Dramatic Arts - Hollywood
1336 N LaBrea Ave, Hollywood CA 90028
Dan Justin, Director of Admissions
800-222-2867 Fax: 323-464-1250
Website: www.aada.org
E-mail: admissions-ca@aada.org

AMERICAN CONSERVATORY THEATER
30 Grant Ave, San Francisco CA 94108-5800
Melissa Smith, Conservatory Director
415-439-2350
Website: www.act-sf.org

Chapman University
One University Drive, Orange CA 92866-1099
Michael Drummy, Assistant Vice President for Enrollment
Services and Chief Admission Officer
714-997-6411 or 888-CUAPPLY Fax: 714-997-6713
Website: www.chapman.edu
E-mail: admit@chapman.edu

Concordia University
1530 Concordia, Irvine CA 92612-3203
Lori McDonald, Executive Director of Enrollment Services
800-229-1200 or 949-854-8002 Fax: 949-854-6894
Website: www.cui.edu
E-mail: admission@cui.edu

Orange Coast College
PO Box 5005, Costa Mesa CA 92628-5005
Kristin Clark, Director of Admissions
714-432-5773 Fax: 714-432-5736
Website: www.orangecoastcollege.edu
E-mail: kclark@cccd.edu

Whittier College
PO Box 634, Whittier CA 90608-0634
Kieron Miller, Director of Admissions
562-907-4200 Fax: 562-907-4870
Website: www.whittier.edu
E-mail: kmiller@whittier.edu

DISTRICT OF COLUMBIA

NATIONAL CONSERVATORY OF DRAMATIC ARTS
1556 Wisconsin Ave NW
Washington DC 20007-2758
Nan Kyle Ficca, Vice President
202-333-2202 Fax: 202-333-1753
Website: theconservatory.org
E-mail: ncdadrama@aol.com

FLORIDA

Florida State University
600 W College Ave, Tallahassee FL 32306-1096
Janice V. Finney, Director of Admissions
850-644-2525 Fax: 850-644-0197
Website: admissions.fsu.edu
E-mail: admissions@admin.fsu.edu

University of South Florida
4202 E Fowler Ave, Tampa FL 33620-6900
J. Robert Spatig, Director of Admissions
813-974-3350 Fax: 813-974-9689
Website: www.usf.edu
E-mail: admissions@admin.usf.edu

IDAHO

Brigham Young University - Idaho
120 Kimball Bldg, Rexburg ID 83460
Gordon Westenskow, Director of Admissions
208-496-1020 Fax: 208-496-1220
Website: www.byui.edu
E-mail: admissions@byui.edu

University of Idaho
Moscow ID 83844-4253
Lloyd Scott, Director of New Student Services
208-885-6163 Fax: 208-885-4477
Website: www.uidaho.edu
E-mail: nss@uidaho.edu

ILLINOIS

Columbia College Chicago
600 S Michigan Ave, Chicago IL 60605-1996
Murphy Monroe, Executive Director of Admissions
312-344-7130 Fax: 312-344-8024
Website: www.colum.edu
E-mail: admissions@colum.edu

North Central College
30 N Brainard St, Naperville IL 60540-4690
Martha Stolze, Director of Admissions
630-637-5800 Fax: 630-637-5819
Website: www.northcentralcollege.edu
E-mail: admissions@noctrl.edu

Roosevelt University
430 S Michigan Ave, Chicago IL 60605
Gwen E. Kanelos, Asst. Vice President for Enrollment Services
877-APPLY-RU Fax: 312-341-4216
Website: www.roosevelt.edu
E-mail: applyru@roosevelt.edu

South Suburban College of Cook County
15800 State St, South Holland IL 60473
Jane Ellen Stocker, Dean of Enrollment Services
708-596-2000 Fax: 708-225-5806
Website: www.southsuburbancollege.edu
E-mail: jstocker@southsuburbancollege.edu

INDIANA

Hanover College
PO Box 108, Hanover IN 47243-0108
William D. Preble, Dean of Admission
800-213-2178 Fax: 812-866-7098
Website: www.hanover.edu
E-mail: admissions@hanover.edu

St. Mary-of-the-Woods College
Saint Mary of the Woods IN 47876-1001
James P. Malley, Jr., Director of Admission
800-926-7692 Fax: 812-535-5010
Website: www.smwc.edu
E-mail: smwcadms@smwc.edu

University of Evansville
1800 Lincoln Ave, Evansville IN 47722-0001
Thomas E. Bear, V.P. of Enrollment Services
800-423-8633 Fax: 812-488-4076
Website: www.evansville.edu
E-mail: admission@evansville.edu

IOWA

Briar Cliff University
PO Box 2100, Sioux City IA 51104-0100
Sharisue Wilcoxon, VP for Enrollment Management
712-279-5200 Fax: 712-279-1632
Website: www.briarcliff.edu
E-mail: admissions@briarcliff.edu

Clarke College
1550 Clarke Dr, Dubuque IA 52001-3198
Andy Schroeder, Director of Admissions
800-383-2345 Fax: 563-584-8666
Website: www.clarke.edu
E-mail: andy.schroeder@clarke.edu

Graceland University
1 University Place, Lamoni IA 50140
Brian Shantz, Vice President for Enrollment and Dean
of Admissions
641-784-5196 Fax: 641-784-5480
Website: www.admissions.graceland.edu
E-mail: admissions@graceland.edu

Iowa Lakes Community College
300 S 18th St, Estherville IA 51334-2721
Anne Stansbury, Asst. Director of Admissions
712-362-7945 Fax: 712-362-8363
Website: www.iowalakes.edu
E-mail: info@iowalakes.edu

Mount Mercy College
1330 Elmhurst Dr NE, Cedar Rapids IA 52402-4797
Jim Krystofiak, Dean of Admission
800-248-4504 Fax: 319-363-5270
Website: www.mtmercy.edu
E-mail: admission@mtmercy.edu

Waldorf College
106 S 6th St, Forest City IA 50436-1713
Steve Lovik, Vice President of Enrollment Management
800-292-1903 or 641-585-8112 Fax: 641-585-8125
Website: www.waldorf.edu
E-mail: loviks@waldorf.edu
See listing under "Universities"

KANSAS

Independence Community College
PO Box 708, Independence KS 67301-0708
Dr. Terry Hetrick, President
800-842-6063 Fax: 620-331-5344
Website: www.indycc.edu
E-mail: admissions@indycc.edu

Newman University
3100 W McCormick St, Wichita KS 67213
Jann Reusser, Admissions Recruitment Coordinator
316-942-4291 ext. 2144 Fax: 316-942-4483
Website: www.newmanu.edu
E-mail: reusserj@newmanu.edu

KENTUCKY

Morehead State University
Morehead KY 40351-1689
Dayna Seelig, Enrollment Services
800-585-6781 Fax: 606-783-5038
Website: www.moreheadstate.edu
E-mail: admissionsug@moreheadstate.edu

MARYLAND

Hagerstown Community College
11400 Robinwood Dr, Hagerstown MD 21742-6590
Dr. Daniel E. Bock, Assistant Director of Admissions
301-790-2800 Fax: 301-791-9165
Website: www.hagerstowncc.edu
E-mail: bockd@hagerstowncc.edu

MASSACHUSETTS

Boston University
121 Bay State Rd, Boston MA 02215
Kelly Walter, Executive Director of Admissions
617-353-2300 Fax: 617-353-9695
Website: web.bu.edu
E-mail: admissions@bu.edu

Emerson College
120 Boylston St, Boston MA 02116-4624
Sara S. Ramirez, Director of Undergraduate Admission
617-824-8600 Fax: 617-824-8609
Website: www.emerson.edu
E-mail: admission@emerson.edu

MICHIGAN

Delta College
University Center MI 48710-0001
Duff Zube, Director of Admissions
989-686-9093 Fax: 989-667-2202
Website: www.delta.edu
E-mail: admit@delta.edu

HILLSDALE COLLEGE
33 E College St, Hillsdale MI 49242-1298
Professor George Angell, Director
517-607-2178 Fax: 517-607-2665
Website: www.hillsdale.edu
E-mail: george.angell@hillsdale.edu

MACOMB COMMUNITY COLLEGE
44575 Garfield Rd, Clinton Township MI 48038-1139
Information Center
586-445-7999
Website: www.macomb.edu
E-mail: answer@macomb.edu

MACOMB COMMUNITY COLLEGE
14500 E 12 Mile Rd, Warren MI 48088-3896
Information Center
586-445-7999
Website: www.macomb.edu
E-mail: answer@macomb.edu

Specs Howard School of Broadcast Arts
19900 W 9 Mile Rd, Southfield MI 48075-3953
Nancy Shiner, Admissions Director
248-358-9000 Fax: 248-746-9772
Website: www.specshoward.edu
E-mail: info@specshoward.edu

MINNESOTA

Bethany Lutheran College
700 Luther Dr, Mankato MN 56001
Don Westphal, Dean of Admissions
507-344-7000 Fax: 507-344-7376
Website: www.blc.edu
E-mail: admiss@blc.edu

Pillsbury Baptist Bible College
315 S Grove Ave, Owatonna MN 55060-3097
Stephen R. Seidler, Director of Admissions
507-451-2710 Fax: 507-451-0156
Website: www.pillsbury.edu
E-mail: steveseidler@pillsbury.edu

SHATTUCK-ST. MARY'S SCHOOL
PO Box 218, Faribault MN 55021-0218
Amy D. Wolf, Director of Admissions
507-333-1618 Fax: 507-333-1661
Website: www.s-sm.org
E-mail: admissions@s-sm.org
See listing under "Preparatory Schools - Coed"

MISSOURI

Truman State University
100 E Normal, Kirksville MO 63501
Office of Admission
660-785-4000 Fax: 660-785-4181
Website: admissions.truman.edu
E-mail: admissions@truman.edu

Webster University
470 E Lockwood Ave, Saint Louis MO 63119-3194
Peter Sargent, Dean, College of Fine Arts
314-968-7006 Fax: 314-963-6102
Website: www.webster.edu
E-mail: sargenae@webster.edu
See listing under "Universities"

William Woods University
1 University Ave, Fulton MO 65251-1098
Jimmy Clay, Director of Admissions
573-642-2251 Fax: 573-592-1146
Website: www.williamwoods.edu
E-mail: admissions@williamwoods.edu
See listing under "Universities"

MONTANA

Rocky Mountain College
1511 Poly Dr, Billings MT 59102-1796
Bonnie Knapp, Director of Admissions
800-877-6259 Fax: 406-657-1189
Website: www.rocky.edu
E-mail: admissions@rocky.edu

NEBRASKA

University of Nebraska at Kearney
905 W 25th St, Kearney NE 68849-0001
Dusty Newton, Director of Admissions
800-KEARNEY Fax: 308-865-8987
Website: www.unk.edu
E-mail: admissionsug@unk.edu

NEW JERSEY

Bergen Community College
400 Paramus Rd, Paramus NJ 07652
Julian Gomez, Asst. Director of Admissions
201-447-7100 Fax: 201-444-7036
Website: www.bergen.edu
E-mail: jgomez@bergen.edu

New Jersey City University
2039 John F Kennedy Blvd
Jersey City NJ 07305-1588
Carmen Panlilio, Asst. V.P. for Admissions and
Financial Aid
201-200-3234 Fax: 201-200-2044
Website: www.njcu.edu
E-mail: admissions@njcu.edu

NEW YORK

American Academy of Dramatic Arts - New York
120 Madison Ave, New York NY 10016-7089
Karen Higginbotham, Director of Admissions
800-463-8990 Fax: 212-685-8093
Website: www.aada.org
E-mail: admissions-ny@aada.org

College of Saint Rose
432 Western Ave, Albany NY 12203-1419
Maryelizabeth Amico, Asst V.P. for Undergraduate
Admissions
518-454-5150 Fax: 518-454-2013
Website: www.strose.edu
E-mail: admit@strose.edu

Long Island University-C. W. Post Campus
720 Northern Blvd, Brookville NY 11548-1300
Joanne Graziano, Executive Director of Admissions
516-299-2900 Fax: 516-299-2137
Website: www.liu.edu/cwpost
E-mail: enroll@cwpost.liu.edu

Molloy College
1000 Hempstead Ave
Rockville Centre NY 11570-1100
Marguerite Lane, Director of Admissions
516-678-5000 ext. 6291 Fax: 516-256-2247
Website: www.molloy.edu
E-mail: admissions@molloy.edu
See listing under "Universities"

St. Joseph's College
245 Clinton Ave, Brooklyn NY 11205-3688
Theresa LaRocca Meyer, V.P. for Enrollment
Management
718-636-6800 Fax: 718-636-8303
Website: www.sjcny.edu
E-mail: tlaroccameyer@sjcny.edu

SUNY Niagara County Community College
3111 Saunders Settlement Rd
Sanborn NY 14132-9487
Kathleen Saunders, Director of Admissions
716-614-6200 Fax: 716-614-6820
Website: www.niagaracc.suny.edu
E-mail: saunders@niagaracc.suny.edu

SUNY Orange County Community College
115 South St, Middletown NY 10940-6437
Margot St. Lawrence, Director of Admissions
845-341-4030 Fax: 845-342-8662
Website: www.sunyorange.edu
E-mail: apply@sunyorange.edu
See listing under "Community and Junior Colleges"

NORTH CAROLINA

Lees-McRae College
PO Box 128, Banner Elk NC 28604-0128
Walt Crutchfield, Dean of Admissions
800-280-4562 Fax: 828-898-8707
Website: www.lmc.edu
E-mail: admissions@lmc.edu

Louisburg College
501 N Main St, Louisburg NC 27549-2399
800-775-0208 or 919-496-2521 Fax: 919-496-1788
Website: www.louisburg.edu
E-mail: admissions@louisburg.edu

Meredith College
3800 Hillsborough St, Raleigh NC 27607-5298
Heidi L. Fletcher, Director of Admissions
919-760-8581 Fax: 919-760-2348
Website: www.meredith.edu
E-mail: admissions@meredith.edu
See listing under "Women's Colleges"

NORTH DAKOTA

Dickinson State University
Dickinson ND 58601-4896
Steve Glasser, Director of Student Recruitment
800-279-4295 Fax: 701-483-2409
Website: www.dickinsonstate.edu
E-mail: dsu.hawks@dickinsonstate.edu

OHIO

Cleveland State University
2121 Euclid Ave RW 204, Cleveland OH 44115
Dr. Richard Arndt, Dean of Undergraduate Recruitment
and College Partnerships
888-CSU-OHIO Fax: 216-687-9210
Website: www.csuohio.edu
E-mail: admissions@csuohio.edu

Mount Vernon Nazarene University
800 Martinsburg Rd, Mount Vernon OH 43050-9509
Timothy Eades, Director of Admissions
866-462-6868 Fax: 740-393-0511
Website: www.gotomvnu.com
E-mail: admissions@mvnu.edu
See listing under "Universities"

The Ohio State University, Department of Theatre
Drake Performance & Event Center
1849 Cannon Dr, Columbus OH 43210
614-292-5821 Fax: 614-292-3222
Website: theatre.osu.edu
E-mail: theatre-ugrad@osu.edu

OKLAHOMA

Oral Roberts University
7777 S Lewis Ave, Tulsa OK 74171-0001
Chris Belcher, Director of Undergraduate Admissions
800-678-8876 Fax: 918-495-6222
Website: www.oru.edu
E-mail: admissions@oru.edu

OREGON

Cascade College
9101 E Burnside St, Portland OR 97216-1599
800-550-7678 Fax: 503-257-1222
Website: www.cascade.edu
E-mail: admissions@cascade.edu

Warner Pacific College
2219 SE 68th Ave, Portland OR 97215-4026
Shannon Mackey, Director of Admissions
503-517-1000 Fax: 503-517-1352
Website: www.warnerpacific.edu
E-mail: admissions@warnerpacific.edu

PENNSYLVANIA

Arcadia University
450 S Easton Rd, Glenside PA 19038-3295
Dennis Nostrand, VP for Enrollment Management
877-ARCADIA (877-272-2342) Fax: 215-881-8767
Website: www.arcadia.edu
E-mail: admiss@arcadia.edu
See listing under "Universities"

Gannon University
109 University Sq, Erie PA 16541-0001
Christopher Tremblay, Director of Admissions
800-GANNON-U Fax: 814-871-5803
Website: www.gannon.edu
E-mail: admissions@gannon.edu

University of the Arts
320 S Broad St, Philadelphia PA 19102-4994
Susan Gandy, Director of Admissions
800-616-2787 Fax: 215-717-6045
Website: www.uarts.edu
E-mail: admissions@uarts.edu

SOUTH CAROLINA

PRESBYTERIAN COLLEGE
503 S Broad St, Clinton SC 29325
Richard Dana Paul, Dean of Admissions
800-476-7272 Fax: 864-833-8481
Website: www.presby.edu
E-mail: admissions@presby.edu

University of South Carolina - Upstate
800 University Way, Spartanburg SC 29303-4932
Donette Stewart, Assistant VC for Enrollment Services
864-503-5246 Fax: 864-503-5727
Website: www.uscupstate.edu
E-mail: dstewart@uscupstate.edu
See listing under "Universities"

TENNESSEE

Lipscomb University
3901 Granny White Pike, Nashville TN 37204-3951
Ricky Holaway, Director of Admissions
800-333-4358 ext. 1776 Fax: 615-269-1804
Website: www.lipscomb.edu
E-mail: admissions@lipscomb.edu

Tennessee State University
3500 John A Merritt Blvd, Nashville TN 37209-1561
John Cade, Dean of Admissions & Records
615-963-5101 Fax: 615-963-2930
Website: www.tnstate.edu
E-mail: jcade@tnstate.edu

TEXAS

Angelo State University
ASU Station 11014, San Angelo TX 76909
Bonnie Stennett, Coordinator of Recruiting
800-946-8627 Fax: 325-942-2078
Website: www.angelo.edu
E-mail: admissions@angelo.edu

Blinn College
902 College Ave, Brenham TX 77833-4098
Dennis K. Crowson, Registrar
979-830-4000 Fax: 979-830-4110
Website: www.blinn.edu
E-mail: recruiting@blinn.edu

KD STUDIO - ACTORS CONSERVATORY
2600 N Stemmons Fwy Ste 117
Dallas TX 75207-2168
T. A. Taylor, Director of Education
877-278-2283 Fax: 214-630-5140
Website: www.kdstudio.com
E-mail: admissions@kdstudio.com
Established 1979. Private. Coed. Accreditation: TEA, NAST, Texas Higher Education Coordinating Board. Tuition: $11,000. Enrollment: 100 full-time. Faculty: 26. Student-faculty ratio: 18:1. Degrees: Applied Associates Degree. Private library Resource Center. This program is aimed at developing camera acting skills as well as stage acting. Faculty are involved as industry professionals. A showcase is performed upon graduation where agents, casting directors and local producers and directors attend. FA available. VA approved.

Texas Woman's University
PO Box 425589, Denton TX 76204-5589
Erma Nieto, Director of Admissions
866-809-6130 Fax: 940-898-3081
Website: www.twu.edu
E-mail: admissions@twu.edu

University of Houston
122 E Cullen Bldg, Houston TX 77204-2023
Office of Admission
713-743-9595
Website: www.uh.edu
E-mail: admissions@uh.edu

University of Texas at Arlington
Box 19111, Arlington TX 76019-0111
Hans Gatterdam, Director of Admission
817-272-6287 Fax: 817-272-3435
Website: www.uta.edu
E-mail: admissions@uta.edu

VERMONT

Bennington College
One College Drive, Bennington VT 05201
Ken Himmelman, Dean of Admissions & Financial Aid
800-833-6845 Fax: 802-440-4320
Website: www.bennington.edu
E-mail: admissions@bennington.edu

VIRGINIA

Radford University
PO Box 6903, Radford VA 24142
David W. Kraus, Director of Admissions
800-890-4265 Fax: 540-831-5038
Website: www.radford.edu
E-mail: ruadmiss@radford.edu

Randolph-Macon Woman's College
2500 Rivermont Ave, Lynchburg VA 24503
Patricia LeDonne, Director of Admissions
434-947-8100 Fax: 434-947-8996
Website: www.rmwc.edu
E-mail: admissions@rmwc.edu

WASHINGTON

Cornish College of the Arts
1000 Lenora St, Seattle WA 98121
Eric Pedersen, Director of Admission
800-726-ARTS (2787) Fax: 206-720-1011
Website: www.cornish.edu
E-mail: admissions@cornish.edu

Gonzaga University
502 E Boone Ave, Spokane WA 99258-0102
Julie McCulloh, Dean of Admission
800-322-2584 or 509-323-6572 Fax: 509-323-5780
Website: www.gonzaga.edu
E-mail: mcculloh@gu.gonzaga.edu

WEST VIRGINIA

Concord University
Athens WV 24712
Michael Curry, Vice President of Financial Aid & Admissions
888-384-5249 Fax: 304-384-3218
Website: www.concord.edu
E-mail: admissions@concord.edu

Davis & Elkins College
100 Campus Dr, Elkins WV 26241-3996
Renee Heckel, Director of Enrollment Management
800-624-3157 Fax: 304-637-1800
Website: www.davisandelkins.edu
E-mail: admiss@davisandelkins.edu

Fairmont State University
1201 Locust Ave, Fairmont WV 26554-2470
Steve Leadman, Director of Admissions
304-367-4892 or 800-641-5678 Fax: 304-367-4789
Website: www.fairmontstate.edu
E-mail: admit@fairmontstate.edu

West Virginia Wesleyan College
59 College Ave, Buckhannon WV 26201-2699
Robert N. Skinner II, Director of Admission
800-722-9933 Fax: 304-473-8108
Website: www.wvwc.edu
E-mail: admission@wvwc.edu

WISCONSIN

St. Norbert College
100 Grant St, De Pere WI 54115
Brian Studebaker, Director of Admission
800-236-4878 Fax: 920-403-4072
Website: www.snc.edu
E-mail: admit@snc.edu

STUDY ABROAD

ALABAMA

Faulkner University
5345 Atlanta Hwy, Montgomery AL 36109-3398
Keith Mock, Director of Admissions
800-879-9816 ext. 7200 or 334-386-7200
Fax: 334-386-7137
Website: www.faulkner.edu
E-mail: admissions@faulkner.edu

ALASKA

University of Alaska Anchorage
PO Box 141629, Anchorage AK 99514-1629
Cecile Mitchell, Director of Enrollment Services
907-786-1480 Fax: 907-786-4888
Website: www.uaa.alaska.edu/
E-mail: enroll@uaa.alaska.edu

University of Alaska Southeast
11120 Glacier Hwy, Juneau AK 99801-8625
Paul Kraft, Dean of Students/Enrollment Management
907-796-6000 Fax: 907-796-6005
Website: www.uas.alaska.edu
E-mail: paul.kraft@uas.alaska.edu

ARIZONA

University of Arizona
Tucson AZ 85721-0040
Paul Kohn, Director of Admissions
520-621-3237 Fax: 520-621-9799
Website: www.admissions.arizona.edu or www.arizona.edu

ARKANSAS

Ouachita Baptist University
410 Ouachita St, Arkadelphia AR 71998-0001
David Goodman, Director of Admissions
870-245-5773 Fax: 870-245-5500
Website: www.obu.edu
E-mail: admissions@obu.edu

CALIFORNIA

Antioch University
801 Garden St Ste 101
Santa Barbara CA 93101-1581
Ankara McPherson, Director of Admissions
805-962-8179 Fax: 805-962-4786
Website: www.antiochsb.edu
E-mail: amcpherson@antiochsb.edu

Chapman University
One University Drive, Orange CA 92866-1099
Michael Drummy, Assistant Vice President for Enrollment
Services and Chief Admission Officer
714-997-6411 or 888-CUAPPLY Fax: 714-997-6713
Website: www.chapman.edu
E-mail: admit@chapman.edu

Concordia University
1530 Concordia, Irvine CA 92612-3203
Lori McDonald, Executive Director of Enrollment Services
800-229-1200 or 949-854-8002 Fax: 949-854-6894
Website: www.cui.edu
E-mail: admission@cui.edu

FIDM/The Fashion Institute of Design & Merchandising
919 S Grand Ave, Los Angeles CA 90015-1421
Director of Admissions
213-624-1201 or 800-624-1200 Fax: 213-624-4799
Website: www.fidm.edu
E-mail: info@fidm.com
See listing under "Community and Junior Colleges"

Orange Coast College
PO Box 5005, Costa Mesa CA 92628-5005
Kristin Clark, Director of Admissions
714-432-5773 Fax: 714-432-5736
Website: www.orangecoastcollege.edu
E-mail: kclark@cccd.edu

Whittier College
PO Box 634, Whittier CA 90608-0634
Kieron Miller, Director of Admissions
562-907-4200 Fax: 562-907-4870
Website: www.whittier.edu
E-mail: kmiller@whittier.edu

DELAWARE

Wesley College
120 N State St, Dover DE 19901-3876
302-736-2300 Fax: 302-736-2301
Website: www.wesley.edu

FLORIDA

Florida State University
600 W College Ave, Tallahassee FL 32306-1096
Janice V. Finney, Director of Admissions
850-644-2525 Fax: 850-644-0197
Website: www.admissions.fsu.edu
E-mail: admissions@admin.fsu.edu

Lynn University
3601 N Military Trl, Boca Raton FL 33431-5598
Brett Ormandy, Director of Admissions
561-237-7078 Fax: 561-237-7100
Website: www.lynn.edu
E-mail: admission@lynn.edu

University of South Florida
4202 E Fowler Ave, Tampa FL 33620-6900
J. Robert Spatig, Director of Admissions
813-974-3350 Fax: 813-974-9689
Website: www.usf.edu
E-mail: admissions@admin.usf.edu

GEORGIA

Savannah College of Art and Design
PO Box 2072, Savannah, GA 31402-2072
PO Box 77300, Atlanta, GA 30357
Phone: 800-869-7223 (Savannah) or 877-722-3285 (Atlanta)
E-mail: admission@scad.edu (Savannah) or sca-datl@scad.edu (Atlanta)

www.scad.edu
SCAD is a private, nonprofit institution accredited by the Commission on Colleges of the Southern Association of Colleges and Schools to award bachelor's and master's degrees. The college offers B.F.A., M.Arch., M.A., M.F.A., and M.U.D. degrees. Enrollment is approximately 7,350; 6 percent are international. More than 30 areas of study. Online programs via SCAD e-Learning.

ILLINOIS

Benedictine University
5700 College Rd, Lisle IL 60532-0900
630-829-6300 or 888-829-6363 Fax: 630-829-6301
Website: www.ben.edu
E-mail: admissions@ben.edu
See listing under "Universities"

CONCORDIA UNIVERSITY
7400 Augusta St, River Forest IL 60305-1402
708-209-3100 Fax: 708-209-3473
Website: www.curf.edu
E-mail: crfadmis.edu

North Central College
30 N Brainard St, Naperville IL 60540-4690
Martha Stolze, Director of Admissions
630-637-5800 Fax: 630-637-5819
Website: www.northcentralcollege.edu
E-mail: admissions@noctrl.edu

NORTHEASTERN ILLINOIS UNIVERSITY
5500 N Saint Louis Ave, Chicago IL 60625-4699
Rubee Fuller, International Programs
773-442-4050 Fax: 773-442-4020
Website: www.neiu.edu
E-mail: r-fuller@neiu.edu

Roosevelt University
430 S Michigan Ave, Chicago IL 60605
Gwen E. Kanelos, Asst. Vice President for Enrollment Services
877-APPLY-RU Fax: 312-341-4216
Website: www.roosevelt.edu
E-mail: applyru@roosevelt.edu

INDIANA

St. Mary-of-the-Woods College
Saint Mary of the Woods IN 47876-1001
James P. Malley, Jr., Director of Admission
800-926-7692 Fax: 812-535-5010
Website: www.smwc.edu
E-mail: smwcadms@smwc.edu

University of Evansville
1800 Lincoln Ave, Evansville IN 47722-0001
Thomas E. Bear, V.P. of Enrollment Services
800-423-8633 Fax: 812-488-4076
Website: www.evansville.edu
E-mail: admission@evansville.edu

IOWA

Briar Cliff University
PO Box 2100, Sioux City IA 51104-0100
Sharisue Wilcoxon, VP for Enrollment Management
712-279-5200 Fax: 712-279-1632
Website: www.briarcliff.edu
E-mail: admissions@briarcliff.edu

Clarke College
1550 Clarke Dr, Dubuque IA 52001-3198
Andy Schroeder, Director of Admissions
800-383-2345 Fax: 563-584-8666
Website: www.clarke.edu
E-mail: andy.schroeder@clarke.edu

Graceland University
1 University Place, Lamoni IA 50140
Brian Shantz, Vice President for Enrollment and Dean of Admissions
641-784-5196 Fax: 641-784-5480
Website: www.admissions.graceland.edu
E-mail: admissions@graceland.edu

Iowa Lakes Community College
3200 College Dr, Emmetsburg IA 50536-1055
Anne Stansbury, Asst. Director of Admissions
712-852-5212 Fax: 712-362-8363
Website: www.iowalakes.edu
E-mail: info@iowalakes.edu

Iowa Lakes Community College
300 S 18th St, Estherville IA 51334-2721
Anne Stansbury, Asst. Director of Admissions
712-362-7945 Fax: 712-362-8363
Website: www.iowalakes.edu
E-mail: info@iowalakes.edu

Iowa Lakes Community College
1900 Grand Ave, Suite 8, Spencer IA 51301
Anne Stansbury, Assistant Director of Admissions
712-262-7141 Fax: 712-262-4047
Website: www.iowalakes.edu
E-mail: info@iowalakes.edu

KANSAS

Newman University
3100 W McCormick St, Wichita KS 67213
Jann Reusser, Admissions Recruitment Coordinator
316-942-4291 ext. 2144 Fax: 316-942-4483
Website: www.newmanu.edu
E-mail: reusserj@newmanu.edu

LOUISIANA

Dillard University
2601 Gentilly Blvd, New Orleans LA 70122-3097
Linda G. Nash, Director of Admissions
Website: www.dillard.edu
E-mail: admissions@dillard.edu

MASSACHUSETTS

Anna Maria College
50 Sunset Ln, Paxton MA 01612
Julie A. Mitchell, Director of Admissions
508-849-3360 Fax: 508-849-3362
Website: www.annamaria.edu
E-mail: admissions@annamaria.edu

Bay Path College
588 Longmeadow St, Longmeadow MA 01106-2292
Lisa Casassa, Director of Admissions
413-565-1331 Fax: 413-565-1105
Website: www.baypath.edu
E-mail: lcasassa@baypath.edu

Boston University
121 Bay State Rd, Boston MA 02215
Kelly Walter, Executive Director of Admissions
617-353-2300 Fax: 617-353-9695
Website: web.bu.edu
E-mail: admissions@bu.edu

Massachusetts Institute of Technology
77 Massachusetts Ave, Cambridge MA 02139-4307
Marilee Jones, Dean of Admission
617-253-1000 Fax: 617-253-4016
Website: my.mit.edu
E-mail: admissions@mit.edu

University of Massachusetts Dartmouth
Old Westport Rd, North Dartmouth MA 02747-2300
Kevin Curow, Academic Advising
508-999-9299 Fax: 508-999-8850
Website: explore.umassd.edu
E-mail: kcurow@umassd.edu

MICHIGAN

Alma College
614 W Superior St, Alma MI 48801-1599
Anne Monroe, Director of Admissions
800-321-ALMA Fax: 989-463-7057
Website: www.alma.edu
E-mail: admissions@alma.edu

Andrews University
Berrien Springs MI 49104-0001
Randall Graves, Director of Recruitment Services
800-253-2874 Fax: 269-471-2670
Website: www.connect.andrews.edu
E-mail: gravesr@andrews.edu

Grand Valley State University
1 Campus Dr, Allendale MI 49401-9403
616-331-2025 Fax: 616-331-2000
Website: www.gvsu.edu
E-mail: go2gvsu@gvsu.edu

HILLSDALE COLLEGE
33 E College St, Hillsdale MI 49242-1298
Dr. Ellen Justice-Templeton, Director
517-607-2442 Fax: 517-607-2208
Website: www.hillsdale.edu
E-mail: ellen.justicf@hillsdale.edu

University of Michigan-Dearborn
4901 Evergreen Rd, Dearborn MI 48128-1491
The Office of Admissions & Orientation
313-593-5100 Fax: 313-436-9167
Website: www.umd.umich.edu
E-mail: admissions@umd.umich.edu

MINNESOTA

Pillsbury Baptist Bible College
315 S Grove Ave, Owatonna MN 55060-3097
Stephen R. Seidler, Director of Admissions
507-451-2710 Fax: 507-451-0156
Website: www.pillsbury.edu
E-mail: steveseidler@pillsbury.edu

MISSOURI

Columbia College
1001 Rogers St, Columbia MO 65216-0001
Regina Morin, Director of Admissions
573-875-7352 Fax: 573-875-7506
Website: www.ccis.edu
E-mail: admissions@ccis.edu

Stephens College
PO Box 2121, Columbia MO 65215-0001
David Adams, Dean of Enrollment Management
573-442-2211 Fax: 573-876-7237
Website: www.stephens.edu
E-mail: dadams@stephens.edu

Truman State University
100 E Normal, Kirksville MO 63501
Office of Admission
660-785-4000 Fax: 660-785-4181
Website: admissions.truman.edu
E-mail: admissions@truman.edu

University of Missouri
1 University Blvd, Saint Louis MO 63121-4499
Tracy Faschingbauer, Coordinator
314-516-5753 Fax: 314-516-6757
Website: www.umsl.edu
E-mail: admissions@umsl.edu

Webster University
470 E Lockwood Ave, Saint Louis MO 63119-3194
Mark Beirn, Study Abroad
314-968-7433 Fax: 314-968-7119
Website: www.webster.edu
E-mail: mbeirn@webster.edu
See listing under "Universities"

William Woods University
1 University Ave, Fulton MO 65251-1098
Jimmy Clay, Director of Admissions
573-642-2251 Fax: 573-592-1146
Website: www.williamwoods.edu
E-mail: admissions@williamwoods.edu
See listing under "Universities"

MONTANA

Rocky Mountain College
1511 Poly Dr, Billings MT 59102-1796
Bonnie Knapp, Director of Admissions
800-877-6259 Fax: 406-657-1189
Website: www.rocky.edu
E-mail: admissions@rocky.edu

NEBRASKA

Nebraska Wesleyan University
5000 Saint Paul Ave, Lincoln NE 68504-2794
Patricia Karthauser, V.P. for University Enrollment
402-466-2371 Fax: 402-465-2177
Website: www.nebrwesleyan.edu
E-mail: admissions@nebrwesleyan.edu

NEW JERSEY

Bergen Community College
400 Paramus Rd, Paramus NJ 07652
Julian Gomez, Asst. Director of Admissions
201-447-7100 Fax: 201-444-7036
Website: www.bergen.edu
E-mail: jgomez@bergen.edu

New Jersey City University
2039 John F Kennedy Blvd
Jersey City NJ 07305-1588
Carmen Panlilio, Asst. V.P. for Admissions and Financial Aid
201-200-3234 Fax: 201-200-2044
Website: www.njcu.edu
E-mail: admissions@njcu.edu

Ramapo College of New Jersey
505 Ramapo Valley Rd, Mahwah NJ 07430-1623
Director of Admissions
201-684-7300 or 201-684-7301 Fax: 201-684-7964
Website: www.ramapo.edu
E-mail: admissions@ramapo.edu

NEW YORK

AMERICAN UNIVERSITY IN CAIRO
420 5th Ave 3rd Floor, New York NY 10018
Student Affairs Office
212-730-8800 Fax: 212-730-1600
Website: www.aucegypt.edu
E-mail: aucegypt@aucnyo.edu

College of Saint Rose
432 Western Ave, Albany NY 12203-1419
Maryelizabeth Amico, Asst V.P. for Undergraduate Admissions
518-454-5150 Fax: 518-454-2013
Website: www.strose.edu
E-mail: admit@strose.edu

Long Island University-C. W. Post Campus
720 Northern Blvd, Brookville NY 11548-1300
Joanne Graziano, Executive Director of Admissions
516-299-2900 Fax: 516-299-2137
Website: www.liu.edu/cwpost
E-mail: enroll@cwpost.liu.edu

Molloy College
1000 Hempstead Ave
Rockville Centre NY 11570-1100
Marguerite Lane, Director of Admissions
516-678-5000 ext. 6291 Fax: 516-256-2247
Website: www.molloy.edu
E-mail: admissions@molloy.edu
See listing under "Universities"

Pratt Institute
200 Willoughby Ave, Brooklyn NY 11205-3899
Heidi Metcalf, Director of Admissions
718-636-3600 Fax: 718-636-3670
Website: www.pratt.edu
E-mail: hmetcalf@pratt.edu

Roberts Wesleyan College
2301 Westside Dr, Rochester NY 14624-1997
Office of Admissions
585-594-6400 Fax: 585-594-6371
Website: www.roberts.edu
E-mail: admissions@roberts.edu

SUNY College at Brockport
350 New Campus Dr, Brockport NY 14420-2997
Bernard S. Valento, Director of Undergraduate Admissions
585-395-2751 Fax: 585-395-5452
Website: www.brockport.edu
E-mail: admit@brockport.edu

Wells College
PO Box 500, Aurora NY 13026
Susan Sloan, Director of Admissions
800-952-9355 Fax: 315-364-3227
Website: www.wells.edu
E-mail: ssloan@wells.edu

NORTH CAROLINA

Meredith College
3800 Hillsborough St, Raleigh NC 27607-5298
Heidi L. Fletcher, Director of Admissions
919-760-8581 Fax: 919-760-2348
Website: www.meredith.edu
E-mail: admissions@meredith.edu
See listing under "Women's Colleges"

Salem College
Winston Salem NC 27108
Dana Evans, Dean of Admissions/Fin. Aid
800-32-SALEM Fax: 336-917-5572
Website: www.salem.edu
E-mail: admissions@salem.edu
See listing under "Women's Colleges"

OHIO

Franciscan University of Steubenville
University Blvd, Steubenville OH 43952
Margaret J. Weber, Director of Admissions
800-783-6220 or 740-283-6226 Fax: 740-284-5456
Website: www.admissions.edu
E-mail: mweber@franciscan.edu

Ursuline College
2550 Lander Rd, Cleveland OH 44124-4398
Sarah E. Sundermeier, Director of Admissions
888-URSULINE Toll Free Fax: 440-684-6138
Website: www.admission.ursuline.edu
E-mail: admission@ursuline.edu

OKLAHOMA

Oklahoma State University
Stillwater OK 74078
Gerry Auel, Program Director
405-744-8569
Website: www.okstate.edu
E-mail: gerry.auel@okstate.edu

OREGON

Cascade College
9101 E Burnside St, Portland OR 97216-1599
800-550-7678 Fax: 503-257-1222
Website: www.cascade.edu
E-mail: admissions@cascade.edu

PENNSYLVANIA

Arcadia University
450 S Easton Rd, Glenside PA 19038-3295
David Larsen, VP and Director
866-927-2234 Fax: 215-881-8767
Website: www.arcadia.edu
Semester and year-long programs in Australia,
England, Equatorial Guinea, France, Greece, Ireland,
Italy, Korea, New Zealand, Northern Ireland, Scotland,
Spain and Wales.
See listing under "Universities"

Art Institute of Philadelphia
1622 Chestnut St, Philadelphia PA 19103-5119
Larry McHugh, Director of Admissions
800-275-2474 Fax: 215-405-6399
Website: www.aiph.aii.edu
E-mail: aiphinfo@aii.edu

Gannon University
109 University Sq, Erie PA 16541-0001
Christopher Tremblay, Director of Admissions
800-GANNON-U Fax: 814-871-5803
Website: www.gannon.edu
E-mail: admissions@gannon.edu

Juniata College
1700 Moore St, Huntingdon PA 16652-2196
Michelle Bartol, Dean of Enrollment
877-JUNIATA Fax: 814-641-3100
Website: www.juniata.edu
E-mail: admissions@juniata.edu

Lebanon Valley College
101 N College Ave, Annville PA 17003-1400
William Brown, Dean of Admissions & Financial Aid
866-LVC-4ADM or 717-867-6181 Fax: 717-867-6026
Website: www.lvc.edu
E-mail: admission@lvc.edu

MOUNT ALOYSIUS COLLEGE

7373 Admiral Peary Hwy, Cresson PA 16630-1999
Frank C. Crouse Jr., Vice President for Enrollment
Management
814-886-6383 or 888-823-2220 Fax: 814-886-6441
Website: www.mtaloy.edu
E-mail: admissions@mtaloy.edu

SOUTH CAROLINA

Columbia International University
PO Box 3122, Columbia SC 29230-3122
John Basie, Director of University Admissions
800-777-2227 Fax: 803-786-4209
Website: www.ciu.edu
E-mail: yesciu@ciu.edu
See listing under "Theological Studies & Religious
Vocations"

PRESBYTERIAN COLLEGE

503 S Broad St, Clinton SC 29325
Richard Dana Paul, Dean of Admissions
800-476-7272 Fax: 864-833-8481
Website: www.presby.edu
E-mail: admissions@presby.edu

TENNESSEE

Lipscomb University
3901 Granny White Pike, Nashville TN 37204-3951
Ricky Holaway, Director of Admissions
800-333-4358 ext. 1776 Fax: 615-269-1804
Website: www.lipscomb.edu
E-mail: admissions@lipscomb.edu

TEXAS

Angelo State University
ASU Station 11014, San Angelo TX 76909
Bonnie Stennett, Coordinator of Recruiting
800-946-8627 Fax: 325-942-2078
Website: www.angelo.edu
E-mail: admissions@angelo.edu

University of Houston
122 E Cullen Bldg, Houston TX 77204-2023
Office of Admission
713-743-9595
Website: www.uh.edu
E-mail: admissions@uh.edu

VERMONT

NORWICH UNIVERSITY

158 Harmon Dr, Northfield VT 05663
Jennifer Hasenfus, International Programs
800-468-6679
Website: www.norwich.edu
E-mail: jhasenfu@norwich.edu

VIRGINIA

Radford University
PO Box 6903, Radford VA 24142
David W. Kraus, Director of Admissions
800-890-4265 Fax: 540-831-5038
Website: www.radford.edu
E-mail: ruadmiss@radford.edu

WASHINGTON

Gonzaga University
502 E Boone Ave, Spokane WA 99258-0102
Julie McCulloh, Dean of Admission
800-322-2584 or 509-323-6572 Fax: 509-323-5780
Website: www.gonzaga.edu
E-mail: mcculloh@gu.gonzaga.edu

WEST VIRGINIA

West Virginia Wesleyan College
59 College Ave, Buckhannon WV 26201-2699
Robert N. Skinner II, Director of Admission
800-722-9933 Fax: 304-473-8108
Website: www.wvwc.edu
E-mail: admission@wvwc.edu

WISCONSIN

St. Norbert College
100 Grant St, De Pere WI 54115
Brian Studebaker, Director of Admission
800-236-4878 Fax: 920-403-4072
Website: www.snc.edu
E-mail: admit@snc.edu

WYOMING

University of Wyoming
Admissions Office
Dept 3435, Laramie WY 82071-3435
Aaron Appelhans, Contact
800-342-5996 Fax: 307-766-4042
Website: www.uwyo.edu
E-mail: why-wyo@uwyo.edu

SUMMER SESSIONS

ALABAMA

Alabama A & M University
PO Box 908, Normal AL 35762
Antonio Boyle, Director of Admissions
256-372-5245 Fax: 256-372-5249
Website: www.aamu.edu
E-mail: aboyle@aamu.edu

CALHOUN COMMUNITY COLLEGE

PO Box 2216, Decatur AL 35609-2216
M. Wayne Tosh, Registrar
256-306-2500 Fax: 256-306-2941
Website: www.calhoun.edu
E-mail: pml@calhoun.edu
See listing under "Community and Junior Colleges"

Faulkner University
5345 Atlanta Hwy, Montgomery AL 36109-3398
Keith Mock, Director of Admissions
800-879-9816 ext. 7200 or 334-386-7200
Fax: 334-386-7137
Website: www.faulkner.edu
E-mail: admissions@faulkner.edu

ALASKA

University of Alaska Anchorage
PO Box 141629, Anchorage AK 99514-1629
Cecile Mitchell, Director of Enrollment Services
907-786-1480 Fax: 907-786-4888
Website: www.uaa.alaska.edu/
E-mail: enroll@uaa.alaska.edu

University of Alaska Southeast
11120 Glacier Hwy, Juneau AK 99801-8625
Paul Kraft, Dean of Students/Enrollment Management
907-796-6000 Fax: 907-796-6005
Website: www.uas.alaska.edu
E-mail: paul.kraft@uas.alaska.edu

ARIZONA

University of Arizona
Tucson AZ 85721-0040
Paul Kohn, Director of Admissions
520-621-3237 Fax: 520-621-9799
Website: www.admissions.arizona.edu or
www.arizona.edu

CALIFORNIA

Chapman University
One University Drive, Orange CA 92866-1099
Michael Drummy, Assistant Vice President for
Enrollment
Services and Chief Admission Officer
714-997-6411 or 888-CUAPPLY Fax: 714-997-6713
Website: www.chapman.edu
E-mail: admit@chapman.edu

Orange Coast College
PO Box 5005, Costa Mesa CA 92628-5005
Kristin Clark, Director of Admissions
714-432-5773 Fax: 714-432-5736
Website: www.orangecoastcollege.edu
E-mail: kclark@cccd.edu

San Diego Christian College
2100 Greenfield Dr, El Cajon CA 92019-1157
Jon Melone, Director of Admissions
800-676-2242 Fax: 619-590-1739
Website: www.sdcc.edu
E-mail: admissions@sdcc.edu

COLORADO

ILIFF SCHOOL OF THEOLOGY

2201 S University Blvd, Denver CO 80210-4798
Stephanie Yahas, Coordinator of Summer School
800-678-3360 or 303-765-3117 Fax: 303-777-0164
Website: www.iliff.edu
E-mail: admissions@iliff.edu

CONNECTICUT

University of New Haven
300 Boston Post Rd, West Haven CT 06516
Part-Time Admissions
203-932-7361 Fax: 203-931-6093
Website: www.newhaven.edu
E-mail: gradinfo@newhaven.edu

DELAWARE

Wesley College
120 N State St, Dover DE 19901-3876
302-736-2300 Fax: 302-736-2301
Website: www.wesley.edu

FLORIDA

International Academy of Design & Technology
5104 Eisenhower Blvd, Tampa FL 33634-6313
Richard Costa, V.P. of Admissions and Marketing
813-880-8092 Fax: 813-881-0008
Website: www.academy.edu
E-mail: admissions@academy.edu

Jones College
5353 Arlington Expy, Jacksonville FL 32211-5588
Dorothy D. Jones, Chief Executive Officer
904-743-1122 Fax: 904-744-4446
Website: www.jones.edu
E-mail: lwade@jones.edu

Jones College
11430 N Kendall Dr Ste 200, Miami FL 33176
Barclay Charles, Contact
305-275-9996 Fax: 305-743-4446
Website: www.jones.edu
E-mail: pcarbone@jones.edu

Lynn University
3601 N Military Trl, Boca Raton FL 33431-5598
Brett Ormandy, Director of Admissions
561-237-7900 Fax: 561-237-7100
Website: www.lynn.edu
E-mail: admission@lynn.edu

SOUTHWEST FLORIDA COLLEGE

1685 Medical Ln, Fort Myers FL 33907-1157
866-SWFC-NOW or 239-939-4766 Fax: 239-936-4040
Website: www.swfc.edu
E-mail: studentinfo@swfc.edu

Trinity Baptist College
800-200 Hammond Blvd, Jacksonville FL 32221
R. Larry Appleby, Director of Admissions
904-596-2400 Fax: 904-596-2531
Website: www.tbc.edu
E-mail: emailtrinity@tbc.edu

University of South Florida
4202 E Fowler Ave, Tampa FL 33620-6900
J. Robert Spatig, Director of Admissions
813-974-3350 Fax: 813-974-9689
Website: www.usf.edu
E-mail: admissions@admin.usf.edu

GEORGIA

Kennesaw State University
1000 Chastain Rd NW, Kennesaw GA 30144-5591
Dr. Ralph Rascati, Dean
770-423-6000
Website: www.kennesaw.edu

North Georgia Technical College
434 Meeks Ave, Blairsville GA 30512-2983
Admissions
706-781-2300 Fax: 706-781-2307
Website: www.northgatech.edu
E-mail: info@northgatech.edu

North Georgia Technical College
8989 Highway 17, Toccoa GA 30577
706-779-5591
Website: www.northgatech.edu
E-mail: info@northgatech.edu

North Georgia Technical College
Clarkesville Campus
PO Box 65, Clarkesville GA 30523-0002
Admissions
706-754-7700 Fax: 706-754-7777
Website: www.northgatech.edu
E-mail: info@northgatech.edu

Savannah College of Art and Design

PO Box 2072, Savannah, GA 31402-2072
PO Box 77300, Atlanta, GA 30357
Phone: 800-869-7223 (Savannah) or 877-722-3285 (Atlanta)
E-mail: admission@scad.edu (Savannah) or sca-datl@scad.edu (Atlanta)
www.scad.edu
    SCAD is a private, nonprofit institution accredited by the Commission on Colleges of the Southern Association of Colleges and Schools to award bachelor's and master's degrees. The college offers B.F.A., M.Arch., M.A., M.F.A., and M.U.D. degrees. Enrollment is approximately 7,350; 6 percent are international. More than 30 areas of study. Online programs via SCAD e-Learning.

TOCCOA FALLS COLLEGE

PO Box 800899, Toccoa Falls GA 30598
Christy Meadows, Director of Admissions
888-785-5624 Fax: 706-282-6012
Website: www.tfc.edu
E-mail: admissions@tfc.edu

ILLINOIS

Benedictine University
5700 College Rd, Lisle IL 60532-0900
630-829-6300 or 888-829-6363 Fax: 630-829-6301
Website: www.ben.edu
E-mail: admissions@ben.edu
See listing under "Universities"

CONCORDIA UNIVERSITY

7400 Augusta St, River Forest IL 60305-1402
708-209-3100 Fax: 708-209-3473
Website: www.curf.edu
E-mail: crfadmis.edu

Roosevelt University
430 S Michigan Ave, Chicago IL 60605
Gwen E. Kanelos, Asst. Vice President for Enrollment Services
877-APPLY-RU Fax: 312-341-4216
Website: www.roosevelt.edu
E-mail: applyru@roosevelt.edu

South Suburban College of Cook County
15800 State St, South Holland IL 60473
Jane Ellen Stocker, Dean of Enrollment Services
708-596-2000 Fax: 708-225-5806
Website: www.southsuburbancollege.edu
E-mail: jstocker@southsuburbancollege.edu

VANDERCOOK COLLEGE OF MUSIC

3140 S Federal St, Chicago IL 60616-3704
Tamara V. Trutwin, Student Recruiter
Kelly Westergaard, Admissions Coordinator
800-448-2655 ext. 230 Fax: 312-225-5211
Website: www.vandercook.edu
E-mail: admissions@vandercook.edu
    Established 1928. Private. Coed. Accreditation: NCA; NASM; Illinois State Board of Higher Learning. Tuition: $7,945 undergrad, $3,960 graduate. Room & Board: $6,500 undergrad, $1,650 graduate. Enrollment: 85 undergraduate. Faculty: 35. Student-faculty ratio: 6:1. Degrees: Bachelor of Music Education, Master of Music Education. The only College in the U.S. solely devoted to the preparation of music educators. There is a 100% placement rate for those seeking a career in music education after graduation.

INDIANA

Ancilla Domini College
Donaldson IN 46513
Erin Wittmeyer, Director of Admissions
574-936-8898 Fax: 574-935-1773
Website: www.ancilla.edu
E-mail: erin.wittmeyer@ancilla.edu

IOWA

Briar Cliff University
PO Box 2100, Sioux City IA 51104-0100
Sharisue Wilcoxon, VP for Enrollment Management
712-279-5200 Fax: 712-279-1632
Website: www.briarcliff.edu
E-mail: admissions@briarcliff.edu

Graceland University
1 University Place, Lamoni IA 50140
Brian Shantz, Vice President for Enrollment and Dean of Admissions
641-784-5196 Fax: 641-784-5480
Website: www.admissions.graceland.edu
E-mail: admissions@graceland.edu

Iowa Lakes Community College
3200 College Dr, Emmetsburg IA 50536-1055
Anne Stansbury, Asst. Director of Admissions
712-852-5212 Fax: 712-362-8363
Website: www.iowalakes.edu
E-mail: info@iowalakes.edu

Iowa Lakes Community College
300 S 18th St, Estherville IA 51334-2721
Anne Stansbury, Asst. Director of Admissions
712-362-7945 Fax: 712-362-8363
Website: www.iowalakes.edu
E-mail: info@iowalakes.edu

Iowa Lakes Community College
1900 Grand Ave, Suite 8, Spencer IA 51301
Anne Stansbury, Assistant Director of Admissions
712-262-7141 Fax: 712-262-4047
Website: www.iowalakes.edu
E-mail: info@iowalakes.edu

KANSAS

Independence Community College
PO Box 708, Independence KS 67301-0708
Dr. Terry Hetrick, President
800-842-6063 Fax: 620-331-5344
Website: www.indycc.edu
E-mail: admissions@indycc.edu

Newman University
3100 W McCormick St, Wichita KS 67213
Jann Reusser, Admissions Recruitment Coordinator
316-942-4291 ext. 2144 Fax: 316-942-4483
Website: www.newmanu.edu
E-mail: reusserj@newmanu.edu

LOUISIANA

Delta School of Business and Technology
517 Broad St, Lake Charles LA 70601-4334
Gary Holt, President
337-439-5765 Fax: 337-436-5151
Website: www.deltatech.edu
E-mail: susan@deltatech.edu

Dillard University
2601 Gentilly Blvd, New Orleans LA 70122-3097
Linda G. Nash, Director of Admissions
Website: www.dillard.edu
E-mail: admissions@dillard.edu

Our Lady of Holy Cross College
4123 Woodland Dr, New Orleans LA 70131-7399
Office of Enrollment Services
504-394-7744 Fax: 504-391-2421
Website: www.olhcc.edu

MARYLAND

Hagerstown Community College
11400 Robinwood Dr, Hagerstown MD 21742-6590
Dr. Daniel E. Bock, Assistant Director of Admissions
301-790-2800 Fax: 301-791-9165
Website: www.hagerstowncc.edu
E-mail: bockd@hagerstowncc.edu

Villa Julie College
1525 Greenspring Valley Rd
Stevenson MD 21153-0641
Mark Hergan, V.P. Enrollment Services
410-486-7001 Fax: 410-602-6600
Website: www.vjc.edu/admissions
E-mail: admissions@mail.vjc.edu

MASSACHUSETTS

The Art Institute of Boston at Lesley University
700 Beacon St, Boston MA 02215-2598
Office of Admissions
617-585-6710 Fax: 617-585-6720
Website: www.aiboston.edu
E-mail: admissions@aiboston.edu

Bristol Community College
777 Elsbree St, Fall River MA 02720-7395
Rodney S. Clark, Director of Admissions
508-678-2811 ext. 2516, 2179 Fax: 508-730-3265
Website: www.bristol.mass.edu
E-mail: admissions@bristol.mass.edu

LANDMARK SCHOOL

PO Box 227, Prides Crossing MA 01965-0227
Director of Admission
978-236-3000 Fax: 978-927-7268
Website: www.landmarkschool.org
E-mail: admission@landmarkschool.org
    Established 1971. Private. Coed. Accreditation: NEASC, NAIS, AISNE, MAAPS. Boarding and day tuitions vary depending on program. Student-faculty ratio: 3:1. Landmark's Summer Programs accepts students 7-20, in grades 1-12, of average to superior intelligence, with a history of healthy, emotional development and a diagnosis of a specific, language-based learning disability. Several five-week programs are offered and include daily 1:1 tutorials.

SCHOOL OF THE MUSEUM OF FINE ARTS, BOSTON

230 The Fenway, Boston MA 02115-5534
Office of Admissions
617-267-1219 Fax: 617-369-3679
Website: www.smfa.edu
E-mail: admissions@smfa.edu
    The SMFA welcomes teens from a variety of backgrounds. At the School you'll find an exciting community of artists and programs that will help you build skills, learn new forms of expression - and free yourself to see things, and do things, differently. The Pre-College Summer Studio for juniors and seniors in high school is a five-week intensive program that focuses on drawing, printmaking, painting, sculpture, ceramics, video, sound, and more while earning college credit. The Young Artists' Program for ages 13-15 gives teens a chance to learn drawing, screenprinting, painting, and mixed media.

University of Massachusetts Dartmouth
Old Westport Rd, North Dartmouth MA 02747-2300
Susan Lane, Associate Vice Chancellor
508-999-9202 Fax: 508-999-8621
Website: explore.umassd.edu
E-mail: slane@umassd.edu

WINCHENDON SCHOOL

172 Ash St, Winchendon MA 01475-1700
J. William LaBelle, Headmaster
800-622-1119 Fax: 978-297-0911
Website: www.winchendon.org
E-mail: admissions@winchendon.org

MICHIGAN

Delta College
University Center MI 48710-0001
Duff Zube, Director of Admissions
989-686-9093 Fax: 989-667-2202
Website: www.delta.edu
E-mail: admit@delta.edu

HILLSDALE COLLEGE

33 E College St, Hillsdale MI 49242-1298
Sam McArthur, Registrar
517-607-2360 Fax: 517-607-2657
Website: www.hillsdale.edu
E-mail: sam.mcarthur@hillsdale.edu

Lawrence Technological University
21000 W 10 Mile Rd, Southfield MI 48075-1058
Jane Rohrback, Director of Admissions
800-225-5588 Fax: 248-204-2228
Website: www.ltu.edu
E-mail: admissions@ltu.edu
See listing under "Universities"

University of Michigan-Dearborn
4901 Evergreen Rd, Dearborn MI 48128-1491
The Office of Admissions & Orientation
313-593-5100 Fax: 313-436-9167
Website: www.umd.umich.edu
E-mail: admissions@umd.umich.edu

MINNESOTA

Hibbing Community College
1515 E 25th St, Hibbing MN 55746-3300
Holly Bigelow, Director of Enrollment
800-224-4HCC or 218-262-7200 Fax: 218-262-6717
Website: www.hibbing.edu
E-mail: admissions@hibbing.edu

National American University
1550 W Highway 36, Roseville MN 55113
Matthew Mottl, Director of Admissions
651-644-1265 Fax: 651-644-0690
Website: www.national.edu
E-mail: mmottl@national.edu

RASMUSSEN COLLEGE - ST. CLOUD

226 Park Ave S, Saint Cloud MN 56301-3713
Admissions
320-251-5600 or 800-852-0460 Fax: 320-251-3702
Website: www.rasmussen.edu
E-mail: stcloud@rasmussen.edu

Ridgewater College-Hutchinson Campus
2 Century Ave SE, Hutchinson MN 55350-3100
Dawn Bjork, Counselor
800-222-4424 Fax: 320-231-7767
Website: www.ridgewater.edu
E-mail: dawn.bjork@ridgewater.edu

Ridgewater College-Willmar Campus
PO Box 1097, Willmar MN 56201-1097
Sally Kerfeld, Director of Admissions
800-722-1151 Fax: 320-231-7677
Website: www.ridgewater.edu
E-mail: skerfeld@ridgewater.edu

MISSISSIPPI

Tougaloo College
500 W County Line Rd, Tougaloo MS 39174-9799
Juno Leggette Jacobs, Director of Admissions
601-977-7768 Fax: 601-977-4501
Website: www.tougaloo.edu
E-mail: jjacobs@tougaloo.edu

MISSOURI

Ozark Christian College
1111 N Main St, Joplin MO 64801-4804
Troy Nelson, Director of Admissions
800-299-4622 Fax: 417-624-0090
Website: www.occ.edu
E-mail: occadmin@occ.edu
See listing under "Universities"

University of Missouri
1 University Blvd, Saint Louis MO 63121-4499
Ms. Linda Silman, Registrar
314-516-5545 Fax: 314-516-7096
Website: www.umsl.edu
E-mail: admissionsu@msx.umsl.edu

William Woods University
1 University Ave, Fulton MO 65251-1098
Jimmy Clay, Director of Admissions
573-642-2251 Fax: 573-592-1146
Website: www.williamwoods.edu
E-mail: admissions@williamwoods.edu
See listing under "Universities"

MONTANA

Rocky Mountain College
1511 Poly Dr, Billings MT 59102-1796
Bonnie Knapp, Director of Admissions
800-877-6259 Fax: 406-657-1189
Website: www.rocky.edu
E-mail: admissions@rocky.edu

NEBRASKA

Mid-Plains Community College
McCook Community College Campus
1205 E 3rd St, Mc Cook NE 69001-2631
Kelly Rippen, Director of Recruitment
800-658-4348 Fax: 308-345-8180
Website: www.mpcc.edu
E-mail: rippenk@mpcc.edu

Mid-Plains Community College
North Platte Community College - North Campus
1101 Halligan Dr, North Platte NE 69101-7659
Kelly Rippen, Director of Recruitment
800-658-4308 ext. 8107 Fax: 308-534-5770
Website: www.mpcc.edu
E-mail: rippenk@mpcc.edu

Mid-Plains Community College
North Platte Community College - South Campus
601 W State Farm Rd, North Platte NE 69101
Kelly Rippen, Director of Recruitment
800-658-4308 ext. 8107 Fax: 308-535-3789
Website: www.mpcc.edu
E-mail: rippenk@mpcc.edu

NEW HAMPSHIRE

Southern New Hampshire University
2500 N River Rd, Hooksett NH 03106-1045
Steve Soba, Director of Admissions
603-645-9611 Fax: 603-645-9693
Website: www.snhu.edu
E-mail: s.soba@snhu.edu

NEW JERSEY

New Jersey City University
2039 John F Kennedy Blvd
Jersey City NJ 07305-1588
Carmen Panlilio, Asst. V.P. for Admissions and Financial Aid
201-200-3234 Fax: 201-200-2044
Website: www.njcu.edu
E-mail: admissions@njcu.edu

Ramapo College of New Jersey
505 Ramapo Valley Rd, Mahwah NJ 07430-1623
Director of Admissions
201-684-7300 or 201-684-7301 Fax: 201-684-7964
Website: www.ramapo.edu
E-mail: admissions@ramapo.edu

NEW YORK

Briarcliffe College
1055 Stewart Ave, Bethpage NY 11714-3545
Theresa Donohue, Director of Admissions
516-918-3600 Fax: 516-470-6020
Website: www.briarcliffe.edu

College of Saint Rose
432 Western Ave, Albany NY 12203-1419
Maryelizabeth Amico, Asst V.P. for Undergraduate Admissions
518-454-5150 Fax: 518-454-2013
Website: www.strose.edu
E-mail: admit@strose.edu

LABORATORY INSTITUTE OF MERCHANDISING

12 E 53rd St, New York NY 10022-5268
Kristina Gibson, Director of Admissions
800-677-1323 or 212-752-1530 Fax: 212-750-3432
Website: www.limcollege.edu
E-mail: admissions@limcollege.edu
See listing under "Universities"

Long Island University-C. W. Post Campus
720 Northern Blvd, Brookville NY 11548-1300
Lee Kelly, Assistant Provost Enrollment Services
516-299-2431 Fax: 516-299-3939
Website: www.liu.edu/cwpost
E-mail: enroll@cwpost.liu.edu

Molloy College
1000 Hempstead Ave
Rockville Centre NY 11570-1100
Marguerite Lane, Director of Admissions
516-678-5000 ext. 6291 Fax: 516-256-2247
Website: www.molloy.edu
E-mail: admissions@molloy.edu
See listing under "Universities"

:: New York Military Academy
78 Academy Ave
Cornwall on Hudson NY 12520-1325
CAPT Robert D. Watts, USN (Ret.), Superintendent
Maureen T. Kelly, Director of Admissions
888-ASK-NYMA Fax: 845-534-7699
Website: www.nyma.org
E-mail: admissions@nyma.ouboces.org
See listing under "Preparatory Schools - Coed"

Pratt Institute
200 Willoughby Ave, Brooklyn NY 11205-3899
Heidi Metcalf, Director of Admissions
718-636-3600 Fax: 718-636-3670
Website: www.pratt.edu
E-mail: hmetcalf@pratt.edu

PURCHASE COLLEGE STATE UNIVERSITY OF NEW YORK (SUNY)

735 Anderson Hill Rd, Purchase NY 10577-1400
Betsy Immergut, Director of Admissions
914-251-6300 Fax: 914-251-6314
Website: www.purchase.edu
See listing under "Universities"

Roberts Wesleyan College
2301 Westside Dr, Rochester NY 14624-1997
Office of Admissions
585-594-6400 Fax: 585-594-6371
Website: www.roberts.edu
E-mail: admissions@roberts.edu

SUNY College at Brockport
350 New Campus Dr, Brockport NY 14420-2997
Bernard S. Valento, Director of Undergraduate Admissions
585-395-2751 Fax: 585-395-5452
Website: www.brockport.edu
E-mail: admit@brockport.edu

NORTH DAKOTA

Williston State College
PO Box 1326, Williston ND 58802-1326
Penny Powell, Director Enrollment Services
701-774-4200 Fax: 701-774-4544
Website: www.wsc.nodak.edu
E-mail: penny.soiseth@wsc.nodak.edu

OHIO

ART ACADEMY OF CINCINNATI

1212 Jackson St, Cincinnati OH 45202
Gregory Allgire Smith, President
513-562-6262 Fax: 513-562-8778
Website: www.artacademy.edu
E-mail: admissions@artacademy.edu
See listing under "Art"

Cleveland State University
2121 Euclid Ave RW 204, Cleveland OH 44115
Dr. Richard Arndt, Dean of Undergraduate Recruitment and College Partnerships
888-CSU-OHIO Fax: 216-687-9210
Website: www.csuohio.edu
E-mail: admissions@csuohio.edu

Columbus College of Art & Design
107 N 9th St, Columbus OH 43215-1700
877-997-CCAD or 614-224-9101
Website: www.ccad.edu
E-mail: admissions@ccad.edu

Owens Community College
300 Davis St, Findlay OH 45840-3631
William J. Ivoska PhD., Vice President of Student Services
567-429-3500 Fax: 567-423-0246
Website: www.owens.edu
E-mail: admissions@owens.edu

Owens Community College
PO Box 10000, Toledo OH 43699-1947
William J. Ivoska, Ph.D, Vice President of Student Services
567-661-7000 Fax: 567-661-7607
Website: www.owens.edu
E-mail: admissions@owens.edu

OKLAHOMA

Oklahoma State University
Stillwater OK 74078
Joan Payne, Associate Registrar
405-744-6876 Fax: 405-744-5285
Website: www.okstate.edu
E-mail: joan.payne@okstate.edu

OREGON

Cascade College
9101 E Burnside St, Portland OR 97216-1599
800-550-7678 Fax: 503-257-1222
Website: www.cascade.edu
E-mail: admissions@cascade.edu

PENNSYLVANIA

Arcadia University
450 S Easton Rd, Glenside PA 19038-3295
Harold W. Stewart, Registrar
215-572-2100 Fax: 215-881-8767
Website: www.arcadia.edu
See listing under "Universities"

Art Institute of Philadelphia
1622 Chestnut St, Philadelphia PA 19103-5119
Larry McHugh, Director of Admissions
800-275-2474 Fax: 215-405-6399
Website: www.aiph.aii.edu
E-mail: aiphinfo@aii.edu

Gannon University
109 University Sq, Erie PA 16541-0001
Christopher Tremblay, Director of Admissions
800-GANNON-U Fax: 814-871-5803
Website: www.gannon.edu
E-mail: admissions@gannon.edu

Holy Family University
9801 Frankford Avenue, Philadelphia PA 19114
Lauren Campbell, Director of Admissions
215-637-3050 Fax: 215-281-1022
Website: www.holyfamily.edu
E-mail: admissions@holyfamily.edu

Juniata College
1700 Moore St, Huntingdon PA 16652-2196
Michelle Bartol, Dean of Enrollment
877-JUNIATA Fax: 814-641-3100
Website: www.juniata.edu
E-mail: admissions@juniata.edu

La Roche College
9000 Babcock Blvd, Pittsburgh PA 15237-5898
Thomas Hassett, Director of Freshman and International Admissions
412-536-1272 or 800-838-4LRC Fax: 412-536-1272
Website: www.laroche.edu
E-mail: admissions@laroche.edu

MOUNT ALOYSIUS COLLEGE

7373 Admiral Peary Hwy, Cresson PA 16630-1999
Frank C. Crouse Jr., Vice President for Enrollment Management
814-886-6383 or 888-823-2220 Fax: 814-886-6441
Website: www.mtaloy.edu
E-mail: admissions@mtaloy.edu

SOUTH CAROLINA

Columbia Biblical Seminary & School of Missions
PO Box 3122, Columbia SC 29230-3122
Michelle MacGregor, Director of University Admissions
800-777-2227 Fax: 803-333-0607
Website: www.ciu.edu
E-mail: yescbs@ciu.edu
See listing under "Theological Studies & Religious Vocations"

Columbia International University
PO Box 3122, Columbia SC 29230-3122
John Basie, Director of University Admissions
800-777-2227 Fax: 803-786-4209
Website: www.ciu.edu
E-mail: yesciu@ciu.edu
See listing under "Theological Studies & Religious Vocations"

Spartanburg Technical College
PO Box 4386, Spartanburg SC 29305-4386
Nancy Garmroth, Dean of Admissions & Financial Aid
864-592-4810 Fax: 864-592-4945
Website: stcsc.edu

SOUTH DAKOTA

NATIONAL AMERICAN UNIVERSITY

321 Kansas City St, Rapid City SD 57701-3692
Angela G. Beck, Director of Enrollment Management
605-394-4800 Fax: 605-394-4871
Website: www.national.edu/rc/index.html
E-mail: rcadmissions@national.edu

National American University
2801 S Kiwanis Ave Ste 100
Sioux Falls SD 57105-4293
605-334-5430 Fax: 605-334-1575
Website: www.national.edu

Presentation College
1500 N Main St, Aberdeen SD 57401-1280
JoEllen Lindner, Dean of Admissions
605-229-8492 Fax: 605-229-8425
Website: www.presentation.edu
E-mail: admit@presentation.edu

TENNESSEE

Lipscomb University
3901 Granny White Pike, Nashville TN 37204-3951
Ricky Holaway, Director of Admissions
800-333-4358 ext. 1776 Fax: 615-269-1804
Website: www.lipscomb.edu
E-mail: admissions@lipscomb.edu

:: THE WEBB SCHOOL
PO Box 488, Bell Buckle TN 37020-0488
Matt Anderson, Director of Operations in Admissions
931-389-6003 Fax: 931-389-6657
Website: www.thewebbschool.com
E-mail: admissions@webbschool.com

TEXAS

Angelo State University
ASU Station 11014, San Angelo TX 76909
Bonnie Stennett, Coordinator of Recruiting
800-946-8627 Fax: 325-942-2078
Website: www.angelo.edu
E-mail: admissions@angelo.edu

University of Houston
122 E Cullen Bldg, Houston TX 77204-2023
Office of Admission
713-743-9595
Website: www.uh.edu
E-mail: admissions@uh.edu

UTAH

:: WASATCH ACADEMY
120 S 100 W, Mount Pleasant UT 84647-1509
Kim Stephens, Director of Admissions
800-634-4690 Fax: 435-462-1450
Website: www.wacad.org
E-mail: admissions@wacad.org

VERMONT

NORWICH UNIVERSITY

158 Harmon Dr, Northfield VT 05663
Registrars Office
800-468-6679
Website: www.norwich.edu
E-mail: nuregstr@norwich.edu
See listing under "Universities"

Southern Vermont College
982 Mansion Dr, Bennington VT 05201-6002
Kathleen James Ring, Director of Admissions
800-378-2782 Fax: 802-447-4695
Website: www.svc.edu
E-mail: admis@svc.edu

VIRGINIA

:: Fishburne Military School
PO Box 988, Waynesboro VA 22980-0722
Colonel William Alexander, Superintendent
Captain Christopher A. Richmond, Director of Admissions
800-946-7773 Fax: 540-946-7738
Website: www.fishburne.org
E-mail: crichmond@fishburne.org

:: FORK UNION MILITARY ACADEMY
PO Box 278, Fork Union VA 23055-0278
Lt. Gen. John E. Jackson Jr., USAF (Ret.), President
Lt. Col. Chip Jones, Director of Summer School
800-462-3862 or 434-842-4213 Fax: 434-842-4300
Website: www.forkunion.com
Private. Men only. Accreditation: VAIS, SACS, NAIS, AMCS, SAIS. Tuition: $3,400. Enrollment: 200. Faculty: 20. Student-faculty ratio: 10:1. Library: 19,000+ volumes. 19 buildings on 1,000 acres. Technology center with over 300 networked multi-media computers. Can register for 1 new or 2 repeat subjects. Non-military.

:: **MASSANUTTEN MILITARY ACADEMY**
614 S Main St, Woodstock VA 22664-1205
Murali Sinnathamby, Director of Admissions
877-466-6222 or 540-459-2167 Fax: 540-459-5421
Website: www.militaryschool.com
E-mail: admissions@militaryschool.com

:: Oak Hill Academy
2635 Oak Hill Rd, Mouth of Wilson VA 24363-3004
Dr. Michael D. Groves, President
276-579-2619 Fax: 276-579-4722
Website: www.oak-hill.net
E-mail: info@oak-hill.net
See listing under "Preparatory Schools - Coed"

Radford University
PO Box 6903, Radford VA 24142
David W. Kraus, Director of Admissions
800-890-4265 Fax: 540-831-5038
Website: www.radford.edu
E-mail: ruadmiss@radford.edu

· Southside Virginia Community College
109 Campus Dr, Alberta VA 23821-2930
Ronald E. Mattox, Dean of Admissions
434-949-1014 Fax: 434-949-7863
Website: www.sv.vccs.edu
E-mail: ronald.mattox@sv.vccs.edu

· Southside Virginia Community College
200 Daniel Rd, Keysville VA 23947
Ronald E. Mattox, Dean of Admissions
434-736-2018 Fax: 434-736-2082
Website: www.sv.vccs.edu
E-mail: ronald.mattox@sv.vccs.edu

WASHINGTON

Wenatchee Valley College
1300 5th St, Wenatchee WA 98801-1799
Marco Azurdia, Dean, Student Development
509-682-6805 Fax: 509-682-6541
Website: www.wvc.edu

WEST VIRGINIA

Concord University
Athens WV 24712
Michael Curry, Vice President of Financial Aid &
Admissions
888-384-5249 Fax: 304-384-3218
Website: www.concord.edu
E-mail: admissions@concord.edu

Davis & Elkins College
100 Campus Dr, Elkins WV 26241-3996
Renee Heckel, Director of Enrollment Management
800-624-3157 Fax: 304-637-1800
Website: www.davisandelkins.edu
E-mail: admiss@davisandelkins.edu

West Virginia Wesleyan College
59 College Ave, Buckhannon WV 26201-2699
Robert N. Skinner II, Director of Admission
800-722-9933 Fax: 304-473-8108
Website: www.wvwc.edu
E-mail: admission@wvwc.edu

WISCONSIN

St. Norbert College
100 Grant St, De Pere WI 54115
Brian Studebaker, Director of Admission
800-236-4878 Fax: 920-403-4072
Website: www.snc.edu
E-mail: admit@snc.edu

WYOMING

University of Wyoming
Admissions Office
Dept 3435, Laramie WY 82071-3435
Aaron Appelhans, Contact
800-342-5996 Fax: 307-766-4042
Website: www.uwyo.edu
E-mail: why-wyo@uwyo.edu

GUAM

University of Guam
UOG Station, Mangilao GU 96923
Deborah Leon Guerrero, Registrar
671-735-2201 or 671-735-2208 Fax: 671-735-2203
Website: www.uog.edu
E-mail: admitme@uog9.uog.edu

TEACHER EDUCATION

ALABAMA

Alabama A & M University
PO Box 908, Normal AL 35762
Antonio Boyle, Director of Admissions
256-372-5245 Fax: 256-372-5249
Website: www.aamu.edu
E-mail: aboyle@aamu.edu

Alabama State University
PO Box 271, Montgomery AL 36101-0271
334-229-4200

Auburn University
Auburn AL 36849
334-844-4000

Auburn University at Montgomery
PO Box 244023, Montgomery AL 36124
334-244-3000

Birmingham-Southern College
900 Arkadelphia Rd, Birmingham AL 35254-0002
800-523-5793

· **CALHOUN COMMUNITY COLLEGE**
PO Box 2216, Decatur AL 35609-2216
M. Wayne Tosh, Registrar
256-306-2500 Fax: 256-306-2941
Website: www.calhoun.edu
E-mail: jmc@calhoun.edu

Faulkner University
5345 Atlanta Hwy, Montgomery AL 36109-3398
Keith Mock, Director of Admissions
800-879-9816 ext. 7200 or 334-386-7200
Fax: 334-386-7137
Website: www.faulkner.edu
E-mail: admissions@faulkner.edu

Huntingdon College
1500 E Fairview Ave, Montgomery AL 36106-2148
334-833-4222

Jacksonville State University
700 Pelham Rd N, Jacksonville AL 36265-1602
256-782-5000

Judson College
302 Bibb St, Marion AL 36756
Michael Scotto, Director of Admissions
800-447-9472 Fax: 334-683-5147
Website: www.judson.edu
E-mail: admissions@judson.edu

Oakwood College
Oakwood Rd NW, Huntsville AL 35896-0001
256-726-7000

Samford University
800 Lakeshore Dr, Birmingham AL 35229-0002
205-726-3673

Spring Hill College
4000 Dauphin St, Mobile AL 36608-1791
334-460-4000

Stillman College
PO Box 1430, Tuscaloosa AL 35403-1430
205-349-4240

Troy University
Troy AL 36082-0001
Jim Hutto, Dean of Enrollment Management
334-670-3175

Troy University Dothan
PO Box 8368, Dothan AL 36304-0368
334-983-6556

Tuskegee University
Tuskegee Institute AL 36088
334-727-8011

University of Alabama
Box 870118, Tuscaloosa AL 35487
Dr. Lisa B. Harris, Director of Admissions
205-348-5666

University of Alabama at Birmingham
Univ Sta, Birmingham AL 35294-0001
205-934-4011

University of Alabama in Huntsville
PO Box 1247, Huntsville AL 35899-0001
Ann Lee, Assoc. Director for Recruiting Program and
Events
1-800-UAH-CALL Fax: 256-824-6073
Website: www.uah.edu
E-mail: leev@uah.edu

University of Mobile
PO Box 13220, Mobile AL 36663-0220
251-675-5990

University of Montevallo
Station 6030, Montevallo AL 35115
205-665-6030

University of North Alabama
Univ Sta, Florence AL 35632-0001
256-760-4100

University of South Alabama
307 University Blvd N, Mobile AL 36688-3053
Melissa Haab, Director of Admissions
251-460-6141 Fax: 251-460-7876
Website: www.southalabama.edu
E-mail: admiss@usouthal.edu

University of West Alabama
Hwy 11, Livingston AL 35470
205-652-3400

ALASKA

Sheldon Jackson College
801 Lincoln St, Sitka AK 99835-7651
800-478-4556

University of Alaska Anchorage
PO Box 141629, Anchorage AK 99514-1629
Cecile Mitchell, Director of Enrollment Services
907-786-1480 Fax: 907-786-4888
Website: www.uaa.alaska.edu/
E-mail: enroll@uaa.alaska.edu

University of Alaska Fairbanks
PO Box 757480, Fairbanks AK 99775
907-474-7581

University of Alaska Southeast
11120 Glacier Hwy, Juneau AK 99801-8625
Paul Kraft, Dean of Students/Enrollment Management
907-796-6000 Fax: 907-796-6005
Website: www.uas.alaska.edu
E-mail: paul.kraft@uas.alaska.edu

ARIZONA

Arizona State University
PO Box 870112, Tempe AZ 85287-0112
480-965-9011

Southwestern College
2625 E Cactus Rd, Phoenix AZ 85032-7097
Admissions/Financial Aid Office
800-247-2697 or 602-992-6101 Fax: 602-404-2159
Website: www.swcaz.edu
E-mail: admissions@swcaz.edu

University of Arizona
Tucson AZ 85721-0040
Paul Kohn, Director of Admissions
520-621-3237 Fax: 520-621-9799
Website: www.admissions.arizona.edu or
www.arizona.edu

ARKANSAS

Arkansas State University
PO Box 1630, State University AR 72467-1630
870-972-2100

Arkansas Tech University
215 W O St, Russellville AR 72801-2222
479-968-0389

Harding University
900 E Center Ave, Searcy AR 72149
501-279-4000

Henderson State University
1100 Henderson St, Arkadelphia AR 71999-0001
870-230-5000

Hendrix College
1600 Washington Ave, Conway AR 72032-3080
501-329-6811

John Brown University
2000 W University St, Siloam Springs AR 72761-2121
877-JBU-INFO

Lyon College
PO Box 2317, Batesville AR 72503-2317
Dan Rutledge, Director of Admissions
870-793-9813

Ouachita Baptist University
410 Ouachita St, Arkadelphia AR 71998-0001
David Goodman, Director of Admissions
870-245-5110 Fax: 870-245-5500
Website: www.obu.edu
E-mail: admissions@obu.edu

Philander Smith College
812 W 13th St, Little Rock AR 72202-3799
501-375-9845

· Phillips Community College of the University of Arkansas
PO Box 785, Helena AR 72342-0785
Dr. Steven Murray, Chancellor
Lynn Boone, Vice Chancellor for Student Services /
Registrar
870-338-6474 Fax: 870-338-7542
Website: www.pccua.edu
E-mail: lboone@pccua.edu

Southern Arkansas University
100 E University, Magnolia AR 71753
870-235-4000

University of Arkansas at Fayetteville
1 University of Arkansas, Fayetteville AR 72701-1201
479-575-2000

University of Arkansas at Little Rock
2801 S University Ave, Little Rock AR 72204-1000
501-569-3000

University of Arkansas at Monticello
PO Box 3600, Monticello AR 71656
870-367-6811

University of Arkansas at Pine Bluff
1200 University Dr, Pine Bluff AR 71601-2799
870-543-8000

University of Central Arkansas
201 Donaghey Ave, Conway AR 72035-5003
501-450-5000

University of the Ozarks
415 N College Ave, Clarksville AR 72830-2880
Jim Decker, Director of Admissions
479-979-1000

CALIFORNIA

American College of California
760 Market St Ste 1009
San Francisco CA 94102-2305
Sherris Goodwin, Director
415-677-9717 Fax: 415-677-9810
Website: www.acca.edu
E-mail: info@acca.edu

Antioch University
801 Garden St Ste 101
Santa Barbara CA 93101-1581
Ankara McPherson, Director of Admissions
805-962-8179 Fax: 805-962-4786
Website: www.antiochsb.edu
E-mail: amcpherson@antiochsb.edu

Antioch University Southern California
400 Corporate Pointe, Culver City CA 90230-7615
Admissions Office
800-7-ANTIOCH Fax: 310-821-6032
E-mail: admissions@antiochla.edu
Master of Arts in Education and Teacher Credentialing
Program.

Azusa Pacific University
901 E Alosta Ave, Azusa CA 91702
626-969-3434

Biola University
13800 Biola Ave, La Mirada CA 90639-0001
562-903-6000

California Baptist University
8432 Magnolia Ave, Riverside CA 92504-3297
951-689-5771

California State University-Bakersfield
9001 Stockdale Hwy, Bakersfield CA 93311-1022
661-664-2011

California State University-Chico
Chico CA 95929-0001
530-898-6116

California State University-Dominguez Hills
1000 E Victoria St, Carson CA 90747-0001
310-243-3300

California State University-East Bay
25800 Carlos Bee Blvd, Hayward CA 94542-3001
510-885-3000

California State University-Fresno
Fresno CA 93740-0001
559-278-4240

California State University-Fullerton
PO Box 34080
Fullerton CA 92634
714-278-2011

California State University-Los Angeles
5151 State University Dr, Los Angeles CA 90032
323-343-3000

California State University-Northridge
18111 Nordhoff St, Northridge CA 91330-0001
818-677-1200

California State University-San Bernadino
5500 University Pkwy
San Bernardino CA 92407-2393
Olivia Rosas, Director of Admissions
909-880-5000 Fax: 909-880-7034
Website: enrollment.csusb.edu
E-mail: orosas@csusb.edu

California State University-San Marcos
San Marcos CA 92096-0001
760-750-4000

California State University-Stanislaus
801 W Monte Vista Ave, Turlock CA 95382-0256
Lisa Bernardo, Director of Admissions
209-667-3357

Chapman University
One University Drive, Orange CA 92866-1099
Michael Drummy, Assistant Vice President for
Enrollment
Services and Chief Admission Officer
714-997-6411 or 888-CUAPPLY Fax: 714-997-6713
Website: www.chapman.edu
E-mail: admit@chapman.edu

CONCORDIA UNIVERSITY

1530 Concordia, Irvine CA 92612-3203
Lori McDonald, Executive Director of Enrollment
Services
800-229-1200 or 949-854-8002 Fax: 949-854-6894
Website: www.cui.edu
E-mail: admission@cui.edu

Fresno Pacific University
1717 S Chestnut Ave, Fresno CA 93702-4798
559-453-2000

HEBREW UNION COLLEGE - JEWISH INSTITUTE OF RELIGION

3077 University Ave, Los Angeles CA 90007-3796
Dr. Matt Albert, Regional Director of Admissions and
Recruitment
213-749-3424 Fax: 213-747-6128
Website: www.huc.edu
E-mail: malbert@huc.edu

Holy Names University
3500 Mountain Blvd, Oakland CA 94619-1699
Dr. Hoffman-Marr, Director of Admissions
510-436-1010

Humboldt State University
1 Harpst St, Arcata CA 95521-8299
707-826-3011

INTERNATIONAL CHRISTIAN EDUCATION COLLEGE

Early Childhood Education
3807 Wilshire Blvd Ste 730
Los Angeles CA 90010-3108
Dr. Charles Chong Y. Lee, President
213-368-0316 Fax: 213-368-0318
E-mail: icec@sbcglobal.net

La Sierra University
4700 Pierce St, Riverside CA 92515-8247
Bobby Brown, Director of Admissions
800-874-5587

Loyola Marymount University
7900 Loyola Blvd, Los Angeles CA 90045-2699
310-338-2700

Mills College
5000 MacArthur Blvd, Oakland CA 94613-1000
510-430-2255

Mt. St. Mary's College
12001 Chalon Rd, Los Angeles CA 90049-1599
310-954-4000

Notre Dame de Namur University
1500 Ralston Ave, Belmont CA 94002-1997
Martin Bednarek, Director of Admissions
800-263-0545

Orange Coast College
PO Box 5005, Costa Mesa CA 92628-5005
Kristin Clark, Director of Admissions
714-432-5773 Fax: 714-432-5736
Website: www.orangecoastcollege.edu
E-mail: kclark@cccd.edu

Pacific Union College
1 Angwin Ave, Angwin CA 94508-9797
707-965-6311

PEPPERDINE UNIVERSITY

Graduate School of Education and Psychology
6100 Center Dr, Los Angeles CA 90045
Fionnbarr Kelly, Director of Admissions
310-568-5744 Fax: 310-568-5755
Website: www.gsep.pepperdine.edu
E-mail: gsep@pepperdine.edu
*Master of Arts in Education and/or Teaching Credential
*Master of Arts in Educational Technology (Online)
*Master of Science in Administration and Preliminary Administrative Services Credential
*Master of Science in Workplace Learning and Performance
*Doctor of Education in Educational Leadership, Administration, and Policy
*Doctor of Education in Educational Technology
*Doctor of Education in Organization Change
*Doctor of Education in Organizational Leadership

Point Loma Nazarene University
3900 Lomaland Dr, San Diego CA 92106-2810
Eric Groves, Director of Admissions
800-733-7770

San Diego Christian College
2100 Greenfield Dr, El Cajon CA 92019-1157
Jon Melone, Director of Admissions
800-676-2242 Fax: 619-590-1739
Website: www.sdcc.edu
E-mail: admissions@sdcc.edu

San Diego State University
5500 Campanile Dr, San Diego CA 92182-0002
619-594-5200

San Francisco State University
1600 Holloway Ave, San Francisco CA 94132-1722
415-338-1111

San Jose State University
1 Washington Sq, San Jose CA 95192-0001
408-924-1000

Santa Clara University
500 El Camino Real, Santa Clara CA 95053-0001
408-554-4000

Sonoma State University
1801 E Cotati Ave, Rohnert Park CA 94928-3609
Louis T. Levy, Senior Director Enrollment Services
707-664-2880

Stanford University
520 Lasuen Mall Union 232, Stanford CA 94305-3005
650-723-2300

University of California
Santa Barbara CA 93106
805-893-8000

University of Judaism
15600 Mulholland Dr, Los Angeles CA 90077-1599
Bryan Pisetsky, Director of Undergraduate Admissions
310-476-9777

University of La Verne
1950 3rd St, La Verne CA 91750-4443
800-876-4858

University of San Diego
5998 Alcala Park, San Diego CA 92110-2492
Admissions
619-260-4506

University of the Pacific
3601 Pacific Ave, Stockton CA 95211-0197
209-946-2011

Vanguard University of Southern California
55 Fair Dr, Costa Mesa CA 92626-6597
714-556-3610

COLORADO

Adams State College
Alamosa CO 81102
Matt Gallegos, Director of Admissions
800-824-6494

Colorado College
14 E Cache La Poudre St
Colorado Springs CO 80903-3243
719-389-6344

Colorado State University
102 Administration, Fort Collins CO 80523-0001
970-491-1101

Colorado State University - Pueblo
2200 Bonforte Blvd, Pueblo CO 81001-4990
719-549-2461

Mesa State College
1100 North Ave, Grand Junction CO 81501
970-248-1020

Metropolitan State College
PO Box 173362, Campus Box 21
Denver CO 80217-3362
303-556-6228

NORTHEASTERN JUNIOR COLLEGE

100 College Ave, Sterling CO 80751-2399
Judy Giacomini, Interim Chief Administrative Officer
Tina Joyce, Director of Admissions
970-521-7000 or 970-521-6752 Fax: 970-521-6801
Website: www.njc.edu
E-mail: tina.joyce@njc.edu

Regis University
3333 Regis Blvd, Denver CO 80221-1099
303-458-4900

University of Colorado
Boulder CO 80309-0001
303-492-1411

University of Colorado
1420 Austin Bluffs Pkwy
Colorado Springs CO 80918-3735
719-262-3000

University of Colorado at Denver and Health Sciences
Center
Downtown Denver Campus
PO Box 173364, Denver CO 80217-3364
303-556-2717 Fax: 303-556-4479
Website:
www.cudenver.edu/academics/colleges/school+of+education

University of Northern Colorado
Greeley CO 80639
Allen Huang, Interim Dean of Education
970-351-2817

Western State College of Colorado
Gunnison CO 81231-0001
Director of Admissions
800-876-5309

CONNECTICUT

Albertus Magnus College
700 Prospect St, New Haven CT 06511-1189
Richard Lolatte, Dean of Admission
203-773-8501 or 800-578-9160 Fax: 203-773-5248
Website: www.albertus.edu
E-mail: admissions@albertus.edu

Eastern Connecticut State University
83 Windham St, Willimantic CT 06226-2295
860-456-5000

Fairfield University
1073 N Benson Rd, Fairfield CT 06824-5171
203-254-4000

Quinnipiac University
275 Mount Carmel Ave, Hamden CT 06518-1905
Joan Isaac Mohr, VP & Dean of Admissions
203-582-8600

Sacred Heart University
5151 Park Ave, Fairfield CT 06825-1023
203-371-7999

St. Joseph College
1678 Asylum Ave, West Hartford CT 06117-2791
860-232-4571

Southern Connecticut State University
501 Crescent St, New Haven CT 06515-1355
203-392-5200

University of Bridgeport
126 Park Ave, Bridgeport CT 06604-5620
Barbara L. Maryak, Dean of Admissions
203-576-4552

University of Connecticut
Storrs CT 06269-0001
860-486-2000

University of Hartford
200 Bloomfield Ave, West Hartford CT 06117-1599
860-768-4100

University of New Haven
300 Boston Post Rd, West Haven CT 06516
Asst. Director of Undergraduate Admissions
203-932-7329 Fax: 203-932-7137
Website: www.newhaven.edu
E-mail: gradinfo@newhaven.edu

Western Connecticut State University
181 White St, Danbury CT 06810-6826
203-837-8200

DELAWARE

Delaware State University
1200 N DuPont Hwy, Dover DE 19901-2275
302-857-6060

University of Delaware
Newark DE 19711
302-831-2000

Wesley College
120 N State St, Dover DE 19901-3876
302-736-2300 Fax: 302-736-2301
Website: www.wesley.edu

DISTRICT OF COLUMBIA

Catholic University of America
620 Michigan Ave NE, Washington DC 20064-0001
202-319-5000

Gallaudet University
800 Florida Ave NE, Washington DC 20002-3695
Charity Reedy Hines, Director of Admissions
202-651-5750

George Washington University
2035 H St NW, Washington DC 20052-0002
202-994-1000

Trinity University
125 Michigan Ave NE, Washington DC 20017-1090
202-884-9000

University of the District of Columbia
4200 Connecticut Ave NW
Washington DC 20008-1174
LaVerne M. Hill-Flanagan, Director of Admissions
202-274-5100

FLORIDA

THE BAPTIST COLLEGE OF FLORIDA
5400 College Dr, Graceville FL 32440-1831
Christopher M. Bishop, Director of Admissions
800-328-2660 Fax: 850-263-9026
Website: www.baptistcollege.edu
E-mail: admissions@baptistcollege.edu

Barry University
11300 NE 2nd Ave, Miami Shores FL 33161-6695
800-695-2279

Bethune-Cookman College
640 Dr Mary McLeod Bethune Blvd
Daytona Beach FL 32114-3099
Edwin Coffie, Director of Admissions
800-448-0228

CARLOS ALBIZU UNIVERSITY
2173 NW 99th Ave, Miami FL 33172-2209
Gerardo Alvarado, MBA, Director of Admissions,
Recruitment & Outreach
305-593-1223 ext. 137 Fax: 305-593-1854
Website: www.mia.albizu.edu
E-mail: admissions@albizu.edu

City College
2000 W Commercial Blvd, Fort Lauderdale FL 33309
Britt Carpenter, Director of Admissions
954-492-5353 Fax: 954-491-1965
Website: www.citycollege.edu
E-mail: bcarpenter@citycollege.edu

Clearwater Christian College
3400 Gulf To Bay Blvd, Clearwater FL 33759-4595
727-726-1153

Eckerd College
4200 54th Ave S, Saint Petersburg FL 33711
727-867-1166

Flagler College
PO Box 1027, Saint Augustine FL 32085-1027
904-829-6481

Florida A&M University
Tallahassee FL 32307
850-599-3000

Florida Atlantic University
PO Box 3091, Boca Raton FL 33431-0991
800-299-4328

Florida Southern College
111 Lake Hollingsworth Dr, Lakeland FL 33801-5607
Robert B. Palmer, V.P., Dean of Enrollment
Management
863-680-4131

Florida State University
600 W College Ave, Tallahassee FL 32306-1096
Janice V. Finney, Director of Admissions
850-644-2525 Fax: 850-644-0197
Website: admissions.fsu.edu
E-mail: admissions@admin.fsu.edu

Jones College
5353 Arlington Expy, Jacksonville FL 32211-5588
Dorothy D. Jones, Chief Executive Officer
904-743-1122 Fax: 904-744-4446
Website: www.jones.edu
E-mail: lwade@jones.edu

Jones College
11430 N Kendall Dr Ste 200, Miami FL 33176
Barclay Charles, Contact
305-275-9996 Fax: 305-743-4446
Website: www.jones.edu
E-mail: pcarbone@jones.edu

Lynn University
3601 N Military Trl, Boca Raton FL 33431-5598
Brett Ormandy, Director of Admissions
561-237-7900 Fax: 561-237-7100
Website: www.lynn.edu
E-mail: admission@lynn.edu

Palm Beach Atlantic University
PO Box 24708, West Palm Beach FL 33416-4708
561-803-2000

Rollins College
1000 Holt Ave, Winter Park FL 32789
407-646-2000

Saint Leo University
PO Box 6665, Saint Leo FL 33574
Deborah Bandy, Director of Admissions
352-588-8200 or 800-334-5532 Fax: 352-588-8257
Website: www.saintleo.edu
E-mail: admission@saintleo.edu

St. Thomas University
16401 NW 37th Ave, Miami Gardens FL 33054
Fr. Edward Blackwell, Contact
800-367-9010 or 305-628-6546 Fax: 305-628-6591
Website: www.stu.edu
E-mail: signup@stu.edu

Stetson University
421 N Woodland Boulevard, De Land FL 32720-3761
386-822-7000

Trinity Baptist College
800-200 Hammond Blvd, Jacksonville FL 32221
R. Larry Appleby, Director of Admissions
904-596-2400 Fax: 904-596-2531
Website: www.tbc.edu
E-mail: emailtrinity@tbc.edu

University of Central Florida
PO Box 160111, Orlando FL 32816
407-823-3000

University of Florida
PO Box 114000, Gainesville FL 32611-4000
352-392-3261

University of Miami
PO Box 248006, Coral Gables FL 33124-8006
305-284-2211

University of North Florida
4567 Saint Johns Bluff Rd S
Jacksonville FL 32224-2645
904-620-1000

University of South Florida
4202 E Fowler Ave, Tampa FL 33620-6900
J. Robert Spatig, Director of Admissions
813-974-3350 Fax: 813-974-9689
Website: www.usf.edu
E-mail: admissions@admin.usf.edu

University of Tampa
401 W Kennedy Blvd, Tampa FL 33606-1490
813-253-3333

University of West Florida
11000 University Pkwy, Pensacola FL 32514-5750
850-474-2000

Warner Southern College
5301 US Highway 27 S, Lake Wales FL 33859-8725
863-638-1426

GEORGIA

Albany State University
504 College Dr, Albany GA 31705-2796
229-430-4600

Armstrong Atlantic State University
11935 Abercorn St, Savannah GA 31419-1997
Kim West, Asst. Dean and Registrar Enrollment
Services
912-927-5277 Fax: 912-921-5462
Website: www.armstrong.edu
E-mail: admissions@mail.armstrong.edu

Augusta State University
2500 Walton Way, Augusta GA 30904-4562
706-737-1400

Berry College
2277 Martha Berry Hwy NE
Mount Berry GA 30149-0149
706-232-5374

Brewton-Parker College
Highway 280, Mount Vernon GA 30445
800-342-1087

Clayton State University
5900 N Lee St, Morrow GA 30260
770-961-3500

Columbus State University
4225 University Ave, Columbus GA 31907-5645
706-568-2001

Emory University
200B Jones Center, Atlanta GA 30322
404-727-6123

Fort Valley State University
1005 State University Dr, Fort Valley GA 31030-3298
478-825-6307

Georgia College and State University
231 W Hancock St, Milledgeville GA 31061-3371
478-445-5350

Georgia Southern University
PO Box 8024, Statesboro GA 30460
Admissions Office
912-681-5532

Georgia Southwestern State University
800 Wheatley St, Americus GA 31709-4635
229-928-1279

Georgia State University
PO Box 4009, Atlanta GA 30302-4009
404-651-2365

Kennesaw State University
1000 Chastain Rd NW, Kennesaw GA 30144-5591
Yiping Wan, Dean of College of Education
770-423-6117
Website: www.kennesaw.edu

LaGrange College
601 Broad St, LaGrange GA 30240-2955
Andy Geeter, Director of Admission
800-593-2885

Mercer University in Macon
1400 Coleman Ave, Macon GA 31207-0003
John P. Cole, Sr. Assoc. V.P. for Admissions
478-301-2650

North Georgia College & State University
Dahlonega GA 30597-0001
706-864-1400

Oglethorpe University
4484 Peachtree Rd NE, Atlanta GA 30319-2797
Kelly Gosnell, Director of Admission
404-261-1441 Fax: 404-364-8491
Website: www.oglethorpe.edu
E-mail: admission@oglethorpe.edu

Paine College
1235 15th St, Augusta GA 30901-3182
800-476-7703

Piedmont College
PO Box 10, Demorest GA 30535-0010
800-277-7020

Shorter College
315 Shorter Ave, Rome GA 30165-4267
800-868-6980

Spelman College
350 Spelman Ln SW, Atlanta GA 30314-4395
800-982-2411

Thomas University
1501 Millpond Rd, Thomasville GA 31792-7478
Darla M. Glass, Director of Student Affairs
229-226-1621

TOCCOA FALLS COLLEGE
PO Box 800899, Toccoa Falls GA 30598
Christy Meadows, Director of Admissions
888-785-5624 Fax: 706-282-6012
Website: www.tfc.edu
E-mail: admissions@tfc.edu

University of Georgia
Athens GA 30602-0001
706-542-3000

University of West Georgia
Carrollton GA 30118-0001
770-836-6500

Valdosta State University
N Patterson St, Valdosta GA 31698-0001
229-333-5952

Wesleyan College
4760 Forsyth Rd, Macon GA 31210-4462
800-447-6610

HAWAII

Brigham Young University
55-220 Kulanui St, Laie HI 96762-1293
808-293-3211

Chaminade University of Honolulu
3140 Waialae Ave, Honolulu HI 96816-1510
Joy Bouey, Dean of Enrollment Management
808-739-4619

Kauai Community College
3-1901 Kaumualii Hwy, Lihue HI 96766-9500
808-245-8255 Fax: 808-245-8297
Website: kauai.hawaii.edu
E-mail: arkauai@hawaii.edu

IDAHO

Boise State University
1910 University Dr, Boise ID 83725-0399
208-426-1011

Brigham Young University - Idaho
120 Kimball Bldg, Rexburg ID 83460
Gordon Westenskow, Director of Admissions
208-496-1020 Fax: 208-496-1220
Website: www.byui.edu
E-mail: admissions@byui.edu

Idaho State University
PO Box 8270, Pocatello ID 83209-0001
208-282-0211

Lewis-Clark State College
500 8th Ave, Lewiston ID 83501-2698
Steve Bussolini, Director of Admissions
800-933-5272

Northwest Nazarene University
623 Holly St, Nampa ID 83686-5897
208-467-8011

University of Idaho
Moscow ID 83844-4253
Lloyd Scott, Director of New Student Services
208-885-6163 Fax: 208-885-4477
Website: www.uidaho.edu
E-mail: nss@uidaho.edu

ILLINOIS

AMERICAN INTERCONTINENTAL UNIVERSITY ONLINE
5550 Prairie Stone Parkway Suite 400
Hoffman Estates IL 60192
Admissions Department
877-701-3800
Website: www.aiuonline.edu
E-mail: info@aiuonline.edu

ARGOSY UNIVERSITY/CHICAGO
350 N Orleans St, Merchandise Mart
Chicago IL 60654
Ashley Delaney, Director of Admissions
800-626-4123 Fax: 312-777-7750
Website: www.argosyu.edu
E-mail: adelaney@argosyu.edu

Augustana College
639 38th St, Rock Island IL 61201-2296
309-794-7000

Aurora University
347 S Gladstone Ave, Aurora IL 60506-4892
Carol R. Dunn, Ed.D., Vice President for Enrollment
800-742-5281 Fax: 630-844-5535
Website: www.aurora.edu
E-mail: admission@aurora.edu

Benedictine University
5700 College Rd, Lisle IL 60532-0900
630-829-6300 or 888-829-6363 Fax: 630-829-6301
Website: www.ben.edu
E-mail: admissions@ben.edu

Bradley University
1501 W Bradley Ave, Peoria IL 61625-0002
800-447-6460

Chicago State University
9501 S King Dr, Chicago IL 60628-1598
773-995-2000

CONCORDIA UNIVERSITY
7400 Augusta St, River Forest IL 60305-1402
708-209-3100 Fax: 708-209-3473
Website: www.curf.edu
E-mail: crfadmis.edu

De Paul University
1 E Jackson Blvd, Chicago IL 60604-2287
Carlene Klaas, Director of Admissions
312-362-8000

De Paul University
2323 N Seminary Ave, Chicago IL 60614-3298
312-362-8000

Eastern Illinois University
600 Lincoln Ave, Charleston IL 61920-3099
217-581-5000

Elmhurst College
190 S Prospect Ave, Elmhurst IL 60126-3296
630-279-4100

Eureka College
300 E College Ave, Eureka IL 61530-1500
309-467-3721

Illinois College
1101 W College Ave, Jacksonville IL 62650-2299
217-245-3000

Illinois State University
Normal IL 61790-0001
309-438-2111

Knox College
Galesburg IL 61401
309-341-7100

Lewis University
One University Parkway, Romeoville IL 60446
800-897-9000

Loyola University - Mundelein College
6525 N Sheridan Rd, Chicago IL 60626-5311
773-262-8100

Loyola University of Chicago
820 N Michigan Ave, Chicago IL 60611-2103
312-915-6000

MacMurray College
447 E College Ave, Jacksonville IL 62650-2590
217-479-7000

Millikin University
1184 W Main St, Decatur IL 62522-2084
Lin Stoner, Dean of Admission
800-373-7733

Monmouth College
700 E Broadway, Monmouth IL 61462-1963
Kristi Hippen, Director of Admission
309-457-2131

National-Louis University
2840 Sheridan Rd, Evanston IL 60201-1796

North Central College
30 N Brainard St, Naperville IL 60540-4690
Martha Stolze, Director of Admissions
630-637-5800 Fax: 630-637-5819
Website: www.northcentralcollege.edu
E-mail: admissions@noctrl.edu

NORTHEASTERN ILLINOIS UNIVERSITY
5500 N Saint Louis Ave, Chicago IL 60625-4699
Maureen Gillette, Dean
773-442-4050 Fax: 773-442-4020
Website: www.neiu.edu

Northern Illinois University
DeKalb IL 60115
815-753-1000

North Park College & Theological Seminary
3225 W Foster Ave, Chicago IL 60625-4810
773-244-6200

Olivet Nazarene University
1 University Ave
Bourbonnais IL 60914
815-939-5011

Principia College
Elsah IL 62028-9799
618-374-2131

Quincy University
1800 College Ave, Quincy IL 62301-2670
217-222-8020

Rockford College
5050 E State St, Rockford IL 61108-2393
William Laffey, Director of Admission
800-892-2984

Roosevelt University
430 S Michigan Ave, Chicago IL 60605
Gwen E. Kanelos, Asst. Vice President for Enrollment
Services
877-APPLY-RU Fax: 312-341-4216
Website: www.roosevelt.edu
E-mail: applyru@roosevelt.edu

Southern Illinois University
Carbondale IL 62901-4400
618-453-2121

Southern Illinois University Edwardsville
Edwardsville IL 62026-0001
618-650-3705

South Suburban College of Cook County
15800 State St, South Holland IL 60473
Jane Ellen Stocker, Dean of Enrollment Services
708-596-2000 Fax: 708-225-5806
Website: www.southsuburbancollege.edu
E-mail: jstocker@southsuburbancollege.edu

Trinity Christian College
6601 W College Dr, Palos Heights IL 60463-0929
Joshua Lenarz, Director of Admissions
708-597-3000

Trinity International University
2065 Half Day Rd, Deerfield IL 60015-1241
847-945-8800

University of Illinois at Springfield
One University Plaza, Springfield IL 62794
217-206-4847

University of St. Francis
500 Wilcox St, Joliet IL 60435
800-735-7500

Western Illinois University
1 University Cir, Macomb IL 61455-1390
309-295-1414

Wheaton College
501 College Ave, Wheaton IL 60187-5571
630-752-5000

INDIANA

Ancilla Domini College
Donaldson IN 46513
Erin Wittmeyer, Director of Admissions
574-936-8898 Fax: 574-935-1773
Website: www.ancilla.edu
E-mail: erin.wittmeyer@ancilla.edu

Anderson University
1100 E 5th St, Anderson IN 46012-3495
765-649-9071

Ball State University
2000 W University Ave, Muncie IN 47306-0002
765-285-5555

Bethel College
1001 W McKinley Ave, Mishawaka IN 46545-5591
Office of Admissions
574-257-3339

Butler University
4600 Sunset Ave, Indianapolis IN 46208-3443
317-940-8000

Calumet College of St. Joseph
2400 New York Ave, Whiting IN 46394-2195
219-473-7770

DePauw University
313 S Locust St, Greencastle IN 46135-1736
800-447-2495

Earlham College and Earlham School of Religion
801 National Rd W, Richmond IN 47374-4095
765-983-1200

Franklin College
101 Branigin Blvd, Franklin IN 46131
Jacqueline S. Acosta, Director of Admissions
800-852-0232 Fax: 317-738-8274
Website: www.franklincollege.edu
E-mail: admissions@franklincollege.edu

Goshen College
1700 S Main St, Goshen IN 46526-4794
574-535-7000

Grace College
200 Seminary Dr, Winona Lake IN 46590-1224
800-54-GRACE

Hanover College
PO Box 108, Hanover IN 47243-0108
William D. Preble, Dean of Admission
800-213-2178 Fax: 812-866-7098
Website: www.hanover.edu
E-mail: admissions@hanover.edu

Huntington College
2303 College Ave, Huntington IN 46750-1299
260-356-6000

Indiana State University
Terre Haute IN 47809-0001
Richard Toomey, Director of Admissions
812-237-6311

Indiana University
300 N Jordan Ave, Bloomington IN 47405-1106
812-855-4848

Indiana University at Kokomo
PO Box 9003, Kokomo IN 46904-9003
765-453-2000

Indiana University at South Bend
PO Box 7111, South Bend IN 46634-7111
574-237-4111

Indiana University East
2325 Chester Blvd, Richmond IN 47374-1289
765-973-8200

Indiana University Northwest
3400 Broadway, Gary IN 46408-1101
219-980-6500

Indiana University-Purdue University at Fort Wayne
2101 E Coliseum Blvd, Fort Wayne IN 46805-1445
260-481-6100

Indiana University Southeast
4201 Grant Line Rd, New Albany IN 47150-2158
812-941-2000

Indiana Wesleyan University
4201 S Washington St, Marion IN 46953-4974
765-674-6901

Manchester College
604 E College Ave, North Manchester IN 46962-1276
260-982-5000

Marian College
3200 Cold Spring Rd, Indianapolis IN 46222-1997
317-955-6000

Oakland City University
138 N Lucretia St, Oakland City IN 47660
Brian J. Baker, Director of Admissions
800-737-5125 Fax: 812-749-1433
Website: www.oak.edu
E-mail: bbaker@oak.edu
See listing under "Universities"

Purdue University
2200 169th St, Hammond IN 46323
219-989-2993

Purdue University
475 Stadium Mall Dr, West Lafayette IN 47907
765-494-4600

Purdue University
1401 S US Highway 421, Westville IN 46391-9542
219-785-5200

St. Joseph's College
PO Box 890, Rensselaer IN 47978-0890
219-866-6000

St. Mary-of-the-Woods College
Saint Mary of the Woods IN 47876-1001
James P. Malley, Jr., Director of Admission
800-926-7692 Fax: 812-535-5010
Website: www.smwc.edu
E-mail: smwcadms@smwc.edu

St. Mary's College
46 Madeliva, Notre Dame IN 46556
574-284-4000

Taylor University
500 W Reade Ave, Upland IN 46989-1002
765-998-2751

University of Evansville
1800 Lincoln Ave, Evansville IN 47722-0001
Thomas E. Bear, V.P. of Enrollment Services
800-423-8633 Fax: 812-488-4076
Website: www.evansville.edu
E-mail: admission@evansville.edu

University of Indianapolis
1400 E Hanna Ave, Indianapolis IN 46227-3697
317-788-3368

University of Southern Indiana
8600 University Blvd, Evansville IN 47712-3591
812-464-8600

Valparaiso University
Valparaiso IN 46383
219-464-5000

IOWA

Briar Cliff University
PO Box 2100, Sioux City IA 51104-0100
Sharisue Wilcoxon, VP for Enrollment Management
712-279-5200 Fax: 712-279-1632
Website: www.briarcliff.edu
E-mail: admissions@briarcliff.edu

Buena Vista University
610 W 4th St, Storm Lake IA 50588-1798
712-749-2235

Clarke College
1550 Clarke Dr, Dubuque IA 52001-3198
Andy Schroeder, Director of Admissions
800-383-2345 Fax: 563-584-8666
Website: www.clarke.edu
E-mail: andy.schroeder@clarke.edu

Coe College
1220 1st Ave NE, Cedar Rapids IA 52402-5092
319-399-8000

Cornell College
600 1st St NW, Mount Vernon IA 52314-1098
319-895-4100

Dordt College
498 4th Ave NE, Sioux Center IA 51250-1697
Quentin Van Essen, Executive Director of Admissions
800-343-6738

Graceland University
1 University Place, Lamoni IA 50140
Brian Shantz, Vice President for Enrollment and Dean of
Admissions
641-784-5196 Fax: 641-784-5480
Website: www.admissions.graceland.edu
E-mail: admissions@graceland.edu

Grand View College
1200 Grandview Ave, Des Moines IA 50316-1599
515-263-2800

Grinnell College
PO Box 805, Grinnell IA 50112-0805
641-269-4000

Iowa Lakes Community College
3200 College Dr, Emmetsburg IA 50536-1055
Anne Stansbury, Asst. Director of Admissions
712-852-5212 Fax: 712-362-8363
Website: www.iowalakes.edu
E-mail: info@iowalakes.edu

Iowa Lakes Community College
300 S 18th St, Estherville IA 51334-2721
Anne Stansbury, Asst. Director of Admissions
712-362-7945 Fax: 712-362-8363
Website: www.iowalakes.edu
E-mail: info@iowalakes.edu

Iowa Lakes Community College
1900 Grand Ave, Suite 8, Spencer IA 51301
Anne Stansbury, Assistant Director of Admissions
712-262-7141 Fax: 712-262-4047
Website: www.iowalakes.edu
E-mail: info@iowalakes.edu

Loras College
1450 Alta Vista St, Dubuque IA 52001-4399
Tim Hauber, Director of Admissions
800-245-6727

Luther College
700 College Dr, Decorah IA 52101-1045
563-387-2000

Morningside College
1501 Morningside Ave, Sioux City IA 51106-1717
712-274-5000

Mount Mercy College
1330 Elmhurst Dr NE, Cedar Rapids IA 52402-4797
Jim Krystofiak, Dean of Admission
800-248-4504 Fax: 319-363-5270
Website: www.mtmercy.edu
E-mail: admission@mtmercy.edu

Northwestern College
101 7th St SW, Orange City IA 51041-1996
712-737-7000

University of Dubuque
2000 University Ave, Dubuque IA 52001-5099
563-589-3000

Upper Iowa University
PO Box 1857, Fayette IA 52142-1857
563-425-5200

- Waldorf College
106 S 6th St, Forest City IA 50436-1713
Steve Lovik, Vice President of Enrollment Management
800-292-1903 or 641-585-8112 Fax: 641-585-8125
Website: www.waldorf.edu
E-mail: loviks@waldorf.edu
See listing under "Universities"

Wartburg College
PO Box 1003, Waverly IA 50677-0903
Brent Matthias, Interim Director of Admissions
319-352-8200 Fax: 319-352-8579
Website: www.wartburg.edu
E-mail: admissions@wartburg.edu

KANSAS

Baker University
PO Box 65, Baldwin City KS 66006-0065
785-594-6451

Barclay College
607 N Kingman, Haviland KS 67059
Herb Frazier, Director of Admissions
800-862-0226 Fax: 620-862-5242
Website: www.barclaycollege.edu
E-mail: admissions@barclaycollege.edu

Benedictine College
1020 N 2nd St, Atchison KS 66002-1499
913-367-5340

Bethany College
421 N 1st St, Lindsborg KS 67456-1897
785-227-3311

Bethel College
300 E 27th St, North Newton KS 67117-8061
316-283-2500

Emporia State University
1200 Commercial St, Emporia KS 66801-5087
620-343-1200

Fort Hays State University
600 Park St, Hays KS 67601-4099
785-628-4000

Friends University
2100 W University Ave, Wichita KS 67213-3397
316-261-5800

Kansas State University
Manhattan KS 66506
785-532-6250

McPherson College
PO Box 1402, Mc Pherson KS 67460-1402
620-241-0731

Newman University
3100 W McCormick St, Wichita KS 67213
Jann Reusser, Admissions Recruitment Coordinator
316-942-4291 ext. 2144 Fax: 316-942-4483
Website: www.newmanu.edu
E-mail: reusserj@newmanu.edu

Ottawa University
1001 S Cedar St, Ottawa KS 66067-3399
785-242-5200

Pittsburg State University
1701 S Broadway St, Pittsburg KS 66762-7500
620-231-7000

Southwestern College
100 College St, Winfield KS 67156-2499
620-229-6000

Tabor College
400 S Jefferson St, Hillsboro KS 67063-1758
Rusty Allen, Dean of Enrollment Management
620-947-3121 Fax: 620-947-6276
Website: www.tabor.edu
E-mail: admissions@tabor.edu

University of Kansas
Lawrence KS 66045-0001
Karen Gallagher, Dean

University of Saint Mary
4100 S 4th St, Leavenworth KS 66048-5023
913-682-5151

Washburn University
1700 SW College Ave, Topeka KS 66621-0001
785-231-1010

Wichita State University
1845 N Fairmount St, Wichita KS 67260-0124
Gina Crabtree, Director of Admissions
316-978-3085

KENTUCKY

Alice Lloyd College
100 Purpose Rd, Pippa Passes KY 41844-9005
John Mills, Director of Admissions
888-280-4252

Asbury College
1 Macklem Dr, Wilmore KY 40390-1198
859-858-3511

Bellarmine University
2001 Newburg Rd, Louisville KY 40205-1877
502-452-8000

Berea College
Berea KY 40404-0001
859-985-3000

Campbellsville University
1 University Dr, Campbellsville KY 42718-2799
Scott Necessary, Coordinator of Undergraduate Admissions
270-789-5000

Eastern Kentucky University
521 Lancaster Ave, Richmond KY 40475-3102
859-622-1000

Kentucky State University
400 E Main St, Frankfort KY 40601-2334
502-597-6000

Kentucky Wesleyan College
3000 Frederica St, Owensboro KY 42301-6055
800-999-0592

Morehead State University
Morehead KY 40351-1689
Dayna Seelig, Enrollment Services
800-585-6781 Fax: 606-783-5038
Website: www.moreheadstate.edu
E-mail: admissions@moreheadstate.edu

Murray State University
Murray KY 42071
Phil Bryan, Director of Admissions
270-762-3011

Northern Kentucky University
Newport KY 41099-0001
859-572-5100

Pikeville College
147 Sycamore St, Pikeville KY 41501
606-218-5250

Spalding University
851 S 4th St, Louisville KY 40203-2188
502-585-9911

Transylvania University
300 N Broadway, Lexington KY 40508-1776
859-233-8242 Fax: 859-233-8797
Website: www.transy.edu
E-mail: admissions@transy.edu

Union College
310 College St, Barbourville KY 40906-1499
Joretta Nelson, Vice President for Enrollment Management
800-489-8646

University of Kentucky
Lexington KY 40506-0001
Don Witt, Director of Admissions
859-257-9000

University of Louisville
2301 S 3rd St, Louisville KY 40292-2001
502-852-5555

Western Kentucky University
1 Big Red Way, Bowling Green KY 42101
270-745-0111

LOUISIANA

Centenary College of Louisiana
PO Box 41188, Shreveport LA 71134-1188
318-869-5011

Dillard University
2601 Gentilly Blvd, New Orleans LA 70122-3097
Linda G. Nash, Director of Admissions
Website: www.dillard.edu
E-mail: admissions@dillard.edu

Grambling State University
PO Box 864, Grambling LA 71245
318-274-3811

Louisiana College
PO Box 560, Pineville LA 71359-0001
Mary Wagner, Director of Admissions
318-487-7259

Louisiana State University
1 University Pl, Shreveport LA 71115-2301
318-797-5000

Louisiana State University and A & M College
Louisiana State Univ, Baton Rouge LA 70803-0001
225-578-3202

Louisiana Tech University
PO Box 3168, Ruston LA 71272-0001
318-257-0211

McNeese State University
4100 Ryan St, Lake Charles LA 70605-4510
337-475-5000

Nicholls State University
University Station, Thibodaux LA 70310-0001
985-446-8111

Northwestern State University
Natchitoches LA 71497-0001
Jana Lucky, Director of Enrollment Services
318-357-4503

Our Lady of Holy Cross College
4123 Woodland Dr, New Orleans LA 70131-7399
Office of Enrollment Services
504-394-7744 Fax: 504-391-2421
Website: www.olhcc.edu

Southeastern Louisiana University
PO Box 784, Hammond LA 70404-0784
985-549-2000

Southern University A&M College
Southern University, Baton Rouge LA 70813-0001
225-771-4500

University of Louisiana at Lafayette
PO Box 44672, Lafayette LA 70504
337-482-6678

University of Louisiana at Monroe
700 University Ave, Monroe LA 71209-9001
318-342-1000

University of New Orleans
New Orleans LA 70148-0001
504-280-6000

MAINE

Bowdoin College
Brunswick ME 04011
207-725-3000

HUSSON COLLEGE

One College Cir, Bangor ME 04401-2999
Jane Goodwin, Director of Admissions
800-4HU-SSON or 207-941-7100 Fax: 207-941-7935
Website: www.husson.edu
E-mail: admit@husson.edu
See listing under "Universities"

- Southern Maine Community College
2 Fort Rd, South Portland ME 04106-1698
Dr. James Ortiz, President
Scott MacDonald, Director of Financial Aid
207-741-5500 Fax: 207-741-5671
Website: www.smccme.edu
E-mail: oharmon@maine.rr.com

Thomas College
180 W River Rd, Waterville ME 04901-5097
207-859-1111

University of Maine
246 Main St, Farmington ME 04938
Sharon M. Oliver, Director of Admissions
207-778-7000

University of Maine
9 OBrien Ave, Machias ME 04654-1321
207-255-1200

University of Maine
Orono ME 04469-0001
207-581-1110

University of Maine at Fort Kent
23 University Dr, Fort Kent ME 04743
888-TRY-UMFK

University of Maine at Presque Isle
181 Main St, Presque Isle ME 04769-2844
207-768-9532

University of Southern Maine
PO Box 9300, Portland ME 04104-9300
207-780-4141

MARYLAND

Bowie State University
14000 Jericho Park Rd, Bowie MD 20715-9465
301-464-3000

Coppin State University
2500 W North Ave, Baltimore MD 21216-3698
410-951-3000

Frostburg State University
Frostburg MD 21532-1001
301-687-4000

Goucher College
1021 Dulaney Valley Rd, Baltimore MD 21204-2780
410-337-6000

::: Griggs University
PO Box 4437, Silver Spring MD 20914-4437
Anita L. Jacobs, Director of Admissions
301-680-6570 Fax: 301-680-6583
Website: www.griggs.edu
E-mail: registrar@griggs.edu

Hood College
401 Rosemont Ave, Frederick MD 21701
301-663-3131

Morgan State University
1700 E Cold Spring Ln, Baltimore MD 21251-0002
443-885-3000

Mt. St. Mary's University
16300 Old Emmitsburg Rd
Emmitsburg MD 21727-7799
301-447-6122

University of Maryland
College Park MD 20742-0001
301-405-1000

University of Maryland Eastern Shore
Princess Anne MD 21853
Edwina Morse, Director of Admissions
410-651-6410

Villa Julie College
1525 Greenspring Valley Rd
Stevenson MD 21153-0641
Mark Hergan, V.P. Enrollment Services
410-486-7001 Fax: 410-602-6600
Website: www.vjc.edu/admissions
E-mail: admissions@mail.vjc.edu

Washington College
300 Washington Ave, Chestertown MD 21620-1197
410-778-2800

MASSACHUSETTS

Anna Maria College
50 Sunset Ln, Paxton MA 01612
Julie A. Mitchell, Director of Admissions
508-849-3360 Fax: 508-849-3362
Website: www.annamaria.edu
E-mail: admissions@annamaria.edu

Assumption College
500 Salisbury St, Worcester MA 01609-1294
Kathleen Murphy, Dean of Enrollment
508-767-7000 Fax: 508-799-4412
Website: www.assumption.edu
E-mail: admiss@assumption.edu

Atlantic Union College
PO Box 1000, South Lancaster MA 01561-1000
Office of Enrollment Services
800-282-2030

Bay Path College
588 Longmeadow St, Longmeadow MA 01106-2292
Lisa Casassa, Director of Admissions
413-565-1331 Fax: 413-565-1105
Website: www.baypath.edu
E-mail: lcasassa@baypath.edu

Bay State College
122 Commonwealth Ave, Boston MA 02116-2901
Craig Pfannenstiehl, President
617-217-9000 Fax: 617-536-1735

Becker College
Campuses in Worcester and Leicester, MA
61 Sever St, Worcester MA 01609-2165
Karen H. Schedin, Director of Admissions
508-791-9241 Fax: 508-890-1500
Website: www.becker.edu
E-mail: admissions@becker.edu
See listing under "Universities"

Boston College
140 Commonwealth Ave
Chestnut Hill MA 02467-3800
617-552-8000

Boston University
121 Bay State Rd, Boston MA 02215
Kelly Walter, Executive Director of Admissions
617-353-2300 Fax: 617-353-9695
Website: web.bu.edu
E-mail: admissions@bu.edu

Bridgewater State College
Bridgewater MA 02325-0001
508-697-1237

Bristol Community College
777 Elsbree St, Fall River MA 02720-7395
Rodney S. Clark, Director of Admissions
508-678-2811 ext. 2516, 2179 Fax: 508-730-3265
Website: www.bristol.mass.edu
E-mail: admissions@bristol.mass.edu

Curry College
1071 Blue Hill Ave, Milton MA 02186-2395
Bruce Weckworth, Director of Admissions
617-333-2210

Eastern Nazarene College
23 E Elm Ave, Quincy MA 02170-2999
617-773-6350

Elms College
291 Springfield St, Chicopee MA 01013-2839
800-255-3567

Fisher College
118 Beacon St, Boston MA 02116-1501
Stephen Carter, Director of Admissions
800-446-1226

Hampshire College
Amherst MA 01002
Karen S. Parker, Director of Admissions
413-559-5471

Harvard University
8 Garden St, Cambridge MA 02138-3630
617-495-1000

Lasell College
1844 Commonwealth Ave, Newton MA 02466-2716
617-243-2225

Lesley University
29 Everett St, Cambridge MA 02138-2790
Jane Raley, Director of Admissions
617-349-8800

Massachusetts College of Liberal Arts
375 Church St, North Adams MA 01247-4100
413-662-5381

Merrimack College
315 Turnpike St, North Andover MA 01845-5800
978-683-7111

Mt. Holyoke College
50 College St, South Hadley MA 01075-1424
413-538-2000

Northeastern University
360 Huntington Ave, Boston MA 02115-5000
617-373-2000

Pine Manor College
400 Heath St, Chestnut Hill MA 02467-2332
Bill Nichols, Dean of Admission
617-731-7167

Regis College
235 Wellesley St, Weston MA 02493-1571
781-768-2000

Salem State College
352 Lafayette St, Salem MA 01970-5353
978-741-6000

School of the Museum of Fine Arts, Boston
230 The Fenway, Boston MA 02115-5534
Office of Admissions
617-369-3626 or 800-643-6078 Fax: 617-369-4264
Website: www.smfa.edu
E-mail: admissions@smfa.edu
See listing under "Universities"

Springfield College
263 Alden St, Springfield MA 01109-3788
Mary DeAngelo, Director of Admissions
800-343-1257

Stonehill College
320 Washington St, Easton MA 02357-5610
508-565-1373

Suffolk University
8 Ashburton Pl, Boston MA 02108-2770
617-573-8460

Tufts University
520 Boston Ave, Medford MA 02155-5555
617-628-5000

University of Massachusetts
Amherst MA 01003
413-545-0111

University of Massachusetts Boston
100 William T Morrissey Blvd, Boston MA 02125-3393
Liliana Mickle, Director of Undergraduate Admissions
617-287-6000

University of Massachusetts Dartmouth
Old Westport Rd, North Dartmouth MA 02747-2300
Steven T. Briggs, Director of Admissions
508-999-8605 Fax: 508-999-8755
Website: explore.umassd.edu
E-mail: sbriggs@umassd.edu

University of Massachusetts Lowell
1 University Ave, Lowell MA 01854-2893
978-934-4000

Western New England College
1215 Wilbraham Rd, Springfield MA 01119-2655
413-782-1321

Westfield State College
PO Box 1630, Westfield MA 01086
Michelle Mattie, Associate Dean, Admission and
Enrollment Services
413-572-5300
Website: www.wsc.ma.edu
E-mail: admission@wsc.ma.edu

Wheelock College
200 Riverway, Boston MA 02215-4176
617-734-5200

Worcester State College
486 Chandler St, Worcester MA 01602-2597
508-929-8000

MICHIGAN

Albion College
611 E Porter St, Albion MI 49224-1831
800-858-6770

Alma College
614 W Superior St, Alma MI 48801-1599
Anne Monroe, Director of Admissions
800-321-ALMA Fax: 989-463-7057
Website: www.alma.edu
E-mail: admissions@alma.edu

Andrews University
Berrien Springs MI 49104-0001
Randall Graves, Director of Recruitment Services
800-253-2874 Fax: 269-471-2670
Website: www.connect.andrews.edu
E-mail: gravesr@andrews.edu

Aquinas College
1607 Robinson Rd SE, Grand Rapids MI 49506-1799
Paula Meehan, Dean of Admissions
616-732-4460

Baker College of Jackson
2800 Springport Rd, Jackson MI 49202-1230
Kelli Hoban, Director of Admissions
517-789-6123

Calvin College
3201 Burton St SE, Grand Rapids MI 49546-4388
800-688-0122

Central Michigan University
100 Warriner Hall, Mount Pleasant MI 48859-0001
989-774-4000

Concordia University
4090 Geddes Rd, Ann Arbor MI 48105-2797
Gary Neumann, Director of Admissions
734-995-7300 Fax: 734-995-4610
Website: www.cuaa.edu
E-mail: admissions@cuaa.edu

Delta College
University Center MI 48710-0001
Duff Zube, Director of Admissions
989-686-9093 Fax: 989-667-2202
Website: www.delta.edu
E-mail: admit@delta.edu

Eastern Michigan University
Ypsilanti MI 48197
800-GO-TO-EMU

Ferris State University
901 S State St, Big Rapids MI 49307-2295
231-591-2000

Grand Valley State University
1 Campus Dr, Allendale MI 49401-9403
616-331-2025 Fax: 616-331-2000
Website: www.gvsu.edu
E-mail: go2gvsu@gvsu.edu

HILLSDALE COLLEGE
33 E College St, Hillsdale MI 49242-1298
Dr. Kathy Connor, Chairperson
517-607-2424 Fax: 517-437-3923
Website: www.hillsdale.edu
E-mail: kathy.conner@hillsdale.edu

Hope College
PO Box 9000, Holland MI 49422-9000
616-395-7000

Lawrence Technological University
21000 W 10 Mile Rd, Southfield MI 48075-1058
Jane Rohrback, Director of Admissions
800-225-5588 Fax: 248-204-2228
Website: www.ltu.edu
E-mail: admissions@ltu.edu
See listing under "Universities"

Madonna University
36600 Schoolcraft Rd, Livonia MI 48150-1173
734-432-5300

Marygrove College
8425 W McNichols Rd, Detroit MI 48221-2599
313-927-1200

Michigan Technological University
1400 Townsend Dr, Houghton MI 49931-1200
Nancy Rehling, Director of Admissions
906-487-2335

Northern Michigan University
1401 Presque Isle Ave, Marquette MI 49855-5301
906-227-1000

Oakland University
2200 N Squirrel Rd, Rochester MI 48309
Eleanor L. Reynolds, Assistant Vice President &
Director of Admissions
248-370-2100
Website: www.oakland.edu
E-mail: ouinfo@oakland.edu

Olivet College
300 S Main St, Olivet MI 49076-9724
269-749-7000

Saginaw Valley State University
7400 Bay Rd, University Center MI 48710-0001
989-790-4000

Siena Heights University
1247 E Siena Heights Dr, Adrian MI 49221-1796
517-263-0731

Spring Arbor University
106 E Main St, Spring Arbor MI 49283-9799
517-750-1200

University of Detroit-Mercy
PO Box 19900, Detroit MI 48219-0900
313-993-1000

University of Michigan-Dearborn
4901 Evergreen Rd, Dearborn MI 48128-1491
The Office of Admissions & Orientation
313-593-5100 Fax: 313-436-9167
Website: www.umd.umich.edu
E-mail: admissions@umd.umich.edu

Wayne State University
5980 Cass Ave, Detroit MI 48202-3489
313-577-2424

Western Michigan University
Kalamazoo MI 49008
269-387-1000

MINNESOTA

ARGOSY UNIVERSITY / TWIN CITIES
1515 Central Pkwy, Eagan MN 55121-1756
O. Jeanne Stoneking, Director of Admissions
651-846-2882 Fax: 651-994-7956
Website: www.argosy.edu
E-mail: tcadmissions@argosyu.edu

Augsburg College
2211 Riverside Ave, Minneapolis MN 55454-1350
612-330-1000

Bemidji State University
1500 Birchmont Dr NE, Bemidji MN 56601-2699
877-236-4354

Bethany Lutheran College
700 Luther Dr, Mankato MN 56001
Don Westphal, Dean of Admissions
507-344-7000 Fax: 507-344-7376
Website: www.blc.edu
E-mail: admiss@blc.edu

Bethel College
3900 Bethel Dr, Saint Paul MN 55112-6999
651-638-6400

Carleton College
1 N College St, Northfield MN 55057-4044
800-995-2275 or 507-646-4190 Fax: 507-646-4526
Website: www.carleton.edu
E-mail: admissions@acs.carleton.edu

College of Saint Benedict
37 College Ave S, Saint Joseph MN 56374-2099
320-363-5011

College of St. Catherine
2004 Randolph Ave, Saint Paul MN 55105-1789
651-690-6000

College of Saint Scholastica
1200 Kenwood Ave, Duluth MN 55811-4199
Brian Dalton, V.P. of Enrollment Management
800-447-5444

Concordia College
901 8th St S, Moorhead MN 56562-0002
Dr. Marilyn Guy, Chairperson
218-299-3004

Concordia University-Saint Paul
275 Syndicate St N, Saint Paul MN 55104-5494
651-641-8278

Gustavus Adolphus College
800 W College Ave, Saint Peter MN 56082-1485
Mark H. Anderson, Dean of Admission
800-GUSTAVUS Fax: 507-933-7474
Website: www.gustavus.edu
E-mail: admission@gustavus.edu

Hamline University
1536 Hewitt Ave, Saint Paul MN 55104-1284
651-523-2800

Macalester College
1600 Grand Ave, Saint Paul MN 55105-1899
651-696-6000

Minnesota State University Mankato
228 Wiecking Center, Mankato MN 56001
507-389-1866

Minnesota State University Moorhead
1104 7th Ave S, Moorhead MN 56563-0002
218-236-2011

Pillsbury Baptist Bible College
315 S Grove Ave, Owatonna MN 55060-3097
Stephen R. Seidler, Director of Admissions
507-451-2710 Fax: 507-451-0156
Website: www.pillsbury.edu
E-mail: steveseidler@pillsbury.edu

Ridgewater College-Willmar Campus
PO Box 1097, Willmar MN 56201-1097
Sally Kerfeld, Director of Admissions
800-722-1151 Fax: 320-231-7677
Website: www.ridgewater.edu
E-mail: skerfeld@ridgewater.edu

St. Cloud State University
720 4th Ave S, Saint Cloud MN 56301-4442
877-654-7278

St. Mary's University of Minnesota
700 Terrace Hts Ste 2, Winona MN 55987-1321
507-452-4430

St. Olaf College
1500 Saint Olaf Ave, Northfield MN 55057-1001
507-646-2222

Southwest Minnesota State University
1501 State St, Marshall MN 56258-1598
507-537-7678

University of Minnesota
10 University Dr, Duluth MN 55812-2496
Beth Esselstrom, Director of Admissions
218-726-7171

University of Minnesota
231 Pillsbury Dr SE, Minneapolis MN 55455-0230
612-625-2008

University of Minnesota - Morris
600 E 4th St, Morris MN 56267-2132
Rodney Oto, Director
800-992-8863

University of St. Thomas
2115 Summit Ave, Saint Paul MN 55105-1096
651-962-5000

Winona State University
PO Box 5838, Winona MN 55987-0838
507-457-5000

MISSISSIPPI

Alcorn State University
PO Box 359, Lorman MS 39096
601-877-6147

Belhaven College
1500 Peachtree St, Jackson MS 39202-1789
601-968-5927

Delta State University
Hwy 8 W, Cleveland MS 38733
662-846-3000

Jackson State University
1440 J.R. Lynch St, Jackson MS 39217
Stephanie Chatman, Director of Admissions
601-979-2100

Millsaps College
PO Box 15495, Jackson MS 39210
601-974-1000

Mississippi College
PO Box 4086, Clinton MS 39058-0001
601-925-3000

Mississippi State University
PO Box J, Mississippi State MS 39762-5509
662-325-2323

Mississippi University for Women
1100 College St Unit W1613, Columbus MS 39701
Terri Heath, Director of Admissions
877-GO-2-THEW

Mississippi Valley State University
14000 Highway 82 W Box 7222
Itta Bena MS 38941-1401
Office of Admissions
662-254-3347

Tougaloo College
500 W County Line Rd, Tougaloo MS 39174-9799
Juno Leggette Jacobs, Director of Admissions
601-977-7768 Fax: 601-977-4501
Website: www.tougaloo.edu
E-mail: jjacobs@tougaloo.edu

University of Mississippi
University MS 38677
662-232-7226

University of Southern Mississippi
PO Box 5165, Hattiesburg MS 39406-1000
601-266-5000

MISSOURI

Calvary Bible College & Theological Seminary
15800 Calvary Rd, Kansas City MO 64147-1341
Robert M. Reinsch, Director of Admissions
800-326-3960 Fax: 816-331-4474
Website: www.calvary.edu
E-mail: admissions@calvary.edu

Central Missouri State University
Warrensburg MO 64093-8888
Charles Petentler, Associate Director of Admissions
800-956-0177

Columbia College
1001 Rogers St, Columbia MO 65216-0001
Regina Morin, Director of Admissions
573-875-7352 Fax: 573-875-7506
Website: www.ccis.edu
E-mail: admissions@ccis.edu

Culver-Stockton College
1 College Hl, Canton MO 63435-1299
Betty Smith, Director of Enrollment Services
800-537-1883

Drury University
900 N Benton Ave, Springfield MO 65802-3791
417-873-7879

Harris-Stowe State University
3026 Laclede Ave, Saint Louis MO 63103-2199
LaShanda R. Boone, Director of Admissions
314-340-3300 Fax: 314-340-3555
Website: www.hssu.edu
E-mail: admissions@hssu.edu

Lincoln University
820 Chestnut St, Jefferson City MO 65101-3500
573-681-5000

Lindenwood University
209 S Kingshighway St
Saint Charles MO 63301-1695
Sheryl Guffey, Director of Admissions
636-949-2000 Fax: 636-949-4989
Website: www.lindenwood.edu

Maryville University of St. Louis
13550 Conway Rd, Saint Louis MO 63141-7299
314-529-9300

Missouri Southern State University - Joplin
3950 Newman Rd, Joplin MO 64801-1512
417-625-9300

Missouri Valley College
500 E College St, Marshall MO 65340-3197
Dr. Dennis Ehlert, Division Dean
660-831-4170

Missouri Western State College
4525 Downs Dr, Saint Joseph MO 64507-2294
800-662-7041

Northwest Missouri State University
800 University Dr, Maryville MO 64468-6001
660-562-1212

Ozark Christian College
1111 N Main St, Joplin MO 64801-4804
Troy Nelson, Director of Admissions
800-299-4622 Fax: 417-624-0090
Website: www.occ.edu
E-mail: occadmin@occ.edu
See listing under "Universities"

Park University
8700 NW River Park Dr, Parkville MO 64152-3795
816-741-2000

Southeast Missouri State University
1 University Plz, Cape Girardeau MO 63701-4710
573-651-2000

Southwest Baptist University
1600 University Ave, Bolivar MO 65613-2597
417-328-5281

Stephens College
PO Box 2121, Columbia MO 65215-0001
David Adams, Dean of Enrollment Management
573-442-2211 Fax: 573-876-7237
Website: www.stephens.edu
E-mail: dadams@stephens.edu

Truman State University
100 E Normal, Kirksville MO 63501
Office of Admission
660-785-4000 Fax: 660-785-4181
Website: admissions.truman.edu
E-mail: admissions@truman.edu

University of Missouri
5100 Rockhill Rd, Kansas City MO 64110-2446
816-235-1000

University of Missouri
1 University Blvd, Saint Louis MO 63121-4499
Dr. Charles D. Schmitz, Dean College of Education
314-516-5109 Fax: 314-516-5227
Website: www.umsl.edu
E-mail: admissions@umsl.edu

Washington University in St. Louis
1 Brookings Dr, Saint Louis MO 63130-4899
314-935-5000

Webster University
470 E Lockwood Ave, Saint Louis MO 63119-3194
Dr. Brenda Fyfe, Dean, School of Education
314-968-7090 Fax: 314-968-7115
Website: www.webster.edu
E-mail: fyfebv@webster.edu
See listing under "Universities"

Westminister College
501 Westminster Ave, Fulton MO 65251-1299
573-642-3361

William Jewell College
500 College Hill, Liberty MO 64068-1896
800-753-7009

William Woods University
1 University Ave, Fulton MO 65251-1098
Jimmy Clay, Director of Admissions
573-642-2251 Fax: 573-592-1146
Website: www.williamwoods.edu
E-mail: admissions@williamwoods.edu
See listing under "Universities"

MONTANA

Carroll College
1601 N Benton Ave, Helena MT 59625-0002
Cynthia Thornquist, Director of Admissions &
Enrollment Operations
406-447-4384

Montana State University - Billings
1500 University Dr, Billings MT 59101-0252
Karen Everett, Director
800-565-MSUB

Montana State University - Bozeman
103 Culbertson Hall, Bozeman MT 59715-5072
406-994-2452

Rocky Mountain College
1511 Poly Dr, Billings MT 59102-1796
Bonnie Knapp, Director of Admissions
800-877-6259 Fax: 406-657-1189
Website: www.rocky.edu
E-mail: admissions@rocky.edu

University of Montana
Missoula MT 59812-0001
406-243-0211

University of Montana - Western
710 S Atlantic St, Dillon MT 59725-3598
406-683-7011

NEBRASKA

Chadron State College
1000 Main St, Chadron NE 69337-2690
308-432-6000

College of Saint Mary
7000 Mercy Rd, Omaha NE 68106
Lorin Werth, V.P. for Enrollment
800-926-5534 or 402-399-2407 Fax: 402-399-2412
Website: www.csm.edu
E-mail: lwerth@csm.edu

Concordia University
800 N Columbia Ave, Seward NE 68434-1594
402-643-3651

Creighton University
2500 California Plz, Omaha NE 68178-0001
402-280-2700

Dana College
2848 College Dr, Blair NE 68008-1099
James Lynes, Director of Admissions
800-444-3262

Doane College
1014 Boswell Ave, Crete NE 68333-2421
402-826-2161

Hastings College
PO Box 269, Hastings NE 68902-0269
402-463-2402

Nebraska Wesleyan University
5000 Saint Paul Ave, Lincoln NE 68504-2794
Patricia Karthauser, V.P. for University Enrollment
402-466-2371 Fax: 402-465-2177
Website: www.nebrwesleyan.edu
E-mail: admissions@nebrwesleyan.edu

Peru State College
PO Box 10, Peru NE 68421-0010
Office of Admissions
800-742-4412 Fax: 402-872-2296
Website: www.peru.edu
E-mail: admissions@oakmail.peru.edu

Union College
3800 S 48th St, Lincoln NE 68506-4300
Buell Fogg, V.P. for Enrollment Services
800-228-4600

University of Nebraska
14th & R Sts, Lincoln NE 68588
402-472-7211

University of Nebraska at Kearney
905 W 25th St, Kearney NE 68849-0001
Dusty Newton, Director of Admissions
800-KEARNEY Fax: 308-865-8987
Website: www.unk.edu
E-mail: admissionsug@unk.edu

University of Nebraska at Omaha
60th and Dodge St, Omaha NE 68182-0001
402-554-2800

Wayne State College
1111 Main St, Wayne NE 68787-1172
402-375-7000

NEVADA

GREAT BASIN COLLEGE
1500 College Pkwy, Elko NV 89801-5032
Julie G. Byrnes, Director of Enrollment Management
775-753-2271 Fax: 775-753-2311
Website: www.gbcnv.edu
E-mail: bjulie@gbcnv.edu

University of Nevada
Reno NV 89557-0001
775-784-1110

University of Nevada Las Vegas
4505 S Maryland Pkwy, Las Vegas NV 89154-9901
800-334-8658

NEW HAMPSHIRE

Antioch University New England
40 Avon St, Keene NH 03431-3516
David Caruso, President
Leatrice A. Johnson, Director of Admissions
603-357-6265 Fax: 603-357-0718
Website: www.antiochne.edu
E-mail: admissions@antiochne.edu

Colby-Sawyer College
100 Main St, New London NH 03257-4648
603-526-3000

Dartmouth College
Hanover NH 03755
603-646-1110

Franklin Pierce College
20 College Rd, Rindge NH 03461
800-437-0048

Keene State College
229 Main St, Keene NH 03435-0002
603-358-2276

New England College
26 Bridge St, Henniker NH 03242-3297
603-428-2211

Plymouth State University
17 High St, MSC #44, Bagley House
Plymouth NH 03264-1595
603-535-5000

Rivier College
420 S Main St, Nashua NH 03060-5086
David Boisvert, Director of Undergraduate Admissions
603-897-8507

St. Anselm College
100 Saint Anselms Dr, Manchester NH 03102-1310
603-641-7000

Southern New Hampshire University
2500 N River Rd, Hooksett NH 03106-1045
Steve Soba, Director of Admissions
603-645-9611 Fax: 603-645-9693
Website: www.snhu.edu
E-mail: s.soba@snhu.edu

NEW JERSEY

Bergen Community College
400 Paramus Rd, Paramus NJ 07652
Julian Gomez, Asst. Director of Admissions
201-447-7100 Fax: 201-444-7036
Website: www.bergen.edu
E-mail: jgomez@bergen.edu

Caldwell College
9 Ryerson Ave, Caldwell NJ 07006-6195
973-618-3000

College of New Jersey
PO Box 7718, Ewing NJ 08628-0718
609-771-1855

College of Saint Elizabeth
2 Convent Rd, Morristown NJ 07960-6923
973-292-4000

Felician College
262 S Main St, Lodi NJ 07644-2198
973-559-6000

Kean University
1000 Morris Ave, Union NJ 07083-7133
908-527-2000

Monmouth University
400 Cedar Ave, West Long Branch NJ 07764-1890
732-571-3400

Montclair State University
Montclair State University, Montclair NJ 07043-1624
973-655-4000

New Jersey City University
2039 John F Kennedy Blvd
Jersey City NJ 07305-1588
Carmen Panlilio, Asst. V.P. for Admissions and
Financial Aid
201-200-3234 Fax: 201-200-2044
Website: www.njcu.edu
E-mail: admissions@njcu.edu

Ramapo College of New Jersey
505 Ramapo Valley Rd, Mahwah NJ 07430-1623
Director of Admissions
201-684-7300 or 201-684-7301 Fax: 201-684-7964
Website: www.ramapo.edu
E-mail: admissions@ramapo.edu

Richard Stockton College of New Jersey
PO Box 195, Pomona NJ 08240
609-652-1776

Rider University
2083 Lawrenceville Rd, Lawrenceville NJ 08648-3099
Susan Christian, Director of Admissions
609-896-5042

Rowan University
201 Mullica Hill Rd, Glassboro NJ 08028-1700
856-256-4000

St. Peter's College
2627 John F Kennedy Blvd, Jersey City NJ 07306
888-SPC-9933

Seton Hall University
400 S Orange Ave, South Orange NJ 07079-2697
973-761-9000

William Paterson University
300 Pompton Rd, Wayne NJ 07470-2103
973-720-2000

NEW MEXICO

New Mexico Highlands University
PO Box 9000, Las Vegas NM 87701
James Abreu, Contact
505-454-3357

New Mexico State University
PO Box 30001, Las Cruces NM 88003-8001
505-646-0111

University of New Mexico
1 University Campus, Albuquerque NM 87131-0001
505-277-0111

NEW YORK

Adelphi University
Garden City NY 11530
516-877-3100

Alfred University
1 Saxson Dr, Alfred NY 14802
607-871-2111

Cazenovia College
Cazenovia NY 13035-1084
Robert Croot, Dean of Admissions & Financial Aid
800-654-3210

College of New Rochelle
29 Castle Pl, New Rochelle NY 10805-2339
914-654-5000

College of Saint Rose
432 Western Ave, Albany NY 12203-1419
Maryelizabeth Amico, Asst V.P. for Undergraduate
Admissions
518-454-5150 Fax: 518-454-2013
Website: www.strose.edu
E-mail: admit@strose.edu

CUNY City College
Convent Ave at 138th St, New York NY 10031
Celia Lloyd, Interim Director of Admissions
212-650-6977

CUNY College of Staten Island
2800 Victory Blvd, Staten Island NY 10314-6600
718-982-2000

CUNY Hunter College
695 Park Ave, New York NY 10021
Aaron Gibbs, Assistant Director of Recruitment
212-772-4497 Fax: 212-650-3336
Website: www.hunter.cuny.edu
E-mail: aaron.gibbs@hunter.cuny.edu

CUNY York College
9420 Guy R Brewer Blvd, Jamaica NY 11451-0001
718-262-2000

Daemen College
4380 Main St, Amherst NY 14226-3592
Donna Shaffner, Director of Admissions
800-462-7652 or 716-839-8225 Fax: 716-839-8229
Website: www.daemen.edu
E-mail: admissions@daemen.edu
See listing under "Universities"

Dominican College of Blauvelt
470 Western Hwy, Orangeburg NY 10962-1210
845-359-7800

Dowling College
150 Idle Hour Blvd, Oakdale NY 11769-1999
631-244-3000

D'Youville College
320 Porter Ave, Buffalo NY 14201-1084
716-829-7600

Elmira College
1 Park Pl, Elmira NY 14901-2099
Gary Fallis, Dean of Admissions
607-735-1724

FIVE TOWNS COLLEGE
305 N Service Rd, Dix Hills NY 11746-5871
631-424-7000 ext. 2110 Fax: 631-656-2172
Website: www.fivetowns.edu
E-mail: admissions@ftc.edu
See listing under "Universities"

Fordham University
441 E Fordham Rd, Bronx NY 10458-9993
John W. Buckley, Dean of Admissions
718-817-4000

Fordham University - Lincoln Center
113 W 60th St, New York NY 10023-7484
Regis G. Bernhardt PhD, Dean
212-636-6000

Hofstra University
100 Hofstra University, Hempstead NY 11549-1000
516-463-6600

Houghton College
PO Box 128, Houghton NY 14744-0128
585-567-9200

Iona College
715 North Ave, New Rochelle NY 10801-1890
Tom Weede, Director of Admissions
914-633-2000

Ithaca College
953 Danby Rd, Ithaca NY 14850-7002
607-274-3011

Keuka College
PO Box 98, Keuka Park NY 14478-0098
315-536-4411

Le Moyne College
1419 Salt Springs Rd, Syracuse NY 13214-1301
800-333-4733

Long Island University-C. W. Post Campus
720 Northern Blvd, Brookville NY 11548-1300
Joanne Graziano, Executive Director of Admissions
516-299-2900 Fax: 516-299-2137
Website: www.liu.edu/cwpost
E-mail: enroll@cwpost.liu.edu

Long Island University
Rockland Graduate Campus
70 Route 340, Orangeburg NY 10962-2219
Kelly J. McCafferty, M.S., Director of Admissions
845-359-7200

Long Island University - Southampton College
239 Montauk Hwy, Southampton NY 11968
631-283-4000

Manhattan College
4513 Manhattan College Pkwy
Riverdale NY 10471-4099
Dr. William Merriman, Dean of Education
718-862-7200

Manhattanville College
2900 Purchase St, Purchase NY 10577-2132
914-694-2200

Marymount College at Fordham University
100 Marymount Ave, Tarrytown NY 10591-3796
914-631-3200

Medaille College
18 Agassiz Cir, Buffalo NY 14214-2695
716-884-3281

Mercy College
555 Broadway, Dobbs Ferry NY 10522-1189
Kathleen Jackson, Director of Admissions
800-MERCY-NY

Molloy College
1000 Hempstead Ave
Rockville Centre NY 11570-1100
Marguerite Lane, Director of Admissions
516-678-5000 ext. 6291 Fax: 516-256-2247
Website: www.molloy.edu
E-mail: admissions@molloy.edu
See listing under "Universities"

Mt. St. Mary College
330 Powell Ave, Newburgh NY 12550-3494
845-561-0800

Nazareth College of Rochester
4245 East Ave, Rochester NY 14618-3790
585-389-2525

New York Institute of Technology
PO Box 8000, Old Westbury NY 11568-8000
516-686-7516

Niagara University
PO Box 2011, Niagara University NY 14109-2011
George Pachter, Dean of Admissions & Records
800-462-2111

Nyack College
1 South Boulevard
Nyack NY 10960-3698
845-358-1710

Pratt Institute
200 Willoughby Ave, Brooklyn NY 11205-3899
Heidi Metcalf, Director of Admissions
718-636-3600 Fax: 718-636-3670
Website: www.pratt.edu
E-mail: hmetcalf@pratt.edu

Roberts Wesleyan College
2301 Westside Dr, Rochester NY 14624-1997
Office of Admissions
585-594-6400 Fax: 585-594-6371
Website: www.roberts.edu
E-mail: admissions@roberts.edu

Russell Sage College
45 Ferry St, Troy NY 12180-4115
518-244-2000

St. Bonaventure University
Saint Bonaventure NY 14778-9999
585-375-2000

St. John Fisher College
3690 East Ave, Rochester NY 14618-3597
585-385-8000

St. John's University
8000 Utopia Pkwy, Queens NY 11439
Office of Admission
718-990-2000 or 888-9-STJOHNS Fax: 718-990-2096
Website: www.stjohns.edu
E-mail: admissions@stjohns.edu
See listing under "Universities"

St. Joseph's College
245 Clinton Ave, Brooklyn NY 11205-3688
Theresa LaRocca Meyer, V.P. for Enrollment
Management
718-636-6800 Fax: 718-636-8303
Website: www.sjcny.edu
E-mail: tlaroccameyer@sjcny.edu

St. Joseph's College
155 W Roe Blvd, Patchogue NY 11772
631-447-3200

St. Lawrence University
2501 Saint Lawrence Univ, Canton NY 13617-1475
315-229-5011

Skidmore College
815 N Broadway, Saratoga Springs NY 12866-1698
518-580-5000

SUNY at Albany
1400 Washington Ave, Albany NY 12222-1000
Jonathan Bartow, Director of Graduate Studies
518-442-3980

SUNY College at Brockport
350 New Campus Dr, Brockport NY 14420-2997
Bernard S. Valento, Director of Undergraduate
Admissions
585-395-2751 Fax: 585-395-5452
Website: www.brockport.edu
E-mail: admit@brockport.edu

SUNY College at Buffalo
1300 Elmwood Ave, Buffalo NY 14222-1004
716-878-4000

SUNY College at Old Westbury
PO Box 210, Old Westbury NY 11568-0210
516-876-3000

SUNY College at Potsdam
Potsdam NY 13676
Thomas W. Nesbitt, Director of Admissions
315-267-2000

SUNY Niagara County Community College
3111 Saunders Settlement Rd
Sanborn NY 14132-9487
Kathleen Saunders, Director of Admissions
716-614-6200 Fax: 716-614-6820
Website: www.niagaracc.suny.edu
E-mail: saunders@niagaracc.suny.edu

SUNY Orange County Community College
115 South St, Middletown NY 10940-6437
Margot St. Lawrence, Director of Admissions
845-341-4030 Fax: 845-342-8662
Website: www.sunyorange.edu
E-mail: apply@sunyorange.edu
See listing under "Community and Junior Colleges"

Touro College
27 W 23rd St Ste 33, New York NY 10010-4202
212-463-0400

Trocaire College
360 Choate Ave, Buffalo NY 14220-2003
Paul B. Hurley, Ph.D., President
716-826-1200 Fax: 716-828-6107
Website: www.trocaire.edu
E-mail: info@trocaire.edu
See listing under "Community and Junior Colleges"

University at Buffalo, The State University of New York
15 Capen Hall, Buffalo NY 14260-1660
Patricia G. Armstrong, Director of Admissions
888-UB-ADMIT

University of Rochester
Meliora Hall, Rochester NY 14627
585-275-2121

Wagner College
One Campus Rd, Staten Island NY 10301
Leigh Ann DePascale, Director of Admissions
718-390-3411

NORTH CAROLINA

Appalachian State University
ASU Station, Boone NC 28608-0001
828-262-2000

Barton College
PO Box 5000, Wilson NC 27893
252-399-6300

Belmont Abbey College
100 Belmont Mount Holly Rd
Belmont NC 28012-1802
888-222-0110 Fax: 704-825-6670
Website: www.belmontabbeycollege.edu
E-mail: admissions@bac.edu

Bennett College
900 E Washington St, Greensboro NC 27401-3298
336-273-4431

Campbell University
PO Box 546, Buies Creek NC 27506-0546
Herbert V. Kerner, Jr., Director of Admissions
800-334-4111

Catawba College
2300 W Innes St, Salisbury NC 28144-2488
Gordon A. Kirkland, Associate Director of Admissions
704-637-4402

Davidson College
PO Box 7156, Davidson NC 28035-7156
Chris Gruber, Acting Dean of Admission
800-768-0380

Duke University
Durham NC 27706-8001
919-684-8111

East Carolina University
Speight 154, Greenville NC 27858
Dr. Marilyn Sheerer, Dean

Elizabeth City State University
1704 Weeksville Rd, Elizabeth City NC 27909-7806
252-335-3400

Fayetteville State University
1200 Murchison Rd, Fayetteville NC 28301-4298
910-486-1111

Gardner-Webb University
PO Box 817, Boiling Springs NC 28017
704-406-2361

Greensboro College
815 W Market St, Greensboro NC 27401-1875
336-272-7102

Guilford College
5800 W Friendly Ave, Greensboro NC 27410-4173
Randy Doss, Dean of Enrollment
336-316-2100

Haywood Community College
185 Freedlander Dr, Clyde NC 28721
Debbie Rowland, Coordinator of Admissions
828-627-4500 Fax: 828-627-4513
Website: www.haywood.edu
E-mail: drowland@haywood.edu

High Point University
933 Montlieu Ave, High Point NC 27262-3598
336-841-9000

Johnson C. Smith University
100 Beatties Ford Rd, Charlotte NC 28216-5302
704-378-1000

Lees-McRae College
PO Box 128, Banner Elk NC 28604-0128
Walt Crutchfield, Dean of Admissions
800-280-4562 Fax: 828-898-8707
Website: www.lmc.edu
E-mail: admissions@lmc.edu

Lenoir-Rhyne College
7th Ave and 8th St, Hickory NC 28603
828-328-1741

Livingstone College
701 W Monroe St, Salisbury NC 28144-5298
704-797-1000

Louisburg College
501 N Main St, Louisburg NC 27549-2399
800-775-0208 or 919-496-2521 Fax: 919-496-1788
Website: www.louisburg.edu
E-mail: admissions@louisburg.edu

Mars Hill College
Mars Hill NC 28754
Chad Holt, Dean of Enrollment
866-MHC-4-YOU Fax: 828-689-1473
Website: www.mhc.edu
E-mail: cholt@mhc.edu

Meredith College
3800 Hillsborough St, Raleigh NC 27607-5298
Heidi L. Fletcher, Director of Admissions
919-760-8581 Fax: 919-760-2348
Website: www.meredith.edu
E-mail: admissions@meredith.edu
See listing under "Women's Colleges"

Methodist College
5400 Ramsey St, Fayetteville NC 28311-1498
910-630-7000

Montreat College
PO Box 1267, Montreat NC 28757-1267
800-622-6968

Mt. Olive College
634 Henderson St, Mount Olive NC 28365
Tim Woodard, Director of Admissions
919-658-2502 Fax: 919-658-9816
Website: www.moc.edu
E-mail: admissions@moc.edu
See listing under "Universities"

North Carolina A&T State University
1601 E Market St, Greensboro NC 27411
Lee Young, AVC Enrollment
336-334-7500 Fax: 336-334-7478
Website: www.ncat.edu
E-mail: uadmit@ncat.edu

North Carolina Central University
PO Box 19617, Durham NC 27707-0022
919-560-6100

North Carolina State University
PO Box 7001, Raleigh NC 27695-0001
919-515-2011

North Carolina Wesleyan College
3400 N Wesleyan Blvd, Rocky Mount NC 27804-8677
252-985-5100

Pfeiffer University
PO Box 960, Misenheimer NC 28109-0960
704-463-1360

Queens University of Charlotte
1900 Selwyn Ave, Charlotte NC 28274-0002
704-337-2212

St. Andrews Presbyterian College
1700 Dogwood Mile St, Laurinburg NC 28352-5521
Glenn Batten, Vice President for Enrollment
910-277-5554

St. Augustine's College
1315 Oakwood Ave, Raleigh NC 27610-2298
919-516-4000

Salem College
Winston Salem NC 27108
Dana Evans, Dean of Admissions/Fin. Aid
800-32-SALEM Fax: 336-917-5572
Website: www.salem.edu
E-mail: admissions@salem.edu
See listing under "Women's Colleges"

Shaw University
118 E South St, Raleigh NC 27601-2399
919-546-8200

University of North Carolina
1 University Hts, Asheville NC 28804-3251
828-251-6600

University of North Carolina
Chapel Hill NC 27599-0001
919-962-2211

University of North Carolina
9201 University City Blvd, Charlotte NC 28223
704-547-2000

University of North Carolina
601 S College Rd, Wilmington NC 28403-3201
910-962-3000

University of North Carolina at Greensboro
1000 Spring Garden St, Greensboro NC 27412-0001
336-334-5243

University of North Carolina at Pembroke
PO Box 1510, Pembroke NC 28372-1510
910-521-6000

Wake Forest University
PO Box 7305, Winston Salem NC 27109-7305
336-759-5000

Warren Wilson College
PO Box 9000, Asheville NC 28815-9000
Richard Blomgren, Dean of Admissions
828-298-3325

Western Carolina University
University Dr, Cullowhee NC 28723-9646
828-227-7211

Wingate University
201 E Wilson St, Wingate NC 28174-9600
704-233-8000

Winston-Salem State University
601 S Mrtn Lther King Jr Dr
Winston Salem NC 27110-0003
336-750-2000

NORTH DAKOTA

Dickinson State University
Dickinson ND 58601-4896
Steve Glasser, Director of Student Recruitment
800-279-4295 Fax: 701-483-2409
Website: www.dickinsonstate.edu
E-mail: dsu.hawks@dickinsonstate.edu

Jamestown College
6000 College Ln, Jamestown ND 58405-0002
701-252-3467

Mayville State University
330 3rd St NE, Mayville ND 58257-1299
Dr. Pamela Balch, President
Brian Larson, Director of Enrollment Services
800-437-4104

Minot State University
500 University Ave W, Minot ND 58707-0002
Dennis Parisien, Enrollment Services Rep.
800-777-0750 ext. 3350

North Dakota State University
Fargo ND 58105
701-237-7211

Sitting Bull College
1341 92nd St, Fort Yates ND 58538
Melody Azure, Director of Admissions / Registrar
701-854-3861 Fax: 701-854-3403
Website: www.sittingbull.edu
E-mail: melodya@sbci.edu

University of Mary
7500 University Dr, Bismarck ND 58504-9652
701-255-7500

University of North Dakota
Box 8193 University Station, Grand Forks ND 58203
701-777-2011

Valley City State University
101 College St SW, Valley City ND 58072-4024
Dan Klein, Director of Enrollment Services
800-532-8641 ext. 7101 Fax: 701-845-7299
Website: www.vcsu.edu
E-mail: enrollment.services@vcsu.edu
See listing under "Universities"

OHIO

Antioch College
795 Livermore St, Yellow Springs OH 45387-1697
937-754-5000

Ashland University
401 College Ave, Ashland OH 44805-3799
419-289-4142

Baldwin-Wallace College
275 Eastland Rd, Berea OH 44017-2088
440-826-2900

Bowling Green State University
110 McFall Center, Bowling Green OH 43403-0001
866-CHOOSE-BGSU

Capital University
2199 E Main St, Columbus OH 43209-2394
614-236-6011

Cedarville University
251 N Main St, Cedarville OH 45314
937-766-2211

Cleveland State University
2121 Euclid Ave RW 204, Cleveland OH 44115
Dr. Richard Arndt, Dean of Undergraduate Recruitment and College Partnerships
888-CSU-OHIO Fax: 216-687-9210
Website: www.csuohio.edu
E-mail: admissions@csuohio.edu

College of Wooster
Wooster OH 44691-2363
Paul J. Deutsch, Dean of Admissions
800-877-9905

Defiance College
701 N Clinton St, Defiance OH 43512-1695
419-784-4010

Denison University
PO Box B, Granville OH 43023-0603
740-587-0810

Franciscan University of Steubenville
University Blvd, Steubenville OH 43952
Margaret J. Weber, Director of Admissions
800-783-6220 or 740-283-6226 Fax: 740-284-5456
Website: www.admissions.edu
E-mail: mweber@franciscan.edu

Heidelberg College
310 E Market St, Tiffin OH 44883-2462
418-448-2000

John Carroll University
20700 N Park Blvd, Cleveland OH 44118-4581
216-397-1886

Kent State University
PO Box 5190, Kent OH 44242-0001
Paul Deutsch, Director of Admissions
330-672-2444

Lake Erie College
391 W Washington St, Painesville OH 44077-3389
440-352-3361

Malone College
515 25th St NW, Canton OH 44709-3897
John Chopka, Dean of Admissions
330-471-8100

Miami University
E High St, Oxford OH 45056
513-529-2531

Mt. Union College
1972 Clark Ave, Alliance OH 44601-3929
Vincent Heslop, Director of Admissions
800-334-6682

Mount Vernon Nazarene University
800 Martinsburg Rd, Mount Vernon OH 43050-9509
Timothy Eades, Director of Admissions
866-462-6868 Fax: 740-393-0511
Website: www.gotomvnu.com
E-mail: admissions@mvnu.edu
See listing under "Universities"

Muskingum College
147 Center St, New Concord OH 43762-1193
740-826-8211

Ohio Dominican University
1216 Sunbury Rd, Columbus OH 43219-2099
614-253-2741

OHIO NORTHERN UNIVERSITY
525 S Main St, Ada OH 45810-1555
Tena Roepke, Director of the Center for Teacher Education
419-772-2118
Website: www.onu.edu
E-mail: admissions-ug@onu.edu
See listing under "Universities"

The Ohio State University
School of Teaching and Learning
Arps Hall, 1945 North High St, Columbus OH 43210
614-292-2581 Fax: 614-292-7695
Website: coe.ohio-state.edu
E-mail: edtl-oas@osu.edu

Ohio State University-Marion
1465 Mount Vernon Ave, Marion OH 43302-5695
740-389-6786

Ohio University - Zanesville Branch
1425 Newark Rd, Zanesville OH 43701-2695
740-588-1439

Otterbein College
78 W Home St, Westerville OH 43081-1489
614-890-3000

Owens Community College
300 Davis St, Findlay OH 45840-3631
William J. Ivoska PhD., Vice President of Student Services
567-429-3500 Fax: 567-423-0246
Website: www.owens.edu
E-mail: admissions@owens.edu

Owens Community College
PO Box 10000, Toledo OH 43699-1947
William J. Ivoska, Ph.D, Vice President of Student Services
567-661-7000 Fax: 567-661-7607
Website: www.owens.edu
E-mail: admissions@owens.edu

Shawnee State University
940 2nd St, Portsmouth OH 45662-4344
740-354-3205

University of Akron
381 Buchtel Mall, Akron OH 44304-1584
330-972-7111

University of Cincinnati
2700 Clifton Ave, Cincinnati OH 45220-2873
513-556-6000

University of Dayton
300 College Park, Dayton OH 45469-1300
Robert F. Durkle, Director of Admissions
800-837-7433 Fax: 937-229-4729
Website: admission.udayton.edu
E-mail: admission@udayton.edu

University of Findlay
1000 N Main St, Findlay OH 45840-3695
419-422-8313

University of Rio Grande
General Delivery, Rio Grande OH 45674-9999
H. Paul Lloyd, Dean
740-245-5353 ext. 7328

University of Toledo
2801 W Bancroft St, Toledo OH 43606-3390
419-530-4636

Urbana University
579 College Way, Urbana OH 43078
937-484-1301

Ursuline College
2550 Lander Rd, Cleveland OH 44124-4398
Sarah E. Sundermeier, Director of Admissions
888-URSULINE Toll Free Fax: 440-684-6138
Website: www.admission.ursuline.edu
E-mail: admission@ursuline.edu

Walsh University
2020 E Maple St, North Canton OH 44720
800-362-9846

Wilmington College
251 Ludovic St, Wilmington OH 45177
937-382-6661

Wittenberg University
PO Box 720, Springfield OH 45501-0720
937-327-6231

Wright State University
3640 Colonel Glenn Hwy, Dayton OH 45435-0002
937-775-3333

Youngstown State University
Sweeney Welcome Ctr, One University Plz
Youngstown OH 44555-0002
Sue Davis, Contact
877-GO-TO-YSU

OKLAHOMA

Bacone College
2299 Old Bacone Rd, Muskogee OK 74403-1568
Jerrett Phillips, Director of Admissions
918-781-7340

Cameron University
2800 W Gore Blvd, Lawton OK 73505-6377
580-581-2200

East Central University
1100 E 14th St
Ada OK 74820-6999
Pamla Armstrong, Director of Admissions
580-332-8000

Langston University
PO Box 907, Langston OK 73050-0907
405-466-2231

Mid-America Christian University
3500 SW 119th St, Oklahoma City OK 73170-4504
Haley Hope, Director of Admissions
405-691-3800 Fax: 405-692-3165
Website: www.macu.edu
E-mail: info@macu.edu

Northeastern State University
600 N Grand Ave, Tahlequah OK 74464-2301
918-456-5511

Northwestern Oklahoma State University
709 Oklahoma Blvd, Alva OK 73717
580-327-1700

Oklahoma Baptist University
500 W University St, Shawnee OK 74804-2590
405-275-2850

Oklahoma Christian University
PO Box 11000, Oklahoma City OK 73136-1100
405-425-5000

Oklahoma City University
2501 N Blackwelder Ave
Oklahoma City OK 73106-1493
Shery Boyles, Director of Admissions
405-521-5050

Oklahoma Panhandle State University
PO Box 430, Goodwell OK 73939-0430
580-349-2611

Oklahoma State University
Stillwater OK 74078
Kathy.Boyer, Coordinator
405-744-6350
Website: www.okstate.edu
E-mail: kathy.boyer@okstate.edu

Oklahoma Wesleyan University
2201 Silver Lake Rd, Bartlesville OK 74006-6299
918-333-6151

Oral Roberts University
7777 S Lewis Ave, Tulsa OK 74171-0001
Chris Belcher, Director of Undergraduate Admissions
800-678-8876 Fax: 918-495-6222
Website: www.oru.edu
E-mail: admissions@oru.edu

Southeastern Oklahoma State University
Station A, Durant OK 74701
580-924-0121

Southern Nazarene University
6729 NW 39th Expy, Bethany OK 73008-2694
405-789-6400

Southwestern Oklahoma State University
100 Campus Dr, Weatherford OK 73096-3098
580-772-6611

University of Central Oklahoma
100 N University Dr, Edmond OK 73034-5209
405-974-2000

University of Oklahoma at Norman
660 Parrington Oval, Norman OK 73019-3070
405-325-0311

University of Sciences & Arts of OK
PO Box 82345, Chickasha OK 73018
405-224-3140

University of Tulsa
600 S College Ave, Tulsa OK 74104-3126
Earl Johnson, Dean of Admission
918-631-2307 Fax: 918-631-5003
Website: www.utulsa.edu
E-mail: admission@utulsa.edu

OREGON

Cascade College
9101 E Burnside St, Portland OR 97216-1599
800-550-7678 Fax: 503-257-1222
Website: www.cascade.edu
E-mail: admissions@cascade.edu

Corban College
5000 Deer Park Dr SE, Salem OR 97317-9330
503-581-8600

Lewis & Clark College
0615 SW Palatine Hill Rd, Portland OR 97219-7899
503-768-7000

Linfield College
900 SE Baker St, Mc Minnville OR 97128-6894
503-472-2200

Oregon State University
Corvallis OR 97333-9800
541-737-0123

Pacific University
2043 College Way, Forest Grove OR 97116-1797
Karen M. Dunston, Executive Director of Admissions
800-635-0561 Fax: 503-352-2975
Website: www.pacificu.edu
E-mail: admissions@pacificu.edu

Portland State University
PO Box 751, Portland OR 97207-0751
503-725-3000

Southern Oregon University
1250 Siskiyou Blvd, Ashland OR 97520-5010
541-552-7672

Warner Pacific College
2219 SE 68th Ave, Portland OR 97215-4026
Shannon Mackey, Director of Admissions
503-517-1000 Fax: 503-517-1352
Website: www.warnerpacific.edu
E-mail: admissions@warnerpacific.edu

Western Oregon University
345 Monmouth Ave N, Monmouth OR 97361-1314
David McDonald, Dean, Admission, Retention & Enrollment Management
877-877-1593 Fax: 503-838-8067
Website: www.wou.edu
E-mail: wolfgram@fsa.wou.edu

PENNSYLVANIA

Albright College
PO Box 15234, Reading PA 19612-5234
610-921-2381

Allegheny College
520 N Main St, Meadville PA 16335-3902
814-332-3100

Alvernia College
400 Saint Bernardine St, Reading PA 19607
610-796-8200

Arcadia University
450 S Easton Rd, Glenside PA 19038-3295
Dennis Nostrand, VP for Enrollment Management
877-ARCADIA (877-272-2342) Fax: 215-881-8767
Website: www.arcadia.edu
E-mail: admiss@arcadia.edu
See listing under "Universities"

Bloomsburg University of Pennsylvania
400 E 2nd St, Bloomsburg PA 17815-1399
570-389-4000

California University of Pennsylvania
250 University Ave, California PA 15419-1394
724-938-4000

Carlow University
3333 5th Ave, Pittsburgh PA 15213-3165
412-578-6000

Cedar Crest College
100 College Dr, Allentown PA 18104-6196
Judith A. Neyhart, Vice President Enrollment
800-360-1222

Chatham College
Woodland Rd, Pittsburgh PA 15232-2826
412-365-1100

Chestnut Hill College
9601 Germantown Ave, Philadelphia PA 19118-2693
Jodie King, Director of Admissions
215-248-7001

Cheyney University of Pennsylvania
PO Box 200, Cheyney PA 19319-0200
610-399-2275

Clarion University of Pennsylvania
840 Wood St, Clarion PA 16214-1232
William Bailey, Dean of Enrollment Management
814-393-2306 Fax: 814-393-2030
Website: www.clarion.edu
E-mail: admissions@clarion.edu

College Misericordia
301 Lake St, Dallas PA 18612-1008
Admissions
570-674-6400

Drexel University
3141 Chestnut St, Philadelphia PA 19104-2875
Dana R. Davies, Director of Undergraduate Enrollment
800-2-DREXEL

Duquesne University
600 Forbes Ave, Pittsburgh PA 15282-0001
Paul-James Cukanna, Director of Admissions
412-396-5000

Eastern University
1300 Eagle Rd, Saint Davids PA 19087-3696
610-341-5800

East Stroudsburg University of PA
200 Prospect St
East Stroudsburg PA 18301
570-424-3211

Edinboro University of Pennsylvania
Edinboro PA 16444-0001
814-732-2000

Elizabethtown College
1 Alpha Dr, Elizabethtown PA 17022-2298
717-361-1000

Gannon University
109 University Sq, Erie PA 16541-0001
Christopher Tremblay, Director of Admissions
800-GANNON-U Fax: 814-871-5803
Website: www.gannon.edu
E-mail: admissions@gannon.edu

Geneva College
3200 College Ave, Beaver Falls PA 15010-3599
724-846-5100

Gratz College
7605 Old York Rd, Melrose Park PA 19027
Jill Sigman, Director of Admissions
215-635-7300 Fax: 215-635-7320
Website: www.gratzcollege.edu
E-mail: admissions@gratz.edu

Gwynedd-Mercy College
1325 Sumneytown Pike, Gwynedd Valley PA 19437
Dennis Murphy, V.P. Enrollment Management
800-DIAL-GMC

Holy Family University
9801 Frankford Avenue, Philadelphia PA 19114
Lauren Campbell, Director of Admissions
215-637-3050 Fax: 215-281-1022
Website: www.holyfamily.edu
E-mail: admissions@holyfamily.edu

Immaculata University
Immaculata PA 19345
Women's College Office of Admissions
610-647-4400

Indiana University of Pennsylvania
Indiana PA 15705-0001
724-357-2100

Juniata College
1700 Moore St, Huntingdon PA 16652-2196
Michelle Bartol, Dean of Enrollment
877-JUNIATA Fax: 814-641-3100
Website: www.juniata.edu
E-mail: admissions@juniata.edu

King's College
133 N River St, Wilkes Barre PA 18711-0801
Michelle Lawrence-Schmude, Director of Admission
570-208-5900 Fax: 570-208-5971
Website: www.kings.edu
E-mail: admissions@kings.edu

Kutztown University of Pennsylvania
Kutztown PA 19530
610-683-4000

Lancaster Bible College
901 Eden Rd, Lancaster PA 17601-5036
Joanne M. Roper, Associate VP for Admissions
866-LBC-4YOU or 717-560-8271 Fax: 717-560-8213
Website: www.lbc.edu
E-mail: admissions@lbc.edu
See listing under "Theological Studies & Religious Vocations"

La Roche College
9000 Babcock Blvd, Pittsburgh PA 15237-5898
Thomas Hassett, Director of Freshman and International Admissions
412-536-1272 or 800-838-4LRC Fax: 412-536-1272
Website: www.laroche.edu
E-mail: admissions@laroche.edu

La Salle University
1900 W Olney Ave, Philadelphia PA 19141-1199
Robert Voss, Dean of Admissions
215-951-1500

Lebanon Valley College
101 N College Ave, Annville PA 17003-1400
William Brown, Dean of Admissions & Financial Aid
866-LVC-4ADM or 717-867-6181 Fax: 717-867-6026
Website: www.lvc.edu
E-mail: admission@lvc.edu

Lock Haven University
Lock Haven PA 17745
James C. Reeser, Dean of Admissions
570-893-2027

Lycoming College
700 College Pl, Williamsport PA 17701-5192
570-321-4000

Mansfield University of Pennsylvania
Academy St, Mansfield PA 16933
570-662-4000

Marywood University
2300 Adams Ave, Scranton PA 18509-1598
570-348-6211

Mercyhurst College
501 E 38th St, Erie PA 16546-0001
800-825-1926

Millersville University of Pennsylvania
PO Box 1002, Millersville PA 17551-0302
717-872-3024

MOUNT ALOYSIUS COLLEGE
7373 Admiral Peary Hwy, Cresson PA 16630-1999
Frank C. Crouse Jr., Vice President for Enrollment
Management
814-886-6383 or 888-823-2220 Fax: 814-886-6441
Website: www.mtaloy.edu
E-mail: admissions@mtaloy.edu

Muhlenberg College
2400 W Chew St, Allentown PA 18104-5586
610-821-3100

Neumann College
1 Neumann Dr, Aston PA 19014-1298
Dennis Murphy, Director of Admissions
610-459-0905 Fax: 610-558-5652
Website: www.neumann.edu
E-mail: neumann@neumann.edu

Pennsylvania State University
Broadhead Rd, Monaca PA 15061
724-773-3500

Pennsylvania State University
201 Shields Bldg PO Box 300
University Park PA 16802-3000
814-865-4700

Point Park University
201 Wood St, Pittsburgh PA 15222-1984
Philip Clarke, Associate Director of Admissions
412-392-3430

Robert Morris College
600 5th Ave, Pittsburgh PA 15219-3010
412-227-6800

Robert Morris University
881 Narrows Run Rd, Coraopolis PA 15108-1169
412-262-8200

Rosemont College
1400 Montgomery Ave, Rosemont PA 19010-1699
Ms. Rennie Andrews, Director of Admissions
610-526-2966

St. Francis University
PO Box 600, Loretto PA 15940-0600
814-472-3000

St. Vincent College
300 Fraser Purchase Rd, Latrobe PA 15650-2690
724-539-9761

Seton Hill University
Greensburg PA 15601-1599
Mary Kay Cooper, Director of Admissions and Adult
Student Services
800-826-6234

Shippensburg University
1871 Old Main Dr, Shippensburg PA 17257-2299
717-477-7447

Slippery Rock University
14 Maltby Dr, Slippery Rock PA 16057-1326
724-738-9000

Susquehanna University
514 University Ave, Selinsgrove PA 17870-1164
570-374-0101

Temple University
Broad St & Montgomery Ave, Philadelphia PA 19122
215-204-7000

Thiel College
75 College Ave, Greenville PA 16125-2181
724-589-2000

University of Pennsylvania
3400 Spruce St, Philadelphia PA 19104-4274
215-898-5000

University of Pittsburgh
1150 Mount Pleasant Rd
Greensburg PA 15601-5860
Brandi S. Darr, Director of Admissions and Financial
Aid
724-836-9880 Fax: 724-836-7160
Website: www.upg.pitt.edu
E-mail: upgadmit@pitt.edu

University of Pittsburgh at Bradford
300 Campus Dr, Bradford PA 16701-2812
Alexander Nazemetz, Director of Admissions
814-362-7555

University of Scranton
800 Linden St, Scranton PA 18510-4501
570-941-7400

University of the Arts
320 S Broad St, Philadelphia PA 19102-4994
Susan Gandy, Director of Admissions
800-616-2787 Fax: 215-717-6045
Website: www.uarts.edu
E-mail: admissions@uarts.edu

Villanova University
800 E Lancaster Ave, Villanova PA 19085
610-519-4500

Washington & Jefferson College
60 S Lincoln St, Washington PA 15301-4801
Alton E. Newell, Vice President for Enrollment
724-223-6025 Fax: 724-223-6534
Website: www.washjeff.edu
E-mail: admission@washjeff.edu

Waynesburg College
51 W College St, Waynesburg PA 15370-1222
Robin L. Moore, Dean of Admissions
800-225-7393

West Chester University of Pennsylvania
S High St, West Chester PA 19383-0001
610-436-1000

Widener University
1 University Pl, Chester PA 19013-5792
610-499-4000

Wilkes University
170 S Franklin St, Wilkes Barre PA 18766-0001
570-408-5000

York College of Pennsylvania
PO Box 15199, York PA 17405-7199
717-846-7788

RHODE ISLAND

Providence College
549 River Ave, Providence RI 02918-0002
401-865-1000

Rhode Island College
600 Mount Pleasant Ave, Providence RI 02908-1924
401-456-8000

Salve Regina University
100 Ochre Point Ave, Newport RI 02840-4192
401-847-6650

University of Rhode Island
Kingston RI 02881
401-874-1000

SOUTH CAROLINA

Benedict College
1600 Harden St, Columbia SC 29204-1086
Phyllis L. Thompson, Director of Admissions
803-253-5143

Charleston Southern University
PO Box 118087, Charleston SC 29423-8087
Cheryl Burton, Director of Admissions
800-947-7474

The Citadel
171 Moultrie St, Charleston SC 29409-0002
843-953-5000

Clemson University
105 Sikes Hall, Clemson SC 29634
864-656-2287

Coastal Carolina University
PO Box 261954, Conway SC 29528-6054
Office of Admissions
800-277-7000 Fax: 843-349-2127
Website: www.coastal.edu
E-mail: admissions@coastal.edu

College of Charleston
66 George St, Charleston SC 29424-1407
Suzette Stille, Admissions
843-953-5670

Columbia College
1301 Columbia College Dr, Columbia SC 29203-5998
Elizabeth G. Quackenbush, Director of Admissions
803-786-3871

Columbia International University
PO Box 3122, Columbia SC 29230-3122
John Basie, Director of University Admissions
800-777-2227 Fax: 803-786-4209
Website: www.ciu.edu
E-mail: yesciu@ciu.edu
See listing under "Theological Studies & Religious
Vocations"

Converse College
580 E Main St, Spartanburg SC 29302-0006
864-596-9000

Erskine College & Seminary
PO Box 176, Due West SC 29639
Bart Walker, Director of Admissions
864-379-8838 Fax: 864-379-3048
Website: www.erskine.edu
E-mail: admissions@erskine.edu

Francis Marion University
PO Box 100547, Florence SC 29501-0547
843-661-1362

Furman University
3300 Poinsett Hwy, Greenville SC 29613-0002
864-294-2000

Lander University
320 Stanley Ave, Greenwood SC 29649-2099
Jonathan Reece, Director of Admissions
888-4-LANDER

Limestone College
1115 College Dr, Gaffney SC 29340-3799
Chris Phenicie, V.P. for Enrollment
864-489-7151 Fax: 864-488-8206
Website: www.limestone.edu
E-mail: cphenicie@limestone.edu

Morris College
100 W College St, Sumter SC 29150-3599
803-934-3200

Newberry College
2100 College St, Newberry SC 29108-2197
800-845-4955

North Greenville University
PO Box 1892, Tigerville SC 29688-1892
Dr. Robin Johnson, Dept. Chair
Website: www.ngc.edu
See listing under "Universities"

PRESBYTERIAN COLLEGE
503 S Broad St, Clinton SC 29325
Richard Dana Paul, Dean of Admissions
800-476-7272 Fax: 864-833-8481
Website: www.presby.edu
E-mail: admissions@presby.edu

South Carolina State University
PO Box 7127, Orangeburg SC 29117-0001
Lillian M. Adderson, Director of Admissions
803-536-7185

Southern Wesleyan University
PO Box 1020, Central SC 29630-1020
864-644-5000

University of South Carolina
Columbia SC 29208-0001
803-777-7700

University of South Carolina - Upstate
800 University Way, Spartanburg SC 29303-4932
Donette Stewart, Assistant VC for Enrollment Services
864-503-5246 Fax: 864-503-5727
Website: www.uscupstate.edu
E-mail: dstewart@uscupstate.edu
See listing under "Universities"

Winthrop University
701 W Oakland Ave, Rock Hill SC 29733-0001
803-323-2211

Wofford College
429 N Church St, Spartanburg SC 29303-3663
864-597-4000

SOUTH DAKOTA

Augustana College
29th and South Smt, Sioux Falls SD 57197-0001
605-274-0770

Black Hills State University
1200 University St, Spearfish SD 57799-0002
605-642-6011

Dakota State University
820 N Washington Ave, Madison SD 57042-1799
605-256-5112

Dakota Wesleyan University
1200 W University Ave, Mitchell SD 57301
605-995-2600

Mt. Marty College
1105 W 8th St, Yankton SD 57078-3724
605-668-1514

South Dakota State University
PO Box 2201, Brookings SD 57007-0001
605-688-4151

University of Sioux Falls
1101 W 22nd St, Sioux Falls SD 57105-1699
605-331-5000

University of South Dakota
414 E Clark St, Vermillion SD 57069-2307
605-677-5011

TENNESSEE

Aquinas College
4210 Harding Pike, Nashville TN 37205-2086
Diane C. LeJeune, Director of Admissions
615-297-7545 ext. 460 Fax: 615-297-7970
Website: www.aquinas-tn.edu
E-mail: lejeuned@aquinas-tn.edu

Austin Peay State University
601 College St, Clarksville TN 37044-0002
931-221-7011

Belmont University
1900 Belmont Blvd, Nashville TN 37212-3757
615-460-6000

Bryan College
PO Box 7000, Dayton TN 37321-7000
423-775-2041

Carson-Newman College
1646 Russell Ave, Jefferson City TN 37760
865-471-4000

Christian Brothers University
650 E Parkway S, Memphis TN 38104-5568
901-321-3000

East Tennessee State University
PO Box 70685, Johnson City TN 37614
Dr. Martha Collins, Dean of Education
423-439-7626

Freed-Hardeman University
158 E Main St, Henderson TN 38340-2398
731-989-6000

King College
1350 King College Rd, Bristol TN 37620-2635
423-968-1187

Lee University
PO Box 3450, Cleveland TN 37320-3450
Debbie Murray, Dean of the College of Education
800-533-9930

Le Moyne-Owen College
807 Walker Ave, Memphis TN 38126-6595
901-774-9090

Lincoln Memorial University
PO Box 2012, Harrogate TN 37752
423-869-3611

Lipscomb University
3901 Granny White Pike, Nashville TN 37204-3951
Ricky Holaway, Director of Admissions
800-333-4358 ext. 1776 Fax: 615-269-1804
Website: www.lipscomb.edu
E-mail: admissions@lipscomb.edu

Maryville College
502 E Lamar Alexander Pkwy
Maryville TN 37804-5919
865-981-8000

Middle Tennessee State University
1301 E Main St, Murfreesboro TN 37132-0001
615-898-2300

Milligan College
1 Milligan College, Milligan College TN 37682
423-461-8700

Peabody College of Vanderbilt University
Box 327, Nashville TN 37203
615-322-8410

Tennessee State University
3500 John A Merritt Blvd, Nashville TN 37209-1561
John Cade, Dean of Admissions & Records
615-963-5101 Fax: 615-963-2930
Website: www.tnstate.edu
E-mail: jcade@tnstate.edu

Tennessee Technological University
PO Box 5006, Cookeville TN 38505-0001
931-372-3101

Tennessee Temple University
1815 Union Ave, Chattanooga TN 37404-3587
423-493-4100

Trevecca Nazarene University
333 Murfreesboro Rd, Nashville TN 37210-2834
615-248-1200

Tusculum College
PO Box 5051, Greeneville TN 37743
Melissa Ripley, Associate Director of Admissions
800-729-0256 Fax: 423-798-1622
Website: www.tusculum.edu
E-mail: mripley@tusculum.edu

Union University
1050 Union University Dr, Jackson TN 38305
731-668-1818

University of Memphis
Memphis TN 38152-0001
901-678-2000

University of Tennessee
615 McCallie Ave, Chattanooga TN 37403-2504
Yancy Freeman, Director of Admissions
423-425-4111 Fax: 423-425-4157
Website: www.utc.edu
E-mail: Yancy-Freeman@utc.edu

University of Tennessee
527 Andy Holt Tower, Knoxville TN 37996-0001
865-974-1000

University of Tennessee
Martin TN 38238-0001
731-587-7000

TEXAS

Angelo State University
ASU Station 11014, San Angelo TX 76909
Bonnie Stennett, Coordinator of Recruiting
800-946-8627 Fax: 325-942-2078
Website: www.angelo.edu
E-mail: admissions@angelo.edu

Arlington Baptist College
3001 W Division St, Arlington TX 76012-3425
Janie Taylor, Director of Admissions
817-461-8741 Fax: 817-274-1138
Website: www.abconline.edu
E-mail: jhall@abconline.org

Austin College
900 N Grand Ave, Sherman TX 75090-4400
903-813-2000

Baylor University
Po Box 97008, Waco TX 76798-7008
254-710-1011

Concordia University
3400 N I H 35, Austin TX 78705-2702
512-486-2000

Dallas Baptist University
3000 Mountain Creek Pkwy, Dallas TX 75211-9209
214-333-7100

East Texas Baptist University
1209 N Grove St, Marshall TX 75670-1498
903-935-7963

Lamar State College-Orange
410 W Front St, Orange TX 77630-5899
Rebecca Campbell, Registrar
409-883-7750 Fax: 409-882-3055
Website: www.lsco.edu
E-mail: becky.campbell@lsco.edu

Lamar University
PO Box 10009, Beaumont TX 77710-0009
409-880-8661

Midwestern State University
3410 Taft Blvd, Wichita Falls TX 76308-2096
940-397-4000

Our Lady of the Lake University
411 SW 24th St, San Antonio TX 78207-4666
Mary Kay Cooper, Dean of Enrollment
210-434-6711 Fax: 210-431-4013
Website: www.ollusa.edu
E-mail: admission@lakeollusa.edu

Prairie View A&M University
PO Box 188, Prairie View TX 77446
936-857-3311

St. Edward's University
3001 S Congress Ave, Austin TX 78704-6489
512-448-8400

St. Mary's University of San Antonio
1 Camino Santa Maria St
San Antonio TX 78228-8500
210-436-3011

Sam Houston State University
PO Box 2026, Huntsville TX 77341
936-294-1111

Schreiner University
2100 Memorial Blvd, Kerrville TX 78028-5697
Todd D. Brown, Director of Admissions
800-343-4919

Southern Methodist University
PO Box 750181, Dallas TX 75275-0181
Ron Moss, Dean of Admission
214-768-2058

Stephen F. Austin State University
PO Box 6078, Nacogdoches TX 75962-0001
936-468-2011

Texas A&M University
College Station TX 77843-0001
979-845-3211

Texas A&M University
700 University Blvd, Kingsville TX 78363
361-593-2111

Texas A&M University - Corpus Christi
6300 Ocean Dr, Corpus Christi TX 78412-5503
361-825-5700

Texas Christian University
TCU Box 297013, Fort Worth TX 76129
817-257-7000

Texas Lutheran University
1000 W Court St, Seguin TX 78155-5978
830-372-8000

Texas Southern University
3100 Cleburne St, Houston TX 77004-4583
713-313-7011

Texas Tech University
1 Texas Tech University, Lubbock TX 79409-0001
806-742-2011

Texas Wesleyan University
1201 Wesleyan St, Fort Worth TX 76105-1536
Stephanie Boatner, Director of Freshman Admission
800-580-8980

Texas Woman's University
PO Box 425589, Denton TX 76204-5589
Erma Nieto, Director of Admissions
866-809-6130 Fax: 940-898-3081
Website: www.twu.edu
E-mail: admissions@twu.edu

Trinity University
715 Stadium Dr, San Antonio TX 78212-7200
210-999-7011

University of Dallas
1845 E Northgate Dr, Irving TX 75062-4736
972-721-5000

University of Houston
122 E Cullen Bldg, Houston TX 77204-2023
Office of Admission
713-743-9595
Website: www.uh.edu
E-mail: admissions@uh.edu

University of Houston-Clear Lake
2700 Bay Area Blvd, Houston TX 77058-1025
281-283-2500

University of Mary Hardin-Baylor
UMHB Station Box 8001, Belton TX 76513
254-295-8642

University of St. Thomas
3800 Montrose Blvd, Houston TX 77006-4626
Eduardo Prieto, Director of Admissions
713-522-7911 Fax: 713-525-3558
Website: www.stthom.edu
E-mail: prietoe@stthom.edu

University of Texas at Arlington
Box 19111, Arlington TX 76019-0111
Hans Gatterdam, Director of Admission
817-272-6287 Fax: 817-272-3435
Website: www.uta.edu
E-mail: admissions@uta.edu

University of Texas at Austin
0 the Univ of Texas, Austin TX 78712
512-471-3434

University of Texas at San Antonio
6900 N Loop 1604 W, San Antonio TX 78249-1130
210-458-4011

University of Texas at Tyler
3900 University Blvd, Tyler TX 75701-6622
Jim Hutto, Dean Enrollment Management
800-888-9537

University of the Incarnate Word
4301 Broadway St, San Antonio TX 78209-6318
210-829-6000

Wayland Baptist University
1900 W 7th St, Plainview TX 79072-6998
806-296-5521

West Texas A & M University
WTAMU Box 907, Canyon TX 79016-0001
806-651-2000

UTAH

Brigham Young University
Provo UT 84602-0001
801-378-5000

Southern Utah University
351 W Center St, Cedar City UT 84720-2470
Prent Klag, Dept. Chair
435-586-7803

University of Utah
1460 E 201 S, Salt Lake City UT 84112
801-581-7200

Utah State University
Logan UT 84322-0001
435-797-1000

Westminster College
1840 S 1300 E, Salt Lake City UT 84105-3617
801-832-2200

VERMONT

Bennington College
One College Drive, Bennington VT 05201
Ken Himmelman, Dean of Admissions & Financial Aid
800-833-6845 Fax: 802-440-4320
Website: www.bennington.edu
E-mail: admissions@bennington.edu

Castleton State College
Castleton VT 05735
William Allen Jr., Dean of Enrollment
800-639-8521

College of St. Joseph
71 Clement Rd, Rutland VT 05701-3899
802-773-5900

Goddard College
121 Pitkin Rd, Plainfield VT 05667
802-454-8311

Green Mountain College
1 College Cir, Poultney VT 05764-1199
802-287-8000

Johnson State College
337 College Hill, Johnson VT 05656
802-635-2356

Lyndon State College
PO Box 919, Lyndonville VT 05851
802-626-6200

NORWICH UNIVERSITY
158 Harmon Dr, Northfield VT 05663
Dr. Diane Byrne, Program Director
800-468-6679 Fax: 802-485-2364
Website: www.norwich.edu
E-mail: dbryne@norwich.edu

Saint Michael's College
One Winooski Park, Colchester VT 05439-0001
Jacqueline Murphy, Director
802-654-3000

University of Vermont
194 S Prospect St, Burlington VT 05401-3518
802-656-3131

VIRGINIA

Averett University
420 W Main St, Danville VA 24541-3692
804-791-5600

Bluefield College
3000 College Dr, Bluefield VA 24605-1799
276-326-3682

Bridgewater College
402 E College St, Bridgewater VA 22812-1599
540-828-8000

Christopher Newport University
1 University Pl, Newport News VA 23606
757-594-7000

College of William and Mary
PO Box 8795, Williamsburg VA 23187-8795
757-221-4000

Eastern Mennonite University
1200 Park Rd, Harrisonburg VA 22802-2404
540-432-4000

Emory & Henry College
PO Box 947, Emory VA 24327-0947
276-944-4121

Ferrum College
PO Box 1000, Ferrum VA 24088-9001
Gilda Q. Woods, Director of Admissions
800-868-9797

George Mason University
4400 University Dr, Fairfax VA 22030-4444
Dr. Jack Levy, Chairperson
703-993-2144

Hampton University
Hampton VA 23669
757-727-5000

James Madison University
800 S Main St, Harrisonburg VA 22807-0002
540-568-6211

Liberty University
PO Box 20000, Lynchburg VA 24506-8001
804-582-2000

Longwood University
201 High St, Farmville VA 23909-1801
804-395-2000

Lynchburg College
1501 Lakeside Dr, Lynchburg VA 24501-3199
804-544-8100

Mary Baldwin College
Staunton VA 24401
Lisa A. Branson, Executive Director of Admissions and Financial Aid
800-468-2262 Fax: 540-887-7292
Website: www.mbc.edu
E-mail: admit@mbc.edu

Marymount University
2807 N Glebe Rd, Arlington VA 22207-4299
703-522-5600

Norfolk State University
700 Park Ave, Norfolk VA 23504
Michelle Marable, Director of Admissions
757-823-8600

Old Dominion University
1 Old Dominion University, Norfolk VA 23529-1000
757-683-3000

Radford University
PO Box 6903, Radford VA 24142
David W. Kraus, Director of Admissions
800-890-4265 Fax: 540-831-5038
Website: www.radford.edu
E-mail: ruadmiss@radford.edu

Randolph-Macon College
PO Box 5005, Ashland VA 23005-5505
804-752-7200

Randolph-Macon Woman's College
2500 Rivermont Ave, Lynchburg VA 24503
Patricia LeDonne, Director of Admissions
434-947-8100 Fax: 434-947-8996
Website: www.rmwc.edu
E-mail: admissions@rmwc.edu

Roanoke College
221 College Ln, Salem VA 24153-3794
540-375-2500

St. Paul's College
406 Windsor Ave, Lawrenceville VA 23868-1202
804-848-3111

Shenandoah University
1460 University Dr, Winchester VA 22601-5195
Michael D. Carpenter, Director of Admissions
800-432-2266

Southside Virginia Community College
109 Campus Dr, Alberta VA 23821-2930
Ronald E. Mattox, Dean of Admissions
434-949-1014 Fax: 434-949-7863
Website: www.sv.vccs.edu
E-mail: ronald.mattox@sv.vccs.edu

Southside Virginia Community College
200 Daniel Rd, Keysville VA 23947
Ronald E. Mattox, Dean of Admissions
434-736-2018 Fax: 434-736-2082
Website: www.sv.vccs.edu
E-mail: ronald.mattox@sv.vccs.edu

University of Richmond
Richmond VA 23173
804-289-8000

University of Virginia
PO Box 400160, Charlottesville VA 22904
804-924-0311

University of Virginia College at Wise
1 College Ave, Wise VA 24293
276-328-0100

Virginia Commonwealth University
901 W Franklin St, Richmond VA 23284
804-828-0100

Virginia Intermont College
1013 Moore St, Bristol VA 24201-4225
540-669-6101

Virginia Polytechnic Institute & State University
Blacksburg VA 24061
540-231-6000

Virginia State University
1 Hayden Dr, Petersburg VA 23806-0001
804-524-5000

Virginia Wesleyan College
1584 Wesleyan Dr, Norfolk VA 23502-5599
757-455-3200

WASHINGTON

Antioch University
2326 6th Ave, Seattle WA 98121
Pam Smith Mentz, Director of Enrollment Services
888-268-4477

BATES TECHNICAL COLLEGE
1101 S Yakima Ave, Tacoma WA 98405-4895
David Borofsky, President
253-680-7000 Fax: 253-680-7101
Website: www.bates.ctc.edu
E-mail: info@bates.ctc.edu

Central Washington University
400 E University Way, Ellensburg WA 98926
William Swain, Director of Admissions
509-963-3001

City University
11900 NE 1st St, Bellevue WA 98005-3030
800-426-5596

Eastern Washington University
Cheney WA 99004
509-359-6200

Gonzaga University
502 E Boone Ave, Spokane WA 99258-0102
Julie McCulloh, Dean of Admission
800-322-2584 or 509-323-6572 Fax: 509-323-5780
Website: www.gonzaga.edu
E-mail: mcculloh@gu.gonzaga.edu

Pacific Lutheran University
12180 Park Ave S, Tacoma WA 98447-0014
David E. Gunovich, Director of Admissions
253-535-7151

St. Martin's University
5300 Pacific Ave SE, Lacey WA 98503-1297
360-491-4700

Seattle Pacific University
3307 3rd Ave W, Seattle WA 98119-1997
206-281-2000

Seattle University
900 Broadway, Seattle WA 98122-4340
206-296-6000

University of Puget Sound
1500 N Warner St, Tacoma WA 98416-0005
253-879-3100

Walla Walla College
204 S College Ave, College Place WA 99324-1198
509-527-2615

Washington State University
1 SE Stadium Way, Pullman WA 99164-0001
509-335-3564

Wenatchee Valley College
1300 5th St, Wenatchee WA 98801-1799
Marco Azurdia, Dean, Student Development
509-682-6805 Fax: 509-682-6541
Website: www.wvc.edu

Western Washington University
516 High St, Bellingham WA 98225-5996
360-650-3000

Whitworth College
300 W Hawthorne Rd, Spokane WA 99251-0001
Fred Pfursich, Dean of Admissions & Financial Aid
800-533-4668

WEST VIRGINIA

Alderson-Broaddus College
Philippi WV 26416
Eric A. Ruf, Director of Admissions
800-263-1549

Bethany College
Bethany WV 26032
304-829-7000

Bluefield State College
219 Rock St, Bluefield WV 24701-2198
304-327-4000

Concord University
Athens WV 24712
Michael Curry, Vice President of Financial Aid & Admissions
888-384-5249 Fax: 304-384-3218
Website: www.concord.edu
E-mail: admissions@concord.edu

Davis & Elkins College
100 Campus Dr, Elkins WV 26241-3996
Renee Heckel, Director of Enrollment Management
800-624-3157 Fax: 304-637-1800
Website: www.davisandelkins.edu
E-mail: admiss@davisandelkins.edu

Fairmont State University
1201 Locust Ave, Fairmont WV 26554-2470
Steve Leadman, Director of Admissions
304-367-4241 or 800-641-5678 Fax: 304-367-4789
Website: www.fairmontstate.edu
E-mail: admit@fairmontstate.edu

Glenville State College
200 High St, Glenville WV 26351-1200
304-462-4128

Marshall University
400 Hal Greer Blvd, Huntington WV 25755-0003
304-696-3170

Salem International University
PO Box 500, Salem WV 26426-0500
304-782-5011

University of Charleston
2300 MacCorkle Ave SE, Charleston WV 25304-1099
304-357-4800

West Liberty State College
PO Box 295, West Liberty WV 26074
304-336-5000

West Virginia State University
PO Box 1000, Institute WV 25112-1000
304-766-3000

West Virginia University
PO Box 6001, Morgantown WV 26506-6001
304-293-0111

West Virginia Wesleyan College
59 College Ave, Buckhannon WV 26201-2699
Robert N. Skinner II, Director of Admission
800-722-9933 Fax: 304-473-8108
Website: www.wvwc.edu
E-mail: admission@wvwc.edu

WISCONSIN

Alverno College
PO Box 343922, Milwaukee WI 53234-3922
Mary Kay Farrell, Director of Admissions
414-382-6100 Fax: 414-382-6354
Website: www.alverno.edu
E-mail: admissions@alverno.edu

Beloit College
700 College St, Beloit WI 53511-5596
Thomas Warren, Chairperson
608-363-2336

Cardinal Stritch University
6801 N Yates Rd, Milwaukee WI 53217-3985
414-410-4000

Carroll College
100 N East Ave, Waukesha WI 53186-5593
James Wiseman, Dean of Admissions
800-CARROLL

Carthage College
2001 Alford Park Dr, Kenosha WI 53140-1994
262-551-6000

Concordia University
12800 N Lake Shore Dr, Mequon WI 53097-2402
262-243-5700

Edgewood College
1000 Edgewood College Dr, Madison WI 53711
608-663-4861

Lakeland College
PO Box 359, Sheboygan WI 53082-0359
Nathan Dehne, Director of Admission
920-565-1100 Fax: 920-565-1215
Website: www.lakeland.edu
E-mail: admissions@lakeland.edu

Marian College of Fond du Lac
45 S National Ave, Fond du Lac WI 54935-4621
Eric Peterson, Dean of Admission
800-262-7426 ext. 7650

Marquette University
PO Box 1881, Milwaukee WI 53201-1881
Robert Blust, Director of Admissions
414-288-7302 Fax: 414-288-3764
Website: www.mu.edu
E-mail: admissions@marquette.edu

Mount Mary College
2900 N Menomonee River Pkwy
Milwaukee WI 53222-4597
414-256-1219

Northland College
1411 Ellis Ave, Ashland WI 54806-3999
800-753-1840

Ripon College
PO Box 248, Ripon WI 54971-0248
920-748-8115

St. Norbert College
100 Grant St, De Pere WI 54115
Brian Studebaker, Director of Admission
800-236-4878 Fax: 920-403-4072
Website: www.snc.edu
E-mail: admit@snc.edu

Silver Lake College
2406 S Alverno Rd, Manitowoc WI 54220-9319
920-684-6691

University of Wisconsin
PO Box 4004, Eau Claire WI 54702
715-836-2637

University of Wisconsin
PO Box 2000, Kenosha WI 53141-2000
262-595-2345

University of Wisconsin
1 University Plz, Platteville WI 53818-3001
Angela Udelhofen, Recruitment Manager
608-342-1200

University of Wisconsin
410 S 3rd St, River Falls WI 54022
715-425-3911

University of Wisconsin
PO Box 2000, Superior WI 54880
715-394-8101

University of Wisconsin
800 W Main St, Whitewater WI 53190-1705
262-472-1234

University of Wisconsin Green Bay
2420 Nicolet Dr, Green Bay WI 54311-7003
Pamela Harvey-Jacobs, Interim Director of Admissions
920-465-2111

University of Wisconsin in La Crosse
115 Graff Main Hall, La Crosse WI 54601
Tim Lewis, Director of Admissions
608-785-8939

University of Wisconsin - Oshkosh
800 Algoma Blvd, Oshkosh WI 54901-8602
920-424-0202

University of Wisconsin-Stout
124 Bowman Hall, Menomonie WI 54751-2662
715-232-1123

Viterbo University
815 9th St S, La Crosse WI 54601-8802
608-796-3000

WYOMING

University of Wyoming
Admissions Office
Dept 3435, Laramie WY 82071-3435
Aaron Appelhans, Contact
800-342-5996 Fax: 307-766-4042
Website: www.uwyo.edu
E-mail: why-wyo@uwyo.edu

GUAM

Guam Community College
PO Box 23069, G.M.F. GU 96921-0307
Virginia Charfauros Tudela, Ph.D., Registrar
671-735-5531 Fax: 671-734-5238
Website: www.guamcc.edu
E-mail: Webmaster@guamcc.edu

University of Guam
UOG Station, Mangilao GU 96923
Deborah Leon Guerrero, Registrar
671-735-2201 or 671-735-2208 Fax: 671-735-2203
Website: www.uog.edu
E-mail: admitme@uog9.uog.edu

PUERTO RICO

Bayamon Central University
PO Box 1725, Bayamon PR 00960-1725
787-786-3030

Pontifical Catholic University of Puerto Rico
2250 Ave Las Americas, Ponce PR 00717-0777
787-841-2000

Universidad Adventista de las Antillas
PO Box 118, Mayaguez PR 00919-0118
Evelyn Del Valle Rivera, Director of Admissions
787-834-9595 Fax: 787-834-9597
Website: www.uaa.edu
E-mail: admissions@uaa.edu

University of Puerto Rico
R Ave Antonio R Barcelo, Cayey PR 00736-5534
787-738-2161

University of Puerto Rico
CUH Station Rd 908 Bo Tejas, Humacao PR 00791
787-850-0000

University of Puerto Rico
PO Box 23303, Rio Piedras PR 00931-3303
787-764-0000

University of Puerto Rico at Arecibo
PO Box 4010, Arecibo PR 00614
787-815-0000

University of Puerto Rico at Ponce
PO Box 7186, Ponce PR 00732-7186
787-844-6161

University of Puerto Rico
Bayamn University College
Carretera 174, Km 2.8, Bayamn PR 00959
787-786-2885

THEOLOGICAL STUDIES & RELIGIOUS VOCATIONS

ALABAMA

Faulkner University
5345 Atlanta Hwy, Montgomery AL 36109-3398
Keith Mock, Director of Admissions
800-879-9816 ext. 7200 or 334-386-7200
Fax: 334-386-7137
Website: www.faulkner.edu
E-mail: admissions@faulkner.edu

HUNTSVILLE BIBLE COLLEGE
PO Box 3493, Huntsville AL 35810
John Clay, Contact
256-539-0834 Fax: 256-539-0854
Website: www.huntsvillebiblecollege.com
E-mail: hbc@huntsvillebiblecollege.com

Judson College
302 Bibb St, Marion AL 36756
Michael Scotto, Director of Admissions
800-447-9472 Fax: 334-683-5147
Website: www.judson.edu
E-mail: admissions@judson.edu

Southeastern Bible College
2545 Valleydale Rd, Birmingham AL 35244
Lynn Gannett-Malick, Director of Enrollment
Management
800-749-8878 Fax: 205-970-9207
Website: www.sebc.edu
E-mail: admissions@sebc.edu

ALASKA

ALASKA BIBLE COLLEGE
PO Box 289, Glennallen AK 99588-0289
907-822-3201 Fax: 907-822-5027
Website: www.akbible.edu
E-mail: info@akbible.edu

ARIZONA

Southwestern College
2625 E Cactus Rd, Phoenix AZ 85032-7097
Admissions/Financial Aid Office
800-247-2697 or 602-992-6101 Fax: 602-404-2159
Website: www.swcaz.edu
E-mail: admissions@swcaz.edu

ARKANSAS

Ouachita Baptist University
410 Ouachita St, Arkadelphia AR 71998-0001
David Goodman, Director of Admissions
870-245-5110 Fax: 870-245-5500
Website: www.obu.edu
E-mail: admissions@obu.edu

CALIFORNIA

AMERICAN BAPTIST SEMINARY OF THE WEST
2606 Dwight Way, Berkeley CA 94704-3029
510-841-1905 Fax: 510-841-2446
Website: www.absw.edu
E-mail: admissions@absw.edu

Chapman University
One University Drive, Orange CA 92866-1099
Michael Drummy, Assistant Vice President for
Enrollment
Services and Chief Admission Officer
714-997-6411 or 888-CUAPPLY Fax: 714-997-6713
Website: www.chapman.edu
E-mail: admit@chapman.edu

CHURCH DIVINITY SCHOOL OF THE PACIFIC
2451 Ridge Rd, Berkeley CA 94709-1217
Kathleen Crisp, Director of Admissions and
Recruitment
510-204-0715 Fax: 510-204-0749
Website: www.cdsp.edu
E-mail: admissions@cdsp.edu

COMMUNITY CHRISTIAN COLLEGE
251 Tennessee St, Redlands CA 92373
909-335-8863 Fax: 909-335-9101
Website: www.cccollege.net
E-mail: admin@cccollege.net

Concordia University
1530 Concordia, Irvine CA 92612-3203
Lori McDonald, Executive Director of Enrollment
Services
800-229-1200 or 949-854-8002 Fax: 949-854-6894
Website: www.cui.edu
E-mail: admission@cui.edu

DOMINICAN SCHOOL OF PHILOSOPHY & THEOLOGY
2301 Vine St, Berkeley CA 94708
John Knutsen, Director of Admissions
888-450-DSPT or 510-883-2073 Fax: 510-849-1372
Website: www.dspt.edu
E-mail: admissions@dspt.edu

GRADUATE THEOLOGICAL UNION
2400 Ridge Rd, Berkeley CA 94709-1212
Kathleen Kook, Assistant Dean for Admissions
800-826-4488 Fax: 510-649-1730
Website: www.gtu.edu
E-mail: gtuadm@gtu.edu

HEBREW UNION COLLEGE - JEWISH INSTITUTE OF RELIGION
3077 University Ave, Los Angeles CA 90007-3796
Dr. Matt Albert, Regional Director of Admissions and
Recruitment
213-749-3424 Fax: 213-747-6128
Website: www.huc.edu
E-mail: malbert@huc.edu

JESUIT SCHOOL OF THEOLOGY AT BERKELEY
1735 LeRoy Ave, Berkeley CA 94709-1193
Rev. Joseph P. Daoust SJ, President
Patricia Abracia, Director of Admissions
800-824-0122 or 510-549-5000 Fax: 510-841-8536
Website: www.jstb.edu
E-mail: admissions@jstb.edu
See listing under "Graduate Schools"

San Diego Christian College
2100 Greenfield Dr, El Cajon CA 92019-1157
Jon Melone, Director of Admissions
800-676-2242 Fax: 619-590-1739
Website: www.sdcc.edu
E-mail: admissions@sdcc.edu

Simpson University
2211 College View Dr, Redding CA 96003-8606
Jim Herberger, Director of Admissions
888-9-SIMPSON Fax: 530-226-4861
Website: www.simpsonuniversity.edu
E-mail: admissions@simpsonuniversity.edu
See listing under "Liberal Arts and Sciences"

SOUTHERN CALIFORNIA SEMINARY
2075 E Madison Ave, El Cajon CA 92019
Ed Herrelko, Director of Student Services
619-442-9841 Fax: 619-442-4510
Website: www.socalsem.edu
E-mail: info@socalsem.edu

COLORADO

Denver Seminary
6399 S Santa Fe Dr, Littleton CO 80120
Robert Fomer, VP Student Services
303-762-6982 Fax: 303-783-3122
Website: denverseminary.edu
E-mail: bob.fomer@denverseminary.edu

ILIFF SCHOOL OF THEOLOGY
2201 S University Blvd, Denver CO 80210-4798
Peggy Blocker, Director of Admissions
800-678-3360 or 303-765-3112 Fax: 303-777-0164
Website: www.iliff.edu
E-mail: admissions@iliff.edu

Nazarene Bible College
1111 Academy Park Loop
Colorado Springs CO 80910-3717
Dr. Laurel Matson, VP for Enrollment & Student
Development
719-596-5110 Fax: 719-884-5199
Website: www.nbc.edu
E-mail: admissions@nbc.edu

CONNECTICUT

HARTFORD SEMINARY
77 Sherman St, Hartford CT 06105-2260
Kelton Cobb, Seminary Academic Advisor
860-509-9513 Fax: 860-509-9509
Website: www.hartsem.edu
E-mail: info@hartsem.edu

FLORIDA

THE BAPTIST COLLEGE OF FLORIDA
5400 College Dr, Graceville FL 32440-1831
Christopher M. Bishop, Director of Admissions
800-328-2660 Fax: 850-263-9026
Website: www.baptistcollege.edu
E-mail: admissions@baptistcollege.edu

NORTH TENNESSEE BIBLE INSTITUTE AND SEMINARY
556 W Bayshore Dr, Eastpoint FL 32328
Dr. Celeste Wall, President
850-927-4711
Website: www.ntbis.com
E-mail: drwhc@ntbis.com

Saint Leo University
PO Box 6665, Saint Leo FL 33574
Deborah Bandy, Director of Admissions
352-588-8200 or 800-334-5532 Fax: 352-588-8257
Website: www.saintleo.edu
E-mail: admission@saintleo.edu

St. Thomas University
16401 NW 37th Ave, Miami Gardens FL 33054
Dr. Thomas Ryan, Department Chair
800-367-9010 or 305-628-6546 Fax: 305-628-6591
Website: www.stu.edu
E-mail: signup@stu.edu

St. Vincent DePaul Regional Seminary
10701 S Military Trl, Boynton Beach FL 33436-4899
Rev. Steven O'Hala, Academic Dean
561-732-2424 ext. 151 Fax: 561-732-8808
Website: www.svdp.edu
E-mail: sohala@svdp.edu
M.Div and M.A.

Trinity Baptist College
800-200 Hammond Blvd, Jacksonville FL 32221
R. Larry Appleby, Director of Admissions
904-596-2400 Fax: 904-596-2531
Website: www.tbc.edu
E-mail: emailtrinity@tbc.edu

TRINITY COLLEGE OF FLORIDA
2430 Welbilt Blvd, Trinity FL 34655-4401
Dr. David Colburn, VP of Enrollment & Adult Education
727-376-6911 Fax: 727-376-0781
Website: www.trinitycollege.edu
E-mail: tquest2@trinitycollege.edu
See listing under "Universities"

GEORGIA

BEULAH HEIGHTS BIBLE COLLEGE
PO Box 18145, Atlanta GA 30316-0145
Dr. James B. Keiller, V.P. & Dean of Academic Affairs
404-627-2681 Fax: 404-627-0702
Website: www.beulah.org
E-mail: bhbc@beulah.org

INTERDENOMINATIONAL THEOLOGICAL CENTER
700 Martin Luther King Jr Dr SW
Atlanta GA 30314-4143
Walter Cabassa, Recruitment Coordinator
404-527-7792 Fax: 404-527-0901
Website: www.itc.edu
E-mail: wcabassa@itc.edu

Luther Rice University
3038 Evans Mill Rd, Lithonia GA 30038
Russ Sorrow, Director of Enrollment Management
770-484-1204 Fax: 770-484-1155
Website: www.lru.edu
E-mail: admissions@lru.edu

TOCCOA FALLS COLLEGE
PO Box 800899, Toccoa Falls GA 30598
Christy Meadows, Director of Admissions
888-785-5624 Fax: 706-282-6012
Website: www.tfc.edu
E-mail: admissions@tfc.edu

HAWAII

HAWAII THEOLOGICAL SEMINARY
PO Box 861754, Wahiawa HI 96786
Kevin Gilbert, President
808-622-4487 Fax: 808-595-4779
Website: www.hits.edu
E-mail: info@hits.edu

IDAHO

Brigham Young University - Idaho
120 Kimball Bldg, Rexburg ID 83460
Gordon Westenskow, Director of Admissions
208-496-1020 Fax: 208-496-1220
Website: www.byui.edu
E-mail: admissions@byui.edu

ILLINOIS

CONCORDIA UNIVERSITY
7400 Augusta St, River Forest IL 60305-1402
708-209-3100 Fax: 708-209-3473
Website: www.curf.edu
E-mail: crfadmis.edu

LUTHERAN SCHOOL OF THEOLOGY AT CHICAGO
1100 E 55th St, Chicago IL 60615-5199
Rev. Brian Halverson, Director of Admissions
800-635-1116 ext. 726 or 773-256-0726
Fax: 773-256-0782
Website: www.lstc.edu
E-mail: admissions@lstc.edu

MCCORMICK THEOLOGICAL SEMINARY
5460 S University Ave, Chicago IL 60615
Rev. Craig Howard, Director of Recruitment and
Admissions
800-228-4687 Fax: 773-288-2612
Website: www.mccormick.edu
E-mail: admit@mccormick.edu

North Central College
30 N Brainard St, Naperville IL 60540-4690
Martha Stolze, Director of Admissions
630-637-5800 Fax: 630-637-5819
Website: www.northcentralcollege.edu
E-mail: admissions@noctrl.edu

NORTHERN BAPTIST THEOLOGICAL SEMINARY
660 E Butterfield Rd, Lombard IL 60148-5698
Charles Dresser, Executive Director of Enrollment Management
630-620-2180 Fax: 630-620-2190
Website: www.seminary.edu
E-mail: admissions@seminary.edu

Spertus College
618 S Michigan Ave, Chicago IL 60605-1901
312-922-9012 Fax: 312-922-6406
Website: www.spertus.edu
E-mail: college@spertus.edu

INDIANA

ASSOCIATED MENNONITE BIBLICAL SEMINARIES
3003 Benham Ave, Elkhart IN 46517-1947
Randall C. Miller, Director of Admissions
800-964-2627 Fax: 574-295-0092
Website: www.ambs.edu
E-mail: admissions@ambs.edu

BETHANY THEOLOGICAL SEMINARY
615 National Rd W, Richmond IN 47374-4019
Dr. Eugene F. Roop, President
800-287-8822 Fax: 765-983-1840
Website: www.brethren.org/bethany
E-mail: bethanysem@aol.com

CHRISTIAN THEOLOGICAL SEMINARY
1000 W 42nd St, Indianapolis IN 46208-3301
Edward L. Wheeler, President
Mary L. Harris, Associate Dean for Student Services
800-585-0508 or 317-931-2300 Fax: 317-923-1961
Website: www.cts.edu
E-mail: admissions@cts.edu
  Private. Coed. Accreditation: ATS. Tuition: $325/hr. En-rollment: 140 full-time, 140 part-time. Faculty: 19. Student-faculty ratio: 14:1. Degrees: M.Div; MTS; MAMFT; MAPF. Ecumenical seminary committed to strong ministerial leadership with creative programs in the arts, counseling and worship.

Hanover College
PO Box 108, Hanover IN 47243-0108
William D. Preble, Dean of Admission
800-213-2178 Fax: 812-866-7098
Website: www.hanover.edu
E-mail: admissions@hanover.edu

Oakland City University
138 N Lucretia St, Oakland City IN 47660
Brian J. Baker, Director of Admissions
800-737-5125 Fax: 812-749-1433
Website: www.oak.edu
E-mail: bbaker@oak.edu
ATS Accredited.
See listing under "Universities"

St. Mary-of-the-Woods College
Saint Mary of the Woods IN 47876-1001
James P. Malley, Jr., Director of Admission
800-926-7692 Fax: 812-535-5010
Website: www.smwc.edu
E-mail: smwcadms@smwc.edu

University of Evansville
1800 Lincoln Ave, Evansville IN 47722-0001
Thomas E. Bear, V.P. of Enrollment Services
800-423-8633 Fax: 812-488-4076
Website: www.evansville.edu
E-mail: admission@evansville.edu

IOWA

Briar Cliff University
PO Box 2100, Sioux City IA 51104-0100
Sharisue Wilcoxon, VP for Enrollment Management
712-279-5200 Fax: 712-279-1632
Website: www.briarcliff.edu
E-mail: admissions@briarcliff.edu

Graceland University
1 University Place, Lamoni IA 50140
Brian Shantz, Vice President for Enrollment and Dean of Admissions
641-784-5196 Fax: 641-784-5480
Website: www.admissions.graceland.edu
E-mail: admissions@graceland.edu

UNIVERSITY OF DUBUQUE THEOLOGICAL SEMINARY
2000 University Ave, Dubuque IA 52001-5050
800-369-8387 Fax: 563-589-3110
Website: udtseminary.net
E-mail: udtsadms@dbq.edu

Waldorf College
106 S 6th St, Forest City IA 50436-1713
Steve Lovik, Vice President of Enrollment Management
800-292-1903 or 641-585-8112 Fax: 641-585-8125
Website: www.waldorf.edu
E-mail: loviks@waldorf.edu
See listing under "Universities"

Wartburg College
PO Box 1003, Waverly IA 50677-0903
Brent Matthias, Interim Director of Admissions
319-352-8200 Fax: 319-352-8579
Website: www.wartburg.edu
E-mail: admissions@wartburg.edu

WARTBURG THEOLOGICAL SEMINARY
PO Box 5004, Dubuque IA 52004-5004
Heather Devine, Director of Admissions
563-589-0200 Fax: 563-589-0333
Website: www.wartburgseminary.edu
E-mail: admissions@wartburgseminary.edu

KANSAS

Barclay College
607 N Kingman, Haviland KS 67059
Herb Frazier, Director of Admissions
800-862-0226 Fax: 620-862-5242
Website: www.barclaycollege.edu
E-mail: admissions@barclaycollege.edu

Newman University
3100 W McCormick St, Wichita KS 67213
Jann Reusser, Admissions Recruitment Coordinator
316-942-4291 ext. 2144 Fax: 316-942-4483
Website: www.newmanu.edu
E-mail: reusserj@newmanu.edu

Tabor College
400 S Jefferson St, Hillsboro KS 67063-1758
Rusty Allen, Dean of Enrollment Management
620-947-3121 Fax: 620-947-6276
Website: www.tabor.edu
E-mail: admissions@tabor.edu

KENTUCKY

LEXINGTON THEOLOGICAL SEMINARY
631 S Limestone, Lexington KY 40508-3288
Erika Smith, Director of Admissions
859-252-0361 Fax: 859-281-6042
Website: www.lextheo.edu
E-mail: esmith@lextheo.edu

Louisville Presbyterian Seminary
1044 Alta Vista Rd, Louisville KY 40205-1798
Kerry Rice, Director of Admissions
502-895-3411 or 800-264-1839 Fax: 502-992-9399
Website: www.lpts.edu
E-mail: admissions@lpts.edu
Degrees offered MDiv, MA, DMin, ThM

MID-CONTINENT UNIVERSITY
99 E Powell Rd, Mayfield KY 42066-9007
Butch Booth, Director of Admissions
800-894-8878 or 270-247-8521 ext. 244
Fax: 270-247-3115
Website: www.midcontinent.edu
E-mail: admissions@midcontinent.edu

Transylvania University
300 N Broadway, Lexington KY 40508-1776
859-233-8242 Fax: 859-233-8797
Website: www.transy.edu
E-mail: admissions@transy.edu

MARYLAND

::: Griggs University
PO Box 4437, Silver Spring MD 20914-4437
Anita L. Jacobs, Director of Admissions
301-680-6570 Fax: 301-680-6583
Website: www.griggs.edu
E-mail: registrar@griggs.edu

MAPLE SPRINGS BAPTIST BIBLE COLLEGE & SEMINARY
4130 Belt Rd, Capitol Heights MD 20743-5711
Rev. Percy V. Coker, Director of Admissions and Records
301-736-3631 Fax: 301-735-6507
Website: www.msbbcs.edu

MASSACHUSETTS

Anna Maria College
50 Sunset Ln, Paxton MA 01612
Julie A. Mitchell, Director of Admissions
508-849-3360 Fax: 508-849-3362
Website: www.annamaria.edu
E-mail: admissions@annamaria.edu

Assumption College
500 Salisbury St, Worcester MA 01609-1294
Kathleen Murphy, Dean of Enrollment
508-767-7000 Fax: 508-799-4412
Website: www.assumption.edu
E-mail: admiss@assumption.edu

Boston University
121 Bay State Rd, Boston MA 02215
Kelly Walter, Executive Director of Admissions
617-353-2300 Fax: 617-353-9695
Website: web.bu.edu
E-mail: admissions@bu.edu

Gordon College
255 Grapevine Rd, Wenham MA 01984-1899
Nancy Mering, Director of Admissions
866-464-6736 Fax: 978-867-4682
Website: www.gordon.edu
E-mail: admissions@gordon.edu

WESTON JESUIT SCHOOL OF THEOLOGY
3 Phillips Pl, Cambridge MA 02138-3418
Gustav A. Garzon, Director of Admissions
617-492-1960 Fax: 617-492-5833
Website: www.wjst.edu
E-mail: admissioninfo@wjst.edu
  Established 1922. Private. Coed. Accreditation: ATS. Tuition: $15,460 full-time/year. Fees: $600. Enrollment: 161 full-time, 55 part-time. Faculty: 19. Degrees: Master of Arts (MA), Master of Divinity (MDiv), Master of Theological Studies (MTS), Master of Theology (ThM), Licentiate in Sacred Theology (STL), Doctorate in Sacred Theology (STD). Library: 266,000 volumes. Roman Catholic seminary, sponsored by the Society of Jesus. Accepts lay people, women and men religious. Member of the Boston Theological Institute. Harvard Square location. International Theology Center.

MICHIGAN

Alma College
614 W Superior St, Alma MI 48801-1599
Anne Monroe, Director of Admissions
800-321-ALMA Fax: 989-463-7057
Website: www.alma.edu
E-mail: admissions@alma.edu

Andrews University
Berrien Springs MI 49104-0001
Randall Graves, Director of Recruitment Services
800-253-2874 Fax: 269-471-2670
Website: www.connect.andrews.edu
E-mail: gravesr@andrews.edu

CALVIN THEOLOGICAL SEMINARY
3233 Burton St SE, Grand Rapids MI 49546-4301
Greg Janke, Director of Admissions
616-957-6036 Fax: 616-957-8621
Website: www.calvinseminary.edu
E-mail: admissions@calvinseminary.edu

Concordia University
4090 Geddes Rd, Ann Arbor MI 48105-2797
Gary Neumann, Director of Admissions
734-995-7300 Fax: 734-995-4610
Website: www.cuaa.edu
E-mail: admissions@cuaa.edu

SAINTS CYRIL AND METHODIUS SEMINARY
3535 Indian Trl, Orchard Lake MI 48324-1623
Karen Shirilla, Academic Dean
248-683-0312 Fax: 248-738-6735
Website: www.orchardlakeseminary.org
E-mail: sscms.dean@comcast.net

MINNESOTA

LUTHER SEMINARY
2481 Como Ave, Saint Paul MN 55108-1496
Rev. Ronald Olson, Contact
800-588-4373 Fax: 651-641-3521
Website: www.luthersem.edu
E-mail: admissions@luthersem.edu

Pillsbury Baptist Bible College
315 S Grove Ave, Owatonna MN 55060-3097
Stephen R. Seidler, Director of Admissions
507-451-2710 Fax: 507-451-0156
Website: www.pillsbury.edu
E-mail: steveseidler@pillsbury.edu

UNITED THEOLOGICAL SEMINARY OF THE TWIN CITIES
3000 5th St NW, New Brighton MN 55112-2598
Sandra H. Casmey, Director of Admissions
651-255-6107 or 800-937-1316 Fax: 651-633-4315
Website: www.unitedseminary-mn.org
E-mail: admissions@unitedseminary-mn.org

MISSISSIPPI

MAGNOLIA BIBLE COLLEGE
PO Box 1109, Kosciusko MS 39090-1109
Garvis Semore, President
800-748-8655 Fax: 662-289-1850
Website: www.magnolia.edu
E-mail: gsemore@magnolia.edu

Tougaloo College
500 W County Line Rd, Tougaloo MS 39174-9799
Juno Leggette Jacobs, Director of Admissions
601-977-7768 Fax: 601-977-4501
Website: www.tougaloo.edu
E-mail: jjacobs@tougaloo.edu

WESLEY COLLEGE
PO Box 1070, Florence MS 39073-1070
Beverly Porter, V.P. for Academic Affairs
601-845-2265 Fax: 601-845-2266
Website: www.wesleycollege.edu
E-mail: admissions@wesleycollege.edu

MISSOURI

ASSEMBLIES OF GOD THEOLOGICAL SEMINARY
1435 N Glenstone Ave, Springfield MO 65802-2131
Dr. Mario Guerreiro, Director of Enrollment Management
800-467-AGTS Fax: 417-268-1001
Website: www.agts.edu
E-mail: agts@agseminary.edu

Calvary Bible College & Theological Seminary
15800 Calvary Rd, Kansas City MO 64147-1341
Robert M. Reinsch, Director of Admissions
800-326-3960 Fax: 816-331-4474
Website: www.calvary.edu
E-mail: admissions@calvary.edu

CENTRAL BIBLE COLLEGE
3000 N Grant Ave, Springfield MO 65803-1096
Scott Lindner, Executive Director of Enrollment Services
800-831-4222 ext. 1290 Fax: 417-833-5141
Website: www.cbcag.edu
E-mail: cbcinfo@cbcag.edu

COVENANT THEOLOGICAL SEMINARY
12330 Conway Rd, Saint Louis MO 63141-8697
Dr. Bryan Chapell, President
800-264-8064 Fax: 314-434-4819
Website: www.covenantseminary.edu
E-mail: admissions@covenantseminary.edu

KENRICK SCHOOL OF THEOLOGY
5200 Glennon Dr, Saint Louis MO 63119-4330
Msgr. Ted L. Wojcicki, President-Rector
314-792-6100 Fax: 314-792-6500
Website: www.kenrick.edu
E-mail: registrar@kenrick.edu

MIDWEST THEOLOGICAL SEMINARY
851 Parr Rd, PO Box 365, Wentzville MO 63385-0365
Dr. James Song, President
636-327-4645 Fax: 636-327-4715
Website: www.midwest.edu
E-mail: inf@midwest.edu

NAZARENE THEOLOGICAL SEMINARY
1700 E Meyer Blvd, Kansas City MO 64131-1263
Roger L. Hahn, Dean of the Faculty
816-333-6254 Fax: 816-333-6271
Website: www.nts.edu
E-mail: rlhahn@nts.edu

OZARK CHRISTIAN COLLEGE
1111 N Main St, Joplin MO 64801-4804
Troy Nelson, Director of Admissions
800-299-4622 Fax: 417-624-0090
Website: www.occ.edu
E-mail: occadmin@occ.edu
See listing under "Universities"

William Woods University
1 University Ave, Fulton MO 65251-1098
Jimmy Clay, Director of Admissions
573-642-2251 Fax: 573-592-1146
Website: www.williamwoods.edu
E-mail: admissions@williamwoods.edu
See listing under "Universities"

MONTANA

LUSTRE CHRISTIAN HIGH SCHOOL
HC 66 Box 57, Lustre MT 59225-9705
Al Leland, Supervising Teacher
406-392-5735 Fax: 406-392-5765
Website: www.lustrechristian.com
E-mail: 2lchs@nemontel.net
See listing under "Preparatory Schools - Coed"

NEBRASKA

Midland Lutheran College
900 N Clarkson St, Fremont NE 68025-4200
Todd Hansen, Associate Director of Admissions
402-941-6501 Fax: 402-941-6513
Website: www.mlc.edu
E-mail: admissions@mlc.edu

NEW YORK

ALLIANCE THEOLOGICAL SEMINARY
350 N Highland Ave, Nyack NY 10960-1416
Heather Rosenberg, Director of Admissions
845-353-2020 Fax: 845-348-3912
Website: www.nyack.edu/ats
E-mail: admissions.ats@nyack.edu

COLGATE ROCHESTER CROZER DIVINITY SCHOOL
1100 S Goodman St, Rochester NY 14620-2589
Robert Jones, V.P. of Enrollment Services
585-271-1320 or 888-937-3732 Fax: 585-271-8013
Website: www.crcds.edu
E-mail: admissions@crcds.edu

College of Saint Rose
432 Western Ave, Albany NY 12203-1419
Maryelizabeth Amico, Asst V.P. for Undergraduate Admissions
518-454-5150 Fax: 518-454-2013
Website: www.strose.edu
E-mail: admit@strose.edu

DAVIS COLLEGE
400 Riverside Dr, Johnson City NY 13790
Brian Murphy, VP of Enrollment Management
607-729-1581 Fax: 607-729-2962
Website: www.davisny.edu
E-mail: admissions@davisny.edu

Jewish Theological Seminary of America
3080 Broadway, New York NY 10027-4650
Jan Michael Skidds, Associate Director of Admissions
212-678-8000 Fax: 212-280-6022
Website: www.jtsa.edu
E-mail: lcadmissions@jtsa.edu

Molloy College
1000 Hempstead Ave
Rockville Centre NY 11570-1100
Marguerite Lane, Director of Admissions
516-678-5000 ext. 6291 Fax: 516-256-2247
Website: www.molloy.edu
E-mail: admissions@molloy.edu
See listing under "Universities"

NEW YORK THEOLOGICAL SEMINARY
475 Riverside Suite Ste 500, New York NY 10115
Yon Su Kang, Contact
212-870-1211 Fax: 212-870-1236
Website: www.nyts.edu
E-mail: online@nyts.edu

Roberts Wesleyan College
2301 Westside Dr, Rochester NY 14624-1997
Office of Admissions
585-594-6400 Fax: 585-594-6371
Website: www.roberts.edu
E-mail: admissions@roberts.edu

St. John's University
8000 Utopia Pkwy, Queens NY 11439
Office of Admission
718-990-2000 or 888-9-STJOHNS Fax: 718-990-2096
Website: www.stjohns.edu
E-mail: admissions@stjohns.edu
See listing under "Universities"

UNION THEOLOGICAL SEMINARY
3041 Broadway, New York NY 10027-5792
Joseph C. Hough, Jr., President
212-662-7100 Fax: 212-280-1416
Website: www.uts.columbia.edu
E-mail: admissns@uts.columbia.edu

WORD OF LIFE BIBLE INSTITUTE
PO Box 129, Pottersville NY 12860-0129
518-494-4723 Fax: 518-494-7474
Website: www.wol.org

NORTH CAROLINA

APEX SCHOOL OF THEOLOGY
5104 Revere Rd, Durham NC 27713-2421
Dr. J.E. Perkins, President
919-572-1625 Fax: 919-572-1762
Website: www.apexsot.edu
E-mail: info@apexsot.edu

Belmont Abbey College
100 Belmont Mount Holly Rd
Belmont NC 28012-1802
888-222-0110 Fax: 704-825-6670
Website: www.belmontabbeycollege.edu
E-mail: admissions@bac.edu

Heritage Bible College
PO Box 1628, Dunn NC 28335
910-892-3178 Fax: 910-892-1809
Website: www.heritagebiblecollege.org
E-mail: generalinfo@heritagebiblecollege.org

HOOD THEOLOGICAL SEMINARY
1810 Lutheran Synod Dr, Salisbury NC 28144
Albert J. D. Aymer, President
704-636-6823 Fax: 704-636-7699
Website: www.hoodseminary.edu
E-mail: dstewart@hoodseminary.com

JOHN WESLEY COLLEGE
2314 N Centennial St, High Point NC 27265-3197
Dr. Brian Donley, President
Greg Workman, Admissions Officer
336-889-2262 ext. 127 Fax: 336-889-2261
Website: www.johnwesley.edu
E-mail: admissions@johnwesley.edu
Established 1932. Private. Coed. Accreditation: ABHE. Tuition: $7,810. Room and board: $1,990. Enrollment: 173. Student-faculty ratio: 12:1. Degrees: AA, BA, Bth. Library: 47,000 volumes. 2 buildings on 25 acres. John Wesley College offers specialized studies in the area of Christian ministries; pastoral, Bible/theology, counseling (psychology), elementary christian school teacher education, youth & childrens ministry, missions, music, management and ethics, and pre-seminary. Distance education is offered. A christian college with a distinctly personal and practical approach to Bible based education, located in the center of the fast growing Piedmont area of North Carolina.

Lees-McRae College
PO Box 128, Banner Elk NC 28604-0128
Walt Crutchfield, Dean of Admissions
800-280-4562 Fax: 828-898-8707
Website: www.lmc.edu
E-mail: admissions@lmc.edu

Mt. Olive College
634 Henderson St, Mount Olive NC 28365
Tim Woodard, Director of Admissions
919-658-2502 Fax: 919-658-9816
Website: www.moc.edu
E-mail: admissions@moc.edu
See listing under "Universities"

NEW LIFE THEOLOGICAL SEMINARY
PO Box 790106, Charlotte NC 28206
Judith Mann, Registrar
704-334-6882 Fax: 704-334-6885
Website: www.nlts.org

SOUTHEASTERN BAPTIST THEOLOGICAL SEMINARY
Southeastern College at Wake Forest
PO Box 1889, Wake Forest NC 27588-1889
Jerry L. Yandell, Director of Admissions
919-761-2280 or 800-284-6317 Fax: 919-556-0998
Website: www.sebts.edu
E-mail: admissions@sebts.edu

NORTH DAKOTA

Oak Grove Lutheran School
124 N Terrace N, Fargo ND 58102-3899
Rachel Mathson, Director of Admissions
701-237-0212 Fax: 701-237-4217
Website: www.oakgrovelutheran.com
E-mail: oakgrove.lutheranschool@sendit.nodak.edu

OHIO

BEXLEY HALL SEMINARY
583 Sheridan Ave, Columbus OH 43209-2325
John Kevern, Dean & President
614-231-3095 Fax: 614-231-3236
Website: www.bexley.edu
E-mail: columbus@bexley.edu or
rochester@bexley.edu

Franciscan University of Steubenville
University Blvd, Steubenville OH 43952
Margaret J. Weber, Director of Admissions
800-783-6220 or 740-283-6226 Fax: 740-284-5456
Website: www.admissions.edu
E-mail: mweber@franciscan.edu

GOD'S BIBLE SCHOOL AND COLLEGE
1810 Young St, Cincinnati OH 45202-6838
Aaron Profitt, Director of Admissions
513-721-7944 Fax: 513-721-1357
Website: www.gbs.edu
E-mail: admissions@gbs.edu

Mount Vernon Nazarene University
800 Martinsburg Rd, Mount Vernon OH 43050-9509
Timothy Eades, Director of Admissions
866-462-6868 Fax: 740-393-0511
Website: www.gotomvnu.edu
E-mail: admissions@mvnu.edu
See listing under "Universities"

PAYNE THEOLOGICAL SEMINARY
PO Box 474, Wilberforce OH 45384-0474
Dr. Leah Gaskin Fitchue, Contact
937-376-2946 Fax: 937-376-3330
Website: www.payne.edu
E-mail: lfitchue@payne.edu

TEMPLE BAPTIST COLLEGE
11965 Kenn Rd, Cincinnati OH 45240
Dr. Tanmay Pramanik, Dean of Student Affairs
513-851-3800 Fax: 513-589-3052
Website: www.templebaptistcollege.com
E-mail: tanmay.pramanik@templebaptistcollege.com

United Theological Seminary
4501 Denlinger Rd, Trotwood OH 45426
Betty J. Stutler, Director of Admissions
800-322-5817 Fax: 937-529-2292
Website: www.united.edu
E-mail: admissions@united.edu

University of Dayton
300 College Park, Dayton OH 45469-1300
Robert F. Durkle, Director of Admissions
800-837-7433 Fax: 937-229-4729
Website: admission.udayton.edu
E-mail: admission@udayton.edu

Ursuline College
2550 Lander Rd, Cleveland OH 44124-4398
Sarah E. Sundermeier, Director of Admissions
888-URSULINE Toll Free Fax: 440-684-6138
Website: www.admission.ursuline.edu
E-mail: admission@ursuline.edu

OKLAHOMA

Mid-America Christian University
3500 SW 119th St, Oklahoma City OK 73170-4504
Haley Hope, Director of Admissions
405-691-3800 Fax: 405-692-3165
Website: www.macu.edu
E-mail: info@macu.edu

Oral Roberts University
Adult Learning Service Center
7777 S Lewis Ave, Tulsa OK 74171-0001
888-900-4678 Fax: 918-495-7965
Website: www.oru.edu
E-mail: alsc@oru.edu

Southwestern Christian University
PO Box 340, Bethany OK 73008-0340
Megan Miles, Director of Admissions
405-789-7661 Fax: 405-495-0078
Website: www.swcu.edu
E-mail: jean@swcu.edu

OREGON

Cascade College
9101 E Burnside St, Portland OR 97216-1599
800-550-7678 Fax: 503-257-1222
Website: www.cascade.edu
E-mail: admissions@cascade.edu

Concordia University
2811 NE Holman St, Portland OR 97211-6099
Bobi Swan, Director of Admissions
503-288-9371 Fax: 503-280-8531
Website: www.cu-portland.edu
E-mail: cu-admissions@cu-portland.edu

Marylhurst University
17600 Pacific Hwy (Hwy 43)
Marylhurst OR 97036-0261
Director of Admissions
800-634-9982 ext. 6268 Fax: 503-635-6585
Website: www.marylhurst.edu
E-mail: studentinfo@marylhurst.edu

Warner Pacific College
2219 SE 68th Ave, Portland OR 97215-4026
Shannon Mackey, Director of Admissions
503-517-1000 Fax: 503-517-1352
Website: www.warnerpacific.edu
E-mail: admissions@warnerpacific.edu

PENNSYLVANIA

Baptist Bible College and Seminary
538 Venard Rd, Clarks Summit PA 18411-1297
Glen Amos, Director of Admissions
570-586-2400 Fax: 570-585-9299
Website: www.bbc.edu
E-mail: admissions@bbc.edu

BIBLICAL THEOLOGICAL SEMINARY
200 N Main St, Hatfield PA 19440-2421
Pamela J. Smith, VP for Student Advancement
800-235-4021 Fax: 215-368-7002
Website: www.biblical.edu
E-mail: admissions@biblical.edu

DeSales University
2755 Station Ave, Center Valley PA 18034-9565
610-282-1100 Fax: 610-282-2342
Website: www.desales.edu

EVANGELICAL SCHOOL OF THEOLOGY
121 S College St, Myerstown PA 17067-1299
Tom Maiello, Dean of Admissions
800-532-5775 Fax: 717-866-4667
Website: www.evangelical.edu
E-mail: admissions@evangelical.edu

Gannon University
109 University Sq, Erie PA 16541-0001
Christopher Tremblay, Director of Admissions
800-GANNON-U Fax: 814-871-5803
Website: www.gannon.edu
E-mail: admissions@gannon.edu

Gratz College
7605 Old York Rd, Melrose Park PA 19027
Jill Sigman, Director of Admissions
215-635-7300 Fax: 215-635-7320
Website: www.gratzcollege.edu
E-mail: admissions@gratz.edu

Juniata College
1700 Moore St, Huntingdon PA 16652-2196
Michelle Bartol, Dean of Enrollment
877-JUNIATA Fax: 814-641-3100
Website: www.juniata.edu
E-mail: admissions@juniata.edu

King's College
133 N River St, Wilkes Barre PA 18711-0801
Michelle Lawrence-Schmude, Director of Admission
570-208-5900 Fax: 570-208-5971
Website: www.kings.edu
E-mail: admissions@kings.edu

LANCASTER BIBLE COLLEGE
901 Eden Rd, Lancaster PA 17601-5036
Dr. Peter W. Teague, President
Joanne M. Roper, Associate VP for Admissions
866-LBC-4YOU or 717-560-8271 Fax: 717-560-8213
Website: www.lbc.edu
E-mail: admissions@lbc.edu

Established 1933. Private. Coed. Accreditation: MSA, AABC, ACSI approval. Tuition $12,510. Room and board: $5,710. Fees: $570. Enrollment: 589 full-time, 240 part-time. Faculty: 86. Student-faculty ratio: 18:1. Degrees: AS in Bible, BS in Bible, BS in Education. Library: 176,566 volumes. 16 buildings on 100 acres. Departments: Biblical Counseling, Church & Ministry Leadership, Christian Education, Health, Physical Ed & Athletics, Intercultural Studies, Music, Office Administration, Teacher Education.

La Roche College
9000 Babcock Blvd, Pittsburgh PA 15237-5898
Thomas Hassett, Director of Freshman and International Admissions
412-536-1272 or 800-838-4LRC Fax: 412-536-1272
Website: www.laroche.edu
E-mail: admissions@laroche.edu

Lebanon Valley College
101 N College Ave, Annville PA 17003-1400
William Brown, Dean of Admissions & Financial Aid
866-LVC-4ADM or 717-867-6181 Fax: 717-867-6026
Website: www.lvc.edu
E-mail: admission@lvc.edu

LUTHERAN THEOLOGICAL SEMINARY
7301 Germantown Ave, Philadelphia PA 19119-1794
Rick Summy, Director of Admissions
800-286-4616 Fax: 215-248-4577
Website: www.ltsp.edu
E-mail: admissions@ltsp.edu

LUTHERAN THEOLOGICAL SEMINARY AT GETTYSBURG
61 Seminary Ridge, Gettysburg PA 17325-1795
Nancy E. Gable (Diaconal Minister), Assoc. Dean of Church Vocations
800-MLU-THER Fax: 717-334-3469
Website: www.ltsg.edu
E-mail: admissions@ltsg.edu

MORAVIAN THEOLOGICAL SEMINARY
1200 Main St, Bethlehem PA 18018
Rev. Melissa Johnson, Director of Admissions
610-861-1516 Fax: 610-861-1569
Website: www.moravianseminary.edu
E-mail: seminary@moravian.edu

Neumann College
1 Neumann Dr, Aston PA 19014-1298
Dennis Murphy, Director of Admissions
610-459-0905 Fax: 610-558-5652
Website: www.neumann.edu
E-mail: neumann@neumann.edu

PITTSBURGH THEOLOGICAL SEMINARY
616 N Highland Ave, Pittsburgh PA 15206-2525
Sherry Sparks, Director of Admissions
412-362-5610 ext. 2115 or 800-451-4194 Admissions only
Fax: 412-363-3260
Website: www.pts.edu
E-mail: sparks@pts.edu

Established 1794. PTS is affiliated with the Presbyterian Church, U.S.A. and serves students of any denomination. Our primary mission is to train lay and ordained leaders for the Church through rigorous academic and practical experience. Special emphases are urban, educational and counseling ministries. Degrees offered: Master of Divinity, MA, Master of Sacred Theology, Doctor of Ministry and three dual degrees in social work, law, and public policy. Part-time and evening programs, child care and financial aid available. We are located on a 13 acre park-like campus in an urban setting between the Highland Park and East liberty area of Pittsburgh.

ST. TIKHON'S ORTHODOX THEOLOGICAL SEMINARY
PO Box 130, South Canaan PA 18459-0130
Metropolitan Herman, President
Bishop Tikhon, Rector
Very Rev. Michael G. Dahulich, Ph.D., Dean
570-937-4411 Fax: 570-937-3100
Website: www.stots.edu
E-mail: stots@stots.edu

Talmudical Yeshiva of Philadelphia
6063 Drexel Rd, Philadelphia PA 19131-1296
Rabbi Uri Mandelbaum, Director of Admissions
215-477-1000 Fax: 215-477-5065
E-mail: typ@attglobal.net

Westminster College
New Wilmington PA 16172-0001
Doug Swartz, Director of Admissions
724-946-7100 Fax: 724-946-6171
Website: www.westminster.edu
E-mail: swartzdl@westminster.edu

RHODE ISLAND

ZION BIBLE COLLEGE
27 Middle Hwy, Barrington RI 02806-1296
Director of Recruiting
401-246-0900 Fax: 401-246-0906
Website: www.zbc.edu
E-mail: recruiting@zbc.edu

SOUTH CAROLINA

Bob Jones University
1700 Wade Hampton Blvd
Greenville SC 29614-0001
David Christ, Director of Admissions
800-BJ-AND-ME Fax: 800-2-FAX-BJU
Website: www.bju.edu
E-mail: admissions@bju.edu
See listing under "Universities"

Columbia Biblical Seminary & School of Missions
PO Box 3122, Columbia SC 29230-3122
Michelle MacGregor, Director of University Admissions
800-777-2227 Fax: 803-333-0607
Website: www.ciu.edu
E-mail: yescbs@ciu.edu
See listing under "Theological Studies & Religious Vocations"

COLUMBIA INTERNATIONAL UNIVERSITY
PO Box 3122, Columbia SC 29230-3122
Phone 800-777-2227, Fax: 803-786-4209
Dr. George W. Murray, President
John Basie, Director of University Admissions
Website: www.ciu.edu
E-mail: yesciu@ciu.edu

Established 1923. Multidenominational. Coed. Privately supported, nonprofit. Accredited by The Commission on Colleges of the Southern Association of Colleges and Schools (SACS). Bible College accredited by the Accrediting Association of Bible Colleges (AABC) and Seminary by the Association of Theological Schools (ATS). Graduate School is approved for Teacher Education programs by the South Carolina Department of Education, Division of Teacher Education and Certification, which is affiliated with the National Association of State Directors of Teacher Education and Certification (NASDTEC) and by the Association of Christian Schools International (ACSI).

CIU Graduate School: Enrollment (Fall 2003) 80 students. Tuition: $375 per credit for semesters and summer and winter short terms. Curriculum: Master of Education, Curriculum and Instruction (Generalist, School Technology, Learning Disabilities, Christian School Guidance, ESL); Master of Education, Educational Administration; Master of Arts in Bible Teaching; Master of Arts in Teaching for State Certification; Master of Arts in Counseling; Master of Arts in Teaching English as a Foreign Language; Fall 2006 has 2 Ed.D. programs: Doctor of Education in Educational Leadership (Christian School Education, Christian Higher Education). Admissions: Christian testimony, baccalaureate degree, transcripts with 3.0 GPA for MA in Counseling or upper 50% GRE score, PPST (MAT only), essay, and references.

Bible College: Enrollment (Fall 2005) 550 students. Tuition: $6,603 for each semester (two). Curriculum: one year Bible Certificate, AA, BS, BA. Bible major combines with one of the following: Applied English, Bible Teaching, Biblical Languages, Business and Organizational Leadership, Communication, Deaf Ministry, Family & Church Education, General Studies, Humanities, Intercultural Studies (Missions), Middle Eastern Studies, Music, Nursing (cooperative program through General Studies), Outdoor Leadership, Pastoral Ministries, Psychology, Radio Broadcasting, Teacher Education, Teaching English as a Foreign Language (TEFL), Video Production, Youth Ministry. Admission: Christian testimony, SAT or ACT and HS transcripts or GED required, references, essay.

Columbia Biblical Seminary & School of Missions: Enrollment (Fall 2005) 134 students. Tuition: $400 per credit hour for semesters and short terms. Curriculum: Biblical Ministry Certificate; Master of Arts (General); Master of Arts in Bible Exposition; Master of Arts in Educational Ministries; Master of Arts in Pastoral Counseling and Spiritual Formation; Master of Arts in Leadership for Evangelism and Mobilization; Master of Arts in Intercultural Studies; Master of Divinity with the following tracks: Intercultural Studies, Academic Ministries, Bible Exposition, Educational Ministries, Pastoral Counseling and Spiritual Formation; Doctor of Ministry with concentrations in Pastoral Leadership, Missions, Member Care, and Preaching. Flexible training for college graduates, with or without Bible training, and for pastors or missionaries. Admission: Christian testimony, baccalaureate degree transcripts with 2.5 GPA essay, references. Separate housing for single graduate students, on campus mobile home park for some married students. Faculty to student ratio: 1:18. No admissions deadline. Located on scenic 400 acre campus, seven miles from state capital.

CIU serves Christ and His church by inspiring, developing and equipping people for lifelong pursuit of God and servant leadership in His global cause.

Erskine College & Seminary
PO Box 176, Due West SC 29639
Bart Walker, Director of Admissions
864-379-8838 Fax: 864-379-3048
Website: www.erskine.edu
E-mail: admissions@erskine.edu

North Greenville University
PO Box 1892, Tigerville SC 29688-1892
Dr. Walter Johnson, Dept. Chair
Website: www.ngc.edu
See listing under "Universities"

TENNESSEE

EMMANUEL SCHOOL OF RELIGION
One Walker Dr, Johnson City TN 37601-9438
David Fulks, Director of Admissions
423-461-1535 or 800-933-3771 Fax: 423-926-6198
Website: www.esr.edu
E-mail: admissions@esr.edu

Free Will Baptist Bible College
3606 W End Ave, Nashville TN 37205
Ryan Lewis, Director of Recruitment
800-76-FWBBC Fax: 615-269-6028
Website: www.fwbbc.edu
E-mail: recruit@fwbbc.edu

Lipscomb University
3901 Granny White Pike, Nashville TN 37204-3951
Ricky Holaway, Director of Admissions
800-333-4358 ext. 1776 Fax: 615-269-1804
Website: www.lipscomb.edu
E-mail: admissions@lipscomb.edu

NORTH TENNESSEE BIBLE INSTITUTE AND SEMINARY
PO Box 3797, Clarksville TN 37043-3797
Dr. William Corley, Chancellor
931-552-1510 Fax: 931-552-1464
Website: www.ntbis.com
E-mail: drwhc@ntbis.com

TEXAS

Arlington Baptist College
3001 W Division St, Arlington TX 76012-3425
Janie Taylor, Director of Admissions
817-461-8741 Fax: 817-274-1138
Website: www.abconline.edu
E-mail: jhall@abconline.org

BAPTIST MISSIONARY ASSOCIATION THEOLOGICAL SEMINARY
1530 E Pine St, Jacksonville TX 75766-5407
Charley Holmes, President
903-586-2501 Fax: 903-586-0378
Website: www.bmats.edu
E-mail: bmatsem@bmats.edu

BAPTIST UNIVERSITY OF THE AMERICAS
8019 S Panam Expy, San Antonio TX 78224-1336
Mary Ranjel, Director of Admissions
800-721-1396 Fax: 210-924-2701
Website: www.bua.edu
E-mail: mranjel@bua.edu

DALLAS THEOLOGICAL SEMINARY
3909 Swiss Ave, Dallas TX 75204-6411
Greg Hatteberg, Director of Admissions
214-841-3661 or 866-DTS-WORD Fax: 214-841-3664
Website: www.dts.edu
E-mail: admissions@dts.edu

HOUSTON GRADUATE SCHOOL OF THEOLOGY
2501 Central Parkway Suite A19, Houston TX 77092
Keith A. Jenkins, Ph.D., President
Daniel K. Dunlap, Ph.D., Dean of the Faculty
713-942-9505 or 877-TRY-HGST Fax: 713-942-9506
Website: www.hgst.edu
E-mail: mevans@hgst.edu

Established 1983. Private. Coed. Evangelical, Multicultural and Ecumenical. Accreditation: ATS (Association of Theological Schools in the US & Canada).

Degrees offered: MA, MA in Counseling (LPC & LMFT), M Div, D Min, and D Min in Military Chaplaincy (approved by Army & Navy Chiefs of Chaplains); Certificate Program in Spiritual Formation; DMin also offered in Korean language. Undergraduate Degree Required.

Full-time 2006-07 Tuition: $8,550. Fees: $300. Rolling Application Deadlines - Fee: $50. Federal & Private financial aid available. Institutional Application & FAFSA required. Approved by Veterans Administration. Approximately 240 students. Faculty: 11 full-time, 21 part-time (90% with terminal degrees).

Fall, Bridge, Spring, May, and Summer I & II Terms. Classes taught day & evening, seven days a week. Campus conveniently located near center of 4th largest metropolitan area in the U.S.

KINGS WAY MISSIONARY INSTITUTE
401 S 35th St, Mc Allen TX 78501
Don Russell, President - BOD
956-682-6187 Fax: 956-682-9030
Website: www.kingswaymissionary.com
E-mail: kingswaymissionary@aol.com

University of St. Thomas
3800 Montrose Blvd, Houston TX 77006-4626
Eduardo Prieto, Director of Admissions
713-522-7911 Fax: 713-525-3558
Website: www.stthom.edu
E-mail: prietoe@stthom.edu

VIRGINIA

Catholic Distance University
120 E Colonial Hwy, Hamilton VA 20158-9012
Marianne Evans Mount, Executive VP
888-254-4CDU Fax: 540-338-4788
Website: www.cdu.edu
E-mail: tcashen@cdu.edu

GRAHAM BIBLE COLLEGE
PO Box 1630, Bristol VA 24203-1630
Dr. Philip R. Blevins, President
423-968-4201 Fax: 423-968-4266
Website: www.grahambiblecollege.com
E-mail: info@grahambiblecollege.com

UNION THEOLOGICAL SEMINARY AND PRESBYTERIAN SCHOOL OF CHRISTIAN EDUCATION
3401 Brook Rd, Richmond VA 23227-4597
Pat Morgan, Associate Director of Admissions
800-229-2990 Fax: 804-355-3919
Website: www.union-psce.edu
E-mail: admissn@union-psce.edu

WASHINGTON

BAKKE GRADUATE UNIVERSITY OF MINISTRY
1013 8th Ave, Seattle WA 98104-1222
Judi Melton, Registrar
206-264-9100 Fax: 206-264-0613
Website: www.bgu.edu
E-mail: bgu@bgu.edu

Gonzaga University
502 E Boone Ave, Spokane WA 99258-0102
Julie McCulloh, Dean of Admission
800-322-2584 or 509-323-6572 Fax: 509-323-5780
Website: www.gonzaga.edu
E-mail: mcculloh@gu.gonzaga.edu

WEST VIRGINIA

Davis & Elkins College
100 Campus Dr, Elkins WV 26241-3996
Renee Heckel, Director of Enrollment Management
800-624-3157 Fax: 304-637-1800
Website: www.davisandelkins.edu
E-mail: admiss@davisandelkins.edu

West Virginia Wesleyan College
59 College Ave, Buckhannon WV 26201-2699
Robert N. Skinner II, Director of Admission
800-722-9933 Fax: 304-473-8108
Website: www.wvwc.edu
E-mail: admission@wvwc.edu

WISCONSIN

Lakeland College
PO Box 359, Sheboygan WI 53082-0359
Nathan Dehne, Director of Admission
920-565-1100 Fax: 920-565-1215
Website: www.lakeland.edu
E-mail: admissions@lakeland.edu

Marquette University
PO Box 1881, Milwaukee WI 53201-1881
Robert Blust, Director of Admissions
414-288-7302 Fax: 414-288-3764
Website: www.mu.edu
E-mail: admissions@marquette.edu

NASHOTAH HOUSE
2777 Mission Rd, Nashotah WI 53058-9793
The Very Rev. Robert S. Munday, Ph.D., Dean and President
262-646-6500 Fax: 262-646-6504
Website: www.nashotah.edu
E-mail: nashotah@nashotah.edu

St. Norbert College
100 Grant St, De Pere WI 54115
Brian Studebaker, Director of Admission
800-236-4878 Fax: 920-403-4072
Website: www.snc.edu
E-mail: admit@snc.edu

WYOMING

University of Wyoming
Admissions Office
Dept 3435, Laramie WY 82071-3435
Aaron Appelhans, Contact
800-342-5996 Fax: 307-766-4042
Website: www.uwyo.edu
E-mail: why-wyo@uwyo.edu

PUERTO RICO

COLEGIO PENTECOSTAL MIZPA
PO Box 20966, Rio Piedras PR 00928
Rev. Nereida Torres, Dean of Students
787-720-4476 Fax: 787-720-2012
Website: www.colmizpa.edu
E-mail: decanatoestudiante@colmizpa.edu

Universidad Adventista de las Antillas
PO Box 118, Mayaguez PR 00919-0118
Evelyn Del Valle Rivera, Director of Admissions
787-834-9595 Fax: 787-834-9597
Website: www.uaa.edu
E-mail: admissions@uaa.edu

UNIVERSITIES AND COLLEGES

ALABAMA

Alabama A & M University
PO Box 908, Normal AL 35762
Antonio Boyle, Director of Admissions
256-372-5245 Fax: 256-372-5249
Website: www.aamu.edu
E-mail: aboyle@aamu.edu

Alabama State University
PO Box 271, Montgomery AL 36101-0271
334-229-4200

Athens State University
300 N Beaty St, Athens AL 35611-1902
256-233-8100

Auburn University
Auburn AL 36849
334-844-4000

Auburn University at Montgomery
PO Box 244023, Montgomery AL 36124
334-244-3000

Birmingham-Southern College
900 Arkadelphia Rd, Birmingham AL 35254-0002
800-523-5793

Concordia College
1804 Green St, Selma AL 36703
Evelyn Pickens, Director of Enrollment Management and Placement
334-874-5700

Faulkner University
5345 Atlanta Hwy, Montgomery AL 36109-3398
Keith Mock, Director of Admissions
800-879-9816 ext. 7200 or 334-386-7200
Fax: 334-386-7137
Website: www.faulkner.edu
E-mail: admissions@faulkner.edu

Herzing College
280 W Valley Ave, Homewood AL 35209-4816
Kim Conway, Director of Admissions
205-916-2800 Fax: 205-916-2807
Website: www.herzing.edu/birmingham
E-mail: info@bhm.herzing.edu

Huntingdon College
1500 E Fairview Ave, Montgomery AL 36106-2148
334-833-4222

HUNTSVILLE BIBLE COLLEGE
PO Box 3493, Huntsville AL 35810
John Clay, Contact
256-539-0834 Fax: 256-539-0854
Website: www.huntsvillebiblecollege.com
E-mail: hbc@huntsvillebiblecollege.com

Jacksonville State University
700 Pelham Rd N, Jacksonville AL 36265-1602
256-782-5000

Judson College
302 Bibb St, Marion AL 36756
Michael Scotto, Director of Admissions
800-447-9472 Fax: 334-683-5147
Website: www.judson.edu
E-mail: admissions@judson.edu

Miles College
PO Box 3800, Birmingham AL 35208
205-929-1654

Oakwood College
Oakwood Rd NW, Huntsville AL 35896-0001
256-726-7000

Samford University
800 Lakeshore Dr, Birmingham AL 35229-0002
205-726-3673

Selma University
1501 Lapsley St, Selma AL 36701
334-872-2533

Southern Christian University
1200 Taylor Rd, Montgomery AL 36117
800-351-4040

Spring Hill College
4000 Dauphin St, Mobile AL 36608-1791
334-460-4000

Stillman College
PO Box 1430, Tuscaloosa AL 35403-1430
205-349-4240

Strayer University
3570 Grandview Pkwy, Birmingham AL 35243
205-453-6300

Talladega College
627 Battle St W, Talladega AL 35160-2354
256-362-0206

Troy University
Troy AL 36082-0001
Jim Hutto, Dean of Enrollment Management
334-670-3175

Troy University Dothan
PO Box 8368, Dothan AL 36304-0368
334-983-6556

Troy University Montgomery
PO Box 4419, Montgomery AL 36103-4419
334-834-1400

Troy University - Phenix City
1 University Pl, Phenix City AL 36869
334-297-1007

Tuskegee University
Tuskegee Institute AL 36088
334-727-8011

University of Alabama
Box 870118, Tuscaloosa AL 35487
Dr. Lisa B. Harris, Director of Admissions
205-348-5666

University of Alabama at Birmingham
Univ Sta, Birmingham AL 35294-0001
205-934-4011

University of Alabama in Huntsville
PO Box 1247, Huntsville AL 35899-0001
Ann Lee, Assoc. Director for Recruiting Program and Events
1-800-UAH-CALL Fax: 256-824-6073
Website: www.uah.edu
E-mail: leev@uah.edu

University of Mobile
PO Box 13220, Mobile AL 36663-0220
251-675-5990

University of Montevallo
Station 6030, Montevallo AL 35115
205-665-6030

University of North Alabama
Univ Sta, Florence AL 35632-0001
256-760-4100

University of South Alabama
307 University Blvd N, Mobile AL 36688-3053
Melissa Haab, Director of Admissions
251-460-6141 Fax: 251-460-7876
Website: www.southalabama.edu
E-mail: admiss@usouthal.edu

University of West Alabama
Hwy 11, Livingston AL 35470
205-652-3400

Virginia College
65 Bagby Dr, Birmingham AL 35209
205-802-1200

ALASKA

ALASKA BIBLE COLLEGE
PO Box 289, Glennallen AK 99588-0289
907-822-3201 Fax: 907-822-5027
Website: www.akbible.edu
E-mail: info@akbible.edu

Alaska Pacific University
4101 University Dr, Anchorage AK 99508-4672
Ernie Norton, Director of Admissions
800-252-7528

Charter College
2221 E Northern Lights Blvd Ste 120
Anchorage AK 99508-4157
907-276-7712

Sheldon Jackson College
801 Lincoln St, Sitka AK 99835-7651
800-478-4556

University of Alaska Anchorage
PO Box 141629, Anchorage AK 99514-1629
Cecile Mitchell, Director of Enrollment Services
907-786-1480 Fax: 907-786-4888
Website: www.uaa.alaska.edu/
E-mail: enroll@uaa.alaska.edu

University of Alaska
Bristol Bay Campus
PO Box 1070, Dillingham AK 99576-1070
907-842-5109

University of Alaska
Chuchi Campus
PO Box 297, Kotzebue AK 99752-0297
907-442-3400

University of Alaska Fairbanks
PO Box 757480, Fairbanks AK 99775
907-474-7581

University of Alaska Interior Campus
PO Box 756720, Fairbanks AK 99775-6720
907-474-7211

University of Alaska Matanuska-Susitna
PO Box 2889, Palmer AK 99645-2889
907-745-9712

University of Alaska Southeast
11120 Glacier Hwy, Juneau AK 99801-8625
Paul Kraft, Dean of Students/Enrollment Management
907-796-6000 Fax: 907-796-6005
Website: www.uas.alaska.edu
E-mail: paul.kraft@uas.alaska.edu

University of Alaska Southeast-Ketchikan
2600 7th Ave, Ketchikan AK 99901-5728
907-225-6177

University of Alaska
Tanana Valley Campus
PO Box 758000, Fairbanks AK 99775-8000
907-474-7400

ARIZONA

American Indian College of the Assemblies of God
10020 N 15th Ave, Phoenix AZ 85021-2199
Steve Clindaniel, Director of Admissions
602-944-3335

Apollo College
630 W Southern Ave, Mesa AZ 85210-5005
480-831-6585

Apollo College
8503 N 27th Ave, Phoenix AZ 85051-4063
602-864-1571

Apollo College
2701 W Bethany Home Rd, Phoenix AZ 85017-1705
602-433-1333

Apollo College
3550 N Oracle Rd, Tucson AZ 85705
520-888-5885

Arizona State University
PO Box 870112, Tempe AZ 85287-0112
480-965-9011

Arizona State University Polytechnic
7001 E Williams Field Rd, Mesa AZ 85212
480-727-3278

Arizona State University West
PO Box 37110, Phoenix AZ 85069-7110
602-543-5500

Collins College: A School of Design and Technology
(Formerly Al Collins Graphic Design School)
1140 S Priest Dr, Tempe AZ 85281-5240
Toby Craver, Director of National Admissions
800-876-7070 Fax: 480-829-0183
Website: www.collinscollege.edu
E-mail: nationaladmissions@collinscollege.edu

The Conservatory of Recording Arts & Sciences
2300 E Broadway Rd, Tempe AZ 85282-1707
Tonya Visconti, Director of Admissions
800-562-6383 or 480-858-9400 Fax: 480-829-1332
Website: cras.org
E-mail: info@cras.org
See listing under "Music"

Grand Canyon University
3300 W Camelback Rd, Phoenix AZ 85017-1097
602-249-3300

International Baptist College
2150 E Southern Ave, Tempe AZ 85282
480-838-7070

International Institute of the Americas
925 S Gilbert Rd Ste 201, Mesa AZ 85204-4440
Meredith Kiljan, Director
480-545-8755 Fax: 480-926-1371
Website: www.iia.edu
E-mail: mjensen@iia.edu

International Institute of the Americas
6049 N 43rd Ave, Phoenix AZ 85019-1600
Lynn McConnell, Director
602-242-6265 Fax: 602-589-1353
Website: www.iia.edu
E-mail: lmcconnell@iia.edu

International Institute of the Americas
4136 N 75th Ave Ste 211, Phoenix AZ 85033-3169
Dr. Lori Ebert, Director
623-849-8208 Fax: 623-849-0110
Website: www.iia.edu
E-mail: nsabino@iia.edu

International Institute of the Americas
5441 E 22nd St, Tucson AZ 85710
Leigh Anne Pechota, Director
520-748-9799 Fax: 520-748-9355
Website: www.iia.edu
E-mail: lpechota@iia.edu

Midwestern University
19555 N 59th Ave, Glendale AZ 85308-6814
James Walter, Director of Admissions
623-572-3275

Northcentral University
505 W Whipple St, Prescott AZ 86301
928-541-7777

Northern Arizona University
PO Box 4084, Flagstaff AZ 86011-0001
520-523-9011

Phoenix First Pastors College
1220 E Rosemonte Dr, Phoenix AZ 85024-2921
602-867-4587

Phoenix Seminary
4222 E Thomas Rd Ste 400, Phoenix AZ 85018
602-850-8000

Prescott College
220 Grove Ave, Prescott AZ 86301-2912
928-778-2090

Remington College
875 W Elliot Rd #126, Tempe AZ 85284-1133
Joe Drennen, President
800-395-4322

Southwestern College
2625 E Cactus Rd, Phoenix AZ 85032-7097
Admissions/Financial Aid Office
800-247-2697 or 602-992-6101 Fax: 602-404-2159
Website: www.swcaz.edu
E-mail: admissions@swcaz.edu

University of Advancing Technology
2625 W Baseline Rd, Tempe AZ 85283
Lary Dougherty, Director of Admissions
800-658-5744

University of Arizona
Tucson AZ 85721-0040
Paul Kohn, Director of Admissions
520-621-3237 Fax: 520-621-9799
Website: www.admissions.arizona.edu or
www.arizona.edu

University of Phoenix
4615 E Elwood St, Phoenix AZ 85040-1908
480-966-9577

Western International University
9215 N Black Canyon Hwy, Phoenix AZ 85021-2718
602-943-2311

ARKANSAS

ARKANSAS BAPTIST COLLEGE
1600 Bishop St, Little Rock AR 72202-6067
501-372-6883 Fax: 501-372-0321

Arkansas State University
PO Box 1630, State University AR 72467-1630
870-972-2100

ARKANSAS STATE UNIVERSITY MOUNTAIN HOME
1600 S College St, Mountain Home AR 72653
Tonya Sexton, Director of Marketing & Public Relations
870-508-6109 Fax: 870-508-6287
Website: www.asumh.edu
E-mail: tsexton@asumh.edu

Arkansas Tech University
215 W O St, Russellville AR 72801-2222
479-968-0389

Central Baptist College
1501 College Ave, Conway AR 72032
501-329-6872

Ecclesia College
9653 Nations Dr, Springdale AR 72762
800-735-9926

Harding University
900 E Center Ave, Searcy AR 72149
501-279-4000

Henderson State University
1100 Henderson St, Arkadelphia AR 71999-0001
870-230-5000

Hendrix College
1600 Washington Ave, Conway AR 72032-3080
501-329-6811

John Brown University
2000 W University St, Siloam Springs AR 72761-2121
877-JBU-INFO

Lyon College
PO Box 2317, Batesville AR 72503-2317
Dan Rutledge, Director of Admissions
870-793-9813

Ouachita Baptist University
410 Ouachita St, Arkadelphia AR 71998-0001
David Goodman, Director of Admissions
870-245-5110 Fax: 870-245-5500
Website: www.obu.edu
E-mail: admissions@obu.edu

Philander Smith College
812 W 13th St, Little Rock AR 72202-3799
501-375-9845

Southern Arkansas University
100 E University, Magnolia AR 71753
870-235-4000

University of Arkansas at Fayetteville
1 University of Arkansas, Fayetteville AR 72701-1201
479-575-2000

University of Arkansas at Little Rock
2801 S University Ave, Little Rock AR 72204-1000
501-569-3000

University of Arkansas at Monticello
PO Box 3600, Monticello AR 71656
870-367-6811

University of Arkansas at Pine Bluff
1200 University Dr, Pine Bluff AR 71601-2799
870-543-8000

University of Arkansas for Medical Sciences
4301 W Markham St, Little Rock AR 72205-7101
501-686-5000

University of Central Arkansas
201 Donaghey Ave, Conway AR 72035-5003
501-450-5000

University of the Ozarks
415 N College Ave, Clarksville AR 72830-2880
Jim Decker, Director of Admissions
479-979-1000

Williams Baptist College
PO Box 3665, Walnut Ridge AR 72476-3665
Angela Flippo, Vice President for Enrollment
Management
800-722-4434

CALIFORNIA

American Institute of Health Science
3501 Atlantic Ave, Long Beach CA 90807
562-988-2278

American InterContinental University
12655 W Jefferson Blvd, Los Angeles CA 90066
310-302-2000

Antioch University
801 Garden St Ste 101
Santa Barbara CA 93101-1581
Ankara McPherson, Director of Admissions
805-962-8179 Fax: 805-962-4786
Website: www.antiochsb.edu
E-mail: amcpherson@antiochsb.edu

Antioch University Southern California
400 Corporate Pointe, Culver City CA 90230-7615
Admissions Office
800-7-ANTIOCH Fax: 310-821-6032
E-mail: admissions@antiochla.edu

Argosy University
San Francisco Bay Area Campus
999A Canal Blvd, Point Richmond CA 94804-3547
Cynthia Sirkin, Associate Director of Admissions
510-215-0277

Armstrong University
1301 Marina Village Pkwy Suite 340
Alameda CA 94601-1084
510-865-1336

Art Institute of California - Inland Empire
630 E Brier Dr, San Bernardino CA 92408
909-915-2100

The Art Institute of California - San Francisco
1170 Market St, San Francisco CA 94102-4908
Director of Admissions
888-493-3261 Fax: 415-863-6344
Website: www.aicasf.aii.edu
E-mail: aisfadm@aii.edu

Azusa Pacific University
901 E Alosta Ave, Azusa CA 91702
626-969-3434

Bethany University
800 Bethany Dr, Scotts Valley CA 95066-2896
831-438-3800

Bethesda Christian University
730 N Euclid St, Anaheim CA 92801-4132
Dr. Grace Sung Cho, D.D., Chancellor
714-517-1945

Biola University
13800 Biola Ave, La Mirada CA 90639-0001
562-903-6000

Brooks Institute of Photography
801 Alston Rd, Santa Barbara CA 93108-2399
Inge B. Kautzmann, Director of Admissions
805-966-3888 ext. 217 or 218

California Baptist University
8432 Magnolia Ave, Riverside CA 92504-3297
951-689-5771

California Christian College
4881 E University Ave, Fresno CA 93703-3599
559-251-4215

CALIFORNIA COAST UNIVERSITY
700 N Main St, Santa Ana CA 92701
Admissions Office: 888-CCU-UNIV or 714-547-9625
Fax: 714-547-5777
Dr. Thomas Neal, President
Dr. Cynthia Teeple, Academic Vice President
Website: www.calcoast.edu
E-mail: info@calcoast.edu
Established 1973. Proprietary. Coed. Accreditation: California Coast University holds accreditation through the Accrediting Commission of the Distance Education and Training Council (DETC). The DETC is an educational association located in Washington, D.C. Founded in 1926, it is the standard setting agency for distance education institutions. Approval: Bureau for Private Postsecondary and Vocational Education - State of California, charter member California Association of State Approved Colleges & Universities, member Association for Adult & Continuing Education, member The Alliance for Private Post Secondary Academic Institutions.
Tuition: $2,805-$12,070. California Coast University has selected the SLM Corporation, commonly known as Sallie Mae, to help the university provide financing for its students. Sallie Mae is the nation's leading provider of education funding. Sallie Mae also allows students to borrow additional loan amounts to cover additional expenses, such as textbooks, equipment, or living expenses.
Enrollment: 30,000. California Coast University is approved by the California State Approving Agency to enroll veterans or other eligible persons under Title 38, U.S. Code. California Coast University holds a Memorandum of Understanding with Defense Activity for Non-Traditional Education Support (DANTES) as an external degree provider.
A private college offering off-campus independent study programs in the traditional areas of business administration, management, psychology, education. Admissions: enroll year round, requires official transcripts, letters of recommendation, detailed curriculum vita or occupational history.
Process: evaluation of prior academic work followed by analysis of occupational history, including participation in workshops, seminars, training programs, specialized projects for credit. Credit is demonstrated by accelerated learning guides or study guides.
Residency: All course work may be completed off campus, utilizing correspondence methods. Interest free loans available to students.

California College of the Arts
1111 Eighth St, San Francisco CA 94107
Robynne Royster, Director of Admission
800-447-1-ART or 415-703-9523 Fax: 415-703-9539
Website: www.cca.edu
E-mail: enroll@cca.edu

California College of the Arts
Oakland Campus
5212 Broadway, Oakland CA 94618-1487
Robynne Royster, Director of Admission
800-447-1-ART Fax: 415-703-9539
Website: www.cca.edu
E-mail: enroll@cca.edu

California Institute of Technology
1200 E California Blvd, Pasadena CA 91106
626-395-6341

California Lutheran University
60 W Olsen Rd, Thousand Oaks CA 91360-2787
805-492-2411

California Polytechnic State University
San Luis Obispo CA 93407
805-756-1111

California State Polytechnic University
3801 W Temple Ave, Pomona CA 91768-2557
909-869-2000

California State University-Bakersfield
9001 Stockdale Hwy, Bakersfield CA 93311-1022
661-664-2011

California State University Channel Isle
1 University Dr, Camarillo CA 93012
805-437-8400

California State University-Chico
Chico CA 95929-0001
530-898-6116

California State University-Dominguez Hills
1000 E Victoria St, Carson CA 90747-0001
310-243-3300

California State University-East Bay
25800 Carlos Bee Blvd, Hayward CA 94542-3001
510-885-3000

California State University-Fresno
Fresno CA 93740-0001
559-278-4240

California State University-Fullerton
PO Box 34080
Fullerton CA 92634
714-278-2011

California State University-Long Beach
1250 N Bellflower Blvd, Long Beach CA 90840-0006
562-985-4111

California State University-Los Angeles
5151 State University Dr, Los Angeles CA 90032
323-343-3000

California State University-Monterey Bay
100 Campus Center, Seaside CA 93955-8000
831-582-3000

California State University-Northridge
18111 Nordhoff St, Northridge CA 91330-0001
818-677-1200

California State University-Sacramento
6000 J St, Sacramento CA 95819-2605
916-278-6011

California State University-San Bernadino
5500 University Pkwy
San Bernardino CA 92407-2393
Olivia Rosas, Director of Admissions
909-880-5000 Fax: 909-880-7034
Website: enrollment.csusb.edu
E-mail: orosas@csusb.edu

California State University-San Marcos
San Marcos CA 92096-0001
760-750-4000

California State University-Stanislaus
801 W Monte Vista Ave, Turlock CA 95382-0256
Lisa Bernardo, Director of Admissions
209-667-3070

Chapman University
One University Drive, Orange CA 92866-1099
Michael Drummy, Assistant Vice President for
Enrollment
Services and Chief Admission Officer
714-997-6411 or 888-CUAPPLY Fax: 714-997-6713
Website: www.chapman.edu
E-mail: admit@chapman.edu

Charles R. Drew University of Medicine & Science
1621 E 120th St, Los Angeles CA 90059
323-563-4800

Claremont McKenna College
500 E 9th St, Claremont CA 91711-5903
909-621-8000

COGSWELL COLLEGE
1175 Bordeaux Dr, Sunnyvale CA 94089-1210
Patricia Del Rio, Director of Admissions
800-264-7955 or 408-541-0100 Fax: 408-747-0764
Website: www.cogswell.edu
E-mail: info@cogswell.edu
Established in 1907. Private. Nonprofit. Coed. WASC
accredited. Fusion of Art and Engineering. Bachelor of
Arts Degrees: Digital Art and Animation (DAA), Digital
Motion Picture (DMP). Bachelor of Science Degrees:
Digital Audio Technology (DAT), Digital Arts Engineering
(DAE), Electrical Engineering (EE), Software Engineering
(SE), Fire Science (distance learning). Hands-on creative
environment. Student-teacher ratio 12:1. Professional-
quality software programs. Internships. Portfolio required
for DAA, DAT and DMP majors.

COLEMAN COLLEGE
8888 Balboa Ave, San Diego CA 92123-1506
Sheryl L. Ridens, Dean of Academics
858-499-0202 Fax: 858-499-0233
Website: www.coleman.edu
E-mail: admissions@coleman.edu

Coleman College
1284 W San Marcos Blvd Suite 110
San Marcos CA 92069-4073
760-747-3990

COMMUNITY CHRISTIAN COLLEGE
251 Tennessee St, Redlands CA 92373
909-335-8863 Fax: 909-335-9101
Website: www.cccollege.net
E-mail: admin@cccollege.net

Concordia University
1530 Concordia, Irvine CA 92612-3203
Lori McDonald, Executive Director of Enrollment
Services
800-229-1200 or 949-854-8002 Fax: 949-854-6894
Website: www.cui.edu
E-mail: admission@cui.edu

Concord Law School
10866 Wilshire Blvd Ste 1200, Los Angeles CA 90024
800-439-4794

Design Institute of San Diego
8555 Commerce Ave, San Diego CA 92121-2610
Paula Parrish, Director of Admissions
858-566-1200

Dominican University of California
50 Acacia Ave, San Rafael CA 94901-2298
Office of Admissions
888-323-6762

Emmanuel Bible College
1605 E Elizabeth St, Pasadena CA 91104
626-791-2575

Expression College for Digital Arts
6601 Shellmound St, Emeryville CA 94608
510-654-2934

Fashion Careers College
1923 Morena Blvd, San Diego CA 92110-3555
Tanya McAnear, Director of Admissions
619-275-4700 Fax: 619-275-0635
Website: www.fashioncareerscollege.com
E-mail: info@fashioncareerscollege.com
See listing under "Fashion Art"

FIDM/The Fashion Institute of Design & Merchandising
17590 Gillette Ave, Irvine CA 92614
Director of Admissions
949-851-6200 or 888-974-3436 Fax: 949-851-6808
Website: www.fidm.edu
E-mail: info@fidm.com
See listing under "Community and Junior Colleges"

FIDM/The Fashion Institute of Design & Merchandising
919 S Grand Ave, Los Angeles CA 90015-1421
Director of Admissions
213-624-1201 or 800-624-1200 Fax: 213-624-4799
Website: www.fidm.edu
E-mail: info@fidm.com
See listing under "Community and Junior Colleges"

FIDM/The Fashion Institute of Design & Merchandising
1010 2nd Ave, San Diego CA 92101-4903
Director of Admissions
619-235-2049 or 800-243-3436 Fax: 619-232-4322
Website: www.fidm.edu
E-mail: info@fidm.com
See listing under "Community and Junior Colleges"

FIDM/The Fashion Institute of Design & Merchandising
55 Stockton St, San Francisco CA 94108-5829
Director of Admissions
415-675-5200 or 800-422-3436 Fax: 415-296-7299
Website: www.fidm.edu
E-mail: info@fidm.com
See listing under "Community and Junior Colleges"

Fresno Pacific University
1717 S Chestnut Ave, Fresno CA 93702-4798
559-453-2000

Golden Gate University
536 Mission St, San Francisco CA 94105-2967
415-442-7000

Harvey Mudd College
Claremont CA 91711-3104
Peter Osgood, Contact
909-621-8011 Fax: 909-607-7046
Website: www.hmc.edu
E-mail: admission@hmc.edu

Holy Names University
3500 Mountain Blvd, Oakland CA 94619-1699
Dr. Hoffman-Marr, Director of Admissions
510-436-1010

Hope International University
2500 Nutwood Ave, Fullerton CA 92831-3104
714-879-3901

Humboldt State University
1 Harpst St, Arcata CA 95521-8299
707-826-3011

Humphreys College
6650 Inglewood Ave, Stockton CA 95207-3896
209-478-0800

Institute of Computer Technology
3200 Wilshire Blvd, Los Angeles CA 90010-1308
Director of Admissions
213-381-3333

Interior Designers Institute
1061 Camelback St, Newport Beach CA 92660-3228
949-675-4451

ITT Technical Institute
9680 Granite Ridge Dr, San Diego CA 92123-2657
858-571-8500

John F. Kennedy University
100 Ellinwood Way, Pleasant Hill CA 94523-4817
Ellena Bloedorn, Director of Admissions
925-969-3300

The Kings College and Seminary
14800 Sherman Way, Van Nuys CA 91405
818-779-8040

Laguna College of Art and Design
2222 Laguna Canyon Rd
Laguna Beach CA 92651-1136
Anthony Padilla, V.P. of Enrollment
800-255-0762

La Sierra University
4700 Pierce St, Riverside CA 92515-8247
Bobby Brown, Director of Admissions
800-874-5587

Life Pacific College
1100 W Covina Blvd, San Dimas CA 91773-3298
800-356-0001

Lincoln University
401 15th St, Oakland CA 94612-2801
510-628-8010

Loma Linda University
Loma Linda CA 92350-0001
Richard Weismeyer, Director
800-422-4558

Loyola Marymount University
7900 Loyola Blvd, Los Angeles CA 90045-2699
310-338-2700

Master's College and Seminary
21726 Placerita Canyon Rd, Newhall CA 91321-1235
661-259-3540

Menlo College
1000 El Camino Real, Atherton CA 94027-4300
650-688-3753

Mt. St. Mary's College
12001 Chalon Rd, Los Angeles CA 90049-1599
310-954-4000

National Hispanic University
14271 Story Rd, San Jose CA 95127-3889
Outreach & Recruitment
408-273-2680

National University
11255 N Torrey Pines Rd, La Jolla CA 92037-1011
858-642-8000

New College School of Law
50 Fell St, San Francisco CA 94102-5206
415-241-1300

Newschool of Architecture and Design
1249 F St, San Diego CA 92101-6634
Gilbert D. Cooke, AIA, Dean
Barbara Wingate, Director of Admissions
619-235-4100 ext. 123

Northwestern Polytechnic University
47671 Westinghouse Dr, Fremont CA 94539
Dr. P. Hsu, Contact
510-657-5913 Fax: 510-657-8975
Website: www.npu.edu
E-mail: npuadm@npu.edu

Notre Dame de Namur University
1500 Ralston Ave, Belmont CA 94002-1997
Martin Bednarek, Director of Admissions
800-263-0545

Occidental College
1600 Campus Rd, Los Angeles CA 90041-3314
323-259-2500

Otis College of Art and Design
9045 Lincoln Blvd, Los Angeles CA 90045-3505
Samuel Hoi, President
310-665-6800

PACIFIC STATES UNIVERSITY
1516 S Western Ave, Los Angeles CA 90006-4299
Dr. Brandon Kim, Associate University Dean
323-731-2383 Fax: 323-731-7276
Website: www.psuca.edu
E-mail: admissions@psuca.edu
Established 1928. Private. Coed. Accreditation: Accrediting Council for Independent Colleges & Schools
(ACICS). Tuition: BBA - $7,920, MBA - $8,400. Fees:
$1,910. Enrollment: 200. Faculty: 22. Student-faculty ra-
tio: 8:1. Degrees: BBA, MBA, BSCIS, MSCS, MSIS. Library: 15,000 volumes. 7 buildings. International student
body & faculty. Located in the great metropolitan city of
Los Angeles. Financial aid and scholarships are available.

Pacific Union College
1 Angwin Ave, Angwin CA 94508-9797
707-965-6311

Patten University
2433 Coolidge Ave, Oakland CA 94601-2699
Dr. Gary Moncher, President
Inez Bailey, Director of Admissions
510-261-8500

Pepperdine University
24255 Pacific Coast Hwy, Malibu CA 90263-0002
310-456-4000

Pitzer College
1050 N Mills Ave, Claremont CA 91711-6101
909-621-8219

PLATT COLLEGE
6250 El Cajon Blvd, San Diego CA 92115-3916
Carly Westerfield, Admissions Coordinator
619-265-0107 or 866-752-8826 Fax: 619-308-0570
Website: www.platt.edu
E-mail: info@platt.edu
Established 1980. Private. Coed. Accreditation:
ACCSCT. Tuition: Approximately $16,000. Fees: $100.
Enrollment: 350. Faculty: 25. Student-faculty ratio: 14:1.
Library: 1,700 volumes + online. 2 buildings. Design
school offering BS, AAS and diploma programs. "Hands
on" programs in Graphic Design, Multimedia Design,
Animation, Digital Video Production, and Web page design. Full range of General Education courses required to
complete AAS + BS degrees. Classes offered morning,
afternoon and evening. Job placement and financial aid
services available. Visit www.platt.edu.

Point Loma Nazarene University
3900 Lomaland Dr, San Diego CA 92106-2810
Eric Groves, Director of Admissions
800-733-7770

Pomona College
333 N College Way, Claremont CA 91711-4429
Peter W. Stanley, President

Remington College
123 Camino De La Reina #100N
San Diego CA 92108-3002
Christopher Tilley, Campus President
619-686-8600

St. Mary's College
1928 Saint Marys Rd, Moraga CA 94556-2744
925-631-4000

Samuel Merritt College
370 Hawthorne Ave, Oakland CA 94609-3108
Anne Seed, Assoc. Director of Admission
510-869-6610

San Diego Christian College
2100 Greenfield Dr, El Cajon CA 92019-1157
Jon Melone, Director of Admissions
800-676-2242 Fax: 619-590-1739
Website: www.sdcc.edu
E-mail: admissions@sdcc.edu

San Diego State University
5500 Campanile Dr, San Diego CA 92182-0002
619-594-5200

SAN FRANCISCO ART INSTITUTE
800 Chestnut St, San Francisco CA 94133
Paula Farmer, Director of Admission
800-345-SFAI Fax: 415-749-4503
Website: www.sfai.edu
E-mail: admissions@sfai.edu
Founded in 1871, SFAI offers one of the most innovative and interdisciplinary environments in higher education. Offering accredited Bachelor of Fine Arts (BFA), Bachelor of Arts (BA), Master of Fine Arts (MFA), Summer Master of Fine Arts (SMFA), Post-Baccalaureate (PB), and Master of Arts (MA) programs, SFAI is committed to furthering the relationship between the practices and theories of contemporary art. SFAI's School of Studio Practice centers on the development of the artist's vision and consists of the departments of: Design+Technology, Film, New Genres, Painting, Photography, Printmaking, and Sculpture. SFAI's School of Interdisciplinary Studies offers BA and MA programs in History and Theory of Contemporary Art, Urban Studies, and Exhibition and Museum Studies (MA only). Together the two schools provide an inclusive model to address contemporary art and culture, and the programs prepare students to be creative practitioners in a variety of professional fields. The Summer MFA program has the same rigor as the Academic Year MFA, yet is designed for those who choose an alternate academic schedule. The Post-Baccalaureate program is an excellent way to prepare for entrance into an MFA program or to enhance skills and knowledge. SFAI's faculty is comprised of active artists, curators, writers, and scholars. Dean of Academic Affairs is renowned curator and critic Okwui Enwezor. Dean of Graduate Studies is artist and filmmaker Renee Green. Director of Exhibitions and Public Programs is curator Hou Hanru. Visiting artists and scholars play a significant role in education at SFAI, with recent visitors including Matthew Barney, William Kentridge, Raqs Media Collective, and others. All students have 24-hour access to the SFAI campus. SFAI's main campus includes painting, photography, sculpture, and printmaking studios, post-production facilities, and the first high-definition video research lab in the Bay Area. The Diego Rivera Gallery, an open-air amphitheater, and a 250-seat theater are also available to students for exhibiting and screening work. SFAI's library collection includes more than 26,000 volumes with emphasis on modern and contemporary art, over 200 current periodicals, and an extensive image, video, and audio archive available only to SFAI students. The 62,000 square-foot Graduate Center includes a digital lab, film and sound studios, darkrooms, a woodshop, and a gallery for student work. SFAI has rolling application deadlines, and there are competitive and need-based scholarships available to undergraduates, a fellowship program for graduate students, and community college scholarships for transfer students. Visit the SFAI website for specific application requirements.

SAN FRANCISCO CONSERVATORY OF MUSIC
50 Oak St, San Francisco CA 94102
Alexander Brose, Director of Admission
800-899-7326 Fax: 415-503-6299
Website: www.sfcm.edu
E-mail: admit@sfcm.edu

San Francisco State University
1600 Holloway Ave, San Francisco CA 94132-1722
415-338-1111

San Jose State University
1 Washington Sq, San Jose CA 95192-0001
408-924-1000

Santa Clara University
500 El Camino Real, Santa Clara CA 95053-0001
408-554-4000

Shasta Bible College & Graduate School
2951 Goodwater Ave, Redding CA 96002
530-221-4275

SOKA UNIVERSITY OF AMERICA
1 University Dr, Aliso Viejo CA 92656
Eric Hauber, Ph.D., Dean of Student Recruitment
949-480-4150 Fax: 949-480-4151
Website: www.soka.edu
E-mail: hauber@soka.edu

Sonoma State University
1801 E Cotati Ave, Rohnert Park CA 94928-3609
Louis T. Levy, Senior Director Enrollment Services
707-664-2880

Southern California Institute of Architecture
960 E 3rd St, Los Angeles CA 90013-1822
Wenona Colinco, Director of Admissions
213-613-2200

SOUTHERN CALIFORNIA SEMINARY
2075 E Madison Ave, El Cajon CA 92019
Ed Herrelko, Director of Student Services
619-442-9841 Fax: 619-442-4510
Website: www.socalsem.edu
E-mail: info@socalsem.edu

Stanford University
Hopkins Marine Station, Pacific Grove CA 93950
831-373-0464

Stanford University
520 Lasuen Mall Union 232, Stanford CA 94305-3005
650-723-2300

Thomas Aquinas College
10000 Ojai Rd, Santa Paula CA 93060-9621
800-634-9797

Touro University International
5665 Plaza Dr 3rd Floor, Cypress CA 90630
714-816-0366

Trinity Life Bible College
5225 Hillsdale Blvd, Sacramento CA 95842
916-348-4689

University of California
110 Sproul Hall, Berkeley CA 94720-5804
510-642-6000

University of California
1 Shields Ave, Davis CA 95616
530-752-1011

University of California
Irvine CA 92697-0001
949-824-5011

University of California
9500 Gilman Dr, La Jolla CA 92093
858-534-2230

University of California
Los Angeles CA 90095-0001
310-825-4321

University of California
900 University Ave, Riverside CA 92521-0001
951-827-1012

University of California
Santa Barbara CA 93106
805-893-8000

University of California-Davis
2315 Stockton Blvd, Sacramento CA 95817-2201
916-453-3096

University of California-Irvine Med. Ctr
101 The City Dr S, Orange CA 92868-3201
714-456-5678

University of California Los Angeles
Center for the Health Sciences
10833 Le Conte Ave, Los Angeles CA 90095-3075
310-825-5654

University of California Medical Center
200 W Arbor Dr #H-910C, San Diego CA 92103-1911
619-543-6654

University of California-Santa Cruz
Santa Cruz CA 95064
831-459-0111

University of Judaism
15600 Mulholland Dr, Los Angeles CA 90077-1599
Bryan Pisetsky, Director of Undergraduate Admissions
310-476-9777

University of La Verne
1950 3rd St, La Verne CA 91750-4443
800-876-4858

University of Redlands
PO Box 3080, Redlands CA 92373-0999
909-793-2121

University of San Diego
5998 Alcala Park, San Diego CA 92110-2492
Admissions
619-260-4506

University of San Francisco
2130 Fulton St, San Francisco CA 94117-1050
415-422-5555

University of Southern California
Univ Park, Los Angeles CA 90089-0001
213-740-2311

University of the Pacific
3601 Pacific Ave, Stockton CA 95211-0197
209-946-2011

UNIVERSITY OF THE WEST
1409 N Walnut Grove Ave, Rosemead CA 91770
Grace Hsiao, Registrar & Admissions Officer
626-571-8811 Fax: 626-571-1413
Website: www.uwest.edu
E-mail: graceh@uwest.edu

Vanguard University of Southern California
55 Fair Dr, Costa Mesa CA 92626-6597
714-556-3610

Westmont College
955 La Paz Rd, Santa Barbara CA 93108-1099
Joyce Luy, Director of Admissions
805-565-6200

Westwood College
3250 Wilshire Blvd Fl 4, Los Angeles CA 90010
213-739-9999

Whittier College
PO Box 634, Whittier CA 90608-0634
Kieron Miller, Director of Admissions
562-907-4200 Fax: 562-907-4870
Website: www.whittier.edu
E-mail: kmiller@whittier.edu

William Jessup University
1190 Saratoga Ave Ste 210, San Jose CA 95129
408-278-4343

Woodbury University
7500 N Glenoaks Blvd, Burbank CA 91504-1099
818-767-0888

World Mission University
500 Shatto Pl Ste 600, Los Angeles CA 90020
213-385-2322

COLORADO

Adams State College
Alamosa CO 81102
Matt Gallegos, Director of Admissions
800-824-6494

American University of Paris
950 S Cherry St Ste 240, Denver CO 80246
303-757-6333

Art Institute of Colorado
1200 Lincoln St, Denver CO 80203-2172
David Zorn, President
Brian A. Parker, Director of Admissions
800-275-2420 Fax: 303-860-8520
Website: www.artinstitutes.edu
E-mail: baparker@aii.edu

CollegeAmerica - Colorado
Main Campus
1385 S Colorado Blvd 5th Floor
Denver CO 80222-3304
Barbara Thomas, President
303-691-9756

CollegeAmerica - Colorado Springs
3645 Citadel Dr S, Colorado Springs CO 80909
719-637-0600

CollegeAmerica - Fort Collins
4601 S Mason St, Fort Collins CO 80525-3740
Anna DiTorrice-Mull, Director of Admissions
970-223-6060

College for Financial Planning
8000 E Maplewood Ave, Greenwood Vlg CO 80111
303-220-1200

Colorado Christian University
180 S Garrison St, Lakewood CO 80226-1053
800-44-FAITH

Colorado College
14 E Cache La Poudre St
Colorado Springs CO 80903-3243
719-389-6344

Colorado School of Mines
1500 Illinois St, Golden CO 80401
Bill Young, Director of Enrollment Management
303-273-3220

COLORADO SCHOOL OF TRADITIONAL CHINESE MEDICINE
1441 York St Ste 202, Denver CO 80206
David DiBrigida, Administrative Director
303-329-6355 Fax: 303-388-8165
Website: www.cstcm.edu
E-mail: admin@cstcm.edu

Colorado State University
102 Administration, Fort Collins CO 80523-0001
970-491-1101

Colorado State University - Pueblo
2200 Bonforte Blvd, Pueblo CO 81001-4990
719-549-2461

Colorado Technical University
4435 N Chestnut St
Colorado Springs CO 80907-3895
719-598-0200

DeVry Institute of Technology
5775 DTC Blvd, Greenwood Village CO 80111
303-694-6600

Fort Lewis College
1000 Rim Dr, Durango CO 81301-3999
970-247-7010

JONES INTERNATIONAL UNIVERSITY
9697 E Mineral Ave, Centennial CO 80112-3446
Education Center
800-811-5663 Fax: 303-784-8547
Website: www.jonesinternational.edu
E-mail: info@international.edu

Mesa State College
1100 North Ave, Grand Junction CO 81501
970-248-1020

Metropolitan State College
PO Box 173362, Campus Box 16
Denver CO 80217-3362
William S. Hathaway-Clark, Director of Admissions
303-556-3058

Naropa University
2130 Arapahoe Ave, Boulder CO 80302-6697
303-546-3572

National American University
5125 N Academy Blvd
Colorado Springs CO 80918-4001
Jeanne Liepe, Campus Director
719-277-0588

National American University
1325 S Colorado Blvd #100, Denver CO 80222-3308
Nathan Larson, Regional President
303-758-6700

Nazarene Bible College
1111 Academy Park Loop
Colorado Springs CO 80910-3717
Dr. Laurel Matson, VP for Enrollment & Student Development
719-596-5110 Fax: 719-884-5199
Website: www.nbc.edu
E-mail: admissions@nbc.edu

Regis University
3333 Regis Blvd, Denver CO 80221-1099
303-458-4900

ROCKY MOUNTAIN COLLEGE OF ART & DESIGN
1600 Pierce St, Lakewood CO 80214
Marianna Bagge, Director of Admissions
800-888-2787 Fax: 303-759-4970
Website: www.rmcad.edu
E-mail: admissions@rmcad.edu

Teikyo Loretto Heights University
3001 S Federal Blvd, Denver CO 80236-2711
303-936-8441

United States Air Force Academy
USAF Academy CO 80840
719-333-1110

University of Colorado
Boulder CO 80309-0001
303-492-1411

University of Colorado
1420 Austin Bluffs Pkwy
Colorado Springs CO 80918-3735
719-262-3000

University of Colorado at Denver and Health Sciences Center
Downtown Denver Campus
PO Box 173364, Denver CO 80217-3364
303-556-5600
Website: www.cudenver.edu

University of Colorado at Denver and Health Sciences Center
Health Sciences Program
4200 E 9th Ave Box C245, Denver CO 80262
Phoebe Lindsey Barton, Ph.D., Director
Website: www.uchsc.edu

University of Denver
2199 S University Blvd, Denver CO 80208-0001
303-871-2000

UNIVERSITY OF DENVER UNIVERSITY COLLEGE
2211 S Josephine St, Denver CO 80208
Dr. James R. Davis, Dean
303-871-3354 Fax: 303-871-4047
Website: www.universitycollege.du.edu
E-mail: ucolinfo@du.edu

University of Northern Colorado
Greeley CO 80639
Gary Gullickson, Director of Admissions
970-351-2881

University of Phoenix
Colorado Division
10004 Park Meadows Dr, Lonetree CO 80124-5453
303-755-9090

Western State College of Colorado
Gunnison CO 81231-0001
Director of Admissions
800-876-5309

Yeshiva Toras Chaim Talmudic Seminary
1555 Stuart St, Denver CO 80204
303-629-8200

CONNECTICUT
Albertus Magnus College
700 Prospect St, New Haven CT 06511-1189
Richard Lolatte, Dean of Admission
203-773-8501 or 800-578-9160 Fax: 203-773-5248
Website: www.albertus.edu
E-mail: admissions@albertus.edu

ALLEN INSTITUTE CENTER FOR INNOVATIVE LEARNING
PO Box 100, Hebron CT 06248
866-666-6910
Website: www.alleninstitute.info
E-mail: info@alleninstitute.info

Beth Benjamin Academy of Connecticut
132 Prospect St, Stamford CT 06901-1284
203-325-4351

Central Connecticut State University
1615 Stanley St, New Britain CT 06053-2439
860-832-3200

Connecticut College
270 Mohegan Ave, New London CT 06320-4150
860-447-1911

Eastern Connecticut State University
83 Windham St, Willimantic CT 06226-2295
860-456-5000

Fairfield University
1073 N Benson Rd, Fairfield CT 06824-5171
203-254-4000

Hartt Community Division
200 Bloomfield Ave, West Hartford CT 06117
Michael Yaffe, School Director
860-768-7768

Holy Apostles College and Seminary
33 Prospect Hill Rd, Cromwell CT 06416-2027
860-632-3000

Paier College of Art
20 Gorham Ave, Hamden CT 06514-3902
203-287-3032

Post University
800 Country Club Rd, Waterbury CT 06708-3240
Sandra M. Fernandes, Associate Director of Admissions
Will Johnson, Associate Director of Admissions
203-596-4520

Quinnipiac University
275 Mount Carmel Ave, Hamden CT 06518-1905
Joan Isaac Mohr, VP & Dean of Admissions
203-582-8600

Sacred Heart University
5151 Park Ave, Fairfield CT 06825-1023
203-371-7999

Southern Connecticut State University
501 Crescent St, New Haven CT 06515-1355
203-392-5200

Trinity College
300 Summit St, Hartford CT 06106-3186
Larry Dow, Dean of Admissions & Financial Aid
860-297-2180

United States Coast Guard Academy
15 Mohegan Ave, New London CT 06320-4195
800-883-8724

University of Bridgeport
126 Park Ave, Bridgeport CT 06604-5620
Barbara L. Maryak, Dean of Admissions
203-576-4552

University of Connecticut
1084 Shennecossett Rd, Groton CT 06340-6048
860-486-4444

University of Connecticut
Storrs CT 06269-0001
860-486-2000

University of Connecticut
32 Hillside Ave, Waterbury CT 06710-2217
203-757-1231

University of Connecticut
1800 Asylum Ave, West Hartford CT 06117-2699
860-241-4700

University of Connecticut Health Center
263 Farmington Ave, Farmington CT 06032-1956
860-679-2000

University of Hartford
200 Bloomfield Ave, West Hartford CT 06117-1599
860-768-4100

University of New Haven
300 Boston Post Rd, West Haven CT 06516
Director of Undergraduate Admissions
203-932-7319 Fax: 203-931-6093
Website: www.newhaven.edu
E-mail: adminfo@newhaven.edu

Wesleyan University
Middletown CT 06459-0001
860-685-2000

Western Connecticut State University
181 White St, Danbury CT 06810-6826
203-837-8200

Yale University
38 Hillhouse Ave, New Haven CT 06511
203-432-4771

DELAWARE
Delaware State University
1200 N DuPont Hwy, Dover DE 19901-2275
302-857-6060

Goldey-Beacom College
4701 Limestone Rd, Wilmington DE 19808-1993
Stacey Schwartz, Assistant Director of Admissions
302-998-8814 Fax: 302-996-5408
Website: www.gbc.edu
E-mail: admissions@gbc.edu

University of Delaware
Newark DE 19711
302-831-2000

Wesley College
120 N State St, Dover DE 19901-3876
302-736-2300 Fax: 302-736-2301
Website: www.wesley.edu

Wilmington College
320 N DuPont Hwy, New Castle DE 19720-6491
302-328-9401

DISTRICT OF COLUMBIA
American University
4400 Massachusetts Ave NW
Washington DC 20016-8200
202-885-1000

Catholic University of America
620 Michigan Ave NE, Washington DC 20064-0001
202-319-5000

CORCORAN COLLEGE OF ART AND DESIGN
500 17th St NW, Washington DC 20006-4804
Elizabeth Paladino, Director of Admission
202-639-1814 or 888-CORCORAN Fax: 202-639-1830
Website: www.corcoran.edu
E-mail: admissions@corcoran.org

Gallaudet University
800 Florida Ave NE, Washington DC 20002-3695
Charity Reedy Hines, Director of Admissions
202-651-5750

Georgetown University
37th and O St NW, Washington DC 20057-0001
202-687-0100

George Washington University
2035 H St NW, Washington DC 20052-0002
202-994-1000

Howard University
2400 6th St NW, Washington DC 20059-0002
202-806-6100

Potomac College
4000 Chesapeake St NW, Washington DC 20016
Florence Tate, President
202-686-0876 Fax: 202-686-0818
Website: www.potomac.edu
E-mail: ftate@potomac.edu

Southeastern University
501 I St SW, Washington DC 20024-2788
Sean Jamieson, Director of Admissions
202-478-8210 Fax: 202-488-8093
Website: www.seu.edu
E-mail: admissions@admin.seu.edu

Strayer University
1133 15th St NW, Washington DC 20005
202-419-0400

University of the District of Columbia
4200 Connecticut Ave NW
Washington DC 20008-1174
LaVerne M. Hill-Flanagan, Director of Admissions
202-274-5100

FLORIDA
American InterContinental University
8151 Peters Rd Ste 1000, Plantation FL 33324-4005
954-835-0939

Argosy University/Sarasota
5250 17th St, Sarasota FL 34235-8242
800-331-5995

Art Institute of Tampa
4401 N Himes Ave Ste 150, Tampa FL 33614
813-873-2112

Asbury Theological Seminary
Florida Campus
8401 Valencia College Ln, Orlando FL 32825
Rev. Eric Currie, Assistant Director of Admissions
407-482-7500

Ave Maria University
1025 Commons Cir, Naples FL 34119
877-283-8648

THE BAPTIST COLLEGE OF FLORIDA
5400 College Dr, Graceville FL 32440-1831
Christopher M. Bishop, Director of Admissions
800-328-2660 Fax: 850-263-9026
Website: www.baptistcollege.edu
E-mail: admissions@baptistcollege.edu

Barry University
11300 NE 2nd Ave, Miami Shores FL 33161-6695
800-695-2279

Beacon College
105 E Main St, Leesburg FL 34748-5162
Carolyn Scott, Director of Admissions
352-787-7660

Bethune-Cookman College
640 Dr Mary McLeod Bethune Blvd
Daytona Beach FL 32114-3099
Edwin Coffie, Director of Admissions
800-448-0228

CARLOS ALBIZU UNIVERSITY
2173 NW 99th Ave, Miami FL 33172-2209
Gerardo Alvarado, MBA, Director of Admissions, Recruitment & Outreach
305-593-1223 ext. 137 Fax: 305-593-1854
Website: www.mia.albizu.edu
E-mail: admissions@albizu.edu

City College
2000 W Commercial Blvd, Fort Lauderdale FL 33309
Britt Carpenter, Director of Admissions
954-492-5353 Fax: 954-491-1965
Website: www.citycollege.edu
E-mail: bcarpenter@citycollege.edu

Clearwater Christian College
3400 Gulf To Bay Blvd, Clearwater FL 33759-4595
727-726-1153

Eckerd College
4200 54th Ave S, Saint Petersburg FL 33711
727-867-1166

Edison College
PO Box 60210, Fort Myers FL 33906-6210
Billee Silva, Director Student Development
239-489-9054

Edward Waters College
1658 Kings Rd, Jacksonville FL 32209-6199
904-355-3030

EVERGLADES UNIVERSITY (MAIN CAMPUS)
5002 T-Rex Ave Suite 100, Boca Raton FL 33431
Kristi Mollis, President
888-772-6077 Fax: 561-912-1191
Website: www.evergladesuniversity.edu
E-mail: admissions-boca@evergladesuniversity.edu
Private. Coed. Accreditation: ACCSCT. Tuition: $406 per credit. Enrollment: 725. Faculty: 125. On campus student-faculty ratio: 8:1. Online student to faculty ratio: 18:1. Classes are offered on campus and online, small student-faculty ratio, courses are taught one subject per month, monthly start dates. Financial aid to those who qualify, placement assistance available upon graduation.

EVERGLADES UNIVERSITY
Orlando Campus (Branch Campus)
5600 Lake Underhill Rd Suite 200, Orlando FL 32807
Shirley Long, Vice President
866-289-1078 Fax: 407-482-9801
Website: www.evergladesuniversity.edu
E-mail: admissions-orl@evergladesuniversity.edu
Private. Coed. Accreditation: ACCSCT. Tuition: $406 per credit Enrollment: 725. Faculty: 125. Student-faculty ratio: 8:1. Classes are offered on campus, small student-faculty ratio, courses are taught one subject per month, monthly start dates. Financial aid to those who qualify, placement assistance available upon graduation.

EVERGLADES UNIVERSITY
Sarasota Campus (Branch Campus)
6001 Lake Osprey Dr, Sarasota FL 34240
Brad Brewer, Vice President
866-907-2262 Fax: 941-907-6634
Website: www.evergladesuniversity.edu
E-mail: admissions-sar@evergladesuniversity.edu
Private. Coed. Accreditation: ACCSCT. Tuition: $406 per credit. Enrollment: 725. Faculty: 125. Student-faculty ratio: 8:1. Classes are offered on campus and on-line, small student-faculty ratio, courses are taught one subject per month, monthly start dates. Financial aid to those

who qualify, placement assistance available upon graduation.

Flagler College
PO Box 1027, Saint Augustine FL 32085-1027
904-829-6481

Florida A&M University
Tallahassee FL 32307
850-599-3000

Florida Atlantic University
PO Box 3091, Boca Raton FL 33431-0991
800-299-4328

Florida Gulf Coast University
10501 FGCU Blvd, Fort Myers FL 33965-0001
239-590-1000

Florida Institute of Technology
150 W University Blvd, Melbourne FL 32901-6975
Judi Marino, Director of Admissions
800-888-4348

Florida International University
Tamiami Trl, Miami FL 33199-0001
305-348-2000

Florida International University
Biscayne Blvd and 151st St, North Miami FL 33181
305-940-5625

Florida Memorial University
15800 NW 42nd Ave, Opa Locka FL 33054-6199
305-626-3600

Florida Metropolitan University
225 N Federal Hwy, Pompano Beach FL 33062
Fran Heaston, Director of Admissions
800-468-0168

Florida Metropolitan University-Brandon
3924 Coconut Palm Dr, Tampa FL 33619-1354
Marty Baca, Director of Admissions
877-338-0068 (Toll Free)

Florida Metropolitan University-Lakeland Campus
995 E Memorial Blvd Ste 110
Lakeland FL 33801-1973
Jodi De La Garza, Director of Admissions
863-686-1444

Florida Metropolitan University
Melbourne Campus
2401 N Harbor City Blvd, Melbourne FL 32935
321-253-2929

Florida Metropolitan University
Orlando College - North
5421 Diplomat Cir, Orlando FL 32810-5601
Charlene Donnelly, Director of Admissions
800-628-5870

Florida Metropolitan University
Orlando South
9200 Southpark Center Loop, Orlando FL 32819
Annette Cloin, Contact
407-851-2525 Fax: 407-851-1477
Website: www.fmu.edu
E-mail: acloin@cci.edu

FLORIDA METROPOLITAN UNIVERSITY
Pinellas Campus
2471 N McMullen Booth Rd
Clearwater FL 33759-1359
Sandra Williams, Director of Admissions
800-353-3687 or 727-725-2688 Fax: 727-725-3827
Website: www.fmu.edu
E-mail: sawilliams@cci.edu

Florida Metropolitan University
Tampa Campus
3319 W Hillsborough Ave, Tampa FL 33614-5801
Donnie Broughton, Director of Admissions
813-879-6000

Florida Southern College
111 Lake Hollingsworth Dr, Lakeland FL 33801-5607
Robert B. Palmer, V.P., Dean of Enrollment Management
863-680-4131

Florida State University
600 W College Ave, Tallahassee FL 32306-1096
Janice V. Finney, Director of Admissions
850-644-2525 Fax: 850-644-0197
Website: admissions.fsu.edu
E-mail: admissions@admin.fsu.edu

HERZING COLLEGE
1595 S Semoran Blvd #1501
Winter Park FL 32792-5509
Kathy Nagle, Director of Admissions
407-478-0500 Fax: 407-478-0501
Website: www.herzing.edu
E-mail: info@orl.herzing.edu

Hobe Sound Bible College
PO Box 1065, Hobe Sound FL 33475-1065
772-546-5534

International Academy of Design & Technology
5104 Eisenhower Blvd, Tampa FL 33634-6313
Richard Costa, V.P. of Admissions and Marketing
813-880-8092 Fax: 813-881-0008
Website: www.academy.edu
E-mail: admissions@academy.edu

INTERNATIONAL ACADEMY OF DESIGN AND TECHNOLOGY
5959 Lake Ellenor Dr, Orlando FL 32809-4633
Dr. John Dietrich, VP of Admissions
877-753-0007 Fax: 407-251-0465
Website: www.iadt.edu
E-mail: info@iadt.edu

INTERNATIONAL COLLEGE
4501 Colonial Blvd, Fort Myers FL 33966
Rita Lampus, Vice President of Enrollment Management
800-466-0019 or 239-482-0019 Fax: 239-938-7891
Website: www.internationalcollege.edu
E-mail: cmorrison@internationalcollege.edu

INTERNATIONAL COLLEGE
2655 Northbrooke Dr, Naples FL 34119
Rita Lampus, Vice President of Enrollment Management
800-466-8017 or 239-513-1122 Fax: 239-598-6254
Website: www.internationalcollege.edu
E-mail: admit@internationalcollege.edu
Established 1990. Private. Coed. Accreditation: SACS. Tuition: $12,960 (including summer term). Fees: $190/semester. Enrollment: 984 full-time, 620 part-time. Faculty: 109. Student-faculty ratio: 19:1. Degrees: Associate in Science, Bachelor of Science, Master of Business Admin, Master of Public Admin, Master of Science. Library: 35,725 volumes. 2 buildings. 3 miles from the Gulf of Mexico.

Jacksonville University
2800 University Blvd N, Jacksonville FL 32211-3394
904-744-3950

Johnson & Wales University
1701 NE 127th St, North Miami FL 33181-2518
Jeff Greenip, Director of Admissions
305-892-7000

Jones College
5353 Arlington Expy, Jacksonville FL 32211-5588
Dorothy D. Jones, Chief Executive Officer
904-743-1122 Fax: 904-744-4446
Website: www.jones.edu
E-mail: lwade@jones.edu

Jones College
11430 N Kendall Dr Ste 200, Miami FL 33176
Barclay Charles, Contact
305-275-9996 Fax: 305-743-4446
Website: www.jones.edu
E-mail: pcarbone@jones.edu

Lake Erie College of Osteopathic Medicine
5000 Lakewood Ranch Blvd
Bradenton FL 34211-4909
June Flaim, Student Affairs Coordinator
941-756-0690

Lynn University
3601 N Military Trl, Boca Raton FL 33431-5598
Brett Ormandy, Director of Admissions
561-237-7900 Fax: 561-237-7100
Website: www.lynn.edu
E-mail: admission@lynn.edu

Miami International University of Art & Design
1501 Biscayne Blvd, Miami FL 33132
Elsia Suarez, Director of Admissions
800-225-9023

New College of Florida
5700 N Tamiami Trl, Sarasota FL 34243-2146
941-359-4310

NORTH TENNESSEE BIBLE INSTITUTE AND SEMINARY
556 W Bayshore Dr, Eastpoint FL 32328
Dr. Celeste Wall, President
850-927-4711
Website: www.ntbis.com
E-mail: drwhc@ntbis.com

Northwood University
2600 N Military Trl, West Palm Beach FL 33409-2999
Jack Letvinchuk, Director of Admissions
800-458-8325 Fax: 561-640-3328
Website: www.northwood.edu
E-mail: fladmit@northwood.edu

Nova Southeastern University
3301 College Ave, Davie FL 33314-7796
954-262-7300

Nova Southeastern University Health Profession
3200 S University Dr, Davie FL 33328-2018
Marla Frohlinger, Director of Admissions
954-262-1101 Fax: 954-262-2282
Website: www.nova.edu
E-mail: marlaf@nsu.nova.edu

Palm Beach Atlantic University
PO Box 24708, West Palm Beach FL 33416-4708
561-803-2000

Pensacola Christian College
PO Box 18000, Pensacola FL 32523-9160
850-478-8496

Polytechnic University of the Americas
8180 NW 36th St, Doral FL 33166
305-418-4220

Ringling School of Art & Design
2700 N Tamiami Trl, Sarasota FL 34234-5812
James H. Dean, Dean of Admissions
941-351-5100

Rollins College
1000 Holt Ave, Winter Park FL 32789
407-646-2000

Saint Leo University
PO Box 6665, Saint Leo FL 33574
Deborah Bandy, Director of Admissions
352-588-8200 or 800-334-5532 Fax: 352-588-8257
Website: www.saintleo.edu
E-mail: admission@saintleo.edu

St. Thomas University
16401 NW 37th Ave, Miami Gardens FL 33054
Andre Lightbourn, Director of Admissions
800-367-9010 or 305-628-6546 Fax: 305-628-6591
Website: www.stu.edu
E-mail: signup@stu.edu

Schiller International University
453 Edgewater Dr, Dunedin FL 34698-7532
Markus Leibrecht, Director of Admissions
727-736-5082

Southeastern University
1000 Longfellow Blvd, Lakeland FL 33801-6099
863-667-5000

South University
1760 N Congress Ave
West Palm Beach FL 33409-5178
Steven A. Schwab, President
561-697-9200 Fax: 561-697-9944
Website: www.southuniversity.edu
E-mail: wpb@southuniversity.edu
SACS Accreditation.

Stetson University
421 N Woodland Boulevard, De Land FL 32720-3761
386-822-7000

Strayer University
6302 E Martin Luther King Blvd Ste 450
Tampa FL 33619
813-663-0100

Strayer University
4902 Eisenhower Blvd Ste 100, Tampa FL 33634
813-882-0100

Trinity Baptist College
800-200 Hammond Blvd, Jacksonville FL 32221
R. Larry Appleby, Director of Admissions
904-596-2400 Fax: 904-596-2531
Website: www.tbc.edu
E-mail: emailtrinity@tbc.edu

TRINITY COLLEGE OF FLORIDA
2430 Welbilt Blvd, Trinity FL 34655-4401
Dr. David Colburn, VP of Enrollment & Adult Education
800-388-0869 Fax: 727-569-1410
Website: www.trinitycollege.edu
E-mail: admissions@trinitycollege.edu
Established 1932. Bachelor of Arts in Biblical Studies. Associates of Arts. Certificate Programs. Majors: Church Ministries, Counseling, Missions, Elementary Education. Quest Adult Completion Program. Bachelor of Science. Majors: Leadership and Ministry, Management and Ethics, Counseling and Mediation, Elementary Education. Accreditation: ABHE. Financial Aid for those who qualify.

University of Central Florida
PO Box 160111, Orlando FL 32816
407-823-3000

University of Florida
PO Box 114000, Gainesville FL 32611-4000
352-392-3261

University of Miami
PO Box 248006, Coral Gables FL 33124-8006
305-284-2211

University of Miami
4600 Rickenbacker Cswy, Miami FL 33149-1031
305-361-4000

University of North Florida
4567 Saint Johns Bluff Rd S
Jacksonville FL 32224-2645
904-620-1000

University of South Florida
140 7th Ave S, Saint Petersburg FL 33701-5001
727-893-9536

University of South Florida
4202 E Fowler Ave, Tampa FL 33620-6900
J. Robert Spatig, Director of Admissions
813-974-3350 Fax: 813-974-9689
Website: www.usf.edu
E-mail: admissions@admin.usf.edu

University of Tampa
401 W Kennedy Blvd, Tampa FL 33606-1490
813-253-3333

University of West Florida
11000 University Pkwy, Pensacola FL 32514-5750
850-474-2000

Warner Southern College
5301 US Highway 27 S, Lake Wales FL 33859-8725
863-638-1426

Webber International University
PO Box 96, Babson Park FL 33827-0096
863-638-1431

Yeshiva Gedolah Rabbinical College
1140 Alton Rd, Miami Beach FL 33139
305-673-5664

GEORGIA

Albany State University
504 College Dr, Albany GA 31705-2796
229-430-4600

American InterContinental University
3330 Peachtree Rd NE, Atlanta GA 30326-1016
404-965-5700

American InterContinental University
6600 Peachtree Dunwoody Rd
500 Embassy Row, Atlanta GA 30328
404-965-6500

Armstrong Atlantic State University
11935 Abercorn St, Savannah GA 31419-1997
Kim West, Asst. Dean and Registrar Enrollment Services
912-927-5277 Fax: 912-921-5462
Website: www.armstrong.edu
E-mail: admissions@mail.armstrong.edu

Art Institute of Atlanta
6600 Peachtree Dunwoody Rd
100 Embassy Row, Atlanta GA 30328-1649
Donna Scott, Director of Admissions
800-275-4242

Atlanta Christian College
2605 Ben Hill Rd, East Point GA 30344-1999
404-761-8861

Augusta State University
2500 Walton Way, Augusta GA 30904-4562
706-737-1400

BEACON UNIVERSITY
6003 Veterans Pkwy, Columbus GA 31909
Admissions Department
706-323-5364 Fax: 706-323-3236
Website: www.beacon.edu
E-mail: beacon@beacon.edu

Berry College
2277 Martha Berry Hwy NE
Mount Berry GA 30149-0149
706-232-5374

BEULAH HEIGHTS BIBLE COLLEGE
PO Box 18145, Atlanta GA 30316-0145
Dr. James B. Keiller, V.P. & Dean of Academic Affairs
404-627-2681 Fax: 404-627-0702
Website: www.beulah.org
E-mail: bhbc@beulah.org

Brewton-Parker College
Highway 280, Mount Vernon GA 30445
800-342-1087

Carver Bible College
PO Box 4335, Atlanta GA 30302-4335
800-262-4253

Clark Atlanta University
223 James Brawley Dr SW, Atlanta GA 30314
404-880-8000

Clayton State University
5900 N Lee St, Morrow GA 30260
770-961-3500

Columbus State University
4225 University Ave, Columbus GA 31907-5645
706-568-2001

Covenant College
14049 Scenic Hwy, Lookout Mountain GA 30750
706-820-1560

Emmanuel College
PO Box 129, Franklin Springs GA 30639-0129
800-860-8800

Emory University
200B Jones Center, Atlanta GA 30322
404-727-6123

Fort Valley State University
1005 State University Dr, Fort Valley GA 31030-3298
Gerri McCord, Dean of Admissions & Enrollment
478-825-6307

Georgia College and State University
231 W Hancock St, Milledgeville GA 31061-3371
478-445-5350

Georgia Institute of Technology
225 North Ave NW, Atlanta GA 30332-0002
404-894-2000

Georgia Southern University
PO Box 8024, Statesboro GA 30460
Admissions Office
912-681-5532

Georgia Southwestern State University
800 Wheatley St, Americus GA 31709-4635
229-928-1279

Georgia State University
PO Box 4009, Atlanta GA 30302-4009
404-651-2365

Herzing College
3355 Lenox Rd NE Ste 100, Atlanta GA 30326-1332
Richard Hinton, Director of Admissions
404-816-4533

ITT Technical Institute
1000 Cobb Place Blvd NW, Kennesaw GA 30144
770-426-3000

Kennesaw State University
1000 Chastain Rd NW, Kennesaw GA 30144-5591
Dr. Ralph Rascati, Dean
770-423-6000
Website: www.kennesaw.edu

LaGrange College
601 Broad St, LaGrange GA 30240-2955
Andy Geeter, Director of Admission
800-593-2885

Life University
1269 Barclay Cir SE, Marietta GA 30060-2903
Dr. Deborah E. Heairlston, Director of New Student Development
770-426-2884 Fax: 770-426-2895
Website: www.life.edu
E-mail: admissions@life.edu

Luther Rice University
3038 Evans Mill Rd, Lithonia GA 30038
Russ Sorrow, Director of Enrollment Management
770-484-1204 Fax: 770-484-1155
Website: www.lru.edu
E-mail: admissions@lru.edu

Medical College of Georgia
1120 15th St, Augusta GA 30912-0004
706-721-2725

Mercer University in Atlanta
3001 Mercer University Dr, Atlanta GA 30341-4155
678-547-6000

Mercer University in Macon
1400 Coleman Ave, Macon GA 31207-0003
John P. Cole, Sr. Assoc. V.P. for Admissions
478-301-2650

Morehouse School of Medicine
720 Westview Dr SW, Atlanta GA 30310-1495
404-752-1500

North Georgia College & State University
Dahlonega GA 30597-0001
706-864-1400

North Metro Technical College
5198 Ross Rd SE, Acworth GA 30102-3129
Missy Cusack, Director of Admissions
770-975-4000 Fax: 770-975-4142
Website: www.northmetrotech.edu
E-mail: info@northmetrotech.edu

Oglethorpe University
4484 Peachtree Rd NE, Atlanta GA 30319-2797
Kelly Gosnell, Director of Admission
404-261-1441 Fax: 404-364-8491
Website: www.oglethorpe.edu
E-mail: admission@oglethorpe.edu

Oxford College of Emory University
100 Hamill St
Oxford GA 30054-2291
Jennifer B. Taylor, Director of Admissions
770-784-8888

Paine College
1235 15th St, Augusta GA 30901-3182
800-476-7703

Piedmont College
PO Box 10, Demorest GA 30535-0010
800-277-7020

Reinhardt College
7300 Reinhardt College Cir, Waleska GA 30183-2981
770-720-5600

Savannah College of Art and Design
PO Box 2072, Savannah, GA 31402-2072
PO Box 77300, Atlanta, GA 30357
Phone: 800-869-7223 (Savannah) or 877-722-3285 (Atlanta)
E-mail: admission@scad.edu (Savannah) or sca-datl@scad.edu (Atlanta)
www.scad.edu
   SCAD is a private, nonprofit institution accredited by the Commission on Colleges of the Southern Association of Colleges and Schools to award bachelor's and master's degrees. The college offers B.F.A., M.Arch., M.A., M.F.A., and M.U.D. degrees. Enrollment is appoximately 7,350; 6 percent are international. More than 30 areas of study. Online programs via SCAD e-Learning.

Savannah College of Art and Design
PO Box 77300, Atlanta GA 30357
877-722-3285

Savannah College of Art and Design
3219 College St, Savannah GA 31404-5255
912-356-2187

Shorter College
315 Shorter Ave, Rome GA 30165-4267
800-868-6980

Southern Polytech State University
1100 S Marietta Pkwy SE, Marietta GA 30060-2855
770-528-7200

South University
709 Mall Blvd, Savannah GA 31406-4881
912-201-8000

Strayer University
3101 TowerCreek Pkwy SE Ste 700
Atlanta GA 30339
770-612-2170

Thomas University
1501 Millpond Rd, Thomasville GA 31792-7478
Darla M. Glass, Director of Student Affairs
229-226-1621

TOCCOA FALLS COLLEGE
PO Box 800899, Toccoa Falls GA 30598
Christy Meadows, Director of Admissions
888-785-5624 Fax: 706-282-6012
Website: www.tfc.edu
E-mail: admissions@tfc.edu

University of Georgia
Athens GA 30602-0001
706-542-3000

University of West Georgia
Carrollton GA 30118-0001
770-836-6500

Valdosta State University
N Patterson St, Valdosta GA 31698-0001
229-333-5952

HAWAII

Brigham Young University
55-220 Kulanui St, Laie HI 96762-1293
808-293-3211

Chaminade University of Honolulu
3140 Waialae Ave, Honolulu HI 96816-1510
Eric Nemoto, Director Financial Aid
800-735-3733

Clayton University
1160 North King St-MSC-106
Honolulu HI 96817-3455

Hawaii Business College
33 S King St 4th Floor, Honolulu HI 96813-4316
Roger Ramos, Director of Admissions
808-524-4014

Hawaii Pacific University
1164 Bishop St, Honolulu HI 96813
808-544-0200

Hawaii Pacific University
45-045 Kamehameha Hwy, Kaneohe HI 96744-5297
808-235-3641

HAWAII THEOLOGICAL SEMINARY
PO Box 861754, Wahiawa HI 96786
Kevin Gilbert, President
808-622-4487 Fax: 808-595-4779
Website: www.hits.edu
E-mail: info@hits.edu

University of Hawaii at Hilo
200 W Kawili St, Hilo HI 96720-4075
808-933-3301

University of Hawaii at Manoa
2444 Dole St, Honolulu HI 96822-2302
808-956-5280

University of Hawaii - West Oahu
96-129 Ala Ike St, Pearl City HI 96782
808-454-4700

IDAHO

Albertson College of Idaho
2112 Cleveland Blvd, Caldwell ID 83605-4432
208-459-5000

Boise Bible College
8695 W Marigold St, Boise ID 83714-1220
800-893-7755

Boise State University
1910 University Dr, Boise ID 83725-0399
208-426-1011

Brigham Young University - Idaho
120 Kimball Bldg, Rexburg ID 83460
Gordon Westenskow, Director of Admissions
208-496-1020 Fax: 208-496-1220
Website: www.byui.edu
E-mail: admissions@byui.edu

Idaho State University
PO Box 8270, Pocatello ID 83209-0001
208-282-0211

Lewis-Clark State College
500 8th Ave, Lewiston ID 83501-2698
Steve Bussolini, Director of Admissions
800-933-5272

New Saint Andrews College
PO Box 9025, Moscow ID 83843
208-882-1566

Northwest Nazarene University
623 Holly St, Nampa ID 83686-5897
208-467-8011

University of Idaho
Moscow ID 83844-4253
Lloyd Scott, Director of New Student Services
208-885-6163 Fax: 208-885-4477
Website: www.uidaho.edu
E-mail: nss@uidaho.edu

ILLINOIS

AMERICAN INTERCONTINENTAL UNIVERSITY ONLINE
5550 Prairie Stone Parkway Suite 400
Hoffman Estates IL 60192
Admissions Department
877-701-3800
Website: www.aiuonline.edu
E-mail: info@aiuonline.edu

Augustana College
639 38th St, Rock Island IL 61201-2296
309-794-7000

Aurora University
347 S Gladstone Ave, Aurora IL 60506-4892
Carol R. Dunn, Ed.D., Vice President for Enrollment
800-742-5281 Fax: 630-844-5535
Website: www.aurora.edu
E-mail: admission@aurora.edu

BENEDICTINE UNIVERSITY
5700 College Rd, Lisle IL 60532-0900
Kari Gibbons, Dean of Enrollment
630-829-6300 or 888-829-6363 Fax: 630-829-6301
Website: www.ben.edu
E-mail: admissions@ben.edu
   Established 1887. Private. Coed. Accreditation: North Central Association of Colleges & Schools. Tuition: $18,700. Room & board: $6,393. Fees: $510. Enrollment: 1,728 full-time, 1,504 part-time. Faculty: 142. Student-faculty ratio: 14:1. Degrees: AA, BA, BBA, BS, MAEd, MBA, MEd, MPH, MS, PhD, EdD. Library: 162,000 volumes. 10 buildings on 108 acres plus a new Sports Complex. Located 25 miles west of Chicago in the heart of the DuPage County Research and Development Corridor. Recreational, educational and cultural facilities of the city are easily accessible.

Blackburn College
700 College Ave, Carlinville IL 62626-1498
217-854-3231

BLESSING-RIEMAN COLLEGE OF NURSING
PO Box 7005, Quincy IL 62305-7005
Erin Flesner, Admission Counselor
Heather Mutter, Admission Counselor
217-228-5520 Fax: 217-223-4661
Website: www.brcn.edu
E-mail: admissions@brcn.edu

Bradley University
1501 W Bradley Ave, Peoria IL 61625-0002
800-447-6460

Chicago State University
9501 S King Dr, Chicago IL 60628-1598
773-995-2000

Christian Life College
400 E Gregory St, Mount Prospect IL 60056
847-259-1840

Columbia College Chicago
600 S Michigan Ave, Chicago IL 60605-1996
Murphy Monroe, Executive Director of Admissions
312-344-7130 Fax: 312-344-8024
Website: www.colum.edu
E-mail: admissions@colum.edu

CONCORDIA UNIVERSITY
7400 Augusta St, River Forest IL 60305-1402
708-209-3100 Fax: 708-209-3473
Website: www.curf.edu
E-mail: crfadmis.edu

De Paul University
1 E Jackson Blvd, Chicago IL 60604-2287
Carlene Klaas, Director of Admissions
312-362-8000

De Paul University
2323 N Seminary Ave, Chicago IL 60614-3298
312-362-8000

Dominican University
7900 Division St, River Forest IL 60305-1066
708-366-2490

Eastern Illinois University
600 Lincoln Ave, Charleston IL 61920-3099
217-581-5000

East-West University
816 S Michigan Ave, Chicago IL 60605-2103
312-939-0111

Elmhurst College
190 S Prospect Ave, Elmhurst IL 60126-3296
630-279-4100

Eureka College
300 E College Ave, Eureka IL 61530-1500
309-467-3721

Governors State University
1 University Pkwy, University Park IL 60466-0975
708-534-5000

Greenville College
315 E College Ave, Greenville IL 62246-1199
618-664-1840

HARRINGTON COLLEGE OF DESIGN
200 W Madison St, Chicago IL 60606-3433
Wendi Franczyk, VP of Admissions
877-939-4975 Fax: 312-697-8032
Website: www.harringtoncollege.com
E-mail: wfranczyk@interiordesign.edu

Since 1931, Harrington College of Design has been providing the career development skills and training that are essential to those who want to break into the dynamic, growing field of design. Accredited by the Accrediting Council for the Independent Colleges and Schools (ACICS) and the National Association of Schools of Art and Design (NASAD), Harrington delivers interior design, digital photography and communication design programs - Bachelor of Fine Arts in Interior Design, Bachelor of Fine Arts in Communication Design, and an Associate of Applied Science in Interior Design and Digital Photography. At Harrington, you can gain valuable hands-on experience with industry-current equipment and technology. Flexible scheduling options, year-round schooling and evening options allow you to complete your education at a pace that fits your lifestyle and budget. Financial aid available for those who qualify.

Hebrew Theological College
7135 Carpenter Rd, Skokie IL 60077-3263
Schmuel Schuman, Registrar
847-982-2500

Illinois College
1101 W College Ave, Jacksonville IL 62650-2299
217-245-3000

The Illinois Institute of Art
1000 N Plaza Dr, Schaumburg IL 60173-4942
847-619-3450

Illinois Institute of Art, The
350 N Orleans St Lbby 136, Chicago IL 60654-1510
312-280-3500

Illinois Institute of Technology
3300 S Federal St, Chicago IL 60616-3793
Brent Benner, Director of Admissions
312-567-3000

Illinois State University
Normal IL 61790-0001
309-438-2111

Illinois Wesleyan University
PO Box 2900, Bloomington IL 61702-2900
James R. Ruoti, Dean of Admissions
309-556-3031

International Academy of Design and Technology
1 N State St #400, Chicago IL 60602-3300
877-ACADEMY

Judson College
1151 N State St, Elgin IL 60123-1498
847-695-2500

Kendall College
900 N North Branch St, Chicago IL 60622
Office of Admissions
877-588-8860

Knox College
Galesburg IL 61401
309-341-7100

Lake Forest College
555 N Sheridan Rd, Lake Forest IL 60045-2399
847-234-3100

Lakeview College of Nursing
903 N Logan Ave, Danville IL 61832-3731
217-443-5238

Lewis University
One University Parkway, Romeoville IL 60446
800-897-9000

LEXINGTON COLLEGE
310 S Peoria St, Chicago IL 60607-3534
Elizabeth Searby, Admissions Counselor
312-226-6294 Fax: 312-226-6405
Website: www.lexingtoncollege.edu
E-mail: admissions@lexingtoncollege.edu

Lincoln Christian College
100 Campus View Dr, Lincoln IL 62656-2167
217-732-3168

Loyola University
6525 N Sheridan Rd, Chicago IL 60626-5385
773-508-2320

Loyola University
2160 S 1st Ave, Maywood IL 60153-3304
708-216-3229

Loyola University of Chicago
820 N Michigan Ave, Chicago IL 60611-2103
312-915-6000

MacMurray College
447 E College Ave, Jacksonville IL 62650-2590
217-479-7000

McKendree College
701 College Rd, Lebanon IL 62254-1299
618-537-6830

MENNONITE COLLEGE OF NURSING AT ILLINOIS STATE UNIVERSITY
PO Box 5810, Normal IL 61790-5810
Nancy Ridenour, Dean and Professor
309-438-7400 Fax: 309-438-2620
Website: www.mcn.ilstu.edu
E-mail: mcninfo@ilstu.edu

Midstate College
411 W Northmoor Rd, Peoria IL 61614-3595
309-692-4092

Midwestern University
555 31st St, Downers Grove IL 60515-1235
Raelene Brower, Director of Admissions
630-969-4400

Millikin University
1184 W Main St, Decatur IL 62522-2084
Lin Stoner, Dean of Admission
800-373-7733

Monmouth College
700 E Broadway, Monmouth IL 61462-1963
Kristi Hippen, Director of Admission
309-457-2131

Moody Bible Institute
820 N La Salle Dr, Chicago IL 60610-3263
800-967-4624

National-Louis University
2840 Sheridan Rd, Evanston IL 60201-1796

North Central College
30 N Brainard St, Naperville IL 60540-4690
Martha Stolze, Director of Admissions
630-637-5800 Fax: 630-637-5819
Website: www.northcentralcollege.edu
E-mail: admissions@noctrl.edu

NORTHEASTERN ILLINOIS UNIVERSITY
5500 N Saint Louis Ave, Chicago IL 60625-4699
Janice Harring-Hendon, Executive Director of Enrollment Services
773-442-4050 Fax: 773-442-4020
Website: www.neiu.edu
E-mail: jharringhendon@neiu.edu

Northern Illinois University
DeKalb IL 60115
815-753-1000

North Park College & Theological Seminary
3225 W Foster Ave, Chicago IL 60625-4810
773-244-6200

Northwestern University
303 E Chicago Ave, Chicago IL 60611-3008
312-503-6950

Northwestern University
1801 Hinman Ave, Evanston IL 60208-1260
847-491-3741

Olivet Nazarene University
1 University Ave
Bourbonnais IL 60914
815-939-5011

Principia College
Elsah IL 62028-9799
618-374-2131

Quincy University
1800 College Ave, Quincy IL 62301-2670
217-222-8020

Robert Morris College
905 Meridian Lake Dr, Aurora IL 60504-4904
630-375-8000

Robert Morris College
1000 Tower Ln #200, Bensenville IL 60106-1040
630-787-7800

Robert Morris College
401 S State St, Chicago IL 60605-1229
312-935-6800

Robert Morris College
43 Orland Square Dr, Orland Park IL 60462-3206
708-226-3800

Robert Morris College
3101 Montvale Dr, Springfield IL 62704-4260
217-793-2600

Rockford College
5050 E State St, Rockford IL 61108-2393
William Laffey, Director of Admission
800-892-2984

Roosevelt University
430 S Michigan Ave, Chicago IL 60605
Gwen E. Kanelos, Asst. Vice President for Enrollment Services
877-APPLY-RU Fax: 312-341-4216
Website: www.roosevelt.edu
E-mail: applyru@roosevelt.edu

Roosevelt University
1400 N Roosevelt Blvd, Schaumburg IL 60173
847-619-8600

Rush University
College Admission Services
600 S Paulina St #440, Chicago IL 60612-3806
Hicela Castruita, Director
312-942-7100

Saint John's College
Department of Nursing
421 N 9th St, Springfield IL 62702
217-525-5628

St. Xavier University
3700 W 103rd St, Chicago IL 60655-3199
773-298-3000

Shimer College
PO Box 500, Waukegan IL 60079-0500
Bill Paterson, Contact
847-249-7195

Southern Illinois University
Carbondale IL 62901-4400
618-453-2121

Southern Illinois University
PO Box 19621, Springfield IL 62794
217-545-8000

Southern Illinois University Edwardsville
Edwardsville IL 62026-0001
618-650-3705

Trinity Christian College
6601 W College Dr, Palos Heights IL 60463-0929
Joshua Lenarz, Director of Admissions
708-597-3000

Trinity College of Nursing & Health Sciences
2122 25th Ave, Rock Island IL 61201-5317
Joanne Cunningham, Director of Admissions
309-779-7700 Fax: 309-799-7748
Website: www.trinitycollegeqc.edu
E-mail: con@trinityqc.com

Trinity International University
2065 Half Day Rd, Deerfield IL 60015-1241
847-945-8800

University of Chicago
5801 S Ellis Ave, Chicago IL 60637-1476
773-702-1234

University of Illinois
901 W Illinois St, Urbana IL 61801
217-333-1000

University of Illinois at Chicago
PO Box 5220, Chicago IL 60680-5220
312-996-3000

University of Illinois at Springfield
One University Plaza, Springfield IL 62794
217-206-4847

University of St. Francis
500 Wilcox St, Joliet IL 60435
800-735-7500

VANDERCOOK COLLEGE OF MUSIC
3140 S Federal St, Chicago IL 60616-3704
Tamara V. Trutwin, Student Recruiter
Kelly Westergaard, Admissions Coordinator
800-448-2655 ext. 230 Fax: 312-225-5211
Website: www.vandercook.edu
E-mail: admissions@vandercook.edu

Established 1928. Private. Coed. Accreditation: NCA; NASM; Illinois State Board of Higher Learning. Tuition: $7,945 undergrad, $3,960 graduate. Room & Board: $6,500 undergrad, $1,650 graduate. Enrollment: 85 undergraduate. Faculty: 35. Student-faculty ratio: 6:1. Degrees: Bachelor of Music Education, Master of Music Education. The only College in the U.S. solely devoted to the preparation of music educators. There is a 100% placement rate for those seeking a career in music education after graduation.

Western Illinois University
1 University Cir, Macomb IL 61455-1390
309-295-1414

West Suburban College of Nursing
3 Erie Ct, Oak Park IL 60302
Admissions
708-763-6530

Wheaton College
501 College Ave, Wheaton IL 60187-5571
630-752-5000

INDIANA

Anderson University
1100 E 5th St, Anderson IN 46012-3495
765-649-9071

Art Institute of Indianapolis
3500 Depauw Blvd, Indianapolis IN 46268
317-613-4800

Ball State University
2000 W University Ave, Muncie IN 47306-0002
765-285-5555

Bethel College
1001 W McKinley Ave, Mishawaka IN 46545-5591
Office of Admissions
574-257-3339

Butler University
4600 Sunset Ave, Indianapolis IN 46208-3443
317-940-8000

Calumet College of St. Joseph
2400 New York Ave, Whiting IN 46394-2195
219-473-7770

Crossroads Bible College
601 N Shortridge Rd, Indianapolis IN 46219-4912
Nathan McGuire, Director of Admissions
317-352-8736 ext. 30

Davenport University
8200 Georgia St, Merrillville IN 46410-6128
800-748-7880

DePauw University
313 S Locust St, Greencastle IN 46135-1736
800-447-2495

Earlham College and Earlham School of Religion
801 National Rd W, Richmond IN 47374-4095
765-983-1200

Franklin College
101 Branigin Blvd, Franklin IN 46131
Jacqueline S. Acosta, Director of Admissions
800-852-0232 Fax: 317-738-8274
Website: www.franklincollege.edu
E-mail: admissions@franklincollege.edu

Goshen College
1700 S Main St, Goshen IN 46526-4794
574-535-7000

Grace College
200 Seminary Dr, Winona Lake IN 46590-1224
800-54-GRACE

Hanover College
PO Box 108, Hanover IN 47243-0108
William D. Preble, Dean of Admission
800-213-2178 Fax: 812-866-7098
Website: www.hanover.edu
E-mail: admissions@hanover.edu

HOLY CROSS COLLEGE
PO Box 308, Notre Dame IN 46556-0308
Vincent M. Duke, Director of Admissions
574-239-8400 Fax: 574-239-8323
Website: www.hcc-nd.edu
E-mail: admissions@hcc-nd.edu

Huntington College
2303 College Ave, Huntington IN 46750-1299
260-356-6000

Indiana Institute of Technology
1600 E Washington Blvd, Fort Wayne IN 46803-1297
260-422-5561

Indiana State University
Terre Haute IN 47809-0001
Richard Toomey, Director of Admissions
812-237-6311

Indiana University
300 N Jordan Ave, Bloomington IN 47405-1106
812-855-4848

Indiana University at Kokomo
PO Box 9003, Kokomo IN 46904-9003
765-453-2000

Indiana University at South Bend
PO Box 7111, South Bend IN 46634-7111
574-237-4111

Indiana University East
2325 Chester Blvd, Richmond IN 47374-1289
765-973-8200

Indiana University Northwest
3400 Broadway, Gary IN 46408-1101
219-980-6500

Indiana University-Purdue University at Fort Wayne
2101 E Coliseum Blvd, Fort Wayne IN 46805-1445
260-481-6100

Indiana University-Purdue University at Indianapolis
355 Lansing St, Indianapolis IN 46202-2815
317-274-5555

Indiana University Southeast
4201 Grant Line Rd, New Albany IN 47150-2158
812-941-2000

Indiana Wesleyan University
4201 S Washington St, Marion IN 46953-4974
765-674-6901

International Business College
5699 Coventry Ln, Fort Wayne IN 46804
260-459-4500 Fax: 260-436-1896
Website: www.ibcfortwayne.edu
E-mail: skinzer@ibcfortwayne.edu

Manchester College
604 E College Ave, North Manchester IN 46962-1276
260-982-5000

Marian College
3200 Cold Spring Rd, Indianapolis IN 46222-1997
317-955-6000

Martin University
PO Box 18567, Indianapolis IN 46218-0567
317-543-3235

Mid-America Reformed Seminary
229 Seminary Dr, Dyer IN 46311
219-864-2400

OAKLAND CITY UNIVERSITY
138 N Lucretia St, Oakland City IN 47660
Brian J. Baker, Director of Admissions
800-737-5125 Fax: 812-749-1433
Website: www.oak.edu
E-mail: bbaker@oak.edu
 Established 1865. Private. Coed. Accreditation: North
Central Association of Colleges and Schools, NCATE.
Tuition: $15,060. Room & board: $5,030. Fees: $1,860.
Enrollment: 600 full-time, 54 part-time. Faculty: 51.
Student-faculty ratio: 17:1. Degrees in: Business, Educa-
tion, Music, Art, Religious Studies, Computer Sciences.
Library: 83,000 volumes. 15 buildings on 16 acres.

Purdue University
2200 169th St, Hammond IN 46323
219-989-2993

Purdue University
475 Stadium Mall Dr, West Lafayette IN 47907
765-494-4600

Purdue University
1401 S US Highway 421, Westville IN 46391-9542
219-785-5200

Rose-Hulman Institute of Technology
5500 Wabash Ave, Terre Haute IN 47803-3920
James A. Goecker, Dean of Admissions
812-877-8213 Fax: 812-877-8941
Website: www.rose-hulman.edu
E-mail: admis.ofc@rose-hulman.edu

St. Joseph's College
PO Box 890, Rensselaer IN 47978-0890
219-866-6000

Taylor University
1025 W Rudisill Blvd, Fort Wayne IN 46807-2197
260-744-8600

Taylor University
500 W Reade Ave, Upland IN 46989-1002
765-998-2751

Tri-State University
Angola IN 46703
260-665-4100

University of Evansville
1800 Lincoln Ave, Evansville IN 47722-0001
Thomas E. Bear, V.P. of Enrollment Services
800-423-8633 Fax: 812-488-4076
Website: www.evansville.edu
E-mail: admission@evansville.edu

University of Indianapolis
1400 E Hanna Ave, Indianapolis IN 46227-3697
317-788-3368

University of Notre Dame
220 Main Building, Notre Dame IN 46556
574-631-5000

University of St. Francis
2701 Spring St, Fort Wayne IN 46808-3994
Matthew P. Nettleton, Director of Admissions
260-434-3279

University of Southern Indiana
8600 University Blvd, Evansville IN 47712-3591
812-464-8600

Valparaiso University
Valparaiso IN 46383
219-464-5000

IOWA

Briar Cliff University
PO Box 2100, Sioux City IA 51104-0100
Sharisue Wilcoxon, VP for Enrollment Management
712-279-5200 Fax: 712-279-1632
Website: www.briarcliff.edu
E-mail: admissions@briarcliff.edu

Buena Vista University
610 W 4th St, Storm Lake IA 50588-1798
712-749-2235

Central College
812 University St, Pella IA 50219-1999
641-628-9000

Clarke College
1550 Clarke Dr, Dubuque IA 52001-3198
Andy Schroeder, Director of Admissions
800-383-2345 Fax: 563-584-8666
Website: www.clarke.edu
E-mail: andy.schroeder@clarke.edu

Coe College
1220 1st Ave NE, Cedar Rapids IA 52402-5092
319-399-8000

Cornell College
600 1st St NW, Mount Vernon IA 52314-1098
319-895-4000

DIVINE WORD COLLEGE SEMINARY
102 Jacoby Dr SW, Epworth IA 52045
Len Uhal, Director of Admissions
563-876-3332 Fax: 563-876-5515
Website: www.svdvocations.org
E-mail: dwm@mwci.net

Dordt College
498 4th Ave NE, Sioux Center IA 51250-1697
Quentin Van Essen, Executive Director of Admissions
800-343-6738

Drake University
2507 University Ave, Des Moines IA 50311-4505
Laura Linn, Director of Admissions
515-271-2011

Emmaus Bible College
2570 Asbury Rd, Dubuque IA 52001-3096
563-588-8000

Faith Baptist Bible College
1900 NW 4th St, Ankeny IA 50023-2192
515-964-0601

The Franciscan University
400 N Bluff Blvd, Clinton IA 52732-3910
563-242-4023

Graceland University
1 University Place, Lamoni IA 50140
Brian Shantz, Vice President for Enrollment and Dean
of Admissions
641-784-5196 Fax: 641-784-5480
Website: www.admissions.graceland.edu
E-mail: admissions@graceland.edu

Grand View College
1200 Grandview Ave, Des Moines IA 50316-1599
515-263-2800

Grinnell College
PO Box 805, Grinnell IA 50112-0805
641-269-4000

Hamilton College
7009 Nordic Dr, Cedar Falls IA 50613
Tim Cole, Campus President
319-277-0220 Fax: 319-363-3812
Website: www.hamiltonia.edu
E-mail: ticole@hamiltoncf.com

Hamilton College
3165 Edgewood Pkwy SW, Cedar Rapids IA 52404
Susan Spivey, Campus President
319-363-0481 Fax: 319-363-3812
Website: www.hamiltonia.edu
E-mail: spiveys@hamiltonia.edu

Hamilton College
2570 4th St SW, Mason City IA 50401-4665
Joe Albers, Executive Director
641-423-2530 Fax: 641-423-7512
Website: www.hamiltonia.edu
E-mail: jalbers@hamiltonia.edu

Hamilton College
4655 121st St, Urbandale IA 50323-2311
Ed Rogan, Campus President
515-727-2100 Fax: 515-727-2115
Website: www.hamiltonia.edu
E-mail: erogan_dm@hamiltonia.edu

Hamilton Technical College
1011 E 53rd St, Davenport IA 52807-2653
Mark Christy, Director
563-386-3570 Fax: 563-386-6756
Website: www.hamiltontechcollege.com
E-mail: mchristy@hamiltontechcollege.com
See listing under "Career Schools"

Iowa State University
Ames IA 50011-0001
515-294-4111

Iowa Wesleyan College
601 N Main St, Mount Pleasant IA 52641-1398
Donald G. Hapward, Director of Admissions
319-385-8021

Kaplan University
1801 E Kimberly Rd #1, Davenport IA 52807-2095
563-355-3500

Loras College
1450 Alta Vista St, Dubuque IA 52001-4399
Tim Hauber, Director of Admissions
800-245-6727

Luther College
700 College Dr, Decorah IA 52101-1045
563-387-2000

Maharishi University of Management
1000 N 4th St, Fairfield IA 52557-0002
641-472-7000

MERCY COLLEGE OF HEALTH SCIENCES
928 6th Ave, Des Moines IA 50309-1225
Susan Rhoades, Dean Enrollment & Student Services
515-643-3180 Fax: 515-643-6698
Website: www.mchs.edu
E-mail: srhoades@mercydesmoines.org

Morningside College
1501 Morningside Ave, Sioux City IA 51106-1717
712-274-5000

Mount Mercy College
1330 Elmhurst Dr NE, Cedar Rapids IA 52402-4797
Jim Krystofiak, Dean of Admission
800-248-4504 Fax: 319-363-5270
Website: www.mtmercy.edu
E-mail: admission@mtmercy.edu

Northwestern College
101 7th St SW, Orange City IA 51041-1996
712-737-7000

St. Ambrose University
518 W Locust St, Davenport IA 52803-2898
563-333-6000

Simpson College
701 N C St, Indianola IA 50125-1297
515-961-6251

University of Dubuque
2000 University Ave, Dubuque IA 52001-5099
563-589-3000

University of Iowa
107 Calvin Hall, Iowa City IA 52242-1315
319-335-3500

University of Northern Iowa
Cedar Falls IA 50614-0001
319-273-2311

Upper Iowa University
PO Box 1857, Fayette IA 52142-1857
563-425-5200

Vennard College
PO Box 29, University Park IA 52595-0029
800-686-8391

WALDORF COLLEGE
106 S 6th St, Forest City IA 50436-1713
Steve Lovik, Vice President of Enrollment Management
800-292-1903 or 641-585-8112 Fax: 641-585-8125
Website: www.waldorf.edu
E-mail: loviks@waldorf.edu
 Established 1903. 4 year Private. Coed. Accreditation:
North Central Association of Colleges and Schools. Tui-
tion: $15,885. Room & board: $5,270. Fees: $785. Enroll-
ment: 510 full-time, 90 part-time. Faculty: 36 full-time, 15
part-time. Student-faculty ratio: 13:1. Degrees: BA/BS in
Biology, Business, Communications, Elementary Education K-6, Secondary Education, Music Education, Foundation of Education, English, History, Humanities,
Computer Information Systems, Music, Psychology,
Physical Science (also will receive BS in Chemical Engineering from Iowa State University in this dual degree),
Theatre Arts, and Wellness. Library: 36,000 volumes,
5,863 bound periodicals. 13 buildings on 40+ acres. All
incoming students receive a laptop computer to use for
the 4 years they are here. Accelerated Bachelor's program - 3 years.

Wartburg College
PO Box 1003, Waverly IA 50677-0903
Brent Matthias, Interim Director of Admissions
319-352-8200 Fax: 319-352-8579
Website: www.wartburg.edu
E-mail: admissions@wartburg.edu

William Penn University
201 Trueblood Ave, Oskaloosa IA 52577-1757
641-673-1012

KANSAS

Baker University
PO Box 65, Baldwin City KS 66006-0065
785-594-6451

Baker University School of Nursing
1500 SW 10th Ave, Topeka KS 66604-1301
888-866-4242

Barclay College
607 N Kingman, Haviland KS 67059
Herb Frazier, Director of Admissions
800-862-0226 Fax: 620-862-5242
Website: www.barclaycollege.edu
E-mail: admissions@barclaycollege.edu

Benedictine College
1020 N 2nd St, Atchison KS 66002-1499
913-367-5340

Bethany College
421 N 1st St, Lindsborg KS 67456-1897
785-227-3311

Bethel College
300 E 27th St, North Newton KS 67117-8061
316-283-2500

Central Christian College of Kansas
PO Box 1403, Mc Pherson KS 67460-1403
Dr. David Ferrell, Director of Admissions
800-835-0078

Emporia State University
1200 Commercial St, Emporia KS 66801-5087
620-343-1200

Fort Hays State University
600 Park St, Hays KS 67601-4099
785-628-4000

Friends University
2100 W University Ave, Wichita KS 67213-3397
316-261-5800

Kansas State University
Manhattan KS 66506
785-532-6250

Kansas State University - Salina
College of Technology & Aviation
2310 Centennial Rd, Salina KS 67401-8058
785-826-2640

Kansas Wesleyan University
100 E Claflin Ave, Salina KS 67401-6196
785-827-5541

Manhattan Christian College
1415 Anderson Ave, Manhattan KS 66502-4081
785-539-3571

McPherson College
PO Box 1402, Mc Pherson KS 67460-1402
620-241-0731

Mid-America Nazarene University
2030 E College Way, Olathe KS 66062-1851
913-782-3750

Newman University
3100 W McCormick St, Wichita KS 67213
Jann Reusser, Admissions Recruitment Coordinator
316-942-4291 ext. 2144 Fax: 316-942-4483
Website: www.newmanu.edu
E-mail: reusserj@newmanu.edu

Ottawa University
1001 S Cedar St, Ottawa KS 66067-3399
785-242-5200

Pittsburg State University
1701 S Broadway St, Pittsburg KS 66762-7500
620-231-7000

Southwestern College
100 College St, Winfield KS 67156-2499
620-229-6000

Sterling College
125 W Cooper St, Sterling KS 67579
Cal White, V.P. Enrollment Services
800-346-1017

University of Kansas
Lawrence KS 66045-0001
Alan Cerveny, Director of Admissions

University of Kansas Medical Center
3901 Rainbow Blvd, Kansas City KS 66160-0001
913-588-5000

University of Saint Mary
4100 S 4th St, Leavenworth KS 66048-5023
913-682-5151

Washburn University
1700 SW College Ave, Topeka KS 66621-0001
785-231-1010

Wichita State University
1845 N Fairmount St, Wichita KS 67260-0124
Gina Crabtree, Director of Admissions
316-978-3085

KENTUCKY

Alice Lloyd College
100 Purpose Rd, Pippa Passes KY 41844-9005
John Mills, Director of Admissions
888-280-4252

Asbury College
1 Macklem Dr, Wilmore KY 40390-1198
859-858-3511

Bellarmine University
2001 Newburg Rd, Louisville KY 40205-1877
502-452-8000

Berea College
Berea KY 40404-0001
859-985-3000

Brescia University
717 Frederica St, Owensboro KY 42301-3023
Sr. Mary Austin Blank, OSB, Director of Admissions
877-BRESCIA

Campbellsville University
1 University Dr, Campbellsville KY 42718-2799
Scott Necessary, Coordinator of Undergraduate Admissions
270-789-5000

Centre College
600 W Walnut St, Danville KY 40422-1394
859-238-5200

Clear Creek Baptist Bible College
300 Clear Creek Rd, Pineville KY 40977-9752
606-337-3196

Eastern Kentucky University
521 Lancaster Ave, Richmond KY 40475-3102
859-622-1000

Embry-Riddle Aeronautical University
300 High Rise Dr Suite 392, Louisville KY 40213-3253
J. Michael Novak, Director of Enrollment Management
888-409-3728

Frontier School of Midwifery & Family Nursing
PO Box 528, Hyden KY 41749
606-672-2312

Georgetown College
400 E College St, Georgetown KY 40324-1696
502-863-8011

Kentucky Christian University
100 Academic Pkwy, Grayson KY 41143-2205
606-474-3000

Kentucky Mountain Bible College
PO Box 10, Vancleve KY 41385-0010
800-879-5622

Kentucky State University
400 E Main St, Frankfort KY 40601-2334
502-597-6000

Kentucky Wesleyan College
3000 Frederica St, Owensboro KY 42301-6055
800-999-0592

Lindsey Wilson College
210 Lindsey Wilson St, Columbia KY 42728-1223
270-384-8100

MID-CONTINENT UNIVERSITY
99 E Powell Rd, Mayfield KY 42066-9007
Butch Booth, Director of Admissions
800-894-8878 or 270-247-8521 ext. 244
Fax: 270-247-3115
Website: www.midcontinent.edu
E-mail: admissions@midcontinent.edu

Morehead State University
Morehead KY 40351-1689
Dayna Seelig, Enrollment Services
800-585-6781 Fax: 606-783-5038
Website: www.moreheadstate.edu
E-mail: admissions@moreheadstate.edu

Murray State University
Murray KY 42071
Phil Bryan, Director of Admissions
270-762-3011

Northern Kentucky University
Newport KY 41099-0001
859-572-5100

Pikeville College
147 Sycamore St, Pikeville KY 41501
606-218-5250

Spalding University
851 S 4th St, Louisville KY 40203-2188
502-585-9911

Sullivan University
PO Box 998, Fort Knox KY 40121-0998
502-942-8500

Sullivan University
2355 Harrodsburg Rd, Lexington KY 40504-3307
800-467-6281

Sullivan University
3101 Bardstown Rd, Louisville KY 40205-3000
800-844-1354

Thomas More College
333 Thomas More Pkwy, Crestview Hills KY 41017
859-341-5800

Transylvania University
300 N Broadway, Lexington KY 40508-1776
859-233-8242 Fax: 859-233-8797
Website: www.transy.edu
E-mail: admissions@transy.edu

Union College
310 College St, Barbourville KY 40906-1499
Joretta Nelson, Vice President for Enrollment Management
800-489-8646

University of Kentucky
Lexington KY 40506-0001
Don Witt, Director of Admissions
859-257-9000

University of Louisville
2301 S 3rd St, Louisville KY 40292-2001
502-852-5555

University of the Cumberlands
6178 College Station Dr
Williamsburg KY 40769-1372
606-549-2200

Western Kentucky University
1 Big Red Way, Bowling Green KY 42101
270-745-0111

LOUISIANA

Centenary College of Louisiana
PO Box 41188, Shreveport LA 71134-1188
318-869-5011

Dillard University
2601 Gentilly Blvd, New Orleans LA 70122-3097
Linda G. Nash, Director of Admissions
Website: www.dillard.edu
E-mail: admissions@dillard.edu

Grambling State University
PO Box 864, Grambling LA 71245
318-274-3811

Louisiana College
PO Box 560, Pineville LA 71359-0001
Mary Wagner, Director of Admissions
318-487-7259

Louisiana State University
1 University Pl, Shreveport LA 71115-2301
318-797-5000

Louisiana State University and A & M College
Louisiana State Univ, Baton Rouge LA 70803-0001
225-578-3202

Louisiana State University at Alexandria
8100 Highway 71 S, Alexandria LA 71302-9121
318-445-3672

Louisiana State University Health Sciences Center
433 Bolivar St, New Orleans LA 70112-2223
504-568-4808

Louisiana Tech University
PO Box 3168, Ruston LA 71272-0001
318-257-0211

Loyola University New Orleans
6363 Saint Charles Ave, New Orleans LA 70118-6143
504-865-2011

McNeese State University
4100 Ryan St, Lake Charles LA 70605-4510
337-475-5000

Newcomb College of Tulane University
1229 Broadway St, New Orleans LA 70118-5210
504-865-5594

Nicholls State University
University Station, Thibodaux LA 70310-0001
985-446-8111

Northwestern State University
Natchitoches LA 71497-0001
Jana Lucky, Director of Enrollment Services
318-357-4503

Northwestern State University
1800 Line Ave, Shreveport LA 71101-4653
Norann Planchock, Director
318-677-3100

OUR LADY OF THE LAKE COLLEGE
7434 Perkins Rd, Baton Rouge LA 70808
Marvell Nesmith, Director of Admissions
225-768-1700 Fax: 225-768-1726
Website: www.ololcollege.edu
E-mail: mnesmith@ololcollege.edu

St. Joseph Seminary College
Saint Benedict LA 70457
Dr. Russ Pottle, Director of Admissions
985-867-2225

Southeastern Louisiana University
PO Box 784, Hammond LA 70404-0784
985-549-2000

Southern University A&M College
Southern University, Baton Rouge LA 70813-0001
225-771-4500

Southern University in New Orleans
6400 Press Dr, New Orleans LA 70126-1009
504-286-5000

Tulane University
6823 Saint Charles Ave, New Orleans LA 70118-5698
504-865-4000

University of Louisiana at Lafayette
PO Box 43370, Lafayette LA 70504
337-482-6729

University of Louisiana at Monroe
700 University Ave, Monroe LA 71209-9001
318-342-1000

University of New Orleans
New Orleans LA 70148-0001
504-280-6000

William Carey College
3939 Gentilly Blvd Box 309, New Orleans LA 70126
Tom Huebner, Director of Admissions
504-865-1502

Xavier University
1 Drexel Dr, New Orleans LA 70125-1098
504-486-7411

MAINE

Bates College
1 Bates College, Lewiston ME 04240
207-786-6000

Bowdoin College
Brunswick ME 04011
207-725-3000

Colby College
150 Mayflower Hill Dr, Waterville ME 04901-4799
207-872-3000

College of the Atlantic
105 Eden St, Bar Harbor ME 04609-1198
207-288-5015

HUSSON COLLEGE
One College Cir, Bangor ME 04401-2999
William Beardsley, President
Jane Goodwin, Director of Admissions
800-4-HUSSON or 207-941-7100 Fax: 207-941-7935
Website: www.husson.edu
E-mail: admit@husson.edu
    Established 1898. Private. Coed. Accreditation: NEASC, NLN. Tuition: $11,520. Room and board: $6,240. Fees: $250. Enrollment: 1,605 full-time, 372 part-time.

Faculty: 100. Student-faculty ratio: 21:1. Degrees: associate's, bachelor's, master's. Library: 37,871 volumes. 8 buildings on 200 acres, new Center for Family Business building. New Clara L. Swan Fitness Center. Gym. Pool. International Center for Language Studies (ICLS). The Commons. Programs include accounting, business administration, computer information systems, nursing and physical therapy, occupational therapy, physical education, master of science in business, health care management and nurse practitioner, science and humanities, biology, elementary education, hospitality management, paralegal studies, psychology, criminal justice.

Maine College of Art
97 Spring St, Portland ME 04101-3987
Jodie Lane, Director of Admissions
800-639-4808

Maine Maritime Academy
Battle Ave, Castine ME 04420-0001
Jeff Wright, Director of Admissions
207-326-2206

St. Joseph's College of Maine
278 Whites Bridge Rd, Standish ME 04084-5263
Vincent Kloskowski, Dean of Admissions
800-338-7057 Fax: 207-893-7862
Website: www.sjcme.edu
E-mail: admission@sjcme.edu

Thomas College
180 W River Rd, Waterville ME 04901-5097
207-859-1111

Unity College
HC 78 Box 1, Unity ME 04988-9502
207-948-3131

University of Maine
46 University Dr, Augusta ME 04330
207-621-3000

University of Maine
246 Main St, Farmington ME 04938
Sharon M. Oliver, Director of Admissions
207-778-7000

University of Maine
9 OBrien Ave, Machias ME 04654-1321
207-255-1200

University of Maine
Orono ME 04469-0001
207-581-1110

University of Maine at Fort Kent
23 University Dr, Fort Kent ME 04743
888-TRY-UMFK

University of Maine at Presque Isle
181 Main St, Presque Isle ME 04769-2844
207-768-9532

University of New England
11 Hills Beach Rd, Biddeford ME 04005-9526
207-283-0171

University of Southern Maine
PO Box 9300, Portland ME 04104-9300
207-780-4141

Westbrook College
716 Stevens Ave, Portland ME 04103-2693
207-797-7261

MARYLAND

Baltimore Hebrew University
5800 Park Heights Ave, Baltimore MD 21215-3996
410-578-6900

BALTIMORE INTERNATIONAL COLLEGE

17 Commerce St, Baltimore MD 21202-3230
Kristin Ciarlo, Director of Admissions
410-752-4710 ext. 120 Fax: 410-752-3730
Website: www.bic.edu
E-mail: admissions@bic.edu
Founded in 1972, Baltimore International College is an independent college regionally accredited by the Commission on Higher Education, Middle States Association of Colleges and Schools. The college offers specialized masters, baccalaureate and associate's degrees, and a certificate program through its School of Culinary Arts, School of Hotel Restaurant and Catering Management, and School of Graduate Studies. The college's programs include a master of science in Hospitality Management degree, bachelor's degrees in Culinary Management, Hospitality Management, Hospitality Management with Marketing Concentration; associate's degrees in Professional Cooking, Professional Cooking and Baking and Professional Baking and Pastry; and certificates in Professional Culinary Arts.
The college has a campus in Baltimore, MD., just two blocks from Baltimore's famous Inner Harbor and within easy walking distance of many of the city's major attractions. The college also has Virginia Park, a sprawling 100-acre preserve along the shore of Lough Ramor in Virginia, County Cavan, Ireland. The Virginia Park campus is home to the Park Hotel and a golf course, pleasure gardens, and 15 miles of walking paths. Students may take courses at the Virginia Park campus studying under European-educated chefs and hoteliers.
The mission of Baltimore International College is to provide qualified students with the education and experience they need to pursue progressive careers within the international foodservice and lodging industry.

Bowie State University
14000 Jericho Park Rd, Bowie MD 20715-9465
301-464-3000

Capitol College
11301 Springfield Rd, Laurel MD 20708-9759
Darnell Edwards, Director of Admissions
800-950-1992

Columbia Center
6740 Alexander Bell Dr, Columbia MD 21046-2100
410-290-1777

Columbia Union College
7600 Flower Ave, Takoma Park MD 20912-7794
301-891-4000

Coppin State University
2500 W North Ave, Baltimore MD 21216-3698
410-951-3000

Frostburg State University
Frostburg MD 21532-1001
301-687-4000

Goucher College
1021 Dulaney Valley Rd, Baltimore MD 21204-2780
410-337-6000

ITT Technical Institute
11301 Red Run Blvd, Owings Mills MD 21117
443-394-7115

Johns Hopkins University
600 N Wolfe St, Baltimore MD 21287-0005
410-955-3182

Johns Hopkins University
3400 N Charles St, Baltimore MD 21218-2680
410-516-8000

Loyola College
4501 N Charles St, Baltimore MD 21210-2694
410-617-2000

MAPLE SPRINGS BAPTIST BIBLE COLLEGE & SEMINARY

4130 Belt Rd, Capitol Heights MD 20743-5711
Rev. Percy V. Coker, Director of Admissions and Records
301-736-3631 Fax: 301-735-6507
Website: www.msbbcs.edu

Maryland Institute College of Art
1300 W Mount Royal Ave, Baltimore MD 21217-4191
Theresa Lynch Bedoya, VP, Dean of Admissions & Financial Aid
410-225-2222

McDaniel College
2 College Hl, Westminster MD 21157-4303
410-848-7000

Morgan State University
1700 E Cold Spring Ln, Baltimore MD 21251-0002
443-885-3000

Mt. St. Mary's University
16300 Old Emmitsburg Rd
Emmitsburg MD 21727-7799
301-447-6122

National Labor College
1000 New Hampshire Ave, Silver Spring MD 20903
301-431-6400

ST. JOHN'S COLLEGE

PO Box 2800, Annapolis MD 21404-2800
John Christensen, Director of Admissions
800-727-9238 Fax: 410-269-7916
Website: www.stjohnscollege.edu
E-mail: admissions@sjca.edu

St. Mary's College of Maryland
18952 E Fisher Rd, Saint Marys City MD 20686
301-862-0200

Salisbury University
1101 Camden Ave, Salisbury MD 21801-6837
410-543-6000

Sojourner-Douglass College
500 N Caroline St, Baltimore MD 21205-1898
410-276-0306

Strayer University
1520 Jabez Run Ste 100, Millersville MD 21108
410-923-4500

Strayer University
4 Research Pl Ste 100, Rockville MD 20850
301-548-5500

Towson State University
8000 York Rd, Towson MD 21252-0002
410-830-2000

United States Naval Academy
121 Blake Rd, Annapolis MD 21402
410-293-1000

University of Baltimore
1420 N Charles St, Baltimore MD 21201-5779
410-837-4200

University of Maryland
520 W Lombard St, Baltimore MD 21201
410-706-3100

University of Maryland
1000 Hilltop Cir, Baltimore MD 21250-0001
410-455-1000

University of Maryland
College Park MD 20742-0001
301-405-1000

University of Maryland
Univ Blvd And Adelphi Rd
College Park MD 20742-0001
301-985-7000

University of Maryland Eastern Shore
Princess Anne MD 21853
Edwina Morse, Director of Admissions
410-651-6410

Villa Julie College
1525 Greenspring Valley Rd
Stevenson MD 21153-0641
Mark Hergan, V.P. Enrollment Services
410-486-7001 Fax: 410-602-6600
Website: www.vjc.edu/admissions
E-mail: admissions@mail.vjc.edu

Washington College
300 Washington Ave, Chestertown MD 21620-1197
410-778-2800

MASSACHUSETTS

American International College
1000 State St, Springfield MA 01109-3155
Peter Miller, Dean of Admissions
413-737-7000

Amherst College
PO Box 5000, Amherst MA 01002
413-542-2000

Anna Maria College
50 Sunset Ln, Paxton MA 01612
Julie A. Mitchell, Director of Admissions
508-849-3360 Fax: 508-849-3362
Website: www.annamaria.edu
E-mail: admissions@annamaria.edu

The Art Institute of Boston at Lesley University
700 Beacon St, Boston MA 02215-2598
Office of Admissions
617-585-6710 Fax: 617-585-6720
Website: www.aiboston.edu
E-mail: admissions@aiboston.edu

Assumption College
500 Salisbury St, Worcester MA 01609-1294
Kathleen Murphy, Dean of Enrollment
508-767-7000 Fax: 508-799-4412
Website: www.assumption.edu
E-mail: admiss@assumption.edu

Atlantic Union College
PO Box 1000, South Lancaster MA 01561-1000
Office of Enrollment Services
800-282-2030

Babson College
PO Box 57310, Babson Park MA 02457-0310
781-235-1200

Bay State College
122 Commonwealth Ave, Boston MA 02116-2901
Craig Pfannenstiehl, President
617-217-9000 Fax: 617-536-1735

BECKER COLLEGE

Campuses in Worcester and Leicester, MA
61 Sever St, Worcester MA 01609-2165
Karen H. Schedin, Director of Admissions
508-791-9241 Fax: 508-890-1500
Website: www.becker.edu
E-mail: admissions@becker.edu
Established 1887. Private. Coed. Accreditation: New England Association of Schools and Colleges, Inc. Tuition: $18,000. Room & board: $8,000. Fees: $610. Enrollment: 843 full-time, 171 part-time. Student-faculty ratio: 15:1. Degrees: AS, BA, BS. Library: 75,000 volumes. 47 buildings on 100 acres. One campus in Worcester (city) and one campus in Leicester (country). On-site Preschool and Child Development Center, Veterinary Clinic. State-of-the-art Health Sciences facilities. Joint BS/JD program. Army ROTC program. Study abroad in Grimsby, England. NCAA Division III Athletics. Financial aid for those who qualify. Member of the Colleges of the Worcester Consortium.

Benjamin Franklin Institute of Technology
41 Berkeley St, Boston MA 02116-6307
Norman Kraft, Dean of Enrollment
617-423-4630 ext. 121 Fax: 617-482-3706
Website: www.bfit.edu
E-mail: admissions@bfit.edu

Bentley College
175 Forest St, Waltham MA 02452-4705
781-891-2000

Berklee College of Music
1140 Boylston St, Boston MA 02215-3693
Damien S. Bracken, Director of Admissions
800-BERKLEE or 617-747-2222 Fax: 617-747-2047
Website: www.berklee.edu
E-mail: admissions@berklee.edu

Boston Architectural Center
320 Newbury St, Boston MA 02115-2795
617-262-5000

Boston Baptist College
950 Metropolitan Ave, Boston MA 02136
617-364-3510

Boston College
140 Commonwealth Ave
Chestnut Hill MA 02467-3800
617-552-8000

Boston Conservatory
8 Fenway, Boston MA 02215-4099
617-536-6340

Boston University
121 Bay State Rd, Boston MA 02215
Kelly Walter, Executive Director of Admissions
617-353-2300 Fax: 617-353-9695
Website: web.bu.edu
E-mail: admissions@bu.edu

Boston University Medical Center
100 E Newton St, Boston MA 02118-2308
617-638-5300

Brandeis University
415 South St, Waltham MA 02453-2700
781-736-3500

Bridgewater State College
Bridgewater MA 02325-0001
508-697-1237

Clark University
950 Main St, Worcester MA 01610-1473
508-793-7711

College of the Holy Cross
1 College St, Worcester MA 01610-2322
508-793-2011

Curry College
1071 Blue Hill Ave, Milton MA 02186-2395
Bruce Weckworth, Director of Admissions
617-333-2210

Eastern Nazarene College
23 E Elm Ave, Quincy MA 02170-2999
617-773-6350

Elms College
291 Springfield St, Chicopee MA 01013-2839
800-255-3567

Emerson College
120 Boylston St, Boston MA 02116-4624
Sara S. Ramirez, Director of Undergraduate Admission
617-824-8600 Fax: 617-824-8609
Website: www.emerson.edu
E-mail: admission@emerson.edu

Emmanuel College
400 Fenway, Boston MA 02115-5798
617-277-9340

Fisher College
118 Beacon St, Boston MA 02116-1501
Stephen Carter, Director of Admissions
800-446-1226

Fitchburg State College
160 Pearl St, Fitchburg MA 01420-2697
978-345-2151

Framingham State College
PO Box 9101, Framingham MA 01704-0101
508-620-1220

Franklin W. Olin College of Engineering
Olin Way, Needham MA 02492
781-292-2300

Gordon College
255 Grapevine Rd, Wenham MA 01984-1899
Nancy Mering, Director of Admissions
866-464-6736 Fax: 978-867-4682
Website: www.gordon.edu
E-mail: admissions@gordon.edu

Hampshire College
Amherst MA 01002
Karen S. Parker, Director of Admissions
413-559-5471

Harvard University
8 Garden St, Cambridge MA 02138-3630
617-495-1000

Hebrew College
160 Herrick Rd, Newton Centre MA 02459-2237
617-559-8610

Hellenic College/Holy Cross Greek Orthodox School of
Theology
50 Goddard Ave, Brookline MA 02445-7415
Sonia Belcher, Director
617-731-3500

ITT TECHNICAL INSTITUTE
333 Boston Providence Tpke
Norwood MA 02062-3932
Tom Ryan, Director of Recruiting
800-879-TECH (8324) Fax: 781-278-0766
Website: www.itt-tech.edu
E-mail: tryan@itt-tech.edu
Established 1990. Private. Coed. Accreditation: ACICS. Enrollment: 300. Student-faculty ratio: 11:1. Associate Degrees offered: Computer Drafting & Design, Computer Electronics Technology, Computer Network Systems, Multimedia.

Lasell College
1844 Commonwealth Ave, Newton MA 02466-2716
617-243-2225

Massachusetts College of Art
621 Huntington Ave, Boston MA 02115-5801
617-232-1555

Massachusetts College of Liberal Arts
375 Church St, North Adams MA 01247-4100
Denise Richardello, Vice President for Enrollment and
External Relations
413-662-5410

Massachusetts Institute of Technology
77 Massachusetts Ave, Cambridge MA 02139-4307
Marilee Jones, Dean of Admission
617-253-1000 Fax: 617-253-4016
Website: my.mit.edu
E-mail: admissions@mit.edu

Massachusetts Maritime Academy
Cape Cod
101 Academy Dr, Buzzards Bay MA 02532-3400
CDR. Keith D. Rabine, Dean of Enrollment Services
800-544-3411

Merrimack College
315 Turnpike St, North Andover MA 01845-5800
978-683-7111

Mt. Ida College
777 Dedham St, Newton Center MA 02459-3323
617-969-7000

Nichols College
Dudley MA 01571-5000
Kimberly A. Kossuth, Director of Admissions
508-943-1560

Northeastern University
360 Huntington Ave, Boston MA 02115-5000
617-373-2000

Pine Manor College
400 Heath St, Chestnut Hill MA 02467-2332
Bill Nichols, Dean of Admission
617-731-7167

Regis College
235 Wellesley St, Weston MA 02493-1571
781-768-2000

Richmond University, London, England
343 Congress St Ste 3100, Boston MA 02210-1214
617-450-5617

Salem State College
352 Lafayette St, Salem MA 01970-5353
978-741-6000

SCHOOL OF THE MUSEUM OF FINE ARTS, BOSTON
230 The Fenway, Boston MA 02115-5534
Office of Admissions
617-369-3626 or 800-643-6078 Fax: 617-369-4264
Website: www.smfa.edu
E-mail: admissions@smfa.edu

The School of the Museum of Fine Arts, Boston (SMFA), is a fine arts college that offers students the opportunity to design their own individualized course of study and tailor a program that best suits their needs and goals. Similar to an artists' colony, the Museum School's focus is on creative investigation, risk-taking, and exploration of individual vision.

A division of the Museum of Fine Arts, Boston, and in partnership with Tufts University, the SMFA, or Museum School, offers a diverse curriculum with a full range of studio and academic resources. The School's extensive interdisciplinary studio curriculum is developed continually in order to incorporate new media and new approaches, concepts, and theories. A large faculty of working artists and an intimate student-faculty ratio of 9:1 provide each student extensive opportunities for individual consultation and dialogue.

Program options include the all-studio Diploma, Bachelor of Fine Arts, Bachelor of Fine Arts in Art Education, five-year combined degree program (BFA and BS or BA), Master of Fine Arts, Master of Arts in Teaching in Art Education, and the Post-Baccalaureate certificate program and Fifth Year certificate program. All students in degree programs are jointly enrolled at the Museum School and Tufts University and receive a Tufts degree.

Students at the Museum School have the city of Boston as their campus, where a short walk can span many different landscapes, including Copley Square, Fenway Park, Newbury Street, and Chinatown. The more than 60 major universities and colleges in the Boston area make this coastal city a mecca for students. The city is devoted to the arts. Along with the Museum of Fine Arts (which is adjacent to the School) are the Isabella Stewart Gardner Museum, the Institute of Contemporary Art, and the Photographic Resource Center. Across the Charles River in Cambridge are the List Center, associated with the Massachusetts Institute of Technology, and the many museums associated with Harvard University, including the Fogg Museum, the Busch-Reisinger Museum, the Sackler Museum, the Carpenter Center, and the Harvard University Museum. Boston also has a lively gallery scene, with spaces ranging from the traditional to the most avant-garde.

Simon's Rock College of Bard
80 Alford Rd, Great Barrington MA 01230-1559
413-528-0771

Springfield College
263 Alden St, Springfield MA 01109-3788
Mary DeAngelo, Director of Admissions
800-343-1257

Stonehill College
320 Washington St, Easton MA 02357-5610
508-565-1373

Suffolk University
8 Ashburton Pl, Boston MA 02108-2770
617-573-8460

Tufts University
520 Boston Ave, Medford MA 02155-5555
617-628-5000

University of Massachusetts
Amherst MA 01003
413-545-0111

University of Massachusetts at Worcester
55 Lake Ave N, Worcester MA 01655-0001
508-856-8989

University of Massachusetts Boston
100 William T Morrissey Blvd, Boston MA 02125-3393
Liliana Mickle, Director of Undergraduate Admissions
617-287-6000

University of Massachusetts Dartmouth
Old Westport Rd, North Dartmouth MA 02747-2300
Steven T. Briggs, Director of Admissions
508-999-8605 Fax: 508-999-8755
Website: explore.umassd.edu
E-mail: sbriggs@umassd.edu

University of Massachusetts Lowell
1 University Ave, Lowell MA 01854-2893
978-934-4000

Wentworth Institute of Technology
550 Huntington Ave, Boston MA 02115-5998
David C. Planchard, Director of Admissions
617-442-9010
Website: www.wit.edu/apply
E-mail: planchardd@wit.edu

Western New England College
1215 Wilbraham Rd, Springfield MA 01119-2655
413-782-1321

Westfield State College
PO Box 1630, Westfield MA 01086
Michelle Mattie, Associate Dean, Admission and
Enrollment Services
413-572-5300
Website: www.wsc.ma.edu
E-mail: admission@wsc.ma.edu

Wheaton College
26 E Main St, Norton MA 02766-2322
Gail Berson, Dean of Admissions & Student Aid
800-394-6003

Wheelock College
200 Riverway, Boston MA 02215-4176
617-734-5200

Williams College
Williamstown MA 01267
413-597-3131

Worcester Polytechnic Institute
100 Institute Rd, Worcester MA 01609-2280
Edward J. Connor, Director of Admissions
508-831-5286 Fax: 508-831-5875
Website: admissions.wpi.edu
E-mail: admissions@wpi.edu

Worcester State College
486 Chandler St, Worcester MA 01602-2597
508-929-8000

MICHIGAN

Adrian College
110 S Madison St, Adrian MI 49221-2575
517-265-5161

Albion College
611 E Porter St, Albion MI 49224-1831
800-858-6770

ALMA COLLEGE
614 W Superior St, Alma MI 48801-1599
Anne Monroe, Director of Admissions
800-321-ALMA Fax: 989-463-7057
Website: www.alma.edu
E-mail: admissions@alma.edu

Andrews University
Berrien Springs MI 49104-0001
Randall Graves, Director of Recruitment Services
800-253-2874 Fax: 269-471-2670
Website: www.connect.andrews.edu
E-mail: gravesr@andrews.edu

Aquinas College
1607 Robinson Rd SE, Grand Rapids MI 49506-1799
Paula Meehan, Dean of Admissions
616-732-4460

Ave Maria College
300 W Forest Ave, Ypsilanti MI 48197
Joshua McCallen, Director of Admissions
866-866-3030

Baker College of Auburn Hills
1500 University Dr, Auburn Hills MI 48326-2642
248-340-0600

Baker College of Cadillac
9600 E 13th St, Cadillac MI 49601-9574
Mike Tisdale, Director of Admissions
231-876-3100

Baker College of Clinton Township
34950 Little Mack Ave
Clinton Township MI 48035-4701
586-791-6610

Baker College of Flint
1050 W Bristol Rd, Flint MI 48507-5508
810-767-4000

Baker College of Jackson
2800 Springport Rd, Jackson MI 49202-1230
Kelli Hoban, Director of Admissions
517-789-6123

Baker College of Muskegon
1903 Marquette Ave, Muskegon MI 49442-1453
231-726-4904

Baker College of Owosso
1020 S Washington St, Owosso MI 48867-4400
989-729-3300

Baker College of Port Huron
3403 Lapeer Rd, Port Huron MI 48060-2597
Dan Kenny, Director of Admissions
888-262-2442

Calvin College
3201 Burton St SE, Grand Rapids MI 49546-4388
800-688-0122

Central Michigan University
100 Warriner Hall, Mount Pleasant MI 48859-0001
989-774-4000

Cleary University - Livingston Campus
3750 Cleary Dr, Howell MI 48843
517-548-3670

Cleary University - Washtenaw Campus
3601 Plymouth Rd, Ann Arbor MI 48105-2659
734-332-4477

College for Creative Studies
201 E Kirby St, Detroit MI 48202-4048
Julie Hingelberg, Dean of Enrollment Services
313-664-7425
Website: www.ccscad.edu

Concordia University
4090 Geddes Rd, Ann Arbor MI 48105-2797
Gary Neumann, Director of Admissions
734-995-7300 Fax: 734-995-4610
Website: www.cuaa.edu
E-mail: admissions@cuaa.edu

Cornerstone University
1001 E Beltline Ave NE
Grand Rapids MI 49525-5897
616-949-5300

Davenport University
415 Fulton St E, Grand Rapids MI 49503-4407
Lynnae Selberg, Director of Enrollment
616-451-3511

Davenport University
5300 Bay Rd, Saginaw MI 48604
989-799-7800

Davenport University - Central Region
3555 E Patrick Rd, Midland MI 48642-5891
989-835-5588

Davenport University - Eastern Region
4801 Oakman Blvd, Dearborn MI 48126-3799
313-581-4400

DAVENPORT UNIVERSITY - WARREN
27650 Dequindre Rd, Warren MI 48092
Tracey Schaffer, Director of Enrollment Services
586-558-8700 Fax: 586-558-7868
Website: www.davenport.edu
E-mail: tracey.schaffer@davenport.edu

Eastern Michigan University
Ypsilanti MI 48197
800-GO-TO-EMU

Ferris State University
901 S State St, Big Rapids MI 49307-2295
231-591-2000

Grace Bible College
PO Box 910, Grand Rapids MI 49509-0910
800-968-1887

Grand Valley State University
1 Campus Dr, Allendale MI 49401-9403
Jodi Chycinski, Director of Admissions
616-331-6611 Fax: 616-331-2000
Website: www.gvsu.edu
E-mail: go2gvsu@gvsu.edu

Great Lakes Christian College
6211 W Willow Hwy, Lansing MI 48917-1231
517-321-0242

HILLSDALE COLLEGE
33 E College St, Hillsdale MI 49242-1298
Jeffrey S. Lantis, Director of Admissions
517-607-2327 Fax: 517-607-2223
Website: www.hillsdale.edu
E-mail: admissions@hillsdale.edu

Hope College
PO Box 9000, Holland MI 49422-9000
616-395-7000

Kalamazoo College
1200 Academy St, Kalamazoo MI 49006-3295
269-337-7000

Kendall College of Art & Design
17 Fountain St NW, Grand Rapids MI 49503-3002
Dr. Oliver H. Evans, President
800-676-2787 or 616-451-2787 Fax: 616-831-9689
Website: www.kcad.edu
E-mail: brittons@ferris.edu

Lake Superior State University
1000 College Dr, Sault Sainte Marie MI 49783-1637
906-632-6841

LAWRENCE TECHNOLOGICAL UNIVERSITY
21000 W 10 Mile Rd, Southfield MI 48075-1058
Jane Rohrback, Director of Admissions
800-225-5588 Fax: 248-204-2228
Website: www.ltu.edu
E-mail: admissions@ltu.edu
   Established 1932. Private. Coed. Accreditation: North Central Association plus all professional programs hold additional accreditation. Undergraduate Tuition: $17,000 - $21,000. Graduate Tuition: $7,000 - $10,000. Room & board: $7,227. UG Fees: $250 - $280; Grad Fees: $200. Enrollment: 1,625 full-time, 2,523 part-time. Faculty: 415. Student-faculty ratio: 12:1. Degrees offered: DBA, DMIT, DEMS, MS, MSEd, ME, MBA, BS, BFA, AS. Library: 126,000 volumes plus numerous CD-ROM and Internet database search systems. 10 buildings on 125 acres. Over 60 degree programs are offered. "Real world" student projects augment most of Lawrence Tech's programs, contributing to a remarkable 90% placement rate. Lawrence Tech is Michigan's first wireless laptop campus. High end Laptops are provided to all undergraduates and included in tuition. A Standard & Poors survey ranks LTU in the top third of U.S. colleges which supply the leaders of America's most successful corporations.

Madonna University
36600 Schoolcraft Rd, Livonia MI 48150-1173
734-432-5300

Marygrove College
8425 W McNichols Rd, Detroit MI 48221-2599
313-927-1200

Michigan Jewish Institute
25401 Coolidge Hwy, Oak Park MI 48237
248-414-6900

Michigan State University
450 Administration Bldg, East Lansing MI 48824
517-355-1855

Michigan Technological University
1400 Townsend Dr, Houghton MI 49931-1200
Nancy Rehling, Director of Admissions
906-487-2335

Northern Michigan University
1401 Presque Isle Ave, Marquette MI 49855-5301
906-227-1000

Northwood University
4000 Whiting Dr, Midland MI 48640
Daniel F. Toland, Dean of Admissions
800-457-7878 Fax: 989-837-4490
Website: www.northwood.edu
E-mail: miadmit@northwood.edu

Oakland University
2200 N Squirrel Rd, Rochester MI 48309
Eleanor L. Reynolds, Assistant Vice President & Director of Admissions
248-370-2100
Website: www.oakland.edu
E-mail: ouinfo@oakland.edu

Olivet College
300 S Main St, Olivet MI 49076-9724
269-749-7000

Reformed Bible College
3333 E Beltline Ave NE
Grand Rapids MI 49525-9749
Nate Vander Stelt, Director of Enrollment Management
616-988-3621

Rochester College
800 W Avon Rd, Rochester Hills MI 48307-2764
248-218-2000

Saginaw Valley State University
7400 Bay Rd, University Center MI 48710-0001
989-790-4000

Siena Heights University
1247 E Siena Heights Dr, Adrian MI 49221-1796
517-263-0731

Spring Arbor University
106 E Main St, Spring Arbor MI 49283-9799
517-750-1200

University of Detroit-Mercy
PO Box 19900, Detroit MI 48219-0900
313-993-1000

University of Michigan-Ann Arbor
1220 Student Activities Bldg, Ann Arbor MI 48109
734-764-1817

University of Michigan-Ann Arbor
400 N Ingalls St, Ann Arbor MI 48109-2029
Elaine Cosme-Petersen, Marketing, Recruiting Coordinator
734-764-7188

University of Michigan-Dearborn
4901 Evergreen Rd, Dearborn MI 48128-1491
The Office of Admissions & Orientation
313-593-5100 Fax: 313-436-9167
Website: www.umd.umich.edu
E-mail: admissions@umd.umich.edu

University of Michigan-Flint
303 E Kearsley St, Flint MI 48502-1950
810-762-3000

Walsh College of Accountancy & Business Administration
PO Box 7006, Troy MI 48007-7006
Diane Zalapi, Asst. V.P., Student Services
248-823-1610

Wayne State University
5980 Cass Ave, Detroit MI 48202-3489
313-577-2424

Western Michigan University
Kalamazoo MI 49008
269-387-1000

MINNESOTA
ARGOSY UNIVERSITY / TWIN CITIES
(formerly Minnesota School of Professional Psychology and Medical Institute of Minnesota)
1515 Central Pkwy, Eagan MN 55121-1756
O. Jeanne Stoneking, Director of Admissions
651-846-2882 Fax: 651-994-7956
Website: www.argosy.edu
E-mail: tcadmissions@argosyu.edu

Augsburg College
2211 Riverside Ave, Minneapolis MN 55454-1350
612-330-1000

Bemidji State University
1500 Birchmont Dr NE, Bemidji MN 56601-2699
877-236-4354

Bethany Lutheran College
700 Luther Dr, Mankato MN 56001
Don Westphal, Dean of Admissions
507-344-7000 Fax: 507-344-7376
Website: www.blc.edu
E-mail: admiss@blc.edu

Bethel College
3900 Bethel Dr, Saint Paul MN 55112-6999
651-638-6400

Carleton College
1 N College St, Northfield MN 55057-4044
800-995-2275 or 507-646-4190 Fax: 507-646-4526
Website: www.carleton.edu
E-mail: admissions@acs.carleton.edu

College of Saint Scholastica
1200 Kenwood Ave, Duluth MN 55811-4199
Brian Dalton, V.P. of Enrollment Management
800-447-5444

College of Saint Scholastica
340 Cedar St, Saint Paul MN 55101
651-298-1015

College of Visual Arts
344 Summit Ave, Saint Paul MN 55102-2124
L. Tanaka, Director of Student Affairs
651-224-3416

Concordia College
901 8th St S, Moorhead MN 56562-0002
Thomas Thomsen, President
Scott Ellingson, Director of Admissions
218-299-3004

Concordia University-Saint Paul
275 Syndicate St N, Saint Paul MN 55104-5494
651-641-8278

Crossroads College
920 Mayowood Rd SW, Rochester MN 55902-2382
Ralph Anderson, Director of Admissions
800-456-7651

Crown College
8700 College View Dr, Saint Bonifacius MN 55375
Mitch Fisk, Director of Admissions
952-446-4142

Gustavus Adolphus College
800 W College Ave, Saint Peter MN 56082-1485
Mark H. Anderson, Dean of Admission
800-GUSTAVUS Fax: 507-933-7474
Website: www.gustavus.edu
E-mail: admission@gustavus.edu

Hamline University
1536 Hewitt Ave, Saint Paul MN 55104-1284
651-523-2800

Macalester College
1600 Grand Ave, Saint Paul MN 55105-1899
651-696-6000

Martin Luther College
1995 Luther Ct, New Ulm MN 56073-3300
Rev. Earle Treptow, Director of Admissions
507-354-8221

MCNALLY SMITH COLLEGE OF MUSIC
19 Exchange St East, St. Paul MN 55101
Debbie Sandridge, Director of Admissions
800-594-9500 or 651-291-0177 Fax: 651-291-0366
Website: www.mcnallysmith.edu
E-mail: dsandridge@mcnallysmith.edu
   Established 1985. Private. Coed. Accreditation: National Association of Schools of Music. Tuition: $13,920 per year. Fees: vary. Faculty: 50. Student-faculty ratio: 8:1. Bachelor of Music Degree in Music Performance (emphasis in Guitar, Bass, Drums, Keyboard, Voice, or Brass & Woodwinds). Bachelor of Arts Degree in Music (Business). AAS Degrees in Recording Technology, Music Production, Music Business, and Music Performance. Diploma programs available. Campus located in downtown St. Paul, in the heart of the Twin Cities music scene. State of the art studios, concert stage and theater, music library, and rehearsal rooms. World class faculty.

Metropolitan State University
700 7th St E, Saint Paul MN 55106-5000
Rosa Rodriguez, Admissions Director
651-793-1300 Fax: 651-793-1546
Website: www.metrostate.edu
E-mail: rosa.rodriguez@metrostate.edu

Minnesota State University Mankato
228 Wiecking Center, Mankato MN 56001
507-389-1866

Minnesota State University Moorhead
1104 7th Ave S, Moorhead MN 56563-0002
218-236-2011

NATIONAL AMERICAN UNIVERSITY
112 W Market, Bloomington MN 55425-5521
Seamus White, Director of Admissions
952-883-0439 Fax: 952-883-0106
Website: www.national.edu
E-mail: swhite@national.edu

NATIONAL AMERICAN UNIVERSITY
6120 Earle Brown Dr Suite 100
Brooklyn Center MN 55430
Jeffrey Allen, PhD, Campus Vice President
763-560-8377 Fax: 763-549-9955
Website: www.national.edu
E-mail: jallen@national.edu

National American University
1550 W Highway 36, Roseville MN 55113
Matthew Mottl, Director of Admissions
651-644-1265 Fax: 651-644-0690
Website: www.national.edu
E-mail: mmottl@national.edu

North Central University
910 Elliot Ave, Minneapolis MN 55404-1391
612-343-4779

Northwestern College
3003 Snelling Ave N, Saint Paul MN 55113-1598
Dr. Douglas Huffman, Dean of Admissions
651-631-5111

Oak Hills Christian College
1600 Oak Hills Rd SW, Bemidji MN 56601-8826
Dan Hovestol, Admissions Director
218-751-8670

Pillsbury Baptist Bible College
315 S Grove Ave, Owatonna MN 55060-3097
Stephen R. Seidler, Director of Admissions
507-451-2710 Fax: 507-451-0156
Website: www.pillsbury.edu
E-mail: steveseidler@pillsbury.edu

St. Cloud State University
720 4th Ave S, Saint Cloud MN 56301-4442
877-654-7278

St. Mary's University of Minnesota
700 Terrace Hts Ste 2, Winona MN 55987-1321
507-452-4430

St. Olaf College
1500 Saint Olaf Ave, Northfield MN 55057-1001
507-646-2222

Southwest Minnesota State University
1501 State St, Marshall MN 56258-1598
507-537-7678

University of Minnesota
2900 University Ave, Crookston MN 56716-5001
218-281-6510

University of Minnesota
10 University Dr, Duluth MN 55812-2496
Beth Esselstrom, Director of Admissions
218-726-7171

University of Minnesota
231 Pillsbury Dr SE, Minneapolis MN 55455-0230
612-625-2008

University of Minnesota - Morris
600 E 4th St, Morris MN 56267-2132
Rodney Oto, Director
800-992-8863

University of Minnesota Rochester
855 30th Ave SE, Rochester MN 55904-4945
Dick Westerlund, Program Director
507-280-2838

University of St. Thomas
2115 Summit Ave, Saint Paul MN 55105-1096
651-962-5000

Winona State University
PO Box 5838, Winona MN 55987-0838
507-457-5000

MISSISSIPPI

Alcorn State University
PO Box 359, Lorman MS 39096
601-877-6147

Belhaven College
1500 Peachtree St, Jackson MS 39202-1789
601-968-5927

Delta State University
Hwy 8 W, Cleveland MS 38733
662-846-3000

Jackson State University
1440 J.R. Lynch St, Jackson MS 39217
Stephanie Chatman, Director of Admissions
601-979-2100

MAGNOLIA BIBLE COLLEGE
PO Box 1109, Kosciusko MS 39090-1109
Garvis Semore, President
800-748-8655 Fax: 662-289-1850
Website: www.magnolia.edu
E-mail: gsemore@magnolia.edu

Millsaps College
PO Box 15495, Jackson MS 39210
601-974-1000

Mississippi College
PO Box 4086, Clinton MS 39058-0001
601-925-3000

Mississippi State University
PO Box J, Mississippi State MS 39762-5509
662-325-2323

Mississippi University for Women
1100 College St Unit W1613, Columbus MS 39701
Terri Heath, Director of Admissions
877-GO-2-THEW

Mississippi University for Women-Tupelo
1918 Briar Ridge Rd, Tupelo MS 38804-5904
Kay Brown, Contact
662-844-0284

Mississippi Valley State University
14000 Highway 82 W Box 7222
Itta Bena MS 38941-1401
Office of Admissions
662-254-3347

Rust College
150 Rust Ave, Holly Springs MS 38635-2330
662-252-8000

Southeastern Baptist College
4229 Highway 15 N, Laurel MS 39440-1096
601-426-6346

Tougaloo College
500 W County Line Rd, Tougaloo MS 39174-9799
Juno Leggette Jacobs, Director of Admissions
601-977-7768 Fax: 601-977-4501
Website: www.tougaloo.edu
E-mail: jjacobs@tougaloo.edu

University of Mississippi
University MS 38677
662-232-7226

University of Mississippi Medical Center
2500 N State St, Jackson MS 39216-4500
601-984-1010

University of Southern Mississippi
PO Box 5165, Hattiesburg MS 39406-1000
601-266-5000

University of Southern Mississippi
730 E Beach Blvd, Long Beach MS 39560
228-865-4500

WESLEY COLLEGE
PO Box 1070, Florence MS 39073-1070
Beverly Porter, V.P. for Academic Affairs
601-845-2265 Fax: 601-845-2266
Website: www.wesleycollege.edu
E-mail: admissions@wesleycollege.edu

William Carey College
1856 Beach Dr, Gulfport MS 39507-1508
228-867-9201

William Carey College
498 Tuscan Ave, Hattiesburg MS 39401-5461
800-962-5991

MISSOURI

Avila University
11901 Wornall Rd, Kansas City MO 64145-1698
816-942-8400

Baptist Bible College
628 E Kearney St, Springfield MO 65803-3498
800-228-5754

Calvary Bible College & Theological Seminary
15800 Calvary Rd, Kansas City MO 64147-1341
Robert M. Reinsch, Director of Admissions
800-326-3960 Fax: 816-331-4474
Website: www.calvary.edu
E-mail: admissions@calvary.edu

CENTRAL BIBLE COLLEGE
3000 N Grant Ave, Springfield MO 65803-1096
Scott Lindner, Executive Director of Enrollment
Services
800-831-4222 ext. 1290 Fax: 417-833-5141
Website: www.cbcag.edu
E-mail: cbcinfo@cbcag.edu

Central Christian College of the Bible
911 E Urbandale Dr, Moberly MO 65270-1923
Troy Titus, Director of Admissions
888-263-3900

Central Methodist University
411 Central Methodist Sq, Fayette MO 65248-1198
660-248-6247

Central Missouri State University
Warrensburg MO 64093-8888
Charles Petentler, Associate Director of Admissions
800-956-0177

Clayton University
11939 Manchester Road #123, Saint Louis MO 63131

College of the Ozarks
Point Lookout MO 65726
417-334-6411

Colorado Technical University
520 E 19th Ave, North Kansas City MO 64116-3614
Michael Murdie, Director of Admissions
816-472-7400

Columbia College
1001 Rogers St, Columbia MO 65216-0001
Regina Morin, Director of Admissions
573-875-7352 Fax: 573-875-7506
Website: www.ccis.edu
E-mail: admissions@ccis.edu

Cox College of Nursing & Health Sciences
1423 N Jefferson Ave, Springfield MO 65802-1917
417-269-3401

Culver-Stockton College
1 College Hl, Canton MO 63435-1299
Betty Smith, Director of Enrollment Services
800-537-1883

DEACONESS COLLEGE OF NURSING
6150 Oakland Ave, Saint Louis MO 63139-3215
Michelle McGrail, Dean of Enrollment and Student
Affairs
314-768-3044 Fax: 314-768-5673
Website: www.deaconess.edu
E-mail: michelle.mcgrail@deaconess.edu

Drury University
900 N Benton Ave, Springfield MO 65802-3791
417-873-7879

Evangel University
1111 N Glenstone Ave, Springfield MO 65802-2191
Charity Fahlstrom, Director of Admissions
417-865-2811 Fax: 417-520-0545
Website: www.evangel.edu
E-mail: fahlstromc@evangel.edu

Fontbonne University
6800 Wydown Blvd, Saint Louis MO 63105-3098
314-889-1419

GRACELAND UNIVERSITY
1401 W Truman Rd, Independence MO 64050
Patricia K. Trachsel, Dean of Independence Campus
816-833-0524 Fax: 816-833-2990
Website: www.graceland.edu
E-mail: trachsel@graceland.edu

Hannibal-LaGrange College
2800 Palmyra Rd, Hannibal MO 63401-1999
573-221-3675

Harris-Stowe State University
3026 Laclede Ave, Saint Louis MO 63103-2199
LaShanda R. Boone, Director of Admissions
314-340-3300 Fax: 314-340-3555
Website: www.hssu.edu
E-mail: admissions@hssu.edu

Kansas City Art Institute
4415 Warwick Blvd, Kansas City MO 64111-1820
800-522-5224

Lincoln University
Truman Educ Center Bldg 499
Fort Leonard Wood MO 65473
573-681-5421

Lincoln University
820 Chestnut St, Jefferson City MO 65101-3500
573-681-5000

Lindenwood University
209 S Kingshighway St
Saint Charles MO 63301-1695
Sheryl Guffey, Director of Admissions
636-949-2000 Fax: 636-949-4989
Website: www.lindenwood.edu

Maryville University of St. Louis
13550 Conway Rd, Saint Louis MO 63141-7299
314-529-9300

Missouri Baptist University
1 College Park Dr, Saint Louis MO 63141-8698
314-434-1115

Missouri Southern State University - Joplin
3950 Newman Rd, Joplin MO 64801-1512
417-625-9300

Missouri State University
901 S National Ave, Springfield MO 65897
417-836-5000

Missouri State University - West Plains
128 Garfield, West Plains MO 65775
417-255-7255

Missouri Tech
1167 Corporate Lake Dr, Saint Louis MO 63132
314-569-3600

Missouri Valley College
500 E College St, Marshall MO 65340-3197
J. Kenneth Bryant, President
660-831-4108

Missouri Western State College
4525 Downs Dr, Saint Joseph MO 64507-2294
800-662-7041

National American University
3620 Arrowhead Ave, Independence MO 64057-1791
Janet Miller, Director of Admission
816-353-4554

Northwest Missouri State University
800 University Dr, Maryville MO 64468-6001
660-562-1212

OZARK CHRISTIAN COLLEGE
1111 N Main St, Joplin MO 64801-4804
Troy Nelson, Director of Admissions
800-299-4622 or 417-624-2518 Fax: 417-624-0090
Website: www.occ.edu
E-mail: occadmin@occ.edu
  Established 1942. Private. Coed. Accreditation: ABHE.
Tuition: $7,840. Room & board: $2,025. Fees: $480. En-
rollment: 712 full-time, 135 part-time. Faculty: 43.
Student-faculty ratio: 20:1. Degrees: Bachelors Degrees
in Theology; Biblical Literature with majors in Bible and
Psychology, Bible and Deaf Ministry; Christian Educa-
tion; Bible and Ministry; Bible and Missions; Music Minis-
try and Music and Worship. Associate degrees in Bible,
Elementary, Middle School, Secondary Education, or
Nursing. Coop degree programs with Missouri Southern
State College in Joplin, Mo., Pittsburg State University in
Pittsburg, KS., and Fort Hays State University, Hays, KS.
96% of graduates enter degree-related fields.

Park University
8700 NW River Park Dr, Parkville MO 64152-3795
816-741-2000

Ranken Technical College
4431 Finney Ave, Saint Louis MO 63113-2898
Elizabeth M. Keserauskis, Director of Admissions
314-371-0233 Fax: 314-371-0241
Website: www.ranken.edu
E-mail: admissions@ranken.edu

Research College of Nursing
2525 E Meyer Blvd, Kansas City MO 64132
816-995-2800

Rockhurst University
1100 Rockhurst Rd, Kansas City MO 64110-2561
Mark Kopenski, VP of Enrollment Management
816-501-4000

St. Louis Christian College
1360 Grandview Dr, Florissant MO 63033-6499
Dr. Ronald L. Oakes, Academic Dean
Rick Fordyce, Registrar
314-837-6777

ST. LOUIS COLLEGE OF PHARMACY
4588 Parkview Pl, Saint Louis MO 63110-1088
Penny Bryant, Director of Admissions/Registrar
314-367-8700 Fax: 314-446-8310
Website: www.stlcop.edu

St. Louis University
221 N Grand Blvd, Saint Louis MO 63103-2097
314-977-2222

Saint Luke's College
8320 Ward Parkway Suite 300
Kansas City MO 64114
Josh Richards Asst. Director of Admissions
816-932-2367 Fax: 816-932-9064
Website: www.saintlukescollege.edu
E-mail: slc-admissions@saint-lukes.org

Southeast Missouri State University
1 University Plz, Cape Girardeau MO 63701-4710
573-651-2000

Southwest Baptist University
1600 University Ave, Bolivar MO 65613-2597
417-328-5281

Southwest Baptist University
4431 S Fremont Ave, Springfield MO 65804-7307
417-841-5046

Truman State University
100 E Normal, Kirksville MO 63501
Office of Admission
660-785-4000 Fax: 660-785-4181
Website: admissions.truman.edu
E-mail: admissions@truman.edu

University of Missouri
228 Jesse Hall, Columbia MO 65211-0001
573-882-2121

University of Missouri
5100 Rockhill Rd, Kansas City MO 64110-2446
816-235-1000

University of Missouri
102 Parker, Rolla MO 65409
Lynn Stichnote, Director of Admission
573-341-4164

University of Missouri
1 University Blvd, Saint Louis MO 63121-4499
John Kundel, Director of Admissions
314-516-5451 Fax: 314-516-5310
Website: www.umsl.edu
E-mail: admissions@umsl.edu

Washington University in St. Louis
1 Brookings Dr, Saint Louis MO 63130-4899
314-935-5000

WEBSTER UNIVERSITY
470 E Lockwood Ave, Saint Louis MO 63119-3194
Niel DeVasto, Director of Admissions
Website: www.webster.edu
E-mail: admit@webster.edu
800-753-6765
314-968-7100 Fax: 314-968-7116 (graduate)
314-968-6991 Fax: 314-968-7115 (undergraduate)
  Established 1915. Private. Coed. Accreditation:
NCACS. Tuition: $18,240. Room and board: $7,300. Enrollment: 2,460 full-time, 1,153 part-time. Faculty: 160,
Student-faculty ratio: 15:1. Degrees: BA, BFA, BM,
BMEd, BS, BSN, MA, MBA, MAT, MSN, DMGT. Library:
400,000 volumes. 36 buildings on 45 acres. Nationally
recognized programs in the performing arts and communications. Regionally recognized programs in education
and business. Students from 40 states and 30 countries.
Beautiful suburban campus in a wooded community of
20,000. Average class size of 15. New Residence Halls
for 320 additional students open in 2006. Campuses in
four European countries, China and Thailand.

Westminister College
501 Westminster Ave, Fulton MO 65251-1299
573-642-3361

William Jewell College
500 College Hill, Liberty MO 64068-1896
800-753-7009

WILLIAM WOODS UNIVERSITY
1 University Ave, Fulton MO 65251-2388
Jimmy Clay, Director of Admissions
573-592-4296 Fax: 573-592-1146
Website: www.williamwoods.edu
E-mail: admission@williamwoods.edu
Established 1892. Private. Coed. Accreditation: North Central Association of Colleges & Schools, Higher Learning Commission. Tuition: $14,300. Room & board: $2,625 room, $2,625 board. Enrollment: 1,025. Student-faculty ratio: 14:1. Degrees: BA, BS, BSW, AA Paralegal, MED, MBA. Equestrian Science, Equine Administration, Interpreting and Sign Language, Sports Management, Human Administration.

MONTANA

Carroll College
1601 N Benton Ave, Helena MT 59625-0002
Dr. Thomas J. Trebon, President
Cynthia Thornquist, Director of Admissions & Enrollment Operations
406-447-4384

Montana State University - Billings
1500 University Dr, Billings MT 59101-0252
Karen Everett, Director
800-565-MSUB

Montana State University - Bozeman
103 Culbertson Hall, Bozeman MT 59715-5072
406-994-2452

Montana State University Northern
PO Box 7751, Havre MT 59501-7751
406-265-3700

Montana Tech of the University of Montana
1300 W Park St, Butte MT 59701-8997
800-445-TECH

Rocky Mountain College
1511 Poly Dr, Billings MT 59102-1796
Bonnie Knapp, Director of Admissions
800-877-6259 Fax: 406-657-1189
Website: www.rocky.edu
E-mail: admissions@rocky.edu

University of Great Falls
1301 20th St S, Great Falls MT 59405-4996
Cathy Day, Director of Admissions
406-791-5200

University of Montana
Missoula MT 59812-0001
406-243-0211

University of Montana - Western
710 S Atlantic St, Dillon MT 59725-3598
406-683-7011

NEBRASKA

Bellevue University
1000 Galvin Rd S, Bellevue NE 68005-3098
Mary Hawkins, V.P. of Enrollment
800-756-7920

Chadron State College
1000 Main St, Chadron NE 69337-2690
308-432-6000

Clarkson College
101 S 42nd St, Omaha NE 68131-2715
Sara Bonney, Director of Admissions
402-552-3100 Fax: 402-552-6057
Website: www.clarksoncollege.edu
E-mail: admiss@clarksoncollege.edu

Concordia University
800 N Columbia Ave, Seward NE 68434-1594
402-643-3651

Creighton University
2500 California Plz, Omaha NE 68178-0001
402-280-2700

Dana College
2848 College Dr, Blair NE 68008-1099
James Lynes, Director of Admissions
800-444-3262

Doane College
1014 Boswell Ave, Crete NE 68333-2421
402-826-2161

Grace University
1311 S 9th St, Omaha NE 68108-3629
402-449-2800

Hastings College
PO Box 269, Hastings NE 68902-0269
402-463-2402

Midland Lutheran College
900 N Clarkson St, Fremont NE 68025-4200
Todd Hansen, Associate Director of Admissions
402-941-6501 Fax: 402-941-6513
Website: www.mlc.edu
E-mail: admissions@mlc.edu

Nebraska Christian College
1800 Syracuse Ave, Norfolk NE 68701-2458
Jason Epperson, Admissions
402-379-5000

Nebraska Wesleyan University
5000 Saint Paul Ave, Lincoln NE 68504-2794
Patricia Karthauser, V.P. for University Enrollment
402-466-2371 Fax: 402-465-2177
Website: www.nebrwesleyan.edu
E-mail: admissions@nebrwesleyan.edu

Peru State College
PO Box 10, Peru NE 68421-0010
Office of Admissions
800-742-4412 Fax: 402-872-2296
Website: www.peru.edu
E-mail: admissions@oakmail.peru.edu

Union College
3800 S 48th St, Lincoln NE 68506-4300
Buell Fogg, V.P. for Enrollment Services
800-228-4600

University of Nebraska
14th & R Sts, Lincoln NE 68588
402-472-7211

University of Nebraska at Kearney
905 W 25th St, Kearney NE 68849-0001
Dusty Newton, Director of Admissions
800-KEARNEY Fax: 308-865-8987
Website: www.unk.edu
E-mail: admissionsug@unk.edu

University of Nebraska at Omaha
60th and Dodge St, Omaha NE 68182-0001
402-554-2800

Wayne State College
1111 Main St, Wayne NE 68787-1172
402-375-7000

York College
912 Kiplinger Ave, York NE 68467-2631
402-363-5600

NEVADA

Art Institute of Las Vegas
2350 Corporate Cir, Henderson NV 89074-7737
702-369-9944

GREAT BASIN COLLEGE
1500 College Pkwy, Elko NV 89801-9930
Julie G. Byrnes, Director of Enrollment Management
775-753-2271 Fax: 775-753-2311
Website: www.gbcnv.edu
E-mail: bjulie@gbcnv.edu
Public. Coed. Accreditation: Northwest Association of Schools & Colleges. Tuition: $51-$75 per credit plus non-resident tuition of $2,457.50 per semester if applicable. Enrollment: 861 full-time, 1,759 part-time. Faculty: 64 full time and adjunct 120. Student-faculty ratio: 18:1. Degrees: Associate and some Baccalaureate. 12 buildings plus residence halls on 44 acres. GBC is the major provider of post-secondary education in central and northeastern Nevada and has been from its first days as an upstart college thirty-eight years ago.

Morrison University
10315 Professional Circle Suite 201
Reno NV 89521-4826
Charles Timinsky, Director of Enrollment
775-850-0700 Fax: 775-850-0711
Website: www.morrisonuniversity.com

Sierra Nevada College-Lake Tahoe
999 Tahoe Boulevard, Incline Village NV 89451
Dr. Ben Solomon, President
800-332-8666

University of Nevada
Reno NV 89557-0001
775-784-1110

University of Nevada Las Vegas
4505 S Maryland Pkwy, Las Vegas NV 89154-9901
800-334-8658

NEW HAMPSHIRE

Colby-Sawyer College
100 Main St, New London NH 03257-4648
603-526-3000

Daniel Webster College
20 University Dr, Nashua NH 03063-1323
Paul LaBarre, Director of Enrollment Services
603-577-6600

Dartmouth College
Hanover NH 03755
603-646-1110

Franklin Pierce College
5 Chenell Dr, Concord NH 03301-8540
603-228-1155

Franklin Pierce College
17 Bradco Rd, Keene NH 03431-3900
603-357-0079

Franklin Pierce College
670 N Commercial St Ste 206, Manchester NH 03101

Franklin Pierce College
73 Corporate Dr, Portsmouth NH 03801-2847
603-433-2000

Franklin Pierce College
20 College Rd, Rindge NH 03461
800-437-0048

Granite State College
8 Old Suncook Rd, Concord NH 03301-6400
603-228-3000

Hesser College
3 Sundial Ave, Manchester NH 03103-7245
603-668-6660

Hesser College - Division of Continuing Education
25 Hall St, Concord NH 03301
Stanley Post, Director of Admissions
603-225-9200

Hesser College - Division of Continuing Education
410 Amherst St, Nashua NH 03063-1286
Bruce Thompson, Director of Admissions
603-883-0404

Hesser College - Division of Continuing Education
170 Commerce Way, Portsmouth NH 03801-3245
Heidi Hale, Director of Admissions
603-436-5300

Hesser College - Division of Continuing Education
11 Manor Pkwy, Salem NH 03079
Valerie Sager, Director of Admissions
603-898-3480

Keene State College
229 Main St, Keene NH 03435-0002
603-358-2276

Magdalen College
511 Kearsarge Mountain Rd, Warner NH 03278
603-456-2656

New England College
26 Bridge St, Henniker NH 03242-3297
603-428-2211

Plymouth State University
17 High St, MSC #44, Bagley House
Plymouth NH 03264-1595
603-535-5000

Rivier College
420 S Main St, Nashua NH 03060-5086
David Boisvert, Director of Undergraduate Admissions
603-897-8507

St. Anselm College
100 Saint Anselms Dr, Manchester NH 03102-1310
603-641-7000

Southern New Hampshire University
2500 N River Rd, Hooksett NH 03106-1045
Steve Soba, Director of Admissions
603-645-9611 Fax: 603-645-9693
Website: www.snhu.edu
E-mail: s.soba@snhu.edu

Thomas More College of Liberal Arts
6 Manchester St, Merrimack NH 03054-4855
603-880-8308

University of New Hampshire
Durham NH 03824
603-862-1234

University of New Hampshire
400 Commercial St, Manchester NH 03101-1113
603-668-0700

NEW JERSEY

Berkeley College
44 Rifle Camp Rd, West Paterson NJ 07424-3367
800-446-5400

Bloomfield College
467 Franklin St, Bloomfield NJ 07003
973-748-9000

Caldwell College
9 Ryerson Ave, Caldwell NJ 07006-6195
973-618-3000

Centenary College
400 Jefferson St, Hackettstown NJ 07840-2100
Glenna Warren, Director of Admissions
908-852-1400 Fax: 908-852-3454
Website: www.centenarycollege.edu
E-mail: warreng@centenarycollege.edu

College of New Jersey
PO Box 7718, Ewing NJ 08628-0718
609-771-1855

Drew University
36 Madison Ave, Madison NJ 07940-1493
973-408-3000

Fairleigh Dickinson University
285 Madison Ave, Madison NJ 07940-1099
800-338-8803

Fairleigh Dickinson University
1000 River Rd, Teaneck NJ 07666-1996
201-692-2000

Felician College
262 S Main St, Lodi NJ 07644-2198
973-559-6000

Georgian Court University
900 Lakewood Ave, Lakewood NJ 08701-2697
732-364-2200

Kean University
1000 Morris Ave, Union NJ 07083-7133
908-527-2000

Monmouth University
400 Cedar Ave, West Long Branch NJ 07764-1890
732-571-3400

Montclair State University
Montclair State University, Montclair NJ 07043-1624
973-655-4000

New Jersey City University
2039 John F Kennedy Blvd
Jersey City NJ 07305-1588
Carmen Panlilio, Asst. V.P. for Admissions and Financial Aid
201-200-3234 Fax: 201-200-2044
Website: www.njcu.edu
E-mail: admissions@njcu.edu

New Jersey Institute of Technology
University Heights, Newark NJ 07102
973-596-3000

Princeton University
Princeton NJ 08544-0001
609-258-3000

Rabbi Jacob Joseph School
1 Plainfield Ave, Edison NJ 08817-4476
732-985-6533

Ramapo College of New Jersey
505 Ramapo Valley Rd, Mahwah NJ 07430-1623
Director of Admissions
201-684-7300 or 201-684-7301 Fax: 201-684-7964
Website: www.ramapo.edu
E-mail: admissions@ramapo.edu

Richard Stockton College of New Jersey
PO Box 195, Pomona NJ 08240
609-652-1776

Rider University
2083 Lawrenceville Rd, Lawrenceville NJ 08648-3099
Susan Christian, Director of Admissions
609-896-5042

Rowan University
200 N Broadway, Camden NJ 08102-1102
856-757-2857

Rowan University
201 Mullica Hill Rd, Glassboro NJ 08028-1700
856-256-4000

Rutgers-The State University of New Jersey
Camden Campus
311 N 5th St, Camden NJ 08102-1405
856-225-6026

Rutgers-The State University of New Jersey
Newark Campus
Newark NJ 07102
973-353-5568

Rutgers-The State University of New Jersey
New Brunswick Campus
35 College Ave, New Brunswick NJ 08901
732-932-4636

St. Peter's College
Hudson Terrace, Englewood Cliffs NJ 07632
201-568-7730

St. Peter's College
2627 John F Kennedy Blvd, Jersey City NJ 07306
888-SPC-9933

Seton Hall University
400 S Orange Ave, South Orange NJ 07079-2697
973-761-9000

SOMERSET CHRISTIAN COLLEGE
PO Box 9035, Zarephath NJ 08890
Anthony Viscioni, VP of Enrollment Management &
Communications
800-234-9305 Fax: 732-356-4846
Website: www.somerset.edu
E-mail: info@somerset.edu

Stevens Institute of Technology
Castle Point on Hudson, Hoboken NJ 07030
201-216-5100

Thomas Edison State College
101 W State St, Trenton NJ 08608-1101
609-984-1100

UMDNJ-School of Health Related Professions
65 Bergen St, Newark NJ 07107-3001
973-972-5453

UMDNJ-School of Nursing
30 Bergen St, Newark NJ 07107
973-972-4322

UMDNJ-University of Medicine and Dentistry of New
Jersey
65 Bergen St, Newark NJ 07107-3001
973-972-4300

Westminster Choir College of Rider University
101 Walnut Ln, Princeton NJ 08540-3819
Matthew T. Kadlubowski, Director of Admissions
609-921-7144

William Paterson University
300 Pompton Rd, Wayne NJ 07470-2103
973-720-2000

NEW MEXICO

Apollo College
5301 Central Ave NE Ste 101
Albuquerque NM 87108-1514
800-368-7246

College of Santa Fe
1600 Saint Michaels Dr, Santa Fe NM 87505-7634
505-473-6011

College of the Southwest
6610 N Lovington Hwy, Hobbs NM 88240-9129
505-392-6561

Eastern New Mexico University
Portales NM 88130
800-367-3668

Institute of American Indian Arts
83 A Van Nu Po, Santa Fe NM 87508-1300
Myra Garro, Manager of Enrollment & Admissions
505-424-2328 Fax: 505-424-4500
Website: www.iaia.edu
E-mail: recruitment@iaia.edu

International Institute of the Americas
4201 Central Ave NW Suite J
Albuquerque NM 87105-1649
Ed Sigman, Director
505-880-2877 Fax: 505-352-0199
Website: www.iia.edu
E-mail: syelton@iia.edu

Metropolitan College
8100 Mountain Rd NE Ste 200
Albuquerque NM 87110-7800
Jessica M. Quinonez, Director of Admissions
505-888-3400

National American University
4775 Indian Sch Rd NE #200
Albuquerque NM 87110-3976
505-265-7517

National American University
1601 Rio Rancho Dr SE #200
Rio Rancho NM 87124-1093
505-891-1111

National College of Midwifery
209 State Road 240, Taos NM 87571
505-758-8914

New Mexico Highlands University
PO Box 9000, Las Vegas NM 87701
Director of Student Recruitment
800-338-NMHU

New Mexico Institute of Mining & Technology
801 Leroy Pl, Socorro NM 87801-4750
505-835-5011

New Mexico State University
PO Box 30001, Las Cruces NM 88003-8001
505-646-0111

St. John's College
1160 Camino Cruz Blanca, Santa Fe NM 87505-4599
L. Clendenin, Director of Admissions
800-331-5232 Fax: 505-984-6162
Website: www.stjohnscollege.edu
E-mail: admissions@sjcsf.edu

Southwestern College
PO Box 4788, Santa Fe NM 87502-4788
Kristine Schmidt BA, Director of Admissions
877-471-5756 ext. 26

University of New Mexico
1 University Campus, Albuquerque NM 87131-0001
505-277-0111

University of Phoenix
New Mexico Division
7471 Pan Amrcan West Fwy NE
Albuquerque NM 87109-4645
505-821-4800

Western New Mexico University
PO Box 680, Silver City NM 88062-0680
505-538-6011

NEW YORK

Adelphi University
Garden City NY 11530
516-877-3100

Alfred University
1 Saxson Dr, Alfred NY 14802
607-871-2111

Alfred University - New York State College of Ceramics
2 Pine St, Alfred NY 14802-1214
607-871-2411

AMERICAN UNIVERSITY IN CAIRO
420 5th Ave 3rd Floor, New York NY 10018
Student Affairs Office
212-730-8800 Fax: 212-730-1600
Website: www.aucegypt.edu
E-mail: aucegypt@aucnyo.edu

Bard College
Annandale on Hudson NY 12504
845-758-6822

Berkeley College - Westchester Campus
99 Church St, White Plains NY 10601-1505
800-446-5400

Boricua College
186 N 6th St, Brooklyn NY 11211-3209
718-782-2200

Boricua College
3755 Broadway, New York NY 10032-1599
212-694-1000

Briarcliffe College
1055 Stewart Ave, Bethpage NY 11714-3545
Theresa Donohue, Director of Admissions
516-918-3600 Fax: 516-470-6020
Website: www.briarcliffe.edu

Canisius College
2001 Main St, Buffalo NY 14208-1098
716-883-7000

Cazenovia College
Cazenovia NY 13035-1084
Robert Croot, Dean of Admissions & Financial Aid
800-654-3210

Central Yeshiva Tomchei Tmimim Lubavitz
841 Ocean Pkwy, Brooklyn NY 11230-2700
Joseph Wilmowsky, Registrar
718-434-0784

Clarkson University
PO Box 5500, Potsdam NY 13699
315-268-6400

Colgate University
13 Oak Dr, Hamilton NY 13346-1386
Gary Ross, Director of Admissions
315-228-7401

College of Mount Saint Vincent
6301 Riverdale Ave, Riverdale NY 10471-1093
718-405-3200

College of New Rochelle
755 Co Op City Blvd, Bronx NY 10475-1601
718-320-0300

College of New Rochelle
332 E 149th St, Bronx NY 10451-5606
718-665-1310

College of New Rochelle
1368 Fulton St, Brooklyn NY 11216-2600
718-638-2500

College of New Rochelle
29 Castle Pl, New Rochelle NY 10805-2339
914-654-5000

College of New Rochelle
125 Barclay St, New York NY 10007-2199
212-815-1710

College of New Rochelle
144 W 125th St, New York NY 10027-4423
212-662-7500

College of Saint Rose
432 Western Ave, Albany NY 12203-1419
Maryelizabeth Amico, Asst V.P. for Undergraduate
Admissions
518-454-5150 Fax: 518-454-2013
Website: www.strose.edu
E-mail: admit@strose.edu

Columbia University
2960 Broadway, New York NY 10027-6900
212-854-1754

Columbia University
168th & Broadway, New York NY 10032
212-305-5756

Concordia College
171 White Plains Rd, Bronxville NY 10708-1998
914-337-9300

Cooper Union
30 Cooper Sq, New York NY 10003
212-353-4100

Cornell University
410 Thurston Ave, Ithaca NY 14850-2432
607-255-2000

CUNY Bernard M. Baruch College
17 Lexington Ave, New York NY 10010-5518
212-802-2000

CUNY Brooklyn College
2900 Bedford Ave, Brooklyn NY 11210-2814
718-951-5000

CUNY City College
Convent Ave at 138th St, New York NY 10031
Celia Lloyd, Interim Director of Admissions
212-650-6977

CUNY College of Staten Island
2800 Victory Blvd, Staten Island NY 10314-6600
718-982-2000

CUNY Hunter College
695 Park Ave, New York NY 10021
Aaron Gibbs, Assistant Director of Recruitment
212-772-4497 Fax: 212-650-3336
Website: www.hunter.cuny.edu
E-mail: aaron.gibbs@hunter.cuny.edu

CUNY John Jay College of Criminal Justice
899 10th Ave, New York NY 10019-1029
212-237-8000

CUNY Lehman College
250 Bedford Park Blvd W, Bronx NY 10468-1527
718-960-8000

CUNY Medgar Evers College
1650 Bedford Ave, Brooklyn NY 11225-2010
718-270-4900

CUNY Queens College
6530 Kissena Blvd, Flushing NY 11367-1575
718-997-5000

CUNY York College
9420 Guy R Brewer Blvd, Jamaica NY 11451-0001
718-262-2000

DAEMEN COLLEGE
4380 Main St, Amherst NY 14226-3592
Donna Shaffner, Director of Admissions
800-462-7652 or 716-839-8225 Fax: 716-839-8229
Website: www.daemen.edu
E-mail: admissions@daemen.edu
Established 1947. Private. Coed. Tuition: $16,020.
Room & board: $7,300. Degrees: BA, BS, BFA, DPT, MS,
tDPT. Library: 135,000 volumes. Situated on a 39 acre
site in suburb of Buffalo, NY. Daeman College is a private,
independent, co-educational college offering extensive
liberal arts and preprofessional programs. The College
awards bachelor's degrees in more than 40 major fields
including Art, Business, Natural Sciences, Education,
English, History and Government, and Nursing. Daemen
is eminently known for its Physician Assistant (BS/MS)
and Physical Therapy (BS/DPT) programs.

DAVIS COLLEGE
400 Riverside Dr, Johnson City NY 13790
Brian Murphy, VP of Enrollment Management
607-729-1581 Fax: 607-729-2962
Website: www.davisny.edu
E-mail: admissions@davisny.edu

Dominican College of Blauvelt
470 Western Hwy, Orangeburg NY 10962-1210
845-359-7800

Dowling College
150 Idle Hour Blvd, Oakdale NY 11769-1999
631-244-3000

D'Youville College
320 Porter Ave, Buffalo NY 14201-1084
716-829-7600

Elmira College
1 Park Pl, Elmira NY 14901-2099
Gary Fallis, Dean of Admissions
607-735-1724

Excelsior College
7 Columbia Cir, Albany NY 12203-5156
518-464-8500

Farmingdale SUNY
2350 Broadhollow Rd, Farmingdale NY 11735
631-420-2200

Fashion Institute of Technology
227 W 27th St, New York NY 10001-5992
212-217-7999

FIVE TOWNS COLLEGE
305 N Service Rd, Dix Hills NY 11746-5871
631-424-7000 ext. 2110 Fax: 631-656-2172
Website: www.fivetowns.edu
E-mail: admissions@ftc.edu
Founded in 1972. Private, co-ed college offering 2-
year, 4-year and graduate degree programs. Accreditation: MSACS and NYS Board of Regents. Tuition: $15,200
per year ($635 per credit, plus fees). Enrollment: 1,000
students. Faculty: 85. Degrees: AA, AS, AAS, BFA, BMus,
BPS, BS, MusM, MS in Education, DMA. Rolling admissions. 5 buildings on 40 wooded acres. Library: 35,000
volumes and music archives. Majors: Accounting, Audio
Recording Technology, Broadcasting, Business Management, Childhood Education, Communications, Computer Business Applications, Jazz/Commercial Music,

Liberal Arts, Marketing/Retailing, Music Business, Music Composition/Songwriting, Music Education, Music Performance, Musical Theatre, Theatre Arts, and Film/Video Production. Financial aid, Internships program and Career Services available.

Fordham University
441 E Fordham Rd, Bronx NY 10458-9993
Karen Pellegrino, Director of Admissions
800-FORDHAM

Fordham University - Lincoln Center
113 W 60th St, New York NY 10023-7484
Robert Grimes, S.J., Ph.D., Dean
212-636-6000

Globe Institute of Technology
291 Broadway Fl 2, New York NY 10007-1814
212-349-4330

Hamilton College
198 College Hill Rd, Clinton NY 13323-1295
Richard Fuller, Dean of Admissions
315-859-4421

Hartwick College
West St
Oneonta NY 13820
607-431-4000

Hilbert College
5200 S Park Ave, Hamburg NY 14075-1597
Timothy Lee, Director of Admissions
716-649-7900 Fax: 716-649-0702
Website: www.hilbert.edu
E-mail: tlee@hilbert.edu

Hobart & William Smith Colleges
Pulteney St, Geneva NY 14456
John Young, Director of Admissions
315-789-5500 Fax: 315-781-3654
Website: www.hws.edu
E-mail: young@hws.edu

Hofstra University
100 Hofstra University, Hempstead NY 11549-1000
516-463-6600

Houghton College
PO Box 128, Houghton NY 14744-0128
585-567-9200

Houghton College
910 Union Rd, West Seneca NY 14224-3499
716-674-6363

Iona College
715 North Ave, New Rochelle NY 10801-1890
Tom Weede, Director of Admissions
914-633-2000

Iona College
PO Box 1522, Pearl River NY 10965-8522
845-620-1350

Ithaca College
953 Danby Rd, Ithaca NY 14850-7002
607-274-3011

Jewish Theological Seminary of America
3080 Broadway, New York NY 10027-4650
Jan Michael Skidds, Associate Director of Admissions
212-678-8000 Fax: 212-280-6022
Website: www.jtsa.edu
E-mail: lcadmissions@jtsa.edu

Juilliard School
60 Lincoln Center Plz, New York NY 10023-6588
Lee Cioppa, Associate Dean for Admissions
212-799-5000 Fax: 212-769-6420
Website: www.juilliard.edu
E-mail: admissions@juilliard.edu

Keller Graduate School of DeVry University
120 W 45th St Rm 200, New York NY 10036
Jennifer Blumberg, Admissions Representative
212-556-0002

Keuka College
PO Box 98, Keuka Park NY 14478-0098
315-536-4411

LABORATORY INSTITUTE OF MERCHANDISING
12 E 53rd St, New York NY 10022-5268
Kristina Gibson, Director of Admissions
800-677-1323 or 212-752-1530 Fax: 212-750-3432
Website: www.limcollege.edu
E-mail: admissions@limcollege.edu
Established 1939. Private. Coed. Accreditation: Middle States Association of Schools & Colleges. Tuition: $17,250. Fees: $450. Enrollment: 1,000. Faculty: 115. Student-faculty ratio: 9:1. Degrees offered: BBA, BPS, AAS. Library: 12,000 volumes. 2 five week internships, full semester work co-op, weekly fashion industry field trips, weekly fashion industry guest lectures, over 90% career placement within 90 days of graduation.

Le Moyne College
1419 Salt Springs Rd, Syracuse NY 13214-1301
800-333-4733

Long Island University
2nd Ave, Brentwood NY 11717
Marlyne Hynds, Asst. Provost
631-273-5112

Long Island University
555 Broadway, Dobbs Ferry NY 10522-1134
914-693-4500

Long Island University-Brooklyn Campus
1 University Plz, Brooklyn NY 11201-5372
718-488-1000

Long Island University-C. W. Post Campus
720 Northern Blvd, Brookville NY 11548-1300
Joanne Graziano, Executive Director of Admissions
516-299-2900 Fax: 516-299-2137
Website: www.liu.edu/cwpost
E-mail: enroll@cwpost.liu.edu

Long Island University
Rockland Graduate Campus
70 Route 340, Orangeburg NY 10962-2219
Kelly J. McCafferty, M.S., Director of Admissions
845-359-7200

Long Island University - Southampton College
239 Montauk Hwy, Southampton NY 11968
631-283-4000

Manhattan College
4513 Manhattan College Pkwy
Riverdale NY 10471-4099
William J. Bisset Jr., Asst. V.P. for Enrollment Management
718-862-7200

Manhattan School of Music
120 Claremont Ave, New York NY 10027-4698
Amy A. Anderson, Director of Admission & Financial Aid
212-749-2802 ext. 2

Manhattanville College
2900 Purchase St, Purchase NY 10577-2132
914-694-2200

Marist College
3399 North Rd, Poughkeepsie NY 12601
Jay E. Murray, Director of Admissions
845-575-3000

Marymount Manhattan College
221 E 71st St, New York NY 10021-4501
212-517-0400

Medaille College
18 Agassiz Cir, Buffalo NY 14214-2695
716-884-3281

Mercy College
1200 Waters Pl, Bronx NY 10461-2704
718-798-8952

Mercy College
555 Broadway, Dobbs Ferry NY 10522-1189
Kathleen Jackson, Director of Admissions
800-MERCY-NY

Mercy College
277 Martine Ave, White Plains NY 10601
914-948-3666

Mercy College
2651 Strang Blvd, Yorktown Heights NY 10598-2997
914-245-6100

Mercy College - Manhattan Campus
66 W 35th St, New York NY 10001
212-615-3351

Metropolitan College of New York
75 Varick St, New York NY 10013-1919
212-343-1234

MOLLOY COLLEGE
1000 Hempstead Ave
Rockville Centre NY 11570-1100
Marguerite Lane, Director of Admissions
516-678-5000 ext. 6291 Fax: 516-256-2247
Website: www.molloy.edu
E-mail: admissions@molloy.edu
Established 1955. Private. Coed. Accreditation: MSACS, NLN, Board of Regents of New York, CSWE. Tuition: $15,150. Fees: $500. Enrollment: 1,808 full-time, 704 part-time, 840 graduate. Faculty: 303. Student-faculty ratio: 11:1. Degrees: AA, AAS, BA, BS, MBA in Accounting and Business, MS in Education, Nursing. Library: 133,500 volumes. 4 buildings on 30 acres.

Monroe College
2501 Jerome Ave, Bronx NY 10468-4305
Evan Jerome, Director of Admissions
718-933-6700 Fax: 718-364-3552
Website: www.monroecollege.edu
E-mail: ejerome@monroecollege.edu

Mt. St. Mary College
330 Powell Ave, Newburgh NY 12550-3494
845-561-0800

Nazareth College of Rochester
4245 East Ave, Rochester NY 14618-3790
585-389-2525

New School University
66 W 12th St, New York NY 10011-8603
212-229-5600

New York City College of Technology CUNY
300 Jay St, Brooklyn NY 11201-1909
Joe Lento, Director of Admissions
718-260-5000

NEW YORK COLLEGE OF HEALTH PROFESSIONS
6801 Jericho Tpke, Syosset NY 11791
Barbara Carver, Senior Vice President
800-9-CAREER Fax: 516-364-0989
Website: www.nycollege.edu
E-mail: bcarver@nycollege.edu

New York Institute of Technology
PO Box 8000, Old Westbury NY 11568-8000
516-686-7520

New York Institute of Technology
PO Box 8000, Old Westbury NY 11568-8000
516-686-7516

New York Institute of Technology
Central Islip Campus
211 Carleton Ave, Central Islip NY 11722
631-348-3000

New York Institute of Technology
Manhattan Campus
1855 Broadway, New York NY 10023-7602
212-261-1508

NEW YORK SCHOOL OF INTERIOR DESIGN
170 E 70th St, New York NY 10021-5110
David Sprouls, Director of Admissions
800-33-NYSID or 212-472-1500 Fax: 212-472-1867
Website: www.nysid.edu
E-mail: admissions@nysid.edu
Established 1916. Private. Coed. College devoted to Interior Design education. Tuition: $20,460 per year. Fees: $110. Enrollment: 750. Faculty: 95. Accreditation: NASAD, FIDER. Four programs offered: Master of Fine Arts, 4-year Bachelor degree, 2-year Associate degree, 1-year non-degree Basic Interior Design. Located in Manhattan's historic Upper East Side near center of interior design industry. Faculty consists of Designers, Architects and Artists.

New York University
70 Washington Sq S, New York NY 10012-1019
212-998-1212

New York University Medical Center
550 1st Ave, New York NY 10016-6481
212-263-5111

Niagara University
PO Box 2011, Niagara University NY 14109-2011
George Pachter, Dean of Admissions & Records
800-462-2111

Nyack College
1 South Boulevard
Nyack NY 10960-3698
845-358-1710

Pace University
1 Pace Plz, New York NY 10038-1502
212-346-1200

Pace University
861 Bedford Rd, Pleasantville NY 10570-2799
914-773-3200

Pace University
White Plains Campus
78 N Broadway, White Plains NY 10603
914-442-4000

Parsons School of Design
66 5th Ave, New York NY 10011-8802
212-229-8953

Paul Smith's College
Paul Smiths NY 12970
Amber DeBeer, Assistant Director of Admissions
800-421-2605 Fax: 518-327-6016
Website: www.paulsmiths.edu
E-mail: admiss@paulsmiths.edu

Polytechnic University
6 Metrotech Ctr, Brooklyn NY 11201-3840
718-260-3600

Polytechnic University
105 Maxess Rd Suite 201N, Melville NY 11747-3857
631-755-4300

Pratt Institute
200 Willoughby Ave, Brooklyn NY 11205-3899
Heidi Metcalf, Director of Admissions
718-636-3600 Fax: 718-636-3670
Website: www.pratt.edu
E-mail: hmetcalf@pratt.edu

PURCHASE COLLEGE STATE UNIVERSITY OF NEW YORK (SUNY)
735 Anderson Hill Rd, Purchase NY 10577-1400
Thomas Schwarz, President
Betsy Immergut, Director of Admissions
914-251-6300 Fax: 914-251-6314
Website: www.purchase.edu
E-mail: admisn@purchase.edu
Established in 1967. Public. Coed. Accreditation: MSACS, NY State Board of Regents. Tuition: $4,350 for NYS residents, $10,610 for non-residents. Room and board: $7,310. Fees: $1,091.50. Enrollment: 3,302 full-time, 518 part-time, with 65% of total living on campus. Faculty: 341. Student-faculty ratio: 13.8:1. 36 buildings designed by celebrated architects. Located on 550 acres in a semi-rural setting less than an hour from New York City.
Curriculum: The Liberal Arts and Sciences divisions offer a traditional Liberal Arts program leading to BA and BS (within Natural Sciences) degrees in Humanities (Art History, Cinema Studies, Creative Writing, Drama Studies, History, Journalism, Language and Culture, Literature, and Philosophy), Natural Sciences (Biology, Chemistry, Environmental Science, Mathematics-with a concentration in Computer Science, New Media, and Psychology-with a concentration in Psychobiology), Social Sciences (Anthropology, Economics-with a concentration in Business Economics, Political Science, and Sociology), and Interdisciplinary programs (Asian Studies, Liberal Arts - with concentrations in lesbian/gay studies, liberal studies, and media, society, and the arts, Media Studies, and Women's Studies). Nationally ranked conservatories of Dance, Music, Theater Arts and Film, and The School of Art+ Design offer professional training programs with BFA degrees in Acting, Arts Management, Dance, Dramatic Writing, Film, Theatre Design/Technology, Visual Arts, and a Mus.B in Music. The Conservatories also offer MFA degrees in Dance, Theatre Design/Tech. and Visual Arts, an MM in Music, and an MA degree in Art History. The BFA, Mus.B, MM and MFA programs are only offered to full-time, daytime students. The Music Conservatory also offers a two-year Artist's Diploma, and a one-year Performer's Certificate. Continuing Education offers certificate programs in Arts Management, Child Care, Early Childhood Development, Computer Languages with Business Applications, Computer Science, Data Processing, Economics, Environmental Management, and General Business.
Purchase College is unique in that it has the largest Visual Arts facility in the U.S., the only dance building in the country designed specifically for the training and performance of dance, and a large science research center. In addition, Purchase has a Performing Arts Center which

houses four theatres, ranging from a 1,400 seat concert hall to an experimental black box theatre; and the Neuberger Museum, the sixth largest university museum in the U.S. with a permanent collection that exceeds 14,000 works.

The Library holds 273,483 volumes, 1,975 subscriptions, 14,375 records and CD's and 237,277 microforms. It has a computerized card catalog which can access an inter-library loan system, with local institutions and other SUNY colleges; and a microcomputer lab.

For more information please call, or make a reservation for our information sessions - most Mondays and Fridays at 9:30 A.M or 2:00 P.M.

Rensselaer Polytechnic Institute
110 8th St, Troy NY 12180-3590
518-276-6000

Roberts Wesleyan College
2301 Westside Dr, Rochester NY 14624-1997
Office of Admissions
585-594-6400 Fax: 585-594-6371
Website: www.roberts.edu
E-mail: admissions@roberts.edu

Rochester Institute of Technology
1 Lomb Memorial Dr, Rochester NY 14623-5603
585-475-2411

ROCHESTER INSTITUTE OF TECHNOLOGY NATIONAL TECHNICAL INSTITUTE FOR THE DEAF (NTID)

52 Lomb Memorial Dr, Rochester NY 14623-5604
Robert Borden, Director of NTID Admissions
585-475-6700 (v/TTY) Fax: 585-475-2696
Website: www.rit.edu/ntid/getinfo
E-mail: NTIDAdmissions@rit.edu

Established 1965. Private. Coed. Tution $8,559 (NTID or NTID supported students only). Room & Board: $8,748. Fees: $642. Enrollment: 1,100. Faculty: 210. Degrees offered: MS, BS, AS, AAS, AOS. Library: 800,000 volumes. 237 buildings on 1,300 acres. Qualified deaf and hard-of-hearing students can earn bachelor's or master's degrees in more than 200 programs offered by RIT's seven other colleges - Applied Science and Technology, Business, Computing and Information Sciences, Engineering, Imaging Arts and Sciences, Liberal Arts, and Science. They also can earn associate degrees in more than 30 accredited NTID programs including: Accounting Technology, Administrative Support Technology, Applied Computer Technology, Applied Optical Technology, Art and Business Technology, Automation Technologies - Robotics, Computer Design, Computer Aided Drafting Technology, Computer Integrated Machining Technology, Digital Imaging & Publishing Technology, and Laboratory Science Technology. Additionally NTID offers degrees in American Sign Language-English Interpretation and a Master's of Science in Secondary Education of Students who are Deaf or Hard of Hearing.

St. Bonaventure University
Saint Bonaventure NY 14778-9999
585-375-2000

St. Francis College
180 Remsen St, Brooklyn NY 11201-4398
718-522-2300

St. John Fisher College
3690 East Ave, Rochester NY 14618-3597
585-385-8000

St. John's University
101 Murray St, New York NY 10007-2165
212-962-4111

ST. JOHN'S UNIVERSITY

8000 Utopia Pkwy, Queens NY 11439
Matthew Whelan, Director of Admission
718-990-2000 or 888-9-STJOHNS Fax: 718-990-2096
Website: www.stjohns.edu
E-mail: admissions@stjohns.edu

Established 1870 by the Vincentian Community. Roman Catholic. Campuses in Queens, Staten Island, and Manhattan, NY. Additional locations in Oakdale, NY, and Rome, Italy. Accreditation: Middle States Association of Colleges and Schools; AACSB International - The Association to Advance Collegiate Schools of Business; American Association for Accreditation of Laboratory Animal Care; American Bar Association; American Chemical Society; American Council on Pharmaceutical Education; American Library Association; American Psychological Association; American Speech-Language-Hearing Association; Association of American Law Schools.

Tuition: $22,800. Room and board: $11,000. Full-time Undergraduate Enrollment: 12,111. Total University Enrollment: 19,813. Male: 40%, Female: 60%. More than 90% of students receive financial aid.

Modern, on-campus housing is available at St. John's 105-acre campus in Queens, NY, and its 16.5 acre campus on Staten Island, NY. The Manhattan campus offers limited housing. Resident students: 2,555. Library: 1.7 million volumes. Academic facilities include microcomputer laboratories, 17 microcomputer classrooms, 104 multimedia classrooms, and a television and radio production center. Big East athletic facilities include lacrosse and baseball fields, tennis courts, basketball courts, weight rooms, a cardiovascular fitness center, a new soccer stadium, and a new University fieldhouse. More than 180 academic clubs, fraternities, and sororities.

Faculty: 1,333 full-time faculty, 90% with Ph.D. or other terminal degree. Student-faculty ratio: 18:1.

Undergraduates earn B.A., B.S., or B.F.A. degrees in nearly 100 majors, including arts and sciences, business, education, and fine arts. Also offered: six-year Pharm.D. program, B.A./M.A. and B.S./M.S. in selected areas. Pre-professional programs: administrative studies, advertising communications, communication arts, computer science, criminal justice, cytotechnology, funeral service administration, health services administra-

tion, hospitality management, journalism, legal studies, medical technology, physician assistant, sport management, telecommunications, television and film, toxicology. Army ROTC is available. Graduate degrees: M.A., M.S., M.B.A., J.D., D.A., Ph.D., Ed.D.

Admission requirements: institutional application and $30 processing fee (fee is waived for those who apply on-line at www.stjohns.edu/apply), FAFSA, high school transcript (college transcript for transfers), and official scores on SAT or ACT. TOEFL and declaration of finances for foreign students. Rolling Admission policy except for Pharm.D. program, which has a February 1st deadline for Fall admission.

The Queens and Staten Island campuses are in residential areas a short distance from New York City's cultural, financial, and entertainment centers. Beaches, parks, and other recreational sites are nearby.

St. John's University
300 Howard Ave, Staten Island NY 10301-4496
718-447-4343

St. Joseph's College
245 Clinton Ave, Brooklyn NY 11205-3688
Theresa LaRocca Meyer, V.P. for Enrollment Management
718-636-6800 Fax: 718-636-8303
Website: www.sjcny.edu
E-mail: tlaroccameyer@sjcny.edu

St. Joseph's College
155 W Roe Blvd, Patchogue NY 11772
631-447-3200

St. Lawrence University
2501 Saint Lawrence Univ, Canton NY 13617-1475
315-229-5011

St. Thomas Aquinas College
125 Route 340, Sparkill NY 10976-1050
845-398-4000

Sarah Lawrence College
1 Meadway, Bronxville NY 10708
914-337-0700

School of Visual Arts
209 E 23rd St, New York NY 10010-3994
212-592-2000

Siena College
515 Loudonville Rd, Loudonville NY 12211-1462
Ned Jones, Director of Admissions
518-783-2300

Skidmore College
815 N Broadway, Saratoga Springs NY 12866-1698
518-580-5000

SUNY at Albany
1400 Washington Ave, Albany NY 12222-1000
Thomas Flemming, Associate Director of Admissions
518-442-5435

SUNY at Binghamton
PO Box 6001, Binghamton NY 13902-6001
607-777-2000

SUNY at Stony Brook
Stony Brook NY 11794-0001
631-689-6000

SUNY College at Brockport
350 New Campus Dr, Brockport NY 14420-2997
Bernard S. Valento, Director of Undergraduate Admissions
585-395-2751 Fax: 585-395-5452
Website: www.brockport.edu
E-mail: admit@brockport.edu

SUNY College at Buffalo
1300 Elmwood Ave, Buffalo NY 14222-1004
716-878-4000

SUNY College at Cortland
PO Box 2000, Cortland NY 13045-0900
Mark Yacavone, Assistant Director
607-753-4711

SUNY College at Fredonia
Fredonia NY 14063
716-673-3111

SUNY College at Geneseo
1 College Cir, Geneseo NY 14454-1401
585-245-5211

SUNY College at New Paltz
75 S Manheim Blvd Ste 1, New Paltz NY 12561-2400
845-257-2121

SUNY College at Old Westbury
PO Box 210, Old Westbury NY 11568-0210
516-876-3000

SUNY College at Oneonta
Oneonta NY 13820
607-436-3500

SUNY College at Oswego
Oswego NY 13126
315-312-2500

SUNY College at Plattsburgh
Plattsburgh NY 12901
518-564-2000

SUNY College at Potsdam
Potsdam NY 13676
Thomas W. Nesbitt, Director of Admissions
315-267-2000

SUNY College of Agriculture & Technology
107 Schenectady Ave, Cobleskill NY 12043
Clayton A. Smith, Director of Admissions
800-295-8988

SUNY College of Agriculture & Technology
Morrisville NY 13408
Thomas Ver Dow, Dean of Enrollment Management
800-258-0111

SUNY College of Environmental Science & Forestry
1 Forestry Dr, Syracuse NY 13210-2712
315-470-6500

SUNY College of Technology
Alfred NY 14802
Deborah J. Goodrich, Director of Admissions
800-4AL-FRED Fax: 607-587-4299
Website: www.alfredstate.edu
E-mail: admissions@alfredstate.edu

SUNY Empire State College
617 Main St Fl 3, Buffalo NY 14203-1416
716-853-7700

SUNY Empire State College
200 N Central Ave, Hartsdale NY 10530-1925
914-948-6206

SUNY Empire State College
21 British American Blvd, Latham NY 12110-1405
518-783-6203

SUNY Empire State College
325 Hudson St Flr 5, New York NY 10013-1005
212-647-7800

SUNY Empire State College
PO Box 130, Old Westbury NY 11568-0130
516-997-4700

SUNY Empire State College
1475 Winton Rd N, Rochester NY 14609-5803
585-244-3884

SUNY Empire State College
1 Union Ave, Saratoga Springs NY 12866-4309
518-587-2100

SUNY Empire State College
219 Walton St Fl 1, Syracuse NY 13202-1226
315-472-5799

SUNY Institute of Technology Utica/Rome
PO Box 3050, Utica NY 13504-3050
315-792-7100

SUNY Maritime College
6 Pennyfield Ave, Bronx NY 10465-4127
718-409-7200

SUNY Upstate Medical University
750 E Adams St, Syracuse NY 13210
315-464-5540

SWEDISH INSTITUTE

College of Health Sciences
226 W 26th St, New York NY 10001-6700
Leslie Kielson, Dean of Admissions
212-924-5900 ext. 125 Fax: 212-924-7600
Website: www.swedishinstitute.edu
E-mail: admissions@swedishinstitute.edu

Established 1916. Private. Coed. Degrees: Associate in Occupational Studies in Massage Therapy. Master of Science in Acupuncture. Focused program in massage therapy features Western & Eastern approaches. Can be completed in 16 months full-time. The Master of Science in Acupuncture focuses on classical Chinese Acupuncture. Full time students can complete the degree in three years.

Syracuse University
Syracuse NY 13244-0001
315-443-1870

Touro College
27 W 23rd St Ste 33, New York NY 10010-4202
212-463-0400

Touro College
240 E 123rd St, New York NY 10035-2038
212-722-1575

Union College
Schenectady NY 12308
518-388-6000

United States Merchant Marine Academy
300 Steamboat Rd, Kings Point NY 11024-1699
516-773-5000

United States Military Academy West Point
646 Swift Rd, West Point NY 10996-1905
Colonel Michael L. Jones, Director of Admissions
845-938-4041 Fax: 845-938-8121
Website: admissions.usma.edu
E-mail: admissions@usma.edu

University at Buffalo, The State University of New York
15 Capen Hall, Buffalo NY 14260-1660
Patricia G. Armstrong, Director of Admissions
888-UB-ADMIT

University of Rochester
Meliora Hall, Rochester NY 14627
585-275-2121

Utica College
1600 Burrstone Rd, Utica NY 13502-4857
315-792-3111

Utica School of Commerce
201 Bleecker St, Utica NY 13501-2280
Cindy Delaney, Director of Admissions
315-733-2307 Fax: 315-733-9281
Website: www.uscny.edu
E-mail: admissions@uscny.edu

Vassar College
124 Raymond Ave, Poughkeepsie NY 12604-0002
845-437-7000

VAUGHN COLLEGE OF AERONAUTICS AND TECHNOLOGY

8601 23rd Ave, Flushing NY 11369-1037
Vincent Papandrea, Director of Admissions
800-776-2376 Fax: 718-429-0671
Website: www.vaughn.edu
E-mail: admitme@vaughn.edu

Established 1932. Private. Coed. Accreditation: MSACS, ABET. Tuition: $13,400. Fees: $280. Enrollment: 842 full-time, 284 part-time. Faculty: 59. Student-faculty ratio: 11:1. Degrees: BS, AAS, AOS. Library: 62,000 vols. Offering bachelor and associate degrees in airport management, aviation maintenance, flight training, electronic technology, engineering, general management, mechatronic engineering, pre-engineering and computerized

design/animated graphics. Hands-on training. Extensive career development services and financial aid available.

Wagner College
One Campus Rd, Staten Island NY 10301
Leigh Ann DePascale, Director of Admissions
718-390-3411

Webb Institute
298 Crescent Beach Rd, Glen Cove NY 11542-1321
William Murray, Director of Admissions
516-671-2213

Wells College
PO Box 500, Aurora NY 13026
Susan Sloan, Director of Admissions
800-952-9355 Fax: 315-364-3227
Website: www.wells.edu
E-mail: ssloan@wells.edu

WORD OF LIFE BIBLE INSTITUTE
PO Box 129, Pottersville NY 12860-0129
518-494-4723 Fax: 518-494-7474
Website: www.wol.org

Yeshiva and Kolel Bais Medrash Elyon
73 Main St, Monsey NY 10952-3013
845-356-7064

Yeshiva Derech Chaim
1573 39th St, Brooklyn NY 11218-4413
718-438-5476

Yeshiva Gedolah Bais Yisroel
2002 Avenue J, Brooklyn NY 11210-3645
718-258-7400

Yeshiva Gedolah Imrei Yosef D'Spinka
1460 56th St, Brooklyn NY 11219-4617
718-972-1989

Yeshiva Novominsk
1569 47th St, Brooklyn NY 11219-2742
718-438-2727

Yeshiva University
500 W 185th St, New York NY 10033-3299
212-960-5400

NORTH CAROLINA

APEX SCHOOL OF THEOLOGY
5104 Revere Rd, Durham NC 27713-2421
Dr. J.E. Perkins, President
919-572-1625 Fax: 919-572-1762
Website: www.apexsot.edu
E-mail: info@apexsot.edu

Appalachian State University
ASU Station, Boone NC 28608-0001
828-262-2000

Barber-Scotia College
145 Cabarrus Ave W, Concord NC 28025-5187
704-789-2900

Barton College
PO Box 5000, Wilson NC 27893
252-399-6300

Belmont Abbey College
100 Belmont Mount Holly Rd
Belmont NC 28012-1802
888-222-0110 Fax: 704-825-6670
Website: www.belmontabbeycollege.edu
E-mail: admissions@bac.edu

Brevard College
400 N Broad St, Brevard NC 28712
828-883-8292

CABARRUS COLLEGE OF HEALTH SCIENCES
401 Medical Park Dr, Concord NC 28025
Mark Ellison, Director of Admissions
704-783-1556 Fax: 704-783-2077
Website: www.cabarruscollege.edu
E-mail: admissions@cabarruscollege.edu
Established: 1942. Private. Coed. Accreditation: Southern Association of Colleges & Schools. Tuition: $7,500. Enrollment: 380. Degrees Offered: Baccalaureate in Health Services Management, Medical Imaging, Nursing. Associates in Medical Assistant, Nursing, Occupational Therapy Assistant, Surgical Technology. Affiliated with Northeast Medical Center, a magnet hospital.

Campbell University
PO Box 546, Buies Creek NC 27506-0546
Herbert V. Kerner, Jr., Director of Admissions
800-334-4111

Carolinas College of Health Sciences
PO Box 32861, Charlotte NC 28232-2861
Elizabeth West, Admissions Officer
704-355-5043 Fax: 704-355-9336
Website: www.carolinascollege.edu
E-mail: elizabeth.west@carolinascollege.edu
See listing under "Nursing"

Catawba College
2300 W Innes St, Salisbury NC 28144-2488
Gordon A. Kirkland, Associate Director of Admissions
704-637-4402

Chowan College
PO Box 1848, Murfreesboro NC 27855
252-398-6500

Davidson College
PO Box 7156, Davidson NC 28035-7156
Chris Gruber, Acting Dean of Admission
800-768-0380

Duke University
Durham NC 27706-8001
919-684-8111

East Carolina University
1000 E 5th St, Greenville NC 27858

Elizabeth City State University
1704 Weeksville Rd, Elizabeth City NC 27909-7806
252-335-3400

Elon University
2700 Campus Box, Elon NC 27244
Susan C. Klopman, Dean of Admissions
800-334-8448

Fayetteville State University
1200 Murchison Rd, Fayetteville NC 28301-4298
910-486-1111

Gardner-Webb University
PO Box 817, Boiling Springs NC 28017
704-406-2361

Gardner-Webb University
PO Box 908, Statesville NC 28687-0908
704-872-3664

Greensboro College
815 W Market St, Greensboro NC 27401-1875
336-272-7102

Guilford College
5800 W Friendly Ave, Greensboro NC 27410-4173
Randy Doss, Dean of Enrollment
336-316-2100

High Point University
933 Montlieu Ave, High Point NC 27262-3598
336-841-9000

Johnson & Wales University
801 W Trade St, Charlotte NC 28202
980-598-1000

Johnson C. Smith University
100 Beatties Ford Rd, Charlotte NC 28216-5302
704-378-1000

JOHN WESLEY COLLEGE
2314 N Centennial St, High Point NC 27265-3197
Greg Workman, Admissions Officer
336-889-2262 ext. 127 Fax: 336-889-2261
Website: www.johnwesley.edu
E-mail: admissions@johnwesley.edu
See listing under "Theological Studies & Religious Vocations"

Lees-McRae College
PO Box 128, Banner Elk NC 28604-0128
Walt Crutchfield, Dean of Admissions
800-280-4562 Fax: 828-898-8707
Website: www.lmc.edu
E-mail: admissions@lmc.edu

Lee University Charlotte Center
1209 Little Rock Rd, Charlotte NC 28214-2310
Thomas Tatum, Center Director
704-394-2307

Lenoir-Rhyne College
7th Ave and 8th St, Hickory NC 28603
828-328-1741

Livingstone College
701 W Monroe St, Salisbury NC 28144-5298
704-797-1000

Mars Hill College
Mars Hill NC 28754
Chad Holt, Dean of Enrollment
866-MHC-4-YOU Fax: 828-689-1473
Website: www.mhc.edu
E-mail: cholt@mhc.edu

Meredith College
3800 Hillsborough St, Raleigh NC 27607-5298
Heidi L. Fletcher, Director of Admissions
919-760-8581 Fax: 919-760-2348
Website: www.meredith.edu
E-mail: admissions@meredith.edu
See listing under "Women's Colleges"

Methodist College
5400 Ramsey St, Fayetteville NC 28311-1498
910-630-7000

Montreat College
PO Box 1267, Montreat NC 28757-1267
800-622-6968

MT. OLIVE COLLEGE
634 Henderson St, Mount Olive NC 28365-1299
Tim Woodard, Director of Admissions
919-658-2502 Fax: 919-658-9816
Website: www.moc.edu
E-mail: admissions@moc.edu
Private. Coed. Accreditation: Commission on Colleges of the Southern Association of Colleges and Schools. Tuition: $11,520. Room & board: $4,800. Fees: $280. Enrollment: 1946 full-time, 884 part-time. Faculty: 215. Student-faculty ratio: 15:1. Degrees offered: Bachelor of Arts, Bachelor of Science, Bachelor of Applied Science, Associate in Arts, Associate in Science. Library: 66,000 volumes. 13 buildings on 135 acres.

North Carolina A&T State University
1601 E Market St, Greensboro NC 27411
Lee Young, AVC Enrollment
336-334-7500 Fax: 336-334-7478
Website: www.ncat.edu
E-mail: uadmit@ncat.edu

North Carolina Central University
PO Box 19617, Durham NC 27707-0022
919-560-6100

North Carolina School of the Arts
1533 S Main St, Winston Salem NC 27127
Sheeler Lawson, Director of Admissions
336-770-3290

North Carolina State University
PO Box 7001, Raleigh NC 27695-0001
919-515-2011

North Carolina Wesleyan College
3400 N Wesleyan Blvd, Rocky Mount NC 27804-8677
252-985-5100

Peace College
15 E Peace St, Raleigh NC 27604-1194
Laura C. Bingham, President
800-PEACE-47

Pfeiffer University
PO Box 960, Misenheimer NC 28109-0960
704-463-1360

Piedmont Baptist College
716 Franklin St, Winston Salem NC 27101-5197
Ronnie Mathis, Director of Admissions
800-937-5097

Queens University of Charlotte
1900 Selwyn Ave, Charlotte NC 28274-0002
704-337-2212

Roanoke Bible College
715 N Poindexter St, Elizabeth City NC 27909-4054
252-334-2070

St. Andrews Presbyterian College
1700 Dogwood Mile St, Laurinburg NC 28352-5521
Glenn Batten, Vice President for Enrollment
910-277-5554

St. Augustine's College
1315 Oakwood Ave, Raleigh NC 27610-2298
919-516-4000

Shaw University
118 E South St, Raleigh NC 27601-2399
919-546-8200

Strayer University
3200 Spring Forest Rd, Raleigh NC 27616
919-878-9900

University of North Carolina
1 University Hts, Asheville NC 28804-3251
828-251-6600

University of North Carolina
Chapel Hill NC 27599-0001
919-962-2211

University of North Carolina
9201 University City Blvd, Charlotte NC 28223
704-547-2000

University of North Carolina
601 S College Rd, Wilmington NC 28403-3201
910-962-3000

University of North Carolina at Greensboro
1000 Spring Garden St, Greensboro NC 27412-0001
336-334-5243

University of North Carolina at Pembroke
PO Box 1510, Pembroke NC 28372-1510
910-521-6000

Wake Forest University
PO Box 7305, Winston Salem NC 27109-7305
336-759-5000

Warren Wilson College
PO Box 9000, Asheville NC 28815-9000
Richard Blomgren, Dean of Admissions
828-298-3325

Western Carolina University
University Dr, Cullowhee NC 28723-9646
828-227-7211

Wingate University
201 E Wilson St, Wingate NC 28174-9600
704-233-8000

Winston-Salem Bible College
PO Box 777, Winston Salem NC 27102-0777
336-774-0900

Winston-Salem State University
601 S Mrtn Lther King Jr Dr
Winston Salem NC 27110-0003
336-750-2000

NORTH DAKOTA

Dickinson State University
Dickinson ND 58601-4896
Steve Glasser, Director of Student Recruitment
800-279-4295 Fax: 701-483-2409
Website: www.dickinsonstate.edu
E-mail: dsu.hawks@dickinsonstate.edu

Jamestown College
6000 College Ln, Jamestown ND 58405-0002
701-252-3467

Mayville State University
330 3rd St NE, Mayville ND 58257-1299
Dr. Pamela Balch, President
Brian Larson, Director of Enrollment Services
800-437-4104

Medcenter One College of Nursing
512 N 7th St, Bismarck ND 58501-4425
Mary Smith, Director of Student Services
701-323-6271

Minot State University
500 University Ave W, Minot ND 58707-0002
Dennis Parisien, Enrollment Services Rep.
800-777-0750 ext. 3350

North Dakota State University
Fargo ND 58105
701-237-7211

Trinity Bible College
50 6th Ave S, Ellendale ND 58436-7150
Jerry A. Grimshaw, Enrollment Manager
701-349-3621

University of Mary
7500 University Dr, Bismarck ND 58504-9652
701-255-7500

University of North Dakota
Box 8193 University Station, Grand Forks ND 58203
701-777-2011

VALLEY CITY STATE UNIVERSITY
101 College St SW, Valley City ND 58072-4024
Dan Klein, Director of Enrollment Services
800-532-8641 ext. 7101 Fax: 701-845-7299
Website: www.vcsu.edu
E-mail: enrollment.services@vcsu.edu
Established 1890. Public. Coed. 532 women, 481 men; 34% live on campus. Accreditation: NCACS, NCATE,

NASM. 69% of students received financial assistance in 2005-2006. Tuition: $125.10/credit in-state, $136.36/credit MN; $156.36/credit SD, MT, KS, MI, MO, NE, Manitoba, Saskatchewan; $187.65/credit WUE States; $334.02/credit other out of state and international. Room and Board: $3,446. Four residence halls. Each room individually wired for internet and TV cable. Family student housing also available. Numerous student organizations, some academic based, a fraternity and a sorority. BS, BA in 35 areas spanning Business Administration, Computer Information Systems, Communication Arts, Social Science, Education (including M.Ed.), Psychology, Fine Arts, Health and Physical Education, Mathematics, and Science. VCSU first in North Dakota, second in the US to provide a laptop computer to each student and faculty. Student model is IBM R40 Series ThinkPad computer; software and hardware updates on regular basis. Unlimited access to information 24 hours a day seven days a week. Student to faculty ratio is 12:1. Campus has 29 historic and modern buildings on 64 acres. High-speed wired and wireless internet access throughout campus. Rhoades Science Center has science labs throughout, a planetarium, photo lab, and greenhouse. Athletic facilities include a swimming pool in Student Center, a physical ed building, a 2,500 seat field-house with a new wood floor, synthetic 400 meter outdoor track surrounding the football field with bench seating in the stadium, tennis courts, racquetball courts, a baseball and softball fields. Two nine-hole golf courses offering student discounts. Fine arts facilities include a ceramics building, a 220 seat performance auditorium in the music building, an historic 850 seat Vangstad auditorium, and a theatre in the round for more intimate settings. The four-level library has 91,346 volumes, 59,400 microfilms, 15,624 aud/vid, records, and CDs, 1,937 periodical subscriptions, over 1,500 of these on-line. Campus is in a rural town of about 7,000 with a wooded hill to the south and a meandering river on the north side of the campus. A historic footbridge connects the campus to Valley City, ND which is located about 50 minutes west of Fargo, ND. The climate consists of warm to hot summers and cold winters. To be admitted, students must have completed four units of high school English and three units in each subject of Math, Lab Science, and Social Science. International students must complete the TOEFL and declare financial ability. A $35 application fee, high school transcript, college transcripts, proof of immunization are also required of all applicants.

OHIO

Allegheny Wesleyan College
2161 Woodsdale Rd, Salem OH 44460
800-292-3153

Antioch College
795 Livermore St, Yellow Springs OH 45387-1697
937-754-5000

Antioch University McGregor
800 Livermore St, Yellow Springs OH 45387
937-767-6321

Art Institute of Ohio - Cincinnati
1011 Glendale Milford Rd, Cincinnati OH 45215
513-771-2829

Ashland University
401 College Ave, Ashland OH 44805-3799
419-289-4142

Athenaeum of Ohio
6616 Beechmont Ave, Cincinnati OH 45230-2000
513-231-2223

Baldwin-Wallace College
275 Eastland Rd, Berea OH 44017-2088
440-826-2900

Bluffton University
1 University Dr, Bluffton OH 45817
419-358-3000

Bowling Green State University
110 McFall Center, Bowling Green OH 43403-0001
866-CHOOSE-BGSU

Capital University
2199 E Main St, Columbus OH 43209-2394
614-236-6011

Case Western Reserve University
10900 Euclid Ave, Cleveland OH 44106
216-368-2000

Cedarville University
251 N Main St, Cedarville OH 45314
937-766-2211

Central State University
PO Box 1004, Wilberforce OH 45384-1004
937-376-6011

Cincinnati Christian University
PO Box 4320, Cincinnati OH 45204
Erin Oppy, Executive Director of Undergraduate Admissions
513-244-8141

Cincinnati College of Mortuary Science
645 W North Bend Rd, Cincinnati OH 45224-1428
Dr. Dan Flory, President
513-761-2020

Circleville Bible College
PO Box 458, Circleville OH 43113-0458
800-701-0222

Cleveland Institute of Art
11141 East Blvd, Cleveland OH 44106-1700
216-421-7000

CLEVELAND INSTITUTE OF MUSIC
11021 East Blvd, Cleveland OH 44106-1705
William Fay, Director of Admission
216-795-3107
Website: www.cim.edu

Cleveland State University
2121 Euclid Ave RW 204, Cleveland OH 44115
Dr. Richard Arndt, Dean of Undergraduate Recruitment and College Partnerships
888-CSU-OHIO Fax: 216-687-9210
Website: www.csuohio.edu
E-mail: admissions@csuohio.edu

College of Mount Saint Joseph
5701 Delhi Rd, Cincinnati OH 45233-1669
513-244-4200

College of Wooster
Wooster OH 44691-2363
Paul J. Deutsch, Dean of Admissions
800-877-9905

Columbus College of Art & Design
107 N 9th St, Columbus OH 43215-1700
877-997-CCAD or 614-222-3261 Fax: 614-232-8344
Website: www.ccad.edu
E-mail: admissions@ccad.edu

Davis College
4747 Monroe St, Toledo OH 43623-4389
Dana Stern, Admissions Director
419-473-2700 Fax: 419-473-2472
Website: www.daviscollege.edu
E-mail: learn@daviscollege.edu

Defiance College
701 N Clinton St, Defiance OH 43512-1695
419-784-4010

Denison University
PO Box B, Granville OH 43023-0603
740-587-0810

Franciscan University of Steubenville
University Blvd, Steubenville OH 43952
Margaret J. Weber, Director of Admissions
800-783-6220 or 740-283-6226 Fax: 740-284-5456
Website: www.admissions.edu
E-mail: mweber@franciscan.edu

Franklin University
201 S Grant Ave, Columbus OH 43215-5399
614-341-6300

GOD'S BIBLE SCHOOL AND COLLEGE
1810 Young St, Cincinnati OH 45202-6838
Aaron Profitt, Director of Admissions
513-721-7944 Fax: 513-721-1357
Website: www.gbs.edu
E-mail: admissions@gbs.edu

Heidelberg College
310 E Market St, Tiffin OH 44883-2462
418-448-2000

Hiram College
PO Box 96, Hiram OH 44234-0096
800-362-5280

Hocking College
3301 Hocking Pkwy, Nelsonville OH 45764-9704
Diane K. Wolf, Assistant Director of Admissions Information
800-282-4163

John Carroll University
20700 N Park Blvd, Cleveland OH 44118-4581
216-397-1886

Kent State University
PO Box 5190, Kent OH 44242-0001
Paul Deutsch, Director of Admissions
330-672-2444

Kenyon College
1 Kenyon College, Gambier OH 43022-9623
740-427-5000

Kettering College of Medical Arts
3737 Southern Blvd, Kettering OH 45429-1299
David Lofthouse, Director of Enrollment Services
800-433-5262

Lake Erie College
391 W Washington St, Painesville OH 44077-3389
440-352-3361

Laura & Alvin Siegal College of Judaic Studies
26500 Shaker Blvd, Cleveland OH 44122-7116
216-464-4050

Lourdes College
6832 Convent Blvd, Sylvania OH 43560-2898
800-878-3210

Malone College
515 25th St NW, Canton OH 44709-3897
John Chopka, Dean of Admissions
330-471-8100

Marietta College
215 5th St, Marietta OH 45750-4047
740-376-4600

MEDCENTRAL COLLEGE OF NURSING
335 Glessner Ave, Mansfield OH 44903-2265
Christopher M. Harris, Director for Enrollment Management
419-520-2600 Fax: 419-520-2610
Website: www.medcentral.edu
E-mail: charris@medcentral.edu

Miami University
E High St, Oxford OH 45056
513-529-2531

Mount Carmel College of Nursing
127 S Davis Ave, Columbus OH 43222-1504
800-556-6972

Mt. Union College
1972 Clark Ave, Alliance OH 44601-3929
Vincent Heslop, Director of Admissions
800-334-6682

MOUNT VERNON NAZARENE UNIVERSITY
800 Martinsburg Rd, Mount Vernon OH 43050-9509
Timothy Eades, Director of Admissions
866-462-6868 Fax: 740-393-0511
Website: www.gotomvnu.com
E-mail: admissions@mvnu.edu
   Mount Vernon Nazarene University is a private, four-year, intentionally Christian teaching university for traditional students, graduate students and working adults. U.S. News & World Report ranks MVNU in the Top 50 Best in the Midwest (Bachelor's). With a 400 acre main campus in Mount Vernon, Ohio, and six satellite campuses, MVNU emphasizes academic excellence, spiritual growth, service to community and church. We offer an affordable education to more than 2,450 students from 24 states and 11 countries. With a variety of on-campus activities, nearly 40 student-run organizations, and competitive intercollegiate athletics, students enjoy an active and fun campus environment. See why MVNU is Life Changing!

Muskingum College
147 Center St, New Concord OH 43762-1193
740-826-8211

Myers University
3813 Euclid Ave, Cleveland OH 44115
Ronald G. Brown, Vice President for Enrollment Management
216-432-8992
Website: www.myers.edu
E-mail: rgbrown@myers.edu

Oberlin College
Carnegie Bldg, Oberlin OH 44074
Debra Chermonte, Dean of Admissions & Financial Aid

Ohio Dominican University
1216 Sunbury Rd, Columbus OH 43219-2099
614-253-2741

OHIO NORTHERN UNIVERSITY
525 S Main St, Ada OH 45810-1555
Karen P. Condeni, V.P. & Dean of Admissions & Financial Aid
888-408-4668 Fax: 419-772-2313
Website: www.onu.edu
E-mail: admissions-ug@onu.edu
   Established 1871. Private. Coed. Accreditation: Higher Learning Commission & Member of NCA, ACS, CAAHEP, NASM, EAC of ABET, ACPE, AALS, ABA, AACSB International, NCATE, Ohio Dept. of Education. 2005-06 Tuition: $27,045 - $30,390. Room & board: $6,720. Fees: $210. Enrollment: 3,275 full-time, 113 part-time. Faculty: 316. Student-faculty ratio: 12:1. Degrees offered: BA, BFA, BM, BS, BSCLS, BSBA, BSCE, BSCPE, BSEE, BSN, BSME, PharmD, MET, JD. Over 45 buildings on 285 acres. Colleges of: Arts & Sciences, Business Administration, Engineering, Pharmacy & Law; Direct Entry Pharmacy Program.

The Ohio State University
Enarson Hall, 154 W 12th Ave
Columbus OH 43210-1390
Dr. Mabel Freeman, Asst. V.P., Undergraduate Admissions and First Year Experience
614-292-3980 Fax: 614-292-4818
Website: www.osu.edu
E-mail: freeman.9@osu.edu

Ohio State University-Lima Campus
4240 Campus Dr, Lima OH 45804-3576
Garlene Smithson, Dir. Enrollment Services
419-995-8396

Ohio State University-Mansfield Campus
1680 University Dr, Mansfield OH 44906-1547
419-755-4011

Ohio State University-Marion
1465 Mount Vernon Ave, Marion OH 43302-5695
740-389-6786

Ohio State University-Newark
1179 University Dr, Newark OH 43055-1797
740-366-3321

Ohio University
PO Box 640, Athens OH 45701-0640
740-593-1000

Ohio University
Chillicothe Campus
PO Box 629, Chillicothe OH 45601
Student Services
740-774-7200 Fax: 740-774-7295
Website: www.ohiou.edu/chillicothe/

Ohio University
Eastern Campus
45425 National Rd W
Saint Clairsville OH 43950-9724
740-695-1720

Ohio University
Lancaster Campus
1570 Granville Pike, Lancaster OH 43130-1097
740-654-6711

Ohio University
Southern Campus
1804 Liberty Ave, Ironton OH 45638-2279
740-533-4600

Ohio University - Zanesville Branch
1425 Newark Rd, Zanesville OH 43701-2695
740-588-1439

OHIO WESLEYAN UNIVERSITY
61 S Sandusky St, Delaware OH 43015-2398
Director of Admission
740-368-3020 Fax: 740-368-3314
Website: www.owu.edu
E-mail: owuadmit@owu.edu

Otterbein College
78 W Home St, Westerville OH 43081-1489
614-890-3000

PAYNE THEOLOGICAL SEMINARY
PO Box 474, Wilberforce OH 45384-0474
Dr. Leah Gaskin Fitchue, Contact
937-376-2946 Fax: 937-376-3330
Website: www.payne.edu
E-mail: lfitchue@payne.edu

Rosedale Bible College
2270 Rosedale Rd, Irwin OH 43029
740-857-1311

Shawnee State University
940 2nd St, Portsmouth OH 45662-4344
740-354-3205

TEMPLE BAPTIST COLLEGE
11965 Kenn Rd, Cincinnati OH 45240
Dr. Tanmay Pramanik, Dean of Student Affairs
513-851-3800 Fax: 513-589-3052
Website: www.templebaptistcollege.com
E-mail: tanmay.pramanik@templebaptistcollege.com

Union Institute & University
440 E McMillan St, Cincinnati OH 45206-1925
513-861-6400

University of Akron
381 Buchtel Mall, Akron OH 44304-1584
330-972-7111

University of Cincinnati
2700 Clifton Ave, Cincinnati OH 45220-2873
513-556-6000

University of Cincinnati
OMI College of Applied Science
2220 Victory Pkwy, Cincinnati OH 45206-2839
Rita K. Hessley, PhD, Dean
513-556-6567

University of Dayton
300 College Park, Dayton OH 45469-1300
Robert F. Durkle, Director of Admissions
800-837-7433 Fax: 937-229-4729
Website: admission.udayton.edu
E-mail: admission@udayton.edu

University of Findlay
1000 N Main St, Findlay OH 45840-3695
419-422-8313

University of Northwestern Ohio
1441 N Cable Rd, Lima OH 45805-1498
Rick Morrison, Director of Admissions
419-998-3120

University of Rio Grande
General Delivery, Rio Grande OH 45674-9999
Dr. Chris Pines, Dean
740-245-5353 ext. 7426

University of Toledo
2801 W Bancroft St, Toledo OH 43606-3390
419-530-4636

Urbana University
579 College Way, Urbana OH 43078
937-484-1301

Ursuline College
2550 Lander Rd, Cleveland OH 44124-4398
Sarah E. Sundermeier, Director of Admissions
888-URSULINE Toll Free Fax: 440-684-6138
Website: www.admission.ursuline.edu
E-mail: admission@ursuline.edu

Walsh University
2020 E Maple St, North Canton OH 44720
800-362-9846

Wilberforce University
PO Box 1001, Wilberforce OH 45384-1001
937-376-2911

Wilmington College
251 Ludovic St, Wilmington OH 45177
937-382-6661

Wittenberg University
PO Box 720, Springfield OH 45501-0720
937-327-6231

Wright State University
3640 Colonel Glenn Hwy, Dayton OH 45435-0002
937-775-3333

Xavier University
3800 Victory Pkwy, Cincinnati OH 45207-1092
513-745-3000

Youngstown State University
Sweeney Welcome Ctr, One University Plz
Youngstown OH 44555-0002
Sue Davis, Contact
877-GO-TO-YSU

OKLAHOMA
Bacone College
2299 Old Bacone Rd, Muskogee OK 74403-1568
Jerrett Phillips, Director of Admissions
918-781-7340

Cameron University
2800 W Gore Blvd, Lawton OK 73505-6377
580-581-2200

East Central University
1100 E 14th St
Ada OK 74820-6999
Pamla Armstrong, Director of Admissions
580-332-8000

Family of Faith College
PO Box 1805, Shawnee OK 74802
405-273-5331

Hillsdale Free Will Baptist College
PO Box 7208, Moore OK 73153
405-912-9000

ITT Technical Institute
1900 NW Expressway St #305R
Oklahoma City OK 73118
405-810-4100

Langston University
PO Box 907, Langston OK 73050-0907
405-466-2231

Metropolitan College
1900 Northwest Expressway R302
Oklahoma City OK 73118
Pam Picken, Director of Admissions
405-843-1000

Mid-America Christian University
3500 SW 119th St, Oklahoma City OK 73170-4504
Haley Hope, Director of Admissions
405-691-3800 Fax: 405-692-3165
Website: www.macu.edu
E-mail: info@macu.edu

Northeastern State University
600 N Grand Ave, Tahlequah OK 74464-2301
918-456-5511

Northwestern Oklahoma State University
709 Oklahoma Blvd, Alva OK 73717
580-327-1700

Oklahoma Baptist University
500 W University St, Shawnee OK 74804-2590
405-275-2850

Oklahoma Christian University
PO Box 11000, Oklahoma City OK 73136-1100
405-425-5000

Oklahoma City University
2501 N Blackwelder Ave
Oklahoma City OK 73106-1493
Shery Boyles, Director of Admissions
405-521-5050

Oklahoma Panhandle State University
PO Box 430, Goodwell OK 73939-0430
580-349-2611

Oklahoma State University
Stillwater OK 74078
Paul Carney, Director of Undergraduate Admissions
405-744-7275 Fax: 405-744-7092
Website: www.okstate.edu
E-mail: admit@okstate.edu

Oklahoma Wesleyan University
2201 Silver Lake Rd, Bartlesville OK 74006-6299
918-333-6151

Oral Roberts University
7777 S Lewis Ave, Tulsa OK 74171-0001
Chris Belcher, Director of Undergraduate Admissions
800-678-8876 Fax: 918-495-6222
Website: www.oru.edu
E-mail: admissions@oru.edu

Rogers State University - Claremore Campus
1701 W Will Rogers Blvd, Claremore OK 74017-3259
Joe Wiley, President
918-343-7777

St. Gregory's University
1900 W MacArthur St, Shawnee OK 74804-2499
405-878-5100

Southeastern Oklahoma State University
Station A, Durant OK 74701
580-924-0121

Southern Nazarene University
6729 NW 39th Expy, Bethany OK 73008-2694
405-789-6400

Southwestern Christian University
PO Box 340, Bethany OK 73008-0340
Megan Miles, Director of Admissions
405-789-7661 Fax: 405-495-0078
Website: www.swcu.edu
E-mail: jean@swcu.edu

Southwestern Oklahoma State University
100 Campus Dr, Weatherford OK 73096-3098
580-772-6611

SPARTAN COLLEGE OF AERONAUTICS AND TECHNOLOGY
8820 E Pine St, Tulsa OK 74115-5802
Director of Admissions
800-331-1204 Fax: 918-831-8609
Website: www.spartan.edu
E-mail: spartan@mail.spartan.edu
Established 1928. Coed. Accredited member school: ACCSCT. Providing Technical training and education in Avionics, Instruments, and Maintenance; Nondestructive Testing and Quality Control. Complete flight training program. Offering Diplomas, Associate of Applied Science and Bachelor of Science in Aviation Technology Management.

University of Central Oklahoma
100 N University Dr, Edmond OK 73034-5209
405-974-2000

University of Oklahoma at Norman
660 Parrington Oval, Norman OK 73019-3070
405-325-0311

University of Oklahoma Health Sciences
1000 Stanton L Young Blvd
Oklahoma City OK 73190
405-271-4000

University of Sciences & Arts of OK
PO Box 82345, Chickasha OK 73018
405-224-3140

University of Tulsa
600 S College Ave, Tulsa OK 74104-3126
Earl Johnson, Dean of Admission
918-631-2307 Fax: 918-631-5003
Website: www.utulsa.edu
E-mail: admission@utulsa.edu

OREGON
Apollo College
2004 Lloyd Ctr Fl 3, Portland OR 97232-1309
503-761-6100

The Art Institute of Portland
1122 NW Davis St, Portland OR 97209-2911
503-228-6528

Birthingway College of Midwifery
12113 SE Foster Rd, Portland OR 97266
503-760-3131

Cascade College
9101 E Burnside St, Portland OR 97216-1599
800-550-7678 Fax: 503-257-1222
Website: www.cascade.edu
E-mail: admissions@cascade.edu

Concordia University
2811 NE Holman St, Portland OR 97211-6099
Bobi Swan, Director of Admissions
503-288-9371 Fax: 503-280-8531
Website: www.cu-portland.edu
E-mail: cu-admissions@cu-portland.edu

Corban College
5000 Deer Park Dr SE, Salem OR 97317-9330
503-581-8600

Eastern Oregon University
One University Blvd, La Grande OR 97850
Sherri Edualson, Director of Admissions
800-452-8639

George Fox University
414 N Meridian St, Newberg OR 97132-2625
503-538-8383

Gutenberg College
1883 University St, Eugene OR 97403
541-683-5141

ITT Technical Institute
6035 NE 78th Ct, Portland OR 97218-2852
503-255-6500

Lewis & Clark College
0615 SW Palatine Hill Rd, Portland OR 97219-7899
503-768-7000

Linfield College
900 SE Baker St, Mc Minnville OR 97128-6894
503-472-2200

Linfield College
2215 NW Northrup St, Portland OR 97210-2982
503-229-7161

Marylhurst University
17600 Pacific Hwy (Hwy 43)
Marylhurst OR 97036-0261
Director of Admissions
800-634-9982 ext. 6268 Fax: 503-635-6585
Website: www.marylhurst.edu
E-mail: studentinfo@marylhurst.edu

Multnomah Bible College and Biblical Seminary
8435 NE Glisan St, Portland OR 97220-5898
Daniel R. Lockwood, President
800-275-4672

Northwest Christian College
828 E 11th Ave, Eugene OR 97401-3745
541-343-1641

OREGON COLLEGE OF ART & CRAFT
8245 SW Barnes Rd, Portland OR 97225-6399
Barry Beach, Director of Admissions
503-297-5544 or 800-390-0632 Fax: 503-297-9651
Website: www.ocac.edu
E-mail: admissions@ocac.edu

Oregon Institute of Technology
3201 Campus Dr, Klamath Falls OR 97601-8801
541-885-1000

Oregon State University
Corvallis OR 97333-9800
541-737-0123

Pacific Northwest College of Art
1241 NW Johnson St, Portland OR 97209-3023
Rebecca Haas, Director of Admissions
503-821-8972

Pacific University
2043 College Way, Forest Grove OR 97116-1797
Karen M. Dunston, Executive Director of Admissions
800-635-0561 Fax: 503-352-2975
Website: www.pacificu.edu
E-mail: admissions@pacificu.edu

Portland State University
PO Box 751, Portland OR 97207-0751
503-725-3000

Reed College
3202 SE Woodstock Blvd, Portland OR 97202-8139
503-771-1112

Southern Oregon University
1250 Siskiyou Blvd, Ashland OR 97520-5010
541-552-7672

University of Oregon
1217 University of Oregon, Eugene OR 97403
541-346-1000

University of Portland
5000 N Willamette Blvd, Portland OR 97203-5798
503-943-7911

Walla Walla College School of Nursing
10345 SE Market St, Portland OR 97216
503-251-6115

Warner Pacific College
2219 SE 68th Ave, Portland OR 97215-4026
Shannon Mackey, Director of Admissions
503-517-1000 Fax: 503-517-1352
Website: www.warnerpacific.edu
E-mail: admissions@warnerpacific.edu

Western Oregon University
345 Monmouth Ave N, Monmouth OR 97361-1314
David McDonald, Dean, Admission, Retention & Enrollment Management
877-877-1593 Fax: 503-838-8067
Website: www.wou.edu
E-mail: wolfgram@fsa.wou.edu

Willamette University
900 State St, Salem OR 97301-3931
503-370-6300

PENNSYLVANIA

Albright College
PO Box 15234, Reading PA 19612-5234
610-921-2381

Allegheny College
520 N Main St, Meadville PA 16335-3902
814-332-3100

Alvernia College
400 Saint Bernardine St, Reading PA 19607
610-796-8200

ARCADIA UNIVERSITY
450 S Easton Rd, Glenside PA 19038-3295
Dr. Jerry M. Greiner, President
Dennis Nostrand, VP for Enrollment Management
877-ARCADIA (877-272-2342) Fax: 215-881-8767
Website: www.arcadia.edu
E-mail: admiss@arcadia.edu
　　Established 1853. Independent. Coed. Accreditation: MSACS. Tuition: $23,990. Room and board: $9,300. Enrollment: Approx. 1,750 full-time undergraduate resident and commuter students; 1,450 graduate and 235 part-time students. Student-faculty ratio: 12:1. Degrees: BA, BS, BFA, DPT, MA, MEd, MS. Eighteen buildings on 71 acres, including the expanded Landman Library, a state-of-the-art residence hall designed to house 120 students in suite-style accomodations, and Grey Towers Castle, a national historic landmark. Located 25 minutes by train from center city Philadelphia, which offers theaters, museums, concerts, shops, sporting events and all the other diverse resources of a major metropolitan area. Also 2 hours from New York City and Washington DC as well as the New Jersey beaches. Special programs include: internships or co-op programs for every field of study; honors program; Distinguished Scholarships and Achievement Awards; 4 + 2.5 Doctorate in Physical Therapy (DPT), a 4 + 2 Master of Medical Science: Physician Assistant program, and a 4 + 2 Master of Arts in International Peace and Conflict Resolution; student/faculty research and publication; nationally recognized study abroad program; "London and Scotland Previews," unique opportunities for first-year students in good standing to spend spring break in London or Scotland for $245.

Art Institute of Philadelphia
1622 Chestnut St, Philadelphia PA 19103-5119
Larry McHugh, Director of Admissions
800-275-2474 Fax: 215-405-6399
Website: www.aiph.aii.edu
E-mail: aiphinfo@aii.edu

THE ART INSTITUTE OF PITTSBURGH
The College for Creative Minds
420 Boulevard Of The Allies, Pittsburgh PA 15219
Newton I. Myvett, VP/Director of Admissions
800-275-2470 or 412-263-6600 Fax: 412-263-6667
Website: www.aip.aii.edu
E-mail: pahughes@aii.edu
　　Established in 1921. Known as a leader in creative education. College is located in the heart of downtown, surrounded by limitless cultural, educational, and recreational opportunities. Licensed by the State of PA and accredited by the Accrediting Council for Independent Colleges and Schools to confer Associate of Science and Bachelor of Science degrees. Approved for training of veterans and eligible veteran's dependents. Authorized by federal law to enroll non-immigrant alien students.
　　Enrollment: 2700+ students; Co-ed.
　　Financial Aid available to qualified students through various federal and state programs. Awards based on individual need and availability of funds. Other Institute scholarship programs are available. Information regarding eligibility can be obtained by contacting an admissions representitive at 1-800-275-2470.
　　Student Housing: School sponsored housing available in the form of furnished apartments.
　　Bachelor degrees available in: Advertising, Culinary Management, Game Art and Design, Digital Media Production, Graphic Design, Industrial Design, Interactive Media Design, Interior Design, Media Arts and Animation, Photography, Visual Effects and Motion Graphics.
　　Associate Degrees available in: Culinary Arts, Graphic Design, Industrial Design, Interactive Media Design, Photography, Video Production.
　　Diploma programs include: The Art of Cooking, Digital Design, Residential Planning, Web Design. Some classes available evenings, Saturdays, and online.
　　Admissions: Prospective students must be a high school graduate or hold a General Educational Development (GED) Certificate. High school students who have not yet graduated should submit a partial transcript that indicates their expected graduation date, SAT and ACT testing not required for admission, however, may be used to determine the student's preparedness for college-level course work in English and/or mathematics.
　　Faculty: 98 full-time and 47 part-time instructors.
　　Facilities: 10 floors of fully networked computer labs and specialty facilities such as editing suites, digital photography labs, a television production studio, an industrial design machine shop, fully equipped culinary kitchens and more.

Baptist Bible College and Seminary
538 Venard Rd, Clarks Summit PA 18411-1297
Glen Amos, Director of Admissions
570-586-2400 Fax: 570-585-9299
Website: www.bbc.edu
E-mail: admissions@bbc.edu

Bloomsburg University of Pennsylvania
400 E 2nd St, Bloomsburg PA 17815-1399
570-389-4000

Bryn Athyn College of the New Church
PO Box 717, Bryn Athyn PA 19009
215-938-2543

Bucknell University
Lewisburg PA 17837
570-577-2000

Cabrini College
610 King of Prussia Rd, Radnor PA 19087-3698
Mark T. Osborn, VP for Enrollment Management
610-902-8100

California University of Pennsylvania
250 University Ave, California PA 15419-1394
724-938-4000

Carnegie Mellon University
5000 Forbes Ave, Pittsburgh PA 15213-3890
412-268-2000

Central Pennsylvania College
College Hill & Valley Rds, Summerdale PA 17093
Katie Bogovic, Admissions Director
800-759-2727 Fax: 717-728-2505
Website: www.centralpenn.edu
E-mail: katie.bogovic@centralpenn.edu

Chestnut Hill College
9601 Germantown Ave, Philadelphia PA 19118-2693
Jodie King, Director of Admissions
215-248-7001

Cheyney University of Pennsylvania
PO Box 200, Cheyney PA 19319-0200
610-399-2275

Clarion University of Pennsylvania
840 Wood St, Clarion PA 16214-1232
William Bailey, Dean of Enrollment Management
814-393-2306 Fax: 814-393-2030
Website: www.clarion.edu
E-mail: admissions@clarion.edu

Clarion University - Venango Campus
1801 W 1st St, Oil City PA 16301
814-676-6591

College Misericordia
301 Lake St, Dallas PA 18612-1008
Admissions
570-674-6400

Curtis Institute of Music
1726 Locust St, Philadelphia PA 19103-6187
215-893-5252

Delaware Valley College
700 E Butler Ave, Doylestown PA 18901-2697
Stephen W. Zenko, Director of Admissions
800-2-DEL-VAL

DeSales University
2755 Station Ave, Center Valley PA 18034-9565
610-282-1100 Fax: 610-282-2342
Website: www.desales.edu

Dickinson College
PO Box 1773, Carlisle PA 17013-2896
717-243-5121

Drexel University
3141 Chestnut St, Philadelphia PA 19104-2875
Dana R. Davies, Director of Undergraduate Enrollment
800-2-DREXEL

Duquesne University
600 Forbes Ave, Pittsburgh PA 15282-0001
Paul-James Cukanna, Director of Admissions
412-396-5000

Eastern University
1300 Eagle Rd, Saint Davids PA 19087-3696
610-341-5800

East Stroudsburg University of PA
200 Prospect St
East Stroudsburg PA 18301
570-424-3211

Edinboro University of Pennsylvania
Edinboro PA 16444-0001
814-732-2000

Elizabethtown College
1 Alpha Dr, Elizabethtown PA 17022-2298
717-361-1000

Franklin and Marshall College
PO Box 3003, Lancaster PA 17604-3003
717-291-3911

Gannon University
109 University Sq, Erie PA 16541-0001
Christopher Tremblay, Director of Admissions
800-GANNON-U Fax: 814-871-5803
Website: www.gannon.edu
E-mail: admissions@gannon.edu

Geneva College
3200 College Ave, Beaver Falls PA 15010-3599
724-846-5100

Gettysburg College
300 N Washington St, Gettysburg PA 17325-1483
Gail Sweezey, Director of Admissions
717-337-6100

Gratz College
7605 Old York Rd, Melrose Park PA 19027
Jill Sigman, Director of Admissions
215-635-7300 Fax: 215-635-7320
Website: www.gratzcollege.edu
E-mail: admissions@gratz.edu

Grove City College
100 Campus Dr, Grove City PA 16127-2104
Jeffrey C. Mincey, Director of Admissions
724-458-2100

Gwynedd-Mercy College
1325 Sumneytown Pike, Gwynedd Valley PA 19437
Dennis Murphy, V.P. Enrollment Management
800-DIAL-GMC

Haverford College
370 Lancaster Ave, Haverford PA 19041-1392
Jess Lord, Dean of Admission
610-896-1000 Fax: 610-896-1338
Website: www.haverford.edu
E-mail: admission@haverford.edu

Holy Family University
9801 Frankford Avenue, Philadelphia PA 19114
Lauren Campbell, Director of Admissions
215-637-3050 Fax: 215-281-1022
Website: www.holyfamily.edu
E-mail: admissions@holyfamily.edu

Holy Family University - Newtown
Newtown PA 18940
Karen Galardi, Executive Director
215-504-2000 Fax: 215-504-2050
Website: www.holyfamily.edu
E-mail: kgalardi@holyfamily.edu

Holy Family University - Woodhaven
1311 Bristol Pike, Bensalem PA 19020
Honour Moore, Associate VP for Extended Learning
215-637-7700 ext. 5008 Fax: 215-633-0558
Website: www.holyfamily.edu
E-mail: hmoore@holyfamily.edu

Immaculata University
Immaculata PA 19345
Women's College Office of Admissions
610-647-4400

Indiana University of Pennsylvania
Indiana PA 15705-0001
724-357-2100

ITT Technical Institute
760 Moore Rd, King of Prussia PA 19406
610-491-8004

Juniata College
1700 Moore St, Huntingdon PA 16652-2196
Michelle Bartol, Dean of Enrollment
877-JUNIATA Fax: 814-641-3100
Website: www.juniata.edu
E-mail: admissions@juniata.edu

King's College
133 N River St, Wilkes Barre PA 18711-0801
Michelle Lawrence-Schmude, Director of Admission
570-208-5900 Fax: 570-208-5971
Website: www.kings.edu
E-mail: admissions@kings.edu

Kutztown University of Pennsylvania
Kutztown PA 19530
610-683-4000

Lafayette College
High St, Easton PA 18042
610-330-5000

Lake Erie College of Osteopathic Medicine
1858 W Grandview Blvd, Erie PA 16509-1025
Elaine Morse, Admissions Coordinator
814-866-6641

La Roche College
9000 Babcock Blvd, Pittsburgh PA 15237-5898
Thomas Hassett, Director of Freshman and
International Admissions
412-536-1272 or 800-838-4LRC Fax: 412-536-1272
Website: www.laroche.edu
E-mail: admissions@laroche.edu

La Salle University
33 University Dr, Newtown PA 18940
215-579-7335

La Salle University
1900 W Olney Ave, Philadelphia PA 19141-1199
Robert Voss, Dean of Admissions
215-951-1500

Lebanon Valley College
101 N College Ave, Annville PA 17003-1400
William Brown, Dean of Admissions & Financial Aid
866-LVC-4ADM or 717-867-6181 Fax: 717-867-6026
Website: www.lvc.edu
E-mail: admission@lvc.edu

Lehigh University
27 Memorial Dr West, Bethlehem PA 18015-3094
Eric Kaplan, Dean of Admissions
610-758-3100

Lincoln University
Lincoln University PA 19352
Michael C. Taylor, Director of Admissions
800-790-0191 Fax: 610-932-1209
Website: www.lincoln.edu
E-mail: mtaylor@lu.lincoln.edu

Lock Haven University
Lock Haven PA 17745
James C. Reeser, Dean of Admissions
570-893-2027

Lycoming College
700 College Pl, Williamsport PA 17701-5192
570-321-4000

Mansfield University of Pennsylvania
Academy St, Mansfield PA 16933
570-662-4000

Marywood University
2300 Adams Ave, Scranton PA 18509-1598
570-348-6211

Mercyhurst College
501 E 38th St, Erie PA 16546-0001
800-825-1926

Messiah College
1 S College Ave, Grantham PA 17027
717-766-2511

Messiah College
2026 N Broad St, Philadelphia PA 19121-2305
215-769-2526

Millersville University of Pennsylvania
PO Box 1002, Millersville PA 17551-0302
717-872-3024

Moravian College
1200 Main St, Bethlehem PA 18018-6650
610-861-1300

MORAVIAN THEOLOGICAL SEMINARY
1200 Main St, Bethlehem PA 18018
Rev. Melissa Johnson, Director of Admissions
610-861-1516 Fax: 610-861-1569
Website: www.moravianseminary.edu
E-mail: seminary@moravian.edu

MOUNT ALOYSIUS COLLEGE
7373 Admiral Peary Hwy, Cresson PA 16630-1999
Frank C. Crouse Jr., Vice President for Enrollment
Management
814-886-6383 or 888-823-2220 Fax: 814-886-6441
Website: www.mtaloy.edu
E-mail: admissions@mtaloy.edu

Muhlenberg College
2400 W Chew St, Allentown PA 18104-5586
610-821-3100

Neumann College
1 Neumann Dr, Aston PA 19014-1298
Dennis Murphy, Director of Admissions
610-459-0905 Fax: 610-558-5652
Website: www.neumann.edu
E-mail: neumann@neumann.edu

Pennsylvania College of Art and Design
PO Box 59, Lancaster PA 17608-0059
Susan Matson, Director of Enrollment Management
717-396-7833 Fax: 717-396-1339
Website: www.pcad.edu
E-mail: admissions@pcad.edu

Pennsylvania College of Technology
1 College Ave, Williamsport PA 17701-5778
570-326-3761

Pennsylvania State University
777 W Harrisburg Pike, Middletown PA 17057
717-948-6000

Pennsylvania State University
Broadhead Rd, Monaca PA 15061
724-773-3500

Pennsylvania State University
3550 7th St Rd, New Kensington PA 15068-1765
Patricia K. Brady, Director of Admissions
724-334-5466

Pennsylvania State University
201 Shields Bldg PO Box 300
University Park PA 16802-3000
814-865-4700

Pennsylvania State University
The Behrend College
5091 Station Rd, Erie PA 16563-0002
814-898-6000

Philadelphia Biblical University
200 Manor Ave, Langhorne PA 19047-2943
Josh Edwards, Contact
800-366-0049

Philadelphia University
4201 Henry Ave, Philadelphia PA 19144-5409
215-951-2700

Point Park University
201 Wood St, Pittsburgh PA 15222-1984
Philip Clarke, Associate Director of Admissions
412-392-3430

Reconstructionist Rabbinical College
1299 Church Rd, Wyncote PA 19095-1898
Rabbi Daniel Aronson, Dean of Admissions
215-576-0800

THE RESTAURANT SCHOOL AT WALNUT HILL COLLEGE
4207 Walnut St, Philadelphia PA 19104-5296
Karl D. Becker, Admissions Director
215-222-4200 ext. 3011 Fax: 215-222-4219
Website: www.walnuthillcollege.com
E-mail: info@walnuthillcollege.com

Robert Morris College
600 5th Ave, Pittsburgh PA 15219-3010
412-227-6800

Robert Morris University
881 Narrows Run Rd, Coraopolis PA 15108-1169
412-262-8200

Rosemont College
1400 Montgomery Ave, Rosemont PA 19010-1699
Ms. Rennie Andrews, Director of Admissions
610-526-2966

St. Francis University
PO Box 600, Loretto PA 15940-0600
814-472-3000

St. Joseph's University
5600 City Ave, Philadelphia PA 19131-1376
610-660-1000

St. Vincent College
300 Fraser Purchase Rd, Latrobe PA 15650-2690
724-539-9761

St. Vincent Seminary
300 Fraser Purchase Rd, Latrobe PA 15650
724-537-4592

Seton Hill University
Greensburg PA 15601-1599
Mary Kay Cooper, Director of Admissions and Adult
Student Services
800-826-6234

Shippensburg University
1871 Old Main Dr, Shippensburg PA 17257-2299
717-477-7447

Slippery Rock University
14 Maltby Dr, Slippery Rock PA 16057-1326
724-738-9000

Strayer University
3600 Horizon Blvd Ste 100, Trevose PA 19053
215-953-5999

Susquehanna University
514 University Ave, Selinsgrove PA 17870-1164
570-374-0101

Swarthmore College
500 College Ave, Swarthmore PA 19081-1390
610-328-8000

Temple University
Broad St & Montgomery Ave, Philadelphia PA 19122
215-204-7000

Temple University
3307 N Broad St, Philadelphia PA 19140-5101
215-787-7000

Temple University Ambler
Ambler PA 19002
Michael Schlotterbeck, Contact
215-283-1252

Temple University Center City
1515 Market St, Philadelphia PA 19102
215-204-8822

Temple University Tyler School of Art
Beech and Penrose Aves, Elkins Park PA 19027
215-782-2875

Thiel College
75 College Ave, Greenville PA 16125-2181
724-589-2000

Thomas Jefferson University
111 S 11th St, Philadelphia PA 19107-4824
215-955-6000

University of Pennsylvania
3400 Spruce St, Philadelphia PA 19104-4274
215-898-5000

University of Pittsburgh
1150 Mount Pleasant Rd
Greensburg PA 15601-5860
Brandi S. Darr, Director of Admissions and Financial
Aid
724-836-9880 Fax: 724-836-7160
Website: www.upg.pitt.edu
E-mail: upgadmit@pitt.edu

University of Pittsburgh
4200 5th Ave, Pittsburgh PA 15260-3583
412-624-4141

University of Pittsburgh at Bradford
300 Campus Dr, Bradford PA 16701-2812
Alexander Nazemetz, Director of Admissions
814-362-7555

University of Pittsburgh at Johnstown
450 Schoolhouse Rd, Johnstown PA 15904-2990
814-269-7000

University of Pittsburgh at Titusville
504 E Main St #287, Titusville PA 16354-2010
814-827-4400

University of Scranton
800 Linden St, Scranton PA 18510-4501
570-941-7400

University of the Arts
320 S Broad St, Philadelphia PA 19102-4994
Susan Gandy, Director of Admissions
800-616-2787 Fax: 215-717-6045
Website: www.uarts.edu
E-mail: admissions@uarts.edu

University of the Sciences in Philadelphia
600 S 43rd St, Philadelphia PA 19104-4418
215-596-8800

Ursinus College
PO Box 1000, Collegeville PA 19426-1000
610-409-3000

Villanova University
800 E Lancaster Ave, Villanova PA 19085
610-519-4500

Washington & Jefferson College
60 S Lincoln St, Washington PA 15301-4801
Alton E. Newell, Vice President for Enrollment
724-223-6025 Fax: 724-223-6534
Website: www.washjeff.edu
E-mail: admission@washjeff.edu

Waynesburg College
51 W College St, Waynesburg PA 15370-1222
Robin L. Moore, Dean of Admissions
800-225-7393

West Chester University of Pennsylvania
S High St, West Chester PA 19383-0001
610-436-1000

Westminster College
New Wilmington PA 16172-0001
Doug Swartz, Director of Admissions
724-946-7100 Fax: 724-946-6171
Website: www.westminster.edu
E-mail: swartzdl@westminster.edu

Widener University
1 University Pl, Chester PA 19013-5792
610-499-4000

Wilkes University
170 S Franklin St, Wilkes Barre PA 18766-0001
570-408-5000

York College of Pennsylvania
PO Box 15199, York PA 17405-7199
717-846-7788

RHODE ISLAND
Brown University
1 Prospect St, Providence RI 02912
401-863-1000

Bryant University
1150 Douglas Pike, Smithfield RI 02917-1287
401-232-6000

Johnson & Wales University
8 Abbott Park Pl, Providence RI 02903-3775
401-598-1000

New England Institute of Technology
2500 Post Rd, Warwick RI 02886-2244
Michael Kwiatkowski, Director of Admissions
401-739-5000 Fax: 401-738-5122
Website: www.neit.edu
E-mail: eflynn@neit.edu

Providence College
549 River Ave, Providence RI 02918-0002
401-865-1000

Rhode Island College
600 Mount Pleasant Ave, Providence RI 02908-1924
401-456-8000

Rhode Island School of Design
2 College St, Providence RI 02903-2717
401-454-6100

Roger Williams University
1 Old Ferry Rd, Bristol RI 02809-2921
Michelle Beauregard, Director of Freshman Admission
800-458-7144 ext. 3500 Fax: 401-254-3557
Website: www.rwu.edu
E-mail: mbeauregard@rwu.edu

Roger Williams University
150 Washington St, Providence RI 02903-3300
401-274-2200

Salve Regina University
100 Ochre Point Ave, Newport RI 02840-4192
401-847-6650

University of Rhode Island
Kingston RI 02881
401-874-1000

ZION BIBLE COLLEGE
27 Middle Hwy, Barrington RI 02806-1296
Director of Recruiting
401-246-0900 Fax: 401-246-0906
Website: www.zbc.edu
E-mail: recruiting@zbc.edu

SOUTH CAROLINA
Allen University
1530 Harden St, Columbia SC 29204-1085
803-376-5701

Anderson College
316 Boulevard, Anderson SC 29621-4035
864-231-2000

Benedict College
1600 Harden St, Columbia SC 29204-1086
Phyllis L. Thompson, Director of Admissions
803-253-5143

BOB JONES UNIVERSITY
1700 Wade Hampton Blvd
Greenville SC 29614-0001
Stephen Jones, President
David Christ, Director of Admissions
800-BJ-AND-ME Fax: 800-2-FAX-BJU
Website: www.bju.edu
E-mail: admissions@bju.edu
Established 1927. Private. Coed. Tuition: $8,580.
Room and board: $4,860. Enrollment: 2,861 boarding,
1,438 day. Faculty: 232 full-time, 150 part-time. Degrees:
AAA, AAS, BA, BFA, BMus, BS, BSN, EdS, MA, MAT,
MBA, MDiv, MEd, MME, MMin, MMus, MS, DMin, SMin,
DpasTh, PhD, EdD. Library: 294,000 volumes. 73 build-
ings on 225 acres. Gym. Pool. 2 & 3 year trade programs
available. Unusual Films produces outstanding Christian
films. University Press produces Christian and educational texts.

Charleston Southern University
PO Box 118087, Charleston SC 29423-8087
Cheryl Burton, Director of Admissions
800-947-7474

Claflin University
700 College Ave, Orangeburg SC 29115-4477
803-535-5000

Clemson University
105 Sikes Hall, Clemson SC 29634
864-656-2287

Coastal Carolina University
PO Box 261954, Conway SC 29528-6054
Office of Admissions
800-277-7000 Fax: 843-349-2127
Website: www.coastal.edu
E-mail: admissions@coastal.edu

Coker College
300 E College Ave, Hartsville SC 29550-3797
843-383-8000

College of Charleston
66 George St, Charleston SC 29424-1407
Suzette Stille, Admissions
843-953-5670

Columbia International University
PO Box 3122, Columbia SC 29230-3122
John Basie, Director of University Admissions
800-777-2227 Fax: 803-786-4209
Website: www.ciu.edu
E-mail: yesciu@ciu.edu
See listing under "Theological Studies & Religious
Vocations"

Erskine College & Seminary
PO Box 176, Due West SC 29639
Bart Walker, Director of Admissions
864-379-8838 Fax: 864-379-3048
Website: www.erskine.edu
E-mail: admissions@erskine.edu

Francis Marion University
PO Box 100547, Florence SC 29501-0547
843-661-1362

Furman University
3300 Poinsett Hwy, Greenville SC 29613-0002
864-294-2000

Greenville Technical College
PO Box 5616, Greenville SC 29606-5616
Martha White, Director of Admissions
800-723-0673 (US) or 800-922-1183 (SC)
Website: www.greenvilletech.com

Lander University
320 Stanley Ave, Greenwood SC 29649-2099
Jonathan Reece, Director of Admissions
888-4-LANDER

Limestone College
1115 College Dr, Gaffney SC 29340-3799
Chris Phenicie, V.P. for Enrollment
864-489-7151 Fax: 864-488-8206
Website: www.limestone.edu
E-mail: cphenicie@limestone.edu

Morris College
100 W College St, Sumter SC 29150-3599
803-934-3200

Newberry College
2100 College St, Newberry SC 29108-2197
800-845-4955

NORTH GREENVILLE UNIVERSITY
PO Box 1892, Tigerville SC 29688-1892
Charles "Buddy" Freeman, Exec. Director of
Admissions & Financial Planning
864-977-7001 Fax: 864-977-7177
Website: www.ngc.edu
E-mail: bfreeman@ngc.edu
    Established 1892. Private. Coed. Accreditation: SACS.
Tuition: $10,760. Room and Board: $6,190. Fees: $200.
Enrollment: 1,649 full-time, 195 part-time. Faculty: 73
full-time, 74 part-time. Student-faculty ratio: 18:1. Majors:
Accounting, Applied Gerontology, Biology, Business Ad-
ministration, Christian Studies, Church Music, Elemen-
tary/Early Childhood Education, Elementary Education,
English, History/Political Science, Intercultural Studies
(Missions), Interdisciplinary Studies, International Busi-
ness, Management, Mass Communications, Mathemat-
ics, Music Composition, Music Education, Music
Performance, Outdoor Leadership, Psychology, Social
Studies, Sports Management, Youth Ministry. Minors: Ac-
counting, American Studies, Art, Biology, Broadcasting,
Business Administration, Christian Studies, Computer
Science, Counseling/Psychology, Economics, Educa-
tion, English, History, International Business, Journalism,
Management, Marketing, Mass Communications, Music,
Natural Science, Spanish, Sports Management, Theatre,
Visual Arts, Youth Ministry. Associates Degrees: Arts,
Fine Arts, Science.

PRESBYTERIAN COLLEGE
503 S Broad St, Clinton SC 29325
Richard Dana Paul, Dean of Admissions
800-476-7272 Fax: 864-833-8481
Website: www.presby.edu
E-mail: admissions@presby.edu

South Carolina State University
PO Box 7127, Orangeburg SC 29117-0001
Lillian M. Adderson, Director of Admissions
803-536-7185

Southern Methodist College
PO Box 1027, Orangeburg SC 29116-1027
Gary Briden, President
803-534-7826

Southern Wesleyan University
PO Box 1020, Central SC 29630-1020
864-644-5000

South University
9 Science Court, Columbia SC 29203
Trish Wade, Contact
803-799-9082 Fax: 803-799-9038
Website: www.southuniversity.edu
E-mail: twade@southuniversity.edu

Strayer University
200 Center Point Cir # 300, Columbia SC 29210
803-750-2500

University of South Carolina
471 University Pkwy, Aiken SC 29801
803-648-6851

University of South Carolina
Columbia SC 29208-0001
803-777-7700

University of South Carolina Beaufort
801 Carteret St, Beaufort SC 29902-4601
Anita M. Folsom, Director of Admissions
843-521-4101

UNIVERSITY OF SOUTH CAROLINA - UPSTATE
800 University Way, Spartanburg SC 29303-4932
Donette Stewart, Assistant VC for Enrollment Services
864-503-5246 Fax: 864-503-5727
Website: www.uscupstate.edu
E-mail: dstewart@uscupstate.edu
    Public. Coed. Accredited by the Commission on Col-
leges of the Southern Association of Colleges and
Schools. Tuition: $7,437. Room & board: $3,200 - $4,500.
Fees: $175. Enrollment: 3,707 full-time, 681 part-time.
Faculty: 336. Student-faculty ratio: 18:1. Degrees of-
fered: Bachelor of Arts, Bachelor of Sciences, Master's of
Education. Library: 215,000+ volumes. 12 buildings on
300 acres. Small class size, Metropolitan mission, all pro-
fessional schools are Nationally Accredited, Scholarships available, Modern expanding campus facilities,
NCAA Division II Athletics.

Voorhees College
Voorhees Rd, Denmark SC 29042
803-793-3351

Winthrop University
701 W Oakland Ave, Rock Hill SC 29733-0001
803-323-2211

W.L. Bonner Bible College
4430 Argent Ct, Columbia SC 29203
803-754-3950

Wofford College
429 N Church St, Spartanburg SC 29303-3663
864-597-4000

SOUTH DAKOTA

Augustana College
29th and South Smt, Sioux Falls SD 57197-0001
605-274-0770

Black Hills State University
1200 University St, Spearfish SD 57799-0002
605-642-6011

Dakota State University
820 N Washington Ave, Madison SD 57042-1799
605-256-5112

Dakota Wesleyan University
1200 W University Ave, Mitchell SD 57301
605-995-2600

Mt. Marty College
1105 W 8th St, Yankton SD 57078-3724
605-668-1514

National American University
1270 Ryan St - 28 MSS/DPE, Ellsworth AFB SD 57706
605-923-5856

NATIONAL AMERICAN UNIVERSITY
321 Kansas City St, Rapid City SD 57701-3692
Angela G. Beck, Director of Enrollment Management
605-394-4800 Fax: 605-394-4871
Website: www.national.edu/rc/index.html
E-mail: rcadmissions@national.edu

National American University
2801 S Kiwanis Ave Ste 100
Sioux Falls SD 57105-4293
605-334-5430 Fax: 605-334-1575
Website: www.national.edu

Northern State University
1200 S Jay St, Aberdeen SD 57401-7198
605-626-3011

Oglala Lakota College
PO Box 490, Kyle SD 57752-0490
605-455-2321

Presentation College
1500 N Main St, Aberdeen SD 57401-1280
JoEllen Lindner, Dean of Admissions
605-229-8492 Fax: 605-229-8425
Website: www.presentation.edu
E-mail: admit@presentation.edu

Sinte Gleska University
PO Box 105, Mission SD 57555-0105
605-856-5880

South Dakota School of Mines and Technology
501 E Saint Joseph St, Rapid City SD 57701-3901
605-394-2511

South Dakota State University
PO Box 2201, Brookings SD 57007-0001
605-688-4151

University of Sioux Falls
1101 W 22nd St, Sioux Falls SD 57105-1699
605-331-5000

University of South Dakota
414 E Clark St, Vermillion SD 57069-2307
605-677-5011

TENNESSEE

American Baptist College
1800 Baptist World Center Dr
Nashville TN 37207-4994
Marcella Lockhart, Executive Asst. for Administration
615-256-1463

AQUINAS COLLEGE
4210 Harding Pike, Nashville TN 37205-2148
Diane C. LeJeune, Director of Admissions
615-297-7545 ext. 460 Fax: 615-297-7970
Website: www.aquinas-tn.edu
E-mail: lejeuned@aquinas-tn.edu

Austin Peay State University
601 College St, Clarksville TN 37044-0002
931-221-7011

Baptist Memorial College of Health Science
1003 Monroe Ave, Memphis TN 38104-3104
Office of Admissions
866-575-2247

Belmont University
1900 Belmont Blvd, Nashville TN 37212-3757
615-460-6000

Bethel College
325 Cherry Ave, McKenzie TN 38201-1735
Tina L. Hodges, Director of Admissions
731-352-4030

BLAIR SCHOOL OF MUSIC OF VANDERBILT UNIVERSITY
2400 Blakemore Ave, Nashville TN 37212-3406
Dwayne Sagen, Assistant Dean for Admissions
615-322-7679 Fax: 615-343-0324
Website: www.vanderbilt.edu
E-mail: dwayne.p.sagen@vanderbilt.edu

Bryan College
PO Box 7000, Dayton TN 37321-7000
423-775-2041

Carson-Newman College
1646 Russell Ave, Jefferson City TN 37760
865-471-4000

Christian Brothers University
650 E Parkway S, Memphis TN 38104-5568
901-321-3000

Cumberland University
1 Cumberland Sq, Lebanon TN 37087-3408
Jason Brewer, Director of Admissions
615-444-2562

East Tennessee State University
PO Box 70731, Johnson City TN 37614-1326
Dr. Linda Doran, Vice Provost

Fisk University
1000 17th Ave N, Nashville TN 37208-3051
William Carter, Director of Admissions
615-329-8766

Freed-Hardeman University
158 E Main St, Henderson TN 38340-2398
731-989-6000

Free Will Baptist Bible College
3606 W End Ave, Nashville TN 37205
Ryan Lewis, Director of Recruitment
800-76-FWBBC Fax: 615-269-6028
Website: www.fwbbc.edu
E-mail: recruit@fwbbc.edu

International Academy of Design & Technology
1 Bridgestone Park, Nashville TN 37214
615-232-7384

ITT TECHNICAL INSTITUTE
2845 Elm Hill Pike, Nashville TN 37214-3717
James Royster, Director of Recruitment
615-889-8700 Fax: 615-872-7209
Website: www.itt-tech.edu
E-mail: jroyster@itt-tech.edu

King College
1350 King College Rd, Bristol TN 37620-2635
423-968-1187

Lambuth University
705 Lambuth Blvd, Jackson TN 38301-5296
731-425-2500

Lane College
545 Lane Ave, Jackson TN 38301-4598
731-426-7500

Lee University
PO Box 3450, Cleveland TN 37320-3450
Dale W. Goff, V.P. Institutional Advancement
800-533-9930

Le Moyne-Owen College
807 Walker Ave, Memphis TN 38126-6595
901-774-9090

Lincoln Memorial University
PO Box 2012, Harrogate TN 37752
423-869-3611

Lipscomb University
3901 Granny White Pike, Nashville TN 37204-3951
Ricky Holaway, Director of Admissions
800-333-4358 ext. 1776 Fax: 615-269-1804
Website: www.lipscomb.edu
E-mail: admissions@lipscomb.edu

Maryville College
502 E Lamar Alexander Pkwy
Maryville TN 37804-5919
865-981-8000

Memphis College of Art
1930 Poplar Ave, Memphis TN 38104-2764
901-272-5100

Middle Tennessee State University
1301 E Main St, Murfreesboro TN 37132-0001
615-898-2300

Milligan College
1 Milligan College, Milligan College TN 37682
423-461-8700

NORTH TENNESSEE BIBLE INSTITUTE AND SEMINARY
PO Box 3797, Clarksville TN 37043-3797
Dr. William Corley, Chancellor
931-552-1510 Fax: 931-552-1464
Website: www.ntbis.com
E-mail: drwhc@ntbis.com

O'More College of Design
423 S Margin St, Franklin TN 37064-2816
Dr. K. Mark Hilliard, President
Chris Lee, Director of Enrollment Management
615-794-4254 Fax: 615-790-1662
Website: www.omorecollege.edu
E-mail: clee@omorecollege.edu

Peabody College of Vanderbilt University
Box 327, Nashville TN 37203
615-322-8410

Rhodes College
2000 N Parkway, Memphis TN 38112-1624
901-843-3000

South College
3904 Lonas Dr, Knoxville TN 37909
Walter Hosea, Director of Admissions
865-251-1800

Southern Adventist University
PO Box 370, Collegedale TN 37315-0370
423-238-2111

Strayer University
2620 Thousand Oaks Blvd, Memphis TN 38118-2427
901-369-0835

Strayer University
6211 Shelby Oaks Dr, Memphis TN 38134
901-383-6750

Strayer University
30 Rachel Dr Ste 200, Nashville TN 37214
615-871-2260

Tennessee State University
3500 John A Merritt Blvd, Nashville TN 37209-1561
John Cade, Dean of Admissions & Records
615-963-5101 Fax: 615-963-2930
Website: www.tnstate.edu
E-mail: jcade@tnstate.edu

Tennessee Technological University
PO Box 5006, Cookeville TN 38505-0001
931-372-3101

Tennessee Temple University
1815 Union Ave, Chattanooga TN 37404-3587
423-493-4100

Tennessee Wesleyan College
PO Box 40, Athens TN 37371-0040
423-745-7504

Trevecca Nazarene University
333 Murfreesboro Rd, Nashville TN 37210-2834
615-248-1200

Tusculum College
PO Box 5051, Greeneville TN 37743
Melissa Ripley, Associate Director of Admissions
800-729-0256 Fax: 423-798-1622
Website: www.tusculum.edu
E-mail: mripley@tusculum.edu

Union University
1050 Union University Dr, Jackson TN 38305
731-668-1818

University of Memphis
Memphis TN 38152-0001
901-678-2000

University of Tennessee
615 McCallie Ave, Chattanooga TN 37403-2504
Yancy Freeman, Director of Admissions
423-425-4111 Fax: 423-425-4157
Website: www.utc.edu
E-mail: Yancy-Freeman@utc.edu

University of Tennessee
527 Andy Holt Tower, Knoxville TN 37996-0001
865-974-1000

University of Tennessee
Martin TN 38238-0001
731-587-7000

University of Tennessee Health Science Center
800 Madison Ave, Memphis TN 38163-0002
901-448-5500

University of the South
735 University Ave, Sewanee TN 37383-1000
931-598-1000

Vanderbilt University
W End Ave, Nashville TN 37240-0001
615-322-7311

Watkins College of Art and Design
and The Watkins Film School
2298 Metrocenter Blvd, Nashville TN 37228-1306
Connie Baer, V.P. for Admissions, Marketing, and
Enrollment Management
615-383-4848

Williamson Christian College
200 Seaboard Ln, Franklin TN 37067
615-771-7066

TEXAS

Abilene Christian University
ACU Box 29000, Abilene TX 79699-0001
325-674-2000

Amberton University
1700 Eastgate Dr, Garland TX 75041-5511
972-279-6511

Angelo State University
ASU Station 11014, San Angelo TX 76909
Bonnie Stennett, Coordinator of Recruiting
800-946-8627 Fax: 325-942-2078
Website: www.angelo.edu
E-mail: admissions@angelo.edu

Argosy University/Dallas
8080 Park Ln Ste 400, Dallas TX 75231
214-890-9900

Arlington Baptist College
3001 W Division St, Arlington TX 76012-3425
Janie Taylor, Director of Admissions
817-461-8741 Fax: 817-274-1138
Website: www.abconline.edu
E-mail: jhall@abconline.org

Austin College
900 N Grand Ave, Sherman TX 75090-4400
903-813-2000

Austin Graduate School of Theology
1909 University Ave, Austin TX 78705-5610
Mark Martin, Registrar
512-476-2772

BAPTIST UNIVERSITY OF THE AMERICAS
8019 S Panam Expy, San Antonio TX 78224-1336
Mary Ranjel, Director of Admissions
800-721-1396 Fax: 210-924-2701
Website: www.bua.edu
E-mail: mranjel@bua.edu

Baylor University
Po Box 97008, Waco TX 76798-7008
254-710-1011

Brazosport College
500 College Dr, Lake Jackson TX 77566-3199
979-230-3000

COLLEGE OF SAINT THOMAS MORE
3020 Lubbock Ave, Fort Worth TX 76109
Maria Stromberg, Registrar
817-923-8459 Fax: 817-924-3206
Website: www.cstm.edu
E-mail: pflores@cstm.edu

Concordia University
3400 N I H 35, Austin TX 78705-2702
512-486-2000

The Criswell College
4010 Gaston Ave, Dallas TX 75246-1537
Tommy Weir, VP Institutional Advancement
800-899-0012

Dallas Baptist University
3000 Mountain Creek Pkwy, Dallas TX 75211-9209
214-333-7100

Dallas Christian College
2700 Christian Pkwy, Dallas TX 75234-7299
800-688-1029

East Texas Baptist University
1209 N Grove St, Marshall TX 75670-1498
903-935-7963

Hardin-Simmons University
2200 Hickory St, Abilene TX 79601-2345
325-670-1000

Houston Baptist University
7502 Fondren Rd, Houston TX 77074-3298
David Melton, Director of Admissions
281-649-3000

Howard Payne University
1000 Fisk Ave, Brownwood TX 76801-2715
325-646-2502

Huston-Tillotson University
900 Chicon St, Austin TX 78702-9997
512-505-3000

Jarvis Christian College
PO Box 1470, Hawkins TX 75765-1470
903-769-5700

Lamar University
PO Box 10009, Beaumont TX 77710-0009
409-880-8888

Le Tourneau University
PO Box 7001, Longview TX 75607-7001
903-233-3000

Lubbock Christian University
5601 19th St, Lubbock TX 79407-2099
806-796-8800

McMurry University
14th and Sayles, Abilene TX 79697-0001
325-793-3800

Midwestern State University
3410 Taft Blvd, Wichita Falls TX 76308-2096
940-397-4000

Northwood University
1114 W FM 1382, Cedar Hill TX 75104-1204
Sylvia Correa, Director of Admissions
800-927-WOOD Fax: 972-291-3824
Website: www.northwood.edu
E-mail: ray@northwood.edu

Our Lady of the Lake University
411 SW 24th St, San Antonio TX 78207-4666
Mary Kay Cooper, Dean of Enrollment
210-434-6711 Fax: 210-431-4013
Website: www.ollusa.edu
E-mail: admission@lakeollusa.edu

Paul Quinn College
3837 Simpson Stuart Rd, Dallas TX 75241-4398
214-376-1000

Prairie View A&M University
PO Box 188, Prairie View TX 77446
936-857-3311

Rice University
6100 Main St, Houston TX 77005-1892
800-527-6957

Rio Grande Bible Institute
4300 S US Highway 281, Edinburg TX 78539-9699
956-380-8100

St. Edward's University
3001 S Congress Ave, Austin TX 78704-6489
512-448-8400

St. Mary's University of San Antonio
1 Camino Santa Maria St
San Antonio TX 78228-8500
210-436-3011

Sam Houston State University
PO Box 2026, Huntsville TX 77341
936-294-1111

Schreiner University
2100 Memorial Blvd, Kerrville TX 78028-5697
Todd D. Brown, Director of Admissions
800-343-4919

Southern Methodist University
PO Box 750181, Dallas TX 75275-0181
Ron Moss, Dean of Admission
214-768-2058

Southwestern Adventist University
PO Box 567, Keene TX 76059-0567
800-433-2240

Southwestern Assemblies of God University
1200 Sycamore St, Waxahachie TX 75165-2397
Pat Thompson, Admissions Counselor
972-937-4010

Southwestern Baptist Theological Seminary
PO Box 22000, Fort Worth TX 76122
817-923-1921

Southwestern Christian College
PO Box 10, Terrell TX 75160-9002
972-524-3341

Southwestern University
PO Box 740, Georgetown TX 78627
512-863-6511

Stephen F. Austin State University
PO Box 6078, Nacogdoches TX 75962-0001
936-468-2011

Sul Ross State University
Alpine TX 79832-0001
432-837-8032

Tarleton State University
PO Box T0030, Stephenville TX 76402
254-968-9000

Texas A&M at Galveston
PO Box 1675, Galveston TX 77553-1675
409-740-4400

Texas A&M International University
5201 University Blvd, Laredo TX 78041
956-326-2000

Texas A&M University
College Station TX 77843-0001
979-845-3211

Texas A&M University
700 University Blvd, Kingsville TX 78363
361-593-2111

Texas A&M University - Commerce
PO Box 3011, Commerce TX 75429
903-886-5102

Texas A&M University - Corpus Christi
6300 Ocean Dr, Corpus Christi TX 78412-5503
361-825-5700

Texas A&M University - Texarkana
PO Box 5518, Texarkana TX 75505-5518
903-223-3000

TEXAS CHIROPRACTIC COLLEGE
5912 Spencer Hwy, Pasadena TX 77505-1699
Sandra Hughes, D.C.; Director of Admission
281-487-1170 Fax: 281-991-4871
Website: www.txchiro.edu
E-mail: shughes@txchiro.edu

Texas Christian University
TCU Box 297013, Fort Worth TX 76129
817-257-7000

Texas College
2404 N Grand Ave, Tyler TX 75702
903-593-8311

Texas Lutheran University
1000 W Court St, Seguin TX 78155-5978
830-372-8000

Texas Southern University
3100 Cleburne St, Houston TX 77004-4583
713-313-7011

Texas State University - San Marcos
601 University Dr, San Marcos TX 78666-4685
512-245-2111

Texas Tech University
1 Texas Tech University, Lubbock TX 79409-0001
806-742-2011

Texas Tech University Health Science Center
Lubbock TX 79430
806-743-3111

Texas Wesleyan University
1201 Wesleyan St, Fort Worth TX 76105-1536
Stephanie Boatner, Director of Freshman Admission
800-580-8980

Trinity University
715 Stadium Dr, San Antonio TX 78212-7200
210-999-7011

University of Dallas
1845 E Northgate Dr, Irving TX 75062-4736
972-721-5000

University of Houston
122 E Cullen Bldg, Houston TX 77204-2023
Office of Admission
713-743-9595
Website: www.uh.edu
E-mail: admissions@uh.edu

University of Houston-Clear Lake
2700 Bay Area Blvd, Houston TX 77058-1025
281-283-2500

University of Houston-Downtown
1 Main St, Houston TX 77002-1014
713-221-8000

University of Houston-Victoria
3007 N Ben Wilson St, Victoria TX 77901
361-570-4848

University of Mary Hardin-Baylor
UMHB Station Box 8001, Belton TX 76513
254-295-8642

University of North Texas
PO Box 305309, Denton TX 76203-5309
940-565-2000

University of St. Thomas
3800 Montrose Blvd, Houston TX 77006-4626
Eduardo Prieto, Director of Admissions
713-522-7911 Fax: 713-525-3558
Website: www.stthom.edu
E-mail: prietoe@stthom.edu

University of Texas at Arlington
Box 19111, Arlington TX 76019-0111
Hans Gatterdam, Director of Admission
817-272-6287 Fax: 817-272-3435
Website: www.uta.edu
E-mail: admissions@uta.edu

University of Texas at Austin
0 the Univ of Texas, Austin TX 78712
512-471-3434

University of Texas at Brownsville
80 Fort Brown, Brownsville TX 78520
956-544-8200

University of Texas at Dallas
PO Box 830688, Richardson TX 75083-0688
972-690-2111

University of Texas at El Paso
500 W University Ave, El Paso TX 79968-8900
915-747-5000

University of Texas at San Antonio
6900 N Loop 1604 W, San Antonio TX 78249-1130
210-458-4011

University of Texas at Tyler
3900 University Blvd, Tyler TX 75701-6622
Jim Hutto, Dean Enrollment Management
800-888-9537

University of Texas Health Science Center
PO Box 20036, Houston TX 77225-0036
713-500-4472

University of Texas Health Science Center
7703 Floyd Curl Dr, San Antonio TX 78229
210-567-7000

UNIVERSITY OF TEXAS-HOUSTON
6901 Bertner Ave, Houston TX 77030-3901
William D. Stewart, Coordinator of Admissions
713-500-2104 Fax: 713-500-2107
Website: http://son.uth.tmc.edu
E-mail: william.stewart@uth.tmc.edu

University of Texas of the Permian Basin
4901 E University Blvd, Odessa TX 79762-8122
432-552-2020

University of Texas-Pan American
1201 W University Dr, Edinburg TX 78539-2909
956-381-2011

University of Texas Southwestern Medical Center
5323 Harry Hines Blvd, Dallas TX 75390-7208
214-648-3111

University of the Incarnate Word
4301 Broadway St, San Antonio TX 78209-6318
210-829-6000

Wayland Baptist University
1900 W 7th St, Plainview TX 79072-6998
806-296-5521

West Texas A & M University
WTAMU Box 907, Canyon TX 79016-0001
806-651-2000

Wiley College
711 Wiley Ave, Marshall TX 75670-5199
903-927-3300

UTAH

Brigham Young University
Provo UT 84602-0001
801-378-5000

ITT TECHNICAL INSTITUTE
920 Levoy Dr, Murray UT 84123-2500
Gary Wood, Director of Recruitment
801-263-3313 Fax: 801-263-3497
Website: www.itt-tech.edu
E-mail: gwood@itt-tech.edu

Southern Utah University
351 W Center St, Cedar City UT 84720-2470
D. Mark Barton, Asst. VP Student Services
435-586-7715

Stevens Henager College
PO Box 9428, Ogden UT 84409-0428
Cindy Williams, Director of Admissions
801-394-7791 Fax: 801-621-0866
Website: www.stevenshenager.edu
E-mail: shcogden@yahoo.com

University of Utah
1460 E 201 S, Salt Lake City UT 84112
801-581-7200

Utah State University
Logan UT 84322-0001
435-797-1000

Weber State University
1001 University Cir, Ogden UT 84408
801-626-6000

Westminster College
1840 S 1300 E, Salt Lake City UT 84105-3617
801-832-2200

VERMONT

Bennington College
One College Drive, Bennington VT 05201
Ken Himmelman, Dean of Admissions & Financial Aid
800-833-6845 Fax: 802-440-4320
Website: www.bennington.edu
E-mail: admissions@bennington.edu

Castleton State College
Castleton VT 05735
William Allen Jr., Dean of Enrollment
800-639-8521

Champlain College
PO Box 670, Burlington VT 05402-0670
802-860-2727

College of St. Joseph
71 Clement Rd, Rutland VT 05701-3899
802-773-5900

Goddard College
121 Pitkin Rd, Plainfield VT 05667
802-454-8311

Green Mountain College
1 College Cir, Poultney VT 05764-1199
802-287-8000

Johnson State College
337 College Hill, Johnson VT 05656
802-635-2356

Lyndon State College
PO Box 919, Lyndonville VT 05851
802-626-6200

Marlboro College
PO Box A, Marlboro VT 05344
802-257-4333

Middlebury College
Middlebury VT 05753-6200
802-443-5000

New England Culinary Institute
48 1/2 Park St, Essex VT 05452
Dawn Hayward, Director of Admissions
877-223-6324 Fax: 802-225-3280
Website: www.neci.edu
E-mail: Admissions@neci.edu
See listing under "Career Schools"

New England Culinary Institute
250 Main St, Montpelier VT 05602
Dawn Hayward, Director of Admissions
877-223-3211 Fax: 802-225-3280
Website: www.neci.edu
E-mail: Admissions@neci.edu
See listing under "Career Schools"

NORWICH UNIVERSITY
158 Harmon Dr, Northfield VT 05663
Shelby Wallace, Director of Admissions
LTC Skip Davison, Director of Recruitment
800-468-6679 Fax: 802-485-2032
Website: www.norwich.edu
E-mail: nuadm@norwich.edu
    Established 1819. Nations first private Military College.
Accreditation: NEASC.
    Student Body: Coed. 1,100 Cadets, 450 residential
students, 375 commuter day students.
    Tuition: $20,088. Exceptional opportunities for aca-
demic, leadership and merit scholarships.
    Student Housing: Room and board: $7,374. Nine on-
campus dormitories with off-campus housing available in
the local community.
    Curriculum: 30 Academic majors with specialized pro-
grams in Architecture, Business, Computer Science, Information Assurance, Engineering, Nursing, Math and
Science. Online Masters programs offered in Business
Administration, Civil Engineering, Diplomacy, Justice
Administration, and Information Assurance.
    Admission requirements include application, $35 fee,
academic record, SAT/ACT scores, personal essay, letters of recommendation and extracurricular activities.
Those applying for the Corps of Cadets must meet physical standards. TOEFL and declaration of finances for international students required. Rolling admissions.
    Faculty: 144 full-time, 104 part-time. ROTC: Army,
Navy, Air Force and Marine Corps.
    Facilities: 42 buildings on 1,200 acres. Library:
300,000+ volumes. 4 athletic facilities. Ice Hockey Arena,
Student Lounge, Nautilus and Weight Rooms, Indoor
Swimming Pool, and Computer Labs in all teaching facilities, dorms are wired.
    Environment: Norwich is located in the middle of ski-
country in Vermont. Stowe, Sugarbush and Killington ski
resorts are located within an hour's drive. Northfield is
10-miles south of the state capital of Montpelier. Burlington International Airport is an hour drive. Boston and
Montreal are a 3-hour drive from campus.

Saint Michael's College
One Winooski Park, Colchester VT 05439-0001
Jacqueline Murphy, Director
802-654-3000

Southern Vermont College
982 Mansion Dr, Bennington VT 05201-6002
Kathleen James Ring, Director of Admissions
800-378-2782 Fax: 802-447-4695
Website: www.svc.edu
E-mail: admis@svc.edu

University of Vermont
194 S Prospect St, Burlington VT 05401-3518
802-656-3131

Woodbury College
660 Elm St, Montpelier VT 05602-4017
Kathleen Moore, Director of Admissions
800-639-6039 Fax: 802-229-2141
Website: www.woodbury-college.edu
E-mail: admiss@woodbury-college.edu

VIRGINIA

American Military University
10648 Wakeman Ct, Manassas VA 20110
703-330-5398

APPALACHIAN SCHOOL OF LAW
PO Box 2825, Grundy VA 24614-1825
Nancy Pruitt, Director of Student Services
800-895-7411 Fax: 276-935-8261
Website: www.asl.edu
E-mail: npruitt@asl.edu

The Art Institute of Washington
1820 N Fort Myer Dr, Arlington VA 22209
Larry McHugh, Director of Admissions
703-358-9550

Averett University
420 W Main St, Danville VA 24541-3692
804-791-5600

Bluefield College
3000 College Dr, Bluefield VA 24605-1799
276-326-3682

Bridgewater College
402 E College St, Bridgewater VA 22812-1599
540-828-8000

::: Catholic Distance University
120 E Colonial Hwy, Hamilton VA 20158-9012
Marianne Evans Mount, Executive VP
888-254-4CDU Fax: 540-338-4788
Website: www.cdu.edu
E-mail: tcashen@cdu.edu

Christendom College
134 Christendom Dr, Front Royal VA 22630
540-636-2900

Christopher Newport University
1 University Pl, Newport News VA 23606
757-594-7000

College of William and Mary
PO Box 1346, Gloucester Point VA 23062
804-642-7000

College of William and Mary
PO Box 8795, Williamsburg VA 23187-8795
757-221-4000

Eastern Mennonite University
1200 Park Rd, Harrisonburg VA 22802-2404
540-432-4000

Emory & Henry College
PO Box 947, Emory VA 24327-0947
276-944-4121

Ferrum College
PO Box 1000, Ferrum VA 24088-9001
Gilda Q. Woods, Director of Admissions
800-868-9797

George Mason University
4400 University Dr, Fairfax VA 22030-4444
Eddie Tallent, Director of Admissions
703-993-2400

GRAHAM BIBLE COLLEGE
PO Box 1630, Bristol VA 24203-1630
Dr. Philip R. Blevins, President
423-968-4201 Fax: 423-968-4266
Website: www.grahambiblecollege.com
E-mail: info@grahambiblecollege.com

Hampton University
Hampton VA 23669
757-727-5000

James Madison University
800 S Main St, Harrisonburg VA 22807-0002
540-568-6211

Jefferson College of Health Sciences
Formerly Community Hospital
PO Box 13186, Roanoke VA 24031-3186
Judith McKeon, Director of Admissions
540-985-8483

Liberty University
PO Box 20000, Lynchburg VA 24506-8001
804-582-2000

Longwood University
201 High St, Farmville VA 23909-1801
804-395-2000

Lynchburg College
1501 Lakeside Dr, Lynchburg VA 24501-3199
804-544-8100

Marymount University
2807 N Glebe Rd, Arlington VA 22207-4299
703-522-5600

Norfolk State University
700 Park Ave, Norfolk VA 23504
Michelle Marable, Director of Admissions
757-823-8600

Old Dominion University
1 Old Dominion University, Norfolk VA 23529-1000
757-683-3000

PATRICK HENRY COLLEGE
1 Patrick Henry Cir, Purcellville VA 20132
540-338-1776 Fax: 540-338-8707
Website: www.phc.edu
E-mail: admissions@phc.edu

Radford University
PO Box 6903, Radford VA 24142
David W. Kraus, Director of Admissions
800-890-4265 Fax: 540-831-5038
Website: www.radford.edu
E-mail: ruadmiss@radford.edu

Randolph-Macon College
PO Box 5005, Ashland VA 23005-5505
804-752-7200

Roanoke College
221 College Ln, Salem VA 24153-3794
540-375-2500

St. Paul's College
406 Windsor Ave, Lawrenceville VA 23868-1202
804-848-3111

Shenandoah University
1460 University Dr, Winchester VA 22601-5195
540-665-4500

Southern Virginia University
1 University Hill Dr, Buena Vista VA 24416
540-261-8400

Stratford University
7777 Leesburg Pike #100 South
Falls Church VA 22043
Keith Evans, Contact
703-821-8570 Fax: 703-734-5335
Website: www.stratford.edu
E-mail: admissions@stratford.edu

Strayer University
45150 Russell Branch Pkwy, Ashburn VA 20147
703-729-8800

Strayer University
700 Independence Pkwy Ste 400
Chesapeake VA 23320
757-382-9900

Strayer University
9990 Battleview Pkwy, Manassas VA 20109-2368
703-330-8400

Strayer University
PO Box 487, Newington VA 22122
703-339-1850

UNIVERSITY OF MANAGEMENT AND TECHNOLOGY
1901 Fort Myer Dr Ste 700, Arlington VA 22209
703-516-0035 Fax: 703-516-0985
Website: www.umtweb.edu
E-mail: info@umtweb.edu

University of Mary Washington
1301 College Ave, Fredericksburg VA 22401-5300
Dr. Martin A. Wilder, Jr., Director of Admissions
540-654-2000 Fax: 540-654-1857
Website: www.umw.edu
E-mail: admit@umw.edu

University of Richmond
Richmond VA 23173
804-289-8000

University of Virginia
PO Box 400160, Charlottesville VA 22904
804-924-0311

University of Virginia College at Wise
1 College Ave, Wise VA 24293
276-328-0100

Virginia Commonwealth University
901 W Franklin St, Richmond VA 23284
804-828-0100

Virginia Intermont College
1013 Moore St, Bristol VA 24201-4225
540-669-6101

Virginia Polytechnic Institute & State University
Blacksburg VA 24061
540-231-6000

Virginia State University
1 Hayden Dr, Petersburg VA 23806-0001
804-524-5000

Virginia Union University
1500 N Lombardy St, Richmond VA 23220-1711
804-257-5600

Virginia University of Lynchburg
2058 Garfield Ave, Lynchburg VA 24501
434-528-5276

Virginia Wesleyan College
1584 Wesleyan Dr, Norfolk VA 23502-5599
757-455-3200

Washington & Lee University
Lexington VA 24450
540-463-8400

WASHINGTON

Antioch University
2326 6th Ave, Seattle WA 98121
Pam Smith Mentz, Director of Enrollment Services
888-268-4477

Apollo College
10102 E Knox Ave, Spokane WA 99206-4146
509-532-8888

Central Washington University
400 E University Way, Ellensburg WA 98926
William Swain, Director of Admissions
509-963-3001

City University
11900 NE 1st St, Bellevue WA 98005-3030
800-426-5596

Cornish College of the Arts
1000 Lenora St, Seattle WA 98121
Eric Pedersen, Director of Admission
800-726-ARTS (2787) Fax: 206-720-1011
Website: www.cornish.edu
E-mail: admissions@cornish.edu

CROWN COLLEGE
8739 S Hosmer St, Tacoma WA 98444-1836
John Wabel, CEO
253-531-3123 Fax: 253-531-3521
Website: www.crowncollege.edu
E-mail: jwabel@crowncollege.edu

DIGIPEN INSTITUTE OF TECHNOLOGY
5001 150th Ave NE, Redmond WA 98052
Admissions
425-558-0299 Fax: 425-558-0378
Website: www.digipen.edu
E-mail: admissions@digipen.edu

Eastern Washington University
Cheney WA 99004
509-359-6200

Evergreen State College
2700 Evergreen Pkwy NW, Olympia WA 98505-0005
360-866-6000

Gonzaga University
502 E Boone Ave, Spokane WA 99258-0102
Julie McCulloh, Dean of Admission
800-322-2584 or 509-323-6572 Fax: 509-323-5780
Website: www.gonzaga.edu
E-mail: mcculloh@gu.gonzaga.edu

Henry Cogswell College
3002 Colby Ave, Everett WA 98201-4012
Jane Buckman, Director of Admissions
866-411-4221 Fax: 425-257-0405
Website: www.henrycogswell.edu
E-mail: admissions@henrycogswell.edu

Heritage University
3240 Fort Rd, Toppenish WA 98948-9599
509-865-8500

Intercollegiate Center for Nursing Education
2917 W Fort Gorge Wright Dr, Spokane WA 99204
509-324-7360

Northwest Baptist Seminary
4301 N Stevens St, Tacoma WA 98407-6699
253-759-6104

Northwest College of Art
16464 State Highway 305 NE
Poulsbo WA 98370-8625
Craig Freeman, President
360-779-9993

Northwest University
PO Box 579, Kirkland WA 98083-0579
Myles Corrigan, Associate V.P. - Enrollment
425-889-5209

Pacific Lutheran University
12180 Park Ave S, Tacoma WA 98447-0014
David E. Gunovich, Director of Admissions
253-535-7151

Puget Sound Christian College
PO Box 13108, Everett WA 98206-3108
425-257-3090

St. Martin's University
5300 Pacific Ave SE, Lacey WA 98503-1297
360-491-4700

Seattle Pacific University
3307 3rd Ave W, Seattle WA 98119-1997
206-281-2000

Seattle University
900 Broadway, Seattle WA 98122-4340
206-296-6000

Trinity Lutheran College
4221 228th Ave SE, Issaquah WA 98029-9264
425-392-0400

University of Puget Sound
1500 N Warner St, Tacoma WA 98416-0005
253-879-3100

University of Washington
Seattle WA 98195-0001
206-543-2100

Walla Walla College
204 S College Ave, College Place WA 99324-1198
509-527-2615

Washington State University
1 SE Stadium Way, Pullman WA 99164-0001
509-335-3564

Western Washington University
516 High St, Bellingham WA 98225-5996
360-650-3000

Whitman College
345 Boyer Ave, Walla Walla WA 99362-2083
509-527-5111

Whitworth College
300 W Hawthorne Rd, Spokane WA 99251-0001
Fred Pfursich, Dean of Admissions & Financial Aid
800-533-4668

WEST VIRGINIA

Alderson-Broaddus College
Philippi WV 26416
Eric A. Ruf, Director of Admissions
800-263-1549

Appalachian Bible College
PO Box ABC, Bradley WV 25818-1353
Rita K. Pritt, Director of Admissions
800-678-9222

Bethany College
Bethany WV 26032
304-829-7000

Bluefield State College
219 Rock St, Bluefield WV 24701-2198
304-327-4000

Concord University
Athens WV 24712
Michael Curry, Vice President of Financial Aid & Admissions
888-384-5249 Fax: 304-384-3218
Website: www.concord.edu
E-mail: admissions@concord.edu

Davis & Elkins College
100 Campus Dr, Elkins WV 26241-3996
Renee Heckel, Director of Enrollment Management
800-624-3157 Fax: 304-637-1800
Website: www.davisandelkins.edu
E-mail: admiss@davisandelkins.edu

Fairmont State University
1201 Locust Ave, Fairmont WV 26554-2470
Steve Leadman, Director of Admissions
304-367-4892 or 800-641-5678 Fax: 304-367-4789
Website: www.fairmontstate.edu
E-mail: admit@fairmontstate.edu

Glenville State College
200 High St, Glenville WV 26351-1200
304-462-4128

Marshall University
400 Hal Greer Blvd, Huntington WV 25755-0003
304-696-3170

MOUNTAIN STATE UNIVERSITY
Box 9003, Beckley WV 25802-9003
866-FOR-MSU1 or 304-929-1433 Fax: 304-253-5072
Website: www.mountainstate.edu
E-mail: gomsu@mountainstate.edu
Established 1933. Private. Coed. Accreditation: The Higher Learning Commission of North Central Association of Colleges and Schools. 2005-06 Tuition & Fees: $7,350. Room & board: $4,980 - $6,916. Enrollment: 4,107. Faculty: 85 full-time, 131 part-time. Student-faculty ratio: 27:1. Degrees: AA, AS, BA, BS, BSN, BSW, MA, MCJA, MS, MHS, MSN, MSPA, MSSL. Library: 95,500 volumes. Largest private college in West Virginia; extensive financial aid package; same tuition for in-state or out-of-state students; extensive health science programs.

Ohio Valley University
1 Campus View Dr, Vienna WV 26105
800-678-6780

Salem International University
PO Box 500, Salem WV 26426-0500
304-782-5011

Shepherd University
PO Box 3210
Shepherdstown WV 25443
304-876-5000

University of Charleston
2300 MacCorkle Ave SE, Charleston WV 25304-1099
304-357-4800

West Liberty State College
PO Box 295, West Liberty WV 26074
304-336-5000

West Virginia State University
PO Box 1000, Institute WV 25112-1000
304-766-3000

West Virginia University
PO Box 6001, Morgantown WV 26506-6001
304-293-0111

West Virginia University at Parkersburg
300 Campus Dr, Parkersburg WV 26101
304-424-8220

West Virginia University Institute of Technology
405 Fayette Pike, Montgomery WV 25136-2436
304-442-3071

West Virginia Wesleyan College
59 College Ave, Buckhannon WV 26201-2699
Robert N. Skinner II, Director of Admission
800-722-9933 Fax: 304-473-8108
Website: www.wvwc.edu
E-mail: admission@wvwc.edu

Wheeling Jesuit University
316 Washington Ave, Wheeling WV 26003-6295
304-243-2000

WISCONSIN

Alverno College
PO Box 343922, Milwaukee WI 53234-3922
Mary Kay Farrell, Director of Admissions
414-382-6100 Fax: 414-382-6354
Website: www.alverno.edu
E-mail: admissions@alverno.edu

BELLIN COLLEGE OF NURSING
PO Box 23400, Green Bay WI 54305-3400
Penny Croghan, Director of Admissions
920-433-5803 Fax: 920-433-7416
Website: www.bcon.edu
E-mail: admissio@bcon.edu

Beloit College
700 College St, Beloit WI 53511-5596
James Zielinski, Director of Admissions
608-363-2500

Cardinal Stritch University
6801 N Yates Rd, Milwaukee WI 53217-3985
414-410-4000

Carroll College
100 N East Ave, Waukesha WI 53186-5593
James Wiseman, Dean of Admissions
800-CARROLL

Carthage College
2001 Alford Park Dr, Kenosha WI 53140-1994
262-551-6000

Columbia College of Nursing
2121 E Newport Ave, Milwaukee WI 53211-2952
414-961-3530

Concordia University
12800 N Lake Shore Dr, Mequon WI 53097-2402
262-243-5700

Edgewood College
1000 Edgewood College Dr, Madison WI 53711
608-663-4861

HERZING COLLEGE
5218 E Terrace Dr, Madison WI 53718-8340
Donald Madelung, President
Rebecca Abrams, Director of Admissions
800-582-1227 or 608-249-6611 Fax: 608-249-8593
Website: www.herzing.edu
E-mail: info@msn.herzing.edu
Established 1948. Private. Coed. Accreditation: NCA. Tuition: $7,600 - $8,600 (2 semesters). Fees: $75 - $600. Enrollment: 590 full-time, 87 part-time. Faculty: 29. Student-Faculty ratio: 23:1. Degrees offered: AS, BS in Computer Information Systems; AS, BS in Computer Network & Security Technology; CAD Drafting; Computers, Electronics and Telecommunications Technology; BS in Technology Management & Information Technology; AS, BS in Business Administration; BS in Homeland Security & Public Safety; AS in Interactive & Graphic Arts; Diploma & AAS in Medical Billing & Insurance Coding. Minors in Business Management, Accounting, Legal Studies & Healthcare.
Founded in 1948 as one of the nation's first electronics schools. Certification preparation inbedded in curriculum: A+, Net+, MCSE, CCNA, Certified Electronics Technician and Associate. Three-year bachelor degree. Bachelor-completion program available online.
No dorms, but housing and job assistance to new and existing students.

Lakeland College
PO Box 359, Sheboygan WI 53082-0359
Nathan Dehne, Director of Admission
920-565-1100 Fax: 920-565-1215
Website: www.lakeland.edu
E-mail: admissions@lakeland.edu

Lawrence University
PO Box 599, Appleton WI 54912-0599
920-832-7000

Maranatha Baptist Bible College
745 W Main St, Watertown WI 53094-7638
920-261-9300

Marian College of Fond du Lac
45 S National Ave, Fond du Lac WI 54935-4621
Eric Peterson, Dean of Admission
800-262-7426 ext. 7650

Marquette University
PO Box 1881, Milwaukee WI 53201-1881
Robert Blust, Director of Admissions
414-288-7302 Fax: 414-288-3764
Website: www.mu.edu
E-mail: admissions@marquette.edu

Milwaukee Institute of Art & Design
273 E Erie St, Milwaukee WI 53202-6003
Mark Fetherston, Director of Admissions
414-291-8070

Milwaukee School of Engineering
1025 N Broadway, Milwaukee WI 53202-3109
414-277-7300

Northland Baptist Bible College
W10085 Pike Plains Rd, Dunbar WI 54119
715-324-6900

Northland College
1411 Ellis Ave, Ashland WI 54806-3999
800-753-1840

Ottawa University - Milwaukee
300 N Corporate Dr Ste 110
Brookfield WI 53045-5865
262-879-0200

Ripon College
PO Box 248, Ripon WI 54971-0248
920-748-8115

St. Norbert College
100 Grant St, De Pere WI 54115
Brian Studebaker, Director of Admission
800-236-4878 Fax: 920-403-4072
Website: www.snc.edu
E-mail: admit@snc.edu

Silver Lake College
2406 S Alverno Rd, Manitowoc WI 54220-9319
920-684-6691

State Laboratory of Hygiene
465 Henry Mall, Madison WI 53706-1578
Lynn Sterud, Ed. Coordinator
608-262-2802

University of Wisconsin
PO Box 4004, Eau Claire WI 54702
715-836-2637

University of Wisconsin
PO Box 2000, Kenosha WI 53141-2000
262-595-2345

University of Wisconsin
716 Langdon St, Madison WI 53706-1481
608-262-1234

University of Wisconsin
PO Box 413, Milwaukee WI 53201-0413
414-229-1122

University of Wisconsin
1 University Plz, Platteville WI 53818-3001
Angela Udelhofen, Recruitment Manager
608-342-1200

University of Wisconsin
410 S 3rd St, River Falls WI 54022
715-425-3911

University of Wisconsin
2100 Main St, Stevens Point WI 54481-3871
715-346-0123

University of Wisconsin
PO Box 2000, Superior WI 54880
715-394-8101

University of Wisconsin
800 W Main St, Whitewater WI 53190-1705
262-472-1234

UNIVERSITY OF WISCONSIN BARABOO/SAUK CO.

1006 Connie Rd, Baraboo WI 53913-1015
Tom Martin, Asst. Dean for Student Services
608-356-8351 Fax: 608-356-0752
Website: www.baraboo.uwc.edu
E-mail: boouinfo@uwc.edu

University of Wisconsin Green Bay
2420 Nicolet Dr, Green Bay WI 54311-7003
Pamela Harvey-Jacobs, Interim Director of Admissions
920-465-2111

University of Wisconsin in La Crosse
115 Graff Main Hall, La Crosse WI 54601
Tim Lewis, Director of Admissions
608-785-8939

University of Wisconsin - Oshkosh
800 Algoma Blvd, Oshkosh WI 54901-8602
920-424-0202

University of Wisconsin-Stout
124 Bowman Hall, Menomonie WI 54751-2662
715-232-1123

Viterbo University
815 9th St S, La Crosse WI 54601-8802
608-796-3000

Wisconsin Indianhead Technical College
505 Pine Ridge Dr, Shell Lake WI 54871
Miriam Crandall, Dean of Student Services
800-243-9482 Fax: 715-468-2819
Website: www.witc.edu
E-mail: mcrandal@witc.edu
Campuses in Ashland, New Richmond, Rice Lake, Superior.

Wisconsin Lutheran College
8800 W Bluemound Rd, Milwaukee WI 53226-4626
414-443-8800

WYOMING

University of Wyoming
Admissions Office
Dept 3435, Laramie WY 82071-3435
Aaron Appelhans, Contact
800-342-5996 Fax: 307-766-4042
Website: www.uwyo.edu
E-mail: why-wyo@uwyo.edu

GUAM

Pacific Islands Bible College
PO Box 22619, Barrigada GU 96921
671-472-8716

University of Guam
UOG Station, Mangilao GU 96923
Deborah Leon Guerrero, Registrar
671-735-2201 or 671-735-2208 Fax: 671-735-2203
Website: www.uog.edu
E-mail: admitme@uog9.uog.edu

PUERTO RICO

American University of Puerto Rico
PO Box 2037, Bayamon PR 00960-2037
787-798-2040

Atlantic College
PO Box 1774, Guaynabo PR 00970-1774
Zaida Perez, Director of Admissions
787-720-1022 Fax: 787-720-1092
Website: www.atlanticcollege-pr.com
E-mail: atlancol@coqui.net

Bayamon Central University
PO Box 1725, Bayamon PR 00960-1725
787-786-3030

Caribbean University
PO Box 493, Bayamon PR 00960-0493
787-780-0070

Colegio Biblico Pentecostal de Puerto Rico
PO Box 901, Saint Just PR 00978-0901
787-761-0640

COLEGIO PENTECOSTAL MIZPA

PO Box 20966, Rio Piedras PR 00928
Rev. Nereida Torres, Dean of Students
787-720-4476 Fax: 787-720-2012
Website: www.colmizpa.edu
E-mail: decanatoestudiante@colmizpa.edu

CONSERVATORY OF MUSIC

350 Calle Rafael Lamar, San Juan PR 00918
Eutimia Santiago, Director of Admissions
787-751-0160 ext. 275 Fax: 787-758-8268
Website: www.cmpr.edu
E-mail: admisiones@cmpr.edu

Electronic Data Processing College
PO Box 192303, Hato Rey PR 00919-2303
787-765-3560

ESCUELA DE ARTES PLASTICAS PUERTO RICO

PO Box 9021112, San Juan PR 00902-1112
Marine's Lopez-Lopez, Dean Student Affairs
Juan Negroni, Admissions Officer
787-729-0007 Fax: 787-721-3798
Website: www.eap.edu.pr
E-mail: eap@coqui.net

Inter American University
Call Box 20000, Aguadilla PR 00605
787-891-0925

Inter American University of Puerto Rico
PO Box 4050, Arecibo PR 00614
787-878-5475

Inter American University of Puerto Rico
PO Box 517, Barranquitas PR 00794-0517
787-857-3600

Inter American University of Puerto Rico
500 Road 830, Bayamon PR 00957
787-279-1912

Inter American University of Puerto Rico
PO Box 70003, Fajardo PR 00738
787-863-2390

Inter American University of Puerto Rico
PO Box 10004, Guayama PR 00785
787-864-2222

Inter American University of Puerto Rico
PO Box 191293, Hato Rey PR 00919
787-250-1912

Inter American University of Puerto Rico
104 Turpo Industrial Park Rd #1, Mercedita PR 00715
787-284-1912

Inter American University of Puerto Rico
PO Box 5100, San German PR 00683
787-264-1912

Pontifical Catholic University of Puerto Rico
PO Box 144045, Arecibo PR 00614
787-881-1212

Pontifical Catholic University of Puerto Rico
5 Calle Santiago Palmer S, Guayama PR 00784-4965
787-864-0550

Pontifical Catholic University of Puerto Rico
PO Box 1326, Mayagez PR 00681
787-834-5151

Pontifical Catholic University of Puerto Rico
2250 Ave Las Americas, Ponce PR 00717-0777
787-841-2000

SAN JUAN BAUTISTA SCHOOL OF MEDICINE

PO Box 4968, Caguas PR 00726-4968
Lissette Torres, Registrar
787-743-3038 Fax: 787-746-3093
Website: www.sanjuanbautista.edu
E-mail: ltorres@sanjuanbautista.edu

Universidad Adventista de las Antillas
PO Box 118, Mayaguez PR 00919-0118
Evelyn Del Valle Rivera, Director of Admissions
787-834-9595 Fax: 787-834-9597
Website: www.uaa.edu
E-mail: admissions@uaa.edu

Universidad Central Del Caribe
PO Box 60327, Bayamon PR 00960-6032
787-798-3001

Universidad Del Turabo
PO Box 3030, Gurabo PR 00778
787-743-7979

Universidad Metropolitana
PO Box 21150, San Juan PR 00928-1150
787-766-1717

Universidad Politecnica de Puerto Rico
PO Box 192017, San Juan PR 00919-2017
787-754-8000

University of Puerto Rico
PO Box 4800, Carolina PR 00984-4800
787-257-0000

University of Puerto Rico
R Ave Antonio R Barcelo, Cayey PR 00736-5534
787-738-2161

University of Puerto Rico
CUH Station Rd 908 Bo Tejas, Humacao PR 00791
787-850-0000

University of Puerto Rico
PO Box 9020, Mayaguez PR 00681
787-832-4040

University of Puerto Rico
PO Box 23303, Rio Piedras PR 00931-3303
787-764-0000

University of Puerto Rico
PO Box 365067, San Juan PR 00936-5067
787-758-2525

University of Puerto Rico at Arecibo
PO Box 4010, Arecibo PR 00614
787-815-0000

University of Puerto Rico at Ponce
PO Box 7186, Ponce PR 00732-7186
787-844-8181

University of Puerto Rico
Bayamn University College
Carretera 174, Km 2.8, Bayamn PR 00959
787-786-2885

University of the Sacred Heart
PO Box 12383, Santurce PR 00914
787-728-1515

VIRGIN ISLANDS

University of the Virgin Islands
2 John Brewers Bay, Saint Thomas VI 00802
340-776-9200

University of the Virgin Islands
RR 2 Box 10000
Kingshill VI 00850
340-776-9200

VETERINARY MEDICINE

ALABAMA

Judson College
302 Bibb St, Marion AL 36756
Michael Scotto, Director of Admissions
800-447-9472 Fax: 334-683-5147
Website: www.judson.edu
E-mail: admissions@judson.edu

CALIFORNIA

Chapman University
One University Drive, Orange CA 92866-1099
Michael Drummy, Assistant Vice President for
Enrollment
Services and Chief Admission Officer
714-997-6411 or 888-CUAPPLY Fax: 714-997-6713
Website: www.chapman.edu
E-mail: admit@chapman.edu

Western Career College
7301 Greenback Ln Bldg A, Citrus Heights CA 95621
Jim Murphy, Contact
916-722-8200 Fax: 916-722-6883
Website: www.westerncollege.edu

Western Career College
380 Civic Dr Ste 300, Pleasant Hill CA 94523-1984
LaShawn Wells, Contact
925-609-6650 Fax: 926-609-6666
Website: www.westerncollege.edu

Western Career College
8909 Folsom Blvd, Sacramento CA 95826-3203
Sue Smith, Contact
916-361-1660 Fax: 916-361-6666
Website: www.westerncollege.edu

Western Career College
6201 San Ignacio Ave, San Jose CA 95119
Steve Ashab, Director of Admissions
408-360-0840 Fax: 408-360-0848
Website: www.westerncollege.edu

Western Career College
15555 E 14th St Ste 500, San Leandro CA 94578
Julie Elmquist, Contact
510-276-3888 Fax: 510-276-3653
Website: www.westerncollege.edu

Western Career College
1313 W Robinhood Dr Ste B, Stockton CA 95207
Dave Semrau, Contact
209-956-1240 Fax: 209-956-1244
Website: www.westerncollege.edu

COLORADO

Bel-Rea Institute of Animal Technology
1681 S Dayton St, Denver CO 80247-3048
Paulette Kaufman, Administrator
303-751-8700 Fax: 303-751-9969
Website: www.bel-rea.com
E-mail: admissions@bel-rea.com

NORTHEASTERN JUNIOR COLLEGE

100 College Ave, Sterling CO 80751-2399
Judy Giacomini, Interim Chief Administrative Officer
Tina Joyce, Director of Admissions
970-521-7000 or 970-521-6752 Fax: 970-521-6801
Website: www.njc.edu
E-mail: tina.joyce@njc.edu

IOWA

Briar Cliff University
PO Box 2100, Sioux City IA 51104-0100
Sharisue Wilcoxon, VP for Enrollment Management
712-279-5200 Fax: 712-279-1632
Website: www.briarcliff.edu
E-mail: admissions@briarcliff.edu

KANSAS

Newman University
3100 W McCormick St, Wichita KS 67213
Jann Reusser, Admissions Recruitment Coordinator
316-942-4291 ext. 2144 Fax: 316-942-4483
Website: www.newmanu.edu
E-mail: reusserj@newmanu.edu

MASSACHUSETTS

Becker College
Campuses in Worcester and Leicester, MA
61 Sever St, Worcester MA 01609-2165
Karen H. Schedin, Director of Admissions
508-791-9241 Fax: 508-890-1500
Website: www.becker.edu
E-mail: admissions@becker.edu
See listing under "Universities"

MICHIGAN

MACOMB COMMUNITY COLLEGE

44575 Garfield Rd, Clinton Township MI 48038-1139
Information Center
586-445-7999
Website: www.macomb.edu
E-mail: answer@macomb.edu

MINNESOTA

Duluth Business University
4724 Mike Colalillo Dr, Duluth MN 55807-2723
Bonnie Kupczynski, Director
800-777-8406 Fax: 218-628-2127
Website: www.dbumn.edu
E-mail: info@dbumn.edu

MISSOURI

Truman State University
100 E Normal, Kirksville MO 63501
Office of Admission
660-785-4000 Fax: 660-785-4181
Website: admissions.truman.edu
E-mail: admissions@truman.edu

William Woods University
1 University Ave, Fulton MO 65251-1098
Jimmy Clay, Director of Admissions
573-642-2251 Fax: 573-592-1146
Website: www.williamwoods.edu
E-mail: admissions@williamwoods.edu
See listing under "Universities"

MONTANA

Rocky Mountain College
1511 Poly Dr, Billings MT 59102-1796
Bonnie Knapp, Director of Admissions
800-877-6259 Fax: 406-657-1189
Website: www.rocky.edu
E-mail: admissions@rocky.edu

NEBRASKA

VATTEROTT COLLEGE

11818 I St, Omaha NE 68137
Todd S. Clark, Director
402-891-9411 Fax: 402-891-9413
Website: www.vatterott-college.edu
E-mail: tclark@vatterott-college.edu

NEW YORK

Roberts Wesleyan College
2301 Westside Dr, Rochester NY 14624-1997
Office of Admissions
585-594-6400 Fax: 585-594-6371
Website: www.roberts.edu
E-mail: admissions@roberts.edu

SUNY College of Technology
Alfred NY 14802
Deborah J. Goodrich, Director of Admissions
800-4AL-FRED Fax: 607-587-4299
Website: www.alfredstate.edu
E-mail: admissions@alfredstate.edu

NORTH CAROLINA

Lees-McRae College
PO Box 128, Banner Elk NC 28604-0128
Walt Crutchfield, Dean of Admissions
800-280-4562 Fax: 828-898-8707
Website: www.lmc.edu
E-mail: admissions@lmc.edu

Louisburg College
501 N Main St, Louisburg NC 27549-2399
800-775-0208 or 919-496-2521 Fax: 919-496-1788
Website: www.louisburg.edu
E-mail: admissions@louisburg.edu

OHIO

The Ohio State University
College of Veterinary Medicine
127 Vet Med Acad Bldg, 1900 Coffey Rd
Columbus OH 43210
614-292-8831 Fax: 614-292-6989
Website: vet.osu.edu
E-mail: graham.194@osu.edu

OHIO WESLEYAN UNIVERSITY

61 S Sandusky St, Delaware OH 43015-2398
Director of Admission
740-368-3020 Fax: 740-368-3314
Website: www.owu.edu
E-mail: owuadmit@owu.edu

Ursuline College
2550 Lander Rd, Cleveland OH 44124-4398
Sarah E. Sundermeier, Director of Admissions
888-URSULINE Toll Free Fax: 440-684-6138
Website: www.admission.ursuline.edu
E-mail: admission@ursuline.edu

OKLAHOMA

Oklahoma State University
Stillwater OK 74078
Michael Lorenz, Dean
405-744-6651
Website: www.okstate.edu
E-mail: michael.lorenz@okstate.edu

PENNSYLVANIA

Johnson College
3427 N Main Ave, Scranton PA 18508-1495
Dr. Ann L. Pipinski, President & CEO
Melissa Ide, Director of Enrollment Management
800-2WE-WORK or 570-342-6404 ext. 125
Fax: 570-348-2181
Website: www.johnson.edu
E-mail: admit@johnson.edu

Juniata College
1700 Moore St, Huntingdon PA 16652-2196
Michelle Bartol, Dean of Enrollment
877-JUNIATA Fax: 814-641-3100
Website: www.juniata.edu
E-mail: admissions@juniata.edu

VET TECH INSTITUTE

125 7th St, Pittsburgh PA 15222-3410
Cheri Yaworski, Director of Admissions
800-570-0693 Fax: 412-232-4348
Website: www.vettechinstitute.com
E-mail: cyaworski@vettechinstitute.com

SOUTH DAKOTA

NATIONAL AMERICAN UNIVERSITY

321 Kansas City St, Rapid City SD 57701-3692
Angela G. Beck, Director of Enrollment Management
605-394-4800 Fax: 605-394-4871
Website: www.national.edu/rc/index.html
E-mail: rcadmissions@national.edu

TEXAS

University of St. Thomas
3800 Montrose Blvd, Houston TX 77006-4626
Eduardo Prieto, Director of Admissions
713-522-7911 Fax: 713-525-3558
Website: www.stthom.edu
E-mail: prietoe@stthom.edu

WASHINGTON

Gonzaga University
502 E Boone Ave, Spokane WA 99258-0102
Julie McCulloh, Dean of Admission
800-322-2584 or 509-323-6572 Fax: 509-323-5780
Website: www.gonzaga.edu
E-mail: mcculloh@gu.gonzaga.edu

WEST VIRGINIA

West Virginia Wesleyan College
59 College Ave, Buckhannon WV 26201-2699
Robert N. Skinner II, Director of Admission
800-722-9933 Fax: 304-473-8108
Website: www.wvwc.edu
E-mail: admission@wvwc.edu

WISCONSIN

St. Norbert College
100 Grant St, De Pere WI 54115
Brian Studebaker, Director of Admission
800-236-4878 Fax: 920-403-4072
Website: www.snc.edu
E-mail: admit@snc.edu

WYOMING

University of Wyoming
Admissions Office
Dept 3435, Laramie WY 82071-3435
Aaron Appelhans, Contact
800-342-5996 Fax: 307-766-4042
Website: www.uwyo.edu
E-mail: why-wyo@uwyo.edu

WOMEN'S COLLEGES

ALABAMA

Judson College
302 Bibb St, Marion AL 36756
Michael Scotto, Director of Admissions
800-447-9472 Fax: 334-683-5147
Website: www.judson.edu
E-mail: admissions@judson.edu

CALIFORNIA

Mills College
5000 MacArthur Blvd, Oakland CA 94613-1000
510-430-2255

Mt. St. Mary's College
12001 Chalon Rd, Los Angeles CA 90049-1599
310-954-4000

Mt. St. Mary's College - Doheny Campus
10 Chester Pl, Los Angeles CA 90007-2518
213-746-0450

Scripps College
1030 Columbia Ave, Claremont CA 91711-3948
909-621-8000

CONNECTICUT

Hartford College for Women
1265 Asylum Ave, Hartford CT 06105-2299
860-236-1215

St. Joseph College
1678 Asylum Ave, West Hartford CT 06117-2791
860-232-4571

DISTRICT OF COLUMBIA

Trinity University
125 Michigan Ave NE, Washington DC 20017-1090
202-884-9000

GEORGIA

Agnes Scott College
141 E College Ave, Decatur GA 30030-3770
404-471-6000

Brenau College
1 Centennial Cir, Gainesville GA 30501-3668
770-534-6299

Spelman College
350 Spelman Ln SW, Atlanta GA 30314-4395
800-982-2411

Strayer University
3355 Northeast Expy NE Ste 100, Atlanta GA 30341
770-454-9270

Wesleyan College
4760 Forsyth Rd, Macon GA 31210-4462
800-447-6610

ILLINOIS

Loyola University - Mundelein College
6525 N Sheridan Rd, Chicago IL 60626-5311
773-262-8100

INDIANA

St. Mary-of-the-Woods College
Saint Mary of the Woods IN 47876-1001
James P. Malley, Jr., Director of Admission
800-926-7692 Fax: 812-535-5010
Website: www.smwc.edu
E-mail: smwcadms@smwc.edu

St. Mary's College
46 Madeliva, Notre Dame IN 46556
574-284-4000

KENTUCKY

Midway College
512 E Stephens St, Midway KY 40347-1120
800-755-0031

MARYLAND

College of Notre Dame of Maryland
4701 N Charles St, Baltimore MD 21210-2404
410-435-0100

Hood College
401 Rosemont Ave, Frederick MD 21701
301-663-3131

MASSACHUSETTS

Bay Path College
588 Longmeadow St, Longmeadow MA 01106-2292
Lisa Casassa, Director of Admissions
413-565-1331 Fax: 413-565-1105
Website: www.baypath.edu
E-mail: lcasassa@baypath.edu

Lesley University
29 Everett St, Cambridge MA 02138-2790
Jane Raley, Director of Admissions
617-349-8800

Mt. Holyoke College
50 College St, South Hadley MA 01075-1424
413-538-2000

Pine Manor College
400 Heath St, Chestnut Hill MA 02467-2332
Bill Nichols, Dean of Admission
617-731-7167

Regis College
235 Wellesley St, Weston MA 02493-1571
781-768-2000

Simmons College
300 Fenway, Boston MA 02115-5898
617-521-2000

Smith College
Northampton MA 01063-0001
Debra Shaver, Director of Admissions
800-383-3232 Fax: 413-585-2527
Website: www.smith.edu
E-mail: admission@smith.edu

Wellesley College
106 Central St, Wellesley MA 02481-8203
Board of Admission
781-283-2270

MINNESOTA

College of Saint Benedict
37 College Ave S, Saint Joseph MN 56374-2099
320-363-5011

College of St. Catherine
2004 Randolph Ave, Saint Paul MN 55105-1789
651-690-6000

MISSISSIPPI

Blue Mountain College
PO Box 160, Blue Mountain MS 38610
800-235-0136

Mississippi University for Women
1100 College St Unit W1613, Columbus MS 39701
Terri Heath, Director of Admissions
877-GO-2-THEW

Mississippi University for Women-Tupelo
1918 Briar Ridge Rd, Tupelo MS 38804-5904
Kay Brown, Contact
662-844-0284

MISSOURI

Cottey College
1000 W Austin Blvd, Nevada MO 64772-2790
417-667-8181

Stephens College
PO Box 2121, Columbia MO 65215-0001
David Adams, Dean of Enrollment Management
573-442-2211 Fax: 573-876-7237
Website: www.stephens.edu
E-mail: dadams@stephens.edu

NEBRASKA

College of Saint Mary
7000 Mercy Rd, Omaha NE 68106
Lorin Werth,V.P. for Enrollment
800-926-5534 or 402-399-2407 Fax: 402-399-2412
Website: www.csm.edu
E-mail: lwerth@csm.edu

NEW JERSEY

College of Saint Elizabeth
2 Convent Rd, Morristown NJ 07960-6923
973-292-4000

NEW YORK

Barnard College
3009 Broadway, New York NY 10027-6598
212-854-5262

Marymount College at Fordham University
100 Marymount Ave, Tarrytown NY 10591-3796
Gerard Reedy, S.J., Ph.D., Dean
914-631-3200

Russell Sage College
45 Ferry St, Troy NY 12180-4115
518-244-2000

NORTH CAROLINA

Bennett College
900 E Washington St, Greensboro NC 27401-3298
336-273-4431

MEREDITH COLLEGE
3800 Hillsborough St, Raleigh NC 27607-5298
Heidi L. Fletcher, Director of Admissions
919-760-8581 or 800-MEREDITH Fax: 919-760-2348
Website: www.meredith.edu
E-mail: admissions@meredith.edu
   Established in 1891. Private Women's College. Accredited by the Commission on Colleges of the Southern Association of Colleges and Schools. Enrollment: 2,400 students. Projected tuition and fees for 2005-2006: $20,000. Projected room and board for 2005-2006: $5,600. Students required to live on campus freshman and sophomore year, unless special permission is granted. Federal, state, and institutional financial aid available. Institutional application and FAFSA required.
   Undergraduates BA, BM, BS, and BSW available in over 40 majors plus pre-professional programs in dentistry, law, medicine, pharmacy, physical therapy, physician assistant, and veterinary medicine. Graduate degrees: Master of Business Administration, Master of Education, Master of Music, and Master of Nutrition.
   Evening and summer courses are available. Degree completion program for women over age 23.
   Admission requirements include application and $40 fee, ACT or SAT scores, high school transcripts (college transcripts for transfers), teacher recommendation, and guidance counselor recommendation. TOEFL and declaration of finance for international students. Early decision deadline is October 15. Rolling decision recommended deadline is February 15.
   Faculty: 279 full and part-time, 84% of full-time faculty have doctoral degrees. Student-faculty ratio: 10:1. 225 acre campus, 7 residence halls, Carlyle Campbell Library (156,703 volumes), music library, art galleries, research greenhouse, music practice rooms, 600-seat auditorium, theater, concert hall, student center, computer labs, child care lab, learning center, autism lab, astronomy observation deck, indoor swimming pool, fitness center, dance studio, lighted outdoor tennis courts, putting green, softball field and soccer field and basketball court.
   Moderate climate, convenient to beaches and mountains. Located in North Carolina's capital city of Raleigh. Excellent opportunities for co-ops and internships with local companies. Wide range of student activities including social and service clubs, religious organizations, class events, and traditional events.

Peace College
15 E Peace St, Raleigh NC 27604-1194
Laura C. Bingham, President
800-PEACE-47

SALEM COLLEGE
Winston Salem NC 27108-0548
Dana Evans, Dean of Admissions/Fin. Aid
800-32-SALEM Fax: 336-917-5572
Website: www.salem.edu
E-mail: admissions@salem.edu
   Established 1772. Moravian. Enrollment: 1,000. Comprehensive fee for boarding students: $26,226, day students: $16,975, plus $215 Student Government Association fee for boarding and day students. Four year, liberal arts, residential college for women conferring Bachelor of Arts, Bachelor of Science and Bachelor of Music degrees with majors in American studies, accounting, art, arts management, biology, business administration, chemistry, communication, economics, English, French, German, history, interior design, international business, international relations, mathematics, medical technology, music, music education, philosophy, psychology, religion, sociology, and Spanish. Teacher certification is offered in early childhood, ESL, middle grades, secondary and learning disabilities.
   Admissions: College recognizes that variations in school curricula, methods of teaching, and aptitudes of students make it difficult for any one pattern of entrance standards to be required. It is recommended that candidates present 16 academic units which include 4 in English, 2 in a foreign language, 2 in history, 3 in math, and 3 in science. SAT and/or ACT are required. Transfer students must have a 2.0 GPA. Committee on Admissions considers each application individually and bases its decision on the general excellence of the candidate's school record, test scores, extracurricular activities, and personal qualifications of the applicants. The College welcomes students of different racial, ethnic, religious, and geographic backgrounds.
   Financial Aid: Salem offers both need-based financial assistance and competitive, no-need scholarships. Every effort is made to assist as many students as funds will permit. Approximately 70% receive financial aid, which consists of a combination of grant, loan and/or work. The competitive scholarships range from $5,000-$16,975 per year.
   Accreditation: Southern Association of Colleges and Secondary Schools, National Association of Schools of Music, National Council for the Accreditation of Teacher Education; course in medical technology recognized by the American Medical Association and the American Society of Clinical Pathologists.

OHIO

Ursuline College
2550 Lander Rd, Cleveland OH 44124-4398
Sarah E. Sundermeier, Director of Admissions
888-URSULINE Toll Free Fax: 440-684-6138
Website: www.admission.ursuline.edu
E-mail: admission@ursuline.edu

PENNSYLVANIA

Bryn Mawr College
101 N Merion Ave, Bryn Mawr PA 19010-2899
610-526-5000

Carlow University
3333 5th Ave, Pittsburgh PA 15213-3165
412-578-6000

Cedar Crest College
100 College Dr, Allentown PA 18104-6196
Judith A. Neyhart, Vice President Enrollment
800-360-1222

Chatham College
Woodland Rd, Pittsburgh PA 15232-2826
412-365-1100

Moore College of Art and Design
20th & Race St, Philadelphia PA 19103-1178
215-568-4000

Rosemont College
1400 Montgomery Ave, Rosemont PA 19010-1699
Ms. Rennie Andrews, Director of Admissions
610-526-2966

Wilson College
1015 Philadelphia Ave
Chambersburg PA 17201-1285
717-264-4141

SOUTH CAROLINA

Columbia College
1301 Columbia College Dr, Columbia SC 29203-5998
Elizabeth G. Quackenbush, Director of Admissions
803-786-3871

Converse College
580 E Main St, Spartanburg SC 29302-0006
864-596-9000

TEXAS

Texas Woman's University
PO Box 425589, Denton TX 76204-5589
Erma Nieto, Director of Admissions
866-809-6130 Fax: 940-898-3081
Website: www.twu.edu
E-mail: admissions@twu.edu

VIRGINIA

Hollins University
PO Box 9707, Roanoke VA 24020
800-456-9595

Mary Baldwin College
Staunton VA 24401
Lisa A. Branson, Executive Director of Admissions and
Financial Aid
800-468-2262 Fax: 540-887-7292
Website: www.mbc.edu
E-mail: admit@mbc.edu

Randolph-Macon Woman's College
2500 Rivermont Ave, Lynchburg VA 24503
Patricia LeDonne, Director of Admissions
434-947-8100 Fax: 434-947-8996
Website: www.rmwc.edu
E-mail: admissions@rmwc.edu

Sweet Briar College
Sweet Briar VA 24595
804-381-6100

WISCONSIN

Alverno College
PO Box 343922, Milwaukee WI 53234-3922
Mary Kay Farrell, Director of Admissions
414-382-6100 Fax: 414-382-6354
Website: www.alverno.edu
E-mail: admissions@alverno.edu

Mount Mary College
2900 N Menomonee River Pkwy
Milwaukee WI 53222-4597
414-256-1219

WOMEN'S STUDIES

ALABAMA

University of Alabama in Huntsville
PO Box 1247, Huntsville AL 35899-0001
Ann Lee, Assoc. Director for Recruiting Program and
Events
1-800-UAH-CALL Fax: 256-824-6073
Website: www.uah.edu
E-mail: leev@uah.edu

ALASKA

University of Alaska Anchorage
PO Box 141629, Anchorage AK 99514-1629
Cecile Mitchell, Director of Enrollment Services
907-786-1480 Fax: 907-786-4888
Website: www.uaa.alaska.edu/
E-mail: enroll@uaa.alaska.edu

ARIZONA

University of Arizona
Tucson AZ 85721-0040
Paul Kohn, Director of Admissions
520-621-3237 Fax: 520-621-9799
Website: www.admissions.arizona.edu or
www.arizona.edu

FLORIDA

Florida State University
600 W College Ave, Tallahassee FL 32306-1096
Janice V. Finney, Director of Admissions
850-644-2525 Fax: 850-644-0197
Website: admissions.fsu.edu
E-mail: admissions@admin.fsu.edu

University of South Florida
4202 E Fowler Ave, Tampa FL 33620-6900
J. Robert Spatig, Director of Admissions
813-974-3350 Fax: 813-974-9689
Website: www.usf.edu
E-mail: admissions@admin.usf.edu

ILLINOIS

Roosevelt University
430 S Michigan Ave, Chicago IL 60605
Gwen E. Kanelos, Asst. Vice President for Enrollment
Services
877-APPLY-RU Fax: 312-341-4216
Website: www.roosevelt.edu
E-mail: applyru@roosevelt.edu

MASSACHUSETTS

Boston University
121 Bay State Rd, Boston MA 02215
Kelly Walter, Executive Director of Admissions
617-353-2300 Fax: 617-353-9695
Website: web.bu.edu
E-mail: admissions@bu.edu

University of Massachusetts Dartmouth
Old Westport Rd, North Dartmouth MA 02747-2300
Jeanette Riley, Assistant Professor
508-999-8279 Fax: 508-999-8621
Website: explore.umassd.edu
E-mail: jlriley@umassd.edu

MICHIGAN

University of Michigan-Dearborn
4901 Evergreen Rd, Dearborn MI 48128-1491
The Office of Admissions & Orientation
313-593-5100 Fax: 313-436-9167
Website: www.umd.umich.edu
E-mail: admissions@umd.umich.edu

MINNESOTA

Carleton College
1 N College St, Northfield MN 55057-4044
800-995-2275 or 507-646-4190 Fax: 507-646-4526
Website: www.carleton.edu
E-mail: admissions@acs.carleton.edu

Pillsbury Baptist Bible College
315 S Grove Ave, Owatonna MN 55060-3097
Stephen R. Seidler, Director of Admissions
507-451-2710 Fax: 507-451-0156
Website: www.pillsbury.edu
E-mail: steveseidler@pillsbury.edu

MISSOURI

Columbia College
1001 Rogers St, Columbia MO 65216-0001
Regina Morin, Director of Admissions
573-875-7352 Fax: 573-875-7506
Website: www.ccis.edu
E-mail: admissions@ccis.edu

University of Missouri
1 University Blvd, Saint Louis MO 63121-4499
Dr. Mark Burkholder, Dean-College of Arts & Sciences
314-516-5501 Fax: 314-516-5415
Website: www.umsl.edu
E-mail: admissions@umsl.edu

NEBRASKA

Nebraska Wesleyan University
5000 Saint Paul Ave, Lincoln NE 68504-2794
Patricia Karthauser, V.P. for University Enrollment
402-466-2371 Fax: 402-465-2177
Website: www.nebrwesleyan.edu
E-mail: admissions@nebrwesleyan.edu

NEW JERSEY

New Jersey City University
2039 John F Kennedy Blvd
Jersey City NJ 07305-1588
Carmen Panlilio, Asst. V.P. for Admissions and
Financial Aid
201-200-3234 Fax: 201-200-2044
Website: www.njcu.edu
E-mail: admissions@njcu.edu

NEW YORK

College of Saint Rose
432 Western Ave, Albany NY 12203-1419
Maryelizabeth Amico, Asst V.P. for Undergraduate
Admissions
518-454-5150 Fax: 518-454-2013
Website: www.strose.edu
E-mail: admit@strose.edu

CUNY Hunter College
695 Park Ave, New York NY 10021
Aaron Gibbs, Assistant Director of Recruitment
212-772-4497 Fax: 212-650-3336
Website: www.hunter.cuny.edu
E-mail: aaron.gibbs@hunter.cuny.edu

PURCHASE COLLEGE STATE UNIVERSITY OF NEW YORK (SUNY)

735 Anderson Hill Rd, Purchase NY 10577-1400
Betsy Immergut, Director of Admissions
914-251-6300 Fax: 914-251-6314
Website: www.purchase.edu
See listing under "Universities"

SUNY College at Brockport
350 New Campus Dr, Brockport NY 14420-2997
Bernard S. Valento, Director of Undergraduate
Admissions
585-395-2751 Fax: 585-395-5452
Website: www.brockport.edu
E-mail: admit@brockport.edu

Wells College
PO Box 500, Aurora NY 13026
Susan Sloan, Director of Admissions
800-952-9355 Fax: 315-364-3227
Website: www.wells.edu
E-mail: ssloan@wells.edu

NORTH CAROLINA

Meredith College
3800 Hillsborough St, Raleigh NC 27607-5298
Heidi L. Fletcher, Director of Admissions
919-760-8581 Fax: 919-760-2348
Website: www.meredith.edu
E-mail: admissions@meredith.edu
See listing under "Women's Colleges"

Salem College
Winston Salem NC 27108
Dana Evans, Dean of Admissions/Fin. Aid
800-32-SALEM Fax: 336-917-5572
Website: www.salem.edu
E-mail: admissions@salem.edu
See listing under "Women's Colleges"

OHIO

The Ohio State University
Department of Women's Studies
286 University Hall, 230 N Oval Mall
Columbus OH 43210
614-292-1021 Fax: 614-292-0276
Website: womens-studies.osu.edu
E-mail: womstd.info@osu.edu

University of Dayton
300 College Park, Dayton OH 45469-1300
Robert F. Durkle, Director of Admissions
800-837-7433 Fax: 937-229-4729
Website: admission.udayton.edu
E-mail: admission@udayton.edu

PENNSYLVANIA

MOUNT ALOYSIUS COLLEGE

7373 Admiral Peary Hwy, Cresson PA 16630-1999
Frank C. Crouse Jr., Vice President for Enrollment
Management
814-886-6383 or 888-823-2220 Fax: 814-886-6441
Website: www.mtaloy.edu
E-mail: admissions@mtaloy.edu

TEXAS

Texas Woman's University
PO Box 425589, Denton TX 76204-5589
Erma Nieto, Director of Admissions
866-809-6130 Fax: 940-898-3081
Website: www.twu.edu
E-mail: admissions@twu.edu

University of Houston
122 E Cullen Bldg, Houston TX 77204-2023
Office of Admission
713-743-9595
Website: www.uh.edu
E-mail: admissions@uh.edu

VERMONT

Bennington College
One College Drive, Bennington VT 05201
Ken Himmelman, Dean of Admissions & Financial Aid
800-833-6845 Fax: 802-440-4320
Website: www.bennington.edu
E-mail: admissions@bennington.edu

VIRGINIA

Radford University
PO Box 6903, Radford VA 24142
David W. Kraus, Director of Admissions
800-890-4265 Fax: 540-831-5038
Website: www.radford.edu
E-mail: ruadmiss@radford.edu

WASHINGTON

Gonzaga University
502 E Boone Ave, Spokane WA 99258-0102
Julie McCulloh, Dean of Admission
800-322-2584 or 509-323-6572 Fax: 509-323-5780
Website: www.gonzaga.edu
E-mail: mcculloh@gu.gonzaga.edu

WYOMING

University of Wyoming
Admissions Office
Dept 3435, Laramie WY 82071-3435
Aaron Appelhans, Contact
800-342-5996 Fax: 307-766-4042
Website: www.uwyo.edu
E-mail: why-wyo@uwyo.edu

INDEX

Explanation

Schools are listed alphabetically. Each entry has the school name, state abbreviation and a three letter classification code. For example Aaker's Business College, ND (TCT) is found in the **Career Schools** "(TCT)" classification in the state of North Dakota "ND".

Classification codes and their corresponding classifications:

(AAT)	Aeronautics, Aviation and Space	(MED)	Medicine
(AGR)	Agriculture	(MIL)	Military Science
(AHS)	Allied Health Science	(MKD)	Marketing and Distribution
(ARC)	Architecture	(MNC)	Men's Colleges
(ART)	Art	(MTH)	Mathematics
(BIO)	Biological Science	(MUS)	Music
(BKS)	Ethnic Studies	(NRS)	Nursing
(BUS)	Business and Management	(OPT)	Optometry
(CPC)	Chiropractic Medicine	(OST)	Osteopathic Medicine
(CTS)	Construction Trades	(PBH)	Public Health
(DNT)	Dentistry	(PHR)	Pharmacy
(EGN)	Engineering	(PHS)	Physical Science
(EGT)	Engineering Technology	(PHT)	Photography
(EMB)	Personal and Miscellaneous Services	(POD)	Podiatric Medicine
(FRS)	Conservation/Renewable Natural Resources	(PPT)	Precision Production Trades
		(PRB)	Preparatory Schools for Boys
		(PRC)	Preparatory Schools Coeducational
(FSA)	Fashion Art	(PRG)	Preparatory Schools for Girls
(GRD)	Graduate Schools	(PSY)	Psychology
(HME)	Home Economics	(PTS)	Protective Services
(HMS)	Home Study and Correspondence	(SCT)	Business - Administrative Support
(HND)	Handicapped, Schools for the	(SCW)	Social Science
(IFS)	Computer and Information Science	(SPD)	Speech and Drama
(INT)	Interior Design	(SSS)	Summer Sessions
(JRC)	Community and Junior Colleges	(STA)	Study Abroad
(JRN)	Communications	(TCT)	Career Schools
(LAS)	Liberal Arts and Sciences	(TED)	Teacher Education
(LAW)	Law	(TSR)	Theological & Religious Vocations
(LBS)	Library Science		
(LND)	Landscape Architecture	(UNC)	Universities and Colleges
(LTR)	Letters	(VET)	Veterinary Medicine
(MBA)	Master of Business Administration	(WMC)	Women's Colleges
(MCR)	Mechanics and Repairers	(WMS)	Women's Studies

A

Aakers College, ND (TCT)
Aaron's Academy of Beauty, MD (TCT)
Abbott Acad of Cosmetology Arts/Sciences, MO (TCT)
Abdill Career College, OR (TCT)
ABI - AccuTech Business Institute, MD (TCT)
Abilene Christian University, TX (UNC)
Abington Memorial Hospital, PA (AHS)
Abraham Baldwin Agriculture College, GA (JRC)
Academia Maison D'Esthetique, PR (TCT)
Academia Serrant, PR (TCT)
Academia Vocacional Del Turabo, PR (TCT)
Academy at Charlemont, MA (PRC)
Academy College, MN (TCT)
Academy Education Services, CA (TCT)
Academy for Five Element Acupuncture, FL (GRD)
Academy for Practical Nursing/Health Occ, FL (TCT)
Academy of Art University, CA (ARC)
Academy of Beauty Arts, TN (TCT)
Academy of Beauty Culture, CO (TCT)
Academy of Chinese Culture & Health Sci., CA (GRD)
Academy of Cosmetology, MT (TCT)
Academy of Cosmetology, OK (TCT)
Academy of Cosmetology, SC (TCT)
Academy of Court Reporting, MI (TCT)
Academy of Court Reporting, OH (TCT)
Academy of Creative Hair Design, LA (TCT)
Academy of Creative Hair Design, PA (TCT)
Academy of Hair Design, KS (TCT)
Academy of Hair Design, NV (TCT)
Academy of Hair Design, OR (TCT)
Academy of Hair Design, PA (TCT)
Academy of Hair Design, TX (TCT)
Academy of Hair Design, WA (TCT)
Academy of Hair Design #1, MS (TCT)
Academy of Hair Design #3, MS (TCT)
Academy of Hair Design #4, MS (TCT)
Academy of Hair Design #6, MS (TCT)
Academy of Hair Design #7, MS (TCT)
Academy of Hair Technology, SC (TCT)
Academy of Healing Arts Massage, FL (TCT)
Academy of Massage Therapy, NJ (TCT)
Academy of Medical Arts and Business, PA (TCT)
Academy of Oriental Medicine at Austin, TX (GRD)
Academy of Our Lady of Guam, GU (PRG)
Academy of the Holy Family, CT (PRG)
Academy of the New Church Boys School, PA (PRB)
Academy of the New Church Girls School, PA (PRG)
Academy of the Sacred Heart, LA (PRG)
Academy Pacific Travel College, CA (TCT)
Accelerated Schools Foundation, CO (PRC)
Accotink Academy, VA (HND)
Aces-Full Academy for Casino Dealers, NV (TCT)
ACT College, VA (TCT)
Acupuncture & Massage College, FL (GRD)
Acupuncture & Integrative Medicine Coll., CA (GRD)
A Cut Above Beauty College, IN (TCT)
Adams State College, CO (UNC)
Adcon Technical Institute, CA (TCT)
Adelphi University, NY (UNC)
Adirondack Beauty School, NY (TCT)
Adler Graduate School, MN (GRD)
Adler School of Professional Psychology, IL (GRD)
Admiral Farragut Academy, FL (PRC)
Adrian College, MI (UNC)
Adrian's Beauty College of Turlock, CA (TCT)
Advanced/Basic Hair Design Training Ctr, FL (TCT)
Advanced Barber College and Hair Design, TX (TCT)
Advanced College, CA (TCT)
Advanced Software Analysis, NY (TCT)
Advanced Technology Institute, VA (TCT)
Advanced Training Associates, CA (TCT)
Advance Science Institute, FL (TCT)
Advance Tech College, PR (TCT)
Adventist HealthCare Health Careers Ctr, MD (TCT)
Advocate Illinois Masonic, IL (TCT)
Advocate Trinity Hospital, IL (TCT)
Aesthetics Institutes of Cosmetology, MD (TCT)
Agnes Scott College, GA (WMC)
Aguadilla Technical College, PR (TCT)
AIB College of Business, IA (JRC)
Aiken Preparatory School, SC (PRC)
Aiken Technical College, SC (JRC)
Ailano School of Aesthetics, MA (TCT)
Ailano School of Cosmetology, MA (TCT)
AIMS Academy, TX (TCT)
Aims Community College, CO (JRC)
Airman Proficiency Center, OR (TCT)
Akron General Medical Center, OH (AHS)
Akron Institute, OH (TCT)
Akron Machining Institute, OH (TCT)
AKS Massage School, VA (TCT)
Alabama A & M University, AL (UNC)
Alabama Institute for the Deaf and Blind, AL (HND)
Alabama Southern Community College, AL (JRC)
Alabama State College of Barber Styling, AL (TCT)
Alabama State University, AL (UNC)
Aladdin Beauty College, NM (TCT)
Alamance Community College, NC (JRC)
Alameda Beauty College, CA (TCT)
Alaska Bible College, AK (UNC)
Alaska Pacific University, AK (UNC)
Alaska Vocational Technical School, AK (TCT)
Albany College of Pharmacy, NY (AHS)
Albany Law School of Union University, NY (GRD)
Albany State University, GA (UNC)
Albany Technical College, GA (TCT)
Albert Einstein Medical Center, PA (AHS)
Albertson College of Idaho, ID (UNC)
Albertus Magnus College, CT (UNC)
Albion College, MI (UNC)
Albright College, PA (UNC)
Albuquerque Barber College, NM (TCT)
Albuquerque TVI Community College, NM (TCT)
Alcorn State University, MS (UNC)
Alderson-Broaddus College, WV (UNC)
Alexandria Academy of Beauty, LA (TCT)
Alexandria Technical College, MN (JRC)
Alfred G. Glassell School of Art, TX (TCT)
Alfred University, NY (UNC)
Alfred Univ.-NY State Coll. of Ceramics, NY (UNC)
Alhambra Beauty College, CA (TCT)
Alice Lloyd College, KY (UNC)
Allan Hancock College, CA (JRC)
Allegany College of Maryland, MD (JRC)
Allegheny College, PA (UNC)
Allegheny Valley Hospital, PA (AHS)
Allegheny Wesleyan College, OH (UNC)
Allen Academy, TX (PRC)
Allen College, IA (TCT)
Allen County Community College, KS (JRC)
Allen Inst. Ctr. for Innovative Learning, CT (UNC)
Allen School, NY (TCT)
Allentown School of Cosmetology, PA (TCT)
Allen University, SC (UNC)
Alliance Theological Seminary, NY (TSR)
Alliant International University, CA (GRD)
Allied Business School, CA (HMS)
Allied College - North, MO (TCT)
Allied College - South, MO (TCT)
Allied Health Careers, TX (TCT)
Allied Medical & Technical Careers, PA (TCT)
Allied Medical & Technical Institute, PA (JRC)
All Saints' Episcopal School, MS (PRC)
All Saints Healthcare System, WI (AHS)
All-State Career School, MD (TCT)
All-State Career School, PA (TCT)
Alma College, MI (UNC)
Alpena Community College, MI (JRC)
Altamaha Technical College, GA (TCT)
Altoona Beauty School, PA (TCT)
Altoona Hospital, PA (AHS)
Alvareita's College of Cosmetology, IL (TCT)
Alvernia College, PA (UNC)
Alverno College, WI (UNC)
Alvin Community College, TX (JRC)
Amarillo College, TX (JRC)
Amarillo College of Hairdressing, TX (TCT)
Amberton University, TX (UNC)
Ambler Beauty Academy, PA (TCT)
Americana Beauty College II, CO (TCT)
American Academy McAllister Institute, NY (JRC)
American Academy of Acupuncture, MN (TCT)
American Academy of Art, IL (ART)
American Academy of Cosmetology, CT (TCT)
American Academy of Dramatic Arts, CA (TCT)
American Academy of Dramatic Arts, NY (TCT)
American Academy of Hair Design, KS (TCT)
American Baptist College, TN (UNC)
American Baptist Seminary of the West, CA (GRD)
American Barber Institute, NY (TCT)
American Beauty Academy, MD (TCT)
American Beauty Academy, PA (TCT)
American Beauty College, CA (TCT)
The American Boychoir School, NJ (PRB)
American Business Academy, NJ (TCT)
American Business College, PR (TCT)
American Business College of Puerto Rico, PR (TCT)
American Career College, CA (TCT)
American Career Institute, NV (HMS)
American College, PA (GRD)
American College of Acupuncture, TX (GRD)
American College of California, CA (TCT)
American College of Hair Design, MO (TCT)
American College of Hairstyling, IA (TCT)
American College of Health Professions, CA (TCT)
American College of Medical Technology, CA (TCT)
American Coll of Traditional Chinese Med, CA (GRD)
American Commercial College, TX (TCT)
American Conservatory Theater, CA (GRD)
American Educational College, PR (TCT)
American Film Institute, CA (ART)
American Floral Art School, IL (TCT)
American Graduate University, CA (GRD)
American Health Information Management, IL (HMS)
American Health Science University, CO (HMS)
American Indian Coll of Assemblies/God, AZ (UNC)
American Inst. of Alternative Medicine, OH (TCT)
American Institute of Applied Science, NC (HMS)
American Institute of Baking, KS (TCT)
American Institute of Health Science, CA (UNC)
American Inst. of Medical-Dental Tech., UT (TCT)
American Institute of Technology, AZ (TCT)
American Institute of Technology, NV (TCT)
American InterContinental University, CA (UNC)
American InterContinental University, FL (UNC)
American InterContinental University, GA (UNC)
American Intercontinental Univ Online, IL (UNC)
American International College, MA (UNC)
American Military Academy, PR (PRC)
American Military University, VA (UNC)
American Professional Institute, AR (TCT)
American Professional Institute, GA (TCT)
American Public University, WV (HMS)
American Red Cross Blood Services, GA (AHS)
American River College, CA (JRC)
American Samoa Community College, AS (JRC)
American School, IL (HMS)
American School for the Deaf, CT (HND)
American School of Business, LA (TCT)
American School of Technology, OH (TCT)
American Sentinel University, AL (HMS)
American Technological College, PR (TCT)
American University, DC (UNC)
American University in Cairo, NY (UNC)
American University of Paris, CO (UNC)
American University of Puerto Rico, PR (UNC)
Americare School of Nursing, FL (TCT)
Ameritech College, UT (TCT)
Amherst College, MA (UNC)
Ancilla Domini College, IN (JRC)
Anderson College, SC (UNC)
Anderson County Beauty College, TX (TCT)
Anderson Memorial Hospital, SC (AHS)
Anderson University, IN (UNC)
Andover College, ME (JRC)
Andover Newton Theological School, MA (GRD)
Andrew College, GA (JRC)
Andrew Jackson University, AL (HMS)
Andrews School, OH (PRG)
Andrews University, MI (UNC)
A New Beginning School of Massage, TX (TCT)
Angelina College, TX (JRC)
Angelo State University, TX (UNC)
Anna Maria College, MA (UNC)
Anne Arundel Community College, MD (JRC)
Annie Wright School, WA (PRG)
Anoka-Ramsey Community College, MN (JRC)
Anoka Technical College, MN (JRC)
Anson College of Cosmetology, NC (TCT)
Antelope Valley College, CA (JRC)
Antilles School of Technical Careers, PR (TCT)
Antioch College, OH (UNC)
Antioch University, CA (UNC)
Antioch University, WA (UNC)
Antioch University McGregor, OH (UNC)
Antioch University New England, NH (GRD)
Antioch University Southern California, CA (UNC)
Antonelli College, MS (TCT)
Antonelli College, OH (TCT)
Antonelli Institute - Art & Photography, PA (JRC)
Antonelli Medical & Professional Inst, PA (TCT)
Apex School of Beauty Culture, IN (TCT)
Apex School of Theology, NC (UNC)
Apex Technical School, NY (TCT)
Apollo College, AZ (UNC)
Apollo College, NM (UNC)
Apollo College, OR (UNC)
Apollo College, WA (UNC)
Apollo College Boise, ID (TCT)
Appalachian Bible College, WV (UNC)
Appalachian School of Law, VA (UNC)
Appalachian State University, NC (UNC)
Appalachian Technical College, GA (TCT)
Applied Professional Training, CA (HMS)
Apprentice Sch. - Northrop Grumman, VA (TCT)
Aquinas College, MI (UNC)
Aquinas College, TN (UNC)
Aquinas Institute of Theology, MO (GRD)
ARAMARK Healthcare Support Services, PA (AHS)
ARAMARK Healthcare Support Services SW, MO (AHS)
Arapahoe Community College, CO (JRC)
Arcadia University, PA (UNC)
Archmere Academy, DE (PRC)
Argosy University/Atlanta, GA (GRD)
Argosy University/Chicago, IL (GRD)
Argosy University/Chicago Northwest, IL (GRD)
Argosy University/Dallas, TX (UNC)
Argosy University/Hawaii, HI (GRD)
Argosy University/Orange County, CA (GRD)
Argosy University/Phoenix, AZ (GRD)
Argosy University/Sarasota, FL (UNC)
Argosy University/Seattle, WA (GRD)
Argosy University/Tampa, FL (GRD)
Argosy University/Twin Cities, MN (UNC)
Argosy University/Washington DC, VA (GRD)
Argosy University/San Francisco Campus, CA (UNC)
Ari Ben Aviator, FL (TCT)
Arizona Academy of Beauty, AZ (TCT)
Arizona Academy of Beauty - North, AZ (TCT)
Arizona Automotive Institute, AZ (TCT)
Arizona College of Allied Health, AZ (TCT)
Arizona Sch of Dentistry & Oral Health, AZ (DNT)
Arizona School of Health Sciences, AZ (GRD)
AZ State School for the Deaf & Blind, AZ (HND)
Arizona State University, AZ (UNC)
Arizona State University Polytechnic, AZ (UNC)
Arizona State University West, AZ (UNC)
Arizona Western College, AZ (JRC)
Arkadelphia Beauty College, AR (TCT)
Arkansas Aviation Technologies Center, AR (TCT)
Arkansas Baptist College, AR (UNC)
Arkansas Beauty School, AR (TCT)
Arkansas Beauty School - Conway, AR (TCT)
Arkansas Career Training Institute, AR (TCT)
AR College of Barbering & Hair Design, AR (TCT)
Arkansas Northeastern College, AR (JRC)
Arkansas School for the Blind, AR (HND)
Arkansas School for the Deaf, AR (HND)
Arkansas State University, AR (UNC)
Arkansas State University - Beebe, AR (JRC)
Arkansas State University Mountain Home, AR (UNC)
Arkansas State University - Newport, AR (JRC)
Arkansas State University Searcy Campus, AR (TCT)
Arkansas Tech University, AR (UNC)
Arkansas Valley Technical Institute, AR (TCT)
Arlington Baptist College, TX (UNC)
Arlington Career Institute, TX (TCT)
Arlington Medical Institute, TX (TCT)
Armstrong Atlantic State University, GA (UNC)
Armstrong County Memorial Hospital, PA (AHS)
Armstrong University, CA (UNC)
Army and Navy Academy, CA (PRB)
Arnold/Padrick's Univ of Cosmetology, GA (TCT)
Arnold's Beauty School, TN (TCT)
Arnot-Ogden Medical Center, NY (TCT)
Arrowhead Regional Medical Center, CA (TCT)
Art Academy of Cincinnati, OH (ART)
Art Center College of Design, CA (ART)
The Art Center Design College, AZ (ART)
The Art Center Design College, NM (ART)
Angelo School of Cosmetology Hair Design, RI (TCT)
Arthur James Cancer Hospital, OH (AHS)
Arthur's Beauty College, AR (TCT)
Art Institute of Atlanta, GA (UNC)
The Art Inst. of Boston at Lesley Univ., MA (UNC)
Art Institute of California, CA (TCT)
Art Institute of CA Inland Empire, CA (UNC)
Art Institute of California, CA (ART)
Art Institute of California, CA (TCT)
Art Institute of California - San Fran, CA (UNC)
Art Institute of Charlotte, NC (TCT)

Art Institute of Cincinnati, OH (ART)
Art Institute of Colorado, CO (UNC)
Art Institute of Dallas, TX (TCT)
Art Institute of Fort Lauderdale, FL (TCT)
Art Institute of Houston, TX (JRC)
Art Institute of Houston - Culinary, TX (TCT)
Art Institute of Indianapolis, IN (UNC)
Art Institute of Las Vegas, NV (UNC)
Art Institute of New York City, NY (TCT)
Art Institute of Ohio - Cincinnati, OH (UNC)
Art Institute of Philadelphia, PA (UNC)
Art Institute of Phoenix, AZ (TCT)
Art Institute of Pittsburgh, PA (UNC)
Art Institute of Portland, OR (UNC)
Art Institute of Seattle, WA (TCT)
Art Institute of Tampa, FL (UNC)
Art Institute of Washington, VA (UNC)
Art Institutes International Minnesota, MN (JRC)
Art Instruction Schools, MN (HMS)
Artistic Academy of Hair Design, NJ (TCT)
Artistic Beauty College, AZ (TCT)
Artistic Beauty College, CO (TCT)
Asbury College, KY (UNC)
Asbury Theological Seminary, FL (UNC)
Asbury Theological Seminary, KY (GRD)
Ascension College, LA (TCT)
Asheville Buncombe Technical Comm. Coll., NC (JRC)
Asheville School, NC (PRC)
Ashland Community and Technical College, KY (JRC)
Ashland County-West Holmes Career Center, OH (TCT)
Ashland Theological Seminary, OH (GRD)
Ashland University, OH (UNC)
Ashworth College, GA (HMS)
Asian American Intl Beauty College, CA (TCT)
Asian Institute of Medical Studies, AZ (GRD)
ASM Beauty World Academy, FL (TCT)
Asnuntuck Community College, CT (JRC)
Aspen University, CO (HMS)
Assemblies of God Theological Seminary, MO (GRD)
Associated Mennonite Biblical Seminaries, IN (GRD)
Associated Pathologist Laboratories, NV (AHS)
Associated Technical College, CA (TCT)
Assumption College, MA (UNC)
Assumption College for Sisters, NJ (JRC)
Astoria Beauty College, OR (TCT)
Astrodome Dental Career Center, TX (TCT)
Athenaeum of Ohio, OH (UNC)
Athenian School, CA (PRC)
Athens State University, AL (UNC)
Athens Technical College, GA (JRC)
ATI Career Training Center, FL (TCT)
ATI Career Training Center, TX (TCT)
ATI College of Health, FL (JRC)
ATI Health Education Center, TX (AHS)
ATI Technical Training Center, TX (TCT)
Atlanta Area School for the Deaf, GA (HND)
Atlanta Christian College, GA (UNC)
Atlanta Institute of Music, GA (JRC)
Atlanta Job Corps Center, GA (TCT)
Atlanta Medical Center, GA (TCT)
Atlanta Metro College, GA (JRC)
Atlanta School of Massage, GA (TCT)
Atlanta Technical College, GA (TCT)
Atlantic Cape Community College, NJ (JRC)
Atlantic College, PR (UNC)
Atlantic Co. Vocational Technical School, NJ (AHS)
Atlantic Institute of Oriental Medicine, FL (GRD)
Atlantic Technical Center, FL (TCT)
Atlantic Union College, MA (UNC)
Atlantic University, VA (HMS)
Atlantic University of Chinese Medicine, NC (GRD)
ATS Institute of Technology, OH (TCT)
Auburn Adventist Academy, WA (PRC)
Auburn University, AL (UNC)
Auburn University at Montgomery, AL (UNC)
Audio Recording Technology Institute, FL (TCT)
Augsburg College, MN (UNC)
Augusta Medical Center, VA (TCT)
Augustana College, IL (UNC)
Augustana College, SD (UNC)
Augusta State University, GA (UNC)
Augusta Technical College, GA (JRC)
Aultman Hospital, OH (AHS)
Aurora Health Care, WI (TCT)
Aurora University, IL (UNC)
Austin Beauty School, NY (TCT)
Austin Business College, TX (TCT)
Austin College, TX (UNC)
Austin Community College, TX (JRC)
Austine School for the Deaf, VT (HND)
Austin Graduate School of Theology, TX (UNC)
Austin Peay State University, TN (UNC)
Austin Presbyterian Theological Seminary, TX (GRD)
Australasian College of Health Sciences, OR (HMS)
Automotive Training Center, PA (TCT)
Avalon Beauty College, CA (TCT)
Avance Beauty College, CA (TCT)
Aveda Institute, LA (TCT)
Aveda Institute, MN (TCT)
Aveda Institute, TX (TCT)
Ave Maria College, MI (UNC)
Ave Maria University, FL (UNC)
Averett University, VA (UNC)
Aviation & Electronic School of America, CA (TCT)
Aviation Institute of Maintenance, GA (TCT)
Aviation Institute of Maintenance, IN (TCT)
Aviation Institute of Maintenance, MO (TCT)
Aviation Institute of Maintenance, PA (TCT)
Aviation Institute of Maintenance, TX (TCT)
Aviation Institute of Maintenance, VA (TCT)
Avila University, MO (UNC)
Avon Old Farms School, CT (PRB)
Award Beauty School, MD (TCT)
Ayers Institute, LA (TCT)
AZ School of Acupuncture & Oriental Med, AZ (GRD)
Azusa Pacific University, CA (UNC)

B

Babel University Professional School, HI (HMS)
Babson College, MA (UNC)
Bacone College, OK (UNC)
Bahner College of Hairstyling, NE (TCT)
Bainbridge College, GA (JRC)
Baker College of Auburn Hills, MI (UNC)
Baker College of Cadillac, MI (UNC)
Baker College of Clinton Township, MI (UNC)
Baker College of Flint, MI (UNC)
Baker College of Jackson, MI (UNC)
Baker College of Muskegon, MI (UNC)
Baker College of Owosso, MI (UNC)
Baker College of Port Huron, MI (UNC)
Bakersfield College, CA (JRC)
Baker University, KS (UNC)
Baker University School of Nursing, KS (UNC)
Bakke Graduate University of Ministry, WA (GRD)
Baldwin Beauty School #5, TX (TCT)
Baldwin Beauty School - North, TX (TCT)
Baldwin-Wallace College, OH (UNC)
Ball Memorial Hospital, IN (TCT)
Ball State University, IN (UNC)
Baltimore City Community College, MD (JRC)
Baltimore Hebrew University, MD (UNC)
Baltimore International College, MD (UNC)
Baltimore School of Massage, MD (TCT)
Baltimore School of Massage-York Campus, PA (TCT)
Baltimore Studio of Hair Design, MD (TCT)
Bamberg Job Corps Center, SC (TCT)
Bancroft School of Massage Therapy, MA (TCT)
Bangor Theological Seminary, ME (GRD)
Bank Street College of Education, NY (GRD)
Baptist/St. Vincent's Health System, FL (TCT)
Baptist Bible College, MO (UNC)
Baptist Bible College and Seminary, PA (UNC)
The Baptist College of Florida, FL (UNC)
Baptist Health System, AL (TCT)
Baptist Health System, TX (AHS)
Baptist Hospital, TX (AHS)
Baptist Hospital of Southeast Texas, TX (AHS)
Baptist Medical Center, AL (TCT)
Baptist Medical Center, SC (AHS)
Baptist Medical Centers, FL (TCT)
Baptist Memorial Coll. of Health Science, TN (UNC)
Baptist Memorial Hospital, TN (AHS)
Baptist Missionary Theological Seminary, TX (GRD)
Baptist School of Nursing-NW, AR (NRS)
Baptist School of Nursing-SE, AR (NRS)
Baptist Schools of Allied Health, AR (TCT)
Baptist Theological Seminary, VA (GRD)
Baptist University of the Americas, TX (UNC)
Baran Institute of Technology, CT (TCT)
Barber-Scotia College, NC (UNC)
Barclay College, KS (UNC)
Bard College, NY (UNC)
Barnard College, NY (WMC)
Barnes-Jewish College of Nursing, MO (NRS)
BarPalma Beauty Careers Academy, VA (TCT)
Barrett & Company School of Hair Design, KY (TCT)
Barry University, FL (UNC)
Barstow Community College, CA (JRC)
Barton College, NC (UNC)
Barton County Community College, KS (JRC)
Bass Memorial Academy, MS (PRC)
Bastrop Beauty School #1, LA (TCT)
Bastyr University, WA (GRD)
Bates College, ME (UNC)
Bates Technical College, WA (TCT)
Batesville Job Corps Center, MS (TCT)
Baton Rouge Community College, LA (JRC)
Baton Rouge General Medical Center, LA (AHS)
Baton Rouge School of Computers, LA (TCT)
Bauder College, GA (JRC)
Bayamon Central University, PR (UNC)
Bayamon Community College, PR (TCT)
Bay de Noc Community College, MI (JRC)
Bayfront Medical Center, FL (TCT)
Bayhealth Medical Center, DE (AHS)
Baylor College of Medicine, TX (GRD)
Baylor School, TN (PRC)
Baylor University, TX (UNC)
Baylor University Medical Center, TX (GRD)
Bay Medical Center, FL (GRD)
Bay Mills Community College, MI (JRC)
Bayonne Hospital School of Nursing, NJ (NRS)
Bay Path College, MA (WMC)
Bayshire Beauty Academy, MI (TCT)
Bay State College, MA (AHS)
Bay State College, MA (UNC)
Bay State School of Technology, MA (TCT)
Bay Vista College of Beauty, CA (TCT)
Beacon College, FL (UNC)
Beacon University, GA (UNC)
Beal College, ME (JRC)
Beatrice Academy of Beauty, OH (TCT)
Beaufort County Community College, NC (JRC)
Beau La Reine College of Beauty Culture, UT (TCT)
Beau Monde College Acad of Cosmetology, OR (TCT)
Beau Monde College of Hair Design, OR (TCT)
Beauty and Barber Academy, FL (TCT)
Beauty College of America, GA (TCT)
The Beauty Institute, TN (TCT)
Beauty School of Middletown, NY (TCT)
Beauty Schools of America, FL (TCT)
Beauty Technical College, OK (TCT)
Beaver Falls Beauty Academy, PA (TCT)
Becker College, MA (UNC)
Beckfield College, KY (TCT)
Beckley Beauty Academy, WV (TCT)
Beebe Medical Center School of Nursing, DE (TCT)
Bee-Jay's Hairstyling Academy, AR (TCT)
Behold! Beauty Academy, TX (TCT)
Beis Medrash Heichal Dovid, NY (MNC)
Belhaven College, MS (UNC)
Bellarmine University, KY (UNC)
Bellevue Community College, WA (JRC)
Bellevue Hospital Center, NY (AHS)
Bellevue University, NE (UNC)
Bellin College of Nursing, WI (UNC)
Bellingham Beauty School, WA (TCT)
Bellingham Technical College, WA (TCT)
Bellin Hospital, WI (TCT)
Bellvue Beauty School, WA (TCT)
Belmont Abbey College, NC (UNC)
Belmont Hill School, MA (PRB)
Belmont Technical College, OH (JRC)
Belmont University, TN (UNC)
Beloit College, WI (UNC)
Bel-Rea Institute of Animal Technology, CO (TCT)
The Bement School, MA (PRC)
Bemidji State University, MN (UNC)
Benedict College, SC (UNC)
Benedictine College, KS (UNC)
Benedictine University, IL (UNC)
Benefits Health Care-West Campus, MT (AHS)
Benes International School of Beauty, FL (TCT)
Benjamin Franklin Inst. of Technology, MA (JRC)
Ben Lippen School, SC (PRC)
Bennett Beauty Institute, DC (TCT)
Bennett College, NC (WMC)
Bennington College, VT (UNC)
Ben Taub Hospital, TX (AHS)
Bentley College, MA (UNC)
Berdan Institute, NJ (TCT)
Berea College, KY (UNC)
Berean Institute, PA (TCT)
Bergen Community College, NJ (JRC)
Berkeley City College, CA (JRC)
Berkeley College, NJ (JRC)
Berkeley College, NJ (UNC)
Berkeley College - Westchester Campus, NY (UNC)
Berkeley Divinity School, CT (GRD)
Berklee College of Music, MA (UNC)
Berkshire Community College, MA (JRC)
Berkshire Medical Center, MA (AHS)
Berkshire School, MA (PRC)
Berks Technical Institute, PA (TCT)
Berk Trade School, NY (TCT)
Berry College, GA (UNC)
Bessemer State Technical College, AL (JRC)
Best Care Training Institute, NJ (TCT)
Beta Tech, SC (TCT)
Beta Tech, VA (TCT)
Beta Tech West, VA (TCT)
Bethany College, KS (UNC)
Bethany College, WV (UNC)
Bethany Lutheran College, MN (UNC)
Bethany Theological Seminary, IN (GRD)
Bethany University, CA (UNC)
Beth Benjamin Academy of Connecticut, CT (UNC)
Bethel College, IN (UNC)
Bethel College, KS (UNC)
Bethel College, MN (UNC)
Bethel College, TN (UNC)
Bethel Seminary, MN (GRD)
Bethel Seminary of the East, PA (GRD)
Bethesda Christian University, CA (UNC)
Bethesda Memorial Hospital, FL (TCT)
Beth HaMedrash Shaarei Yosher, NY (MNC)
Beth HaTalmud Rabbinical College, NY (MNC)
Beth Israel Healthcare, MA (AHS)
Beth Medrash Govoha, NJ (MNC)
Bethune-Cookman College, FL (UNC)
Beulah Heights Bible College, GA (UNC)
Bevill State Community College, AL (JRC)
Bexley Hall Seminary, NY (GRD)
Bexley Hall Seminary, OH (GRD)
Biblical Theological Seminary, PA (GRD)
Bidwell Training Center, PA (TCT)
Big Bend Community College, WA (JRC)
Bill Hill's College of Cosmetology, IA (TCT)
Bill Priest Inst. Economic Development, TX (TCT)
Biola University, CA (UNC)
Birmingham-Southern College, AL (UNC)
Birthingway College of Midwifery, OR (UNC)
Bishop Clarkson Memorial Hospital, NE (AHS)
The Bishop's School, CA (PRC)
Bishop State Community College-Central, AL (JRC)
Bishop State Community College-Carver, AL (TCT)
Bishop State Community College-Main, AL (JRC)
Bishop State Community College, AL (TCT)
Bismarck State College, ND (JRC)
BJ's Beauty & Barber College, WA (TCT)
Blackburn College, IL (UNC)
Blackfeet Community College, MT (JRC)
Black Hawk College, IL (JRC)
Blackhawk Technical College, WI (JRC)
Black Hills Beauty College, SD (TCT)
Black Hills State University, SD (UNC)
Black River Technical College, AR (TCT)
Bladen Community College, NC (JRC)
Blades School of Hair Design, MD (TCT)
Blaine The Beauty Career School, MA (TCT)
Blair Academy, NJ (PRC)
Blair College, CO (JRC)
Blair School of Music of Vanderbilt U., TN (UNC)
Blessed John XXIII National Seminary, MA (GRD)
Blessing Hospital, IL (TCT)
Blessing-Rieman College of Nursing, IL (UNC)
Blinn College, TX (JRC)
Blood Center of SE Wisconsin, WI (AHS)
Bloomfield College, NJ (UNC)
Bloomington Hospital, IN (AHS)
Bloomington-Normal School of Radiography, IL (AHS)
Bloomsburg University of Pennsylvania, PA (UNC)
Blue Cliff College, LA (TCT)
Blue Cliff College, MS (TCT)
Blue Cliff School of Therapeutic Massage, AL (TCT)
Bluefield College, VA (UNC)
Bluefield Regional Medical Center, WV (AHS)
Bluefield State College, WV (UNC)
Bluegrass Community & Technical College, KY (JRC)
Blue Mountain College, MS (WMC)

C

Central Carolina Technical College, SC (JRC)
Central Catholic High School, TX (PRB)
Central Christian College of Kansas, KS (UNC)
Central Christian College of the Bible, MO (UNC)
Central Christian School, OH (PRC)
Central College, IA (UNC)
Central College of Cosmetology, MO (TCT)
Central Community College, NE (JRC)
Central Connecticut State University, CT (UNC)
Central Florida Blood Bank, FL (TCT)
Central Florida College, FL (TCT)
Central Florida Community College, FL (JRC)
Central Florida Institute, FL (TCT)
Central Georgia Technical College, GA (TCT)
Centralia College, WA (JRC)
Central Institute for the Deaf, MO (HND)
Central Kentucky Technical College, KY (TCT)
Central Lakes College, MN (JRC)
Central Maine Community College, ME (JRC)
Central Maine Medical Center, ME (JRC)
Central Medical Education, IL (AHS)
Central Methodist University, MO (UNC)
Central Michigan University, MI (UNC)
Central Missouri State University, MO (UNC)
Central Ohio Technical College, OH (JRC)
Central Oregon Community College, OR (JRC)
Central Pennsylvania College, PA (UNC)
Central Piedmont Community College, NC (JRC)
Central State Beauty Academy, OK (TCT)
Central State University, OH (UNC)
Central Suffolk Hospital, NY (AHS)
Central Texas Beauty College, TX (TCT)
Central Texas Beauty College #2, TX (TCT)
Central Texas College, TX (JRC)
Central Texas Commercial College, TX (TCT)
Central Virginia Community College, VA (JRC)
Central Washington University, WA (UNC)
Central Wyoming College, WY (JRC)
Central Yeshiva Tomchei Tmimim Lubavitz, NY (UNC)
Centre College, KY (UNC)
Centro de Capacitacion y Asesoramiento, PR (TCT)
Centro de Estudios Multidisciplinarios, PR (TCT)
Centura-St. Anthony Hospital, CO (TCT)
Centurion Professional Training, NY (TCT)
Century College, MN (JRC)
Century College, PR (TCT)
Century School of Cosmetology, OH (TCT)
Cerritos College, CA (JRC)
Cerro Coso Community College, CA (JRC)
Certified Careers Institute, UT (TCT)
CFS The School at Church Farm, PA (PRB)
Chabot College, CA (JRC)
Chadron State College, NE (UNC)
Chaffey College, CA (JRC)
Chaminade College Preparatory School, MO (PRB)
Chaminade University of Honolulu, HI (UNC)
Champlain College, VT (UNC)
Champlain Valley Physicians Hospital, NY (AHS)
Chandler-Gilbert Community College, AZ (JRC)
Chaparral College, AZ (TCT)
Chapel Hill-Chauncy Hall School, MA (PRC)
Chapman School of Seamanship, FL (TCT)
Chapman University, CA (UNC)
Charity-Delgado School of Nursing, LA (HME)
Charles of Italy Beauty College, AZ (TCT)
Charles R. Drew Univ. of Med. & Science, CA (UNC)
Charles Stewart Mott Community College, MI (JRC)
Charles Stuart School of Locksmithing, NY (TCT)
Charleston Cosmetology Institute, SC (TCT)
Charleston School of Beauty Culture, WV (TCT)
Charleston Southern University, SC (UNC)
Charlie & Sue's School of Hair Design, TX (TCT)
Charlotte Technical Center, FL (TCT)
Charter College, AK (UNC)
Charter Oak State College, CT (HMS)
Chase College, CA (TCT)
Chatfield College, OH (JRC)
Chatham College, PA (WMC)
Chatham Hall, VA (PRG)
Chattahoochee Technical College, GA (JRC)
Chattahoochee Valley Community College, AL (JRC)
Chattanooga State Tech. Comm. College, TN (JRC)
Cheeks Intl Academy of Beauty Culture, CO (TCT)
Cheeks Intl Academy of Beauty Culture, WY (TCT)
Chemeketa Community College, OR (JRC)
Cheryl Fell's School of Business, NY (TCT)
Chesapeake College, MD (JRC)
Cheshire Academy, CT (PRC)
Chester College of New England, NH (JRC)
Chestnut Hill College, PA (UNC)
Cheveux School Hair Design and Hairport, NC (TCT)
Cheyney University of Pennsylvania, PA (UNC)
Chicago School of Massage Therapy, IL (TCT)
Chicago Sch. of Professional Psychology, IL (GRD)
Chicago State University, IL (UNC)
Chicago Theological Seminary, IL (GRD)
Chic University of Cosmetology, MI (TCT)
Chief Dull Knife College, MT (JRC)
CHI Institute, PA (TCT)
CHI Institute/RETS Campus, PA (TCT)
Child Development Ctr. of Northern VA, VA (HND)
Children's Hospital, MA (AHS)
Children's Hospital & Medical Center, OH (AHS)
Children's Hospital of Los Angeles, CA (TCT)
Chillicothe Beauty Academy, MO (TCT)
Chipola College, FL (JRC)
Chippewa Valley Technical College, WI (JRC)
C.H. McCann Technical School, MA (TCT)
Choate Rosemary Hall School, CT (PRC)
Chowan College, NC (UNC)
Chris' Beauty College, MS (TCT)
Christchurch School, VA (PRB)
Christendom College, VA (UNC)
Christ Hospital, OH (AHS)
Christ Hospital School of Nursing, NJ (TCT)
Christiana Care Health Services, DE (AHS)
Christian Brothers University, TN (UNC)
Christian Life College, IL (UNC)
Christian Theological Seminary, IN (TSR)
Christopher Newport University, VA (UNC)
Christ School, NC (PRB)
Christ the King Seminary, NY (GRD)
Chubb Institute, IL (TCT)
Chubb Institute, NJ (TCT)
Chubb Institute, NY (TCT)
Chubb Institute-Keystone School, PA (TCT)
Church Divinity School of the Pacific, CA (GRD)
Church of God Theological Seminary, TN (GRD)
Cincinnati Christian University, OH (UNC)
Cincinnati College of Mortuary Science, OH (UNC)
Cincinnati State Technical & Comm Coll, OH (JRC)
Circle J Beauty School, TX (TCT)
Circleville Bible College, OH (UNC)
Cisco Junior College, TX (JRC)
The Citadel, SC (MNC)
Citizens General Hospital, PA (NRS)
Citizen's High School, FL (HMS)
Citizens Medical Center, TX (AHS)
Citrus College, CA (JRC)
Cittone Institute, NJ (TCT)
Cittone Institute, PA (TCT)
City College, FL (JRC)
City College, FL (TCT)
City College, FL (UNC)
City College of San Francisco, CA (JRC)
City of Hope Medical Center, CA (TCT)
City University, WA (UNC)
Columbia Biblical Seminary, SC (GRD)
Clackamas Community College, OR (JRC)
Claflin University, SC (UNC)
Claremont Graduate University, CA (GRD)
Claremont McKenna College, CA (UNC)
Claremont School of Theology, CA (GRD)
Claremore Beauty College, OK (TCT)
Clarendon College, TX (JRC)
Clare's Beauty College, WA (TCT)
Clarion University of Pennsylvania, PA (UNC)
Clarion University - Venango Campus, PA (UNC)
Clarita Career College, CA (TCT)
Clark Atlanta University, GA (UNC)
Clark College, WA (JRC)
Clarke College, IA (UNC)
Clarksburg Beauty Academy, WV (TCT)
Clarkson College, NE (UNC)
Clarkson University, NY (UNC)
Clark State Community College, OH (JRC)
Clark University, MA (UNC)
Class Act I School of Cosmetology, MO (TCT)
Classic College of Hair Design, KS (TCT)
Clatsop Community College, OR (JRC)
Clayton State University, GA (UNC)
Clayton University, HI (UNC)
Clayton University, MO (UNC)
Clear Creek Baptist Bible College, KY (UNC)
Clearfield Beauty Academy, PA (TCT)
Clearfield Hospital, PA (AHS)
Clearwater Christian College, FL (UNC)
Cleary University - Livingston Campus, MI (UNC)
Cleary University - Washtenaw Campus, MI (UNC)
Clemson University, SC (UNC)
Cleveland Chiropractic College, MO (BIO)
Cleveland Chiropractic College of LA, CA (BIO)
Cleveland Clinic Foundation, OH (TCT)
Cleveland Community College, NC (JRC)
Cleveland Institute of Art, OH (UNC)
Cleveland Institute Dental Medical Asst., OH (TCT)
Cleveland Institute of Electronics, OH (JRC)
Cleveland Institute of Music, OH (UNC)
Cleveland State Community College, TN (JRC)
Cleveland State University, OH (UNC)
Cleveland Veterans Affairs Medical Ctr, OH (AHS)
Clinton Community College, IA (JRC)
Clinton Community College, NY (JRC)
Clinton Junior College, SC (JRC)
Cloud County Community College, KS (JRC)
Clover Park Technical College, WA (TCT)
Clovis Community College, NM (JRC)
Cloyd's Beauty School #1, LA (TCT)
Cloyd's Beauty School #2, LA (TCT)
Cloyd's Beauty School #3, LA (TCT)
Coachella Valley Technical Skills Center, CA (TCT)
Coahoma Community College, MS (JRC)
Coastal Bend College, TX (JRC)
Coastal Carolina Community College, NC (JRC)
Coastal Carolina University, SC (UNC)
Coastal Georgia Community College, GA (JRC)
Coastline Community College, CA (JRC)
Cobb Beauty College, GA (TCT)
Cochise College, AZ (JRC)
Cochran School of Nursing, NY (TCT)
Coconino Community College, AZ (JRC)
Coe College, IA (UNC)
Coffeyville Community College, KS (JRC)
Cogswell College, CA (UNC)
Coker College, SC (UNC)
Colburn School, CA (TCT)
Colby College, ME (UNC)
Colby Community College, KS (JRC)
Colby-Sawyer College, NH (UNC)
Colegio Biblico Pentecostal De PR, PR (UNC)
Colegio Educativo Tecnologico Industrial, PR (TCT)
Colegio Mayor de Technologia, PR (TCT)
Colegio Pentecostal Mizpa, PR (UNC)
Colegio Tecnico de Electricidad Galloza, PR (TCT)
Colegio Tecnico Metropolitano, PR (TCT)
Colegio Tecnologico y Comercial, PR (TCT)
Coleman College, CA (UNC)
Colgate Rochester Crozer Divinity School, NY (GRD)
Colgate University, NY (UNC)
Colleen O'Hara's Beauty Academy, CA (TCT)
CollegeAmerica, AZ (TCT)
CollegeAmerica - Colorado, CO (UNC)
CollegeAmerica - Colorado Springs, CO (UNC)
CollegeAmerica - Fort Collins, CO (UNC)
College for Creative Studies, MI (UNC)
College for Financial Planning, CO (UNC)
College Misericordia, PA (UNC)
College of Alameda, CA (JRC)
College of Art Advertising, OH (TCT)
College of Automotive Management, CA (TCT)
College of Biblical Studies, TX (JRC)
College of Business & Technology, FL (TCT)
College of Career Training, CA (TCT)
College of Charleston, SC (UNC)
College of Coiffure Art, MT (TCT)
College of Cosmetology, OR (TCT)
College of Court Reporting, IN (TCT)
College of DuPage, IL (JRC)
College of Eastern Utah, UT (JRC)
College of Hair Design, IA (TCT)
College of Hair Design, KS (TCT)
College of Hair Design, NE (TCT)
College of Hair Design Careers, OR (TCT)
College of Information Technology, CA (TCT)
College of Lake County, IL (JRC)
College of Legal Arts, OR (TCT)
College of Marin, CA (JRC)
College of Menominee Nation, WI (JRC)
College of Micronesia, FM (JRC)
College of Mount Saint Joseph, OH (UNC)
College of Mount Saint Vincent, NY (UNC)
College of New Jersey, NJ (UNC)
College of New Rochelle, NY (UNC)
College of Notre Dame of Maryland, MD (WMC)
College of Office Technology, IL (TCT)
College of Saint Benedict, MN (WMC)
College of Saint Catherine, MN (WMC)
College of Saint Elizabeth, NJ (WMC)
College of Saint Joseph, VT (UNC)
College of Saint Mary, NE (WMC)
College of Saint Rose, NY (UNC)
College of Saint Scholastica, MN (UNC)
College of Saint Thomas More, TX (UNC)
College of San Mateo, CA (JRC)
College of Santa Fe, NM (UNC)
College of Southern Idaho, ID (JRC)
College of Southern Maryland, MD (JRC)
College of the Albemarle, NC (JRC)
College of the Atlantic, ME (UNC)
College of the Canyons, CA (JRC)
College of the Desert, CA (JRC)
College of the Holy Cross, MA (UNC)
College of the Humanities and Sciences, AZ (HMS)
College of the Mainland, TX (JRC)
College of the Marshall Islands, MH (JRC)
College of the Ozarks, MO (UNC)
College of the Sequoias, CA (JRC)
College of the Siskiyous, CA (JRC)
College of the Southwest, NM (UNC)
College of Visual Arts, MN (UNC)
The College of Westchester, NY (JRC)
College of William and Mary, VA (UNC)
College of Wooster, OH (UNC)
Collin County Community College, TX (JRC)
Collins Career Center, OH (TCT)
Collins College School of Design & Tech., AZ (UNC)
Collins School of Cosmetology, KY (TCT)
Colorado Academy, CO (PRC)
Colorado Ctr for Medical Laboratory Sci., CO (TCT)
Colorado Christian University, CO (UNC)
Colorado College, CO (UNC)
Colorado Institute of Taxidermy, CO (TCT)
Colorado Mountain College, CO (JRC)
Colorado Northwestern Community College, CO (JRC)
Colorado Rocky Mountain School, CO (PRC)
Colorado School for the Deaf and Blind, CO (HND)
Colorado School of Healing Arts, CO (TCT)
Colorado School of Mines, CO (UNC)
Colorado Sch. of Professional Psychology, CO (GRD)
Colorado School of Trades, CO (TCT)
CO Sch of Traditional Chinese Medicine, CO (UNC)
The Colorado Springs School, CO (PRC)
Colorado State University, CO (UNC)
Colorado State University - Pueblo, CO (UNC)
Colorado Technical University, CO (UNC)
Colorado Technical University, MO (UNC)
Colorado Technical University, SD (JRC)
Colorado Timberline Academy, CO (PRC)
Columbia Basin College, WA (JRC)
Columbia Beauty Academy, MO (TCT)
Columbia Beauty School, SC (TCT)
Columbia Center, MD (UNC)
Columbia Centro Universitario, PR (JRC)
Columbia Centro Universitario, PR (TCT)
Columbia College, CA (JRC)
Columbia College, IL (UNC)
Columbia College, MO (UNC)
Columbia College, SC (WMC)
Columbia College Hollywood, CA (TCT)
Columbia College of Nursing, WI (UNC)
Columbia Commonwealth University, WY (HMS)
Columbia-Greene Beauty School, NY (TCT)
Columbia-Greene Community College, NY (JRC)
Columbia HealthOne, CO (AHS)
Columbia Hospital, WI (AHS)
Columbia International University, SC (TSR)
Columbia Southern University, AL (HMS)
Columbia State Community College, TN (JRC)
Columbia Theological Seminary, GA (GRD)
Columbia Union College, MD (UNC)
Columbia University, NY (UNC)
Columbus College of Art & Design, OH (UNC)
Columbus Regional Hospital, IN (AHS)
Columbus State Community College, OH (JRC)
Columbus State University, GA (UNC)
Columbus Technical College, GA (JRC)
Comanche Co. Memorial Hospital, OK (AHS)
Commercial Driver Training School, NY (TCT)
Commonwealth Institute / Funeral Service, TX (JRC)
Commonwealth Technical Institute, PA (JRC)
Community Business College, CA (TCT)
Community Christian College, CA (UNC)
Community College of Allegheny County, PA (JRC)
Community College of Aurora, CO (JRC)

Fork Union Military Academy, VA (PRB)
Forman School, CT (PRC)
Forrest General Hospital, MS (AHS)
Forrest Junior College, SC (JRC)
Forsyth Technical Community College, NC (JRC)
Fort Belknap College, MT (JRC)
Fort Berthold Community College, ND (JRC)
Fort Hays State University, KS (UNC)
Fort Lewis College, CO (UNC)
Fort Peck Community College, MT (JRC)
Fort Pierce Beauty Academy, FL (TCT)
Fort Sanders School of Nursing, TN (NRS)
Fort Scott Community College, KS (JRC)
Fort Valley State University, GA (UNC)
Fort Wayne School of Radiography, IN (AHS)
Fort Worth Beauty School, TX (TCT)
Foster's Cosmetology College, MS (TCT)
Fountain Valley School of Colorado, CO (PRC)
Four-D College, CA (TCT)
Four Seasons Salon and Day Spa School, WI (TCT)
Fox College, IL (TCT)
Foxcroft School, VA (PRG)
Fox Institute of Business, CT (TCT)
Fox Valley Technical College, WI (JRC)
Framingham State College, MA (UNC)
Fran Brown College of Beauty, UT (TCT)
Franciscan School of Theology, CA (GRD)
Franciscan University, IA (UNC)
Franciscan University of Steubenville, OH (UNC)
Francis Marion University, SC (UNC)
Francois D. Hair Design Academy, UT (TCT)
Frankford Hospital, PA (NRS)
Franklin & Marshall College, PA (UNC)
Franklin Beauty School #2, TX (TCT)
Franklin Career College, CA (TCT)
Franklin Career Institute, NY (TCT)
Franklin College, IN (UNC)
Franklin Pierce College, NH (UNC)
Franklin Pierce Law Center, NH (GRD)
Franklin Technology - MSSU, MO (TCT)
Franklin University, OH (UNC)
Franklin W. Olin College of Engineering, MA (UNC)
Frank Lloyd Wright Sch of Architecture, AZ (GRD)
Frank Phillips College, TX (JRC)
Frederick and Charles Beauty College, CA (TCT)
Frederick Community College, MD (JRC)
Freed-Hardeman University, TN (UNC)
Free Will Baptist Bible College, TN (UNC)
French Culinary Institute, NY (TCT)
Fresno City College, CA (JRC)
Fresno Pacific University, CA (UNC)
Friends University, KS (UNC)
Froedtert Memorial Lutheran Hospital, WI (AHS)
Frontier Community College, IL (JRC)
Frontier School of Midwifery, KY (UNC)
Front Range Community College, CO (JRC)
Frostburg State University, MD (UNC)
Fryeburg Academy, ME (PRC)
Fuller Theological Seminary, CA (GRD)
Fullerton College, CA (JRC)
Full Sail - Real World Education, FL (TCT)
Fulton-Montgomery Community College, NY (JRC)
Furman University, SC (UNC)
Futures International High School, CA (HMS)

G

Gadsden Business College, AL (TCT)
Gadsden State Community College, AL (JRC)
Gainesville College, GA (JRC)
Gaither Beauty College, AL (TCT)
Galen College Medical & Dental Assts., CA (TCT)
Galen College of Nursing, KY (NRS)
Galen Health Institute School of Nursing, TX (NRS)
Galen Health Institute, FL (NRS)
Gallaudet University, DC (UNC)
Gallipolis Career College, OH (TCT)
Gallipolis State Institute, OH (HND)
Gal Mar Academy of Hairdressing, CT (TCT)
Galveston College, TX (JRC)
Gamla College, NY (JRC)
Gannon University, PA (UNC)
Garden City Community College, KS (JRC)
Gardner-Webb University, NC (UNC)
Garnet Career Center, WV (TCT)
Garrett College, MD (JRC)
Garrett Evangelical Theological Seminary, IL (GRD)
Garrison Forest School, MD (PRG)
Gary Job Corps Center, TX (TCT)
Gaston College, NC (JRC)
Gates College, CA (TCT)
Gateway Community & Technical College, KY (TCT)
Gateway Community College, AZ (JRC)
Gateway Community College, CT (JRC)
Gateway Technical College, WI (JRC)
Gavilan Community College, CA (JRC)
GECAC Training Institute, PA (TCT)
Geisinger Medical Center, PA (AHS)
Gem City College, IL (JRC)
Gemological Institute of America, CA (TCT)
Gemological Institute of America, NY (TCT)
Gem State Academy, ID (PRC)
Gene Juarez Academy of Beauty, WA (TCT)
General Theological Seminary, NY (GRD)
Genesee Community College, NY (JRC)
Geneva College, PA (UNC)
George C. Wallace State Comm College, AL (JRC)
George Fox University, OR (GRD)
George Fox University, OR (UNC)
George Mason University, VA (UNC)
George School, PA (PRC)
George Stone Vocational Technical Ctr., FL (TCT)
George T. Baker Aviation School, FL (TCT)
Georgetown College, KY (UNC)
Georgetown Preparatory School, MD (PRB)
Georgetown University, DC (UNC)
George Washington University, DC (UNC)
Georgia Academy for the Blind, GA (HND)
Georgia Aviation Technical College, GA (TCT)
Georgia Career Institute, GA (TCT)
Georgia Career Institute, TN (TCT)
Georgia College & State University, GA (UNC)
Georgia Driving Academy, GA (TCT)
Georgia Highlands College, GA (JRC)
Georgia Institute of Cosmetology, GA (TCT)
Georgia Institute of Technology, GA (UNC)
Georgia Medical Institute, GA (TCT)
Georgia Military College, GA (JRC)
Georgian Court University, NJ (UNC)
Georgia Perimeter College, GA (JRC)
Georgia School for the Deaf, GA (HND)
Georgia Southern University, GA (UNC)
Georgia Southwestern State University, GA (UNC)
Georgia State University, GA (UNC)
Gerber Akron Beauty School, OH (TCT)
Germanna Community College, VA (JRC)
Gettysburg College, PA (UNC)
Ghent Beauty Academy, VA (TCT)
Gibbs College, CT (JRC)
Gibbs College, NJ (JRC)
Gibbs College - Northern Virginia, VA (TCT)
Gibbs College of Boston, MA (TCT)
Gibson's Barber & Beauty College, MS (TCT)
Gill-Tech Academy of Hair Design, WI (TCT)
Gilmour Academy, OH (PRC)
Girard College School, PA (PRC)
Glendale Career College, CA (TCT)
Glendale Community College, AZ (JRC)
Glendale Community College, CA (JRC)
Glen Dow Academy of Hair Design, WA (TCT)
Glen Oaks Community College, MI (JRC)
Glens Falls Hospital, NY (AHS)
Glenville State College, WV (UNC)
Glenwood Beauty Academy, CO (TCT)
Global Business Institute, NY (TCT)
Global University, MO (HMS)
Globe College, MN (TCT)
Globe Institute of Technology, NY (UNC)
Globelle Technical Institute, PR (TCT)
Gloden Hall Health Care Center, NY (AHS)
Gloucester County College, NJ (JRC)
Goddard College, VT (UNC)
God's Bible School and College, OH (UNC)
Gogebic Community College, MI (JRC)
Golden Gate Baptist Theological Seminary, CA (GRD)
Golden Gate University, CA (UNC)
Golden State College, CA (AHS)
Golden West College, CA (JRC)
Goldey-Beacom College, DE (UNC)
Golf Academy of Arizona, AZ (TCT)
Golf Academy of Hawaii, HI (TCT)
Golf Academy of San Diego, CA (TCT)
Golf Academy of the Carolinas, SC (TCT)
Golf Academy of the South, FL (TCT)
Gonzaga University, WA (GRD)
Gonzaga University, WA (UNC)
Good Samaritan Hospital, IN (TCT)
Good Samaritan Hospital, OH (AHS)
Goodwin College, CT (AHS)
Goodwin Institute, CT (TCT)
Goodwin Institute Business School, CT (TCT)
Gordon College, GA (JRC)
Gordon College, MA (UNC)
Gordon-Conwell Theological Seminary, MA (GRD)
Goshen College, IN (UNC)
Goucher College, MD (UNC)
Gould Academy, ME (PRC)
Governor Baxter School for the Deaf, ME (HND)
Governor Dummer Academy, MA (PRC)
The Governor French Academy, IL (PRC)
Governors State University, IL (UNC)
Gow School, NY (PRB)
Grabber School of Hair Design, MO (TCT)
Grace Bible College, MI (UNC)
Grace College, IN (UNC)
Grace Theological Seminary, IN (GRD)
Grace Hospital, MI (AHS)
Graceland University, IA (UNC)
Graceland University, MO (UNC)
Grace University, NE (UNC)
Graduate Institute of Applied Linguistic, TX (GRD)
Graduate Theological Union, CA (GRD)
Grady Health System, GA (AHS)
Grafton School, VA (HND)
Graham Bible College, VA (UNC)
Graham Hospital, IL (TCT)
Graham Webb Intl. Academy of Hair, VA (TCT)
Grambling State University, LA (UNC)
Grand Canyon University, AZ (UNC)
Grand Rapids Community College, MI (JRC)
Grand River Academy, OH (PRB)
Grand Valley State University, MI (UNC)
Grand View College, IA (UNC)
Granite State College, NH (UNC)
Grantham University, MO (HMS)
Gratz College, PA (UNC)
Grays Harbor College, WA (JRC)
Grayson County College, TX (JRC)
Great Basin College, NV (JRC)
Greater Baltimore Medical Center, MD (AHS)
Greater Johnstown Area Voc Tech School, PA (TCT)
Greater West Town School, IL (TCT)
Great Lakes Christian College, MI (UNC)
Great Lakes College, MI (JRC)
Great Lakes Institute of Technology, PA (TCT)
Great Plains Area Voc. Tech. School, OK (TCT)
Greenfield Community College, MA (JRC)
Green Mountain College, VT (UNC)
Green Mountain Valley School, VT (PRC)
Green River Community College, WA (JRC)
Greensboro College, NC (UNC)
Greenville College, IL (UNC)
Greenville Technical College, SC (JRC)
Greenwood Academy of Hair Design, WA (TCT)
Gretna Career College Training Institute, LA (TCT)
Grier School, PA (PRG)
Griffin Technical College, GA (TCT)
Griggs International Academy, MD (HMS)
Griggs University, MD (HMS)
Grinnell College, IA (UNC)
Grossmont College, CA (JRC)
Groton School, MA (PRC)
Grove City College, PA (UNC)
Guadalupe Vocational Institute, FL (TCT)
Guam Adventist Academy, GU (PRC)
Guam Community College, GU (JRC)
Guaynabo Technical College, PR (TCT)
Guilford College, NC (UNC)
Guilford Technical Community College, NC (JRC)
Gulf Coast College, FL (TCT)
Gulf Coast Community College, FL (JRC)
Gulf Coast Regional Blood Center, TX (AHS)
Gulf Coast Trades Center, TX (TCT)
Gulfport Job Corps Center, MS (TCT)
Gunderson Medical Foundation, WI (AHS)
The Gunnery, CT (PRC)
Gunston Day School, MD (PRC)
Gupton-Jones College of Funeral Service, GA (EMB)
Gustavus Adolphus College, MN (UNC)
Gutenberg College, OR (UNC)
Guy's Shreveport Academy of Cosmetology, LA (TCT)
Gwinnett College of Business, GA (TCT)
Gwinnett Technical College, GA (JRC)
Gwynedd-Mercy College, PA (UNC)

H

Hacienda LaPuente Valley Adult Education, CA (TCT)
Hackensack Univ Medical Center, NJ (AHS)
Hackley School, NY (PRC)
Hadley School for the Blind, IL (HND)
Hagerstown Business College, MD (JRC)
Hagerstown Community College, MD (JRC)
Hair Academy, MD (TCT)
Hair Academy, OH (TCT)
Hair Arts Academy, IN (TCT)
Hair Design Institute at Fifth Avenue, NY (TCT)
Hair Design School, KY (TCT)
The Hair Design School, KY (TCT)
Hair Dynamics Education Center, CO (TCT)
Hair in Motion Beauty Academy, MA (TCT)
Hairitage College of Beauty, UT (TCT)
Hairitage Hair Academy, UT (TCT)
Hairmasters Institute of Cosmetology, IL (TCT)
Hair Masters University of Beauty, CA (TCT)
Hair Professionals Academy, IL (TCT)
Hair Professionals Acad of Cosmetology, IL (TCT)
Hair Professionals Career College, IL (TCT)
Hair Professionals School of Cosmetology, IL (TCT)
Hairstyling Institute of Charlotte, NC (TCT)
Hairstylist Academy, NC (TCT)
Halifax Community College, NC (JRC)
Halifax Medical Center, FL (TCT)
Hallmark Institute of Aeronautics, TX (TCT)
Hallmark Institute of Photography, MA (TCT)
Hallmark Institute of Technology, TX (TCT)
Hamilton College, IA (UNC)
Hamilton College, NE (JRC)
Hamilton College, NY (UNC)
Hamilton College - Lincoln Campus, NE (TCT)
Hamilton Technical College, IA (TCT)
Hamline University, MN (UNC)
Hammer United World College, NM (PRC)
Hampden-Sydney College, VA (MNC)
Hampshire College, MA (UNC)
Hampshire Country School, NH (PRB)
Hampton University, VA (UNC)
Hamrick Truck Driving School, OH (TCT)
Hancock Memorial Hospital, IN (AHS)
Hanger Orthopedic Group, CT (HMS)
Hannibal Area Voc. Technical School, MO (TCT)
Hannibal-LaGrange College, MO (UNC)
Hanover College, IN (UNC)
Hanover Park College of Beauty Culture, IL (TCT)
Happy Valley School, CA (PRC)
Harcum Junior College, PA (JRC)
HARDI Home Study Institute, OH (HMS)
Harding Academy, AR (PRC)
Harding University, AR (UNC)
Harding University Grad Sch of Religion, TN (GRD)
Hardin-Simmons University, TX (UNC)
Harford Community College, MD (JRC)
Hargrave Military Academy, VA (PRB)
Harker School, CA (PRC)
Harlem School of Technology, NY (TCT)
Harold S. Washington College, IL (JRC)
Harper Hospital, MI (AHS)
Harpers Ferry Job Corps, WV (TCT)
Harrington College of Design, IL (UNC)
Harrisburg Area Community College, PA (JRC)
Harrisburg Institute of Trade & Tech., PA (TCT)
Harris Hospital, TX (AHS)
Harrison Career Institute, DE (TCT)
Harrison Career Institute, MD (TCT)
Harrison Career Institute, NJ (TCT)
Harrison Career Institute, PA (TCT)
Harris School of Business, NJ (TCT)
Harris-Stowe State University, MO (UNC)
Harry S. Truman College, IL (JRC)
Harry Wendelstedt Umpire School, FL (TCT)
Hartford College for Women, CT (JRC)
Hartford Conservatory, CT (TCT)
Hartford Hospital, CT (TCT)
Hartford Seminary, CT (GRD)
Hartnell College, CA (JRC)
Hartt Community Division, CT (UNC)
Hartwick College, NY (UNC)
Harvard University, MA (UNC)
Harvey Mudd College, CA (UNC)
Harvey School, NY (PRC)
Haskell Indian Nations University, KS (JRC)
Hastings College, NE (UNC)
Hattiesburg Radiology Group, MS (AHS)
Haverford College, PA (UNC)

International School of Cosmetology, CA (TCT)
International School of Skin/Nailcare, GA (TCT)
International Technical College, PR (TCT)
International Theological Seminary, CA (TSR)
International Training Careers, FL (TCT)
International Yacht Restoration School, RI (TCT)
Inver Hills Community College, MN (JRC)
Iona College, NY (UNC)
Iona College at Blue Hill, NY (UNC)
Iowa Braille and Sight Saving School, IA (HND)
Iowa Central Community College, IA (JRC)
Iowa Lakes Community College, IA (JRC)
Iowa Methodist Medical Center, IA (AHS)
Iowa School for the Deaf, IA (HND)
Iowa School of Beauty, IA (TCT)
Iowa State University, IA (UNC)
Iowa Wesleyan College, IA (UNC)
Iowa Western Community College, IA (JRC)
Irvine Valley College, CA (JRC)
Island Drafting & Technical Institute, NY (JRC)
Isothermal Community College, NC (JRC)
Itasca Community College, MN (JRC)
Itawamba Community College, MS (JRC)
Ithaca College, NY (UNC)
ITI Technical College, LA (TCT)
ITT Technical Institute, AL (JRC)
ITT Technical Institute, AR (TCT)
ITT Technical Institute, AZ (TCT)
ITT Technical Institute, CA (JRC)
ITT Technical Institute, CA (TCT)
ITT Technical Institute, CA (UNC)
ITT Technical Institute, CO (JRC)
ITT Technical Institute, FL (JRC)
ITT Technical Institute, FL (TCT)
ITT Technical Institute, GA (UNC)
ITT Technical Institute, ID (JRC)
ITT Technical Institute, IL (JRC)
ITT Technical Institute, IL (TCT)
ITT Technical Institute, IN (JRC)
ITT Technical Institute, IN (TCT)
ITT Technical Institute, KY (TCT)
ITT Technical Institute, LA (TCT)
ITT Technical Institute, MA (TCT)
ITT Technical Institute, MA (UNC)
ITT Technical Institute, MD (UNC)
ITT Technical Institute, MI (JRC)
ITT Technical Institute, MO (BUS)
ITT Technical Institute, MO (JRC)
ITT Technical Institute, NE (JRC)
ITT Technical Institute, NM (JRC)
ITT Technical Institute, NV (TCT)
ITT Technical Institute, NY (TCT)
ITT Technical Institute, OH (JRC)
ITT Technical Institute, OH (TCT)
ITT Technical Institute, OK (UNC)
ITT Technical Institute, OR (UNC)
ITT Technical Institute, PA (TCT)
ITT Technical Institute, PA (UNC)
ITT Technical Institute, SC (TCT)
ITT Technical Institute, TN (JRC)
ITT Technical Institute, TN (TCT)
ITT Technical Institute, TN (UNC)
ITT Technical Institute, TX (JRC)
ITT Technical Institute, TX (TCT)
ITT Technical Institute, UT (UNC)
ITT Technical Institute, VA (JRC)
ITT Technical Institute, WA (JRC)
ITT Technical Institute, WA (TCT)
ITT Technical Institute, WI (JRC)
Iverson Business School, GA (TCT)
Ivory Dental Technology College, CA (TCT)
Ivy Tech Community College - Bloomington, IN (TCT)
Ivy Tech Community College Central IN, IN (JRC)
Ivy Tech Community College North Central, IN (JRC)
Ivy Tech Community College - Columbus, IN (JRC)
Ivy Tech Community College East Central, IN (TCT)
Ivy Tech Community College - Kokomo, IN (TCT)
Ivy Tech Community College - Lafayette, IN (TCT)
Ivy Tech Community College - Northeast, IN (TCT)
Ivy Tech Community College - Northwest, IN (TCT)
Ivy Tech Community College - Richmond, IN (TCT)
Ivy Tech Community College - Southeast, IN (TCT)
Ivy Tech Community College - Southern, IN (JRC)
Ivy Tech Community College - Southwest, IN (TCT)
Ivy Tech Community College Wabash Valley, IN (TCT)
Ivy Tech State College, IN (JRC)

J

J & J Hair Design College, MS (TCT)
J & M Academy of Cosmetology, KY (TCT)
Jack Mabley Development Center, IL (HND)
Jackson Community College, MI (JRC)
Jackson Memorial Medical Center, FL (TCT)
Jackson State Community College, TN (JRC)
Jackson State University, MS (UNC)
Jacksonville College, TX (JRC)
Jacksonville State University, AL (UNC)
Jacksonville University, FL (UNC)
Jacobs Creek Job Corps Civilian Center, TN (TCT)
James Albert School of Cosmetology, CA (TCT)
James A. Rhodes State Coll, OH (JRC)
James Haley Veteran's Hospital, FL (AHS)
James H. Faulkner State Comm. College, AL (JRC)
James Madison High School, GA (HMS)
James Madison University, VA (UNC)
Jameson Memorial Hosp School of Nursing, PA (NRS)
James Sprunt Community College, NC (JRC)
Jamestown Business College, NY (TCT)
Jamestown College, ND (UNC)
Jamestown Community College, NY (JRC)
Jarvis Christian College, TX (UNC)
Javelin Technical Training Center, GA (TCT)
Jay's Technical Institute, TX (TCT)
Jean Madeline Educ. Ctr. for Cosmetology, PA (TCT)
Je Boutique College of Beauty, CA (TCT)
Jefferson College, MO (JRC)
Jefferson College of Health Sciences, VA (UNC)
Jefferson Community & Technical College, KY (JRC)
Jefferson Community College, NY (JRC)
Jefferson Community College, OH (JRC)
Jefferson Davis Community College, AL (JRC)
Jefferson Davis Community College, AL (TCT)
Jefferson Regional Medical Center, AR (TCT)
Jefferson State Community College, AL (JRC)
Jefferson Technical College, KY (TCT)
Jenks Beauty College, OK (TCT)
Jennie Edmundson Memorial Hospital, IA (AHS)
Jenny Lea Academy of Cosmetology, KY (TCT)
Jerry's School of Hairstyling, MO (TCT)
Jersey Shore Medical Center, NJ (AHS)
Jesuit School of Theology at Berkeley, CA (GRD)
Jewish Theological Seminary of America, NY (UNC)
J. F. Drake State Technical College, AL (JRC)
J. F. Ingram State Technical College, AL (JRC)
JNA Institute of Culinary Arts, PA (TCT)
Joe Kubert Sch of Cartoon & Graphic Arts, NJ (TCT)
John A. Gupton College, TN (JRC)
John A. Logan College, IL (JRC)
John Amico's School of Hair Design, IL (TCT)
John Brown University, AR (UNC)
John Carroll University, OH (UNC)
John Dewey College, PR (TCT)
John F. Kennedy Memorial High School, WA (PRC)
John F. Kennedy University, CA (UNC)
John Jay Beauty College, LA (TCT)
John Jay Kenner Academy, LA (TCT)
John Jay Slidell Beauty College, LA (TCT)
John Marshall Law School, IL (GRD)
Johns Hopkins University, DC (GRD)
Johns Hopkins University, MD (UNC)
Johnson & Wales University, CO (TCT)
Johnson & Wales University, FL (UNC)
Johnson & Wales University, NC (UNC)
Johnson & Wales University, RI (UNC)
Johnson Bible College, TN (GRD)
Johnson College, PA (JRC)
Johnson County Community College, KS (JRC)
Johnson C. Smith University, NC (UNC)
Johnson State College, VT (UNC)
Johnston Community College, NC (JRC)
John Tracy Clinic, CA (HMS)
John Tyler Community College, VA (JRC)
John Wesley College, NC (TSR)
John Wesley Intl. Barber/Beauty Coll, CA (TCT)
John Wood Community College, IL (JRC)
Jolie Hair and Beauty Academy, MA (TCT)
Joliet Junior College, IL (JRC)
Jones Beauty College, TX (TCT)
Jones Beauty College #2, TX (TCT)
Jones College, FL (UNC)
Jones County Junior College, MS (JRC)
Jones International University, CO (UNC)
Jon Louis School of Beauty, NY (TCT)
Jon Nave University of Cosmetology, TN (TCT)
Josef's School of Hair Design, ND (TCT)
Joseph's College of Beauty, NE (TCT)
Joseph's of Kearney Sch of Hair Design, NE (TCT)
Joy's School of Hair Design, NJ (TCT)
JPS Inst. for Health Career Development, TX (AHS)
J. Sargeant Reynolds Community College, VA (JRC)
Judson College, AL (UNC)
Judson College, IL (UNC)
Juilliard School, NY (UNC)
June Buchanan School, KY (PRC)
Jung Tao School of Chinese Medicine, NC (GRD)
Juniata College, PA (UNC)

K

Kaiser Permanente Medical Center, CA (TCT)
Kalamazoo College, MI (UNC)
Kalamazoo Valley Community College, MI (JRC)
Kambly School/Developmentally Impaired, MI (HND)
Kankakee Community College, IL (JRC)
Kansas City Art Institute, MO (UNC)
Kansas City Kansas Community College, KS (JRC)
KC Univ. of Medicine and Biosciences, MO (GRD)
Kansas School for the Deaf, KS (HND)
Kansas State School for the Blind, KS (HND)
Kansas State University, KS (UNC)
Kansas Wesleyan University, KS (UNC)
Kapiolani Community College, HI (JRC)
Kaplan University, IA (UNC)
Kaskaskia College, IL (JRC)
Katharine Gibbs School, NJ (TCT)
Katharine Gibbs School, NY (TCT)
Katharine Gibbs School, RI (TCT)
Kauai Community College, HI (JRC)
Kaufman Beauty School, KY (TCT)
KAW Area Technical School, KS (TCT)
Kaye Beauty College, IN (TCT)
Kay Harvey Hairdressing Academy, MA (TCT)
KD Studio - Actors Conservatory, TX (TCT)
Kean University, NJ (UNC)
Keck Graduate Institute, CA (GRD)
Kee Business College, VA (TCT)
Keene Beauty Academy, NH (TCT)
Keene State College, NH (UNC)
Kehilath Yakov Rabbinical Seminary, NY (MNC)
Keio Academy of New York, NY (PRC)
Keiser Career College, FL (TCT)
Keiser College, FL (JRC)
Keller Graduate School of Management, CA (BUS)
Keller Graduate School, IL (BUS)
Keller Graduate School of DeVry Univ., IL (MBA)
Keller Graduate School, IL (BUS)
Keller Graduate School, IL (MBA)
Keller Graduate School, MO (MBA)
Keller Graduate School, NY (UNC)
Keller Graduate School, OH (BUS)
Keller Graduate School, VA (MBA)
Keller Graduate School, WI (MBA)
Keller Graduate School of Management, AZ (BUS)
Keller Graduate School of Management, AZ (MBA)
Keller Graduate School of Management, CA (BUS)
Kellogg Community College, MI (JRC)
Kenai Peninsula College, AK (JRC)
Kendall College, IL (UNC)
Kendall College of Art & Design, MI (UNC)
Kendall's Academy of Beauty Arts/Science, UT (TCT)
Kennebec Valley Community College, ME (JRC)
Kennedy-King College, IL (JRC)
Kennesaw State University, GA (UNC)
Kenneth Shuler's School of Cosmetology, SC (TCT)
Kenrick School of Theology, MO (GRD)
Kensington College, CA (TCT)
Kent Career/Technical Center, MI (TCT)
Kent School, CT (PRC)
Kents Hill School, ME (PRC)
Kent State University, OH (UNC)
Kent State University-Ashtabula Campus, OH (JRC)
Kent State University-East Liverpool, OH (JRC)
Kent State University-Geauga Campus, OH (JRC)
Kent State University-Salem Campus, OH (JRC)
Kent State University-Stark Campus, OH (JRC)
Kent State University-Trumbull Campus, OH (JRC)
Kent State University, OH (JRC)
Kentucky Christian University, KY (UNC)
Kentucky Mountain Bible College, KY (UNC)
Kentucky School for the Blind, KY (HND)
Kentucky School for the Deaf, KY (HND)
Kentucky State University, KY (UNC)
Kentucky Wesleyan College, KY (UNC)
Kenyon College, OH (UNC)
Kettering College of Medical Arts, OH (UNC)
Kettering University, MI (EGN)
Keuka College, NY (UNC)
Key College, FL (TCT)
KeySkills Learning, NJ (TCT)
Keystone College, PA (JRC)
Keystone National High School, PA (HMS)
Kildonan School, NY (PRC)
Kilgore College, TX (JRC)
Kilian Community College, SD (JRC)
Kim Anh Academy of Beauty, CA (TCT)
Kimball Union Academy, NH (PRC)
King College, TN (UNC)
The Kings Academy, TN (PRC)
King's College, NC (JRC)
King's College, PA (UNC)
The Kings College and Seminary, CA (UNC)
King's Daughter's Hospital, IN (AHS)
Kings Way Missionary Institute, TX (TCT)
Kingwood College, TX (TCT)
Kirkland Beauty School, WA (TCT)
Kirksville Coll. of Osteopathic Medicine, MO (GRD)
Kirkwood Community College, IA (JRC)
Kirtland Community College, MI (JRC)
Kishwaukee College, IL (JRC)
The Kiski School, PA (PRB)
Kittanning Beauty School, PA (TCT)
Klamath Community College, OR (JRC)
Knowledge Systems Institute, IL (IFS)
Knox College, IL (UNC)
Knox County Career Center, OH (TCT)
Knox School, NY (PRC)
Knox Theological Seminary, FL (GRD)
Kodiak College, AK (JRC)
Kol Yaakov Torah Center, NY (MNC)
Kutztown University of Pennsylvania, PA (UNC)

L

LaBaron Hairdressing Academy, KS (TCT)
LaBaron Hairdressing Academy, MA (TCT)
La Belle Beauty Academy, FL (TCT)
La Belle Beauty School, FL (TCT)
Labette Community College, KS (JRC)
Laboratory Institute of Merchandising, NY (UNC)
Lac Courte Oreilles Ojibwa Comm College, WI (JRC)
Lackawanna College, PA (JRC)
Lacy Cosmetology School, SC (TCT)
Lafayette Beauty Academy, IN (TCT)
Lafayette College, PA (UNC)
Lafayette General Medical Center, LA (AHS)
La Grange College, GA (UNC)
LaGuardia Community College / CUNY, NY (JRC)
Laguna College of Art and Design, CA (UNC)
La' James College of Hairstyling, IA (TCT)
La' James College of Hairstyling, IL (TCT)
Lake Area Technical Institute, SD (TCT)
Lake Charles Memorial Hospital, LA (AHS)
Lake City Community College, FL (JRC)
Lake College, CA (TCT)
Lake Erie College, OH (UNC)
Lake Erie College\Osteopathic Medicine, FL (UNC)
Lake Erie College\Osteopathic Medicine, PA (UNC)
Lake Forest Academy, IL (PRC)
Lake Forest Beauty College, CA (TCT)
Lake Forest College, IL (UNC)
Lake Forest Graduate Sch. of Management, IL (GRD)
Lake Grove School-Maple Valley, MA (HND)
Lake Grove School, NY (HND)
Lake Grove School at Durham, CT (HND)
Lake Land College, IL (JRC)
Lakeland College, WI (UNC)
Lakeland Community College, OH (JRC)
Lakeland Regional Medical Center, FL (TCT)
Lakeland Village School, WA (HND)
Lake Michigan College, MI (JRC)
Lake Region State College, ND (JRC)
Lakeshore Medical Lab Training Programs, IN (TCT)
Lakeshore Technical College, WI (TCT)
Lakeside School of Massage Therapy, WI (TCT)
Lake-Sumter Community College, FL (JRC)
Lake Superior College, MN (JRC)
Lake Superior State University, MI (UNC)
Lake Tahoe Community College, CA (JRC)
Lake Technical Center, FL (TCT)
Lakeview College of Nursing, IL (UNC)
Lake Washington Technical College, WA (TCT)
La Lumiere School, IN (PRC)
Lamar Community College, CO (JRC)

Pat Goins Ruston Beauty School, LA (TCT)
Pat Goins Shreveport Beauty School, LA (TCT)
Pathology and Cytology Laboratories, KY (TCT)
Pathway School, PA (HND)
Patricia Stevens College, MO (TCT)
Patrick Henry College, VA (UNC)
Patrick Henry Community College, VA (JRC)
Patsy & Rob's Academy of Beauty, MO (TCT)
Patten University, CA (UNC)
The Patterson School, NC (PRC)
Patton State Hospital, CA (AHS)
Pat Wilson Beauty College, KY (TCT)
Paul D. Camp Community College, VA (JRC)
Paul Mitchell The School, CA (TCT)
Paul Quinn College, TX (UNC)
Paul Smith's College, NY (UNC)
Payne Theological Seminary, OH (UNC)
P.B. Cosmetology Education Centre, NJ (TCT)
PCI Dealers School, NV (TCT)
PCI Health Training Center, TX (TCT)
PC Professor, FL (TCT)
Peabody College of Vanderbilt University, TN (UNC)
Peabody Institute Johns Hopkins Univ., MD (GRD)
Peace College, NC (UNC)
Pearl River Community College, MS (JRC)
Peddie School, NJ (PRC)
Peirce College, PA (JRC)
Pelican Flight Training Center, FL (TCT)
Pellissippi State Technical Comm. Coll., TN (JRC)
Peninsula Academy, VA (HND)
Peninsula College, WA (JRC)
Penn Commercial Business/Technical Sch., PA (TCT)
Pennco Tech, NJ (TCT)
Pennco Tech, PA (TCT)
Pennington School, NJ (PRC)
Penn State Cosmetology Academy, PA (TCT)
Penn State Dickinson School of Law, PA (GRD)
Penn State Fayette Eberly Campus, PA (JRC)
Penn State Great Valley School, PA (GRD)
PA Academy of Cosmetic Arts & Sciences, PA (TCT)
Pennsylvania Academy of the Fine Arts, PA (TCT)
Pennsylvania College of Art and Design, PA (UNC)
Pennsylvania College of Optometry, PA (GRD)
Pennsylvania College of Technology, PA (JRC)
Pennsylvania College of Technology, PA (UNC)
Pennsylvania Culinary Institute, PA (JRC)
Pennsylvania Gunsmith School, PA (TCT)
Pennsylvania Highlands Community College, PA (JRC)
Pennsylvania Hospital, PA (AHS)
Pennsylvania Institute of Taxidermy, PA (TCT)
Pennsylvania Institute of Technology, PA (JRC)
Pennsylvania School for the Deaf, PA (HND)
Pennsylvania School of Business, PA (JRC)
Penn State Hershey College of Medicine, PA (GRD)
Pennsylvania State University, PA (JRC)
Pennsylvania State University, PA (UNC)
Penn Valley Community College, MO (JRC)
Penrose-St. Francis Health System, CO (TCT)
Pensacola Christian College, FL (UNC)
Pensacola Junior College, FL (JRC)
Pepperdine University, CA (PSY)
Pepperdine University, CA (UNC)
Performance Training, NJ (TCT)
Perkins School for the Blind, MA (HND)
Perkiomen School, PA (PRC)
Perry Technical Institute, WA (TCT)
Peru State College, NE (UNC)
Pfeiffer University, NC (UNC)
Phagans' Beauty College, OR (TCT)
Phagans' Central Oregon Beauty College, OR (TCT)
Phagans' Grants Pass College of Beauty, OR (TCT)
Phagans' Medford Beauty School, OR (TCT)
Phagans' Newport Academy of Cosmetology, OR (TCT)
Phagans' Orchards Beauty School, WA (TCT)
Phagans' School of Beauty, OR (TCT)
Phagans' School of Hair Design, OR (TCT)
Phagans' Tigard Beauty School, OR (TCT)
The Phelps School, PA (PRB)
Philadelphia Biblical University, PA (UNC)
Philadelphia Coll. Osteopathic Medicine, PA (GRD)
Philadelphia University, PA (UNC)
Philander Smith College, AR (UNC)
Phillips Academy, MA (PRC)
Phillips Beth Israel School of Nursing, NY (TCT)
Phillips Comm. Coll. of the Univ. of AR, AR (JRC)
Phillips Exeter Academy, NH (PRC)
Phillips Graduate Institute, CA (GRD)
Phillips Hairstyling Institute, NY (TCT)
Phillips Theological Seminary, OK (GRD)
Phlebotomy Learning Center, CO (TCT)
Phoenix College, AZ (JRC)
Phoenix East Aviation, FL (TCT)
Phoenix First Pastors College, AZ (UNC)
Phoenix Institute of Herbal Medicine, AZ (GRD)
Phoenix Seminary, AZ (UNC)
Photographic Center Northwest, WA (TCT)
PIA School of Specialized Technology, PA (AAT)
Pickens Technical Center, CO (TCT)
Piedmont Baptist College, NC (UNC)
Piedmont College, GA (UNC)
Piedmont Community College, NC (JRC)
Piedmont Technical College, SC (JRC)
Piedmont Virginia Community College, VA (JRC)
Pierce College, WA (JRC)
Pierre's School of Cosmetology, ME (TCT)
Pikes Peak Community College, CO (JRC)
Pikeville College, KY (UNC)
Pillsbury Baptist Bible College, MN (UNC)
Pima Community College, AZ (JRC)
Pima Medical Institute, AZ (TCT)
Pima Medical Institute, CA (TCT)
Pima Medical Institute, CO (TCT)
Pima Medical Institute, NM (TCT)
Pima Medical Institute, NV (TCT)
Pima Medical Institute, WA (TCT)
Pine Crest School, FL (PRC)
Pine Forge Academy, PA (PRC)
Pinellas Technical Education Center, FL (TCT)
Pine Manor College, MA (UNC)
Pine Ridge School, VT (PRC)
Pine Technical College, MN (JRC)
Pineville Beauty School, LA (TCT)
Piney Woods School, MS (PRC)
Pinnacle Career Institute, KS (TCT)
Pinnacle Career Institute, MO (TCT)
Pioneer Pacific College, OR (TCT)
Pipo Academy of Hair Design, TX (TCT)
Pitt Community College, NC (JRC)
Pittsburgh Institute of Mortuary Science, PA (JRC)
Pittsburgh Technical Institute, PA (TCT)
Pittsburgh Theological Seminary, PA (TSR)
Pittsburg State University, KS (UNC)
Pitzer College, CA (UNC)
Pivot Point Cosmetology Research Center, IL (TCT)
Pivot Point International, IL (TCT)
Pivot Point the Masters, AL (TCT)
PJA School, PA (TCT)
PJ's College of Cosmetology, IN (TCT)
PJs College of Cosmetology, KY (TCT)
Platt College, CA (TCT)
Platt College, CA (UNC)
Platt College, CO (JRC)
Platt College, OK (TCT)
Platte Valley Academy, NE (PRC)
Plaza Beauty School, TN (TCT)
Plaza College, NY (TCT)
Plaza School of Beauty Culture, SC (TCT)
Plymouth State University, NH (UNC)
Point Loma Nazarene University, CA (UNC)
Point Park University, PA (UNC)
Point Park Univ.-St. Francis Med. Ctr., PA (AHS)
Politec Institute, PR (TCT)
Polk Community College, FL (JRC)
Polytechnic Institute, TX (TCT)
Polytechnic University, NY (GRD)
Polytechnic University, NY (UNC)
Polytechnic University of the Americas, FL (UNC)
Pomfret School, CT (PRC)
Pomona College, CA (UNC)
Ponca City Beauty College, OK (TCT)
Ponce Paramedical College, PR (TCT)
Ponce School of Medicine, PR (GRD)
Pontifical Catholic Univ. of Puerto Rico, PR (UNC)
Pontifical College Josephinum, OH (MNC)
Porter and Chester Institute, CT (TCT)
Porter and Chester Institute, MA (TCT)
Porter Memorial Hospital, IN (AHS)
Porterville College, CA (JRC)
Porterville Development Center, CA (TCT)
Portfolio Center, GA (TCT)
Port Huron Hospital, MI (AHS)
Portland Community College, OR (JRC)
Portland State University, OR (UNC)
Port St. Lucie Beauty Academy, FL (TCT)
Portsmouth Abbey School, RI (PRC)
Portsmouth Beauty School of Hair Design, NH (TCT)
Post University, CT (UNC)
Poteau Beauty College, OK (TCT)
Potomac Academy of Hair Design, VA (TCT)
Potomac College, DC (UNC)
Potomac State College of West Virginia U, WV (JRC)
Pottsville Hospital School of Nursing, PA (TCT)
Poway Academy of Hair Design, CA (TCT)
Powder Springs Beauty College, GA (TCT)
Poynter Institute for Media Studies, FL (TCT)
Prairie State College, IL (JRC)
Prairie View A&M University, TX (NRS)
Prairie View A&M University, TX (UNC)
Pratt Community College, KS (JRC)
Pratt Institute, NY (UNC)
The Praxis Institute, FL (TCT)
The Praxis Institute, FL (TCT)
Precision Technical Institute, CA (TCT)
Premiere Career College, CA (TCT)
Premier Hair Academy, UT (TCT)
Presbyterian College, SC (UNC)
Presbyterian Hospital, NC (AHS)
Presbyterian Hospital, TX (AHS)
Presbyterian Pan American School, TX (PRC)
Prescott College, AZ (UNC)
Presentation College, SD (UNC)
Pressley Ridge School, PA (HND)
Prestonsburg Community College, KY (JRC)
Prince George's Community College, MD (JRC)
Prince Institute of Professional Studies, AL (JRC)
Prince Regional Vocational Tech School, CT (TCT)
Princeton Information Technology Center, PA (TCT)
Princeton Theological Seminary, NJ (GRD)
Princeton University, NJ (UNC)
Prince William Sound Community College, AK (JRC)
Principia College, IL (UNC)
Principia School, MO (PRC)
Proctor Academy, NH (PRC)
Professional Beauty School, WA (TCT)
Professional Business College, NY (TCT)
Professional Career Development Inst, GA (HMS)
Professional Career Institute, CA (TCT)
Professional Careers Institute, IN (TCT)
Professional Choice Hair Design Academy, IL (TCT)
Professional Cosmetology Education Ctr, AR (TCT)
Professional Cosmetology Institute, IA (TCT)
Professional Electrical School, PR (TCT)
Professional Golfers Career College, CA (TCT)
Professional Hair Design Academy, WI (TCT)
Professional Institute of Beauty, CA (TCT)
Professional Massage Training Center, MO (TCT)
Professional Skills Institute, OH (TCT)
Professional Technical Institute, PR (TCT)
Professional Training Center, FL (TCT)
Protestant Episcopal Theologcl. Seminary, VA (GRD)
Provena United Samaritans Medical Center, IL (TCT)
Providence College, RI (UNC)
Providence Hospital, MI (AHS)
Provo College, UT (TCT)
Pro Way Hair School, GA (TCT)
Pruonto's Hair Design Institute, PA (TCT)
Pryor Beauty College, OK (TCT)
The Psychological Studies Institute, GA (GRD)
Public Health Foundation Enterprises, CA (TCT)
Pueblo Community College, CO (JRC)
Puerto Rico Technical Jr College, PR (TCT)
Puget Sound Christian College, WA (TSR)
Pulaski Technical College, AR (TCT)
Punxy Beauty School of Cosmetology Arts, PA (TCT)
Purchase College SUNY, NY (UNC)
Purdue University, IN (UNC)
Purnell School, NJ (PRG)
Putney School, VT (PRC)
Pyramid Career Institute, IL (TCT)

Q

Quantum Helicopters, AZ (TCT)
Queen City College, TN (TCT)
Queen of Peace Hospital, SD (AHS)
Queen of the Holy Rosary College, CA (JRC)
Queens University of Charlotte, NC (UNC)
Quincy College, MA (JRC)
Quincy University, IL (UNC)
Quinebaug Valley Community College, CT (JRC)
Quinnipiac University, CT (UNC)
Quinsigamond Community College, MA (JRC)

R

Rabbi Isaac Elchanan Theological Sem., NY (GRD)
Rabbi Jacob Joseph School, NJ (UNC)
Rabbinical Academy Mesivta Rabbi Chaim, NY (MNC)
Rabbinical College Beth Shraga, NY (MNC)
Rabbinical Coll. Bobovr Yeshiva Bnei Zn., NY (MNC)
Rabbinical Coll. Ch' San Sofer of NY, NY (MNC)
Rabbinical College of America, NJ (MNC)
Rabbinical College of Long Island, NY (MNC)
Rabbinical College of Ohr Shimon Yisroel, NY (MNC)
Rabbinical College of Telshe, OH (MNC)
Rabbinical Seminary Adas Yereim, NY (MNC)
Rabbinical Seminary M'Kor Chaim, NY (MNC)
Rabbinical Seminary of America, NY (MNC)
Rabun Gap-Nacoochee School, GA (PRC)
Radford M. Locklin Technical Center, FL (TCT)
Radford University, VA (UNC)
Radiation Therapy Services, FL (TCT)
Rainier School, WA (HND)
RainStar University, AZ (TCT)
Rainy River Community College, MN (JRC)
Ralph's Virginia School of Cosmetology, VA (TCT)
Ramapo College of New Jersey, NJ (UNC)
Ramirez College of Business Technology, PR (TCT)
Randolph Community College, NC (JRC)
Randolph-Macon Academy, VA (PRC)
Randolph-Macon College, VA (UNC)
Randolph-Macon Woman's College, VA (WMC)
Randolph School, AL (PRC)
Ranger College, TX (JRC)
Ranken Technical College, MO (JRC)
Raphael's School of Beauty Culture, OH (TCT)
Rapid City Regional Hospital, SD (AHS)
Rapides Regional Medical Center, LA (AHS)
Rappahannock Community College, VA (JRC)
Raritan Bay Medical Center, NJ (NRS)
Raritan Valley Community College, NJ (JRC)
Raritan Valley Flying School, NJ (TCT)
Rasmussen College, MN (TCT)
Ravenscroft Beauty College, IN (TCT)
Razzle Dazzle College of Hair Design, ID (TCT)
R.D. Hairstyling College, ND (TCT)
Reading Area Community College, PA (JRC)
Reading Hospital & Medical Center, PA (AHS)
Reconstructionist Rabbinical College, PA (UNC)
Recording Workshop, OH (TCT)
The Rectory School, CT (PRB)
Redemption Christian Academy, NY (PRC)
Redlands Community College, OK (JRC)
Red Rocks Community College, CO (JRC)
Redwoods Community College, CA (JRC)
Reed College, OR (UNC)
Reedley College, CA (JRC)
Reformed Bible College, MI (UNC)
Reformed Episcopal Seminary, PA (GRD)
Reformed Presbyterian Theological Sem., PA (GRD)
Reformed Theological Seminary, FL (GRD)
Reformed Theological Seminary, MS (GRD)
Reformed Theological Seminary, NC (GRD)
Reformed Theological Seminary, VA (GRD)
Refrigeration School, AZ (TCT)
Regency Beauty Academy, MN (TCT)
Regent University, VA (GRD)
Regional West Medical Center, NE (AHS)
Regis College, MA (UNC)
Regis University, CO (UNC)
Reid Hospital & Health Care Services, IN (AHS)
Reid State Technical College, AL (JRC)
Reignbow Beauty Academy, NJ (TCT)
Reignbow Hair Fashion Institute, NJ (TCT)
Reinhardt College, GA (UNC)
Remington College, AL (TCT)
Remington College, AR (TCT)
Remington College, AZ (UNC)
Remington College, CA (UNC)
Remington College, CO (HMS)
Remington College, CO (TCT)
Remington College, FL (TCT)
Remington College, HI (TCT)
Remington College, LA (TCT)
Remington College, OH (TCT)
Remington College, TN (JRC)
Remington College, TN (TCT)
Remington College, TX (JRC)
Remington College, TX (TCT)
Rend Lake College, IL (JRC)
Reno Tahoe Job Training Academy, NV (TCT)
Rensselaer at Hartford, CT (GRD)
Rensselaer Polytechnic Institute, NY (UNC)
Renton Technical College, WA (JRC)

Reppert School of Auctioneering, IN (TCT)
Research College of Nursing, MO (UNC)
Research Medical Center, MO (AHS)
Restaurant School at Walnut Hill College, PA (UNC)
RETS Electronic School, MA (TCT)
RETS Technical Center, OH (TCT)
Reuben Allen College, TN (TCT)
Rhodec International, MA (HMS)
Rhode Island College, RI (UNC)
Rhode Island Hospital, RI (AHS)
Rhode Island School of Design, RI (UNC)
Rhodes College, TN (UNC)
Rice Memorial Hospital, MN (AHS)
Rice University, TX (UNC)
Richard Bland College, VA (JRC)
Richard J. Daley College, IL (JRC)
Richard Milburn High School, VA (HMS)
Richard's Beauty College, CA (TCT)
Richard Stockton College of New Jersey, NJ (UNC)
Richland College, TX (JRC)
Richland Community College, IL (JRC)
Richmond Community College, NC (JRC)
Richmond University London England, MA (UNC)
Rich Mountain Community College, AR (JRC)
Rider University, NJ (UNC)
Ridge Vocational-Technical Center, FL (TCT)
Ridgewater College-Hutchinson Campus, MN (JRC)
Ridgewater College-Willmar Campus, MN (JRC)
Ridley-Lowell Business & Technical Inst., CT (TCT)
Ridley-Lowell Business & Technical Inst., NY (TCT)
Riggs Le Mar Beauty College, OH (TCT)
Ringling School of Art & Design, FL (UNC)
Rio Grande Bible Institute, TX (UNC)
Rio Hondo College, CA (JRC)
Rio Salado Community College, AZ (JRC)
Ripon College, WI (UNC)
Rising Spirit Inst. of Natural Health, GA (TCT)
Rita's Moorhead Beauty College, MN (TCT)
Riverland Community College, MN (AHS)
Riverland Community College, MN (TCT)
Riverland Technical College, MN (TCT)
River Parishes Community College, LA (JRC)
Riverside Community College, CA (JRC)
Riverside Hairstyling Academy, FL (TCT)
Riverside Hospital, OH (AHS)
Riverside Military Academy, GA (PRB)
Riverside School of Health Careers, VA (TCT)
Rivertown School of Beauty, GA (TCT)
Rivier College, NH (UNC)
Rizzieri Aveda School, NJ (TCT)
Roane State Community College, TN (JRC)
Roanoke Bible College, NC (UNC)
Roanoke-Chowan Community College, NC (JRC)
Roanoke College, VA (UNC)
The Robert B. Adams/LabCorp CLS Program, AL (AHS)
Robert Louis Stevenson High School, CA (PRC)
Robert Morgan Educational Center, FL (TCT)
Robert Morris College, IL (UNC)
Robert Morris College, PA (UNC)
Robert Morris University, PA (UNC)
Roberto-Venn Guitar Making School, AZ (TCT)
Robert Packer Hospital, PA (AHS)
R. Paul Academy of Cosmetology Arts/Sci, MD (TCT)
Roberts Wesleyan College, NY (UNC)
Robeson Community College, NC (JRC)
Rob Roy Academy, MA (TCT)
Rob Roy Academy Fall River Campus, MA (TCT)
Rob Roy Academy Taunton Campus, MA (TCT)
Rochester Business Institute, NY (TCT)
Rochester College, MI (UNC)
Rochester Community & Technical College, MN (JRC)
Rochester Community & Technical College, MN (TCT)
Rochester General Hospital, NY (AHS)
Rochester Institute of Technology, NY (UNC)
Rochester Institute of Technology (NTID), NY (JRC)
Rochester School for the Deaf, NY (HND)
Rockefeller University, NY (GRD)
Rockford Business College, IL (TCT)
Rockford College, IL (UNC)
Rockford Memorial Hospital, IL (AHS)
Rockhurst University, MO (UNC)
Rockingham Community College, NC (JRC)
Rockingham Memorial Hospital, VA (TCT)
Rock Point School, VT (PRC)
Rock Valley College, IL (JRC)
Rocky Mountain College, MT (UNC)
Rocky Mountain College of Art & Design, CO (UNC)
Roffler Moler Hairstyling College, GA (TCT)
Roger's Academy of Hair Design, IN (TCT)
Rogers State University, OK (UNC)
Roger Williams University, RI (UNC)
Rogie's School of Beauty Culture, PR (TCT)
Rogue Community College, OR (JRC)
Rolf Institute of Structural Integration, CO (TCT)
Rollins College, FL (UNC)
Roman Academy of Beauty Culture, NJ (TCT)
Ronnie & Dorman's School of Hair Design, LA (TCT)
Roosevelt University, IL (UNC)
R. Franklin University of Medicine, IL (GRD)
Roseburg Beauty College, OR (TCT)
Rosedale Bible College, OH (UNC)
Rosedale Technical Institute, PA (TCT)
Rose-Hulman Institute of Technology, IN (UNC)
Rosel School of Cosmetology, IL (TCT)
Rosemead Beauty School, CA (TCT)
Rosemont College, PA (WMC)
Rose State College, OK (JRC)
Ross Medical Education Center, FL (TCT)
Ross Medical Education Center, MI (TCT)
Rowan-Cabarrus Community College, NC (JRC)
Rowan Technical College, KY (TCT)
Rowan University, NJ (UNC)
Roxborough Memorial Hospital, PA (TCT)
Roxbury Community College, MA (JRC)
Royal Beauty Careers, TX (TCT)
Royale College of Beauty, CA (TCT)
Royer-Greaves School for Blind, PA (HND)
RSHT Training Center, VA (TCT)
Rudae's School of Beauty Culture, IN (TCT)
Rudy & Kelly Academy of Hair & Nails, VA (TCT)
Rumsey Hall School, CT (PRC)
Rush University, IL (UNC)
Russell Sage College, NY (WMC)
Russell Sage Graduate School, NY (GRD)
Rust College, MS (UNC)
Rutgers-The State University of N.J., NJ (UNC)
Rutland Regional Medical Center, VT (AHS)

S

Sacramento City College, CA (JRC)
Sacramento Medical Foundation Blood Bank, CA (AHS)
Sacred Heart Hospital, PA (AHS)
Sacred Heart Hospital, SD (AHS)
Sacred Heart Hospital, WI (AHS)
Sacred Heart Major Seminary, MI (MNC)
Sacred Heart Medical Center, WA (AHS)
Sacred Heart Preparatory School, CA (PRC)
Sacred Heart School of Theology, WI (GRD)
Sacred Heart University, CT (UNC)
Saddleback College, CA (JRC)
Saddlebrook Preparatory School, FL (PRC)
SAE Institute Nashville, TN (TCT)
Safford College of Beauty Culture, AZ (TCT)
Sage College, CA (TCT)
Sage College of Albany, NY (JRC)
Sage Technical Commerical Driving School, MT (TCT)
Sage Technical School, WY (TCT)
Sage Technical Services, ID (TCT)
Saginaw Chippewa Tribal College, MI (JRC)
Saginaw Valley State University, MI (UNC)
St. Albans School, DC (PRB)
St. Alexius Medical Center, ND (AHS)
St. Alphonsus Regional Medical Center, ID (AHS)
St. Ambrose University, IA (UNC)
St. Andrews Presbyterian College, NC (UNC)
St. Andrew's School, DE (PRC)
St. Andrew's School, FL (PRC)
St. Andrew's School, GA (PRC)
St. Andrew's School, RI (PRC)
St. Andrew's-Sewanee School, TN (PRC)
St. Anne's-Belfield School, VA (PRC)
St. Anselm College, NH (UNC)
St. Anthony College of Nursing, IL (TCT)
St. Anthony Medical Center, IL (AHS)
St. Augustine College, IL (JRC)
St. Augustine's College, NC (UNC)
St. Barnabas Medical Center, NJ (AHS)
St. Bernard's Sch of Theology & Ministry, NY (GRD)
St. Bonaventure University, NY (UNC)
St. Catharine College, KY (JRC)
St. Catherines Military School, CA (PRB)
St. Catherine's School, VA (PRG)
St. Charles Borromeo Seminary, PA (MNC)
St. Charles Community College, MO (JRC)
St. Charles Hospital, OH (AHS)
St. Clair County Community College, MI (JRC)
St. Cloud Hospital, MN (AHS)
St. Cloud Regency Beauty Academy, MN (TCT)
St. Cloud State University, MN (UNC)
St. Cloud Technical College, MN (JRC)
St. Coletta School, WI (HND)
St. Croix Lutheran High School, MN (PRC)
St. Dominic-Jackson Memorial Hospital, MS (AHS)
St. Edward's University, TX (UNC)
St. Elizabeth College of Nursing, NY (TCT)
St. Elizabeth Hospital, IL (TCT)
St. Elizabeth Hospital, OH (AHS)
St. Elizabeth Hospital, TX (AHS)
St. Elizabeth Hospital, WI (AHS)
St. Elizabeth Medical Center, KY (TCT)
St. Elizabeth School of Nursing, IN (TCT)
St. Francis Career College, CA (TCT)
St. Francis College, NY (UNC)
St. Francis High School, HI (PRG)
St. Francis Hospital, IL (TCT)
St. Francis Hospital, NJ (NRS)
St. Francis Hospital, OK (AHS)
St. Francis Hospital, WI (AHS)
St. Francis Hospital Center, IN (TCT)
St. Francis Medical Center, IL (TCT)
St. Francis Medical Center, LA (AHS)
St. Francis Medical Center, NJ (AHS)
St. Francis Medical Ctr. Coll./Nursing, IL (TCT)
St. Francis Seminary, WI (GRD)
St. Francis University, PA (UNC)
St. George's School, RI (PRC)
St. Gregory's Academy, PA (PRB)
St. Gregory's University, OK (UNC)
St. James Mercy Hospital, NY (AHS)
St. James School, MD (PRC)
St. John Fisher College, NY (UNC)
St. John of God Community Services, NJ (HND)
St. Johnsbury Academy, VT (PRC)
St. John's College, IL (UNC)
St. John's College, MD (UNC)
St. John's College, NM (UNC)
St. John's Hospital, IL (AHS)
St. John's Hospital, MI (AHS)
St. John's Mercy Medical Center, MO (AHS)
St. John's Military School, KS (PRB)
St. John's Northwestern Military Academy, WI (PRB)
St. John's Preparatory School, MA (PRB)
St. John's Preparatory School, MN (PRC)
St. John's Regional Health Center, MO (AHS)
St. John's Regional Medical Center, CA (TCT)
St. John's Regional Medical Center, MO (AHS)
St. John's River Community College, FL (JRC)
St. John's School of Nursing, MO (NRS)
St. John's University, MN (MNC)
St. John's University, NY (UNC)
St. John Vianney College Seminary, FL (MNC)
St. Joseph College, CT (WMC)
St. Joseph Hospital, CA (AHS)
St. Joseph Hospital & Health Center, IN (AHS)
St. Joseph Hospital/Marshfield Clinic, WI (AHS)
St. Joseph's College, IN (UNC)
St. Joseph's College, NY (UNC)
St. Joseph's College of Maine, ME (UNC)
St. Joseph's Hospital College of Nursing, NY (TCT)
St. Joseph Seminary College, LA (UNC)
St. Joseph's Hospital, GA (TCT)
St. Joseph's Hospital, KY (AHS)
St. Joseph's Hospital, PA (AHS)
St. Joseph's Hospital, RI (AHS)
St. Joseph's Institute for the Deaf, MO (HND)
St. Joseph's Seminary, NY (GRD)
St. Joseph's University, PA (UNC)
St. Lawrence Seminary High School, WI (PRB)
St. Lawrence University, NY (UNC)
St. Leo University, FL (UNC)
St. Louis Christian College, MO (UNC)
St. Louis College of Health Careers, MO (TCT)
St. Louis College of Pharmacy, MO (UNC)
St. Louis Community College, MO (JRC)
St. Louis Hair Academy, MO (TCT)
St. Louis University, MO (UNC)
St. Luke's College, IA (JRC)
St. Luke's College, MO (UNC)
St. Luke's Hospital, MA (AHS)
St. Luke's Hospital, PA (NRS)
St. Luke's Hospital/Mayo Clinic, FL (AHS)
St. Luke's Medical Center, OH (AHS)
St. Luke's Medical Center, WI (AHS)
St. Luke's Midland Regional Medical Ctr., SD (AHS)
St. Margaret Hospital, IN (AHS)
St. Margaret Hospital School of Nursing, PA (TCT)
St. Margaret's School, VA (PRG)
St. Mark's School, MA (PRC)
St. Martin's University, WA (UNC)
St. Mary of Providence School, IL (HND)
St. Mary-of-the-Woods College, IN (WMC)
St. Mary's Campus Coll. of St. Catherine, MN (JRC)
St. Mary's College, CA (UNC)
St. Mary's College, IN (WMC)
St. Mary's College of Maryland, MD (UNC)
St. Mary Seminary/Graduate Sch. Theology, OH (TSR)
St. Mary's Hall, TX (PRC)
St. Mary's Hospital, CT (AHS)
St. Mary's Hospital, OK (AHS)
St. Mary's Hospital, VA (AHS)
St. Mary's Hospital/Mayo Medical Center, MN (AHS)
St. Mary's Medical Center, MI (AHS)
St. Mary's Medical Center, WV (TCT)
St. Mary's Preparatory High School, MI (PRB)
St. Mary's School, NC (PRG)
St. Mary's School for the Deaf, NY (HND)
St. Mary's Seminary & University, MD (GRD)
St. Mary's University of Minnesota, MN (GRD)
St. Mary's University of Minnesota, MN (UNC)
St. Mary's University of San Antonio, TX (UNC)
St. Meinrad School of Theology, IN (GRD)
St. Michael's College, VT (LAS)
St. Michael's Prepartory School, CA (PRB)
St. Norbert College, WI (UNC)
St. Olaf College, MN (UNC)
St. Patrick Hospital, MT (AHS)
St. Patrick's Hospital, LA (AHS)
St. Patrick's Seminary & University, CA (GRD)
St. Paul College, MN (JRC)
St. Paul Lutheran High School, MO (PRC)
St. Paul School of Theology, MO (GRD)
St. Paul's College, VA (UNC)
St. Paul's School, NH (PRC)
St. Petersburg College, FL (JRC)
St. Petersburg Theological Seminary, FL (GRD)
St. Peter's College, NJ (UNC)
St. Phillip's College, TX (JRC)
St. Rita School for the Deaf, OH (HND)
SS. Cyril and Methodius Seminary, MI (GRD)
St. Stanislaus College Prep, MS (PRB)
St. Stephen's Episcopal School, TX (PRC)
St. Thomas Academy, MN (PRB)
St. Thomas Aquinas College, NY (UNC)
St. Thomas Choir School, NY (PRB)
St. Thomas Hospital, TN (AHS)
St. Thomas More School, CT (PRB)
St. Thomas University, FL (UNC)
St. Tikhon's Orthodox Theological Sem., PA (GRD)
St. Timothy's School, MD (PRG)
St. Vincent Catholic Medical Center, NY (TCT)
St. Vincent College, PA (UNC)
St. Vincent DePaul Regional Seminary, FL (MNC)
St. Vincent Hospital, WI (AHS)
St. Vincent Hospital & Medical Center, OR (AHS)
St. Vincent Infirmary Medical Center, AR (AHS)
St. Vincent's College, CT (JRC)
St. Vincent Seminary, PA (UNC)
St. Vincent's Hospital & Health Center, MT (AHS)
St. Vincent's Hospital & Medical Center, NY (AHS)
St. Vincent's Medical Center, NY (AHS)
St. Vladimir's Orthodox Theological Sem., NY (GRD)
St. Xavier University, IL (UNC)
Salem Academy, NC (PRG)
Salem College, NC (WMC)
Salem College of Hairstyling, MO (TCT)
Salem Community College, NJ (JRC)
Salem International University, WV (UNC)
Salem State College, MA (UNC)
Salina Area Vocational Technical School, KS (TCT)
Salisbury School, CT (PRB)
Salisbury University, MD (UNC)
Salish Kootenai College, MT (JRC)
Salter School, MA (TCT)
Salt Lake Community College, UT (JRC)
Salve Regina University, RI (UNC)
Samaritan Hospital School of Nursing, NY (TCT)
Samaritan Medical Center, NY (AHS)
Samford University, AL (UNC)
Sam Houston State University, TX (UNC)
Sampson Community College, NC (JRC)
Samra University of Oriental Medicine, CA (GRD)
Samuel Merritt College, CA (UNC)
San Antonio Beauty College #3, TX (TCT)

San Antonio Beauty College #4, TX (TCT)
San Antonio College, TX (JRC)
San Antonio College Medical Dental Asst., TX (TCT)
San Bernardino Valley College, CA (JRC)
Sandersville Technical College, GA (TCT)
Sandhills Community College, NC (JRC)
San Diego Christian College, CA (UNC)
San Diego City College, CA (JRC)
San Diego Mesa College, CA (JRC)
San Diego Miramar College, CA (JRC)
San Diego State University, CA (UNC)
San Domenico School, CA (PRG)
Sand Springs Beauty College, OK (TCT)
Sandy Spring Friends School, MD (PRC)
San Fernando Beauty Academy, CA (TCT)
Sanford-Brown College, IL (TCT)
Sanford-Brown College, MO (TCT)
Sanford-Brown College, OH (TCT)
Sanford-Brown Institute, FL (TCT)
Sanford Brown Institute, FL (TCT)
Sanford-Brown Institute, NY (TCT)
Sanford-Brown Institute Houston, TX (JRC)
San Francisco Art Institute, CA (UNC)
San Francisco Conservatory of Music, CA (UNC)
San Francisco State University, CA (UNC)
San Francisco Theological Seminary, CA (GRD)
San Jacinto College, TX (JRC)
San Joaquin College of Law, CA (GRD)
San Joaquin Delta College, CA (JRC)
San Joaquin General Hospital, CA (TCT)
San Joaquin Valley College, CA (JRC)
San Jose City College, CA (JRC)
San Jose State University, CA (UNC)
San Juan Basin Technical College, CO (TCT)
San Juan Bautista School of Medicine, PR (UNC)
San Juan College, NM (JRC)
San Marcos Baptist Academy, TX (PRC)
Santa Ana College, CA (JRC)
Santa Barbara Business College, CA (JRC)
Santa Barbara Business College, CA (TCT)
Santa Barbara City College, CA (JRC)
Santa Barbara Coll. of Oriental Medicine, CA (GRD)
Santa Barbara Cottage & Gen. Hosp., CA (TCT)
Santa Catalina School, CA (PRG)
Santa Clara University, CA (UNC)
Santa Fe Community College, FL (JRC)
Santa Fe Community College, NM (JRC)
Santa Monica College, CA (JRC)
Santa Rosa Junior College, CA (JRC)
Santiago Canyon College, CA (JRC)
Sarah Lawrence College, NY (UNC)
Sarasota County Technical Institute, FL (TCT)
Sarasota Memorial Hospital, FL (AHS)
Sarasota School of Massage Therapy, FL (TCT)
Sauk Valley Community College, IL (JRC)
Savannah College of Art & Design, GA (UNC)
Savannah College of Art and Design, GA (UNC)
Savannah River College, GA (TCT)
Savannah State University, GA (UNC)
Savannah Technical College, GA (TCT)
Sawyer College, IN (TCT)
Sawyer School, CT (TCT)
Sawyer School, RI (TCT)
Saybrook Graduate School, CA (GRD)
Scattergood Friends School, IA (PRC)
Scenic Mountain Medical Center, TX (AHS)
Schenck Civilian Conservation Center, NC (TCT)
Schiller International University, FL (UNC)
Schilling-Douglas School of Hair Design, DE (TCT)
Schoolcraft College, MI (JRC)
School for International Training, VT (GRD)
School for the Deaf, NY (HND)
School of Advertising Art, OH (TCT)
School of Art & Design @ Montgomery Coll, MD (JRC)
School of Automotive Machinists, TX (TCT)
School of Communication Arts, NC (TCT)
School of Creative Hair Design, MI (TCT)
School of Hair Design, KY (TCT)
School of Hair Design, OK (TCT)
The School of Hairstyling, ID (TCT)
The School of Health Careers, FL (TCT)
School of Health Management, MO (GRD)
School of the Art Institute of Chicago, IL (GRD)
School of the Museum of Fine Arts, MA (UNC)
School of Urban Missions, LA (JRC)
School of Visual Arts, NY (UNC)
Schreiner University, TX (UNC)
Schuylkill Institute of Business & Tech., PA (TCT)
Scientific College of Beauty/Barbering, WI (TCT)
Scot Lewis Beauty School, MN (TCT)
Scot Lewis School, MN (TCT)
Scot Lewis School of Cosmetology, MN (TCT)
Scott & White Memorial Hospital & Clinic, TX (TCT)
Scott Cole Academy, AZ (TCT)
Scott College of Cosmetology, WV (TCT)
Scott Community College, IA (JRC)
Scottsdale Community College, AZ (JRC)
Scottsdale Culinary Institute, AZ (TCT)
Scranton State School for the Deaf, PA (HND)
Scripps College, CA (WMC)
Scripps Memorial Hospital, CA (TCT)
Scripps Research Institute, CA (GRD)
Seabury Hall, HI (PRC)
Seabury-Western Theological Seminary, IL (TSR)
Searcy Beauty College, AR (TCT)
Seattle Central Community College, WA (JRC)
Seattle Institute of Oriental Medicine, WA (GRD)
Seattle Pacific University, WA (UNC)
Seattle University, WA (UNC)
Seattle University School of Law, WA (GRD)
Sebring Career School, TX (TCT)
Seguin Beauty College, TX (TCT)
Selma University, AL (UNC)
Seminary Ext. Independent Study Inst., TN (HMS)
Seminary of the Immaculate Conception, NY (GRD)
Seminole Community College, FL (JRC)
Seminole State College, OK (JRC)
Sentara School of Health Professions, VA (AHS)
Sequoia Institute, CA (TCT)
Serbia's Technical College, PR (TCT)
SER Business and Technical Institute, IL (TCT)
SER Business and Technical Institute, MI (TCT)
Sessions.edu Online School of Design, NY (HMS)
Seton Hall University, NJ (UNC)
Seton Hall University School of Law, NJ (GRD)
Seton Hill University, PA (UNC)
Settlement Music School, PA (MUS)
Seward County Community College, KS (JRC)
Sewickley Valley Hospital, PA (AHS)
Shady Side Academy, PA (PRC)
Shadyside Hospital, PA (AHS)
Shands Jacksonville Medical Center, FL (TCT)
Shannon West Texas Memorial Hospital, TX (AHS)
Sharon Regional Health System, PA (AHS)
Sharps Academy of Hairstyling, MI (TCT)
Shasta Bible College & Graduate School, CA (UNC)
Shasta College, CA (JRC)
Shattuck-St. Mary's School, MN (PRC)
Shawnee Beauty College, OK (TCT)
Shawnee Community College, IL (JRC)
Shawnee State University, OH (UNC)
Shaw University, NC (UNC)
Shear Ego Intl School of Hair Design, NY (TCT)
Sheldon Jackson College, AK (UNC)
Shelton State Community College, AL (JRC)
Shenandoah University, VA (UNC)
Shenandoah Valley Academy, VA (PRC)
Shepherd University, WV (UNC)
Sheridan College, WY (JRC)
Sheridan Technical Center, FL (TCT)
Sherman College of Straight Chiropractic, SC (GRD)
Shimer College, IL (UNC)
Shippensburg University, PA (UNC)
Shore Beauty School, NJ (TCT)
Shoreline Community College, WA (JRC)
Shore Memorial Hospital, NJ (AHS)
Shorter College, GA (UNC)
Shor Yoshuv Institute, NY (MNC)
Shreveport Job Corps Center, LA (TCT)
Sidney's Hairdressing College, KS (TCT)
Siena College, NY (UNC)
Siena Heights University, MI (UNC)
Sierra Academy of Aeronautics, CA (TCT)
Sierra College, CA (JRC)
Sierra College of Beauty, CA (TCT)
Sierra Nevada College-Lake Tahoe, NV (UNC)
Sierra Valley Business College, CA (TCT)
Silver Lake College, WI (UNC)
Simi Valley Adult Education, CA (TCT)
Simmons College, MA (WMC)
Simmons Institute of Funeral Service, NY (TCT)
Simon's Rock College of Bard, MA (UNC)
Simpson College, IA (UNC)
Simpson University, CA (LAS)
Sinclair Community College, OH (JRC)
Sinte Gleska University, SD (UNC)
Sioux Valley Hospital, SD (AHS)
Sisseton Wahpeton Community College, SD (JRC)
Sisters of Charity Medical Center, NY (AHS)
Si Tanka University, SD (TCT)
Sitting Bull College, ND (JRC)
Skagit Valley College, WA (JRC)
Skidmore College, NY (UNC)
SkillSource Office & Technology Center, WA (TCT)
Skin Works School of Advanced Skin Care, UT (TCT)
Skyline College, CA (JRC)
Slippery Rock University, PA (UNC)
Smith College, MA (WMC)
Snead State Community College, AL (JRC)
Snow College, UT (JRC)
Sodexho Marriott Healthcare Mid-Atlantic, MD (AHS)
Sodexho Marriott Services, MA (AHS)
Sojourner-Douglass College, MD (UNC)
Soka University of America, CA (UNC)
Solano Community College, CA (JRC)
Solebury School, PA (PRC)
Somerset Christian College, NJ (UNC)
Somerset Community College, KY (JRC)
Somerset Community Hospital, PA (AHS)
Sonoma College, CA (TCT)
Sonoma College - San Francisco, CA (TCT)
Sonoma State University, CA (UNC)
Sonoran Desert Institute, AZ (HMS)
Sotheby's Institute of Art, NY (TCT)
South Arkansas Community College, AR (JRC)
South Baylo University, CA (GRD)
South Carolina Criminal Justice Academy, SC (TCT)
South Carolina School for Deaf and Blind, SC (HND)
South Carolina State University, SC (UNC)
South Central College, MN (JRC)
South Coast College, CA (TCT)
South College, NC (JRC)
South College, TN (UNC)
South Dakota School for the Deaf, SD (HND)
South Dakota School Visually Handicapped, SD (HND)
South Dakota School Mines and Technology, SD (UNC)
South Dakota State University, SD (UNC)
Southeast Alabama Medical Center, AL (TCT)
Southeast Applied Technology College, UT (TCT)
Southeast Arkansas College, AR (TCT)
Southeast Community College, NE (JRC)
Southeastern Baptist College, MS (UNC)
Southeastern Baptist Theological Sem., NC (GRD)
Southeastern Beauty School, GA (TCT)
Southeastern Bible College, AL (TSR)
Southeastern Business College, OH (TCT)
Southeastern Career College, TN (TCT)
Southeastern Career Institute, TX (TCT)
Southeastern Community College, IA (JRC)
Southeastern Community College, NC (JRC)
Southeastern Illinois College, IL (JRC)
Southeastern Louisiana University, LA (UNC)
Southeastern Oklahoma State University, OK (UNC)
Southeastern School of Cosmetology, AL (TCT)
Southeastern School of Neuromuscular, FL (TCT)
Southeastern School of Neuromuscular, NC (TCT)
Southeastern School of Neuromuscular, SC (TCT)
Southeastern Technical College, GA (TCT)
Southeastern Technical Institute, MA (TCT)
Southeastern University, DC (BUS)
Southeastern University, FL (UNC)
Southeast Kentucky Community/Tech Coll, KY (JRC)
Southeast MO Hospital College of Nursing, MO (TCT)
Southeast Missouri State University, MO (UNC)
Southeast School of Cosmetology, KY (TCT)
Southeast Technical Institute, SD (TCT)
Southern Adventist University, TN (UNC)
Southern Arkansas University, AR (UNC)
Southern Arkansas University Tech, AR (JRC)
Southern Baptist Theological Seminary, KY (GRD)
Southern California College of Optometry, CA (GRD)
Southern California Inst. Architecture, CA (UNC)
Southern California Institute of Tech, CA (TCT)
Southern CA Regional Occupational Center, CA (TCT)
Southern California Seminary, CA (UNC)
Southern CA University of Health Science, CA (GRD)
Southern Careers Institute, TX (TCT)
Southern Christian University, AL (UNC)
Southern College of Optometry, TN (GRD)
Southern Community College, AL (JRC)
Southern Connecticut State University, CT (UNC)
Southern Evangelical Seminary, NC (GRD)
Southern Illinois University, IL (UNC)
Southern Illinois Univ. Edwardsville, IL (UNC)
Southern Institute of Cosmetology, AR (TCT)
Southern Institute of Cosmetology, TN (TCT)
Southern Maine Community College, ME (JRC)
Southern Methodist College, SC (UNC)
Southern Methodist University, TX (UNC)
Southern Nazarene University, OK (UNC)
Southern Nevada Univ of Cosmetology, NV (TCT)
Southern New England School of Law, MA (GRD)
Southern New Hampshire University, NH (UNC)
Southern Oregon University, OR (UNC)
Southern Polytech State University, GA (UNC)
Southern Regional Medical Center, GA (AHS)
Southern School of Beauty, OK (TCT)
Southern State Community College, OH (JRC)
Southern Union State Community College, AL (AHS)
Southern Union State Community College, AL (JRC)
Southern University A&M College, LA (UNC)
Southern University at Shreveport, LA (JRC)
Southern University in New Orleans, LA (UNC)
Southern Utah University, UT (UNC)
Southern Vermont College, VT (UNC)
Southern Virginia University, VA (UNC)
Southern Wesleyan University, SC (UNC)
Southern WV Community & Technical Coll., WV (JRC)
South Florida Community College, FL (JRC)
South Florida Institute of Technology, FL (TCT)
South Georgia College, GA (JRC)
South Georgia Technical College, GA (TCT)
South Hills Beauty Academy, PA (TCT)
South Hills School of Business & Tech., PA (TCT)
South Kent School, CT (PRB)
South Louisiana Beauty College, LA (TCT)
South Louisiana Community College, LA (JRC)
South Mountain Community College, AZ (JRC)
South Piedmont Community College, NC (JRC)
South Plains College, TX (JRC)
South Puget Sound Community College, WA (JRC)
South Seattle Community College, WA (JRC)
Southside Regional Medical Center, VA (AHS)
Southside Virginia Community College, VA (JRC)
South Suburban College of Cook County, IL (JRC)
South Texas Barber College, TX (TCT)
South Texas College, TX (JRC)
South Texas College of Law, TX (GRD)
South Texas Vocational-Technical Inst., TX (TCT)
South University, AL (JRC)
South University, FL (UNC)
South University, GA (UNC)
South University, SC (UNC)
Southwest Acupuncture College, NM (GRD)
Southwest Applied Technology College, UT (TCT)
Southwest Baptist University, MO (UNC)
Southwest Coll of Naturopathic Medicine, AZ (GRD)
Southwestern Academy, CA (PRC)
Southwestern Adventist University, TX (UNC)
Southwestern Assemblies of God Univ., TX (UNC)
Southwestern Baptist Theological Sem., TX (UNC)
Southwestern Christian College, TX (UNC)
Southwestern Christian University, OK (UNC)
Southwestern College, AZ (UNC)
Southwestern College, CA (JRC)
Southwestern College, KS (UNC)
Southwestern College, NM (UNC)
Southwestern College, OH (JRC)
Southwestern College of Business, KY (TCT)
Southwestern College of Business, OH (JRC)
Southwestern College of Business, OH (TCT)
Southwestern Community College, IA (JRC)
Southwestern Community College, NC (JRC)
Southwestern Illinois College, IL (JRC)
Southwestern Indian Polytechnic Inst., NM (JRC)
Southwestern Michigan College, MI (JRC)
Southwestern Oklahoma State University, OK (JRC)
Southwestern Oklahoma State University, OK (UNC)
Southwestern Oregon Community College, OR (JRC)
Southwestern Professional Institute, TX (TCT)
Southwestern University, TX (UNC)
Southwestern University School of Law, CA (GRD)
Southwest Florida College, FL (JRC)
Southwest General Hospital, OH (AHS)
Southwest Georgia Technical College, GA (TCT)
Southwest Institute of Healing Arts, AZ (TCT)
Southwest Institute of Technology, TX (TCT)
Southwest Kansas Technical School, KS (TCT)
Southwest Minnesota State University, MN (UNC)
Southwest Mississippi Community College, MS (JRC)
SW Mississippi Regional Medical Center, MS (AHS)
SW School of Business & Tech Careers, TX (TCT)
Southwest Tennessee Community College, TN (JRC)
Southwest Texas Junior College, TX (JRC)

Trinity Christian College, IL (UNC)
Trinity College, CT (UNC)
Trinity College of Florida, FL (UNC)
Trinity College of Nursing, IL (UNC)
Trinity College of Puerto Rico, PR (TCT)
Trinity Episcopal School for Ministry, PA (GRD)
Trinity Evangelical Divinity School, IL (GRD)
Trinity International University, FL (GRD)
Trinity International University, IL (UNC)
Trinity Life Bible College, CA (UNC)
Trinity Lutheran College, WA (UNC)
Trinity Lutheran Seminary, OH (GRD)
Trinity Medical Center, ND (AHS)
Trinity Medical Center East, OH (NRS)
Trinity-Pawling School, NY (PRB)
Trinity University, DC (WMC)
Trinity University, TX (UNC)
Trinity Valley Community College, TX (JRC)
Triple Cities School of Beauty Culture, NY (TCT)
Tri-State Business Institute, PA (TCT)
Tri-State College of Acupuncture, NY (GRD)
Tri-State College of Massotherapy, OH (TCT)
Tri-State Cosmetology Institute, TX (TCT)
Tri-State University, IN (UNC)
Triton College, IL (JRC)
Trocaire College, NY (JRC)
Troy School of Beauty Culture, NY (TCT)
Troy University, AL (UNC)
Troy University Montgomery, AL (UNC)
Troy University - Phenix City, AL (UNC)
Truck Driving Academy, CA (TCT)
Truckee Meadows Community College, NV (JRC)
Truck Marketing Institute, CA (HMS)
Truett McConnell College, GA (JRC)
Truman Medical Center, MO (AHS)
Truman State University, MO (UNC)
Trumbull Business College, OH (TCT)
Tucson College, AZ (TCT)
Tufts University, MA (GRD)
Tufts University, MA (UNC)
Tulane University, LA (UNC)
Tulare Beauty College, CA (TCT)
Tulsa Community College, OK (JRC)
Tulsa County Area Voc Tech District 18, OK (TCT)
Tulsa Welding School, FL (TCT)
Tulsa Welding School, OK (TCT)
Tunxis Community College, CT (JRC)
Turner Job Corps Center, GA (TCT)
Turtle Mountain Community College, ND (JRC)
Tusculum College, TN (UNC)
Tuskegee University, AL (UNC)
Tuttle Vocational Technical Center, OK (TCT)
Twin City Beauty College, MI (TCT)
Tyler Junior College, TX (JRC)

U

Uintah Basin Applied Technology College, UT (TCT)
Ulster County Community College, NY (JRC)
Ultrasound Diagnostic School, GA (TCT)
Ultrasound Diagnostic School, MA (TCT)
Ultrasound Diagnostic School, MD (TCT)
Ultrasound Diagnostic School, NJ (TCT)
Ultrasound Diagnostic School, NY (TCT)
Ultrasound Diagnostic School, PA (TCT)
Ultrasound Diagnostic School, TX (TCT)
UMDNJ Grad. Sch. of Biomedical Sciences, NJ (GRD)
UMDNJ-New Jersey Dental School, NJ (GRD)
UMDNJ-New Jersey Medical School, NJ (GRD)
UMDNJ-Robert Wood Johnson Medical School, NJ (GRD)
UMDNJ-Sch. of Health Related Professions, NJ (UNC)
UMDNJ-School of Nursing, NJ (UNC)
UMDNJ School of Public Health, NJ (GRD)
UMDNJ-University of Medicine & Dentistry, NJ (UNC)
Umpqua Community College, OR (JRC)
Undergraduate School of Cosmetology, IL (TCT)
Unification Theological Seminary, NY (GRD)
Uni Health America/Glendale Mem Hospital, CA (AHS)
Union College, KY (UNC)
Union College, NE (UNC)
Union College, NY (UNC)
Union County College, NJ (JRC)
Union Institute & University, OH (UNC)
Union Institute & University, VT (GRD)
Union Memorial Hospital, MD (NRS)
Union Springs Academy, NY (PRC)
Union Theological Seminary, NY (GRD)
Union Theological Sem. & Presbyterian, VA (GRD)
Union University, TN (UNC)
Unitech Training Academy, LA (TCT)
United Beauty College, CA (TCT)
United Health Services Hospital, NY (AHS)
United Hospital Center, WV (AHS)
United Regional Health Care System, TX (TCT)
United States Air Force Academy, CO (UNC)
United States Coast Guard Academy, CT (UNC)
United States Merchant Marine Academy, NY (UNC)
United States Military Academy, NY (UNC)
United States Naval Academy, MD (UNC)
United States Sports Academy, AL (GRD)
United Talmudical Seminary, NY (MNC)
United Theological Seminary, OH (GRD)
United Theological Seminary/Twin Cities, MN (GRD)
United Tribes Technical College, ND (JRC)
United Truck & Car Driving School, CA (TCT)
Unity College, ME (UNC)
Universal Career Counseling, PR (TCT)
Universal Career Counseling Center, PR (TCT)
Universal College of Beauty, CA (TCT)
Universal College of Beauty, NC (TCT)
Universal Technical Institute, AZ (TCT)
Universal Technical Institute, CA (TCT)
Universal Technical Institute, IL (TCT)
Universal Technical Institute, MA (TCT)
Universal Technical Institute, PA (TCT)
Universal Technical Institute, TX (TCT)
Universal Technology College, PR (TCT)
Universal Therapeutic Massage Institute, NM (TCT)
Universal Training Center, CA (TCT)
Universidad Adventista de las Antillas, PR (UNC)
Universidad Central Del Caribe, PR (UNC)
Universidad del Este, PR (TCT)
Universidad Del Turabo, PR (UNC)
Universidad FLET, FL (HMS)
Universidad Metropolitana, PR (UNC)
Universidad Politecnica de Puerto Rico, PR (UNC)
University at Buffalo SUNY, NY (GRD)
University at Buffalo SUNY, NY (UNC)
University College of San Juan, PR (JRC)
University Health Center, PA (AHS)
University Hospital, TX (AHS)
University Hospital Health System, GA (AHS)
University Hospital of Cleveland, OH (AHS)
University Hospital of Oklahoma City, OK (AHS)
University Medical Center, LA (AHS)
University of Advancing Technology, AZ (UNC)
University of Akron, OH (UNC)
University of Akron-Wayne College, OH (JRC)
University of Alabama, AL (UNC)
University of Alabama at Birmingham, AL (UNC)
University of Alabama Hospital, AL (AHS)
University of Alabama in Huntsville, AL (UNC)
University of Alaska Anchorage, AK (UNC)
University of Alaska Bristol Bay Campus, AK (UNC)
University of Alaska Chuchi Campus, AK (UNC)
University of Alaska Fairbanks, AK (UNC)
University of Alaska Interior Campus, AK (UNC)
University of Alaska Kuskokwim Campus, AK (JRC)
University of Alaska Matanuska-Susitna, AK (JRC)
University of Alaska Northwest Campus, AK (JRC)
University of Alaska Sitka Campus, AK (JRC)
University of Alaska Southeast, AK (UNC)
University of Alaska Southeast-Ketchikan, AK (JRC)
University of Alaska Tanana Valley Cmps, AK (UNC)
University of Arizona, AZ (UNC)
University of Arizona Medical Center, AZ (MED)
University of Arkansas at Fayetteville, AR (UNC)
University of Arkansas at Fort Smith, AR (JRC)
University of Arkansas at Little Rock, AR (UNC)
University of Arkansas at Monticello, AR (UNC)
University of Arkansas at Pine Bluff, AR (UNC)
University of Arkansas Community College, AR (JRC)
University of Arkansas/Medical Sciences, AR (UNC)
University of Arkansas - Monticello, AR (TCT)
University of Baltimore, MD (UNC)
University of Bridgeport, CT (UNC)
University of California, CA (GRD)
University of California, CA (UNC)
University of California-Davis, CA (UNC)
University of CA Hastings College of Law, CA (GRD)
University of California-Irvine Med. Ctr, CA (UNC)
UCLA Center for the Health Sciences, CA (UNC)
University of California Medical Center, CA (UNC)
University of California-Santa Cruz, CA (UNC)
University of Central Arkansas, AR (UNC)
University of Central Florida, FL (UNC)
University of Central Oklahoma, OK (UNC)
University of Charleston, WV (UNC)
University of Chicago, IL (UNC)
Univ. of Chicago Hospital/Roosevelt U., IL (AHS)
University of Cincinnati, OH (JRC)
University of Cincinnati, OH (UNC)
Univ. of Cincinnati Coll. Allied Health, OH (JRC)
University of Cincinnati/OMI College, OH (UNC)
University of Cincinnati, OH (JRC)
University of Colorado, CO (UNC)
University of Colorado at Denver, CO (UNC)
University of Colorado Health Sciences, CO (UNC)
University of Connecticut, CT (UNC)
University of Connecticut Health Center, CT (UNC)
University of Cosmetology Arts & Science, TX (TCT)
University of Dallas, TX (UNC)
University of Dayton, OH (UNC)
University of Delaware, DE (UNC)
University of Denver, CO (UNC)
University of Denver University College, CO (UNC)
University of Detroit-Mercy, MI (UNC)
University of Dubuque, IA (UNC)
University of Dubuque Theological Sem., IA (GRD)
University of East West Medicine, CA (GRD)
University of Evansville, IN (UNC)
University of Findlay, OH (UNC)
University of Florida, FL (UNC)
University of Georgia, GA (UNC)
University of Great Falls, MT (UNC)
University of Guam, GU (UNC)
University of Hartford, CT (UNC)
University of Hawaii at Hilo, HI (UNC)
University of Hawaii at Manoa, HI (UNC)
University of Hawaii - West Oahu, HI (UNC)
University of Houston, TX (UNC)
University of Houston-Clear Lake, TX (UNC)
University of Houston-Downtown, TX (UNC)
University of Houston-Victoria, TX (UNC)
University of Idaho, ID (UNC)
University of Illinois, IL (GRD)
University of Illinois, IL (UNC)
University of Illinois at Chicago, IL (UNC)
University of Illinois at Springfield, IL (UNC)
University of Indianapolis, IN (UNC)
University of Iowa, IA (UNC)
University of Judaism, CA (UNC)
University of Kansas, KS (UNC)
University of Kansas Medical Center, KS (UNC)
University of Kentucky, KY (UNC)
Univ. of Kentucky Chandler Medical Ctr., KY (AHS)
University of La Verne, CA (UNC)
University of Louisiana at Lafayette, LA (UNC)
University of Louisiana at Monroe, LA (UNC)
University of Louisville, KY (UNC)
University of Maine, ME (UNC)
University of Maine at Presque Isle, ME (UNC)
University of Management and Technology, VA (UNC)
University of Mary, ND (UNC)
University of Mary Hardin-Baylor, TX (UNC)
University of Maryland, MD (UNC)
University of Maryland Eastern Shore, MD (UNC)
University of Mary Washington, VA (UNC)
University of Massachusetts, MA (UNC)
University of Massachusetts at Worcester, MA (UNC)
University of Massachusetts Boston, MA (UNC)
University of Massachusetts Dartmouth, MA (UNC)
University of Massachusetts Lowell, MA (UNC)
UMDNJ-School of Osteopathic Medicine, NJ (GRD)
University of Memphis, TN (UNC)
University of Miami, FL (UNC)
University of Michigan-Ann Arbor, MI (UNC)
University of Michigan-Dearborn, MI (UNC)
University of Michigan-Flint, MI (UNC)
University of Minnesota, MN (UNC)
University of Minnesota Rochester, MN (UNC)
University of Mississippi, MS (UNC)
University of Mississippi Medical Center, MS (UNC)
University of Missouri, MO (UNC)
University of Mobile, AL (UNC)
University of Montana, MT (UNC)
Univ of Montana Missoula College of Tech, MT (JRC)
University of Montana - Western, MT (UNC)
University of Montevallo, AL (UNC)
University of Nebraska, NE (UNC)
University of Nebraska at Kearney, NE (UNC)
University of Nebraska at Omaha, NE (UNC)
University of Nebraska Medical Center, NE (GRD)
University of Nevada, NV (UNC)
University of Nevada Las Vegas, NV (UNC)
University of New England, ME (UNC)
University of New Hampshire, NH (UNC)
University of New Haven, CT (UNC)
University of New Mexico, NM (JRC)
University of New Mexico, NM (UNC)
University of New Orleans, LA (UNC)
University of North Alabama, AL (UNC)
University of North Carolina, NC (UNC)
University of North Carolina at Pembroke, NC (UNC)
University of North Carolina Hospitals, NC (AHS)
University of North Dakota, ND (UNC)
University of Northern Colorado, CO (UNC)
University of Northern Iowa, IA (UNC)
University of Northern Virginia, VA (GRD)
University of North Florida, FL (UNC)
University of North Texas, TX (UNC)
University of N Texas Health Science Ctr, TX (GRD)
University of Northwestern Ohio, OH (UNC)
University of Notre Dame, IN (UNC)
University of Oklahoma at Norman, OK (UNC)
University of Oklahoma Health Sciences, OK (UNC)
University of Oregon, OR (UNC)
University of Pennsylvania, PA (UNC)
University of Phoenix, AZ (UNC)
University of Phoenix, CO (UNC)
University of Phoenix-NM Division, NM (UNC)
University of Pittsburgh, PA (UNC)
University of Pittsburgh at Bradford, PA (UNC)
University of Pittsburgh at Johnstown, PA (UNC)
University of Pittsburgh at Titusville, PA (UNC)
University of Portland, OR (UNC)
University of Puerto Rico, PR (UNC)
University of Puerto Rico - Aguadilla, PR (JRC)
University of Puerto Rico at Arecibo, PR (UNC)
University of Puerto Rico at Ponce, PR (UNC)
University of Puerto Rico at Utuado, PR (JRC)
Univ. of Puerto Rico/Bayamon Univ. Coll., PR (UNC)
University of Puget Sound, WA (UNC)
University of Redlands, CA (UNC)
University of Rhode Island, RI (UNC)
University of Richmond, VA (UNC)
University of Rio Grande, OH (UNC)
University of Rochester, NY (UNC)
University of Rochester Medical Center, NY (MED)
Univ. of St. Augustine for Health Sci., FL (HMS)
University of St. Francis, IL (UNC)
University of St. Francis, IN (UNC)
University of Saint Mary, KS (UNC)
University of St. Mary of the Lake, IL (GRD)
University of St. Thomas, MN (UNC)
University of St. Thomas, TX (UNC)
University of San Diego, CA (UNC)
University of San Francisco, CA (UNC)
University of Sciences & Arts of OK, OK (UNC)
University of Scranton, PA (UNC)
University of Sioux Falls, SD (UNC)
University of South Alabama, AL (UNC)
University of South Carolina, SC (JRC)
University of South Carolina, SC (UNC)
University of South Dakota, SD (UNC)
University of Southern California, CA (GRD)
University of Southern California, CA (UNC)
University of Southern Indiana, IN (UNC)
University of Southern Maine, ME (UNC)
University of Southern Mississippi, MS (UNC)
University of South Florida, FL (GRD)
University of South Florida, FL (UNC)
University of Tampa, FL (UNC)
University of Tennessee, TN (UNC)
Univ. of Tennessee Health Science Center, TN (UNC)
University of Tennessee Medical Center, TN (TCT)
University of Texas, TX (UNC)
University of Texas at Austin, TX (UNC)
University of Texas at Brownsville, TX (UNC)
University of Texas at Dallas, TX (UNC)
University of Texas at El Paso, TX (UNC)
University of Texas at San Antonio, TX (UNC)
University of Texas at Tyler, TX (UNC)
University of TX Health Science Center, TX (UNC)
University of Texas Health Science Ctr., TX (UNC)
University of Texas-Houston, TX (UNC)
University of Texas Anderson Cancer Ctr., TX (TCT)
University of Texas Medical Branch, TX (GRD)
University of Texas of the Permian Basin, TX (UNC)
University of Texas-Pan American, TX (UNC)
University of Texas S.W. Medical Center, TX (UNC)
University of the Arts, PA (UNC)
University of the Cumberlands, KY (UNC)

University of the District of Columbia, DC (UNC)
University of the D.C. School of Law, DC (GRD)
University of the Incarnate Word, TX (UNC)
University of the Ozarks, AR (UNC)
University of the Pacific, CA (GRD)
University of the Pacific, CA (UNC)
University of the Sacred Heart, PR (UNC)
University of the Sciences Philadelphia, PA (UNC)
University of the South, TN (UNC)
University of the Virgin Islands, VI (UNC)
University of the West, CA (UNC)
University of Toledo, OH (UNC)
University of Tulsa, OK (UNC)
University of Utah, UT (UNC)
University of Vermont, VT (UNC)
University of Virginia, VA (UNC)
University of Virginia College at Wise, VA (UNC)
University of Washington, WA (UNC)
University of West Alabama, AL (UNC)
University of West Florida, FL (UNC)
University of West Georgia, GA (UNC)
University of West Los Angeles, CA (GRD)
University of Wisconsin, WI (UNC)
University of Wisconsin Baraboo/Sauk Co., WI (UNC)
Univ. of Wisconsin Center-Barron County, WI (JRC)
University of Wisconsin Center, WI (JRC)
University of Wisconsin, WI (UNC)
University of Wisconsin - LaCrosse, WI (UNC)
University of Wisconsin Marathon County, WI (JRC)
University of Wisconsin-Marinette, WI (JRC)
Univ. of Wisconsin - Marshfield/Wood Co., WI (JRC)
University of Wisconsin, WI (UNC)
University of Wisconsin Waukesha, WI (JRC)
University of Wyoming, WY (UNC)
U.P. Academy of Hair Design, MI (TCT)
UPMC School of Medical Imaging, PA (TCT)
Upper Columbia Academy, WA (PRC)
Upper Iowa University, IA (UNC)
Upper Valley Teacher Institute, NH (TCT)
Urbana University, OH (UNC)
Urban College of Boston, MA (JRC)
Ursinus College, PA (UNC)
Ursuline College, OH (UNC)
Utah Career College, UT (TCT)
Utah Schools for the Deaf and the Blind, UT (HND)
Utah State University, UT (UNC)
Utah Valley Regional Medical Center, UT (AHS)
Utah Valley State College, UT (JRC)
UTA Mesivta of Kiryas Joel, NY (MNC)
Utica College, NY (UNC)
Utica School of Commerce, NY (JRC)
Utica School of Commerce, NY (TCT)
Utica School of Commerce, NY (UNC)

V

Valdosta State University, GA (UNC)
Valdosta Technical College, GA (TCT)
Valencia Community College, FL (JRC)
Valencia Community College East Campus, FL (JRC)
Valley Beauty School, OH (TCT)
Valley Beauty School, WV (TCT)
Valley City State University, ND (UNC)
Valley College of Technology, WV (JRC)
Valley College of Technology, WV (TCT)
Valley Forge Christian College, PA (BUS)
Valley Forge Military Academy, PA (PRB)
Valley Forge Military College, PA (MNC)
Valley Hospital, NJ (AHS)
Valley View Regional Hospital, OK (AHS)
Valparaiso University, IN (UNC)
Vance-Granville Community College, NC (JRC)
Vanderbilt University, TN (UNC)
VanderCook College of Music, IL (UNC)
Vanguard Institute of Technology, TX (TCT)
Vanguard University of Southern CA, CA (UNC)
Vassar College, NY (UNC)
Vatterott College, IA (TCT)
Vatterott College, IL (TCT)
Vatterott College, KS (TCT)
Vatterott College, MO (TCT)
Vatterott College, NE (TCT)
Vatterott College, OH (TCT)
Vatterott College, OK (TCT)
Vatterott College, TN (TCT)
Vaughn College of Aeronautics and Tech, NY (UNC)
Vee's School of Beauty Culture, IL (TCT)
Velma B's Beauty Academy, TX (TCT)
Velvatex College of Beauty Culture, AR (TCT)
Vennard College, IA (UNC)
Ventura College, CA (JRC)
Venus Beauty Academy, PA (TCT)
Verde Valley School, AZ (PRC)
Vermillion Community College, MN (JRC)
Vermont Academy, VT (PRC)
Vermont College of Cosmetology, VT (TCT)
Vermont Law School, VT (GRD)
Vermont Technical College, VT (JRC)
Vernon College, TX (JRC)
Vernon's Kansas School of Cosmetology, KS (TCT)
Veterans Administration Hospital, WV (AHS)
Veterans Administration Medical Center, MA (AHS)
Veterans Administration Medical Center, OR (AHS)
Veterans Affairs Medical Center, CA (AHS)
Veterans Affairs Medical Center, NY (AHS)
Veterans Affairs Medical Center, TX (AHS)
Veterans Affairs Medical Center, UT (AHS)
Vet Tech Institute, PA (TCT)
Vici Beauty School, WI (TCT)
Victoria Beauty College, TX (TCT)
Victoria College, TX (JRC)
Victor Valley Beauty College, CA (TCT)
Victor Valley Community College, CA (JRC)
Vidalia Beauty School, LA (TCT)
Villa Julie College, MD (UNC)
Villa Maria College of Buffalo, NY (JRC)
Villanova Prep School, CA (PRC)
Villanova University, PA (UNC)
Vincennes Beauty College, IN (TCT)
Vincennes University, IN (JRC)
Virgil's Beauty College, OK (TCT)
Virginia Career Institute, VA (TCT)
Virginia College, AL (TCT)
Virginia College, AL (UNC)
Virginia College, MS (TCT)
Virginia College of Osteopathic Medicine, VA (GRD)
Virginia Commonwealth University, VA (UNC)
Virginia Episcopal School, VA (PRC)
Virginia Farrell Beauty School, MI (TCT)
Virginia Highlands Community College, VA (JRC)
Virginia Home for Boys, VA (HND)
Virginia Intermont College, VA (UNC)
Virginia Marti College of Art & Design, OH (TCT)
Virginia Military Institute, VA (MNC)
Virginia Polytechnic Inst. & State Univ., VA (UNC)
Virginia School Center, CA (TCT)
Virginia School for the Deaf and Blind, VA (HND)
Virginia School of Hair Design, VA (TCT)
Virginia School of Massage, VA (TCT)
Virginia School of Technology, VA (TCT)
Virginia State University, VA (UNC)
Virginia Union University, VA (UNC)
Virginia University of Lynchburg, VA (UNC)
Virginia Wesleyan College, VA (UNC)
Virginia Western Community College, VA (JRC)
Viterbo University, WI (UNC)
Volunteer Beauty Academy, TN (TCT)
Volunteer State Community College, TN (JRC)
Von Curtis Academy of Hair Design, UT (TCT)
Voorhees College, SC (UNC)
Vortex Helicopters, LA (TCT)

W

Wabash College, IN (MNC)
Wabash Valley College, IL (JRC)
Wade College Dallas Market Center, TX (JRC)
Wadley Regional Medical Center, TX (AHS)
Wagner College, NY (UNC)
Wake Forest University, NC (GRD)
Wake Forest University, NC (UNC)
Wake Technical Community College, NC (JRC)
Walden University, MN (GRD)
Waldorf College, IA (UNC)
Wallace Community College Sparks Campus, AL (JRC)
Wallace State Community College, AL (JRC)
Walla Walla College, WA (UNC)
Walla Walla College School of Nursing, OR (UNC)
Walla Walla Community College, WA (JRC)
Walnut Hill School, MA (PRC)
Walsh Coll. Accountancy & Bus. Admin., MI (UNC)
Walsh University, OH (UNC)
Walter Boswell Memorial Hospital, AZ (AHS)
Walter Reed Medical Center, DC (TCT)
Walters State Community College, TN (JRC)
Wards Corner Beauty Academy, VA (TCT)
Warner Pacific College, OR (UNC)
Warner Southern College, FL (UNC)
Warren County Community College, NJ (JRC)
Warren Wilson College, NC (UNC)
Wartburg College, IA (UNC)
Wartburg Theological Seminary, IA (GRD)
Warwick Academy of Beauty Culture, RI (TCT)
Wasatch Academy, UT (PRC)
Washburn University, KS (UNC)
Washington & Jefferson College, PA (UNC)
Washington & Lee University, VA (UNC)
Washington Adventist Hospital, MD (AHS)
Washington Bible College, MD (MUS)
Washington College, MD (UNC)
Washington Conservatory of Music, DC (TCT)
Washington County Adult Skill Center, VA (TCT)
Washington County Community College, ME (JRC)
Washington Holmes Technical Center, FL (TCT)
Washington Hospital, PA (NRS)
Washington Hospital Center, DC (TCT)
Washington State Community College, OH (JRC)
Washington State School for the Blind, WA (HND)
Washington State School for the Deaf, WA (HND)
Washington State University, WA (UNC)
Washington Theological Union, DC (GRD)
Washington University in St. Louis, MO (UNC)
Washtenaw Community College, MI (JRC)
Watkins Institute-College of Art/Design, TN (UNC)
Watkinson School, CT (PRC)
Waubonsee Community College, IL (JRC)
Waukesha County Technical College, WI (JRC)
Wausau Hospital Center, WI (AHS)
Waycross College, GA (JRC)
Wayland Academy, WI (PRC)
Wayland Baptist University, TX (UNC)
Wayne Community College, NC (JRC)
Wayne County Community College, MI (JRC)
Waynesburg College, PA (UNC)
Wayne State College, NE (UNC)
Wayne State University, MI (UNC)
Weatherford College, TX (JRC)
Webber International University, FL (UNC)
Webb Institute, NY (UNC)
The Webb School, TN (PRC)
The Webb Schools, CA (PRC)
Weber State University, UT (UNC)
Webster College, FL (JRC)
Webster College, WV (JRC)
Webster University, MO (UNC)
Weill Medical College of Cornell Univ, NY (GRD)
Welborn Baptist Hospital, IN (AHS)
Welder Training & Testing Institute, PA (TCT)
Wellesley College, MA (WMC)
Wells College, NY (UNC)
Wenatchee Valley College, WA (JRC)
Wentworth Institute of Technology, MA (UNC)
Wentworth Military Academy, MO (JRC)
Wentworth Military Academy, MO (PRC)
Wesleyan College, GA (WMC)
Wesleyan University, CT (UNC)
Wesley Biblical Seminary, MS (GRD)
Wesley College, DE (UNC)
Wesley College, MS (UNC)
Wesley Theological Seminary, DC (GRD)
West Boca Medical Center, FL (AHS)
Westbrook College, ME (UNC)
West Central Technical College, GA (TCT)
Westchester Community College, NY (JRC)
Westchester County Medical Center, NY (AHS)
Westchester School of Beauty Culture, NY (TCT)
West Chester University of Pennsylvania, PA (UNC)
West Coast Training, WA (TCT)
West Coast Ultrasound Institute, CA (TCT)
Westech College, CA (TCT)
Western Business College, OR (TCT)
Western Business College, WA (TCT)
Western Career College, CA (TCT)
Western Carolina University, NC (UNC)
Western College of Southern California, CA (TCT)
Western Connecticut State University, CT (UNC)
Western Culinary Institute, OR (TCT)
Western Dakota Technical Institute, SD (TCT)
Western Governors University, UT (HMS)
Western Hills Sch of Beauty & Hair Dsgn., OH (TCT)
Western Illinois University, IL (UNC)
Western International University, AZ (UNC)
Western Iowa Tech Community College, IA (JRC)
Western Kentucky University, KY (UNC)
Western Michigan University, MI (UNC)
Western Nebraska Community College, NE (JRC)
Western Nevada Community College, NV (JRC)
Western New England College, MA (UNC)
Western New Mexico University, NM (UNC)
Western Oklahoma State College, OK (JRC)
Western Oregon University, OR (UNC)
Western Pacific Truck School, CA (TCT)
Western Pacific Truck School, WA (TCT)
Western Pennsylvania Hospital, PA (TCT)
Western Pennsylvania School for Blind, PA (HND)
Western Pennsylvania School for the Deaf, PA (HND)
Western Piedmont Community College, NC (JRC)
Western Reserve Academy, OH (PRC)
Western Reserve Care System, OH (AHS)
Western School of Health & Bus. Careers, PA (TCT)
Western Seminary, OR (GRD)
Western State College of Colorado, CO (UNC)
Western States Chiropractic College, OR (GRD)
Western State University College of Law, CA (GRD)
Western Technical College, TX (TCT)
Western Texas College, TX (JRC)
Western Theological Seminary, MI (GRD)
Western University of Health Sciences, CA (AHS)
Western Washington University, WA (UNC)
Western Wisconsin Technical College, WI (JRC)
Western Wyoming Community College, WY (JRC)
Westfield State College, MA (UNC)
West Georgia Technical College, GA (TCT)
West Hills Community College, CA (JRC)
West Jersey Health System, NJ (AHS)
West Kentucky Comm. & Technical College, KY (JRC)
Westlawn Institute of Marine Technology, CT (HMS)
West Liberty State College, WV (UNC)
West Los Angeles College, CA (JRC)
West Los Angeles VA Medical Center, CA (AHS)
West Michigan Coll of Barbering & Beauty, MI (TCT)
Westminister College, MO (UNC)
Westminster Choir College of Rider Univ., NJ (UNC)
Westminster College, PA (UNC)
Westminster College, UT (UNC)
Westminster School, CT (PRC)
Westminster Theological Seminary, CA (GRD)
Westminster Theological Seminary, PA (GRD)
Westmont College, CA (UNC)
Westmoreland County Community College, PA (JRC)
West Nottingham Academy, MD (PRC)
Weston Distance Learning, CO (HMS)
Weston Jesuit School of Theology, MA (TSR)
Westover School, CT (PRG)
West Park Hospital, WY (AHS)
West Shore Community College, MI (JRC)
West Suburban College of Nursing, IL (UNC)
West Tennessee Business College, TN (TCT)
West Texas A & M University, TX (UNC)
Westtown School, PA (PRC)
West Valley College, CA (JRC)
West Virginia Business College, WV (TCT)
West Virginia Career Institute, PA (TCT)
West Virginia Junior College, WV (TCT)
West Virginia Northern Community College, WV (JRC)
West Virginia Sch./Osteopathic Medicine, WV (GRD)
West Virginia Schools/Deaf and Blind, WV (HND)
West Virginia State University, WV (UNC)
West Virginia University, WV (UNC)
West Virginia University at Parkersburg, WV (UNC)
West Virginia University Hospital, WV (AHS)
West Virginia University Inst of Tech., WV (UNC)
West Virginia Wesleyan College, WV (UNC)
Westwood Aviation Institute, TX (TCT)
Westwood College, CA (TCT)
Westwood College, CA (UNC)
Westwood College, GA (TCT)
Westwood College, IL (TCT)
Westwood College, TX (TCT)
Westwood College - Denver North, CO (TCT)
Westwood College - Denver South, CO (TCT)
Westwood College - Houston South, TX (TCT)
Westwood College - Inland Empire, CA (TCT)
Westwood College of Aviation Technology, CA (TCT)
Westwood College of Aviation Technology, CO (TCT)
Westwood College of Technology, IL (TCT)
Westwood College of Technology, TX (TCT)
Westwood College - South Bay Campus, CA (TCT)
Wharton County Junior College, TX (JRC)
Whatcom Community College, WA (JRC)
Wheaton College, IL (UNC)
Wheaton College, MA (UNC)
Wheeling Hospital, WV (AHS)
Wheeling Jesuit University, WV (UNC)